D1219049

Who's Who in America®

Who'sWho in America®

2003

MARQUIS
Who'sWho
21st Century Editions
Since 1899
The Chronicle of Human Achievement

57th Edition
Volume 2
L-Z

MARQUIS Who'sWho®
121 Chanlon Road
New Providence, NJ 07974 U.S.A.
www.marquiswhoswho.com

Who'sWho in America®

Marquis Who's Who®

Published by Marquis Who's Who, a member of the Lexis-Nexis Group.

President and Chief Executive Officer John Lawler
Vice President and Chief Financial Officer Philip T. Evans
Chief Information Officer John Roney

For information, contact:
Marquis Who's Who
121 Chanlon Road
New Providence, New Jersey 07974
1-908-673-1000
www.marquiswhoswho.com

International Standard Book Number 0-8379-6966-2 (Set, Classic Edition)
0-8379-6967-0 (Volume 1, Classic Edition)
0-8379-6970-0 (Set, Deluxe Edition)
0-8379-6971-9 (Volume 1, Deluxe Edition)
International Standard Serial Number 0083-9841

Manufactured in the United States of America.

Table of Contents

Volume 1

Volume 2

Volume 3

Preface

"WHO'S WHO IN AMERICA *shall endeavor to list those individuals who are of current national reference interest and inquiry either because of meritorious achievement or because of the position they hold."*

Albert Nelson Marquis
Founder, 1899

A Standard Reference Work

When the first edition of *Who's Who in America* appeared in 1899, it presented itself as a new and untried experiment in the field of American reference book publishing. It was the first publication ever issued which claimed to be, in any comprehensive degree, a general biographical directory of notable American contemporaries. During the generations that have passed, *Who's Who in America* has garnered a worldwide reputation for presenting the most accurate, current biographical data available. Quickly establishing itself as a standard reference work, it has grown steadily in public favor, and today is recognized globally as the premier reference pertaining to notable living Americans.

The 57th Edition upholds the guiding principle set forth by A.N. Marquis in 1899: The editors of *Who's Who in America* continue to strive to identify and chronicle the achievements of men and women who have become the leaders in our society's political, cultural, and economic affairs.

One Principle Governs Selection

In 1899, Marquis Biographees numbered 8,602, or one person per 10,000 of U.S. population. In this 57th Edition, Marquis Who's Who proudly presents the biographies of over 128,000 outstanding individuals. While our Biographees have grown in number, our selection standards remain stringent. Fewer than four in 10,000 people are included in *Who's Who in America.*

Selection is based solely on reference value. Individuals become eligible for listing by virtue of their positions and/or noteworthy achievements that have proven to be of significant value to society. An individual's desire to be listed is not sufficient reason for inclusion. Similarly, wealth or social position are not criteria. Of course, Marquis Who's Who has never charged a fee for publishing a biography, nor is purchase of the book ever a factor in the selection of Biographees.

Compiling the Most Accurate Biographical Data

Through fifty-seven editions, the basic *Who's Who in America* compilation process has remained unchanged. Potential Biographees are identified by Marquis researchers and editors. Candidates are sent data forms and are invited to submit complete biographical and career information. These data are reviewed to confirm that candidates meet the stringent selection criteria. Sketches are then prepared and sent to Biographees for prepublication checking.

In some cases, Marquis staff members compile and/or verify the biographical data through independent research. Sketches compiled in this manner are denoted by asterisks. For a small number of cases, where detailed information is not available at publication, the editors have written brief sketches with current career information; these are also indicated by asterisks.

To maintain its reputation for currency, and at the same time to adhere to space limitations, *Who's Who in America* undergoes meticulous review of selection criteria with each edition. Deletion of some names is inevitable; such deletion is not arbitrary. For example, if a Biographee has retired from active participation in a career or public life, the sketch may be excluded. In large part, it is career development that determines inclusion and continuation.

Annual publication enables *Who's Who in America* to bring users more new names and update more existing entries each edition. In all, over 33,000 new names appear in the 57th Edition.

Responding to Your Reference Needs

Who's Who in America provides a number of useful reference features. As a complement to the biographical profiles, the Geographic and Professional Indexes make *Who's Who in America* an even more productive research tool. Through these indexes, users can identify and locate individuals in any of thirty-eight professional categories, as well as by country, state, or city.

This edition also contains a cumulative Retiree Index of persons whose names were deleted from the 54th through 56th Editions because they have retired from active work. This index enables the user to locate the last published biographical sketch of each listee.

There is also a Necrology of Biographees whose sketches appeared in the previous Edition and whose deaths were reported prior to the closing of this edition. The sketches have been removed from the book. (For those Biographees whose deaths were reported prior to May 2002, complete biographical information, including date of death and place of interment, can be found in Volume XIV of *Who Was Who in America*.)

Finally, many of the women and men profiled in *Who's Who in America* have included in their biographies a listing of their avocations, thus providing additional insights into their personal lives and interests. Some of the sketches also end with an italicized feature, "Thoughts on My Life." The statement is written by the Biographees and reflects their own principles, goals, ideals, and values that have been guidelines for their success and achievement.

Our Challenge

Putting together a reference source as comprehensive as *Who's Who in America* is a monumental challenge. Over our long history, Marquis Who's Who researchers and editors have exercised diligent care in preparing each sketch for publication. Despite all precautions, however, errors do occasionally occur. Users of this directory are invited to notify the publisher of any such errors so that corrections can be made in a subsequent edition.

Board of Advisors

Marquis Who's Who gratefully acknowledges the following distinguished individuals who have made themselves available for review, evaluation, and general comment with regard to the publication of the 57th Edition of *Who's Who in America*. The advisors have enhanced the reference value of this edition by the nomination of outstanding individuals for inclusion. However, the Board of Advisors, either collectively or individually, is in no way responsible for the selection of names appearing in this volume, nor does the Board of Advisors bear responsibility for the accuracy or comprehensiveness of the biographical information or other material contained herein.

Mindy Aloff
Freelance Writer

William C. Anderson
Executive Director
American Academy of Environmental Engineers
Annapolis, Maryland

Steven C. Beering
President Emeritus
Purdue University
West Lafayette, Indiana

Willard L. Boyd
President Emeritus
Field Museum of Natural History

Dr. Thomas C. Dolan
President and CEO
American College of Healthcare Executives

Charles C. Eldredge
Hall Distinguished Professor of American Art
University of Kansas
Lawrence, Kansas

Barbara Haskell
Curator
Whitney Museum of American Art

Thomas R. Horton
Former Chairman
American Management Association

Jill Krementz
Author and Photographer

Charles F. Larson
President
Industrial Research Institute, Inc.

Andrew Leckey
Syndicated Investment Columnist
The Chicago Tribune

Judith P. Lotas
Founding Partner
Lotas Minard Patton McIver, Inc.

Martin E. Marty
Professor Emeritus
University of Chicago Divinity School

Robert G. McKinnell
Former President
International Society of Differentiation, Inc.
University of Minnesota
St. Paul, Minnesota

Jeremiah P. Ostriker
Provost
Princeton University
Princeton, New Jersey

Louis Rukeyser
Economic Commentator
Host, Louis Rukeyser's Wall Street

James B. Sales
Former Senior Partner
Fulbright & Jaworski
Houston, Texas

Catharine R. Stimpson
University Professor
New York University

John Fox Sullivan
President and Publisher
National Journal

Elie Wiesel
Author
Professor of Philosophy
Boston University

Standards of Admission

The foremost consideration in determining who will be admitted to the pages of *Who's Who in America* is the extent of an individual's reference interest. Reference value is based on either of two factors: (1) the position of responsibility held or (2) the level of significant achievement attained in a career of noteworthy activity. The majority of Biographees qualify for admission on the basis of the first factor, a specific position of responsibility. Incumbency in the position makes the person someone of high reference interest. The factor of position includes the following categories:

1. High-ranking members of the executive, legislative, and judicial branches of the United States government. This group includes, for example, the President of the United States, members of Congress, cabinet secretaries, chief administrators of selected federal agencies and commissions, and justices of the federal courts.

2. Military officers on active duty with the rank of Major General or higher in the Army, Air Force, and Marine Corps, and of Rear Admiral or higher in the U.S. Navy.

3. Specified state government officials. Among these are governors, lieutenant governors, secretaries of state, attorneys general, and treasurers. Also included under this standard are presidents of state senates, state university system administrators, chief state health officers, and officials of American territories.

4. Judges of state and territorial courts of the highest appellate jurisdiction.

5. High-level officials of principal cities, based on population. These officials include mayors, police chiefs, school superintendents, and other selected positions.

6. Leading government officials of Canada and Mexico. In Canada, this group includes the prime minister, premiers of the provinces, ministers of departments of the federal government, and justices of the highest courts. Examples in the Mexican government are the president of the country and cabinet secretaries of the national government.

7. Principal officers of major national and international businesses as defined by several quantitative criteria.

8. Ranking administrative officials of major universities and colleges. Some of the officers included in this category are president, provost, dean, and selected department heads.

9. Heads of leading philanthropic, cultural, educational, professional, and scientific institutions and associations. These institutions include, for example, selected foundations, museums, symphony orchestras, libraries, and research laboratories.

10. Selected members of certain honorary and professional organizations, such as the National Academy of Sciences, the National Academy of Design, the American College of Trial Lawyers, and the Royal Society of Canada.

11. Chief ecclesiastics of the principal religious denominations.

12. Recipients of major national and international awards, such as the Nobel and Pulitzer Prizes, the Academy Awards and the Antoinette Perry, or Tony Awards. Also included are winners of important professional awards, such as the American Institute of Architecture's Gold Medal for Architecture.

Admission by the second factor—significant achievement—is based on the application of objective criteria established for each field. An artist whose works are included in major museums qualifies for admission for noteworthy accomplishment. The professor who has made important research contributions in his field is of reference interest because of his outstanding achievements. Qualitative standards determine eligibility for every field.

In many instances there is considerable overlap between the two factors used for inclusion in *Who's Who in America*. For example, the head of a major library is in the book because of position, but reaching that responsibility also signifies important achievement. Similarly, a state governor not only holds a position that warrants inclusion; attaining that post also represents significant achievement in the political world. In both cases, the reference value of the biographical sketch is significant. Whether the person has been selected because of position or as a mark of achievement, the Biographee in *Who's Who in America* has noteworthy accomplishments beyond those of the vast majority of contemporaries.

Key to Information

[1] **GIBSON, OSCAR JULIUS,** [2] physician, medical educator; [3] b. Syracuse, N.Y., Aug. 31, 1937; [4] s. Paul Oliver and Elizabeth H. (Thrun) G.; [5] m. Judith S. Gonzalez, Apr. 28, 1968; [6] children: Richard Gary, Matthew Cary, Samuel Perry. [7] BA magna cum laude, U. Pa., 1960; MD, Harvard U., 1964. [8] Diplomate Am. Bd. Internal Medicine, Am. Bd. Preventive Medicine. [9] Intern Barnes Hosp., St. Louis, 1964-65, resident, 1965-66; clin. assoc. Nat. Heart Inst., NIH, Bethesda, Md., 1966-68; chief resident medicine U. Okla. Hosps., 1968-69; asst. prof. cmty. health Okla. Med. Ctr., 1969-70, assoc. prof., 1970-74, prof., chmn. dept., 1974-80; dean Coll. Medicine U. Okla., 1978-82; v.p. med. staff affairs Bapt. Med. Ctr., Oklahoma City, 1982-86, exec. v.p., 1986-88, chmn., 1988-95, chmn, CEO, 1995—; [10] mem. governing bd. Ambulatory Health Care Consortium, Inc., 1979-80; mem. Okla. Bd. Medicolegal Examiners, 1985—; mem. Okla. Bd. of Med. Ethics, 1994—. [11] Contrb. articles to profl. jours. [12] Bd. dirs., v.p. Okla. Arthritis Found., 1982—; trustee N. Ctrl. Mental Health Ctr., 1985—. [13] Served U.S. Army, 1955-56. [14] Recipient R.T. Chadwick award Overlook Hosp., 1968; Am. Heart Assn. grantee, 1985-86, 88, 1995-96. [15] Fellow Assn. Tchrs. Preventive Medicine; mem. AAAS, AMA, Am. Fedn. Clin. Rsch., Assn. Med. Colls., Masons, Shriners, Sigma Xi. [16] Republican. [17] Roman Catholic. [18] Avocations: swimming, weight lifting, travelling. [19] Home: 6060 N Ridge Ave Oklahoma City OK 73126 [20] Office: Bapt Med Ctr 1986 Cuba Hwy Oklahoma City OK 73120

KEY

[1] Name
[2] Occupation
[3] Vital statistics
[4] Parents
[5] Marriage
[6] Children
[7] Education
[8] Professional certifications
[9] Career
[10] Career-related
[11] Writings and creative works
[12] Civic and political activities
[13] Military
[14] Awards and fellowships
[15] Professional and association memberships, clubs and lodges
[16] Political affiliation
[17] Religion
[18] Avocations
[19] Home address
[20] Office address

Table of Abbreviations

The following abbreviations and symbols are frequently used in this book.

******An asterisk following a sketch indicates that it was researched by the Marquis Who's Who editorial staff and has not been verified by the Biographee.*

A

A Associate (used with academic degrees only)
AA, A.A. Associate in Arts, Associate of Arts
AAAL American Academy of Arts and Letters
AAAS American Association for the Advancement of Science
AACD American Association for Counseling and Development
AACN American Association of Critical Care Nurses
AAHA American Academy of Health Administrators
AAHP American Association of Hospital Planners
AAHPERD American Alliance for Health, Physical Education, Recreation, and Dance
AAS Associate of Applied Science
AASL American Association of School Librarians
AASPA American Association of School Personnel Administrators
AAU Amateur Athletic Union
AAUP American Association of University Professors
AAUW American Association of University Women
AB, A.B. Arts, Bachelor of
AB Alberta
ABA American Bar Association
ABC American Broadcasting Company
AC Air Corps
acad. academy, academic
acct. accountant
acctg. accounting
ACDA Arms Control and Disarmament Agency
ACHA American College of Hospital Administrators
ACLS Advanced Cardiac Life Support
ACLU American Civil Liberties Union
ACOG American College of Ob-Gyn
ACP American College of Physicians
ACS American College of Surgeons
ADA American Dental Association
a.d.c. aide-de-camp
adj. adjunct, adjutant
adj. gen. adjutant general
adm. admiral
adminstr. administrator
adminstrn. administration
adminstrv. administrative
ADN Associate's Degree in Nursing
ADP Automatic Data Processing
adv. advocate, advisory
advt. advertising
AE, A.E. Agricultural Engineer
A.E. and P. Ambassador Extraordinary and Plenipotentiary
AEC Atomic Energy Commission
aero. aeronautical, aeronautic
aerodyn. aerodynamic
AFB Air Force Base
AFL-CIO American Federation of Labor and Congress of Industrial Organizations
AFTRA American Federation of TV and Radio Artists
AFSCME American Federation of State, County and Municipal Employees
agr. agriculture
agrl. agricultural
agt. agent
AGVA American Guild of Variety Artists
agy. agency
A&I Agricultural and Industrial
AIA American Institute of Architects
AIAA American Institute of Aeronautics and Astronautics
AIChE American Institute of Chemical Engineers
AICPA American Institute of Certified Public Accountants
AID Agency for International Development
AIDS Acquired Immune Deficiency Syndrome
AIEE American Institute of Electrical Engineers
AIM American Institute of Management
AIME American Institute of Mining, Metallurgy, and Petroleum Engineers
AK Alaska
AL Alabama
ALA American Library Association
Ala. Alabama
alt. alternate
Alta. Alberta
A&M Agricultural and Mechanical
AM, A.M. Arts, Master of
Am. American, America
AMA American Medical Association
amb. ambassador
A.M.E. African Methodist Episcopal
Amtrak National Railroad Passenger Corporation
AMVETS American Veterans of World War II, Korea, Vietnam
ANA American Nurses Association
anat. anatomical
ANCC American Nurses Credentialing Center
ann. annual
ANTA American National Theatre and Academy
anthrop. anthropological
AP Associated Press
APA American Psychological Association
APGA American Personnel Guidance Association
APHA American Public Health Association
APO Army Post Office
apptd. appointed
Apr. April
apt. apartment
AR Arkansas
ARC American Red Cross
arch. architect
archeol. archeological
archtl. architectural
Ariz. Arizona
Ark. Arkansas
ArtsD, ArtsD. Arts, Doctor of
arty. artillery
AS American Samoa
AS Associate in Science
ASCAP American Society of Composers, Authors and Publishers
ASCD Association for Supervision and Curriculum Development
ASCE American Society of Civil Engineers
ASHRAE American Society of Heating, Refrigeration, and Air Conditioning Engineers
ASME American Society of Mechanical Engineers
ASNSA American Society for Nursing Service Administrators
ASPA American Society for Public Administration
ASPCA American Society for the Prevention of Cruelty to Animals
assn. association
assoc. associate
asst. assistant
ASTD American Society for Training and Development
ASTM American Society for Testing and Materials
astron. astronomical
astrophys. astrophysical
ATLA Association of Trial Lawyers of America
ATSC Air Technical Service Command
AT&T American Telephone & Telegraph Company
atty. attorney
Aug. August
AUS Army of the United States
aux. auxiliary
Ave. Avenue
AVMA American Veterinary Medical Association
AZ Arizona
AWHONN Association of Women's Health Obstetric and Neonatal Nurses

B

B. Bachelor
b. born
BA, B.A. Bachelor of Arts
BAgr, B.Agr. Bachelor of Agriculture

Balt. Baltimore
Bapt. Baptist
BArch, B.Arch. Bachelor of Architecture
BAS, B.A.S. Bachelor of Agricultural Science
BBA, B.B.A. Bachelor of Business Administration
BBB Better Business Bureau
BBC British Broadcasting Corporation
BC, B.C. British Columbia
BCE, B.C.E. Bachelor of Civil Engineering
BChir, B.Chir. Bachelor of Surgery
BCL, B.C.L. Bachelor of Civil Law
BCLS Basic Cardiac Life Support
BCS, B.C.S. Bachelor of Commercial Science
BD, B.D. Bachelor of Divinity
bd. board
BE, B.E. Bachelor of Education
BEE, B.E.E. Bachelor of Electrical Engineering
BFA, B.F.A. Bachelor of Fine Arts
bibl. biblical
bibliog. bibliographical
biog. biographical
biol. biological
BJ, B.J. Bachelor of Journalism
Bklyn. Brooklyn
BL, B.L. Bachelor of Letters
bldg. building
BLS, B.L.S. Bachelor of Library Science
BLS Basic Life Support
Blvd. Boulevard
BMI Broadcast Music, Inc.
BMW Bavarian Motor Works (Bayerische Motoren Werke)
bn. battalion
B.&O.R.R. Baltimore & Ohio Railroad
bot. botanical
BPE, B.P.E. Bachelor of Physical Education
BPhil, B.Phil. Bachelor of Philosophy
br. branch
BRE, B.R.E. Bachelor of Religious Education
brig. gen. brigadier general
Brit. British, Brittanica
Bros. Brothers
BS, B.S. Bachelor of Science
BSA, B.S.A. Bachelor of Agricultural Science
BSBA Bachelor of Science in Business Administration
BSChemE Bachelor of Science in Chemical Engineering
BSD, B.S.D. Bachelor of Didactic Science
BSEE Bachelor of Science in Electrical Engineering
BSN Bachelor of Science in Nursing
BST, B.S.T. Bachelor of Sacred Theology
BTh, B.Th. Bachelor of Theology
bull. bulletin
bur. bureau
bus. business
B.W.I. British West Indies

C

CA California
CAA Civil Aeronautics Administration
CAB Civil Aeronautics Board
CAD-CAM Computer Aided Design–Computer Aided Model
Calif. California
C.Am. Central America
Can. Canada, Canadian
CAP Civil Air Patrol
capt. captain
cardiol. cardiological
cardiovasc. cardiovascular
CARE Cooperative American Relief Everywhere
Cath. Catholic
cav. cavalry
CBC Canadian Broadcasting Company
CBI China, Burma, India Theatre of Operations
CBS Columbia Broadcasting Company
C.C. Community College
CCC Commodity Credit Corporation
CCNY City College of New York
CCRN Critical Care Registered Nurse
CCU Cardiac Care Unit
CD Civil Defense
CE, C.E. Corps of Engineers, Civil Engineer
CEN Certified Emergency Nurse
CENTO Central Treaty Organization
CEO chief executive officer
CERN European Organization of Nuclear Research
cert. certificate, certification, certified
CETA Comprehensive Employment Training Act
CFA Chartered Financial Analyst
CFL Canadian Football League
CFO chief financial officer
CFP Certified Financial Planner
ch. church
ChD, Ch.D. Doctor of Chemistry
chem. chemical
ChemE, Chem.E. Chemical Engineer
ChFC Chartered Financial Consultant
Chgo. Chicago
chirurg. chirurgical
chmn. chairman
chpt. chapter
CIA Central Intelligence Agency
Cin. Cincinnati
cir. circle, circuit
CLE Continuing Legal Education
Cleve. Cleveland
climatol. climatological
clin. clinical
clk. clerk
C.L.U. Chartered Life Underwriter
CM, C.M. Master in Surgery
CM Northern Mariana Islands
CMA Certified Medical Assistant
cmty. community
CNA Certified Nurse's Aide
CNOR Certified Nurse (Operating Room)
C.&N.W.Ry. Chicago & North Western Railway
CO Colorado
Co. Company
COF Catholic Order of Foresters
C. of C. Chamber of Commerce
col. colonel
coll. college
Colo. Colorado
com. committee
comd. commanded
comdg. commanding
comdr. commander
comdt. commandant
comm. communications
commd. commissioned
comml. commercial
commn. commission
commr. commissioner
compt. comptroller
condr. conductor
Conf. Conference
Congl. Congregational, Congressional
Conglist. Congregationalist
Conn. Connecticut
cons. consultant, consulting
consol. consolidated
constl. constitutional
constn. constitution
constrn. construction
contbd. contributed
contbg. contributing
contbn. contribution
contbr. contributor
contr. controller
Conv. Convention
COO chief operating officer
coop. cooperative
coord. coordinator
CORDS Civil Operations and Revolutionary Development Support
CORE Congress of Racial Equality
corp. corporation, corporate
corr. correspondent, corresponding, correspondence
C.&O.Ry. Chesapeake & Ohio Railway
coun. council
CPA Certified Public Accountant
CPCU Chartered Property and Casualty Underwriter
CPH, C.P.H. Certificate of Public Health
cpl. corporal
CPR Cardio-Pulmonary Resuscitation
C.P.Ry. Canadian Pacific Railway
CRT Cathode Ray Terminal
C.S. Christian Science
CSB, C.S.B. Bachelor of Christian Science
C.S.C. Civil Service Commission
CT Connecticut
ct. court
ctr. center
ctrl. central
CWS Chemical Warfare Service
C.Z. Canal Zone

D

D. Doctor
d. daughter
DAgr, D.Agr. Doctor of Agriculture
DAR Daughters of the American Revolution
dau. daughter
DAV Disabled American Veterans
DC, D.C. District of Columbia
DCL, D.C.L. Doctor of Civil Law
DCS, D.C.S. Doctor of Commercial Science
DD, D.D. Doctor of Divinity

DDS, D.D.S. Doctor of Dental Surgery
DE Delaware
Dec. December
dec. deceased
def. defense
Del. Delaware
del. delegate, delegation
Dem. Democrat, Democratic
DEng, D.Eng. Doctor of Engineering
denom. denomination, denominational
dep. deputy
dept. department
dermatol. dermatological
desc. descendant
devel. development, developmental
DFA, D.F.A. Doctor of Fine Arts
D.F.C. Distinguished Flying Cross
DHL, D.H.L. Doctor of Hebrew Literature
dir. director
dist. district
distbg. distributing
distbn. distribution
distbr. distributor
disting. distinguished
div. division, divinity, divorce
divsn. division
DLitt, D.Litt. Doctor of Literature
DMD, D.M.D. Doctor of Dental Medicine
DMS, D.M.S. Doctor of Medical Science
DO, D.O. Doctor of Osteopathy
docs. documents
DON Director of Nursing
DPH, D.P.H. Diploma in Public Health
DPhil, D.Phil. Doctor of Philosophy
D.R. Daughters of the Revolution
Dr. Drive, Doctor
DRE, D.R.E. Doctor of Religious Education
DrPH, Dr.P.H. Doctor of Public Health, Doctor of Public Hygiene
D.S.C. Distinguished Service Cross
DSc, D.Sc. Doctor of Science
DSChemE Doctor of Science in Chemical Engineering
D.S.M. Distinguished Service Medal
DST, D.S.T. Doctor of Sacred Theology
DTM, D.T.M. Doctor of Tropical Medicine
DVM, D.V.M. Doctor of Veterinary Medicine
DVS, D.V.S. Doctor of Veterinary Surgery

E

E, E. East
ea. eastern
E. and P. Extraordinary and Plenipotentiary
Eccles. Ecclesiastical
ecol. ecological
econ. economic
ECOSOC Economic and Social Council (of the UN)
ED, E.D. Doctor of Engineering
ed. educated
EdB, Ed.B. Bachelor of Education
EdD, Ed.D. Doctor of Education
edit. edition
editl. editorial
EdM, Ed.M. Master of Education
edn. education
ednl. educational
EDP Electronic Data Processing
EdS, Ed.S. Specialist in Education
EE, E.E. Electrical Engineer
E.E. and M.P. Envoy Extraordinary and Minister Plenipotentiary
EEC European Economic Community
EEG Electroencephalogram
EEO Equal Employment Opportunity
EEOC Equal Employment Opportunity Commission
E.Ger. German Democratic Republic
EKG Electrocardiogram
elec. electrical
electrochem. electrochemical
electrophys. electrophysical
elem. elementary
EM, E.M. Engineer of Mines
EMT Emergency Medical Technician
ency. encyclopedia
Eng. England
engr. engineer
engring. engineering
entomol. entomological
environ. environmental
EPA Environmental Protection Agency
epidemiol. epidemiological
Episc. Episcopalian
ERA Equal Rights Amendment
ERDA Energy Research and Development Administration
ESEA Elementary and Secondary Education Act
ESL English as Second Language
ESPN Entertainment and Sports Programming Network
ESSA Environmental Science Services Administration
ethnol. ethnological
ETO European Theatre of Operations
Evang. Evangelical
exam. examination, examining
Exch. Exchange
exec. executive
exhbn. exhibition
expdn. expedition
expn. exposition
expt. experiment
exptl. experimental
Expy. Expressway
Ext. Extension

F

F.A. Field Artillery
FAA Federal Aviation Administration
FAO Food and Agriculture Organization (of the UN)
FBA Federal Bar Association
FBI Federal Bureau of Investigation
FCA Farm Credit Administration
FCC Federal Communications Commission
FCDA Federal Civil Defense Administration
FDA Food and Drug Administration
FDIA Federal Deposit Insurance Administration
FDIC Federal Deposit Insurance Corporation
FE, F.E. Forest Engineer
FEA Federal Energy Administration
Feb. February
fed. federal
fedn. federation
FERC Federal Energy Regulatory Commission
fgn. foreign
FHA Federal Housing Administration
fin. financial, finance
FL Florida
Fl. Floor
Fla. Florida
FMC Federal Maritime Commission
FNP Family Nurse Practitioner
FOA Foreign Operations Administration
found. foundation
FPC Federal Power Commission
FPO Fleet Post Office
frat. fraternity
FRS Federal Reserve System
FSA Federal Security Agency
Ft. Fort
FTC Federal Trade Commission
Fwy. Freeway

G

G-1 (or other number) Division of General Staff
GA, Ga. Georgia
GAO General Accounting Office
gastroent. gastroenterological
GATE Gifted and Talented Educators
GATT General Agreement on Tariffs and Trade
GE General Electric Company
gen. general
geneal. genealogical
geod. geodetic
geog. geographic, geographical
geol. geological
geophys. geophysical
geriat. geriatrics
gerontol. gerontological
G.H.Q. General Headquarters
GM General Motors Corporation
GMAC General Motors Acceptance Corporation
G.N.Ry. Great Northern Railway
gov. governor
govt. government
govtl. governmental
GPO Government Printing Office
grad. graduate, graduated
GSA General Services Administration
Gt. Great
GTE General Telephone and Electric Company
GU Guam
gynecol. gynecological

H

HBO Home Box Office
hdqs. headquarters
HEW Department of Health, Education and Welfare
HHD, H.H.D. Doctor of Humanities
HHFA Housing and Home Finance Agency
HHS Department of Health and Human Services

HI Hawaii
hist. historical, historic
HM, H.M. Master of Humanities
HMO Health Maintenance Organization
homeo. homeopathic
hon. honorary, honorable
Ho. of Dels. House of Delegates
Ho. of Reps. House of Representatives
hort. horticultural
hosp. hospital
H.S. High School
HUD Department of Housing and Urban Development
Hwy. Highway
hydrog. hydrographic

I

IA Iowa
IAEA International Atomic Energy Agency
IATSE International Alliance of Theatrical and Stage Employees and Moving Picture Operators of the United States and Canada
IBM International Business Machines Corporation
IBRD International Bank for Reconstruction and Development
ICA International Cooperation Administration
ICC Interstate Commerce Commission
ICCE International Council for Computers in Education
ICU Intensive Care Unit
ID Idaho
IEEE Institute of Electrical and Electronics Engineers
IFC International Finance Corporation
IGY International Geophysical Year
IL Illinois
Ill. Illinois
illus. illustrated
ILO International Labor Organization
IMF International Monetary Fund
IN Indiana
Inc. Incorporated
Ind. Indiana
ind. independent
Indpls. Indianapolis
indsl. industrial
inf. infantry
info. information
ins. insurance
insp. inspector
insp. gen. inspector general
inst. institute
instl. institutional
instn. institution
instr. instructor
instrn. instruction
instrnl. instructional
internat. international
intro. introduction
IRE Institute of Radio Engineers
IRS Internal Revenue Service
ITT International Telephone & Telegraph Corporation

J

JAG Judge Advocate General
JAGC Judge Advocate General Corps
Jan. January
Jaycees Junior Chamber of Commerce
JB, J.B. Jurum Baccalaureus
JCB, J.C.B. Juris Canoni Baccalaureus
JCD, J.C.D. Juris Canonici Doctor, Juris Civilis Doctor
JCL, J.C.L. Juris Canonici Licentiatus
JD, J.D. Juris Doctor
jg. junior grade
jour. journal
jr. junior
JSD, J.S.D. Juris Scientiae Doctor
JUD, J.U.D. Juris Utriusque Doctor
jud. judicial

K

Kans. Kansas
K.C. Knights of Columbus
K.P. Knights of Pythias
KS Kansas
K.T. Knight Templar
KY, Ky. Kentucky

L

LA, La. Louisiana
L.A. Los Angeles
lab. laboratory
L.Am. Latin America
lang. language
laryngol. laryngological
LB Labrador
LDS Latter Day Saints
LDS Church Church of Jesus Christ of Latter Day Saints
lectr. lecturer
legis. legislation, legislative
LHD, L.H.D. Doctor of Humane Letters
L.I. Long Island
libr. librarian, library
lic. licensed, license
L.I.R.R. Long Island Railroad
lit. literature
litig. litigation
LittB, Litt.B. Bachelor of Letters
LittD, Litt.D. Doctor of Letters
LLB, LL.B. Bachelor of Laws
LLD, L.L.D. Doctor of Laws
LLM, L.L.M. Master of Laws
Ln. Lane
L.&N.R.R. Louisville & Nashville Railroad
LPGA Ladies Professional Golf Association
LPN Licensed Practical Nurse
LS, L.S. Library Science (in degree)
lt. lieutenant
Ltd. Limited
Luth. Lutheran
LWV League of Women Voters

M

M. Master
m. married
MA, M.A. Master of Arts
MA Massachusetts
MADD Mothers Against Drunk Driving
mag. magazine
MAgr, M.Agr. Master of Agriculture
maj. major
Man. Manitoba
Mar. March
MArch, M.Arch. Master in Architecture
Mass. Massachusetts
math. mathematics, mathematical
MATS Military Air Transport Service
MB, M.B. Bachelor of Medicine
MB Manitoba
MBA, M.B.A. Master of Business Administration
MBS Mutual Broadcasting System
M.C. Medical Corps
MCE, M.C.E. Master of Civil Engineering
mcht. merchant
mcpl. municipal
MCS, M.C.S. Master of Commercial Science
MD, M.D. Doctor of Medicine
MD, Md. Maryland
MDiv Master of Divinity
MDip, M.Dip. Master in Diplomacy
mdse. merchandise
MDV, M.D.V. Doctor of Veterinary Medicine
ME, M.E. Mechanical Engineer
ME Maine
M.E.Ch. Methodist Episcopal Church
mech. mechanical
MEd., M.Ed. Master of Education
med. medical
MEE, M.E.E. Master of Electrical Engineering
mem. member
meml. memorial
merc. mercantile
met. metropolitan
metall. metallurgical
MetE, Met.E. Metallurgical Engineer
meteorol. meteorological
Meth. Methodist
Mex. Mexico
MF, M.F. Master of Forestry
MFA, M.F.A. Master of Fine Arts
mfg. manufacturing
mfr. manufacturer
mgmt. management
mgr. manager
MHA, M.H.A. Master of Hospital Administration
M.I. Military Intelligence
MI Michigan
Mich. Michigan
micros. microscopic, microscopical
mid. middle
mil. military
Milw. Milwaukee
Min. Minister
mineral. mineralogical
Minn. Minnesota
MIS Management Information Systems
Miss. Mississippi
MIT Massachusetts Institute of Technology
mktg. marketing
ML, M.L. Master of Laws
MLA Modern Language Association
M.L.D. Magister Legnum Diplomatic
MLitt, M.Litt. Master of Literature, Master of Letters

MLS, M.L.S. Master of Library Science
MME, M.M.E. Master of Mechanical Engineering
MN Minnesota
mng. managing
MO, Mo. Missouri
moblzn. mobilization
Mont. Montana
MP Northern Mariana Islands
M.P. Member of Parliament
MPA Master of Public Administration
MPE, M.P.E. Master of Physical Education
MPH, M.P.H. Master of Public Health
MPhil, M.Phil. Master of Philosophy
MPL, M.P.L. Master of Patent Law
Mpls. Minneapolis
MRE, M.R.E. Master of Religious Education
MRI Magnetic Resonance Imaging
MS, M.S. Master of Science
MS, Ms. Mississippi
MSc, M.Sc. Master of Science
MSChemE Master of Science in Chemical Engineering
MSEE Master of Science in Electrical Engineering
MSF, M.S.F. Master of Science of Forestry
MSN Master of Science in Nursing
MST, M.S.T. Master of Sacred Theology
MSW, M.S.W. Master of Social Work
MT Montana
Mt. Mount
MTO Mediterranean Theatre of Operation
MTV Music Television
mus. museum, musical
MusB, Mus.B. Bachelor of Music
MusD, Mus.D. Doctor of Music
MusM, Mus.M. Master of Music
mut. mutual
MVP Most Valuable Player
mycol. mycological

N

N. North
NAACOG Nurses Association of the American College of Obstetricians and Gynecologists
NAACP National Association for the Advancement of Colored People
NACA National Advisory Committee for Aeronautics
NACDL National Association of Criminal Defense Lawyers
NACU National Association of Colleges and Universities
NAD National Academy of Design
NAE National Academy of Engineering, National Association of Educators
NAESP National Association of Elementary School Principals
NAFE National Association of Female Executives
N.Am. North America
NAM National Association of Manufacturers
NAMH National Association for Mental Health
NAPA National Association of Performing Artists
NARAS National Academy of Recording Arts and Sciences
NAREB National Association of Real Estate Boards
NARS National Archives and Record Service
NAS National Academy of Sciences
NASA National Aeronautics and Space Administration
NASP National Association of School Psychologists
NASW National Association of Social Workers
nat. national
NATAS National Academy of Television Arts and Sciences
NATO North Atlantic Treaty Organization
NATOUSA North African Theatre of Operations, United States Army
nav. navigation
NB, N.B. New Brunswick
NBA National Basketball Association
NBC National Broadcasting Company
NC, N.C. North Carolina
NCAA National College Athletic Association
NCCJ National Conference of Christians and Jews
ND, N.D. North Dakota
NDEA National Defense Education Act
NE Nebraska
NE, N.E. Northeast
NEA National Education Association
Nebr. Nebraska
NEH National Endowment for Humanities
neurol. neurological
Nev. Nevada
NF Newfoundland
NFL National Football League
Nfld. Newfoundland
NG National Guard
NH, N.H. New Hampshire
NHL National Hockey League
NIH National Institutes of Health
NIMH National Institute of Mental Health
NJ, N.J. New Jersey
NLRB National Labor Relations Board
NM New Mexico
N.Mex. New Mexico
No. Northern
NOAA National Oceanographic and Atmospheric Administration
NORAD North America Air Defense
Nov. November
NOW National Organization for Women
N.P.Ry. Northern Pacific Railway
nr. near
NRA National Rifle Association
NRC National Research Council
NS, N.S. Nova Scotia
NSC National Security Council
NSF National Science Foundation
NSTA National Science Teachers Association
NSW New South Wales
N.T. New Testament
NT Northwest Territories
nuc. nuclear
numis. numismatic
NV Nevada
NW, N.W. Northwest
N.W.T. Northwest Territories
NY, N.Y. New York
N.Y.C. New York City
NYU New York University
N.Z. New Zealand

O

OAS Organization of American States
ob-gyn obstetrics-gynecology
obs. observatory
obstet. obstetrical
occupl. occupational
oceanog. oceanographic
Oct. October
OD, O.D. Doctor of Optometry
OECD Organization for Economic Cooperation and Development
OEEC Organization of European Economic Cooperation
OEO Office of Economic Opportunity
ofcl. official
OH Ohio
OK Oklahoma
Okla. Oklahoma
ON Ontario
Ont. Ontario
oper. operating
ophthal. ophthalmological
ops. operations
OR Oregon
orch. orchestra
Oreg. Oregon
orgn. organization
orgnl. organizational
ornithol. ornithological
orthop. orthopedic
OSHA Occupational Safety and Health Administration
OSRD Office of Scientific Research and Development
OSS Office of Strategic Services
osteo. osteopathic
otol. otological
otolaryn. otolaryngological

P

PA, Pa. Pennsylvania
P.A. Professional Association
paleontol. paleontological
path. pathological
PBS Public Broadcasting System
P.C. Professional Corporation
PE Prince Edward Island
pediat. pediatrics
P.E.I. Prince Edward Island
PEN Poets, Playwrights, Editors, Essayists and Novelists (international association)
penol. penological
P.E.O. women's organization (full name not disclosed)
pers. personnel
pfc. private first class
PGA Professional Golfers' Association of America
PHA Public Housing Administration
pharm. pharmaceutical

PharmD, Pharm.D. Doctor of Pharmacy
PharmM, Pharm.M. Master of Pharmacy
PhB, Ph.B. Bachelor of Philosophy
PhD, Ph.D. Doctor of Philosophy
PhDChemE Doctor of Science in Chemical Engineering
PhM, Ph.M. Master of Philosophy
Phila. Philadelphia
philharm. philharmonic
philol. philological
philos. philosophical
photog. photographic
phys. physical
physiol. physiological
Pitts. Pittsburgh
Pk. Park
Pky. Parkway
Pl. Place
P.&L.E.R.R. Pittsburgh & Lake Erie Railroad
Plz. Plaza
PNP Pediatric Nurse Practitioner
P.O. Post Office
PO Box Post Office Box
polit. political
poly. polytechnic, polytechnical
PQ Province of Quebec
PR, P.R. Puerto Rico
prep. preparatory
pres. president
Presbyn. Presbyterian
presdl. presidential
prin. principal
procs. proceedings
prod. produced (play production)
prodn. production
prodr. producer
prof. professor
profl. professional
prog. progressive
propr. proprietor
pros. atty. prosecuting attorney
pro tem. pro tempore
PSRO Professional Services Review Organization
psychiat. psychiatric
psychol. psychological
PTA Parent-Teachers Association
ptnr. partner
PTO Pacific Theatre of Operations, Parent Teacher Organization
pub. publisher, publishing, published
pub. public
publ. publication
pvt. private

Q

quar. quarterly
qm. quartermaster
Q.M.C. Quartermaster Corps
Que. Quebec

R

radiol. radiological
RAF Royal Air Force
RCA Radio Corporation of America
RCAF Royal Canadian Air Force
RD Rural Delivery
Rd. Road
R&D Research & Development
REA Rural Electrification Administration
rec. recording
ref. reformed
regt. regiment
regtl. regimental
rehab. rehabilitation
rels. relations
Rep. Republican
rep. representative
Res. Reserve
ret. retired
Rev. Reverend
rev. review, revised
RFC Reconstruction Finance Corporation
RFD Rural Free Delivery
rhinol. rhinological
RI, R.I. Rhode Island
RISD Rhode Island School of Design
Rlwy. Railway
Rm. Room
RN, R.N. Registered Nurse
roentgenol. roentgenological
ROTC Reserve Officers Training Corps
RR Rural Route
R.R. Railroad
rsch. research
rschr. researcher
Rt. Route

S

S. South
s. son
SAC Strategic Air Command
SAG Screen Actors Guild
SALT Strategic Arms Limitation Talks
S.Am. South America
san. sanitary
SAR Sons of the American Revolution
Sask. Saskatchewan
savs. savings
SB, S.B. Bachelor of Science
SBA Small Business Administration
SC, S.C. South Carolina
SCAP Supreme Command Allies Pacific
ScB, Sc.B. Bachelor of Science
SCD, S.C.D. Doctor of Commercial Science
ScD, Sc.D. Doctor of Science
sch. school
sci. science, scientific
SCLC Southern Christian Leadership Conference
SCV Sons of Confederate Veterans
SD, S.D. South Dakota
SE, S.E. Southeast
SEATO Southeast Asia Treaty Organization
SEC Securities and Exchange Commission
sec. secretary
sect. section
seismol. seismological
sem. seminary
Sept. September
s.g. senior grade
sgt. sergeant
SHAEF Supreme Headquarters Allied Expeditionary Forces
SHAPE Supreme Headquarters Allied Powers in Europe
S.I. Staten Island
S.J. Society of Jesus (Jesuit)
SJD Scientiae Juridicae Doctor
SK Saskatchewan
SM, S.M. Master of Science
SNP Society of Nursing Professionals
So. Southern
soc. society
sociol. sociological
S.P.Co. Southern Pacific Company
spkr. speaker
spl. special
splty. specialty
Sq. Square
S.R. Sons of the Revolution
sr. senior
SS Steamship
SSS Selective Service System
St. Saint, Street
sta. station
stats. statistics
statis. statistical
STB, S.T.B. Bachelor of Sacred Theology
stblzn. stabilization
STD, S.T.D. Doctor of Sacred Theology
std. standard
Ste. Suite
subs. subsidiary
SUNY State University of New York
supr. supervisor
supt. superintendent
surg. surgical
svc. service
SW, S.W. Southwest
sys. system

T

TAPPI Technical Association of the Pulp and Paper Industry
tb. tuberculosis
tchg. teaching
tchr. teacher
tech. technical, technology
technol. technological
tel. telephone
Tel. & Tel. Telephone & Telegraph
telecom. telecommunications
temp. temporary
Tenn. Tennessee
Ter. Territory
Ter. Terrace
TESOL Teachers of English to Speakers of Other Languages
Tex. Texas
ThD, Th.D. Doctor of Theology
theol. theological
ThM, Th.M. Master of Theology
TN Tennessee
tng. training
topog. topographical
trans. transaction, transferred
transl. translation, translated
transp. transportation
treas. treasurer
TT Trust Territory
TV television

TVA Tennessee Valley Authority
TWA Trans World Airlines
twp. township
TX Texas
typog. typographical

U

U. University
UAW United Auto Workers
UCLA University of California at Los Angeles
UDC United Daughters of the Confederacy
U.K. United Kingdom
UN United Nations
UNESCO United Nations Educational, Scientific and Cultural Organization
UNICEF United Nations International Children's Emergency Fund
univ. university
UNRRA United Nations Relief and Rehabilitation Administration
UPI United Press International
U.P.R.R. United Pacific Railroad
urol. urological
U.S. United States
U.S.A. United States of America
USAAF United States Army Air Force
USAF United States Air Force
USAFR United States Air Force Reserve
USAR United States Army Reserve
USCG United States Coast Guard
USCGR United States Coast Guard Reserve
USES United States Employment Service
USIA United States Information Agency
USMC United States Marine Corps
USMCR United States Marine Corps Reserve
USN United States Navy
USNG United States National Guard
USNR United States Naval Reserve
USO United Service Organizations
USPHS United States Public Health Service
USS United States Ship
USSR Union of the Soviet Socialist Republics
USTA United States Tennis Association
USV United States Volunteers
UT Utah

V

VA Veterans Administration
VA, Va. Virginia
vet. veteran, veterinary
VFW Veterans of Foreign Wars
VI, V.I. Virgin Islands
vice pres. vice president
vis. visiting
VISTA Volunteers in Service to America
VITA Volunteers in Technical Assistance
vocat. vocational
vol. volunteer, volume
v.p. vice president
vs. versus
VT, Vt. Vermont

W

W, W. West
WA Washington (state)
WAC Women's Army Corps
Wash. Washington (state)
WATS Wide Area Telecommunications Service
WAVES Women's Reserve, US Naval Reserve
WCTU Women's Christian Temperance Union
we. western
W. Ger. Germany, Federal Republic of
WHO World Health Organization
WI Wisconsin
W.I. West Indies
Wis. Wisconsin
WSB Wage Stabilization Board
WV West Virginia
W.Va. West Virginia
WWI World War I
WWII World War II
WY Wyoming
Wyo. Wyoming

Y

YK Yukon Territory
YMCA Young Men's Christian Association
YMHA Young Men's Hebrew Association
YM & YWHA Young Men's and Young Women's Hebrew Association
yr. year
YT, Y.T. Yukon Territory
YWCA Young Women's Christian Association

Z

zool. zoological

Alphabetical Practices

Names are arranged alphabetically according to the surnames and under identical surnames according to the first given name. If both surname and the first given name are identical, names are arranged alphabetically according to the second given name.

Surnames beginning with De, Des, Du (however capitalized or spaced) are recorded with the prefix preceding the surname and arranged alphabetically under the letter D.

Surnames beginning with Mac and Mc are arranged alphabetically under M.

Surnames beginning with Saint or St. appear after names that begin Sains, and are arranged according to the second part of the name, e.g., St. Clair before Saint Dennis.

Surnames beginning with Van, Von, or von are arranged alphabetically under the letter V.

Compound surnames are arranged according to the first member of the compound.

Many hyphenated Arabic names begin Al-, El-, or al-. These names are alphabetized according to each Biographee's designation of last name. Thus Al-Bahar, Neta may be listed either under Al- or under Bahar, depending on the preference of the listee.

Also, Arabic names have a variety of possible spellings when transposed to English. Spelling of these names is always based on the practice of the Biographee. Some Biographees use a Western form of word order, while others prefer the Arabic word sequence.

Similarly, Asian names may have no comma between family and given names, but some Biographees have chosen to add the comma. In each case, punctuation follows the preference of the Biographee.

Parentheses used in connection with a name indicate which part of the full name is usually deleted in common usage. Hence Chambers, E(lizabeth) Anne indicates that the usual form of the given name is E. Anne. In such a case, the parentheses are ignored in alphabetizing and the name would be arranged as Chambers, Elizabeth Anne. However, if the name is recorded Chambers, (Elizabeth) Anne, signifying that the entire name Elizabeth is not commonly used, the alphabetizing would be arranged as though the name were Chambers, Anne. If an entire middle or last name is enclosed in parentheses, that portion of the name is used in the alphabetical arrangement. Hence Chambers, Elizabeth (Anne) would be arranged as Chambers, Elizabeth Anne.

Where more than one spelling, word order, or name of an individual is frequently encountered, the sketch has been entered under the form preferred by the Biographee, with cross-references under alternate forms.

Who'sWho in America®

Biographies L-Z

LAALY, HESHMAT OLLAH, chemist, science administrator, consultant; b. Kermanshah, Iran, June 23, 1927; came to Germany, 1951, Can., 1967, U.S., 1984; s. Jacob and Saltanat (Afshani) L.; m. Parvaneh Modarai, Oct. 7, 1963; (div. 1971); children: Ramesh, Edmond S.; m. Parivash M. Farahmand, Feb. 7, 1982. BS in Chemistry, U. Stuttgart, Germany, 1955; MS in Chemistry, U. Stuttgart, Republic of Germany, 1958, PhD in Chemistry, 1962. Chief chemist Kress Sohne, Krefeld, Germany, 1963-67; analytical chemist Gulf Oil Research Ctr., Montreal, Que., Can., 1967-70; material scientist Bell-Northern Research, Ottawa, Ont., Can., 1970-71; research officer NRC of Can., 1972-84; pres. Roofing Materials Sci. and Tech., L.A., 1984—. Patentee in field. Author: The Science and Technology of Traditional and Modern Roofing Systems, 1992 (World Lifetime Achievement award Am. Biog. Inst. 1992); patentee bi-functional photovoltaic single ply roofing membrane. Mem. ASTM, Inst. Roofing and Waterproofing Cons., Single-Ply Roofing Inst., Am. Chem. Soc., Constrn. Specifications Inst., Nat. Roofing Contractors Assn., UN Indsl. Devels. Orgn., Internat. Conf. Bldg. Ofcls., Roofing Cons. Inst., Inst. for Roofing and Waterproofing Cons., Can. Standard Assn., Can. Gen. Standards Bd., The Engineered Wood Assn., Am. Plywood Assn. Office: Roofing Materials Sci & Tech 9037 Monte Mar Dr Los Angeles CA 90035-4235 Fax: 310-559-6090. E-mail: RMSTLaaly@aol.com.

LAANANEN, DAVID HORTON, mechanical engineer, educator; b. Winchester, Mass., Nov. 11, 1942; s. Joseph and Helen Katherine (Horton) L.; m. Mary Ellen Storck, Sept. 9, 1967 (div. 1981); children: Gregg David, Robin Kaye; m. Delores Ann Talbert, May 21, 1988. BS in Mech. Engring., Worcester Poly. Inst., 1964; MS, Northeastern U., 1965, PhD, 1968. Project engr. Dynamic Sci., Phoenix, 1972-74; asst. prof. Pa. State U., State College, 1974-78; mgr. R&D Simula Inc., Phoenix, 1978-83; assoc. prof. Ariz. State U., Tempe, 1983-97, prof., 1997—, dir. aerospace rsch. ctr., 1992-93, dir. Airworthiness Assurance Ctr. of Excellence, 1997-2000. Referee: Jour. Aircraft, Jour. Composite Materials; contbr. articles to Jour. Aircraft, Jour. Am. Helicopter Soc., Jour. Thermoplastic Composite Materials, Composites Sci. and Tech., others. Fellow AIAA (assoc.; design engring. tech. com.); mem. ASME, Am. Helicopter Soc., Sigma Xi, Sigma Gamma Tau, Pi Tau Sigma. Democrat. Achievements include research in aircraft crash survivability, composite structures. Office: Ariz State U Dept Mech Aerospace En Tempe AZ 85287 E-mail: david.laananen@asu.edu.

LAANE, JAAN, chemistry educator; b. Paide, Estonia, June 20, 1942; came to U.S., 1949. s. Robert Freidrich and Linda (Treufeldt) L.; m. Tiiu Virkhaus, Sept. 3, 1966; children: Christina J., Lisa A. BS in Chemistry, U. Ill., 1964; PhD in Chemistry, MIT, 1967; Doctorate (hon.), U. Tartu, Estonia, 2000. Asst. prof. of chemistry Tufts U., Medford, Mass., 1967-68, Tex. A&M U., College Station, 1968-72, assoc. prof. of chemistry, 1972-76, prof. of chemistry, 1976—, chmn. div. of physical and nuclear chemistry, 1977-87, 93-94, dir. Inst. for Pacific Asia, 1987-90, assoc. dean sci., 1994-97; dep. exec. dir., sr. policy advisor Tex. A&M U./Koriyama, 1990-94; editor Jour. Molecular Structure, 1994—. Reviewer numerous profl. jours. and grant agys., 1968—; cons. indsl. and govt. orgns., 1970—; vis. prof. U. Bayreuth, Fed. Republic Germany, 1979-80; speaker Tex. A&M Faculty Senate, College Station, 1985-86; dir. NATO Advanced Rsch. Workshop, Ulm, Germany, 1992. Contbr. numerous articles to profl. jours.; lectr. numerous sci. presentations. Pres., founder College Station Assn. for Gifted and Talented, 1982-83. Recipient 10 rsch. grants Robert A. Welch Found., 1970-97, 10 rsch. grants NSF, 1976-97, U.S. Sr. Scientist award Alex Von Humboldt Found., Fed. Republic Germany, 1979, Disting. Tchg. award Tex. A&M Assn. Former Students; elected to Estonian Acad. Sci., 1995; Robert A. Welch Found. lectr., 1998-99. Fellow Am. Inst. Chemists, Am. Phys. Soc.; mem. Am. Chem. Soc. (sect. pres. 1977-78), Soc. for Applied Spectroscopy, Alexander von Humboldt Assn. Am. (pres. Tex. chpt. 2000-01), Coblentz Soc. (bd. dirs., treas. 1986-89), Tex. A&M Faculty Club (pres. 1987-88), Phi Beta Delta (pres. 1990-91). Achievements include research in molecular spectroscopy and vibrational potential energy functions of molecules, laser Raman spectroscopy, laser induced fluorescence spectroscopy, ft-infrared spectroscopy. Home: 1906 Comal Cir College Station TX 77840-4818 Office: Tex A&M U Chemistry Dept College Station TX 77843-0001 Fax: 409-845-3154. E-mail: laane@mail.chem.tamu.edu.

LAAS, VIRGINIA JEANS, historian, educator; b. Joplin, Mo., Oct. 1, 1943; d. Virgil Edward and Virginia (Kring) Jeans; m. Frederick Hulett Laas, June 22, 1963; children: Andrew, Matthew, Gilbert. BA in History, Kans. State Coll., 1964, MA in History, 1966; PhD in History, U. Ark., 1993. Cert. secondary tchr., history. Jr. high tchr. Joplin (Mo.) Pub. Schs., 1964-65; instr. Mo. So. State Coll., Joplin, 1988-92, asst. prof., 1992-97, assoc. prof., 1997—. Part-time instr. Pitts. State U., 1980-88, Mo. So. State Coll., 1984-88. Author: Love and Power in the Nineteenth Century: The Marriage of Violet Blair, 1998 (Best Book award Mo. Conf. on History 1999); co-author: Lincoln's Lee: The Life of Rear Admiral Samuel Phillips Lee, 1986 (John Lyman Book award of N. Am. Soc. for Oceanic History, 1986, Phi Alpha Theta Best Book award 1986); editor: Wartime Washington: The Civil War Letters of Elizabeth Blair Lee, 1991, Bridging Two Eras: The Autobiography of Emily Newell Blair, 1877-1951, 1999; contbr. articles to hist. jours. Recipient Southern Outstanding Tchr. award, 1994; named Mo. Prof. of Yr., Carnegie Found./Case, 2000; rsch. grantee Huntington Libr., 1991, F.D.R. Libr., 1996, State Hist. Soc. Libr., 1996. Mem. Orgn. Am. Historians, So. Hist. Assn., Mo. Hist. Assn., Assn. for Documentary Editing, So. Assn. for Women Historians, State Hist. Soc. of Mo. (trustee 1996—). Office: Mo So State Coll 3950 Newman Rd Joplin MO 64801-1512

LAATSCH, AUDREY FRIEDA, volunteer, consultant; b. Milw., Aug. 4, 1929; d. Edwin David and Rose Margaret (Kurz) L. BA, U. Wis., 1953; MSW, U. Calif., Berkeley, 1956; cert. child psychotherapy, Inst. for Psychoanalysis, Chgo., 1968; AA in Interior Design, Milw. Area Tech. Coll., 1990. Trainee, social work Wis. Dept. Pub. Welfare, Stevens Point, Wis., 1953-54, caseworker Fond du Lac, 1956-59; therapist Lakeside Children's Ctr., Milw., 1959-62, dir. of therapy, 1962-70, assoc. dir., therapy, 1970-77; assoc. dir. Lakeside Children's Ctr. now Lakeside Child and Family Ctr., 1977-84; dir. treatment foster care Lakeside Child & Family Ctr., 1984-88; vol. pres. Seth Peterson Cottage Conservancy, Mirror Lake, Lake Delton, Wis., 1989-93; corr. sec. Seth Peterson Cottage Conservancy, Mirror Lake, Lake Delton, from 1993. Treas. Seth Peterson Cottage Conservancy, 1995-97, sec., 1997—; sec. Frank Lloyd Wright/Wis. Heritage Program, 1991-95. Contbr. articles to profl. jours. Bd. dirs. Friends of Campus, U. Wis.-Baraboo-Sauk County, 1995—, Friends of Wis. State Parks, 1996—, Frank Lloyd Wright/Wis. Heritage Program, 1991—; mem. Wis. Heritage Tourism Adv. Bd., 1995—; bd. dirs. Friends of Mirror Lake State Park. Mem. Am. Assn. Children's Residential Ctrs. (life mem., program chmn. 1972-73, treas. 1974-75, chmn. nominating com. 1977-79), Assn. Child Psychotherapists, Phi Beta Kappa, Phi Kappa Phi. Democrat. Lutheran. Home: Wisconsin Dells, Wis. Deceased.

LABA, MARVIN, management consultant; b. Newark, Mar. 17, 1928; s. Joseph Abraham and Jean Cecil (Saunders) L.; m. Sandra Seltzer, Apr. 16, 1961 (div. May 1974); children: Stuart Michael, Jonathan Todd; m. Elizabeth Luger, June 11, 1974 (div. 1979). BBA, Ind. U., 1951. Buyer Bamberger's (Macy's N.J.), Newark, 1951-67; v.p., mdse. adminstr. Macy's N.Y., 1967-73; v.p., gen. mdse. mgr. Howland/Steinback, White Plains, N.Y., 1973-75, Pomeroy's, Levittown, Pa., 1975-76; v.p., gen. mdse. mgr., sr. v.p., exec. v.p. May Co. Calif., North Hollywood, 1976-79; pres., chief exec. officer G. Fox & Co. (div. of the May dept. stores), Hartford, Conn., 1979-82; pres. Richard Theobald & Asocs., L.A., 1983; pres., chief exec. officer Marvin Laba & Assocs., 1983—. With U.S. Army, 1946-48. Avocations: coins, tennis, theatre, travel. Office: Marvin Laba & Assoc 16030 Ventura Blvd Ste 660 Encino CA 91436

LABALME, PATRICIA HOCHSCHILD, foundation administrator; b. N.Y.C., Feb. 26, 1927; d. Walter and Kathrin (Samstag) Hochschild; m. George Labalme, Jr., June 6, 1958; children: Jennifer R., Henry G., Lisa G., Victoria A. BA magna cum laude, Bryn Mawr Coll., 1948; MA, Harvard U., 1950, PhD, 1958. Instr. history Wellesley Coll., Mass., 1952-57; tchr. history Brearley Sch., N.Y.C., 1957-59; lectr. Barnard Coll., 1961-77; adj. assoc. prof. history Hunter Coll., 1979; lectr. NYU, 1980-82, adj. prof. history, 1986-87; assoc. dir. Inst. for Advanced Study, Princeton, N.J., 1982-88, sec. corp., 1982-92, asst. to dir., 1992-97, visitor Sch. Hist. Studies, 1997-98; mem. adv. bd. Gladys Krieble Delmas Found., N.Y.C., 1976—79, trustee, 1979—. Trustee Am. Acad. in Rome, N.Y.C., 1979—99; exec. dir. Renaissance Soc. Am., N.Y.C., 1982—85, trustee, 1982—89, N.Y.C., 1998—. Author: Bernardo Giustiniani: A Venetian of the Quattrocento, 1969; contbg. editor: Beyond Their Sex: Learned Women of the European Past, 1980, A Century Recalled: Essays in Honor of Bryn Mawr College, 1987; contbr. articles to profl. jours. and publs. Trustee Brearley Sch., 1975-83, pres., 1978-82, hon. trustee, 1983—; trustee Lawrenceville Sch., 1985-96, trustee emerita, 1996—. Recipient Caroline A. Wilby prize Radcliffe Coll., 1958 Mem. Am. Hist. Assn., Soc. for Renaissance Studies, Renaissance Soc. Am., Ateneo Veneto, Cosmopolitan Club, Harvard Club (N.Y.C.), Cream Hill Lake Assn. (West Cornwall, Conn.), Phi Beta Kappa. Office: Gladys Krieble Delmas Found 521 Fifth Ave Ste 1612 New York NY 10175-1699

LABAN, MYRON MILES, physician, administrator; b. Detroit, Mar. 9, 1936; s. Larry Max and Mary Marsha (Harris) LaB.; m. Rita Joyce Hochman, Aug. 17, 1958; children: Terry, Amy, Craig BA, U. Mich., Ann Arbor, 1957, MD, 1967; M.Med. Sci., Ohio State U., Columbus, 1965. Diplomate Am. Bd. Phys. Medicine and Rehab. Intern Sinai Hosp., Detroit, 1961-62; resident Ohio State U. Hosp., 1962-65; assoc. dir. phys. medicine and rehab. Letterman Gen. Hosp., San Francisco, 1965-67; dir. phys. medicine and rehab. William Beaumont Hosp., Royal Oak, Mich., 1967—; Licht lecturer Ohio State U., 1986, clin. prof., 1993. Clin. prof. Wayne State U., Detroit, 1990, clin. prof. Oakland U., Rochester, Mich., 1983, Ohio State U., Columbus, 1992; bd. dirs. Oakland County Med. Bd., Birmingham, Mich., 1982-87; rep. to Commn. on Phys. Medicine and Rehab., Mich. State Med. Soc. Contbr. chpts. in books, articles to profl. publs. Med. dir. Oakland County March of Dimes, Mich., 1969-83. Served to capt. U.S. Army, 1965-67 Fellow Am. Acad. Phys. Medicine and Rehab. (bd. dirs. 1980, pres. 1985-86, Bernard Baruch Rsch. award 1961, R. Rosenthal Rsch. award 1982, Zeiter lectureship, Disting. Clinician award 1991, "Top Doc" PM&R Detroit Monthly 1993, 96, Frank H. Krusen award 1997); mem. AMA, Am. Congress Rehab. Medicine, Am. Assn. Electromyography and Electrodiagnosis (program dir. 1972), Oakland County Med. Soc. (treas. 1983, pres.-elect 1987, pres. 1988-89), Mich. State Med. Soc., Mich. Acad. Phys. Med. and Rehab. (pres. 1982-84, jud. commr. 1991-95, mem. editl. bd. Jour. Phys. Med. and Rehab.). Republican. Jewish. Avocations: gardening; ship modeling. Office: LMT Rehabilitation Assocs 3535 W 13 Mile Rd Rm 703 Royal Oak MI 48073-6710 E-mail: myjoy@comcast.net.

LABARDI, JILLIAN GAY, financial planner, insurance agent; b. Terre Haute, Ind., Feb. 24, 1945; d. Frank Moses and Joan (Forster) Pierson; m. Jack Alexander Labardi, June 24, 1968. Student, Am. Coll., Paris, 1963; Student, U. Madrid, 1964, Am. U., Washington, 1965, U. Florence, Italy, 1966, Cen. Piedmont Community Coll., Charlotte, N.C., 1984-86; student, Am. Coll., Bryn Mawr, Pa., 1982-89. Chartered fin. cons., CLU; registered investment advisor. Interpreter Desesco Internat.-Export Co., Florence, Italy, 1966-67; tri-lingual sec. U.S. Topographical Team, Livorno, Italy, 1967-68; mgr. internat. sales Whitin Internat., Charlotte, 1968-81; internat. sales cons. Concord (N.C.) Warehousing, 1981-82; agt., fin. planner Prin. Fin. Group, Charlotte, 1982-97; assoc. Consol. Planning, 1997—. Ind. intrepreter-translator, Charlotte, 1968-2000; instr. Italian, Cen. Piedmont C.C., 1970-80. Vol. Internat. House, Charlotte, 1986-2000. Mem. Internat. Assn. Fin. Planning, Am Soc. CLUs, Am. Soc. Chartered Fin. Cons., Nat. Assn. Life Underwriters (Nat. Quality award 1984, 86-2000, Nat. Sales Achievement award 1986-2000), Women Bus. Owners (charter, treas. 1986-2000), life mem. Million Dollar Round Table, Charter Prospectors Club, Charlotte Sales and Mktg. Club, Christopher Columbus Carolinas (founder, pres., bd. dirs.). Democrat. Roman Catholic. Home: 221 Scottridge Dr Charlotte NC 28217-4045 Office: Consolidated Planning Inc 4201 Congress St Ste 350 Charlotte NC 28209-4622 E-mail: jillabardi@aol.com.

LABAREE, BENJAMIN WOODS, history educator; b. New Haven, July 21, 1927; s. Leonard Woods and Elizabeth Mary (Calkins) L.; m. Linda Carol Prichard, June 27, 1959; children: Benjamin Woods Jr., Jonathan Martin, Sarah Calkins Churchill. BA, Yale U., 1950; AM, Harvard U., 1953, PhD, 1957. Instr. history Conn. Coll., New London, 1957-58; from instr. to asst. prof. history, Allston Burr Sr. tutor Harvard U., Cambridge, Mass., 1958-63; dean Williams Coll., Williamstown, 1963-67, assoc. to prof. history, 1963-77, Ephraim Williams Prof. Am. History, 1972-77; dir. Williams Coll.-Mystic Seaport Program/Mystic Seaport Mus., Mystic, Conn., 1977-89; dir. Ctr. for Environ. Studies Williams Coll., 1989-91, prof. history and environ. studies, 1989-92; prof. emeritus, 1992—. Vis. prof. Trinity Coll., Conn., 1993, Williams Coll., 1994, Clark U., 1997, Tufts U. Fletcher Sch. Law and Diplomacy, 1998; dir. Munson Inst. Am. Maritime Studies, Mystic, 1974-96; mng. editor Essex Inst. Hist . Collections, Salem, Mass., 1956-60; co-dir. summer inst. Am. and the Sea NEH, 1996. Author: Patriots and Partisans, 1962, The Boston Tea Party, 1964, America's Nation-Time, 1972, Colonial Massachusetts, 1979; co-author: New England and The Sea, 1972, The Atlantic World of Robert G. Albion, 1975, Empire or Independence, 1976, America and the Sea, 1998; editor: The William Gottlieb Schauttler Family in America, 2002; mem. editl. bd.: American Neptune, 1996—. Mem. Mt. Greylock Regional H.S. Com., Williamstown, 1971-74; bd. dirs. Newburyport Maritime Soc., 1991-99, Lowell's Boat Shop trust, 1992-99. With USNR, 1945-46. Recipient Wilbur Cross award Conn. Humanities Coun., 1990, Samuel Eliot Morison award USS Constitution Mus., 1993, Citation of Honour, Soc. Colonial Wars, 1978; co-recipient John Lyman award N.Am. Soc. Oceanic History, 1999. Mem. Am. Hist. Assn. (com. 1971-73), Am. Antiquarian Soc., Colonial Soc. Mass., Mass. Hist. Soc., Inst. for Early Am. History and Culture (coun. mem. 1983-86), others. Democrat. Unitarian-Universalist. Avocations: sailing, rowing, swimming. Home and Office: 2 Andrews Ln Amesbury MA 01913-4102

LABAREE, DAVID FLEMING, educator; b. Phila., May 17, 1947; s. Benjamin and Jean Ridgley L.; m. Mary Elizabeth Murray, June 10, 1979 (div. Mar. 1987); m. Diane Marie Churchill, Oct. 10, 1992. BA, Harvard Coll., 1970; MA, U. Pa., 1978, PhD, 1983. Asst. prof. Mich. State U., East Lansing, 1985-88, assoc. prof., 1988-98, prof., 1998—. Author: The Making of an American High School, 1988, How to Succeed in School Without Really Learning, 1997. Office: Mich State U 116R Erickson Hall East Lansing MI 48824-1034

LABARGE, CHRISTOPHER W. priest; b. Pittsfield, Mass., May 9, 1953; s. Paul Willson LaB. and Nanette Marie Passier. BA in Sacred Theology, St. Francis de Sales Coll., Milw., 1979; STB, MDiv, St. Mary's Sem. and U., Balt., 1985; STL, St. Mary's Sem. and Univ., Balt., 1986. Ordained priest Roman Cath. Ch., 1985. Assoc. pastor Our Lady of Fatima, New Castle , Del., 1985—88, St. Elizabeth's , Wilmington, 1988—92, Holy Cross, Dover, 1992—95; adminstr. Immaculate Conception, Marydel, Md., 1995—96, pastor, 1996—. Chaplain Wilmington Fire Dept., 1989—92; leadership W.W. Marriage Encounter, Wilmington, 1992—95. Bd. dirs. Choptank Cmty. Health, Denton, Md., 2000—, Social Svcs. Adv. Bd., Denton, 1998—. Mem.: KC (friar 4th degree 1993—, Del. state chaplain 1998—2000). Home: 517 Main St PO Box 411 Marydel MD 21649 Office: Immaculate Conception PO Box 399 Marydel MD 21649

LABARGE, MARGARET WADE, medieval history educator; b. N.Y.C., July 18, 1916; arrived in Can., 1940; d. Alfred Byers and Helena (Mein) Wade; m. Raymond C. Labarge, June 20, 1940 (dec. May 1972); children: Claire Labarge Morris, Suzanne, Charles, Paul. BA, Radcliffe Coll., 1937; LittB, Oxford (Eng.) U., 1939; LittD (hon.), Carleton U., Ottawa, Ont., Can., 1976; LLD (hon.), U. Waterloo, Ont., Can., 1993. Lectr. history U. Ottawa, Carleton U., 1950-62; adj. prof. history Carleton U., Ottawa, 1983—. Author: Simon de Montfort, 1962, A Baronial Household, 1965, Gascony, 1980, A Small Sound of the Trumpet, 1987, A Medieval Miscellany, 1997, others; contbr. articles to profl. jours. Bd. dirs. St. Vincent's Hosp., Ottawa, 1969-81; chmn. 1977-79; pub. rep. bd. dirs. Can. Nurses Assn., 1980-83; bd. dirs. Carleton U., 1984-93, Coun. on Aging, 1986-93 (pres., 1989-91). Recipient Alumnae Recognition award Radcliffe Coll., 1987. Fellow Royal Soc. Can.; mem. Medieval Acad., Soc. of Can. Medievalists (pres. 1993-94), Order of Can., Phi Beta Kappa. Roman Catholic. Avocations: traveling, reading, walking. Home and Office: 402-555 Wilbrod St Ottawa ON Canada K1N 5R4 E-mail: mwlabarge@sympatico.ca.

LABARGE, RICHARD ALLEN, financial analyst, educator; b. Salt Lake City, May 6, 1934; s. Oza Joseph and Mae (Erdman) LaB.; m. Catherine Eulalie Laurent, June 10, 1953 (div. 1979); children: R. Allen Jr., Catherine, Joseph Laurent, Nedra Anne, Eve Marie, Mary Evangeline, Louis E.R.; m. Karin Louise Peterson, June 28, 1980; 1 child, Robert E.J. AB, U. Mich., 1954; MA, Tulane U., 1955; PhD, Duke U., 1960. Chartered fin. analyst, 1982. Asst. prof. So. Methodist U., Dallas, 1957-60; treas., fin. analyst, spl. legis. analyst world hdqrs. Ford Motor Co., Dearborn, 1960-65; assoc. prof. Fla. State U., Tallahassee, 1965-67; prof. econs. and fin. U. New Orleans, 1967-89, chair dept., 1967-73; prof. Rutgers U., Camden, N.J., 1990-92; prin. Capital Choices, Inc., 1992—. Fin. economist U.S. SEC, Washington, summer, 1977; cons. bd. regents State U. System Fla., Tallahassee, Miami, 1989; lectr. Fin. Analysts' Rev., Raleigh, N.C., 1989-92, Zurich, Switzerland, 1990, Bangkok, Thailand, 1993. Author: (monograph) Impact of United Front on Economic Development of Guatemala, 1960; contbr. articles to internat. profl. jours. Rsch. tng. fellow Social Sci. Rsch. Coun., Washington, 1956-57, Sr. Fulbright-Hays prof., Mexico, 1973-74. Mem. Assn. for Investment Mgmt. Rsch. N.Y. Soc. Security Analyst, Nat. Assn. Bus. Economists (New Orleans chpt., pres. 1972-73, 75-76), Mich. Alumni Assn. (New Orleans chpt., pres. 1985-89). Republican. Avocations: computer programming, travel. Home: 160 Ardmore Ave Haddonfield NJ 08033-1428 Office: Capital Choices Inc 160 Ardmore Ave Haddonfield NJ 08033-1428

LABARR, THOMAS C. electrical engineer, consultant; s. Charles D. and Jane E. (Persbacker) LaBarr; m. Aimee Marie Hubbard, Jan. 2, 1986. Electronic technician Siemens, Scottsdale, Ariz., 1972—77; sr. electronic technician Lorlin, Danbury, Conn., 1977—82, electronic engr., 1982—87, mgr. quality control/assurance, 1987—90; electronic support engr. SUNY , New Paltz, NY, 1991—. Author: (quality control) Quality Control in Semiconductor Test Equipment, 1989. Bd. mem. Beacon Landing Project, Beacon, NY, 2002—02; v.p. Fishkill Ridge Caretakers, Fishkill, 1999—2002. Seaman USN, 1968—71. Mem.: Union Concerned Scientists, Fishkill Ridge Caretakers (v.p. 1999—2002), Beacon Sloop Club (pres. 1980—83, v.p. 2001—02, chmn. environ. edn./action com. 1983—2002). Liberal. Avocations: gardening, hiking, sailing. Home: 1347 Route 9D Beacon NY 12508 Personal E-mail: labarrt@engr.newpaltz.edu. E-mail: labarrt@engr.newpaltz.edu.

LABARRE, CARL ANTHONY, retired government official; b. Sherwood, N.D., July 16, 1918; s. William Paul and Josephine K. LaB.; m. Persis Wester, Sept. 9, 1941; 1 son, William Paul, II. Student. U. Mont., 1936-40; postgrad., Naval Acad. Postgrad. Sch., 1945-46; grad., Naval War Coll., 1958-59, Advanced Mgmt. Program, Harvard U. Commd. ensign U.S. Navy, 1941, advanced through grades to capt., 1971; served in various fin., inventory control systems and purchasing assignments, to 1971; insp. gen. (Naval Supply Systems Command), to 1971; ret., 1971; dep. dir. materials mgmt. service GPO, Washington, 1971-75, dir. materials mgmt. service, 1975, asst. public printer, supt. documents, 1975-82. Decorated Navy Commendation medal with V, Joint Service commendation medal, Legion of Merit with gold star; recipient Public Printers Disting. Service award, 1977, 81 Mem.: Harvard Bus. Sch. (Washington).

L'ABATE, LUCIANO, psychologist; b. Brindisi, Italy, Sept. 19, 1928; came to U.S., 1948; s. Govanni and Alma (Zaccaro) L'A.; m. Bess Lukas, Aug. 30, 1958; children: John W., Elisabeth L. BA, Tabor Coll., 1950, MA, Wichita State U., 1953; PhD, Duke U., 1956. Diplomate Am. Bd. Profl. Psychologists; lic. psychologist, Ga. Psychologist Pitt County Health Dept., Greenville, N.C., 1956-57; USPH fellow Michael Reese Hosp., Chgo., 1958-59; asst. prof. Washington U. Med. Sch., St. Louis, 1959-64; assoc. prof. Emery U. Med. Sch., Atlanta, 1964-65; prof. Ga. State U., 1965-90, prof. emeritus, 1991—; dir., owner Workbooks for Better Living, 1997—. Author: Principles of Clinical Psychology, 1964, (with L.T. Curtis) Teaching the Exceptional Child, 1975, Understanding and Helping the Individual in the Family, 1976, Enrichment: Structured Interventions with Couples, Families, and Groups, 1977, (with B.L. L'Abate) How to Avoid Divorce: Help for Troubled Marriages, 1977, (with G. Rupp) Enrichment: Skill Training for Family Life, 1981, (with J.C. Hansen) Approaches to Family Therapy, 1982, (with G. Weeks) Paradoxical Therapy: Theory and Practice with Individuals, Couples and Families, 1982, Family Psychology: Theory, Therapy and Training, 1983, (with S. McHenry) Handbook of Marital Interventions, 1983, (with R.S. Sauber and G. Weeks) Family Therapy: Basic Concepts and Terms, 1985, Systematic Family Therapy, 1986, (with G. Ganahl and J.C. Hansen) Methods of Family Therapy, 1986, Family Psychology II: Theory, Therapy, Enrichment, and Training, 1987, (with S.E. Weinstein) Structured Enrichment Programs for Couples and Families, 1987), (with L. Young) Casebook of Structured Enrichment Programs for Couples and Families, 1987, Building Family Competence: Primary and Secondary Prevention Strategies, 1990, Programmed Writing: A Self-Administered Approach for Interventions with Individuals, Couples and Families, 1992; editor: Values, Ethics and Legalities in Family Therapy, 1982, Handbook of Family Psychology and Therapy, vols. I and II, 1985; editor (with M. Milan) Handbook of Social Skills Training and Research, 1985, (with Jack E. Farrar and Dan A. Serritella) Handbook of Differential Treatments for Addictions, 1992, (with D.A. Bagarozzi) Sourcebook of Marriage and Family Evaluation, 1993, (with S.R. Sauber, G. Weeks & W. Buchanan) Dictionary of Family Psychology and Family Therapy, 1993, A Theory of Personality Development, 1994, Handbook of Developmental Family Psychology and Psychopathology, 1994, Family Evaluation: A Psychological Approach, 1994, The Self in the Family: Toward a Classification of Personality, Criminality, and Psychopathology, 1997, Family Psychopathology: The Relational Roots of Dysfunctional Behavior, 1998, Distance Writing and Computer-Assisted Interventions in Psychiatry and Mental Health, 2001, Family Psychology III. Theory-Building and Theory Testing, Prevention, and Psychotherapy, 2002, Beyond Psychotherapy: Programmed Writing and Computer-Assisted Interventions, 2003, Workbooks in Mental Health, 2003; contbr. over 250 articles to profl. jours. Recipient Rsch. awards USPHS,

Greenville, N.C., 1956-58, St. Louis, Mo., 1959-62. Fellow AAAS, APA, Internat. Acad. Family Psychology (co-founder, pres. 1990-91), others. Address: 2079 Deborah Dr NE Atlanta GA 30345-3917 Office: 2079 Deborah Dr NE Atlanta GA 30345-3917

LABAY, EUGENE BENEDICT, lawyer; b. El Campo, Tex., July 20, 1938; s. Ben F. and Cecelia M. (Orsak) L.; m. Katherine Sue Ermis, Dec. 29, 1962; children: Michael, Joan, John, Paul, David, Patrick, Steven. BBA, St. Mary's U., San Antonio, 1960; JD, St. Mary's U., 1965. Bar: Tex. 1965, U.S. Dist. Ct. (we. dist.) Tex. 1968, U.S. Dist. Ct. (no. dist.) Tex. 1973, U.S. Dist. Ct. (ea. dist.) Tex. 1986, U.S. Ct. Appeals (5th cir.) 1968, U.S. Ct. Appeals (11th cir.) 1981, U.S. Supreme Ct. 1980. Briefing atty. Supreme Ct. Tex., Austin, 1965-66; assoc. Cox & Smith Inc., San Antonio, 1966-71, ptnr., 1972-83, v.p., 1972-94; pvt. practice, 1994—. Contbr. articles to profl. jours. Served to 1st lt. U.S. Army, 1960-62. Mem. ABA, State Bar Tex. (chmn. sect. internat. law 1979-80), San Antonio Bar Assn., Fed. Bar Assn., Am. Judicature soc., Cath. Lawyers Guild San Antonio, KC (coun. grand knight 1982-83), Phi Delta Phi. Home: 31720 Post Oak Trl Boerne TX 78015-4133 Office: PO Box 15244 112 W Craig Pl San Antonio TX 78212-3416

LABAYEN, LOUIE ANTHONY LOPEZ, information analyst, consultant; b. Manila, Jan. 17, 1960; came to U.S., 1976; s. Wilfredo Lizares and Rose Jocelyn Ocampo (Lopez) L.; m. Rosalinda Maglonzo Torres, June 6, 1987; children: John Gustav Torres, James Daniel Torres. BA, De La Salle U., Manila, 1981; MusM, U. No. Colo., 1986. Mgr. Network Mgmt. Corp., Kansas City, Mo., 1988-90; sr. analyst Blue Cross Blue Shield, 1990-94; v.p. Patriot Mortgage Co., 1994; team leader Tapestry Computing, 1994-95; sr. cons. Oracle Corp., 1995; devel. mgr. Uniband, Inc., 1995-96; mng. prin. Paladin Data Sys., Inc., 1996—; ind. bus. owner Quixtar, 1999—. Lectr. Mt. Carmel Coll., Baler, Philippines, 1982-83; project leader Blue Cross Blue Shield, 1991-94. Mem. Am. Symphony Orch. League, 1985—. Mem. IEEE, Internat. Oracle Users Group, Mu Phi Epsilon, Rotary (exch. student Antwerp, Ohio 1976), K.C. Avocations: photography, gourmet cooking, sailing, golf, architecture. Home and Office: 152 Madrona Dr NW Gig Harbor WA 98335-5927

LABBE, ARMAND JOSEPH, curator, anthropologist; b. Lawrence, Mass., June 13, 1944; s. Armand Henri and Gertrude Marie (Martineau) L.; m. Denise Marie Scott, Jan. 17, 1969 (div. 1972). BA in Anthropology, Univ. Mass., 1969; MA in Anthropology, Calif. State U., 1986; lifetime instr. credential in anthropology, State Calif. Curator collections Bowers Mus., Santa Ana, Calif., 1978-79, curator anthropology, 1979-86, chief curator, 1986—, dir. rsch. and collections, 1991—. Instr. prof. Santa Ana Coll., 1981-86, U. Calif., Irvine, 1983, 87, 91, 93, Calif. State U., Fullerton, 1982, 83, 88, 97, 98, 99, part-time faculty, appt. rsch. assoc. dept. anthropology, 1997—, Calif. State U., Fullerton; trustee Balboa Arts Conservation Ctr., San Diego, 1989-97, Ams. Found., Greenfield, Mass., 1985-94, Quintcentenary Festival Discovery, Orange County, Calif., 1990-91, Mingei Internat. Mus., La Jolla, Calif., 1993—, treas. bd. dirs. 1996—; inaugural guest lectr. Friends of Ethnic Art, San Francisco, 1988; hon. bd. dirs., Ethnic Arts Coun., L.A.; mem. Orange County 46th Congressional Dist. Art Bd., 1997—. Author: Man and Cosmos, 1982, Ban Chiang, 1985, Colombia Before Columbus, 1986 (1st prize 1987), Leigh Wiener: Portraits, 1987, Colombia Antes de Colón, 1988 (honored at Gold Mus. Bogotá, Colombia, 1988), Images of Power: Master Works of the Bowers Museum of Cultural Art, 1992, Pre-Columbian Art: Marine Animal Forms, 2001; co-author Tribute to The Gods: Treasures of the Museo del Oro, Bogotá, 1992, Guardians of the Life Stream: Shamans, Art and Power In Prehispanic Central Panama, 1995, Shamans, Gods, and Mythic Beasts: Colombian Gold and Ceramics in Antiquity, 1998; contbg. author: What Is A Shaman: Shamans and Medicine Men From A Western Point of View, 1999. Hon. bd. dirs. Ethnic Arts Coun. L.A.; cons. Orange County Coun. on History and Art, Santa Ana, 1981-85; mem. Task Force on County Cultural Resources, Orange County, 1979; cons., interviewer TV prodn. The Human Journey, Fullerton, 1986-89; treas., bd. trustees Mingei Internat. Mus., San Diego, 1996—; mem. art bd. Orange County 46th Congl. Dist., 1997—. With USAF, 1963-67. Recipient cert. of Recognition Orange County Bd. Suprs., 1982, award for outstanding scholarship Colombian Community, 1987, Distinguished Citizens for the Arts award NAACP, 1999, cert. of recognition Calif. State Senate, 1999; honored for authorship Friends of Libr., 1987, 88; grantee Nat. Endowment for Arts, 1994, NEH, 2000. Fellow Am. Anthrop. Assn.; mem. AAAS, Am. Assn. Mus., N.Y. Acad. Scis., S.W. Anthrop. Assn. Avocations: photography, travel. Home: 2854 Royal Palm Dr Apt C Costa Mesa CA 92626-3828 E-mail: labbe@bowers.org.

LABBE, SLUGGER, race car driver; Crew chief Kenny Irwin (driver) Dale Earnhardt Inc, Mooresville, NC, 1998—2001, crew chief Michael Waltrip (driver), 2001—. Office: Dale Earnhardt Inc 1675 Coddle Creek Hwy Mooresville NC 28115-8245

LABBETT, JOHN EDGAR, senior financial executive; b. Chesham, Bucks, Eng., June 19, 1950; came to U.S., 1987; s. Gordon F. and Sylvia (Dalton) L.; m. Mary McGagh, Jan. 30, 1976; children: Jennifer F., Alexander T. Audit clk. White Withers and Co., Bexhill, Eng., 1966-71; auditor Peat Marwick Mitchell, London, 1971-73; chief acct. Guild S&V Ltd., 1973-74; from fin. analyst to contr. Roneo Vickers Ltd., 1974-81; fin. contr. Cambridge (Eng.) Instruments Ltd., 1981-82; fin. dir. Linfood C&C Ltd. subsid. Dee Corp., Milton Keynes, U.K., 1982-85; fin. controller Dee Corp., Milton Keines, 1985-87; exec. v.p., chief fin. officer Hermans Sporting Goods, Inc., Carteret, N.J., 1987-93; v.p., CFO The Petfood Giant, Inc., 1994-95; exec. v.p., chief fin. officer House of Fabrics, Inc., Sherman Oaks, Calif., 1995-98; exec. v.p., CFO Egghead.com, Inc., Menlo Park, 1998-2001; CFO Millenium Networks, Inc., North Hollywood, 2001, New.Net, Sherman Oaks, 2002—. Fellow Inst. Chartered Accts. Eng. and Wales. Mem. Ch. Eng. Home: 80 Stagecoach Rd Bell Canyon CA 91307-1042

LABBE-WEBB, ELIZABETH GERALYN, arts administrator, theatre artist; b. Akron, Ohio, Oct. 7, 1966; d. Edward James and Ruth Carolyn (Petree) L. BA in Theatre Arts, Kent State U., 1989. Contract prodn. technician Players' Theatre Columbus, Ohio, 1989-91; asst. prodn./co. mgr. Phila. Festival Theatre, 1991-92; costume asst. Am. Music Theatre Festival, Phila., 1991-92; office asst. Players' Theatre Columbus, 1992-93; audio description coord. Ohio Theatre Alliance, Columbus, 1993-94; sr. devel. assoc., grants mgr. Opera Assn. Ctrl. Ohio, 1994-99, assoc. dir. devel., 1998-2000; freelance stage mgr., freelance acting tchr., 1994—; project mgr. The Bus. of Art, 2000—02. V.p. Rosebriar Shakespeare Co., Columbus, 1995-96, pres. 1997-98. Chpt. leader, chpt. arts officer Soc. for Creative Anachronism, 1995-2002; adv., vol. Canine Companions for Independence; creative cons. Found. for Environ. Edn., 2001-02; fundraising cons. Columbus Light Opera, 2000-2001. Personal Devel. grant Jefferson Ctr. for the Arts, 1994. Mem. Ohio Prospect Rsch. Network (bd. dirs. 1997-2001).

LABE, ROBERT BRIAN, lawyer; b. Detroit, Sept. 2, 1959; s. Benjamin Mitchell and Gloria Florence (Wright) L.; m. Mary Lou Budman, Nov. 12, 1989; two children: Bridget and Katherine. BA with high honors, Mich. State U., 1981; JD, Wayne State U., 1984; LLM, Boston U., 1985. Bar: Mich. 1984, U.S. Dist. Ct. Mich. 1985, U.S. Tax Ct. 1985. Assoc. Weingarden & Hauer, P.C., Bingham Farms, Mich., 1988-92, shareholder, 1992-94; prin. Robert B. Labe, P.C., Southfield, 1994—2002; mem. Dickinson Wright, PLLC, Bloomfield Hills, 2002—. Adj. prof. taxation and estate planning Walsh Coll., Troy, Mich., 1990-92; lectr. and presenter in field. Author: Research Edge-Taxation Guide, 1994, Bus. Succession Planning, 1996, Family Limited Liability Cos. and Limited Partnerships, 1998; mem. publ. adv. bd. Inst. Continuing Legal Edn. U. Mich., 1993—; contbr. articles to profl. jours. Bd. dirs. Oakland Bar, Oakland County Bar Found. Avocations: tennis, spectator sports. Office: Dickinson Wright PLLC 38525 Woodward Ave # 2000 Bloomfield Hills MI 48304 E-mail: labelaw1@home.msen.com.

LABELLE, THOMAS JEFFREY, academic administrator; b. Owen, Wis., Sept. 21, 1941; s. Wendell Allen and Katherine (Dolan) LaB.; m. Nancy Reik, June 16, 1966 (dec. 1981); children: Katherine Anne, Jeanette Marie AA, Pierce Coll., Woodland Hills, Calif., 1962; BA, Calif. State U., Northridge, 1964; MA, U. N.Mex., Albuquerque, 1967, PhD, 1969. Prof. UCLA, 1969-86, asst. dean edn., 1971-79, assoc. dean grad. div., 1980-86; prof. comparative and internat. edn. U. Pitts., 1986-90, dean Sch. Edn., 1986-90; v.p. acad. programs, provost Ga. State U., Atlanta, 1990-93; provost, v.p. acad. affairs and rsch. W.Va. U., Morgantown, 1993-96; provost v.p. acad. affairs San Francisco State U., 1996—2002; exec. dir. internat. and area studies U. Calif., Berkeley, Calif., 2002—. Cons. InterAm. Found., U.S. AID, Ford Found., CBS, Acad. Ednl. Devel., Juarez and Assocs. Author: Education and Development in Latin America, 1972, Nonformal Education in Latin America and the Caribbean, 1986, Stability, Reform or Revolution, 1986, Education and Intergroup Relations, 1985, Multiculturalism and Education, 1994, Ethnic Studies and Multiculturalism, 1996. Vol. Peace Corps, Colombia, 1964-66. Grantee Fulbright Found., 1983, 96, InterAm. Found., Latin America, 1984; recipient Andres Bello award 1st Class, Venezuela, 1987. Fellow Soc. Applied Anthropology; mem. Comparative and Internat. Edn. Soc. (pres. 1981), Coun. on Anthropology and Edn. (bd. dirs. 1977), Inter-Am. Found. (chmn. learning fellowship on social change), Golden Key, Omicron Delta Kappa, Phi Kappa Phi. Democrat. Office: U California IAS 360 Stephens Hall Berkeley CA 94720-2300

LABENSKY, SARAH ROSS, culinary educator; b. Murray, Ky., Mar. 16, 1958; d. James Mason and Lucille Thomson Ross; m. Steven Jay Labensky, Oct. 14, 1983 (div. May 1995); m. Louis David Moline, Sept. 3, 1995. BS, Murray (Ky.) State U., 1980; JD, Vanderbilt U., 1983; cert., Scottsdale C.C., 1986. Atty. Hocker and Axford, Tempe, Ariz., 1983-85; cook/chef Phoenix, 1985-90; prof. Scottsdale C.C., 1990-98; dir. Miss. U. for Women Culinary Arts Inst., Columbus, 1998—. Author: On Cooking, 1995, 2d edit., 1999 (IACP nominee 1995), Webster's N.W. Dictionary of Culinary Arts, 1997, 2d edit., 2000, Applied Math for Food Service, 1998. Mem. Am. Culinary Fedn., Internat. Assn. Culinary Profls. (bd. dirs. 1999—, sec.-treas., 2002, cert. culinary profl.). Office: Miss Univ for Women Box W-1639 Columbus MS 39701

LABENZ-HOUGH, MARLENE, dispute resolution professional; b. St. Edward, Nebr., May 25, 1954; d. Ralph Labenz and Lorene (Laudenklos); m. Jeff Hough, Mar. 5, 1983. Assocs., Platte Coll., 1974; BS in Social Work magna cum laude, U. Nebr., 1976; MA in Clin. Psychology, Trinity U., 1980. Adminstrv. asst., mgmt. analyst II City of San Antonio Dept. Human Resources and Svcs., 1980, adminstrv. asst. II, 1980-82, casework supr., Victims of Crime Program, 1982-89, program coord., Children's Resources Dvsn., 1989-90; asst. dir. Bexar County Dispute Resolution Ctr., San Antonio, 1990-92, dir., 1992—. Bd. dirs. KidShare, 1993-96, YWCA, 1990-93; mem. ADR sect. coun. State Bar Tex., 1996-99. Mem.: Assn. Family and Conciliation Cts., Tex. Mediators Credentialing Assn., Alamo Area Mediators Assn., Tex. Dispute Resolution Ctrs. Dirs. Coun., Tex. Mediation Trainers' Roundtable, Assn. Conflict Resolution, Conflict Resolution and Peer Mediation Coun., Nat. Assn. Cmty. Mediation (founding dir.), Soc. Profls. in Dispute Resolution (co-chair S.W. region chpt. 1993, co-chair nat. conf. 1995, Profl. Dedication award 1994), Acad. Family Mediators, Tex. Assn. Mediators (chair conf. 1999, bd. dirs. 1999—2002), Coll. Tex. Mediators, Alpha Xi Delta. Home: 2518 Ashton Village Dr San Antonio TX 78248-2200

LABER, DAMIAN ABEL, internist, hematologist, oncologist, educator; b. Buenos Aires, Feb. 28, 1968; came to U.S., 1994; s. Manuel and Juana Felisa Laber; m. Rosalia Laber, Sept. 7, 1996. MD, U. Buenos Aires, 1992. Diplomate Am. Bd. Internal Medicine, subspecialty hematology and med. oncology. Intern in internal medicine to resident Meridia Huron Hosp., Cleve., 1994-97; fellow hematology, oncology Baylor Coll. Medicine, Houston, 1997—; asst. prof. medicine, asst. scientist, dir. genito-urinary clin. rsch. program U. Louisville, 2001—, dir. med. oncology and hematology fellowship program, 2001—. Office: U Louisville James Graham Brown Cancer Ctr 529 S Jackson St Ste 205 Louisville KY 40202

LABER, JERI LIDSKY, writer, human rights activist; b. N.Y.C., May 19, 1931; d. Louis and Mae (Zias) Lidsky; m. Austin A. Laber, Oct. 3, 1954 (div. 1982); children: Abigail, Pamela, Emily; m. Charles M. Kuskin, June 19, 1994. BA, NYU, N.Y.C., 1952; MA, cert. Russian Inst., Columbia U., 1954. Fgn. editor Current Digest of Soviet Press, 1954-56; publs. dir. Inst. for Study of USSR, N.Y.C., 1958-70; free-lance author, journalist, 1970-77; exec. dir. Internat. Freedom to Publish Com., Assn. Am. Pubs., N.Y.C., 1977—; dir. Fund for Free Expression, 1977-79; exec. dir. Helsinki Watch, 1979-95; sr. adviser Human Rights Watch, 1995-2001. Vice-chair Internat. Helsinki Fedn., Vienna, Austria, 1986-93; mem. vis. com. New Sch. U., N.Y.C., 1990-96. Author: The Courage of Strangers: Coming of Age with the Human Righs Movement, 2002; co-author: A Nation is Dying-Afghanistan Under the Soviets, 1979-87, 1987, Cooking for Carefree Weekends, 1976; co-author, editor numerous cookbooks including Fannie Farmer Cookbook, 1979; contbr. more than 100 articles to profl. jours. and newspapers. Decorated Order of Merit of the Czech Republic; recipient rsch. and writing award John D. and Catherine T. MacArthur Found., 2001. Mem. Coun. on Fgn. Rels. Avocations: gardening, cooking, needlework. Home: 67 Riverside Dr New York NY 10024-6135

LABINE, CATHERINE WILDER, civic worker; b. Springfield, Mass., Oct. 11, 1938; d. William Wallace and Edith (Russell) Wilder; m. Richard Armand Labine; children: Sherry Labine Donovan, Todd Richard, Alyssa Labine Collins. BS in Math., U. Mass., 1960. Committeewoman Mass. Rep. Com., 1980—; mem. Mass. Gov.'s Commn. on Women's Issues, 1991-94; mem., vice chmn. Mass. State Coll. Bldg. Authority, 1992—; chmn. acad. and campus affairs com. Mass. Bd. Higher Edn., Boston, 1992—. Methodist. Avocations: tennis, golf, art, music, investments. Home: 10 Highridge Rd Wilbraham MA 01095-2307

LA BLANC, ROBERT EDMUND, consulting company executive; b. N.Y.C., Mar. 21, 1934; s. Charles Wesley and Anne R. (Dobson) La B.; m. Elizabeth Lammers, 1962; children: Elizabeth, Robert, Jeanne Marie, Paul, Michelle. B.E.E., Manhattan Coll., 1956; DHL honoris causa (hon.), Manhattan Coll., 1997; MBA, NYU, 1962. With Bell System, 1956-69; mem. tech. staff Bell Telephone Labs., 1961-62; seminar leader AT&T Long Lines, Cooperstown, N.Y., 1965-67; mktg. supr. AT&T Hdqrs., N.Y.C., 1967-68; planning engr. N.Y. Telephone, 1968-69; mgr. Salomon Bros., N.Y.C., 1969-73, v.p., 1973-75, gen. partner, 1975-79; vice chmn. Continental Telephone Corp., N.Y.C., 1979-81; pres. Robert E. LaBlanc Assocs., Inc., 1981—. Bd. dirs. Chartered Semicondr. Mfg. Ltd., Singapore, Computer Assocs. Internat., Inc., Storage Tech. Corp., Titan Corp., Prudential Diversified Series-High Conservative Growth, Prudential Diversified Series-High Growth, Prudential Diversified Series-Moderate Growth, Global Utility Fund, Target Portfolio Trust, Target Large Capitalization Value Portfolio, Target Large Capitalization Growth Portfolio, Target US Gov. Money Market Portfolio, Target Internat. Bond Portfolio, Target Internat. Equity Portfolio, Target Intermediate Equity Portfolio, Target Intermediate Term Bond Portfolio, Target Mortgate Backed Securities Portfolio, Target Small Capitalization Growth Portfolio, Target Small Capitalization Value Portfolio, Target Funds: Target Internat. Equity, Target Total Return Bond, Target Large Cap Growth, Target Large Cap Value, Target Small Cap Growth, Target Small Cap Value, Prudential World Fund-Internat. Value Fund, Prudential World Fund-Global Growth Fund, Prudential Jennison Internat. Growth Fund, Prudential Natural Resources Fund, Prudential Global Genesis Fund, Prudential Pacific Growth Fund, Prudential L.Am. Equity Fund, Prudential Developing Markets Equity, Prudential European Growth Fund, Prudtneial MoneyMarket Assets, PILP, Prudential Tax Free Money, Spl. Money Market, Cash Accumulation Trust-Liquid Assets Fund, Cash Acculuation Trust-Nat. Money Market Fund, Command Money Fund, Command Govt. Fund, Command Tax-Free Fund. Vice chmn. bd. trustees Manhattan Coll., 1987-93, trustee, 1994—. Served to 1st lt. USAF, 1956-59. Named Wall St. Leading Analyst Instl. Investor Mag., 1973-78 Fellow: Fin. Analysts Fedn.; mem.: Assn. for Computing Machinery, NY Soc. Security Analysts (sr.), Econ. Club, Univ. Club, Equestrian Order Holy Sepulchre of Jerusalem (knight). Republican. Roman Catholic. E-mail: rLaBlanc@aol.com.

LABODA, GERALD, oral and maxillofacial surgeon; b. Phila., Aug. 15, 1936; s. Lewis and Rose (Waldman) L.; m. Sheila Lois Plasky, Aug. 2, 1956; children: Amy, Michèle, Alane, Bruce. Student, Temple U., 1954-56, DMD, 1960; postgrad., U. Pa., 1960-61. Diplomate Am. Bd. Oral and Maxillofacial Surgery. Resident physician in oral and maxillofacial surgery Jefferson U. Hosp., Phila., 1961-63; pvt. practice oral and maxillofacial surgery S.W. Fla. Oral and Facial Surgery Assocs., Ft. Myers, 1965—. Bd. dirs Nationsbank, S.W. Fla., 1974-99; chmn. bd. trustees S.W. Fla. Regional Med. Ctr., Ft. Myers, 1989-94, sec. bd. trustees, 1974-89; med. dir. S.W. Fla. divsn. Columbia/HCA Healthcare Corp., 1994-99; trustee East Pointe Hosp. Lehigh, Fla., Gulf Coast Hosp., Ft. Myers; v.p. Flordeco, Inc.; chmn. bd. dirs. Procraft Industries, L.L.C. Contbr. articles to profl. jours. Pres. YMCA of Lee County, 1976; pres., bd. dirs. Found. for LEe County Pub. Schs., Ft. Myers, Fla., 1981, Fla. Gulf Coast Univ. Found.; vice chmn. Downtown Redevel. Agy., Ft. Myers, 1985—93; chmn., 1993—; bd. dirs. United Way of Lee County, 1981, Fla. Repertory Theater, 1999—, chmn., 2001—; mem. bd. dentistry State of Fla., 1999—. Fellow Am. Assn. Oral and Maxillofacial Surgeons (trustee Dist. III 1984-87, v.p. 1987-88, pres. 1989-90); mem. Fla. Soc. Oral and Maxillofacial Surgeons (pres. 1980-81), Fla. Dental Soc. of Anesthesiology (pres. 1978-79), S.W. Fla. Dental Soc. (pres. 1974), Southeastern Soc. Oral and Maxillofacial Surgery Found. (bd. dirs. 1993—, vice chmn. 1997, chmn. 1998-2000), bd. Dentistry, State of Fla., 1999—. Republican. Jewish. Avocations: flying, skiing, scuba diving, white water rafting. Office: SW Fla Oral Facial Surg Assocs Summerlin Med Park 5285 Summerlin Rd Fort Myers FL 33919-7602 E-mail: Splaboda@aol.com.

LABONTÉ, C(LARENCE) JOSEPH, financial and marketing executive; b. Salem, Mass. children: Linda, Joseph. BS, AME, Northeastern U.; MBA with distinction (Baker scholar), Harvard U. With H.P. Hood & Sons, Boston; project engr., mktg. coordinator Market Forge Co., Everett, Mass.; with ARA Services, Inc., Phila., exec. asst. to pres., v.p., exec. v.p.; pres. Western Co., Los Angeles; pres., chief operating officer, dir. Twentieth Century-Fox Film Corp., Beverly Hills, Calif.; chmn., chief exec. officer The Vantage Group Inc.; pres., chief operating officer Reebok Internat. Ltd., Canton, Mass.; also bd. dirs. Reebok Internat., Stoughton; chmn., CEO, Vantage Group, Inc., Palos Verdes, Calif.; pres., CEO, Jenny Craig, Internat., La Jolla, also bd. dirs., mem. exec. com. Del Mar. Bd. dirs. several cos.; founder Am. Bus. Initiative for Free South Africa; bd. dirs. U.S.-SALEP, Washington; mem. com. for econ. devel., Washington. Founding dir. South African Free Elections Fund; nat. bd. dirs. Big Bros. Am., 1970-74, pres.; bd. dirs. L.A. Philharm. Assn., 1990-94, pres., CEO, chmn. bd. dirs.; trustee Northeastern U.; mem. Harvard U. Bus. Sch. Fund; trustee Orthop. Hosp., L.A. Mem. Harvard U. Bus. Sch. Assn., Husky Assocs. Northeatern U., Huntington Soc., Human Rights Watch (Calif. exec. com.), Phila. Country Club Down Town Club, Vesper Club, Bankers Club San Francisco, 100 Club L.A. Office: The Vantage Group Inc PO Box 9488 Rancho Santa Fe CA 92067-4488 E-mail: vantagegroup@cox.net.

LABOON, LAWRENCE JOSEPH, personnel consultant; b. St. Louis, Aug. 4, 1938; s. Joseph Warren and Ruth (Aab) LaB.; children: Lindsey Beth, Allison Ruth; m. Glynys M. Brown, Sept. 16, 1989; children: Lawrence Bradley, Meredith Ashley. BS magna cum laude, Tex. Wesleyan U., 1962. Cert. pers. cons., 1968. Operating mgr. Firestone Tire & Rubber Co., Akron, Ohio, 1962-66; pres., CEO, Met. Pers., Inc., Phila., 1966—, chmn., 2000—; pres. Metro Tech, Valley Forge, 1977—, Metro Temps, Valley Forge, 1978—, Metro Med. , Valley Forge, Pa., 2001—, Transport Tng. Corp., Valley Forge, 1993—; dir. Alpha-Indian Rock Savs. and Loan Assn., chmn. compensation com., 1986-90; chmn. pvt. employment agy. adv. coun. Pa. Dept. Labor and Industry, 1973-82. Guest lectr. Drexel U., 1976-91; human resources del. to USSR, Citizen Amb. Program, 1991. Mem. People to People Internat. Mission to Vietnam and Asia, 1993; mem. exec. bd. Valley Forge Profl. Ctr., 2001—. With USAF, 1954—60. Mem. Nat. Employment Assn. (cert., state certification bd. chmn. 1969-71, bd. dirs. 1972-74, chmn. bd. regents 1973), Pa. Assn. Pers. Svcs. (pres. 1971-72, Blanchet Meml. award 1973), Nat. Assn. Pers. Cons., Am. Soc. Pers. Adminstrn., Mid-Atlantic Assn. Temporary Svcs. (pres. 1983-84), TEMPNET (bd. dirs. 1986-88), Nat. Assn. Profl. Employers, Exec. Riders Ltd. (pres. 1986-88), Glenhardie Condominium Assn. (non-resident exec. bd. 1989-91), Alpha Chi. Republican. Lutheran. Home: 255 Country Ln Phoenixville PA 19460-1708 Office: 1260 Valley Forge Rd Valley Forge PA 19482-0641 E-mail: ljl@metpersnl.com.

LABOON, ROBERT BRUCE, lawyer; b. St. Louis, June 14, 1941; s. Joseph Warren LaBoon and Ruth (Aab) LaBoon Freling; m. Ramona Ann Hudgins, Aug. 24, 1963; children: John Andrew, Robert Steven. BSc, Tex. Christian U., 1963; LLB cum laude, So. Meth. U., 1965. Bar: Tex. 1965. Ptnr. Locke Liddell & Sapp LLP, Houston, 1965-86, 88—; vice chmn. and gen. counsel Tex. Commerce Bancshares, Inc., 1986-88. Bd. dirs. Tex. Med. Ctr., Tex. Children's Hosp. Bd. dirs., chair The Greater Houston Partnership, Houston area ARC; trustee The Kayser Found.; mem. bd. visitors M.D. Anderson Cancer Ctr.-U. Cancer Found. Fellow Tex. Bar Found., Am. Coll. of Trust and Estate Counsel; mem. ABA, AM. Law Inst., Tex. Assn. of Bank Counsel, Houston Bar Assn., State Bar Tex., Houston Club, River Oaks Country Club. Office: Locke Liddell & Sapp LLP 600 Travis St Ste 3500 Houston TX 77002-3095

LABOR, EARLE GENE, English language educator; b. Tuskahoma, Okla., Mar. 3, 1928; s. Earle Labor and Sylvia Kirkpatrick Steger; m. Betty Garrett, Sept. 21, 1952 (dec. Aug. 1989); children: Royce, Kirk, Kyle, Isabel; m. Gayle Johnson, May 25, 1996; 1 child, Andrea. AB, So. Meth. U., Dallas, 1949, MA, 1952; PhD, U. Wis., Madison, 1961. Instr. English So. Meth. U., Dallas, 1950-52; asst. sales mgr. Haggar Co., 1954-55; instr. English Centenary Coll., Shreveport, La., 1955-56, asst. prof. English, 1959-62, George A. Wilson prof. Am. Lit. La., 1966—; tchg. asst. U. Wis., Madison, 1956-59; head dept. English, chmn. dept. Humanities Adrian (Mich.) Coll., 1962-66. Adv. bd. Jack London Found., Glen Ellen, Calif., 1973—. Author: Jack London, 1974, 96; co-author: A Handbook of Critical Approaches to Literature, 1966, 74, 92, 96; co-editor: The Letters of Jack London, 1988, The Complete Short Stories of Jack London, 1993; editor: Viking Portable Jack London, 1996. Fulbright prof., Denmark, 1973-74; named Jack London Man of Yr. Jack London Found., 1975, Humanist of Yr. La. Endowment for Humanities, 1991. Mem. MLA, Coll. English Assn. (editor 1967-75, pres. 1977-79, Disting. Svc. award 1983, Lifetime Membership award 1990), Internat. Assn. Univ. Profs. of English, Jack London Soc. (bd. dirs. 1990—), Nat. Assn. Scholars and Critics. Avocation: photography.

LABOR, GAYLE JOHNSON, English language educator; b. Chgo., July 22, 1949; d. Arthur Wilbur and Gene Adele (Gehrung) Johnson; m. Earle Gene Labor, May 25, 1996. BA in English cum laude, Centenary Coll., 1971; MA in Am. Studies, Bowling Green (Ohio) State U., 1972. Lectr. in English Centenary Coll., Shreveport, La., 1973-75; assoc. prof. English Bossier Parish Community Coll., Bossier City, 1975—. Mem. Humane Soc. of the U.S., 1984—, Shreveport Regional Arts Coun., 1985—. Mem. MLA, Coll. English Assn., North La. Hist. Assn. (Max Bradbury award 1994), Am. Studies Assn., Cambridge Club. Democrat. Presbyterian. Avocations: travel, reading, modern dance, dog obedience training. Home: 2505 Melrose Ave Bossier City LA 71111-5931 Office: Bossier Parish Coll 2719 Airline Dr Bossier City LA 71111-5801

LABORDE, TERRENCE LEE, audit consultant, negotiator; b. DuBois, Pa., June 20, 1947; s. Donald Leo and Anna Lee (Wise) LaB.; m. Brenda Sue Roberts, May 16, 1970 (div. 1975); 1 child, Terrence Lee II; m. Elisa Jean Meenan, Sept. 12, 1975; children: Marc Elliott, Dawn Ann. BS, Nat. Coll., 1973. Sr. auditor Def. Contract Audit Agy., State Coll., Pa., 1973-84; contract negotiator Pa. State U., 1984-88, subcontract adminstr., 1988-91, mgr. grant & subcontract adminstrn., 1991-92; pres., CEO Keystone for Future Decisions, Inc., Pennsylvania Furnace, Pa., 1992-98; sr. contract adminstr. Concurrent Technologies Corp., Johnstown, 2002—. Owner LaBorde Enterprises, 1984-98; subcontrats adminstr. United Def., Chambersburg, Pa., 1997-99—; fin. cons. mil. programs, Altoona, Pa., 2000—. Sgt. USAF, 1966-70. Democrat. Lutheran. Avocations: hunting, fishing, landscaping, financial and educational consulting. Home and Office: PO Box 325 121 N Bedford St Newry PA 16665-0325 E-mail: exfed17@cs.com.

LABOVITZ, PRISCILLA, lawyer; b. Lynn, Mass., May 4, 1946; d. Jack Oscar and Barbara Helene (Small) L.; m. Joseph Cirincione, June 25, 1978; children: Amy Labovitz Cirincione, Peter Vincent Labovitz Cirincione. BA, Wellesley Coll., 1968; JD, Northeastern U., 1972. Bar: Mass. 1973, U.S. Ct. Appeals (D.C. cir.) 1983. Ptnr. Geller, Miller, Taylor, Weinberg & Labovitz, Cambridge, Mass., 1973-78; assoc. Bastone & Kaplan, Boston, 1978-81, Law Offices of Jan Pederson, Washington, 1981, Paul Shearman Allen & Assocs., Washington, 1982-84; pvt. practice law, 1988—. Contbr. articles to profl. jours. Literacy and homeless vol. Mem. NOW, Am. Immigration Lawyers Assn., Amnesty Internat. (legis. coord. 1990-96). Office: 6856 Eastern Ave NW Ste 354 Washington DC 20012-2165

LABOWITZ, SHONI, writer, lecturer; b. Balt., Oct. 29, 1946; d. Herschel and Nechama (Rabinowitz) Leibowitz; m. Phillip Abraham Labowitz, July 4, 1966; children: Marc Ian, Arik Zev. BS, Barry U., 1980; MA, Norwich U., 1985; postgrad., 1965-66. Ordained rabbi, Shalom'l B'Nai Or Rabbinical Program, 1987. Photographic journalist Barton Gillette Art Agy., Balt., 1966; coord. program devel. dept. cont. edn. Broward C. C., Ft. Lauderdale, 1982-85; dir. Women's Ctr. dept. cont. edn., 1982-85; stress reduction cons. Ctr. Psychol. Svcs., Ft. Lauderdale, 1986; chaplain Hospice, Inc., 1987-90; rabbi Temple Adath Or, 1987—. Creator, pres. (spiritual health spa programs) Living Waters, 1995—; radio host Spiritual Focus, WNN-AM, Boca Raton, 1998; lectr. in field. Author: MiraculousLiving: A Guided Journey in Kabbalah, 1996, God, Sex & Women of the Bible: Discovering Our Sensual, Spiritual Senses, 1998; co-author: An Invitation to Prayer, 2000. Vol. Life Enhancement for Adolescent Females, Hollywood, Fla., 1998. Mem. Assn. Rabbis for Jewish Renewal, Aleph: Alliance for Jewish Renewal, Network Jewish Renewal Cmties. Avocations: painting, hiking, travel, reading. Office: Temple Adath Or 10400 Griffin Rd # 302 Davie FL 33328 E-mail: shonilabowitz@bellsouth.net.

LABRECQUE, RICHARD JOSEPH, retired industrial executive; b. Lawrence, Mass., Dec. 19, 1938; s. Eugene N. and Ludivine M. (Roy) L.; m. Janet Marie Michaud, July 16, 1960; children: David R., Lisa M., Susan M. BSEE, Tufts U., 1962; MS in Indsl. Adminstrn., Union U., 1971. Mgr. mfg. engring. GE Aircraft Engine Group, Lynn, Mass., 1962-68; with Colt Industries, 1969-81; pres. FM Pump div., Kansas City, Kans., 1973-78, Quincy (Ill.) Compressor div., 1979-81; with ITT Industries, Inc., 1982-2000, pres. fluid handling div., 1982-95, sr. v.p., 1996-98; pres., CEO ITT Fluid Tech. Corp., Upper Saddle River, N.J., 1996-2000; exec. v.p. ITT Industries, 1998-2000, ret., 2000—. Bd. dirs. Big Machines Inc. Campaign chmn. United Way Wyandotte County, Kansas City, 1979. Mem. Hydraulic Inst. (bd. dirs. 1976—, pres. 1979, 96, chmn. 1997).

LABRIOLA, ANGELINA MARIE, librarian; b. Jersey City, Nov. 24, 1946; d. Pasquale Michael and Antonia Maria (DeFelice) L. AA, Felician Coll., 1996, BA in English, 2002. Cardiology tech., nursing asst. St. Joseph Hosp., Phila., 1984-88; nursing asst., aide Our Lady of Lourdes Infirmary, Lodi, NJ, 1988-92; receptionist St. ignatius Home, Phila., 1992-93; libr. Immaculate Conception High Sch., Lodi, 1993-98; asst. to curriculum libr. Felician Coll., 1998—2002, dir. comm. curriculum, 2002—. Mem. Felician Sisters, 1981—. Roman Catholic. Avocations: reading, writing, praying, walking, tutoring.

LA BRUNA, VINCENT VITO, orthodontist; b. Regalbuto, Italy, Sept. 4, 1933; came to the U.S., 1935; s. Nunzio and Vincenza (Termine) L.B.; m. Nina La Bruna, June 29, 1958; children: Vincent A., Anthony N. BS, St. John's Coll., 1954; DDS, NYU, 1958; cert. of splty. in orthodontics, Columbia U., 1961. Lic. dentist, N.Y. Pvt. practice, N.Y.C., 1961—. Dir. dentistry Cabrini Med. Ctr., N.Y.C., 1981—; pres. Met. Rsch. Inst., N.Y.C., 1966—. Contbr. articles to profl. jours. Chmn. orthodontists ARC, N.Y.C., 1970-72; vol. oral cancer screening Am. Cancer Soc., N.Y.C., 1981—; nominated by mayor to Environ. Control Bd., N.Y.C., 1971; mem. adv. coun. N.Y. State Planning Commn., 1974-75. Recipient UN Medal, Pope Paul II, 1995, Man of Yr. award State Cmty. Mayors, 1988, Ellis Island medal of honor, 1998. Fellow Am. Coll. Dentistry, Internat. Coll. Dentistry; mem. 1st Dist. Dental Soc. (pres. 1995), Eastern Dental Soc. (pres. 1978), N.Y. State Dental Assn. (gov. 1998--), Columbia Orthodontic Soc. (pres. 1973, del. to ADA 1994-2000), Italian Am. Profl. and Bus. Assn. (pres. 1985—), Equestrian Order of Holy Sepulchre (knight comdr. 1970—), Sovereign Order of Cypress (knight comdr. 1977—). Roman Catholic. Avocations: architectural restorations, antiques. Home and Office: 829 Park Ave New York NY 10021-2846

LABRUYERE, THOMAS EDWARD, health facility administrator; b. St. Louis, Aug. 2, 1955; s. Thomas Edward and Daisy Lillian (Nussbaum) LaB.; m. Annette Sue Gusoskey, Oct. 27, 1979; children: Thomas Edward III, Christopher John, Sarah Elizabeth. AAS, Maryville Coll., 1979, BS in Mgmt. with honors, 1990; MBA, Maryville U., 1993. Registered respiratory therapist. Coord. insvc. edn. Normandy Hosp., St. Louis, 1977-79; mgr. dept. Lifemark Cardiopulmonary, Houston, 1979-81; from asst. supr. respiratory therapy to adminstrv. dir. St. Anthony's Med. Ctr., St. Louis, 1981-95, adminstrv. dir. Cardiopulmonary and Radiology, 1995—. Mem. respiratory care adv. com. Forest Park C.C., St. Louis, 1993—; bd. dirs. Nalco Credit Union, vice chmn., 1995—, mem. supervisory com., 1991-93. Asst. scoutmaster Boy Scouts Am., St. Louis, 1995-96, asst. cubmaster, 1993, 94, troop com. chmn., 1996—; coach CYC Baseball, St. Louis, 1993-96, CYC Soccer, 1993-97. Mem. Am. Coll. Healthcare Execs. (assoc.), Am. Coll. Cardiovascular Adminstrs., Am. Assn. Respiratory Care. Avocations: 2nd dan blackbelt Tae Kwon Do (black belt), camping. Home: 3036 Armona Dr Saint Louis MO 63129-5202 Office: Saint Anthony's Med Ctr 10010 Kennerly Rd Saint Louis MO 63128-2106

LABSVIRS, JANIS, economist, educator; b. Bilska, Latvia, Mar. 13, 1907; s. Karlis and Kristina L.; Mag.Oec., Latvian State U., 1930; MS, Butler U., 1956; PhD, Ind. U., 1959; Dr. hist. (hon.), Latvian Acad. Scis., 1994. Tchr., Latvia, 1930-36; dir. dept. edn. Fedn. Latvian Trade Unions, 1936-37; v.p. Kr. Baron's U., Extension, Riga, Latvia, 1938-40, also exec. v.p. Filma, Inc., 1939-40; with UNRRA and Internat. Refugee Orgn., Esslingen, Germany, 1945-50; asst. prof. econs. Ind. State U., Terre Haute, 1959-62, assoc. prof., 1963-68, prof., 1969-73, prof. emeritus, 1973—; head dept. pub. and social affairs Latvian Ministry for Social Affairs, 1938-40; dir. Sch. of Commerce and Gymnasium, Tukums, Latvia, 1941-44. Danforth grantee, 1961; Ind. State U. research grantee, 1966; Mem. Am. Latvian Assn., Am. Assn. Advancement Slavic Studies, Assn. Advancement Baltic Studies, Am. Econ. Assn., Royal Econ. Soc. Lutheran. Author: Local Government's Accounting and Management Practices, 1947, 2d edit. 1992; A Case Study in the Sovietization of the Baltic States: Collectivization of Latvian Agriculture 1944-1956, 1959, 2d & 3d edit., 1988, 4th edit. 1989; Atminas un Pardomas, 1984, reprinted in Latvia, 3d edit., 1993, Kurp Ejam ?, 1996, reprinted in Latvia, 1997; Karlis Ulmanis, 1987, reprinted in Latvia, 2d edit., 1991, Kam Drosme Ir, 1990, reprinted in Latvia, 5th edit., 1992; contbr. articles profl. jours. Recipient Triju Zvaigznu Ordenis highest civilian medal President of Latvia, 1995. Home: 2617 Bridgeview Way Apt 1A Indianapolis IN 46220-1438

LABUDDE, ROY CHRISTIAN, lawyer; b. Milw., July 21, 1921; s. Roy Lewis and Thea (Otteson) LaB.; m. Anne P. Held, June 7, 1952; children: Jack, Peter, Michael, Susan, Sarah. AB, Carleton Coll., 1943; JD, Harvard U., 1949. Bar: Wis. 1949, U.S. Dist. Ct. (ea. and we. dists.) Wis. 1950, U.S. Ct. Appeals (7th cir.) 1950, U.S. Supreme Ct. 1957. Assoc. Michael, Best & Friedrich, Milw., 1949-57, ptnr., 1958—. Dir. DEC-Inter, Inc., Milw. Western Bank, Western Bancshares, Inc., Superior Die Set Corp., Aunt Nellie's Farm Kitchens, Inc. Bd. dirs. Wis. Hist. Soc. Found.; chmn., bd. dirs. Milw. div. Am. Cancer Soc. Served to lt. j.g. USNR, 1943-46. Mem. Milw. Estate Planning Coun. (past pres.), Wis. Bar Assn., Wis. State Bar Attys. (chmn. tax sch., bd. dirs. taxation sect.), Univ. Club, Milw. Club, Milw. Country Club. Republican. Episcopalian. Home: 4201 W Stonefield Rd Mequon WI 53092-2771 Office: Michael Best & Friedrich 100 E Wisconsin Ave Ste 3300 Milwaukee WI 53202-4108

LABUDOVIC, MARKO, research scientist, consultant; b. Podgorica, Yugoslavia, Sept. 7, 1967; came to U.S., 1998; s. Saleta and Stanislava Labudovic; m. Natasa Labudovic. BSc, U. Montenegro, Podgorica, 1992, MSc, 1995, PhD in Metallurgy & Materials Sci., 1998; PhD in Mech. Engring., So. Meth. U., 2001. Asst. lectr. U. Montenegro, 1992-96, 97-98; rsch. scientist Brunel U., London, 1996-97, So. Meth. U., Dallas, 1998-2000; rsch. devel. Corning Lasertron, Bedford, 2000—. Contbr. articles to Metall. Transactions, Jour. Mfg. Sci., Math. Sci. & Tech. Recipient 19 Dec. award County of Podgorica, 1990, LUCA award, 1986, Univ. award, 1992, British Sch. Trust, 1996, Grad. Assistance in Areas of Nat. Needs, 1998, Frederik E. Terman award, 2000. Office: 11 Oak Park M/S L2-727 Bedford MA 01730

LABUNSKI, STEPHEN BRONISLAW, professional society administrator; b. Jordanow, Poland, Sept. 24, 1924; came to U.S., 1928, naturalized, 1943; s. Wiktor and Wanda (Mlynarski) L.; m. Betty E. Marley, Oct. 2, 1947 (div. June 1963); children: Linda, Richard, Roger; m. Jeralyn LeBrun, Aug. 28, 1967. Student, U. Kansas City, Mo., 1946-49, George Washington U., 1950. Adminstrv. asst. to U.S. Congressman Richard W. Bolling, 1949-51; with Storz Broadcasting Co., 1954-57; v.p. ABC radio network, 1957; head broadcast div. Crowell Collier Pub. Co., 1958; v.p., gen. mgr. WMCA Radio/Straus Broadcasting Group, N.Y.C., 1958-65; pres. radio div. NBC, 1965-69; mng. dir. WMCA Radio, 1969-71; v.p., partner Chuck Blore Creative Services, 1971-75; exec. v.p. Merv Griffin Group Radio, 1975-77; exec. dir. Internat. Radio and TV Soc., N.Y.C., 1978-94, Circles Spl. Events, N.Y.C., 1994-98; dir. spl. events Cahners Bus. Info., 1998—. Bd. dirs. Radio Advt. Bur., 1965-69, Nat. Assn. Broadcasters, 1965-67 Chmn. adv. com. Voice of Am., 1987-89; Democratic candidate for Mo. Legislature, 1948. With AUS and USAAF, 1943-46. Mem. Advt. Council. Home: 30 E 37th St New York NY 10016-3019 Office: Cahners Bus Info 245 W 17th St New York NY 10011-5300

LABUZ, RONALD MATTHEW, design educator; b. Utica, N.Y., Nov. 17, 1953; s. Emil John and Elsie (Pritchard) L.; m. Carol Ann Altimonte, Sept. 5, 1975. BA, SUNY, Oswego, 1975; MA, Ohio State U., 1977; MPhil, Syracuse U., 1993, MA, 1994, PhD, 1997. Acquisition dir. Collegiate Pub., Columbus, Ohio, 1977-78; pres. Advt., Pub. and Avatar Media Advt. Agy., 1978-80; prodn. specialist Am. Ceramic Soc., 1980-81; assoc. prof. advt. Mohawk Valley C.C., Utica, 1981-85, prof. dept. art, 1985—. Author: Typography and Typesetting, 1988, Contemporary Graphic Design, 1991, The Computer in Graphic Design, 1994, Digital Design, 2000, and 9 other books. Recipient Chancellor's award for excellence, SUNY, 1989, 2002, faculty exch. scholar, 1990. Mem. Printing History Soc., Am. Printing History Assn., Graphic Design Educators Assn. (bd. dirs. 1989-94, treas. exec. bd. 1992-94), Am. Ctr. for Design, Am. Inst. Graphic Arts, N.Y. State Assn. Two-Yr. Colls. (bd. dirs. 1990-91). Office: Mohawk Valley CC 1101 Sherman Dr Utica NY 13501-5308 E-mail: rmlabuz@cs.com., rlabuz@mvcc.edu.

LAC, MING Q. Information technology and electronics executive; b. Canton, Peoples Republic China, Sept. 14, 1948; came to U.S., 1971; s. N.V. Lac and Hang-Yung; m. Sally W.F. Shih, July 14, 1973; children: Daisy Nice, Anne F., Larry M. BSEE, Nat. Taiwan U., Taipei, 1971; MS, Ohio State U., 1973, postgrad., 1975. Research assoc. Ohio State U., Columbus, Ohio, 1971-74, programmer, 1974-76; mgr., firmware engr. MI Square Corp., 1976-78; sr. engr. Diebold Inc., Hebron, Ohio, 1978-81; v.p. products ID Systems Corp., Dublin, 1981-84; v.p., engring. GTECH Corp., Providence, 1984-89, cons., 1990—91, dir. Far East, 1991—97; pres. Champion Sys., Warwick, 1998—. Mem. IEEE, R.I. Council Tech. (tech. com.). Home: 360 Spring Valley Dr East Greenwich RI 02818-1912 Office: Champion Sys 5 Division St Warwick RI 02818

LA CAGNINA, HENRY, artist; b. Bklyn., Apr. 9, 1909; s. Leonardo and Giulia (Schimentti) La Cagnina; m. Alice R.J. La Cagnina, 1936 (dec. Jan. 1999); children: David H., Giulia R., Michael L. Student, Cooper Union, N.Y.C., 1925—26. Coord./designer Spl. Skills sect. Dept. Agr., Washington, 1936—38, P.R. Devel. Co., San Juan, 1943—45; tchr. dept. art St. Paul's Sch., Concord, NH, 1946—49. Design cons. Baker Furniture Co., Holland, Mich., 1960—61. Murals, screens, curtains, mural, ceiling murals, enamel and woodcarving. Mem. jury of selection N.H. League of Arts and Crafts, Concord, 1947—49; tchr. Internat. Upholsterers Union, 1957—59. Episcopalian. Home: 621 Franklin Rd Highlands NC 28741

LACAGNINA, MICHAEL ANTHONY, judge; b. Rochester, N.Y., July 6, 1932; s. Frank and Josephine (LoMaglio) L.; m. Mary Laura Mantle, June 8, 1952; children: John Michael, Gina Laura, Frank Anthony. BS in Bus. Adminstrn, U. Ariz., 1955, LL.B., 1957. Bar: Ariz. 1957. Asst. U.S. atty., Tucson, 1958-60; partner firm Bilby, Shoenhair, Warnock & Dolph, 1960-83, of counsel, 1983-84; judge divsn. II Ariz. Ct. Appeals, 1984-95; vice chief judge Div. II, Ariz. Ct. Appeals, 1985-87, chief judge, 1987-89. Served with USMCR, 1950-52. Fellow Am. Coll. Trial Attys., Ariz. Bar Found. (chmn. fellows 1986-87); mem. ABA, Ariz. Bar Assn., Pima County Bar Assn. (pres. 1981), Nat. Assn. R.R. Trial Attys., Am. Bd. Trial Advs. (nat. exec. com., nat. sec. 1981, nat. pres. 1983), Ariz. Judges Assn. (exec. com. 1985-95), Tucson Def. Attys. (pres.), Los Charros del Desierto, Phi Delta Phi, Alpha Kappa Psi. Democrat. Episcopalian. Home: 7100 E River Canyon Rd Tucson AZ 85750-2110

LACAPRA, DOMINICK CHARLES, historian, educator; b. N.Y.C., July 13, 1939; s. Joseph and Mildred (Sciascia) LaC.; m. Anne-Marie Hlasny, June 15, 1965 (div.); 1 dau., Veronique. BA, Cornell U., 1961; PhD, Harvard U., 1970. Tutor Harvard U., Cambridge, Mass., 1967-69; asst. prof. history Cornell U., Ithaca, N.Y., 1969-74, assoc. prof., 1974-79, prof. history, 1979—, Goldwin Smith prof. European intellectual history, 1985-92, Bryce and Edith M. Bowmar prof. humanistic studies, 1992—. Assoc. dir. Sch. of Criticism and Theory Cornell U., 1997-2000; dir. Sch. Criticism and Theory, 2000—. Author: Emile Durkheim, 1972, A Preface to Sartre, 1978, "Madame Bovary" on Trial, 1982, Rethinking Intellectual History, 1983, History and Criticism, 1985, History, Politics and the Novel, 1987, Soundings in Critical Theory, 1989, Representing the Holocaust, 1994, History and Memory after Auschwitz, 1998, History and Reading: Tocqueville, Foucault, French Studies, 2000, Writing History, Writing Trauma, 2001. Fulbright fellow France, 1961-62, Woodrow Wilson fellow Harvard U., 1962-63, sr. fellow NEH, 1979, Sch. Criticism and Theory; recipient Disting. Tchg. award Coll. Arts and Scis. Cornell U., 1979. Mem. MLA, Am. Hist. Assn., Internat. Assn. Philosophy and Lit., Soc. Phenomenological and Existential Philosophy, Am. Comparative Lit. Assn., Soc. for the Humanities (dir.). Home: 624 Highland Rd Ithaca NY 14850 Office: Cornell U History Dept McGraw Hall Ithaca NY 14853 E-mail: DCL3@cornell.edu.

LA CAVA, DONALD LEON, communications executive; b. Fair Lawn, N.J., July 11, 1928; s. Paul and Angela (Viviano) La C.; m. Mary A. Morrison (div. 1980); children: Anita, Mark, Brigid, Kevin, Christopher, Peter, David, Daniel. BA in English, UCLA, 1982. V.p. Batjac Prodns., Hollywood, Calif., 1956-69; pres. Markab Mgmt., Beverly Hills, 1969-73, Triton Prodns., Encino, 1973-86; v.p. Jet Charter Am., Inc., 1986-97; mng. dir. No. Global Fin. & Investment, Reno, 1997-98. V.p. Internat. Jet Airways, 1986—, LaCava Aviation, 1996—. Served to lt. USNR, 1951-63, Korea. Mem. Dirs. Guild Am. Avocation: aviation. Home: 16936 Burbank Blvd Apt 127 Encino CA 91316-1814

LACER, ALFRED ANTONIO, lawyer, educator; b. Hammonton, N.J., Feb. 14, 1952; s. Vincent and Carmen (Savall) L.; m. Kathleen Visser, June 15, 1974; children: Margaret, James, Matthew. BA in Polit. Sci., Gordon Coll., 1974; JD, Cath. U. Am., 1977. Bar: Md. 1977, U.S. Dist. Ct. Md. 1980, U.S. Ct. Appeals (4th cir.) 1980, U.S. Supreme Ct. 1997. Law clk. to Honorable Joseph A. Mattingly, Sr. Cir. Ct. St. Mary's County, Leonardtown, Md., 1977-78; ptnr. Lacer, Sparling, Densford & Reynolds PA and predecessors, Lexington Park, 1978-99; county atty. St. Mary's County, 1999-2000, CEO, county adminstr., 2000—. Adj. prof. bus. law Fla. Inst. Tech., Patuxent, Md., 1989-92, 95-99; vis. instr. St. Mary's Coll. of Md., 1988, 91; mem. bd. edn. St. Mary's County (Md.) Pub. Schs., 1989-94, pres., 1991-92; mem. inquiry panel Atty. Grievance Commn. of Md., 1984-90. Bd. dirs. St. Mary's Hosp., Leonardtown, 1982-88, v.p., 1985-88; bd. dirs. So. Md. Cmty. Action, Inc., Hughsville, Md., 1982-84, St. Mary's County Tech. Coun., 1997-99. Mem. ABA, Md. Bar Assn. (com. on jud. appointments 1982-85), St. Mary's County Bar Assn. (v.p. 1979-80, pres. 1980-81). Episcopalian. Office: Office of the County Adminstr PO Box 653 Leonardtown MD 20650-0653

LACERDA, ALEX H. physicist, researcher; b. June 2, 1962; m. Andrea Labouriau, Feb. 7, 1962; children: Hugo Labouriau-Lacerda. PhD(hon.) , Univ. Joseph Fourier, 1990. Program dir. Los Alamos Nat. Lab., Los Alamos, N.Mex., 1995—. Office: Los Alamos National Laboratory Mail Stop E536 Los Alamos NM 87544 Business E-Mail: lacerda@lanl.gov.

LACERENZA, JOSEPH CHARLES, research scientist; b. Stamford, Conn., Feb. 4, 1958; s. Vito Vincent and Rose Marie (Schinella) Lacerenza. Degree in physics, Saint Basil's, Stamford, 1976; student, U. Conn., 1978. Cert. tech. applications for transmissions of combined energy force. With tech. comms. sci. City of Stamford, 1980—85; with tech., mech. sci. U.S. Govt., Norman, 1986—87. Head R&D Unique Techs., Stamford , 1987—, engaged in sci. of recovery of electronic components subjected to adverse environ.l conditions , Stamford, 1991—. Author: (prose) 1- 2- 3 -4 , 1996 (Personal Achievement award, 1974). Rsch. / nat. security RNC, Washington, 2001—02. Mem.: KC. Office: Unique Techs 22 Highview Ave Stamford CT 06907 Home Fax: 203-968-9796; Office Fax: 203-968-9796. Business E-Mail: jhunted7667@yahoo.com.

LACEY, AARON MICHAEL, actor, director, screenwriter, executive producer; b. Washington, May 26, 1969; Advanced cert., Nat. Conservatory Drama Arts, 1993. CEO AML Productions, Washington, 1987—. Appearances include: (tv series) In Our Lives, 1987-94, (tv primetime spls.) Running Out of Time, 1989, Fatal Mix, 1990, (films) Major League II, 1993, Twelve Monkeys, 1995, Shadow Conspiracy, 1996; assoc. prodr., story writer, screenwriter, Edge, 1997; exec. prodr., story writer, screen writer, dir. Sync, 2000; screen plays include: (tv) (In Our Lives) Gangs, 1993, (films) Crimson Road, 1989, Cumulus Nine, 1990, Mind Walker, 1991. Supporter Anti Defamation League, People for Ethical Treatment of Animals, MADD, Wash. Regional Alcohol Program. Recipient Capital Region Emmy awards NATAS, 1991. Mem. Screen Actors Guild, Actors Equity Assn., Am. Fedn. TV Radio Artists. Avocation: karate (first-degree black belt). E-mail: amlfilms@aol.com.

LACEY, CLOYD EUGENE, retired insurance company executive; b. New Lexington, Ohio, Mar. 12, 1918; s. Russell Anderson and Freda (Bahr) L.; m. Jane Linn Williams, Sept. 12, 1941; children: Thomas, Melinda Lacey Houfek, Janene Lacey Paulus. BS in Bus. Adminstrn., Ohio State U., 1941. Acct., asst. treas. Pioneer Mut. Causualty Co., Columbus, Ohio, 1945-51; various corp. fin. positions Nationwide Ins. Cos., 1951-73, v.p., asst. controller, 1973-75, v.p., corp. controller, 1975-78, v.p. Office of Treas., controller, 1978-81, sr. v.p. fin., 1981-82, ret., 1982. Served with U.S. Army, 1943-45. Republican. Methodist. *I believe in God and put my trust in him. I believe in treating other people fairly and in giving them credit for accomplishments. I believe in maintaining a high degree of integrity. I believe in diligence and determination in performing a task. I believe in striving for excellence.*

LACEY, DOROTHY ELLEN, theology studies educator, religious organization administrator; b. Urbancrest, Ohio, Feb. 24, 1931; d. Charles Franklin Nesbitt and Clifford (Dickerson); m. Joseph W. Lacey; 1 child Michael Clifford. B in Christian Edn., M in Christian Edn., Grace Internat. Coll., 1996. Ednl. dir. Emmanuel Tempe Ch. of Rochester N.Y., Inc., 1962—, adminstr., 1985—. Women's ministry evangelistic seminar tchr. Pentecostal Assemblies of the World, Indpls., 1960—; pres., founder Lacey's Travel Agy., Rochester, 1983—88; pres. women's ministry N.Y. Coun., 1990—96. Mem.: NAACP, Profl. Bus. Women, Urban League. Pentecostal Assemblies. Avocations: singing, playing musical instruments. Home: 3500 Brown Rd PO Box 148 Caledonia NY 14423 Office: Emmanuel Temple Ch Rochester 1 Seneca Pkwy Rochester NY 14613

LACEY, EDWARD MARTIN, fire chief; b. Oak Park, Ill., Sept. 4, 1948; s. Martin Joseph and Delores Mary (Molitor) L.; m. Kathleen Ann Flight, Oct. 6, 1973; children: Patrick, Brian. BA, Western Ill. Univ., 1986. Cert. fire officer, fire inspector. Probationary fireman Schaumburg (Ill.) Fire Dept., 1970-71, fireman, 1971-72, act. lt., 1972-76, lt., 1976-80, capt., 1980-83, dir. of fire prevention, 1983-86, battalion chief, 1986-90, acting chief, 1990-91, chief, 1991—. Com. mem. Streamwood Ill. Fire Dept. Deputy Chief Screening com., 1991. Co-author village ordinances, 1981, 88. Com. mem. Shelter, Inc., Schaumburg, 1991. Recipient Appreciation award VFW, 1984, Fire Prevention Achievement award Ill. Fire Inspectors Assn., 1988. Mem. Internat. Assn. Fire Chiefs, Ill. Fire Chiefs Assn., Northeastern Ill. Fire Chiefs Assn., Irish Fellowship Club Chgo., Ancient Order Hibernians (trustee), KC (past pres., past grand knight). Roman Catholic. Avocations: golf, history, geneology. Office: Schaumburg Fire Dept 1601 N Roselle Rd Schaumburg IL 60195-3612

LACEY, HENRY BERNARD, lawyer; b. Aurora, Colo., Nov. 30, 1963; s. Leonard Joseph and Colleen Trece (Ryan) L. BS, Ariz. State U., 1988, JD, 1991. Bar: Ariz. 1991, Oreg. 1996; U.S. Dist. Ct. Ariz. 1991, U.S. Ct. Appeals (9th cir.) 1992, U.S. Dist. Ct. Oreg. 1999. Jud. law clk. to Hon. Cecil F. Poole U.S. Ct. Appeals 9th Cir., San Francisco, 1991-92; assoc. Kimball & Curry, P.C., Phoenix, 1992-93; atty. Law Office of Henry B. Lacey, 1993-94, Portland, Oreg., 1996-99, Flagstaff, Ariz., 1999—; vis. fellow Natural Resources Law Inst. Northwestern Sch. Law, Lewis and Clark Coll., Portland, 1994-95; chief counsel Colo. Plateau Wildlands Def. Coun., Inc., 2001—. Counsel/environ. group adv. bd. dirs. Coalition to Reform the Ctrl. Ariz. Project, Phoenix, 1993; vol. lawyer Land and Water Fund of the Rockies, Boulder, Colo., 1993—; vol. lawyer Portland Audubon Soc., 1996-99; adj. prof. No. Ariz. U., 2000—; bd. dirs. Brite, Inc., Phoenix, Common Ground, Flagstaff, Habitat for Humanity, Flagstaff. Gen. counsel Maricopa County, Ariz. Dem. Party, 1992-94. Mem.: Order of Coif, Phi Delta Phi. Roman Catholic. Avocations: hiking, bicycling, reading, photography. Office: 120 N San Francisco St Flagstaff AZ 86001 E-mail: henry.lacey@azbar.org.

LACEY, HOWARD RAYMOND, food technologist; b. Mar. 18, 1919; s. Clarence Frederick and Sarah Lovisa (Hancock) L.; m. Dorothy Louise Daulton, Aug. 23, 1947; children: Howard R. Jr., Janet H. Lacey Wanink. BS in Chemistry, U. Mass., 1942. Processed foods inspector USDA, various locations, 1942-46; tech. dir. P.J. Ritter Co. (now Curtice-Burns, Inc.), Bridgeton, N.J., 1946-67; gen. mgr., v.p. food mfg. Brooks Foods (now Curtice-Burns, Inc.), Mt. Summit, Ind., 1967-74, tech. dir., 1974-85; pres. Lacey Assocs., Inc., 1985-96. Cons. Cape May Canners, N.J., Party Tyme Corp., N.Y.C.; instr. Better Process Control Sch., Purdue U., West Lafayette, Ind., 1981-85. Inventor 100% corn sweetener added to catsup, improved method for firming diced red peppers, Stannous chloride added to asparagus. Asst. mgr. Little League Baseball, Bridgeton, 1958-61; merit badge counselor Cub Scouts, Boy Scouts Am., 1957-67; contbg. mem. U.S. Senatorial Rep. Club, Washington, 1978—, Rep. Nat. Com., 1982—; vol. Ind. Basketball Hall of Fame, 1990—; cons. Jr. Achievement, 1991-98. Recipient New Foods award Canner/Packer Mag., 1969, Outstanding Svc. to Food Processing Industry award Ind. Food Processors Assn., 1985. Mem. Inst. Food Tech. (nat., Hoosier chpt., quality assurance sect.), Phi Tau Sigma (local, nat., internat.), Toastmasters (Bridgeton), Masons, Elks. Avocations: travel, tennis, reading, big band music, bicycling. E-mail: hrlacey@kiva.net.

LACEY, HUGH MATTHEW, philosophy educator; b. Sydney, Australia, Sept. 7, 1939; came to U.S., 1972; s. Owen Charles and Margaret Jane (Devine) L.; m. Maria Ines Rocha E. Silva, Aug. 14, 1966; children: Andrew David, Daniel Carlos. BA, U. Melbourne, Australia, 1962, MA, 1964; PhD, Ind. U., 1966. Tutor in math. U. Melbourne, 1961-63; lectr. history and philosophy of sci. U. Sydney, 1966-68; prof. philosophy U. São Paulo, Brazil, 1969-72, Swarthmore (Pa.) Coll., 1972, chmn. dept. philosophy, 1973-83, Eugene M. Lang Rsch. Prof. of Philosophy, 1993-97, The Scheuer Family prof. humanities, 2000—. Vis. prof. Temple U., Phila., spring 1983, Villanova U., fall 1984, Instituto de Teologia, São Paulo, spring 1988, fall, 1992, Ctrl. Am. U., El Salvador, summer 1991, U.Pa., fall 1995, U. Melbourne, spring 1996, U. São Paulo, fall 1996, fall 2000; Dyason lectr. Australasian Assn. History Philosophy and Social Studies of Sci., 1996. Author: A Linguagem Do Espaco E do Tempo, 1972, Valores e Atividade Cientifica, 1998, Is Science Value Free? Values and Scientific Understanding, 1999, Psicologia Experimental e Natureza Humana, 2001; co-author: Behaviorism, Science and Human Nature, 1982; co-editor: Towards a Society That Serves Its People: The Thought of El Salvador's Murdered Jesuits, 1991; cons. editor: Jour. for Theory of Social Behavior, 1977—, Behavior and Philosophy, 1987—, Jour. for Peace and Justice Studies, 1987—. Bd. dirs. Chester-Swarthmore Coll. Cmty. Coalition, 1993—2001. NSF fellow, 1975, 79, 83, 2000; Fulbright grantee, 1963; Research Found. of State of São Paulo grantee, 1969, 73, 96, 2000. Mem. Philosophy of Sci. Assn., Am. Philos. Assn., Am. Psychol. Assn. (commn. on behavior modification 1974-77). Roman Catholic. Home: 336 Park Ave Swarthmore PA 19081-2013 Office: Dept Philosophy Swarthmore 500 College Ave Swarthmore PA 19081-1306 E-mail: hlacey1@swarthmore.edu.

LACEY, JAMES FRANCIS, American studies educator; b. N.Y.C., Oct. 15, 1933; s. James Francis and Edna Mildred Lacey; m. Barbara Anne Ellson, Aug. 17, 1958; children: Christopher, Elizabeth. BA, St. Peter's Coll., 1955; MA, Boston Coll., 1959; PhD, NYU, 1968. Instr. St. Francis Coll., Bklyn., 1958-62, asst. prof., 1963-67; assoc. prof. Eastern Conn. State U., Willimantic, 1968-71, prof., 1972—, dir. honors program, 1992—. Mem. adv. bd. Conn. Rev., New Britain, 1990—; cons. Houghton Mifflin, Inc., Boston, 1993. Contbr. articles and revs. to profl. jours. Elected mem. Zoning Bd. of Appeals, Windham, Conn., 1982-85; bd. dirs. Henry Barnard Found., New Britain, 1994—. 1st lt. USAR, 1955-57. German Acad. Exch. Svc. fellow, 1965, 68, NEH fellow, 1978. Mem. Am. Studies Assn., Nat. Collegiate Honors Coun., Deutscher Gesellschaft Fuer Amerika-Studien, Windham Hist. Soc. (bd. dirs.

1997—, pres.-elect Nat. Collegiate Honors Coun., N.E. Region 1999-2000, pres. 2000-2001), Willimantic Country Club, Columbia Canoe Club, Windham Yacht Club, Sigma Tau Delta, Omicron Delta Kappa. Democrat. Avocations: golf, sailing, canoeing. Home: 305 Prospect St Willimantic CT 06226-2207 Office: Eastern Conn State U Willimantic CT 06226

LACEY, JOHN IRVING, psychologist, physiologist, educator; b. Chgo., Apr. 11, 1915; s. David and Cecelia (Burnstein) L.; m. Beatrice Lucile Cates, Apr. 16, 1938; children— Robert Arnold, Carolyn Ellen. AB, Cornell U., 1937, PhD, 1941. Instr. Queen's Coll., Flushing, N.Y., 1941-42; mem. faculty Antioch Coll., 1946-77, prof. psychophysiology, 1956-77; mem. staff Fels Research Inst., Yellow Springs, Ohio, 1946-82, chief sect. behavioral physiology, 1946-82; Fels prof. psychiatry Wright State U. Med. Sch., 1977-82, prof. emeritus, 1982—. Cons. USPHS, 1957-82, FDA, 1977-82; mem. bd. sci. counselors Nat. Inst. Aging, NIH, 1977-80 Cons. editor Jour. Comparative and Physiol. Psychology, 1953-69, Jour. Psychosomatic Medicine, 1962-65, Jour. Psychophysiology, 1964-69, Jour. Physiol. Psychology; contbr. articles to profl. jours. Served to capt. USAAF, 1942-46 Centennial scholar Johns Hopkins U., 1976; recipient Psychol. Sci. Gold medal Am. Psychol. Found., 1985. Fellow Am. Psychol. Soc. (William James fellow 1989); mem. Soc. Psychophysiol. Research (award for disting. contbns. 1970, pres. 1961-62, dir. 1965-68), Am. Psychosomatic Soc. (bd. dirs. 1959-62), Soc. Exptl. Psychologists, Am. Psychol. Assn. (pres. div. physiol. and comparative psychology 1969-70, mem. council 1964-68, 70-73, 78-79, bd. dirs. 1974-77, Disting. Sci. Contbn. award 1976), AAAS (chmn. sect. 1985-86), Psychonomic Soc., Soc. for Neurosci., Acad. Behavioral Medicine Rsch., Internat. Brain Rsch. Orgn., Nat. Acad. Scis. (chair com. new techs. in cognitive psychophysiology with NRC 1988), Sigma Xi, Phi Kappa Phi. Home: 70-260 Mottle Cir Rancho Mirage CA 92270 E-mail: jilacey@aol.com.

LACEY, JOHN WILLIAM CHARLES, management consultant; b. London, May 1, 1930; came to U.S., 1956; s. William J. and Florence (Farbus) L.; m. Edna Winifred Burns, July 28, 1951; children: Jonathan Charles, Erika Jane. BA with honors, Oxford (Eng.) U., 1952, MA with honors, 1956. Sr. sci. officer Govt. of U.K., 1952-60; U.S. liaison officer Brit. embassy, Washington, 1956-60; mgr. research and devel., spl. systems Control Data Corp., Bloomington, Minn., 1960-63, dir. ops., 1963; pres. Control Data subs. Control Corp., 1964-65, gen. mgr. Devel. and Standard Systems div., 1965, v.p. computer equipment group, 1966-67, v.p. corp. devel., 1967-71, v.p., sr. staff officer corp. plans and controls, 1971-73, sr. v.p. corp. plans and controls, chmn. mgmt. com., 1973-77; pres. Control Data Edn. Co., 1977-79, Control Data Info. and Edn. Systems Co., 1979-82; exec. v.p. Control Data Corp., 1982-86. Cons. in field, 1986-2000; chmn. bd. Control Corp., Adcomp Corp., 1963-66; dir. Instron Corp., 1987-99. Bd. dirs. Jr. Achievement Greater Mpls., 1966-76, Mpls. Acquatennial, 1975-82, Guthrie Theater, 1983-88; bd. dirs. Computer Mus., 1982-86, trustee, 1986-93. With Brit. Royal Navy, 1948-49. E-mail: jwlacey@aol.com.

LACEY, MARTHA JANE, social worker; b. Clarkston, Mich., July 15, 1931; d. Hazen S. and Jeannette A. (Knox) Atkins; m. Thomas J. Lacey, Aug. 17, 1957; children: Eileen, Tod, Kathleen. BA, Mich. State U., 1952; MS Social Work, U. Wis., 1960. Cert. social worker, Ill., Acad. Cert. Social Workers, supervisory endorsement, Ill. Youth dir. YWCA, Aurora, Ill., 1956-58; social worker Community Consolidated Sch. Dist. 15, Palatine, 1973-88; ret. Vol. Campfire Girls, Cub Scouts, PTA, local Sunday sch., Arlington Heights, Ill., 1966-73; mem. admistrv. bd. Los Ministerios Hispanos de los Suburbios Noroeste, Palatine, 1984-97; active United Meth. Ch., Stoughton, Wis. Mem. Campaign for Children Com. United Meth. Women (chair 1988-97), Commn. for Ch. and Society (social concerns chair 1990-92). Avocation: travel. Home: 1998 Skyline Dr Stoughton WI 53589-3254

LACEY, PEELER GRAYSON, diagnostic radiologist; b. Kosciusko, Miss., June 16, 1954; s. Dick Grayson and Beatrice (Peeler) L.; m. Holley Anne Westbrook, July 8, 1978; children: Peeler Grayson Jr., Lauren Elizabeth. BA in Chemistry, Emory U., 1975; MD, U. Miss., 1979. Diplomate Am. Bd. Radiology. Intern U. Miss Med. Ctr., Jackson, 1979-80, resident in diagnostic radiology, 1980-83; diagnostic radiologist South Cen. Regional Med. Ctr., Laurel, Miss., 1983—, Jasper Gen. Hosp., Bay Springs, 1983—. V.p., ptnr. Radiology Assocs., Laurel, 1983— Past asst. scoutmaster Troop 32, exec. bd. mem. Pine Burr Area coun. Boy Scouts Am.; chmn. Chickasawhay dist. Boy Scouts Am.; Sun. sch. tchr., deacon. First Bapt. Ch., Laurel. Named one of Outstanding Young Men of Am., 1987; recipient Silver Beaver award Boy Scouts Am. Mem. AMA, NRA (life), Radiol. Soc. N.Am., So. Radiology Soc., Am. Coll. Radiology, Am. Heart Assn., Miss. State Med. Assn., Miss. Radiol. Soc., South Miss. Med. Soc. (pres. 1992), South Cen. Regional Med. Ctr. (pres. 1994), Roentgen Ray Soc., Miss. Bowhunters Assn. (life), Found. N.Am. Wild Sheep, Nat. Eagle Scout Assn. (life, past chmn. Pine Burr area coun.), Cum Laude Soc., Safari Club Internat. (life), Boone and Crockett Club (life assoc.), Sigma Chi (life loyal Sig.). Avocations: hunting, fishing, reading. Home: 2432 Ridgewood Dr Laurel MS 39440-2147 Office: Radiology Assocs 235 S 12th Ave # 2427 Laurel MS 39440-4324

LACEY, ROBERTA BALAAM, emergency room nurse, pediatrics nurse; b. Houston, Aug. 22, 1970; d. Edwin Carnall and Clara Hideko (Fujita) Balaam; m. Wayne Robert Lacey, Dec. 31, 1991. BSN, U. Wash., 1993. RN, Wash., Hawaii; PALS, cert. pediat. nurse; ACLS; ENPC. Clinic nurse Valley Family Practice Clinic, Renton, 1991-93; nursing technician II Swedish Hosp., Seattle, 1992-93; staff nurse Kapiolani Med. Ctr. for Women and Children, Honolulu, 1993-97, Geary Cmty. Hosp., Junction City, Kans., 1997—2001; pediatric nurse Kaiser Permanente Med. Ctr., Honolulu, 2001—. Mem. Emergency Nurses Assn., Sigma Theta Tau. Democrat. Avocations: snow skiing, hiking, camping, kayaking. Home: 94-369 Keehuhiwa St Mililani HI 96789 Office: Kaiser Moanalua Med Ctr 3288 Moanalua Rd Honolulu HI 96819

LACEY, RONALD LEE, II, film and video producer, director; b. Indpls., Feb. 17, 1964; s. Ronald Lee Sr. and Loretta Delores (Webb) L.; children: Vannari L., Edward A., Ariel N. BA in Telecom., Ind. U., Indpls., 1992. Videographer, editor Ind. Black Exp, Indpls., 1986-87; freelance videographer ESPN, 1989-90; freelance Madame C. J. Walker, Bristol, Conn., 1990; prodr. and dir. Sta. WFMB-TV, Indpls., 1990-91; freelance Unitel Video, Pitts., 1992; audio visual technician AhL Comm., Indpls., 1992-93; prodn. asst. Sta. WTHR-TV, 1994-96; prodr. and dir. Marcus Media, 1995-97, Fade II Black Filmworks, Indpls., 1997—. Writer, prodr., and dir. (documentary) Debra Wynn: Portrait of an Interracial, 1990, Minority Television in Indianapolis, 1991; appeared in TV shows Silk Stockings and Renegade, 1993-94; freelance in filming for various commls., 1996. Freelance office comm. Disciples of Christ, 1987-92; mem. 100 Black Men, Indpls., 1997—. Mem. Nat. Black Programming Consortium (producer), Black Filmmaker Found. (profl. mem.), Black Filmmakers Hall of Fame, Ind. Film Soc. Office: Fade II Black Filmworks 4501 E 38th St Indianapolis IN 46218-1525 E-mail: hollywood-indiana@excite.com.

LACH, ALMA ELIZABETH, food and cooking writer, consultant; b. Petersburg, Ill. d. John H. and Clara E. Satorius; m. Donald F. Lach; 1 child, Sandra Judith. Diplome de Cordon Bleu, Paris, 1956. Feature writer Children's Activities mag., 1954-55; creator, performer childrens cooking TV show Let's Cook, 1955; food editor Chgo. Daily Sun-Times, 1957-65; hostess weekly food program on CBS, 1962-66; pres. Alma Lach Kitchens, Inc., Chgo., 1966—; performer TV show Over Easy, PBS, 1977-78. Dir. Alma Lach Cooking Sch., Chgo.; lectr. U. Chgo. Downtown Coll., Gourmet Inst., U. Md., 1963, Modesto (Calif.) Coll., 1978, U. Chgo., 1981; resident master Shoreland Hall, U. Chgo., 1978-81; food cons. Food Bus. Mag., 1964-66, Chgo.'s New Pump Room, Lettuce Entertain You, Bitter End Resort, Brit. V.I., Midway Airlines, Flying Food Fare, Inc., Berghoff Restaurant, Hans' Bavarian Lodge, Unocal '76, Univ. Club Chgo. Author: A Child's First Cookbook, 1950, The Campbell Kids at Home, 1953, Let's Cook, 1956, Candlelight Cookbook, 1959, Cooking a la Cordon Bleu, 1970, Alma's Almanac, 1972, Hows and Whys of French Cooking, 1974, reprint, 1998; contbr. to World Book Yearbook, 1961-75, Grolier Soc. Yearbook, 1962; columnist Modern Packaging, 1967-68, Travel & Camera, 1969, Venture, 1970, Chicago mag., 1978, Bon Appetit, 1980, Tribune Syndicate, 1982; inventor: Curly-Dog Cutting Bd., 1995, Alma's Walker Tray, 1996. Recipient Pillsbury award, 1958, Grocery Mfrs. Am. Trophy award, 1959, certificate of Honor, 1961, Chevalier du Tastevin, 1962, Commanderie de l'Ordre des Anysetiers du Roy, 1963, Confrerie de la Chaine des Rotisseurs, 1964, Les Dames D'Escoffier, 1982, Culinary Historians of Chgo., 1993. Mem. Am. Assn. Food Editors (chmn. 1959), Tavern Club, Quadrangle Club (Chgo.). Home and Office: 5750 S Kenwood Ave Chicago IL 60637-1744 Fax: 773-363-2875. E-mail: alma@almalach.com. *The art of cooking rests upon one's ability to taste, to reproduce taste, and to create taste. To achieve distinction the cook must taste everything, study cookbooks of all kinds, and experiment constantly in the kitchen. I stress in my writing and teaching the logic of food preparation, for the cook who possesses logic, knows how to create dishes rather than being content merely to duplicate the recipes of others.*

LACH, DANIEL EMILE, mergers and acquisitions consultant; b. Montreal, Que., Can., June 9, 1958; arrived in Eng., 1989; s. Emile and Mary Lach; m. Nicola Mary Menzies, May 28, 1995; children: Michael, Thomas. B Engring., McGill U., Montreal, 1981; MBA, York U., Toronto, Ont., Can., 1984. Cons. Deloitte Haskins & Sells, Toronto, 1986-88; exec. Enskilda Securities, London, 1989-92; asst. dir. BZW, 1993-95; dir. Credit Lyonnais, 1995-96; cons., 1997—. Cons. Navia ASA, Trondheim, Norway, 1996-98, Endress & Hauser AG, Reinach, Switzerland, 1998, Eltek ASA, Drammen, Norway, 1999, Ziton SA (PTY) Ltd, Capetown, South Africa, 2000. Home and Office: Little Braxted Burgh Hill E Sussex Etchingham TN19 7PB England

LACH, JOSEPH THEODORE, physicist; b. Chgo., May 12, 1934; s. Joseph and Kate (Ziemba) L.; m. Barbara Ryan, June 26, 1965; children— Michael, Elizabeth AB, U. Chgo., 1953, MS, 1956; PhD, U. Calif.-Berkeley, 1963. Rsch. assoc. in physics Yale U., Hew Haven, 1963-65, asst. prof. physics, 1966-69; physicist Fermi Nat. Accelerator Lab., Batavia, Ill, 1969—, chmn. dept. physics, 1974-75; chmn. Gordon Rsch. Conf. in Elem. Particle Physics, 1975. Mem. joint rsch. program with USSR and People's Republic of China. Fellow Am. Phys. Soc., Physicians for Social Responsibility, Ill. Geol. Survey (rsch. affiliate). Home: 28w364 Indian Knoll Trl West Chicago IL 60185-3013 Office: Fermilab PO Box 500 Batavia IL 60510-0500 E-mail: lach@fnal.gov.

LACH, PETER, humanities educator; b. Indianapolis, Ind., Aug. 14, 1944; s. Theodore and Madge Marie Lach; life ptnr. Bruce F. Betts (dec.). M.F.A., U. of Iowa, Iowa City, Iowa, 1971—73; MA, DePauw U., Greencastle, Indiana, 1966—68, BA, 1962—66. Scenic Artist United Scenic Artist, Local 350, IL, 1972. Chair, sch. of fine arts Fairmont State Coll., Fairmont, W.Va., 2002—; chair, theatre arts dept. U. of the Pacific, Stockton, Calif., 1995—2002; asst. prof. of theatre Shaw U., Raleigh, NC, 1993—95; assoc. dean and prof. Calif. State U., Dominguez Hills, Carson, Calif., 1974—83; instr. Calif. State U., Chico, Chico, 1973—74, Elmira Coll., Elmira, NY, 1968—71. Panel mem., communication and the costume design process Communication Assn. of Am., Seatle, Wash., 2000—00; cons., audience bldg. strategies Calif. State U., Hayward, Hayward, Calif., 1996—97; presented paper, strategies for bldg. and maintaining audiences Am. Theatre Assn., New York, NY, 1979—79, workshop, scene design for comedy, San Francisco, 1980—80. Designer (play) The Moon Over Buffalo (Ellie Award, 2002), (play at the homegrown theatre, new york) The First Jewish Boy in the Ku Klux Klan, (outdoor pageant, weber point stockton) Stockton, The Dream Lives On, (play, New 42nd St. Theatre, New York) Bridges, (play, Asian American Repertory Theatre) Maiden Voyages. Artistic dir. and/or mem. Stockton Opera Assn., Stockton, Calif., 1996—2001. Mem.: Who's Who in Am. Edn. Achievements include Published Production Photographs, THE ENJOYMENT OF THEATRE; Published Production Photographs, EARLY AMERICAN DRAMATISTS; Published Production Photographs, SHAKESPEARE'S COMEDIES. Avocations: travel, theatre, theatre, theatre. Home: 1408 Far Meadows Morgantown WV 26508 Office: Fairmont State College 1201 Locust Avenue Fairmont WV 26554 Personal E-mail: plach@fscwv.edu. E-mail: plach@fscwv.edu.

LACHANCE, JANICE RACHEL, former federal agency administrator, lawyer; b. Biddeford, Maine, June 17, 1953; d. Ralph L. and Rachel A. (Desnoyers) L. BA, Manhattanville Coll., 1974; JD, Tulane U., 1978. Bar: Maine 1978, D.C. 1982, U.S. Supreme Ct. 1999. Staff dir. subcom. on antitrust Ho. of Reps., Washington, 1982-83; adminstrv. asst. Congresswoman Katie Hall, 1983-84; asst. pres. sec. Mondale-Ferraro Campaign, Washington, 1984; press sec. Congressman Tom Daschle, 1985; ptnr. Lachance and Assocs., Washington, 1985-87; dir. communications and polit. action Am. Fedn. Govt. Employees (AFL-CIO), 1987-93; dir. policy and communications U.S. Office Pers. Mgmt., 1993-96, chief of staff, 1996-97, dep. dir., 1997, dir., 1997—2001; mgmt. consultant Analytica Inc., Alexandria, Va., 2001. Vis. scholar Cornell U., 1972-73. Editor newsletter Govt. Standard, 1987-93. Mem. Delta Delta Delta, Phi Alpha Delta; fellow Nat. Acad. Pub. Admin. Democrat. Roman Catholic. Office: 302 Lamond Pl Alexandria VA 22314*

LACHANCE, PAUL ALBERT, food science educator, clergyman; b. St. Johnsbury, Vt., June 5, 1933; s. Raymond John and Lucienne (Landry) Lachance; m. Therese Cecile Cote; children: Michael P, Peter A, M-Andre, Susan A. BS, St. Michael's Coll., 1955; postgrad., U. Vt., 1955-57; PhD, U. Ottawa, 1960; cert. in pastoral counseling, N.Y. Theol. Sem., 1981; DSc (hon.), St. Michael's Coll., 1982. Ordained deacon Roman Cath Ch, 1977. Assigned to St. Paul's Ch., Princeton, N.J.; aerospace biologist Aeromed. Research Labs., Wright-Patterson AFB, Ohio, 1960-63; lectr. dept. biology U. Dayton, 1963; flight food and nutrition coordinator NASA Manned Spacecraft Center, Houston, 1963-67; assoc. prof. dept. food sci. Rutgers U., New Brunswick, N.J., 1967-72, dir. Sch. Feeding effectiveness research project, 1969-72, prof., 1972—, faculty rep. to bd. trustees, 1988-90, dir. grad. program food sci., 1988-91, chmn. food sci. dept., 1991-97, chmn. univ. senate, 1990-93, faculty rep. to bd. govs., 1990-94, exec. dir. The Nutraceuticals Inst., 1997—. Consult Nutritional Aspects Food Processing, Nutraceuticals; mem nutrition adv comt Whitehall-Robins/Centrum Consumer div, 1989—2000; mem sci adv bd Roche chem div Hoffmann La Roche Co, 1976—88; mem nutrition policy comt Beatrice Food Co, 1979—86; trustee religious ministries comt Princeton Med Ctr; bd dirs J R Short Milling Co. Mem. editl. adv. bd.: Nutrition Reports Internat., 1963—83, mem. editl. adv. bd.: Sch. Food Svc. Rsch. Rev., 1977—82, mem. editl. adv. bd.: Profl. Nutritionist, 1977—80, mem. editl. adv bd.: Jour. Med. Consultation, 1985—2002, mem. editl. adv bd.: Jour. Medicinal Foods, 1998—2002, mem. editl. adv bd.: Food and Chem. Toxicology, 2000—, mem. editl. adv bd.: Jour. Nutraceuticals Functional & Health Foods, 2000—; contbr. articles to profl. jours. Served to capt USAF, 1960—63. Recipient Endel Karmas award for excellence in tchg. food sci., 1988. Fellow: Am Soc Nutritional Sci, Am Col Nutrition, Inst Food Technologists (William Cruess award for excellence in tchg. 1991, Babcock-Hart award 2001); mem.: NY Inst Food Technologists (chmn 1977—78), AAAS, Sociedad Latino Americano de Nutricion, Nat Asn Cath Chaplains, Am Pub Health Asn, Soc Nutrition Educ, Am Dietetic Asn, NY Acad Sci, Am Soc Clin Nutrition, Am Asn Cereal Chemists, Delta Epsilon Sigma, Sigma Xi. Home: 34 Taylor Rd Princeton NJ 08540-9521 Office: Rutgers U Food Sci 65 Dudley Rd New Brunswick NJ 08901-8520 E-mail: lachance@aesop.rutgers.edu.

LACHAPELLE, CLEO EDWARD, real estate broker; b. West Warwick, R.I., Aug. 16, 1925; s. Wilfrid Maxim and Alice (Michaud) L.; m. Ann Wilcox, July 17, 1954; children: Linda, Susan. BA in Sociology, St. Bonaventure U., 1950. Real estate broker, R.I.; lic. social worker. Probation officer R.I. Dept. Social Welfare, Cranston, 1951-53; prevention coord. R.I. Juvenile and Family Cts., Providence, 1953-63; asst. dir. Providence Youth Progress Bd., Inc., 1963-64, exec. dir., 1965-67, Progress for Providence, Inc., 1967-70; adminstr. Marathon House, Inc., Providence, 1970-77; dir. Washingtonian Hosp. and Ctr. for Addictions, Boston, 1977-80; state refugee coord. R.I. Office Refugee Resettlement, Cranston, 1980-85; broker, owner C.E. Lachapelle Real Estate Agy., Warwick, 1986—. Ret. social svcs. cons. VA Hosp., 1971-72, Nat. Ctr. Urban Ethnic Affairs, Washington, 1974-76, City of Providence, 1976-77, HHS, 1985, NIMH, 1985, and others; part-time detached youth worker Providence Recreation Dept., 1953-63; mem. mayor's adv. bd. City of Providence Model Cities Program, 1968-70; mem. adv. panel Nat. Inst. Drug Abuse, Rockville, Md., 1978; chair gov.'s study com. spl. needs population State of R.I., 1982-85; chair refugee policy Northeastern Regional Consultations, Boston, 1983; active U.S. Refugee Coodinators Policy Adv. Group, Washington, 1983, and others. Sgt. USAF, 1943-46, PTO. Mem. Nat. Assn. Realtors, R.I. Assn. Realtors, Kent Washington Bd. Realtors, Audubon Soc., Nat. Trust for Hist. Preservation. Roman Catholic. Avocations: reading, golf, gardening, structure restoration and environment preservation. Home: 39 Winslow Ave Warwick RI 02886-4724 Office: CE Lachapelle Real Estate 2905 Post Rd Warwick RI 02886-3117

LA CHAPELLE, DOLORES, environmentalist, writer; b. Louisville, July 4, 1926; d. John A. and Anna May (Kelly) Greenwell; divorced. BA, Denver U., 1947. Co-founder Deep Ecology; dir. Way of Mountain Learning Ctr., Silverton, Colo.; workshops leader, 1981—. Workshop presenter U. Utah, Salt Lake City, 1981-94, U. Wis., La Crosse, 1988-91, Notre Dame U., 1989, U. North Tex., Denton, 1990. Author: Earth Festivals, 1976, Earth Wisdom, 1978, rev. edit., 1984, also German translation, Sacred Land, Concerning Deep Ecology and Celebrating Life, rev. ed. 1992, also German translation, Deep Powder Snow, 1993, also Italian translation, D.H. Lawrence: Future Primitive, 1996. Mem. various environ. orgns., 1976—. Mem. Phi Beta Kappa. Avocations: teaching skiing, leading mountain climbing and outdoor rituals. Home: Box 542 Silverton CO 81433 Office: Way of the Mountain Ctr PO Box 542 Silverton CO 81433

LACHAR, DAVID, psychologist, educator; b. Washington, Dec. 14, 1946; s. George Peter Lachar and Harriet Zukav; m. Barbara Leeser, June 23, 1968; children: Ruth Wintz, Greg. BA, Wayne State U., 1966; PhD, U. Minn., 1970. Diplomate Am. Bd. Assessment Psychology (exec. com. mem. 1996—). Dir. divsn. psychology Lafayette Clinic Wayne State U., Detroit, 1978-85; dir. psychology tng. and rsch. Inst. Behavioral Medicine Good Samaritan Med. Ctr., Phoenix, 1985-87; prof. dept. psychiatry U. Tex. Houston Med. Sch., Houston, 1987—. Cons. editor: Jour. Cons. and Clin. Psychology, 1984-87, Psychological Assessment, 1991-2000, Jour. Clin. Child Psychology, 1984-96, Jour. Personality Assessment, 1979—, Assessment, 1993—, Jour. Sch. Psychology, 1986-92; contbr. articles to profl. jours., chpts. to books. Fellow APA, Soc. Personality Assessment, Am. Psychological Soc. Office: U Tex Houston Med Sch 1300 Moursund Houston TX 77030-3497 Fax: 713-500-2530. E-mail: david.lachar@uth.tmc.edu.

LACHCIK, NANCY LOU MARSHALL, lawyer, educator; b. Biloxi, Miss., July 25, 1957; d. Joseph John and Ruth Elaine (Glidden) Marshall; m. Joseph A. Lachcik. AA, St. Clair County C.C., 1977; BA, U. Mich., 1979; JD, Thomas M. Cooley Law Sch., 1982. Bar: Mich. 1983. Assoc. Dietrich & Cassavaugh, Port Huron, Mich., 1983-84; atty., referee St. Clair County Probate Ct., 1984-94; substitute tchr. Fraser (Mich.) Area Schs., Mich., 2000—. Deaconess 1st Congl. Ch., Port Huron, 1975-77; campaign worker William T. Fischer for County Commr., 1983; active Pleasant Valley Schs. PTO; mem. Pleasant Valley Sch. Edn. in Excellence Bd. Mem. ABA, ATLA, Mich. Bar Assn., St. Clair County Bar Assn., St. Clair County Coun. for Prevention Child Abuse and Neglect, Women Lawyers Assn. (treas. Blue Water region), Phi Theta Kappa. Republican.

LACHENAUER, ROBERT ALVIN, retired school superintendent; b. Newark, Apr. 1, 1929; s. Alvin Frederick and Helen Louise (Bowers) L.; m. Patricia McConnell, June 14, 1952; children: Jane, Nancy, Robert. AB, Montclair State U., 1951, MA, 1956; EdS, Seton Hall U., 1983. Diplomate in sch. adminstrn., 1988; cert. sch. adminstr., N.J., sch. bus. adminstr., N.J., tchr., N.J., supr., N.J., secondary sch. prin., N.J. Tchr. Bd. Edn., Union, N.J., 1951-52, 54-57, asst. bd. sec., 1957-61; dep. supt. New Providence (N.J.) Sch. Dist., 1961-76, supt., 1976-91, interim dir. of transp., 2002. Interim bus adminstr. Morris Union Joint Commn. 2000. Vice pres. Rigorous Ednl. Assistance Deserving Youth Found., 1991-93; treas. sch. monies Morris-Union Jointure Commn., 1987-93; pres. Union County Sch. Bus. Ofcls., 1967-68; chmn. Title IV State Adv. Coun., Trenton, N.J., 1976-78; pres. Morris-Union Jointure Commn., N.J., 1981-83, Union County Supts. Roundtable, 1983-84; adv. bd. Summit Bank, 1971-86; elder treas. Presbyn. Ch., New Providence, 1958-62; treas. New Providence Hist. Soc., 1966-76 pres. United Way, New Providence, 1978; property mgr. Providence Presbyn. Ch., Hilton Head Island, 1993-98, elder, 1995-97. Served as seaman USN, 1952-54. Named Disting. Scholar of the Acad., Nat. Acad. for Sch. Execs., 1990. Mem. N.J. Assn. Sch. Adminstrs. (exec. bd. 1986-91, Dedicated and Disting. Svc. 1991), N.J. Assn. Sch. Bus. Ofcls. (pres. 1974-75), Assn. Sch. Bus. Ofcls. U.S. (professionalization com. 1974, membership chmn. 1976), N.J. Assn. Ednl. Secs. (adv. bd. 1976=91, Outstanding Adminstr. of Yr. 1987), Rotary (pres. 1980-81). Home: Amherst Mews 17 Dickinson Rd Basking Ridge NJ 07920-4905 E-mail: rapmlach@aol.com.

LACHENBRUCH, ARTHUR HEROLD, geophysicist, researcher; b. New Rochelle, N.Y., Dec. 7, 1925; s. Milton Cleveland and Leah (Herold) L.; m. Edith Bennett, Sept. 7, 1950; children: Roger, Charles, Barbara. BA, Johns Hopkins U., 1950; MA, Harvard U., 1954, PhD, 1958. Registered geophysicist and geologist, Calif. Research geophysicist U.S. Geol. Survey, 1951—. Vis. prof. Dartmouth Coll., 1963; mem. numerous adv. coms. and panels. Contbr. articles to sci. jours. Mem. Los Altos Hills (Calif.) Planning Commn., 1966-86. Served with USAAF, 1943-46. Recipient Spl. Act award U.S. Geol. Survey, 1970, Meritorious Service award, 1972, Disting. Service award U.S. Dept. Interior, 1978. Fellow AAAS, Am. Geophys. Union (Walter H. Bucher medal 1989), Royal Astron. Soc., Geol. Soc. Am. (Kirk Bryan award 1963), Arctic Inst. N.Am.; mem. Nat. Acad. Sci. Achievements include current work: solid-earth geophysics, terrestial heat flow, tectonophysics, permafrost; sub-specialties: tectonics, geophysics. Office: US Geol Survey 345 Middlefield Rd Menlo Park CA 94025-3591

LACHENICHT-BERKELEY, ANGELA MARIE, marketing professional; b. St. Louis, Feb. 3, 1955; d. Bernard J. and Dolores B. (Vaughn) L.; m. David L. Fuller, Sept. 6, 1974 (div. Mar. 1987); m. John Berkeley, Apr. 22, 1991. A in Bus. Adminstrn., Meremac Community Coll., St. Louis, 1983; chancellor cert., U. Mo., St. Louis, 1989; cert. of tng. in employment law, U. Mo. St. Louis, St. Louis, 1990. P.B.X. operator Arthur Enterprises, St. Louis, 1971-73; credit mgr. Watson Furniture, 1973-80; owner, operator Action Video World, 1980-85; regional dir. retention and telemktg. Charter Comms., 1985—. Coord. Am. Cablevision, St. Louis, 1988; cons. Thomas Construction, St. Louis, 1987-90. Author, editor: (guide) Cencom Insider, 1989-91. Telemarketing coord. Comic Relief/Health Care for Homeless Coalition, St. Louis, 1988-92; cons. Non-Profit Employment Liaison Com., St. Louis, 1989-90. Recipient Emmy award, St. Louis chpt. NATAS, 1988, Civic Commendation, Health Care for the Homeless Coalition, St. Louis, 1989, 90, 91, 92. Mem. Women in Cable, Nat. Cable TV Assn. Democrat. Roman Catholic. Avocations: reading, creative writing, traveling, gourmet cooking, dancing. Office: Charter Comms 941 Charter Commons Town And Country MO 63017-0609

LACHER, THOMAS EDWARD, JR. tropical ecologist; b. Pitts., Aug. 9, 1949; s. Thomas Edward and Mary Catherine (McMullen) L.; m. Susana Ulisses Teixeira, Mar. 9, 1978; children: Iara Luiza, Lais Maria. BS, U. Pitts., 1972, PhD, 1980. Teaching asst. U. Pitts., 1972-78; asst. prof. U. de Brasilia, Brazil, 1979-81, Western Wash. U., Bellingham, 1981-87, assoc. prof., 1987-89; full prof. Clemson (S.C.) U., 1989—. Vis. prof. Fed. U. Minas Gerais, Belo Horizonte, Brazil, 1986; mem. area adv. com. Fulbright Commn., Washington, 1991-94; mem. species survival com. Internat. Union for Conservation of Nature and Natural Resources, Gland, Switzerland, 1989—. Author: Comparative Social Behavior of Caviid Rodents, 1981; editor: The Population Ecology and Wildlife Toxicology of Agricultural Pesticide Use, 1993; contbr. articles to Biosci., Jour. Mammalogy, Ecology, Am. Naturalist. Best Paper award Assn. S.E. Naturalists, 1983; grantee Am. Cyanamid Co., 1989, U.S. Forest Svc., 1989, 90, USAID, 1992. Mem. Am. Soc. Mammalogists (chair internat. rels. com., 1991—), Assn. Tropical Biology, Am. Soc. Naturalists, Ecol. Soc. Am., Sigma Xi. Democrat. Roman Catholic. Achievements include research in community ecology in tropical savannahs, foraging ecology of tropical primates and rodents, and territoriality in small mammals. Office: Clemson U Archbold Tropical Rsch Ctr 126 Lehotsky Hl Clemson SC 29634-0001

LACHMAN, MARGUERITE LEANNE, real estate investment advisor; b. Vancouver, B.C., Can., Mar. 16, 1943; came to U.S., 1955; d. Wilfred Harry and Claire Elisha (Silverthorn) L. BA, U. So. Calif., 1964; MA, Claremont U., 1966. With Real Estate Rsch. Corp., 1965-87, sr. v.p., 1977-79, pres., CEO, 1979-87; mng. dir. Schroder Real Estate Assocs., 1987-99, Schroder Mortgage Assocs., 1992-98; prin. Lend Lease Real Estate Investments, 1999—. Bd. dirs. Lincoln Nat. Corp., Liberty Property Trust; frequent lectr. seminars and profl. groups; exec.-in-residence Columbia Bus. Sch., 2000—. Author: (with Al Smith and Anthony Downs) Achieving Effective Desegregation, 1973, (with

Susan Olson) Tax Delinquency in the Inner City, 1976, Emerging Trends in Real Estate, 1981, 82, 83, 84, 85, 86, 87, Decade to Decade, 1988, Real Estate's Demographic Puzzle, 1995; contbr. articles to profl. jours. Gov. Urban Land Found. Mem. Urban Land Inst., N.Y. Women's Forum, Inc., Comml. Real Estate Women-N.Y. Office: Lend Lease 909 3rd Ave Fl 8 New York NY 10022-4731 E-mail: llachman@lendleaserei.com.

LACHMANN, DAVID GEORGE, legislative staff; b. N.Y.C., Dec. 28, 1958; s. Karl and Lotte Lachmann. BA in Philosophy and Polit. Sci., Boston U., 1984. Chief of staff N.Y. State Assemblywoman Eileen C. Dugan, Bklyn. and Albany, N.Y., 1985-89; legis. asst. Congressman Stephen J. Solarz, Washington, 1989-93; legis. dir. Congressman Jerrold Nadler, 1993-97; minority profl. staff subcom. on comml. and adminstrv. law U.S. Ho. Reps., 1997-2001, minority profl. staff subcom. on the Constitution, 2001—. Campaign staff Solarz for Congress, Bklyn., 1992; recording sec. Ind. Neighborhood Dems., Bklyn., 1986-89; vol. Stephen D. Brenza for Coun., Bklyn., 1985, Nadler for Congress, N.Y.C., 1994, 96; vol. Dem. Assembly campaign com., 1985-89. Jewish. Office: Com on Jud US Ho of Reps B 336 Rayburn HOB Washington DC 20515 E-mail: David.Lachmann@mail.house.gov.

LACHMANN, ELISABETH AMANDA, physician; b. Middletown, N.Y., Sept. 12, 1961; d. Erich Frederick and Christa Luise Lachmann; m. Kevin Charles Hunt, July 11, 1992; children: Lars Christian Hunt, Elisabeth Alexandra Hunt. AB, Bryn Mawr (Pa.) Coll., 1983; MD, Med. Coll. Pa., 1987. Intern in internal medicine North Shore U. Hosp., Manhasset, N.Y., 1987-88; resident in phys. medicine and rehab. N.Y. Hosp.-Cornell Med. Ctr., 1988-91; attending physiatrist N.Y. Presbyn. Hosp., 1991—, assoc. attending physiatrist, 1999—; clin. assoc. prof. Weill Medical Coll. Cornell Univ., N.Y.C., 1991—2001, prof., 2001—; pvt. practice, 2001—. Program dir. Dept. Rehab. Medicine N.Y. Presbyn. Hosp., 1991-99, quality assurance rep., 1991-2001; advisor Weill Med. Coll. of Cornell U., 1995—. Author: (with others) Clinical Oncology, 1995, 00, Principles/Practice Supportive Oncology, 1998, 2001, Physical Medicine and Rehabiliation, The Complete Approach, 1999. Recipient Conrad Jobst Found award Am. Congress of Rehab. Medicine, 1990. Mem. AMA, Am. Acad. of Phys. Medicine and Rehab. (mem. spl. interest group cancer rehab.), Office of Women in Medicine (sr. advisor). Republican. Lutheran. Home: 17 Hungerford Rd Briarcliff Manor NY 10510-1308 Office: 115 E 64st St 1st Fl New York NY 10021

LACHMANN, FRANK MICHAEL, psychologist, psychoanalyst; b. Breslau, Silesia, Germany, Dec. 9, 1929; came to U.S., 1938; s. Hans and Käte (Landsberg) L.; m. Annette Schamroth, July 15, 1962; children: Suzanne, Peter. BA, NYU, 1951; PhD, Northwestern U., 1955. Diplomate Am. Bd. Examiners in Profl. Psychology; cert. psychologist, N.Y., Mass. Pvt. practice psychoanalysis and psychotherapy, N.Y.C., 1964—. Mem. founding faculty Inst. for Psychoanalytic Study of Subjectivity, N.Y.C. Co-author: Psychoanalysis of Developmental Arrests, 1980, Self and Motivational Systems, 1994, The Clinical Exchange, 1996, Transfering Aggression, 2001, Infant Research and Adult Treatment, 2002. Mem. Internat. Coun. for Psychoanalytic Self Psychology. Avocations: bicycling, skiing. Office: 393 West End Ave New York NY 10024-6138 E-mail: framlach@aol.com.

LACHMAYR, KAREN LINDA, microbiologist, researcher; b. Agusta, ME, Apr. 1, 1975; d. Horst Lachmayr, Hella Lachmayr. Student, Harvard U., 1998—. Rsch. asst. New Eng. Biolabs, Beverly, Mass., 1995—98; rsch. specialist Harvard Sch. Pub. Health, Boston, 2000—01; tchg. asst. Harvard U., 2000—02, proctor Cambridge, 2001—. Teaching assistant Harvard University, Boston, 2000—02, Proctor, Cambridge, MA, 2001—pres. Mem.: Am. Soc. Microbiology. Avocations: sailing, skiing. Home: 2683 Harvard Yard Mail Ctr Cambridge MA 02138

LACIVITA, MICHAEL JOHN, safety engineer; b. Youngstown, Ohio, June 26, 1924; s. John and Carmela (Cacciavillani) L.; m. Margaret Mary Savoia, May 17, 1952; children: Linda Marie Lacivita Krieger, Sandra Marie Lacivita Vicarel. BSBA, Youngstown State U., 1951. Quality control techncian, supr. Republic Rubber div. Aeroquip Corp., Youngstown, 1951-65, mgr. quality control, 1965-67, prodn. supt., 1967-71; quality control mgr. Comml. Shearing Inc., 1971-75, dir. corp. safety, 1975-79, dir. corp. safety and security, 1979-86. Contbr. articles to profl. jours. and newspapers; patentee in field of bicycles; one-man photography shows include Butler Inst. Am. Art, 1984, 89, 92, Apple Gallery, Youngstown, 1985, Youngstown State U. Libr., 1986, Bank One, Youngstown, 1988. With USN, 1943-46. Named to Ohio Sr. Citizens Hall of Fame, 1996, Nat. Honor Soc., 1942. Mem. Am. Soc. Safety Engrs. (safety profl. of yr. award Ohio-Pa. chpt. 1984), Forging Industry Assn. (nat. safety and health com. 1980-83), Youngstown-Warren Inventors Assn. (pres. 1994-95). Home: 3220 Eldora Dr Youngstown OH 44511-1252 *Personal philosophy: My staff of life has been one of a never ending yearn to learn.*

LACK, LARRY HENRY, small business owner; b. Richland, Wash., Aug. 27, 1952; s. Eugene Herman and Myrtle (Wellman) L.; m. Patricia Ann Henry, Aug. 19, 1978; children: Vicki Marie, Rachel Ann. Enlisted USAF, 1970, disabled vet., 1978; aircraft mechanic Ill., S.C., Okla. AFBs., 1970-78; profl. inventor, prin. Lack Industries, Inc., Shreveport, La., 1979-85, Phoenix, 1985—; CEO Stellar Internat., 1991—. Cons. U.S. Air Force, Altus AFB, 1978-80, Cates & Phillips Patent Attys., Phoenix, 1985—; pres. La. Innovators Tech., Shreveport, 1981-82; lectr. Glendale Community Coll. 1987-88; guest lectr. Ariz. State U., 1989-90; authored legislation to regulate invention promotion cos. in Ariz., 1989. Patentee in field. Names to America's 2000 Most Notable Men. Mem. Internat. Platform Assn. Republican. Achievements include invention of Anasazi submersible, downhole positive displacement pump, the SunFlow solar pump, the Pegasus wind-driven pump, the scuba HeadLight, SS Telectric arc welder, Earth bore 2000 Drilling Rig, Stellar Compact Crude Oil Recovery System, others. Avocations: scuba diving, parachuting, hunting, rock climbing, flying. Home: PO Box 7632 Phoenix AZ 85011-7632 Office: 6332 W Oraibi Dr Glendale AZ 85308-5200 Fax: 623-376-9967. E-mail: stellar1@qwest.net.

LACK, LEON, pharmacology and biochemistry educator; b. Bklyn, Jan. 7, 1922; s. Jacob and Yetta (Wolf) L.; m. Pauline Kaplan, Feb. 14, 1948; children: Elias David, Joshua Morris, Johanna Elaine, Adina Roberta, Evonne Clara. BA, Bklyn. Coll., 1943; MS, Mich. Stae Coll., 1948; PhD, Columbia U., 1953; postgrad. (Univ. postdoctoral fellow), Duke U., 1954-55. Instr. in pharmacology and exptl. therapeutics Johns Hopkins U. Sch. Medicine, 1955-59, asst. prof. pharmacology and exptl. therapeutics, 1959-63; asst. prof. physiology and pharmacology Duke U. Med. Center, 1964-66, prof. pharmacology, 1966-92, prof. emeritus pharmacology, 1992—, chief biochemist to clin. research, 1966-70. Cons. E.I. DuPont de Nemours and Co., 1990-91, Monsanto, 1992-93. Contbr. numerous articles to profl. publs. Served with USAAF, 1943-46, PTO. Grantee NIH, 1960-90, OSHA, Ctr. for Disease Control, 1991-93. Mem. Am. Soc. Biol. Chemists, Am. Soc. Pharmacology and Exptl. Therapeutics. Jewish. Achievements include rsch. in pharmacology of cholesterol and lipids, pharmacology of intestinal bile salt transport, enzyme inhibitors relevant to prostatic cancer. Home: 2936 Welcome Dr Durham NC 27705-5556 Office: Duke U Med Ctr PO Box 3185 Durham NC 27715-3185

LACK, PATRICIA ANN, drilling and pumping company executive, consultant; b. Phoenix, Oct. 15, 1946; d.J.V. and Vivian Margaret Henry; m. Ronald Lee Jackson, Mar. 6, 1964 (div. May 1969); 1 child, Vicki Marie Snyder; m. Larry Henry Lack, Aug. 19, 1978. Student, Glendale (Ariz.) C.C., 1985-86. Enlisted USAF, 1973, advanced through grades to E-6, 1984; equipment mgr. Supply Squadron, Eglin AFB, Fla., 1973-74; supr. inventory mgmt. 3d Supply Squadron, Clark Air Base, The Philippines, 1974-77; chief supply sr. advisor 443d Supply Squadron, Altus AFB, Okla., 1977-79; instr., br. chief curriculum devel. SAC Non-Commd. Officers Acad., Barksdale AFB, La., 1979-84; resigned, 1984; pres. Lack Industries, Inc., Phoenix, 1984-90; chmn. bd. Stellar Innovations, LLC, 1996—. Freelance cons. and trainer, Phoenix, 1984-90; sexual discrimination recognition, protection, prevention trainer Glendale C.C. and to cos., Phoenix, 1984-90; cons. on career motivation enhancement to bus., Phoenix, 1984-95; counselor sexual assault recovery workshops, Phoenix, 1993—. Author: (novel) Willowman, 1993. Pub. spkr. to various women's groups and bus., Phoenix, 1990—. Mem. DAV (life), NRA (life), NRA Inst. for Legis. Action (life, honor roll 1995), Women Entrepreneurs Ariz. Republican. Avocations: flying, scuba diving, sport shooting, reading, camping. Office: Stellar Innovations LLC PO Box 7632 Phoenix AZ 85011-7632 Office Fax: 602-866-1561.

LACKENMIER, JAMES RICHARD, college president, priest; b. Lackawanna, N.Y., May 15, 1938; s. Harold and Margaret (Murphy) L. AB, Stonehill Coll., 1961; STL, Pontifical Gregorian U., Rome, 1965; AM, U.N.C., 1968; MA, U. Chgo., 1970. Ordained priest, Roman Catholic Ch. Tchr. English Notre Dame High Sch., Bridgeport, Conn., 1965-66, St. Peter's High Sch., Gloucester, Mass., 1966-68; chaplain St. Xavier Coll., Chgo., 1969-71; dir. collegiate formation Moreau Sem., Notre Dame, Ind., 1971-73; dir. campus ministry King's Coll., Wilkes-Barre, Pa., 1974-75, dir. devel., 1975-81, pres., 1981-99. Program dir. U. Portland Ctr., Salzburg, Austria, 1999-2001; treas. Holy Cross Fathers, 2000—. Bd. regents U. Portland, 1993-99; bd. trustees Mercy Hosp., 1989-95; bd. dirs. Pa. Ednl. Telecom. Exch. Network, 1994-99, Com. on Econ. Growth, Earth Conservancy, 1992-99, Pa. Ind. Coll. and Univ. Rsch. Ctr., 1995-99, Ctr. for Agile Pa. Edn., 1994-99, Greater Wilkes-Barre Partnership, Inc.; mem. United Way Campaign Cabinet, 1995-99; adv. bd. Pa. Mountains coun. Boy Scouts Am., Tuition Acct. Program, Office of Gov., Commonwealth Pa., 1992-96, 97-99; chmn. United Way Wyoming Valley, 1986; treas. Congregation of Holy Cross, Eastern Providence, 2001; corp. mem. Holy Cross Family Ministries, bd. dirs., 2001—; bd. dirs. Pius XII Youth and Family Svcs., 2001—. Mem. Rotary Internat. Lodges: Rotary Internat.; K.C. Democrat.

LACKEY, DEBORAH K. art educator; b. Gainesville, Ga., Nov. 1, 1952; d. R.G. Jr. and Florine L. BS in Art Edn., U. Ga., 1978, M in Art Edn., 1985, EdS, 1992, EdD, 1997. Cert. elem. tchr., Ga. Elem. art specialist Clarke County Bd. of Edn., Athens, Ga., 1979-80, Fulton County Bd. of Edn., Atlanta, 1980—. Adj. instr. Ga. State U., Atlanta, 1983-91, Clayton State Coll., Morrow, Ga., 1985-86, Mercer U., Atlanta, 1986—; curriculum chair elem. art edn. curriculum for Fulton County Schs., 1986; mem. Ga. tchr. cert. test revision com., Atlanta, 1990-94; adj. prof. Brenau U., 1998—. Mem. Gov.'s Fine Arts Edn. Adv. Coun., 1993—; mem. tchr. adv. panel High Mus. Art, Atlanta, 1995—; chair Art Edn. & Tech. Com., Fulton County Bd. Edn., 1995—. Mem. Nat. Art Edn. Assn. (rep.-elect southeast region elem. divsn. 1991-93, dir. 1993-95, southeastern elem. art educator 1998, nat. elem. art educator 1999), Ga. Art Edn. Assn. (bd. dris. 1985—, pres. 1991-93, Ga. Art Educator of Yr. 1991, Ga. Elem. Art Educator of the Yr. 1997), Ga. Citizens for the Arts, Gold Key, Phi Kappa Phi, Kappa Delta Pi, Phi Lambda Theta. Office: Roswell North Elem 10525 Woodstock Rd Roswell GA 30075-2939

LACKEY, JAMES FRANKLIN, JR. civil engineer; b. Tatum, N.Mex., Jan. 3, 1932; s. James Franklin and Florence Estelle (Morris) L.; m. Sue Linda Shockley Lackey, Sept. 22, 1953; children: James Franklin III, Dale Robert, John Patrick, Patricia Marie. BS in Civil Engring., Okla. State U., 1962. Registered profl. engr., Calif., Okla., Tex., Ariz., Nebr., Wash., Utah, Idaho, Colo. Engr. Morrison-Knudsen Sedalia, Mo., 1962-63; asst. civil engr. Internat. Engring. Co., Inc., San Francisco, 1963-64, assoc. civil engr., 1964-67, sr. civil engr., 1969-73, prin. engr., 1973-74, chief civil engr., 1974-77, chief engr., 1978-82, design mgr., 1983-86; mgr. spl. projects Morrison-Knudsen Engrs., 1986-90, mgr. projects, infrastructure Dallas, 1991-94; v.p., COO gen. constrn. divsn. Balfour Beatty Construction, Atlanta, 1994-96; pres. Sun Cities Area Transit System, Inc., 1997—. Capt. U.S. Army, 1952-59. Recipient Commendation medal with oak leaf, U.S. Army; named Kavanaugh Community Bldg. award scholar, 1961. Mem. ASCE (life), NSPE, Ga. Soc. Profl. Engrs., Ariz. Soc. Profl. Engrs. Home: 19820 N Willowcreek Cir Sun City AZ 85373-1236 Office: Balfour Beatty Construction Inc 999 Peachtree St NE Atlanta GA 30309-3915

LACKEY, JIMMIE R. government agency administrator; b. Birmingham, Ala. B in Bus. and Sociology, Okla. Coll. Liberal Arts; M in Computer Engring., Kans. State U.; MPA, Shippensburg U., Pa.; postgrad., U.S. Army Command and Gen. Staff Coll., U.S. Army War Coll. Commd. U.S. Army, advanced through grades to col., ret., 1997; command assignments include warhead detachment Turkey; artillery bn. 1st cavalry divsn. Tex.; 25th infantry divsn. artillery Hawaii; staff assignments include key opers and plans positions at bn., divsn. artillery, major Army command, Army staff; project mgr. major computer sys.; svc. sch. instr.; tours of duty in Germany, Turkey, Vietnam; key assignments in Asia-Pacific region; project dir. Asia-Pacific Ctr. Security Studies, Honolulu, 1995—97, exec. dir., 1997—. Decorated Legion of Merit (3rd), Bronze Star. Mem.: Japan-Am. Soc. Hawaii, Pacific and Asian Affairs Coun., Rotary. Office: Asia-Pacific Ctr Security Studies 2058 Maluhia Rd Honolulu HI 96815*

LACKEY, KAYLE DIANN, elementary education educator; b. Willard, Ill., Oct. 22, 1937; d. Lon Edward and Eldora Grace (Pecord) Ogborn; m. Joseph Donald Lackey, Nov. 29, 1958; 1 child, Dana Lyn Embree. BA in History, Asbury Coll., Wilmore, Ky., 1958; MA with honors, Webster U., 1975, cert. reading specialist, 1977; cert. gifted and talented educator, So. Ill. U., Edwardsville, 1990. Ltd. cert. elem. edn., Ill; cert. pub. sch. tchr. (life), Mo.; cert. reading specialist, Mo.; registered profl. real estate salesperson, Mo. Tchr. kindergarten Dist. # 196, Dupo, Ill., 1959-63, reading specialist, 1973-79, tchr. 2d grade, 1979-84, tchr. 4th grade, 1985-93, tchr. gifted and talented, 1990-92; tchr. 1st grade Mehlville R-9 Dist., St. Louis, 1963-65, substitute tchr., 1965-72, 1993—. Clin. coop. tchr. So. Ill. U., Edwardsville, 1989; salesperson Coldwell Banker Real Estate, St. Louis, 1985-2000. Rep. for tchrs. Am. Fedn. Tchrs., Dupo, 1975-77, mem. negotiation com., 1981; tchr. U.S. Divsn. Laubach Literacy Internat., St. Louis, 1987-89; author, tchr. gifted and talented enrichment summer program, 1991; participant Asbury Coll. travel seminary on Near-Eastern studies, 1985; rep. ecumenical com. Cmty. Resource Svcs., 1986-89, trustee 2000, 01—; chmn. bd. edn. presch. Zion United Meth., St. Louis, 1987-88, 2000-01, trustee, 1986-90, mem. adminstrv. bd. religion and race, ch. and soc., 1989-93, fin. sec., 1999, bd. dirs., 2000; active voter registration Gephardt for Congress, St. Louis, 1993-95; mem. Ill. Tchrs. Retirement Sys., 1993—; vol. Am. Cancer Soc., 2000. Recipient Appreciation for Tchg. Excellence award Bd. Edn., Dupo, 1993, Ill. Math. and Sci. Acad. award of Excellence, 1999. Mem. St. Louis Zoo Soc., Mo. Bot. Soc. Avocations: piano, travel, writing, reading, political campaign volunteerism. Home: 6511 Towne Woods Dr Saint Louis MO 63129-4521

LACKEY, LARRY A., JR. civil engineer; b. Fairfax, Va., Dec. 3, 1964; s. Larry Alton Sr. and Ilene Jane Lackey; m. Rebecca Sue Owen, Feb. 14, 1987; children: Bryan, Benjamin, Daniel, Carolyn. BSCE, U. South Fla., 1994. Registered profl. engr., N.C., Ga. Engring. designer Camp Dresser & McKee, Inc., Clearwater, Fla., 1987-94; project mgr. Mosby Engring. Assocs., Inc., Sarasota, 1994-96; project engr. McGill Assocs., P.A., Asheville, N.C., 1996-98; dir. engring. and pub. works Macon County, Franklin, 1998—. Pres. First Regency Developers, Inc., Franklin.; advisor planning com. Macon County Pub. Schs.; instr. Southwestern C.C., Franklin, 1998—. Sr. comdr. Royal Rangers, Franklin, 1998—. Mem. ASCE, Am. Water Work Assn., Water Environ. Fedn., Chi Epsilon. Office: Macon County 109 Sierra Dr Franklin NC 28734-0762 Fax: (828) 349-2185. E-mail: allackey@dnet.net.

LACKEY, MARY MICHELE, physician assistant; b. Johnson City, N.Y., Dec. 22, 1955; d. Joseph Charles and Jane Ann (Weston) Reardon; m. Donald V. Lackey Jr., Oct. 27, 1979 (div. Nov. 1995); m. Shane R. Russell, Mar. 27, 1999. AAS in Nursing, Broome Community Coll., Binghamton, N.Y., 1978; cert. family nurse practitioner, Albany Med. Coll., 1982; BS in Psychology and Sociology, U. State of N.Y., Albany, 1989. Cert. physician asst., family nurse practitioner, nurse midwife; RN, N.Y., Conn. Physician asst. Streit, Hickey & Lasky MD, P.C., Saratoga Springs, N.Y., 1982-85, Litchfield Hills Ob/Gyn., Sharon, Conn., 1986-89, Dutchess Med. Practice, PC, Amenia, N.Y., 1991-2001. Physican asst. Vassar Coll. Health Svcs., Poughkeepsie, N.Y., 1990—. Leader, instr. Girl Scouts U.S.A., Dutchess County, N.Y., 1990-98. Lt. col. U.S. Army, 1975-98 (ret.). Fellow: Am. Coll. Nurse Midwives, Am. Acad. Physician Assts.; mem.: Militia Assn. N.Y., N.G. Assn. U.S., Phi Theta Kappa. Roman Catholic. Avocations: breeding exhbn. poultry and geese, gourmet cooking, collect early med. books and equipment. Home: 262 Davis Rd Salt Point NY 12578-3122

LACKI, ALLAN VINCENT, industrial engineer; b. Kearny, N.J., Apr. 6, 1953; s. John Theodore and Jenny (Biondo) L.; m. Joan Terese Blake, Apr. 15, 1978; children: Karen Marie, Brian Cameron. BS in Indsl. Engring., N.J. Inst. Tech., 1975, MS in Mgmt. Engring., 1982. Indsl. engring. intern St. Luke's Hosp. Ctr., N.Y.C., 1974; sales engring. assoc. Faber Assoc., Clifton, NJ, 1975; plant indsl. engr. trainee Am. Can Co., Union, 1975, staff indsl. engr. Greenwich, Conn., 1976; methods engring. supr. Jersey Cen. Power, Morristown, 1976—81; ops. analyst sr. III, FirstEnergy, Parsippany, NJ, 1982—93, transp. engring. supr. Morristown, 1994—96, power contracts specialist Reading, Pa., 1997—2000, transmission investment engr., 2000—01, sr. bus. analyst Pa., 2001—. Cons. in field. Contbr. articles to profl. jours. Event organizer Mine Hill (N.J.) Day Com., 1987-88. Mem. Inst. Indsl. Engrs. (chpt. v.p. 1999—; webmaster and competition dir. 2000—), Soc. Automotive Engrs., Corvair Soc. Am., N.J. Assn. Corvair Enthusiasts (sec. 1988-96; webmaster 2000—), Lincoln Highway Heritage Corridor Assn., Northeast Corvair Coun. (webmaster 2000—, dir. competition), Phi Eta Sigma, Tau Beta Pi, Alpha Pi Mu (pres. local chpt. 1974-75). Achievements include development of transmission contracts for new electric power plants, power purchase contracts, management information systems and construction equipment. Avocations: antique auto restoration, writing, camping, web-site design. Home: 102 Atlantic Ave Sinking Spring PA 19608-9343 Office: FirstEnergy Rt 183 & Van Reed Rd Reading PA 19605 E-mail: alacki@gpu.com., redbat01@aol.com.

LACKLAND, JOHN, lawyer; b. Parma, Idaho, Aug. 29, 1939; AB, Stanford U., 1962; JD, U. Wash., 1964; master gardener, Colo. State U., 1996. Bar: Wash. 1965, U.S. Dist. Ct. (we. dist.) Wash. 1965, (ea. dist.) Wash. 1973, U.S. Ct. Appeals (9th cir.) 1965, Conn. 1981, U.S. Dist. Ct. Conn. 1983, U.S. Supreme Ct. 1973, U.S. Dist. Ct. (so. dist.) N.Y. 1988. Assoc. firm Lane Powell Moss & Miller, Seattle, 1965-69; asst. atty. gen. State of Wash., 1969-72; asst. chief State of Wash. (U. Wash. div.), 1969-72; v.p., sec., gen. counsel Western Farmers Assn., Seattle, 1972-76, Fotomat Corp., Stamford, Conn., 1976-80; ptnr. Leepson & Lackland, 1981-88, Lackland and Nalewaik, 1988-92; pvt. practices Westport, Conn., 1992-94; prin. Lackland Assocs., Grand Junction, Colo., 1994—2002. Bd. dirs. Mercer Island (Wash.) Congl. Ch., 1967-70, pres. bd. dirs., 1970; mem. land use plan steering com. City of Mercer Island, 1970-72; bd. dirs. Mercer Island Sch. Dist., 1970-73, v.p. bd. dirs., 1972, pres. 1973; trustee Mid-Fairfield Child Guidance Ctr., 1982-84, Norfield Congl. Ch., 1982-84; bd. dirs. Grand Junction Symphony Orch., 1995-99.

LACKLAND, THEODORE HOWARD, lawyer; b. Chgo., Dec. 4, 1943; s. Richard and Cora Lee (Sanders) L.; m. Dorothy Ann Gerald, Jan. 2, 1970; 1 child, Jennifer Noel. BS, Loyola U., Chgo., 1965; MA, Howard U., 1967; JD, Columbia U., 1975; grad., U.S. Army Ranger Sch., 1968. Bar: N.J. 1975, U.S. Dist. Ct. N.J. 1975, Ga. 1982, U.S. Tax Ct. 1983, U.S. Supreme Ct. 1979, U.S. Dist. Ct. (no. dist.) Ga. 1982, U.S. Dist. Ct. (mid. dist.) Ga. 1985. Assoc. Dewey, Ballantine, Bushby, Palmer & Wood, N.Y.C., 1975-78; asst. U.S. atty. Dist. N.J., Newark, 1978-81; ptnr. Arnall Golden & Gregory, Atlanta, 1981-93, Lackland & Assoc., Atlanta, 1993-95, Lackland & Heyward, Atlanta, 1995-2000, Lackland & Assocs., LLC, Atlanta, 2000—. Adj. prof. law Ga. State U. Law Sch., 1989-99. Assoc. editor Columbia Human Rights Law Rev., 1974-75; contbr. articles to profl. jours. Adv. dir. Atlanta Bus. Devel. Ctr., Minority Bus. Devel. Coun., Atlanta, 1983-91; mem. exec. com. Leadership Atlanta, 1986, 1990-91. Capt. U.S. Army, 1967-71. Decorated Bronze Star with 1 oak leaf cluster, Purple Heart, Air medal. Mem.: Atlanta Bar Assn., Gate City Bar Assn., Fed. Bar Assn., Ga. Bar Assn., ABA. Democrat. Roman Catholic. Home: 4400 Oak Ln Marietta GA 30062-6355 Office: Lackland & Assocs LLC 230 Peachtree St NW Atlanta GA 30303-1562

LACKNER, JAMES ROBERT, aerospace medicine educator; b. Virginia, Minn., Nov. 11, 1940; s. William and Lillian Mae (Galbraith) L.; m. Ann Martin Graybiel, Aug. 26, 1970. BSc, MIT, 1966, PhD, 1970. Asst. prof. psychology Brandeis U., Waltham, Mass., 1970-74, assoc. prof. psychology, 1974-79, Riklis prof. physiology dept. psychology, 1977—, chmn. dept. psychology, 1975-83, provost, dean faculty, 1986-89, dir. Ashton Graybiel Spatial Orientation Lab., 1982—. Research assoc. dept. psychology and clin. research ctr. MIT, Cambridge, 1970-80; sci. adv. bd. Space Biomed. Research Inst., Houston, 1982—, Aphasia Research Ctr. Boston U. Sch. Med., 1977-82, Eunice Kennedy Shriver Ctr. Harvard U. Med. Sch., Cambridge, 1980-90; sci. adv. panel astronaut longitudinal health program Johnson Space Ctr., NASA, 1983, exec. sec. space adaptation syndrome steering com., 1982-84, preadaption trainer working group, 1986—, artificial gravity working group, 1987—; fabricant com. life scis. experiments for a space sta., 1982; space scis. bd. sensory motor panel NAS, 1984-86; com. on hearing, bioacoustics and biomechanics NRC, 1985-89, com. on vision, 1987-92, com. on space, biology and medicine, 1991-99, mem. com. virtual reality rsch. and devel., 1992-95. Mem. editorial bd. Presence, 1992—, Jour. Vestibular Rsch., 1991-2001, Jour. Neurophysiology, 1995—, Exptl. Brain Rsch., 1997—, Jour. Exptl. Psychology, 2001—; contbr. more than 200 articles to sci. jours. Mem. Am. Soc. for Gravitational and Space Biology, Aerospace Med. Assn. (Arnold B. Tuttle award), Soc. for Neurosci., Psychonomics Soc., Internat. Brain Research Orgn., Barany Soc. (hon.), Internat. Acad. Astronautics (hon.). Achievements include research in human sensory-motor coordination and spatial orientation. Home: Boyce Farm Rd Lincoln MA 01773-4813 Office: Brandeis U Ashton Graybiel Lab 415 South St Waltham MA 02453-2728

LACKOFF, MARTIN ROBERT, engineer, physical scientist, researcher; b. Queens, N.Y., Oct. 6, 1946; s. Samuel K. and Esther (Soifer) L.; m. Mara Lee Feinstein, Oct. 29, 1989; 1 child, Blythe Ann. BSEE, U. R.I., 1969, MS in Ocean Engring., 1971, PhD in Ocean Engring., 1974. With tech. staff Stein Assocs., Inc., Waltham, Mass., 1974; tech. staff to dir. of tech. Naval Underwater Systems Ctr., New London, Conn., 1975-77, tech. staff advanced systems tech., 1977-79; staff to mgr. Computing Systems div. Analogic Corp., Wakefield, Mass., 1980-83; staff to mgr. signal processing dept. Equipment div. Raytheon Co., Wayland, 1983-85; lead engr. The Mitre Corp., Bedford, 1985-97; sr. prin. engr. Raytheon Sys. Co., 1997—. Instr. EE Dept. Hartford (Conn.) Grad. Ctr., 1977-80. Mem. Am. Geophys. Union, Tau Beta Pi, Phi Kappa Phi. Office: Raytheon Electronic Systems 180 Hartwell Rd Bedford MA 01730-2498 E-mail: mlackoff@worldnet.att.net.

LACLAIR, PATRICIA MARIE, physical education director, paramedic; b. East Liverpool, Ohio, Dec. 29, 1958; d. James Herbert and Irene Marie (Ruthledge) LaC. BS in Edn., Youngstown State U. Cert. paramedic, lic. Tex. Dept. Health, cert. BLS instr., basic trauma life support advanced, ACLS, Tex. Sch. Bus. Driver Safety Tng. Cert. Dir. elem. phys. edn. Trinity (Tex.) Ind. Sch. Dist., 1985—; instr. CPR AHA, Bryan, Tex., 1985—, instr. phys. edn., 1989—; emergency med. technician Express Care EMS, 1999—2001; paramedic Prime Care EMS. Emergency med. svcs. program instr., 1994—, emergency med. svcs. program examiner, 1994—, basic critical incident stress mgmt. trainer, 1994—; instr. Trinity Peninsula Ambulance Svc., 1994-95; sec. bd. dirs. Trinity Emergency Med. Svc., 1990-95, mgr. 1986-95; instr., trainer Primecare Emergency Med. Svc., 1996-99, Jacksonville Fire Dept. Emergency Med. Svcs., 1996—; instr.-examiner Tex. Emergency Med. Svc., 1992-99. Vol. EMT, 1985-95. Home: 206 Valley Ln Crockett TX 75835-1328 Address: 206 Valley Ln Crockett TX 75835-1328

LACOMBE, MICHAEL, information technology executive; Grad., Ecole Supérieure Libre des Sciences Commerciales Appliquées, 1977. Sales engr. Sharp Electronics Corp.; retail sales mgr. Microsoft, Redmond, Wash., 1983, dep. gen. mgr. sales and mktg. ops., 1984, regional dir. So. Europe, 1991; v.p. Microsoft Europe; sr. v.p., chmn. Microsoft Europe, Middle East and Africa. Office: Microsoft One Microsoft Way Redmond WA 98052-6399*

LACOMB-WILLIAMS, LINDA LOU, community health nurse; b. Galion, Ohio, Oct. 1, 1948; d. Horace Allen and Roberta May (Black) Braden; m. Robert Earl LaComb, Feb. 1, 1970 (div. Aug. 1984); children: Robin Marie, Patrick Alan; m. Robert Allen Williams, Aug. 30. 1991; children Erin, Megan. BSN, Capitol U., 1970; MPH, U. South Fla., 2002. RN, Fla., Ohio. Staff nurse St. Anne's Hosp., Columbus, Ohio, 1970; pub. health nurse Hillsborough County Dept. Health, Tampa, Fla., 1970-80, community health nurse supr., 1980-87; sr. community health nurse Polk County Dept. Health, Lakeland, 1987-88; sr. RN supr. Children's Med. Svcs., Tampa, 1988-91, Lakeland, 1991-99; sr. cmty. health nurse supr. Polk County Health Dept., Fla., 1999—. 1st lt. flight nurse res. USAF, 1971-75. Recipient Boss of Yr. award, Straberry chpt. Am. Bus. Women's Assn., 1985. Mem.: ARC, ANA, Fla. Nurses Assn. (grievance rep. state employees profl. bargaining unit 1976, pres. 1984—87, 1st v.p. 1989—91, dist. 2d v.p. 1998, Undine Sams award 1987, Nurse of Yr. award Dist. Four 1987), Eta Sigma Gamma, Sigma Theta Tau, Phi Kappa Phi.

Republican. Presbyterian. Avocations: walking, nurses' rights. Home: PO Box 1491 Valrico FL 33595-1491 Office: Polk County Health Dept Lakeland Office 3241 Lakeland Hills Blvd Lakeland FL 33805-2266 E-mail: lacombwilliams@aol.com.

LACOSTE, PAUL, lawyer, educator, university official; b. Montreal, Que., Can., Apr. 24, 1923; s. Emile and Juliette (Boucher) L.; m. Louise Marcil, Aug. 31, 1973 (div.); children: Helene, Paul-André, Anne-Marie. BA, U. Montreal, 1943, MA, 1944, Licenciate in Philosophy, 1946, Licenciate in Law, 1960; postgrad., U. Chgo., 1946-47; Docteur de l'Universite, U. Paris, 1948; LLD (hon.), McGill U., 1975, U. Toronto, 1978; D Univ. (hon.), Laval U., 1986. Bar: Que. 1960. Prof. philosophy U. Montreal, 1946-86, prof. law, 1960-68, 1985-87, vice rector, 1966-68, exec. vice rector, 1968-75, rector, 1975-85, prof. emeritus, 1987—. Moderator, commentator CBC, 1956-63; mem. firm Lalande, Brière, Reeves, Lacoste et Paquette, Montreal, 1964-66; mem. Royal Commn. on Bilingualism and Biculturism, 1963-71, Que. Superior Coun. Edn., 1964-68, Que. Coun. Univs., 1969-77; mem. Conf. Rectors and Prins. Que. Univs., 1967-85, pres. 1977-79; chmn. Fed. Commn. and Coms. for Environ. Projects, 1991-98. Author: (with others) La crise de l'enseignement au Canada Francais, 1961, Justice et Paix scolaire, 1962, A Place of Liberty, 1964, Le Canada au seuil du siecle de l'abondance, 1969, Education permanente et potentiel universitaire, 1977; contbr. articles to profl. jours. Mem. Corp. de l'Ecole des Hautes Etudes Commerciales, 1975-85, Ecole Polytechnique, 1975-85, Corp. du Coll. Marie de France; bd. dirs. Clin. Rsch. Inst. of Montreal, 1975-85; pres. Assn. des universités partiellement ou entièrement de langue française, 1978-81. Mem. Assn. Univs. and Colls. of Can. (mem. com. of pres. 1975-85, v.p. 1977, pres. 1978-79), Assn. Commonwealth Univs. (dir. 1977-80) Home: 2820 Willowdale Montreal QC Canada H3T 1H5 Office: Université de Montréal CP 6128 Pavillon 2910 bur 6 Montreal QC Canada H3C 3J7

LA COUR, LOUIS BERNARD, lawyer; b. Columbus, Ohio, Aug. 12, 1926; s. Louis and Cleo (Carter) La C.; m. Jane Lee McFarland, Mar. 24, 1950; children: Lynne Denise, Avril Rose, Cheryl Celeste. BA, Ohio State U., 1951; LLB, Franklin U., 1961; JD, Capital U., Columbus, 1967. Bar: Ohio 1962. Land commr. U.S. Dist. Ct. (so. dist.) Ohio, Columbus, 1981, spl. master, 1983-87; spl. counsel City of Columbus Atty.'s Office, 1986—. Contbr. articles to profl. jours. Cons. NAACP, N.Y.C., 1975-80; mem. Greater Columbus Arts Coun., Model State Legis. Com.; sec. Mid-Ohio Regional Planning Commn., Columbus, 1978; vice-chmn. Columbus Civic Ctr. Commn., 1979; mem. rural zoning commn. Franklin County, 1994; mem. Ohio Elected Ofcls. Commn.; mem. Franklin Soil and Water Conservation Dist. Mem. ABA, , Franklin County Rural Zoning Commn., Columbus Bar Assn., Am. Planning Assn. (task force), Ohio Elected Ofcls. Commn., New Albany C.C., Franklin Soil and Water Conservation, Sigma Pi Phi, Lambda Boulé. Democrat. Roman Catholic. Avocations: tennis, cooking, theatre, jazz. Home: 1809 N Cassady Ave Columbus OH 43219-1520 Office: 500 S Front St Ste 1140 Columbus OH 43215-7628

LACOURSIERE, ROY BARNABY, psychiatrist; b. Windsor, Ont., Can., Aug. 9, 1937; s. Lionel and Cecile (Robinet) L.; m. Marilyn E. Marshall, Sept. 9, 1961 (div. Apr. 1974); children: Jacqueline, Joan, Colette; m. Joanna Durrance, Sept. 25, 1982; 1 adopted child, Eric. BA with honors, U. Windsor, 1962; MD, McGill U., Montreal, Can., 1966. Diplomate Am. Bd. Psychiatry and Neurology, Diplomate Am. Bd. Forensic Psychiatry; cert. in alcoholism Am. Soc. Addiction Medicine. Intern then resident Menninger Sch. Psychiatry, Topeka, 1966-71; dir. community service office Menninger Found., 1971-74; chief chem. problems treatment unit, extended care/ geriatric psychiatry unit VA Hosp., 1975-97, cons. psychiatry, 1972-74; practice medicine specializing in forensic psychiatry, 1973—; vis. prof. Washburn U. Law Sch., 1974—. Author: The Life Cycle of Groups, 1980, (with others): Patients, Psychiatrists and Lawyers: Law and the Mental Health System, 2d edit., 1997; contbr. articles to profl. jours. Vestry St. David's Episc. Ch., Topeka, 1985-88 Fellow Am. Psychiat. Assn., ACP, Royal Coll. Physicians and Surgeons Can.; mem. Am. Acad. Psychiatry and Law, Am. Acad. Forensic Scis. Avocations: travel, reading, writing. Office: 3600 SW Burlingame Rd Topeka KS 66611-2053

LACOUTURE, PETER GEORGE, medical researcher; b. Worcester, Mass., Oct. 26, 1951; s. Paul Arthur and Virginia Rose Lacouture; m. Sheila Foy Lacouture, Apr. 29, 1978; children: Alyssa Lynne, Bryan Peter, Timothy Scott. AB Chemistry, Holy Cross Coll., 1973; MS Pharm., Mass. Coll. Pharm., 1981, PhD Pharm., 1986. Cons. Mass. Poison Control, Boston, 1977—87; cons. epidemiology unit Boston U., 1980—87; sr. rsch. asst. Harvard Sch. Pub. Health, 1980—85; rsch. affiliate Children's Hosp., 1985—87; instr. pediatrics Harvard Med. Sch., 1988—89; asst. dir. Wyeth-Ayerst Rsch., Radnor, Pa., 1988—94; sr. dir. rsch. & devel. Purdue Pharma LP, Stamford, Conn., 1992—2001; pres. Magidom Discovery, LLC, Westport, 2001—. Adj. asst. prof. Brown U., Providence, 1994—, U. Pa., Phila., 2000—. Contbr. articles to profl. jours. Coach Newtown Babe Ruth, Conn., 1995—2000; coord., coach Newtown Soccer Club, 1993—2001. Scholar Powers scholar, Holy Cross Coll., 1970—73, Bradbury-White scholar, Mass. Coll. Pharm., 1974, 1984. Mem.: Am. Acad. Neurology, Am. Acad. Asthma, Allergy & Immunology, Am. Soc. Anesthesiology, Am. Coll. Rheumatology, Am. Thoracic Soc., Am. Acad. Clin. Toxicology. Roman Catholic. Achievements include patents for prolonged anesthesia in joints. Avocations: woodworking, gardening, architecture. Office: Magidom Discovery LLC 1771 Post Rd E #228 Westport CT 06880

LACOVARA, PHILIP ALLEN, lawyer; b. N.Y.C., July 11, 1943; s. P. Philip and Elvira Lacovara; m. Madeline E. Papio, Oct. 14, 1961; children: Philip, Michael, Christopher, Elizabeth, Karen, Daniel, Andrew. AB magna cum laude, Georgetown U., 1963; JD summa cum laude, Columbia U., 1966. Bar: N.Y. 1967, D.C. 1974, U.S. Supreme Ct. 1970. Law clk. to presiding justice U.S. Ct. Appeals D.C. Cir., 1966-67; asst. to solicitor gen. U.S. Washington, 1967-69; assoc. Hughes Hubbard & Reed, N.Y.C., 1969-71, ptnr. N.Y.C. and Washington, 1974-88; v.p., sr. counsel GE, Fairfield, Conn., 1988-90; mng. dir, gen. counsel Morgen Stanley & Co., N.Y.C., 1990-93; ptnr. Mayer, Brown & Platt, N.Y.C. and Washington, 1993—. Spl. counsel to N.Y.C. Police Commr., 1971-72; dep. solicitor gen. U.S. Dept. Justice, Washington, 1972-73; counsel to spl. prosecutor Watergate Spl. Prosecution Force, 1973-74; lectr. law Columbia U.; adj. prof. Georgetown U. Law Ctr.; vis. lectr. various colls., univs.; mem. Jud. Conf. D.C. Circuit, 1973—; chmn. commn. on admissions and grievances U.S. Ct. Appeals for D.C. Circuit, 1980-86; spl. counsel U.S. Ho. of Reps. Com. on Standards Ofcl. Conduct, 1976-77; chmn. bd. trustees Public Defender Service for D.C., 1976-81; sec. exec. com. bd. visitors Columbia U. Sch. Law; pres. Columbia U. Sch. Law Alumni Assn., 1986-88; bd. govs. D.C. Bar, 1981-84, gen. counsel, 1985-87, pres., 1988-89, mem. legal ethics com., 1976-81, chmn. code subcom., 1977-81. Contbr. articles to profl. jours. Co-chair, Washington Lawyers Com. for Civil Rights Under Law, 1982-84; mem. D.C. Jud. Nomination Commn., 1981-86; bd. dirs. Legal Aid Soc. of N.Y.C., 1992—. Fellow Am. Coll. Trial Lawyers; mem. ABA (ho. of dels. 1978-89, vice-chmn. sect. individual rights and responsibilities 1985-87, 89-91, chmn. 1991-92), Am. Law Inst., Practicing Law Inst. (trustee), Cath. Interracial Coun. N.Y., Lawyers Com. for Human Rights (trustee 1991—), Legal Aid Soc. N.Y.C. (bd. dirs. 1992-98), London Ct. of Internat. Arbitration, Lotos Club, Knights of Malta. Roman Catholic. Home: 1137 Smith Ridge Rd New Canaan CT 06840-2333 Office: 1675 Broadway New York NY 10019-5820

LACROIX, CHRISTIAN MARIE MARC, fashion designer; b. Arles, Bouches du Rhône, France, May 16, 1951; s. Maxime and Jeannette (Bergier) L. Grad., U. Valery, Montpelier, France, 1973. Asst. Hermes Co., Paris, 1978-79, Guy Paulin Co., Paris, 1980-81; chief designer Jean Patou Co., 1982-87; prin. Christian Lacroix Co., 1987—. Author: Pieces of a Pattern, 1992, The Diary of a Collection, 1996; illustrator: Style d'aujourd hui, 1995. Decorated officier des Arts et Lettres, chevalier de la Legion d'Honneur (France); recipient Golden Thimble award, 1986, 88, Coun. Fashion Designer Am. award, 1987, Prix Balzac, 1989, Das Goldene Spinnrad award Kreffeld, R.F.A., 1990, Molière Best Costumes award for Phédre, 1996; decorated Comdr. de L'Order des Arts et des Lettres, 1998, Chevalier de la Legion d'honneur, 2002. Roman Catholic. Office: Christian Lacroix 73 Faubourg Saint-Honoré 75008 Paris France

LA CROIX, SUMNER JONATHAN, economics educator; b. Hartford, Conn., Dec. 28, 1954; s. Harold Francis and Miriam Alma (McDermott) La C. BA, U. Va., 1976; MA, U. Wash., 1979, PhD, 1981. Asst. prof. dept. econs. U. Hawaii, Honolulu, 1981-86, assoc. prof., 1986-90, prof., 1990—, chair dept. econs., 2001—; Alena Wels Hirshorn prof. Barnard Coll., Columbia U., N.Y.C., 1998—2000; sr. fellow rsch. program East-West Ctr., Honolulu, 2001—. Vis. lectr. U. Canterbury, Christchurch, New Zealand, 1984, Australian Grad. Sch. Mgmt., Sydney, 1987; vis. prof. Fudan U., Shanghai, 1990; vis. scholar U. Calif., Berkeley, 1995. Co-editor: Emerging Patterns of East Asian Investment in China, 1995, Japan's New Economy, 2001; contbr. articles to econ. jours. Treas. Life Found., Honolulu, 1984-86; chmn. Hawaii Names Project, Honolulu, 1988-90. Recipient Puhlick Vol. award Life Found., Honolulu, 1991, Robert W. Clopton award U. Hawaii, 1995. Mem. Am. Econ. Assn., Western Econ. Assn., Econ. History Assn., Cliometric Soc. Democrat. Avocations: running, swimming, history. Office: U Hawaii Saunders Hall 542 2424 Maile Way Honolulu HI 96822 E-mail: lacroix@hawaii.edu.

LACY, ALAN JASPER, retail executive; b. Cleveland, Tenn., Oct. 19, 1953; BSIM, Ga. Inst. Tech., 1975; MBA, Emory U., 1977. CFA. Fin. analyst Holiday Inns, Inc., Memphis, 1977-79; mgr. investor rels. Tiger Internat., L.A., 1979-80, Dart Industries, L.A., 1980-81; dir. corp. fin. Dart & Kraft, Northbrook, Ill., 1981-82, asst. treas., 1982-83, treas., v.p., 1984-86, v.p. fin. and adminstrn. internat., 1987-88; v.p., treas., CFO Minnetonka Corp., Bloomington, Minn., 1988-89; sr. v.p. strategy and devel. Kraft Gen. Foods, Glenview, Ill., 1989-90, sr. v.p. fin., 1990-92, sr. v.p. fin., strategy, sys., 1992-93; v.p. fin. svcs. and sys. Philip Morris Cos., 1993-95; exec. v.p., CFO Sears, Roebuck & Co., 1995-97, pres., credit svcs., 1997-99, CEO, pres., chmn., 2000—. Mem. Econ. Club (Chgo.). Office: Sears Roebuck 3333 Beverly Rd Hoffman Estates IL 60179*

LACY, ALEXANDER SHELTON, lawyer; b. South Boston, Va., Aug. 18, 1921; s. Cecil Baker and Lura Elizabeth (Byram) L.; m. Carol Jemison, Aug. 8, 1952; children: John Blakeway, Joan Elizabeth Chancey, Alexander Shelton. BS in Chemistry, U. Ala., 1943; LL.B., U. Va., 1949. Bar: Ala. 1949, U.S. Ct. Appeals (5th, 11th and D.C. cirs.) 1981, U.S. Supreme Ct. 1979. Assoc. Bradley, Arant, Rose & White, Birmingham, Ala., 1949-54; with Ala. Gas Corp., 1954-86; v.p., asst. sec., atty. Ala. Gas Corp./Energen Corp., 1969-86; v.p., sec., atty. Ala. Gas Corp., 1974-86; with Patrick and Lacy, Birmingham, 1986-96. Pres., chmn. bd. Birmingham Symphony Assn., 1964-67; chmn. Birmingham-Jefferson Civic Center Authority, 1965-71. Served with USN, 1943-46. Mem. ABA, Ala. Bar Assn. (chmn. energy law com. 1984-86), Birmingham Bar Assn., Am. Gas Assn. (chmn. legal sect. 1983-85), Fed. Energy Bar Assn., Fed. Bar Assn., Am. Judicature Soc., Mountain Brook Club, Phi Gamma Delta, Phi Delta Phi. Episcopalian. Home: 3730 Montrose Rd Birmingham AL 35213-3824

LACY, ALLEN WAYNE, economics educator; b. Oct. 14, 1938; s. Allen Luther and Betty Isabelle (Sharp) Lacy; m. Nancy Jean Cira, Apr. 2, 1960; children: Valerie Lynn Lacy Allen, Stuart Scott. BS, Auburn U., 1966, MS, 1968; PhD, Iowa State U., 1971. Grad. asst. Auburn U., Ala., 1966—68, asst. prof. econs., 1971—76; instr. Iowa State U., Ames, 1968—71; spl. instr. Ctrl. Coll., Pella, 1971; prof., head econs. Auburn U.-Montgomery, Ala., 1976—98, prof. emeritus, 1998—. Cons. to bus. Editor: Ala. Bus. and Econs. Reports, 1977—98, So. Bus. and Econ. Jour., 1986—. With USAF, 1961—65. Recipient Faculty Svc. award, Alumni Auburn U. at Montgomery, 1981. Mem.: Ctrl. Ala. Purchasing Mgmt. Assn. (chmn. bd. dirs. 1998—2000), Ala. Acad. Sci. (chmn. 1975—78), Mid-South Acad. Econ. and Fin., So. Econs. Assn., Am. Econ. Assn., Beta Gamma Sigma, Omicron Delta Epsilon, Phi Kappa Phi (S.E. regional v.p. 1998—). Avocations: amateur dramatics, racquetball. Home: 415 N Moye Dr Montgomery AL 36109-4615 Office: Auburn U at Montgomery Dept Econs 7300 University Dr Montgomery AL 36117-3531

LACY, ANDRE BALZ, industrial executive; b. Indpls., Sept. 12, 1939; s. Howard J. II and Edna B. (Balz) L.; m. Julia Lello, Feb. 23, 1963; children: John Andre, Mark William, Peter Lello. BA Econs., Denison U.; DEng (hon.), Rose-Hulman Inst. Various mgmt. positions U.S. Corrugated, Indpls., 1961-69, exec. v.p., 1969-72; exec. v.p., chief ops. officer Lacy Diversified Industries, 1972-78, chmn. bd. subs., 1973-78, pres., chief ops. officer, 1978-83; pres., chief exec. officer Lacy Diversified Industries, now LDI, Ltd., 1983—, chmn., 1992. Bd. dirs. Herff Jones, Inc., Indpls., Patterson Dental Co., Mpls., Finish Master, Inc., Nat. Bank Indpls. Mem. bd. mgrs. Rose-Hulman Inst., Terre Haute, Ind.; pres. Indpls. Bd. Sch. Commn., Indpls., 1985-86; hon. mem. 500 Festival Assocs., Inc., Indpls.; chmn. United Way Greater Indpls., 1989-91; bd. dirs. Hudson Inst., Indpls. Conv. and Visitors Assn., 1996; dir. Ctrl. Ind. Corp. Partnership, Indpls. Downtown, Inc. Mem. Nat. Assn. Wholesaler Distbrs. (dir.), Young Pres. Orgn., Ind. C. of C. (bd. dirs. 1989), Ind. Pres. Orgn., Kiwanis Club of Indpls., Skyline Club, Columbia Club, Meridian Hills Golf and Country Club (Indpls.), Lost Tree Club. Republican. Episcopalian. Avocation: sailing. Home: 450 E Vermont St Indianapolis IN 46202-3680 Office: LDI Ltd 54 Monument Cir Ste 800 Indianapolis IN 46204-2928

LACY, BILL, college president, architect; b. Madill, Okla., Apr. 16, 1933; s. Leon and Eunice L.; m. Susan Cavert Butler, Dec. 27, 1992; children: Jan, Kate, Shawn, Ross, Jessica. BArch, Okla. State U., 1955, MArch, 1958; DFA (hon.), Miami U., Oxford, Ohio, 1985. Design architect Caudill, Rowlett, Scott, Houston, 1958-61; prof., assoc. chmn. dept. architecture Rice U., 1961-65; prof., dean sch. architecture U. Tenn., Knoxville, 1965-70; v.p. Omniplan, Dallas, 1970-71; dir. architecture and environ. arts Nat. Endowment Arts, Washington, 1971-77, dir. fed. design program, 1972-77; pres. Am. Acad. in Rome, N.Y.C., 1977-80, The Cooper Union, N.Y.C., 1980-88; pres. Purchase Coll. SUNY, 1993—. Archtl. cons. Fgn. Bldgs. Ops., Dept. State Author: 100 Contemporary Architects, 1991, Angels and Franciscans, 1992; contbr. articles, designs to profl. jours. Bd. dirs. Internat. Design Conf. Aspen, 1973-92; bd. dirs. Tiffany Found., Am. Archtl. Found.; cons. Rothschild Found., J. Paul Getty Trust; exec. dir. Pritzker Architecture Prize. With U.S. Army, 1955-57. Loeb fellow Harvard U., 1973; Getty scholar, 1991. Fellow AIA; mem. Univ. Club. Office: 735 Anderson Hill Rd Purchase NY 10577-1402 E-mail: lacy@purchase.edu.

LACY, CAROLYN JEAN, elementary education educator, secondary education educator; b. Marshall, Ark., Apr. 6, 1944; d. Charles Ira Bolch and Edna Rebecca Cherry; 1 child, Kelli Jean. AA with distinction, Riverside City Coll., 1980; BA, U. Calif., Riverside, 1982, postgrad., 1983; MEd, U.S. Internat. U., 1993. Cert. social sci. tchr., Calif. Educator Perris (Calif.) Elem. Sch. Dist., 1984-89, Rialto (Calif.) Unified Sch. Dist., 1989—. Instr. Developing Capable People, Riverside, Calif., 1986-89; presenter, lectr. Jurupa Unified Sch. Dist., Riverside, 1990, Rialto Unified Sch. Dist., 1990; developer peer tutor program Perris Elem. Sch. Dist., 1989; dir. chess club Dollahan Elem. Sch., 1995-98, computer chmn., 1995-97; dir. chess club Rialto Mid. Sch., 1998. Editor: (newsletter) Perris Lights, 1989. Active Students in Environ. Action, Riverside, 1978; mem. Riverside County Task Force for Self-Esteem. Named Mentor Tchr. State of Calif., 1988. Mem. AAUW, NEA, Calif. Tchrs. Assn., U. Calif. Alumni Assn., Phi Delta Kappa, Alpha Gamma Sigma. Democrat. Mem. Lds Ch. Avocations: painting, writing, gardening, reading, travel. Home: 4044 Wallace St Riverside CA 92509-6809

LACY, CLAUD HAROLD SANDBERG, astronomer, educator; b. Shawnee, Okla., June 5, 1947; s. Lester Claud and Leola Chrstine (Hinton) L.; m. Patricia Kathryn McCoy, Apr. 1, 1971 (div. 1984); m. Patricia Alison Sandberg, Dec. 19, 1988; children: Adrian R., Kathryn Mia Rose. MS in Physics, U. Okla., Norman, 1971; PhD in Astronomy, U. Tex., 1978. Vis. asst. prof. Tex. A&M U., College Station, Tex., 1978-80; asst. prof. astronomy U. Ark., Fayetteville, 1980-86, assoc. prof., 1986-99, prof., 1999—. Author: Astronomy Laboratory Exercises, 1981; contbr. articles to Astron. Jour. With U.S. Army, 1971-73. NSF grantee, 1981-84, 2000—. Mem. Am. Astron. Soc., Internat. Astron. Union. Achievements include determination of accurate absolute properties for stars in over 28 eclipsing binary star systems, photometric orbits of 611 eclipsing binary stars in the Large Magellanic Cloud; discovery of 40 new double-lined eclipsing binaries. Office: U Ark Dept Physics Fayetteville AR 72701 E-mail: clacy@uark.edu.

LACY, ELIZABETH BERMINGHAM, state supreme court justice; b. 1945; BA cum laude, St. Mary's Coll., Notre Dame, Ind., 1966; JD, U. Tex., 1969; LLM, U. Va., 1992. Bar: Tex. 1969, Va. 1977. Staff atty. Tex. Legis. Coun., Austin, 1969-72; atty. Office of Atty. Gen., State of Tex., 1973-76; legis. aide Va. Del. Carrington Williams, Richmond, 1976-77; dep. atty. gen. jud. affairs div. Va. Office Atty. Gen., 1982-85; mem. Va. State Corp. Commn., 1985-89; justice Supreme Ct. Va., 1989—. Office: Va Supreme Ct 100 North 9th Street, 5th Floor Richmond VA 23219*

LACY, GREGORY LAWRENCE, protective services official; b. Long Beach, Calif., June 12, 1949; s. George Lawrence and Pauline L. (Smith) L.; m. Cheryl Ann Carey, Apr. 16, 1987 (div. May 1990); children: Megan Lee, Tess Jordan; adopted children: Randy J., Jennie A.; m. Suphan Wongruan, June 4, 1991 (div. May 1999). AS in Forestry, Bottineau (N.D.) Sch. Forestry, 1967; cert. law enforcement, N.D. Police Acad., Bismarck, 1967; AS in Engring., N.D. State Sch. Sci., 1972. Cert. EMT, emergency trauma tech., law enforcement, N.D., Alaska. Law enforcement officer Langdon (N.D.) Police Dept., 1972-77; law enforcement officer, tng. officer Smith Security - Spl. Divsn., Anchorage, 1977-80; security officer, field tng. officer AHTNA-Am. Guard & Alert Security Co., 1980—. Tng. officer Langdon Police Dept., 1973-77. Active Campaign for Sheriff Re-election, Cavalier County, Langdon, 1973-77; pub. fire arms tng. Langdon Police Dept., 1973-77. Mem. NRA (life), Air Couriers Assn., Gold Prospectors Assn. (life). Baptist. Avocations: hunting, fishing, photography, hiking, computers. Home: 3705 Arctic Blvd # 622 Anchorage AK 99503-5774 Office: Doyon Universal Svcs 701 W 8th Ave Ste 500 Anchorage AK 99501-3468

LACY, HERMAN EDGAR, management consultant; b. Chgo., June 21, 1935; s. Herman E. and Florence L.; m. Mary C. Lacy; children: Frederick H., Carlton E., Douglas H., Jennifer S., Victoria J., Rebecca M. BS in Indsl. Engring., Bradley U., 1957; MBA, U. Chgo., 1966. Cert. mgmt. cons. Plant mgr., indsl. engring. supr. Hammond Organ Co., Chgo., 1961-66; mgr. corp. indsl. engring. Consol. Packaging Corp., 1966-68; mgr. mgmt. cons. Peat, Marwick, Mitchell & Co., 1968-70; dir. ops. Wilton Enterprises, Inc., 1970-77; v.p., gen. mgr. Intercraft Industries Corp., 1978-79; pres. Helmco Cons. Assocs., Glenview, Ill., 1979—. Instr. Roosevelt U., Oakton Coll., Harper Coll. Served to capt. USAF, 1957-61. Mem. Inst. Indsl. Engrs. (past pres., founder north suburban Ill. chpt.), Am. Mgmt. Assn., Nat. Coun. Phys. Distbn. Mgmt., Soc. Mfg. Engrs., Inst. Mgmt. Cons. Office: Helmco Cons Assocs PO Box 18747 Fountain Hills AZ 85269-8747

LACY, JOHN FORD, retired lawyer; b. Dallas, Sept. 11, 1944; s. John Alexander and Glenda Arcenia (Ford) L.; m. Cece Smith, Apr. 22, 1978. BA, Baylor U., 1965; JD, Harvard U., 1968. Bar: Tex. 1968. Assoc. atty. Akin, Gump, Strauss, Hauer & Feld L.L.P., Dallas, 1968-72, ptnr., 1973-82; pres. Ford Lacy PC (affiliated with Akin, Gump et al.), 1982-99. Co-founder, pres. rsch. coun. U. Tex. Southwestern Med. Ctr., Dallas, 1985-91; bd. dirs. Vis. Nurse Assn. Tex., 1994-2001, 1st vice chmn., 2000-01. With U.S. Army, 1968-74. Home: 3710 Shenandoah St Dallas TX 75205-2121 E-mail: ford@fordlacy.com.

LACY, JOHN RUSSELL, retired state government administrator, public affairs counselor; b. Trenton, N.J., June 12, 1938; s. J(ohn) Russell and Mary Grey (Snedeker) L.; m. Joanne Ida Fitzpatrick, Apr. 20, 1963; 1 child, Shannon Rae. BA, Rutgers U., 1961; MA, St. Regis U., 2000. Pers. technician N.J. Dept. Civil Svc., Trenton, 1962-63; pub. info. dir. Internat. Hdqrs. Babe Ruth Baseball, 1963-68; comms. mgr. Univac Divsn.-Sperry Rand Corp., Blue Bell, Pa., 1968-69; dir. membership rels. N.J. Taxpayers Assn., Trenton, 1969-71; exec. asst. to state treas. N.J. Dept. Treasury, 1971-73; exec. v.p. N.J. Retail Mechts. Assn., 1973; owner Lacy Comms., J.R. Lacy Assocs., Hamilton, NJ, 1973—; pub. Mercer Messenger, 1983-88; dep. dir. N.J. State Lottery Commn., Trenton, 1988-90; dir. spl. projects/alumni affairs Mercer County C.C., 1990-99; dir. N.J. Human Resource Devel. Inst., 1999—2002. Mem. Hamilton Twp. Coun., Hamilton, 1976-99, N.J. League of Municipalities, Elected Ofcls. Hall of Fame; pres. Hamilton YMCA, 1974-75; chmn. Hamilton Twp. Econ. Devel. Commn., 1973-75; pres. Mercer County League Municipalities, Hamilton, 1995-99; bd. dirs. Project Freedom, Inc.; pres. Hamilton Little Bigger League Grads., Inc., 2002--. Named Humanitarian of Yr., Animals in Distress, Inc., 1990, Outstanding Chpt. Pres. in Mercer County, N.J. Jaycees, 1971. Mem. Hamilton Twp. Optimist Club (charter mem.), Ancient Order of Hibernians, VFW (hon.), DAV (life), Tau Kappa Epsilon. Republican. Methodist. Avocations: team sports, historical fiction and biographies, restoring antique furniture. Home: 9 Compton Way Hamilton NJ 08690-3920 Office: JR Lacy Assocs PO Box 3489 Hamilton NJ 08619 E-mail: Jrlacy@aol.com.

LACY, MARJORIE ANN, writer; b. Heber Springs, Ark., Mar. 20, 1951; d. Lewis Otto and Mildred Louise (Hilton) L.; m. Travis Lee Bishop, Aug. 16, 1969 (div. Aug. 1992); children: Barrett LeRoy, April Annette Bishop Roberts. BA, U. Ark., 1995, postgrad., 1997—. Editl. asst. Leisure Arts, Little Rock, 1988-91, editl. writer, 1995-96, mng. editor, 1996-99; health sci. writer U. Ark. Med. Schs., 1999—. Mem. Nat. Fedn. Press Women, Internat. Assn. Bus. Communicators, Soc. Tech. Comm. Avocations: ballrom dancing, rock collecting, travel. Home: 26 Ivy Dr Little Rock AR 72209-2107

LACY, NORRIS J. literature educator; b. Hopkinsville, Ky., Mar. 8, 1940; s. Edwin V. Lacy and Lillian Louise Joiner; m. Susan Houston, Jan. 6, 1984. AB, Murray State U., 1962; MA, Ind. U., 1963, PhD, 1967. From asst. prof. to prof. French U. Kans., Lawrence, 1966-88; prof. French and comparative lit. Washington U., St. Louis, 1988-98; Edwin Erle Sparks prof. French Pa. State U., University Park, 1998—. Vis. assoc. French UCLA, 1975-76; editor-in-chief Summa Publs., Birmingham, Ala., 1981-86; editl. dir. Arthurian Studies, Cambridge, Eng., 1999—; editor: Arthurian Archives, Cambridge, 1996—, Arthurian Characters and Themes, N.Y.C., 1994—. Author: Craft of Chrétien de Troyes, 1980, Arthurian Handbook, 1988 (Choice Outstanding Book award), Reading Fabliaux, 1993, 99, 24 others; editor Arthurian Encyclopedia, 1986, Lancelot-Grail, 1993-96; contbr. articles to profl. jours. Knighted French Govt., 1988. Mem. MLA, Am. Assn. French Tchrs., Medieval Acad. Am., Internat. Arthurian Soc. (hon. pres.). Office: Pa State U Dept French University Park PA 16802 E-mail: NJL2@psu.edu.

LACY, ROBINSON BURRELL, lawyer; b. Boston, May 7, 1952; s. Benjamin Hammett and Jane (Burrell) L. AB, U. Calif., Berkeley, 1974; JD, Harvard U., 1977. Bar: N.Y. 1978, U.S. Dist. Ct. (so. and ea. dists.) N.Y. 1979, U.S. Dist. Ct. (we. dist.) N.Y. 1992, U.S. Ct. Appeals (2d cir.) 1983, U.S. Ct. Appeals (10th cir.) 1990, U.S. Ct. Appeals (3d cir.) 2002, U.S. Supreme Ct. 1986. Law clk. to judge U.S. Dist. Ct. (so. dist.) N.Y., N.Y.C., 1977-78; law clk. to chief justice Warren Burger U.S. Supreme Ct., Washington, 1978-79; assoc. Sullivan & Cromwell, N.Y.C., 1979-85, ptnr., 1985—. Mem. ABA, Assn. of Bar of City of N.Y., N.Y. State Bar Assn. Office: Sullivan & Cromwell 125 Broad St Fl 28 New York NY 10004-2489

LACY, WILLIAM B. academic administrator; b. Wellsville, Ny, Apr. 27, 1942; s. Edred Earl and Gertrude Lacy; m. Laura Jane Robinson; children: Donovan, Kristin. BS, Cornell Univ., Ithaca, NY, 1964; MS, Colgate Univ., Hamilton, NY, 1965; MA, Univ. Mich., Ann Arbor, MI, 1971, PhD, 1975; MS, Colgate Univ., Hamilton, NY, 1965; MA, Univ. Mich., Ann Arbor, MI, 1971, PhD, 1975. Instr. to full prof. Univ. Ky., Lexington, Ky., 1974—89; asst. dean/asst. dir. Penn State Univ., University Park, Pa., 1989—94; assoc. dean Cornell Univ., Ithaca, 1994—99; vice provost/prof. Univ. Calif. Davis, Davis, 1999—. Pres. AG, Food, & Human Values Soc., 1992—93, Rural Sociol. Soc., 1998—99; panel mem. NRC, Washington, 1993—95, Washington, 1999—. Co-author: (book) Science, AG, & Politics of Science, Plants, Power, & Profit, Making Nature, Shaping Culture. Mem. Pres. Clinton's Coun., 1994—95. 1st leut. US Army, 1965—67, Korea. Fellow: Am. Assoc. for Advancement of Sci.; mem.: Nat. 4-H Coun. (bd. of trustees 1996—98). Home: 1114 Purdue Drive Davis CA 95616-1736 Office: Univ California Office of the Provost One Shields Ave Davis CA 95616

LADAGE, LINDA ROLF, special education educator; b. Decatur, Ill., Jan. 9, 1960; d. Frank Henry and Joan Louise (Adams) Rolf; m. Steven Charles Ladage, Oct. 25, 1986; children: John Henry, Jane Marie, Rebecca Lynn, Daniel Rolf. BS in Edn., Ill. State U., 1982, cert. in elem. edn., 1985; cert. in EMH, Western Ill. U. & So. Ill. U., 1985. Tchr. of children with multiple handicaps Taylorville (Ill.) Sch. Dist., 1982-86; lead tchr. of children with multiple handicaps Circle Project, U. N.C. and St. Mark's Ctr., Charlotte, 1987-88; tchr. of young adults with severe handicaps Dwight (Ill.) Community Sch. for Multi-handicapped, 1988-89; pvt. tutor Dwight, 1990-92, Bloomington, Ill., 1992-95; sub. tchr., 1996—. Sprk. in field. Supt. Sunday sch. Emmanuel Luth. Ch., Dwight, 1990. Mem. Philanthropic Edn. Orgn. (v.p. 1989-90, pres. 1993-96). Avocations: camping, crafts, writing, piano. Home: 405 Woodland Ave Bloomington IL 61701-5671

LADANYI, BRANKA MARIA, chemist, educator; b. Zagreb, Croatia, Sept. 7, 1947; came to U.S., 1969; d. Branko and Nevenka (Zilic) L.; m. Marshall Fixman, Dec. 7, 1974. BSc, McGill U., Montreal, Can., 1969; M in Philosophy, Yale U., 1971, PhD, 1973. Vis. prof. of chemistry U. Ill., 1974; postdoctoral research assoc. Yale U., 1974-77, research assoc., 1977-79; asst. prof. chemistry Colo. State U., Ft. Collins, 1979-84, assoc. prof. chemistry, 1985-87, prof. chemistry, 1987—. Vis. fellow Joint Inst. for Lab. Astrophysics, 1993-94. Assoc. editor Jour. Chem. Physics, 1994—; referee and contbr. articles to profl. jours. Fellow Sloan Found., 1982-84, Dreyfus Found., 1983-87; grantee NSF, NATO, 1983-89. Fellow Am. Phys. Soc.; mem. AAAS, Am. Chem. Soc. (PRF grantee 1979-82, 1989-91, 95-98), Sigma Xi. Office: Colo State U Dept Chemistry Fort Collins CO 80523-1872 E-mail: bl@lamar.colostate.edu.

LADANYI, BRANKO, civil engineer, educator; b. Zagreb, Croatia, Dec. 14, 1922; emigrated to Can., 1962, naturalized, 1967; s. Adalbert and Zora (Kniewald) L.; m. Nevenka Zilic, Dec. 14, 1946; children: Branka, Thomas, Marc. BCE, U. Zagreb, 1947; PhD in Soil Mechanics, U. Louvain, Belgium, 1959. Design engr. Dept. Transp., Zagreb, 1947-52; teaching asst. U. Zagreb, 1952-58; research engr. Belgian Geotech. Inst., Ghent, 1958-62; asso. prof., then prof. civil engring. Laval U., Quebec, Can., 1962-67; prof. civil engring. Ecole Poly., U. Montreal, 1967-94, prof. emeritus, 1994—, dir. North Engring. Centre, 1972—. Author papers in geotech. field, chpts. in books. Recipient Que. sci. award Que. Ministry Edn., 1974, De Beer Geotech. award Belgian Geotech. Soc., 1986, Elbert F. Rice Meml. award ASCE and U. Alaska, Fairbanks, 1991, North Sci. award Govt. of Can., 1996. Fellow ASCE (amity award 1995), Royal Soc. Can., Can. Acad. Engring., Engring. Inst. Can., Can. Soc. Civil Engring.; mem. ASTM, Order Engrs. Que., Can. Geotech. Soc. (R.F. Legget geotech. award 1981, Roger J.E. Brown meml. award 1993), Can. Inst. Mining and Metallurgy. Office: Ecole Polytech Box 6079 Succ Centre-Ville Montreal QC Canada H3C3A7 *There is no end to learning.*

LADAR, JERROLD MORTON, lawyer; b. San Francisco, Aug. 2, 1933; AB, U. Wash., 1956; LLB, U. Calif., Berkeley, 1960. Bar: Calif. 1961, U.S. Supreme Ct. 1967. Law clk. to judge U.S. Dist. Ct. (no. dist.) Calif., 1960-61; asst. U.S. atty. San Francisco, 1961-70; chief criminal div., 1968—71; mem. firm MacInnis & Donner, San Francisco, 1971—73; prof. criminal law and procedure U. San Francisco Law Sch., 1962-83; pvt. practice San Francisco., 1971—; ptnr. Ladar & Ladar, San Francisco, 1994—. Lectr. Hastings Coll. Law, Civil and Criminal Advocacy Programs, 1985-2002; chair pvt. defender panel U.S. Dist. Ct. (no. dist.) Calif., 1980-90; ct. apptd. chair stats. and tech. subcom. Fed. Civil Justice Reform Act Com. (no. dist.) Calif., 1990-95; ct. apptd. mem. Fed. Ct. Civil Local Rules Revision Com. (no. dist.) Calif., 1994—; ct. apptd. chmn. Criminal Local Rules Revision Com. (no. dist.) Calif., 1991-99; mem. continuing edn. of bar criminal law adv. com. U. Calif., Berkeley, 1978-83, 89-2001; panelist, mem. nat. planning com. ABA Nat. Ann. White Collar Crime Inst., 1996—; ct. apptd. mem. Local Disciplinary Rule Draft com., 1998-99 Author: (with others) Selected Trial Motions, Grand Jury Practice, Asset Forfeiture, 6 edits., California Criminal Law and Procedure Practice, 3d edit. 4th edit., 5th edit., 6th edit., 2002, Direct Examination-Tips and Techniques, 1982, Collateral Effects of Federal Convictions, 1997, Insult Added to Injury: The Fallout From Tax Conviction, 1997, Give Me A Break-Finding Federal Misdemeanors, 1998, The Court: We're Here to Seek the Truth; Defense Counsel: Excuse Me, That's Not My Job, 1999, A Day At The Grand Jury, 2000, The Tale of Daubert at the Gates: Use A Trojan Horse, 2001, The Art of Direct Examination, 2002. Trustee Tamalpais Union High Sch. Dist., 1968-77, chmn. bd., 1973-74; mem. adv. com. Nat. PTA Assn., 1972-78; apptd. mem. criminal justice act com. U.S. Ct. Appeals (9th cir). Fellow Am. Bd. Criminal Lawyers; mem. ABA, San Francisco Bar Assn. (editor in Re 1974-76), State Bar Calif. (pro-tem disciplinary referee 1976-78, vice chmn. pub. interest and edn. com. criminal law sect., mem. exec. com. criminal law sect. 1980-87, editor Criminal Law Sect. News 1981-87, chmn. exec. com. 1983-84), Am. Inns. of Ct. (exec. com. 1994-97), Fed. Bar Assn. (panelist), Nat. Sentencing Inst. (contbr.) Office: 1916 Vallejo St San Francisco CA 94123-4918

LADD, CHARLES CUSHING, III, civil engineering educator; b. Bklyn., Nov. 23, 1932; s. Charles Cushing and Elizabeth (Swan) L.; m. Carol Lee Ballou, June 11, 1954; children: Melissa, Charles IV, Ruth, Matthew. AB, Bowdoin Coll., 1955; SB, MIT, 1955, SM, 1957, ScD, 1961. Asst. prof. civil engring. MIT, 1961-64, assoc. prof., 1964-70, prof., 1970-94, dir. Ctr. Sci. Excellence in Offshore Engring., 1983-94, Edmund K. Turner prof., 1994-2001, Edmund K. Turner prof. emeritus, 2001—. Gen. reporter 9th Internat. Conf. Soil Mechanics and Found. Engring., Tokyo, 1977; co-gen. reporter 11th Internat. Conf. Soil Mechanics and Found. Engring., San Francisco, 1985; mem. geotech. bd. NRC, 1992-94. Contbr. articles to profl. jours. Mem. Concord (Mass.) Republican Town Com., 1968-82; commr. Concord Dept. Pub. Works, 1965-78, chmn., 1972-74. Fellow ASCE (rsch. prize 1969, Croes medal 1973, Norman medal 1976, Terzaghi lectr. 1986, exec. com. geotech. engring. divsn. 1989-96, chmn. 1993-94, Geo-Inst. bd. govs. 1996-98, hon. mem. 1995, Middlebrooks award 1996, 2002, Karl Terzaghi award 1999); mem. NAE, ASTM (Hogentogler award 1990), NSPE, Boston Soc. Civil Engrs. (bd. govs. 1972-81, pres. 1977-78, Arthur Casagrande Meml. lectr. 2000), Transp. Rsch. Bd., Internat. Soc. Soil Mechanics and Geotech. Engring., Am. Soc. Engring. Edn., Assn. Engring. Firms Practicing in the Geoscis., AAUP, Brit. Geotech. Soc., Can. Geotech. Soc. Home: 7 Thornton Ln Concord MA 01742-4107 Office: MIT Dept Civil & Environ Engrng Cambridge MA 02139 E-mail: ccladd@MIT.edu.

LADD, CULVER SPROGLE, secondary education educator; b. Bismarck, N.D., Nov. 15, 1929; s. Culver Sprogle and Eleanor (Pearson)L. BS, U. Md., 1953; MA, Am. U., 1963, PhD, 1984; postgrad., Harvard U., summer 1963, Oxford (Eng.) U., 1975-76; cert. by correspondence, Nat. Def. U., Thailand, 1972. Clk.-photographer Dept. Justice, FBI, Washington, 1946-54; intercept controller Dept. of Def., USAF, 1954-56; asst. office mgr. Covington & Burling, Lawyers, Washington, 1956-62; tchr. Internat. Sch. Bangkok, Thailand, 1964-66; lectr. U. Md., Thailand, 1966-67, 71-74; project dir. Bus. Rsch. Ltd., Thailand, 1966-67, 72-74; spl. lectr. Payap U., Chiang Mai, Thailand, 1974-75, 2000-2001; tchr. D.C. Pub. Schs., 1978-2000. Cons. USAID, Thailand, 1973-74; vis. scientist Brookhaven Nat. Labs., L.I., 1988; master tchr. Woodrow Wilson Fellowship Found., 1989. Rep. candidate Md. Senate 29th Legislative Dist., 1998. Capt. USAFR, 1953-72. Recipient Appreciation award Payap U. 1987. Mem. Mid-Atlantic Region Assn. for Asian Studies, Acad. Polit. Sci., Nat. Capital Area Polit. Sci. Assn., Nat. Coun. Tchrs. Math., Mid. States Coun. Social Studies, Aircraft Owners and Pilots Assn., Omicron Delta Kappa, Pi Sigma Alpha. Republican. Presbyterian. Avocations: gardening, flying. Office: POACRE Airfield 845 Crystal Rock Rd PO Box 2084 Lusby MD 20657-1884 E-mail: CSLADD@juno.com.

LADD, DIANE, actress; b. Meridian, Miss., Nov. 29, 1942; m. Bruce Dern (div.); 1 child, Laura; m. William Shea, Jr. (div.); m. Robert C. Hunter, Feb. 14, 1999. Grad., St. Aloysius Acad. Appearances include (films) The Wild Angels, 1966, The Reivers, 1969, Macho Callahan, 1970, Rebel Rousers, 1970, WUSA, 1970, White Lightning, 1973, Alice Doesn't Live Here Anymore, 1974, Chinatown, 1974, Embryo, 1976, The November Plan, 1976, All Night Long, 1981, Something Wicked This Way Comes, 1983, Black Widow, 1987, Plain Clothes, 1988, National Lampoon's Christmas Vacation, 1989, Wild at Heart, 1990, A Kiss Before Dying, 1991, Rambling Rose, 1991, Cemetery Club, 1992, Hold Me, Thrill Me, Kiss Me, 1992, Code Name: Chaos, 1992, Carnosaur, 1993, Father Hood, 1993, Spirit Realm, 1993, Obsession, 1994, Mrs. Munck (also dir.), 1994, The Haunted Heart, 1995, Raging Angels, 1995, Ghosts of Mississippi, 1996, Mother, 1996, Citizen Ruth, 1996, James Dean: Race With Destiny, 1997, Primary Colors, 1998, Daddy N Them, 1999; (TV series) Alice, 1980-81, Rain, 2001, Law of Enclosures, 2001; (TV movies) The Devil's Daughter, 1973, Thaddeus Rose and Eddie, 1978, Black Beauty, 1978, Willa, 1979, Guyana Tragedy: The Story of Jim Jones, 1980, Desperate Lives, 1982, Grace Kelly, 1983, I Married a Centerfold, 1984, Crime of Innocence, 1985, Celebration Family, 1987, Bluegrass, 1988, The Lookalike, 1990, Rock Hudson, 1990, Shadow of a Doubt, 1991, Hush Little Baby, 1994, Ruby Ridge: An American Tragedy, 1996, Breach of Faith: Family of Cops II, 1997, The Waiting Game, 1997, The Staircase, 1998; (TV mini-series) Cold Lazarus, 1996, Aftermath, 2001, Damage Care, 2001. Recipient award Brit. Acad., Spirit award, Golden Globe award, 3 Acad. award nominations, 4 Golden Globe nominations, 3 Emmy nominations for Guest Actress in a Series (Grace Under Fire), 1994, Dr. Quinn, Medicine Woman, Touched by an Angel.

LADD, HELEN FRANCIS, social sciences educator, researcher; b. Boston, Aug. 27, 1945; d. Joseph Alvah Locke and Helen Francis Summers; m. Dudley Howe Ladd, Sept. 7, 1968 (div. Feb. 1993); children: Ethan Atterburg, Haven Francis; m. Edward Bogardus Fiske, June 29, 1997. BA, Wellesley Coll., 1967; MSc, London Sch. Econs., 1968; PhD, Harvard U., 1974. Asst. prof. Wellesley (Mass.) Coll., 1974—77; asst. and assoc. prof. Harvard U., Cambridge, Mass., 1977—86; prof. Duke U., Durham, NC, 1986—. Vis. lectr. Dartmouth Coll., Hanover, NH, 1968—69; co-chair com. edn. fin. Nat. Acad. Scis., Washington, 1996—99; vis. sr. fellow Brookings Instn., Washington, 1994—95. Contbr. articles to profl. jours. Active Eno River Unitarian Universalist, Durham, NC, 1989—. Grantee Fulbright grant to New Zealand, Fulbright Assn., 1998, Fulbright grant to South Africa, 2002. Mem.: Assn. Pub. Policy Analysis adn Mgmt., Nat. Tax Assn. (pres. 1994—95, v.p.), Am. Econ. Assn. Democrat. Unitarian Universalist. Avocations: tennis, sailing, travel. Office: Duke U Sanford Inst Box 90243 Durham NC 27705

LADD, JAMES ROGER, international business executive and consultant; b. San Diego, Mar. 5, 1943; s. Robert Dwinell and Virginia Ruth (Dole) L.; m. Sharon Patricia Smith, Aug. 22, 1964; children— Brian Andrew, Jennifer Louise, Casey James AB, Duke U., 1964. CPA, CMC. With Deloitte Haskins & Sells, Seattle, 1964-79, mng. ptnr. Tokyo, 1979-84, dir. human resources N.Y.C., 1984-86, area mng. ptnr. Seattle, 1986-89; mng. dir. Deloitte & Touche, 1989-92; pres. Ladd Pacific Cons., 1992-97; pres., CEO EnCompass Globalization Inc., Kirkland, 1997—2001; sr. v.p. fin. & ops. BSquare Corp., Bellevue, 2002—. Bd. dirs., treas. Seattle Found., 1988—97; trustee Duke U., 1991—93; chair global bus. adv. bd. U. Wash., 1995—97, 2001—; trustee United Way of King County Endowment Fund, 1993—, Wash. CPA Found., 2001—; treas. United Way of King County, 1990—93. Mem. AICPA, Japan Am. Soc. State Wash. (chmn. 1996-98), Wash. Soc. CPAs, Duke Alumni Assn. (nat. pres. 1991-92), Inst. Mgmt. Cons., Rainier Club.

LADD, JOSEPH CARROLL, retired insurance company executive; b. Chgo., Jan. 26, 1927; s. Stephen C. and Laura (McBride) L.; m. Barbara Virginia Carter, June 5, 1965; children: Carroll, Joseph Carroll, Barbara, Virginia, William. BA, Ohio Wesleyan U., 1950; CLU, Am. Coll., Bryn Mawr; D in Bus. Adminstrn. (hon.), Spring Garden Coll., 1985. Agt. Conn. Gen. Life Ins. Co., Chgo., 1950-53, staff asst., 1953-54, mgr. Evanston (Ill.) br. office, 1954-60, dir. agys., 1960-62, mgr. Los Angeles br. office, 1963; v.p. sales Fidelity Mut. Life Ins. Co., Phila., 1964-67, sr. v.p. sales, 1968, exec. v.p., 1969-71, pres., chief exec. officer, dir., 1971-84, chmn., chief exec. officer, dir., 1984-89, chmn., dir., 1989-91; ret. Bd. dirs. Corestates Fin., Phila. Suburban Corp., Phila. Electric Co. Trustee Bryn Mawr Hosp.; trustee United Way of S.E. Pa.; trustee Phila. United Way, also gen. chmn. 1978 campaign; bd. dirs. Phila. YMCA. Served with USNR, 1945-46. Recipient Civic Achievement award Am. Jewish Com., 1978, Achiever's award WHEELS Med. and Specialized Transp., 1978, Ohio Wesleyan U. Life Achievement award Delta Tau Delta, 1982, William Penn award, Greater Phila. C. ofC. and PENJERDEL Coun., 1988, Robert Morris Citizenship award Valley Forge Coun. Boy Scouts Am., 1988; named YMCA Man of Yr., 1979, William Penn Found. Disting. Pennsylvanian, 1980. Mem. Greater Phila. C. of C. (dir., chmn. 1979, 83-84), Phila. Country Club, Union League Club (Phila.), Summer Beach (Fla.) Country Club.

LADD, LOUISE, writer; b. Montclair, N.J. d. Chester Reed and Marion Louise Ladd; m. Doug Taylor; m. Calvin E. Cordulack, June 14, 1965 (div. Mar. 1977); children: Julianne Louise Gemmell, Christopher Donald Cordulack, Jeffrey Joseph Cordulack. BA, Wellesley Coll., 1965; student, actors workshop, Fairfield U., 1975—84. Prodr. Conn. Ctr. Acting Ensemble, Fairfield, 1976—95; tchr., Writers' Workshop Fairfield (Conn.) U. Sch. Continuing Edn., 1990—; part-time librarian Darien (Conn.) Pub. Libr., 1985—93, Fairfield Pub. Libr., 1993—96; freelance editor, 1993—. Spkr. various schs., orgns. and confs., Fairfield County, 1987—. Author: Miracle Island, 1995, Castle in Time, 1995, Lost Valley, 1996, Cherry Blossom Moon, 1996, Call Me Just Plain Chris, 1998, The Wrangler's Secret, 1998, Prize-Winning Horse--Maybe, 1998, The Perfect Horse, 1998, Home for Christmas, 1998, Rodeo!, 1999, Me, My Mare and the Movie, 1999, Belle's Foal, 1999, Stage Fright, 1993, Island of Secrets, 1994, Captive Heart, 1995; editor (with Doug Taylor): Sandy Dennis: A Personal Memoir, 1997; author: A Whole Summer of Weird Susan, 1987, The Double Fudge Dare, 1989; contbr. chapters to books, articles to mags. Mem.: Women Writing the West, Authors Guild, Sc. Childrens Book Writers and Illustrators, Nat. League PEN Women. Democrat. Mem. Soc. Of Friends. Avocations: reading, gardening, ice skating, snorkeling. Home and Office: 27 Bloomfield Dr Fairfield CT 06825

LADD, LOUISE ELIZABETH, investments company executive; b. Waco, Tex., Sept. 17, 1950; d. Ludwig Nitter and Rae Elizabeth (Skibrek) L. BA, U. Wis., 1972. CFP. Mktg. rep. Marine Bank (Banc One), Milw., 1973-74; sales specialist Xerox, Wauwatosa, 1974-78; account exec. Dean Witter (now Morgan Stanley), 1978-82, assoc. v.p. investments, 1982-85, v.p. investments, 1985-96, 1st v.p. investments, 1996-98, sr. v.p. investments, 1998—. Bd. dirs. Presdl. Dimensions. Past bd. dirs. Nex Door Found., Milw. Am. Field Svc. scholar, 1967. Mem. Inst. Cert. Fin. Planner, Profl. Dimensions, Milw. Found. Womens Fund, Milw. Bond Club. Avocations: skiing, traveling, golf. Office: Morgan Stanley 1200 N Mayfair Rd Ste 400 Milwaukee WI 53226-3286 E-mail: louise.ladd@morganstanley.com.

LADD, MARCIA LEE, medical equipment and supplies company executive; b. Bryn Mawr, Pa., July 22, 1950; d. Edward Wingate and Virginia Lee (McGinnes) Mullinix; children: Joshua Wingate, McGinnes Lee; m. Leroy D. Werley, III, Aug. 5, 2000. BA, U. Pa., 1972; MEd, U. Va., 1973; MA, Emory U., 1979. Rsch. assoc. N.C. Tng. and Standards Coun., Raleigh, 1973-75; dir. counseling svc. N.C. State Youth Svcs. Agy., 1975-76; acad. dean Duke U., Durham, N.C., 1976-77; prin. Ladd & Assocs. Mgmt. Cons., Chapel Hill, 1979-88; v.p. adminstrn. CompuChem Corp., Research Triangle Park, 1988-91; v.p. mktg. Prentke Romich Co., Wooster, Ohio, 1991-94; v.p. ops. Exec. Staffing Svcs., Inc., Cary, N.C., 1994; pres., CEO, owner Triangle Aftercare, Durham, 1994—. Bd. dirs. Home Med. Svcs. Bd. dirs. Oackwood Hist. Soc. , Raleigh, 1981—84; mem. bd. vis. Carolina Friends Sch., Durham, 1986—89; bd. dirs. Orange Enterprises, 2000—; Stephen min. Univ. Presbyn. Ch., Chapel Hill, 1994—97, youth group leader, 1995—97, 2000—02, trustee, 1998—2000; bd. dirs. Wayne County Arts Coun., Wooster, 1992, Stoneridge/Sedgefield Swim/Racquet Club, Chapel Hill, 1985—88. Decorated Order of Long Leaf Pine Gov. of N.C., 1976; named one of Impact 100 Most Influential People, Research Triangle, N.C., 1997. Presbyterian. Office: Triangle Aftercare 105 W NC Hwy 54 Ste 267 Durham NC 27713

LADDAGA, LAWRENCE ALEXANDER, lawyer; b. New Hyde Park, N.Y., Aug. 12, 1957; s. Carmine Michael and Adeline (Lauricella) L.; m. Beth Jane Goodlove, Nov. 12, 1983; children: Amanda May, Rachel. BA cum laude, U. S.C., 1978, JD, 1981. Bar: S.C. 1981, U.S. Dist. Ct. S.C. 1981, U.S. Ct. Appeals (4th cir.) 1981, U.S. Tax Ct. 1982, U.S. Supreme Ct. 1989. Assoc. Wise & Cole, P.A., Charleston, S.C., 1981-83; founding shareholder, sr. ptnr. Laddaga-Garrett PA, 1983—; adj. asst. prof. dept. health adminstrn. and policy Med. U. S.C., 1999—. Bd. dirs., 1st v.p. Charleston chpt. Am. Cancer Soc., 1987-88. Fellow Healthcare Fin. Mgmt. Assn. (advanced mem., bd. dirs. 1991-94, sec., v.p. 1991-95, pres. 1997-98, nat. principles and practices bd. 2002—), S.C. Bar Assn. (chairperson health care law com. 1995-97), Charleston County Bar Assn., Am. Health Lawyers Assn., S.C. Hosp. Assn., Order Ky. Cols., Kiwanis, Elks, Masons, Phi Beta Kappa. Home: 1391 Madison Ct Mount Pleasant SC 29466-7961 Office: 5300 International Blvd Ste B 203 North Charleston SC 29418 E-mail: LADDAGA@sehealthlaw.com.

LADEHOFF, LEO WILLIAM, metal products manufacturing executive; b. Gladbrook, Iowa, May 4, 1932; s. Wendell Leo and Lillian A. L.; m. Beverly Joan Dreessen, Aug. 1, 1951; children: Debra K., Lance A. BS, U. Iowa, 1957. Supt. ops. Square D Co., 1957-61; mfg. mgr. Fed. Pacific Electric Co., 1961; v.p. ops. Avis Indsl. Corp., 1961-67; pres. energy products Group Gulf & Western Industries, Inc., 1967-78; chmn. bd., pres., chief exec. officer, dir. Amcast Indsl. Corp., Ohio, 1978-95, chmn. bd. dirs., 1995—97, 2001—. With USAF, 1951—54, Korea. Mem. Soc. Automotive Engrs., U. Iowa Alumni Assn., Forest Highlands Country Club, The Estancia Club. Republican. Home: 27276 N 103d Way Scottsdale AZ 85255 Office: Amcast Indsl Corp PO Box 98 Dayton OH 45401-0098 also: Elkhart Products Corp 1255 Oak St Elkhart IN 46514-2277 E-mail: lladehoff@aol.com.

LADEN, BEN ELLIS, economist, writer; b. Savannah, Ga., Mar. 4, 1942; s. Bernard and Fannie Rachel (Cooper) L.; m. Susan Sherman, Aug. 16, 1964; children: Francine, Jonathan, Paul. AB, Princeton U., 1963; PhD, Johns Hopkins U., 1969. Asst. prof. econs. Ohio State U., 1967-71; economist Fed. Res. Bd., 1971-74; v.p., chief economist T. Rowe Price Assocs., Balt., 1974-87; dir. fin. instns. regulation staff HUD, Washington, 1990-94; pres. Bel Assocs., 1994—. Author: Economic Trend, 1974-87; also articles. Fellow Nat. Assn. Bus. Economists (dir. 1981-87, pres. 1984-85); mem. Am. Econs. Assn. Jewish. Home: 3111 Rittenhouse St NW Washington DC 20015-1614 E-mail: benladen@prodigy.net. *Each person has to find his own unique formula for success. My greatest achievements have come from the following elements. 1. A clear concept of priorities with persistent concentration on the highest priority. 2. Building structures which will continue to payoff in the future, rather than trying for immediate results. 3. Identifying those areas where my contribution could be the greatest and could be unique. 4. Always striving for the highest quality in my work. 5. Most important, learning from the experience of others and respecting the individual ways of other people.*

LADENDORFF, LINDA HARDIN-REED, early childhood education educator; b. Gunnison, Colo., Nov. 21, 1941; d. L. Douglas and Gertrud (Helmecke) Hardin; m. Robert Henry Ladendorff, dec. 20, 1964; children: Noma Ladendorff Collins, Lisa Wordelman. BA in Elem. Edn., U. Ariz., 1964; MA in Reading and Learning Disabilities, No. Ariz. U., 1986. Cert. in elem. edn., pre-sch., spl. edn. and adult edn., also cert. reading specialist, Ariz. Kindergarten tchr. St. Johns (Ariz.) Unified Schs., 1977-84; tchr., dir. Escuela Para Los Ninas Pre-Sch., St. Johns/Springerville, Ariz., 1985-88; instructional specialist Inst. for Human Devel./No. Ariz. U., Flagstaff, 1989, Alcohol Misuse Prevention Project/U. Mich., Ann Arbor, 1990; tchr. 1st grade Miami (Ariz.) Area Schs., 1991—. Bd. dirs., sec. Apache County Guidance Clinic, St. Johns, 1981; mem. spl. edn. adv. com. Ariz. Dept. Edn., Phoenix, 1986, 87, 88. Mem. adv. com. to City Coun., Victoria, Tex., 1974-75; membership sec. Fine Arts Assn., Victoria, 1973-75; sec. Cmty. Action Com., Victoria, 1974. U.S. Dept. Edn. spl. edn. grantee, 1984, 85, 86, other grants. Mem. TESOL, Ariz. Reading Assn. (bd. dirs.), Gila County Reading Assn. (pres.), Ariz. Assn. Lifelong Learners, Internat. Reading Assn., Delta Kappa Gamma. Methodist. Avocations: needlework, gardening, travel. Home: 1308 Crestwood Dr Globe AZ 85501-1517 Office: Inspiration Addition Sch 929 Rose Rd Miami AZ 85539-1160

LADENHEIM, JULES CALVIN, neurosurgeon; b. Union Hill, N.J., Apr. 21, 1923; s. Solomon and Miriam (Preminger) L.; m. Janet Bloom, Feb. 15, 1959; children: Eric, Fred (dec.), Karen. AB, Harvard U., 1944; MD, N.Y. Med. Coll., 1947. Diplomate Am. Bd. Surgery, Am. Bd. Neurologic Surgery. Intern Queens Gen. Hosp., N.Y.C., 1947-48; resident in gen. surgery N.Y. Med. Coll., 1948-50, Pitts. Med. Ctr., 1952-53, Mt. Sinai, Cleve., 1953-54; resident in neurosurgery Serafimer Hosp., Stockholm, 1954-56, Med. Coll. Va., Richmond, 1956-57, Neurology Inst. N.Y., 1957-58, Mary Hitchcock, Hanover, N.H., 1958-60; pvt. practice Hackensack, N.J., 1960—. Staff neurosurgeon Hackensack U. Hosp., 1960—, Holy Name Hosp., Teaneck, N.J., 1960—, Meadowland Hosp., Secaucus, N.J., 1987—, St. Mary Hosp., Hoboken, 1987—. Co-author: Arteriovenous Aneurysm, 1956; author: Intraventric Meningiomas, 1961, Leonard Bertapaglia, 1991, Firearms and Ballistics, 1996. Lt. USNR, 1950-52. Decorated Navy and Marine Corp medal. Mem. Abraham Lincoln Soc. (pres. 1993-94), Harvard Club N.Y. Office: 664 River Rd Teaneck NJ 07666-1642 E-mail: julescalvin@aol.com.

LADENSON, MARK LAWRENCE, economist, educator; b. Chgo., Dec. 12, 1941; s. Alex and Inez (Sher) L.; m. Joyce Ruddel, Aug. 14, 1971; 1 child, Sharon. *Mark Ladenson's father, Alex, was chief librarian at Chicago Public Library from 1966-1975 and editor of American Library Laws. He led a successful effort to prevent the demolition of the landmark, former main library building, and convert it to the magnificent Chicago Culture Center. His wife, Joyce, is a professor of American Thought and Language, and one of the founders and director (1981-2001) of the Women's Studies Program at Michigan State University. Mark's brother, Robert has been a Professor of Philosophy at Illinois Institute of Technology in Chicago since 1984, is the author of three books, and established the Intercollegiate Ethics Bowl in 1993. His daughter, Sharon, is currently a bibliographer at Michigan State University Library.* BA, U. Wis., 1963; MBA, U. Chgo., 1965; PhD, Northwestern U., 1970. Asst. prof., then assoc. prof. econs. Mich. State U., East Lansing, 1970-84, prof. econs., 1984—. Vis. scholar Ga. State U., Atlanta, 1975-76; faculty fellow, supervising economist U.S. GAO, Washington, 1978-80. Book rev. bd. editors Atlantic Econ. Jour., Edwardsville, Ill., 1986—; contbr. numerous articles to profl. jours. Mem. Am. Econ. Assn., Midwest Econs. Assn., Atlantic Econ. Assn., Internat. Assn. Jazz Record Collectors (best article award 1988), Jazz Photographers Assn. Home: 230 Oxford Rd East Lansing MI 48823-2627 Office: Mich State Univ Dept Econs East Lansing MI 48824

LADER, LAWRENCE, writer; b. N.Y.C., Aug. 6, 1919; s. Ludwig and Myrtle (Powell) L.; m. Jean MacInnis, Aug. 24, 1942 (div. Jan. 1946); m. Joan Summers, Sept. 27, 1961; 1 dau., Wendy Summers. AB, Harvard U., 1941. With press dept. ABC, 1941-42; contbg. editor Coronet mag., 1946; feature editor Glamour mag., 1953; lectr. NYU, 1957-59, Philips Brooks Assn., Harvard, 1962—; regular contbr. Am. Heritage, Reader's Digest, N.Y. Times mags., others, 1941—; exec. dir. Hugh Moore Fund, 1966-67; fgn. corr. Arab-Israel War, 1948, other overseas assignments, 1951, 55, 57; adj. assoc. prof. journalism NYU, 1967-72. Author: Margaret Sanger, 1955, The Bold Brahmins, New England's War Against Slavery, 1961, Abortion, 1966, juvenile Margaret Sanger, 1969, Breeding Ourselves to Death, 1971, Foolproof Birth Control, 1972, Abortion II: Making the Revolution, 1973, Power on the Left: American Radical Movements since 1946, 1979, Politics, Power and the Church, 1987, RU 486, 1991, A Private Matter, 1995, Ideas Triumphant, 2002. Chmn. exec. com. Nat. Abortion Rights Action League, 1969-72, chmn. bd., 1972-76; pres. Abortion Rights Mobilization, 1976— . Served to lt. AUS, 1942-46; officer-in-charge N.Y. Troop Information, Armed Forces Radio Service. Recipient Benjamin Franklin Mag. award, 1969, Cert. Distinction, NOW, 1989; named Feminist Majority Feminist of Yr., 1992. Mem. Authors Guild. Clubs: Harvard, Century Assn. (N.Y.C.). Home: 51 5th Ave New York NY 10003-4320

LADER, MALCOLM HAROLD, pharmaceutical consultant; b. Liverpool, England, Feb. 27, 1936; s. Abe and Minnie (Sholl) L.; m. Susan Ruth Packer, Apr. 16, 1961; children: Deborah, Vicki, Charlotte. BSc, U. Liverpool, 1956, MB, ChB, 1959; PhD, U. London, 1963; MD, U. Liverpool, 1964; DSc, U. London, 1978. Rsch. staff MRC, England, 1966—2001. Cons. Maudsley Hosp., 1970-2001; prof. emeritus clin. psychopharmacology, U. London, 1978-2001, emeritus prof., 2001—; advisor WHO. Author: Biological Treatments in Psychiatry, 1996; contbr. articles to profl. jours. Decorated Order of Brit. Empire, 1996. Fellow: Acad. Med. Scis., Royal Soc. Psychiatrists, Soc. for Study of Addiction (hon.), Am. Coll. Psychiatry (hon.), Brit. Assn. Psychopharmacology (hon.). Avocations: antiques, paintings. Home: 11 Kelsey Way Kent BR3 3LP England E-mail: m.lader@iop.kcl.ac.uk.

LADER, PHILIP, lawyer, government official, diplomat, business executive, university president; b. Jackson Heights, N.Y., Mar. 17, 1946; BA, Duke U., 1966; MA, U. Mich., 1967, Oxford U., England, 1968; JD, Harvard U., 1972; 14 Hon. Doctorates, from Brit. and Am. Univs. Bar: Fla. 1972, D.C. 1973, S.C. 1979. Atty. Sullivan & Cromwell, N.Y.C., 1972; law clk. to U.S. cir. judge, 1973; pres. Sea Pines Co., Hilton Head Island, 1979-83, Winthrop U., Rock Hill, S.C., 1983-85; exec. v.p. Sir James Goldsmith's US Holding Co.,

1986-88; pres. Bus. Execs. for Nat. Security, Washington, 1990—91; pres., vice chancellor Bond U., Queensland, Australia, 1991-93; adminstr. SBA, Washington, 1994-97; mem. President's Cabinet, 1994-97; U.S. amb. to Ct. of St. James, 1997-2001; chmn. WPP plc, 2001—; sr. advisor Morgan Stanley Internat., 2001—; ptnr. Nelson Mullins Riley & Scarborough, 2001—. Dep. dir. for mgmt. Office Mgmt. and Budget Exec. Office Pres., 1993; dep. chief of staff White House, asst. to Pres., 1993-94; chmn. Pres.'s Coun. on Integrity and Efficiency, 1993, chmn. Pres.'s Mgmt. Coun.; chmn. policy com. Nat. Performance Rev., 1993; dir. RAND Corp., AES Corp., Marathon Oil. Candidate for gov. of S.C., 1986; chmn. bd. visitors Duke U. Sanford Inst. Pub. Policy; bd. dirs. ARC, 1996-97; founder Renaissance Inst.; bd. trustees Brit. Mus.; chmn. Am. Assn. Royal Acad. Art; trustee Ditchley Found.. Hon. fellow Pembroke Coll., Oxford U., London Bus. Sch., John Moores U.; hon. bencher Mid. Temple. Mem. Coun. Fgn. Rels., Chief Execs. Orgn., D.C. Met. Club, World Pres.'s Orgn., Harvard Club N.Y.C., Soc. Internat. Bus. Fellows, Royal Soc. Arts (mem. adv. bd. Prince of Wales Trust, trustee Windsor Leadership Forum), Mfrs. and Sci. (Benjamin Franklin medal 2001), Phi Beta Kappa. Episcopalian. Office: Liberty Ctr 151 Meeting St Ste 600 Charleston SC 29401

LADERMAN, CAROL C. anthropologist, educator; b. Bklyn., Oct. 25, 1932; d. Philip and Sylvia (Sugarman) Ciavati; m. Gabriel Laderman, Feb. 12, 1953; children: Raphael, Michael. BA with honors, Hunter Coll., 1972; MA, Columbia U., 1975, PhD with distinction, 1979. Vis. lectr. Yale U., New Haven, 1980-82; asst. prof. Fordham U., Bronx, N.Y., 1982-88, assoc. prof., 1988-90; prof. anthropology City Coll.-CUNY, N.Y.C., 1990—, chmn. dept., 1990-96, 99—. External assessor Acad. of Malay Studies, U. Malaya. Author: Wives and Midwives, 1983, Taming the Wind of Desire, 1991, Main Peteri: Malay Shamanism, 1991; editor: Techniques of Healing in Southeast Asia, 1988, The Performance of Healing, 1996; mem. editl. bd. Anthropology and Humanism. Cons. N.Am. Conf. on Ethiopian Jewry, N.Y.C. Social Sci. Rsch. Coun. fellow, 1975-78, John Simon Guggenheim fellow, 1987-88; NEH grantee, 1982-85, 87-90; Resident scholar Rockefeller Found., 1989. Mem. Am. Anthropol. Assn., Am. Ethnological Assn., Soc. for Med. Anthropology, Coun. on Nutritional Anthropology (exec. bd. 1985-89), Internat. Assn. for Study of Traditional Asian Medicine (sec.-gen. 1992-96). Avocations: music, art. Office: City Coll/CUNY Dept Anthropology New York NY 10031

LADEROUTE, CHARLES DAVID, engineer, economist, consultant; b. Helena, Mo., Aug. 2, 1948; s. Estel and Anna Maude (Stuart) L.; m. Linda Dodd, June 8, 1985; 1 child, Lindsay; 1 stepchild, Erik. BS in Engring. Mgmt., U. Mo., Rolla, 1971, BS in Econs., 1972; MA in Econs., Ea. Mich. U., 1980; postgrad., Harvard U., 1979-81. Sr. rate analyst Consumers Power Co., Jackson, Mich., 1972-79; prin. cons. Chas. T. Main, Inc., Boston, 1979-81; pres., chief exec. officer Charles D. Laderoute, Ltd., St. Joseph, Mo., 1981—, also chmn. bd. dirs. Mem. supplemental faculty Jackson Community Coll., 1974-78; course dir. Ctr. for Profl. Advancement, East Brunswick, N.J., 1981—; ptnr. Knowledge Applications Software, LP, Acton, Mass., 1986—; lectr. in field. Contbr. articles to profl. jours. Mem. Nat. Rep. Senatorial Com., 1990-91, Rep. Nat. Com., 1990—; charter mem. Rep. Campaign Coun., 1991; mem. fin. com., chair Town of Boxford, computer study com. chair and clk., capital budgeting com., sch. tech. com., Tri-Town Sch. Union Ctrl. Office Bookkeeping Rev. Com., bd. commrs. trust funds; chair, treas. Rep. Town Com. Mem. Am. Econs. Assn., Am. Meteorol. Soc., Nat. Assn. Bus. Economists, Nat. Soc. Rate of Return Analysts, Internat. Assn. Energy Economists (charter, pres. N.E. chpt. 1984-86), Am. Soc. Engring. Mgmt. (charter, life), Planning Engrs. Desktop Computer Users Group (charter, pres. 1987-88), ABA (assoc.), Am. Gas. Assn. (assoc.), Can. Gas. Assn. (assoc.), Assn. Energy Engrs., Demand-Side Mgmt. Soc. (charter), Assn. Demand-Site Mgmt. Profls. (charter), Essex Club (dir.), Omicron Delta Epsilon. Republican. Achievements include creation of Relative System Utilization method used in utility industry for allocation of demand related costs; research in effect of weather and possible global warming on energy sales and peak demands. Office: Charles D Laderoute Ltd 5114 Amazonia Rd Saint Joseph MO 64505-3163

LADIN, EUGENE, communications company executive; b. N.Y.C., Oct. 26, 1927; s. Nat and Mae (Cohen) L.; m. Millicent Dolly Frankel, June 27, 1948; children: Leslie Hope, Stephanie Joy. BBA, Pace U., 1956; MBA, Air Force Inst. Tech., 1959; postgrad., George Washington U., 1966-69. Cost engr. Rand Corp., Santa Monica, Calif., 1960-62; mgr. cost and econ. analysis Northrop Corp., Hawthorne, 1962-66; dir. financial planning Communications Satellite Corp., Washington, 1966-70; treas., chief fin. and adminstrv. officer Landis & Gyr, Inc., Elmsford, N.Y., 1970-76; v.p., treas., comptroller P.R. Telephone Co., San Juan, 1976-77; v.p. fin. Comtech Telecommunications Corp., Smithtown, N.Y., 1977—; acting pres. Comtech Antenna Corp., St. Cloud, Fla., 1978-80; chmn., chief exec. officer Telephone Interconnect Enterprises/Sunshine Telephone Co., Balt., Md. and Orlando, 1980-82; pres. Ladin and Assocs., Cons. and Commodity Traders, Maitland, 1982-84; pres., chief fin. officer Braintech Inc., South Plainfield, N.J., 1984; sr. v.p. fin., chief fin. officer Teltec Savs. Communications Co., Miami, Fla., 1984-88; chief fin. officer Hurwitz Group Inc., North Miami Beach, 1988-91; cons. pvt. practice, 1991-98; v.p., CFO Ginsite Materials, Inc., Plantation, Fla., 1998-99. Assoc. prof. acctg. So. Ill. U., East St. Louis, 1960; asso. prof. bus. U. Md., 1969-70; adj. prof. George Washington U., 1969-70; vis. prof. acctg. Pace U., 1970; cons. E. Ladin, Pembroke Pines, Fla., 1999—. Served to capt. USAF, 1951-60. Decorated Air Force Commendation medal; recipient Air Force Outstanding Unit award. Avocations: golf, sailing. Home and Office: 13355 SW 16th Ct Apt 401E Hollywood FL 33027-2429 *An individual must have sufficient self esteem to sustain the courage of his convictions, a high degree of professional integrity, and his individual character. Society has adopted a philosophy of "walk the middle road".*

LADJEVARDI, HABIB, historian; b. Tehran, Iran, May 28, 1938; came to U.S., 1950; s. Seyed Mahmoud and Tahereh (Kashani) L.; m. Mina Nassirzadeh, Aug. 3, 1962 (div. June 1979); children: Mahmoud, Mariam, Leila. BS, Yale U., 1961; MBA, Harvard U., 1963; DPhil, Oxford U., 1981. Personnel dir. Behshahr Ind. Group, Tehran, 1963-65, mktg. dir., 1966-69; pres. Paxan Corp., 1969-70; chmn. bd. dirs. Container Corp. of Iran, 1969-79; founder, v.p. Iran Ctr. Mgmt. Studies, Tehran, 1970-79; sr. rsch. assoc. Harvard U. Bus. Sch., Cambridge, Mass., 1980-81; rsch. assoc. Harvard U. Ctr. for Middle Eastern Studies, 1981—, assoc. dir., 1987-90, dir. Iranian oral history project, 1981—. Mem. acceptance coms. Tehran Stock Exch., 1973-76; lectr. Iran Ctr. for Mgmt. Studies, 1975-79; vis. fellow Oxford (Eng.) Ctr. Mgmt. Studies, 1976-79; v.p. exec. coun. Harvard U. Bus. Sch., 1978-79; exec. sec. Soc. for Iranian Studies, Cambridge, 1982-87; chmn. Iranian Studies Harvard U. Ctr. for Middle Eastern Studies, 1990—, chmn. pubs. com., 1990—. Author: Labor Unions & Autocracy in Iran, 1985, Guide to the Iranian Oral History Collection, 1993, Memoirs of Ali Amini, 1995, Memoirs of Shapour Bakhtiar, 1996, Memoirs of Hamid Kadjar, 1996, Memoirs of M.E. Amirteymour, 1997, Memoirs of Abdolmajid Madjidi, 1998, Memoirs of Fatemeh Pakravan, 1998, Memoirs of Jafar Sharif-Emami, 1999, Memoirs of M.A. Modjtahedi, 2000; contbr. articles to profl. jours., chpts. to books. Mem. coun. of state Adminstrv. and Employment Affairs of Iran, 1972-76; dir. devel. and investment Bank of Iran, 1972-79; mem. ctrl. coun. Pres. of Univs. and Colls. of Iran, 1971-78; pres. Tahereh Found., Cambridge, Mass., 1982—. NEH grantee, 1984-87. Mem. Am. Hist. Assn., Young Presidents Orgn., Acad. Polit. Sci., N.Y. Acad. Scis., Iranian Assn. of Boston (founder, pres. 1988-91), Yale U. Class Coun., Yale Club of N.Y. Democrat. Avocations: skiing, grandchildren, gardening. Office: Harvard U Ctr Mid Eastern Studies 1737 Cambridge St Cambridge MA 02138 E-mail: ladjevar@fas.harvard.edu.

LADJEVARDI, HAMID, fund manager; b. Tehran, Iran, June 11, 1948; came to U.S., 1948; s. Ahmad and Banoo (Barzin) L.; children: Adella, Lilly. BA in Econs., BA in Polit. Sci., U. Calif., Berkeley, 1971; MBA, Harvard U., 1973. Dep. mng. dir. Behshahr Indsl. Group, Tehran, 1974-79; vice-chmn., fin. dir. Akam Group of Cos., 1975-79; investment mgr., v.p. Morgan Stanley & Co., N.Y.C., 1980-92; mgr. Baltic Fund 1 LLC, N.Y., 1994—. Instr. Fairleigh Dickinson U., Rutherford, N.J., 1984; mem. supervisory coun. Lindeks, Latvia, Kinnisvara Ekspress, Estonia; chmn. Baltic Fund Hotels, Vilnius, 1996—. Vice-chmn. U.S. Baltic Found.; trustee Zimmerli Art Mus. Mem. Fgn. Policy Assn., Carnegie Coun. on Ethics and Internat. Affairs, U.S. Senatorial Club, Harvard Club, Nat. Arts Club. Home: 11 Gramercy Park S Apt 3 New York NY 10003-1753 Office: Baltic Fund 1LP 15 E 26th St Ste 1809 New York NY 10010-1505 E-mail: Hamid@balticfund.com.

LADMAN, A(ARON) J(ULIUS), anatomist, educator; b. Jamaica, N.Y., July 3, 1925; s. Thomas and Ida (Sobin) L.; m. Barbara Powers, 1948 (div. 1980); children: Susan Elizabeth, Thomas Frederick; m. Patricia A. Bergbauer, 1982; 1 child, Peter John. Student, Miami U., Oxford, Ohio, 1942-43; AB, NYU, 1947; postgrad., U. Cin., 1948-49; PhD, Ind. U., 1952. Teaching fellow anatomy U. Cin., 1948-49, Ind. U., 1949-52; with Harvard Med. Sch., 1952-61, assoc., 1955-61; assoc. prof. U. Tenn. Med. Units, 1961-64; vis. assoc. prof. Yale, 1964; prof., chmn. dept. anatomy U. N.Mex. Sch. Medicine, Albuquerque, 1964-81; prof. anatomy Hahnemann U., Phila., 1981-94, Med. Coll. Pa. and Hahnemann U. Sch. Medicine, Phila., 1995; adj. prof. neurobiology and anatomy Allegheny U., 1996; adj. prof. neurobiology & anatomy MCP Hahnemann U., 1996—2002, dean Sch. Allied Health Professions, 1981-86. Adj. prof. neurobiology and anatomy Drexel U. Coll. Medicine, 2002—. Assoc. editor Anat. Record, 1967-68, editor-in-chief, 1968-98, cons. editor, 1998—; contbr. articles to profl. jours. Recipient Rsch. Career Devel. award USPHS, 1962-64; rsch. fellow Am. Cancer Soc., 1952-55, spl. rsch. fellow USPHS, 1955-57, 71-72. Fellow AAAS; mem. Am. Assn. Anatomists (exec. com. 1972-76, 2d v.p. 1980-81, 1st v.p. 1981-82), Am. Soc. for Cell Biology, Nat. Inst. Gen. Med. Scis. (rsch. cancer awards com. 1967-71), Electron Microscope Soc. Am. (exec. coun. 1974-76), Coun. Biol. Editors (sec. 1977-82), Histochem. Soc. Home: 103 Arbor Way Lansdale PA 19446-6433 E-mail: ajl0031@aol.com.

LADMER, WILLIAM EDWARD, food product engineering executive; b. N.Y.C., Jan. 21, 1942; s. Alfred Harold and Lucille (Peyser) L.; children: Lisa Beth, David. BSME magna cum laude, U. Ctrl. Ariz., 1966, MSIE, 1969. Registered profl. engr.; cert. plant engr. Engr. mgr. Boeing Corp., Seattle, 1966-72; pres. Ladmer Engring., San Diego, 1972-80, Allentown, Pa., 1982-90; engr. mgr. Sohio Petroleum, San Francisco, 1980-82; plant engr. mfg. Kraft Foods, Champaign, Ill., 1990-93; corp. engring. group mgr. McKee Foods, Collegedale, Tenn., 1993-97, E2M, Atlanta, 1997-98; plant engring. mgr. Pontiac Foods, Columbia, S.C., 1998—. Author: Design Build-What Can You-What Should You Expect, 1996, Project Engineering-Food Plants, 1991, Food Plant Sanitation, 1984. Firefighter Tri Cmty. Vol. Fire Dept., Collegedale, 1993-97. With U.S. Army, 1961-63. Mem. Inst. of Indsl. Engrs. (sr. mem.), Inst. of Plant Engrs. (sr. mem.), Soc. of Mfg. Engrs. (sr. mem.). Achievements include 2 patents on the method of 2 sided welding, application of leaded glass on substrate. Home: 30 Rosewalk Ln Elgin SC 29045-9407 E-mail: bladmer@msm.com.

LADNER, ANN-MARIE CALVO, special education educator; b. Hartford, Conn., Feb. 6, 1949; d. Vincent J. and Mary S. (Santangelo) Calvo; m. R. Martin Ladner, June 19, 1971; children: Mary-Lorraine Amy Cox, R. Vincent, Michelle A. AS, Belleville Area Coll., 1983; BS in Speech and Theater, So. Ill. U., Edwardsville, 1985, MS in Edn., 1986; EdS, Auburn U. Montgomery, 1993. Cert. specific learning disabilities, Ala., psychometrist, Ala., sch. adminstr., Ala. Tchr. merchandising Skadron Coll. Bus., San Bernardino, Calif., 1981-82; tchr. English as second lang. Turkish-Am. Assn., Ankara, Turkey, 1986; tchr. speech and computers Ozel Atilim Lisesi, 1987-88; tchr. English and reading St. Jude H.S., Selma, Ala., 1989-90; tchr. spl. edn. Selma Sch. Dist., 1990-92, Montgomery (Ala.) County Schs., 1992—93, tchr. spl. edn., 1995—98; tchr. spl. edn. Dept. Youth Svcs., Jemison, Ala., 1993-95; founder, adminstr. Exploratorium Acad. Inc., Montgomery, 1999—. Libr. bd. dirs. City of Millbrook, Ala., 1992-94; bd. dirs. Turkish-Am. Assn., Ankara, 1987-88, Millbrook YMCA, 1993-95; judge, coach Nat. Forensics League, Belleville, Ill., 1985. Named Competent Toastmaster, Toastmasters Internat., 1985; mini-grantee Montgomery Area Cmty. Found., 1992. Mem. Nat. Coun. Tchrs. Math., Mensa, Kappa Delta Pi. Avocations: internet, reading, collecting educational materials. Home: 844 Brookland Curv Montgomery AL 36117-4548

LADNER, BENJAMIN, university president; b. Mobile, Ala. m. Nancy Bullard Ladner; 4 children. BA, Baylor U.; BD, Southern Seminary; PhD, Duke U.; D (hon.), Elizabethtown (Pa.) Coll., SookMyung Women's U., South Korea. Prof. dept. philosophy and religious studies U. N.C., Greensboro; pres. Nat. Faculty of Humanities, Arts & Scis., Atlanta, Am. U., Washington, 1994—. Office: Am Univ 4400 Massachusetts Ave NW Washington DC 20016-8060*

LADOW, C. STUART, retired consultant financial services; b. Warren, Pa., Apr. 21, 1925; s. Clyde and Glendine (Bentley) LaD.; m. Donna Elizabeth Miller, Aug. 21, 1993; 1 child, Paul Stuart. BA, Cornell U., 1947. With Gen. Electric Co., 1947-50; mgr. N.Y. region Gen. Electric Credit Corp., N.Y.C., 1950-80, v.p. Stamford, Conn., 1971-80; pres. GECC Fin. Services, 1975-78, Color Tyme TV Rental div. Curtis Mathes Corp., Athens, Tex., 1980; sr. v.p. Yegen Assocs., Inc., Paramus, N.J., 1981-85, exec. v.p., 1985-87; pres. Yegen Equity Loan Corp., N.J., 1987; fin. svcs. cons. Allison Park, Pa., 1988-99; dir. Nat. Capital Holdings, 1997-98; ret., 1999. Bd. dirs. Puritan Life Ins. Co., Providence. V.p., bd. dirs. Jr. Achievement of Stamford, Inc., 1973-80; exec. budget com., chmn. budget panel United Way of Stamford, 1973-80; chmn. Stamford chpt. Am. Cancer Soc., 1977; pres. Spring Meadow Condominium Assn., Wyckoff, N.J., 1983, trustee, 1983-88; moderator Emmanuel Bapt. Ch., Ridgewood, N.J., 1985-86; trustee North Hills Community Baptist Ch., 1988-91; dir. Hampton Twsp. Mcpl. Authority, Allison Park, Pa., 1991-97, dir., treas. Baptist Homes of Western Pa., 1992-98, pres. Arbors Homeowners Assn., Allison Park, 1992-93; pres. Cornell U. Class of 1947, 1992-97. Recipient Cmty. Svc. award Gen. Electric Credit Corp., 1976. Mem. Nat. Second Mortgage Assn. (pres. 1987-88, Outstanding Service award, Meritorious Svc. award 1989), Nat. Consumer Finance Assn. (certificate of appreciation), Masons, Shriners, Cornell Club of Pitts. Republican. Baptist. Home and Office: 4211 Latour Ct Allison Park PA 15101-2968 *Ours is a great country that deserves the devotion and strong support of those who call it home. There can be few satisfactions in life greater than assisting in the moral, spiritual and career growth of those whom we have the opportunity to know and possibly influence.*

LA DU, BERT NICHOLS, JR. pharmacology educator, physician; b. Lansing, Mich., Nov. 13, 1920; s. Bert Nichols and Natalie (Kerr) La D.; m. Catherine Shilson, June 14, 1947; children: Elizabeth, Mary, Anne, Jane. BS, Mich. State Coll., 1943; MD, U. Mich., 1945; PhD in Biochemistry, U. Calif., Berkeley, 1952. Intern Rochester (N.Y.) Gen. Hosp., 1945-46; research asso. N.Y.U. Research Service, Goldwater Meml. Hosp., N.Y.C., 1950-53; sr. asst. surgeon USPHS, Nat. Heart Inst., 1954-57; surgeon, later sr. surgeon, med. dir. Nat. Inst. Arthritis and Metabolic Disease, 1957-63; prof., chmn. dept. pharmacology N.Y.U. Med. Sch., 1963-74; prof. pharmacology U. Mich. Med. Sch., Ann Arbor, 1974-89, prof. emeritus, 1989—, chmn. dept., 1974-81. Contbr. articles to profl. jours. Served with AUS, 1943-45. Mem. AAAS, Am. Chem. Soc., N.Y. Acad. Sci. (pres.), Am. Soc. Biol. Chemistry, Am. Soc. Pharmacol. Therapeutics (pres.), Am. Soc. Human Genetics, Biochem. Soc. (Gt. Britain). Home: 505 E Huron St Apt 702 Ann Arbor MI 48104-1541 Office: U Mich Med Sch 7422 MSRB3 Ann Arbor MI 48109-0632 E-mail: bladu@umich.edu.

LADUE, EDDY LORAIN, economist, educator; b. Middlesex, N.Y., June 23, 1939; s. George Jay and Ester (Eddy) LaDue; m. Lorraine Judith Frankish, June 27, 1964; children: Steven George, Scott Philip, Shelley Ester. BS, Cornell U., 1964, MS, 1966; PhD, Mich. State U., 1972. Farm owner, operator George LaDue and Sons, Canandaigua, NY, 1959—62; extension assoc. Cornell U., Ithaca, 1965—67, asst. prof. agrl. econs., 1971—76, assoc. prof. agrl. econs., 1976—84, prof. agrl. econs., 1984—98, W.F. Myers Prof. Agrl. Fin., 1998—. Agrl. economist U.S. Dept. Agr., 1977—78; cons. Congl. Budget Office, Washington, 1979; cons. in field; assoc. editor Jour. Agrl. Fin. Rev., 1983—90, co-editor, 1992—96, editor, 1991, 1997—. Mem.: Northeastern Agr. and Resource Econs. Assn., Am. Agr. Econs. Assn., Phi Kappa Phi. Republican. Avocations: golf, fishing, gardening. Home: 1132 Snyder Hill Rd Ithaca NY 14850-8802 Office: Cornell U 357 Warren Hall Ithaca NY 14853-7801 E-mail: ell4@Cornell.edu.

LADUNGA, ISTVAN (STEVE LADUNGA), computational molecular biologist; b. Budapest, Hungary, Nov. 8, 1951; came to U.S., 1993; s. Istvan and Emily (Balogh) L.; m. Lidia Szatmari, Aug. 16, 1976 (dec. 1985); children: Sylvia, Nick; m. Katalin Halász, Nov. 6, 1986. MS in Biology and Chemistry, Eötvös U., Budapest, 1976, PhD in Biology, 1978. Jr. rsch. fellow U. Agr., Gödöllö, Hungary, 1976-77; jr. sch. assoc. to rsch. assoc. Inst. Computer Sci., Budapest, 1977-89; head dept. Nat. Com. Technol. Devel., 1986-89; rsch. assoc. genetics Eötvös U., 1989-93; vis. rsch. assoc. math. Stanford (Calif.) U., 1993-94; rsch. assoc. molecular and human genetics Baylor Coll. Medicine, Houston, 1994-96; asst. dir. SmithKline Beecham Pharms., King of Prussia, Pa., 1996-2000; sr. scientist Celera Genomics Corp., Foster City, Calif., 2000—. Author software on classification of proteins, 1990-92, pattern database search, 1994-97, physicochem. sequence analysis, 1996-97, Rev. on Secreted Proteins, 2000, Tutorials on Sequence Database Searches; contbr. articles to profl. jours.; patentee in field. Recipient Grand Prix, Hungarian Ministry Edn., Budapest, 1977, Spl. prize Hungarian Biol. Soc., Budapest, 1977. Office: PE Celera Genomics 850 Lincoln Centre Dr Foster City CA 94404-1128 Personal E-mail: ladunga@yahoo.com. Business E-Mail: steven.ladunga@fc.celera.com.

LADWIG, HAROLD ALLEN, neurologist; b. Manilla, Iowa, May 11, 1922; s. Ernest and Iva Marie (Allen) L.; m. Marjorie Lois Foster, June 26, 1946; children: Stephen H., Rosemary A. BA, U. Iowa, 1952, MD, 1947. Intern St. Joseph Hosp., Sioux City, Iowa, 1947-48; pvt. practice U. Minn., 1948-49, resident, 1949-50; pvt. practice Nebr., 1954-83, N.C., 1983—; pres. Omaha Neurol. Clinic, 1972-83. Contbr. articles to profl. jours. Bd. dirs. Boys and Girls Club, Wilson, N.C., 1995—, Salvation Army, Wilson, 1996—, Country Drs. Mus., Bailey, N.C., 1995-2002, Mental Health Bd., Wilson, 1995—. Comdr. USNR, 1950-52. Fellow Am. Coll. Physicians, Am. Acad. Neurology; mem. AMA, Am. Assn. Electrodiagnostic Medicine, Am. Soc. Electroencephalography and Neurophysiology, Wilson County Med. Soc. (sec. 1993, v.p. 1994, pres. 1995), Wilson Meml. Hosp. Found. (pres. 1993—), Douglas County Med. Soc. (exec. bd. 1960-63), Kiwanis (pres. Wilson chpt. 1995, Kiwanian of Yr. award 1992-93), Phi Beta Kappa, Beta Beta Beta. Methodist. Avocation: computers. Home: PO Box 3164 Wilson NC 27895-3049 E-mail: hladwig@nc.rr.com.

LAEL, RICHARD L. humanities educator; b. Hickory, NC, Sept. 16, 1946; m. Ann Sisac. BA, Lenoir-Rhyne Coll., Hickory, 1968; MA, U. NC, 1972, PhD, 1976. Instr. NC State U., Raleigh, 1975—77, vis. asst. prof., 1977—78; asst. prof. dept. humanities Westminster Coll., Fulton, Mo., 1978—84, assoc. prof., 1984—90, prof., 1990—. Author: The Yamashita Precedent, 1982 (Mo. Conf. History Disting. Book award, 1983), Arrogant Diplomacy, 1987; co-author: Versailles and After, 1983; contbg. author: The Rating Game in American Politics, 1987, contbg. author: The War of 1898 and U.S. Interventions, 1994; contbr. articles to profl. jours. Recipient Mo. Gov.'s award for excellence in tchg., 2000. Mem.: Soc. for Historians of Am. Fgn. Rels., Soc. for Mil. History, Orgn. Am. Historians. Office: Westminster Coll 501 Westminster Ave Fulton MO 65251-1299 E-mail: laelr@jaynet.wcmo.edu.

LAESSIG, RONALD HAROLD, preventive medicine and pathology educator, state official; b. Marshfield, Wis., Apr. 4, 1940; s. Harold John and Ella Louise L.; m. Joan Margaret Spreda, Jan. 29, 1966; 1 child, Elizabeth Susan. BS, U. Wis., Stevens Point, 1962; PhD, U. Wis., 1965. Jr. faculty Princeton (N.J.) U., 1966; chief clin. chemistry Wis. State Lab. Hygiene, Madison, 1966-80, dir., 1980—; asst. prof. preventive medicine U. Wis., 1966-72, assoc. prof., 1972-76, prof., 1976—, prof. pathology, 1980—. Cons. Ctr. Disease Control, Atlanta; dir. Nat. Com. for Clin. Lab. Stds., Villanova, Pa., 1977-80; chmn. invitro diagnostic products adv. com. FDA, 1974-75; mem. rev. com. Nat. Bur. Stds., 1983-86 Mem. editl. bd. Med. Electronics, 1970—, Analytical Chemistry, 1970-76, Health Lab. Sci., 1970—; contbr. articles to profl. jours. Mem. State of Wis. Tech. Com. Alcohol and Traffic Safety, 1970-88. Sloan Found. grantee, 1966; recipient numerous grants Mem. APHA (Difco award 1974), Am. Assn. Clin. Chemistry (chmn. safety com. 1984-86, bd. dirs. 1986-89, Natelson award 1989, Contbns. Svc. to Profession award 1990, Reiner award 1998, Eiler award 1999), Am. Soc. for Med. Tech., Nat. Com. Clin. Lab. Stds. (pres. 1980-82, bd. dirs. 1984-87), Sigma Xi Avocation: woodworking. Office: State Lab Hygiene 465 Henry Mall Madison WI 53706-1578 E-mail: rhl@mail.slh.wisc.edu. *If you are doing something you really enjoy and it affords you the opportunity to really help your fellow man--you're really blessed (like I am).*

LAESSIG, WALTER BRUCE, publishing executive; b. Englewood, N.J., Aug. 11, 1941; s. George Bruce Laessig and Eileen May (Codling) Roma; m. Susan Lamme, June 13, 1964; children: Katherine Anne, Sarah Eileen, Matthew Lamme. AB in History, Cornell U., 1963, MBA in Fin., LLB, Cornell U., 1966. Bar: N.Y. 1966, D.C. 1968. Atty. Nixon, Hargrave, Devans & Doyle, Rochester, N.Y., 1966-68, Martin, Whitfield & Thaler, Washington, 1968-70; minority economist, counsel Joint Econ. Com., U.S. Congress, 1971-75; minority tax counsel Com. on Ways and Means, U.S. Ho. Reps., 1975-77; gen. counsel Nat. Assn. REITs, 1977-79; atty. Laessig, Brown, Hearn & Clohan, 1979-84; v.p. Warren, Gorham & Lamont, N.Y.C., 1984-85, exec. v.p., 1986, pres., chief exec. officer, 1987-89; exec. v.p., chief oper. officer Thomson Profl. Pub., Stamford, Conn., 1989-90; pres., chief exec. officer The Argus Group, Washington, 1990—. Republican. Presbyterian. Office: The Argus Group 1101 Vermont Ave NW Ste 400 Washington DC 20005-3521

LA FALCE, JOHN JOSEPH, congressman, lawyer; b. Buffalo, Oct. 6, 1939; s. Dominic E. and Catherine M. (Stasio) La F.; m. Patricia Fisher, 1979. BS, Canisius Coll., 1961; JD, Villanova U., 1964; LLD (hon.), Niagara U., 1979, St. Johns U., 1989; LHD (hon.), Canisius Coll., 1990; LLD (hon.), Villanova U., 1991. Bar: N.Y. 1964. Mem. N.Y. State Legislature, 1971-74, 94th-107th Congresses representing 29 dist. N.Y., 1975—; ranking minority mem. House Banking & Fin. Svcs. Com., Washington. Capt. adj. gen. corps AUS. Democrat. Office: US Ho of Reps Rm 2310 Rayburn House Off Bldg Washington DC 20515-0001*

LA FARGE, TIMOTHY, retired plant geneticist; b. N.Y.C., Mar. 14, 1930; s. Louis Bancel and Hester Alida (Emmet) La F.; m. Anne Blackstone, Oct. 16, 1960 (div. Mar. 1964); m. Frances Madelyne Holst, Aug. 6, 1966 (dec. 1992); 1 child, Jason Emmet; m. Nkem R. Salako, Dec. 4, 1993 (div. Oct. 1998); m. Frances W. Stott, Sept. 5, 2002. BA in Dance, Black Mountain Coll., 1952; BSc in Forestry, U. Maine, 1964; M in Forestry, Yale U., 1965; PhD, Mich. State U., 1971. Forestry aid Forest Svc., Orono, Maine, 1962-64; lab. technician geology dept. Yale U., New Haven, 1965; rsch. forester USDA Forest Svc., Macon, Ga., 1965-69, plant geneticist Southea. Sta., 1970-82, plant geneticist Nat. Forest Sys. Atlanta, 1982-2000, ret., 2000; consulting assoc. Daniels and Assocs., Inc., Forest Genetics Cons., San Francisco, 2000—. Contbr. articles to profl. jours. Recipient Certs. of Merit, USDA Forest Svc., Atlanta, 1986, 88. Mem. AAAS, Soc. Am. Foresters. Democrat. Achievements include demonstration that backcrossing and hybridization between shortleaf pine and loblolly pine can effectively produce fast-growing back-cross hybrids that are resistant to fusiform rust; application of Best Linear Prediction to analysis of unbalanced or messy progeny test data. Home: 863 Foerster St San Francisco CA 94127-2307 E-mail: tlafrg@aol.com.

LAFARGUE, MELBA FAYE FULMER, financial manager, real estate consultant; b. Baton Rouge, July 13, 1937; d. Harry Geon and Alice (Peters) Fulmer; m. Leo Wallace LaFargue, Aug. 13, 1953 (div. Aug. 1983). BS in Acctg., La. State U., 1959; postgrad., Am. Sch. Banking, 1962. Cert. fin. mgr., realtor. Co-owner Newspaper Crossroads, Kinder, La., 1958-74; loan officer Great So. Mktg. and Loan, 1959-60; office mgr. Savant Constrn. Co., Kinder, 1960-74; cons. Baton Rouge Recreation and Park Commn., 1975-77; realtor Sherwood Realty, Inc., Baton Rouge, 1974—; service mgr. Campus Fed. Credit Union, 1980—. Fin. counselor Displaced Homemakers, Baton Rouge, 1983. Mem. Women in Politics, Baton Rouge; cons. fin. Cath. Daus. Am., 1960—. Mem. Nat. Assn. of Bank Women, Nat. Assn. Realtors, Am. Mgmt. Assn., Investors Assn. Democrat. Roman Catholic. Home: 2506 Shadowbrook Dr Baton Rouge LA 70816-2850 Office: AmSouth Investment Svcs Inc 201 NW Railroad Ave Hammond LA 70401-3249

LAFARO, ANGELO JOHN, small business owner; b. Poteau, Okla., June 2, 1949; s. Angelo John Sr. and Nettie Marie (Stephens) LaF.; m. Lydia Elizabeth Camozzo, June 9, 1979. BA, Northeastern Okla. State U., 1978; postgrad., Okla. State U., 1980-85. Cert. Data Processor. Successively applications programmer, systems analyst, project leader, EDP strategic planner Phillips Petroleum Co., Bartlesville, Okla., 1978-86, mgr., 1982-86; dir. Data Resources div. Maricopa County Govt., Phoenix, 1986-89; mgr. govt. accts., dir.

govt. and edn. accounts, regional mgr. Computerland Corp., 1989-92, Boeing acct. mgr. Seattle, 1992-94; dir. telephony integration Fujitsu Corp., Tokyo, 1994-98; chmn., CEO The Lighthouse Group, Phoenix, 1998—. Creator, marketer copyrighted Boone Busters T-Shirt, 1985. V.p. Green County March of Dimes, Bartlesville, 1982-84. Served with USAF, 1969-72. Fellow NSF, Boulder, Colo., 1977, Rotary Found., Taiwan, 1983. Mem. Rotary (treas. Phoenix Sunrise club 1987-89). Republican. Roman Catholic. Avocations: travel, reading, investments, photography. Home: 1131 E Stephens Dr Tempe AZ 85283-4709 Office: The Lighthouse Group Renaissance at the Galleria 1131 E Stephens Dr Ste 11 Tempe AZ 85283-4709 E-mail: aj_ml@hotmail.com.

LAFAVE, ALAN DEAN, dean, educator; s. Lonnie Dean and Irene Mae LaFave; m. Kari Jean Laubach, June 8, 1985; children: Ashley, Alexis. MusB in Edn., No. State U., Aberdeen, S.D., 1985; MusM, D in Musical Arts, Ariz. State U., Tempe, 1990. Dir. of bands No. State U., Aberdeen, SD, 1991—2002, dean, sch. of fine arts, 2000—. Mem.: S.D. Music Educators Assn. (band chair 1996—2002). Office: Northern State U 1200 South Jay St Aberdeen SD 57401

LAFAVE, RICHARD, engineer, consultant; b. Detroit, June 6, 1944; s. Arthur Victor and Marie Anne (Regan) L.; m. Carole Anne Mutch, June 26, 1971; children: Laura, David, Daniel. B in Welding Engring., Ohio State U., 1968, MBA, 1974; Diploma in Internat. Welding Engring., IIW/IIS, 2002. Registered profl. engr., Ohio, Pa. Indsl. engr. Jeffrey Mining Machinery Co., Columbus, Ohio, 1968-73; sr. research engr. Westinghouse Electric Co., Pitts., 1974-76; sr. cons. engr. Elliott Co., Jeannette, Pa., 1976—. Tech. advisor Gateway Sch. Dist., 1987. Editor Pitts. Profl. Engr., 1992-95; co-inventor welding consumable, 1977; inventor welding method, 1999. Lay advisor Westmoreland County Community Coll., Youngwood, Pa.; mem. Pitts. Symphony Soc., 1987-89, Carnegie Inst., Pitts., 1987-89; parent advisor Gateway Sch. Dist., Monroeville, Pa., 1981. Recipient Highest Honors award Ohio Soc. Profl. Engrs., Columbus, 1968, 73, Arc Welding award J.F. Lincoln Found., Cleve., 1979, A.F. Davis Silver medal, 1995, Minnotte-Cable Svc. award, 2000. Mem. Am. Welding Soc. (tech. coms. 1979-01), Am. Council Internat. Inst. Welding, Nat. Soc. Profl. Engrs. (state dir.), Pa. Soc. Profl. Engrs. (state dir.), Chi Phi (Sparks medal 1968). Democrat. Roman Catholic. Office: Elliott Co N 4th St Jeannette PA 15644-1473 E-mail: rlafave@elliott-turbo.com.

LAFEBER, WALTER FREDERICK, history educator, author; b. Walkerton, Ind., Aug. 30, 1933; s. Ralph N. and Helen (Lidecker) LaF.; m. Sandra Gould, Sept. 11, 1955; children: Scott Nichols, Suzanne Margaret Kahl. BA, Hanover Coll., 1955; MA, Stanford, 1956; PhD, U. Wis., 1959. Asst. prof. history Cornell U., 1959-63, assoc. prof., 1963-67, prof., 1967-68, Noll prof. history, 1968—, Weiss Presdl. Tchg. fellow, 1994—; Commonwealth lectr. U. London, Eng., 1973; Callander lectr. U. Aberdeen, 1987; Shaw lectr. Johns Hopkins U., 1989; Landmark prof. Am. U., 1992; Jefferson lectr. U. Calif., Berkeley, 1992. Mem. adv. com. hist. div. State Dept., 1971-75. Author: The New Empire...1860-1898, 1963, 2d edit., 1998, America, Russia and the Cold War, 1966, 9th edit., 2002, The Panama Canal, The Crisis in Historical Perspective, 1978, expanded edit., 1979, 2d edit., 1989, Inevitable Revolutions: The U.S. in Central America, 1983, 2d edit., 1992, The American Age...1750 to the Present, 1989, 2d edit., 1994, The American Search for Opportunity, 1865-1913, 1993, The Clash: U.S. Japanese Relations Throughout History, 1997, Michael Jordan and the New Globalism Capitalism, 1999, 2d edit., 2002; co-author: The American Century, 5th edit., 1997, America in Vietnam, 1985; editor: John Quincy Adams and American Continental Empire, 1965, America in the Cold War, 1969, also others; co-editor: Behind the Throne, Essays in Honor of Fred Harvey Harrington, 1993; mem. editorial adv. bd. : Polit. Sci. Quar.; cons., appeared on PBS programs on Theodore Roosevelt, Harry Truman, 1900, War of 1898 and others. Recipient Gustavus Myers prize, 1985, Bancroft prize, 1998; Guggenheim fellow, 1990. Mem.: Soc. Historians of Am. Fgn. Rels. (pres. 1999—2000), Am. Acad. Arts and Scis., The Hist. Soc., Am. Hist. Assn. (Albert Beveridge prize 1962), Orgn. Am. Historians (Hawley prize 1998). Office: Cornell U Dept History McGraw Hall Ithaca NY 14853-4601 E-mail: wfl3@cornell.edu.

LAFEMINA, GERRY, writing and literature educator; b. Bklyn., Aug. 11, 1968; s. Robert Joseph and Antoinette Veronica LaFemina; m. Mary Ann Samyn, July 16, 1999; 1 child from previous marriage, Alexander. AB, Sarah Lawrence Coll., 1990; MA in Lit., MFA in Creative Writing, Western Mich. U., 1993. Instr. writing and lit. Kirtland C.C., Roscomon, Mich., 1994—. Author: (poems) 23 Below, 1994, City of Jazz and Punk, 1995, A Print of Wildflowers, 1996, Shattered Hours: Poems, 1997, Zarathrustra in Love: Prose Poems, 2001. Emerging Artist fellow Irving Gilmore Found., 1993; creative artist grantee Art Serve Mich., 1998. Mem. MLA, Assoc. Writing Programs (bd. dirs. 2000—). Buddhist. Avocation: vintage cars. E-mail: lafeming@kirtland.cc.mi.us.

LAFER, FRED SEYMOUR, data processing company executive; b. Passaic, N.J., Mar. 17, 1929; s. Abraham David and Pauline (Braer) L.; m. Barbara Bernstein, Apr. 4, 1954; children: Deborah, Gordon, Diana. BIE, NYU, 1950, JD, 1961; LHD (hon.), William Paterson Coll., 1987. Bar: N.J. 1961. Sec. to Justice Hayden Proctor, N.J. Supreme Ct., 1961-62; partner firm Hoffman Humphreys Lafer, Wayne, N.J., 1962-67; sec., gen. counsel Automatic Data Processing, Inc., Clifton, 1967-97, v.p., 1968-81, sr. v.p., 1981-96; pres. N.J. Nets Profl. Basketball Team, 1984. Pres. Taub Found., 1996—. Chmn. United Jewish Appeal Fedn. North Jersey, 1973-74; pres. Jewish Fedn. North Jersey, 1976-77; v.p. N.J. Bd. Edn., 1967-68; bd. dirs. Chilton Meml. Hosp., Pompton Plains, N.J., 1970-72; trustee William Paterson Coll., 1974—, vice-chmn. bd., 1977, chmn. bd., 1978-80; pres. Am. Friends of Hebrew U., 1985-89; exec. com. Washington Inst. Near East Policy, sec.-treas., 1993-99, pres., 2000—. Served to lt. USAF, 1951-52. Recipient honorary doctorate Hebrew U. of Jerusalem, 1995. Mem. Computer Law Assn. (pres. 1972-74), Assn. Data Processing Service Orgns. (chmn. 1983), ABA Office: ADP Inc 1 Adp Blvd Ste 1 Roseland NJ 07068-1786

LA FERLA, FRANK MICHAEL, b. Phila., July 28, 1963; s. Paul La Ferla and Michelangela Corridore; m. Carolyn T. Spadea, Aug. 22, 1987; children: Caroline, Monica. BS, St. Joseph's U., 1985; PhD, U. Minn., 1990. Postdoctoral fellow ARC, Rockville, Md., 1990-95; prof. U. Calif., Irvine, 1995—. Roman Catholic. Office: U Calif 1109 Gillspie Rsch Facility Irvine CA 92697

LAFEVER, HOWARD NELSON, plant breeder, geneticist, educator; b. Wayne County, Ind., May 13, 1938; s. Samuel L. and Flossie B. (Ellis) L.; m. Kay M. Schutz, Aug. 30, 1958; children: Julie, Jeff BS, Purdue U., 1959, MS, 1961, PhD, 1963. Instr. Wis. State U., LaCrosse, 1963; assoc. prof. Purdue U., West Lafayette, Ind., 1963; research geneticist USDA-Agrl. Research Service, Starkville, Miss., 1963-65; plant breeder, prof. agronomy Ohio State U., Ohio Agr. Research and Devel. Ctr., Wooster, 1965-91; owner Sunbeam Extract Co., 1991—. Patentee Becker, Cardinal, Dynasty, Freedom Hopewell and Bravo wheats and developer of 35 other small grain varieties; contbr. numerous articles to profl. jours. Fellow Am. Soc. Agronomy (bd. dirs. 1982-84, assoc. editor 1982-85); mem. Assn. Ofcl. Seed Certifying Agys., Ohio Seed Improvement Assn. (dir. 1968-83, grantee 1975-91). Presbyterian. Avocations: woodworking; golf. Home: 500 Danberry Dr Wooster OH 44691-5211 E-mail: wheatbreeding@aol.com.

LAFFERTON, MACKIE V. (MAKKI V. LAFFERTON), artist; b. Gallina, N.Mex., Dec. 11, 1933; d. Jose Melquiades and Maria Ruperta (Serrano) Valdez; m. Henry Imre Lafferton, July 31, 1959 (div. Dec. 1983); children: Sandra Marie, Henry James, Jacqueline Margit. Student, N.Mex. State U., 1977, 82, San Juan Coll., 1983, 84, Art Masters Acad., Albuquerque, N. Mex., 1995—. Owner, mgr. Bloomfield (N.Mex.) Plumbing and Heating, Inc., 1971-83, Central Apts., Bloomfield, 1981-93, Fine Arts By Makki, Albuquerque, 1995—. mem., fundraiser Bloomfield C. of C., 1972-84. Tailor, designer ready-made clothing (numerous awards 1971-80); artist: represented in private and pub. collections throughout the U.S. and abroad; in permanent collections: Multi-Cultural Ctr. of Bloomfield, N. Mex., Cath. Social Svcs. of Albuquerque, Casa Esperanza, Inc., Albuquerque, Salmon Ruins Mus., Bloomfield; exhbns. and awards include: Portraiture and figurative painting and drawings: 1st prize, Farmington, N. Mex., 1987, numerous shows at the Civic Ctr. of Farmington, N. Mex., 1993, People's Choice award, N. Mex. Art League, Albuquerque, 1995, Hon. Mention Marco Polo Art Exhibit, Nairobi, Kenya, 1995, Jurors Selection award of recognition Minature Arts Bardean, Albuquerque, 1996, 25th Nat. Small Painting Exhibition Jurors Selection N. Mex. Art League, Albuquerque, 1996. Mem. N.Mex. Watercolor Soc., N.Mex. Art League, Knickerbocker Artists, Pastel Soc. N.Mex. Republican. Roman Catholic. Avocations: world-wide travel, art. Home: Fine Arts By Makki 109 Rosemont St Albany NY 12203-2423

LAFFERTY, BEVERLY LOU BROOKOVER, retired physician, consultant; b. Newark, Aug. 15, 1938; d. Lawrence William and Rosie (Rey) Brookover; children: Marla Michele, William Brookover, Wesley Voris, Latour Rey. BS, Ohio State U., 1959, MD, 1963. Diplomate Am. Bd. Family Practice. Intern Grant Hosp., Columbus, Ohio, 1963-64; pvt. practice medicine West Union, 1964-75, Sun City Center, Fla., 1975-79, Brandon, 1979-95. Mem. staff Adams County Hosp., v.p., 1971-72, chief of staff, 1973-75; mem. staff Brandon Regional Med. Ctr., 1977—, chmn. dept. family practice, 1984-86, hosp. trustee, 1984-92, chief of staff elect, 1986-88, chief of staff, 1988-90; physician adv. utilization mgmt. dept. South Bay Hosp., Sun City Ctr., Fla., 1995—, Brandon Regional Hosp., 1995—, physician adv., 1994—. Mem. Am. Acad. Family Physicians, Fla. Med. Assn., Fla. Acad. Family Physicians, Hillsborough County Med. Assn., Alpha Lambda Delta, Alpha Epsilon Iota, Alpha Epsilon Delta (sec. 1958-59).

LAFFERTY, JAMES MARTIN, retired physicist; b. Battle Creek, Mich., Apr. 27, 1916; s. James V. and Ida M. (Martin) L.; m. Eleanor J. Currie, June 27, 1942; children: Martin C., Ronald J., Douglas J., Lawrence E. Student, Western Mich. U., 1934-37; BS in Engring. Physics, U. Mich., 1939, MS in Physics, 1940, PhD in Elec. Engring, 1946. Physicist Eastman Kodak Research Lab., Rochester, N.Y., 1939; physicist Gen. Electric Research Lab., Schenectady, 1940, 42-81, mgr. power electronics lab., 1972-81; with Carnegie Instn., Washington, 1941-42. Past pres. Internat. Union Vacuum Sci. Technique and Applications, 1980-83; People to People citizen ambassador program group leader for Vacuum Sci. and Tech. delegation to Europe, 1984, China, 1986, Australia, 1988, Soviet Union, 1990. Editor, contbg. author: Scientific Foundations of Vacuum Technique (Dushman), 1962; editor: Vacuum Arcs, Theory and Applications, 1980, Foundations of Vacuum Science and Technology, 1997; assoc. editor Jour. Vacuum Sci. and Tech, 1966-69; mem. editl. bd. Internat. Jour. Electronics, 1968-89; contbr. articles to profl. jours.; patentee in field. Mem. greater consistory Ref. Ch.; trustee Schenectady Museum, 1967-73, sec., 1971-72, pres., 1972-73. Recipient Devel. award Bur. Naval Ordnance, 1946; Distinguished Alumnus citation U. Mich., 1953; IR-100 award, 1968 Fellow AAAS, IEEE (Lamme medal 1979), Am. Phys. Soc.; mem. Nat. Acad. Engring., Am. Vacuum Soc. (hon. life mem.; dir. 1962-70, sec. 1965-67, pres. 1968-69), U.S. Power Squadrons (comdr. Lake George squadron 1975-76, comdr. Dist. 2 1981-82, nat. rear comdr. 1987-91, treas. Ednl. Fund 1992—), Sigma Xi, Phi Kappa Phi, Iota Sigma, Tau Beta Pi. Achievements include inventing lanthanum boride cathode, 1950, hot cathode magnetron ionization gauge, 1961, triggered vacuum gap, 1966. Home: 1202 Hedgewood Ln Niskayuna NY 12309-4605

LAFFERTY, JOYCE G. ZVONAR, retired middle school educator; b. Balt., July 9, 1931; d. George S. and Carolyn M. (Bothe) Greener; children: Barbara Z. Gunter, John G. Zvonar, David A. Zvonar. BS, Towson State, 1963; M. equivalent, Md. Inst. Coll. of Art, 1978. Cert. tchr., Md. Tchr., dept. chmn. Hampstead Hill. Jr. High Annex, Balt.; tchr. Forest Park Sr. High; tchr., dept. chmn. Roland Park Mid. Sch. Mem. Nat. Art Edn. Assn., Internat. Soc. Artists, Balt. Tchrs. Union. Home: 1101 Gilcrest Ct Baltimore MD 21234-5924

LAFIELD, KAREN WOODROW, science educator, demographer; b. Fairfield, Ill., Oct. 14, 1950; d. Raymond and Margaret Ann (Simpson) Woodrow; m. William E. Mason, June 13, 1970 (div. July 1976); m. William L. Lafield, July 16, 1991. BA, U. Ill., Chgo., 1972; MA, U. Tenn., 1976; PhD, U. Ill., 1984. Demographic statistician U.S. Census Bur., Suitland, Md., 1983-92; adj. rsch. assoc. Ctr. for Social and Demographic Analysis SUNY, Albany, 1993-96; sr. rsch. analyst U.S. Commn. on Immigration Reform, Washington, 1994-95; rsch. scientist U. Tex., Austin, 1995-96; asst. prof. Miss. State U., Starkville, 1996-99, assoc. prof., 1999—. Cons. NIH, Washington, 1994-99; cons.-rschr. Mex.-U.S. Binat. Migration Study, 1995-97; expert U.S. Immigration and Naturalization Svc., Washington, 1999—. Contbr. chpts. to books Migration Between Mexico and United States, 1998, Illegal Immigration: A Reference Handbook, 1999; mem. editl. bd.: Population Rsch. and Policy Rev., Columbia, S.C., 1999—; contbr. articles to profl. jours. Rsch. grantee Nat. Insts. of Child Health and Human Devel., 1998-01 Mem. AAUS, Am. Sociol. Assn., Population Assn. Am., Am. Statis. Assn. (program com. 2000-01), So. Demographic Assn., N.Y. Acad. Scis. Office: Miss State U 200 Bowen Hall Hardy Rd Mississippi State MS 39762 E-mail: KarenWLafield@cs.com.

LAFILI, ELLEN YOST See YOST, ELLEN G.

LA FLARE, MARY J. DICKINSON, librarian; b. N.Y.C., Apr. 12, 1929; d. Lambert Francis and Mary Catherine (Mosher) Dickinson; m. Joseph P. La Flare, 1951 (div. 1969); children: Joseph P., Mary Ellen, Lizanne La Flare Krol, Patricia La Flare Santella. BA, Coll. Mt. St. Vincent, Riverdale, N.Y., 1950; MLS, St. John's U., Queens, N.Y., 1971. Cert. pub. libr., N.Y. Libr., rschr. Info. and Retrieval Ctr. Levittown (N.Y.) Union Free Sch. Dist., 1969-71; grad. asst. dept. L.S. St. John's U., 1969-71; mktg. rsch. libr. Sperry & Hutchinson, N.Y.C., 1971-76, project mgr. mktg. rsch., 1977-82; reference libr. Uniondale (N.Y.) Pub. Libr., 1985-86; reference libr., community libr. Farmingdale (N.Y.) Pub. Libr., 1986—. Adj. prof. Nassau C.C., Garden City, N.Y., 1982-92, Hofstra U., Hempstead, N.Y., 1983-85; reading cons. Daleview Nursing Home, Farmingdale, 1993-94. St. Johns U. fellow, 1969-71. Mem. Coll. Mt. St. Vincent Alumnae (mem. capital fund com. 1985), Acad. St. Joseph Alumnae. Republican. Roman Catholic. Home: 142 Jervis Ave Farmingdale NY 11735-2426 Office: Farmingdale Pub Libr 116 Merritts Rd Farmingdale NY 11735-3251

LA FLÈCHE, ÉRIC RICHER, retail executive; MBA, Harvard U. Sr. dir. real estate Metro Inc., sr. v.p., gen. mgr. Super C Division; pres. Loeb Can. Inc. Office: Metro Inc 11011 Maurice-Duplessis Blvd Montreal QU Canada H1C 1V6*

LAFLER, KIRK PAUL, computer information scientist; b. Penn Yan, N.Y., Feb. 27, 1956; s. Paul Alton and Eleanor Theresa (Gombar) L.; m. Darlynn Joan Lasky, July 7, 1984. BS, U. Miami, 1978, MS, 1982. Pvt. practice computer cons., Miami, Fla., 1976-78; jr. programmer analyst Rydacom Inc., 1978-79; systems engr. Electronic Data Systems Corp., Washington, 1979-81; programmer analyst Great Am. Fed., San Diego, 1981-82; systems analyst San Diego Gas and Electric Co., 1982-83; pres., chief exec. officer Software Intelligence Corp., San Diego, 1984—. Instr. info ctr. So. Calif. Edison Co., Rosemead, 1983-85; computer seminar speaker, San Diego, 1983—. Contbr. articles to profl. jours. Sponsor and contbr. Children Inc., Richmond, Va., 1980—, Muscular Dystrophy Assn., N.Y.C., 1985—, Am. Heart Assn., San Diego, 1987—, St. Jude Children's Rsch., 1989—. Recipient Commendation award U.S. Dept. Energy, 1981. Mem. Am. Assn. for Artificial Intelligence, So. Calif. SAS Users Group (chmn., pres. 1989—), The Internat. Platform Assn., Assn. Computing Machinery. Republican. Roman Catholic. Avocations: sailing, scuba diving, marine biology, computers, music. Office: Software Intelligence Corp PO Box 1390 Spring Valley CA 91979-1390

LAFLEUR, KENNETH CHARLES, ophthalmologist; b. Lawtell, La., Aug. 22, 1941; s. Abram George and Mary Irene (Olivier) L.; m. Patricia Ione McNamara, Aug. 3, 1963; children: James Mathew, Suzanne Annette, Caroline Marie. BS, U. So. La., 1963; MD, Tulane U., 1966. Diplomate Am. Bd. Ophthalmology. Intern Hermann Hosp., Houston, 1966-67; ophthalmology resident U. Tex., 1967-70; practice medicine specializing in ophthalmology Opelousas, La., 1972—. Clin. asst. prof. La. State U. Eye Ctr., New Orleans, 1983—. Trustee St. Landry Roman Cath. Ch., Opelousas, 1979-99. Maj. U.S. Army Med. Corps, 1970-72. Fellow Am. Acad. Ophthalmology, Soc. Mil. Ophthalmologists; mem. Am. Intraocular Implant Soc., Elks, K.C. (Knight of Yr. award 1984). Avocation: fishing. Office: 1110 Dr AC Terrence Blvd Opelousas LA 70570 E-mail: klafleur@cybermp.net.

LAFLEUR, KENNETH GORDON, retired minister; b. Waterville, Maine, Dec. 14, 1933; s. Daniel Kenneth and Louise May LaFleur; m. Helen Faith Myrick; children: Margaret. MDiv, Bangor Theol. Seminary, 1951—56; BA, U. Maine, Orono, 1961; MA, Brandeis U., 1969—70. Ordained Unitarian Universalist Assn., 1956. Min. Unitarian Ch., Castine, Maine, 1954—58, First Parish, Northboro, Mass., 1958—60, Wayland, 1962—69, Hingham, 1972—85, min. emeritus, 1985—2002; lectr. in history Northeastern U., Boston, 1985—87. Bd. mem. Ombudsman Bd. for the Elderly, Plymouth County, 1973—75; pres. Hingham (Mass.) Clergy Assn., 1978—81. Contbr. articles. Founding dir. of Dayspring (AIDS support service) Kennebec Valley Regional Health Agy., Waterville, 1988; bd. mem. Vassalboro (Maine) Pub. Libr., 1988—90, All Souls Universalist Ch., Oakland, 2000—. Mem.: Phi Beta Kappa (Delta of Maine chap.). Democrat. Unitarian Universalist. Avocations: electronics, photography, music. Home: Main St PO Box 110 East Vassalboro ME 04935 Personal E-mail: lafleur@pivot.net.

LAFLEUR, LAURETTE CARIGNAN, artist; b. Manchester, N.H., Nov. 14, 1939; d. Henri Marie-Louis and Emelia Adelaide Carignan; m. Donald J. Lafleur, May 28, 1960; children: Thomas R., Elaine P., Claudette M., Judith M., Robert G., David P. Student, Notre Dame Coll., 1976-77, 79-80. Cashier Pru-Bache Securities, Manchester, 1986; office mgr. Shockley & Assoc. Advt., Amherst, N.H., 1987-88; acctg. clk. State of N.H. Adminstrv. Svcs., Concord, 1993-96; artist, 1976—. One-woman shows include Hooksett Pub. libr., 1999, N.H. chpt. Am. Mothers, Inc., 1999, Barnes and Noble Bookstore, 1996, Ocean Park Art Assn., 1996, Augusta Merchants Bus. Adminstrn., 1995, Ogunquit C. of C., 1993, Saco merchants Assn., 1994, jury. Recipient Hon. mention Am. Mothers, Inc. Creative Arts Competition, 1999. Mem.: Keene Art Assn., Nashua Artists Assn., Manchester Artists Assn. (sec., pres.). Roman Catholic. Avocations: avid reading, cross-country skiing, bicycling, traveling, sewing. E-mail: LauretteL@juno.com.

LAFLEY, ALAN FREDERICK, retired banker; b. Stamford, Conn., Aug. 26, 1922; s. Alan George and Clara (Petersen) L.; m. Kathryn Margaret Irwin, Mar. 1, 1946; children: Alan George, Nora Kathryn, Jo Anne, Mary Patricia. BBA, Clarkson U., Potsdam, N.Y., 1946; MBA, U. Mich., 1948. Asst. prof. Sch. of Bus.; placement dir. Clarkson U., 1948-50, Sch. Bus., Ind. U., Bloomington, 1950-51; with Gen. Electric Co., 1951-73, mgr. exec. personnel and compensation, 1968-73; v.p. personnel Clark Equipment Co., Buchanan, Mich., 1973-75; exec. v.p. human resources Chase Manhattan Bank, N.Y.C., 1975-84; mng. dir. Korn Ferry Internat., 1984-86. Exec. in residence, vis. prof. U. Mich. Sch. Bus., Ann Arbor, 1984-85; cons., advisor, lectr., human resources mgr. Mem. adv. Bus. Leadership coun., Clarkson U. Served to 1st lt. U.S. Army and USAAF, 1942-46. Fellow Human Resources Policy Inst., Boston U.

LAFLEY, ALAN G. consumer products company executive; b. Keene, N.H., June 13, 1947; AB, Hamilton Coll., 1969; MBA, Harvard Bus. Sch., 1977. Brand asst. Joy Procter & Gamble, 1977-78, sales tng. Denver Sales Dist., 1978-80, asst. brand mgr. Tide, 1978-80, brand mgr. Dawn & Ivory Snow, 1980-81, brand mgr. spl. assignment and Ivory Snow, 1981-82, brand mgr. Cheer, 1982-83, assoc. advt. mgr. PS&D Divsn. to advt. mgr., 1983-86, 86-88, gen. mgr. laundry products PS&D Divsn., 1988-91, v.p. laundry and cleaning products, 1991-92, group v.p., pres. laundry and cleaning products, 1992-94, group v.p., pres. Far East Divsn., 1994-95, exec. v.p., pres. Asia Divsn., 1995-98, exec. v.p., pres. N.Am. Divsn., 1998-99, pres. Global Beauty Care and North Am., 1999-2000; pres. & CEO Proctor & Gamble, 2000—. Trustee Hamilton Coll., Cin. Playhouse in the Park, Cin. Symphony Orchestra, Cin. Inst. of Fine Arts, The Seven Hills Sch.; past mem. Am. C. of C. in Japan, adv. coun. Schulich Sch. of Bus., York U., Toronto. With USN, 1970-75. Mem. Hamilton Club of So. Ohio, Harvard Club of Cin., Met. Club, Commonwealth Club of Cin. Office: The Proctor & Gamble Co 1 Procter And Gamble Plz Cincinnati OH 45202-3315*

LA FOLLETTE, DOUGLAS J. secretary of state; b. Des Moines, June 6, 1940; s. Joseph Henry and Frances (Van der Wilt) LaF. BS, Marietta Coll., 1963; MS, Stanford U., 1964; PhD, Columbia U., 1967. Asst. prof. chemistry and ecology U. Wis.-Parkside, 1969-72; mem. Wis. Senate, 1973-75; sec. state State of Wis., Madison, 1975-79, 83—. Author: Wisconsin's Survival Handbook, 1971, The Survival Handbook, 1991. Mem. Council Econ. Priorities; mem. Lake Michigan Fed., Wis. Environ. Decade, 1971, S.E. Wis. Coalition for Clean Air, Dem. candidate for U.S. Congress, 1970, for Wis. lt. gov., 1978, for U.S. Senate, 1988. Recipient Environ. Quality EPA, 1976 Mem. Am. Fedn. Tchrs., Fedn. Am. Scientists, Phi Beta Kappa Office: Office Sec State of Wis PO Box 7848 Madison WI 53707-7848

LAFOND, EMMANUEL F. scientist; b. Saint Omer, Pas De Cal, France, Mar. 17, 1970; came to U.S., 1997; s. Alain R. Lafond and Dominique O. Martel. B of Fundamental Physics, U. Paris XI, Orsay, 1990, M in Optics and Photonics, 1992, PhD in Optics and Photonics, 1995. Rsch. and devel. scientist EADS Corp., Suresnes, France, 1995-96; quality ins. inspector Iris Quality & Tech., Leuna, Germany, 1997; asst. scientist Inst. Paper Sci., Atlanta, 1997-99; assoc. scientist Inst. Paper Sci. and Tech., 1999—. Patentee in field; contbr. articles to profl. jours. Mem.: Optical Soc. Am., Optical Soc. France. Office: Inst Paper Sci and Tech 500 10th St NW Atlanta GA 30318-5794 E-mail: emmanuel.lafond@ipst.edu.

LAFOND, THOMAS JOSEPH, lawyer; b. Chgo., Feb. 25, 1941; s. Charles J. and Marie F. (Lane) LaF.; m. Karen Kent, June 13, 1964; children: Julia, Jennifer, Laura, Susan. BSBA, John Carroll U., 1963; JD, Case Western Res. U., 1966. Assoc. Henderson, Quail, Schneider & Smeltz, Cleve., 1968-75; ptnr. Schneider, Smeltz, Ranney & LaFond, 1975—. Pres. Citizens League, Cleve., 1984-86; grad. Leadership Cleve., 1985. Capt. U.S. Army, 1966-68. Mem. ABA, Ohio State Bar Assn., Cleve. Bar Assn. (bd. trustees 1983-86, chmn. young lawyers 1972, ethics com. 1979, profl. trends com. 1982, pres. 1991—). Office: Schneider Smeltz Ranney & LaFond 1111 Superior Ave E Ste 1000 Cleveland OH 44114-2568 E-mail: tlafond@ssrl.com.

LAFONT, CRISTINA, educator; b. Valencia, Spain, Feb. 8, 1963; came to U.S., 1995; d. Julio and Maria (Hurtado) L. BA, MA, U. Valencia, Spain, 1986; PhD, U. Frankfurt, Germany, 1992. Teaching asst. U. Valencia, Spain, 1988—89; instr. U. Frankfurt, Germany, 1993—95; rschr. Inst. Philosophy, Madrid, 1992—95; asst. prof. Northwestern U., Evanston, Ill., 1995—2001, assoc. prof., 2001—. Adj. prof. U. Mex., Mexico City, 1994. Author: La Razon Como Lenguaje, 1993, Sprache und Welterschlissung, 1994, The Linguistic Turn in Hermeneutic Philosophy, 1999, Heidegger, Language, and World-Disclosure, 2000; cons. editor Philosophy and Social Criticism Jour., 1996—; assoc. editor Isegoria Jour., Madrid, 1993—. Nat. Ctr. Scientific Rsch.grantee, Germany, 1987-90; DAAD fellow U. Frankfurt, 1990-92; U. Valencia fellow, 1985-86. Mem. Am. Philosophical Assn., Soc. Phenomenology & Existential Philosophy. Office: Northwestern U 1818 Hinman Ave Evanston IL 60208-0810

LAFONT, WILLIAM HAROLD, lawyer,farmer; b. Plainview, Tex., May 14, 1940; s. Harold Matthews and Jane Powell L.; m. Susan Chandler, 1961 (div. Oct. 1964); m. Ellie Agnus Dardis, Dec. 27, 1984; children: Christopher Chapman, Emily, Christopher Lafont, Nicole Smock, Matthew. BBA, U. Tex., 1961, JD, 1964. Bar: Tex. 1964, Am. Bar, Ctrl. Plains Bar. Ptnr. Lafont, Tunnell & Formby, Plainview, Tex., 1964—. Pres. Ctrl. Plains, Plainview, 1980-82. Pres. Plainview C. of C., Plainview, 1964—, Optimist Club, Plainview, 1975. Mem. Toastmasters Internat. (pres. 1964-78), YMCA (dir. 1998—), Plainview Country Club (pres. 1998—). Democrat. Methodist. Home: 310 Mesa Cir Plainview TX 79072-6508 Office: Lafont Tunnell Formby Lafont Skaggs Bldg 701 Broadway St Fl 1 Plainview TX 79072-7353

LAFONTAINE, DIANE ELAINE, retired elementary education educator, computer specialist; b. Gadsden, Ala., Jan. 3, 1944; d. William Edward and Adele Helen (Plasman) Frantz; m. Robert L. Lafontaine, Jan. 13, 2001. BS, Jacksonville (Ala.) State U., 1965; MEd, Ga. State U., 1972; cert. 6th yr. specialist in adminstrn., Troy State U., 1996. Cert. adminstr., supr., tchr. math, Ala., Ga. Actuarial clk. Life Ins. Co. Ala., Gadsden, 1965-66; tchr. Trinity Pvt. Sch., Columbus, Ga., 1968-69, Phenix City (Ala.) Sch. Sys., 1969-71; tchr. mid. grades Post Dependent Schs., Ft. Benning, Ga., 1970-82, chair dept. math., 1973-85, coord. curriculum, 1980-84, instr. staff devel., 1985—, tchr. math. grade 7, 1991-96, tchr. math. grade 8, 1996-2001, edn. technologist, 1997-2001, ret., 2001. Adj. prof. math. Troy State U., 2000—; chairperson negotiation contract com. Post Dependent Schs., Ft. Benning, Ga., 1993—, mediation trainer, 1994, mem. salary negotiations team, 1993—, faculty rep., 1992—; owner computer bus., 1984-85; active Tchr. in Space Program NASA, 1985; sch. sys. rep. to survey Rand Corp., 1987; pres. Fla. Instrnl. Computing Conf. for Computer Using Educators, 1988, North Cook Ednl. Svc. Ctr., St.

Charles, Ill., 1990, Ga. Tech. Conf., Columbus; liaison Nat. Coun. Tchrs. Math. and Chattahoochee Coun. Tchrs. Math., 1996; mem. joint stds. com. Dept. Def. Edn. Activity, 1998—. Contbr. to curriculum guide, 1969, vignette to text book. Sec. PTA, 1979-80, Columbus Cmty. Concerts, 1983; usher Springer Theater, Columbus, 1984. Mem. ASCD, NEA (del. 1998—), Nat. Coun. Tchrs. Math. (guest spkr. 1979, 70, contact person 1996), Profl. Assn. Ga. Educators, Ga. Coun. Tchrs. of Math., Benning Edn. Assn. (sec. 1973-77, v.p. 1992—, treas. 2000-2001), Fed. Edn. Assn. Methodist. Avocations: bridge, travel, shopping. Home: PO Box 10 Houston AL 35572 E-mail: delaf489@aol.com.

LAFONTAINE, THOMAS E. chemical engineer; b. North Adams, Mass., Jan. 2, 1952; s. Omer Charles and Isabella Frances (Luczinski) LaF.; m. Catherine Hackett, July 9, 1981; children: Christina, Colima. Dir. tech. internat. Cameron-Yakima (Wash.), Inc., 1981-87; dir. engring. Agro Industries de Tecoman S.A., Tecoman, Mexico, 1987-88; pres., owner Teltech Engring., Yakima, 1988—; tech. dir., v.p. Intercon Pacific, Inc., Portland, 1989-2001; pres., CEO Bridge Techs., Inc., 1997—. Cons. Phillippine Govt. Contbr. articles to profl. jours. Mem. Am. Water Works Assn., Air Pollution Control Assn., Internat. Carbon Soc. Achievements include development of specially treated activated carbons for specific use, conversion of cubi nut shells into activated carbon; design of installation and startup of activated carbon manufacturing plants in Philippines, China, Mexico, Malaysia and U.S. E-mail: telaf@aol.com.

LA FORCE, JAMES CLAYBURN, JR. economist, educator; b. San Diego, Dec. 28, 1928; s. James Clayburn and Beatrice Maureen (Boyd) La F.; m. Barbara Lea Latham, Sept. 23, 1952; children: Jessica, Allison, Joseph. BA, San Diego State Coll., 1951; MA, UCLA, 1958, PhD, 1962. Asst. prof. econs. UCLA, 1962-66, assoc. prof., 1967-70, prof., 1971-93, prof. emeritus, 1993—, chmn. dept. econs., 1969-78, dean Anderson Sch. Mgmt., 1978-93; acting dean Hong Kong U. Sci. & Tech., 1991-93. Bd. dirs. Jacobs Engring. Group Inc., The Timken Co., The Black Rock Funds, Payden & Rygel Investment Trust, Providence Investment Coun. Mut. Funds, Trust Investment Mgrs.; chmn. adv. com. Calif. Workmen's Compensation. Author: The Development of the Spanish Textile Industry 1750-1800, 1965, (with Warren C. Scoville) The Economic Development of Western Europe, vols. 1-5, 1969-70. Bd. dirs. Nat. Bur. Econ. Rsch., 1975-88, Found. Francisco Marroquin, Lynde and Harry Bradley Found., Pacific Legal Found., 1981-86; trustee Found. for Rsch. in Econs. and Edn., 1970—, chmn., 1977—; mem. bd. overseers Hoover Inst. on War, Revolution and Peace, 1979-85, 86-93; mem. nat. coun. on humanities NEH, 1981-88; chmn. Pres.'s Task Force on Food Assistance, 1983-84. Social Sci. Research Council research tng. fellow, 1958-60; Fulbright sr. research grantee, 1965-66; Am. Philos. Soc. grantee, 1965-66 Mem.: Mont Pelerin Soc., Econ. History Assn., Phi Beta Kappa. Office: UCLA Anderson Grad Sch Mgmt 405 Hilgard Ave Los Angeles CA 90095-9000

LA FORCE, PIERRE JOSEPH, lawyer; b. Berlin, Mar. 29, 1936; s. F. Maurice and Marie R. (Montminy) La F. AB, St. Anselm Coll., 1957; JD, Georgetown U, 1960. Bar: D.C. 1960, U.S. Supreme Ct. 1972, U.S. Ct. Appeals (D.C. Cir.) 1960, (6th Cir.) 1976, (9th Cir.) 1984, Fed. Cir. 1966. Assoc. Hogan & Hartson, D.C., 1960-69; ptnr. Wilkinson, Cragun & Barker, 1970-82, Baenen, Timme, 1982-84, Wilkinson, Barker, Knauer LLP, 1984—. Mem. ABA, D.C. Bar Assn., Barristers, Univ. Club. Republican. Roman Catholic. Avocations: tennis, squash. Office: Wilkinson Barker Knauer LLP 2300 N St NW Ste 700 Washington DC 20037-1191

LAFOREST, LANA JEAN, lawyer; b. Providence, Apr. 14, 1952; d. Harold Joseph Ecker and Nettie Jean (Starks) Page; children: Timothy Charles, Tisha DeAnne. AA in Humanities and Social Scis., Niagara County C. C., 1989; BA in English Lit. magna cum laude, Buffalo State Coll., 1990, MA in English Lit., 1999; JD, SUNY Buffalo Sch. Law, 1994. Bar: Fla. Property mgr. Personal Income Property Mgmt., Lockport, 1976—; sales assoc. John F. Collins Realty, 1979-83, Town Crier Clark Nodine Realty, Lockport, 1983-90, McKnight, Hogan & Noonan, Lockport, 1990-91, H. Potter Realty, Lockport, 1991-93; advocate Family Court Resource Project Haven House, 1994-99; advocate domestic violence clinic U. Buffalo Law Sch., 1994; pvt. practice East Amherst, N.Y., 1994—. Owner, operator Custom Crafts by Lana, Lockport, 1975-79; adv. domestic violence clinic U. Buffalo Law Sch., 1994. Editor: (lit. mag.) Writer's Revue, 1989; corr. Union-Sun and Jour., summer 1989. Girl scouts coord. Niagara County Coun. Girl Scouts, Sanborn, N.Y., 1978-84; clover clan 4-H club leader Niagara County Coop. Extension, Lockport, 1984-87; with Project Dandelion, Neighborhood Legal Svcs., 1994-96. Mem. ABA, MLA, Mensa, N.Y. State Bar Assn., Niagara Linguistics Soc., Nat. Assn. Realtors, Univ. Buffalo Law Sch. Alumni Assn., Buffalo State Coll. Alumni Assn., Niagara County Community Coll. Alumni Assn., U. Buffalo Assn. Women Law Students, Erie County Bar Assn., Women's Bar Assn. Erie County, Phi Alpha Delt. Avocations: writing, sewing, gourmet cooking, painting. Address: 2705 29th Ave W Bradenton FL 34205-3723 Fax: 941-753-3636. E-mail: Lana@unforgettable.com.

LAFORGE, ROBERT G. epidemiologist, educator, researcher; b. June 3, 1953; ScD, Johns Hopkins U, 1977. Asst. prof. Brown U., Providence, 1988-91; dir. survey rsch. Cancer Prevention Rsch. Ctr. U. R.I., Kingston, 1991—, prof. Cancer Prevention Rsch. Ctr., 1991—. Prin. investigator rsch. grantee A Proactive Individualize Program for Coll. Drinking, 1999, A Stage Matched Alcohol Intervention for Managed Care, 2000—. Inventor Windows-based survey mgmt. sys., 1996. Treas. troop 2 Boy Scouts Am., East Greenwich. Mem. Am. Pub. Health Assn., Soc. Epidemiologic Rsch. Office: Cancer Prevention Rsch Ctr U RI 2 Chaffee Rd Kingston RI 02881-2017

LAFORTE, GEORGE FRANCIS, JR. lawyer; b. Oak Lawn, Ill., Dec. 15, 1970; s. George Francis and Nancy Ruth (Avery) LaF. BS, No. Ill. U., 1992; JD, John Marshall Law Sch., Chgo., 1996. Bar: Ill. 1996. Ptnr. Bishop, Rossi & Scarlati, Ltd., Oakbrook Terrace, Ill., 1996—; of counsel Law Offices George F. LaForte, Olympia Fields, 1996—. Adminstrv. hearing officer Village of Frankfort, Ill., 1997-98. Mem. ATLA, Ill. Bar Assn., DuPage County Bar Assn. (arbitrator 1997—). Republican. Roman Catholic. Avocation: sports. Office: Bishop Rossi & Scarlati Ltd 2 TransAm Plaza Dr Ste 200 Oakbrook Terrace IL 60181 E-mail: glafortejr@bishoprossi.com.

LAFORTUNE, BILL, mayor; State asst. atty. gen. City of Tulsa, 1990—93; spl. judge State of Okla. for 14th Judicial Dist., 1993; dist. atty. Tulsa County, 1995; mayor City of Tulsa, Okla., 2002—. Dir. Gilcrease Mus. Assn., Child Abuse Network, Inc. Mem.: Tulsa County Bar Assn. Office: City Hall 200 Civic Ctr Tulsa OK 74103*

LAFRAMBOISE, JOAN CAROL, middle school educator; b. Bklyn., June 23, 1934; d. Anthony Peter and Nellie Eva (Zaleski) Ruggles; m. Albert George Laframboise, Aug. 5, 1961; children: Laura J., Brian A. BS in Edn., Springfield (Mass.) Coll., 1956. Cert. tchr. social sci., and mid. sch.; cert. tchr. support specialist; cert. tchr. gifted. Tchr. Meml. Jr. H.S., Wilbraham, Mass., 1956-61, Midland Park (N.J.) Jr./Sr. H.S., 1961-63, Luke Garrett Middle Sch., Austell, Ga., 1983-93; tchr. lang. arts Pine Mountain Middle Sch., Kennesaw, 1993-2001; ret., 2001. Coun. pres. Knights of Lithuania, Westfield, Mass., 1973-75, Holyoke, Mass., 1975-76, New Eng. dist. pres., 1976-77; mem. Wistariahurst Mus. Assocs., Holyoke, 1975-77. Jr. League mini-grantee, 1991. Mem. ASCD, NEA, Ga. Assn. Educators, Cobb County Assn. Educators, Nat. Coun. Tchrs. English, Nat. Coun. Social Studies. Home: 2891 Dara Dr Marietta GA 30066-4009

LAFREDO, STEPHEN, systems associate; b. Lansdale, Pa., Aug. 21, 1962; s. Frank Joseph and Yuriko (Mizuo) L. BS in Microbiology, Pa. State U., 1984; AAS magna cum laude, AS magna cum laude, Montgomery County C.C., 1992. Rsch. technician Thomas Jefferson Sch. Medicine, Phila., 1984-86; rsch. assoc. Temple Sch. Medicine, 1986-88, R.W. Johnson Pharm. Rsch. Inst., Raritan, N.J., 1988-91; clin. rsch. assoc. Rhone-Poulenc Rorer Ctrl. Rsch., Collegeville, Pa., 1991-93; advanced programmer/analyst Shared Med Systems, Malvern, 1993-95; sr. cons. KPMG Peat Marwick LLP, Radnor, 1995-96; tech. designer Computer Scis. Corp., Cons. & Sys. Integration, Berwyn, 1996-97; sys. assoc. Merck & Co., Inc., West Point, 1997—. Contbr. articles to profl. jours. Sgt. U.S. Army N.G., 1983-89. Mem. Fraternal Order of Police (assoc.). Avocations: autocross, bicycling, reading, stunt-kite flying, English steel tip darts. Home: 311 Jamestown Ct Lansdale PA 19446-4377

LAGACE, PAUL ALFRED, college educator; b. Lewiston, Maine, July 27, 1957; s. Lucien Alfred and Claire (Malo) L.; m. Robin Lea Pare, July 9, 1983. SB, MIT, 1978, SM, 1979, PhD, 1982. Rsch. fellow MIT, Cambridge, Mass., 1978-82, Draper asst. prof., 1982-86, assoc. prof. aeronautics and astronautics, 1986-91, prof., dir. Tech. Lab. for Advanced Composites, 1986—, exec. officer dept. aeronautics and astronautics, 1990-92, assoc. dir. engring. sys. divsn., 1999-2001. Cons. Foster-Miller, Inc., Waltham, Mass., 1983-95, McClellan AFB, Sacramento, Calif., 1983-90, Raytheon, Mass., 1985—; co-dir. Leaders Manufacturing Program and Sys. Desing and Mgmt. Program, 1998—; chmn. scientific adv. bd. Am. Composite Tech. Editor Jour. Composites Tech. and Rsch., 1990-91; contbr. articles to profl. jours. Hertz Found. fellow, 1978. Fellow AIAA (sr.); mem. ASTM, Internat. Com. on Composite Materials (pres. 1993-99; world fellow), Soc. for Advancement of Material and Process Engring., Am. Soc. for Composites, Am. Composite Tech. Assn. (chmn. sci. adv. bd. 1987—), Sigma Xi, Tau Beta Pi. Avocations: football officiating, softball. Home: 10 Wilton Dr Wilmington MA 01887-2216 Office: 77 Massachusetts Ave Cambridge MA 02139-4301 E-mail: pal@mit.edu.

LAGALLY, MAX GUNTER, physics educator; b. Darmstadt, Germany, May 23, 1942; came to U.S., 1953, naturalized, 1960; s. Paul and Herta (Rudow) L.; m. Shelley Meserow, Feb. 15, 1969; children: Eric, Douglas, Karsten BS in Physics, Pa. State U., 1963; MS in Physics, U. Wis.-Madison, 1965, PhD in Physics, 1968. Registered profl. engr., Wis. Instr. physics U. Wis., Madison, 1970-71, asst. prof. materials sci., 1971-74, assoc. prof., 1974-77, prof. materials sci. and physics, 1977—, dir. thin-film deposition and applications ctr., 1982-93, John Bascom Prof. materials sci., 1986—, E.W. Mueller Prof. materials sci. and physics, 1993—. Gordon Godfrey vis. prof. physics, U. New South Wales, Sydney, Australia, 1987; cons. in thin films, 1977—; vis. scientist Sandia Nat. Lab., Albuquerque, 1975; founder, pres. Piezomax Techs., Inc. (now nPoint, Inc.), 1997—, now chmn.. Editor: Kinetics of Ordering and Growth at Surfaces, 1990, (with others) Methods of Experimental Physics, 1985, Evolution of Surface and Thin-Film Microstructure, 1993, Morphological Organization in Epitaxial Growth and Removal, 1998; mem. editorial bd., also editor spl. issue Jour. Vacuum Sci. and Tech., 1978-81; prin. editor Jour. Materials Rsch., 1990-93; mem. editorial bd. Surface Sci., 1994-2001, Revs. Sci. Instruments, 1997-2000, Diffusion and Defect Data, 1997—; contbr. articles to profl. jours.; patentee in field. Max Planck Gesellschaft fellow, 1968, Alfred P. Sloan Found. fellow, 1972, H.I. Romnes fellow, 1976, Humboldt Sr. Rsch. fellow, 1992, 93; grantee fed. agys. and industry; recipient Outstanding Sci. Alumnus award Pa. State U., 1996. Fellow AAAS, Am. Phys. Soc. (D. Adler award 1994, Davisson-Germer prize 1995), Australian Inst. Physics, Am. Vacuum Soc. (M.W. Welch prize 1991, trustee 1995-97); mem. Materials Rsch. Soc. (medal 1994), Leopoldina-German Acad. Scis., Nat. Acad. Engring. Home: 5110 Juneau Rd Madison WI 53705-4744 Office: U Wis Materials Sci & Engring 1509 University Ave Madison WI 53706-1538 E-mail: lagally@engr.wisc.edu., lagally@npoint.com.

LAGANGA, DONNA BRANDEIS, sales and marketing executive; b. Bklyn., June 27, 1950; d. Sidney L. and Sylvia (Herman) Brandeis; m. Thomas LaGanga, Aug. 11, 1974. BS in Bus. Edn., Ctrl. Conn. State Coll., 1972, MS, 1975; EdD in Ednl. Adminstrn.-C.C. Leadership, U. Tex., 1999. Various secretarial positions, 1969-72; tchr. bus. Lewis S. Mills Regional H.S., Burlington, Conn., 1972-78; cons. nat. accounts Southwestern Pub. Co., Pelham Manor, N.Y., 1978-84, dist. sales mgr., 1984-89; pres. DBL Industries, Inc., Torrington, Conn., 1989—. Nat. accounts mgr. South-Western Pub. Co., Cin., 1989—93, from sr. sales and mktg. mgr. to nat. career sch. mgr., 1993—95; dir. admissions and records Tunxis C.C.-Bristol Career Ctr., Farmington, Conn., 1995—, dir. cmty. alliances, Conn., 1992—2002; v.p. adminstrv. svcs. Human Resource Devel. Assocs., 1996—; co-owner Colonial Welding Svc., seminar condr., 1980—; pres. DBL Industries, Inc.; mem. adv. bd. secretarial sci. dept. LaGuardia C.C., L.I. City, NY, 1982—95; mem. adv. bd. Krissler Bus. Inst. EDPA grantee, 1973; mem. non-partisan ednl. reform task force Pres. George Bush; dir. continuing edn. and workforce alliances, 2002—. Mem. NAFE, Assn. Info./Sys. Profls., Am. Mgmt. Assn., Nat. Bus. Edn. Assn., Profls. Secs. Internat., Eastern Bus. Edn. Assn., Conn. Bus. Edn. Assn., New Eng. Bus. Edn. Assn., Profl. Secs. Assn., N.Y., Nat. Assn. Cert. Profls. Secs. (cert. profl. sec.), U.S. Golf Assn., Delta Pi Epsilon, Phi Kappa Phi. Avocations: reading, bicycling, golf. Home: 2929 Torringford St Torrington CT 06790-2332 Office: 430E N Main St Bristol CT 06010

LAGASSE, BRUCE KENNETH, retired structural engineer; b. Bklyn., Feb. 1, 1940; s. Joseph F. Lagasse and Dora S. Gould. BSME, U. Calif., Berkeley, 1964. Structures engr. Rockwell Internat., Canoga Park, Calif., 1964-69; mem. tech. staff Hughes Aircraft Co., Los Angeles, 1969-70; scientist/engr. Hughes Aircraft Co. (now Raytheon Sys. Co.), El Segundo, Calif., 1972-97; sr. engr. Litton Ship Systems, Los Angeles, 1971-72; prin. mech. engr. Raytheon Systems Co., El Segundo, 1997-2000; ret. Lectr., tech. edn. class coord. Hughes Aircraft Co., El Segundo, 1980-97; cons. in field, Van Nuys, Calif., 1979—. Libertarian state chmn., L.A., 1977-79, nat. committeeman, Washington, 1979-81; chair Libertarian Judicial Com. (state and national), 1996—. Mem. ASME. Avocations: reading, jogging, hiking, symphonic music, photography. Home: 1029 Ringneck Way Sparks NV 89436 E-mail: bkl1776@aol.com.

LAGDAMEO-HOGAN, MARIA-ELENA, lawyer; b. Manila, Jan. 18, 1969; came to U.S., 1983; d. Antonio Manuel and Maria-Linda (Floirendo) Lagdameo; m. Brian F. Hogan, Dec. 13, 1996. BA in Govt., Smith Coll., Northampton, Mass., 1990; JD, Bklyn. Law Sch., 1993; LLM in Internat. Trade & Bus. Law, Fordham U., N.Y.C., 1996. Bar: N.J. 1994, N.Y. 1996. Assoc., Franklin Lakes, N.J. Home: 908 Mohawk Rd Franklin Lakes NJ 07417-2837

LAGE, CRISTINA, communications executive; b. Buenos Aires, Nov. 13, 1954; d. Ib Lage and Else (Olsen) H.; m. Poul Ingemann, 1978. BSc in Econs., Copenhagen Bus. Sch., 1977, MSc in Econs., 1980. Asst. v.p. Privatbanken, Copenhagen, 1982-85, v.p., 1985-87; sr. v.p., group treas. Internat. Svc. Systems, 1987-92; fin. dir. Copenhagen Cultural Capital, 1992-94; group fin. dir. ISS Scandinavia, Copenhagen, 1994-96; dir. Louisiana Mus. of Modern Art, Humlebaek, Denmark, 1996-2000; CEO TV2/Danmark, Odense, 2000—. Office: TV2/Danmark Rugaardsvej 25 DK 5100 Odense C Denmark E-mail: raad@tv2.dk.

LAGEMANN, ELLEN CONDLIFFE, history and education educator; b. N.Y.C., Dec. 20, 1945; d. John Charles and Jane Grace (Rosenthal); m. Jonathan Kord Lagemann, June 28, 1969; 1 child, Nicholas Kord. AB cum laude, Smith Coll., 1967; MA, Columbia U., 1968, PhD with distinction, 1978. Tchr. Roslyn H.S., Roslyn, NY, 1967-69; exec. dir. WMCA: Call for Action, N.Y.C., 1969-71; asst. dir. Bank Street Sch. for Children, 1971-72; tchng. and rsch. asst. Inst. Phil. and Politics of Edn., Tchrs. Coll. Columbia U., 1974-78; asst. prof., then assoc. prof. Tchrs. Coll. Columbia U. Dept. Hist., 1978-87, prof. history and edn., 1987-94, NYU, N.Y.C., 1994—2000; pres. Spencer Found., 2000—02; Charles Warren prof. history of edn., dean Harvard Grad. Sch. Edn., Cambridge, Mass., 2002—. Dir. Markle Found., N.Y.C.; trustee, Russell Sage Found., N.Y.C.; former trustee Center for Advanced Study in Behavioral Scis., Standford, CA; mem. gov. coun. Rockefeller Archive Ctr.; former mem. adv. com. Ctr. Nonprofits and Philanthropy, Urban Inst., Washington; affiliate dept. history Faculty of Arts and Sci. Author: A Generation of Women: Education in the Lives of Progressive Reformers, 1979, Private Power for the Public Good (Outstanding Book award), 1983, The Politics of Knowledge, 1989, An Elusive Science: The Troubling History of Education Reserach, 2000; editor: Nursing History: New Perspectives, New Possibilities, 1983, Jane Addams on Education, 1985, Teachers College Record, 1990-95, Brown v. Bd. of Education: The Challenge for Today's Schools, 1996, Philanthropic Foundations: New Scholarship, New Possibilities, 1999, Issues in Educational Research, Problems and Possibilities, 1999; many articles and book chpts. Grantee Carnegie Corp., Spencer Found, Carnegie Found. for Advancement of Teaching, Kettering Found., Lilly Endowment, fellow Ctr. for Advanced Study in Behavioral Scis. Mem. Nat. Acad. Edn. (pres. 1998-2001), History of Edn. Soc. (pres. 1987-88), Am. Hist. Assn., Orgn. Am. Historians, Am. Ednl. Rsch. Assn., Century Assn., Cosmopolitan Club, Home: 61 Grazier Rd Cambridge MA 02138 Office: Harvard Grad Sch Edn Dean's Office Appian Way Cambridge MA 02138

LAGERSTROM, THOMAS JAY, engineering executive; b. Ames, Iowa, Sept. 12, 1955; s. John Emil Lagerstrom and Shirley Jean Bantin; m. Teresa Neal, 1990; children: Katherine Marie, Ian Thomas. BSEE, U.S. Naval Acad., 1977; JD, U. Nebr., 1984, PhD in Indsl. Engring., 1991. Registered profl. engr., Nebr.; Bar: Nebr. Tchg./rsch. asst. U. Nebr., Lincoln, 1985-92, asst. prof. engring., 1992-96; sr. engring. mgr. Square D Co., 1997—. Capt. USNR, 1977—. Home: 4115 Red Deer Dr Lincoln NE 68516-3068 Office: Square D Co 1717 Center Park Rd Lincoln NE 68512-1290 E-mail: tjlgrstrm@aol.com.

LAGIN, NEIL, landscape designer, consultant; b. Bronx, N.Y., Jan. 10, 1942; s. Barney and Helen (Goldberg) L. Cert. Xeriscape instr. South Fla. Water Mgmt. Buyer Alexanders, N.Y.C., 1961-69; sales mgr. Halldon, Ltd., 1969-79; mgr., ptnr. in concession Michele Craig, Westbury, N.Y., 1979-85; ptnr. ALW Trading, "9", N.Y.C., 1985-87; owner, operator Accent Foliage, Delray Beach, Fla., 1987-89; pres. Neil Lagin Property Mgmt., Neil's Landscape Svc., Boca Raton, 1988-97; landscape dir. Am. Heritage Sch., Boca Raton, Delray Beach; ptnr. All Star Landscaping, 1997-99; landscape mgmt. cons., 1999-2001; landscape dir. Every Bloomin' Thing Ltd., Cayman Islands, 2001—02; landscape cons., 2002—. Author poetry; exhibitor photography shows, Ward Nasse Gallery-Salon, 1975-79, Timothy Blackburn Gallery, 1978, Washington Art Show and others. Notary pub., Fla., 1990-95; mem. nursery adv. bd. Habilitation Ctr. for the Handicapped, Boca Raton, 1991—; mem. overall adv. com. Palm Beach County Ext., 1992—, sec., chair program rev. com.; bd. dirs. Greater Palm Beach Area Alzheimers Assn., 1993; mem. Environ. Resource Landscape Team; mem. Boca Raton Postal Customer Adv. Coun., 1994-96; memb. bd. dirs. Pheasant Walk Homeowners Assoc., 1996-97; adv. ocun. Plant the Planet TV series, 1997. Named Fla. Master Gardener, Inst. Food and Agrl. Scis., U. Fla., 1989, Best Landscaper in Boca Raton, South Fla. Newspaper Network, 1991, Best Local Vol. in Boca Raton, 1994, Outstanding Master Gardener, State of Fla., 1995. Mem. Internat. Palm Soc. (Palm Beach chpt.), Rare Fruit Coun. Internat. (Palm Beach chpt.), Boca Raton C. of C. (grad. leadership program 1991). Office: c/o Neil's Landscape Service 189 Giant Oak Ave Thousand Oaks CA 91320-3455 E-mail: eblomint@candw.ky.

LAGLE, JOHN FRANKLIN, lawyer; b. Kansas City, Mo., Jan. 22, 1938; s. Ernest J. and Hilda B. Lagle; m. Nina E. Weston, Aug. 1, 1959; m. Diana G. Fogle, July 14, 1962 (dec. 1992); children: Robert, Gregory. BBA, UCLA, 1961, JD, 1967. Bar: Calif. 1967, U.S. Dist. Ct. (no. dist.) Calif. 1967. Assoc. Hindin, McKittrick & Marsh, Beverly Hills, Calif., 1967-70, Macco Corp., Newport Beach, 1970, Rifkind & Sterling, Beverly Hills, 1971; mem. Fulop & Hardee, and predecessor firm, 1971-82; ptnr. Leff & Stephenson, 1983; sole practice Los Angeles, 1984; ptnr. Barash & Hill (formerly Wildman, Harrold, Allen, Dixon, Barash & Hill) L. A., 1985-91; of counsel Barbosa Garcia, 1998—2000, Hill, Farrer & Burrell, LLP, 2000—01; atty. pvt. practice, 1991—. Arbitrator NASD Regulation, Inc. Contbr. to Practice Under the California Corporate Securities Law of 1978. Served with U.S. Army, 1961-63. Mem. ABA, Arbitration Assn. (arbitrator), Calif. Bar Assn., Los Angeles County Bar Assn. Republican. E-mail: j. Office: 16750 Marquez Ave Pacific Palisades CA 90272-3240 E-mail: lagle@msn.com.

LAGOWSKI, BARBARA JEAN, writer, book editor; b. Adams, Mass., Nov. 9, 1955; d. Frank Louis and Jeanette (Wanat) L.; m. Richard Dietrich Mumma III, Oct. 11, 1980; 1 child, Adam Dietrich. BA, U. South Fla., 1977; MA, Johns Hopkins U., 1978. Asst. editor Fred Jordan Books Grossett and Dunlap Pubs., N.Y.C., 1978-80; mng. editor Methuen Inc., 1980-81; mng. assoc., sr. editor Bobb-Merrill Co Inc., 1981-84; editor New Am. Libr., 1984-85. Poet-in-the-schs. Hillsborough County Arts Council, Tampa., Fla., 1976-77; poet-in-residence Cloisters Children's Mus., Balt., 1977-78 Author: Silver Skates series, 1988—89; co-author: Good Spirits, 1986, Teen Terminators, 1989, How to Get the Best Public School Education for Your Child, 1991, The Sports Curmudgeon, 1993, How to Attract Anyone, Anytime, Anyplace, 1993, Daily Negotiations: A Malcontent's Book of Meditations for Every Interminable Day of the Year, 1996, 101 Ways to Flirt: How to Get More Dates and Meet Your Mate, 1997, Cyberflirt: How to Attract Anyone, Anywhere on the World Wide Web, 1999; singer: Angel Signs: A Celestial Guide to the Powers of Your Own Guardian Angel, 2002. Mem. Authors Guild, Phi Kappa Phi Home: 237 Lenox Ave Long Branch NJ 07740-5022 E-mail: blagowski@aol.com.

LAGRAND, KENNETH, technology products company executive; b. 1941; married. BS in Mech. Engring., Mich. State U., 1964. Dir. mktg. Grayson Divsn. Robertshaw Controls Co., 1975-79; v.p., gen. mgr. Simicon Divsn. Robertshaw Controls Co., Holland, Mich., 1979-87; exec. v.p., dir. Gentex, 1987—. Mem. Soc. Automotive Engrs. Office: Gentex Corp 600 N Centennial St Zeeland MI 49464-1318

LAGRECA, THOMAS RICHARD, flooring company executive, lawyer; b. N.Y.C., Dec. 16, 1957; s. Jack Charles and Gloria LaG.; m. Joanne Baio, Nov. 25, 1989; children: Jack, Jessica, Joseph. BA, Pa. State U., 1979; JD, St. John's U., 1983. Atty. Dewey Ballatine, N.Y.C., 1983-85, Nynex Corp., N.Y.C., 1985-90; prin. Concourse Floors, Inc., Bklyn., 1990-97, Spectrum Flooring, Ltd., Bklyn., 1997—. Editor-in-chief St. John's Law Rev., 1982-83; contbr. poetry and short stories to profl. publs. Mem. Tau Kappa Epsilon. Avocations: reading, music. Home: 788 Winding Way Rivervale NJ 07675

LAGUE, ROBERT ALFRED, music educator; b. Woonsocket, R.I., June 18, 1947; s. Alfred George Lague and Olga Lapchinski; m. Nancy Greenshade, Aug. 24, 1968 (div. 1974); children: Michael, Jennifer; m. Nancy Louise Brown, Feb. 18, 1979; children: Jessica, Juliana. B in Music Edn., New Eng. Conservatory, 1968, MusM in Applied Piano, 1971. Cert. music tchr. Mass., adminstr. Mass. Tchr. Lexington (Mass.) Pub. Schs., 1968—84, Andoren (Mass.) Pub. Schs., 1985—99; tchr., adminstr. Stoneham (Mass.) Pub. Schs., 1999—. Choir dir., organist First Congl. Ch., Natick, 1971—; chorus dir. Lexington Pope Chorus, 1981—2002; ofcl. organist Mass. Tchrs. Assn., Boston, NEA, Washington. Author: Directing Broadway Musicals-Secondary Teachers, 1998. Scholar, Beethoven Club, Woonsocket, R.I., 1968. Mem.: NEA (founder, treas. fine arts caucus 1977—), Am. Choral Dirs. Assn. (Bass-Bicentennial Chorus 1976), Mass. Music Edn. Assn. (mem. exec. bd. N.E. dist., historian, Lowell Mason award 1999). Democrat. Congregationalist. Avocations: reading, swimming, camping, travel, concerts. Home: 9 Cronin Way Woburn MA 01801 Office: Stoneham Pub Schs 149 Franklin St Stoneham MA 02180

LAGUEUX, RONALD RENE, federal judge; b. Lewiston, Maine, June 30, 1931; s. Arthur Charles and Laurette Irene (Turcotte) L.; m. Denise Rosemarie Boudreau, June 30, 1956; children: Michelle Simone, Gregory Charles, Barrett James. AB, Bowdoin Coll., 1953; LLB, Harvard U., 1956. Assoc. then ptnr. Edwards and Angell Law Firm, Providence, 1956-68; assoc. justice Superior Ct. State of R.I., 1968-86; judge U.S. Dist. Ct., 1986—; chief judge, 1992-99. Exec. counsel to Gov. Chafee, R.I., 1963-65. Rep. candidate for U.S. Senate, 1964; corporator R.I. Hosp., Providence, 1965-01; solicitor Southeastern New Eng. Province United Way, 1957-68. Mem. Bowdoin Coll. Alumni Council (past v.p., pres.), Am.-French Geneal. Soc. Home: 90 Greenwood Ave Rumford RI 02916-1934 Office: US Dist Ct 1 Exchange Ter Providence RI 02903-1744

LAGUNAS-SOLAR, MANUEL CLAUDIO, research radiochemist; b. Valparaiso, Chile, Dec. 23, 1941; came to U.S., 1970; s. Manuel and Alejandria (Solar) Lagunas; children: Claudio Lagunas, Rodrigo Lagunas. Lic. in chemistry and edn., Cath. U. Valparaiso, 1968; MS in Chemistry, U. P.R., Mayaguez, 1970; PhD in Chemistry, U. Calif., Davis, 1974. Lectr. chemistry Cath. U. Valparaiso, 1965-68; rsch. & tchg. asst. P.R. Nuc. Ctr., Mayaguez, 1968-69; instr. phys. chemistry U. P.R., 1969-70; asst. rsch. chemist U. Calif. Crocker Nuc. Lab., Davis, 1973-80, assoc. rsch. chemist, 1980-89, rsch. chemist, 1989—. Scientific collaborator/advisor Chilean Exporters Assn., Santiago, 1985—, Hortifrut S.A., Santiago, 1997—; scientific advisor Titan Beta Devel. Co., Dublin, Calif., 1993-96, SteriGenics, Inc., Fremont, Calif., 1992—. Patentee in field. Mem. Am. Chem. Soc., Soc. Nuc. Medicine, Inst. Food Technology, Chilean Soc. Nuc. Medicine & Biology. Roman Catholic. Avocations: tennis, soccer, skiing, sailing. Office: U Calif Crocker Nuc Nab 1 Shields Ave Davis CA 95616-5200 Fax: (530) 754-8246. E-mail: solar@crocker.ucdavis.edu.

LAGUNOFF, DAVID, physician, educator; b. N.Y.C., N.Y., Mar. 14, 1932; s. Robert and Cieele (Lipman) L.; m. Susan P. Powers, Mar. 8, 1958; children: Rachel, Liza, Michael. MD, U. Chgo., 1957. Rsch. asst. microbiology U.

Miami, Coral Gables, Fla., 1951-53; intern U. Calif. San Francisco Hosp., 1957-58; postdoctoral fellow dept. pathology U. Wash., Seattle, 1958-59, trainee in pathology, 1959-60, instr. pathology, 1960-62, asst. prof., 1962-65, assoc. prof., 1965-69, prof., 1969-79; prof. dept. pathology St. Louis U., 1979—, chmn. dept. pathology, 1979-89, 91-96, asst. v.p., 1989-93. Assoc. dean rsch. St. Louis U. Sch. Medicine, 1989—96; vis. lectr. dept. pathology Sackler Sch. Medicine, Tel Aviv, 1988; vis. prof. dept. pathology U. Wash., Seattle, 2001—02. Nat. Heart Inst. fellow Carlsberg Laboratorium, Copenhagen, 1962-64, Nat. Cancer Inst. fellow Sir William Dunn Sch. Pathology, Oxford, Eng., 1970. Mem.: AAUP, AAAS, Am. Soc. Investigative Pathologists, Am. Soc. Cell Biology. Office: St Louis Univ Sch Medicine Dept Pathology 1402 S Grand Blvd Saint Louis MO 63104-1004 E-mail: lagunofd@slucare1.sluh.edu.

LAHAIE, UTE SUSANNE, language educator; b. Stuttgart, Germany, Feb. 16, 1960; d. Hans and Hiltrud Klappenecker; m. L. Scot Lahaie, Jan. 25, 1995; children: Michèle Aimée, Isabelle Bernice. Diploma, Justus-Liebig U., Giessen, Germany, 1985, PhD, 1995. Lang. and culture instr. U.S. Army Edn. Ctr., Giessen, 1984-85; adj. lectr. City Coll. Chgo., 1985-87; adj. instr. Open Univ., Lich, Germany, 1984-88; dir. Child Devel. Ctr. U.S. Army Mil. Cmty., Giessen, 1987-89; rsch. assoc. Justus-Liebig U., 1990-95; adj. lectr. U. Mary-Hardin Baylor, Belton, Tex., 1995-96; dir. Lang. Acquistion Ctr. Baylor U., Waco, 1996—, asst. prof. German, 1996—. Mem. Coun. Internat. Edn., Waco, 1998-99. Co-translator (play) The Beloved, 1990. Mem.: Computer Assisted Lang. Instrn. Consortium, South Ctrl. Assn. Lang. Learning Tech. (pres.-elect), Am. Assn. Tchrs. German, Internat. Assn. Lang. Learning Tech. E-mail: Ute_Lahaie@baylor.edu.

LAHART, DANIEL KENNETH, priest, educational administrator; b. Park Ridge, Ill., Oct. 3, 1961; s. F. Vern and Eileen (Ryan) L. BSBA, Georgetown U., 1983; MDiv, Weston Sch. Theology, 1993; MEd, Boston Coll., 1994; MBA, Stanford U., 1996. Ordained priest, 1994. Faculty Scranton (Pa.) Prep. Sch., 1987-90; v.p. fin. and adminstrn. Gonzaga Coll. H.S., Washington, 1996-2001; asst. provincial secondary edn. Md. Province, Soc. of Jesus, Balt., 1997-2001; pres. Strake Jesuit Coll. Prep., Houston, 2001—. Bd. regents Georgetown U., Washington, 1993—. Trustee Trinity Coll., Washington, 2000—, Dallas Jesuit Coll. Prep., Dallas, 2001—; mem. Jesuit Vol. Corps, Houston, 2002—. Mem. Alpha Sigma Nu (nat. pres. 1997—). Roman Catholic. Avocations: travel, water sports, people. Home and Office: 8900 Bellaire Blvd Houston TX 77036 Fax: 713-271-3407. E-mail: lahart_d@strakejesuit.org.

LAHEY, REGIS HENRY, bank executive; b. Pitts., July 15, 1948; s. Michael Patrick and Henrietta (Szczesny) L. Diploma in Indsl. Mgmt., Ednl. Inst. Pitts., 1968; BS, Robert Morris Coll., Pitts., 1981; grad., Bucknell U., 1991. Corp. trustee Union Nat. Bank, Pitts., 1968-70; asst. supr. Mellon Bank, N.A., 1978-80, supr., 1980-83, unit mgr., 1983-84, asst. ops. officer, 1984-86, ops. officer, 1986-87, trust and investment officer, 1987-93, asst. v.p., 1993-94, sect. mgr., 1994-97, mgr. tax reclaim and check issuance divsn., 1997—, v.p., 2000—. Instr. cash mgmt. Master Trust U., Pitts., 1987—. Mem. Am. Mgmt. Assn. Republican. Roman Catholic. Avocations: photography, jogging. Office: Mellon Bank One Mellon Ctr Pittsburgh PA 15258-0001

LAHEY, RICHARD THOMAS, JR. nuclear engineer, fluid mechanics engineer; b. St. Petersburg, Fla., Feb. 20, 1939; married, 1961; 3 children. BS, U.S. Merchant Marine Acad., 1961; MS, Rensselaer Polytechnic Inst., 1964; ME, Columbia U., 1966; PhD in Mechanical Engring., Stanford U., 1971. Engr. Knolls Atomic Power Lab., 1961-64; rsch. assoc. Columbia U., 1964-66; mgr. core & safety devel. nuclear energy divsn. Gen. Electric, 1966-75; chmn. dept. nuclear engring. Rensselaer Poly. Inst., Troy, N.Y., 1975-87, prof. nuclear engring. and engring. physics, 1987—, prof. dept. chem. engring., 1987—, Edward E. Hood, Jr. prof. engring., 1989—, dir. ctr. multiphase rsch., 1991-94, dean engring., 1994-98. Bd. mem. PJM Internat., LLC, 1997-; mem. sci. adv. com. EG&G Idaho, Inc., 1976-83; mem. Advanced Code Rev. Group & LOFT Rev. Group U.S. Nuclear Regulatory Commn., 1976-84; commr. Engring. Manpower Commn., 1981-84; pres. R.T. Lahey, Inc., 1981-83; adj. prof. U. Pisa, Italy and Claude Bernard U., France, 1987; Alexander von Humboldt Sr. scientist fellow, 1994-95. Editor: Jour. Nuclear Engring. & Design, 1983-94. Recipient Arthur Holly Compton award, 1989, Glenn T. Seaborg medal, 1992, E. O. Lawrence Meml. award U.S. Dept. Energy, 1988; Fulbright fellow Magdalen Coll., Oxford U., 1983-84. Fellow ASME, Am. Nuclear Soc. (Tech. Achievement award 1985), N.Y. Acad. Scis., Am. Soc. Engring. Edn. (Glen Murphy award 1985), Sigma Xi; mem., Nat. Acad. Engring., Russian Acad. Sci. (fgn. mem. Bashkorstan, Russia). Achievements include research in two-phase flow and boiling heat transfer technology; nuclear reactor thermal-hydraulics and safety. Office: Rensselaer Poly Inst Jonsson Engring Ctr 110 8th St Troy NY 12180-3522

LAHIFF, MARILYN J. nursing administrator; b. Youngstown, Ohio; d. Jack L. and Lila J. (Webb) Mills; m. Lawrence C. Lahiff, Apr. 26, 1974. AAS, Lorain County C.C., Elyria, Ohio, 1973; student, Youngstown U., 1960-61. RN, Fla., Ohio; lic. rehab. svc. provider, Fla.; cert. rehab. nurse, cert. ins. rehab. specialist, cert. case mgr. Team leader pediatrics Lakewood (Ohio) Hosp., 1973-75; adminstr. Upjohn HealthCare Svcs., Reno, 1977-78, 83-84; occupational health/sch. nurse Medina (Ohio) County Achievement Ctr., 1979-83; regional mgr. Beverly Enterprises, Torrance, Calif., 1984-87; program mgr. RehabCare Corp., Cleve., 1988-89; supr. med./vocat.rehab Feisco, Sarasota, Fla., 1989-92; cons., med. case mgmt. Riscorp, 1993-94; chief operating officer Prime Managed Care Svcs., Inc., 1994—. Mem. editl. bd. Directions in Rehab. Counseling, 1994. Mem. Assn. Rehab. Nurses, Fla. State Assn. Rehab. Nurses, Phi Theta Kappa. Avocations: boating, reading. Home: 30051 Center Ridge Rd Apt C Westlake OH 44145-5163

LAHIRI, DEBOMOY KUMAR, molecular neurobiologist, educator; b. Varanasi, Uttar Pradesh, India, Sept. 9, 1955; came to U.S. 1983. s. Benoy Kumar and Nilima Rani (Moitra) L.; m. Mithu Mukherjee, Dec. 15, 1991; 1 child, Niloy K. MS, Benaras Hindu U., India, 1975, PhD, 1980. Rsch. fellow Benaras Hindu U., Varanasi, 1975-79; jr. scientist Indian Coun. of Agrl. Rsch., New Delhi, India, 1979-81; postdoctoral fellow McMaster U. Sch. Medicine, Hamilton, Ont., Can., 1982; asst. rsch. scientist NYU, N.Y.C., 1983-86; rsch. assoc. N.Y. State Inst. for Basic Rsch., Staten Island, N.Y., 1987; asst. prof. Mt. Sinai Sch. Medicine, N.Y.C., 1988-90; asst. prof., chief molecular neurogenetics lab. Inst. Psychiat. Rsch. Ind. U. Sch. Medicine, Indpls., 1990—, asst. prof. med. & molecular genetics, 1994-96, assoc. prof. med. neurobiology and med. & molecular genetics, 1996—. Presenter in field. Contbr. articles to profl. jours. U.P. Govt. Merit scholar, 1970-75; Univ. Grants Commn. New Delhi jr. rsch. fellow, 1975-79; grantee NIH, 1991—, Alzheimer's Assn., Chgo., 2000—. Mem. AAAS, Am. Soc. Cell Biology, Am. Soc. Human Genetics, Am. Soc. for Neurochemistry, Am. Soc. Biochemistry and Molecular Biology, Genetics Soc. Am., Internat. Soc. for Neurochemistry, Soc. Biol. Psychiatry, Soc. for Neurosci., N.Y. Acad. Scis. Democrat. Hindu. Achievements include the molecular cloning and sequencing a cDNA for a major hnRNP (heterogenous nuclear ribonuceoprotein particle) core protein; determination of the presence of beta amyloid precursor protein (APP) in different regions of human brain, and alternatively spliced APP transcripts in different tissues and various cell types; demonstration of a relationship between cholinergic agonists and the processing of APP; elucidation of the role of cholinesterase inhibitor on the processing of APP, first demonstration that tacrine can alter the secretion/metabolism of APP in cultured cells; first characterization of the beta amyloid gene promoter; and an enhancer like element in the beta amyloid gene promoter; research related to the origin and biogenesis of Alzheimer amyloid plaque and the general areas of gene regulation and genetics of Alzheimer's Disease, development of a rapid, economical, non-enzymatic and non-organic method for DNA extraction, elucidation of the genetic basis of neuropsychiatric disorders by the linkage studies using molecular genetic methods and PCR (polymerase chain reaction) based genotyping, RFLP (restriction fragment length ploymorphism) and candidate gene studies in families ascertained through the NIMH Genetics Initiative in order to confirm association between the inheritance of a molecular marker with the member of the family sharing the illness, development of a sensitive radioimmunoassay to measure melatonin in human plasma samples, bipolar patients have an increased sensitivity to the effects of light on the circadian rhythm of melatonin secretion, and the risk of mood disorder seems to be related to this hypersensitivity to light, the suppression of melatonin by light may be a trait marker for bipolar affective disorder; demonstration pineal hormone melatonin can regulate the processing of Alzheimer's amyloid precursor protein in cultured cells. Home: 5731 Arabian Run Indianapolis IN 46228-1684 Office: Inst Psychiat Rsch Ind Univ 791 Union Dr Indianapolis IN 46202-2873

LAHIRI, KAJAL, economics educator; b. Kulti, West Bengal, India, June 16, 1947; came to U.S., 1971; s. Samarendra Nath and Dipali (Sanyal) L.; m. Maitra Nandini, Sept. 12, 1979; 1 son, Indraneil. BA, U. Calcutta, 1967, MA, 1970; MA, U. Rochester, 1974, PhD, 1975. Faculty mem. SUNY-Albany, 1976—; assoc. prof., 1979-81, prof. econs., 1981—, bd. dir. Econometric Rsch. Tng. Inst., 1982—; vis. scholar Internat. Monetary Fund, 1988—; cons. The World Bank, 1988-89. Author: (with A. Datta, P. Basu) Economics of Education, 1974, Econometrics of Inflationary Expectations, 1981, (with G.H. Moore) Leading Economic Indicators; contbr. articles to profl. jours. Merit scholar Govt. West Bengal, 1969; U. Rochester research fellow, 1971-75, NSF grantee, 1982, NAS grantee, 1982. Mem. Am. Econ. Assn., Econometric Soc., Am. Statis. Assn. Mem. editorial bd. Atlantic Econ. jour., 1982—, Jour. Econometrics, 1990—; reviewer Math. Revs., 1984—. Hindu. Home: 1 Aspen Hts Slingerlands NY 12159-9745

LAHMANN, ROBERT OSCAR, artist, retired; b. Port Washington, Wis., July 4, 1923; s. Oscar Otto and Edna Mildred Lahmann; m. Lorraine Loretta Lahmann, Apr. 14, 1956; children: Robert Charles, Ellen Jeyne Lahmann Christensen, Peter William, Emily Arlene Lahmann Boysa. Grad. in Art, Layton Sch. Art, Milw., 1950; student in Portrait Painting, Acad. Fine Arts, Chgo., 1956-57; studied with Guitano Busalacchi, Milw., 1957-65. Tchr. art, 1962-64. Tchr. art Delafield, Wis., Pewaukee Wis.; pvt. tchr., 1962-64. Exhibited in group shows U. Wis., 1947 (1st prize), Layton Sch. Art, 1948-49, Bay Shore Exhibit, 1952, Bresslers Gallery Exhibit, 1960, Ramsburg Gallery, Oconomowoc, Wis., 1960, Watertown Open Show, 1961, Maple Dale Sch. Exhibit, 1977, Sentinal Art Show, 1979-80, North Lake Art Show, 1979-80, County Fair, 1979, 80, 81 (prize winner 1979, 80, 81), West Bend Gallery, 1981, 15th Ann. Arts Festival, 1981-82, Paine Gallery, 1998; sculptor Milw. County Zoo, 1960; artist stain glass, 1962; represented in permanent collections Landmark Gallery, Marquett U., City of Port Washington, St. John's Ch., Milw. Electric Tool Corp.; paintings donated to Friends of Channel 10-36. Recipient Andrew Clark award Wis. Regional Art Show Assn., 1979, Award of Excellence League of Artists, 1979, 80, 99, Best of Show award League of Artists, 1980, Purchase award Waukesha County Ct., 1981-85, Aaron Bohrod award Wis. Regional Art Show Assn., 1984-87. Mem. Wis. Regional Artist Assn., League Milw. Artists, West Bend Friends of Art.

LAHOOD, MARVIN JOHN, English educator; b. Auburn, N.Y., Mar. 21, 1933; s. Salem and Anna (Mahfoud) L.; m. Marjorie Braun, Aug. 22, 1959; children: John, Melissa, Mark. BS, Boston Coll., 1954; MA in English, U. Notre Dame, 1958, PhD in English, 1962. Instr. Niagara U., 1960-61, assoc. prof., 1962-64, Buffalo (N.Y.) State Coll., 1964-67, prof., 1967-71, prof. ind. study, 1968-69, prof., assoc. for acad. devel., 1969-71, prof., 1978-95, Disting. tchg. prof., 1995—; prof., acad. dean Coll. Misericordia, 1971-72, Salem State Coll., 1972-75; prof., dean faculty D'Youville Coll., 1975-78. Chair Burchfield Poets and Writers Com., 1985—; manuscript reviewer Prentice Hall, 1986-88; lectr. U. Dortmund, Germany, 1986, Lille U., France, Cath. U. Lille, 1991; chair SUNY Senate Ops. Com., 1994-97, chair, Undergrad Com., 1999-2002. Author: Conrad Richter's America, 1974, State University College at Buffalo, A History: 1946-1972, 1980; editor: Latvian Literature, 1964, Tender Is the Night: Essays in Criticism, 1969, Stories of Tragedy and Triumph, 1997; contbr. Grad. Degrees column Notre Dame Mag., 1996--; contbr. articles to profl. jours. Pres. Mt. St. Mary Acad. Bd. Trustees, 1990-94. SUNY Faculty Rsch. fellow, 1967, 68, USOE fellow Inst. on Ednl. Media, 1967, SUNY fellow Inst. for Devel. Black Studies, 1969; SUNY Faculty Exch. scholar, 1969—; recipient SUNY Chancellor's award Excellence in Teaching, 1985, Boston Coll. Alumni award for Excellence in Edn., 1997, Tchr. of Yr. award Buffalo State Coll. United Student Govt., 1999. Mem. F. Scott Fitzgerald Soc. (bd. dirs. 1999-02). Office: Buffalo State College 1300 Elmwood Ave Buffalo NY 14222-1095 E-mail: lahoodmj@buffalostate.edu.

LAHOOD, MARY ANNE, real estate investor; b. Grosse Pointe Farms, Mich., Aug. 23, 1947; d. Tom and Melania (Simon) LaH.; children: Lila, Michael. BA, Wayne State U., 1972. Ptnr. LaHood Lanes, Inc., St. Clair Shores, Mich., 1972-89, LaHood Properties, Grosse Pointe Shores, 1972—. Patron Detroit Inst. of Arts, Grosse Pointe Yacht Club; sec. environ. group NYCE, Detroit Hist. Soc. Avocations: fiction writing, art collecting, long distance walking, sailing, tennis. Home: 20 Stillmeadow Ln Grosse Pointe Shores MI 48236-1118 E-mail: lahood@aol.com.

LAHOOD H. RAY, congressman; b. Peoria, Ill., Dec. 6, 1945; m. Kathleen (Kathy) Dunk LaHood; children: Darin, Amy, Sam, Sara. Student, Canton Jr. Coll., Ill.; BS in Edn. and Sociology, Bradley U., 1971. Tchr. Catholic and pub. jr. high schs., 1971-77; dist. administrv. asst. to congressman Tom Railsback, 1977; mem. Ill. Ho. of Reps., 1982; Chief of Staff Ho. of Reps.; mem. 106th Congress from 18th Ill. dist., 1995—. Mem. Intelligence Com., Appropriations Com., Budget Com. Bd. dirs. Economic Devel. Coun.; pres. sch. bd. Spalding and Notre Dame H.Schs., Bradley U. Nat. Alumni Bd.; svc. to Children's Hosp. Bd., Peoria Area Retarded Citizens Bd.; dir. Rock Island County Youth Svcs. Bur. Mem. ITOO Soc., Downtown Rotary Club, Holy Family Ch. (Peoria), Peoria Area C. of C. Roman Catholic. Office: US House Reps 1424 Longworth HOB Washington DC 20515-1318 also: 100 NE Monroe St Ste 100 Peoria IL 61602-1003*

LAHOUD, NINA JOSEPH, lawyer, international organization assistant; b. Littleton, N.H., July 10, 1956; d. Joseph and Loretta Lahout. Student, Smith Coll., 1975-76; BA, Harvard U., 1978; JD, U. Pa., 1981; postgrad., Am. U., Cairo, 1982. Bar: N.Y. 1981. Assoc. Shearman & Sterling, N.Y.C., 1982-83; legal advisor Office of the Force Comdr., UN Interim Force in Lebanon, Naqoura, 1983-86; dep. legal advisor UN Transition Assistance Group in Namibia, Windhoek, 1989-90; sr. legal officer UN Transitional Authority in Cambodia, Phnom Penh, 1992-93; spl. asst. to asst. sec.-gen. for mgmt. and coordination UN Peace Forces in the Former Yugoslavia, Zagreb, Croatia, 1995-96; legal officer Office of Legal Affairs, UN Hdqrs., N.Y.C., 1986-93, sr.legal officer, 1993-97; spl. asst. to asst. sec.-gen. for planning and support Dept. Peacekeeping Ops., UN Hdqrs., 1997-98, 2000—, spl. asst. to undersec.-gen. for peacekeeping ops., 1998—2001, chief of peacekeeping best practices unit Office of Under Sec.-Gen. for Peacekeeping Ops., 2001—. Chief of staff to Spl. Rep. of Sec.-Gen. in Kosovo, UN Mission in Kosovo, Jan.-Sept. 2000; dir. to dep. spl. rep. of sec.-gen. in East Timor, UN Transitional Adminstrn. in East Timor, 2001 . Contbr. articles to profl. jours. Mem. Assn. Bar City N.Y. (com. on internat. human rights 1987-90, com. on internat. law 1996—), Internat. Law Assn. (human rights com. 19837), Am. Soc. Internt. Law, U. Pa. Law Sch. Alumni Assn., Harvard U. Alumni Assn. E-mial. Office: Un Hdqrs Dept Peacekeeping Ops One Un Plz Rm S-22705 New York NY 10017 E-mail: lahoud@un.org.

LAHOWCHIC, NICHOLAS JOHN, retail specialty company executive; b. N.Y.C., Apr. 11, 1947; s. Nicholas and Mary Ellen (Dunn) La H.; m. Diane Forrest; children: Tara Anne, Nicole Marie. Student, Marquette U., 1964-66; BS in Acctg., Fairleigh Dickinson U., 1970; MBA, Pace U., 1980. Acct. Okonite Cable Corp., Passaic, N.J., 1966-68; cost analyst Philips Broadcast Equip. Corp., Paramus, 1968-69; corp. acct. Thomas J. Lipton, Inc., Englewood Cliffs, 1969-70, fin. systems analyst, 1970-72, mgr. cash mgmt., 1972-73, mgr. hdqrs. distbn. svcs., 1974-76, mgr. distbn. and sales svcs., 1976-77, mgr. ops. planning, 1977-79; gen. mgr. McGraw Hill Book Co., N.Y.C., 1979-81; dir. inventory mgmt. Nabisco Brands, Inc., Parsippany, N.J., 1981-84, dir. inventory mgmt. and logistics planning, 1984-85, dir. logistics planning, systems and adminstrn., 1985-87; dir. logistics Colgate-Palmolive, Inc., N.Y.C., 1987-89, dir. customer svc. and logistics, 1989-91; v.p. corp. logistics Becton Dickinson & Co., Franklin Lakes, N.J., 1991-95; pres. Becton Dickinson Supply Chain Svcs., 1995-97; pres., CEO Ltd. Logistics Svcs., Inc., Columbus, Ohio, 1997—. Bd. dirs. Express Scipts, Inc., Swift Rivers, Inc.; cons. in field. Mem. editl. adv. bd. Supply Chain Mgmt. Rev., Med. Product Sales mag; contbr. articles to bus. publs. Trustee United Way, Greater Columbus, Ohio. Recipient Harry Salzburg medallion award, 1997. Mem. Nat. Assn. Accts., Am. Mgmt. Assn., Am. Prodn. and Inventory Control Soc. (dir. 1979-80), Nat. Coun. Phys. Distbn. Mgmt. (v.p. 1982-83), Health Industry Distbn. Assn. (bd. dirs. 1997-2001), Health Industry Mfrs. Assn., Health Industry Bar Code Coun., Grocery Mfrs. Assn. (chmn. distbn. ops. steering com.), Coun. Logistics Mgmt., Internat. Materials Mgmt. Soc. Pace U., Columbus C. of C. (bd. dirs.). Home: 13 New Albany Farms Rd New Albany OH 43054-9000 Office: Ltd Logistics Svcs Inc Two Limited Pky PO Box 182199 Columbus OH 43218-2199 Fax: 614-415-6809. E-mail: NLAHowchic@limited-logistics.com.

LAHR, JOHN WILLIAM, optometrist; b. June 11, 1950; s. Willard Keith and Verly Marion (Westfall) L.; m. Mary Jo Geffert, Sept. 11, 1976; children: Brian, Jennifer, Suzanne. BS, Ind. U., 1972, OD, 1974. Assoc. Dr. Earl Doelle, Grand Rapids, Minn., 1974-75, Dr. G.T. Gibbons, Cambridge, 1975-77; pres. Cambridge Eye Clinic, 1977-98; prin. cons. Edmonds, Lahr, Peters Consulting, Phila.; dir. primary eye svcs. STAAR Surg., 1999—; med. dir. Eye Med. Vision Plan, 2001—. Cons. Grand Rapids Vocat. Tech. Inst., 1974-75, Cambridge State Hosp., St. Cloud Vocat. Tech. Inst., 1979-87, Sandstone Fed. Corr. Inst., 1982—; dir. mktg. Am.'s Doctors of Optometry, Tracy, Minn., 1982-87. Fellow Am. Acad. Optometry; mem. Am. Optometric Assn. (eyecare benefits com. 1988-98, chmn. 1996-98, chmn. coding subcom., fed. health care entitlement com. 1990-98, clin. guidelines com. 1994-98, chmn. eye care benefits ctr. 1996—), Minn. Optometric Assn. (pres. 1987-88, Optometrist of Yr. 1990-91), Met. Dist. Optometric Soc., (pres. 1982-83), Cambridge C. of C.. Republican. Methodist. Home and Office: 707 Sunset Ln Cambridge MN 55008-1019 E-mail: jwlahr@earthlink.net.

LAHTINEN, SILJA LIISA, artist; b. Lumivaara, Finland; came to U.S., 1978; d. Vaino Lambertinpoika and Katri Elisa (Tirri) Talikka; m. Pentti Kalervo Lahtinen; children: Karoliina, Katriina, Antti. BFA, MA, U. Helsinki, Finland, 1969; BFA, Atlanta Coll. Art, 1983; MFA, Md. Inst. Coll. Art, 1986. Tchr. Teknillinen Oppilaitos, Lahti, Finland, 1969-78; teaching asst. Md. Inst., Coll. of Art, Balt., 1986; artist, owner Siljas Fine Art Studio, Marietta, Ga., 1987—. V.p., creative advisor Pentec Internat. Inc., Marietta, Ga., 1994—; tchr. etching, painting Atlanta Coll. Art, 1997—. Solo exhbns. include Ariel Gallery, N.Y.C., 1987, 350th Anniversary Swedish/Finnish Art, Atlanta, Ga., 1988, Callanwolde Arts Ctr., Atlanta, 1988, Morin-Miller Gallery, N.Y.C., 1989, La Chapelle de la Sorbonne, Paris, 1990, TaideArt Gallery Helsinki, 1987, 88, 91, 92, Internat. Exhbn., Ward-Nasse Gallery, N.Y.C., 1991, Pihagalleria, Lahti, Finland, 1995, Ars Arrakoski, Padasjoki, Finland, 1999, 2000, Nuutti Galleria, Virrat, Finland, 2002; group exhbns. include Scandinavian Artists, Savannah Coll. Art & Design, 1989, La Chapelle de la Sorbonne, Paris, 1990, Ariel Gallery Group Exhbns., N.Y.C., 1987, 89, 90, Med. Coll. Ga., Augusta, 1992, 93, 94, Abney Gallery, N.Y.C., 1993, U. Alaska, Anchorage, 1993, Ward-Nasse Gallery, N.Y.C., 1989-99, Ward-Nasse Gallery Yr. Round Salon, 1999-2002, New Visions Gallery, Atlanta, 1993, Seaside Art Gallery, Nags Head, N.C., 1993, Spruill Ctr. Gallery, Atlanta, 1993, New Ams. Selected by Coca Cola Co., 1996, Telfair Mus. Art, Savannah, 1995, Albany Mus. Art, 1994, San Bernardino Art Mus., 1995, Orgn. of Ind. Artists, N.Y.C., 1995, Rutgers Nat., 1994, Stedman Gallery, City of Atlanta Gallery, Chastain Pk., 1994, Rolling Stone Press Gallery, Printmakers Renaissance, 1996, Atlanta Coll. of Art Juried Alumni Exhbn., 1987, 96, Chattahoochee Valley Art Mus., La Grange, Ga., 1997, Barbara Archer Gallery, Atlanta, 2001, Fabulous Finishes, Inc. and Biasucci Co., 2002, other shows; selected collections include Barbara Archer Gallery, 2001, Trinity Sch., Dr. Weisman Ctr., Lahden Rautateollisuus, Rauma, Vuorineuvos Tauno Matomaki, Helsinki, Pentec Internat. Inc., Markku af Herlin, Helena Jaakonmaki Collection, Hugh and Sirkka Barbour, Boston and others; contbr. various articles to profl. jours. Recipient Internat. Art Competition, Cert. of Excellence in Printmaking, N.Y.C., 1988, Award from FINNAIR to transport exhibit round trip Finland/USA, The State of Ga. award for achievement Ga. Women in the Visual Arts, 1997, Avery Gallery, 2 Painting awards, 1988. Mem.: Womens Caucus Art, Ward Nasse Gallery, Four Winds Soc., Roswell Fine Arts Alliance, Orgn. Ind. Artists, Am. Art Therapy Assn. Lutheran. Avocations: shamanism, trance dance, Zen Buddhism, haiku, yoga. Office: Siljas Fine Art Studio 5220 Sunset Trl Marietta GA 30068-4740

LAI, ERIC PONG SHING, family physician, educator; b. Kowloon, Hong Kong, May 20, 1946; s. Man Hoi and Lai Ming (Chiu) L.; m. Mimi Maria Mak Lai, Sept. 11, 1972; children: Gordon, Jennifer. BSc, Acadia U., Wolfville, Nova Scotia, 1971; MB, B CH, LRCS, LLMRCP, U. Ireland, Dublin, 1977; DFM, Chinese U. Hong Kong, 1989. Med. diplomate, Ireland, UK, Hong Kong. Rsch. fellow Med. Sch. McGill U., Montreal, Can., 1971; resident in medicine Chesterton Hosp. Cambridge (Eng.) U., 1977; resident New Addenbrooke Hosp., Cambridge, 1978; resident in gynecology Princess Margaret Hosp., Kowloon, Hong Kong, 1979-81; pvt. practice family physician Hong Kong, 1981-2001. Bd. dirs. First Med. Mgmt. Ltd., Calgary, Alta., Can., 1989; found. dir. Chinese Recreation Assn., Calgary; lectr. Hong Kong U., 1986-92, Chinese U. Hong Kong, 1986-92; facilitator Hong Kong Coll. Gen. Practitioners, 1986-92; internat. dir. World Orgn. Health Promotion, 1993-2002; cons. G-Way Holdings Internat. Inc., 1993-2002; internat. med. dir. G-Way Health Centre, Can., 1995-2002. Mem. Hong Kong Dem. Found., 1990-92, Hong Kong Bd. Edn. Coll. Gen. Practitioners, 1986-92, chmn., 1991-92, com. chmn. refresher course, 1991-92; vice chmn. found. Kidney Ctr. Precious Blood Hosp., 1991; adviser S.E. Asia Rsch. Inst., 1992; mem. Pub. Edn. Com., 1993-95; med. cons. World Orgn. Health Promotion, Can., 1993-2002. Named Henry Burton De Wolfe scholar to McGill U., 1971. Mem. Internat. Lions Club (v.p. Mt. Cameron chpt. 1986-90, pres. 1990-91, zone chmn. Internat. Club 1991-92, Melvin Jones fellow 1991-2002). Democrat. Avocations: reading, meditation, writing poetry, walking, boxing.

LAI, FENG-QI, instructional designer; b. Shanghai, China, Mar. 25, 1948; came to U.S., 1992; d. Zheng-Zhong Lai and Yao-Zhang Zhu; m. Qun Zhang, Oct. 22, 1984. BA, Changsha (China) Railway Inst., 1982; MS, Purdue U., 1994, PhD, 1997. Asst. lectr. Shanghai Tiedao U., 1982-86, lectr., assoc. dir., 1986-91; instrnl. designer Nat. Edn. Tng. Group, Naperville, Ill., 1998; sr. instr., dir. tng. Advanced Tech. Support, Inc., Schaumburg, 1998-2000; sr. instrnl. designer Cognitive Concepts, Inc., Evanston, 2000—02; asst. prof. Ind. State U., Terre Haute, Ind., 2002—. Transl.: Writing Scientific Papers in English, 1983; co-author: Applied Cryptography, 1999. Mem. Phi Kappa Phi. Avocations: music, reading, Chinese poetry, photography, crafts.

LAI, HUNG-CHANG, computer scientist; s. Shi-Shon Lai and Zho-Zon Lee. MS, Columbia U., 1996. Unix sys. engr. Alliance Capital, N.Y.C., 1996—99; Unix sys. cons. Goldman Sachs, 1999—.

LAI, JUEY HONG, chemical engineer; b. Taipei, Taiwan, Dec. 4, 1936; came to U.S., 1961, naturalized, 1976; s. Kwo-Wang and Chin-Feng L.; m. Li-Huey Chang, June 30, 1968; children: Eric Yo-Ping, Bruce Yo-Sheng. BS in Chem. Engring., Nat. Taiwan U., 1959; MS in Chem. Engring., U. Wash., 1963, PhD in Phys. Chemistry, 1969. Rsch. specialist dept. chemistry U. Minn., 1969-73; prin. research scientist Honeywell Phys. Scis. Ctr., Honeywell, Inc., Bloomington, Minn., 1973-78, sr. prin. research scientist, 1978-83; staff scientist Honeywell Tech. Ctr., Honeywell, Inc., 1983-87; pres. Lai Labs., Inc., Burnsville, Minn., 1988—. Lectr. SUNY, New Paltz, 1983; mem. spl. emphasis rev. panel Nat. Inst. Dental and Craniofacial Rsch./NIH, 2000—01. Author/editor: Polymers for Electronic Applications, 1989; contbr. articles on solid state chemistry, polymer chemistry and dental materials to tech. jours.; rschr. on polymer materials for electronics, gas removal tech., solid state chemistry and dental materials; holder 9 patents in electronic and dental materials. Bd. dirs. Chinese Am. Assn. Minn., 1977-79, Minn. Taiwanese Assn., 1995-97, 1998-2001. Recipient H.W. Sweatt Tech. award, Honeywell, Inc., 1980, Small Bus. Innovation Rsch. award, Dept. Health and Human Svcs., 1990, 1993—95, 1997, 1999. Fellow: Am. Inst. Chemists; mem.: Am. Chem. Soc., Am. Assn. Dental Rsch., Phi Lambda Upsilon, Sigma Xi. Office: Lai Labs Inc 12101 16th Ave S Burnsville MN 55337-2982 E-mail: jlai@aol.com.

LAI, W(EI) MICHAEL, mechanical engineer, educator; b. Amoy, Fukien, China, Nov. 29, 1930; naturalized U.S. citizen, 1967; m. Linda Yu-ling Chu, Dec. 21, 1963. BSCE, Nat. Taiwan U., 1953; MS in Engring. Mech., U. Mich., 1959, PhD, 1962. Asst. prof. mechanics Renssalaer Poly. Inst., Troy, N.Y., 1961-66, assoc. prof., 1967-77, prof., 1978-87, acting dept. chmn., 1986-87; prof. mech. engring. and orthopaedic bioengring. Columbia U., N.Y.C., 1987—, acting chmn. dept. mech. engring., 1995-96, chmn. dept. mech. engring., 1996—. Author: Elements of Elasticity, 1965, Introduction to

Continuum Mechanics, 1974, 3rd edit., 1993. Fellow: ASME (chmn. bioengring. divsn. 1996—97, Melville medal for best paper 1982, Best Paper award bioengring. divsn. 1991, Lissner medal for outstanding achievement in bioengring. 2001), Am. Inst. Med. and Biol. Engring.; mem.: AAAS, Orthopaedic Rsch. Soc., Am. Soc. Biomechanics. Home: 215 W 95th St Apt 9H New York NY 10025-6355 Office: Columbia U Dept Mech Engring W 120th St Mail Code 4703 New York NY 10027

LAI, YOUNG-JOU, industrial engineer; b. Changhou, Taiwan, July 30, 1960; s. Ching-Yen and Ching (Chang) Lai; m. Jochun Wu, July 7, 1990; children: Sunny Yen-Wen, Tony Yen-An. BBA in Indsl. Mgmt. Sci., Nat. Cheng-Kang U., 1983; MS in Indsl. Engring., Kans. State U., 1989, PhD in Ops. Rsch., 1991. Asst. prof. Kans. State U., Manhattan, 1991-96; ops. rsch. analyst HCL Internat., Inc., 1992-96; economist, ops. rsch. specialist Phillips Petroleum Co., Bartlesville, Okla., 1996—2001; economist specialist Phillips China Inc., Beijing, 2001—. Adj. prof. Kansas State U., 1996—; spkr. in field. Author: Fuzzy Mathematical Programming, 1992, Fuzzy Multiple Objective Decision Making, 1994; mem. editl. bd. Computers and Ops. Rsch. Jour.; contbr. articles to profl. jours. including Computers and Ops. Rsch., European Jour. of Operational Rsch., Fuzzy Sets and Systems, IIE Transaction, Internat. Jour. of Prodn. Rsch., Jour. of the Operational Rsch. Soc., Quality and Reliability Engring., others. Recipient 1997 Annual Wingman award of Refinery, Mktg., Transp., Phillips Petroleum Co. Mem. Inst. for Ops. Rsch. and Mgmt. Sci., Internat. Fuzzy Systems Assn., Prodn. and Ops. Mgmt. Soc., Phi Kappa Phi. Avocations: golfing, fishing, running, reading. E-mails. Office: Phillips Petroleum Co PO Box 7000 Bartlesville OK 74004-7000 Home: 936 River Gdn Ea Side Baixinzhuang Vill Housha Yu Shunyi District Beijing 101300 China Office: Phil Petrol Co Rm 1201 Hyundai Millenium Tower 38 Xiaoyun Rd Chaoyang Dist Beijing 100027 China E-mail: yjlai@ppco.com., yjlai@aol.com.

LAIBLE, JON MORSE, retired mathematics educator, dean; b. Bloomington, Ill., July 25, 1937; s. Russell James and Margaret (Herold) L.; m. Jo Ann Ivens, June 14, 1959; children: Kathy Jo, Kenneth Russell, Jackie Ann Laible Muhs, Michael Howard. Student, Carleton Coll., 1955-57; BS, U. Ill., 1959; MA, U. Minn., 1961; PhD, U. Ill., 1967. Asst. prof. Western Ill. U., Macomb, 1962-64; asst. prof., assoc. prof. then prof. math. Ea. Ill. U., Charleston, 1964-80, dean Coll. Liberal Arts and Scis., 1980-93, dean Coll. Scis., 1993-94; ret., 1994. Vis. prof. math. Millikin U., Decatur, Ill., 1994-97. Chmn. citizens cons. coun. Unit #1 Pub. Schs., Charleston, 1975-78; adv. com. Sarah Bush Lincoln Health Ctr., Charleston, 1986; bd. dirs. Ea. Ill. U. Found., 1995-1999, v.p., 1996-98, exec. officer, 1998—, pres., 1998-99; pres. Tarble Arts Ctr. Adv. Bd., 1996-98. Recipient Outstanding Faculty Merit award Ea. Ill. Univ., 1978, Univ. Svc. award, 1991. Mem. Math. Assn. Am. (bd. govs. 1977-80, chmn. com. vis. lectrs. and cons. 1980-88, Disting. Svc. award Ill. sect. 1985), Ill. Sect. Math. Assn. Am. (chmn. 1975, 94), Sigma Xi. Democrat. E-mail: cfjml1@eiu.edu.

LAIBLE-WHITE, SHERRY LYNNE, welfare reform administrator; b. Peoria, Ill., Apr. 7, 1958; d. Elwood Gynne and Virginia Marie (Tiezzi) L.; m. Michael Robert White, Oct. 17, 1992. BS, Ill. State U., 1980; M in Leadership Human Svc. Adminstrn., Bradley U., 1999. V.p. pub. rels., devel. Goodwill Industries Ctrl. Ill., Peoria, 1988-92; mktg. employment specialist Dept. Human Svcs., Office Rehab., 1992-98; employment and tng. splst. Dept. Human Svcs., State of Ill., 1998—. Bd. dirs. Pvt. Industry Coun., Peoria. Mem. Rep. Nat. Orgn. Disability, Washington, 1990-97; mem. alumni bd. Ill. State U., 1992-98. Recipient Peoria Area Bus. Adv. Coun. Leadership award, 1997; named among 40 leaders Under 40 award WMBD Radio, 1997. Mem. Nat. Soc. Fundraising Execs. (vice chair external affairs 1990-91), Women in Mgmt. (v.p. pub. rels. 1991), Leadership Ill. (participant, spkr. 1991-95), Rotary (projects com. chair 1996-98). Independent. Roman Catholic. Avocations: walking, jogging, biking, gardening, canning, decorating. Home: 6332 N Devonshire Dr Peoria IL 61615-2513 Office: Divsn of Cmty Ops Region III 1115 N North St Ste B Peoria IL 61606-1959 E-mail: SLaibleW@aol.com.

LAIBMAN, DAVID, economist, educator; b. New York, N.Y., Dec. 25, 1942; s. Erwin Milton Laibman, Beatrice Rosenberg Laibman; m. Marcia Elaine Klugman; children: Anthony Klugman, Leslie, Raquel Klugman. PhD in Econ., New Sch. for Social Rsch., 1973. Prof. of econ. CUNY, N.Y.C., 1982—. Author: Value, Technical Change and Crisis: Explorations in Marxist Economic Theory, 1992, Capitalist Macrodynamics: A Systematic Introduction, 1997; editor: Science & Society, 1991—. Recipient Edith Henry Johnson Meml. award in Econ., New Sch. for Social Rsch., 1973. Mem.: Union for Radical Polit. Econ. Avocation: Acoustic guitar (ragtime); folk music. Home: 50 Plaza Street E #2C Brooklyn NY 11238 Office: Graduate School CUNY 365 Fifth Avenue New York NY 10016 Personal E-mail: dlaibman@netzero.net.

LAIDIG, WILLIAM RUPERT, retired paper company executive; b. Sterling, Ill., Feb. 3, 1927; s. George and Margaret Anne (Gnewuch) Laidig; m. Lorraine Mae Grom, Jan. 2, 1952 (dec.); children: Ann Marie, Mary Katherine, Margaret Anne, William Andrew. BSM.E., Marquette U., 1949. Registered profl. engr., Ga., Ala., Wis., Ark. Engr. Inland Steel Products, 1949-50, Nekoosa Papers Inc., Port Edwards, Wis., 1950-62, mgr., 1962-66, Ashdown, Ark., 1966-72, mill mgr. Port Edwards, Wis., 1972-75; v.p., resident mgr. Gt. So. Paper Co., Cedar Springs., Ga., 1975-80, sr. v.p., 1979-80, pres., 1980-84; exec. v.p. Gt. No. Nekoosa Corp., Stamford, Conn., 1980-84, pres., chief exec. officer, chmn., dir., 1984-90; chmn. Jaakko Pöyry (USA), Inc., Raleigh, N.C., 1991-92; ret. Pres. Village of Port Edwards, Wis., 1966-67; trustee Marquette U., Milw.; bd. dirs. Tasman Chile Ltd., 1993. Lt. USN, 1952-53. Mem.: Eagle Creek Country (Fla.), K.C., Elks. Roman Catholic. Home: 764 Eagle Creek Dr Apt 301 Naples FL 34113-8012

LAIDLAW, ANDREW R. lawyer; b. Durham, N.C., Aug. 28, 1946; BA, Northwestern U., 1969; JD, U. N.C., 1972. Bar: Ill. 1972. Chair exec com., mem. Seyfarth, Shaw, Chgo., CEO Chicago. Contbr. articles to profl. jours. Mem. ABA (antitrust and securities law coms. 1982—), Barristers. Office: Seyfarth Shaw Mid Continental Plz 55 E Monroe St Ste 4200 Chicago IL 60603-5863

LAIDLAW, HARRY HYDE, JR. entomology educator; b. Apr. 12, 1907; s. Harry Hyde and Elizabeth Louisa (Quinn) L.; m. Ruth Grant Collins, Oct. 26, 1946; 1 child Barbara Scott Laidlaw Murphy. BS, La. State U., 1933, MS, 1934; PhD, U. Wis., 1939. Tchg. asst. La. State U., 1933—34, rsch. asst., 1934—35; prof. biol. sci. Oakland City (Ind.) Coll., 1934—91; state apiarist Ala. Dept. Agr. and Industries, Montgomery, 1941—42; entomologist First Army, N.Y.C., 1946—47; asst. prof. entomology, asst. apiculturist U. Calif., Davis, 1947—53, assoc. prof. entomology, assoc. apiculturist, 1953—59, prof. entomology, apiculturist, 1959—74, prof. entomology emeritus, apiculturist emeritus, 1974; assoc. dean Coll. Agr., 1960—64, chair agr. faculty, staff, 1965—66. Coord. U. Calif.-Egypt Agrl. Devel. Program AID, 1979—83. Author (with J.E. Eckert): Queen Rearing, 1950; author: Instrumental Insemination of Honey Bee Queens, 1977, Contemporary Queen Rearing, 1979, (slide set) Instrumental Insemination of Queen Honey Bees, 1976; author: (with R.E. Page Jr.) Queen Rearing and Bee Breeding, 1998. Trustee Yolo County (Calif.) Med. Soc. Scholarship Com., 1965—83. Capt. AUS, 1942—46, capt. AUSR, 1952, maj. AUSR, 1952, LTC AUSR, 1956. Named honored guest, Tamagawa U., Tokyo, 1980; recipient Cert. of Merit, Am. Bee Jour., 1957, Merit award, Calif. Ctrl. Valley Bee Club, 1974, We. Apicultural Soc., 1980, Gold Merit award, Internat. Fedn. Beekeepers' Assns., 1986, Disting. Svc. award, Ariz. Beekeepers Assn., 1987, Cert. of Appreciation, Calif. State Beekeeper's Assn., 1987, award, Alan Clemson Meml. Found., 1989, Award of Distinction, Coll. Agrl. and Environ. Scis. U. Calif. Davis, 1997; fellow Genetics fellow, Alumni Rsch. Found.; grantee, Rockefeller Found., Brazil, 1954—55, NIH, 1963—66, NSF, 1966—74. Fellow: Soc. Am., Entomol. Soc. Am. (honoree spl. symposium 1990, C.W. Woodworth award Pacific br. 1981), AAAS; mem.: Ret. Officers Assn. (2nd v.p. Sacramento chpt. 1984—86), Nat. Assn. Uniformed Svcs., Am. Soc. Integrative Biology, Am. Inst. Biol. Scis., Scabbard and Blade, Sigma Xi (treas. Davis chpt. 1959—60, v.p. chpt. 1966—67), Alpha Gamma Rho (pres. La. chpt. 1933—34, counsellor We. Province 1960—66). Democrat. Presbyterian. Achievements include determination of cause of failure of attempts to artificially inseminate queen honey bees; invention of instruments and procedures to consistently accomplish same; elucidation of genetic relationships of individuals of polyandrous honey bee colonies; design of genetic procedures for behavioral study and breeding of honey bees for general and specific uses. Home: 761 Sycamore Ln Davis CA 95616-3432 Office: U Calif Dept Entomology Davis CA 95616

LAIDLAW, ROBERT RICHARD, publishing company executive; b. Berwyn, Ill., Mar. 25, 1923; s. John and Mabel Josephine (Howard) L.; m. Evangeline Rene Harrelson, Aug. 12, 1944; children— Andrew Robert, Kimberly, Lisa; m. Marilyn C. Carlson, Sept. 7, 1998. Student, Dartmouth Coll., 1941-42; AB, U. N.C., 1947, JD, 1950. Sales rep. Laidlaw Bros. (textbook pubs.), River Forest, Ill., 1950-58, sales mgr., 1958-60, exec. v.p., 1960-68, pres., 1968-85. Served with USNR, 1942-45. Congregationalist.

LAIDLAW, SAUNDRA See WESTON, SAUNDRA

LAIDLER, DAVID ERNEST WILLIAM, economics educator; b. Tynemouth, Northumberland, Eng., Aug. 12, 1938; s. John Alphonse and Leonora (Gosman) L.; m. Antje Charlotte Breitwisch, Jan. 29, 1965; 1 dau., Nicole Joanna; m. Frances Joan Hutner, Aug. 1960 (div. 1964). B.Sc., London Sch. Econs., 1959; MA, U. Syracuse, 1960; PhD, U. Chgo., 1964; MA, U. Manchester, Eng., 1973. Temporary asst. lectr. London Sch. Econs., 1961-62; asst. prof. U. Calif.-Berkeley, 1963-66; lectr. econs. U. Essex, Colchester, Eng., 1966-69; prof. econs. U. Manchester, 1969-75; vis. prof. econs. Brown U., Providence, 1973; prof. econs. U. Western Ont., London, Can., 1975—. Chair Bank of Montreal, 2000—; mem. econ. adv. panel to Marc Lalonde, minister fin., Ottawa, Ont., 1982-84; research coord. Macdonald Royal Commn., 1984-85; scholar in residence C.D. Howe Inst., 1990-91, adj. scholar, 1991—, Canadian Bankers' Assn. scholar, 2000—; mem. econs. com. Social Sci. Research Council, Gt. Britain, 1972-75; mem. program adv. com. Carnegie-Rochester Pub. Policy Conf. Series, Rochester, Pitts., 1978-79; Lister lecter. Brit. Assn. Advancement Sci., 1972; spl. advisor Bank of Can., 1998-99. Author: The Demand for Money - Theories and Evidence, 1969, Introduction to Microeconomics, 1974, Essays on Money and Inflation, 1975, Monetarist Perspectives, 1982, Taking Money Seriously, 1990, The Golden Age of the Quantity Theory, 1991, (with W. Robson) The Great Canadian Disinflation, 1993, Money and Macroeconomics, Selected Essays, 1997; Fabricating the Keynesian Revolution, 1999; mem. editl. bd. Rev. Econ. Studies, 1970-75, Am. Econ. Rev., 1976-78, Can. Jour. Econs., 1977-79, Jour. Econ. Lit., 1978-91; assoc. editor: Jour. Money, Credit and Banking, 1979—. Rsch. grantee NSF, 1964-66, Social Sci. Rsch. Coun., 1971-76, Social Scis. and Humanities Rsch. Coun. Can., 1977-81, 94-99, 94—, Bradley Found., 1991-96. Fellow Royal Soc. Can., mem. Am. Econ. Assn., Can. Econ. Assn. (exec. com. 1980-83, pres. 1987-88, Douglas Purvis Meml. prize 1994). Home: 345 Grangeover Ave London ON Canada N69 4K8 Office: U Western Ont Dept Econs London ON Canada N6A 5C2 E-mail: Laidler@uwo.ca.

LAIN, DAVID CORNELIUS, health scientist, researcher; b. Savannah, Ga., May 17, 1955; s. Marion Cornelius and Sandra (Weatherly) L.; m. Brenda Kay Gastin, May 24, 1980; children: Candace, Heather. BS, MS, Columbia Pacific U., 1985, PhD, 1987; JD, Newport U., 1996. Diplomate Am. Bd. Forensic Examiners, Am. Bd. Forensic Medicine; lic. respiratory care practitioner. Instr. dept. continuing edn. Ga. So. U., Statesboro, 1983; rsch. devel. coord. Meml. Med. Ctr. Inc., Savannah, Ga., 1983-87; rsch. coord., asst. prof. dept. allied health sci. Med. Coll. Ga., Augusta, 1987—; clin. mgr. Ohmeda Respiratory Care, Columba, Md., 1990-95; clin. mgr., v.p. clin. and program devel. Respironics, Inc., Murrysville, Pa., 1995-2001; pres. Lain Med. Consultants, Inc., Kennesaw, Ga., 1997-2000; pres., CEO Nationwide Sleep Cons., Inc., Murrysville, Cleve., 2001—. Bd. dirs. Ga. Soc. Cardiopulmonary Tech., Atlanta, 1987; mem. Respiratory Therapy Adv. Com., Augusta, 1987-90; cons. Aero-Med. Internat., 1987; rsch. affiliate Siemen Elem., Schaumburg, Ill., 1986; manuscript reviewer Am. Assn. Respiration Therapy, Dallas, 1988, Am. Col. Chest Disease, 1990. Contbr. articles to profl. jours. Recipient Appreciation award Am. Heart Assn., 1985, Outstanding Achievement award Calif. Coll. Health Sci., 1986. Mem. AAAS, So. Med. Assn., N.Y. Acad. Sci., Am. Assn. Respiratory Care, Nat. Bd. Respiratory Care (registered respiratory therapist). Democrat. Achievements include 9 inventions; researchon reduction of peak inspiratory pressure during acute lung injury to reduce latrogenic progression of lung pathology; diagnosis and treatment of newborn jaundice. Home and Office: 5121 Scenic Dr Murrysville PA 15668-1560

LAINCZ, BETSY ANN, nurse; b. Phila., Feb. 7, 1949; d. Harry Ellsworth and Betty Mary (Minton) Henderson; m. Douglas Dardaris, 1968 (div. 1975); children: Amy, Christopher; m. Fred J. Laincz, Jan. 12, 1982; children: Joshua, Emily, Michael. Student, Bucks County C.C., Newtown, 1969-87, Temple U., Phila., 1973, Upper Bucks Sch. of Nursing, Perkasie, 1983, Internat. Sch. of Shiatsu, Doylestown, 1995-96, LaSalle U., 2000—. Lic. nurse, Pa. Staff nurse, mental health technician Doylestown (Penn.) Hosp., 1983-85, data abstractor med. records, 1988-89; nurse, coun., asst. mgr. NutriSystem, Warrington, Pa., 1985-88; nurse Independence Court, Quakerstown, 1991; health svcs. supr. Bucks County Assn. Retarded Citizens, 1992-95; nurse Penn Found. Drug and Alcohol Recovery Ctr., 1996-2000; owner, founder, operator Willow Agy., Perkasie, Pa., 1996—. Mem. supports and standards com. Bucks County Assn. Retarded Citizens, 1995; territory mgr. Healthskil, Fairless Hills and Conshohocken, Pa., 2000—, regional mgr., Pa., 2001—. Editor (newsletter) Serendipity, 1996-98. Mem. United Friends Sch., co-chair fundraising, 1989-97, nominating com., 1995-2000, ann. auction com. 1990-97, devel. com, 1991-92, 98—; active Individual's Person Centered Planning Team, 1994—, Inst. of Noetic Scis., 1993—. Mem. Buck Womens Investment Club (v.p. 1995-2002), The Smithsonian Instn., Libr. of Congress Assn., Nat. Assn. of Investers Corp., Co-op Am., Sierra Club. Republican. Mem. United Ch. Christ. Avocations: reading, writing, art, antiques. Home: 532 W Market St Perkasie PA 18944-1419 E-mail: blaincz@healthskil.com.

LAINE, CLEO (CLEMENTINA DINAH DANKWORTH), singer; b. Southall, Middlesex, Eng., Oct. 28, 1927; d. Alexander and Minnie (Bullock) Campbell; m. George Langridge, 1947 (div.); m. John Philip William Dankworth, 1958; children: Stuart, Alec, Jackie MA (hon.), Open U., 1975; MusD (hon.), Berklee Coll. Music, 1982. Vocalist Dankworth Orch., 1953-58; lead role in Seven Deadly Sins, Edinburgh, Scotland Festival and Sadlers Wells, 1961, in Showboat, 1972; acting roles Edinburgh Festival, 1966, 67, Colette, 1980; appeared in A Time to Laugh, Hedda Gabler, The Women of Troy, The Mystery of Edwin Drood, 1986 (Theatre World award, Tony award nomination), Into the Woods, 1989 (L.A. Drama Critics award nomination); guest appearances symphony orchs. Eng. and abroad; numerous TV appearances and record albums; most recent albums That Old Feeling, 1985, Cleo Sings Sondheim, 1988, Woman to woman, 1989, Jazz, 1991, Nothing Without You (with Mel Torme), 1992, Smilin' Through (with Dudley Moore), 1992, Cleo at Carnegie, 1993, Born on Friday, 1993, A Beautiful Thing, 1994, Blue and Sentimental, 1994, Solitude (with John Dankworth), 1997, The Very Best of Cleo Laine, 1999, A Quintessential Cleo, 2001, Live in Manhattan, 2001; gold records: Feel the Warm, I'm a Song, Live at Melbourne; Platinum records: (with James Galway) Best Friends, Sometimes When We Touch; author: Cleo, an autobiography, 1994. Decorated Order Brit. Empire, Dame Order Brit. Empire; recipient Golden Feather award Los Angeles Times, 1973, Edison award, 1974, Grammy award for best female jazz vocal, 1985, Theatre World award, 1986; named Show Bus. Personality of Yr., Variety Club, 1977, Singer of Yr., TV Times, 1978; Tony nominee, 1986; recipient Theatre World award, 1986, Lifetime Achievement award N.A.R.M., 1990, Brit. Jazz award for best female vocalist, 1990. Office: care Sonoma-Hope Inc 10 Bank St # 55 Rockaway NJ 07866-3428

LAINE, IRIS RUTH, minister, public relations/advertising executive; b. Aurora, Ill., Feb. 8, 1925; d. Herman Carl Butke and Ella Stallman; m. Steven Laine, Nov. 4, 1970; 1 child, Leah Reich; stepchildren: Karen McGivney, David, Mark. BA, Fla. Atlantic U., 1981; postgrad., Harvard Div. Sch., 1983, St. Vincent de Paul Sem., 1985-86; MDiv, Luth. Sem., 1988. Ordained to Evangelical Luth. Ch., 1988. Advt. writer, prodr. Chgo. Advt. Agys. and Sears Roebuck & Co., Chgo., 1950-61; promotion copy chief Chgo. Sun-Times/Daily News, 1962-65; trade rels. dir. Smith, Bucklin & Assocs., Inc., Chgo., 1966—78; v.p., treas. Stirco, Inc., Boca Raton, 1979-82; pastor, preacher Evang. Luth. Ch. in Am., Fla., 1987-95. Author: Getting to Know God, 2001; co-author: Promotion in Foodservice, 1972. Mem. Cmty. Interfaith Coalition, Boca Raton, 1992-94, Women in Ministry, Boca Raton, 1988-90, Tradewinds Conf. Mins., Palm Beach/Martin counties, Fla., 1987-92, Synodical Coun., Evang. Luth. Ch. in Am., Fla., 1989-90; dir. Coun. on Hotel, Restaurant and Instnl. Edn., 1969; dir., sec. Internat. Food Editl. Coun., Nat. Orgn., 1968; vol. Rep. Orgns., Palm Beach County, 1996—. Recipient Award Art Dirs. Club of Chgo., 1964; named Top Ten in TV Pharms. award Am. TV Commls. Festival, 1960. Mem. Rotary Internat., Phi Kappa Phi, Alpha Sigma Lambda. Avocations: writing, social service. Home: 500 S Ocean Blvd Apt 904 Boca Raton FL 33432 Fax: 561-392-4822. E-mail: irislaine@aol.com.

LAINE, KATIE MYERS, communications consultant, executive coach; b. Bluffton, Ohio, Oct. 2, 1947; d. George Emerson and Eleanore (Keeney) Myers; m. Donald Edward Laine (div. Feb. 1990); 1 child, Brett Edward. BS in Edn., S.W. Tex. State U., 1970. Dir. vols. Austin (Tex.) Ctr. for Attitudinal Healing, 1983-86; talk show host Austin Cablevision, 1986-89; community rels. officer Laguna Gloria Art Mus., Austin, 1989-90; spl. events mgr. Ann Richards for Gov. Campaign, 1990—. Profl. TV talk show host Katie Laine and Friends. Mem. Mayor's Adv. Coun., Austin, 1989—, Austin Women's Polit. Caucus, 1989—, Emily's List, 1989—; vol. Mayor Lee Cooke Campaign, 1988, Ann Richards Campaign for Gov., 1989; tchr. Divorce Recovery Clinic; co-chair tng. team Coun. Cmty. Reconcilliation, 1999. Mem. NOW, Women in Communications, Nat. Assn. for Corp. Speaker Activities, Paramount Producers. Avocations: speaking, TV prodn., reading, dancing. Home: 8703 United Kingdom Dr Austin TX 78748-6400

LAING, JAMES THOMAS, retired charitable association administrator; b. Charleston, W.Va., Jan. 2, 1934; s. James Tamplin and Claire (Lenila) Laing; m. Patricia Ann Boehmer, June 25, 1955 (div. Mar. 1976); children: Michael Thomas, Susan Kay; m. Barbara Jean Crossman, Apr. 11, 1981. AB, Kent (Ohio) State U., 1955, MA, 1956. Asst. exec. dir. United Cmty. Svcs., Lorain, Ohio, 1959-64; assoc. exec. sec. United Fund, Canton, 1964-69, exec. dir. St. Joseph, Mo., 1969-73, United Way, South Bend, Ind., 1973-76, United Way of Oakland County, Pontiac, Mich., 1976-97, pres., 1997-99; ret., 1999. Instr. sociology Kent State U., St. Mary's Coll., South Bend, Oakland U., Rochester, Mich., 1959-80; field cons. United Health Founds., N.Y.C., 1967-71; mem. profl. adv. com. United Way Am., Alexandria, Va., 1979-84; mem. profl. adv. bd. United Way Internat., 1981-96. Bd. dirs. Internat. Bluegrass Music Mus., Owensboro, Ky., 1994—, treas. bd., 1999-2001; bd. dirs. United Way Mich., 1999-2000; v.p. United Way Nat. Retiree Assn., 2000—, bd. dirs., 1998—, v.p. 2000—. 1st lt. USAF, 1956-59. Mem. Rotary (past pres.), Blue Key, Phi Sigma Kappa, Alpha Kappa Delta, Pi Gamma Mu. Methodist. Avocations: bluegrass music, golf, photography. Home: 3254 Angelus Dr Waterford MI 48329-2512

LAING, KAREL ANN, magazine publishing executive; b. Mpls., July 5, 1939; d. Edward Francis and Elizabeth Jane Karel (Templeton) Hannon; m. G. R. Cheesebrough, Dec. 19, 1959 (div. 1969); 1 child, Jennifer Read; m. Ronald Harris Laing, Jan. 6, 1973; 1 child, Christopher Harris Grad., U. Minn., 1960. With Guthrie Symphony Opera Program, Mpls., 1969-71; account supr. Colle & McVoy Advt. Agy., Richfield, Minn., 1971-74; owner The Cottage, Edina, 1974-75; salespromotion rep. Robert Meyers & Assocs., St. Louis Park, 1975-76; cons. Webb Co., St. Paul, 1976-77, custom pub. dir., 1977-89; pres. K.L. Publs., Inc., Bloomington, Minn., 1989—. Contbr. articles to profl. jours. Community vol. Am. Heart Assn., Am. Cancer Soc., Edina PTA; charter sponsor Walk Around Am., St. Paul, 1985 Mem. Bank Mktg. Assn., Fin. Instn. Mktg. Assn., Advt. Fedn. Am., Am. Bankers Assn., Direct Mail Mktg. Assn., Minn. Mag. Pub. Assn. (founder, bd. govs.), St. Andrews Soc. Republican. Presbyterian. Avocations: painting; gardening; reading; traveling. Office: KL Publs 2001 Killebrew Dr Minneapolis MN 55425-1865

LAING, MALCOLM BRIAN, geologist, consultant; b. Apr. 4, 1955; s. Alexander Duncan and Joan (Dawson) L.; m. Vicki Lynne; children: Megan Jenè, Brian Duncan. BS in Geology, Tex. Christian U., 1978. Geologist Electro-Seise, Inc., Ft. Worth, 1978-79, Exploration Logging Co., Houston, 1979-80, Thomas-Powell Royalty Co., Ft. Worth, 1980-82, Lentex Petroleum Inc., Abilene, Tex., 1982-84; cons., 1984-90, Tex. Dept. Health, 1990-92, Tex. Water Commn., 1992-93, Tex. Natural Resource Conservation Commn., 1993—. World wide cons. on WWII German aircraft. Co-author: FW-190D Walk Around, FW 190A/F Walkaround. Dir. Caprock chpt.; bd. dirs. Tex. Air Mus., 1995—, Cactus Air Force, 2000—. Mem. Am. Assn. Petroleum Geologists, West Tex. Wing Confederate Air Force (past fin. officer, past CAF check pilot, past ops. officer). Republican. Methodist. Office: 4630 50th St Ste 600 Lubbock TX 79414-3520

LAING, THOMAS DALLAS, JR. marine surveyor, salvage consultant; b. Biloxi, Miss., Oct. 17, 1943; s. Thomas Dallas and Norma Lee (Wininger) L.; m. Judy Marcela Ledesma, Apr. 4, 1981; 1 child, Robyn Jessica; 1 child from previous marriage, Thomas Dallas III. Student in drafting, ship constrn., Jackson County Jr. Coll., 1963-64; student in marine and indsl. welding and constrn., Southmost Coll., 1976. Lic. U.S. Mcht. Marine 3000 Gross Ton master. From deckhand to capt. various comml. fishing trawlers, Gulf of Mex., 1962-63; ship fitter Ingalls Shipbldg., Pascagoula, Miss., 1963-64; various positions including port capt. Wm. B. Rudolf, Inc., New Orleans, 1965-73; port capt. Black Gold Marine, Inc., 1973-74; marine surveyor Rivers and Gulf Marine, Inc., New Orleans and Brownsville, Tex., 1975-76; owner T. Laing and Assocs. and Tex. Torpedo, Inc., Brownsville, 1976-80; marine surveyor John L. Kingston and Assocs., Inc., Houston, 1980-83; owner Comml. Marine Service, 1983—. Marine surveyor and cons. to various marine ins. cos., 1974—; loss control cons. Gulf Coast Towboat Assn., Houston, 1985—; marine salvage cons. Otis Engring., New Orleans, 1986—; qualified expert witness on marine-related cases U.S. Fed. Ct., Tex., 1980-86, Tex. Dist. Ct., 1986, USCG, 1987; apptd. to comml. fishing industry adv. com. Sec. of Transp., 1989-91, chmn. sub-com., 1989-91. Inventor round type double twin shrimp trawl separator, 1977; originator ship engine exhaust system; contbg. author: Gulf Coast Fishing Manual. Mem. Nat. Assn. Marine Surveyors (cert.; bd. dirs., West Gulf regional v.p. 1988-92, nat. v.p. 1996-98, nat. pres. 1998-2000), Soc. Naval Architects and Marine Engrs., Am. Yacht and Boat Coun., Tex. A&M U. Sea Grant Program, Nat. Coun. Fishing Vessel Safety and Ins., Houston Mariners Club. Avocations: model sailing ships, guitar, sailing. Office: Comml Marine Svc PO Box 33836 Seattle WA 98133-0836

LAINGEN, LOWELL BRUCE, diplomat; b. Odin Twp., Minn., Aug. 6, 1922; s. Palmer K. and Ida Mabel (Eng) L.; m. Penelope Babcock, June 1, 1957; children: William Bruce, Charles Winslow, James Palmer. BA cum laude, St. Olaf Coll., 1947; MA in Internat. Relations, U. Minn., 1949. Internat. rels. officer State Dept., 1949-50; joined U.S. Fgn. Svc., 1950; vice consul Hamburg, Germany, 1951-53; 3d sec. embassy Teheran, Iran, 1953-54; consul Meshed, Iran, 1954-55; asst., then officer chargé Greek affairs State Dept., 1956-60; 2d sec., then 1st sec. embassy Karachi, Pakistan, 1960-64; with Pakistan/Afghanistan affairs bur. State Dept., 1964-67; assigned Nat. War Coll., 1967-68; dep. chief mission to Afghanistan Kabul, 1968-71; country dir. Pakistan, Afghanistan and Bangladesh, State Dept., 1971-73, India, Nepal, Sri Lanka and the Maldives, 1973-74, acting dep. asst. sec. state for Near Eastern and South Asian affairs, 1974-75, dep. asst. sec. state for European affairs, 1975-76; ambassador to Malta, 1977-79; chargé d'affaires Am. Embassy, Teheran, Iran, 1979; held hostage by Iranian student militants, 1979-81; v.p. Nat. Def. U., Ft. McNair, Washington, 1981-86; exec. dir. Nat. Commn. Pub. Service, Washington, 1987-90; pres. Am. Acad. Diplomacy, 1991—. Lectr. Security Overseas Seminar, Fgn. Svc. Inst., 1995-2000; Sol Linowitz chair in internat. rels. Hamilton Coll., 1998. Recipient Fgn. Svc. cup, 1998. Home: 5627 Old Chester Rd Bethesda MD 20814-1035

LAINWALA, SHABNAM, pediatrician; b. Bombay, India, Nov. 26, 1965; d. Hannan and Hafiza Lainwala; m. Anjum Majeed. MB BChir, Grant Med. Coll., Bombay, 1989; PhD, Clark U., 1995. Rsch. asst. Clark U., Worcester, Mass., 1990—95, tchg. staff, 1990—95; postdoctoral fellow Beth Israel Hosp., Boston, 1995—96; house staff Maimonides Med. Ctr., N.Y.C., 1996—99; fellow New Eng. Med. Ctr., Boston, 1999—. Recipient Greater Bombay Tchrs. Assn. award, 1983, Natalie Zucker Women's Found. award, 2000. Mem.: Am. Acad. Pediats. Home: #E34 15 Spencer Rd Acton MA 01719 Office: New Eng Med Ctr 750 Washington St Acton MA 01719 Home Fax: 978-266-2905; Office Fax: 617-636-1456. Personal E-mail: slainwala@hotmail.com. Business E-mail: slainwala@lifespan.org.

LAIOU, ANGELIKI EVANGELOS, history educator; b. Athens, Greece, Apr. 6, 1941; came to U.S., 1959; d. Evangelos K. and Virginia I. (Apostolides) Laios; m. Stavros B. Thomadakis, July 14, 1973; 1 son, Vassili N. BA, Brandeis U., 1961; MA, Harvard U., 1962, PhD, 1966. Asst. prof. history

Harvard U., Cambridge, Mass., 1969-72, Dumbarton Oaks prof. Byzantine history, 1981—; assoc. prof. Brandeis U., Waltham, 1972-75; prof. Rutgers U., New Brunswick, N.J., 1975-79, disting. prof., 1979-81; chmn. Gennadeion com. (Am. Sch. Classical Studies), Athens, Greece, 1981-84; dir. Dumbarton Oaks, 1989-98; prof. history Harvard U., Cambridge, 1998—. Mem. Greek Parliament, 2000—2002. Author: Constantinople and the Latins, 1972, Peasant Society in the Late Byzantine Empire, 1977, Mariage, amour et parenté à Byzance, XIe-XIIIe siècles, 1992, Gender, Society and Economic Life in Byzantium, 1992, Consent and Coercion to Sex and Marriage in Ancient and Medieval Societies, 1993. Guggenheim Found. fellow, 1971-72, 79-80, Dumbarton Oaks sr. fellow, 1983—, Am. Coun. Learned Socs. fellow, 1988-89. Fellow Am. Acad. Arts and Scis., Medieval Acad., Acad. Athens; mem. Am. Hist. Assn., Medieval Acad. Am., Societa Ligure di Storia Patria, Greek Com. Study of South Eastern Europe. Office: Harvard U Dept History Cambridge MA 02138 E-mail: laiou@fas.harvard.edu.

LAIRD, BETTY ANN, writer, researcher, actress; b. Grand Island, Nebr., Dec. 19, 1925; d. Myron E. and Anna L. (Youtsey) Olson; m. Roy D. Laird, Sept. 3, 1946; children: Claude M., David A., Heather L. BA cum laude, Hastings (Nebr.) Coll., 1948. Tchr. Walnut Jr. H.S., Grand Island, 1949-50; curriculum advisor U. Wash., Seattle, 1955-56; asst. instr. English U. Kans., Lawrence, 1958-63, adminstr. Polish program, 1972-73, guest rsch. asst., 1982-83; ind. rsch. analyst, 1970—; co-founder Parker-Laird Enterprises, Overbrook, Kans., 1976-2000, also bd. dirs. Author: Tea and Empathy: The University Women's Club Centennial History, 1999; co-author: (with Roy D. Laird) Soviet Communism and Agrarian Revolution, 1970, To Live Long Enough: The Memoirs of Naum Jasny, Scientific Analyst, 1976, A Soviet Lexicon: Important Concepts and Phrases, 1988, (with Martha Parker) Soil of our Souls: Histories of Clinton Lake Area Communities, 1976, 5th edit., 1994; co-editor: The Future of Agriculture in the Soviet Union and Eastern Europe, 1977, The Political Economy of Collectivized Agriculture: A Comparative Study of Communist and Non-Communist Systems, 1979; contbr. articles to K.C. Times and Okla. Today; prodr. mus. exhibits and plays; actress various T.V. movies and commercials. Bd. dirs. Douglas County Hist. Soc., Lawrence, 1987-94, Douglas County Rural Water Dist., 1987-92; mem. Douglas County Bd. Zoning Appeals, 1981-83. Grantee Naum Jasny Family Found., 1974. Mem. SAG. Avocations: folk singing, gardening. E-mail: MIRovna@aol.com.

LAIRD, CLEVE W. biomedical researcher, consultant; b. Montclair, N.J., Mar. 29, 1938; s. George Alvin and Cecily Watrous Laird; m. Elizabeth Fort Cortelyou; children: Kevin, Brian. BA, Gettysburg Coll., 1957—61; MS, U. Neb., 1961—63; PhD, Rutgers State U., 1963—68. Cert. radiation biology 1967. Dir. biol. rsch. Hycel, Inc., Houston, 1971—74; rsch. biologist Bioresearch Inst., Boston, 1974—76; dir. biol. rsch. Block Engring., Cambridge, 1976—81; new product devel. Internat. Remote Imaging Sys., Chatsworth, Calif., 1986—89; pres. & CEO Drial Con., Inc., Simi Valley, 1987—2001; exec. v.p. Tech. Chem. & Prod. Inc., Fort Lauderdale, Fla., 1991—97; dir. new product devel. Union Carbide, Terrytown, NY. Contbr. jour., scientific papers tech. book chpt. Fellow NIH predoctoral fellow, NIH, 1963—71. Mem.: Nat. Rifle Assn. (instr., coach 1958—2001). Avocations: wood working, marine models, shooting. Office: Drial Cons Inc 2139 Tapo St Simi Valley CA 93063 Office Fax: 805-522-1526. Personal E-mail: Diabetes@ix.netcom.com. Business E-Mail: Diabetes@ix.netcom.com.

LAIRD, DAVID, humanities educator emeritus; b. Marshfield, Wis., Oct. 17, 1927; s. Melvin Robert and Helen Melissa (Connor) L.; m. Helen Astrid Lauritzen, Sept. 10, 1955; 1 child, Vanessa Ann. PhB, U. Chgo., 1947; BA with highest honor, U. Wis., 1950, MA, 1951, PhD, 1955; postgrad., Courtauld Inst., 1953. Instr. to asst. prof. Oberlin Coll., 1955-58; mem. faculty Calif. State U., L.A., 1958—, chmn. dept. English, 1969-73, chmn. dept. Am. studies, 1977-79. Nat. Humanities Inst. fellow U. Chgo., 1978-79; sr. Fulbright lectr. U. Tunis, Tunisia, 1979-80; fellow Folger Shakespeare Libr., 1982; Fulbright lectr. Odense U. (Denmark), 1983-84; vis. prof. U. Ottawa, 1984-85; cons. to Choice. Mem. editorial bd. Jour. Forest History; contbr. articles on Shakespeare, Am. lit. and cultural history to profl. jours. Mem. Western Shakespeare Seminar, Friends of Huntington Libr. Recipient Outstanding Prof. award Calif. State U., 1987, Nat. Endowment for the Humanities Summer Seminar award Northwestern U., 1989; Uhrig Found. grantee, 1964-65; Fulbright fellow, 1953-54. Mem. MLA, Malone Soc., Am. Studies Assn., Phi Beta Kappa. Home: 208 S Cherry Ave Marshfield WI 54449-3732 Office: Calif State U Humanities Dept Los Angeles CA 90032

LAIRD, DORIS ANNE MARLEY, humanities educator, musician; b. Charlotte, N.C., Jan. 15, 1931; d. Eugene Harris and Coleen (Bethea) Marley; m. William Everette Laird Jr., Mar. 13, 1964; children: William Everette III, Andrew Marley, Glen Howard. MusB, Converse Coll., Spartanburg, S.C., 1951; opera cert., New Eng. Conservatory, Boston, 1956; MusM, Boston U., 1956; PhD, Fla. State U., 1980. Leading soprano roles S.C. Opera Co., Columbia, 1951-53, Plymouth Rock Ctr. of Music and Art, Duxbury, Mass., 1953-56; soprano Pro Musica, Boston, 1956, New Eng. Opera Co., Boston, 1956; instr. Stratford Coll., Danville, Va., 1956-58, Sch. Music Fla. State U., Tallahassee, 1958-60, dept. humanities, 1960-68; tchr. Fla. State U., 1973-79; asst. prof. Fla. A&M U., Tallahassee, 1979-89, assoc. prof., 1990—. Vis. scholar Cornell U., 1988; participant So. Conf. on Afro-Am. Studies, Inc. Author: Colin Morris: Modern Missionary, 1980; contbr. articles to profl. jours. Soprano Washington St. Meth. Ch., Columbia, S.C., 1951-53, Copley Meth. Ch., Boston, 1953-56; soloist Trinity United Meth. Ch., Tallahassee, 1983—; mem. Saint Andrews Soc., Tallahassee, 1986—; judge Brain Bowl, Tallahassee, 1981-84. Named subject of article in Glamour mag., 2001; recipient NEH award, 1988, Disting. Alumna award, Converse Coll., 2001; scholar Phi Sigma Tau, 1960. Mem. AAUP, AAUW, Nat. Art Educators Assn., Tallahassee Music Tchrs. Assn., Tallahassee Music Guild, Am. Guild of Organists, DAR (mus. rep. 1984-85), Colonial Dames of 17th Century (music dir. 1984-85), Nat. Assn. Humanities Edn., U. Wyo. Women's Club. Democrat. Avocations: travel, dancing. Home: 1125 Mercer Dr Tallahassee FL 32312-2833 Office: Fla A&M U Dept Humanities Room 405 Tucker Hall Tallahassee FL 32307 Personal E-mail: wlaird@garnet.acns.fsu.edu. Business E-Mail: dorislaird@famu.edu.

LAIRD, FRANK N. political science educator; b. Ashtabula, Ohio, Dec. 12, 1952; s. Frank Earl and Mary Yolanda (Fiori) L.; m. Pamela Walker, June 17, 1989. BA, Middlebury Coll., 1975; postgrad., Edinburgh (Scotland) U., 1975-76; PhD, MIT, 1985. Postdoctoral rsch. fellow Harvard U., Cambridge, Mass., 1985-87; asst. prof. U. Denver, 1987-94; assoc. prof., 1994—. Cons. Sigma Xi, New Haven, Conn., 1985. Contbr. articles to profl. jours. Rsch. grantee NSF. Mem. Am. Polit. Sci. Assn., AAAS, Soc. for Risk Analysis, Assn. for Pub. Policy Analysis and Mgmt., Soc. for Social Studies of Sci. Office: U Denver Grad Sch Internat Studies Denver CO 80208-0001

LAIRD, JEAN ELOUISE RYDESKI (MRS. JACK E. LAIRD), author, adult education educator; b. Wakefield, Mich., Jan. 18, 1930; d. Chester A. and Agnes A. (Petranek) Rydeski; m. Jack E. Laird, June 9, 1951; children: John E., Jayne E., Joan Ann P., Jerilyn S., Jacquelyn T. Bus. Edn. degree, Duluth (Minn.) Bus. U., 1948; postgrad., U. Minn., 1949-50. Tchr. Oak Lawn (Ill.) H.S. Adult Evening Sch., 1964-72, St. Xavier Coll., Chgo., 1974—. Lectr., commencement address cir.; writer newspaper column Around The House With Jean, A Woman's Work, 1965-70, Chicagotown News column The World As I See It, 1969, hobby column Modern Maturity mag., travel column Travel/Leisure mag., beauty column Ladycom mag., Time and Money Savers column Lady's Circle mag., consumerism column Ladies' Home Jour. Author: Lost in the Department Store, 1964, Around the House Like Magic, 1968, Around the Kitchen Like Magic, 1969, How to Get the Most from Your Appliances, 1967, Hundreds of Hints for Harassed Homemakers, 1971, The Alphabet Zoo, 1972, The Plump Ballerina, 1971, The Porcupine Story Book, 1974, Fried Marbles and Other Fun Things to Do, 1975, Hundreds of Hints for Harassed Homemakers: The Homemaker's Book of Time and Money Savers, 1979, Homemaker's Book of Energy Savers, 1981; also 427 paperback booklets; contbr. articles to mags. Mem.: Marist, Mt. Assissi Acad., St. Linus Guild, Queen of Peace Parents Clubs, Oak Lawn Bus. and Profl. Women's Club, Canterbury Writers Club Chgo. Roman Catholic. Home: 10540 Lockwood Ave Oak Lawn IL 60453-5161 also: Vista De Lago Lake Geneva WI 53147 also: Harbor Towers Yacht Club Siesta Key FL 34242

LAIRD, MARY See WOOD, LARRY

LAIRD, WILBUR DAVID, JR. bookseller, editor; b. Kansas City, Mo., Mar. 15, 1937; s. Wilbur David and Alma Blanche (Turner) L.; children: Wendy, Cynthia, Brian Andrew, David Alexander; m. Helen M. Ingram, July 12, 1984. Student, U. Wichita, 1959-60; BA, UCLA, 1965, MLS, 1966. Reference libr. U. Calif., Davis, 1966-67; acquisitions libr. U. Utah, 1967-70, asst. dir. for tech. svcs., 1970-71, assoc. dir., 1971-72; univ. libr. U. Ariz., Tucson, 1972-90; pres. Books West S.W., 1990—. Author: Hopi Bibliography, 1977; editor: Books of the Southwest, 1977-97. Bd. dirs. Westerners Internat., 1974-87, Tucson Civic Ballet, 1975-76, S.W. Pks. and Mon. Assn., 1993—. With USN, 1955-59. Mem. ALA, Ariz. State Libr. Assn. (pres. 1978-79), Western History Assn., Western Lit. Assn., Guild Ariz. Antiquarian Booksellers. Office: Books West Southwest Inc 4749 E San Francisco St Tucson AZ 85712 E-mail: wdlbks@cox.net.

LAIRD, WILLIAM EVERETTE, JR. economics educator, administrator; b. Hattiesburg, Miss., Feb. 4, 1934; s. William Everette and Mildred Alva (Howard) L.; m. Doris Anne Marley, Mar. 13, 1964; children: William Everette III, Andrew Marley, Glen Howard. BS, Stetson U., 1956; MA, George Washington U., 1958; PhD, U. Va., 1962. Asst. prof. Fla. State U., Tallahassee, 1960-66, assoc. prof., 1966-71, prof., 1971—, chmn. dept. econs., 1974-97, SERVICE prof., 1997—2002, prof. emeritus, 2002—. Contbr. articles to profl. jours. DuPont fellow, 1959-60; recipient awards Fla. State U. Grad. Research Council, 1965, 66, Faculty Devel. awards Fla. State U., 1971 Mem. Am. Econs. Assn., So. Econ. Assn., Plantagenet Soc. Magna Charta Barons Club, Jamestowne Soc., St. Andrew Soc., Order of First Families of Va. Methodist. Home: 1125 Mercer Dr Tallahassee FL 32312-2833 Office: Fla State U Dept Econs Tallahassee FL 32306-2180 E-mail: wlaird@garnet.acns.fsu.edu.

LAISURE, THOMAS JAMES, artist, sculptor; b. Kansas City, Mo., Dec. 17, 1960; s. Thomas Edward and Bette Anne (Stewart) L. BFA, Kans. State U., Manhattan, 1984. Illustrator, designer Ho. Lloyd, Grandview, Mo., 1984; designer So. Hemisphere Aerostat Rsch. Expedition., Lenexa, Kans., 1986-88; sculptor Kansas City, 1985—. Judge Shooting Stars Recognition and Scholarship awards, Johnson County, Kans., 1999, 2000. Prin. works include Into Thy Hand, Shawnee Mission Med. Ctr., 1992, Glory Unto God, 1996, Black Swans, McPherson Meml. Hosp., 1996; designer board game BrainTwister, 1988 (named One of Top 25 Games Chgo. Tribune 1988). Recipient purchase award Lenexa Arts Coun., 1988, People's Choice award Nat. 3-Dimentional Art Show, 1989, 1st place award Trinity Lutheran Religious Art Show, Mission, Kans., 2000. Avocations: golf, tennis, indoor soccer, fencing, snow skiing.

LAIT, HAYDEN DAVID, lawyer; b. Bangor, Maine, Dec. 18, 1947; s. Saul and Marion (Pepper) L.; m. Kay Scruggs, Mar. 10, 1982; children: Erin Middleton, David Middleton. BBA, U. Okla., 1969; JD, Memphis State U., 1975. Bar: Tenn., U.S. Dist. Ct. (we. dist.) Tenn. Pvt. practice, Memphis, 1975—. Instr. constitutional law Shelby State Coll., Memphis, 1977-78; vol. U.S. Peace Corps, Kuala Lumpur, Malaysia, 1969-71; pres. Memphis State U. Law, Alumni Nat. Chpt., 1988; adj. prof. law U. Memphis Sch. Law., 1998—. Dir. Shelby Residential and Vocat., Memphis, 1987-89. Fellow Am. Coll. Civil Trial Mediators; mem. Memphis Bar Assn., Memphis Trial Lawyers (bd. govs. 1977). Office: 266 S Front St # 206 Memphis TN 38103-3803

LAITIN, DAVID DENNIS, political science educator; b. Bklyn., June 4, 1945; s. Daniel and Frances (Blumenkranz) L.; m. Delia Fortune; children: Marc Oliver, Anna Elizabeth. BA, Swarthmore Coll., 1967; PhD, U. Calif., Berkeley, 1974. Instr. Nat. Tchr. Edn. Ctr., Afgoy, Somalia, 1969; master Grenada Boys' Secondary Sch., West Indies, 1970-71; asst. prof. dept. polit. sci. U. Calif.-San Diego, La Jolla, 1975-79, prof., 1984-87, chmn., 1986-87; reader dept. polit. sci. U. Ife, Nigeria, 1979-80; prof. polit. sci., dir. Wilder House Ctr. for Study Politics, History and Culture U. Chgo., 1987-99, William R. Kenan, Jr. prof., 1992-99; prof. polit. sci. Stanford (Calif.) U., 1999—. Expert witness fgn. affairs subcom. U.S. Ho. Reps., 1981; resident Rockefeller Found., Bellagio Ctr., Sept. 1996. Author: Politics, Language and Thought: The Somali Expereience, 1977, Hegemony and Culture: Politics and Religious Change Among the Yoruba, 1986, Somalia: A Nation in Search of a State, 1987, Language Repertoires and State Construction in Africa, 1992, Identity in Formation: The Russian-Speaking Populations of the Near Abroad, 1998. Fellow NEH, 1979-80, Howard Found., 1984-85, German Marshall Fund, 1984-85, John Simon Guggenheim Found., 1995-96, Harry F. Guggenheim Found., 1997—, Ctr. for Advanced Study in Behavioral Scis., 19989-2000; co-prin. investigator award NSF, 1993-95, 2002—; recipient award Am. Assn. for the Advancement of Slavic Studies, Dogan award Soc. for Comparative Rsch.; co-prin. investigator award Carnegie Found., 2000-01. Mem. Am. Polit. Sci. Assn. (2 awards), Am. Acad. Arts and Scis., Coun. Am. Polit. Sci. Assn. Office: Stanford U Dept Polit Sci Stanford CA 94305 E-mail: dlaitin@stanford.edu.

LAJE, ZILIA L. writer, publisher, translator; b. Havana, Cuba, Feb. 1, 1941; came to U.S., 1961; d. Luis B. Laje and Zilia Isabel Bello; divorced; 1 child, Alberto Luis Dominguez. Comml. acct., Escuela Profl. de Comercio, Havana, 1959-61; AA in Bus. Adminstrn., Miami-Dade C.C., 1989. Export documentation clk. Pittsburgh Plate Glass Internat., Havana, 1959-60; agy. sec. Occidental Life Ins. Co., Miami, 1962-67; sec. to v.p./br. mgr. Chgo. Title Ins. Co., 1972-76; corp. banking asst. S.E. Bank, N.A., Miami Springs, Fla., 1978-90; writer, transl. Miami, 1991—. Exhibitor Miami Book Fair Internat., 1995—. Author: La Cortina de Bagazo, 1995, The Sugar Cane Curtain, 2000, Cartas Son Cartas, 2001. Mem.: PEN Ctr. for Writers in Exile, Writer's N.Y., Cuban Writers in Miami (founder, assoc.), Women's Nat. Book Assn. (corr.). Republican. Roman Catholic. Avocations: needlepoint, photography, travel. Office: Escritores Cubanos de Miami PO Box 45-1732 Miami FL 33245-1732 E-mail: guarinapub@juno.com.

LAJEUNESSE, RAYMOND JOHN, JR. lawyer; b. Glens Falls, N.Y., Dec. 6, 1942; s. Raymond John and Frances Louise (Bigonesse) L.; m. Jade Christine West, Aug. 16, 1975. BA in Humanities, cum laude, Providence Coll., R.I., 1964; LLB, Washington and Lee U., Lexington, Va., 1967. Bar: Va., D.C. Rsch. dir. United Republicans of Am., Washington, 1967-68; political rsch. cons. pvt. practice, 1969-71; legis. asst. Va. House of Delegates, Richmond, 1972-73; staff atty. Nat. Right to Work Legal Defense Found., Springfield, Va., 1971-2001, v.p., legal dir., 2001—. Contbr. articles to profl. jours. Advisor labor-related agys., Office Pres.-Elect, Washington, 1980; mem. Arlington Co. Manpower Planning Coun., 1976-82, Arlington Co. Bd. Legis. Adv. Com., 1971-72, Va. Republican State Ctrl. Com., Richmond, 1973-83. Mem.: Federalist Soc. (exec. com. labor and employment practice group 2000—). Office: Nat Right to Work Legal Def Found 8001 Braddock Rd Ste 600 Springfield VA 22160-0001 E-mail: rjl@nrtw.org.

LAJINESS-POLOSKY, DANINE THERESA, psychiatric-mental health nurse, pediatric nurse; b. Toledo, Oct. 16, 1961; d. Ambrose Joseph and Sharon Joyce (Montrie) Lajiness; m. John Daniel Polosky III, Apr. 21, 1990. BSN, U. Detroit-Mercy, 1984; student, U. Toledo, 1988, Med. Coll. of Ohio, 1988; MN, U. Phoenix, 1994. Cert. psychiat.-mental health; RN cert. Adult psychiat. nurse St. Charles Hosp., Oregon, Ohio, 1984-87; adult psychiat. clin. instr. Med. Coll. of Ohio, Toledo, 1987-88; crisis unit supr. New Rescue Crisis Svcs., 1987-88; adult med. nurse Mercy-Meml. Hosp., Monroe, Mich., 1988; child pscyhiat. nurse Charter Hosp. of Aurora (Colo.), 1989-90, asst. dir. nursing, 1990; pediatric float nurse Children's Hosp., Denver, 1991, clin. coord. After Hours Care Program, 1991-95; v.p. quality improvement Six County, Inc., Zanesville, Ohio, 1995—. Republican. Roman Catholic.

LAJOHN, LAWRENCE ANTHONY, research scientist; b. Jamestown, N.Y., Apr. 23, 1949; s. Anthony Raymond and Anne Theresa La John. BA, Ohio No. U., 1971; MS, George Washington U., 1976, Clarkson U., 1988, PhD, 1990. Chemist NIH, Bethesda, Md., 1972-76; rsch. asst. Miles Labs., Elkhart, Ind., 1976-77; U. Notre Dame, South Bend, 1977-78; So. Ill. U., Carbondale, 1978-82; Queen's U., Can., 1982-84; Clarkson U., 1985-90; postdoctoral fellow Dept. Applied Math., U. Western Ont., London, 1990-93; rsch. scientist dept. physics & astronomy U. Pitts., Pa., 1993—. Physics instr. U. Pitts., Carnegie Mellon U., Duquesne U. Contbr. articles to profl. jours. Mem. AAAS, Am. Chem. Soc., Am. Math. Soc., Am. Phys. Soc., Math. Assn. Am., N.Y. Acad. Sci., Sigma Xi. Avocations: weight lifting, baseball, bowling. Office: Dept Physics & Astronomy Univ Pitts Pittsburgh PA 15260 E-mail: lajohn@stribor,phyast.pitt.edu.

LAJOIE, RANDY, race car driver; Race car driver NASCAR. Achievements include all-time money won leader Busch Series; Busch North Series champion, 1985; Busch Series champion, 1996, 97; winner Daytona season opener, 2001. Office: c/o Evans Motorsports PO Box 177 128 S Iredell Indsl Pk Rd # 7 Mooresville NC 28115*

LAJOIE, RICHARD JOHN, JR. information technology executive; b. Kansas City, Mo., Apr. 10, 1947; s. Richard John Lajoie and Julia Hortense Bush; m. Mary Alice Herod, Aug. 21, 1971; children: Richard, Molly. BBA in Fin., U. Notre Dame, 1969; MBA, Xavier U., 1972. CPA Va. Staff acct. Peat Marwick Mitchell (KPMG), Washington, Cin., 1972—77; internal audit mgr., dir. fin. acctg., v.p. and contr. plastics divsn. Clopay Corp., Cin., 1977—87; v.p., corp. contr. Structural Dynamics Rsch. Corp., Milford, 1987—94; CFO Cad Cam Inc., Dayton, 1995—96, Gen. Revenue Corp., Cin., 1996—97; CFO, CIO, pres. info. tech. divsn., pers. multi-media svs. divsn. Belcan Corp., 1997—. Bd. dirs. Applied Tech. Cons., Cleve., Gen. Revenue Corp., Cin. Mem. adv. bd. No. Ky. C. of C., Ft. Mitchell, 2001—; co. coord. United Way, Fine Arts Fund, Cin., 1997—; mem. steering com. Connect Ky. Statewide Ky. Innovation Commn., Ctr. for Info. Tech. Enterprise Inc., Bowling Green, 2001—. 1st lt. U.S. Army, 1969—71, Vietnam. Decorated Bronze Star with three bronze oak leaf clusters. Mem.: Fin. Execs. Inst., Assn. Corp. Growth, Leadership Club No. Ky. and Greater Cin. (founding mem.). Avocations: physical fitness activities, golf, collecting memorabilia, reading. Home: 8163 Lyndhurst Ct Cincinnati OH 45249 Office: Belcan Corp 10200 Anderson Way Cincinnati OH 45242 Office Fax: 513-985-7250. Business E-Mail: dlajoie@belcan.com.

LAJOUS, ROBERTA, diplomat, editor; b. Mexico City, Feb. 6, 1954; d. Adrian and Luz (Vargas) Lajous. Licenciatura Relaciones Internacionales, El Colegio de Mexico, 1975; MA, Stanford U., 1976, postgrad., 1976-77. Dep. dir. bilingual edn. Secretaria Educacion Publica, Mexico City, 1977-78; dep. dir. Secretaria de Relaciones Exteriores, 1978-83, dir. gen. for N. Am. affairs, 1983-86, dir. gen. for European affairs, 1986-88; dir. Examen mo. pub., Mexico City, 1989-94; sec. de Asuntos Internat. Partido Revolucionario Instnl., 1992-93; amb. to Austria, permanent rep. to UN Vienna, 1995-99; dir. Matias Romero Ctr. Diplomatic Studies and Rsch. of Mex., 1999-2001; alt. permanent rep. to UN N.Y.C., 2001—. Adviser internat. affairs presdl. candidate Dr. Ernesto Zedillo, 1994—; mem. adv. group to Boutros Boutros-Ghali for Women's Conf., 1994—; lectr. in field. Author: The Foreign Policy of Porfirio Diaz 1876-1910; contbr. articles to profl. jours. Mem. Comision de Relaciones Internacionales, PRI, 1989—; dir. Revista Mex. de Politica Exterior, 1999-2001. Mem. Mexican Fgn. Svc. Assn., Fondo de Apoyo Infantil Mex., Centro Tepoztlan Mex., Stanford U. Alumni Assn. Home: Anatole France No 14 Mexico City 11560 Mexico 01900

LAKAH, JACQUELINE RABBAT, political scientist, consultant; b. Cairo, Apr. 14, 1933; came to U.S., 1969, naturalized, 1975; d. Victor Boutros and Alice (Mounayer) Rabbat; m. Antoine K. Lakah, Apr. 8, 1951; children: Micheline, Mireille, Caroline. BA, Am. U. Beirut, 1968; MPh, Columbia U., 1974; cert., Mid. East Inst., 1975, PhD, 1978. Adj. asst. prof. polit. sci. and world affairs Fashion Inst. Tech., N.Y.C., 1978-88, asst. prof., 1988-93, assoc. prof., 1993-97, prof., 1997—, asst. chair dept. social scis., 1989-95, chair dept. social scis., 1995-97, acting dean liberal arts, 1998-2000. Asst. prof. grad. faculty polit. sci. Columbia U., N.Y.C., summer 1979, vis. scholar, 1982-83, also mem. seminar on Mid. East, 1978—; guest faculty Sarah Lawrence Coll., 1981-82; cons. on Mid. East; faculty rsch. fellow SUNY, summer 1982. Columbia Faculty fellow, 1970-73, NDEA Title IV fellow, 1971-72; Mid. East Inst. scholar, 1976; Rockefeller Found. scholar, 1967-69. Mem. European Cmty. Studies Assn., Am. Polit. Sci. Assn., Fgn. Policy Assn., Internat. Studies Assn., Internat. Polit. Sci. Assn. Roman Catholic. Home: 41-15 94th St Flushing NY 11373-1745 E-mail: jlakah@nyc.rr.com.

LAKATOS, SUSAN CAROL, investment banker, artist; b. N.Y., 1960; BA, Georgetown U., 1981; MBA, Columbia U., 1989. CFA. Economist Washington Analysis Corp., 1980-84; v.p., economist Kidder, Peabody & Co., Inc., N.Y.C., 1984-89, investment strategist, 1989-92; pres. Ananda Advisors, 1992-2000; dir. rsch. Veronis Suhler, N.Y.C., 2000—. Bd. dirs., chair com. on prices, Bus. Rsch. Adv. Coun., Washington, 1983-92. One person shows include Stables Art Ctr., Taos, 1996-98, Bareiss Gallery, Taos, 1998. Mem. fin. com. Columbia Bus. Sch. Mem. Assn. Investment Mgmt. and Rsch., N.Y. Soc. Securities Analysts, Fin. Womens Assn. N.Y. Office: 350 Park Ave New York NY 10022-6022

LAKDAWALA, SHARAD R. psychiatrist; b. Broach, India, Oct. 7, 1949; came to U.S., 1977; s. Ramprasad D. and Kailasben Lakdawala; m. Bhavna B. Khatri, Jan. 2, 1978; children: Viraj, Ravi. BJ, Med. Coll., Ahmedabad, India, 1972. Diplomate Am. Bd. Psychiatry and Neurology, Am. Bd. Geriat. Psychiatry. Intern Civil Hosp., Ahmedabad, 1972-73; resident in psychiatry B.J. Med. Coll. and Civil Hosp., 1974-75; med. officer in-charge psychiat. unit Kasama (Zambia) Gen. Hosp., 1975-77; rotating intern NYU Med. Ctr., 1977-78, Bellevue Hosp., 1977-78; resident CUNY/Mt. Sinai Svcs., 1978-81; pvt. practice, Tampa and Brandon, Fla., 1981—; dir. mental health svcs. Tampa Gen. Hosp., 1988-93, chmn. dept. psychiatry, 1990-93; med. dir., svc. dir. adult psychiatry Charter Hosp. Tampa Bay, 1993—2000; sys. med. dir. Charter Behavioral Health Sys. Tampa Bay, 1996=2000. Chmn. dept. psychiatry Tampa Gen. Hosp.; past pres. med. staff Charter Hosp. Tampa Bay, svc. dir. adult psychiatry; mem. St. Joseph's Hosp.; systems med. dir. Charter Behavioral Health Sys. Tampa Bay; assoc. divisional med. dir. Charter Behavioral Health Sys., 1998—; cons. in field. Fellow Am. Psychiat. Assn., Fla. Psychiat. Soc., Tampa Psychiat. Assn. (v.p. 1989-90, pres. 1990-91), Am. Assn. Psychiatrists India (pres-elect Fla. chpt.) Office: 2908 W Waters Ave Ste 101 Tampa FL 33614-1855 also: 505 Eichenfeld Dr Ste 106 Brandon FL 33511-5956

LAKE, BRUCE MENO, applied physicist; b. L.A., Nov. 22, 1941; s. Meno Truman and Jean Ivy (Hancock)_L. BS in Engring., Princeton U., 1963; MS, Calif. Inst. Tech., 1965, PhD, 1969. Mem. tech. staff advanced instrumentation dept. TRW Corp., Redondo Beach, Calif., 1969-73, head exptl. hydrodynamics sect., 1973-81, asst. mgr. dept. fluid mechanics, 1977-81, mgr. dept. fluid mechanics, 1981-96, mgr. computational physics bus. area, 1996-2000. Contbr. articles to profl. jours. and books. Ford Found. fellow, 1964-65, TRW tech. fellow. Mem. Am. Phys. Soc., Nat. Acad. Engring. Office: 41650 Calle Pino Murrieta CA 92562

LAKE, DAVID ALAN, investments lawyer; b. El Campo, Tex., Jan. 15, 1938; s. Cortus L. and Ottis W. (Noland) L.; m. Shirley L. Hill, Dec. 20, 1966; children: Joel, Jonathan, Jeffrey Kyle, Kristi. BA, Baylor U., 1960; BD, Southwestern Seminary, 1963; JD, So. Methodist U., 1966. Bar: Tex. 1966. Lawyer Nickerson & Lake, Pittsburg, Tex., 1966-68; pvt. practice Tyler, 1967—. Gen. ptnr. Colonial Manor, Tyler, 1968-90, Golden Manor, Pittsburg, 1968-82; pres. Gardendale, Inc., Jacksonville, Tex., 1973-93, Am. Health Svcs., Inc., Tyler, 1977—, N.E. Tex. Contracting Co., Tyler, 1982—; sec., bd. dirs. Sunset Care Ctr., Jacksonville, 1973-79; chmn. bd. dirs. Cypress Bank, Fed. Savs. Bank, Pittsburg. Bd. dirs. Way of Life, Inc., Tyler, 1972-75, Smith County Heart Assn., Tyler, 1974-75; bd. dirs., chmn. Smith County Red Cross, Tyler, 1972-77; deacon, Sunday sch. tchr. 1st Bapt. Ch., Tyler, 1972—; bd. dirs., v.p. Tex. Health Care Assn., 1975-76; trustee East Tex. Bapt. U., Marshall, 1993-99. Mem. Tex. and Smith County Bar Assn., Baylor Univ. Devel. Coun., Jacksonville Jaycees (bd. dirs. 1965-66), Petroleum Club, Emerald Bay club, Lee Booster Club (pres. 1987-88), Rotary Internat. (Paul Harris fellow 1990—, bd. dirs. South Tyler chpt. 1971-74, pres. 1978-79). Avocations: reading, fishing, hunting. Home: 815 Pinedale Pl Tyler TX 75701-9645 Office: 6101 S Broadway Ave Ste 450 Tyler TX 75703-4400 E-mail: D-Slake@Tyler.net.

LAKE, JAMES RONALD, behavioral neuroscience researcher; b. Dallas, Apr. 8, 1959; BA in Biology, BA in Psychology, U. Dallas, 1982; MA in Gen. Clin. Psychology, U. Houston-Clear Lake, 1993. Histology tech. St. Joseph's Hosp., Houston, 1983-87; rsch. assoc. behavioral neurosci. U. Houston-Clear Lake, 1987—. Adj. faculty behavioral scis. U. Houston-Clear Lake, 1989—. Mem. APA, Soc. Neurosci., Internat. Behavioral Neurosci. Soc., Am. Psychol. Soc., Am. Art Therapy Assn., Assn. for Humanistic Psychology, Inst. Noetic Scis. Avocations: nutrition, spirituality, yoga, sculpture, dance. Office: U Houston Clear Lake 2700 Bay Area Blvd Box 22 Houston TX 77058-1002 E-mail: lake@cl.uh.edu.

LAKE, JOHN RICHARD, gastroenterologist; b. Cloquet, Minn., Aug. 15, 1953; s. John Romain and Agnes (Dagny) L.; m. Mamiko Lake, Mar. 3, 1979; children: Katrina, Chelsea, Natalie. BS in Biochemistry, U. Minn., 1975, MD, 1979. Diplomate Am. Bd. Internal Medicine with subspecialty in gastroenterology. Intern and resident in internal medicine U. Calif., San Francisco, 1979-82, from asst. to assoc. prof., 1986-98; prof. medicine and surgery U. Minn., Mpls., 1998—; dir. liver transplant program Fairview Univ. Med. Ctr., 1998—. Mem. sci. adv. bd. Vitagen Inc., LaJolla, Calif., 1995—. Author/editor: Comprehensive Clinical Hepatology, 1999; assoc. editor Am. Jour. Transplantation, 2001—. Bd. dirs. United Network for Organ Sharing, Richmond, Va., 2000—; bd. dirs. Am. Liver Found., San Francisco chpt., 1990-98. Recipient Young Investigator award Am. Soc. Transplant Physicians, 1997, Clin. Investigator award, 1998. Mem. AASCD, Am. Soc. Transplantation (bd. dirs., pres. 1999-2000, com. head 1997-2001), Internat. Liver Transplant Soc., Western Soc. for Clin. Investigation, Alpha Omega Alpha. Avocations: skiing, golf. Office: Univ of Minnesota Med Sch Mayo A-543 420 Delaware St SE Minneapolis MN 55455-0374 E-mail: lakex009@tc.umn.edu.

LAKE, JOSEPH EDWARD, ambassador; b. Jacksonville, Tex., Oct. 18, 1941; s. Lloyd Euel and Marion Marie (Allen) L.; m. Sarah Ann Bryant (div.); children: Joseph Edward, Mary Elizabeth; m. Jo Ann Kessler, June 12, 1971; 1 child, Michael Allen. BA summa cum laude, Tex. Christian U., 1962, MA, 1967. 3rd sec. U.S. Embassy, Taipei, Taiwan, 1963-65, Bur. of European Affairs Dept. State, 1966-67; second sec. U.S. Embassy, Cotonou, Dahomey, 1967-69; with bur. intelligence and rsch. Dept. State, 1969-71; second sec. U.S. Embassy, Taipei, Taiwan, 1971-76; with office Philippine affairs Dept. State, 1976-77; second sec. U.S. Embassy, Lagos, Nigeria, 1977-78; prin. officer and consul U.S. Consulate, Kaduna, Nigeria, 1978-81; with Fgn. Svc. Inst., Washington, 1981-82; first sec. U.S. Embassy, Sofia, Bulgaria, 1982-84, charge d'affaires Bulgaria, 1984, counselor, dep. chief mission Bulgaria, 1984-85; dep. dir. regional affairs , bur. East Asian and Pacific Affairs Dept. State, 1985-86; advisor U.S. delegation 41st UN Gen. Assembly, 1986; dir. ops. ctr. Dept. State, Washington, 1987-90; amb. to Rep. of Mongolia, Ulaanbaatar, 1990-93, Rep. of Albania, Tirana, 1994-96; dep. asst. sec. of state for info. mgmt. Dept. State, Washington, 1996-97; dir. internat. affairs City of Dallas, 1997—2002; rsch. assoc. Tower Ctr. So. Meth. U. Mem. adv. bd. Asian studies program So. Meth. U. Contbr. articles to profl. jours. Mem. exec. com., bd. dirs. Dallas Coun. on World Affairs; mem. Dallas Com. on Fgn. Rels.; mem. adv. bd. internat. program U. Dallas Grad. Sch. Mgmt. Mem. Am. Fgn. Svc. Assn., Greater Dallas Asian Am. C. of C. (adv. bd.), French C. of C., Brit. Am. Comml. Assn., Tex. Dist. Export Coun. Home: 6145 Highgate Ln Dallas TX 75214-2155 E-mail: joelake@hotmail.com.

LAKE, KATHLEEN COOPER, lawyer; b. San Antonio, Jan. 11, 1955; d. Herschel Taliaferro and Virginia Mae (Hylton) Cooper; m. Randall Brent Lake, Apr. 9, 1977; 1 child, Ethan Taliaferro. AB in Polit. Sci. magna cum laude, Middlebury Coll., 1977; JD with high honors, U. Tex., 1980. Bar: Tex. 1980, U.S. Ct. Appeals (5th cir.) 1981, U.S. Ct. Appeals (D.C. and 3rd cirs.) 1984. Assoc. atty. Vinson & Elkins, Houston, 1980-88; ptnr. Vinson & Elkins, LLP, 1989—. Bd. advisors, columnist Utilities, Y2K Advisor, 1998-99. Adult leader, com. mem. Sam Houston Area Coun.-Golden Arrow dist. Boys Scouts Am., 1993—, chair troop com., 1998-2001. Recipient Unit Svc. award Sam Houston Area Coun.-Golden Arrow dist. Boy Scouts Am., 1996, 98. Fellow Tex. Bar Found. (life), Houston Bar Found.; mem. ABA (vice-chair com. 1997-99), Energy Bar Assn., State Bar Tex., Tex. Law Rev. Assn. (life), Houston Bar Assn., Middlebury Coll. Alumni Assn. (com. mem. 1980-2000, Houston com. chair 2001—), Order of Coif, Phi Beta Kappa, Phi Kappa Phi. Office: Vinson & Elkins LLP 2300 First City Tower 1001 Fannin St Houston TX 77002-6760 E-mail: klake@velaw.com.

LAKE, KEVIN BRUCE, medical association administrator; b. Seattle, Jan. 25, 1937; s. Winston Richard and Vera Emma (Davis) L.; m. Suzanne Roto, Oct. 25, 1986; children from previous marriage: Laura, Kendrick, Wesley. BS, Portland State U., 1960; MD, U. Oreg., 1964. Intern Marion County Gen. Hosp. and Ind. Med. Ctr., Indpls., 1964-65; resident U. Oreg. Hosps. and Clinics, 1968-70, fellow in infectious and pulmonary diseases, 1970-71; fellow in pulmonary diseases U. So. Calif., 1971-72, instr. medicine, 1972-75, asst. clin. prof., 1975-79, assoc. clin. prof., 1979-84, clin. prof., 1986—. Dir. med. edn. and research La Vina Hosp., 1972-75; dir. respiratory therapy Methodist Hosp., Arcadia, Calif., 1975— ; mem. staff Los Angeles County/U. So. Calif. Med. Center, Santa Teresita Hosp., Duarte, Calif., Huntington Meml. Hosp., Pasadena, Calif.; attending physician, mem. med. adv. bd. Foothill Free Clinic, Pasadena. Contbr. articles to profl. jours. Mem. exec. com. Profl. Staff Assn. U. So. Calif. Sch. Medicine; 2d v.p. bd. mgmt. Palm St. br. YMCA, Pasadena, 1974, 1st v.p., 1975, chmn., 1976-78, met. bd. dirs., 1976-84; bd. dirs. Mendenhall Ministries, La Vie Holistic Ministries, Hospice of Pasadena, Hastings Found. co-pres. PTA, Allendale Grade Sch., Pasadena, 1975-76; deacon Pasadena Covenant Ch., 1976-79. Served to lt. U.S. Navy, 1965-68. NIH grantee, 1971-72. Fellow ACP, Am. Coll. Chest Physicians; mem. Am. Thoracic Soc., Calif. Thoracic Soc., Oreg. Thoracic Soc., Trudeau Soc., Am. Soc. Microbiology, N.Y. Acad. Scis., Calif. Med. Assn., L.A. County Med. Assn. Democrat. Home: 875 S Madison Ave Pasadena CA 91106-4404 Office: 444 N Altadena Dr Pasadena CA 91107-2501

LAKE, NANCY JEAN, nursing educator, operating room nurse; b. Sandborn, Ind., May 13, 1942; d. Thomas Malone and Vivian Pearl (Meek) Wills; divorced; children: Brian, Deanna, Patrick. AS, Cleve. State Community Coll., 1972. RN, Ky., Ind., N.Y., Ark. Staff nurse geriatric unit Regional Hosp., Ft. Smith, Ark., 1973-74; pub. health staff nurse, 1974; staff nurse Bradley County Hosp., Cleveland, Tenn., 1972-73; staff nurse recovery room and oper. room St. Anthony Hosp., Terre Haute Regional Hosp., Terre Haute, Ind., 1974-76; staff nurse oper. room, emergency room, med.-surg. fl. Washington County Hosp., Salem, 1976-77; oper. room. staff nurse Floyd County Hosp., New Albany, 1977-78; staff nurse oper. room Good Samaritan Hosp., Vincennes, 1978-82; staff nurse oper. room and thoriac cardio vascular coord. Winthrope Univ. Hosp., Mineola, N.Y., 1982-86; staff nurse oper. room Humana Hosp., Audubon, 1986-92; staff nurse oper. rm. Jewish Hosp. Healthcare Ctr., 1990—, staff nurse, organ retrivial nurse, nurse in sterile processing, 2000—. Home: 515 S Chestnut St Seymour IN 47274-3043

LAKE, SIM, federal judge; b. Chgo., July 4, 1944; BA, Tex. A&M, 1966; JD, U. Tex., 1969. Bar: Tex. 1969, U.S. Dist. Ct. (so. dist.) Tex. 1969, U.S. Ct. Appeals (5th cir.) 1969, U.S. Supreme Ct. 1976. From assoc. to ptnr. Fulbright & Jaworski, Houston, 1969-70, 72-88; judge U.S. Dist. Ct. (so. dist.) Tex., 1988—. Past editor Houston Lawyer. Capt. U.S. Army., 1970-71. Fellow Tex. Bar Found., Houston Bar Assn., State Bar Tex., Am. Law Inst. Office: US Courthouse 515 Rusk Ave Rm 9535 Houston TX 77002-2605

LAKE, STANLEY JAMES, security consulting company executive, motel chain executive, locksmith; b. Oklahoma City, June 3, 1926; s. Clyde Edward Lake and Helene Frances (Herndon) Hunnicut; m. Lila Marguarite Mosley, Mar 29, 1947 (div. Aug. 1952); children: Katherine, Marilyn, Stanley James II; m. Norma Jean Phelps, Jan. 21, 1960. Student, Mont. State U., 1946-48. Owner, mgr. Lake Oil Co., Glendive, Mont., 1949-53, Lake Mining Co., Salt Lake City, 1954-57, Lake Realty Co., Denver, 1958-63, Stanlake Corp., Denver, 1964—, Stanlake Luxury Budget Motels, Denver, 1979—, Lake's Security and Lock Svc., Englewood, Colo., 1979—. Co-owner, instr. Colo. Karate Assn., Denver, 1965-73, 2d degree black belt. Originator modular budget motel concept, 1963. Chmn. bd. for karate Rocky Mountain region AAU, 1972-73. With USAAC, 1945-46. Recipient Presdl. award for teaching karate to disadvantaged and civic orgns., 1972, numerous others. Mem. Assn. Locksmiths Am. (cert. master locksmith), Rocky Mountain Locksmiths Assn., Japan Karate Assn. Rocky Mountain Area (chmn. bd. 1970-73), Masons, Shriners. Republican. Methodist. Avocations: computers, skiing, reading, investing, airplane pilot. Home: 6026 S Elizabeth Way Littleton CO 80121-2816 Office: Lake's Security & Lock Svc 6200 S Syracuse Way Ste 125 Englewood CO 80111-4745 E-mail: stan1926@qwest.net.

LAKE, SUZANNE, singer, teacher; b. Palisade, N.J., June 26, 1929; d. Mayhew Lester and Suzanne Louise (Robin) L.; m. George A. De Vos, Nov. 19, 1974. Pvt. tchr., Oakland, Calif., 1976-86, univ. extension U. Calif., Sacramento State U., 1981-84. Featured roles opera, N.Y.C., 1948-51; appeared in Broadway plays The King and I, 1951-54, History of Musical Comedy with Leonard Bernstein, 1957, Flower Drum Song, 1960-61; featured singer with Guy Lombardo, 1964, 65; concert and supper club appearances in U.S., Can., Carribbean, Japan, Republic of Korea, and Europe, 1955-91, recs. include the Soul of Chanson, Potpourri, others; also TV appearances. Mem. Actors Equity, AFTRA, Am. Guild Mus. Artists, Am. Guild Variety Artists. Home: 2835 Morley Dr Oakland CA 94611-2547

LAKE, TRACY MARIE GRACE, accountant; b. Fort McMurray, Alta., Can., Feb. 16, 1974; came to the U.S., 1984; d. David Stanley Austin and Faye Aaron Hales. BS in Acctg., So. Ill. U., 1997. Asst. office mgr. So. Ill. U. Press, Carbondale, 1994-97; staff acct. Pepsi Cola Bottling, Marion, Ill., 1997-99; acct. I So. Ill. U., 1999—. Vol. Arthritis Found., Carbondale, 1996-97, Herrinfest, Herrin, Ill., 1998-2000. Mem. Future Bus. Leaders Am.-Phi Beta Lambda (profl. 1997-00, Ill. Phi Beta Lambda divsn. pres.-elect 2000) Home: 447 N Seba Hurst IL 62949 E-mail: tlake@siu.edu.

LAKE, VICTOR HUGO, former manufacturing company executive; b. Quincy, Mass., Nov. 11, 1919; s. Victor Hugo and Edna Beatrice (Blott) L.; m. Jeannette Elzena Stewart, Apr. 26, 1942; children: Victor Stewart, Valerie Jean; m. 2d, Jacqueline Rose Davis, July 4, 1975. Student, Lawrence Inst. Tech., 1939-42, U. Maine, 1943. Asst. supt. Taylor Winfield Corp., Detroit, 1938-43; prodn. control mgr. Fed. Machine & Welder Co., Warren, Ohio, 1944-49; with Am. Welding & Mfg. Co., 1949-82, mgr. materials, 1969-82; ret., 1982. Served with AUS, 1943-44. Mem. Am. Soc. Metals, Trumbull County Indsl. Mgmt. Assn. (pres. 1972-73). Republican. Methodist. Home: 9042 Tiara Ct New Port Richey FL 34655-1532 E-mail: victorlake@msn.com.

LAKE, WESLEY WAYNE, JR. internist, allergist, educator; b. New Orleans, Oct. 11, 1937; s. Wesley Wayne and Mary McGehee (Snowden) L.; m. Abby F. Arnold, Aug. 1959 (div. 1974); children: Courtenay B., Corinne A., Jane S.; married Melissa Bowman, Mar. 1999. AB in Chemistry, Princeton U., 1959; MD, Tulane U., 1963. Diplomate Am. Bd. Internal Medicine, Am. Bd. Allergy and Immunology. Intern Charity Hosp. of La., New Orleans, 1963-64, resident internal medicine, 1966-69; NIH fellow allergy and immunology La. State U. Med. Ctr., 1969-70; instr. dept. medicine Tulane U., New Orleans, 1967-69; fellow dept. medicine La. State U., 1969-70, instr. dept. medicine, 1970-73, asst. clin. prof. medicine, 1973-77; chief allergy clinic La. State U. Svc. Charity Hosp. La., 1970-77; assoc. clin. prof. medicine Tulane U., 1978—93. Temp. staff positions various hosps., 1963-70, including Baton Rouge Gen. Hosp., Our Lady of the Lake Hosp., Glenwood Hosp., St. Francis Hosp., Monroe, La., Lallie Kemp Charity Hosp., Independence, La., Huey P. Long Hosp., Pineville, La.; gen. med. officer outpatient clinic Hunter AFB, Savannah, Ga., 1964-65, gen. med. officer internal medicine svc., 1965-66; cons. physician Seventh Ward Gen. Hosp., Hammond, La., 1971-77, Slidell (La.) Meml. Hosp., 1971-89, St. Tammany Parish Hosp., Covington, La., 1977-85; cons. physician East Jefferson Hosp., Metairie, La., 1971-77, staff physician, 1990—; asst. vis. physician Charity Hosp. New Orleans, 1970-75, staff physician, 1975-77, vis. phys. Tulane divsn., 1979-93; assoc. physician So. Bapt. Hosp., New Orleans, 1970-75, chmn. dept. medicine, chmn. internal medicine com., 1982-84, chmn. pharmacy and therapeutics, 1980-82, mem. investigative rev. com., 1984-85, mem. internal medicine quality assurance com., 1989-94; staff physician Kenner (La.) Regional Med. Ctr. (formerly St. Jude Med. Ctr.), 1985-99, chmn. quality assurance com., 1987-89. Author: (with others) Infiltrative Hypersensitivity Chest Diseases, 1975; contbr. articles to profl. jours. including Jour. Immunology, Internat. Archives Allergy and Applied Immunology, Jour. Allergy and Clin. Immunology; also chpts. in books concerning chest diseases. Fellow ACP, Am. Coll. Allergy, Sigma Xi; mem. New Orleans Acad. Internal Medicine, Musser-Burch Soc., S.E. Allergy Soc., La. Allergy Soc. (sec. 1975-76, v.p. 1976-77, pres. 1977-78). Republican. Episcopalian. Home: 4636 Perrier St New Orleans LA 70115-3920 Office: 4224 Houma Blvd Ste 250 Metairie LA 70006-2935

LAKE-BRUSE, KRISTY DEAN, pharmacologist, toxicologist, researcher, educator; b. Riverside, Calif., Dec. 22, 1958; BS in Biology, U. Mo., 1982; MS in Biology, Southwest Mo. State U., 1986; PhD in Pharmacology, Toxicology, Va. Commonwealth U., 1996. Vet. asst. Emergency Vet. Clinic, Overland Park, Kans., 1981-83; vet. asst., office mgr. Stanley (Kans.) Vet. Clinic, 1982-83; vet. asst. Sunset Animal Clinic, Suisun City, Calif., 1987, Berkeley (Calif.) Dog and Cat Hosp., 1987-88, Alameda County Emergency Animal Hosp., San Leandro, Calif., 1988-89; tchg. asst. Clover Hill High Sch., Richmond, Va., 1996; postdoctoral fellow Univ. Iowa, Iowa City, 1997—2001; staff pharmacologist WIL Rsch., Inc., Ashland, Ohio, 2001—. Rschr. U. Calif., Davis , 1987, Syntex, Palo Alto, Calif., 1988—92, Scios Nova, Inc., Mountain View, Calif., 1992—93; vis. prof. U. Iowa, 1999, Kirkwood Cmty. Coll., Cedar Rapids, Iowa, 1999. Contbr. articles to profl. jours. Mentor Thomas Jefferson High Sch., Richmond, Va., 1994-95, 95-96; sci. fair judge West Valley Elem. Sch., Cupertino, Calif., 1990, 91, 92, 93, Santa Clara Valley Sci. and Engring. Fair, San Jose, Calif., 1991, 92, Greater Metro Richmond (Va.) Sci. Fair, 1995, 96, Va. Jr. Acad. Sci., 1994, 95, 96. Recipient Young Investigator's award Am. Heart Assn., Incline Village, Nev., 1998, Caroline tumSuden/Frances A. Hellebrandt Profl. Opportunity award Am. Physiological Soc., San Francisco, 1998. Avocations: softball, scuba diving. Home: 423 US Rte 42 Polk OH 44866 Office: WIL Rsch 1407 George Rd Ashland OH 44805 Fax: 419-289-3650. E-mail: Kbruse@wilresearch.com.

LAKES, DIANA MARY, artist; b. Sussex, N.J., Aug. 12, 1948; d. Renato and Lillian Vezzetti; m. Roderic S. Lakes, Aug. 14, 1971. BA, Russell Sage Coll., 1970. Artist Gallerie Je Reviens, Westport, Conn., 1996-2001. Exhibitions include Swen Parson Gallery, Dekalb, Ill., 1987, Wright Mus. Art, Beloit, Wis., 1987, Tarble Arts Ctr., Charleston, Ill., 1988, Purdue U. Galleries, West Lafayette, Ind., 1988, Midwest Mus. Am. Art, Elkhart, Ind., 1988, Yolanda Fine Arts, Chgo., 1989, McCormick Place, 1990, Sonje Mus. Contemporary Art, Kyongju, Korea, 1992, China World Trade Ctr., Beijing, 1995, Chgo. Ctr. Self-Taught, 1996, U.S. Embassy, Montevideo, Uruguay, 1998—2001, Pittori Naifs a Guiglia 5th Salone Internazionale, Modena, Italy, 1999, The Naive Painters in Castelvetro, Italy, 2001, Cedar Rapids Mus. of Art, Iowa, 2002—, Represented in permanent collections Musee d'Art Naif Max Fourny, Paris, Daryl Hannah, Musee Internat. d'Art Naif Yvon-M. Diagle, Que., others. Home: 1225 Edgehill Dr Madison WI 53705-1414 E-mail: dianaspalette@powercom.net.

LAKHANPAL, SHARAD, physician; b. Lucknow, India, Oct. 15, 1951; came to U.S., 1980; s. Rajendra Nath and Indra (Kalia) L.; m. Rashmi Sharma, Nov. 17, 1980; children: Akshai, Shuchi, Virad. Student, Colvin Coll., Lucknow, 1969; MB, BS, K.G. Med. Coll., Lucknow, 1974, Dr.med., 1977. Diplomate Am. Bd. Internal Medicine, Am. Bd. Rheumatology. Rotating intern Gandhi Meml. and Assocs. Hosps., King George's Med. Coll., 1974, resident in medicine, 1975-78; sr. house officer in internal medicine Sunderland Hosp., Hemlington Hosp., Poole Hosp., Eng., 1979-80; resident in internal medicine Meml. Hosp., U. Mass. Med. Sch., Worcester, 1980-82; fellow Mayo Clin., Rochester, Minn., 1983-86; attending physician St. Paul Med. Ctr., Dallas, 1987—; asst. prof. medicine Southwestern Med. Sch., 1989-96, assoc. prof. medicine, 1996—, clin. prof. medicine, 2002—. Instr. Southwestern Med. Sch., Dallas, 1987-89; referee to numerous med. jours. Sr. editor Jour. Biol. and Chem. Rsch., 1987—; mem. editl. bd. Jour. Indian Rheumatism Assn., 1999—; contbr. chpt. to book and articles to profl. jours. Bd. dirs. North Tex. chpt. Arthritis Found., 1992-98; trustee DFW Hindu Temple, Dallas, 1994-99; bd. dirs. United Way of Met. Dallas, 1995-97, mem. exec com., 1995-96. Recipient Platinum Jubilee Gold medal King Georges Med. Coll., 1986; Am. Rheumatism Assn. fellow, 1984, 85, scholar, 1986; Philips Hench scholar, 1986. Fellow ACP, Am. Rheumatism Assn. (founding), Am. Coll. Rheumatology; mem. Indian Rheumatism Assn. (editl. bd.), Arthritis Found. (sci. com. and chmn. profl. edn. com. North Tex. chpt., also bd. dirs. 1992-98), Lupus Found. Am. (med. adv. bd.), Tex. Med. Assn., Dallas County Med. Soc., Tex. Indo-Am. Physicians Soc. (pres. 1994-95), King George Med. Coll. Alumni Assn. in Am. (sec.-treas. 1988-89, v.p. 1991-92, pres. 1993-94), Dallas-Ft. Worth Rheumatology Club (organizing sec.), Am. Assn. Physicians of Indian Origin (sec. 2000—). Hindu. Avocations: running, travel, tennis. Office: Rheumatology Assocs 5939 Harry Hines Blvd Ste 400 Dallas TX 75235-5360

LAKIN, JAMES DENNIS, allergist, immunologist, director; b. Harvey, Ill., Oct. 4, 1945; s. Ora Austin and Annie Pitranella (Johnson) L.; m. Sally A. Stuteville, July 22, 1972; children: Margaret K., Matthew A. PhD, Northwestern U., 1968, MD, 1969; MBA in Med. Group Mgmt., U. St. Thomas, 1996. Diplomate Am. Bd. Internal Medicine, Am. Bd. Allergy and Immunology. Dir. allergy rsch. Naval Med. Rsch. Inst., Bethesda, Md., 1974-76; clin. prof. U. Okla., Oklahoma City, 1976-89; dir. lab., chmn. allergy and immunology dept. Oxboro Clinics, Bloomington, Minn., 1989—; dir. Fairview Allergy and Asthma Svcs., 1995-2001; mng. ptnr. Minn. Allergy and Asthma Consultants, LLP, 2001—. Bd. dirs. Okla. Med. Rsch. Found., Oklahoma City, 1980-89; regional cons. Diver Alert Network, Duke U., Chapel Hill, N.C., 1987—; cert. diving med. officer NOAA, 1988. Co-author: Allergic Diseases, 1971, 3d edit., 1986; contbr. articles, revs. to profl. publs. Councilperson Our Lord's Luth. Ch., Oklahoma City, 1978-88, Faith Luth. Ch., Lakeville, Minn., 1990-91. Lt. comdr. USN, 1970-76. Fellow ACP, Am. Acad. Allergy and Immunology, Am. Coll. Chest Physicians, Am. Coll. Med. Practice Execs. (E.B. Stevens Article of Yr. award 1998); mem. Am. Assn. Immunologists, Med. Group Mgmt. Assn., Am. Coll. Physician Execs. Achievements include research in characterization of the immunoglobulin system of the rhesus monkey, alterations in allergic reactivity during immunosuppression. Office: Minn Allergy and Asthma Cons LLP 600 W 98th St Bloomington MN 55420-4773

LAKRITZ, ESTHER, retired English language educator; b. Milw., Apr. 11, 1928; d. Alexander Himmelman and Mildred Hoffman; children: Simeon, Naomi, David. BS in Secondary Edn., Milw. State Tchrs. Coll., 1949; MLS, U. Wis., 1976. Author: (children's book) Randy Visits Doctor, 1962, (workbook) Developing Library Skills, 1989, (romantic suspense) To Track a Copycat, 1995, (mystery) Battlelines, 1999. Avocation: freelance writing. Home: 17460 Plaza Otonal San Diego CA 92128-1830

LAKRITZ, JEFFREY, veterinary educator; b. Hanford, Calif., Oct. 17, 1959; s. Simon and Mary Elizabeth L.; m. Antoinette Elisa Marsh, oct. 1, 1994. BS, U. Calif., Davis, 1981, DVM, 1987, PhD, 1996. Diplomate Am. Coll. Vet. Internal Medicine. Postgrad. rschr. U. Calif., Davis, 1996-98; asst. prof. U. Mo., Columbia, 1998—. Vet. cons. Robert L. Young, Ft. Lauderdale, Fla., 1990—. Author (contbg.): 5 Minute Veterinary Consult, 1999, 2002, Current Veterinary Therapy, 1996, Current Veterinary Therapy Equine, 2000. Mem.: AAAS, Am. Assn. Equine Practitioners, Am. Coll. Vet. Internal Medicine, Am. Soc. Microbiology, Mo. Vet. Med. Assn., Am. Vet. Med. Assn., Soc. Toxicology. Office: Univ Mo-Columbia 379 E Campus Dr Columbia MO 65211-0001

LAKSHMAN, VENKATESH, gastroenterologist, researcher, gastroenterologist, educator; b. Bangalore, Karnataka, India, Mar. 12, 1967; s. Jagga Chinna and Kousalya Lakshman. MBBS, St. Georges Hosp. Med. Sch., London, 1990, DIC, 1988; Msc, Imperial Coll. Sch. Medicine, London, 1998. Diplomate Am. Bd. Internal Medicine with subsplty. in gastroenterology. Rsch. fellow Hammersmith Hosp., ICSM, London, 1997-98; gastroenterologist Christchurch (N.Z.) Pub. Hosp., 1999, Mid. Ctrl. Health, Palmerston North, N.Z., 1999-2000, Hammersmith Hosp., London, 2000-2001; asst. prof. gastroenterology U. Iowa Hosp. and Clinic, Iowa City, 2001; William and Sondra Myers Family prof. medicine U. Iowa Coll. Medicine, 2002—. Fellow: Royal Soc. Medicine London; mem.: Am. Soc. Gastrintestinal Endoscopy, Am. Gastroenterol. Assn., Am. Coll. Gastroenterologists. Achievements include co-inventor self propelling endoscope. Office: Cdd-Jcp 200 Hawkins Dr Iowa City IA 52242-1009 E-mail: venkatesh_lakshman@uiowa.edu., venklakshman@hotmail.

LAKSHMANA, VISWANATH, computer and information systems executive; b. Trivandrum, Kerala, India, Mar. 3, 1958; arrived in U.S., 1980; s. Lakshmana and Lakshmy L.; m. Rukmani, July 15, 1985; children: Avinash, Abiram. MS in Computer Sci., Iowa State U., 1987; MS in Meterology, S.D. Sch. Mines and Tech., 1982. Contract programmer Iowa State U., 1984-87, software cons., 1984-87; coord. academic computing SUNY, Cortland, N.Y., 1987-91; dir. computer and info. systems Pa. State U., Harrisburg, 1991-95; dir. computer and telecomm. svcs. Texas A&M Internat. U., 1995—. Contbr. articles to profl. jours. Office: TAMIU 5201 University Blvd Laredo TX 78041-1920 Home: 2009 Manzanares Dr Laredo TX 78045-6308

LAKSHMIKANTHAM, VANGIPURAM, mathematics educator; b. Hyderabad, India, Aug. 8, 1926; came to U.S., 1960, naturalized, 1966; s. Soroja Bukkapatnam, Feb. 22, 1942; children: Sreekantham, Neerada, Nirupama. MA, Osmania U., Hyderabad, 1955, PhD, 1958. Mem. faculty UCLA, 1960-61, Math. Rsch. Ctr., U. Wis., Madison, 1961-62; mem. Rsch. Inst. Advanced Studies, Balt., 1962-63; assoc. prof. U. Alta., Calgary, Can., 1963-64; prof., chmn. dept. math. Marathwada U., Aurangabad, India, 1964-66, U. R.I., Kingston, 1966-73, U. Tex., Arlington, 1973-88; prof., head dept. math. scis. Fla. Inst. Tech., Melbourne, 1989—. Author 33 books; founder, editor: Jour. Nonlinear Analysis, A-Series and B-Series, Nonlinear Studies, Stochastic Analysis and Applications, Mathematical Problems in Engring., Hybrid Systems and Applications; assoc. editor other jours.; contbr. over 400 rsch. articles to profl. publs. Mem. Am. Math. Soc., Indian Math. Soc., Soc. Indsl. and Aplied Math., Nat. Acad. Sci. India, Internat. Fedn. Nonlinear Analysts (founder). Office: Fla Inst Tech Dept Math Scis 150 W University Blvd Melbourne FL 32901-6975 E-mail: lakshmik@winnie.fit.edu.

LAKSHMIVARAHAN, SIVARAMAKRISHNAN, computer science educator; b. Karaikurichi, Tamil Nadu, India, June 12, 1944; came to U.S., 1975; s. Sankaran Sivaramakrishna and Subbulakshmi (Narayanan) Iyer; m. Shantha Sitaram Varahan, Feb. 5, 1973; children: Subha, Bharathram. BSc in Physics with distinction, U. Madras, India, 1964; BE in Elec. Tech. with distinction, Indian Inst. Sci., Bangalore, 1967, ME in Applied Electronics, 1969, PhD in Learning Algorithms, 1973. Rsch. asst. dept. elec. engring. Indian Inst. Sci., Bangalore, 1969-73; project asst. Sch. Automation Indian Inst. Tech., 1973, lectr., asst. prof. dept. computer sci. Madras, 1973-75; vis. asst. prof. div. applied math. Brown U., Providence, 1975-76; asst. prof. dept. engring. and applied sci. Yale U., New Haven, 1976-78; assoc. prof. Sch. Elec. Engring. and Computer Sci., U. Okla., Norman, 1978-84, prof., 1984-92, prof. Sch. Computer Sci., 1992—, Hallibuurton disting. lectr. Coll. Engring., 1984-86, Assocs. disting. lectr., 1986-87, George Lynn Cross rsch. prof., 1995. Vis. prof. U. Bonn, 1980, 82, U. Laval, Quebec City, Can., 1982, AMOCO Prodn. Rsch. Ctr., Tulsa, summer 1983, Nat. Inst. Standards and Tech., Gaithersburg, Md., summer 1985, Tech. Inst. for Higher Studies Monterrey, Mex., 1988, 90, 93, Nat. Tsing-Huo U., Hinshu, Taiwan, 1992, Indian Inst. Sch., Bangalore, 1993; cons. AMOCO Prodn. Rsch. Ctr., Nat. Inst. Standards and Tech.; colloquium speaker in field. Author: Lectures on Automata Theory, 1974, Learning Algorithms: Theory and Application, 1982, (with S.K. Dhall) Analysis and Design of Parallel Algorithms, 1990, Parallel Prefix Computations, 1994; editor: Procs. of Workshop on Parallel Processing using Heterogeneous Element Processor, 1985, spl. issue Info. Scis.-Internat. Jour., 1987; contbr. numerous articles to sci. jours., chpts. to books. Recipient Regents award for rsch. and creative activities U. Okla., 1982, Regents award for superior teaching, 1992; grantee NSF, 1981-83, 85, 86-87, 89-93, U. Okla. Office Rsch. Adminstrn., 1981, AMOCO, summers 1983-86, 1985-85, 87-88, U. Okla. Energy Resource Inst., 1984-86, Denelcor, Inc., 1985, Okla. Gov.'s Coun. on Sci. and Tech., 1986, More Okla. Sci. and Tech. Fellow IEEE (citation for contbns. to learning algorithms, parallel computing and their applications 1993), IEEE Computer Soc. (vice chmn. Oklahoma City chpt. 1982-83, chmn. 1983-85), Assn. for Computing Machinery (editl. bd. Applied Computing Rev. 1993—, nat. lectr. selection com. 1992-93, nat. lectr. 1989-92, faculty advisor student chpt. U. Okla. 1987-89, citation for contbns. to learning and parallel algorithms). Avocation: Indian classical music. Office: U Okla Sch Computer Sci Norman OK 73019-0001

LAL, DEVENDRA, nuclear geophysics educator; b. Varanasi, India, Feb. 14, 1929; s. Radhe Krishna and Sita Devi L.; m. Aruna Damany, May 17, 1955 (dec. July 1993). BS, Banaras Hindu U., Varanasi, 1947, MS, 1949, DSc (hon. causa), 1984; PhD, Bombay U., 1960. Research student Tata Inst. of Fundamental Research, Bombay, 1949-60, research fellow, fellow, assoc. prof., 1960-63, prof., 1963-70, sr. prof., 1970-72; dir. Phys. Research Lab., Ahmedabad, India, 1972-83, sr. prof., 1983-89; vis. prof. UCLA, 1965-66, 83-84; prof. Scripps Instn. Oceanography, La Jolla, Calif., 1967—. Editor: Early Solar System Processes and the Present Solar System, 1980, Biogeochemistry of the Arabian Sea, 1995. Recipient K.S. Krishnan Gold medal Indian Geophys. Union, 1965, S.S. Bhatnagar award for Physics, Govt. of India, 1971, award for Excellence in Sci. and Tech., Gedn. of Indian Chamber Com., 1974, Pandit Jawaharlal Nehru award for Scis., 1986, Group Achievement award NASA, 1986, Raman Birth Centenary award, 1996, V.M.

Goldschmidt medal, 1997. Fellow AAAS, Royal Soc. London, Indian Nat. Sci. Acad., Indian Acad. Scis., Geol. Soc. India (hon.), Phys. Rsch. Lab. Ahmedabad, Tata Inst. Fundamental Rsch., Geochem. Soc. USA; mem. NAS U.S.A. (fgn. assoc.), Third World Acad. Scis. (founding mem.), Indian Geophys. Union, NAS India, Royal Astron. Soc. (assoc.), Internat. Acad. Aeronautics, Internat. Union of Geodesy and Geophysics (pres. 1984-87), Am. Acad. Arts and Scis. (fgn., hon. mem.), Internat. Assn. Phys. Sci. of Ocean (hon. mem., pres. 1979-83). Hindu. Avocations: chess, photography, painting, math. puzzles. Office: U Calif Scripps Inst Oceanography GRD-0244 La Jolla CA 92093-0244 Fax: (858) 822-3310. E-mail: dlal@ucsd.edu.

LALA, DOMINICK J. manufacturing company executive; b. N.Y.C., June 2, 1928; s. Joseph and Mary (Billera) L.; m. Nancy Bosco, Nov. 30, 1957; children: John, Steven, James, Thomas, Patrice. BS, NYU, 1951. Mem. staff BDO/Seidman (CPAs), N.Y.C., 1951-62; v.p., contr. Universal Am. Corp., 1962-68; sr. v.p. fin. Paramount Pictures Corp., 1968-70; exec. v.p. Gould Paper Corp., N.Y.C., 1970—2002. With AUS, 1946-47. Mem. AICPA, N.Y. State Soc. CPAs, Fin. Execs. Inst. Home: 10 Burnham Pl Manhasset NY 11030-2709

LALA, PEEYUSH KANTI, medical scientist, educator; b. Chittagong, Bengal, India, Nov. 1, 1934; came to U.S., 1963, to Can., 1967. s. Sudhangshu Bimal and Nani Bala (Chaudhuri) L.; m. Arati Roy-Burman, July 7, 1962 (dec.); children: Probal, Prasun; m. Shipra Bhattacareya, Nov. 6, 1992. MB, BS, Calcutta (India) U., 1957, PhD in Med. Biophysics, 1961, MD, 1962. Demonstrator in pathology Calcutta Med. Coll., 1959-60, NRS Med. Coll., Calcutta, 1961-62; resident rsch. assoc. biol. and med. rsch. divsn. Argonne (Ill.) Nat. Lab., 1963-64; rsch. scientist, asst. prof. Lab. Radiobiology, U. Calif. Med. Ctr., San Francisco, 1964-66; rsch. scientist Biol. and Health Physics div. Chalk River (Ont., Can.) Nuclear Lab., 1967-68; from asst. prof. to assoc. prof. dept. anatomy McGill U., Montreal, Que., Can., 1968-77, prof. dept. anatomy Can., 1977-83; prof. dept. anatomy and cell biology U. Western Ont., London, 1983-2000, chmn. dept. anatomy and cell biology, 1983-93, prof. dept. oncology, 1990-2000; prof. emeritus dept. anatomy and cell biology, dept. oncology, microbiology and immunology, 2000—. Mem. grants panel MRC Can., Ottawa, Ont., 1983-87, 93-96, NIH U.S.A., Bethesda, Md., 1977-95, Nat. Cancer Inst. Can., Toronto, 1987-90, Cancer Rsch. Soc., Montreal, 1987-90; mem. Cannaught Com., Toronto, 1990-91; vis. prof. Walter and Eliza Hall Inst. Med. Rsch., U. Melbourne, Australia, 1977-78. Mem. editl. bd.: Exptl. Hematology, 1974—77, mem. editl. bd.: Leukemia Rsch., 1977—86, mem. editl. bd.: Am. Jour. Reproductive Immunology, 1989—93, mem. editl. bd.: Early Pregnancy: Biology and Medicine, 1995—, mem. editl. bd.: Placenta, 1996—, mem. editl. bd.: Biology of Reproduction, 2001—, assoc. editor: Am. Jour. Anatomy, 1987—90, guest editor: Cancer and Metastasis Revs., Vol. 17, 1998; contbr. Chmn. Bengali Cultural Ctr., Montreal, 1978-83. Fellow, Fulbright Found., 1962; grantee, MRC Can. (now CIHR), 1968—, NCI Can., 1968—, NIH, 1976—79, Cancer Rsch. Soc., 1978—96, U.S. Army Med. Rsch., 1996—. Mem. Am. Assn. Cancer Research, Am. Assn. Anatomists, Can. Assn. Anatomists, Cell Biologists and Neurobiologists (chmn. awards com. 1987-89, v.p. and pres. elect 1989-90, pres. 1991-93, J.C.B. Grant award 1990), Internat. Soc. Exptl. Hematology, Soc. Leukocyte Biology, Am. Assn. Immunologists, Can. Soc. Immunologists, Internat. Soc. Reproductive Immunology (councillor 1986-89), Am. Soc. Reproductive Immunology (v.p. 1985-86), Soc. Study Reprodn. Achievements include discovery of of new mode of cancer immunotherapy resulting in a successful phase two human trial; of mode of treatment of interleukin-2 therapy induced side effects of capillary leakage; of mechanism responsible for nitric oxide-mediated stimulation of breast cancer progression; production of normal, precancerous and cancerous trophoblast cell lines from first trimester human placentae; identification control mechanisms in the protection of the uterus from placental invasion and their derangements during tumorigenesis. Office: U Western Ont Dept Anatomy London ON Canada N6A 5C1

LALE, CISSY STEWART (LLOYD LALE), freelance writer; b. Port Arthur, Tex., Jan. 15, 1924; d. Lloyd M. and May (Cowart) Stewart; m. Max Sims Lale, Oct. 9, 1983. BJ, U. Tex., 1945. Reporter Record-News, Wichita Falls, Tex., 1945, News-Messenger, Marshall, 1945-47; editor Times-Rev., Cleburne, 1947-49; women's editor, columnist Star-Telegram, Ft. Worth, 1949-87; freelance writer Children's Promise mag., Health-Scope mag., 1987-89. Author: Sweetie Ladd's Historic Fort Worth, 1999. Bd. dirs. Trinity Terr. Retirement Community, 1991-94. Recipient Ballard Heritage award North Tex. Hist. Soc.; Cissy Stewart Day proclaimed by Ft. Worth City Coun., 1987, portrayed in outdoor mural City of Ft. Worth, 1987. Mem. Women in Comm., Inc. (nat. pres. 1968-71), Tex. State Hist. Assn. (pres. 1996-97), East Tex. Hist. Assn. (pres. 1994), Tex. Heritage, Inc. (bd. dirs. Ft. Worth chpt. 1990), Womans Club Ft. Worth, Ft. Worth Garden Club (v.p. 1995-96). Episcopalian. Home: # 101 3900 White Settlement Rd Fort Worth TX 76107-7822

LA LIBERTE, ANN GILLIS, graphic artist, consultant, designer, educator; b. St. Paul, Nov. 10, 1942; d. Edward Robert and Frances Caroline (Sullivan) Gillis; m. Paul Henry La Liberte, Aug. 22, 1964; children: Paul E., Elizabeth La Liberte Collins, Stephen A., Helen La Liberte Gallagher, Peter N., Marc H. Student, Am U., 1963-64, Cardinal Stritch Coll., Milw., 1960-63; BA, Coll. St. Catherine, St. Paul, 1985. Artist, owner Ann La Liberte Papers and Posters, Minnetonka, Minn., 1968-71, A.L. Graphic Design and Drawings, Minnetonka, 1987-2001; artist-in-residence Tara Tonka Studio, 1987-2001, Tara Claire Studio, Gordon, Wis., 2001—. Artist Arts in Schs., Minn., 1985-2001; pvt. art tchr., dir. creativity and problem solving seminars, 1991—. Liturgical design cons. Midwest, 1977—; paintings, drawings, photography and sculpture exhibited Mpls. and St. Paul area, 1983—; sculpture Life Exhibit, Paul VI Inst. for the Arts, Washington, 1988, on tour Vt., Ohio, Mo., Ill., Wis., 1988. Del. Minn. Ind. Reps., 1969, vice chmn. Minnetonka, 1970; promotional artist Soc. for Preservation Human Dignity, Palatine, Ill., 1973, Minn. Citizens Concerned for Life, 1980-88, Secular Franciscans, St. Paul, 1985; deanery rep. pastoral coun. Archdiocese of St. Paul and Mpls., 1978-82; chmn. devel. task force out-reach program Resurrection Ch., Mpls., 1980-81, cons. artist, 1983-87; dir. liturg. design Ch. of Immaculate Heart of Mary, Minnetonka, 1989-2001; liturgical art and environ. cons. Mem. Nat. Assn. Liturgical Mins., Mpls. Inst. of Arts, Nat. Mus. Women in Arts (charter), Walker Art Ctr., Minnetonka Ctr. for Arts, Coll. of St. Catherine Alumna Assn., Artists for Life Nat. Slide Registry, Delta Phi Delta. Roman Catholic. Avocations: art history, swimming, hiking, travel, sculpture. Studio: Tara Claire Studio 13706 S Fowler Cir Gordon WI 54838-9039 E-mail: taraclaire01@hotmail.com.

LALIBERTE, RICK, member of parliament; Mem. parliament House of Commons, Ottawa, Canada. Office: House of Commons Ottawa ON U1A 0A6 Canada also: Sister Simard Centre Beaver St Box 490 Beauval Saskatchewan S0M 0J0 Canada*

LALIKOS, JANICE FAY, surgeon; b. Hamilton, Mass., Nov. 2, 1962; d. Stephen Michael and Florence (Pavles) L.; m. Nicola Antonio Francalancia, Sept. 2, 1989. BA, Case Western Reserve U., 1984; MD, Johns Hopkins U., 1988, MA, 1989. Diplomate Am. Bd. Surgery, Am. Bd. Plastic and Reconstructive Surgery. Intern Vanderbilt U. Med. Ctr., Nashville, 1988-89, resident, 1989-91, 92-94; resident plastic surgery U. Mass. Sch. Med. Ctr., Worcester, 1994-96; fellow craniofacial surgery U. Pitts., 1991-92; instr. U. Mass. Sch. Medicine, Worcester, 1996-97; asst. prof. Divsn. Plastic Surgery East Carolina U., Greenville, N.C., 1997-2000, assoc. prof. divsn. plastic surgery, 2000—. Home: 506 Guilder Ln Greenville NC 27858-6580 Office: East Carolina U PCMH 600 Medical Dr Greenville NC 27834-7503 E-mail: lalikosj@mail.ecu.edu.

LALL, B. KENT, civil engineering educator; b. Feb. 4, 1939; m. Margaret Vivienne Boult, Nov. 30, 1970; 1 child, Niren Nicolaus. BS in Civil Engring., Panjab Engring. Coll., Chandigarh, India, 1961; ME in Hwy. Engring., U. Roorkee, India, 1964; PhD in Transp., U. Birmingham, Eng., 1969. Registered profl. engr. Commonwealth scholar U. Birmingham, 1966-69; lectr. Indian Inst. Tech., New Delhi, 1964-72, asst. prof., 1972-75; assoc. prof. U. Man., Winnipeg, Can., 1975-77; assoc. prof. civil engring. Portland (Oreg.) State U., 1977-84, prof., 1984—. Vis. prof. U. Adelaide, South Australia, 1985; cons. Nat. Rds. Bd., Ministry of Works, Wellington, New Zealand, 1986. Editor procs., co-author: Transportation Engineering; contbr. articles to profl. jours. Vol. Meals on Wheels, Portland, 1991—. Fellow ASCE (chmn. transp. congress 1995, exec. com. urban transp. divsn. 1994-95, pub. transp. com. 1988-91, mem. high speed ground transport com.), Inst. Transp. Engrs., Transp. Rsch. Bd., Rotary (bd. dirs. S.W. Portland 1990-91, 95-2000, pres. 1998-99), Intelligent Transp. Soc. Am. Office: Portland State U Dept Civil Engring PO Box 751 Portland OR 97207-0751 E-mail: kent@cecs.pdx.edu.

LALLEY, FRANK EDWARD, computer company executive; b. Woonsocket, R.I., Jan. 11, 1944; s. Frank Edward III and Lois Eva (Parkin) L.; m. Joyce Lynne Rynkiewicz, June 11, 1983; children: Jonathan, Robert, Adrienne, Andrea. B in Mgmt. Engring., Rensselaer Poly. Inst., 1965; MBA, So. Ill. U., 1971; postgrad., George Washington U., 1972-75. Ops. rsch. analyst U.S. Army, 1969-74; energy analyst FEA, Washington, 1974-77; dir. petroleum supply div. U.S. Dept. Energy, 1977-87; dir. Office Info., Mgmt. and Stats. U.S. Dept. Vets. Affairs, 1987-90, assoc. dep. asst. sec. Info. Resources Policies and Oversight, 1990-94, assoc. dep. asst. sec. Telecom., 1994-98; asst. commr. Fed. Tech. Svc., Gen. Svcs. Adminstrn., Fairfax, Va., 1998—2002; pres., CEO Computer Equity Corp., Chantilly, 2002—. Co-chmn. publ. U.S. Refining Industry, Nat. Petroleum Coun., 1986, govt. liaison publ. U.S. Oil and Gas Outlook, 1987; mem. Nat. Performance Review, 1993; chmn. Interagency Com. Info. Resources Mgmt., 1994-95, chmn. Interagency Mgmt. Coun., 1997-98; mem. Nat. Comm. Sys. Com. of Principals, 1994-98. Capt. USAF, 1965-69. Recipient Pres. Meritorious Exec. award, 2001. Office: Computer Equity Corp 4500 Southgate Pl Ste 300 Chantilly VA 20151

LALLI, MICHAEL ANTHONY, lawyer; b. N.Y.C., Sept. 14, 1955; s. Joseph and Maria (Magnacca) L.; m. Marigrace Ann Esposito, May 19, 1979; children: Elena Marie, Marissa Ann. BA, Fordham Coll., 1976, JD, 1979; LLM, NYU, 1984. Bar: N.Y. 1980, U.S. Dist. Ct. (so. dist.) N.Y. 1981. Assoc. counsel Equitable Life Assurance Soc. U.S., N.Y.C., 1979-85; sr. tax atty. Chevron Texaco Corp., White Plains, NY, 1985—. Mem. moot ct. bd. 1977-79. Mem. Fordham Urban Law Jour., 1977-79. Mem. ABA, N.Y. State Bar Assn., Phi Beta Kappa, Pi Sigma Alpha. Roman Catholic. Home: 16 Thomas St Scarsdale NY 10583-1031 Office: Chevron Texaco Corp 2000 Westchester Ave West Harrison NY 10604-3692

L'ALLIER, JAMES JOSEPH, educational multimedia company executive, instructional designer; b. St. Paul, June 24, 1945; s. Charlemagne Joseph and Mildred Marie (LeVasseur) L'A.; m. Susan Kay Margulies, Apr. 28, 1973. BS magna cum laude, U. Wis., River Falls, 1969, MS, 1973; PhD, U. Minn., 1980. Instr. English, multimedia specialist River Falls Sr. High Sch., 1969-71; instr. English Stillwater (Minn.) Sr. High Sch., 1971-80; mgr. computer assisted instrn. Wilson Learning Corp., Mpls., 1980-83, dir. R&D, 1983-86; v.p. R&D Wilson Learning Interactive Tech. Group, Santa Fe, 1986-89; v.p. product devel. Nippon Wilson Learning, Tokyo, 1989-90; v.p. instructional design Whole Systems International, Cambridge, Mass., 1990-93; v.p. product devel. Thomson NETg, A Thomson Learning Co., Naperville, 1993-98; v.p. R&D NETg, A Harcourt Brace Co., Ill., 1998-2000, v.p. R&D, chief learning officer, 2000—. Expert witness Universal Tng., Chgo., 1989-91; bd. dirs. Info. Tech. Tng. Assn., chair standards com. 2000—. Author: (video prodns.) Who Shot the Terminal?, 1984, The Tenth Woman, 1987, Working Toward the Future, 1991, America's Workforce: A Vision for the Future, 1992; mem. editorial bd. Learning Age, Mpls., 1987-89, CLO Mag., Chgo., 2002-; product reviewer Ednl. Tech., N.Y.C., 1981-83; assoc. editor Performance and Instrn., Washington, 1983-85; inventor Interactive Learning System-Skill Builder; holder 240 copyrights; inventor, patent for interactive learning sys. Skill Builder. Curriculum chair Total Info. Ednl. Systems, St. Paul, 1971-76; fund raiser U. Minn. Alliance, Mpls., 1983-89; contbr. Am. Cancer Soc., Washington, 1987—; mem. pub. svc. com. Instructional Systems Assn., Sunset Beach, Calif., 1988—; reviewer William H. Donner Found., Inc., N.Y.C., 1993—. U. Minn. Grad. Sch. Edn. sr. fellow, 1984; U.S. Dept. Labor grantee, 1991. Mem. U. Wis. Alumni Assn., Instructional Systems Assn. (conf. chair 1980, 84), U. Minn. Alumni Assn., Boston Computer Soc., Pres.'s Club U. Minn., Heritage Soc. U. Wis. Avocations: reading, photography, music. Office: Thomson NETG 1751 W Diehl Rd Naperville IL 60563-1840

LALLINGER, E. MICHAEL, savings and loan association executive; b. St. Louis, Aug. 17, 1915; s. Michael N. and Clara (Neiderhoff) L.; m. Johnetta Claire Ward, Jan, 14, 1948; children: Michael John, John Ward, Mary Jeanne. Student, Jefferson Coll., St. Louis, 1937. With RFC, 1941—51, asst. mgr. Dallas office, 1950—51; asst. regional commr. IRS, Dallas, 1952—56; exec. v.p. Gibraltar Savs. Assn., Houston, 1956—63, pres., chmn. bd., CEO, 1963—85, pres., 1963—90, chmn. bd., chief exec. officer, 1980—88, ret., 1988, also dir.; pres., CEO, dir. Imperial Corp. Am., 1980—. Dir. First Internat. Bank, Houston, Fed. Home Loan Mortgage Corp., Washington, First Tex. Savs. Assn.; tchr. individual and corp. tax acctg. Jefferson Coll., 1939—40; chmn. Fin. Commn., State of Tex., 1977, 81. Capt., inf. AUS, 1942-46, ETO. Decorated Silver Star, Bronze Star, Purple Heart; recipient Order Leopold Belgium, Croix de Guerre Belgium. Mem. Nat. League Insured Savs. Assn., U.S. Savs. and Loan League, U.S. C. of C., Houston C. of C. Home: 2121 Kirby Dr Apt 52 Houston TX 77019-6065 Office: 1770 Saint James Pl Ste 605 Houston TX 77056-3500

LALLO, LARRY JONATHON, economic developer; b. Akron, Ohio, Aug. 2, 1953; s. Laddie Lallo and Vera Simpson; m. Susan Lallo; 1 child, Jason. BA, Akron U., 1980; postgrad., Tiffin U., 2001—. Cert. econ. developer. Regional planner Allen County Planning, Lima, Ohio, 1980-82; devel. officer Akron Housing Authority, 1983-89; exec. dir. Barberton (Ohio) Cmty. Devel., 1990—. Cons. Renkert Devel., Canton, Ohio, 1990-93; trsutee roads and bridges Willowdale Latie Club, North Canton, Ohio, 1996-98. Rsch. analyst: An Atlas of India, 1976. Constrn. team leader Mercy Teams, Nicaragua, 1998; mem. missions bd. High Mill Ch., North Canton, 1999. Master USCG. Named Outstanding Bus. Leader of Yr., South Summit C. of C., 2000. Mem. Am. Econ. Devel. Coun., Ohio Devel. Assn., Downtown Barberton Inc. (bd. dirs. 1998). Office: Barberton Cmty Devel Corp 104 3rd St NW Barberton OH 44203-8223 E-mail: llallo@cs.com.

LALLY, MARGARET MATES, English educator, poet; b. Cleve., Aug. 5, 1941; d. Edward Frank and Claire Christine Mates; m. Thomas Robert Lally, Oct. 21, 1961 (div. Sept. 1976); children: Patrick John, Michael James. BA in English, Case Western Res. U., 1972, MA in English, 1974, PhD in English, 1982. Tchr. Cleve. Pub. Sch. Sys., 1960-63; lectr. English, Cleve. State U., 1975-77, Case Western Res. U., Cleve., 1976-83, U. Akron, Ohio, 1982-87; assoc. prof. English, The Citadel, Charleston, S.C., 1987—. Mem. The Poet's Prize Com., N.Y.C., 1990—. Author: (poems) Juliana's Room, 1988. Recipient ind. artist's award Ohio Arts Coun., 1984. Home: PO Box 30494 Charleston SC 29417-0494 Office: The Citadel Dept English Charleston SC 29409-0001 E-mail: lallym@citadel.edu.

LALLY, MICHAEL DAVID, writer, actor; b. Orange, N.J., May 25, 1942; s. James A. and Irene I. (Dempsey) L.; m. Lee Fischer, 1964 (dec. 1986); children: Caitlin Maeve, Miles Aaron; m. Jaina Flynn, 1997; 1 child, Flynn Albert James; m. BA, U. Iowa, 1968, MFA, 1969. Instr. Trinity Coll., Washington, 1969-74; book reviewer Washington Post, 1974-77; editor Franklin Library div. Franklin Mint, 1976-79; editor, pub. various newspapers and presses including Iowa Defender, Some of Us Press, The Washington Review of the Arts, 1966-80, Venice mag., 1988-91, The Hollywood Rev., 1991. Bd. dirs. The Print Center, Bklyn., 1972-75, Washington Film Classroom, 1970-72 Actor: (films) Last Rites, 1980, The Nesting, 1981, White Fang, 1991, Cool World, 1992, Basic Instinct, 1992, Not Again, 1996, Last Grave, 2002, (stage) The Heroes, 1981, Balm in Gilead, 1983, The Rhythm of Torn Stars, 1988-89, Short Eyes, 1994, (TV) Cagney and Lacey, 1984, Berrengers, 1985, Hardcastle and McCormick, 1986, L.A. Law, 1989, Father Dowling's Mysteries, 1991, Caught in the Act, 1993, Diagnosis Murder, 1994, NYPD Blue, 1995, 97, 99, Brooklyn South, 1997, JAG, 1997, 98, Law and Order, 2000, Ed, 2001; freelance writer, reviewer, actor, N.Y.C., 1975-82; screenwriter, actor, L.A., 1982-99, screenwriter, actor, N.Y.C., 1999—; author 20 books including Rocky Dies Yellow, 1974, German edit., 1982, Dues, 1974, Catch My Breath, 1976, 95, Just Let Me Do It, 1978, Attitude, 1982, Hollywood Magic, 1982, Cant Be Wrong, 1996, Of, 1999, It's Not Nostalgia, 1999, It Takes One to Know One, 2001; author, dir. (one-act play) Four Grown Men, N.Y.C., 1982, Hollywood Magic, L.A., 1983; co-author (play) The Rhythm of Torn Stars, 1988-89; 3 short plays, 1995; recorded poems on CD, What You Find There, 1994; contbr. articles and poetry to profl. jours., newspapers, mags. Served with USAF, 1962-66. Nat. Endowment for Arts fellow, 1974, 81; recipient Discovery award N.Y. Poetry Ctr., 1972, award Poets Found., 1974, Lit. Prize award Pacificus Found., 1996, Am. Book award, 2000. Mem. SAG, AFTRA, Writers Guild Am., P.E.N. (Oakland Josephine Miles award for excellence in lit. 1997).

LALLY, NORMA ROSS, retired federal agency administrator; b. Crawford, Nebr., Aug. 10, 1932; d. Roy Anderson and Alma Leona (Barber) Lively; m. Robert Edward Lally, Dec. 4, 1953 (div. Mar. 1986); children: Robyn Carol Murch, Jeffrey Alan, Gregory Roy. BA, Boise (Idaho) State U., 1974, MA, 1976; postgrad., Columbia Pacific U., 1988—. With grad. admissions Boise State U., 1971-74; with officer programs USN Recruiting, Boise, 1974; pub. affairs officer IRS, Boise and Las Vegas, 1975-94; ret., 1994. Speaker in field, Boise and Las Vegas, 1977—. Contbr. articles to newspapers. Mem. task force Clark County Sch. Dist., Las Vegas, 1986-96, Las Vegas Art Mus. Staff sgt. USAF, 1950-54. Mem.: NAFE, Women in Mil. Svc. Am. (charter), Mensa, Marine's Meml. Club (life), Am. Legion (life). Avocations: writing, dancing, music, golf, swimming. Home: 3013 Hawksdale Dr Las Vegas NV 89134-8967 E-mail: norlally@aol.com.

LALLY, RICHARD FRANCIS, aviation security consultant, former association executive, former government official; b. Newark, Nov. 23, 1925; s. Francis J. and Helen (Fennesy) L.; m. Doris P. Yasko, Sept. 10, 1949; children: Barbara J. Lally-Dittler, Joan E. Lally Turton. BS, Upsala Coll., 1950. Spl. agt. FBI, Atlanta, Cin. and Washington, 1951-60; area dir., chief gen. investigations Dept. Labor, Newark and Washington, 1960-63; dep. dir. compliance and security FAA, Washington, 1963-65, dir. compliance and security, 1965-67; dir. investigations and security Dept. Transp., Washington, 1967-70, dir. equal opportunity, 1967-70, dir. civil rights, 1970-72, dir. transp. security, 1972-74; dir. civil aviation security FAA, 1974-82; v.p. security Air Transport Assn. Am., 1982-91; aviation security consultant, 1991—. Served with AC U.S. Army, 1944-46. Recipient Exceptional Svc. citation Dept. Trans., 1969, Meritorious Achievement award, 1970, Sec.'s award, 1973, Superior Achievement award, 1970, Sec.'s award, 1973, Superior Achievement award, 1973, 76, Superior Achievement in Equal Opportunity award, 1977, Disting. Alumnus award Upsala Coll., 1979, Presdl. Rank Sr. Exec. award, 1980, Extraordinary Svc. award FAA, 1991, Internat. Security Mgmt. Assn. J. Paul Breslin Recognition award, 1993. Home and Office: Bay Colony 25 Indian River Dr Dagsboro DE 19939-3201 E-mail: rfldpl@aol.com.

LALLY, VINCENT EDWARD, atmospheric scientist; b. Brookline, Mass., Oct. 13, 1922; s. Michael James and Ellen Teresa (Dolan) L.; m. Marguerite Mary Tibert, June 5, 1949; children: Dennis V., Marianne Baugh, Stephen J. BS in Meteorology, U. Chgo., 1944; BSEE, MIT, 1948, MS in Engring. Adminstrn., 1949. Engr. Bendix-Friez, Balt., 1949-51; chief metall. equip. devel. Air Force Cambridge Rsch. Labs., Bedford, Mass., 1951-58; rsch. dir. Teledynamics, Phila., 1958-61; dir. Nat. Sci. Balloon Facility Nat. Ctr. for Atmospheric Rsch., Boulder, Colo., 1961-66, sr. scientist, 1966-91, sr. scientist emeritus, 1991—. Contbr. articles to sci. jours., chpt. to handbook in field. 1st lt. USAAC, 1942-46. Fellow Am. Meteorol. Soc. (Cleveland Abbe award 1990); mem. Inst. Navigation, Sigma Xi. Achievements include 7 patents for space inflatables, superpressure balloons, rocket instruments, communications techniques; made first balloon flight around the world, longest balloon flight; pioneered technology in measurements from radiosondes, aircraft and rockets. Avocations: running, golf, application of Monte Carlo techniques to gaming. Home: 4875 Sioux Dr Apt 304 Boulder CO 80303-3765 Office: Nat Ctr Atmospheric Rsch PO Box 3000 Boulder CO 80307-3000

LALLY-GREEN, MAUREEN ELLEN, superior court judge, law educator; b. Sharpsville, Pa., July 5, 1949; d. Francis Leonard and Charlotte Marie (Frederick) Lally; m. Stephen Ross Green, Oct. 5, 1979; children: Katherine Lally, William Ross, Bridget Marie. BS, Duquesne U., 1971, JD, 1974. Bar: Pa. 1974, D.C., U.S. Dist. Ct. (we. dist.) Pa. 1974, U.S. Ct. Appeals (3d cir.) 1974, U.S. Supreme Ct. 1978. Atty. Houston Cooper, Pitts., 1974-75, Commodity Futures Trading Comm., Washington, 1975-78; counsel Westinghouse Electric Corp., Pitts., 1978-83; adj. prof. law Duquesne U., 1983-86, 2000—, prof. law, 1986-2000; judge Superior Ct, 1998, Superior Ct., 2000—. Fed. dist. ct. arbitrator; mem. criminal procedure rules com. Supreme Ct. Pa., 1994-97; dir. European Union Law Conf., Dublin, 1995-97, Intellectual Law Conf., Italy, 1997; panel Disciplinary Bd. of Commonwealth of Pa.; adj. prof. law Duquesne U., 2000—. Chair Cranberry Twp. Zoning Hearing Bds., Pa., 1983-98; counsel Western Pa. Ptnrs. of Ams., 1987-90, pres. 1993-95, bd. dirs., 1995—; active Elimination of World Hunger Project, 1977-85, Bishop's Com. on Dialogue with Cath. Univs.; co-chair Millenium com. Duquesne U., 1997-2000. Fellow Kellogg Found. (for Ptnrs. of Ams.), 1990-92. Mem. Pa. Bar Assn. (ethics com. 1987-94, commn. on women in the law 1994—, co-chair quality of work life com. 2001, mem. exec. com., chair 2002), Allegheny County Bar Assn. (women in law com., professionalism com., ethics com., sec. bd. dirs. 1992-2001), Duquesne U. Alumni Assn. (bd. dirs. 1982-89, sec. 1988-89, gov. of bd.), Duquesne U. Law Alumni Assn. (bd. dirs. 1987, treas. 1991, v.p. 1992). Republican. Roman Catholic. Avocations: children's activities, sports. Office: 2420 Grant Bldg 330 Grant St Pittsburgh PA 15219-2202

LALONDE, BERNARD JOSEPH, educator; b. Detroit, June 3, 1933; s. John Bernard and Fannie (Napier) LaL.; m. Barbara Elaine Eggenberger, Sept. 6, 1958; children— Lisa Renee, Michell Ann, Christopher John. AB, U. Notre Dame, 1955; MBA, U. Detroit, 1957; PhD, Mich. State U., 1961. Asst. prof. mktg. U. Colo., Boulder, 1961-65; assoc. prof. Mich. State U., East Lansing, 1965-69; James R. Riley prof. mktg. and logistics Ohio State U., Columbus, 1969-85, Raymond E. Mason prof. transp. and logistics, 1985-95, prof. emeritus, 1995. Author: Physical Distribution Management, 2d edit, 1968, Customer Service: A Management Perspective, 1988; Editor: Jour. Bus. Logistics; Jour. book and monographs editor, Am. Mktg. Assn.; Contbr. articles to profl. jours. Pres. Transp. Research Found. Recipient John Drury Sheehan award, 1976; Formerly Ford scholar; Gen. Electric fellow. Mem. Am. Marketing Assn., Regional Sci. Assn., Council Logistic Mgmt., Soc. Logistics Engrs., Beta Gamma Sigma, Alpha Kappa Psi. Roman Catholic. Home: 8538 Pitlochry Ct Dublin OH 43017-9770 Office: Ohio State U Coll Bus Supply Chain Mgmt Rsch Grp 421 Hagerty Hall Columbus OH 43210

LALONDE, FERNAND, lawyer; Counsel Leduc, Leblanc, Inc., Montreal, Canada. Bd. dirs., vice-chmn. ISee3D, Inc.; interim pres. Quebec Securities Commn., Canada; mem. Assembly Nat. Quebec, Canada, solicitor gen., house leader of the offcl. oppositon; bd. dirs. AirCanada, Inc. Past pres. Montreal Mus. Fine Arts; bd. dirs. Theatre du Nouveau Monde. Mem.: Soc. Energy Foster Wheeler (chmn. bd.). Office: Leduc Leblanc Inc 407 St Laurent Montreal H2Y 2Y5 Canada*

LALONDE, FRANCINE, member of parliament; b. Ste.-Hyacinthe, Que., Aug. 24, 1940; children: Dominique, Philippe, Julien. Degree in edn. psychology, École normale Cardinal-Lé; lic. in history, U. Montreal. Instr. occupl. health and safety, history and adminstrn. U. Montreal, U. Que., Montreal, Chicoutimi, école Hautes Études Commls.; mem. Can. Parliament for Bloc Québécois for Mercier, 1993—. Ofcl. opposition critic on human resources and lit., v.p. standing com. on human resources devel., 1993-97; critic on industry, employment and econ. devel. Bloc Québécois, 1997-99, critic on fgn. affairs, mem. standing com. fgn. affairs and internat. trade, 1999—. Dir. info. and prs. CEGEP sect. CSN, 1969-83, 1st woman v.p., pres. Nat. Tchrs.' Fedn., chair coordinating com. pvt. sector fedns.; coord. Soc. Coop. Produits Électriques et Moteurs, 1984; minister responsible for status of women Govt. Que., 1985; cand. for presidency Parti Québécois, 1985, mem. nat. exec. coun., 1988, program advisor, 1991. Office: House of Commons 907 Confederation Bldg Ottawa ON Canada K1A 0A6 E-mail: 1alonf@parl.gc.ca.

LALONDE, MARC, lawyer, former Canadian government official; b. Ile Perrot, Que., Can., July 26, 1929; s. J. Albert and Nora (St-Aubin) L.; m. Claire Tetreau, Sept. 8, 1955; children: Marie, Luc, Paul, Catherine. BA, Coll. St. Laurent, Montreal, 1950; LLB, U. Montreal, 1964, LLM, 1955; MA in Econs. and Polit. Sci., Oxford (Eng.) U., 1957; PhD honoris causa, Limburg U., The Netherlands, 1989, DhD. Bar: Que. 1955, Queen's Coun. 1971, Order of Can, 1988. Prof. bus. law and econs. U. Montreal, 1957-59; spl. asst. to Minister of Justice, Ottawa, Ont., Can., 1959-60; partner firm Gelinas, Bourque, Lalonde & Benoit, Montreal, 1960-68; policy adviser to Prime Minister Lester B. Pearson, Ottawa, 1967-68; prin. sec. to Prime Minister

Pierre E. Trudeau, 1968-72; elected to House of Commons for Montreal-Outremont, 1972; minister of nat. health and welfare, 1972-77; minister of state for fed.-provincial relations, 1977-78; minister responsible for status of women, 1975-78; minister of justice and atty. gen. Can., 1978-79; minister of energy, mines and resources, 1980-82; minister of finance, 1982-84; sr. counsel Stikeman, Elliott, Montreal. Bd. dirs. Citibank of Can., O&Y Properties, Inc., Sherritt Power, Inc., Oxbow Equities Corp.; ad hoc judge Internat. Ct. Justice, 1995—. Author: The Changing Role of the Prime Minister's Office, 1971. Decorated officer Order of Can.; Queen's Counsel; recipient Dana award APHA, 1978. Mem. Internat. Coun. on Comml. Arbitration, Am. Arbitration Assn., London Ct. Internat. Arbitration, Privy Coun. Can. Mem. Liberal Party. Home: 1477 boul Perrot Ile Perrot QC Canada J7V 7P2 E-mail: mlalonde@mte.stikeman.com.

LALONDE, ROBERT FREDERICK, state senator, retired; b. Bay City, Mich., Dec. 1, 1922; s. Joseph and Mildred Amanda (Brimmer) LaL.; m. Betty Ellen Schwartz, Aug. 2, 1941; 1 child, Rose Marie. BGE in Bus., U. Omaha, 1965. Airport mgr. Jackson (Wyo.) Hole Airport, Jackson, Wyo., 1972-80; county commr. Teton County, 1982-86, rental property owner, 1970-88; Wyo. state senator, 1989-95. Author: The Dangerous Trilogy, 1973. Chmn. Teton County Rep. Com., Jackson, 1975-77; del. Rep. Nat. Conv., Detroit, 1980; mem. Electoral Coll., Cheyenne, Wyo., 1980; sec. Wyo. Rep. party, 1980-82; chmn. Teton County Planning Commn., Jackson, 1973-78. Col. USAF, 1943-70. Mem. Am. Legion (comdr. 1989-94), Wyo. Airport Operators Assn. (founder, pres. 1973-75, Disting. Svc. award 1979), Jackson Hole C. of C. (pres. 1977-79, Citizen of Yr. 1975, Disting. Svc. award 1980), Rotary (pres. 1976-77). Christian Scientist. Avocations: hunting, fishing. Home: PO Box 1707 Jackson WY 83001-1707

LALOR, DANIEL KEVIN, judge; b. Catskill, N.Y., June 14, 1944; s. Edward and Anna (O'Grady) L.; m. Susan Munn, Aug. 18, 1968; children: Atticus Edward, Becket Colin, Clement Munn. AB, Georgetown U., 1966, JD, 1969. Bar: N.Y. 1969, U.S. Dist. Ct. (no. and so. dists.) N.Y., D.C. 1974, Fla. 1977, U.S. Supreme Ct. 1978. Atty. Met. Life Ins. Co., N.Y.C., 1969-72; ptnr. law firm Meadow Ruf and Lalor, P.C., Catskill, 1972-87; pub. defender Greene County, 1972-76, 1st asst. dist. atty., 1978-88, dist. atty., 1988-90, family, country and surrogate ct. judge, 1991—. Counsel Village of Catskill, 1972-80, Village of Coxsackie, 1983-88, Town of Greenville, 1980, Rheedlen Found. Recipient McCahill medal, 1969. Mem. ABA, Greene County Bar Assn. (sec. 1975, treas. 1976, v.p. 1977, pres. 1978), Nat. Dist. Attys. Assn., N.Y. State Bar Assn., Nat. Legal Aide and Defenders Assn., N.Y. State Defenders Assn. (bd. dirs. 1973-78), D.C. Bar Assn., Assn. of Bar of City of N.Y., Fla. Bar Assn., Royal Cork Yacht Club, Elks. Roman Catholic. Home: 58 William St Catskill NY 12414-1419 Office: County Courthouse 320 Main St Catskill NY 12414-1816 E-mail: dlalor@courts.state.ny.us.

LAM, ARTHUR M. anesthesiologist, educator; b. Hong Kong, Oct. 13, 1949; came to U.S., 1987; s. Pui-Kit Lam and Siu-Fan Wong; m. Annie Y. Lu, Nov. 9, 1974; children: Derek, Jessica, Michelle. MD, U. Western Ont., London, Can., 1974. Diplomate Am. Bd. Anesthesiology. Intern St. Joseph's Hosp., London, 1974-75; resident U. Western Ont., 1975-77, 78-79, U. Toronto, Toronto Gen. Hosp., Hosp. for Sick Children, 1977-78; lectr. dept. anesthesia U. Western Ont., 1979-82, asst. prof., 1982-86, assoc. prof., 1986-87; chief anesthesia St. Joseph's Hosp., London, 1986-87; assoc. prof. anesthesia U. Wash., Seattle, 1987-91, prof. anesthesiology, prof. neurol. surgery, 1991—. Head neuroanesthesia Harborview Med. Ctr., Seattle, 1987—. Co-author: Essentials of Anesthesia, 1983; editor: Anesthetic Management of Acute Head Injury, 1995; contbr. over 100 articles to profl. jours., 25 chpts. to textbooks; patentee on transcranial doppler frame. Fellow Royal Coll. Physicians and Surgeons Can.; mem. Am. Soc. Anesthesiology, Internat. Anesthesia Rsch. Soc., N.Y. Acad. Scis., Soc. Neurosurg. Anesthesia and Supportive Care (pres. 1997-98), Wash. State Soc. Anesthesiologists. Avocations: skiing, basketball, tennis. Home: 8116 SE 77th Pl Mercer Island WA 98040-5937 Office: Harborview Med Ctr 325 9th Ave Seattle WA 98104-2420

LAM, CEDRIC FUNG, electrical engineer, researcher; b. Kunming, Yunnan, China, Nov. 21, 1970; s. Shing-wu Lam, Wai-yin Chan. BEE, U.Hong Kong, 1993; PhD in Elec. Engring., U.Calif., L.A., 1999. Rsch. asst. U. Hong Kong, Hong Kong, China, 1992, tchg. asst., 1993—94; tchg. assoc. U. Calif., L.A., Calif., 1996, instr., 1996—98, rsch. asst., 1995—99; sr. tech. staff AT&T Lab., Middletown, NJ, 1999—. Conf. chmn. Co-author: Future Trends in Microelectronics: The Road Ahead, 1999, Optical Fiber Telecommunications, 2002; contbr. articles to profl. jours.; editor: Jour. Optical Networking, 2001—. Fellow Sir Edward Youde fellowship, Hong Kong Govt., 1994—97, Non-resident Student fellowship, U. Calif., Los Angeles, 1995—99. Mem.: IEEE. Home: 202 Knollwood Dr. Middletown CA 07748 Office: AT&T Labs Research 200 S. Laurel Ave. Middletown CA 07748 Office Fax: 732-368-9477. Personal E-mail: cflam@ieee.org. Business E-Mail: cflam@research.att.com.

LAM, CHEUNG-WEI, electrical engineer; b. Hong Kong, Mar. 5, 1965; came to U.S., 1987; s. Yeung-Tak and Sau-Jin (Wong) L.; m. Hoi-Man Sarah Hui, May 29, 1993; children: Isaac Samuel, Grace Sally. BS, Chinese U. Hong Kong, 1987; MS, MIT, 1989, PhD, 1993. Rsch. asst. MIT, Cambridge, 1988-93; rschr. Schlumberger-Doll Rsch, Ridgefield, Conn., 1990; prin. engr. Viewlogic Systems, Inc., Camarillo, Calif., 1993-98, Transcendent Design Tech., Inc., Camarillo, 1998-99; sr. EMC engr. Apple Computer, Inc., Cupertino, Calif., 1999—. Mem. com. Soc. Automotive Engrs./Electromagnetic Compatibility Modeling Task Force, 1994, IEEE EMC TC-9, 1995—. Contbr. articles to Jour. Superconductivity, IEEE, Jour. Electromagnetic Waves and Applications. Bank of Am. scholar, 1985, Du Pont scholar, 1986. Mem. IEEE (prize 1987, best paper award 1996), Sigma Xi. Achievements include design of efficient electromagnetic interference simulator, nonlinear models for superconducting transmission lines; research in high-speed electronic interconnection and packaging, acoustic logging in borehole structures. Home: 6969 Calabazas Creek Cir San Jose CA 95129-3709 Office: Apple Computer Inc 1 Infinite Loop # Ms26A Cupertino CA 95014-2084 E-mail: lam@alum.mit.edu.

LAM, CHUN HUNG, finance educator, consultant; b. Kowloon, Hong Kong, Oct. 6, 1947; came to U.S., 1966; s. Wing Cheong and Choi Chu (Chan) L.; m. Wai-Fung Edith Kong, June 14, 1975; children: Jon, Jay, Rick. BS in Edn., Duke U., 1971, MBA, 1974, PhD, 1977; MS in Edn., Princeton U., 1972. Bus. analyst Corning Internat., Corning, N.Y., 1974; instr. Duke U., Durham, N.C., 1976-77; asst. prof. Sch. Bus. Tulane U., New Orleans, 1977-81; assoc. prof. Cox Sch. Bus. So. Meth. U., Dallas, 1981—, chmn. Dept. Fin. Cox Sch. Bus., 1988-91. Bd. dirs. Pacific Southwest Bank, Corpus Christi, Tex., 1990—, North Tex. Mesbic, Inc., Dallas, 1990-93, 1st Internat. Bank, Dallas, 1992—; mem. adv. bd. Trinity Christian Acad., Addison, Tex., 1992—; faculty senate exec. com. So. Meth. U., 1996-98. Author: Microcomputer Application in Banking, 1986; contbr. articles to profl. jours. Recipient Howard Wissner Teaching award Tulane U., 1981, James B. Duke fellowship, 1976. Mem. Fin. Mgmt. Assn., Fin. Assn., Phi Beta Kappa, Tau Beta Pi. Office: Cox Sch Bus So Meth U Dallas TX 75275

LAM, GALEN KA-RON, electrical engineer; b. Winnipeg, Man., Can., May 18, 1969; arrived in Japan, 1993; s. Peter Kuen-Yui and Sau-Yin (Ng) Lam; m. Mamiko Nishiguchi, Mar. 25, 1997. BSc in Elec. Engring., U. Calgary, Alta., 1991. Sys. planning engr., overseas plant engring. dept. NEWJEC, Inc., Osaka, Japan, 1993-97; facilities planning, power sys. engr. TransAlta Utilities Corp., Calgary, Alta., Can., 1997-98; transmission adminstr., tech. svcs. group ESB Internat., Alta., Can., 1998—. Mem.: IEEE, Geologists and Geophysicists Alta., Assn. Profl. Engrs. Achievements include numerous pre-feasibility and feasibility studies on coal thermal, hydro and combined cycle plants, pumped storage, and nuclear power projects in numerous countries. Avocations: bicycling, music, reading, tennis. Office: ESBI Alberta Ltd 900 736-8th Ave SW Calgary AB Canada T2A 7W3 E-mail: galen.lam@shaw.ca., galen.lam@eal.ab.ca.

LAM, PAULINE POHA, library director; b. Hong Kong, Oct. 21, 1950; came to U.S., 1971; d. Cheung and Kam-Chun (Mo) Li; m. Frank Sung-Lun Lam, Nov. 28, 1973; children: Candace See-Win Lam, Megan See-Kay Lam. BA, U. B.C., 1977; MLS, U. Tex., 1980; cert. City Mgmt. Acad., Austin C.C., 1994. Libr. dir. City of Cedar Park (Tex.). Bd. dirs. Cedar Park Pub. Libr. Found., 1994—. Mem. Work Force Literacy Com. Literacy Coun. of Williamson County, 1995; bd. dirs. ARC of Ctrl. Tex., Austin, 1995-97. Mem. ALA, Tex. Libr. Assn., Tex. Mcpl. League Libr. Dir. Assn. Avocations: reading, crocheting, painting. Office: Cedar Park Pub Libr 550 Discovery Blvd Cedar Park TX 78613-2200

LAM, SIMON SHIN-SING, computer science educator; b. Macao, July 31, 1947; came to U.S., 1966; s. Chak Han and Kit Ying (Tang) L.; m. Amy Leung, Mar. 29, 1971; 1 child, Eric BSE.E. with distinction, Wash. State U., 1969; MS in Engring., UCLA, 1970, PhD, 1974. Research engr. ARPA Network Measurement Ctr., UCLA, Los Angeles, 1971-74; research staff mem. IBM Watson Research Ctr, Yorktown Heights, N.Y., 1974-77; asst. prof. U. Tex.-Austin, Austin, 1977-79, assoc. prof., 1979-83, prof. computer sci., 1983—; David S. Bruton Centennial prof. U. Tex., 1985-88, anonymous prof., 1988-2001, chmn. dept. computer sci., 1992-94, regents chair computer sci., 2001—. Editor-in-chief IEEE/ACM Transactions on Networking, 1995-99; editor: Principles of Communication and Networking Protocols; contbr. articles to profl. jours. Recipient William R. Bennett prize, 2001; NSF grantee, 1978—; Chancellor's Teaching fellow UCLA, 1969-73 Fellow IEEE (Leonard G. Abraham prize 1975, William R. Bennett prize 2001), ACM (program chmn. symposium 1983). Avocations: tennis, swimming, skiing, travel. Office: Univ Tex Dept Comp Sci Austin TX 78712

LAMAGNA, JOSEPH, author; b. Yonkers, N.Y., June 27, 1934; s. Angelo and Lina (Scariati) L. Grad. h.s., Yonkers. Probation investigator, enforcement officer Westchester County, Yonkers, N.Y., 1964-89; ret., 1989; owner Lamagna Pubs., Yonkers, 1970—. Guest spkr. various radio and TV talk shows, 1980—; instr./lectr. writing courses. Author: Wild Game Cookbook and Other Recipes, 3rd edit., 1997, Coins: The Collector's Guide, 2nd edit., 1997, Trout Fishing USA, 1997, Write Right: Not, Almost Right, 1996, God's Last Will & Testament for Earth, 1999, Rip Van Winkle's New Saga, 1999; contbr. short stories to Kaatskill Life Mag., Entertainer Mag., N.Y. State Outdoor Recreation Guide, So. N.Y. Sportsman, Westchester Life Notes, Yonkers Home News and Times, others. Mem. NRA, Ret. Pub. Employees Assn. (life), N.Y. State Probation Officers Assn., Mt. Carmel Cath. Men's Club (life). Republican. Avocations: fishing, hunting, photography. Office: Lamagna Pubs PO Box 882 Yonkers NY 10702-0882

LAMALFA, JOACHIM JACK, retired clinical psychologist; b. Milw., Aug. 10, 1915; s. Salvatore and Josephine (Foti) L.; m. Constance Zarcone, Dec. 27, 1944; children: Constance Joanne, John Cibik, Jacquelyn Grace, Houston Lee Browne. BS, Marquette U., 1938; MS, U. Wis., 1941; PhD, U. Mich., 1949. Lic. psychologist, Wis. Research asst. U. Mich., Ann Arbor, 1946-47; psychol. intern Milw. County Hosp. for Mental Diseases, 1947-49; instr. psychology Marquette U., Milw., 1951-52; pvt. practice psychology, 1949-2001. Founder, chmn. dept. psychology Milw. County Hosp. for Mental Diseases, 1947, Marquette U. Dept. Psychology, 1947, St. Michael's Hosp. Mental Health Clinic, 1952; mem. affiliate staff St. Mary's Hosp., Ozaukee, Wis., 1994—. Author: (with Henry Viet) Psychosis with Cerebral Arterioschlerosis as Affected by Adrenal Cortical Extract. Mem. Am. Psychol. Assn., Wis. Psychol. Assn., Soc. Clin. Psychologists, Milw. Psychol. Assn., Nat. Register Health Service Providers in Psychology, Phi Kappa Phi, Phi Delta Kappa Republican. Roman Catholic. Home: 7821 N Lake Dr Milwaukee WI 53217-2911

LAMALIE, ROBERT EUGENE, retired executive search company executive; b. Fremont, Ohio, June 3, 1931; s. Glennis and Mildred M. (Hetrick) L.; m. Dorothy M. Zilles, June 20, 1953; children: Deborah, Dawn, Elaine. BA, Capital U., Columbus, Ohio, 1954; postgrad., Case Western Res. U. Asst. dir. recruiting Xerox Corp., 1959-62; mgr. orgn. planning and profl. recruiting Glidden Co., 1962-65; search cons. Booz, Allen & Hamilton, Inc., Cleve., 1965-67; pres., chief exec. officer Lamalie Assocs., Inc., Tampa, Fla., 1967-84, chmn. bd. dirs., chief exec. officer, 1984-87, chmn. bd. dirs., 1987-88; pres. Robert Lamalie, Inc., Marco Island, 1988-90, ret., 1990. Served with U.S. Army, 1954-56, Korea.

LAMAN, JERRY THOMAS, mining company executive; b. Muskogee, Okla., Mar. 1, 1947; s. Thomas J. and Juanita J. (Pittman) L.; m. Lenora J. Laman, July 1, 1972; children: Troy T., Brian D. Silver Diploma, Colo. Sch. Mines, 1969, Exec. MBA, 2000. Refinery engr. ARCO, Torrance, Calif., 1969-71; chem. engr. Cleveland-Cliffs Iron Co., Mountain City, Nev., 1971-73, asst. mine supt., 1973-77, chief uranium metallurgist Casper, Wyo., 1977-83; project mgr. In-Situ, Inc., Laramie, 1983-85, v.p., 1985-98, also bd. dirs.; pres. Solution Mining Corp., Laramie, Wyo., 1990-2000, also bd. dirs., 1990-2000. Mem.: Petroleum Engrs. Tex. Avocations: golf, fishing. E-mail: jerry_laman@yahoo.com.

LAMANET LALONDE, SHARI, artist, art educator; b. San Francisco, Sept. 29, 1949; d. Alfred Paul and Marjorie Theodora (Hibschle) L.; m. Philip Martin Lalonde, Sept. 28, 1974; children: Sydney Lamanet, Paul Braque. BFA, San Francisco Art Inst., 1971, MFA, 1979. Mem. painting faculty San Francisco Art Inst., 1981—. Group shows include Emmanuel Walter Gallery San Francisco Art Inst., 1980, 83, 87, Rental Gallery San Francisco Mus. Modern Art, 1980, 93, 96, Sierra Nevada Mus. Art, Reno, Nev., 1980, Minot (N.D.) State Coll., 1981 (Hon. Mention), San Francisco Mus. Modern Art, 1981, Stedman Art Gallery Rutgers U., Camden, N.J., 1981-82, So. Exposure Gallery, San Francisco, 1983, Slant Gallery, San Francisco, 1984, Alternative Mus., N.Y.C., 1984, Ian Birkstad Gallery, London, 1985, Musavi Gallery, N.Y.C., 1985 (First Place Drawing), ARCO Visual Arts Ctr., Anchorage, Alaska, 1985-86, Fairbanks (Alaska) Art Assn., 1985-86, Alaska State Mus., Juneau, 1985-86, Koslow Gallery, L.A., 1988, 89, Camerawork Gallery, San Francisco, 1988 (Phelan award 1987), Downey Mus. Art, L.A., 1989, John Michael Kohler Arts Ctr., Sheboygan, Wis., 1990, U. San Diego, 1990, Redding (Calif.) Mus. Art and History, 1991, San Francisco Art Inst., 1992, 93, 96, Opts Arts, San Francisco, 1994, Ctr. Visual Arts, Oakland, Calif., 1994, Jernigan Wicker Gallery, San Francisco, 1997, numerous others; one person shows include Bruce Velick Gallery, San Francisco, 1984, 86, 88, Sheppard Gallery, U. Nev., Reno, 1984, Slant Gallery, 1985, Monterey (Calif.) Mus. Art, 1986. Bd. dirs. San Francisco Children's Art Ctr., 1990-92; mem. fine arts com. Schs. of the Sacred Heart, San Francisco, 1995-96. Home: 2475 Pacific Ave San Francisco CA 94115-1237 Office: San Francisco Art Inst 800 Chestnut St San Francisco CA 94133-2206

LAMANTIA, CHARLES ROBERT, management consulting company executive; b. N.Y.C., June 12, 1939; s. Joseph Ferdinand and Catherine (Perniciaro) LaM.; m. Ann Christine Carmody, Sept. 16, 1961; children: Elise, Matthew. BA, Columbia U., 1960, BS, 1961, MS, 1962, ScD, 1965; grad. advanced mgmt. program, Harvard Bus. Sch., 1979. Cons. staff Arthur D. Little, Inc., Cambridge, Mass., 1967-77, v.p., 1977-81, pres., COO, 1987-88, pres., CEO, 1988-98, chmn., CEO, 1998-99, also bd. dirs.; pres., CEO Koch Process Sys., Westboro, Mass., 1981-86. Mem. adv. coun. Sch. Engring. Columbia U., 1990-98; mem. adv. bd. Sch. Mgmt. Boston Coll., 1995—; bd. dirs. State St. Corp., 1994—, Marathon Techs., 2001—; trustee Meml. Dr. Trust, 1988-99; bd. govs. New Eng. Med. Ctr., 1989-95; bd. advisors StoneGate Ptnrs., 2000-01, IntellectExchange.com, 2000—. Mem. Corp. Woods Hole Oceanog. Inst., 1996—; mem. bd. overseers Mus. Sci., Boston, 1988-94, Sta. WGBH-TV, 1990—, mem. Conf. Bd., 1989-99; mem. Mass. Gov.'s Coun., Mass. Bus. Roundtable, 1992-99, bd. dirs. 1998-99; bd. dirs. Boston Pub. Libr. Found., 1997-2001. Lt. USN, 1965-67. Sloan Found. fellow, 1962, NSF fellow, 1965. Mem. AIChE.

LAMANTIA, PAUL CHRISTOPHER (W. ZOMBEK), artist; b. Chgo., Jan. 20, 1938; BFA, Chgo. Art Inst., 1966, MFA, 1968. Exhibited in numerous one-man and group shows; represented in permanent collections Chgo. Art Inst., Mus. Contemporary Art, Chgo., Nat. Mus. Am. Art, Smithsonian Inst., Washington, Madison Art Ctr., Wis., David and Alfred Smart Mus. of Art, U. Chgo., Sonia Zaks Gallery, Cin. Art Mus., Ukrainian Inst. Modern Art, Chgo., pvt. collection, Paris. Recipient Mr. and Mrs. Frank G. Logan medal, Chgo. Art Inst., 1984.

LAMAR, HORACE BEASELY, JR. university dean; b. Mobile, Ala., June 12, 1955; m. Danielle Kennedy; children: Horace Lamar III, Kennedy O'Neil Lamar. BS, Miss. Valley State U., 1977; MA, U. Minn., 1979; PhD in Music Edn., U. So. Miss., 1989. Tchr. music LeFlore H.S., Mobile, Ala., 1979-88; asst. prof. music Ala. A&M U., Normal, 1988-91, Ala. State U., Montgomery, 1991-95, dean Sch. Music, 1995—. Band and choral clinician, music edn. cons., performer S.Ea. U.S. Home: 137 Oldfield Dr Montgomery AL 36117-3937 Office: Alabama State University PO Box 271 Montgomery AL 36101-0271 E-mail: hlamar@asunet.alasu.edu.

LAMAR, HOWARD ROBERTS, educational administrator, historian; b. Tuskegee, Ala., Nov. 18, 1923; s. John Howard and Elma (Roberts) L.; m. Doris Shirley White, Sept. 3, 1959; children: Susan Kent, Sarah Howard. BA, Emory U., 1944; MA, Yale U., 1945, PhD, 1951; LHD (hon.), Emory U., 1975; LLD (hon.), Yale U., 1993; LittD (hon.), U. Nebr., 1994. Instr. U. Mass., 1945-46, Wesleyan U., Middletown, Conn., 1948-49; mem. faculty Yale U., 1949-94, prof. Am. History and history Am. West, 1964-94, W.R. Coe prof. Am. history, 1979-87, Sterling prof. history, 1987—, chmn. history dept., 1962-63, 67-70, dir. history grad. studies, 1964-67, fellow Ezra Stiles Coll., 1961-94, dean, 1979-85, pres., 1992-93, Sterling prof. history emeritus, 1994—. Author: Dakota Territory, 1861-1889, 1956, 97, The Far Southwest, 1846-1912, A Territorial History, 1966, 2d edit., 2000; also articles, reviews.; Editor: (Joseph Downey) Cruise of the Portsmouth, 1958, Western Americana Series, 1961— , New Encyclopedia of the American West, 1998, Gold Seeker: Adventures of A Belgian Argonaut in California, 1985, paperback 1998; co-author, co-editor The Frontier in History: North America and Southern Africa Compared, 1981, History of the American Frontier Series, 1976—. Alderman, New Haven, 1951-53. Mem. Orgn. Am. Historians, Western History Assn. (pres. 1971-72), Am. Antquarian Soc., Elihu Soc., Conn. Acad. of Arts and Scis., Phi Beta Kappa. Democrat. Home: 1747 Hartford Tpke North Haven CT 06473-1249 Office: Yale U Dept History New Haven CT 06520

LAMAR, JASON RANDOLPH, multimedia designer; b. Muncie, Ind., June 3, 1974; s. William Gregg and Andrea Lynn LaMar. BS in Journalism, Ball State U., 1996. Asst. coord. The Ind. Acad. Office Outreach Programs, Muncie, 1996-98, asst. dir. comm. and devel., 1998-99; dir. web svcs. Ohio Wesleyan U., Delaware, 1999—. Founder, creative dir. LightVibe Studios, Columbus, Ohio. Project dir. (ednl. web sites) Smithsonian Nat. Mus. Natural History, 1997, 98, San Francisco Exploratorium, 1997, BBC WebGuide, 1998, The Chgo. Field Mus., 1999 (Bonus.com Editor's Choice award 1999), The Newseum, 1998. Web dir. Carter for County Commr., Delaware County, Ohio, 2000. Recipient Coolest Sci. Site Nat. Acad. Press, 1997-98. Avocations: MIDI music composition, creative writing, digital art and illustration. Office: Ohio Wesleyan U Mowry Alumni Ctr Delaware OH 43015

LAMARRE, BERNARD, engineering, contracting and manufacturing advisor; b. Chicoutimi, Que., Can., Aug. 6, 1931; s. Emile J. and Blanche M. (Gagnon) L.; m. Louise Lalonde, Aug. 30, 1952; children: Jean, Christine, Lucie, Monique, Michèle, Philippe, Mireille. BSc, Ecole Poly., Montreal, Que., Can., 1952; MSc, Imperial Coll., U. London, 1955; LLD, St. Francis Xavier U., N.S., Can., 1980; D in Engring. (hon.), U. Waterloo, Ont., 1984; LLD (hon.), U. Concordia, Montreal, 1985; D in Engring. (hon.), U. Montreal, 1985; D in Applied Sci. (hon.), U. Sherbrooke, Que., 1986; D in Bus. Adminstrn. (hon.), U. Chicoutimi, Que., 1987; D in Sci. (hon.), Queen's U., Kingston, Ont., 1987; D in Engring. (hon.), U. Ottawa, Ont., 1988, Tech. U. N.S., 1989, Royal Mil. Coll., Kingston, 1990; PhD in Sci. (hon.), McGill U., 2001. Structural and founds. engr. Lalonde-Valois, Montreal, 1955-60, chief engr., 1960-62; ptnr., gen. mgr., pres. Lalonde, Valois, Lamarre, Valois, 1962-72; chmn., chief exec. officer Lavalin Group, 1972-91; sr. advisor SNC-Lavalin Inc., 1991-99. Chmn. Soc. du Vieux Port de Montreal, Bellechasse Santè, Fre Composite Inc., Soc. de la Faune et des Parcs du Quebec (FAPAC), Ecole Polytechnique de Montreal; bd. dirs. Tembec Inc., Microcell Inc., Acier Leroux Inc., Tolus Solutions d'Affairs, Inc., Capital Internat. CDPQ. Bd. dirs. U. of Montreal, Montreal Design Inst.; chmn. Montreal Mus. Fine Arts. Decorated officer Ordre nat. du Québec, Order of Can.; Athlone fellow, 1952. Fellow Engring. Inst. Can., Can. Soc. Civil Engring.; mem. ASCE, Order Engrs. Que., Mont-Royal Club, St. Denis Club, Laval-sur-le Lac Club. Roman Catholic. Home: 4850 Cedar Crescent Montreal QC Canada H3W 2H9 E-mail: gbsi@dsuper.net.

LAMAS, GERVASIO ANTONIO, cardiologist, educator; b. Jan. 10, 1952; BA, Harvard U., 1974; MD, NYU, 1978. Diplomate Am. Bd. Cardiology. Fellow Harvard/Brigham Hosp., 1978-84; asst. prof. Harvard U., Cambridge, Mass., 1987-93; assoc. prof. U. Miami, Miami Beach, Fla., 1993—. Hon. prof., Argentina; dir. cardiovasc. rsch. Mt. Sinai Med. Ctr., Miami, 1999. Contbr. articles to profl. jours. Mem.: Am. Coll. Cardiology (dist. rep. 1995—98), Am. Heart Assn. (bd. dirs. 1999—, pres. Miami Dade 2000—01). Office: Cardiovasc Assocs of Miami 4300 Alton Rd Ste 207 Miami Beach FL 33140-2800 E-mail: glamas@msmc.com.

LAMAS, LORENZO, actor, director; b. Santa Monica, Calif., Jan. 20, 1958; s. Fernando Lamas and Arlene Dahl; children: Alvaro Joshua, Shayne Dahl, Paton Lee, Alexandra Lyn, Victoria Arlene. Grad., Farragut Acad., Pine Beach, N.J., 1975, Jim Russel Sch. Motor Racing, 1985. Cert. instrument rated pilot. Ptnr. LeConte Driving Sch., Willow Springs, Calif., 1985—; driver Phil Conte Racing, Paramount, 1985—, driver competition in Internat. Motor Sports Assn. prototypes, 1988, 89. Appeared in films, Grease, 1978, Take Down, 1978, Tilt, 1979, Body Rock, 1984, Snake Eater, 1989, The Killing Streets, 1991, Night of the Warrior, 1991, also co-prodr. Snake Eater II: The Drug Buster, 1991, Final Impact, 1992, C.I.A., Code Name Alexa, 1992, Snake Eater III: His Law, 1992, Final Round, 1993, Bounty Tracker, 1993, The Swordsman, 1993, C.I.A. II: Target Alexa, 1994 (also dir.), Terminal Justice, 1995, Gladiator Cop II: The Swordsman, 1995, The Rage, 1996, Mask of Death, 1996, Undercurrent, 1998; (TV movies) Detour to Terror, 1980, Bad Blood, 1994; appeared in TV series, California Fever, 1979, Midland Heights, 1980, Falcon Crest, 1981-90, Dancin' to the Hits, 1986, Renegade, 1992, Air Am., 1998-99, The Immortal, 2000. Winner Toyota Grand Prix of Long Beach, 1985. Avocations: surfing, flying, golf, motorcycles, karate. Office: No Rain Prodns Inc care L & L Bus Mgmt 3727 W Magnolia Blvd # 807 Burbank CA 91505-2818

LAMAZE, JEAN-HUGHES DE, equity analyst executive; b. Paris, Apr. 11, 1965; s. Jean and Cecile (De Franclieu) De L.; m. Aude de Chassey, May 15, 1993. LLB, U. Paris II-Assas, 1987; diploma, Inst. Superieur de Gestion, Paris, 1988, Ctr. Formation Fin. Analysis, 1992, Franco-Brit. C. of C., 1986; Internat. Exec. Programme, INSEAD, 2000. Trainee analyst Enskilda Securities, London, 1987; trainee fund mgr. Cholet-Dupont, Paris, 1988; equity analyst Enskilda Societe de Bourse, 1989-96; dir., head French equity rsch. and European utilities rsch. Credit Suisse First Boston, London, 1996—2002; exec. dir. global investment rsch. Goldman Sachs, 2002—. Head young mems. Parti Republicain, Paris, 1985. Lt. French Light Cavalry, 1988-89. Recipient Nat. Def. medal French State, 1989. Mem. French Soc. Fin. Analysts (diploma 1992), Insead Alumni Assn., Cercle du Bois de Boulogne. Avocations: theater actor, mountains, politics. Home: 14 Onslow Gardens London SW7 3AW England Office: Goldman Sachs Internat Peterborough Ct 133 Fleet St London EC4A 2BB England E-mail: jean-hughes.delamaze@gs.com.

LAMB, BRUCE DOUGLAS, lawyer; b. Miami, Fla., Mar. 21, 1955; s. Jean Altman and Irene Gloria Lamb; married, July 31, 1981; 1 child, Alison Marie. BA, U. South Fla., 1977; JD, Fla. State U., 1980, MA, 1981. Bar: Fla. 1981. Staff atty. Dept. Profl. Regulation, Tallahassee, 1981-83, sr. atty., 1983-88, gen. counsel, 1988, chief atty. Tampa, 1988-91; assoc. Shear Newman Hahn & Rosenkranz PA, 1991-92; shareholder Shear, Newman, Rosenkranz, Burton and Lamb, P.A., 1992-2000; ptnr. Ruden, McClosky, Smith, Schuster and Russell, P.A., 2000—. Contbr. articles to profl. jours. Mem. Fla. Bar Assn. (treas. health law sect. 1998-99, chair 2000-2001, exec. coun.). Avocation: scuba. Office: Ruden McClosky Smith Schusta and Russell PA Ste 2700 401 E Jackson St Tampa FL 33602-5841 E-mail: bruce.lamb@ruden.com.

LAMB, CHARLES F. educator, retired minister; b. Maryville, Tenn., Dec. 18, 1934; s. C. Fred and Sadie Ellen (Tedder) L.; children: Elizabeth Susan, Linda Louise, Jennifer Janet; m. Betty Jane Zimmerman, Dec. 29, 1979. BA, Maryville Coll., 1956; MDiv, Grad. Sem. of Phillips U., 1961; D in Ministry, N.Y. Theol. Sem., 1990. Ordained to ministry Christian Ch., 1961. Pastor East Aurora Christian Ch., N.Y., 1961-71; assoc. regional min. Christian Ch., Disciples of Christ, Northeastern Region, Buffalo, 1971-75, regional min., 1975-99; ret., 1999; tchr. religion Niagara U., 1999—; asst. to minister First Presbyn. Ch., Youngstown, N.Y., 1999—. Mem. orgns. clergy and coun. of chs. Trustee Village of East Aurora, 1968-73; active environ. groups Conf. Mayors and Village Ofcls. N.Y., 1968-73; adj. prof. Niagara U., 1999—; asst.

to the minister First Presbyn. Ch., Youngstown, N.Y., 1999—. Author: Doc's Diary, 1996, More Meanderings from Doc's Diary, 2000. Pres. Coll. Regional Mins., 1997-99; mem. adminstrv. com. Gen. Bd. of Christian Ch., Disciples of Christ, 1997-99. Mem. Conf. Regional Ministers and Moderators of the Disciples of Christ (pres. 1997-99), Sierra Club (mem. exec. com. Niagara group 2001-). Democrat. Home: 335 Walnut Ln Youngstown NY 14174-1348 E-mail: clamb0@prodigy.net.

LAMB, CHARLES MOODY, political science educator, researcher; b. Murfreesboro, Tenn., Mar. 1, 1945; s. Edward Clay and Opal Irene (Tune) L. B.S., Middle Tenn. State U., 1967; M.A., U. Ala., 1970, Ph.D., 1974. Adminstrv. specialist NASA, Washington, 1971; research scientist George Washington U., Washington, 1973-75; equal opportunity specialist U.S. Commn. on Civil Rights, Washington, 1975-77; asst. prof. polit. sci. SUNY-Buffalo, 1977-84, assoc. prof., 1984— ; cons. U.S. Congress Office Tech. Assessment, Washington, 1974-75, 84. Co-editor, contbg. author: Supreme Court Activism and Restraint, 1982 (Choice Outstanding Acad. Book award 1983); Implementation of Civil Rights Policy, 1984; Judicial Conflict and Consensus, 1986. Served to 1st lt. U.S. Army, 1972. Recipient awards in field; grantee NSF, 1974-75, Office Tech. Assessment, 1974-75, SUNY Research Found., 1982. Mem. N.Y. State Polit. Sci. Assn. (pres. 1985-86), Am. Polit. Sci. Assn. (exec. com. sect. on law cts. and jud. process 1984-86), N.E. Polit. Sci. Assn. (exec. council 1983-85), Common Cause, Law and Soc. Assn., Leadership Conf. on Civil Rights, Midwest Polit. Sci. Assn., Pi Sigma Alpha, Pi Gamma Mu, Pi Sigma Beta. Democrat. Presbyterian. Avocations: tennis; swimming. Home: 58 Ruskin Rd Snyder NY 14226-4254 Office: SUNY Dept Polit Sci 520 Park Club Ln Buffalo NY 14221-5013

LAMB, DARLIS CAROL, sculptor; b. Wausa, Nebr. d. Lindor Soren and June Berniece (Skalberg) Nelson; m. James Robert Lamb; children: Sherry Lamb Sobh, Michael, Mitchell. BA in Fine Arts, Columbia Pacific U., San Rafael, Calif., 1988, MA in Fine Arts, 1989. Exhibitions include Nat. Arts Club, N.Y.C., 1983 (Catherine Lorillard Wolfe award sculpture , 1983, Catherine Lorillard Wolfe award sculpture , 1997, C.L. Wolfe Horse's Head award , 1994, Anna Hyatt Huntington cash award, 1995, honorable mention , 1996, medal of honor, 1998, Anna Hyatt Huntington bronze medal, 2000, Paul Manship Meml. award, 2001), 1985, 1989, 1991—93, 1995—97, 1998, 2000, 2001, N.Am. Sculpture Exhibit, Foothills Art Ctr., Golden, Colo., 1983—84 (Pub. Svc. Co. of Colo. sculpture award , 1990), 1986—87, 1990—91, Nat. Acad. of Design, 1986, Nat. Sculpture Soc., 1985 (C. Percival Dietch Sculpture prize , 1991), 1991, 1995, 1997, Loveland Mus. and Gallery, 1990—91, Audubon Artists, 1991, Allied Artists Am., 1992, 1995, Pen and Brush, 1993 (Roman Bronze award , 1995), 1995—97, 1999, 2000, 2001, Colorado Springs Fine Arts Mus., 1996 (Award of Merit), 1998, 2000, All Colo. Exhibit, 2001 (1st prize sculpture), Represented in permanent collections Nebr. Hist. Soc., Am. Lung Assn. of Colo., Benson Park Sculpture Garden, Loveland, U.S. Space Found., Colorado Springs Osteo. Found., one-woman shows include Curtis Arts & Humanities Ctr., Greenwood Village, Colo., 2002. Mem. Catherine Lorillard Wolfe Art Club, N.Am. Sculpture Soc., Pen & Brush. Office: PO Box 9043 Englewood CO 80111-8000 E-mail: dlambsculpture@usa.net.

LAMB, DAVID ALAN, mathematician; b. Tucson, Aug. 21, 1964; s. Paul Arthur and Elsie Ann (Saar) L.; m. Jennifer Hutto; 1 child, Katherine Hutto. BS in Math., George Mason U., 1985; PhD of Math., U. Wis., 1992. Mathematician U.S. Army, Warren, Mich., 1994—. Recipient Eagle Scout award Boy Scouts Am., 1982. Mem. Am. Math. Soc., Math. Assn. Am. Methodist. Office: US Army TA Com-TARDEC Amsta Tr D Mail Stop 157 Warren MI 48397-0001 Home: 44010 Donley Dr Sterling Heights MI 48314-2636 E-mail: lambd@tacom.army.mil.

LAMB, DEBORAH KATHLEEN, music educator, consultant; b. Mpls., Aug. 12, 1953; d. Douglas Francis and Alexandria Marie (Mansour) L.; m. Doug Winters. BS, U. Minn., 1976; MS, U. Ill., 1982. Cert. vocal music tchr. Minn, mastery in Orff Schulwerk, mastery in Kodaly edn. Tchr. elem. vocal music Mound (Minn.) Pub. Schs., 1977-81; tchr. elem. music methods U. Ill., Champaign-Urbana, 1981-82; tchr. elem., secondary vocal music, humanities Mounds Park Acad., Maplewood, Minn., 1982-84; tchr. elem. vocal music Mpls. Pub. Schs., 1984-85, Elk River Pub. Schs., Rogers, Minn., 1985, St. Louis Park (Minn.) Pub. Schs., 1986—. Co-planner profl. devel. plan fellowship program Minn. State Dept. Edn., Mpls., 1989-90. Contbr. article to profl. jours.; conductor St. Louis Park (Minn.) Youth Choir, 1990-98, St. Louis Park Children's Choir, 1992—; guest conductor: Children's Choirs, U.S. Minn. State Dept. Edn. fellow, 1988-89. Mem. Am. Choral Dirs. Assn., Orgn. Am. Kodály Educators (cert. mastery, conf. chair 1994-95), Midwest Kodály Music Educators Am. (pres. 2001-2003), Music Educators Nat. Conf., Sigma Alpha Iota, Pi Kappa Lambda. Avocations: quilting, reading, creative writing, fiber art. Office: St Louis Pk Spanish Immersion Sch 6300 Walker St Minneapolis MN 55416

LAMB, EDWARD ALLEN, JR. business owner; b. Elgin, Ill., Oct. 5, 1957; s. Edward Allen and Sara Dina (Mirs) L. Sr.; m. Alice Craig, Sept. 19, 1977 (div. Sept. 1980); 1 child, Jeremy Edward; m. Cynthia Lee Gray, Mar. 24, 1990; children: Brittany Mary Sarah, Benjamin Allen Douglas. Student, Devry Inst., Chgo., 1975-77. Svc. mgr. Stereo Studio, Arlington Heights, Ill., 1977-79; co-founder, svc. mgr. Ariz. Instrument Inc., Tempe, 1979-90; prin. owner Lamb Tech. Svcs., Gilbert, Ariz., 1991—. Bd. dirs. Odor Control Com./Water Environment Fedn., Alexandria, Va., 1987—. Contbr. articles to profl. jours. Mem. Water Environment Fedn. Achievements include use of monitoring instrumentation to reduce public nuisance/How to Complaints. Office: Lamb Tech Svcs 23622 S Cloverland Ct Chandler AZ 85248-6233

LAMB, ELIZABETH SEARLE, freelance writer, poet; b. Topeka, Jan. 22, 1917; d. Howard Sanford and Helen Baker (Shaver) Searle; m. F. Bruce Lamb, Dec. 11 1941 (dec. Dec. 1992); 1 child, Carolyn. BA, U. Kans., Lawrence, 1939, BMus, 1940. Canon City corr. Pueblo (Colo.) Chieftan, 1957-59; editor Frogpond: Quar. Haiku Jour./Haiku Soc. Am., N.Y.C., 1984-91, 94. Author: Today and Every Day, 1970, Inside Me, Outside Me, 1974, In This Blaze of Sun, 1975, Picasso's Bust of Sylvette, 1977 (HSA Merit Book award), 39 Blossoms, 1982 (HSA Merit Book award), Casting into a Cloud: Southwest Haiku, 1985 (HSA Merit Book award), Lines for My Mother, Dying, 1988, (in Chinese) The Light of Elizabeth Lamb: 100 American Haiku, 1993, Ripples Spreading Out, 1997, (in Polish/English) Petals of Iris, 1998, Across the Windharp: Collected and New Haiku, 1999 (HSA Merit Book award); assoc. editor Haiku S.W., Santa Fe, 1993; author numerous poems. Bd. dirs. Pub. Libr., Canon City, 1957-58; sec. Friends of the Pub. Libr., Santa Fe, 1979-82; 1st hon. curator Am. Haiku Archive, Calif. State Libr., Sacramento, 1996-97. Recipient 2d place award Ruben Dario Meml. Poetry Contest, OAS, 1967, awards Nat. League Am. Pen Women, Haiku Soc. Am., Mus. Haiku Lit., Tokyo, Mainichi Daily News, Tokyo, Poetry Soc. Japan, 55th Ann. Basho Festival, Ueno, Japan, numerous others. Mem. Haiku Soc. Am. (pres. 1971), Poetry Soc. Am., Haiku Internat. Assn. (Japan), Haiku Can. Democrat. Christian. Avocations: chamber music, harp. Home: 970 Acequia Madre Santa Fe NM 87505 E-mail: eslamb@earthlink.net.

LAMB, H. RICHARD, psychiatry educator; b. Phila., Sept. 18, 1929; s. Julius R. and Lillian (Beerman) L.; m. Doris Murial Koehn, Feb. 10, 1969; children: Jonathan Howard, Carolyn Elizabeth, Thomas Warren. BA, U. Pa., 1950; MD, Yale U., 1954. Diplomate Am. Bd. Psychiatry and Neurology. Chief rehab. svcs. San Mateo (Calif.) County Mental Health Svcs., 1960-76; prof. psychiatry U. So. Calif. Sch. Medicine, L.A., 1976—. Vis. prof. U. Wales, Coll. Medicine, Cardiff, 1991; chmn. Hosp. & Comty. Psychiatry Inst. Program Planning Com., 1990-95. Editor: New Directions for Mental Health Services, 1979—; mem. editl. bd.: Psychiat. Svcs., 1981-90, 96—, Psychosocial Rehab. Jour., 1982—, Internat. Jour. Social Psychiatry, 1988—; author 6 books; contbr. chpts. to books, articles to profl. jours. Capt. U.S. Army, 1958-60. Named Exemplary Psychiatrist, Nat. Alliance for Mentally Ill, 1992. Fellow Am. Psychiat. Assn. (chmn. task force on homeless mentally ill 1983-84, Presdl. Commendation 1985, coun. on psychiat. svcs. 1996—, van Ameringen award in psychiat. rehab. 1998), Am. Coll. Psychiatrists. Office: U So Calif Dept Psychiatry 2020 Zonal Ave Los Angeles CA 90033-1011

LAMB, IRENE HENDRICKS, medical researcher; b. Ky., May 9, 1940; d. Daily P. and Bertha (Hendricks) Lamb; m. Edward B. Meadows (dec.). Diploma in nursing, Ky. Bapt. Hosp., Louisville; student, Berea (Ky.) Coll., Calif. State U., L.A. RN, Ky. Charge nurse, head nurse acute medicine, med. ICU, surgical ICU, emergency room various med. ctrs., 1963-67; staff nurse rsch. CCU U. So. Calif./L.A. County Med. Ctr., 1968; nurse mgr. clin. rsch. ctr. U. So. Calif./Los Angeles County Med. Ctr., L.A., 1969-74; sr. rsch. nurse cardiology Stanford (Calif.) U. Sch. Medicine, 1974-85, rsch. coord. pvt. clin., 1988; dir. clin. rsch. San Diego Cardiac Ctr., 1989-92; sr. cmty. health nurse Madison County Health Dept., Berea, 1993-97; sr. clin. rsch. mgr. stroke program U. Ky. Coll. Medicine, Lexington, 1997-2001. Co-contbr. numerous articles to med. jours.; contbr. articles to nursing jours., chpts. to med. books. Bd. dirs. Ky. Stroke Assn., 1998-2000. Avocations: photography, hand weaving. Home: 107 Lorraine Ct Berea KY 40403-1317 *Choose work situations that stimulate your intellect and force learning...and when that situation becomes easy move forward to more difficult work. Along the way read, read, read.*

LAMB, JAMES P. advertising executive; b. Queens, N.Y., Nov. 4, 1968; BA, U. Albany, N.Y., 1991; MA, John Jay Coll., N.Y.C., 1998. Cert. transp. practitioner U.S. Dept. Transp., 1999. Motor carrier investigator N.Y. State Dept. Transp., N.Y.C., 1993—98; excise tax investigator N.Y. State Tax Endorsement, 1998; grant adminstr. N.Y. State DCJS, Albany, 1999; security mgr. Mail.com, Inc., N.Y.C., 2000—01; dir. of privacy and compliance Exact Advertising, 2002—. Dir., chmn. DOT Authority.com, N.Y.C., 2001—; dir. Dippikill, Inc., Albany, 2001—; cons. BBI Cons. Svcs., N.Y.C., 1998—2001. Dep. inspector Suffolk Aux. Police, Babylon, NY, 1997—98. Recipient Exceptional Pub. Svc. award, FBI, 2001. Mem.: High Tech Crime Consortium, High Tech Crime Investigation Assn. Avocations: camping, songwriting. Home: PO Box 319 New York NY 10274

LAMB, JAMIE PARKER, JR. retired mechanical engineer, educator; b. Boligee, Ala., Sept. 21, 1933; s. Jamie Parker and Cletus (Hixson) L.; m. Nancy Catherine Flaherty, June 11, 1955; children: David Parker, Stephen Patrick. BS, Auburn U., 1954; MS, U. Ill., 1958, PhD, 1961. Asst. prof. engrng. mechanics N.C. State U., Raleigh, 1961-63; mem. faculty dept. mech. engrng. U. Tex., Austin, 1963-2001, prof., 1970-2001, chmn. dept., 1970-76, 96-01, assoc. dean engrng., 1976-81, prof. faculty aerospace engrng., 1981-88; prof. emeritus, 2001—; chmn. dept. U. Tex., 1981-88, Ernest Cockrell Jr. Meml. prof., 1981-2001; dir. engrng. program U. Tex.-Pan Am., 1993-94. Cons. LTV Aerospace Corp., Dallas, Marshall Space Flight Center, Huntsville, Ala., Tracor, Inc., Austin, Rocketdyne, McGregor, Tex., ARO, Inc., Tullahoma, Tenn., Tex. Gas Transport Co., Austin; spl. cons. U. São Paulo, Brazil, 1974; cons. Mobil Oil Corp., Dallas, Gilbarco, Inc., Greensboro, N.C.; mem. bd. boiler rules Tex. Dept. Labor and Standards, 1977-81; mem. rev. panel postdoctoral assoc. NRC, 1981-95, mem. U.S. nat. com. on theoretical and applied mechanics, 1985-89; chmn. 10th U.S. Nat. Congress Applied Mechanics, 1986 Assoc. tech. editor: Jour. Fluids Engrng., 1976-79; contbr. articles to profl. jours. Served to 1st lt. USAF, 1955-57. Recipient Joe J. King Profl. Engrng. Achievement award U. Tex. at Austin, 1984, Disting. Alumnus award U. Ill. Dept. Mech. and Indsl. Engrng., 1985, Centennial Alumnus award Auburn U. Dept. Mech. Engrng., 1986. Fellow ASME (chmn. fluid mechanics tech. com. 1982-84, Founder's award Central Tex. sect. 1975, Leadership award 1976, 81, Centennial award 1980); assoc. fellow AIAA; mem. Am. Soc. Engrng. Edn. (chmn. summer faculty programs com. 1978-80, chmn. mech. engrng. div. 1979-80, bd. dirs. Profl. Interest Council I, 1981-82), Nat. Soc. Profl. Engrs., Sigma Xi, Pi Tau Sigma, Tau Beta Pi, Sigma Gamma Tau. Baptist. Home: 2605 Pinewood Ter Austin TX 78757-2136 E-mail: jplamb@mail.utexas.edu.

LAMB, SISTER JANE MARIE, bereavement counselor, nurse; b. Aud, Mo., Aug. 24, 1936; d. James Earl Sr. and Hada Lavenia (Mantle) L. BSN, St. Louis U., 1968; MA in Health Ministry, Sangamon State U., 1981; diploma, St. John's Hosp. Sch. Nursing, Springfield, Ill., 1961. Joined Order of St. Francis, Roman Catholic Ch., 1954. Maternity nurse Sacred Heart Hosp., Eau Claire, Wis., 1961-62; pediatric head nurse St. Mary's Hosp., Decatur, Ill., 1962-66; maternity supr. St. John's Hosp., Sprinfield, 1968-69, chaplain Springfield, 1977-82; founder grief support program SHARE, 1977; program facilitator SHARE St. John's Hosp., Springfield, 1982-87; acting dir. St. Monica's, 1973; organizer, dir. pastoral care St. Mary's Hosp., Decatur, 1974-77; nat. dir. SHARE St. Elizabeth's Hosp., Belleville, Ill., 1988-91; with St. Francis Convent, Springfield, 1991-92; pastoral assoc. St. Agnes Parish, Hillsboro, Ill., 1992-95; coord. lay assoc. program for hosp. Sisters of St. Francis, Springfield, 1995—, mem. leadership team, 1999—. Adj. instr. So. Ill. U. Sch. Medicine, Springfield, 1979-87; lectr., presenter, 1978-88, workshop condr., 1978-91. Author: How to Start Your Own SHARE, 1979, 5th edit., 1991; editor: Bittersweet. . .Hellogoodbye, 1988; exec. producer (videos) To Touch Today, 1979, Memories, 1982, Alive Again, 1985; editor, pub. newsletter SHARE; contbr. articles on grief and mourning to publs. in field. Bd. dirs. Pregnancy Care Ctr., Springfield, 1982-85, St. Johns Sch. of Dietetics, 1984-87; mem. SIDS Edn. Com., State of Ill. Recipient citation award Cath. Health Assn., Boston, 1982. Mem. Nat. Assn. Cath. Chaplains (cert. pastoral assoc.), Assn. of Death Edn. and Counseling (cert. profl. grief counselor and death educator), Pregnancy, Infant Loss Am. Alliance (bd. dirs.), THANATOS (bd. dirs.), UNITE (bd. dirs.). Avocations: guitar, boating, geneology.

LAMB, JEFFRY EARL, civil engineer; b. Shelbyville, Ill., Aug. 23, 1951; s. Earl Leroy and Barbara Jean (Allison) L.; m. Arlene Kay Smith, Aug. 28, 1971; children: Tricia Nicole, Gregory Earl. BSCE, U. Ill., 1973. Registered profl. engr., Ill., Ind. Engr. Archtl. and Engring. Svcs., Decatur, Ill., 1974-79; engr. assoc. Shaffer, Krimmel, Silver & Assocs., 1979-85; supr. civil/structural engring. Ill. Power Co., 1985—. Designer, author 53rd Am. Power Conf. Proceedings, 1991. Chmn. Mt. Zion (Ill.) Park Found.-Devel. Com., 1990-93; bd. dirs. Mt. Zion Youth Baseball, 1988-93. Mem. ASCE, Chi Epsilon. Office: Ill Power Co 500 S 27th St Decatur IL 62521-2200

LAMB, MARGARET WELDON, lawyer; b. Arlington, Mass., June 26, 1935; d. Hubert Weldon and Lydia Cazneau (Baker) L. BA, U. Denver, 1959; JD, Boston Coll., 1964. Bar: Mass. 1964, N.M. 1969. Pvt. practice, Taos County, N.Mex., 1971-76; dist. atty. N.Mex. 8th Jud. Dist., Taos, 1978-80; pvt. practice specializing in aviation adminstrv. law, 1981-98; founder Sunshine Aviation Safety Studies, 1989—. Air safety investigator, writer, flight instr., 1981—; faculty assoc. Johns Hopkins Univ. Ctr. for Inquiry Rsch. and Policy, 1994—. Contbr. articles on aviation safety to profl. publs. Mem. AIAA, Am. Meteorol. Soc., Aerospace Med. Assn., Lawyer-Pilots Bar Assn., Nat. Assn. Flight Instrs., NTSB Bar Assn. Achievements include research in microscale mountain weather and aircraft crashes; organizing clinics for flight instructors and pilots in U.S. and New Zealand. Home and Office: PO Box 718 Alamosa CO 81101

LAMB, MARY ANGELA, hospital patient educator, nurse; b. Cin., June 17, 1939; d. Harry C. and Victoria Rose (Wich) Vogelsang; div.; children: Ronald, Catherine, Rod. Diploma in Nursing, Mercy Sch. Nursing, 1960; BSN, Thomas More Coll., 1985. RN Ohio, Ky., cert. CDE, CWOCN. Staff nurse St. Francis Hosp., Cin., 1960-61, Flagler Hosp., St. Augustine, Fla., 1961, St. Vincent Hosp., Jacksonville, 1961-63, North Miss. Community Hosp., Tupelo, 1963, Moline (Ill.) Pub. Hosp., 1964-66; staff nurse, head nurse Good Samaritan Hosp., Cin., 1966-72, patient educator, 1973—. Cons. United Ostomy Assn., Cin., 1975—. Vol., speaker Am. Cancer Soc., Cin., 1975—; vol. Am. Diabetic Assn., Cin., 1970—. Mem. Am. Assn. Diabetic Edn., Diabetic Educators of Cin. Area (treas. 1992, 96), Toastmasters Internat. Roman Catholic. Avocations: crafts-embroidery, exercise. Home: 5611 Old Blue Rock Rd Cincinnati OH 45247-2723 Office: Good Samaritan Hosp 375 Dixmyth Ave Cincinnati OH 45220-2489 E-mail: Angie_Lamb@trihealth.com.

LAMB, MICHAEL E. psychology researcher; b. Lusaka, Zambia, Oct. 22, 1953; came to U.S., 1973; s. Francis B. and Michelle M. (de Lestang) L.; m. Kathleen J. Sternberg; children: Jeanette M., Philip D.; children from previous marriage: Damon G., Darryn N.; 1 stepchild, Aya Lewkowicz. BA, U. Natal, Durban, Republic of South Africa, 1972; MA, Johns Hopkins U., 1974; MS, MPhil, Yale U., 1975, PhD, 1976; PhD honoris causa, U. Göteborg, Sweden, 1995. Asst. prof. psychology U. Wis., Madison, 1976-78; asst. prof. U. Mich., Ann Arbor, 1978-80; prof. psychology, psychiatry, pediatrics U. Utah, Salt Lake City, 1980-87; sr. scientist and sect. chief NIH, Bethesda, Md., 1987—. Vis. prof. U. Haifa, Israel, 1980, Hokkaido U., Sapporo, Japan, 1985, U. Osnabruck, Germany, 1989, Martin Luther U., Halle, Germany, 1997. Editor: The Role of the Father in Child Development, 1976, rev. edit., 1981, 97, Social and Personality Development, 1978, Social Interaction Analysis, 1978, Advances in Developmental Psychology vol. I, 1981, vol. 2, 1982, vol. 3, 1984, vol. 4, 1986, Infant Social Cognition, 1981, Sibling Relationships, 1982, Nontraditional Families, 1982, Adolescent Fatherhood, 1986, The Father's Role: Applied Perspectives, 1986, The Father's Role: Cross-Cultural Perspectives, 1987, Developmental Psychology: An Advanced Textbook, 1982, rev. edits., 1988, 92, 99, Infant Development: Perspectives from German Speaking Countries, 1991, Child Care in Context: Cross-Cultural Perspectives, 1992, Adolescent Problem Behaviors, 1994, Parenting and Child Development in Nontraditional Families, 1999, others; co-author: Development in Infancy, 1982, rev. edits., 1987, 92, 2002, Socialization and Personality Development, 1982, Infant-Mother Attachment, 1985, Child Psychology Today, 1986, Investigative Interviews of Children, 1998. Recipient Young Psychologist award Am. Psychol. Assn., 1976, Boyd McCandless award Am. Psychol. Assn., 1978, Superior Rsch. award U. Utah, 1985, Disting. Rsch. award U. Utah, 1986. Fellow Am. Psychol. Soc.; mem. Soc. Rsch. in Child Devel., Internat. Soc. for Study of Behavioral Devel., Am. Profl. Soc. on Abuse of Children. E-mail: Michael. Office: NICHD Sect Social and Emotion Ste 8048 6705 Rockledge Dr Bethesda MD 20892 E-mail: Michael_Lamb@nih.gov.

LAMB, MILDRED SHIMONISHI, retired administrative secretary; b. Vacaville, Calif., May 12, 1913; d. Yojiro and Noriye (Takei) Kubota; m. Toshio Shimonishi, June 19, 1938 (dec. Apr. 1963); children: Don (dec.), Joyce Takanashi, Sam (dec.), Naomi Terashima, Cheri Mitsuno; m. William L. Lamb, Jan. 29, 1974 (dec. Aug. 1977). AA, Long Beach (Calif.) Jr. Coll., 1935. Sec. to security officer U.S. Naval Air Stat., Japan, 1955-57; sec. to provost marshal U.S. Marine Corp Facility, Japan, 1957-58; stenographer-receptionist Calif. State Disability Ins., Long Beach, 1958-76; retired, 1976. Author: And Then a Rainbow, 1990. Mem. Woman's Club Bellflower (fin. sec. and treas. 1983-92, Woman of Yr. award 1989-90), Gen. Fedn. Women's Club. Republican. Presbyterian. Avocations: knitting, sewing, reading, travel, collect lady bug ornaments. Home: 4484 Driving Range Rd Corona CA 92883-0662 E-mail: mililamb@aol.com.

LAMB, PATRICK JOHN, financial consultant, state official; b. Charleston, W.Va., Oct. 22, 1938; s. Charles Bernard and Grace Frances (Jackson) L.; m. Kathleen Campbell, May 5, 1962; children: Christine M., Mary K., Charles P., Michael J., Karen P. BSBA, W.Va. State Coll., 1962; MBA, W.Va. Coll. Grad. Studies, 1984. Auditor W.Va. Tax Dept., Charleston, 1961-63; acct. The Diamond, 1963-66, W.Va. Water Co., Charleston, 1966-69; sr. rsch. assoc., comptroller W.Va. Rsch. League, 1969-97; assoc. dir., comptr. Putnam County Devel. Authority, Hurrican, W.Va., 1997-98; prin. Patrick Lamb, Fin. Cons., Charleston, 1998—. Acct., auditor W.Va. Solid Waste Mgmt. Bd., Charleston, 1999—. Author: The Economic Impact of the Arts in West Virginia. Mem. W.Va. Pub. Accts. Assn., Nat. Assn. Accts., KC (grand knight 1986-88, 94-96, Cath. layman 1981, dist. dep. 1988-93, state warden 1993-95, state advocate 1995-96, state treas. 1996-98, state sec. 1998-2000, state dep. 2000-02). Republican. Roman Catholic. Home and Office: 1403 Jackson St Charleston WV 25301-1909

LAMB, PETER JAMES, meteorology educator, researcher, consultant; b. Nelson, New Zealand, June 21, 1947; came to U.S., 1971; s. George Swan and Dorothy Elizabeth (Smith) L.; children: Karen Deborah Lockwood, Brett Timothy. BA, U. Canterbury, Christchurch, New Zealand, 1969, MA with honors, 1971; PhD, U. Wis., 1976; DSc, U. Canterbury, 2002. Asst. lectr. U. Canterbury, 1971; rsch. asst. U. Wis., Madison, 1971-76, rsch. assoc., 1976; lectr. U. Adelaide, Australia, 1976-79; sr. scientist Ill. Water Survey, Champaign, 1979-91, sect. head, 1984-90; prof. U. Okla., Norman, 1991—, George Lynn Cross rsch. prof., 2001—. Vis. rsch. assoc. U. Miami, Fla., 1978-79; adj. prof. U. Ill., Urbana, 1983-94; dir. Coop. Inst. Mesoscale Meteorol. Studies, Norman, 1991—; dir. Internat. Ctr. Disaster Rsch., 1994-99; assoc. dir. Weather Ctr. Programs, Norman, 1996—; cons. Dept. State, Dept. Energy, Agy. Internat. Devel., NOAA, NSF, World Meteorol. Orgn., Kingdom of Morocco, U. Wis., U. Adelaide, U. Witwatersrand, Univs. Space Rsch. Assn., Stratus Cons., Inc., EPA, 1983—; site sci. atmospheric radiation measurement program Dept. Energy, 1992—. Contbr. articles to profl. jours. Coach Champaign Youth Soccer Orgn., 1983-91. Grantee NSF, EPA, Dept. Energy, NOAA, AID, World Meteorol. Orgn., MacArthur Found., Ins. Inst. Property Loss Reduction, Inst. Bus. and Home Safety, The Williams Cos., Japan Marine Sci. and Tech. Ctr. Fellow Am. Meteorol. Soc. (chief editor Jour. Climate 1989-95); mem. Am. Geophysicial Union, Royal Meteorol. Soc. (Margary lectr. 1991), Sigma Xi. Achievements include research on heat transport by the Atlantic Ocean; investigations into the in causes of droughts in Sahelian Africa and Morocco; study of N.Am. precipitation patterns; assessment of economic value of weather and climate information. Home: 3616 Burlington Dr Norman OK 73072-3647 Office: Univ of Oklahoma CIMMS-Sarkeys Energy Ctr 100 E Boyd St Rm 1110 Norman OK 73019-1015 E-mail: plamb@ou.edu.

LAMB, REBECCA ANN, software engineer; b. Urbana, Ill., Nov. 19, 1948; d. Marvin Curtis and Elizabeth Ann (Schumacher) Tyler; m. Gary Lynn Lamb, Aug. 22, 1970; children: James Tyler, Jonathan Curtis. BS, Bowling Green State U., 1971. Programmer Reynolds & Reynolds Co., Dayton, Ohio, 1972-73, systems analyst, 1973-75, project leader, 1975-77, programming supr., 1977-82, sr. quality analyst, 1982-86, sr. quality coord., 1986-88; lead software engr. Mead Data Cen., Miamisburg, 1988-89, staff software engr., 1989-93; sr. staff software engr. Computer Scis. Corp., Dayton, 1994-97, quality specialist, 1995-96, quality mgr., 1996—. Author papers in field. Charter orgn. rep. Boy Scouts Am., Kettering, Ohio, 1989—; coach Young Am. Bowling Alliance, Dayton, 1989—. Mem. IEEE, Am. Soc. for Quality Control (chmn. Dayton sect. 1989-90), Assn. for Computing Machinery (sec. chpt. 1970-71),. Dayton Advs. for Computing Women (v.p.), Toastmasters (club pres. 1991). Presbyterian. Avocations: bowling, volleyball. Office: Computer Scis Corp 2300 Paramount Pl Fairborn OH 45324

LAMB, ROBERT EDWARD, retired diplomat, professional society administrator; b. Atlanta, Nov. 17, 1936; s. T. E. and Lois (Harris) Lamb; m. Lucille Trujillo, Jan. 13, 1962; children: Robert Edward, Anne Gretchen, Michael David. BA in Internat. Rels., U. Pa., 1962. Joined Fgn. Svc. Dept. State, Washington, 1963, dir. fin. services, 1975-77, dir. passport office, 1977-79; adminstrv. counsellor U.S. Embassy, Bonn, Germany, 1979-83; asst. sec. of state for adminstrn. Dept. State, Washington, 1983-85; asst. sec. of state Diplomatic Security, 1985-89; U.S. Amb. to Cyprus Cyprus, 1990-93; spl. Cyprus coord., 1993-94; exec. dir Am. Philatelic Soc., State Coll., Pa., 1994—. Pub.: Index of American Philatelic Literature, 1999—2001. With USMC, 1958—61. Mem.: Am. Fgn. Svc. Assn. (governing bd. 1999—2001). Home and Office: PO Box 8068 State College PA 16803-8068 E-mail: relamb@stamps.org.

LAMB, RONALD ALFRED, editor; b. Seattle, Mar. 17, 1948; s. Lowell Rendall and Esther Irene (Fischer) L.; m. Nancy Sandine, Apr. 20, 1973; children: Braden Daniel, Kirsten Marie. AA, Highline Coll., 1968; BA, U. Wash., 1970. Sports writer Federal Way/Des Moines (Wash.) News, 1972-74, Skagit Valley Herald, Mt. Vernon, Wash., 1975-77, reporter, 1977-79, Bremerton (Wash.) Sun, 1979-84; editor Microsoft Press, Bellevue and Redmond, Wash., 1984-98. Editor: Command Performance: Microsoft Excel, 1986 (Achievement award Puget Sound chpt. Soc. Tech. Comm. 1986), Computer Lib/Dream Machines, 1987 (Non-fiction Computer Book of Yr. award Computer Press Assn. 1988), Variations in C, 2d edit., 1989 (Merit award Puget Sound chpt. Soc. Tech. Comm. 1989), Inside OLE 2, 1994 (Merit award Puget Sound chpt. Soc. Tech. Comm. 1994), Word 6 for Windows Companion, 1994 (Excellence award Puget Sound chpt. Soc. Tech. Comm. 1994), The Ultimate Windows 95 Book, 1995 (Disting. award Puget Sound Chpt. Soc. Tech. Comm. 1995-96, Achievement award Internat. Tech. Publs. Competition 1996; Official Microsoft Internet Explorer Book, 1996 (Merit award Puget Sound chpt. Soc. Tech. Comm. 1996-97); contbg. author: Tukwila: Community at the Crossroads, 1991 (1st place non-fiction books history Wash. Press Assn., 1992). Del. to state conv. Wash. State Dem. Party, Tacoma, 1984; sec. South Ctrl. Schs. Adv. Coun., Tukwila, 1987-88; mem. Foster Friends of Libr., Tukwila, 1988—; chmn. South Ctrl. 2000 Com., Tukwila, 1987-89, Foster Annexation Com., Tukwila, 1988-89; bd. dirs. South Ctrl. Sch. Dist., Tukwila, 1989-93, chmn. bd. dirs., 1991-93. Mem. Soc. Profl. Journalists, King County Dirs. Assn. (bd. dirs. 1992-93), Wash. State Sch. Dirs. Assn. (urban schs. com.

1993), Highline C.C. Found. (bd. dirs. 2000-01). Democrat. Avocations: hiking, reading, theater, gardening, genealogy. Home: 4251 S 139th St Tukwila WA 98168-3260 E-mail: lambtownwest@msn.com.

LAMB, STACIE THOMPSON, elementary school educator; b. Abilene, Tex., Nov. 9, 1965; d. George Lyman and Shirley Elizabeth (Burton) T.; m. Dennis A. Lamb; children: Lane, Logann. BS in Edn., Lubbock Christian Coll., 1986; postgrad., Tex. Tech U. Elem. Edn. grades 1-6, Tex. 1st grade tchr. Lubbock (Tex.) I.S.D. Brown Elem., 1986-87; 3rd grade tchr., chairperson Morton (Tex.) I.S.D., 1987-89; 5th grade lang. arts tchr. Whiteface (Tex.) C.I.S.D., 1990—. Mem. ASCD, Classroom Tchrs. Assn. (sec. 1988-89, elem. rep. 1991-92). Office: PO Box 117 Whiteface TX 79379-0117 Home: 7324 93rd St Lubbock TX 79424-4938

LAMB, SYDNEY MACDONALD, linguistics and cognitive science educator; b. Denver, May 4, 1929; s. Sydney Bishop and Jean Louisa (MacDonald) L.; m. Sharon Reese Rowell, June 17, 1956 (div. 1971); children: Christina, Sarah, Nancy; m. Susan Ellen Jones, May 15, 1977. BA, Yale U., 1951; PhD, U. Calif., Berkeley, 1958. From asst. to assoc. prof. linguistics U. Calif., Berkeley, 1958-64; from assoc. to prof. Yale U., New Haven, 1964-77; mng. ptnr. Semionics Assocs., Houston, 1977-93; prof. Rice U., 1980—. Fellow Ctr. for Advanced Study in Behavioral Scis., Stanford, Calif., 1973-74. Author: Outline of Stratificational Grammar, 1966, (with others) Sprung from Some Common Source, 1991, Pathways of the Brain: The Neurocognitive Basis of Language, 1999; inventor associative computer memory, 1977, 80, 4 patents; contbr. articles to profl. jours. NSF grantee, 1959-64, 66-70; Am. Council of Learned Soc. grantee, 1973-74. Mem. Linguistic Soc. Am. (exec. com. 1966-68), Linguistics Assn. of Can. and U.S. (pres. 1983-84, chmn. bd. dirs. 1995—), Houston Philos. Soc. (pres. 1992-93). Avocations: singing, songwriting. Office: Rice U Dept Linguistics Houston TX 77251 E-mail: lamb@rice.edu.

LAMB, WILLIS EUGENE, JR. physicist, educator; b. L.A., July 12, 1913; s. Willis Eugene and Marie Helen (Metcalf) Lamb; m. Ursula Schaefer, June 5, 1939 (dec. Aug. 1996); m. Bruria Kaufman, Nov. 29, 1996. BS, U. Calif., 1934, PhD, 1938; DSc (hon.) , U. Pa., 1953, Gustavus Adolphus Coll., 1975, Columbia U., 1990; MA, Oxford (Eng.) U., 1956, Yale U., 1961; LHD (hon.) , Yeshiva U., 1965; Dr.rer.nat. (hon.) , U. Ulm., Germany, 1997. Mem. faculty Columbia U., 1938—52, prof. physics, 1948—52, Stanford U., 1951—56; Wykeham prof. physics and fellow New Coll., Oxford U., 1956—62; Henry Ford 2d prof. physics Yale U., 1962—72, J. Willard Gibbs prof. physics, 1972—74; prof. physics and optical scis. U. Ariz., Tucson, 1974—, Regents prof., 1990—. Morris Loeb lectr. Harvard U., 1953—54; Gordon Shrum lectr. Simon Fraser U., 1972; cons. Philips Labs., Bell Telephone Labs., Perkin-Elmer, NASA; vis. com. Brookhaven Nat. Lab. Recipient Rumford premium, Am. Acad. Arts and Scis., 1953, award, Rsch. Corp., 1954, (with P. Kusch) Nobel prize in Physics, 1955, Yeshiva award, 1962, Einstein Medal, Soc. for Optical & Quantum Electronics, 1992, Nat. medal of Sci., 2000; fellow Guggenheim, 1960—61, sr. Alexander von Humboldt, 1992—94. Fellow: Royal Sci. Edinburgh, N .Y. Acad. Scis., Optical Soc. Am., Am. Phys. Soc., Inst. Physics and Phys. Soc. (hon. Guthrie lectr. 1958); mem.: NAS, Sigma Xi, Phi Beta Kappa. Office: U Ariz Optical Scis Ctr Meinel Bldg 1630 E University Blvd Tucson AZ 85721-0094*

LAMBE, JAMES PATRICK, lawyer; b. Washington, June 4, 1952; s. John Joseph and Patricia Ann (Job) Lambe; m. Marie Barbara Giardino, May 21, 1977; children: Katherine Mary, Joseph Patrick. AB with distinction, U. Mich., 1974; JD, U. Ill., 1977. Bar: Calif. 1977, U.S. Dist. Ct. (ea. dist.) Calif. 1977, U.S. Ct. Appeals (9th cir.) 1978, U.S. Supreme Ct. 1981, U.S. Dist. Ct. (ctrl. dist.) Calif. 1983, D.C. 1985; cert. specialist in criminal law State Bar Calif. Bd. Legal Specialization; cert. specialist in criminal trial advocacy Nat. Bd. Trial Advocacy. Assoc. Wagner & Wagner, Fresno, Calif., 1978-79, Parichan, Renberg, Crossman & Eliason, Fresno, 1979; claims atty. CIGNA Corp., 1979-85; dep. city atty. City of Fresno, 1985-86; dep. pub. defender County of Fresno, 1986—. Cons., author Continuing Edn. of the Bar, U. Calif./State Bar Calif., Berkeley, 1992—; judge pro tem Fresno County Superior Ct., 2000—; instr. Summer Trial Skills Inst., San Diego, 2001—. Cons. to books: California Criminal Law Procedure and Practice, update, 1992, 3rd edit., 1996, California Criminal Law Forms Manual, 1995, rev., 2001; co-author: California Criminal Law Procedure and Practice, 6th edit., 2002. Mem.: Calif. Pub. Defenders Assn., State Bar Calif. (conf. of dels. 1996—99, criminal law sect. exec. com. 2001—), Nat. Assn. Criminal Def. Lawyers, Fresno County Bar Assn. (bd. dirs. 1998—99), D.C. Bar, Calif. Attys. for Criminal Justice, Phi Alpha Delta. Democrat. Avocation: distance running. Office: Fresno County Pub Defenders Office 2220 Tulare St Ste 300 Fresno CA 93721-2130

LAMBERG, JOHN DAVID, internist; b. Seattle, Jan. 9, 1944; MD, U. Wash., 1971. Diplomate Am. Bd. Internal Medicine, Am. Bd. Med. Oncology and Hematology. Intern Boston U., 1971-72, resident, 1972-73; fellow in hematology/oncology Nat. Cancer Inst., 1973-76. Mem. Am. Soc. Clin. Oncology. Office: Doctors Clinic Bremerton 2512 Wheaton Way Bremerton WA 98310-3399

LAMBERG-KARLOVSKY, CLIFFORD CHARLES, anthropologist, archaeologist; b. Prague, Czechoslovakia, Oct. 2, 1937; came to U.S., 1939; s. Carl Othmar von Lamberg and Bellina Karlovsky; m. Martha Louise Veale, Sept. 12, 1959; children: Karl Emil Othmar, Christopher William. AB, Dartmouth Coll., 1959; MA (Wenner-Gren fellow), U. Pa., 1964, PhD, 1965; MA (hon.), Harvard U., 1970. Asst. prof. sociology and anthropology Franklin and Marshall Coll., 1964-65; asst. prof. anthropology Harvard U., 1965-69, prof., 1969-90, Stephen Phillips prof. archaeology, 1991—; curator Near Eastern archaeology Peabody Museum Archaeology and Ethnology, 1969—, mus. dir., 1977-90. Assoc. Columbia U., 1969—; trustee Am. Inst. Iranian Studies, 1968-98, Am. Inst. Yemeni Studies, 1976-77; dir. rsch. Am. Sch. Prehist. Rsch., 1974-79, 94—, Centro di Richerche Ligabue, 1984; Reckitt archaeol. surveys in Syria, 1965, excavation projects at Tepe Yahya, Iran, 1967-75, Sarazm, Tadjikistan, USSR, 1985, archaeol. surveys in Saudi Arabia, 1977-80, USSR, 1990-91; dir. survey and excavations Anau, Turkmenistan, 1992-97; corr. fellow Inst. Medio and Extremo Orient, Italy; mem. UNESCO com. for sci. study of mankind, 1989-97. Author: (with J. Sabloff) Ancient Civilizations: The Near East and Mesoamerica, 1979; editor: (with J. Sabloff) The Rise and Fall of Civilizations, 1973, Ancient Civilizations and Trade, 1975, Hunters, Farmers and Civilization, 1979, Archaeological Thought in America, 1988, Beyond the Tigris and Euphrates, 1996; author, gen. editor: Tepe Yahya: The Early Periods, 1986. Recipient medal Iran-Am. Soc., 1972; NSF grantee, 1966-75, 78-80, 93, Nat. Endowment for Arts grantee, 1977—, NEH grantee, 1977—. Fellow AAAS (chmn. USA/USSR archaeol. exch. program), Am. Acad. Arts and Scis., Soc. Antiquaries Gt. Britain and Ireland (sec. N.Am. chpt. 1985-93), Am. Anthrop. Assn., N.Y. Acad. Sci., USSR Acad. Sci., Soc. Am. Archaeology, Archeol. Inst. Am.; mem. German Archaeol. Inst., Danish Archaeol. Inst., Brit. Archaeol. Inst., Tavern Club (Boston). Office: Peabody Mus Archaeology & Ethnology 11 Divinity Ave Cambridge MA 02138-2019 E-mail: karlovsk@fas.harvard.edu.

LAMBERSON, JOHN ROGER, insurance company executive; b. Aurora, Mo., Aug. 16, 1933; s. John Oral Lamberson and Golda May (Caldwell) Tidwell; m. Virginia Lee, Aug. 10, 1957; 1 child, John Clinton. BA, U. Calif., Berkeley, 1954. Coach, tchr. Thousand Palms (Calif.) Sch., 1954-55; underwriter trainee Fireman's Fund Ins. Co., San Francisco, 1955; surety mgr. Safeco Ins. Co. (formerly Gen. Ins. Co.), San Francisco and Sacramento, Calif., 1957-61; pres., COO Willis Corroon Corp., N.Y.C., 1966-92, also bd. dirs., chmn. constrn. industry div., mem. exec. com., aquisition com.; pres., chmn., CEO Lamberson Consulting LLC, San Francisco, 1992—. Bd. dirs. Willis Cornoon Group PLC, London, Consumers Benefit Life Ins. Co., Constrn. Inst. Mem. ASCE (bd. dirs. Construction Institute), Nat. Assn. Heavy Engring. Constructors (bd. dirs. 1985—, Golden Beavers award for outstanding svc. to industry), Constrn. Fin. Mgmt. Assn. (bd. dirs. 1987-91, exec. com.), Assoc. Gen. Contractors Am. (membership devel. com., past chmn. bd. dirs. nat. assoc. mems. coun.), Assoc. Gen. Contractors Calif. (bd. dirs. 1976), Nat. Assn. Surety Bond Prodrs. (past nat. pres., regional v.p.), Am. Inst. Contractors, Soc. Am. Mil. Engrs., The Moles-Heavy Engring. Constrn. Soc., Young Pres. Orgn. (sem. leader), Bankers Club, Sharon Heights Golf and Country Club, Bermuda Dunes Country Club, Rockaway Hunting Club, Villa Taverna Club, Bldg. Futures Coun. Home: 85 Greenoaks Dr Atherton CA 94027-2160 Office: Lamberson Consulting LLC 580 California St Ste 500 San Francisco CA 94104-1000 E-mail: jrlamberson@mindspring.com.

LAMBERT, ABBOTT LAWRENCE, retired accountant; b. N.Y.C., Mar. 19, 1919; s. Woolf W. and Estelle (Wittcover) L.; m. Natalie Rosenberg, Mar. 19, 1950 (dec.); m. Lois H. Ribman, Oct. 9, 1958 (dec.); children: Nancy Lambert Rodgers, Jane Lambert Peck. BA, Columbia U., 1940, MS in Acctg., 1946. CPA, N.Y. Acct., N.Y.C., 19440-42, 46-48; v.p. Chopak Mills, Inc., 1948-71; pres. Carthage Fabrics Corp., N.C., 1964-71; pres., dir. 1025 Fifth Ave. Corp., N.Y.C., 1965-71, dir., 1975-78, 81-82. Trustee Associated Camps, 1972—, v.p., 1985—, Fedn. Jewish Philanthropies N.Y., 1958-75, life 1975-86; founding mem. coun. Overseers UJA Fedn., N.Y., 1986; life rep. assembly Domestic Affairs Divsn. UJA Fedn., 1986—; trustee Assn. Jewish Sponsored Camps, 1964—, pres., 1964-67, 76-79, hon. pres., 1990—. Capt. AUS, 1942-46. Decorated Bronze Star. Mem. N.Y. State Soc. CPAs, Zeta Beta Tau. Home: 1025 5th Ave New York NY 10028-0134

LAMBERT, DALE JOHN, lawyer; b. Lethbridge, Alberta, Can., Mar. 1, 1946; s. Theron M. and Verl (Johansen) L.; m. Janice Noreen Clitheroe, July 29, 1975; children: Kristin, Kimberly, Tamara. BS, Brigham Young U., 1970; JD, U. Utah, 1973. Bar: Utah 1973, U.S. Dist. Ct. Utah 1975, U.S. Supreme Ct 1991, U.S. Ct. Appeals (10th cir.) 1976. Legis. asst. Congressman Gunn McKay, Washington, 1973-75; dir. Christensen Jensen P.C., Salt Lake City, 1978—. Contbr. articles to profl. jours.; presenter legal seminars. State chmn. Utah State Dem. Party, 1979—81, chmn. platform com., 1982, chmn. state conv., 1983; councilman Salt Lake City, 2002—; bd. trustees Dixie State Coll., St. George, Utah, 1983—93. Recipient Golden Key award Gov.'s Commn. on Employment, 1978; named one of Outstanding Young Men of Am., Jr. C. of C., 1979. Fellow Am. Coll. Trial Lawyers; mem. Internat. Assn. of Def. Counsel, ABA (litigation sect.), Utah State Bar Assn. (litigation sect.), Def. Rsch. Assn. (Utah chair 1989-90), Internat. Assn. Def. Counsel (state chair 2001—). Mem. Lds Ch. Avocations: golf, teaching, traveling. Home: 2563 Maywood Dr Salt Lake City UT 84109-1657 Office: Christensen & Jensen 50 S Main St Ste 1500 Salt Lake City UT 84144-2044 E-mail: dale.lambert@chrisjen.com.

LAMBERT, DEBORAH KETCHUM, public relations executive; b. Greenwich, Conn., Jan. 22, 1942; d. Alton Harrington and Robyna (Neilson) Ketchum; m. Harvey R. Lambert, Nov. 23, 1963 (div. 1985); children: Harvey Richard Jr., Eric Harrington. BS, Columbia U., 1965. Researcher, writer The Nowland Orgn., Greenwich, Conn., 1964-67; model Country Fashions, 1964-67; freelance writer to various newspapers and mags., 1977-82; press sec. Va. Del. Gwen Cody, Annandale, Va., 1981-82; assoc. editor Campus Report, Washington, 1985—; adminstrv. asst. Accuracy in Media, Inc., 1983-84, dir. pub. affairs, 1985—. TV producer weekly program The Other Side of the Story, 1994—; bd. dirs. Accuracy in Academia, Washington; film script cons. The Seductive Illusion, 1988-89. Columnist: The Eye, The Washington Inquirer, 1984—, Squeaky Chalk, Campus Report, 1985—; contbr. articles to various mags.; producer: The Other Side of the Story, 1993—. Co-founder, mem. Va. Rep. Forum, McLean, 1983—; mem. Rep. Women's Fed. Forum. Mem. Am. Bell Assn., Pub. Rels. Soc. Am., DAR., World Media Assn., Am. Platform Assn. Republican. Presbyterian. Home: 809 Gatestone St Gaithersburg MD 20008 Office: Accuracy in Media Inc 4455 Connecticut Ave NW Washington DC 20008-2328 E-mail: DLam530483@aol.com.

LAMBERT, EDYTHE RUTHERFORD, retired language educator, civic volunteer; b. Candler, N.C., Oct. 6, 1921; d. John William and Addie Bell (Holcombe) Rutherford; m. Robert Stansbury Lambert, Mar. 7, 1946; children: Margaret Anne, Dorothy Lee (dec.). BA, U. N.C., Greensboro, 1942; MA, Clemson U., 1970. Tchr. French Linden (N.C.) High Sch., 1942-43; lab. tech. Am. Enka (N.C.) Corp., 1943-44; reporter Asheville (N.C.) Citizen-Times Co., 1944-46; with pub. relations dept. Shorter Coll., Rome, 1955; instr. Clemson (S.C.) U., 1966-68. Docent hist. house mus. Pendleton Hist. Found., 1974—; pres. Clemson Area Arts Council, 1978-79, Pickens County Friends of the Arts, S.C., 1981-82, Clemson Council Human Relations, 1987; bd. dirs. Clemson Child Devel. Ctr., 1976—. Recipient Algernon Sydney Sullivan award for community svcs. Clemson U., 1990, Human Rights award Baha'is of Pickens County, 1991. Mem. AAUW (pres. 1985—, Named Gift Recipient 1979, 86, fellow 1964, editor The Palmetto Leaf, 1984-86), Phi Kappa Phi. Clubs: Clemson U. Woman's (v.p. membership 1984-85). Democrat. Methodist. Avocations: bridge, reading, travel, antiques.

LAMBERT, ETHEL GIBSON CLARK, secondary school educator; b. Atlanta, Apr. 18, 1943; d. Robert Harold and Ethel (Gibson) Clark; m. Hugh Felder Lambert, June 27, 1964 (div. Nov. 3, 1988); children: Courtney, Elizabeth, Hugh Lambert Jr. BA, Oglethorpe U., Atlanta, 1965; MEd, Kennesaw State U., Marietta, Ga., 1992; EdS, State U. West Ga., Carrollton, 1997. Lic. tchr. T-6, Ga. Tchr. Clayton County Bd. Edn., Jonesboro, Ga., 1965-66, Fulton County Bd. Edn., Atlanta, 1966-67; tchr. pre-sch. weekday program First Bapt. Ch., Gainesville, Ga., 1984-88; tchr. remedial edn. program Riverdale H.S./Clayton County Bd. Edn., 1990—. Author: The Impact of Geography on the Campaigns of the Civil War Fought in Georgia, 1993, The Utilization of Georgia Historical Sites as Teaching Methodology in MIddle Grades Education, 1993, (juvenile) Obnoxious Bill, 1993, Research on Academic Motivation of Elementary, Middle and Secondary School Students in America, 1993, Reading Strategies that Address the Reluctant Reader in America's Public Middle and High Schools, 1995, Mathematics: Tying Together the World of School and the World of Work, 1996, A Martin Family History: An Interview of Aunt Clyde: "I look back..., 1999. Den leader Cub Scouts Am., Gainesville, 1980-83; mem. Christian Businessmen's Prayer Breakfast, Atlanta, 1990-95, 96. Mem. Profl. Assn. Ga. Educators, Order Ea. Star, College Park Women's Club, College Park Hist. Soc., Pi Lambda Theta. Baptist. Avocations: swimming, skating, reading, walking, genealogy. Home: 1881 Myrtle Dr SW Apt 711 Atlanta GA 30311-4919 Office: Riverdale High Sch 160 Roberts Dr Riverdale GA 30274-3302 E-mail: elambert@rhs.ccps.ga.net.

LAMBERT, EUGENE KENT, oncologist, hematologist; b. Hinsdale, Ill., Feb. 13, 1944; s. Eugene Nelson and Dorothy Louise (Diedrichson) L.; m. Maria Natalie Gonzalez,June 19, 1971; children: Carlotta Pilar, Danielle Suzanne, Jori Marie. BA, North Ctrl. Coll., Naperville, Ill., 1966; MD, U. Ill., Chgo., 1970. Diplomate Am. Bd. Internal Medicine, Am. Bd. Hematology, Am. Bd. Med. Oncology. Fellow in hematology Michael Reese Hosp., Chgo., 1976; fellow Northwestern U., 1979; oncologist Wichita (Kans.) Clinic, 1979-81, Dreyer Med. Clinic, Aurora, Ill., 1981-86, Fond du Lac (Wis.) Clinic, 1986—. Med. dir. at large Wis. divsn. Am. Cancer Soc., 1991-96. Bd. dirs. Girl Scouts Am., Aurora, Ill., 1985-86, El Centro, Aurora, 1985-86, Fond du Lac Regional Clinic, 1992. Lt. USNR, 1971-73. Mem. AMA, ACP, Am. Soc. Hematology, Am. Soc. Clin. Oncologists. Avocations: music, volley ball, reading, cross country skiing. Office: Fond du Lac Clinic 480 E Division Fond Du Lac WI 54935-3734

LAMBERT, EUGENE LOUIS, engineer, manufacturing executive; b. Providence, Jan. 26, 1948; s. Louis Eugene and Concetta (Russo) L.; m. Maureen McHugh, Feb. 1, 1969 (div. June 1979); children: Kenneth Patrick, Margaret-Mary; m. Julia Coy Hadeka, Dec. 21, 1988. BS in Elec. Engring., U. R.I., 1969; MBA, N.H. Coll., 1981. Registered profl. engr., N.Y., N.H., Mass., Maine, La., N.J. Elec. engr. Kaiser Aluminum, Bristol, R.I., 1969-70; plant engr. Milliken & Co., Exeter, N.H., 1971-81; consulting engr. Jones & Beach, Engrs., Stratham, 1981-82; salesman Simplex Wire & Cable Co., Newington, 1982; sales engr. The Valve Co., Portsmouth, 1982-83; engring. mgr. TVC Systems, 1983-90; mgr. elec. and instrument engring. Herzog-Hart Corp., Boston, 1990-94; v.p. Dumont Assocs., Inc., Nashua, N.H., 1994-99; New England regional ops. dir. TAVA Tech. (now Real Enterprise Solutions), Exeter, NH, 1999—2001; prin. engr. Wunderlich-Malec Engrs., Portsmouth, 2001—. Cons. Automation & Power Elec. Engrs., Exeter, N.H., 1982—; guest lectr., U. N.H., Durham, 1987, 88; faculty mem. work curriculum com. Boston Archtl. Ctr., 1991-97. Capt. U.S. Army, 1970-71. Mem. IEEE (sr. mem.), Am. Inst. Plant Engrs. (cert.), Instrument Soc. Am. (sr. mem.), Am. Prodn. and Inventory Control Soc., Am. Soc. Quality, Internat. Dist. Heating and Cooling Assn. (chmn. controls com. 1988-89), Internat. Soc. for Pharm. Engrs., Kiwanis (bd. dirs. Exeter, N.H. 1981), Am. Soc. Quality. Office: Wunderlich-Malec Engrs 200 International Dr Ste 185 Portsmouth NH 03801

LAMBERT, FREDERICK WILLIAM, lawyer, educator; b. Millburn, N.J., Feb. 12, 1943; m. Barbara E. Fogell, Aug. 13, 1965; children: Elisabeth, Mark. BA, U. Mich., 1965, JD, 1969. Bar: Ohio 1969, Fla. 1973, Calif. 1973, U.S. Supreme Ct. 1975. Law clk. to Stanley N. Barnes, U.S. Cir. Judge U.S. Cir. Ct., L.A., 1969-70; atty. advisor Office Legal Counsel U.S. Dept. Justice, Washington, 1970-71; law clk. to Justice William H. Rehnquist U.S. Supreme Ct., 1971-72; pvt. practice L.A., 1973-90; acting gen. counsel Itel Corp., San Francisco, 1981-82; ptnr. Adams, Duque & Hazeltine, L.A., 1985-90, chmn. bus. law dept., 1989-90; assoc. prof. Hastings Coll. Law, U. Calif., San Francisco, 1993-99, prof. law, 1999—. Vis. prof. U. Mich. Law Sch., Ann Arbor, 1990-91, Duke Law Sch., Durham, N.C., 1992-93. Mem. Am. Law Inst., Am. Law and Econs. Assn., Econ. Round Table of L.A., Calif. State Bar Assn., Half Moon Bay Yacht Club. Home: 1100 Pilarcitos Ave Half Moon Bay CA 94019-1459

LAMBERT, GEORGE ROBERT, lawyer, real estate broker; b. Muncie, Ind., Feb. 21, 1933; s. George Russell and Velma Lou (Jones) L.; m. Mary Virginia Alling, June 16, 1956; children: Robert Allen, Ann Holt, James William. BS, Ind. U., Bloomington, 1955; JD, IIT Chgo., 1962. Bar: Ill. 1962, U.S. Dist. Ct. (no. dist.) Ill. 1962, Iowa 1984, Pa. 1988, Ind. 1999. V.p., gen. counsel, sec. Washington Nat. Ins. Co., Evanston, Ill., 1970-82; v.p., gen. counsel Washington Nat. Corp., 1979-82; sr. v.p., sec., gen. counsel Life Investors Inc., Cedar Rapids, Iowa, 1982-88; v.p., gen. counsel Provident Mut. Life Ins. Co., Phila., 1988-95; pres. Lambert Legal Consulting, Inc., Wilmington, Del., 1995—; realtor Coldwell Banker, North Palm Beach, Fla., 1996—2001, Cressy and Everett GMAC Real Estate, South Bend, Ind., 1999-2000; owner, broker Lambert Realty, Granger, 2001—. Alderman Evanston City Coun., 1980-82. Served to lt. USAF, 1955-57. Mem. Ill. State Bar Assn., Ind. Bar Assn., Iowa Bar Assn., Assn. of Life Ins. Counsel (past pres.), Nat. Assn. Realtors, Ind. Assn. Realtors, Greater South Bend-Mishawaka Assn. Realtors, Inc. Home: 51702 Stoneham Way Granger IN 46530-8493

LAMBERT, JEAN MARJORIE, health care executive; b. Bay City, Mich., Mar. 19, 1943; d. Richard William and Fidelis Rena (LeVasseur) L. BA, Madonna U., Livonia, Mich., 1967; MA, Ea. Mich. U., 1975. Cert. in Shiatsu; bd. cert. reflexology. Dir. religious edn. Archdiocese of Detroit, 1970-75, dir. evaluation, 1975-77; assoc. dir. programming Intermedia Found., Santa Monica, Calif., 1977-78; acad. dean St. John Provincial Sem., Plymouth, Mich., 1978-84; asst. dir. quality mgmt. Sisters of Mercy Health Corp., Farmington Hills, 1984-87; sr. cons. Mercy Collaborative, Livonia, mich., 1987-88; v.p. Mission Mercy Health Sys., Cin., 1988-91, Mission Sisters Providence Health Sys., Springfield, Mass., 1991-99; sr. v.p. Mission Integration Humility of Mary Health Ptnrs., Youngstown, Ohio, 1999—. Asst. prof. homiletics St. John Sem., Plymouth, Mich., 1978—85, St. Mary of the Woods Coll. , Terre Haute, Ind., 1985, St. Meinrad Sem., Ind., 1984; bd. dirs. Combined Health Appeal of Mass., Providence Ministries, New Eng. Conf. Cath. Healthcare; mem. Am. Reflexology Cert. Bd.; reflexology and therapeutic touch practitioner. Editor Religious Edn., 1975-77. Nat. Cath. Edn. Assn.-Assn. Theol. Schs. for U.S. and Can. grantee, 1983. Mem. NAFE, Groundwork, Network, Am. Hosp. Assn., Am. Mgmt. Assn., Mental Health Assn., Cath. Health Assn. (bd. dirs. New Eng. Conf.), Acad. Leadership in Cath. Health Care, Providence Ministries (bd. dirs.). Roman Catholic. Avocations: woodcarving, photography, continuing education, shiatsu, reflexology. Office: Humility of Mary Health Ptnrs 1044 Belmont Ave Youngstown OH 44504-1006

LAMBERT, JEREMIAH DANIEL, lawyer, educator; b. N.Y.C., Sept. 11, 1934; s. Noah D. and Clara (Ravage) L.; m. Vicki Anne Asher, July 25, 1959 (div.); children: Nicole Stirling, Alix Stewart, Leigh Asher; m. Sanda Kayden, Dec. 3, 1983; children: Clare Kayden, Hilary Kayden. AB magna cum laude, Princeton U., 1955; LL.B., Yale U., 1959. Bar: N.Y. 1960, D.C. 1964, U.S. Ct. Appeals (5th cir.) 1964, U.S. Supreme Ct. 1964. Assoc. Cravath, Swaine & Moore, N.Y.C., 1959-63; sr. ptnr. Peabody, Lambert & Meyers, Washington, 1969-84; ptnr. Shook, Hardy & Bacon, 1997—2002; dir. Global Crossing, Ltd., 2002—. Adj. prof. law Georgetown U., Washington, 1978-79; trustee Internat. Law Inst., Washington, 1983-88; mem. adv. com. on Electricity Futures Contracts, N.Y. Merc. Exch., 1994-95; mem. bd. govs. Yale Law Jour., 1958-59. Author (editor): (Marketing Books) Economica and Political Incentives to Petroleum Development , 1990; author: Creating Competitive Markets: The PJM Model, 2001; co-author (with Lawrence White): Handbook of Modern Construction Law, 1982; mem. editl. adv. bd., contbr. (Econ. Book) The Impact of Competition, 2000; contbr. articles to legal publs. 1st lt. USAR, 1963-66. Fulbright scholar U. Copenhagen, 1955-56. Mem. ABA, Am. Soc. Internat. Law, D.C Bar Assn., Bar Assn. of City of N.Y., Cosmos Club, Princeton Club, Yale Club, Chevy Chase Club, Phi Beta Kappa. Office: Law Firm of Jeremiah D. Lambert Ste 450 1615 L St, NW Washington DC 20036-5666 E-mail: jlambert@shb.com.

LAMBERT, JOAN DORETY, elementary education educator; b. Trenton, N.J., Oct. 21, 1937; d. John William and Margaret (Fagan) Dorety; m. James E. Lambert Sr., June 25, 1960; children: Margi, Karen, James E., Kevin. BA, Georgian Ct. Coll., Lakewood, N.J., 1958. Cert. tchr., Pa., N.J. Tchr. 2d and 3d grades combined Washington Elem. Sch., Trenton, 1958-61; tchr. kindergarten music St. Genevieve Sch., Flourtown, Pa., 1968-78, tchr. 3d grade, 1978—. Producer, dir. musical shows for St. Genevieve Sch., 1970-78; demonstration classroom for writing process on computers Chestnut Hill Coll. Mem. Jr. League of Trenton, 1960-68, Jr. League of Phila., 1968-70. Teleflex Internat. grantee, 1989-92, Anna B. Stokes Meml. scholar, 1960, Met. Opera grantee, 1958-60. Mem. NEA. Republican. Roman Catholic. Avocations: walking, theater, reading, swimming, family activities. Home: 33 Coventry Ct Blue Bell PA 19422-2528 Office: St Genevieve Sch 1237 Bethlehem Pike Flourtown PA 19031-1902

LAMBERT, JOHN BOYD, chemical engineer, consultant; b. Billings, Mont., July 5, 1929; s. Jean Arthur and Gail (Boyd) L.; m. Jean Wilson Bullard, June 20, 1953 (dec. 1958); children: William, Thomas, Patricia, Cathy, Karen; m. Ilse Crager, Sept. 20, 1980 (dec. 1995). BS in Engring., Princeton U., 1951; PhD, U. Wis., 1956. Rsch. engr. E.I. DuPont de Nemours Co., Wilmington, Del., 1956-69; sr. rsch. engr. Fansteel, Inc., Balt., 1969, mktg. mgr., plant mgr. North Chicago, Ill., 1970-73, mgr. mfg. engring. Waukegan, 1974-80, corp. tech. dir. North Chicago, 1980-86, gen. mgr. metals, 1987-90, v.p., corp. tech. dir., 1990-91. IESC vol., Brazil, 1995; ind. cons., Lake Forest, Ill., 1991—. Contbr. articles to profl. jours. Recipient Charles Hatchett medal Inst. Metals, London, 1986. Mem. AIChE, Am. Chem. Soc., Am. Soc. Metals, Sigma Xi. Episcopalian. Achievements include patents in field of dispersion-strengthened metals, refractory metals, chemical vapor deposition, both products and processes. Home and Office: 617 Greenbriar Ln Lake Forest IL 60045-3214 Fax: 847-234-7649. E-mail: drjbl@aol.com.

LAMBERT, JON KELLY, mechanical engineer; b. Seattle, Nov. 4, 1954; s. William Edward and Irene Myrtle (Paulson) Lambert; m. Karen Dawn Drake, May 11, 2002; children from previous marriage: Kelly Renee, Juliette Kristine. Cert. nuclear lead auditor. Nuclear quality control inspector various orgns., 1981-87; dir. quality Tanco, Inc., Houston, 1987; welding engr. Joy Technologies, Inc., Thompson, 1987; quality inspector Townsend & Bottum Svcs. Group, 1987-88; welding engr. M.K. Ferguson Co., Bridgman, Mich., 1988, quality engr. Aiken, S.C., 1988-90; welding engr. Westinghouse Savannah River Co., 1990-95; quality assurance mgr. Mitsubishi Heavy Industries Am., Inc., Newport Beach, Calif., 1995-96; with Am. Welding Soc., 1996-98; asst. dir. certification, staff engr. Bechtel Internat., Campeche, Mexico, 1998—2000; welding supr. HMT, Inc., 2001—02; welding engr. Energy Steel & Supply Co., 2002—. Cons., expert witness, 2001—. Mem. Am. Welding Soc. (cert. welding insp., mem. sub-com. structural welding code-steel, charter com. stainless steel welding code 1990—). Achievements include work on safety of nuclear power plants, defense nuclear facilities, offshore oil and gas production platforms. E-mail: jon20013@hotmail.com.

LAMBERT, JOSEPH EARL, state supreme court chief justice; b. Berea, Ky., May 23, 1948; s. James Wheeler and Ruth (Hilton) L.; m. Debra Hembree, June 25, 1983; children: Joseph Patrick, John Ryan. BS in Bus. and

Econs., Georgetown Coll., 1970; JD, U. Louisville, 1974; PhD (hon.) , Eastern Ky. U., 1999, Georgetown Coll., 1999, Northern Ky. U., 2002. Bar: Ky. 1974. Staff Sen. John Sherman Cooper U.S. Senate, Washington, 1970-71; law clk. to judge U.S. Dist. Ct., Louisville, 1974-75; ptnr. Lambert & Lambert, Mt. Vernon, Ky., 1975-87; justice Supreme Ct. Ky., Frankfort, 1987-98, chief justice, 1998—. Chmn. Jud. Form Retirement Commn., 1996—. Mem. Bd. Regents Eastern Ky. U., Richmond, 1988-92. Recipient Disting. Alumni award U. Louisville Sch. Law, 1988; named Outstanding Judge of Ky., 2000. Mem.: ABA, Ky. Bar Assn. Republican. Baptist. Office: State Ky State Capitol Bldg Office Chief Justice Rm 231 Frankfort KY 40601 E-mail: cjlambert@mail.aoc.state.ky.us.*

LAMBERT, JOSEPH BUCKLEY, chemistry educator; b. Ft. Sheridan, Ill., July 4, 1940; s. Joseph Idus and Elizabeth Dorothy (Kirwan) L.; m. Mary Wakefield Pulliam, June 27, 1967; children: Laura Kirwan, Alice Pulliam, Joseph Cannon. BS, Yale U., 1962; PhD (Woodrow Wilson fellow 1962-63, NSF fellow 1962-65), Calif. Inst. Tech., 1965. Asst. prof. chemistry Northwestern U., Evanston, Ill., 1965-69, assoc. prof., 1969-74, prof. chemistry, 1974-91, Clare Hamilton Hall prof. chemistry, 1991—, Charles Deering McCormick prof., 1999—, chmn. dept., 1986-89, dir. integrated sci. program, 1982-85. Vis. assoc. Brit. Mus., 1973, Polish Acad. Scis., 1981, Chinese Acad. Scis., 1988. Author: Organic Structural Analysis, 1976, Physical Organic Chemistry through Solved Problems, 1978, The Multinuclear Approach to NMR Spectroscopy, 1983, Archaeological Chemistry III, 1984, Introduction to Organic Spectroscopy, 1987, Recent Advances in Organic NMR Spectroscopy, 1987, Acyclic Organonitrogen Stereodynamics, 1992, Cyclic Organonitrogen Stereodynamics, 1992, Prehistoric Human Bone, 1993, Traces of the Past, 1997, Organic Structural Spectroscopy, 1998; audio course Intermediate NMR Spectroscopy, 1973; editor in chief Journal of Physical Organic Chemistry; contbr. articles to sci. jours. Recipient Nat. Fresenius award, 1976, James Flack Norris award, 1987, Fryxell award, 1989, Nat. Catalyst award, 1993; Alfred P. Sloan fellow, 1968-70, Guggenheim fellow, 1973, Interacad. exch. fellow (U.S.-Poland), 1985, Air Force Office sci. rsch. fellow, 1990. Fellow AAAS, Japan Soc. for Promotion of Sci., Brit. Interplanetary Soc., Ill. Acad. Sci. (life); mem. Am. Chem. Soc. (chmn. history of chemistry divsn., 1996, F.S. Kipping award 1998), Royal Soc. Chemistry, Soc. Archaeol. Scis. (pres. 1986-87), Phi Beta Kappa, Sigma Xi (hon. lectr. 1997-98). Home: 1956 Linneman St Glenview IL 60025-4264 Office: Northwestern University Dept of Chemistry 2145 Sheridan Rd Evanston IL 60208-3113

LAMBERT, JOSEPH PARKER, retired dentist; b. Bronte, Tex., Oct. 6, 1921; s. Joseph P. and Mary Josephine (Robison) L.; m. Jean Molesworth, Dec. 8, 1945; children: Jean Elizabeth, Mary Catherine, Helen Patricia, Thomas Joseph, Charlotte Anne. DDS, Baylor U., 1952. Cert. Tex. State Bd. Dental Examiners, Wyo. State Bd. Dental Examiners, 1952. Instr. Baylor U. Coll. Dentistry, Dallas, 1952-56, from asst. prof. to prof., dept. chmn., 1957-86, prof. emeritus, 1986—. With USN, 1942-45. Fellow Am. Coll. Dentists; mem. ADA, Tex. Dental Assn., Dallas County Dental Assn., Omicron Kappa Upsilon. Republican. Methodist. Avocations: church work, gardening.

LAMBERT, JUDITH A. UNGAR, lawyer; b. N.Y.C., Apr. 13, 1943; d. Alexander Lawrence and Helene (Rosenson) Ungar; m. Peter D. Leibowits, Aug. 22, 1965 (div. 1971); 1 child, David Gary. BS, U. Pa., 1964; JD magna cum laude, U. Miami, 1984. Bar: N.Y. 1985, Fla. 1990. Assoc. Proskauer Rose Goetz & Mendelsohn, N.Y.C., 1984-86, Taub & Fasciana, N.Y.C., 1986-87, Hoffinger Friedland Dobrish Bernfeld & Hasen, N.Y.C., 1987-88; pvt. practice, 1988—. Mem. ABA, N.Y. State Bar Assn., Assn. Bar of City of N.Y., N.Y. Women's Bar Assn. (family law and trusts and estates com.), N.Y. County Lawyers Assn. Avocations: travel, music, theater. Office: 245 E 54th St New York NY 10022-4707

LAMBERT, KIRSTEN SCHNOOR, public relations executive, writer; b. Chgo., Dec. 26, 1963; d. Walter Karl and Irmgard (von Stockhausen) Schnoor; m. Christopher Jay Lambert, May 25, 1996. BA in Liberal Arts, DePaul U., 1995. Editl. and prodn. asst. Kraft Inc., Glenview, Ill., 1986-89; comm. assoc. Budget Rent A Car, Chgo., 1989-91; spl. events asst. Chgo. Sun-Times, 1992-94; editl. asst. Chgo. Reader, 1994-95; freelancer DonTech Corp., Chgo., 1995-96; comm. mgr. The Sherwood Group, Inc., Northbrook, 1996-00; mktg. and comm. mgr. Am. Orthopaedic Assn., Rosemont, 2000—. Author: Chicago '96 Democratic National Convention Visitors' Guide, 1996; editor newsletter Interactions, 1999 (Circle of Excellence award Am. Soc. Assn. Execs, 1999). Support mgr. Howard Brown Meml. Clinic, Chgo., 1987-91. Mem. Internat. Assn. Bus. Communicators (chpt. membership com. 1989-91). Avocations: writing, music, dancing. Office: Am Orthopaedic Assn 6300 N River Rd Rosemont IL 60018-4206 E-mail: lambert@aoassn.org.

LAMBERT, LECLAIR GRIER, writer, lecturer, consultant, state government public information administrator; b. Miami, Fla. s. George F. and Maggie (Grier) L. BS, Hampton Inst., 1959; postgrad., Harvard U., 1959, U. Munich, 1965-66. Rschr., copy reader Time-Life Books, 1961-64; tchr. biology and Eng. lit., secondary level U.S. Dependent's Schs. Overseas, Tripoli, Libya, 1964-65; biology editor H.S. textbooks Holt, Rinehart & Winston, N.Y.C., 1966-69; biology editor and writer Ency. Britannica, 1969; copy editor Russian sci. monographs The Faraday Press, 1970-71; writer Med. World News, 1971; pub. rels. writer Nat. Found./March of Dimes, White Plains, N.Y., 1972. Lectr. cmty. and human rels. Black Cultural heritage at local schs. and colls., 1977-87; guest lectr. Liberty Sq. (Fla.) 50th Anniversary, 1986, Black History Month Minn. Ho. of Reps., 1987-96, creator and coord. student spkr. Ho. of Reps. Youth Forum, 1992; radio commentator Sta. KEEY, 1975-80; reporter Twin Cities Courier, Mpls., 1976-86. Author: Reflections of Life--Poems, Prose and Essays, 1981, A Learning Journey Through Black History, 1982; editor, writer: Minnesota's Black Community, 1977; editor: Art in Development: A Nigerian Perspective, 1983; freelance writer and designer of brochures and pamphlets, 1974—; contbr. articles to profl. jours. Dir. comm. St. Paul Urban League, 1972-80, asst. to exec. dir., 1985-86, bd. dirs., 1992—, sec. bd., 1999—, co-chair 75th Anniversary Celebration; mem. adv. bd. Archie Givens Found. for African Am. Lit. Rare Books Collection, U. Minn., 1988—; exec. dir. African Am. Mus. Art and History, 1980-86; info. officer Mpls. Urban League, 1978-79; co-founder, bd. dirs. Summit-Univ. Free Press, 1974-79, U. Minn. Black Learning Resource Ctr., 1980-83; past mem. Roy Wilkins Meml., Com. Civic Ctr., St. Paul, 1985; mem. state meml. com. Martin Luther King Celebration Com., 1987-96; mem. Ethiopian Famine Relief Com.; mem. rev. com. Twin Cities Mayors' Pub. Art Awards, 1981; co-founder W. Suburban Annual Black History Month Celebration Com., 1983-86; mem. St. Paul Civic Ctr. Authority Bd., 1985-97, vice chair, 1991-97, bd. rep. pub. art, bldg. expansion com., bd. rep. "Am.'s Smithsonian" exhbn.; mem. St. Paul City Art Plan Com., 1987-88, Minn. Mus. Am. Art orgnl., exhibits plan coms., 1989-91, trustee, 1991-96, v.p., 1992-93, pres., 1993-94, chair, 1994-95; adv. bd. YMCA Youth in Govt., 1997—; sgt-at-arms, officer Minn. Ho. of Reps., 1987-96, coord. ednl. programs, mem. cultural diversity tng. task force, 1992—, dir. pub. info., 1996—; pub. weekly column Reflections, Session Weekly; trustee Coll. Visual Arts, 1997—; mem. St. Paul-Mpls. com. on fgn. rels., 1998-2000; cons. ARD/USAID staff tng. Palestinian Legis. Coun., Curr. tng. plan for Birzeit U., West Bank, 1997; bd. dirs. Minn. Landmarks, 2001—; commr., St. Paul Human Rights Commn., 1999—; bd. dirs. St. Paul Visitors and Conv. Bur., 1990-93. Served to 1 lt., Chem. Corps., U.S. Army, 1959-61. Recipient Cmty. Martin Luther King Comm. award, 1978, Spl. Recognition award Mpls. St. Acad., 1983, Spl. Achievement award Roosevelt H.S., 1985, Spl. Recognition award Twin Cities African Am. Mus., 1985, Liberty Sq. Tenants' Spl. Recognition award, 1986, Vol. Svc. award St. Paul Urban League, 1988, Spl. Recognition award Palestine Journalists Assn., 1997, Hubert H. Humphrey Inst. Internat. Fellows Program, 1998; LeClair Lambert Day proclaimed by City of St. Paul, 1997. Mem. Pub. Rels. Soc. Am., African-Am. Mus. Assn. (mem. nat. legis. edn. com. 1983, exec. coun., Midwest region rep. 1984-89, Achievement award 1985). Office: Minn Ho Reps 100 Constitution Ave Saint Paul MN 55155-1298

LAMBERT, LINDA MARGARET, reading specialist; b. Livingston County, Ky., Jan. 17, 1941; d. Wiley Jackson and Florence Allie (Davidson) Stallions; m. Leland Dawson Lambert; children: Sharon Kay, Sheila Lynn, Wiley Lee. AA, Yuba Coll., 1970; BLS, Mary Washington Coll., 1980; MEd, U. Va., 1986. Cert. tchr., Va. Elem. tchr. Stafford (Va.) County Schs., 1979-91, reading specialist, 1991—, reading recovery tchr., 1997—. Mem. com. Devel. Elem. Counselors, Stafford, 1987-89, Devel. Appropriate Assessment, Stafford, 1993-94. Sponsor Ghostwriter Mystery Club, Garrisonwoods Estates, 1993-97; mem. Fairview Bapt. Ch., Stafford Dem. Com., 1996—; del. Va. State Dem. Convention. Mem. NEA, Reading Recovery Coun. N.Am., Va. Edn. Assn., Stafford County Edn. Assn., Internat. Reading Assn., Va. State Reading Assn., Rappahanook Reading Coun., Hist. Fredericksburg Antique Automobile Club. Democrat. Avocations: swimming, reading, antiques. Home: 203 Rumford Rd Fredericksburg VA 22405-3206 Office: Hampton Oaks Elem Sch 107 Northampton Blvd Stafford VA 22554-7660

LAMBERT, LLOYD LAVERNE, minister; b. Agusta, Ill., June 5, 1925; s. Charles N. Sr. and Lena (Johnson) L.; m. Dorothy Mae Spaar, June 22, 1946; children: Rebecca, Toby, Michael, Corey. Student, Millikin U., 1948-49, Anderson (Ind.) Coll., 1953-54, student, 1956-57. Ordained to ministry Ch. of God (Anderson, Ind.), 1955. Founder, exec. dir. The Christian Ctr., Anderson, 1956—. Chaplain Madison County Detention Ctr. Bd. dirs. Habitat for Humanity, Anderson, Recovery in Christ, Sowers of Seeds, Inc., Counselors for Alcohol and Other Drug Abuses; past chmn. Nursing Home Ministries; past pres. Madison County Svcs. Coun.; past dep. sheriff Madison County Sheriff's Dept.; mem. adv. bd. for drug abuse St. John's Hosp.; chmn. Human Rels. Commn., City of Anderson, 1981-84; founder Home for Alcoholics, Anderson. With F.A., U.S. Army, 1943-46; PTO. Recipient spl. recognition Exchange Club Anderson, 1971, recognition Ind. Dept. Corrections, 1972, Liberty Bell award ABA, 1973, Outstanding Citizenship award Ind. Elks, 1973-74, Svc. to Mankind award Sertoma Club, 1980, 98, 99, Chief Anderson award, 1986, Elmo A. Funk Ideal of Svc. award, 1990; named as one of top people of the century Anderson Newspaper and Madison County, 1999, Sagamore of the Wabash Gov. State Ind. Frank O'Bannon. Mem. Anderson Ministerial Assn., Internat. Union Gospel Missions (past pres., sec.-treas. midwestern dist.), Rotary (past sargeant-at-arms and sec., pres. Anderson club 1975-76, Community Image award 1973, 80, Internat. Paul Harris fellow 1983). Home: 146 Stacey Ln Anderson IN 46016-5894 Office: The Christian Ctr 625 Main St PO Box 743 Anderson IN 46015-0743

LAMBERT, LYN DEE, library media specialist, law librarian; b. Fitchburg, Mass., Jan. 5, 1954; m. Paul Frederick Lambert, Aug. 11, 1979; children: Gregory John, Emily Jayne, Nicholas James. BA in History, Fitchburg State Coll., 1976, MEd in History, 1979; JD, Franklin Pierce Law Ct., 1983; MLS, Simmons Coll., 1986. Law libr. Fitchburg Law Libr., Mass. Trial Ct., 1985-96; media specialist libr. Samoset Sch., Leominster, Mass., 1996—. Instr. paralegal studies courses Fisher Coll., Fitchburg, 1989-94, Anna Maria Coll., Paxton, Mass., 1995—, Atlantic Union Coll., Lancaster, Mass., 1995—, pre-law coll. courses Fitchburg State Coll., 1995—; tech. com. City of Leominster Shc., Net Day Participant and trainer/leader, Leominster H.S., Northwest, Johnny Appleseed, Fall Brook, Southeast and Samoset. Mem. Am. Legion Band, Fitchburg, 1959—, Westminster (Mass.) Town Band, 1965—, Townsend Town Band, 1999—; appt. to Mass. Strategic Plan Com. for delivery of libr. svcs. among multi-type librs. within the commonwealth; mem. Patrick S. Gilmore Cmty. Honor Band, Hatch Shell, Boston, 2000, 2001. Recipient Community Leadership award Xi Psi chpt. Kappa Delta Pi-Fitchburg State Coll. chpt., 1993. Mem. ALA, Am. Assn. Law Librarians (copyright com. 1987-89, publs. rev. com. 1990-92, state, ct. and county law librs. spl. interest sect. publicity com. 1993—), Law Librarians New Eng. (conf. com. 1988), Mass. Libr. Assn. (edn. chair 1991-93, freedom of info. com., legislation com.), New Eng. Libr. Assn., New Eng. Microcomputer Users Group (profl. assoc.), North Cen. Mass. Libr. Alliance (newsletter editor 1990—), Spl. Libr. Assn., Beta Phi Mu, Phi Alpha Delta, Phi Delta Kappa (newsletter editor Montachusett chpt. 1998-2000, pres. Montachusett chpt. 2000-02). Avocations: singing, guitar, clarinet, hiking, camping. Office: Samoset Libr Media Ctr 100 Decicco Dr Leominster MA 01453-5161

LAMBERT, LYNDA JEANNE, humanities and arts educator, artist; b. Ellwood City, Pa., Aug. 27, 1943; d. William Joseph McKinney and Esther Louella Kirker; m. Charles Robert Lambert, April 14, 1961; children: Salome Yaromey, Heidi McClure, Victoria Jacques, Ilsa Barry, R. Andrew. BFA, Slippery Rock U. of Pa., 1989, MA in English, 1994; MFA, W.Va. U., 1991. Gallery mgr., instr. W.Va. U., Morgantown, 1989-91; grants specialist West Valley Coll., Saratoga, Calif., 1991-92; exec. dir. Hoyt Inst. of Fine Arts, New Castle, Pa., 1992-96; asst. prof. fine art and humanities Geneva Coll., Beaver Falls, 1997—. Site surveyor Am. Assn. Mus., Washington, 1998—; panel mem. Pa. Ptnrs. in the Arts, Loretto, 1997-2000; conf. workshop presenter Christians in the Visual Arts, 1997. Author: Concerti: Psalms for the Pilgrimage, 2002. Active workshop on printmaking Girl Scouts, Geneva Coll., 1999. Recipient Woman of Distinction award Beaver Castle Girl Scouts, Pa., 1995, Cash award Carnegie Mus. Art, Pitts., 1999, 2000, award of excellence in scholarship Geneava Coll., 2000, award of excellence Beaver Valley Internat. Art Festival, 2002; permanent exhibit includes Ambassadors Residence, Papua New Guinea, 2001—. Mem. Nat. Assn. Women Artists, Womens Caucus for Art, Associated Artists Pitts. (mem. exhbn. com.). Avocations: antique collecting, viking glass research, riding motorcycles. Home: 104 River Rd Ellwood City PA 16117-2607 Office: Geneva Coll 3200 College Ave Beaver Falls PA 15010-3557 E-mail: llambert@ccia.com., llambert@geneva.edu.

LAMBERT, MARY CLARK, civic volunteer; b. Havre de Grace, Md., Apr. 27, 1931; d. John Noble Clark and Mary Eleanor (Fahey) Clark Leffler; m. René Arthur Lambert, May 14, 1955; children: Karen, Mark, John. BS in Edn., U. Del., 1954. Tchr. New Castle (Del.) Schs., 1954-55, Harford County (Md.) Schs., 1955-56; owner, dir. Sch. of Horsemanship, Harford County, 1954-76. Contbr. tech. and gen. interest articles to mags. and newspapers, 1949—. 4-H Club leader, 1970; docent Susquehanna Mus., Havre de Grace, 1982—; vol. Decoy Mus., 1986—; sec. Hist. Dist. Commn., 1983—89; mem. Hist. Preservation Commn., chmn., 1999—2001, sec., 2001—; mem. local planning and zoning commn., 1987—92, vice chair, 1990—92. Republican. Avocations: photography, classical music, writing, theater, restoring old homes. Home and Office: 115 S Union Ave Havre De Grace MD 21078-3111

LAMBERT, MEG STRINGER, construction executive, architect, interior designer; b. Selma, Ala., Aug. 10, 1941; d. John Bryant and Margaret Vandiver (Clark) Stringer; m. George Edward Buchner, June 30, 1962 (div. 1972); children: Susan Mayo Buchner, George Bryant Buchner, Robert Carson Buchner; m. Joseph Smith Lambert, June 20, 1975. BS, Auburn U., 1961, postgrad., 1972-73. Lic. real estate broker Ala., home builder Ala., master builder cert. Nat. Assn. Home Builders, cert. constrn. assoc. Nat. Assn. Women in Constrn. Math tchr. Selma (Ala.) Pub. Sch., 1961-62, Oscoda (Mich.) Pub. Sch., 1963-64; real estate sales Stower's Gallery of Homes, Montgomery, Ala., 1974-75; constrn. mgr. Lambert Constrn. Co., Inc., 1975-80, home builder, designer Prattville, 1984—; sec. estimating dept. Aesco Steel Co., Montgomery, 1981-82; steel bridge estimator and sales assoc. Trinity Industries, 1983-84; pres. Home Touch Builders, Inc., 2000—. Chmn. parade homes Prattville/Millbrook chpt. Home Builders, 1985—87, program chmn., 1985—90; masonry adv. bd. Prattville Vocat. Sch., Prattville, 1994—2001. Author: (book) A History of the Pleasant Hill Baptist Church (1840-1990), 1990. Vice-chmn. Prattville Planning Commn., 1992—95; mem. land use com. City Comprehensive Plan, 1994—95; mem. leadership steering com. Autagua County, 1995—98, bd. equalization, 1995—99; chmn. health and welfare com. 1st United Meth. Ch., 1993; mem. beautificiation com. Prattville C. of C., 1992—95; pres. Pleasant Hill Cemetary Assn., 1990—98, 2000—02, South Dallas Hist. Preservation Assn., 2002—. Named Woman of the Yr., Montgomery chpt. Nat. Women in Constrn., 1990. Mem.: Greater Montgomery Home Builders Assn. (mem. longe range planning com. 1986, bd. dirs., exec. com. 2001, Named Builder of the Yr. 1989), Autauga County Heritage Assn. (pres. 1992). Republican. Avocations: genealogy, painting, historical preservation activities, working in political campaigns. Home: 394 Kingston Ridge Rd Prattville AL 36067-1725 Office: Lambert Construction Co Inc PO Box 680656 Prattville AL 36068-0656

LAMBERT, NADINE MURPHY, psychologist, educator; b. Ephraim, Utah; m. Robert E. Lambert, 1956; children— Laura Allan, Jeffrey. PhD in Psychology, U. So. Calif., 1965. Diplomate Am. Bd. Profl. Psychology, Am. Bd. Sch. Psychology. Sch. psychologist Los Nietos Sch. Dist., Whittier, Calif., 1952-53, Bellflower (Calif.) Unified Sch. Dist., 1953-58; research cons. Calif. Dept. Edn., Los Angeles, 1958-64; dir. sch. psychology tng. program U. Calif., Berkeley, 1964—, asst. prof. edn., 1964-70, asso. prof., 1970-76, prof., 1976—, assoc. dean for student svcs., 1988-94. Mem. Joint Com. Mental Health of Children, 1967-68; cons. state depts. edn., Calif., Ga., Fla.; cons. Calif. Dept. Justice; mem. panel on testing handicapped people Nat. Acad. Scis., 1978-81. Author: School Version of the AAMD Adaptive Behavior Scale, 3d edit., 1993; co-author: (with Wilcox and Gleason) Educationally Retarded Child: Comprehensive Assessment and Planning for the EMR and Slow-Learning Child, 1974, (with Hartsough and Bower) Process for Assessment of Effective Functioning, 1981, (with Windmiller and Turiel) Moral Development and Socialization -- Three Perspectives, 1979; assoc. editor Am. Jour. Orthopsychiatry, 1975-81, Am. Jour. Mental Deficiency, 1977-80, (with McCombs) How Students Learn-Reforming Schools Through Learner-Centered Education, 1998, others. With Hartsough and Sandoval Children's Attention and Adjustment Survey, 1990. Recipient Dorothy Hughes award for outstanding contbn. to ednl. and sch. psychology NYU, 1990, Tobacco Disease Related Rsch. award U. Calif., 1990-94, NIDA, 1994-2001; grantee NIMH, 1965-87, Calif. State Dept. Edn., 1-72, 76-78, NHSTE Dept. Transportation, 1995. Fellow APA (coun. reps. divsn. sch. psychologists, bd. dirs. 1984-87, mem. bd. profl. affairs 1981-83, bd. ednl. affairs 1991-94, chmn. 1992-94, exec. com. divsn. sch. psychology 1994-96, mem. commn. for recognition of specialities and professions in psychology 1993-97, Disting. Svc. award 1980, award for disting. profl. contbns. 1986, award for disting. career contbns. of applications of psychology to edn. and tng. 1999), Nat. Assn. of Sch. Psychologists (hon., Legend in Sch. Psychology 1998), Am. Orthopsychiat. Assn.; mem. NEA, Calif. Assn. Sch. Psychologists (pres. 1962-63, Sandra Goff award 1985). Office: U Calif Dept Education Berkeley CA 94720-0001 E-mail: nlambert@socrates.berkeley.edu.

LAMBERT, REBECCA FOTOUHI, communications executive; b. Binghamton, N.Y., Jan. 31, 1947; d. Abol Hassan and Eleanor Margaret (Page) Fotouhi; m. Edward S. Bent, June 20, 1987; 1 child, Maxwell S. Student, Simmons Coll., 1965-68; BA, Williams Coll., 1969; A.M.P., Harvard Bus. Sch., 1982. V.p., treas. Champlain Properties, Stowe, Vt., 1971-75; adminstrv. asst. Nat. Rep. Senatorial Com., 1975-76; strategist Wallop for U.S. Senate Campaign, Washington, 1976-77; chief of staff Senator Malcolm Wallop, 1977-80; dep. asst. sec. U.S. Dept. Energy, 1981-82; assoc. dep. sec. U.S. Dept. Commerce, 1982-83; dir. corp. info. CBS Inc., N.Y.C., 1983; govt. relations cons. law firm Wiley & Rein, 1984-85; pres. Lambert Broadcasting, Inc., N.Y.C., 1988—. Chmn., chief exec. officer Healthcare Satellite Broadcasting. Mem. Reagan Transition Team, 1980, Am. Coun. Young Polit. Leaders; pres. Bellevue Hosp. Assn., 1986—; assoc. mem. med. ctr. bd. NYU. Van Lear fellow, 1978 Mem. Am. Coun. Young Polit. Leaders, Bellevue Hosp. Assn. (pres. 1986—). Episcopalian. Office: Healthcare Satellite Broadcasting 119 W 57th St Ste 1100 New York NY 10019-2401 also: 2 Old New Milford Rd Brookfield CT 06804-2426

LAMBERT, RICHARD BOWLES, JR. festival administrator; b. Clinton, Mass., Apr. 20, 1939; s. Richard Bowles and Dorothy Elisabeth (Peck) L.; m. Sherrill Faye Smith, July 4, 1964; 1 child, Lisa Beth Lauren. AB in Physics, Lehigh U., 1961; ScM in Physics, Brown U., 1964, PhD in Physics, 1966; postgrad., Goethe Inst., Germany, 1966, NATO Internat. Sch., 1966, Max Planck Inst. for Physics & Astrophysics, 1966. Fulbright fellow Inst. for Stromungsmechanik Tech. Hochschule, Munich, Germany, 1966-67; asst. prof. U. R.I. Grad. Sch. Oceanography, 1968-74, assoc. prof., 1974; program dir. physical oceanography program NSF, Washington, 1975-77; rsch. oceanographer Sci. Applications Internat. Corp., 1977-79, mgr. ocean physics divsn., 1979-83, asst. v.p., 1980-83, sr. rsch. oceanographer, 1983-84; assoc. program dir. physical oceanography program NSF, Washington, 1984-91, program dir. physical oceanography program, 1991-99; dir. ops. Master Works Festival, 1997—. Adv. com. NOAA; assoc. dir. U.S. TOGA Project Office 1985-91; delegate Intergovernmental TOGA Bd., 1985-91; delegation head Intergovernmental WOCE Panel; co-investigator, chief scientist on oceanographic rsch. cruises, 1971-74. Interim editor Jour. Geophys. Rsch.-Oceans, 1999-2000; contbr. articles to profl. jours. including Jour. Fluid Mech. Bd. dirs. Christian Performing Artist's Fellowship, Haymarket, Va., 1993—. Mem. Am. Geophys. Union (Ocean Scis. award 1999), The Oceanography Soc. (life), Phi Beta Kappa, Sigma Xi. E-mail: rblambert@erols.com.

LAMBERT, RICHARD WILLIAM, mathematics educator; b. Gettysburg, Pa., May 1, 1928; s. Allen Clay and Orpha Rose (Hoppert) L.; m. Phyllis Jean Bain, Sept. 2, 1949 (div. May 1982); children: James Harold, Dean Richard; m. Kathleen Ann Waring, Aug. 30, 1982; stepchildren: Gregory Scott Gibbs, LeAnn Marie Gibbs. BS, Oreg. State U., 1952; MA in Teaching Math., Reed Coll., 1962. Instr. Siuslaw High Sch., Florence, Oreg., 1954-55, David Douglas High Sch., Portland, 1955-67, Mt. Hood Community Coll., Gresham, 1967-87, ret., 1987. NSF grantee, 1959, 60, 62. Mem. Nat. Coun. Tchr. Math., Am. Math Soc., Math. Assn. Am., Am. Math. Assn. of Two Yr. Colls., Oreg. Coun. Tchrs. Math. Democrat. Methodist. Avocations: travel, camping, home improvements, reading. Home: 11621 SE Lexington St Portland OR 97266-5933

LAMBERT, ROBERT FRANK, electrical engineer, consultant; b. Warroad, Minn., Mar. 14, 1924; s. Fred Joseph and Nutah (Gibson) L.; m. June Darlene Flatten, June 30, 1951; children: Cynthia Marie, Susan Ann, Katherine Cheryl. B.E.E., U. Minn., 1948, MS in Elec. Engring, 1949, PhD, 1953. Asst. prof. U. Minn. Inst. Tech., Mpls., 1953-54, assoc. prof., 1955-59, prof. elec. engring., 1959-94, prof. emeritus, 1994; dir. propagation research lab. U. Minn., 1968-87; assoc. dean U. Minn. (Inst. Tech.), 1967-68; asst. prof. Mass. Inst. Tech., 1954-55. Cons. elec. engr., also in acoustics, 1953—; guest scientist Third Phys. Inst., Göttingen, Fed. Republic Germany, 1964; vis. scientist NASA, Hampton, Va., 1979; dir. Inst. Noise Control Engring., Washington, 1972-75 Contbr. numerous articles to tech. jours. Served with USNR, 1943-46. Fellow IEEE, Acoustical Soc. Am. (assoc. editor jour. 1985-93); mem. Am. Soc. Engring. Edn., Am. Soc. Engring. Sci., AAAS, Inst. Noise Control Engring. (dir., John C. Johnson Meml. award), Sigma Xi, Tau Beta Pi, Eta Kappa Nu, Gamma Alpha. Lutheran. Achievements include rsch. in acoustics, communication tech. random vibrations. Home: 2503 Snelling Curv N Saint Paul MN 55113 Office: U Minn Inst Tech Dept Elec Engring Minneapolis MN 55455

LAMBERT, ROBERT LOWELL, scientific investigator; b. Mpls., Jan. 3, 1923; s. Luell E. and Amy (Schwerin) L.; m. Jean Louise Zavodney, Mar. 19, 1949; children: Thomas R., John N. Student, U. Utah, 1941-42, Tex. A&M Coll., 1943-44, Biarritz (France) Am. U., 1945; BS, UCLA, 1947, MBA, 1948; grad. student, U. Minn., 1948-50; PhD, U. Beverly Hills, 1982. Instr. bus. adminstrn. U. Minn., 1948-50; with Budget Pack, Inc., Los Angeles, 1950-55, v.p., 1954-55; with Riverside Cement Co. div. Amcord, Inc., Los Angeles, 1955-61, treas., 1960- 61; finance dir. Amcord, Inc., 1961-72, treas., 1965-72, 75-80, v.p., 1967-72, sec., 1972-74, sr. v.p., 1972-80; pres., dir. Inst. for Bus. Edn., Newport Beach, Calif., 1981-83; ind. investigator, author in field of chronobiological epidemiology, 1984—. Former dir., officer various subsidiaries Amcord, Inc. Contbr. articles to profl. jours. Vice pres. Amcord Found., 1958-80. Served with inf. AUS, World War II, ETO. Decorated Combat Inf. badge, Bronze star with oak leaf cluster, Presdl. Unit citiation, Belgian Fourragere. Mem. Tau Kappa Epsilon, Beta Gamma Sigma, Alpha Kappa Psi. Clubs: Big Canyon Country (Newport Beach); Palm Desert Resort Country. Home: 13 Cool Brk Irvine CA 92612-3412

LAMBERT, STEVEN CHARLES, lawyer; b. Kingsport, Tenn., Aug. 22, 1947; s. M. Charles and Janet (Sultner) L.; children: Shelley Elizabeth, Charles Burnette. BA, Duke U., 1969; JD, Georgetown U., 1974. Bar: D.C. 1975, U.S. Ct. Fed. Claims, U.S. Ct. Appeals (fed. cir.), U.S. Tax Ct. Law clk. to Chief Judge Wilson Cowen, U.S. Ct. Claims, Washington, 1974-75; assoc. Wilkinson, Cragun & Barker, 1975-80, ptnr., 1980-82, Hamel & Park, Washington, 1982-88, Hopkins & Sutter, Washington, 1988-2001, Foley & Lardner, Washington, 2001—. Chmn. adv. coun. U.S. Ct. Claims, 1982-86, mem. adv. coun., 1986—, chmn. bicentennial commn., 1987-91. Co-author: Tax Ideas Desk Book, 1980; contbr. articles to profl. jours. Chmn. bd. trustees Ferrum Coll.; pres. bd. pensions United Meth. Ch.; mem. bd. govs., Wesley Sem., 2000—. With U.S. Army, 1970-72. Fellow Am. Bar Found.; mem. ABA (sec. litigation and natural resources), Am. Arbitration Assn., Claims Ct. Bar

Assn. (pres. 1990-91, bd. dirs. 1999—), Fed. Cir. Bar Assn. (bd. dirs. 1986-88), Bar Assn. D.C. (bd. dirs. 1981-83). Methodist. Avocations: boating, fishing, tennis. Office: Foley & Lardner 3000 K St NW Ste 500 Washington DC 20007-5143

LAMBERT, TOBIAS P. music educator; b. Fairview Park, Ohio, Apr. 29, 1973; s. Dennis M. and Carol M. Lambert. B of Music Edn., B of Music Composition, Cleve. State U., 1997. Asst. band dir. Fairview Park City Schs., 1991—97; music tchr. Columbia Station (Ohio) Sch. Dist., Columbia Station, 1997—2000, Bethel (Alaska) Regional H.S., 2000—01, Colony Mid. Sch., Palmer, 2001—. Mem. East 21 St. Brass Quintet, Cleve., 1995—97, Lorain (Ohio) County Cmty. Band, 1997—2000, Mat-Su Cmty. Band, Wasilla, Alaska, 2001—. Editor: Alaska Music Educator, 2001—. Active Bethel Arts Coun., Alaska, 2000—01, Camai Festival, 2000—01. Named Educator of Month, Lorain County Edn. Svc. Ctr., 2000. Mem.: Alaska Music Educator Assn. (state editor 2000—), Ohio Music Educator Assn. (properties mgr. 1997—2000), Ohio Collegiate Music Educator Assn. (pres. Cleve. state chpt. 1991—97, state sec.). Avocations: caving, hiking, music, movies. Home: PO Box 2171 Palmer AK 99645

LAMBERT, WILLIAM JESSE, III, writer; b. Spokane, Wash., May 22, 1942; s. William Jesse Jr. and Olive Nellie Mae (Brown) L. BA in Bus. Adminstrn., Wash. State U., 1964. Free-lance writer, Spokane, Wash., 1965—. Author: Adonis, 1969, Adonis at Actum, 1970, Adonis at Bomasa, 1970, Five Roads to Tlen, 1970, Maneaters of Malibu, 1971, Their Husbands are at War, 1971, Starship Intercourse, 1971, Faculty Wife, 1971, Too Beautiful, 1972, Big Guns, 1972, Sex Intrigue, 1972, Dog-Collar Boys, 1972, Male Sex Idol, 1972, The Erection, 1972, Blackballed, 1972, Mountain Men, 1972, Joint Hunger, 1973, Making the Jock, 1973, E-Mission, 1974, Beat the Man Down, 1975, Bugger Boy, 1975, Trucker Sucker, 1975, Stud Maker, 1975, Bondage Boy, 1976, Leather Bound, 1976, Brother in Bondage, 1976, B&D Boys, 1976, Strung and Hung, 1976, Boy in Bondage, 1977, Hotel Hustlers, 1977, The Secret of the Phallic Stone, 1977, In the Hole, 1977, Animal Man, 1978, Incestuous Summer, 1978, Lessons for Mother, 1978, The Gang-Ravaged Teacher, 1978, Love's Courage, 1979, Hung Father, 1979, Oil-Rig Boys, 1979, Enlisted Man, 1979, Love's Emerald Flame, 1980, Vanessa in White Marble, 1980, House of Brave Bulls, 1980, The Last Galaxy Game, 1980, Voyage of the Trigon, 1981, The Galactic Arena, 1981, Michael: The Master, 1981, Well-Hung Hustler, 1981, Heavy Cruisers, 1982, Masters and Slaves, 1982, In Stocks and Bondage, 1982, Golden Shower Slave, 1982, Love's Golden Spell, 1983, Emerald-Silk Intrigue, 1987, Jungle-Quest Intrigue, 1987, Moon-Stone Intrigue, 1988, CircuSex, 1997, Diary of a Hustler, 1997, Slaves, 1997, Young Cruisers, 1997, California Creamin', 1998, Summer Sweat, 1999, A Slip to Die For, 1999, When Summer Comes, 2001, numerous others; contbr. articles to various publs. With U.S. Army, 1964-67. Mem. Northwest Playwrights Guild. Avocations: collecting art, knives and swords and Tarzan comic books.

LAMBERT, WILLIE LEE BELL, mobile equipment company owner, educator; b. Texas City, Tex., Oct. 23, 1929; d. William Henry and Una Oda (Stafford) Bell; m. Eddie Roy Lambert, July 2, 1949; (dec. Mar. 1980); children: Sondra Kay Lambert Bradford, Eddie Lee. Degree in bus., Met. Bus. Coll., 1950; AAS, Coll. of Mainland, 1971; BS, Sam Houston U., 1976. Cert. hand and foot reflexologist, Hatha Yoga instr. Sec. Judges Reddell & Hopkins, Texas City, 1945-47, Union Carbide Chemicals, Texas City, 1947-48, John Powers Modeling, 1948—49, Charles Martin Petroleum, Texas City, 1948-50; acct. Goodyear Co., La Marque, Tex., 1968-70; instr. Coll. of the Mainland, Texas City, 1970—, serials libr., 1970-77, instr., 1970; exec. dir., office mgr. Mobile Air Conditioning, La Marque, 1977-80; owner Kivert, Inc., 1982—; ptnr., exec. dir. A/C Mobile Equipment Corp., 1988—94. Owner Star Bell Ranch, 1985—. Vol. Union Carbide Chems., Texas City, 1970—, Carbide Retiree Corp., Inc., Texas City, 1980—, Hospice, Galveston, Tex., 1985—, various polit. campaigns, Texas City, 1951-62, MD Anderson Cancer Inst., U. Tex., 1995—; v.p. Coalition on Aging Galveston County, Tex. City, 1990-92; vol. Baylor Coll. Medicine, Houston, 1990—; mem. adv. coun. bd. Galveston County Sr. Citizens, Galveston, 1990—; mem. planning bd. Heart Fund and Cancer Fund, Texas City, 1953-62, Santa Fe (Tex.) St. Citizens, 1990—; benefactor mem. Mainland Mus., Texas City, Tex., 1994—; sec. YMCA, 1947-55; sec. Ladies VFW, 1950-59; leader Girl Scouts Am., 1958-65; v.p. PTA, 1957-60; counselor Bapt. Ch. Camp, 1960-64; v.p. Santa Fe Booster Club, 1963-67; mem. Internat. Platform Assn., 1995—. Named Vol. of Yr., Heights Elem. Sch., Texas City Sch. Dist., 1959, Most Glamorous Grandmother, 1985, Mother of Yr., Texas City/La Marque C. of C., 1990, Unsung Hero award Texas City, 1995, 96, 97, 99, 2001, 02; named to Tex. Women's Hall of Fame, 1984. Mem. Internat. Platform Assn. Republican. Baptist. Avocations: making porcelain dolls and soft sculpture dolls, painting china portraits, sewing, needlework, volunteer work. Home: PO Box 1253 Santa Fe TX 77510-1253

LAMBERTI, MARJORIE, history educator; b. New Haven, Sept. 30, 1937; d. James and Anna (Vanacore) L. BA, Smith Coll., 1959; MA, Yale U., 1960, PhD, 1965. Prof. history Middlebury Coll., Vt., 1964—, Charles A. Dana prof., 1984—. Author: Jewish Activism in Imperial Germany, 1978, State, Society and the Elementary School in Imperial Germany , 1989, The Politics of Education: Teachers and School Reform in Weimar Germany, 2002; mem. editl. bd.: History of Edn. Quar., 1992—94; contbr. articles. Mem. exec. com. Friends of Smith Coll. Librs., 1995—2001. NEH fellow, 1968-69, 81-82, Inst. for Advanced Study, Princeton, 1992-93, The Woodrow Wilson Ctr., Washington, 1997-98; German Acad. Exch. Svc. rsch. grantee, 1988. Mem. Am. Hist. Assn., Conf. Group for Ctrl. European History, Leo Baeck Inst., Phi Beta Kappa. Home: 8 S Gorham Ln Middlebury VT 05753-1002 Office: Middlebury Coll Dept History Middlebury VT 05753

LAMBERTON, LOWELL H. business educator; b. Portland, Oreg., Aug. 6, 1944; s. Forest H. Lamberton and Frances Ruth (Carrier) Love; m. Ruth Althea Lenzen, Dec. 14, 1991; 1 child, L. Heather. BA, Walla Walla Coll., 1966; MA, U. Nebr., Linocln, 1968; MBA, Suffolk U., 1977, advanced profl. cert., 1987. Grad. asst. U. Nebr., Lincoln, 1966-68; instr. English Atlantic Union coll., South Lancaster, Mass., 1968-69; asst. prof. English Cen. N.Eng. Coll., Worcester, 1969-74; bus. instr. Wenatchee (Wash.) Valley Coll., 1978-81; prof. bus. Cen. Oreg. C.C., Bend, 1981—. Cons. U.S. Forestry Svc., 1984-89, various small cos. and corps., 1981—; pres. bd. dirs. Consumer Credit Counseling, 1996-98. Author: Human Relations: Strategies for Success 1995, Working with People: H.R. Guide, 1997. Mem. Faculty Assn. (pres. local chpt. 1997-98). Baptist. Home: 2081 NE Hollowtree Ln Bend OR 97701-6552 Office: Cen Oreg CC 2600 NW College Way Bend OR 97701-5933

LAMBERTSEN, CHRISTIAN JAMES, environmental physiologist, physician (family or general practice ONLY), educator; b. Westfield, N.J., May 15, 1917; s. Christian and Ellen (Stevens) Lambertsen; m. Naomi Helen Hill, Feb. 5, 1944; children: Christian James, David Lee, Richard Hill, Bradley Stevens. BS, Rutgers U., 1939; MD, U. Pa., 1943; DSc, Northwestern U., 1977. Prof. pharmacology and exptl. therapeutics, prof. medicine U. Pa. Sch. Medicine, 1946—87, Markle scholar in med. sci., 1948—53; founding dir. Inst. for Environ. Medicine, U. Pa. Med. Ctr., 1968—, disting. prof. environ. medicine, 1985—; mem. adv. panel on med. scis. Office of Asst. Sec. Defense, 1954—61; sec. basic scis. Nat. Bd. Med. Examiners, 1955—71; mem. Pres.'s Space Panel, 1967—70; mem. oceanographic adv. bd. Office of Asst. Sec. of Navy for R & D, 1968—77; mem. marine bd. Nat. Acad. Engring., 1973—77. Dir. Environ. Biomed. Stress Data Ctr., 1992—; adviser Office of Marine Resources, NOAA, 1972—76; med. adviser Ocean Sys. Inc., Houston, 1960—83; med. dir. SubSea Intern, 1984—; chmn. com. Man in Space; with Space Sci. Bd., NAS, 1960—62; chmn. life scis. adv. bd. McDonnell-Douglas Aircraft Corp., St. Louis, 1960—67; sr. life scis. adviser Union Carbide Corp., Buffalo, Westinghouse Elec. Corp., Annapolis, Md., 1972—74, Air Products and Chems. Corp., Allentown, Pa., 1983—87; pres. Ecosystems, Inc., Phila., 1972—. Editor: Underwater Physiology Symposium, II, III, IV, V, 1963—76; mem. editl. bd.: Marine Tech. Soc. Jour., 1977—85; contbr. articles to med. and sci. jours. Maj. AUS, OSS, 1944—46. Decorated Legion of Merit U.S. Army; recipient Lindback award for disting. tchg., 1967, Tuttle award, Aerospace Med. Assn., 1970, Undersea Med. Behnke award, 1970, Dept. Def. Disting. Pub. Svc. medal, 1972, Marine Tech. Soc. award in Ocean Sci. and Engring., 1972, Dept. Navy Commendation Adv. Svc., 1972, award in environ. scis., N.Y. Acad. Scis., 1974, Disting. Pub. Svc. award, USCG, 1976, Disting. Med. Grad. award, U. Pa., 1989, Lifetime Achievement award, UDT-Seal Assn., 1995, Spl. Forces Green Beret award, U.S. Army, 1996, Pioneer award, Hist. Diving Soc., 2001; grantee, NIH, USN, USAF, NASA, NOAA. Fellow: Aerospace Med. Assn. (v.p. 1968); mem.: NAE, Phila. Maritime Mus., U.S. Army Spl. Forces Regiment One, Pa. Med. Soc., Phila. County Med. Soc., Undersea Med. Soc. (founding pres.), Peripatetic Med. Soc., Marine Tech. Soc., USN UDT/Seal Assn. (hon. life mem.), John Morgan Med. Rsch. Soc., Internat. Union Physiol. Scis., Internat. Astronautic Fedn., Internat. Acad. Astronautics, Phila. Coll. Physicians, Assn. Am. Med. Colls., Am. Soc. Clin. Investigation, Am. Physiol. Soc., Am. Soc. Pharmacology and Exptl. Therapeutics, Am. Coll. Clin. Pharmacology and Chemotherapy, Cosmos Club (Washington), Sigma Xi. Home: 3500 W Chester Pike # 129 Newtown Square PA 19073-4101 Office: U PA Med Ctr Inst Envrion Medicine 1 John Morgan Bldg Philadelphia PA 19104-6068

LAMBIRD, PERRY ALBERT, pathologist; b. Reno, Nev., Feb. 7, 1939; s. C. David and Florence (Knowlton) L.; m. Mona Sue Salyer, July 30, 1960; children: Allison Thayer Watson, Jennifer Salyer, Elizabeth Gard, Susannah Johnson. BA, Stanford U., 1958; MD, Johns Hopkins U., 1962; MBA, Okla. City U., 1973. Diplomate Am. Bd. Pathology. Fellow in internal medicine Johns Hopkins Hosp., Balt., 1962-63, resident pathologist, 1965-68, chief resident, 1968-69; med. cons. USPHS, Washington, 1963-65; pathologist Med. Arts Lab., Oklahoma City, 1969-96, chmn., 1998—, Okla. Meml. Hosp., Southwest Med. Ctr., 1974—, Nat. Cancer Inst., 1974-81; chmn. PATHCOR, Inc. 1995—; propr. Lambird Mgmt. Cons. Service, Oklahoma City, 1974—; pres. Ind. Pathology Inst., Inc., 1984-88, chmn. bd. dirs., 1988—; assoc. prof. pathology and orthopedic surgery U. Okla. Coll. Medicine, 1980-90, prof., 1990—; cons. in field. Reviewer Jour. Am. Med. Assn, 1983—; contbr. articles to profl. jours. Pres. Okla. Symphony Orch., 1974-75, Ballet Okla., 1978-79; del. Republican Nat. Conv., 1976, alt. del., 1984; bd. regents Uniformed Svcs. U. Health Scis., 1983-88; mem. task force entitlements and human assistance programs U.S. Ho. of Reps., 1983-88; bd. dirs. Commn. on Office Lab. Assessment, 1988—, chmn., 1992-94. Served to lt. comdr. USPHS, 1963-65. Recipient Exec. Leadership award Oklahoma City U., 1976, Physician's Recognition award AMA, 1969-98, Outstanding Pathologist award Am. Pathology Found., 1984; named Disting. Practioner Nat. Acad. of Practice, 1990. Fellow Am. Soc. Clin. Pathologists, Coll. Am. Pathologists, (gov. 1984-92); mem. AMA (ho. of dels., coun. on med. svc.), Okla. Med. Assn. (ho. of dels., trustee, pres.), Okla. County Med. Soc. (pres.), Okla. Soc. Cytopathology (pres.), Am. Pathology Found. (pres.), Okla. Found. for Peer Rev. (dir.), Arthur Purdy Stout Soc. Surg. Pathologists, Am. Assn. Pathologists, Okla. Assn. Pathologists (pres.), So. Med. Assn., N.Y. Acad. Sci., Am. Soc. Cytology, Okla. Soc. Cytopaths (pres.), Osler Soc., Okla. City Clin. Soc., Johns Hopkins Med. and Surg. Assn., Phi Beta Kappa (Phi Beta Kappa of Yr. 1996), Alpha Omega Alpha. Republican. Methodist. Office: PATHCOR 6761 NE Vinings Way Hillsboro OR 97124-7811 Home: 688 Glenneyre St Laguna Beach CA 92651-2420

LAMBO, MICHELE DIANE, interior designer; b. Jackson, Mich., June 13, 1951; d. Angelo Marko and Florence (Petroff) L. Student Jackson Community Coll., 1970-71; B.A. in Interior Design, Mich. State U., 1975; postgrad. Bowling Green State U., 1978— . With Jacobson's Furniture Galleria, Ann Arbor, Mich., 1976, interior designer, salesperson, Toledo, 1976-77; tchr., coordinator Rogers High Sch., Toledo, 1977-78; interior designer, salesperson Johnson's Fine Furniture, Toledo, 1978-79; interior designer, draftsperson Crown Store Equipment Co., Holland, Ohio, 1980— ; cons. interior design Weight Watchers, Inc., Lansing, Mich., 1984-85, others; lectr. in field. Dancer, Lansing Ballet Co., Mich., 1972-75, Kitka Dance Ensemble, Toledo, 1977-82, Toledo Sch. Ballet, 1980— ; vol. Am. Cancer Soc., Toledo, 1985, Epilepsy Ctr. Northwest Ohio, 1985; blood donor ARC, 1971— . Jackson County Rosequeen Pageant scholar, 1971, 72; Toledo Sch. Ballet scholar, 1983. Mem. Am. Soc. Interior Designers, Inst. Bus. Designers. Club: Ladies Guild (pres. 1983-85). Avocations: dancing; sewing; singing; running; skiing; swimming.

LAMBORN, LEROY LESLIE, law educator; b. Marion, Ohio, May 12, 1937; s. LeRoy Leslie and Lola Fern (Grant) Lamborn. AB, Oberlin Coll., 1959; LLB, Western Res. U., 1962; LLM, Yale U., 1963; JSD, Columbia U., 1973. Bar: N.Y. 1965, Mich. 1974. Asst. prof. law U. Fla., 1965-69; prof. Wayne State U., Detroit, 1970-97, prof. emeritus, 1997—. Vis. prof. State U., Utrecht, 1981. Author: (book) Legal Ethics and Professional Responsibility, 1963; contbr. articles on victimology to profl. jours. Mem.: World Soc. Victimology, Nat. Orgn. Victim Assistance (exec. com. 1982—94, bd. dirs. 1979—88), Am. Law Inst. Home: Apt 2502 1300 E Lafayette St Detroit MI 48207-2924 Office: Wayne State U Law Sch Detroit MI 48202

LAMBRECH, RÉGINE M. college program administrator, language educator; b. White Plains , N.Y., Nov. 21, 1950; arrived in France, 1978; d. Matthew André and Winifred Dorothy (Blaney) L. BA, Ladycliff Coll., 1972; MA, Pa. State U., 1975, PhD, 1985. Tchg. asst. Pa. State U., University Park, Pa., 1972-78; vis. prof. French and English U. Lyon (France) II, 1978-79; asst. prof. French and English U. Lyon III, 1979-83; assoc. prof. French and English École Centrale de Lyon, Écully, France, 1983-2000, dir. internat. rels. France, 1989-2000; dir. internat. edn. Quinnipiac U., Hamden, Conn., 2000—. Cons. internat. rels. U. Timisoara, Romania, 1995, Rector of Poly. U. Lodz, Poland, 1993, U. Warsaw, 1994, Rector of U. Salford, Eng., 1991-92, European Commn.'s Task Force for Human Resources, Edn. and Youth, 1995-2000; adv. bd. humanities dept. U. Salford, 1990—; presenter and invited spkr. in field at various confs. and workshops; bd. dirs. Rhone-Alpes Internat. Enterprises, Lyon Internat. Mem. editl. bd. Jour. Profl. Studies, 1996—, Internat. Jour. of Leadership in Edn., 1998—, Jour. for Acad. Leadership, 2000—; book and manuscript reviewer Lang. Planning and Lang. Learning Jour., 1992—; book manuscript reviewer on 2d lang. acquisition, Cambridge U. Press, 1992—; contbr. articles to profl. jours. and conf. procs. Recipient Disting. Alumna award Pa. State U., 1996, Irena Galewska-Kielbasinski award, Tech. Univ. Darmstadt, Germany, 1993; named Erasmus scholar in residence, French Dept. Trinity College, Dublin, Ireland, 1991; recipient Tchr. of Yr. award Nat. Conservatory of Arts and Profns., 1991. Mem. MLA, NAFSA, Assn. Internat. Educators (overseas ednl. advisors spl. interest group), European Assn. Internat. Edn. (chair internat. rels. mgrs. sect. 1989-94, mem. study abroad and fgn. student advisors/langs. for ednl. mobility profl. sects.; elected bd. lang. educators, chair working group on intercultural issues 1996-98, chair ICT Group), Union des Profs. de Langues Étrangères dans les Grandes Écoles (internat. commn.), Internat. Soc. Intercultural Edn., Tng. and Rsch., Lyon Assn. Dirs. Internat. Rels. (bd. dirs. 1996-2000), Pa. State U. Alumni Club of France (founder, pres. 1985-2000), Phi Sigma Iota, Alpha Mu Gamma, Phi Kappa Phi, Phi Beta Delta (Woman of Achievement award 2002). Roman Catholic. Avocations: reading, sports, crafts, volunteer work. Home: 6 Bayview Ter New Fairfield CT 06812-3402 Office: Quinnipiac U 275 Mount Carmel Ave Hamden CT 06518-1961 E-mail: Regine.Lambrech@quinnipiac.edu.

LAMBRECHT, DOUGLAS A. investment management consultant; b. Bronxville, N.Y. s. George Walter and Muriel Morgan L.; m. Constance Reneé Picotte, Oct. 11, 1997; children: Elliott Morgan, Anna Christine, Laura Barber. BA, Ind. U., 1985. Cert. investment mgmt. cons. Assn. Profl. Investment Consultants; cert. bus. counselor; cert. internat. investment specialist. V.p., fin. cons. Robinson-Humphrey Co., Hilton Head Island, S.C., 1986-97; mng. dir. Lighthouse Investment Advisors, Inc., 1997-99; investment mgmt. cons. Investment Resource Group, LLC, 1999—. Contbr. articles to profl. publs. Founding chmn. Hilton Head Coun. of Estate and Fin. Advisers, 1993-95, pres., 1993-2000. With USAF, 1970-72, Eglin AFB, Fla., 1970-72. Avocations: fly fishing, rafting, travel. Office: Investment Resource Group LLC 304 Waters Edge Shelter Cove Hilton Head Island SC 29928 Fax: 843-842-7973. E-mail: dougl@investmentresource.com.

LAMBRIGHT, STEPHEN KIRK, brewing company executive; b. Kansas City, Mo., Dec. 3, 1942; s. Ray B. and Janet Lambright; m. Gail T. Tabler; children: Stephen K. Jr., James H., Sarah E., Catherine L. BS in Acctg., U. Mo., 1965; JD cum laude, St. Louis U., 1968, MBA in Fin., 1977. Bar: Mo., 1968, Va. 1979, D.C. 1979; CPA, Mo. Tax acct. Arthur Andersen & Co., 1965-69; atty. Lashly, Caruthers, Thies, Rava & Hamel, 1970-77; asst. gen. counsel Anheuser-Busch Cos., St. Louis, 1977-78, exec. asst. chmn. bd., 1978-79, v.p., nat. affairs Washington, 1979-81, v.p., industry and govt. affairs St. Louis, 1981-83, mem. corp. policy com., 1981—, v.p. group exec., 1983—, group v.p., gen. counsel. Mem. Shriner's Hosp. for Crippled Children, Keep Am. Beautiful. Mem. C. of C. of U.S. Presbyterian. Home: 415 Sheffield Estate Dr Saint Louis MO 63141-8523 Office: Anheuser-Busch Cos Inc 1 Busch Pl Saint Louis MO 63118-1852

LAMBRIGHT, WILLIAM HENRY, political science-public administration educator; b. Balt., July 9, 1939; s. William Henry and Nellie Mae (Brown) L.; m. Nancy Greeley Turner, Dec. 21, 1963; children: Henry Dandridge, Nathaniel Greeley. AB, Johns Hopkins U., 1961; MA, Columbia U., 1962, PhD, 1966. Guest scholar Brookings Instn., Washington, 1965-66; spl. asst. NASA, 1970; asst. prof. polit. sci. and pub. adminstrn. Maxwell Sch. Syracuse (N.Y.) U., 1966-69, assoc. prof., 1970-76, prof., 1976—, dir. Ctr. for Environ. Policy and Adminstrn. Maxwell Sch., 1995—. Dir. Sci. and Tech. Policy Ctr. Syracuse Rsch. Corp., 1972-94. Author: Governing Science and Technology, 1976, Technology Transfer to Cities, 1979, Presidential Management of Science and Technology, 1985, Powering Apollo: James E. Webb of NASA, 1995; co-author: Educating the Innovative Public Manager, 1981; editor (with Dianne Rahm): Technology and U.S. Competitiveness: Institutional Focus, 1992; contbr. over 250 articles, reports and papers to profl. jours. Recipient numerous rsch. grants, including NSF, EPA, NASA, HHS, and NIST, 1972—. Mem. AAAS, Am. Polit. Sci. Assn., Am. Soc. for Pub. Adminstrn. (exec. com. for pub. adminstrn. 1987—). Office: Ctr Environ Policy Adminstrn Syracuse U 400 Eggers Hl Syracuse NY 13244-0001

LAMBRIX, WINIFRED MARIE MCFARLANE, retired elementary education educator; b. Phoenix, June 5, 1947; d. James McFarlane and Alice Lucille (McFarlane) Nedoff; m. Leroy Edward Lambrix, May 28, 1976; 1 child, Michael John. Diploma, Grand Rapids Sch. Bible & Music, 1968; BA, Cedarville Coll., 1970; postgrad., Western Mich. U., 1971-72, Grand Valley State Coll., 1974-75, Bakersfield Coll., 1978-80, Calif. State U., Bakersfield, 1987; MS, LaVerne U., 1993. Cert. tchr. art and music K-12, Mich., Calif.; cert. tchr. multiple subjects, Calif.; cert. in pupil pers. svc., Calif.; cert. adminstr., Calif.; cert. resource specialist. Tchr. S.W. Sch., Wyoming (Mich.) Pub. Sch., 1970-75; substitute tchr. Bakersfield area schs., 1976-82; kindergarten tchr. Planz Sch., Greenfield Union Sch. Dist., Bakersfield, 1982-2000; resource specialist Planz Sch., 1994-2000; ret. Paintings exhibited in various group shows, 1977-82 (numerous awards). Bd. dirs., sec. Artisian's Guild, Bakersfield, 1977-82. Avocations: art, music, children's choirs, American sign language.

LAMBRO, DONALD JOSEPH, columnist; b. Wellesley, Mass., July 24, 1940; s. Pascal and Mary (Lapery) L.; m. Jacquelyn Mae Killmon, Oct. 6, 1968; 1 son, Jason Phillip. BS, Boston U., 1963. Reporter, Boston Traveler, 1963; freelance writer Washington, 1965-67; statehouse reporter UPI, Hartford, Conn., 1968-70, reporter Washington, 1970-80; columnist United Feature Syndicate, 1981—; commentator AP Radio Network, 1982-83, Nat. Pub. Radio, 1984-85. Writer, host TV documentary Star Spangled Spenders, 1982; host, co-writer PBS TV documentary Inside the Republican Revolution, 1995; nat. editor Washington Times, 1987-88; chief polit. corr. Washington Times, 1988—. Author: The Federal Rathole, 1975; The Conscience of a Young Conservative, 1976; Fat City: How Washington Wastes Your Taxes, 1980; Washington-City of Scandals, 1984; Land of Opportunity, 1986. Recipient Warren Brookes award for Excellence in Journalism, Am. Legis. Exch. Coun., 1995. Albanian Orthodox. Office: The Washington Times 3600 New York Ave NE Washington DC 20002-1996

LAMDIN, LOIS SYMONS, English educator; b. Pitts., May 17, 1927; d. Louis and Edith Mae Symons; m. Karl Kay Lewin, Apr. 18, 1948 (div. Jan. 1968); m. Ezra Lamdin, June 30, 1969; children: Jeff, Jan, Nancy BA, U. Pitts., 1948, PhD, 1967. Asst. prof. Carnegie-Mellon U., Pitts., 1965-69; assoc. prof., chair English dept. Hostos Cmty. Coll., N.Y.C., 1969-74; prof., assoc. dean Empire State Coll., N.Y., 1974-79; exec. dir. CLEO, Phila., 1980-85; pub. Great Valley Bus. News, Paoli, Pa., 1984-94; exec. dir. Bus. Devel. and Tng. Ctr., 1984-92. Chmn. bd. Disco Cmty. Svcs., N.Y.C., 1989-91; cons., writer Can. and U.S. univs., 1993—. Author: (books) Elder Learning in Aging Society, 1997, Earn College Credit for What You Know, 1997; co-author: (book) Employability, 1993; editor: (book) Roads to Learning Society, 1985. Trustee Maine Coll. of Art, Portland, 1996—, Maine Humanities Coun., Portland, 1998—, Portland Stage Co., Portland, 1997—, Maine League of Women Voters, Augusta, Maine, 1995—. Fellow NEH, Yale U., 1974. Mem. Coun. for Adult and Exptl. Learning (regional mgr. 1981-90), Poets and Writers. Avocations: reading, hiking, canoeing, swimming, gourmet cooking. E-mail: lamdin@ime.net.

LAMEIRO, GERARD FRANCIS, corporate strategist, investment banker; b. Paterson, N.J., Oct. 3, 1949; s. Frank Raymond and Beatrice Cecilia (Donley) L. BS, Colo. State U., 1971, MS, 1973, PhD, 1977. Sr. scientist Solar Energy Rsch. Inst., Golden, Colo., 1977-78; asst. prof. mgmt. sci. and info. systems Colo. State U., Fort Collins, 1978-83, mem. editl. bd. energy engring., 1978-82, editl. bd. energy econs. policy and mgmt., 1981-82; pres. Successful Automated Office Systems, Inc., 1982-84; product mgr. Hewlett Packard, 1984-88, computer networking cons., 1988-89; editl. bd. HP Chronicle, 1986-88, columnist, 1988, mgmt. strategist, 1988-91; dir. Lameiro Rsch. Inst., 1991-97; market developer Hewlett-Packard Co., 1996-97, product mktg. mgr., 1997-98, corp. bus. model strategist, 1998-2000, investment mgr., 2000—. Lectr. dept. computer sci. Colo. State U., 1983, lectr. dept. mgmt., 1983; sr. rsch. fellow, dir. Lameiro Rsch. Inst., 1993-97. Author: Campaign Code of Ethics, 1988, Ten Laws for Creating Wealthy Nations, 1994, Ten Laws for Winning Presidential Elections, 1992, Campaign Code of Ethics, 1988, Ten Laws for Creating Wealthy Nations, 1994; mem. editl. bd. Energy Engring., Policy and Mgmt., 1981-82, Energy Engring., 1978-82; developer LRI Presdl. Electoral Outlook Model, 1992, LRI Gold Model for Projecting Presdl. Elections, 1996; contbr. articles in mgmt. and tech. areas to profl. jours. Mem. Presdl. Electoral Coll., 1980. Recipient Nat. Disting. Svc. award Assn. Energy Engrs., 1981, Honors Prof. award Colo. State U., 1982; Colo. Energy Rsch. Inst. fellow 1976, NSF Postdoctoral fellow 1977. Mem. ASTD, Assn. for Computing Machinery, Assn. Energy Engrs. (pres. 1980, Nat. Disting. Svc. award 1981, internat. bd. dirs. 1980-81), Am. Mgmt. Assn., Am. Mktg. Assn. (exec.), Am. Soc. for Quality Control, IEEE Computer Soc., Inst. Indsl. Engrs., U.S. C. of C., Crystal Cathedral Golden Eagles Club, Platinum Eagles Club, Diamond Eagles Club, The Heritage Found., Sigma Xi, Phi Kappa Phi, Beta Gamma Sigma, Kappa Mu Epsilon. Roman Catholic. Office: Hewlett-Packard Co 3404 East Harmony Rd MS-92-MOD4/16 Fort Collins CO 80528-9599 E-mail: gerry-lameiro@hp.com.

LAMEL, LINDA HELEN, professional society executive, former insurance company executive, former college president, lawyer; b. N.Y.C., Sept. 10, 1943; d. Maurice and Sylvia (Abrams) Treppel; 1 child, Diana Ruth Sands. BA magna cum laude, Queens Coll., 1964; MA, NYU, 1968; JD., Bklyn. Law Sch., 1976. Bar: N.Y. 1977, U.S. Dist. Ct. (3d dist.) N.Y. 1977. Secondary sch. tchr. Farmingdale (N.Y.) Pub. Sch., 1965-73; curriculum specialist Yonkers (N.Y.) Bd. Edn., 1973-75; program dir. Office of Lt. Gov., Albany, N.Y., 1975-77; dep. supt. N.Y. State Ins. Dept., N.Y.C., 1977-83; pres. CEO Coll. of Ins., 1983-88; v.p. Tchr.'s Ins. and Authority Assn., 1988-96; exec. dir. Risk and Ins. Mgmt. Soc., 1997-2000; CEO Claims on Line, Inc., 2000—02. Contbr. articles to profl. jours. Campaign mgr. lt. gov.'s primary race, N.Y. State, 1974; v.p. Ednl. Found., 1997-2000. Mem. ABA (tort and ins. sect. com. chmn. 1985-86), N.Y. State Bar Assn. (exec. com. ins. sect. 1984-88), Assn. of Bar of City of N.Y. (chmn. med. malpractice com. 1989-91, ins. law com. 1997-98), Am. Mgmt. Assn. (ins. and risk mgmt. coun.), Am. Soc. Workers Compensation Profls. (bd. dirs. 1999—), Fin. Women's Assn., Assn. Profl. Ins. Women (bd. dirs. 2002—, Woman of Yr. 1988), Bklyn. Law Sch. Alumni Assn. (pres.-elect), Phi Beta Kappa Assocs. (bd. dirs. 1992—).

LAMENDOLA, WALTER FRANKLIN, technology educator, business executive; b. Donora, Pa., Jan. 29, 1943; BA in English, St. Vincent Coll., 1964; MSWin Community Orgn., U. Pitts., 1966; diploma in Sociology and Social Welfare, U. Stockholm, 1970; PhD in Social Work, U. Minn., 1976. Cmty. svcs. dir. Ariz. tng. programs State Dept. Mental Retardation, Tucson, 1970-73; assoc. prof. social welfare adminstrn. Fla. State U., 1976-77; pres., CEO, Minn. Rsch. and Tech., Inc., 1977-81; assoc. prof., dir. Allied Health Computer Lab. East Carolina U., 1981-84; prof., dir. info. tech. ctr. Grad. Sch. Social Work U. Denver, 1984-87, 99—; cons. info. tech., rsch. human svcs.,

1987-90; v.p. rsch. Colo. Trust, Denver, 1990-93, info. tech. and rsch. cons., 1993—. Cons. European Network Info. Tech. & Human Svcs.; mem. rebldg. communities initiative PODER project Casey Found., 1996-97; mem. adv. bd. ctr. Computers in Tchg. Initiative, U. Southampton, Brit. Rsch. Coun. Univs., Human Svc. Info. Tech. Applications, CREON Found., The Netherlands; lectr. conf., symposia, univs. U.S., Europe; mem. nat. adv. bd. Native Elder Health Resource Ctr., 1994-96; co-founder Denver Free Net, 1993; adj. prof. U. Colo. Health Scis. Ctr., 1996—; dir. tech. GSSU, U. Denver, 1998—; info. tech. cons. Healthy Nations Program Robert Wood Johnson Found, 1993-96; evaluator Nat. Libr. Rsch. Program, Access Colo. grant, 1994, Nat. Info. Infrastructure grant Colo. State Libr.; cons. set up on the Internet for U.S. Cts.-Ct. for Mental Health Svcs., NIH, Frontier Mental Health Svcs. Network grant; collaborating investigator SBIR award Computerized Advance Directives, tech. plan San Mateo County and Seattle Dist. Cts.; keynote spkr. conf. Human Svc. Info. Tech. Applications, Finland, 1996; adj. prof. U. Colo., 1997-98; dir. tech., adj. prof. U. Denver, 1997-98; adj. prof. informatics U. Colo. Health Scis. Ctr., 1998; mem. nat. adv. coun. Ctr. Substance Abuse Prevention Dept. Health & Human Svcs., 1998, co-chair prevention decision support sys. steering group, 1999; pres. ActiveGuide, L.L.C.; mem. nat. design team Decision Support Sys., U.S. Dept. Health & Human Svcs., 1998—, mem. nat. adv. bd. Data Coord. Ctr., 1999—; prin. investigator bridge project Cmty. Tech. Ctr., U.S. Dept. Edn., 2000—; prin. investigator, The Bridge Cmty. Tech. Ctr. Dept. Edn., 2000-03. Co-author: Choices for Colorado's Future, 1993, The Integrity of Intelligence: A Bill of Rights for the Information Age, 1992, Choices for Colorado's Future: Executive Summary, 1991, Choices for Colorado's Future: Regional Summaries, 1991; co-editor: A Casebook of Computer Applications in Health and Social Services, 1989; contbr. numerous articles to profl. jours. Capt. U.S. Army, 1966-69. Recipient Innovative Computer Application award Internat. Fedn. Info. Processing Socs., 1979; Nat. Lib. Rsch. Evaluator grantee, Colo., 1994—, Nat. Info. Infrastructure grantee Dept. Edn., State Libr. and Adult Literacy, 1994-95; Funds & Couns. Tng. scholar United Way Am., 1964-66, Donaldson Fund scholar, 1965-66, NIMH scholar, 1964-66, 73-76, St. Vincent Coll. Benedictine Soc. scholar, 1963-64; vis. fellow U. Southampton, 1992-95. Office: GSSW Univ Denver 2148 South High St Denver CO 80208 also: ActiveGuide LLC PO Box 351 Wheat Ridge CO 80034-0351 E-mail: wlamendo@du.edu.

LAMENSDORF, HUGH, urologist, educator; b. Greenville, Miss., July 20, 1936; s. Jerome Hugh and Rosann (Mundt) Lamensdorf; m. Louise Faye Doernberg, July 6, 1958; children: Jerome Stewart, Marilyn Elizabeth, Bradley Hugh, Jonathan Louis. BS, Tulane U., 1958, MD, 1961. Diplomate Am. Bd. Urology. Intern U. Miss. Hosp., Jackson, 1961—62; resident in urology Ochsner Found. Hosp., New Orleans, 1962—66; mem. staff Urology Clinics of N. Tex., Ft. Worth, 1968—. Chief staff Med. Plaza Hosp., Ft. Worth; prof. surgery Southwestern Med. Sch., Dallas. Served to capt. USAF, 1966—68. Mem.: AMA (del. from Tex., vice chmn., pres. forum for med. affairs 2002), ACS, Pan Am. Med. Assn. (coun.), Tarrant County Med. Assn. (pres. 1986), Tex. Med. Assn. (pres. 1996—97), Tex. Urol. Soc. (pres. 1975), Societe Urologie Internat., Tex. Surg. Soc., Am. Acad. Pediat., Soc. for Pediatric Urology, Am. Fertility Soc., Am. Assn. Clin. Urologists, Am. Urol. Assn., Ft. Worth C. of C. (bd. dirs.). Republican. Home: 1424 Shady Oaks Ln Fort Worth TX 76107-3538 Office: Ste 405 1300 W Terrell Ave Fort Worth TX 76104-2810 Business E-Mail: lamensdorf@urologyclinics.com.

LAMER, ANTONIO, retired Canadian supreme court chief justice; b. Montreal, Can., July 8, 1933; s. Antonio and Florence (Storey) L.; m. Danièle Tremblay; children: Stephane, Melanie, Jean-Frederic. BA, Licentiate in Laws, U. Montreal, 1956; LLD, U. Moncton, 1981, U. Montreal, 1991, U. Toronto, 1992, U. N.B., 1995, Dalhousie U., 1996, U. New Brunswick, 1999; D Univ. (hon.), U. Ottawa, 1987, St. Paul U., 2001. Bar: Que. 1957. Justice Superior Ct. Que., 1969-78, Que. Ct. Appeal, 1978-80, Supreme Ct. Can., 1980-99, chief justice, 1990-2000; vice chmn. Nat. Law Reform Commn. Can., 1971-75, chmn., 1976-78; prof. agrege U. Montreal, 1967—; read law with Cutler, Lamer, Bellemare & Assocs.; lectr. U. Montreal, Can. Jud. Conf.; former sr. ptnr. Cutler, Lamer, Bellemare & Assocs.; Que. Bar rep. govt. interdisciplinary com. on structures U. Que.; chmn. Can. Law Reform Commn., 1975; spl. cons. Stikeman Elliott, 2000—. Assoc. prof. U. Montreal, Montreal, Canada, 2000; chmn. bd. dir. Les Rendez-Vous de la Francophonie ; chmn. adv. coun. Historica , mem. exec. bd. dirs.; pres. adv. coun. Nat. Police Svcs. Bd. dirs. Canadian Human Rights Found., 1974; chmn. bd. dirs. Las Rendez-Vous de la francophonie; chmn. adv. coun. Historica; mem. exec. bd. dirs., pres. adv. coun. Nat. Police Svcs. Served with Can. Army Res., 1950, hon. col. 2nd Field Reg.; nat. chmn. hon. col. and lt. col. ground forces. Decorated companion Order of Can., knight of justice Order of St. John; recipient Order of Merit, U. Montreal, 1991 Mem. Privy Coun. Can., Can. Jud. Coun. (chmn.), Nat. Jud. Inst. (chmn.), Soc. Criminologie Québec (pres. 1974). Office: 50 O'Connor St Ste 1600 Ottawa ON Canada K1P 6L2 E-mail: alamer@ott.stikeman.com.

LAMEY, MARY COCOVE, elementary guidance counselor; b. Cedarville, N.J., Apr. 5, 1941; d. Anthony Sidney Sr. and Mary Grace (Musumeci) Cocove; m. Timothy William Lamey Sr., Dec. 28, 1963; children: Michele Mary Lamey Carr, Timothy William Jr. BA in Elementary Edn., State Coll. Glassboro, 1963; MA in Student Personnel Svcs., Rowan U., 1983. Cert. elem. tchr., student pers. svcs., prin. and supr., dir. of guidance, sch. social worker, N.J. Elem. tchr. West Deptford (N.J.) Bd. Edn., 1963-64, Mantua (N.J.) Bd. Edn., 1964-69, Washington Twp. Bd. Edn., Sewell, N.J., 1969-70; substitute tchr. West Deptford Bd. Edn., 1971-75; creative writing tchr. Elmer (N.J.) Bd. Edn., 1977; elem. tchr. Logan Twp. Bd. Edn., Bridgeport, N.J., 1977-86, elem. prin., 1986-89; elem. guidance counselor West Deptford Bd. Edn., 1989—. Sec. Pitman (N.J.) We Care, 1984-87, Camden County Elem. Counselors, Barrington, N.J., 1991-93; v.p. Spl. Svcs., Glassboro, N.J., 1997—. Author, editor Guiding Light from the Counselor's Desk, 1990—. Facilitator Active Parenting, West Deptford, 1990—; active holiday food drives West Deptford Twp., 1990—; facilitator, tchr. Nat. Program Safety Town, West Deptford, 1992—, mem. drug task force, 1995-97. Named Gloucester County Tchr. of Yr., Sewell, 1986. Mem. NEA, ASCD, N.J. Edn. Assn., Gloucester County Counselors Assn., Alpha Epsilon Lambda (v.p. spl. svcs.), Phi Delta Kappa. Roman Catholic. Avocations: church activities, post card collecting, traveling, reading, family activities. Home: 608 Howard Ave Pitman NJ 08071-1833 Office: Green Fields Sch 15 Hill Ln Woodbury NJ 08096-6302 E-mail: mlamey@wdeptford.k12.nj.us.

LAMIA, THOMAS ROGER, lawyer; b. Santa Monica, Calif., May 31, 1938; s. Vincent Robert II and Maureen (Green) L.; m. Susan Elena Brown, Jan. 10, 1969; children: Nicholas, Katja, Jenna, Tatiana, Carlyn, Mignon. Student, U. So. Calif., 1956, BS, 1961; student, U. Miss., 1957-58; JD, Harvard U., 1964. Bar: Calif. 1965, D.C. 1980, N.Y. 1990, U.S. Dist. Ct. (ctrl. dist.) Calif. 1965, U.S. Dist. Ct. D.C. 1980, U.S. Tax Ct. 1982. Assoc. McCutchen, Black, Verleger & Shea, L.A., 1964-66; lectr. in law U. Ife, Ile-Ife, Nigeria, 1966-67, U. Zambia, Lusaka, 1967-68; assoc. Paul, Hastings, Janofsky & Walker, 1968-72, ptnr., 1972-99, mem. exec. com., 1976-80, mng. ptnr. Washington office, 1980-83; pvt. practice N.Y.C., 1999—. Prin., mgr., gen. counsel Cowan Rentals, LLC, 1997—. Office: 24 W 55th St Ste 7B New York NY 10019-5320 E-mail: trlamia@lamialaw.com.

LAMIS, LEROY, artist, retired educator; b. Eddyville, Iowa, Sept. 27, 1925; s. Leo and Blanche (Bennett) L.; m. Esther Sackler, Aug. 13, 1954; children: Alexander, Jonas. BA, N.Mex. Highlands U., 1953; MA, Columbia U., 1956. Mem. faculty dept. art Ind. State U., 1961— , prof., 1972-89, retired 1989; artist-in-residence Dartmouth Coll., 1970; founder PC ART, 1983 One-man sculpture exhbns. include Staempfli Gallery, N.Y.C., 1966, 69, 73, Gillman Gallery, Chgo., 1967, Tacoma Mus., 1970, Ft. Wayne Art Mus., 1968, Des Moines Art Ctr., 1970, La Jolla Mus., 1970, Ind. State U., 1976, Sheldon Swope Art Mus., Terre Haute, Ind., 1979; kinetic computer art exhbns. at Ben Shahn Gallery, William Patterson Coll., N.J., Ind. State U., 1985, Bronx Mus. Art, 1986, 55 Mercer Gallery, 1990, Indpls. Art Mus., 1992, Evansville Mus. Sci. and Art, 1994, Swope Art Mus., Terre Haute, 1996-97, Fifth Annual N.Y. Digital Salon Sch. Visual Arts, N.Y.C., 1997, Seventh Annual N.Y. Digital Salon Sch. Visual Arts, 99; represented in permanent collections Albright-Knox Mus., Des Moines Art Ctr., Whitney Mus. Am. Art, Joseph H. Hirshorn Collection, Washington, Indpls. Mus., J.B. Speed Mus., Louisville; author: (computer program) Eighty 5, 1985; creator, prodr. various computer software. Served with AUS, 1943. Recipient Award Commn. N.Y. State Coun. of the Arts, 1970. Address: Apt 35 600 S 4th St Terre Haute IN 47807-4333 E-mail: arlamis@ruby.indstate.edu.

LAMISON, ERIC ROSS, lawyer; b. Akron, Aug. 3, 1970; s. Donald Ross and Linda Marie (Alexander) L. BS in Physiology, Mich. State U., 1992; JD magna cum laude, U. Mich., 1995. Bar: Calif. 1995, U.S. Dist. Ct. (ctrl. dist.) Calif. 1996, U.S. Ct. Appeals (9th cir.) 1998, U.S. Dist. Ct. Ariz. 1998, U.S. Dist. Ct. (no. dist.) Calif. 1998, 2000, U.S. Ct. Appeals (Fed. cir.) 1999, U.S. Patent Office 1999. Ptnr. Kirkland & Ellis, L.A., 1995—. Mem. Order of the Coif, ABA (intellectual Property Sect.). Office: Kirkland and Ellis 777 S Figueroa St Los Angeles CA 90017

LAMKIN, FLETCHER M., JR. academic administrator; b. Lakehurst, N.J., Apr. 2, 1942; married; 3 daus. BS, U.S. Mil. Acad., 1964; MS in Engrng., U. Calif., Berkeley; DPhil, U. Wash.; grad., Army Command Gen. Staff Coll., Naval War Coll. Commd. 2d lt. U.S. Army, 1964; early assignments include battery exec. officer 7th bn., 11th field arty., Republic South Vietnam, bn. fire support officer, battery comdr. Republic South Vietnam, 1966-67; comdr. 1st spl. tng. co. Ft. Gordon, Ga., 1967-68; bn. ops. officer 1st bn., 38th field arty., Korea, 1975-76; bn. eaxec. officer, tng. officer, dep. ops. officer 9th infantry divsn., Ft. Lewis, Wash., 1976-80; inspections team chief, Office of Inspector Gen. U.S. Army Europe, Babenhausen, Germany, 1981-83; instr., asst. prof. dep. mechs. U.S. Mil. Acad., West Pt., NY, 1971-74, assoc. prof. dept. engring., 1987-89, prof., dep. head dept. civil and mech. engrng., 1989-92, vice dean acad. bd., 1993-94, prof., head dept. civil and mech. engirng., 1994-95, dean acad. bd., 1995—2000; pres. Westminster Coll., Fulton, Mo., 2000—. Office: Office of the President Westminster College 501 Westminster Ave Fulton MO 65251-1299

LAMKIN, MARTHA DAMPF, lawyer; b. Talladega, Ala., May 20, 1942; d. Keith J. and Neva (Magness) Dampf; m. E. Henry Lamkin Jr., Aug. 28, 1968; children: Melinda Lamkin Magaddino, Matthew Davidson. BA in English summa cum laude, Calif. Baptist U., 1964; MA in English and Am. Lit., Vanderbilt U., 1966; JD, Ind. U., 1970. Bar: Ind. 1970. Assoc. Joseph D. Geeslin, Indpls., 1971-72, Lowe, Gray, Steele & Hoffman, Indpls., 1976-82; field office mgr. U.S. Dept. Housing and Urban Devel., 1982-87; exec. dir., corp. rep. responsibility and govtl. affairs Cummins Engine Co., Inc., Columbus, 1987-91; exec. v.p. corp. advancement USA Group, Inc., Indpls., 1991-2000; pres., CEO, bd. dirs. USA Group Found., Inc., 2000-2001; CEO, pres., bd. dirs. Lumina Foundation for Education Inc., 2001—. Pres., bd. dirs. Cummins Engine Found., 1989-91; bd. dirs. Meridian Mut. Ins. Co., Indpls., USA Group, Inc., USA Group Loan Svcs., Inc., United Student Aid Funds, 1994-2000; bd. dirs. Citizens Gas & Coke Utility, Inc., vice chair, 1990-. Commr., sec., chmn. Indpls. Human Rights Commn., 1971-79; commr. Indpls. Housing Authority, 1979-82; chmn. exec. com. S.K. Lacy Exec. Leadership Alumni, Indpls., 1986-87; chmn. Ind. Leadership Celebration, Indpls., 1985-87; sec. Gov.'s Mansion Commn., Indpls., 1981-89; bd. dirs. Great Indpls. Progress Commn., 1986-87, Indpls. Symphony Orch., 1983-89, 98-99, Indpls. Project, 1986-91, Ind. Fiscal Policy Inst., 1998—, Ind. Colls. Ind., 1997-2000; bd. dirs., sec. COMMIT, Inc., COMMIT Found., 1990-97; chmn. bd. trustees Christian Theol. Sem., Indpls., 1983-93; hon. gov. Richard C. Lugar Excellence Pub. Svc. Series, 1990—; chair, 1997, trustee Indpls. Found., 1992—; mem. exec. com. Mayor's Task Force on Housing, 1987, exec. com., Ind. Sports Corp., 1997-2000; sec., bd. dirs. Indpls. Econ. Devel. Corp., 1997-2000; chair, dir. Ctrl. Ind. Cmty. Found., 1998-; mem. Hoosier Capitol Girl Scouts Adv. Bd., 1996-2002. Recipient Presdl. Rank award 1985, Mental Health Initiative Gov. Ind., 1986, Matrix award Women in Communication, 1987. Mem. State Assembly Women (pres. 1977-79), Indpls. Jr. League, Indpls. C. of C. (bd. dirs. 1986-87). Republican. Mem. Christian Ch. (Disciples Of Christ). Office: Limina Found for Edn 30 S Meridian Ste 700 Indianapolis IN 46204

LAMLE, HUGH ROY, investment advisor, consultant; b. Yonkers, N.Y., July 20, 1945; s. Paul and Lee (Wolf) L.; m. Elizabeth Bowman, Jan. 12, 1969. BA in Polit. Sci. and Econs., Queens Coll., CUNY, 1968; MBA in Fin. and Investment, Baruch Coll., CUNY, 1970. Registered investment advisor. Owner, pres. Investment Rsch. Assocs., N.Y.C., 1967-76; asst. to exec. v.p. Douglas T. Johnston, 1969-70; v.p. F.I. duPont/Lenox Capital Mgmt., 1970-74; prin., dir., pres. M.D. Sass Investors Svcs., 1974—; prin., dir., exec. v.p. M.D. Sass Capital Mgmt. Corp., 1985-87, Sass Elliot & Page, N.Y.C., 1985-87; dir., pres. M.D. Sass Assocs., 1974—; v.p., dir., prin. Corp. Capital Cons., N.Y.C., 1975—; exec. v.p. Sass Southmark Mut. Funds, 1986-89; exec. v.p., dir. Corp. Renaissance Group Inc., 1994-2000; pres. Resurgence Asset Mgmt., 1998—. Pres., chief investment officer Chase & M.D. Sass Ptnrs., 1995—2001; dir. CCC Resources, N.Y.C., CCC Advs., N.Y.C., FINEX; vice chmn., bd. dirs. Coolsavings.com Inc., 1999—2000; bd. dirs. N.Y. Bd. Trade, 2000—; participant in seminars, panels and workshops; expert witness in securities and valuation litigation; lectr. in field; subject of articles and TV programs. Contbr. articles to profl. jours., mags., newspapers, books. Trustee Citizen's Budget Commn. N.Y.C. Fellow Fin. Analysts Fedn.; mem. N.Y. Soc. Security Analysts (Vol. of Yr. 1986), Nat. Instl. Options Soc., Investment Mgmt. Cons. Assn., Beta Gamma Sigma (hon.). Avocations: catamaran racing, windsurfing racing, pistol shooting, skiing. Home: 555 Dune Rd Westhampton Beach NY 11978-2946 also: LG Smith Blvd 494 Aruba Aruba also: 0220 Nottingham Rd #4 Avon CO 81620 Office: MD Sass Investors Svcs 18th Fl 1185 Ave of Americas New York NY 10036

LAMM, CAROLYN BETH, lawyer; b. Buffalo, Aug. 22, 1948; d. Daniel John and Helen Barbara (Tatakis) L.; m. Peter Edward Halle, Aug. 12, 1972; children: Alexander P., Daniel E. BS, SUNY Coll. at Buffalo, 1970; JD, U. Miami (Fla.), 1973. Bar: Fla., 1973, D.C., 1976, N.Y. 1983. Trial atty. frauds sect. civil div. U.S. Dept. Justice, Washington, 1973-78, asst. chief comml. litigation sect. civil div., 1978, asst. dir., 1978-80; assoc. White & Case, 1980-84, ptnr., 1984—. Mem. Sec. State's Adv. Com. Pvt. Internat. law, Secs. Study Com. on Proposal Hague Conv. on Jurisdiction and the Enforcement of Judgements; arbitrator U.S. Panel of Arbitrators, Internat. Ctr. Settlement of Investment Disputes, 1995-2002; mem. com. on pvt. dispute resolution NAFTA. Mem. bd. editors Can./U.S. Rev. Bus. Law, 1987-92; mem. editorial adv. bd. Inside Litigation; contbg. editor: Internat. Arbitration Law Rev., 1997—; contbr. articles to legal pubs. Mem. coun. Holy Trinity Parish; bd. dirs. DC Appleseed Found. Fellow Am. Bar Found.; mem. ABA (chmn. young lawyers divsn., bd. govs. 2002--, rules and calendar com., chmn. house membership com., chmn. assembly resolution com., sec. 1984-85, chmn. internat. litigation com. coun. 1991-94, sect. litigation, ho. dels. 1982—, nomination com. 1984-87, chair 1995-96, past D.C. Cir. mem., standing com. fed. judiciary 1992-95, chmn. com. scope and correlation of work 1996-97, commn. on multidisciplinary practice, bd. govs. 2002--), Am. Arbitration Assn. (bd., arbitrator, adv. com. internat. arbitration, gen. counsel's law com., bd. dirs.), Fed. Bar Assn. (chmn. sect. on antitrust and trade regulation), Bar Assn. D.C. (bd. dirs., sec., found. bd.), D.C. Bar (pres. 1997-98, bd. govs. 1987-93, steering com. litigation sect.), Am. Law Inst. (coun.)(named Women Laywer of the yr., 2002), Women's Bar Assn. D.C., Am. Soc. Internat. Law, Am. Indonesian C. of C. (bd. dirs.), Am. Uzbekistan C. of C. (bd. dirs., sec., gen. counsel), Am. Turkish Friendship Coun. (bd. dirs., chair), Nat. Women's Forum, Columbia Country Club, Manchester Country Club. Democrat. Home: 2801 Chesterfield Pl NW Washington DC 20008-1015 Office: White and Case 601 13th St NW Washington DC 20005-3807 E-mail: clamm@whitecase.com.

LAMM, DONALD STEPHEN, publishing company executive; b. N.Y.C., May 31, 1931; s. Lawrence William and Aleen Antonia (Lassner) L.; m. Jean Stewart Nicol, Sept. 27, 1958; children: Douglas William, Robert Lawrence, Wendy Nicol. BA with honors, Yale, 1953; postgrad., Oxford (Eng.) U., 1956. With W.W. Norton & Co., Inc., N.Y.C., 1956-2000, from v.p. to pres., 1968-94, chmn., 1984-2000, also dir. Also dir. New Direction Pub. Corp.; assoc. Carlisle & Co., N.Y.C.; guest fellow Yale U., 1980, 85, Phi Beta Kappa lectr. 1994; Ida Beam disting. vis. prof. U. Iowa, 1987-88; guest fellow Woodrow Wilson Ctr., 1996; regents lectr. U. Calif., Berkeley, 1998-99; pres. Yale U. Press, 1985-2000; mem. bd. advisors Yale Rev., mem. bd. Control U. Calif. Press; fellow Ctr. for Advanced Study in the Behavioral Scis., 1998-99; mem. editl. bd. Am. Scholar. Author: (with others) The Spread of Economic Ideas, 1989, Beyond Literacy, 1990, Book Publishing in the United States Today, 1997, Perception, Cognition, and Language, 2000; mem. editl. bd. Logos. Mem. Inst. Early Am. History and Culture, Williamsburg, Va. With U.S. Army, 1953-55. Fellow Branford Coll., Yale U. Fellow Am. Acad. Arts and Scis.; mem. Manuscript Soc., Century Assn., Elizabethan Club, Phi Beta Kappa (senator 1990—, exec. com. 1998—). Home: 741 Calle Picacho Santa Fe NM 87505 Office: Carlisle & Co 24 East 64th St New York NY 10021

LAMM, FREDDIE RAY, research agricultural engineer; b. Boonville, Mo., Sept. 11, 1955; s. Henry Silas and Mildred Jean (Pfeiffer) L.; m. Donna Lee Gawith, Dec. 31, 1983; children: Elaine MaDonna, Henry Silas IV, Rachel Alison, Sarah Nicole. BS in Agrl. Engring., U. Mo., 1978, MS in Agrl. Engrng., 1979; PhD in Engring., Kans. State U., 1990. Registered profl. engr., Kans. Instr. Kans. State U., Colby, 1979-90, asst. prof., 1990-94, assoc. prof. agrl. engrng., 1994-2000, prof. agrl. engring., 2000—. Contbr. articles to profl. jours. Mem. Am. Soc. Agrl. Engrs. (chair SW-245 1993-94, Kans. sect. chair 1996-97, Young Mem. of Yr. 1993), Irrigation Assn. (chmn. agrl. irrigation com. 1995-97), Am. Soc. Agronomy, Kans. Acad. Sci., Am. Soc. Plasticulture, Sigma Xi, Alpha Epsilon, Gamma Sigma Delta. Democrat. Baptist. Achievements include research with use of microirrigation on field corn. Avocations: snow skiing, computers. Office: Kansas State Univ 105 Experiment Farm Dr Colby KS 67701-1697 E-mail: flamm@oznet.ksu.edu.

LAMM, HARRIET A. mathematics educator; b. Beeville, Tex., Dec. 4, 1948; d. James R. and Dorothy D. (Kendall) L. BA, Tex. Christian U., 1971; BS in Edn., S.W. Tex. State U., 1973, MEd, 1976; PhD, Tex. A&M U., 1993. Cert. secondary tchr., Tex. Instr. math. South San Antonio Ind. Sch. Dist., San Antonio, 1973-74; teaching asst. in math. S.W. Tex. State U., San Marcos, 1974-76; tchr. math. Seguin (Tex.) Ind. Sch. Dist., 1976-78, George West (Tex.) Ind. Sch. Dist., 1978-83, Lingleville (Tex.) Ind. Sch. Dist., 1983, Northside Ind. Sch. Dist., San Antonio, 1984-87, Beeville (Tex.) Ind. Sch. Dist., 1987-88; teaching asst. Tex. A&M U., College Station, 1991-92; instr. math. Coastal Bend Coll., Beeville, 1988-91, 1992-01; asst. project dir. Tex A&M U., Corpus Christi, 01—. Instr. math. Tarleton State U., Stephenville, Tex., 1983. Mem. Nat. Coun. Tchrs. Math., Tex. Coun. Tchrs. Math., Sch. Sci. and Math. Assn., Math. Assn. Am., Assn. Tex. Educators, Rsch. Coun. for Math. Learning. Avocations: ranching, sculpture, drawing.

LAMM, MICHAEL EMANUEL, pathologist, immunologist, educator; b. Bklyn., May 19, 1934; s. Stanley S. and Rose (Lieberman) L.; m. Ruth Audrey Kumin, Dec. 16, 1961; children— Jocelyn, Margaret Student, Amherst Coll., 1951-54; MD, U. Rochester, 1959; MS in Chemistry, Western Res. U., 1962. Diplomate Am. Bd. Pathology. Intern, asst. resident in pathology Inst. Pathology Western Res. U. and Univ. Hosps. of Cleve., 1959-62; research assoc. NIMH, Bethesda, Md., 1962-64; asst. prof. pathology NYU Sch. Medicine, N.Y.C., 1964-68, assoc. prof., 1968-73, prof., 1973-81; prof. dept. pathology Case We. Res. U. Sch. Medicine, 1981—; chmn. dept. Case Western Res. U. Sch. Medicine, 1981-2001. Vis. sci. dept. biochemistry U. Oxford, 1968; vis. prof. dept. pathology U. Geneva, 1976-77; mem. cancer spl. program adv. com. Nat. Cancer Inst., Bethesda, 1976-79, mem. bd. sci. counselors divsn. cancer biology, diagnosis and ctrs., 1993-95; mem. sci. adv. com. Damon Runyon-Walter Winchell Cancer Fund, N.Y.C., 1978-82; mem. immunol. sci. study sect. NIH, Bethesda, 1988-92; mem. immunotoxicology subcom. NRC, 1989-90; mem. toxin peer rev. panel Am. Inst. Biol. Sci., 1990—; bd. dirs. Univ. Associated for Rsch. and Edn. Pathology. Mem. editl. bd. Procs. Soc. Exptl. Biology and Medicine, 1973-82, Molecular Immunology, 1979-83, Jour. Immunol. Methods, 1980—, Jour. Immunology, 1981-85, Am. Jour. Pathology, 1982-92, Regional Immunology, 1988-95, Modern Pathology, 1989-96; contbr. articles to profl. jours. Recipient for excellence in teaching NYU Sch. Medicine, 1974; named Career Scientist Health Research Council, City of N.Y., 1966-75; NIH grantee, 1965— Fellow N.Y. Acad. Scis.; mem. Am. Assn. Pathologists (councilor 1986-88, sec. treas. 1988-90, v.p. 1990-91, pres. 1991-92), Am. Assn. Immunologists, Am. Soc. Biochemistry and Molecular Biology, Coll. Am. Pathologists, U.S. and Can. Acad. Pathology, Soc. for Exptl. Biol. Medicine, Clin. Immunology Soc., Soc. Mucosal Immunology, Am. Soc. Clin. Pathologists, Harvey Soc., Sigma Xi, Alpha Omega Alpha. Home: Apt 6B 13515 Shaker Blvd Cleveland OH 44120-5602

LAMM, NORMAN, academic administrator, rabbi; b. Bklyn., Dec. 19, 1927; s. Samuel and Pearl (Baumol) L.; m. Mindella Mehler, Feb. 23, 1954; children: Chaye Lamm Warburg, Joshua B., Shalom E., Sara Rebecca Lamm Dratch. BA summa cum laude, Yeshiva Coll., 1949; PhD, Bernard Revel Grad. Sch., 1966; Dr. of Hebrew Letters (hon.), Hebrew Theol. Coll., 1977, Gratz Coll., 1999. Cert. Ordained rabbi 1951. Ordained rabbi, 1951; asst. rabbi Congregation Kehilath Jeshurun, N.Y.C., 1952—53; rabbi Congregation Kodimoh, Springfield, Mass., 1954—58, Jewish Center, N.Y.C., 1958—76; Erna and Jakob Michael prof. Jewish philosophy Yeshiva U., 1966—, pres., 1976—, Rabbi Isaac Elchanan Theol. Sem., N.Y.C., 1976—. Vis. prof. Judaic studies Bklyn. Coll., 1974-75; dir. Union Orthodox Jewish Congregations Am. Author: A Hedge of Roses, 1966, The Royal Reach, 1970, Faith and Doubt, 1971, Torah Lishmah, 1972 (rev. English edition 1989), The Good Society, 1974, Halakot ve'Halikhot: Essays on Jewish Law, 1990, Torah Umadda: The Encounter of Religious Learning and Worldly Knowledge in the Jewish Tradition, 1990, The Shema: Spirituality and Law in Judaism, 1998, The Religious Thought of Hasidism: Text and Commentary, 1999 (Nat. Jewish Book awrd); editor: Library of Jewish Law and Ethics, 1975—; co-editor: The Leo Jung Jubilee Volume, 1962, A Treasury of Tradition, 1967, The Joseph B. Soloveitchik Jubilee Vol., 1984, Halakhot ve'Halikhot (Heb.): Essays on Jewish Law, 1990, Torah Umadda: The Encounter of Religious Learning and Worldly Knowledge in the Jewish Tradition, 1990. Trustee-at-large Fedn. Jewish Philanthropies, N.Y.; mem. exec. com. Assn. for a Better N.Y.; bd. dirs. Am. Friends-Alliance Israelite Universelle; mem. Pres.'s Commn. on the Holocaust, 1978-89; chmn. N.Y. Conf. on Soviet Jewry, 1970; mem. Halakhah Commn., Rabbinical Council Am. Recipient Abramowitz Zeitlin award, 1972 Mem. Assn. Orthodox Jewish Scientists (charter; bd. govs.) Office: Yeshiva U Office of Pres 500 W 185th St New York NY 10033-3201 also: Rabbi Isaac Eichanan Theol Sem 2540 Amsterdam Ave New York NY 10033-2807*

LAMM, RICHARD DOUGLAS, lawyer, former governor of Colorado; b. Madison, Wis., Aug. 3, 1935; s. Arnold E. and Mary (Townsend) L.; m. Dorothy Vennard, May 11, 1963; children: Scott Hunter, Heather Susan. BBA, U. Wis., 1957; LLB, U. Calif., Berkeley, 1961. Bar: Colo. 1962; CPA, Colo. Accountant, Salt Lake City, 1958, Ernst & Ernst, Denver, 1961-62; atty. Colo. Anti-Discrimination Commn., 1962-63, Jones, Meiklejohn, Kilroy, Kehl & Lyons, Denver, 1963-65; sole practice, 1965-74; mem. Colo. Ho. of Reps., 1966-74, asst. minority leader, 1971-74; gov. Colo., 1975-87; now spl. counsel Berliner, Boyle, Kaplan, Zisser & Walter (formerly O'Connor & Hannan), Denver; dir. Ctr. for Pub. Policy & Contempo U. Denver, 1987—. Asso. prof. law U. Denver, from 1969; chmn. natural resource and environ. mgmt. com. Nat. Gov.'s Assn., 1978-79, mem., from 1979, also mem. exec. com. and environment com., and chmn. task force on synthetic fuels. Pres. Denver Young Democrats, 1963; v.p. Colo. Young Democrats, 1964; mem. Conservation Found., Denver Center Performing Arts Center for Growth Alternatives, Central City Opera House Assn. Served as 1st lt. U.S. Army, 1957-58. Office: Berliner Boyle Kaplan Zisser & Walter 1 United Bank Ctr 1700 Lincoln St Denver CO 80203-4500 Mailing: U Denver Ctr for Pub Policy 2199 S Univ Blvd Denver CO 80208

LAMMERS, LAURA BEA, writer, communications executive; b. San Diego, Nov. 22, 1963; d. Lennis Larry and Beatrice Mearlyn Lammers. Student, U. Tulsa, 1981-82; A sum cum laude, Ocean County Coll., 1993; postgrad., Stockton U., 1994-95. Tech. writer SpaceCom, Gaithersburg, Md., 1984-85; computer tng. cons. Portsmouth, N.H., 1985-89; actress, model Foster Fell Agency, N.Y.C., 1989-92; tech. writer Preferred Behavioral Health, Lakewood, N.J., 1992-96, Zellweger Uster, Knoxville, Tenn., 1997-2001, Hampton-Tilley Assocs., Knoxville, 1999-2000; dir. content, bus. devel. Webcortex, Inc., Queens, 2000—. Pres., founder CyberNuts, Inc., Knoxville, 1998—; cons. Maximus, Washington, 1997; German translator The Learning Co., Knoxville, 1998; trade show salesperson, N.Y.C., 1989-92. Author, editor: A Hero Borne, Tribute to John Glenn, 1999, Poetry of the Web, 2000; artist works includes restoration of Embassy of Kuwait, Washington, 1983; adminstr. editor Alliance for Women in History, 1990-97. Vol. CMC Hosp., Toms River, N.J., 1992-96; fundraiser Hurricane David and Kobe Earthquake Relief; sci. officer region 9 Star Trek Orgon, Toms River, 1994-97; host Barnes & Noble Women's Poetry Group, 1998-99. Recipient Poetry award, Am. Collegiate Poets, 1981, 1st pl. French Extemporaneous award, Clemson U.,

1979. Mem.: Nat. Soc. DAR, AITP, NAFE, AAUW, Peoria Tribe Okla., Soc. Tech. Comm., Info. Tech. Bus. Assn., Knoxville Assn. Women Execs., Padi Scuba (cert. mem.), Phi Theta Kappa. Avocations: poetry, art, scuba, piano, travel. Office: CyberNuts Inc DBA APoetBorn.Com PO Box 24238 Knoxville TN 37933-2228 E-mail: docs2hire@yahoo.com.

LAMMERS, LENIS LARRY, management consultant; b. Hardin, Mont., July 16, 1937; s. George Joseph and Mayma Rose (Bolten) L.; m. Bea Marilyn Jones, Nov. 25, 1961; children: Laura Bea, Lennis Steven. BSEE, U.S. Naval Acad., 1960; MS in Ocean Engring., U.S. Naval Postgrad. Sch., 1971; postgrad., Duke U., 1982. Commd. ensign USN, 1960, advanced through grades to capt., 1981, various submarine assignments, 1960-68; ship supt. and docking office Mare Island Naval Shipyard, Vallejo, Calif., 1971-76; repair officer USS L.Y. Spear (AS 36), 1976-78; plan and estimate supt. Charleston Naval Shipyard, Charleston, S.C., 1978-81; Trident ILS officer integrated logistics systems Naval Sea Systems Command, Washington, 1981-82; planning officer Mare Island Naval Shipyard, Vallejo, 1983-84; commanding officer Portsmouth Naval Shipyard, Portsmouth, N.H., 1984-87; dir. plant material and maintenance Oyster Creek NGS, GPU-Nuclear, Forked River, N.J., 1987-94; pres. Plant Reliability Engring. Assoc., Toms River, 1994-96; sr. maintenance cons. Computational Systems Inc., Knoxville, 1996—. Guest lectr., sr. mgr. tng. course Naval Sea Systems Command, Washington, 1984-87, Engring. Duty Officer Sch., Vallejo, 1983-87; host and sponsor Navy League, Portsmouth, 1984-87; founder, lifetime mem. Ports Navy Shipyard Hist. Found., 1985—; founder Shipyard Employees Assn., Portsmouth, 1986. Pres., Navy Relief Soc., Portsmouth, 1984-87; chmn. YMCA Bldg. Fund-Greater Portsmouth area, 1985-87; hon. mem. Police Soc., Portsmouth Naval Shipyard, 1987, Rotary Club, Portsmouth, 1984-87; scoutmaster Boy Scouts Am., Charleston, 1980-81. Mem. Soc. Indsl. Engring., Am. Soc. Naval Engrs., Naval Inst., U.S. Naval Submarine League, U.S. Naval Acad. Alumni Assn. Avocations: trumpet, piano, theatre, golf, hunting. E-mail: len.lammer@compsys.com.

LAMMERT, THOMAS EDWARD, lawyer; b. Pitts., Mar. 26, 1947; s. John Albert and Gladys Irene (Miller) L.; m. Anita N. Kelm, Sept. 25, 1976; children: Brian, Andrew. BS, U. Pitts, 1969; JD, U. Akron, 1976. Bar: Ohio 1976, Fla 1983, U.S. Ct. Appeals (6th cir.) 1983, U.S. Supreme Ct., 1982. Assoc. Guy, Mentzer & Towne, Akron, Ohio, 1976-84, ptnr., 1984-85, Guy, Lammert & Towne, Akron, 1985—. Mem. ABA, Ohio State Bar Assn., Fla. Bar Assn., Stark County Bar Assn., Akron Bar Assn. Republican. Office: Guy Lammert & Towne 2210 1st National Towers Akron OH 44308

LAMMIE, JAMES LOUIS, engineering executive, retired military officer; b. 1931; BS, U.S. Mil. Acad., 1953; MSE, Purdue U., 1957; MSBA, George Washington U., 1969. Commd. U.S. Corps of Engrs. U.S. Army, 1953, advanced through grades to col., ret., 1953—74; with Atlantic Transit Sys. Parsons Brinckerhoff, Inc., N.Y.C., 1975—82, COO, 1982—90, dir., 1983—2000, CEO, 1990—96, sr. exec., 2000—. Office: Parsons Brinckerhoff Inc One Penn Plz Fl 2 New York NY 10119-0021

LAMMING, JOHN HAROLD, lawyer; b. Evanston, Ill., July 20, 1951; s. John Hunter and Alice Eleanor (Michalek) L.; m. Anne Carter Seddon, July 31, 1981; children: Ian Alexander, Colin Douglas, Sarah Anne Carter. BA in English and French, U. Mo., 1976; JD, Washington U., St. Louis, 1980, BS in Chemistry, 1992; MS in Chemistry, St. Louis U., 1995. Bar: Mo. 1980, U.S. Dist. Ct. (ea. and we. dists.) Mo. 1980, Ill. 1981, U.S. Ct. Appeals (8th cir.) 1981, U.S. Patent and Trademark Office 1990, Canadian Patent Office 1995. Pvt. practice, St. Louis, 1980-84; patent litigation atty. affiliated with Monsanto Co., 1984-86; foreclosure supr. Citicorp Mortgage, Inc., 1987-88; patent atty. U.S. Army Materiel Command, 1988-97; assoc. gen. counsel Washington U., 1997—. Mem. Brentwood (Mo.) Planning and Zoning Commn., 1981-83. Mem. ABA (award pub. contract law sect. 1991), Nat. Assn. Coll. and Univ. Attys., Am. Chem. Soc., Amateur Speedskating Union of the U.S., Alliance Francaise, Internat. Union of Pure and Applied Chemistry, Assn. of Univ. Tech. Mgrs., Phi Sigma Iota. Episcopalian. Office: Washington U Sch Med Campus Box 8037 660 S Euclid Ave Saint Louis MO 63110-1010

LAMON, HARRY VINCENT, JR. lawyer, director; b. Macon, Ga., Sept. 29, 1932; s. Harry Vincent and Helen (Bewley) L.; m. Ada Healey Morris, June 17, 1954; children: Hollis Morris, Kathryn Gurley. BS cum laude, Davidson Coll., 1954; JD with distinction, Emory U., 1958. Bar: Ga. 1958, D.C. 1965. Of counsel Troutman Sanders LLP, Atlanta, 1995—. Adj. prof. law Emory U., 1960-79. Contbr. articles to profl. jours. Mem. adv. bd. Metro Atlanta Salvation Army, 1963-97, chmn., 1975-79, life mem., 1997—, mem. nat. adv. bd., 1976-96, chmn. 1991-93, emeritus, 1996—; mem. adv. coun. on employee welfare and pension benefit plans U.S. Dept. Labor, 1975-79; mem. pension and benefits reporter adv. bd. Bur. Nat. Affairs, 1972-; mem. bd. visitors Davidson Coll., 1979-89; trustee, pres. So. Fed. Tax Inst., Inc., 1965—; trustee Am. Tax Policy Inst., Inc., 1989-96, Embry-Riddle Aero U., 1989-2001, emeritus, 2001—, Cathedral of St. Philip Endowment Fund, Atlanta, 1989—. 1st lt. AUS, 1954-56. Recipient Others award Salvation Army, 1979, Centennial honoree, 1990. Fellow Am. Bar Found. (life), Am. Coll. Trust and Estate Counsel, Am. Coll. Tax Counsel, Internat. Acad. Estate and Trust Law, Ga. Bar Found. (life), Am. Coll. Employee Benefits Counsel (charter); mem. ABA, Atlanta Bar Assn. (life), Am. Bar Retirement Assn. (bd. dirs. 1989-96, pres. 1994-95), Am. Law Inst. (life), Am. Employee Benefits Conf., So. Employee Benefits Conf. (pres., 1972, hon. life mem.), State Bar Ga. (chmn. sect. taxation 1969-70, vice chmn. comm on continuing lawyer competency 1982-89, emeritus 2002), Am. Judicature Soc., Atlanta Tax Forum, Lawyers Club Atlanta, Nat. Emory U. Law Sch. Alumni Assn. (pres. 1967), Practicing Law Inst., ALI-ABA Inst., CLUs Inst., The Group, Inc. (hon. life), Kiwanis Club Atlanta (hon. mem.; pres. 1974), Peachtree Racket Club (pres. 1986-87), Atlanta Coffee House Club, Capital City Club, Cosmos Club (Washington), Phi Beta Kappa (fellow), Omicron Delta Kappa, Phi Delta Phi, Phi Delta Theta (chmn. nat. cmty. svc. day 1969-72, legal commr. 1973-76, province pres. 1976-79, Golden Legion 2001). Episcopalian. Home: 4415 Paces Battle NW Atlanta GA 30327-3023 Office: Lamon & Sherman Consulting LLC 1950 N Park Pl Ste 125 Atlanta GA 30339 Fax: 770-933-0065. E-mail: Harry.Lamon@Lamonsherman.com.

LAMON, RICHARD PAUL, emergency physician, family practice physician; b. Mpls., Nov. 12, 1946; s. Robert A. and Ann M. Lamon; m. Joan F. Lamon, Aug. 25, 1968; 2 children. MD, Loma Linda U., 1972. Bd. cert. emergency medicine and family practice. Intern San Bernardino County Hosp., 1972-73, resident family practice, 1973-75; physician Regions Med. Ctr. (formerly St. Paul-Ramsey Med. Ctr.). Clin. asst. prof. emergency medicine U. Minn. Mem. ACEP, SAEM, Am. Acad. Family Practice. Office: Regions Med Ctr 640 Jackson St Saint Paul MN 55101-2502

LAMOND, SHARON ANN, health administrator; b. Providence, Sept. 23, 1948; d. John and Alice M. (Ulczukiewicz) Dec; m. William F. Lamond Jr., Nov. 18, 1972; 1 child Kristin. AS in Nursing, Community Coll. R.I., 1969; BSN, Stonehill Coll., 1987. RN Mass., R.I., cert. cmty. health nurse, ANCC. Pub. health nurse Town Carver Mass., 1980-85; branch mgr., supr. Colonial Nursing Assoc., Plymouth, Mass., 1985-87; quality assurance mgr. Staff Builders Home Care, Boston, 1987-90; dir. profl. svcs., adminstr. Olsten Kimberly Quality Care, Providence, 1990-92; supr. family practice Harvard Pilgrim Health Care of N.E., Swansea, Mass., 1992, mem. triage dept. pediats. Warwick, R.I., 1993-95; corp. peer rev. Blue Cross & Blue Shield Mass., Boston, 1996-98; quality assurance/infection control coord. Natick (Mass.) VNA, Inc., 2000—. Recipient Student Recognition award, Stonehill Coll., 1987. Mem.: Am. Profls. Infection Control, Mass. Assn. Pub. Health Nurses, Mass. Assn. Pub. Health Nurses, Am. Profls. in Infection Control, Am. Assn. for Continuity of Care, Alpha Sigma Lambda. Home: #1939 50 Abbott Run Valley Cumberland RI 02864-3261 Office: TLC 380 Broadway Providence RI 02909 E-mail: slamond@cox.net.

LAMONICA, SERGIO, financial consulting company executive; b. Rome, Sept. 4, 1943; s. Roberto and Teresa (Neri) L.; m. Antonietta Abazia (div. 1970); m. Marilena Ervo Bruschi, Sept. 10, 1999; stepchildren: Giorgia, Ginevra. Degree in econs., U. Naples, Italy, 1966; postgrad., Am. Studies Ctr., Ann Arbor, Mich., 1966; degree in pub. rels. with honors, ISIRP, Rome, 1971; degree in fin. analysis, Bocconi U., Milan, Italy, 1976. CPA; ofcl. state auditor's chpt.; econ. journalist. Office mng. ptnr. Arthur Andersen, Bologna, Italy, 1982-87, audit practice dir. Italy and Greece Milan, 1987-89; bus. cons. country ptnr. Arthur Andersen MBA, 1987-89, corp. fin. country ptnr., 1989-91, chmn., mng. dir., 1991-97, chmn., 1997-2000. Chmn. adv. bd. Andersen Worldwide, Chgo., 1985-86, mem. Japanese Internat. Network, Tokyo, 1987-93; chmn., mng. dir. Omniconsult, 2000—. Italian edn. coord. Vital Signs, 1997; author: Euro: The Effects on Corporate Businesses, 1998; contbr. articles on bus. to Italian fin. newspaper Il Sole 24Ore, 1990—. Mem. Assn. Italiana Analisti Finanziari (dirs. coun. 1991—), Assn. Nazionale Direttori Amministrazione e finanza (statutory auditor 1994—), Ordine Commercialisti, Ordine Giornalisti, Italian Fedn. Pub. Rels. Profls. Avocations: sailing, skiing, travel, photography, model cars. Home: Vaile Sabotino 19/2 20135 Milan Italy Office: Omniconsult SRL Via Andegari 18 20121 Milan Italy

LAMONSOFF, NORMAN CHARLES, psychiatrist; b. Bklyn., Sept. 16, 1936; s. Isidore and Kate (Wolfe) L.; m. Sheila R. Kaplan, Aug. 27, 1961; children: Karen M., Jacob D. BA, Cornell U., 1958; MD, SUNY, 1962. Diplomate Am. Bd. Psychiatry and Neurology. Medical internship Bklyn. Jewish Hosp., 1963; residency psychiatry Kings County Hosp., Bkyln., 1963-66; sr. supervising psychiatrist St. Vincent's Hosp. of Richmond, Staten Island, N.Y., 1968-70; cons. psychiatrist Staten Island Hosp., 1968-87; dir. psychiatry N.Y.C. Dept. Mental Health and Mental Retardation Svcs., 1970-74; attending psychiatrist Jersey City (N.J.) Medical Ctr., 1974-76; program dir. addiction svcs. unit Jersey City Medical Ctr., 1974-76; medical dir. Somerset County Com. Mental Health Ctr., Somerville, N.J., 1976-83, Helene Fuld Crisis Ctr., Trenton, 1984-87; chmn. psychiatry Helene Fuld Med. Ctr.; medical dir. Bristol-Bensalem Human Svcs. Ctr., Newportville, Pa., 1987—. Clinical supr. residency training The Trenton Psychiatric Hosp., clinical asst. prof. N.J. Coll. Medicine. Contbr. articles to profl. jours. With U.S. Army, 1966-68. Decorated Army Commendation medal; recipient Exemplary Psychiatrist award Bucks County area chpt., Nat. Alliance for the Mentally Ill., 1994. Mem. N.Y. Soc. Clinical Psychiatry, Am. Psychiatry Assn., Am. Medical Assn., Mercer County Medical Soc. Home: 121 Trappe Ln Langhorne PA 19047-1432 Address: PO Box L-27 Langhorne PA 19047 Office: 1051 Lindenhurst Rd Yardley PA 19067-5412

LAMONT, ALICE, accountant, consultant; b. Houston, July 19; d. Harold and Bessie Bliss (Knight) L. BS, Mont. State U.; MBA in Taxation, Golden Gate U., 1983. CPA; registered fin. advisor. Tchr. London Ctrl. H.S., 1974-80; acct. Signetics, Sunnyvale, Calif., 1980-82; propr. Alice Lamont Ltd., 1985—. Mem. Atlanta Hist. Soc., 1985-93, High Mus. Art, 1986-89, Atlanta Botanical Garden, Brit. Am. Bus. Group (mem. com. 1993-97), Friend of Atlanta Opera, Jeannette Rankin Found.; mem. Atlanta organizing com. Nat. Osteoporosis Found., 1997-2000. Mem.: AAUW (life; mem. audit chmn. Atlanta br. 1993—95, mem. scholarship com. 1994—), Atlanta Tax Study Assn., Ga. Soc. CPAs (chmn. Acctg. Inst. 1995—97), Women's Commerce Club (mem. adv. bd. 1994—98), Atlanta Woman's Club (co-chair ways and means com. 1985—86, asst. treas. 1986—88, treas. 1990, 1992—94).

LAMONT, GENE, professional baseball coach, former professional baseball team manager; b. Rockford, Ill., Dec. 25, 1946; m. Melody; children: Melissa, Wade. Student, No. Ill. U., Western Ill. U. Player various minor league teams Detroit Tigers, 1965-73, 75-77, with major league team, 1970-75; mgr. minor league team Kansas City Royals, Fort Myers, Fla., 1977-79, Jacksonville, 1979-84; coach Pitts. Pirates, 1986-91; mgr. Chgo. White Sox, 1991-95, Pittsburgh Pirates, 1995—2001; coach Houston Astros, 2001—. Named Southern League Mgr. of Yr., 1982. Office: Houston Astros PO Box 288 Houston TX 77001*

LAMONT, LANSING, journalist, public affairs executive, author; b. N.Y.C., Mar. 13, 1930; s. Thomas Stilwell and Elinor (Miner) L.; m. Ada Jung, Sept. 18, 1954; children: Douglas Ranlet, Elisabeth Jung Lamont Wolcott, Virginia Alden Lamont Cazedessus, Thomas Stilwell II. AB, Harvard U., 1952; MS in Journalism with honors, Columbia U., 1958. Reporter, Washington Star, 1958-59; Washington corr. Worcester (Mass.) Gazette, also other New Eng. papers, 1959-60; sci. reporter Washington bur. Time mag., 1961-63, polit. reporter, 1964-68, corr., dep. chief London bur., 1969-71, chief Can. corr., chief Ottawa bur., 1971-73; chief corr. UN bur. Time mag., N.Y.C., 1973-74; v.p., mng. dir. Can. Affairs The Americas Soc., 1981-91, sr. fellow, 1991-94. Author: Day of Trinity (alt. selection Lit. Guild Am.), 1965, Campus Shock, 1979, Journey to the Last Empire: The Soviet Union in Transition, 1991, Breakup: The Coming End of Canada and the Stakes for America, 1994 (Notable Books of Yr., N.Y. Times), Sand and Glitter: Exploring the Ancient Middle East, 1994-95, In the Land of Sangria and Sorrows: Spain, 1997, No Twilight About Me: A Life in Letters, 1999; co-ed itor Private Letters of John Masefield, 1979, Friends So Different: Essays on Canada and U.S. in the 1980's, 1989. Mem. alumni bd. dirs. Harvard U., also chmn. nominating com. for overseers; trustee Milton Acad., Am. Mus. Natural History, N.Y.C., Nat. Inst. for Music Theatre; pres. Am. Trust for the Brit. Libr.; pres. Century Assn. Archives Found.; mem. Can.-Am. Com., 1984-94, Coun. Fgn. Rels. 1985—. Served to 1st lt., inf. U.S. Army, 1954-57. William Cullen Bryant fellow Met. Mus. Art, 1984— . Mem. Century Assn. (N.Y.C.), Harvard Club (N.Y.C.). Episcopalian. Office: 133 E 80th St New York NY 10021-0317

LAMONT, LEE, music management executive; b. Queens, N.Y. m. August Tagliamonte, Apr. 30, 1951; 1 child, Leslie Lamont. With Nat. Concerts & Artists Corp., N.Y.C., 1955-58; asst. Sol Hurok Concerts, 1958-67; person rep. for concerts, rec. and TV Isaac Stern, 1968-76; v.p. ICM Artists Ltd., 1976-85; pres. ICM Artists Ltd. and ICM Artists (London) Ltd., 1985-95, chmn. bd. dirs., 1995—. Former mem. adv. com. Hannover (Germany) Internat. Violin Competition. Former mem. bd. overseers Curtis Inst. Music. Mem. Ams. for the Arts, Japan Soc., Asia Soc., Am. Symphony Orch. League (bd. dirs.), Bohemian Club. Avocations: painting, sculpture. Office: ICM Artists Ltd 40 W 57th St Fl 16 New York NY 10019-4098 E-mail: llamont@icmtalent.com.

LAMONT, MICHELE, sociologist, educator; b. Toronto, Ont., Can., Dec. 15, 1957; came to U.S., 1983; d. Jacques and Jeanine (Page) L.; m. Frank Richardson Dobbin, June 6, 1987. BA, Ottawa U., Ont., 1977, MA, 1978; Doctorate, U. Paris, 1983. Postdoctoral fellow Stanford (Calif.) U., 1983-85; asst. prof. U. Tex., Austin, 1985-87, Princeton (N.J.) U., 1987-93, assoc. prof., 1993—. Author: Money, Morals and Manners, 1992, Cultivating Differences, 1992; co-editor: Cultivating Differences: Symbolic Boundaries and the Making of Inequality, 1992, The Dignity of Working Men, 2000, Rethinking Comparative Cultural Sociology, 2000. Grantee NSF, 1992-94, 2000-, German Marshall Funds U.S., 1992-93, Spencer Found., 1994-95, Guggenheim Found., 1996—, Russell Sage Found., 1996—. Mem. Am. Sociol. Assn. (chair cultural sect. 1993-94). Home: 67 Rosedale Rd Princeton NJ 08540-6701 Office: Princeton U Sociology Dept Princeton NJ 08544-0001

LAMONT, OWEN AUSTIN, economist; b. Boston, May 18, 1966; s. Austin Lamont and Sarah Robinson Newcomb; m. Elizabeth Bernier, March 11, 1995; children: Robinson, Duncan. BA with honors, Oberlin Coll., 1988; postgrad., MIT, 1990-94. Rsch. asst. The Boston Co. Econs. Advisors, Inc., 1988-89, assoc. economist, 1989-90; asst. prof. dept. econs. Princeton U., 1994-95; asst. prof. fin. Grad. Sch. Bus. U. Chgo., 1995-98, assoc. prof. fin., 1998—. NSF fellow, 1990-93, Sloan fellow, 1993-94. Mem. Am. Econ. Assn., Nat. Bur. Econ. Rsch. Office: U Chgo Grad Sch Bus 1101 E 59th St Chicago IL 60637

LAMONT, ROSETTE CLEMENTINE, Romance languages educator, theatre journalist, translator; b. Paris; came to U.S., 1941, naturalized, 1946; d. Alexandre and Loudmilla (Lamont) L.; m. Frederick Hyde Farmer, Aug. 9, 1969. BA, Hunter Coll., 1947; MA, Yale U., 1948, PhD, 1954. Tutor Romance langs. Queens Coll., CUNY, 1950-54, instr., 1954-61, asst. prof., 1961-64, assoc. prof., 1965-67, prof., 1967-96; mem. doctoral faculties, comparative lit., theatre, French and women's studies cert. program CUNY, 1968-96, prof. emeritus PhD program in theater, 1996—. State Dept. envoy Scholar Exch. Program, USSR, 1974; rsch. fellow, 1976; lectr. Alliance Francaise, Maison Francaise of NYU; vis. prof. Sorbonne, Paris, 1985-86; vis. prof. theatre Sarah Lawrence Coll., 1994—. Author: The Life and Works of Boris Pasternak, 1964, De Vive Voix, 1971, Ionesco, 1973, The Two Faces of Ionesco, 1978, Ionesco's Imperatives: The Politics of Culture, 1993, Women on the Verge, 1993; translator: Days and Memory, 1990, Auschwitz and After, 1995 (ALTA prize), Brazen, 1996, The Storm, 1999; also contbr. to various books; author, guest editor The Metaphysical Farce issue Collages and Bricolages, 1996-97; mem. editl. bd. Western European Stages, also contbg. editor; European corr. Theatre Week: Columbia Dictionary of Modern European Literature; fgn. corr. Stages; reviewer France-Amérique-Le Figaro. Decorated chevalier, then officier des Palmes Academiques, officier des Arts et Lettres (France); named to Hunter Coll. Hall of Fame, 1991; Guggenheim fellow, 1973-74; Rockefeller Found. humanities fellow, 1983-84. Mem. PEN, MLA, Am. Soc. Theatre Research, Internat. Brecht Soc., Drama Desk (voting mem.), Internat. Assn. Theatre Critics, Phi Beta Kappa, Sigma Tau Delta, Pi Delta Phi. Clubs: Yale. Home: 260 W 72nd St Apt 9D New York NY 10023-2822 *An educator does not merely impart knowledge: he or she communicates an attitude, a way of looking at the world. So does the writer. Through each creative mind the world is born anew.*

LAMONT-HAVERS, RONALD WILLIAM, physician, research administrator; b. Wymondham, Norfolk, Eng., Mar. 6, 1920; came to U.S., 1955, naturalized, 1964; s. William Fredrick L.-H.; m. Gabrielson, Oct. 16, 1965; children— Wendy, Melinda, Ian. BA, U. B.C., 1942; MD, U. Toronto, 1946; diploma in internal medicine, McGill U., 1953. Intern Vancouver (B.C., Can.) Gen. Hosp., 1946-48; resident in internal medicine Queen Mary Vets. Hosp., Montreal, Que., Can., 1949-51; Canadian Arthritis and Rheumatism Soc. fellow Columbia Presbyterian Hosp., Coll. Physicians and Surgeons, Columbia U., N.Y.C., 1951-53; med. dir. Canadian Arthritis and Rheumatism Soc., B.C. div., Vancouver, 1953-55, Arthritis and Rheumatism Found., N.Y.C., 1955-64; instr. in medicine Coll. Physicians and Surgeons, Columbia U., 1955-64; assoc. dir. extramural programs NIAMD, Bethesda, Md., 1964-68, dep. dir., 1972-74; assoc. dir. extramural programs NIH, 1968-72, acting dir., dep. dir. Md., 1974-76, acting dir., 1975, dep. dir., 1974-76; dep. to gen. dir. for rsch. policy and adminstrn. Mass. Gen. Hosp., Boston, 1976-87, v.p. rsch. and tech. affairs, 1987-90, sr. cons. for rsch., 1990-99; dep. dir. Cutaneous Biology Rsch. Ctr. Mass. Gen. Hosp. and Harvard U., 1990—. Del. USSR-Arthritis Exchange Program, 1964; U.S. coordinator U.S.-USSR Coop. Program in Arthritis, 1973-75. Served with M.C. Royal Canadian Army, 1944-46. Recipient Golden Pen award Jour. Am. Phys. Therapy Assn., 1965; Superior Service award HEW, 1973; Spl. citation Sec. HEW, 1975 Fellow Royal Coll. Physicians (Can.); mem. Am. Coll. Rheumatology (dir. Met. Washington sect. 1964-66), N.Y. Rheumatism Assn. (pres. 1960), Arthritis Found. (dir., governing mem. 1966-80, pres. Mass. chpt. 1987-89), Am. Acad. Orthopaedic Surgeons (hon.), Am. Gastroent. Assn. (affiliate), Alpha Omega Alpha. Office: Mass Gen Hosp 13th St Bldg 149 Charlestown MA 02129-2000 E-mail: rlh@chrc2.mgh.harvard.edu.

LAMOREAUX, LAURA ELÁN, artist, writer; b. Manhattan, N.Y., Nov. 5, 1955; d. Marilyn Jeanne L.; m. Michael Edward Hilleman. AS (with honors), Columbia Greene Coll., 1973; student, UCLA, Westwood, 1983, Otis Palson Sch. Design, L.A., 1984-88. RN, Calif. Design artist (CD cover and 8 record labels) The Message Is in the Music, 1994. Recipient Creative award Internat. Art Show, Paris, 1994. Avocations: gardening, reading, hiking, mediation, writing poetry. Home and Office: 151 Westlake Blvd Malibu CA 90265-2442

LAMOREAUX, PHILIP ELMER, geologist, hydrogeologist, consultant; b. Chardon, Ohio, May 12, 1920; s. Elmer I. and Gladys (Rhodes) L.; m. Ura Mae Munro, Nov. 11, 1943; children: Philip E Jr., James W., Karen L. BA, Denison U., 1943, PhD (hon.), 1972; MS, U. Ala., 1949. Registered profl. geologist, Ga., N.C., S.C., Tenn., Ind., Ariz., Ark., Fla., Wyo., Pa., Mo., Ala. Geologist U.S. Geol. Survey, Tuscaloosa, Ala., 1943-45, dist. geologist Groundwater Office, 1945-57, divsn. hydrologist water resources programs, 1957-59, chief ground water br. Washington, 1959-61; state geologist, oil and gas supr. Ala. Geol. Survey, Tuscaloosa, 1961-76; pres. P.E. LaMoreaux & Assocs. Inc., 1976-87, chmn. bd. dirs., 1987-90, sr. hydrologist, 1990—. Lectr. Am. Geol. Inst. Coll. Program, 1969-71, Am. Geophys. Union Coll. Program, 1961—, NSF, Ala. Acad. Sci. H.S. Program, 1961—, No. Engring. and Testing, Salt Lake City, 1985, Ga. State U., Fla. State U., Vanderbilt U., Denison U., Auburn U., U. of Montpellier, France, U. Christ Church, New Zealand, U. Praetoria, South Africa; hydrogeology cons. to 30 fgn. countries. Editor in chief Jour. Environ. Geology, 1982—; editor in chief: Annotated Bibliography Carbonate Rocks, vols. 1-5; contbr. articles to profl. jours. Active Nat. Drinking Water Adv. Coun. EPA, 1984-88; tech. rev. group Oak Ridge Nat. Lab., 1984-88; trustee Denison U.; adv. Boy Scouts Am. Black Warrior Coun., 1993—. Recipient Comdrs. medal C.E., 1990. Mem.: AAAS, NAS (nat. rsch. coun. geotech. bd. 1990—92, water sci. and tech. bd. 1990—97, bd. earth scis. and resources 1992—97, earth resources com. 1995—97, nat. landslide hazard mitigation strategy com. 2001—02), AIME, ASTM, NAE, Ala. C. of C. (Pres.'s adv. com., Rep. of Energy 1980), Southeastern Geol. Soc., Soil Conservation Soc. Am., Soc. Econ. Paleontologists and Mineralogists, Soc. Econ. Geologists, Nat. Ground Water Assn. (group 2020 2001—), Nat. Water Well Assn., Nat. Water Resources Assn., Nat. Speleological Soc., Nat. Rivers and Harbors Congress, Nat. Assn. Geology Tchrs., Miss. Geol. Soc., Interstate Oil Compact Commn. (vice chmn. 1963, chmn. rsch. com.), Internat. Water Resources Assn. (Karst Commn. 1961—), Internat. Assn. Hydrogeologists (pres. 1977—80, v.p. 1973—77, com. on water rsch. 1978—80, chmn. hydrology hazardous waste commn. 1983—91, mem. com. thermal and mineral waters 1994—, adv. to pres. 1995—), Geol. Soc. London, Geol. Soc. Am. (1st. chmn. hydrogeology group 1963, chmn. O.E. Meinzer award com. 1965, cons. membership S.E. sect. 1967—68, chmn. nominating com., bd. dirs., bd. trustees, publs. com., chmn.), Assn. Am. State Geologists (statistician 1966—69), Am. Inst. Profl. Geologists (chmn. com. on rels. with govtl. agencies 1967—70, bd. dirs. 1969—70, chmn. liaison com. fed. agencies 1968—70, pres.), Am. Inst. Hydrology, Am. Geophys. Union, Am. Geol. Inst. (chmn. com. on publs. 1968—70, pres. 1971—72, chmn. environ. geosci. adv. com. 1994—, mem. AGI Found., bd. trustees, Ian Campbell award 1990, William B. Heroy award 1995), Am. Assn. Petroleum Geologists (acad. liaison com., Ho. of Dels. 1970—72, com. preservation samples and cores 1998—, chmn. divsn. geosci. hydrogeology com., mem. pubs. com. 1998—), Ala. Geol. Soc., Ala. Acad. Sci. Republican. Presbyterian. Avocations: photography, stamp collecting, coin collecting, gardening. Office: PE LaMoreaux 2626 1/2 University Blvd Tuscaloosa AL 35401-1508 Fax: 205-391-3534. E-mail: pela@dbtech.net.

LAMOTHE, ARTHUR J. lawyer; b. Augusta, Maine, June 20, 1962; s. Roland J. and Kathleen A. (Small) L., Sept. 29, 1990; children: Joel T., Matthew G., Kimberlee A. JD, U. Maine, 1987. Bar: Maine 1987, U.S. Dist. Ct. Maine 1987, U.S. Ct. Appeals (1st cir.) 1998. In-house atty. Cen. Maine Power Co., Augusta, 1987-90; assoc. Friedman & Babcock, Portland, Maine, 1990-97; pvt. practice Brunswick, 1997—. Mem. Communities of MerryMeeting Bay Bus. Assn.; active MerryMeeting Micro-Loan Rev. Bd., 2000—; bd. dirs. Big Bros./Big Sisters, Portland, 1994—97, Brunswick, 1997—, chair, 1999—. Mem. ABA, Maine State Bar Assn., Cumberland Bar Assn., Bath-Brunswick Bar Assn., Phi Beta Kappa. Office: PO Box 425 Brunswick ME 04011-0425 E-mail: art@lamothelaw.com.

LAMOTHE, DONAT ROMEO, music educator; b. Keene, N.H., Oct. 14, 1935; s. Romeo Paul and Gabrielle Jeannette (Drouin) L. MA, St. John's U., Collegeville, Minn., 1969; MusM, Boston U., 1973; PhD, U. Strasbourg, France, 1980. Ordained priest, Roman Cath. Ch., 1962. Prof. music Assumption Coll., Worcester, Mass., 1963—. Editor music edition: Matins at Cluny, 1986, 24 Etudes Permodales, 1989, Pseaumes a III Voix, C. LeJeune, 2000. Office: Assumption Coll 500 Salisbury St Worcester MA 01609-1265

LAMOTHE, IRENE ELISE, television producer, distributor; b. Berlin, Sept. 13, 1949; d. Wilfred J. and Estelle Bertha (Lefevre) L.; divorced. Diploma/Med. Lab. Tech., Naval Med. Sch., Bethesda, Md., 1971; Diploma/Communications, Leland Powers Sch., Boston, 1973. Pvt. pilot airplane, 1974, comml. pilot rotorcraft-helicopter, 1982. Owner, operator New Eng. Security Agy., Milan, 1974-78; adminstr., instr. Kahana's Stunt Sch., Chatsworth, Calif., 1980-83; project devel. specialist Galaxy Mountain Music Prodns., Van Nuys, 1984-87; writer, prodr. Lance-Cara Pub. Co./Wilby Records, Mission Hills, 1988—; exec. producer LCJ Prodns., Studio City, 1989—; chief exec. officer Zemoz Entertainment, 1992—. Ind. stunt woman, major studios, 1978-85. Producer: (ednl. video) Discover Yourself In Hollywood, 1992 (Angel award for Excellence in Media 1993, Parent's Choice award for ednl. video 1995); producer, co-writer, Safety is No Accident, 1991; producer (TV series) Hollywood Structured, 1989—, Inside California Country, 1986; writer/producer: New Highland Thunder, 1999, A Good Day, 1999, (Christmas songs) Wilby the X-mas Tree, 1988, A Christmas Waltz, 1988; co-creator: (multi-media project) GB the Cosmic Snoball, 1985. With USN,

1967-72. Recipient Angel Award for Excellence in Media Hollywood Structured, 1991, 92, Angel Award for Ednl. Video, 1993, Bronze award Worldfest Houston, 1992. Mem. Lemurian Order. Office: LCJ Prodns 3841 Eureka Dr Studio City CA 91604-3107 E-mail: ilamothe@worldnet.att.net.

LAMOTTA, CONNIE FRANCES, communications consultant; b. Bronx, N.Y., Oct. 10, 1942; d. Salvatore Charles and Mary Moscatiello LaMotta; children: Raphael, Peter, David. BA, SUNY, Albany, 1969. Activities coord. San Diego Assn. for the Retarded, 1970-72; edn. program dir. Edn. Ctrs. of Newark Archdiocese, 1973-79; dir. comm. tng. Riverside Eating Disorder Clinic, Secaucus, N.J., 1979-84; comm. coord. Sun Chem. Corp., N.Y.C., 1984-86; pub. rels. dir. Nat. Coffee Assn., 1986-87; v.p. pub. rels. comms. Direct Mktg. Assn., 1987-99, sr. v.p. pub. rels. comms., 1987-99; pres. La Motta Strategic Comms., Inc., 1999—. Mem.: Women in Comms., Direct Mktg. Assn. E-mail: connie@lamottastrategic.com.

LAMOTTE, JANET ALLISON, retired management specialist; b. Norfolk, Va., Mar. 3, 1942; d. Charles Nelson Jr. and Geneva Elizabeth (Baird) Johnson; m. Larry LaMotte, Aug. 30, 1964 (div. Aug. 1979); children: Lisa Renee LaMotte Buchholz, Lori Louise. AA, Rose State Coll., 1982; BA, U. Ctrl. Okla., 1984; MA in Human Rels., U. Okla., 1986. Clk./typist U.S. Army, Washington, 1960, Fort Belvoir, Va., 1961, Dallas, 1961, IRS, Dallas, 1962, Richmond, Va., 1962-63, DLA, Alexandria, 1978, IRS, Oklahoma City, 1978-79, Tinker AFB, 1979; sec. IRS, Richmond, 1963-64, Tinker AFB, 1981-82; pers. asst. State Bd. Control, Austin, Tex., 1964-65; procurement clk. FAA, Oklahoma City, 1965-66; acctg. clk. Tinker AFB, 1980-81; clk./stenographer, 1980-81; supply specialist, 1982-87; worldwide inventory mgmt. specialist, 1987-98. Safety chmn. Kensler Elem. Sch. PTA, Wichita, 1974-75; vol. CONTACT Crisis Helpline, 1986-89. Federally Employed Women scholar, 1984. Mem.: AARP, AAUW, Tinker (Okla.) Mgmt. Assn. (membership, ticket monitor 1994—98), Okla. Air Force Assn. (v.p. comms. 1995—97, exec. sec. 1996—97, Okla. Mem. of Yr. 1996, Nat. Exceptional Svc. award 1996), Air Force Assn. (v.p. pub. rels. Gerrity chpt. 1994, v.p. comm. 1995—98, Nat. medal of Merit 1995, Exceptional Svc. awrd 1996, Chpt. Exceptional Svc. award 1998), Nat. Assn. Ret. Fed. Employees, Am. Bus. Women's Assn. (v.p. membership downtown reflections chpt. 1992—93), Toastmasters (area gov. 1991—92, area editor K-3 Newsletter 1992—93, pres. Tinker chpt. 1989, edn. v.p. 1988, awards), Rural Retreat (Va.) Hist. Soc., Morrow County (Ohio) Geneal. Soc., Pulaski County (Ky.) Hist. Soc., Nat. Trust for HIst. Preservation. Methodist. Avocations: history, writing, genealogy, crafts, reading. Home: 9525 Ridgeview Dr Oklahoma City OK 73120-3419 E-mail: jlamott99@msn.com.

LA MOTTE, LOUIS COSSITT, JR. medical scientist, consultant; b. Clinton, S.C., Jan. 21, 1928; s. Louis Cossitt Sr. and Sarah (Hunter) La M.; m. Lila Jean Magruder, Dec. 31, 1948; children: Barbara Jones, Robert, Nancy Warren, Diane, Cynthia Love. AB, Duke U., 1948; MS in Pub. Health, U. N.C., 1951; ScD, Johns Hopkins U., 1958. Bacteriologist N.C. State Lab. Hygiene, Raleigh, 1948-51; virologist U.S. Army Chem. Corps, Ft. Detrick, Md., 1951-58; chief virus investigations unit Communicable Disease Ctr., Greeley, Colo., 1958-66, asst. chief disease ecology sect., 1965-66, chief cmty. studies br. Atlanta, 1966-69; dir. microbiology divsn. Ctr. for Disease Control, 1969-73, dir. tech. evaluation and assistance divsn., 1973-86. Mem. dean's alumni coun. Sch. Hygiene and Pub. Health, Johns Hopkins U., Balt., 1995—; cons. Divsn. Pub. Health Ga., Atlanta, 1994; mem. recombinant adv. com. NIH, Bethesda, Md., 1970; mem. exec. com. Am. Com. on Arthropod-borne Viruses, Atlanta, 1964-66. Author: (with others) Federal Legislation & the Clinical Laboratory, 1981; contbr. articles to profl. jours. Trustee Ga. Fed. Mil. Retiree Coalition, Atlanta, 1990-93; coord. Neighborhood Watch Assn., Dunwoody, Ga., 1986—; advisor Sch. Pub. Health, Emory U., Atlanta, 1994—. Recipient Superior Svc. award USPHS, 1981. Republican. Presbyterian. Avocation: computer utilization. Home: 4820 Leeds Ct Dunwoody GA 30338-5026

LAMOUREUX, GLORIA KATHLEEN, nurse, retired air force officer, consultant; b. Billings, Mont., Nov. 2, 1947; d. Laurits Bungaard and Florence Esther (Nielsen) Nielsen; m. Kenneth Earl Lamoureux, Aug. 31, 1973 (div. Feb. 1979). BS, U. Wyo., 1970; MS, U. Md., 1984. Staff nurse, ob-gyn DePaul Hosp., Cheyenne, Wyo., 1970; enrolled USAF, 1970, advanced through grades to col.; staff nurse ob-gyn dept. 57th Tactical Hosp., Nellis AFB, Nev., 1970-71, USAF Hosp., Clark AB, Republic Philippines, 1971-73; charge nurse ob-gyn dept. USAF Regional Hosp., Sheppard AFB, Tex., 1973-75, staff nurse ob-gyn dept. MacDill AFB, Fla., 1976-79; charge nurse ob-gyn dept. USAF Med. Ctr., Andrews AFB, Md., 1979-80, MCH coord., 1980-82; chief nurse USAF Clinic, Eielson AFB, Alaska, 1984-86, Air Force Systems Command Hosp., Edwards AFB, Calif., 1986-90; comdr. 7275th Air Base Group Clinic, Italy, 1990-92, 42d Med. Group, Loring AFB, Maine, 1992-94; 347th Med. Group, Moody AFB, Ga., 1994-96; chief nursing svcs. divsn. Hdqrs. Air Edn. and Tng. Command, Randolph AFB, Tex., 1996-2000. Ind. cons. Customers First Cons., Universal City, 2000—, v.p., 2000—; sr. cons. Karta Tech., Inc., San Antonio, 2002—. Mem. Assn. Women's Health, Obstetric, and Neonatal Nurses (sec.-treas. armed forces dist. 1986-88, vice-chmn. armed forces dist. 1989-91), Air Force Assn., Bus. and Profl. Women's Assn. (pub. rels. chair Prince George's County chpt. 1981-82), Sigma Theta Tau. Republican. Lutheran. Avocations: reading, needlework, piano, photography. Home: 13515 Thessaly Universal City TX 78148-2810 Office: # 103-164 1645 Pat Booker Rd Universal City TX 78148 E-mail: glamoureux@satx.rr.com., customersfirst2@satx.rr.com.

LAMOUREUX, WILLIAM ALBERT, poet; b. Montreal, Que., Can., Aug. 15, 1938; came to U.S., 1938, naturzliaed, 1952; s. William C. and Beatrice (Benoit) L. BA, Tufts U., 1964; postgrad., Boston U., 1964-65, U. Hawaii, 1974. Ptnr. Lamoureux Funeral Home, Gardner, Mass., 1949-76; founder, propr. Librairie Francaise, Santurce, P.R., 1970-73; broker, salesman Portner & Portner, Inc., Realtors, Hollywood, Fla., 1978-82; right-of-way agt. Fla. Dept. Transp., 1978-80. Works include (poetry) La lumiere se retire du bord de la terrasse..., 1960, Comme je traversais le pays des licornes, 1961, Un oranger, supreme emeraude, 1962. Mem. Mensa. Republican. Roman Catholic. Home and Office: 4601 Highway A1A Apt 401 Vero Beach FL 32963-1353 E-mail: wlamoureux@hotmail.com.

LA MOY, JUNE INEZ, graphic designer; b. Las Vegas, Nev., June 8, 1961; d. Peter Henry and Patsy Joan Lamoy. Student, U. South Fla., Santa Monica Coll. New accts. adminstr. Pacific Nat. Bank; legal svc. adminstr. Candle Corp.; office mgr. Coast Litho; owner La Moy Design. Contbr. to Just Us Express jour. Mem. Habitat for Humanity. Mem. AAAS, Los Angeles County Mus. Art (patron), Nature Conservancy,. Friends of the Griffith Obs., Toastmasters (cert.). Avocations: hand crafts, philosophy.

LAMP, BENSON J. tractor company executive; b. Cardington, Ohio, Oct. 7, 1925; m. Martha Jane Motz, Aug. 21, 1948; children: Elaine, Marlene, Linda, David. BS in Agr. and B in Agrl. Engring., Ohio State U., 1949, MS in Agrl. Engring., 1952; PhD in Agrl. Engring., Mich. State U., 1960. Registered profl. engr., Ohio. Prof. agrl. engring. Ohio State U., Columbus, 1949-61, 87-91, prof. emeritus, 1991—; product mgr. Massey Ferguson Ltd., Toronto, Can., 1961-66; product planning mgr. Ford Tractor Ops. div. Ford Motor Co., Troy, Mich., 1966-71, mktg. mgr., 1971-76, bus. planning mgr., 1978-87; v.p. mktg. and devel. Ford Aerospace div. Ford Motor Co., Dearborn, 1976-78. Author: Corn Harvesting, 1962. Served to 2d lt. USAF, 1943-45. Fellow Am. Soc. Agrl. Engrs. (pres. 1985-86, Gold medal 1993); mem. Nat. Acad. Engring., Country Club at Muirfield Village (Dublin, Ohio). Avocations: golf, tennis, bridge. Office: BJM Company Inc 6128 Inverurie Dr E Dublin OH 43017-9472

LAMP, FREDERICK JOHN, museum curator; b. Malvern, Pa., Nov. 20, 1944; s. Clyde Herman and Grace Ebersole (Landis) L.; m. Diane Frank, May 18, 1974 (div. 1984). BS, Kent State U., 1967; MA, Ohio U., 1971; PhD, Yale U., 1982. Adminstr., lectr. Mus. African Art, Washington, 1973-77; curator Balt. Mus. Art, 1981—. Author: Art of Baga, La Guinee, African Art of W Atlantic Coast; contbr. articles to profl. jours. Nat. Mus. Act degree fellow, 1977-79; rsch. grantee Nat. Endowment Arts, 1976-85, Social Sci. Rsch. Coun., 1979-81, 88, Smithsonian Instn., 1985, Fulbright, 1991-92, Nat. Gallery Art, 1995-96. Mem. Coll. Art Assn., African Studies Assn. (Arts council). Democrat. Avocations: collecting African art. Office: Balt Mus Art Art Museum Dr Baltimore MD 21218-3898 E-mail: flamp@artmba.org.

LAMPARELLO, PATRICK JOHN, surgeon, educator; b. Jersey City, Mar. 22, 1951; s. Patrick John and Julia Josephine (Castro) L.; m. Alexis Jane Rich, July 27, 1974; children: Patrick, Tracy, Emily, Ashley. BA magna cum laude, U. Pa., 1973; MD, Albert Einstein Coll. Medicine, 1976. Diplomate Am. Bd. Gen. and Vascular Surgery. From resident to chief resident Montefiore Med. Ctr., Bronx, 1976-80; fellow vascular surgery NYU Med. Ctr., N.Y.C., 1980-81, attending surgeon, 1981—, assoc. prof. surgery, 1991—; chief vascular surgery Manhattan VA Hosp., 1985-88; dir. vascular surgery Bellevue Hosp. Ctr., 1990—98; dir. vasc. surgery NYU Sch. Medicine, 1997—. Author: Current Therapy in Vascular Surgery, 1994; author book chpts. Coach Old Tappan (N.J.) Baseball Assn., 1984-93, Old Tappan Soccer League, 1986-90; team physician Northern Valley Jr. Football League, Bergen County, N.J., 1990-91. Named to Best Doctors Metro Area, Castle and Connolly, Best Doctor, N.Y. mag. Fellow Am. Coll. Surgeons: mem. N.Y. Vascular Soc. (coun. 1984—), Am. Assn. Vascular Surgeons, Ea. Vascular Soc., Perepheral Vascular Soc., N.Y. Cardiovascular Soc. (v.p. 1990—), Soc. Vascular Surgery, Ridgewood Country Club, Phi Beta Kappa. Roman Catholic. Avocations: golf, tennis, skiing. Office: NYU Med Ctr 530 1st Ave # 6F New York NY 10016-6402

LAMPARTER, WILLIAM C. printing and publishing consultant, digital printing and information systems specialist; b. Bklyn., July 13, 1929; s. William C. and Nadine (Lesch) L.; m. Ann E. Martyn; children: Ellen, Susan, David. BS, Springfield (Mass.) Coll., 1951; MS, Boston U., 1952. V.p., gen. mgr. Mead Digital Systems, 1975-78; pres. Nat. Assn. Printers and Lithographers, Teaneck, N.J., 1978-82, PrintCom Cons. Group, 1982—. Mem. adv. com. to Sch. of Printing Mgmt. and Scis., Rochester Inst. Tech., adv. to Graphic Arts Tech. and Edn. Ctr., bd. dirs. CIMSPrint, Inc.; internat. lectr. in field, prin. speaker Comprint Internat. Printing and Pub. Conf., Scotland, 1998; conf. organizer and prin. speaker Exec. Outlook NPES (assn. suppliers printing and pub tech.), Chgo. 1997—. Author: Forecast of Long-Term Business and Technological Trends in the Graphic Arts, 1968, transl. into Polish, Russian, 1973, The Electronic Superhighway Revolution 1994-1997-2000-2010, 1994, The Impact of the Information Superhighway on Traditional Print Media, 1995, Critical Trends Update - An Overview of Printing Industry Trends in the Year of the Digital Drupa, 1996, 2000, Management Guide to Digital Printing, 1996; prin. economist, author Printing Industry Quar. Bus. Indicator Report, 1979-85, Ann. Tech. Impact Rev., 1985, Interpretative Tech. Analysis, 1986, Printing Industry Materials Mgmt. Newsletter, 1985-86; pub., prin. editor FYI/HarbingerWatch, 1995—; contbg. editor Am. Printer mag., 1990—. Served with U.S. Army. Recipient Tech. Leadership award Nat. Assn. Printers and Lithographers, 1995, Neil Richards Visionary Leadership award Graphic Arts Mktg. Info. Svc., 2001. Mem. Graphic Arts Tech. Found. (Soc. of Fellows), Printing Industries Am. Inc., Nat. Assn. Printers and Lithographers, Tech. Assn. Graphic Arts, Rsch. and Engring. Coun. of Graphic Arts Industry Inc. (mem. exec. com. John L. Kronenberg Leadership award 1999), Assn. for Graphic Arts Tng., World Future Soc., Am. Soc. Quality Control, Soderstrom Soc., Inst. of Printing (London), Nat. Printing Equip. Assn. (former bd. mem.), Sigma Delta Chi. Office: 1020 Farm Creek Rd Waxhaw NC 28173-7793 E-mail: printcom@aol.com. *Commitment, developing people and combining their skills with the advantages of knowldege-based process control in a bottom-line oriented but innovative entrepreneurial atmosphere are the keys to success in today's changing business environment.*

LAMPE, HENRY OSCAR, securities trader; b. Bremen, Germany, Apr. 8, 1927; , parents U.S. citizens; s. Henry D. and Dorothea C. (Gatje) Lampe; m. Virginia Harvey, July 18, 1953 (dec. 1984); m. Margaret Sanger Marston, Mar. 4, 1989. BS with honors, Am. U., 1952. Investigator pub. safety Office Mil. Govt., Berlin, 1947-49; methods examiner Butr. Consular Affairs, Dept. State, 1952-53; investigator USIA, Office Security, 1953-55; budget examiner Resources and Civil Works divsn. Bur. Budget, Washington, 1955-58; v.p., br. mgr. Birely & Co., Washington and Arlington, Va., 1959-66; v.p. Thomson McKinnon Securities, Inc., Arlington, 1967-89, Prudential-SEcurities, Inc., Vienna, 1989-94; dir., treas. Med.-Tech., Inc. Cons., lectr. in field. Co-author: (book) Faculty Handbook, George Mason U., 1985. Mem. Joint George Mason U./Arlington County Adv. Bd., 1995—; active Arlington Sister City Assn., 1993—; past chmn. Arlington Com. 100, 1963; mem. bd. Arlington Sister City Commn., 1993—99; trustee Arlington Hosp. Found., 1986—89, sec., treas., 1988—89; trustee Arlington Hosp. Adv. Bd., 1991—96, Arlington Hosp., 1976—86, chmn., 1982—85; mem. bd. vis. George Mason U., 1980—88; vice chmn. Home Health Svcs. Co. Va., 1984—86; campaign chmn. Arlington Va. United Way, 1981; trustee United Way Met. D.C., 1982—90; mem. Va. Adv. Bd. Aging, 1971—78, White Ho. Conf. Aging, 1971, Arlington County Manpower Commn., 1974—76, No. Va. Regional Planning Commn., 1967—69; vice chmn. Va. Met. Areas Transp. Study Commn., 1970—74; mem. Va. Legis., 1970—72. With USN, 1945—46. Named Arlington County Man of the Yr., 1985; recipient Merit citation, U.S. Office Mil. Govt., Berlin, 1949, Lifetime Achievement award, Am. U., 1987, Voice and Vision award, 1996. Mem.: Bus. Roundtable, Arlington C. of C. (bd. dirs. 1985—92, exec. com. 1986—92, pres. 1990), Bond Club Washington Rep., Lions (Arlington). Lutheran. Avocation: gardening. Home: 2459 N Wakefield Ct Arlington VA 22207-3555

LAMPE, MARGARET SANGER, community activist; b. Tucson, Nov. 19, 1941; d. Stuart and Barbara (Peabody) Sanger; m. Donn Richard Marston, Mar. 21, 1961 (dec. 1988); children: Peggy Marston Van Cleave, Nancy Marston Skidmore, Michael Peabody Marston (dec.); m. Henry Oscar Lampe, Mar. 4, 1989. Student, U. Ariz., 1959-61, George Washington U., 1961-62. Office adminstr. L.T. Delyannis & Assocs., Arlington, Va., 1978-81, Bean, Kinney, Korman, Arlington, 1985-91. Pres., v.p., mem. PTA, Arlington, 1970-79; mem. task force delinquency prevention, Richmond, Va., 1976-78; mem., com. chair Va. Congress PTA, Richmond, 1975-79; mem., vice chair Va. Bd. Edn., Richmond, 1979-87; chmn. task force Nat. Inst. Edn., Washington, 1983; mem. Nat. Commn. Excellence in Edn., Washington, 1981-83; vice chair govt. affairs Nat. Assn. State Bds. Edn., Washington, 1984-85; bd. visitors Va. Poly. Inst. and State U., Blacksburg, 1988-92; mem. Arlington County Sch. Bd., 1995-96; v.p. Planned Parenthood Met. Washington, 1978-79, 99—; mem. women's com. Nat. Symphony, 1978-80; pres. Arlington Com. of 100; chmn. Arlington County Bicentennial Celebration Task Force, 2000-2001. Recipient Outstanding Citizen award Arlington County Schs., 1978, 84, Outstanding Svc. Plaque Pres. Reagan, 1984, Outstanding Woman in Press Va. Press Corp., 1986-87, Cmty. Voice & Vision award Cable TV, 1996, Arlington County Commn. on Statues of Women award, 2001, Woman of Vision award, 2001. Mem. Jr. League No. Va. (chair), Women's Econ. Roundtable, Rock Spring Garden Club, Commonwealth Cir., Neighbors' Club, Arlington Com. of 100 (chair 1999-2000). Avocations: travel, cooking, gardening. Home: 2459 N Wakefield Ct Arlington VA 22207-3555

LAMPE, RICHARD PAUL, biology educator; b. Albert City, Iowa, Mar. 30, 1947; s. Elwood Carl and Verna M. Lampe; m. Maxine Beth Lampe, Aug. 2, 1968; children: Nichole Lynn Johnson, Michael Richard. BS, Buena Vista Coll., Storm Lake, Iowa, 1969; MA, U. Kans., 1971; PhD, U. Minn., 1976. Asst. prof. biology Buena Vista Coll., 1976-81, assoc. prof. biology, 1981-88, prof. biology, 1988-91, dean, Sch. of Sci., 1986-91, dean of faculty, 1992-97; exec. v.p. Buena Vista U., Storm Lake, 1996-97, prof. biology, 1998—. Chair, Buena Vista Healthcare Found., 2000—, mem. Buena Vista Swan Restoration com., 1998—. Lutheran. Avocations: racquetball, hunting, fly fishing, fly tying, rod building. E-mail: lamper@bvu.edu.

LAMPEN, RICHARD JAY, lawyer, investment banker; b. New Brunswick, N.J., Nov. 12, 1953; s. J. Oliver and Miriam (Walsh) L.; m. Susan Matson, June 8, 1975; children: Katharine, Caroline. BA, Johns Hopkins U., 1975; JD, Columbia U., 1978. Bar: Fla. 1978, U.S. Dist. Ct. (so. dist.) Fla. 1978. From assoc. to ptnr. Steel Hector & Davis, Miami, Fla., 1978-86, co-chmn. corp. dept., 1992-95; mng. dir. Salomon Bros. Inc., N.Y.C., 1986-92; exec. v.p., gen. counsel New Valley Corp., Miami, Fla., 1995—; exec. v.p. Vector Group Ltd., 1996—. Bd. dir. New Valley Corp., Thinking Machines Corp., CDSI Holdings Inc., Ladenburg Thalmann Fin. Svcs. Inc. Pres. Miami Children's Mus.; bd. dir. Ransom-Everglades Sch. Mem. Fla. Bar Assn. (chmn. securities law com. 1985-86), City Club, Riviera Club. Office: New Valley Corp 100 SE 2nd St Fl 32 Miami FL 33131-2158 E-mail: rlampen@vectorgroupltd.com.

LAMPERT, ELEANOR VERNA, retired human resources specialist; b. Porterville, Calif., Mar. 23; d. Ernest Samuel and Violet Edna (Watkins) Wilson; m. Robert Mathew Lampert, Aug. 23, 1935; chidren: Sally Lu Winton, Lary Lampert, Carol R. John. Student in bus. fin., Porterville Jr. Coll., 1977-78; grad., Anthony Real Estate Sch., 1971; student, Laguna Sch. of Art., 1972, U. Calif., Santa Cruz, 1981. Bookkeeper Porterville (Calif.) Hos., 1956-71; real estate sales staff Ray Realty, Porterville, 1973; sec. Employment Devel. Dept. State of Calif., 1973-83; orientation and tng specialist CETA employees, 1976-80. Sec. Employer Adv. Group, 1973-80, 81—. Author: Black Bloomers and Han-Ga-Ber, 1986. Mem. U.S. Senatorial Business Adv. Bd., 1981-84, Rep. Nat. congl. Com., 1982-88, Sierra View Hosp. Vol. League, 1988-89 (pres.); charter mem. Presdl. Republican Task Force, 1981—, Republican National Committee; vol. Calif Hosp. Assn., 1983-89, Calif. Spl. Olympics Spirit Team, Sonora Community Hospital Oak Plus League, Special Olympics Northern Calif. partner. Recipient Merit Cert., Gov. Pat Brown, State of Calif., 1968. Mem. Lindsay Olive Growers, Sunkist Orange Growners, Am. Kennel Club, Internat. Assn. Personnel in Employment Security, Calif. State Employes Assn. (emeritus Nat. Wildlife Fedn., NRA, Friends of Porterville Library, Heritage Found., DAR (Kaweah chpt. rec. sec. 1988—), Internat. Platform Assn., Dist. Fedn. Women's Clubs (recording sec. Calif. chpt. 1988—), Ky. Hist. Soc., Women's Club of Calif. (pres. Porterville chpt. 1988-89, dist. rec. sec. 1987-89), Mo. Rep. Women of Taney County, Internat. Sporting and Leisure Club. Ladies Aux, VFW (No. 5168 Forsyth,Mo.), Ozark Walkers League, Women of the Moose Lodge, Humane Soc. U.S. Republican.

LAMPERT, LEONARD FRANKLIN, mechanical engineer; b. Mpls., Nov. 13, 1919; s. Arthur John Lampert and Irma (Potter) Smith. BME, U. Minn., 1943, B in Chem. Engring., 1959, MS in Biochemistry, 1964, PhD in Biochemistry, 1969. Registered profl. engr., Minn. With flight measurement rsch. dept. Douglas Aircraft Corp., El Segundo, Calif., 1943-47; researcher, tchr. U. Minn., Mpls., 1947-83; with rsch. engring. dept. Mpls. Honeywell Corp., 1950-55; info. scientist Control Data Corp., Mpls., 1982-88; mech. engr. Leonard Lampert Co., White Bear Lake, Minn., 1988—. Scientist Eurasion Watermilfoil Control, White Bear Lake, 1989—; stockholder rep. Lampert Lumber Co., St. Paul, 1988—. Contbr. articles to profl. jours. Mem. Am. Inst. Chem. Engrs. (award 1959), Am. Chem. Soc., U. Minn. Alumni Assn. (advisor) MIT Alumni Assn. (advisor), Phi Gamma Delta (advisor), Gamma Alpha, Phi Lambda Upsilon. Republican. Avocations: Ballroom dancing competitions, snow and water skiing, biking, geography, travel. Home and Office: 2467 S Shore Blvd Saint Paul MN 55110-3820

LAMPERT, MICHAEL ALLEN, lawyer; b. Phila., May 6, 1958; s. Arnold Leonard and Marilyn Lampert; 1 child, David Max. AB in Econs. cum laude, U. Miami, Coral Gables, Fla., 1979, postgrad., 1980; JD, Duke U., 1983; LLM in Taxation, NYU, 1984. Bar: Fla. 1983, D.C. 1984, Pa. 1984, U.S. Tax Ct. 1984, U.S. Ct. of Appeals for the Armed Forces 1995; U.S. Dist. Ct. (S. Dist. Fla.), 2000, bd. cert. tax lawyer, Fla. Bar. Assoc. Cohen, Scherer, Cohn & Silverman, P.A., North Palm Beach, Fla., 1984-88; instr. divsn. continuing edn. Fla. Atlantic U., Boca Raton, 1988—98; prin. Jacobson & Lampert, P.A., 1988—91; pvt. practice West Palm Beach, 1991—. Mem. editl. bd. South-eastern Tax Alert, 1993-97, Sales and Use Tax Alert, 1997—. Instr., trainer, past chpt. vice-chair, sect. bd. dirs. ARC, Palm Beach County, Fla.; bd. dirs. Jewish Fedn. Palm Beach County, 1989-91, 97-99, Jewish Family and Children's Svc. Palm Beach County, 1988—, treas., 1991-94, pres., 1997-99; pres. Jewish Residential and Family Svc., Inc., 1997—, T & M Ranch Cmty., Inc., 2000--; commr. Commn. for Jewish Edn.-Palm Beach, 1997-99; past mem. nat. planned giving com. Weismann Inst., Israel; mem. exec. bd., past v.p. planned giving Am. Soc. for Tech., Palm Beach. Recipient Young Leadership award, 1988, Safety award ARC, 1989, Cert. of Merit, Am. Radio Relay League, West Palm Beach Club, 1988, Cert. of Appreciation for Leadership, ARC Disaster Svcs., Palm Beach County, 1989, Disaster Svc. award, 1994, Human Resources award, 1993, Tax Law award Legal Aid Soc. of Palm Beach County and Palm Beach County Bar Assn., 1993, Young Leadership award Jewish Fedn. of Palm Beach County, 1998. Mem. Palm Beach Tax Inst. (pres., bd. dirs. 1993-94), Fla. Bar (exec. coun., mem. dirs. com. tax sect.), Palm Beach County Bar Assn. (chair bus. and corp. continuing legal edn. com. 1989-90, chair legal asst. com. 1988-91, Tax Law award 1993), Legal Aid Soc. of Palm Beach County, Inc. Avocations: aquatics, amateur radio, running. Office: Ste 900 1655 Palm Beach Lakes Blvd West Palm Beach FL 33401-2211 E-mail: lamperttaxlaw@att.net.

LAMPERT, S. HENRY, retired dentist; b. Bklyn., Mar. 10, 1929; s. Joseph and Sadie (Bass) L.; m. Jacqueline Adler, Mar. 27, 1955; children: Karen Ann, Beth Robin, Judith Ellen. BA, U. Ill., 1950; DDS, NYU, 1954. Intern in dentistry Mt. Sinai Hosp., N.Y.C., 1954-55; gen. practice dentistry Essex Junction, Vt., 1957-95; ret., 1995. Dir. Temporo Mandibular Joint Program, Med. Ctr. Hosp. Vt., Burlington, 1970-76, attending staff 1957-92, peer rev. com., 1978-92; mem. staff Fanny Allen Hosp., Winooski, Vt., 1961-89 ; assoc. prof. Sch. Allied Health Scis., U. Vt., Burlington, 1963-73, clin. instr. Coll. Medicine, 1974-75, clin. instr. dept. oral surgery, 1986-96. Sec., Vt. Bd. Dental Examiners, 1973-76, pres., 1976-77; instr. photography Church St. Ctr. for Cmty. Edn., U. Vt., until 1998; mem. N.E. Regional Bd. Dental Examiners, 1973-84, 96-98, cons. and examiner, 1996; lectr. in field; CPR instr. Vt. Heart Assn., 1977-2000; photographer Essex (Vt.) Reporter, 1997—; instr. photography Essex Town Parks and Recreation Dept., 1999—. Contbr. articles to profl. jours., photographs pub. in numerous mags. and jours. Capt. AUS, 1955-57. Fellow Internat. Coll. Dentists; mem. ADA (standard setting com. of coun. on nat. bd. exams. 1978-81), Champlain Valley (pres. 1961-62), Acad. Operative Dentistry, Vt. Dental Soc., Masons, Rotary, Alpha Omega. Jewish (bd. govs. synagogue 1967-70, 72-73, chmn. bd. edn.). Home: PO Box 667 Essex Junction VT 05453-0667 E-mail: jackie_ejvt@aol.com.

LAMPERT, WAYNE MORRIS, corporate financier; b. N.Y.C., Feb. 4, 1941; s. William B. and Fagel (Lefrak) L.; m. Sara Joyce Kirsch, Sept. 11, 1966 (div. 1978); children: Marcie Lynn, Warren Harris. BA, Syracuse U., 1962; LLD, Fordham U., 1965; MArch, U. Houston, 1992. Bar: N.Y. 1966, Fla. 1976, Tex. 1987, U.S. Customs Ct., U.S. Supreme Ct. Mgmt. intern Gen. Svcs. Adminstrn., Washington, 1965-66; atty. Legal Aid Soc., N.Y.C., 1966-67; asst. dist. atty. Kings County Dist. Atty.'s Office, Bklyn., 1967-69; pvt. practice Queens, N.Y., 1969-71, Miami, Fla., 1976-86; law sec. N.Y. State Ct. Claims, N.Y.C., 1971-73; chmn. bd. dirs. Texam Exploration Co., Inc., Houston, 1986-88; owner Vision Travel, Inc., Coral Gables, Fla., 1977-2000; dir., v.p. Lenway Mgmt., Inc., Fort Lauderdale, 1996—; pres. New Vision Travel Inc., 2000—. Tchr. law Charron Williams Coll., Miami, 1976-78. Bd. dirs. LeFrak Found., Queens, 1962-70, Youth Ednl. Coun., Ft. Lauderdale, Fla., 1965—; campaign mgr. Morris Kirsch for Bklyn. Borough Pres., 1973; pres. Boathouse of Hendricks Isle Condo Assn., 1999—. Fellow Met. Mus. Art; mem. Lawrence Yacht Club (treas. 1972-73), Sunshine Athletic Assn. Scuba Club (pres. 2001—), Neptune Flamingo Yacht Club (chaplain 1977-78, commdr. St. Thomas U.S. power squadron 1994-96), Kappa Phi Kappa, Phi Alpha Delta, Tau Sigma Delta. Republican. Avocations: fishing, boating, gardening. Office: 2400 E Las Olas Blvd # 124 Fort Lauderdale FL 33301

LAMPERT, ZOHRA, actress; b. N.Y.C. d. Morris and Rose (Eriss) L. BA, U. Chgo.; MA, CUNY; studies with Mira Rostova. Actress: (stage prodns.) Dancing in the Chequered Shade, 1955, Venice Preserv'd, 1955-56, Diary of a Scoundrel, 1956, Major Barbara, 1956, Maybe Tuesday, 1958, Look: We've Come Through, 1961 (Tony nomination), First Love, 1961, Mother Courage and Her Children, 1963 (N.Y. Drama Critics award 1973, Tony nomination), After the Fall, 1964, Marco Millions, 1964, The Natural Look, 1967, Lovers and Other Strangers, 1968, The Sign in Sidney Brustein's Window, 1972, Unexpected Guests, 1977, Drinks Before Dinner, 1978-79, Gifted Children, 1983, My Poppa's Wine, 1986, The Diary of Anne Frank, 1987, Mr. Gogol and Mr. Preen, 1991, A Day in New York, 1994-95, Krinsky, 1996, (feature films) Splendor in the Grass, 1961, A Fine Madness, 1966, Bye Bye Braverman, 1968, Let's Scare Jessica to Death, 1971, Opening Night, 1977, Alphabet City, 1984, The Cafeteria, 1986, Fakebook, 1989, Alan and Naomi, 1991, The Eden Myth, 1998 (TV series) Where the Heart is, 1970-71, The Girl with Something Extra, 1973-74, Doctors' Hospital, 1975-76, (TV movies) The Connection, 1972, Ladies of the Corridor, 1975, The Girl, The Gold Watch and Everything, 1979, Izzy & Moe, 1985, (TV spl.) Leonard Bernstein's Carmen for Omnibus; (TV episodes) Better Luck Next Time, 1964, The F.B.I., 1970, Love, American Style, 1972-73, The Bob Newhart Show, 1973, Kojak (Emmy award), 1975,

Quincey, 1979, others, also radio and TV commls. (Andy award). Recipient Ralph Weiler prize for painting, Louis La Beaume prize for painting Nat. Acad. Design. Mem. Actors' Equity Assn., AFTRA, AGVA, Nat. Acad. N.Y. Address: care David Williams Don Buchwald Agy 10 E 44th St New York NY 10017-3601

LAMPERTI, JOHN WILLIAMS, mathematician, educator; b. Montclair, N.J., Dec. 20, 1932; s. Frank A. and Louise (Williams) L.; m. Claudia Jane McKay, Aug. 17, 1957; children— Matthew, Steven, Aaron, Noelle. BS, Haverford Coll., 1953; PhD, Calif. Inst. Tech., 1957. Instr., then asst. prof. math. Stanford (Calif.) U., 1957-62; rsch. assoc. Rockefeller Inst., 1962-63; faculty Dartmouth Coll., Hanover, N.H., 1963-98, prof. math., 1968-98, prof. emeritus, 1998—. Sci. exch. visitor to USSR, 1970; vis. prof. U. Aarhus, Denmark, 1972-73, Nicaraguan Nat. U., 1990; cons. Am. Friends Svc. Com., 1980, 85, 91. Author: Probability: A Survey of the Mathematical Theory, 1966, 2d edit., 1996, Stochastic Processes: A survey of the Mathematical Theory, 1977, What Are We Afraid Of? An Assessment of the "Communist Threat" in Central America, 1988. Fellow Inst. Math. Stats.; mem. ACLU, War Resisters League, Peace Action, Amnesty Internat., Fedn. Am. Scientists. Home: Upper Loveland Rd Norwich VT 05055 Office: Dartmouth Coll Dept Math Hanover NH 03755 E-mail: j.lamperti@dartmouth.edu.

LAMPI, RAUNO ANDREW, food engineer; b. Gardner, Mass., Aug. 12, 1929; s. Oiva Anders and Olga (Tapola) L.; m. Betty Martha Noponen, Sept. 22, 1951; children: Steven R., Martin A., Karin O., Eric T. BS in Food Tech., U. Mass., 1951, MS in Food Tech., 1955, PhD in Food Tech., 1957. Registered profl. engr., Mass. Instr. U. Mass., Amherst, 1954-57; asst. mgr. food divsn. Foxboro (Mass.) Co., 1957-59; tech. dir. New England Apple Products Co. (now Veryfine Products, Inc.), Littleton, Mass., 1959-62; mgr. food tech. sect. Cen. Engring. Lab., FMC Corp., Santa Clara, Calif., 1962-66; packaging technologist Natick (Mass.) Rsch., Devel. and Engring. Ctr., U.S. Army, 1966-68, rsch. phys. scientist, 1968-76, supervising mech. engr., 1976-88, phys. sci. adminstr., 1988-89; ind. cons. food engr. Westboro, Mass., 1990—. Cons. Food and Agro Systems, Sunnyvale, Calif., 1990—, Orgn. Am. States, Campinas, Brazil, 1979, 81; lectr. NSF food engring. workshop, 1975, 2nd Internat. Congress Food and Engring., Helsinki, Finland, 1979, 2nd Internat. Symposium Catering Systems Design, Harrogate, Eng., 1979, Danish Soc. Food Tech. and Hygiene, Copenhagen, 1980, 11th Internat. Food Symposium, Japan External Trade Orgn., Tokyo, 1982, Inst. Food Technologists food svc. seminar, Chgo., 1989; R & D advisor Dept. Def., 1976-89. Contbr. chpt. to: Fundamentals of Food Canning Technology, 1979, Foodservice Systems, 1979, 3 others; contbr. articles to sci. publs.; inventor I-R detection of seal defects; patentee in field. 1st lt. USAF, 1951-53, Saudi Arabia. Recipient Col. Rohland Isker award R & D Assocs., 1969, Sr. award IEEE, 1974, Underwood-Prescott Meml. Symposium lectr. honor MIT, 1980, U.S. Army Exceptional Civilian Svc. medal; named Nat. Restaurant Assn. Newsmaker, 1979. Fellow Inst. Food Technologists (emeritus, Indsl. Achievement award 1978, Riester-Davis award 1995). Democratic. Lutheran. Avocations: motor homing, reading, walking, wood working. Home and Office: 20 Wheeler Rd Westborough MA 01581-3533

LAMPINEN, JOHN A. newspaper editor; b. Waukegan, Ill., Nov. 26, 1951; s. Walter Valentine and Patricia Mae Irene (Pruess) L.; m. Belinda Walter, Oct. 20, 1973; children: Amanda Michelle, Heidi Elizabeth. BS in Comm., U. Ill., 1973. Staff writer Paddock Cir. Newspapers, Libertyville, Ill., 1973-75; regional editor The Jour., New Ulm, Minn., 1975-76; various positions Daily Herald, Arlington Heights, Ill., 1976-90, asst. v.p., mng. editor, 1990-97, asst. v.p., exec. editor, 1997-99, v.p., exec. editor, 1999—. Adj. prof. Medill Sch. Journalism, Northwestern U., Evanston, Ill., 1995-98. Mem. Assoc. Press Mng. Editors, Soc. Profl. Journalists, Am. Soc. Newspaper Editors. Avocations: baseball, long-distance running, coaching girls softball, sports memorabilia. Office: Daily Herald 155 E Algonquin Rd Arlington Heights IL 60005-4617*

LAMPKIN, RALPH, JR. vocalist, nightclub consultant, producer, writer, coach; b. N.Y.C., Apr. 29, 1957; s. Ralph Sr. and Betty Jane (Rothschild) L. Vocalist Alice Tully Hall, Carnegie Hall, Copacabana, Grand Finale, Boltax, Arthur's Scene One, Small's Paradise, Parkwest, Rivera, Beefsteak Charlie's, His-n-Her's, Orphans, Centry Ctr., Gentry of Chgo., La cage aux Folles, 1971-85; booking mgr. Showcase One, Chgo., 1985; writer Jam Sessions, 1986; bd. dirs. Edgar Rd. Theatre Co., 1988; bus. mgr. Beaux-Arts Design Studio, South Bend, Ind., 1989-91, Serendipity Studios, South Bend, 1991—. Nightclub cons. Debbie Burrell, N.Y.C., 1979-81, Terry Burrell, N.Y.C., 1979-81, Denise Tomasello, Chgo., 1988-91, Michael DeLorenzo, 1978-81; song plugger Amanda McBroom, Alan Rich, David Freidman, Tom Snow, Tom Anderson, 1984—; with sound and lights team Michael Calabrese & Pudgy, Chgo., 1988—; sound team Michiana Arts Coun., South Bend, 1989, dir. Carnival of Arts, 1989-97; voice coach, Danny Lerman, South Bend, 1990; lyricist Frank DePaul, Ester Hana, Louis Montelione, Danny Lerman, Renee Lopez, 1980—; producer, engr. Danny Lerman, Wendy Como, Loretta Del Los Rios, Kristen Gustafson, Audrey Morris, Ester Hana, Bob Solone, Bob Moreen, Joel Barry, Alexandra Billings, Martha Lorin, Patti Morabito, Suzanne Petri, David Gurland, 1990—, Patti Morabito, Robin Kay; record prodr. Being Alive, Come Walk With Me, 2000; co-prodr. Cabaret on Record, 2001; prodr. nightclub appearances Alexandra Billings, Beckie Menzie, Cory Jamison, Patti Morabito, Tom Michael, Christianna Moffa, Lee Stevens, Sheree Sand, others; stage mgr. South Bend Civic Theatre, 1990—, bd. dirs., 1994-2001, dir. mus. series, 1995—. Midwest corr. (column) Cabaret Scenes, 1995-99; prodr. A Holiday Cabaret, Mercury Theatre, Chgo., 1999, A Holiday Cabaret, Chgo. Bailiwick Arts Ctr., 2000, Gypsy, Bailiwick Arts Ctr., Chgo., 2001; co-prodr. The Gershwin Concert, 1996, 97, Largely Live Starring Hinton Battle, Apollo Theatre, 1999 A Holiday Cabaret 2000, Bailiwick Theatre, 2000, Gypsy, Bailiwick Theatre, 2001; prodr. nightclub debut Alexandra Billings, 1997, 99, 2000, 01, Beckie Menzie, 1997, Cory Jamison, 1998, Patti Morabito, 1998, Tom Michael, 2000. Vol. Chgo. House, 1985-88; tech. dir. Stop AIDS Orgn., Chgo., 1989, 90, 91; produr. concert Muscular Dystrophy Assn., South Bend, 1990; stage dir. Follies 1989 to benefit St. Joseph and Michiana Hosp.; co-producer Aids Found. Benefit, 1999. Mem. ASCAP (6 spl. awards 1995-2000), Nat. Acad. Recording Arts and Scis., Manhatt an Assn. Cabarets. Home: 1614 S Taylor St South Bend IN 46613-2028

LAMPKY, JAMES ROBERT, bacteriology and mycology educator; b. Battle Creek, Mich., June 19, 1927; s. Howell Clayton and Viva Fay (McNally) L.; m. Shirley Ann Kellett, Dec. 28, 1971; children— Dawne, Diane, Judi, Lynda, Richard, Mark. B.S., Eastern Mich. U., 1955-59; M.A., U. Mo., 1961, Ph.D., 1966. Asst. prof. U. Wis.-Whitewater, 1962-66; from asst. prof. to prof. bacteriology and mycology Central Mich. U., Mt. Pleasant, 1966— . Contbr. articles to profl. jours. Fungal identification person Western Mich. Poison Control Ctr., Grand Rapids, 1978— . Served with U.S. Army, 1945-46. Mem. Am. Soc. Microbiology, Mich. Acad., Mycol. Soc., Soc. Indsl. Microbiology. Avocations: golfing, hunting, fishing, fine furniture making. Home: PO Box 20127 Myrtle Beach SC 29575-0020 Office: Central Michigan Univ Biolog Mount Pleasant MI 48859-0001

LAMPL, LEE ANN, internet marketing professional; b. Harrisburg, Pa. BA in Comm., U. Tex., Arlington, 1991. Sales assoc., customer svc. rep. Dillards Dept. Store, Arlington, Tex., 1991-92; inside sales rep. Doak Schoenemann & Co., Dallas, 1992, outside sales rep., 1993; sr. sales rep. John H. Harland Co., Irving, Tex., 1993-96; owner, operator McKinney (Tex.) Café, 1996-97; owner, artist Art Glass Kitchen, Dallas, 1997—; regional sales mgr. Kelly Svcs., 1997-98, Houston tech. support bus. mgr., 1998-99; outside sales rep. Houston Cellular Co., 1999—. Vol. The Family Pl., Dallas; vol. publicity dir. Tex. Visual Arts Assn., Dallas, 1990-91. Home: # B 1216 Welch St Houston TX 77006-1133 E-mail: leel@wt.net.

LAMPL, PEGGY ANN, public policy administrator; b. N.Y.C., Dec. 12, 1930; d. Joseph and Alice L. BA, Bennington Coll., 1952. Dir. program devel. dept. mental health AMA, Chgo., 1962-66; spl. asst. NIMH, HEW, Washington, 1967-69; public relations dir. LWV, 1969—73, exec. dir., 1973—78, exec, dur, 1984; dep. asst. Sec. of State for congressional relations Dept. State, 1978-81; dep. dir. Iris Systems Devel., 1982-83; exec. dir. Children's Def. Fund, Washington, 1984-89, LWV, Washington, 1989-98; project mgr. Crimes of War, W.W. Norton, 1999; founder Project Vote Smart, Washington, 1993—; bd. dirs. Crimes of War Project, 1998—. Home: 2500 Q St NW Washington DC 20007-4373

LAMPORT, ANTHONY MATTHEW, investments and venture capitalist; b. N.Y.C., Dec. 8, 1935; s. Harold and Golden (Siwek) L.; m. Cynthia Hullinger, 1961; children: Sarah, Aaron. BA, Harvard U., 1957, MBA, 1959. With Drexel Burnham Lambert, N.Y.C., 1959-90; pres. Lambda Fund, Mgmt., 1990—. Bd. dirs. Super Shuttle Internat., Prophesy Software, Sr. Bridge Family Cos. Trustee Securities Industry Assn. Found. Econ. Edn., N.Y.C., 1976—. Office: Lambda Fund Mgmt Inc 380 Lexington Ave New York NY 10022

LAMPSON, BUTLER WRIGHT, computer scientist; b. Washington, Dec. 23, 1943; s. Edward Tudor and Mary Caroline (Wright) L.; m. Lois Helen Alterman, Sept. 23, 1967; children: Michael Alterman, David Wright AB, Harvard U., 1964; PhD, U. Calif.-Berkeley, 1967; D.Sc. (hon.), Eidgenossiche Technische Hochschule, Zurich, 1986; D in Info. (hon.), U. Bologna, 1996. Asst. prof. U. Calif.-Berkeley, 1967-70, assoc. prof., 1970-71; dir. system devel. Berkeley Computer Corp., 1969-71; prin. scientist Xerox Research Ctr., Palo Alto, Calif., 1971-75, sr. research fellow, 1975-84; sr. cons. engr. Digital Equipment Corp., 1984-86, corp. cons. engr., 1986-93, sr. corp. cons. engr., 1993-95; arch. Microsoft Corp., Cambridge, Mass., 1995—, disting. engr., 2000—. Adj. prof. elec. engring. and computer sci. MIT, 1987—. Contbr. articles to profl. jours. Patentee in field Recipient IEEE Computer Pioneer award, 1996, Nat. Computer Sys. Security award NIST/NSA, 1998, von Neumann medal IEEE, 2001. Fellow AAAS, Assn. Computing Machinery (Software System award 1984, A.M. Turing award 1992); mem. NAE. E-mail: blampson@microsoft.com.

LAMPSON, NICK, congressman; b. Beaumont, Tex., Feb. 14, 1945; m. Susan Lampson; children: Hillary, Stephanie. BA, Lamar U., 1968, MA, 1974. Biology tchr. Beaumont Pub. Schs.; tax assessor-collector Jefferson County, Tex.; mem. U.S. Congress from 9th Tex. dist., 1997—; mem. sci., transp. and infrastructure coms. Del. White Ho. Conf. Aging, 1995; dir. Area Agy. Aging; active Am. Heart Assn., Land Manor, Young Men's Bus. Assn.; chair Bishop's Faith Appeal St. Jude Cath. Ch., 1995. Named Outstanding Young Man of Beaumont Tex. Jaycees, 1978. Office: US Ho of Reps 417 Cannon Ho Office Bldg Washington DC 20515-4309*

LAMS, EDMOND GEORGE, special education educator; b. Detroit, Jan. 30, 1941; s. Edmond Julius and Irene Margaret (Hornfischer) L.; m. Gabriela Helen Dudzinski, June 13, 1969; children Theresa Ann, Catherine Helene. AA, Macomb Community Coll., Warren, Mich., 1962; BS, Wayne State U., 1964, MEd, 1968. Cert. elem. spl. edn. tchr., tchr. cons., work study coord., social worker, Mich. Spl. edn. tchr. Roseville (Mich.) Community Schs., 1964-69; exec. dir. Macomb Assn. for Retarded Children, Mt. Clemens, Mich., 1969-76; tchr., coord. Edwin Denby Children's Home, Detroit, 1977-82; social worker, activity dir. Alexander Continuing Care Ctr., Royal Oak, Mich., 1983-84; spl. edn. tchr. Sanilac Intermediate Sch. Dist., Sandusky, 1984-91; work study coord., tchr. cons., transition specialist, rehab. coord., Medicaid coord., 1991—. Seminar tchr. Macomb Community Coll., Mt. Clemens, Mich., 1972; assoc. exec. Boy Scouts Am., Detroit, 1977. Tchr. Sacred Heart Ctr. Exceptional Children, Roseville, 1964-69; pres. Macomb Assn. Emotionally Disturbed, Roseville, 1967-69; scout master Boy Scouts Am. (handicapped troop), Warren, 1976-84. Recipient Spl. Tribute Mich. State Senate, 1975, Merit award Boy Scouts Am., Detroit, 1980. Mem. NEA, Mich. Edn. Assn., Sanilac Intermediate Edn. Assn., Coun. for Exceptional Children (charter mem. Pioneer Div.), Mich. Assn. Work Study Coords., KC. Roman Catholic. Avocations: gardening, experimental rose growing. Home: 1149 S Loree Rd Carsonville MI 48419-9323 Office: Sanilac Intermediate Schs 46 N Jackson St Sandusky MI 48471-1196

LAMSON, EVONNE VIOLA, therapist, health care administrator, consultant, pastor, Christian educator; b. Ithaca, Mich., July 8, 1946; d. Donald and Mildred (Perdew) Guild; m. James E. Lamson, Nov. 2, 1968; 1 child, Lillie D. A in Math., Washtenaw C.C., Ypsilanti, Mich., 1977; BS, Ea. Mich. U., 1989; MA in Pastoral Counseling, Ashland (Ohio) Theol. Sem., 1993. Lic. profl. counselor Mich.; cert. addiction counselor. Data base mgr. ERIM, Ann Arbor, Mich., 1978-81; mgr. product svcs. Comshare, 1981-90, project leader, tng. course designer info. techs., 1991-93; founder, pres. G & L Consultants, Brighton, Mich., 1982—; clin. supr. Brighton (Mich.) Hosp., 1993-99, 1016 Treatment Ctrs., Midland, Mich., 1999; program dir. Choices, Mt. Pleasant, 1999; chem. specialist Bay/Arenac Behavioral Health, Standish. Tng. specialist Comshare, Ann Arbor, 1990-93; assoc. pastor, dir. Christian edn. Keystone Cmty. Ch., Saline, Mich., 1993-95; founder Living Waters Counseling, 1993—. Study leader Brighton Wesleyan Ch., 1981-93; lic. minister Wesleyan Ch. Am., 1993-95; program dir. Wesleyan Womens Assn. of Brighton, 1983-91; clin. staff counselor Women's Resource Ctr., Howell, Mich., 1991-94; clin. counselor Livingston Counseling and Assessment, 1994-99, clin. team leader, 1995-97, clin. supr., 1997-99. Mem. AACD, NAFE, AACC, Am. Mgmt. Assn., Fairbanks Family of Am., Internat. Platform Assn. Avocations: skiing, motivational speaking, reading. Home: 3351 N Lakeside Dr Sanford MI 48657-9473 Office: 1000 W Cedar St Standish MI 48658-9421

LAMSON, GEORGE HERBERT, economics educator; b. Hartford, Conn., Feb. 21, 1940; s. Arroll Liscomb and Marguerite (Brechbuhler) L.; m. Susan Kathryn Lippert, Sept. 7, 1968; children: Scott, Brandon. AB, Princeton U., 1963; MA, Northwestern U., 1966, PhD, 1971. Research asst. Northwestern U. Econ. Survey of Liberia, Monrovia, 1962-63; instr. dept. econs. Loyola U., Chgo., 1967-68, U. Conn., Storrs, 1968-69; asst. prof. then assoc. prof. dept. econs. Carleton Coll., Northfield, Minn., 1969-80, Williams prof., 1981—, chmn. dept., 1978-84, 99-00. Cons. Minn. Higher Edn. Coordinating Com., St. Paul, 1971-72; textbook reviewer John Wiley & Sons, N.Y.C., 1979-82; reviewer NSF grad. fellowship program, 1988-90; vis. prof. U. Internat. Bus. and Econs., Beijing, China, 1994, 98; dir. Carleton Oversees seminar in econs. Cambridge, U.K., 1986, 91, 97, 2002; vis. scholar Chinese Acad. Social Scis., Beijing, 2001. Intersocietal studies fellow Northwestern U., 1966-67; recipient Faculty Devel. awards 1979, 90-91. Mem. Am. Econ. Assn., Midwest Econ. Assn., Minn. Econ. Assn. (bd. dirs. 1981-83, pres. 1984) Home: 4485 Detelemark Rd Dundas MN 55019-4050 Office: Carleton Coll Dept Econs Northfield MN 55057 E-mail: glamson@carleton.edu.

LAMSON, ROBERT WOODROW, retired school system administrator; b. L.A., Dec. 28, 1917; s. Ernest K. and Mabel (Mahoney) L.; m. Jeannette Juett, July 22, 1949; children: Robert Woodrow Jr., Nancy Virginia, Kathleen Patricia. BA, Occidental Coll., 1940; MA, U. So. Calif., 1955. Cert. tchr., prin., supt., Calif. Tchr. El Monte (Calif.) Sch. Dist., 1940-43, L.A. City Sch. Dist., 1945—78, prin., 1949-55, supr., 1955-57, adminstrv. asst., 1957-59, area supt., 1959-78; ret., 1978; agt. Keilholtz Realtors, La Canada, Calif. Instr. various colls. and univs. so. Calif.; one of founders, v.p., bd. dirs. U.S. Acad. Decathlon, Cerritos, Calif., 1981-86. Bd. dirs. 10th Dist. PTA, L.A., 1965-70; chmn. Scout-O-Rama, Gt. Western coun. Boy Scouts Am., 1980. Lt. comdr. USNR, 1943-46, mem. Res. ret. Mem. Am. Assn. Sch. Adminstrs., Assn. Adminstrs. L.A., Alumni Occidental Coll. in Edn. (a founder, past pres., bd. dirs.), Town Hall, Nat. PTA (hon. life), Calif. PTA (hon. life, bd. dirs. 1978-80), 31st Dist. PTA (hon. life, bd. dirs. 1965-78, auditorium named in his honor 1978), Phi Beta Kappa, Alpha Tau Omega. Republican. Avocations: gardening, reading. Home: 4911 Vineta Ave La Canada Flintridge CA 91011-2624 Office: Richard Keilholtz Realtors 727 Foothill Blvd La Canada Flintridge CA 91011-3405

LAMUNIÈRE, CAROLINE PARKER, artist; b. Cleve., Nov. 22, 1942; d. Lorand Victor Johnson and Dorothy (Strom) Ussher; m. Robert Parker, Sept. 7, 1966; children: Robert F. Parker Jr., Juliana Johnson; m. Jean Marie Lamunière, Oct. 23, 1991. BA in Art History, Skidmore Coll., 1965. Exhibited in group shows at Berkshire Mus., Pittsfield, Mass., 1977, Peel Gallery, Danby, Vt., 1980, 83, 85, 87-88, 91, Elain Starkman Gallery, N.Y.C., 1980, 84-86, Brocton (Mass.) Mus., 1982, Hood Coll., Frederick, Md., 1982, Albright Knox Mus., Buffalo, 1984, 87, Nat. Soc. for Painters in Acrylic & Casein, 1984, 86, 88, Franz Bader Gallery, Washington, 1987-89, 91; Gallaudet U., Washington, 1988, Ariel Gallery, N.Y.C., 1990-92, Lois Hodes Gallery, Balt., 1992, XX c. Art Gallery, 1992, 96-98, Hand Artes Gallery, Truchas, N.Mex., 1997, Woman Made Gallery, Chgo., Elaine eckwith Gallery, Jamaica, Vt., 1998, The Best of Acrylic Painting, 1996, Joyce Robbins Gallery, Santa Fe. N.Mex., 1999, Munson Gallery, Santa Fe, 2002. Address: 2953 Plaza Blanca Santa Fe NM 87507-6518

LAMY, M(ARY) REBECCA, land developer, former government official; b. Ft. Bragg, N.C., Nov. 21, 1929; d. Charles Joseph and Sarah Esther (Koonce) L. BA, U. N.C., Greensboro, 1952. Procurement analyst Air Force Mil. Interdept. Purchase Request Mgmt. Office, Washington, 1958-60, procurement and fiscal officer, 1960-68; budget analyst Naval Air Sys. Command, 1968-69, indsl. specialist, 1969-71, Armament Devel. and Test Ctr., Eglin AFB, Fla., 1971-74, Def. Logistics Agy., Alexandria, Va., 1974-81; logistics mgmt. specialist Strategic Sys. Project Office, Dept. Navy, Washington, 1981-82; procurement analyst Hdqrs. Dept. Army, 1982-85. Emeritus mem. Onslow Mus. Found. Bd., Richlands, NC, Onslow Meml. Hosp. Aux., Jacksonville, 1985—91. Recipient Outstanding Performance awards USAF, 1956, 65, 72, 73, Quality award Def. Logistics Agy., 1979, Outstanding Performance award, 1978, 79, Exceptional Svc. award, 1983, 84, 85, Comdr.'s award Hdqrs. Dept. Army, 1985, others. Mem. U. N.C. at Greensboro Alumni Assn.

LAN, DONALD PAUL, JR. lawyer; b. Orange, N.J., July 19, 1952; s. Donald Paul and Hannah Paula (Resnik) L.; m. Deborah Sue Rothenberg, Aug. 20, 1978; children: Jennifer Robyn, Adam Christopher, Eric Jacob. BS in Acctg., U. R.I., 1974; JD, Rutger U., 1977; LLM in Taxation, Georgetown U., 1982. Bar: N.J. 1977, D.C. 1978, Tex. 1983, U.S. Dist. Ct. N.J. 1977, U.S. Dist. Ct. (no., so., we. and ea. dists.) Tex. 1983, U.S. Ct. Claims 1978, U.S. Tax Ct. 1977, U.S. Ct. Appeals (fed. cir.) 1978, U.S. Ct. Appeals (5th cir.) 1984, U.S. Ct. Appeals (8th cir.) 1997. Clk. to spl. trial judge U.S. Tax Ct., Washington, 1977-78; trial atty. tax div. U.S. Dept. Justice, 1978-82; assoc., ptnr. Shank, Irwin & Conant, Dallas, 1982-87; ptnr. Finley, Kumble Wagner et al, 1987, Strasburger & Price, Dallas, 1988-96; shareholder Kroney, Mincey, Inc., 1996—. Adj. prof. law So. Meth. U., 1990—; lectr. on tax controversy and litigation, 1983—. Named Outstanding Atty. tax div. U.S. Dept. Justice, 1980. Mem.: ABA (ct. procedures com. tax sect. 1987—, stds. in tax practice com. tax sect. 1992—, chair 2001—), D.C. Bar Assn., Dallas Bar Assn., State Bar Tex. (chmn. ct. procedures com. tax sect. 1995—97, coun. mem. 1997—2000), Beta Gamma Sigma, Beta Alpha Psi, Phi Kappa Phi. Jewish. Avocation: all sports. Office: Kroney Mincey 12221 Merit Dr Ste 1210 Dallas TX 75251-2244

LAN, KEJIAN ALLAN, physicist, researcher, educator; b. China, Dec. 30, 1937; s. Chunlin Lan and Alice Wu; m. Yafei Chen, Sept. 27, 1967; 1 child, Di Lan. BS, Tsinghua U., 1961, MS, 1963. Asst. prof. Tsinghua U., Beijing, 1974-80, assoc. prof., 1980-87; chief engr., v.p. Huahai New Tech. Co., 1985-87; vis. rsch. scientist U. Houston, 1987-92, sr. rsch. scientist, 1992—. Co-author: Nuclear Electronics, 1986. Mem. IEEE (transactions on nuclear sci. sect.). Avocation: photography. Office: U Houston Dept Physics 4800 Calhoun Rd Houston TX 77204-5506

LAN, XUEKUI, engineer; came to U.S., 1991; BS, Xi'an (China) Jiaotong U., 1983, MS, 1986; PhD, Auburn U., 1995. Tchg. asst. Xi'an Jiaotong U., 1986-88, lectr., 1988-91; R&D engr. R&D Ctr. Beloit Corp., Rockton, Ill., 1995-98, product engr. R&D Ctr., 1998-2000; sr. project engr. ICEM CFD Engring., Livonia, Mich., 2000—. Contbr. articles to profl. jours. Mem. ASME (assoc.), Tech. Assn. Pulp and Paper Industry. Achievements include inventor of method and apparatus for coating a travelin paper web.

LA NATRA, JODI ANN, music educator, educator; b. Bklyn., Aug. 30, 1943; d. Claude and Rose (Cipolla) Pellegrino; m. George Salvatore La Natra, Dec. 10, 1966; children: Danielle, Nicole. BA, Bklyn. Coll., 1966; postgrad., Kean Coll., 1991—. Primary tchr. N.Y.C. Bd. Edn., Bklyn., 1966-72; pvt. practice music instr. Millburn, N.J., 1973—; early childhood, music literacy tchr. Music Preludes, Inc., 1981-89; early childhood, music literacy dir. Musically Yours, Inc., 1989—. Co-author: (music/early childhood literacy curriculum) Music Preludes, 1981. Recipient Comprehensive Musicianship cert. Internat. Piano Teaching Found. Mem. Music Educators Assn., Piano Tchrs. Soc. N.J. (exec. bd. mem. 1983—, judge of music evaluations 1984-86, high honor tchr. award 1982, 83, 84, 86). Roman Catholic. Avocations: reading, painting, traveling. Office: Musically Yours Inc 875 Ridgewood Rd Millburn NJ 07041-1412

LANC, JOHN JAN, civil and geodetic engineer, land surveyor; b. Prague, Czechoslovakia, Sept. 6, 1941; came to U.S., 1969; s. Frantisek Lanc and Marie (Bouchner) Kaderabek; 1 child, John R. Engring. diploma, Czechoslovakia Tech. U., 1963. Registered profl. engr. N.Y., N.J., Pa., Conn., Tex.; cert. profl. land surveyor N.Y., N.J., Pa., Conn.; cert. profl. planner N.J. Geodetic and civil engr. Konstruktiva, Prague, 1964-68; land surveyor Eustance & Horowitz, P.C., Circleville, N.Y., 1969-71, proj. engr., land surveyor, 1972-73, v.p., prin. engr., 1973-85; pres., prin. engr. Lanc & Tully Engring. and Surveying, P.C., Goshen, 1985—. Cons. engr. various villages, towns, cities N.Y. state, 1973—. Active Nat. Ski Patrol, N.Y., 1985—. Fellow Am. Congress on Surveying & Mapping; mem. ASCE, NSPE, Orange County & Sullivan Counties chpt. NSPE (pres. 1981-82), Profl. Engrs. in Pvt. Practice. Avocations: skiing (mem. Nat. Ski Patrol), sailing, tennis, kayaking. Home: 90 Susan Ln Circleville NY 10919-3250 Office: Lanc & Tully PO Box 687 Goshen NY 10924-0687

LANCASHIRE, DOUGLAS SAMUEL, mechanical engineer; b. Berea, Ohio, Aug. 4, 1967; s. Richard B. and Marilou (Cook) L.; m. Maria Santiago, March 9, 1991; children: Allen Michael, Derek Miguel, Stephen Samuel. BME, Ga. Inst. Tech., 1990. Registered profl. engr., Ohio. From design engr. to dept. mgr. The Osborn Engring. Co., Cleve., 1990-94, project mgr., 1994—, mgr. mech. engring., 1998—. Green Lights Surveyor Ally U.S. EPA, 1997—; spkr. in field. Author in field. Stewardship, promotion commn. officer Fairview (Ohio) Cmty. Ch., 1996—. Mem. Assn. Energy Engrs. (life), Am. Soc. Heating, Refrigerating, Air Conditioning Engrs., Inc., Order of the Engr. Am. Baptist. Achievements include leadership and technical expertise in the field of energy conservation; has performed energy audits at facilities across the U.S.; project mgr. for the implementation of the U.S. EPA's Energy Star Bldg. Showcase Program at the Frank J. Lausche State Office Bldg. in Cleve., Ohio. The award winning project resulted in an annual energy savings of more than 35% for the building, one of only 25 bldgs. selected nationwide to participate in this pilot program. Office: The Osborn Engineering Co 1300 E 9th St Ste 1500 Cleveland OH 44114-1573

LANCASTER, ALDEN, educational and management consultant; b. Balt., Feb. 25, 1956; d. Henry Carrington and Martha (Roe) L. BA magna cum laude, Duke U., 1977; MA, George Washington U., 1979. Program designer, coord. Duke U. and George Washington U., Durham, N.C., 1977-79; mgr. profl. devel. programs Nat. Assn. Coll. and Univ. Bus. Officers, Washington, 1979-80; assoc. dir. refugee relief agy. Ch. of the Saviour, Bangkok, Thailand, 1980-81; dir. cmty. svcs. U.S. Cath. Conf. Refugee Resettlement Agy., San Diego, 1981-82; nat. project dir. Bread for the World Ednl. Fund, Washington, 1982-83; edn. dir., exec. dir. Ptnrs. for Global Justice, 1983-85; dir. adult edn. programs, tchr. Spanish Ednl. Devel. Ctr., 1983-86; exec. dir., cons. Samaritan Ministry Greater Washington, 1985-87; career counselor, tng. cons. Rockport Inst., Washington, 1985—; dir. nat. literacy tng., ednl. cons. Assn. for Community Based Edn., 1987—; mgmt. cons. Women's Tech. Assistance Project, Ctr. Cmty. Change, 1988-89; ednl. cons. George Washington U., 1989-93, Pub./Pvt. Ventures, Phila., Savannah, Ga., Ft. Lauderdale, Fla., 1990-91; sr. cons., dir. nat. literacy projects Wider Opportunities for Women, Washington, 1991-94. Mem. nat. adv. bd. Project Lifelong Learning, Pa. State U. Inst. for Study Adult Literacy, 1992-93; sr. ednl. cons. United Way of Am., 1992—; curriculum devel. cons. Eckerd Family Youth Alternatives, Clearwater, Fla., 1993-94; sr. literacy staff devel. and evaluation cons. Nat. Inst. Literacy, 1993—; sr. program and staff devel. cons. Ramah Navajo Sch. Bd., Pine Hill, N.Mex., 1993—; adj. assoc. prof. George Washington U. Grad. Sch. Edn., 1993; sr. cons. State of Utah Dept. Edn., 1994; sr. contextual literacy cons. Friends of the Family, Inc., Balt., 1994—; sr. literacy staff devel. participatory evaluation cons. State of Maine, 1994-96; sr. contextual literacy cons. State of S.C. Literacy Resource Ctr., 1995-96; staff devel. cons. Centro de Estudios de Espanol Pop Wuj, Quetzaltenango, Guatemala, 1995; sr. adult literacy expert Atlantic Resources Corp., Manassas, Va., 1995-97; tng. of trainers cons. Neighborhoods, Inc., Battle Creek, Mich., 1995-96; sr. adult literacy advisor Am. Inst. for Rsch.—CIR, Roslyn, Va., 1996—; trainer of trainers, author, evaluator D.C. Literacy Resource Ctr., 1996—; ednl. TV outreach cons., Mars Hill and York TV Assocs., 1996—; sr. cons. mgmt. and orgnl. devel., tng. and career devel. McNeil Techs. for Dept. Energy, Energy Efficiency and Renewable Energy, 1997—, and for Dept. of Commerce, Office of Civil Rights, 1999; new sch. proposal expert reviewer D.C. Pub. Charter Sch. Bd., Washington, 1997—; mgmt. devel. cons. Laubach Lit. Action, Syracuse, N.Y., 1997—. Co-author: National Institute for Literacy 1992-93 National Literacy Grants Final Report, 1995; author: An Introduction to Intergenerational Literacy, 1992; co-author: (with Thomas G. Sticht) Functional Context Education: A Primer for Program Providers, 1992; editor, primary author: Literacy for Empowerment: A Resource Handbook for Community Based Educators, 1989. Democrat. Mem. Soc. Friends. Home and Office: 6708 Poplar Ave Takoma Park MD 20912-4810

LANCASTER, BARBARA MAE, management consulting company executive; b. Stafford Springs, Conn., Feb. 18, 1930; d. Harold D. and Ruth (Bristol) Stebbins; m. Colin T. Lancaster, June 5, 1948 (div. July 1979); children: Wayne, Sharon, Kevin, Karen, Kim. BS in Commerce, Rider Coll., 1981, MBA, 1984. CPA, N.J.; cert. fin. planner, life underwriter; chartered fin. cons. Acct. Electro Mech. Research, Princeton Junction, N.J., 1963-70; treas. Raritan Valley Ceilings, Inc., Monmouth Junction, 1970-78; adminstrv. asst. Total Enterprises, Princeton, 1979-81; pres. Lancaster Mgmt., Inc., Monmouth Junction, 1981—. Tchr. Adult Sch., South Brunswick, N.J., 1986-94; adj. prof. Rutgers U., 1989, also vis. prof.; speaker in field. Author: Entrepreneurial Training Institute Course I-Business Plan, 1994, Guide to Living Styles for Retirees-Professional Education, 1995. Mem. small bus. adv. com. Princeton C. of C., 1984-90; mem. adv. bd. Small Bus. Devel.Ctr., Newark, 1986-96, Nat. Coun. Aging, 1995—; chair N.J. Devel. Authority for Small Bus., Minorities and Women's Enterprises, 1991-94. Named Advocate of Yr., U.S. SBA, N.J., 1987. Mem. Nat. Assn. Women Bus. Owners (treas. N.J. chpt. 1987—), N.J. Assn. Women Bus. Owners (pres. 1986-88), Women Life Underwriters Conf. (pres. 1987-88, nat. pres. 1991-92), Bus. and Profl. Women, Mid-Atlantic Venture Capital (v.p. 1988). Democrat. Avocations: dancing, playing piano. Home and Office: 112 Appletree Ct Monmouth Junction NJ 08852-2102 E-mail: blanc@superlink.net.

LANCASTER, CARROLL TOWNES, JR. business executive; b. Waco, Tex., Mar. 14, 1929; s. Carroll T. and Beatrice (Hollaman) L.; m. Catherine Virginia Frommel, May 29, 1954; children: Loren Thomas, Barbara, Beverly, John Tracy. Student, U. Tex., 1948-51, 52-53. Sales coord. Union Tank div. Butler Mfg. Co., Houston, 1954-56, sales rep. New Orleans, 1956-57, br. mgr., 1957-60; asst. to exec. v.p. Maloney-Crawford Mfg. Co., Tulsa, 1960-62; mktg. cons., sr. assoc. Market/Product Facts, 1962-63; market devel. asst. Norriseal Controls divsn. Dover Corp., Houston, 1963-66; area dir. Arthritis Found., 1966-69, regional dir., 1969-71; exec. dir. United Cerebral Palsy, Tex. Gulf Coast, 1971-74, Leukemia Soc. Am., Gulf Coast, 1974-76, Lancaster & Assocs., 1976—. Christian edn. tchr., 1970, supr. 1971, asst. youth football coach, Bellaire, 1967-68, 70-71; mem. Houston-Galveston Area Health Commn. Study Group, 1972-76, co-chmn. 1976; dir. essayist Tex. Low Vision Coun., 1976-79, sec.-treas., 1978-81, pres. 1981-85; pres. Bellaire Civic Action Club, 1987-88, del. Houston Interfaith Sponsoring Com., 1979-81; bd. dirs. Coun. Chs. Greater Houston, 1966-68, v.p. 1968. With USNR, 1946-48, 51-52. Recipient award for securing free blood for indigent Harris County Hosp. Dist., 1968. Mem. Am. Mktg. Assn., Huguenot Soc., Military Order of Stars and Bars, San Marcos Acad., Ex-Students Assn. (pres. 1982-84), SAR, Delta Sigma Phi. Episcopalian (vestryman 1975-78). Home: 6900 County Road 261 Zephyr TX 76890-3779

LANCASTER, H(AROLD) MARTIN, former congressman, former presidential advisor, academic administrator; b. Patetown Community, N.C., Mar. 24, 1943; s. Harold Wright and Eva (Pate) L.; m. Alice Matheny; children: Ashley Elizabeth, Mary Martin. AB, U. N.C., 1965, JD, 1967. Asst. staff judge adv. 12th Naval Dist., San Francisco, 1968; staff judge adv. USN, USS Hancock, 1968-70; ptnr. Baddour, Lancaster, Parker, Hine & Keller P.A., Goldsboro, N.C., 1970-86; rep. N.C. Gen. Assembly, Raleigh, 1978-86; mem. 100th-103rd Congresses from 3d N.C. dist., Washington, 1987-94; spl. advisor to the President on chem. weapons, 1995; asst. sec. of the Army, 1996-97; pres. N.C. Cmty. Coll. Sys., 1997—. Mem. armed svcs. com., readiness subocm., mil. pers. subcom.; chmn. morale, welfare and recreation panel; small bus. com. Mcht. Marine and Fisheries com.; chmn. judiciary com. N.C. Ho. of Reps., 1983-86; chmn. hwy. safety com., 1981-83; chmn. congrl. study group on Germany, 1994, North Atlantic Assembly, 1989-94; former mem. numerous other coms.; bd. dirs. Nat. Ctr. Family Literacy, 1998—, Global Transpark Auth., 1997—, N.C. Global Ctr., N.C. Pub. Sch. Forum, 1997—. Chmn. N.C. Arts Coun., 1977-81, Goldsboro Wayne Bicentennial Commn., 1975-76; pres. Community Arts Coun., 1973-74, Wayne Community Concert Assn., 1972-73; chmn. bd. trustees Wayne County Pub. Libr., 1979-80; chmn. Wayne chpt. ARC, 1978-79; mem. adv. bd. Z. Smith Reynolds Found.; deacon First Presbyn. Ch., 1972-75, elder, 1980-86; elder White Meml. Presbyn. Ch., 2002—, chmn. worship com., 2002—. Recipient Disting. Svc. award Goldsboro Jaycees, 1977, N.C. Crime and Justice award Gov.'s Crime Commn., 1984, Spl. award Gov.'s Adv. Coun. for Persons with Disabilities, 1985, Valand award Mental Health Assn. N.C., 1985, Outstanding Legislators awards Neuse River Coun. Govts., N.C. Assn. Sch. Counselors, Nat. Security Leadership award, 1987, 89, 90, 91, 92, Sound Dollar award, 1988, 89, 90, Spirit of Enterprise award U.S. C. of C., 1989, 92, 93, Doer of Deeds award House Leadership, 1989, Pub. Health Svc. award N.C. Primary Care Assn., 1991, Charles Dick Medal of Merit, U.S. Nat. Guard Assn., 1992, Tad Davis Meml. award, U.S. Mil. Sports Assn., 1992; named N.C. and U.S. Alumnus of Yr., 4-H, 1987, Knight Comdr. of the Ct. of Honor, 1994, 33 degree Mason Scottish Rite, 1997, Silver Order of the de Fleuriers (Corps of Engrs.), 1997, Tar Heel of the Week, Raleigh News and Observer, 2000, Outstanding Alumnus U. NC Sch. of Law, 2002. Mem. ABA, Assn. Trial Lawyers Am., N.C. Bar Assn. (bd. govs.), Eighth Jud. Dist. Bar Assn., N.C. Acad. Trial Lawyers (Outstanding Legislator award), Wayne County Hist. Soc. Lodges: Masons (33d degree), Shriners, Elks. Office: NC Cmty Coll Sys 200 W Jones St Raleigh NC 27603-1378 E-mail: martinl@nccs.cc.nc.us.

LANCASTER, JEANETTE (BARBARA LANCASTER), dean, nursing educator; BSN, U. Tenn.; MSN, Case Western Res. U.; PhD, U. Okla. Staff nurse U. Tenn.; nurse clinician Univ. Hosps. of Cleve.; assoc. prof. psychiat. nursing Tex. Christian U.; coord. cmty. health nursing U. Ala., Birmingham, chair master's degree program Sch. Nursing; dean, prof. Sch. Nursing Wright State U., Dayton, Ohio; now dean, prof. nursing U. Va., Charlottesville; assoc. dir. patient care svcs. U. Va. Health Scis. Ctr. Former chmn. bd. dirs. Va. Statewide Area Health Edn. Ctr.; former pres. Charlottesville and Albemarle divsn. Am. Heart Assn.; presenter in field. Author: Community and Public Health Nursing: Nursing Issues in Leading and Managing Change; editor: Family and Cmty. Health; contbr. Bd. dirs. U. Va. Women's Ctr., Hospice of the Piedmont. Recipient Disting. Alumni award Frances Payne Bolton Sch. Nursing, Case We. Res. U., 1984, Outstanding Alumni award, U. Tenn. Coll. Nursing, 1985, honored with establishment of Jeanette Lancaster Professorship in Nursing, 1999. Fellow: Am. Acad. Nursing; mem.: Am. Assn. Colls. Nursing and Hospice Piedmont (bd. dirs.), Am. Assn. Colls. Nursing (bd. dirs.). E-mail: lancaster@virginia.edu.

LANCASTER, JOHN HOWARD, civil engineer, consultant; b. Bklyn., July 3, 1917; s. George York and Alice Eliot (Littlejohn) L.; m. Phyllis Elaine Metcalf, June 1, 1938; children: Judith Ann, Barbara Jean, Marylin Sharon, Kathryn Joy, Debra Elizabeth. BS, Worcester (Mass.) Poly. Inst., 1939. Registered profl. engr., N.Y., N.Mex.; lic. master mariner USCG. Engr. Austin Co., N.Y.C., 1939-40; engr. C.E., 1940-42, asst. to divsn. engr., 1942-43; chief engrng. and constrn. AEC, Upton, N.Y., 1946-54; chief project engr. Brookhaven Nat. Lab., 1954-72; asst. dir. Nat. Radio Astronomy Obs. and program mgr. very large array radiotelescope program, Socorro, N.Mex., 1972-81; propr. John H. Lancaster & Assocs. (cons. engrs.), 1950-72; cons. NRAO/Associated Univs. Inc., 1981—. Cons. in field, 1970—; bd. dirs., sec. corp. Seven Seas Cruising Assn., 1994-96; cons. NSF, 1970, Cornell U., 1971, Fermi Nat. Accelerator Lab., 1980. Bd. dirs. Good Samaritan Nursing Home; treas. Socorro Pub. Libr. With USNR, 1942-46. Recipient Meritorious Service award NSF, 1976 Mem. NSPE, N.Y. Soc. Profl. Engrs., N.Mex. Soc. Profl. Engrs., N.Mex. Tech. Club, Rotary, Masons, Scottish Rite, Shriners, Ea. Star, Sigma Xi, Alpha Tau Omega. E-mail: lancastereja@aol.com.

LANCASTER, JOHN LYNCH, III, lawyer; b. Dallas, Nov. 10, 1936; s. John Lynch Jr. and Loretta Charlotte (Delaney) L.; m. Jane Frances Riddle, Sept. 5, 1959; children: Delaney, John, Jim, Student, Washington and Lee U., 1954-56; BA, U. Tex., 1958, LLB, 1960. Bar: Tex. 1960; diplomate Am. Bd. Trial Advs. Ptnr. Jackson Walker, L.L.P., Dallas, 1962—. Mayor Town of Highland Park, Tex., 1984-86. Fellow Am. Coll. Trial Lawyers; mem. Inn of Ct. (master). Office: Jackson Walker LLP 901 Main St Ste 6000 Dallas TX 75202-3797

LANCASTER, KENNETH G. lawyer; b. Stafford Springs, Conn., Dec. 6, 1949; s. Talbot Augustin and Helen Collier (McRae) L.; m. Margaret Jane Royer, Aug. 25, 1973; children: Kimberly Jane, John Talbot, Christopher Andrew. BA, U. Miami, 1971, JD, 1974. Bar: Fla. 1974, U.S. Dist. Ct. (so. dist.) Fla. 1975, U.S. Dist. Ct. (mid. dist.) Fla. 1976. Adminstr. Met. Dade County, Miami, Fla., 1971-73; assoc. Robert A. Spiegel, Coral Gables, 1973-78; sole practice South Miami, 1978-80; ptnr. Clark, Dick & Lancaster, 1980-87, King & Lancaster PA, South Miami, 1987—. Cons. 1st City Bank Dade County, Miami, 1983-84; dir. U. Miami Bus. Sch. Bd. dirs., pres.-elect U. Miami Hall Fame, Coral Gables, 1984—, mem. U. Miami endowment com., 1982—; mem. Atty.'s Title Ins. Fund, 1982—. Mem. ABA, Fla. Bar Assn., Dade County Bar Assn. (Disting. Svc. award 1984), Dade County Attys. Real Property Coun., Hurricane Club/U. Miami (bd. dirs. 1984—, pres. 1996-97). Home: 10241 SW 141st St Miami FL 33176-7005 Office: King & Lancaster PA 5975 Sunset Dr Ste 703 Miami FL 33143-5198

LANCASTER, KIMBERLY MEIRON (KC LANCASTER), artist; b. D.C., Jan. 28, 1965; d. James Edward and Donna Jeanne (Wilmot) Chase; m. William Christopher Rolls Lancaster, Apr. 21, 1990. Line worker Teledyne Waterpik, Ft. Collins, Colo., 1983-84; key operator Miracle Printer, 1984-85, Kwik Kopy, Lakewood, Colo., 1985-86, Copy Boy, Denver, 1986-87; supr. Kinko's Copies, Boulder, Colo., 1988-95; owner, operator Kirin Graphics, Northglenn, 1995—. Artist White Mountain (Colo.) Souvenir Co., 1996-97; art dir., artist Alderac Entertainment Group, Inc., 1997—. Author, artist: Night Shade, Ltd., 1996. Mem. Soc. Creative Anachronism (illuminator-chronicler Ft. Collins, Denver 1982-84, craftsperson 1984-94), Internat. Fantasy Gaming Soc. Democrat. Avocations: crafts, painting, writing, reading, exercise.

LANCASTER, LISA MARIE, law enforcement officer; b. Worcester, Mass., Nov. 13, 1966; d. William Peter Ben and Willie Mae (Blyther) L.; m. James T. Spencer, Jr., July 15, 1987 (div. July 1988). Student, Lincoln U., 1984-85, U. S.C., 1986; B, Community Coll., Dover, Del., 1991; A in Criminal Justice, C.C. of the Air Force, Wilmington Coll., 1990; BS in Behavioral Sci., Wilmington Coll., 1996; postgrad., Wesley Coll., 1991—, Wilmington Coll. E-1 3743 BMTS USAF, Lackland AFB, Tex., 1985-86; E-2, E-3 363 SPS USAF, Shaw AFB, S.C., 1986-88; E-4 8th SPS USAF, Kunsan Air Base, Korea, 1989-90; E-5 436 SPS USAF, Dover, 1990—; D.A.R.E. instr. Sch. Ill. Police Acad., 1993; police officer New Castle County Police, New Castle, Del., 1994—. Pres. dorm coun. 363 SPS, Shaw AFB, 1986-88; K-55 radar cert. 436 SPS, Dover, 1991—; drug identifier Del. State Police Acad., Dover, 1991—. Rep. Worcester (Mass.) Youth Games, 1982-84; counselor Worcester City Boys & Girls Camp, 1983-84; social worker Shelter for Abused Children, Sumter, S.C., 1987-88; vol. Shelter for Homeless, Kunsan, 1989-90; tchr. Drug Abuse Resistance Edn., 1993; active Big Sister program; asst. girls basketball coach Pauda Acad., 1996-97. Mem. NAACP (Del. charter), 436 Security Policy Booster Club (sec. 1990—). Democrat. Baptist. Avocations: basketball, running, horseback riding, bicycling, tennis. Office: 3601 N Dupont Hwy New Castle DE 19720-6315 Home: 927 S 13th Ct Nashville TN 37206-3161

LANCASTER, MICHAEL DEAN, artist, marketing executive; b. Sarasota, Fla., Nov. 9, 1955; s. Stuart Guage Lancaster and Betty Deane Warren; m. Barbara Wood Harnack, Aug. 29, 1981; 1 child, Amrit Ringling. Founder, pres. Malen Bridge (N.Y.) Pottery, 1979-87; pres. Malden Bridge Art Ctr., 1981-87; head of ceramics Malden Bridge Sch. of Art, 1981-87; pres. Historic Malden Bridge Playhouse Soc., 1983-86; v.p. New World Subliminals, Santa Fe, 1987-89; co-dir. Children's Workshop, Cerrillos, 1993-96. Pres. N.J. Lancaster Fine Art, Madrid, 1987-98; pres., curator N.J. Lancaster, 1998—. Bd. dirs. Internat. Friends of Transformative Art, Scottsdale, Ariz., 1991-93; vol. Kitchen Angels, Santa Fe, 2001. Avocations: studio pottery, architecture and design. E-mail: njlancaster@iglide.net.

LANCASTER, RALPH IVAN, JR. lawyer; b. Bangor, Maine, May 9, 1930; s. Ralph I. and Mary Bridget (Kelleher) L.; m. Mary Lou Pooler, Aug. 21, 1954; children: Mary Lancaster Miller, Anne, Elizabeth Peoples, Christopher, John, Martin. AB, Coll. Holy Cross, 1952; LLB, Harvard U., 1955; LLD (hon.), St. Joseph's Coll., 1991. Bar: Maine 1955, Mass. 1955. Law clk. U.S. Dist. Ct. Dist. Maine, 1957-59; ptnr. firm Pierce Atwood, Portland, Maine, 1961—, mng. ptnr., 1993-96; ind. counsel In Re Herman apptd. by spl. divsn. D.C. Ct. Appeals, 1998—2001. Condr. trial advocacy seminar Harvard U.; lectr. U. Maine; chmn. merit selection panel U.S. Magistrate for Dist. of Maine, 1982, 88; bd. visitors U. Maine Sch. Law, 1991-96, chair, 1991-93; spl. master by appointment U.S. Supreme Ct. in State of N.J. vs. State of Nev. et al, 1987-88; mem. 1st Ctr. Adv. Com. on Rules, 1991-96, legal adv. bd. Martindale Hubbell, Lexis Nexis, 1990—; represented U.S. in Gulf of Maine in World Ct. at The Hague, 1984; U.S. Supreme Ct. apptd. spl. master Commonwealth of Va. vs. State of Md., 2000—. Former mem. Diocese of Portland Bur. Edn. With U.S. Army, 1955-57. Mem. Maine Jud. Coun., Am Coll. Trial Lawyers (chmn. Maine 1974-79, bd. regents 1982-87, treas. 1985-87, pres. 1989-90), Maine Bar Assn. (pres. 1982), Cumberland County Bar Assn., Canadian Bar Assn. (hon.). Republican. Roman Catholic. Home: 162 Woodville Rd Falmouth ME 04105-1120 Office: 1 Monument Sq Portland ME 04101-4033 E-mail: RLancaster@PierceAtwood.com.

LANCASTER, SALLY RHODUS, non-profit consultant; b. Gladewater, Tex., June 28, 1938; d. George Lee and Milly Marie (Meadows) Rhodus; m. Olin C. Lancaster, Jr., Dec. 23, 1960; children: Olin C. III, George Charles, Julie Meadows. BA magna cum laude, So. Meth. U., 1960, MA, 1979; PHD, Tex. A&M, Commerce, 1983. Tchr. English pub. schs., 1960-61, 78-79; exec. v.p., sr. advisor Meadows Found., Inc., Dallas, 1979-96, also trustee and dir. Trustee So. Meth. U., 1980—88, East Tex. State U., regent, 1987—93; Tex. del. White House Conf. on Tourism, 1995; dir. Inst. Nautical Archaeology, 1988—2001; dir. emeritus Meadows Found.; mem. adv. bd. Cmtys. Found. Tex. Named Disting. Alumni, So. Meth. U., Tex. A&M Commerce; recipient Ruth Lester award Tex. Hist. Commn., 1998; grantee-making and evaluations coms. Jacksonville Cmty. Found., 2000-01. Mem. Plantation Ladies Assn. (pres. 2000-01), Philos. Soc. Tex., Phi Beta Kappa. Presbyterian. E-mail: srhodusl@aol.com.

LANCASTER, TINA, real estate executive, small business owner, rancher; b. Austin, Tex., July 21, 1939; d. Ernest Thomas and Dorothy A. (Loya) Prado; children from a previous marriage: Christina M., Joseph P., M. Kathleen. Student, U. Notre Dame, St. Mary's Coll., South Bend, Ind., 1958-62, U. Pa., Austin Sch. of Bus./Real Estate, 1982-86. Cert. realtor, Tex.; inernat. cert. yoga instr. Owner, pres. Diversified Properties, Austin, 1972—; owner, publisher Austin Home & Gardens, 1978-84, San Antonio Homes & Gardens, 1978-84, The Catholic Journal, Austin, 1978-84; owner, pres. Diversified Prodns., 1978—; owner Escondido Internat. Bazaar, 1984—, Escondido Ranch, Austin, 1984—; owner, dir. Women's Health & Fitness Ctr., 1986-93, Diversified, USA, water purification and desalianation R & D; Diversified Cos.; Diversified Worldwide. Freelance hist. writer. Bd. dirs. Mayor's Alternative Sources of Income Com., Austin, 1982, Bowie High Sch., Austin, 1989-90; mem. adv. bd., exec. com., sec. City of Austin Parks and Recreation; mem. adv. bd. South Austin Sr. Activity Ctr. Named Most Successful Woman, Mexican-Am. Profl. Women's Assn., 1981. Mem. U.S. Bd. of Realtors, Tex. Bd. of Realtors, Austin Bd. of Realtors, Headliner's Club, Austin Club. Avocations: photography, writing, painting, traveling. Home: 217 Capri Lakeway Resort Austin TX 78734-4305

LANCE, ALAN GEORGE, state attorney general; b. McComb, Ohio, Apr. 27, 1949; s. Cloyce Lowell and Clara Rose (Wilhelm) Lance; m. Sheryl C. Holden, May 31, 1969; children: Lisa, Alan Jr., Luke. BA, S.D. State U., 1971; JD, U. Toledo, 1973. Bar: Ohio 1974, U.S. Dist. Ct. (no. dist.) Ohio 1974, U.S. Ct. Mil. Appeals 1974, Idaho 1978, U.S. Supreme Ct. 1996. Asst. pros. atty. Fulton County, Wauseon, Ohio, 1973—74; ptnr. Foley and Lance, Chartered, Meridian, Idaho, 1978—90; prin. Alan G. Lance, 1990—94; rep. Idaho Ho. of Reps., Boise, 1990—94, majority caucus chmn., 1992—94; atty. gen. State of Idaho, 1995—. Capt. U.S. Army, 1974—78. Mem.: Idaho Trial Lawyers Assn., Idaho Bar Assn., Ohio Bar Assn., Nat. Assn. Attys. Gen. (vice-chmn. conf. western attys. gen. 1998, chmn. 1999), Meridian C. of C. (pres. 1983), Elks, Am. Legion (judge adv. 1981—90, state comdr. 1988—89, alt. nat. exec. com. 1992—94, nat. exec. com. 1994—96, chmn. nat. fgn. rels. commn. 1996—97, ex-officio mem. nat. POW/MIA com. 1996—, nat. comdr. 1999—2000, chmn. nat. adv. com. 2000—01). Republican. Avocation: fishing. Home: 1370 Eggers Pl Meridian ID 83642-6528 Office: Office of the ttorney General 700 West Jefferson Street PO Box 83720 Boise ID 83720-3720

LANCE, LEONARD, state legislator; b. Easton, Pa., June 25, 1952; s. Wesley L. and Anne (Anderson) L.; m. Heidi A. Rohrbach. BA, Lehigh U., 1974; JD, Vanderbilt U., 1977; MPA, Princeton U., 1982. Law clk. to judges Warren County Ct., Belvidere, N.J., 1977-78; asst. counsel Office of Gov., State of N.J., Trenton, 1983-90; mem. N.J. Gen. Assembly, 1991—2002, N.J. State Senate, 2002—. Mem. Grandin Libr. Bd., Clinton, N.J., 1990-2000, N.J. Coun. for Humanities, Trenton, 1994—; trustee Newark Mus., 1995—, Centenary Coll., Hackettstown, N.J., 1998—, McCarter Theatre, 1998—. Mem. Princeton Club N.Y., Phi Beta Kappa. Republican. Home: PO Box 5240 Clinton NJ 08809-0240 Office: NJ State Senate 119 Main St Flemington NJ 08822-1615

LANCE, SEAN P. pharmaceutical executive; Formerly with Noristan Group of Cos. Ltd.; from various positions to exec. chmn. Boots Co. Pty Ltd., South Africa, 1982-85; from various mgmt. positions to COO internat. ops., chief exec. designate Glaxo Wellcome Plc, 1985—97; pres., CEO Chiron Corp., Emeryville, Calif., 1998—, chmn. bd. dirs., 1999—; pres. International Federation of Pharma. Mfr. Assoc., Geneva, 1996—98. Office: Chiron Corp 4560 Horton St Emeryville CA 94608-2916*

LANCE, STEVEN, clinical hypnotherapist, hypnocounselor, author; BA in English, Upsala Coll., 1976. Cert. advanced clin. hypnotherapist, master hypnocounselor. Dir. mktg. Monmouth County Arts Coun.-Count Basie Theatre, Red Bank, N.J., 1990; entertainment columnist The Two River Times, 1991-93; founder, exec. dir. Silent Running Soc., 1985—; founder, mng. editor (online svc.) www.PlanetShowbiz.com, www.Planet007.com, www.PlanetSuperman.com, www.HollywoodNJ.com. Host Names in the News, WHTG (FM), Eatontown, N.J., 1993-96. Author: Written Out of Television: The Encyclopedia of Cast Changes and Character Replacements, 1945-94, 1996, Written Out of Television: A TV Lover's Guide to Cast Changes 1945-94, 1996; rsch. asst. (Vincent Terrace) Television Character and Story Facts, 1993, (Vincent Terrace) Television Specials, 1995, (James Robert Parish) Rose: Rosie O'Donnell's Biography, 1997, others; actor Star Trek: The Motion Picture, 1980, Stardust Memories, 1981. Office: VEGR 4057 Hwy 9 N Howell NJ 07731-3307 Fax: 732-364-1705. E-mail: StevenLance@netscape.net.

LANCELLA, EILEEN M. social worker; b. Bklyn. d. Nicholas and Rose (Mazzarella) L. MSW, Columbia U., 1978. Field instr. SUNY, Stony Brook; supr. social work Little Flower Children's Svcs., Bklyn. Mem. NASW, Acad. Cert. Social Workers (cert.). Address: 2650 Ocean Pky Brooklyn NY 11235-7749

LANCELLOTTA, JOHN JERRY-LOUIS, foundation administrator; b. Providence, Aug. 25, 1953; s. Joseph Ralph and Mary Grace (DeGregory) L. AS in Polit. Sci. cum laude, Roger Williams U., 1983, BS in Pub. Adminstrn. cum laude, 1984. academically cert. in paralegal studies, Roger Williams Coll,. 1982. Contractor, estimator Ctr. Contractors, West Warwick, R.I., 1975-79; staff trainer econ. dept. City of Warwick, 1982; legis. aide to U.S. Senator Pell, Providence, 1983-85; ombudsman/investigator Atty. Gen., 1985-91; exec. dir. Jaycee Found., West Warwick, 1991—. Adviser Narragansett Bay Commn., Providence, 1982—89; cons. Mcpl. Affairs, West Warwick, Coventry, RI, 1979—93. Candidate Town Coun., West Warwick, 1976-92; com. Rep. Dist. 39, West Warwick, 1984-86; mem. Comprehensive Plan Commn., West Warwick, 1990-92; exec. bd. Citizens Adv. Com., v.p. 1979-86; mem. R.I. and Pawtuxet Valley Ch. Couns., 1972-92; 1st tree bd. commr. Town of West Warwick, 1999; cons. Jr. Achievement R.I., 2000; mem. Nat. Arbor Day Found., 1989. Recipient Cert. of Appreciation, CARE, 1985, Cmty. Leadership At Risk Children Letter of Achievement, Lt. Gov. R.I., 1989, letters of commendation U.S. Pres. Bush and Clinton, 1992-96, Proclamation Gov. of R.I., 1990, 1st Civic Pride citation Town of West Warwick, 1989, Environ. citation Gov. of R.I., 1998-99, Svc. Above Self award, Pawtuxet Valley Rotary Internat., 1999, Congl. citation for outstanding pub. svc. U.S. Rep. James R. Langevin, 2001, Congl. citation of congratulations U.S. Rep. Patrick J. Kennedy, 2001, Cert. of Accomplishment U.S. Sen. Jack Reed, 2001, Excellence in Cmty. Svc. award Town of West Warwick, 2001, Disting. Cmty. Leadership award Mayor City of Providence, 2001, Meritorious Cmty. Involvement award, Mayor City of Cranston, 2001, Pub. Svc. Achievement award Gov., Lt. Gov. and Atty. Gen. State of R.I., 2001. Mem.: ACLU, Am. Inst. Cancer Rsch., Acad. Polit. Sci., Diocese of Providence and Cmty. Affairs Vicariate (Cert. 1988), Am. Soc. Pub. Adminstrn. (contbr. 1984—99, Letter of Excellence 1986), Am. Indian Youth, Am. Life League, U.S. Jaycees Alumni Club. Democrat. Roman Catholic. Avocations: animal rescue, horticultural digs, walking club, spiritual outings, disabled visitations. Home: 32 River Ave West Warwick RI 02893-1820 Office: Jaycee Found PO Box 348 West Warwick RI 02893-0348

LANCHNER, BERTRAND MARTIN, lawyer, advertising executive; b. Boston, Oct. 3, 1929; s. Abraham Joseph and Mina (Grossman) L.; m. Nancy Nelson, Apr. 26, 1979; 1 son by previous marriage, David; 1 stepdau., Renate. BA, Stanford U., 1951; postgrad., Columbia U. Grad. Sch. Bus., 1951-52, U. Vienna, Austria, summer 1955; JD, Harvard U., 1955. Bar: N.Y. bar 1956. Asso. firm Sage, Gray, Todd & Sims, N.Y.C., 1955-57; atty. Warner Bros. Pictures, 1957-59; asst. gen. counsel Dancer-Fitzgerald-Sample, 1959-62; gen. counsel Lawrence C. Gumbinner Advt. Agy., 1962-63; dir. bus. affairs and sports contract negotiations CBS-TV, 1963-69; gen. counsel, exec. v.p. Videorecord Corp. Am., Westport, Conn., 1969-73; sr. v.p., sec., gen. counsel N.W. Ayer, Inc., N.Y.C., 1973-97, also bd. dirs.; with Lanchner Law Firm, 1997—. Bd. dirs. 170 E. 79th St. Corp., Advt. Info. Services Inc., N.Y.C.; guest lectr. Yale U. Law Sch. Mem. adv. bd.: Communications and the Law. Mem. ABA, N.Y. State Bar Assn., Assn. of Bar of City of N.Y. (chmn. subcom. advt. agy. 1981-83), Copyright Soc. U.S., Am. Assn. Advt. Agys. (chmn. legal com. 1986-89, 95-97), Am. Corp. Counsel Assn. (chair advt. com. 1996—), Am. Advt. Fedn. (mem. legal com.), Harvard Club N.Y.C., East Hampton Tennis Club, Tennisport Club., Green Hollow Tennis Club. Office: Lanchner Law Firm 170 E 79th St New York NY 10021-0436

LANCIONE, BERNARD GABE, lawyer; b. Bellaire, Ohio, Feb. 3, 1939; s. Americus Gabe and June (Morford) L.; m. Rosemary C., Nov. 27, 1976; children: Amy, Caitin, Gillian, Bernard Gabe II, Elizabetta Marie. BS, Ohio U., 1960; JD, Capitol U., 1965. Bar: Ohio 1965, U.S. Dist. Ct. (so. dist.) Ohio 1967, U.S. Supreme Ct. 1969, U.S. Ct. Appeals (4th cir.) 1982, U.S. Dist. Ct. (no. dist.) Ohio 1989. Pres. Lancione Law Office, Co., L.P.A., Bellaire, Ohio, 1965-87; mng. atty. Cichon Lancione Co., L.P.A., St. Clairsville, 1982-85; of counsel Ward, Kaps, Bainbridge, Maurer, Bloomfield & Melvin, Columbus, 1987-88; Ohio Asst. Atty. Gen., 1988-91; sole practice, 1991—. Spl. counsel Ohio Atty. Gen's. Office, 1991-95; solicitor Bellaire City (Ohio), 1968-72; asst. prosecutor County of Belmont (Ohio), 1972-76. Pres. Young Dems. Ohio, 1970-72; pack com. chmn. Pack 961, Westerville, Ohio Cub Scouts Am., 1992-93. Mem. ABA, Assn. Trial Lawyers Am., Ohio State Bar Assn., Columbus Bar Assn., Ohio Acad. Trial Lawyers (award of merit 1972). Democrat. Roman Catholic. Home: 1108 Acillom Dr Westerville OH 43081-1104 Office: 647 Park Meadow Rd # E Westerville OH 43081-2878 E-mail: blancion@columbus.rr.com.

LANCKTON, ARTHUR VAN CLEVE, lawyer; b. New London, Conn., Sept. 7, 1942; m. Alice Elizabeth Keidan, Aug. 31, 1967; children: Benjamin E., Samuel F. BA cum laude, Yale U., 1964; JD cum laude, Harvard U., 1967. Bar: Mass. 1967, U.S. Dist. Ct. Mass. 1968, U.S. Tax Ct. 1969, U.S. Ct. Appeals (1st cir.) 1982, U.S. Supreme Ct. 1986. Atty., dir. Harvard Law Sch. Community Legal Assistance Office, Cambridge, Mass., 1967-71; teaching fellow Harvard Law Sch., 1970-71; dep. gen. counsel Mass. Exec. Offices of Human Svcs., Boston, 1971-75; gen. counsel Dept. of Pub. Welfare, 1975-78;

assoc. Bingham, Dana & Gould, 1978-83, Craig and Macauley, Boston, 1983-85, ptnr., 1985—. Democrat. Jewish. Office: Craig and Macauley 600 Atlantic Ave Ste 2900 Boston MA 02210-2215 E-mail: lanckton@craigmacauley.com.

LANCLOS, RITCHIE PAUL, petroleum engineer; b. Opelousas, La., Sept. 20, 1964; s. Curley Joseph and Velma Marie (Folks) L.; m. Courtney Thereśe Brennan, Mar. 26, 1994. BS in Petroleum Engring., U. Southwestern La., 1987; MS in Petroleum Engring. cum laude, Tex. A&M U., 1990. Registered profl. engr., La. Petroleum engr. exploration and prodn. Mobil Oil Corp., New Orleans, 1987-89, Conoco, Inc., New Orleans, 1990-93; petroleum engr. property acquisitions WRT Energy Corp., The Woodlands, Tex., 1994; petroleum engr. reservoir engring. Petrobras Am., Inc., Houston, 1995-97; asset engr. Texaco E&P, New Orleans, 1997—2001; sr. reservoir engr. Dominion E&P, 2001—. Bd. dirs. Big Bros./Big Sisters, New Orleans, 1991-94, Boys/Girls Club, Lafayette, La., 1992-94, Vol. Instrs. Teaching Adults (VITA), Lafayette, 1991-94; loaned exec. United Way, New Orleans, 1993-94. Scholar Am. Petroleum Inst., Lafayette, 1985-86, scholar Texaco Rsch. Ctr., Texaco Inc., College Station, Tex., 1989-90; fellow Petroleum Engring., 1989-90. Mem. Soc. Petroleum Engrs., Tex. A&M U. Petroleum Engring. Alumni (v.p. 1994-95, thesis adv. com.). Republican. Roman Catholic. Achievements include developments in the field of reservoir fluid characterization. Avocations: traveling, golfing, reading. Home: 1329 State St Mandeville LA 70448-1030 E-mail: ritchie_p_lanclos@dom.com.

LANCOUR, KAREN LOUISE, secondary education educator; b. Cheboygan, Mich., June 2, 1946; d. Clinton Howard and Dorothy Marie (Passeno) L. AA, Alpena Community Coll., 1966; BA, Ea. Mich. U., 1968, MS, 1970. Teaching asst. Ea. Mich. U., Ypsilanti, 1968-70; tchr. sci. Utica (Mich.) Community Schs., 1970-98, ret., 1998. Editor Sci. Olympiad Nat. Dir.'s Man., 2000—. Nat. event supr. Sci. Olympiad, 1986—, mem. nat. rules com., 1987—, Mich. state event supr., 1986—, regional dir., 1987, state bd., 1998—. Recipient Disting. Svc. award Nat. Sci. Olympiad, 1995. Mem. Nat. Sci. Tchrs. Assn., Mich. Sci. Tchrs. Assn., Nat. Assn. Biology Tchrs., Met. Detroit Sci. Tchrs. Assn. (Outstanding Sci. Educator award 1997), Smithsonian Inst., Nat. Geographic Soc., Edison Inst., Mortar Bd., Internat. Biograph. Soc., Am. Biograph. Inst. Rsch. Assn. (dep. gov.), Internat. Platform Assn., Phi Theta Kappa, Kappa Delta Phi. Home: 312 W Bosley St Alpena MI 49707-2126

LAND, ALLAN STEPHEN, surgeon; b. Balt., Nov. 24, 1938; MD, U. Md., 1965. Diplomate Am. Bd. Surgery. Intern Sinai Hosp., Balt., 1965-66, resident in surgery, 1966-70. Chief surg. svcs., chief utilization review South Shore Hosp., Miami, Fla.; clin. assoc. prof. U. Miami; med. dir. Worldnet Svcs. Corp.; emeritus Mt. Sinai Hosp., Miami Heart Inst. Fellow ACS; mem. Southeastern Surg. Congress.

LAND, GEORGE A. philosopher, writer, educator, consultant, speaker; b. Hot Springs, Ark., Feb. 27, 1933; s. George Thomas Lock and Mary Elizabeth Land; m. Jo A. Gunn, 1957 (dec. 1969); children— Robert E., Thomas G., Patrick A.; m. Beth Smith Jarman, 1987. Student, Millsaps Coll., 1952-54, U. Veracruz, Mexico, 1957-59; numerous hon. degrees U.S. and abroad. Program dir. Woodall TV Stas. of Ga., Columbus, 1951-52; ops. mgr. Lamar Broadcasting, Jackson, Miss., 1952-54; anthrop. research Cora, Huichole and Yaqui tribes, Latin Am. Mexico, 1955-60; dir. gen. Television del Norte (NBC), Mexico, 1960-62; v.p. Roman Corp., St. Louis, 1962-64; chmn. Transolve Inc., Cambridge, Mass., and St. Petersburg, Fla., 1964-68; chief exec., chmn. Innotek Corp., N.Y.C.; also pres. Hal Roach Studios, Los Angeles and N.Y.C., 1969-71; chmn. emeritus Turtle Bay Inst., N.Y.C., 1971-80; vice chmn. Wilson Learning Corp., Mpls., 1980-86; chmn., CEO Leadership 2000 The Farsight Group, Phoenix, 1986—; prof. Mankato State U., 1973-74; sr. fellow U. Minn., 1982—. Cons.-in-residence Synplex Inc., N.Y.C., AT&T, Forest Hosp., Des Plaines, Social Systems Inc., Chapel Hill, N.C., Children's Hosp., Nat. Med. Ctr., Washington, Herman Miller Inc., Arthur Anderson & Co., strategy cons. Intermedics Orthopedics; mem. Nat. Action Com. on Drug Edn., 1974-75, sr. exec. svc. U.S. Govt. 2000-2001, Assn. Non-profit mgmt., 1999, The Congerence Bd. 1999, 2000, Ctr.; co-chmn. Syncon Conf., So. Ill. U., 1972-74; keynoter Emerging Trends in Edn. Conf., Minn., 1974, 75, Bicentennial Conf. on Limits to Growth, So. Ill. U., 1976, No. States Power Conf., 1975, U.S. Office Edn., Nat. Conf. Improvements in Edn., 1979, World Conf. on Gifted, 1977, S.W. Conf. on Arts, 1977, World Symposium on Humanity, 1979, Internat. Conf. Internal Auditors, 1977, Four Corners Conf. on Arts, 1977, Chautaugua Inst., 1977, 78, Conf. Am. Art Tchrs. Assn., 1979, Internat. Conf. on Gifted, 1982, Japan Mgmt. Assn., Nat. Conf. Art Curators, Chgo., 1985, others; keynoter, Nat. Conf. on Econ. Devel., Mex., 1988, Credit Union Roundtable, Tampa, Fla., 1988, Internat. Bihai Conf., Princeton, N.J., 1982, co-chmn. com. on society World Conf. Peace and Poverty, St. Joseph's U., Phila., 1968, Internat. Bahai Conf. Princeton U., 1987, Gov.'s Trade Corridor Conf., Phoenix, 1994, Cath. Hosp. Assn., Phila, 1994, Am. Assn. Adminstrs., 1994, Inst. Pub. Execs., 1994, Fed. Conf. Quality, Washington, 1994, MAC IS Nat. Conf., Ont., 1994, Innovative Thinking Conf., 1994, Ventana Groupware Conf., 1994, Assn. Non-Profit Orgs., 1998, The Conf. Bd., 1999, 2000, Strategic Innovation Conf., 1999, Tng. Dirs. Forum, 1999, Young Pres.' Orgn., Cannes, 1993, Assn. Convn. and Visitors Bureau, Phoenix, 1993, Profession Conv. Mgmt. Assn., Atlanta, Internat. Assn. Law Enforcement, 1995, Cath. Health Assn., 1995, Excellence in Govt. Fellows, 1996, U.S. Govt. Sr. Exec. Svc., 2000, 01, Chautauqua Instn., 2001, many others; mem. Nat. Security Sem., U.S. Dept. Def., 1975; cons. keynoter corp. policy strategic sems. The Bell System, AT&T, 1978—; mem. faculty Edison Electric Grad. Mgmt. Inst., 1972-78; lectr., seminarian in transformation theory, strategic planning and interdisciplinary rsch. Menninger Found., U. Ga., Emory U., Waterloo (Can.), Office of Sec. HEW, Jamestown (N.Y.) Coll., Hofstra U., U.S. Office Edn., Calif. Dept. Edn., St. Louis U., Coll. William and Mary, Webster Coll., St. Louis, Wash. State Dept. Edn., U. Ky., So. Ill. U., St. John's U., Harvard U., U. South Fla., MIT, U. Veracruz, Children's Hosp. D.C., Gov.'s Sch. N.C., Scottsdale (Ariz.) Ctr. Arts, Humbolt U., East Berlin, AAAS, others; advanced faculty Creative Problem SolvingInst., SUNY, 1965—, S, Conn. Coll.; disting. lectr. Northwestern State U., La., SUNY, Coll. of the Lakes, Ill.; cons. govt., industry and instrns. in U.S. and abroad including AT&T, IBM, Dow Chem, Dow Corning, DuPont, Hughes, TRW, 3Mm OAS, Fed. Quality Inst., U.S. Dept. Commerce, U.S. Dept. Agr., Office Patent & Trademarks, U.S. Gen. Svc. Adminstrn., Gen Mills, GM, Moore Corp., Branch Corp., Credit Union Nat. Assn., USDA, Excellence in Govt. Fed. Quality Cons. Group, U.S. Dept. Energy, Lockheed Martin, Dept. Housing and Urban Devel., Wescorp, PEMEX, Petroleos de Venezuela, Am. Medicas Sys., Def. Evaluation and Rsch. Agy (U.K.)., Stanford U., others. Author: Innovation Systems, 1967, Innovation Technology, 1968, Four Faces of Poverty, 1968, (as George T.L. Land) Grow or Die: The Unifying Principle of Transformation, 1973, Creative Alternatives and Decision Making, 1974, The Opportunity Book, 1980, (with Vaune E. Ainsworth), Breakpoint and Beyond, 1994, (with Beth Jarman) New Paradigm in Business, 1994, Community Building in Business, 1995, Forward to Basics; contbr. to profl. jours. and gen. mags. Sr. fellow U. Mich. Fellow: World Bus. Acad., NY Acad. Scis.; mem.: Authors League Am., Authors Guild, Com. for Future (colleague), World Future Soc., Am. Soc. Value Engrs. (past dir.), Creative Edn. Found. (trustee, Lifetime Achievement award 1993), Am. Soc. Cybernetics (past v.p.), Soc. Gen. Sys. Rsch. Achievements include research on interdisciplinary unification, orginated transformation theory. Inventor computer-assisted group creative thinking processes, "The Innovator," "CoNexus," "TeamWare" and others. Home: 7470 E San Miguel Ave Scottsdale AZ 85250-6446 Office: Leadership 2000 6619 N Scottsdale Rd Scottsdale AZ 85250 *I was fortunate enough in my youth to experience and learn what has been the most important idea and principle in my life, the natural law of enrichment through diversity. This concept means that change and growth come about more by combining differentnesses than by adding likenesses. As in the biological world, where such behavior produces the vitality of hybrids, and as in chemistry, where the co-valent bonds of carbon make life possible, in human life we can also benefit immeasurably from using our differences as a creative way to grow anew. Thus, we can evolve beyond polarizations such as nationalism, racism, sexism, institutionalism and other obstacles that separate us and stunt our ability to realize the full community of Man.*

LAND, IRENE STOKVIS, marketing executive; b. N.Y.C., Sept. 29, 1939; d. Joseph William and Beatrice Winifred (Turetsky) Stokvis; m. Paul Ivan Land, Nov. 5, 1965; 1 child, Jonathan Brock. BA, CUNY, Queens, 1961. Assoc. book rev. editor Library Jour., N.Y.C., 1961-76; mgr. advt. and promotion Elsevier Sci. Pub. Co., 1980-86; mgr. promotion Springer-Verlag, 1986-88; freelance personal mgr. for actors, 1988-92; freelance mktg. and media comm., 1992—. Avocations: painting, piano, writing. Home: 401 E 34th St Apt N5B New York NY 10016-4921

LAND, JUDITH BROTEN, stockbroker; b. Newark, July 27, 1951; d. Robert Allan and Marjorie (Frederickson) Broten; m. Andre Paul Land, Jan. 6, 1973; children: Ian Sherard, Margo Caryn. Student, Hood Coll., 1969-70, Denver U., 1970-71, Monmouth Coll., 1971-72, Fla. Atlantic U., 1976-77. Lic. ins. agt., Fla. Ops. dept. Fahnestock & Co., Red Bank, N.J., 1973; with ops. dept. Thomson McKinnon, South Orange, 1973-75, br. ops. rep. Boca Raton, Fla., 1977-80; sales asst., trainee Butcher & Singer Inc., 1980-81, stockbroker, 1981-85, A.G. Edwards & Sons, Inc., Boca Raton, 1985—. Lectr. Palm Beach County Schs., Boca Raton, 1987-95, Palm Beach County Librs., 1990-91; daily stock market radio reporter Sta. WDBF-AM, Delray Beach, Fla., 1979-81. Community theatre performer; song composer. Mem. Singing Pines Children's Mus., Boca Raton, 1985-89, Young Women of the Arts, Boca Raton, 1989, C. of C., 1990-92. Republican. Episcopalian. Avocations: golf. Office: AG Edwards & Sons Inc 1900 Glades Rd Ste 451 Boca Raton FL 33431-8548

LAND, JUDY M. real estate broker; b. Phoenix, Oct. 6, 1945; d. Sanford Karl Land and Latanne (Hilburn) Land Krauss; divorced; children: Neal McNeil III, Latanne Tahnee. AA in Econs., Merritt Coll., 1967; MBA, Brklyn Bus. Sch., 1984. Cert. real estate developer, broker and appraiser. With real estate sales dept. Odmark/Welch Co/Mesa Realty, San Diego, 1971-76; v.p. Brehm Communities, 1977; mgr. investment div. Ayers Realty, Encinitas, Calif., 1978-79; asst. v.p. Harry L. Summers Inc., La Jolla, 1982-85; pres. The Land Co., Carlsbad, 1979-90; nat. mktg. dir. Nat. Safety Assocs., San Diego, 1990—; pres. Coldwell Banker-The Land Divsn., Rancho Santa Fe, Calif., 1996—. Fundraiser Hunger Project, 1979-86, Youth at Risk, 1984-86, Multiple Sclerosis Soc., 1984; mem. exec. com. U.S. Olympics, 1984; bd. dirs. Polit. Policies Com., San Diego, 1986. Mem. Nat. Assn. Real Estate Appraisers, Nat. Assn. Women Execs., Nat. Assn. Home builders, Home Builders Council (pres. 1985), Building Industry Assn. San Diego (bd. dirs. 1985, sale and mktg. coun.), Econ. Devel. Corp. San Diego (membership com. 1984), Women Comml. Real Estate, Life Spike Club. Avocations: tennis, skiing, swimming. Office: Coldwell Banker Land Divsn PO Box 2274 Rancho Santa Fe CA 92067-2274

LAND, KENNETH CARL, sociology educator, demographer, statistician, consultant; b. Llano, Tex., Aug. 19, 1942; s. Otto Carl and Tillie (Lindemann) L.; m. Jacqueline Yvette Apere, Mar. 22, 1969; 1 child, Kristoffer Carl. BA, Tex. Luth. Coll., 1964; MA, U. Tex., 1966, PhD, 1969. Staff assoc. Russell Sage Found., N.Y.C., 1969-73; lectr. Columbia U., 1970-73; assoc. prof. U. Ill., Urbana, 1973-76, prof., 1976-81; prof. sociology U. Tex., Austin, 1981-86; prof., chmn. dept. sociology Duke U., Durham, N.C., 1986-97, John Franklin Crowell prof. sociology, 1990—. Editor: Social Indicator Models, 1975, Social Accounting Systems, 1981, Multidimensional Mathematical Demography, 1982, Forecasting in the Social and Natural Sciences, 1987; contbr. articles to profl. jours. Fellow AAAS, Am. Statis. Assn., Internat. Soc. Quality Life Studies; mem. Sociol. Rsch. Assn., Am. Sociol. Assn. (Paul F. Lazersfeld award methodology sect. 1997), Population Assn. Am., Am. Soc. Criminology. Lutheran. Office: Duke U Dept Sociology Durham NC 27708-0088

LAND, KENNETH DEAN, test and balance agency executive, energy and environmental consultant; b. Central City, Nebr., Oct. 5, 1931; s. Adrew Kenneth Land and Marie Eveline (Weaver) Gehrke. Grad., El Camino Coll., Gardena, Calif., 1954-56; student, Long Beach City Coll., 1958, Calif. State Coll., Long Beach, 1959. Cert. quality assurance inspector for smoke removal and life safety systems; cert. test & balance engr. for bldg., environ. sys. Gen. mgr. Air Heat Engrs., Inc., Santa Fe Springs, Calif., 1956-61; sales and estimating engr. Thermodyne Corp., Los Alamitos, 1962-64; pres., founder Air Check Co., Inc., Santa Ana, 1964-69; chief engring. technician Nat. Air Balance Co., Los Angeles, 1969-73; gen. mgr. B&M Air Balance Co., South El Monte, Calif., 1973-78; chief exec. officer, founder Land Air Balance Tech. (LABTECH), Las Vegas, Nev., 1978—. Founder, bd. dirs. Energy Resources and Mgmt., Inc., San-I-Pac, Internat., Inc., Energy Equities Group, Inc., Utility Connection, 1990—. Active Las Vegas Founders Club-Las Vegas Invitational PGA Tournament, 1983—, player, 1992; former trustee Assoc. Air Balance Coun.-Sheet Metal Workers Internat. Apprenticeship Tng. Fund; mem. Citizens Against Govt. Waste, 1990—, YNOT Night for YMCA, 1987—; co-founder The Golf Com., operators charity golf tournament for Am. Cancer Soc., 1990, 91, Am. Diabetes Assn., 1992, Nev. Child Seekers, 1992—. With USN, 1951-54, journalist. Mem. ASHRAE (pres. so. Nev. chpt. 1983-84, editor chpt. bull. 1979-89, Citizen of Yr. 1989), CSI (co-founder Las Vegas chpt., pres. 1989-90, editor, founder chpt. bull. 1987-90, S.W. regional mem. chmn. 1990-91), Assn. Energy Engrs., Am. Soc. Profl. Cons., Associated Air Balance Coun. (cert. test and balance engr. 1966—, internat. pres. 1988-89, bd. dirs. 1982-90, mem. numerous coms.), Sheet Metal Workers Internat. Tng. Fund, Internat. Conf. Bldg. Officials, Internat. Assn. Plumbing and Mech. Officials, Nat. Fedn. Ind. Businessmen, Rotary (So. El Monte Calif. Club 1977-78, Las Vegas S.W. Nev. Club 1978-94, bd. dirs. 1983-85, 88-90, photographer 1987-90, chmn. internat. svc., 4 Paul Harris fellowships, charter mem. Las Vegas West Club, Nev., 1994—), Citizens for Pvt. Enterprise, Nev. Taxpayers Assn., UNLV Golf Found., UNLV Presdl. Assocs. Group, Nev. Devel. Assn., Nev. Nuclear Waste Study Com. adv. coun., Sheet Metal and Air Conditioning Contractors Assn. (nat. and so. Nev. chpt. bd. dirs.), Associated Gen. Contractors (nat. and Las Vegas chpt.), Nat. Energy Mgmt. Inst. (cert., co-chmn. Nev. adv. coun., instr. Energy Mgmt. Tng. 1991), Las Vegas C. of C., Nat. Inst. Bldg. Scis., Nev. Assn. Ind. Businessman, Nat. Fire Protection Assn., Am. Soc. Hosp. Engrs., Nev. Profl. Facility Mgrs. Assn., 1992—, Las Vegas Country Club. Avocations: golf, dancing, racquetball, collecting jazz, swing and big band music. Fax: 702-382-3299. E-mail: Ken@landairbalance.com.

LAND, MING HUEY, college dean; b. Hsinchu, Taiwan, July 10, 1940; came to U.S., 1966; s. Jin-tu an Jen (Huang) L.; m. Whei-ing Yang, July 30, 1970; children: Judy Karen, Michael Henry. BS, Taiwan Normal U., 1963; MS, No. Ill. U., 1968; EdD, Utah State U., 1970; postgrad. mgmt. devel. program, Harvard U., 1993. Tchr. Hsinchu (Taiwan) High Sch., 1963-66; asst. prof. Ea. Ill. U., Charleston, 1970-71; prof. Miami U., Oxford, Ohio, 1971-83; chairperson Appalachian State U., Boone, N.C., 1983-89, dean, 1989—2002, prof. tech., 2002—. Fulbright vis. prof. Chungnam Nat. U., Taejon, S. Korea, 1981-82; mem. Fulbright Lectureship Coun. Internat. Excahnge Scholars, 1981. Contbr. over 50 articles to profl. jours. Named hon. prof., Northeast U. (China), 1986; recipient Laureate citation Epsilon Pi Tau, 1987, Disting. Svc. citation, 1998, Disting. Alumni award Coll. Engring., Utah State U., 2001. Mem. Am. Soc. Engring. Edn., Internat. Tech. Edn. Assn. (Spl. Recognition award 1990, Lockette/Monroe Humanitarian award 1998), Nat. Assn. Indsl. Tech. (univ. divsn. pres. 1997-98, Outstanding Regional Dir. award 1994-95), Internat. Coun. of Fine Arts Deans. Avocations: travel, hiking, music. Home: 320 University Cir Boone NC 28607-4383 Office: Dept Technology Appalachian State U Boone NC 28608-2122

LAND, REBEKAH RUTH, marriage and family therapist; b. Columbus, Ga., Feb. 5, 1946; d. Roland Irving and Thelma Rebekah (Gibbins) Van Hooser; m. Richard Dale Land, Sr., May 29, 1971; children: Jennifer Rebekah, Richard Dale Jr., Rachel Elisabeth. AB, Samford U., 1967; M in Religious Edn., New Orleans Bapt. Theol. Sem., 1970; MSW, Tulane U., 1971; PhD, Tex. Woman's U., 1988. Lic. profl. counselor; lic. marital and family therapist; lic. clin. social worker; diplomate Am. Bd. Sexology. Sch. social worker Chattanooga Pub. Schs., 1967-68; edn. and youth dir. Trinity Bapt. Ch., New Orleans, 1968-69; caseworker Youth Study Ctr., 1972; adj. prof. Criswell Coll., Dallas, 1976-89; counselor First Bapt. Ch., 1982-85; psychotherapist Minirth-Meier Clinic, Richardson, Tex., 1985-87; asst. dir. counseling Dallas Theol. Sem., 1987-89; pvt. practice Nashville, 1989—; coord. Trilogy Program Parthenon Pavilion Psychiat. Hosp., 1990-94. Mem. ACA, Am. Assn. Marriage and Family Therapy (clin.), Am. Assn. Sex Educators (cert. sex therapist), Counselors and Therapists, Assn. for Religious Values in Counseling Republican. Baptist. Avocation: crafts. Office: Parkview Towers 210 25th Ave N Ste 1010 Nashville TN 37203-1674 Fax: 615-327-1653. E-mail: horns@earthlink.net.

LAND, REGINALD BRIAN, library administrator; b. Niagara Falls, Ont., Can., July 29, 1927; s. Allan Reginald and Beatrice Beryl (Boyle) L.; m. Edith Wyndham Eddis, Aug. 29, 1953; children— Mary Beatrice, John Robert Eddis. BA, U. Toronto, Ont., Can., 1949, BLS, 1953, MLS, 1956, MA, 1963. Catalogue copy editor T. Eaton Co. Ltd., Toronto, 1950-51; reference librarian Toronto Pub. Library, 1953-55; cataloguer U. Toronto Library, 1955-56, asst. librarian, 1959-63, assoc. librarian, 1963; head div. bus. and industry Windsor Pub. Library, Ont., Can., 1956-57; asst. editor Canadian Bus. Mag., Montreal, Que., Can., 1957-58, assoc. editor Can., 1958-59; exec. asst. to Minister Fin. of Can., Ottawa, Ont., 1963-64; prof. library sci. U. Toronto, 1964-78, part-time prof., 1978-93, prof. emeritus, 1993—, dean Faculty Library Sci., 1964-72; exec. dir. Ont. Legis. Library, Toronto, 1978-93. Author: Sources of Information for Canadian Business, 1962, 4th rev. edit., 1985, Eglinton: The Election Study of a Federal Constituency, 1965; founder, gen. editor: Directory of Associations in Canada, 1974, 18th rev. edit., 1997. Mem. Canadian Radio-TV and Telecommunications Commn., 1973-78, Ont. Hist. Soc. Decorated Knight Hospitaller Order of St. John of Jerusalem; recipient Kenneth R. Wilson Meml. award Bus. Newspapers Assn. Can., 1959, Disting. Achievement award Ont. Library Trustees Assn., 1968, Queen Elizabeth IIs Silver Jubilee medal, 1977, Spl. Librarianship award Can. Assn. for Spl. Librs. and Info. Svcs., 1991, 125th Anniversary Confederation Can. medal, 1992, Alumni Jubilee award U. Toronto Libr. & Info. Sci. Alumni Assn., 1994. Mem. ALA (chmn. com. on accreditation 1973-74), Assn. Parliamentary Librs. in Can. (pres. 1982-84), Can. Libr. Assn. (pres. 1975-76), Ont. Libr. Assn. (1st v.p. 1962-63), Ont. Govt. Librs. Coun. (chmn. 1984-85), Assn. for Libr. and Info. Sci. Edn. (pres. 1973-74), Can. Assn. for Grad. Edn. in Libr. Archival and Info. Studies (pres. 1966-67), Can. Coun. Libr. Schs. (chmn. 1971-72), Ex Libris Assn. (bd. dirs. 1994-99, pres. 1998), Inst. Profl. Librs. Ont. (pres. 1961-62), Ont. Coun. Libr. Schs. (chmn. 1968-72), Spl. Librs. Assn. (Mem. of Yr. award Toronto chpt. 1986), Ont. Geneal. Soc., Ont. Coll. and Univ. Librs. Assn. (merit award 1992), Ont. Hist. Soc., United Empire Loyalists' Assn. Can. Mem. Anglican Ch. Home: 9 Wild Rose Court Guelph ON Canada N1G 4X7

LAND, RICHARD DALE, minister, religious organization administrator; b. Houston, Nov. 6, 1946; s. Leggette Sloan and Marilee (Welch) L.; m. Rebekah Ruth Van Hooser, May 29, 1971; children: Jennifer, Richard Jr., Rachel. BA, Princeton U., 1969; ThM, New Orleans Bapt. Theol. Sem., 1972; D.Phil., U. Oxford, Eng., 1980. Ordained to ministry So. Bapt. Conv., 1969. Pastor S. Oxford Bapt. Ch., Oxford, Eng., 1972-75; prof. theology and ch. history Criswell Coll., Dallas, 1975-76, acad. dean, 1976-80, v.p. for acad. affairs, 1980-88; pres. ethics and religious liberty commn. So. Bapt. Conv., Nashville, 1988—. Mem. exec. com. Nat. Coalition against Pornography, Cin., 1989—; bd. dirs. Bapt. Joint Com. Pub. Affairs, Washington, 1987-91, Nat. Pro-Life Religious Coun., Washington; host nationally syndicated daily radio program For Faith & Family, 1998—, daily radio commentary 1999—; host weekly call-in talk show Richard Land Live, 2002—; appointed by Pres. Goerge W. Bush to U.S. Comn. on Internat. Religious Freedom, 2000—. Cons. editor Criswell Study Bible, 1979. Mem. Gov.'s Task Force on Welfare Reform, Austin, Tex., 1988, Pres.'s Campaign for a Drug-Free Soc., Washington, 1991—; bd. dirs. Nat. Law Ctr., Arlington, Va., 1991—. Recipient Disting. Alumnus award New Orleans Bapt. Theol. Sem., 1997. Mem. Bapt. World Alliance (spl. com. on racism 1992, gen. bd. 1993, v. chmn. christian ethics com. 1995—). Office: Ethics & Religious Liberty Commn 901 Commerce St Ste 550 Nashville TN 37203-3600

LAND, ROBERT DONALD, business consultant; b. Niagara Falls, Ont., Can., Feb. 16, 1926; came to the U.S., 1953; s. Allan Reginald and Beatrice Beryl (Boyle) L.; m. Beverly Grace Hook, July 23, 1955 (div. Nov. 1977); children: Brian, Diane, Susan. BA, U. Toronto, Ont., Can., 1948. Assoc. Life Office Mgmt. Assn. Inst.; cert. profl. bus. cons., Inst. Profl. Bus. Cons. Investment analyst Toronto Gen. Trusts, 1948-50; actuarial acct. Crown Life Ins. Co., Toronto, 1950-53; pres. PM Detroit, Inc., Southfield, Mich., 1953-87, PM Group-Don Land & Assocs., Southfield, 1988—. Pres., dir. Practice Mgmt. Assocs., Toronto, 1969—. Mem., vol. Jaycees, Detroit, 1954-56; coach Royal Oak (Mich.) Hockey Assn., 1974-76. Seaman Royal Can. Navy, 1944-46. Mem. Nat. Assn. Accts., Nat. Assn. Healthcare Cons., Nat. Assn. Tax Profls., Inst. Cert. Bus. Cons. (trustee 1975-76), Nautical Rsch. Guild, U.S. Naval Inst., Soc. Nautical Rsch., Ind. Accts. Mich. Republican. Episcopalian. Avocations: nautical research, photography, boating. Home: 180 Leslie Ln Apt 246 Waterford MI 48328-4849

LANDA, ESTHER ROSENBLATT, volunteer; b. Salt Lake City, Dec. 25, 1912; d. Simon and Sylvia Gertrude (Liberman) Rosenblatt; m. Jerome Joseph Landa, Sept. 26, 1943; children: Carol Leslie, Howard Simon, Terry Ellen. BA, Mills Coll., 1933, MA, 1937, HHD (hon.), 1980, LLD (hon.), U. Utah, 1978; HLD (hon.), Westminster Coll., 1982. Pub. rels. Mills Coll., Calif., 1934-39, Bennington (Vt.) Coll., 1941; account exec. Constnace Hope Assocs., N.Y.C., 1941-42; iinfo. specialist various agys. U.S. Govt., 1942-43; cons. burs. Cmty. Devel. and Indian Svcs., U. Uta, 1962-65; dir. women's programs U. Utah, 1965-71; nat. pres. Nat. Coun. Jewish Women, 1975-79; mem. Pres.'s Adv. Com. Women, 1978-80, Pres.'s Commn. for Nat. Agenda for 80's, 1979-80. Mem. Salt Lake City Bd. Edn.; 1958-70, Utah State Bd. Edn., 1970-74; sec.-treas. Nat. Assn. State Bds. Edn., 1973-74; pres. Salt Lake County Cmty. Action Program, 1968-70; pres. LWV SAlt Lake City, 1956-58; chairperson task force on equal opportunity for women Nat. Jewish Cmty. Rels. Adv. Coun., 1977-83; bd. dirs. Coun. of Jewish Fedns. N.Am., Planned Parenthood Assn. of Utah; mem. planning com. White House Conf. on Children, 1970; Utah del. White House Conf. on Families, 1980; U.S. del. World Conf. UN Decade for Women, Copenhagen, 1980; mem. adv. coun. Grad. Sch. Social work U. Utah, mem. Utahns United Versus Nuclear Arms Race; pub. mem. Commn. on Accreditation, Coun. on Social Work Edn., 1984-86. Author Pres.'s column Nat. Coun. Jewish Women Jour., 1975-79; contbg. editor for UN end of decade women's conf. Good Housekeeping mag., 1985, Nairobi, Kenya. Named to Salt Lake Coun. of Women Hall of Fame, 1958; hon. life mem. PTA, 1963; recipient Liberty Bell award Utah Bar Assn., 1963; Utah Woman of Yr., AAUW, 1965; Woman of Yr. B'nai B'rith, 1965; Man of Yr. in Utah Edn., Phi Delta Kappa, 1967; Civil Rights Worker of Yr. award NAACP, 1968; Disting. Svc. award Utah Sch. Bds. Assn., 1969, 72; U. Utah Alumni Merit award, 1976; Disting. Woman awrd U. Utah, 1978; Susa Young Gates award Nat. Women's Polit. Caucus, 1979; U. Utah Disting. Alumni award, 1984; Citation Utah chpt. NCCJ, 1980; Citizen of Yr. award Nat. Women Assn. Social Work. Mem. Nat. Coun. Jewish Women, LWV, NOW, Nat. Women's Polit. Caucus, ACLU, Hadassah, B'nai B'rith Women, ORT, Phi Beta Kappa, Delta Kappa Gamma. Democrat. Jewish. Home: 515 S 1000 E # 1001 Salt Lake City UT 84102-3003

LANDA, GEORGE, cardiologist, internist; b. Czechoslavakia, Nov. 22, 1947; MD, SUNY, 1972. Intern Long Island Jewish Hosp., 1972-73, resident medicine, 1973-75, Queens Gen. Hosp., 1974-75; fellow cardiology N.Y. Med., 1975-77; staff Nyack Hosp., Suffern, N.Y., Good Samaritan Hosp., Suffern. Fellow Am. Coll. Cardiology; mem. Am. Coll. Physicians. Office: 8 Med Park Dr Pomona NY 10970-3516

LANDA, HOWARD MARTIN, lawyer, business executive; b. Bklyn., Oct. 12, 1943; s. George and Lilli (Skolnik) L.; m. Nori Neinstein, Mar. 14, 1971; children— Alyson, David. BA (N.Y. State Regents scholar), Bklyn. Coll., 1964; JD (tuition scholar), U. Chgo., 1967. Bar: N.Y. 1968. Pvt. practice, N.Y.C., 1968-69; assoc. Garfield, Solomon & Mainzer, 1969-70, Szold, Brandwen, Meyers & Altman, N.Y.C., 1970-74; v.p., sec., gen. counsel IPCO Corp., White Plains, N.Y., 1974-90, also bd. dirs.; pres., mng. dir. Martin Hand Assocs., Inc., Greenwich, Conn., 1990-92, also bd. dirs.; owner Law Offices of Howard M. Landa, N.Y.C., 1990-94; counsel Rand Rosenzweig Smith Radley Gordon & Burstein LLP, 1994—. Lectr. Dental Lab. Conf., 1977. Contbr. articles to profl. jours. Mem. Mayor N.Y.C. Panel to Study Dept. Gen. Services' Div. Mcpl. Supplies, 1978-79; vice-chmn. So. N.Y. chpt. Nat. Multiple Sclerosis Soc., 1984—, bd. dirs., 1984—. Mem.: ABA, Bus. Network Internat. (chpt. pres. 1998—2000). Office: 605 3rd Ave New York NY 10158-0180 E-mail: hlanda@randrose.com.

LANDAHL, HERBERT DANIEL, biophysicist, mathematical biologist, researcher, consultant; b. Fancheng, China, Apr. 23, 1913; (parents Am. citizens); s. Carl W. and Alice (Holmberg) L.; m. Evelyn Christine Blomberg, Aug. 23, 1940; children: Carl David, Carol Ann Landahl Kubai, Linda C. Landahl Shidner. Student, U. Minn., 1931-32; AB, St. Olaf Coll., Northfield,

Minn., 1934; SM, U. Chgo., 1936, PhD, 1941. Rsch. asst. psychometric lab. U. Chgo., 1937-39, rsch. asst. math. biophysics, 1938-41, instr., 1942-45, asst. prof. com. on math. biology, 1945-48, assoc. prof., 1949-56, prof., 1956-68, acting. chmn., 1965-67; prof. biophysics and math. U. Calif., San Francisco, 1968-80, prof. emeritus, 1980—. Cons. Respiratory Project, U. Chgo., 1944-46, toxicity lab. U. Chgo., 1947-51, USAF radiation lab., U. Chgo., 1951-67, dept. biomath. U. Tex., Houston, 1968-89; mem. NIH com. on epidemiology and biometry, Bethesda, Md., 1960-64. Co-author: Mathematical Biophysics of Central Nervous System, 1945; contbr. approximately 190 sci. papers to various jours.; chief editor Bull. Math. Biology, 1973-80; mem. editl. Computers in Biology and Medicine, 1971-90. Recipient Career Devel. award NIH, 1962-67, Career Achievement award Soc. Toxicology, 1987; grantee NIH, 1963-67. Fellow AAAS; mem. Biophys. Soc., Biometric Soc. (charter), Bioengring. Soc. (charter), Latin Am. Biomath. Soc. (charter), Soc. for Math. Biology (founding, pres. 1981-83). Home: 472 Lansdale Ave San Francisco CA 94127-1617 Office: U Calif PO Box 970 San Francisco CA 94143-0001

LANDAR, HERBERT JAY, linguistics educator, writer; b. N.Y.C., Dec. 7, 1927; s. Leo and Mildred (Mann) L.; m. Muriel Anne Epstein; children: Clifford, Nancy, Stephen. BA, Queens Coll., 1949; MA, Yale U., 1955, PhD, 1960. Mem. S.W. project in comparative psycholinguistics Social Sci. Rsch. Coun., 1955-56; instr. Reed Coll., Portland, Oreg., 1957-59; predoctoral fellow Social Sci. Rsch. Coun., 1959-60; mem. dept. pub. health and preventive medicine Cornell U. Med. Coll, Navajo-Cornell Clinic, Ariz., 1959-60; prof. linguistics Calif. State U., L.A., 1960-91, prof. emeritus, 1991—. Vis. prof. Ind. U., Bloomington, 1976-77, U. Blaise Pascal, Clermont-Ferrand, France, 1987-88. Author: Language and Culture, 1966, (in Japanese) Kotoba-To Bunka, 1977; contbr. articles to profl. jours. With U.S. Army, 1950-52. Guggenheim Found. fellow, 1967-68; Fulbright Commn. grant, 1987-88. Fellow AAAS, Am. Anthrop. Assn., Royal Anthrop. Inst. Gt. Britain and Ireland; mem. Ling. Soc. Am., N.Y. Acad. Scis., Assn. Computational Linguistics, Soc. Américanistes Paris. Home: 220 San Anselmo Ave San Francisco CA 94127-2030

LANDAU, BERNARD ROBERT, biochemistry educator, physician; b. Newark, June 24, 1926; s. Morris Harry and Estelle (Kirsch) L.; m. Lucille Slosberg, Jan. 11, 1956; children: Steven Brian, Deborah Louise (dec.), Rodger Martin. S.B., MIT, 1947; PhD, Harvard U., 1950, MD, 1954; MD (hon.), Karolinska Inst., 1993. Diplomate: Am. Bd. Internal Medicine. Intern Peter Bent Brigham Hosp., Boston, 1954-55; clin. assoc. Nat. Cancer Inst., Bethesda, Md., 1955-57; fellow in biochemistry Harvard U., 1957-58; sr. resident Peter Bent Brigham Hosp., 1958-59; asst. prof. medicine Case Western Res. U., 1959-62, assoc. prof., 1962-67, prof., 1969—, prof. biochemistry, 1979—, physician Univ. Hosps., 1969—. Dir. dept. biochemistry Merck and Co., Rahway, N.J., 1967-69 Contbr. articles to profl. jours. Fellow Commonwealth fund, 1965-66, Fogarty Sr. Internat. fellow 1986-87, 93-94; grantee Am. Heart Assn., 1959-64; recipient William B. Peck Postgrad. Research award, 1961 Fellow AAAS; mem. Am. Fedn. Clin. Research, Am. Soc. Clin. Investigation, Assn. Am. Physicians, Am. soc. Biol. Chemists, Am. Physiol. Soc., Endocrine Soc., Central Soc. Clin. Research, Am. Diabetes Assn., Sigma Xi, Alpha Omega Alpha Home: 19501 S Woodland Rd Cleveland OH 44122-2834 Office: University Hosps Cleveland 11100 Euclid Ave Cleveland OH 44106-1736 E-mail: brl@po.cwru.edu.

LANDAU, ELLIS, gaming company executive; b. Phila., Feb. 24, 1944; s. Manfred and Ruth (Fischer) L.; m. Kathy Suzanne Thomas, May 19, 1968 (div.); children: Rachel, David; m. Yvette Ehr Cohen, Nov. 1, 1992. BA in Econs., Brandeis U., 1965; MBA, Columbia U., 1967. Fin. analyst SEC, Washington, 1968-69; asst. treas. U-Haul Internat., Phoenix, 1969-71; v.p., treas. Ramada, Inc., 1971-90; CFO Boyd Gaming Corp., Las Vegas, Nev., 1990—. Home: 7571 Silver Meadow Ct Las Vegas NV 89117-2986 Office: Boyd Gaming Corp 2950 Industrial Rd Las Vegas NV 89109-1100 E-mail: ellislandau@boydgaming.com.

LANDAU, ELVITA ANN, library director; b. Sept. 7, 1949; BA, Fort Hays State U., Kans., 1971; MLS, Emporia State U., Kans., 1973. Dir. Hays (Kans.) Pub. Libr., 1975-79; head adult svcs. Salina (Kans.) Pub. Libr., 1980-84; libr. Sch. of Music, Univ. Idaho, Moscow, 1984-85; from asst. dir. to dir. Brookings (S.D.) Pub. Libr., 1985—. Office: Brookings Pub Libr 515 3d St Brookings SD 57006-2077 E-mail: elandau@sdln.net.

LANDAU, EMANUEL, epidemiologist; b. N.Y.C., Nov. 28, 1919; s. Meyer and Annie (Heller) L.; m. Davetta Goldberg, Sept. 5, 1948; children: Melanie (dec.), Elizabeth. BA, CCNY, 1939; Phd, Am. U., 1966. Supervisory analytical statistician Calif. Dept. Public Health, 1957-59, chief biometry sect., divsn. air pollution, 1959-62; head lab. and clin. trials sect. Nat. Cancer Inst., 1962-65; statis. adviser Nat. Air Pollution Control Adminstrn., 1965-69; epidemiologist Environ. Health Svc., 1969-71; chief epidemiologic studies br. Bur. Radiol. Health, 1971-74; project dir., sci. cons. Am. Pub. Health Assn., Washington, 1975—. Cons., adv. in field, including WHO adv. on air quality criteria, Geneva, 1967, Karolinska Inst., Stockholm, 1968. Contbr. articles to profl. jours. Vol. White House Health Care Reform Corr. With AUS, 1942-46, capt. USPHS Res. Decorated Belgian Fourragere; recipient Superior Svc. award HEW, 1963. Fellow Am. Pub. Health Assn., Royal Soc. Health; mem. Soc. Epidemiologic Rsch., Am. Statis. Assn. (chmn. com. on stats. and environ.), Cosmos Club. Democrat. Jewish. Home: 4601 N Park Ave Apt 208 Chevy Chase MD 20815-4575 Office: Am Pub Health Assn 800 I Street NW Washington DC 20001-3710

LANDAU, FELIX, lawyer; b. Hof/Salle, Germany, June 29, 1947; came to U.S., 1950; s. Fiszel and Ursula (Wahncau) Landau; children: Erik Lloyd, Kelly Anne, Kristine Marie. BS, U. Colo., 1969; MA, U. Northern Colo., 1972; JD cum laude, Gonzaga U., 1982. Bar: Wash. 1983, Wis. 1988. Assoc. Liebman, Conway, Olejniczak and Jerry, S.C., Green Bay, Wis., 1987-90; pvt. practice, Bellevue, Wash., 1990—. Assoc. editor Gonzaga U. Law Rev., 1981-82; author: Accident Investigation - Documenting the Facts, WSTLA Automobile Accident Litigation Deskbook, 2000. Founder, head coach Bellevue Eagles Track and Cross Country Team. Capt. USAF, 1983-87. Mem. ABA, Wash. Bar Assn., Wash. State Trial Lawyers Assn. (Eagle mem., chmn. Eastside roundtable 1995-98), East King County Trial Lawyers Assn., Wis. Bar Assn., Phi Delta Phi. Avocations: sports, golf, basketball, tennis, jogging, coaching USA Track and Field and Cross Country Running. Office: 14670 NE 8th St Bellevue WA 98007-4127 Business E-mail: landaulawoffice@aol.com.

LANDAU, HERMAN, newspaperman retired; b. Louisville, Apr. 12, 1911; s. Oscar Hayim and Rebecca (Fuhrer) L.; m. Leah Seligman, Apr. 15, 1946 (dec. 1974); children: Kay Landau Miller, Rebecca Landau Greenfield; m. Helen Berman Landau, June 15, 1975; children: Margaret Berman Goldberg, Susan Berman Rogers, Joseph. B in Liberal Studies, U. Louisville, 1985. Makeup editor The Courier-Jour., Louisville, 1928-52, The Louisville Times, 1952-75; ret., 1975; founder, contbr. Cmty., Louisville, 1977-91, editor emeritus, 1991—. Author: (book) Adath Louisville, 1981. Bd. dirs. Jewish Cmty. Ctr., 1945-72, Jewish Cmty. Fedn., 1970—, B'nai B'rith Louisville Lodge #14, 1937—, Jewish Edn. Assn., N.Y.C., 1980. Recipient Vol. of Yr. award Jewish Cmty. Ctr., Louisville, 1959, Jewish Cmty. Fedn., 1991, Outstanding Participation award, Bonds for Israel, 1981, Jewish Person of Yr. award B'nai B'rith, 1997. Democrat. Jewish. Home: 2637 Drayton Dr Louisville KY 40205-2331

LANDAU, LAURI BETH, accountant, tax consultant; b. Bklyn., July 21, 1952; d. Jack and Audrey Carolyn (Zuckernick) L. BA, Skidmore Coll., 1973; postgrad., Pace U., 1977-79. CPA, N.Y. Mem. staff Audrey Z. Landau, CPA, Suffern, N.Y., 1976-78, Ernst & Whinney, N.Y.C., 1979-80, mem. sr. staff, 1980-82, supr., 1982-84; mgr. Arthur Young & Co., 1984-87, prin., 1987-89; sr. mgr. Ernst & Young, 1989-92; ptnr. Landau & Landau, Pomona, N.Y., 1992—. Ptnr. Audrey Z. Landau & Co., Wilmington, Vt., 1995—; spkr. World Trade Inst., N.Y.C., 1987—, Nat. Fgn. Trade Coun., N.Y.C., 1989—. Composer songs. Career counselor Skidmore Coll., Saratoga Springs, N.Y., 1977—; mem. leadership com. Class of 1973, 83-85, pres., 1985-93, fund chmn., 1987-88, mem. planned gift com., 1989—. N.Y. State Regents scholar, 1970. Mem. Nat. Conf. CPA Practitioners, N.Y. State Soc. CPAs, Rockland Bus. Assn., Skidmore Coll. Alumni Assn. (mem. nominating com. 1989-92). Skidmore Alumni Club. Democrat. Avocations: music, ballet, photography, sports. Office: 26 Firemans Memorial Dr Pomona NY 10970-3553 E-mail: lauri@landauandlandau.com.

LANDAU, LISA, investment banker; b. N.Y.C., June 1, 1967; d. Norman Joseph and Marjorie Lou L. BA, Columbia U., 1989; MBA, Harvard U., 1994. Analyst Drexel Burnham, N.Y.C., 1989-1990, Bear Sterns, N.Y.C., 1990-1991, Wasserstein Perella, N.Y.C., 1991-1992; assoc. Merrill Lynch, 1994-1997, v.p., 1998-1999, dir., 1999—. Woman of the Yr. award Columbia Coll. Women, 1997. Mem. Columbia Coll. Alumni Assn. (dir. and v.p.), Columbia Coll. Bd. Visitors. Avocations: running, hiking, traveling. Home: 25 Central Park W New York NY 10023-7253 Office: Merrill Lynch World Financial Ctr New York NY 10281

LANDAU, MARTIN, actor; b. Bklyn., June 20, 1934; m. Barbara Bain (div.); children: Susie, Juliet. Student, Art Students League, Actors Studio. Staff artist, cartoonist N.Y. Daily News. Star TV series Mission: Impossible, 1966-69 (Golden Globe award 1967), Space 1999, 1974-77, others; TV appearances include Omnibus, Playhouse 90, G.E. Theatre, Gunsmoke, Twilight Zone; also TV movies Welcome Home, Johnny Bristol, 1972, Savage, 1973, The Death of Ocean View Park, 1979, The Harlem Globetrotters on Gilligan's Island, 1981, The Fall of the House of Usher, 1982, The Neon Empire, 1989, By Dawn's Early Light, 1990, Something to Live For: The Alison Gertz Story, 1992, Legacy of Lies, 1992 (Ace award), 12:01, 1993, miniseries Joseph, 1995; films include Pork Chop Hill, North by Northwest, 1959, Stagecoach to Dancer's Rock, 1961, Cleopatra, 1962, Hallelujah Trail, 1964, The Greatest Story Ever Told, 1965, Nevada Smith, 1966, They Call Me Mr. Tibbs, 1970, Operation SNAFU, 1970, A Town Called Hell, 1971, Johnny Bristol, 1971, Black Gunn, 1972, Strange Shadows in an Empty Room, 1977, Meteor, 1979, The Last Word, 1979, Without Warning, 1980, Operation Moonbase Alpha, 1980, Earthright, 1980, Beauty and the Beast, 1981, Alone in the Dark, 1982, Trail by Terror, 1983, Tucker: The Man and His Dreams, 1988 (Acad. Award nominee 1988), Crimes and Misdeameanors, 1989 (Golden Globe award 1989, Acad. award nominee 1989), Paint It Black, 1990, Real Bullets, 1990, Firehead, 1991, Eye of the Widow, 1991, Mistress, 1992, Silver, 1993, Intersection, 1994, Ed Wood, 1994 (Best Supporting Actor Acad. award 1994, Golden Globe award 1994, SAG award 1994, Am. Comedy award 1994, N.Y. Film Critics award 1994, L.A. Film Critics award 1994, Chgo. Film Critics award 1994, Nat. Soc. Film Critics award 1994, Boston Film Critics award 1994, Tex. Film Critics award 1994, Lifetime Achivement award Houston Film Festival 1994, Lifetime Achivement award Charleston Film Festival 1994), The Elevator, 1996, City Hall, 1996, The Adventures of Pinocchio, 1996, Legend of the Spirit Dog (voice), 1997, Animals, 1997, B*A*P*S, 1997, The Long Way Home (voice), Winter, 1998, The Joyrides, 1998, The X Files: Fight the Future, 1998, Rounders, 1998, ED-TV, 1999, Carlo's Wake, 1999, The Joyriders, 1999, The Commission, 1999, (miniseries) The Life and Times of Joe Bonnano, 1999, The New Adventures of Pinocchio, 1999, In the Beginning, 2000, Haven, 2000, Very Mean Men, 2000, The Majestic, 2001; stage appearances include Middle of the Night, Uncle Vanya, Stalag 17, Wedding Breakfast, First Love, The Goat Song, Dracula. Emmy nominee; recipient Lifetime Achievement award San Diego Film Festival, 1998. Mem. Acad. Motion Picture Arts and Scis., Actors Studio (W. Coast dir.) Office: 23717 Long Valley Rd Calabasas CA 91302-2409

LANDAU, MARTIN, political science educator; b. N.Y.C., July 12, 1921; s. User Noah and Clara (Markowitz) L.; m. Bernice Feldman, July 11, 1943; children— Madeline, Claudia. AB, Bklyn. Coll., 1947; MA in Pub. Adminstrn, N.Y. U., 1948; PhD, 1952; Docteur Honoris Causa, U. Paris, Dauphine, 1993. Vis. research prof. U. Calif. at Berkeley, 1969-71, prof. polit. sci., 1972—; Distinguished prof. City U. N.Y., Bklyn., 1970-72; lectr. orgn. and decision theory Fgn. Service Inst., U.S. Dept. State, Washington, 1969-72. Cons. in field; chancellor Grad. Sch. Pub. Adminstrn., U. P.R., San Juan, 1970-71; Berkeley Exch. prof., Peking U., 1985; Phi Beta Kappa Nat. Lectr., 1984; dir. Berkeley-Hong Kong Project, 1984—. Author: Political Theory and Political Science; Studies in the Methodology of Political Inquiry, 1972; Chmn. editorial bd.: Polit. Sci, 1971— ; mem. editorial bd.: Jour. Comparative Adminstrv. Studies, 1969— , Comparative Politics, 1970—, Jour. Theoretical Politics, 1988—, Jour. Behavioral Decision Making, 1988—. Served with Signal Corps AUS, 1941-45. Recipient Distinguished Teaching award Bklyn. Coll., 1963, E. Harris Harbison award gifted teaching Danforth Found., 1969-70, William E. Mosher award distinguished scholarship Soc. Pub. Adminstrn., 1970, 79; John Simon Guggenheim fellow, 1976-77; fellow Center Advanced Study in Behavioral Sci., 1976-77 Fellow Nat. Acad. Public Adminstrn.; mem. Am. Polit. Sci. Assn., Philosophy of Sci. Assn. Home: 1410 Summit Rd Berkeley CA 94708-2215 Office: U Calif Dept Polit Sci Berkeley CA 94720-0001

LANDAU, MICHAEL B. law educator, musician, writer; b. Wilkes-Barre, Pa., July 3, 1953; s. Jack Landau and Florence (Rabitz) Simon. BA, Pa. State U., 1975; JD, U. Pa., 1988. Vis. prof. law Dickinson Sch. Law, Pa. State U., Carlisle; assoc. Cravath, Swaine and Moore, N.Y.C., 1988-90, Skadden, Arps, N.Y.C., 1990-92; assoc. prof. Coll. Law Ga. State U., Atlanta, 1992-99, prof. law, 1999—. Vis. prof. law U. Ga. Law Sch., 1998; guest lectr. Johannes Kepler U., Linz, Austria, summer 1994, 95, 96; vis. scholar Univ. Amsterdam, 2000. Contbr. articles to law jours. on copyright, art, patent, entertainment law. Mem. ABA, N.Y. State Bar Assn., Internat. Bar Assn., Vol. Lawyers for Arts, Am. Fedn. Musicians, Am. Intellectual Property Law Assn., Copyright Soc. U.S. Am., Phi Kappa Phi, Omicron Delta Epsilon. Democrat. Avocations: photography, jazz guitar, jazz piano. Office: Ga State U Coll Law University Pla Atlanta GA 30303 E-mail: mlandau@gsu.edu.

LANDAU, PETER EDWARD, editor; b. N.Y.C., July 16, 1933; s. Edward and Charlotte (Schmidt) L. AB, Duke U., 1955; MS in Econs., Columbia U., 1959. Editl. asst. Newsweek mag., N.Y.C., 1955-57, asst. editor, 1958-61, assoc. editor, 1962-67; v.p. Tiderock Corp., 1967; sr. editor Instl. Investor, N.Y.C., 1968, mng. editor, 1968-70, editor, 1971-91, editor-at-large, 1991-97; historian St. Andrew's Golf Club, 1993—. Co-author: Presidential Lies: The Illustrated History of White House Golf, 1996. Home: 10 Old Jackson Ave Unit 11 Hastings On Hudson NY 10706

LANDAU, SIDNEY IVAN, lexicographer; b. N.Y.C., Apr. 11, 1933; s. Emanuel and Sadie Mildred (Halpern) L.; m. Sarah Gaston Bradford, June 19, 1959; children: Paul, Amy. BA in English, Queens Coll., 1954; MFA in Creative Writing, U. Iowa, 1959. Instr. English Miami U., Oxford, Ohio, 1959-61; editor, then editor-in-chief dictionaries Funk & Wagnalls, N.Y.C., 1961-70; editor-in-chief Doubleday Dictionary, Doubleday Roget's Thesaurus Doubleday & Co., 1975-77; editor-in-chief Internat. Dictionary of Medicine and Biology, John Wiley & Sons, 1977-88, mgr. med. jours., 1982-84, exec. editor medicine, 1985-87, pub. chemistry and life scis. sci.-tech. div., 1987-88; edtl. dir. N.Am. br. Cambridge U. Press, 1988-93; editor-in-chief Cambridge Dictionary of Am. English, 2000. Author: Dictionaries: The Art and Craft of Lexicography, 1984, 2d edit., 2001; contbr. numerous articles to profl. jours. With U.S. Army, 1954-56. Fellow: Dictionary Soc. N.Am. (pres. 1993—95); mem.: Am. Dialect Soc. Home: 50 W 96th St Apt 2A New York NY 10025-6527

LANDAU, WALTER LOEBER, lawyer; b. New Orleans, Sept. 9, 1931; s. Walter Loeber and Mae (Wilzin) L.; m. Barbara Jane Gordon, June 23, 1954; children: Donna Hardiman, Blair Trippe, Gordon Loeber. BA, Princeton U., 1953; LLB, Harvard U., 1956. Bar: N.Y. 1956, U.S. Dist. Ct. (so. dist.) N.Y. 1962, U.S. Supreme Ct. 1971. Assoc. firm Sullivan & Cromwell, N.Y.C., 1959-65, ptnr., 1966-98, sr. counsel, 1999—. Trustee Reece Sch., N.Y.C.; mem. Met. Opera Assn.; bd. dirs., treas. Opera Orch. N.Y., bd. dirs. N.Y.C. Opera; bd. dirs., sec. Manhattan Theatre Club. Fellow Am. Bar Found.; mem. ABA, N.Y. State Bar Assn., Assn. Bar City N.Y., Am. Law Inst. Republican. Office: Sullivan & Cromwell 125 Broad St Fl 24 New York NY 10004-2400 E-mail: landaul@sullcrom.com.

LANDAUER, ELVIE ANN WHITNEY, humanities educator, writer; b. Detroit, Dec. 10, 1937; d. Augustus and Leona (Green) Moore; m. Thomas Whitney, 1963 (div. 1978); m. Ernest Landauer, Dec. 31, 1987. BA, Calif. State U., L.A., 1978; MA, San Francisco State U., 1989; postgrad., U. N.Mex. Dep. dir. Calif. Arts Coun., Sacramento, 1976-79; exec. dir. Mothers Emergency Svc., 1979-82; assoc. dir. San Francisco Cmty. Bds., 1982-83; adminstr. San Francisco Rsch. Project, 1983-86; exec. dir. East Bay Ctr. for Performing Arts, Richmond, Calif., 1987-89; instr. English Calif. C.C.s, Pittsburg, Fremont & Hayward, 1990-93; instr. Am. studies U. N.Mex., Albuquerque, 1993-94; instr. humanities New Coll., San Francisco, 1994-95. Bus. owner, pub. Academics of Course! Books, Berkeley, Calif., 1997—; rschr. L.A. Cmty. Arts Alliance, 1972. Author: (drama anthology) The Disinherited, 1971, The Uptown Mrs. Carrie, 1989; prodr. Meat Theater Co., 1970-72. Bd. dirs. Richmond (Calif.) Arts Coun., 1986-89; workshop coord. L.A. Writers Workshop, 1966-69, Sacramento Civic Theater, 1980; project coord. City Spirit Project, Pasadena, Calif., 1972-75. With USN, 1958-61. Recipient Woman of Yr. award Iota Phi Lambda, Sacramento, 1981. Home: 100 Kathy Ellen Ct Vallejo CA 94591- Fax: 510-845-9351.

LANDAUER, SUSAN E. artist; b. Oakland, Calif., July 31, 1958; AB, U. Calif., Berkeley, 1982; MA in History of Art, Yale U., 1984, PhD in History of Art, 1992. Ind. curator/author, 1992—96; asst. curator L.A. County Mus., L.A., 1996; founding co-dir. S.F. Ctr. for the Book, 1996—97; Katie and Drew Gibson Chief Curator San Jose Mus. of Art, Calif., 1999—. Author: (novels) Elmer Bischolf: The Ethics of Paint, 2001, California Impressionists, 1996, The San Francisco Sch of Abstract Expressionism, 1996, Obatas Yosemite, 1993. Office: San Jose Mus of Art 110 S Market San Jose CA 95113

LANDAW, STEPHEN ARTHUR, physician, educator; b. Paterson, N.J., June 20, 1936; s. Louis and Ida (Machowsky) L.; children: Jared Lawrence, Nicole Renee. BS, U. Wis., 1955; MD, George Washington U., 1959; PhD, U. Calif., Berkeley, 1969. Intern Mt. Sinai Hosp., N.Y.C., 1959-60, resident in internal medicine, 1960-61; fellow in hematology Med. Coll. Va., 1962-63; fellow in nuclear medicine Donner Lab., U. Calif., 1963-69, asst. physician, 1970-73; chief isotope lab. Highland-Alameda County Hosp., Oakland, Calif., 1970-73; asso. prof. SUNY, Syracuse, 1973-78, prof., 1978-99; assoc. chief staff research and devel. VA Med. Center, Syracuse, 1973-94; chief, hematology VA Med. Ctr., 1997-99; vis. prof. Rockefeller U., N.Y.C., 1988; vis. physician Rockefeller U. Hosp., 1988; dep. editor, hematology Uptodate, Inc., Wellesley, Mass., 1999—. Pres. Ctrl. N.Y. Rsch. Corp., 1989-94. Contbr. in field. Served with U.S. Army, 1961-62. VA grantee, 1973-93; NASA grantee, 1976-82; recipient NASA Kosmos Achievement awards, 1975, 77 Fellow ACP; mem. Am. Soc. Hematology, Am. Fedn. Clin. Rsch., Soc. Pediat. Rsch., Soc. Exptl. Biology and Medicine, N.Y. Acad. Sci., Sigma Xi, Alpha Omega Alpha. Jewish. Home: 241 Perkins St Apt F103 Jamaica Plain MA 02130-4058 Office: Uptodate Inc 34 Washington St Ste 200 Wellesley MA 02481-1903 E-mail: slandaw@uptodateinc.com.

LANDE, JAMES AVRA, lawyer; b. Chgo., Oct. 2, 1930; s. Theodore and Helen C. (Hamburger) L.; m. Ann Mari Gustavsson, Feb. 21, 1959; children: Rebecca Susanne, Sylvia Diane. BA, Swarthmore Coll., 1952; JD, Columbia U., 1955. Bar: N.Y. 1958, Calif. 1967. Assoc. Rein, Mound & Cotton, N.Y.C., 1957-59; atty. VA, Seattle, 1959-61, Weyerhaeuser Co., Tacoma, 1961-63, Lande Assocs., San Francisco, 1963-67, NASA, Ames Rsch. Ctr., Moffett Field, Calif., 1967-70; house counsel Syntex Corp., Palo Alto, 1970-73; dir. contracts dept. Electric Power Rsch. Inst., 1973-81; corp. atty., dir. contracts Lurgi Corp., Belmont, 1981-82; contracts mgr. Bechtel Corp., San Francisco, 1982-92; sr. contract mgr. Bay Area Rapid Transit Dist., Millbrae, Calif., 1992—. Adj. prof. U. San Francisco Sch. Law, 1972-73; lectr. law U. Santa Clara Sch. Law, 1968-82; pres. Syntex Fed. Credit Union, 1971-72. Served with U.S. Army, 1955-57. Mem. Calif. Bar Assn., Nat. Contract Mgmt. Assn. (past pres., dir. Golden Gate chpt.), Lawyers Club San Francisco. Home: 1330 33rd Ave San Francisco CA 94122-1305 Office: Bay Area Rapid Transit Dist 979 Broadway Millbrae CA 94030-1912

LANDE, ROGER LEE, lawyer; b. Lake Mills, Iowa, Nov. 7, 1936; s. Carl Johann and Gladys Kathryn (Schmidthuber) Lande; m. Sarah Dunkerton Lande, Aug. 20, 1960; children: Margaret Ann, Roger Christopher. BA, JD, U. Iowa, 1961. Bar: Iowa 1961. Pres., CEO Stanley, Lande & Hunter, Muscatine, Iowa, 1961—. Mem. editl. bd. U. Iowa Jour. Corp. Law, 1976-98. Mem. Iowa State Bd. Regents, 1996—2001; bd. dirs. Iowa Law Sch. Found., Iowa City, 1989—, Muscatine Devel. Corp., 1990—; chair Iowa Assn. Bus. and Industry, 1991—92. Mem. Iowa State Bar Assn. (pres. 1981-82, bd. govs. 1977-79), Rotary, Union League Club Chgo., Des Moines Club. Office: Stanley Lande & Hunter 301 Iowa Ave Ste 400 Muscatine IA 52761-3881 E-mail: RLande@slhlaw.com.

LANDE, RUTH HARRIET, photographer, language educator; b. N.Y.C., May 17, 1929; d. Julius Dewey and Josie (Rosenberger) Schlesenger; m. Bernard Lande, Dec. 21, 1951 (div. 1983); 1 child, Stephen. BS, Adelphi U., 1964; MS, Hofstra U., 1988. Cert. tchr., N.Y. Tchr. E. N.Y. Vocat. High Sch., Bklyn., 1968-70; freelance photographer Muttontown and Great Neck, N.Y., 1979—; adj. prof. English as 2d lang. C.W. Post Coll., Brookville, 1989—; tchr. photography Bethpage Adult Edn., 1991-95, Port Washington (N.Y.) Adult Edn., 1995, Mineola Adult Edn., 1999. Recipient Pell grant, Hofstra U., 1986. Mem. Nassau Assn. Continuing Community Edn., Syosset Camera Club (sec. 1987-89), Great Neck Color Camera Club, Nassau Counselors Assn., Rockport Art Assn., Boothbay Region Art Found., Maine Art Gallery, Art League of Long Island. Avocations: walking, swimming, photography. Home: 1 Ipswich Ave Apt 209 Great Neck NY 11021-3261

LANDEGGER, CARL CLEMENT, machinery and pulp manufacturing executive; b. Vienna, Austria, Sept. 20, 1930; came to U.S., 1937, naturalized, 1947; s. Karl F. and Helena (Berger) L.; children: Christine, Claudia, Cary, Celia, Gregory. BS in Social Sci., Georgetown U., 1951. Vice chmn. Parsons and Whittemore, Inc., N.Y.C., 1953—; with Black Clawson Co., 1956—, exec. v.p., 1959-65, pres., 1965—, chmn., 1967—. Chmn. Black Clawson Co. Inc., United Container Machinery Inc., St. Anne Nackawic Pulp & Paper Co.; vice chmn. Ala. River Pulp Co., Monroeville, Ala. Bd. dirs. Georgetown U., Gregorian U. Found. 1st lt. USAF, 1951-53. Mem. Explorers Club, Road Runners Club (bd. dirs.). Office: Black Clawson Co 150 E 52d St New York NY 10022

LANDEN, ROBERT GERAN, retired historian, educator, university administrator; b. Boston, July 13, 1930; s. Harry James and Evelyn Gertrude (Geran) L.; m. Patricia Kizzia, July 19, 1958; children— Michael Geran, Robert Kizzia, Jill Arnett, Amy Patricia. AB, Coll. of William and Mary, 1952; MA, U. Mich., 1953; A.M., Princeton U., 1958, PhD (Ford Found. fellow), 1961. Asst. prof. social sci. Ball State U., Muncie, Ind., 1959-60; asst. prof. near eastern studies U. Mich., Ann Arbor, 1960-61; asst. prof. history Dartmouth, Hanover, N.H., 1961-66, asst. dean of freshmen, 1963-64, asso. prof. history, 1966-67; prof., head dept. history Va. Poly. Inst. and State U., Blacksburg, 1967-69; prof. history U. S.C., Columbia, 1969-75, asso. vice provost, 1971-72, asso. provost, 1972-73; dean U. S.C. (Coll. of Social and Behavioral Scis.), 1972-75; prof. history U. Tex. at Arlington, 1975-77; dean U. Tex. at Arlington (Coll. Liberal Arts), 1975-77; prof. history U. Tenn., Knoxville, 1977-86; dean Coll. Liberal Arts, 1977-85; prof. history, v.p. acad. affairs, provost U. Montevallo, 1986-88; prof. history and humanities, dir. programs in the humanities Va. Poly Inst. and State U., Blacksburg, 1988-95, prof. emeritus history and humanities, 1995—. Author: Oman Since 1856, 1967, The Emergence of the Modern Middle East, 1970, (with Abid Al-Marayati) The Middle East, Its Governments and Politics, 1972; contbr. articles to profl. jours. and book revs. to hist. publs. Served with AUS, 1953-55. Am. Coun. Learned Socs. fellow, 1965-66, Comparative Studies Ctr. Faculty fellow, 1965-66, Malone fellow, 1988. Fellow Middle East Studies Assn. of N. Am.; mem. Theta Delta Chi, Phi Kappa Phi. Roman Catholic. Home: 108 Edgewood Ln Williamsburg VA 23185-3213

LANDER, GREGG, lawyer; b. Victoria, Tex., Sept. 3, 1965; s. B.E. Leissner Jr. and Reed Johnston. BBA in Mktg., Tex. A&M U., 1989; JD, Calif. Western Sch. Law, 1997. Law clk. Law Office of Kenneth S. Greenfield, San Diego, 1996-97; legal asst. Disney Interactive, Glendale, 1998; assoc. Bolden & Martin LLP, L.A., 1998-99, Kiesel, Boucher & Larson LLP, Beverly Hills, Calif., 1999—2001; with Law Offices of Kevin T. Barnes, L.A., 2001—. Mem.: ATLA, ABA, Beverly Hills Bar Assn., Los Angeles County Bar Assn., Calif. State Bar Assn. Avocations: multimedia, photography, nature. Home: 1546 S Fairfax Ave #1 Los Angeles CA 90019 Office: Law Offices of Kevin T Barnes 5670 Wilshire Blvd Ste 1460 90036 E-mail: gregglander@email.com.

LANDER, HORACE NORMAN, genetics consultant, materials consultant; b. Cambridge, Mass., May 28, 1923; s. Norman and Emily Ann (Rolls) L.; m. Donna Ruth Packer, Oct. 14, 1943 (dec. May 1983); children: Karen D. Sanders (dec.), Jeffrey B., Kathleen E. Silver, Gregory N., Caroline E. Shaw; m. Ingrid Elisabet Roslund, Apr. 9, 1985. BS in Metallurg. Engring., MIT,

1951, ScD in Metallurgy, 1955; postgrad., Harvard U., 1970. Materials engr. Metal Hydrides, Inc., Beverly, Mass., 1954-56; supr. process devel. Jones & Laughlin Steel Corp., Pitts., 1956-60; asst. dir., dir. R & D Youngstown (Ohio) Steet & Tube Co., 1960-70; v.p. rsch. Amax, Inc., Greenwich, Conn., 1970-71, v.p. rsch. and market devel., 1971-83, sr. v.p rsch. and market devel., 1983-85; materials engr. Nippon Steel USA, N.Y.C., 1985-96; pres. Scangen, Inc., Beaufort, S.C., 1996—. Mem. sci. and tech. com. Indsl. Rsch. Inst., N.Y.C., 1975-83; genetics cons. ProteGene, Inc., Tokyo, 1994—; mem. indsl. adv. bd. MIT, Cambridge, Mass., Pa. State U., State College, U. Conn., Storrs, 1975-83. Contbr. 15 technical articles to profl. jour. 1st lt. USAF, 1943-46. Fellow Am. Smelting and Refining Co., 1952-55. Fellow Am. Soc. Metals; mem. MIT Club of Boston, Sigma Xi, Tau Beta Pi (hon.). Avocations: writing poetry, golf, walking, swimming, computer applications. Home: 245 Dataw Dr Saint Helena Island SC 29920-3810 Office: ScanGen Inc 245 Dataw Dr Saint Helena Island SC 29920-3810

LANDER, JAMES ALBERT, retired military officer, comptroller; b. Abbeville, S.C., Apr. 9, 1930; s. William Jones and Annie (Cheatham) L.; m. Jolene Patricia Smith, June 8, 1952; children: Theresa (dec.), Britt, Leslie, Victoria (dec.), Gail, Jean, David. BS, Lander Coll., 1986; LLD (hon.), Lander U., 2000. Technician S.C. Nat. Guard, Abbeville, 1952-53; life ins. salesman Gulf Life Pilot, Met., Anderson, S.C., 1953-66; maj. U.S. Army, 1966-71; plans and ops. officer, chief of staff S.C. Army N.G., Columbia, 1971-85, maj. gen. mil., 1988-91; mem. S.C. Senate, 1993-99; elected state comptr. State of S.C., 1999—. Chmn. RSVP Adv. Com., 1991—, Newberry County Literacy Assn., 1991-93; deacon Newberry 1st Bapt. Ch., 1981; past chmn. Boy Scouts Am., Newberry. Decorated Bronze Star, Legion of Merit; recipient Arc Legis. award, 1999, Order of Palmetto State of S.C., 1985, Palmetto Cross, 1991, Silver Beaver award Boy Scouts Am., 1990; named Legislator of Yr. S.C. Assn. Counties and S.C. Assn. Deaf, 1994. Mem.: MOWW, ROA, VVA, Sheiner, C. of C. Newberry, Assn. U.S. Army, Exch. Club (pres.), Masons, VFW, Am. Legion. Democrat. Baptist. Avocations: reading, gardening. Home: 2029 Main St Newberry SC 29108-3521 Office: SC Comptr Gen 305 Wade Hampton Office Columbia SC 29201 E-mail: cgoffice@cg.state.sc.us.

LANDER, JOYCE ANN, nursing educator, medical/surgical nurse; b. Benton Harbor, Mich., July 27, 1942; d. James E. and Anna Mae Remus LPN, Kalamazoo Practical Nursing, Ctr., 1967; AAS, Kalamazoo Valley C.C., 1981, Grad. Massage Therapy Program, 1995. LPN-RN Bronson Meth. Hosp., Kalamazoo, 1972-82; RN med./surg. unit Borgess Med. Ctr., 1982-84; RN pediatrics Upjohn Home Health Care, 1984-88; supr. nursing lab Kalamazoo Valley Community Coll., 1982—. Therapeutic massage therapist in client homes with Business Kneading Peace Therapeutic Massage, Kalamazoo, 1995—; nursing asst., instr. State of Mich. Observer, 1990-96. Author: What Is A Nurse, 1980. Address: 3300 Woodstone Dr E Apt 108 Kalamazoo MI 49008-2548

LANDER, RUTH A. medical group and association administrator; b. Fitchburg, Mass., Dec. 13, 1948; d. H. Allison and Violet K. (Erickson) Linné; m. C. Stephen Lander, June 28, 1968; children: Timothy, Mary. BA, Ohio State U., 1978; postgrad., Kennedy-Western U., 1995—. Dir. fin. Luth. Svc. Assn. New England, Natick, Mass., 1973-76; gen. mgr. Logos, Columbus, 1976-87; practice adminstr. Columbus Oncology Assocs., Inc., 1987—. Sec., treas. Adminstrs. in Oncology Hematology Assembly, Englewood, Colo., 1994-95, legis. liaison, 1994-95, pres.-elect, 1995-96, pres., 1996-97; spkr. on med. group mgmt. issues. Editor Adminstrs. in Oncology Hematology Assembly News, 1994-95; mem. editl. bd. Oncology Issues Mag., 1998-2000; mem. editl. adv. bd. for coding and reimbursement Oncology & Hematology, 2001; contbr. articles to profl. jours. Mem. Vineyard Christian Fellowship, Westerville, Ohio; grass roots legis. group Ohio Med. Group Mgmt. Assn., Columbus, 1994—. Fellow Med. Group Mgmt. Assn., Am. Coll. Med. Practice Execs. (nat. chair membership devel. com. 1999); mem. Nat. Oncology Soc. Network, Mid-Ohio Med. Group Mgmt. Assn (pres. 1993-94, sec. 1992-93, program dir. 1991-92, exec. com. 1990-97), Assn. Cmty. Cancer Ctr. (mem. editl. bd. mag. 1998-2000), Ohio Med. Group Mgmt. Assn. (exec. com. 1994-2001, sec. 1995-96, pres.-elect 1997, pres. 1998), Ohio Oncology Med. Group Mgmt. Assn. (pres. 1997), Ohio State Med. Assn. (mem. group practice task force 2000-02). Republican. Avocations: reading, computers, crafts, knitting, Bible study. Office: Columbus Oncology Assocs 810 Jasonway Ave Ste A Columbus OH 43214-2329

LANDERCASPER, JEFFREY, surgeon; b. Cozad, Nebr., Feb. 24, 1954; s. Dale Louis and Barbara L.; m. Betty Niall, June 12, 1976; children: Samuel Gene, Christopher Dale. BA, U. Denver, 1976; MD, U. Colo., 1980. Chmn. dept. surgery Gundersen/Luth., LaCrosse, Wis., 1993-2001. Fellow Am. Coll. Surgeons. Office: Gundersen Luth 1836 South Ave La Crosse WI 54601-5429

LANDERS, PATRICIA GLOVER, reading specialist; b. Pine Bluff, Ark., Nov. 15, 1945; d. Maurice Alexander Glover and Ruth Wells-Glover Wimberly; children: Wendolynn. BS in Edn., Ark. State U., 1967; MS in Edn., OBU, 1976; postgrad., U. of Ark., 1980—81, U. of Ariz., 1980—81, Ariz. State U., 1983—88, U. Phoenix, 1988—89. Cert. tchr. English, reading specialist K-12 Ariz., C.C., English, lang. arts, composition Ariz. Elem. music supr. Greene County Tech. Schs., Paragould, Ark., 1967—68; band & choir dir. Naylor (Mo.) Schs., 1968—70; elem. tchr. Poughkeepsie (Ark.) Schs., 1970—72; reading specialist Sheridan (Ariz.) Schs., 1975—82, CGUHS, Casa Grande, 1982—; assoc. prof. Pima C.C., Tucson, 1982—94, Centra Ariz. Coll., Coolidge, 1983—93; English tchr. CGUHS Alternative, Casa Grande, 1994—2001; owner Landers' Tutoring Svc., 2001—. Test supr. SAT , ACT Testing Svcs., Casa Grande, 1997—. Author: Making English Make Sense, 1996. Invited rep. U.S. to China People to People Amb. Program, 2000; French hornist CAC Cmty. Concert Band, Coolidge, Ariz., 1984—2000; organist North Trekell Bapt. Ch., Casa Grande, 1996—, founder instrumental music founds. group, 2001; chair babysitting com. CGRMC, 1995—98. Mem.: IRA, NEA, SEA (pres. 1978—79), Ark. Reading Coun., Ctrl. Ariz. Reading Coun., Ariz. Reading Coun., Ariz. Edn. Assn., Casa Grande Edn. Assn. (pres. 1985—86, Outstanding Svc. award 1985—86), CGRMC Aux. (com. chairperson 1995—98, Vol. of Month 1995). Democrat. Baptist. Avocations: reading, jogging, musical instruments. Home: P.O. Box 589 Arizona City AZ 85223 Office: CGUHS 2730 N Trekell Rd Casa Grande AZ 85222 Fax: 520-316-3353. Personal E-mail: patriciaglove90@hotmail.com. Business E-Mail: planders@cguhs.org.

LANDERS, STEVEN E. lawyer; b. N.Y.C., May 23, 1947; BA, Antioch Coll., 1969; JD, Harvard U., 1973. Gen. counsel N.Y. State Exec. adv. com. Sentencing, 1978-79; sec. N.Y. State adv. commn. Adminstrn. Justice, 1981-83; ptnr. Paul, Weiss, Rifkind, Wharton & Garrison, N.Y.C. and Paris. Mem. Internat. Bar Assn., Assn. Bar City N.Y., Am. C. of C. in France (chmn. pres.'s coun. 1995-97). Office: Paul Weiss et al 62 rue Faubourg St Honore 75008 Paris France E-mail: slanders@paulweiss.com.

LANDERS, TERESA PRICE, librarian; b. N.Y.C., Dec. 28, 1954; d. Stanley and June Ethel (Novick) Price; m. Gary David Landers, Sept. 2, 1979; children: Joshua Price, Alisha Rose. BA in History cum laude, Williams Coll., 1976; MA in LS, U. Denver, 1978; postgrad., Ctrl. Wash. U., 1980; MA in Orgnl. Mgmt., U. Phoenix, 1999. Libr., asst. analyst Earl Combs, Inc., Mercer Island, Wash., 1979; reference libr. Yakima (Wash.) Valley Regional Libr., 1981-83, coord. youth svcs., 1983-84; libr. Tempe (Ariz.) Pub. Libr., 1984-85; supervisory libr. Mesa (Ariz.) Pub. Libr., 1985-90; head telephone reference Phoenix Pub. Libr., 1990-91, head bus. and scis., 1991-95, info. svcs. mgr., 1995-99; dep. dir. Corvallis-Benton County Pub. libr., 1999—. Cons. Fed. Dept. Corrections, Phoenix, 1993. Mem. ALA, Oreg. Libr. Assn., Nat. Wildlife Fedn. (life), Altrusa, Beta Phi Mu. Democrat. Unitarian Universalist. Avocations: cooking, horseback riding, gardening. Office: Corvallis-Benton County Pub Libr 645 NW Monroe Ave Corvallis OR 97330-4722 E-mail: teresa.landers@ci.corvallis.or.us.

LANDERS, VERNETTE TROSPER, writer, educator, association executive; b. Lawton, Okla., May 3, 1912; d. Fred Gilbert and LaVerne Hamilton (Stevens) Trosper; m. Paul Albert Lum, Aug. 29, 1952 (dec. May 1955); 1 child, William Tappan; m. 2d Newlin Landers, May 2, 1959 (dec. Apr. 1990); children: Lawrence, Marlin. AB with honors, UCLA, 1933, MA, 1935, EdD, 1953; Cultural doctorate (hon.), Lit. World U., Tucson, 1985. Tchr. secondary schs. Secondary Schs., Montebello, Calif., 1935-45, 48-50, 51-59, 1935-45, 48-50, 51-59; prof. Long Beach City Coll., 1946-47; asst. prof. L.A. State Coll., 1950; dean girls Twenty-Nine Palsm (Calif.) H.S., 1960-65; dist. counselor Morongo (Calif.) Unified Sch. Dist., 1965-72, coord. adult edn., 1965-67, guidance project dir., 1967; clk.-in-charge Landers (Calif.) Post Office, 1962-82, ret., 1982. Participant Yucca Valley Cowboy Poetry and Music Gathering, 1996, 98; grand marshall Yucca Valley Grubstake Parade, 1999. Author: Impy, 1974, Talkie, 1975, Impy's Children, 1975, Nineteen O Four, 1976, Little Brown Bat, 1976, Sio-Go, 1977, Owls Who and Who Who, 1978, Sandy, The Coydog, 1979, The Kit Fox and the Walking Stick, 1980; contbr. articles to profl. jours., poems to anthologies. V.p., sec. Landers Assn., 1965—; sec. Landers Vol. Fire Dept., 1972—; life mem. Hi-Desert Playhouse Guild, Hi-Desert Meml. Hosp. Guild; bd. friends Copper Mountain Coll., 1990-91; bd. dirs., sec. Desert Emergency Radio Svc.; mem. Rep. Senatorial Inner Cir., 1990-92, Regent Nat. Fedn. Rep. Women, 1990-92, Nat. Rep. Congl. Com., 1990-91, Presdl. Task Force, 1990-92; lifetime mem. Girl Scouts USA, 1991. Recipient internat. diploma Creativity award Internat. Pers. Rsch. Assn., 1972, award Goat Mt. Grange No. 818, 1987; cert. of merit for disting. svc. to edn., 1973; Order of Rose, 1978, Order of Pearl, 1989, Alpha Xi Delta; poet laureate Ctr. of Internat. Studies and Exchanges, 1981; diploma of merit in letters U. Arts, Parma, Italy, 1982; Golden Yr. Bruin UCLA, 1983; World Culture prize Nat. Ctr. for Studies and Rsch., Italian Acad., 1984; Golden Palm Diploma of Honor in poetry Leonardo Da Vinci Acad., 1984; Diploma of Merit and titular mem. internat. com. Internat. Ctr. Studies and Exchanges, Rome, 1984; Recognition award San Gorgonio coun. Girl Scouts USA, 1984—; Cert. of Appreciation Morongo Unified Sch. Dist., 1984, 89; plaque for contbn. to postal svc. and cmty. U.S. Postal Svc., 1984; Biographee of Yr. award for outstanding achievement in the field of edn. and svc. to cmty. Hist. Preservation of Am.; named Princess of Poetry of Internat. Ctr. Cultural Studies and Exchange, Italy, 1985; cmty. dinner held in her honor for achievement and svc. to cmty., 1984; Star of Contemporary Poetry Masters of Contemporary Poetry, Internat. Ctr. Cultural Studies and Exchanges, Italy, 1984; named to honor list of leaders of contemporary art and lit. and apptd. titular mem. of Internat. High Com. for World Culture & Arts Leonardo Da Vinci Acad., 1987; named to honor list Foremost Women 20th Century for Outstanding Contbn. to Rsch., IBC, 1987; Presdl. Order of Merit Pres. George Bush-Exec. Coun. of Nat. Rep. Senatorial Com., Congl. cert. of Appreciation U.S. Ho. of Reps.; other awards and certs. Guest of hon. ground breaking ceremony Landers Elementary Sch. 1989, dedication ceremony, 1991. Fellow Internat. Acad. Poets (life), World Lit. Acad.; mem. Am. Pers. and Guidance Assn., Internat. Platform Assn., Nat. Ret. Tchrs. Assn., Calif. and Nat. Assn. for Counseling and Devel., Am. Assn. for Counseling and Devel. (25-Yr. Membership pin 1991), Nat. Assn. Women Deans and Adminstrs., Montebello Bus. and Profl. Women's Club (pres.), Nat. League Am. Pen Women (sec. 1985-86), Leonardo Da Vinci Acad. Internat. (Winged Glory diploma of honor in letters 1982), Landers Area C. of C. (sec. 1985-86, Presdl. award for Outstanding Svcs., Internat. Honors Cup 1992-93), Desert Nature Mus., Whittier Toastmistress Club (Calif.) (pres. 1957), Homestead Valley Women's Club (Landers), Soroptimists (sec. 29 Palms chpt. 1962, life mem. 1983, Soroptimist of Yr. local chpt. 1987-88), Phi Beta Kappa, Pi Lambda Theta (Mortar Bd., Prytanean UCLA, UCLA Golden Yr. Bruin 1983), Sigma Delta Pi, Pi Delta Phi. Home: PO Box 3839 Landers CA 92285-0839

LANDERSMAN, STUART DAVID, engineer; b. Bklyn., May 26, 1930; s. Joseph David and Thelma (Domes) L.; m. Martha Britt Morehead, Sept. 2, 1955; children: David Wesley, Mark Stuart. BA, Dakota Wesleyan U., Mitchell, S.D., 1953; MS, George Washington U., 1967. Lic. USCG master mariner. Commd. ensign USN, 1953, advanced through grades to capt., 1974, ret., 1982; engr. Applied Physics Lab., Johns Hopkins U., Laurel, Md., 1982-2000; facilitator Marine Safety Internat., San Diego, 2000—. Convoy commodore USN, Royal Navy, Can. Armed Forces, 1984-92. Author books on shiphandling, naval tactics, principles of naval warfare; contbr. articles to mags.; developer shiphandling simulators, procs. for naval protection of merchant shipping. Decorated Bronze Star, (3) Legion of Merit. Home: 93 Antigua Ct San Diego CA 92118-3313 E-mail: stulanders@aol.com.

LANDES, GEORGE MILLER, biblical studies educator; b. Kansas City, Mo., Aug. 2, 1928; s. George Y. and Margaret B. (Fizzell) L.; m. Carol Marie Dee, Aug. 30, 1953; children: George Miller Jr., Margaret Dee, John Christopher. AB, U. Mo., 1949; M.Div., McCormick Theol. Sem., 1952; PhD, Johns Hopkins U., 1956. Minister to youth Second Presbyn. Ch., Balt., 1952-53, Govans Presbyn. Ch., Balt., 1953-56; instr. Old Testament Union Theol. Sem., N.Y.C., 1956-58, asst. prof. Old Testament, 1958-62, assoc. prof., 1962-70, prof., 1970-95; prof. emeritus Union Theol. Sem, 1995—. Ann. prof. Am. Sch. Oriental Research, Jersusalem, Israel, 1967-68 Author: Building Your Biblical Hebrew Vocabulary, 2001; editor, author: Report on Archaeological Work, 1975. Nettie F. McCormick fellow, 1952-54; Am. Council Learned Socs. fellow, 1967-68 Mem. Soc. Bibl. Lit., Amman Ctr. Archaeol. Rsch. (v.p. 1969-79), Am. Schs. Oriental Rsch. (sec. 1972-94), Phi Beta Kappa. E-mail: glandes@attmail.com.

LANDES, JASON R. music educator; b. Tuscola, Ill., Nov. 20, 1973; s. Phillip L. and Judith E. Landes; m. Lynda C. Newhart, June 17, 1995; 1 child Ellie. B in Music Edn., Ill. Wesleyan U., 1996; M in Music Edn., Ill. State U., 2000. Tchg. cert. Ill. Instrumental and vocal music dir. Lexington Cmty. Schs. #7, Lexington, Ill., 1996—2002. Home: 1703 Truman Dr Normal IL 61761 Office: Lexington Cmty Schs #7 PO Box 67 Wall and Cherry Sts Lexington IL 61753 Personal E-mail: jlelnds@mtco.com. Business E-Mail: jlandes@lexington.k12.il.us.

LANDES, WILLIAM ALAN, publishing executive; b. Bronx, Apr. 27; s. Sidney H. and June Dorothy (Heal-Gordon) L.; m. Sharon, Dec. 14, 1991 (div. Apr. 1995); children: Wendy, Paula. BA & BS, Hunter Lehman Coll., 1968; MS, NYU, 1969; MA, Calif. State U., 1972; PhD, UCLA, 1989. Mgr. Jay's, N.Y.C., 1967-69; assoc. producer New World Prodns., Hollywood, Calif., 1971-72; entertainment editor Showcase Mag., 1972-75; artistic dir., dir. theatre Players U.S.A., San Gabriel, 1975-78; artistic dir. Merrick Studios, Hollywood, 1978-79; producer, dir. Empire Entertainment, Studio City, Calif., 1979—; CEO, chmn. Players Press, Inc., 1980—. Capt. USAF, 1962-67. Mem. SAG, AFTRA, AEA, DGA, SSDC, Writers Guild. Avocations: writing, painting.

LANDES, WILLIAM M. law educator; b. 1939. AB, Columbia U., 1960, PhD in Econs., 1966. Asst. prof. econs. Stanford U., 1965-66; asst. prof. U. Chgo., 1966-69; asst. prof. Columbia U., 1969-72; assoc. prof. Grad. Ctr., CUNY, 1972-73; now prof. U. Chgo. Law Sch.; founder, chmn. Lexecon Inc., 1977-98, chmn. emeritus, 1998—; mem. bd. examiners GRE in Econs., ETS, 1967-74. Mem. Am. Econ. Assn., Am. Law and Econ. Assn. (v.p. 1991-92, pres. 1992-93), Mont Pelerin Soc. Author: (with Richard Posner) The Economic Structure of Tort Law, 1987; editor: (with Gary Becker) Essays in the Economics of Crime and Punishment, 1974; editor Jour. Law and Econs., 1975-91, Jour. Legal Studies, 1991—. Office: U Chgo Sch Law 1111 E 60th St Chicago IL 60637-2776 also: Lexecon Inc 332 S Michigan Ave Ste 1300 Chicago IL 60604-4406

LANDESMAN, HOWARD M. academic administrator; b. Bklyn., 1938; m. Lynne Landesman; 1 child Lori. BS, UCLA, 1958; DDS, U. So. Calif., 1962, MS in Edn., 1971. Co-dir., grad. prosthodontics program U. So. Calif., chair, dept. restorative dentistry, assoc. dean, academic and faculty affairs, exec. assoc. dean, Sch. Dentistry, dean, Sch. Dentistry; dean. Sch. Dentistry U. Colo., 1999—. Office: 4200 E 9th Ave Box C284 Denver CO 80262*

LANDESS, FRED STONE, lawyer; b. Memphis, Jan. 27, 1933; s. Sterling Stone and Beulah Elizabeth (Melton) L.; m. Catherine Sue Lee, Dec. 27, 1953; children— Susan Elinor, Charles Barton, Catherine Elizabeth Student, Wake Forest Coll., 1951-53; AB, George Washington U., 1955; LL.B., U. Va., 1958. Bar: Va. 1958. Enforcement atty. NLRB, Washington, 1958-60; assoc., then ptnr. McGuire, Woods, Battle & Boothe LLP, Charlottesville, VA., 1960-99, ret., 1999. Sec. Bd. Zoning Appeals, City of Charlottesville, Va., 1967-69; bd. dirs. YMCA, Charlottesville, 1975, Westminster Child Care Ctr., Charlottesville, 1978 Fellow Am. Coll. Real Estate Lawyers; mem. Charlottesville-Albemarle Bar Assn. (pres. 1983-84), Va. Bar Assn. (real estate com.), Va. State Bar (7th dist. disciplinary com. 1986-88, sec. 1987, chmn. 1987-88), Charlottesville-Albemarle Bd. Realtors (assoc.), Blue Ridge Homebuilders Assn. (assoc.). Clubs: Boar's Head Sports (Charlottesville). Democrat. Presbyterian. Avocations: tennis, sailing, gardening. Home: 515 Wiley Dr Charlottesville VA 22903-4650

LANDESS, MIKE (MALCOLM LEE LANDESS III), television news anchorman; b. Houston, June 20, 1946; s. Malcolm Lee Jr. Landess and Joyce Ardis (Halley) Quitter; children: Kristen and Jennifer. Grad., Robert E. Lee H.S., Tyler, Tex. Radio reporter WFAA-AM, Dallas, 1969-70; TV reporter WFAA-TV, 70-72, KTRK-TV, Houston, 1972-73; noon anchor, reporter KYW-TV, Phila., 1973-74; NBC news anchor WKYC-TV, Cleve., 1974-77; news anchor KUSA-TV, Denver, 1977-93; Gannett anchor WXIA-TV, Atlanta, 1993—. Anchor, reporter, producer: (TV documentary) Wednesday's Child, 1978, Fight of His Life, 1982; anchor, reporter (TV spl.) Say "NO" to Strangers, 1979. Bd. dirs. Am. Cancer Soc., Denver, 1982-86, Colo. Head Injury Assn., Denver, 1990-93, Brain Injury Assn Ga., Atlanta, 1994—. Recipient numerous Emmy awards: Outstanding Achievement Anchor, 1988, 91, Outstanding Achievement Children's Programming, 1983, TV Programming Excellence, 1995, Outstanding Achievement award Luth. Social Svcs., Am. Cancer Soc. Mem. NATAS, Radio & TV News Dir. Assn., Atlanta Press Club, Sigma Delta Chi. Baptist. Avocations: vintage guitars, motorsports. Office: WXIA-TV 1611 W Peachtree St NE Atlanta GA 30309-2664

LANDFIELD, JAMES SEYMOUR, small business owner; b. Fargo, N.D., Sept. 12, 1950; s. Seymour and Ruth D'Vora (Goldberg) L.; 1 child, Melissa; m. Diane Gingold. Diploma, U. Salamanca, Spain; BA in Econs., Brandeis U.; MA in Internat. Rels., U. Chgo.; MBA in Fin. and Internat. Bus., Columbia U. Various fin. mgmt. positions, N.Y.C., Washington, 1974-84, Chevy Chase, Md., 1984-90; v.p. fin. Realty Ptnrs. Corp., McLean, Va., 1984-85; mgr. acctg. Steptoe & Johnson, Washington, 1985-88; dir. acctg. Nat. Coffee Svc. Assn., Fairfax, Va., 1990-91; dep. exec. dir. Svs. Corp. Ret. Execs., Washington, 1992-94; pres. Bus. Help Inc., McLean, Va., 1995—. Home: 730 Lawton St Mc Lean VA 22101-1510

LANDFIELD, RICHARD, lawyer; b. Chgo., Jan. 16, 1941; s. Joseph D. and Donna (Mayberg) L.; m. Ilona Kiraldi, Aug. 6, 1965; children: Anne, Katharine, Sarah. BA, Amherst Coll., 1962; LLB cum laude, Harvard U., 1965. Bar: N.Y. 1966, D.C. 1972. Asoc. Breed, Abbott & Morgan, N.Y.C., 1965-66, 69-72, Washington, 1972-75; ptnr. Dunnells, Duvall & Porter, 1975-79, Landfield, Becker & Green, Washington, 1979-89, Breed, Abbott & Morgan, 1989-92, Landfield & Becker, Chartered, 1992-94; shareholder Sanders, Schnabel, Brandenburg & Zimmerman, P.C., 1995-97; ptnr. Berliner, Corcoran & Rowe, L.L.P., 1997—. Bd. dirs. Carlson Holdings Corp., 1984-89; gen. counsel The European Inst.; active numerous Amherst Coll. alumni groups; mem. lawyers com. The Washington Opera, 1984-86, 87—; trustee Holton-Arms Sch., Bethesda, Md., 1984-86, 87-96, chmn. bldgs., grounds com., 1985-91, chmn. fin com., 1993-95, past pres. Parents' Assn., trustee emeritus, 1996—. 1st lt. U.S. Army, 1966-69. Decorated Army Commendation medal; John W. Simpson Law fellow Amherst, 1963. Mem. ABA, N.Y. State Bar Assn., Met. Club (Washington), Kenwood Country Club (Bethesda). Republican. Home: 5101 Baltan Rd Bethesda MD 20816-2309 Office: Berliner Corcoran & Rowe LLP 1101 17th St NW Ste 1100 Washington DC 20036-4798 E-mail: rlandfield@bcr-dc.com.

LANDGARTEN, HELEN BARBARA, art psychotherapist, educator; b. Detroit, Mar. 4, 1921; d. Samuel and Lena (Lindenbaum) Tapper; m. Nathan Landgarten, Oct. 10, 1942. BFA, UCLA, 1963; MA in Marriage, Family and Child Counseling, Goddard Coll., 1972; D in Art Therapy (hon.), Norwich U., 1998. Cert. art therapist Art Therapy Credentials Bd., Inc. Coord. art psychotherapy Cedars-Sinai Med. Ctr., L.A., 1967-90; chmn., dir. clin. art therapy Immaculate Heart Coll., 1972-80; chmn., prof. dept. clin. art therapy Loyola Marymount U., 1980-88, prof. emeritus, 1988—. Cons. U.S. Dept. Defense, Germany, 1982-86; pres. Internat. Art Therapy Consultation, L.A., 1989-92; staff rsch. assoc. Rsch. and Edn. Inst. Harbor UCLA Med. Ctr., Beit T'shuvah Residence for Addiction Behaviors, 1999—. Author: Clinical Art Therapy, 1980, Family Art Psychotherapy, 1988; editor Adult Art Psychotherapy 1991 Mag., Photo Collage, 1993; contbr. articles to profl. jours. Founder L.A. County Art Mus., 1983—, L.A. Contemporary Mus., 1983—; v.p. Calif. Beach Art Corp., 2000—. Fellow Soc. Psychopathology of Expression; mem. Am. Art Therapy Assn. (hon., life, registered art therapist, bd. dirs. 1969-71, 84-86, treas. 1984-86), So. Calif. Art Therapy Assn. (hon., life, pres. 1972-74). E-mial. E-mail: tandelini@aol.com.

LANDGREBE, DAVID ALLEN, electrical engineer; b. Huntingburg, Ind., Apr. 12, 1934; s. Albert E. and Sarah A. L.; m. Margaret Ann Swank, June 7, 1959; children: James David, Carole Ann, Mary Jane. BSEE, Purdue U., 1956, MSEE, 1958, PhD, 1962. Mem. tech. staff Bell Telephone Labs., Murray Hill, N.J., 1956; electronics engr. Interstate Electronics Corp., Anaheim, Calif., 1958, 59, 62; mem. faculty Purdue U., West Lafayette, Ind., 1962—, dir. lab. for applications of remote sensing, 1969-81, prof. elec. engring., 1970—, assoc. dean engring., 1981-84, acting head sch. elec. and computer engring., 1995-96. Rsch. scientist Douglas Aircraft Co., Newport Beach, Calif., 1964; dir. Univ. Space Rsch. Assn., 1975-78. Author: (with others) Remote Sensing: The Quantitative Approach, 1978. Recipient medal for exceptional sci. achievement NASA, 1973, William T. Pecora award NASA/U.S. Dept. Interior, 1990. Fellow IEEE (pres. Geosci. and Remote Sensing Soc. 1986-87, Sci. Achievement award 1992), AAAS, Am. Soc. Photogrammetry and Remote Sensing; mem. Am. Soc. for Engring. Edn., Sigma Xi, Tau Beta Pi, Eta Kappa Nu. Office: Purdue U Dept Elec Engring West Lafayette IN 47907-1285 E-mail: landgreb@ecn.purdue.edu.

LANDGREBE, JOHN ALLAN, chemistry educator; b. San Francisco, May 6, 1937; s. Herbert Frederick and Janet Miller (Allan) L.; m. Carolyn Jean Thomson, Dec. 23, 1961; children— Carolyn Janet, John Frederick BS, U. Calif.-Berkeley, 1959; PhD, U. Ill., 1962. Asst. prof. U. Kans., Lawrence, 1962—67, assoc. prof., 1967—71, prof., 1971—2002, prof. emeritus, 2002—, dept. chmn., 1970—80. Vis. prof. U. Calif.-Berkeley, 1974 Author: Theory and Practice in the Organic Laboratory, 1973, 4th edit., 1993. NSF fellow, 1960-62; E. Watkins Faculty fellow U. Kans., 1963; recipient Career Tchg. award Chancellors Club, 1999. Mem. Am. Chem. Soc., Royal Soc. of Chemistry, Phi Lambda Upsilon Republican. Lutheran. Avocations: shade and water gardening, camping, hiking. Home: 1125 Highland Dr Lawrence KS 66044-4523 Office: U Kansas Dept Chemistry Lawrence KS 66045-0001

LANDGREBE, MARILYN ANN, nutritionist, electrochemical company executive; b. N.Y.C., June 8, 1935; d. Charles J. and Marie L. Osterwald; m. Albert R. Landgrebe, June 14, 1958; children: Marie Pilz, Albert C. PhD, U. Md., 1977. Nutritionist Children's Brain Rsch. Clinic, Washington, 1974-80; dir. rsch. Almar Rsch. Lab., Beltsville, Md., 1980-88; v.p. Internat. Electrochem. Systems & Tech., Long Neck, Del., 1990—. Cons. Autistic Soc., 1974-77. Contbr. articles to profl. jours. Pres PTA, Calverton, Md., 1967. Mem. Am. Assn. Ret. Persons, Mariner's Cove Assn. (beautiful and landscape com. 1999). Avocations: gardening, boating, reading, travel. Home and Office: Internat Electrochem Systems & Tech B14 Sussex Ln Long Neck DE 19966-9634 E-mail: albert@dmv.com.

LANDI, DALE MICHAEL, industrial engineer, academic administrator; b. Cleve., July 8, 1938; s. Lawrence Roy and Lillian (Caramell) L.; m. Mary Margaret Lipke, Mar. 23, 1974; children: Michael Kenneth, Kristin Marie. BS, Northwestern U., 1960, MS, 1963, PhD, 1965. Systems analyst Gen. Electric Corp., Chgo., 1960-61; research specialist Rand Corp., Santa Monica, Calif., 1965-68, assoc. dept. head, 1968-70, program dir., 1973-78, v.p., chief scientist, 1978-87; asst. budget dir. N.Y.C., 1970-71; asst. police commr. N.Y.C., 1971-73; v.p. SUNY, Buffalo, 1987—. Home: 238 Brantwood Rd Buffalo NY 14226-4306 Office: SUNY at Buffalo 544 Capen Hall Buffalo NY 14260-1600 E-mail: landi@research.buffalo.edu.

LANDI, DIANE MARIE, graphic designer, consultant; b. Paterson, N.J., Apr. 27, 1952; d. Mario Gustave and Josephine (Ryba) L. Cert. media completion, Sch. Visual Arts, N.Y.C., 1972. Reiki practitioner 2nd degree. Ptnr. R-Art Corp., N.Y.C., 1972; chief designer Medallion Industries, Paterson, 1972-77; designer Equitable Bag, L.I. City, N.Y., 1977-82; owner Landi Graphics, N. Bergen, N.J., 1982—, Landi Liquidators, 2000—. Mem. Graphic

Artists Guild, Amnesty Internat., MENSA, Humane Soc. U.S., Beethoven Soc., Hudson County Animal League. Libertarian. Avocations: playing piano, composing, painting, designing clothes.

LANDINI, RICHARD GEORGE, university president emeritus, English educator; b. Pitts., June 4, 1929; s. George R. and Alice (Hoy) L.; m. Phyllis Lesnick, Nov. 26, 1952 (dec. Mar. 1992); children: Richard, Gregory, Matthew, Cynthia, Vincent; m. Barbara Lee Shockley, Oct. 5, 1996. AB, U. Miami, 1954, MA, 1956; PhD, U. Fla., 1959; D in Civil Law, Quincy Coll., 1985; LLD, U. Miami, 1980, Baiko Jo Gakuin Coll., Japan, 1987, Ind. State U., 1996. From asst. prof. to prof. English Ariz. State U., 1959-70, dean, 1968-70; prof. English, acad. v.p. U. Mont., 1970-75; pres. Ind. State U., 1975-92, prof. English, 1975—. Author: Owls and Sycamores, 2000; contbr. articles on lit. and higher edn. to profl. jours. Served with U.S. Army, 1948-51. Decorated Sagamore of the Wabash, 1977; comdr. Knight of the Holy Sepulchre Jerusalem, 1996. Mem. Phi Beta Kappa, Phi Delta Kappa, Phi Alpha Theta, Phi Kappa Phi, Sigma Tau Delta. Roman Catholic. Office: Ind State Univ Dept English Root Hl # A-288 Terre Haute IN 47809-0001 E-mail: ejlandi@root.indstate.edu.

LANDIS, CAROLYN PRESS, corporate executive; b. Chgo., Mar. 24, 1943; d. John Elmer and Betty (Grace) P.; m. Mark Landis, Aug. 12, 1965; children: Jennifer, Jonathan, Deborah, Meredith. BS in Biochemistry, Cornell U., 1965; MA in Polit. Sci., Rutgers U., 1967; MPA in Urban Affairs, Princeton U., 1969. Chemistry tchr. Lower Merion High Sch., Ardmore, Pa., 1965-66; program officer N.J. Dept. Higher Edn., Trenton, 1969-70; v.p. EDUCOM, Princeton, N.J., 1970-83; pres. Internat. Ins. Holdings Corp., 1983—, also bd. dirs.; pres. Per Scholas, N.Y.C., 1995-96, also bd. dirs., 1995—; CEO IIHC Mgmt. Cons., 1996—; v.p. Catalyst Ptnrs., LLC, 1997—. Bd. dirs. MSM Regional Coun., exec. com., chmn. nominating com. 1983-95, Hers, Mid-Am., chmn. 1976—; trustee Cedar Crest Coll., Allentown, Pa., 1982-95, vice-chmn., chmn. fin. com., 1985-86, chmn., 1986-89; trustee N.J. Inst. Tech., 1988-97; commr. Commn. Higher Edn. Middle States Assn., 1985-94, vice-chmn., 1987, exec. com., 1987-94; adv. bd. Carnegie Bank, N.J., 1988-94; proposal reviewer NSF, 1979-82; prin. investigator for ednl. rsch. study Nat. Inst. Edn., Washington, 1977; cons. in field; bd. dirs. Joint Venture South Fla., 1995-98. Author: (with others) Contracting for Computing, 1975, 73, Teaching Law with Computers, 1978, Financial Planning Models, 1979, 4th Inventory of Computing, 1980, Proceedings of Univac UA, 1979. Coordinator Princeton Area NOW, 1973-75; screening bd. Rockefeller Pub. Service Awards Program, Princeton, 1979-82. Russell Sage Found. grantee, 1973. Mem. Assn. Computing Machinery (editor 1974-77, chmn. nominating com. 1979), AAAS, Am. Assn. for Higher Edn., IEEE Computer Soc., Am. Mgmt. Assn. Unitarian Universalist. Avocations: travel, water sports, skiing, gardening. Home and Office: 251 Crandon Blvd # Th-161 Key Biscayne FL 33149-1541

LANDIS, DAVID MORRISON, state legislator; b. Lincoln, Nebr., June 10, 1948; m. Melodee Ann McPherson, June 6, 1969; children: Matthew, Melissa. BA, U. Nebr., 1970, JD, 1971, M. in Cmty. Regional Planning, 1995; MPA, U. Nebr., Omaha, 1984. Bar: Nebr. 1972. Practice law, Lincoln, 1972-74; mem. Nebr. Legislature from 46th dist., 1978—; chmn. govt. mil. and vets. affairs com. Nebr. Legislature, 1983-87, chmn. banking, commerce and ins., 1988—. Instr. Coll. Law, U. Nebr., 1990—; adj. faculty mem. dept. pub. adminstrn. U. Nebr., Omaha, 1984—; adj. faculty mem. Nebr. Wesleyan U., 1995—96, 1999—; adj. mem. faculty Doane Coll., 1985—95. Bd. dirs. Lower Platte S. Natural Resources Dist., 1971—78; adminstrv. law judge Dept. Labor, 1977—78; officer PTA, 1979—80; mem. Nebr. Humanities Coun., 1990—96, Nebr. Repertory Theatre. Named Tchr. of the Yr., Doane Coll., 1987, 1988, 1992; named to Hall of Fame, Nebr. Repertory Theatre, 2002. Mem. Innocents Soc. (hon.), Golden Key Soc. (hon., U. Nebr.), Pi Alpha Alpha (hon. U. Nebr. at Omaha), Tau Sigma Delta (hon. U. Nebr., Lincoln). Office: Nebr State Legislature Rm 1116 State Capitol Lincoln NE 68509 E-mail: dlandis@unicam.state.ne.us.

LANDIS, DONNA MARIE, nursing administrator, women's health nurse; b. Lebanon, Pa., Sept. 5, 1944; d. James O.A. and Helen Joan (Fritz) Muench; m. David J. Landis, Jan. 1, 1967 (div. Jan. 1985); children: Danielle M. Landis Barry, David J., Derek J.; m. John C. Broderick, Jan. 1, 1990 (div. Jan. 1995). Diploma, St. Joseph's Hosp. Sch. Nursing, Reading, Pa., 1965. RN Md., cert. densitometry technologist. Head nurse med.-surg. unit Hosp. of U. Pa., 1965-67; nurse various hosps. and physician's offices, Md., Pa., 1965-85; clin. dir., clin. rsch. study coord., DEXA technologist Osteoporosis Diagnostic and Monitoring Ctr., Laurel, Md., 1985-95, owner, 1995—; clin. dir., clin. rsch. study coord. Osteoporosis Assessment Ctr., Wheaton, 1985-95; clin. dir./owner Women's Health Rsch. Ctr., Laurel, 1996—. Cons. Osteoporosis and DEXA Merck Pharm., 1995—, Eli Lilly Pharms., 1998—, Nat. Nurses Panel Osteo., 1998—. Mem. task force on osteoporosis State of Md., 1996—. Mem.: Balt. Bone Club, Washington Met. Bone Club (steering com. 1996, bd. dirs. 1999—2001, sec. 1999—2001), Nat. Osteoporosis Risk Assessment Project (specialist practice and technologist trainer 1997—98), Allied Health Profls./Arthritis Found., Nat. Osteoporosis Found. (pub. policy contact), Internat. Soc. Clin. Densitometry (steering com. 1993—96, contbg. editor SCAN newsletter 1994—, sci. adv. com. 1996—99, cert. and credentialing com. technologists and physicians 1995—98, technologist edn. subcom. 2000—, trustee 1999—2002), St. Joseph's Hosp. Alumni Assn., Kiwanis Club (pres. Prince George's County 2000—01, bd. dirs.). Office: 14201 Laurel Park Dr Ste 104 Laurel MD 20707-5203 Fax: 301-776-5972. E-mail: dmlandis@whrc.net.

LANDIS, EDGAR DAVID, business consultant; b. Myerstown, Pa., Jan. 7, 1932; s. Edgar Michael and Anna Irene (Dubble) L.; m. Patricia Ann Leininger, June 13, 1953; children: Susan, Jean. BS, Lebanon Valley Coll., 1953; MBA, U. Pa., 1957. C.P.A. Acct., audit supr. Peat, Marwick, Mitchell & Co. (now KPMG), Phila., 1957-64; corp. controller, div. exec. v.p. Carlisle Corp., Pa., 1964-73; v.p., sr. v.p., exec. v.p. CDI Corp., Phila., 1973-97, also dir.; dir. affiliates in U.S. and Europe; dir., vice chmn. Allegiance Bank of N.A., Bala Cynwyd, Pa., 1998—. Cons. to CDI Corp., Phila., 1998—. Bd. dirs. Carlisle Sch. Dist., 1967-71, Carlisle City Airport, 1968-71, YMCA, Ardmore, Pa., 1981-87, chmn., 1984-86, YMCA, Phila., 1988-97, vice chmn. 1991-97, YMCA, Sarasota, Fla., 1998—. With U.S. Army, 1954-56, Japan. Mem. Lebanon Valley Coll. Alumni Assocs. (regional chmn. 1977-82) Republican. Methodist. Home: 988 Blvd Of The Arts Sarasota FL 34236-4872

LANDIS, FRED, mechanical engineering educator; b. Munich, Mar. 21, 1923; came to U.S., 1947, naturalized, 1954; s. Julius and Elsie (Schulhoff) L.; m. Billie H. Schiff, Aug. 26, 1951 (dec. Jan. 10, 1985); children: John David, Deborah Ellen, Mark Edward. B.Eng., McGill U., 1945; S.M., MIT, 1949, Sc.D., 1950. Design engr. Canadian Vickers, Ltd., Montreal, Can., 1945-47; asst. prof. mech. engring. Stanford U., 1950-52; research engr. Northrop Aircraft, Inc., Hawthorne, Calif., 1952-53; asst. prof. NYU, 1953-56, assoc. prof., 1956-61, prof., 1961-73, chmn. dept. mech. engring., 1963-73; dean, prof. mech. engring. Poly. U., Bklyn., 1973-74; dean Coll. Engring. and Applied Sci., U. Wis., Milw., 1974-83, prof. mech. engring., 1984-94; emeritus prof. U. Wis., 1994—. Staff cons. Pratt & Whitney Aircraft Co., 1957-88. Cons. editor, Macmillan Co., 1960-68; cons. editorial bd.: Funk & Wagnalls Ency., 1969-90 , Compton's Ency., 1984-94; contbr. numerous rsch. articles to profl. jours. and encys., including Ency. Britannica. Mem. Dobbs Ferry (N.Y.) Bd. Edn., 1965-71, v.p. 1966-67, 70-71, pres., 1967-68; bd. dirs. Westchester County Sch. Bds. Assn., 1969-70, v.p., 1970, pres., 1970-71; bd. dirs. Engring. Found., 1988-94. Fellow AIAA (assoc.), ASME (hon. mem., divsn. exec. com. 1965-73, policy bd. 1973-89, v.p. 1985-89, 92-95, bd. govs. 1989-91), Am. Soc. Engring. Edn.; mem. Sigma Tau, Tau Beta Pi, Pi Tau Sigma. Home: 2420 W Acacia Rd Milwaukee WI 53209-3306

LANDIS, JOHN WILLIAM, engineering and construction executive, government advisor; b. Kutztown, Pa., Oct. 10, 1917; s. Edwin Charles and Estella Juliabelle (Barto) L.; m. Muriel Trayes Souders, July 5, 1941; children: Maureen Lucille, Marcia Millicent BS in Engring. Physics summa cum laude, Lafayette Coll., Easton, Pa., 1939, ScD (hon.), 1960. Registered profl. engr., Calif. Research engr. Eastman Kodak Co., Rochester, N.Y., 1939-43; cons. Navy Dept., Washington, 1946-50; head sci. and engring. dept. Ednl. Testing Service, Princeton, N.J., 1948-50; reactor engr. AEC, Washington, 1950-53; dir. customer relations atomic energy div. Babcock & Wilcox Co., N.Y.C., 1953-55, asst. mgr. atomic energy div. Lynchburg, Va., 1955-62, mgr. atomic energy div., 1962-65, gen. mgr. Washington ops., 1965-68; regional v.p. Gulf Gen. Atomic Co., Washington, 1968-69, group v.p. LaJolla, Calif., 1969-70, pres., dir. subs., 1970-74; pres. Power Systems Co., Gen. Atomic Partnership, 1974-75; sr. v.p., dir., pres. subs. Stone & Webster Engring. Corp., Boston, 1975-92, pvt. cons., 1992—. Founding dir. Cen. Fidelity Banks, Inc., Richmond, Va.; founding gov. Nat. Materials Property Data Network, Inc., Phila.; chmn. adv. com. isotopes and radiation devel. and four other adv. coms. AEC, Washington, 1957-70; chmn. coms., co. rep. Atomic Indsl. Forum (now U.S. Nuclear Energy Inst.), Washington, 1953-95; mem. N.Y. State Adv. Com. on Atomic Energy, 1956-59, Va. State Adv. Com. on Nuclear Energy, 1959-68; vice chmn. mgmt. com. Nat. Environ. Studies Project, Washington, 1974-89; dir., v.p., pres., chmn. bds. and coms., trustee Internat. Fund, Am. Nat. Standards Inst., N.Y.C., 1957—; vice chmn. ISO-9000 Registration Com.; dir., chmn. Fusion Power Assocs., Gaithersburg, Md., 1981-98; chmn. U.S. Fusion Industry Coun., Internat. Thermonuclear Exptl. Reactor Industry Coun., 1994-98; chmn. com. on energy-related atmospheric pollution World Energy Conf., London, 1984-90, N.Am. coord. global energy study, 1989-93; dir., chmn. com. on protection of environ. U.S. Energy Assn., Washington, 1981-98; mem. fusion adv. panel U.S. Ho. Reps., Washington, 1979-87; charter mem. magnetic fusion adv. com. U.S. Dept. Energy, Washington, 1982-84, chmn. internat. rsch. and devel. panel, chmn. civilian nuclear power panel, vice chmn., chmn. energy rsch. advisory bd., 1984-90; mem. adv. bd. Sec. of Energy, 1990-93, fusion energy adv. com., 1994-99; advisor Carnegie-Mellon U., Pitts., 1971-73, Pa. State U., State College, 1980-83, U. Calif. San Diego, 1974-82, U. Fla., Gainesville, 1984—; vis. and sustaining fellow MIT, Cambridge, 1971-90; chmn. bus. adminstrn. adv. bd. U. San Diego, 1972-75; chmn. engnring. adv. com. Lafayette Coll., 1988-98. Co-author: six books; contbr. articles to profl. and trade jours. Trustee, chmn. Randolph-Macon Woman's Coll., Lynchburg, Va., 1963—; trustee Lafayette Coll., Easton, Pa., 1962—. Va. Poly. Inst. and State U., Blacksburg, 1966-70; bd. dirs. Va. Poly. Inst. Ednl. Found., Blacksburg, 1968-80; mem. U. Calif. Pres.'s Coun. on the Nat. Labs., 1993-99; chmn. MIT Reactor Com., 1995—; mem. Sr. Rev. Group, Amarillo Nat. Resource Ctr. for Plutonium, 1994-99; mem. Va. Adv. Bd. on Indsl. Devel. and Planning, Richmond, 1962-72; bd. dirs. Va. Engring. Found., Charlottesville, 1962-65; trustee Seven Hills Sch., Lynchburg, Va., 1960-65; dir. Harvard U. Ctr. for Blood Rsch., 1992-99; mem. Mayor's Com. on Energy, San Diego, 1973-75; chmn., mem. six coms. Nat. Rsch. Coun., 1976-96. Served to lt. USN, 1943-46, ETO. Decorated Letter of Commendation, two battle stars; recipient Gen. of Industry award State of Okla., 1971, George Washington Kidd award, Joseph E. Bell award Lafayette Coll., Lehigh Valley Favorite Son award State of Pa., 1976, Dwight D. Eisenhower Award of Honor, 1990, Winston Churchill Medal of Wisdom, 1988, Disting. Career award Fusion Power Assocs., 1991, Howard Coonley medal Am. Nat. Standards Inst., 1991, Exceptional Pub. Svc. award U.S. Dept. Energy, 1992, Henry DeWolf Smyth Nuclear Statesman award Am. Nuclear Soc. and Nuclear Energy Inst., 1996; named Hon. Citizen City of Dallas, 1973, Alumni fellow Lafayette Coll., 1984; elected to Soc. d'Honneur Lafayette Coll., 1989; elected to Wisdom Hall of Fame, 1987. Fellow ASME, Am. Nuclear Soc. (pres. 1971-72, v.p. 1970-71, treas. 1964-68, chmn. coms. 1956—, bd. dirs. 1956-74), Am. Soc. Macro-Engring. (pres. 1985-88, chancellor 1988—, charter bd. dirs. 1983—); mem. NAE, Internat. Assn. Macro-Engring. Socs. (founding dir. 1987—, treas. 1989—, pres. 1999—), San Diego Hall Sci. (life), Phi Beta Kappa, Sigma Xi, Tau Beta Pi, Pi Delta Epsilon, Omicron Delta Kappa. Avocations: photography, landscaping, book-collecting, hiking. Home: 2131 Chestnut Oak Ct SW Roanoke VA 24018-2118

LANDIS, LARRY SEABROOK, marketing and communications consultant; b. Princeton, N.J., Nov. 2, 1945; s. Donald Edward and Caroline Ann (Magalhaes) L.; m. Carol Louise Butz, Sept. 28, 1974; 1 child, Christopher Seabrook. AB cum laude, Wabash Coll., 1967; postgrad., U. N.C., 1967-68, Ind. U., 1969-70. Asst. to mayor Richard G. Lugar (now U.S. Senator, R-Ind.), Indpls., 1969-71; press sec. to Otis R. Bowen (Rep. candidate for gov., Ind.), 1972; dir. mktg. svcs. Garrison, Jasper Rose & Co., 1972-76; v.p. mktg. and media services Hickman & Assoc., 1976—80; v.p. corp. advt. Am. Fletcher Nat. Bank (Bank One Indpls., N.A.), 1980-84; dir. comm. PALLM, Inc., 1984—85; v.p., dir. acct. planning Handley & Miller, Inc., 1985—91; pres. Marketrends, Inc., 1991—; mng. ptnr., COO Am. Grassroots, LLC, 2000—. Lectr. polit. sci. Ind. U./Purdue U., Indpls., 1969-71; bd. dirs. Event Techs., Inc., 1994-96. Co-author: How To, 1974; contbr. articles to profl. jours. Active gov.-elect Ad Hoc Com. on Ednl. Fin., Indpls., 1972-73, campaign mgr. Salin for Congress Com., Ft. Wayne, Ind., 1971-72; mem. exec. com. statewide Rep. legis. campaign Victory '90, Ind., 1989-90; mem. mktg. com. United Way Ctrl. Ind., 1992-93; mem. mktg. adv. com. Indpls. Symphony Orch., 1992-97; bd. dirs. USCO Adult Edn. Program, Indpls., 1975-82, pres., 1980-82, Citizens Environ. Coun., Inc., Zionsville, Ind., 1984-86, v.p., 1986-96; rsch. dir. Ruckelshaus for U.S. Senate, 1968; mem. exec. com. Blankenbaker for Congress, 1995-96, 97-98; gov.'s adv. panel Children's Health Ins. Program, 1998-99. With U.S. Army, 1968-69. Mem. Am. Mktg. Assn., Am. Water Works Assn., Acad. Health Svcs. Mktg., Bank Mktg. Assn., Greater Wabash Found., Ind. C. of C., Indpls. Assn. Wabash Men (bd. dirs.), Indpls. C. of C., Indpls. Advt. Club, Ind. Hist. Soc. (life, trustee 1995—, exec. com. 1996-2000, 02–), Indpls. Press Club, Columbia Club, Econ. Club, Entrepreneurs' Alliance, Indsl. Computing Soc. (founding), Ind. Tech. Partnership, Ind. Info. Tech. Assn., Nature Conservancy, English-Speaking Union, Pi Delta Epsilon, Delta Sigma Rho/Tau Kappa Alpha, Phi Kappa Psi. Republican. Methodist. Avocations: photography, woodworking, gardening. Home: 9560 Huntington Ln Indianapolis IN 46260 Office: Marketrends Inc Circle Tower Bldg 55 Monument Circle Ste 522 Indianapolis IN 46204-5911

LANDIS, RICHARD GORDON, retired food company executive; b. Davenport, Okla., Apr. 5, 1920; s. John William and Venna Marie (Perrin) L.; m. Beth Throne, Nov. 6, 1943; children: Gary Perrin, Dennis, Michael, Kay Ellen. BA, U. LaVerne, 1942; postgrad., Claremont Grad. Sch., 1947; LLD (hon.), U. LaVerne, 1981. Mgmt. Delmonte Corp, San Francisco, 1942-83, pres., 1971-77, pres. & chief exec. officer, 1977-78, chmn. & chief exec. officer, 1978-81; pres. Pacific div. R.J. Reynolds, Inc., 1981-83; former chancellor U. LaVerne, Calif. Bd. dirs. Stanford Rsch. Internat., Menlo Park, Calif. Mem. Commn. of Calif., 1984-90; chmn. Pacific Basin Econ. Coun., 1975-83; officer Boy Scouts Am., 1946—, Invest in Am.; Lt. USAF, 1942-46. Mem. Pacific Union Club, Bohemian Club, Peachtree C. of C. Republican. Avocations: golf, edn. activities, youth programs. Office: 120 Montgomery St Ste 1880 San Francisco CA 94104-4321

LANDIS, ROBERT KUMLER, III, investment banker, lawyer; b. Dayton, Ohio, June 20, 1953; s. Robert Kumler Landis Jr. and Rebecca (McCall) Baird; m. Robin Lee Taylor, June 2, 1979; children: Robert Kumler IV, Taylor McCall, Samuel Tufts. AB, Princeton (N.J.) U., 1975; JD, Harvard U., 1978. Bar: N.Y. 1978. Assoc. Simpson Thacher & Bartlett, N.Y.C., 1978-83; dir. Merrill Lynch & Co., 1984-94; mng. dir. Schooner Capital Internat., Boston, 1994-96; pres. Northern Lights Investors, LLC, 1996—. Dir. River Gold Mines Ltd., Toronto, Western Quebec Mines, Inc., Montreal. Republican.

LANDMAN, DEBORAH TRACY, real estate company executive, fitness trainer; b. Weymouth, Dorset, Eng., Aug. 24, 1969; came to U.S., 1997; d. Charles Denison and Helen Joy Bate; m. Michael Trevor Webb, May 31, 1992 (div.); m. William Scott Landman, Aug. 30, 1997. Pers. adminstr. RAF, Uxbridge, Eng., 1987-92; pres. Bodytalk Fitness, Ltd., Haslemere, Eng., 1992-97, Elite Retail Leasing, Inc., Parkland, Fla., 1997—. Actress, model. Contbr. articles on fitness to mags.; prodr. workout video Bodytalk Step Workout Video, 1992. Organizer charity events Starlight Found., 1995. Mem. Aerobics Orgn. Gt. Britain, Fitness Profls. U.K., Nat. Register Personal Trainers, IDEA Fitness Profls. Anglican. Avocations: fitness, horseback riding, dressage, travel, running. Office: Elite Retail Leasing Inc 5251 NW 80th Ter Parkland FL 33067-1137 E-mail: elitelease@aol.com., ukactress@aol.com.

LANDO, HARRY ALAN, psychology educator; b. New Haven, Conn., Sept. 6, 1946; s. Harry and Anne Lindsey (Wolf) L.; m. Lois Irene Hamilton, June 1, 1978; children— Elizabeth Anne, Ruth Ellen. B.A., George Washington U., 1968; Ph.D., Stanford U., 1973. Asst. prof. Iowa State U., Ames, 1972-77, assoc. prof., 1977-81, prof. psychology, 1981— ; cons. Nat. Heart, Lung, Blood Inst., Bethesda, Md., 1979— , Nat. Inst. on Drug Abuse, Rockville, Md., 1982— . Contbr. chpts. to profl. jours. Co-campaign chmn. Hamilton for County Supr., Story County, Iowa, 1982; mem. Substance Abuse Adv. Bd., Ames, 1981-83; mem. smoking com. Lung Assn., Des Moines, 1981— , Heart Assn. Risk Factors Subcom., Des Moines, 1982— . Recipient Psi Chi psychology hon. award George Washington U., 1967; Stanford U. fellow, 1968, 71. Fellow Am. Psychol. Assn.; mem. Am. Cancer Inst. (grant review com. 1983-87, cons. 1979—), AAAS, Sigma Xi (sci. hon.). Democrat. Home: 1303 Jefferson St Ames IA 50010-4242 Office: Iowa State U Dept Psychology Ames IA 50011-0001

LANDO, JEROME BURTON, macromolecular science educator; b. Bklyn., May 23, 1932; s. Irving and Ruth (Schwartz) L.; m. Geula Ahroni, Dec. 2, 1962; children: Jeffrey, Daniel, Avital. AB, Cornell U., 1953; PhD, Poly. Inst. Bklyn., 1963. Chemist Camille Dreyfus Lab., Research Triangle Inst., Durham, N.C., 1963-65; asst. prof. macromolecular sci. Case Western U., Cleve., 1965-68, assoc. prof., 1968-74, prof., 1974—; chmn. dept. Case Western, 1978-85; pres., CEO Edison Polymer Inovation Corp., 2000—. Erna and Jakob Michael vis. prof. Weizmann Inst. Sci., Rehovot, Israel, 1987; Lady Davis vis. prof. Technion, Haifa, Israel, 1992-93. Author: (with S. Maron) Fundamentals of Physical Chemistry, 1974; mem. editl. adv. bd. Polymers for Advanced Techs. Served to lt. U.S. Army, 1953-55. Named Alexander Von Humboldt Sr. Am. Scientist U. Mainz, Germany, 1974, disting. alumnus Poly. U., 1990. Fellow Am. Phys. Soc.; mem. Am. Chem. Soc., Am. Crystallographic Assn., Soc. Plastics Engrs. (rsch. award 1994, edn. award 1999), Sigma Xi. Jewish. Home: 21925 Byron Rd Cleveland OH 44122-2942 Office: Case Western Res U Dept Macromolecular Sci Kent Hale Smith Bldg 321 Cleveland OH 44106

LANDON, JAMES HENRY, lawyer; b. Atlanta, Oct. 24, 1945; s. Ralph Henry and Gertrude Leola (Rew) L. BA, Vanderbilt U., Nashville, 1967; JD, Harvard U., Cambridge, Mass., 1970. Bar: Ga. 1971, U.S. Dist. Ct. (no. dist.) Ga. 1971, U.S. Ct. Claims 1972, U.S. Supreme Ct. 1976, U.S. Tax Ct. 1980. Assoc. Hansell & Post, Atlanta, 1971-76, ptnr., 1976-89, Jones, Day, Reavis & Pogue, Atlanta, 1989—. Adj. prof. Emory Law Sch., Atlanta, 1983-84; dir. TRC Staffing Svc., Inc., Atlanta, 1987—; mem. steering com. So. Pension Conf., Atlanta, 1985-88. Co-author: Transportation Politics in Atlanta, 1970; contbr. article to profl. jour. Trustee Atlanta Symphony Orch., 1981-87, 89-92, Atlanta Hist. Soc., 1983-98, 99—, Ctr. for Puppetry Arts, Inc., 1995-2001, Atlanta Bot. Garden, 1998—; mem. cmty. adv. bd. Jr. League of Atlanta, 1987-90; gen. counsel Woodruff Arts Ctr., Inc., 1993—; trustee Atlanta Med. Heritage, Inc., 1993—, pres., 1996-97; trustee The Hambidge Ctr., 1994-99, chmn. 1998-99; trustee Cherokee Garden Libr., 2000—. Mem. ABA, Ga. Bar Assoc., Atlanta Bar Assoc., Explorers Club of N.Y.C., Phi Beta Kappa. Presbyterian. Avocations: mountain climbing, hiking. Home: 1327 Peachtree St NE Apt 503 Atlanta GA 30309-3254 Office: Jones Day Reavis & Pogue SunTrust Plz 303 Peachtree St NE Ste 3500 Atlanta GA 30308-3242

LANDON, JANE KEYTE, music educator; b. Montoursville, Pa., Feb. 6, 1934; d. M. Robb Keyte Sr. and Frances Helen Entz; m. Eugene Earl Landon, Aug. 22, 1955; 1 child, Benjamin Eugene. BA cum laude, Lycoming Coll., 1955. Instr. piano Lycoming Coll., Williamsport, Pa., 1956-62; music tchr. Montoursville H.S., 1962-64; min. of music Bethany Luth. Ch., Montoursville, 1964-71; pvt. piano instr., 1962—. Adjudicator Pa. Fedn. Music Clubs. Mem. Messiah Luth. Ch., sanctuary choir mem., mem. Madrigal Singers, dir. men's quartet. Mem. Music Tchrs. Nat. Assn., Nat. Guild Piano Tchrs. (chmn. Williamsport 1965—), Pa. Music Tchrs. Assn. (pres. Williamsport local 1970—), Williamsport Music Club (past pres.), The Clio Club (corr. sec. 1997—), DAR. Republican. Avocations: concerts, antiques, gardening, cooking. Home: 144 Quaker State Rd Montoursville PA 17754-7608

LANDON, JOHN CAMPBELL, research and development company executive; b. Hornell, N.Y., Jan. 3, 1937; s. Earl Shephard and Eleanor (Crane) Landon; m. Nancy Ann Bachenheimer, Aug. 24, 1958; children: David Bachenheimer, Martha Susan, Katherine Ellen, Peter Crane. BA in Biology, Alfred (N.Y.) U., 1959; MS in Biology, George Washington U., Washington, 1962, PhD in Biology, 1967. Biologist Nat. Cancer Inst., NIH, Bethesda, Md., 1960-65; from virologist to dir. Litton Bionetics, Kensington, 1965-75; pres., dir. EG&G Mason Rsch. Inst., Worcester, Mass., 1975-82; pres., CEO Bioqual, Inc., Rockville, Md., 1982—; founder, v.p., co-owner Brewster (Mass.) Book Store, Inc., Brewster, Mass, 1982—; pres., CEO Sema, Inc., Rockville, 1986-91, BIOQUAL Inc. (formerly Diagnon Corp.), Rockville, 1986—, also chmn. bd. dirs.; founder, pres., CEO Enhanced Therapeutics, Inc., 1994—. Cons. EG&G, Worcester, Mass., 1982—85; reviewer ad hoc com. NIH, Bethesda, Md., 1981—; nat. coun. arts and scis. George Washington U., 1996—; mem. credit com. Potomac Cmty. Fed. Credit Union, 1982—85. Contbr. articles to profl. jours. Bd. dirs. Found. Comparative and Conservation Biology, Peirce Warwick Adoption Svc., Washington, 1970—79, pres., 1972—75; bd. dirs. Venture Expenditionary, 1979—83, pres., 1981—83. Mem.: AAAS, N.Y. Acad. Scis., Am. Soc. Microbiology, Am. Soc. Cell Biology, NIH Alumni Assn. (bd. dirs. 2002—), Sigma Xi. Office: Bioqual Inc 9600 Medical Center Dr Rockville MD 20850-3336 also: Brewster Bookstore 2648 Main St Brewster MA 02631-1958 E-mail: jlandon@bioqual.com.

LANDON, JOJENE BABBITT, special education educator; b. Boise, Idaho, Feb. 7, 1940; d. Clarence Ray and Mary (McHenry) Babbitt; m. James Wallace Landon, Dec. 8, 1963; children: Sharon Jene, John Charles, Franklin Thomas, Jonathan Kennette. BA in Far Ea. History, U. Md., 1968; MEd in Spl. Edn., Bowie (Md.) State Coll., 1974; MS in Reading, Johns Hopkins U., 1978; postgrad., Calif. State U., Sacramento, 1987-92. Cert. tchr. for severely handicapped and learning handicapped, also reading specialist, resource specialist, multiple subject and social sci., Calif. Spl. edn. resource tchr. Anne Arundel County, Glen Burnie, Md., 1974-80; tchr. severely emotionally disturbed Leeward Dist., Ewa Beach, Hawaii, 1980-84, North Valley Schs. Inc., Stockton, Calif., 1984-85, Stockton Unified Sch.Dist., 1985-87, Serene Community Sch., Sacramento, 1987-90; tchr. spl. edn. Sacramento Unified Sch. Dist., 1990; tchr. spl. edn., dept. chair Rio Tierra Jr. High Sch., Sacramento, 1990—. Developer, presenter project Ho'okoho U. Hawaii and Hawaii Dept. Edn., Honolulu, 1982-84. Supt. protestant Sunday schs. Pearl Harbor (Hawaii) Naval Sta. Chapel, 1983; lay speaker United Meth. Ch., 1989—. With U.S. Army, 1961-64. Named Grant Dist. Tchr. of Yr., 1997. Mem. Coun. Exceptional Children. Republican. Avocations: Biblical studies, ancient history. Home: 8941 Lake Grove Ct Elk Grove CA 95624-2722 E-mail: jojenelandon@hotmail.com.

LANDON, MICHAEL DE LAVAL, historian, educator; b. St. John, N.B., Can., Oct. 8, 1935; came to U.S., 1960; s. Arthur Henry Whittington and Elizabeth Worthington (Fair) L.; m. Doris Lee Clay, Dec. 31, 1959 (div. May 1980); children: Clay de Laval, Letitia Elizabeth; m. Carole Marie Prather, Feb. 28, 1981. BA, Oxford (Eng.) U., 1958, MA, 1961, U. Wis., 1962, PhD, 1966. Asst. master Manor House Sch., Horsham, Eng., 1957, Dalhousie Sch., Ladybank, Scotland, 1958, Lakefield (Ont.) Coll. Sch., 1958-60; asst. prof. history U. Miss., Oxford, 1964-67, assoc. prof., 1967-72, prof., 1972-2000, acting dir. librs., 1986-87, acting chair modern langs., 1996-99, prof. emeritus, 2000—. Author: The Triumph of the Lawyers, 1970, The Honor and Dignity of the Profession, 1979, Erin and Britannia, 1980, The Challenge of Service, 1995. Commr. City Housing Authority, Oxford, 1983—, chmn., 1993—; lay Eucharistic minister Episcopal Ch. Am. Philos. Soc. Rsch. grantee, 1967, 74. Fellow Royal Hist. Soc. (U.K.); mem. Am. Soc. for Legal History (sec.-treas. 1988-97), Phi Kappa Phi, Eta Sigma Phi, Phi Alpha Theta, Pi Delta Phi. Episcopalian. Avocation: bird feeding. Home: 219 Bramlett Blvd Oxford MS 38655-3434 Office: Univ of Miss Dept History PO Box 1848 University MS 38677-1848 E-mail: hslandon@olemiss.edu.

LANDON, MICHAEL LEE, religious studies educator; b. Enid, Okla., Nov. 7, 1956; s. William Frank and Eleanor Fern Landon; m. Susan Kay McFarland, Apr. 12, 1979; children: Angela, Cynthia, Michael. BS, BA, Okla. Christian U., 1979; MA, Harding Grad. Sch. Religion, Memphis, 1983; PhD, Trinity Evang. Div. Sch., Deerfield, Ill., 1997. Missionary Ch. of Christ, Sao Paulo, Brazil, 1982—90; bench chemist Drug and Lab. Disposal Co., Plainwell, Mich., 1991—94; minister West Ch. Ch. of Christ, Hammond, La., 1994—95, Ch. of Christ, Pratt, Kans., 1997—98; asst. prof. Barclay Coll., Haviland, 1998—2001; prof. dept. religion Southwestern Christian Coll., Terrell, Tex., 2001—. Mem. steering com. for self study Barclay Coll., Haviland, 2000—01. Contbr. articles. Pres. bd. dirs. Ginger Ford Habitat for Humanity, Hammond, Ind., 1996—97. Mem.: Assn. of Profs. of Missions, Am. Soc. Missiology, Am. Anthropol. Assn., Alpha Chi. Mailing: Southwestern Christian Coll PO Box 10 Terrell TX 75160

LANDON, ROBERT GRAY, retired manufacturing company executive; b. Portsmouth, Ohio, Dec. 22, 1928; s. Herman Robert and Hazel Ruth Landon; m. Carole A. Beaumont, Aug. 30, 2001; children: Geoffrey, Suzanne. Student, Cornell U., 1947-49; BA in Econs., U. Pa., 1955; grad. advanced mgmt. program, Harvard Sch. Bus., 1978. Loan officer Nat. City Bank, Cleve., 1955-60; SEC adminstr. Smith Kline Corp., 1960-64; controller, treas. Grumman Allied Industries, Inc., Garden City, N.Y., 1964-76, v.p., 1977-82; v.p. investment mgmt. Grumman Corp., Bethpage, N.Y., 1978-79; pres. Grumman Ohio Corp., Worthington, Ohio, 1979-88. Served with AC, USN, 1949-53. Mem. The Oaks Club.

LANDON, ROBERT KIRKWOOD, philanthropist, retired insurance company executive; b. N.Y.C., Apr. 27, 1929; s. Kirk A. and Edith (Ungar) L.; children: Chris, Kathleen Landon Staley, Kellyann Landon Spears. Student, U. Va., 1946-48; BS, Ga. Inst. Tech., 1950. With Am. Bankers Life Assurance Co., Miami, Fla., 1952-99, pres., 1960-74, 95, chmn., chief exec. officer, 1974-99; chmn. bd., CEO Am. Bankers Ins. Group Inc., Miami, 1980-95, chmn. bd., 1980-99; pres. Landon Corp., Dover, Del., 1971-99; charter mem. advisory bd. Fla. Internat. U., 1972-74. Trustee Kirk A. and Dorothy P. Landon Found., 1969—. Barry U. Lt. (j.g.) USNR, 1950-53. Mem. World Bus. Coun., Scabbard and Blade, Phi Gamma Delta. Republican. Congregationalist. Home: 10 Edgewater Dr Apt 16E Coral Gables FL 33133-6969 Office: The Kirk Found 255 Alhambra Cir Ste 820 Coral Gables FL 33134-7412 E-mail: kirk_landon@assurant.com.

LANDON, SUSAN MELINDA, petroleum geologist; b. Mattoon, Ill., July 2, 1950; d. Albert Leroy and Nancy (Wallace) L.; m. Richard D. Dietz, Jan. 24, 1993. BA, Knox Coll., 1972; MA, SUNY, Binghamton, 1975. Cert. profl. geologist; cert. petroleum geologist. Petroleum geologist Amoco Prodn. Co., Denver, 1974-87; mgr. exploration tng. Amoco, Houston, 1987-89; ind. petroleum geologist Denver, 1990—. Instr. petroleum geology & exploration Bur. of Land Mgmt., U.S. Forest Svc., Nat. Park Svc., 1978-86. Editor: Interior Rift Basins, 1993. Mem., chmn. Colo. Geol. Survey Adv. Com., Denver, 1991-98; mem. bd. on Earth Sci. and Resources-NRC, 1992-97, chair com. on earth resources, 1998—; mem. Nat. Coop. Geologic Mapping Program Fed. Adv. Com., 1997—. Recipient Disting. Alumni award Knox Coll., 1986, Disting. Svc. award Rocky Mountain Assn. Geologists, 1986, Disting. Pub. Svc. to Earth Sci. award Rocky Mountain Assn. Geologists, 1998. Mem. Am. Assn. Petroleum Geologists (hon., treas., Disting. Svc. award 1995), Am. Inst. Profl. Geologists (pres. 1990, Martin Van Couvering award 1991), Am. Geol. Inst. (pres. 1998), Rocky Mtn. Assn. Geologists (pres. 2000). Achievements include frontier exploration for hydrocarbons in U.S. Home: 780 Ballantine Rd Golden CO 80401-9503 Office: Thomasson Ptnr Assocs 1410 High St Denver CO 80218-2609 E-mail: susanlandon@att.net.

LANDON, WILLIAM J. intelligence officer; b. Menno, S.D., June 23, 1939; s. Helmuth Samuel and Violet A. (McPherson) Neuharth. LLB, Blackstone Sch. Law, 1962, JD, 1968; AA in Bus. Mgmt., Coastline C.C., 1984; postgrad., Am. Mil. U., 2001—. Criminal investigator Internat. Acad. Police Sci., Oklahoma City, Southwestern Inst. Criminology, Lawton; criminal investigator, intelligence officer ASI divsn. Internat. Investigators and Police, St. John, N.B., Can., 1964-94; intelligence officer, analyst Internat. Investigators & Police, Rapid City, SD, 1990—2001, ret., 2001. Student Am. Mil. U., Manassas Park, Va., 2000—. Sponsor Robin Anne Syperda Benedict meml. scholarship Calif. State U., Fullerton, 1990—. With USMC, 1957-65. Mem. Internat. Assn. Study Organized Crime, Internat. Investigators Police Assn., Internat. Assn. Law Enforcement Intelligence Analysts, Assn. Former Intelligence Officers, Am. Soc. Criminology, Nat. Mil. Intelligence Assn. Avocations: martial arts, classical music, fencing.

LANDOVSKY, ROSEMARY REID, figure skating school director, coach; b. Chgo., July 26, 1933; d. Samuel Stuart and Audrey Todd (Lyons) Reid; m. John Indulis Landovsky, Feb. 20, 1960; children: David John, Linette. BA in Psychology, Colo. Coll., 1956. Profl. skater Holiday on Ice Touring Show, U.S., Mex., Cuba, 1956-58; skating dir. and coach Paradice Arena, Birmingham, 1958-62, Les Patineurs, Huntsville, Ala., 1960-62; coach competitive (Ice Skating Inst. Am., U.S. Figure Skating Assn.) Michael Kirby and Assocs., River Forest, Chgo., Ill., 1962-63; rink mgr., skating dir. Lake Meadows Ice Arena, Chgo., 1963-68; coach (ISIA, USFSA) Rainbo Arena, 1968-73; skating dir. Northwestern U. Skating Sch., Evanston, Ill., 1968-73, Robert Crown Ice Ctr., Evanston, 1973-75; dir. instl. programs Skokie (Ill.) Park Dist., 1975-87. Competition dir. ISIA All America Competition, 1985-86. Dir., producer, choreographer Ice Show: Nutcracker Ballet, 1973, Ice Extravaganza III, 1985, Ice Lights '86, '87. Election judge, worker, Ind. Dems., Chgo., 1964-68. Mem. AAUW, Profl. Skaters Guild, Ice Skating Inst. Am., Coll. Coll. Alumni Assn., Gamma Phi Beta. Avocations: building cabin, travel, golf, tennis, hiking.

LANDOW-ESSER, JANINE MARISE, lawyer; b. Omaha, Sept. 23, 1951; d. Erwin Landow and Beatrice (Hart) Appel; m. Jeffrey L. Esser, June 2, 1974; children: Erica, Caroline. BA, U. Wis., 1973; JD with honors, George Washington U., 1976. Bar: Va. 1976, DC 1977, Ill. 1985. Atty. U.S. Dept. Energy, Washington, 1976-83, Bell, Boyd & Lloyd, Chgo., 1985-86, Seyfarth, Shaw, Fairweather & Geraldson, Chgo., 1986-88, Holleb & Coff, Chgo., 1988-2000, Quarles & Brady, Chgo., 2000—. Contbr. articles to profl. jours. Bd. dirs. Bernard Zell Anshe Emet Day Sch. Parent-Tchr. Orgn., 1991-95. Mem. ABA, Chgo. Bar Assn. (vice chmn. environ. law com. 1990-91, chmn. 1991-92), Am. Jewish Congress (bd. dirs., pres. Midwest Region 2001--). Office: Quarles & Brady 500 W Madison St Ste 3700 Chicago IL 60661-2592 E-mail: je3@quarles.com.

LANDPHAIR, TED, broadcaster, author; b. Cleve., Sept. 12, 1942; s. Wallace Harold and Louise U. (McQuown) L.; m. Carolyn J. Bolan, June 15, 1964(div. Jan. 1988); children: Jeannette, Juliette, Nicole, Robert; m. Carol M. Highsmith, June 11, 1988. BS, Ohio U., 1964; MA, U. Iowa, 1965. Journalism instr. Midwestern U., Wichita Falls, Tex., 1965-67; newspaper reporter The Nat. Observer, Washington, 1967-70; broadcaster WMAL-AM Radio, 1970-79, KFWB-AM, L.A., 1979; newspaper editor New Orleans Bus. NP, 1980-85; broadcaster The Voice of Am., Washington, 1986—. Co-author 30 photog. tour books on cities, states and regions, also Pennsylvania Avenue: America's Main Street, 1989, Union Station: A Decorative History, 1991, Embassies of Washington, 1993, America Restored, 1993, Forgotten No More, 1994. Recipient Peabody award George Foster Peabody Com., 1976, several New Orleans Press Club awards, 1982-85. Methodist. Avocations: gardener, writer, bottle collector. Office: Voice of Am 330 Independence Ave SW Washington DC 20237-0001 E-mail: tland@voanews.com.

LANDRAM, CHRISTINA LOUELLA, librarian; b. Dec. 10, 1922; d. James Ralph and Bertie Louella (Jordan) Oliver; m. Robert Ellis Landram, Aug. 7, 1948; 1 child, Mark Owen. BA, Tex. Woman's U., 1945, BLS, 1946, MLS, 1951. Preliminary cataloger Libr. of Congress, Washington, 1946-48; cataloger U.S. Info. Ctr., Tokyo, 1948-50, U.S. Dept. Agr., Washington, 1953-54; libr. Yokota (Japan) AFB, 1954-55, St. Mary's Hosp., West Palm Beach, Fla., 1957-59, Jacksonville (Ark.) H.S., 1959-61; coord. Shelby County Librs., Memphis, 1961-63; head catalog dept. Ga. State U. Libr., 1963-86, libr., assoc. prof. emeritus, 1986—. Contbr. articles to libr. jours. Mem. ALA (chmn. cataloging norms 1979-80, nominating com. 1977-78), Ga. Libr. Assn. (chmn. resources and tech. svcs. sect. 1969-71), Metro-Atlanta Libr. Assn. (pres. 1967-68), Southeastern Libr. Assn. (mem. govtl. rels. com. 1975-78, intellectual freedom com. 1984-86, mem. Rothrock awards com. 1987-90). Presbyterian. Home: 15201 Olive Blvd Apt 495 Chesterfield MO 63017-1819 E-mail: bobland2@juno.com.

LANDRIEU, MARY L. senator; b. Nov. 23, 1955; m. E. Frank Snellings. BA, La. State U., 1977. Real estate agt.; La. state rep. from dist. 90, 1979-89; La. state treas., 1987-95; U.S. senator from La., 1997—; mem. armed svcs. com.; mem. nutrition and forestry com.; mem. energy and natural resources com.; mem. small business com. Del., Dem. Nat. Conv., 1980 Mem. LWV, Women Execs. in State Govt., Fedn. Dem. Women, Delta Gamma. Roman Catholic. Office: 724 Hart Senate Off Bldg Washington DC 20510-0001*

LANDRIGAN, PHILIP JOHN, epidemiologist, educator; b. Boston, June 14, 1942; s. John Joseph and Frances Joan (Conlin) Landrigan; m. Mary Florence Magee, Aug. 27, 1966; children: Mary Frances, Christopher Paul, Elizabeth Marie. AB, Boston Coll., 1963; MD, Harvard U., 1967; MS, DIH, London Sch. Hygiene and Tropical Medicine, 1977. Diplomate Am. Bd. Pediat., Am. Bd. Preventive Medicine, Am. Bd. Occupl. Medicine, Am. Coll. Epidemiology. Intern Cleve. Met. Gen. Hosp., 1967—68; resident in pediatrics Children's Hosp. Med. Ctr., Boston, 1968—70; fellow in pediatrics Harvard U. Med. Sch., 1969—70; clin. instr. pediatrics Emory U. Sch. Medicine, Atlanta, 1970—71; epidemic intelligence service officer Ctrs. for Disease Control, 1970—73, dir. research and devel. smallpox erradication program, 1973—74, chief environ. hazards activity, 1974—79; dir. div. Surveillance, Hazard Evaluations and Field Studies Nat. Inst. for Occupational Safety and Health, Cin., 1979—85; prof. community medicine and pediatrics Mt. Sinai Sch. Medicine, N.Y.C., 1985—, dir. div. environ. and occupational medicine, 1985—90; prof., chmn. dept. community and preventative medicine, 1990—. Mem. bd. on toxicology and environ. health hazards NAS, Washington, vice chmn., 1981—86; clin. prof. environ. health Sch. Pub. Health U. Wash., Seattle, 1983—. Contbr. numerous articles to prlfl. jours.; cons. editor: Archives of Environ. Health, 1982—, cons. editor: Am. Jour. Indsl. Medicine, 1979—, editor-in-chief: Environ. Rsch., 1987—. Recipient Vol. award, Dept. HEW, 1973, Pub. Health Svc. Career Devel. award, 1975, group citation as mem. of Ctr. for Disease Control beryllium rev. panel, 1978, Meritorious Svc. medal, USPHS, 1985. Fellow: Royal Soc. Medicine; mem.: AAAS, APHA, Soc. for Epidemiologic Rsch., Am. Epidemiol. Soc., Inst. of Medicine Internat. Commn. on Occupl. Health. Home: 915 Stuart Ave Mamaroneck NY 10543-4124 Office: Mt Sinai Sch Medicine Dept Community Medicine 1 Gustave L Levy Pl # 1057 New York NY 10029-6500

LANDRON, MICHEL JOHN, lawyer; b. Santurce, P.R., June 15, 1946; s. Francis Xavier and Francisca (Carretero) Healy; m. Carol McQuade, Apr. 22, 1989; children: Michael Francis, Ryan McQuade. BA, Lehman Coll., 1968, postgrad., 1969-73; JD, Fordham U., 1977. Bar: N.Y. 1978, U.S. Dist. Ct. (so. dist.) N.Y. 1978, U.S. Dist. Ct. (ea. dist.) N.YU. 1978. Asst. atty. gen. Office of Atty. Gen., N.Y. State Dept. Law, N.Y.C., 1978-80; enforcement atty. N.Y. Stock Exch., 1980-81; pvt. practice, 1981-82, 84—; mem. Leaf, Duell, Drogin P.C., N.Y.C., 1982-84; gen. counsel Rockcom, Inc., 1985-87; adminstrv. law judge City of N.Y., 1987; counsel Berger and Paul, N.Y.C., 1984-85; assoc. area counsel Digital Equipment Corp., 1988-89. Adj. instr. N.Y. Law Sch., Ramapo Coll.; master arbitrator, Am. Arbitration Assn., U.S. Dist. Ct. (ea. dist.) N.Y.; mediator U.S. Dist. Ct. (ea. dist.) N.Y.; guest lectr. Lehman Coll.; cons. in field; arbitrator Civil Ct. N.Y.C., No Fault Ins. Panel State of N.Y., Nat. Assn. Securities Dealers, Inc.; arbitrator, mem. arbitration appeals panel Am. Arbitration Assn. Author: Conflicts of Law, 1992; (with others) Personal Injury: Actions, Defenses and Damages, 1992, Choice of Law; contbr. chpts. to books, articles to profl. jours. Mem. Assn. Arbitrators City of N.Y., Am. Judges Assn., KC, Phi Alpha Delta (Disting. Svc. award 1977). Republican. Roman Catholic. Avocations: music, reading, sports. Office: SI Bank & Trust Trust Dept 1535 Richmond Ave Staten Island NY 10314

LANDRUM, FRANK WOOLSON, library/media educator; b. Phila., Feb. 13, 1939; s. William Rutherford and Eleanor Marley Landrum; m. Jane Wright, Jan. 28, 1967 (div. Sept. 1999); children: Amy Elizabeth Bray, Wesley Wright. BS in Edn., Millersville State U., 1962; MSLS, Villanova U., 1970; cert., U. Oreg., 1985. Cert. media specialist, adminstr., Oreg., Md. Sch. librarian Susquenita Sch. Dist., Duncannon, Pa., 1962-63; elem. sch. librarian Price George's County Schs., Upper Marlboro, Md., 1966-67, libr. specialist, 1967-76, asst. supr. libr., 1976-82; part-time instr. Western Md. Coll., Westminster, 1978-80; media svcs. supr. Lane Edn. Svc. Dist., Eugene, Oreg., 1982—2001, dir. curriculum and staff devel., 1999-2000; project mgr. Oreg. Sch. Libr. Info. Sys., 2001—. Copyright cons. Portland Pub. Schs., 1995; coord. chmn. Big Six Skills Conf., Portland, 1998; founder Lane County Student Video Festival, 1984-2000. Contbr. articles to profl. publs. Bd. dirs. Lane Edn. Found., Eugene, 1998-99; mem. task force adv. bd. Pub. Safety Coord. Com., Lane County, 1999; vol. baseball coach Churchill H.S., Eugene, 1990-93, 95; mem. edn. bd. Cable Access Adv. Com., Lane County, 1983-87; sec.-treas. Lane-Douglas Libr. Consortium, 1983-86. With U.S. Army, 1964-66. Mem. Assn. Regional Media Ctrs. of Oreg. (chmn. 1987-88, 98-2000), Confedn. oreg. Sch. Adminstrs. (regional rep. 1995-98), Oreg. Edn. Media Assn. (mem. conf. com. 1999). Avocations: sports, toy trains. Office: Lane Edn Svc Dist PO Box 2680 Eugene OR 97402 Home: 2635 E Wilshire Dr Eugene OR 97405-1228 E-mail: fwlandrum@aol.com.

LANDRUM, LARRY JAMES, computer engineer; b. May 29, 1943; s. Floyd Joseph and Jewel Helen (Andreska) L.; m. Ann Marie Hartman, Aug. 25, 1963 (div.); children: Larry James, David Wayne, Andrei Mikhail, Donal Wymore; m. Mary Kathleen Turner, July 27, 1980. Student, N.Mex. Inst. Mining and Tech., 1961-62, N.Mex. State U., 1963-65; AA in Data Processing, Ea. Ariz. Coll., 1971; BA in Computer Sci., U. Tex., 1978. Tech. svc. rep. Nat. Cash Register, 1966-73; with ASC super-computer project Tex. Instruments, Austin, 1973-80, computer technician, 1973-75, tech. instr., 1975-76, product engr., 1976-78, operating sys. programmer, 1978-80; computer engr. Ariz. Pub. Svc., Phoenix, 1980-84, sr. computer engr., 1984-87, lead computer engr., 1987-88, sr. computer engr., 1988-90, sr. control sys. engr., 1990-94; software engr. CDI Corp., 1996-98; project engr. Sargent & Lundy LLC, 1998-00; sr. engr. Westinghouse Electric Corp., 2000—. Instr. computer fundamentals Ea. Ariz. Coll., 1972-73, Rio Salado C.C., Phoenix, 1985-86. Mem. bd. trustees Epworth United Meth. Ch., 1987-89, chmn., 1988; mem. cmty. devel. adv. com. City of Glendale, Ariz., 1988-90, chmn., 1991-92; local arrangements chmn. Conf. on Software Maintenance, 1988. Mem. IEEE Computer Soc., Assn. Computing Machinery, Mensa, Phi Kappa Phi. Methodist. Office: PO Box 580 Carlsbad NM 88221-0580

LANDRUM-BITTLES, JENITA, artist, educator; b. Jackson, Mich., Dec. 25, 1959; d. Bennie C. Landrum and Maxine A. Johnson; m. Roland Bittles, June 28, 1995; 1 child, Cory Mychal. BFA, Ariz. State U., 1991; MFA, Ohio State U., 1997. Art coord., grad. tchg. asst. Ohio State U., Columbus, 1997-98, vis. lectr., 1997—. Instr. art Columbus State Coll., 1997—, Cultural Arts Ctr., Columbus, 1997, Columbus Mus. Art, 1997; artist in residence Fort Hays Visual Arts Sch., Columbus, 1997, Skowhegan, N.Y.C., 1996. Solo exhbns. include Maine Daily News, 1996, The Lantern, 1996, 97, Ft. Hayes Shot Tower Gallery, Columbus, 1997, ACE Gallery, Columbus, 1998; contbr. articles to profl. jours. Grantee Liquitex, 1995, Edith Fergus Gilmore, 1997; Albert Murray Family scholarship, 1995-97; Ohio State U. fellow, 1997. Mem. Nation Women's Art Caucus, Black Women's Task Force (chairperson 1994—), Coll. Art Assn. Address: 3789 Towne Center Blvd Columbus OH 43219-3106

LANDRY, FRANCES LEGGIO, lawyer; b. Baton Rouge, Aug. 11, 1908; d. George and Josephine (Loicano) Leggio; m. Jules F. Landry, Aug. 9, 1934; 1 child, Frances Harriet Landry Borghardt. BA, La. State U., 1926, JD, 1934. Bar: La. 1934. Ptnr. Landry & Landry, Baton Rouge, 1934-90; sole practice, 1990—. Atty. to assist tax collector East Baton Rouge Parish, 1940-46; lectr. law sch. La. State U., Baton Rouge, 1942-43. Mem. Baton Rouge Beautification Com., 1963-66; pres. bd. control East Baton Rouge Library, 1964-84, hon. mem. 1984—; bd. dirs. Lafayette Gallery, Baton Rouge, 1969—; past v.p. West Baton Rouge Parish Mus.; past mem. bd. dirs. Anglo-Am. Mus., Baton Rouge; hon. mem. bd. dirs. La. State U. Art Mus. Mem. ABA, La. Bar Assn., Baton Rouge Bar Assn. (past WA chmn. membership. com.), Inter-Am. Bar Assn. (former mem.), Cath. Daus. Am., Equestrian Order of Holy Sepulchre, Women's Club (past pres.), Quota (past internat. pres.). Avocations: historical preservation, art galleries. Home: 2036 Lake Hills Pky Baton Rouge LA 70808-1453 Office: 348 Lafayette St Baton Rouge LA 70801-1206

LANDRY, FRANCIS RODERICK, medical librarian; b. Dorchester, Mass., July 29, 1950; s. Francis A. and Anna M. Landry; m. Joan E. Halpin, June 4, 1988. BA in English, U. Mass., Boston, 1974; MLS, Simmons Coll., 1985, postgrad., 1994—. Acad. Health Info. Profls., 1993—. With libr., coord. continuing med. edn. Boston Coll. Libr. System, Chestnut Hill, Mass., 1974-86; asst. libr. Mt. Auburn Hosp., Cambridge, 1986-89; chief med. libr. Waltham-Weston Hosp. and Med. Ctr., 1989-93; med. libr. Heywood Hosp., Gardner, 1993-98, U. Mass. Meml. Health Alliance, Leominster and Fitchburg, 1998—. Corr. sec. Consortium for Info. Resources, Mass., 1990-91; teaching asst. computer lab. Boston Coll., 1986-89; instr. Nat. Libr. of Medicine software, Waltham, 1990-93. Mem. Med. Libr. Assns., Spl. Librs. Am. (sci. and tech. divsn., on-line divsn.), Mass. Health Scis. Libr. Network, Ctrl. Mass. Consortium Hosp. Rsch. Librs., Basic Health Sci. Librs., Worcester Area Cooperating Librs. Roman Catholic. Office: U Mass Meml Health Alliance Leominster Campus 60 Hospital Rd Leominster MA 01453-2205

LANDRY, JOEL DANIEL, II, lawyer; b. Washington, Oct. 18, 1963; s. Joel Daniel and Mary Ann (DiMario) L.; m. Lisa Roseann Giuliano, Oct. 24, 1993. BA, U. R.I., 1986; JD, New Eng. Sch. Law, 1989. Bar: R.I., 1989; U.S. Dist. Ct. R.I., 1990. Spl. asst. atty. gen. State of R.I., Providence, 1989-90; asst. city solicitor City of Providence, 1990-92; pvt. practice Providence, 1990—; ptnr. Voccola & Landry Law Offices. Bd. dirs. DiMario Motors, Inc., Providence. Vice chmn. Providence Water Supply Bd., 1992—. Mem. ABA, Am. Trial Lawyers Assn., Order Sons of Italy in Am., Nat. Italian Am. Bar Assn., Justinian Law Soc. (bd. dirs. 1994). Roman Catholic. Home: 16 Lladnar Dr Lincoln RI 02865-4013 Office: Voccola & Landry 454 Broadway Ste 201 Providence RI 02909-1650

LANDRY, JOHN MARSDALE, non-profit organization consultant; b. New London, Conn., July 2, 1962; s. Robert Normand and Elaine Ruth (Marsdale) L. BA in English Lit., Coll. of the Holy Cross, 1984; postgrad., Jesuit Novitiate of New Eng., 1984-85; MPA, Harvard U., 1998. Info. and referral coord. United Way of Mass. Bay, Boston, 1985-87; capital fundraising cons. Ketchum, Inc., Pitts., 1989-93; maj. gifts officer MIT, Cambridge, 1993-94, assoc. dir. resource devel., 1994-97; pres. John Landry Inc. Capital Fundraising, Palm Beach, Fla., 1997—. Bd. trustees Cheverus H.S., Portland, Maine, 1993-97; co-chmn. devel. com. Boston Living Ctr., 1993-94; presenter Cath. Sch. Devel. Conf., Worcester, Mass., 1993, 94, Case Dist. Conf., 1996. Del. State of Maine Dem. Conv., Portland, 1988; fundraising capt. Human Rights Campaign Fund, Washington, 1993-95; mem. Fed. Adv. Network, Washington, 1994—. Mem. Nat. Soc. Fund-Raising Execs., Coun. for Advancement and Support of Edn., Cath. Sch. Devel. Assn., Planned Giving Group New Eng.. Roman Catholic. Avocations: music (guitar, piano), compose original liturgical and folk music.

LANDRY, JOSEPH L., JR. retired affirmative action specialist; b. Woodlawn, La., Dec. 23, 1940; s. Joseph L. Landry and Clara Desmairis; widowed; children: Alan Joseph, Kevin Dale. Student, Northwestern State U. La., 1959-61, McNeese State U., 1961-62, Hosp. Corps. Sch., Great Lakes, Ill., 1962, Cardiopulmonary Technique Sch., Bethesda, Md., 1964, Instr. Tng. Sch., Norfolk, Va., 1968, Pers. Adminstrn. & Career Counseling Sch., San Diego, 1973, Disease Vector Ecology Control Ctr. Sch., Jacksonville, Fla., 1974; AA, Prince George's C.C., Largo, Md., 1975. Gas meter reader Tex. La. Gas Co., Alexandria, La., 1959; hosp. orderly Lake Charles (La.) Meml. Hosp., 1961-62; staff hosp. corpsman Charleston (S.C.) Naval Hosp., 1962-63; staff instr. Cardiopulmonary Technique Sch., U.S. Naval Hosp., Bethesda, Md., 1964-66, chief respiratory therapy dept., 1967-70; staff pulmonary technologist VA Hosp., Washington, 1966-67, staff cardiopulmonary technologist, 1970-74; clin. instr. Respiratory Therapy Sch., Washington Technical Inst., D.C. U., 1970-74; cardiopulmonary technologist divsn. coal mine workers' compensation U.S. Dept. Labor, Washington, 1974-82; program analyst Office Fed. Contract Compliance Programs, 1982-84, equal opportunity specialist, 1984-96; ret., 1996. Co-writer guidelines for Freedom of Info. Act and Privacy Act; cons. Peopleclick, New Orleans, 1996—; lectr. in field. Acting chairperson citizens adv. com. Reston Police Dist., 1986; past pres., bd. dirs. Deepwood Homeowners' Assn.; bd. dirs., "F" lic. coach Reston Soccer Assn.; mem. PTA and Booster Club of South Lakes High Sch.; bd. mem., v.p. amateur divsn. La. Soccer Assn.; past asst. dist. dir., past dist. dir. Boy Scouts Am., St. Tammany Parish.; cert. referee USSF. With USN, 1962-66, USNR, 1966-89, ret. 1989. Mem. Nat. Assn. Fed. Retirees (pres. chpt. #1428 2001-2002), Am. Legion (adjutant), Am. Heart Assn. Democrat. Roman Catholic. Home: PO Box 8823 Mandeville LA 70470-8823 E-mail: jllandry@earthlink.net.

LANDRY, MARK EDWARD, podiatrist, researcher; b. Washington, May 24, 1950; s. John Edward and Daphne (Fay) L.; m. Mary Ann Kotey, Sept. 7, 1974; children: John Ryan, Christopher John, Jessica Marie. D in Podiatry, Ohio Coll. Podiatric Medicine, 1975; MS in Edn., U. Kans., 1982. Diplomate Am. Bd. Podiatric Surgery, Am. Bd. Podiatric Orthopedics and Primary Podiatric Medicine. Gen. practice podiatry, Kansas City, Mo., 1977—, Overland Park, Kans., 1980—; clin. asst. prof. U. Health Scis., Kansas City, 1985-98; clin. assoc. prof. Coll. Podiatric Medicine and Surgery U. Osteo. Medicine and Health Scis., Des Moines, 1985-92; clin. instr. Sch. Medicine U. Mo., Kansas City, 1987-95. Founder, bd. dirs. Kansas City Podiatric Residency Program, Kansas City, 1982-91; adv. bd. Rockport Shoe Co.; chmn. podiatry dept. Park Lane Med. Ctr., Kansas City, Mo., 1995-97; dir. continuing edn. Kans. Podiatric Med. Assn., 1997—. Contbr. articles to profl. jours. Cons. Mid-Am. Track and Field Assn., Lenexa, Kans., 1978-88; com. chmn. Boy Scouts Am., Overland Park, Kans.; coach Johnson County Soccer League, 1987-90; head coach 6th and 7th grade girls' Cath. Youth Orgn. Basketball, 1995-96, 97; sponsor 8 & 11 Baseball League, 1987-90. 1st lt. USAF, 1975-77. Recipient Pres.'s award Ohio Sch. Podiatric Medicine, 1975; USAF scholar Armed Forces Health Professions, 1973-75. Fellow Am. Coll. Foot Surgeons, Acad. Podiatric Sports Medicine, Am. Coll. Primary Podiatric Medicine & Podiatric Orthopedics; mem. Kans. Podiatric Med Assn. (bd. dirs. 1997—), Brit. Podiatry Assn. (hon.), Am. Bd. Primary Podiatric Medicine (founding dir., bd. examiner 1994—), Holy Cross Social Club (pres. 1983-84), Prairie Life Club, Leukemia Assn. of Am. (team in tng. 1997-2000, team capt. 1999, K.C. corp. challenge participant 1997-99), K.C. (4th degree 1995—, chancellor 1998, 99), KC Ski Club (trip capt. 1999). Republican. Roman Catholic. Avocations: triathlon training (completed Grand Floridian Ironman competition, 1998, Ironman Fla., 1999), skiing. Home: 8120 W 99th St Overland Park KS 66212-3444 Office: 10550 Quivira Rd Ste 260 Overland Park KS 66215-2375 E-mail: mlandry398@aol.com.

LANDRY, MICHAEL GERARD, investment company executive; b. Ottawa, Ont., Can., July 20, 1946; came to U.S., 1982; s. Edmund Oscar and Clarice (St. Germain) L.; m. Barbara Trebbi, Dec. 15, 1996; children: Noel Michael, Adam Jonah. BA in Econ., Carleton U., 1969. V.p. MD Mgmt. Ltd., Ottawa, 1977-82; sr. v.p. Templeton Investment Counsel, Ft. Lauderdale, Fla., 1982-87; v.p. Templeton Galbraith Hansberger, Nassau, 1986-87; dir. Templeton Global Growth Fund Ltd., Australia, 1987; pres., CEO Mackenzie Investment Mgmt. Inc., Boca Raton, Fla., 1987-99, The Mackenzie Group of Funds, Boca Raton, 1987-99, The Ivy Funds, 1992-99; mem. exec. com. Mackenzie Fin. Corp., Toronto, 1994-99; pres. Gray Rocks Asset, 1999; v.p., CFO BMC Fund, Inc., 2000—. Bd. dirs. BMC Fund. Bd. dirs., chmn. fin. com. Children's Place/Connor's Nursery (chmn. fin. com. 1997, bd. dirs. 1993-98, pres. 1997-98). Mem. Internat. Soc. Fin. Analysts (former bd. dirs.), Assn. Can. Pension Mgmt. (bd. dirs. 1986-89), Fin. Analysts Fedn. Roman Catholic. Office: GrayRocks Asset Mgmt 305 S Andrews Ave Ste 503 Fort Lauderdale FL 33301

LANDRY, PAUL LEONARD, lawyer; b. Mpls., Nov. 23, 1950; s. LeRoy Robert Landry and Alice Ruth (Swain) Stephens; m. Lisa Yvonne Yeo, Dec. 13, 1984; children: Marc, Lauren, Matthew. BA, Macalester Coll., 1974; postgrad., Georgetown U., 1976-77; JD, Boston U., 1977. Bar: Va. 1977, D.C. 1978, Minn. 1984, U.S. Dist. Ct. D.C., U.S. Dsit. Ct. Va., U.S. Dist. Ct. Minn., U.S. Ct. Appeals (D.C., 2d, 4th and 8th cirs.). Dancer Dance Theater Harlem, N.Y.C., 1971-72; prin. dancer Dance Theatre Boston, 1972-75; atty. EPA, Washington, 1976-77; assoc. Reed, Smith, Shaw & McClay, 1977-83; officer, shareholder Fredrikson & Byron, P.A., Mpls., 1984—. Adj. prof. law William Mitchell Coll. Law, St. Paul, 1985-89. Bd. dirs. Ind. Sch. Dist. 284, Wayzata, Minn., 1989-96, 2002-, chmn., 1992-93; bd. dirs. Walker Art Ctr., Mpls., 1992—; bd. dirs., vice chair Greater Twin Cities Youth Symphonies, 1999-2001; advisor Kevin McCary Scholarship Fund. Mem. ABA (conf. of minority ptnrs. adv. com.), Nat. Bar Assn., Minn. State Bar Assn. (art and entertainment sect., labor and employment sect.), D.C. Bar, Hennepin Conty Bar Assn., Black Entertainment and Sports Lawyers Assn., Barristers. Avocations: golf, music, basketball. Office: Fredrikson & Byron PA 900 2nd Ave S Ste 1100 Minneapolis MN 55402-3328 E-mail: plandry@fredlaw.com.

LANDRY, RICHARD, ballet dancer; b. Edmonton, Alta., Can. Student, Nat. Ballet Sch., Toronto, Ont., Can. Mem. Nat. Ballet Can., Toronto, 1992—97, second soloist, 1997—. Office: Walter Carsen Ctr for Nat Ballet Can 470 Queens Quay W Toronto ON Canada M5V 3K4 Office Fax: 416-345-8323.*

LANDRY, ROBERT JOSEPH, physicist; b. Taftville, Conn., Mar. 14, 1935; s. Philip Camille and Alice Marie (Vautour) L.; m. Cathryn Anne Campana, June 22, 1963; children: Robert A., Michele M. Hinkle, Kenneth A. AS in Gen. Studies, Mitchell Coll., 1959; BS in Physics, U. Conn., 1961, MS in Physics,

1963. Sr. rsch. scientist Am. Optical Corp., Southbridge, Mass., 1964-73; commd. lt. USPHS, 1973, advanced through grades to capt., 1981; optical physicist FDA, Rockville, Md., 1973-77, chief electro-optics br., 1977-91, sr. scientist, 1991—. Sec. TC-76 laser std. tech. com. Internat. Electro-Tech. Com., 1980-83; co-chair ANSI com. photobiol. safety of lamps and lamp sys., 1989-97, Illumination Engring. SoN.Am., 1989-97. Contbr. 20 articles to profl. jours., chpts. to book. Achievements include numerous patents including patents for photochemotherapy dosimeter, method for apparatus for monitoring optical radiation. Home: 2442 Merchant St Frederick MD 21701-3201 Office: Electro-Optics Br FDA HFZ 134 9200 Corporate Blvd Rockville MD 20850-3229 E-mail: rjl@cdrh.fda.gov.

LANDRY, WALTER JOSEPH, lawyer; b. Willswood, La., Jan. 23, 1931; s. John Theodore and Lelia Lucille (Peltier) L.; m. Carolyn Margaret Kruschke, Nov. 24, 1962; children: Celeste, John, Joseph, Catherine, Walter Jr., James. BSME, U. Notre Dame, 1952; JD, Tulane U., 1958; MA, Am. U., 1969, PhD, 1975. Bar: La. 1958, U.S. Supreme Ct. 1961. Legis asst. to U.S. Sen. Russell B. Long, Washington, 1956-57; pvt. practice law New Orleans, 1958-61; fgn. svc. officer Dept. State, 1961-70; mem., action officer U.S. del. to San Jose Conf. Am. Conv. on Human Rights, 1969; ptnr. Landry, Poteet, and Landry, 1979-90; Futures Broker, 1990-99, U.S. Patent Office, 1999—2001. Asst. prof. U. Southwestern La., 1970-74; chmn. U.S. Lang. Policy Conf., Chgo., 1983; pres. Fedn. Am. Cultural and Lang. Communities, Inc., 1984—. Editor: La. Donkey, 1977-79; contbr. articles to profl. jours. Mem. Lafayette Parish Dem. Exec. Com., 1971—, chmn., 1976-83; mem. Dem. State Ctrl. Com. La., 1971—, past state co-chmn. affirmative action, 1975-76; counsel Bill of Rights Com. La. Constnl. Conv., 1973-74; del. Dem. Nat. Mid-Term Conf., 1974, 78, alt. del. Dem. Nat. Conv., 1980; organizer La. Assn. Parish Dem. Exec. Coms., 1976-77, pres., 1977-78; chmn. Dem. Caucus, 7th Congl. Dist. La., 1985-87. Maj. USMCR, Korea. Mem. Internat. Rels. Assn. of Acadiana (pres. 1974-75), ABA (internat. law working group 1971-76), Am. Soc. Internat. Law, Internat. Good Neighbor Coun. (organizer, pres. Acadiana chpt. 1978-81), Think-Tank for Nat. Self-Determination (exec. dir. 1994—). Home and Office: 3835 9th St N # 201E Arlington VA 22203-1910

LANDS, ROBERT FRED, private investigator; b. Texarkana, Ark. s. Dudley Buel and Ima Sue Lands; m. Linda Kay Lands; children: Robert Jennifer, Samuel Lisa. Internet Rsch. Specialist, Pulaski Tech. Coll., Little Rock, 2002. Cert. pvt. investigator Tex., 1990, Ark., 1998, locomotive engr. 1979, master cert. internat web designer 2000, Microsoft profl. 2000, computer graphic artist 1999, ins. agt. Ark., 1998, real estate agt. Tex., 1977. Locomotive engr. Pine Bluff/San Antonio divsns. Cotton Belt / So. Pacific R.R., 1979—88; rr. safety inspector Lands Investigations Co., North Little Rock, Ark., 1994—. Author: Investigating Railroad Related Injuries and Accident Reconstruction, 1998. Mem. BL of E PAC, Cleve., 1979—2000. Mem.: Brotherhood of Locomotive Engrs., Nat. Assn. R.R. Safety Cons. and Investigators. Baptist. Avocations: golf, hunting, fishing, camping. Office: Lands Investigations Company 4900 Stratford Rd North Little Rock AR 72116 Personal E-mail: rflands@yahoo.com. Business E-Mail: landsinvestigationscompany@yahoo.com.

LANDSBERG, BRIAN KEITH, law educator; b. Sacramento, Oct. 27, 1937; s. Morris and Dorothy K. Landsberg; m. Dorothy S. Landsberg, June 11, 1967; children: Elizabeth, Rachel, Joshua. BA, U. Calif., Berkeley, 1959, LLB, 1962; cert. African law, U. London, 1963. Bar: Calif. 1963, U.S. Ct. Appeals (4th cir.) 1969, U.S. Ct. Appeals (9th cir.) 1970, D.C. 1972, U.S. Ct. Appeals (7th and 10th cirs.) 1972, U.S. Ct. Appeals (8th and D.C. cirs.) 1975, U.S. Ct. Appeals (3rd cir.) 1977, U.S. Ct. Appeals (2nd cir.) 1979, U.S. Ct. Appeals (5th cir.) 1980. Atty. U.S. Dept. Justice, Washington, 1964-86, chief edn. sect., civil rights divsn., 1969-74, chief appellate sect., civil rights divsn., 1974-86, acting dep. asst. atty. gen. civil rights divsn., 1993-94; prof. law McGeorge Sch. Law, Sacramento, 1986—, assoc. dean, 2001—. Mem. ethics com. D.C. Bar Assn., Washington, 1981-84; dir. Civil Rights Divsn. Assn., Washington, 1992—; vis. prof. law U. Calif., Berkeley, 1995, 97; trustee Lawyers Com. for Civil Rights Under Law, Washington, 1996—. Author: Enforcing Civil Rights, 1997; contbr. articles to profl. jours. Mem. Pub. Access Programming Task Force, Sacramento, 1992; bd. mem. Jewish Cmty. Rels. Coun., Sacramento, 1993—, chair, 1998-99; bd. mem. Aids Housing Alliance, Sacramento, 1993-95; mem. exec. bd. Congregation B'nai Israel, v.p., 1996-98; pres. Sacramento Jewish Fedn., 2001—. With USNR, 1954-62. Summer fellow NEH, Washington, 1979. Mem. ABA, Order of Coif. Democrat. Jewish. Office: McGeorge Sch Law 3200 5th Ave Sacramento CA 95817-2799 E-mail: blandsberg@uop.edu.

LANDSBERG, GARY MILLER, law firm investigator; b. Pasadena, Calif., Oct. 13, 1953; s. Henry and Patricia Ann Landsberg; m. Judy E. Caine, Nov. 21, 1979; children: Briana, Nicole. AS, Portland C.C., 1982. Investigator Freelance Legal Inst., Portland, Oreg., 1981-82, Martin, Bischoff, et al, Portland, 1983—. Profl. musician and rec. artist, bass player, drummer, 1975-90. Coach/mgr. area youth soccer orgn. Mem. Internat. Soc. Air Safety Investigators. Office: Martin Bischoff et al 888 SW 5th Ave Ste 900 Portland OR 97204-2023

LANDSBERG, GERALD, educator, consultant; b. N.Y.C., July 15, 1942; s. Louis and Sadie L.; m. Claire Warga Landsberg, Mar. 24, 1974; 1 child, Joshua. MSW, NYU, 1967, MPA, 1979; DSW, CUNY, 1979. Dir. rsch. Maimonides Hosp. CMHC, Bklyn., 1968-79; commr. Ulster County Mental Health Svcs., Kingston, N.Y., 1979-87; assoc. commr. N.Y.C. Dept. Mental Health, 1987-91; prof. chair social policy NYU Sch. of Social Work, 1991—. Editor: Forensic Mental Health,-2001, Interional Forensic, 2001, (newsletter) Community Mental Health Report, 2000. Mem. N.Y. Nat. Assn. of Social Workers (v.p. 1999-2001). Office: NYU Sch of Social Work One Washington Sq N New York NY 10003

LANDSBERG, JILL WARREN, lawyer, educator; b. N.Y.C., Oct. 11, 1942; d. George Richard and Evelyn (Schepps) Warren; m. Lewis Landsberg, June 14, 1964; children: Alison, Judd Warren. BA, George Washington U., Washington, 1964; MAT, Yale U., 1965; JD, Boston Coll., 1976. Bar: Mass., 1977, Ill., 1991. Assoc., dir. (ptnr.) Widett, Slater & Goldman PC, Boston, 1976-90; pvt. practice Chgo., 1991-94; faculty Med. Sch. Ethics and Human Values Dept. Northwestern U., 1991-94; exec. asst. spl. counsel for child welfare svcs. Office of the Gov., 1994-95, acting spl. counsel for child welfare svcs., 1995-96; cons. in field, 1996—2002; adj. prof. law Northwestern U. Govt. agys. cons.; mem. Legis. Com. on Juvenile Justice, Chgo., 1995—96, Task Force on Violence Against Children, Chgo., 1995—99, Citizens Com. on the Juvenile Ct., Chgo., 1995—. Tutor Ptnrs. in Edn., 4th Presbyn. Ch., Chgo., 1993—; mem. steering com. Ill. Ct. Improvement Program, 1995-99; Ill. Jud. Inquiry Bd., 2000—; adv. bd. Libr. Internat. Rels., Chgo., 1993-94; bd. trustees Children's Home and Aid Soc. of Ill. Mem. ABA, Chgo. Bar Assn., Ill. State Bar Assn., Phi Beta Kappa, Order of the Coif. Home and Office: 70 E Cedar St Chicago IL 60611-1179

LANDSBERG, LEWIS, dean, endocrinologist, medical researcher; b. N.Y.C., Nov. 23, 1938; AB, Williams Coll., 1960; MD, Yale U., 1964. From instr. to asst. prof. medicine Sch. Medicine Yale U., 1969-72; from asst. prof. to assoc. prof. Harvard Med. Sch., 1972-77, from assoc. prof. to prof., 1977-86; Irving S. Cutter prof., chmn. dept. medicine Med. Sch. Northwestern U. Med. Sch., 1990—2000; dir. Ctr. Endocrinology, Metabolism & Nutrition Northwestern U., 1990-93; dean, v.p. for medical affairs Northwestern U. Med. Sch., Chicago, Ill., 2000—. Assoc. physician Yale-New Haven Hosp., 1969-71, attending physician, 1971-72, Beth Israel Hosp., 1974-79, physician, 1979-88, sr. physician, 1988-90; attending physician West Haven VA Hosp., 1970-72; assisting physician Boston City Hosp., 1972-73, assoc. vis. physician, 1973-74; physician-in-chief dept. medicine Northwestern Meml. Hosp., 1990—. Fellow ACP, AAAS; mem. Am. Fedn. Clin. Rsch., Endocrine Soc., N.Y. Acad. Scis., AHA, Am. Soc. Pharmacology and Exptl. Therapeutics, Am. Physiology Soc., Am. Soc. Clin. Investigators, Am. Clin. and Climatological Assn., Assn. Am. Physicians. Achievements include rsch. in catecholamines and the sympathoadrenal system, nutrition and the sympathetic nervous system, obesity and hypertension. Office: Northwestern Univ Med Sch Morton 4-656 310 East Superior St Chicago IL 60611-2958*

LANDSBERG, MICHELE, journalist; b. Toronto, July 12, 1939; d. Jack and Naomi Leah Landsberg; m. Stephen Lewis, May 30, 1963; children: Ilana Naomi, Avram David, Jenny Leah. BA, U. Toronto, 1962. Reporter Globe & Mail, Toronto, 1962-65, columnist, 1985-89; freelancer, 1965-71; editor, feature writer Chatelaine, 1971-78; columnist The Toronto Star, 1978-84, 89—, Globe and Mail, Toronto, 1985-88. Author: Women & Children First, 1982, Reading for the Love of It, 1986, This is New York, Honey! A Homage to Manhattan in Love & Rage, 1989. Recipient Nat. Newspaper award (columns), 1980, (feature writing) 1981, Gov.-Gen.'s Persons' awrd, 2002; co-recipient Florence Bird award, 1997. Office: Toronto Star 1 Yonge St Toronto ON Canada M5E 1E6

LANDSBERGER, JOSEPH FRANK, academic administrator; b. St. Paul, May 6, 1945; s. Claude Edward and Blanche Evelyn (Dvorak) L. MA, U. Minn., 1981; M in Internat. Mgmt., U. St. Thomas, 1990. Mgr. learning ctr. U. St. Thomas, St. Paul, 1976—. Vol. educator U.S. Peace Corps, Soutouboua, Togo, 1968-71. Author: Study Guides and Strategies (also website). Vol. park developer Dept. Parks & Recreation, St. Paul, 1995—. Mem. Assn. Edn., Comm. & Technology. Mem. Soc. Friends. Avocations: garden design, website development, international travel. Office: U St Thomas 2115 Summit Ave Saint Paul MN 55105 E-mail: jflandsberge@stthomas.edu.

LANDSBERGER, KURT, scientific and medical products executive; b. Prague, Czechoslovakia, Dec. 28, 1920; came to U.S., 1939; s. Ernest and Helen (Hoffman) L.; m. Anny Terkel, July 25, 1943; children: David I., Allen S. Grad., Handelsakademie, Vienna, Austria, 1938. Founder Bel-Art Products, Maddak Inc., Applied Coatings, Pequannock, NJ, 1946—, chmn. bd., 1982—. Author: William Steinitz, Chess Champion: A Biography, 1997, Between the 1st and 2nd Mountain: Daring to Be Different, 2001, The Steinitz Papers, 2002; patentee in field. Chmn. planning bd. Borough of Verona, N.J., 1982-85; pres. Verona Dem. Com., 1954-58; mem. Bahamas Nat. Trust: trustee Beth Ahm Congregation, 1986-90; bd. dirs. West Essex Rehab. Ctr., 1986-92; mem. Essex County Handicapped Adv. Bd., 1986-93; founder, chmn. Save the Mountains. Served with U.S. Army, 1942-46. Mem. Verona C. of C. (pres. 1962), N.J. Conservation Found., Internat. Wildlife Fedn., N.J. Hist. Soc., Montclair Art Mus., Newark Mus., Nat. Trust Historic Preservation, Kiwanis (pres. 1962). Jewish.

LANDSBERGER, SHELDON, nuclear engineer, educator, radiation engineer, educator; b. Petach-Tikva, Israel, Apr. 5, 1950; PhD, U. Toronto, 1982; MS, Concordia U., Montreal, Can., 1976, Salford U., Salford, Eng., 1973; BS, Sir George Williams U., Montreal, Canada, 1972. Prof. U. Tex. at Austin, Austin, Tex., 1997—2002, U. Ill., Urbana-Champaign, 1987—97; rsch. scientist McMater U., Hamilton, Canada, Canada, 1983—86; post doctoral fellow NRC Can., Ottawa, Canada. Cons. Internat. Atomic Energy Agy., Vienna, 1987—2002. Editor: Elemental Analysis of Airborne Particles, 1999. Mem.: Am. Chem. Soc., Am. Nuc. Soc. Office: U Tex at Austin NETL Pickle Rsch Campus R-9000 Austin TX 78712 Home Fax: (512) 471-4589; Office Fax: (512) 471-4589. Personal E-mail: s.landsberger@mail.utexas.edu. Business E-Mail: s.landsberger@mail.utexas.edu.

LANDSBURG, STEVEN ELLIOT, economics and mathematics educator; b. Phila., Feb. 24, 1954; s. Norman and Vivian Leatrice (Klein) L.; divorced; 1 child, Cayley Elizabeth. MA, U. Rochester, 1974; PhD, U. Chgo., 1979. Asst. prof. U. Iowa, Iowa City, 1981-85; vis. asst. prof. U. Rochester (N.Y.), 1986-88; assoc. prof. Colo. State U., Ft. Collins, 1989—. Vis. asst. prof. Cornell, Ithaca, N.Y., 1983, U. Rochester, 1983-84, assoc. prof. 1991—; rsch. assoc. Inst. for Def. Analysis, Princeton, N.J., 1987, Queens U., Kingston, Ont., Can., 1986; visitor Inst. for Advanced Study, Princeton, 1982, 83, 88; mem. Rochester Ctr. for Econ. Rsch., Rochester, 1987—; bd. dirs. Hutchinson Tech. Author: Price Theory & Applications, 1988, The Armchair Economist, 1993, Microeconomics, 1996, Fair Play, 1997; columnist Forbes mag., 1994—, Slate mag., 1996-; contbr. articles to math., philos. and econs. jours. Avocations: book collecting, poetry. Home: 109 Edgewood Ave Rochester NY 14618-3103 Office: U Rochester Dept Econs Rochester NY 14627

LANDSMAN, RICHARD, investment company executive, finance educator; b. N.Y.C., Oct. 31, 1949; s. Irving and Shirley (Siegel) L.; m. Wendy Benfield, Apr. 19, 1988; 1 child, Nerys. BS, Queens Coll., 1970, MS, 1971; MSW, Hunter Coll., 1977; MBA, Pace U., 1982. Exec. dir. CoPay Inc., Great Neck, N.Y., 1972-84; sr. v.p. Smith Barney Inc., N.Y.C., 1984-89, 92-96; v.p. Shearson Lehman Inc., 1989—92; sr. v.p. Prudential Securities, Garden City, N.Y., 1996; pres. Nottinghill Capital Mgmt. Inc., Roslyn, NY, 1997—. Prof. Grad. Sch. Bus. Columbia U., N.Y.C., 1996—; disting. adj. prof. St. Johns U. Grad. Sch. Bus., N.Y.C., 1999—. Author numerous articles on security analysis and equity evaluation. Named Rising Young Star of Wall St., Crains Bus News, 1984. E-mail: nhillcap@aol.com.

LANDSTROM, ELSIE HAYES, retired editor; b. Kuling, Kiangsi, China, June 22, 1923; came to the U.S., 1935; d. Paul Goodman and Helen Mae (Wolf) Hayes; m. Victor Norman Landstrom, Jan. 21, 1953 (dec. Oct. 1989); children: Peter S., Ruth H. BA, Hamline U., 1945. Writer, editor adminstrv. staff Am. Friends Svc. Com., Phila., 1946-52, MIT, Cambridge, Mass., 1952-53; mem. editl. bd. Approach Mag., Phila. and Needham, 1947-67; sr. editor Word Guild, 1976-82; freelance writer and editor Conway, Mass., 1976-98; ret., 1998. Author: Closing the Circle—An American Family in China, 1998; editor: Propaganda and Aesthetics, 1979, Taoism and Chinese Religion, 1981, Hyla Doc in China 1924-1949, 1991, Hyla Doc in Africa 1950-1961, 1994; exhibited Chinese paintings, 1996, 97. Newsletter editor, draft resisters support com. Wellesley (Mass.) Friends Meeting; chair Fair Housing Com., Needham. Avocations: birding, reading, painting. Home: 86 Kendal Dr Kennett Square PA 19348-2327

LANDWEHR, ARTHUR JOHN, minister; b. Northbrook, Ill., Mar. 8, 1934; s. Arthur John Sr. and Alice Eleanor (Borchardt) L.; m. Avonna Lee, Sept. 19, 1953; children: Arthur J. III, Andrea Lea Parrish. BA, Drake U., 1956; BD, Garrett-Theol. Sem., 1959; DD (hon.), North Cen. Coll., 1980. Ordained to ministry Meth. Ch., 1959. Pastor Lyndon (Ill.) United Meth. Ch., 1956-59, Marseilles (Ill.) United Meth. Ch., 1959-65, Faith United Meth. Ch., Lisle, Ill., 1965-69; sr. minister First United Meth. Ch., Elmhurst, 1969-75, Evanston, 1975-88, Grace United Meth. Ch., Naperville, 1988-2000, sr. min. emeritus, 2000—. Trustee Garrett-Evang. Theol. Sem., Evanston, 1976-2000, life trustee, 2000—, 1st v.p. bd. trustees, 1977-86, Arthur J. Landwehr endowed scholarship, 1999; del. to gen. conf. United Meth. Ch., 1976, 80, 84, 88, World Meth. Conf., Nairobi, Kenya, 1986; Wilson lectr., 1987; preacher Adams Sermon Bloomington, Ind., 1991, N.Mex. Ann. Conf., 1992, N.W. Tex. Conf., 1992, East Ohio Conf., 1997. Author: In the Third Place, 1972, Lessons on Pastoral Epistles, 1997, Cokesbury Press, Working Well: Vocation in Business, 2000, United Methodist History: A Brief History of the Northern Illinois Conference, 1999; creator Landart.50mags.com, 2001; contbr. articles to profl. jours. Convenor Blue Ribbon Com. for Referendum on Expanded Gambling in Ill., 1994; coun. mem. United Meth. Ch., 1996. Recipient citation for human rels. City of Lisle, 1969, Most Disting. Alumni award Garrett-Evang. Theol. Sem., 2002; study grantee World Coun. Chs., Sri Lanka, 1983, Ecumenical Inst. for Advanced Studies, Tantur, Israel, 1977; scholarship named in his honor Garrett-Evangelical Theol. Sem., 1999. Mem. AAAS, Am. Acad. Religion, Am. Theol. Soc., Ill. Bar Assn. (interprofl. cooperation com. 1991-95), Order of St. Luke, Rotary (pres. 1963), Univ. Club (Evanston, Ill., pres. 1986-87). Home: 2260 Petworth Ct Unit 101A Naperville IL 60565-3031 Office: Grace United Meth Ch 300 E Gartner Rd Naperville IL 60540-7424 *It is evident to me that life is a gift surrounded in mystery. Like most mysteries, we wait for the moment of revelation in which there is a profound understanding. I've learned that without a radical lane life has no future.*

LANDY, BURTON AARON, lawyer; b. Chgo., Aug. 16, 1929; s. Louis J. and Clara (Ernstein) L.; m. Eleonora M. Simmel, Aug. 4, 1957; children: Michael Simmel, Alisa Anne. Student, Nat. U. Mex., 1948; BS, Northwestern U., 1950; postgrad. scholar, U. Havana, 1951; JD, U. Miami, 1952; postgrad. fellow, Inter-Am. Acad. Comparative Law, Havana, Cuba, 1955-56. Bar: Fla. 1952. Practice law in internat. field, Miami, 1955—; ptnr. firm Ammerman & Landy, 1957-63, Paul, Landy, Beiley & Harper, P.A. and predecessor firm, 1964-94, Steel Hector & Davis, 1994-97; ptnr. firm, chmn. emeritus Internat. Practice Group Akerman, Senterfitt & Eidson, P.A., 1997—. Lectr. Latin Am. bus. law U. Miami Sch. Law, 1972-75; also internat. law confs. in U.S. and abroad; mem. Nat. Conf. on Fgn. Aspects of U.S. Nat. Security, Washington, 1958; mem. organizing com. Miami regional conf. Com. for Internat. Econ. Growth, 1958; mem. U.S. Dept. Commerce Regional Export Expansion Council, 1969-74, mem. Dist. Export Council, 1978— ; mem. U.S. Sec. State Adv. Com. on Pvt. Internat. Law; dir. Fla. Council Internat. Devel., 1977—, chmn. 1986-87, 99; mem. U. Miami Citizens Bd., 1977— ; chmn. Fla. del. S.E. U.S.-Japan Assn., 1980-82; mem. adv. com. 1st Miami Trade Fair of Ams., 1978; dir., v.p. Greater Miami Fgn. Trade Zone, Inc., 1978—; mem. organizing com., lectr. 4 Inter-Am. Aviation Law Confs.; bd. dirs. Inter-Am. Bar Legal Found.; participant Aquaculture Symposium Sci. and Man in the Ams., Mexico City, Fla. Gov's Econ. Mission to Japan and Hong Kong, 1978; mem. bd. exec. advisors Law and Econs. Ctr.; mem. vis. com., internat. adv. bd. U. Miami Sch. Bus.; mem. internat. fin. council Office Comptroller of Fla.; founding chmn. Fla.-Korea Econ. Coop. Com., 1982— , Southeast U.S.-Korea Econ. Com., 1985—; chmn. Expo 500 Fla.-Columbus Soc., 1985-87; founding co-chmn. So. Fla. Roundtable-Georgetown U. Ctr. for Strategic and Internat. Studies, 1982-85; chmn. Fla. Gov.'s Conf. on World Trade, 1984— ; founding gen. counsel Fla. Internat. Bankers Assn.; dir., former gen. counsel Fla. Internat. Ins. and Reins. Assn., chmn. Latin Am. Carribbean Bus. Promotion Adv. Counc. to U.S. Sec. of Commerce and Aid Adminstr; appointee Fla. Internat. Trade and Investment Coun.; mem. steering com. Summit of Ams., 1994—, co-chair post summit planning com.; strategic planning com. Mayor Miami Dade County Internat. Trade Commn. Contbg. editor Econs. Devel. Lawyers of the Ams., 1969-74; contbr. numerous articles to legal jours. in U.S. and fgn. countries. Chmn. City of Miami Internat. Trade and Devel. Com., 1984-86; chmn. internat. task force Beacon Coun. of Dade County, Fla., 1985, dir., chmn., 1991—; bd. dirs., exec. com. Internat. Comml. Dispute Resolution Ctr., Miami Internat. Arbitration and Mediation Inst.; chmn. Comml. Dispute Resolution Ctr. for the Ams., Miami, 1995—; apptd. by Gov. of Fla. to Internat. Currency and Barter Commn., 1986; lectr. U. Miami Inter-Ban course for Latin Am. bankers; steering com. Summit of the Americas, Miami, 1994, co-chair post Summit Planning Com., 1994; co-chair mayor Miami-Dade County Strategic Planning for Internat. Trade, 1998—; co-chair strategic planning com. Mayor of Miami Dade County Internat. Trade Commn.; bd. dirs. Trade Mission Ctr. Am., 2000—; mem. internat. adv. com. Enterprise Fla., 2000—. With JACGC, USAF, 1952-54, Korea; to maj. Res. Named Internat. Trader of Yr., Fla. Council Internat. Devel., 1980, Bus. Person of Yr., 1986; recipient Pan Am. Informatica Comunicaciones Expo award, 1983, Lawyer of Americas award U. Miami, 1984, Richard L. McLaughlin award Fla. Econ. Devel. Coun., 1993; named hon. consul gen. Republic of Korea, Miami, 1983-88, State of Fla., 99—, recipient Heung-in medal (Order of Diplomatic Service), 1986, Ministerial Citation, Min. of Fgn. Affairs, 1988; apptd. Hon. consul Ft. Lauderdale, Fla., 1991-98; apptd. Hon. consul gen. State of Fla., 1999—. Fellow ABA Found. (chmn. com. arrangements internat. and comparative law sect. 1964-65, com. on Inter-Am. affairs of ABA 1985-87); mem. Inter-Am. Bar Assn. (asst. sec.-gen. 1957-59, treas. 11th conf. 1959, co-chmn. jr. bar sect. 1963-65, mem council 1969—, exec. com. 1975—, pres. 1982-84, Diploma de Honor 1987, William Roy Vallance award 1989), Spanish Am. Bar Assn., Fla. Bar Assn. (vice chmn. adminstrv. law com. 1965, vice chmn. internat. and comparative law com. 1967-68, chmn. aero. law com. 1968-69), Dade County Bar Assn. (chmn. fgn. laws and langs com. 1964-65), Internat. Ctr. Fla. (World Trade Ctr., pres. 1981-82), World Peace Through Law Ctr., Miami Com. Fgn. Relations, Inst. Ibero Am. Derecho Aero., Am. Soc. Internat. Law, Council Internat. Visitors, Am. Fgn. Law Assn. (pres. Miami 1958), Bar of South Korea (hon. mem.), Greater Miami C. of C. (bd. govs. 1986—), Colombian-Am. C. of C. (bd. dirs. 1986—), Peruvian-Am. C. of C. (bd. dirs.), Norwegian Am. C. of C. (bd. dirs.), Phi Alpha Delta. Home: 605 Almeria Ave Coral Gables FL 33134-5602 Office: One SE Third Ave 28th Flr Miami FL 33131 E-mail: blandy@akerman.com.

LANDY, JOANNE VEIT, foreign policy and health policy reform analyst; b. Chgo., Oct. 15, 1941; d. Fritz and Lucille (Stearns) Veit; m. Seymour Landy, Mar., 1959 (div. 1962); m. Nelson Lichtenstein, Mar., 1972 (div. 1976). BA in History, U. Calif., Berkeley, 1968, MA in History, 1970; MPH, Columbia U., 1982. Dir. N.Y. Met. Office, U. Chgo., N.Y.C., 1977-80; pres. Campaign for Peace and Democracy, 1982—98; exec. dir. Physicians for a Nat. Health Program NY Chpt., 2000—. Editor: Peace and Democracy, 1984-1996; mem. editl. bd. New Politics, 1986—. Recipient grant for rsch. and writing John D. and Catherine T. Mac Arthur Fedn., Program on Peace and Internat. Cooperation, Chgo., 1990-91. Mem. Coun. on Fgn. Rels., Phi Beta Kappa. Home: 2785 Broadway Apt 7A New York NY 10025-2850

LANDY, LEIGH (HARRY LEIGH LANDY), music educator, composer; b. Bronxville, N.Y., Nov. 23, 1951; s. Robert Jay Landy and Joan Lila (Aaron) Shapiro; m. Evelyn Carnduff Jamieson, Aug. 15, 1996; 1 child, Marissa. BSc, Columbia U., 1972, MA, 1974; PhD, SUNY, Buffalo, 1977. Univ. Hoofddocent Univ. van Amsterdam, The Netherlands, 1977-93; head of music dept. Univ. Coll. Bretton Hall, Wakefield, Eng., 1993-97; head of contemporary arts Manchester Met. U., Eng., 1997-99; rsch. prof. contemporary music De Montfort U., Leicester, Eng., 1999—. Bd. dirs. Composers Desktop Project, Chippenham, Wiltshire, England, 1992—, Phoenix Arts, Leicester; performing arts advisor North West Arts Bd., Manchester, ACE, 1998; artistic dir. Idée Fixe: Exptl. Sound and Movement Theatre, Crewe; composer in residence Dutch Nat. Theatre Co., The Hague, 1988—89. Author: What's the Matter with Experimental Music, 1991, Experimental Music Notebooks, 1994, Devising Dance and Music Idée Fixe, 2000; European editor: Ear Mag., 1981—85; co-editor: Organised Sound: an Internat. Jour. of Music Tech. , 1995—; music editor: Avant Garde, 1987—, music editor: Avante Garde, 1998—, composer video music theater pieces, others. British Coun. Rsch. fellow, U. York, 1991; Fulbright scholar, Amsterdam, 1976-77. Mem. Sonic Arts Network. Office: De Montfort U Clephan Bldg Leicester LE1 9BH England E-mail: llandy@dmu.ac.uk.

LANDY, LISA ANNE, lawyer; b. Miami, Fla., Apr. 20, 1963; d. Burton Aaron and Eleonora Maria (Simmel) L. BA, Brown U., 1985; JD cum laude, U. Miami, 1988. Bar: Fla. 1988, U.S. Dist. Ct. (so. dist.) Fla. 1988. Atty. Paul, Landy, Beiley & Harper, P.A., Miami, Fla., 1988-94, Steel Hector & Davis, Miami, 1994-97, ptnr., 1996-97; shareholder Akerman Senterfitt & Eidson P.A., Miami , 1997—. Bd. dirs. Miami City Ballet, 1992-97, pres., 1996; bd. dirs. Women in Internat. Trade, Miami, 1992—, pres., 1994; bd. dirs. Orgn. Women in Internat. Trade, 1994—, v.p., 1997, 98, pres. 1998-2000; bd. dirs. Women in Tech. Internat. South Fla, The Next Step Youth Cmty. Ctr., Inc., IT Women, Inc., 2002—. Mem. ABA, Inter-Am. Bar Assn. (asst. sec. 1997-2000). Avocations: sports, arts, fluent in Spanish, French.

LANDY, RICARDO LOPEZ, humanities educator; b. Guatemala City, Guatemala, Sept. 17, 1949; came to U.S., 1963; s. Lino and Mercedes (Villaverde) L. BA, U. Tex. El Paso, 1970; MA, U. Tex. Austin, 1972, PhD, 1976. Cert. tchr., Tex. Instr. U. Tex., Austin, 1970-76; asst. prof. Tex. A&M U., College Station, 1976-77, Harvard U., Cambridge, Mass., 1977-82; lectr. Spanish UCLA, 1983-84; asst. prof. Grambling (La.) State U., 1992-93; coord. Spanish Tarleton State U., Stephenville, Tex., 1994-95; dir., cons. Pacific Basin Internat., El Paso, 1995—. Spl. vis. faculty agr., pedagogy in Spanish, Calif. State U., Stanislaus, 1999-2000. Author: El espacio Novelesco en Galdós, 1984, Journey to Montserrat, 1996, (play) La chamaca brava, 1988, El gran magnate, (novel), 1998. Mem. Sigma Delta Pi. Avocations: painting, photography. E-mail: seabird. Office: Pacific Basin Internat 304 Carnival Dr El Paso TX 79912-5704 E-mail: virgoyorix@aol.com.

LANE, ADELAIDE IRENE, computer systems specialist, researcher; b. Bronx, N.Y., Sept. 27, 1939; d. Anton John and Constance Mary (Fogle) Pospisil; m. Robert Walton Lane, Sept. 26, 1964; children: Frank Anton, Miriam Helen, Robin Ann. BS in Edn. cum laude, SUNY, Oneonta, 1961; MS in Edn., Hofstra U., 1963; MS in Computer Sci., Rensselaer Poly. Inst., 1983. Cert. tchr., N.Y., Vt. Tchr. Island Trees Jr. H.S., Levittown, N.Y., 1961-64; copy editor, typesetter Pennysaver & Press, Bennington, Vt., 1976-77; tchr. Mt. Anthony Jr./Sr. H.S., 1977-80; computer operator Rensselaer Poly. Inst., Troy, N.Y., 1981-82, graphics application programmer, 1982-87, sr. graphics application programmer, 1987-92, mgr. instrnl. computing, 1992-94, mgr. instrn. multimedia, dir. new media ctr., 1994-96; pres. IDEA Cons., Onancock, Va., 1996—. Tchr. computer sci. Russell Sage Coll., Troy, 1984-85; cons. Union Coll., Schenectady, 1990. Editor: The Rock Ribs of Bennington Town, 1977; contbr. articles to profl. jours. Asst. coach Bennington Swim Team, 1972-75; troop leader Girl Scouts U.S., Hoosick Falls, N.Y., 1973-79; tchr. Hoosick Falls Ice Skating Club, 1975-80. Interuniv. Consortium for Ednl. Computing fellow, 1984. Mem. IEEE (affiliate), Nat. Computer Graphics

Assn., Ednl. Uses of Info. Tech./EDUCOM (mem. Joe Wyatt Challenge selection com. 1990-91). Republican. Roman Catholic. Avocations: sailing, multimedia computing, weaving, watercolor painting. E-mail: lanea@esva.net.

LANE, ALFRED THOMAS, medical educator; b. Dayton, Ohio, July 17, 1947; BS, U. Dayton, 1969; MD, Ohio State U., 1973. Diplomate Am. Bd. Pediatrics, Am. Bd. Dermatology; lic. physician, Calif. Intern, resident pediatrics Children's Hosp. L.A., 1973-76; pvt. practice Pleasant Valley Pediatric Med. Group, Camarillo, Calif., 1976-79; resident dermatology U. Colo. Sch. Medicine, Denver, 1979-82; asst. prof. dermatology and pediatrics U. Rochester (N.Y.) Med. Ctr., 1982-88; attending physician Strong Meml. Hosp., 1982-90; staff dermatologist Rochester Gen. Hosp., 1985-90; dir. Dermatology Clinic VA, Rochester, 1985-90; assoc. prof. dermatology and pediatrics U. Rochester Med. Ctr., 1988-90; staff physician in dermatology and pediatrics Stanford (Calif.) U. Med. Ctr., Stanford Children's Hosp., 1990—, dir. pediatric dermatology, 1990—; assoc. prof. dermatology and pediatrics Stanford U. Med. Ctr., 1990-96; prof. dermatology Stanford (Calif.) U. Med. Ctr., 1996—; acting chmn. dept. dermatology Stanford U. Med. Ctr., 1995-96, chmn. dermatology, 1996—; chief dermatology svc. Stanford U. Med. Ctr., Stanford Health Svcs., 1995—. Author: with W.L. Weston) Color Textbook of Pediatric Dermatology, 1991; (with W.L. Weston and J.G. Morelli) Color Textbook of Pediatric Dermatology, 1995; contbr. articles to profl. jours. Recipient Buswell fellowship U. Rochester, 1982-83, Clin. Investigator award NIH, 1983-88. Fellow Am. Acad. Pediatrics, Am. Acad. Dermatology (mem. task force on pediatric dermatology 1987-92, mem. adv. coun. 1988-90, mem. Presdl. Commn. on Melanoma/Skin Cancer 1988-92, mem. task force on youth edn. 1989-94); mem. Soc. Pediatric Dermatology (bd. dirs. 1986-93, pres. elect 1990-91, pres. 1991-92), Soc. Investigative Dermatology (com. on pub. rels. 1990-94, com. on govt. and pub. rels. 1992-94), Soc. Pediatric Rsch., Am. Dermatol. Assn., Am. Soc. Laser Medicine and Surgery. Office: Stanford U Med Ctr Dept Dermatology 900 Blake Wilbur Dr Dept W71 Palo Alto CA 94304-2201

LANE, ALVIN HUEY, JR. management consultant; b. Dallas, May 2, 1942; s. Alvin Huey and Marianne (Halsell) L.; m. Melanie Kadane, June 21, 1963; children— Alvin Huey, III, Michael, Lance, Marianne. BA, Rice U., Houston, 1964, BS, 1965. Mgmt. positions with Procter & Gamble Mfg. Co., 1965-68; mgmt. cons. Ernst & Young, CPA's, Dallas, 1968-69; v.p. fin., sec. Balanced Investment Dynamics Co., 1969-72, Dr Pepper Co., Dallas, 1972-80, sr. v.p. fin., sec., 1980-83; pres. Lane & Assocs., Dallas, 1983—. Bd. dirs. Love Bottling Co., Muskogee, Okla., Marketplace Christian Network, Dallas. Western Electric scholar Rice U., 1964, J. Venn Leeds scholar, 1964. Mem. Lakewood Country Club. Home: 3415 Colgate Ave Dallas TX 75225-4830 Office: Lane and Assocs 10440 N Central Expy Ste 610 Dallas TX 75231-2227 E-mail: alane@laneassociates.net.

LANE, ALVIN S. lawyer; b. Englewood, N.J., June 17, 1918; s. Martin Lane and Nettie (Gans) Daniels; m. Terese P. Lyons, Apr. 24, 1949; children: Mary-Jo, Judith Lyons. Ph.B., U. Wis., 1940; LL.B., Harvard U., 1943. Bar: N.Y. 1947. Sr. ptnr. Wien, Lane & Malkin, 1954-83; chmn. Rapidata, Inc., 1967-82; Mem. adv. bd. to N.Y. atty. gen. on art legis., 1966-71. Contbr. articles to art publs. and legal jours. Mem. bd. mgmt. Henry Ittleson Rsch. Ctr. Disturbed Children, Riverdale, N.Y., 1961-70; fellow Brandeis U., 1966—, nat. adv. coun. 20th Century Art Soc. High Mus. of Art, 1986-95; sec., trustee Aldrich Mus. Contemporary Art, Inc., 1969-76; trustee Lexington Sch. Deaf, 1971; v.p., trustee Soho Ctr. Visual Artists, Inc., 1974-83; dir. Creative Artists Pub. Svc. Program, Inc., 1982-84; mem. drawing com. Whitney Mus. Am Art, 1991-93; mem. The Elvehjem Mus. Art Coun., 1992—. Served as lt. USNR, 1942-46. Mem. Assn. of Bar of City of N.Y. (chmn. com. art 1963-65), N.Y. Artists Equity Assn. (dir. 1982-84) Clubs: Harvard (N.Y.C.), Riverdale Yacht. Home: 5251 Independence Ave Bronx NY 10471-2825 Office: 35 E 38th St New York NY 10016-2529

LANE, ARTHUR ALAN, lawyer; b. N.Y.C., Dec. 2, 1945; s. George and Delys L.; m. Jane Ficocella, Dec. 30, 1972; 1 child, Eva B. BA, Yale U., 1967; JD, Columbia U., 1970, MBA, 1971. Bar: N.Y. 1971. Assoc. Webster, Sheffield, Fleischmann, Hitchcock & Brookfield, N.Y.C., 1971-72; asst. to divsn. counsel Liggett & Myers, Inc., 1973; assoc. Wickes, Riddell, Bloomer, Jacobi & McGuire, 1974-78, Morgan, Lewis & Bockius, N.Y.C., 1979; ptnr. Eaton & Van Winkle, 1980—94, DeForest & Duer, N.Y.C., 1994-99, Lamb & Barnosky, Melville, 1999—. Mem. ABA, Assn. of Bar of City of N.Y. Avocation: gardening. Home: 103 Brooksite Dr Smithtown NY 11787-4456 Office: Lamb & Barnosky 534 Broadhollow Rd Melville NY 11747

LANE, BARBARA MILLER (BARBARA MILLER-LANE), humanities educator; b. N.Y.C., Nov. 1, 1934; d. George Ross Rede and Gertrude Miller; m. Jonathan Lane, Jan. 28, 1956; children: Steven Gregory, Eleanor. BA, U. Chgo., 1953, Barnard Coll., 1956; MA, Radcliffe Coll., 1957; PhD, Harvard U., 1962. Tutor history and lit. Harvard U., Cambridge, Mass., 1960-61; lectr. to prof. history Bryn Mawr Coll., Bryn Mawr, Pa., 1962-75, dir. Growth and Structure of Cities Program, 1971-89, Andrew W. Mellon prof. humanities, 1981-99, Katherine McBride prof., 1999—. Vis. prof. Architecture, Columbia U., 1989; cons. NEH sr. fellowships, Washington, 1971-73, Time-Life Books, N.Y.C., 1975; advisor Macmillan Ency. of Architects, N.Y.C., 1979-82; vis. examiner U. Helsinki, 1991; vis. lectr. Technische Universität, Berlin, 1991 Author: (books) Architecture and Politics in Germany, 1968, 1985, 1973, 1986; co-author: Nazi Ideology Before 1933, 1978, National Romanticism and Modern Architecture in Germany and the Scandinavian Countries, 2000; author (contbg.): Growth and Transformation of the Modern City, 1979, Macmillan Encyclopedia of Architects, 1982, Urbanisierung im 19. und 20. Jahrhundert, 1983, Perspectives in American History, 1984, The Evidence of Art: Images and Meaning in History, 1986, Art and History, 1988, Nationalism in the Visual Arts, 1991, Moderne Architektur in Deutschland: Expressionismus und Neue Sachlichkeit, 1994, Ultra terminum vagari: Scritti in onore di Carl Nylander, 1997; contbg. editor: Urbanism Past and Present, 1980—85; bd. editors (journal) Archtl. History Found., 1988—, Ctrl. European History, 1992—97; contbr. articles. Co-founder, dir., chmn. bd. dirs. New Gulph Child Care Ctr., Bryn Mawr, 1971-75; mem. Middle Atlantic Regional Com., Mellon Fellowships in the Humanities, 1985-87; mem. vis. com. Harvard U. Dept. History, 1986-92, Berlin Stadtforum (adv. coun. to Senator for Urban Devel. and Environment), 1991-96; mem. nat. screening com. Inst. Internat. Edn., 1999—; mem. com. NEH sr. fellowships, 2000—. Recipient Lindback award for excellence in tchg., 1988, medal of honor U. Helsinki, 1996; fellow AAUW, 1959-60, Fels Found., 1961-62, Am. Council Learned Socs., 1967-68, Guggenheim Found., 1977-78, sr. fellow Ctr. for Advanced Study in Visual Arts, Nat. Gallery Art, Washington, 1983; Am. Scandinavian Found. fellow, 1989, Wissenschaftskolleg zu Berlin fellow, 1990-91; NEH grantee, summer 1989; NEH sr. fellow, 1998. Mem. Soc. Archtl. Historians (bd. dirs. 1977-80, Alice Davis Hitchcock award 1968, chmn. awards coms. 1976, 82, chmn. jour. com. 1982-83), Conf. Group on Central European History (bd. dirs. 1977-79, chmn. awards com. 1987), Am. Hist. Assn. (mem. coun. 1979-82, chmn. com. on Popular Mag. of History 1982), Coll. Art Assn., Phi Beta Kappa Office: Bryn Mawr Coll Bryn Mawr PA 19010

LANE, BENNIE R. mathematician, educator; b. Deming, N.Mex., July 2, 1935; s. William V. Lane and Neva Ruth Durham; m. Josephine G. Green, Aug. 18, 1956; children: Margaret, Joseph, Ruth, Rebekah Barnett. PhD, George Peabody Coll., 1962. Asst. prof. U. Chattanooga, 1959—61; instr. Vanderbilt U., Nashville, 1961—62; asst. prof. Colo. State Coll., Greeley, 1962—63; assoc. prof. George Peabody Coll., Nashville, 1963—66; chair dept. math. Ea. Ky. U., Richmond, 1966—78, prof. math., 1978—97.

LANE, BRUCE STUART, lawyer; b. New London, Conn., May 15, 1932; s. Stanley S. and Frances M. (Antis) L.; m. Ann Elizabeth Steinberg, Aug. 10, 1958; children: Sue Ellen, Charles M., Richard I. Student, Boston U., 1948-49; AB magna cum laude, Harvard U., 1952, JD, 1955. Bar: Ohio 1955, D.C. 1966, U.S. Ct. Claims 1960, U.S. Tax Ct. 1961, U.S. Supreme Ct. 1961. Assoc. Squire, Sanders & Dempsey, Cleve., 1955-59; sr. trial atty. tax div. Dept. Justice, Washington, 1959-61; tax atty. Dinsmore, Shohl, Barrett, Coates & Deupree, Cin., 1961-65; sec., asst. gen. counsel corp. and tax matters Communications Satellite Corp., Washington, 1965-69; v.p., gen. counsel Nat. Corp. Housing Partnerships, 1969-70; pres. Lane and Edson P.C., 1970-89; ptnr. Kelley Drye & Warren, 1989-93, Peabody & Brown, Washington, 1993-99, Nixon Peabody LLP, Washington, 1999-2000, sr. cousnel, 2001—. Co-editor-in-chief Housing and Devel. Reporter; author publs. and articles on tax, partnership and real estate. Incorporator, bd. dirs., past pres. D.C. Inst. Mental Health; past chmn. citizens Com. sect. 5 Chevy Chase, Md.; past mem. Montgomery County Hist. Preservation Commn., Md.; mem. chmn. coun. Crow Canyon Archeol. Ctr., Cortez, Colo. Maj. JAG, USAR, 1952-68. Mem. ABA, Am. Law Inst., Am. Coll. Real Estate Lawyers (pres. 1986-87), Anglo-Am. Real Property Inst., Phi Beta Kappa. Home: 3711 Thornapple St Chevy Chase MD 20815-4111 Office: Nixon Peabody LLP 401 9th St NW Ste 900 Washington DC 20004-2134

LANE, CHARLOTTE KNOX, association executive; b. Washington, July 1, 1918; d. Robert Welch and Sarah (Chaney) K.; m. Perry Mehaffey Lane Sr., Apr. 13, 1940; children: Penelope K. Snyder, Sarah Lane Sutherland, Perry Mehaffey Jr., Gregory Scott (dec.). Student, Sweet Briar Coll., 1936-38, Miss Conley's Sch., 1938-39. Sec. Washington County Blind Assn., Pa., 1967; office mgr. Washington County Tourism, 1967-69, exec. dir., 1969-92. V.p. Washington County History and Landmarks, 1983—; sec. Bradford House Assn., Washington, 1985—; mem. Pa. Bd. Hist. Preservation, Harrisburg, 1983-85. Recipient award for significant contbn. Washington County Arts Council, 1987. Mem. Nat. Tour Assn., Travel Pa. Assn. (bd. dirs. 1975—, sec. 1975-80), Pa. Travel Council, Duncan Glass Soc. (bd. dirs. 1984—). Lodges: Zonta (bd. dirs. Washington). Democrat. Presbyterian. Home: 3463 Route 40 Washington PA 15301-8569 Office: Washington County Tourism BOO Sta S Main St Washington PA 15301

LANE, DAVID OLIVER, retired librarian; b. Flint, Mich., Oct. 17, 1931; s. Clinton Ellis and Mary Ailene (Sanders) L. BA, U. Mich., 1958, A.M. in L.S, 1959; doctoral fellow, U. Chgo., 1968. Various library assignments, 1959-63; asst. dir. libraries Boston U., 1963-67; asst. univ. librarian U. Calif., San Diego, 1968-69; chief librarian, prof., dept. chmn. Hunter Coll., N.Y.C., 1969-90. Dir. NSF funded study of library acquisitions, 1967-68; chmn. Council Chief Librarians, City U. N.Y., 1972-75; trustee N.Y. Met. Reference Library Agy., 1978-87. Author: Study of the Decision Making Procedures for the Acquisition of Science Library Materials, 1968. Mem. A.L.A. (life), Assn. Coll. and Research Libraries, Beta Phi Mu. Home: 27D E Hill Dr Somers NY 10589

LANE, DAVID ALLAN, network and database professional; b. Toronto, Ont., Can., May 2, 1966; s. Robert Howard and Barbara Jean (Jacques) L.; m. Dianne Marie Brower, Nov. 10, 1990. BA in Geography, George Washington U., 1989. Cert. NetWare engr. Sys. analyst Global Mgmt. Sys., Bethesda, Md., 1993-95; field svc. engr. Compucel Svc., Inc., Laurel, 1995; network and database mgr. The Aluminum Assn., Washington, 1995-96; sr. network engr. Intermetrics, Inc., 1996-97; technical dir. ManTech Internat. Corp., Fairfax, Va., 1997—. Recipient Hon. Mention award Art Dirs. Guild of DC, 1985. Mem. Network Profl. Assn. Avocations: rock climbing, mountain biking, scuba diving. Office: ManTech Internat Corp 12015 Lee Jackson Hwy Ste 300 Fairfax VA 22033-3300

LANE, DOROTHY SPIEGEL, preventive medicine physician; b. Bklyn., Feb. 17, 1940; d. Milton Barton and Rosalie (Jacobson) Spiegel; m. Bernard Paul Lane, Aug. 5, 1962; children: Erika, Andrew, Matthew. BA, Vassar Coll., 1961; MD, Columbia U., 1965, MPH, 1968. Diplomate Am. Bd. Preventive Medicine, Am. Bd. Family Practice. Resident in preventive medicine N.Y.C. Dept. Health Dist., 1966-68, project dir. children and youth project Title V, HHS, 1968-69; med. cons. Maternal and Child Health Svc. HHS, Rockville, Md., 1970-71; asst. prof. preventive medicine Sch. Medicine SUNY, Stony Brook, 1971-76, assoc. prof., 1976-92, prof., 1992—2002, assoc. dean, 1986—; chair dept. cmty. medicine, dir. med. edn. Brookhaven Meml. Hosp. Med. Ctr., Patchogue, N.Y., 1972-86; chair. Am. Bd. Preventive Medicine, Schiller Park, IL; disting. svc. prof. SUNY, 2002—. Contbr. articles to profl. jours. Mem. nat. assembly LI divsn. Am. Cancer Soc., 1996—2001, exec. com., 1975—96; corp. mem. Nassau Suffolk Health Sys. Agy, 1977—97; nat. bd. dir. LI divsn. Am. Cancer Soc., 1994—96; bd. dir. Cmty. Health Plan Suffolk, Hauppauge, NY, 1986—91. Grantee HHS-USPHS, 1977—, Nat. Cancer Inst., 1987—. Fellow: APHA, Am. Bd. Preventive Medicine (trustee 1991—2000, chair 1998—2000), NY Acad. Medicine, Am. Acad. Family Physicians, Am. Coll. Preventive Medicine (regent 1988—96, sec.-treas. 1994—96, pres. 2001—), Assn. Tchrs. Preventive Medicine (pres. 1996—98); mem.: Home Accreditation Coun. for Continuing Med. Edn. Office: SUNY at Stony Brook Sch Medicine Health Scis Ctr L 4 Stony Brook NY 11794-0001

LANE, DOUGLAS CALDER, investment counsel; b. Bklyn., Nov. 2, 1945; s. John Burns and Elizabeth Ann (Fuller) L.; m. Susan Leslie, June 20, 1967 (div. 1989); children: John, Matthew, Sarah, Todd; m. Gay Trimbach, Oct. 2, 1993. BS, Lehigh U., Bethlehem, Pa., 1967; MBA, U. Mich., 1968. Cert. fin. analyst; chartered investment counsel. Ptnr. Brundage, Story & Rose, N.Y.C., 1968—; pres. Lane Capital Mgmt., 1994—. Trustee, chmn. investment com., vice chmn. fin. com. Lehigh U., Bethlehem, Pa. Mem. N.Y. Soc. Security Analysts, Saucon Valley Country Club, Downtown Athletic Club, Essex County Country Club, Bradford Bath & Tennis Club (gov.). Avocations: tennis, squash, golf. Home: 6 Bradford Way Cedar Grove NJ 07009-1934

LANE, EDWARD WOOD, JR. retired banker; b. Jacksonville, Fla., Apr. 4, 1911; s. Edward Wood and Anna Virginia (Taliaferro) L.; m. Helen Spratt Murchison, Oct. 16, 1948; children: Edward Wood III, Helen Palmer, Anna Taliaferro, Charles Murchison. AB, Princeton, 1933; LL.B., Harvard U., 1936. Bar: Fla. 1936. Partner firm McCarthy, Lane & Adams (and predecessors), Jacksonville, 1941-60; pres., CEO Atlantic Nat. Bank, 1961-76, chmn., 1976-85, First Union Nat. Bank of Fla. (formerly Atlantic Nat. Bank), Jacksonville, 1985-86, ret., 1986. Served to lt. comdr. USNR, World War II. Mem. Phi Beta Kappa. Clubs: Florida Yacht (Jacksonville), Timuquana Country (Jacksonville), River (Jacksonville), Univ. (Jacksonville); Ponte Vedra. Home and Office: 3790 Ortega Blvd Jacksonville FL 32210-4333

LANE, ELIZABETH ANN, genealogist, researcher; b. Horton, Kans. , Mar. 9, 1957; d. Dale D. Sheets and Marlene E. Kletchka; m. Rex L. Lane; children: Laura, Catherine. BSW, U. Kans., 1983. Dir. CASA, Atchison, Kans., 1997—98; asst. dir. Juvenile Intake and Assessment, Oskaloosa, 1998—2001. Mem.: AAUW, Atchison Preservation Alliance (mem. bd. dirs. 1999—2001), Friends Atchison Libr. (pres. 2001—02), Atchison County Hist. Soc. (pres. 2001—02). Avocations: gardening, reading, music, travel. Home: EA Lane Rsch Svcs 841 S Fourth St Atchison KS 66002-2904 Personal E-mail: llane1@charter.net.*

LANE, ERIC JAY, retail executive; BA in Econs., U. Calif., Santa Barbara. With Macy's, The Men's Wearhouse, Inc., Fremont, Calif., 1988—, v.p. store ops., 1990-93, sr. v.p. merchandising, 1993-97, COO, 1997-2000, pres., COO, 2001—. 1st lt. USAR, 1982. Office: The Mens Wearhouse Inc 40650 Encyclopedia Cir Fremont CA 94538

LANE, EVELYN PROCTER CONANT, computer operator; b. Gloucester, Mass., May 14, 1919; d. Daniel Moody and Edith Procter (Morrow) Conant; m. Rodney Harris Lane, Aug. 24, 1945; children: Stephen Mark, Stephanie May, Robert Michael. Student, Gloucester C.C., 1937. Office clk. LePage's Inc., Gloucester, 1937-41, computer operator, 1947-53; operator tabulating equipment dept. USN, Boston, 1941-44, War Assets Adminstrn., Boston, 1944-47; computer operator Peter Smith Publ. Inc., Magnolia, Mass., 1962—. Compiler Index of Surnames Early Mass., 1990, (books) Towne Family in Early Mass., 1990, Nurse/Esty Families in Early Mass., 1991, Procter Family in Early Mass., 1991, Bishop & Burroughs Families in Early Mass., 1991, Carrier/Currier Families in Early Mass., 1992. Active Peabody & Essex Mus., Salem, Mass.; brail translator during WWII Mem. New Eng. Hist. & Geneaol. Soc., Cape Ann Hist. Assn. Methodist. Avocations: genealogy, knitting. Home: Bldg 1 4 Chebacco Ter Essex MA 01929-1228

LANE, FIELDING H. lawyer; b. Kansas City, Mo., May 6, 1926; s. Ralph Fielding and Nancy Lee (Greene) L.; m. Patricia Cecil Parkhurst, Jan. 25, 1980 BS in Bus. Adminstrn., U. Mo.-Columbia, 1948; LL.B. cum laude, Harvard U., 1951. Bar: Mo. 1951, Calif. 1956. Assoc. Watson Ess Marshall & Enggas, Kansas City, Mo., 1951-55; assoc. Thelen Marrin Johnson & Bridges, San Francisco, 1955-66, ptnr., 1967-95, of counsel, 1996—. Served with USN, 1944-46; PTO; lt. comdr. Res. (ret.) Home: PO Box 1495 Aptos CA 95001-1495 Office: Thelen Reid & Priest LLP 101 2d St Ste 1800 San Francisco CA 94105 E-mail: fhlane@thelenreid.com.

LANE, FRANK JOSEPH, JR. lawyer; b. St. Louis, May 10, 1934; s. Frank Joseph and Virginia Laurette (Hausman) L.; m. Margaret Ann Dwyer, Mar. 2, 1957; children: Mary, Stephen, Thomas, Michael. BS in Commerce, JD, St. Louis U., 1956; LLM, Georgetown U., 1960; grad. Parker Sch. Internat. Law, Columbia U., 1970; cert., Coll. Fin. Planning, Denver, 1988. Bar: Mo. 1956, U.S. Dist. Ct. (ea. dist.) Mo. 1956, U.S. Ct. Appeals (8th cir.) 1960, U.S. Supreme Ct. 1959, U.S. Ct. Mil. Appeals, 1957. Ptnr. Goldenhersh, Goldenhersh, Fredericks, Newman & Lane, St. Louis, 1960-64, Lane & Leadlove, St. Louis, 1964-66, Dill & Lane, St. Louis, 1978-79; counsel Ralston Purina Co., 1966-78; pres.'s adv. bd., 1967-69; of counsel Petrolite Corp., St. Louis, 1979-83; v.p., trust officer Gravois Bank, 1983-85; regional v.p., trust officer Merc Bank N.A., 1985-89; of counsel Dill, Wamser, Bamvakais & Newsham PC, 1989—. Instr. internat. law St. Louis U., 1979. Bd. dirs. Met. St. Louis Sewer Dist., 1965-73, chmn., 1968-69; bd. dirs. Webster Groves KC Home Assn., 1999-01; mem. St. Louis Regional Commerce & Growth Assn. environ. com., 1978-82; mem. planned giving com. Am. Heart Assn., St. Louis, 1986-88, St. Louis Soc. for Crippled Children, 1991; bd. dirs. Midwestern Braille Vols., Inc., chmn., 1995—; atty. St. Louis Geneal. Soc., 1996—; pres. Ozark Cmties. Coun. St. Louis County, 1964-65. Capt. U.S. Army JAGC, Pentagon, 1957-60. Mem. Mo. Bar Assn., Met. St. Louis Bar Assn. (chmn. rels. with law schs. com. 1961-62, enrollment com. 1962-63, chmn. office practice com. 1963-64, elected admissions com. 1967), Estate Planning Coun. St. Louis, Rotary (bd. dirs. Crestwood, Mo. chpt. 1988-89), KC (grand knight 1964-66, adv. West County 1983-90, Webster Groves 1991-2001). Republican. Roman Catholic. Avocations: oil painting, golf, travel, investment analysis. Home: 520 Lering Dr Ballwin MO 63011-1588 Office: 9939 Gravois Rd Saint Louis MO 63123-4211 E-mail: frank_j_lane@juno.com.

LANE, GARY MATTHEW, lawyer; b. Fairfield, Iowa, Oct. 12, 1944; m. Gerda C. Murra; children: Matthew P., Stephen W. BA, U. Iowa, 1967, JD with distinction, 1969. Bar: Iowa 1969, U.S. Dist. Ct. (so. dist.) Iowa 1969, U.S. Dist. Ct. (no. dist.) Iowa 1977. Asst. county atty. Scott County, Davenport, Iowa, 1969-78; ptnr. Wehr, Berger, Lane & Stevens and predecessors, 1969—. Bd. dirs., past pres. HELP, Legal Svcs. Corp., Davenport, Iowa, 1972—; founding dir., past pres. Legal Svcs. Corp. Iowa, Des Moines, 1977-93. Pres. Davenport Diocesan Lay Coun., Iowa, 1980-82; trustee Quad City Symphony Orch., Davenport, 1980-89; pres. Marriage and Family Counseling Svc., Davenport, 1985-87; chmn. Davenport Neighborhood Task Force, 1991; pres. bd. Assumption H.S., 1994-96. Fellow Iowa Acad. Trial Lawyers; mem. ATLA (Disting. Mem. award 1989), Iowa Trial Lawyers Assn. (bd. govs. 1980-88, Outstanding Key Mem. 1988), Iowa Bar Assn., Scott County Bar Assn. Office: Wehr Berger Lane & Stevens Ste 900 Kahl Bldg 326 W 3d St Davenport IA 52801

LANE, GILBERT MANUEL, retired educational administrator; b. N.Y.C., Jan. 27, 1938; s. Herbert Daniel and Margaret Ann (Massenberg) L.; m. Norma Beane Lalor, Aug. 22, 1970; 1 child, Gilbert Manuel Jr. BA in Liberal Arts, CCNY, 1962; MA in Edn., CUNY, 1974. Tchr. Jr. High Sch. 117 Bd. Edn., N.Y.C., 1963-88; asst. dir. Key Sch. - Bd. Edn., 1988-93; ret., 1993. Pres. Lane & Lane Enterprise, N.Y.C., 1991—. Inventor utility cart, 1978, family game Family Ladder, 1987, geog. game Flagships, 1990; contbr. poems to Dance on the Horizon, 1994. Mem. Manhattan Coun. for Devel. Disabled, Cardinal Hayes H.S. Alumni Assn., St. Thomas the Apostle Alumni Assn. Roman Catholic. Avocation: inventing. Home and Office: 4017 Secor Ave Bronx NY 10466-2411 E-mail: secor40lane17@webTV.net.

LANE, GLORIA JULIAN, foundation administrator; b. Chgo., Oct. 6, 1932; d. Coy Berry and Katherine (McDowell) Julian; m. William Gordon Lane (div. Oct. 1958); 1 child, Julie Kay Rosewood. BS in Edn., Cen. Mo. State U., 1958; MA, Bowling Green State U., 1959; PhD, No. Ill. U., 1972. Cert. tchr. Assoc. prof. William Jewell Coll., Liberty, Mo., 1959-60; chair forensic div. Coral Gables (Fla.) High Sch., 1960-64; assoc. prof. No. Ill. U., DeKalb, 1964-70; prof. Elgin (Ill.) Community Coll., 1970-72; owner, pub. Lane and Assocs, Inc., San Diego, 1972-78; prof. Nat. U., 1978-90; pres., chief exec. officer Women's Internat. Ctr., 1982—. Founder, dir. Living Legacy Awards, San Diego, 1984—. Author: Project Text for Effective Communications, 1972, Project Text for Executive Communication, 1980, Positive Concepts for Success, 1983; editor Who's Who Among San Diego Women, 1984, 85, 86, 90—, Systems and Structure, 1984. Named Woman of Accomplishment, Soroptimist Internat., 1985, Pres.'s Coun. San Diego, 1986, Center City Assn., 1986, Bus. and Profl. Women, San Diego, 1991, Woman of Yr., Girls' Clubs San Diego, 1986, Woman of Vision, Women's Internat. Ctr., 1990, Wonderwoman 2000 Women's Times Newspaper, 1991; recipient Angel in Action award, 1999, Independence award Ctr. for Disabled, 1986, Founder's award Children's Hosp. Internat., Washington, 1986, Making Difference for Women award, Soroptimist Internat., 1998, Women Who Mean Business Courage Award San Diego Bus. Jour., 1998. Avocations: computers, painting, writing. Home and Office: 6202 Friars Rd Unit 311 San Diego CA 92108-5000

LANE, GRETCHEN GAINES, social worker, bereavement counselor; b. Shreveport, La., May 21, 1942; d. Merrel Ennis and Josephine (Lingle) Gaines; m. Kenneth P. Lane, 1965; 1 child, Christina. BA, Trinity U., 1964; MA, Union Theol. Sem., 1967; MSW, Cath. U., 1980. Cert. social worker, Md. Program coord. Washington Episcopal Diocese Aging, 1967-68; counselor Family Svc. Cen. Va., Lynchburg, 1976-77; cons. N.W. Community Mental Health Ctr., Reston, Va., 1980; clin. social worker Johns Hopkins Hosp., Balt., 1981-83; bereavement counselor Hospice of No. Va., Arlington, 1983-84, bereavement coord., 1984-88; pediatric oncology social worker Georgetown U. Hosp., Washington, 1988-90. Bereavement cons. Life with Cancer, Fairfax Hosp., 1990—; children's bereavement cons. Montgomery Hospice Soc., Rockville, Md., 1990—. Author: My Memory Book: A Journal for Bereaved Children, 1995, Children and End of Life Issues in End of Life Nursing Care, 2001; co-author: Psychosocial Concerns of Hand and Upper Limb Tumour Patient, 1991. Co-founder Com. to Establish Self-Esteem Task Force in Md. Legis., Silver Spring, 1987-90. Alden Dow Creativity fellow, 2000. Mem. NASW, Assn. Cert. Social Workers, Trinity U. Alumni Assn. Presbyterian.

LANE, HOLLY DIANA, artist; b. Cleve., Sept. 13, 1954; d. Edwin Joseph and Ursula Anna (Neustadt) Selyem; m. L.A. Lane, Apr. 20, 1975. AA in 2-Dimensional Art, Cuesta Coll., San Luis Obispo, Calif., 1982; BFA with great distinction, San Jose State U., 1986, MFA in Pictorial Art, 1988. One-woman shows include Ivory/Kimpton Gallery, San Francisco, 1989, Rutgers Barclay Gallery, Santa Fe, 1990, Bingham Kurts Gallery, Memphis, 1992, (solo survey show with catalog) Art Mus. of S.E. Tex., Beaumont, 1995, Natalie & James Thompson Gallery, San Jose State U., 2001, Yellowstone Art Museum, 2001, Lyman Allyn Museum of Art, 2001,(6 major solo shows) Schmidt Bingham Gallery, N.Y.C., 1991, 93, 95, 97, 99; 2001, group mus. shows include Eiteljorg Mus., Indpls., 1995, 00, Yerba Buena Ctr. for the Arts, San Francisco, 1994, Knoxville (Tenn.) Mus. Art, 1993-94, Fine Arts Ctr. U. R.I., Kingston, 1992, The Contemporary Mus., Honolulu, 1993, 2002, Boise (Idaho) Art Mus., 1994, Castle Gallery-Coll. New Rochelle, N.Y., 1996, Kennedy Mus. Am. Art, Athens, Ohio, 1996, Calif. Ctr. for the Arts Escondido Mus., 1996, Samuel P. Harn Mus., U. Fla., Gainesville, 1996, Whitney Mus. Am. Art, Champion, Conn., 1997-98, Arnot Art Mus., Elmira, N.Y., 1997-98, Susan H. Arnold Art Gallery Lebanon Valley Coll., Anniville, Pa., 1997-98, Pelham (N.Y.) Art Ctr, 1998, Art Mus. Western Va., 1999-00, San Jose Mus. Art, 1999-2000, Art Mus. Western Va., 1999-2000, Santa Cruz Art Museum, 2000, Brevard Mus. Art and Sci., Melbourne, Fla., 2000, Gallery of Contemporary Art, Sacred Heart U., Fairfield, Conn., 2002, others; represented in permanent collections in Art Mus. S.E. Tex., The Contemporary Mus., Honolulu, A.R.A. Svcs., Phila., Dow Jones & Co., N.Y.C., Detroit Zool. Gardens, Prin. Fin. Group, Des Moines, IDS, Mpls., Memphis Cancer Ctr.; works reproduced in books, mags., calendars, jours., including ARTNews, Art in America, N.Y. Times, Art Papers, Art & Antiques, New Yorker Mag., Christian Sci. Monitor, Pvt. Arts, Forensic Examiner, NYarts Mag., The Wilson Quar., Review Mag., NYC, 1999, Women Artists calendar 1996-98, San Raphael, Calif., The Sciences, N.Y. Acad. Scis., 1992, 93, (textbook) Artist and Audience, (London) 1996, Dreams 1900-2000: Sci., Art and the Unconscious Mind (book), 1999, Wilson Quarterly, 1998, Rev. Mag., 1999, Dreamworks: Twentieth-Century Artistic and Psychological Perspectives,

1999; works presented and discussed in TV documentaries, including Welcome to Nocturnia, 1993, Women in Art, Time-Warner, Manhattan Cable, N.Y.C., 1993, 94; in books accompanying TV show Bill Moyers Genesis, A Living Tradition, PBS, 1996, Healing and the Mind, 1993. Named Alumna of Yr., Cuesta Coll., 1992; pres.'s scholar San Jose State U., 1986, Johanna Rietz scholar Art Assn. of Morro Bay, Calif., 1981; recipient honorable mention Western States Arts Fedn., Santa Fe, 1994. Mem. Coll. Art Assn. (scholarship 1981). Avocations: nature walks, contemplation, reading. Home: 182 Brian Ln Santa Clara CA 95051-6704 Address: care Forum Gallery 745 Fifth Ave 5th Fl New York NY 10151 E-mail: hlane42@earthlink.net.

LANE, JAMES F. software engineer; b. Jersey City, Nov. 6, 1953; s. Francis Robert and Margaret Ellen Lane. BS in Computer Sci., Worcester Poly. Inst., 1971-75; postgrad., U. Colo., 1978. Sr. software engr. Digital Group, Denver, 1977; systems software designer, project leader Microsoft, Redmond, Wash., 1978-85; pres. Elvyn Software, Inc., 1985-87; mgr. PDL group, mgr. software engring. dept. Hanzon Data Inc., Bothell, 1985-90; owner Novelty Hill Software, Inc., Redmond, 1987—; ptnr. Mare Crisium, LLC, 2000—. Avocations: Lindy Hop, Argentine Tango. Home: 22006 NE 114th St Redmond WA 98053-5701 Office: Novelty Hill Software Inc Redmond WA 98053

LANE, JAMES MCCONKEY, retired investment executive; b. Pitts., July 9, 1929; s. Mortimer Bliss and Mary (Knapp) L.; m. Arlyne Ruth Nelson, Dec. 16, 1950; children: James, Theodore, Thomas, Karen, David. BA, Wheaton Coll., 1952; MBA, U. Chgo., 1953; postgrad., NYU, 1956, U. Buffalo, 1960. Credit corr. John Plain & Co., Chgo., 1951; trainee Chase Manhattan Bank, N.Y.C., 1953-55, account mgr. investment adv. divsn., 1955-59, investment officer, 1959-62, 2d v.p., 1962-64, v.p., mgr. corp. pension trust investments, 1964-66, v.p. divsn. exec. pension trust investment divsn., 1966-68, chmn. investment policy com., 1968-78, sr. v.p., investment group exec., 1968-70, exec. v.p. fiduciary investment dept., 1970-78; pres., dir. Chase Investors Mgmt. Corp., 1972-78; mng. dir. Cyrus J. Lawrence Inc., 1978-82; sr. v.p., chief investment officer, head trust investment divsn. NBD Bank N.A., Detroit, 1982-94, sr. mgmt., 1984-94; ret., 1994. Bd. dirs. Chateau Communities, Inc., NAIC Growth Fund, Inc. Bd. dirs. Christian Camps Inc., 1978—, Baseball Chapel Inc., 1994—, William Tyndale Coll., 1985—, chmn., 1995—99; trustee Wheaton Coll., 1971—; chmn. Wheaton Coll. Trust Co., 2000—. Mem. Stone Harbor Golf Club, Boca Raton Resort and Club, Premier Club. Home and Office: 3700 S Ocean Blvd Unit 1006 Highland Beach FL 33487 also: 2 86th St Stone Harbor NJ 08247-1607

LANE, JERRY ROSS, alcohol and drug abuse service counselor; b. Pampa, Tex., June 3, 1944; s. Wilbur Howard and Christina Lavina (Hendrix) L.; m. Mary Lou Jetton, July 9, 1966; children: Jeffrey Ross, Tamara Noel. BS, McMurry U., 1968; MS in Counseling Psychology, Emmanuel Bapt. U., 1988, D in Counseling Psychology, 1991. Cert. and registered hypnotherapist, CHt. Tchr. Fannin Elem., Abilene, Tex., 1968-70, Tierra Blanca Elem., Hereford, 1970-72; acctg. and sales staff Lane and Co., Inc., Panhandle, 1972-74; min. music and edn. Memphis (Tex.) United Meth. Ch., 1974-75, First United Meth. Ch., McAllen, Tex., 1975-79; chaplain cancer treatment ctr. McAllen (Tex.) Br. M.D. Anderson Hosp., 1977-79; owner, counselor Snelling and Snelling Employment, Pampa, 1979-83; tchr. Travis Elem., 1983-89; student asst. program coord. Pampa (Tex.) Ind. Sch. Dist., 1989-92; counselor, dir. drug/alcohol program Clarendon Coll. Pampa (Tex.) Ctr., 1992-96; owner dir., Hi-Plains Hypotherapy/Counseling Inst., 1997—. Trainer Developing Capable People, Provo, Utah, 1990—; trainer family cmty. leadership Tex. Extension Svc., Amarillo, Tex., 1990—; parenting cons. Region XVI Edn. Svc. Ctr., Amarillo, 1991—, adv. bd. drug/alcohol, 1992—; cons. Cal Farley's Family Living Ctr., Borger, Tex., 1992—. Bd. dirs. Pampa (Tex.) Fine Arts, 1980-83, Pampa United Way, 1996; chmn. bd. Salvation Army, Pampa, 1982; bd. pres. Civic Ballet, Pampa, 1984; choir mem., bd. dirs. First United Meth. Ch.; vol. grief counselor Hospice of Panhandle. Named Family of Yr., Mormon Ch., Pampa, 1981, Top Gun, Tex. Tech. Dads and Moms Assn., Lubbock, Tex., 1990; grantee Tex. Coun. Assn. Drug/Alcohol, Pampa (Tex.) Ind. Sch. Dist., 1989-93. Mem. Am. Assn. Christian Counselor, Nat. Christian Counselor Assn., Tex. Christian Counselors Assn., Panhandle Christian Counselors Assn., Tex. Jr. Coll. Tchrs. Assn., Pampa C. of C. Avocations: interior decorating, writing, horticulture. Home: 2007 Williston St Pampa TX 79065-3632 Office: Clarendon Coll Pampa Ctr 900 N Frost St Pampa TX 79065-5456

LANE, JOAN FLETCHER, educational administrator; b. San Francisco, May 7, 1928; d. Howard French and Kathryn Elizabeth (Kraft) Fletcher; m. Melvin Bell Lane, Feb. 15, 1953; children: Whitney Lane-Miller, Julie Lane-Gay. AB, Smith Coll., 1949. Staff World Affairs Coun. No. Calif., San Francisco, 1949-51, Inst. Internat. Edn., Stanford, Calif., 1952; spl. asst., dean Sch. H&S Stanford U., 1982-93, spl. asst. bd. trustees, 1993—. Bd. dirs. McClatchy Newspapers, Sacramento; dir. The James Irvine Found., San Francisco, 1990-02. Trustee San Francisco Found., 1984-92; trustee Smith Coll., Northampton, Mass., 1978-85, chmn. bd. trustees, 1982-85, v.p. alumnae assn., 1975-78; bd. dirs. Internat. House, U. Calif., Berkeley, 1971-80; pres., assoc. coun. Mills Coll., Oakland, Calif., 1974-78. Recipient John M. Greene award Smith Coll., 1988. Avocations: hiking, gardening. Home: 99 Tallwood Ct Atherton CA 94027-6431

LANE, JOHN DENNIS, lawyer; b. Norwalk, Conn. s. John J. and Theresa A. (Donnelly) L.; m. Elizabeth J. Galliher, Apr. 28, 1949; children: Elizabeth J., John Dennis, Margaret A., Robert E., Paul G. BS, Georgetown U., 1943, JD, 1948. Bar: D.C. 1948, Conn. 1950. Atty. Office Chief Counsel, Bur. Internal Revenue, Washington, 1948-49; exec. sec. to U.S. Senator Brien McMahon, 1949-50; adminstrv. asst., 1950-52; pvt. practice Washington and Norwalk, 1953-2001; ptnr. Hedrick & Lane, 1954— 82, Wilkes, Artis, Hedrick & Lane, 1982-2000, Wilkes Artis, 2000-2001. Mem. council Adminstrv. Conf. U.S., 1961; bd. regents Georgetown U., 1979—. Served to capt. USMCR, 1943-45. Recipient Citation of Merit. Fellow Am. Bar Found.; mem. ABA (chmn. standing com. unauthorized practice of law 1971-73, chmn. standing com. nat. conf. groups 1973-75, D.C. cir. mem. standing com. on fed. judiciary 1984-86, Fed. cir. mem. 1987-90), Fed. Commn. Bar Assn. (pres.-elect 1990, pres. 1991-92, alt. rep. to UN 1997-99), Am. Law Inst., Met. Club, Columbia Country Club (Chevy Chase, Md.). Home: 5045 Van Ness St NW Washington DC 20016-1960 Office: 8th Fl 1200 New Hampshire Ave NW Washington DC 20036-6802 E-mail: ilane@dlalaw.com.

LANE, JOHN RODGER, art museum director; b. Evanston, Ill., Feb. 28, 1944; s. John Crandall Lane and Jeanne Marie (Rodger) L. Moritz; m. Inge-Lise Eckmann, 1992. BA, Williams Coll., 1966; MBA, U. Chgo., 1971; AM, Harvard U., 1973, PhD, 1976; DFA (hon.), San Francisco Art Inst., 1995. Asst. dir. Fogg Art Mus., Cambridge, Mass., 1974; exec. asst. to dir., adminstr. curatorial affairs, asst. dir. curatorial affairs Bklyn. Mus., N.Y.C., 1975-80; dir. Carnegie Mus. Art, Pitts., 1980-86, San Francisco Mus. Modern Art, 1987-97, Dallas Mus. Art, 1999—. Vis. com. Williams Coll. Mus. Art, 1998—. Author: Stuart Davis: Art and Art Theory, 1978; co-editor: Abstract Painting and Sculpture in America, 1927-1944, 1983, Carnegie International, 1985; exec. editor: The Making of a Modern Museum/SFMOMA, 1995. Trustee Fountain Valley Sch., Colorado Springs, 1999—. Served to lt. USNR, 1966-69. Nat. Endowment Arts Mus. fellow, 1974-75 Mem. Assn. Art Mus. Dirs. (trustee 2000—), Am. Assn. Museums, Internat. Council Museums, Coll. Art Assn. E-mail: jlane@dm-art.org.

LANE, KENNETH EDWIN, retired advertising agency executive; b. Orange, N.J., Sept. 30, 1928; s. Clarence Edwin and Erma Catherine (Kinser) L.; children by previous marriage— Kenneth, Laura, Linda, Katherine; m. Susan Spafford Zimmer, Sept. 13, 1980; stepchildren— Todd and Margaret Zimmer. BA, U. Chgo., 1947, MA, 1950. Mgr. media Toni div. Gillette Co., 1953-63; media dir. MacParland-Aveyard Co., 1963-64; assoc. media dir. Leo Burnett Co., Chgo., 1964-71, mgr. media dept., 1971-75, sr. v.p. media services, 1975-84. Bd. dirs. Traffic Audit Bur. Maj. USAR, ret. Mem. Am. Assn. Advt. Agys., Media Dirs. Council., Phi Beta Kappa Office: Leo Burnett Agy 35 W Wacker Dr Chicago IL 60601-1614

LANE, KENNETH ROBERT, producer, distributor; b. N.Y.C., N.Y., Dec. 3, 1942; s. Carl Lane and Freda Rosalind; m. Marjory Horowitz, Dec. 1965 (div. 1967); m. Nicole Sloan Helguero (div.); m. Yolanda Natalia Bianco, Mar. 1990; 1 child, Jonathan. BA, CUNY, 1965. Cert. engr. Prodn. mgr. Saul Bass & Assocs., Los Angeles, 1968-70; cameraman, prodn. mgr. Nat. Film Bd. Can., Vancouver, 1970-71; producer, distbr. Troma Inc., N.Y.C., 1976-77; prin. Ken Lane Films, 1976—; producer, prodn. mgr. Platinum Prodns./Platinum Pictures, 1977-78, Ganymede Prodns., N.Y.C., 1978-80; cameraman, audio mixer Madison Sq. Garden Network, 1981-82; tech. dir. Sta. WNET Channel 13 (PBS), 1983; cameraman Fox Broadcasting Co., Sta. WNYW, 1981—; audio mixer, engr. ABC, 1982—, CBS, N.Y.C., 1988—, NBC, N.Y.C., 1991—. Producer/distbr.: (motion pictures) Delora, 1977, Legacy of Horror, 1981, The Navy vs. the Night Monsters, 1981, Women of the Prehistoric Planet, 1981. Treas. Washington Market Community Park, N.Y.C., 1985-86. Mem.: Nat. Ct. Reporters Assn. (cert. legal video specialist), Internat. Brotherhood Elec. Workers, Internat. Brotherhood Elec. Workers, Nat. Assn. Broadcast Engrs. Technicians, Internat. Alliance Theatrical and Stage Employees. Jewish. Avocations: tennis, baseball, golf, art collecting. Home: 69-51 Cloverdale Blvd Flushing NY 11364-3121 Office: 80 N Moore St Apt 26G New York NY 10013-2734

LANE, LAURENCE WILLIAM, JR. retired ambassador, publisher; b. Des Moines, Nov. 7, 1919; s. Laurence William and Ruth (Bell) L.; m. Donna Jean Gimbel, Apr. 16, 1955; children: Sharon Louise, Robert Laurence, Brenda Ruth. Student, Pomona Coll., 1938-40, LLD (hon.), 1976; BJ, Stanford U., 1942; DHL (hon.), Hawaii Loa Coll., 1991. Chmn. bd. Lane Pub. Co.; pub. Sunset Mag., Sunset Books and Sunset Films; U.S. amb. to Australia and Nauru, 1985-89; ret., 1990. Bd. dirs. Calif. Water Svc. Co., Crown Zellerbach Corp., Pacific Gas and Electric Co.; bd. dirs. Time Inc.; bd. dirs. Oreg. Coast Aquarium, Internat. Bd. Advice, ANZ Bank; U.S. amb. and commr. Gen. Worlds Fair, Japan, 1975-76; hon. fellow Coll. Notre Dame, 1974. Former mem. adv. bd. Sec. Interior's Bd. Nat. Parks; mem. adv. coun. Grad. Sch. Bus., Stanford U., SRI; mem. Pres.'s Nat. Productivity Adv. Com.; mem. Pacific Basin Econ. Coun.; former bd. dirs. Pacific Forum, CSI, Nat. Parks Found.; vol. The Nat. Ctr.; mem. bd. overseers Hoover Instn. War, Revolution and Peace; mem. exec. com. Ctr. for Australian Studies, U. Tex., Austin. Lt. USNR, World War II, PTO. Decorated officer Order of Australia; recipient Conservation Svc. award Sec. Interior; Theodore and Conrad Wirth award NPF, 1994; Wiliam Penn Mott Jr. Conservationist of Yr. award NPCA, 1995; named hon. prof. journalism Stanford U. Mem. Newcomen Soc. N.Am., Pacific Asia Travel Assn. (life mem., chmn. 1980-81), Coun. of Am. Ambs., Los Rancheros Vistadores, Advt. Club San Francisco, No. Calif. Alumni Assn., Bohemian Club, Pacific Union, Men's Garden Club L.A., Alpha Delta Sigma. Republican. Presbyterian. Office: 3000 Sand Hill Rd Bldg 215 Menlo Park CA 94025-7113

LANE, LEON, anthropologist, sociologist, educator; b. Barberton, Ohio, Mar. 2, 1965; s. Leon P. and Dorthy Lane; children: Katherine. MA, U. of Ky., 1993. Asst. prof. Lexington C.C., Lexington, Ky., 1999—. Contbr. chapters to books. Diversity amb. Mandala Movement, Lexington, 1999—2002. Mem.: Am. Anthrop. Assn. Office: Lexington Community College - SSGT Cooper Drive Lexington KY 40506-0235 Office Fax: 859-257-9578. E-mail: llane01@uky.edu.

LANE, LILLY KATHERINE, museum staff member; b. Inverness, Fla., Mar. 25, 1934; d. Robert Joseph and Edna Lee (Rooks) Lane; children from previous marriage: James D. Nichols, Gayle Patricia Nichols. RN, St. Luke's Hosp., Jacksonville, Fla., 1955; BFA in Ceramics cum laude, U. Fla., 1984, BA in Asian Studies, 1985, MFA in Ceramics, 1994; cert. in mus. studies, Fla. State U., 2000. RN Fla., Va., Ill., Morocco. Swimming tchr., Port Lyautey, Morocco, 1962-63; RN various, 1955-83; English tchr. South China Normal U., Guangzhou, 1987-88; Chinese Calligraphy tchr. St. Augustine, Fla., 1992-93; asst. collections Harn Mus. Art, Gainesville, 1994—. Contbr. articles in Chinese and English to profl. jours. Pres. Naval Officers Wives Club, Washington, 1973—74. Recipient Fed. Nursing traineeship, 1964; scholar Fla. State Nursing, 1963, Winn-Lovett Nursing, 1950. Mem.: UDC, DAR, AAUW, Fla. Assn. Mus., Am. Assn. Mus., Asian Ceramic Rsch. Orgn., Fla. Craftsmen, Asia Soc., Nat. Art Edn. Assn., United Daus. of the Confederacy, Phi Delta Kappa.

LANE, MALCOLM DANIEL, biological chemistry educator; b. Chgo., Aug. 10, 1930; s. Malcolm Daniel Lane and Helga Sofia (Nielsen) Wilke; m. Patricia L. Sonquist, Mar. 17, 1951; children: Claudia J. Lane, M. Daniel Jr. BS, Iowa State U., 1951, MS, 1953; PhD, U. Ill., 1956. Assoc. prof. Va. Poly. Inst., Blackburg, 1956-63, prof. biochemistry, 1963-64; assoc. prof. biochemistry Sch. Medicine N.Y.U., 1964-69, prof. biochemistry Sch. Medicine, 1969-70, Johns Hopkins U., Balt., 1970-78, 97—, DeLamar prof., dir. dept. biol. chemistry, 1978-97. Mem. editl. bd.: Jour. Biol. Chemistry, 1969-74, 79-84, Biochem. et Biophysica Acta, 1968-70, 75-79, Archives Biochemistry and Biophysics, 1977-80, Ann. Revs. Biochemistry, 1980-84; exec. editor: Biochem./Biophys. Rsch. Com., 1986—; contbr. numerous articles to profl. jours. Fellow Am. Acad. Arts and Sci., Am. Soc. for Nutritional Scis.; mem. NAS, Am. Soc. Biochem. Molecular Biology (sec. 1987-89, program chmn. 1990-91, pres., William C. Rose award 1981), Am. Soc. Cell Biology, Am. Inst. Nutrition (Mead-Johnson award 1966), Am. Chem. Soc. Avocations: chamber music, boating, fishing, photography. Office: Johns Hopkins U Sch Medicine 725 N Wolfe St Baltimore MD 21205-2105 E-mail: dlane@jhmi.edu.

LANE, MARGARET ANNA SMITH, real estate property manager, real estate developer; b. Aspinwall, Pa., Nov. 26, 1918; d. Max Charles and Mary Ann (Jones) Smith; m. Frank A. Lane Jr., Feb. 7, 1954; 1 child, Alan Michael. AB, UCLA, 1940; MS, U. So. Calif., 1949. Cert. secondary tchr., Calif. Demonstration and tng. tchr. UCLA and U. Calif., Northridge, 1948-74; pvt. practice Cottonwood, Ariz., 1975—. Tchr. dept. chmn. L.A. City Schs., 1948-74; sec.-treas. Silver Hoof, Inc., Sedona, Stone Pine Gallery, Ltd., Sedona. Mem. Pi Gamma Mu. Avocations: Native American cultures, art. Home: PO Box 4289 West Sedona AZ 86340-4289

LANE, MARGARET BEYNON TAYLOR, librarian; b. St. Louis, Feb. 6, 1919; d. Archer and Alice (Jones) Taylor; m. Horace C. Lane, Jan. 6, 1945; children: Margaret Elizabeth, Thomas Archer. BA, La. State U., 1939, JD, 1942; BS in Libr. Sci., Columbia U., 1941. Reference and circulation asst. Columbia Law Libr., N.Y.C., 1942-44; law libr., asst. prof. U. Conn. Sch. Law, Hartford, 1944-46; law libr. La. State U. Law Sch., Baton Rouge, 1946-48; recorder documents La. Sec. of State's Office, 1949-75; law libr. Lane Fertitta, Lane Janney & Thomas, 1976-96. Mem. depository libr. coun. to Pub. Printer, 1972-77; mem. plan devel. com. La. Fed. Depository Libr., 1982-83. Author: State Publications and Depository Libraries, 1981, Selecting and Organizing State Government Publications, 1987. Treas. Delta Iota House Bd. of Kappa Kappa Gamma, 1965-68; mem. La. Adv. Coun. State Documents Depository Program, 1991—. Inductee La. State U. Law Ctr. Hall of Fame, 1987. Mem.: ALA (interdivisional com. pub. documents 1967—74, chmn. 1967—70, govt. documents round table, state and local documents task force 1972—, coord. 1980—82, James Bennett Childs award 1981, anniversary honor roll 1996, Hoduski Founders award 1997), Baton Rouge Bar Assn., La. Bar Assn., La. Libr. Assn. (Essae M. Culver Disting. Svc. award 1976, Lucy B. Foote award 1986, Margaret T. Lane award named in her honor 1994), Mortar Bd., Baton Rouge Libr. Club, Kappa Kappa Gamma, Phi Delta Delta. Home: 333 Lee Dr Apt 274 Baton Rouge LA 70808 Office: 435 Louisiana Ave Baton Rouge LA 70802-5820 E-mail: mtlane@cox.net.

LANE, MARK, lawyer, educator, writer; b. N.Y.C., Feb. 24, 1927; s. Harry Arnold and Elizabeth Lane; m. Patricia Ruth Erdner, 1987; children: Anne-Marie, Christina. LLB, Bklyn. Law Sch., 1951. Bar: N.Y. 1951, D.C. 1995. Mng. mem. The Lane Law Firm, PLLC, N.Y.C. and Washington, pvt. practice law, founding mem., sr. ptnr., 1952—; founder Mid-Harlem Community Parish Narcotics Clinic, 1953, East Harlem Reform Dem. Club, 1959; prof. law Cath. U., Washington, 1975—76. Founder and dir. Citizens Commn. Inquiry; founder Wounded Knee Legal Def.-Offense Com., 1973, The Covered Wagon, Mountain Home, Idaho, 1971. Author: (books) Rush to Judgment, 1966, A Citizen's Dissent, 1968, Chicago Eye-Witness, 1969, Arcadia, 1970, Conversations with Americans, 1970, Executive Action, 1973, (with Dick Gregory) Code Name Zorro, 1977, The Strongest Poison, 1980, Plausible Denial, 1991, Murder in Memphis, 1993; prodr. films Rush to Judgment, 1967, Two Men in Dallas, 1987, 92; writer, prodr. plays Trial of James Earl Ray, 1978, Plausible Denial, 1992, Winds of Doctrine, 1994; writer, prodr. screenplays, Arcadia, 1992, Slay the Dreamer, 1992, Plausible Denial, 1993; founder publs. Citizens Quar., 1975, Helping Hand, 1971. Mem. N.Y. State Assembly, 1960-62. With AUS, 1945-47. Home and Office: 105 2nd St NE Washington DC 20002-7303 *I do not believe that our fate is pre-ordained. I do believe that women and men, working together, can determine their own destiny and that the people write their own history. What moves me most directly into action is the fact that I hate bullies. What concerns me the most in contemporary America is the influence of the police and spy organizations with the national news media. Together these are bullies to contemplate and oppose.*

LANE, MIHARU QUALKINBUSH, artist, educator; b. Fukuoka, Japan, Apr. 3, 1948; came to U.S., 1958; d. Donald Nelson and Shizuko Moriyama Qualkinbush; m. Edward Anthony Lane, July 10, 1970; children: Adam Shaw, Lauren Belle. BA in Fine Art, East Stroudsburg U., 1991; MFA, Marywood U., 1995. Artist, painter, printmaker Art Spectrum, N.Y.C., 1978-85; artist, printmaker Fine Arts 260, Book of the Month Club, 1978-79, Collector's Guild, Doubleday Co. Inc., N.Y.C., 1978-82, Original Print Collectors Group Ltd., N.Y.C., 1982-85; asst. prof. art East Stroudsburg (Pa.) U., 1996—. Grant evaluator, faculty dept. Pa. State Sys. of Higher Edn., Harrisburg, 1998-99. Exhbns. include Bklyn. Botanic Garden, N.Y., 1984, Middleton Gallery, 1984, 85, 86, Madelon Powers Gallery, East Stroudsburg U., 1980, 92, 2000, Millersville U., 1999, George Mason U., 1997, Pa. State U., 1998, Anton Dutot Mus. and Gallery, Delaware Water Gap, Pa., 2000, Wittaker Ctr. for Scis. and Art, Harrisburg, Pa., 2000, Md. Inst. Coll. Art, 2001. Grantee partnership in the Arts, Monroe County Arts Coun., 1998, East Stroudsburg U. Found., 1999, East Stroudsburg U., 2001; Faculty Devel. grantee East Stroudsburg U., 2001. Fellow Assn. Pa. State Coll. and Univ. Faculties (mem. scholarship com. 2000). Democrat. Office: East Stroudsburg U 200 Prospect St East Stroudsburg PA 18301-2999 E-mail: mlane@po_box.esu.edu.

LANE, NANCY, editor, human rights activist; b. N.Y.C., Dec. 20, 1938; d. Morton and Lillian (Gelb) L. AB in Am. Civilization, Barnard Coll., 1960. Mem. staff N.Y. Times, 1959-61; from asst. to assoc. editor Polit. Sci. Quar. and Procs. Acad. Polit. Sci., Columbia U., N.Y.C., 1962-70; from assoc. editor to mng. editor Am. Hist. Rev. Am. Hist. Assn., 1970-74; from sr. editor to exec. editor Oxford U. Press, N.Y.C., 1974-97; cons., 1997—99. Vol. Bellevue-NYU Program for Survivors of Torture, 1998-99. Mem. ACLU, Amnesty Internat. U.S.A., New Yorkers Against the Death Penalty. Home: 45 W 10th St New York NY 10011-8763

LANE, NANCY LUCILLE, mental health and critical care nurse; b. N.J., Mar. 12, 1943; 1 child, Michael Blumenauer. Diploma, Meml. Hosp. Sch. Nursing, Albany, N.Y., 1964; BSN, SUNY, New Paltz, 1992. Cert. psychiat. and mental health nurse, ANCC. Staff nurse, premature ctr. Children's Hosp., Buffalo, 1964-66; ICU and emergency room nurse Meml. Hosp., 1966-67; intensive care staff nurse St. Peters Hosp., Albany, 1967—89; staff nurse psychiatry VA Hosp., 1989-91, Albany Med. Ctr. Hosp., 1992-96; case mgr. Value Options, 1997-99, Reed Group Ltd., 1999—. Julia O. Wells scholar. Home: 21B Commodore St Albany NY 12205-3023

LANE, ORRIS JOHN, JR. engineer; b. Sigourney, Iowa, Apr. 21, 1932; s. Orris John and Hester Hanna (Hazen) L.; m. Joan Joyce Nelson, June 19, 1954; children: Jerry, Beth, Dona, Seth. BS in Engring., Iowa State U., 1957. Registered profl. engr., Iowa. Spl. investigations engr. Iowa Dept. Transp., Ames, 1962-64, Portland cement concrete engr., 1964-72, 83-87, dist. materials engr. Atlantic, 1972-83, testing engr. Ames, 1987—. Achievements include development of bridge floor repair procedure using bonded concrete, and development of fast-track procedure for concrete pavement opened to early traffic. Home: 1111 Garfield Ave Ames IA 50014-3858 Office: Iowa Dept Transp 800 Lincoln Way Ames IA 50010-6993

LANE, PATRICIA PEYTON, nursing consultant; b. Danville, Ill., Oct. 5, 1929; d. Louis Weldon Sr. and Ruth Jeanette (Meyer) Peyton; m. H.J. Lane, Dec. 23, 1950 (div.); children: Jennifer Lane-Carr, Peter Lane, Amelia Ozog. Diploma, St. Elizabeth Hosp., 1950; BA in Psychology magna cum laude, Rosary Coll., 1974; postgrad., Lakeview Coll. of Nursing, Danville, Ill., 1987-88; student, Triton Jr. Coll., River Grove, Ill., 1969-72. Staff nurse St. Elizabeth Hosp., Danville, Ill., 1950; staff nurse nursery Ill. Rsch. and Ednl. Hosp., Chgo., 1951, charge nurse tumour clinic, 1951-54; res. sch. nurse elem. schs., Oak Park, Ill., 1969-78; sta. mgr. Oak Park-River Infant Welfare, 1972-76; vision and hearing screener suburban elem. schs., 1980-82; sch. nurse West Subrban Assn. Spl. Edn., Cicero, 1978-80; caseworker, counselor Vermilion County Mental Health and Devel. Disabilities, Inc., Danville, 1983-86; case coord., nurse cons. Crosspoint Human Svcs., 1986-88; staff nurse psychiat. acute care unit Community Hosp. of Ottawa, Ill., 1988-89; dir. social svcs. Pleasant View Luther Home, Ottawa, 1989-93; clin. case coord. Access Svcs., Inc., Mendota, Ill., 1993-97; cmty. ombudsman LaSalle County Alternatives for the Older Adult, Peru, 1993-97; ret., 1997. Cons. in field. Recipient Ill. Gov.'s award for Exceptional Achievement in cmty. svc. and svc. to elderly, 1997.

LANE, PEGGY LEE, educator; b. Ferndale, Mich., Jan. 13, 1948; d. Otto Gustave and Ruth Geraldine (Keyser) Kleve; m. Mark Lane, Sept. 7, 1978 (dec. June 1989). BA, Ctrl. Mich. U., 1969, MA, 1972; PhD, U. North. Colo., 1998. Tchr. Potterville (Mich.) Schs., 1969-76, Alpena (Mich.) Pub. Schs., 1976-78, 87-89, Anchor Bay Schs., New Baltimore, Mich., 1978-79; owner Park Lane Jewelry, Glasgow, Mont., 1979-87; county supt. Valley County, 1987; tchr. Littleton (Colo.) Pub. Schs., 1990-97, Cherry Creek Pub. Schs., Colo., 1997—. Mem. ASCD, Am. Psychol. Soc., Am. Edn. Rsch. Assn. Unitarian Universalist. Home: 2905 S Clermont Dr Denver CO 80222-6719

LANE, RICHARD ALLAN, physician, health sciences educator; b. Camp LeJuene, N.C., Feb. 5, 1956; s. Howard Allan and Elizabeth Jane (Fischer) L.; m. Cynthia Diane Gastineau, Jan. 7, 1978; children: Tiffany Marie, Laurel Christina. BS, U. Md., 1978, MD, 1982; MPH in Tropical Medicine, Tulane U., 1986. Diplomate Am. Bd. Preventive Medicine. Intern Md. Gen. Hosp., Balt., 1982-83; squadron flight surgeon, 363rd Tactical Fighter Wing USAF, Shaw AFB, 1983-85, resident in aerospace medicine Brooks AFB, 1986-87, advanced through grades to maj., 1983-87; chief aeromed. svcs. Warner Robins Air Logistics Ctr., Robins AFB, 1987-89; staff physician, microbiology instr. Liberty U., Lynchburg, Va., 1989-91, assoc. prof. health scis., 1991—. Cons., spkr. Liberty Godparent Home, Lynchburg, 1989—; mem. residency adv. bd. Meharry Med. Coll., Nashville, Tenn., 1987-89; adj. faculty health sci. Internat. Health Honduras project James Madison U., Harrisonburg, Va., 1993-2000; adj. clin. prof. nurse practitioner program Old Dominion U., 1997-2000. Contbr. articles to profl. jours. Bd. dirs. Network for Women in Crisis, Lynchburg, 1990-91; exec. bd. Lynchburg chpt. ARC, 1991-93; founder Emmanuel Bapt. Ch., chpt. AWANA, Warner Robins, Ga., 1987-89; trainer Youth at the Crossroads Internat. AIDS Prevention Program, 1996—; med. cons. World Help. Fellow Am. Coll. Preventive Medicine; mem. Gideons Internat. (camp treas. 1988-89), Am. Soc. Tropical Medicine and Hygiene, Aerospace Med. Assn. Republican. Baptist. Home: 103 Village Rd Lynchburg VA 24502-2308 Office: Liberty U Dept Health Svc Lynchburg VA 24506 E-mail: ralane@aol.com.

LANE, RICHARD DANIEL, professional association administrator; b. Eau Claire, Wis., Feb. 13, 1957; s. Edna I Lane; m. Kathleen J. Remund, Apr. 29, 1984; children: Christa, Anna. BBA in Info. Systems, U. Wis., 1979. Various info. systems positions Aid Assn. for Luths., Appleton, Wis., 1979-93, methodology cons., 1993-96, bus. process cons., 1996-97, strategist br. and vol. devel., 1997-99, dir. agy. br. channel support, 1999—2002, leader engagement and growth adminstrn., 2002—. Br. treas. Aid Assn. for Luths., 2001—02. Grant com. chair PTA, Appleton, 1996-97, co-pres., 1998-2000; classroom and website tech. support Highlans Elem. Sch., Appleton, 1999—; mem. Faith Luth. Ch., Sunday sch. tchr., 1998—, past dept. head 5th & 6th grade, elder, deacon, usher, 1985-88, TLC group facilitator, 1997-99, EAP adv. com. publs., 1995-97. Avocations: collector car restoration. Home: 1741 N Eugene St Appleton WI 54914 Office: Aid Assn for Luths 4321 N Ballard Rd Appleton WI 54919-0001 Fax: 920-380-5377. E-mail: RDL0213@aol.com., Dick_Lane@AAL.Org.

LANE, ROBERT W. farm equipment manufacturing executive; b. Washington D.C. BA (high honors), Wheaton (Ill.) Coll., 1972; MBA, U. Chgo. Grad. Sch. Bus., 1974. First Nat. Bank Chgo., Europe; various positions Deere & Co., Moline, Ill., 1982—, CFO, sr. v.p. fin./tax/acctg., 1996—98, sr. v.p., mng.

dir. mfg. mktg. Europe, Africa, Middle East, 1998—99, pres. worldwide agrl. equip. divn., 1999, COO, pres., 2000, chmn. bd., CEO, 2000—. Office: Deere & Co 1 John Deere Rd Moline IL 61265-8098*

LANE, ROBIN, lawyer; b. Kerrville, Tex., Nov. 28 1947; d. Rowland and Gloria (Benson) Richards; m. Stanley Lane, Aug. 22, 1971 (div. 1979); m. Anthony W. Cunningham, Nov. 22, 1980; children: Joshua Lane, Alexandra Cunningham. BA with honors in Econs., U. Fla., 1969; MA, George Washington U., 1971; JD, Stetson U. Coll. Law, 1978. Bar: Fla. 1979, U.S. Ct. Appeals (11th cir.) 1981, U.S. Supreme Ct. 1986, U.S. Ct. Appeals (D.C. cir.) 1992, U.S. Ct. Appeals (3rd cir.) N.Y. 1993. Mgmt. trainee internat. banking Gulf Western Industries, N.Y.C.; internat. rsch. specialist Ryder Systems, Inc., Miami, Fla., 1973, project mgr., 1974; assoc. Wagner, Cunningham, Vaughan & McLaughlin, Tampa, Fla., 1979-85; pvt. practice law, 1985—; guest lectr. med. jurisprudence Stetson U. Coll. Law, 1982-91, also mem. exec. coun. law alumni bd. Contbr. articles to various revs. Recipient Am. Jurisprudence award-torts Lawyers Co-op. Fla., 1979; Scottish Rite fellow, 1968-69. Mem. ABA, Acad. Fla. Trial Lawyers (mem. com. 1983-84), Assn. Trial Lawyers Am., Fla. Bar Assn., Fla. Women's Alliance, Omicron Delta Epsilon. Home: 4934 Saint Croix Dr Tampa FL 33629-4831 Office: PO Box 10155 Tampa FL 33679-0155

LANE, SARAH MARIE CLARK, elementary education educator; b. Conneaut, Ohio, July 27, 1946; d. Robert George and Julia Ellen (Sanford) Clark; m. Ralph Donaldson Lane, May 28, 1977; children: Richard, Laura. BS in Edn., Kent State U., 1977; MS in Edn., Coll. Mt. St. Joseph, 1988. Cert. tchr., Ohio. Coord. newspaper in edn. Tribune Chronicle, Warren, Ohio, 1986-89; tutor MacArthur Found. Project, 1988-89; tchr. chpt. I Lakeview Local Schs., Cortland, 1989—. Freelance writer newspaper Conn. News Herald, 1963-64, Tribune Chronicle, 1980-89; contbr. articles to profl. jours.; author: A Walk Through Historic Cortland, 1994. V.p. Bazetta Cortland Hist. Soc., 1983-85; chmn. com. local history project Lakeview Schs., Cortland, 1992—; mem. Trumbull County Bicentennial Commn., 1996—. George Record Found. scholar, 1964-66. Mem. Internat. Reading Assn. (Ohio coun.), Cortland Community Concert Band (pres. 1991-92), Mem. Christian Ch. (Disciples Of Christ). Avocations: writing, historical research, genealogy, reading. Home: 298 Corriedale Dr Cortland OH 44410-1622 Office: Cortland Elem Sch 264 Park Ave Cortland OH 44410-1098

LANE, SHERYL LEANNE, music educator, organist, violinist, pianist; b. Ft. Worth, Oct. 12, 1962; d. Charles Paul and Ruth Marie (Polston) Rich; m. Ben Harold Lane, Dec. 18, 1984; children: Christopher Paul, Mark William. B of Music Edn., Baylor U., 1984; MusM, N.E. La. U., 1995; postgrad., U. Memphis, 1998—. Accompianist Tex. Girls Choir, Ft. Worth, 1984-85; pvt. music tchr. Memphis, 1984-98; music tchr. Clinton (Okla.) Pub. Schs., 1985-87; violinist Ctrl. Tex. Orch., Temple, 1988-93; organist, pianist Parkview Bapt. Ch., Monroe, 1993-98; violinist Monroe Symphony Orch., 1993-98; piano tchr. Claiborne Christian Sch., West Monroe, La., 1995-98; asst. condr. Monroe (La.) Youth Symphony, 1996-98; orch. rep. Monroe Symphony Orch., 1996—98; instr. music dept. N.E. La. U., 1997-98; pvt. music tchr. Memphis, 1998—; grad. tchg. asst. U. Memphis, 1998—2001; min. music Collierville Christian Ch., 1999—; string tchr. Memphis City Schs., 2001—. Orch. rep. Monroe Symphony Orch., 1996-98. Children's choir coord. Parkview Bapt. Ch., 1994-98; foster parent La. Bapt. Children's Home, Monroe, 1997-98; min. music Collierville Christian Ch. Named one of Outstanding Young Women of Am., 1987. Mem. Nat. Fedn. Music Clubs, Am. Coll. Musicians (local chmn. 1985-98), Monroe Dist. Music Tchrs. Assn. (pres., treas. 1993-98), Artistic Adv. of Monroe Symphony, Memphis Music Tchrs. Assn., Germantown Music Tchrs. Assn., Phi Kappa Phi, Alpha Chi. Republican. Avocations: reading, needlepoint, swimming, travel, camping. Home: 3762 Misty Oak Dr Memphis TN 38125-2449

LANE, SYLVIA, economist, educator; b. N.Y.C. m. Benjamin Lane, Sept. 2, 1939; children: Leonard, Reese, Nancy. AB, U. Calif., Berkeley, 1934, MA, 1936; postgrad., Columbia U., 1937; PhD, U. So. Calif., 1957. Lectr., asst. prof. U. So. Calif., Los Angeles, 1947-60; assoc. prof. econs. San Diego State U., 1961-65; assoc. prof. finance, assoc. dir. Ctr. for Econ. Edn. Calif. State U., Fullerton, 1965-69, chmn. dept. fin., 1967-69; prof. agrl. econs. U. Calif., Davis, 1969-82, prof. emerita, 1982—; prof. emerita and economist Giannini Found., U. Calif.-Berkeley, 1982—; vis. scholar Stanford U., 1975-76. Cons. Calif. Adv. Commn. Tax Reform, 1963, Adv. Office Consumer Affairs, Exec. Office of Pres., 1972-77, FAO, UN, 1983. Author: (with E. Bryant Phillips) Personal Finance, 1963, rev. edit., 1979, The Insurance Tax, 1965, California's Income Tax Conformity and Withholding, 1968, (with Irma Adelman) The Balance Between Industry and Agriculture in Economic Development, 1989; editl. bd. Agrl. Econs., 1986-92; also articles, reports in field. Project economist Los Angeles County Welfare Planning Coun., 1956-59; del. White House Conf. on Food and Nutrition, 1969, Pres.'s Summit Con. on Inflation, 1974; mem. adv. com. Ctr. for Bldg. Tech., Nat. Bur. Stds., 1975-79; bd. dirs. Am. Coun. Consumer Interests, 1972-74; exec. bd. Am. Agr. Econ. Assn. 1976-79. Ford Found. fellow UCLA, 1963; Ford Found. fellow U. Chgo., 1965; fellow U. Chgo., 1968 Fellow Am. Agrl. Econ. Assn. (life, Sylvia Lane Fellowship Fund 1993); mem. Am. Econ. Assn., Am. Coun. Consumer Interests, Omicron Delta Epsilon (pres. 1973-75, trustee 1975-83, chmn. bd. trustees 1982-84). Home and Office: 2231 Caminito Preciosa N La Jolla CA 92037-7231 *Select goals carefully* . . .

LANE, THEODORE, economist; b. N.Y.C., July 17, 1934; s. Simon Harry and Golda Naomie (Lipshitz) L.; m. Susan Alkire, Sept. 1, 1960 (div. 1977); children: Geoffrey Martin Lane, Joshua Edward Lane; m. Cheryl K. Thomas, July 13, 1984. BA, Temple U., 1956; MA, U. Ill., 1959; PhD, U. Wash., 1965. Asst. prof. econs. U. Wis., Milw., 1966-67; exec. v.p. Conserco, Seattle, 1967-68; pres. Human Resources Planning Inst., 1969-77; sr. regional economist White House Conf., Washington, 1978; ptnr. Lane/Langley & Assocs., Seattle, 1979-81; vis. prof. econs. U. Alaska, Anchorage, 1981-84; cons. Econ. Devel. Adminstn. of P.R., San Juan, 1984-86; ptnr. Thomas/Lane & Assocs., Seattle, San Juan, 1986—. Contbr. articles to profl. jours. Commr. Pioneer Sq. Hist. Preservation Commn., Seattle, 1979-81. Mem. Am. Econ. Assn., Western Region Sci. Assn. (pres.-elect, bd. dirs.), Pacific Regional Sci. Coordinating Orgn. (bd. dirs.). Democrat. Avocations: tennis, boating. Office: Thomas/Lane & Assocs 117 E Louisa St # 141 Seattle WA 98102-3203 also: Thomas/Lane & Assocs 1018 Ashford # 7 San Juan PR 00907-1100

LANE, VIVIAN PRYCE, educational counselor; b. Girardville, Pa., May 26, 1938; d. Edward Thomas and Vivian Adelaide (Portz) Davis; m. Franklin L. Lane, Aug. 13, 1960. BS in Edn. cum laude, Kutztown U., 1960; MSW, Temple U., 1981. Lic. social worker, Pa.; cert. counselor, Pa. Counselor Eastern Sch. Dist., Wrightsville, Pa., 1960-62; counselor, tchr. Penn Manor Sch. Dist., Millersville, 1962-70; adminstrv. asst. Cattell Sch., Lancaster, 1970-73; counselor Phila. Sch. Dist., 1982—. Ednl. cons., Phila., 1987—. Active Food Cupboard program Diocese of Phila., 1985, outreach com. Episcopal Social Svcs., Phila., 1987-88, 97—; coord. info. requests Phila. Tourist/Conv. Bur., 1993-94; arboretum asst. Swarthmore Coll., 2001—. Mem. NASW, Am. Assn. Counseling and Devel., Kappa Delta Pi. Democrat. Avocation: cycling. Home: PO Box 186 Clifton Heights PA 19018-0186 Office: Phila Sch Dist N 21st St Philadelphia PA 19104

LANE, WILLIAM LEWIS, civil engineer; b. Helena, Mont., May 27, 1947; s. William Addison and Edith (Swanson) L.; m. Marily Rae Wofford, Jan. 2, 1971; children: Mark Lewis, Timothy James. BSCE, Mont. State U., 1969, MSCE, 1970; PhD in Civil Engring., Colo. State U., 1975. Registered profl. engr., Colo. Sr. river basin modeler U.S. Bur. Reclamation, Denver, 1975-80, sr. hydrologist Boise, Idaho, 1980-82, sr. flood hydrologist Denver, 1982-97; pvt. practice hydrology and water resources engring. cons. Golden, Colo., 1975—. Faculty affiliate Colo. State U., Ft. Collins, 1989—, short course lectr., 1980, 81; moderator, invited lectr. NATO Advanced Study Insts., Portugal, 1988, Spain, 1989; resource person, tech. rep. NAS Coms., 1985-88, 90-92; mem. several nat. coms. on water data, extreme floods, flood frequency and hydrologic modelling. Author: Applied Modeling of Hydrologic Time Series, 1980, (manual) Applied Stochastic Techniques, 1990; contbr. articles to profl. jours. Judge Internat. Sci. Engring Fair, Anaheim Calif., 1978, Orlando Fla., 1991; scoutmaster Boy Scouts Am., Denver, 1985-93; coach, referee U.S. Youth Soccer Assn., Boise and Denver, 1980-89. Mem. ASCE (surface water hydrology com. 1989—), Am. Geophys. Union, Phi Kappa Phi, Tau Beta Pi, Pi Mu Epsilon, Chi Epsilon. Democrat. Roman Catholic. Achievements include development of widely used computer programs for hydrologic time series analysis. Home: 1091 Xenophon St Golden CO 80401-4218

LANE, WILLIAM W. electronics executive; b. Roanoke, Va., Feb. 25, 1934; s. Melvin V. and Cecile (Lane); m. Ronnie G Lane, Sept. 14, 1978; children: Jonathan D., Drew H., Craig M. BA, Bklyn. Coll., 1956; MBA, Cornell U., 1958. V.p. Major Electronics Corp., 1959-70, chmn., dir., 1970; v.p., dir. Internat. Transistor Corp., Burbank, Calif., 1971-73; vice chmn., dir. Internat. Chia Hsin, Taipai, Taiwan, 1973-76; chmn., dir. Emerson (H.K. Ltd.), Hong Kong, from 1976; chmn., CEO, dir. Emerson Radio Corp., North Bergen, N.J., 1974-91; officer, bd. dirs. Star Light Electronics, Ridgefield, NJ. Pres. Majorette Enterprises, from 1961; chmn. MAJ EXCO Imports Inc., 1977-85, Emerson Computer Corp., 1989-91, H.H. Scott, Inc. Cardiac Resuscitator Corp., Portland, Oreg., Emerson Italy, Emerson Spain, Atlantic Shore 400 Cons. Corp., Emerson Investment Corp., Major Realty Corp., Emteck Tech. (U.K.) Ltd.; pres. W. Lane & Assocs. Inc., 1992—. Served with AUS, 1958-59. Mem. bus. adv. bd. U.S. Senate.

LANEGRAN, DAVID ANDREW, geography educator; b. St. Paul, Nov. 27, 1941; s. Walter Bucannon and Lita Evangeline (Wilson) L.; children: Kimberley Rae, Elizabeth Ann, Erik David, Katherin Jane. BA, Macalester Coll., St. Paul, 1963; MA, U. Minn., 1966, PhD, 1970. John S. Holl prof. geography Macalester Coll., 1969—. Pres. Minn. Landmarks, St. Paul, 1988—, mng. dir., 1979-82; program assoc. Gen. Svc. Found., St. Paul, 1980-85; vis. prof. several univs., U.S., 1979-89; chmn. bd. dirs. Geographic Edn. Nat. Implementation Project, 1987-90; coord. Minn. Alliance for Geographic Edn., St. Paul, 1987—; v.p. Nat. Coun. Geographic Edn., 1995—; pres. Nat. Coun. Geographic Edn., 1998. Author: The Saint Paul Experiment: Initiative of the Latimer Administration, 1989, St. Anthony Park: Portrait of a Community, 1987, Grand Avenue: Renaissance of an Urban Street, 1996, (with others) The Legacy of Minneapolis: Preservation Amid Change, 1983, (with Judith Martin) Where We Live: Residential Districts of the Twin Cities, 1983, (with Ernest Sandeen) The Lake District of Minneapolis: A Neighborhood History, 1979, (with P. Kane) St. Paul Omnibus, Images of the Changing City, 1979, (with Risa Palm) An Invitation to Geography, 1978, (with Patrice St. Peter) Geolinks: K-12 Geography Curriculum, 1994. Chmn. St. Paul City Planning Commn., 1982-87; dir. Northwest Area Found., 1988-90, St. Paul Progress Housing Corp., 1984-86. Named one of ten outstanding coll. or univ. tchrs. of geography Ednl. Change Mag., 1977; recipient Award for Excellence Minn. Soc. AIA, 1978, Burlington-No. award for teaching excellence Burlington No. Found., 1988, 96, Thomas Jefferson Teaching and Cmty. Svc. award Robert McConnell Found.; named to South St. Paul Hall of Excellence, 1989. Mem. Assn. Am. Geographers (treas. 1987-89, nat. councilor 1986-89), Nat. Coun. for Geographic Edn. (joint com. for geographic edn. 1983-85, exec. com., v.p. 1995-97, pres. 1998—). Democrat. Presbyterian. Home: 140 Wheeler St S Saint Paul MN 55105-1925 Office: Macalester Coll 1600 Grand Ave Saint Paul MN 55105-1801

LANER, RICHARD WARREN, lawyer; b. Chgo., July 12, 1933; s. Jack E. and Esther G. (Cohon) L.; m. Barbara Lee Shless, Aug. 15, 1954 (dec. Oct. 1997); children: Lynn, Kenneth; m. Daryl Lynn Homer, Sept. 17, 1998. Student, U. Ill., 1951-54; BS, Northwestern U., 1955, LLB, 1956. Bar: Ill. 1956. Assoc. Laner, Muchin, Dombrow, Becker, Levin & Tominberg, Ltd., Chgo., 1956-62, ptnr., 1962-99, of counsel, 1999. Editor Northwestern Law Rev., 1954-56; contbr. articles to profl. jours. Mem. Chgo. Bar Assn. (chmn. com. labor law 1972-73), Chgo. Assn. Commerce and Industry, Order of Coif. Home: 161 E Chicago Ave Unit 41de Chicago IL 60611-2601 Office: Laner Muchin Dombrow Becker Levin & Tominberg Ltd 515 N State St Fl 28 Chicago IL 60610-4325 E-mail: rlaner@lmdblt.com.

LANEROLLE, LYON WERNER JOHN, research scientist, educator; b. Kandy, Sri Lanka, Feb. 1, 1968; arrived in U.S., 1997; s. Neville Anthony John and Rachel Lilian Lanerolle. BSc with honors, U. Birmingham, Eng., 1991; PhD, Oxford (Eng.) U., 1997. Postdoctoral rsch. fellow U. Mass.-Dartmouth, New Bedford, 1997—2001; asst. rsch. prof. Rutgers U., New Brunswick, NJ, 2002—. Scholar Sci. Undergrad. scholar, U. Birmingham, 1989, Wingate scholar, Harold Hyam Wingate Found., London, 1991—93. Avocations: tennis, walking, cooking, sightseeing. Office: IMCS Rutgers The State Univ NJ 71 Dudley Rd New Brunswick NJ 08901

LANEY, JAMES EARL (PETE LANEY), state representative, speaker of the house, farmer; b. Hale Center, Tex., Mar. 20, 1943; s. Wilber and Frances (Wilson) L.; m. Nelda Kay McQuien; children: KaLyn, Jamey Kay, J. Pete. BS, Tex. Tech U., 1965. State rep. State of Tex., Austin, 1973—; 71st speaker Tex. House of Reps., 1993—. House spkr. pro tem; chmn. House State Affairs Com., House Adminstrn. Com.; officer Legis. Budget Bd., Legis. Coun.; mem. governing bd. Coun. of State Govts. Named Texas Tech. Disting. Alumnus. Address: PO Box 900 Hale Center TX 79041-0900*

LANEY, JAMES THOMAS, former ambassador, educator; b. Wilson, Ark., Dec. 24, 1927; s. Thomas Mann and Mary (Hughey) L.; m. Berta Joan Radford, Dec. 20, 1949; children: Berta Joan Vaughan, James T., Arthur Radford, Mary Ruth Laney Reilly, Susan Elizabeth Castle. BA, Yale U., 1950, BD, 1954, PhD, 1966; DD (hon.), Fla. So. Coll., 1977; LHD (hon.), Rhodes Coll., 1979; HHD (hon.), Mercer U., 1980; LLD (hon.), DePauw U., 1985; DD (hon.), Wofford Coll., 1986; LHD (hon.), Millsaps Coll., 1988, Austin Coll., 1990, W.Va. Wesleyan Coll., 1990, Yale U., 1993; DD (hon.), Emory U., 1994; LLD (hon.), U. St. Andrews, Scotland, 1994, Alaska Pacific U., 1994; DD (hon.), Yonsei U., Korea, 1997; LHD (hon.), U. S.C., 1997, Queens Coll., 1998; D in Internat. Affairs, Am. U., 1998; LLD (hon.), Piedmont Coll., 1999; DD (hon.), Kwansei Gakuin U., Japan, 2000; LHD (hon.), LaGrange Coll., 2000, U. Richmond, 2001, LLD (hon.) , 2001. Chaplain Choate Sch., Wallingford, Conn., 1953-55; ordained to ministry Meth. Ch., 1955; asst. lectr. Yale Div. Sch., 1954-55; pastor St. Paul Meth. Ch., Cin., 1955-58; sec. student Christian movement, prof. Yonsei U., Seoul, Korea, 1959-64; asst. prof. Christian ethics Vanderbilt U. Div. Sch., 1966-69; dean Candler Sch. Theology, Emory U., 1969-77, pres. univ., 1977-93; U.S. amb. to Republic of Korea, 1993-97. Vis. prof. Harvard Div. Sch., 1974. Author: The Education of the Heart, 1994; (with J.M. Gustafson) On Being Responsible, 1968; contbr. columns N.Y. Times, Washington Post, L.A. Times. Pres. Nashville Cmty. Rels. Coun., 1968-69; mem. Yale Coun. Com., 1972-77; bd. dirs. Fund Theol. Edn.; chmn. United Bd. Christian Higher Edn. in Asia, 1990-93; bd. dirs. Atlanta Symphony, 1979-91; chmn. bd. overseers com. to visit Harvard Div. Sch., 1980-85; mem. Yale U. Coun. Exec. Com., 1990-93; mem. Carnegie Endowment Nat. Commn. on Am. and the New World; mem. adv. com. Atlanta Project; chmn. so. dist. Rhodes Scholarship Com., 1980-90; bd. dirs. Atlantic Coun., 1987-93. With AUS, 1946-48; mem. tercentenary steering com. Yale U., 1998—2001; co-chmn. Faith & City, Atlanta, Ga. Selected for Leadership Atlanta, 1970-71; recipient Disting. Alumnus award Yale U. Div. Sch., 1979, 93, Kellogg award for leadership in higher edn., 1983, Wilbur Cross medal Yale Grad. Sch., 1996, James Van Fleet award, Korean Soc., 1996, Kangwa medal for disting. diplomatic svc., Rep. Korea, 1997, Dept. Defense medal for disting. pub. svc., U.S. Govt., 1997, 1st Internat. Human Rights award Inst. Human Rights, Korea, 1998; D.C. Macintosh fellow Yale U., 1965-66. Mem. Am. Soc. Christian Ethics, Soc. for Values Higher Edn. (pres. 1987-91), Coun. on Fgn. Rels. (co-chair task force on Korean Peninsula 1997—), Pilgrim Soc., Atlanta C. of C., Commerce Club, Phi Beta Kappa, Omicron Delta Kappa. Office: Emory U Pres Emeritus 1462 Clifton Rd NE Ste 302 Atlanta GA 30322-1000

LANEY, JOHN THOMAS, III, federal judge; b. Columbus, Ga., Mar. 27, 1942; s. John Thomas Jr. and Leila (Davis) L.; m. Louise Pierce, Nov. 23, 1974; children: Thomas Whitfield, Elizabeth Davis. AB, Mercer U., 1964, JD magna cum laude, 1966. Bar: Ga. 1965, U.S. Dist. Ct. (mid. dist.) Ga. 1966, U.S. Ct. Appeals (5th cir.) 1966, U.S. Ct. Mil. Appeals 1967, U.S. Ct. Appeals (11th cir.) 1981. Assoc. Swift, Pease, Davidson & Chapman, Columbus, 1970-73; ptnr. Page, Scrantom, Harris & Chapman, 1973-86; judge mid. dist. Ga. U.S. Bankruptcy Ct., 1986—. Co-editor-in-chief Mercer Law Rev., 1965-66; contbr. articles to profl. jours. Former pres., dir. Metro. Boys Club of Columbus. Capt. U.S. Army, 1966-70. Mem. ABA (judge adminstrv. divsn. Nat. Conf. Fed. Trial Judges), State Bar Ga. (chmn. gen. practice and trial sect. 1983-84, chmn. state disciplinary bd. 1984-85), Am. Judicature Soc., Nat. Conf. Bankruptcy Judges, Columbus Bar Assn., Inc. (pres. 1985-86), Rotary. Presbyterian. Office: US Bankruptcy Ct 1 Arsenal Pl 901 Front Ave Ste 309 Columbus GA 31901-2797 E-mail: k4bai@worldnet.att.net.

LANEY, LEROY OLAN, economist, banker, educator; b. Atlanta, Mar. 20, 1943; s. Lee Edwin and Paula Izlar (Bishop) L.; m. Sandra Elaine Prescott, Sept. 3, 1966; children: Prescott Edwin, Lee Olan III. B Indsl. Engring., Ga. Inst. Tech., 1965; MBA in Fin., Emory U., 1967; MA in Econs., U. Colo., 1974, PhD in Econs., 1976. Budget analyst Martin-Marietta Corp., Denver, 1971-72; economist Coun. Econ. Advisers, Washington, 1974-75; internat. economist U.S. Treasury Dept., 1975-78; sr. economist Fed. Res. Bank Dallas, 1978-88; prof. econs., chmn. dept. Butler U., Indpls., 1989-90; sr. v.p. 1st Hawaiian Bank, Honolulu, 1990-98; prof. econs. and fin. Hawaii Pacific U., 1998—. Chmn. Fed. Res. Com. on Internat. Rsch., Washington, 1981-83; vis. prof. U. Tex., Arlington and Dallas, 1978-85; adj. prof. So. Meth. U., Dallas, 1982-85. Editor bank periodicals, 1975-88; contbr. articles to profl. jours. Mem. Internat. Fin. Symposium, Dallas, 1982-85; Hawaii Coun. on Revenues. Lt. USN, 1967-71. Scholar Ga. Inst. Tech., 1961; rsch. fellow Emory U., 1965-67, teaching fellow U. Colo., 1972-73; rsch. grantee Butler U., 1989-90. Mem. Am. Econ. Assn., Western Econ. Assn., Indpls. Econ. Forum, Plaza Club, Honolulu Rotary, Omicron Delta Epsilon, Lambda Alpha, Kappa Sigma. Avocations: sailing, skiing, reading, fly-fishing. Office: Sch Bus Adminstrn Hawaii Pacific Univ Honolulu HI 96813 E-mail: L09_LANEY@hotmail.com.

LANEY, MICHAEL L. manufacturing executive; b. Los Angeles, Sept. 10, 1945; s. Roy and Wanda Laney; m. Marti Miller, Dec. 31, 1964; children: Tynna, Kristen. BS with honors, Calif. State U., Northridge, 1967; MBA, UCLA, 1969. CPA, Calif. Sr. tax acct. Haskins-Sells, Los Angeles, 1967-69; asst. prof. acctg. Calif. State U., Northridge, 1969-72; tax prin. M. Klaiman Acctg. Corp., Beverly Hills, Calif., 1972-75; pvt. practice, 1975-80; v.p., controller Ducommun, Inc., Los Angeles, 1980-87; sr. v.p., fin. and adminstrn. Monarch Mirror Door Co. Inc., Chatsworth, Calif., 1987-92; v.p. ops. feature animation Walt Disney Pictures and TV (part of The Walt Disney Co.), Glendale, 1992-93; sr. v.p. ops. Warner Bros., 1994-96; pres. Children's Wonderland, Agoura, 1996-97; CFO Dacor, Pasadena, 1997-2001; pres., CEO Cool Roof of Calif., Inc., Calabasas, 2001—. Mem. Fin. Execs. Inst., Tax Execs. Inst., Am. Inst. CPA's, Calif. Soc. CPA's. Office: Laney & Assocs PO Box 8993 Calabasas CA 91372-8993 E-mail: Mlaneyassoc.@yahoo.com.

LANEY, SANDRA EILEEN, service company executive; b. Cin., Sept. 17, 1943; d. Raymond Oliver and Henrietta Rose (Huber) H.; m. Dennis Michael Laney, Sept. 30, 1968; children: Geoffrey Michael, Melissa Ann. AS in Bus. Adminstrn., Thomas More Coll., 1988, BA in Bus. Adminstrn., 1993. Adminstrv. asst. to chief exec. officer Chemed Corp., Cin., 1982, asst. v.p., 1982-84, v.p., 1984-91, v.p., chief adminstrv. officer, 1991-93, sr. v.p., chief adminstrv. officer, 1993-2001, bd. dirs., 1986—, exec. v.p. chief adminstrn. officer, 2001—. Bd. dirs. Omnicare Inc., Covington, Ky. Mem. bd. advisors Sch. Nursing U. Cin., 1992—; bd. overseers Cin. Symphony Orch., 1998; trustee Lower Price Hill Cmty. Sch., Cmty. Land Coop. of Cin. Mem. AAUW, NOW, Internat. Platform Assn., Amnesty Internat., World Affairs Coun., Women's Action Coun. Roman Catholic. Office: Chemed Corp 2600 Chemed Ctr 255 E 5th St Cincinnati OH 45202-4700

LANE-ZUCKER, LAURIE JOHN, communications executive, writer, editor; b. Greenwich, Conn., May 24, 1965; s. Jack Wolf and Jane Lane Lee (Kirby) Zucker; m. Christina Burgess Rahr, Aug. 27, 1994; children: Liam John, Anna Rahr, Silas Malarkey. BA, Middlebury Coll., 1988; postgrad., Columbia U., 1991-92, Bread Loaf Sch. English, 1990-92. Contbg. editor, writer Orion Mag., Great Barrington, Mass., 1991—; co-founder, mng. dir. The Orion Soc., 1991—, exec. dir., 2002—. Organizer Watershed Conf., Libr. Congress, 1996. Editor, writer Orion Afield mag., Great Barrington, 1997—; co-developer OrionOnline mag., 2001—. Organizer Fire and Grit Millennium Conf., Nat. Conservation Tng. Ctr., Shepherdstown, W.Va., 1999. Home: 75 Taconic Ave Great Barrington MA 01230-1709 Office: The Orion Soc 187 Main St Great Barrington MA 01230-1623 E-mail: laneos@orionsociety.org.

LANFEAR, KENNETH JOSEPH, engineering administrator, hydrologist; b. N.Y.C., July 15, 1946; m. Kathleen Lanfear; children: Sara, Meghan, Michael. BCE, Manhattan Coll., 1968; MS in Civil Engring., Stanford U., 1969; MBA, Va. Tech., 1986. Cert. profl. engr., Md. Asst. mgr. Nat. Water Summary Program, U.S. Geol. Survey, Reston, Va., 1983-93, network products coord., 1994-99, Gateway to the Earth program mgr., 2000—. Mem. bd. dirs. No. Va. Youth Symphony Assn., Annandale, Va., 1988-96. Named Cult Hero to River Runners, Outside Mag., Mar. 1999. Mem.: Am. Water Resources Assn. (pres. 2002, Pres.'s award 1993). Home: 1648 Wainwright Dr Reston VA 20190-3431 Office: US Geol Survey MS 605 12201 Sunrise Valley Dr Reston VA 20192 E-mail: lanfear@usgs.gov.

LANFORD, LUKE DEAN, retired electronics company executive; b. Greer, S.C., Aug. 4, 1922; s. John D. and Ethel W. (Ballenger) L.; m. Donna Marie Cellar, Dec. 20, 1945 (dec. Apr. 29, 1984); 1 dau., Cynthia Lea Lanford Brown; m. Jacquelyn Sue Carr Bussell, Feb. 14, 1986 BSE.E., Va. Poly. Inst., 1943. With Western Electric Co., Inc., 1946-78, asst. mgr. tng., 1957-60, mgr. engring. Kansas City, 1960-63, asst. works mgr. Allentown, Pa., 1963-65; plant mgr. Reading, 1965-69; gen. mgr. Indpls., 1969-78. Dir. Met. Indpls. Television Assn., Inc., Sta. WFYI-TV, 1970— , pres., 1975-79 Served with U.S. Army, 1943-46. Mem. IEEE, Telephone Pioneers Am., Jacaranda West Country Club, Eta Kappa Nu, Tau Beta Pi, Phi Kappa Phi. Republican. Presbyterian. Home: 1935 Pebble Beach Ct Venice FL 34293-3830

LANFORD, OSCAR ERASMUS, JR. retired university vice chancellor; b. Louisa County, Va., Dec. 19, 1914; s. Oscar E. and Ruth (Miller) L.; m. Caroline C. Sherman, Aug. 24, 1937 (dec. Jan. 1990); children— Oscar III, Caroline Aldrich (Mrs. William Eastman), Henry C. Sherman, William Armistead, Virginia Bowen (Mrs. Sedruddin Hemani); m. Esther Lund Arroe, Feb. 23, 1991. BS, Va. Mil. Inst., 1934; A.M., Columbia, 1937, PhD, 1939. Research chemist Gold Dust Corp., 1934-36; instr. chemistry Columbia, 1937-40; prof. chemistry, chmn. dept. State U. N.Y. Coll., Albany, 1940-52, dean coll., 1952-61; first dir. Atmospheric Scis. Research Center, 1961; pres. Fredonia Coll., SUNY, 1961-70; dir. panel on univ. purposes and goals, gen. mgr. constrn. fund, vice chancellor SUNY, 1970-83, cons. univ. planning and mgmt., 1983—. Author textbooks, articles in sci. jours. Mem. Sigma Xi, Phi Lambda Upsilon. Clubs: University (Albany, N.Y.). Home and Office: 2567 Brookview Rd Castleton On Hudson NY 12033-9713 E-mail: Elanford@albany.net.

LANG, BRIAN JOSEPH, museum administrator; b. Cleve., June 1, 1969; s. Joseph Francis and Marjorie L.; m. Jennifer Noel Cervantes, May 28, 1994 (div. May 1998). BA, Beloit Coll., 1991; MA, U. Denver, 1997. Exhibits preparator Beloit (Wis.) Coll. Mus., 1987-91; intern New World dept. Denver Art Mus., 1991-93, adminstrv. asst. New World dept., 1993-94, security officer, 1994-95; curator Hiwan Homestead Mus., Evergreen, Colo., 1995-99; mgr. ops. Vance Kirkland Mus. and Found., Denver, 1999-2000; curator Dumbarton House/NSCDA, Washington, 2000—. Mem. Am. Assn. Mus., Soc. for Am. Archaeology, Jefferson County Hist. Soc., Assn. No. Front Range Mus. (sec.-treas. 1997-99), Colo. Arts and Crafts Soc. (bd. dirs. 1997-2000). Avocations: art, antiques, baseball cards, theater, visiting museums. Home: 7111 Woodmont Ave Apt 710 Bethesda MD 20815-6235 Office: Dumbarton House 2715 Que St NW Washington DC 20007-3071 Fax: 202-337-0348. E-mail: brianlang@dumbartonhouse.org.

LANG, CAROL MAX, veterinarian, educator; b. Paris, Dec. 29, 1937; s. Acel G. and O. Nadine (Beaver) L.; m. Sylvia Smith, Jan. 10, 1965; children: Karen E., John A., Susan C. BS, U. Ill., 1959, DVM, 1961. Diplomate Am. Coll. Lab. Animal Medicine. Capt., vet. corp. Walter Reed Army Inst. Research, Washington, 1961-63; asst. prof. Pa. State U. Coll. Medicine, Hershey, 1966-69, assoc. prof., 1969-72, prof., 1972-84, George T. Harrell Jr. prof., 1984—, asst. dean continuing edn., 1984-96. Contbr. more than 160 articles to profl. publs. Served to capt. U.S. Army, 1961-63. Recipient Research award Am. Assn. Lab. Animal Sci., 1980-81, Charles River award Am. Vet. Med. Assn., 1987; Bowman Gray Sch. Med. postdoctoral fellow, 1963-66. Mem. Am. Vet. Med. Assn., Am. Assn. Lab. Animal Sci., Am. Coll. Lab. Animal Medicine (past pres.). Home: 472 Hilltop Rd Hummelstown PA 17036-8512 Office: Pa State U Milton S Hershey Med Ctr PO Box 850 Hershey PA 17033-0850 E-mail: cml7@psu.edu.

LANG, CATHERINE LOU, small business owner; b. Hugo, Okla., June 12, 1946; d. John Wilburn Sr. and Velma Lou (Evans) Freeman; m. Laurence Larry Lang, Nov. 20, 1974; children: Tana Louise, Henry Nathan, Gina Elise; 1 stepchild, Michael. BA in Sociology and Econs., Northeastern State U., 1970. Co-owner C&L Jewelry, Waterford, Mich., 1980—. Landlord of rental home, Novi, Mich., 1977-93. Active Northwest Child Rescue Women Jr. League, 1975—, League of Women of Detroit; mem. PTA Mercy Sch. for Girls, Farmington, Mich., 1990-94, Walled Lake Mich. Schs., 1981—; mem. Great Decisions, active in leadership, 1988; team parent Team Elan Skating Team, 1991-92; mem. Lakes Assn., Novi, 1992; mem. Covenant Bapt. Ch., 1977—, Am. Bapt. Women, Novi PTSA Parent Assn., 1999, Evergreen Coll. Parent Assn., 1998—. Recipient (with son) Arrow of Light pin Cub Scouts. Mem. AAUW (charter, Novi-Northville br., membership/diversity v.p. 1998—, dist. VIII co-chair 1999), MADD, Internat. Fedn. Univ. Women, Nat. Assn. Investors Corp., Detroit Skating Club, Top Stock Stock Club, Lioness of Mich. Democrat. Avocations: ceramic and porcelain dolls, ice skating team supporter, nat. vol. work. Home: 1369 E Lake Dr Novi MI 48377-1442 Office: C&L Jewelry 924 W Huron St Waterford MI 48328-3726

LANG, CECIL YELVERTON, English language educator; b. Walstonburg, N.C., Sept. 18, 1920; s. Wilton Earl and Lillie (Yelverton) L.; m. Violette Noelle Guérin-Lésé, Apr. 2, 1952; 1 child, François-Michel. AB, Duke U., 1941, AM, 1942; MA, Harvard U., 1946, PhD, 1949. Instr., then asst. prof. English Yale U., New Haven, 1949-57; assoc. prof. Claremont (Calif.) Grad. Sch., 1957-59; prof. Syracuse (N.Y.) U., 1959-65, U. Chgo., 1965-67; prof. Ctr. for Advanced Studies U. Va., Charlottesville, 1967-70, Commonwealth prof. English, 1970-84, John Stewart Bryan prof., 1984-91, prof. emeritus, 1991—. Editor: The Swinburne Letters, 6 vols., 1959-62, New Writings of Swinburne, 1964, The Pre-Raphaelites and Their Circle, 1968; co-editor: The Tennyson Letters, 3 vols., 1982-90, The Letters of Matthew Arnold, 1996—. 1st lt. USAAF, 1942-46. Guggenheim fellow, 1951-52; Fulbright fellow, 1951-52, Morse fellow, 1956-57. Fellow Brit. Acad. (corr.), Royal Soc. Lit. Home: 500 Crestwood Dr # 1507 Charlottesville VA 22903-4860 Address: English Department UVA 219 Bryan Hall Charlottesville VA 22903 E-mail: cyl@virginia.edu.

LANG, DANIEL S. artist; b. Tulsa, Mar. 17, 1935; s. Irving and Dorothy D. (Lauterer) L. B.F.A., Tulsa U., 1953; M.F.A., Iowa U., 1959. Asst. prof. art SUNY, Fredonia, 1959-60, Art Inst. Chgo., 1962-64, Washington U., St. Louis, 1964-65; vis. artist Ohio State U., 1968-69, U. South Fla., 1971, U. Utah, spring 1984. Adj. prof. U. Utah, 1984— One-man shows include Boston Mus. Fine Arts, 1961, Arthur Tooth & Sons, London, 1970, 74, Alexandra Monett Gallery, Brussels, Belgium, 1973, 78, Fairweather Hardin Gallery, Chgo., 1971, 77, 80, Il Gabbiano Gallery, Rome, 1975, DM Gallery, London, 1975, Gimpel & Weitzenhofer, N.Y.C., 1976, Fischbach Gallery, N.Y.C., 1977, 79, Graphik Internat. GMBH, Stuttgart, Germany, 1979, Richard Demarco Gallery, Edinburgh, Scotland, 1981, 83, Watson/Willour Gallery, Houston, 1981, David Findlay Gallery, N.Y.C., 1981, 83, Sherry French Gallery, N.Y.C., 1984, Meredith Long Gallery, Houston, 1984, Washington Gallery, Glasgow, 1986, Phillips Gallery, Salt Lake City, 1988, Gilcrease Mus., Tulsa, 1989, Am. Stock Exch., N.Y.C., 1991, Galleria Civica, Seregno, Italy, 1991, The Hokin Gallery, Palm Beach, Fla., 1991, Taylor's Contemporary Gallery, Hot Springs, Ark., 1992, Galleria Delle Art, Cittá di Castello, Italy, 1992, William Hardie Gallery, Glasgow, Scotland, 1992, Civic Gallery, Urbino, Italy, 1992, London Art Fair, 1994, Elliot Smith Gallery, St. Louis, 1994, Alexandre Gallery U. Tulsa, 1995, Galerie Hertz, Louisville, Ky., 1996, Bridgewater/Lustberg Gallery, N.Y., 1997, MD Modern Gallery, Houston, 1999; group shows include Am. Fedn. of Arts travelling exhbn., 1968-69, U. Pa. Inst. Contemporary Art, 1970, Moore Coll. Art, 1971, Boston U., 1972, Joslyn Art Mus., Omaha and Sheldon Meml. Art Galleries, Lincoln, Nebr., 1973-74, Sherry French Gallery, 1983, 85, 86, Ruth Siegel Gallery, N.Y.C., 1989, Antarctica 2-man show sponsored by NSF, organized by Smithsonian Instn., 1976-79, America 1976 travelling exhbn., 1976-78, including stops at Fogg Art Mus. Harvard U., Wadsworth Atheneum, Hartford, Conn. and, Corcoran Gallery Art, Washington, Watson/de Nagy Gallery of Houston travelling exhbn., 1978-79, Hirschl & Adler Gallery, N.Y.C., 1980, Gerald Peters Gallery, 1993, Landfall Press, Chgo., 1993, Cline Fine Art Gallery, Sante Fe, 1994, U. Tulsa, 1994, London Art Fair, 1997, Glasgow Art Fair, 1997, MD Modern Gallery, 1998, MB Modern Gallery, N.Y., 1998, Stewart & Stewart Pubs., N.Y., 1998, Waterman Fine Art Ltd., London, 1998, M.A. Doran Gallery, Tulsa, Okla., 1999; represented in permanent collections including Bklyn. Mus. High Mus. Art, Atlanta, Denver Art Mus., Mus. Modern Art, N.Y.C., Art Inst. Chgo., Library of Congress, Boston Public Library, Calif. Palace Legion of Honor, Nelson Rockefeller Collection, N.Y.C., Victoria and Albert Mus., London, Hunterian Art Gallery, U. Glasgow, Elliot Smith Gallery, St. Louis, 1994, The Cline Fine Art Gallery, Santa Fe, 1994, R. Duane Reed, St. Louis, 1996, Galerie Hertz, Louisville, Ky., 1996, Bridgewater, Lustberg, N.Y., 1999, MB Modern Gallery, N.Y., 2000, Galleria La Loggia, Sansepolcro, Italy, 2002, other pub. and pvt. collections; designer sets for Orfeo, Kent Opera Co., Eng., later filmed by BBC, 1976. Served with U.S. Army, 1954-56. Home: 38 W 56th St New York NY 10019-3814 also: Montone (PG) 06014 Montone Italy

LANG, DANNY ROBERT, urban planner; b. St. Louis, June 4, 1955; s. George Robert and V. Arlene (Underwood) L.; m. Diane Marie Martin, Aug. 14, 1976; children: Douglas Gerald, Derek Robert, Darin Kenneth. BS, U. Mo., 1977. Dir. lakes and pks. Lake Saint Louis (Mo.) Cmty. Assn., 1977-80; environ. planner Harland Bartholomew & Assoc., St. Louis, 1980-81, Booker & Assocs., St. Louis, 1981-87; dir. cmty. devel. City of St. Peters, 1987-95, dir. city devel., 1995—2001; sr. planner Horner & Shifrin, St. Louis, 2000—; dir. city devel. City of St. Charles. Dir. deanery planning St. Charles Deanery-St. Louis Archdiocese. Recipient Eagle Scout Boy Scouts Am., 1972. Mem. Am. Planning Assn. (past pres. Mo. chpt. 1992-97, Excellence in Planning awards 1985, 87, 91, 96), Mo. Tax Increment Fin. Assn. (bd. dirs. 1995-97). Roman Catholic. Avocations: coaching little league baseball, stamp collecting. Office: Horner & Shifrin Inc 5200 Oakland Ave Saint Louis MO 63110

LANG, DOUGLAS STEWART, lawyer; b. St. Louis, July 25, 1947; s. Ervin Jacob and Jacqueline Helen (Kratky) L.; m. Martha Kay Taylor, Aug. 25, 1973; children: Brian Chester and Christopher John (twins), Stewart Taylor. BS BA, Drake U., 1969; JD, U. Mo., 1972. Bar: Mo. 1972, Tex. 1973, U.S. Dist. Ct. (no. dist.) Tex. 1973, U.S. Ct. Appeals (5th cir.) 1977, U.S. Dist. Ct. (ea. dist.) Tex. 1992, U.S. Dist. Ct. (we. dist.) Tex. 1993. Law clk. to Hon. Fred L. Henley Mo. Supreme Ct., St. Louis, 1972-73; assoc. Weber, Baker & Allums, Dallas, 1973-78; ptnr. Gardere, Porter & DeHay, 1978-79, Gardere Wynne Sewell LLP, Dallas, 1979—. Speaker continuing legal edn. seminars.; bd. dirs. Legal Svcs. of North Tex., Inc., 1997—, vice chair, 1998, chair, 1999-2000. Chalice bearer and lay reader Ch. of Incarnation, Dallas, 1984—, vestry mem. 1990-95; campaign chmn., treas. Election Nathan L. Hecht, judge 95th dist. ct., Dallas, 1982; mem. Dallas Mus. Art, 1986—; mem. Dallas Cmty. Rep. Men's Club, 1986—; mem. troops com. Boy Scout Troop 72, Dallas, 1989-97, asst. scoutmaster, 1992-97, order of arrow; v.p. Park Cities Ctrl. Dads' Club, Dallas, 1990-91; pres. Univ. Park Grade Sch. Dad's Club, 1990-91; bd. councillors U. Dallas, 1991-93; bd. dirs. Com. for Qualified Judiciary, 1999-2002; bd. trustees, vice chmn. chair long range planning com., exec. com. Anglican Sch. Theology, 2000—; exec. coun. Episcopal Diocese of Dallas, 2002--. Recipient Outstanding Svc. awd. Legal Svcs. North Tex., Dallas, 1991, Alumni Achievement award, Drake U., Des Moines, Iowa, 1992, Double D award Drake U., 1993. Fellow Tex. Bar Found. (sustaining, life, trustee 1997-2000), Am. Bar Found., Dallas Bar Found (trustee 1991—, sec.-treas. 1994-96, vice chair 1996-98, chair 1998-2001); mem. ABA (litigat. sect. 1974—, mem. exec. coun. Nat. Conf. of Bar Pres. 1995-98, exec. com. Met. Bar Caucus 1991-97, sec.-treas. 1992-93, pres.-elect 1993-94, pres. 1994-95, ho. of dels. 1996-2000), State Bar Tex. (bd. dirs. 1992-95, exec. com. 1994-95, Outstanding Third Yr. Dir. award 1995, Presdl. Citation 1999), Dallas Bar Assn. (bd. dirs. 1976-78, 80-2000, pres. 1991), Dallas Assn. Young Lawyers (bd. dirs. 1975, v.p. 1976, treas. 1975, pres. 1977, Outstanding Young Lawyer in Dallas 1981), Tex. Young Lawyers Assn. (bd. dirs. 1976-78), Tex. Assn. Bank Coun. (bd. dirs. 1990-93, v.p. 1994-95, pres. elect 1995-96, pres. 1996-97), Tex. Assn. Defense Counsel, Am. Inn of Ct. (membership chmn. 1991-95, exec. com. 1991—, counselor 1995-96, pres. 1997-99), Salesmanship Club of Dallas, Tex. Ctr. for Ethics and Professionalism (chair 1999-2002), Drake U. Nat. Alumni Assn. (bd. dirs. 1998—, v.p. programming 2000—). Republican. Episcopalian. Avocations: golf, hiking, rafting, camping. Office: Gardere & Wynne LLP 1601 Elm St Ste 3000 Dallas TX 75201-4761

LANG, ERNST FREDERICK, radiologist; b. Detroit, Dec. 16, 1916; s. Ernst Frederick and Alice Rhoda (Whitehead) L.; m. Virginia Davis, June 14, 1941; children: William, Carolyn, Elizabeth, Barbara. AB with distinction, U. Mich., 1938, MD, 1941. Diplomate Am. Bd. Radiology (radiology and nuclear medicine); lic. physician, Mich. Intern Harper Hosp., Detroit, 1941, resident in radiology, 1942-45, radiologist, 1945—, L. Reynolds Assoc., Detroit, 1945—. Clin. assoc. prof. radiology Wayne State U. Coll. Medicine, Detroit, 1973-82. Asst., assoc., acting editor Am. Jour. Roentgenology, 1971-80. 1st lt. AUS, 1941. Fellow Am. Roentgen Ray Soc. (exec. coun. 1968-77, 1st v.p. 1976-77)); mem. Radiol. Soc. N.Am., Mich. Radiol. Soc. (sec., treas. 1955-58, pres. 1973-75). Avocations: reading, writing, math, computer programming.

LANG, EVERETT FRANCIS, JR. brokerage house executive; b. Providence, Sept. 27, 1942; s. Everett Francis and Catherine Mary (Cuddigan) L.; m. Margaret Letitia McKenna; 1 child, Joseph; m. Frances Marie Biasi. BS, Boston U., 1965; MEd, U. Va., 1972, EdD, 1976. Lic. security broker. Elem. sch. tchr. Henrico County Sch. Systems, Highland Springs, Va., 1970-71, middle sch. tchr., 1971-72; asst. regional dir. Sch. Continuing Edn. U. Va., Charlottesville, 1972-76; assoc. dir. human resources Met Property & Liability Ins. Co., Warwick, R.I., 1976-79; human resources cons. Colonial Penn Group, Phila., 1979-81; v.p. Bankers Trust Co., N.Y.C., 1981-86; v.p. sales BT Brokerage Corp., 1986-90; chmn., pres., chief exec. officer Bankers Trust Brokerage Corp., 1990-92; pres. Nat. Discount Brokers, 1993-95, pres., CEO, 1995-98; pres. of Digital Trading facility WIT Soundview Tech. Group , 1999-2000; exec. v.p. Fleet Securities, 2001—. Capt. USAF, 1965-69, Vietnam. Decorated with Bronze Star, Army Commendation medal. Mem. Phi Delta Kappa, Kappa Delta Pi, Sigma Alpha Epsilon. Avocation: golf. Home: 5 Michele Ct Allendale NJ 07401-1013 Office: Fleet Securities 26 Broadway New York NY 10004

LANG, GEORGE, restaurateur; b. Székesfehérvár, Hungary, July 13, 1924; came to U.S., 1946, naturalized, 1950; s. Simon and Ilona (Lang) Deutsch; m. Jenifer Lang; children: Andrea, Brian, Simon John, Georgina Kathlyn. Student, U. Szeged, Hungary, 1945, Mozarteum, Salzburg, Austria, 1945-46, U. Stranieri, Perugia, Italy, 1950-51; LHD (hon.), Ind. Univ., 1994. Asst. banquet mgr. Waldorf-Astoria, 1953-58; v.p. sales and marketing Brass Rail Orgn., 1958-60; v.p. Restaurant Assocs., 1960-71; pres. George Lang Corp., N.Y.C., 1971-83; owner (with Ronald Lauder) Gundel's Restaurant, Budapest, Hungary, 1990—; co-owner Tokaj and Eger Vineyard. Author: The Cuisine of Hungary, 1971, Lang's Compendium of Culinary Nonsense and Trivia, 1980, The Café des Artistes Cookbook, 1984, Nobody Knows the Truffles I've Seen, A Memoir, 1998; co-author: Gundel Album, 1993; cons. editor Time-Life Book div.'s Foods of the World series, 1966-70; contbr. to Ency. Brit., 1974, also columnist mags. Pub. mem. Am. Revolution Bicentennial Commn., 1969— , mem. exec. com., chmn. Festival U.S.A. coordinating art, internat. exchange and spl. events for Bicentennial celebrations. Address: 33 W 67th St New York NY 10023-6224 E-mail: glang@cafedesartistesnyc.com. *In the great recipe of life, salt is the passion and the spice is enthusiasm.*

LANG, GEORGE EDWARD, lawyer; b. Peekskill, N.Y., Apr. 7, 1932; s. George Louis and Florence (Sheehan) Lang; m. Rose Marie Corrao, June 8, 1953 (dec. Apr. 10, 2000); children: G. Vincent, Kathleen M.; m. Jane Ann Edwards, Sept. 30, 2000. AB, U. Notre Dame, 1954, JD, 1955. Bar: Ky. 1955, U.S. Dist. Ct. Ky. 1956. City atty., Munfordville, Ky., 1958-85, Bonnieville, 1958-85; atty. Hart County, Munfordville, 1962-70; hearing officer Ky. Workmen's Compensation Bd., 1971-79; master commr. Hart Cir. Ct., 1984—. Pres. South Ctr. Ky. Broadcasting Co., Munfordville, 1984-88; v.p. Cub Run (Ky.) Industries, 1986-90. Pres. Munfordville Indsl. Found., 1968-90; bd. dirs. Mammoth Cave (Ky.) Devel. Assn., 1972—; chmn. Hart County Dem. Party, Munfordville, 1972-78. Mem. Ctrl. Ky. Wildlife Fedn. (pres. 1962-64), Munfordville Lions Club (pres. 1966-68), Horse Cave Rotary Club (v.p. 1968-69). Roman Catholic. Office: PO Box 366 Munfordville KY 42765-0366 E-mail: gepl11@yahoo.com.

LANG, GEORGE FRANK, insurance executive, consultant, lawyer; b. Orange, N.J., Aug. 21, 1937; s. Frank W. and Hilda I. (Pierson) L.; m. Grace B. Preisler, Jan. 30, 1960; children: Christine, Gregg, Cynthia; m. Valerie J. Hanson, Nov. 24, 1978. BS, Ill. Wesleyan U., 1960; JD, Ill. Inst. Tech., 1968. Account exec. Scarborough & Co., Chgo., 1960-67; dir. fin. inst. George F. Brown & Sons, 1967-69; v.p., dir. Fin. Ins. Svc., Schaumburg, Ill., 1969-79; pres. City Ins. Svc., Elizabeth, N.J., 1980-84; mng. dir. Res. Fin. Mgmt., Miami, Fla., 1984-85; v.p. Beneficial Ins. Group, Newport Beach, Calif., 1985-86, Ask Ins. Svc., Irvine, 1986-89, cons. product ctr. sales, 1989; cons. Nat. Dealer Ins. Systems, 1989, New Liberty Adminstrn., 1990—, Home Crest Ins., 1991—, Great Western Ins. Agy., 1992—, Dana Harbor Ins. Svcs., Inc., 1995—. Cons. in field. Bd. dirs. Woodview Civic Assn., Mt. Prospect, Ill., 1964-70, pres., bd. dirs., 1969; bd. dirs. Chippendale Assn., Barrington, Ill., 1972-76, v.p., bd. dirs., 1976. Avocations: boating, fishing, traveling. Home: 173 Ave del Poniente San Clemente CA 92672-4647 Office: PO Box 3435 Dana Point CA 92629-2910 E-mail: Danaharbo@AOL.com.

LANG, GORDON, JR. retired lawyer; b. Evanston, Ill., July 27, 1933; s. Gordon and Harriet Kendig Lang; m. Clara Bates Van Derzee, Sept. 26, 1970; children: Elizabeth K., Gordon III, Harriet B. BA, Yale U., 1954; MA in History, U. Ariz., 1958; LLB, Harvard U., 1960. Bar: Ill. 1960. Assoc. Gardner, Carton & Douglas, Chgo., 1960-67, ptnr., 1967-98, ret., 1998. Cons., 1999—. Dir. North Side Boys' Clubs, Chgo., 1961-67, Yale Scholarship Trust Ill., 1966-69, pres., 1967; mem. Assocs. Rush-Presbyn.-St. Luke's Med. Ctr., Chgo., 1962—, Assocs. Northwestern U., Evanston, 1970—; dir. Chgo. Youth Ctrs., 1967—, pres., 1982-84; trustee Chgo. Latin Sch. Found., 1978—, pres., 1995—; trustee Groton (Mass.) Sch., 1982-93; dir. United Way of Chgo., 1984-90, United Way/Crusade of Mercy (Met. Chgo.), 1989-95; apptd. Bush/Cheney elector 2000 presdl. election. 1st lt. USAF, 1955-57. Mem. ABA (sect. bus. law), Ill. State Bar Assn., Chgo. Bar Assn. (mem. corp. law com. 1975-98, mem. fin. instns. com. 1985-98), Chgo. Club (former dir. and sec.), Econ. Club Chgo. (former dir. and sec.), Onwentsia Club, Racquet Club Chgo., Chgo. Commonwealth Club, Yale Club Chgo. (former dir., past pres.). Republican. Episcopalian. Avocations: golf, skiing, hiking. Home: 1520 N Astor St Chicago IL 60610-1610 Office: Gardner Carton & Douglas 321 N Clark St Ste 3400 Chicago IL 60610-4795 E-mail: glang@gcd.com.

LANG, HOWARD LAWRENCE, electrical engineer; b. St. Louis, Nov. 16, 1958; s. William and Hermine L.; m. Karen Friedman, June 26, 1988; children: Arielle Ilyssa, Emily Danielle. BS in Biophysics with high distinction, U. Ill., 1981; MSEE, Cert. Biomedical Engring., Wash. U., St. Louis, 1984; MSE in Computer and Info. Sci., U. Pa., 1990. Registered profl. engr., Pa., N.J., N.Y. Biomedical engr. Midwest Rsch. Inst., Kansas City, Mo., 1983; sr. engr. AT&T Bell Labs., Holmdel, N.J., 1984—. Contbr. articles to profl. jours.; designer fiber optic comm. sys. Chmn. AT&T Magic Club, Holmdel, 1985-88, Illini Emergency Med. Svcs., Urbana, 1979-81. Mem. IEEE (sr., sec. Computer Soc. N.J. coast sect. 1998-99, Service award 1984), NSPE, N.J. Soc. Profl. Engrs., Tau Beta Pi, Phi Eta Sigma. Avocations: magic, cycling. Home: PO Box 200 Holmdel NJ 07733-0200

LANG, JACKIE ANN, nursing consultant; b. Cin., Oct. 10, 1960; d. John Harvey and Sallie Joan (Ralston) Kegley; m. James Edward Lang, Nov. 19, 1988; children: Rachel, Victoria, Rebecca, Stephanie, Michael. BSN, U. Cin., 1983, MSN, 1988. RN, Ohio; cert. quality mgmt. Staff and charge nurse med.-surg. Univ. Hosp., Cin., 1983-86, critical care staff nurse, 1986-88; med.-surg. instr. nursing sch. Good Samaritan Hosp., 1987-89; med.-surg. clin. nurse specialist The Jewish Hosp., 1989-91; cons. Greater Cin. Internal Medicine, 1990—. Contbr. nursing newsletters. Mem. aux. The Jewish Hosp. of Cin., 1993—2001, Parks and REcreation Commn., Montgomery, 2001—; mem. N.E. Cmty. Challenge Coalition, 2001—; first v.p. All Saints PTO, 2000—01, pres., 2001—02. Univ. grad. scholar U. Cin., 1985-86. Mem.: Southwestern Ohio Nurses Assn., Ohio Nurses Assn., ANA, LWV, Montgomery Women's Club (Sunshine chmn. 1996—97, arts dept. chmn. 1997—98, rec. sec. 1998—2000, 2nd v.p. 2000—01), Gen. Fedn. Women's Clubs, Ohio Fedn. Women's Clubs, Sigma Theta Tau, Alpha Chi Omega (pledge pres. 1979—80, 3d v.p. 1981—82, chpt. pres. 1982—83, alumni sec. 1984—86, alumni mem. co-chmn. 1995—99). Roman Catholic. Home: 8884 Castleford Ln Cincinnati OH 45242-6351

LANG, JAMES PATRICK, priest; b. Syracuse, N.Y., Feb. 14, 1949; s. Eugene Adolph and Rita James Lang. BA, Wadhams Hall Seminary Coll., 1971; MDiv, St. Mary's Sem. and Univ., Balt., 1974. Deacon Cathedral of the Immaculate Conception, Syracuse, NY, 1974—75; assoc. pastor Our Lady of Lourdes Ch., Utica, 1975—77, St. Mary of the Assumption Ch., Rome, 1977—81; chaplain and dir. of Hall Newman Ctr. & Chapel of Lady of the Holy Spirit at SUNY, Oswego, 1981—91; chaplain and dir. Alibrandi Cath. Ctr. and Thomas More Chapel at Syracuse U., 1991—98; diocesan dir. Office of Pastoral Planning, Diocese of Syracuse, 1999—; diocesan vicar for parishes Diocese of Syracuse, 2000—. Mem. faculty Formation for Minisry Program, Diocese of Syracuse, 1984—91; mem. Senate of Priests, Diocese of Syracuse, 1984—, mem. exec. com., 1985—98, vice chair exec. com., 1989—93, chair exec. com., 1993—97; mem. Diocesan Pastoral Coun., Syracuse, 1984—; vice chair Diocesan Pastoral Coun, 1992—94; mem. Priests' Coun. State of N.Y., 1986—98; treas., 1987—91; pres., 1991—95; observer Nat. Coun. Cath. Bishops, 1991—95; mem. Diocesan Coll. Consultors, 1996—98; other related appointments. Chmn. adv. com. Psi chpt. Syracuse U. Alpha Phi Omega Nat. Co-Ed Svc. Fraternity, 1991—, chmn. adv. com. Epsilon Nu Chpt. Syracuse U., 1991—; Bd. dirs. Hiawatha Coun. BSA, 1993—99; mem. faculty Nat. Camping Sch. BSA, 1992—, chaplain, 1992—, program instr., 1996—; mem. N.E. Region BSA 2002 Outdoor Program Seminar, 2000—; and others.; bd. dirs. Oneida County Cmty.. Action, Inc. , Utica, NY, 1976—81, fin. chmn., 1980—81, treas., 1981; Bd. dirs. Cath. Charities of Onandaga County, 1993—. Recipient Robert E. Hall award, Oswego (N.Y.) Newman Found.,Inc., 1991, Key to the City, Mayor's Office City of Oswego, 1991, St. George award, Cath. Com. on Scouting, Diocese of Syracuse, 1992, Silver Beaveer award, Hiawatha Coun. BSA, Syracuse, 1998, Silver Antelope award, Northeast Region BSA, 2001, Disting. Svc. Key, Alpha Phi Omega, Phi chpt. Syracuse U., 1998, Chancellor's award for pub. svc., Syracuse U., 1998. Mem.: Nat. Assn. Ch. Personnel Adminstrs., Conf. on Pastoral Planning and Coun. Devel., Theta Alpha Kappa, Theta Chi Beta. Republican. Home: 4845 S Salina St Syracuse NY 13205 Office: Vicar for Parishes Diocese of Syrcuse 340 E Onandaga St PO Box 511 Office Fax: 315-478-4619. E-mail: jplang@aol.com.

LANG, JAMES DEVORE, JR. ministry executive; b. Ft. Lewis, Wash., Apr. 29, 1941; s. James Devore and Margaret Lang; m. Barbara Jo Drury, July 3, 1965; children: Kathrena, Teresa, Christina, Angela. BS, USAF Acad., 1963; postgrad., Pepperdine U., 1977-79. Commd. 2d lt. USAF, 1963, advanced through grades to capt., resigned, 1969; regional dir., v.p. Lorraine L. Blair, Inc., San Francisco, 1969-71; v.p. Capital Planning Assn., San Rafael, Calif., 1971-73; pres. Delger Corp., Novato, 1973-76; chmn., CEO Delger Fin. Corp., 1976-83; pres., chmn., CEO Alternate Energy Corp., 1978-81; pres., CEO Shiloh Resources, 1980-83; sales rep., engr., v.p. Aztec Bldg., Inc., Norman, Okla., 1985-90; pres., CEO Amerex Corp., 1990-93; v.p., exec. dir. Bill Glass Prison Ministries, Inc., Dallas, 1994-99, exec. v.p., 1996-96, pres., 1999-2001; exec. dir. Prison Ministry, 2001—. Elder, pastor Trinity Bapt. Ch., Norman, 1990-93. Author: Real Estate Investment Trusts in Financial Planning, 1973; contbr. numerous articles to profl. publs. Regent Coll. for Fin. Planning, 1974-76. Decorated Air medal with 7 oak leaf clusters, Air Force Commendation medal; Paul Harris fellow Rotary Internat., 1978; recipient Golden Bull award Bank of Marin, 1977. Mem. Internat. Assn. Fin. Planning (nat. pres. 1973-74, chmn. 1974-75). Avocations: church, family, sports, flying. Home: 910 Fairway Dr Duncanville TX 75137-4612 Office: Champions for Life PO Box 761101 Dallas TX 75376-1101

LANG, JANELLE J. accountant; b. Oelwein, Iowa, May 11, 1948; d. Arthur and Esther Louise (Moeller) Andrew; m. Robert Martin Lang, Sept. 4, 1971; children: Sybil, Jacqueline. BA in Bus. and Music Edn., Upper Iowa Coll., 1970; BA in Acctg., Buena Vista Coll., 1993. Tchr. Davenport (Iowa) Cmty. Schs., 1971-72, Bennett (Iowa) Cmty. Schs., 1972-73, Madison (Wis.) Cmty. Schs., 1973-74; acct. Robert M. Lang, M.D., P.C., Ottumwa, Iowa, 1976—. Mem. governing bd. S.E. Iowa Symphony Orch., 1995—; bd. dirs. Ottumwa Civic Music, 1996; violist S.E. Iowa Symphony, 1996—, Ottumwa Symphony Orch., 1996—; worship and music coord. 1st Luth. Ch., Ottumwa, 1995. Mem. NAFE, Am. Mgmt. Assn. Lutheran. Avocation: gardening. Home: 818 E Highland Ave Ottumwa IA 52501-2134 Office: Robert M Lang MD PC 1106 Pennsylvania Ave Ottumwa IA 52501-2109

LANG, JOHN ERNEST, lawyer; b. Arkansas City, Kans., Dec. 27, 1936; s. Ernest R. and Ruth (Evans) L.; m. Joleen C. Jilka, Nov. 22, 1959; children: Jill Kay Lang Gobble, Jeffrey R. BS, U. Kans., 1958; JD, Washburn U., 1962. Bar: Kans. 1962, U.S. Dist. Ct. Kans. 1962, U.S. Ct. Appeals (10th cir.) 1969. Mcpl. judge City of Wamego, Kans., 1967-78; county atty. Pottawatomie County, 1967-70, county counselor, 1977—; pvt. practice, Wamego, 1961—. Bd. dirs. First Nat. Bank, Wamego. Trustee The Stormont Found., Topeka, 1989-95; trustee Wamego City Hosp., 1969-89, chmn. bd. trustees, 1988-89; chair Gov.'s Com. on Instnl. Mgmt. and Comty. Mental Health, Topeka, 1974-80; mem. Gov.'s Adv. Com. on Criminal Adminstrn., Topeka, 1970-72. With USAR, 1956-62. Mem. Kans. Bar Assn., Pottawatomie County Bar Assn. Democrat. Methodist. Avocation: golf. Office: PO Box 2 Wamego KS 66547-0002 E-mail: langlaw@wamego.net.

LANG, JOHN JOSEPH, systems engineer, program manager; b. Franklin, Pa., Feb. 24, 1960; s. Robert Andrew and Mary Jane (Wensel) Lang. BSEE, Marquette U., 1982; MBA, Pepperdine U., 1987. Cert. project mgmt. profl. Project Mgmt. Inst. Mem. tech. staff Hughes Aircraft Co., Fullerton, Calif., 1982-85, sr. project engr., 1991-94, field team leader, test dir. Anaheim Hills, 1985-88, tech. supr., project engr., 1989-90; project mgr. Hughes Info. Tech. Systems, Riyadh, Saudi Arabia, 1994-97; mgr. engring. programs Raytheon Systems Co., 1997-99; dir. Cambridge Technology Ptnrs., Phoenix, 1999—. Contbr. Active Am. Cmty. Svcs., Riyadh, 1994—99, Sch. of Bus. and Mgmt. Scholar Sch. of Bus. and Mgmt. scholar, Pepperdine U., 1986. Mem.: NSPE, NARAS, AAAS, IEEE, Project Mgmt. Inst. (cert. project mgmt. profl.), Engring. Mgmt. Soc., N.Y. Acad. Scis. Avocations: music, nanotechnology. Office: Cambridge Tech Ptnrs 1928 E Highland Av F104/130 Phoenix AZ 85016-4236 E-mail: J.Lang@computer.org.

LANG, JOSEPH HAGEDORN, lawyer; b. Cleve., Sept. 30, 1937; s. Carl Frederick and Martha Clotilda (Hagedorn) L.; m. Elsie A. O'Berry, Aug. 8, 1965; children: Joseph H. Jr., Robert Warren, James O'Berry. AA, St. Petersburg Jr. Coll., 1959; BA, Duke U., 1961; JD, U. Fla., 1963. Bar: Fla. 1964, U.S. Dist. Ct. (mid. dist.) Fla. 1965, U.S. Ct. Appeals (5th cir.) 1965, U.S. Supreme Ct. 1975. Assoc. Baynard McLeod & Overton, St. Petersburg, Fla., 1964-69; ptnr. Baynard McLeod & Lang, 1969-80; pres. Baynard McLeod & Lang, P.C., 1980—. Active Police Cmty. Coun., Cmty. Alliance; chmn. bd. dirs. St. Petersburg Jr. Coll., Pinellas County, 1983-97, trustee, 1977-97, chmn., 1982-89, 92-96, chmn. emeritus, 1997—; mem. State Bd. C.C.'s, 1997-2001, vice chmn. 1998-99, chmn., 1999-2000; vice chmn. Pinellas County Workforce Devel. Bd., 1997-99, sec., 1999-2000; mem. exec. com. Pinellas County Worknet, 2001—. Named Sch. Adv. Com. Mem. of Yr.; recipient Trustee of Yr. award Fla. Assn. Cmty. Coll., 1993, Bob Graham C.C. Disting. Svc. award, 1994, Trustee Leadership award So. Region, ACCT, 1994, Alumni award St. Petersburg Jr. Coll., 1990. Mem. Fla. Bar Assn., St. Petersburg Bar Assn., St. Petersburg C. of C. (Outstanding Mem. award 1990), Suncoasters Club, Dragon Club, Phi Theta Kappa (Disting. Alumni award 1978). Democrat. Roman Catholic. Office: Baynard McLeod & Lang 669 1st Ave N Saint Petersburg FL 33701-3696 Office Fax: 727-343-2547.

LANG, JULES, lawyer; b. Basel, Switzerland, Aug. 30, 1938; came to U.S., 1941; s. Simon and Regina (Fisch) L.; m. Barbara Diane Gottheil, Aug. 28, 1960; 1 child, Erik. BA, U. Conn., 1960; JD with distinction, U. Mich., 1963; LLM, NYU, 1968. Bar: Conn. 1963, U.S. Dist. Ct. Conn. 1964, U.S. Tax Ct. 1964, U.S. Ct. Appeals (2d cir.) 1967, U.S. Supreme Ct. 1969. Ptnr. Lepofsky, Lepofsky & Lang, Norwalk, Conn., 1963—. State trial referee, 1985—, special master, U.S. Dist. Ct. Conn., 1988—. Mem. Norwalk Bd. Edn., 1969-75, chmn. 1973, Norwalk Bd. Estimate and Taxation, 1977-83, chmn. 1979; trustee Conn. Comty.-Tech. Colls., 1977—; pres. Goodman Found., Norwalk, 1988—. Mem. Am. Judicature Soc., Assn. Trial Lawyers Am.,

Norwalk/Wilton Bar Assn. (pres 2001), Greater Norwalk Community Council. Democrat. Jewish. Office: Lepofsky Lepofsky and Lang 7-9 Isaac St Norwalk CT 06850-4102 E-mail: jules.lang@snet.net.

LANG, KEVIN, economics educator; b. Ottawa, Ont., Feb. 16, 1955; came to U.S., 1956; s. Kurt and Gladys (Engel) L.; m. Shulamit Beth Kahn, June 17, 1982; children: Ariella, Jenya. BA and MA, Oxford U., 1976; MS, U. Montreal (Can.), 1978; PhD, MIT, 1982. Prin. investigator Centre de recherches sur l'opinion publique inc., Montreal, 1973-78; asst. prof. U. Calif., Irvine, 1981-87; assoc. prof. econs. Boston U., 1987-90, prof. econs., 1990—, assoc. chmn. econs., 1989-93; vis. scholar MIT, Cambridge, Mass., 1993-94. Cons. World Book, Washington, 1988-89; editor Aldine de Gruyter, Hawthorne, N.Y., 1988—; mem. adv. bd. Can. Econ. Rsch. Forum, 1991—. Editor: Unemployment and the Structure of Labor Markets, 1987; contbr. articles to profl. jours. Bd. dirs. Boston Food Coop., 1980-81, 86-87, mem. fin. com., 1978-81, 86—; Town Meeting mem., Brookline, Mass., 1992—. Faculty rsch. fellow Nat. Bur. Econ. Rsch., Cambridge, 1986-92; Olin Found. fellow, 1986-87; Alfred P. Sloan Found. fellow, 1987-89; Fulbright rsch. fellow N.Z. Inst. Econ. Rsch., 1989; NSF grantee, 1984-89. Mem. Am. Econs. Assn., Can. Econs. Assn. Office: Boston U Dept Econs 270 Bay State Rd Boston MA 02215-1403

LANG, LENORE SCHULMAN, visual artist; b. N.Y.C., Nov. 23, 1927; d. Samuel Woolf and Rose (Horowitz) Rosenberg; m. Jerome Lewis Schulman, June 12, 1948 (div. Oct. 1973); 1 child, Ellen Frances; m. Fred Fulton Lang, Jan. 28, 1975 (dec. Nov. 1991); children: Ellen Frances, Martha Sue; m. Carl Abraham Auerbach, June 22, 1993. BFA, Pratt Inst., Bklyn., 1948; student, Balt. Mus. Art, 1953-54, IIT Sch. Design, Chgo., 1966-67. Designer Norcross, Inc., N.Y.C., 1948-50; tchr. printmaking North Shore Art League, Winnetka, Ill., 1971-73. Juror Art Inst. Chgo., 1985-87. Solo exhbns. include U. Ill. Med. Ctr., Chgo., 1971, Federal Jewish Orgn., Chgo., 1972, Mishkenot Sha'ananim, Jerusalem, 1974, Unicorn Gallery, N.Y.C., 1975, Botanic Gardens, Glencoe, Ill., 1977, Evanston (Ill.) Pub. Libr., 1982, Gruen Gallery, Chgo., 1st Ill. Ctr. bldg. lobby, Chgo., 1985, 101 N. Wacker Dr. bldg. lobby, 1986, East/West Gallery, 1988, Gallery 416, Mpls., 1995, 97; group shows include Art Inst. Chgo., 1978, 79, 87, Peace Mus., Chgo., 1981, Northwestern U., Evanston, 1982, WFMT-Chgo. Mag., 1983, Evanston Art Ctr., 1985, NAB Gallery, Chgo., 1986, Suburban Fine Arts Ctr., Highland Park, Ill., 1988, Spertus Mus., Chgo., 1988, Countryside Gallery, Arlington Heights, Ill., 1989, Chgo. Post Gallery, 1989, Evanston Art Ctr., 1989, State of Ill. Bldg., Chgo., 1989, Artemisia Gallery, Chgo., 1990, Sabbeth Gallery, Glen Cove, N.Y., 1990, Arts Club Chgo., 1991, SCAN Exhibit, Chgo., 1991, Chgo. Cultural Ctr., 1992, Riggs Gallery, La Jolla, Calif., 1992, Beacon St. Gallery, Chgo., 1994, Triangle Gallery, 1995, Ill. State Mus., Springfield, 1995, Mus. Sci. and Industry, Chgo., 1995, Athaneum Music & Art Libr., La Jolla, Calif., 1995, Loyola U., Chgo., 1995, Gallery 416, Mpls., 1995, 96, 97, Ancient Traditions Gallery, 1996, Judy A. Saslow Gallery, Chgo., 1997, Chgo. Cultural Ctr., 1998, So. Calif. Reg. Exhibit, 1998, Sch. of Chgo. Art Inst., 1998, San Diego Art Inst., 1999. Mem. Arts Club Chgo. (profl. mem.), Chgo. Artists Coalition, Cliff Dweller's Club (profl. mem.). Avocations: shell, fossil and rock hunting, concerts, theatre, reading, travel. Home: 1530 Tower Rd Winnetka IL 60093-1627

LANG, LILLIAN OWEN, retired accountant; b. Yorkville, Tenn., Oct. 8, 1915; d. Hugh Preston and Susan (Davis) Owen; 1 child, John Sanford. Student, U. Tenn. Extension, 1956-62, Memphis State U., 1963-64, Memphis Acad. Arts, 1965-66. CPA, Tenn. Shipping clk. Buckeye Cellulose Corp., 1943-46; x-ray technician Memphis and Shelby County Health Dept., 1948-56; acctg. clk. Purex Corp., 1957-59; bookkeeper Electrolock, Inc., 1959-62; sec.-treas. Allied Bruce Terminix Cos., Inc., Mobile, Ala., 1962-80, v.p., 1980-86; also dir.; pvt. practice acctg. Memphis, 1986-2000; ret., 2000. Mem. DAR, Am. Soc. Women Accts. (pres. Mobile chpt. 1977-78, dir. SE area 1979-81). Mem. Christian Ch. (Disciples Of Christ). Home and Office: 5799 Whale Point Ln Rock Hall MD 21661

LANG, LINDA KAY, music educator; b. Scott City, Kans., Mar. 20, 1952; d. Eugene F. and Blanche (Slivey) Carver; m. Paul Lang, Aug. 5, 1978; children: Jenny, Stacy. BMus, Ft. Hays State U., 1974, M. in Elem. Edn., 1980; Orff tchg. cert., Hamline U. Vocal music tchr. Unified Sch. Dist., Grainfield, Kans., 1974-75, Garden City, 1975-78, Hays, 1980—. Mem. Hays Symphony, Ft. Hays State U., 1997—. Adjudicator Jr. High Music Festivals, 1988—; organist Immaculate Heart Mary Parish, Hays, 1985—, religion tchr., 1989-2000. Mem. Kans. Nat. Edn. Assn. (bldg. rep. 1993-94, 2002—), Kans. Music Tchrs. Assn. (pres. dist. IV 1994-95), Kans. Music Edn. Assn. (dist. IV elem. choir chmn., dist. IV Outstanding Elem. Music Tchr. 1999-2000). Avocations: sewing, crocheting, cooking, music. Home: 1601 E 27th Street Ter Hays KS 67601-2114 Office: Lincoln Sch 1906 Ash St Hays KS 67601-3297

LANG, LOTHAR A. engineer; b. Aschaffenburg, Germany, Feb. 13, 1959; s. Horst and Marianne (Ziegler) L.; m. Judith K. Pfeifroth, July 12, 1985; children: Matthias, Thomas, Christina. BS in Chem. Engring., U. Minn., 1983; Diploma in Chem. Engring., Tech. U. Karlsruhe, 1985; PhD in Chem. Engring., U. Stuttgart, Germany, 1991. Process engr. in ctrl. R&D tech. Bayer AG, Leverkusen, Germany, 1990-95, prodn. and plant mgr. in silicone base production Germany, 1995-98, head advanced process control Germany, 1998-2000; engring. fellow Polyol Tech. Ctr. Bayer Corp., Newton Square, Pa., 2000—. Adv. bd. PMC Utrecht, Netherlands, 1996-97. Author publs. in field. Finalist Computerworld-Smithsonian, 1995. Mem. Verein Deutscher Ingenieure. Roman Catholic. Avocations: sports, family, travel. Office: Bayer Corp 3801 West Chester Pike Newtown Square PA 19073-2387 E-mail: Llang587@cs.com., Lothar.Lang.b@bayer.com.

LANG, MABEL LOUISE, classics educator; b. Utica, N.Y., Nov. 12, 1917; d. Louis Bernard and Katherine (Werdge) L. BA, Cornell U., 1939; MA, Bryn Mawr Coll., 1940, PhD, 1943; LittD., Coll. Holy Cross, 1975, Colgate U., 1978; L.H.D., Hamilton Coll. Mem. faculty Bryn Mawr Coll., 1943-91, successively instr., asst. prof., 1943-50, assoc. prof., 1950-59, prof. Greek, 1959-88, chmn. dept., 1960-88, acting dean coll. 2d semester, 1958-59, 60-61; chmn. mng. com. Am. Sch. Classical Studies, Athens, 1975-80, chmn. admissions and fellowship com., 1966-72; Blegen disting. rsch. prof. semester I Vassar Coll., 1976-77; Martin classical lectr. Oberlin Coll., 1982. Co-author: Athenian Agora Measures and Tokens; author: Palace of Nestor Frescoes, 1969, Athenian Agora Graffiti and Dipinti, 1976; Herodotean Narrative and Discourse, 1984, Athenian Agor Ostraka, 1990; contbr. articles profl. jours. Guggenheim fellow, 1953-54; Fulbright fellow Greece, 1959-60 Mem. Am. Philos. Soc., Am. Acad. Arts and Scis., German Archaeol. Inst., Am. Philol. Assn., Soc. Promotion Hellenic Studies (Eng.), Classical Assn. (Eng.). Home: 905 New Gulph Rd Bryn Mawr PA 19010-2941 Office: Dept Greek Bryn Mawr Coll Bryn Mawr PA 19010

LANG, MARGO TERZIAN, artist; b. Fresno, Calif. d. Nishan and Araxie (Kazarosian) Terzian; m. Nov. 29, 1942; children: Sandra J. (Mrs. Ronald L. Carr), Roger Mark, Timothy Scott. Student, Fresno State U., 1939-42, Stanford U., 1948-50, Prado Mus., Madrid, 1957-59, Ariz. State U., 1960-61; workshops with, Dong Kingman, Ed Whitney, Rex Brandt, Millard Sheets, George Post. Maj. exhbns. include, Guadalajara, Mex., Brussels, N.Y.C., San Francisco, Chgo., Phoenix, Corcoran Gallery Art, Washington, internat. watercolor exhbn., Los Angeles, Bicentennial shows, Hammer Galleries, N.Y.C., spl. exhbn. aboard, S.S. France, others, over 80 paintings in various Am. embassies throughout world; represented in permanent collections, Nat. Collection Fine Arts Mus., Smithsonian Instn.; lectr., juror art shows; condr. workshops.; interviews and broadcasts on Radio Liberty, Voice of Am. Bd. dirs. Phoenix Symphony Assn., 1965-69, Phoenix Musical Theater, 1965-69. Recipient award for spl. achievements Symphony Assn., 1966, 67, 68, 72, spl. awards State of Ariz., silver medal of excellence Internat. Platform Assn., 1971; honoree U.S. Dept. State celebration of 25 yrs. of exhbn. of paintings in embassies worldwide, 1989. Mem. Internat. Platform Assn., Ariz. Watercolor Assn., Nat. Soc. Arts and Letters (nat. dir. 1971-72, nat. art chmn. 1974-76), Nat. Soc. Lit. and Arts, Phoenix Art Mus., Friends of Mexican Art, Am. Artists Profl. League, English-Speaking Union, Musical Theater Guild, Ariz. Costume Inst., Phoenix Art Mus., Scottsdale Art Ctr., Ariz. Arts Commn. (fine arts panel 1990-91), Friends of Art and Preservation in Embassies. Home: 6127 E Calle Del Paisano Scottsdale AZ 85251-4212 *As a romantic impressionist I feel a tremendous exhilaration at being able to communicate my philosophy through my paintings. I look for God's beauty and mystery in all things, and as an artist, I feel very fortunate that I can eliminate the ugliness and the negatives and concentrate on the wonders of the universe around us.*

LANG, MELANIE SUE, physician, oral and maxillofacial surgeon; b. Sacramento, Aug. 31, 1965; AS in Health Sci., Union Coll., 1986; DDS, U. Nebr., 1991; cert., U. Wash., 1992; MD, U. Fla., 1996, cert., 1999. Resident U. Wash., Seattle, 1991-92; rsch. fellow U. Nebr., Lincoln, 1992-93; resident U. Fla., Gainesville, 1993-99, resident in gen. surgery, 1997-98, chief resident, 1998-99; cosmetic fellow U. Ala., Birmingham, 1999-2000. Contbr. articles to profl. jours. including Jour. Oral and Maxillofacial Implants, Jour. Oral and Maxillofacial Surgery, Am. Jour. Cosmetic Surgery. Recipient Ishiyaku EuroAmerican, Inc. book award, 1991. Mem.: ADA, AMA, Am. Assn. Hosp. Dentists, Oral and Maxillfacial Found., Am. Coll. Oral and Maxillfacial Surgeons, Am. Assn. Oral and Maxillfacial Surgeons, Omicron Kappa Upsilon (Dr. William S. Kramer award 1990, Scholastic Performance award 1990—91, Janet M. Glasgow Meml. Achievement citation 1996), Alpha Omega Alpha, Phi Kappa Phi, Fla. U. Med. Alumni Assn. Avocations: animals, antiques, biking, coin collecting, family. Home: 4017 S Best Ct Veradale WA 99037-8228 Office: Spokane Oral & Maxillfacial Surgery 12109 E Broadway Ave Bldg C Spokane WA 99206 E-mail: melslang@aol.com.

LANG, NICHOLAS PAUL, surgeon; b. Jonesboro, Ark., Apr. 11, 1947; s. Paul Alexandra and Lula (Cornish) L.; m. Carol Ann Holl, Aug. 1968 (div. May 1978); 1 child, Christopher; m. Helen Felecia Haley, July 25, 1979; children: Patrick, Courtney. Student, U. Ark., 1969; MD, U. Ark. Med. Scis., 1973. Diplomate Am. Bd. Surgery. Resident in surgery U. Ark. Med. Scis., Little Rock, 1973-77, assoc. prof. surgery, 1977-84, 1984-90, prof. surgery, 1990—; rsch. fellow Nat. Cancer Inst., Bethesda, Md., 1977-79; staff surgeon Little Rock VA Hosp. (now Ctrl. Ark. Vets. Healthcare Sys.), 1979-95, chief of surgery, 1995—2002, chief of staff, 2001—. Contbr. articles to profl. publs. Mem. nat. bd. Am. Cancer Soc., Atlanta, 1989-96; bd. dirs. CARTI, Little Rock, 1994—. Grantee Nat. Cancer Inst., 1995—, EPA, 1996—. Fellow ACS, Southwestern Surg. Congress (councillor 1989-95, pres. 2000-2001); mem. AMA, So. Surg. Assn., Assn. for Surg. Edn. (pres. 2000-2001), Am. Assn. Cancer Rsch. Baptist. Avocations: woodworking, gardening. Home: 1323 White Rd Little Rock AR 72211-4019 Office: Ctrl Ark Vets Healthcare Sys # 11-LR 4300 W 7th St Little Rock AR 72205-5446 E-mail: nick.lang@med.va.gov.

LANG, NORMA M. nursing educator; b. Wausau, Wis., Dec. 27, 1939; BSN, Alverno Coll., 1961; MSN, Marquette U., 1963, PhD, 1974. Staff nurse, asst. instr. St. Joseph's Hosp., 1961-62; instr., coord. med.-surg. nursing St. Mary's Sch. Nursing, 1964-65; from instr. to prof. U. Wis. Sch. Nursing, Milw., 1965—92, dean, 1980—92, U. Pa. Sch. Nursing, Phila., 1992—2000, prof., 1992—. Nursing coord. Wis. Regional Med. Program, 1968-73; rsch. assoc. U. Wis., Milw., 1977, ctr. sci. Urban Rsch. Ctr., 1977-79. Contbr. articles to profl. jours. Recipient Ernest A. Codman Award, 2001. Fellow Am. Acad. Nursing; mem. ANA, NAS, AAUP, APHA, Am. Heart Assn. Office: U Pa Sch Nursing 420 Guardian Dr Philadelphia PA 19104-4210*

LANG, NORTON DAVID, physicist; b. Chgo., July 5, 1940; s. Charles and Sadelle (Bilow) L.; m. Enid Asher, June 8, 1969; children: Eugenie, Aaron. AB summa cum laude, Harvard U., 1962, A.M., 1965, PhD, 1968; postgrad. (Knox fellow), London Sch. Economics, 1962-63. Asst. research physicist, lectr. U. Calif., San Diego, 1967-69; mem. staff IBM Research Center, Yorktown Heights, N.Y., 1969—. Erwin W. Mueller meml. lectr., Pa. State U., 1992. Contbr. articles on theoretical physics to profl. jours.; asso. editor: Phys. Rev. Letters, 1980-83. Fellow N.Y. Acad. Scis., Am. Phys. Soc. (chmn. fellowship com. divsn. condensed matter physics 1985-87, Davisson-Germer prize 1977, chmn. Davisson-Germer Prize com. 1990); mem. Am. Chem. Soc., Phi Beta Kappa. Office: IBM Rsch Ctr Yorktown Heights NY 10598

LANG, OTTO, industry executive, former Canadian cabinet minister; b. Handel, Sask., Can., May 14, 1932; s. Otto T. and Maria (Wurm) L.; m. Adrian Ann Merchant, 1963-88; children: Maria (dec.), Timothy, Gregory, Andrew, Elisabeth, Amanda, Adrian; m. Deborah McCawley, 1989; stepchildren: Andrew, Rebecca. BA, U. Sask., 1951, LLB, 1953; BCL (Rhodes scholar), Oxford (Eng.) U., 1955; LLD (hon.), U. Man., 1987. Bar: Sask. 1956, Ont., Yukon and N.W.T 1972, Man. 1988; created Queen's counsel 1972. Mem. faculty Law Sch., U. Sask., 1956-68, assoc. prof. law, 1958-61, prof., dean law, 1961-68; M.P. for Sask.-Humboldt, 1968-79; Canadian min. without portfolio, 1968-69; min. for energy and water, 1969; min. of manpower and immigration, 1970-72; min. of justice, 1972-75, 78-79; min. transport, 1975-79; min.-in-charge Canadian Wheat Bd., 1969-79; exec. v.p. Pioneer Grain Co. Ltd., James Richardson & Sons Ltd., Winnipeg, Manitoba, Can., 1979-88; chmn. Transp. Inst., U. Man., 1988-93; mng. dir. Winnipeg Airports Authority, Inc., 1992-93; vice chmn., 1993—; pres., CEO Centra Gas Manitoba, Inc., Winnipeg, 1993-99; cons., 1999—; sr. counsel G.P.C., 2000—. Mem. Queen's Privy Coun. for Can.; hon. consul gen. for Japan, 1993-97; bd. dirs. Investors Group Trust Co., London Life Trust Co. Editor: Contemporary Problems in Public Law, 1967. V.P. Sask. Liberal Assn., 1956-62, fed. campaign chmn., Sask., 1963-64; campaign chmn. Winnipeg United Way, 1983; chmn. Royal Winnipeg Ballet Captial Campaign, 1996-99. Decorated officer Order of Can. Mem.: St. Charles Golf Club. Roman Catholic. Office: GPC 6 Liss Rd Saint Andrews MB Canada R1A 2X2 Fax: 204-338-1524. E-mail: olang@mb.sympatico.ca.

LANG, PHILIP DAVID, former state legislator, insurance company executive; b. Portland, Oreg., Dec. 16, 1929; s. Henry W. and Vera (Kern) L.; m. Marcia Jean Smith, May 29, 1952 (div. Oct. 1979); 1 son, Philip David, III; m. Virginia Ann Wolf, Feb. 16, 1980. Student, Lewis and Clark Coll., 1951-53, Northwestern Coll. Law, 1956. Police officer Oreg. Dept. State Police, Salem, 1953-55; claims adjuster Glenns Falls Ins. Co., Portland, 1955-57, Oreg. Automobile Ins. Co., Portland, 1959-61; adminstrv. asst. to mayor City of Portland, 1957-58; spl. agt., underwriter North Pacific Ins. Co., Portland, 1961-63, mgr., 1963-65, asst. v.p., 1965-80, v.p., 1980-95; ret., 1995; asst. v.p. Oreg. Automobile Ins. Co., 1965-80, v.p., 1980-95; ret., 1995; appt. chmn. Oreg. Liquor Control Commn., 1998—. Mem. Oreg. Ho. of Reps., 1960-79, speaker, 1975-79; Div. leader Multnomah County (Oreg.) Democratic Com., 1956-60, precinct com., 1956—. With USAF, 1947-50. Mem. Oreg. Ins. Underwriters Assn., VFW, Masons, DeMolay (Legion Honor), Theta Chi. Roman Catholic. Home: 5769 SW Huddleson St Portland OR 97219-6645 Fax: 503-245-2452. *Success is achieved through commitment to, and perserverance in, all that is undertaken; balanced with tolerance and understanding of all persons.*

LANG, STEPHEN NORMAN, orthopedist, surgeon; b. Kankakee, Ill., Feb. 14, 1941; s. Milton and Libby (Winner) L.; m. Rose Virginia Brown, May 24, 1970; children: Libby, Jason, Adam. Student, U. Ill., 1958-61, MD, 1965. Diplomate Am. Bd. Orthopaedic Surgery. Intern Cook County Hosp., Chgo., 1965-66; resident Duke U. Med. Ctr., Durham, N.C., 1966-71, asst. prof. orthopaedic surgery, 1986—; pvt. practice Kankakee, 1971-72; orthopaedic surgeon Triangle Orthopaedic Assocs., Durham, 1972-86. Mem. Medicolegal Com., Durham, 1994—, co-chmn., 1996—; bd. dirs., chmn. grants aid com. Durham Cerebral Palsy Found., 1990-96. Fellow Am. Acad. Orthop. Surgeons; mem. AMA, Ea. Orthop. Assn. (past historian), N.C. Orthop. Assn., N.C. Med. Soc. Avocations: golf, yard work, needlepoint. Home: 1532 Hermitage Ct Durham NC 27707-1666 Office: Duke Univ Med Ctr PO Box 2919 Durham NC 27710-0001 E-mail: lang0001@mc.duke.edu.

LANG, THOMPSON HUGHES, publishing company executive; b. Albuquerque, Dec. 12, 1946; s. Cornelius Thompson and Margaret Miller (Hughes) L. Student, U. N.Mex., 1965-68, U. Americas, Mexico City, 1968-69. Advt. salesman Albuquerque Pub. Co., 1969-70, pres., 1971—; pub., pres., treas., dir. Jour. Pub. Co., 1971—; pres., dir. Masthead, Internat., 1971—; pres. Magnum Systems, Inc., 1973—; pres., treas., dir. Jour. Ctr. Corp., 1979—; chmn. bd., dir. Starline Printing, Inc., 1985—. Chmn. bd. dirs. Corp. Security and Investigation, Inc., 1986—; pres., bd. dirs. Eagle Systems, Inc., 1986—. Mem. HOW Orgn., Sigma Delta Chi. Home: 8643 Rio Grande Blvd NW Albuquerque NM 87114-1301 Office: Albuquerque Pub Co PO Drawer JT 87103 7777 Jefferson St NE Albuquerque NM 87109-4343

LANG, WILLIAM CHARLES, financial executive; b. Bronx, N.Y., Jan. 29, 1944; s. Harold C. and Katherine L. (Pratt) L.; m. Marilyn Warshow, June 27, 1965 (dec.); children: Kenneth William, Pamela Sue. BS magna cum laude, Lehigh U., 1965. C.P.A. Accounting supr. Peat, Marwick, Mitchell & Co., 1965-69; contr. Pueblo Internat., Inc., N.Y.C., 1970-72, v.p. fin., 1972-77; exec. v.p. adminstrn. and fin. Kenyon & Eckhardt, Inc., 1977-85; exec. mng. dir. Finley, Kumble, Wagner, Heine, Underberg, Manley, Myerson & Casey, 1985-88; pres., CO, Furr's Inc., Lubbock, Tex., 1989-92; exec. v.p. fin. and adminstrn., chief fin. officer Duane Reade, N.Y.C., 1993-96, chief adminstrv. officer, 1993-96; exec. v.p. fin, CFO, CAO GAF Materials Corp., Wayne, N.J., 1997-2001; prof. acctg., law and taxation Montclair (N.J.) State U., 2001—. Mem. AICPA, Fin. Execs. Inst., Nat. Acctg. Soc., N.Y. State Soc. CPAs, Beta Gamma Sigma, Sigma Phi. Office: Montclair State University Montclair NJ 07043-1624

LANG, WILLIAM WARNER, physicist; b. Boston, Aug. 9, 1926; s. William Warner and Lilla Gertrude (Wheeler) L.; m. Asta Ingard, Aug. 31, 1954; 1 son, Robert. BS, Iowa State U., 1946, PhD, 1958; MS, MIT, 1949. Acoustical engr. Bolt Beranek and Newman, Inc., Cambridge, Mass., 1949-51; instr. in physics U.S. Naval Postgrad. Sch., Monterey, Calif., 1951-55; cons. engr. E.I. du Pont de Nemours & Co., Wilmington, Del., 1955-57; mem. research staff MIT, 1958; physicist IBM, Poughkeepsie, N.Y., 1958-92, program mgr. acoustics tech., 1976-90, mem. sr. tech. staff, 1990-92; pres. Internat. Inst. Noise Control Engring., Leuven, Belgium, 1988—99. Editor: Designing for Noise Control, 1978. Pres. Noise Control Found., Poughkeepsie, 1975-92, 1994—; adj. prof. physics Vassar Coll., 1979-96; chmn. working group Internat. Orgn. Standardization, 1969—; chmn. tech. com. 29 Internat. Electrotech. Commn., 1975-84. Served with USN, 1944-47, 52. Decorated Meritorious Service medal; recipient Pro Silentio medal Hungarian Optical, Acoustical and Film Tech. Soc., 1989. Fellow AAAS, IEEE (Audio and Electroacoustics Achievement award 1970, dir. 1970-71, Centennial medal 1984), Audio Engring. Soc., Acoustical Soc. Am. (Silver medal 1984, treas. 1994-98), Inst. Acoustics (U.K.) (hon. fellow); mem. Nat. Acad. Engring., Inst. Noise Control Engring./U.S.A. (pres. 1978), Rotary (pres. local club 1975-76). Episcopalian. Home and Office: 29 Hornbeck Rdg Poughkeepsie NY 12603-4205 E-mail: langww@alum.mit.edu.

LANG, WILLIAM EDWARD, mathematics educator; b. Salisbury, Md., Oct. 22, 1952; s. Woodrow Wilson and Clara T. L. BA, Carleton Coll., 1974; MS, Yale U., 1975; PhD, Harvard U., 1978. Vis. mem. Inst. for Advanced Study, Princeton, N.J., 1978-79; exch. prof. Universite de Paris, Orsay, 1980; C.L.E. Moore instr. MIT, Cambridge, 1980-82; asst. prof. U. Minn., Mpls., 1982-83, assoc. prof., 1983-89; vis. assoc. prof Brigham Young U., Provo, Utah, 1988-89, prof., 1989—. Contbr. articles to profl. jours. Fellow NSF 1974-77, 79-80. Mem. Am. Math. Soc., Math. Assn. Am., Math. Scis. Rsch. Inst., Sigma Xi. Republican. Office: Brigham Young Univ Dept Math Provo UT 84602

LANGACKER, PAUL GEORGE, physics educator; b. Evanston, Ill., July 14, 1946; s. George Rollo and Florence (Hinesley) L.; m. Irmgard Sieker, June 25, 1983. BS, MIT, 1968; PhD, U. Calif., Berkeley, 1972; MA, U. Pa., 1981. Postdoctoral assoc. Rockefeller U., N.Y.C., 1972-74, U. Pa., Phila., 1974-75, asst. prof. physics, 1975-81, assoc. prof. physics, 1981-85, prof. physics, 1985-93, 98—, William Smith Term prof. physics, 1993-98, chair, dept. physics and astronomy, 1996-2001. Exec. com. Divsn. Particles & Fields of Am. Phys. Soc., Washington, 1989-91; mem. editorial bd. Phys. Rev., 1986-88, 91-93; sci. dir. Theoretical Advanced Study Inst., Boulder, Colo., 1990, 98. Editor: Testing the Standard Model, 1991, Precision Tests of the Standard Electroweak Model, 1995; divsnl. assoc. editor Phys. Rev. Letters, 1998--. Recipient Humboldt award A.V. Humboldt Soc., 1987-88. Fellow Am. Phys. Soc., AAAS. Office: U of Pa Dept of Physics 2N10 David Rittenhouse Lab Philadelphia PA 19104 E-mail: pgl@electroweak.hep.upenn.edu.

LANGACKER, RONALD WAYNE, linguistics educator; b. Fond du Lac, Wis., Dec. 27, 1942; s. George Rollo and Florence (Hinesley) L.; m. Margaret G. Fullick, June 5, 1966 (dec.); m. Sheila M. Pickwell, Mar. 28, 1998. AB in French, U. Ill., 1963, A.M. in Linguistics, 1964, PhD, 1966. Asst. prof. U. Calif. at San Diego, La Jolla, 1966-70, asso. prof., 1970-75, prof. linguistics, 1975—. Author: Language and its Structure, 1968, Fundamentals of Linguistic Analysis, 1972, Non-Distinct Arguments in Uto-Aztecan, 1976, An Overview of Uto-Aztecan Grammar, 1977, Foundations of Cognitive Grammar I, 1987, Concept, Image and Symbol, 1990, Foundations of Cognitive Grammar II, 1991, Grammar and Conceptualization, 1999; assoc. editor: Lang, 1971-77, Cognitive Linguistics, 1989—; contbr. articles in field to profl. jours. Guggenheim fellow, 1978 Mem. Linguistic Soc. Am., Cognitive Sci. Soc., Soc. for Study Indigenous Langs. of Ams., Internat. Cognitive Linguistics Assn. (pres. 1997-99), AAUP, ACLU. Home: 7381 Rue Michael La Jolla CA 92037-3915 Office: U Calif San Diego Dept Linguistics 0108 La Jolla CA 92093 E-mail: rlangacker@ucsd.edu.

LANGBAUM, ROBERT WOODROW, English language educator, author; b. N.Y.C., Feb. 23, 1924; s. Murray and Nettie (Moskowitz) L.; m. Francesca Levi Vidale, Nov. 5, 1950; 1 child, Donata Emily. AB, Cornell U., 1947; MA, Columbia U., 1949, PhD, 1954. Instr. English Cornell U., 1950-55, asst. prof., 1955-60; assoc. prof. U. Va., Charlottesville, 1960-63, prof. English, 1963-67, James Branch Cabell prof. English and Am. lit., 1967-99, prof. emeritus, 1999—. Vis. prof. Columbia U., summer 1960, 65-66, Harvard U., summer 1965; mem. supervising com. English Inst., 1970-71, chmn., 1972; mem. Christian Gauss Book Award Com., 1984-86; U.S. Info. Svc. lectr. Japan, Taiwan, Hong Kong, 1988. Author: The Poetry of Experience: The Dramatic Monologue in Modern Literary Tradition, 1957 (Spanish trans. 1996), The Gayety of Vision: A Study of Isak Dinesen's Art (Danish trans. 1964), 1964, The Modern Spirit: Essays on the Continuity of Nineteenth and Twentieth Century Literature, 1970, The Mysteries of Identity: A Theme in Modern Literature, 1977, The Word From Below: Essays on Modern Literature and Culture, 1987, Thomas Hardy in Our Time, 1995; editor: The Tempest (Shakespeare), 1964; anthology The Victorian Age: Essays in History and in Social and Literary Criticism, 1967; mem. editl. bd. Victorian Poetry, 1963—, New Lit. History, 1969—, Bull. Rsch. in Humanities, 1977—, Studies in English Lit., 1978—, So. Humanities Rev., 1979—, Studies in Browning and His Circle, 1987—, Victorian Lit. and Culture, 1991—, Symbiosis, 1995—. Served to 1st lt. M.I. AUS, 1942-46. Ford Found. fellow Center for Advanced Study, Stanford, Calif., 1961-62; Guggenheim fellow, 1969-70, Sr. fellow Nat. Endowment for Humanities, 1972-73; Am. Council Learned Socs. grantee, 1961, 75-76; fellow Clare Hall, Cambridge U., Eng., 1978; U. Va. Ctr. Advanced Study fellow, 1982; resident scholar Bellagio Study and Conf. Ctr. Rockefeller Found., Italy, 1987. Mem. MLA (del. assembly 1979-81), AAUP, PEN, Assn. Lit. Scholars and Critics, Phi Beta Kappa. Home: 223 Montvue Dr Charlottesville VA 22901-2022 E-mail: rwl8v@virginia.edu.

LANGBEIN, JOHN HARRISS, lawyer, educator; b. Washington, Nov. 17, 1941; s. I. L. and M. V. (Harriss) L.; m. Kirsti M. Hiekka, June 24, 1973; children: Christopher, Julia, Anne. AB, Columbia U., 1964; LLB, Harvard U., 1968, Cambridge U., 1969, PhD, 1971; MA (hon.), Yale U., 1990. Bar: D.C. 1969, Fla. 1970; barrister-at-law Inner Temple, Eng., 1970. Asst. prof. law U. Chgo., 1971-73, assoc. prof., 1973-74, prof., 1974-80, Max Pam prof. Am. and fgn. law, 1980-90; Goodhart Prof. Legal Sci. Cambridge Univ., 1997-98, Chancellor Kent prof., 1990—2001; Sterling prof. law and legal history Yale U., New Haven, 2001—. Commr. Nat. Conf. Commrs. on Uniform State Laws, 1984—; reporter Uniform Prudent Investor Act; assoc. reporter Restatement of Property (3d): Wills and Other Donative Transfers. Author: Prosecuting Crime in the Renaissance, 1974, Torture and the Law of Proof: Europe and England in the Ancient Regime, 1977, Comparative Criminal Procedure: Germany, 1977; (with L. Waggoner) Selected Statutes on Trusts and Estates, 1987, rev. edits., 1991, 92, 94, 95, 2001; (with B. WolK) Pension and Employee Benefit Law, 1990, 3d edit., 2000, (with R. Helmholz et al.) The Privilege Against Self-Incrimination, 1997, Origins of Adversary Criminal Trial; contbr. numerous articles on law and legal history in profl. jours. Hon. fellow Trinity Hall Cambridge U.; mem. ABA, Am. Acad. Arts and Scis., Am. Coll. Trust and Estate Counsel, Am. Law Inst., Am. Soc. Legal History, Am. Hist. Assn., Selden Soc., Gesellschaft fuer Rechtsvergleichung, Internat. Acad. Estate and Trust Law, Internat. Acad. Comparative Law. Republican. Episcopalian. Office: Yale Univ Sch Law PO Box 208215 127 Wall St New Haven CT 06520-8215 E-mail: john.langbein@yale.edu.

LANGBERT, MITCHELL BERKE, business educator; b. Forest Hills, N.Y., May 29, 1954; s. Sam and Ruth Langbert; m. Enid Wolfe, May 1984 (div. Nov. 1994); m. Freda Bernstein, Apr., 1996. AB, Sarah Lawrence Coll., 1975; MBA, Coll. of Ins., N.Y.C., 1981, UCLA, 1981; PhD, Columbia U., N.Y.C., 1991. Pension adminstr. Inco Ltd., N.Y.C., 1976-79; pension analyst Johnson & Johnson, New Brunswick, N.J., 1981-84; dir. employee benefits City Fed. Savs. and Loan, piscataway, 1984-86; sr. budget analyst ways and means com. staff N.Y. State Assembly, Albany, 1991; asst. prof. bus. Clarkson U., Potsdam, N.Y., 1991-94, Dowling Coll., Oakdale, 1994-96, Iona Coll., New Rochelle, 1996-98; asst. prof. econs. CUNY, Bklyn., 1998—. Mgmt. cons. various orgns., N.Y.C., 1994—; adj. prof. NYU, 1996—. Author: Wellness Programs in Taft Hartley Funds, 1992; contbr. articles to profl. publs. Dem. campaign asst. Bellamy for Comptr., N.Y.C., 1990, Green for Pub. Adv., N.Y.C., 1996-97; campaign vol. Bloomberg for Mayor, 2001. Mem. ASTD, Inst. Mgmt. Cons., Nat. Assn. Scholars, Soc. for Advancement of Socioecons., Assn. Evolutionary Econs., Ind. Rsch. Assn., N.Am. Case Rsch. Assn. Jewish. Office: CUNY 140 Riverside Dr # 16K New York NY 10024-2605 E-mail: Langbert@brooklyn.cuny.edu., mflangbert@aol.com.

LANGBORT, POLLY, retired advertising executive; b. N.Y.C. d. Julius and Nettie (Berman) L. BA, Adelphi U. Sec. Young & Rubicam, Inc., N.Y.C., media buyer, media planner, 1960-65, planning supr., 1965-70, v.p. group supr., 1970-75, v.p., dir. planning devel., 1975-80, sr. v.p., dir. planning, 1980-85, sr. v.p. direct mktg. and media services Wunderman, Worldwide div., 1985-86, exec. v.p. dir. mktg. & media services, 1986-90; assoc. pub. Lear's Mag., 1990-91; ret., 1991. Author: DMA Factbook, 1986; contbr. articles to profl. jours. Spl. gifts chairperson Am. Cancer Soc., N.Y.C., 1985-90. Mem. Boca Raton Resort and Club, Boca Pointe Country Club. Avocations: classical music, outdoor activities. Home: 7614 La Corniche Cir Boca Raton FL 33433-6055 E-mail: pollylang@aol.com.

LANGDALE, EMORY LAWRENCE, physician; b. Walterboro, S.C., Oct. 14, 1919; s. Clint May and Lillian Blanch (Reddish) L.; m. Maggie Lee Herndon (dec. 1971); children: Fred Emory, Betty Marlene, Thomas Wayne, Emory Lawrence, Jr.; m. Annie Newell Smith, Feb. 17, 1973. BS, Coll. Charleston, 1949; MD, Med. U. S.C., 1953. Diplomate Am. Acad. Physical Medicine and Rehab. Resident VA Hosp., Richmond, Va., 1963-66; chief rehab. medicine VA Med. Ctr., Hampton, 1966-69; asst. prof. physical medicine and rehab. Med. Coll. Va., Richmond, 1969-74; med. officer Charleston (S.C.) Regional Naval Hosp., 1974-76; chief rehab. medicine VA Med. Ctr., Augusta, Ga., 1974-81; assoc. prof. Med. U. S.C., 1981-85; med. dir. Rehab. Svc. Colleton Rsch. Hosp., Walterboro, S.C., 1987-91; private practice No. Charleston, 1989—. With Coast Guard, 1942-45, ATO, PTO. Fellow Am. Acad. Physical Medicine and Rehab.; mem. AMA (physician's recognition award 1980), Med. Soc. Va., S.C. Med. Assn., So. Soc. Physical Medicine and Rehab., Charleston County Med. Soc. Republican. Baptist. Avocations: hunting, fishing. Home: 1064 Stonehenge Dr Charleston SC 29406-2417 Office: 1250 Remount Rd Charleston SC 29406-3419

LANGDALE, GEORGE WILFRED, soil scientist, researcher; b. Walterboro, S.C., Sept. 14, 1930; s. Benjamin Hayward and Hazel Ruth (Smith) L.; m. Eugenia Miles Boatwright, Aug. 28, 1955. BS, Clemson U., 1957, MS, 1961; PhD, U. Ga., 1969. Rsch. soil scientist USDA, Agrl. Rsch. Svc., S.C., Ga., Tex., 1957-96; ret., 1996. Conservation tillage and soil erosion. Contbr. chpts. to books and articles to profl. jours. With 27th inf. U.S. Army, 1952-53, Korea. Kellogg fellow Agr. Policy Inst., 1963-64, Melvin Jones fellow Lions Internat., 1998. Fellow Soil and Water Conservation Soc. (chpt. pres. Tex. 1970-71, Ga. 1994-95, H.H. Bennett award 1993), Am. Soc. Agronomy (pres. Ga. chpt. 1986-87), Soil Sci. Soc. Am.; mem. World Assn. Soil and Water Conservation, Internat. Soil Sci. Soc., Sigma Xi. Baptist. Avocations: conservation gardening, small game hunting, genealogy. Home: 125 Orchard Knob Ln Athens GA 30605-3427

LANGDALE, NOAH NOEL, JR. research educator, former university president; b. Valdosta, Ga., Mar. 29, 1920; s. Noah N. and Jessie Katharine (Catledge) L.; m. Alice Elizabeth Cabaniss, Jan. 8, 1944; 1 son, Noah Michael. AB, U. Ala., 1941; LLB, Harvard U., 1948, MBA, 1950; LLD, U. Ala., 1959. Bar: Ga. bar 1951. Asst. football coach U. Ala., 1942; practiced law Valdosta, 1951-57; instr., then asst. prof. econs. and social studies, chmn. dept. accounting, econs., bus. adminstrn. Valdosta State Coll., 1954-57; pres. Ga. State U., Atlanta, 1957-88, Disting. univ. rsch. prof., 1988-89, ret., 1989, pres. emeritus, disting. rsch. prof. emeritus, 1989—. Dir. Guardian Life Ins. Co. Am.; past mem. U.S. Adv. Commn. Ednl. Exchange; former mem. Pres.'s Commn. NCAA. Served to lt. (s.g.) USNR, 1942-46. Recipient 1st Georgian of Year award Ga. Assn. Broadcasters, 1962; Silver Anniversary All-Am. award Sports Illustrated, 1966; Mrytle Wreath award Hadassah, 1970; Salesman of Yr. award Sales and Mktg. Execs. of Atlanta, 1975; Silver Knight of Mgmt. award Lockheed-Ga. chpt. Nat. Mgmt. Assn., 1978; Humanitarian award Nat. Jewish Hosp. and Research Center/Nat. Asthma Center, 1980, Robert T. Jones award Boy Scouts Am. Mem. ABA, Ga. Bar Assn., Ga. Bar Found. (life), Ga. Assn. Colls. (pres. 1962-63), SAR (past v.p. Ga.), Gridiron Soc., Rotary, Phi Beta Kappa, Omicron Delta Kappa, Delta Chi, Phi Kappa Phi. Methodist. Office: Library North Ga State University Atlanta GA 30303

LANGDON, FRANK CORRISTON, political science educator, researcher; b. LaGrange, Ill., June 3, 1919; s. Ernest Warren and Julia Ida (Mondeng) L.; m. Virginia Irene Osborne, Nov. 11, 1922; children: Peter John, Marc Christopher. AB, Harvard U., 1941, A.M., 1949; PhD, U. Calif.-Berkeley, 1953. Japanese Lang. Sch. intelligence officer U.S. Navy, Stillwater, Okla., 1945-46; econ. analyst Hdqrs. SCAP, Fgn. Trade div., Tokyo, 1946-47; instr. polit. sci. U. Calif. Far East Program, Korea, Japan, Guam, 1953-55; sr. lectr. Canberra U. Coll., Australia, 1955-58; prof. polit. sci. Univ. B.C., Vancouver, 1958-84, emeritus prof., 1984—, sr. research assoc. Inst. Internat. Rels., 1984—. Author: Politics in Japan, 1967, Japan's Foreign Policy, 1973, Politics of Canadian-Japanese Economic Relations, 1952-83, 83; co-editor, co-author: Japan in the Post Hegomonic World, 1993; co-editor, contbr.: Superpower Maritime Strategy in the Pacific, 1990; contbr. articles to profl. jours. Served to lt. comdr. USNR, 1941-45. Mem. Internat. House Japan, Internat. Studies Assn., Can. Consortium on Asia Pacific Security, Vancouver Mokuyokai Soc., Japan Studies Assn. of Can. Clubs: Mokuyokai (Vancouver). Democrat. Presbyterian. Home: 4736 W 4th Ave Vancouver BC Canada V6T 1C2 Office: U BC Dept Pol Sci Buchanan C472 1866 Main Mal Vancouver BC Canada V6T 1Z1

LANGDON, HERSCHEL GARRETT, lawyer, director; b. Lowry City, Mo., Oct. 6, 1905; s. Isaac Garrett and Della (Park) L.; m. Ethel Virginia Waterson, May 26, 1931 (dec. Apr. 1979); children: Richard G., Ann Virginia (Mrs. Charles Eugene Willoughby Ward); m. Miriam Pickett, May 17, 1982. BA, U. Iowa, 1930, JD, 1931. Bar: Iowa 1931. Atty. Herrick, Langdon & Langdon (and predecessors), 1935—. Fellow Am. Coll. Trial Lawyers, Am. Bar Found.; mem. Am., Iowa, Polk County bar assns., Phi Beta Kappa, Delta Sigma Rho, Phi Delta Pi. Congressionalist. Club: Mason. Office: 1800 Financial Ctr 7th and Walnut Des Moines IA 50309 Home: 612 Glenview Dr Des Moines IA 50312-2528

LANGDON, ROBERT COLIN, dermatologist, educator; b. Medford, Oreg., Oct. 29, 1954; s. Hector and Marian Louise (Green) L.; m. Beva Ann Nall, July 22, 1979. BS in Biology with honors, U. Oreg., 1976, MD, 1980. Diplomate Am. Bd. Dermatology. Intern in internal medicine Good Samaritan Hosp., Portland, Oreg., 1980-81; postdoctoral fellow in dermatology Sch. Medicine Yale U., New Haven, 1981-82, instr. in dermatology, 1984-85, asst. prof. dermatology, 1985-90, clin. asst. prof. dermatology, 1993—; resident in dermatology Yale-New Haven Hosp., 1982-84, attending physician, 1984-90, 93—; pvt. practice dermatology Westport, Conn., 1984-86, Arcadia and Covina, Calif., 1990-91, Cerritos and Glendale, 1991-92, Madison, Conn., 1992—. Attending physician West Haven (Conn.) VA Med. Ctr., 1992—, Intercommunity Med. Ctr., Covina, 1990-92, Pioneer Hosp., Artesia, Calif., 1991—; founder, moderator of DERM-L, Yale U., 1994—. Reviewer Jour. Investigative Dermatology, 1986—, Jour. Am. Acad. Dermatology, 1988—, Archives of Dermatology, 1989—, Jour. Clin. Investigation, 1989—, Dermatologic Surgery, 1999—; assoc. editor Dermatology Online Jour., U. Calif., Davis, 1995—; contbr. articles to profl. publs. Maulding scholar, 1979. Fellow Am. Acad. Cosmetic Surgery; mem. AAAS, Am. Soc. Dermatologic Surgery, Am. Soc. Laser Medicine and Surgery, Am. Acad. Dermatology, Conn. State Med. Soc., Am. Soc. Liposuction Surgery, Internat. Soc. Cosmetic Laser Surgeons, New Haven County Med. Assn., Phi Beta Kappa. Home: 324 Blake Cir Hamden CT 06517-3300 Office: Shoreline Dermatology 5 Durham Rd Guilford CT 06437 E-mail: rlangdon@cosmeticlaser.com.

LANGE, C. WILLIAM, lawyer, educator; b. St. Louis, June 15, 1946; s. Carl W. and Marion M. (Guenther) L.; m. Catherine L. Janowiak, June 7, 1981; children: Courtney Anne, Carl William IV. BA, Westminster Coll., 1968; MBA, St. Louis U., 1972; JD, Oklahoma City U., 1974. Bar: Mo. 1975, U.S. Dist. Ct. Mo. 1975, U.S. Ct. Appeals (8th cir.) 1986. With claims dept. MFA Ins. Cos., Columbia, Mo., 1968-71; ptnr. Lange & Lange, Cuba, 1976-81; pvt. practice, 1981-88; ptnr. Lange & Lange, 1989—. Pros. atty. Crawford County (Mo.), 1979-80; city atty. City of Cuba, 1978-80, 82-88; prof. mgmt. Maryville U., St. Louis, 1974—; instr. East Central Coll., Union, Mo., 1975. Mem. Crawford County Child Welfare Adv. Com., 1979-88, pres. 1984-86; mem. Crawford County Child Abuse and Neglect Team, 1981-90; treas. Sixteenth Senatorial Dist. Rep. Com., 1993-94. Served with Air N.G., 1967-74. Mem. ABA, Mo. Bar Assn., 42d Jud. Cir. Bar Assn., St. Louis Met. Bar Assn., Cuba C. of C. Lodges: Optimists. Presbyterian. Home: PO Box 88 Cuba MO 65453-0088 Office: Lange and Lange Attys PO Box 280 Cuba MO 65453-0280 E-mail: langelaw@fidnet.com.

LANGE, CARL JAMES, psychology educator; b. Seneca, Pa., June 1, 1925; s. Otto Carl and Rose Marie (Jetter) L.; m. Veronica Szelypecz, Jan. 14, 1950; children: David Carl, Veronica Jean. BS, Duke U., 1945; MS, U. Pitts., 1948, PhD, 1951. Lic. psychologist, Va. Project dir. Human Resources Research Office, George Washington U., 1953-60, dir. research, planning, 1960-69; asst. v.p. research George Washington U., 1969-75, v.p. adminstrn., research, prof. psychology, 1975-88, v.p. rsch., prof. psychology, 1988-89, prof. emeritus, 1989—. Cons. NSF, Ford Found.; bd. dirs. Sch. for Contemporary Edn., Nat. Lab. Higher Edn., Eric Clearinghouse for Higher Edn., Southeastern Univs. Rsch. Assn. Contbr. articles in field to profl. jours.; bd. editors: Research in Higher Education. Served with USN, 1943-45. Fellow Am. Psychol. Assn.; mem. AAAS, Sigma Xi. Home: 7 Clarendon Ct Williamsburg VA 23188-1513 E-mail: cjlange@widowmaker.com.

LANGE, CHRISTOPHER FREDERICK, management consultant; b. Buffalo, Jan. 17, 1963; s. Robert John and Kiulani Susan (Hume) L. BS in Internat. Mktg., Miami U., Oxford, Ohio, 1985. Account exec. Consol. Freightways, Inc., Virginia Beach, Va., 1985-86; pres. Transp. Cons., Inc., 1986-91, Lange Truck Lines, Virginia Beach, 1988-91; v.p. sales and mktg. Givens, Inc., Chesapeake, Va., 1991-92; cons. Andersen Cons., Cleve., 1992—. Mem. Coun. Logistics Mgmt., Am. Prodn. and Inventory Control Soc., Am. Soc. Transp. and Logistics. Episcopalian. Avocations: snow skiing, ice hockey, tennis, cycling.

LANGE, CLIFFORD E. librarian; b. Fond du Lac, Wis., Dec. 29, 1935; s. Elmer H. and Dorothy Brick (Smithers) L.; m. Janet M. LeMieux, June 6, 1959; children: Paul, Laura, Ruth. Student, St. Norbert Coll., 1954-57; BS, Wis. State U., 1959; MSL.S. (Library Services Act scholar), U. Wis., 1960, PhD (Higher Edn. Act fellow), 1972. Head extension dept. Oshkosh (Wis.) Public Library, 1960-62, head reference dept., 1962-63; asst. dir. Jervis Library, Rome, 1962; dir. Eau Claire (Wis.) Public Library, 1963-66; asst. dir. Lake County Public Library, Griffith, Ind., 1966-68; asst. prof. Sch. Library Sci., U. Iowa, 1971-73; dir. Wauwatosa (Wis.) Public Library, 1973-75; asst. prof. U. So. Calif., 1975-78; state librarian N.Mex. State Library, Santa Fe, 1978-82; dir. Carlsbad City Library, Calif., 1982—. Served with U.S. Army, 1958. Mem. ALA, Calif. Libr. Assn. Home: 3575 Ridge Rd Oceanside CA 92056-4952 Office: 1775 Dove Ln Carlsbad CA 92009-4048 E-mail: clang@ci.carlsbad.ca.us.

LANGE, DAVID CHARLES, journalist; b. Natrona Hts., Pa., Oct. 14, 1949; s. Charles Manfred Lange and Helga (Hingst) Faverty; m. Linda Gaiduk, June 29, 1974; children: Erik David, Anthony Charles. BA in Journalism, Kent State U., 1975; postgrad., Akron U., 1980-83. Placement specialist Goodwill Industries Cleve., 1976-77; mng. editor, sports editor Chagrin Valley Times, Chagrin Falls, Ohio, 1977-82; editor Chagrin Valley Times/Solon Times, 1988—; features editor, Sunday editor Lake County Telegraph, Painesville, Ohio, 1982-83; editor Geauga Times Leader, Chardon, 1983-84; editor-in-chief Habitat, Cleve., 1984-88. Asst. swim coach Lake Erie Silver Dolphins/Kenston H.S., 1999—. With USN, 1968-71, Vietnam. Recipient Democracy in Housing award Cleve. Assn. Real Estate Brokers, 1988. Mem. Soc. Profl. Journalists (Excellence in Journalism award human interest reporting 1981, Best Columnist in Ohio 2000), Ohio Newspaper Assn. (Hooper award for editl. writing 1991-92, 94, 96-2002, 2d place 1990, 93, Hooper award for column writing 1993, 97, 2001-02), Chagrin Valley C. of C., Solon C. of C., Cleve. Press Club, Nat. Newspaper Assn., VFW, Am. Legion, Vietnam Vets. Am. Avocations: swimming, skiing, tennis, basketball. Home: 8353 Chagrin Rd Chagrin Falls OH 44023-4757 Office: Chagrin Valley Times PO Box 150 Chagrin Falls OH 44022-0150

LANGE, FREDERICK EDWARD, JR. computer information systems architect; b. Johnstown, Pa., Oct. 21, 1946; s. Frederick Edward and Jean Louise (Huebner) L.; m. Karen Ann Mawson, Mar. 15, 1975; 1 child, Sharon Ann. BA in Social Scis., Cleve. State U., 1969, MA in Econs., 1978. Cert. secondary tchr., Ohio. Vol. Peace Corps, Liberia and Micronesia, 1969-73; tchr. Cleve. Pub. Schs., 1973-74; dir. Westside Inst. Tech., Cleve., 1974-81; systems analyst Case Western Res. U., 1982-83; systems engr. Profl. Support, Inc., Brecksville, 1983-91; analyst Setpoint, 1991-93; prin. cons. Cap Gemini Am., Beechwood, Ohio, 1994-96; sr. prin. cons. Oracle Corp., Cleve., 1996-2000; sr. analyst Nat. City Corp., Highland Hills, 2001—. Bd. dirs. Zoe, Inc., Cleve., Fast Refund Svc. Editor: Fuel Efficiency and Safety, 1979; contbr. Data Mgmt. Rev. Mem. Richmond Heights (Ohio) Civic League, 1986, Northeast Ohio Returned Vol. Assn. (Beyond War award 1987), Cleve., 1978—, Nat. Peace Corps Assn. Mem. Am. Econs. Assn., Data Processing Mgmt. Assn., Assn. Computing Machinery, Instument Soc. Am. (Dedicated Svc. award 1980), Javelin Class Assn. (fleet capt. 1982-83, sec. 1987-88, commodore 1989-91), Forest City Yacht Club. Avocations: sailing, gardening, genealogy. Office: Nat City Corp 23000 Mill Creek Blvd Highland Hills OH 44122 E-mail: lange@acm.org.

LANGE, KATHERINE J. writer; b. Wyandotte, Mich., Feb. 8, 1957; d. James DiDi and Margaret Ann (Kirk) Putman. Student, Normandale Coll., 1980-82. V.p., artist mgr. T.S.J. Prodns., Richfield, Minn., 1975-99; v.p. T.S.J. Literary Agy., 1973-96; mgr., agt. The T.S.J. Booking Agy., 1980-96; asst. editor, author Songwriter U.S.A. mag., Atlanta, 1986-87; staff writer Music Mgmt. and Internat. Promotion mag., Copenhagen, 1983—; pres. Katherine's Greetings, 1994—, Internat. Literary Concepts, Mpls., 1996—. Contbr. articles to Sun Newspapers, Songwriter Connection, Woman's Press. Mem. ASCAP, NAFE, Am. Fedn. Musicians. Democrat. Lutheran. Avocations: building model ships, painting. Home and Office: Internat Literary Concepts 422 Pierce St NE Minneapolis MN 55413-2514

LANGE, LESTER HENRY, mathematics educator; b. Concordia, Mo., Jan. 2, 1924; s. Harry William Christopher and Ella Martha (Alewel) L.; m. Anne Marie Pelikan, Aug. 17, 1947 (div. Oct. 1960); children: Christopher, Nicholas, Philip, Alexander; m. Beverly Jane Brown, Feb. 4, 1962; 1 son, Andrew. Student, U. Calif., Berkeley, 1943-44; BA in Math, Valparaiso U., 1948; MS in Math, Stanford, 1950; PhD in Math, U. Notre Dame, 1960. Instr., then asst. prof. math. Valparaiso U., 1950-56; instr. math. U. Notre Dame, 1956-57, 59-60. Mem. faculty San Jose State U., Calif., 1960—, prof. math., head dept., 1961-70, dean Sch. Natural Scis. and Math., 1970—, dean Sch. Sci., 1972-88, emeritus prof. math., emeritus dean, 1988—; founder Soc. Archimedes at San Jose State U., 1982; now spl. asst. to dir. Moss Landing (Calif.) Marine Labs.; founding bd. dirs. Friends of MLML, Inc. Author text on linear algebra; sr. editor Calif. Math, 1981-84; contbr. to profl. jours. Served with inf. AUS, 1943-46, ETO. Decorated Combat Infantryman's Badge and Bronze Star; Danforth fellow, 1957-58; NSF faculty fellow, 1958-59. Fellow Calif. Acad. Scis.; mem. Math. Assn. Am. (bd. govs., L.R. Ford Sr. award 1972, George Polya award 1993), Calif. Math. Coun., London Math. Soc., Fibonacci Assn. (bd. dirs. 1987-97), Nat. Coun. Tchrs. Home: 308 Escalona Dr Capitola CA 95010-3419 Office: Moss Landing Marine Labs Moss Landing CA 95039 E-mail: lange@cruzio.com.

LANGE, LINDA DIANE, education educator, researcher; b. Muskegon, Mich., Jan. 28, 1950; AB in Edn., U. Mich., 1974, EdS in Edn. and Psychology, 1978, PhD in Edn., 1991. Cert. sch. psychologist, N.J. Dance coach Huron (Mich.) H.S., 1974-75; sch. psychologist Lenawee County Schs., Adrian, Mich., 1979-80; rsch. asst. The Psychol. Corp., San Antonio, 1986-88; asst. prof. edn. Marshall U., Huntington, W.Va., 1991-95. Vis. asst. prof. edn. Sacred Heart U. Fairfield, Conn., 1995-96; ednl. rschr. Collaborative Rsch. Bd. Marshall U., 1992-93; presenter in field. Contbr. articles to profl. jours. Mem. ASCD, APA, Am. Assn. Tchg. and Curriculum, Am. Ednl. Rsch. Assn., Assn. Tchr. Educators, Ea. Ednl. Rsch. Assn., Soc. Rsch. on Adolescence, Soc. for Study of Social Problems, Southeastern Assn. Ednl. Studies, New England Edn. Rsch. Orgn. Lutheran. Avocations: dance, music, art, water sports, skiing. Address: PO Box 416 Bridgeport CT 06601-0416

LANGE, PHIL C. retired education educator; b. North Freedom, Wis., Feb. 26, 1914; s. Richard Samuel and Martha (Grosinske) L.; m. Irene Oyen, June 8, 1940; children— Dena Rae, Richard (dec.). BA, U. Wis., 1934, MA, 1936, PhD, 1941. Tchr. Reeseville (Wis.) Pub. Sch., 1935-37; chmn. English dept. Wayland Jr. Coll. and Acad., Beaver Dam, Wis., 1937-39; instr. English, student teaching supr. Beloit (Wis.) High Sch., 1939-40; asst. instr. U. Wis., Madison, 1940-41, summers 1938, 39; chmn. psychology dept., dean men. Ariz. State Coll., Flagstaff, 1941-42; chmn. edn. dept. SUNY, Fredonia, 1942-50; prof. edn., coordinator student teaching Tchrs. Coll., Columbia U., 1950—. Cons., expert for Dept. State, UNESCO, AID. Author, editor curriculum materials; photographer, columnist Sun City Ctr. News. Coord. Issues and Ideas program Cmty. Ch. Coll. Served with USNR, 1943-46. Recipient Filmstrip award Graphic Arts, 1966; Communication award Nat. Soc. Programmed Instrn., 1968; award Ednl. Press Assn. Am., 1969 Home: Lake Towers Apt 764 101 Trinity Lakes Dr Sun City Center FL 33573-5755 Office: Tchrs Coll Columbia Univ New York NY 10027

LANGE, RICHARD A. medical educator; b. Anchorage, Mar. 1, 1956; s. Richard and Joyce Lange; m. Joy Bobette George; children: David Michael, Jonathan Ryan, Brian Patrick. BS, North Tex. State U., 1978; MD, U. Tex. Southwestern Med. Ctr., 1982. Diplomate Am. Bd. Internal Medicine, Am. Bd. Cardiovascular Disease. Resident Johns Hopkins Hosp., Balt., 1982-85; fellowship U. Tex. Southwestern Med. Ctr., Dallas, 1985-88; assoc. dir. cardiac catherization lab. Parkland Meml. Hosp., 1988-91, dir. cardiac catheterization lab., 1991—, dir. cardiac pacemaker svc., 1991-92; assoc. prof. internal medicine U. Tex. Southwestern Med. Sch., 1992-99, co-dir. adult congential heart disease clinic, 1993—, prof. internal medicine, 1999—; dir. fellowship tng. program. Jonsson-Rogers chair in cardiology, 1994—. Recipient Merit award Am. Heart Assn., 1998, Outstanding Tchr. award, 1999; tng. fellowship NIH, 1986-87, fellowship Chilton Found., 1979. Mem. Alpha Omega Alpha. Office: UT Southwestern Med Ctr 5323 Harry Hines Blvd Rm CS7 102 Dallas TX 75390-7200

LANGE, RICHARD ALAN, music educator; b. Missoula, Mont., May 8, 1956; s. Henry Joseph and Margaret Lange; m. Kim Lange, June 18, 1983. MusB, Coll. Notre Dame, 1978; MFA, U. Minn., 1983, DMA, 1992. Instr. Schmitt Music, Mpls., 1980—85, Crown Coll., St. Bonifacious, 1983—89; tchg. asst. U. Minn., Mpls., 1981—89; prof. Northwestern Coll., St. Paul, 1989—. Mem.: St. Paul Piano Tchrs. Assn., Minn. Music Tchrs. Assn. Avocations: basketball, swimming, crossword puzzles. Home: 3249 Adair Ave N Crystal MN 55422 Office: Northwestern Coll 3003 Snelling Ave N Saint Paul MN 55113

LANGE, RON Q. music educator; b. Waco, Tex., July 18, 1955; s. Leo Clarence and Ouida Joy Lange; m. Sharolyn K. Adams, Sept. 19, 1961; children: Casey, Samantha. B in Music Edn., U. Tex., El Paso, 1979. Tchg. cert. Alaska, Tex. Choral dir. Grand Prairie (Tex.) H.S., 1985—91, Plainview (Tex.) H.S., 1992—94, Chugiak H.S., Eagle River, Alaska, 1995—. Mem. music curriculum com. Anchorage Sch. Dist., 1999—2002; member music book adoption com. Ysleta Ind. Sch. Dist., El Paso, 1981—82; choral dir. First Presbyn. Ch., Anchorage, 2000—02, Joy Luth., Eagle River, 1994—96; commr. Arts Adv. Commn., Anchorage, 2000—02. Named Alaska Tchr. of the Year 1st Alt., Dept. Edn. State of Alaksa, 2001, Tchr. of Excellence, British Petroleum, 1999; recipient CREATE award, Municipality of Anchorage, 1998. Mem.: NEA, Am. Choral Dirs. Assn., Music Educators Nat. Conf., Anchorage Educators Assn., Alaska Choral Dirs. Assn. (president elect 2002—), Alaska Music Educators Assn. (region rep. 2000—02). Home: 17470 Beaujolais Cr Eagle River AK 99577 Office: Chugiak HS S Birchwood Exit Eagle River AK 99577 Office Fax: 907-742-3050. Personal E-mail: lange@gci.net.

LANGE, SCOTT LESLIE, communications company executive, voice professional; b. Chgo., July 10, 1946; s. Harry W. and Evelyn (Udell) L.; m. Linda A. Shoenthal, Mar. 30, 1969; 1 child, Stephen H. BS in Speech, Northwestern U., 1968. Prodn. mgr., announcer WCOG Radio, Greensboro, N.C., 1971-72; writer, producer, dir. ARC, Washington, 1973-78; mgr. audio-visual services Am. Bankers Assn., 1978-79; writer, producer, dir. AT&T Comm., 1979-82, Cin., 1982-84; pres. Lange Comm., Inc., 1984—. Writer, producer, dir. numerous films, videotapes, radio and TV pub. service announcements, slide programs. Served with U.S. Army, 1968-71, Vietnam. Recipient Cert. Outstanding Creativity, U.S. TV Commls. Festival, 1973, 75, Gold Quill of Excellence award Internat. Assn. Bus. Communicators, 1981. Mem. AFTRA, Internat. TV Assn. (pres. D.C. chpt. 1981, Golden Reel of Merit award 1978, Golden Reel of Excellence award 1980), Soc. Motion Picture and TV Engrs. Jewish. Avocations: film and video collector, music enthusiast. Home and Office: Lange Comm Inc 6315 Turpin Hills Dr Cincinnati OH 45244-3560 E-mail: scottlange@worldnet.att.net.

LANGE, TIMOTHY J. priest; b. Crofton, Nebr., July 12, 1933; s. Joseph and Cecilia (Schrempp) Lange. BA in Philosophy, Conception (Mo.) Sem., 1957; BA in Theology, Mt. St. Bernard Sem., Dubuque, Iowa, 1961; MDiv, Creighton U., 1978. Assoc. pastor Archdiocese Omaha, 1961—71; pastor St. Peter & Paul, Butte, 1971—76, St. Rose, Crofton, 1976—86, St. Peter, Stanton, 1986—. Roman Catholic. Avocations: music teaching, playing piano, organ, saxophone. Home: 1509 Ivy Stanton NE 68779 Office: Saint Peters Ch PO Box 557 Stanton NE 68779 Office Fax: 402-439-2149.

LANGE, WILLIAM MICHAEL, lawyer; b. Hammond, Ind., Oct. 9, 1946; s. William Frederick L.; m. Nancy A. White, 1 child, William Robert. BA, Ind. U., 1968; JD, George Washington U., 1974. Bar: D.C. 1975, Colo. 1977, U.S. Ct. Appeals (D.C. cir.) 1975, U.S. Ct. Appeals (10th cir.) 1977, U.S. Ct. Appeals (5th cir.) 1984, U.S. Supreme Ct. 1982, U.S. Ct. Appeals (3d cir.) 1988, U.S. Ct. Appeals (7th cir.) 1989, U.S. Ct. Appeals (6th cir.) 1989, U.S. Ct. Appeals (2d cir.) 1997. Assoc. Wolf & Case, Washington, 1974-75, J.R. Wolf, Washington, 1975-76; atty. Colo. Interstate Gas Co., Colorado Springs, 1976-79, sr. atty., 1979-82, gen. atty., 1982-84, asst. gen. counsel, 1984-87, The Coastal Corp., 1985—87; assoc. gen. counsel ANR Pipeline Co., 1986-87; atty. private practice, 1987; asst. gen. counsel Consumers Energy Co.; gen. coun. Mich. Gas Storage Co., 1987—; asst. gen. coun. CMS Enterprises, 2001—. Lt. (j.g.) USN, 1968-71, Vietnam. Independent. Episcopalian.

LANGE-CONNELLY, PHYLLIS, musician, music educator; b. Elgin, Ill., Oct. 14, 1935; d. William Carl and Freide Ricka Helena (Reimer) Werneke; children: Catherine Mary Gathman, Debra, Mark William. AA, Elgin (Ill.) C.C., 1985; BA, Nat. Lewis U., 1988; MM, No. Ill. U., 1995. Dir. music, organist Bethlehem Luth. Ch., Dundee, Ill., 1961-79, St. John's Luth. Ch., Algonquin, 1979-89, Trinity Luth. Ch., Huntley, 1990-92, St. Paul U.C.C. Ch., Barrington, 1992-94, St. James Episcopal Ch., Dundee, 1994—; assoc. organist, handbell dir. Holy Trinity Luth. Ch., Elgin, 1995-98; dir. worship and music, 1998-99. Para-profl. tutor Sch. Dist. 300, Dundee, Ill., 1979-85; music educator; mem. AGO del. to Ea. Europe through People-to-People Internat., 1998. Mem. United Way Dundee Twp., 1999, Dundee Main St. Orgn. Mem. Am. Guild Organists (dean N.W. chpt. 1999, Fox Valley chpt.), Am. Guild English Handbell Ringers, Music Tchrs. Nat. Assn., Elgin Choral Union (mem. edn./outreach com. 1999), Pi Kappa Lambda Music Soc. Democrat. Episcopalian. Avocations: reading, golf. Home: 4154 Whatehall Ln Algonquin IL 60102

LANGELOH, JEAN KLEPPINGER, interior designer; b. Allentown, Pa., Aug. 2, 1921; d. Samuel Adam Kleppinger and Elsie May Herman; m. Robert H. Langeloh, Feb. 7, 1959 (div. 1986); children: Geoffrey Robert (dec.), Gail Elizabeth. BS in Art Edn., Skidmore Coll., 1943; postgrad., Columbia U.,

1945-46, N.Y. Sch. Interior Design, 1945-46. Interior designer James McCreary, N.Y.C., 1946-47; showroom, sales staff Katzenbach & Warren, 1947-48; owner, interior designer, cons. Jean K. Langeloh Interiors, Beals Island, Maine, 1950—. Interior design instr. YWCA, Greenwich, Conn., 1975-86; owner Island Wreaths, Beals Island, Maine, 1998—. Mem. Am. Soc. Interior Designers (assoc. New England chpt.). Republican. Lutheran. Avocations: reading, gardening, traveling, volunteer work.

LANGENBERG, DONALD NEWTON, retired academic administrator, physicist; b. Devils Lake, N.D., Mar. 17, 1932; s. Ernest George and Fern (Newton) L.; m. Patricia Ann Warrington, June 20, 1953; children: Karen Kaye, Julia Ann, John Newton, Amy Paris. BS, Iowa State U., 1953; MS, UCLA, 1955; PhD (NSF fellow), U. Calif. at Berkeley, 1959; D.Sc. (hon.), U. Pa., 1985, MA (hon.), 1971. Electronics engr. Hughes Research Labs., Culver City, Calif., 1953-55; acting instr. U. Calif. at Berkeley, 1958-59; mem. faculty U. Pa., Phila., 1960-83, prof., 1967-83; dir. Lab. for Research on Structure of Matter, 1972-74; vice provost for grad. studies and research, 1974-79; chancellor U. Ill.-Chgo., 1983-90, U. Md. System, Adelphi, 1990—2002. Maitre de conference associe Ecole Normale Superieure, Paris, France, 1966-67; vis. prof. Calif. Inst. Tech., Pasadena, 1971; guest researcher Zentralinstitut für Tieftemperaturforschung der Bayerische Akademie der Wissenschaften and Technische Universität München, 1974; dep. dir. Nat. Sci. Found., 1980-82 Rschr., contbr. to publs. on solid state and low temperature physics including electronic band structure in metals and semiconductors, quantum phase coherence and nonequilibrium effects in superconductors, sci. and edn. policy and rsch. adminstrn. Recipient John Price Wetherill medal Franklin Inst., 1975, Disting. Contribution to Research Adminstrn. award Soc. Research Adminstrs., 1983, Disting. Achievement Citation, Iowa State Alumni Assn., 1984, Significant Sig award Sigma Chi, 1985; fellow NSF, 1959-60, Alfred P. Sloan Found., 1962-64; Guggenheim Found., 1966-67 Fellow AAAS (pres. 1990), Am. Phys. Soc. (pres. 1993), Sigma Xi. Office: U System Md 3300 Metzerott Rd Adelphi MD 20783-1600*

LANGENBERG, FREDERICK CHARLES, business executive; b. N.Y.C., July 1, 1927; s. Frederick C. and Margaret (McLaughlin) L.; m. Jane Anderson Bartholomew, May 16, 1953; children: Frederick C., Susan Jane; m. Marguerite Cardone, Apr. 13, 1996. BS, Lehigh U., 1950, MS, 1951; PhD, Pa. State U., 1955; postgrad. execs. program, Carnegie-Mellon U., 1962. With U.S. Steel Corp., 1951-53; vis. fellow MIT, 1955-56; with Crucible Steel Corp., Pitts., 1956-68, v.p. research and engring., 1966-68; pres. Trent Tube div. Colt Industries, Milw., 1968-70; exec. v.p. Jessop Steel Co., Washington, 1970, pres., 1970-75; pres., bd. dirs. Am. Iron and Steel Inst., 1975-78; pres. Interlake Corp., Oak Brook, Ill., 1979-81, pres., chmn, chief exec. officer, 1981-91, also bd. dirs.; chmn. Langand Corp., Pitts., 1991—. Bd. dirs. Carpenter Tech., Reading, Pa., The Interlake Corp., Chgo. Contbr. articles to tech. jours.; patentee in field. Served with USNR, 1944-45. Named Oak Brook Bus. Leader of the Yr., 1986, Disting. Bus. Leader, DuPage County, 1988; Alumni fellow Pa. State U., 1977; recipient Disting. Alumni award, Pa. State U., 1989, Lehigh U., 1990. Fellow Am. Soc. Metals (disting. life mem. 1982, trustee, Pitts. Nite lectr. 1970, Andrew Carnegie lectr. 1976; David Ford McFarland award Penn State chpt. 1973); mem. AIME, Am. Soc. Metals, Metals Powder Industry Fedn., Phi Beta Kappa, Sigma Xi, Tau Beta Pi. Clubs: Duquesne, St. Clair Country (Pitts.), Congl., Burning Tree, Chgo. Golf, Chgo., Laurel Valley, Rolling Rock (Ligonier, Pa.), Belleair County Club (Fla.). Office: Langand Corp PO Box 1286 Mc Murray PA 15317

LANGENDOEN, DONALD TERENCE, linguistics educator; b. Paterson, N.J., June 7, 1939; s. Gerrit and Wilhelmina (Van Dyk) L.; m. Sally Wicklund, Aug. 16, 1964 (div. Mar. 1982); 1 child, David; m. Nancy Susan Kelly, July 28, 1984. BS, MIT, 1961, PhD, 1964. Asst. prof. Ohio State U., Columbus, 1964-68; vis. assoc. prof. Rockefeller U., N.Y.C., 1968-69; prof. Bklyn. C. and Grad. Ctr., CUNY, 1969-88, U. Ariz., Tucson, 1988—. Exec. officer grad. linguistics program, CUNY, N.Y.C., 1971-78; head dept. linguistics, U. Ariz., Tucson, 1988-97; vis. prof. City U. Hong Kong, 1998; vis. scientist IBM T.J. Watson Research Ctr., Yorktown Heights, N.Y., 1986-87; sr. lectr. Fulbright, Utrecht, Holland, 1977. Author: The London School of Linguistics, 1968; co-author: The Vastness of Natural Languages, 1984; editor: Linguistics Abstracts, 1997—; co-editor: Optimality Theory: An Overview, 1997; book review editor Linguist List, 2001—. Fellow N.Y. Acad. of Scis., N.Y.C., 1977; named Ptnr. in Edn., Bd. of Edn., N.Y.C., 1982. Mem. AAAS (chair sect. Z 2000), Linguistic Soc. Am. (sec., treas. 1984-88, pres. 1999), Assn. for Computational Linguistics, Assn. for Linguistic and Lit. Computing. Office: U Ariz Dept Linguistics Box 210028 Tucson AZ 85721-0028

LANGENEGGER, ARMIN, radiation physicist; b. Mainburg, Bavaria, Germany, Oct. 12, 1953; came to U.S., 1990; s. Kurt Andreas and Anne Maria (Sommerer) L.; m. Patricia Gail Cross, Feb. 28, 1982; children: Michael, Thomas, Elyse Beth; m. Lisa Marie Nelesen, Oct. 12, 1991; children: Nicholas Kurt, Matthew John. Diploma, Gordon Inst. Tech., Geelong, Victoria, Australia, 1975; BSc, Deakin U., Geelong, 1982; M Biomed. Engring., U. NSW, Sydney, Australia, 1988. Diplomate Am. Bd. Med. Physicists. Physics technologist Prince of Wales Hosp., Sydney, 1976-79, physicist, 1979-82; sr. physicist Royal Prince Alfred Hosp., 1982-87, dep. chief physicist, 1987-88; chief physicist Royal North Shore Hosp., 1988-90; physicist Waukesha (Wis.) Meml. Hosp., 1990-92, chief physicist, 1992-93; physicist St. Marys Med. Ctr., Racine, Wis., 1993—. Dir., cons. Ralode Pty Ltd., Sydney, 1982-88; cons. Biotel Pty. Ltd., Sydney, 1990-91, Radiation Physics Svcs., Milw., 1990—; invited participant Russian trip on radiation protection; invited spkr. Am. Assn. Med. Dosimetrists, 1998. Capt. Neighborhood Watch, Sydney, 1988-89. Mem. Am. Assn. Physicists in Medicine, Australasian Coll. Phys. Scientists and Engrs. in Medicine (sec. 1988-89). Anglican. Achievements include patent procs. couch mounted stereotactic head frame holder; creator inexpensive stereotactic radiosurgery package, dosimetry intercomparison group. Home: 3633 Canada Goose Xing Racine WI 53403-4504 Office: Southea Wis Regional Cancer Ctr All Saints Healthcare Sys 3809 Spring St Racine WI 53405-1667

LANGENHEIM, JEAN HARMON, biology educator; b. Homer, La., Sept. 5, 1925; d. Vergil Wilson and Jeanette (Smith) H.; m. Ralph Louis Langenheim, Dec. 1946 (div. Mar. 1961). BS, U. Tulsa, 1946; MS, U. Minn., 1949, PhD, 1953. Rsch. assoc. botany U. Calif., Berkeley, 1954-59, U. Ill., Urbana, 1959-61; rsch. fellow biology Harvard U., Cambridge, Mass., 1962-66; asst. prof. biology U. Calif., Santa Cruz, 1966-68, assoc. prof. biology, 1968-73, prof. biology, 1973-93, prof. biology emerita, 1993—. Academic v.p. Orgn. Tropical Studies, San Jose, Costa Rica, 1975-78; mem. sci.adv. bd. EPA, Washington, 1977-81; chmn. com. on humid tropics U.S. Nat. Acad. Nat. Research Council, 1975-77; mem. com. floral inventory Amazon NSF, Washington, 1975-87. Author: Botany-Plant Biology in Relation to Human Affairs.; contbr. articles to profl. jours. Grantee NSF, 1966-88; recipient Disting. Alumni award U. Tulsa, 1979. Fellow AAAS, AAUW, Calif. Acad. Scis., Bunting Inst.; mem. Bot. Soc. Am., Ecol. Soc. Am. (pres. 1986-87), Internat. Soc. Chem. Ecology (pres. 1986-87), Assn. for Tropical Biology (pres. 1985-86), Soc. for Econ. Botany (pres. 1993-94). Home: 191 Palo Verde Ter Santa Cruz CA 95060-3214 Office: U Calif Sinsheimer Labs Dept Biol Santa Cruz CA 95064 E-mail: lang@darwin.ucsc.edu.

LANGENHEIM, ROGER ALLEN, lawyer; b. Feb. 21, 1935; s. Elmer L. and Esther L. (Gerkensmeyer) L.; m. Susan C. McMichael, Aug. 31, 1963; children: Ann Elizabeth, Mark Allen, Sara Ann. BS, U. Nebr., 1957, LLB, 1960. Bar: Nebr. 1960, Mo. 1960. Assoc. Stinson, Mag, Thomson, McEvers & Fizzell, Kansas City, Mo., 1960-66; v.p., gen counsel Black, Sivalls & Bryson, Inc., 1966-70; internat. atty. Dresser Industries, Inc., Dallas, 1970-71; group counsel Petroleum & Mineral Group, Houston, 1971-75; gen. counsel Oilfield Products Group, 1975-80; v.p., gen. counsel Magcobar Group, 1980-85; assoc., gen. counsel Dresser Industries, Inc., 1985-87, sr. assoc., gen. counsel, 1987-98, staff v.p., assoc. gen. counsel, 1994-98; gen. counsel Dresser-Rand Co., 2000—. Editor: U. Nebr. Law Rev., 1958-59. Mem. Nebr. Bar Assn., Mo. Bar Assn., Order of Coif. Republican. Roman Catholic. Home: 6172 Haley Ln Fort Worth TX 76132-3875 E-mail: Rlangenheim@worldnet.att.net.

LANGENKAMP, SANDRA CARROLL, retired healthcare policy executive; b. St. Joseph, Mo., Feb. 10, 1939; d. William Harry Minger and Beverly (Carroll) Lee; m. R. Hayden Downie, June 1, 1963 (div. Feb. 1979); children: Whitney, Timothy, Allyson; m. R. Dobie Langenkamp, Aug. 1993. BS, Tex. Women's U., 1960. Adjunctive therapist Menninger Meml. Hosp., Topeka, 1960-66; asst. adminstr. Hillcrest Med. Ctr., Tulsa, 1977-82; dir. Vol. Action Agy., 1982-83; exec. dir. Tulsa Bus. Health Group, 1983-95; v.p. Met. Tulsa C. of C., 1985-95; exec. dir. Tulsa Program for Affordable Health Care, 1986-96; ret., 1996. Cons. mem. Okla. Employment Security Commn., Oklahoma City, 1988—; exec. dir. Tulsa Cmty. Found. for Indigent Health Care, 1986-96, Long-Term Care Authority, 1999—; officer State of Okla. Basic Health Benefits Bd., 1985-96, chmn., 1992-93; exec. dir. Tulsa Program for Affordable Health Care, 1989—; mem. health benefit com. Okla. Ins. Commn., 1994—; mem. Gov.'s Com. on Health Care, 1993; bd. dirs. Exec. Svc. Corps Tulsa, Associated Ctrs. for Therapy. Author: editorial column Point of View, 1985—, Tulsa mag., 1985—. Count commn. appointee Tulsa Met. Area Planning Commn., 1973-81; mayor's appointee Tulsa Housing Authority, 1985-88; pres. Tulsa Met. Ministry, 1980-83; bd. dirs. ARC, Tulsa, 1971-73, 84-85, Okla. Arts Inst., 1995—; vol. Police Svc. Homicide Divsn., Police Svc. Detective Divsn., 1999—; exec. dir. Tulsa Met. Literacy Coalition, 1998—; bd. dirs. Simon Estes Found., 2000—, Tylsa Philharmoni, Inc, 2000—. Mem. Am. C. of C. (exec. dir. Okla. chpt.), Met. Tulsa C. of C. (v.p. 1983-95), Tulsa Tennis Club. Democrat. Roman Catholic. Avocations: reading, gardening, knitting, drawing, pottery.

LANGENWALTER, GARY ALLAN, manufacturing and management consulting company executive; b. Pendleton, Oreg., Jan. 11, 1946; s. Allan Charles and Florine Ruth (Brace) L.; m. Janet Ann Case, Aug. 5, 1972; children: Karl Case, Keith Allan. Diploma, NOIB, Breukelen, The Netherlands, 1966; BA in Mgmt., U. Oreg., 1967; MBA in Mgmt., Mich. State U., 1969. Cert. fellow in prodn. and inventory mgmt.; cert. in integrated resources mgmt. Programmer, analyst Arthur Andersen & Co., Detroit, 1969-72; project mgr. Burroughs Corp., Detroit and Radnor, Pa., 1972-78; mgr. MIS Faultless Caster, Evansville, Ind., 1978-82; mgr. mfg. cons. Peat Marwick Main, Cin. and N.Y.C., 1983-87, Coopers & Lybrand, Boston, 1988; founder, pres. Langenwalter & Assocs., Stow, 1988-95, Mfg. Cons. Ptnrs., Inc., 1995—; CEO, Philips Cryptographic Techs., 2001—. Adj. instr. Nichols Coll., Dudley, Mass., 1989-91, Clark U., 1997—, Northeastern U., 2000—, Suffolk U., 2001--. Co-author: The Handbook of Materials and Capacity Requirements Planning, 1993; author: Scheduling Training Aid, 1998, Lean Manufacturing Methologies, 1999, Enterprise Resources Planning and Beyond: Integrating Your Entire Organization, 2000. Mem. adminstrv. coun. St. Matthew's United Meth. Ch., Acton, Mass., 1989-90, 93-95, 2000—, chair, 2002—, cert. lay spkr., 1999—, lay chaplain , 2001—; capt. Stow Minutemen, 1990-95; pres. Stow Bus. Assn., 1992-94, dir., 1995-96. With U.S. Army, 1969-71. Fellow Am. Prodn. and Inventory Control Soc. (bd. dirs. nat. lean mfg. specific industry group 1993-98, nat. process industry specific industry group 1999—, spkr. internat. conf. 1994-99, spkr. regional chpt. meetings 1979—, instr. lean mgmt. 1995-99); mem. Assn. Mfg. Excellence, Beta Gamma Sigma. Home and Office: 22 Seven Star Ln Stow MA 01775-1449 E-mail: gary.langenwalter@mfgcons.com.

LANGE-OTSUKA, PATRICIA ANN, nursing educator; b. Sandusky, Ohio, June 25, 1959; d. James Henry and Elaine Elnora Lange; m. Lewis Masao Otsuka, Mar. 29, 1994; 1 stepchild, Katrina. Diploma in nursing, Providence Hosp. Sch. Nursing, 1981; BSN, Bowling Green State U., 1984; MSN in Cmty. Health, Med. Coll. Ohio Sch. Nursing, 1991; postgrad. in pharmacology, U. Hawaii, 1996; EdD in Higher Edn., Nova Southeastern U., 1999. RN, Hawaii, Ohio; clin. specialist in cmty. health, ANA; APRN, ANAC, Hawaii, Ohio, Assn. Nurses in AIDS Care, AONE. Hawaii. RN Providence Hosp., Sandusky, Ohio, 1981-91; grad. tchg. asst. Med. Coll. Ohio, Huron, 1989-91; nursing supr. Bellevue (Ohio) Hosp., 1991; asst. prof. nursing Hawaii Loa Coll., Kaneohe, 1991-92, Hawaii Pacific U., Kaneohe, 1992—, acad. coord., 1993-98, nursing grad. program coord., 1998—, assoc. prof., 2000—. NCLEX rev. provider Med. Coll. Pa., Honolulu, 1993, Stanley Kaplan Corp., Honolulu, 1994, LBJ Tropical Med. Ctr., Pago Pago, 1996; freelance edn. cons., Hawaii, 1991—. Recipient Svc. awards Am. Diabetes Assn. Ohio Affiliate, Columbus and Sandusky, 1990. Mem. Assn. Nurse Execs. (treas. Hawaii chpt. 1999-2000), Providence Hosp. Sch. Nursing Alumnae Assn. (pres.-elect, pres. 1988-90), Sigma Theta Tau (Gamma Psi at large, counselor 1993-97, Excellence in Nursing Edn. award 1999), Nat. Orgn. Nurse Practioner Faculty, Hawaii League for Nursing (pres.-elect 2002--. Office: Hawaii Pacific Univ 45-045 Kamehameha Hwy Kaneohe HI 96744-5297

LANGER, BERNHARD, professional golfer; b. Anhausen, Germany, Aug. 27, 1957; m. Vikki Langer; children: Jackie Carol, Stefan Bernhard, Christina Joy. Profl. golfer, 1972—; mem. European Ryder Cup Team, 1981, 83, 85, 87, 89, 91, 93, 95, 97, World Cup Team, 1976, 77, 78, 79, 80, 90, 91, 93, 95, 97; capt. Nissan Cup Team, 1985, 86, Kirin Cup Team, 1987, Four Tours World Championship Team, 1989. Winner 7 German Nat. Opens and 2 German Nat. PGAs, over 50 internat. tournaments including Dunlop Masters, 1980, Colombian Open, 1980, German Open, 1981, 82, 85, 86, Bob Hope Brit. Classic, 1981, Italian Open, 1983, Glasgow Classic, 1983, Johnnie Walker Tournament, 1983, Caslo World, 1983, Irish Open, 1984, 87, Dutch Open, 1984, French Open, 1984, Spanish Open, 1984, Australian Masters, 1985, European Open, 1985, Sun City Challenge, 1985, PGA Championship Eng., 1987, Belgian Classic, 1987, European Epson Match Play, 1988, Peugeot Spanish Open, 1989, German Masters, 1989, Madrid Open, 1990, Benson & Hedges Open, 1991, Heineken Dutch Open, 1992, Honda Open, 1992, Volvo PGA Championship, 1993, European Open, Volvo PGA, 1995, Dunhill Asian Masters, 1996, Italian Open, Benson & Hedges Internat. Czech Open, Linde German Masters, Argentine Masters, 1997; winner Lancome Trophy; leader European Order of Merit, 1981, 84; tour victories include Masters, 1985, 93, Sea Pines Heritage Classic, 1985. Avocations: skiing, soccer.

LANGER, BRUCE ALDEN, lawyer; b. N.Y.C., Mar. 17, 1953; s. Samuel S. and Yvette Langer. BA summa cum laude with distinction, Boston U., 1975, JD cum laude, 1978. Bar: N.Y. 1979, U.S. Dist. Ct. (so. and ea. dists.) N.Y. 1979, U.S. Tax Ct. 1979, U.S. Ct. Appeals (2d cir.) 1983, U.S. Supreme Ct. 1985. Law clk. to presiding chief justice U.S. Bankruptcy Ct. (ea. dist.) N.Y., summers 1976-77; with Breed Abbott & Morgan, N.Y.C., 1978-81, White & Case, N.Y.C., 1981-84, Fishman Forman & Landau, N.Y.C., 1984-85, Fishman Forman & Langer, N.Y.C., 1985-86, Paradise & Alberts, N.Y.C., 1986-89; pvt. practice, 1989—. Editor Boston U. Law Rev., 1977-78; contbg. author: Pensions and Investments, 1979; contbr. articles to profl. jours. Harold C. Case Presdl. scholar, 1974-75. Mem. Phi Beta Kappa, Phi Alpha Theta. Office: 5th Fl 488 Madison Ave New York NY 10022

LANGER, COREY JAY, oncologist; b. Freeport, N.Y., Apr. 21, 1957; s. Leon Irwin and Rita (Frank) L.; m. Mindy Ruth Slavin, Apr. 5, 1981; children: Adina Jocelyn, Micah Philip. BA, MD, Boston U., 1981. Intern Grad. Hosp. of U. Pa., Phila., 1981-82; resident U. Pa., 1982-84; attending physician Fox Chase Cancer Ctr., 1987—, chair pharmacy and therapeutics com., 1989—, co-dir. thoracic oncology, 1994—, co-chair quality mgmt. com., 1995—. Assoc. prof. Temple U. Sch. Medicine, 2000—. Fellow Presbyn. U. Pa. Med. Ctr., 1984-86, Fox Chase Cancer Ctr., 1986-87. Fellow ACP; mem. Am. Assn. for Cancer Rsch., Am. Soc. Clin. Oncology, Am. Soc. Hematology, Internat. Assn. for Study of Lung Cancer, Ea. Coop. Oncology Group, Radiation Therapy Oncology Group, Delaware Valley Poets, Phi Beta Kappa. Avocations: poetry, softball. Office: FCCC 7701 Burholme Ave Philadelphia PA 19111-2412

LANGER, DENNIS HENRY, pharmaceutical company executive; b. N.Y.C., Sept. 8, 1951; s. Nathan and Mira (Kenig) L.; m. Susan D. Follett, Jan. 21, 1980; children: William, Thomas. BA, Columbia U., 1971; MD, Georgetown U., 1975; JD cum laude, Harvard U., 1983. Diplomate Am. Bd. Psychiatry. Intern, resident, chief resident Yale U. Sch. Medicine, New Haven, 1975-78; clin. assoc. Nat. Inst. Mental Health, Bethesda, Md., 1978-80; clin. fellow Harvard Med. Sch., Boston, 1980-82, instr., 1982-83; assoc. clin. investigator Eli Lilly and Co., Indpls., 1983-84; assoc. med. dir. Abbott Lab., North Chicago, 1984-86; product mgr. Abbott Lab, 1986-87, sr. product mgr., 1987-88; sr. group product dir. G.D. Searle and Co., Skokie, Ill., 1988-89, sr. dir. mktg., 1989-91; pres., CEO, dir. Neose Technols. Inc., Horsham, Pa., 1991-94; v.p. bus. strategy-U.S. SmithKline Beecham Pharm., Phila., 1994-96, v.p. health mgmt. svcs., 1996-98; sr. v.p. rsch. and devel. SmithKline Beecham Healthcare Svcs., 1998-99; sr. v.p. product devel. strategy, rsch. and devel. SmithKline Beecham Pharmaceuticals, 1999-2000; sr. v.p. project mgmt. and rsch. and devel. strategy Glaxo SmithKline, 2000—. Cons. Food and Drug Adminstrn., Rockville 1980-82, clin. assoc. prof. Ind. U. Sch. Medicine, Indpls. 1983-84, U. Health Scis. Chgo. Med. Sch., 1984-91. Contbr. articles to profl. jour. Bd. dirs. Epilepsy Svcs. Northeast Ill., 1985-91, v.p., 1986-89, SmithKline Beecham Found., 1996—; bd. vis. Georgetwon U. Sch. medicine, 1998—; bd. regents Georgetown U., 2000—. Mem. Am. Acad. Child and Adolescent Psychiatry (Com. On Rights and Legal Matters), Am. Psychiatric Assn., Am. Soc. Law and Medicine. E-mail: dennis_h_langer@gsk.com.

LANGER, EDWARD L. trade association administrator; b. Cleve., May 8, 1936; s. Edward L. and Evelyn (Palmer) L.; m. Sheila Mary Fitzpatrick, Nov. 5, 1957 (div. Sept. 1976); children— Dennis, Edward, Michael, Thomas, Michele; m. Carol E. Stower, Aug. 4, 1979; children— Tamara, Troy BS, John Carroll U., 1958, MA, 1964; postgrad., Ohio U., 1962, 63, Cleve. State U., 1967-68. Asst. dean admissions and records John Carroll U., University Heights, Ohio, 1964-65; head guidance Wickliffe City Schs., 1965-67; successively dir. mem. relations, mktg., planning, asst. mng. dir. Am. Soc. for Metals, Materials Park, 1967-84, mng. dir., 1984-96; bd. dirs., vice-chmn. Kolene Corp, 1997—. Bd. dirs. Kolene Corp. Author: Solid State Structures and Reactions, 1968 Bd. dirs., vice chmn. Cleve. Conv. Bur., 1984-98. Mem. Am. Soc. Assn. Execs. (bd. dirs., vice chmn. 1988-92), Coun. Engring. and Sci. Soc. Execs. (bd. dirs. 1987-93, pres. 1992), numerous other engring. and sci. socs. Avocations: fishing, golf.

LANGER, ELLEN JANE, psychologist, educator, writer; b. N.Y.C., Mar. 25, 1947; d. Norman and Sylvia (Tobias) L. BA, NYU, 1970; PhD, Yale U., 1974. Cert. clin. psychologist. Asst. prof. psychology The Grad. Ctr. CUNY, 1974-77; assoc. prof. psychology Harvard U., Cambridge, Mass., 1977-81, prof., 1981—. Cons. NAS, 1979-81, NASA; mem. div. on aging Harvard U. Med. Sch., 1979—, mem. psychiat. epidemiology steering com., 1982-90; chair social psychology program Harvard U., 1982-94, chair Faculty Arts and Scis. Com. of Women, 1984-88. Author: Personal Politics, 1973, Psychology of Control, 1983, Mindfulness, 1989, The Power of Mindful Learning, 1997; editor: (with Charles Alexander) Higher Stages of Human Development, 1990, (with Roger Schank) Beliefs, Reasoning and Decision-Making, 1994; contbr. articles to profl. and scholarly jours. Guggenheim fellow; grantee NIMH, NSF, Soc. for Psychol. Study of Social Issues, Milton Fund, Sloan Found., 1982; recipient Disting. Contbn. of Basic to Applied Psychology award APS, 1995. Fellow Computers and Soc. Inst., Am. Psychol. Assn. (Disting. Contributions to Psychology in Public Interest award 1988, Disting. Contributions of Basic Sci. to Applied Psychology 1995); mem. Soc. Exptl. Social Psychology, Phi Beta Kappa, Sigma Xi. Democrat. Jewish. Avocations: theater, horseback riding, tennis. Office: Harvard U Dept Psychology 33 Kirkland St Cambridge MA 02138-2044

LANGER, EVA MARIE, video specialist; b. Oceanside, Calif., Sept. 23, 1958; d. William Frank and Clotilde (Gonzalo) L. BS, San Diego State U., 1980. Audio engr. Peters Prodns., San Diego, 1980-83; news writer Sta. KSDO, 1981-82; audio prodn. engr. Tuesday Prodns., 1983-85; video technician Voice & Video, 1983-84, ednl. sales staff, 1984-85, govt. and ednl. mktg. saleswoman, 1985-86, retail sales mgr., corp. and comml. mktg. saleswoman, 1986-88, med. sales specialist, 1988-93; key account exec. Audio Video Supply, 1993-94; regional mgr. Gen. Projection Sys., 1994-95; dist. sales mgr. Hoffman Video Sys., 1995-96; sr. mgr. video svcs. QUALCOMM Inc., San Diego, 1996—. Ind. radio producer, San Diego, 1984—, ind. music searcher, 1984-85. Prodr.: Persons with AIDS Project, 1984-85, (documentary) Joyu, A Zen Priest, 1987. Camera operator Mothers Embracing Nuclear Disarmament, San Diego, 1985, Reiki Therapist II, 1988; co-chmn. L.L.L.A.C., 1991. Recipient Communicator Crystal award, 1999, 2001, Telly award, 2000. Mem. NAFE, Am. Women in Radio and TV (dir.-at-large 1985, 1st v.p. 1986, editor newsletter 1985-86). Democrat. Home: 4565 Lucille Dr San Diego CA 92115-1924 Office: QUALCOMM Inc 5775 Morehouse Dr San Diego CA 92121-1714

LANGER, JAMES STEPHEN, physicist, educator; b. Pitts., Sept. 21, 1934; s. Bernard F. and Liviette (Roth) L.; m. Elinor Goldmark Aaron, Dec. 21, 1958; children: Ruth, Stephen, David. BS, Carnegie Inst. Tech., 1955; PhD, U. Birmingham, Eng., 1958. Prof. physics Carnegie-Mellon U., Pitts., 1958-82, assoc. dean, 1971-74; prof. physics U. Calif., Santa Barbara, 1982—, dir. Inst. for Theoretical Physics, 1989-95. Contbr. articles to profl. jours. Guggenheim fellow, 1974-75; Marshall scholar, 1955-57 Fellow AAAS, Am. Acad. Arts and Scis., Am. Phys. Soc. (chair divsn. condensed matter physics 1997-98, pres.-elect 1999, pres. 2000, Oliver E. Buckley Condensed-Matter Physics prize 1997); mem. NAS (v.p. 2001—). Democrat. Jewish. Home: 1130 Las Canoas Ln Santa Barbara CA 93105-2331 Office: U Calif Dept Physics Santa Barbara CA 93106 E-mail: langer@physics.ucsb.edu.

LANGER, JUDITH ANN, literacy educator; b. N.Y.C. BA, CUNY, 1962, MSEd, 1965; PhD, Hofstra U., 1978. Asst. prof. L.I. U., 1973-78; asst. prof. dept. ednl. psychology NYU, 1978-80; sr. rschr. lang. behavior rsch. lab. U. Calif., Berkeley, 1980-84; assoc. prof. sch. of edn. Stanford U., 1984-87; prof. SUNY, Albany, 1987—, disting. prof., 2001—. Dir. Nat. Rsch. Ctr. on English Learning & Achievement; co-dir. Nat. Rsch. Ctr. Lit. Tchg. and Learning; trustee Rsch. Found.; task force mem. Nat. Commn. on Edn. Stds. and Testing; adv. com. New Stds. in Edn. Project, Literacy Unit, LRDC and Nat. Ctr. on Edn. and the Economy; adv. bd. Nat. Coun. of Chief State Sch. Officers, Nat. Objective in Reading, Nat. Assessment of Ednl. Progress, Reading and Writing Assessments, 1980—; cons. Calif. Assessment Program, N.C. English Lang. Arts Standards, Calif. State Dept. Edn., Ctr. for Lang. Edn. and Rsch., Ctr. for the Study of Writing, Rev. of Rsch. on Reading and Writing Relationships, Mich. State Edn. Dept. Author: Reader Meets Author/Bridging the Gap, 1982, Understanding Reading and Writing Research, 1985, Children Reading and Writing: Structures and Strategies, 1986, Language, Literacy, and Culture, 1987, Issues of Society and Schooling, How Writing Shapes Thinking: Studies of Teaching and Learning, 1987, Literature Instruction: A Focus on Student Response, 1992, Literature Instruction: Practice & Policy, 1994, Envisioning Literature, 1995, Effective Literacy Instruction: Building Successful Reading and Writing Programs, 2002; contbr. articles to profl. jours.; editor: Research in the Teaching of English, 1984-92; editl. bd. English Internat., Jour. of Reading Behavior, Newsletter, Lab. of Comparative Human Cognition, Jour. of Reading and Writing, Internat. Jour. of Reading and Writing; reviewer in field. Recipient numerous grants; fellow Rockefeller Found., Benton fellow U. Chgo. Fellow Am. Psychol. Assn., Nat. Conf. on Rsch. in English; mem. MLA, Am. Ednl. Rsch. Assn., Am. Psychol. Soc., Conf. on Coll. Composition and Comm., Internat. Reading Assn., Nat. Reading Conf., Nat. Coun. of Tchrs. of English (trustee), Soc. for Rsch. in Child Devel., Soc. for Text and Discourse, Kappa Delta Pi. Office: Univ at Albany 1400 Washington Ave Albany NY 12222-0100

LANGER, LAWRENCE LEE, English educator, writer; b. N.Y.C., June 20, 1929; s. Irving and Esther (Strauss) L.; m. Sondra Weinstein, Feb. 21, 1951; children: Andrew, Ellen. BA, CCNY, 1951; AM, Harvard U., 1952, PhD, 1961. Teaching fellow Harvard U., Cambridge, Mass., 1954-57; instr. English U. Conn., Storrs, 1957-58, Simmons Coll., Boston, 1958-61, asst. prof., 1961-66, assoc. prof., 1966-72, prof., 1972-76, Alumnae prof., 1976-92, Alumnae prof. emeritus, 1992—. Fulbright prof. Am. Lit. U. Graz, Austria, 1963-64. Author: The Holocaust and The Literary Imagination, 1975, The Age of Atrocity, 1978, Versions of Survival, 1982, Holocaust Testimonies, 1991 (Nat. Book Critics Cr. award for Criticism 1991), Art From the Ashes: A Holocaust Anthology, 1995, Admitting the Holocaust: Collected Essays, 1995, Landscapes of Jewish Experience: Paintings of Samuel Bak, 1997, Preempting the Holocaust, 1998, The Game Continues: Chess in the Art of Samuel Bak, 1999, In a Different Light: The Book of Genesis in the Art of Samuel Bak, 2001. Sr. rsch. fellow NEH, 1978-79, 89-90, Koerner fellow for study of the Holocaust, Ctr. for Hebrew and Jewish Studies, Oxford, Eng., 1997; Shapiro Sr. scholar-in-residence Rsch. Inst. U.S. Holocaust Meml. Mus., 1996, Strassler disting. vis. prof. Ctr. for Holocaust and Genocide Studies, Clark U., 2002; resident scholar Rockefeller Found. Study and Conf. Ctr., Bellagio, Italy, 2003. Mem. MLA, PEN. Office: care Yale Univ Press Authors Mail PO Box 209040 New Haven CT 06520-9040 E-mail: llanger@world.std.com.

LANGER, RALPH ERNEST, journalist, newspaper executive and editor; b. Benton Harbor, Mich., July 30, 1937; s. Ralph L. and Mary (Skuda) L.; m. Katherine B. McGuire, June 25, 1960; children: Terri B., Tammi L. Student, Central Mich. U., 1955-57; BA in Journalism, U. Mich., 1957-59. Telegraph editor, reporter Grand Haven (Mich.) Daily Tribune, 1959-60; mng. editor Port Angeles (Wash.) Evening News, 1962-66; copy desk Detroit Free Press, 1966-68; asst. mng. editor Dayton Jour. Herald, 1968, mng. editor, 1968-75; editor Everett (Wash.) Herald, 1975-81; mng. editor Dallas Morning News, 1981-83, exec. editor, 1983-86, v.p., 1986-91, sr. v.p., exec. editor, 1991-96, exec. v.p., editor, 1997-98; ret., 1999; exec.-in-residence So. Meth. U., 1999—2002. Pres. Freedom of Info. Found. Tex., 1985-89, Nat. Freedom of Info. Coalition, 1992-93, Coun. of Presidents, 1991-92.. 1st lt. U.S. Army, 1960-62. Mem. Am. Soc. Newspaper Editors (bd. dirs. 1997—), Press Club Dallas (pres. 1985-86), A.P. Mng. Editors Assn. (bd. dirs. 1980—, sec. 1989, v.p. 1990, pres. 1990-91), Coun. of Pres.'s (founding pres. 1992-93), AP Mng. Editors Assn. Found. (pres. 1991-92), Scabbard and Blade, Alpha Phi Gamma, Sigma Phi Epsilon. E-mail: RalphLanger@att.net.

LANGER, RICHARD J. lawyer; b. Rockford, Ill., June 10, 1944; s. John W. and Dorothy E. (Brunn) Langrehr; m. Audrey A. Russo, Jan. 28, 1967; children: Kathleen M., Michael R. BS, U. Ill., 1967; JD, U. Wis., 1974. Bar: Wis. 1974, U.S. Dist. Ct. (we. dist.) Wis. 1974. Assoc. Ela, Esch, Hart & Clark, Madison, Wis., 1974-76; ptnr. Stolper, Koritzinsky, Brewster & Neider, 1976-91, Michael, Best & Friedrich, Madison, 1991—. Pres. Hospice Care Found., Inc. Author: The Marital Property Classification Handbook, 1986, 2d edit., 1998, Workbook For Wisconsin Estate Planners, 1997, Family Estate Planning in Wisconsin, 1996, also articles. Sec. Combat Blindness Found., Madison, 1988—. Fellow Am. Coll. Trust and Estate Coun.; mem. ABA, State Bar Wis., Madison Estate Coun. Avocations: scuba diving, traveling, bicycling. Home: 1502 Windfield Way Madison WI 53562-3808 Office: Michael Best & Friedrich 1 S Pinckney St Madison WI 53703-2892

LANGER, ROBERT MARTIN, retired chemical engineering company executive, consultant; b. Boston, May 29, 1925; s. Samuel Morton and Ethel (Shlivek) L. B.Engring., Yale U., 1945, D.Engring., 1952; S.M., MIT, 1948. Sales mgr. The Badger Co., Inc., Cambridge, Mass., 1968-70; dep. mng. dir. Badger B.V., The Hague, The Netherlands, 1970-74, mng. dir. The Netherlands, 1974-78; v.p., project adminstrn. The Badger Co., Inc., Cambridge, 1978-80; sr. v.p. Badger Am., Inc., 1981-83; v.p., treas. The Badger Co., Inc., 1983-87. Served to lt. j.g. USNR, 1945-46 Mem. AIChE. Home: 280 Commonwealth Ave Boston MA 02116-2422

LANGER, STEVEN, human resources management consultant and industrial psychologist; b. N.Y.C., June 4, 1926; s. Israel and Anna (Glaisner) L.; m. Jacqueline White, Oct. 11, 1954 (dec. Dec. 1969); children: Bruce, Diana, Geoffrey; m. Elaine Catherine Brewer, Dec. 29, 1979 (dec. Feb. 1992). BA in Psychology, Calif. State U., Sacramento, 1950; MS in Pers. Svcs., U. Colo., 1958; PhD, Walden U., 1972. Lic. psychologist, Ill. Asst. to pers. dir. City and County of Denver, 1956-59; pers. dir. City of Pueblo (Colo.), 1959-60; pers. cons. J.L. JAcobs & Co., Chgo., 1961-64, adminstrv. mgr., 1966-67; sales selection mgr. Reuben H. Donnelly Corp., 1964-66; pres. Abbott, Langer & Assocs., Crete, Ill., 1967—. Vis. prof. mgmt. Loyola U., Chgo., 1969-71; community prof. behavioral scis. Purdue U., Calumet campus, Hammond, Ind., 1973-75. Contbr. articles on indsl. psychology and human resources mgmt. to profl. publs. Mem. Ill. Psychol. Assn. (chmn. sect. indsl. psychologists 1971-72), Chgo. Psychol. Assn. (pres. 1974-75, 94-95), Chgo. Indsl./Orgnl. Psychologists, Soc. Human Resources Mgmt. (accredited, chmn. rsch. award com. 1966-69), World at Work, Chgo. Compensation Assn. (sec. 1976-77), Mensa (pres. Chgo. chpt. 1972-74). Unitarian Universalist. Home: 309 Herndon St Park Forest IL 60466-1132 Office: Abbott Langer & Assoc 548 1st St Crete IL 60417-2199 E-mail: slanger@abbott-langer.com.

LANGERAK, ESLEY OREN, retired research chemist; b. Pella, Iowa, Oct. 28, 1920; s. William Henry and Grace Dena (Vander Linden) L.; m. Elizabeth Jane Rhodes (dec.), Nov. 18, 1944; children— Kristin, Lisbeth, Peter; m. Marian Sawin Stauffer, May 22, 1999. BS in Chemistry, Central Coll., Iowa, 1941; MS, U. Del., 1947, PhD in Organic Chemistry, 1949. High sch. tchr. Garden Grove Consol. Sch., Iowa, 1941-42; research chemist, supr., lab mgr. DuPont Co., Wilmington, Del., 1949-81, compensation mgr. chems. and pigments dept., 1981-85; ret., 1985. Contbr. articles to profl. jours.; patentee in field (3). Served with Ordnance, U.S. Army, 1942-46, PTO. Mem.: DuPont Country. Republican. Presbyterian.

LANGERMANN, JOHN W. R. financial services executive; b. N.Y.C., Aug. 14, 1943; BA with highest honors, Lehigh U., 1965. Ptnr., sales mgr. L.F. Rothschild, Unterberg, Towbin, Boston, 1977-87; sr. v.p. County Nat. West Securities, 1987-90; mng. dir. instl. sales Ladenburg, Thalmann & Co., Inc., 1994-96; mgr. Brown Bros. Harriman & Co., 1996-99; ptnr. Langermann.com, 1999—, Blue River Fin. Consulting Group, 2001—; dir. Whitman and Co., 2001—; pres. Blue River Fin. Consulting Group. Avocations: vintage sports car racing, wu shu. Address: PO Box 391855 Cambridge MA 02139 E-mail: jlangermann@yahoo.com.

LANGEVIN, EDGAR LOUIS, retired humanities educator; b. Hanover, N.H., Dec. 8, 1929; BS, Worcester State Coll., 1952, MEd, 1955; MA, Assumption Coll., 1960; MBA, Anna Maria Coll., 1979, paralegal cert., 1993; Cert. of Advanced Grad. Study, U. Mass., 1989. Substitute tchr. Worcester (Mass.) Pub. Schs., 1953-57; tchr. Providence St. Jr. High, 1957-63, Burncoat High, Worcester, 1963-69; assoc. prof. Framingham (Mass.) State Coll., 1969-96; ret., 1996. Chair Career Day Fgn. Lang. Majors, Framingham State Coll., 1975; prof. emeritus Framingham State Coll., 1996. Active Worcester Dem. City Com., 1992—. Mem. Elks. Home: 39 Carlisle St Worcester MA 01602-3323

LANGEVIN, JAMES R. congressman, former state official; b. Providence, Apr. 22, 1964; s. Richard Raymond and June Katherine (Barrett) L. B Arts and Scis., R.I. Coll., 1990; MPA, Harvard U., 1994. State rep. City of Warwick, R.I., 1988-94; sec. of state State of R.I., Providence, 1995-2001; mem. U.S. Congress from 2d R.I. dist., 2001—; mem. armed svcs. com., small bus. com. Bd. mem. Am. Red Cross, Pawtucket, R.I., 1993—, Tech Access, Providence, 1995, R.I. State House Restoration Com., 1995, March of Dimes, Warwick Shelter, Naval War Coll. Found., Pari Independent Living. Mem. Save the Bay R.I., K.C. Democrat. Roman Catholic. Avocations: reading, public speaking, community involvement. Office: 109 Cannon House Office Bldg Washington DC 20515*

LANGEVIN, THOMAS HARVEY, higher education consultant; b. St. Paul, Mar. 20, 1922; s. Thomas E. and Myrtle (Damsgard) L.; m. Pearl E. Mattfeld, Aug. 29, 1942; children: Dennis, Timothy. BS, Concordia Tchrs. Coll., Seward, Neb., 1947; MA, U. Neb., 1949, PhD, 1951. Quarantine insp. USPHS, 1943-45; grad. asst., asst. instr. U. Neb., 1947-51; prof. Concordia Tchrs. Coll., 1951-63, dean coll., 1961-63, acting pres., 1961-63; dir. long-range planning project Luth. Ch.-Mo. Synod, 1964-65; also cons. Bd. Higher Edn.; acad. v.p. Pacific Luth. U., 1965-69; pres. Capital U., Columbus, Ohio, 1969-79, pres. emeritus, 1979—; pres. Thomas H. Langevin Assoc., Lady-Lake, Fla., 1979—. Prin. Registry for Coll. and Univ. Pres., 1992—; chmn. Luth. Edn. Conf. N.Am., 1980-87; cons. Battelle Inst., 1979-87; cons., vis. fellow Battelle Seattle Rsch. Ctr., 1976. Co-chmn. Tacoma Area Urban Coalition Edn. Task Force, 1967-69; mem., past chmn. Ohio Com. Pub. Programs in Humanities; former exec. com. Fedn. Pub. Programs in Humanities; former mem. Ohio Higher Edn. Facilities Commn.; former mem. Commn. on Future Lutheran Edn., Luth Edn. Conf. N.Am., pres., 1977-78; bd. dirs. Nat. Urban League, 1979-83; mem. Columbus Urban League; former mem. Met. Columbus Sch. Com.; bd. dirs. Tacoma Citizens Com. Pub. TV, 1967-69, Design for Progress Tacoma, 1969, Tacoma Area Urban Coalition, 1967-69; bd. rev. Air U.; former adv. com. Center Sci. and Industry, Columbus; assoc. in urban affairs Nat. Inst. Pub. Affairs; bd. control Concordia Coll., Portland, Oreg., 1965-69; bd. overseers Acad. Contemporary Problems, Columbus, 1972-75; trustee Columbus Symphony Orch., pres., 1979-81; past trustee Columbus Sch. Girls, Columbus Met. Area Community Action; hon. trustee Internat. Council of Mid-Ohio; past bd. govs. Goodwill Industries Central Ohio, Salesian Inner City Boys' Club; past bd. dirs., pres. Blue Cross Central Ohio; bd. dirs. Options, Learning Connections, Franklin County Heart Br., Columbus Area Mental Health Center; bd. dirs. Battelle Meml. Inst. Found., chmn., 1977-78; mem. bd. dirs. Nationwide Corp. Served with USCGR, 1943-45. Recipient Carnegie grant, postdoctoral fellow Center for Study Higher Edn., U. Mich., 1963-64 Mem. Assn. Ind. Colls. and Univs. Ohio (chmn. 1971-74), Orgn. Am. Historians, Nebr., Ohio hist. socs., Am. Assn. Higher Edn., Newcomen Soc. N.Am., Navy League U.S. (past dir. Columbus council), Columbus Area C. of C. (dir. 1971-74) Clubs: Columbus Rotary (dir.). Lutheran. Home: 441 San Pedro Dr Lady Lake FL 32159-8664 E-mail: thlangevin@aol.com.

LANGFELD, PATRICIA ANN, trade association executive, marketing and event planner; b. Washington, Nov. 4, 1942; d. Charles Edwards and Kathryn Marie (Griffin) Junkin; m. Stanley Chaitt Langfeld, May 1, 1981. Grad. high sch., Washington. Cert. in orgn. mgmt. U.S. C. of C. Mgr. adminstrv. svcs. Nat Stone Assn., Washington, 1966-76; dir. comm. Nat. Ice Assn., Bethesda, Md., 1976-77; dir. mem. svcs. Optical Labs. Assn., 1977-82; v.p. confs. and edn. Internat. Franchise Assn., Washington, 1982-94; dir. profl. edn. svc. Congl. Quar. Inc., 1994-98; dir. meetings and exhibits Nat. Assn. Life Underwriters, 1998-2000; v.p. mktg. and devel. Competitive Telecom. Assn., 2000—. Mem. coun. advisors Walt Disney World, Orlando, Fla., 1992-94; mem. bd. advisors Greenbrier Resort, White Sulphur Springs, W.Va., 2001—. Editor, contbr. monthly newsletters Stone News, 1974-76, Ice News, 1976=77, OLA News, 1977-82; contbr. writer Franchising World, 1982-94. Mem. ball exec. com. Nat. Symphony Orch., Washington, 1995—, com. chmn., 1997—, mem. com. for wine tasting and silent auction benefit, 1993-96; mem. campaign leadership bd. Salvation Army Turning Point Ctr. for Homeless Women and Children, Washington, 1996—; mem. fall benefit com. Woodrow Wilson House Armistice Day Event, Washington, 1998—. Mem. Am. Soc. Assn. Execs., Profl. Conv. Mgmt. Assn., Greater Washington Soc. Assn. Execs. (innovate adv. coun. 1997-98, Springtime in Park adv. coun. 1998-2000, profl. women's forum 1998-2000). Republican. Jewish. Avocations: collecting oriental art, classical music, deep sea fishing, travel adventures. Home: 5300 Camberley Ave Bethesda MD 20814 Office: Competitive Telecom Assn 1900 M St NW Washington DC 20036 E-mail: plangfeld@comptel.org.

LANGFELD, STANLEY CHAITT, government executive; b. Harrisburg, Pa., Jan. 10, 1945; s. Millard Ash Jr. and Bessie Chaitt; m. Patricia Ann Junkin, May 1, 1981. BA in History, U. Md., 1968; MS in Real Estate and Urban Devel. Plng., Am. U., 1971. Market analyst The Rouse Co., Columbia, Md., 1971-72; dir. residential and recreational devel. couns. Urban Land Inst., Washington, 1972-74; realty specialist U.S. Gen. Svcs. Adminstrn., 1975-78, sr. realty specialist, 1978-81, program control officer, 1981-83, dep. dir. Office of Program Control, 1983-85, spl. asst. to asst. commr. Office Real Property Mgmt./Safety, 1985-88, spl. asst. to asst. commr. for real property devel., 1988-90, dep. dir. Office Real Estate Pub. Bldgs. Svc., 1990-91, dir. real estate policy divsn. Office Real Estate, 1991-95, dir. real property policy div. Office Governmentwide Policy, 1995—. Mem. bd. editors: Pub. Mgr. Quart. Mag., 1998—; author: (publs.) The Balanced and Orderly Development of a Site in Close Proximity to a Metro Station as a Contributor to a More Viable Urban Environment in the Washington Metropolitan Area, 1971, Federal Real Property Asset Management Principles, 1996, Project Reference Files, Urban Land Institute, 1973. Mem. com. for wine tasting and silent auction benefit Nat. Symphony Orch., Washington, 1993—96; mem. exec. com. Nat. Symphony Orch. Ball, 2000—01; advisor to bd. Salvation Army's Turning Point Ctr. for Homeless Women and Children, Washington, 1996—. Recipient Morris Cafritz Meml. scholar, Am. U., 1970, Dean's scholar, 1970, Hammer award, Nat. Partnership for Reinventing Govt., 1999, Disting. Svc. award, U.S. Govt., 2001; fellow, Urban Transp. Ctr., Urban Mass Transit Adminstrn., U.S. Dept. Transp., 1971. Mem.: Fed. Exec. Inst. Alumni Assn. (bd. dirs., exec. sec., chair 2000—), Cosmos Club (new mem. orientation com. 2000—). Republican. Jewish. Avocations: reading, travel, walking, collecting fine arts and Oriental carpets. Home: 5300 Camberley Ave Bethesda MD 20814 Office: US Gen Svcs Adminstrn 1800 F St NW Washington DC 20405 Office Fax: 202 219 0104. E-mail: stanley.langfeld@gsa.gov.

LANGFIELD, RAYMOND LEE, real estate developer; b. Houtzdale, Pa., Jan. 31, 1921; s. Arthur H. and Sadie L. (Morris) L.; m. Helen Deborah Elion, Oct. 15, 1952; 1 child, Joanna Langfield Rose. BS in Indsl. Engring., Pa. State U., 1942. Registered profl. engr., Conn. Chief mgmt. engr. CIT Fin. Corp., N.Y.C., 1947-50; v.p. Mosler Safe Co., 1950-60; pres. Spicer Fuel Co., Groton, Conn., 1960-86, United Fuel Corp., Groton, 1962-86, Spicer Gas Co., Groton. 1982-86, Conn. Hotel Corp., New London, 1986-94. Mem. Conn. Energy Adv. Bd., Hartford, 1985-87; pres. Grade Arts Ctr., New London, 1985-87. Lt. comdr. USNR, 1941-47. Mem. Southeast Conn. C. of C. (bd. dirs., chmn. bd. 1978-80), Ind. Conn. Petroleum Assn. (chmn. bd. 1973-74, Oil Man of Yr., 1975), New Eng. Fuel Inst. (bd. dirs. 1972-84), Navy League Conn. (bd. dirs. 1985-87). Jewish. Avocations: fresh-water fishing, electronics. Home: 23362 Torre Cir Boca Raton FL 33433-7026

LANGFORD, CECILIA MOTES, nurse educator; b. Saginaw, Mich., Apr. 15, 1950; d. Robert D. and Jeanette K. (Richardson) Grzegorczyk; children: Larry F., Michael A., Christopher J. ADN, Ariz. Western Coll., 1980; BSN, Sonoma State U., 1985; MS in Health, U. North Fla., 1994, postgrad. Cert. BLS instr. Am. Heart Assn. Staff nurse in psychiatry Yuma (Ariz.) Regional Med. ctr., 1980-81; staff nurse, charge nurse Community Hosp., Santa Rosa, Calif., 1981-85; staff nurse Saddleback Hosp., El Toro, 1985-86; sch. health nurse Dept. of Def., Iwakuni, Japan, 1986-87; staff nurse intensive and critical care units Humana Hosp., Orange Park, Fla., 1987-89, nurse educator, 1989-95, Columbia/HCA Specialty Hosp., Jacksonville, 1995-97; mem. staff, patient edn. coord. Shands Jacksonville (formerly Meth. Med. Ctr.), 1997—. Adj. prof. nursing Fla. Community Coll., Jacksonville, 1990-96. Author ednl. materials. Counselor Suicide Prevention, Santa Rosa, 1984; receptionist Navy Relief Soc., Iwakuni, 1986; vol. Am. Heart Assn., Jacksonville, 1992—, HIV/AIDS Buddy Program, 1997—. Mem. AACN (cert.), Jacksonville Area Nurse Insvc. Educators, Nat. Nursing Staff Devel. Orgn., Assn. Rehabilitation Nurses. Office: Shands Jacksonville 580 W 8th St Jacksonville FL 32209-6599

LANGFORD, CHARLES DOUGLAS, state legislator, lawyer; b. Montgomery, Ala., Dec. 9, 1922; s. Nathan G. and Lucy B. (Brown) L. BS, Tenn. State U., Nashville, 1948; LLB, Cath. U. of Am., 1952, JD, 1967. Bar: Ala. 1953, U.S. Dist. Ct. (mid. dist.) Ala. 1954, U.S. Ct. Appeals (5th cir.) 1969, U.S. Supreme Ct. 1976, U.S. Ct. Appeals (11th cir.) 1982. Ptnr. Gray, Langford, Sapp, McGowan, Gray & Nathanson, Montgomery, Ala., 1968—; mem. Ala. State Senate, 1983—. Officer St. John A.M.E. Ch. With U.S. Army, 1943-46. Mem. Elks (past exalter ruler So. Pride lodge), Alpha Phi Alpha. Democrat. Home: 918 E Grove St Montgomery AL 36104-4738 Office: 400 S Union St Ste 205 Montgomery AL 36104-4316

LANGFORD, DEAN TED, lighting and precision materials company executive; b. Princeton, Ill., June 19, 1939; s. Claude Robert and Dorothy Alene (Tuckerman) L.; m. Nancy Hirsch; children: Douglas T., John P. BS in Math. and Aero. Engring., U. Ill., 1962; LHD (hon.), Salem State Coll., 1990. Regional sales mgr. N.E. region ICM, Westport, Conn., 1980-81, corp. dir. mgmt. devel. Armonk, N.Y., 1981-82, group dir. comm. Ryebrook, 1982-83; v.p. mktg. GTE Comm. Sys., Stamford, Conn., 1983-84; pres. GTE Elec. Products, Danvers, Mass., 1984-93; pres., CEO, Osram Sylvania Inc., 1993—2002; ret., 2002. Bd. dirs. Osram Sylvania Inc., 2001. Mem. bd. advisers U. Ill. Sch. Engring., Chgo., 1984-92; mem. adv. bd. Northeastern U., Boston, 1984—; trustee Civic Edn. Found. Lincoln-Filene Ctr., Tufts U.; mem. corp. bd. Mass. Gen. Hosp.; bd. dirs. Nat. Park Found., 2002. Mem. NAM, Nat. Elec. Mfg. Assn. (bd. dirs.), Alliance To Save Energy (co-chmn.), U. Ill. Alumni Assn. (bd. dirs.), Salem Country Club, Las Campanas Country Club, Sawgrass Country Club, Marsh Landing Country Club. Avocations: biking, golf, cross-country skiing. Home: 24617 Harbour View Dr Ponte Vedra Beach FL 32082-1506 E-mail: dean.langford@sylvania.com.

LANGFORD, JACK DANIEL, elementary school educator; b. Cookeville, Tenn., Jan. 15, 1960; s. Sam Harley and Mary Delma (Carr) L.; m. Marilyn Patricia Poteet. BS in Secondary Edn., Tenn. Tech. U., 1983, MA in Ednl. Adminstrn. and Supervision, 1987, MA, 1993, postgrad. Lic. tchr., Tenn. Bus. tchr. Dekalb County H.S., Smithville, Tenn., 1984; social studies tchr. White County Mid. Sch., Sparta, 1985-92; 1st-6th grade title I tchr. Findlay Elem. Sch., 1992—. Chmn. Findlay Improvement Team, Sparta, 1993—, co-chmn. discipline stds. com., 1996—. Vice-pres. White County Natural Resource Conservation Svc.; mem. Nat. Arbor Day Found.; trustee Almyra Meth. Co. Recipient Career Ladder II State of Tenn., 1995. Mem. ASCD, NEA, Tenn. Edn. Assn., Internat. Reading Assn., Nat. Geog. Soc., White County Edn. Assn., Tenn. Cattlemen's Assn., White-Van Buren Cattlemen's Assn., White County Farm Bur., Nat. Arbor Soc., Tenn. Assn. for Supervision and Curriculum Devel., Tenn. Reading Assn., Phi Delta Kappa. Avocations: reading, movies, sight seeing, conversing with friends, visiting. Home: 1404 Lawrence Hudgens Rd Sparta TN 38583-3703

LANGFORD, JAMES JERRY, lawyer; b. Birmingham, Ala., May 19, 1933; S. N.B. and Margaret Elizabeth (Fuller) L.; m. Mary Elizabeth Fryant, Mar. 21, 1958; children: Jan Carol Langford Hammett, Joel Fryant L. BS, U. So. Miss., 1955; JD, U. Miss., 1970. Bar: Miss. 1970, U.S. Dist. Ct. (no. and so. dists.) Miss. 1970, U.S. Ct. Appeals (5th cir.) 1971, U.S. Ct. Appeals (11th cir.). Agt. Met. Life Ins. Co., Jackson, Miss., 1957-58; sales rep. Employers Mut. of Wausau, 1958-64; v.p. Reid-McGee Ins. Co., 1964-67; from assoc. to sr. ptnr., mng. ptnr. Wells Marble & Hurst, 1970-97, sr. ptnr., 1997—. Editor-in-chief Miss. Law Jour., 1969-70. 1st lt. U.S. Army, 1955-57. Fellow. Miss. Bar Found.; mem. ABA, Fed. Bar Assn. (pres. Miss. chpt. 1981-82), Fedn. Def. and Corp. Counsel, Nat. Assn. RR Trial Counsel, Miss. Bar Assn., Miss. Def. Lawyers Assn. (pres. 1992-93), Country Club Jackson, Phi Delta Phi, Omicron Delta Kappa, Pi Kappa Alpha. Presbyterian. Avocations: military history, baseball. Home: 12 Plum Tree Ln Madison MS 39110-9620 Office: Wells Marble & Hurst PO Box 131 Jackson MS 39205-0131 E-mail: jlangfordesq@aol.com. *People respect honesty, trustworthiness, hard work and sincerity. Do what you truly want to do for your vocation, for that is the secret of happiness in a business career.*

LANGFORD, LAURA SUE, ratings analyst; b. Evansville, Ind., Sept. 28, 1961; d. Lee Denmar Miller and Susan E. (Morton) Reitz; m. John E. Langford, May 15, 1992; 1 child Rowan Dian. BFA in Drama, U. So. Calif., L.A., 1983; MBA in Fin. & Pub./Non-Profit, Columbia U., 1992. Credit mgr. Super-Freeze Co., Inc., Burbank, Calif., 1984-86; asst. Salomon Bros. Inc., L.A., 1986-87; rsch. analyst Bank of Calif., N.A., 1987, pub. fin. officer, 1988-90; intern Citizens Budget Commn., N.Y.C., 1991; analyst Standard & Poor's Ratings Group, 1992-93, assoc., 1993-94, assoc. dir., 1994-95, dir., 1996-98; v.p. Duff & Phelps Credit Rating Co., 1998—2000; dir. HypoVereinsbank, 2000—. Contbr. . Fellow Divsn. Rsch. Assn. Student Officer fellow, Columbia U., 1991—92; scholar Pres.'s scholar, U. Evansville, 1979—81. Avocations: skiing, rollercoaster riding, science fiction.

LANGFORD, ROLAND EVERETT, environmental scientist, safety engineer, writer; b. Owensboro, Ky., Apr. 11, 1945; s. John Roland and Mary Helen (Cockriel) L.; m. Son-Hee Shin, Dec. 18, 1971; children: John Everett, Lee Shin. AA, Armstrong State Coll., 1965; BS, Ga. So. Coll., 1967; MS, U. Ga., 1971, PhD, 1974, U. N.C., 1996. Cert. profl. environ. auditor, indsl. hygienist, safety profl., registered hazardous substances profl., sanitarian, State of Ariz., Nat. Environ. Health Assn.; diplomate Am. Acad. Sanitarians. Instr. Savannah (Ga.) Sci. Mus., 1971-72, Bainbridge (Ga.) Jr. Coll., 1973-74; asst. prof. chemistry Ga. Mil. Coll., Milledgeville, 1975-77; asst. prof. Ga. So. Coll., Statesboro, 1977-78; commd. capt. U.S. Army, 1978, advanced through grades to lt. col., 1992; chief chemistry sect. U.S. Army Acad. Health Scis., Ft. Sam Houston, Tex., 1978-79; sanitary engr. U.S. Army Environ. Hygiene Agy., Aberdeen Proving Ground, Md., 1979-81; comdr. environ. sanitation detachment Taegu, Republic of Korea, 1981-83; environ. sci. officer Ft. Huachuca, Ariz., 1984-88; chief occupl. health rsch. U.S. Army Biomed. R&D Lab., Ft. Detrick, Md., 1991-92; comdr. med. rsch. detachment Walter Reed Army Inst. Rsch., Wright-Patterson AFB, Ohio, 1992-98; preventive medicine officer NATO/IFOR, Zagreb, Croatia, Sarajevo, Bosnia-Herzegovina, 1996-97; chief abiotic processes br. Robert S. Kerr Lab. of U.S. EPA, Ada, Okla., 1998; supt. health and safety Huntsman Corp. Jefferson County Ops., Port Neches, Tex., 1998-2000; mgr. indsl. hygiene and product stewardship Huntsman Corp., Houston, 2000—. Mem. panel Comprehensive Assistance to Undergrad. Sci. Edn., NSF, 1975-77; mem. emergency response planning guidelines com. panel Am. Indsl. Hygiene Assn., 1999—; judge Internat. Sci. Fair, San Antonio, 1979; mem. sci. rev. panel NIH, 1986—; adj. faculty St. Leo's Coll., San Antonio, 1978-79, U. Md., Taegu and Pusan, Korea, 1981-83, AFIT, 1993-98, Purdue U., 1995—; mem. submarine atmosphere health assessment U.S. Navy, 2000—. Author: International Book of Units and Measurement Systems, 1999; co-author: Hazardous Materials Training Program for International Union of Operating Engineers, 1988, Fundamentals of Hazardous Materials Incidents, 1990, Substance Abuse in the Workplace, 1994; contbr. articles to profl. jours. Active Boy Scouts Am., Ft. Sam Houston, 1978-79; mem. parish coun., lay minister Holy Family Parish, Ft. Huachuca, 1985-88, lay min., lector 1985-88; advisor Med. Explorer Post, Ft. Huachuca, 1986-88; lay minister St. Thomas More Ch., 1988-91, WPAFB Chapel, 1992-98. Fellow Am. Inst. Chemists; mem. AIChE, Am. Soc. Safety Engrs., Am. Acad. Indsl. Hygiene (cert.), Am. Chem. Soc., Nat. Environ. Health Assn. (cert. hazardous materials profl.), Korean Chem. Soc., Royal Asiatic Soc. (bd. dirs. 1982-83), Assn. Mil. Surgeons U.S., Am. Acad. Sanitarians (cert.), Health Physics Soc., Am. Indsl. Hygiene Assn., Am. Acad. Health Physics (assoc.). Republican. Roman Catholic. Avocations: ham radio, Asian studies, photography. Home: 5627 Heather Run Houston TX 77041-6617 Office: Huntsman Corp 3040 Post Oak Blvd Houston TX 77056-6500 E-mail: Everett_Langford@huntsman.com.

LANGFORD, WALTER MARTIN, retired greeting card and gift wrap manufacturing executive; b. Steubenville, Ohio, Jan. 2, 1931; s. Martin and Ola Belle (Stiff) L.; m. Winifred Claire Major, Mar. 14, 1953 (dec. Oct. 1997); children: Martin B., Janet R., Steven M.; m. Joyce Powell, July 25, 1998. BS in Acctg., U. Kans., 1952; JD, Ill. Inst. Tech., 1971. With Am. Can. Co., 1956-66; internal audit mgr. All-Steel, Inc., Aurora, Ill., 1966-68, div. contr., 1968-71, dir. corp. svcs., 1971-77; v.p. adminstrn. Gibson Greetings, Inc., Cin., 1977-79; sr. v.p. ops. Cleo Wrap Corp. div. Gibson Greetings, Inc., Memphis, 1979-87, exec. v.p., gen. mgr., 1987-90. Bd. dirs., corp. sec., v.p. Gibson Greetings, Inc., Cin., 1978-91. Mem. adv. bd. State Tech. Inst., Memphis, 1986-91; bd. dirs. Jr. Achievement of Memphis, 1985-91, Theatre Memphis, 1994-99, treas., 1997-99; trustee LeMoyne-Owen Coll., 1991-2000, chmn., 1994-98, emeritus, 2000—; adv. bd. Rhodes Coll., 1995-99. Lt. (j.g.) USNR, 1952-56, Korea. Mem. Ill. Bar Assn. Lodges: Rotary. Avocation: book collecting.

LANGGUTH, A(RTHUR) J(OHN), writer, journalism educator; b. Mpls., July 11, 1933; s. Arthur John and Doris Elizabeth (Turnquist) Langguth. BA cum laude, Harvard U., 1955. Corr. Cowles Newsletter, 1959; mem. bur. Look Mag. Bur., Washington, 1959; polit. corr. for Presdl. election Valley Times Cowles Publs., San Fernando Valley, Calif., 1960, corr. Calif. gubernatorial election, 1962; reporter N.Y. Times, Dallas, 1963, NC, 1963, corr. S.E. Asia, 1964, bur. chief Saigon (Vietnam), 1965; spl. assignment N.Y. Times Mag., 1968, 70; reporter N.Y. Times, Miss., 1963, Ala., 1963. Fellow Shaw traveling fellow, Harvard Coll., 1955—56, John Simon Guggenheim Meml. Found., 1976—77. Mem.: Author's Guild. Home: 1922 Whitley Ave Los Angeles CA 90068-3233 Office: U So Calif Asc 102C University Park Los Angeles CA 90089-0001 E-mail: langguth@usc.edu.

LANGGUTH, MARGARET WITTY, health facility administrator, volunteer; b. Evanston, Ill., June 21, 1950; d. LeRoy and Catherine Ann (Conrad) Witty; m. Gregory Bryce Bukar, June 5, 1971 (dec. 1989); children: Michael Bryce, Caroline Nicole; m. Franklin James Langguth, Feb. 2, 2002. BS, DePaul U., 1972, MBA, 1981; MS, Finch U. Health Scis., 1996. Staff med. technologist The Evanston Hosp., 1972-75, immunopathology lab. supr., 1975-77, lab. mgr., 1977-84, dir. lab. adminstrn., 1984-85; bookkeeper Ronald Knox Montessori Sch., Wilmette, Ill., 1986-87; beauty cons. Mary Kay Cosmetics, 1990-96; sec. Northwestern U., Evanston, 1991-94; physician asst. Women's Med. Group, P.C., Skokie, Evanston, Ill., 1996-98; ind. sales assoc. Mannatech, Inc., 1998—2001; adminstrv. dir. clin. lab. Rush North Shore Med. Ctr., Skokie, Ill., 1999—. Den leader Cub Scouts, Boy Scouts Am., Wilmette, 1985—87, den leader coach, 1987—88; active PTA of St. Francis Xavier Sch., 1985—94, chair rummage sale, 1987—88, scouting coord., 1991—92, sch. bd., 1986—90, sec., 1988—89, vice chmn., 1989—90; troop co-leader, song leader Girl Scouts Am., 1992—98; mem. women's bd. Rush North Shore Med. Ctr., 2000—; campaign 2001 com. mem. United Way of Skokie Valley-Rush North Shore, co-chair for campaign 2002; eucharistic min. sick St. Francis Xavier Ch., 1990—93, liturgical song leader, 1993—. Recipient Emily Withrow Stebbins award, Evanston Hosp., 1985. Mem.: NAFE, North Shore Profl. Women's Assn., Clin. Lab. Mgmt. Assn., Am. Soc.

Clin. Pathologists, Wilmette Hist. Soc., Elms Social Club (pres. 1992). Avocations: knitting, interior decorating, reading. Office: Rush North Shore Med Ctr Clin Labs 9600 Gross Point Rd Skokie IL 60076 E-mail: mlangguth@rsh.net.

LANGHAM, GAIL B. writer; b. Cin., Jan. 25, 1944; d. William Henry Brester and Irma Edna Hutzelman; 3 children. BA, North Ctrl. Coll., 1989. Columnist Arts Scene, 1988-92; performing arts critic, features writer SUN Press, Naperville, Ill., 1988-92; freelance theatre critic Cin. City Beat, 1994-96; freelance writer Cin., 1993—. Founding mem. Naperville Writers Group, 1986-92. Avocations: travel, reading.

LANGHAM, NORMA E. playwright, educator, poet, composer, inventor; b. California, Pa. d. Alfred Scrivener and Mary Edith (Carter) L. BS, Ohio State U., 1942; B in Theatre Arts, Pasadena Playhouse Coll. Theatre Arts, 1944; MA, Stanford U., 1956; postgrad., Summer Radio-TV Inst., 1960, Pasadena Inst. Radio, 1944-45. Tchr. sci. California High Sch., 1942-43; asst. office pub. info. Denison U., Granville, Ohio, 1955; instr. speech dept. Westminster Coll., New Wilmington, Pa., 1957-58; instr. theatre. California U., 1959, asst. prof., 1960-62, assoc. prof., 1962-79, prof. emeritus, 1979—, co-founder, sponsor, dir. Children's Theatre, 1962-79. Founder, producer, dir. Food Bank Players, 1985, Patriot Players, 1986, Noel Prodns., 1993. Writer: (plays) Magic in the Sky, 1963, Founding Daughters (Pa., Nat. DAR awards 1991), Women Whisky Rebels (Pa. Nat. DAR awards 1992), John Dough (Freedoms Found. award 1968), Who Am I?, Hippocrates Oath, Gandhi, Clementine of '49, Soul Force, Dutch Painting, Purim, Music in Freedom, The Moon Is Falling, Norma Langham's Job Johnson; composer, lyricist: (plays) Why Me, Lord?, (text) Public Speaking; co-inventor (computer game) Highway Champion. Recipient Exceptional Acad. Svc. award Pa. Dept. Edn., 1975, Appreciation award Bicentennial Commn. Pa., 1976, Gregg award Calif. U. of Pa. Alumni Assn., 1992, Emeriti Faculty award California U. Pa., 2000. Mem. AAUW (co-founder Calif. br., 1st v.p. 1971-72, pres. 1972-73, Outstanding Woman of Yr. 1986, 97), DAR, Internat. Platform Assn. (poetry award 1993, 94, monologue award 1997), California U. Pa. Assn. Women Faculty (founder, pres. 1972-73), California 150, California Hist. Soc., Pa. Assn. Safety Edn., Washington County Hist. Soc., Dramatists Guild, Ctr. in Woods, Mensa, Alpha Psi Omega, Omicron Nu. Presbyterian (elder). Home: 204 Ellsworth St California PA 15419-1206

LANGHANS, EDWARD ALLEN, drama and theater educator; b. Warren, Pa., Mar. 11, 1923; s. Allen Milton and Frances Allen L. BA, U. Rochester, 1948, MA in English, 1949; MA in Theatre, U. Hawaii, 1951; PhD in Theatre, Yale U., 1955. Asst. prof. drama U. Tex., Austin, 1955-57; asst. prof. drama and theatre U. Hawaii, Honolulu, 1957-64, assoc., 1964-71, prof., chmn. dept., 1971-85, assoc. dean arts and humanities, 1987, prof. emeritus, 1988—. Vis. prof. Tufts U., 1967-68; rsch. prof. George Washington U., 1975-76. Author: (with Philip Highfill and Kalman Burnim) A Biographical Dictionary of Actors, Actresses, Musicians, Dancers, Managers and Other Stage Personnel in London 1660-1800, 16 vols., 1973-93, Five Restoration Theatrical Adaptations, 1980, Restoration Promptbooks, 1981, Eighteenth-Century British and Irish Promptbooks, 1987; co-author: An International Dictionary of Theater Language, 1985; contbr. chpt. to book and articles to The New Grove Dictionary of Opera, 4 vols., 1992, International Dictionary of Theatre: Actors, Directors and Designers, 1996, Cambridge and Blackwell Companions to Restoration Drama, 2000, 01; dir., designer numerous plays. Bd. dirs. Honolulu Theatre for Youth, 1958-63, Hawaii Theatre Council, 1965-70, Hawaii Theatre Festival, 1978-82. Served with USAAF, 1942-47. Decorated Air medal, D.F.C.; Nat. Endowment for Humanities grantee, 1975-76, 85-86; Folger Shakespeare Library fellow, 1970-73 Mem. Am. Assn for Theatre in Higher Edn., Soc. Theatre Research, Am. Soc. Theatre Research. Home: 1212 Punahou St Apt 3402 Honolulu HI 96826-1026 E-mail: ealanghans@worldnet.att.net.

LANGHANS, LESTER FRANK, III, construction company executive; b. Corning, N.Y., Apr. 7, 1948; s. Lester Frank and Lois Jane (Keeler) L.; children: Kristen, Daniel, David, Ellen. BS in Bldg. Constrn., Va. Poly. Inst. and State U., 1970. V.p. Cape Assocs., Inc., North Eastham, Mass., 1971-75; treas. Langhall Builders, Inc., East Dennis, 1976-77; project mgr. The Green Co., Inc., East Falmouth, 1977-83, CMJ Builders, Inc., Quincy, 1983-84; project coord. Corcoran Mullins, Jennison, Inc., 1984-85; prin. TEL Assocs., Barnstable, Mass., 1985; dir. devel. LBC, Inc., Rockland, 1985-86, v.p. planning and devel., 1986-88; constrn. and devel. mgr. Olde Forge Realty, Boston, 1988-89; pres., treas. Job Busters, Barnstable, 1990-97; mgr. projects, supt. jobs Cape Assocs., Inc., North Eastham, 1993-97; v.p. Merlang Assocs., Barnstable, 1997-98, pres., 1998-2000; chief estimator, project mgr. No. Heritage Builders, Inc., Nantucket, Mass., 2000, Constrn. Mgmt. Assoc., Inc., Hyannis, 2000—01. Mem. choir East Dennis Cmty. Ch., 1970-79, elder, 1972-75, clk., 1973-74, deacon, 1981-87, treas., 1985-90. With U.S. Army, 1970-71, 2002, with Res., 1971-76, 92—, with USNR, 1982-85. Home: 85 Braggs Ln Barnstable MA 02630-1510 Office: Constrn Mgmt Assoc Inc Ste 3W 218 W Main St Hyannis MA 02601-3778 E-mail: lester1sg@hotmail.com.

LANGHOFF, ERIK, physician, educator; b. Copenhagen, Denmark, Mar. 26, 1952; came to U.S., 1987; s. Svend Andersen and Else Larsen Langhoff; m. Marcia Jean Finegold, Aug. 15, 1992; 1 child, Benjamin V. BA, Soro Acad., Denmark, 1972; MD, U. Copenhagen, 1979, PhD, 1988. Cert. physician nat. Bd. Health, Denmark. Resident, rsch. fellow in internal medicine Rigshospitalet, Copenhagen, 1979-87; assoc. physician, rsch. fellow in cellular physiology and immunology Rockefeller U. Hosp./Rockefeller U., N.Y.C., 1987-89; clin. fellow in nephrology Mass. Gen. Hosp., Boston, 1994-96; instr. pathology Harvard Med. Sch./Dana Farber Cancer Inst., 1989-94; instr. medicine Harvard Med. Sch./Mass. Gen. Hosp., 1994-96, asst. prof. medicine, 1996-97; prof. medicine and nephrology and renal transplant svc. Pa. State U./Hershey Med. ctr., 1997-99, prof. cellular and molecular physiology, 1998-99; chief nephrology Bronx (N.Y.) VA Med Ctr., 1999—; prof. medicine Mt. Sinai Med. Sch., N.Y.C., 1999—. Mem. study section Nat. Inst. Allergy and Infectious Diseases, 1995, Nat. Cancer Inst., 1997-98. Mem. editl. bd., ad hoc referee Jour. Immunology, Jour. Nucleic Acids Rsch., Jour. AMA, Jour. Virology, Jour. Immunopharmacology, and others; contbr. 70 articles to profl. jours. Recipient Friends of Dana Farber award, 1989, Winston and Revson award, 1979. Mem. AMA, Am. Soc. Nephrology, Danish Soc. Nephrology (Mommensen hon. award 1997), Danish Med. Assn. Office: Mt Sinai Hosp Dept Medicine Divsn Nephrology New York NY 10029 also: Bronx VA Med Ctr Dept Nephrology 130 W Kingsbridge Rd Bronx NY 10468-3904

LANGHOLZ, ARMIN PAUL, communications educator; b. St. Paul, June 25, 1929; s. Christian Theodore and Selma Cora (Kamholz) L.; m. Mary Ann Green, Aug. 13, 1955; children: Kevin Dean, Lori Lee Langholz West. BS in Edn., Capital U., 1951; MA, Ohio State U., 1955, PhD, 1965. Instr. Capital U., Columbus, Ohio, 1954-57, asst. prof., 1957-66, assoc. prof., 1966-71, prof., 1971-94, dept. chmn., 1970-75, 80-93, prof. emeritus, 1994—. Dir. comm. Met. Area Ch. Bd., Columbus, 1959-70; cons. Luth. Edn. Conf. of North Am., Washington, 1980-94. Prodr.: (children's TV program) Wonderbox, 1959-70, (religious news program) We Want to Know. Bd. dirs., chmn. Luth. Sr. City, Columbus, 1985-90; bd. dirs. cen. Ohio Luth. Social Svcs., 1990-97. Sgt. 1st class U.S. Army, 1952-54, Korea. Recipient Stellhorn award, Capital U., 1985, Praestantia award for Disting. Teaching, Capital U., 1986. Mem. NATAS (bd. dirs. Columbus/Dayton/Cin. chpt., Disting. Svc. award Ohio Valley chpt. 1994), Speech Comm. Assn., Ohio Speech Comm. Assn., Broadcast Edn. Assn., Nat. Collegiate Players, Tau Kappa Alpha. Avocations: golf, gardening. Home: 1348 Haddon Rd Columbus OH 43209-3101

LANGHOUT-NIX, NELLEKE, artist; b. Utrecht, The Netherlands, Mar. 27, 1939; came to U.S., 1968, naturalized, 1978; d. Louis Wilhelm Frederick and Geertruida Nix; m. Ernst Langhout, July 26, 1958; 1 son, Klaas-Jan Marnix. MFA, The Hague, The Netherlands, 1958. Head art dept. Bush Sch., Seattle, 1969-71; dir. creative projects Project Rsch., 1971-72; artist-in-residence Fairhaven Coll., Bellingham, Wash., 1974, Jefferson Cmty. Ct., Seattle, 1978-82, Lennox Sch., N.Y.C., 1982; dir. NN Gallery, Seattle, 1970—. Guest curator Holland-U.S.A. Bicentennial Show, U. Wash., 1982; project dir. Women in Art Today, Wash., 1989, Wash. State Centennial Celebration; Washington to Washington traveling exhbn., 1989; bd. dirs. Soho 20 Artists Galleries, N.Y.C. Executed wall hanging for King County Courthouse, Seattle, 1974; one-woman shows include Nat. Art Center, 1980, Gail Chase Gallery, Bellevue, Wash., 1979, 80, 83, 84, Original Graphics Gallery, Seattle, 1981, Bon Nat. Gallery, Seattle, 1981, Kathleen Ewing Gallery, Washington, 1986, Ina Broerse Laren, Holland, 1992, Charlotte Daneel Gallery, Holland, 11992, Christopher Gallery, Tucson, 1992, Mercer Island Cmty. Arts Ctr., 1992, Lisa Harris Gallery, Seattle, 1994, Jacques Marchais Mus. Tibetan, S.I., N.Y., 1995, 4th World Conf. on Women, China, 1995, Global Focus, Beijing, 1995, Elite Gallery, Moscow, 1995, Soho 20, N.Y.C., 1998, 99, 2000; exhibited in group shows, including Cheney Cowles Mus., Spokane, 1977, Bellevue Art Mus., 1978, 86, Renwick Gallery, Washington, 1978, Kleinert Gallery, Woodstock, N.Y., 1979, Artcore Meltdown, Sydney Australia, 1979, Tacoma Art Mus., 1979, 83, 86, 87, Ill. State Mus., Springfield, 1979, Plener Sandomierz, Poland, 1980, Western Assn. Art Mus. travel show, 1979-80, Madison Square Garden, N.Y.C., 1981, Exhbn. Space, N.Y.C., 1982, Lisa Harris Gallery (solo exhbns.), 1985, 87, 88, 94, Wash. State Centennial, Tacoma, 1989, Nordic Heritage Mus., Seattle, 1994, Balch Inst. Ethnic Studies, Phila., 1997, Ctr. Contemporary Art, Seattle, 1997, Zaaijer Gallery, Amsterdam, The Netherlands, 1998; solo exhbns. include SoHo20, N.Y.N.Y. Gallery, Plener Collection, Sandomierz, Bell Tel. Co. Collection, Seattle, U. Wash., Seattle, Children's Orthopedic Hosp., Seattle, Nat. Mus. Women in Arts, Washington, D'Ars Studio Gallery, Milan, Italy, 2001, Nat. Mus. Women in Arts, Washington, 2002, Collins Gen. Ctrl. Libr., Portland, Oreg., 2002; installations Tacoma Art Mus; author: (with others) Step Inside the Sacred Circle, 1989, An Artist's Book 1940-45 Remembered, 1991; author: Tsoek: Earthly Writings by a Fourpaw, 1996, Cicada, the Brood of 1996, Zones of Time, Sand and Rain, 2000; writer, designer Papua New Guinea-Where She Invented Bow and Arrow, 1996; pub., editor: (Chelsea Rhodes) A Girl and Her Cat as a Matter of Fact, 2000, (artist's book) Septembereleven o-one, 2002, To Anne Frank, 2002. Bd. dirs. Wing Luke Mus., Seattle, 1978-81, Wash. State Trust Hist. Preservation, 1990-93, Soho 20, 1997-2000; v.p. Denny Regrade Cmty. Coun., 1978-79; mem. Seattle Planning Commn., 1978-84; mem. adv. bd. dirs. Nat. Mus. Women in Arts, Washington, 1996—. Recipient wall hanging award City of Edmonds, Wash., 1974, Renton 83 merit award, 1984; merit award Internat. Platform Assn. Art Exhibit, 1984, silver medal 1st place, 1985, 87, gold medal, 1989; Year 2000 grant Libr. Book Fellows, Nat. Mus. of Women in the Arts, Washington. Mem. Denny Regrade Arts Coun. (co-founder), Internat. Platform Assn., Women in Arts N.Y.C., Nat. Mus. Women in Arts (founding, Libr. fellow, chmn. Wash. State com. 1988-89, mem. nat. adv. bd. 1993—), Seattle-King County Cmty. Arts Network (bd. dirs. 1983-85, chmn. 1984-85), Nat. Artist Equity Assn. Address: PO Box 375 Mercer Island WA 98040-0375 E-mail: nixnelleke@hotmail.com.

LANGLANDS, ROBERT PHELAN, mathematician, educator; b. New Westminster, Can., Oct. 6, 1936; came to U.S., 1960; s. Robert and Kathleen (Phelan) L.; m. Charlotte Lorraine Cheverie, Aug. 13, 1956; children: William, Sarah, Robert, Thomasin. BA, U. B.C., 1957, MA, 1958, DS honoris causa, 1985; PhD, Yale U., 1960; DSc (hon.), McMaster U., 1985, CUNY, 1985; D in Math. (hon.), U. Waterloo, 1988; DSc (hon.), U. Paris, 1989, McGill U., 1991, Toronto U., 1993, U. Montréal, 1997; DSc (hon.) , U. Laval, 2002. From instr. to assoc. prof. Princeton (N.J.) U., 1960-67; prof. math. Yale U., New Haven, 1968-72, Inst. Advanced Study, Princeton, 1972—. Author: Euler Products, 1971, (with H. Jacquet) Automorphic Forms on GL (2), 1970, On the Functional Equations Satisfied by Eisenstein Series, 1976, Base Change for GL (2), 1980, Les Débuts d'une Formule des Traces Stable, 1983. Recipient Wilbur Lucius Cross medal Yale U., 1975, Common Wealth award Sigma Xi, 1984, Mathematics award Nat. Acad. Sci., 1988, Wolf prize in math. Wolf Found., 1995-96, la Grande Médaille d'Or de l'Académie des Scis., 2000. Fellow Royal Soc. London, Royal Soc. Can.; mem. NAS, Am. Math Soc. (Cole prize 1982), Can. Math. Soc. Office: Inst Advanced Study Sch Math Olden Ln Princeton NJ 08540

LANGLEY, BARRY LYNN, dentist; b. Shreveport, La., Sept. 19, 1946; s. Arthur Wilson and Alyne (Heim) L.; m. Joyce Schlecht, May 31, 1969; children: Eric Brandon, Sarah Benne. DDS, Loyola U., 1971. Pvt. practice, Mobile, Ala., 1973—. Trustee Holy Cross Luth. Ch., Mobile; bd. dirs. Ala. Dental Polit. Action Com., 1995-2000, Children's Dental Health Bd., Mobile, Ala., 1980s; dental advisor Mobile Infirm. Sleep Disorders Rev. Panel, 1996-2000. Fellow Acad. Dentistry Internat., Internat. Coll. Dentists; mem. Ala. Dental Assn. (exec. com. 1996-2000, pres. 1999-2000), ADA (alt. del. ann. session 1997-2000), Acad. Gen. Dentistry, Mobile Area Dental Soc. (pres. 1994-95), Mobile Area C. of C. Lutheran. Avocations: backpacking, skydiving, golfing, gardening, cycling, web surfing. Office: 4720 Airport Blvd Mobile AL 36608 E-mail: langbl@aol.com.

LANGLEY, ERNEST (CHRIS LANGLEY), engineer, educator; b. Neptune Township, Nj, Feb. 7, 1955; s. Christopher Greene Langley and Shirley Jean Lachenauer; m. Noreen Etta White, Dec. 31, 1986; children: Kevin Christopher, Patrick William, Michael James, Jeffrey Daniel, Sonja Joy, Marc Jared. BS Indsl. Engring. Tech., Kean Coll., Union Township, NJ, 1996. Cert. Energy Manager, AEE; Teaching Certificate NJ, cert. Hazmat Technician NJ. Plant engr. NP / St. Elias, Cordova, Alaska, 1979—85; hvac shift supr. Merck, Rahway, NJ, 1986—91; chief engr. Tropicana, Jersey City, 1991—99; cogen ops. mgr. JCI/Roche, Nutley; maintenance / utility mgr. Crompton, Perth Amboy, 2001—01; maintenance mgr. Wyeth, Pearl River, NY, 2001—02; sr. utilities engr. Imclone, Branchburg, NJ, 2002—. Lectr. Energy Expo, NJ, 1993—. Mm2 ss / dv USN, 1973—77, Pearl Harbor. Mem.: RSES, ASHRAE. Avocations: camping, fishing, theme parks. Office: Imclone 22 Chubb Way Somerville NJ 08876 E-mail: chris.langley@imclone.com.

LANGLEY, GEORGE ROSS, medical educator; b. Sydney, N.S., Can., Oct. 6, 1931; s. John Goerge Elmer and Freda Catherine (Ross) L.; m. Jean Marie Ballantyne, June 22, 1957; children: Joanne Marie, Mark Ross, Richard Graham. BA, Mt. Allison U., 1952; MD, Dalhousie U., 1957. Intern Victoria Gen. Hosp., Halifax, N.S., 1957, resident, 1958, Toronto (Ont.) Gen. Hosp., 1960, U. Melbourne, Australia, 1961, U. Rochester, N.Y., 1962; John and Mary Markle scholar in acad. medicine Dalhousie U., Halifax, 1963-68, from lectr. to prof. medicine, 1963-69, prof., chmn. dept. medicine, 1974-82; chief of service medicine Camp Hill Hosp., Halifax, 1969-74; head dept. medicine Victoria Gen. Hosp., 1974-82; prof. medicine Dolhouise U., Queen Elizabeth II Hlth. Sci. Ctr., 1982—; exec. dir. Strategic Hlth. Svcs. Dept. Hlth. Provinces, Nova Scotia, Canada, 1998-2000. Chmn. clin. investigation grants com. Med. Research Council, 1976-78; chmn. clin. and epidemiol. research adv. com., bd. dirs. Nat. Cancer Inst. Can., 1978-86 Contbr. articles to sci. jours. Decorated Queen's Jubilee medal, 1977. Fellow Internat. Soc. Hematology, Royal Coll. Physicians and Surgeons (v.p., coun., Wightman vis. prof. 1990), ACP (bd. govs. 1973-78, laureate Atlantic region 1996), Royal Coll. Physicians (Edinburgh); mem. Can. Hematology Soc. (pres. 1976-78), Can. Soc. Clin. Investigation, Am. Soc. Hematology, Can. Soc. Oncology, Alpha Omega Alpha. Mem. United Ch. Can. Home: 6025 Oakland Rd Halifax NS Canada B3H 1N9 Office: Victoria Gen Hosp Ste 8-024 Halifax NS Canada B3H 2Y9 E-mail: Ross.Langley@dal.ca.

LANGLEY, GLEN MARTIN, telecommunications executive, engineering consultant; b. Kansas City, Kans., Feb. 27, 1962; s. Glenn Dale and Nancy Isabelle (Mills) L. BS, Kans. State U., 1985. Profl. umpire Nat. Assn. Profl. Baseball, St. Petersburg, 1986-90; sales mgr. Trilogy Comms., Pearl, Miss., 1991-93, Jerry Conn Assoc., Chambersburg, Pa., 1993-96; reg. mgr. Augat Commn. Products, Kent, Wash., 1996-97. Mem. bd. dirs. Dixie chpt. SCTE, Birmingham, Ala., 1994-95, Music City SCTE, Nashville, 1995-96; assoc. dir. Miss. Cable TV Assoc., Jackson, Miss., 1995-96. Mem. Soc. Cable, Telecomms. Engrs., Tau Kappa Epsilon, Tau Kappa Epsilon Alumni, Kansas State Alumni Assn. Avocations: running, skiing, photography, golf. Home: 201 Acton Ct Columbia SC 29212-8260 Office: Moore Diversified Products Lexington KY 40507

LANGLEY, JAMES EDWARD, music educator; b. Warner Robins, Ga., Nov. 1, 1962; s. Delmer Lee and Norice Ann Langley; m. Tammy Sue Langley, June 21, 1995; children: Josh Stephen, Christopher Aaron. BM Music Edn., U. of Ga., Athens, Georgia, 1985. Music educator Feagin Mill, Warner Robins, Ga., 1996—, Rumble Mid. Sch., Warner Robins, 1992—96, Northside H.S., Warner Robins, 1987—92, Harlem H.S., Harlem, 1985—87. Bd. of directors Cmty. Concert Assn., Warner Robins, Ga., 2002. Mem.: PAGE.

LANGLEY, JIMMY LAWRENCE, explosives/toxic chemical safety specialist, general safety specialist, safety consultant; b. Albertville, Ala., Dec. 18, 1953; s. Arlin Lawrence and Cecile Belle Langley; m. Deborah Kathren Small; children: Shanna Maureen, James Lawrence, Daniel Tsali. BS: Forensic Science/Biology/General Chem, Jacksonville State University, Jacksonville, Alabama, 1977—88; MS: Scouting, Oral Roberts University, Tulsa, Oklahoma, 2001—02; AS: Emergency Med. Tech., Bus. Adminstrn., Gadsden State Jr. Coll., Ala., 1977; Army Mgmt., Army Staff College, Fort Belvoir, Va., 1998; Safety, U.S. Army Safety Center, Fort Rucker, Ala., 1992—93. Cert. National Registered Emergency Med. Tech.-Paramedic 1988; Safety and Health Manager 2001, Professional Clown 1968. Chief Hollis Fire Department, Heflin, Ala., 1979—82; paramedic Oxford (Ala.) Rescue, 1982—88, Anniston(Ala.) Rescue, 1988—90, U.S. Army Chem. Sch., Fort McClellan, Ala., 1990—91; safety specialist (Army Intern Program) Letterkenny Army Depot, Chambersburg, Pa., 1991—93; specialist in explosives and toxic chems. U.S. Army Tech. Ctr. for Explosives Safety, McAlester, Okla., 1993—. Safety Specialist U.S. Army Tech. Ctr. for Explosives Safety, McAlester, OK, 1993—2002; safety supr. personnel in high risk ops. U.S. Army Tech. Ctr. for Explosives Safety, McAlester, 1993—2002, risk assessor, 1993—2002, general safety cons., 1993—2002, safety data rschr., 1993—. Contbr. Action (Civilian Commendation Medal, 2001). Chmn. Frink-Chambers Indian Edn. Com., McAlester, Okla., 2000—02; Cubmaster Pack 403, Indian Nations Coun.l BSA, 1998—2002; 1st Lt. Oxford (Ala.) Emergency Rescue Squad, 1984—86. Named Cubmaster of the Year 1999, BSA Okla.-Tulsa Dist., 1999; recipient State of Alabama, Both Houses Concurring, for Heroism, State of Alabama, 1989, Commendation for Exceptional Performance Rating, U.S. Army, 1991, Award for Service Support (USA MEDDAC STATE-SIDE AIRVAC OPERATIONS) during Operation Desert Storm, U.S. Army MEDDAC, 1992, Achievement Medal for Civilian Service, U.S. Army, 1992, Letter of Recognition from Savanna Army Depot endorsed by USADACS Dir., Savanna Army Depot and Defense Ammunition Ctr., 1995, Special Act Svc. Award, U.S. Army Inspector General, 1998, Service Award, U.S. Army, 1999 - 2000, Achievement Medal for Civilian Svc., 2001. Mem.: Certified Safety and Health Managers (No Office Held), Clowns of America International (No Office Held). Baptist. Avocations: fishing, camping, gardening, hunting, swimming. Office: Defense Ammun Ctr/USATCES 1 C Tree Road, Bldg 35 Mcalester OK 74501-9053 Office Fax: 918-420-8503. Personal E-mail: Jimmy.L@Langley.com. Business E-Mail: Jimmy.Langley@DAC.Army.Mil.

LANGLEY, JOELLEN S. music educator; b. Rocky Mt., N.C., Mar. 12, 1950; d. John Sidney Jr. and Josephine Smith; m. John B. Langley; 1 child, Jillian Joelle Cleghorn. BA in Music Edn., Temple U., 1975. Cert. K-12 music tchr., N.J., Pa. Music dir. Runnemede (N.J.) Pub. Schs., 1978—. Co-owner children's music prodn. co. JJ Creations; spkr. in field. Composer, singer, tchr., adult and children's music; performer Phila. Civic Ctr., 1988; publ. children's music. U.S. rep. to Venezuela by spl. invitation of consul gen. Venezuela and min. fgn. affairs, 1995. Recipient Tchr. of Yr. award Gov. Tom Keane, N.J., 1988.

LANGLEY, JOSEPH JEREMIAH, artist, poet; b. Rocky Mount, N.C., Aug. 15, 1963; s. J. Langley and I. Edwards. DEUG, U. Montpellier, France, 1985; BA, Davidson Coll., 1985; lic., U. Paris-Sorbonne, 1989, maitrise, 1990. Door to door salesman Southwestern Pub. Co., Nashville, 1982; merchandiser Record Bar, Rocky Mount, 1982—83; asst. tchr. English Lycee Clemenceau, Montpellier, 1986—87; comedian, acrobat, singer ZINGARO, Paris, 1987—89; tchr. Glossa Lang. Sch., 1988—89; singer, waiter Hollywood Savoy, 1989—90; exec. sales and mgmt. L'OREAL, 1990—98. Actor: (films) Le Nouveau Monde, 1989, ZINGARO, 1989; , translator diverse textes; singer: (TV series) Presence protestante, 1989; author: (poems) Joseph's GIft, 1996; contbr. book, poems (Poet of Merit, 1997). Vol. Aids Assn., Avignon, France, 1997—99; organizer Charity Gospel Concerts for Needy, 1998. Mem.: Theatre de l'air Nouveau. Avocations: water-skiing, skiing, bicycling. Office: Joseph Langley 104 Avenue de la Republique Hall 2 75011 Paris France

LANGLEY, LESTER DANNY, educator; b. Aug. 7, 1940; BA, West Tex. State U., 1961, MA, 1962; PhD, U. Kans., 1965. Rsch. prof. U. Ga., Athens, 1988-2000, prof. emeritus, 2000—. E-mail: lesterd.langley@verizon.net.

LANGLEY, LYNNE SPENCER, newspaper editor, columnist; b. West Palm Beach, Fla., June 4, 1947; d. George Hosmer and Elwa June (Harries) Spencer; m. William A. Langley, Oct. 10, 1970 (dec. 2001). Student, Glasgow U., Scotland, 1967-68; BA with honors, Coll. of Wooster, 1969. Feature writer, asst. woman's editor Palm Beach Times, West Palm Beach, 1969-70; asst. editor Brunswick (Maine) Times Record, 1971; investigative reporter Maine Times, Topsham, 1971-75; asst. mng. editor York County Coast Star, Kennebunk, Maine, 1976-78; environ. and med. editor, nature columnist Charleston (S.C.) Post and Courier Newspapers, 1979—. Editor Maine Audubon Soc. News, 1975-76; stringer Newsweek mag., 1971-75; speaker in field; freelance writer. Author: Nature Watch, 1987. Mem. Charleston Mus., S.C. chpt. Nature Conservancy. Recipient Media award S.C. Assn. Mentally Retarded, 1985, Media awards Charleston County Parks and Recreation Commn., 1985, Am. Diabetes Assn., S.C. chpt. 1989, Communicator of Yr. award S.C. Wildlife Fedn., 1983, Writing awards S.C. Press Assn., 1987, First Pl. in column writing S.C. Press. Assn., 1998. Mem. Am. Hort. Soc., Nat. Audubon Soc., Charleston Natural History Soc. (Media award 1985), Garden Writers Assn. Am., PEO (sec. chpt. D Maine 1975-76, corr. sec. chpt. J. S.C. 1986-88), Sigma Delta Chi. Home: PO Box 97 Adams Run SC 29426-0097 Office: 134 Columbus St Charleston SC 29403-4809 E-mail: llangley@postandcourier.com.

LANGLEY, PATRICIA COFFROTH, retired psychiatric social worker; b. Pitts., Mar. 1, 1924; d. John Kimmell and Anna (McDonald) Coffroth; m. George J. Langley, May 1, 1946; children: George Julius III, Mary Patricia, Kelly Joan; stepchildren: Robin Spencer, Veronica Bell. BA, Empire State Coll., 1976; MSW, Hunter Coll., 1980. Diplomate Clin. Social Worker; lic. social worker, Conn.; cert. Conn. Psychiat. rehab. worker. Credentialed aloholism treament counselor, supervisor Bronx Mcpl. Hosp. Center, Albert Einstein Med. Coll., 1970-74, case worker, comprehensive alcoholism treatment center, dept. psychiatry, 1974-80; asst. coordinator outpatient psychiat. alcoholism Meridian Ctr., Stamford, Conn., 1980-83, dir. family treatment; pvt. practice and consultation; ret., 2000. Vol. DuBois Day Clinic, Stamford, 1966-67, Greenwich Hosp., 1966-67. Mem. NASW, Conn. Soc. for Clin. Social Workers. Home: 50 Lafayette Pl Greenwich CT 06830-5405

LANGLEY, RICKY LEE, occupational medicine physician; b. Fountain, N.C., Aug. 31, 1957; s. Ernest Lee and Janie Ruth (Fulford) L.; m. Sandra Jane Ward, June 7, 1980; children: Patrick, Nicholas, Megan. BS magna cum laude, N.C. State U., 1979; MD, Bowman Grey Sch. Medicine, 1983; MPH, U. N.C., 1988. Diplomate Am. Bd. Internal Medicine, Am. Bd. Preventive Medicine. Intern East Carolina Sch. Medicine, Greenville, N.C., 1983-84, resident, 1984-86; asst. prof. dept. preventive medicine and health policy East Carolina U., 1989-91, adj. asst. prof. dept. family medicine, 1989-91, adj. asst. prof. dept. environ. health, 1989-98, asst. prof. dept. internal medicine, 1991; fellow Sch. Medicine Duke U., Durham, 1986-88, asst. cons. prof. in occupational medicine, 1989-90, asst. clin. prof. dept. community and family medicine, 1991-96; pvt. practice occupational medicine Health and Hygiene, Inc., Greensboro, 1988-89; med. dir. Mebane (N.C.) Med. Ctr., 1996-98, Kernodle Clinic, Inc., 1998; pub. health physician Occupl. and Environ. Epidemiology, Dept. Health & Human Svc., Raleigh, N.C., 1998—. Adj. asst. prof. dept. biol. and agrl. engring. N.C. State U., 1996—99; cons. in field; mem. planning com. on agrl. safety N.C. State Fair, 1991; mem. task force Agri-Bus. for Gov.'s Commn. on Reduction of Infant Morality, 1992; mem. N.C. State Task Force on Blood-Borne Pathogens N.C. Occupl. Health and Safety Adminstrn., 1991—92; presenter in field.; mem. Nat. Pork Procedures Coun. Task Force on Worker Health and Safety, 1995; occupl. medicine residency program evaluator for NIOSH, 1992—96, mem. spl. emphasis panel, 1996—; mem. agrl. safety and health coun. N.C. Dept. Labor, 1996—; mem. N.C. Pesticide Bd., 1998—; occupl. medicine residency adv. com. Duke U., 1998—; mem. bd. collaborators N.C. Inst. Health and Safety in Agr., Forestry & Fisheries, 2001—. Editor: Safety and Health in Agriculture, Forestry and Fisheries, 1997, (textbook) Animal Handlers; guest editor N.C. Med. Jour., 1992, 93, 95, mem. editl. bd., 1999—; co-editor Environmental Health Secrets, 2001; contbr. articles to profl. jours. Vol. Greenville Cmty. Shelter, 1990, Health Hotline, WITN, 1990, 91, State Employee Wellness Day 1989, Adopt-A-Hwy.

Project, 1989; Dr. of the Day, N.C. State Legislature, 1991; doctor on call blood drive ARC, Greensboro, 1989; vol. Freemont Peoples Clinic, 1993; pub. affairs officer, mem. USCG Aux., 1996-99, flotilla 18-11, 1995-98; hunting safety educator, N.C., 1996—; mem. Alamance County (N.C.) Bd. Adjustment, 1997-99. Lloyd T. Weeks scholar, 1978, Benjamin Elloit Ibie and Benjamin Elliot Ibie Jr. Meml. scholar, 1976. Fellow ACP, Am. Coll. Occupl. and Environ. Medicine (del. 1995-98), Am. Coll. Preventive Medicine; mem. AMA, N.C. Med. Soc. (environ. health subcom. 1991—, vice chair 1999-2000, chair 2000-2001), Am. Occupl. Med. Assn. (mem. med. ctr. occupl. health com. 1990-97), Carolinas Occupl. Med. Assn. (sec.-treas. 1991-92, pres-elect 1992-93, pres. 1993-94, del. 1995-98), N.C. Archeol. Soc. (exec. bd. 1998-2000), Am. Conf. Govt. Indsl. Hygienists, Am. Indsl. Hygiene Assn., Tarheel Archaeology Soc. (edn. chair 1996-2000), Found. for Advanced Lithics Studies (sec.-treas. 2000), Sigma Xi, Phi Kappa Phi, Phi Eta Sigma, Gamma Sigma Delta, Alpha Epsilon Delta. Avocations: astronomy, archeology. Home: 1506 Miles Chapel Rd Mebane NC 27302-9008 Office: Mebane Med Clinic Mebane NC 27302 E-mail: rick.langley@ncmcil.net.

LANGLEY, ROGER RICHARD, editor; b. Amsterdam, N.Y., Aug. 22, 1930; s. Walter B. and Anna Mae (McCaffrey) L.; m. Norma A. Sekinger, Feb. 5, 1960; children: David, Jennifer, Michael. AB, Syracuse U., 1958, AM, 1965; diploma in edn. parish svc., Trinity Coll., 1999. Cert. tchr. N.Y. Salesman Underwood-Olevitti Corp., Syracuse, 1960-61; editor Ind. Newspaper Chain, Marathon, N.Y., 1961-64; reporter Syracuse Herald-Jour., 1964-66; asst. city editor Ithaca (N.Y.) Jour., 1966-68; gen. editor Best Medium Pub., Englewood Cliffs, N.J., 1968-74; chief bur. World News Corp., Washington, 1974-76; syndicated columnist Washington (D.C.) Writers' Syndicate, 1978-82, sr. editor, 1977-95, chief exec. officer, 1982-95, ret., 1995. Instr. U. Md., College Park, Am. U., Washington, George Washington U., Washington, Montgomery Coll., Md.; dean workshops on humor in the workplace, humor and health Comedy Coll.; speaker and tng. cons. Comedy Coll., Washington, 1982-92; mem. White House Press Corp. 1974-84. Author: Wife Beating: The Silent Crisis, 1977, You Can Chart Your Career Path, 1992; author audio tape presentation Speak With Humor; editor: The Great Comedians Joke Book, 1999; contbr. articles to mags. and newspapers. Pres. Woodly Gardens Home Owners Assn., Rockville, Md., 1975; mem. Keep Montgomery County (Md.) Beautiful, 1985-89, Fuel Oil Task Force, Montgomery County, 1985-89, Emergency Mgmt. Com., Montgomery County, 1985-89, Bethesda (Md.) Action Group, 1989-93, mgr. Silver Spring (Md.) urban dist., 1993-97; founder, bd. dirs. First Night Montgomery County; bd. dirs. Montgomery County Conf. and Visitors Bur., Art Gliner Ctr. Humor, U. Md. Served with USN, 1950-54, Korea. Recipient Enterprise Writing award N.Y. A.P., 1967, Nat. Assn. Counties awards, Excellence in Writing award Nat. Assn. Counties. Mem. Nat. Press Club, Am. Legion Post of Nat. Press Club, Toastmasters (various offices Silver Spring, Md. chpt., Toastmaster of Yr. 1986, 91), Beta Theta Pi. Home: 625 Smallwood Rd Rockville MD 20850-1918

LANGLEY, ROLLAND AMENT, JR. retired engineering technology company executive; b. San Francisco, Aug. 22, 1931; s. Rolland Ament and Kathryn Lee (Beals) L.; m. Pamela Winston, May, 15, 1954 (div. 1978); children: Owen C., Cynthia, James R.; m. Chiara Bini-Sexton, Apr. 12, 1978. BS in Engring. and Physics, U. Calif., Berkeley, 1953; MME, U. Pitts., 1961; MBA, Golden Gate U., 1973. Engr. Bettis Atomic Power Lab. of Westinghouse Electric Corp., Pitts., 1957-62; with Bechtel Corp., San Francisco, 1962-71; mgr. refinery and chem. nuclear fuel ops. Bechtel Inc., 1977-78; mgr. projects nuclear fuel ops. Bechtel Nat. Inc., 1979-80, mgr. decontamination and restoration nuclear fuel ops., 1980-81, v.p., mgr. nuclear fuels ops. Oak Ridge, Tenn., 1981-84, sr. v.p., mgr. div. ops., R & D ops. San Francisco, 1985-89; dep. mgr. Uranium Enrichment Assocs., 1972-76; v.p. Uranium Enrichment Tech. Inc., 1976-77; pres., dir. Bechtel Systems Mgmt. Inc., 1988-90; pres., CEO BNFL Inc., 1990-97, 98-99, also bd. dirs., 1994-2000. Bd. dirs. 21st Century Coatings; trustee, pres. World Mem. Fund-U.S.A., 1993-98; chmn., Pajarito Sci. Corp., 1995-97, bd. dirs.; pres. Pacific Nuclear Coun., 1998-2000; mem. Nat. Acad. Sci. panel on nuclear separation and transmutation, 1992-95. Contbr. articles to profl. jours. Trustee Environ. Sci. and Tech. Inst., 1995-98. Capt. USNR. Recipient Bausch and Lomb Sci. award, 1948. Mem. Naval Res Assn. (past pres. Golden Gate chpt.). Achievements include patents in nuclear fuel and reactor systems design; research on uranium enrichment, nuclear waste disposal, fast breeder reactors, and engineering management. Home: PO Box 28 Middleburg VA 20118-0208

LANGLINAIS, JOSEPH WILLIS, educator, chaplain; b. San Antonio, Aug. 12, 1922; s. Joseph Willis and Marie Nellie (St. Julien) L. BS in Edn. U. Dayton, 1943; STD, U. Fribourg, Switzerland, 1954. Joined Soc. Mary of St. Louis, 1940; ordained priest Roman Cath. Ch., 1952. Joined Soc. Mary, 1940; tchr. high schs. in Mo., Ill. and Man., Can., 1943-48; dir. admissions Chaminade Coll. Prep. Sch., St. Louis, 1957-59; dir. Archdiocesan High Sch. Sodality Union St. Louis, 1958-59, Marianist Novitiate, Galesville, Wis., 1959-63; mem. faculty St. Mary's U., San Antonio, 1963—, dean Sch. Arts and Scis., 1964-75, acad. v.p., 1975-81, dir. instnl. self-study, 1970-72, 82-84, chmn. theology dept., 1981-83, dean Sch. Humanities and Social Scis., 1986, chaplain Sch. of Bus., 1988—, Univ. Prof., 1993—; pres. Cen. Cath. Marianist High Sch., 1987-91. Dir. semester in Puebla, Mex. St. Mary's U., 1994; pres. Holy Rosary Sch. Bd., 1995-99; archdiocesan ecumenical rep., 1996—, counselor, 1997—; bd. dirs. Mariological Soc. Am., 1997—. Contbr.: Catholic Encyclopedia America, Encyclopedic Dictionary of Religion, 1979. Pres. United Svcs. Orgn. South Tex., 1985-87, Holy Rosary Elem. Sch., San Antonio, 1997-99; mem. bd. Tex. Bach Choir; pres. sch. bd. Ctrl. Cath. H.S., 1987-91; chaplain Marianist Residence at St. Mary's U., 1999—. Named Champion of Compassion, B'nai B'rith, San Antonio, 1990, Nat. Commn. Comty. and Justice, 2001. Mem. AAUP, Cath. Theol. Soc. Am., Mariological Soc. Am., Archaeol. Soc. Am., Torch Internat., Nat. Soc. Arts and Letters, Rotary. Avocations: horticulture, classical music. Home: 520 Fordham Ave San Antonio TX 78228-8559 E-mail: jwillis@st.marytx.edu.

LANGLOIS, MICHAEL A. financial adviser, consultant; b. Springfield, Mass., July 4, 1956; s. Arthur Edward and Maria (Duchesneau) L.; children: Michelle, Jeffrey; m. Kathleena Iacchei; 1 stepchild, Lisa Massaro. BBA, Bryant Coll., 1978, MBA, 1982. Registered investment adviser. Mfg. supr. Browne & Sharpe, Inc., North Kingstown, R.I., 1978-81; gen. mgr. N.H. Ball Bearing Inc., Peterborough, 1981-84; registered rep. Waddell & Reed, Inc., Cranston, R.I., 1982-86, dist. mgr., 1986-88; devel. mgr. Monarch Fin. Group, Providence, 1988-91; prin., owner Strategic Fin. Group, Cranston, 1993—. Pres. Langlois & Assocs., Cranston, 1986; instr. Bryant Coll. Contbr. articles to profl. jours. Mem. Nat. Assn. Securities Dealers, Nat. Assn. Life Underwriters, Am. Arbitration Assn. (arbitrator), Am. Assn. Individual Investors, Internat. Assn. Fin. Planning, Fin. Planning Assn., Internat. Assn. Registered Fin. Planners, Internat. Bd. Cert. Fin. Planners, Nat. Assn. Estate Planners. Republican. Roman Catholic. Home: 45 Mollie Dr Cranston RI 02921-1415 Office: Langlois & Assocs 1150 New London Ave Ste 320 Cranston RI 02920-3036

LANGMAN, CRAIG BRADFORD, nephrologist; b. Phila., Feb. 15, 1953; s. Ralph Leon and Kate (Freedman) L.; m. Lynne Tylke. BA, Temple U., 1974; MD, Hahnemann U., 1977. Diplomate Nat. Med. Bd. Examiners. Residency in pediatrics Children's Hosp. Phila., 1977-79, fellow in pediatric nephrology, 1979-81; assoc. attending physician divsn. nephrology Michael Reese Hosp. and Med. Ctr., Chgo., 1981-84, attending physician, 1984-85, Children's Meml. Hosp., Chgo., 1985; asst. prof. pediatrics Northwestern U. Sch. Medicine, 1985-87, tenured assoc. prof., 1987-93, tenured prof., 1993; assoc. chair pediatrics rsch. program devel. dept. pediatric Northwestern U. Med. Sch., 1989-93; assoc. dir. gen. clin. rsch. ctr. Northwestern U. Med. Sch. and Northwestern Meml. Hosp., 1991-96, divsn. head pediatric nephrology, 1995—. Mem. editl. bd. Pediatric Endocrinology, 1991—, Pediatric Nephrology, 1994-97; assoc. editor: Primer on Metabolic Bone Diseases, 1st thru 4th edits., 1988—; referee numerous profl. jours.; contbr. articles to profl. jours. Mem. med. adv. bd. Lincoln Park Zoo, 1992—; active Ill. Dept. of Health Coalition on Osteoporosis, 1995—. NIH grantee, 1982-84, 87, 89, 89-90, 90-96. Mem. Soc. for Pediatric Rsch., Am. Fedn. for Clin. Rsch., Am. Soc. Nephrology, Am. Soc. Bone and Mineral Rsch., Midwest Soc. Pediatric Rsch., Internat. Coun. Calcium Regulating Hormones, Internat. Soc. for Renal Nutrition and Metabolism, Assn. Clin. Scientists, Internat. Bone and Mineral Soc., Internat. Pediatric Nephrology Assn., Am. Soc. Pediatric Nephrology, Nat. Kidney Found., Am. Bd. Pediatrics, N.Am. Pediatric Renal Transplant Cooperative Study, Am. Kidney Soc. (pres. coun. 1996-97). Office: Childrens Meml Hosp Divsn Nephrology 2300 N Childrens Plz # 37 Chicago IL 60614-3394

LANGMAN, NANCY, health services administrator; b. Bayshore, N.Y., Mar. 8, 1948; d. Vincent F. and Patricia (Jones) Langman; m. Robert A. Dorwart, June 20, 1976 (dec.); children: Kirsten, Stefan; m. Gary Cogley, Oct. 21, 2000; step-children: Adam, Michael. BS, Wagner Coll., 1970; MS, Boston U., 1973; MPH, Tulane U. Sch. Pub. Health, 1974. RN, Mass.; cert. psychiat. nurse clin. specialist, ANA Advanced Practice Psychiat. Nursing. Assoc. prof. La. State U., New Orleans, 1974-76; dir. consultation Mystic Valley Mental Health, Lexington, Mass., 1976-81; dir. outpatient clinic Human Resources Inst., Lowell, 1981-83; mgr. mental health Harvard Cmty. Health, Brookline, 1983-87, Pvt. Health Care Sys., Lexington, 1987-91; dir. mental health Blue Cross Blue Shield Mass., Boston, 1991-96, clin. dir. Raytheon account, 1995-96; v.p. Care Group, 1997-98; ind. health care cons., 1998-99; v.p. med. affairs The Oak Group, 1999—; cons. Behavioral Healthcare Ptnrs., 1998—99, Brockton Hosp., 2000—01, Brookline Mental Health Ctr., 2001—02. Cons. Neighborhood Health Plan, Boston, 1987-91; mem. adv. bd. Mass. Sch. Profl. Psychology, 1991-98; reviewer Psychiat. Svcs., 1993—; co-chair Nat. Mental Health Conf., Blue Cross Blue Shield Nationwide, 1995-97; steering com. Occupl. Medicine, 1997; bd. dirs. Concord Assabet Adolescent and Family Svcs., 1998—; mem. nat. adv. com. Behavioral Healthcare Ptnrs., 1999—. Contbr. articles to profl. jours., chpt. to book Primary Care Meets Mental Health, 1997. Recipient stipend Nat. Inst. Mental Health, 1969, 70, 73. Mem. Am. Coll. Mental Health Adminstrs., Sigma Theta Tau. Democrat. Avocations: antiques, cooking, decorating, biking, hiking. Office: The Oak Group 888 Worcester St Ste 40 Wellesley MA 02482-3793 E-mail: nlangman@oakgroup.com.

LANGMEAD, JOSEPH MICHAEL, accountant, consultant; b. Balt., Nov. 5, 1944; s. Richard James and Dorothy Kathleen (DeCarlo) L.; m. Judy Kay Kearney, June 26, 1969; children: Maureen Langmead Cochran, Gregory, Benjamin. BSBA, Loyola Coll., 1968, MBA, 1973; postgrad., St. Mary's Sem. and Univ., Balt., 2000—. CPA, Md. Acct. Kushnick & Waldman, Balt., 1965-68; auditor KPMG, 1968-76, ptnr. N.Y.C., 1976-2000; cons. Balt., 2000—. SEC reviewing ptnr. KPMG, London, 1994-2000. Pres. bd. trustees Ctr. Stage, Balt., 1981-88, chmn. capital campaign, 1988-91; chmn. bd. trustees Loyola H.S., Towson, Md., 1983-87; bd. fin. City of Balt., 1988-92; trustee Roland Pk. Country Sch., Balt., 1990-93, Md. State Arts Coun., Balt., 1991-94; chmn. Balt. Arts Stabilization Project Com., 1991-94; bd. dirs. Nat. Arts Stabilization, Balt., 1991-2001, chmn., 2000-01; bd. dirs. Md. chpt. Nat. Multiple Sclerosis Soc., 2002—. With U.S. Army, 1968-70. Mem. AICPA, Md. Assn. CPAs (bd. dirs. 1990-93), Mensa. Democrat. Roman Catholic. Avocations: opera, music, theology, history. Home: 102 Witherspoon Rd Baltimore MD 21212 E-mail: joseph.langmead@verizon.net.

LANGNESS, DAVID GORDON, manufacturing executive; b. New Richmond, Wis., Aug. 28, 1953; s. Gilbert Donald and Helen Lucille (Hanson) L.; m. Cynthia Louise Goulet, July 31, 1982; children: Michael, Nicole, David Jr., Danielle, Benjamin. BA in Biology and Chemistry, Augsburg Coll., 1975; MA in Human Resources Mgmt., Pepperdine U., 1981; MS, MBA, West Coast U., 1986; D of Mgmt., Webster U., 1996. CFP. Commd. 2d. lt. USMC, 1975, advanced through grades to capt., resigned, 1983; group mgr. quality ctrl. Douglas Aircraft, Long Beach, Calif., 1984-86, telecom mgr., 1986-89, McDonnell Douglas, St. Louis, 1989-92, bus. ops. mgr., 1992-95, auditing mgr., 1995-96, prog. mgr., 1996—. Scoutmaster Boy Scouts Am., St. Charles, Mo., 1995—; pres. Webster U. Doctoral Assn., 1997-99. Named honor grad. USMC, Quantico, Va., 1975. Mem. Ind. Assn. Cert. Fin. Planning, Strategic Planning Forum. Avocations: sports, pigeon fancier, woodworking. Home: 4 Bluff View Ct Saint Charles MO 63303-6607 Office: The Boeing Co M/S S270-1345 PO Box 516 Saint Louis MO 63166-0516 E-mail: dlangness@aol.com., david.g.langness@boeing.com.

LANGONE, KENNETH, investment company executive; BA, Bucknell U.; MBA, NYU. Chmn., CEO Invemed Assocs., N.Y.C. Bd. dirs. Choicepoint, Inc., GE, TRICON Global Restaurants, Unifi, Inc., NY Stock Exch. Bd. overseers Stern Sch.; chmn. bd. trustees NYU Med. Sch.; trustee, chmn. nominating com., chmn. endowment com., mem. exec. com. Bucknell U., NY Philharm., Children's Oncology Soc. (Ronald McDonald House), Robin Hood Found. Office: Invemed Assocs 375 Park Ave Ste 2205 New York NY 10152

LANGONI, RICHARD ALLEN, civil engineer; b. Trinidad, Colo., Aug. 7, 1945; s. Domenic and Josephine (Maria) L.; m. Pamela Jill Stansberry, Aug. 19, 1972; children: Kristi, Kerri. A of Applied Sci., Trinidad State Jr. Coll., 1966; BSCE, Colo. State U., 1968; MA, U. No. Colo., 1978. Registered profl. engr., Colo. Civil engr. Dow Chm. Co., Golden, Colo., 1968-71; city engr., dir. pub. works City of Trinidad, 1971-74; civil engr. Clement Bros. Constrn. Co., 1974-75; instr. Trinidad State Jr. Coll., 1975-78; city engr., dir. pub. works City of Durango, Colo., 1978-82; traffic engr. Colo. Dept. Transp., Durango, 1982—. Civil engineer; b. Trinidad, Colo., Aug. 7, 1945; s. Domenic and Josephine (Maria) L.; A of Applied Sci., Trinidad State Jr. Coll., 1966; BSCE Colo. State U., 1968; MA, U. No. Colo., 1978; m. Pamela Jill Stansberry, Aug. 19, 1972; children: Kristi, Kerri. Registered profl. engr. Colo., N.Mex. Civil engr. Dow Chem. Co., Golden, Colo., 1968-71; city engr., dir. public works City of Trinidad, 1971-74; civil engr. Clement Bros. Constrn. Co., 1974-75; instr. Trinidad State Jr. Coll., 1975-78; city engr., dir. public works City of Durango (Colo.), 1978-82; traffic engr. Colo. Dept. Transp., Durango, 1982—. Recipient Meritorious Svc. award City of Durango. Mem. Nat. Soc. Profl. Engrs., ASCE, Am. Public Works Assn., Water Pollution Control Fedn., Profl. Engrs. Colo., Durango C. of C., Nat. Ski Patrol (Purgatory and Wolf Creek), Phi Theta Kappa, Chi Epsilon. Recipient Meritorious Svc. award City of Durango. Mem. ASCE, Nat. Soc. Profl. Engrs., Am. Pub. Works Assn., Water Pollution Control Fedn., Profl. Engrs. Colo., Durange C. of C., Nat. Ski Patrol (Purgatory and Wolf Creek), Phi Theta Kappa, Chi Epsilon. Home: 30 Moenkopi Dr Durango CO 81301-8599 E-mail: Richard.Langoni@dot.state.co.us .

LANGRIDGE, ROBERT, scientist, educator; b. Essex, Eng., Oct. 26, 1933; came to U.S., 1957; naturalized, 1987. s. Charles and Winifred (Lister) L.; m. Ruth Gottlieb, June 26, 1960; children: Elizabeth, Catherine, Suzanne. BSc in Physics (1st class honours), U. London, Eng., 1954, PhD in Crystallography, 1957. Vis. research fellow biophysics Yale, 1957-59; research assoc. biophysics M.I.T., 1959-61; research assoc. pathology Children's Cancer Research Found., Boston; research assoc. biophysics, lectr. biophysics, also tutor biochem. scis. Harvard, 1961-66; research assoc. Project MAC, Lab. for Computer Sci., M.I.T., 1964-66; prof. biophysics and info. scis. U. Chgo., 1966-68; prof. chemistry and biochem. scis. Princeton, 1968-76; prof. pharm. chemistry, biochemistry and biophysics, dir. Computer Graphics Lab. U. Calif., San Francisco, 1976-94, prof. emeritus, 1994—. Vis. prof. computer sci. Stanford U., 1983-84; vis. prof. biochem., biophys. Oreg. State U., 1995-97; mem. computer and biomath. rsch. study sect. NIH, USPHS, 1968-72, chmn., 1975-77, mem. nat. adv. rsch. resources coun., 1992-96, mem. adv. com. to dir., 1993-95; mem. vis. com. biology dept. Brookhaven Nat. Lab., 1977-80, mem. adv. com. neutron diffraction, biology dept., 1980-83; mem. sci. and ednl. adv. com. Lawrence Berkeley Labs., 1988-92; chair U. Calif. Berkeley/U. Calif. San Francisco Grad. Group in Bioengring., 1991-93; mem. computer sci. and telecomm. bd. NRC, NAS, 1988-91. Guggenheim fellow, 1983-84 Fellow AAAS; mem. NAS, Inst. of Medicine. Home: 60 The Crescent Berkeley CA 94708-1702 E-mail: boblangr@socrates.berkeley.edu.

LANGROCK, KARL FREDERICK, former academic administrator; b. Toeterville, Iowa, Jan. 26, 1927; s. Lee Henry and Alice Dora (Grube) L.; m. Rose Marie Meyer, June 4, 1950; children: Laura Sue, Charles Alan. BA, U. No. Iowa, 1949; MA, U. Iowa, 1951; MDiv, Luth. Sch. Theology, Chgo., 1955; LittD (hon.), Grand View Coll., 1989. Pastor Lake Park Luth. Ch., Milw., 1955-57, Resurrection Luth. Ch., Franklin Park, Ill., 1957-62, Luth. Ch of the Holy Spirit, Deerfield, 1962-69; asst. to pres. Berea (Ky.) Coll., 1969-72; pres. Grand View Coll., Des Moines, 1972-88; free-lance writer, 1988—. Mem. Iowa Coll. Aid Commn., Des Moines, 1980-84, Luth. Social Services of Ill., Chgo., 1962-70, pres., 1968-70. Served in USN, 1945-46. Mem. Iowa Assn. Independent Colls. and Univs. (bd. dirs. 1972-87, chmn. 1986-87), Council of Luth. Ch. in Am. Colls. (pres. 1978), Phi Eta Sigma. Address: 6665 W Burnside Rd Apt 456 Portland OR 97210-6669

LANGSLEY, DONALD GENE, psychiatrist, medical board executive; b. Topeka, Oct. 5, 1925; s. Morris J. and Ruth (Pressman) L.; m. Pauline R. Langsley, Sept. 9, 1955; children: Karen Jean, Dorothy Ruth, Susan Louise. BA, SUNY, Albany, 1949; MD, U. Rochester, 1953. Diplomate: Am. Bd. Psychiatry and Neurology (dir. 1976-80), Nat. Bd. Med. Examiners. Intern USPHS Hosp., San Francisco, 1953-54; resident psychiatry U. Calif., 1954-59, NIMH career tchr. in psychiatry, 1959-61; candidate San Francisco and Chgo. insts. for psychoanalysis, 1958-67; asst. prof., assoc. prof. psychiatry U. Colo. Sch. Medicine, 1961-68; prof., chmn. dept. psychiatry U. Calif., Davis, 1968-77, U. Cin., 1977-81; prof. dept. psychiatry Northwestern U. Sch. Medicine, Chgo., 1981—. Mem. psychiatry edn. com. NIMH, 1969-75; exec. v.p. Am. Bd. Med. Spltys., 1981-91; trustee Ednl. Commn. for Fgn. Med. Graduates, 1983-91; mem. adv. com. on Grad. Med. Edn. Dept. Def., 1986-87; bd. govs. EcuMed, 1983-85; bd. dirs. Nat. Resident Matching Program, 1982, sec. 1984-87, 89-91, pres. 1987-89; mem. Ill. Med. Disciplinary Bd., 2000—. Author: The Treatment of Families in Crisis, 1968, Mental Health Education in the New Medical Schools, 1973, Peer Review Manual for Psychiatry, 1976, Handbook of Community Mental Health, 1981, Evaluating the Skills of Medical Specialists, 1983, Legal Aspects of Certification & Accreditation, 1983, Trends in Specialization, 1985, Hospital Privileges & Specialty Medicine, 1986, Hospital Privileges & Specialty Medicine, 2d edit., 1991, How to Evaluate Residents, 1986, How to Select Residents, 1988, Health Policy Issues in Graduate Medicine Education, 1992, Ethics Primer of American Psychiatric Association, 2000; contbr. articles to med. jours. Served with AUS, 1943-46; med. officer USPHS, 1953-54. Recipient Spl. awards Colo. Assn. for Mental Health, 1968, Spl. awards Sacramento Area Mental Health Assn., 1973 Fellow Am. Psychiat. Assn. (Hofheimer award 1971, pres. 1980-81, chmn. peer rev. com. 1975-77, Kiewit lectr. 1990, Adminstrv. Psychiatry award 1993, ethics appeals bd. 1993-99, ethics com. 2000-03), Am. Coll. Psychiatrists; mem. Ctrl. Calif. Psychiat. Soc. (pres. 1973-74), Colo. Psychiat. Soc. (pres.-elect 1967-68), Soc. Med. Adminstrs. Home and Office: 9445 Monticello Ave Evanston IL 60203-1117 E-mail: langsley@northwestern.edu.

LANGSLEY, PAULINE ROYAL, psychiatrist; b. Lincoln, Nebr., July 2, 1927; d. Paul Ambrose and Dorothy (Sibley) Royal; m. Donald G. Langsley, Sept. 9, 1955; children: Karen Jean, Dorothy Ruth Langsley Runman, Susan Louise. BA, Mills Coll., 1949; MD, U. Nebr., 1953. Cert. psychiatrist, Am. Bd. Psychiatry and Neurology. Intern Mt. Zion Hosp., San Francisco, 1954; resident U. Calif., 1954-57, student health psychiatrist Berkeley, 1957-61, U. Colo., Boulder, 1961-68; assoc. clin. prof. psychiatry U. Calif. Med. Sch., Davis, 1968-76; student health psychiatrist U. Calif., 1968-76; assoc. clin. prof. psychiatry U. Cin., 1976-82; pvt. practice psychiatry Cin., 1976-82; cons. psychiatrist Federated States of Micronesia, Pohnpei, 1984-87; fellow in geriatric psychiatry Rush-Presbyn./St. Luke Hosp., Chgo., 1989-91. Mem. accreditation rev. com. Accreditation Coun. for Continuing Med. Edn., 1996-98. Trustee Mills Coll., Oakland, 1974-78, 2001—; bd. dirs. Evanston Women's Club. Fellow Am. Psychiat. Assn. (chair continuing med. edn. 1990-96); mem. AMA, Am. Med. Womens Assn., Ohio State Med. Assn., Ill. Psychiat. Assn. (sec. 1993-95, pres.-elect 1995-96, pres. 1996-97, accreditation coun. 1996-98). Home and Office: 9445 Monticello Ave Evanston IL 60203-1117

LANGSNER, ALAN MICHAEL, pediatric cardiologist; b. N.Y.C., Dec. 21, 1948; s. Herman and Celeste (Prince) L.; m. Hilary Schmidt, Dec. 19, 1971. BA in Psychology, Fairleigh Dickinson U., 1970; MD, U. Autonomia Guadalajara, Jalisco, Mex., 1977; postgrad., NYU, 1977-78. Cert. Am. Bd. Pediat. and Pediat. Cardiology. Resident in pediatrics N.Y. Med. Coll./Met. Hosp. Ctr., N.Y.C., 1978-79, resident in pediatrics-primary care tng. program, 1979-80, chief resident in pediatrics-primary care tng. program, 1980-81; pvt. practice pediatric cardiology, 1983—; attending pediatrics, sr. cons. pediatric cardiology St. Barnabas Med. Ctr., Livingston, N.J., 1983—; assoc. cons. pediatric cardiology St. Vincent's Med. Ctr., S.I., N.Y., 1983—; chief dept. pediatric cardiology Children's Hosp. of N.J. at Newark Beth Israel Hosp., 1999—. Cons. pediatric cardiology, clin. assoc. prof. pediatrics NYU Sch. Medicine, N.Y.C., 1983—, S.I. U. Hosp., 1985—; mem. perinatal rev. com., med. bd. St. Barnabas Med. Ctr.; presenter in field. Contbr. articles to profl. jours. Fellow Am. Coll. Caridology, Am. Acad. Pediatrics; mem. AMA, Essex County Med. Soc. Office: 405 Northfield Ave West Orange NJ 07052-3023

LANGSTAFF, DAVID HAMILTON, aerospace industry executive; b. Paris, June 12, 1954; s. E. Kennedy and Percy (Lee) L.; m. Cynthia Shauer, Aug. 26, 1978; children: Meredith Avery, Christopher Maxim, Thomas Stoddard, William Hamilton. BA cum laude, Harvard U., 1977, MBA, 1981. Assoc. First Boston Internat., Athens, Greece, 1977-78, Blyth Eastman Dillon & Co., Athens, 1978-79; prin. Langstaff Design & Mgmt., Cambridge, Mass., 1980-81; assoc. Inverness Group, Houston, 1981-82, v.p. corp. fin., 1982-83, v.p. corp. fin., mgr. mergers and acquisitions, 1983-84; sr. v.p., CFO, sec., treas., dir. Space Industries Inc., 1984-93; CFO, dir. Calspan SRL Corp., Washington, 1993-95; pres., CEO, vice chmn. Veridian (formerly Calspan), 1995—. Bd. dirs. Barnesville Sch., Washington Revels; moderator The Aspen Inst. Avocations: music, athletics, counseling. Office: Veridian Corp 1200 S Hayes St Ste 1100 Arlington VA 22202-5005

LANGSTAFF, ELEANOR MARGUERITE, retired library science educator; b. Washington, June 21, 1934; d. William Truman and Bernice Louise (Tharpe-Mecum) De Selms; m. David Knox Langstaff, June 19, 1970 (dec. 1984). BA, Colo. State U., Ft. Collins, 1958; MA, Fordham U., 1961; MS, Cath. U. Am., 1970; MPhil, CUNY, 1994, PhD, 1998; cert. in tropical edn., U. London/Makerere Coll., Uganda. Mem. Tchrs. for East Africa program Columbia U., N.Y.C., 1961-64; fgn. svc. officer USIA, 1965-69, acting country pub. affairs officer Bangui, Central African Republic, 1967-68, regional books officer Nigeria, 1968-69; libr. Sch. Libr. and Info. Sci., Pratt Inst., N.Y.C., 1970-72; assoc. prof. libr. sci. Bernard M. Baruch Coll., CUNY, 1973-95, prof., 1996—. Cons. on info. Langstaff-French Assocs., Manchester, Vt., 1982-88; dir. hypermedia devel. project Libr. Svc. and Constrn. Act, U.S. Dept. Edn., 1989-90. Author: Andrew Lang, 1978; (with Thomas V. Atkins) Access to Information: Library Research and Demonstration Methods, 1979, Panama, 1982; co-author: Access Information: Business, 1986, 90, Access Information: Social Sciences and Humanities, 1990; (with others) British Women Writers, 1988. Vol. ARC, Bklyn., 1972—. Recipient excellence in French lit. award French Govt., 1958, Fulbright Lecturing award U. Mauritius, 1992—. Mem. ALA, Libr. Assn. CUNY (v.p. 1974-75, pres. 1975-76), Assn. Coll. and Rsch. Librs., Phi Beta Mu. Episcopalian. Home: 100 Remsen St Brooklyn NY 11201-4256 E-mail: elang2@juno.com.

LANGSTAFF, JOHN MEREDITH, musician; b. Bklyn., Dec. 24, 1920; s. Bridgewater Meredith and Esther Knox (Boardman) Langstaff; m. Diane Guggenheim; 1 child Carol ; m. Nancy Graydon Woodbridge, Apr. 3, 1948; children: John Elliot, Peter Gerry, Deborah Graydon. Student, Curtis Inst. Music, Juilliard Sch. Music, Columbia U. Founder, dir. emeritus Revels, Inc., Watertown, Mass. Mem. faculty Simmons Coll., Boston, 1970—86, Wheelock Coll., Boston, 1974—79, Mass. Coll. Art, 1977, Boston Coll., 1979, U. Conn., 1977—79, Lesley Coll., 1978—99; artistic dir. Young Audiences Mass., 1972—81, adv. bd. mem., 1981—; lectr. in field. Author: Frog Went a-Courtin', 1955, Over in the Meadow, 1957, On Christmas Day in the Morning, 1959, The Swapping Boy, 1960, Ol' Dan Tucker, 1963, Hi! Ho! The Rattlin' Bog, 1969, Jim Along, Josie, 1970, Gather My Gold Together, 1971, The Golden Vanity, 1971, Soldier, Soldier, Won't You Marry Me?, 1972, The Two Magicians, 1973, Shimmy, Shimmy Coke-a-pop!, 1973, St. George and the Dragon, 1973, A-Hunting We Will go, 1974, A Season for Singing, 1974, Sweetly Sings the Donkey, 1976, Hot Cross Buns, 1978, The Christmas Revels Songbook, 1985, Sally Go Round the Moon, 1986, What a Morning!, 1987, Climbing Jacob's Ladder, 1991, I Have a Song to Sing-O, 1994; author: (foreword) Old Christmas, 1996; co-author: Celebrate the Spring, 1998, Celebrate the Winter, 2001; co-author: (film) The Lively Art of Picture Books; dir.(music dept.): Potomac Sch., 1953—68, Shady Hill Sch., 1969—72. 1st lt. inf. AUS, WWII. Recipient Hope S. Dean Meml. award, Found. for Children's Books, 1991, citation, Boston Theater, 1996, award, Kodaly Music Inst., 2001. Mem.: English Folk Song Soc. (founder, dir. Christmas Revels 1956, 1957,

1966, 1970—2000, dir. Spring Revels 1972—97, dir. Sea Revels 1983—94), Country Dance and Song Soc. Am., Actors Equity, Internat. Folk Music Coun. Office: Revels Inc 80 Mount Auburn St Watertown MA 02472-3930

LANGSTON, JAMES LELAND, electronics engineer; b. Atlanta, July 26, 1942; s. Paul T. and Vernie D. (Bridges) L.; m. Alice Jean Evans, 1985; 1 child, Brent Leland. BSEE, So. Meth. U., 1966, postgrad., 1966-67. Registered profl. engr., Tex. Technician Collins Radio, Richardson, Tex., 1961-65, design engr., 1965-67, lead engr., 1967-70, sr. engr., 1970-71, Tex. Instruments, Dallas, 1971-73, project engr., 1973-75, systems engr., 1975-78, mem. tech. staff, 1978-82, sr. mem. tech. staff, 1982-98, disting. mem. tech. staff, 1998-99, engring. fellow, 1999—, program mgr. com. and signal processing, 1986-92, chief engring. comm. and electronic systems, 1992-96; chief tech. officer Crosspan divsn. Raytheon, 1998-2000, mgr. sys. engring. Colo., 2000—. Contbr. articles to profl. jours. Advisor, Jr. Achievement, Highland Park. H.S., 1981. Recipient Group Achievement award NASA, 1976, cash award and cert. of appreciation, 1979, Pub. Svc. award medal, 1981. Mem. IEEE (chair coms.). E-mail: j-langston2@worldnet.att.net, j-langston2@raytheon.com.

LANGSTON, PAUL T. music educator, university dean, composer; b. Marianna, Fla., Sept. 15, 1928; s. Howard McGhee and Rosa (Jeffries) L.; m. Esther Howard, Aug. 12, 1950; children: Claire Beth, Erin, Howard. Pvt. study with Nadia Boulanger, 1962, 63; diploma, Conservatoire Americaine, France; BA, U. Fla., 1950; MS in Music, So. Bapt. Theol. Sem., 1953; SMD, Union Theol. Sem., 1963; DMus (hon.), Stetson U., 1985. Organist-choirmaster St. John's Bapt. Ch., Charlotte, N.C., 1953-60; instr. music theory Davidson Coll., 1959-60; mem. faculty Stetson U., De Land, Fla., 1960-93, dean Sch. Music, 1963-85, William Kenan Jr. prof. music, 1985-93, prof. and dean music emeritus, 1993—; assoc. condr. Charlotte Oratorio Singers, 1954-60. Dir. Fla. Internat. Music Festival, Fla. Internat. Music Festival Inst.; research fellow Inst. Sacred Music, Yale U., 1985 Composer organ, choral works.; oratorio Petros (premier Nov. 1983). Recipient Hand award for outstanding rsch., 1993. Mem.: Assn. Anglican Musicians, Am. Guild Organists (McEniry award for tchg. excellence 1991), Delta Tau Delta, Pi Kappa Lambda, Omicron Delta Kappa. Home: 313 N Salisbury Ave Deland FL 32720-4054 E-mail: plangsto@dnet.net.

LANGSTON, THOMAS SAMUEL, political science educator; b. Louisville, Nov. 25, 1960; s. John Harold and Patricia Marie Langston; m. Mary Anne Sprague, May 15, 1982; children: Jessica, Taylor. Student, Duke U., 1980; BA cum laude, U. Tex., 1982; PhD, MIT, 1989. Tchr. Keystone Sch., San Antonio, 1982-83; vis. instr. SUNY, Geneseo, 1988-89; asst. prof. dept. polit. sci. Tulane U., New Orleans, 1989-95, assoc. prof., 1995—2002, prof., 2003—, chmn. dept. polit. sci., 1999—2002. Chmn. dept. polit. sci. Tulane U., 1999—. Author: Ideologues and Presidents, 1992, With Reverence and Contempt, 1995, Lyndon Baines Johnson, 2002. Vestry mem. St. George's Episcopal Ch., New Orleans, 1995-98, 2001--. Moody grantee Lyndon Johnson Presdl. Libr. Found., 1987, O'Donnell grantee George Bush Presdl. Libr. Found., 2000; John M. Olin fellow Boston U. Inst. for Study of Econ. Culture, 1990-91. Mem. Am. Polit. Sci. Assn. (bd. dirs. Presidency Rsch. Group 2000—, editor Presidency Rsch. Group Report 2000—), Thackeray Soc. Episcopalian. Avocations: golf, skiing. Home: 4616 Prytania St New Orleans LA 70115 Office: Dept Polit Sci Tulane U New Orleans LA 70118 E-mail: langston@tulane.edu.

LANGTON, CLEVE SWANSON, advertising executive; b. N.Y.C., Sept. 1, 1950; s. Raymond Benedict and Viola (Swanson) L.; m. Patricia Scott, July 16, 1976; children: Elizabeth Renwick, Cleve., Jr. BA, NYU, 1972; MBA, Columbia U., 1974. Product mgr. Gen. Foods Corp., White Plains, N.Y., 1974-76; sr. account exec. Dancer Fitzgerald Sample, N.Y.C., 1976-79; v.p., account supr. D'Arcy MacManus Masius, 1979-83; corp. v.p. bus. devel. worldwide DMB&B, 1983-89; corp. sr. v.p. DDB Needham Worldwide, 1990-92; corp. exec., v.p. multinat. nat. client devel., 1993—. Bd. dirs. Grad. Sch. Bus. Columbia U., Weissman Ctr. Internat. Bus. CUNY, Helen Keller Worldwide. Mem. Met. Club. Office: DDB Needham Worldwide Inc 437 Madison Ave New York NY 10022-7001

LANGTON, DANIEL JOSEPH, English, writing educator, poet; b. Paterson, N.J., Sept. 6, 1927; s. Daniel Patrick and Martha Langton; m. Eva Heymann, Feb. 1, 1949; 1 child, Mark. BA, San Francisco State U., 1952, MA, 1954; PhD, U. Calif., Berkeley, 1970. Lifetime tchg. credential, Calif. Tchr. San Rafael (Calif.) H.S., 1963-67; from asst. prof. to prof. English and creative writing San Francisco State U., 1967—. Author: Querenica, 1976 (Devins award 1976), The Hogarth-Selkirk Letters, 1985, The Inheritance, 1990, Life Forms, 1995. Mem. ACLU. Mem. Poetry Soc. Am., Internat. Poetry Soc., Am. Acad. Poets. Democrat. Home: 1673 Oak St San Francisco CA 94117-2013 Office: San Francisco State Univ Coll Humanities San Francisco CA 94132

LANGTON, JANE GILLSON, writer, illustrator; b. Boston, Dec. 30, 1922; d. Joseph Lincoln and Grace Irene (Brown) Gillson; m. William Gale Langton, June 10, 1943 (dec. Apr. 1997); children: Christopher, David, Andrew. BS, U. Mich., 1944, MA, 1945, Radcliffe Coll., 1948. Author: The Transcendental Murder, 1964, Dark Nantucket Noon, 1975, The Memorial Hall Murder, 1978, Natural Enemy, 1982, Emily Dickinson is Dead, 1984, Good and Dead, 1986, Murder at the Gardner, 1989, The Dante Game, 1991, God in Concord, 1992, Divine Inspiration, 1993, The Shortest Day, 1995, Dead as a Dodo, 1996, The Face on the Wall, 1998, The Thief of Venice, 1999, Murder at Monticello, 2001, The Escher Twist, 2002; (children's books) Her Majesty, Grace Jones, 1961, The Boyhood of Grace Jones, Paper Chains, The Diamond in the Window, The Swing in the Summerhouse, The Astonishing Stereoscope, The Fledgling (Newbery Honor book 1980), The Fragile Flag, 1984, The Time Bike, 2000. Home: 9 Baker Farm Rd Lincoln MA 01773-3005 E-mail: jlangton@mindspring.com.

LANGTON, JEFFREY H. judge; b. Hamilton, Mont., Apr. 22, 1953; s. Richard L. and N. Louise (Mittower) L.; m. Patricia L. Stanbery, June 17, 1978 (div. Feb. 1999); children: Melanie, Matthew, Stephen, Thomas. BA in history with high honors, U. Mont., 1975, JD, 1978. Bar: Mont. 1978, U.S. Dist. Ct. Mont. 1978. Assoc. Schultz Law Firm, Hamilton, 1978-82; pvt. practice, 1982-92; dist. judge 21st Dist. Ct., 1993—. Bd. clin. visitors Law Sch., U. Mont., Missoula, 1993-99; Mont. Sentence Review Divsn., 1998-2001, chmn., 2000-01; chmn. self represented litigants Mont. Supr. Ct. Commn., 2000—. Author: The Victor Story, 1985. Bd. dirs. Victor Heritage Mus., 1990-95. Named Man of Yr. Victor Booster Club, 1988, 93. Mem. ABA (Mont. del. 1994—), Am. Jud. Soc., Mont. Bar Assn., Mont. Judges Assn. Presbyterian. Avocations: Montana history, fly fishing, environmental issues. Home: 2975 Mittower Rd Victor MT 59875-9542 Office: 21st Jud Dist 205 Bedford St Hamilton MT 59840-2853

LANGUM, W. SUE, civic worker; b. Kennett, Mo., Jan. 10, 1934; d. Howard S. and Lucille (Hubble) Walker; m. Norman H. Nelson, June 22, 1957 (dec. Sept. 1969); 1 child, Kirby Walker Nelson; m. John K. Langum, Dec. 28, 1972 (dec. Feb. 1998). Student, Northwestern U., 1952-53, Crane Jr. Coll., 1953-54. Svc. rep. Ill. Bell Tel. Co., Chgo., 1956-57; receptionist Tri-City Animal Hosp., Elgin, Ill., 1967-69; rsch. asst. Bus. Econs. Inc., Chgo., 1969-73, dir., 1973—. V.p. Elgin Coun. PTA, 1969-73; bd. dirs. OEO, 1972-73, Meals on Wheels, Elgin, 1972-93, Coloquy Coffee House, 1968-70, Judson Coll. Friends, 1976-87, Elgin Area Hist. Soc., 1982—, Elgin Symphony Orch. Assn., 1984-93, Elgin Symphony League, 1982-93, pres. 1984-86; bd. dirs. United Meth. Women, 1978-93, pres., 1980-84; vol. Fish, 1974-76; bd. dirs., treas. Easter Seal Assn. for Crippled Children, 1977-90; mem. Elgin Beautification Commn., 1986-88, Tuesday Morning Bible Study Club. Mem. Sister Cities Assn. Elgin (bd. dirs. 1990), LWV (v.p. Elgin Club 1965), Tucson Women's Club, Current History Forum Club. Home: 4096 Silverstone Rd Zionville NC 28698-9381

LANGWIG, JOHN EDWARD, retired wood science educator; b. Albany, N.Y., Mar. 5, 1924; s. Frank Irving and Arlene Stone (Dugan) L.; m. Margaret Jacquelyn Kirk, Aug. 31, 1946; 1 dau., Nancy Ann Langwig Davis. BS, U. Mich., 1948; MS, Coll. of Forestry, SUNY, Syracuse, 1968, PhD, 1971. Asst. to supt. Widdicomb Furniture Co., Grand Rapids, Mich., 1948-50; salesman John B. Hauf Furniture, Inc., Albany, N.Y., 1950-51; asst. mgr. furniture dept. Montgomery Ward Co., Menands, 1951-52; office mgr. U.S. Plywood Corp., Syracuse, 1952-65; instr. wood products engring. SUNY Coll. Forestry, 1969-70; asst. prof. wood sci. Okla. State U., Stillwater, 1971-74, prof., head dept. forestry, 1974-81, prof. wood sci., wood products extension specialist, 1982-86, mem. faculty council, 1983-86; mem. Gov.'s Com. on Forest Practices, 1975-77. Contbr. articles to profl. jours. Served with AUS, 1943-45. NSF fellow, 1966-68 Mem. Soc. Am. Foresters, TAPPI, Forest Products Research Soc. (regional bd. dirs. 1983-89, regional rep. to nat. exec. bd. 1983-86), Soc. Wood Sci. and Tech., Okla. Acad. Sci., Okla. Forestry Assn. (bd. dirs. 1982-83), Council Forestry Sch. Execs., Sigma Xi, Xi Sigma Pi., Gamma Sigma Delta, Alpha Zeta, Phi Kappa Phi. Episcopalian. Home: 33 Liberty Cir Stillwater OK 74075-2015 Office: Okla State U Dept Forestry Stillwater OK 74078-0001 *My graduate education began after a seventeen year career in the forest products industry. This additional education broadened my life, and opened up a rich new world of experience beyond my greatest expectations. I commend to all young people the pursuit of a maximum education, as one of life's most worthy efforts.*

LANGWORTHY, EVERETT WALTER, association executive, natural gas exploration company executive; b. West Springfield, Mass., Aug. 17, 1918; s. Walter Carr and Lucy Anne (Laurent) L.; m. Mary Jane Mateer, Nov. 30, 1946 (dec. Oct. 1966); children: John Alan, Jo Ann Langworthy Sears, Robert Carr; m. Joan E. Scott, Feb. 27, 1982; stepchildren: Russell, Michael, Gregory BA, U. Mass., 1940; MA, George Washington U., 1964; grad., Nat. War Coll., 1964. Commd. 2d lt. U.S. Army, 1943; commd. capt. U.S. Air Force, 1947; advanced through grades to col., 1963; ret., 1972; v.p. ops. Meteor Aero Inc., Gaithersburg, Md., 1972-76; sec. contest and record bd. Nat. Aero. Assn., Washington, 1976-80, exec. v.p., 1980—. V.p. LABCO Inc., Martinsburg, W.Va., 1974—; gen. ptnr. M&E Assocs., Gaithersburg, 1976—; dir. Acad. Model Aeronautics, Reston, Va.; cons. FBI, 1992—; cons. FBI; cons., expert witness, 1995—. Contbr. articles and columns on aerospace activities to profl. publs. U.S. rep. Fedn. Aeronautique Internat., Paris, 1980—. Decorated DFC, Air medal African Campaign award, Berlin Air Life medal; recipient Paul Tissandier diploma Fedn. Aeronautique Internationale, 1987. Mem. Nat. Aviation Club (elder statesman aviation 1990), Aero Club Washington, Air Force Assn., Ret. Officers Assn., Soaring Soc. Am. (bd. dirs. 1980—), U.S. Hang Gliding Assn. (bd. dirs. 1980—), VFW. Clubs: Lakewood Country (Rockville, Md.). Republican. Avocations: golf; writing. Home: 610 Gunston Ln Wilmington NC 28405-5317 Office: Nat Aeronautic Assn 1815 Ft Myer Dr Arlington VA 22209-1805 Fax: 910-256-0480. E-mail: ewlang@earthlink.net.

LANGWORTHY, LUCINDA MINTON, lawyer; b. Paris, Jan. 3, 1956; came to U.S. 1958; d. Wilfred Max Mortimer and Florence (Schrey) Minton; m. John Alan Langworthy, Feb. 17, 1989; children: Alan Frederick David, Gary Paul, Maxwell Carr. Student, Univ. Coll., Buckingham, Eng., 1977; BA in Biology and English, Bucknell U., 1978; JD, George Washington U., 1981. Bar: D.C. 1981, U.S. Dist. Ct. D.C. 1984, U.S. Ct. Appeals (D.C. cir. 1986), U.S. Supreme Ct. 2000. Jud. clk. Atomic Safety and Licensing Bd. Panel, U.S. NRC, Washington, 1981-83; assoc. Hunton & Williams, 1983-90, counsel, 1990—. Mem. ABA, Prettyman-Leventhal Am. Inn of Ct. Office: Hunton & Williams 1900 K St NW Washington DC 20006-1110 E-mail: clangworthy@hunton.com.

LANGWORTHY, ROBERT BURTON, lawyer; b. Kansas City, Mo., Dec. 24, 1918; s. Herman Moore and Minnie (Leach) L.; m. Elizabeth Ann Miles, Jan. 2, 1942; children: David Robert, Joan Elizabeth Langworthy Tomek, Mark Burton. AB, Princeton U., 1940; JD, Harvard U., 1943. Bar: Mo. 1943, U.S. Supreme Ct. 1960. Practiced in, Kansas City, 1943—; assoc., then mem. and v.p. Linde, Thomson, Langworthy, Kohn & Van Dyke, P.C., 1943-91; pres., mng. shareholder Blackwood, Langworthy & Schmelzer, P.C., Kansas City, Mo., 1991-96; mng. mem. Blackwood & Langworthy, LC, 1996—. Lectr. on probate, law sch. CLE courses U. Mo., Kansas City. Mem. bd. editors Harvard Law Rev., 1941-43; contbr. chpts. to Guardian and Trust, Powers, Conservatorships and Nonprobate Desk Books of Mo. Bar. Mem. edn. appeal bd. U.S. Dept. Edn., 1982-86; commr. Housing Authority Kansas City, 1963-71, chmn., 1969-71; chmn. Bd. Election Commrs. Kansas City, 1973-77; chmn. bd. West Ctrl. area YMCA, 1969—; mem. bd. Mid-Am. region YMCA, 1970-83, vice chmn., 1970-73, chmn., 1973-78; pres. Met. Bd. Kansas City (Mo.) YMCA (now YMCA of Greater Kansas City), 1965, bd. dirs., 1965—, mem. nat. bd. 1971-78, 79-83; bd. dirs. YMCA of the Rockies, 1974—, bd. sec., 1994-99; chmn. bd. trustees Sioux Indian YMCAs, 1983—; bd. dirs. Armed Svcs. YMCA, 1984-85; pres. Met. Area Citizens Edn., 1969-72; chmn. Citizens Assn. Kansas City (Mo.), 1967, bd. dirs., 1995-96; bd. dirs. Project Equality Kans.-Mo., 1967-80, pres., 1970-72, treas., 1972-73, sec., 1973-76; 1st v.p. Human Resources Corp. Kansas City, 1969-71, 72-73, bd. dirs., 1965-73; hon. v.p. Am. Sunday Sch. Union (now Am. Missionary Fellowship), 1965—; vice chmn. bd. trustees Kemper Mil. Sch., 1966-73; U.S. del. YMCA World Coun., Buenos Aires, 1977, Estes Park, Colo., 1981, Nyborg, Denmark, 1985; bd. dirs. Mo. Rep. Club, 1960—; del., mem. platform com. Rep. Nat. Conv., 1960; Rep. nominee for U.S. Congress, 1964; mem. gen. assembly Com. on Representation Presbyn., 1991-97, moderator, 1993-94; commr. to gen. assembly Presbyn. Ch., 1984, mem. gen. assembly com. on location of hdqs. 1984-87; moderator Heartland Presbyn., 1984. Lt. (j.g.) USNR, 1943-46, capt. Res. ret. Mem.: ABA, Harvard Law Sch. Assn. Mo. (v.p. 1973—74, pres. 1974—75, 1985—87), Lawyers Assn. Kansas City, Mo. State Bar (chmn. probate and trust com. 1983—85, chmn. sr. lawyers com. 1991—93), Kansas City Bar Assn. (chmn. probate law com. 1988—90, 1999—2000, living will com. 1989—91), Kansas City Club. Presbyterian (Elder). Home: Claridge Ct Apt 305 8101 Mission Rd Prairie Village KS 66208-5238 Office: 1220 Washington St Ste 300 Kansas City MO 64105-1439 E-mail: Robertlangworthy@aol.com.

LANGWORTHY, THOMAS ALLAN, microbiologist, educator; b. Oak Park, Ill., Aug. 7, 1943; s. Thomas Earl and Jean Carolyn (Hruby) L.; m. Pamela Joyce Tanis, May 15, 1965 (div. 1985); children; Jocelyn Ann, Jennifer Elise; m. Jane Rae Heckenlively, Sept. 15, 1988. AB, Grinnell Coll., 1965; PhD, U. Kans., 1971. Asst. prof. U. S.D., Vermillion, 1973-78, assoc. prof., 1978-82, prof., 1982-91, prof., chair, 1991-95, prof., 1995—. Alexander von Humboldt preistrager and guest prof. U. Regensburg, Germany, 1984-85; cons. EG&G Idaho, Idaho Falls, 1984—. Contbr. articles to profl. jours. and chpts. to books; mem. editl. bd. Applied and Environ. Microbiology, 1987-96. Fellow Am. Acad. Microbiology; mem. Am. Soc. for Microbiology, AAAS, Internat. Orgn. for Mycoplasmology, Sigma Xi. Office: U SD Sch Medicine 414 E Clark St Vermillion SD 57069-5166 E-mail: tlangwor@usd.edu.

LANGWORTHY, WILLIAM CLAYTON, college official; b. Watertown, N.Y., Sept. 3, 1936; s. Harold Greene and Carolyn (Peach) L.; m. Margaret Joan Amos, Sept. 6, 1958; children: Kenneth, Geneva. BS magna cum laude, Tufts U., 1958; PhD, U. Calif.-Berkeley, 1962. Asst. prof. Alaska Meth. U., Anchorage, 1962-65; asst. prof. chemistry Calif. State U.-Fullerton, 1965-67, assoc. prof., 1967-72, prof., 1972-73, assoc. dean Sch. Letters Arts and Scis., 1970-73; prof. chemistry Calif. Poly. State U., San Luis Obispo, 1973-76, head dept. chemistry, 1973-76; dean Sch. Sci. and Math Calif. Poly State U., 1976-83; v.p. acad. affairs Ft. Lewis Coll., Durango, Colo., 1983-95, prof., 1995-2000. Author: monograph Environmental Education, 1971; contbr. articles to profl. jours. Treas. Coun. Concerned Citizens, Inc., Arroyo Grande, Calif., 1976—83; mem. Clean Air Coalition, San Luis Obispo, 1978—83; active Mozart Festival, 1981—82; mem. Jacksonville Boosters, 2001—, treas., 2002—; mem. Rogue Valley Harmonizers, 2001—; bd. dirs. Durango Choral Soc., 1984—93, San Juan Symphony League, pres, 1997—2000; bd. dirs. Durango Repertory Theatre Co., 1990—96, pres., 1992—94. Mem. AAAS, AAHE, Am. Chem. Soc., Coun. Colls. Arts and Scis. (bd. dirs. 1982), Sierra Club, Phi Beta Kappa, Sigma Xi, Kappa Mu Epsilon, Phi Kappa Phi. Home: PO Box 1570 Jacksonville OR 97530 E-mail: hillsidebill@aol.com.

LANHAM, SALLIE CLAY, artist, educator; b. Louisville, Dec. 15, 1939; d. Watson and Virginia Murphy (Alexander) Clay; m. Jame Forrest Thompson, Aug. 25, 1962 (div. Sept. 1985); children: James Clay, Forrest Clay; m. Charles Robert Lanham Jr., Dec. 27, 1986. Grad., Cin. Art Acad., 1964. Artist Stone Advt. Studio, Lexington, Ky., 1964-65; artist tours dept. Commonwealth of Ky., Frankfort, 1965-70; artist educator Capital Day Sch., 1970-84; adult art tchr. Ky. State U., 1972-74; art dir. Assn. Publs., Inc., Louisville, 1984-88; artist, art dir. Lanham Media Svc., Frankfort & Crystal Lake, Ill., 1988—. One woman show at Ctrl. Bank Gallery, Lexington; exhibited in group shows at Loudoun House, Lexington, Frankfort Arts Art Guild, Ky. Watercolor Soc., Louisville, Ctrl. Ky. Art Guild, Elizabethtown, Ky., Lexington Arts and Cultural Coun., 1998, Arts Pl. Gallery, Lexington, Masterpieces of Maturity, Lexington, 1998, Indpls. Mus. Art Rental Gallery, Totally Transparent, Louisville, Ky. Visions, Frankfort and Somerset, 1998. 1st v.p. Frankfort Arts Found., 1986-87; chmn. County Rep. Party, Franklin County, Ky., 1987—; bd. dirs. King Ctr., Frankfort Arts Found.; 3d v.p. Off Broadway Theater, Frankfort Presbyn. Ch.; pres. Northland Area Art League; bd. dirs., treas. Civic Ctr. Authority, Crystal Lake; mem. steering com. Women's Network. Fellow Va. Ctr. for Creative Arts, 1998; recipient Ky. visions award Project Art Tchr. prize Ky. Art Edn. Assn., Ky. Arts Coun., 1998, 1st pl. award several juried art fairs, Ill.; Arts Showcase grante Frankfort Arts Found., 1999. Mem. Frankfort Area Art Guild (v.p. 1999-2000, bd. dirs. 1986—, chmn. student art show 1987-2000), Ky. Watercolor Soc. (3d pl. award 198&), Lexington Art League, Ctrl. Ky. Art Guild, Colonial Dames Am. (3d v.p. Ky. chpg. 1987—). Presbyterian. Avocation: water sports. Office: Lanham Media Svc 8 Justice Ln Frankfort KY 40601-9495 E-mail: lanham@dcr.net.

LANHAM, SANDRA, conservationist; BA in Social Psychology, We. Mich. U., 1970. Lic. pvt. pilot. Founder, dir. The Desert Sanctuary, Ariz., Environ. Flying Svcs., Tucson, 1991—. Founding bd. mem. Coastal Conservative Found.; bd. dirs. Border Ecology Project. Mem.: Internat. Assn. Natural Resource Pilots. Office: Environ Flying Svcs 250 W Old Ina Rd Tucson AZ 85704*

LANIER, BOB, mayor; b. Baytown, Tex. Chmn. Tex. Hwy. and Pub. Transp. Commn., 1983-87, Met. Transit Authority, Houston, 1987-89; mayor City of Houston, 1992-98. Recipient V.P. Al Gore's Hammer award in recognition of efforts to streamline govt., Outstanding Tex. Leader award John Ben Shepherd Pub. Leadership Found. Office: City of Houston PO Box 1562 Houston TX 77251-1562

LANIER, DOUGLAS MERCER, English language and literature educator; b. Augusta, Ga., Dec. 22, 1955; s. Robert L. and Sarah M. Lanier. BA, Stetson U., 1977; MA, Duke U., 1979, PhD, 1989. Instr. Duke U., Durham, N.C., 1985-86; lectr. UCLA, L.A., 1986-87; asst. prof. Allegheny Coll., Meadville, Pa., 1987-90, U. N.H., Durham, 1990-98, assoc. prof., 1998—, dir. Grad. Studies in English dept., 1998—. Mem. editl. bd. South Atlantic Quar., 1984; author: Shakespeare and Modern Popular Culture, 2002. Mem. MLA, Shakespeare Assn. Am., Renaissance Soc. Am. Office: U NH Dept English Durham NH 03824 E-mail: Doug.Lanier@unh.edu.

LANIER, DREW NOBLE, political science educator; b. Dallas, Dec. 21, 1962; s. J. E. and Jeannine N. Lanier. BA, U. North Tex., 1986, PhD, 1997; JD, DePaul U., 1990. Bar: Tex., U.S. Ct. Appeals (5th cir.). Assoc. atty. Hughes, Watters & Askanase, LLP, Houston, 1990—92; asst. prof. polit. sci. U. Ctrl. Fla., Orlando, 1997—. Contbr. chpts. to scholarly publs. and articles to profl. jours. Mem. Am. Polit. Sci. Assn., So. Polit. Sci. Assn., Midwest Polit. Sci. Assn., Western Polit. Sci. Assn., S.W. Social Sci. Assn. Office: U Ctrl Fla PO Box 161356 Orlando FL 32816 E-mail: dlanier@mail.ucf.edu.

LANIER, GEORGE H. lawyer; b. LaGrange, Ga., Feb. 20, 1944; AB cum laude, Harvard Coll., 1966; LLB, Columbia U., 1970. Bar: Ga. 1971. Ptnr. King & Spalding, Atlanta. Mem. ABA, State Bar Ga., Atlanta Bar Assn. Office: King & Spalding 191 Peachtree St NE Ste 4900 Atlanta GA 30303-1740

LANIER, JACQUELINE RUTH, curator, artist; b. Boston, Dec. 15, 1947; d. John Stanley and Mary Elizabeth (Porter) L.; 1 child, Raymond Rashad Lanier. BS in Edn., Morgan State U., 1976. Drama specialist Day in Arts Boston Symphony, 1971; drama specialist Balt. City Cultural Arts & Urban Svcs., 1974-78; prodr., host Sta. WEAA-FM, 1985-90; with ACTION, 1987-89; R & D implementer Abell Found., 1988-89; developer, curator Lanier Mus. African-Am. History, 1983—; bus. mgr. League for Handicap-Camp Greentop, 1997; cons., development, program coord. Being Reunited with Opportunity, 1998—. Seminar staff developer dept. edn. Balt. Cith Sch., 1988; lectr., presenter IRS, 1988; R & D implementer Lady Md. Found., 1989; lectr. D.C. Pub. Libr., 1990; asst. devel. coord., collections mgr. Heritage Mus. Art, 1990—, Lanier Enterprises Internat., 1997—; curator, lectr. Benjamin Banner Mus. and Park, 1998—; lectr. in field. Prodr. Call of the Ancestor, 1992; exhbts. include Counciling Ctr., 1992, Internat. Black Women Congress, 1992, Morgan State U., 1992, Busterizing, Inc., Md. Commn. African Am. History & Culture, 1992, City Life Mus., 1992, Encore Theatre Co., 1992, Social Security Adminstrn., 1992, New Shiloh Bapt. Ch., 1992, Enon Bapt. Ch., 1992, St. Peter Clavers Ch., 1992, Immaculate Conception Ch., 1994, Martin Luther King Ch., 1994, Heritage Mus. Art, 1994, Chesapeake Coll., 1994, 97, Native Am. Mus., 1994, Nat. Assn. Black Vets., 1994, Dept. Equal Employment Devel., 1994, Perry Point Vets. Hosp., 1994, UN, 1995, D.C. Country Club, 1995, Howard County C.C., 1995, Cambridge Coll., 1995, Johns Hopkins Rsch. Inst., 1995, Hist. Sharp. St. Ch., 1995, Balt. Aquarium, 1996, Chesapeake Coll., 1996, Allaganey County Arts Coun., 1996, Heritage Mus., 1996, Md. Humanities Coun., 1996, Nat. Aquarium Balt. 1996, Mobil Corp. Hdqrs., 1996, 97, Health Care Fin. Adminstrn., 1996, 97, League Serving People with Disabilities, 1997. Mem. exec. com. Broadway East Cmty. Assn.; bd. dirs., 2d dist. rep. Citizen Plabning & Housing Assn.; chmn. East Balt. Coun. Neighborhoods, Inc.; mem. Empowerment Zone Devel. Bd.; gen. ptnr. Gay St. Housing Partnership Ltd.; bd. dirs., pres. Housing Assistance Corp.; v.p. Mid. East Cmty. Devel. Corp.; vol. Balt. City Commn. Women, Urban Svcs. Agy., Balt. City Youth Fair, WAVR Radio; com. mem. Democratic State Ctrl. Com.; mem. substance abuse prevention coun. Mayor's Coordinating Coun. Criminal Justice, Voices of Electorate; mem. Black Single Parents; mem., pres. Ira Aldridge Players; adv. com. minority bus. tourism Md. Dept. Econ. Employment Devel. Office Tourism; mem. Sankofa exhb. adv. com. Md. Hist. Soc., bd. dirs. Seventh Sons Prodn. Co. Recipient Outstanding Svc. award Campfire, Inc., Fifteen Yr. Svc. award, 100 Hours Vol. Svc. award VA, Outstanding Svc. award Md. House Dels., Citation City of Balt. Citizens, Svcs. Agy. & Citizens Balt. award Urban Svcs. Agy., Svc. to Jazz Cmty. award Gemini Prodns., Inc., Outstanding Cmty. Svc. award African Am. Women's Expo, Outstanding Leadership award AFRAM, 1995; inducted into Black Collectors Hall of Fame, 1992, Wall of Fame, 1994, Health Care Fin. Adminstrn., 1997. Mem. Nat. Assn. Fundraising Execs., Nat. Assn. Black Collectors & Dealers, New Gay St. Improvement Assn. (pres.), Black Ethnic Collectibles Mag. (adv. bd.), Transitional Housing Program (adv. com.). Democrat. Lutheran. Avocations: environmentalist, synchronized swimming, writing, reading, storytelling. Home: 3817 Clifton Ave Baltimore MD 21216-2428

LANIER, ROBERT C. (BOB LANIER), real estate owner, developer, former mayor; b. Baytown, Tex., 1925; Student, Lee Coll., Univ. N.Mex.; grad. in law with hons., U. Tex., 1949. Former reporter The Baytown Sun and The Austin Am.-Statesman.; law assoc. Baker & Botts; then pvt. practice; mayor Houston, 1991-97. Chmn. Tex. Highway and Pub. Transp. Commn., Houston Met. Transit Authority; founder Houston Community Coll.; founder, chmn. Bd. Hope Ctr. Wilderness Camp. Office: Ste 3210 909 Fannin St Houston TX 77010-1015

LANIER, WILLIAM JOSEPH, college program director; b. Great Falls, Mont., Dec. 20, 1963; s. Bolder Lanue and Nancy Jo (Kiszczak) L. AS, No. Mont. Coll., 1985, B Tech., 1987, MEd, 1989. Grad. asst. No. Mont. Coll., Havre, 1987-89; dir. residence life Mont. State U. -No. (formerly No. Mont. Coll.), 1989-95, dir. student life, 1995—. Bd. dirs. Havre Encourages Long Range Prevention, 1992-95, Hill County Crimestoppers, 1991-93; adv. bd. No. Ctrl. Mont. Upward Bound, Harlem, 1992—; mem. Nat. Eagle Scout Assn., Irving, Tex., 1991—. Recipient Golden N award student senate No. Mont. Coll., 1992. Mem. Am. Counseling Assn., Am. Coll. Pers. Assn., Nat. Assn. Student Pers. Adminstrs., No. Mont. Coll. Alumni Assn. (bd. dirs 1990—). Avocations: reading, collecting baseball cards. Home: 1236 10th Ave Havre MT 59501 Office: Mont State U PO Box 7751 Havre MT 59501-7751

LANIER, WILLIAM LOVEL, JR. anesthesiologist, educator; b. Statesboro, Ga., June 8, 1955; s. William Lovel Sr. and Nancy (Jones) L.; m. Mary Duckworth, July 15, 1978; children: Elizabeth Brooke, William Hudson. BS, U. Ga., 1976; MD, Med. Coll. of Ga., 1980. Diplomate Am. Bd. Anesthesiology (examiner 1994—, cert. of recertification 2001-). Resident in anesthesiology Wake Forest U. Med. Ctr., Bowman Gray Sch. Medicine, Winston-Salem, N.C., 1980-83; fellow in neurosurg. anesthesia Mayo Grad. Sch. Medicine, Rochester, Minn., 1983-84; cons. in anesthesiology Mayo Clinic,

1984—, prof. anesthesiology, 1995—. Aitken Meml. lectr. U. Western Ont., London, 1993; Marshall Meml. lectr. U. Toronto, 2000. Sect. editor: Jour. Neurosurg. Anesthesiology, 1988—92, editor-in-chief: Mayo Clinic Procs., 1999—; contbr. numerous articles and editls. to profl. publs, chapters to books. Grantee NIH, 1999—. Mem.: Coun. Sci. Editors, Am. Diabetes Assn., Assn. of Univ. Anesthesiologists (mem. sci. adv. bd. 1998—2001), Soc. Neurosurg. Anesthesiology and Critical Care (pres. 1993—94), Am. Soc. Anesthesiologists, First Families of Ga., Phi Kappa Phi, Phi Beta Kappa. Roman Catholic. Avocations: fishing, hunting, reading, boating. Office: Mayo Clinic 200 1st St SW Rochester MN 55905-0002 E-mail: lanier.william@mayo.edu.

LANING, J. HALCOMBE, retired computer scientist; b. Kansas City, Mo., Feb. 14, 1920; s. J. Halcombe and Mary Alice (Knox) L.; m. Betty Arleen Kolb, June 27, 1943; children: Christine, James, Susan, Linda. Student, Kansas City Jr. Coll., 1936-38; SBChemE, MIT, 1940, postgrad., 1941, PhD in Applied Math., 1947; postgrad., Brown U., 1941-42. Engr. Watertown (Mass.) Arsenal Govt. U.S., 1942-45; group leader instrumentation lab. MIT, Cambridge, 1945-73; head dept. C.S. Draper Lab., 1973-88, sr. tech. advisor, 1988-89. Author: Random Processes in Automatic Control, 1956; creator computer programs; patentee in field. C.S. Draper fellow, 1982-85. Mem. NAE, Assn. Computing Machinery, Am. Math. Soc., Soc. for Indsl. and Applied Math., AIAA, IEEE, Inst. Mgmt. Scis. E-mail: hlaning@aol.com.

LANK, EDITH HANDLEMAN, columnist, educator; b. Boston, Feb. 27, 1926; m. Norman Lank; children: Avrum, David, Anna. BA magna cum laude, Syracuse U. Columnist L.A. Times Syndicate, 1976—2000; TV host Sta. WOKR-TV, Rochester, N.Y., 1983-84; radio host Sta. WBBF-AM, 1984-85; columnist Tribune Media Svcs., 2000—. Lectr. St. John Fisher Coll., Rochester, 1977-89; commentator Sta. WXXI-FM, Rochester, 1977—; guest Pub. Radio Internat., St. Paul, 1987—; speaker in field. Author: Home Buying, 1981, Selling Your Home, 1982, Modern Real Estate Practice in New York, 1983, rev. 8th edit., 2001, The Home Seller's Kit, 1988, rev. 4th edit. 1997, The Complete Home Buyer's Kit, 1989, rev. 4th edit., 1997, Dear Edith, 1990, Essentials of New Jersey Real Estate, rev. 4th edit., 2000, 201 Questions Every Homebuyer and Seller Must Ask, 1996, Jane Austen speaks to Women, 2000; co-author: Your Home as a Tax Shelter, 1993; contbr. articles to Time, New Yorker, McCall's, Real Estate Today, Persuasions, Modern Maturity, others. Recipient media award Bar Assn. Monroe County, 1982, Matrix award Women in Ommunications, 1984, Woman of Distinction award Gov. Mario Cumo, N.Y., 1985; named Communicator of Yr., SUNY, Brockport, 1986. Mem. Real Estate Educators Assn. (bd. dirs., Consumer Edn. award 1982, 83, 86, 96, Real Estate Educator of Yr. 1984), Nat. Assn. Real Estate Editors (bd. dirs), Jane Austen Soc. N.Am. (dir.), Phi Beta Kappa. Avocations: scuba diving. Home and Office: 240 Hemingway Dr Rochester NY 14620-3316 E-mail: edithlank@aol.com.

LANKFORD, NEILL STACY, urologist; b. Bicknell, Ind., Mar. 9, 1947; s. Dallas Eugene and Lois Marie (Wampler) L.; m. Suzane Kimble, Aug. 30, 1969; children: Garrick Theodore, Charles Brent, Carmen Marie. BS in Pharmacy, Purdue U., 1970; MD, Ind U., Indpls., 1974. Diplomate Am. Bd. Urology, Nat. Bd. Med. Examiners. Intern Ind. U. Med. Ctr. Hosps., Indpls., 1974-75; resident in gen. surgery Ind. U. Med. Ctr., 1975-76, resident in urology, 1976-79; urologist Urology Assocs. of Elkhart, Ind., 1979—. Pres. Med. Bd. of Ind., Indpls., 1992, 99; mem. Ind. State Licensing Bd., 1992, 95, sec., 1993, v.p., 1993, pres., 1994; staff physician Elkhart Gen. Hosp., 1979—, exec. com., 1984-85, chmn. dept. surgery, 1984-85, dir. med. edn.; vis. staff St. Joseph's Med. Ctr., 1984—; mem. group to develop workshops on use of opiods in chronic pain Pain and Policy Studies Group, 1997—; mem. com. to evaluate licensure exams. Fedn. State Med. Bds., 1998—, nominating com., 1994, 95, cons. to program com., 1995, fin. com., 2000, 01, co-moderator Chgo. meeting, 1995, chmn. com. uniform stds. and procedures, 1996-97, cons. to pain and policy studies group, 1997, bd. dirs., 2002—; mem. credentials com. Ptnrs. Health Plan of Ind., 1998—; assoc. med. dir. Ptnr. Health Plan Ind.; mem. No. Ind. Instnl. Oncology Rev. Bd.; mem. step 3 com. U.S. Med. Lic. Exam., 2001—, mem. com. score validity. Chmn. South Bend (Ind.) Med. Found., 1989-92, Am. heart ride Am. Heart Assn., 2002; peer rev. physician advisor Ind. Found. of Med. Care, 1987-89; physician advisor Sentinel Peer Rev. Orgn., 1989-93; bd. dirs. United Cancer Svcs., YMCA; bd. dirs. No. Ind. region Am. Heart Assn., 2002. Recipient Sagamore of the Wabash award, Gov. Evan Bayh, 1996. Fellow ACS (No. Ind. selection com.); mem. AMA, Am. Urol. Assn. (north ctrl. sect.), Elkhart County Med. Soc. (sec.-treas. 1981-92, pres. 1992), Fedn. of State Med. Bds. (program com. 1994-95, nominating com. 1994-95, del. from Ind. 1996, chmn. spl. com. for uniform stds. and procedures 1997, mem. fin. com. 2000, mem. spl. com. on licensure exams. 1999, 00), Ind. Med. Assn., Elkhart Med. Assn. (bd. dirs.). Avocations: sailing, biking. Home: 21474 Carlton Ave Cassopolis MI 49031-9375 Office: Urology Assocs of Elkhart 105 N Nappanee St Elkhart IN 46514-1994

LANKFORD, THOMAS LEE, governmental relations consultant; b. Rochester, N.Y., Nov. 23, 1963; s. Lee N. and K. Joan Lankford; m. Laurie Ann Lankford, Sept. 21, 1996; children: Cole Alexander, Ethan Lee. BA in Polit. Sci., SUNY, Geneseo, 1985; MA in Internat. Transactions, George Mason U., 1993. Claim adjustor Allstate Ins., Rochester, 1986-87; legis. asst. U.S. Senator Gordon Humphrey, Washington, 1988-90; sr. policy advisor U.S. Senator Bob Smith, 1990-97; v.p. Van Scoyoc Assocs., 1997—.

LANNERS, THOMAS MARTIN, music educator; b. Chgo., July 14, 1965; s. Raymond William and Virginia Lee Lanners; m. Heather Ellen Shea, Oct. 23, 1993; children: Benjamin Thomas, Joel Ethan. MusB summa cum laude, Fla. State U., 1987; MusM, Eastman Sch. Music, 1989, D in Musical Arts, 1991. Instr. music U. Akron, Ohio, 1991—95; assoc. prof. music Okla. State U., Stillwater, 1995—. Presenter in field; adjudicator in field. Mem.: Okla. Music Tchrs. Assn. (chair coll. faculty forum 2002—), Music Tchrs. Nat. Assn., Pi Kappa Lambda, Phi Kappa Phi. Democrat. Avocations: reading, sports. Office: Okla State Univ 132 Seretean Ctr Stillwater OK 74078-4077

LANNERT, ROBERT CORNELIUS, manufacturing company executive; b. Chgo., Mar. 14, 1940; s. Robert Carl and Anna Martha (Cornelius) L.; children: Jacqueline, Krista, Kevin, Meredith. BS in Indsl. Mgmt., Purdue U., 1963; MBA, Northwestern U., 1967; grad. Advanced Mgmt. Program, Harvard U., 1978. With Navistar Internat. Corp. (formerly Internat. Harvester), Chgo., 1963—; staff asst. overseas fin. Navistar Internat. Transp. Corp. (formerly Internat. Harvester), 1967-70; asst. mgr., treas. and contr. IH Finanz AG, Zurich, Switzerland, 1970-72; mgr. overseas fin. corp. hdqrs. Internat. Truck & Engine Co., Chgo., 1972—76, asst. treas., 1976—79, v.p., treas., 1979—90; exec. v.p., chief fin. officer Navistar Internat. Corp., 1990—2002, vice chmn., CFO, 2002—, also bd. dirs. Bd. dirs. NITC, Harbour Assurance Co., Bermuda, Navistar Fin. Corp., Chgo. Mem. Fin. Execs. Inst. Home: 130 N Grant St Hinsdale IL 60521-3334 Office: Navistar Internat Corp 4201 Winfield Rd PO Box 1488 Warrenville IL 60555

LANNES, WILLIAM JOSEPH, III, electrical engineer; b. New Orleans, Oct. 12, 1937; s. William Joseph Jr. and Rhea Helen (Simon) L.; m. Patricia Anne Didier, Jan. 17, 1961; children: David Mark, Kenneth John, Jennifer Anne. BEE, Tulane U., 1959; MEE, U.S. Naval Postgrad. Sch., 1966. Registered profl. engr. Commd. 2d lt. U.S. Marine Corps, 1959, advanced through grades to maj., 1967, served as electronics officer, ops. officer, 1967-70; substation engr. La. Power & Light, New Orleans, 1970-71, utility engr., 1971-76, systems relay engr., 1976-77, systems substation engr., 1977-79, engring. supr. for substation, 1979-83, substation engring. mgr., 1983-86, dir. systems engring., 1986—, v.p. systems engring., 1986-88, with cen. engring., 1988-89; sr. v.p. Energy Supply Fossil, 1989-91; v.p. svc. and support Entergy Corp., 1991-92; assoc. dean rsch. and grad. studies Coll. Engring. U., New Orleans, 1992-97. Dir. U. New Orleans EPRI Cmty. Initiative Ctr., 1993-95; assoc. dir. Ctr. Energy Resources Mgmt., 1993-96, dir. Ctr. Energy Resources Mgmt., 1996-2002; dir. Engring. Mgmt. Program, 1995-2002, chmn. engring. mgmt. dept., 2002—; instr. Delgado Jr. Coll., 1973-74; instr. elec. engring. U. New Orleans, 1979-80; dir. 5th Dist. Savs. and Loan, 1982—; spkr. profl. confs. Contbr. articles to profl. jours. Committeeman New Orleans Area Coun., Boy Scouts Am., 1972-76; vol. United Way 1975, 76, 81; treas. PTA, 1971; vol. tchr. Confraternity of Christian Doctrine, 1972; mem. bus. adv. coun. Our Lady of Holy Cross Coll., 1981-86; chmn. engring. adv. coun. U. New Orleans; bd. dirs. New Life in La.; vol. coach New Orleans Recreation Dept., 1973; mem. La. Employees Com. on Polit. Action, Tulane Univ. Engring. Coun., New Orleans Archdiocesan Pastoral Coun., 1988-91; mem. adv. bd. Bridge House, 1992-95. Decorated Bronze Star; Cross of Gallantry Republic S. Vietnam; recipient Cert. of Merit Mayor New Orleans, 1964; registered profl. engr., La. Fellow IEEE (profl. mem. 1996, Outstanding Svc. award 1976, chmn. New Orleans sect. 1981-82, Edward Freitag award 1988, Region 3 Outstanding Engr. award 1991); mem. Electric Power Rsch. Inst. (industry advisor), Edison Electric Inst. (systems and equipment com.), Soc. Power Rsch. and Implementation (chmn. 1987-94), Southeastern Electric Exch. (substation com. 1977-85), Power Engring. Soc. (Prize Paper award 1988), Sigma Xi, Eta Kappa Nu. Republican. Roman Catholic. Office: Coll Engring U New Orleans New Orleans LA 70148-0001 E-mail: wlannes@uno.edu.

LANNIGAN, ELIZABETH GRIFFIN, occupational therapist, educator; b. Glens Falls, N.Y., Aug. 3, 1952; d. Robert Michael and Rita Anne (McDonnell) Griffin; m. William Edward Lannigan, Apr. 23, 1977; children: Emily Anne, Patrick Michael. BS in Occupl. Therapy, Tufts U., 1974; MA in Occupl. Therapy, NYU, 1984, postgrad. Registered occupl. therapist Am. Occupl. Therapy Assn.; cert. vocat. evaluator Commn. on Cert. of Work Adjustment and Vocat. Evaluation Specialists. Occupl. therapist Fernald State Sch., Waltham, Mass., 1974-75, Meml. Hosp., Worcester, 1975-77, McLean Hosp., Belmont, 1977-78; sr. occupl. therapist Greystone Park (N.J.) Psychiat. Hosp., 1981, prin. occupl. therapist, 1984-85; clin. coord., occupl. therapist Hagedorn Ctr. for Geriatrics, Glen Gardner, N.J., 1986-91; adj. instr. NYU, N.Y.C., 1978-94; asst. prof. occupl. therapy programs sch. health scis. Touro Coll., 1996-97; program dir., asst. prof. occup. therapy program Seton Hall U., South Orange, N.J., 1997-99; pvt. practice Montclair, 1999—. Rehab. cons. Berman Home, Montclair, N.J., 1983, Cedar Grove (N.J.) Residential Ctr., 1984-85, Woodbridge Child Diagnostic and Treatment Ctr., 1987-88, Mt. Carmel Guild, Cath. Cmty. Svcs., Newark, 1994. Mem. Am. Occupl. Therapy Assn., N.J. Occupl. Therapy Assn., Nat. Rehab. Assn., Nat. Alliance for the Mentally Ill, Pi Lambda Theta. Home and Office: 160 Grove St Montclair NJ 07042-4011 E-mail: lglannigan@aol.com.

LANNIGAN, JAMES WILLIAM, voluntary service officer; b. Rochester, N.Y., Mar. 2, 1944; s. Clarence Lannigan and Catherine Weber; m. Margaret E. McLeod, May 19, 1984. Bachelor's degree, Empire State Coll., 1984; MBA, Wichita State U., 1998. News/sports editor Sta. WBTA, Batavia (N.Y.) Broadcasting Inc., 1968-84; therapeutic recreation therapist Lyons (N.J.) VA Med. Ctr., 1984-88; asst. vol. chief Hines (Ill.) VA Hosp., 1988-90; vol. svc. officer Kansas City (Mo.) VA Med. Ctr., 1990—. Mem. com. on profl. devel. and stds. Am. Soc. Vol. Svcs./Am. Hosp. Assn., Chgo., 1991, mem. com. on continuous quality improvement, 1993; mem. task force on disabilities Heart of Am. United Way, Kansas City, Mo., 1994; com. chmn. policies and procedures Mo. Assn. Dir.'s of Vol. Svcs., Jefferson City, 1997. Bd. dirs. Heart of Am. Stand Down Com., Kansas City, Mo., 1994—; adv. bd. S.E. Med. Professions H.S., Kansas City, Mo., 1994—; mem. gov. vol. support network adv. com. Points of Light Found. With USAF, 1963-67. Office: VA Med Ctr 4801 E Linwood Blvd Kansas City MO 64128-2226

LANNIN, DONALD ROWE, oncologist, surgeon; b. Mpls., Feb. 18, 1948; s. Donald and Shirley (Vincent) L. BA, Stanford U., 1970; MD, U. Minn., 1974. Diplomate Am. Bd. Surgery. Intern in gen. surgery U. Minn., Mpls., 1974-75, resident in gen. surgery, 1975-82; from asst. prof. to assoc. prof. Ea. Carolina U. Sch. Medicine, Greenville, N.C., 1982-93, prof., 1993—. Dir. Leo W. Jenkins Cancer Ctr., Greenville, 1992—; univ. policy and rev. com. on human rsch. Ea. Carolina U. Sch. Medicine, 1982-97, AIDS com., 1985-91, promotion and tenure com., 1991-94; mem. N.C. Comprehensive Breast and Cervical Cancer Control Com., 1993—. Edtl. bd. Surgical Oncology, Current Surgery; contbr. articles to profl. jours. Bd. dirs. Am. Cancer Soc., Raleigh, N.C., 1984—. Mem. AMA, AAAS, Am. Coll. Surgeons, Am. Assn. Cancer Rsch., Soc. Surgical Oncology, Assn. Acad. Surgeons, Societe Internationale De Chirurgie, Assn. for Surgical Edn., N.C. Med. Assn., Nat. Surgical Adjuvant Breast Project, Pediat. Oncology Group, Alpha Omega Alpha. Office: Yale U Sch Medicine PO Box 208062 New Haven CT 06520-8062 E-mail: donald.lannin@yale.edu.

LANNON, KATHLEEN MARIA, information consultant; b. Cumberland, Md., Jan. 21, 1949; d. Clifton Miller and Agnes Josephine (Walsh) Marsh; m. Peter Francis Lannon, Apr. 29, 1983. AA cum laude, Mt. Aloysius Jr. Coll., 1969; BA, George Mason U., 1979; postgrad., George Washington U., 1987-88. Mgmt. analyst Nat. Archives and Records Adminstrn., Washington, 1970-80, Gen. Svcs. Adminstrn., Washington, 1980-85, Dept. of State, Washington, 1985-90; prin. Lannon Info. Cons., Vienna, 1990—. Editor college literary magazine, 1969; contbr. articles to profl. jours. Avocations: gardening, aquaria, sailing. Home and Office: 2781 Grovemore Ln Vienna VA 22180-7069

L'ANNUNZIATA, MICHAEL FRANK, chemist, consultant; b. Springfield, Mass., Oct. 14, 1943; s. Michael Peter and Irene M. L'Annunziata; m. Maria del Carmen Elena Monge, Mar. 3, 1973; children: Michael O., Helen, Frank E. BS, St. Edward's U., Austin, Tex., 1965; MS, U. Ariz., 1967, PhD, 1970. Rsch. chemist Amchem Products, Inc., Ambler, Pa., 1971-72; rsch. assoc. U. Ariz., Tucson, 1972-73; prof., sect. head U. Chapingo, Mexico, Mexico, 1973-75; rsch. scientist Nat. Inst. Nuclear Rsch., Mexico City, 1975-77; assoc. officer IAEA, Vienna, 1977-80, 2d officer, 1980-83, 1st officer, head sci. visits program, 1983-86, sr. officer, head fellowships and tng. sect., 1986-91; mng. dir. LMS Internat. Tech. Svcs., Ltd., Coronado, Calif., 1992-95; dir. WorldTech Internat. Tech. Svcs., Oceanside, 1995-99; pres. The Montague Group, 1999—. Bd. dirs. internat. sci. programs Uppsala (Sweden) U.; internat. IAEA cons.; cons., lectr. Forestry Rsch. Inst., Ibadan, Nigeria, 1994, 95, Ministry Edn., Jakarta, Indonesia, 1995, Internat. Sales, Mktg., and Tng., Packard BioScis. Co., Meriden, Conn., 1995-2002, Egypt Atomic Energy Authority, Cairo, 1995, 96, Gezira Rsch. Sta., Wad Medani, Sudan, 1995, Ethopian Sci. and Tech. Commn., Addis Ababa, 1996, Nat. Radiation Commsn., Arusha, Tanzania, 1996; vis. lectr. Advanced Sch. Tropical Agriculture, Cardenas, Mexico, 1973, Atomic Energy Commn. of Ecuador, Quito, 1978, Timiryazev Agrl. Acad., Moscow, 1980, 81, Nuc. Rsch. Inst. in Vet. Medicine, Lalahan, Turkey, 1981, IAEA Seilbersdorf Labs., Seibersdorf, Austria, 1978-82, U. Guanajuato, Mex., 1981, Coll. Montecillo, Chapingo, Mex., 1989, Korea Atomic Energy Rsch. Inst., Seoul, 1991, Nat. Atomic Energy Agy., Jakarta, 1991-94, Zhejiang Agrl. U., Hangzhou, China, 1992, Ctrl. Nuc. "La Reina", Santiago, Chile, 1992, Internat. Atomic Energy Agy., Vienna, 1993, Mt. Makulu Ctrl. Rsch. Sta., Lusaka, Zambia, 1994, Office Atomic Energy Peace, Bangkok, 1995, Swedish Radiation Protection Inst., Stockholm, 1996, CIEMAT, Madrid, 1996, Laguna Verde Nuc. Power Plant, Vera Cruz, Mex., 1996, Oak Ridge (Tenn.) Nat. Labs., 1998, Min. Water and Irrigation, Amman, Jordan, 1998, Wyeth-Ayerst, Pearl River, N.Y., 1998, Chem. Industry Inst. Toxicology, Rsch. Triangle Park, N.C., 1998, Los Alamos Nat. Labs., N.Mex., 2000, U.S. Dept. Energy Idaho Nat. Engring. and Environ. Labs., Idaho Falls, 2000; hon. prof. Zhejiang Agrl. U., 1992. Author: (textbooks) Radiotracers in Agricultural Chemistry, 1979, Radionuclide Tracers, Their Detection and Measurement, 1987; author, editor (with J.O. Legg) Isotopes and Radiation in Agricultural Sciences, Vol. 1, 1984, Vol. 2, 1984, Handbook of Radioactivity Analysis, 1998; contbr. articles to profl. jours. Recipient hon. tchg. diploma, silver plaque Ctrl. U., Ecuador, Quito, 1978. Mem. AAAS, N.Y. Acad. Scis., Am. Nuc. Soc., Sigma Xi, Phi Lambda Upsilon, Gamma Sigma Delta. Roman Catholic. Achievements include discovery of molecular D-chiro-inositol phosphate in soil/plant systems; determination of the biochemical mechanism and pathway involved in the formation of soil chiro-inositol phosphate; discovered microbial epimerization as origin of inositol phosphate isomers in soil; elucidated mechanisms of soil organic phosphorus fixation; separation of the radioactive nuclides Sr-90 from soil surfaces after nuclear fallout; first separation of radioactive nuclides Sr-90 and Y-90 by electrophoresis; execution of over 80 fact-finding, planning, and implementation missions to over 60 countries of Asia, Africa, Europe, Latin America, North America, and the Middle East for United Nations, International Atomic Energy Agy. from 1978 to the present; development of several chemical and instrumental techniques for the analysis of radioactive nuclides. Office: The Montague Group Sorrento Towers North 5355 Mira Sorrento Pl Ste 100 San Diego CA 92121 E-mail: montaguegroup@cs.com.

LANO, CHARLES JACK, retired financial executive; b. Port Clinton, Ohio, Apr. 17, 1922; s. Charles Herbin and Antoinette (Schmitt) L.; m. Beatrice Irene Spees, June 16, 1946 (dec. 1995); children: Douglas Cloyd, Charles Lewis. BS in Bus. Adminstrn. summa cum laude, Ohio State U., 1949. C.P.A., Okla. With U.S. Gypsum Co., 1941-46, Ottawa Paper Stock Co., 1946-47; accountant Arthur Young & Co. (C.P.A.'s), Tulsa, 1949-51; controller Lima div. Ex-Cell-O Corp., 1951-59, electronics div. AVCO Corp., 1959-61, Servomation Corp., 1961; asst. comptroller Scovill Mfg. Co., Waterbury, Conn., 1961-62, comptroller, 1962-67; controller CF&I Steel Corp., Denver, 1967-69, v.p., controller, 1969-70; controller Pacific Lighting Corp., 1970-76; exec. v.p. Arts-Way Mfg. Co., Armstrong, Iowa, 1976-85; mgmt. auditor City of Anaheim, Calif., 1985-96; ret., 1996. Served with USMCR, 1942-45. Mem. Am. Inst. C.P.A.'s, Calif. Soc. C.P.A.'s, Inst. Internal Auditors. Home: 6274 E Calle Jaime Anaheim CA 92807-4005

LANOU, ROBERT EUGENE, JR. physicist, educator; b. Colchester, Vt., Feb. 13, 1928; s. Robert E. and Flora G. (Goyette) L.; m. Cornelia Rockwell Wheeler, May 14, 1960; children: Katharine, Gregory, Elizabeth, Steven. BS, Worcester Poly. Inst., 1952; PhD, Yale U., 1957. Physicist Lawrence Berkeley (Calif.) Lab., 1956-59; asst. prof. physicist Brown U., Providence, 1960-63, assoc. prof., 1963-67, prof., 1967—, chair dept. physics, 1986-92. Cons. Brookhaven Nat. Lab., Upton, N.Y., Los Alamos (N.Mex.) Nat. Lab.; sci. advisor Gov. State of R.I., Providence, 1986-88. Contbr. articles to profl. jours. With USN, 1946-48, ETO. Grantee Dept. Energy, 1960—, NSF, 1995—. Fellow AAAS, Am. Phys. Soc.; mem. Sigma Xi, Tau Beta Pi. Achievements include research in experimental particle physics and astrophysics. Home: 90 Keene St Providence RI 02906-1508 Office: Brown U Dept Physics Providence RI 02906

LA NOUE, TERENCE DAVID, artist, educator; b. Hammond, Ind., Dec. 4, 1941; s. George David and Lois (Lish) L.; children: Daniel, Alexandra. BFA, Ohio Wesleyan U., 1964; Fulbright meister student, Hochschule fur Bildenden Kunste, West Berlin, 1964-65; MFA, Cornell U., 1967; DFA, Ohio Wesleyan U., 1994. Prof. Trinity Coll., Hartford, Conn., 1967-72, CUNY, N.Y.C., 1972-85, NYU, 1987. Works represented in various museums, including Whitney Mus., Guggenheim Mus., Bklyn. Mus., Albright-Knox Mus., Corcoran Gallery Art, Carnegie Inst., Power Inst. Fine Arts, Sydney, Australia, Musé d'Art et Archeologie, Toulon, France, Musée de Strasbourg, France, Mus. Contemporary Art, Teheran, Iran, Mus. Modern Art, N.Y.C.; monograph, Terence La Noue, Ashton Dore, 1992. Grantee Fulbright Found., Berlin, 1964-65, NEA, 1972-73, 83-84, Guggenheim Found., 1982-83. Office: 714 Broadway New York NY 10003-9506

LANSAW, CHARLES RAY, rendering industry executive; b. Middletown, Ohio, Mar. 5, 1927; s. Edward Curtis and Lura (Tyra) L.; m. Joan Betty Kalbaugh, July 4, 1949; children: Charles E., Gail D., Leslie J., Kristi L. Student, Miami U., Oxford, Ohio, 1947-48; student engring., U. Cin., 1949-51. Chief engr., sales mgr. Dupps Co., Germantown, Ohio, 1950-85; pres. C.R. Lansaw, Inc., 1985—. Past mem. Germantown Planing Commn.; past bd. dirs. Germantown Pub. libr., 1991-2001; served with VOCA at Saratov and Volgograd, Russia, 1996, Internat. Exec. Svc. Corps, Alexandria, Egypt, 1993; lay leader Good Shepherd United Meth. Ch. With USNR, 1944-46. Mem. Rotary (pres. Germantown 1987-88, Paul Harris fellow). Avocations: sailing, woodworking, tennis, coin collecting. Home and Office: 73 Sue Dr Germantown OH 45327-1628 E-mail: clansaw@aol.com.

LANSBURY, EDGAR GEORGE, theatrical producer; b. London, Jan. 12, 1930; came to U.S., 1941, naturalized, 1953; s. Edgar Isaac and Charlotte Lillian (McIldowie) L.; m. Rose Anthony Kean, Aug. 12, 1955; children: James, Michael, David, George, Brian, Kate. Ed., UCLA. Designer stock and off-Broadway prodns., 1953-55; art dir. ABC-TV, 1955, CBS-TV, 1955-62, Channel 13, N.Y.C., 1962-63; motion picture art dir., 1963-64; formed Edgar Lansbury Prodns. Inc., for ind. prodn. in theatre and films, 1964—; chmn. The Acting Co. Bd. dirs. drama dept. Story Line Press; chair Russian Mus. Arts Soc. Am. Producer Broadway plays: First One Asleep Whistle, 1966, The Subject Was Roses, 1964, That Summer-That Fall, 1967, The Only Game in Town, 1968, Promenade, 1970, Look to the Lilies, 1970, Engagement Baby, 1971, Godspell, 1971, Elizabeth I, 1972, The Night That Made America Famous, 1974, The Magic Show, 1974, Gypsy, 1975, American Buffalo, 1977, Broadway Follies, 1981, O, Pioneer!, 1989, Club XII, 1990, Amphigorey, 1992, Any Given Day, 1993, Curtains, Grace and Glorie, 1996, In Circles, 1997, As Bees in Honey Drown, 1997, June Moon, 1998; films The Subject was Roses, 1968, Godspell, 1973, The Wild Party, 1974, Squirm, 1976, Blue Sunshine, 1978, He Knows You're Alone, 1980, The Clairvoyant, 1982, Summer Girl, 1983, A Stranger Waits, 1986, Advice from a Caterpillar, 1999, Gypsy "83", 2001; dir. Without Apologies, 1989, All the Queen's Men, 1989, Advice from a Caterpillar, 1990, The Country Club, 1992. Pres. Agni Yoga Soc., Nicholas Roerich Mus., N.Y.C.; bd. govs. League N.Y. Theatres and Prodrs.; chmn. Russian Chamber Chorus, N.Y.C., The Acting Co., N.Y.C. Served with U.S. Army, 1951—53. Recipient N.Y. Art Dirs. award for best comml. film, 1963; N.Y. Outer Critics Circle award, 1965; N.Y. Critics Circle award, 1965; Antoinette Perry award for best produced play, 1965; nomination for Antoinette Perry award for best mus. play, 1977; N.Y. Critics Circle award for best drama, 1977 Office: Edgar Lansbury Prodns 630 9th Ave Ste 214 New York NY 10036-3708

LANSDALE, H. PARKER, minister, historian, non-profit administrator; b. Worcester, Mass., Mar. 18, 1923; s. Herbert P. Jr. and Marjorie M. (McKay) L.; m. Elizabeth Ann MacCollum, Feb. 25, 1945 (div. Jan. 1976); children: Ann T., Kirk M., Todd A.; m. Dorothy Phillips Deschamps, May 26, 1976; children: Thomas A. Deschamps, Margaret D. Sticklen, Brian P. Deschamps, Patricia S. Deschamps. AB, Oberlin Coll., 1944; BD, Yale Div. Sch., 1950; MA, Yale Grad. Sch., 1953, PhD, 1956. Ordained to ministry Presbyn. Ch. (USA), 1950. Boys work sec. YMCA, New Haven, 1948-56; mem. faculty Yale Div. Sch., 1948-56; assoc. gen. sec. YMCA, Wilmington, Del., 1956-59; program dir. YMCA Greater N.Y., N.Y.C., 1959-61; gen. sec. YMCA of Greater Bridgeport, Conn., 1961-69; dir. (on loan from YMCA) Higher Edn. Ctr. for Urban Studies, Bridgeport, 1968-77; cmty. liaison (on loan) Bridgeport Area Found.-United Way, 1977-83; ret., 1983; hon. rsch. assoc. YMCA U.S.A., 1990—. Exec. dir. (on loan) Action for Bridgeport Cmty. Devel., 1964-65; courtesy historian in residence Sarasota-Manatee Campus, U. South Fla.; parish assoc. Hon. Ret. 1st Presbyn. Ch., Sarasota; lectr. in field. Author: (novels) History of the Work of the YMCA with Boys (1900-25), 1992; co-editor There is a Tide, 2000; author and editor: Proc. of the Symposium on the YMCA and its Christian Purpose in the 21st Century., 2001; contbr. articles to profl. jours.; editor in field. Mem. Peace River Presbyn. Ch.; ARC, 1963—70; Bridgeport Model Cities, 1969—74; Park City Hosp., 1970—83; Conn. Health Plan, 1972—80. With USMC, 1942—46. Fellow N.Am. Fellowship YMCA Retirees, World Fellowship YMCA Retirees. Democrat. Avocations: history, writing, volunteer service.

LANSFORD, EDWIN GAINES, accountant; b. Chattanooga, Aug. 20, 1924; s. Frederick Duke Lansford and Edwina (Gaines) Lansford Stone; m. Sue Ann Kemmer, may 29, 1954; children: Virginia Nan, Sue Ann, Edwin Gaines, Jr., James Robert, Frederick Scott. BBA, U. Chattanooga, 1948; LLB, McKenzie Coll., 1958. Mem. Tennessee Bar Assn. Cost acct. Cavalier Corp., Chattanooga, 1948-52; staff acct. O.T. Draewell and H.L. Oakes, 1952-54; own account and various partnerships Crossville & Chattanooga, 1954-98; v.p. Lansford Kawasaki, Inc., Crossville, 1978—; of counsel Lansford, Stephens & Brummett, CPAs, Pikeville and Crossville, Tenn., 1999—. With U.S. Army, 1943-46, ETO. Mem.: NRA, AICPA (hon.), Cumberland County C. of C. (bd. dirs. 1976—79), Tenn. Shooting Sports Assn. (H.P. Rifle Team 1963—64, pres. 1969—71), Nat. Assn. Tax Profls. (bd. dirs. Tenn. chpt. 1996—, treas. 1998—2001), Tenn. Soc. CPA (life; pres. Chattanooga chpt. 1962—63, 1st pres., co-founder Upper Cumberland chpt. 1978—79, sec., various coms.), Elks, Rotary (all offices and bd. dirs. Crossville noon chpt. 1983—, Paul Harris fellow), Lions (treas. Signal Mountain club 1974—75). Methodist. Avocations: hunting, hiking. Office: 92 Rockwood Ave Crossville TN 38555-4610 E-mail: lansford@multipro.com.

LANSING, JEWEL ANNE (JEWEL ANNE BECK), writer, auditor; b. Ronan, Mont., May 13, 1930; d. Lars Martin and Julia Syla Beck; m. Ronald B. Lansing, June 16, 1956; children: Mark, Alyse, Annette. BA in Journalism, U. Mont., 1952; MA in Edn., Stanford U., 1954. CPA, Oreg. Elected auditor

Multnomah County, Portland, Oreg., 1975-82, City of Portland, 1983-86; adj. prof. Lewis and Clark Coll., Portland, 1989-92; interim exec. dir. William Temple Ho., 1994, YWCA, Portland, 1995; interim pres. Oreg. Coll. of Arts and Crafts, 1996; writer, 1987—. Author: Campaigning for Office, 1991, 101 Campaign Tips, 1991, Deadly Games in City Hall, 1997. Candidate state treas. Dem. Party, 1976, 80; pres. Oreg. Fedn. of Dem. Women, 1977-78; city-county consolidation task force City of Portland, 1997-98; active Pacific N.W. local govt. rep. Nat. Intergovtl. Audit Forum, Washington, 1982-85. Recipient Woman of Achievement LWV, 1995, Disting. Leadership award Assn. of Govt. Accts., 1987, Pub. Svc. award Oreg. Soc. of CPAs, 1987, Taxpayers Champion award Oregonians for Cost Effective Govt., 1987. Mem. Womens Investment Network (polit. action com. exec. com., bd. dirs., founder), Oreg. Women's Polit. Caucus (First Woman award 1987), Portland Women's Polit. Caucus (Svc. award 1987), Oreg. Hist. Soc., Oreg. Environtl. Coun., Portland LWV. Unitarian Universalist. Avocations: hiking, playing cards, reading, canoeing, golf.

LANSING, MARK DANIEL, lawyer; b. Albany, N.Y., Feb. 3, 1961; s. Cornelius Hill and Ethel Alice (Haines) L.; m. Nora Ellen Nichols, Oct. 10, 1987. BS, Rensselaer Polytech. Inst., 1983; JD, Union U., 1985; MBA, Rensselaer Poly. Inst., 1998. Bar: D.C., 1989, N.Y., 1985, U.S. Ct. Army Mil. Rev., U.S. Dist. Ct. N.Y., U.S. Supreme Ct. Commd. capt. U.S. Army, 1986; atty. Army Judge Advocate's Gen. Corp., Ft. Ord, Calif., 1986-89; trial atty. tax div. U.S. Dept. Justice, Washington, 1989-93; assoc., then ptnr. Helm Shapiro Anito & McCale P.C., 1993-2001; ptnr. Hiscock & Barclay, Albany, 2001—. Mem. ATLA, N.Y. State Bar Assn., N.Y. State Trial Lawyers Assn., D.C. Bar Assn. Office: Hiscock & Barclay LLP 50 Beaver St Albany NY 12207 E-mail: mlansing@hiscockbarclay.com.

LANSING, SHERRY LEE, motion picture executive; b. Chgo., July 31, 1944; d. Norton and Margo L.; m. William Friedkin. BS summa cum laude in Theatre, Northwestern U., 1966. Tchr. math. public high schs., Los Angeles, 1966-69; model TV commls. Max Factor Co., 1969-70, Alberto-Culver Co., 1969-70; story editor Wagner Internat. Prodn. Co., 1972-74, dir. west coast devel., 1974-75; story editor MGM, 1975-77, v.p. creative affairs, 1977; senior v.p. prodn. Columbia Pictures, 1977-80; pres. 20th Century Fox Prodns., 1980-82; founder Jaffee-Lansing Prodns., 1983—92; chmn. Paramount Motion Pictures Group, L.A., 1992—. Appeared in movies Loving, 1970, Rio Lobo, 1970; ind. producer., Jaffe-Lansing Prodns.; producer Racing With the Moon, 1984,Firstborn, 1984, Fatal Attraction, 1987, The Accused, 1988, Black Rain, 1989, School Ties, 1992, Indecent Proposal, 1993; TV exec. producer When the Time Comes,1987, Mistress, 1992. Office: Paramount Pictures Corp 5555 Melrose Ave Los Angeles CA 90038-3197

LANSKY, JOSHUA MICHAEL, mathematician, educator; b. Cleve., Feb. 17, 1971; s. Lewis and Bettyann Chait L. ScB magna cum laude, Brown U., 1993; AM, Harvard U., 1995, PhD, 1998. Asst. prof. U. Toronto, Canada, 2000—01, Bucknell U., Lewisburg, Pa., 2001—. Vis. asst. prof. U. Rochester, N.Y., 1998-2000. Contbr. articles to profl. jours. Mem. AAUP, Am. Math. Soc., Math. Assn. Am., Sigma Xi. Avocations: chess, computers, biking, basketball. Office: Dept Math Bucknell Univ Lewisburg PA 17837 E-mail: jlansky@bucknell.edu.

LANTER, SEAN KEITH, software engineer; b. Los Alamos, N.Mex., May 8, 1953; s. Robert Jackson and Norma Esther (Jonas) L.; m. Lauri Jane Willand, July 16, 1977; children: Tully Erik, Sarah Elizabeth, Rachel Erin. BA in Physics, U. Utah, 1974, MSME, 1977; MS in Computer Sci., LaSalle U., 1998. Registered profl. engr., Wash. Sr. engr. Boeing Comml. Airplane Co., Seattle, 1977-82; systems analyst Internat. Submarine Tech. Ltd., Redmond, Wash., 1982-83; engr. software Advanced Tech. Labs., Bellevue, 1983-84; engr. contract Rho Co., Redmond, 1984-85; sr. tech. staff Cedar Software Inc., 1985-87; pres. Connexions Engring. and Software, Woodinville, Wash., 1987-88; pres., chief engr. Connexions Engring., Inc., 1990-95; sys. engr. Microrim Software, Inc., Bellevue, Wash., 1998-99. Cons., contract programmer, 1990—. Contbr. articles to profl. jours. Mem. Assn. Computing Machinery, NSPE. Lutheran. Avocations: chamber music, reading, history, baseball. Office: Connexions Engring PO Box 3007 Woodinville WA 98072-3007

LANTHIER, RONALD ROSS, retired manufacturing company executive; b. Montreal, Que., Can., May 2, 1926; s. Emile Edgar and Edith (Martin) L.; m. Jacqueline Barbara Dyment; children: April Carolyn, Bonnie Alice, Ronald Dyment, Andrea Elizabeth, John Elliott. Chartered Accountant, McGill U., 1952. Pub. accountant, 1944-51; chief accountant St. Lawrence Flour Co., 1951-52; controller Canadian Underwriters Assn., 1952-54; div. controller Canadian Aviation Electronics Co., 1954-56; treas. Webb & Knapp, Can., 1956-62; dir. adminstrn., mem. exec. com. Greenshields, Inc. (investment dealers), 1962-67; v.p. finance, treas., mem. exec. com. Canadian Marconi Co., 1967-72; v.p. finance, dir., mem. exec. com. Macdonald Tobacco, Inc., 1972-75; pres. Lanco Mgmt. Ltd., 1975-98; v.p. finance MacDonald Stewart Textiles, 1976-77; v.p. fin., mem. exec. com. Electrolux Can., 1978-79; pres. Robert R. Bramhall & Assos. (Can.) Ltd., 1980-81; sr. v.p. Camflo Mines Ltd., 1981-84; v.p. fin. Starnav Corp., 1984-86; v.p. VR Fin. Svcs., 1987-95. Mem. Inst. Chartered Accts. Que. and Ont., Phi Kappa Pi. Anglican. Home: 100 Westview Dr Aurora ON Canada L4G 7C9 E-mail: jaron@interhop.net.

LANTIGUA, JOSE SALVADOR, computer engineer, consultant; b. Havana, Cuba, Mar. 18, 1953; came to U.S., 1960; s. Jose Gregorio and Hilda Simona (Barrial) L.; m. Pansy Reen Fuller, Mar. 5, 1977; children: Joseph Gabriel, Christina Simone. AA, Miami-Dade C.C., 1973; BA, Northwestern State U. La., 1978, BS, 1979; MA, Pepperdine U., 1980; M Computer Engring., Fla. Atlantic U., 1989. Engr. NASA, Houston, 1973-75; mgr. automation Blue Cross-Blue Shield, Jacksonville, Fla., 1981-83; regional engring. mgr. Victor Techs., 1983-84; dir. sys. integration Abacus Data, Inc., 1984-85; cons. engr. IBM, 1985-93; mng. dir. Furash & Co., Washington, 1993-94; pres. Epi-Tech Corp., Alexandria, Va., 1994-96; v.p. ISS Corp., Stamford, Conn., 1996-97, Renaissance Worldwide, 1997-99; pres., COO Well Credit, Inc., Orange Park, FL, 1999—. Author: Knowledge Rules from Dircted Graphs, 1989; contbr. articles to various publs. Advisor Jr. Achievement, Jacksonville, 1987. Maj. U.S. Army, 1975-80, mem. USAR, 1980—. Mem. IEEE, Am. Assn. for Artificial Intelligence, Assn. for Computing Machinery, Mensa, Phi Theta Gamma. Republican. Roman Catholic. Achievements include development of knowledge acquisition software, business process reengineering methodology, financial application business system architecture. Office: Well Credit Inc PO Box 7078 Orange Park FL 32073-5562

LANTIS, DONNA LEA, retired banker, art educator, artist; b. Medford, Oreg., Oct. 12, 1931; d. James Warren Fader and Amy Bell (Crump) Fader-Snyder; m. Victor Earl Lantis, July 9, 1950 (div. Apr. 1975); children: Deborah Ann Hayes, Diana Lorraine Keaton. BS, So. Oreg. U., 1966; postgrad., Otis Art Inst., L.A., 1969; 5th yr. cert., U. Oreg., 1974. Art tchr., Oreg., Tenn., Ky.; cert. banker Am. Inst. Banking. Banker First Nat. Bank, Ashland, Oreg., 1951-62; tchr. art, history Klamath County Sch. Dist., Klamath Falls, 1966-68; tchr. art Ashland Sch. Dist., 1968-75; banker First Interstate Bank, Medford, Oreg., 1979-92. Supr. student tchrs. So. Oreg. U., Ashland, 1968-75, work with traumatized children, 1968-69. Author illustrated poetry; exhbns. include Oreg. State Fair, So. Oreg. U., Portland, Monmouth Rogue Art Gallery, Medford, Oreg., banks, librs.; dollmaker. Asst. founder lupus support group, Ashland, Oreg., 1977, 78, 79. Elks scholar, 1950, John Dickey Art scholar So. Oreg. U., 1966; recipient Voice of Democracy 1st Place Hon. Mention Broadcasters and Radio Dealers of Am. KWIN, 1949. Mem. AAUW, So. Oreg. Alumni Assn., Libr. of Congress, Women in Arts. Avocations: music, history, writing, gardening, dolls. Home: 604 Newtown St Medford OR 97501-3464

LANTOS, THOMAS PETER, congressman; b. Budapest, Hungary, Feb. 1, 1928; m. Annette Tillemann; children: Annette, Katrina. BA, U. Washington, 1949, MA, 1950; PhD, U. Calif., Berkeley, 1953. Faculty U. Wash., San Francisco State U., 1950-83; TV news analyst, commentator; sr. econ. and fgn. policy adviser to several U.S. senators; mem. Presdl. Task Force on Def. and Fgn. Policy, U.S. Congresses from 12th Calif dist., 1981—; ranking minority mem., internat. rels. subcomm., mem. govt. reform com. Founder study abroad program Calif. State U. and Coll. System. Mem. Millbrae Bd. Edn., 1950-66. Democrat. Office: US Ho of Reps 2217 Rayburn Ho Office Bldg Washington DC 20515-0001*

LANTRIP, IVOLUE MAY, secretary; b. Cherryvale, Kans., Mar. 13, 1929; d. John Franklin Sanders and Treva Jenneve (Rohrbough) McKinnon; m. Truman Leo Lantrip, July 23, 1949; children: Michael Dennis, Richard Oden. Grad. h.s., Benicia, Calif. Sec. Benicia H.S., 1948-54, 62-67, counselors sec., 1961-62; fin. sec., bookkeeper Benicia Unified Sch. Dist., 1967-71, ret. Author: The American Genealogy of the Lantrip Family, 1994. Mem. DAR (Acalanes chpt. historian 1984-86, 88-90, treas. 1986-88), Carquinez Strait Stitchers Quilt Guild (treas. 1996), Ret. Pub. Employees Assn. of Calif. Avocations: oil painting, china painting, quilting/wearable art, genealogy, travel.

LANTZ, JOANNE BALDWIN, academic administrator emeritus; b. Defiance, Ohio, Jan. 26, 1932; d. Hiram J. and Ethel A. (Smith) Baldwin; m. Wayne E. Lantz. BS in Physics and Math., U. Indpls., 1953; MS in Counseling and Guidance, Ind. U., 1957; PhD in Counseling and Psychology, Mich. State U., 1969; LittD (hon.), U. Indpls., 1985; LHD (hon.), Purdue U., 1994; LLD (hon.), Manchester Coll., 1994. Tchr. physics and math. Arcola (Ind.) High Sch., 1953-57; guidance dir. New Haven (Ind.) Sr. High Sch., 1957-65; with Ind. U.-Purdue U., Fort Wayne, 1965—, interim chancellor, 1988-89, chancellor, 1989-94, chancellor emeritus, 1994—. Bd. dirs., hon. dir. Ft. Wayne Nat. Corp.; bd. dirs. Foellinger Found. Contbr. articles to profl. jours. Mem. Ft. Wayne Econ. Devel. Adv. Bd. and Task Force, 1988-91, Corp. Coun., 1988-94; bd. advisors Leadership Ft. Wayne, 1988-94; mem. adv. bd. Ind. Sml. Bus. Devel. Ctr., 1988-90; trustee Ancilla System, Inc., 1984-89, chmn. human resources com., 1985-89, exec. com., 1985-89; trustee St. Joseph's Med. Ctr., 1983-84, pers. adv. com. to bd. dirs., 1978-84, chmn., 1980-84; bd. dirs. United Way Allen County, sec., 1979-80; bd. dirs. Anthony Wayne Vocat. Rehab. Ctr., 1969-75. Mem.: AAUW (internat. fellowship com. 1986—88, program com. 1981—83, Am. women fellowship com. 1978—83, chmn. 1981—83, trust rsch. grantee 1980), APA, Southeastern Psychol. Assn. (referee conv. papers 1987, 1988), Ft. Wayne Ind.-Purdue Alumni Soc. (hon. mem. 1987), Ind. Sch. Women's Club (v.p. program chair 1979—81), Delta Kappa Gamma (editl. bd. 1986—88, gen. chair conv. 1985—86, dir. N.E. region 1982—84, adminstrv. bd. 1982—84, exec. bd. 1982—84, leadership devel. com. 1978—82, bd. trustees ednl. found. 1996—2002), Sigma Xi, Pi Lambda Theta. Avocations: swimming, reading, knitting, boating. E-mail: joalantz@aol.com.

LANTZ, KENNETH EUGENE, consulting firm executive; b. Altoona, Pa., Mar. 9, 1934; s. William Martin and Alice Lucretia (Glass) L.; m. D. Arlene Yocum, Nov. 28, 1959; children: Antonia Marie, Theresa Antoinette. BS cum laude, Fordham U., 1956. Cons. Sutherland Co., 1960-62; spl. rep. IBM, L.A., 1962-67; dir. info. svcs. Loyola-Marymount U., 1967-70; pres. CBIS, 1970-72; mgr. fin. sys. Occidental Life Ins., 1973-77; pres. Kenneth Lantz Assocs., 1977-82; dir. sys. Sayre & Toso, 1982-83; prin. Atwater, Lantz, Hunter & Co., 1983—. Lectr. computing topics Technology Transfer Inst., 1987-88. Author: The Prototyping Methodology, 1984; contbr. articles to profl. jours. 1st lt. USAF, 1957-60. Mem. Future of Automation Roundtable (dir. 1983—), Ins. Acctg. and Sys. Assn. (nat. Merit award 1984). Republican. Roman Catholic. Office: Atwater Lantz Hunter & Co PO Box 572366 Tarzana CA 91357-2366 E-mail: kel@manageknowledge.com.

LANTZ, NORMAN FOSTER, electrical engineer; b. Pekin, Ill., June 8, 1937; s. Norman Gough and Lenore (Elsbury) L.; m. Donnis Maureen Ballinger, Sept. 7, 1958 (div. Aug. 1991); children: Katherine, Deborah, Norman Daniel; m. Judith Eliane Peach, Dec. 7, 1991. BSEE, Purdue U., 1959, MSEE, 1961. System engr. GE Co., Phila., 1961-72; mem. tech. staff The Aerospace Corp., El Segundo, Calif., 1972-75, mgr., 1975-79, dir., 1979-83, prin. dir., 1983-90, sr. project leader, 1991-2000, sys. dir., 2000—. Dir. Internat. Found. for Telemetering, Woodland Hills, Calif., 1985—. 2d lt. U.S. Army, 1960-61. Recipient Pioneer award Internat. Found. for Telemetering. Mem. AIAA (sr.), IEEE, Nat. Def. Indsl. Assn., Am. Mgmt. Assn., Internat. Coun. System Engring. Office: The Aerospace Corp System Director El Segundo CA 90245-4691

LANTZ, PHILLIP EDWARD, corporate executive, consultant; b. Laramie, Wyo., Sept. 21, 1938; s. Everett Delmer and Elizabeth Mary (Stratton) L.; m. Paula Bogel, June 16, 1962; children: Kirk Edward, Eric William. BA in Math., U. Colo., 1960; MA in Math., U. Wyo., 1966; MS in Ops. Rsch., Johns Hopkins U., 1972. Grad. teaching asst. U. Wyo., Laramie, 1964-65; sr. engr. Applied Physics Lab. Johns Hopkins U., Silver Spring, Md., 1965-70; v.p. Ops. Rsch. Inc., 1970-72; dir. Tetra Tech. Inc., Arlington, Va., 1972-74; pres., chief exec. officer Systems Planning and Analysis, Inc., Alexandria, 1974—, also bd. dirs. Lt. USN, 1960-64. Home: 2911 Eddington Ter Alexandria VA 22302-3503 Office: Systems Planning and Analysis Inc Ste 400 2000 N Beauregard St Alexandria VA 22311-1712

LANTZ, ROBERT, literary and talent agent; b. Berlin, July 20, 1914; s. Adolf and Ella (Schloessingk) L.; came to U.S., 1948, naturalized Brit. citizen, 1946; student U. Berlin, 1931-32; m. Feb. 1950; 1 child, Anthony Robin. Story editor Am. film cos., London, 1936-46; talent and lit. agt., N.Y.C., 1948—; pres. The Lantz Office, N.Y.C., 1973—; pres. TARA, N.Y. Mem. British P.E.N. Plays include L'Inconnue de la Seine, Voegelchen, others. Home: 180 E 79th St New York NY 10021-0437 Address: 888 7th Ave New York NY 10106-0001

LANTZ, SUSAN RUPPALT, operating room nurse; b. Balt., July 23, 1948; d. Francis Charles and Eula (Cole) Ruppalt; m. Charles Alan Lantz, Sept. 6, 1969 (div. 1973); 1 child, Heather Leigh; m. Leonard Horne Jr., Oct. 1, 1977; 1 child, Gregory Ryan. BSN, U. N.C., 1973. Cert. nurse operating rm.; BLS, ABLS, TNCC. Clk. patient accounts Meml. Hosp., Chapel Hill, N.C., 1970-71, operating rm. charge nurse vascular, trauma, 1973-76; operating rm. staff nurse Mercy Hosp., Charlotte, 1976-78, operating rm., clin. instr./coord., 1978-80; pvt. scrub Oral Maxillofacial Surgery, 1980-90; operating rm. clin. instr. Presbyn. Sch. Nursing, 1990; operating rm. staff nurse 312th Evacuation hosp., Greensboro, 1990-92; office mgr. Metrolina Power Sweeper Inc., Charlotte, 1979—2001; oper. rm. head nurse 312th Evacuation Hosp., Greensboro, 1992-97; staff nurse oper. rm. Gaston Meml. Hosp., 1997-98, Presbyn. Hosp., 1998-99, Mercy Hosp., 1999—. Lectr. in field. Com. chmn., bd. dirs. Parents Tchr. Student Assn., Charlotte; com. chmn. Cub Scouts, Boy Scouts Am., Charlotte, 1989-90; mem. N.C. Gov.'s Jobs for Vets. Com., 1994-95. Capt. Nurse Corps, USAR, 1990-2000. Decorated Army Commendation medal, Nat. Def. Svc. Medal, S.W. Asia Svc. medal, Kuwait Liberation medal; recipient 1991 Great 100 Nursing Excellence award The Great 100, Inc. Mem. ANA, N.C. Nurses Assn. (steering com. 1992-93), N.C. Coun. Oper. Room Nurses (pres. 1988-92), Assn. Oper. Room Nurses (bd. dirs. Dogwood chpt. 1983-86, 88-90, pres. 1982-83), Am. Legion (2d vice comdr. 1991-92, 1st vice comdr. 1992-93, dist. comdr. 1991-93, com. chmn. 1991-94).

LANYON, WESLEY EDWIN, retired museum curator, ornithologist; b. Norwalk, Conn., June 10, 1926; s. William J. and Frances A. (Merrill) L.; m. Vernia E. Hall, Jan. 29, 1951; children: Cynthia Hall, Scott Merrill. AB in Zoology, Cornell U., 1950; PhD, U. Wis., 1955. Interpretive specialist Nat. Park Service, summers 1947-51; instr. zoology U. Ariz., 1955-56; asst. prof. Miami U., Oxford, Ohio, 1956-57; asst. curator birds Am. Mus. Natural History, N.Y.C., 1957-63, asso. curator, 1963-67, curator, 1967-88; resident dir. Kalbfleisch Field Research Sta., 1958-74. Adj. prof. biology City U. N.Y., 1968-87; expdns. for mus. to, C.Am. and Mexico, 1959, 60, 63, West Indies, 1960, 65, 66, S. Am., 1967-80. Contbr. articles to profl. jours. Fellow Am. Ornithologists Union (Brewster award 1968, pres. 1976-78); mem. Cooper, Wilson ornithol. socs., Eastern Bird Banding Assn., Linnaean Soc. N.Y. Home: PO Box 531 Keene Valley NY 12943-0531 E-mail: wlanyon@aol.com.

LANZA, JOHN FRANCIS, JR. artist, educator; b. Weymouth, Mass., Dec. 31, 1948; s. John Francis and Sadie (Rizzotto) L.; m. Kathy Louise McGill, Aug. 1, 1976; children: Rebecca Elizabeth, Maria Melanie. BA cum laude, Amherst Coll., 1971; MFA, Boston U., 1975. Painting conservator Iso Papo, Brookline, Mass., 1974-86; prof. Art Inst. of Boston, Lesley U., 1978—, coord. drawing and sculpture, 1981-99, acting dept. chair illustration, 1989, acting dept. chair found. dept., 1998. Instr. anatomy Cambridge Ctr. Adult Edn., 1977-85; instr. anatomy and painting South Shore Art Ctr., Cohasset, Mass., 1979-81; instr. Boston Visual Sch., Trieste, Italy, 1988-91, Viterbo, Italy, 1994, Montserrat Coll. Art, Viterbo, 1997; sec., clk. Boston Visual Sch., Dorchester, Mass., 1991-95; jurist South Shore Art Ctr., 1981—; chair curriculum com. Art Inst. of Boston, Lesley Coll., 1985-88, sec., 1988-95, ad hoc faculty com., sec. faculty/staff senate and coun., 1990-99, rep., 1980-88, chair faculty affairs and acad. policies com., 1999-2002. Illustrator: Heritage Collection, The Bragging Tortoise, Theme Books, 1989; one-man show at Helen Bumpus Gallery, 1996, James Libr. and Ctr. for Arts, 2000; exhibited in group shows at Art Inst. Boston, 1979-99, South Shore Art Ctr., 1979-99 (Best Realist award 1988, 2d pl. award for oils 1987), Art Inst. Boston Show, 1980, 84, 90, Boston Visual Sch. Exhibits, 1989, 90, 91, U.S. Extemporaneous Show, 1994, U.S. Extemporaneous Show, Vitorchiano, Italy, 1994, Attleboro Mus., 1998. Libr. vol. Plymouth River Sch., Hingham, Mass., 1988—; worship commn. St. John the Evangelist Ch., Hingham, 1991-99. Recipient Disting. Svc. award, Plymouth River Sch., 1998; fellow Amherst Coll. 1969, Boston U., 1973. Avocations: reading, traveling abroad. Home: 152 Summer St Hingham MA 02043-1062

LANZA, RALPH ANDREW, internist; b. Bklyn., Sept. 15, 1960; s. Ralph Matthew and Isabella Theresa Lanza; m. Carolyn Ann Lanza, Oct. 17, 1987; children: Jessica, Ralph Daniel, Catherine, Matthew. BS, Fairfield U., 1982; MD, U. Rochester, 1986. Diplomate Am. Bd. Internal Medicine. Intern Hosp. of U. Pa., 1986—87, resident, 1987—89; attending physician Bennett Mark Schusser Lanza, Paoli, Pa., 1989-95, Gt. Valley Health, 1996—2001; with Great Valley Med. Assocs., 2001—. Mem. AMA, ACP, KC, Alpha Omega Alpha. Office: Gt Valley Med Assocs 255 W Lancaster Ave Ste 120 Paoli PA 19301 E-mail: lanzar@mlhs.org.

LANZA, ROBERT PAUL, medical scientist; b. Boston, Feb. 11, 1956; s. Samuel and Barbara (Corbett) L. BA, U. Pa., 1978, MD, 1983. Sr. scientist Biohybrid Techs., Shrewsbury, Mass., 1990-93, dir. transplantation biology, 1993-98; clin. assoc. prof. surgery Tufts U., 1994-95; sr. dir. tissue engring. and transplant medicine Advanced Cell Tech., Inc., Worcester, Mass., 1999-2000; med. dir., v.p. med. and sci. devel. Advanced Cell Tech. Group Inc., 1999—. Rschr. Lab. of Richard Hynes, 1975, Gerald Edelman, 1976, Jonas Salk, 1978, B.F. Skinner, 1979-81, Christiaan Barnard, 1981-84; assoc. surgery Harvard Med. Sch., 1991-93. Author: Xeno, 2000; editor: Heart Transplantation, 1984, Medical Science and the Advancement of World Health, 1985, Procurement of Pancreatic Islets I, 1994, Immunomodulation of Pancreatic Islets II, 1994, Immunoisolation of Pancreatic Islets III, 1994, One World, 1996, Tissue Engineering/Cellular Medicine Series, 1995—, Yearbook of Cell and Tissue Transplantation, 1996—, Principles of Tissue Engineering, 1997, 2d edit., 2000, Encapsulated Cell Technology and Therapeutics, 1999, Methods of Tissue Engineering, 2001, Principles of Cloning, 2002; contbr. articles to profl. and lit. jours. Active Conservation Commn., Town of Clinton, 1998—, mem. open space com., 1996-98; founder and dir. South Meadow Pond and Wildlife Assn., 1998—; bd. dirs. Clinton Greenway Conservation Trust, 2001—. Prof. Howe Buck scholar, 1974-75, Benjamin Franklin scholar, 1975-78, Univ. scholar, 1976-83, Fulbright scholar, 1978-79; Hon. Christiaan Barnard fellow, 1981-84, Mry K. Iacocca Transplantation fellow, 1988-90. Achievements include cloned first endangered species; first to reverse aging using nuclear transfer; was part of team that cloned first human embryo. Home: South Meadow Pond Island 35 S Meadow Rd Clinton MA 01510-4327 Office: Advanced Cell Tech 1 Innovation Dr Worcester MA 01605-4307 E-mail: rlanza@advancedcell.com.

LANZAFAME, RAYMOND JOSEPH, surgeon, researcher; b. Rochester, N.Y., Sept. 30, 1952; s. Ray J. and Mary Vera (DeMeis) L.; m. Patricia Marie Volkmar, Apr. 26, 1980; children: Mark Raymond, Karen Elizabeth. BS with honors and distinction, Cornell U., 1974; MD, George Washington U., 1978; MBA, U. Rochester, 1999. Diplomate Nat. Bd. Med. Examiners, Am. Bd. Surgery. Clin. asst. prof. U. Rochester, N.Y., 1983-87, asst. prof., 1987-92, assoc. prof., 1992—. Mem. laser task force N.Y. State Dept. of Health, 1990; dir. laser tng., chmn. laser usage com., Rochester Gen. Hosp. 1983—, dir. surg. laser rsch. lab., 1988—, dir. Laser Ctr., 1984—; bd. dirs. Rochester Gen. Hosp. Found., 1990—. Sr. editor Jour. Clin. Laser Medicine and Surgery, 1987-93, co-editor-in-chief, 1993-96, editor-in-chief, 1996—, referee, 1987—; mem. editl. bd. Laser Medicine and Surgery News and Advances, 1988-90, Jour. Laparoendoscopic Surgery, 1991—, Surgery Alert, 1991-94, Lasers Surg. Medicine, 1995—, Jour. Soc. Laparoendoscopic Surgery, 1996—, Laser Med. Sci., 1997—; referee Jour. Investigative Surgery, 1997—; cons. editor Biomed. Optics, 1992—, mem. editl. bd. Soc. Laparoendoscopic Surg., 1996—, Laser Med. Sci., 1997—; referee J. Invest. Surg., 1997—. Grantee Am. Cancer Soc. Fellow: ACS (councillor upstate N.Y. chpt. 1992—97, young surgeon rep. 1992—, sec.-treas. 1997—98, pres. 1999—); mem.: AMA, Soc. Laparoendoscopic Surgeons (bd. dirs. 2000—), Soc. Univ. Surgeons, Biomed. Optics. Soc., Soc. Photo-Optical Instrumentation Engrs., Ctrl. N.Y. Surg. Soc., Ctrl. Surg. Assn., Soc. for Surgery of Alimentary Tract, Internat. Soc. Surgery, Internat. Soc. for Lasers in Surgery and Medicine, Acad. Surg. Rsch., N.Y. Acad. Scis., Collegium Internat. Chirugie Digestive, Assn. for Acad. Surgery, Am. Soc. for Laser Medicine and Surgery (Mark award 2001), Rochester Acad. Medicine, Rochester Surg. Soc., Monroe County Med. Soc., Med. Soc. State N.Y., Am. Soc. Laser Surgery and Medicine (bd. dirs. 1992—, pres. 1995—96, dir. CME 1999—), Laser Inst. Am. (sr.). Office: 1445 Portland Ave Ste 202 Rochester NY 14621-3095 E-mail: raymond.lanzafame@viahealth.org., raymond.lanzafame@viahealth.org.

LANZEROTTI, LOUIS JOHN, physicist; b. Carlinville, Ill., Apr. 16, 1938; s. Emanuel Louis and Mary Pauline (Orienti) L.; m. Mary Yvonne DeWolf, June 19, 1965; children: Mary Yvonne, Louis DeWolf. BS, U. Ill., 1960; MA, Harvard U., 1963, PhD, 1965. Postdoctoral fellow Lucent Technologies Bell Labs., Murray Hill, N.J., 1965-67; mem. tech. staff AT&T Bell Labs., 1967-82, Disting. mem. tech. staff, 1982—. Adj. prof. U. Fla., Gainesville, 1978-97; mem. polar rsch. bd. NRC, Washington, 1982-91, mem. space sci. bd., 1980-84, chmn. space studies bd., 1988-94, mem. ocean studies bd., 1995-99, chmn. bd. rev. Army Rsch. Lab., 1996-2000, report rev. com., 2000—, chmn. survey com. solar space physics rsch., 2001—; mem. phys. sci. com. NASA, Washington, 1975-79, chmn. space and earth adv. commn., 1984-88, mem. adv. coun., 1984-94; mem. adv. com. on future U.S. space program, 1990, mem. v.p.'s space policy adv. bd., 1992-93, v.p. blue ribbon adv. com. on redesign of space sta., 1993-94; mem. corp. Woods Hole Oceanographic Instn., 1993-2001; mem. governing bd. Am. Inst. Physics, 1997—, mem. exec. com. of governing bd., 2002--. Co-author: Particle Diffusion in Rad. Belts, 1974; co-editor 2 books related to space physics, 1977, 79; contbr. more than 500 tech. papers to profl. jours. V.p. Harding Twp. (N.J.) Sch. Bd., 1982-90, com., 1993—, dep. mayor, 1999—. Recipient Antarctic Svc. medal U.S., 1979, Disting. Pub. Svc. award NASA, 1988, 94, Disting. Sci. medal NASA, 1998, Achievement award Blackburn Coll. Alumni Assn., 1993; mountain named in his honor in Antarctica; minor planet 5504 named in his honor. Fellow AIAA, IEEE, Am. Phys. Soc., Am. Geophys. Union, AAAS; mem. NAE, Internat. Acad. Astronautics, Woods Hole Oceanographic Instn. Office: Bell Labs Lucent Technologies 700 Mountain Ave New Providence NJ 07974-1208 E-mail: ljl@bell-labs.com.

LANZILLOTTI, ROBERT FRANKLIN, economist, educator; b. Washington, June 19, 1921; s. Vincent and Gilda S. (Incutti) L.; m. Patricia Joy Jackson, Oct. 27, 1945; children— Robert J. (dec.), Donna J. Student, Dartmouth Coll., 1943; BA, Am. U., 1946, MA, 1947; PhD, U. Calif., Berkeley, 1953; D.D.L. (hon.), Tampa U., 1979; D.D.S. (hon.), Fla. Inst. Tech., 1979. Teaching fellow U. Calif. at Berkeley, 1947-49; mem. faculty Wash. State U., 1949-61, prof. econs., 1959-61; research assoc. Brookings Instn., 1956-57, 1974-75; prof. econs., chmn. dept. Mich. State U., 1961-69; prof. econs., dean Coll. Bus. Adminstrn., U. Fla., Gainesville, 1969-86, Eminent Scholar chair in Am. econ. instns., 1986-96, dir. Pub. Policy Rsch. Ctr., 1986-99; sr. econ. cons. Infotech, Inc., 1999—; 02655714. Mem. U.S. Price Commn., 1971-72; bd. dirs. Jim Walter Corp., Citizens and So. Bank Corp., Am. Birthright Corp., Catalina Lighting Corp., Fla. Power Corp., Bank of Ormond Beach, Fla., Talquin Corp., Bottom-Line Assoc., Fla. Progress Corp., Southeast Tissue Alliance; chmn. Econ. Adv. Bd. to Gov. Fla., 1973-76; cons. Mich. Bankers Assn., attys. gen. Calif., Wis., Minn., Ill., Fla., Mich., Oreg., Washington; attys. gen. also Fed. Trade Commn., U.S. Dept. Justice, U.S. Govt. Acctg. Office, U.S. Comptroller of the Currency, U.S. Census Bur. Author: Hard-Surface Floor Covering Industry, 1955, Pricing, Production & Marketing Policies of Small Manufacturers, 1964, Banking Structure in Michigan, 1945-63, 1966; co-author: Pricing in Big Business, 1959, Phase II in Review: The Price Commission Experience, 1975, Economic Effects of Government Mandated Costs, 1979; editor: The Conglomerate Corporation, 1981; co-editor: Management Under Government Intervention: The View from Mt. Scopus, 1984; contbr. articles to profl. jours. Served to lt. (j.g.) USNR, 1943-45; lt. comdr. Res. Decorated Bronze Star (2); NATO fellow, 1964 Mem. Am. Econ. Assn., Am. Law and Econ. Assn., So. Econ. Assn. (1st v.p. 1972-73), Fla. Coun. of 100, Internat. Schumpeter Soc. (pres. 2000), Phi Beta Kappa (hon.), Beta Gamma Sigma, Omicron Delta Kappa.

LANZINGER, KLAUS, language educator, educator; b. Woergl, Tyrol, Austria, Feb. 16, 1928; arrived in U.S., 1971, naturalized, 1979; m. Aida Schuessl, June, 1954; children: Franz, Christine. BA, Bowdoin Coll., 1951; PhD, U. Innsbruck, Austria, 1952. Rsch. asst. U. Innsbruck, 1957-67; assoc. prof. modern langs. U. Notre Dame, Ind., 1967-77, prof., 1977-97, prof. emeritus, 1997—. Resident dir. fgn. study program, Innsbruck, 1969-71, 76-78, 82-85; acting chmn. dept. Modern and Classical Languages, U. Notre Dame, fall 1987, chmn. dept. German and Russian, 1989-96. Author: Epik im amerikanischen Roman, 1965, Jason's Voyage: The Search for the Old World in American Literature, 1989; editor: Americana-Austriaca, 5 vols., 1966-83; contbr. numerous articles to profl. jours. Bowdoin Coll. fgn. student scholar, 1950-51; Fulbright rsch. grantee U. Pa., 1961; U. Notre Dame summer rsch. grantee Houghton Libr., Harvard U., 1975, 81; named to Internat. Order of Merit, 2001. Mem. MLA, Deutsche Gesellschaft für Amerikastudien, Thomas Wolfe Soc. (Zelda Gitlin Lit. prize 1993). Home: 52703 Helvie Dr South Bend IN 46635-1215 Office: Dept German Russian Langs & Lits U Notre Dame Notre Dame IN 46556

LANZINO, GIUSEPPE, physician; b. Cosenza, Italy, Jan. 6, 1965; came to U.S., 1992; MD, U. Bologna, Italy, 1989. Rsch. fellow dept. neurosurgery U. Pitts., 1990—91, U. Va., Charlottesville, 1992—94, resident dept. neurosurgery, 1994—97; endovascular fellow dept. neurosurgery U. Buffalo, 1997—99; sr. registrar dept. neurosurgery Plymouth (Eng.) Hosp., 1999—2000; chief resident dept. neurosurgery U. Va., Charlottesville, 2000—01; cerebrovascular fellow Barrow Neurol. Inst., 2001—02; assoc. prof. dept. neurosurgery U. Ill. Coll. Medicine, Peoria, 2002—. Fellow Am. Coll. Angiology; mem. Soc. Critical Care, Am. Heart Assn., N.Y. Acad. Scis. Avocations: history of medicine, history of neurosurgery, soccer. Home: 1324 Independence Ct Metamora IL 61548 Office: Ill Neurol Inst Dept Neurosurgery 530 NE Glen Oak Ave Peoria IL 61637-0001 Office Fax: 309-655-7696. E-mail: glanzino@hotmail.com.

LANZKRON, ROLF WOLFGANG, manufacturing executive; b. Hamburg, Germany, Dec. 9, 1929; arrived in U.S., 1951, naturalized, 1961; s. Aron Artur and Hanna (Farbstein) Lanzkron; m. Amy Virginia Yarri, Mar. 5, 1961; children: Paul Joshua, Sophie Miriam, Lisa Rachel. BS, Milw. Sch. Engring., 1953; MS, U. Wis., 1955, PhD, 1956. Registered profl. engr., Calif. Computer designer Univac Sperry Rand, St. Paul, 1956-58; guidance and control systems integrations staff Martin Marietta, Orlando, Fla., 1958-61, sys. engr. Balt., 1961-68; advanced to chief command and svc. module flight project div. NASA Manned Spacecraft Ctr., Apollo Program, Houston, 1963; graphic ops. mgr. Raytheon Co., Marlborough, Mass., 1968-82, dep. dir. air traffic control, 1982-92, dir. air traffic control, 1992-95; pres. RWL Assocs. Cons., Gloucester, 1995. With Israeli Army, 1948—51. Recipient Outstanding Achievement award, NASA, 1964, Spl. Svc. award, 1966, Clifford Eurto Medallion award, 1995. Mem.: IEEE, AIAA, Am. Mgmt. Assn., Am. Math. Soc., Sigma Xi. Office: RWL Assoc Consulting Firm 2 Mallard Way Gloucester MA 01930-3243 Fax: 978 282-4897.

LANZL, CHRISTINA ANNA, visual artist, arts coordinator; b. L.A., Dec. 19, 1964; d. John and Hanna Elenor (Reichl) L. BA, FHB Stuttgart, Germany, 1987; MA, Boston U., 1991. Rsch. specialist Mass. Coll. Art, Boston, 1987-90; asst. to dir. Boston U. Art Gallery, 1990-91; dir. Bromfield Gallery, Boston, 1991-96; founder, owner Studio 23: Art and Ideas, 1991—; asst. to the project coord. Boston Arts Acad., 1996-97; exec. dir. Brookline (Mass.) Arts Ctr., 1997-2000; resource/project coord. UrbanArts Inst., 2000—. One-woman show includes Radio House Gallery, N.Y.C., 2000. Mem. Am. Assn. Museums, Coll. Art Assn., Women's Caucus for Art (v.p. Boston chpt. 1993-96, exhibitions co-hmn. nat. conf. 1996). E-mail: Christina.Lanzl@massart.edu.

LANZL, ERIC L. social worker; b. Chgo., Jan. 28, 1952; s. Lawrence H. and Elisabeth (Farber) L. BA, DePauw U., 1974; MA Social Svc. Adminstrn., U. Chgo., 1977. Lic. clin. social worker, Ill. Social worker Hines VA Hosp., Maywood, Ill., 1978; clin. therapist City of Chgo., 1978—. Part-time clin. social worker Niles Family Svc., Chgo., 1989—, Fillmore Ctr.'s West Suburban Psychotherapy Assn., 1991. Mem. Ill. Soc. Clin. Social Work, Am. Youth Hostels. Home: 4217 N Paulina St Chicago IL 60613-1239

LAO, LANG LI, nuclear fusion research physicist; b. Hai Duong, Vietnam, Jan. 28, 1954; came to U.S., 1972; s. Thich Cuong and Boi Phan (Loi) L.; m. Ngan Hua, Dec. 22, 1979; children: Bert J., Brian J. BS, MS, Calif. Inst. Tech., 1976; MS, U. Wis., 1977, PhD, 1979. Staff scientist Oak Ridge (Tenn.) Nat. Lab., 1979-81, TRW, Redondo Beach, Calif., 1981-82; mgr. integrated modeling br. Gen. Atomics, San Diego, 1982—. Contbr. articles to sci. jours. Recipient award for Excellence in Plasma Physics Research Am. Physical Society, 1994 Fellow Am. Phys. Soc. (co-recipient excellence in plasma physics rsch. award 1994). Achievements include being world leader in equilibrium analysis of magnetic fusion plasma physics experiments; developed a widely used computer code essential for successful operation and interpretation of tokamak fusion experiments. Office: General Atomics 3550 General Atomics Ct San Diego CA 92121-1122

LAPADOT, SONEE SPINNER, retired automobile manufacturing company official; b. Sidney, Ohio, Apr. 19, 1936; d. Kenneth Lee and Helyn Kathryn (Hobby) Spinner; m. Jan. 13, 1955 (div. Apr. 1970); 1 child, Douglas Cameron Proud; m. Robert Stephen Lapadot, May 4, 1974 (div. Mar. 1994). Student, U. Cin., 1954-56, U. Akron, 1966; BS in Mgmt. Human Resources, Spring Arbor Coll., 1991. Mgr. engring. change implementation Terex divsn. GM, Hudson, Ohio, 1975-77, mgr. prodn. scheduling, 1977-78, gen. adminstr. product purchasing, 1978-79; sr. staff asst. non-ferrous metals GM, Detroit, 1979-80, mgr. tires and wheels, 1980-83, mgr. staff purchasing, 1983-85, mgr. corp. constrn. contracting, 1985-86; mfg. techs. adminstr. Chrysler Motors, 1986-87, mgr. mfg. prodn. control adminstrn. and svcs., 1988, mgr. advanced planning and prodn. systems, 1988-89, mgr. advanced planning and control power train, 1989-90, mgr. Mound Rd. engine prodn. control, 1990-95, mgr. corp. project systems, 1995-96, platform exec. material handling engring., 1996-99, platform exec. spl. projects, 2000-01; ret., 2001. Active fundraising Boy Scouts Am., Grosse Pointe, Mich., 1980-82, Detroit, 1985-96, United Fund, Detroit, 1980-99, Jr. Achievement, Detroit, 1984, 90-96. Mem. NAFE, Soc. Automotive Engrs., Am. Soc. Profl. and Exec. Women, Am. Prodn. and Inventory Control Soc., Automotive Industry Action Group (returnable containers and packaging team), Mensa, Women's Econ. Club of Detroit. Home: 1941 Squirrel Rd Bloomfield Hills MI 48304-1162

LAPALOMBARA, JOSEPH, political science and industrial management educator; b. Chgo., May 18, 1925; s. Louis and Helen (Teutonico) LaP.; m. Lyda Mae Ecke, June 22, 1947 (div.); children— Richard, David, Susan; m. Constance Ada Bezer, June, 1971. AB, U. Ill., 1947, AM, 1950; AM (Charlotte Elizabeth Proctor fellow), Princeton U., 1952, PhD, 1954; student, U. Rome (Italy), 1952-53; MA (hon.), Yale U., 1964. Instr., then asst. prof. polit. sci. Oreg. State Coll., 1947-50; instr. politics Princeton U., 1952; mem. faculty Mich. State U., 1953-64, prof. polit. sci., 1958-64, head dept., 1958-63; prof. polit. sci. Yale U., 1964-96, prof. polit. sci. and mgmt., 1996—2001, Arnold Wolfers prof., 1969—2001, Arnold Wolfers prof. polit. sci. and mgmt. emeritus, 2001—, chmn. dept. polit. sci., 1974-78, 82-85, prof. Sch. Orgn. and Mgmt., 1979—84, 1997—2001; sr. rsch. scholar Yale Ctr. for Comparative Rsch., 2001—; dir. Instn. for Social and Policy Studies, 1987-92; chmn. Coun. Comparative and European Studies, 1966-71; cultural attache, first sec. U.S. embassy, Rome, 1980-81. Vis. prof. U. Florence, Italy, 1957-58, U. Calif.-Berkeley, 1962, Columbia U., 1966-67, U. Turin, 1974, U. Catania, 1974; cons. FCDA, 1956, Carnegie Corp., 1959, Brookings Instn., 1962, Ford Found., 1965-76, Twentieth Century Fund, 1965-69, AID, 1967-68, Fgn. Svc. Inst., 1968-72, 74-76, Ednl. Testing Svc., 1970-75, Alcoa, 1978-80, Rohm & Haas, 1975-76, GE, 1978-80, Union Carbide, 1981-92, Montedison, 1984-85, Ente Nazionale Idrocarburi, 1983-93, Guardian Industries, 1990-93, Praxair, 1992—, Swiss Bank Corp., 1994-99, Athena, 1994-95, Richard Medley Advisors, 1995-2001, Telecom Italia, 1996-99, S.I.A.D., 1999—; sr. rsch. assoc. Conf. Bd. N.Y., 1976-81; pres. Italian-Am. Multimedia Corp. N.Y., 1988—; bd. dirs. Transparency Internat.-U.S.A., 1994—. Author: The Initiative and Referendum in Oregon, 1950, The Italian Labor Movement: Problems and Prospects, 1957, Guide to Michigan Politics, rev. edit, 1960, (with Alberto Spreafico) Elezioni e Comportamento Politico in Italia, 1963, Bureaucracy and Political Development, 1963, Interest Groups in Italian Politics, 1964, Italy: The Politics of Planning, 1966, (with Myron Weiner) Political Parties and Political Development, 1966, Clientela e Parentela, 1967, Burocracia y desarrolo politico, 1970, Crises and Sequences of Political Development, (with others), 1972, Politics Within Nations, 1974, Multinational Corporations and National Elites: A Study in Tensions, 1975, (with Stephen Blank) Multinational Corporations in Comparative Perspective, 1976, Multinational Corporations and Developing Countries, 1979, A Politica nos Interior das Nações, 1982, Democracy, Italian Style, 1987, Democrazia all'italiana, 1988, Die Italiener: oder Demokratie als Lebenskunst, 1988, Democratie à l'italienne, 1990; bd. editors Midwest Jour. Polit. Sci, 1956-57, Yale U. Press, 1965-72, 73-76, ABC-CL10, 1976—, Global Perspectives, 1983-2000; mem. editorial bd. Comparative Politics, 1968—, Jour. Comparative and European Studies, 1969—, Am. Jour. Polit. Sci, 1976-80, Italian Jour., 1988, Yale Rev., 1993—; editor series comparative politics Prentice-Hall Co., 1971-85; editor Jour. Internat. Bus. Edn., 2001-; mem. editorial adv. bd. Jour. Comparative Adminstrn, 1970-74, Adminstrn. and Soc, 1974— ; adv. bd. ABC Polit. Sci; N.Am. editor: Mediterranean Observer, 1981-86; editor in chief Italy, Italy, 1988—; contbr. articles to profl. jours. Mem. exec. com. Inter Univ. Consortium Polit. Rsch., 1966-70; mem. staff Social Sci. Rsch. Coun., 1966-73; chmn. West European fgn. area fellowship program Social Sci. Rsch. Coun.-Am. Coun. Learned Socs., 1972-74; bd. dirs. Mich. Citizenship Clearing House, 1955; mem. internat. coun. Ctr. for Strategic and Internat. Studies, 1990—; mem. Coun. on Fgn. Rels.; U.S. com. Am. Fgn. Policy, 1996—. Decorated knight comdr. Order of Merit, Republic of Italy, Fulbright scholar, 1952-53, 57-58, Penfield scholar U. Pa., 1953; fellow Social Sci. Rsch. Coun., 1952-53, Ctr. Advanced Study Behavioral Scis., 1961-62, Rockefeller Found., 1963-64, Ford Found., 1969, Guggenheim Found., 1971-72, European U. Inst., 1996, Wissenschaftszentrum Berlin, 1996; recipient Guido Dorso prize, Italy, 1984, Medal of Honor, Italian Constitutional Ct., 1993, Presidency of Italian Republic, 1993. Mem. Am. Acad. Arts and Scis., Conn. Acad. Arts and Scis., Am. Acad. in Rome (trustee 1984-90), Social Sci. Research Council (com. comparative politics 1958-72), Am. Polit. Sci. Assn. (exec. coun. 1963-65, exec. com. 1967-68, v.p. 1979-80, mem. conf. group on Italian politics and soc. 1978, conf. pres. 1984-85), Am. Acad. Polit. and Social Sci., Soc. for Italian Hist. Studies, Societá Italiana di Studi Elettorali, Consiglio Italiano di Scienze Sociali, Phi Beta Kappa, Phi Kappa Phi, Phi Eta Sigma. Clubs: Yale of N.Y., Elizabethan, Morys Assn. Home: 50 Huntington St New Haven CT 06511-1333

LAPATIN, KENNETH D.S. archaeologist, art historian; b. Kansas City, Mo., May 4, 1961; s. Arnold Lee and Miriam Fink Shapiro; m. Marina Gemma Belozerskaya, Aug. 17, 1992. AB, U. Calif., 1984; MS, Oxford U., 1986; PhD, U. Calif., Berkeley, 1994. Prof. of art history Boston U., 1994—. Contbr. articles to profl. jours. Postdoctoral fellow J. Paul Getty Trust, 1996-97, Fulbright fellow, Greece, 1988-89, Oscar T. Broneer fellow Am. Acad. in Rome, 1989-90, David E. Finley fellow Nat. Gallery of Art, Washington, 1991-94. Mem. Archaeol. Inst. of Am., Coll. Art Assn. Office: Art History Dept/Boston U 725 Commonwealth Ave # 302 Boston MA 02215-1401 E-mail: lapatin@bu.edu.

LAPE, MICHAEL JOHN, small business owner; b. Phila., Jan. 18, 1943; s. Geo. Frank and Virginia (Magge) L.; m. Lee Coker, Aug. 1996; 1 child, Lynn Lee. AA, U. Pa., 1964, BA, 1966; MBA, U. Md., 1971. Producer, account exec. Burt Claster Prodns., Balt., 1967-69; producer documentaries ABC, N.Y.C., 1969-70; account exec. Westinghouse Broadcasting, Balt., 1970-71, Chgo., 1971-72, N.Y.C., 1972-73, local/gen. sales mgr. Phila., 1973-81; v.p. of sales, mktg. Group W Satellite Communications, Stamford, Conn., 1981-86; gen. mgr., v.p., co-owner Westport-York Ltd. Partnership, York, Pa., 1986-87; ptnr. Internat. Registry of Antiques and Fine Art, Roxbury, Conn., 1990—; CEO TV Am., Denver, 1993-95, Equity Merchant Bank, Dallas, 1998-99. Cons. Burger & Assocs., Glenn Mills, Pa., 1984, Automotive Restorations Vintage Racing, 1988; pres. Shared Info. Techs. for Edn., Washington Depot, Conn., 1999—. Bd. dirs. Merrcer (N.J.) Jr. Coll., 1984—. Mem. Sports Car Club Am., Vintage Sport Car Club Am., Sports Car Vintage Racing Assn. Avocation: vintage car racing.

LAPE, ROBERT CABLE, broadcast journalist; b. Akron, Ohio; s. C. Robert and Mary Elizabeth (Cable) L.; m. Marcia Giesy, (div. Dec. 1969); children: Debra, Robert S., Alida, Douglas; m. Eve Bergman, Feb. 14, 1982. BS in Journalism and Radio Speech, Kent State U., 1955. Reporter, asst. news dir. WCUE Radio, Akron, 1954-56; news dir. WICE Radio, Providence, 1956-61; corr., news dir. WBZ Radio, Boston, 1961-68, WABC-TV, N.Y.C., 1968-82; critic, writer on food and travel, lectr. WABC, WCBS, Crain's N.Y. Bus., N.Y. Law Jour., Agenda N.Y., 1983—, LaCucina Italiana, N.Y. Pocket Guide, The Record (N.J.). Bd. dirs. Internat. Food Media Conf., N.Am., 1986—; anchor The CPA Report, 1999-2000. Author: Epicurean Rendezvous, 1990-96, Bob Lape's Restaurant Index, 1987-91. Nat. judge food March of Dimes, 1991—; spkr., M.C. Crohn's and Colitis Found., N.Y., Nat. Cancer Soc.; judge James Beard Found. Awards. Recipient Emmy award for TV News Coverage, 1980, 1st Ann. Lifetime Achievement award N.Y. State Restaurant Assn., 1998. Mem. SAG, AFTRA, Assn. Italian Sommeliers, Wine Media Guild, Commanderie de Cordon Bleu de France, Compagnons de Beaujolais, Friars Club, Lambs Club. Avocations: travel, reading.

LAPETER, JAMES MICHAEL, real estate executive; b. Troy, N.Y., May 10, 1953; s. Alfred Paul and Grace Martha (Alvarez) L.; m. Susan Marie Brickner, May 31, 1986. BA in Econs. with honors, UCLA, 1975. Sales rep. 3M Co., Los Angeles, 1975-76; pres. Americana Realtors, Bellflower, Calif., 1976— ; real estate instr. Cerritos Coll., Norwalk, Calif., 1980— ; guest lectr. Calif. State U., 1981. Bd. dirs. Cerritos Coll. Real Estate Adv. Bd., Norwalk, 1981— ; mem. Calif. Com. Real Estate Continuing Edn., 1983— . Named Realtor of Yr. Rancho Los Cerritos Bd. Realtors, 1981; Chancellor's Marshal UCLA, 1975; recipient Calif. State Resolution award Calif. Senate and Assembly, 1982. Mem. Calif. C. of C., Calif. Assn. Realtors. (dir. 1978— , exec. com.), Nat. Assn. Realtors, Rancho Los Cerritos Bd. Realtors (pres. 1982, regional v.p.), Blue Key, Lambda Chi Alpha (pres. 1974-75). Republican. Roman Catholic. Home: 3210 E Abbey Ln Orange CA 92867-2009 Office: Americana Realtors PO Box 3801 Ketchum ID 83340-3801

LA PETINA, GARY MICHAEL, lawyer; b. Chgo., Apr. 25, 1955; s. Nicholas J. and Mildred E. (Roth) La P.; m. Donna M. Kulisz, Oct. 9, 1982; children: Patrick James, Nicole Elizabeth. BS, Loyola U., Chgo., 1977; JD, John Marshall Law Sch., Chgo., 1980. Bar: Ill. 1980. Staff atty. Internat. Assn. Lions Clubs, Oak Brook, Ill., 1982-87, gen. counsel, sec., 1987—2001, exec. adminstr., 2001—. Mem.: ABA, Lions. Roman Catholic. Avocations: collectibles, sporting events, reading. Home: 2 S 030 Bristol Ln Warrenville IL 60555 Office: Internat Assn Lions Clubs 300 W 22nd St Oak Brook IL 60523-8815 E-mail: glapetin@lionsclubs.org.

LAPHAM, JERRY L. social services administrator; b. Allegan County, Mich., Aug. 31, 1944; s. Dean D. and Martha Ardise (Pike) L.; m. Judith A. Evans, Aug. 16, 1969. BA, Adrian Coll., 1966; MA, Western Mich. U., 1968. Cert. social worker, Mich. Vocat. rehab. counselor State of Mich., Highland Park, 1967-69; psychology Wayne State Univ., Detroit, 1969-71; exec. dir. Big Brothers Big Sisters, Battle Creek, 1971-81; field rep. to dir. field svcs. Big Brothers Big Sisters of Am., Phila., 1981-91, dir., agency devel., 1991—, dir. tng. and profl. devel. internat., 2001—02; dir. tng. and profl. devel. N.E. Boys and Girls Clubs Am., Macungie, 2002—. Part-time instr. Western Mich. Univ., Wayne State Univ., Albion Coll., Kellogg Cmty. Coll., Monroe County Cmty. Coll., Lehigh Cmty. Coll.; speaker in field. Author: Merger in Big Brothers Big Sisters, 1995, How to Start a Big Brother Big Sister Orgn., 1994, 97, Mentoring Elements of Effective Pres., 1991. Bd. dirs. Ancient Oaks Civic Assn., 1991-93; task force mem. United Meth. Ch., N.Y.C., 1992-94; bd. dirs. Lehigh County Devel., pres., v.p., 1991-97; v.p. program coun. Allenfour United Meth. Ch.; chmn. United Way, 1975; chairperson Pegasus, Inc.; exec. bd. dirs. Calhoun County Juvenile Justice Coord. Coun.; chmn. Calhoun County Runaway Com.; mem. Coalition for Svcs. to Youth Sigma Alpha Epsilon. Recipient Outstanding Campaign Chair award United Way, Phila., 1992-93, 4-H Alumni Assn. award, 4-H, Pa., 1993. Mem. Am. Assn. Counseling and Devel., Nat. Assn. Social Work, Adrian Coll. Alumni Assn. (pres. 1997, v.p. 1995-97), Aspires Connector (pres. 1994-95, founder), Kiwanis (pres., bd. dirs.). Democrat. Methodist. Avocations: genealogy. Office: Boys and Girls Club Am 2011 Aster Rd Macungie PA 18062-8945 Office Fax: 610-398-7381. E-mail: jlapham@bgca.org.

LAPHAM, LEWIS HENRY, editor, author, television host; b. San Francisco, Jan. 8, 1935; s. Lewis Abbot and Jane (Foster) L.; m. Joan Brooke Reeves, Aug. 10, 1972; children: Lewis Andrew, Elizabeth Delphina, Winston Peale. Grad., Hotchkiss Sch., 1952; BA, Yale U., 1956; postgrad., Cambridge U., 1956-57; LLD, Hampden-Sydney Coll., Va. Reporter San Francisco Examiner, 1957-60, N.Y. Herald Tribune, 1960-62; author, editor USA-1, N.Y.C., 1962, Saturday Evening Post, N.Y.C., 1963-67; writer Life mag., Harper's, 1968-70; mng. editor Harper's, 1971-75, editor, 1975-81, 83—. TV host weekly series Bookmark, PBS, also host, author documentary series America's Century. Author: (essays) Fortune's Child, 1980, Money and Class in America, 1988, Imperial Masquerade, 1989, The Wish for Kings, 1993, Hotel America, 1995, Waiting for the Barbarians, 1997, The Agony of Mammon, 1999, Lapham's Rules of Influence, 1999, Lights, Camera, Democracy!, 2001, Theater of War, 2002. Bd. dirs. Librs. for the Future, The Harry Frank Guggenheim Found. Mem. Coun. on Fgn. Rels., Century Assn., The Blind Book Club, Inc. Office: Harper's Mag 666 Broadway Fl 11 New York NY 10012-2394

LAPIDUS, ARNOLD, mathematician, educator; b. Bklyn., Nov. 6, 1933; s. Morris and Mollie L. m. Nancy Beatrice Latner, Aug. 9, 1952 BS, Bklyn. Coll., 1956; MS, PhD, N.Y. U., 1967. Research scientist Courant Inst., N.Y.C., 1956-68; computer application math. analyst Goddard Inst. for Space Studies, 1968-70, math. analyst programming methods, 1970-71, sr. mem. tech. staff computer scis., 1971-73; assoc. prof. quantitative analysis Fairleigh Dickinson U., Teaneck, N.J., 1973-83, prof., chair dept. computer and decision systems, 1983-85; sr. engr. Singer Electronic Systems Corp., Little Falls, 1986-87; owner Advanced Math. Co., Englewood, 1987—2000; pvt. practice, 1987—. Vol. mathematician UMDNJ, Newark, 1998-2001 *Dr. Lapidus tries to follow and promote the precept that the world would be a paradise if we all would make and implement decisions furthering our long term best interests.* Contbr. articles to profl. publs. Mem. AAAS, AAUP, Math. Assn. Am., Am. Math. Soc., Soc. Indsl. and Applied Math. Home and Office: 401 Fergus Way Tobyhanna PA 18466-4068

LAPIDUS, DENNIS, real estate developer; b. Chgo., Oct. 21, 1942; s. Sidney and Mildred (Karlin) L. BSME, Northwestern U., 1964; MBA, Roosevelt U., 1967. Pres., founder Productive Computer Sys., Chgo., 1980-86, MBI Leasing, Chgo., 1986—. Bd. dirs. Anti-Cruelty Soc., New Century Bank. Productive Computer Sys. named to Inc. Mag. 500 Fastest Growing Privately Held Cos., 1986. Mem. Ravisloe Country Club, Medinah Country Club. Avocations: golf, basketball. Home: 1941 N Fremont St Chicago IL 60614-5016 Office: MBI Leasing PO Box 146522 Chicago IL 60614-6400 E-mail: dlap268244@aol.com.

LAPIDUS, JULES BENJAMIN, educational association administrator; b. Chgo., May 1, 1931; s. Leo R. and Lillian D. (Davidson) LaP.; m. Anne Marie Liebman, June 8, 1970; children: Steven, Amy, Mark, Marilyn. BS, U. Ill., 1954; MS, U. Wis., 1957, PhD, 1958. Prof. medicinal and pharm. chemistry Ohio State U., 1958-84; assoc. dean Grad. Sch., 1972-74; dean Grad. Sch., 1974-84; vice provost for research, 1974-82; pres. Council Grad. Schs., 1984-2000. Mem. pharmacology and toxicology tng. com. NIH, 1965-67, pharmacology program com., 1971-74; mem. Grad. Record Examination Bd., 1982-2000. Mem. AAAS.

LAPIDUS, PATRICIA JEAN, social worker; b. Lewiston, Maine, Aug. 13, 1942; d. Frederick Emerson and Hilda Cecile (Small) Mitchell; m. William Spalding Joplin, Jan. 10, 1972 (div. Mar. 1976); 1 child, Benjamin; m. Don Samuel Lapidus, Sept. 19, 1976; children: Noah, Samuel. BA, Ind. U., 1965; MA in Tchg., U. Maine, 1967. Tchr. Bonny Eagle H.S., Standish, Maine, 1965-68, Cape Elizabeth (Maine) H.S., 1968-69; jr. editor Raytheon Corp., Lexington, Mass., 1969-70; tchr. Westford (Mass.) Jr. H.S., 1971-72; crisis intervention worker The Farm, Summertown, Tenn., 1976-79; social worker Head Start, Delawre County, N.Y., 1983-84, Cmty. Maternity Svcs., Oneonta, 1984—. Author: 2000: Here's to Humanity, 2000; contbr. essays and poems to numerous publs. Democrat. Unitarian-Universalist. Office: Cmty Maternity Svcs 9-15 S Main St Oneonta NY 13820-1595

LAPIERRE, DOMINIQUE, writer, historian, philanthropist; b. Chatelaillon, France, July 30, 1931; s. Jean and Luce (Andreota) L.; m. Dominique Conchon, Apr. 5, 1980. Student (Fulbright Exchange scholar), U. Polit. Sci., Paris, 1950-51; BA, Lafayette Coll., Easton, Pa., 1952, LittD (hon.), 1982. Editor Paris Match News mag., 1955-67. Author: The City of Joy, 1985, Beyond Love, 1990, A Thousand Suns, 1999, Five Past Midnight in Bhopal, 2002; co-author: Is Paris Burning?, 1964, Or I'll Dress You In Morning, 1967, O Jersalem, 1971, Freedom at Midnight, 1975, The Fifth Horseman, 1980. Founder, pres. Action Aid for Lepers' Children of Calcutta. Decorated comdr. Order of Tastevin, grand cross Civil Order of Social Solidarity (Spain); recipient Gold medal of the City of Calcutta for humanitarian action, 1987, Rainbow Internat. award UN, 1999; Internat. Prize for Peace Vatican, 1999. Home: 37 rue Charles-Laffitte 92200 Neuilly-sur-Seine France Office: care Morton Janklow Lit Agy 445 Park Ave New York NY 10022-2606 E-mail: d.lapierre@wanadoo.fr.

LAPIN, ANDREW WILLIAM, lawyer; b. Chgo., Feb. 2, 1953; s. Robert Allan and Elaine (Muhlrad) L.; m. Debra Nan Goldberg, July 7, 1979; children: Lauren Elyse, Marisa Anne. BA, Ind. U., 1975; JD, John Marshall Law Sch., 1978. Bar: Ill. 1978, U.S. Dist. Ct. (no. dist.) Ill. 1978. Pvt. practice law, Chgo., 1978-79, 81-87; assoc. Tash & Slavitt, Ltd., 1979-81; of counsel Siegan, Barbakoff & Gomberg, 1987-89, Lapin & Assocs., Chgo., 1989-2000; ptnr. Much, Shelist, Freed, Denenberg, Ament & Rubenstein, P.C., 2000—. Lectr. Nat. Assn. Govt. Guaranteed Lenders. Author: Closing and Funding the SBA Loan. Mem. Nat. Assn. Small Bus. Investment Cos., Chgo. Bar Assn. (real property com., real property fin. subcom.), Ill. Bar Assn., Chgo. Mortgage Attys. Assn. Office: Much Shelist Freed Denenberg Ament & Rubenstein 200 N LaSalle Ste 2100 Chicago IL 60601 E-mail: alapin@muchlaw.com.

LAPIN, HARVEY I. lawyer; b. St. Louis, Nov. 23, 1937; s. Lazarus L. and Lillie L.; m. Cheryl A. Lapin; children: Jeffrey, Gregg. BS, Northwestern U., 1960, JD, 1963. Bar: Ill. 1963, Fla. 1980, Wis. 1985; cert. tax lawyer, Fla.; CPA, Ill. Atty. Office Chief Counsel, IRS, Washington, 1963-65; trial atty. Office Regional Counsel, IRS, 1965-68; assoc., then ptnr. Fiffer & D'Angelo, Chgo., 1968-75; pres. Harvey I. Lapin, P.C., 1975-83; mng. ptnr. Lapin, Hoff, Spangler & Greenberg, 1983-88, Lapin, Hoff, Slaw & Laffey, Chgo., 1989-91; ptnr. Gottlieb and Schwartz, 1992-93; prin. Harvey I. Lapin & Assocs., P.C., Northbrook, Ill., 1993—. Instr. John Marshall Law Sch., 1969—; facility adv. lawyers asst. program Roosevelt U., Chgo.; mem. cemetery adv. bd. Ill. Comptroller, 1974-96, 99—; mem. IRS Great Lakes TE/EO Coun., 2001—. Asst. editor Fed. Bar Jour., 1965-67; contbg. editor Cemetery and Funeral Service Business and Legal Guide; contbr. articles to profl. jours. Mem. ABA, Fla. Bar Assn., Wis. Bar Assn., Ill. Bar Assn., Chgo. Bar Assn., (mem. tax exempt orgns. subcom., sect. taxation 1988-90). Jewish. Office: Harvey I Lapin & Assocs PC PO Box 1327 Northbrook IL 60065-1327

LAPIN, JEFFREY BRENT, lawyer; b. Kansas City, Mo., Dec. 31, 1970; s. Arthur Edward and Bonnie Dubinsky Lapin. BA, U. Kans., 1993; JD with distinction, U. Nebr., 1997. Bar: Kans. 1997, Nebr. 1997. Law clk. Friedman Law Offices, Lincoln, Nebr., 1995-97, atty., 1998—. Tchr. Cmty. Legal Edn. Program, Lincoln, 1997. Recipient Corpus Juris Secundum award in property West Pub., Creighton Coll. Law, 1995; scholar U. Nebr., Lincoln, 1997. Mem. ATLA, Kans. Bar Assn., Nebr. Bar Assn., Nebr. Assn. Trial Lawyers. Republican. Avocations: computers, golf. Office: Friedman Law Offices 633 S 9th St Lincoln NE 68508-2807 Fax: 402-476-8364. E-mail: jlapin@friedmanlaw.com.

LAPIN, SHARON JOYCE VAUGHN, interior designer; b. Lagrange, Mo., July 28, 1938; d. John Nolan and Wilma Emma (Huebotter) Vaughn; m. Byron Richard Lapin, Oct. 14, 1972. BA summa cum laude, U. Wash., Seattle, 1960. Appeared in various Broadway shows, TV commls. and TV shows, 1962-72; mgr. arts and crafts divsn. Convenience Products Clayton Corp., Fenton, Mo. Bd. dirs. St. Louis Conservatory and Schs. for Arts, 1977—92, v.p., 1982—87;

chmn. bd. Studio Set, 1978—81, pres., 1975—78, bd. dirs., 1975—83, Friends of Sci. Mus., 1980—90, v.p., 1984—85; pres. assocs. bd. dirs. St. Louis Sci. Ctr., Inc., 1986-87, 1986—87; bd. dirs. Jr. divsn. St. Louis Symphony Women's Assn., 1973—75; bd. dirs. Women's Assn. St. Louis Symphony, 1988—90. Mem. AFTRA, SAG, AEA, ASID, Phi Beta Phi, Mu Phi Epsilon.

LAPINSKI, FRANCES CONSTANCE, internet product and marketing management; b. Flushing, N.Y., Sept. 19, 1950; d. Frank Stanley and Frances A. (Gaziano) L.; 1 child, Katherine. BS in Edn., SUNY, Oswego, 1972, MS in Edn., 1974; postgrad. in program edn., adminstrn., Syracuse U., 1976; MBA, NYU, 1990. Tchr. Mexico (N.Y.) Boces, 1971-72; chancellor's intern SUNY, Oswego, 1972-74; coordinator housing Lemoyne Coll., Syracuse, 1974-76; project coordinator Am. Assn. State Colls. and Univs., Washington, 1976-79; project mgr. Robt Bell & Co., Balt., 1979-81; asst. treas. Chase Manhattan Bank, N.Y., 1981-84; sr. product mgr. internet svcs. Depository Trust Co., 1984—. Mem. computer security del. to People to People Citizen Amb. Program, China, 1994; mem. corp. adv. bd. Infoworld, 1995—, Tech. Mgrs. Forum, 1996—. Vol. Spl. Olympics, N.J., N.Y., 1984—, Habitat for Humanity, Newark, 1995-98; chmn. Outreach Program, St. Andrew and Holy Communion Ch., South Orange, N.J., 1991-93. Mem. Microcomputer Mgrs. Assn. (vendor liaison 1986-90, bd. dirs. 1991-93, nat. award for excellence 1992, pres. N.Y. chpt. 1994). Avocations: camping, cross country skiing. Home: 11 S Kingman Rd South Orange NJ 07079-2611 E-mail: frances.lapinski@dtcc.com.

LAPLANTZ, DAVID MILTON, artist, retired educator; b. Toledo, June 12, 1944; s. Milton N. LaPlantz and Bernice L. Merle; m. Shereen F. Buckland, Feb. 7, 1970. BS in Edn., Bowling Green State U., 1966; MFA in Metal Smithing, Cranbrook Acad. Art, 1969. Instr. jewelry Inst. Am. Indian Arts, Santa Fe, 1967-68, Flint (Mich.) C.C., 1968-69, Colo. State U., Ft. Collins, 1969-70; asst. prof. art San Diego Sate U., 1970-71; asst. prof. Humboldt State U., Arcata, Calif., 1971-77, prof., 1978—2002. Vis. artist Kent (Ohio) State U., 1977-78. Editor: Jewelry Metalwork Survey 1991: Survey, Visions, Concepts, Communicating, 1991, Jewelry/Metal Work Survey #2: A Way of Communicating, 1992, Jewelry/Metalwork Survey #3: Ideas, Images, Image-makers, 1993; exhibited in group shows at Oliver Art Ctr., Calif. Coll. Arts and Crafts, Oakland, 1990, Connel Gallery, Atlanta, 1990, Great Am. Gallery, Atlanta, 1990, Ont. (Can.) Crafts Coun.'s Craft Gallery, 1993, Nat. Libr., Ottawa, Can., 1993, Gallery Craft Alliance, St. Louis, 1994, Oakland Mus. Art, 1994, Montgomery Coll. Art Gallery, Rockville, Md., 1996, John Waldron Arts Ctr., Bloomington, Ind., 1998, Eloise Pickard Smith Gallery, U. Calif., Santa Cruz, Calif., 1999; represented in permanent collections Am. Craft Mus., N.Y.C., Calif. Crafts Mus., San Francisco, Nat. Mus. Am. Art, Smithsonian Instn., Washington, Nat. Mus. Modern Art, Kyoto, Japan, Oakland Mus. Art, Ont. Crafts Coun., Toronto, Can., Schmuckmuseum, Pforzheim, Germany. Chairperson, mem. adv. com. Sta. KHSU-FM, Humboldt State U., Arcata, 1992-94. Fulbright scholar 1985. Avocations: motorcycles, custom cars, landscaping. Home: 1957 Bartow Rd Mckinleyville CA 95519-4313

LAPOE, WAYNE GILPIN, retired business executive; b. Waynesburg, Pa., July 13, 1924; s. James Lindsay and Mary (Gilpin) LaP.; m. Margaret Louise Clark, Feb. 21, 1953; children: Deborah Jean, Marqui Lynne. BA, Pa. State U., 1947. With personnel and sales depts. Armstrong Cork Co., Lancaster, Pa., 1947-53, Chgo., 1947-53, San Francisco, 1947-53; personnel dir. Safeco Ins. Group., 1953-63, v.p., 1963-86, Safeco Corp., Seattle, 1976-80, sr. v.p., 1980-86; v.p. Gen. Ins. Co. Am., 1963-86, Safeco Ins. Co. Am., 1963-86, Safeco Life Ins. Co., 1963-86, First Nat. Ins. Co. Am., Seattle, 1963-86, Safeco Nat. Ins. Co., St. Louis, 1972-86. Mem. White House Conf. Children and Youth, 1960; bd. dirs. Ind. Colls. Washington. Capt. USAAF, 1943-46, USAF, 1951-52. Decorated D.F.C.; decorated Air medal with three oak leaf clusters Mem. Mus. Flight Seattle, Ocean Liner Mus. N.Y., Am. Polit. Items Collectors (past pres.), Am. Aviation Hist. Soc., SS Hist. Soc. Am., Assn. Des Amis Des Paquebots, Nat. Trust Hist. Preservation, Phi Kappa Tau. Republican. Home: 11986 Lakeside Pl NE Seattle WA 98125-5955

LAPOINTE, LUCIE, Canadian government official; b. Valleyfield, Que., Can., Dec. 23, 1954; d. Paul and Jeannette (Gagné) L.; m. Clive Willis, Apr. 13, 1996; 1 child, Lauren Lapointe-Shaw. BSc in Biol. Scis., McGill U., 1977; MBA, U. Ottawa, Ont., Can., 1982. Tech. officer divsn. biol. scis. NRC, Ottawa, 1977-80, program officer program svcs. secretariat, 1982-84, exec. mgr. pub. rels. and info. svcs., 1984-87, dir. mgmt. svcs. br., 1987-89, sec. gen. exec. offices, 1989—2001; v.p. adminstrn., sec.-treas. Pulp and Paper Rsch. Inst. Can., Poiinte-Claire, 2001—. Office: PAPRICAN 570 boul St-Jean Pointe-Claire QC Canada H9R 3J9

LAPOLT, MARGARET, librarian; b. Austin, Pa., June 9, 1931; d. Thomas Wilbur and Frances Leona (Smith) Bennett; m. Sanford Howard LaPolt, Apr. 14, 1957 (dec. Nov. 1996); children: Cheryl Lynn LaPolt Remson, Mark Alan LaPolt. BSEd, Mansfield (Pa.) U., 1953; MSEd, Western Conn. State U., Danbury, 1963; MSLS, So. Conn. State U., New Haven, 1973. Tchr. 5th grade Bd. Edn., Clearfield, Pa., 1953-54; tchr. 6th grade Emporium (Pa.) Bd. Edn., 1954-58; tchr. 5th grade Darien (Conn.) Bd. Edn., 1958-64; tchr. 3d grade Stratford (Conn.) Bd. Edn., 1965-69, libr., 1969-70, Norwalk (Conn.) Bd. Edn., 1973-92, part-time libr., 1993—2002, ret., 2002. Singer, Norwalk Cmty. Chorus, 1961-73; singer Cmty. Bapt. Ch., Norwalk, 1958—, bd. deacons, 1993-99, trustee, 1981-87. Computer grantee, Norwalk Bd. Edn., 1985. Mem. ALA, Kappa Delta Phi, Kappa Pi. Avocations: knitting, embroidery, travel.

LAPOMARDA, VINCENT A. history educator; b. Portland, Maine, Feb. 28, 1934; s. Pasquale and Mary N. (Bartholomew) L. BA, Boston Coll., Chestnut Hill, Mass., 1957, MA, 1958; Sacred Theology Licentiate, Boston Coll., 1965; PhD in History, Boston U., 1968. Joined S.J. 1951, ordained priest Roman Cath. Ch., 1964. Tchr. Boston Coll. H.S., Dorchester, Mass., 1958-61; asst. prof. history Coll. of Holy Cross, Worcester, 1969-74, assoc. prof., 1974—, coord. Holocaust Collection, 1979—, coord. Italian Am. Collection, 1995—. Author: The Jesuit Heritage in New England, 1977, The Knights of Columbus in Massachusetts, 1982, 2d edit., 1992, The Jesuits and the Third Reich, 1989, The Order of Alhambra, 1994, The Boston Mayor Who Became Truman's Secretary of Labor: Maurice J. Tobin and the Democratic Party, 1995, Charles Nolcini, 1997. Decorated knight Order of Holy Sepulchre, Pilgrim Shell, 1987; Coe fellow Boston Coll., summer 1959, Batchelor faculty fellow Coll. of Holy Cross, 1969, 70; awarded Key to the City of Worcester, Mass., by Mayor, 2001. Mem. Internat. Order Alhambra (historian, chmn. com. on hist. memls. 1981—, Supreme Comdr.'s award 1995, Appreciation award 1999), KC (chaplain Crusader coun. 1980—, fin. sec. 1986—, state historian Mass. 1981—, John J. Spillane award 1989, KC Mass. Coun. award 1996). Avocation: golf. Home: 1 College St Worcester MA 01610-2322 Office: Coll of Holy Cross 1 College St Worcester MA 01610-2395 Fax: 508-793-2624. E-mail: vlapomar@holycross.edu.

LAPONCE, JEAN ANTOINE, political scientist, educator; b. Decize, France, Nov. 1925; s. Fernand and Fernande (Ramond) L.; m. Joyce Price, July, 1950; children: Jean-Antoine, Marc, Patrice; m. Iza Fiszhaut, Apr. 10, 1972; 1 child, Danielle. Diploma, Inst. d'études politiques, Paris, 1947; PhD, UCLA, 1955. Instr. U. Santa Clara, 1956; asst. prof. polit. sci. U. B.C., Can., Vancouver, 1956-61, assoc. prof., 1961-66, prof., 1966—; dir. Inst. Interethnic Rels. U. Ottawa, 1993-2001. Mem. grad. faculty Aichi Shukutoku U., 1994-97. Author: The Protection of Minorities, 1961, The government of France under the Fifth Republic, 1962, People vs Politics, 1970, Left and Right, 1981, Langue et territoire, 1984, Languages and Their Territories, 1987. Fellow Royal Soc. Can. (pres. Acad. Humanities and Social Scis. 1988-91); mem. Can. Polit. Sci. Assn. (pres. 1972-73), Am. Polit. Sci. Assn., French Polit. Sci. Assn., Internat. Polit. Sci. Assn. (pres. 1973-76) Office: U BC Dept Polit Sci Vancouver BC Canada V6T 1Z1

LAPORTE, ADRIENNE AROXIE, nursing administrator; b. Oceanside, N.Y., Sept. 29, 1938; d. Leonide and Grace (Ajamian) LaP. Diploma in nursing, St. John's Episc. Hosp., 1960; BA in Behavioral Scis., Lesley Coll., 1986; MA in Counseling, Liberty U., 1994. RN, N.Y., Fla., Mass., La., Ala.; cert. psychiat./mental health nurse Am. Nurses Credentialing Bd. Supr. Creedmoor State Hosp., Queens Village, N.Y., 1960-66, Taunton (Mass.) State Hosp., 1985-87, Mental Health Resources, Jacksonville, Fla., 1990-92, Staff Builders Home Health Agy., New Bedford, Mass., 1996-99; supr. psychiat. unit Univ. Hosp. of Jacksonville, 1977-79, Parkwood Hosp., New Bedford, 1980-84; dir. nursing Care Unit of Jacksonville Beach, Fla., 1987-90, Bradford Adult & Adolescent, Pelham, Ala., 1992-93, 94-95; program dir. Bowling Green Hosp., Mandeville, La., 1993; nurse mgr./therapist Ctr. for Health and Human Svcs., Inc., New Bedford, Mass., 1999—. Lt. col. Nurse Corps U.S. Army, 1966-87, Vietnam. Decorated Bronze Star, Legion of Merit, Armed Forces Res. medal, Army Commendation medal, Combat Readiness medal, Meritorious Svc. medal, Presdl. and Unit citation, Republic of Vietnam Campaign medal, Vietnam Svc. medal. Mem. ACA, VFW, Nurses Soc. on Addictions, Fla. Nurses Assn., Am. Legion, Vietnam Vets. Am., Internat. Soc. Psychiat.-Mental Health Nurses. Home: 201 McCabe St South Dartmouth MA 02748

LAPORTE, CLOYD, JR. lawyer, retired manufacturing executive; b. N.Y.C., June 8, 1925; s. Cloyd and Marguerite (Raeder) L.; m. Caroline E. Berry, Jan. 22, 1949; children— Elizabeth, Marguerite, Cloyd III. AB, Harvard U., 1946, JD, 1949. Bar: N.Y. 1949. Assoc. mem. firm Cravath, Swaine & Moore, N.Y.C., 1949-56; dir. adminstrn. Metals div. Olin Corp., 1957-66; legal counsel Dover Corp., 1966-93, sec., 1971-93. Dir. Putnam Hosp. Ctr., 2000—. 2d lt. A.C. AUS, WWII. Mem. Harvard Club (N.Y.C.). Home: Gipsy Trail Club Carmel NY 10512

LAPORTE, GERALD JOSEPH SYLVESTRE, lawyer; b. Windsor, Ont., Can., Oct. 16, 1946; came to U.S., 1948, naturalized, 1954; s. Rosaire Joseph and Catherine Rose (Sylvestre) L. BA, Sacred Heart Sem. Coll., 1968; STB, St. Paul U., Ottawa, Ont., 1971; BTh, U. Ottawa, 1971; MA, Georgetown U., 1974; JD, George Washington U., 1976. Bar: Mich. 1976, D.C. 1977. Legis. asst. to U.S. Congressman William J. Randall, Washington, 1971-75; law clk. to U.S. Dist. Judge, 1976-77; assoc. Wilmer, Cutler & Pickering, 1977-82; sr. spl. counsel Office Gen. Counsel, SEC, 1982-85, counsel to commr., 1985-87; assoc. Nutter, McClennen & Fish, 1987; ptnr. Patton Boggs, LLP, 1988-96; counsel Hogan & Hartson LLP, 1996—. Chmn. steering com. sect. corp., fin. and securities law D.C. Bar, 1997-98. Mng. editor George Washington Law Rev., 1975-76. Mem. ABA (sect. on bus. law, fed. regulation of securities com., subcom. SEC adminstrn., budget and legis.), Nat. Assn. Bond Lawyers (vice chmn. securities law and disclosure com. 1994-96), Arlington Hist. Soc. Inc. (pres. 2001—). Democrat. Roman Catholic. Home: 3154 Key Blvd Arlington VA 22201-5037 Office: Hogan & Hartson LLP 555 13th St NW Ste 800E Washington DC 20004-1161 E-mail: GJLaporte@email.com., GJLaporte@hhlaw.com.

LAPORTE, LEO FREDERIC, earth sciences educator, environmental scientist, geophysicist, educator, paleontologist; b. Englewood, N.J., July 30, 1933; s. Leo Frederic and Edea (Giacobbe) L.; married, 1956 (div. 1983); children: Leo G., Eva R.; m. Margaret Liniecki, 1985; 1 child, Noel A. Student, Fordham Coll., 1951-53; AB, Columbia U., 1956, PhD, 1960. From instr. to prof. dept. geol. scis. Brown U., Providence, 1959-71; prof. dept. earth scis. U. Calif.-Santa Cruz, 1971-94, prof. emeritus, 1994, chmn., 1972-75, dean div. natural scis., 1975-76, provost Crown Coll., 1993-98, assoc. vice chancellor for undergrad. edn., 1994-98. Vis. prof., Yale U., 1964; geologist N.Y. State Geol. Survey, 1962-64; petroleum research cons.; mem. com. geol. scis. Nat. Acad. Sci.-NRC, 1970-72; sec. U.S. Nat. Com. Hist. Geology, 1991-93, chair, 1994-96. Author: Ancient Environments, 1968, 79, 89, Encounter with the Earth, 1975, George Gaylord Simpson-Paleontologist and Evolutionist, 2000; prin. author: The Earth and Human Affairs, 1972; editor: Reefs in Time and Space, 1974, Evolution and the Fossil Record, 1978, Simple Curiosity: Family Letters of George G. Simpson, 1987, Establishment of a Geologic Framework for Paleoanthropology, 1990; contbr. articles to profl. jours. Recipient President's award Am. Assn. Petroleum Geologists, 1969; U. Calif. Santa Cruz Alumni Disting. Teaching award, 1980 Fellow AAAS, Geol. Soc. Am., Calif. Acad. Sci.; mem. History of Earth Scis. Soc. (pres. 1994), Soc. Econ. Mineralogists and Paleontologists (chmn. rsch. com., paleontology councilor, editor PALAIOS 1984-89, pres. 1995-96, Hon. Mem. award 1999). E-mail: laporte@cats.ucsc.edu.

LAPORTE, STEPHEN WALTER, police officer; b. Bryn Mawr, Pa., Mar. 30, 1950; s. Walter N. and Margery (Coleman) LaP.; m. Inge L. Loritz, Sept. 8, 1979 (div. Jan. 1990); children: Joseph, Matthew, Sarah. Student, Ripon Coll., 1968-71. Police officer Carol Stream (Ill.) Police Dept., 1973—. Author: Guide to Search and Seizure for Illinois Police, 1994. Vol. Head Start, Carol Stream, 1992—, PTA, Carol Stream, 1988-95; asst. leader Boy Scouts Am., Carol Stream, 1987-95. Recipient Meritorious Svc. award Carol Streams Police Dept., 1977; Valor award DuPage Police Assn., 1990; Valor award Carol Stream Police Dept., 1990. Mem. Fraternal Order of Police. Roman Catholic. Avocations: running, camping, classical music, woodworking, reading. Home: 140 Arrowhead Trl Carol Stream IL 60188-1502 Office: Carol Stream Police Dept 500 N Gary Ave Carol Stream IL 60188-1882

LAPOSATA, JOSEPH SAMUEL, army officer; b. Johnstown, Pa., Oct. 3, 1938; s. Joseph Thomas and Mary Marie (Coco) L.; m. Anita Louise Sabo, Aug. 12, 1961; children: Joseph S. Jr., David G., Matthew M. BS, Indiana U. Pa., 1960; MS, Cornell U., 1968; grad., Command and Gen. Staff Coll., Leavenworth, Kans., 1971, Indsl. Coll. Armed Forces, Washington, 1980. Commd. 2d lt. U.S. Army, 1960, advanced through grades to lt. gen., 1991; asst. chief of staff for logistics 5th Inf. Div., Ft. Polk, La., 1978-79; chief war res. div. Office Dep. Chief of Staff for Logistics, Hdqrs. Dept. Army, Washington, 1980-81; comdr. 8th Support Group, U.S. Army So. European Task Force, Livorno, Italy, 1981-84, dep. comdr., chief of staff Vicenza, Italy, 1984; exec. to dep. chief of staff for logistics Hdqrs. Dept. Army, Washington, 1984-86, dir. plans and ops., dep. chief of staff for logistics, 1986-88; comdg. gen. U.S. Army Material Command-Europe, Heidelberg, Fed. Republic Germany, 1988-89; dep. chief of staff for logistics U.S. Army Europe and 7th Army, 1989-91; chief of staff Allied Forces So. Europe, Naples, Italy, 1991-93; Presdl. appointee as sec. Am. Battle Monuments Commn., Washington, 1994-95; ret. Apptd. diplomatic post as dep. gen. mgr. and dir. logistics ops. and programs NATO Maintenance and Supply Agy., Luxembourg; now ret. Decorated Def. DDSM, DSM (1), Legion of Merit (3), Bronze Star (2); knight comdr. Republic of Italy; recipient Man of Yr. award Interclub Coun., Johnstown, Pa., 1990, Disting. Alumnus award Ind. U. of Pa., 1992, medal for meritorious svc. Am. Battle Monuments Commn., medal for disting. svc., NATO Maint. and Supply Agy., 1999; inducted into Quartermaster Hall of Fame, 1994; named Coll. Emeritus, U.S. Army Q.M. Rgt. Mem. Assn. U.S. Army (pres. European dept. 1989-91), Quartermaster Found. (bd. dirs.), Rotary, Phi Kappa Phi. Roman Catholic. Avocation: golf. Address: 1823 Freedom Dr Melbourne FL 32940-6875 E-mail: jlaposata@cs.com.

LAPOTA, DAVID, oceanographer, marine biologist; b. L.A., June 1, 1949; s. Mathew H. and Jane E. (Cassell) L.; m. Jeannette Harward, June 28, 1975. BS in Zoology, San Diego State U., 1973, MA in Geography, 1982; PhD in Biology, U. Calif., Santa Barbara, 1998. Data analyst San Diego State Found., 1974-79; biologist Naval Ocean Systems Ctr., San Diego, 1979-82, scientist, 1982—. Patentee in field; contbr. articles and abstracts to profl. jours. and chpts. to books. With USAR, 1969-75. Fellow Explorers Club; mem. Am. Geophys. Union, Soc. Environ. Toxicology and Chemistry, European Soc. Environ. Toxicology and Chemistry, Oceanography Soc. Home: 6678 Hemingway Dr San Diego CA 92120-1616 Office: Space Naval Warfare Sys Ctr Marine Environ Br Code D362 San Diego CA 92152-5000 E-mail: lapota@spawar.navy.ml.

LAPP, CHARLES WARREN, internal medicine physician, pediatrician; b. Bklyn., June 10, 1947; s. Warren Anthony and Katherine Emma (Beard) L.; m. Darie Eleanor Conners, Aug. 28, 1971; children: Lauren Michelle, Warren Rutherford. BS, Rensselaer Poly. Inst., 1969, MBME, 1970; MD, Albany Coll. Medicine, 1974. Diplomate Am. Bd. Internal Medicine, Am. Bd. Pediats., Am. Bd. Ind. Med. Examiners. Intern U. N.C., Chapel Hill, 1974-75, resident, 1975-78; med. dir. Hill Haven and Blue Ridge Nursing, Raleigh, N.C., 1978-91; assoc. clin. prof. U. N.C., Chapel Hill, 1978-91, Duke. U. Med. Ctr., 1982—; founder and pres. Piedmont Med. Assn., Raleigh, N.C., 1978-95; med. dir. Cheney Clinic, Charlotte, 1991-95; pres. Hunter-Hopkins Ctr., P.A., 1995—. Cons. TASA Tech. Adviser, Phoenix, 1979—2001; adv. bd. Raleigh Employee Assistance Plan, 1987—89, Health Plus, 1987—89; med. cons. CFIDS Assn. of Am., Charlotte, 1991—. Contbr. articles to profl. jours. including Jour. AMA and Lancet; presenter exhibits to sci. assemblies Pres. Muscular Dystrophy Assn., 1982-84. Named Richard T. Beebe Scholar in Medicine, Albany (N.Y.) Med. Coll.) 1974; Man of the Yr., Jaycees, Raleigh, N.C., 1983. Fellow Am. Acad. Family Physicians, Am. Acad. Pediatrics, Am. Assn. Disability Evaluating Physicians; mem. AMA, N.C. Med. Soc., Am. Assn. for Chronic Fatigue Syndrome (bd. dirs.), Am. Pain Soc. Presbyterian. Avocations: boating, hiking, travel. Office: 10344 Park Rd Ste 300 Charlotte NC 28210-8401 E-mail: drlapp@drlapp.net.

LAPP, JAMES MERRILL, clergyman, marriage and family therapist; b. Lansdale, Pa., July 20, 1937; s. John E. and Edith (Nice) L.; m. Nancy Swartzentruber, Mar. 1, 1936 (dec. Dec. 1998); children: Cynthia Ann, J. Michael; m. Miriam F. Book, Dec. 23, 2000; 1 child, Philip A. BA, Eastern Mennonite Coll., 1960; B.D., Goshen Bibl. Sem., 1963; D.Min., Drew U., 1981. Ordained to ministry Mennonite Ch., 1963. Pastor Belmont Mennonite Ch., Elkhart, Ind., 1961-63; tchr. Christopher Dock Mennonite High Sch., Lansdale, Pa., 1963-70; paster Perkasie Mennonite Ch., 1963-72, Albany Mennonite Ch., Oreg., 1972-81; dir. campus ministries Goshen Coll., Ind., 1981-87; gen. sec., gen. bd. Mennonite Ch., Elkhart, 1987-95; conf. pastor Fraconia Mennonite Conf., Souderton, Pa., 1996—. Moderator Pacific Coast Conf. on Mennonite Ch., Oreg., 1977-79, Mennonite Gen. Assembly, Lombard, Ill., 1985-87. Contbr. articles to Mennonite Ch. publs. Democrat. Avocations: gardening, baking, walking. Home: 443 Penn Oak Ct Harleysville PA 19438 Office: Franconia Mennonite Conf 771 Route 113 Souderton PA 18964-1000

LAPPEN, CHESTER I. lawyer; b. Des Moines, May 4, 1919; s. Robert C. and Anna (Sideman) L.; m. Jon Tyroler Irmas, June 29, 1941; children—Jonathan Bailey, Timothy, Andrea L., Sally Morris. AB with highest honors in Econs, U. Calif., 1940; LL.B. magna cum laude (Faye diploma), Harvard, 1943. Bar: Calif. bar 1943. Practice in, Los Angeles, 1946—; sr. partner firm Mitchell, Silberberg & Knupp, 1949—; advisory bd. Bank Am., 1962-65; chmn. bd., dir. Zenith Nat. Ins. Corp., 1975-77. Bd. dirs. Arden Group, Inc. (chmn. exec. com. 1978), 1963-91, Data Products Corp. (chmn. fin. com.), 1965-93, City Nat. Bank Corp., 1967-92; trustee, pres. Citinat, Devel. Trust; bd. dirs., chmn. bd. Pacific Rim Holding Corp., 1987-94. Editor-in-chief: Harvard Law Rev., 1942-43. Chmn. bd. trustees Immaculate Heart Coll., 1981-88; trustee UCLA Found.; v.p., dir. Ctr. for Childhood. Served as spl. agt. CIA ,U.S. Army, 1943-46. Mem. ABA, Los Angeles Bar Assn. (dir. 1953), Los Angeles Jr. Bar Assn. (pres. 1953), Beverly Hills (Calif.) Bar Assn., Harvard Law Sch. Alumni Assn. So. Calif. (pres. 1973-82), Artus. Republican. Office: Mitchell Silberberg & Knupp 11377 W Olympic Blvd Los Angeles CA 90064-1625

LAPPEN, TIMOTHY, lawyer, investor; b. L.A., Dec. 26, 1947; s. Chester Irwin and Jon Tyroler (Irmas) L.; children: Amy Elizabeth, Jay Robert, Tyler Lewis. AB, U. Calif., Berkeley, 1972; JD, UCLA, 1975. Bar: Calif. 1975, U.S. Dist. Ct. (no. dist.) Calif. 1975, U.S. Ct. Appeals (9th cir.) 1975. Assoc. Lillick, McHose & Charles, San Francisco, 1975-77; ptnr. Lappen & Lappen, L.A., 1977-84; of counsel Jeffer, Mangels, Butler & Marmaro, L.A., San Francisco, 1984—; pres. Lappen Realty and Investment Corp., Santa Monica, Calif., 1987—. Bd. dirs., sec. Dee Constrn. Co., L.A., 1968—. Exec. coms. D.A.R.E., 1992—95; founder, bd. dirs. chmn. Lawyers Against Hunger, 1994—; mem. bd. advisors Am. Acad. for Dance and Kindred Arts, 1995—99; bd. dirs., pres. Santa Monica Protective Assn., Calif., 1981—90, pres., 1991—93; bd. dirs. L.A. Regional Food Bank, 1988—95, pres., 1992—93; trustee Sch. Law UCLA, 1990—94, pres., 1992; mem. bd. dirs. Ctr. for Childhood, 1995—; mem. Chancellor's Assocs. UCLA, 1980—90; exec. coms. L.A. County D.A.'s Office, 1993—2001; former mem. Calif. Lexington Group, L.A. World Affairs Coun. Mem. ABA, Calif. Bar Assn., L.A. County Bar Assn., Century City Bar Assn. Office: Jeffer Mangels Butler & Marmaro # 1000 2121 Avenue of the Stars Los Angeles CA 90067

LAPPENBUSCH, RICHARD W. software company official; b. Bellingham, Wash., Apr. 4, 1968; s. Charles F. and Sylvia (Sullivan) L.; m. Brittany Abbott; children: Vivian Mary, Amelia Jayne. BSBA, U. Redlands, 1990; MPS in Interactive Telecom., NYU, 1993. Program mgr. Continuum Prodns., Bellevue, Wash., 1993; dir. strategic planning Microsaft, Redmond, 1993—. Office: Microsoft One Microsoft Way Redmond WA 98052 Fax: 425-936-7329. E-mail: richlap@microsoft.com., richlap@hotmail.com.

LAPSLEY, JAMES NORVELL, JR. minister, pastoral theology educator; b. Clarksville, Tenn., Mar. 16, 1930; s. James Norvell and Evangeline (Winn) L.; m. Brenda Ann Weakley, June 4, 1953 (dec. May 1989); children: Joseph William, Jacqueline Evangeline; m. Helen Joan Winter, Feb. 24, 1990. BA, Rhodes Coll., 1952; BD, Union Theol. Sem., 1955; PhD (Dv. Sch. fellow, Rockefeller fellow), U. Chgo., 1961. Ordained to ministry Presbyn. Ch., 1955; asst. min. Gentilly Presbyn. Ch., New Orleans, 1955-57; instr. Princeton (N.J.) Theol. Sem., 1961-63, asst. prof., 1963-67, assoc. prof., 1967-76, prof. pastoral theology, 1976-80, Carl and Helen Egner prof. pastoral theology, 1980-92, acad. dean, 1984-89, prof. emeritus, 1992—. Mem. editl. bd. Jour. Pastoral Care, 1966-69, 91—; bd. dirs. N.W. Maricopa UN Assn., 1994-2000, v.p., 1995-96, pres., 1997-98; pres. Critical Issues Coun. of Sun Cities, 1996-97; bd. dirs. Sun Cities Symphony Orch., 1997—, sec. 1999-2001, pres. 2001—. Editor: The Concept of Willing, 1967, Salvation and Health, 1972, Renewal in Late Life Through Pastoral Counseling, 1992; editor: (with B.H. Childs, D.W. Waanders), Festschrift: The Treasure of Earthen Vessels, 1994; chmn. editl. bd. Pastoral Psychology Jour., 1975-84. Bd. dirs. Westminster Found., Princeton U., 1970-76. Danforth fellow Menninger Found., 1960-61 Mem.: Phi Beta Kappa. Presbyterian. Home: 16610 N Meadow Park Dr Sun City AZ 85351-1758 E-mail: lapsley@interacs.com., jlapsley@infomagic.com.

LAPUZ-DE LA PENA, ERLINDA LARON, physician, pathologist, educator; b. Nov. 26, 1933; d. Eriberto Mallari and Teodora Quiero (Laron) Lapuz; m. Cordell De La Pena, Apr. 1, 1957; children: Leslie, Nina, Cordell. MD, U. Santo Tomas, 1957. Diplomate Am. Bd. Pathology. Intern St. John's Hosp., Lowell, Mass., 1959—60; attending physician Tewksbury (Mass.) Hosp., 1960—63; resident in pathology Mercy Hosp., Pitts., 1967—71; instr. pathology U. Pitts. Med. Sch., 1967—71; chief lab. svc. VA Hosp., Clarksburg, W.Va., 1971—, chief of staff, 1983—99; courtesy staff United Hosp. Ctr.; prof. pathology W.Va. U. Sch. Medicine, 1994—; asst. prof. Coll. Nursing Salem (W.Va.) Coll., 1978; asst. prof. Coll. Nursing and Physician Assts. Alderson Broadus Coll., Phillipi. Contbr. articles to med. jours. Fellow: Am. Soc. Clin. Pathology, Am. Coll. Pathologists; mem.: W.Va. Assn. Pathologists (bd. dirs. 1983—, pres. 1987—89, 1997—98), W.Va. Med. Assn., AMA, Clarksburg Country Club. Roman Catholic. Home: 209 Candlelight Dr Clarksburg WV 26301-9725

LAQUINTA, FRED JOHN, healthcare executive; b. Pitts., Nov. 30, 1949; s. John Anthony and Rose Marie (Marino) L.; m. Irene B. Jaszczun, Aug. 12, 1972; children: Diana Rose, Christa Maria. BA in Econs., U. Pitts., 1971, MBA, 1972; grad., U. Mich., 1991. Mgr. benefits adminstrn. Air Products and Chems., Allentown, Pa., 1972-80; benefits planner Exxon Co. U.S.A., Houston, 1980-82; dir. compensation and worldwide benefits Hercules, Inc., Wilmington, Del., 1982-91, dir. human resources planning and devel., 1991-95; v.p. human resources AtlantiCare Health Svs., Pleasantville, NJ, 1995. Cons. 5th grade Jr. Acheivement, Absecon, NJ; founder, past chmn. Del. Health Care Coalition, Wilmington, 1982—86; mem. Gov.'s Health Care Commn., Dover, 1986, 1999—2001, Urban League, Atlantic City; bd. dirs. Rockford Psychiat. Hosp., Wilmington, 1985—86; bd. dirs. Contact-Cape Atlantic (pers. com. ARC Atlantic County). Capt. USAR, 1972—76. Democrat. Roman Catholic. Avocations: family, racquetball. Home: 516 Pelham Dr Absecon NJ 08201

LARABEE, BRENDA J. secondary education educator; b. North Platte, Nebr., Mar. 21, 1966; d. Buster Joy and Patricia Jean (Hopkins) Fear; m. Keith Allen Larabee, July 15, 1989; children: Amanda Jean, Ryan Charles. BS in Edn., Chadron State Coll., 1988. Cert. tchr. Nebr. English/speech/drama 7-12 tchr. Campbell (Nebr.) Pub. Sch., 1988-89, Stuart (Nebr.) Pub. Sch., 1989—. Speech team coach Stuart Pub. Sch., 1989—; dir. plays at dinner theater, 1993-95; one act play coach, 1988—; adj. faculty N.E. Cmty. Coll., Norfolk, Nebr., 1999—. V.p. Town & Country Ext. Club, Stuart, 1995, pres., 1996-97; ch. sch. supt. Stuart Cmty. Ch., 1994-2000; mem. Stuart Cmty. Action Team; sec. Stuart Stock Car Assn., Inc., 2000—. Mem. Nat. Coun. Tchrs. English, Stuart Edn. Assn. (sec./treas.), Atkinson-Stuart Arts Coun. (programming dir.), Nebr. State Edn. Assn., Nebr. Speech Comm. Theater Assn. Republican.

Methodist. Avocations: gardening, parenting, computers, bicycling, reading, cooking. Home: PO Box 155 Stuart NE 68780-0155 Office: Stuart Pub Sch PO Box 99 Stuart NE 68780-0099 E-mail: blarabee@esu8.org.

LARAGH, JOHN HENRY, physician, scientist, educator; b. Yonkers, N.Y., Nov. 18, 1924; s. Harry Joseph and Grace Catherine (Coyne) L.; m. Adonia Kennedy, Apr. 28, 1949; children: John Henry, Peter Christian, Robert Sealey; m. Jean E. Sealey, Sept. 22, 1974. MD, Cornell U., 1948. Diplomate Am. Bd. Internal Medicine. Intern Presbyn. Hosp., N.Y.C., 1948-49, asst. resident, 1949-50; cardiology trainee Nat. Heart Inst., 1950-51; rsch. fellow N.Y. Heart Assn., 1951-52; asst. physician Presbyn. Hosp., 1950-55, asst. attending, 1954-61, assoc. attending, 1961-69, attending physician, 1969-75, pres. elect med. bd., 1972-74; faculty Coll. Physicians and Surgeons Columbia U., 1950-75, prof. clin. medicine, 1967-75, spokesman exec. com. faculty coun., 1971-73; vice-chmn. bd. trustees for profl. and sci. affairs Presbyn. Hosp., 1974-75; dir. Hypertension Ctr., chief nephrology divsn. Columbia-Presbyn. Med. Ctr., 1971-75; Master prof. medicine, dir. Hypertension and Cardiovascular Ctr., N.Y. Hosp.-Cornell Med. Ctr., 1975—, chief cardiology div., 1975-95. Cons. USPHS, 1964—. Editor-in-chief Am. Jour. Hypertension, Cardiovascular Reviews and Reports; Editor: Hypertension Manual, 1974, Topics in Hypertension, 1980, Frontiers in Hypertension Rsch., 1981; editor Hypertension: Pathophysiology, Diagnosis, and Management, 1990, 1995; editorial bd.: Am. Jour. Medicine, Am. Jour. Cardiology, Kidney Internat., Jour. Clin. Endocrinology and Metabolism, Hypertension, Jour. Hypertension, Circulation, Am. Heart Jour., Procs. of Soc. Exptl. Biology and Medicine, Heart and Vessels. Mem. policy adv. bd. hypertension detection and follow-up program Nat. Heart and Lung Inst., 1971, bd. sci. counselor, 1974-79; chmn. U.S.A.-USSR Joint Program in Hypertension, 1977-93. With U.S. Army, 1943-46. Recipient Stouffer prize Med. Rsch., 1969, J.K. Lattimer award Am. Urol. Assn., 1989, Robert Tigerstedt award Am. Soc. Hypertension, 1990, John P. Peters award Am. Soc. Nephrology, 1990, Lifetime Achievement in Medicine award N.Y. Acad. Medicine, 1993, Disting. Alumnus award Cornell U. Med. Coll., 1993, Bristol Myers Squibb award for disting. achievement cardiovalcular rsch., 1996, Disting. Achievement award Coun. for High Blood Pressure Rsch., Am. Heart Assn., 1999; subject of Time Mag. cover story, 1975; Most Frequently Cited Scientist: Top Ten Advances in Cardiopulmonary Medicine, 1946-75. Fellow Am. Coll. Cardiology; mem. ACP (Master), Am. Heart Assn. (chmn. med. adv. bd. coun. high blood pressure rsch. 1968-72), Am. Soc. Clin. Investigation, Assn. Am. Physicians, Assn. Univ. Cardiologists, Endocrine Soc., Am. Soc. Nephrology, Am. Soc. Hypertension (founder, 1st pres. 1986-88), Internat. Soc. Hypertension (pres. 1986-88), Harvey Soc., Kappa Sigma, Nu Sigma Nu, Alpha Omega Alpha, Country Club of Fla., Shinnecock Hills Golf Club (Southampton, N.Y.). Achievements include research on hormones, renin, aldosterone and electrolyte metabolism and renal physiology, mechanisms of edema formation and on causes and treatments of high blood pressure. Home: 5 Sandpiper Dr Village Of Golf FL 33436-5621 Office: NY Hosp-Cornell Med Ctr 525 E 68th St New York NY 10021-4885 E-mail: dczhang@suda.edu.com. *In my research, a key resource has been the ability to perceive everyday clinical phenomena differently, to recognize and develop new ideas and experiments about human physiology and the causes of hypertension and major cardiovascular diseases. These perceptions enable hypotheses and experiments for creation and synthesis of new knowledge that redirects medical thinking.*

LARAMEE, ELAINE R. magazine editor; b. Ogden, Utah, Dec. 8, 1961; d. Richard C. and Valice M. Laramee; m. Rob E. Harrigan, June 29, 1993; 1 child, Jack Laramee Harrigan. BA, Whitman Coll., 1984; postgrad., Harvard U., summer 1984. Editor Savvy Mag., N.Y.C., 1984-86; rsch. editor Sylvia Porter's Personal Fin. Mag., 1986-89; mng. editor Hearst Bus. Books, 1989-94; editor-in-chief N.Y. Life Ins. Co., 1994—. Mem. adv. bd. mil. newspaper, 1999—. Author: Best Mutual Fund Managers, 1994; writer, editor, photo editor: Philip Reisman-The Artist, 1996. Dir., chmn., dist. chmn. Hugh O'Brian Youth Found., N.Y.C., 1987—. Mem. Internat. Assn. Bus. Communicators (writing awards 1994-2000), Life Communicator Assn. Avocations: publishing, theater, arts, golf, writing. Home: 147 Lenox Terrace Maplewood NJ 07040

LARAQUI, SAAD, finance educator; b. Rabat, Morocco, May 14, 1958; arrived in U.S., 1984; s. Abdelkader and Zineb Laraqui; m. Nezha El Fihri, July 31, 1999. Diploma, Inst. Supr. Gestion, Paris, 1982; MBA, U. Tampa, 1985; PhD Mgmt., Rutgers U., 1998; diploma airline acctg. and fin., IATA, Montreal, Canada, 2000. Adj. faculty Rutgers U., Newark, 1987—96; asst. prof. Tel Aviv Internat. Sch. Mgmt., Tel Aviv, 1996—97, Embry Riddle Aero. U., Daytona Beach, Fla., 1998—. Mng. dir. Aviation Cons. Group, Daytona Beach, Fla., 2001—. Contbr. articles to profl. jours., chapters to books. Mem.: Internat. Trade and Fin. Assn., Acad. Mgmt., Acad. Internat. Bus. Avocations: horseback riding, swimming, flying, jogging, biking. Office: Embry Riddle Aeronaut U 600 S Clyde Morris Blvd Daytona Beach FL 32114-3900 Fax: 386-226-6696. Business E-Mail: laraquis@db.erau.edu.

LARAR, GERALD N. physician, research scientist; b. Washington, Feb. 3, 1960; s. Michel E. and Jeanette G. Larar; m. Susan Gamer, May 24, 1992; children: Brendan, Stephanie, Lauren, David. BSEE, Fla. Atlantic U., 1980; MEEE, U. Fla., 1981, PhD in Elec. Engring., 1985; MD, U. Miami, Fla., 1990. Rsch. asst. elec. engring. dept. Mind-Medicine Interaction Rsch. Ctr., U. Fla., 1980-85; tchg. asst. dept. elec. engring. U. Fla., 1981; mem. tech. staff acoustics rsch. dept. AT&T Bell Labs., Murray Hill, N.J., 1985-88; resident joint program in nuclear medicine Harvard Med. Sch., Boston, 1990-92, chief resident, 1991-92, clin. tchg. fellow, 1990-92; diagnostic radiology resident Nassau County Med. Ctr., EAst Meadow, N.Y., 1992-95; abdominal imaging fellow Cleve. Clinic, 1995-96; radiologist Sterling Radiology, 1996-98, Valley Med. Imaging Assocs., 1998-2000, PrimeMed, 2000—. Manuscript reveiwer for various profl. jours. Contbr. articles, abstracts, reports to profl. publs., chpt. to books. Vol. advisor AT&T/N.J. H.S. Sci. Lab. Devel. Program. Mem. AMA, IEEE, Radiol. Soc. N.Am., Soc. Nuclear Medicine, N.J. Assn. Realtors, Am. Coll. Radiology. E-mail: gnlarar@pol.net.

LARA-VALLE, JULIO, medical educator, physician; b. Aug. 13, 1939; MD, U. Peruana Cayetano Heredia, Lima, Peru, 1969. Resident in pediats. Cook County Children's Hosp., Chgo., 1969-72; fellow in asthma, allergy, immunology Coll. Medicine U. Ill., 1972-74, clin. asst. prof. Coll. Medicine, 1975—. Cons. St. Mary of Nazareth Hosp., Chgo., 1975—, Grant-Columbia Hosp., Chgo., 1975—; dir. Scientific Program Silver Anniversary PAMS Convention, Asthma Ctr. Children, 1974—. Mem. AMA, Am. Acad. Pediat., Peruvian Am. Med. Soc. (pres. 2000), Am. Acad. Asthma, Allergy and Immunology, Interasma. Office: 1859 W Chicago Ave Chicago IL 60622-5513 E-mail: jlaravalle@aol.com.

LARBERG, JOHN FREDERICK, wine consultant, educator; b. Kansas City, Mo., Jan. 21, 1930; s. Herman Alvin and Ann (Sabrowsky) L. AA, Kansas City Jr. Coll., 1948; AB cum laude, U. Mo., 1950, postgrad., 1955-56; MSW, Bryn Mawr Coll., 1961. Cert. social worker. With Westinghouse Electric Corp., 1953-56; dir. House of Industry Settlement House, Phila., 1957-61; asst. to exec. dir. Health and Welfare Coun., Inc., Phila., 1961-66; sr. staff cons., 1966-73, dir. Washington office, 1971-72, Nat. Assembly for Social Policy and Devel., Inc., N.Y.C.; nat. dir. community and patient services Nat. Multiple Sclerosis Soc., N.Y.C., 1974-81, nat. dir. spl. projects, 1981-82; adminstrv. v.p. Fedn. Protestant Welfare Agys. N.Y., 1982-86; sr. advisor, 1986-87; exec. dir. Am. Assn. State Social Work Bds., 1987-89; cons. The Wine Aficionado, N.Y., 1990—. Cons. exec. com. Commn. on Vol. Svc. and Action, 1967-76, cons. Met. N.Y. Project Equality, 1968-73, Encampment for Citizenship, 1973-74, Symphony for UN, 1974-77, Lower Eastside Fam. Union, 1984—, Wielenga Psych. Svc., 1993—, Malignant Hyperthermia Assn. U.S., 1994—, Internat. Fedn. Multiple Sclerosis Socs., 1995—, Nat. Multiple Sclerosis Soc., 1997—; bd. dirs. Health Systems Agy. of N.Y., 1984-86; trustee The Riverside Ch., N.Y.C., 1985-89, worship commn., 1992-94, ordination com., 1993—, chmn., 1996—; bd. dirs., mem. exec. com. Metro Assn. United Ch. of Christ, N.Y., 1993—, dir. N.Y. state coun., 1995—, nat. del. Gen. Synod, 1997; mem. Disciples of Christ/United Ch. of Christ N.Y. State Joint Task Force, 1996—; nat. dir. Coun. Soc. Wk. Edn., 1985-86. Served with AUS, 1951-53. Mem. Acad. Cert. Social Workers (charter), Nat. Assn. Social Workers (chpt. legis. com. 1968-70, nat. publs. com. 1968-71, nat. legal regulation com. 1987-89), Internat. Coun. Social Welfare (internat. com. of reps. 1980-84, U.S. com. for Internat. Coun. Social Welfare, bd. dirs. 1983-90, exec. com. 1983-90), Internat. Fedn. Multiple Sclerosis Socs. (vice chmn. patient services com. 1976-81, chmn. 1981-84, mem. individual and family services com. 1984-97, non-govtl. rep. to UN, 1990-96, rep. to Rehab. Internat. Med. Commn. 1976-81), Nat. Conf. Social Welfare (program com. 1966-73, chmn. combined assoc. groups 1969-70, nat. dir. 1971-73, 83-87), Fedn. of Assns. Regulatory Bds. (nat. dir. 1988-89), Malignant Hyperthermia Assn. U.S. (nat. dir. 1984-93, nat. pres. 1985-89, rep. 10th Quad. World Congr. Anesth. Hague 1992), Am. Acad. Polit. and Social Sci., Nat. Urban League (nat. trustee-at-large 1968), Hawk Mountain Sanctuary Assn., Bryn Mawr Social Work Alumni Assn. (pres. 1963-65), Am. Mus. Natural History, N.Y.C. Citizens Union, N.Y. Mcpl. Art Soc., Phi Beta Kappa Assn. N.Y. (pres. 1980-82), Omicron Delta Kappa, QEBH, Alpha Phi Omega, Alpha Pi Zeta, Pi Sigma Alpha, Alpha Kappa Psi. Home and Office: 400 E 58th St Apt 2F New York NY 10022-2333

LARCH, SARA MARGARET, chief operating officer; b. Des Moines, Feb. 14, 1956; d. William Arthur and Beverly Frances (Klanjac) L. BA in Pub. Adminstrn., Miami U., Oxford, Ohio, 1978; M in Health Scis. Adminstrn., Med. Coll. Va., 1992. Personnel clk. City Nat. Bank, Detroit, 1978-79; econ. anlyst asst. Cargill, Inc., Mpls., 1979-81; ob-gyn. adminstr. Ind. U. Med. Ctr., Indpls., 1981-88; adminstr. Georgetown U. Med. Ctr., Washington, 1988-94, dir. quality and capitation sys., 1995; COO Univ. Physicians, Inc. Univ. Md., Balt., 1995—. Mem. Assn. Mgrs. Gynecology and Obstetricians (pres. 1986-87), Med. Group Mgmt. Assn. (bd. dirs. 1995-96, 98—), Acad. Practice Assembly (pres. 1994-95), Am. Coll. Med. Prac. Exec. (fell., 1995). Avocations: piano, reading, traveling, skiing, public speaking. Office: Univ Physicians Inc 419 W Redwood St Ste 220 Baltimore MD 21201-7004

LARDNER, CYNTHIA MARIE-MARTINOVICH, lawyer; b. Detroit, Sept. 20, 1959; m. Michael Lardner, Nov. 5, 1994. BA in Journalism, Mich. State U., 1981; JD magna cum laude, U. Detroit, 1984; postgrad., Wayne State U. Bar: Mich. 1984, U.S. Dist. Ct. (ea. dist.) Mich. 1984. Assoc. Pepper Hamilton & Scheetz, Detroit, 1984-86; pvt. practice law St. Clair Shores, Mich., 1986-89; asst. v.p., atty. NBD Bank NA, Detroit, 1989-93; pvt. practice law, 1993—. Legal writing instr. U. Detroit, 1985—89; bus. law instr. Walsh Coll., Troy, Mich., 1986—87; bd. dirs. Mich. State Bar Jour., Lansing, 1992—; bus. law instr. Macomb C., Fraser, Mich., 1994—2000. Contbr. chpt. to book and articles to profl. jours. Budget adminstrn. and fiscal planning com. City of Ferndale, Mich., 1988-90; mem. fundraising com. Turning Point shelter. Mem. State Bar Mich., Macomb County Bar Assn. Office: 729 Meldrum St Detroit MI 48207-4323

LARDNER, GEORGE, JR. journalist, author; b. N.Y.C., Aug. 10, 1934; s. George Edmund and Rosetta (Russo) L.; m. Rosemary Schalk, July 6, 1957; children: Helen, Edmund, Richard, Charles, Kristin (dec.). AB in Journalism summa cum laude, Marquette U., 1956, MA, 1962. Reporter The Worcester (Mass.) Telegram, 1957-59, The Miami (Fla.) Herald, 1959-63, The Washington Post, 1963-64, 66—, columnist, 1964-65. Chmn. bd. Fund for Investigative Journalism, Washington, 1997—. Author: The Stalking of Kristin, 1995; contbg. author: Deadlock: The Inside Story of America's Closest Election, 2001. Recipient Byline award Marquette U., 1967, Front-page Nat. News award Washington-Balt. Newspaper Guild, 1984, 86, Pulitzer Prize for feature writing, 1993. Mem. Congl. Press Gallery. Roman Catholic. Home: 5604 32nd St NW Washington DC 20015-1623 Office: Washington Post 1150 15th St NW Washington DC 20071-0002

LARDNER, HENRY PETERSEN (PETER LARDNER), insurance company executive; b. Davenport, Iowa, Apr. 5, 1932; s. James Francis and Mary Catharine (Decker) L.; m. Marion Cleaveland White, Dec. 28, 1954; children: Elisabeth, Emily Decker, David, Peter, Sarah (dec.). BSE. (Indsl. Engring.), U. Mich., 1954; MA, Augustana Coll., 1982. C.P.C.U. Indsl. engr. Cutler-Hammer, Milw., 1954; Agt. H.H. Cleaveland Agy., Rock Island, Ill., 1956-60; with Bituminous Ins. Cos., 1960—, exec. v.p., 1968-72, pres., 1972-95, chmn. and CEO, 1984-2000, chmn., 2000—01; pres. Bitco Corp., Rock Island, 1973-95, chmn. bd. dirs., 1973—2001. Bd. dirs. Old Republic Internat.; trustee Underwriters Lab., Inc., 1997—. Bd. govs. State Colls. and Univs., 1971-80; trustee Black Hawk Coll., 1964-72; mem. Ill. Bd. Higher Edn., 1976-77; chmn. Ill. State Scholarship, 1982-85. Served with AUS, 1954-56. Home: 3227 29th Ave Rock Island IL 61201-5568 E-mail: peter.lardner@verizon.net.

LARDY, HENRY A(RNOLD), biochemistry educator; b. Roslyn, S.D., Aug. 19, 1917; s. Nicholas and Elizabeth (Gebetsreiter) L.; m. Annrita Dresselhuys, Jan. 21, 1943; children: Nicholas, Diana, Jeffrey, Michael. BS, S.D. State U., 1939, DSc (hon.), 1979; MS, U. Wis., 1941, PhD, 1943. Asst. prof. U. Wis., Madison, 1945-47, assoc. prof., 1947-50, prof., 1950-88, Vilas prof. biol. sci., 1966-88, prof. emeritus, 1988—. Henry Lardy annual lectr. S.D. State U., Brookings, 1985. Edtl. bd. Archives Biochemistry and Biophysics, 1957-60, Jour. Biol. Chemistry, 1958-64, 80-85, Biochem. Preparations, Methods of Biochem. Analysis, Biochemistry, 1962-73, 75-81; contbr. over 450 articles to profl. jours. Pres. Citizens vs McCarthy, Wis., 1950. Recipient Neuberg medal Am. Soc. European Chemists, 1956, Wolf Found. award in Agr., 1981, Nat. award Agrl. Excellence, 1982. Fellow Wis. Acad. Arts and Scis.; mem. Am. Chem. Soc. (chmn. biol. divsn. 1958, Paul-Lewis Labs. award 1949), Am. Soc. Biol. Chemists (pres. 1964, William Rose award 1988), Am. Acad. Arts and Scis. (Amory prize 1984), Am. Philos. Soc., Am. Diabetes Assn., Nat. Acad. Scis., Biochem. Soc. Great Britain, Harvey Soc., Soc. for Study of Reprodn. (Carl Hartman award 1984), The Endocrine Soc., Japanese Biochem. Soc. (hon.), Golden Retriever Club Am. (pres. 1964). Democrat. Achievements include patents for steroid compounds and lab. apparatus. Home: 1829 Thorstrand Rd Madison WI 53705-1052 Office: U Wis 1710 University Ave Madison WI 53705-4087

LARDY, LEONARD ANTHONY, English educator; b. Sentinel Butte, N.D., July 16, 1933; s. Peter Aloysius and Elizabeth Julia (Dietz) L.; m. Joan Frances Ehrmantraut, Aug. 25, 1956; children: Timothy John, Ronald Anthony, Rebecca Jo Manzano, Lisa Anne Hall. BS in Edn., Dickinson (N.D.) State U., 1955; MA in English, U. Mont., Missoula, 1959; postgrad., Calif. State U., U. Wyo., Laramie. Tchr. Hazen (N.D.) H.S., 1955-57, Williston (N.D.) H.S., 1957-58, Dickinson (N.D.) Ctrl. H.S., 1959-61, Eisenhower H.S., Rialto, Calif., 1961-65, San Gorgonio H.S., San Bernardino, 1965-69; assoc. prof. San Bernardino Valley C.C., 1969-94, prof. emeritus, 1994—. Active Calif. Dem. Com. Mem. NEA (ret.), Calif. Tchrs. Assn. (ret.), Shoreline Beagle Club, Mt. Baldy Beagle Club, Am. Kennel Club. Democrat. Roman Catholic. E-mail: LeonardALardy@aol.com. Home: 33727 Liberty Rd Yucaipa CA 92399-2363

LARDY, NICHOLAS RICHARD, economics educator; b. Madison, Wis., Apr. 8, 1946; s. Henry Arnold and Annrita (Dresselhuys) L.; m. Barbara Jean Dawe, Aug. 29, 1970; children: Elizabeth Brooke, Lillian Henry. BA, U. Wis., 1968; MA, U. Mich., 1972, PhD, 1975. Asst. prof. Yale U., New Haven, 1975-79, assoc. prof., 1979-83, asst. dir. econ. growth ctr., 1979-82; assoc. prof. U. Wash., Seattle, 1983-85, chair China program, 1984-89, prof., 1985-95, dir. The Henry M. Jackson Sch. Internat. Studies, 1991-95; sr. fellow The Brookings Instn., Washington, 1995—; Frederick Frank adj. prof. in internat. trade and fin. Yale U. Sch. Mgmt., New Haven, 1997-2000. Bd. dirs. Nat. Com. on U.S.-China Rels., N.Y.C., Comm. in Internat. Rels. Studies with China, 1989-92, Program for Internat. Studies in Asia, 1993-95; chmn. Com. on Advanced Study in China; vice chmn. com. on scholarly comm. with China NAS, Washington, 1991-95; mem. bd. mgrs. The Blakemore Found., 1993-95; founding mem. Pacific Coun. on Internat. Policy, 1995—; mem. Coun. on Fgn. Rels. Author: Economic Growth and Distribution in China, 1978, Agriculture in China's Modern Economic Development, 1983, (policy study) Economic Policy Toward China in the Post-Reagan Era, 1989, Foreign Trade and Economic Reform in China, 1978-1990, 1992, China in the World Economy, 1994, China's Unfinished Economic Revolution, 1998, Integrating China into the Global Economy, 2002; mem. editl. bd.: The China Quar. (London), mem. editl. bd.: China Econ. Rev., mem. editl. bd.: Jour. Asian Bus., mem. editl. bd.: Jour. Contemporary China. Rsch. fellow Am. Coun. Learned Socs., 1976, 78-79, 89-90, Henry Luce Found., Inc., 1980-82; faculty rsch. grantee Yale U., 1976, 78. Mem. Am. Econ. Assn., Assn. for Asian Studies (nominating com. 1986-87), Assn. for Comparative Econ. Studies (exec. com. 1986-88). Avocations: skiing, squash, tennis, sailing. Home: 2811 Albemarle St NW Washington DC 20008-1037 Office: The Brookings Instn 1775 Massachusetts Ave NW Washington DC 20036-2103 E-mail: nlardy@brook.edu.

LARET, MARK R. CEO; BS, regents scholar, UCLA; M, Haynes Found. fellow, U. Southern Calif. CEO U. Calif., San Francisco, 2000—, U.C. Irvine Med. Ctr., Orange; dep. dir. UCLA Med. Ctr.; CEO UCLA Med. Group. Office: UCSF Med Ctr 500 Parnassus Ave San Francisco CA 94143*

LAREW, H. GORDON, engineering educator, consultant; b. Independence, W.Va., June 5, 1922; s. Hiram G. Larew and Lula Margaret Stemple; m. Mary Jo Thompson, Nov. 22, 1946; children: Jane Jo, Hiram G., Elizabeth T. BS Civil Engring., W.Va. U., 1944; MS Civil Engring., Purdue U., 1952, PhD Civil Engring., 1960. Profl. engr., Va. Jr. engr. N.Y. Ctrl. Sys., N.Y.C., 1946; instr. engring. Purdue U., West Lafayette, Ind., 1947—56; prof. civil engring. U. Va., Charlottesville, 1956—92, prof. emeritus, 1992—. Cons. engr. H. Gordon Larew Cons. Engr., Charlottesville, Va., 1956—. Contbg. author (novels) Structural Engineers Handbook , 1992; contbr. articles to profl. jours. Mem. bd. zoning appeals City of Charlottesville. Fellow: ASCE (pres. Va. sect.); mem.: Chi Epsilon (hon.), Tau Beta Pi (hon.). Avocations: hunting, fishing, stamp collecting. Office: 2500 Hillwood Pl Charlottesville VA 22901-2923

LARGE, G. GORDON M. computer software company executive, retired; b. Phila., Apr. 4, 1940; s. James M. and Sarah Morris (Ellison) L.; m. Janet G. Leith, 1964 (div. 1998); children: Christopher M., Allison G. (dec. Aug. 1998); m. Theresa A. M. Misiorek, Nov. 30, 1978. BA, Princeton U., 1962; MBA, U. Pa., 1963. V.p. Smith, Barney & Co., Inc., N.Y.C., 1964-73; adminstr. N.J. State Energy Office, Trenton, 1974-75; exec. dir. N.J. Cabinet Energy Com., 1974-75; v.p. Mathematica, Inc., Princeton, N.J., 1975-81, Mathematica Products Group, Inc., Princeton, 1981-84, Martin Marietta Data Sys., Greenbelt, Md., 1984-86; sr. v.p., CFO Palladian Software, Inc., Cambridge, Mass., 1986-88, Pansophic Sys., Inc., Lisle, Ill., 1988-91; sr. v.p., fin. and adminstrn. CFO Sys. Ctr. Inc., Reston, Va., 1992-93; exec. v.p., CFO Card Establishment Svcs., Inc., Melville, N.Y., 1993-95, Interleaf Inc., Waltham, Mass., 1995-96, Phase Forward Inc., Waltham, 1999-2000, ret., 2000. Avocations: running, tennis, photography, music, golf.

LARGE, JOHN ANDREW, library and information service educator; b. Mexborough, Yorkshire, Eng., Mar. 27, 1947; arrived in Can., 1989; s. Gordon and Winifred Mary (Tompkins) L.; m. Valerie Merle Wilson, Aug. 30, 1972; children: Amanda Fiona, Kirsty Jane. BSc in Econs., London U., 1968, diploma in libr., 1973; PhD, Glasgow U., Scotland, 1973. Asst. libr. Glasgow U. Libr., 1973-74; libr. Inst. Soviet and East European Studies, Glasgow U., 1974-78; prin. lectr. Coll. Librarianship Wales, Aberystwyth, 1978-89; prof., dir. Grad. Sch. Libr. and Info. Studies McGill U., Montreal, Que., Can., 1989-98, CN-Pratt-Grinstad prof. of info. studies Can., 1998—. Vice chmn. U.K. Online User Group, London, 1987-89; chmn. Can. Coun. Libr. Schs., 1991-93, 97-98; external examiner U. W.I., 1991-99, U. Ibadan, Nigeria, 1992-95; bd.d irs. Atwater Libr. and Computer Ctr., 1999—. Author: The Foreign-Language Barrier, 1983, The Artificial Language Movement, 1985, Japanese edit., 1995, A Modular Curriculum for Information Studies, 1987; co-author: Online Searching: Principles and Practice, 1990, Information Seeking in the Online Age, 1999; editor: Manual of Online Search Strategies, 1988, 3d edit., 2001, CD-ROM Information Products: An Evaluative Guide vol. 1, 1990, vol. 2, 1991, vol. 3, 1992, World Info. Report, 1997, ICT for Library and Information Professionals: A Training Package-Modules 1-2, 2001; mem. editl. adv. bd. Jour. Librarianship and Info. Sci., 1992—, Jour. of Universal Lang., 2000—, South African Jour. Libraries and Info. Sci., 2002—; editor jour. Edn. for Info., 1983—, Treasures of Islam, 1999, CD-ROM Info. Products, 1993. Rsch. grantee Brit. Libr. R&D Dept., 1981-82, 85-86, European Space Agy., 1983-85, Nat. Libr. Can., 2002; IBM Acad. Info. Exch. fellow, 1991-92, Social Sci. and Humanities Rsch. Coun. fellow, 1991-94, 96-98, 98-99; recipient Commemorative medal for 125th Anniversary of the Confedn. of Can., 1992. Avocation: music listening and playing. Office: McGill U Grad Sch Libr and Info Studies 3459 McTavish Montreal QC Canada H3A 1Y1

LARGE, MARY MITCHELL WESTALL, volunteer; b. Asheville, N.C., July 20, 1916; d. James and Mary Mitchell (Wiley) Westall; m. Edwin Kirk Large Jr., Sept. 4, 1937; children: Marianne M. Large Newman, Catherine L. O'Shea, John R. Large. AB summa cum laude, Randolph-Macon Woman's Coll., 1936; MA, Columbia U., N.Y.C., 1937; student, Princeton Theol. Seminary, 1973-74. With sales dept. Bamberger's Store, Newark, 1937; advt. rschr. Vick Chem. Co., N.Y.C., 1937-40; substitute tchr., tutor Hunterdon County (N.J.) Schs., 1946-73. Guest spkr. Girl Scouts USA, 1999. Editor: James Joyce & Heraldry, 1986, Beyond This Darkness, 1993. Active Girl Scouts Am., 1944—, bd. dirs. Rolling Hills Coun., 1970—, pres. 1960-62, pres. Flemington, N.J., 1952-54; dir. edn. 1st Alexandria Presbyn. Ch., Mt. Pleasant, N.J., 1974-76; elder Presbyn. Ch., 1959—; bd. dirs. mission coun. Presbyn. New Brunswick, N.J, various other coms. Recipient Thanks award Girl Scouts Am., 1994, Woman of Achievement award, 1999, Golden award Hunt County C. of C., 1996. Mem. Phi Beta Kappa. Republican. Avocations: hospital volunteering, teaching, public speaking, reading, writing. Home: 4275 Owens Rd Apt 601 Evans GA 30809-3307

LARGE, TIMOTHY WALLACE, religious organization administrator; b. Palo Alto, Calif., Feb. 23, 1942; s. Charles Delano Henry and Jean Eleanor (Parker) L.; m. Vickie Lee Olson, Aug. 6, 1978; children: Jonathan Jeffrey, Sarah Jean. BSBA, Menlo Coll., 1964; MBA, U. Santa Clara, 1966; cert., Multnomah Sch. Bible, Portland, Oreg., 1973; M of Div., Talbot Theol. Sem., La Mirada, Calif., 1978. CPA, Calif. Acct. Bramer Accountancy Corp., Santa Fe Springs, Calif., 1974-76; instr. Biola Coll., La Mirada, 1978; acct. Conservative Bapt. Assn. So. Calif., Anaheim, 1978-83; CPA H. Canaday, P.A., Santa Fe Springs, 1983—; adminstr. Temple Baptist Ch., Perris, Calif., 1985-87; treas. Inst. Evangelico, La Puenta, 1987—. Cons. Exec. Leasing, La Mirada, 1976—. Treas. Founders chpt. Kidney Found. So. Calif., Orange County, 1974-76; chaplain Christian Hosp. Med. Ctr., Perris, 1985—. Served with U.S. Army, 1965-69. Fellow Nat. Assn. Ch. Bus. Adminstrs.; mem. AICPA, Am. Mgt. Assn., Christian Ministries Mgt. Assn. Republican. Baptist. Avocations: bowling, ping pong, travel. Home: 26928 Potomac Dr Sun City CA 92586-3164 Office: 14864 Valley Blvd La Puente CA 91746-3225

LARGEN, JOSEPH, retailer, furniture manufacturer, book wholesaler; b. Union, N.J., June 13, 1940; s. Fred and Wilma Largen; children: Lori, Lisa. BS in Econs, U. Mo., 1963. Mgmt. trainee R.R. Donnelly Corp., Chgo., 1964-67; distbn. mgr., material control and distbn. Warwick Electronic Co., Niles, Ill., 1967-69; with Brodart, Inc., 1969—, v.p. prodn. Pa., 1973-75, exec. v.p., 1975-78, pres., 1978—. Served with USCG, 1963-64. Home: 2000 1st Ave Apt 2602 Seattle WA 98121-2172 Office: Brodart Co 500 Arch St Williamsport PA 17701-7809

LARGENT, MARGIE, architect; b. Adrian, Mo., Feb. 28, 1923; d. Arlie Everett Largent and Ruby Lacey Grosshart; m. Creighton A. Anderson, May 10, 1954; children: Michael Creig, Jon William Everett. Student, Capital Bus. Coll., 1942, Art Ctr. Sch. of Design, Pasadena, Calif., 1944, 45, 46, Willamette U., 1946-47; BArch, U. Oreg., 1950. Registered arch., Wash., Oreg., Alaska. Sr. structural draftsman Stone & Webster Engrs., L.A. and Boston, 1950-52; prodn. coord. Jon Konigshofer, Carmel, Calif., 1953-54, Daniel-Mann-Johnson, Archs., L.A., 1954-55, Gordon Cochran, Arch., Portland, Oreg., 1956-57, John Groom, Arch., Salem, 1958-60; designer Largent & Anderson, Lake Oswego, 1961-63; arch. Margie Largent, 1964—. Prin. works include Shon Tay Profl. Ctr., Lake Oswego, 1965-78, Jackson Residence, Warm Springs Reservation, Oreg., 1974, Crosby-Earth Shelter, San Juan Island, Wash., 1975, Anderson Tri-Plex, Cordova, Alaska, 1983. Active Land Use Com., Lake Oswego, 1970—, Park Adv. Bd., Clacksmas County, Oreg., 1975-79, Bldg. Bd. Appeals, Lake Oswego, 1978-98; pres. Associated C. of C., Clackamas County, 1970. Mem. Constrn. Specifications Inst. (Portland chpt. pres. 1977, 86, editor 1979, 84, archivist 1980, Capital chpt. archivist 1995—). Home: 535 Boone Rd SE Salem OR 97306-1844 Office: Margie Largent Arch PO Box 1291 Lake Oswego OR 97035-0528

LARGENT, STEVE, former congressman, former professional football player; b. Tulsa, Sept. 28, 1954; m. Terry Largent; children: Kyle, Kelly, Kramer, Casie BS in biology, U. Tulsa, 1976. Wide receiver Seattle Seahawks,

NFL, Kirkland, Wash., 1976-89; player Pro Bowl, 1979, 80, 82, 85-88; mktg. cons. Sara Lee Corp., 1991-94; mem. 103rd-106th Congresses from 1st Okla. dist., Washington, 1995—2002, mem. budget com., mem. health care task force, mem. sci. com., mem. energy & environ. and space & aeronautics subcoms., mem. commerce com.; candidate for Governor, Okla., 2002. Mem. commerce com., energy and power subcom., telecomms., trade and consumer protection com., fin. and hazardous materials subcom. Holder NFL record for passes caught in consecutive games, also for career receiving yardage, receptions; named to NFL Hall of Fame, 1995.*

LARGMAN, THEODORE, consultant; b. Phila., Nov. 16, 1923; s. Max and Rose Largman; m. Doris Citrin (dec. Dec. 1990); children: Susan Slotnick, Robert, Richard, Michele. BA, Temple U., 1948; PhD, Ind. U., 1952. Chemist Allied Chem. and Dye Corp., Phila., 1952-60; sr. chemist Allied Chem., Morristown, N.J., 1960-62, sr. scientist, 1963-65; sr. rsch. scientist Allied/Signal, 1965-89; pres., founder Triad Industries, 1990-95, cons., 1995—. One man shows include Morris County First Night Celebration, Morristown, N.J., 1996, Diviane Galleries, Randolph, N.J., 1997, Art Gallery, Marantz Gallery, West Orange, N.J., 1998, Art Gallery, County Coll. of Morris, Randolph, 1999. Pres., founder Renaissance Group, Morristown, 1990-93; chmn. Environ. Commn., Morristownship, 1998—. With Signal Corps, 1943-46. Achievements include patents for novel fibers, pesticides, flame retardants, polymers, polyster, nylon fibers. Avocations: gardening, tennis, traveling. Office: Triad Industries 7 Upperfield Rd Morristown NJ 07960-4923

LARIC, MICHAEL VICTOR, management and marketing administrator; b. Split, Yugoslavia, Feb. 8, 1945; came to U.S., 1971; s. Joseph and Ljubica (Abraham) L.; m. Roberta Kine; children: Shai Samuel, Pnina Leora, Ari Nathaniel. BA in Econs. and Polit. Sci., Hebrew U. of Jerusalem, 1968, MA in Bus., 1971; PhD, CUNY, 1976. Economist Israel Hotel & Motel Owners, Tel Aviv, 1968-69; gen. mgr. Galia Laundries, Jerusalem, 1969-71; economist Risk Analysis Corp., Alpine, N.J., 1971-72; lectr. CUNY, N.Y.C., 1972-73; asst. prof. Rutgers U., State U. N.J., Newark, 1974-75, U. Conn., Storrs, 1975-81; prof. mktg. U. Balt., 1981—, acad. assoc. dean, 1992-95, area coord. mktg., 1995-2000, co-dir. Ctr. Tech. Comm., 1995—, chair mktg., 2000—. Course dir. Data Tech. Inst., Clifton, N.Y., 1986-92, Frost & Sullivan, N.Y.C. and Eng., 1990—; cons. Ecomares Internat., Ellicott City, Md., 1981—. Author: Marketing Management: Analysis Using Spreedsheets, 1988, Lotus Exercises for Principles of Marketing, 1986, 14 other books; contbr. numerous articles, monographs and cases to profl. jours. Named Outstanding Young Man of The Yr. Jaycees, 1979, 80. Mem.: Am. Econs. Assn., Product Devel. and Mgmt. (charter, bd. dirs. 1981, 1982), Am. Mktg. Assn. (bd. dirs. Balt. chpt. 1976—82, Outstanding Contbr. of Conn. 1978), Beta Gamma Sigma. Home: 4609 Morning Ride Ct Ellicott City MD 21042-5927 Office: U Balt 1420 N Charles St Baltimore MD 21201-5720 E-mail: mlaric@ubmail.ubalt.edu.

LARIO, FRANK M., JR. lawyer, judge; b. Phila., July 1, 1937; s. Frank M. and Marie Ann (Mandarino) L.; m. Kathleen A. Cowan, July 1, 1961; children: Michael James, Kathleen Marie, Frank M. III. AB cum laude, Georgetown U., 1959; postgrad., Harvard U., 1959; JD cum laude, Rutgers U., 1962. Bar: N.J. 1962, U.S. Dist. Ct. N.J. 1963, U.S. Ct. Appeals (3d cir.) 1978, U.S. Supreme Ct. 1969. Law sec. to assoc. justice Vincent S. Haneman N.J. Supreme Ct., 1962-63; ptnr. Lario, Nardi & Gleaner, Haddonfield, N.J., 1973-93; mcpl. judge Borough of Magnolia, 1969-93, Borough of Audubon Park, 1970-93, Borough of Woodlynne, 1971-76, Borough of Bellmawr, 1976-93; superior ct. judge State of N.J., 1993—. Instr. estate planning Inst. Continuing Legal Edn., 1962-69, instr. legal ethics, 1973-78; com. on mcpl. cts. N.J. Supreme Ct., 1980-92, com. on character, 1983-92; bd. govs. Georgetown U., 1978-81, alumni senate, 1981—. Mem. editl. bd. Rutgers Law Rev., 1961-62. Mem. ABA, N.J. Bar Assn. (chmn. mcpl. cts. of N.J. com. 1978-81), Camden County Bar Assn. (bd. mgrs. 1973-76, chmn. immigration and naturalization com. 1974-83, long range planning com. 1976-78, sec. 1979-80, treas. 1980-81, v.p. 1982-83, pres. 1984-85), Camden County Mcpl. Judges Conf. (sec. 1975, pres. 1976-77), Rutgers U. Law Sch. Alumni Assn. (chmn. scholarship com. 1971-82), Rutgers U. Law Sch. Alumni Assn. South Jersey (chancellor 1968-69, bd. mgrs. 1970-82), Georgetown U. Alumni Assn. (gov. 1976—), Men of Malvern (assoc. capt. 1968—), Vesper Club (Phila.), Tavistock Country Club (Haddonfield), Union League of Phila., KC, Georgetown U. Alumni South Jersey (pres. 1970-72). Office: Hall of Justice 101 S Fifth St Camden NJ 08103-4001

LARIVIERE, GENE ROBERT, surgeon; b. Amarillo, Tex., Feb. 3, 1959; MD, U. Tex. Diplomate Am. Bd. Surgery. Resident in gen. surgery Wesley Med. Ctr., Wichita, Kans., 1985-90; pvt. practice Iowa City. Mem. staff Welborn Bapt. Hosp., Evansville, Ind., 1990-94, Mercy Hosp., Iowa City, 1994—. Office: Surg Svcs 1040 William St Iowa City IA 52240-6633

LARIVIERE, RICHARD WILFRED, university administrator, educator, consultant; b. Chgo., Jan. 27, 1950; s. Wilfred Francis and Esther Irene Lariviere; m. Janis Anne Worcester, June 5, 1971; 1 child, Anne Elizabeth. BA, U. Iowa, 1972; PhD, U. Pa., 1978. Lectr. U. Pa., Phila., 1978-79; asst. prof. U. Iowa, Iowa City, 1980-82; prof. U. Tex., Austin, 1982—, Ralph B. Thomas Regents prof. Asian studies, 1993—, assoc. v.p., 1995-99, dean Coll. Liberal Arts, 1999—. Dir. Sinha & Lariviere Ltd., Austin; founder Doing Bus. in India seminar; cons. Perot Sys. Corp., Dallas, 1993—; bd. dirs. HCL/Perot Sys., Amsterdam; chmn. Coun. Am. Overseas Rsch. Ctrs., Washington. Author: Ordeals in Hindu Law, 1981, Narada Smrti, 1989; gen. editor Studies in South Asia. Fellow NEH, 1979-83. Fellow Royal Asiatic Soc.; mem. Am. Oriental Soc., Am. Inst. Indian Studies (sr.fellow 1989, 95, v.p. 1990), Assn. Asian Studies. Lutheran. Home: 3415 Cactus Wren Way Austin TX 78746-6636

LARIZADEH, M(OHAMMED) R(EZA), business educator; b. Tehran, Iran, Apr. 14, 1947; came to U.S., 1966; s. Hassan and Nosrat (Saremi) L.; m. Dianne Ellen Pincus, Mar. 25, 1973; children: Dariush, Darya Anna. BA in Econs., Bus., UCLA, 1972, cert. in acctg., 1974. Cert. colls. teaching credential, Calif. (life); lic. real estate agent, Calif. Auditor Peat, Marwick & Mitchell, L.A., 1972-74; controller Petromain Constrn. Co., Tehran, 1975-77; v.p. fin. Pilary Marine Shipping Co., 1977-79; prof. Iranian Inst. Banking, 1975-78; pres. Audicount Acctg. and Auditing Group, L.A., 1984—; prof. bus. and acctg. East L.A. Coll., 1980-87, vice-chmn. dept. bus. and acctg., 1987—, chmn. dept. bus. adminstrn., 1988—; prof. acctg. Santa Monica (Calif.) Coll., 1987—. Mgmt. cons. L.P. Assocs. Mfg. Co., L.A., 1981—; mng. dir. Barrington Enterprises, L.A.; prof. Santa Monica Coll., 1987. Author/translator: Accounting/Auditing, 1975. Mem. NEA, Internat. Fedn. Bus. Edn., Am. Mgmt. Assn., Am. Acctg. Assn., Faculty Assn. Calif. C.C.s, Am. Fedn. Tchrs., Calif. Tchrs. Assn., Am. Entrepreneur Assn., Nat. Assn. Realtors, Am. Assn. Pub. Accts., Calif. Assn. Bus. Educators, Calif. Assn. Realtors, Nat. Soc. Pub. Accts., Calif. Bus. Edn. Assn., Internat. Fedn. Bus. Edn., Inst. Mgmt. Accts., UCLA Alumni Assn. (life), Alpha Kappa Psi.

LARK, M. ANN, management consultant, strategic planner, naturalist; b. Denver, Feb. 28, 1952; d. Carl Eugene and Arlena Elizabeth (Bashor) Epperson; m. Larry S. Lark, Apr. 1, 1972 (div. 1979). Asst. corp. sec., savs. dir. Imperial Corp. dba Silver State Savs. & Loan, Denver, 1972-75; client svcs. mgr. 1st Fin. Mgmt. Corp., Englewood, Colo., 1977-81; regional account mgr. Ericsson Info. Systems, Chatsworth, Calif., 1981-82; ind. cons. Denver, 1982-84; regional account mgr. InnerLine/Am. Banker, Chgo., 1984-85; chief info. officer Security Pacific Credit Corp., San Diego, 1985-88; prin. The Genessee Group, Thousand Oaks, Calif., 1988—. Avocations: tennis, gardening, hiking, bicycling, writing, sketching. Home and Office: 1144 El Monte Dr Thousand Oaks CA 91362-2117

LARK, RAYMOND, artist, art scholar; b. Phila., June 16, 1939; s. Thomas and Bertha (Lark) Crawford. Student, Phila. Mus. Sch. Art, 1948-51, L.A. Trade Tech. Coll., 1961-62; BS, Temple U., 1961; LHD, U. Colo., 1985. Ednl. dir. Victor Bus. Sch., L.A., 1969-71; pub. rels. exec. Western States Svc. Co., 1968-70; owner, mgr. Raymond Lark's House of Fine Foods, 1962—67; exec. sec. to v.p. Physicians Drug and Supply Co., Phila., 1961-67. Lectr. L.A. Trade Tech. Coll., 1973, Compton (Calif.) Coll., 1972, Nat. Secs. Assn., Hollywood, Calif., 1970, UCLA, 1983, U. Utah, Salt Lake City, 1993, others. One-man shows include, Distinctive African Am. Art Ctr., Salt Lake City, 2002, Dalzell Hatfield Galleries, L.A., 1968-86, Arthur's Gallery Masterpieces and Jewels, Beverly Hills, Calif., 1971, Dorothy Chandler Pavillion Music Center, L.A., 1974, Honolulu Acad. Arts, 1975, UCLA, 1983, U. Colo. Mus., 1984, Albany State Coll. Art Gallery, Albany, Ga., 1988, Utah Mus. Fine Arts, Salt Lake City, 1989, Mind's Art Gallery, Dickinson U., Dickinson, N.D., 1989, Trinton Mus. Art, Santa Clara, Calif., Greenville (N.C.), 1991, Mus. of Art, 1993, Springfield (Mo.) Art Mus., 1995, Washington County Museum of Fine Arts, Hagerstown, Md., 1996, The Peninsula Fine Arts Center, Newport News, Va., 1996, N.C. State U., Raleigh, 1998-99, others; group exhbns. include, Smithsonian Instn., 1971, N.J. State Mus., Trenton, 1971, Guggenheim Mus., N.Y.C., 1975, Met. Mus. Art, 1976, La Galerie Mauffe, Paris, 1977, Portsmouth (Va.) Mus., 1979, Ava Dorog Galleries, Munich, W. Ger., 1979, Academia Italia, Parma, 1980, Ames Art Galleries and Auctioneers, Beverly Hills, 1980, Le Salon des Nations at Centre International d'Art Contemporain, Paris, 1983, Tivolio Gallery, Salt Lake City, 1991, Hyatt Regency Hotel, Capitol Hill, Washington, 1993, Alexandria Mus. Art, La., 1998, Hill country Arts Found., Ingram, Tex., 1998, Biblical Arts Ctr., Dallas, 1999, Yerba Buena Ctr. The Arts, San Francisco, 2000, others; represented in permanent collections, Library of Congress, Ont. Coll. Art, Toronto, Mus. African and African Am. Art and Antiquities, Buffalo, Carnegie Inst., The State Mus. Pennsylvania, numerous others; art commns. for TV and film studios include, All in the Family, Carol Burnett Show, Maude, The Young and the Restless, Universal City Studios, Palace of the Living Arts, Movie Land Wax Mus.; author works in field; author and contbr. more than 50 scholarly treatises on art, edn. and the hist. devel. of Black Ams., chpts. to encyclopedias and textbooks, articles to jours., introductions to mus. exhbn. catalogues. Recipient gold medal Acad. Italia, 1980, also numerous best of show awards, 3 presdl. proclamations; award Internat. Platform Assn.; Dr. Raymond Lark Day proclaimed by State of Md., 1994, Dr. Raymond Lark Day proclaimed by City of Raleigh, N.C., 1988; grantee Nat. Endowment Arts, ARCO Found., Colo. Humanities Program, Adolph Coors Beer Found. Mem. Art West Assn. (pres. 1968-70) Address: PO Box 76169 Los Angeles CA 90076-0169 E-mail: smithlarkwright@cs.com. *I was telling people that I was Black, proud, and beautiful long before it became fashionable to be very dark. I never felt, "I am the greatest." However, I never had an inferiority complex. I always knew that I had God-given talent, character, and good common sense. In addition, I have always had great confidence in God and in myself. While I am not a soothsayer and never will be a braggart, I knew my art would be recognized. For whatever recognition I have received, I have worked extremely hard and have paid my dues.*

LARKAM, BEVERLEY MCCOSHAM, clinical social worker, family therapist; b. Vancouver , Can., Mar. 3, 1928; came to U.S., 1951; d. William Howard and Marjorie Isobel (Jerome) McCosham; children: Elizabeth, Charles, Daphne, Peter, John. Assoc. Royal Conservatory of Mus., U. Toronto, Toronto, 1948; BA, U. B.C., Can., 1949; BSW, U. B.C., 1950, MSW, 1951. Bd. cert. Diplomate in Clin. Social Work; lic. master social worker, advanced clin. practitioner, marriage and family therapist, Tex. Psychiat. social worker Brackenridge Hosp., 1952-54; chmn. dept. sr. high. sch. Univ. Presbyn. Ch., Austin, Tex., 1952-55, mem. Christian edn. com., 1961-67, bd. dirs. developing and organizing nursery sch., 1967-70; social worker Counseling-Psychol. Svcs. Ctr., U. Tex., 1971-72; psychiat. social worker, chief supr. Adult, Children's Mental Health Human-Devel. Ctr.-South, Austin, Tex., 1972-79; pvt. practice marriage and family therapy, sex therapy and individual and group psychotherapy, 1975—. Field supr. Sch. Social Work U. Tex.; cons. in field. Mem. cmty. orgn. to establish classes for mentally retarded children, 1966-68; mem. City of Austin Commn. for Women, 1978—, chmn., 1982-84, emeritus, 1985—; organizer Austin Assn. for Marriage and Family Therapy, 1980-82, bd. mem. Tex. Assn. for Marriage and Family Therapy, 1980-82, bd. dirs. Nat. Assn. Commns. for Women, 1985-88, Am. Assn. for Marriage and Family Therapy Com. on Racial, Ethic and Cultural Diversity, 1992-95; vol. usher Austin Symphony Orch. Soc., 1972—; mem. Heritage Soc. Austin, Georgetown Heritage Soc., Women's Symphony League of Austin, Austin Art Mus. Mem. Am. Assn. Marriage and Family Therapy (approved supr.), Am. Group Psychotherapy Assn. (cert. group psychotherapist), Southwestern Group Psychotherapy Soc. (sr. faculty), Am. Assn. Sex Educators, Counselors and Therapists (cert. sex therapist, supr.), Acad. Cert. Social Workers, Nat. Assn. Social Workers, Register Clin. Social Workers, Diplomate Internat. Conf. Advancement of Pvt. Practice of Clin. Social Work, Tex. Soc. for Clin. Social Work (bd. dirs. 1990—, pres. 1997-99), Clin. Social Work Fedn., Toastmasters Internat., PEO Sisterhood, Austin Womans Forum (pres. 2002—). Presbyterian (elder, session of Univ. Presbyterian Ch. 1997—). Home and Office: 2102 Raleigh Ave Austin TX 78703-2128 also: 207 E 9th St Georgetown TX 78626-5908

LARKIN, ALEXANDER C. minister; b. San Francisco, Dec. 27, 1941; s. Alexander Larkin, Margaret H. Vogeler. MA, U.San Francisco, 1977; MDiv, St. Patrick Seminary, Menlo Pk., 1967. Episcopal vicar Diocese of San Jose, San Jose, Calif., 1992—96; pastor Sacred Heart Parish, Saratoga, 1996—. Recipient Prelate of Honor award, His Holiness, Pope John Paul II, 2001. Mem.: Cath. Jewish Dialog of Santa Clara County. Office: Sacred Heart Parish 13716 Saratoga Ave Saratoga CA 95070-5432

LARKIN, BARRY LOUIS, professional baseball player; b. Cin., Apr. 28, 1964; m. Lisa Davis. Student, U. Mich., 1982-85. Baseball player Cincinnati Reds, 1986—. First baseball player twice named MVP of Big Ten Athletic Conf.; two-time All-Am. honors; named MVP of National League, 1995, Rookie of Yr. and to All-Star team, 1988-95, to Topps' Triple-A All-Star team, 1986, All-Star teams by Sporting News, 1988-92, 94-95, AP, 1990, UPI, 1990, Maj. League Baseball, 1988-91, 93, to N.L. Silver Slugger team Sporting News, 1988-92, 95; recipient Gold Glove award, 1994-96. Achievements include mem. U.S. Olympic Baseball Team, 1984, World Series Team, 1990. Office: Cin Reds 100 Cinergy Fld Cincinnati OH 45202-3543*

LARKIN, EUGENE DAVID, artist, educator; b. Mpls., June 27, 1921; s. John Peter and Martha Lavinia (Vandevere) L.; m. Audrey Jean Krueger, Jan. 29, 1947; children: Andrew, Alan. BA, U. Minn., 1946, MA, 1949. Mem. faculty dept. art Kans. State Coll., Pittsburg, 1949-54; head printmaking dept., chmn. divsn. fine arts Mpls. Sch. Art, 1954-69; prof. design dept. U. Minn., St. Paul, 1969—, prof. emeritus design, housing and apparel, 1991—. One man exhbns. include, Mpls. Inst. Arts, 1957, 60, 68, Syracuse U., 1962, Walker Art Center, Mpls., 1967, New Forms Gallery, Athens, Greece, 1967, U. Kans., 1972, Macalester Coll., 1974, U. Minn., St. Paul, 1973, 78, 87, 91; group exhbns. include, Phila. Printmakers Club, 1966, 20 American Artists, Geneva, Switzerland, 1964, Big Prints, N.Y. U., 1968, Midwestern Printmakers, Walker Art Center, 1973, Cabo Frio Internat. Print Biennial, Brazil, 1983, Nat. Works on Paper, Minot State Coll., 1986, 17th Annual Works on Paper SW State U., San Marcos, Tex., 4th Annual North Coast Coll. Soc. Exhbn., Hiram Coll., Hudson, Ohio, 1988, 20th Annual Works on Paper Dulin Nat. Knoxville, Knoxville Mus. Art, 1988, Paepcke Meml. Bldg. Gallery, 1993, Aspen Inst. and Music Assoc. of Aspen, 1993, U. St. Thomas, Mpls./St. Paul, 1999; represented in permanent collections, Mus. Modern Art, N.Y.C., Nat. Mus. S.Africa, Capetown, Library Congress, Chgo. Art Inst., Mpls. Inst. Arts, U. Minn. Gallery, Des Moines Art Center, U. Tenn., Kans. State Tchrs. Coll., Minn. Mus. Art, Nat. Collection Fine Arts, Smithsonian Instn; author: Design: The Search for Unity, 1988. Recipient juror's award Rockford Internat. Print and Drawing Biennale, 1983 Mem. Coll. Art Assn. Am. Home: 64 Groveland Ter Minneapolis MN 55403-1103

LARKIN, GREGORY LUKE, emergency physician, educator; b. Pitts., Oct. 18, 1961; MS, Pa. State U., 1987, MD, 1989; MPH, U. Mich., 1996; BSChE, U. Notre Dame. Diplomate Am. Bd. Emergency Medicine. Resident in emergency medicine William Beaumont Hosp., Royal Oak, Mich., 1993; adj. prof. U. Pitts., 1993; prof. surgery, emergency medicine and pub. health U. Tex. Southwestern, Dallas, 2002—; dir. acad. devel., divsn. emergency medicine Parkland Meml. Hosp., 2002—, med. dir. Violence Intervention and Prevention Ctr., 2002—. Clin. ethics cons.; expert on injury control in domestic violence, automotive crash rsch., bioethics, biostats. and internat. emergency care and pub. health. Bd. dirs. Emergency Internat., World Walk Found. Mem. AMA, Am. Coll. Emergency Physicians (chair sect. on injury control and prevention), Soc. Acad. Emergency Medicine. Office: U Tex Southwestern Med Ctr at Dallas 5323 Harry Hines Blvd Rm CS2.122 Dallas TX 75390-8579

LARKIN, JOAN, poet, English educator; b. Boston, Apr. 16, 1939; d. George Joseph and Celia Gertrude (Rosenberg) Moffitt; m. James A. Larkin, Dec. 23, 1966 (div. 1969); 1 child, Kate. BA, Swarthmore Coll., 1960; MA, U. Ariz., 1969. Asst. prof. English CUNY-Bklyn. Coll., 1969—94, ret., 1994, adj. faculty MFA program, 1997—98; assoc. faculty MFA program Goddard Coll., 1994—96, 2002. mem. guest faculty poetry writing Sarah Lawrence Coll., Bronxville, N.Y., 1984-86, fall 1988, 97—; vis. instr. Manhattan Theatre Club, Oneonta, Gainesville, Tenants Harbor and Cummington workshops; poet-in-residence Writers Community, Manhattan, West Side YMCA. Author: (poems) Housework, 1975, A Long Sound, 1986, Cold River, 1997, (rec. poetry reading) A Sign I Was Not Alone, 1980, (prose) If You Want We Have, 1998, Glad Day, 1998; co-editor: Gay and Lesbian Poetry in Our Time: An Anthology, 1988 (Lambda Lit. award 1988), Amazon Poetry, 1975, Lesbian Poetry, 1981; editor: The Women Writers Calendar, 1982, 83, 84, A Woman Like That, 1999; co-translator: Sor Juana's Love Poems, 1997; contbr. poems to periodicals including Am. Poetry Rev., Conditions, Ms., Paris Rev., Sinister Wisdom, The Village Voice, Aphra, Endymion, The Lamp in the Spine, Global City Rev., Am. Rev., Genesis West, Sojourner. NEA fellow in poetry, 1987-88, 96, N.Y. Found. for Arts fellow in poetry, 1987-88; Creative Artists Pub. Svc. Program grantee N.Y. State Coun. Arts, 1976, 80; Mass. Cultural Coun. grantee in playwriting, 1995.

LARKIN, JOHN EDWARD, JR. orthopedic surgeon; b. St. Paul, Nov. 8, 1930; s. John E. and Ann G. (Wedebrand) L.; m. Colles Baxter, June 16, 1981. BS, U. Minn., 1953, MD, 1960. Intern Detroit Receiving Hosp., 1960-61; resident Harvard Surgery Svc./Boston City Hosp., 1961-62, Children's Hosp., Boston, 1963-66, Mass. Gen. Hosp., Boston, 1963-66; pvt. practice St. Paul, 1966-98; emeritus asst. prof. orthopedic surgery U. Minn., 1998—. Pres. Orthop. Surgery, P.A., St. Paul, 1966-98. Bd. dirs. Minn. Coun. for Quality Edn., 1970-79, Minn. Opera, 1974-79, Minn. Mus. Art, St. Paul, 1971-86, 94-95, Irish Am. Cultural Inst., 1974—, U. Minn. Arboretum, 1998—, James Ford Bell Libr., 2000—; trustee Mpls. Inst. of Art, 1980-89; mem. accessiions com. Mpls. Inst. Art, 1979—. With U.S. Army, 1953-55. Fellow Am. Bd. Orthop. Surgery; mem. AMA, N.Am. Spine Soc., Minn. State Med. Assn., Minn. Orthop. Soc., Ramsey County Med. Soc., Min-Da-Mann Orthop. Soc., Irish Am. Orthop. Soc., Twin City Orthop. Soc., New Eng. Orthop. Soc. (hon.), Irish Orthop. Soc. (hon.). Office: Orthop Surgery PA 111 Kellogg Blvd E Ste 300 Saint Paul MN 55101-1235

LARKIN, LAWRENCE ALBERT, retired computer engineer; b. Kansas City, Mo., Jan. 5, 1937; BS, U. Kans., 1959, M Engring., 1960; PhD, U. Mich., 1964. Lic. Profl. Civil Engr. State of Kans. Asst. prof. SUNY, Buffalo, 1964—70; cons. engr. A. O. Smith Corp., Milw., 1970—89, The MacNeal-Schwendler Corp., Milw., 1989—91; v.p. structural engring. STM Cons. Inc., 1991—98.

LARKIN, LEE ROY, retired lawyer; b. Oklahoma City, Aug. 11, 1928; s. William Patrick and Agnes (Matthis) L.; m. Mary Jane Langston, Apr. 17, 1965; children— James William, John Patrick (dec.). BS, Oklahoma A&M U., Stillwater, 1950; MA, Vanderbilt U., 1952; LLB, William Mitchell U., St. Paul, 1959. Bar: Minn. 1959, Tex. 1963, D.C. 1963. Economist U.S. Dept. Agr., Washington, 1953; economist, lawyer Pillsbury, Mpls., 1953-62; ptnr. Harris & Larkin, Houston, 1963-65; sr. ptnr. Andrews & Kurth, 1966-93; retired, 1994. Speaker Continuing Legal Edn. Officer Sharpstown Civic Assn., Houston, 1966-94; elder St. Philip Presbyn. Ch., Houston; moderator Presbytery of New Covenant, Houston, 1980. Served to capt. USAR, 1951-58. Fellow Tex. Bar Found., Houston Bar Found.; mem. ABA, State Bar Tex., Houston Bar Assn., Riverbend Country Club, Rotary (pres. 1978-79), Delta Theta Phi. Avocations: golf, tennis, travel. Home: 3725 Wickersham Ln Houston TX 77027-4013

LARKIN, MARY SUE, financial planner; b. Kansas City, Kans., Sept. 29, 1948; d. Claude Dewey Jr. and Mildred Elaine (Foster) Wyrick; m. James Donald Larkin, June 5, 1971; children: Michael James, David Kirk. BA in Elem. Edn., Baker U., 1970; MA in Edn., Ariz. State U., 1980. Tchr. Bonner Springs (Kans.) Unified Sch. Dist., 1970-71, Finney County Unified Sch. Dist., Garden City, Kans., 1971-73, Deer Valley Unified Sch. Dist., Phoenix, 1974-80; fin. planner Larkin & Assocs., Sun City, Ariz., 1980—; co-founder, registered rep. Fin. Network Investment Corp., Torrance, Calif., 1983, co-regional dir., 2000—. Co-author: The Larkin Guide-Enjoying the Riches of Retirement, 1987. Bd. dirs. Mingus Mountain Estate Residential Ctr., Inc., 1993, sec., 1994—. Recipient creative programming award Nat. Univ. Continuing Edn. Assn., 1994, Fin. Network Circle of Achievement award, 1999. Mem. Altrusa (pres. Sun City 1987-89), Fin. Planning Assn. Republican. Roman Catholic. Office: 17220 N Boswell Blvd Ste L200 Sun City AZ 85373-2000

LARKIN, MICHAEL JOHN, newspaper editor, journalist; b. Boston, Sept. 27, 1950; s. Alfred Sinnott and Lillian Louise L.; m. Sarah Jane Wood, July 6, 1970 (div. 1985); children— Jonathan Michael, Joshua Stuart; m. Alison Rose Biggs, June 1, 1986. BA in English, U. Mass., 1973. News copy editor Boston Globe, 1974-76, sports copy editor, 1976-80, asst. bus. editor, 1980-82, Sunday editor, 1982, mag. editor, 1982-85, living/arts editor, 1985-89, sr. asst. met. editor zoned editions, 1989-92, Sunday editor, 1992-95, asst. mng. editor, 1995-2000, dep. mng. editor/news ops., 2001—. Contbr. BBC, 1997-99. Mem., editl. com., New England Newspaper Assn., 1998—. Office: Boston Globe PO Box 2378 Boston MA 02107-2378

LARKIN, THOMAS ERNEST, JR. investment management company executive; b. Wilkes-Barre, Pa., Sept. 29, 1939; s. Thomas Ernest and Margaret (Gorman) L.; m. Margaret Giban, Nov. 2, 1979; 1 child, Thomas Ernest III. BA in Econs., U. Notre Dame, 1961; postgrad., Grad. Sch. Bus., NYU, 1962-66. New bus. rep. Mfrs. Hanover Trust Co., 1963-66; mgr. pension dept. Eastman Dillon, Union Securities, 1966-69; v.p. Shearson Hayden Stone, Inc., N.Y.C., 1969-75; sr. v.p. Bernstein Macaulay Inc., 1969-75, Crocker Investment Mgmt. Corp., San Francisco, 1975-77, Trust Co. of the West, L.A., 1977, mng. dir., 1982—, pres., COO, 1989-2000; vice chmn. The TCW Group, Inc., 2000—. Trustee U. Notre Dame, Loyola Marymount U., Mt. St. Mary's Coll., Harvard Westlake Sch., Childrens Hosp. L.A., Performing Arts Ctr. of Los Angeles County, L.A. Orthopaedic Hosp. Found. Served with U.S. Army, 1961-63. Mem. Assn. Investment Mgmt. Sales Execs., Internat. Fedn. Employee Benefit Plans, Investment Counsel Assn. Am., Calif. Club, Jonathan Club, Wilshire Country Club, Bel Air Bay Club, Regency Club, L.A., Tennis Club, Olympic Club, N.Y. Athletic Club, Westchester Country Club, L.A. Country Club. Republican. Roman Catholic. Office: TCW Group 865 S Figueroa St Ste 1800 Los Angeles CA 90017-2593

LARKIN, WILLIAM VINCENT, JR. company executive; b. N.Y.C., July 19, 1953; s. William Vincent and Gloria Ann (Stone) L.; m. Margaret Catherine Gunn, Nov. 12, 1988; children: William Vincent III, Jeremy Stone. AB cum laude, Harvard U., 1976; MBA, Yale U., 1980. Intern White House, 1975; staff acct. Price Waterhouse & Co., N.Y.C., 1976-78; mktg. asst. AMF Ben Hogan Co., Ft. Worth, 1980-81; asst. to pres. AMF Biol. & Diagnostic Co., Seguin, 1981-82; mktg. mgr. AMF Tuboscope, Houston, 1982-83, mgr. mill divsn., 1983-84; v.p. Tuboscope Inc., 1984-91; pres., COO Tuboscope Vetco Internat., 1991-93, pres., CEO, 1993-96; pres., COO Galtney Group, Inc., 1996-98; pres., CEO Travis Internat., Inc., 1999—2002. Bd. dirs. Family Svc. Ctr., Houston chpt. Am. Diabetes Assn., Arthritis Found.-Western Region. Mem. Young Pres.'s Orgn. (chpt. vice-chmn.), Yale Sch. Mgmt. Alumni Assn. (chmn. nominating com. 1980-82), A.D. Club (Cambridge, Mass.), Harvard Club (N.Y.C.), Yale Club (Houston). Republican. Episcopalian. Avocations: woodworking, golf, tennis. Home: 369 Piney Point Rd Houston TX 77024

LARNER, DANIEL M. theater educator, playwright, author; b. Olean, N.Y., Apr. 15, 1939; s. Martin L. and Clara Bronstein) L.; m. Margaret Dreher, Mar. 22, 1964 (div. May 1991); children: Eve Larner Bohn, Benjamin; m. Pandora Michael, Mar. 21, 1992; children: Richard Parkes, Elizabeth Parkes. AB in History and Sci., Harvard U., 1960; MS in History of sci., U. Wis., 1962, PhD in Speech in Theatre, 1968. Tutor St. John's Coll., Annapolis, Md., 1962-65; asst./assoc. prof. English, Speech, Theatre Western Wash. U., Bellingham, 1968-81, prof. theatre, 1981—, acting chmn. dept. theatre, 1980-81, dir. grad. study in theatre, 1976-82, founding dir. new playwrights theater, 1973-82, dean Fairhaven Coll., 1982-89. Cons. R.F. McCann & Co., Theatre Architects, Seattle, 1983. Author: (plays) The Death of Christopher Marlowe, 1973, War Dance, 1978; contbr. numerous articles to profl. jours.; assoc. editor Religion and Theatre, 1980. Chmn. facilities/bldg. com. Mt. Baker Theatre Ctr., Bellingham, 1984-91, 98—, bd. dirs., 1984-94, 98—; bd. dirs. ACLU of Wash., Seattle, 1969-80, 89—. Recipient Mayor's Arts award City of

Bellingham, 1987; numerous grants Nat. Endowment for the Arts, Wash. Arts Commn., Matsushita Found., Wash. Ctr. for Improvement of Undergrad. Edn., Western Wash. U., others. Mem. MLA, Assn. for Theatre in Higher Edn., Dramatists Guild (assocs.), Am. Soc. for Theatre Rsch., Popular Culture Assn. (nat. theatre area chmn. 1980-83), Theatre Comms. Group, Eugene O-Neill Soc. (bd. dirs. 1998—), Deutsche Shakespeare Gesellschaft, Wash. Athletic Club. Office: Western Washington Univ Fairhaven Coll MS-9118 Bellingham WA 98225-9118 E-mail: larner@cc.wwu.edu.

LARO, DAVID, judge; b. Flint, Mich., Mar. 3, 1942; s. Samuel and Florence (Chereton) L.; m. Nancy Lynn Wolf, June 18, 1967; children: Rachel Lynn, Marlene Ellen. BA, U. Mich., 1964; JD, U. Ill., 1967; LLM, NYU, 1970 Bar: Mich. 1968, U.S. Dist. Ct. (ea. dist.) Mich. 1968, U.S. Tax Ct. 1971. Ptnr. Winegarden Booth Shedd and Laro, Flint, Mich., 1970-75; sr. ptnr. Laro and Borgerson, 1975-86; prin. David Laro, P.C., 1986-92; apptd. judge U.S. Tax Ct., Washington, 1992—. Of counsel Dykema Gossett, Ann Arbor, Mich., 1989-90; pres., CEO, Durakon Industries, Inc., Ann Arbor, 1989-91, chmn., Lapeer, Mich., 1991—; chmn. Republic Bank, 1986—, vice chmn. Republic Bancorp, Inc., Flint, 1986—; instr. Nat. Inst. Trial Advocacy, vis. prof. U. San Diego Law Sch., adj. prof. law Georgetown Law Sch., 1994—; cons. lectr. on tax reform and litigation in Moscow Harvard U., 1997, Ga. State U., 1998. Regent U. Mich., Ann Arbor, 1975-81; mem. Mich. State Bd. Edn., 1982-83; chmn. Mich. State Tenure Commn., 1972-75; commr. Civil Svc. Commn., Flint, 1984—. Mem. Am. Coll. Tax Counsel, State Bar Mich., Phi Delta Phi. Republican. Office: US Tax Ct 400 2nd St NW Rm 217 Washington DC 20217-0002

LA ROCCA, ISABELLA, artist, educator; b. El Paso, Apr. 14, 1960; d. Remo and Alicia Estela (Gonzalez) La R. BA, U. Pa., 1984; MFA, Ind. U., 1993. Freelance photographer, N.Y.C., 1986-90; assoc. instr. Ind. U., Bloomington, 1991-93; instr. Herron Sch. Art, Indpls., 1992; vis. asst. prof. Ind. U., 1994—; asst. prof. DePauw U., Greencastle, Omd/. 1994-95; vis. asst. prof. Bloomsburg (Pa.) U., 1995-96; freelance photographer, designer, animator San Francisco, 1996—. Instr. art Vista C.C., 1998—, Coll. of Marin, 1999—2000, Calif. State U., Hayward, 1999—2001, City Coll. San Francisco, 2000—. One-woman shows include Haas Gallery, Bloomsburg, Pa., 1996, Ctr. Photography Woodstock, N.Y., Moore Coll., Pa., 1994, Emison Art Ctr., Greencastle, Ind., 1996; exhibited in group shows at 494 Gallery, N.Y.C., 1993, Kala Art Inst., Berkeley, Calif., 2000. Ind. U. CIC Minority fellow, 1990-91; Jewish Found. Edn. Women scholar, 1990; recipient Friends Photography Ferguson award, 1993. Recipient Serpent Source Grant for Women Artists, 1998. E-mail: ilarocca@mac.com.

LAROCCA, PATRICIA DARLENE MCALEER, middle school mathematics educator; b. Aurora, Ill., July 12, 1951; d. Theodore Austin and Lorraine Mae (Robbins) McAleer; m. Edward Daniel LaRocca, June 28, 1975; children: Elizabeth S., Mark E. BS in Edn./Math., No. Ill. U., 1973, postgrad., 1975. Tchr. elem. sch. Roselle (Ill) Sch. Dist., 1973-80; instr. math. Coll. DuPage, Glen Ellyn, Ill., 1988-90; tchr. math. O'Neill Mid. Sch., Downers Grove, 1995—. Pvt. cons., math. tutor, Downers Grove, Ill., 1980-88, 90-95. Bd. dirs. PTA, Hillcrest Elem. Sch., Downers Grove; active Boy Scouts Am.; mem. 1st United Meth. Ch. Ill. teaching scholar, 1969. Methodist. Avocations: antiques, softball, organ, dance. Home and Office: 5648 Dunham Rd Downers Grove IL 60516-1246

LA ROCCA, RENATO VINCENZO, medical oncologist, clinical researcher; b. Cin., June 16, 1957; m. Margaret Carolyn Cauthron, Sept. 5, 1987; children: Alessandra, Marcello, Victoria, Chae, Marcio. MS, Liceo Sci. Statale, Turin, Italy, 1976; postgrad., U. Padua, Italy, 1976-80; MD, Cornell U., 1982. Diplomate Nat. Bd. Med. Examiners, Am. Bd. Internal Medicine, Am. Bd. Oncology. Resident in internal medicine N.Y. Hosp.-Cornell Med. Ctr., N.Y.C., 1982-85; med. oncology fellow medicine br. Nat. Cancer Inst., Bethesda, Md., 1985-88, sr. investigator medicine br., 1988-90; pvt. practice Kentuckiana Med. Oncology Assocs., PSC, Louisville, 1990-97; dir. Kentuckiana Cancer Inst. (KCI), 1997—. Assoc. Clin.(part-time faculty) U. Louisville Sch. Medicine, clin. assoc. prof. medicine U. Ky. Coll. Medicine; spkrs. bur. RPR Pharmaceuticals, Eli Lilly, Rita medial, guest rschr. med. br. Nat. Cancer Inst., NIH, Bethesda; mem. steering com. Ky. Cancer Pain Initiative; mem. adv. bd. Hospice Louisville; chmn. cancer com. Jewish Hosp., Louisville. Author: (chpts. in books) Molecular and Cellular Biology of Prostate Cancer, Molecular Foundations Oncology; contbr. articles to profl. jours.; patentee in field. Chairperson Louisville Lung Cancer Symposium, 2000. Recipient USPHS Commendation medal, 1990, Leadership award Am. Cancer Soc., 1995, Meml. award ACS-WHAS, 2001. Fellow ACP; mem. Am. Soc. Clin. Oncology, Am. Assn. Cancer Rsch., European Soc. Med. Oncology, Am. Cancer Soc. (v.p. Ky. divsn., Meml. award 2001), Am. Coll. Physician Inventors, Am. Pain Soc., Soc. Neuro-Oncology, Jefferson County Med. Soc., Ky. Oncology Soc., Ky. Med. Assn., Ind. Med. Assn., Alpha Omega Alpha. Avocations: sailing, computers, astronomy, skiing, political science. Office: Kentuckiana Cancer Institute PLLC 100 E Liberty St Ste 502 Louisville KY 40202-1427 E-mail: rvl@kuivs.com.

LAROCCO, ELIZABETH ANNE, management information systems professional; b. Bethpage, N.Y., Feb. 15, 1957; d. Alfred Joseph and Teresa Lucille (Scalzo) Bott. BBA, Hofstra U., 1979, MBA, 2000. Programmer Computerland, Westbury, N.Y., 1980-82; software cons., propr. E.A. LaRocco, Ronkonkoma, 1982-85; from bus. programmer to mgr. mgmt. info. sys. corp. applications NEC America, Inc., Melville, 1984-99; product cons. Computer Assocs. Internat., Inc., Islandia, NY, 2000—02; sr. applications engr. SSA Global Technologies, 2002—.

LAROCHE, GÉRARD LAURENT, adult education educator, writer; b. Cambridge, Mass., June 20, 1920; s. J. Arthur and Juliette Anne (Lajeunesse) LaRoche; m. Joyce Iris Cynthia Latchem, Oct. 18, 1947; children: Marianne Aimée, Jerôme Augustin, David Gerard. BA, Boston Coll., 1942, MA, 1943, Harvard U., 1947, postgrad, 1950. Instr. French Tufts U., Medford, Mass., 1948—51; rsch. analytic specialist, translator, br. chief, lectr. linquistics Nat. Security Agy., Ft. Meade, Md., 1952—79; ret., 1979. Asst. professorial lectr. George Washington U., Washington, 1962—65; rsch. assoc. Cath. U. Am., Washington, 1966—74; lectr. linguistics Grad. Sch., Dept. Agr., Washington, 1974—76; guest lectr. music history U. Md., College Park, 1967; lectr. calligraphy Montpelier Cultural Arts Ctr., Laurel, Md., 1997—2000; lectr. music/arch. various high schs., 1967—75. Author: (book) The Memoirs of Gérard LaRoche, 1995; drawings. Choir dir. St. Ambrose Ch., Cheverly, Md., 1964—89. Sgt. U.S. Army, 1943—45. Named Hon. Citizen, Bourginestre and Coun., Ohey and Hasselt, Belgium, 1985; grantee O'Malley Tchg. fellow, Boston Coll., 1942—43. Republican. Roman Catholic. Avocations: violin, photography, historical restoration, cabinet and model making, sound recording. Home: 2426 Lake Ave Cheverly MD 20785

LAROCHE, JANE LAWTON, emergency physician; b. Camden, S.C., Jan. 24, 1948; d. Ripon Wilson and Florence Alexander (Savage) LaRoche. BA, Winthrop U., 1969, BS, 1970; MD, Med. U. S.C., 1975. Cert. internal medicine and geriat. Am. Bd. Internal Medicine, diplomate Am. Bd. Emergency Medicine. Intern then resident Tulane Hosp., New Orleans, 1975-78; emergency rm. physician St. Eugene Hosp., Dillon, S.C., 1978-80; pvt. practice internal medicine Kershaw County Meml. Hosp., Camden, 1980-85; staff physician acute care Byrnes Med. Ctr. Dept. Mental Health, Columbia, S.C., 1985-86; staff physician acute care, mem. decubitis team C.M. Tucker Human Resources-Dowdy Gardner, 1986-94; urgent care physician Doctor's Care, 1992-94; emergency room staff physician PEEDEE Emergency Med. Marlboro Park Hosp. Assn., Bennettsville, S.C., 1995—; physician MDA, 1999—. Clin. asst. prof. geriat. medicine U. S.C. Sch. Medicine, 1990—94; student advisor to faculty U. S.C., Charleston, 1974. Flutist Camden Cmty. Concert Band, 1980—, Camden Cmty. Theater, 1985—, 1st Bapt. Ch. Orch., Camden, 1996—99; mem. ann. loyalty fund com. Winthrop U., 1998—. Fellow: ACP; mem.: Am. Assn. Physicians and Surgeons (bd. cert.), Am. Soc. Internal Medicine, Am. Geriat. Soc. Republican. Episcopalian. Avocation: Avocations: playing flute, flowers.

LAROCHE, LINDA, writer; b. Pasadena, Calif., Oct. 19, 1954; d. Octavio Martinez, Benilde Castro. BA Sociology, Calif. State U. L.A., 1982. Set decorator CBS-TV, L.A., 1988—91; proofreader KFW Bank, Berlin, 1991—93; prodr., writer Paris Prodns., N.Y.C., 1994—97; journalist The Write Words, Pasadena, Calif., 1997—2000; columnist San Gabriel Valley Tribune, West Corina, 2000—. Bd. dirs. Hispanic Women's Coun., L.A., 1985—86. Nominee Children's Fantasy screenplay, Nicholl Found., 1997; recipient Silver Star award, 1990; grantee Media grant, L.A. City Cultural Affairs, 1989, Multi-Cultural grant, Calif. Commn. of Arts, 1989, AFI ind. filmmaker grant, Nat. Endowment Arts, 1989. Mem.: L.A. Opera (spkr.'s bur. 2001—). Jewish.

LAROCHE, ROGER RENAN, psychiatrist; b. St. Paul, July 12, 1960; s. Gerard Auguste and Carolyn Mae (Seese) L.; m. Elizabeth Ann Tollerud, June 25, 1988; children: Austin, Hope, Cordon. BA, Bethel Coll., St. Paul, 1982; MD, U. Minn., 1987. Diplomate Nat. Bd. Med. Examiners, Am. Bd. Psychiatry and Neurology, Am. Soc. Addiction Medicine, Geriatric Psychiatry, Addiction Psychiatry. Med. intern Hennepin County Med. Ctr., Mpls., 1987-88; resident dept. psychiatry Mayo Clinic Grad. Sch. Medicine, Rochester, Minn., 1988-91, fellowship addiction medicine dept. psychiatry, 1991-92; med. dir. dept. psychiatry Bradford (Pa.) Regional Med. Ctr., 1992—; med. dir. Cattaraugus County Coun. on Alcoholism and Substance Abuse, 1995—. Psychiat. cons. Beacon Light Behavioral Health Sys. for Children and Adolescents, 1998—; forensic psychiatrist cons. McKeon County Fed. Corrections Inst., 2000—; rotating med. student educator Mayo Med. Sch., 1987-92; contract forensic psychiatrist U.S. Bur. Prisons, Fed. Med. Ctr., Rochester, 19890-91; prin. investigator for carbamazepine in smoking cessation Mayo Clinic, Rochester, 1991-92, psychiatric rsch. com. cons., 1991-92; pvt. and consulting psychiatrist, Bradford, Pa., 1992—; staff sec.-treas. Bradford Regional Med. Ctr., 1995—, med. staff v.p., 1996, pres. med. staff, 1997-98, chmn. credentials com., 2001—; chmn. Bradford Nursing Pavillion's Utilization Reviews Com., 1999-, vice chairperson bd. of the Twin Tiers Pregnancy Care Ctr., 2002-. Contbr. articles to profl. jours. County del. Rep. Party Conv., Rochester, 1990; bd. dirs. Twin Tiers Pregnancy Care Ctr. Recipient Medtronic Corp.'s Med. Fellow scholarship of excellence in leadership and acads., 1983, Acad. Writing Excellence award Mayo Clinic, 1991; Mayo Clinic Grad. Sch. Medicine grantee, 1991-92. Mem. AMA (resident physician sect. nat. del. 1990, 91), Am. Psychiat. Assn., Am. Soc. Addiction Medicine, Minn. Med. Assn. (del. ho. of dels. 1990, 91, resident physician sect. state governing officer 1990, 91), Pa. Med. Assn., Pa. Psychiat. Soc., Pa. Soc. Addiction Medicine, McKean County Med. Soc. Avocations: violist, vocal soloist, oil painting, weight training, distance biking. Home: 46 Stone Ave Bradford PA 16701-1050 Office: Med Arts Bldg 199 Pleasant St Bradford PA 16701-1098

LAROCHELLE, RICHARD C. tanning company executive; b. Lewiston, Maine, July 21, 1945; s. Paul H. and Jeannette D. (Jean) L.; children: Anne Marie, Paul, Christine, Marc, Peter. BA, U. Maine, 1971; MBA, Northea. U., 1976. Cert. mgmt. acct. V.p., treas. Nat. Tanning and Trading Corp., Peabody, 1976-79; exec. v.p. Hermann Loewenstein Inc., Johnstown, N.Y., 1980-82; pres. Irving Tanning Co., Hartland, Maine, 1982—, CEO, 1992—. Bd. dirs. Hussey Seating Corp. Com. chmn. Boy Scouts Am., Johnstown, 1981-82; trustee YMCA, Johnstown, 1982; treas. Boys/Girls Club, Waterville, Maine, 1985; co-chmn. Maine Govs. Internat. Adv. Bd., 1995-97; bd. dirs. Mid-State Econ. Devel. Corp., 1995-98, Maine Internat. Trade tr.; chmn. Colby Leadership Inst.; mem. bd. advisors U. Maine Sch. Bus., 1995—. With USN, 1965-69. Mem. Leather Industries Am. (chmn. bd. dirs. 1984-86, mem. exec. com. 1982—), Footwear Industries Am. (bd. dirs. 1996—, exec. com. 1998—, vice chair 2000--). Avocations: personal investing, person computing. Home and Office: PO Box 369 Hartland ME 04943-0369 E-mail: dickl5@aol.com.

LAROCK, BRUCE EDWARD, civil engineering educator; b. Berkeley, Calif., Dec. 24, 1940; s. Ralph W. and Hazel M. L.; m. Susan E. Gardner, June 17, 1968; children: Lynne M., Jean E. BS in Civil Engring., Stanford U., 1962, MS in Civil Engring., 1963, PhD, 1966. Registered profl. engr., Calif. Asst. prof. U. Calif., Davis, 1966-72, assoc. prof., 1972-79, prof., 1979—. Sr. vis. fellow U. Wales, Swansea, 1972-73; U.S. sr. scientist Tech. U., Aachen, Germany, 1986-87. Author: (with D. Newnan) Engineer-in-Training Examination Review, 3d edit., 1991, (with R. Jeppson and G. Watters) Hydraulics of Pipeline Systems, 1999; contbr. over 80 tech. articles to profl. jours. Mem. ASCE, Sigma Xi, Tau Beta Pi. Lutheran. Avocation: duplicate bridge. E-mail: ucdavis.edu. Office: Dept Civil Environ Engring U Calif Davis CA 95616-5294

LAROCK, TERRANCE EDMOND, health facility administrator; b. Detroit, Aug. 29, 1952; s. Wendell and Donna Jean (Elliott) LaR.; m. Bonnie Jo Campbell, July 21, 1979; 1 child, Andrew Thomas. A.A., Ohlone Jr. Coll., 1972; postgrad. Calif. State U.-Hawyard, 1976, U. N.Y., 1984; B. Polit. Sci., San Jose State U., 1974. Project planner Gould Inc., Santa Clara, Calif., 1977-79; materials mgr. Stanford Assocs., Menlo Park, Calif., 1979, Delta Assocs., Milpitas, Calif., 1979-81, Masstor Systems, Sunnyvale, Calif., 1981-84; purchasing/planning mgr. Fairchild ATS, San Jose, Calif., 1984—; v.p. ops. REDIFAB, San Jose, 1984-86, v.p. USA ops. Prodstar America, 1986-89, San Jose Med. Ctr., 1990—; group v.p. purchasing Berlex Labs, Inc., Richmond, Calif., 1994—; mgr. Tandy Corp., San Jose, 1976-78; city mgr. Thrifty Rent-A-Car, San Francisco, 1975-76, Softbank Expos, 1996—. Author: Manufacturing Terms and Definition, 1978. Recipient Region 7 & 10 Excellent award, Am. Prodn. & Inventory Control, 1983, Edn. award, 1980, Membership award, 1979. Mem. Am. Prodn. and Inventory Control Soc. (region 10 edn., pres. 1980-81, v.p. bd. dirs. 1986-88), Purchasing Mgmt. Assn. Republican. Lutheran.

LA ROCQUE, EUGENE PHILIPPE, bishop; b. Windsor, Ont., Can., Mar. 27, 1927; s. Eugene Joseph and Angeline Marie (Monforton) LaR. BA, U. Western Ont., 1948; MA, Laval U., 1956. Ordained priest Roman Catholic Ch., 1952, consecrated bishop, 1974; asst. parish priest Ste. Therese Ch., Windsor, 1952-54; registrar, then dean men, lectr. Christ The King Coll., U. Western Ont., 1956-64; asst. spiritual dir. St. Peter's Sem., 1964-65; prin., dean King's Coll., 1965-68; pastor St. Joseph's Ch., Rivière-aux-Canards, Ont., 1968-70, Ste. Anne's Ch., Tecumseh, 1970-74; bishop of Alexandria-Cornwall, Ont., 1974—. Dean Essex County, 1970-73; trustee Essex County Roman Cath. Separate Sch. Bd., 1972-74; 1st chmn. liaison com. Can. Jewish Congress Can. Coun. Chs. and Can. Cath. Conf. Bishops, 1977-84, mem. pro-life com., 1992-94; pres. Ont. Conf. Cath. Bishops, 1992-96; pres. Fedn. Couns. Priests of Can., 1973-74. Mem. KC (3d degree, chaplain Ont. 1977-87). Address: 222 Montreal Rd Box 1388 Cornwall ON Canada K6H 5V4 *Belief in God, who creates my unique human life and has a loving plan and concern for each of his children, sustains me amidst the strains, challenges and turmoils of life.*

LAROCQUE, LINDA LOU, interior designer, educator, playwright; b. Lake Odessa, Mich., May 10, 1944; d. Emory Eugene and Lillian Martha Blakslee; m. Robert Bonte, Feb. 29, 1980 (div. May 15, 1989); children: Timothy. Interior design educator Kalamazoo Valley Coll., Kalamazoo, 1973—77; interior designer Jacobson Store Home, 1974—76; owner, operator Linda LaRocque Interiors, 1976—99; interior design educator Civic and Art Groups throughout Mich. and Fla., 1973—. Author: (play) Aint Tina Turner Classical Music (Second Pl., 1998), Revival at Possum Creek Community Church (Second Pl., 2000), Joyce's Choices (First Pl., 2000). Active Ministry Cmty., Kalamazoo, 1991—97. Mich. Maritime Mus., South Haven, 1994—99. Recipient Writer of the Yr., Am. Christian Writers Assn., 1997, Second Pl. Prodn., Mich. Play Festival, 1997, Third Pl. Prodn., 2001. Mem.: South Haven Ctr. Arts, Douglas Writers Club, Cmty. Theatre Assn. Mich., Scott Club Writers Group. R-Conservative. Roman Catholic. Avocations: rehabilitating distressed real estate, rehabilitating distressed real estate, rehabilitating distressed real estate, rehabilitating distressed real estate, theatre. Home: 118 Superior Street South Haven MI 49090

LA ROSA, FRANCISCO GUILLERMO, pathologist, researcher, educator; b. Lima, Peru, Jan. 17, 1949; came to U.S., 1981; s. Anibal and Carmen (de la Pascua) La R.; m. Clara Ann Dufficy, May 21, 1989; children: David, Anamaria, Joseph. MD, U. Nacional Federico Villarreal, Lima, 1975. cert. (AP/CP), 1995. Instr. U. Nacional Federico Villarreal, Lima, 1973-79, asst. prof., 1979-81; resident in clin. pathology U. de San Marcos, 1977-79; postdoctoral fellow in immunology U. Colo., Denver, 1981-85, instr., 1985-87, asst. prof., 1987-94, resident in pathology, 1992-95, fellow in lung pathology, 1995-96; lab. dir. Miners Colfax Med. Ctr., Raton, N.Mex., 1996—2000; clin. asst. prof. dept path., immunology U. Colo. Health Sci. Ctr., 1996—. Pathologist Sterling Regional Med. Ctr., 1996-2000, Longmont (Colo.) United Hosp., 2002—; pres. Pathology Cons., PC, 1995—, Telepathology Cons., PC, 1996—; cons. Ortho Pharm., Lima, 1979-81, Reaads Med. Products, Inc., Denver, 1991. Contbr. chpts. to books, revs. and articles to profl. jours. Krock Found. fellow, 1985-86, Juvenile Diabetes Found. fellow, 1985-86; NIH grantee, 1988-91; recipient Enrique Leon Garcia Best MD Thesis award Peruvian Pediat. Soc., Lima, 1975, award Diabetes Rsch. and Edn. Found., 1987-88. Mem. AMA, The Transplantation Soc., Soc. Española Immunologia, Am. Assn. Immunologists, Coll. Am. Pathologists, Am. Soc. Clin. Pathologists, Peruvian Soc. Clin. Pathology, Peruvian Soc. Immunology and Allergy, Colo Med. Soc., N.Mex. Med. Soc. Roman Catholic. Avocations: photography, videotaping, stained glass, telepathology. Home: 2663 S Nelson Ct Lakewood CO 80227-2767 Office: Univ of Colo HSC 4200 E 9th Ave # C321 Denver CO 80220-3706 Fax: 413-910-4489. E-mail: LAROSA@TELEPATHOLOGY.com.

LAROSA, JULIUS, engineering company official; b. Jacksonville, Fla., Aug. 11, 1956; s. John Wesley and Mandy (McKinnon) LaR.; m. Elnora Elizabeth Bradford, July 26, 1980; children: Jason Christopher, Steven Andrew, Kristie Renee. Student, Lincoln (Pa.) U., 1976-79. Salesman Kaufmann's Dept. Store, Monroeville, Pa., 1980-81, 83-87; commn. salesman Montgomery Ward Dept. Store, 1981-82; mgr. reprodn. dept. Salvucci Engrs., Inc., Pitts., 1981-87; supr. adminstrv. svcs., mgr. reprodn. dept., supr. document control Eichleay Engrs. Inc., 1987-2000; prodn. mgr. Tri-State Reprographics, 2000—. Printing cons. NAACP, Monroeville, 1986-88. Mem. In-Plant Mgrs. Assn. Democrat. Baptist. Avocations: art, carving, basketball, badminton, camping. Office: Tri-State Reprographics 907 Penn Ave Pittsburgh PA 15222 E-mail: tristate@stargate.net.

LAROSE, KEITH VERNON, lawyer; b. Jacksonville, N.C., Apr. 11, 1953; s. Barton I. and Helen (Zuckor) LaR.; m. Shelley Ann Garbut, Dec. 10, 1978; children: Stephanie Paula, Michael Scott. BS in Journalism, Northwestern U., 1975; JD magna cum laude, Syracuse U., 1978. Bar: N.Y. 1979, U.S. Dist. Ct. (so. and ea. dist.) N.Y. 1979. Legal cons. Fred C. Hart Assocs., N.Y.C., 1978-80; ptnr. Moran, Spiegel, Pergament & Brown, Poughkeepsie, N.Y., 1980-88, Petito and LaRose, Poughkeepsie, 1989-95, LaRose & LaRose, Poughkeepsie, 1996—. Fellow Assn. Trial Lawyers Am.; mem. N.Y. State Trial Lawyers Assn., N.Y. State Bar Assn., Dutchess County Bar Assn. (membership chmn. 1985-86). Avocations: tennis, sailing, skiing. Office: LaRose and LaRose 12 Raymond Ave Poughkeepsie NY 12603-2354

LAROSE, LAWRENCE ALFRED, lawyer; b. Lowell, Mass., Oct. 26, 1958; s. Alfred M. and Rita B. (Plunkett) L.; m. Janet G. Yedwab, Aug. 12, 1984. BA summa cum laude, Tufts U., 1980; JD magna cum laude, Georgetown U., 1983. Bar: N.Y. 1984. Assoc. Sullivan & Cromwell, N.Y.C., 1983-85, 87-90, Melbourne, Australia, 1985-87, Cadwalader, Wickersham & Taft, N.Y.C., 1990-92, ptnr., 1993-2001, King & Spalding, N.Y.C., 2001—. Vis. fellow Faculty of Law, U. Melbourne, 1986-87. Co-author: Public Companies, 2002; contbr. articles to profl. publs. Mem. ABA, N.Y. State Bar Assn., N.Y. County Lawyers Assn., Assn. Bar City N.Y., Am. Soc. Internat. Law, Georgetown U. Nat. Law Alumni Bd. (exec. com., sec.), Down Town Assn. in City of N.Y., Phi Beta Kappa. Avocations: art collecting, art history. Office: King & Spalding 1185 Ave of the Americas New York NY 10036-4003

LAROSE, ROGER, former pharmaceutical company executive, former university administrator; b. Montreal, Que., Can., July 28, 1910; s. Alfred Fervac and Anna (Contant) L.; m. Rita Dagenais, Aug. 10, 1936 (dec. Oct. 1960); 1 child, Louise Larose Cuddihy; m. Julienne Begin, Aug. 3, 1961. BA, U. Montreal, 1929, B.Sc. in Pharmacy, 1932; Licentiate in Social, Polit., and Econ. Scis, 1934. Asst. prof. pharmacy U. Montreal, 1934; dean Faculty Pharmacy, 1960-65, vice rector, 1969-79; with Ciba Co. Ltd., Montreal, 1936-71, v.p., 1958-68, pres., 1968-71, dir., 1958-71; pres. Ciba-Geigy Can. Ltd., 1971-73, dep. chmn. bd., 1973-78, chmn. bd., 1978-82. Vice chmn. bd., mem. exec. com. Bank Canadian Nat., 1969-80; mem. Sci. Council Can., 1966-71; pres. com. Sci. Council on Health Scis., 1969-73. Bd. dirs. Institut recherches cliniques de Montreal, 1968-95, pres. of found. 1995-96; bd. dirs. Hotel-Dieu de Montreal, 1969-79; pres. Hopital St. -Luc de Montreal, 1978-88; bd. govs. Can. Bankers Inst., 1973-80; pres. Montreal Symphony Orch., 1978-79, pres. and mng. dir., 1979-81; pres. Chamber Orch. I Musici de Montreal, 1984-88; bd. dirs. Que. Hosp. Assn. Decorated officer Order Can., 1973. Mem. Acad. Pharmacy (France) (hon.), Pharm. Soc. Gt. Britain (hon.), Can. Hosp. Assn. (bd. dirs. 1985-89, George Findlay Stephen award 1990), St.-Denis Club (Montreal). Roman Catholic. Home: 404-205 Côte Ste Catherine Rd Outremont QC Canada H2V 2A9

LA ROSSA, JAMES M(ICHAEL), lawyer; b. Bklyn., Dec. 4, 1931; s. James Vincent and Marie Antoinette (Tronolone) La R.; m. Dominique Bazin-Thall, Aug. 11, 1998; children: James M., Thomas, Nancy, Susan. BS, Fordham U., 1953, JD, 1958. Bar: N.Y. 1958, U.S. Dist. Ct. N.Y. 1961, U.S. Supreme Ct. 1969. Pvt. practice law, N.Y.C., 1958-62, 67-74, 76—; asst. U.S. atty. Eastern Dist. N.Y., Bklyn., 1962-65; ptnr. firm Lefkowitz & Brownstien, N.Y.C., 1965-67, La Rossa, Shargel & Fishetti, N.Y.C., 1974-76, La Rossa, Brownstein & Mitchell, N.Y.C., 1980-82, La Rossa, Axenfeld & Mitchell, N.Y.C., 1982-84, La Rossa, Cooper, Axenfeld, Mitchell & Bergman, N.Y.C., 1984-85, 86-98; now ptnr. Larossa & Ross; participant Debate on Legal Ethics Criminal Cts. Bar Assn. Queens County, N.Y., 1978. Criminal Trial Advocacy Workshop, Harvard U. Law Sch., 1978; ptnr. LaRossa, Mitchell & Ross, 1986—98, LaRossa & Ross, 1998—2001; owner Law Offices of James M. LaRossa, 2001—. Author: White Collar Crimes: Defense Strategies, 1977, Federal Rules of Evidence in Criminal Matters, 1977, White Collar Crimes, 1978. Served to 1st lt. USMC, 1953-55. Recipient Guardian of Freedom award B'nai B'rith, 1979, Career Achievement awardN.Y. Coun. Def. Lawyers, 1996; Ann. honoree N.Y. Criminal Bar Assn., 1999. Mem. ABA, N.Y. State Bar Assn. (Criminal Law Practitioner of Yr. 1990), Fed. Bar Counsel, Assn. Bar City N.Y. Office: LaRossa 1790 Broadway Ste 1501 New York NY 10019-1412

LAROUNIS, GEORGE PHILIP, manufacturing company executive; b. Bklyn., Mar. 19, 1928; s. Philip John and Helen (Cormentelou) L.; m. Mary G. Efthymiatou, Jan. 13, 1958; 1 child, Daphne H. B.E.E., U. Mich., 1950, postgrad. in Law; JD, N.Y. U., 1954. Electronics engr. in research and devel. Columbia U. Electronics Research Lab., 1952-54; assoc. firm Pennie, Edmonds, Morton, Barrows & Taylor, N.Y.C., 1954-58; fgn. patent atty. Western Electric Co., 1958-60; asst. dir. Bendix Internat., Paris, 1960, dir. licensing and indsl. property rights, to 1974; v.p. staff ops. Bendix Europe, 1974-77; v.p. Bendix Internat. Fin. Corp.; v.p. Europe, Middle East and Africa Bendix Corp., Paris, 1977-82; pres. Bendix Internat. Cons. Corp., 1974-86; v.p., group exec. Allied Automotive, 1982-85; pres. Allied-Signal Fibers Europe S.A.; v.p. Allied-Signal Internat., 1985-93. Bd. dirs. Hellenic Link, Inc., CopyTele, Inc., Delphi Soc., Am. Farm Sch., Greece. With U.S. Army, 1946-47. Decorated chevalier Legion of Honor (France). Mem. N.Y. Patent Bar Assn., Fed. Patent Bar Assn., Licensing Execs. Soc., Am. C. of C. in France and Greece (dir., pres., exec. com. European Coun.), Polo Club de Paris, Papagou Tennis Club (Athens), Tau Beta Pi, Eta Kappa Nu. Home: 15-17 A Tsoha St Athens 11521 Greece E-mail: mglar@compulink.gr.

LAROUSSI, MOUNIR, electrical engineer; b. Sfax, Tunisia, Aug. 9, 1955; came to U.S., 1981; s. Habib and Manana (Jeloul) L.; m. Nicole Christine Mache, Aug. 28, 1986; children: Alexander Habib, Alyssa Jehan, Zackary Max. BS in Elec. Engring., Tech. Faculty Sfax, 1979; MS in Elec. Engring., Nat. Sch. Radio and Elec., Bordeaux, France, 1981; PhD in Elec. and Computer Engring., U. Tenn., 1988. Grad. teaching asst. dept. elec. and computer engring. U. Tenn., Knoxville, 1983-85, rsch. asst. plasma sci. lab., 1984-88; asst. prof. Nat. Sch. Engring., Sfax, 1988-89; assoc. prof. Faculty Scis., 1989-90; rsch. assoc. Plasma Sci. Lab. U. Tenn., Knoxville, 1990-94, rsch. asst. prof., 1995-98; rsch. assoc. prof. Old Dominion U. Applied Rsch. Ctr., Newport News, Va., 1998—. Assoc. editor Physics Essays; contbr. articles to profl. jours. Recipient award Air Force Office Sci. Rsch., Washington, 1991, Advanced Tech. award Inventors Clubs of Am., 1996. Mem. IEEE (sr. mem., Millenium Gold medal 2000), IEEE Nuclear and Plasma Scis. Soc., Sigma Xi (rsch. award 1987). Achievements include contbns. and inventions in the fields of plasma heating, microwave-plasma interactions, atmospheric pressure plasmas and their industrial applications, and plasma cloaking. Office: Old Dominion Univ Applied Rsch Ctr Newport News VA 23606 E-mail: laroussi@jlab.org.

LARPENTEUR, JAMES ALBERT, JR. lawyer; b. Seattle, Aug. 6, 1935; s. James Albert and Mary Louise (Coffey) L.; m. Hazel Marie Arntson, Apr. 23, 1965 (div. 1983); children: Eric James, Jason Clifford; 1 adopted child, Brenda Mon Fong; m. Katherine Annette Bingham, Nov. 8, 1986. BS in Bus., U. Oreg., 1957, LLB, 1961. Bar: Oreg. 1961, U.S. Dist. Ct. Oreg. 1961, U.S. Tax Ct. 1962, U.S. Ct. Appeals (9th cir.) 1962, U.S. Supreme Ct. 1965. Assoc. Schwabe Williamson & Wyatt, Portland, Oreg., 1961-69, ptnr., 1969-82, sr. ptnr., 1982—, mem. exec. com., 1989-92. Dir. exec. com. Portland Rose Festival Assn., 1975—, pres., 1987; ex-officio dir. Portland Visitors Assn., 1981—; bd. dirs., mem. exec. com. Providence Child Ctr. Found., 1983-94, chmn. exec. com., 1986-87; bd. dirs. Willamette Light Brigade, 1987—, Cath. Charities Portland, 1989-92; bd. dirs. Albertina Kerr Ctrs., 1996—, Japanese Garden Soc., 2000—. Mem. Oreg. Bar Assn. (editor, writer, speaker numerous continuing legal edn. programs, chmn. bus. law sect. 1986-87, real estate, estate planning, securities regulation sects.), Multnomah Athletic Club (pres. 1984), Univ. Club of Portland, Waverley Country Club, Astoria Golf and Country Club, City Club of Portland, Thunderbird Country Club of Rancho Mirage. Avocation: golf. Office: Schwabe Williamson & Wyatt 1211 SW 5th Ave Ste 1800 Portland OR 97204-3713 E-mail: jlarpenteur@schwabe.com.

LARR, PETER, retired banker; b. Indpls., Jan. 17, 1939; s. David and Marjorie Kathleen (Hearne) L.; m. Rosamond Holmes Woodfield, July 7, 1962; children— Alexia Aisha, Diana Kirsten, David Hearne BA, Princeton U., 1960. Asst. mgr. London and Beirut brs. Chase Manhattan Bank, 1961-67, v.p., div. exec. land transp., 1976-78, v.p., group exec. credit tng. and devel., 1978-80, v.p., div. exec. commodity fin., 1980-83; sr. v.p., bus. exec. nat. corr. banking Chase Manhattan Bank, N.Y.C., 1983-85, sr. v.p., exec. domestic instl. banking, 1985-90, sr. v.p., risk asset rev. exec., 1990-97, sr. v.p. sr. credit and porfolio mgmt. exec. Asia, 1997—; mgr. dir. group credit officer Global Bank, 1997-2000; ret., 2000—. Assoc. vestry Christ Ch., Rye, N.Y., 1983-85; planning commr., City of Rye, 1992-94, 97—. Mem. Assn. Res. City Bankers (assoc., bank pay sys. com. 1984-90), Am. Bankers Assn. (chmn. corp. banking divsn. 1988-94), Robert Morris Assn. N.Y. (pres. 1994), Am. Yacht Club, Apawamis Club. Avocations: tennis, golf, geneaological rsch.

LARRABEE, BARBARA PRINCELAU, retired intelligence officer; b. Oakland, Calif., Sept. 21, 1923; d. Paul and Mary Emilie (Rueger) Princelau; m. John Joseph Boyle, Oct. 21, 1950 (dec.); m. Donald Richard Larrabee, Nov. 2, 1996. BA, U. Calif., Berkeley, 1948. Intelligence officer CIA, Langley, Va., 1954-82. Bd. dirs. The Thift Shop, Washington, 1988-92; mem. Women's Bd. Columbia Hosp. for Women, Washington, 1986-2001, mem. exec. com., 1989-91, 96-98; mem. com. Washington Antiques Show, 1989—; active Rep. Womens Fed. Forum, Washington, League of Rep. Women of D.C., Inc. Recipient Cert. of Distinction CIA, 1982. Mem.: Assn. Former Intelligence Officers (bd. dirs. 1993—99, v.p. 1997—99, exec. com. 1997—99), Ctrl. Intelligence Retiree Assn., Evergreen Garden Club (v.p. 2001—02), Sulgrave Club, Nat. Press Club, U. Calif. Berkeley Alumni Club of Washington (rec. sec. 1976—77, v.p. 1984—86), Sigma Kappa (v.p. No. Va. alumnae 1992—95, devel. com. Sigma Kappa Found., Inc. 1993—95). Episcopalian. Avocations: aerobics, needlework, travel. Home: 4956 Sentinel Dr Apt 304 Bethesda MD 20816-3562

LARRABEE, DONALD RICHARD, publishing company executive; b. Portland, Maine, Aug. 8, 1923; s. Henry Carpenter and Marion (Clapp) L.; m. Mary Elizabeth Rolfs, Oct. 9, 1948 (dec. Feb. 1996); children: Donna Louise (Mrs. John Palmer), Robert Rolfs; m. Barbara Princelau Boyle, Nov. 2, 1996. Student, Syracuse U., 1941-43. Reporter Portland Press Herald, 1941-43, Syracuse Post Standard, 1943; reporter Griffin-Larrabee News Bur., Washington, 1946-54, mng. editor, 1954-67, bur. chief, 1967-69, owner, 1969-78; dir. Washington office, State of Maine, 1978-89. Dir. Nat. Press Bldg. Corp., 1973-85 Bd. dirs. Nat. Press Found., 1978— . Served with USAAF, 1943-45. Mem.: Assn. Former Intelligence Officers (bd. dirs. 1999—2002), Corrs. for Congl. Press Galleries, Maine Soc. Washington (pres. 1950—53), Chevy Chase Club, Nat. Press Club (Washington) (sec. 1953—54, treas. 1966—67, chmn. bd. 1969, pres. 1973), Gridiron Club (Washington). Episcopalian. Home and Office: 4956 Sentinel Dr #304 Bethesda MD 20816-3562

LARRABEE, MARTIN GLOVER, biophysics educator; b. Boston, Jan. 25, 1910; s. Ralph Clinton and Ada Perkins Miller L.; m. Sylvia Kimball, Sept. 10, 1932 (div. 1944); 1 son, Benjamin Larrabee Scherer; m. Barbara Belcher, Mar. 25, 1944 (dec. 1996); 1 son, David Belcher Larrabee; m. Sarah B. Galloway, July 11, 1998. BA, Harvard U., 1932; PhD, U. Pa., 1937; MD (hon.), U. Lausanne, Switzerland, 1974. Research asst., fellow U. Pa., Phila., 1934-40, assoc. to assoc. prof., 1941-49; asst. prof. physiology Cornell U. Med. Coll., N.Y.C., 1940-41; assoc. prof. Johns Hopkins U., Balt., 1949-63, prof. biophysics, 1963-99, prof. emeritus biophys., 1999—. Contbr. articles to scientific jours. Mem. Am. Physiol. Soc., Biophys. Soc., Am. Soc. Neurochemistry, Internat. Neurochem. Soc., Nat. Acad. Scis., Soc. for Neurosci. (treas. 1970-75), Physiol. Soc. (asso., Eng.), Appalachian Mountain Club, Phi Beta Kappa. Clubs: Appalachian Mountain, Sierra, Mountain of Md. Achievements include research in circulatory, respiratory and nervous systems of animals, especially on synaptic and metabolic mechanisms in sympathetic ganglia, 1934-99; wartime research on oxygen lack, decompression sickness, nerve injury, infrared viewing devices, 1941-45. Home: 11630 Glen Arm Rd Glen Arm MD 21057-9403

LARRABEE, WAYNE FOX, JR. facial plastic surgeon; b. Ft. Benning, Ga., May 10, 1945; s. Wayne Fox and Ruth (Truex) L.; children: Shane, Sascha, Kai, Gregory. BS in Math., Midland Coll., 1967; postgrad., U. Edinburgh, 1965-66; MD, MPH in Epidemiology, Tulan U., 1971. Diplomate Am. Bd. Otolaryngology; lic. MD, Wash. Intern Letterman Gen. Hosp., San Francisco, 1971-72; resident in surgery Tulane U. Svc. Charity Hosp., New Orleans, 1975-76, resident in otolaryngology and maxillofacial surgery, 1976-79; head sect. reconstructive and aesthetic plastic surgery Va. Mason Med. Ctr., Seattle, 1986-88, head sect. otolaryngology, 1985-88. Instr. dept. surgery Tulane Med. Sch., 1975-79, instr. dept. otolaryngology, 1976-79; clin. prof. U. Wash., 1979-88; clin. prof., U. Wash., 1988-2001; pres. med. bd. Virginia Mason Rsch. Ctr., 1985-88; observations fellowship Moorfields Eye Hosp., London, 1988; presenter in field; pres. Am. Bd. Facial Plastic Surgery, 2000-01). Author: Surgical Anatomy of the Face, 1993, Principles of Facial Reconstruction, 1995, Roslyn A Town's Portrait, 2d edit., 1999; mem. editl. bd. Jour. AMA, 1999—; editor Archives of Facial Plastic Surgery, 1999—. Maj. U.S. Army Med. Corps, 1972-75, Panama Canal Zone. Fellow Am. Coll. Surgeons, Am. Acad. Facial Plastic and Reconstructive Surgery (pres. 1996), Am. Soc. Head and Neck Surgery, Triological Soc., Am. Bd. Otolaryngology (bd. dirs.); mem. King County Med. Soc., Am. Acad. Otolaryngology-Head and Neck Surgery, Northwest Acad. Otolaryngology-Head and Neck Surgery (program chmn. 1984-86, sec./treas. 1984-86, pres. 1988—). Avocations: photography, poetry. Office: Ctr for Facial Plastic Surgery 600 Broadway # 280 Seattle WA 98122 E-mail: larrabee@u.washington.edu.

LARRIMORE, RANDALL WALTER, wholesale company executive; b. Lewes, Del., Apr. 27, 1947; s. Randall A. and Irene Larrimore; m. Judith Cutright, Aug. 29, 1970; children: Jacob, Alex. BS, Swarthmore (Pa.) Coll., 1969; MBA, Harvard U., 1971. Product mgr. Richardson-Vick, Wilton, Conn., 1971-75; sr. engagement mgr. McKinsey & Co., N.Y.C., 1975-80; pres. Pepsi-Cola Italia, Rome, 1980-83, Beatrice Home Specialties, Inc. (later acquired by Am. Brands), Skokie, Ill., 1983-87; pres., CEO, MasterBrand Industries, Inc. (subs. of Am. Brands, Inc.), 1988-97; v.p. Am. Brands, Inc., 1988-95; chmn. Moen Inc., 1990-97, chief exec. officer, 1990-94; chmn., chief exec. officer Master Lock Co., 1996-97; pres., CEO United Stationers, Des Plaines, Ill., 1997—, also bd. dirs., 1997—. Bd. dirs. Winnetka Congl. Ch., 1989-90; exec. com. hardware/home improvement coun. City of Hope, 1991-97, pres. 1991-93; exec. com. office products coun. City of Hope, 1997, pres., 2000—; commr. Landmark Preservation Coun., Winnetka, 1992-98; bd. dirs. Olin Corp., 1998—, Evanston Hosp. Corp., 1996—, Students In Free Enterprise, 1998—; trustee Lake Forest Acad., 2002--. Capt. USAR, 1971-79. Named Exec. of Yr., Office Products Internat., 1999. Mem. Plumbing Mfg. Inst. (bd. dirs. 1991-93), Nat. Assn. of Wholesalers (adv. bd. 1999—). Office: United Stationers 2200 E Golf Rd Des Plaines IL 60016-1257 E-mail: rlarrimore@ussco.com.

LARROCA, RAYMOND G. lawyer; b. Jan. 5, 1930; s. Raymond Gil and Elsa Maria (Morales) L.; m. Barbara Jean Strand, June 21, 1952 (div. 1974); children: Denise Ann Sheehan, Gail Ellen, Raymond Gil, Mark Talbot, Jeffrey William. BSS, Georgetown U., 1952; JD, 1957. Bar: Dc. 1957, U.S. Supreme Ct. 1960. Assoc. Kirkland, Fleming, Green, Martin & Ellis, Washington, 1957-64; ptnr. Kirkland, Ellis, Hodson, Chaffetz & Masters, 1964-67, Miller, Cassidy, Larroca & Lewin, Washington, 1967-2000, Baker Botts, Washington, 2000—. Served with arty. U.S. Army, 1948-49, to 1st lt., inf., 1952-54. Mem. ABA, D.C. Bar, Bar Assn. D.C., The Barristers. Republican. Roman Catholic. Club: Congl. Country (Potomac, Md.). Office: Baker Botts LLP 1299 Pennsylvania Ave NW Washington DC 20004-2400 E-mail: ray.larroca@bakerbotts.com.

LARRY, R. HEATH, lawyer, director; b. Huntingdon, Pa., Feb. 24, 1914; s. Ralph E. and Mabel (Heath) L.; m. Eleanor Ketler, Sept. 10, 1938; children: David Heath, Dennis Ketler, Thomas Richard. AB, Grove City Coll., 1934, LL.D., 1964; JD, U. Pitts., 1937. Bar: Pa. 1937, D.C. 1937. Pvt. practice, 1937-38; atty. Nat. Tube Co., 1938-44, sec., dir., 1944-48; gen. atty. U.S. Steel Corp., Pitts., 1948-52, asst. gen. solicitor, 1952-58, adminstrv. v.p. labor relations, 1958-66, exec. v.p., asst. to chmn., 1966-69, vice chmn. bd., 1969-77; pres. N.A.M., 1977-80; of counsel Reed Smith Shaw & McClay, Washington, 1980—. Dir. emeritus Textron, Inc. Trustee emeritus Grove City Coll.; former trustee Conf. Bd. Mem. Am. Iron and Steel Inst. Clubs: Met. (Washington); Economic (N.Y.C.); Gulf Stream Golf, Delray Beach Yacht, Gulf Stream Bath and Tennis, Little. Presbyterian. Home: 4333 N Ocean Blvd Apt A53 Delray Beach FL 33483-7559

LARSEN, ANITA DONICE, writer, consultant, speaker; b. Hastings, Nebr., Dec. 29, 1942; d. Donald S. and Zelda L. L.; m. Brian L. Gustafson, Aug. 25, 1963 (div. Nov. 1984). BA, Buena Vista Coll., 1967; MA, Drake U., 1973. Tchr. Alta (Iowa) H.S., 1967-68; lectr. Drake U., Des Moines, 1972-74; copywriter CMF& Z Adv. Agy., 1983; writer, editor Larsen Assocs., 1980-95, St. Paul, 1985-91, Taos, N.Mex., 1991-94, Albuquerque, 1994-99, Mpls., 1999—. Speechwriter What's Cookin': Pillsbury Study of Trends in American Eating Behaviors, 1988, others. Author: Psychic Sleuths, 1994, The Magus Doll, 1993 (Best Children's novel Southwestern Writers 1993), True Crimes and How They Were Solved, 1993, Lost..and Never Found I, 1984, II, 1991, Guilty or Innocent, many others; author, packager, editor: History's Mysteries Series, 1992, Some Feet Have Noses, 1983; playwright: Felix Culpa, 1973, Hungerbear, 1974, Fish of April, 1974, Tale of the Mouse, 1976; author:(CD ROM on tape) George Lucas, 1999; contbr. articles to profl. jours. Organizer St. Paul Pub. Libr. Youth Svcs. Dept. Event, 1988. Prodn. grantee Iowa State Art Coun. Fox Boy's Night Vision, 1982. Mem. Mpls. Screenwriters Workshop, Sigma Tau Delta, Alpha Psi Omega. Avocations: gardening, cooking, dogs.

LARSEN, CARLTON KEITH, academic administrator; b. L.A., Feb. 17, 1958; s. Richard Keith and Anita Jean (Younce) L.; m. Angela Dawn Young, July 10, 2000. BA, U. Calif., San Diego, 1980; MA in Polit. Sci., Rutgers U., 1985, PhD in Polit. Sci., 1990; grad. Mgmt. Devel. Program, Harvard U., 2000. Vis. lectr. Rutgers U., New Brunswick, N.J., 1985-86; vis. instr. Seton Hall U., South Orange, 1988-89; asst. prof. Centre Coll., Danville, Ky., 1989-96, Drake U., Des Moines, 1996-97; assoc. dir. acad. affairs Pa State U., Altoona, 1997—. Grantee N.J. Inst. on Conflict Resolution, New Brunswick, 1986; grantee, Louis Bevier fellow Rutgers U., New Brunswick, 1986. Mem. NAFSA: Internat. Educators, Internat. Soc. for Study of European Ideas, Am. Assn. Higher Edn., Am. Polit. Sci. Assn. Avocation: retired chef. Office: Pa State Altoona 3000 Ivyside Park Altoona PA 16601-3760 E-mail: ckl7@psu.edu.

LARSEN, DAVID LEONARD, retired religion educator; b. Mpls., Apr. 16, 1931; s. David Paul and Myrtle Grunnet Larsen; m. Jean Cecelia Johnson, May 31, 1957; children: Lorrie, Thomas, Daniel. BA, Stanford (Calif.) U., 1953; MDiv, Fuller Theol. Sem., 1956; DD (hon.), Trinity Coll., 1986. Ordained Evangelical Covenant Ch., 1958. Pastor The Neighborhood Ch., South San Gabriel, Calif., 1953-60, First Covenant Ch., San Francisco, 1960-63, Elim Covenant Ch., Mpls., 1963-69, First Evang. Covenant Ch., Rockford, Ill., 1969-73, First Covenant Ch., Mpls., 1973-81; prof. practical theology, dept. chair Trinity Evang. Divinity Sch., Deerfield, 1981-96, prof. emeritus, 1996. Author: The Anatomy of Preaching, 1989, Telling the Old, Old Story: An Evangelical Approach to Narrative Preaching, 1995, Caring for the Flock: Pastoral Ministry in the Local Congegation, 1991, The Evangelism Mandate, 1992, The Company of the Preacher: A History of Biblical Preaching, 1998, The Company of the Creative: A Christian Reader's Guide to Great Literature, 1999, Biblical Spirituality, 2001, Charles Haddon Spurgeon and The Conspiracy, 2002. Republican. Avocations: reading, walking, travel. Home: 853 Sutton Ct Lincolnshire IL 60069-3431 Office: Trinity Evang Div Sch 2065 Half Day Rd Deerfield IL 60015-1241 E-mail: davlrsn@aol.com.

LARSEN, DAVID WAYNE, telecommunications industry executive; b. Teaneck, N.J., Nov. 27, 1952; s. Robert Louis and Mildred Alfreda (Kraus) L.; m. Victoria Coates, Feb. 18, 1978. BS in Applied Physics, Ga. Tech. U., 1974; ThM, Dallas Theology Sem., 1978, postgrad., 1986-87. Assoc. pastor Clear Lake Cmty. Ch., Houston, 1978-80; sr. pastor Grace Bible Ch., Shawnee, Okla., 1980-86; founder, CEO TIV, Inc., Dallas, Hong Kong, 1987-98; CEO TIV, LLC, Dallas, Hong Kong, Manila, Sydney, Honolulu, 1996—. Cons. Malaysia Hotel Assn., Kuala Lumpur, 1995, Hong Kong Hotel Assn., 1996. Home: 4 Spyglass Ct Frisco TX 75034-6807 Office: TIV LLC Ste 300 5300 Town And Country Blvd Frisco TX 75034-6898

LARSEN, ERIK, art history educator; b. Vienna, Austria, Oct. 10, 1911; arrived in U.S., 1947, naturalized, 1953; s. Richard and Adrienne (Schapringer de Csepreg) L.; m. Lucy Roman, Oct. 4, 1932 (dec. 1981); children: Sigurd-Yves, Annik-Eve., Erik-Claude (dec.); m. Anna Gallup Moses, May 8, 1982 (div. Sept. 1986); m. Katharina Ehling, Oct. 21, 1989. Candidate, Institut Superieur d'Histoire de l'Art et d'Archéologie, Brussels, 1931; Licentiate, Louvain (Belgium) U., 1941; Docteur en Archéologie et Histoire de l'Art, 1959; D. honoris causa, Janus Pannonius U., Pécs, Hungary, 1992. Dir., editor-in-chief on semi-ofcl. cultural mission for Belgian Govt. Pictura, art. mag., Brussels, Rio de Janeiro, Brazil, 1946-47; research prof. art Manhattanville Coll. of Sacred Heart, 1947-55; instr. CCNY, 1948-55; lectr, then vis. prof. Georgetown U., 1955-58, assoc. prof. fine arts, 1958-63, prof., 1963-67, head dept. fine arts, 1960-67; prof. history of art U. Kans., 1967-80, prof. emeritus, 1980—. Dir. Center for Flemish Art and Culture, 1970-80; cons. old masters' paintings, guest-prof. U. Salzburg, Austria, 1988. Author: books, the most recent being La Vie, Les Ouvrages et Les Eleves de Van Dyck, 1975, Calvinistic Economy and 17th Century Dutch Art, 1979, rev. edit., 1999, Anton van Dyck, 1980, Rembrandt, Peintre de Paysages: Une Vision Nouvelle, 1983, Japanese edit., 1992; Seventeenth Century Flemish Painting, 1985, The Paintings of Anthony van Dyck, 2 vols., 1988, Jan Vermeer. Catalogo completo, 1996 (Am. edit., 1998), Hieronymus Bosch, Catalogo completo, 1998 (Am. edit., 1998); contbr. numerous articles, revs. to profl. publs., newspapers. Mem. Kans. Cultural Arts Commn., 1971-73; mem. Kans. Cultural Arts Adv. Council, 1973-79. Served with Belgian Underground, 1942-45. Decorated knight's cross Order Leopold, knight's cross Order of Crown, officer Order Leopold (Belgium); officer Order of Rio Branco (Brazil), Knight's Cross Mex. Order of Law, Culture, and Peace (Mex.); recipient Medal Marques de Olinda for Univ. Merit, Fed. U. of Pernambuco, Brazil, 2001, prix Thorlet, Laureate Inst. France, Académie des sciences morales et politiques, 1962; Internat. Hon. Citizen, New Orleans, 1989; named hon. Ky. col., 1977. Fellow Soc. Antiquaries of Scotland; mem. Appraisers Assn. Am., Association des Diplomés en Histoire de l'Art et Archéologie de L'Université Catholique de Louvain, Académie d'Aix-en Provence (France) (corr.), Académie de Mâcon (France) (assoc.), Académie d'Alsace (France) (hon.), Comité Cultural Argentino (hon.), Schweizerisches Institut fuer Kunstwissenschaft (Zurich, Switzerland), Academia di Belle Arti Pietro Vanucci (Perugia, Italy) (hon.), Royal Soc. Arts (London) (Benjamin Franklin fellow); correspondent-academician Real Academia de Bellas Artes de San Telmo (Malága, Spain), Real Academia de Bellas Artes de San Jorge (Barcelona, Spain), Accademia Tiberina (Rome), Académie Royale D'Archéologie de Belgique (fgn. assoc.). Home: 511 S Washington St Beverly Hills FL 34465-4312

LARSEN, ETHEL PAULSON, retired secondary school educator; b. Superior, Wis., Jan. 24, 1918; d. Ole Peter Paulson and Petra Marie (Boardsen) Gilbertson; m. James Eugene Larsen, June 13, 1943; children: Robert, Karen Larsen DePalermo, Deborah Larsen Farmer, Candice Larsen Herrera. AA, Kendall Coll., 1940; student, U. Wis., 1940-44; BS, SW Tex. U., 1960; postgrad., U. Tex., 1961-67. Tchr. Lakefield (Minn.) Pub. Schs., 1944-46; credit mgr. Sagebiel's Automotive Parts, Seguin, Tex., 1948-49; supervisory clk. supply Edward Gary AFB, San Marcos, 1951-56; property/acctg. chief Gary Army Air Field, 1956-59; tchr. Seguin High Sch., 1960-80; substitute tchr. Seguin Pub. Schs., 1981-83; reporter, photographer Seguin Citizen newspaper, 1981; now ret. Developer speech-journalism curriculum, Minn. State Bd. Edn., 1945; pres. AAUW, Seguin, 1965-66, Seguin Classroom Tchrs., 1971-72; del. to Tex. State Tchrs. Assn., Austin, 1970. Founding mem. York Creek Flood Prevention Dist. for Hays, Comal and Guadalupe counties, 1953-54; Voice of Democracy chair VFW Aux., Geronimo, Tex., 1970-78; writer radio scripts for improved farm-city rels., 1956; vol. tax aide, Seguin, 1987-90; Circle leader 1st United Meth. Ch., Seguin, 1989—; mem. T.B. Bd. Guadalupe County, 1954-57. Mem. Nat. Writers Club, Seguin Garden Club, Seguin-Guadalupe County Ret. Tchrs. (pres. 1990—), Nat. Coun. State Garden Clubs, Inc. (life), Tex. Garden Clubs, Inc. (life, horticulture chmn. Dist. VII 1997-98), Inc. (life), Tex. State Garden Clubs (life, Tex. dist. VII), Tex. Agrl. Ext. Svc. (master gardener), Order Ea. Star, Oakwood Art Group, Delta Kappa Gamma (Theta Kappa chpt. pres. 1978-80). Avocations: writing, art, photography, farm management. Home: 109 Old Campbell Rd Seguin TX 78155-8432

LARSEN, GARY LOY, physician, researcher; b. Wahoo, Nebr., Jan. 10, 1945; s. Allan Edward and Dorothy Mae (Hengen) L.; m. Letitia Leah Hoyt, Dec. 22, 1967; children: Kari Lyn, Amy Marie. BS, U. Nebr., 1967; MD, Columbia U., 1971. Diplomate Am. Bd. Pediatrics, Am. Bd. Pediatric Pulmonology (chmn. 1990-92)/. Pediatric pulmonologist Nat. Jewish Med. and Rsch. Ctr., Denver, 1978—; mem. faculty U. Colo. Sch. Medicine, 1978—, dir. sect. of pediatric pulmonary medicine, 1987—, prof. pediatrics, 1990—; head dept. respiratory medicine The Children's Hosp., 2002—. Contbr. articles to prof. jours. Mem. sci. adv. panel Nat. Urban Air Toxics Rsch. Ctr., 1998—. Maj. M.C., U.S. Army, 1974-76. NIH med. rsch. grantee NIH, 1981—. Mem. AM. Thoracic Soc. (chmn. pediatric assembly 1987-88), Soc. Pediatric Rsch., Phi Beta Kappa, Alpha Omega Alpha, N.Y. Acad. Scis., Chilean Respiratory Soc. (hon.). Lutheran. Office: Nat Jewish Med & Rsch Ctr 1400 Jackson St Denver CO 80206-2761 E-mail: larseng@njc.org.

LARSEN, GLEN ALBERT, JR. finance educator; b. St. Louis, Nov. 9, 1947; s. Glen Albert Sr. and Jane (Steuby) L.; m. Nancy Ann McMahon, Mar. 30, 1980; children: Erik Paul, Colleen Elizabeth. BS in Ceramic Engring., U. Mo., Rolla, 1970; MS in Materials Engring., Purdue U., 1973; MS in Bus. Adminstrn., Ind. U., 1982, DBA in Fin., 1989. Registered profl. engr., Ill.; CFA. Plant ceramic engr. U.S. Steel Corp.-South Works, 1971-73, gen. foreman constrn. svcs., 1973-74; mgr. tech. svc. Merkle Engrs., Inc., 1974-76; gen. foreman U.S. Steel-Gary (Ind.) Works, 1976-80, asst. supt., 1980-83; pres. G.A. Larsen Co., Homewood, Ill., 1983-86; instr. Ind. U., Bloomington, 1986-89, vis. asst. prof. fin., 1989-90; asst. prof. fin. U. Tulsa, 1990-94, assoc. prof. fin., 1994-96; chairperson undergrad. program, assoc. prof. fin. Ind. U., Kelley Sch. Bus., 1996—. Presenter in field. Contbr. articles to profl. jours. 2nd lt. USAR N.G., 1970-76. Mem. Am. Fin. Assn., Fin. Mgmt. Assn. Home: 115 Lynn Ct Zionsville IN 46077-1026 Office: Ind Univ Kelley Sch Bus 801 W Michigan St Indianapolis IN 46202-5199

LARSEN, GWYNNE E. computer information systems educator; b. Omaha, Sept. 10, 1934; d. Melvin and Vernetta (Allen) Bannister; m. John M. Larsen, June 8, 1958; children: Bradley Allen, Blair Kevin, Randall Lawrence. A in Bus. Adminstrn., Denver U., 1956, MBA, 1975, PhD, 1979; BS, Met. State Coll., 1971. Instr. Met. State Coll. Denver, 1979-81, asst. prof., 1981-85, assoc. prof., 1985-88, prof., 1989—, acting chair computer dept., 1991-92. Book reviewer McGraw Hill, 1991, Harcourt Brace Jovanovich, 1991, Macmillan Pub. Co., 1993, Southwestern Pub. Co., 1993; presenter Mountain Plains Mgmt. conf., Denver, 1982, Rocky Mountain Bus. Expo, Denver, 1982, Red Rocks C.C., 1984, Colo.-Wyo. Acad. Sci. conf., 1985, Boulder, 1986, Colorado Springs, 1987; local coord. John Wiley & Sons, Denver, 1982, 83; panel chmn. on office automation Assn. for Computing Machinery, Denver, 1985; spkr. ASTD, 1986, Am. Pub. Works Assn., 1986; participant numerous presentations and confs. Author: (with others) Computerized Business Information Systems Workbook, 1983, Collegiate Microcomputer, 1992, (with Verlene Leeberg) Word Processing: Using WordPerfect 5.0, 1989, Word Processing: Using WordPerfect 5.1, 1991, First Look at WordPerfect 5.1, 1991, First Look at DOS, 1991, First Look at NetWare, 1992, Using WordPerfect for Windows, 1993, (with Marold and Shaw) Using Microsoft Works: An Introduction to Computing, 1993, Using Microsoft Works, An Introduction to Computing, 1993, First Look at WordPerfect 6.0 for Windows, 1994, Using WordPerfect 6.0 for Windows, 1994, Using Microsoft Works for Windows, An Introduction to Computing, 1996, Beyond the Internet, 1996, (with Marold) Using Microsoft Works 4.0, 1997, (with Marold) Internet Navigation and Exploration, 2001; co-author: Microsoft Office 97 Online Course; apptd. editl. bd. Jour. Mgmt. Sys., 1988, Jour. Microcomputer Sys. Mgmt., 1989, Info. Resources Mgmt. Jour., 1991; mem. editl. rev. bd. Jour. Info. Resources Mgmt. Sys., 1985—, Jour. Mgmt. Info. Sys., 1986—, Jour. Database Mgmt. Sys., Jour. Database Mgmt. Sys., 1987—, Jour. End User Computing, 1990—; contbr. articles to profl. jours. Mem. Info. Resources Mgmt. Assn., Colo.-Wyo. Acad. Scis. Avocations: walking, aerobics, reading detective stories. Home: 8083 S Adams Way Littleton CO 80122-3603 Office: Met State Coll Denver Campus Box 45 PO Box 173362 Denver CO 80217-3362

LARSEN, JEANNE, English language educator, writer; b. Washington, Aug. 9, 1950; d. George Edward and Hope Harrin Larsen; m. Thomas Hugh Mesner, Aug. 13, 1977; stepchildren: Scot T. Mesner, Kili J. Mesner. BA, Oberlin Coll., 1971; MA, Hollins Coll., 1972; PhD, U. Iowa, 1983. Lectr. Tunghai U., Taichung, Taiwan, 1972-74; from asst. prof. to assoc. prof. Hollins Coll., Roanoke, Va., 1980-92; prof. English Hollins Coll. (now Hollins U.), 1992—. Author: (novels) Silk Road, 1989, Bronze Mirror, 1992, Manchu Palaces, 1996; (poetry book) James Cook in Search of Terra Incognita, 1979; mem. editl. bd.: Jour. of Fantastic in Arts; contbg. editor: The Hollins Critic. Fellow in transl. NEA, 1995, fiction fellow Va. Commn. for Arts, 1998, Creative Artists Exch. fellow Japan/U.S. Friendship Commn., 1999. Mem. PEN, Internat. Assn. for the Fantastic in Arts (Crawford award 1990), Assn. for Asian Studies, Authors Guild. Office: Hollins U PO Box 9542 Roanoke VA 24020

LARSEN, JONATHAN ZERBE, journalist; b. N.Y.C., Jan. 6, 1940; s. Roy Edward and Margaret (Zerbe) L.; m. Katharine Wilder, May 28, 1966; m. Jane Amsterdam, Aug. 31, 1985 (div. 2000); 1 child, Edward Roy. BA, Harvard U., 1961, MAT, 1963; DHL, Cambridge Coll., 1997. Contbg. editor Time mag., N.Y.C., 1965-66, corr. Chgo., 1966-68, Los Angeles, 1968-70, bur. chief Saigon, Vietnam, 1970-71, asso. editor, 1972-73; editor New Times mag., N.Y.C., 1974-79; Nieman fellow Harvard U., 1979-80; news editor Life mag., 1980-81, sr. editor, 1981-82; free-lance writer, 1982-88; editor-in-chief The Village Voice, N.Y.C., 1989-94. Mem. editl. bd. Columbia Journalism Rev.; chmn. editl. bd. OnEarth Mag. Trustee Natural Resources Def. Council.; vice chmn. Cambridge Coll.; bd. dirs. Larsen Fund. Recipient Clarion award, 1986. Home: 310 West End Ave New York NY 10023

LARSEN, KENNETH MARSHALL, art and human services advocate, consultant; b. San Francisco, June 5, 1946; s. Frank and Klara Margaret (Ashman) L.; m. Nancy Della Rossa Tallent, Sept. 17, 2000. BA, Antioch Coll., 1968; postgrad., U. Calif., Davis, 1976. Lectr. U. Calif., Davis, 1976-78; assoc. pres. Hooper Billstein & Assocs., Oakland, Calif., 1978-80; dir. Rural Arts Svcs., Mendocino, 1980-88; assoc. dir. Calif. Confedn. of the Arts, Sacramento, 1988-96; adj. lectr. Golden Gate U., San Francisco, 1996—; dir. legislation Friends' Com. on Legislation, Sacramento, 1997-2001; dir. pub. policy Calif. Assn. Nonprofits, Sacto., 2001—. Cultural planner City and County of Sacramento, 1995; cultural planning advisor 15 Calif. cities and counties; book rev. editor Ridge Rev., Mendocino, 1980-95. Editor mags. ARC: The Rural Arts Newsletter, 1980-88, Radius: Resources for Local Arts, 1985-91, Calif. Arts Advocate, 1990-94, Sacramento Arts Reporter, 1996—; contbr. articles to state and nat. trade publs. Mem. cultural awards panel

Sacramento Arts Commn., 1995—; mem. interarts grants panel Nat. Endowment for the Arts, 1988-91; mem. grants orgn. Calif. Arts coun., 1981-86. Recipient Statewide Svc. awrd Arts-in-Corrections, 1993, Enabled Artists United, 1992. Mem. Calif. Assn. Nonprofits (bd. dirs. 1995-2001), Nonprofit Policy Coun. (bd. dirs. 1996—), Inst. for Cultural Democracy (bd. dirs. 1990—), Calif Lawyers for the Arts (arbitration and mediation svc. bd. 1996—). Office: CAN PO Box 188947 Sacramento CA 95818-8947 E-mail: klarsen@canonprofits.org.

LARSEN, LAWRENCE BERNARD, JR. priest, pastoral psychotherapist; b. Yonkers, N.Y., Jan. 24, 1937; s. Lawrence Bernard and Astrid Charlotte (Bjorkgren) L.; m. Marion Davidson Hines, Nov. 29, 1968; children: Lawrence Bernard III, Hannah Hines, Sarah Astrid. BA, Trinity Coll., 1958; MDiv, The Gen. Theol. Sem., N.Y.C., 1961; diploma candidate, C.G. Jung Inst., Zurich, Switzerland, 1975; MSW, U. Tenn., 1989; training program, Diocese N.Y. Interim Ministry, 1996. Ordained priest Episcopal Ch., 1961; cert. social worker. Curate Christ Episcopal Ch., Poughkeepsie, N.Y., 1961-63; asst. Episcopal chaplain Vassar Coll., 1961-63; vicar All Saints Episcopal Ch., East Hartford, Conn., 1963-66; asst. to rector Trinity Ch., Southport, 1966-69; chaplain Chatham (Va.) Hall Sch., 1969-72, tchr. bible and religion, 1969-72; Jungian psychotherapist pvt. practice Lookout Mountain, Tenn., 1975-89; priest assoc. Good Shepherd Episcopal Ch., 1975-85; interim rector Episcopal Ch. Nativity, Ft. Oglethorpe, Ga., 1985-86; priest-in-charge St. Barnabas Episcopal Ch., Trion, 1987-89; staff psychotherapist Mid Hudson Consultation Ctr., Wappingers Falls, N.Y., 1989-96; pastoral psychotherapist Northeast Counseling Ctr., Katonah, 1989-96; pastoral care coord. Hospice of No. Westchester, Mt. Kisco, 1995; interim rector Christ Ch. Tarrytown, 1996-97; assoc. priest St. Wilfred's Episcopal Ch., Sarasota, Fla., 1998-99. Asst. for pastoral care St. Wilfred's Episc. Ch., 2000—; asst. Episcopal chaplain Vassar Coll., Poughkeepsie, 1961-63; assoc. priest Good Shepherd Episc. Ch., Lookout Mountain, Tenn., 1975-85, faciltator Mutual Study Ministry, 1996-97. Mem. War on Poverty com. U.S. Office Econ. Opportunity, Hartford, Conn., 1965-66. Republican. Avocations: reading, crossword puzzles, politics. Home: 7623 Preserves Ct Sarasota FL 34243-3769 E-mail: mhlandlbl@msn.com.

LARSEN, LOREN JOSEPH, retired pediatric orthopedic surgeon; b. Idaho Falls, Idaho, Oct. 10, 1914; s. Charles Wilford and Marie (Jacobsen) L.; m. June Elmer, Mar. 20, 1943; children: Mary Ann, Loren J. Jr. BA, U. Utah, 1939; MD, U. Chgo., 1941. Intern Alameda County Hosp., 1942; resident orthopedic surgery Samuel Merit Hosp., Oakland, Calif., 1943-44; postgrad. tng. U. Calif., 1944-46, San Francisco Gen. Hosp., 1946-47; clin. prof. orthopedic surgery U. Calif., San Francisco, 1957-60; chmn. emeritus dept. orthopedic surgery Children's Hosp., 1957-88; chief of staff emeritus Shriner's Hosp. Crippled Children, 1968-80; pvt. practice. Cons. orthopedics U.S. Army Letterman Gen. Hosp., San Francisco, 1959—, U.S. Naval Hosp., Oakland, Calif., 1960-75, King Faisal Hosp., Ridyaah, Saudi Arabia, 1968. Contbr. 37 articles to profl. jours. Mem. Scoliosis Rsch. Soc. (founding), Am. Orthopedic Foot and Ankle Soc. (founding). Republican. Achievements include discovery of reporting syndrome, later named Larsen Syndrome; genetic research to determine the location of the chromosome and genes responsible for inheritance characteristics. Office: 3838 California St San Francisco CA 94118-1522 Home: 826 Wood Ln Petaluma CA 94954-4354

LARSEN, LYNN BECK, lawyer; b. Salt Lake City, Feb. 26, 1945; BA in Math. magna cum laude, U. Utah, 1969; MS in Engring., U. Wash., 1971; JD with honors, George Washington U., 1975. Bar: Va. 1975, U.S. Dist. Ct. (ea. dist.) Va. 1975, D.C. 1976, U.S. Dist. Ct. D.C. 1976, U.S. Ct. Appeals (4th and D.C. cirs.) 1976, U.S. Claim Ct. 1977, Calif. 1978, U.S. Dist. Ct. (cen. dist.) Calif. 1978, U.S. Dist. Ct. (so. dist.) Calif. 1979, U.S. Ct. Appeals (9th cir.) 1979, Utah 1983, U.S. Dist. Ct. Utah 1983, U.S. Ct. Appeals (fed. cir.) 1983, U.S. Ct. Appeals (10th cir.) 1988. Engr. Boeing Co., Seattle, 1969-70; engring analyst CIA, Washington, 1971-73, contracting officer, 1973-74; ptnr. Wickwire Gavin, P.C., Washington, Los Angeles and Salt Lake City, 1974-86, Larsen & Wilkins, Salt Lake City, 1986—88, Larsen & Stewart, 1988—94, McKay, Burton & Thurman, 1995-2000, Project Analysts, Salt Lake City, 2000—. Chmn. legal adv. com. Associated Gen. Contractors Calif. 1983, Associated Gen. Contractors Utah. Contbr. articles to profl. jours. Mem. Phi Beta Kappa. Mem. Lds Ch. Office: Project Analysts 505 E 200 S Ste 400 Salt Lake City UT 84102-2818 E-mail: lynn@projan.com.

LARSEN, MARK A. internet strategy management consultant, lawyer; b. Oak Park, Ill., July 17, 1963; s. Donald R. and Barbara A. Larsen; m. Maria Larsen, May 16, 1992; children: Alexandra, Mitchell, Maxwell. BS, So. Ill. U., 1985; MBA, Dominican U., 1993; JD, John Marshall Law Sch., 1992. Security mgr. Lord & Taylor, Aurora, Ill., 1985-87; claim adjustor Am. Family, Schaumburg, 1987-88; field adjuster Atlantic Mut., Chgo., 1988-90; regional mgr. Am. Internat. Group, 1990-96; nat. dir. of claims Zurich-Am. Ins., Schaumburg, 1996-98; mgmt. cons. Watson Wyatt Worldwide, Chgo., 1998-2000, Zefer, Chgo., 2000, Maxxcap Group, 2000—. Chmn. alumni adv. bd. Dominican U., River Forest, Ill., 1993—. Mem. ABA, Ill. Bar Assn., Inst. Mgmt. Cons., Chgo. Bar Assn., Better Bus. Bur. Republican. Roman Catholic. Avocation: golf. Home: 2240 Buckthorn Dr Algonquin IL 60102-4219 E-mail: Mark.Larsen@maxxcap.com.

LARSEN, MARY ANN INDOVINA, counselor, English educator; b. Chgo., Aug. 9, 1929; d. Michael and Mary Rosalie (Tamaizzo) Indovina; m. Arthur F. Larsen, Jan. 28, 1956 (dec. June 1989); children: Deborah M. Larsen McIlvain, Michael A., Suzanne M. Larsen Channell. BA, DePaul U., 1951, MA, 1986. 1st grade tchr., music tchr. Whittier Sch., Blue Island, Ill., 1951-53, Graham Sch., Chgo., 1953-59; kindergarten tchr. Twain Sch., 1958-59; dental bus. asst. Glenwood, Ill., 1964-88; counselor Glenwood (Ill.) Sch. for Boys, 1987-89; counselor, coord. for special needs South Suburban Coll, South Holland, Ill., 1989-96, instr. English, 1988-93, counselor, instr., 1995—. Mem. Chgo. Archdiocesal Choral Festival, ch. choir. Mem. Ill. Counseling Assn. (writer critiques for manuscripts 1987-90), AACD (book reviewer 1988-91), Ill. Sch. Counselors Assn. (membership com. 198-91—), Phi Kappa Delta, Kappa Delta Pi. Roman Catholic. Avocations: singing, piano, reading, music, opera. Office: South Suburban Coll 15800 State St South Holland IL 60473-1200 E-mail: mlarsen@ssc.cc.il.45.

LARSEN, PHILLIP NELSON, electrical engineer; b. Montrose, Colo., Feb. 27, 1929; s. Virgil Clair and Katherine (Alarid) L.; m. Patricia June Swayze, Aug. 30, 1951; children: James Phillip, Lynn Katherine Larsen Johnston. BSEE, Colo. A&M Coll., 1950; MSEE, U. Ill., 1953, PhDEE, 1956; MSBA, George Washington U., 1967. Registered profl. engr., Colo. Commd. lt. USAF, 1950, advanced through grades to brig. gen., 1973; assoc. prof. elec. engring. USAF Acad., Colo., 1961-66; comdr. OLAA 12th Spl Ops Squadron, Vietnam, 1967-69; spl. asst. to dir. and to prin. dir. def. rsch. and engring. Office Sec. Def., Washington, 1969-72; comdr. Rome (N.Y.) Air Devel. Ctr., 1972-73; vice comdr. Electronic Systems Div. Hanscom AFB, Md., 1973-75; dep. chief staff/systems Hdqrs. Air Force System Command, Andrews AFB, 1975-77; ret. USAF, 1977; v.p. Western Union Telegraph Co., McLean, Va., 1977-80, Systems & Applied Scis. Corp., Riverdale, Md., 1980-81; sr. mem. exec. staff Computer Scis. Corp., Falls Church, Va., 1981-90. Decorated D.S.M., Silver Star, Legion of Merit with 1 oak leaf cluster, D.F.C., Meritorious Svc. medal, Air medal with 11 oak leaf clusters, Air Force Commendation medal, Vietnamese Cross of Gallantry with Gold Star, Vietnamese Cross of Gallantry with Palm. Fellow IEEE, AAAS; mem. Air Force Assn., Masons. Republican. Lutheran. Avocations: fishing, leathercraft. Home: 10719 Oak Pl Fairfax VA 22030-2817

LARSEN, POUL STEEN, library educator; b. Copenhagen, Jan. 30, 1940; s. Kaj Poul and Inger Elise (Seligmann) L.; m. Marianne Pugdahl, July 27, 1963; children: Maria, Anne. Exam.Phil., U. Copenhagen, 1961. Lectr. Copenhagen Coll. Engring., 1961-73, Royal Sch. Librarianship, Denmark, 1971-73, libr. Denmark, 1972, asst. dept. head, assoc. prof. Denmark, 1973-76, head dept. info. media, prof. Denmark, 1976—, chmn. faculty Denmark, 1992-99. Chmn. Danish Best Books of Yr. Com., 1982-89, Danish Standards Com. Phys. Characteristics of Media, 1988-2001; vice-chmn. ISO com. Terminology of Info. and Documentation, 1993-2001; convenor ISO Expert Group Standardization of Graphic Materials, 1991-2001; vis. prof. UCLA, 1983. Author: Contemporary Danish Book Art, 1986, 3d edit., 2002; co-author: Informationsordbogen (Danish Standards Dictionary of Information Terms), 1991, 2d. edit., 1996; contbg. author: Danish Dictionary of National Biography, 1978-85, Danish Handbook of Cultural History, 1991, Danish National Ency., 1993-2000, ISO 5127 Information and Documentation-Vocabulary, 2001; contbr. articles to profl. jours.; editor, book designer, designer typefaces for digital typesetting: LIBER, 1993, MEGA, 1996, COLONNA, 1996; mem. editl. bd. The Libr. Quar., U. Chgo., 1999—. Yale U. fellow, 1984. Home: Vasevej 85 DK-3460 Birkerod Denmark Also: Kirkebyen 11 DK 3790 Hasle Denmark Office: Royal Sch Libr/Info Sci 6 Birketinget DK-2300 Copenhagen Denmark E-mail: psl@psl.dk.

LARSEN, RALPH IRVING, environmental research engineer; b. Corvallis, Oreg., Nov. 26, 1928; s. Walter Winfred and Nellie Lyle (Gellatly) L.; m. Betty Lois Garner, Oct. 14, 1950 (dec. Feb. 1989); children: Karen Larsen Cleeton, Eric, Kristine Larsen Burns, Jan Alan; m. Annie Harmon King, Aug. 3, 1991; children: Vikki King Ball, Terri King Blankenship, Cindi King King (dec.). BSCE, Oreg. State U., 1950; MS, Harvard U., 1955, PhD in Air Pollution and Indsl. Hygiene, 1957. San. engr. divsn. water pollution control USPHS, Washington, 1950-54; chief tech. svc. state and cmty. svc. sect. Nat. Air Pollution Control Adminstrn., Cin., 1957-61; with EPA and Nat. Air Pollution Control Adminstrn., 1961—; environ. rsch. engr. Nat. Exposure Rsch. Lab., Rsch. Triangle Park, N.C., 1971—. Air pollution cons. to Poland, 1973, 75, Brazil, 1978; condr. seminars for air pollution researchers, Paris, Vienna and Milan, 1975; adj. lectr. Inst. Air Pollution Tng., 1969—; Falls of Neuse cmty. rep. City of Raleigh (N.C.), 1974—. Contbr. over 55 articles to profl. jours. Elder Christian and Missionary Alliance Ch. Recipient Commendation medal USPHS, 1979. Mem. Air and Waste Mgmt. Assn. (mem. editl. bd. jour. 1971-88), Conf. Fed. Environ. Engrs., USPHS Commd. Officers Assn. (past br. pres.), Sigma Xi. Republican. Home: 4012 Colby Dr Raleigh NC 27609-6045 *God issued me a 1928-model body. It works best, for others and me, as I read a chapter of the Owner's Manual (The Holy Bible) first thing each morning.*

LARSEN, RALPH S(TANLEY), retired pharmaceutical company executive; b. Bklyn., Nov. 19, 1938; s. Andrew and Gurine (Henningsen) L.; m. Dorothy M. Zeitfuss, Aug. 19, 1961; children: Karen, Kristen, Garret. BBA, Hofstra U., 1962. Mfg. trainee, then supr. prodn. and dir. mfg. Johnson & Johnson, New Brunswick, NJ, 1962-77; v.p. ops., v.p. mktg. McNeil Consumer Products Co. div. Johnson & Johnson, Ft. Washington, Pa., 1977-81; pres. Becton Dickenson Consumer Products, Paramus, NJ, 1981-83; pres. Chicopee div. Johnson & Johnson, New Brunswick, 1983-85, co. group chmn., 1985-86, vice chmn., exec. com., bd. dirs., 1986-89, chmn. bd., pres., CEO, 1989—2002, also bd. dirs., mem. exec. com. Bd. dirs. Xerox Corp., AT&T Wireless, Gen. Electric. Mem. Bus. Roundtable (policy com.). Republican. Avocations: skiing, boating, art. Office: 100 Albany St Ste 200 New Brunswick NJ 08901

LARSEN, RICHARD GARY, accounting firm executive; b. Tampa, Fla., Nov. 28, 1948; s. Dagfinn T. Larsen and Elizabeth M. (Koch) Thompson; m. Harriet Taylor Jones, Dec. 19, 1970; children— Jonathan Daniel, Alice Taylor BBA in Acctg., George Washington U., 1971, JD, 1974; postgrad., Columbia U., 1985. Bar: Va. 1974; CPA, D.C., Va. Mem. staff U.S. Senate, Washington, 1967-73; ptnr. Ernst & Young, 1973—; adj. prof. U. Md., College Park, 1976-78, Am. U., Washington, 1977-78. Mem. ABA, Va. Bar Assn., AICPAs, Md. Soc. CPAs, Univ. Club (Washington), Coral Beach and Tennis Club (Bermuda), Chatham Beach and Tennis Club, Eastward Ho Country Club (Chatham), Columbia Country Club (Chevy Chase), Belle Haven Country Club. Home: 319 S St Asaph St Alexandria VA 22314-3745 Office: Ernst & Young 1225 Connecticut Ave NW Washington DC 20036-2621 E-mail: richard.larsen@ey.com.

LARSEN, RICHARD LEE, former mayor and city manager, business, municipal and labor relations consultant, arbitrator; b. Jackson, Miss., Apr. 16, 1934; s. Homer Thorsten and Mae Cordelia (Amidon) L.; m. Virginia Fay Alley, June 25, 1955; children: Karla, Daniel, Thomas (dec.), Krista, Lisa. BS in Econs. and Bus. Adminstrn, Westminster Coll., Fulton, Mo., 1959; postgrad., U. Kans., 1959-61. Fin. dir. Village of Northbrook, Ill., 1961-63; city mgr. Munising, Mich., 1963-66, Sault Ste. Marie, 1966-72, Ogden, Utah, 1972-77, Billings, Mont., 1977-79; mcpl. cons., 1979—; pub./pvt. sector labor rels. cons., arbitrator, 1979—. Mayor City of Billings, Mont., 1990-95; dep. gen. chmn. Greater Mich. Found., 1968. Bd. dirs. Ctrl. Weber Sewer Dist., 1972-77; chmn. labor com. Utah League Cities and Towns, 1973-77, Mont. League Cities and Towns, 1977-79; bd. dirs., coach Ogden Hockey Assn., 1972-77, Weber Sheltered Workshop, 1974-77, Billings YMCA, 1980-86, Rimrock Found., 1980-86; chmn. cmty. rels. coun. Weber Basin Job Corps Ctr., 1973-77; bishop LDS Ch. With USCG, 1953-57. Recipient Cmty. Devel. Disting. Achievement awards Munising, 1964, Cmty. Devel. Disting. Achievement awards Sault Ste. Marie, 1966-70, Citizen award Dept. of Interior, 1977, Alumni Achievement award Westminster Coll., 1990, Dist. award of merit Boy Scouts Am., 1993, Silver Beaver award Boy Scouts Am., 1994; named Utah Adminstr. of Yr., 1976. Mem. Internat. City Mgmt. Assn. (L.P. Cookingham career devel. award 1974, Clarence Ridley in-service tng. award 1979), Utah City Mgrs. Assn. (pres. 1972-74), Greater Ogden C. of C. (dir.), Rotary (pres. Billings 1997-98), Phi Gamma Delta. Home and Office: 1733 Parkhill Dr Billings MT 59102-2358 E-mail: rlarsen@wtp.net.

LARSEN, RICK, congressman; b. Arlington, Wash. m. Tiia; children: Robert, Per. BA, Pacific Luth. U.; MPA, U. Minn. Dir. public affairs Wash. State Dental Assn.; econ. devel. official Port of Everett; councilman Snohomish County, Wash., County Coun. chair, 1999; congressman Wash. State Second Congressional Dist. Mem. Congressional coms. Transportation and Infrastructure com., Highways and Transit subcom., Railroad subcom., Agriculture com. Office: 1529 Longworth House Office bldg Washington DC 20515*

LARSEN, ROBERT LEROY, artistic director; b. Walnut, Iowa, Nov. 28, 1934; s. George Dewey and Maine M. (Mickel) L. MusB, Simpson Coll., Indianola, Iowa, 1956; MusM, U. Mich., 1958; MusD, Ind. U., 1972. Music prof. Simpson Coll., 1957—, chmn. music dept., 1965-99. Founder, artistic dir. Des Moines Met. Opera, 1973—; mus. and stage dir. over 100 prodns. Mus. coach Tanglewood, Lenox, Mass., 1963, Oglebay Pk. (W.Va.) Opera, 1965, Chgo., N.Y. studios; condr., stage dir. Simpson Coll., Des Moines Met. Opera, Miss. Opera, U. Ariz.; solo pianist, song recital coach and accompanist; adjudicator Met. auditions and competitions, Mpls., Chgo., Kansas City, Mo., Tulsa, San Antonio; stage dir., condr. operas, Simpson Coll., Des Moines Met. Opera, 1973—; editor Opera Anthologies by G. Schirmer; piano rec. artist for G. Schirmer Libr. Recipient Gov's. award State of Iowa, 1974, Iowa Arts award for long term commitment to excellence in the arts, 1998. Mem. Am. Choral Dir. Assn., Nat. Opera Assn., Music Tchrs. Nat. Assn., Pi Kappa Lambda, Phi Kappa Phi, Phi Mu Alpha Sinfonia (faculty advisor). Presbyterian. Avocations: reading, theatre, coaching students. Office: Des Moines Metro Opera 106 W Boston Ave Indianola IA 50125-1836

LARSEN, ROBERT RAY, healthcare executive, surgeon; b. Cushing, Nebr., May 11, 1935; s. Almus Olvier and Margaret Evelyn (Christensen) L.; m. Norma Ruth Fry Fulkerson, June 20, 1962 (div. 1978); m. Rebecca Yasuko Takahashi, Aug. 29, 1982; children: Micaela Brown, Kamala Evora, Karolee Mathison. BA in Biology, Bucknell U., 1956; MD, Temple U., 1960; postgrad., U. Calif., Irvine, 1987. Cert. in med. mgmt.; lic. physician, Calif., Colo. Med. supt. Nekursini (India) Christ Hosp., 1963-68; chief of surgery Platte Valley Med. Ctr., Brighton, Colo., 1971-85; chief of staff, surgeon FHP Hosp., Fountain Valley, Calif., 1985-86; med. dir. FHP Healthcare, 1986-94, v.p. med. affairs, 1994-96; v.p. managed care svcs. McGraw Hill Pub., Mpls., 1996-97; CEO, pres. MD Execs., Inc., Lake Forest, 1996-97. Assoc. prof. U. Calif., Irvine, 1986—; trustee U. Sioux Falls, S.D., 1990—, HealthReform Action Plan, Santa Ana, Calif., 1996—. Contbr. chpt. to book, articles to profl. jours. Group leader St. Andrews Presbyn. Ch., Newport Beach, Calif., 1991—; med. advisor GHAA, Washington, 1993-95, Inst. of Medicine, Washington, 1994. Named Med. Staff Exec. of Yr., Am. Coll. Med. Staff Execs., Atlanta, 1994. Fellow ACS, Southwestern Surg. Congress, Am. Coll. Physician Execs., Healthcare Info. Mgmt. Soc.; me. AMa, Nat. Assn. Managed Care Physicians. Avocations: writing, woodworking, photography, gardening, speaking. Home: 21772 Tahoe Ln Lake Forest CA 92630-1931 E-mail: rlarsen@pol.net.

LARSEN, SAMUEL HARRY, minister, educator; b. Sterling, Kans., Feb. 3, 1947; s. Harold Julius and Edna Marguerite (Wasson) L.; m. Natalie Louise Mahlow, June 21, 1969; children: Samuel Eric, Kristen Joy, Hans Joseph. BS, U.S. Naval Acad., 1969; MDiv, Covenant Theol. Sem., 1979; D of Ministry, Reformed Theol. Sem., 1989; PhD, Trinity Internat. U., 1998. Ordained to ministry Presbyn. Ch., 1981. Ops. officer USS O'Hare USN, Norfolk, Va., 1969-71; sr. advisor River Interdiction divsn. 42 U.S. Naval Adv. Group, Vietnam, 1971-72; instr. U.S. Naval Acad., Annapolis, Md., 1972-75; pastoral intern Community Presbyn. Ch., Nairobi, Kenya, Africa, 1977-78; officer-in-charge Naval Res. Shipboard Simulator Lab. and Sch., New Orleans, 1979-81; church planter Mission to the World, Brisbane, Australia, 1982-84, team coord. Queensland, Australia, 1984-86, regional dir. Australia, 1986-89; squadron chaplain Destroyer Squadron Five, San Diego, 1989-92; chaplain Naval Air Sta. Whidbey Island, Oak Harbor, Wash., 1992-95; acad. mentor Chesapeake Theol. Sem., Linthicum Heights, Md., 1996; assoc. prof. missions Reformed Theol. Sem., Jackson, Miss., 1998—. Dean Westminster Theol. Coll., Brisbane, 1986-88; del. La. Congress on World Evangelism, Manila, 1989. Pres. Covenant Sem. Student Assn., St. Louis, 1976-77; chaplain Chs. Soccer Assn., Sunshine Coast, Australia, 1984-86; tutor Logan Elem. Sch., San Diego, 1991-92; mem. adv. bd. YMCA, Oak Harbor, 1992-95. Recipient Meritorious Svc. medal Sec. of Navy, 1981, 96. Avocations: chess, astronomy, history, anthropology. Office: Reformed Theol Sem 5422 Clinton Blvd Jackson MS 39209-3004 E-mail: slarsen@rts.edu.

LARSEN, STEVEN, orchestra conductor; b. Oak Park, Ill., Feb. 10, 1951; s. Edwin Earnest and Sylvia Nila Larsen; divorced; children: Vanessa, Krista; m. Martha Jane Bein, Mar. 21, 1993. MusB, Am. Conservatory Music, Chgo., 1975; MusM, Northwestern U., 1976. Cert. Nederlandse Dirigenten Kursus. Instr. music theory, chair instrumental dept Am. Conservatory Music, Chgo., 1976-82, orch. dir., 1978; music dir. Opera Theatre of San Antonio, 1987-90; orch. dir. Rockford (Ill.) Symphony Orch., 1991—. Music dir., acting artistic dir. Chgo. Opera Theater, 1981-92; interim artistic dir. Dayton (Ohio) Opera, 1996; music dir. Champaign-Urbana (Ill.) Symphony, 1996—; lectr. opera performance Chgo. Mus. Coll., 1989-96. Recipient Disting. Svc. award Rockford Park Dist., 1997, Condr. of Yr., Ill. Coun. of Orchs., 1998-99, Mayor's Arts award Rockford Area Arts Coun., 1999. Mem. Rockford Downtown Rotary (bd. dirs. 2000-2002). Office: Rockford Symphony Orch 711 N Main St Rockford IL 61103-7204 E-mail: steve@larsenbein.com.

LARSEN, TRACI LYN, interior designer; b. Pasadena, Calif., Sept. 29, 1961; d. Douglas O. and Beverly Ann Albright; 1 child, Christina Nicole. AA in Art, Pasadena City Coll., 1981; cert. in art/interior design, UCLA, Westwood, 1984. Interior designer The Designing Women, La Canada, Calif., 1979-92, Scherrer and Assocs., Pasadena, 1992-95; founder Traci Larsen Interiors, 1996—. Interior designer Pasadena JR. Philharmonic Showcase House of Interior Design, 1986—89, 1991—92, 1994—95, 1997, 1999—2000. Photography Designers West mag., 1988, Traditional Home Mag. Mem. Am. Soc. Interior Designers, Nat. Coun. Interior Designers. Avocations: skiing, tennis, remodeling homes, reading. Office: Traci Larsen Interiors 646 Durwood Dr La Canada CA 91011-2664

LARSEN, WILLIAM LAWRENCE, materials science and engineering educator; b. Crookston, Minn., July 16, 1926; s. Clarence M. and Luverne (Carlisle) L.; m. Gracie Lee Richey, June 19, 1954; children— Eric W., Thomas R. B.M.E., Marquette U., 1948; MS, Ohio State U., 1950, PhD, 1956; postgrad., U. Chgo., 1950-51. Registered profl. engr., Iowa. Research assoc. Ohio State U., Columbus, 1951-56; research metallurgist E. I. duPont de Nemours & Co., Wilmington, Del., 1956-58; metallurgist Ames Lab., AEC, Iowa, 1958-73; assoc. prof. Iowa State U., Ames, 1958-73, prof. materials sci. and engring., 1973-93; prof. emeritus, 1993—. Cons. metallurgical engring., 1960— Contbr. articles to profl. jours. Served with USNR, 1944-46 Mem.: NSPE, NACE Internat. (cert.), ASTM, ASM Internat. (life). Home and Office: 2332 Hamilton Dr Ames IA 50014-8201

LARSGAARD, MARY LYNETTE, librarian, writer; b. Dickinson, N.D., Aug. 4, 1946; d. Martin Vilhelm and Helen Maud (Brooks) L. BA in Geology, Macalester Coll., 1968; MALS, U. Minn., 1969; MA in Geography, U. Oreg., 1978. Asst. documents/maps libr. Ctlr. Wash. State Coll., Ellensburg, 1969-76; map libr. Colo. Sch. Mines, Golden, 1978-86, asst. head spl. collections, 1986-88; asst. head map & imagery lab. U. Calif., Santa Barbara, 1988—. Author: Map LIbrarianship: an Introduction, 1978, 3d edit., 1998, Topographic Mapping of the Americas, Australia and New Zealand, 1984, Topographic Mapping of Africa, Australia & Eurasia, 1992. Mem. ALA (Honors award 1983), We. Assn. Map Librs. (pres. 1975-76), Phi Beta Kappa, Beta Phi Mu. Avocations: walking, reading, dancing. Office: U Calif Santa Barbara Davidson Libr Map and Imagery Lab Santa Barbara CA 93106 E-mail: mary@library.ucsb.edu.

LARSON, ADA COPP, artist; b. Lake City, Minn., Jan. 29, 1922; d. Archer John and Grace Elnora (Geppert) Copp; m. Warren Eugene Larson, Aug. 2, 940 (dec. May 1995); children: Constance Ada, Patricia Ann, Robert Warren. State Tchr. Tng. Cert., Red Wing, Minn., 1939; AA, C.C., Rochester, Minn., 1990; BA magna cum laude, Winona State, 1991. Registered profl. artist. Elem. sch. tchr. State of Minn., Rural Lake City, 1939-41; owner rooming house, Rochester, Minn., 1942-55; co-owner, sec. Queen City Decorators, 1947-60; pvt. art tchr., 1950-99; records keeper scrap books for display Pub. Schs., Rochester, 1950-60; floral designer Bandow-Larson Flowers, 1960-68. Mem. working adv. bd. creation of Art Ctr., Rochester, 1945-65. Author, illustrator: With Clipped Wings I Flew, 2000; illustrator: Pre-Primer Text Book, 1949; prin. works include murals for comml. bldgs., 1952-65; group shows include Artists Equity Assn. Minn. chpt., Minn Artists Assn. Minn. chpt.; designer program cover Symphony Orch., Rochester, 1963. Art instr. Girl Scouts USA, Boy Scouts Am., Rochester, 1963; mem. Rochester/Meth. Hosp. Aux., lobby desk, 1984—2002. Original works grantee Southeastern Minn. Arts Coun., 1996. Mem. Zonta Internat. (book cover), Minn. Citizens for the Arts (arts adv., Minn. Citizen for Art). Democrat. Avocations: gardening, reading, classical music, writing poetry, studying antiques.

LARSON, ALAN PHILIP, federal official; b. Osage, Iowa, July 19, 1949; s. Philip Harold and Marilyn (Lack) L.; m. Nancy Ruth Naden, June 3, 1972; children: NAthan Christopher, Lara Marie, Philip Gardner. BA, U. Iowa, 1971, MA, 1978, PhD, 1982. Econ. officer U.S. Embassy Dept. of State, Kinshasa, Zaire, 1975-77, dep. dir. Washington, 1978-82, counselor for econ. and comml. affairs U.S. Embassy Kingston, Jamaica, 1982-84, exec. asst. to undersec. Washington, 1984-86, dep. asst. sec. for internat. energy, 1986-87, prin. dep. asst. sec. for econs. and bus., 1987-90; U.S. amb. to OECD Paris, 1990-94; dep. asst. sec. for internat. fin. and devel. Washington, 1994-96; asst. sec. economics & business affairs Dept. of State, 1996-99; undersec. econs., bus. and agrl. affairs Dept. State, 1999—. Office: Dept State 2201 C St NW Washington DC 20520-0001*

LARSON, ALLAN LOUIS, political scientist, educator, lay church worker; b. Chetek, Wis., Mar. 31, 1932; s. Leonard Andrew and Mabel (Marek) L. BA magna cum laude, U. Wis., Eau Claire, 1954; PhD, Northwestern U., 1964. Instr. Evanston Twp. (Ill.) High Sch., 1958-61; asst. prof. polit. sci. U. Wis., 1963-64; asst. prof. Loyola U., Chgo., 1964-68, assoc. prof., 1968-74, prof., 1974—. Author: Comparative Political Analysis, 1980, Soviet Society in Historical Perspective: Polity, Ideology and Economy, 2000, (essay) The Human Triad: An Introductory Essay on Politics, Society, and Culture, 1988; (with others) Progress and the Crisis of Man, 1976; contbr. articles to profl. jours. Assoc. mem. Paul Galvin Chapel, Evanston, Ill. Norman Wait Harris fellow in polit. sci. Northwestern U., 1954-56 Mem. AAAS, ASPCA, AAUP, Humane Soc. U.S., Northwestern U. Alumni Assn., Am. Polit. Sci. Assn., Am. Acad. Polit. and Social Sci., Acad. Polit. Sci., Midwest Polit. Sci. Assn., Spiritual Life Inst., Anti-Cruelty Soc., Nat. Wildlife Fedn., N.Am. Butterfly Assn., Acad. of Am. Poets (assoc.), Policy Studies Orgn., Noetic Scis. Inst., Humane Soc. U.S., Kappa Delta Pi, Pi Sigma Epsilon. Roman Catholic. Home: 4169 112th St Chippewa Falls WI 54729-6626 Office: Loyola U 6525 N Sheridan Rd Damen Hall Rm 915 Chicago IL 60626 *We are each of us mysteries to ourselves. We are on a life-long search for meaning: questions about where we have come from, what we are doing and where we are going. The deepest desires of a person embody the spiritual quest. The Kingdom of God tells us where to place our priorities. Life is short. No one is untouched by tragedy. We are reminded every day of our finiteness. We care because it is our nature to care. Christianity teaches a reverence for life that urges us to transcend narcissism and selfishness.*

LARSON, ARVID GUNNAR, electrical engineer; b. July 26, 1937; s. Arvid G. and Marion Edith (Parker) L.; m. Gladys Lorraine Anderson, June 6, 1959 (dec. 1987); 1 child, Gregory Monte; m. Nicole Sours, Aug. 26, 1989. BSEE, Ill. Inst. Tech., Chgo., 1959; MSEE, Stanford (Calif.) U., 1966, PhD in Elec. Engring., 1973. Registered profl. engr., Calif., Va. Rsch. engr. Stanford Rsch. Inst., Menlo Park, Calif., 1964-74; mgr. advanced rsch. Planning Rsch. Corp., McLean, Va., 1974-78; project mgr. Sys. Planning Corp., Arlington, 1978-80; mgr. Washington divsn. Advanced Rsch. and Applications Corp., Vienna, 1980-85; v.p. Analytical Disciplines Inc., 1985-86; prin. Booz, Allen and Hamilton, Inc., 1986-90; sr. v.p. JJH Inc., Arlington, 1990-91; chmn. Nicole Larson Assocs., McLean, 1991—. Rsch. prof. George Mason U., Fairfax, Va., 1991-93; chmn. bd. dirs. Electronics and Aerospace Sys. Conf., 1982-84; bd. dirs. Rsch. Inst. in Info. Scis. and Engring., 1978-99; chmn. 3d NATO Advanced Study Inst. in Info. Scis., 1978. Author: Information Science in Action: System Design, 1983; contbr. numerous elec. engring. articles to profl. publs. Lt. USN, 1959-63. Fellow IEEE (chmn. def. R&D com. 1985-86, chmn. No. Va. sect. 1986-87, vice-chmn. tech. activities com. 1986-87, chmn. new tech. issues com. 1987-89, chmn. fed. govt. activities 1989-90, gen. chmn. U.S. Tech. Policy Conf., 1988, 89, inst. editl. bd. 1986-88, editl. bd. jour. Spectrum 1988-91, Centennial medal 1984, Profl. Achievement award 1987, chmn. U.S. activities 1992, v.p. 1992, bd. dirs. 1992, chmn. govt. fellow com. 1997-98); mem. Am. Assn. Engring. Socs. (chmn. R&D task force 1996-99), Armed Forces Comms. and Electronics Assn., U.S. Naval Inst., Sigma Xi, Cosmos Club (chmn. fin. com. 1993-96, treas. 1997-00, mem. bd. mgmt. 1997-00), Shady Oaks Yacht Club (commodore 1991-93). Home: 3802 Riviera Dr # 3 San Diego CA 92109-6304 E-mail: larsons@n2.net.

LARSON, BENNETT CHARLES, solid state physicist, researcher; b. Buffalo, Oct. 9, 1941; s. Floyd Everet and Gladys May (Hogen) L.; m. Piola Anne Taliaferro, June 6, 1969; children: Christopher Charles, Andrea Kay BA in Physics, Concordia Coll., Moorhead, Minn., 1963; MS in Physics, U. N.D., 1965; PhD in Physics, U. Mo., 1970. Rsch. physicist, group leader x-ray diffraction, sect. head thin films and microstructures solid state div. Oak Ridge Nat. Lab., Tenn., 1969—. Contbr. numerous articles to profl. jours. Recipient Sidhu award Pitts. Diffraction Soc., 1974 Fellow Am. Phys. Soc.; mem. Am. Crystallographic Assn. (Bertram E. Warren Diffraction Physics award 1985), Materials Research Soc. Office: Oak Ridge Nat Lab Solid State Divsn PO Box 2008 Oak Ridge TN 37831-2008 E-mail: bcl@ornl.gov.

LARSON, BEVERLY ROLANDSON, elementary education educator; b. Oklee, Minn., May 30, 1938; d. Orville K. and Belle A. (Anderson) Rolandson; m. Roland K. Larson, June 29, 1962; children: Amy Jo, Ann Marie, Carl Lee. BS, Concordia Coll., 1962; MA, Mankato State U., 1984. Cert. elem., spl. edn. tchr., Minn. Tchr. Hudson Sch. Dist., LaPuente, Calif., 1961-62, Thief River Falls (Minn.) Sch. Dist., 1962-63, Sch. Dist. 271, Bloomington, Minn., 1964-69, 71-72, Valley View Sch., Bloomington, 1989—; spl. edn. tchr. Sch. Dist. 271, 1975-79, 86-89. Youth leader, Sunday sch. tchr. Christ the King Luth. Ch., Bloomington, 1969-82; precinct co-chair Rep. Party, Bloomington, alt., del. Recipient Svc. award Walk for Mankind, 1976, Golden Apple Achiever award Ashland Oil, 1994. Mem. NEA, Assn. Childhood Edn. (pres. Bloomington br. 1992-94), Minn. Edn. Assn., Nat. Learning Disabilities Assn., Minn. Learning Disabilities Assn., Bloomington Edn. Assn. Republican. Lutheran. Avocations: crafts, reading, plays and musicals, golf. Home: 7800 Pickfair Dr Bloomington MN 55438-1380 Office: Valley View Sch 351 E 88th St Bloomington MN 55420-2909

LARSON, BRIAN FOIX, architect; b. Eau Claire, Wis., July 6, 1935; s. Albert Foix and Dorothy Jean (Thompson) L.; m. Mildred Anne Nightswander, Feb. 13, 1961; children: Urban Alexander, Soren Federick. BArch, U. Ill., 1959. Registered architect, Wis., Minn., Colo., Mass., N.H., Fla. Architect-in-tng. Geometrics, Inc., Cambridge, Mass., 1959-60, Bastille Halsey Assoc., Boston, 1960-62; ptnr. Larson, Playter, Smith, Eau Claire, 1962-72; v.p. Larson, Hestekins, Smith, Ltd., 1962-80, Ayres Assocs., Eau Claire, 1980—. Sec. Wis. Bd. Archtl. Examiners, 1985-88, chmn., 1988-89; master juror Nat. Coun. Archtl. Reg. Bd. Bldg. Design Exam, 1987-96. Prin. works include One Mill Plaza, Laconia, N.H. (Honor award New Eng. Regional Council AIA 1974), Eau Claire County Courthouse, Wis., (Honor award Wis. Soc. Architects 1978), St. Croix County Courthouse, Wis., Dunn County Jud. Ctr. Mem. Hist. Bldg. Code Adv. Com., Wis., 1985. Mem. AIA (bd. dirs. 1996-98), Wis. Soc. Architects (pres. 1983), Wis. Architects Found. (bd. dirs. 1992-98), Soc. Archtl. Historians. Home: 215 Roosevelt Ave Eau Claire WI 54701-4065 Office: Ayres Assocs PO Box 1590 Eau Claire WI 54702-1590 E-mail: larsonb@ayresassociates.com.

LARSON, BRUCE ROBERT, lawyer, educator; b. Whittier, Calif., Jan. 14, 1955; s. Robert Edward and Ruth Marie (Peterson) L.; m. Judith Elaine Sword, Oct. 30, 1982; children: Seth Julius, Gregory Bruce. BA magna cum laude, Gustavus Adolphus Coll., 1977; JD cum laude, U. Minn., 1980. Bar: Minn. 1980, U.S. Dist. Ct. Minn. 1980, U.S. Ct. Appeals (8th cir.) 1980, Ga. 1986, Va. 2000. Immigration officer U.S. Immigration & Naturalization Svc., Mpls., 1977-81; atty. Bd. Immigration Appeals U.S. Dept. Justice, Washington, 1981-85; assoc. Powell, Goldstein, Frazer & Murphy, Atlanta, 1986-89, ptnr., 1990-96, Littler, Mendelson, Atlanta, 1996-98; hon. consul of Sweden, 1996-2000; ptnr. Paul, Hastings, Janofsky, Walker, 1998-99, Flippin, Densmore, Morse & Jessee, Roanoke, Va., 1999—2001, of counsel, 2001—; dir. internat. pers. office, atty. legal dept. Mayo Found., Rochester, Minn., 2001—. Adj. prof. immigration law U. Ga., 1991-99; legal advisor Tonka Babe Ruth Baseball League, Minnetonka, Minn., 1980-81. Asst. organist Apostles Luth. Ch., Atlanta, 1986-99, mem. coun., 1994-96, pres. 1995; coach Tonka Babe Ruth and Little Leagues, Minnetonka, 1973-81; bd. govs., Scandinavian Am. Found. Ga., Atlanta, 1992-2000, chmn., 1993-97; bd. dirs. Scandinavian Festival, Inc., 1994-96; asst. dir. Masterworks Chorale, Atlanta, 1988-95; bd. dirs. Swedish Coun. Am., 1998—; mem. bd. advs. Atlanta Internat. Museum, 1997-99; asst. organist, choir dir. St. John Luth. Ch., Roanoke, 1999-2001, interim dir. Praise Ministry, 1999-2000; bd. dirs. Roanoke Symphony Orch., 2000-2001; state coord. for musicians serving Evangelical Luth. Ch., 2001; asst. organist, choir dir. Good Shepherd Luth. Ch., Rochester, 2002 —. Recipient Cert. of Merit, U.S. Atty. Gen., 1982-85. Mem. Am. Immigration Lawyers Assn. (chpt. pres. 1991-93, nat. bd. govs.), Swedish-Am. C. of C., Vasa Order of Am., Iota Delta Gamma. Avocations: music, tennis, bridge, baseball. Office: Mayo Found Internat Pers Office Siebens 5 200 First St SW Rochester MN 55905 E-mail: larson.bruce@mayo.edu.

LARSON, BRYAN A. lawyer; s. Byron Ancedus and Betty Marilyn Larson; m. Kathy Stevenett; children: Aaron, Adam, Conor, Kaden, Sara, Aubrey. BA, Brigham Young U., 1980, JD, 1983. Bar: Utah 1983. Assoc. Christensen, Jensen & Powell, Salt Lake City, 1983-86, McKay, Burton & Thurman, Salt Lake City, 1986-91; ptnr. Larson, Jenkins & Halliday, 1991-95, Larson, Kirkham & Turner, Salt Lake City, 1995-99, Larson, Turner, Fairbanks and Dalby, Salt Lake City, 1999—. Editor newsletter Backtalk, 1995. Mem. ALTA (mem. polit. action com. 1991—), Utah Bar Assn. (com. chmn. 1990-92), Utah Trial Lawyers Assn. (polit. action com. 1991—), Order of Barristers. Mem. Lds Ch. Avocations: boating, snow skiing. Office: Larson Turner Fairbanks & Dalby 1218 W South Jordan Pkwy Ste B South Jordan UT 84095

LARSON, CARL SHIPLEY, engineering educator, consultant; b. Chgo., Sept. 23, 1934; s. Carl Uno and Marion Jean Larson; m. Vivian Phylis Peuckert, Dec. 28, 1957; children: Carl, Michael, Daniel. BSME, U. Ill., 1956, MSME, 1958, PhD, 1965. Registered profl. engr., Ill. Engr. Western Electric, Chgo., 1955-56; from instr. to asst. prof. U. Ill., Urbana, 1965-72, assoc. prof., 1972-91, asst. dean, 1974—, prof., 1991-94, prof. emeritus, 1994—. Bd. dirs. Capsonic Corp., Elgin, Ill. Contbr. articles to profl. jours. Bd. dirs. United Way, Urbana, 1987. Teaching Fellowship Nat. Sci. Found, Urbana, 1960-64. Mem. Am. Soc. Engring. Edn. (sect. chmn. 1990-91), Nat. Coun. Examiners Engring. (coms., vice-chmn. 1989-92). Office: 411 E Mumford Dr Urbana IL 61801-6230 also: U of Ill 206 Engring Hall 1308 W Green St Urbana IL 61801-2936 E-mail: c-larson@uiuc.edu.

LARSON, CAROLE ALLIS, library and information scientist, educator; b. Dayton, Ohio, Aug. 31, 1945; d. Harold Arthur and Myra Barbara Larson; m. Lowell Wilson Eyer, Jr., Nov. 16, 1985. BA in Sociology, Carleton Coll., 1967; MA in Edn., Washington U., 1968; MA in Asian Studies, U. Oregon, 1975; MA in Libr. Sci., U. Denver, 1977. Reference libr. instrnl. svcs. U. Nebr., Kearney, 1978-80; campus libr. Met. Comty. Coll., Omaha, 1980-81; asst. prof. social scis., reference libr. U. Nebr., 1981-85, assoc. prof., 1985—2001, ret., 2001. Cons. Bellevue Coll. Libr., Omaha, 1982-83 Contbr. articles to profl. jours. Co-recipient Reference Svc. Press award Am. Libr. Assn. Reference and Adult Svcs. Divsn., 1995; Washington U. fellow. Mem. ALA, Assn. Coll. and Rsch. Librs., Nebr. Libr. Assn. Democrat. E-mail: researchercl@yahoo.com.

LARSON, CHARLES FRED, consultant; b. Gary, Ind., Nov. 27, 1936; s. Charles F. and Margaret J. (Taylor) Larson; m. Joan Ruth Grupe, Aug. 22, 1959; children: Gregory Paul, Laura Ann. BSME, Purdue U., 1958; MBA summa cum laude, Fairleigh Dickinson U., 1973. Registered profl. engr., N.J. Project engr. Combustion Engring., Inc., East Chicago, Ind., 1958-60; sec. Welding Rsch. Council, N.Y.C., 1960-70, asst. dir., 1970-75; exec. dir. Indsl. Rsch. Inst., Inc., Washington, 1975-99, pres., 1999—2001, Innovation Rsch. Internat., Washington, 2001—. Mem. mech. engring. adv. bd. Purdue U.; mem. selection com. Nat. Inventors Hall of Fame. Assoc. editor: Jour. Pressure Vessel Tech., 1973—75, mem. bd. advisors: Who's Who in Am. Mem. Wyckoff (N.J.) Bd. Edn., 1973—78, pres., 1976—77; reader In Touch Networks, Inc., N.Y.C., 1979—89; chmn. 43d Nat. Conf. Advancement Rsch. Fellow: ASME, AAAS; mem.: Kenwood Club, Univ. Club, Sigma Xi. Republican. Methodist.

LARSON, CHARLES ROBERT, naval officer; b. Sioux Falls, S.D., Nov. 20, 1936; s. Eldred Charles and Gertrude Edythe (Jensen) L.; m. Sarah Elizabeth Craig, Aug. 19, 1961; children: Sigrid Anne, Erica Lynn, Kirsten Elizabeth. BS in Marine Engring., U.S. Naval Acad., 1958. Commd. ensign USN, 1958, advanced through grades to adm., 1990; naval aviator, attack pilot, 1958-63; nuclear power, submarine tng., 1963-64; assigned nuclear subs., 1964-76; naval aide to the Pres., 1969-71; comdg. officer USS Halibut, 1973-76; comdr. submarine devel. group one, head operational deep submergence program, 1976-78; chief naval ops. staff Strategic Submarine Programs, 1978-79; dir. long range planning group Washington, 1978-82; comdr. submarines Mediterranean, 1982-83; supt. U.S. Naval Acad. Annapolis, Md., 1983-86; comdr. 2d Fleet, 1986-88; dir. plans, policies and ops. DCNO, 1988-90; comdr. U.S. Pacific Fleet, 1990-91, U.S. Pacific Command, Hawaii, 1991-94; supt. U.S. Naval Acad., 1994-98; v.p. U.S. Naval Inst., 1994-98; sr. fellow The CNA Corp., Alexandria, Va., 1998—. Bd. dirs. Northrop Grumman, Unocal, Constellation Energy Group. Mem. USO Coun., Honolulu, 1990-92; mem. Honolulu area coun. Boy Scouts Am., 1990-94. Decorated Def. D.S.M., Navy D.S.M. (7), Legion of Merit (3), Bronze Star, others; White House fellow, 1968-69. Mem. NAS (com. on internat. security and arms control), Coun. on Fgn. Rels. Home: 591 Coover Rd Annapolis MD 21401-6921 Office: The CNA Corp 4825 Mark Ctr Dr Alexandria VA 22311-1850

LARSON, CHUCK, JR. state representative; m. Jennifer Eileen Larson. Doctorate, Uinv. Iowa, 1996; BA in Econ. with hon., Univ. Iowa, 1992. State chmn. Rep. Party of Iowa, 2001—; coun. ESCO Group, Cedar Rapids, Iowa, 1999—; asst. atty. Jones County, 1997—99; state rep. Iowa House Dist. 55, 1992—. State vice chair George W. Bush for Pres., 1999—2000; chmn. House Judiciary Com., 1992—; chair Economic Devel. Com.; mem. Res. Officers Assn. Bd. dirs. Salvation Army. Capt. USAR, 1987—. Mem.: Iowa State Bar Assn., Am. Legion, Rotary, Phi Beta Kappa. Republican. Office: 521 E Locust Ste 200 Des Moines IA 50309*

LARSON, DAVID ALLEN, law educator; b. Libertyville, Ill., Nov. 5, 1954; s. Allen John and Mary Jane (Williams) L.; m. Patricia Pierman. BA magna cum laude, DePauw U., Greencastle, Ind., 1976; JD, U. Ill., 1979; LLM, U. Pa., Phila., 1987. Bar: Minn. 1979, U.S. Dist Ct. Minn. 1980, U.S. Ct. Appeals (8th cir.) 1980, Ill. 1982, U.S. Dist. Ct. (no. dist.) Ill. 1982, Nebr. 1989, U.S. Supreme Ct. 1990. Assoc. Meagher & Geer, Mpls., 1979-81; asst. prof. Loyola U. Chgo. Sch. Bus. Adminstrn., 1981-83; assoc. prof. Millsaps Coll. Sch. Mgmt., Jackson, Miss., 1983-87; prof. Creighton U. Sch. Law, Omaha, 1987-90, 91-99; prof.-in-residence appellate div. EEOC, Washington, 1990-91; dir. Dispute Resolution Inst., 1999-2000, sr. fellow, 2000—; prof. law Hamline U., St. Paul, 1999—. Hearing examiner Nebr. EEOC, 1997-2000; vis. scholar Macalester Coll., Sch. Law Hamline U., St. Paul, 1997-98; arbitrator, mediator, expert witness, editor-in-chief Jour. of Alternative Dispute Resolution in Employment. Contbr. articles to profl. jours. Rsch. scholar Lund (Sweden) U. Law Sch., 1985, 88, 89. Mem. ABA (vice chmn. sect. on internat. law and practice, employment law com., vice-chmn. dispute resolution sect., legal edn. com.), Phi Beta Kappa. Avocations: classical music, theater, cinema, profl. sporting events, fishing. Office: Hamline Univ Sch Law 1536 Hewitt Ave Saint Paul MN 55104-1205 Fax: (651) 523-2236. E-mail: davidallenlarson@hotmail.com.

LARSON, DAVID CHRISTOPHER, lawyer; b. Spencer, Iowa, Sept. 4, 1955; s. Leonard and Margaret Rozanne Larson; m. Carol Ann Kuntz, Sept. 17, 1983. BS in Constrn. Engring., Iowa State U., 1978; JD, Creighton U., 1981. Bar: Iowa 1981, U.S. Patent Office 1981, U.S. Dist. Ct. (no. dist.) Iowa 1981, U.S. Ct. Appeals (8th cir.) 1981. Law clk. Henderson & Sturm, Omaha, 1981; ptnr. Stoller & Larson, Spirit Lake, Iowa, 1981-84; pvt. practice, 1984-98; alt. dist. assoc. judge Iowa Jud. Dist. 3A, 1983-98, dist. assoc. judge, 1998—. Mem. Iowa State Bar Assn. (com. on patents, trademarks and copyrights 1982-86), Iowa Judges Assn., Dist. 3A Bar Assn. (pres. 1983-84), DIckinson County Bar Assn. (chmn. Am. citizen com. 1982-83, pres. 1983-84), Iowa Patent Law Assn., Iowa Great Lakes C. of C. (amb. 1982-86), Okoboji Yacht Club (trophy chmn. 1984-88, bd. dirs. 1987—), Kiwanis (chmn. fin. com. 1983, bd. dirs. 1984, pres. 1987), Masons, Order Eastern Star. Republican. Methodist. Office: PO Box 246 Spirit Lake IA 51360-0246 E-mail: dlarson@ncn.net.

LARSON, DAVID LEE, surgeon; b. Kansas City, Mo., Dec. 9, 1943; s. Leonard Nathaniel and Mary Elizabeth (Stuck) L.; m. Sherrill Ankli, Apr. 16, 1977; children: Jeffrey David, Dawn Elizabeth, Bradley Jesse. BS, Bowling Green State U., 1965; MD, La. State U., 1969. Diplomate Am. Bd. Plastic Surgery (bd. dirs. 1996—, sec.-treas. 1998—). Intern Charity Hosp. of La., New Orleans, 1969-70; resident otolaryngology Baylor Coll. Medicine, Houston, 1972-76; plastic surgery resident Ind. U., Indpls., 1976-78; surgeon M.D. Anderson Cancer Ctr., Houston, 1978-85; prof., chmn. dept. plastic and reconstructive surgery Med. Coll Wis., Milw., 1986—. Alano J. Ballantyne prof. in head and neck surgery, M.D. Anderson Cancer Ctr., Houston, 1985; sec.-treas. Am. Bd. Plastic Surgery, 1996-2002. Editor: Cancer in the Neck, 1987, Essentials of Head and Neck Oncology, 1998. Capt. USNR, 1991—. Mem. Am. Assn. Plastic Surgeons, Nat. Inst. Healthcare Rsch. (chmn. bd. dirs. 1995-2000), Plastic Surgery Ednl. Found. (pres. 2001—). Avocations: reading, family, exercise. Home: 13510 Braemar Dr Elm Grove WI 53122-2509 Office: Med Coll Wis 9200 W Wisconsin Ave Milwaukee WI 53226-3522 E-mail: dlarson@mcw.edu.

LARSON, DAVID MITCHELL, English studies educator, writer; b. Marshall, Minn., Oct. 21, 1944; s. Clarence I. and Alyce I. Larson; 1 child, Brian. BA, U. Minn., 1966, MA, 1969, PhD, 1973. Prof. English Franklin & Marshall Coll., Lancaster, Pa., 1971-75, Cleve. State U., 1975—. Contbr. editor: Heath Anthology of American Literature, 1990; contbr. author: Encyclopedia of American Literature, 1999; contbr. articles to profl. jours., short stories to lit. mags. Mem. Human Rights Campaign, Gay Lesbian Ctr., Cleve.; mem. Interweave, Cleve. City Country Dancers, Brothers' Keepers. Mem. AAUP (pres., 2000—, v.p. Cleve. State U. chpt. 1998-2000, sec. 1994-96). Democrat. Unitarian Universalist. Avocations: reading, attending plays, camping. Home: 15105 Lake Ave Apt 2 Lakewood OH 44107-1326 Office: Cleve State U Dept English Euclid at East 24th St Cleveland OH 44115

LARSON, DIANE LAVERNE KUSLER, principal; b. Fredonia, N.D., July 28, 1942; d. Raymond Edwin and LaVerne (Mayer) Kusler; m. Donald Floyd Larson, Aug. 14, 1965. BS, Valley City (N.D.) State U., 1964; MS, Mankato (Minn.) State U., 1977; EdS, U. Minn., 1987. Cert. tchr., Minn. Tchr. elem. Cokato (Minn.) Elem. Sch., 1962-64, Lakeview Elem. Sch., Robbinsdale, Minn., 1964-66; vocal tchr. Wheaton (Minn.) High Sch., 1966-67; tchr. Owatonna (Minn.) Elem. Sch., 1967-88, prin., 1988—. V.p. Cannon Valley Uniserv, Mankato, 1981-83; NEA del. World Confederation of Orgns. of the Teaching Professions, Melbourne, 1988. Named Woman of Yr., Owatonna Bus. and Profl. Women, 1990. Mem. NEA (bd. dirs. 1986-88), Minn. Edn. Assn. (bd. dirs. 1983-88, Outstanding Woman in Leadership award 1983), Minn. Reading Assn. (bd. dirs. 1983-97, Pres. award 1984), Internat. Reading Assn. (coord. for Minn. 1990-97, bd. dirs. 1997-2000, Celebrate Literacy award 1998), Minn. Elem. Prins. Assn., Valley City State U. Alumni Assn. (Cert. of Merit 1998), Delta Kappa Gamma (legis. chmn. 1986-88, pres. 1992, Woman of Achievement award 1989, Tau leadership chair, Tau State 1st v.p. 1997-99). Congregationalist. Home: 19654 Bagley Ave Faribault MN 55021-2246 Office: Washington Sch 338 E Main St Owatonna MN 55060-3096 E-mail: pianodl@clear.lakes.com.

LARSON, DOROTHY ANN, business educator; b. Nekoosa, Wis., Feb. 27, 1934; d. Edwin E. and Ruby E. (Burch) L.; children: Jean Marie Harkey, Kenneth Lee Fitz, Cynthia Ann Anderson. BS with high distinction in Bus. and English, No. Ariz. U., 1969; MA in English, 1971; EdD in Bus., Ariz. State U., 1980. Tchr. English, Cottonwood (Ariz.) Oak Creek Elem. Sch., 1969-70; tchr. bus. and English, Mingus Union High Sch., Cottonwood, 1970-79, dir. vocat. edn., 1976-79; mem. faculty dept. bus. adminstrn. Yavapai Coll., 1979-94, chairperson bus. divsn., 1981-86, prep. coord. Yavapai Tech., 1994-95; cons. Ariz. Dept. Edn.; curriculum specialist Northern Ariz. U., 1995-98; mem. adv. coun. Gov's. Coun. Practitioners. Mem. Ariz. Bus. Edn. Assn. (pres. 1980-81), Nat. Bus. Edn. Assn., Am. Vocat. Assn., Ariz. Edn. Assn., NEA, Nat. Tech. Prep. Network, Pi Omega Pi, Delta Pi Epsilon, Phi Kappa Phi, Alpha Delta Kappa, Phi Delta Kappa. Republican. Editor Ariz. Bus. Edn. Newsletter, 1972-74. Home: 542 S Marina Dr Gilbert AZ 85233-6610

LARSON, EDWARD, state supreme court justice; m. Mary Loretta Thompson; children: Sarah, John, Mary Elizabeth. BS, Kans. State U., 1954; JD, Kans. U., 1960. Pvt. practice, Hays, Kans., 1960—87; judge Kans. Ct. Appeals, 1987—95; justice Kans. Supreme Ct., Topeka, 1995—. Mcpl. judge City of Hays, 1965—72. 2d lt. USAF. Office: Kans Supreme Ct 301 W 10th Rm 388 Topeka KS 66612*

LARSON, EDWARD JOHN, law educator, lawyer, historian; b. Mansfield, Ohio, Sept. 21, 1953; s. Rex and Jean (Uncapher) Larson; m. Lucy Marie Kaiser, July 28, 1990; children: Sarah Marie, Luke Anders. BA, Williams, 1974; MA, U. Wis., 1976, PhD, 1985; JD, Harvard U., 1979. Bar: Wash. 1979, U.S. Dist. Ct. (we. dist.) Wash. 1979, U.S. Ct. Appeals (9th cir.) 1979, U.S. Tax Ct. 1981, U.S. Supreme Ct. 1984. Atty. Davis, Wright & Tremaine, Seattle, 1979—82; assoc. counsel U.S. House Com. on Edn. and Labor, Washington, 1983—86; counsel U.S. Office Edn. Rsch. and Improvement, 1986—87; Richard B. Russell prof. history and law Univ. Ga., Athens, 1987—, chair history dept., 2001—. Panelist human genome project NIH, Washington, 1990—2002; adv. U.S. Dept. Edn., Washington, 1987—93; vis. prof. Univ. Jean Moulin, Lyon, France, 1996; lectr. Templeton Found., 1997; John Adams chair Fulbright program U. Leiden, The Netherlands, 2000—01. Author: Trial & Error, 1985, Sex, Race & Science, 1995, Summer for the Gods, 1997, A Different Death, 1998, Evolution's Workshop, 2001. Counsel Wash. State House Reps., Olympia, 1981—82; analyst Wis. State Senate, Madison, 1974—76. Recipient Pulitzer prize for history, 1998, Templeton Found. Article prize, 1997, George Sarton award, AAAS, 2000; scholar, Rockefeller Found., 1996. Mem.: Forum History Sci. Am. (exec. com. chair 1992—94), History Sci. Soc. (com. chair 1994—97), Wash. State Bar Assn. Avocations: travel, hiking, bicycling, birdwatching. Home: 253 Cobb St Athens GA 30601-2407 Office: Univ Ga LeConte Hall Athens GA 30602 E-mail: edlarson@uga.edu.

LARSON, EDWARD WILLIAM, civil engineering educator, aerospace engineer; b. New Haven, Apr. 17, 1923; s. Edward W. and Clara (Garlick) L; m. Lila Mae Adkinson, Apr. 26, 1952; children: John Edward, Susan Diane. BSCE, Ind. Tech. Coll., 1943; MSCE, Northwestern U., 1948, PhD, 1953. Mgr. turbomachinery Rocketdyne div. Rockwell Internat., Canoga Park, Calif., 1966-68, mgr. engring., 1968-78, assoc. chief engring., 1978-79, dir. design tech., 1979-84, assoc. program mgr., 1984-86; lectr. in engring. Calif. State U., Northridge, 1986-92. With USAAF, 1946-47. Mem. AIAA, Nat. Mgmt. Assn. (Silver Knight award 1984), Inst. Cert. Profl. Mgrs. (chmn. bd. regents 1975-77), Soc. Exptl. Mechanics, Am. Soc. Engring. Edn., Sigma Xi. Home: 18621 Ringling St Tarzana CA 91356-4510

LARSON, ERIC B. hospital administrator; MD, Harvard U., 1973; MPH, U. Wash., 1977. Intern in medicine Beth Israel Hosp., Harvard U., Boston, 1973—74; resident in medicine, RWJ Clin. Scholar Harvard U., 1974—75; adj. prof. health svcs. U. Wash., assoc. dean clin. affairs, prof. medicine; med dir. U. Wash. Med. Ctr., 1989—. Contbr. articles to profl. jours. Fellow: Am. Coll. Physicians; mem.: Am. Soc. Clin. Investigation, Am. Geriatrics Soc., Assn. Am. Physicians, Phi Beta Kappa. Office: U Wash Med Ctr 1959 Pacific St Box 356330 Seattle WA 98195-6330*

LARSON, GARY, cartoonist; b. Tacoma, Aug. 14, 1950; s. Vern and Doris Larson; married. BA in Communications, Wash. State U., 1972. Jazz musician, 1973-76; with music store, Seattle, 1976-77, Humane Soc., Seattle, 1978-80; cartoonist Seattle Times, 1978-79; syndicated cartoonist The Far Side Chronicle Features Syndicate, San Francisco, 1979-84; syndicated cartoonist The Far Side cartoon panel Universal Press Syndicate, Kansas City, Mo., 1984-94; cartoonist, 1994—. Prodr. books, calendars, greeting cars, t-shirts, day runner organizers, computer calendars, screen savers, coffee mugs.; since The Far Side was retired in 1994, it still appears syndicated in over 200 newspapers in fgn. market by Creators Syndicate Internat. Exhbns. include The Far Side of Sci. (exhibited at Calif. Acad. Scis., 1987, Smithsonian Instn., 1987, Denver Mus. Natural History, L.A. County Mus., Shedd Aquarium, Chgo., other mus.), The Far Side of the Zoo, Washington Park Zoo, Portland, Oreg., 1987; author: (cartoon collections) The Far Side, 1982, Beyond The Far Side, 1983, In Search of The Far Side, 1984, Bride of The Far Side, 1985, Valley of the Far Side, 1985, It Came from The Far Side, 1986, The Far Side Observer, 1987, Hound of the Far Side, 1984, Night of the Crash-Test Dummies, 1988, Wildlife Preserves, 1989, The Prehistory of the Far Side: A 10th Anniversary Exhibit, 1989, Weiner Dog Art, 1990, Unnatural Selections, 1991, Cows of Our Planet, 1992, The Chickens are Restless, 1993, The Curse of Madame "C", 1994, Last Chapter and Worse, 1996, (cartoon anthologies) The Far Side Gallery, 1984, The Far Side Gallery II, 1986, The Far Side Gallery III, 1988, The Far Side Gallery IV, 1993, The Far Side Gallery V, 1995, There's A Hair in My Dirt! A Worm's Story, 1998; animated film and CBS TV Halloween spl. Gary Larson's Tales from The Far Side, 1994 (Grand prix Annecy Film Festival, 1995), 2d animated film Gary Lason's Tales from The Far Side II, 1997. Recipient award for Best Humor Panel, Nat. Cartoonists Soc., 1986, Reuben award for Outstanding Cartoonist of Yr. Nat. Cartoonists Soc., 1991, 94, Max and Moritz prize for best internat. comic strip panel Internat. Comics Salon, 1993, other awards. Avocation: jazz music. Address: Creators Syndicated Internat 5777 W Century Blvd Ste 700 Los Angeles CA 90045 also: care Andrews McMeel Pub 4520 Main St Ste 700 Kansas City MO 64111-7701

LARSON, GARY ARTHUR, farmer, financial consultant; b. Madison, Minn., Dec. 16, 1959; s. Alvin J. and Leona L.; m. Ingrid Carol Bellows, Aug. 9, 1986; children: Brent, Sonja. BS in Agrl. Bus., S.D. State U., 1982. Farmer Gary A. Larson Farm, Canby, Minn., 1981—; loan officer, computer programmer Farm Credit Svcs., Canby and Madison, 1983-85, credit analyst, computer programmer Wilmar and Marshall, 1986-91, computer sys. coord. Wilmar, 1992-93. Fin., computer cons. Larson Cons., Canby, 1993—; cons. Small Bus. Adminstr., Brookings, S.D., 1982. Inventor windpower model/report, 1978; patent for planting toolbar. Chmn. parish coun. St. James Ch., Dawson, Minn., 1995-99; mem., worker PTA, Dawson, 1997-2000; mem., telethon worker Pioneer Pub. TV, Appleton, Minn., 1988-2001. Finalist Top 100 Best Managed Farms, Farm Futures Mag., 2001; named one of, 1993—2001; recipient 1st place for wheat yield, Nat. Assn. Wheat Growers, 1990. Mem. Corn Growers Assn., Wheat Growers Assn., Soybean Growers Assn., Mortar Bd., Alpha Zeta (vice chmn. 1981-82). Avocations: restoring classic cars and tractors, hunting, reading. Office: Gary A Larson Farm RR# Box 150 Canby MN 56220

LARSON, GEORGE STANLEY, English educator; b. Willmar, Minn., July 28, 1939; s. George Eric and Alfrieda Charlotte (Forsell) L.; m. Mary Kathryn Engan, May 2, 1971. BA, Augsburg Coll., 1961; MA, Duke U., 1962; PhD, U. Mass., 1969. Prof. English Concordia Coll., Moorhead, Minn., 1962—. Contbr. articles to profl. jours. Woodrow Wilson Found. fellow, 1961-62, U.S.A. Nat. Def. Edn. Act. fellow, 1966-68. Mem. MLA, Nat. Assn. Tchrs. English, Dickens Soc. Lutheran. Avocations: classical music, travel, reading, antiques. Office: Concordia Coll 901 8th St S Moorhead MN 56562

LARSON, GEORGE CHARLES, magazine editor, writer; b. Mar. 31, 1942; s. George Lester and Mildred Caroline (Frehner) L.; m. Valarie Ann Thompson, Aug. 20, 1946; children: Evan Richard; Alice Lynn and Keely Mae (twins). BA, Harvard U., 1964. Staff writer Scholastic Mag., N.Y.C., 1971; regional editor, mng. editor Flying Mag., 1972-78; tech. editor Bus. & Comml. Aviation Mag., White Plains, N.Y., 1980-85; editor Air & Space/Smithsonian Mag., Washington, 1985—. Author: Fly on Instruments, The Blimp Book. Served with U.S. Army, 1966-70, Vietnam. Office: Air & Space Mag PO Box 37012 MRC 951 Washington DC 20013-7012

LARSON, HARRY THOMAS, electronics engineer, executive, consultant; b. Berkeley, Calif., Oct. 16, 1921; s. Harry Homer and Edna Clara (Petersen) L.; m. Merry Evelyn Otteson, Dec. 26, 1956 (div. Dec. 1975); children: Kristin Eve Beltz, Margit Merry Mills, Megan Marie Hoyt. BSEE summa cum laude, U. Calif., Berkeley, 1947; MSEE, UCLA, 1954. Computer engr. Inst. for Numerical Analysis Nat. Bur. Standards, L.A., 1949-51; mem. tech. staff Advanced Electronics Lab. Hughes Aircraft Co., Culver City, Calif., 1951-54; dept. mgr. bus. applications of computers Ramo-Wooldridge Co., Inglewood, 1954-56; asst. divsn. dir. command and control systems Aero. divsn. Philco-Ford Co., Newport Beach, 1956-68; asst. div. dir. software and computing ctr. TRW Systems, Redondo Beach, 1968-69; dir. planning Calif. Computer Products, Anaheim, 1969-74; sr. scientist Hughes Aircraft, Fullerton, Calif., 1978-87; pres. Larbridge Enterprises Cons., Laguna Hills, 1970—. Mem. Army Sci. Bd., Washington, 1988-92; contbd. to NASA's Mission Control Ctr. in Houston for Gemini, Apollo, Skylab and shuttle missions, Field Army tactical command and control system, first random access computer memory, early airborne digital computer, first keyboard and cathode ray tube data entry device (terminal), first-of-a-kind applications of computers in banks, factories, pension trust funds, payroll, acctg., truck scheduling, R.R. car routing, car body design and manufacture, automobile assembly plant inventory control, electrical power distbn. network, steel hot roll mill, computer programming methodologies (modularization, report generator, table-driven software), founds. for display tech. and large screen displays; lectr., organizer, chair confs., workshops, conf. sessions, 1954-74. Editor Proc. Inst. Radio Engrs., 1961; editor, pub. The Labridge Letter, 1973-76; co-editor Handbook of Automation, Computation and Control, 1959; contbr. articles to profl. jours., computer publs.; patentee in field. 1st lt. USAF, 1942-45. Fellow IEEE (life; Centennial medal); mem. IEEE Computer Soc. (co-fouder, nat. chmn. 1954-55, chmn. Social Implications of Computers, 1956-70), Soc. for Info. Display, Am. Fedn. Info. Processing Soc. (bd. govs. 1956-60), Sigma Xi, Tau Beta Pi, Eta Kappa Nu. Avocations: writing, photography. Home and Office: Larbridge Enterprises 236 Calle Aragon Unit A Laguna Beach CA 92653-3492

LARSON, JANE WARREN, ceramist; b. San Francisco, June 2, 1922; d. Stafford Leak and Viola (Lockhart) Warren; m. Clarence Ernest Larson, Apr. 21, 1957; children: Lawrence Ernest, Lance Stafford, Robert Edward. Student, Swarthmore Coll., 1939-41; BA with honors, U. Rochester, 1943; MFA in Ceramics, Antioch Coll., 1982. Sci. reporter, tech. editor Tenn. Eastman Corp., Oak Ridge, 1943-46; chief Tech. Info. Ctr. Carbide & Carbon Chem. Corp., 1946-51; tech. editor physics div. Rand Corp., Santa Monica, Calif., 1954-55, tech. libr. Washington, 1955-57; ceramist Janeware, Santa Monica, 1953-55; pres., bldg. founder Oak Ridge Community Art Ctr., 1963-66, ceramic tchr., 1965-69; ceramic tchr. Inst. Learning in Retirement Am. U., Washington, 1985-88, 94. One-person shows at AAAS, Washington, 1990, Studio Gallery, Washington, 1992, 95, Cosmos Club, Washington, 1998, others 1973—, Creative Ptnrs. Gallery, Bethesda, Md., 1996; group shows at Bader Gallery and others, 1971—, Internat. Sculpture Conf., Washington, 1990, U. Md. Sculpture Show, 1994-95; vanishing diversity murals with water Guest Quarters Hotel gardens, Bethesda, Md., 1987, Oak Ridge Com. Art Ctr. garden, energy and life murals, 1992, Fed. City Shelter, Washington, 1988, U. Md. Chemistry Bldg., 1997; columns: Johns Hopkins Ctr. Internat. Studies, Washington, 1990, NAE, Beckman Ctr., Irvine, Calif., 1990, Asia Nora Restaurant, Washington, 1994; permanent collections include U. Md., College Park, (sculpture) AAAS, Am. Ctr. Physics, College Park, Renwick Gallery Nat. Mus. Am. Art; commns. include 4 murals 20 vases Germaines Restaurant, Washington, 1978, East Wind Restaurant, Alexandria, Va., 1980; lobby murals Nat. Milk Producers Assn., Rosslyn, Va., 1983, U. Md. Chem. Bldg., 10 Molecules that Shaped the World, 1997, 10 Molecules that Matter to Medicine, 1998, NIH Libr. Medicine, The Arrow of Time, 1999, Arlington County Libr., Ubby Blake H.S., 2000; contbr. articles to profl. jours. Commr. Cable TV Commn., Montgomery County, Rockville, Md., 1989-90. Recipient Tile Heritage award, Tile Heritage Found., 2001. Mem. Ind. Agy. Women (pres. 1964-65), Kiln Club Washington (1st prize ann. show 1993), Achievement Rewards Coll. Sci., Inc. (v.p. 1980-81), Artists Equity, Internat. Sculpture Ctr., Bethesda Ceramic Guild (1st prize ann. show 1994, 95), Phi Beta Kappa. Avocation: writing poetry. Home and Office: 9707 Old Georgetown Rd 1420 Bethesda MD 20814

LARSON, JANICE TALLEY, computer science programmer; b. Houston, Sept. 29, 1948; d. Hiram Peak Talley and Jennie Edna Donahoo; m. Harold Vernon Larson, Apr. 8, 1977; children: Randall Neil, Christopher Lee. AA in Computers, San Jacinto Coll., 1981; BA in Computer Info. Systems, U. Houston, Clear Lake, 1984, MA in Computer Info. Systems, 1988; EdD in Instrnl. Tech., U. Houston, 1999. Programmer Control Applications, Houston, 1985-86, Tex. Eastern Pipeline, Houston, 1988-90; instr. computer sci. San Jacinto Coll., 1990-94; computer sci. reader Ednl. Testing Svc., Clear Lake, 1996-2000; programmer for shuttle cockpit avionics upgrade United Space Alliance, 2000—02. Adj. instr. U. Houston, Clear Lake, Tex., 1996, 99; sponsor Computer Sci. Club, Houston, 1992-94. Mem.: IEEE (assoc.), U. Houston Alumni Assn., Kappa Delta Pi, Phi Delta Kappa.

LARSON, JERRY LEROY, state supreme court justice; b. Harlan, Iowa, May 17, 1936; s. Gerald L. and Mary Eleanor (Patterson) L.; m. Debra L. Christensen; children: Rebecca, Jeffrey, Susan, David. BA, State U. Iowa, 1958, JD, 1960. Bar: Iowa. Partner firm Larson & Larson, 1961-75; dist. judge 4th Jud. Dist. Ct. of Iowa, 1975-78; justice Iowa Supreme Ct., 1978—. Office: Supreme Ct Iowa PO Box 109 Des Moines IA 50319-0001

LARSON, JOHN BARRY, congressman, insurance executive; b. Hartford, Conn., July 22, 1948; s. Raymond and Pauline (Nolan) L.; m. Leslie Best, Sept. 20, 1981; children: Carolyn, Laura, one son. BS, Cen. Ct. State U., 1971. Mem. Conn. Senate, 1984-98; pres. Senate, 1986-93; mem. U.S. Congress from 1st Conn. dist., 1999—; mem. armed svcs. com.; mem. sci. com. Recipient Outstanding Alumni award East Hartford High Sch. Nat. Honor Soc., 1985, Legis. Leadership award Conn. Assn. Human Svcs., 1987, Disting. Alumni award Cen. Conn. State U., 1987; Legislator of Yr. award Jr. League Conn., 1988, Conn. Valley Girl Scouts, 1989, Cath. Charities/Cath. Family Svcs., 1989; Man of Yr. award United Irish Socs., 1990, Champion for Children award Conn. Commn. on Children, 1990, recognition award Alzheimer's Assn. Greater Hartford, 1991, appreciation award Conn. AIDS Consortium/United Way Conn., 1991, Child Advocacy Legis. Leadership award Conn. Coalition for Children, 1991, others. Mem. Hartford Club. Democrat. Roman Catholic. Office: Ho of Reps 1419 Longworth Hob Washington DC 20515-0001 also: 221 Main Street, 2nd Floor Hartford CT 06106*

LARSON, JOHN DAVID, insurance company executive, lawyer; b. Madison, Wis., July 6, 1941; s. Lawrence John and Anna Mathilda (Furseth) Larson; m. Evelyn Vie Smith, Jan. 22, 1966 (div. Apr. 1980); children: Eric John, Karen Annette; m. Nancy Jay With, Nov. 29, 1980 (div. Dec. 1998); stepchildren: Andrew Zachary Jay, Anne Elizabeth Jay, Christopher Allen Jay; m. Sherri Ann Kliczak, July 12, 2002; 1 stepchild Cristopher Howard Kliczak. BBA, U. Wis., 1964, JD, 1965, MBA, 1966. CPA Wis.; CLU; bar: Wis. 1965, U.S. Ct. Mil. Appeals 1966; chartered fin. cons. With Nat. Guardian Life Ins. Co., Madison, 1969—, exec. v.p., treas., 1973, pres., dir., 1974—, pres., chief exec. officer, 1989—. Bd. advisors U.S. Bank, Madison; bd. dirs. TV Wis., Inc., KELAB, Inc. Chmn. Madison chpt. ARC, 1974—75; pres. United Way Dane County, 1975, Wis. N.G. Assn., 1992—96; trustee Village of Maple Bluff, 1997—. With U.S. Army, 1966—69, brig. gen. Wis. Army N.G., 1998. Named Disting. Bus. Alumnus, U. Wis.-Madison, 1996; recipient Know Your Madisonian award, Wis. State Jour., 1973. Mem.: ABA, Am. Soc. Fin. Svc. Profls., State Bar Wis., U. Wis. Bus. Alumni (bd. dirs. 1986—90), Madison C. of C. (dir. 1976—80), Maple Bluff Club (bd. dirs. 1974—80), Rotary. Lutheran. Home: 401 New Castle Way Madison WI 53704-6070 Office: PO Box 1191 Madison WI 53701-1191

LARSON, JOHN HYDE, retired utilities executive; b. Phila., Sept. 15, 1930; s. Roy Frank and Olive (Alden) L.; m. Priscilla Hibbs Beane; children: Michael Alden, Christopher Hibbs, Cynthia Ann. BA, Trinity Coll., 1953; M City Planning, MIT, 1955. Vice-pres. The Potomac Edison Co., Hagerstown, Md., 1969-72; treas. Allegheny Power System, Inc., N.Y.C., 1973-79; v.p. fin. Conn. Energy Corp., Bridgeport, Conn., 1980-85, pres., chief exec. officer, 1985-89; exec. v.p., chief operating officer So. Conn. Gas. Co., 1981-85, pres., chief exec. officer, 1985-89; acting dir. fin. City of Bridgeport, 1989-90, chmn. mgmt. adv. com., 1990—93; chmn. selectman's com. on ops. improvement Westport, 1991; chmn. oversight and audit com., pres. trustees Epis Diocese, Vt., 1998—. Mem. Internat. Exec. Svc. Corps., Vladimir, Russia, 1996; bd. dirs. Bolt Tech., Inc., Norwalk Conn. Vice chmn. Bridgeport Hosp., 1991-93; chmn. Nova Med. Corp., 1991-95; hon. chmn. capital funds drive Family Svcs. Woodfield, 1988; treas. Christ Episcopal Ch., Bethel, Vt., 1995-98; trustee Clara Martin Ctr.; pres. Barnard Edn. Found., Inc., 2000-02. Lt. (SC) USNR. Recipient Corp. Leadership award MIT, 1987, Century Svc. award Bridgeport Boys and Girls Club, 1991, Richard P. Bodine Community Leadership award, 1993. Mem. New Eng. Gas Assn. (chmn. 1988-89). Home: Mount Hunger Rd Barnard VT 05031

LARSON, JOHN WILLIAM, lawyer; b. Detroit, June 24, 1935; s. William and Sara Eleanor (Yeatman) L.; m. Pamela Jane Wren, Sept. 16, 1959; 1 dau., Jennifer Wren. BA with distinction, honors in Economics, Stanford, 1957; LLB, Stanford U., 1962. Bar: Calif. 1962. Assoc. Brobeck, Phleger & Harrison, San Francisco, 1962-68, ptnr., 1968-71, 73—, CEO, mng. ptnr., 1988-92, chmn. of firm, CEO, 1993-96; asst. sec. Dept. Interior, Washington, 1971-73; exec. dir. Natural Resources Com., 1973; counsellor to chmn. Cost of Living Coun., 1973. Faculty Practising Law Inst.; bd. dirs. Sangamo Bio Scis., Inc. Mem. 1st U.S.-USSR Joint Com. on Environment; mem. bd. visitors Stanford U. Law Sch., 1974-77, 85-87, 95-96; pres. bd. trustees The Katherine Branson Sch., 1980-83. With AUS, 1957-59. Mem. ABA, Calif. Bar Assn., San Francisco C. of C. (bd. dirs., chmn. 1996), Bay Area Coun., Calif. Acad. Sci., Order of Coif, Pacific Union Club, Burlingame Country Club, Bohemian Club, Lagunitas Country Club. Home: PO Box 349 Ross CA 94957-0349 Office: Brobeck Phleger & Harrison Spear St Tower 1 Market Plz San Francisco CA 94105-1420

LARSON, JOSEPH STANLEY, environmentalist, educator, researcher; b. Stoneham, Mass., June 23, 1933; s. Gustave Adolph and Marian (Kelly) L.; m. Wendy Nichols, Nov. 23, 1958; children: Marion Elizabeth, Sandra Frances. BS, U. Mass., 1956, MS, 1958; PhD, Va. Poly. Inst., 1966. Registered profl. forester, Maine. Exec. sec. Wildlife Conservation, Inc., Boston, 1958-59; state ornithologist Mass. Divsn. Fisheries and Wildlife, 1959-60; head conservation edn. divsn. Natural Resources Inc., U. Md., Annapolis, 1960-62; rsch. asst. prof. LaVale, 1965-67; wildlife rsch. biologist U.S. Fish and Wildlife Svc., Amherst, Mass., 1967-69; prof., dir. The Environ. Inst., U. Mass., 1969-2000, prof. emeritus natural resources conservation, 2000—. Cons. in field. Contbr. articles to profl. jours. Apptd. by gov. to Mass. Fisheries and Wildlife Bd., 2000—. Recipient Chevron Conservation award, 1990, Dir.'s award N.E. Sci. Ctr., Nat. Marine Fisheries Svc., 2000; named Conservationalist of Yr., Mass. Wildlife Fedn., 1997; grantee in field. Mem. AAUP (pres. Mass. chpt. 1976-77), AAAS, Wildlife Soc. (cert. wildlife biologist), Ecol. Soc. Am. (cert. sr. ecologist), Am. Assn. Mammalogists, Nat. Wetlands Tech. Coun. (exec. chmn.), Soc. Wetland Scientists (profl. wetland scientist), Internat. Union for Conservation of Nature and Natural Resources (commn. on ecosystem mgmt., Switzerland), Faculty Univ. Club (pres. 2001--), Cosmos Club, Sigma Xi, Xi Sigma Pi, Phi Sigma. Congregationalist. Home: 27 Arnold Rd Pelham MA 01002-9757 Office: U Mass Environ Inst Blaisdell House Amherst MA 01003-0820 E-mail: larson@tei.umass.edu.

LARSON, KENNETH OSCAR, occupational therapist; b. Encino, Calif., Apr. 8, 1961; s. Charles Louis and Susan Lee (Beitzel) L.; m. Linda Martha McKenney, July 17, 1993. BA, San Jose U., 1986; MA, NYU, 1992. Cert. geriatric occupl. therapist. Occupational therapist N.Y. Hosp., Payne Whitney Clinic, N.Y.C., 1987-92, INOVA Alexandria (Va.) Hosp., 1993—. Co-chair mental health spl. interest group N.Y. Occupational Therapy Assn., 1990-92. Author: (book) The Role of Occupational Therapy with the Elderly, 1997; prin. rschr. (assessment tool) The Role Adaptation Bereavement Inventory, 1992. Mem. Jackson Heights Beautification Group, N.Y.C., 1989—92; pres. Cove Creek Land Assn., 1997—2001. Recipient Mary Booth scholarship San Jose State U., 1986. Mem. Am. Occupational Therapy Assn. (mem. ethics jud. coun. 1997-99, editor Gerontology Spl. Interest Newsletter 1992-95, Svc. award 1995), Va. Occupational Therapy Assn., Nat. Alliance for the Mentally Ill., Am. Mental Health Counselors Assn. Avocations: gardening, carpentry, bicycling, music. Home: 517 N Armistead St Apt T2 Alexandria VA 22312-2885 Office: INOVA Alexandria Hosp 4320 Seminary Rd Alexandria VA 22304-1500

LARSON, KERMIT DEAN, accounting educator; b. Algona, Iowa, Apr. 7, 1939; s. Loren L. and Hansena Laurena (Andersen) L.; m. Nancy Lynne Weber, June 17, 1961; children: Julie Renee, Timothy Dean, Cynthia Lynne. AA, Ft. Dodge Jr. Coll., 1960; BBA, U. Iowa, 1962, MBA, 1963; DBA, U. Colo., 1966. CPA, Tex. Faculty U. Tex., Austin, 1966-94, Arthur Andersen & Co. Alumni prof. emeritus, 1997—, chmn. dept. acctg., 1971-75. Vis. assoc. prof. Tulane U., New Orleans, 1970-71; cons. sales tax audit litigation, pvt. anti-trust litigation, expropriation ins. arbitration. Author: (with John Wild and Barbara Chiappetta) Fundamental Accounting Principles, 1978, 16th edit., 2002, Financial Accounting, 7th edit., 1997, (with Charlene Spoede and Paul Miller) Fundamentals of Financial and Managerial Accounting, 1994; contbr. articles to profl. jours. Mem. AICPA, Am. Acctg. Assn. (v.p. 1978-79), Tex. Soc. CPAs, Beta Gamma Sigma, Beta Alpha Psi. Baptist. Home: 1310 Falcon Ledge Dr Austin TX 78746-5120 E-mail: kermlarson@aol.com.

LARSON, KURT PAUL, fire chief; b. Arlington, Va., Jan. 6, 1958; s. Leonard Paul and June Audrey (Kruck) L.; m. Linda Kay Black, Sept. 21, 1991. BS, U. Colo., 1980; MEd, U. Ariz., 1988; exec. fire officer, Nat. Fire Acad., 1996. Firefighter Wheat Ridge (Colo.) Fire Dept., 1986-89, fire marshal, 1989-90, lt., 1989-90, dep. fire chief, 1991-95, fire chief, 1997-98; performer Up With People Internat., Broomfield, Colo., 1987-98; fire investigator Castlewood Fire Dept., Englewood, 1990-91; fire chief Denver, 1993-97; pres. fire svc. data, tng. and organizational cons. N Command, Gulf Breeze, Fla. Fire svc. lectr., instr., author, Wheat Ridge, 1989-98; bd. dirs. Wheat Ridge Fire Dept.; cons. Wheat Ridge, 1989-98; cons. Pensacola, Fla., 1998—. Mem. Nat. Youth Com., Muscular Dystrophy Assn., 1979; chmn. Easter Seal Soc. Youth Program, 1980, Named Legion of Honor Am. Legion, Denver, 1968, Chevalier Internat. Order of DeMolay, Denver, 1990, Hon. Fire Chief SW Colo. Firefighters Assn., Durango, 1992. Mem. Internat. Assn. Arson Investigators, Internat. Assn. Fire Chiefs, Colo. Fire Chiefs Assn., Nat. Fire Protection Assn., Nat. Fire Acad. Alumni Assn. (fla. coord. N.W. Fla. 1999—), Scottish Rite of Freemasonry (officer 1982-90, Scottish rite officer 1982-96), York Rite of Masonry, Wheat Ridge Masons (presiding officer 1982-94, past master 1992), Fire Safety Educators (treas. 1988-92), Fire Marshals Assn. Colo., Up With People. Republican. Home: 2225 Inverness Dr Pensacola FL 32503-5028 Office: N Command 2225 Inverness Dr Pensacola FL 32503-5028

LARSON, L. JEAN, educational administrator; b. Sioux City, Iowa, Jan. 27, 1934; d. Marion A. and Lola J. (Willenborg) Robey; m. Herbert L. Larson, June 25, 1955; 1 child, Joan Irene. BA with honors, U. No. Iowa, 1954; MEd, U. Ariz., 1959. Cert. adminstr., elem. tchr., Ariz., cert. speech therapist, K-12 tchr., Iowa. Tchr. Tucson Unified Sch. Dist., counselor, prin.; dir. Tucson Hebrew Acad. Dir. Children's Ministries. Mem. Internat. Reading Assn., Ariz. Reading Assn., Tucson Reading Assn., ASCD, PTA, NEA, NAFE, Altrusa, Delta Kappa Gamma, Kappa Delta, Delta Sigma Rho, Kappa Delta Pi (Purple Arrow award). Home: 7041 E Hawthorne St Tucson AZ 85710-1232

LARSON, LARRY, librarian; b. El Dorado, Ark., July 18, 1940; s. Willie Lee and Myrtle Elizabeth (McMaster) L.; m. Dorothy Ann Bing, Apr 23, 1966; 1 child, Larisa Ann. BS, Ouachita Baptist U., 1962; MLS, George Peabody Coll., 1967. Asst. librarian, media specialist Hall High Sch., Little Rock, 1962-65; asst. librarian, circulation Ark. Tech. U., Russellville, 1965-67; asst librarian reference Hendrix Coll., Conway, Ark., 1967-73; head librarian U. Ark., Monticello, 1973-75; librarian, dir. N. Ark. Regional Library, Harrison, 1975-85, Ft. Smith (Ark.) Pub. Library, 1985—. Mem. adv. bd. Sparks Regional Med. Ctr., 1998—. Bd. dirs. Ft. Smith Hist. Soc., 1986-90, Info. Network Ark., 1997—; treas. bd. dirs. Pub. Awareness Com., Ft. Smith, Ark., 1986—. Mem.: ALA, Ark. Adminstrs. Pub. Libr. (chair 1988—89, del. Ark. govs. conf. on librs. 1990), Ark. Libr. Devel. Dist. (chair 1985—87), Ark. Libr. Assn. (vice chair membership com. 1968, chair pub. libr. divsn. 1993, Disting. Svc. award 1985), Info. Network Ark. (bd. dirs. 1997—2001), Noon Exch. Club. Democrat. Baptist. Avocations: gardening, woodworking. Home: 3114 S Enid St Fort Smith AR 72903-4445 Office: Ft Smith Pub Libr 3201 Rogers Ave Fort Smith AR 72903-2953 E-mail: llarson@fspl.lib.ar.us.

LARSON, LEWIS HENRY, JR. anthropologist, researcher, retired archaeologist; b. St. Paul, Jan. 24, 1927; s. Thelma Mae (Brunson) Larson. BA in Anthropology, U. of Minn., 1949; MA in Anthropology, U. of Mich., 1951, PhD in Anthropology, 1969. Asst. prof. of anthropology U. of Ark., Fayetteville, 1952—53; archaeologist Ga. Hist. Commn., Atlanta, 1953—59; assoc. prof. of anthropology Ga. State U., 1960—67; prof. of anthropology State U. of West Ga., Carrollton, 1971—98; Ga. state archaeologist Ga. Dept. of Natural Resources, Atlanta, 1972—98; ret., 1998. Author: (anthropology) Aboriginal Subsistance Technology on the Southeastern Coastal Plain During the Late Prehistoric Period, 1980. Mem. Ga. Rev. Bd. for the Nation Register of Hist. Places, Atlanta, 1972—98. With USN, 1944—46, PTO. Recipient Ga. Governor's Award in the Humanities, Ga. Gov. Zell Miller, 1996. Mem.: Soc. for Am. Archaeology, Am. Anthrop. Assn., Phi Kappa Phi, Sigma Xi.

LARSON, LLOYD WARREN, economist; b. Barrett, Minn., Sept. 2, 1920; s. John Arthur and Jennie Constance (Nygren) L.; m. Laurene J. Tibbitts, June 10, 1995; B.A., U. Minn., 1946, M.A., 1947; postgrad. U. Minn., George Washington U. Assoc. prof. history and polit. sci. Carthage (Ill.) Coll., 1948-49; with Dept. Labor, Washington, 1950-78; chief div. state workers' compensation standards, 1974-78; mem. research faculty Cornell U. Sch. Indsl. and Labor Relations, 1979-81; writer, cons. U.S. Task Force on Safety, 1968, Interdeptl. Workers Compensation Task Force, 1974-77, Nat. Commn. on State Workmen's Compensation Laws, 1971-72; pres. dept. labor credit union, 1960-62; officer, mem. exec. bd. local Am. Fedn. Govt. Employees, 1962-73. Served with U.S. Army, 1942-46. Mem. Am. Polit. Sci. Assn., Center for Study of Presidency, Internat. Soc. Polit. Psychology, Nat. Peace Found., Internat. Platform Assn., Am. Legion (past post comdr.), Order Ky. Cols. Lutheran. Author books, reports, bulls., papers in field. Home: # 304 1007 E 14th St Minneapolis MN 55404-1314

LARSON, MARILYN J. retired elementary music educator; b. Lindstrom, Minn., July 20, 1933; d. Reuben and Dorothy (Holm) L.; m. Harold P. Cohen, Aug. 4, 1957 (div. Dec. 1975); children: Paul, Morrie, Robert. BS with distinction, U. Minn., 1955, MA with honors, 1957. Nat. cert. tchr. music; cert. tchr., Minn.; lic. realtor. Tchr. U. Minn., Mpls., 1955-57, Mpls. Jr. High Sch., 1957-60; piano tchr. pvt. studio, Fridley, Minn.; tchr. Mpls. Pub. Schs., 1976-78, St. Paul Pub. Schs., 1978-97. Designed music curriculum Mpls. Pub. Schs.; mem. INS Roundtable, 2000-01; accompanist Adult Day Care, St. Mary's Home, 2001; piano music for vets., 2000-01. Accompanist U. Minn. Chorus, 1953-56, Berkshire Music Ctr. at Tanglewood, Mass., 1953. Mem. Music Tchrs. Nat. Assn., Fedn. for Am. Immigration Reform, Minnesotans for Immigration Reform (founder, exec. dir. 1999—). Independent. Luth. Avocations: reading, music. Home: 5890 Stinson Blvd Fridley MN 55432-6002 E-mail: marilynmusic@webtv.net.

LARSON, MARK DEVIN, communications executive; b. Rockford, Ill., Aug. 6, 1955; s. Burdette D. Larson and Inga Mae Sandberg; m. Marcia L. Sutton, Feb. 14, 1976; children: Jeffrey, Brandon, Kristin. Grad. high sch., Rockford, 1973. Announcer WRWC Radio, Rockton, Ill., 1971-72; announcer, asst. prodn. dir. WRRR-AM, Rockford, 1972-73; prodn. dir., afternoon host WROK-AM, 1973-76; announcer KFMB-AM, San Diego, 1976-77, asst. program dir., 1977-78, program and ops. mgr., afternoon personality, 1978-94; gen. mgr. KPRZ-AM Radio, 1994—2002, Sta. KPRZ-AM and Sta. KCBQ-AM Radio, San Diego, 1999—2002; talk show host Sta. KCBQ and KPRZ, 1995—2002, mgr., program cons., 2002—; guest host for Michael Medved, Dennis Prager and Hugh Hewitt, Network Radio Talk Shows, 2000—. Co-founder The Program Group, San Diego, 1984-94; co-owner, cons. KISN AM/FM, Salt Lake City, 1985-95; founder, pres. Mark Larson Media Svcs. Inc., El Cajon, Calif., 1985—; nat. program dir./radio Midwest TV, 1988-93; morning talk show host Sta. KRLA-AM, L.A., 2002—, Sta. KCBQ-AM, San Diego, 2002—. Creator (audio seminar series) Personal Program Power, 1985-93; host (TV show) KTTY-TV, 1993-94 (Emmy award 1993); columnist Daily Californian, 1995-2000. Chmn., co-founder Family Heritage Found., 1988—, FHF chmn., 1994—, Prison Fellowship, San Diego, 1990-96; comm. chmn. San Diego County Rep., 1995; active San Diego Youth for Christ, 1987-97; nat. bd. dirs., mem. global leadership coun. Heart to Heart Internat., 2002—; mem. Salem Comm. Polit. Action Com. Named Citizen of Yr., San Diego City Club and Jaycees, 1995, Best Talk Show Host, Achievement in Radio awards, 2002. Mem. Media Fellowship Internat. (chmn. 1998—), San Diego Radio Broadcasters Assn. (pres. 1998—), San Diego Aerospace Mus., City Club San Diego. Avocations: collecting rare books, collecting political autographs and memorabilia, family activities, internat. relief efforts, travel, writing. Office: Mark Larson Media Svc Inc 4370 La Jolla Village Dr #400 San Diego CA 92122 E-mail: mark@marklarson.com.

LARSON, MARK EDWARD, JR. lawyer, educator, financial advisor; b. Oak Park, Ill., Dec. 16, 1947; s. Mark Edward and Lois Vivian (Benson) L.; m. Patricia Jo Jekerle, Apr. 14, 1973; children: Adam Douglas, Peter Joseph, Alex Edward, Gretchen Elizabeth. BS in Acctg., U. Ill., 1969; JD, Northwestern U., 1972; LLM in Taxation, NYU, 1977. Bar: Ill. 1973, N.Y. 1975, D.C. 1976, Minn. 1982, Tex. 1984, U.S. Dist. Ct. (no. dist.) Ill. 1973, U.S. Dist. Ct. (so. dist.) N.Y. 1975, U.S. Ct. Appeals (2d cir.) 1975, U.S. Ct. Appeals (7th cir.) 1976, U.S. Dist. Ct. D.C. 1977, U.S. Ct. Appeals (D.C. cir.) 1977, U.S. Dist. Ct. Minn. 1982, U.S. Ct. Appeals (8th cir.) 1982, U.S. Tax Ct. 1976, U.S. Supreme Ct. 1976; CPA, Ill. Acct. Deloitte & Touche (formerly Haskins & Sells), N.Y.C., 1973—76, Chgo., 1978—81; atty., ptnr. Larson, Perry & Ward and former firms, 1983—; prin. Winfield Fin. Svcs. and affiliates, Houston, Austin and Chgo., 1986—. Adj. faculty U. Minn., Mpls., 1983, Aurora (Ill.) U., 1990-98, St. Xavier U., Chgo., 2000—; exec. dir. Fin. Svcs. Inst. Chgo., St. Xavier U., 1996—. Contbr. articles to profl. jours. Mem. ABA, AICPA, AHLA, Am. Assn. Atty.-CPAs, Acad. Molecular Imaging, Acad. Fin. Svcs., Am. Acctg. Assn., Acad. Molecular Imaging. Office: 1212 S Naper Blvd Ste 119-131 Naperville IL 60540-7349 E-mail: larsgen@usa.net.

LARSON, MARLENE LOUISE, hotel consultant; b. Racine, Wis., Oct. 15, 1952; d. Louis Charles Larson and Mollie Esther (Mauter) Larson Bertana. BS, U. Wis., Whitewater, 1974, MS, 1978; BS, U. Nev., Las Vegas, 1982; MS, U.Wis., Whitewater, 1978; MBA, Calif. Coast U., 1993, postgrad., 1999. Cert. wine steward, restaurant orgnl. exec., food expert, hospitality educator; nat. front desk cert. Tchr. Gilman (Wis.) H.S., 1974-75, Head Start Child Devel., Kenosha, Wis., 1975-78, U. Wis., Whitewater, 1977-78; librarian, tchr. Kenosha Unified Schs., 1978-80; editor U. Nev.-Las Vegas Fedn. Hoteliers, 1981-83; food and beverage clk. MGM Casino & Hotel, Las Vegas, 1983-84; food and beverage controller Congress Hotel, Chgo., 1984-89; prof. Mt. Mary Coll., Milw., 1990—; cons. Congress Hotel, Chgo., 1990-98. Mem. Nat. Restaurant Assn., Coun. on Hotel, Restaurant, and Instl. Edn. Avocations: whitewater rafting and canoeing, school, travel. Office: Mt Mary Coll 2900 N Menomonee River Pky Milwaukee WI 53222-4545 E-mail: mllarson@wi.rr.com.

LARSON, MARY BEA, elementary education educator; b. Brookings, S.D., Apr. 19, 1946; d. Theodore Orville and Doris Rose (Conway) Larson; children: Christie DiRé, Corey DiRe. BA, Wash. State U., 1968, Portland State U., 1973; MA, U. Guam, 1975; postgrad., Seattle Pacific U., 1980-85, Western Wash. U., Oxford U. Cert. tchr., Wash. Tchr. early childhood and creativity Chemeketa C. C., Salem, Oreg., 1971-73; tchr. kindergarten-1st grade Govt. Guam, Agana, 1973-75; tchr. kindergarten, 3rd grade Canal Zone Govt., Balboa, Panama, 1975-78; tchr. kindergarten, 2d-4th grades, elem. art specialist Marysville (Wash.) Sch. Dist., 1978-2001, ret., 2001. Mem. profl. adv. bd.

coll. edn. Western Wash. U., 1989-96. Active Snohomish County Arts Coun. Mem. NEA (del. to Nat. Rep. Assembly, Washington 1992, San Francisco 1993), Wash. Edn. Assn., Marysville Edn. Assn. (pres. 1990-92), Nat. Mus. Women in Arts (founder), Seattle Art Mus. (landmark), Alpha Delta Kappa (state sgt.-at-arms 1990-92, state chaplain 1992-94, state v.p. 1994-96). Home: 15605 N Spring Tree Ct SE Mill Creek WA 98012-5825

LARSON, MAUREEN INEZ, rehabilitation consultant; b. Madison, Minn., Mar. 10, 1955; d. Alvin John and Leona B. (Bornhorst) Larson; m. Michael Earl Klemetsrud, July 7, 1979 (div. Sept. 1988). BA in Psychology & Fine Arts cum laude, U. Minn., 1977; MA in Counseling & Guidance, U. N.D., 1978. Cert. rehab. counselor, ins. specialist; disability analyst. Employment counselor II, coordinator spl. programs Employment Security div. State of Wyo., Rawlins, 1978-80; employment interviewer Employment Security divsn. State of Wash., Tacoma, 1980; lead counselor Comprehensive Rehab. Counseling, 1980-81; dir. counseling Cascade Rehab. Counseling, 1981-87, dist. mgr., 1987-90; regional mgr. Rainier Case Mgmt., 1991-92; owner Maureen Larson and Assocs., Gig Harbor, Wash., 1992—. State capt. legis. div. Provisions Project Am. Personnel and Guidance Assn., 1980. Advocate Grand Forks (N.D.) Rape Crisis Ctr., 1977-78; mem. Pierce County YMCA; bd. dirs. Boys and Girls Clubs of Tacoma, 1991-98, chairperson sustaining drive, 1991-98, sec.-treas., 1992-93, pres., 1994, auction com. and spl. events com.; founding bd. dirs., bd. devel. chair, ballroom dance chair, vice chair Literacy Plus!, 1999-2001. State of Minn. scholar, 1973-77; recipient Alice Tweed Tuohy award U. Minn., 1977, Nat. Disting. Svcs. Registry award Libr. of Congress, 1987; named bd. mem. vol. of Yr. Boys and Girls Clubs of Tacoma, 1992. Mem.: Profls. in Workers Compensation Orgn., Nat. Rehab. Adminstrs. Assn. (bd. dir. 1993), Nat. Rehab. Counseling Assn. (bd. dir. 1993, State of Wash. Counselor of Year 1991, Pacific Region Counselor of Year 1992), Nat. Rehab. Assn. (bd. dir. Olympic chpt. 1988—97, pres. 1990—91, chmn. state conf. planning com. 1990, 1993, 1996), Nat. Fedn. Bus. & Profl. Women (rec. sec. 1978—80, runner-up Young Careerists' Program 1980), Washington Self-Insured Assn., Gig Harbor Yacht Club, Rotary Midday Club, Pi Gamma Mu. Avocations: sailing, aerobics, ballet, arts. Office: M Larson & Assocs 13504 82nd Ave NW Gig Harbor WA 98329-8642 E-mail: mlarsonassoc@msn.com

LARSON, MICHAEL LEN, newspaper editor, hospital administrator; b. St. James, Minn., Feb. 3, 1944; s. Leonard O. and Lois O. (Holte) L.; m. Kay M. Monahan, June 18, 1966; children: Christopher, David, Molly. BA, U. Minn., 1966; MBA, Mankato State U., 1986. Mng. editor Paddock Circle Inc., Libertyville, Ill., 1972-74, New Ulm (Minn.) Journal, 1974-76, Republican-Eagle, Red Wing, Minn., 1976-79, Mankato (Minn.) Free Press, 1979-84, editor, 1984-95, editor of editl. page, 1995-97; editor Minot (N.D.) Daily News, 1997-2000; bus. editor St. Cloud (Minn.) Times, 2000—01; asst. adminstr. Melrose Area Hosp. Complex, 2001—. Bd. dirs. Minot Area Devel. Corp. D. dirs. Valley Indsl. Devel. Corp., Mankato, 1985-95, also treas.; adv. bd. Mankato State U. Bus. Sch. With U.S. Army, 1966-68, Vietnam. Recipient First Place award for investigative reporting Minn. Newspaper Assn., 1969, 71, 72, 76, 78, First Place award for feature writing, Suburban Newspapers Am., 1974. Mem. Minn. AP (pres. 1988—), Kiwanis. Roman Catholic. Avocation: bicycling. Home: 1808 N Eighth St Sartell MN 56377-1697 Office: Melrose Area Hosp Complex 111 N 5th Ave W Melrose MN 56352

LARSON, NANCY CELESTE, computer systems manager; b. Chgo., July 17, 1951; d. Melvin Ellsworth and Ruth Margaret (Carlson) L. BS in Music Ed., U. Ill., 1973, MS in Music Edn., 1976; postgrad., Purdue Univ., 1982-86. Vocal music educator Consol. Sch. Dist., Gilman, Ill., 1975-77; elem. vocal music tchr. Sch. Dist. 161, Flossmoor, 1977-87; instr. Vander Cook Coll., Chgo., 1980-88; systems programmer analyst Sears, Roebuck & Co., 1987-92, tech. instr., 1989-90, project leader, 1990-91, sr. systems analyst, 1991-92, Trans Union LLC, Chgo., 1992-94, mgr., 1994—. Tchr. adult computer edn. Homewood-Flossmoor High Sch., 1986-90. Chmn. Faith Luth. Ch., 1982-87, pres. bd., 1988-91, vocal soloist and voice-over performer. Mem. Ill. Music Educators Assn., Music Educators Nat. Conf., Ill. Educators Assn., Nat. Educators Assn., Am. ORFF Schulwerk Assn., Flossmoor Edn. Assn. (negotiator 1983-86). Republican. Lutheran. Avocations: swimming, skiing, reading, antique hunting. Home: Apt 904 1960 N Lincoln Park W Chicago IL 60614-5440 Office: Trans Union LLC 555 W Adams St Fl 4 Chicago IL 60661-3696

LARSON, PAUL MARTIN, lawyer; b. Tacoma, June 8, 1949; s. Charles Philip and Margeret (Kobervig) L.; m. Kristina Simonson, June 19, 1971; children: Kristin Ilene, Paul Philip, Erika Louise. AB, Stanford U., 1971; JD, Gonzaga U., 1974. Bar: Wash. 1975, U.S. Dist. Ct. (we. dist.) Wash. 1975, U.S. Dist. Ct. (ea. dist.) Wash. 1978, U.S. Ct. Appeals (9th cir.) 1981. Assoc. Hoff & Cross, Tacoma, 1975-76; ptnr., prin. Brooks & Larson, P.S., Yakima, Wash., 1976-87; ptnr. Bogle & Gates, 1987-93, Larson & Perkins, 1994—. Author: (with others) Commercial Law Deskbook, 1981. Pres. Cardio & Pulmonary Inst., Yakima, 1981; bd. dirs. Yakima YMCA, 1981-98, pres.-elect bd. dirs. 2000, pres., 2001—; bd. dirs. Yakima Youth Commn., 1989-93, Yakima Valley chpt. ARC, 1990-93; bd. dirs. Sisters of Providence Med. Ctr.-Yakima Found., 1986-96, pres., 1992-93, Area Svc. bd. mem., 2000—; bd. dirs. Yakima Schs. Found., 1993-2000, pres., 2000. Fellow ABA (standing com. lawyer's responsibility for client protection 1984-89); mem. Wash. State Bar Assn. (spl. dist. counsel, 1985-96, pres. corp. bus. and banking sect. 1987-88, chmn. unauthorized practice of law task force 1995-96), Yakima Estate Planning Coun. (pres. 1981), Rotary. Avocations: tennis, fishing. Office: Larson & Perkins PO Box 550 Yakima WA 98907-0550 E-mail: paul@lplaw.com.

LARSON, PAUL MELVIN, physics researcher; b. Decorah, Iowa, Apr. 10, 1972; s. Joseph Paul and Deanna Marie L. BA in Maths./Physics, St. Olaf Coll., 1994; PhD in Physics, Mich. State U., 2001. Tchg. asst. St. Olaf Coll., Northfield, Minn., 1991-94, rsch. asst., 1993; tchg. asst. Mich. State U., East Lansing, 1995-97, rsch. asst., 1997-2001; postdoctoral rschr. Naval Rsch. Lab., Washington, 2001—. Contbr. articles to profl. jours. Mem. Am. Phys. Soc., Material Rsch. Soc., Phi Beta Kappa, Phi Kappa Phi. Lutheran. Avocations: antique reading, singing, travel. Office: Code 6391 4555 Overlook Ave Washington DC 20375

LARSON, PAUL WILLIAM, public relations executive; b. Wilmington, N.C., May 28, 1956; s. Robert William and Helen Joyce (Hillen) L. BA, U. Calif., Berkeley, 1981; MS in Journalism Medill Sch. of Journalism, Northwestern U., Evanston, Ill., 1991. Reporter Turlock (Calif.) Daily Jour., 1982-84; writer, editor Paul Larson Commns., Modesto, Calif., 1984-90; dir. external affairs and publs. Medill Sch. Journalism, Northwestern U., Evanston, Ill., 1991-96; mgr. strategic com. AMA, Chgo., 1996-98, dir. membership com., 1998-2000, v.p. mem. and bus. comms., 2000—. Adj. lectr. Medill Sch. Journalism, Evanston, 1991-97; assoc. master Commns. Residential Coll., Northwestern U., Evanston, 1993-96. Bd. dirs. Housing Options for Mentally Ill, Evanston, 1993-2000, chmn. comm. com. 1995-2000; docent Evanston Hist. Soc., 1992-95. Recipient Rotary Group Study Exchg. award Rotary Internat., 1986, Rotary Found. Dist. Svc. award, 1995, Leadership Evanston Evanston Cmty. Rels., 1995-96, Vol. of the Yr. award Evanston McGaw YMCA, 1995. Mem. Rotary (bd. dirs. Evanston 1991-95). Office: AMA 515 N State St Chicago IL 60610-4325

LARSON, PETER L. legal assistant, investigator; b. Chgo., June 24, 1941; s. Allan M. and Harriet G. (Lans) L.; m. Carole J. Dierking, Feb. 4, 1961; children: Lori, Lance, Lynn, Lee. Assoc. Bus. Adminstrn., Muskegon Bus. U., 1961. South Tex. area mgr. So. Detectives, Inc., Houston, 1976-78; pres. Confidential Investigation Agy., 1978-85; sr. legal asst. Leger, Coplen & Jefferson, PC, 1985—; pres. Tex. Inc. Citizens' Property Rights Orgn. Chmn. Tri-County Foster Parents, Muskegon, 1974; committeeman Boy Scouts Am., Ravenna, Mich., 1972. Staff sgt. USAF, 1961-64. Mem. ATLA (paralegal affiliate), Nat. Assn. Legal Assts. (cert.), Nat. Assn. Legal Investigators (cert., Editor/Pubs. award 1994), Tex. Bd. Legal Specialization (L.A. divsn. stds. cert. civil, personal injury). Avocations: photography/videography, stamps, antique woodworking tools, target pistols, art. Home: 4810 Innsbruk Dr Houston TX 77066-4355 Office: Tex Citizen Property Rights Org 5847 San Felipe St Ste 2440 Houston TX 77057-3009 E-mail: repeter_cia@email.com.

LARSON, REED EUGENE, foundation administrator; b. Smith County, Kans., Sept. 27, 1922; s. George Christian and Edith Hazel (Whitney) L.; m. Marjorie Jeanne Hess, Aug. 31, 1947; children: Patricia Kay Larson Sween, Barbara Ann Larson Finnegan, Marcia Lynn Larson Craig. Student, Kans. Wesleyan U., 1940-41, Ohio State U., 1943-44; BS in E.E, Kans. State U., 1947. Design engr. Stein Labs., Atchison, Kans., 1947-48; processing engr. Coleman Co., Wichita, 1948-54; exec. v.p. Kansans for the Right to Work, 1954-58, Nat. Right-to-Work Com., Washington, 1959-76, pres., 1976—; exec. v.p. Nat. Right-to-Work Legal Def. Found., 1968-73, pres., 1973—. Chmn. Hallmark Bank & Trust, 1984-96; vice chmn. F&M Bank-No. Va., 1996-99. Served with AUS, 1943-46. Recipient Seldon Waldo award U.S. Jaycees, 1956; Silver Anvil award Public Relations Soc. Am., 1966; James J. Kilpatrick award Internat. Platform Assn., 1980; Awarded Doctor of Laws Campbell U., 1988. Mem. Mont Pelerin Soc., Phila. Soc., Eta Kappa Nu, Tau Beta Pi. Clubs: Kansas Jaycees (pres. 1953-54), Rotary, Am. Legion. Baptist. Home: 105 Robert Cole Ct Williamsburg VA 23185-3385 Office: 8001 Braddock Rd Springfield VA 22160-0001 E-mail: rlwmbg@nrtw.org, larson@nrtw.org.

LARSON, RICHARD EVERETT, lab technician; b. New London, Conn. s. Everett Richard and Rachel (Amendola) L. BS, U. Conn., Storrs, 1977, MS, 1981; student, U. R.I., Kingston, 1982-83. With USCG, 1990—. Episcopalian. Avocations: golf, fishing. Office: US Coast Guard Acad 27 Mohegan Ave New London CT 06320-8101 E-mail: RLarson@cga.uscg.mil.

LARSON, RICHARD JAMES, computer network systems executive; b. Davenport, Iowa, Dec. 13, 1954; s. James Kruse and Carol Darlene (Bush) L.; m. Laurel Mae Johnson, Sept. 11, 1982; children: Paul, Jason, Christine. BA in Mass Communications, St. Ambrose Coll., 1977. Audio technician Boom Audio Inc., Davenport, 1971-75; fire equipment insp. Per Mar Security, 1975; computer operator Lee Enterprise, 1976-77; dir. acad. computer utilization St. Ambrose Coll., 1977-78; tech. programmer Montgomery Elevator (name now Montgomery KONE Inc.), Moline, Ill., 1978-87, computer sys. mgr. R & D, 1987-90; adminstr. Computer Wide Area Network (WAN), 1990-96; desktop support mgr. Computer Scis. Corp., 1996-98; infrastructure analyst Deere and Co., 1998—. Owner Creative Photography Color Lab. and Studio, Coal Valley, Ill., 1990—. Mem. Nat. Rifle Assn., Masons. Republican. Methodist. Avocations: photography, coin collecting, shooting. Home: PO Box 35 Coal Valley IL 61240-0035 Office: Deere and Company 400 19th St Moline IL 61265-1373 E-mail: rlarson@revealed.net.

LARSON, RICHARD SMITH, pathologist, researcher; b. Ithaca, N.Y., Aug. 27, 1962; s. Richard Ingwald and Judith Ann (Larsen) L.; m. Blaire Martin, June 4, 1989. AB in Chemistry summa cum laude, U. N.C., 1984; MD, PhD, Harvard U., 1990. Cert. anatomic and clin. pathologist Am. Bd. Pathology. Pathologist, resident Barnes Hosp., St. Louis, 1990-93; hematopathology fellow Vanderbilt U., Nashville, 1993-96; assoc. prof., chief clin. ops. U. N.Mex., 1996—. Contbr. articles to numerous jours. and books. Recipient Lansky award, UNM Regents' lectureship; named designated investigator for Coaches Against Cancer, Hoops for Lymphoma, Am. Cancer Soc.; grantee Am. Cancer Soc., Am. Heart Assn., NIH. Mem. Coll. Am. Pathologists, Am. Soc. Hematology, Assn. Molecular Pathologists, Southwest Oncology Group, Phi Beta Kappa. Achievements include several patents including anti-inflamatory drugs.

LARSON, ROBERT WILLIAM, education educator, consultant; b. Iowa City, Feb. 8, 1935; s. Robert William and Mary Alice (Scannell) L.; m. Aug. 8, 1997 (div. Nov. 23, 1997). BS, U. Wyo., Laramie; MA, EdD, U. N. Colo., Greeley. Advt., pub. rels. dir. Blue Cross/Blue Shield, Cheyenne, Wyo., 1976-83; mktg. cons. Stress Mgmt. Inst., 1983-86; asst. prof. U. Minn. at Moorhead, 1986-90; mktg. cons. Ad Pro, Duluth, Ga., 1990-92; assoc. prof. Brendau U., Gainesville, 1990-92; asst. prof. Pitts. State U., 1992-96, Northwestern Okla. State, 1998—. Image and mktg. comm., Pitts. State U., 1998. Editor: Campaign Cooking, 2000; contbr. Wild Horses, 1963. Dir. Joplin (Mo.) Advt., 1996-98; county coord. Sally Thompson Senate, Pittsburg, Pans., 1996; states coord., Kathy Kaplan Sec. of State, Cheyenne, Wyo., 1996. Maj. USMC, 1958-62, USMCR, 1963-85. Mem. Alva C. of C., Pittsburg C. of C., Moorhead C. of C. Democrat. Methodist. Avocations: triathlons, waterskiing, basketball, remodeling houses, racquetball. Office: Northwestern Okla State 709 Oklahoma Blvd Alva OK 73717 E-mail: rwlarson@nwosuo.edu.

LARSON, ROLAND ELMER, health care executive; b. Chgo., Jan. 21, 1939; s. Elmer Gustav and Anna (Alphida) L.; children: Eric R., Jennifer L., Melissa K. BA, Augustana Coll., 1961; MHA, U. Iowa, 1963; postgrad., Harvard U., 1978. Adminstrv. asst. U. Vt. Med. Ctr., Burlington, 1962-64; assoc. adminstr. Roger Williams Hosp., Providence, 1964-73; v.p. adminstrn. Norwalk (Conn.) Hosp., 1973-81; pres., chief exec. officer Nashoba Community Hosp., Ayer, Mass., 1981-88; v.p. Charles River Assn., Boston, 1988-90; cons. Charles River Assocs., 1990-93; ind. healthcare cons. Harvard, Mass., 1990—. Chmn. Harvard (Mass.) Coalition Against Drugs and Alcohol, Opportunities, Inc., Providence, 1966-68, Greater Norwalk Community Coun., 1980; bd. dirs. Nat. Arthritis Found., N.Y.C., 1967-71, Am. Cancer Soc., Stamford, Conn., 1978-81. Fellow Am. Coll. Healthcare Execs.; mem. Cen. Mass. Hosp. Coun. (chmn. 1987-88), Rotary. Avocations: sailing, bicycling, golf, squash, woodworking. Home and Office: Larson & Assocs PO Box 602 Boylston MA 01505-0602

LARSON, ROY, journalist, publisher; b. Moline, Ill., July 27, 1929; s. Roy W. and Jane (Beall) L.; m. Dorothy Jennisch, June 7, 1950; children: Mark, Bruce, Jodie, Bradley. AB, Augustana Coll., Rock Island, Ill., 1951; M.Div., Garrett Theol. Sem., 1955. Ordained to ministry Methodist Ch., 1956; min. Covenant United Meth. Ch., Evanston, Ill., 1963-68, First United Meth. Ch., Elmhurst, 1968-69; religion editor Chgo. Sun-Times, 1969-85; pub. The Chgo. Reporter, 1985-94; exec. dir. Garrett-Medill Ctr. for Religion and News Media, Evanston, Ill., 1995—. Home: 1508 Hinman Ave Evanston IL 60201-4664 Office: Garrett-Medill Ctr 2121 Sheridan Rd Evanston IL 60201-2926

LARSON, RUSSELL GEORGE, magazine publisher; b. Waukesha, Wis., May 4, 1942; s. George Arthur and Dorothy Edna (Hanneman) L.; m. Barbara Kay Krsek, Aug. 1, 1964; children— Eric, Craig, Denise AAS, Milw. Sch. Engring., 1962. Tech. writer various publs., 1962-69; assoc. editor Model Railroader Mag., Milw., 1969-75, mng. editor, 1975-77, editor, 1977-93, v.p. editorial, 1989-93, sr. v.p. editorial, 1993—. Pub. Model Railroader Mag., Classic Toy Trains Mag., The Writer, Plays, Garden Railways Mag., Milw. Author: N Scale Primer, 1973, Beginner's Guide to N Scale Model Railroading, 1990, Beginner's Guide to Large Scale Model Railroading, 1994. Lutheran. Avocations: golf, model railroading, reading, travel. Office: Kalmbach Pub Co PO Box 1612 21027 Crossroads Cir Waukesha WI 53186-4055

LARSON, RUSSELL EDWARD, university provost emeritus, consultant agriculture research and development; b. Mpls., Jan. 2, 1917; s. Karl Sam and Belle (Wing) L.; m. Margaret Agnes Johnson, Aug. 19, 1939; children: Gayle Margaret, Beverly Jean, Russell Troy. BS, U. Minn., 1939, MS, 1940, PhD, 1942; DSc (hon.), Delaware Valley Coll. Sci. and Agr., 1966. Asst. prof. U. R.I., Kingston, 1941-44, Pa. State U., University Park, 1944-45, assoc. prof., 1945-47, prof., 1947-77, head dept. horticulture, 1952-62, dean Coll. Agriculture, 1963-72, provost, 1972-77. Sci. advisor Am. Cocoa Rsch. Inst., McLean, Va., 1975-87; cons. Agriculture R & D, State Coll. Pa., 1977—. Contbr. 46 tech. articles on plant sci. to profl. jours. Recipient Outstanding Alumnus award U. Minn., 1961. Fellow AAAS, Am. Soc. Hort. Sci. (pres. 1963-64, L.H. Vaughan award 1948); mem. Am. Genetic Assn., Am. Inst. Biol. Sci., Sigma Xi. Republican. Lutheran. Avocations: gardening, golf, fishing. Home: 608 Elmwood St State College PA 16801-7053 Office: Pa State U 6 Tyson Bldg University Park PA 16802-4202

LARSON, RUSTIN LEE, writer, educator; b. Des Moines, Aug. 19, 1959; s. Virgil Eugene and Leona Helen L.; m. Caroline Godwin, Aug. 14, 1983; children: Katharine, Sarah, Julia. BA, Maharishi U., 1982; MFA, Vt. Coll., 1986. Instr. Des Moines Area C.C., 1986-88, Maharishi U., Fairfield, Iowa, 1988-90, Indian Hills C.C., Ottuma, 1990—2001. Author: Loving the Good Driver, 1996, Lord of the Apes, 1999, Tiresias Strung Out, 1993; editor The Contemporary Rev., 1988—; poet-in-the-schs. Iowa Arts Coun., Des Moines, 1992—; poetry editor The Iowa Source, 1994-2000. Recipients 1st Editors prize Rhino Poetry Forum, 2000. Lutheran. Avocations: drawing, guitar, investing, hiking, cooking. Home: PO Box 1721 Fairfield IA 52556-0029 Office: Maharishi U. 1000 N 4th Fairfield IA 52557 E-mail: rustinlarson@go.com.

LARSON, SHARON LYNN, oncological nurse; b. Mercer, Pa., Sept. 30, 1953; d. Donald and Mary E. (Tesh) Sines; m. Paul A. Larson, Mar. 7, 1981; 1 child, Kristin M. Diploma, Sharon Gen. Hosp. Sch. Nursing, 1974; BSN, Pa. State U., 1982; MSN, Gannon U., 1992. Head nurse, outpatient oncology Greenville (Pa.) Regional Hosp., 1979-82, head nurse, inpatient oncology, 1987-90, mgr. oncology div., 1990-93; dir. oncology and IV therapy Horizon Hosp. System, Greenville, 1994-97, dir. med.-surg. nursing, 1997-99; dir. oncology svcs. UPCI@UPMC Horizon, 1999—. Mem. edn. com. Mercer County divsn. Am. Cancer Soc., bd. dirs., 1993—. Mem. Oncology Nursing Soc., N.W. Pa. Affiliated Orgn. Nurse Mgrs. (pres. 1994), N.W. Pa. Orgn. Nurse Leaders. Home: 223 Hopper Rd Transfer PA 16154-2703 E-mail: larsonsl@msx.upmc.edu.

LARSON, THOMAS WALLIN, editor, writer; b. Neenah, Wis., Sept. 8, 1949; s. John Joseph Milton and Dorothy Wallin L.; life ptnr. Suzanna Martin Neal; children: Jeremy, Blake. BMus, U. N.Mex., 1982; M in English and Am. Lit., U. Calif., San Diego, 1986. Editor City Works Lit. Jour., San Diego, 1993-2000; prof. English San Diego City Coll., 1990—2001; contbg. writer San Diego Reader, 1999—. Contbr. articles to profl. and lit. jours. Recipient fellow Ragdale Artist's Colony, 1996. Democrat. Avocations: travel, walking, vetgetarianism. Home: 3230 Ogalala Ave San Diego CA 92117-1743 Fax: 858-273-4806. E-mail: tlarson@adnc.com.

LARSON, TROY ALLAN, music educator; b. Cudahy, Wis., Apr. 21, 1974; s. Gerald Arthur and Sonja Lynn Larson. Bachelors of Music, West Tex. A&M U., Canyon, TX, 1998. Tchr., jr. high Dumas Ind. Sch. Dist., Dumas, Tex., 1998—99; tchr., k-12 Channing Ind. Sch. Dist., Channing, 1999—2000; tchr., h.s. Albuquerque Pub. Schools - LaCuera H.S., Albuquerque, 2000—. N.mex choral v.p. NMMEA, Albuquerque, 2002—. Recipient Outstanding Choral Award, Heritage Festivals, 2002. Mem.: Music Educators Nat. Conf., N.Mex Educators Assn. R-Consevative. Luthern. Avocation: voice lessons. Home: 11609 Lexington Avenue NE Albuquerque NM 87112 Personal E-mail: troy_larson1@msn.com.

LARSON, VICKI LORD, communication disorders; b. Prentice, Wis., Sept. 21, 1944; d. Edward A. and Stella Mae (Hilton) Lord; m. James Roy Larson, Sept. 3, 1966. BSEd, U. Wis., Madison, 1966, MS, 1968, PhD, 1974. Speech-lang. pathologist Coop. Ednl. Svc. Agy. 2, Minoqua, Wis., 1967—69; instr. U. Wis., Whitewater, 1969—71, rsch. asst. Madison, 1971—73, asst. prof. Eau Claire, 1973-77, assoc. prof., 1977—81, prof. communication disorders, 1981—91, dept. chair, 1978—83, asst. dean grad. studies and univ. rsch., 1984—89, assoc. dean grad. studies and univ. rsch., 1989—91, prof. comm. Oshkosh, 1991—2000, dean Grad. Sch. Rsch., 1991—94; provost, vice chancellor acad. affairs, 1994—2000. Acquistions editor Thinking Publs., Eau Claire, 2001—. Author: Adolescents: Communication Development and Disorder, 1983, Communication Assessment and Intervention Strategies for Adolescents, 1987; contbr. Handbook of Speech-Language Pathology and Audiology, 1988, Language Disorders in Older Students, 1995. Fellow: Am. Speech, Lang., Hearing Assn. (councilor); mem.: Wis. Speech, Lang., Hearing Assn. (pres. 1976, honors 1991), Phi Kappa Phi, Omicron Delta Kappa. Avocations: traveling, quilting, reading. E-mail: larsonvl@northnet.net.

LARSON, WANDA Z(ACKOVICH), writer, poet; b. Cle Elum, Wash., Aug. 27, 1926; d. Stanley Aloysius and Anele (Valente) Zackovich; m. Glen B. Larson, Nov. 18, 1950 (div. Mar. 1967); children: Karen Holk, Margot Huffman, Lisa Larson Landrey (dec. 1998). BA, U. Wash., 1949. Columnist North Bend Herald, Snoqualmie, Wash., 1955-61, Goldendale (Wash.) Sentinel, 1962-67; news editor West Seattle Herald, 1950-51; editor employee newsletter Alaska Steamship Co., Seattle, 1951; editl. asst. Associated Publs., Portland, Oreg., 1970-72, staff writer, 1974-78; pub., editor Blue Unicorn Press Inc., 1990—; poet, host program Sta. KOPB, 1991—2002. Author: Portlandia, 1991, Miracle at Blowing Rock, 1992, Elisabeth: A Biography, 1997, Our Flag - Born Through Valor, 1999, Bird Woman/Mojave (Sacajawea), 2001, The Legend of Something More, 2002. Co-recipient 2nd pl. award Poetry Forum Quar., 1990; hon. mention Still Water Press, 1990, Internat. Mss, 1990. Baptist. Avocations: cooking, humanitarian interests, archaeology. Home: PO Box 40300 Portland OR 97240-0300 E-mail: UnicornPapers@aol.com.

LARSON, WILFRED JOSEPH, chemical company executive; b. N.Y.C., July 12, 1927; s. Fred Wilfred and Mabel Louise (Messier) L.; m. Joan Jesslyn Tilford, Sept. 4, 1949; children: Linda Sue, Robert Wilfred. BS in Econs., U. Pa., 1951; postgrad., U. Chgo., 1958-59, Seton Hall U., 1960-61, U. Cin., 1964-65. With Ward Foods, N.Y.C., 1953-63, contr., chief fin. officer, 1961-63; with Drackett Co., Cin., 1963-79, fin. v.p., 1966-67, adminstrv. v.p., 1967-68, exec. v.p., 1969-79; pres. Bristol-Myers Products Can., 1977-79; v.p. Bristol-Myers Squibb Co., 1981-92; pres. Westwood Squibb Pharms., Inc., 1979-92. Past chmn. Western N.Y. Tech. Devel. Ctr.; bd. dirs. M&T Bank Corp., M&T Bank, Bryant & Stratton, Horus Therapeutics Inc., Imokalee Fedn. Pres., trustee Cin. Adolescent Clinic, Inc., 1968-80; trustee, past chmn. Women's & Children's Rsch. Found., Children's Hosp.; past chmn., bd dirs. Greater Buffalo YMCA; trustee, past treas. Studio Arena Theatre; chmn. SUNY-Buffalo Sch. Pharmacy Centennial, 1986; past trustee Calspan/UB Rsch. Ctr.; past vice chmn., bd. dirs. Buffalo Children's Hosp.; chmn. bd. dirs. Buffalo Philharm. Orch. Soc., Inc., 1986-91; vice chmn. bd. dirs. Greater Buffalo Devel. Found., 1987-92; bd. dirs. Buffalo Fine Arts Acad., 1988-91, Am. Symphony Orch. League, 1989-91, U. at Buffalo Found., 1990-94; mem. cmty. coun. Roswell Park Meml. Inst., 1988-94; bd. dirs. Save the Bays, Naples, Fla., 1990—, Immokalee Found., Naples, 1999--. With USNR, 1945-47, AUS, 1951-53. Named Buffalo/Niagara Sales and Mktg. Exec. of Yr., 1985, Disting. Citizen of Yr. Boy Scouts Am., 1987, Ann. Alumni award Niagara Frontier Exec. of Yr., U. Buffalo Sch. Mgmt., 1987; recipient Disting. Pub. Svc. award SUNY Buffalo Alumni Assn., 1986, Outstanding Citizens award Buffalo News, 1987, Man of Yr. award West Side Bus. and Taxpayers Assn., 1989, Bus. Exec. of Yr. award Nat. Assn. Accts. Buffalo chpt., 1989. Mem. Fin. Execs. Inst. (treas., sec. 1965-68), Greater Buffalo C. of C. (bd. dirs. 1989-92, We. New Yorker of Yr. award 1992, Patron of Arts award 1993), Leland (Mich.) Country Club, Moorings Country Club (Naples, Fla.), Commonwealth Club Cin., Buffalo Club, Royal Poinciana Golf Club (Naples), Naples Yacht Club. Republican. Episcopalian (vestryman, treas. 1966-69). Home: 200 Bahia Pt Naples FL 34103-3511 also: PO Box 742 Leland MI 49654-0742

LARSON-EMISON, JANE BALE, interior design firm executive; b. Dickinson, N.D., Sept. 30, 1946; d. Stanley Walter and Hazel Eleanor (Bartow) Bale; B.S., N.D. State U., 1968. Home fashion coordinator Montgomery Wards, Mpls., 1968-69; staff interior designer McClain, Hedman & Schultz, St. Paul, 1969-72; sales, design mgr. Dayton's Contract Interiors, Mpls., 1972-73; v.p., contract mgr. Contemporary Designs, Inc., Mpls., 1973-79; pres., owner J.B. Larson Assocs., Inc., Mpls., 1979— , Jane Larson-Emison Designs, Deephaven, Minn., 1983-85. Mem. adv. bd. design dept. U. Minn. Coll. Home Econs., 1982-84. Recipient Merit award Minn. Soc. of AIA, 1979, Architecture Minn. Pubs. Design award, 1980, Architecture Minn. Advt. award excellence, 1981. Mem. Inst. Bus. Designers, Mpls. C. of C. (cultural activities com. 1980), Fashion Group. Club: Mpls. Woman's Boys and Girls (sec.), Women's Bd. Home and Office: 3340 Hill Ln Wayzata MN 55391-2602

LARSON MATTERN, JULIA A. music educator, musician; b. Lansing, Mich., Jan. 25, 1961; d. Glen Martin and Bonnie Lou L. BM, Mich. State U., 1984; MM, U. Md., 1986, D in Mus. Arts, 1990. Asst. prof. flute Miss. State U., Starkville, 1989-92; assoc. prof. flute Ball State U., Muncie, Ind., 1992—. Contbr. articles to profl. jours.; prin. flute Muncie Symphony, 1992—; flutist Musical Arts Quintet, 1992—. Mem.: Chamber Music Am., Music Tchrs. Nat. Assn., Coll. Music Soc., Nat. Flute Assn. (competition judge 1992—2002, workshop coord. 1992—94, mem. pedagogy com. 1994—99, advt. editor 1994—99), Nat. Assn. Coll. Wind and Percussion Instrs., Am. Fedn. Musicians. Office: Ball State U Sch Music Muncie IN 47306-0001

LARSSON, PER OLOF, management consultant; b. Uppsala, Sweden, Aug. 8, 1957; arrived in London, 1991; Pvt. practice mgmt. cons., Stockholm, 1983-85; mgmt. cons. EuroConsultants Aps, Copenhagen, 1986-91, Callahan Internat. Ltd., Cork, Ireland, 1992-96; project devel. mgr. Servisair plc, London, 1996-97; mng. dir. Citicentral Ltd., 1998—; dir. IT Resultat Sverige AB, Stockholm, Sweden, 1998—, Forgon AB, Stockholm; dir. EDU Danmark ApS, Copenhagen; dir. IT Sverige AB, Stockholm, 2000—. Mng. dir.

Whitehall Cons. Ltd., London, 1994—; dir. Citicentral AB, Stockholm, 1998—, Differo Konsult AB, Stockholm, 1998-2001, Workman Event AB, Stockholm; dir. Ahrsjö & Ptnrs. Mgmt. Cons. AB, Stockholm, 2000—; chmn. The Bicycle Trader, Inc., Ashland, Oreg., 1995-98, Am. Cyclery LLC, San Francisco, 1997-98, AB Servicestyrkan-IMA, 1996-98, Objekt Inredningsproduktion AB, Stockholm, 200—. Alternate city councillor City of Uppsala, Sweden, 1981; sec.-gen. Swedish Nat. Youth Assn. for Cooperation between the Nordic Countries, 1980-84; counsellor to internat. grand comdr. Ordo Supremus Militaris Temple Hierosolymitani. Decorated knight comdr. Royal Mil. Order Our Lady of the Immaculate Conception of Vila Vizosa, companion Royal House of O'Conor, knight grand cross Order of St. Stanislaus, Commander with Plaque of Royal Order of Dom Carlos Primeiro, Companion of Order of Merit of The Sovereign Mil. Order of the Temple of Jerusalem. Mem. Inst. of Dirs. Home and Office: 48 Quadrant Close The Burroughs NW4 3BY London England E-mail: peroloflarsson@compuserve.com.

LARUCCIA, STEPHEN DOMINIC, university official; b. N.Y.C., July 1, 1945; s. Dominic and Josephine M. (Zaccara) Laruccia; m. Barbara Truncali Stone, Oct. 6, 2001. BA, Manhattan Coll., 1967; MA, U. Mich., 1968, PhD, 1975. Cert. fund raising exec. Instr. classics Thiel Coll., Greenville, Pa., 1969-74; lectr. classics U. Mich., Ann Arbor, 1975-76; instr. history Aspen (Colo.) Country Day Sch., 1977-79; program dir. Cmty. Counseling Svc., Inc., N.Y.C., 1979-83; dir. campaign planning Manhattan Coll., Riverdale, N.Y., 1983-89; dir. spl. programs Pratt Inst., Bklyn., 1989-90; dir. ann. giving St. John's U., Jamaica, N.Y., 1990-98; dir. corp. found. rels. William Paterson U., Wayne, N.J., 1998—. Contbr. articles to profl. jours. Bd. dirs. Belmont Italian Am. Playhouse. U. Mich. fellow, 1967-69; Vergilian Soc. scholar, Cumae, Italy, 1972; Am. Sch. Classical Studies scholar, Athens, 1976. Mem.: Assn. Fundraising Profls., Coun. for Advancement and Support of Edn., Vergilian Soc., Columbia Club. Democrat. Roman Catholic. Avocations: skiing, travel, reading, antiques. Office: William Paterson U 300 Pompton Rd Wayne NJ 07470-2152 E-mail: laruccias@aol.com.

LA RUE, CARL FORMAN, lawyer; b. Ann Arbor, Mich., Aug. 4, 1929; s. Carl D. and Evelina F. La R.; children: Steven, Edward; m. Ann Williams Lindbloom, June 28, 1971; stepchildren: Eric, Sarah Relyea. AB, Harvard U., 1952; LL.B., U. Mich., 1957. Bar: Ohio 1957, Ill. 1964, Calif. 1969. Assoc. firm Fuller & Henry, Toledo, 1957-59; asst. U.S. atty. for Northwestern Ohio, Dept. Justice, 1959-61; staff atty. Aeroquip-Vickers, Inc. (then Libbey-Owens-Ford Co., now part of Eaton Corp.), Toledo, 1961-64; sr. atty. Armour and Co., Chgo., 1964-68; asst. gen. counsel Rockwell Internat., L.A., 1968-78; v.p., gen. counsel, sec. Aeroquip-Vickers, Inc. (then Trinova Corp.), Toledo, 1978-87; of counsel Marshall & Melhorn, 1988-96. With U.S. Army, 1952-54. Mem.: Toledo Tennis Club, Toledo Club. Home: 3553 Brookside Rd Toledo OH 43606-2610

LA RUE, HENRY ALDRED, consultant, former oil company executive; b. Denver, Aug. 13, 1927; s. Robert Hughes and Leona Spencer (Wood) La R.; m. Marion Hardin Klein, Aug. 22, 1954. BS in Bus. Adminstrn., U. Kans., 1951. Pres. Pacific Gulf Oil Co., Tokyo, 1973-74; exec. v.p. Gulf Oil Middle East Co., Pitts., 1974-75, Gulf Sci. and Tech. Co., Pitts., 1975-82; pres. Gulf Research and Devel. Co., 1975-82, Pitts. Applied Rsch. Corp., U. Pitts. Applied Rsch. Ctr., 1986-88; vice chmn. Pitts. Applied Rsch. Ctr., 1988-92; chief exec. officer Alle-Kiski Revitalization Corp., 1989-90. Cons. in field. Bd. dirs. Gulf Oil Corp. Found., Pitts., 1976-82, Franklin Rsch. Ctr., Phila., 1981-86, Colo. Sch. Mines Rsch. Inst., Golden, 1981-87; v.p., dir. Bio Rsch. Ctr. Co., Tokyo, 1973-84; mem. adv. bd. Mellon Inst., Pitts., 1977-83;; sec. Salvation Army Greater Pitts., 1980—; mem. Bell Acres Borough Coun., 1992, vice chmn., 1994. Recipient achievement award indsl. research Slippery Rock U. Mem. Am. Petroleum Inst., Am. C. of C. (pres. Seoul, Korea 1970-71, 1st v.p. Taipei, Taiwan 1972-73), Duquesne Club, Edgeworth Club, Sewickley Heights Golf Club, Beta Theta Pi, Delta Sigma Pi Republican. Episcopalian. Home: 129 Woodcock Drive Rd Sewickley PA 15143-8356 Office: Pitts Applied Research Corp 100 William Pitt Way Pittsburgh PA 15238-1327

LARUE, JAN (PIETERS) (ADRIAN LARUE), musicologist, educator, writer; b. Kisaran, Sumatra, Indonesia, July 31, 1918; s. Carl Downey and Evelina Brown (Forman) LaRue; m. Helen Claire Robison, Aug. 21, 1940 (dec. Aug. 1998); children: Charlotte LaRue Isaacs, Christine LaRue Honig; m. Marian C. Green, Jan. 25, 2000. SB, Harvard, 1940, PhD, 1952; M.F.A., Princeton, 1942. Instr. music Wellesley Coll., 1942-43, 46-48, asst. prof., 1948-50, asso. prof., 1950-57, chmn. dept. music, 1950-57; prof. NYU, 1957-88; prof. emeritus N.Y. U., 1988—, exec. dean arts and sci., 1962-63, chmn. dept. music, 1970-73, dir. grad. studies in music, 1973-80. Vis. prof. UCLA, 1947, U. Mich., 1962, Bar Ilan U., Israel, 1980, Queens U., Ont., 1996; first musicologist-in-residence Mozart Festival, The Kennedy Ctr., Washington, 1975. Author: Guidelines for Style Analysis, 1970, 2d edit., 1992, A Catalogue of 18th Century Symphonies, 1988, Vol. 1, Thematic Identifier; co-author: (with M. Ohmiya) Methods and Models for Comprehensive Style Analysis, 1988; contbg. author: Die Musik in Geschichte und Gegenwart, 1968, Grove's Dictionary of Music and Musicians, 1980, Festschriften Hans Albrecht, 1976, Karl Vötterle, 1977, Charles Cudworth, 1978, Eileen Southern, 1988, Leonard Ratner, 1990, Alan Tyson, 1998; editor: Congress Report of the Internat. Musicol. Soc., 2 vols., 1961, Festschrift Otto Erich Deutsch, 1963, Festschrift Gustave Reese: Aspects of Medieval and Renaissance Music, 1966, Festschrift Bathia Churgin, 2000; contbr. numerous articles on 18th century symphony and concerto, mus. analysis, watermarks, music manuscripts and computer applications to profl. jours. Mem. coun. Smithsonian Instn., 1967-73; mem. Zentralinstitut für Mozartforschung, Salzburg (Austria) Mozarteum, 1969—. 1st lt. Transp. Corps, AUS, 1943-46. Fellow Ford Found., 1954, Fulbright Found., 1954-56, Am. Coun. Learned Socs., 1964, Guggenheim Found., 1965; grantee NEH, 1978, 80-84; honored with publ. of Studies in Musical Sources and Style: Essays in Honor of Jan LaRue, 1990. Mem. Music Libr. Assn., Soc. Ethnomusicology, Am. Musicol. Soc. (hon.; pres. 1966-68), Am. Soc. Eighteenth-Century Studies (exec. bd. 1978-80), Phi Beta Kappa. Home: 103 Woods End Rd New Canaan CT 06840-4030 Office: New York Univ Dept Music New York NY 10003-6757

LARUE, PAUL HUBERT, lawyer; b. Somerville, Mass., Nov. 16, 1922; s. Lucien H. and Germaine (Choquet) LaR.; m. Helen Finnegan, July 20, 1946; children: Paul Hubert, Patricia Seward, Mary Hogan. PhB, U. Wis., 1947, JD, 1949. Bar: Ill. 1955, Wis. 1949, U.S. Supreme Ct. 1972. Grad. asst. instr. polit. sci. dept. U. Wis., 1947-48; mem. staff Wis. Atty. Gen., 1949-50; trial atty., legal advisor to commr. FTC, 1950-55; pvt. practice Chgo.; mem. Chadwell & Kayser, Ltd., 1958-90; ptnr. Vedder, Price, Kaufman & Kammholz, 1990-93; of counsel, 1993-99. Spkr. profl. meetings; mem. Com. Modern Cts. in Ill., 1964; mem. Com. for Constl. Conv. Ill., 1968, Better Govt. Assn., 1966-70 Contbr. articles to profl. jours. Mem. lawyers com. Met. Crusade of Mercy, 1967-68, United Settlement Appeal, 1966-68; apptd. pub. mem. Ill. Conflict of Interest Laws Commn., 1965-67. With AUS, 1943-45, ETO; capt. JAGC, USAFR, 1950-55. Fellow Ill. Bar Found. (life); mem. ABA (mem. coun. sect. antitrust law 1980-83, chmn. Robinson-Patman Act com. 1975-78), Ill. State Bar Assn., Chgo. Bar Assn. (chmn. antitrust com. 1970-71), Wis. State Bar, Rotary. Roman Catholic. Home: 250 Cuttriss Pl Park Ridge IL 60068 E-mail: phlarue@aol.com.

LARUE, RENEE, educator; b. Burlington, Vt., Oct. 21, 1971; d. John Lawrence and Carol Ann (Werking) LaR. AS in Aviation Bus. Adminstrn., Embry-Riddle Aero. U., Daytona Beach, Fla., 1991; BS in Secondary Edn., U. Vt., Burlington, 1995; MA, Goddard Coll., 1999. Cert. secondary and mid. level tchr., Vt. Staff mem. Peace and Justice Coalition, Burlington, 1993-95, 99; day care cons. UNICEF, Georgetown, Guyana, 1995; emergency respite care giver First Call, Burlington, 1996-98, 2001—; middle level educator Browns River Mid. Sch., Underhill, Vt., 1996-97, U32 Jr. Sr. H.S., Montpelier, 1997-99; dir. svc. coord. Family Connection Ctr., Burlington, 1999-2000; tchr. Vt. Adult Learning, 2001—; instr. C.C. of Vt., 2001—. Bd. dirs. Burlington/Puerto Cabezas Sister City Orgn., 1995-97; mem. steering com. Vt. Anti-Racism Action Team, Montpelier, 1996-98; U.S. rep. Internat. Assn. Educators for Peace, 1996-99. Mem. Nat. Coalition Edn. Activists. Avocations: sewing, hiking, snowboarding, camping, rollerblading.

LARUE, RITA RENEA, musician; b. Houston, Feb. 22, 1957; AA, Cumberland Jr. Coll., Lebanon, Tenn., 1976; MusB, Houston Bapt. U., 1980. Music asst. Baptist Temple Ch., Houston, 1973-77; music assoc. W. U. Bapt. Ch., 1979-85; minister of music Autumn Creek Bapt. Ch., 1986-87; exec. asst. GeoQuest Internat., Inc., 1985—. Music coordinator, festival adjudicator, Union Bapt. Assn., Houston, Bapt. Gen. Conv. of Tex.; coordinator Tex. Bapt. All-State Choir Auditions, Houston. Recipient music scholarship, Cumberland Jr. Coll., 1975, Houston Bapt. U., 1976-80, Heights Kiwanis Club scholarship, 1975, Heights Rotary Club scholarship, 1975. Mem. Am. Choral Dirs. Assn., Ch. Music Conf. of the So. Bapt. Conv., Nat. Assn. Female Execs., Sigma Alpha Iota. Home: 4062 Falkirk Ln Houston TX 77025-2908 Office: Andrews & Kurth Law Firm 4200 Texas Commerce Towers Houston TX 77002 Address: 4062 Falkirk Ln Houston TX 77025-2908

LARUE, WILLIAM DAVID, television critic; b. Potsdam, N.Y., Oct. 12, 1957; s. Kenneth James and Carol Marie LaRue; m. Kathleen Lyons, Sept. 24, 1988; children: Brittany, John. BA in English, SUNY, Potsdam, 1979; MA in Pub. Comms., Syracuse U., 1981. Copyeditor Poughkeepsie (N.Y.) Jour., 1981-82, reporter, 1982-84; copyeditor USA Today Update, Alexandria, Va., 1984-85; reporter Post Std., Syracuse, N.Y., 1985-91, TV critic, 1991—. Author: (web site) Collecting Simpsons!, 1996—, (book) Collecting Simpsons!, 1999. Recipient AP Depth Reporting award, Poughkeepsie, 1983, AP Writing Contest award, Syracuse, 1988, 89. Office: Syracuse Newspapers 1 Clinton Sq Syracuse NY 13202-1026

LARUSSA, JOSEPH ANTHONY, optical company executive; b. N.Y.C., May 10, 1925; s. Ignacio and Jennie (Bellone) LaR.; m. Stella M.A. Braconnier, July 2, 1946; children— Joseph, Raymond Paul, Debra Marie. BME, CCNY, 1949; MS, Columbia U., 1955, postgrad. math., mechanics, 1955-59; postgrad. math., physics, NYU, 1959-62; diploma in Infrared Tech, U. Mich. Registered profl. engr., N.Y. V.p.. charge advanced engring. Farrand Optical Co., Inc., Valhalla, N.Y., 1952, sr. v.p., tech. dir., 1952-88; pres., chief oper. officer Tech. Innovation Group Inc, Pleasantville, 1988-90, Electro Visual Engring. Inc., Yorktown Heights, 1991—. Designed Mercury, Gemini, Apollo LM visual spaceflight simulators for NASA; designed space shuttle Aft and Ohd visual simulators for NASA, others for USAF. Patentee in fields of simulation, optics, holography and medical devices; contbr. articles profl. publs. Served with inf. AUS, World War II, ETO. Recipient NASA Lifetime Achievement award, 1998. Mem. AIAA (DeFlorez award 1968), Tau Beta Pi, Pi Tau Sigma. Address: 97 Roosevelt Dr Poughquag NY 12570

LA RUSSA, TONY, JR. (ANTHONY LA RUSSA JR.), professional baseball manager; b. Tampa, Fla., Oct. 4, 1944; m. Elaine Coker, Dec. 31, 1973; 2 daus.: Bianca, Devon. Student, U. Tampa; BA, U. So. Fla., 1969; LLB, Fla. State U., 1978. Bar: Fla., 1979. Player numerous major league and minor league baseball teams, 1962-77; coach St. Louis Cardinals orgn., 1977; mgr. minor league team Knoxville, 1978, Iowa, 1979; coach Chgo. White Sox, 1978, mgr., 1979-86, Oakland A's, 1986-95, St. Louis Cardinals, 1996—. Mgr. A.L. champion Oakland A's, 1988, 89, 90, World champions, 1989; mgr. All-Star team, 1988, coach, 1984, 87. Named Am. League Mgr. of Yr. Baseball Writers' Assn. Am., 1983, 88, 92, AP, 1983, Sporting News, 1983, Am. League Mgr. of Yr., 1988, 92. Office: St Louis Cardinals Busch Stadium 250 Stadium Plz Saint Louis MO 63102-1722*

LARUSSO, ANTHONY CARL, company executive, educator; b. May 5, 1949; s. Nicholas and Rose (Ruspini) LaR.; m. Marianne Elizabeth Baviello, Apr. 4, 1971; children: Anne, Tony. BA, Fordham U., 1971; MBA, NYU, 1972. Cert. mgmt. acct. Sr. project mgr. Office Mgmt. and Control N.Y.C. Dept. Human Resources, 1972-73; mgr. econ. planning Trans World Airlines, N.Y.C., 1973-76; mgr. planning and analysis AMAX, Inc., Greenwich, Conn., 1976-81, mgr. corp. devel., 1981-84, v.p. planning and mktg. metals, 1984-86, v.p. metal refining ops., 1986-87, pres. metal refining ops., 1987-89, pres. climax performance materials corp., 1990-93; gen. mgr. CRI-MET, White Plains, N.Y., 1994-95; pres. Elkem Metals Co., Pitts., 1996—. Adj. prof. mgmt. Pace U., 1975-96. Contbr. articles to profl. jours. Officer local homeowners assn., Pa.; former chmn. local homeowners assn., Mahopac, N.Y.; asst. to chmn. ann. cookie sale Girl Scouts USA, Shrub Oak, N.Y.; coach/safety dir. Am. Youth Soccer Orgn., Yorktown, N.Y. Mem. Acad. Mgmt., Am. Mgmt. Assn., Chief Exec. Network, Inst. Mgmt. Acctg., Orgn. Devel. Inst., Soc. Mining Engrs., Strategic Mgmt. Soc., Ferroalloys Assn. (officer 1996—), Soc. for Advancement of Mgmt., Inc. Republican. Roman Catholic. Avocations: racquetball, swimming, fishing. Home: Woodland Farms 323 Scarlet Cir Wexford PA 15090 Office: Elkem Metals Co PO Box 266 Pittsburgh PA 15230-0266

LARUSSO, JOSEPH, retired musician; b. New York City, Ny, Nov. 21, 1935; s. Jack and Carolyn LaRusso; m. Marian LaRusso; children: Daniel, Kate LaRusso Roman, B Annie Wright. MusB, Manhattan Sch. of Music, New York, 1958, MusM, 1959. First chair tuba 552nd Air Force Band, New York, NY, 1958—64; music dir. Cherry Valley Ctrl. Sch., 1959—61; instrumental music Kingston City Schools, Kingston, 1961—96. Performance - tuba Tudor Brass Quintet, NY, 1965—. Bd. mem. Ulster Performing Arts, Kingston, NY; mem. Ulster County Music Educators Assn. Airman first class Air Force, 1958—64, New York. Mem.: NY State Music Assn., MENC, Am. Fedn. of Musicians, NY State United Teachers. Home: 410 Adams Court Hurley NY 12443

LARY, BANNING KENT, video producer, publisher; b. Chgo., Aug. 27, 1949; s. Banning Gray and Katherine Lee (Tedrow) L.; m. Janice Ann, Dec. 22, 1974 (div. Aug. 1977); 1 child, Venus Ayn Katherine; m. Valerie Maria Dalli, Dec. 28, 1987; children: Alexandra Lee, Kristin Gray. BJ, U. Tex., 1970. Editor-in-chief Beach & Town, Miami, Fla., 1976-77; gen. contractor Larydome Inc., 1977-80; exec. dir. Legal Devel. Resources, Austin, 1989—; pres. Promedion, Inc., 1990—, Am. Multimedia Pubs., Austin, 1996—. Dir., 1985—; freelance writer, 1970—; creative troubleshooter, writer, editor various orgns.; video pub., 1987—. Author: Twist of Faith, 1996; writer, prodr., dir. Robbery! The Aftermath, 1988, Ten Commandments of Avoiding Legal Malpractice, 1989, Ten. Procedures for Avoiding Medical Malpractice, 1990, The Belli Tapes: Winning at Trial, 10 vols., 1991, Childproof: Home Safety Checklist, 1991, Webmaster Secret Internet Marketing Strategies, 1999; video prodr. Bad Paper, 1987, Extortion Set, 1988; prodr. The Sexual Harassment Prevention Kit, 1992, Teens-At-Risk Series, 8 vols., 1998, and many others; prodr. numerous TV commls.; contbr. articles to mags.; author: Twist of Faith, 1996; editor: How to Win Your Case in Court, 1996; pub. Do What You Want to Do, 1996, Gold Medal Performance Without Dangerous Steroids, 1997; editor, prodr.: Living Well Past 50, 1998; prodr., dir.: Heroin Story, Please Remember Suzi, 1998 (silver award), Teen Drinking, 1998 (gold award), Human Communications Theory, 1998 (bronze award), Teen Finances (bronze apple), 1999, Psychology of Criminal Behavior, 2001; inventor roller washer II, golf swing muscle articulator. Mem. bd. Alpha Nu House Corp., Austin. Recipient Gold award for video prodn., 1987, silver award, 1988, 91, Prize Stories Anthology award, 1989, O'Henry awards, Best of Austin award Internat. Assn. Bus. Communicators, 1986, 93, Disting. Achievement award Am. Soc. Ind. Security-Video, 1987, 1st pl. U.S.A. Hometown Video Festival, 1991, award of excellence ACTV, 1992, Bronze award Charleston Internat. Film Festival, 1993, Bronze award Worldfest, 1995, Gold award Flagstaff Internat. Film Festival, 1998, Pegasus award, 1998, Crystal award of Excellence, 1999; named to Top 100 Multimedia Prodrs. Am. Mem. Am. Acad. Poets, Tex. Writers League, Austin Writers League, Amnesty Internat., Sigma Chi. Avocations: photography, painting, philosophy, securities analysis, films. Office: Am Visionary Artists PO Box 3551 Austin TX 78764-3551

LARZELERE, KATHY LYNN HECKLER, paralegal; b. Sellersville, Pa., Dec. 4, 1955; d. Harold Tyson and Hannah Ruth (Wile) Heckler; m. Lawrence Sollanek, Nov. 1984 (div.); m. Loel Harry Larzelere, Aug. 27, 1992; 1 stepdaughter, Lindsie M. AAS magna cum laude, Columbus State C.C., 1991. From sales person to dept. mgr. Macy's New York, North Wales, Pa., 1977-83; store mgr. Bathtique, Wilmington, Del., Towson, Md., 1983-86; customer svc. person Marshall Fields, Chgo., 1987; word processor Franklin County Children Svcs., Columbus, Ohio, 1988-89; legal sec., paralegal M. Cohen and Assocs., 1989-94; paralegal Calig and Handelman LPA, 1994-97, Weltman, Weinberg & Reis, Columbus, 1997—. Author: (poetry) American High School Poets, 1973. Ward coord. Amelia Salerno for City Coun., Columbus, 1993; co-chmn. Columbus Christmas in Apr. Home Amb. Com., Columbus Christmas in Apr. Materials and In-Kind Donations Com.; vol. Ohio Bicentennial Commn. Mem. award Phi Theta Kappa. Mem. Paralegal Assn. Cen. Ohio (writer newsletter The Citator, co-chair student outreach com. 1994-95, chair 1995-97, 1st v.p. 1995-97, 2000-2001, pres. 1997-99, mem. adv. bd. 1999-2000, chair student outreach com. 1999-2000), Columbus Bar Assn. (assoc.). Lutheran. Avocations: handcrafts, reading, walking, watercolor painting, counted cross-stitch. Home: 2119 Kingsglen Dr Grove City OH 43123-1252 Office: Weltman Weinberg & Reis 175 S 3rd St Ste 900 Columbus OH 43215-5177 E-mail: klarzele@columbus.rr.com., klarzelere@weltman.com.

LASAGNA, LOUIS CESARE, medical educator; b. N.Y.C., Feb. 22, 1923; s. Joseph and Carmen (Boccignone) Lasagna; m. Helen Chester Gersten; children: Nina, David, Maria, Kristin, Lisa, Lisa, Peter, Christopher. BS, Rutgers U., 1943; MD, Columbia U., 1947; DSc (hon.) , Hahnemann U., 1980; DSc (hon.) , Rutgers U., 1983. Asst. prof. medicine Johns Hopkins U., Balt., 1954—57, asst. prof. pharmacology, 1954—59, assoc. prof. medicine, 1957—70, assoc. prof. pharmacology, 1959—70; prof. pharmacology and toxicology U. Rochester, 1970—86, prof. medicine, 1970—94; dean Sackler Sch. Med., Tufts U., 1984—, prof. pharmacology and psychiatry, 1984—. Author: The Doctors' Dilemmas, 1962, Life, Death and the Doctor, 1968, Phenylpropanolamine, A Review, 1988; editor: Controversies in Therapeutics, 1980. Sr. asst. surgeon USPHS, 1952—54. Named Disting prof., Tufts U., 1994; recipient Oscar B. Hunter award, Am. Soc. Clin. Pharmacology, 1975, ASPET award, Am. Soc. Pharmacology and Exptl. Therapeutics, 1976, Lilly prize, Brit. Pharm. Soc., 1985, Rutgers U., 1993, Allyn Taylor Internat. prize in Medicine, 1996. Mem.: Am. Coll. Neuropsychopharmacology (pres. 1979—80), Inst. Medicine. Republican. Roman Catholic. Home: 256 Woodland Rd Auburndale MA 02466-2707 Office: Tufts U Sackler Sch Grad Biomed Sci 136 Harrison Ave Boston MA 02111-1800

LASAK, JOHN JOSEPH, lawyer; b. Moosic, Pa., Jan. 18, 1944; s. Frank J. and Ann (Grudzinski) L.; m. Julilee Werteen, Mar. 17, 1973; children: Jennifer Ann, James Michael, Jessica Lee, Jill Emily. AB cum laude, U. Pa., 1965; JD, Harvard U., 1968. Bar: Pa. 1968. Assoc. Crumlish & Kania, Phila., 1968, Kania & Garbarino, Rosemont, Pa., 1971-76, ptnr. Bala Cynwyd, 1977-82, Kania, Lindner, Lasak & Feeney, Bala Cynwyd, 1982—. Mem. Haverford Twp. Planning Commn., 1981-83, vice-chmn., 1983; mem. Radnor Twp. (Pa.) Zoning Bd., 1985-92, 94—, vice chmn., 1987-91, 96, 2000, 02, chmn., 1992, 97, 2001; mem. Radnor Twp. Planning Commn., 1993; co-chmn. Delaware County Transition Coun., 1995-98, sec. Advanced Voting Solutions, Inc., 2001—. Mem. ABA, Pa. Bar Assn., Phila. Bar Assn., Harvard-Radcliffe Club (Phila.), Phi Beta Kappa. Republican. Roman Catholic. Office: 2 Bala Plz Ste 525 Bala Cynwyd PA 19004-1501 E-mail: Jlasak2@aol.com.

LASALA, KENNETH PAUL, engineer, consultant; b. Bronx, N.Y., Sept. 21, 1945; s. Accursio and Agnes LaS.; m. Rebecca Anne Whelan, Nov. 29, 1969; children: Kenneth P. Jr., Gregory T. BS in Physics, Rensselaer Polytech. Inst., 1967; MS in Physics, Brown U., 1971; PhD in Reliability Engring., U. Md., 1993. Engr. Dept. Navy, Washington, 1968-84; chief engring. divsn. Dept. Army, Alexandria, Va., 1984-86; chief reliability engring. divsn. Dept. Air Force, Washington, 1986-91; chief maintenance br. Def. Mapping Agy., Merrifield, Va., 1991-93; staff engr. sys. engring. NOAA Dept. Commerce, Silver Spring, Md., 1993—. Instr., rsch. advisor U. Md., College Park, 1984, 95—. Co-author: Handbook of Reliability Engineering and Management, 1988; contbr. articles to profl. jours. Recipient Field award Reliability & Maintainability Soc. Logistics Engrs., San Jose, Calif., 1989, Washington Chpt. Reliability & Maintainability award, 1989; Reliability Divsn. scholar Am. Soc. Quality Control, 1992. Mem. IEEE (chpt. chmn., ADCOM mem.). Avocations: tennis, painting, model building. Home: 703 Cannon Rd Silver Spring MD 20904-3323

LA SALLE, ARTHUR EDWARD, historic foundation executive; b. New Orleans, Aug. 9, 1930; s. Rene Charles and Jeanne Matilda (Senac) La S.; divorced; children— Carl Alan, Adam David, Jeanne Ambre Victoria. Student Holy Name of Jesus Coll. Founder, pres. Am. R.R. Equipment Assn., Asheville, N.C., 1960— ; founder Trains of Yesterday Mus., Hilliard, Fla., 1964-73; owner, restorer Brush Hill mansion, Irwin, Pa., 1973-77; lessee, restorer Springfield mansion, Fayette, Miss., 1977— ; founder, pres. Hist. Springfield Found., Fayette, 1977— ; cons. Smithsonian Instn., 1959, 75, Japanese Nat. Rys., Tokyo, 1968, Henry Ford Mus., 1975 City of Natchez, Miss., 1985, Old South Soc., Church Hill, Miss., 1985— ; cons. in field; lectr. in field. Author: The Marriage of Andrew Jackson at Springfield Plantation; contbr. articles to profl. jours. Mem. Ry. and Locomotive Hist. Soc., Nat. Trust for Historic Preservation, Natchez Hist. Soc., U.S. Naval Inst. Avocations: historical preservation and study; writing; painting. Home and Office: Springfield Plantation RR 1 Box 201 Fayette MS 39069-9527

LA SALLE, PETER, English educator, writer; b. Providence, May 27, 1947; s. A. Norman and Hope (Conroy) L. BA, Harvard U., 1969; MA, U. Chgo., 1972. Lectr. creative writing Johnson State Coll., Vt., 1974-76; asst. prof. English in creative writing Iowa State Univ., 1977-80; from asst. to full prof. English in creative writing Univ. Tex., Austin, 1980—, Susan Taylor McDaniel Regents prof. creative writing, 2001—; vis. faculty mem. Harvard U. Summer Sch., 1985-97. Author: The Graves of Famous Writers, 1980, Strange Sunlight, 1984, Hockey Sur Glace, 1996. Democrat. Roman Catholic. Office: U Tex Austin Dept English Austin TX 78712

LASATER, ERIC MARTIN, neurobiologist; b. Stuttgart, Fed. Republic Germany, Jan. 6, 1953; (parents Am. Citizens); s. Gene Martin and Naomi Ruth (Krahn) L.; m. Jill Ann Smith, Aug. 6, 1977; children: Brandon, Brent. BS, Colo. State U., 1975; MS, U. Calif., Davis, 1977; PhD, U. Tex. Med. Branch, Galveston, 1980. Postdoctoral fellow Harvard U., Cambridge, Mass., 1980-83, research assoc., 1983-84, biology lectr., 1984-85; asst. prof. U. Utah Health Scis. Ctr., Salt Lake City, 1985-88, assoc. prof., 1988-92, vice chmn., dir. rsch. dept. ophthalmology, 1992—, prof., 1993—. Contbr. articles to jours. Rsch. to Prevent Blindness Inc. William and Mary Greve Internat. rsch. scholar, 1991-94, Lew Wasserman merit award, 2001. Mem. AAAS, Assn. for Research Vision Ophthalmology, Neurosci. Soc., Internat. Soc. for Eye Rsch., Sigma Xi (excellence in research award 1980). Office: U Utah Health Scis Ctr 50 N Medical Dr Salt Lake City UT 84132-0001

LASCELLES, SUSAN, artist; b. Chgo., Jan. 29, 1958; d. Robert John and Donna Lee (Hjorth) L.; m. David Linn Hekelnkaemper, Apr. 17, 1998; children: Michael Lascelles DiCenzo, Max Lascelles Hekelnkaemper. Student, Ohio State U., 1984-87; BA, Empire State Coll., 1990. Artist, painter, photographer, stained glass, animator (film) Uncut, 1981; group shows include The Little Gallery, Springfield, Ohio, 1981, Millennium, N.Y.C., 1981, Rosenmarkt, Zurich, Switzerland, 1982, Upper Arlington Pub. Libr., Columbus, Ohio, 1987, The Dance Circle, Ithaca, N.Y., 1989, Dodajk Internation, Tucson, 1990, New Doors of the Arts, Tucson, 1993, Orts Theatre of Dance, Tucson, 1995, 96, 97, 98, Urban Picnic and Art Auction, Tucson, 1998, Daturo Studios and Gallery, Tucson, 1999, others; represented in permanent collections Corning Mus. Glass Film Libr., Empire State Coll., Färber Hüsli, Hallau, Switzerland, Fred and Pat Crain, Mechanicsburg, Ohio. Acad. merit scholar Scarlet and Gray, Ohio State U., Columbus, 1985, 87; grantee Changes Inc., N.Y.C., 1993. Avocations: gardening, pets, horses, music. Home: 7151 S Sandpiper Ave Tucson AZ 85746-6531

LASCHENSKI, JOHN PATRICK, accountant; b. Darby, Pa., Nov. 20, 1937; s. Sigmund Joseph and Mary (Oldham) L. BS in Physics, Holy Cross Coll., 1959; MS in Physics, U. Wis., 1965; MBA, Rochester Inst. Tech., 1978. CPA N.Y. Engr., mgr. IBM, N.Y., 1964-72; system engr. mgr. Xerox Corp., Rochester, 1972-78, div. controller, 1978-82; pvt. practice acctg., 1982-85; ptnr. Heveron, Laschenski & Walpole, 1985-92; pvt. practice, 1992—; lectr. SUNY, Geneseo, 1993-95. Adj. prof. Rochester Inst. Tech., 1983-94; nat. lectr. in finance and acctg. Am. Mgmt. Assn., 1994—. Lt. USN, 1959-63. Mem. N.Y. State Soc. CPAs (bd. dirs. Rochester 1986-93), Am. Inst. CPAs. Republican. Home and Office: 974 Rousseau Dr Webster NY 14580-4120 E-mail: jackpl@att.net.

LASCHER, ALAN ALFRED, lawyer; b. N.Y.C., Dec. 8, 1941; s. Morris Julius and Sadie Lillian (Chassen) L.; m. C. Amy Weingarten, July 12, 1969; children: David, Lauren, Alexandra, Carlyn. BS, Union Coll., 1963; LLB, Bklyn. Law Sch., 1967. Bar: N.Y. 1967. Assoc. Kramer, Leven et al, N.Y.C., 1969-75; ptnr. real estate dept. Weil, Gotshal & Manges, 1975—. Mem. law com. N.Y. Real Estate Bd., N.Y.C., 1981—; bd. advisors Chgo. Title Ins. Co., 1995—; Leasing Com. Am. Coll. Real Estate Lawyers 2002-. Served to sgt.

USAF, 1968-69. Named Real Estate Lawyer of Yr. Am. Lawyer, 1982. Mem. Am. Coll. Real Estate Lawyers (mem. Resolution Trust Corp. and Bankruptcy coms.). Office: Weil Gotshal & Manges 767 5th Ave Fl Concl New York NY 10153-0119

LASER, CHARLES, JR. oil company executive; b. Redford Twp., Mich., July 8, 1933; s. J.C. and Gertrude L.; m. Glenda Johnson, Sept. 27, 1972; 1 child, Susan Faye. Student, Mich. Tech. U., 1952-54, Ctrl. Mich. U., 1959-60; DD (hon.), Palm Beach Theol. Sem. Coll., 1991; LLD (hon.), Northwood U., 2000. With Retail Credit Co., 1958-60; exec. dir. Saginaw County Rep. Com., 1960-65, Rep. Com. D.C., 1967; fin. dir. San Joaquin Rep. Party, Stockton, Calif., 1968; owner Laser Advt., Bay City, Mich., 1969-75; exec. v.p. Vindell Petroleum, Inc., Midland, 1972-75, Geo Spectra Corp., Ann Arbor, 1977-86; pres. Laser Exploration Inc., Deerfield Beach, Fla. Task force Domestic Violence Gov. Jeb Bush, 1999—; adv. bd. Union Bank, Boca Raton, Fla. Chmn. Genesee County Rep. Com., 1981-82, mem. Broward County Rep. Exec. Com., 1987-88, indsl. bond screening com. Deerfield Beach, 1992; chmn. U.S. Senator Connie Mack Palm Beach County Round Table; bd. dirs. Palm Beach County Libr. Found., Shepherd Care Ministries, Hollywood, Foa., 1991—; adv. com. Tall Pines coun. Boy Scouts Am., mem. adv. bd. Gulf Stream Coun., 1980; mem. gov. prevention adv. com. Juvenile Justice Deliquency, Fla., 1988-96; mem. adv. bd. Humanitarian Soc., 1989—; bd. dirs., life mem. Large Freedoms Found., Valley Forge Broward County, Fla. chpt., 1995—; bd. govs. Northwood U., West Palm Beach, Fla., 1997; chmn. emeritus Fla. Symphonic Pops Orch., 1998; apptd. mem. Task Froce on Domestic Violence. With U.S. Army, 1954-58. Mem. Deerfield Beach C. of C. (v.p.), World Trade Coun. (Palm Beach, Fla. chpt.), Detroit Econ. Club, Bankers Club (Boca Raton), Humanitarian Soc. (adv. bd.), Rep. Men's Club (past pres., v.p. Boca Raton chpt.), Gold Coast Venture Capital Club (Delray Beach chpt.), Palm Beach Roundtable (bd. dirs., chmn. exec. com., sec. 1994-2002), Hillsboro Cove Condominium Assn. (pres. 1994), Rotary, Elks. Home: PO Box 8604 1523 E Hillsboro Blvd Apt 131 Deerfield Beach FL 33441-4301

LASERSOHN, PETER NATHAN, linguist, educator; b. Cleve., June 9, 1959; s. William Bock Lasersohn and Nancy Elizabeth (Moore) Ruskin; m. Sharon Lee Haworth. BA, Earlham Coll., 1981; MA, Ohio State U., 1985, PhD, 1988. Lectr. U. Tex., Austin, 1988-89; postdoctoral tchg. fellow U. Calif., Santa Cruz, 1989-91; asst. prof. U. Rochester (N.Y.), 1991-96, U. Ill., Urbana, 1996-2000, assoc. prof., 2000—. Author: A Semantics for Groups and Events, 1990, Plurality, Conjunction and Events, 1995. Arthur Charles fellow Earlham Coll, 1981, Ohio State U. fellow, 1982, Ohio State U. presdl. fellow, 1987. Mem. Linguistic Soc. Am., Phi Kappa Phi. Mem. Soc. Of Friends. Office: Dept Linguistics U Ill 4088 Fgn Langs Bldg Urbana IL 61801

LASH, JAMES, radiologist; b. N.Y.C., 1930; MD, SUNY, Downstate, 1956. Diplomate Am. Bd. Radiology. Intern Beth Israel Hosp., N.Y.C., 1956-57; resident in radiology Jewish Hosp., Bklyn., 1959-62; ptnr. Marine Park Radiology PC, 1962—. Attending physician Peninsula Hosp. Ctr., Far Rockaway, N.Y. Mem. AMA, Am. Coll. Radiology, Bklyn. Radiol. Soc., N.Y. State Radiol. Soc., Radiol. Soc. N.Am. Office: Marine Park Radiology 2270 Kimball St Brooklyn NY 11234-5139

LASH, MYLES PERRY, hospital administrator, consultant; b. Detroit, May 31, 1946; s. Irving and Rose (Simkovitz) L.; m. Linda Pauline Borger, June 19, 1968; children: Alissa Beth, David Howard. BS, Wayne State U., 1968; M.Hosp. Adminstrn., U. Mich., 1970. Asst. to exec. dir. Peoples Community Hosp. Authority, Wayne, Mich., 1970-72; asst. prof. Grad. Program Hosp. Adminstrn., Ohio State U., Columbus, 1970-72; adminstr. Ohio State U. Hosps., 1973-79; exec. dir. Med. Coll. Va., Richmond, 1979-85; nat. dir. health care Arthur Young Co., Washington, 1985-86; pres. Lash Group-Health Care Cons., 1986-99, Provenance Health Ptnrs., 1999—. Contbr. articles to profl. jours. Bd. dirs. Univ. Hosp. Consortium, 1980-85, pres., 1985. Mem. U. Mich. Hosp. Adminstrn. Alumni Assn. (pres.), Am. Hosp. Assn., Am. Coll. Hosp. Adminstrs. (Robert S. Hudgens Meml. award 1982). Home: 6708 Bonaventure Ct Bethesda MD 20817-4026 Office: 555 13th St NW Ste 380 E Washington DC 20004-1109 E-mail: mlash@provenancehealth.com.

LASH, STEPHEN SYCLE, auction company executive; b. Boston, Feb. 10, 1940; s. Samuel George and Carolyn Virginia (Sycle) L.; m. Wendy Lehman, Oct. 29, 1967; children: Abigail Sycle, William Lehman. BA, Yale U., 1962; MBA, Columbia U., 1966. V.p. Bali Footwear, Inc., Marlborough, Mass., 1962-64, 66-68, S.G. Warburg and Co., London, N.Y.C., 1968-76, Christies, N.Y.C., 1976-80, sr. v.p., 1980-84, exec. v.p., 1984-93, vice chmn., 1993-2000, chmn., 2000—; also bd. dirs. Christies Internat. PLC & Christies Fine Art Ltd. Co-author: A Vision of Paradise: Robertson Ward and the Mill Reef Club. Mem. coun. Nat. Trust for Historic Preservation, 2002—; founder, pres. Ocean Liner Mus., 1983—88, co-chmn., 1988—96; commr. N.Y.C. Landmarks Preservation Commn., 1973—76; bd. dirs. N.Y. Landmarks Conservancy, 1975—95, 1997—, chmn., 1992—95; bd. dirs. Preservation League N.Y., Albany, 1986—, Peabody-Essex Inst., Salem, Mass., 2000—, Nat. Bldg. Mus., Washington, 2001—. Pan Am. Union fellow, 1965. Mem. Yale U. Alumni Assn. Metro N.Y. (pres. 1987-90), River Club, Mill Reef Club, Century Assn., Wadawanuck Club (Stonington, Conn.). Home: 151 E 79th St New York NY 10021-0417 Office: Christies 20 Rockefeller Plz New York NY 10020-1902

LASH, WILLIAM HENRY, III, federal agency administrator, law educator, lawyer; b. Jersey City, Jan. 21, 1961; s. William H. Jr. and Vivian G. Lash; m. Sharon K. Zackula, Dec. 31, 1992; 1 child, William H. IV. BA, Yale U., 1982; JD, Harvard U., 1985. Bar: N.J. 1986, Washington 1988. Law clk. Justice Alan B. Handler, Trenton, N.J., 1985-86; assoc. Fried, Frank, Harris et al, Washington, 1986-88, 88-89; counsel to chmn. U.S. Internat. Trade Commn., 1988; asst. prof. law Western New Eng. Coll., Springfield, Mass., 1989-90, St. Louis U., 1990-93; prof. law George Mason U., Arlington, Va., 1993—; asst. sec. commerce Dept. Commerce, Washington, 2001—. Dir. Nostalgia TV Network, Washington, 1993-98, Carlton Maritime Fund; mem. adv. bd. World TV Program, Washington, 1998; disting. sr. fellow Ctr. for Study of Am. Bus., St. Louis, 1993—; bd. dirs. Virtual Credit Svcs.; adj. fellow Citizens for a Sound Economy, 2000—01. Author: Regulating Securities, 1996, International Trade Law, 1998. Bd. dirs., treas. Internat. Law Students Assn., 1996-2001; vice chmn. fin. instns. Federalist Soc., Washington, 1997-2001; mem. Va. Commn. for Environ., Richmond, 1996; bd. dirs. Trade Policy Ctr. Cato Inst.; adj. fellow Citizens Sound Economy. Mem. ABA (editl. bd. Bus. Law for Today 1997—), Yale Club N.Y.C. Republican. Lutheran. Office: US Dept of Commerce 14th & Constitution Washington DC 20593

LASHBROOKE, ELVIN CARROLL, JR. law educator, consultant; b. Dec. 14, 1939; s. Elvin Carroll Sr. and Lois Lenora (Weger) L.; m. Margaret Ann Jones, Dec. 19, 1964; children: Michelle Ann, David C. BA, U. Tex., 1967, MA, 1968, JD, 1972, LLM, 1977; PhD, Mich. State U., 1993. Bar: Tex. 1972, Fla. 1973. Legis. counsel Tex. Legis. Coun., Austin, 1972-75; pvt. practice law, 1975-77; asst. prof. coll. of law DePaul U., Chgo., 1977-79, Stetson U., St. Petersburg, Fla., 1979-80; assoc. prof. sch. law Notre Dame, Ind., 1981-85; prof., chmn. bus. law dept. Mich. State U., East Lansing, 1985-95; assoc. dean adminstrn. Eli Broad Coll. Bus., 1993-97; pvt. practice cons., 1986-97; dean Coll. Bus. U. Nev., Las Vegas, 1997-99; assoc. dean Broad Grad. Sch. of Mgmt., Mich. State U., East Lansing, 1999—2001, dir. study abroad and e-learning initiatives, 2001—. Instr. St. Edward's U., Austin, 1975-76. Author: Tax Exempt Organizations, 1985, The Legal Handbook of Business Transactions, 1987; contbr. articles to profl. jours. Mem. Tex. Bar Assn., Fla. Bar Assn. Avocation: computers. Home: 6405 Ridgepond Pl East Lansing MI 48823-9777 Office: Mich State Univ Broad Grad Sch of Mgmt East Lansing MI 48824-1122

LASHER, CRAIG RICHARD, policy analyst; b. Newfane, N.Y., Jan. 21, 1959; s. Keith Arlen and Charlotte Marie (Cash) L. AB, Hamilton Coll., 1981; MA, Am. U., 1986. Policy analyst, legis. asst. Population Action Internat., Washington, 1983-89, sr. policy analyst, 1989—. Mem. mgmt. team Campaign to Preserve U.S. Global Leadership, 1998—, mem. political adv. com. League of Conservation Voters, 1998—, mem. leadership coun. Voters for Choice, Washington, 1992—. Grad. fellow United Meth. Ch., 1982; named All-Am. Swimmer Coll. Swimming Coaches Assn. Am., 1978, Eagle Scout Boy Scouts Am., 1974. Mem. SAR, Masons (33 degree), Shriners, Scottish Rite, York Rite, Delta Upsilon. Methodist. Avocations: swimming, bicycling, running. Office: Population Action Internat 1300 19th St NW Fl 2 Washington DC 20036-1609 E-mail: clasher@popact.org.

LASHER, HIRAM NELSON, entrepreneur; b. Catskill, N.Y., Feb. 8, 1920; s. Nelson Frederick and Elizabeth Esther (Palmer) L.; m. Bertha Mae Van Vlierden, Dec. 12, 1948; children: Steven Hiram (dec.), Douglas Nelson, Sandra Elizabeth, Hiram Dennis, Denise Helen, Michael Clark, Michele Betty. DVM, Cornell U., 1942; AAS, Del. Tech. C.C., 1978. Hon. diplomate Am. Coll. Poultry Vets.; lic. vet., Del., N.Y. Pvt. practice, Catskill, 1942-48; poultry pathologist State Bd. Agr., Millsboro and Frankford, Del., 1948-50; founder, pres. Del. Poultry Labs./Sterwin Labs., 1950-79, Inter-Continental Biologics, Inc. (Intervet Am.), Millsboro, 1979-82, Lasher Assocs., Inc., Millsboro, 1982—. Lasher Dining Hall named in his honor Boy Scouts Am., Wilmington, 2000, Lasher Lab., U. Del. named in his honor, 1997; recipient Disting. Citizen award Delmarva Poultry Industry, Inc., 2000, Svc. to Agr. award U. Del., 1999, Order of 1st State, Del. Gov. Tom Carper, 1994, Disting. Leadership award U. Del., 1993, Medal of Achievement, Delmarva Poultry Industry, Inc., 1998, Health Care award Beebe Med. Ctr., 1989, Spl. Svc. award U. Ga., 2001; founder Caswell S. Eidson Eminent scholar program U. Gal. Coll. Vet. Medicine, 2001. Mem.: NY Acad. Scis., Poultry Sci. Assn., Am. Assn. Avian Pathologists (charter mem.) (Spl. Svc. award 2001). Republican. United Methodist. Avocations: philanthropic activities, Capital campaigns and scholarships. Home: 5 Betts Pond Ridge Millsboro DE 19966 Office: Lasher Assocs Inc DuPont Hwy Millsboro DE 19966 Office Fax: 302-934-8745. E-mail: lasherinc@mchsi.com.

LASHER, ROBERT L. retired surgeon; b. Erie, Pa., June 15, 1924; MD, Temple U., 1947. Diplomate Am. Bd. Surgery. Intern St. Vincent's Hosp., Erie, 1947-48; resident in surgery Western Pa. Hosp., Pitts., 1948-49, Aspinwall VA Hosp., 1949-50, 52; ret., 1994. Mem. staff St. Vincent Health Ctr., Erie. Fellow ACS; mem. AMA, Am. Assn. R.R. Surgeons.

LASHLEY, CURTIS DALE, lawyer; b. Urbana, Ill., Nov. 3, 1956; s. Jack Dale and Janice Elaine (Holman) L.; m. Tamara Dawn Yahnig, June 14, 1986. BA, U. Mo., Kansas City, 1978, JD, 1981. Bar: Mo. 1981, U.S. Dist. Ct. (we. dist.) Mo. 1981, U.S. Tax Ct. 1982, U.S. Ct. Appeals (8th cir.) 1992. Assoc. Melvin Heller, Inc., Creve Coeur, Mo., 1982; ptnr. Domjan & Lashley, Harrisonville, 1983-86; asst. gen. counsel Mo. Dept. Revenue, Independence, 1986-89, assoc. gen. counsel, 1989-92, sr. counsel, 1992—, adminstrv. hearing officer, 1995—; spl asst. atty. gen., 1986—; spl. asst. prosecutor Jackson County, Mo., 1990—. City atty., Adrian and Strasburg, Mo., 1985-86. V.p. Cass County Young Reps., Harrisonville, 1985. Recipient honor Senate Resolution 830 and Mo. Ho. Resolution 2314, 2001, Cert. of Appreciation, Kansas City Bd. Police Commrs., 2001, Legis. Resolution honor, Jackson County Mo., 2001. Mem. ABA, NRA, Kiwanis (treas. Harrisonville chpt. 1985-86, Harrisonville Disting. Svc. award 1985), Phi Alpha Delta. Republican. Presbyterian. Office: Mo Dept Revenue 16647 E 23rd St S Independence MO 64055-1922 E-mail: CurtisL752@excite.com.

LASHLEY, FELISSA R. dean, nursing educator, researcher; b. N.Y.C., Apr. 6, 1941; d. Jack and Ruth (Dorbin) Lashley; divorced; children: Peter, Heather, Neal. BS, Adelphi Coll., 1961; MA, NYU, 1965; PhD, Ill. State U., 1973. Cert. Am. Bd. Med. Genetics., Am. Coll. Med. Genetics. Dean Sch. of Nursing So. Ill. U., Edwardsville, Ill. Author: Clinical Genetics in Nursing Practice, 1998 (book of yr. award); editor: The Person with AIDS: Nursing Perspectives, 1987 (Book of Yr. award), Tuberculosis: A Sourcebook for Nursing Practice and Women, Children and HIV/AIDS (Book of Yr. award , 1993), Emerging Infectious Diseases: Trends and Issues, 2002, The Person with HIV/AIDS: Nursing Perspectives, 2000. Mem.: AAAS, ANA (coun. nurse researchers), Am. Coll. Med. Genetics, Ill. Nurses Assn., Midwest Nursing Rsch. Soc., Nat. League Nursing, Am. Acad. Nursing, Am. Soc. Human Genetics. E-mail: flashle@siue.edu.

LASHLEY, LENORE CLARISSE, lawyer; b. N.Y.C., June 3, 1934; d. Leonard Livingston and Una Ophelia (Laurie) L.; children: Donna Bee-Gates, Michele Bee, Maria Bee. BA, CUNY, 1956; MSW, U. Calif., Berkeley, 1970, MPH, 1975; JD, U. Calif., San Francisco, 1981. Bar: Calif. 1981. Atty. W.O.M.A.N., Inc., San Francisco, 1982-84; pvt. practice San Francisco Law Office, 1984-87; dep. dist. atty. Monterey Dist. Atty., Salinas, Calif., 1987-89; trial atty. State Bar of Calif., L.A., 1989; dep. dist. atty. L.A. Dist. Atty., 1989; dep. city atty. Office of City Atty., L.A., 1989—. Chair, bd. dirs. St. Anthony's Dining Room, San Francisco, 1986-87; sec., bd. dirs. NAACP, Monterey, 1987-88; bd. dirs. Childrens Home Soc., Oakland, Calif., 1966-68. Recipient Cert. of Merit, Nat. Assn. Naval Officers, 1987. Mem. L.A. County Bar Assn. (del. to state bar 1992, 93). Roman Catholic. Avocations: running, reading, animal welfare, volunteer work with people with AIDS. Office: City Atty LA 200 N Main St Ste 1700 Los Angeles CA 90012-4110 E-mail: llashle@atty.lacity.org.

LASHLEY, MARK ALAN, physician assistant; b. Balt., Sept. 17, 1959; s. William George and Verna Joan (Buterbaugh) L.; m. Mary Ellen Cadogan, June 21, 1986; children: Christina Marie, Meredith Anne, Heather Nicole, Christopher Mark. BA in Biology, U. Md., Balt., 198l; AA in Physician Asst., Essex (Md.) Community Coll., 1984; MBA, Loyola Coll., Balt., 1987. Cert. physician asst., Md. Emergency room registrar Church Hosp., Balt., 1980-84; surg. physician asst. Baltimore County Gen. Hosp., 1984, South Balt. Gen. Hosp., 1984-85; physician asst. supr. Union Meml. Hosp., 1985-93; asst. prof. Essex C.C., Balt., 1993-95, asst. prof. part-time, 1995—; physician asst. Union Meml. Hosp. and Good Samaritan Hosp., 1995—. Part-time physician asst. Union Meml. Hosp., 1993—, Good Samaritan Hosp., 1995—, Mercy Hosp., 1995—; guest speaker dept. nursing Towson State U., Balt., 1987—; part-time faculty Essex C.C., 1990—. Deacon Loch Raven Bapt. Ch. U.S. Senate scholar, 1977. Fellow Am. Acad. Physician Assts., Md. Acad. Physician Assts. (pres. 1994). Republican. Baptist. Home: 2513 Tally Ho Rd Fallston MD 21047-1220 Office: Essex CC PA Program 7201 Rossville Blvd Baltimore MD 21237-3855

LASHLEY, VIRGINIA STEPHENSON HUGHES, retired computer science educator; b. Wichita, Kans., Nov. 12, 1924; d. Herman H. and Edith M. (Wayland) Stephenson; m. Kenneth W. Hughes, June 4, 1946 (dec.); children: Kenneth W. Jr., Linda; m. Richard H. Lashley, Aug. 19, 1954; children: Robert H., Lisa Lashley Van Amberg, Diane Lashley Tan. BA, U. Kans., 1945; MA, Occidental Coll., 1966; PhD, U. So. Calif., 1983. Cert. info. processor, tchr. secondary and community coll., Calif. Tchr. math. La Canada (Calif.) High Sch., 1966-69; from instr. to prof. Glendale (Calif.) Coll., 1970-92, chmn. bus. div., 1977-81, coord. instructional computing, 1974-92, prof. emeritus, 1992—; sec., treas., dir. Victory Montessori Schs., Inc., Pasadena, Calif., 1980—; pres. The Computer Sch., 1983-92. Pres. San Gabriel Valley Data Processing Mgmt. Assn., 1977-79, San Gabriel Valley Assn. for Systems Mgmt., 1979-80; chmn. Western Ednl. Computing Conf., 1980, 84. Editor Jour. Calif. Ednl. Computing, 1980. NSF grantee, 1967-69, EDUCARE scholar U. So. Calif., 1980-82; John Randolph and Dora Haynes fellow, Occidental Coll., 1964-66; student computer ctr. renamed Dr. Virginia S. Lashley Ctr., 1992. Mem. AAUP, AAUW, DAR (scholarship chair), Calif. Edn. Computing Consortium (bd. dirs. 1979—, v.p. 1983-84, pres. 1985-87), Orgn. Am. Historians, San Marino Women's Club, Colonial Dames, XVII Century (scholarship chair), Nat. Geneal. Soc., New Eng. Hist. Geneal. Soc., Town Hall, World Affairs Coun., Phi Beta Kappa, Pi Mu Epsilon, Phi Alpha Theta, Phi Delta Kappa, Delta Phi Upsilon, Gamma Phi Beta. Republican. Congregationalist. Home: 1240 S San Marino Ave San Marino CA 91108-1227

LASHLEY, WILLIAM BARTHOLOMEW, county official; b. Dayton, Ohio, Jan. 2, 1952; s. William Bartholomew and Reta Carolyn (Reicken) L.; m. Loukia Simopoulos, June 30, 1973; children: Nichole E., Felicite D. BA in Econs., Wright State U., 1976; opthomol. sci. degree, Regis U., 1982. Asst. mgr. First Nat. Bank, Dayton, Ohio, 1973-77; mgr. store Kroger Co., 1977-80; cashier Frontier Bank, Denver, 1980-82; asst. v.p. Empire Savs., 1982-85; mgr. investor acctg. Security Pacific Mortgage Corp., 1985-88; corp. acct. investors Crossland Mortgage Corp., Salt Lake City, 1988-89; fiscal officer Montgomery County Cts., Dayton, 1989—. Mem. Montgomery County Fiscal Task Force, Dayton, 1990—. Mem. ABA (assoc.), Am. Bankers Assn., Govt. Fin. Officers Assn. (mem. select review com.), Mortgage Bankers Assn., Ohio State Bar Assn. (assoc.). Home: 3307 Waltham Ave Kettering OH 45429-3529 Office: Montgomery County Cts 41 N Perry St Dayton OH 45402-1431

LASHMAN, L. EDWARD, arbitrator, mediator, consultant; b. New Orleans, June 6, 1924; s. L. Edward and Edith Ruth (Deutsch) L.; m. Elizabeth Gitt Fichman, June 6, 1948 (dec. Aug. 1984); children: Deborah, Rebekah, David W. (dec. Feb. 1993), Judith; m. Joyce Blicher Schwartz, July 25, 1987. Student, U. N.C., 1940-42, Tulane U., 1942-43. Ptnr. Caire Assocs., New Orleans, 1946-51; with CIO and AFL-CIO, 1951-67; asst. to sec., dir. cong. liason HUD, Washington, 1967-69; mng. ptnr. Urban Housing Assocs., Denver, 1969-70; v.p. U. Mass., 1970-75; dir. external affairs, sr. planning counselor Harvard U., Cambridge, Mass., 1975-89; sec. adminstrn. and fin. Commonwealth of Mass., Boston, 1989-91, chmn. Mass. bd. regents pub. higher edn., 1986-88; chmn. Mass. Housing Fin. Agy., 1977-79, Commonwealth Land Bank, Boston, 1975-77; ret., 1991. Acting exec. dir. (pro bono) Mass. State Lotterty, 1999; contract mediator U.S. Equal Employment Opportunity Commn.; contract arbitrator U.S. Postal Svc. Exec. com. Denver County Dem. Party, 1952-64; chmn. Colo. Urban League, Denver, 1961-63; acting COO (pro bono) Judge Baker Children's Ctr., Boston, 1993-94; dir. Nat. Housing Conf., Washington, 1969-75; v.p. Handel & Haydn Soc., Boston, 1982-84. With U.S. Army, 1943-46, ETO. Mem. Am. Arbitration Assn., Mass. Assn. Mediation Programs, Norfolk and Suffolk County Superior Ct. Mediation Panels, Joint Labor Mgmt. Com. Mediation Panel. Avocations: fly fishing, cooking, photography. Home and Office: 236 Conant Rd Weston MA 02493-1654

LASHMAN, SHELLEY BORTIN, retired judge; b. Camden, N.J., Aug. 18, 1917; s. William Mitchell and Anna (Bortin) L.; m. Ruth Horn, Jan. 3, 1959; children: Karen E. Lashman Hall, Gail A. McBride, Mitchell A., Christopher R. BS, William and Mary Coll., 1938; postgrad., Columbia U., 1938, 39; JD, U. Mich., 1946. Bar: N.Y. 1947, N.J. 1968. Judge N.J. Workers Compensation, 1981-2001. With USNR, 1940-70. Mem. Atlantic County Bar Assn., Am. Judges Assn., Atlantic County Hist. Soc., Am. Judicature Soc., Ret. Officers Assn., U.S. Navy League, Fleet Res. Assn., USS Yorktown CV-5 Club, Mil. Order World Wars. Republican. Home: 1209 Old Zion Rd Egg Harbor Township NJ 08234-7667 Home Fax: 609-653-6686.

LASHNER, MARILYN AUERBACH, communication content analyst, forensic expert; b. Phila., Dec. 11, 1929; d. Jacob and Mildred (Goodrich) Auerbach; m. Melvin Lashner, Aug. 19, 1951; children: Bret Auerbach Lashner, Jane Leslie Lashner, William Mark Lashner, Suzanne Lashner Dayanim. BS in English and Edn., U. Pa., 1950, MS in English and Edn., 1954; PhD in Communications., Temple U., 1979. Cert. secondary English tchr., Pa. Tchr. English, dir. dramatics Cheltenham High Sch., Elkins Park, Pa., 1951-54; instr. English, Pa. State U., Abington, 1967-75; tchr. effective English communication Tng. div. U.S. Civil Svc., Phila., 1974; pres., dir. rsch. Inst. for News Media Analysis, Meadowbrook, Pa., 1979-84; asst. prof. communications Temple U., Phila., 1980-81; prin. rschr. Media Analysis & Comms. Rsch., Meadowbrook, 1984—. Forensic expert on meaning and interpretation of communication content in cases of libel, slander, invasion of privacy, prejudicial publicity, change of venue, fraudulent advertising, copyright infringement, contract interpretation, discourse analysis, indentification of authorship. Author: The Chilling Effect in TV News: Intimidation by the Nixon White House, 1984; also articles. Recipient 1st place nat. award for First Amendment essay Nat. Assn. Broadcasters, 1977; fellow Temple U., 1976-79. Mem. Nat. Forensic Ctr. for Disting. Experts, Am. Acad. Forensic Scientists, Pi Delta Theta. E-mail: malashner@aol.com.

LASHOF, JOYCE COHEN, public health educator; b. Phila. d. Harry and Rose (Brodsky) Cohen; m. Richard K. Lashof, June 11, 1950; children: Judith, Carol, Dan. AB, Duke U., 1946; MD, Women's Med. Coll., 1950; DSc (hon.) , Med. Coll. Pa., 1983. Dir. Ill. State Dept. Pub. Health, 1973—77; dep. asst. sec. for health programs and population affairs Dept. Health, Edn., and Welfare, Washington, 1977—78; sr. scholar in residence IOM, 1978; asst. dir. office of tech. assessment U.S. Congress, 1978—81; dean sch. pub. health U. Calif., Berkeley, 1981—91; prof. pub. health U. Calif. Sch. Pub. Health, 1981—94, prof. emeritus, 1994—. Co-chair Commn. on Am. after Roe vs. Wade, 1991—92; mem. Sec.'s Coun. Health Promotion and Disease Prevention, 1988—91; chair Pres.'s Adv. Com. on Gulf War Vets. Illnesses, 1995—97. Mem. editl. bd.: Wellness Letter, 1993—, mem. editl. bd.: Ann. Rev. of Pub. Health, 1987—90. Recipient Alumni Achievement award, Med. Coll. Pa., 1975, Sedgewick Meml. medal, APHA, 1995. Avocation: hiking. Home: 601 Euclid Ave Berkeley CA 94708-1331 Office: U Calif Sch Pub Health 140 Earl Warren Hl Berkeley CA 94720-7360

LASHUTKA, GREGORY S. mayor, lawyer; b. N.Y.C., 1944; m. Catherine Adams; children: Stephanie, Michael, Nicholas, Lara. BS, Ohio State U., 1967; JD, Capital U., 1974. Bar: Ohio, 1974, Fla., D.C., 1975. Former ptnr. Squire, Sanders & Dempsey, Columbus, Ohio; elected mayor City of Columbus, 1991-99; former Columbus City Atty.; sr. v.p. corp. rels. Nationwide, Columbus, 2000—. Past chmn. Columbus-Area Sports Devel. Corp.; pres. Nat. League of Cities; comentator of the Ohio State U. Football Color, 1983-90; active civic and charitable orgns.; bd. dirs Simon Kenton coun. Boy Scouts Am.; bd. dirs. Columbus Assn. of Performing Arts, Cath. Social Svcs., Columbus chpt. Am. Heart Assn. Served to lt., USN. Named Mcpl. Leader of the Yr., Am. City and County mag., 1993. Mem. Nat. Acad. Pub. Adminstrs. Office: Nationwide One Nationwide Plz Columbus OH 43215-2220

LASICH, VIVIAN ESTHER LAYNE, secondary education educator; b. Hopewell Twp., Pa., Dec. 17, 1935; d. Charles McClung and Harriette Law (George) Layne; m. William G. Lasich, Apr. 10, 1958; children: C. Laurence, Celeste M., Michelle R. AB, Geneva Coll., 1956; MA in Edn., No. Mich. U., 1970, postgrad. Secondary tchr. Freedom (Pa.) High Sch., 1956-57; elem. educator Gilbert Elem. Sch., Gwinn, Mich., 1967-69; lang. arts educator Gwinn Mid. Sch., 1970-99; ret., 1999. Adv. bd. panel Mich. Dept. Edn./Arts, 1976-79; mem. sch. improvement team, 1988-91, 93-94, co-chair, 1995-98; mid sch. concept team, 1992-98, mid sch. at-risk coord. dist. curriculum coord. coun., 1995-96; dist. curriculum strategy action team, 1993-94; dist. profl. devel. strategy action team, 1993-94; mem. sounding bd. Mid. Sch., 1994-98, dist. sch. improvement team, 1994-98; lang. arts curriculum design com., 1997-98; rep. Gwinn Edn. Assn. Mid. Sch., 1995-98. Author: Prophets Without Honor: Teachers, Students, & Trust, 1991. V.p. Marquette (Mich.) Community Theatre, 1962-63 bd. dirs. 1963-74, mem. 1961-92; pres. Marquette Arts Coun. 1973-74, v.p. 1972-73, bd. dirs. 1970-78, mem. 1970-84; pres. Upper Peninsula Arts Coordinating Bd. 1976-78, v.p. 1974-76, bd. dirs. 1978-84; bd. dirs. Mich. Community Theatre Assn. 1972-73; bd. dirs. Mich Community Arts Agys., 1976-79. Recipient Committment to Excellence award Marquette Community Theatre, 1965. Devotion to Arts Development award Upper Peninsula (Mich.) Arts Coord. Bd. 1979. Mem. ASCD, NEA, AAUW, Mich. Edn. Assn., Phi Delta Kappa. Presbyterian. Avocations: rsch., writing, theatrical direction and performance, vocal music. Home: 508 Pine St Marquette MI 49855-3838 Office: Gwinn Area Community Schs Gwinn MI 49841

LASKA, PAUL ROBERT, protective services official, writer, educator; b. Torrington, Conn., Oct. 27, 1951; s. Paul and Geraldine Louise (Musselman) L.; m. Patricia T. Millner, July 19, 2000. BS in Criminology, Fla. State U., 1973. Officer Belle Glade (Fla.) Police Dept., 1974-77; investigator Martin County Sheriff's Office, Stuart, Fla., 1977—, State Fire Marshall, West Palm Beach, 1981. Instr. Indian River C.C., Ft. Pierce, Fla., 1979—, Fla. Inst. Tech., Jensen Beach, 1982-86. Columnist Law Enforcement Tech. Mag.; contbr. articles to profl. jours. Mem. Internat. Assn. Identification, Internat. Assn. Bomb Technicians and Investigators, Internat. Soc. Explosive Engrs., Fla. Internat. Assn. Identification (dir. dist. 1985-88), Fingerprint Soc., Canadian Identification Soc. Republican. Roman Catholic. Avocations: firearms, photography. Home: PO Box 1423 Palm City FL 34991-6423 Office: Martin County Sheriff's Office 800 SE Monterey Rd Stuart FL 34994-4599 E-mail: bdtcop@hotmail.com., plaska@sheriff.martin.fl.us., dactylographer@yahoo.com.

LASKE, JACOB, business executive, career officer, retired; b. Krefeld, Rheinland, Germany, Mar. 5, 1925; s. Chaim Abraham and Jehudith (Stromwasser) L.; m. Edith Batia Goldstein; children: Chaya, Moshe, Amiram. Degree in bus. mgmt., Am. Sch., 1964; B in Law, Am. Sch., 1965. Enlisted

Israel Army, 1947-67, lt. col., 1960-68, ret., 1968; area mgr. Champion Motors VW, Haifa, 1967-70; comml. mgr. Israel Motors, 1970-72, Wires & Cables, Haifa, 1972-74; clearing customs agt., 1974—; pres. Edlas, 1980—. Avocations: crosswords, bridge. Office: Edlas PO Box 386 31003 Haifa Israel

LASKER, GABRIEL WARD, anthropologist, educator; b. York, Eng., Apr. 29, 1912; s. Bruno and Margaret Naomi (Ward) L.; m. Bernice Kaplan, July 31, 1949; children: Robert Alexander, Edward Meyer, Ann Titania. Student, U. Wis., 1928-30; AB, U. Mich., 1934; A.M., Harvard U., 1940, PhD, 1945; DSC (hon.), U. Turin, Italy, 2000. Instr. English Chiao T'ung U., Peking, China, 1936-37; teaching fellow in anatomy Harvard Med. Sch., 1941-42; mem. faculty dept. anatomy Wayne State U. Sch. Medicine, Detroit, 1946—, asst. prof., 1947-55, assoc. prof., 1955-64, prof., 1964-82, prof. emeritus, 1982—; fellow commoner Churchill Coll., Cambridge U., 1983-84. Conducted Wayne U.-Viking Fund field trip to Mexico to study effects of migration on phys. characteristics of Mexicans, 1948 Author: Physical Anthropology, The Evolution of Man, Surnames and Genetic Structure, Happenings and Hearsay: Experiences of a Biological Anthropologist, 1999; editor: Yearbook of Phys. Anthropology, 1945-51, Human Biology, 1953-87, Research Strategies in Human Biology: Field and Survey Studies, 1993; contbr. articles to profl. jours. Fellow Am. Anthrop. Assn., AAAS (v.p. 1968); mem. Am. Assn. Phys. Anthropologists (sec.-treas. 1947-51, v.p. 1960-62, pres. 1963-65, Charles Darwin award 1993), Am. Assn. Anatomists, Human Biology Assn., (pres. 1982-84, First Franz Boas Prize, 1996), Soc. Study Human Biology (U.K.), Asociación Mexicana de Antropología Biológica, Sigma Xi. Office: 540 E Canfield St Detroit MI 48201-1928

LASKER, JONATHAN LEWIS, artist; b. Jersey City, July 30, 1948; s. Lester and Henrietta Selma (Gross) L. Student, Sch. Visual Arts, N.Y.C., 1975-77, Calif. Inst. Arts, 1977. One-man shows include Landmark Gallery, N.Y., Gunnar Kaldeway, Dusseldorf, Fed. Republic Germany, 1981, Annette Gmeiner, Kirchzarten, Fed. Republic Germany, 1984, Tibor de Nagy, N.Y.C., 1984, 1986, Michael Werner, Cologne, Fed. Republic Germany, 1986, 1987, 1990, Massimo Audiello, N.Y.C., 1986, 1988, 1989, Anders Tornberg, Lund, Sweden, 1987, 1990, Gian Enzo Sperone, Rome, 1988, 1991, Sperone Westwater Gallery, N.Y.C., 1991, 1993, 1996, 1999, 2002, Lars Bohman, Stockholm, 1991, 1994, 2001, Inst. Contemporary Art U. Pa., Phila., 1992, Thaddaeus Ropac Gallery, Paris, 1992, 1997, 2000, Witte de With Ctr. Contemporary Art, Rotterdam, 1993, Rhona Hoffman Gallery, Chgo., 1993, Soledad Lorenzo, Madrid, 1995, 1998, L.A. Louver Gallery, 1995, Kunsthalle Bielefeld, Germany, 1997, Stedelijk Mus., Amsterdam, Holland, 1998, Kunstverein St. Gallen, Switzerland, 1998, Timothy Taylor, London, England, 1998, Forum for Contemporary Art, St. Louis, Mo., The Power Plant Contemporary Art Gallery, Toronto, Canada, 1999, Rose Art Mus. Brandeis U., Waltham, Mass., 2000, Thomas Schulte, Berlin, 2002, numerous others, exhibited in group shows at Mus. Ludwig, Cologne, Wacoal Art Ctr., Tokyo, 1985, Rose Art Mus. Brandeis U., Waltham, Mass., 1986, 1999, Corcoran Gallery Art, Washington, 1987, Roos Mus., Malmo, Sweden, U. N. Tex., Denton, J.B. Speed Mus., Louisville, Alta. Coll. Art, Edmonton, Can., Contemporary Arts Ctr., Cin., Santa Fe Community Coll., Gainesville, Fla., Met. Mus. Art, N.Y.C., 1988, Stedelijk Mus., Amsterdam, The Netherlands, 1989, Marc Richards Gallery, L.A., Scott Hansen Gallery, N.Y.C., 1990, Pace Gallery, 1990, Sperone Westwater Gallery, 1991, 1994, 1995, 1996, 1997, 1998, Gallery Modern Art, Bologna, Italy, 1991, Hirshhorn Mus. and Sculpture Garden, Washington, 1991, Mus. Contemporary Art of Dayton Art Inst., 1992, Documenta IX, Kassel, Germany, Gallerie Nächst Sankt Stephan, Vienna, 1992, Thaddaeus Ropac Gallery, Paris, 1992, 1999, Ruth Bloom Gallery, L.A., 1993, Hayward Gallery, London, 1994, Ctr. for the Fine Arts, Miami, 1994, Va. Mus. Fine Arts, Richmond, 1995, Mus. Contemporary Art, Helsinki, Folkwang Mus., Essen, Germany, 1995, Mus. Reina Sofia, Madrid, 1996, Kunsthalle Zurich, Switzerland, 1996, Musée D'Art Moderne, St. Etienne France, 1997, Mus. Am. Art of Pa. Acad. Fine Arts, Phila., 1998, Malmø Konsthall, Sweden, 1998, Menil Collection, Houston, 1999, Aargauer Kunsthaus, Aarau, Switzerland, 2000, Palazzo Cavour, Turin, Italy, 2000, Michael Hue-Williams, London, England, 2000, Rudolfinum Ctr for Contemporary Art, Prague, Czech Republic, 2001, Kunstverein St. Gallen in Kunstmuseum, Switzerland, 2001, Yale U. Art Gallery, New Haven, Conn., 2002, numerous others, Represented in permanent collections Corcoran Gallery, Hirshhorn Mus. and Sculpture Garden, Washington, Mus. Ludwig, Cologne, Wacoal Art Ctr., Tokyo, Whitney Mus. Am. Art, N.Y.C., Moderna Museet, Stockholm, Fond Nat. d'Art Contemporain, Paris, High Mus., Atlanta, Museo de Arte Contemporaneo, Seville, Spain, La Fundacion Caja De Pensiones, Barcelona, Albright Knox Art Gallery, Buffalo, N.Y., Los Angeles County Mus. Art, Calif., Museo Nacional Centro de Arte Reina Sofia, Madrid; critic (numerous art books, catalogs, mags. including) Beyond Boundaries: New York's New Art (Jerry Saltz), N.Y. Art Now, The Saatchi Collection (Dan Cameron), The Silent Baroque (Christian Leigh editor), Interpreting Contemporary Art (Rainer Crone and David Moos), Art at the End of the Social (Collins and Milazzo), Art Since Mid-Century: 1945 to the Present (Daniel Wheeler), Jonathan Lasker, Telling the Tales of Painting (Rainer Crone and David Moos), The 20th Century Art Book (Tony Godfrey, Melissa Larner, et al), Hist. Modern Art (H.H. Arnason and Marla Prather) 4th edit., Art of the 20th Century (Ingo Walther, editor) Taschen Verlag, Modern Art (Sam Hunter, John Jacobus, Daniel Wheeler) 3d rev. edit., Carravaggio on the Beach: Essays on Art in the 1990's (Richard Milazzo), Art News (Feb. 1990, Apr. 1992), Le Monde (June 1992), Art in America, (Apr. 1995), Comtemporary Visual Arts (Apr.-May 2000). NEA fellow, 1987, 89. Office: care Sperone Westwater Gallery 142 Greene St New York NY 10012-3236

LASKER, MORRIS E. judge; b. Hartsdale, N.Y., July 17, 1917; m. Helen M. Schubach; 4 children. BA magna cum laude, Harvard U., 1938; LLB, JD, Yale U., 1941. Bar: N.Y. 1941. Atty. Nat. Def. Com., U.S. Senate, 1941-42, Battle, Fowler, Jaffin & Kheel, 1946-68; fed. judge U.S. Dist. Ct. (so. dist.) N.Y., 1968-94, U.S. Dist. Ct., Boston, 1994—. Contbr. articles to profl. jours. Hon. trustee, bd. dirs. Vera Inst. Justice. Maj. U.S. Army, 1942-46. Recipient Learned Hand medal Fed. Bar Coun., Edward Weinfeld award N.Y. County Lawyers Assn. Mem. ABA, Assn. of Bar of City of N.Y. (exec. com. 1985-89). Avocations: gardening, reading, history, English and American literature. Office: US Dist Ct US Courthouse 1 Courthouse Way Boston MA 02210-3002

LASKEY, FRANCES M. business executive; b. Passaic, N.J., Oct. 30, 1944; d. John and Stella (Galka) Pollack; m. Richard A. Laskey, June 29, 1975. BA, William Paterson Coll., 1966. Tchr. high sch. English, Clifton (N.J.) Pub. Schs., 1966-99; office and bus. ops. adminstr. Chesapeake Atlantic Devel. Group L.L.C., Virginia Beach, Va., 2000-01; sales asst. ABC Family Channel, 2001—. Coach, advisor state championship consumer bowl team Clifton H.S.; apptd. spl. adv. commn. on electronic govt. Office of the Mayor, Virginia Beach, 2000. Recipient Profl. awards Soc. Consumer Affairs, 1999. Mem. NEA, NCTE, N.J. Edn. Assn., Clifton (N.J.) Tchrs. Assn., Passaic County Edn. Assn. Home: 3576 Storm Bird Loop Virginia Beach VA 23453-2265 E-mail: laskey@eudoramail.com.

LASKEY, JAMES HOWARD, lawyer; b. N.Y.C., Dec. 19, 1953; s. Herbert M. and Mina (Yohalem) L.; m. Mary C. Jacobson, Oct. 1, 1983; children: Michael Henry, Kevin Connor, Katherine Anne. BS, MIT, 1975; JD, Yale U., 1978. Bar: N.J. 1978, U.S. Tax Ct. 1982. Law sec. to Hon. Sidney M. Schreiber N.J. Supreme Ct., Newark, 1978-79; atty. antitrust divsn. U.S. Dept. Justice, Washington, 1979-82; assoc. Rosen, Gelman & Weiss, Newark, 1982-84, Norris, McLaughlin & Marcus, Somerville, N.J., 1984-86, ptnr., 1986—. Contbr. articles to profl. jours. Mgmt. com. RideWise Raritan Valley, Somerville, N.J., 1993—. Mem. ABA (mem. antitrust sect., pub. utility law sects.), N.J. State Bar Assn. (chair pub. utility law sect. 1997-98), Somerset County C. of C. (bd. dirs. 1997—), Fed. Comms. Bar Assn., Yale Law Sch. N.J. Alumni Assn. (pres.). Office: Norris McLaughlin & Marcus 721 Rt 202-206 PO Box 1018 Somerville NJ 08876-1018 E-mail: jlaskey@nmmlaw.com.

LASKEY, RICHARD ANTHONY, biomedical device executive; b. N.Y.C., Oct. 24, 1936; s. Charles Lewis and Gertrude Ann (Stolzenhaler) L.; m. Frances M. Pollack, June 29, 1975; children: Victoria Ann, Deborah Lea. Student, CCNY; BS in Chemistry, MS in Organic Chemistry, Ohio; PhD in Organic Chemistry, Sussex (Eng.) U., 1970; LLB, U. Chgo., 1972; MD (hon.), Med. Coll. S.A., 1975, fellow psychiatry, 1976; postgrad. in ob-gyn., U. Pa., 1989-99. Diplomate Am. Bd. Examiners in Psychotherapy. Head sec. med. products, lab. mgr. Hydron Labs., North Brunswick, N.J., 1967-73; v.p. biomed. rsch. Datascope Corp., Paramus, 1973-82; pres., rsch. Millbrook Labs., Inc., Rochelle Park, 1982-2000. Cons. in field; inventor, patentee. Recipient Doctor's award Chgo. Med. Coll., 1975; fellow Am. Acad. Behavioral Sci., 1976. Fellow Am. Inst. Chemists; mem. NRA, AAAS, Md. Med. Soc., Idaho Med. Soc., Nat. Med. Soc., Internat. Coll. Physicians and Surgeons, Am. Inst. Chemist, Am. Psychotherapy Assn., Nat. Psychol. Assn., Assn. Advancement Med. Instrumentation, Soc. Rsch. Adminstrs. Biomed. E-mail: docrichard@yahoo.com.

LASKIN, DANIEL M. oral and maxillofacial surgeon, educator; b. Ellenville, N.Y., Sept. 3, 1924; s. Nathan and Flora (Kaplan) L.; m. Eve Pauline Mohel, Aug. 25, 1945; children: Jeffrey, Gary, Marla. Student, NYU, 1941-42; BS, Ind. U., 1947; MS, U. Ill., 1951; DSc (hon.) , Ind. U., 2001. Diplomate Am. Bd. Oral and Maxillofacial Surgery, Am. Dental Bd. Anesthesiology. Mem. faculty U. Ill., Chgo., 1949-84, prof. dept. oral and maxillofacial surgery, 1960-84, head dept., 1973-84, clin. prof. surgery, 1961-84, dir. temporomandibular joint and facial pain research center, 1963-84; prof., chmn. dept. oral and maxillofacial surgery Med. Coll. Va., Richmond, 1984—2002; dir. temporomandibular joint and facial pain rsch. ctr. MCV, 1984—2002; head dept. dentistry MCV Hosp., 1986—2002; former attending oral surgeon Edgewater, Swedish Covenant, Ill. Masonic, Skokie Valley Community hosps., all Chgo.; former chmn. dept. oral surgery Cook County Hosp., Chgo. Cons. oral surgery to Surgeon Gen. Navy, 1977-83; dental products panel FDA, 1988-92, cons., 1993-95; Francis J. Reichmann Lectr., 1971, Cordwainer lectr., London, 1980, Donald B. Osborn Meml. lectr., 1999. Author: Oral and Maxillofacial Surgery, Vol. I, 1980, Vol. II, 1985; contbr. articles to profl. jours.; editor-in-chief: Jour. Oral and Maxillofacial Surgery, 1972-2002; mem. editl. bd. Internat. Jour. Oral and Maxillofacial Surgery, 1978-88, Topics in Pain Mgmt., Densat, Internat. Jour. Oral and Maxillofacial Implants, Quintessence Internat., Revista Latino America Cirugia Traumatologia Maxilofacial, Va. Dental Jour., Jour. Dental Rsch.; mem. internat. editl. bd. Headache Quar.; mem. editl. bd. Greek Jour. Oral and Maxillofacial Surgery, Electronic Jour. Dentistry; assoc. editor Odontology. Nat. hon. chmn. peer campaign A.A.O.M.S. Edn. and Rsch. Found., 1990; bd. dirs. Internat. Assn. Oral and Maxillofacial Surgeons Found.; chmn. Nat. Acad. Dentistry, 1997-99; pres.-elect Nat. Acad. of Practice, 1999, pres., 2002—. Recipient Disting. Alumni Svc. award Ind. U ., 1975, William J. Gies editl. award hon. mention, 1975-77, 80, 88, 90, 91, 93, 95, 1st prize, 1978-79, 84, 87, 89, 92, 96, 2001, spl. editl. citation Internat. Coll. Dentists, 1999, Simon P. Hullihen Meml. award, 1976, Arnold K. Maislen Meml. award, 1977, Thomas P. Hinman medallion, 1980, W. Harry Archer Achievement award for rsch., 1981, Heidbrink award, 1983, Disting. Alumnus award Ind. U. Sch. Dentistry, 1984, Rene Lefort medal, 1985, Semmelweis medallion Semmelweis Med. U., 1985, Golden Scroll award Internat. Coll. Dentists, 1986, Internat. award Friends Sch. Dental Medicine, U. Conn. Health Ctr., Donald B. Osbon award, 1991, Achievement medal Alpha Omega, 1992, Norton M. Ross Excellence in Clin. Rsch. award, 1993, Va. Commonwealth U. Faculty award of excellence, 1994; named Zendium Lectr., 1989, Edward C. Hinds Lectr., 1990, Disting. Practitioner Nat. Acads. Practice, 1992, Hon. Diplomate, Am. Soc. Osseointegration, 1992; fellow in gen. anesthesia Am. Dental Soc. Anesthesiology, fellow in dental surgery Royal Coll. Surgeons Eng., Glasgow Royal Coll. Physicians and Surgeons (hon.). Fellow: AAAS, Am. Acad. Implant Prosthodontists (academia), Internat. Coll. Dentists, Am. Coll. Dentists, Acad. Internat. Dental Studies (hon.), Internat. Assn. Oral and Maxillofacial Surgeons (hon.; exc. com. 1980—95, pres. 1983—86, sec. gen. 1989—95, exec. dir. 1995—99, gen. chmn. 14th Internat. Conf. on Oral and Maxillofacial Surg. 1999); mem.: ADA (adv. com. advanced edn. in oral surgery 1968—75, cons. Coun. on Dental Edn. 1968—82, mem. Commn. on Accreditation 1975—76), Odontographic Soc., William F. Harrigan Soc., Nat. Chronic Pain Outreach Assn. (adv. bd.), Am. Dental Bd. Anesthesiology (pres. 1983—92), Royal Soc. Medicine, Can. Assn. Oral and Maxillofacial Surgeons (hon.), Brazilian Coll. Oral and Maxillofacial Surgery and Traumatology (hon.), Chilean Soc. Oral and Maxillofacial Surgery (hon.), Hellenic Assn. Oral Surgery (hon.), Sadi Fontaine Acad. (hon.), Internat. Congress Oral Implantologists (hon.), Soc. Maxillofacial and Oral Surgeons South Africa (hon.), Japanese Soc. for Temporomandibular Joint (hon.), Am. Soc. Laser in Dentistry (hon.), Internat. Study Group for Advancement of TMJ Arthroscopy (hon.), Japanese Soc. Oral and Maxillofacial Surgeons (hon.), Am. Assn. Dental Editors, Am. Soc. Exptl. Pathology, Am. Dental Soc. Anesthesiology (pres. 1976—78), Internat. Assn. Dental Rsch., Am. Assn. Oral and Maxillofacial Surgeons (editor Forum 1965—96, pres. 1976—77, editor AAOMS Today 1996—, Disting. Svc. award 1972, rsch. recognition award 1978, William J. Gies award 1979, dedication 73d ann. meeting and sci. sessions 1991), Ill. Splty. Bd. Oral Surgery, Sigma Xi, Omicron Kappa Upsilon. Rsch. and publs. on connective tissue physiology and pathology, particularly cartilage and bone metabolism, craniofacial growth, oral maxillofacial surgery, and pathology of temporomandibular joint. Office: Va Commonwealth U Dept Oral/Maxillofac Surg PO Box 980566 Richmond VA 23298-0566 E-mail: dmlaskin@vcu.edu.

LASKIN, LEE B. judge, lawyer, state senator; b. Atlantic City, June 30, 1936; m. Andrea Solomon; 1 dau., Shari. Student, Am. U., Temple U., Rutgers U., 1960. Bar: N.J. Asst. U.S. atty., N.J., 1964-68; mem. N.J. Gen. Assembly, 1968-70, Camden County Bd. Chosen Freeholders, 1970-73, N.J. Senate, 1977-92; judge N.J. Superior Ct., 1994—. Mcpl. atty. Audubon, Berlin Borough, Berlin Twp., Clementon, Laurel Springs, Mt. Ephraim and Waterford, N.J., and Winslow Twp.; counsel Bellmawr Bd. Edn., Berlin Zoning Bd., Camden County Welfare Bd., Non-Resident Taxpayers Assn., Animal Welfare Assn., Brith Sholom Fed. Credit Union, Camden Hebrew Fed. Credit Union, Union Fed. Savs. and Loan Assn., Div. 880 Amalgamated Transit Union, Local 18 of Am. Fed. Tech. Engrs., Camden Fire Officers Assn., Am. Postal Workers Union, Fuel Mchts. Assn., Shamong Twp. Bd. Edn., Cherry Hill Zoning Bd.; field counsel Fed. Nat. Mortgage Assn.; founder, 1st chmn. Glendale Nat. Bank. Del. Rep. Nat. Conv., 1984. With USMC, 1957-64, USMCR. Office: Camden County Hall Justice 5th and Mickle Blvd Camden NJ 08003-2090

LASKO, ALLEN HOWARD, pharmacist; b. Chgo., Oct. 27, 1941; s. Sidney P. and Sara (Hoffman) L.; m. Janice Marilynn Chess, Dec. 24, 1968 (div. Aug. 1993); children: Stephanie Paige, Michael Benjamin. BS, U. Ill., 1964. Staff pharmacist Michael Reese Hosp. and Med. Ctr., Chgo., 1964-68; clin. pharmacist City of Hope Med Ctr., Duarte, Calif., 1968-73; chief pharmacist Monrovia (Calif.) Cmty. Hosp, 1973-74; chief pharmaicst Santa Fe Meml. Hosp., L.A., 1974-77; pvt. investor, 1977-93; clin. pharmacist Foothill Presbyn. Hosp., Glendora, Calif., 1993—. Author: Diabetes Study Guide, 1972, A Clinical Approach to Lipid Abnormalities Study Guide, 1973, Jet Injection Tested As an Aid in Physiologic Delivery of Insulin, 1973. Mem. Magic Castle. Recipient Roche-Hosp. Pharmacy rsch. award, 1972-73; James scholar U. Ill. Mem. Mensa, Rho Pi Phi. Jewish. Home: 376 Hill St Monrovia CA 91016-2340 Office: Foothill Presbyn Hosp 250 S Grand Ave Glendora CA 91741-4218 E-mail: allenlasko@aol.com.

LASKO, JOEL, company executive; b. N.Y.C., Nov. 1, 1932; s. Max Lasko and Charlotte Parker; m. Mary Anne Thune, Dec. 19, 1973; children: Elizabeth, Andrew. BS in Mktg., Syracuse U., 1955; MBA in Mktg. Mgmt., CCNY, 1957. Br. mgr. Olivetti Corp., Washington, 1958-70; pres. Washington Photocopy, 1970—. Recipient Mktg. medal Am. Mktg. Assn., 1957. Avocations: tennis, skiing. Office: Washington Photocopy 4380 Macarthur Blvd NW Washington DC 20007-2594

LASKO, NATASHA B. psychologist; b. St. Petersburg, Russia, Feb. 12, 1946; d. Boris Mendelevich Golzberg and Zoya Mitrofanovna Andreeva; m. Mark Vladimir Lasko, Mar. 24, 1972; 1 child, Dennis Mark. MA in Clin. Psychology, St. Petersburg U., Russia, 1969, PhD in Clin. Psychology, 1978. Clin. psychologist Bekhterev Psychoneurol. Inst., St. Petersburg, 1969-80; instr. psychology Harvard Med. Sch., Boston, 1990—2001, asst. prof. psychology, 2001—; asst. rsch. Mass. Gen. Hosp., 1998—; psychodiagnostician VA Rsch. Svc., Manchester, N.H., 1989—. Cons. in field. Mem. APA, N.Y. Acad. Scis., Mass. Mental Health Counselors Assn., Russian Soc. Traumatic Stress Studies, Internat. Soc. Traumatic Stress Studies Republican. Avocation: travel. Office: Harvard Med Sch 228 Maple St Manchester NH 03103

LASKOWSKI, EDWARD JOHN, chemist; b. Milw., Dec. 24, 1950; s. Ervin Joseph and Florence Margaret Laskowski; m. Mary Ann Rizzo, July 16, 1988; 1 child, David Edward. BS with honors in Chemistry, U. Wis., 1972; PhD in Inorganic Chemistry, U. Ill., 1976. Postdoctoral rsch. asst. Stanford U., Palo Alto, Calif., 1976-78; mem. tech. staff Lucent Techs. Bell Labs., Murray Hill, N.J., 1978—. Contbr. articles to profl. jours. Mem. Environ. Def. Fund, 1990—, Humane Soc. U.S., 1990—; leader Boy Scouts Am., 1981-88. Mem. Am. Chem. Soc., Alpha Chi Sigma. Roman Catholic. Achievements include patents relating to etching of compound semiconductors, patent for fabrication of an electro-optic sampling probe, patents for fabrication of optical waveguides. Avocations: golf, nature study, minerology, gardening, wildlife protection. Office: Lucent Techs Bell Labs 600 Mountain Ave New Providence NJ 07974-2008 E-mail: ejl@lucent.com.

LASKOWSKI, LEONARD FRANCIS, JR. microbiologist; b. Milw., Nov. 16, 1919; s. Leonard Francis and Frances (Cyborowski) L.; m. Frances Bielinski, June 1, 1946; children— Leonard Francis III, James, Thomas. BS, Marquette U., 1941, MS, 1948; PhD, St. Louis U., 1951. Diplomate: Am. Bd. Microbiology. Instr. bacteriology Marquette U., 1946-48; mem. faculty St. Louis U., 1951—, prof. pathology and internal medicine, Div. Infectious Diseases, 1969-90, prof. emeritus, 1990—, assoc. prof. internal medicine, 1977-90—. Dir. clin. microbiology sect. St. Louis U. Hosps. Labs., 1965— ; cons. clin microbiology Firmin Desloge Hosp., St. Louis U. Group Hosps., St. Marys Group Hosps.; cons. bacteriology VA Hosp.; asst. dept. chief Pub. Health Lab., St. Louis Civil Def., 1958— ; cons. St. Elizabeths Hosp., St. Louis County Hosp., St. Francis Hosp. Contbr. articles to profl. jours. Health and tech. tng. coordinator for Latin Am. projects Peace Corps, 1962-66. Served with M.C. AUS, 1942-46. Fellow Am. Acad. Microbiology; mem. Soc. Am. Bacteriologists, N.Y. Acad. Scis., Am., Mo. pub. health assns., AAUP, Med. Mycol. Soc. Am., Alpha Omega Alpha. Home: 6229 Robertsville Rd Villa Ridge MO 63089-2617 Office: 1402 S Grand Blvd Saint Louis MO 63104-1004

LASKOWSKI, MICHAEL, JR. chemist, educator; b. Warsaw, Poland, Mar. 13, 1930; came to U.S., 1947, naturalized, 1955; s. Michael and Maria (Dabrowska) L.; m. Joan Claire Heyer, Nov. 29, 1957; children: Michael Christopher, Marta Joan. BS magna cum laude, Lawrence Coll., 1950; PhD (NIH fellow), Cornell U., 1954, postgrad., 1954-55, Yale U., 1955-56. Research asst. Marquette U., 1949-50; instr. Cornell U., 1956-57; asst. prof. chemistry Purdue U., 1957-61, asso. prof., 1961-65, prof., 1965—. Chmn. Gordon Rsch. Conf. Physics and Phys. Chemistry Biopolymers, 1966, Proteolytic Enzymes and Their Inhibitors, 1982; mem. study sect. NIH, 1967-71, NSF, 1989, sci. adv. bd. Receptor, Inc., 1993-94, Khepri Pharms., Inc., 1993-95, BioNona Dynamics, 2002-. Mem. editorial bd. Archives Biochemistry and Biophysics, 1972-90, Biochemistry, 1973-78, Jour. Protein Chemistry, 1981-97, Jour. Biol. Chemistry, 1983-88; mem. expert sci. coun. Protein Identification Resource, 2000—; contbr. articles to profl. jours. Recipient McCoy award Purdue U., 1975; co-recipient award in biol. scis. Alfred Jurzykowski Found., 1977 Mem. Am. Chem. Soc. (chmn. sect. 1968-69, treas. div. biol. chemistry 1981-84, councillor 1985-88), Am. Soc. Biol. Chemists, Biophys. Soc., Protein Soc., AAAS, AAUP, Polish Acad. Arts, Sci. Am., ACLU, Sigma Xi. Home: 222 E Navajo St West Lafayette IN 47906-2155 Office: Purdue U Dept Chemistry West Lafayette IN 47907 Office Fax: 765-494-0239. E-mail: michael.laskowski.1@purdue.edu. *A scientist who claims a small subfield of science as his personal fief should strive to leave it simpler and more coherent than he originally found it.*

LASKY, MOSES, lawyer; b. Denver, Nov. 2, 1907; s. Juda Eisen and Ida (Grossman) L.; m. Ruth Helen Abraham, July 6, 1933; children: Morelle, Marshall. AB magna cum laude, U. Colo., 1926, JD, 1928; LHD (hon.), 1996; LL.M., Harvard U., 1929. Bar: Calif. 1930, U.S. Supreme Ct 1947. Asst. dept. econs. U. Colo., 1925-26; salesman, local sales mgr. R.C. Barnum Co., Cleve., 1927-28; assoc. Brobeck, Phleger & Harrison, San Francisco, 1929-41, partner, 1941-79, Lasky, Haas, Cohler & Munter, San Francisco, 1979-94; Lasky, Haas & Cohler, from 1994. Instr. Golden Gate Law Sch., 1934-35; sr. adv. bd. U.S. Ct. Appeals (9th cir.), 1984-90, chmn., 1989-90; vis. prof. law as disting. practitioner in residence Sch. Law, U. Colo., 1995. Contbr. articles in legal field and on Jewish life to jours. and mags. Pres. bd. dirs. San Francisco Mus. Modern Art, 1963, 64, now life trustee; pres. Regional Arts Coun. San Francisco, 1963-64; v.p. bd. dirs. San Francisco Art Inst., 1964; trustee War Meml. San Francisco, 1969-75; co-chmn. San Francisco Crime Com., 1968-71; bd. dirs. The Exploratorium, San Francisco, 1979-96, dir. emeritus, 1996—; bd. overseers L.A. br. Hebrew Union Coll.; nat. exec. com. Am. Jewish Com., 1947-55. Recipient Disting. Alumnus award U. Colo. Law Sch., 1977, U. Colo. medal, 1983, 50 Yr. award Am. Bar Found., 1989. Fellow Am. Coll. Trial Lawyers; mem. ABA, Phi Beta Kappa, Delta Sigma Rho. Home: San Francisco, Calif. Died Apr. 7, 2002.

LASKY, RICHARD DONALD, psychoanalyst, educator; b. N.Y.C., Jan. 22, 1943; s. Sidney Lasky and Alice Presser; m. Judith Faye Sherman. PhD in Psychology, NYU, 1970, postdoctoral cert., 1974. Lic. psychologist, N.Y.; diplomate Am. Bd. Profl. Psychology. Jr. rsch. scientist Rsch. Found. State N.Y., Downstate Med. Ctr., SUNY, Bklyn., 1964-68; asst. prof. L.I. Univ., Greenvale, N.Y., 1969-74; clin. assoc., supr. psychologist doctoral program psychology CUNY, N.Y.C., 1975—; chmn. of faculty Inst. for Psychoanalytic Tng. and Rsch., 1985-2000; clin. prof. psychology postdoctoral program NYU, 1990—. Author: Multiple Personality and the Related Dissociative Disorders, 1984, Dynamics of Development and the Therapeutic Process, 1993; editor: Symbolization and Desymbolization: Essays in Honor of Norbert Freedman, 2002. Rsch. fellow VA, 1968, NIMH fellow, 1969-71. Fellow Acad. of Psychoanalysis; mem. APA, Internat. Psycho-Analytical Assn., Am. Psychoanalytic Assn., Nat. Register of Health Care Providers in Psychology. E-mail: richardlasky@nyc.rr.com.

LASLEY, CHARLES HADEN, cardiovascular surgeon, health and fitness consultant; b. Lewisburg, Ky., Dec. 16, 1921; s. Marion Grinter and Helen May (Murray) L.; m. Mary Brown, June 14, 1946 (div. 1966); children: Mary Ann, Charles H., Jr., Robert Murray, David Marion; m. Janet Elizabeth Evans, Jan. 28, 1967; children: Tiffany Jean, Phillip Evans. BS in chemistry, biology, U. Fla., 1939-43; MD, Harvard Med. Sch., 1944-47. Diplomate Am. Bd. Thoracic Surgery, Am. Bd. Surgery. Intern in surgery Grady Hosp., Atlanta, 1947-48, asst. resident in surgery, 1948-49; resident in surgery Gorgas Hosp., Ancon, Canal Zone, 1950, sr., chief resident surgery, 1951, staff surgeon, chief gen. surgery, 1952-53; asst. chief orthopedic surgery USAH Ft. Carson, Colorado Springs, Colo., 1953-54; resident in cardiac surgery City of Hope Med. Ctr., L.A., 1954-55; resident in thoracic, cardiovascular surgery VAH Oteen, Asheville, N.C., 1955-56; pvt. practice thoracic, cardiovascular surgery Morton Plant Hosp., Clearwater, Fla., 1956-79. Chief of surgery Morton Plant Hosp., 1971-72, chief thoracic, cardiovascular surgery, 1977-78; med. dir. Longevity Clin., Clearwater, 1977-78; med. cons. Wellness Ctr. Morton Plant Hosp., 1996—; lectr. in field. Author: Veritas, 1996, 120 Years of Healthy Longevity...it's possible...here's how!, 2002. Jazz drummer Red Suspenders Jazz Band, 1991—; mem. Calvary Bapt. Ch. With US Army, 1949-54. Mem. Am. Assn. for Thoracic Surgery, Am. Coll. of Sports Medicine, Soc. of Thoracic Surgeons, So. Thoracic Surgery Assn., Fla. Soc. of Thoracic and Cardiovascular Surgeons (president 1972), Suncoast Dixieland Jazz Society. Republican. Avocations: distance running (21 marathons and 42 triathlons), triathlons, handball, dixieland jazz. Home: Unit 4 Pelican Pl 672 Poinsettia Rd Belleair FL 33756-1525

LASLEY, THOMAS J., II, education educator; b. Delaware, Ohio, July 23, 1947; s. Thomas J. and Anna F. (Cooper) L.; m. Janet L. Olney, Apr. 21, 1973; children: Julianne Marie, Elizabeth Ann. BS, Ohio State U., 1969, MA, 1972, PhD, 1978. Cert. tchr. and adminstr. Ohio. Tchr. Upper Arlington, Ohio, 1969-75; rsch. assoc. Ohio State U., 1975-77. Cons. Ohio Dept. Edn., 1977-80, asst. dir. tchr. edn. and cert., 1980-83; prof. U. Dayton (Ohio), 1983—, chmn. dept., 1983-92, dean Sch. Edn., 1998—; cons. on sch. research and disruptive student behavior. Author: Issues in Teacher Education, 1986, Dynamics of Change in Teacher Education, 1986, Teaching Peace, 1994, Strategies for Teaching in a Diverse Society: Instructional Models, 1997, Strategies for Effective Teaching, 2000; contbr. articles to profl. jours. Mem. Am. Edni. Rsch. Assn., Phi Delta Kappa. Office: U Dayton Chaminade Hall Dayton OH 45469 E-mail: thomas.lasley@notes.udayton.edu.

LASORDA-SIVIERI, HELEN MARIE, school social worker; b. Norristown, Pa. d. John Anthony and Helen M. Lasorda; m. Gino J. Sivieri, Aug. 25, 1990. AS, Burlington County Coll., 1982; BS, Hahnemann U., 1984, MS,

1987. Cert. sch. social worker; crisis psychotherapist, student assistance counselor, psychologist. Mental health worker Crisis House, Mt. Holly, N.J., 1984-85; crisis therapist Screening and Crisis Intervention Program, 1985-86, coord., 1986-87; social worker, peer group coord. No. Burlington County Regional Sch. Dist., Columbus, N.J., 1987—; sch. social worker Chesterfield (N.J.) Elem. Sch., 1988—. Developer peer group counseling program, leader peer group No. Burlington Sch., Columbus, 1987—. Recipient Best Practices/Star Schs. Program award, N.J. State Dept. Edn., 1995. Mem. Am. Group Psychol. Assn., Del. Valley Group Psychotherapy Assn., Nat. Sch. Social Worker Assn., N.J. Sch. Social Worker Assn. Home: 305 Island Rd Columbus NJ 08022 Office: No Burlington Regional Sch Dist 160 Mansfield Rd E Columbus NJ 08022

LASOWSKI, ANNE-MARIE F. federal agency administrator; b. Coronado, Calif. d. Donald Thomas Lasowski and Janine Josette Cotta. BA in Polit. Sci. summa cum laude, Wheaton Coll., 1986; M Govt. Adminstrn., MA in Polit. Sci., U. Pa., 1988. Profl. analyst Nat. Govs.' Assn., Washington, 1987; asst. to exec. dir. Fellowship Commn., Phila., 1987; staff evaluator U.S. Gen. Acctg. Office, 1988-94, sr. evaluator nat. security and internat. affairs divsn. Washington, 1994-2000, asst. dir. acquisition & sourcing mgmt., 2000—. Mem. ASPA, Acad. Polit. Sci., Assn. Gen. Accts., Soc. Internat. Affairs, Phi Beta Kappa. Home: 1200 N Veitch St Arlington VA 22201-5818

LASPAGNOLETTA, BENJAMIN JOSEPH, infosystems specialist; b. Rochester, N.Y., Apr. 9, 1946; s. Joseph and Madeline (Scioria) LaS.; m. Susan Ann Appelt, Sept. 6, 1975. AS cum laude, Rochester Bus. Inst., 1967; BS cum laude, U. Rochester, 1972. Computer programmer U. Rochester, 1969-72; systems analyst Blue Cross and Blue Shield, Rochester, 1972-73; assoc. cons. Xerox Corp., 1973-94; sys. engr. Electronic Data Sys., 1994-99. Mem. Data Processing Mgmt. Assn. Republican. Roman Catholic. Avocations: golf, cross country skiing, horseback riding. Home: 9C Greenleaf Meadows Rochester NY 14612-4335 E-mail: laspagnoletta@yahoo.com.

LASPAGNOLETTA, SUSAN ANN, nurse; b. Penn Yan, N.Y., Dec. 24, 1950; d. Herbert Ewald and Virginia Jeanne (Seabury) Appelt; m. Benjamin Joseph LaSpagnoletta, Sept. 6, 1975. Diploma, Craig State Sch., Sonyea, N.Y., 1972. RN, N.Y.; cert. RN in ophthalmology, CRNO, 1993. With med./surg. unit St. Mary's Hosp., Rochester, N.Y., 1972-87, mgr., ophthalmology coord., 1989-98; ophthalmology RN U. Rochester residency program, 1998-99; gen. surgery office nurse Unity Health Sys., Rochester, N.Y., 1999—, RN in long term and transitional care, 2000—. Home: 9C Greenleaf Medows Rochester NY 14612-4335 E-mail: laspagnoletta@yahoo.com.

LASPINA, PETER JOSEPH, computer resource educator; b. Bay Shore, N.Y., June 28, 1951; s. Peter Celestine and Barbara Elizabeth (Rodee) L.; m. Julia Mary Gunther, July 10, 1982; 1 child; Joseph Peter. BMus with high honors, Performer's Cert. on Piano, N.Y. State Coll., Potsdam, 1973; MS in Music Edn., L.I. U., 1978; MS in Tech. Sys. Mgmt., SUNY, Stony Brook, 1987; postgrad., Nova Southeastern U., 1995-97. Tchr. music E. Meadow (N.Y.) pub. schs., 1974-75, Northport-East Northport Pub. Schs., 1975-86, computer resource tchr., 1986—. Adj. faculty SUNY, Stony Brook, 1991—; writer master trainer N.Y. State Edn. Dept., Albany, 1987-88; cons. ednl. tech., Smithtown, N.Y., 1987—; invited del. U.S./China Joint Conf. on Edn., Beijing, 1992, 95-96, and conf. presenter. Contbr. articles to profl. jours. Mem. Am. Fedn. Tchrs., N.Y. State United Tchrs., Suffolk County Music Educators Assn., Nat. Assn. Sci., Tech. and Soc., N.Y. State Assn. Computers and Techs. (mem. conf. com. 1994), Internat. Soc. for Tech. in Edn., Assn. Ednl. Comm. and Tech., Assn. for Advancement of Computers in Edn. Presbyterian. Avocations: reading, oenology, home repair, travel. Home: 21 Knolltop Dr Nesconset NY 11767-2221 Office: SUNY Tech And Soc Program Stony Brook NY 11794-0001 E-mail: plaspina@notes.sunysb.edu.

LASS, NANCY ANNE, physician; b. Chgo., June 18, 1956; d. Edward C. and Betty D. Lass. BS summa cum laude, George Williams Coll., 1977; MD, Chgo. Med. Sch., 1981. Diplomate Am. Bd. Pediat. Resident in pediat. U. Chgo., 1981-84, neonatology fellow, 1984-88, clin. pharmacology fellow, 1985-88; instr. pediat. Washington U., St. Louis, 1988-90; asst. prof. pediat. St. Louis U., 1990-93; attending neonatologist DuPage Neonatology Assocs., Hinsdale, Ill., 1993-94; asst. prof. pediat., clin. pharmacology U. Chgo., 1994-98, lectr. dept. medicine and clin. pharmacology, 1998—; assoc. dir. R&D clin. safety G.D. Searle Co., Skokie, Ill., 1998-99, assoc. dir. R&D clin. rsch., 1999-2001; assoc. dir. product safety Takeda Pharms. N.Am., Lincolnshire, 2001—02; pres. NL Splty. Cons., Inc., 2002—. Dir. high risk infant follow-up program U. Chgo., 1997-98. Contbr. articles to profl. jours. Chair bd. dirs. Luths. in Med. Missions, St. Louis, 1994-2000, advisor to bd. dirs., 2000-2001; active Assn. Luth. Devel. Execs., 1996—, St. Louis Chamber Chorus, 1988-93, Chgo. Symphony Chorus, 2000— Recipient Nat. Rsch. Svc. award NIH, 1985-88. Fellow Am. Acad. Pediatrics, Am. Coll. Clin. Pharmacology; mem. AAAS, AMA, APHA, Am. Coll. Forensic Examiners, Am. Fedn. Med. Rsch., Am. Soc. Clin. Pharm. and Therapeutics, Nat. Assn. for Edn. Young Children, Ill. Med. Soc., Chgo. Med. Soc., Drug. Info. Assn. Avocations: music, reading, public speaking. Office: NL Splty Cons Inc 2609 Burton Dr Westchester IL 60154

LASSAN, DIANE K. librarian; b. Youngstown, OH, Aug. 11, 1954; d. Nickolas and Elizabeth Ann K.; m. Timothy John Lassan, May 28, 1983. BA, Kent State U., 1982, postgrad, 1991. Library shelver Kent State U. Circ. Dept., Kent, OH, 1975-81; media tech. asst. Kent State U. library Serials Dept., 1989-95; library assoc. Kent State U. Govt. Docs., 1986-1989; cataloger Kent State U. Cataloging Dept., 1989-95; sr. library assoc. Kent State U. Govt. Docs., 1995—. Antique dealer. Antique dealer Vol. Coleman Profl. Svcs. (Mental Health Facility), Kent, Ohio, 1998—2001; rep. Support Staff Adv. Com., 1999—2001. Mem. Kent Historical Soc., Nat. Trust Historic Preservation, Nat. Mus. Women inthe Arts. Democrat. Avocations: writing, designing costumes, gift wraps, displays, reading. Office: Kent State U Univ Libraries Media Svc Kent OH 44242-0001 E-mail: DLASSAN@LMS.KENT.EDU.

LASSEN, BETTY JANE, educator; b. Topeka, Apr. 19, 1923; d. Harvey Leroy and Anna Elizabeth (Day) Rose; m. Emil Lassen Jr., June 5, 1944 (dec. Sept. 1989); 1 child, Emil III. Instr., guide YMCA-YWCA, Albuquerque, 1975-84, U. N.Mex. Continuing Edn., Albuquerque, 1979—, Ft. Lewis Coll. Continuing Edn., Durango, Colo., 1992-93. Liaison, asst. coord. San Juan Coll. Elder Hostel, Farmington, N.Mex., 1993-94; owner, pres. Outdoor Adventure Tours, Inc., Albuquerque, 1982—; mem. curriculum com., human svcs. tng. coun. gerontology divsn. continuing edn. U. N.Mex., 1979-82; spkr. in field. Designer ski equipment; contbr. articles, poetry to profl. publs. Vol. instr., guide for disabled Easter Seals Soc., Albuquerque, 1983; vol. campground host Nat. Park Svc., Chaco Canyon Ruins, N.Mex., 1990; campaign vol. Dem. Party, Albuquerque, 1976. Recipient Appreciation award Easter Seals Soc., 1983. Mem. Puerto Del Sol Ladies Golf Assn. (pres. 1976-77), N.Mex. Outfitters/Guides, N.Mex. Cross-Country Ski Club (sec. 1973-76), N.Mex. Mountain Club. Avocations: cross-country skiing, hiking, bicycling, golf, ballroom dancing. Home: Apt 212 13991 E Marina Dr Aurora CO 80014-3787

LASSEN, JOHN KAI, development company executive; b. Youngstown, Ohio, Mar. 28, 1942; s. Kai Kierulff and Helen Susanne (Elsaesser) L.; m. Marion duPont McConnell, Sept. 26, 1987; children: Christian K., Laura Wick, William duPont, James Tyler. BA, Yale U., 1964; JD, U. Pa., 1967. Bar: Del. 1971, U.S. Dist. Ct. Del. 1972. Ptnr. Morris, Nichols, Arsht & Tunnel, Wilmington, Del., 1977-83, Lassen, Smith Katzenstein & Furlow, Wilmington, 1984-91; pres. Chesapeake Industries, Inc., 1992—2001; vice-chmn., COO Krapfcandoit Co., 1995-2000; pres. Southern Sr. Devel. Svcs., Inc., 2000—. Lt. UNSR, 1967-70. Mem.: ABA, Del. World Affairs Coun., Del. Bar Assn. (chmn. decedents, estate and trusts 1979—81), Friends of Winterthur, SAR, Soc. Mayflower Descs. (dep. gov. 1990—93), Soc. Colonial Wars, Yale Club N.Y.C., Lincoln Club, Ocean Reef Club, Vicmead Hunt Club, Wilmington Country Club, Wilmington Club, Rotary. Episcopalian. Home: Crooked Billet PO Box 3712 3510 Kennett Pike Wilmington DE 19807-3019 also: Shore Winds 19 Hall Ave Rehoboth Beach DE 19971-2512

LASSER, GAIL MARIA, psychologist, educator; b. Saddle River, N.J., Feb. 29, 1956; d. Dominick A. and Genevieve M. Sanzo; children: Michael, Jason, Jonathan. B.A., Seton Hall U., 1971; teaching cert. William Paterson Coll., 1973; M.A., Montclair State Coll., 1975; postgrad. Seton Hall U., 1975-77; cert. staff psychologist, N.J., 1977; lic. real estate agt., N.J.; notary pub. Public relations rep. European Health Spa, 1970-71; med. asst. Sci. Prevention and Rehab. Assn., 1973; grad. teaching and research asst. Montclair State Coll., 1973-74; clin. asst. Dr. Brower, 1974; instr. psychology Essex County Coll., 1976-77; clin. psychologist intern Community Mental Health Center, Mt. Carmel Guild, Newark, 1976-77; lectr. St. Michaels Med. Center-N.J. Coll. Medicine, 1977-80; instr. psychology Bergen Community Coll., Paramus, N.J., 1977— ; asst. to ct. adminstr. Bergen County Cts., 1977-78; cons. telecom., 1994—. Active Am. Heart Assn. Mem. Am. Psychol. Assn., Am. Soc. for Physical Research, Pi Lambda Theta, Psi Chi. Home: 234 E Saddle River Rd Saddle River NJ 07458-2614

LASSER, HOWARD GILBERT, chemical engineer, consultant; b. N.Y.C., Nov. 24, 1926; s. Milton and Tessie (Rosenthal) L.; m. Barbara Ann Katz, Aug. 24, 1950; children: Cathy, Ellen Lasser-LeVee, Alan. BSChemE, Lehigh U., 1950; postgrad., Columbia U., 1951; Dr.Ing., Darmstadt Tech. Inst., Germany, 1956. Registered profl. engr., D.C., Va., Calif. Chem. engr. Belvoir Rsch. Engring. & Devel. Ctr., Ft. Belvoir, Va., 1951-55, 58-72, Naval Sea Systems Command, Washington, 1955-56; materials engr. GSA, 1956-57; chem. engr. Naval Facilities Engring. Command, Alexandria, Va., 1972-82, Materials Rsch. Cons., Alexandria & Springfield, 1982—. Author: Design of Electroplating Facilities, 1990; contbr. articles to profl. jours. Fellow AAAS, Oil and Colour Chemists Assn., Am. Inst. Chemists; mem. Am. Electroplaters and Surface Finishers Soc., AIChE, NACE Internat. (cert.), ASM Internat., SSPC Coatings Soc., Am. Watch Makers Soc., Nat. Watch and Clock Collectors Assn., Tau Beta Pi, Sigma Xi, Alpha Chi Sigma, Pi Delta Epsilon. Achievements include 6 patents in electroplating and metal finishing; description of thermodynamic properties of carbon dioxide; development of thermotropic dyes for aluminum oxides; development of dyes to match laser wavelengths to enhance etching of substrates used in the electronics industry and medicine; over 500 publs. in materials and chemical engineering. Home: 5912 Camberly Ave Springfield VA 22150-2438 Office: Materials Rsch Cons 1121 King St Alexandria VA 22314-2924 E-mail: mareco@erols.com.

LASSER, JOSEPH ROBERT, investment company executive; b. N.Y.C., Sept. 25, 1923; s. Milton and Tessie (Rosenthal) L.; m. Ruth Jean Pollak, May 4, 1925; children: James, Carol Lasser Kornblith, Jean. BS, Lehigh U., 1946; MBA, NYU, 1951. Sr. analyst Lewisohn and Co., N.Y.C., 1946-51; dir. research Walston and Co., 1951-55, Wertheim and Co., N.Y.C., 1956-67; ptnr. Shufro, Rose, Ehrman, and Stanley Marks, Lasser & Co., 1967-75; sr. portfolio mgr. C.J. Lawrence, 1975-76; prin., sr. portfolio mgr. Neuberger & Berman, 1977—2002. Treas. Bronx House, N.Y., 1978-95; past trusteee United Jewish Appeal/Fedn. Jewish Philanthropies, mem. bd. overseers. 1st lt. USAF, 1943-45. Decorated Air medal with three bronze oak leaf clusters, one silver oak leaf cluster; recipient 1st Lit. award Soc. Paper Money, 1976. Mem. Am. Numismatic Soc. (councillor 1990-93), N.Y. Soc. Security Analysts, Chartered Fin. Analysts Assn., Phi Beta Kappa, Princeton Club (N.Y.C.), Quaker Ridge (Scarsdale N.Y.). Home: 119 Cushman Rd Scarsdale NY 10583-3405 Office: 605 3rd Ave 43d Fl New York NY 10158-3698

LASSETER, JOHN P. film director, computer animator; b. Hollywood, Calif., Jan. 12, 1957; BA in Fine Arts in Film, Calif. Inst. Arts. Exec. v.p. creative Pixar Animation Studios, Richmond, Calif. Director, writer: Luxo Jr., 1986 (Silver Berlin Bear award Berlin Internat. Film Festival, 1986, nominated Oscar for Best Short Films, Animated Films, 1986), Red's Dream, 1987, Tin Toy, 1988 (Best Short Films, Animated Films Acad. award 1988), Knickknack, 1989 (Best Short Film award Seattle Internat. Film Festival 1989), Toy Story, 1995 (nominated Oscar for Best Writing, Screenplay written Directly for Screen 1995), A Bug's Life, 1998, For the Birds, 2000, Mike's New Car, 2002; director: Adventures of Andre and Wally B., 1984, Toy Story 2, 1999; exec. prodr.: Luxo Jr.; exec. prodr. Geri's Game, 1997, Toy Story 2, Monsters Inc., 2001; actor: Computer Illusions, 1998. Recipient Spl Achievement award 1996 Acad. Awards; also Humanitarian award ShoWest Conv., 1997, Spl. award outstanding achievement, 1996. Office: c/p Pixar Animation Studios 1001 W Cutting Blvd Richmond CA 94804-2028*

LASSETER, KENNETH CARLYLE, pharmacologist; b. Aug. 12, 1942; s. James and Retta (Shad) L.; m. Kathy G. Marks, Aug. 6, 1977; children: Kenneth C. III, Susan, Frank L. BS, Stetson U., 1963; MD, U. Fla., 1967. Diplomate Am. Bd. Clin. Pharmacology. Intern, resident in medicine U. Ky. Med. Ctr., 1967-71; asst. prof., assoc. prof. pharmacology and medicine U. Miami (Fla.) Med. Sch., 1971-81, clin. assoc. prof., 1981—. Adj. assoc. prof. pharmacology, Barry U., 1986—; v.p., dir. Clin. Pharmacology Assos., Inc., Miami, 1981—. Contbr. articles to profl. jours. With USAR, 1971-76. Recipient William B. Peck Sci. Rsch. award Interstate Postgrad. Med. Assn., 1976, Rsch. award Alpha Omega Alpha, 1967. Fellow Am. Coll. Clin. Pharmacology; mem. ACP, Am. Soc. Pharmacology and Exptl. Therapeutics, Am. Soc. Clin. Pharmacology and Therapeutics, Sigma Xi. Republican. Office: Clin Pharmacol Assocs 2060 NW 22nd Ave Miami FL 33142-7338 E-mail: lasseter@clinpharm-miami.com.

LASSETER, ROBERT HAYGOOD, electrical engineering educator, consultant; b. Miami, Fla., Apr. 4, 1938; s. J. Haygood and Elsiemae (Davis) L.; m. Lucy Taylor, Sept. 2, 1979; children: Courtney M., Malahn P., Robert M., Lauren L. BS in Physics, N.C. State U., 1963, MS in Physics, 1967; PhD in Physics, U. Pa., 1971; postdoctoral work, U. Pa., Phila., 1971-73. Cons. engr. GE Co., Phila., 1973-80; from asst. prof. to assoc. prof. U. Wis., Madison, 1980-85, assoc. chmn., 1984-85, prof., 1985—. Dir. power sys. Engring. Rsch. Ctr.- Wis., 1994—; cons. engr. Siemens AG, Germany, 1985-86; cons. Elec. Power Rsch. Inst., Palo Alto, Calif., 1990—, others; expert advisor Conf. Internat. des Grands Réseaux Electriques, 1982—. Contbr. numerous papers to profl. socs. Fellow IEEE. Achievements include pioneering work in application of digital methods to the design of high voltage direct current power systems; basic development of analytical methods for design and study of power electronic controllers in power systems; creating a concept of Microgrids as applied to distributed resources in power systems. Office: Univ Wisconsin Electrical & Computer Engineering 1415 Engineering Dr Madison WI 53706-1607

LASSITER, DARRYL D. television production executive, owner entertainment company; b. Sept. 4, 1963; s. Robert and Johnnye (Patton) L. BA in Comm., Ala. State U., 1986. Assoc. prodr. Good Morning Ala. WKAB-TV 32 (ABC), Montgomery, Ala., 1984-85; news prodn. technician WAKA-TV 8 (CBS), 1985-86; announcer, asst. music dir. WQIM Radio 94.5 FM, 1986-87; program-music dir., announcer WIGO Radio 1340 AM, Atlanta, 1987-92; writer-prodr., dir. TV-16 (Library Channel), 1988-94; prodn. technician WGNX-TV 46 (CBS), 1994—. Mem. bd. adv. So. Music Hall of Fame; sportscaster, cameraman Storer Cable TV-3, Montgomery; set prodn. asst. (TV series) In The Heat Of The Night (CBS) MGM; announcer, prodn. asst. WVAS RADIO 90.7 FM; cameraman Ga. Pub. TV, Atlanta; studio cameraman WHSG-TV 63 (Trinity Broadcasting); marching band clinician McNair H.S.; set prodn. asst. music videos Classic Concepts Films Prodns., N.Y.; promotions dir. (TV show) In The Mix Greenhouse Prodns.; customer svc. rep. Atlanta Jour.-Constitution. Ind. creator; (films) Catch The Reading Express, Atlanta Braves-Library Summer Reading Special, My Life With Martin Luther King: By Coretta King, Spotlight on Jackie Wilson, The Milner Awards, (commercials) MCI, Atlanta Braves, High Mus., Seven Stages, Scitrek Mus., Music Videos. Mem. NAACP, Nat. Fedn. for Musicians, Internat. TV Assn., Black Filmmaker Found., Young Black Programmer's Corp., Image Film & Video. Home: PO Box 50374 Atlanta GA 30302-0374 also: PO Box 50374 Atlanta GA 30302-0374 Office: WGNX TV-46 (CBS) 1810 Briarcliff Rd NE Atlanta GA 30329-4097

LASSITER, DOROTHY TATE, library director; b. New Brunswick, N.J., Nov. 3, 1922; d. Nelson Thomas and Dorothy Octavia (Clements) T.; m. Cleveland Frissell Lassiter, Dec. 16, 1945; children: Mark Frissell, Keith Allan, Brian Eugene. BA in Sociology cum laude, Va. Union U., 1944; MS in Libr. Svc., Columbia U., 1960. Cert. libr., media specialist, N.Y.; cert. libr. dir., media specialist, Ga. Proof clk. Chase Manhattan Bank, N.Y.C., 1956-57; br. libr. Queensborough Pub. Libr., Jamaica, N.Y., 1958-65; head children's dept. White Plains (N.Y.) Pub. Libr., 1965-68; libr. Greenburgh Sch. Dist. 7, Harstdale, N.Y., 1968-69; ref. libr. Mamaroneck (N.Y.) Free Libr., 1969-71; adult svcs. libr. Ossining (N.Y.) Pub. Libr., 1972-73; libr. media specialist Mt. Vernon (N.Y.) High Sch., 1973-79; ref. libr. Pace U., White Plains, N.Y., 1979-80; libr. Atlanta-Fulton County Pub. Libr., 1981-82; libr. dir. Greenforest Bapt. Ch. Libr., Decatur, Ga., 1982—. Libr. Portfolio Ctr., Atlanta, 1982-83; instr. Spelman Coll., Atlanta, 1984-85; substitute tchr. DeKalb County Bd. Edn., Decatur, 1984-88; libr. media specialist Greenforest Christian Academic Ctr., Decatur, 1989—. 1st Headstart libr. Designated storyteller 1965 N.Y. World's Fair. N.Y. Libr. Assn. scholar, 1950. Mem. ALA, NAACP (membership chmn.), Westchester Black Women's Polit. Caucus, UN Assn., Ch. and Synagogue Libr. Assn., Va. Union U. Alumni Assn. (Met. Atlanta chpt., regional v.p.), Alpha Kappa Alpha. Democrat. Baptist. Avocations: reading, story telling, theater, traveling. Home: 4215 Abilene Ct Decatur GA 30034-6025 Office: Greenforest Bapt Ch Libr 3250 Rainbow Dr Decatur GA 30034-1713

LASSITER, KENNETH T. photography educator, consultant; b. Richmond, Va., Jan. 2, 1935; s. B. Taylor and Euzelia (Duke) L.; m. Carol Lester, Apr. 9, 1960; children: Karen, Keith. BS, Va. Tech. U., 1957; MS (hon.), Brooks Inst. Photography, 1992. Engr. Eastman Kodak Co., Rochester, N.Y., 1957-60, tech. editor, 1960-69, dir. publs., 1970-84, dir. photo trade rels., 1984-93, mgr. photo edn., 1986-93; retired, 1993; mng. dir. Palm Beach (Fla.) Photo Workshops, 1993-94. Mem. pres.'s coun. Internat. Ctr. Photography, N.Y.C., 1985-93; dir. Photographic Art & Sci. Found., Oklahoma City, 1984-95. Author: Executive Producer: Techniques of the Masters Videoconference Series; author or editor numerous Kodak publs. Mem. Soc. for Imaging Sci. and Tech. (sr., bd. dirs. 1965-90), Friends of Photography, Nat. Press Photographers Assn., Soc. for Photographic Edn., Photo Imaging Edn. Assn. Republican. Presbyterian. Avocations: travel, photography, music, computers.

LASSLO, ANDREW, medicinal chemist, educator; b. Mukacevo, Czechoslovakia, Aug. 24, 1922; came to U.S., 1946, naturalized, 1951; s. Vojtech Laszlo and Terezie (Herskovicova) L.; m. Wilma Ellen Reynolds, July 9, 1955; 1 child, Millicent Andrea. MS, U. Ill., 1948, PhD, 1952, MLS, 1961. Rsch. chemist organic chems. div. Monsanto Chem. Co., St. Louis, 1952-54; asst. prof. pharmacology, divsn. basic health scis. Emory U., 1954-60; prof. and chmn. dept. med. chemistry Coll. Pharmacy, U. Tenn. Health Sci. Ctr., 1960-90, Alumni Disting. Svc. prof. and chmn., dept. medicinal chemistry, 1989-90, professor emeritus, 1990—. Cons. Geschickter Fund for Med. Research Inc., 1961-62; rsch. contractor U.S. Army Med. R & D Command, 1964-67; dir. postgrad. tng. program sci. librarians USPHS, 1966-72; chmn. edn. com. Drug Info. Assn., 1966-68, bd. dirs., 1968-69; dir. postgrad. tng. program organic medicinal chemistry for chemists FDA, 1971; exec. com. adv. council S.E. Regional Med. Library Program, Nat. Library of Medicine, 1969-71; chmn. regional med. library programs com. Med. Library Assn., 1971-72; mem. pres.'s faculty adv. council U. Tenn. System, 1970-72; chmn. energy authority U. Tenn. Center for Health Scis., 1975-77, chmn. council departmental chmn., 1977, 81; chmn. Internat. Symposium on Contemporary Trends in Tng. Pharmacologists, Helsinki, 1975. Producer, moderator (TV and radio series) Health Care Perspective, 1976-78; author: Travel at Your Own Risk-Reflections on Science, Research and Education, 1998, Molecules, Miracles and Medicine, 2000; editor: Surface Chemistry and Dental Integuments, 1973, Blood Platelet Function and Medicinal Chemistry, 1984; contbr. numerous articles to sci. and profl. jours.; mem. editl. bd. Jour. Medicinal and Pharm. Chemistry, 1961, U. Tenn. Press, 1974-77; composer (work for piano) Synthesis in C Minor, 1968; patentee in field. Trustee 1st Bohemian Meth. Ch., Chgo., 1951-52, mem. bd. stewards, 1950-52; mem. ofcl. bd. Grace Meth. Ch., Atlanta, 1955-60; mem. adminstrv. bd. Christ United Meth. Ch., Memphis, 1964-72, 73-75, 77-79, 81-83, 88-90, chmn. commn. on edn., 1965-67, chmn. bd. Day Sch., 1967-68. 1st lt. USAR, 1953-57, capt., 1957-62. Recipient Research prize U. Ill. Med. Ctr. chpt. Sigma Xi, 1949, Honor Scroll Tenn. Inst. Chemists, 1976, Americanism medal DAR, 1976; U. Ill. fellow, 1950-51; Geschickter Fund Med. Research grantee, 1959-65, USPHS Research and Tng. grantee, 1958-64, 66-72, 82-89, NSF research grantee, 1964-66, Pfeiffer Research Found. grantee, 1981-87. Fellow AAAS, Am. Assn. Pharm. Scientists, Am. Inst. Chemists (nat. councilor for Tenn. 1969-70), Acad. Pharm. Rsch. and Sci.; mem. ALA (life), Am. Chem. Soc. (sr.), Am. Pharm. Assn., Am. Soc. Pharmacology and Exptl. Therapeutics (chmn. subcom. pre and postdoctoral tng. 1974-78, exec. com. ednl. and profl. affairs 1974-78), Sigma Xi (pres. elect U. Tenn. Ctr. for Health Sci. chpt. 1975-76, pres. 1976-77, Excellence in Rsch. award 1989), Beta Phi Mu, Phi Lambda Sigma, Rho Chi. Methodist. Achievements include 7 U.S. and 11 foreign patents in field; identification of platelet aggregation-inhibitory specific functions in synthetic organic molecules; design and synthesis of novel human blood platelet aggregation inhibitors, novel compound for mild stimulation of central nervous system activity; research on relationships between structural features of synthetic organic entities, their physicochemical properties and their effects on biologic activity. Home and Office: 5479 Timmons Ave Memphis TN 38119-6932 E-mail: alasslo.memphis.24822@worldnet.att.net. *Of all the pleasures a human being can savor, none exceeds the satisfaction of a genuine sense of accomplishment. It undergirds all elements of creative living and surmounts vicissitudes exceeding conventional human endurance.*

LASSMAN, MARTIN R. musician, educator; b. Newark, July 26, 1949; s. Samuel and Myrtle Kotkin Lassman, Florence Rubin Lassman (Stepmother); m. Dorilyn English, July 1, 2001; children: Michael Evans, James Alan; children: Liam McWilliams, Keara Kathryn English. MS in Music Edn., U. of Iowa, Iowa City, Iowa, 1973—74; BM in Music Educatiom, U. of Del., Newark, DE, 1967—72. Music Education K-12 DE, 1972. Band dir. Wilmington Friends Sch., Wilmington, Del., 1974—92; vocal music tchr. Cab Calloway Sch. of the Arts, 1992—. Musician pianist, conductor. Bd. mem. CCSA Bord of Directors, Wilmington, Del., 1992—2001. Recipient Mid. Sch. Tchr. of the Yr., RCCSD, 1998. Mem.: ACDA (state mid. sch. r&s chair 1999), MENC (all-state coord.), IAJE. Home: 44 Weilers Bend Wilmington DE 19810 Office: Cab Calloway School of the Arts 100 N DuPont Road Wilmington DE 19807 Personal E-mail: jazzchord@aol.com.

LASSNER, FRANZ GEORGE, educator; b. Leipzig, Germany, May 6, 1926; s. Oscar and Marga (Treskow) L.; m. Marguerite Sansone, Aug. 18, 1961; children: Alexander Nicholas, John Paul. AB in History, Rutgers U., 1947; MA in History, Georgetown U., 1951, PhD in Govt., 1960. With rsch. projects Georgetown U., Washington, 1951-62; rsch. supt. Russian Studies Project, 1956-57; rsch. assoc., curator spl. collections Hoover Inst., Stanford, Calif., 1962-63; dir. Herbert Hoover Presdl. Libr., West Branch, Iowa, 1963-67; dir. archives Hoover Inst., Stanford, 1969-74, spl. rep., 1974-90; dir. devel. Phila. Coll. Textiles and Sci., 1974-76; sr. v.p. programs Freedoms Found., Valley Forge, 1977-91. Adj. prof. history Temple U., Phila., 1992-93, Atlantic C.C., N.J., 1992-95, Bundesheer Rsch. Project, Vienna, Austria, 1997-98. Adv. bd. Internat. Telecomm. Inst., Houston, 1984-89; bd. dirs. St. Lawrence Inst., Montreal, 1985-89. Mem. World Affairs Coun. Greater Valley Forge (bd. dirs. 1991-93), Lambda Chi Alpha, Delta Phi Alpha. Roman Catholic. Home: 1069 Michigan Ave Cape May NJ 08204-2541 E-mail: lassner.1@starpower.net.

LASSWELL, ANITA DIANE, nutrition educator; b. Springfield, Mass., May 16, 1952; d. Robert Louis and Florence (Menchel) Blitz; m. William Lonzo Lasswell Jr., Dec. 29, 1974. BS, Fla. State U., 1974; MS, Fla. Internat. U., 1975; PhD, U. Md., 1995. Registered dietitian; cert. diabetes educator. Pub. health nutritionist Memphis and Shelby County Health Dept., Memphis, 1975-76; clin. dietitian St. Joseph Hosp. East, 1976-77; project coord., instr. Ea. Ky. U., Richmond, 1977-78; clin. dietitian Kent County Meml. Hosp., Warwick, R.I., 1978-80; nutritionist, clin. instr. dept. family medicine Brown U. Sch. of Medicine, Providence, 1980-89; clin. asst. prof. depts. family med./clin. preventive med. U. Md. Sch. Medicine, Balt., 1989-94; rsch. asst. prof., project devel. dir. dept. nutrition U. N.C., Chapel Hill, 1995-97; assoc. prof. dept. dietetics and nutrition Fla. Internat. U., Miami, 1997-98; pres. Creative Nutrition Cons., Vero Beach, Fla., 1998—. Advisor Med. Nutrition Curriculum Initiative U. N.C., Chapel Hill, 1997—99; bd. dirs. Meducation, Durham, NC, Creative Healthcare Cons., Vero Beach, Fla. Author: (textbook) Nutrition for Family and Primary Care Practitioners, 1986, (ednl. CD-ROMs) Nutritional Anemias, 1996 (Bronze Apple award Nat. Ednl. Media Assn. 1997), Nutritional Management of Diabetes Mellitus, 1996, Nutrition and Cancer, 1997, Diet, Obesity and Cardiovascular Disease, 1998, (web-based nutrition edn. module) Nutrition in Preventive Medicine, 2001. Recipient Bronze Apple award Nat. Edn. Media Assn., 1998; named Ky. Col., Gov. Paul E. Patton, 1997. Mem. APHA, Am. Dietetic Assn. (chmn. dietetic practice group dietitians in med. and dental edn. 1985-88, Young Dietitian of Yr. 1982,

Outstanding Svc. award 1988), R.I. Dietetic Assn. (pres. 1984-85, Young Dietitian of Yr. 1982), Soc. for Nutrition Edn., Phi Kappa Phi. Avocations: arts and crafts, gardening, interior decorating. Fax: 772-231-8431. E-mail: lasswell@earthlink.net.

LASSWELL, MARCIA LEE, psychologist, educator; b. Oklahoma City, July 13, 1927; d. Lee and Stella (Blackard) Eck; m. Thomas Lasswell, May 29, 1950 (div. July 1990); children: Marcia Jane, Thomas Ely, Julia Lee. BA, U. Calif., Berkeley, 1949; MA, U. So. Calif., 1952; postgrad., U. Calif., Riverside, U. So. Calif., U. N.C. Individual practice psychotherapy, marriage/family therapy, Claremont, Calif.; asst. prof. Pepperdine Coll., Los Angeles, 1959-60; asst. prof. psychology behavioral sci. dept. Calif. State U., Pomona, 1960-64, asso. prof., 1965-69, prof., 1970—, chmn. dept., 1964-69; asso. clin. dir. Human Relations Center, U. So. Calif., 1975—. Vis. assoc. prof. Scripps Coll., 1968-69, U. So. Calif., 1969-70, Occidental Coll., 1971-72; lectr. various Calif. univs.; mem. staff spl. project alcoholics and narcotics offenders Calif. Prison System, 1970-73; mem. Calif. Accreditation Com. Secondary Schs. and Colls., 1965—; mem. commn. accreditation for marriage and family tng. U.S. Dept. Edn., 1981-87. Author: College Teaching of General Psychology, 1967, Love, Marriage and Family, 1973, No-Fault Marriage, 1976, Styles of Loving, 1980, Marriage and Family, 1982, rev. edit., 1987, 91, Equal Time, 1983. Recipient Outstanding Tchrs. award Calif. State U., 1971, Outstanding Contbn. to Marriage and Family Therapy, 1991, Disting. Clin. Mem. award Calif. Assn. Marriage and Family Therapists, 1995, award Outstanding Marriage and Family Therapy Orgn., 1999. Fellow Am. Assn. Marital and Family Therapy (bd. dirs. 1970-72, 87-91, pres. elect 1993-95, pres. 1995-97, past pres. 1997-98); mem. AAAS, Nat. Coun. Family Rels. (exec. com. 1978-80), Am. Acad. Family Therapy, So. Calif. Assn. Marital and Family Therapy (pres. 1972-73), Groves Family Conf. Acad. (sec. 2000—), Groves Family Conf. (sec. 2001-2003), Alpha Kappa Delta, Phi Delta Gamma, Pi Gamma Mu. Home: 800 W 1st St Apt 2908 Los Angeles CA 90012-2444 Office: 250 W First St # 352 Claremont CA 91711 E-mail: mlass@aol.com.

LAST, MARIAN HELEN, social services administrator; b. L.A., July 2, 1953; d. Henry and Renee (Kahan) Last. BA, Pitzer Coll., 1975; postgrad., U. So. Calif., 1975-84; MS, Long Beach State U., 1980. Lic. marriage therapist. Coordinator City of El Monte, Calif., 1975-76, project dir., 1976—; pvt. practice psychotherapist Long Beach, 1982—; div. mgr. City of El Monte, 1982—. Cons. U. So. Calif. Andrus Ctr., L.A., 1977-78; bd. dirs. Coord. Coun., City of El Monte, 1975—, Sr. Pres.'s Coun., 1982—; Congl. del. White House Conf. on Aging, 1995; chair Nutrition Focus Group, L.A. Co. Area Agy. On Aging, 1993—. Co-author rape survival guide, 1971. Dir., co-founder Rape Response Program, Pomona, San Gabriel Valley, Calif., 1971-80; cons. on sexual assault Pitzer Coll., Claremont, Calif., 1975-78; past pres. El Monte-South El Monte Coord. Coun. Recipient Susan B. Anthony award NOW, Pomona, 1976, Gold award Calif. Emergency Svcs. Assn., 1995, Founders award Project Sister sexual assault ctr., 2002. Mem. Am. Soc. on Aging, Calif. Assn. Sr. Ctr. Dirs. (dist. dir. XIII), Calif. Parks and Recreation Soc. (Profl. Citation award 1993), Calif. Assn. Marriage and Family Therapists, Emergency Resources Assn. (bd. dirs.), Women's Club, Civitan, Chi Kappa Rho Gamma. Democrat. Jewish. Avocations: golf, advocating rights of elderly. Office: City of El Monte 3120 N Tyler Ave El Monte CA 91731-3354

LAST, MICHAEL P. lawyer; b. Chgo., July 31, 1946; s. Jules Hilbert and Muriel Esther (Ruekberg) L.; m. Yong-Hee Chyun, Dec. 1970 (div.); m. Jane Antoinette Nooy Bunnell, May 29, 1983. BA magna cum laude, Lawrence U., 1968; JD cum laude, Harvard U., 1971. Bar: Mass. 1971. Ptnr., head real estate, environ. law dept. Warner & Stackpole, Boston, 1972-84; ptnr., head environ. law dept. Gaston & Snow, 1984-91; ptnr., co-chair environ. law sect. Mintz, Levin, Cohn, Ferris, Glovsky and Popeo P.C., 1991-99; mng. dir. ML Strategies, Inc., 1991-99, v.p., 1999; co-counsel Rackemann, Sawyer & Brewster, 1999—; prin. Nexus Environtl. Ptnrs., 1999—. Bd. dirs. Newell Enterprises Inc., 1983-87; co-chair Am. Law Inst./ABA Ann. Course Study Minimizing Liability for Hazardous Waste Mgmt.; lectr. in field. Contbr. articles to profl. jours. Chair wetlands regulation rev. bd. Mass. Dept. Environ. Quality Engring., 1983-85, Town Wellesley Wetlands Protection Com., 1980-82; mem. Town Wellesley Planning Bd., 1983-88; rep. Town Meeting, Wellesley; mem. rev. bd. Mass. Dept. Environ. Protection, 1991-92; mem. bd. environ. mgmt. Mass. Dept. Environ. Mgmt., 1991—, chmn., 1994-97, 2000—; founder, pres. Santa Fe Coun. Environ. Excellence, 1991—; founder, pres. Berkshire Inst., Inc.; mem. corp. gifts com. Boston Mus. Fine Arts Capital Fund Dr., 1979; vice chair open space plan implementation com. Town Wellesley, 1978-79; trustee, bd. govs. New Eng. Aquarium, 1995—, chmn. David B. Stone award com.; trustee Mass. Eye and Ear Infirmary, 1990-98, Mt. Kearsarge Indian Mus., 1997—; trustee, bd. govs., exec. com. Newton-Wellesley Hosp., 1987-94, hon. trustee, 1994—, chmn. joint trustee staff com., 1992-93; mem. corp. Ptnrs. Healthcare Sys., Inc., 1999—; bd. dirs. Environ. Bus. Coun. New Eng., Inc., 1997—, chmn. Brownfields Com., chmn. ann. retreat, mem. exec. com., 2001—. 1st lt. USAF, 1971-72. Warren Hurst Stevens scholar Lawrence U., 1964. Mem. ABA (standing com. environ. law 1989-91, natural resources sect., corp., banking, bus. law sect., real property, probate, trust law sect.), Boston Bar Assn. (bd. dirs. 1984-87, chair environment com. 1979-81, chair urban affairs sect. 1983-87, co-chair mcpl. planning process com. 1983-87), Greater Boston C. of C. (real estate devel. com. 1979-80, co-chair Boston 2000 project review com. 1982-90, Boston 2000 steering com. 1983-90, co-chair adv. com. Devel. Design Guideline Study Downtown Boston 1983-92), Phi Beta Kappa. Avocations: canoeing, cross country skiing, camping. Office: One Financial Center Boston MA 02111 E-mail: mlast@lastlaw.com.

LAST, RUTH EDITH, actress; b. N.Y.C., May 31, 1934; d. Max Abraham and Fannie (Litt) L.; m. Morton Lazarus, Nov. 7, 1960 (div. Nov., 1970); 1 child, Adam Last Lazarus. BS, NYU, 1955. Actress movies, TV, radio, stage, commls., 1956—. Appeared in films including Endless Love, 1980, Fort Apache, The Bronx, 1982, Manhattan Murder Mystery, 1993, Hollywood Ending, 2002; appeared on TV in Texas, 1980, All My Children, 1995, Ryans Hope, 1989, As the World Turns, 1990, Saturday Night Live, Funhouse, 2001; voice over and on camera in commls. Pres. AFTRA-Heller Meml. Found., 1991-2000; officer Park River Ind. Dems., 1995-2000. Mem.: SAG, AFTRA (v.p. 2001), Actors Equity Assn., Screen Actors Guild. Democrat. Jewish. Home: 440 W End Ave New York NY 10024-5358

LASTER, ATLAS, JR. psychologist; b. Canalou, Mo., Apr. 18, 1948; s. Atlas Sr. and Rose Ella (Brown) L.; m. Janet Lee Rowe, Aug. 22, 1973; Children: Cedric, Marcus, Rosa, Sophia, Leah, Rachel. Student, Wash. U., 1966-69; BD, Union Theology Sem., 1971; MEd, U. Pitts., 1973, PhD, 1976. Diplomate Am. Bd. Disability Analysts, Am. Bd. Profl. Psychology, Am. Bd. Psychol. Specialties. Staff psychologist Mon-Yough Mental Health Svcs., McKeesport, Penn., 1975-76; cons. psychologist DePaul Health Ctr. Care Unit, Bridgeton, Mo., 1977; program dir. Dept. Corrections, Menard, Ill., 1978; mgmt. cons. Univ. Pk. Group, Palm Beach, Fla., 1980; counseling coord. So. Ill. U., 1981-82; mgr. Comprehensive Counseling and Cons. Svcs., Pitts., 1982-84; dir. of christian edn. Pilgrim Congl. Ch., St. Louis, 1985-86; cons. psychologist Div. of Family Svcs., 1986—; asst. prof. Psychology Mo. Bapt. Coll., 1991—; vocat. rehab. counselor Mo. Divsn. Vocat. Rehab., 1991-93; program mgr., mentor Ill. Mentor, Inc., 1997—99; pvt. practice Clayton, 1993—. Sr. cons. Hanley, Harsche, Rottman and Druch, St. Louis, 1979-80; cons. Dept. Mental Health, St. Louis, 1986—, St. Louis Pub. Schs., 1989—, Ill. Dept. Children and Family Svcs., East St. Louis, 1990—, Health Mgmt. Svcs. Am., East Detroit, Mich., 1990—, Divsn. Children and Family Svcs., Spokane, Wash., 1990—, Decatur, Ga., 1990—. Contbr. articles to profl. jours. Cons. Congress of Racial Equality St. Louis, 1987—. Mem. APA, Am. Coll. Forensic Examiners, Nat. Assn. Sch. Psychologists, Mo. Psychol. Assn., Clayton C. of C. (bd. dirs.). Baptist. Avocation: photography. Office: PO Box 16693 Saint Louis MO 63105-1193

LASTER, LEONARD, physician, consultant, author; b. N.Y.C., Aug. 24, 1928; s. Isaac and Mary (Ehrenreich) L.; m. Ruth Ann Leventhal, Dec. 16, 1956; children: Judith Eve, Susan Beth, Stephen Jay. AB, Harvard U., 1949, MD, 1950. Diplomate Nat. Bd. Med. Examiners, Am. Bd. Internal Medicine (gastroenterology). From intern to resident in medicine Mass. Gen. Hosp., Boston, 1950-53; fellow gastroenterology Mass. Meml. Hosp., 1958-59; vis. investigator Pub. Health Rsch. Inst., N.Y.C., 1953-54; lt. commd. USPHS, 1954, advanced through grades to asst. surgeon gen. (rear adm.), 1971; mem. staff Nat. Inst. Arthritis, Metabolic and Digestive Diseases, NIH, Bethesda, Md., 1954-73, chief digestive and hereditary diseases br., 1969-73; from spl. asst. to asst. dir. human resources President's Office Sci. and Tech., 1969-73; exec. dir. Assembly Life Scis., also div. med. scis. NAS-NRC, 1973-74; ret. USPHS, 1973; v.p. acad. affairs and clin. affairs Med. Ctr., also dean Coll. Medicine, prof. medicine Downstate Med. Ctr., SUNY, Bklyn., 1974-78; pres., prof. medicine Oreg. Health Scis. U., Portland, 1978-87; chancellor U. Mass. Med. Ctr., Worcester, 1987-90, disting. prof. medicine and health policy, 1990—, chancellor emeritus, 1990—. Bd. dirs. TEI Biosci., Boston, Photo Electron Corp., Lexington, Mass.; cons. mgmt. and productivity of R&D programs for pharm. corps., R&D strategic planning orgn. corp. health care programs for multinat. paper corp. and pvt. rsch. found.; lab. investigator Marine Biol. Lab., Woods Hole, Mass., 1962—69, chmn. organizer symposia on nat. policy and biomed. scis., 1971—72, libr. reader, 1973—76; chmn. steering com. Falmouth Forum, 1994—2002. Author: Life After Medical School, 32 Doctors Describe How They Shaped Their Medical Careers, 1996; contbr. articles on gastrointestinal disease, inborn errors of metabolism, devel. biology to profl. jours.; contbr. op-ed column and other pieces to Washington Post, essays to Hosp. Practice and MD Mag.c columnist Cape Cod Times, 2002—. Active Found. Advanced Edn. Scis., Bethesda, 1965-69, Bedford Stuyvesant Family Health Ctr., Bklyn., 1975-78, Med. Rsch. Found., Oreg., 1979-87, Oreg. Symphony, 1979-85, Oreg. Contemporary Theatre, 1981-83; pres. Burning Tree Elem. Sch. PTA, Bethesda, 1972-73; bd. dirs. Internat. Artists Series, Worcester, 1988-91, Mass. Biotech. Ctrs. for Excellence, Boston, 1988-96, Mass. Biotech. Rsch. Inst., Worcester, 1988-90, Worcester Bus. Devel. Corp., 1988-91; co-chmn. United Way Ctrl. Mass., COMEC Campaign, 1989; mem. exec. com. Worcester Econ. Club, 1988-91; mem. citizen gov. bd. Worcester Fights Back, 1990-95; chmn. corp. liaison com. Marine Biol. Lab., 1991-92; mem. Worcester Com. Fgn. Rels. (affiliated with Coun. Fgn. Rels.), 1992-96. Fellow ACP; mem. Am. Fedn. Clin. Rsch., Am. Gastroenterol. Assn., Am. Soc. Biol. Chemists, Am. Soc. Clin. Investigation (emeritus), Marine Biol. Lab. Corp., Portland C. of C. (dir. 1980-84), Mass. Med. Soc., Worcester Dist. Med. Soc., Cosmos Club (Washington), Harvard Club (N.Y.C.), Harvard Club (Boston), Phi Beta Kappa, Sigma Xi. Home: 8 Lawrence Farm Rd Woods Hole MA 02543-1416 Office: U Mass Med Sch 55 Lake Ave N Worcester MA 01655-0002 *Education is nurturing excellence in others and facilitating its spread as an infectious disease.*

LASTER, RICHARD, biotechnology executive, consultant; b. Vienna, Austria, Nov. 10, 1923; came to U.S., 1940, naturalized, 1944; s. Alan and Caroline (Harband) L.; m. Liselotte Schneider, Oct. 17, 1948; children: Susan Laster Rubenstein, Thomas. Student, U. Wash., 1941-42; BChE cum laude, Poly. Inst. Bklyn., 1943; postgrad., Stevens Inst. Tech., 1945-47. With Gen. Foods Corp., 1944-82, corp. R & D N.J., 1944-58, ops. mgr. Franklin Baker divsn., 1958-64, ops. mgr. Atlantic gelatin divsn. Woburn, Mass., 1958-64, mgr. R & D Jell-O divsn. White Plains, N.Y., 1967-68, exec. v.p. Maxwell House divsn., 1968-69, pres. Maxwell House divsn., 1969-71, corp. v.p., 1971-73, exec. v.p., 1974-82, also dir. R & D and food-away-from-home, 1975-82. Bd. dirs. DNA Plant Tech. Corp., 1982-94, chmn., 1988-94, CEO, 1982-92, pres., 1982-91; mgmt. cons., 1994—; bd. dirs. RiceTec; bd. dirs., chmn. WellGen, Inc. Contbr. articles to profl. publs.; patentee in field. Mem. Sch. Bd., Chappaqua, NY, 1971—74, pres., 1973—74; chmn., bd. dirs., 1st v.p. United Way of Westchester, 1978; chmn. adv. com. Poly. Inst. Westchester, 1977; trustee Poly. Inst. N.Y., 1978—; mem. coll. coun. SUNY Purchase, Purchase Coll. Found., 1986—; mem. corp. N.Y. Bot. Garden; mem. subcom. export adminstrn. Pres.'s Export Coun., 1995; chmn. Westchester Edn. Coalition, 1992—2001; chmn. Westchester Holocaust Commn., 1994—; chmn. Am. Soc. Plant Physiologists Edn. Found., 1995—2000; mem. New Castle Town Bd., 1996—2001. Recipient Disting. Alumnus award, 1996, Disting. Sc. award NCCJ; Poly Inst. N.Y. fellow. Mem. AAAS, AIChE (Food and Bioengring. award 1972), N.Y. Acad. Scis., Am. Chem. Soc., Am. Inst. Chemists, Tau Beta Pi, Phi Lambda Upsilon. Home: 23 Round Hill Rd Chappaqua NY 10514-1622 Office: Richard Laster 103 S Bedford Rd Mount Kisco NY 10549-3440 E-mail: rilaster@aol.com.

LASTMAN, MELVIN D. mayor; b. Toronto, Ont., Can., Mar. 9, 1933; s. Louis and Rose L.; m. Marilyn Lastman, Nov. 15, 1953; children— Dale, Blayne LLD (hon.), York U., 1997. Pres. Bad Boy Furniture & Appliances, Toronto, 1955-76; mayor North York, Ont., 1972-97, City of Toronto, 1998—. Bd. govs. North York Gen. Hosp.; commr. York-Finch Gen. Hosp. Found. With Pride of Israel Synagogue, Sunnybrook Med. Ctr., Ont. Men's ORT, Can. ORT Orgn., Parents Against Drugs, North York YMCA, Vol. Ctr. Met. Toronto, North York Mental Health Coun., North York Srs. Ctr., North York Hydro Commn., North York chpt. Heart and Stroke Found. Ont., Can. Found. for Ileitis and Colitis, Ont., March of Dimes, Shalom Food Project, Can. Assn. for Riding for the Disabled, St. John Ambulance Canine Therapy Program, Metro Toronto; patron Kidney Found. Can.; hon. chmn. Children's Wish Found. Ont., Drug and Alcohol Network North York, Bloorview MacMillan Ctr., Leukemia Rsch. Fund, St. John's Rehab. Hosp.; with Chi-Ping Dance Group, North York Singers. Recipient Ursaki award Can. Sales and Mktg. Execs., C. of C. Lifetime Achievement award, 1995; named Temple Sinai Brotherhood Humanitarian of Yr., 1995. Mem. North York C. of C., Older Adult Ctrs. Assn., B'nai Brith Can., Juvenile Diabetes Found. Can., Can. Cancer Soc. (Willowdale Unit), Caritas Project, Can. Soc. Yad Vashem (bd. dirs.), Assn. Children with Learning Disabilities, North York Symphony, Kiwanis Club of North York, Kinsmen Club, North York Civitan Club, Rotary. Home: 19 Wideford Pl North York ON Canada M2M 4H3 Office: Mayor's Office City Toronto 100 Queens St West 2d Fl Sta 1070 Toronto ON Canada M5H 2N2

LASTOWKA, JAMES ANTHONY, former federal agency executive, lawyer; b. Chester, Pa., Oct. 1, 1951; s. Joseph Edward and Mary A. (O'Malley) L.; m. Sandra L. Pugh, Apr. 28, 1979; children: Conor David, Carey Anna, Austin Tucker. BA in Econs. cum laude, Syracuse U., 1973; JD, Georgetown U., 1976. Bar: Pa. 1976, D.C. 1990, U.S. Ct. Appeals (4th, 5th, 9th, 10th, 11th, D.C. cirs.) 1981. Staff atty. U.S. Occupational Safety and Health Rev. Commn., Washington, 1976-78, asst. gen. counsel, 1979-80; supervisory atty. Fed. Mine Safety and Health Rev. Commn., 1978-79, dep. gen. counsel, 1980-81, gen. counsel, 1981-84, commr., 1984-90; with Jones, Day, Reavis & Pogue, 1990-92, McDermott, Will & Emery, Washington, 1992—. Contbr. editor Occupational Hazards Mag. Mem. ABA (mem. labor law sect., com. occupational safety and health law). Office: McDermott Will & Emery 600 13th St NW Fl 12 Washington DC 20005-3096

LASURE, JOHN EDWARD, JR. systems analyst; b. N.Y.C., Jan. 15, 1962; s. John Edward Sr. and Olga V. LaSure; children: Ashley Elizabeth, John Edward III. Student, Union Coll., 1983-85. With IBM/Computer Assocs.; computer ops., trust ops. United Nat. Bank, Branchburg, N.J., 1984-86, computer ops. data processing dept., 1986-87, ops. mgr., 1987, jr. systems analyst, 1988-89, systems analyst, 1989-91, sr. systems analyst, 1991-92, network systems mgr., 1992, systems officer, 1992-95, v.p. systems tech., 1995—. Vice chmn. Amigoes! Comm., 1990-91, dir. 1992—. Mem. Computer Task Force Coun. to Mountainside (N.J.) and Plainfield police depts., 1992-93. Served in USAF, 1979-83. Mem. Nat. Systems Programmers Assn., Systems Programmers N.J. (mem. com.), Guide Internat. Corp. Avocations: motorcycling, bicycling, golf, tennis. Office: United Nat Bank PO Box 6000 Bridgewater NJ 08807-0010

LASYS, JOAN, medical nurse, writer, educator, publisher; b. Siauliai, Lithuania, Sept. 1, 1924; arrived in Can., 1948; came to U.S., 1960; d. Joseph-Apolinarius and Elena (Šlapokaite) Barcevičius; m. Bill Lasys, July 31, 1949. RN degree, Lithuanian Red Cross Sch. Nurs, 1945; student, Ariz. State U., 1981-86, Ea. Ariz. Coll., 1981-86. RN, Can., Nebr.; cert. nursing tchr., Ariz. Staff RN St. Mary's Hosp., Montreal, Can., 1949-51, Montreal Gen. Hosp., 1951-53, 1959-60; pvt. duty Nurses Registry, Montreal, 1953-56; Can. civil svc. RN R.H.O. Ctr. Dept. Vets. Affairs, Ottawa, Can., 1956-57, Queen Mary Vets. Hosp., Montreal, 1957-58; staff RN St. Joseph's Hosp., Omaha, 1968-69, Meryvale Hosp., Phoenix, 1969-71, Valley View Hosp., Youngtown, Ariz., 1971-72, Boswell Hosp., Sun City, 1972-76; RN Kivel Care Ctr., Phoenix, 1986-93. Past v.p. and officer Pine-Strawberry (Ariz.) Health Svcs.; columnist/reporter Payson (Ariz.) Roundup. Pub. (mag.) Small Town U.S.A.; prodr. audio tapes: Time Management, Nursing Communications. Life mem. Pine-Strawberry and Gila County Homemakers, Payson Regional Med. Ctr. Aux. Mem.: AAUW, Libr. Congress, Nat. Mus. Women in the Arts, Payson Libr., Rep. Residential Task Force, Kince Geriatric Ctr. Aux. (life), County Attys. and Sheriffs Assn. (hon.), Arbor Day Found., Nature Conservancy, Cooking Club of Am. (charter). Republican. Roman Catholic. Avocations: writing poetry, public speaking, arts and crafts. Home: 506 N William Tell Cir Payson AZ 85541-4050

LASZEWSKI, BOLESLAW TADEUSZ, civic volunteer; b. Gora Ropczycka, Poland, Nov. 22, 1912; s. Jozef and Katarzyna (Toton) L.; m. Sophie Kinel, Sept. 26, 1947 (div. 1968); children: Barbara, Marzena, Dorothy; m. Christine Gaszynski. BSBA, CUNY, 1957; MS, Columbia U., 1956; MA, Jagiellonian U., 1937. Co-founder, hon. pres. Polish Assistance, N.Y.C., 1952—. Co-founder, pres., Polish Combatants Assn., London, 1945-50; v.p. Worldwide Orgn. Poles Abroad, London, 1947-80; mem. Kostiuszko Found., N.Y.C., 1952—; co-founder, pres. Polish Daily News, N.Y.C., 1970—; pres. Polish Am. Army Veterans Assn., 1985—; exec. dir. Polish Inst. Arts & Scis., N.Y.C., 1986-90; v.p., dir. Polish Am. Congress, 1986-88; pres. Polish Fed. Credit Union, Bklyn., 1985-90. Author: From Army to Civilian Life, 1984, Krakow, 1985, East West Russia—USSR—USA—Poland, 1986, Diary of a Soldier, 2000.

LATANÉ, BIBB, social psychologist; b. N.Y.C., July 19, 1937; s. Henry Allen and Felicite Gillman (Bibb) L.; children: Julia Gillman, Claire Augusta, Henry Arbiter. BA, Yale U., 1958; PhD, U. Minn., 1963. Mem. faculty dept. social psychology Columbia U., N.Y.C., 1962-68; prof. psychology, dir. behavioral scis. lab. Ohio State U., Columbus, 1968-82; prof. psychology, dir. Inst. Research Social Sci. U.N.C.-Chapel Hill, 1982-90; prof. psychology Fla. Atlantic U., Boca Raton, 1990—2000. Pres. Social Sci. Confs., Inc.; founder Nags Head Conf. Ctr., Latané Ctr. Human Scis. Contbr. articles to profl. jours. Guggenheim fellow, 1974-75; James McKeen Cattell fellow, 1981-82; NSF, Office of Naval Research grantee. Mem. Am. Psychol. Assn. (council rep. 1971-75), Soc. Personality and Social Psychology (pres. 1976-79, Campbell award 1986), Midwestern Psychol. Assn. (pres. 1981-84), Acad. Mgmt., AAAS (Socio-Psychol. prize 1968, 80), Soc. Exptl. Soc. Psychol. (Disting. Scientist award, 1998), Am. Sociol. Assn., Animal Behavior Soc. Home: 4521 S Ocean Blvd Boca Raton FL 33487-4278 E-mail: latane@seafrolic.org. *We know so much, yet have so much to learn about each other that the science of behavior will continue to vitalize and be vital.*

LATANISION, RONALD MICHAEL, materials science and engineering educator, consultant; b. Richmondale, Pa., July 2, 1942; s. Stephen and Mary (Kopach) L.; m. Carolyn Marie Domenig, June 27, 1964; children: Ivan, Sara. BS, Pa. State U., 1964; PhD in Metall. Engring., Ohio State U., 1968. Postdoctoral fellow Nat. Bur. Standards, Washington, 1968-69; research scientist Martin Marietta, Balt., 1969-73, acting head materials sci., 1973-74; dir. H.H. Uhlig Corrosion Lab. MIT, Cambridge, 1975—. Shell Disting. prof. materials sci. and engring., 1983-88, dir. Materials Processing Ctr., 1984-91; co-founder ALTRAN Materials Engring. Corp., Boston, 1992—. Mem. tech. adv. bd. Modell Devel. Corp., Framingham, Mass., 1987-94; sci. advisor com. on sci. and tech. U.S. Ho. of Reps., 1982-83; chmn. ad hoc com. Mass. Advanced Materials Ctr., Boston, 1985—; mem. adv. bd. Mass. Office Sci. and Tech.; co-PI, NSF/SSI project PALMS; chmn. MIT Coun. on Primary and Secondary Edn. Editor: Surface Effects in Crystal Plasticity, 1977, Atomistics of Fracture, 1983, Chemistry and Physics of Fracture, 1987, Advances in Mechanics and Physics of Fracture, 1981, 83, 86; contbr. articles to profl. jours. Recipient sr. scientist award Humboldt Found., 1974-75, David Ford McFarland award Pa. State U., 1986; named Henry Krumb lectr. AIME, 1984, Disting. Alumnus, Ohio State U. Coll. Engring., 1991, hon. alumnus MIT, 1992; Centennial fellow Coll. Earth and Mineral Scis., Pa. State U., 1996. Fellow Am. Soc. Metals Internat. (govt. and pub. affairs com. 1984), Nat. Assn. Corrosion Engrs. (A.B. Campbell award 1971, Willis R. Whitney award 1994); mem. New Eng. Sci. Tchrs. (founder, co-chmn.), Nat. Acad. Engring., Am. Acad. Arts and Scis., Nat. Materials Adv. Bd., Masons. Roman Catholic. Office: MIT Materials Sci & Engring 77 Mass Ave Rm 8202 Cambridge MA 02139-4307

LATCHUM, JAMES LEVIN, federal judge; b. Milford, Del., Dec. 23, 1918; s. James H. and Ida Mae (Robbins) L.; m. Elizabeth Murray McArthur, June 16, 1943; children: Su-Allan, Elizabeth M. AB cum laude, Princeton U., 1940; JD, U. Va., 1946. Bar: Va. 1942, Del. 1947. Assoc. Berl, Potter & Anderson, Wilmington, 1946-53, partner, 1953-68; judge U.S. Dist. Ct. Del., Wilmington, 1968-73, chief judge, 1973-83, sr. judge, 1983—. New Castle County atty. Del. Hwy. Dept., 1948-50; asst. U.S. atty., 1950-53; atty. Del. Interstate Hwy. Div., 1955-62, Delaware River and Bay Authority, 1962-68 Chmn. New Castle County Democratic Com., 1953-56, Wilmington City Com., 1959-63. Served to maj. Insp. Gen. Corps AUS, 1942-46, PTO. Mem. ABA, Del. Bar Assn., Va. Bar Assn., Order of Coif, Sigma Nu Phi. Clubs: Wilmington, Univ. Presbyterian. Office: US Dist Ct 844 N King St # 34 Wilmington DE 19801-3519

LATHAM, JAMES RICHARD, research scientist; b. Pomona, Calif., July 1, 1946; s. James Richard and Norma Elizabeth (Mills) L.; m. Pamela June Staley Latham, Aug. 31, 1968, 1 child, Joan Elizabeth Latham. AS in Electronics and Computer Tech., AS in Electronics and Telecom. Sys., Las Positas Coll., Livermore, Calif., 1999; student, Chabot Coll., Hayward, Calif., 1965-68, U. Calif., Berkeley, 1964-65. Technician Coast Mfg./Hexel Co., Livermore, Calif., 1966-69, Crown Zellerbach Co., San Leandro, 1969-70; sr. rsch. technician Kaiser Aluminum & Chem. Corp., Pleasanton, 1970-82; sr. technician Clorox Tech. Ctr., 1982-99; sr. info. systems technician Clorox Svcs. Co., 1999—; asst. aux. comms. svc. officer Calif. Dept. Emergency Svcs., 2001—02. Patentee in field. Asst. ACS officer Calif. State DES, 2001—. Named Merit Scholarship Finalist; recipient Naval Res. Officers Training Corp. scholarship. Mem. Am. Chemical Soc. Div. Chemical Technicians (treas. 1993-94), Am. Radio Relay League (asst. sect. mgr. 2000—, dist. emergency coord. 2001—), Livermore Amateur Radio Klub (sec. 1997), Alameda County Sheriff's Comms. Team (asst. ops. officer 1999-2000, ops. officer 2001—). Mem. Lds Ch. Avocations: sailing, amateur radio (KE6QJV).

LATHAM, JOSEPH AL, JR. lawyer; b. Kinston, N.C., Sept. 16, 1951; s. Joseph Al and Margaret Lee (Tyson) L.; m. Elaine Frances Kramer, Dec. 19, l981; children: Aaron Joshua, Adam Daniel. BA, Yale U., 1973; JD, Vanderbilt U., 1976. Bar: Calif. 1976, U.S. Dist. Ct. (cen. dist.) Calif. 1977, U.S. Ct. Appeals (9th cir.) 1977, U.S. Dist. Ct. (no. and so. dists.) Calif. 1978, Ga. 1980, U.S. Dist. Ct. (no. dist.) Ga. 1981, U.S. Ct. Appeals (5th and 11th cirs.) 1981, U.S. Dist. Ct. (mid. dist.) Ga. 1982, D.C. 1984. Assoc. Paul, Hastings, Janofsky & Walker, Orange County and L.A., 1976-80, Atlanta, 1980-83, ptnr. Orange County and L.A., 1987—; chief counsel to bd. mem. NLRB, Washington, l983-85; staff dir. U.S. Commn. on Civil Rights, 1985-86. Instr. advanced profl. program U. So. Calif. Law Ctr., 1988, lectr. law, 1989—. Articles editor Vanderbilt Law Rev., 1975-76; editorial asst. Employment Discrimination Law, 2d edit., 1983; contbr. articles to Barron's, ABA Jour., Litigation, Employee Rels. Law Jour. Mem. Calif. Bar Assn., Ga. Bar Assn., D.C. Bar Assn., Order of Coif. Republican. Episcopalian. Office: Paul Hastings Janofsky & Walker 555 S Flower St Fl 23 Los Angeles CA 90071-2300

LATHAM, JOSEPH WILLIAM, judge; b. June 13, 1947; MPA, JD, Syracuse U., 1974. Surrogate ct. judge Steuben County, Bath, N.Y., 1997, County Ct. judge, Family Ct. judge, acting Supreme Ct. judge, 1999—. Chmn. bd. trustees N.Y. State Supreme Ct. Libr., Bath.

LATHAM, JOYCE EILEEN, writer/editor, poet, photojournalist; b. Lexington, Ky., Apr. 19, 1943; d. Henry Cooper and Lucy (Duncan) L. BA, U. Ky., 1967; postgrad., Swarthmore Coll., 1981, Am. U., 1982, Johns Hopkins U., 1990-93. Pub. mgr. NSF, 1981-93, U.S. Dept. Interior, 1993-96. Freelance clients include FDA, NIMH, AARP, Am. Diabetes Assn., Johns Hopkins U. Press, Peace Corps, Smithsonian Instn., Sci. mag., Nat. Trust Hist. Preservation, George Washington U., U. Md. Med Sch., Ralph Nader groups, World Bank, Washington, Balt., Phila., 1972-81, 96—. Author: Runaway Youth in the Washington (D.C.) Area, 1974; author: (newsletter) Integrated Sr. Care, 1997-98; editor Intro to Health Planning, 1978, Econ. Benefits of Preserving Older Buildings, 1977; chair, editl. bds. 3 fed. newsletters, 1987-93, video narrator, 1991; film and book reviewer Video Times, Washington Living, Wilson Quar., Jour. Pop Culture; contbr. poetry to anthologies, jours. Union Steward Am. Fedn. Govt. Employees, 1972-73, 92; co-founder 1st child care ctr., 1st union local HUD, 1972; co-leader media project, NOW and Fed.

Comm. Commn., 1972-73; leader D.C. neighborhood crime control project, 1977; presenter testimony on nursing homes, Washington City Coun. subcom., 1987; nursing home ombudsman, 1985-93. Recipient 14 awards Soc. Tech. Comms., Nat. Assn. Govt. Comms., 1982-92, 6 awards for vol. cmty. svcs. AARP and others. Mem. AARP, Amnesty Internat. Democrat. Roman Catholic. Avocations: poetry, pottery, film, animals. E-mail: jlcomm@erols.com.

LATHAM, LAVONNE MARLYS, physical education educator; b. Garrison, Iowa, Mar. 17, 1942; d. Harry August and Vona Irene (Loveless) Hilmer; m. Robert Allen Latham Jr., July 21, 1979. BA, U. Iowa, 1964; postgrad., No. Ill. U., 1985, Western Ill. U., 1970-88, Bemidji State U., 1979. Cert. tchr., Ill. Tchr. phys. edn., elem. computer coord. Erie (Ill.) Community Unit 1, 1964—. Head counselor Camp Lenore Owaissa, Hinsdale, Mass., 1964-78. Mem. NEA, AAHPER, Ill. Assn. Health, Phys. Edn. and Recreation, U. Iowa Alumni Assn., Ill. Edn. Assn., Erie Tchrs. Assn. (pres. 1982-83), Nat. Audubon Soc., Nature Conservancy, Delta Kappa Gamma. Baptist. Avocations: violin, computers, photography, travel, outdoor activities. Home: 1002 6th St Erie IL 61250 Office: Erie Community Unit 1 605 6th Ave Erie IL 61250-9452

LATHAM, PATRICIA HORAN, lawyer; b. Hoboken, N.J., Sept. 5, 1941; d. Patrick John and Rosemary (Moller) Horan; m. Peter Samuel Latham, June 12, 1965; children: John Horan, Kerry Patricia. BA, Swarthmore Coll., 1963; JD, U. Chgo., 1966. Bar: D.C. 1967, U.S. Dist. Ct. D.C. 1967, U.S. Ct. Appeals 1967, U.S. Supreme Ct. 1970, Va. 1989, U.S. Dist. Ct. (ea. dist.) Va. 1989, U.S. Dist. Ct. Md. 1991. Assoc. Fried, Frank, Harris, Shriver & Kampelman, Washington, 1966-69; atty. Office of Gen. Counsel, SEC, 1969-71; assoc. Martin & Smith, 1971—, ptnr., 1974-85, Latham & Latham, Washington, 1986—. Lectr. Columbus Sch. Law, Cath. U. Am., Washington, 1978-92; mem. panel of arbitrators N.Y. Stock Exch., 1985—; co-founder, co-dir. Nat. Ctr. Law and Learning Disabilities, 1992—; mem. disability adv. com. GED Testing Svc., 1999—. Co-author: Attention Deficit Disorder and the Law, 1992, Attention Deficit Disorder and the Law, 2d edit., 1997, Learning Disabilities and the Law, 1993, Learning Disabilities and the Law, 2d edit., 2000, Succeeding in the Workplace, 1994, Higher Education Services for Students with Learning Disabilities and Attention Deficit Disorder: A Legal Guide, 1994, Documentation and the Law, 1996, Tales from the Workplace, 1997, Terrorism and the Law: Bringing Terrorists to Justice, 2002; contbg. author: ADD and the College Student, 1993, contbg. author: A Comprehensive Guide to ADD in Adults, 1995, contbg. author: Managing Attention and Learning Disorders in Late Adolescence and Adulthood, 1996, contbg. author: Textbook of Pediatric Neuropsychiatry, 1998, contbg. author: Learning Disabilities and Employment, 1997, contbg. author: ADD in Children and Adults, 1999. Co-founder, trustee Beacon Coll., 1989-93, chmn. bd. trustees, 1990-92; mem. adv. bd. Disability Law Reporter Svc., 1996—. Mem.: ABA, Learning Disabilities Assn. Am. (nat. adv. bd. 1996—2000, nat. bd. dirs. 2000—), Nat. Attention Deficit Disorders Assn. (bd. dirs. 1993—98, nat. adv. bd. 1998—), Am. Arbitration Assn. (panel arbitrators and mediators 1982—), Va. Bar Assn., DC Bar Assn., Ft. Myer and Ft. McNair Club. Roman Catholic. Home: 7000 Loch Edin Ct Potomac MD 20854-4844

LATHAM, PETER SAMUEL, lawyer; b. Boston, July 23, 1940; s. Earl Gansen and Margaret (Perrier) L.; m. Patricia Ann Horan, Sept. 5, 1941; children: John Horan, Kerry Patricia. BA with honors, Swarthmore Coll., 1962; LLB, U. Pa., 1965. Bar: D.C. 1966, U.S. Ct. Appeals (D.C. cir.) 1982, U.S. Dist. Ct. Md. 1991. Atty. SEC, Washington, 1965-66; assoc. firm Vom Baur, Coburn, Simmons & Turtle, 1969-71; mem. firm Wachtel, Ross and Matzkin, 1971-80; ptnr. Latham & Latham and predecessor firms, 1980—. Arbitrator Am. Arbitration Assn., 1978—. Author: Government Contract Disputes, 1981, 86; co-author: Attention Deficit Disorder and the Law: A Guide for Advocates, 1992, Learning Disabilities and the Law, 1993, Succeeding in the Workplace, 1994, Higher Education Services for Students with Learning Disabilities and Attention Deficit Disorder: A Legal Guide, 1994, Documentation and the Law, 1996, Tales from the Workplace, 1997, Attention Deficit Disorder and the Law, 2d edit., 1997, Learning Disabilities and the Law, 2d edit., 2000, Terrorism and the Law-Bringing Terrorists to Justice, 2002; contbg. author ADD and the College Student, 1993, A Comprehensive Guide to ADD in Adults, 1995, Managing Attention and Learning Disorders in Late Adolescence and Adulthood, 1996, Textbook of Pediatric Neuropsychiatry, 1998, Learning Disabilities and Employment, 1997, ADD in Children and Adults, 1999; producer, dir. The ABC's of ADD, other videos on legal topics. Co-founder, trustee Beacon Coll., 1989-93; co-founder Nat. Ctr. for Law and Learning Disabilities. Lt. USN, 1966-69. Decorated Navy Achievement medal with combat V. Mem. ABA, Nat. Attention Deficit Disorders Assn. (bd. dirs. 1993-97), DC Procurement Reform Taskforce (mem. Alternate Dispute Resolution subcom. 1995—), Ft. Myer and Ft. McNair Club. Republican. Roman Catholic. Avocations: tennis, swimming. Home: 7000 Loch Edin Ct Potomac MD 20854-4844 Office: Latham and Latham PO Box 40157 Washington DC 20016-0157

LATHAM, TOM, congressman; b. Hampton, Iowa, July 14, 1948; s. Willard and Evelyn L.; m. Kathy Swinson, 1975; children: Justin, Jennifer, Jill. Student, Watrburg Coll., Iowa State U. Bank teller, bookkeeper, Brush, Colo., 1970-72; ind. ins. agent Fort Lupton, 1972-74; mktg. rep. Hartford Ins. Co., Des Moines, 1974-76; with Latham Seed Co., Alexander, Iowa, 1976—, now v.p., co-owner; mem. 104th-106th Congress from 5th Iowa dist., 1994—. Sec. Republican Party of Iowa; rep. 5th dist. Republican State Ctrl. com.; co-chair Francklin County Republican Ctrl. com.; whip Iowa del. Republican Nat. Conv., 1992. Past chair Franklin County Extension Coun.; mem. Nazareth Lutheran Ch., past pres.; citizens adv. coun. Iowa State U. Mem. Am. Soybean Assn., Am. Seed Trade Assn., Iowa Farm Bur. Fedn., Iowa Soybean Assn., Iowa Corn Growers Assn., Iowa Seed Assn., Agribusiness Assn. of Iowa. Lutheran. Office: US House Reps 440 Cannon Hob Washington DC 20515-1505*

LATHAM, WELDON HURD, lawyer; b. Bklyn., Jan. 2, 1947; s. Aubrey Geddes and Avril (Hurd) L.; m. Constantia Beecher, Aug. 8, 1948; children: Nicole Marie, Brett Weldon. BA, Howard U., 1968; JD, Georgetown U., 1971; postgrad., George Washington U., 1975-76. Bar: D.C. 1972, U.S. Ct. Appeals (D.C. cir.) 1972, U.S. Ct. Mil. Appeals 1974, U.S. Ct. Claims 1975, U.S. Supreme Ct. 1975, Va. 1981, U.S. Ct. Appeals (fed. cir.) 1988. Mgmt. cons. Checchi & Co., Washington, 1968-71; atty. Covington & Burling, 1971-73; sr. atty. Fed. Energy Adminstrn., 1974; asst. gen. counsel Exec. Office Pres. Office Mgmt. and Budget The White House, 1974-76; atty. Hogan & Hartson, 1976-79; gen. dep. asst. sec. HUD, 1979-81; v.p., gen. counsel Sterling Sys., Inc. (subs. PRC.); exec. asst., counsel to chmn., CEO and assoc. gen. counsel Planning Rsch. Corp., McLean, Va., 1981-86; mng. ptnr. Reed, Smith, Shaw & McClay, 1986-91; sr. ptnr. Shaw Pittman, Washington, 1992-2000; sr. ptnr., practice area leader corp. diversity counseling Holland & Knight, 2000—. Adj. prof. Howard U. Law Sch., Washington, 1972-82; guest prof. U. Va., Charlottesville, 1976-90; mem. Va. Govs. Bus. and Industry Adv. Com. on Crime Prevention, 1983-85, Va. Govs. Regulatory Reform Adv. Bd., 1982-84; chmn. task force SBA, 1982; legal counsel Md. Mondale for Pres. Campaign, 1984; mem. editorial adv. bd. Washington Bus. Jour., 1985-87; gen. counsel Nat. Coalition Minority Bus., 1993—; trustee The Am. Univ., 1999; bd. dirs. Metro Washington Airports Authority, Telecomms. Sys., Inc.; bd. govs. Joint Ctr. Polit. and Econ. Studies, 1998--. Columnist Minority Bus. Entrepreneur Mag., 1991—, Diversity Jour., 2002--; mem. editl. bd. Washington Bus. Jour., 1985-87. Washington steering com. NAACP Legal Def. Fund, 1975-95, Fairfax County Airports Adv. Com., 1987-88; bd. dirs., gen. counsel Northern Va. Minority Bus. and Profl. Assn., 1985-92; trustee Va. Commonwealth U., Richmond, 1986-90, George Mason U., Fairfax, Va., 1990-94; bd. dirs. Washington Urban League, 1986-90, U. D.C. Found., 1982-87, Washington Coun. Lawyers, 1973, Profl. Svcs. Coun., 1983-88, Minority Bus. Enterprise Legal Def. and Edn. Fund, 1989-91, Wash. Hosp. Ctr. Found., 1996-98; appointee Greater Washington Bd. Trade, Blue Ribbon Task Force on Rule, 1985-86, bd. dirs., exec. com., chmn. regional affairs com., corp. sec. Greater Wash. Bd. Trade, 1990-95; adv. bd. First Union Nat. Bank, 1995-99; civilian aide to Sec. of Army, 1995-2000; mem. Small Bus. Adminstrn. Nat. Adv. Coun., 1993—, Burger King Corp. Diversity Action Coun., 1996-98, Diversity Best Practices Coun., 2001--, Md. Econ. Devel. Commn., 1996-98, Gov. Bd. Transition Team, 1995, Dem. Nat. Com., 1996, Platform Drafting Com., 1996; prin. coun. for Excellence in Govt., 1989-95; at-large mem. Dem. Nat. Com., 2001--; mayor D.C. Internat. Ins. Adv. Commn., 1994-95; chmn. D.C. Mayors Bus. Adv. Coun., 1994-96; vice-chmn. Dem. Bus. Coun. DNC, 1994-98; co-chmn. UNCF Sportsfest Fundraiser, 1994; hon. vice-chmn. Clinton-Gore Campaign, 1996; mem. corp. adv. coun. Congrl. Black Caucus Found., 1999—; gen. counsels Honors Program Office Sec. Capt. USAF, 1973-74. Recipient SES Effective Mgr. award HUD, 1980, Nat. Assn. for Equal Achievement Opportunity in Higher Edn. award, 1987, A. Philip Randolph award Amtrak, 2001. Mem. ABA (vice-chmn. subcom. pub. contract law sect. 1988-93), Fed. Bar Assn., Nat. Bar Assn., D.C. C. of C. (gen. counsel 1979), State Va. Bar Assn., Washington Bar Assn.(elected to Hall of Fame, 2001), Bar Assn. D.C., Nat. Contract Mgmt. Assn., Econ. Club Washington. Home: 7004 Natelli Woods Ln Bethesda MD 20817-3924 Office: Holland & Knight LLP 2099 Pennsylvania Ave NW Washington DC 20006-1813

LATHAM, WILLIAM PETERS, composer, former educator; b. Shreveport, La., Jan. 4, 1917; s. Lawrence L. and Eugenia (Peters) L.; m. Joan Seyler, Apr. 18, 1946; children: Leslie Virginia, William Peters, Carol Jean. Student, Asbury Coll., Wilmore, Ky., 1933-35, Cin. Conservatory Music, 1936-38; BSc in Music Edn, U. Cin., 1938; BMus, Coll. Music Cin., 1940, MusM, 1941; PhD, Eastman Sch. Music, 1951; pupil composition with, Eugene Goossens, Howard Hanson, Herbert Elwell. Mem. faculty N. Tex. State Tchrs. Coll., 1938-39, Eastern Ill. State Tchrs. Coll., 1946, State Coll. Iowa, 1946-65, prof. music, 1959-65; prof. composition Sch. Music, U. N. Tex., Denton, 1965-84, dir. grad. studies, 1969-84, disting. prof., 1978-84, prof. emeritus, 1984—. Composer numerous works, 1938—, including works for orch., band, chorus, chamber groups, soloists, one opera and one ballet; compositions since 1980 include (chorus) Gaudeamus Academe, 1981, Bitter Land, 1985, My Heart Sings, 1988, Missa Novella, 1989, Only in Texas!, 1994; (chamber music) Ion, The Rhapsode for clarinet and piano, 1985, Metaphors, three songs for soprano, 1988, A Green Voice, cantata for soprano and tenor, 1989, (three songs for high voice) Requiem for My Love, 1994, (orch.) The Sacred Flame, Cantata for Baritone and Orch., 1990, Excelsior K-2 for Orch., 1994, (band) Suite Summertime, three movements for band, 1995,, Y2K, The New Millennium March for Concert Band, 1999 (scenic cantata for orch., chorus, soloists and ballet) Orpheus out West, 1997. Served to 2d lt. AUS, 1942-46. Scholar in composition Cin. Coll. Music, 1939-41; recipient numerous awards and commns. Mem. ASCAP (ann. awards 1962—), Coll. Mus. Soc., Phi Mu Alpha, Pi Kappa Lambda. Home: PO Box 50373 Denton TX 76206-0373

LATHE, ROBERT EDWARD, management and financial consultant; b. Balt., Apr. 8, 1945; s. Warren Calvin Sr. and Margaret Mary (Cavey) L.; m. Hermina Yeghnazarian, Apr. 13, 1967; children: Michelle Gayaneh, Mellina Margaret. MSc in Mgmt., U. Dublin Trinity Coll., 1985. Metrology/field engr. Bendix Field Engring. Corp., Balt., 1967-68; quality assurance supr. space seismology lab. Bendix Aerospace Systems Divsn., Ann Arbor, Mich., 1968-72; programs mgr. Iran Aircraft Industries, Tehran, 1972-76; mgmt. cons. Alexander Proudfoot Co., Chgo., 1977-78; program mgr., field engr. Harris-PRD Electronics Divsn., Syosset, N.Y. & Isfahan, Iran, 1978-80; ops. dir. Airmotive Ireland Ltd., Dublin, 1980-84; project mgr. Handley-Walker Co., Inc., Valencia, Calif., 1986-87; owner, pres. Hyrel Bus. Svcs., Glendale, 1987-90; fin. planner, investment advisor IDS Fin. Svcs. Inc., 1990-94; co-founder, sr. ptnr. Calif. Connection, 1994—. Sgt. USAF, 1963-67, Vietnam. Mem. Am. Legion, Internat. Platform Assn. Avocations: microcomputers, public speaking, golf, swimming, ten-pin bowling. Home: 11014 Mountair Ave Tujunga CA 91042 E-mail: relathe@aol.com., ccesthetique@aol.com.

LATHI, BHAGAWANDAS PANNALAL, retired electrical engineering educator; b. Bhokar, Maharashtr, India, Dec. 3, 1933; came to U.S., 1956; s. Pannalal Rupchand and Tapi Pannalal (Indani) L.; m. Rajani Damodardas Mundada, July 27, 1962; children: Anjali, Shishir. BEEE, Poona U., 1955; MSEE, U. Ill., 1957; PhD in Elec. Engring., Stanford U., 1961. Rsch. asst. U. Ill., Urbana, 1956-57, Stanford (Calif.) U., 1957-60; rsch. engr. Gen. Electric Co., Syracuse, N.Y., 1960-61; cons. to semicondr. industry India, 1961-62; assoc. prof. elec. engring. Bradley U., Peoria, Ill., 1962-69, U.S. Naval Acad., Annapolis, Md., 1969-72; prof. elec. engring. Campinas (Brazil) State U., 1972-78, Calif. State U., Sacramento, 1979—2001, prof. emeritus, 2002—. Vis. prof. U. Iowa, Owa City, 1979. Author: Signals, Systems and Communication, 1965, Communication Systems, 1968 (transl. into Japanese 1977), Random Signals and Communication Theory, 1968, Teoria Signalow I Ukladow Telekomunikacyjnych, 1970, Sistemy Telekomunikacyjne, 1972, Signals, Systems and Controls, 1974, Sistemas de Comunicacion, 1974, 86, Sistemas de Comunicacao, 1978, Modern Digital and Analog Communication Systems, 1983, 89 (transl. into Japanese 1986, 90), Signals and Systems, 1987, Linear Systems and Signals, 1992, Signal Processing and Linear Systems, 1998; contbr. articles to profl. jours. Fellow IEEE. Office: Calif State U 6000 J St Sacramento CA 95819-2605

LATHON, SHERAINE, clergyman; b. Chicago Heights, Feb. 20, 1952; d. Roosevelt Willingham and Norma L. Cobb; m. Willie Lathon, Jr., June 11, 1983; children: Eric, Christopher. AAS, Prairie State Jr. Coll., 1972; BS, Friends Internat. U., 1992, MS, 1994, PhD, 1997. Ordained to ministry, 1999. Collection mgr. Donnelley Directory, Chgo., 1973-87; ch. adminstr. Liberty Temple Full Gospel Ch., 1987—, sr. pastor, 1999—. Assoc. prof. Logos Ministerial Tng. Inst., Friends Internat. U. Co-author: Recovery, 2000. Sec.-treas. Bushido-Kan Acad.; pres. Sheraine Lathon Evangelistic Ministries. Mem. NAFE. Office: Liberty Temple Full Gospel Ch 2233 W 79th St Chicago IL 60620-5803 E-mail: slathon1063@aol.com.

LATHROP, IRVIN TUNIS, retired academic dean, educator; b. Platteville, Wis., Sept. 23, 1927; s. Irvin J. and Marian (Johnson) L.; m. Eleanor M. Kolar, Aug. 18, 1951; 1 son, James I. BS, Stout State Coll., 1950; MS, Iowa State U., 1954, PhD, 1958. Tchr. Ottumwa (Iowa) High Sch., 1950-55; mem. faculty Iowa State U., 1957-58, Western Mich. U., 1958-59, Calif. State Coll., 1959-88, prof. indsl. arts, 1966-88, chmn. dept. indsl. edn., 1969-88, assoc. dean extended edn., 1978-88, prof. emeritus, 1988—. Cons. Naval Ordnance Lab., Corona, Calif., 1961-63 Author: (with Marshall La Cour) Photo Technology, 1966, rev. edit., 1977, Photography, 1979, rev. edit., 1992, The Basic Book of Photography, 1979, Laboratory Manual for Photo Technology, 1973, (with John Lindbeck) General Industry, 1969, rev. edit., 1977, 86, (with Robert Kunst) Photo-Offset, 1979; edit. cons. Am. Tech. Soc; contbr. articles to profl. jours. Mem. adv. com. El Camino and Orange Coast Coll.; mem. Orange County Grand Jury, 1989-90, Orange County Juvenile Justice Commn., 1991—. Mem. Nat. Soc. for Study Edn., Am. Council Indsl. Arts Tchr. Edn., Am. Vocat. Assn., Nat. Assn. Indsl. and Tech. Tchrs., Internat. Tech. Assn., Am. Ednl. Research Assn., Epsilon Pi Tau, Psi Chi, Phi Delta Kappa, Phi Kappa Phi. Home: PO Box 3430 Laguna Hills CA 92654-3430 Office: 1250 N Bellflower Blvd Long Beach CA 90840-0006 E-mail: ilathrop@ix.netcom.com.

LATHROP, KAYE DON, nuclear scientist, educator; b. Bryan, Ohio, Oct. 8, 1932; s. Arthur Quay and Helen Venita (Hoos) L.; m. Judith Marie Green, June 11, 1957; children: Braxton Landess, Scottfield Michael. BS, U.S. Mil. Acad., 1955; MS, Calif. Inst. Tech., 1959, PhD, 1962. Staff mem. Los Alamos Sci. Lab., 1962-67; group leader methods devel. Gen. Atomic Co., San Diego, 1967-68; asst. div. leader theoretical div. Los Alamos Sci. Lab., 1973-75, assoc. div. leader reactor safeguards and reactor safety and tech. div., 1975-77, alt. div. leader energy div., 1977-78, div. leader computer sci. and svcs. div., 1978-79, assoc. dir. for engring. scis., 1979-84; assoc. lab dir., prof. applied rsch. Stanford Linear Accelerator Ctr. Stanford U., 1984-94, prof. emeritus, 1994—. Vis. prof. U. N.Mex., 1964-65, adj. prof., 1966-67; guest lectr. IAEA, 1969; mem. adv. com. reactor physics ERDA, 1973-77; mem. reactor physics vis. com. Argonne Nat. Lab., 1978-83; mem. mgmt. adv. com. y-12 divsn. Union Carbide Corp., 1979-82; mem. engring. nat. adv. com. U. Mich., 1983-92; mem. steering com. Joint MIT-Idaho Nat. Engring. Lab. Rsch. Program, 1985-89; mem. external adv. com. Nuclear Tech. and Engring. divsn. Los Alamos Sci. Lab., 1988-91, 92-93; mem. com. on material control and acctg. for spl. nuclear materials NRC, 1988-89; mem. energy rsch. adv. bd. panel on new prodn. reactor tech. assessment Dept. of Energy, 1988; mem. electric power/energy sys. engring. peer com. NAE, 1992-94, chair, 1994, mem. com. on membership, 1994-97, mem. presdl. nominating com., 1996-97, mem. membership policy com., 1997-99; chair divsn. rev. com. tech. and safety assessment divsn. Los Alamos Nat. Lab., 1994-97, mem. divsn. rev. com. tech. and safety assessment, 1997-99, divsn. rev. com. applied theoretical and computational physics divsn., 1997—; mem. burn code rev. panel Dept. Energy, 2000—; mem. U. Calif. Pres.'s Coun. on Nat. Labs., 1995-99, mem. sci. and tech. panel, 1993-99, mem. nat. sec. panel, 1996-99. Author reports, papers, chpts. to books; mem. editorial adv. bd. Progress in Nuclear Energy, 1983-85 Served to 1st lt. C.E. U.S. Army, 1955-58. Spl. fellow AEC, 1958-61; R.C. Baker Found. fellow, 1961-62; recipient E.O. Lawrence Meml. award ERDA, 1976; Disting. Svc. award Los Alamos Nat. Lab., 1984 Fellow Am. Nuclear Soc. (chmn. math. and computation div. 1970-71, nat. dir. 1973-76, 79-82, treas. 1977-79, Outstanding Performance award 1980); mem. Am. Phys. Soc., Nat. Acad. Engring. Republican. Episcopalian. Home: 190 Cedar Ln E Ridgway CO 81432 E-mail: klathrop@independence.net.

LATHROP, LAWRENCE ERWIN , JR. retired business owner, retired state forest ranger; b. L.A., Dec. 4, 1942; s. Lawrence Erwin and Anna Maxine (Cypert) L.; m. Elaine Dorothy Baudin, May 16, 1964; 1 child, Lawrence Erwin III. AA in Forestry, Lassen Coll., Susanville, Calif., 1968; BA in Pub. Adminstrn., U. San Francisco, 1976. Cert. fire investigator, coll. instr. Forest firefighter Calif. Dept. Forestry and Fire Protection, Santa Clara, 1961, fire apparatus engr. Belmont and Yreka, 1962-64, fire capt. Riverside County, 1964-73, fire prevention officer Clearlake, 1973, state forest ranger I Ione, 1973-82, state forest ranger II Susanville, 1982-93, retired, 1993; cons. pvt. practice Calif., 1993—2000; co-owner Secret Air Aviation Svcs., Janesville, 1994—2000; owner Larry Lathrop Enterprises, 1993—2000. Fire investigation and tng. cons. Nev. Dept. Forestry, Carson City, 1985—2000, U.S. Bur. Land Mgmt., Elko and Winnemuca, Nev., 1985—2000. Author, editor: Tailgate Safety Bull., 1984—91; author: numerous in-svc. tng. programs, including Helicopter Safety, Air Attack, Powerline Inspections, 1978—82. Advisor Demolay, Amador County, Calif., 1976-78; active PTA, Amador County, 1975-82, Lassen County Arson Task Force, 1985-93, State Arson Unit, 1974-93. Master: Masons; mem.: Elks. Republican. Presbyterian. Avocations: hunting, fishing, flying. Home: PO Box 717 Janesville CA 96114-0717

LATHROP, MITCHELL LEE, lawyer; b. L.A., Dec. 15, 1937; s. Alfred Lee and Barbara (Mitchell) L.; m. Lynn Mara Dalton; children: Christin Lorraine Newlon, Alexander Mitchell, Timothy Trewin Mitchell. BSc, U.S. Naval Acad., 1959; JD, U. So. Calif., 1966. Bar: D.C. 1966, Calif. 1966, U.S. Supreme Ct. 1969, N.Y. 1981; cert. arbitrator Nat. Arbitration Forum, ARIAS-US; cert. civil trial specialist Nat. Bd. Trial Advocacy. Dep. counsel L.A. County, Calif., 1966-68; with Brill, Hunt, DeBuys and Burby, L.A., 1968-71; ptnr. Macdonald, Halsted & Laybourne, L.A. and San Diego, 1971-80; sr. ptnr. Rogers & Wells, N.Y.C., San Diego, 1980-86; sr. ptnr., exec. com. Adams, Duque & Hazeltine, L.A., San Francisco, N.Y.C., San Diego, 1986-94, firm chmn., 1992-94; sr. ptnr. Luce, Forward, Hamilton & Scripps, San Diego, N.Y.C., San Francisco, L.A., 1994—. Presiding referee Calif. Bar Ct., 1984-86, mem. exec. com., 1981-88; lectr. law Calif. Judges Assn., Practicing Law Inst. N.Y., Continuing Edn. of Bar, State Bar Calif., ABA, others. Author: State Hazardous Waste Regulation, 1991, Environmental Insurance Coverage, 1991, Insurance Coverage for Environmental Claims, 1992; mem. editl. bd. Def. Counsel Jour., 1997—; editl. bd., Jous. Ins. Coverage. Western Regional chmn. Met. Opera Nat. Coun., 1971—81, v.p., mem. exec. com., 1971—, now chmn; trustee Honnold Libr. at Claremont Colls., 1972—80; sec. Music Ctr. Opera Assn., 1974—80; v.p. San Diego Opera Assn., 1985—89, pres.-elect, 1993, pres., 1994—96; bd. dirs. Music Ctr. Opera Assn., L.A., San Diego Opera Assn., 1980—, Met. Opera Assn., N.Y.C. Mem. ABA, N.Y. Bar Assn., Fed. Bar Assn., Fed. Bar Council, Calif. Bar Assn., D.C. Bar Assn., San Diego County Bar Assn. (chmn. ethics com. 1980-82, bd. dirs. 1982-85, v.p. 1985), Assn. Bus. Trial Lawyers, Am. Intellectual Property Law Assn., Assn. So. Calif. Def. Counsel, Los Angeles Opera Assos. (pres. 1970-72), Soc. Colonial Wars in Calif. (gov. 1970-72), Order St. Lazarus of Jerusalem, Friends of Claremont Coll. (dir. 1975-81, pres. 1978-79), Am. Bd. Trial Advocates, Judge Advocates Assn. (dir. Los Angeles chpt. 1974-80, pres. So. Calif. chpt. 1977-78), Internat. Assn. Def. Counsel, Brit. United Services Club (dir. Los Angeles 1973-75), Mensa Internat., Calif. Soc., S.R. (pres. 1977-79), Calif. Club (Los Angeles), Valley Hunt Club (Pasadena, Calif.), Met. Club (N.Y.C.), The Naval Club (London), Phi Delta Phi. Republican. Home: 3355 Valemont St San Diego CA 92106-2430 Office: Luce Forward Hamilton and Scripps 600 W Broadway Fl 26 San Diego CA 92101-3311 also: Citicorp Ctr 153 E 53rd St 26th Fl New York NY 10022-4611 E-mail: mlathrop@luce.com.

LATHROP, RICHARD HAROLD, computer science educator; b. San Luis Obispo, Calif., Oct. 20, 1954; s. Richard Grant and Ann Lathrop. BA, Reed Coll., 1978; MSEE, MIT, 1983, PhD, 1990. Prodn. control supr. U.S. Postal Svc., Anchorage, 1974-75; computer programmer Solid State Electronics, Lower Hutt, New Zealand, 1980; cons. Gould/AMI Rsch. Lab, Twain Harte, Calif., 1984-91; co-founder Arris Pharm. Corp., South San Francisco, 1989-93; rsch. scientist artificial intelligence lab. MIT, Cambridge, Mass., 1993-95; prof. computer sci. U. Calif., Irvine, 1995—, vice chair, 2000—02. Mem. sci. adv. bd. Combichem Inc., San Diego, 1997-99, Genformatics, San Diego, 2001-; reviewer U.S. Nat. Sci. Found., Washington, 1997-2000; reviewer U.S NIH, 2000-. Guest editor: IEEE Intelligent Systems, 2001; Contbr. articles to profl. jours. Tournament judge Mathcounts, Irvine, Calif., 1996—. Grad. fellow U.S. Nat. Sci. Found., 1980. Mem. Internat. Soc. Computational Biology (bd. dirs., treas. 1996—), Am. Assn. Artificial Intelligence (life). Avocations: calligraphy, sailing, hot tubbing, chess, SCUBA. Office: Info and Computer Sci Dept #3425 U Calif Irvine CA 92697-3425 E-mail: rickl@uci.edu.

LATHROP, ROBERT W, music educator; s. Ralph and Linda Lathrop; m. Merri-Lynn Lois Roques, Mar. 7, 1999. MusB Edn., Gordon Coll., Wenham, MA, 1993. Music tchr. Triton Regional H.S., Byfield, Mass., 1995—; music dir. Byfield Parish Ch., Georgetown, 1995. Mem.: Am. Choral Dirs. Assn., Music Educators Nat. Conf.

LATHROP, THOMAS ALBERT, language educator, educator; b. L.A., Apr. 18, 1941; s. Donald C. and Ethel M. (Challacombe) L.; m. Constance Ellen Cook, Aug. 30, 1969; 1 child, Aline. BA, UCLA, 1964, MA, 1965, PhD, 1970. Mem. faculty Romance langs. UCLA, 1964-66, U. Wyo., 1966-68, Transylvania U., 1973-76, Lafayette Coll., 1976-80; assoc. prof. Romance langs. U. Del., Newark, 1980—. Editor Juan de la Cuesta Hispanic Monographs, 1978—; co-editor The Cabrilho Press, 1974-89; pres. Linguatext, Ltd., 1989—; asst. editor Cervantes Bull. of the Cervantes Soc. Am., 1980-90. Author: The Legend of the Siete Infantes de Lara, 1972; (with F. Jensen) The Syntax of the Old Spanish Subjunctive, 1973, La Vie Saint Eustace, 2000; Espanol--Lengua y cultura de hoy, 1974; The Evolution of Spanish, 1980; De Acuerdo! and Tane Mejor, 1986; (with E Dias) Portugal, Lingua e Cultura, 1978, 2d edit., 1995, Curso de gramatica historica espanola, 1984, 89, (with E. Dias) Brasil: Lingua e Cultura, 1992, student edit. Don Quijote, others; editor: European Classics, 2001-. AID grantee, 1968; Nat. Endowment for Humanities grantee, 1976, 81; Gulbenkian Found. grantee, 1973; Del Amo Found. grantee, 1972. Mem. MLA, Cervantes Soc. Am., Internat. Assn. Hispanists, Am. Coun. on Tchg. of Fgn. Lag., Am. Assn. Tchrs. Spanish and Portugues. Home: 270 Indian Rd Newark DE 19711-5204 Office: U Del Dept Lang Newark DE 19716 E-mail: lathrop@udel.edu.

LATHROPE, DANIEL JOHN, law educator; BSBA, U. Denver, 1973; JD, Northwestern U., 1977; LLM, NYU, 1979. Bar: Ariz. 1977, Calif. 1978. Assoc. Evans, Kitchel & Jenckes, Phoenix, 1977-78; instr. law NYU, 1979-80; assoc. prof. U. Calif. Hastings Coll. Law, San Francisco, 1980-86, prof., 1986—. Assoc. acad. dean U. Calif. Hastings Coll. Law, San Francisco, 1986-87, acting dean, 1987-88, acad. dean, 1988-90; prof., assoc. dean, dir. grad. tax program U. Fla. Coll. Law, Gainesville, 1995-96. Co-author: (with Lind, Schwarz and Rosenberg) Fundamentals of Corporate Taxation, 5th edit., 2002, (with Lind, Schwarz and Rosenberg) Fundamentals of Business Enterprise Taxation, 1997, 2nd edit., 2002, (with Lind, Schwarz and Rosenberg) Fundamentals of Partnership Taxation, 6th edit., 2002, (with Schwarz) Black Letter on Federal Taxation of Corporations and Partnerships, 3d edit., 2002, (with Freeland, Lind and Stephens) Fundamentals of Federal Income Taxation, 12th edit., 2002; author: The Alternative Minimum Tax-Compliance and Planning with Analysis, 1994. Mem. Order of Coif, Beta Gamma Sigma.

LATIES, VICTOR GREGORY, psychology educator; b. Racine, Wis., Feb. 2, 1926; s. Simon Gregory and Rima (Kapnik) L.; m. Martha Ann Fisher, July 29, 1956; children: Nancy, Andrew, Claire. AB, Tufts U., 1949; PhD, U. Rochester, N.Y., 1954. Ford Found. teaching intern Brown U., 1954-55; instr., asst. prof. dept. pharmacology Johns Hopkins U. Sch. Medicine, 1955-65;

assoc. prof. U. Rochester Sch. Medicine and Dentistry, 1965-71, prof. dept. biophysics, psychology, pharmacology, 1971-93, dir. toxicology tng. program, 1978-91, 95-96, dir. environ. studies program, prof. dept. environ. medicine, 1992—. Mem. preclinical psychopharmacology research rev. com. NIMH, 1967-71; mem. bd. on toxicology and environ. health hazards Nat. Acad. Sci.-NRC, 1977-80, mem. toxicology info. program com., 1981-85; mem. sci. rev. com. for health research EPA, 1981-89. Editor: Jour. Exptl. Analysis of Behavior, 1972-76, exec. editor, 1966-72, 76—; editor: (with B. Weiss) Behavioral Toxicology, 1975, Behavioral Pharmacology, 1976; mem. editorial bd.: Jour. Pharmacology and Exptl. Therapeutics, 1965-71, Psychopharmacology, 1968-78, 81-89, The Behavior Analyst, 1980-82, Experimental and Clinical Psychopharmacology, 1993-99; contbr. articles to profl. jours. Served with USN, 1944-46. Fellow Am. Psychol. Assn. (pres. div. psychopharmacology 1968-69, div. exptl. analysis of behavior 1979-82, bd. sci. affairs 1983-85), Behavioral Pharmacology Soc. (pres. 1966-68), Am. Soc. Pharmacology and Exptl. Therapeutics, Assn. for Behavior Analysis, Soc. Toxicology, Am. Psychol. Soc., Soc. for Exptl. Analysis of Behavior (sec.-treas. 1966—). Home: 55 Dale Rd E Rochester NY 14625-2137 Office: U Rochester Medical Ctr Dept Environ Medicine Box EHSC Rochester NY 14642

LATIFUR RAHAMAN, RASUL BOAKSH, legal profession executive; b. Kushita, Bangladesh, Jan. 1, 1945; arrived in India, Jan. 3, 1945; s. Fazlur Rahman and Rabya Khatun Ruby Rabia Khatun; married; children: Rassel, Boaksel. Diploma, Kushtia Coll., 1963, LLB, 1966; M Commerce, Dhaka U., 1967. Headmaster Talberia High Sch., Kushtia Dist., 1961; head asst. Indsl. Promo Svcs., Dacca, 1966-67; income tax cons. Bangladesh Bar Assn., Segun Bagicha/Dacca, 1967-69; pres. Kushtia Income Tax Bar Assn., 1970-90, Padma Devel., Kushtia, 1980—. Chmn. Bangladesh Coms., Padma, Kushtia, 1971—; chmn. Cen. Capital, Padma; leader of party/chmn., Bangladesh Internat. Moisen Order Internat. Command Party, Padma, 1980—; chmn. Ctrl. Capital of Bangladesh, Padma, 299100; trade consulate Bangladesh Trade, Padma, 1980—; chmn. Bazar com., Padma. Mem. Pub. Libr., Kushtia, 1965-66. Office: The Income Tax Bar Assn B06000 Kushtia Padma Bangladesh

LATIMER, ALLIE B. retired lawyer; b. Coraopolis, Pa. d. Lawnye S. and Bennie Latimer BS, Hampton Inst., 1947; JD, Howard U., 1953, MDiv, 1986, DMin, 1988; LLM, Cath. U., 1958; postgrad., Am. U., 1960-61. Bar: N.C. bar 1955, D.C. bar 1960. Vol. in projects Am. Friends Service Com., N.J. and, Europe, 1948-49; correctional officer Fed. Reformatory for Women, Alderson, W.Va., 1949-51; personnel clk. NIH, Bethesda, 1953-55; realty officer Mitchell AFB, N.Y., 1955-56; with Office Gen. Counsel, GSA, Washington, 1957-76, chief counsel, after 1966, asst. gen. counsel, 1971-76, gen. counsel, 1977-87; asst. gen. counsel NASA, 1976-77; spl. counsel Gen. Svcs. Adminstrn., Washington, 1987-96. Past chmn. central office com. Fed. Women's Program, GSA; mem. membership and budget com. Health and Welfare Council, 1967-72 Bd. dirs. D.C. Mental Health Assn., pres., 1977-79; bd. dirs. Friendship House, Washington; elder Presbyn. Ch.; mem. com. on office of Gen. Assembly, Presbyn. Ch. USA; pres. Interacial Council, 1964-75; chmn. Presbyn. Econ. Devel. Corp., 1975-81; mem. governing bd. Nat. Council Chs. of Christ in U.S.A.; bd. trustees Johnson C. Smith Theol. Sem. Recipient GSA Sustained Superior Service award, 1959, Meritorious Service award, 1964, Commendable Service award, 1964, Pub. Service award, 1971, Outstanding Performance award, 1971, Presdl. Rank award, 1983, Disting. Service award, 1984. Mem. ABA, Nat. Bar Assn. (sec. 1966-74, Hall of Fame award 1999), Fed. Bar Assn., Washington Bar Assn. (Ollie M. Cooper award 1998), N.C. Bar Assn., Nat. Bar Found. (dir. 1970-71, pres. 1974-75), Hampton Alumni Assn. (pres. Washington chpt. 1970-71), Howard Law Alumni Assn. (v.p. 1962-63) alumni assns), Links (pres. Washington chpt. 1971-74, nat. v.p. 1976-80), Federally Employed Women (founder, 1st pres.) Home: 1721 S St NW Washington DC 20009-6117

LATIMER, HEATHER, writer; b. East Anglia, England; d. Robin and Jessie L.; m. Walther B. Neubauer, Aug. 24, 1957 (dec. Apr. 1976). Student, Pitmans Coll., London, 1943-46. Photographers Head & Shoulders model, London, 1946-53; asst. to pres. W.H. Schneider Advt., N.Y.C., 1965-67; patron rels. Met. Opera, 1968-70; asst. to dir. Bide-A-Wee Animal Protection Assn., 1970-72; contbg. editor Dogs Mag., 1972-77; freelance writer, 1971-94, Las Vegas, 1994—. Author: (novels) How to make Money as a professional Party Organizer in the Great Leisuretime Market, 1971, Tidypet: How to Make Your Dog an Indoor Toilet and Train Your Puppy or Grown Dog to Use It, 1972, Dogs: Everything You Need to Know to Care for Your Pet, 1979, Cats: Everything You Need to Know to Care for Your Pet, Louis Wain -- King of the Cat Artists, 1860-1939, 1982, One is Fun: Guide to a Happy and Rewarding Single Lifestyle, 1996, Is Forever Too Long?, 2d edit., 2000, Hospitality Jill/Hospitality Jack: How to Approach, Greet and Win Over Strangers in Groups, Twos and Ones: A Guide for Employees, Volunteers and Singles, 7 sects., 2000, How to be an Outstanding Tour Guide or Docent, 2001, The English Cat Artist: Louis Wain, 2002, (audio books) In the Eyes of the Cats, 1997, The Artist, 1992, Curse of the Painted Cats, 1994. Vol. docent N.Y. Botanical Garden, N.Y.C., 1989-94; pres. Internat. League N.Y., N.Y.C., 1957-67; docent Treasures of Russia and the Czars, 1998-99. Mem.: Nat. League of Am. Pen Women, English Speaking Union, Las Vegas Social Register, Princeton Univ. Club (N.Y.C.). Anglican. Avocation: ballroom dancing. Office: PO Box 27383 Las Vegas NV 89126-1383

LATIMER, JAMES HAROLD, percussionist, conductor, composer, consultant, educator; b. Tulsa, June 27, 1934; s. Sylvester and Maria Louise (Wilson) L. MusB, Ind. U., 1956; MusM, Boston U., 1964; postgrad., Harvard U., 1968. Instr., asst. dir. bands Fla. A&M U., Tallahassee, 1957-62; freelance performer Boston, 1963-68; prof. music-percussion U. Wis., Madison, 1968-99; music dir. Wis. Youth Symphony Orchs., 1972-78. Timpanist Madison Symphony Orch., 1968-99; clinician Ludwig Industries, Chgo., 1971—; condr. Capitol City Band, Madison, 1981—; marimbist Madison Marimba Quartet, 1981—; Fulbright lectr. Cairo Conservatoire, 1984-85; Commonwealth vis. prof. Radford (Va.) U., 1985-87. Percussionist Boston Pops Orch., 1968-74; contbr. Inquiring About Communities, 1971; composer, arranger various titles for music-percussion and bands. Mem. ASCAP, Percussive Arts Soc., Am. Fedn. Musicians, Wis. Federated Music Club (hon. life mem.), Rotary (Madison chpt.), Phi Mu Alpha, Kappa Kappa Psi, Phi Beta (hon.). Mem. Soc. Of Friends. Avocations: amateur radio, electronics, woodworking, collecting. Home: 4399 County Rd A Oregon WI 53575-2905

LATIMER, KENNETH ALAN, lawyer; b. Chgo., Oct. 26, 1943; s. Edward and Mary (Schiller) L.; m. Carole Ross, June 23, 1968; children: Cary, Darren, Wendy. BS, U. Wis., 1966; JD with honors, George Washington U., 1969. Bar: D.C. 1969, Ill. 1970. Atty. U.S. Office of Comptroller, Washington, 1969-70; assoc. Berger, Newmark & Fenchel, Chgo., 1970-74, ptnr., 1975-86, Holleb & Coff, Chgo., 1986-99, Duane, Morris LLP, Chgo., 1999—. Guest speaker Ill. Inst. for Continuing Legal Edn., Chgo., 1975-87; lectr. Banking Law Inst., 1996—. Pres. North Suburban Jewish Cmty. Ctr., Highland Park, Ill., 1985; bd. dirs. Jewish Cmty. Ctrs. Chgo., 1985-95. Mem. ABA Fellows, Ill. Bar Assn. (chmn. sect. coun. on comml. banking and bankruptcy 1990-91), ABA (com. on banking and comml. finance), Chgo. Bar Assn. (com. on fin. instns.), Comml. Fin. Assn. Ednl. Found. (founders coun.), Assn. Comml. Fin. Attys. (bd. regents), Am Coll. Comml. Fin Attys., Standard Club. Avocations: jogging, travel. Office: Duane Morris LLC 227 W Monroe St Ste 3400 Chicago IL 60606-5098 E-mail: kalatmer@duane.morris.com.

LATIMER, MARGARET PETTA, retired nutrition and dietetics educator; b. Sacramento, Aug. 17, 1932; d. Rosario and Helen (Sclafani) Petta; m. Westford Ramos Latimer, June 18, 1978. BS, U. Calif., Berkeley, 1954; MA, Calif. State U., Sacramento, 1982. Registered dietitian, Calif.; life teaching credential, Calif. Therapeutic dietitian U. Calif. Med. Ctr., San Francisco, 1955—65; dietitian Roseville (Calif.) Cmty. Hosp., 1966—67, Mercy San Juan Hosp., Carmichael, Calif., 1967—69; substitute tchr. San Juan Unified Sch. Dist., Sacramento, 1970—75, tchr. adult edn., 1971—74; instr. dietetics American River Coll., 1975—77, San Joaquin Delta Coll., Stockton, 1975—95; ret., 1995. Cons. dietitian, Sacramento, 1973-78. Mem.: AAUW (gourmet chmn. 1981—82, editor AAUW Book of Favorite Recipes 1982, membership treas. 1999—), Calif. Dietetic Assn. (pres. Golden Empire dist. 1974—75), Nutrition Today, Am. Dietetic Assn. Republican. Roman Catholic. Avocation: travel.

LATIMER, PAUL JERRY, non-destructive testing engineer; b. Springfield, Tenn., July 21, 1943; s. Paul Daniel and Juanita Inez (Richey) L.; m. Sylvia Susan Cole, June 6, 1966; children: Zachary Nathaniel, Matthew Jason. BS in Physics with honors, U. Tenn., 1966, MS in Physics, 1979, PhD in Physics, 1983. Devel. engr. Oak Ridge (Tenn.) Nat. Lab., 1980-81; faculty rsch. assoc. Ohio State U., Columbus, 1981; rsch. asst. U. Tenn., Knoxville, 1981-83; sr. rsch. engr. McDermott Techs. Inc. R&D divsn. Lynchburg Rsch. Ctr., Va., 1983-98; sr. engr. MAST Automation, Inc., Lynchburg, 1998—2001; physicist, scientist Naval Surface Warfare Ctr., Indian Head, Md., 2001—. *Senior NDT (nondestructive testing) physicist/engineer with over twenty years of experience in the academic community, national labs, and industry. Present work involves systems development and the research development of nondestructive techniques to inspection problems in industry. These ultrasonic applications include the use of both conventional ultrasonic methods and electromagnetic acoustic transducers (EMATs). Active in innovation, as inventor or co-inventor with 12 patents in the field of nondestructive testing. Also, author or co-author of numerous presentations and professional publications. Applications in the areas of aerospace, manufacturing, and fossil utilities.* Contbr. articles to profl. jours.; patentee in field. Co-leader cub pack Lynchburg Area coun. Boy Scouts Am., 1983-84; vol. United Way, 1994; mem. Pacer Club for United Way Support, 1993-98. Mem. ASTM, Am. Soc. Metals, Am. Soc. Non-destructive Testing (cert. Level III untrasonic methods), Am. Welding Soc., Sigma Pi Sigma. Avocations: martial arts, hiking, lapidary, mineral collecting. Home: 376 Juniper Dr Lynchburg VA 24502-5661 Office: Naval Surface Warfare Ctr Bldg 1576-Code 330 PL 101 Strauss Ave Indian Head MD 20640 E-mail: latimerpj@ih.navy.mil.

LATIMER, RONALD GORDON, surgeon; b. Salt Lake City, 1936; MD, George Washington U., 1961. Diplomate Am. Bd. Surgery. Intern George Washington U., 1961-62; resident in surgery Latter Day Saints Hosp., Salt Lake City, 1965-68, 69-70, U. Utah, Salt Lake City, 1968-69, fellow in transplant surgery, 1968-69. Fellow ACS; mem. Am. Assn. Endo. Surgery, Soc. Surgery Alimentary Tract, Pacific Coast Surg. Assn. Office: Sansun Santa Barbara Med Found Clinic PO Box 1200 Santa Barbara CA 93102-1200

LATIMER, ROY TRUETT, museum executive; b. Albany, Tex., Aug. 23, 1928; s. Charles Lee and Zora Neil (Brock) L.; m. Judith Gail Johnson, Nov. 26, 1955 (div. 1975); children: Jeff, Laura, Tiffany; m. Harriet Calvin, Nov. 20, 1976. BA, Hardin-Simmons U., 1951, LLD, 1996. Owner Gen. Ins. Agy., Abilene, Tex., 1951-55; alumni dir. Hardin-Simmons U., 1955-62; dir. pub. relations Tex. Assn. of Realtors, Austin, 1962-65; exec. dir. Tex. Hist. Commn., 1965-81, Tex. Hist. Found., Austin, 1972-81; v.p. pub. relations and mktg. Spaw Glass, Inc., Houston, 1981-85; pres. Houston Mus. Natural Sci., 1986—2001. Pres. Nat. Conf. State Hist. Preservation Officers, 1974-75; bd. advisors Nat. Trust for Hist. Preservation, Washington, 1981-88; bd. dirs. Houston Conv. and Tourist Bur. Mem. Tex. Ho. Reps., Austin, 1952-62; bd. devel. Hardin-Simmons U., 1974—, pres. 1999—; bd. dirs. Downtown Houston Assn., 1983—, past pres.; bd. dirs. Rice Design Alliance, Houston, 1983-87; chmn. S. Main Ctr. Assn., 1991-93. Mem. South Main Ctr. Assn. (bd. dirs. 1988—, pres. 2000—), Giant Screen Theater Assn. (v.p. 1999-2000, pres. 2001-02). Presbyterian. Avocations: running, canoeing, backpacking, travel. Home: 9 Bash Pl Houston TX 77027-5601 E-mail: tlatimer@hmns.org.

LATIMER, STEPHEN MARK, lawyer; b. Bklyn., July 15, 1939; s. Ted and Martha (Goldberg) L.; m. Judith R. Shulman, June 3, 1964 (dec. Mar. 29, 1984); 1 child, Gary. BA, Tufts U., 1961; JD, NYU, 1968. Bar: N.Y. 1968, N.J. 1979, U.S. Dist. Ct. (so. dist.) N.Y. 1970, U.S. Dist. Ct. (ea. dist.) N.Y. 1972, U.S. Dist. Ct. N.J. 1979, U.S. Dist. Ct. (we. dist.) N.Y. 1984, U.S. Dist. Ct. (no. dist.) Tex. 1992, U.S. Ct. Appeals (2d cir.) 1974, U.S. Ct. Appeals (3rd cir.) 1981, U.S. Ct. Appeals (5th cir.) 1986, U.S. Supreme Ct. 1975, U.S. Dist. Ct. (we. dist.) Tex. 2002. Clk. Burke & Parsons, N.Y.C., 1966-67; mng. clk. Otterbourg, Steindler, Houston & Rosen, 1967-68, assoc., 1968-69, Halpern, Schivitz, Scholer and Steingut, N.Y.C., 1969-71; dir. supervised pre-trial release project N.Y. Lawyers Com. for Civil Rights Under Law, 1972-73; dir. cmty. devel. and law reform Bronx Legal Svcs., 1973-79, acting mng. atty., 1974; dir. litigation Camden (N.J.) Regional Legal Svcs., Inc., 1979-81, acting dir., 1981-82; statewide litigation coord. Legal Svcs. of N.J., New Brunswick, 1982-84; sr. litigation atty. Prisoners' Legal Svcs. of N.Y., N.Y.C., 1984-94; asst. dep. pub. defender N.J. Pub. Defender, Newark, 1994-95; ptnr. Loughlin & Latimer, Hackensack, N.J., 1995—. Lectr. Rutgers U. Law Sch., 1975-90. Contbr. articles to profl. jours. Trustee ACLU of N.J., 1982-2001, exec. com. 1984-99, N.J. Assn. Correction, 1986—, Planned Parenthood of Middlesex County, 1981-85. Lt. USN, 1961-66, USNR, 1966-68. Instr. U.S. Marine Acad., Kings Point, N.Y., 1964-66. Mem. N.J. Bar Assn. (vice chmn. individual rights 1998-99, chmn. individual rights, 1999-2001). Home: 120 Floyd Ave Bloomfield NJ 07003-5610 Office: Loughlin & Latimer 131 Main St Hackensack NJ 07601-7140 E-mail: slatimer@mindspring.com.

LATINO, MARK VINCENT, rapid transit executive; b. Bklyn., July 9, 1965; s. Vincent Michael and Rose Anne Latino; m. Arielle Anne Wanser. BS, St. John's U., 1988. Assoc. transit mgmt. analyst MTA N.Y.C. Transit, Bklyn., 1993—99, dir. claims investigation, 1999—. Author: (screenplays) Sluggers, 2002.

LATIOLAIS, MINNIE FITZGERALD, nurse, hospital administrator, retired; b. Dec. 26, 1921; d. Thomas Ambrose and Mildred Surita (Nagle) Fitzgerald; m. Joseph C. Latiolais Jr., July 19, 1947; children: Felisa, Diana, Sylvia, Mary, Amelia, Joseph Clifton III. RN, New Orleans. Asst. night supr. Touro Infirmary, New Orleans, 1943; orthopaedic surg. nurse Ochsner Clinic, 1943-47; asst. DON Ochsner Found. Hosp., 1947; supr. Lafayette (La.) Gen. Hosp., 1960-64; adminstrv. asst., supr. oper. rm. Abbeville (La.) Gen. Hosp., 1964-68; gen. mgr., neurol. surg. nurse J. Robert Rivet, neurol. surgeon, Lafayette, 1968-78; hosp. cons. assoc. B.J. Landry & Assocs.; hosps. cons. Lafayette, 1979-90; DON Acadia St. Landry Hosp., Church Point, 1981-82; supr. supplies, processing and distbn. Univ. Med. Ctr., Lafayette, 1982-90, ret., 1990. Pres. SW La. Rehab. Assn., 1979-80; mem. Mid-La. Health Systems Agy., 1977-82, project rev. chmn., 1978-80; vice chmn. Acadica Regional Clearing House, 1984-86; mem. crafts and practical nurse com. Lafayette Regional Vocat.-Tech. Inst., 1980-84, chmn. 1983-84. Roman Catholic.

LATNER, BARRY P. pathologist; b. L.A., Oct. 8, 1957; m. Claudia Pinilla, Sept. 3, 1988. BA, UCLA, 1979; MD, Chgo. Med. Sch., 1984. Diplomate Am. Bd. Pathology. Intern/resident Calif. Pacific Med. Ctr., San Francisco, 1984-89; pathologist Mt. Diablo Med. Ctr., Concord, Calif., 1989—; asst. clin. prof. U. Calif., Berkeley, 1989—. Contbr. articles to profl. jours. Fellow Coll. Am. Pathologists; mem. Am. Soc. Clin. Pathologists, Am. Assn. Clin. Chemists, Calif. Soc. Pathologists, South Bay Pathology Soc. Office: Mt Diablo Med Ctr 2540 East St Concord CA 94520-1906

LATNO, ARTHUR CLEMENT, JR. telephone company executive; b. Ross, Calif., May 14, 1929; s. Arthur Clement and Marie (Carlin) L.; m. Dorothy Sheldon Guess, June 27, 1953; children— Jeannine Marie, Michele Claire, Arthur Clement III, Mary Suzanne, Patrice Anne. BS, Santa Clara U., 1951. With Pacific Tel. & Tel. Co., San Francisco, 1952-92, v.p., 1972-78, exec. v.p., 1978-92; former amb. accorded by Ronald Reagan, 1988. Chmn. U.S. Delegation to World Telecom. Conf., Australia; bd. dirs. WestAm. Bank, WestAm. Bancorp. Chm. bd. dirs. Marin Cmty. Health; bd. dirs., former chmn. Calif. Inst. Fed. Policy Rsch.; former chmn. adv. bd. Berkeley program in bus. and social policy U. Calif.; former chmn. bd. trustees St. Mary's Coll. Calif. Mem. Meadow Club, Knights of Malta, Alpha Sigma Nu. Home: 67 Convent Ct San Rafael CA 94901-1333

LATONI, ALFONSO RAFAEL, sociology and political science educator; b. Coral Gables, Fla., Feb. 9, 1958; s. Alfonso and Olga (Rodriguez) L.; m. Carmen Sol Ramirez, Nov. 1, 1996; children: Elena Isabel, Angelica Rocio. BA in Polit. Sci., U. P.R., 1979; MA, Georgetown U., 1981; PhD, Boston Coll., 1993. Rsch. asst. Smithsonian Instn., Washington, 1979; asst. fgn. student advisor Georgetown U., 1980-81; tchg. fellow dept. sociology Boston Coll., 1982-83; prof. sociology Interam. U. P.R., San German, 1983-86, cons. for planning new courses, 1983-84, assoc. dean studies, 1985-86; prof. sociology and polit. sci. U. P.R., Mayaguez, 1986—, asst. chmn. dept. social scis., 1988-91. Faculty rep. bd. dirs. Nat. Collegiate Conf. Assn.-Nat. Model U.N., 1994-96; pres. univ. srch. com. for pres. U. P.R., 1994, faculty srch. com. for chancellor U. PR., Mayaguez, 1996. Mem. Arts and Cultural Workshop, Adjuntas, P.R., 1984—; tchr. Labor inst. for Worker Edn., Mayaguez, 1983; asst. organizer United Elec. Radio and Machine Workers of Am., Boston, 1982; cons. to pres. U. P.R. for faculty rsch. scholarships in the Caribbean, 1994—. Mem. City Commn. for the Endowment of the Arts and Culture, Mayaguez, 1995—. Named to Outstanding Young Men of Am., 1988-91; U. P.R. grad. presdl. scholar, 1979; Boston Coll. grantee, 1982, 83. Mem. Am. Sociol. Assn. (chmn. MOST program 1998—), Soc. for Study of Social Problems, Phi Delta Kappa. Avocations: camping, hiking, reading, gardening. Home: 531 Ext Villa Fontana Mayaguez PR 00681 Office: U PR Mayaguez Campus Dept Social Sci Mayaguez PR 00681

LATORRACA, JOSEPH PAUL, writer; b. Montclair, N.J., May 3, 1942; s. Joseph N. and Isabelle E. Latorraca; m. Sharon Hutter, July 3, 1971 (div. June 1976). BA, Rutgers U., 1964, MEd, 1975. Tchr. French East Brunswick H.S., NJ, 1964—79; prin. St. Malachy Cath. Sch., Tamarac, Fla., 1984—88; aquatics dir. Woodmont Country Club, 1979—84, 1989—96; profl. writer, 1996—. Contbr. Usher St. Bernard's Cath. Ch., Sunrise, Fla., 1997—. Recipient 1st Place for Children's Fiction, Foster City Arts and Cultural Coun., Calif., 1999. Roman Catholic.

LATORRE, ROBERT GEORGE, naval architecture and engineering educator; b. Toledo, Jan. 9, 1949; s. Robert James and Madge Violette (Roy) L.; m. Irina Korol, 2000. BS in Naval Architecture and Marine Engrng. with honors, U. Mich., 1971, MS in Engrng., 1972; MSE in Naval Architecture, U. Tokyo, 1975, PhD. in Naval Architecture, 1978. Asst. prof. U. Mich., Ann Arbor, 1979-83; assoc. prof. U. New Orleans, 1984-87, prof. naval architecture and marine engrng., 1987—, chmn. dept., 1989-95. Assoc. prof. mech. engrng., U. Tokyo, 1986-87; rsch. scientist, David Taylor Naval R & D Lab., Bethesda, Md., 1980, 81, Bassin d'Essais des Carenes, Paris, 1983; cons. in field. Contbr. to profl. publs. Mem. Soc. Naval Architects, Royal Inst. Naval Archtects Gt. Britain, ASME, Soc. NAval Architects Japan, Am. Soc. engring. Edn. (program chmn. ocean engrng. divsn. 1989-9O, Japan Club New Orleans. Roman Catholic. Office: U New Orleans 911 Engring Bldg New Orleans LA 70148-0001 E-mail: rglna@uno.edu.

LATOURETTE, STEVEN C. congressman; b. Cleve., July 22, 1954; married; 4 children. BA in Hist., U. Mich., 1976; JD, Cleve. State U., 1979. Asst. pub. defender Lake County Pub. Defender's Office, 1980-83; assoc. Cannon, Stern, Aveni & Krivok, Painesville, 1983-86; with Baker, Hackenberg & Collins, 1986-88; prosecuting atty. Lake County Prosecutor Office, 1988-93; mem. U.S. Ho. of Reps., Washington, 1994—, mem. Com. on Transp. & Infrastructure, subcom. pub. bldgs. & econ. devel., hwys. and transit, & water resources and environ., mem. govt. reform and oversight com., mem. fin. svcs. com., mem. U.S. Holocaust Meml. Coun., trans. & infrastructure, 1995—. Office: US House Reps 2453 Rayburn HOB Washington DC 20515-3519*

LATOURRETTE, JAMES THOMAS, retired electrical engineering and computer science educator; b. Miami, Ariz., Dec. 26, 1931; s. Emery Everest and Carrie D. (Hoffman) LaT.; m. Muriel Ashe, Aug. 28, 1955; children: Mary Beth, John Emery, James Thomas, Joanne. BS, Calif. Inst. Tech., 1953; MA (Gen. Communication Co. fellow), Harvard U., 1954, PhD (NSF fellow), 1958. Research assoc., lectr. physics Harvard U., 1957-59; physicist Gen. Electric Research Lab., Schenectady, 1960-62; sr. supervisory scientist TRG, Inc., Melville, N.Y., 1962-66; sect. head TRG div. Control Data Corp., 1966-67; prof. elec. engrng. and computer sci. Poly. U. (formerly Poly. Inst. Bklyn. and Poly. Inst. N.Y.), Farmingdale, N.Y., 1967-93, prof. emeritus, 1993. Assoc. dir. Weber Rsch. Inst., Poly. U., 1987-90. Contbr. articles to profl. jours. NSF postdoctoral fellow Physikalisches Institut der U. Bonn, Germany, 1959-60 Mem. IEEE, N.Y. Acad. Sci., Assn. for Computer Machinery, Sigma Xi, Tau Beta Pi. Home: 2 Candlewood Ct Huntington NY 11743-1827 Office: Poly Univ Rt 110 Farmingdale NY 11735

LATOURRETTE, KATHRYN, family therapist, counselor, artist; b. Camp Atterbury, Ind., Nov. 16, 1942; d. Herbert Cecil and Goldie Ann (Wright) Little; m. Robert William LaTourrette, Dec. 22, 1964; children: Robert Scott, Bradley Talon, Todd Lawson. BS in Elem. Edn. and Psychology, N.Mex. State U., 1964; MS in Counseling, Troy State U., 1985. Lic. marriage and family therapist, N.Mex. Counseling and Therapy Practice Bd. Elem. tchr. Univ. Hills Elem., Las Cruces, N.Mex., 1964-65; substitute tchr. Mesa (Ariz.) Sch. Sys., 1974-75; counselor Las Vegas (Nev.) Rape Crisis Ctr., 1985-86; group facilitator Nev. State Dept. Corrections, Las Vegas, 1985-86; counselor and family therapist Drug Abuse Comprehensive Coordinating Office, Tampa, Fla., 1989-91, Pinon Hills Hosp., Santa Fe, 1991-99; pvt. practice Jefferson Davis, MD, 1999—. Instr. Abuse Shelter, Okinawa, Japan, 1987-89. Works exhibited Albuquerque Art Soc., 1968-71, Old Town Gallery, Alexandria, Va., 1977-78 (Best in Show award 1977), Conquistador Gallery, Taos, N.Mex., 1982-84. Cub Scout leader, Hahn, Germany, 1965-66; hon. chmn. ARC, Okinawa, 1986-88; advisor Kadina Officers Wives Club, Okinawa, 1986-89. Mem. Am. Assn. Marriage and Family Counselors, Gamma Beta Phi. Presbyterian. Avocations: art, hiking, brass rubbing, gardening. Home: 10648 Weybridge Dr Tampa FL 33626-1824

LATOVICK, PAULA R(AE), lawyer, educator; b. Detroit, Feb. 17, 1954; d. Raymond and Marjorie Camille (Peters) L.; m. William P. Weiner, Aug. 17, 1985; children: Jeffrey Devon, Robert Stirling. BA in Personnel with high honor, Mich. State U., 1976; JD cum laude, U. Mich., 1980, LLM, 1999. Bar: Mich. 1980, U.S. Dist. Ct. (ea. dist.) Mich. 1980, U.S. Dist. Ct. (we. dist.) Mich. 1981, U.S. Ct. Appeals (6th cir.) 1985. Assoc. Fraser, Trebilcock, Davis & Foster P.C., Lansing, Mich., 1980—86, ptnr., 1986—92, chmn. hiring com., 1987—92, chmn. govt. law dept., 1988—90; assoc. prof. Thomas M. Cooley Law Sch., 1992—97, prof., 1998—2001, chair property law dept., 2000—01; ret., 2001. Adj. prof. Thomas M. Cooley Law Sch., Lansing, 1984-86. V.p. YWCA, Lansing, 1988, pres., 1989—91, chmn. bldg. com., 1989—91; head advisor law explorers Boy Scouts Am., 1982—84; mem. Capitol Area Women's Network, 1988; rec. sec. Friends of Kresge Art Mus., 1992—93, corr. sec., 1993—94, 1st v.p., 1994—95, pres., 1995—96; treas. Cub Scouts Pack 107, Boy Scouts Am., 1998—2002; co-chair Friends Greater Lansing Symphony, 2000—01; pres. William Donley Elem. Sch. Parent Coun., 2001—. Named One of Outstanding Young Women of Am., 1985. Fellow Mich. State Bar Found.; mem. NOW, Mich. Bar Assn. (mem. young lawyers exec. coun. 1984-86, mem. com. character and fitness dist. F 1991-2000, subcom. chairperson 1994-2000), Women Lawyers Assn. Mich., Ingham County Bar Assn. (chairperson hist. com. 1984-87, mem. young lawyers bd. 1981-84, pres. 1983, mem. com. on jud. qualifications 1990-93, bd. dirs. 1990-92), Thomas M. Cooley Legal Authors Soc., U. Mich. Alumni Assn. (life), Mich. State U. Alumni Assn., Zonta (rec. sec. local club 1985-86, chmn. membership com. 1988-89). Democrat. Roman Catholic.

LATSHA, TIMOTHY JAMES, music educator, musician; b. Herndon, Pa., Aug. 2, 1969; s. Roger Dale Latsha and Marietta Barbara Wilt; m. Jennifer Elizabeth Peters, Feb. 4, 1994; children: Elizabeth Jane, Olivia Eva. Bachelor Music Edn., Mansfield U., Mansfield, PA, 1991. Tchr. elem. schools, Bloomsburg, Pa., 1991—. Accompanist Marywood U., Scranton, Pa., 1998—99, Bucknell U., Lewisburg, Pa., 2001—. Guest presenter Lebanon Valley Coll. Student PMEA, Lebanon, Pa., 2001; guest condr. PMEA Dist. 8 North Songfest, 2001, PMEA Dist. 8 South Songfest, 2002; worship leader, 2002—02; dvbs coord. and cantana dir., 2002—02. Scholar Thomas Houser Scholarship, Marywood U. Mem.: Columbia County Choral Directors Assn. (pres. 1995—2002), Am. Choral Dist. Assn. (region coord. 1998—98), Pa, Music Educators Assn. Achievements include development of One of the founding fathers of Columbia County Choral Director Association. Office: Bloomsburg Area School District 1200 Railroad Street Bloomsburg PA 17815

LATSHAW, JOHN, entrepreneur, director; b. Kansas City, Dec. 10, 1921; s. Ross W. and Edna (Parker) L.; m. Barbara Haynes, Nov. 13, 1954 (div. Dec. 1975); children: Constance Haynes, Elizabeth Albright. Student, Kansas City Jr. Coll., 1938-40; BS, Mo. U., 1942. Mgr. trading dept. Harris, Upham & Co., 1943-49; ptnr. Uhlmann & Latshaw, 1949-53, E.F. Hutton & Co. (merger with Uhlmann & Latshaw), 1954-87, exec. v.p., mgn. dir., 1987—. Chmn. bd. dirs., chief exec. officer B.C. Christopher & Co., 1987-89, chmn. emeritus, 1989-90; chmn., chief exec. officer Conchemco Inc.; chmn., chief exec. officer, mng. dir. Latshaw Enterprises, 1990—; chmn. bd. dirs. Bus. Communications, Inc., Install, Maintain and Repair, Inc., Interior Designs, Inc.; mem. Kansas City Bd. Trade; gov. Midwest Stock Exchange, 1966-68; moderator, opening speaker Plenary Panel on Needs and Opportunities in Key Bus. Sectors, Miami Conf. on the Caribbean, 1980; pres. World Cable Ltd. Past Chmn. Key Men's

Council; past pres. Friends of Zoo, 1970; mem. exec. com. Religious Heritage Am., Starlight Theatre, Performing Arts Kansas City; v.p., mem. exec. bd. Am. Cancer Soc., 1970, 71; mem. Jackson County and Crusade Adv. Com., Gov.'s Com. on Higher Edn.; bd. dirs. Kansas City Theatre Guild Council, The Curry Found., Am. Urban Devel. Found., Kansas City Crime Commn.; trustee City Employees Pension Plan, St. Andrew's Episcopal Ch. Meml. and Res. Trust Fund, U. Mo., Kansas City; bd. govs. Am. Royal, Agrl. Hall of Fame, 1976-77; exec. bd. Kansas City Area council Boy Scouts Am., 1970-72, adv. bd., 1973, chmn. patriotism program, 1970; hon. bd. dirs. Rockhurst Coll.; past pres. Kansas City Soccer Club, Inc.; mem. exec. com. N.Am. Soccer League, 1968, 69; bd. govs. Invest-In-Am. Nat. Council; mem. Central Region exec. com.; regional chmn. Invest-in-Am. Week Liaison, 1958— ; mem. fin. com. Mayor's Profl. Theater; mem. Univ. Assos. of U. Mo. of Kansas City; chmn. hon. trustees YWCA, 1968-69; trustee Midwest Research Inst.; mem. chancellor's adv. council Met. Community Colls., 1976-77; mem. pres.'s council bd. hon. trustees Kansas City Art Inst.; mem. Pres.' Scholarship Club Avila Coll.; bd. dirs., mem. fin. com. Mayor's Christmas Tree Assn.; chmn. bd. trustee Conservatory of Music; community adv. com. U. Mo. Kansas City Sch. Nursing; mem. Civic Council Greater Kansas City; chmn. Brotherhood Citation Dinner for NCCJ, 1980; trustee Westminster Coll., 1981; hon. bd. govs. Hyman Brand Hebrew Acad.; adv. com. Metro Energy Ctr., 1982; mem. NASA adv. bd. to Pres. U.S., 1983-86. Recipient citation of merit U. Mo., 1957, Golden Eagle award Nat. Invest in Am. Coun., 1970, Chaturathabhorn of Most Exalted Order of White Elephant award, Thailand, 1983; named hon. consul Thailand, Royal Consulate Gen., 1986, The Knight Comdr. of the Most Noble Order of the Crown of Thailand, 1993; decorated Knight Hospitaller of Malta Sovereign Order St. John Jerusalem. Mem. Internat. Trade Assn. (chmn. bd.), Kansas City C. of C. (dir., past pres.), Bus. and Profl. Assn. Western Mo. (mem. adv. bd.), Kansas City Security Traders Assn. (past pres.), Nat. Security Traders Assn. (past exec. v.p.), Wine Soc. of World, Order Jim Daisy, Sigma Nu. Episcopalian (trustee). Clubs: Carriage, Mission Hills Country. Home: 5049 Wornall Apt 2C Kansas City MO 64112-2409 also: 4530 Gulf Shore Blvd N unit 152 Naples FL 34103 Office: 800 W 47th St Ste 716 Kansas City MO 64112-1249

LATSIOS, BARBARA LYNN, government official; b. Phila., Jan. 25, 1954; d. Stephen and Helen Valentina (Matweychuk) Sameruck; m. George Latsios, Aug. 29, 1976; 1 child, Cassandra. Clk., stenographer Nat. Park Svc., Phila., 1971-72, park ranger, 1972-79, supervisory park ranger, 1979-85, purchasing agt., 1985-87; contract specialist EPA, 1987-90, program analyst, 1990—. Mem. Nat. Contract Mgmt. Assn., AFL-CIO (sec. Local 2058 Phila. 1973-75, 2d v.p. 1976-79). Republican. Russian Orthodox. Office: EPA Region III 1650 Arch St Philadelphia PA 19103-2029 E-mail: latsios.barbara@epamail.epa.gov.

LATSON, RICHARD CHARLES, audio-visual specialist; b. Nov. 13, 1947; s. Robert Lee and Ruby (Kent) Latson; m. Sherilyn Day (div.). BA in Radio and TV Comm., Tex. Tech U., 1970. Radio-TV broadcaster, 1967-70; TV prodn. specialist Naval Acad., Annapolis, Md., 1974-79; mgr. TV prodn. Walter Reed Army Med. Ctr., Washington, 1979-87; audio visual mgmt. officer Dept. Army, 1987-90; mgr. audio visual prodn. and distbn. program Dept. Def., Alexandria, Va., 1990—. Mem. fed. audiovisual com. Office Mgmt. and Budget, Washington, 1990—96; U.S. judge Internat. Mil. Film Festival, Argentina, 1998, Bracciano, Italy, 2001, U.S. del. , Rome, 1998; mgr. DoD Audiovisual Prodn. Awards Program, 1998—. Mem. NATO Mil. Audiovisual Working Group, Joint Svcs. Adv. Group Advanced Distributed Learning, 1995—; judge U.S. Army Audiovisual Prodn. Competition, 2000, 2001, 2002, USN Audiovisual Prodn. Competition, 2001. 1st lt. USAF, 1970—74. Decorated Air Force commendation medal. Mem.: NATAS, Brit. & Commonwealth Soc. N.Am. (past pres.), Internat. Imaging Industry Assn. (stds. mgmt. bd. 1992—), Am. Nat. Stds. Inst. (imgae tech. stds. bd. 1990—98, info. sys. stds. bd. 1990—), Gentry Soc. Avocations: old time radio programs, big band music, collecting art. Home: 3344 Hewitt Ave Apt 76 Silver Spring MD 20906-5425 Office: Am Forces Info Svc 601 N Fairfax St Ste 230 Alexandria VA 22314-2007 E-mail: rclatso@hq.afis.osd.mil.

LATTA, DIANA LENNOX, retired interior designer; b. Lahaina, Maui, Hawaii, Aug. 5, 1936; d. D. Stewart and Jean Marjorie (Anderson) Lennox; m. Arthur McKee Latta, Jan. 26, 1957 (dec.); children: Mary-Stewart, Marion McKee Davidson. *Following their marriage, Diana Latta's husband became co-owner/director of the McKee Jungle Garden, Florida's third oldest major tourist attraction; which his grandfather, Cleveland industrialist, Arthur G. McKee had founded in 1931. The Garden continued operations until1976, after which the property was sold for development. Mrs. Latta's daughters have pursued vital career paths. Marion serves as Senior Vice President of Marketing for Montblanc North America. For over ten years, Mary-Stewart has held the position of lodging and hospitality Technology Support Specialist with Sea Island Company in Sea Island, Georgia. Her entry into the hospitality industry began at The Breakers hotel in Palm Beach, Florida.* Grad., The Bishop's Sch., La Jolla, Calif., 1954; student, U. Wash., 1954—56. Dir. Vero Beach (Fla.) br. of Wellington Hall Ltd., Thomasville, NC, 1970—72; asst. to chief designer Rablen-West Interiors, Vero Beach, 1972—75; design and adminstrv. asst. to pres. Design Studio Archtl. & Interior Design Concepts, Inc., 1975—82; owner, designer The Designery, 1983—87; designer's asst. Frank J. Lincoln Interiors, Inc., Vero Beach, Locust Valley, NY, 1987—90; sr. staff designer Chancellor's Inc., Bellingham, Wash., 1992—93; v.p., sec. JADSL Corp., Mill Creek, 1999—. *In 1989, Mrs. Latta's efforts to preserve an 18-acre remnant portion of the McKee Jungle Gardens Preservation Society were instrumental in bringing the work of the Society to the attention of the Trust for Public Land. This linkage enabled the Society to enlarge its vision. In 2001 the reclaimed and faithfully restored McKee Botanical Garden re-opened to the public. The Garden is now listed on the National Register of Historic Places. Throughout her design career, Mrs. Latta was involved with highly diversified commissions, which include assisting with a new marketing concept for the footwear industry, which was implemented in two small stores in New Jersey.* Leading actress (Vero Beach Theatre Guild prodns) The Laughmaker, 1964, Oklahoma, 1966, model Holly Fashion Show, Vero Beach, 1962—69. Mem. Indian River Meml. Hosp. Women's Aux., Vero Beach, 1957—70, chmn., 1960, v.p., 1962—64; founding mem. Indian River Land Trust, 1989—90; chmn. Mill Creek for Youth Com., 1994; advisor to steering com. The Malt Shoppe after-sch. program, Mill Creek, 1995—97; mem. coun. Snohomish County Federated Health and Safety Network, 1999—; bd. dirs., chmn. hospitality com. Vero Beach Mut. Concert Assn., 1973—76; mem. adv. bd. Indian River 4-H Horsemaster's Club, 1973—76; treas., bd. dirs. McKee Jungle Gardens Preservation Soc., Inc., chmn. fundraising com., pub. rels. com.; bd. dirs. Vero Beach Theatre Guild, 1964; mem. adv. com. Safe and Drug Free Schs. Edmonds (Wash.) Sch. Dist., 1996—2002; mem. key leaders bd. Cmtys. That Care Project Edmonds Sch. Dist., 2001—. Mem.: Internat. Platform Assn., Riomar Bay Yacht Club (chmn. tennis com. 1964—66, club tennis champion 1964, 1966), Kappa Kappa Gamma (mem. adv. bd. U. Wash., Seattle chpt. 1997—2000, founding mem. N. Sound Alumnae Assn. 2002—, founding mem. Indian River Alumnae Club 1968). Republican. Episcopalian. Home: 16018 Village Green Dr # B Mill Creek WA 98012-5874

LATTA, GEORGE HAWORTH, III, neonatologist; b. Chattanooga, Sept. 4, 1960; s. George Haworth Jr. and Charlotte (Major) L. BS in Physics, Ga. Inst. Tech., 1982; MD, East Tenn. State U., 1986. Cert. in pediats., neonatology. Intern, resident in pediat. Dartmouth (N.H.) U., 1986-88; resident in pediat. Stanford (Calif.) U., 1988-89; fellow in neonatology Vanderbilt U., Nashville, 1989-90, U. Tenn., Memphis, 1990-92; attending neonatologist Rose Med. Ctr., Denver, 1992-94, Forrest Gen. Hosp., Hattiesburg, Miss., 1994-95, Meth. Hosps., Memphis, 1995-99; neontalogist Intermountain Healthcare, Provo, Utah, 2000—. NIH pulmonary trainee grantee Vanderbilt U., 1989; March of Dimes scholar East Tenn. State U., 1984, Johnny J. Jones scholar, 1981. Fellow Am. Acad. Pediat.; mem. Phi Eta Sigma. Roman Catholic. Avocations: snow skiing, camping, jazz music, aquariums, scuba diving. Home: 1032 S Slate Canyon Dr Provo UT 84606-6455 Office: Utah Valley Regional Med Ctr Intermountain Healthcare 1034 N 500 W Provo UT 84604-3380 E-mail: ghlatta3@earthlink.net., uvglatta@ihc.com.

LATTA, JEAN CAROLYN, financial analyst, chemist; b. Chgo., Oct. 11, 1943; d. John Oscar and Katherine Helen (Schnitzer) Latta. BS in Chemistry, U. Ill., 1966; MS in Chemistry, IIT, 1970; MBA, U. Chgo., 1976. chemist, Gillette Co., Chgo., 1966-67; asst. research chemist, 1969-73; product designer Bunker-Ramo Corp., Chgo., 1973-75; staff exec. George S. May Internat. Co., Park Ridge, Ill., 1977; controller, ind. cons. Bayou City Service Co., Houston, 1978; staff acct. Chemtrust Industries, Franklin Park, Ill., 1979; fin. analyst U. Chgo., 1979-84; sr. price/cost analyst Northrop Corp., Pico Rivera, Calif., 1984-85, pricing coord., engrng. cost analyst Hawthorne, Calif., 1989-96; mem. tech. staff The Aerospace Corp., 1997—. Patentee in electronic field. Democrat. Roman Catholic. E-mail: jclx@aol.com.

LATTA, THOMAS ALBERT, lawyer; b. Tulsa, Nov. 3, 1931; s. Albert Lloyd and Myrtle Irene (Lay) L.; m. Shirley Elaine Glauser, June 20, 1965 (div. 1985); children: Thomas Albert, John Montgomery, Shannon Elaine. Student, Carnegie Mellon U., 1949-52; BA, U. Tex., 1955; JD, U. Tulsa, 1959. Bar: Okla. 1959, Ariz. 1964, D.C. 1965, Calif. 1974. Atty. U.S. Dept. Justice, 1960, Securities and Exchange Commn., 1961—64; pvt. practice San Francisco, 1974, Phoenix, 1975; dir., shareholder Wentworth & Lundin, P.A., 1975-86, San Francisco, 1980-84; of counsel Whitehead, Porter & Gordon LLP, 1997—. Mem. Ariz. Bd. Accountancy, Phoenix, 1979-83. Capt. JAGC, USAR, 1959-60. Avocation: sailing. Office: Whitehead Porter & Gordon LLP 220 Montgomery St Ste 1850 San Francisco CA 94104-3419 E-mail: tal@wpglaw.com.

LATTANZIO, STEPHEN PAUL, astronomy educator; b. Yonkers, N.Y., June 29, 1949; s. Anthony Raymond and Anella Lattanzio; m. Barbara Regina Knisely, Aug. 14, 1976; children: Gregory Paul, Timothy Paul. BA in Astronomy, U. Calif., Berkeley, 1971; MA in Astronomy, UCLA, 1973, postgrad., 1973-75. Planetarium lectr. Griffith Obs., Los Angeles, 1973-75; instr. astronomy El Camino Coll., Torrance, Calif., 1974-75; planetarium lectr. Valley Coll., Los Angeles, 1975; prof. astronomy Orange Coast Coll., Costa Mesa, Calif., 1975—, planetarium dir., 1975—. Mem. adv. commn. Natural History Found. Orange County, Calif., 1988-91; scientific advisor instructional TV series Universe: The Infinite Frontier, 1992—. Contbr. articles to profl. jours. Mem. Astron. Soc. Pacific, The Planetary Soc., Sigma Xi (assoc.), Phi Beta Kappa. Avocation: astronautics. Office: Orange Coast Coll 2701 Fairview Rd Costa Mesa CA 92626-5563 E-mail: slattanzio@cccd.edu.

LATTES, JANE FLAX, museum director; b. Selma, Ala., Nov. 13, 1935; d. Nathan Flax and Dorothy Goldman; m. Conrad G. Lattes, June 28, 1958 (dec. Oct. 1987); children: Lisa, Abigail, Conrad, Jane; m. Norbert Swislocki, Apr. 9, 1991. BA, Swarthmore (Pa.) Coll., 1957; MA, Harvard U., 1958; MS, Bank St. Grad. Sch. Edn., N.Y.C., 1981. Vol. coord. N.Y. Hist. Soc., 1985-90; vol. mgr. Mus. of the City of N.Y., N.Y.C., 1990-91; dir. vols. Solomon R. Guggenheim Mus., 1991-93; dir. vol. svcs. Am. Mus. of Natural History, 1993—2002. Trustee Morris-Jumel Mansion, N.Y.C., 1985—; bd. dirs. N.Y. Mus. Coun., 1986—89, Rockland Ctr. for the Arts, 2001—. Mem. ICOM, Am. Assn. of Mus., Assn. for Vol. Adminstrn. Home: 262 River Rd Nyack NY 10960 E-mail: jflattes@yahoo.com.

LATTIMER, GARY LEE, physician; b. Nanticoke, Pa., Dec. 4, 1939; s. Paul Floyd and Gene Elizabeth L.; m. Patricia Sara Weise, June 14, 1958; children: Toni Jo, Gregory Weise. MD, Temple U., 1966; postgrad., Jefferson Med. Coll., 1970-72. Intern Allentown (Pa.) Hosp.; resident Presbyn.-Univ. Hosp., Phila., 1969-70, Jefferson Med. Coll. Hosp., Phila., 1970-71, chief med. resident, 1971-72; chief infectious diseases Allentown-Sacred Heart Hosp. Center, 1972-80; assoc. prof. medicine U. N.D., 1980-81, chief infectious diseases, 1980-81, New Britain (Conn.) Gen. Hosp., 1981—; assoc. prof. medicine U. Conn., 1981-83; dir. infectious diseases Williamsport Hosp., Divine Providence Hosp., 1983—. Author: Legionnaires' Disease, 1981; contbr. articles to profl. jours. Served with M.C. U.S. Army, 1967-69. Decorated Bronze Star; recipient Disting. Service award Pa. chpt. Am. Legion. Fellow ACP; mem. Am. Soc. Microbiology, AAAS, Nat. Found. Infectious Diseases, Am. Legion. Office: 904 Campbell St Williamsport PA 17701-3166 E-mail: glattimer@shscares.org.

LATTIMORE, BARBARA, healthcare administrator, consultant; b. Birmingham, Ala., June 11, 1961; d. Butler and Alfreda (Kelley) Jackson; m. Ernest Eugene Lattimore, June 7, 1980; children: Kendra, Kimberly, Kandis. BS in Psychology, U. Md., 1988; MEd in Counseling, Boston U., 1990; MSA in Health Svcs., Ctrl. Mich. U., 1998. Lic. profl. counselor; nat. cert. counselor. Sta. mgr. ARC, Hanau, GErmany, 1986-89; program mgr. Sci. Applications Internat., 1989-93; behavioral health clinician South Fulton Mental Health, East Point, Ga., 1993-96; program mgr. Child and Adolescent Program, Atlanta, 1996-98; dir. substance abuse Alcohol and Drug Treatment Ct., 1998—. Founder, CEO, Alternative R&D, Decatur/Stone Mountain, Ga., 1993-99; CEO, Therapeutic Managed Care, Decatur/Stone Mountain, 1999—; cons. Gwinnett County Juvenile Ct., Lawrenceville, Ga., 1998—, Daus. Endowed With Wisdom, Decatur, 1998—, ACE Check Casing, Inc., Atlanta, 1999—, Social Work Svcs., Frankfurt, Germany, 1991-93. Treas., NAACP, Hanau, 1990, v.p., 1991, pres., 1992; troup leader Girl Scouts U.S., Mannheim, Germany, 1989-92; Sunday sch. tchr. Christ Temple Fellowship, 1980—. Recipient Comdr.'s award for cmty. svc. U.S. Army, 1990. Mem. Am. Coll. Healthcare Execs., Sigma Iota Epsilon, Delta Sigma Theta. Home: 7052 Shore Rd Lithonia GA 30058-8214 Office: Fulton County Alcohol and Drug Treatment Ctr 265 Boulevard NE Atlanta GA 30312-1284

LATTIMORE, VERGEL LYRONNE, minister, educator, counselor; b. Charlotte, N.C., Mar. 6, 1953; s. Vergel and Perlia Equilla (Gray) L.; m. Joy Renee Powell, Dec. 16, 1978; children: V. Alston, Adam Victor, Alia Joy. BA, Livingstone Coll., 1975; MDiv, Duke U. Div. Sch., 1977; PhD, Northwestern U., 1984; grad., Air War Coll., Air U., Maxwell AFB, 1998. Ordained to ministry Meth. Ch., 1975. Campus min. Duke U. Chapel, Durham, N.C., 1976-77; asst. dean Duke U., 1977-79; dir. chaplain svcs. Community Hosp., Evanston, Ill., 1979-80; staff cpimse;pr Garrett Evang. Theol. Sem., 1980-83; staff counselor Pastoral Psychotherapy Inst., Park Ridge, Ill., 1980-82; minority student advisor, resident dir. Kendall Coll., Evanston, 1980-83; pastoral counsel Onondaga Pastoral Counseling Ctr. Inc., Syracuse, N.Y., 1983-88; dir. counseling Syracuse Community Health Ctr. Inc., 1988-90; assoc. prof. Meth. Theol. Sch., Delaware, Ohio, 1990-93, prof. pastoral care, 1993—. Regional coord. Nat. Black Student Consultation Southwest U.S.A., 1978-80; rsch. cons. Nat. Acad. Peace and Conflict Resolution, Washington, 1979-80; chairperson Martin Luther King Community Celebration, Syracuse, 1985-90; pres. bd. dirs. PEACE Inc., Syracuse, 1989-90; Goodling Meml. lectr., Duke U. Divinity Sch., 1993; mem. accreditation com. Ohio Credentialing Bd. for Chem. Dependency Profls., 1998—; mem. profl. consultation com., Ohio State U. Med. Ctr., 1994—, Mt. Carmel Med. Ctr., 1996—, Children's Hosp., 1997—; mem. Air N.G. Chaplain Svcs. Divsn. Exec. Team, 1996—. Mem. Human Rights Commn., Syracuse, 1986-90, Social Svcs. Adv. Coun., Syracuse, 1988-90, City of Syracuse/Onondaga County Drug Abuse Commn., 1990, Ohio Coun. Chs. Criminal Justice Task Force, Columbus, 1991—, Hartford Sem. leadership edn. program for sem. execs., 1991-93. Air N.G. asst. to the command chaplain, Langley AFB, Va., 1999-2001. Named Mover and Shaker in Religion, Syracuse Herald Jour., 1988. Fellow Am. Assn. Pastoral Counselors (chmn. rsch. com. 1985-87); mem. AAUP, Am. Assn. Marriage and Family Therapy (clin. mem.), Ohio State U. Nat. Coun. on Alcoholism Summer Inst. on Addiction Studies, Livingstone Coll. Alumni Assn. (pres. Columbus and Ctrl. Ohio chpt. 1993—), Alpha Phi Alpha. Avocations: biking, jogging, jazz, chess. Home: 610 Olde North Church Rd Westerville OH 43081-3133 Office: Meth Theol Sch in Ohio PO Box 8004 3081 Columbus Pike Delaware OH 43015-3211 E-mail: vlattimore@mtso.edu.

LATTIN, ALBERT FLOYD, banker; b. Everett, Wash., May 23, 1950; s. Albert S. and Erma Victoria (Hunt) L. Student, U. Nairobi, Kenya, 1970-71, Am. U. Cairo, Egypt, 1972; BA, Antioch U., 1973; MA, NYU, 1979; MBA, Columbia U., 1984. Asst. curator The Bklyn. Mus., 1973-76, assoc., 1976-79; sec. of the mus. Solomon R. Guggenheim Mus., N.Y.C., 1979-80, cons. in arts, 1980-83; banker Bankers Trust Co., 1984-93; v.p. CS 1st Boston, 1993-95, Credit Suisse First Boston Corp., N.Y.C., 1995—. Bd. dirs., chief investment officer Praedium Recovery Fund, N.Y.C., 1994—; mng. mem. The Praedium Group, L.P., 1999—. Editor, researcher book and catalogue Africa in Antiquity: The Arts of Ancient Nubia and the Sudan, 1978; organizer exhibition/movie The Heritage of Islam, 1982. Dir., trustee Mus. Holography, N.Y.C., 1980-87; mem. bd. advisors Gallery Assn. N.Y., 1988-98; treas. Theban Found., 1991—; mem. Bklyn. Hist. Soc., Brooklyn Heights Assn., 1986—. Mem. Am. Banking Assn., Urban Land Inst., Internat. Council of Mus., Am. Assn. Mus., Internat. Assn. Egyptologists, Roundout Valley Country Club, Columbia Club. Home: Box 206 Lucas Turnpike Accord NY 12404-0206 Office: Credit Suisse First Boston Corp 11 Madison Ave New York NY 10010-3698

LATTING, JEAN KANTAMBU, social worker, educator; b. Dec. 25, 1944; d. A.A. Latting and Marietta Ish Bass; m. Diallo Kantambu; 1 child. BA, Douglass Coll., 1965; MS, Columbia U., 1971; DrPH, U. N.C., 1980. LCSW. Caseworker and cmty. organizer, 1965—71; asst. prof. Grad. Sch. Social Work U. Houston, 1980—88, assoc. prof. Grad. Sch. Social Work, 1988—95, prof. Grad. Sch. Social Work, 1995—. Cons. and rschr. in motivational and reward systems, orgn. devel., workplace diversity. Contbr. articles to profl. jours. Recipient Cachet award for Outstanding Educator, 1994, Faculty of Yr. award, ASSW, 1987; fellow Urban Leadership Tng. Program, Columbia U., 1977—79. Mem.: NASW, Requisite Orgn. Internat. Inst., Assn. Rsch. on Nonprofit Orgns. and Vol. Action, Nat. Assn. Black Social Workers. Home: 1419 Oak Stream Dr Houston TX 77043-3410 Office: U Houston Grad Sch Social Work Houston TX 77004

LATTMAN, LAURENCE HAROLD, retired academic administrator; b. N.Y.C., Nov. 30, 1923; s. Jacob and Yetta (Schwartz) L.; m. Hanna Renate Cohn, Apr. 12, 1946; children— Martin Jacob, Barbara Diane. BSChemE, Coll. City N.Y., 1948; MS in Geology, U. Cin., 1951, PhD, 1953. Instr. U. Mich., 1952-53; asst. head photogeology sect. Gulf Oil Corp., Pitts., 1953-57; asst. prof. to prof. geomorphology Pa. State U., 1957-70; prof., head dept. geology U. Cin., 1970-75; dean Coll. of Mines U. Utah, 1975-83, dean Coll. Engring., 1978-83; pres. N.Mex. Tech., Socorro, 1983-93, pres. emeritus, 1993—. Bd. dirs. Pub. Svc. Co. of N.Mex.; cons. U.S. Army Engrs., Vicksburg, Miss., 1965-69, also major oil cos. Author: (with R.G. Ray) Aerial Photographs in Field Geology, 1965, (with D. Zillman) Energy Law; Contbr. articles to profl. jours. Mem. N.Mex. Environ. Improvement Bd., 1995—. With AUS, 1943-46. Fenneman fellow U. Cin., 1953. Fellow Geol. Soc. Am.; mem. Am. Assn. Petroleum Geologists, Am. Soc. Photogrammetry (Ford Bartlett award 1968), Soc. Econ. Paleontologists and Mineralogists, AIME (Disting. mem. 1981, Mineral Industries Edn., award 1986—), Assn. Western Univs. (chmn. bd. dirs. 1986-87), Sigma Xi. Home: 11509 Penfield Ln NE Albuquerque NM 87111-6526

LATTO, LEWIS M. broadcasting company executive; b. Duluth, Minn., Jan. 21, 1940; s. Lewis M. and Ethel S. L.; divorced; children: Aaron, Caroline. BA, U. Minn., 1963. Owner, mgr. Sta. KXTP, Duluth, 1965-94, Sta. WAKX-FM, 1974-94; owner Sta. KRBT-AM, WEVE-FM, Eveleth, Minn., 1978—, Sta. KGPZ-FM, Grand Rapids, 1995—. Mem. Duluth City Council, 1969-75, pres., 1974. Mem. Nat. Radio Broadcasters Assn. (dir.), Minn. Broadcasters Assn. (pres. 1992-93). Republican. Methodist. Office: Northland Radio Stas 5732 Eagle View Dr Duluth MN 55803-9498 E-mail: lewlatto@aol.com.

LATUSKY, WILLIAM JOHN, investment banker; b. Spokane, Wash., Jan. 12, 1943; s. William Eric and Alvina M. (Heinen) L.; m. Christine Janick, Oct. 25, 1969. BA in Econs., St. Mary's Coll., 1966; student, U. Minn., 1966-67. Fed. funds trader, bond portfolio acct. First Nat. Bank St. Paul, 1967-71, div. asst. bond. portfolio, 1971-74, bond portfolio officer, 1974-77; v.p. investments portfolio, chief investment officer First Western Savs. Assn., Las Vegas, Nev., 1977-89, sr. v.p., 1989-94; fin. advisor Morgan Stanley Dean Witter, 1995—. Mem. investment adv. com. Bd. of Regents U. Nev., Carson City, 1983. Active United Way, St. Paul, 1975-76; bd. dirs. Am. Cancer Soc., 1976-77. Mem. Fin. Mgrs. Soc. for Savs. and Loans, Nat. Corp. Cash Mgmt. Assn., Kiwanis (treas. 1981-85, bd. dirs. 1985-87, edn. chmn. Calif.-Nev. Hawaii dists. 1983-84). Republican. Roman Catholic. Avocation: photography. Home: 3155 E Rochelle Ave Las Vegas NV 89121-5114

LATZA, BEVERLY ANN, accountant; b. Pompton Plains, N.J., June 10, 1960; d. George and Helen Mae (Ryan) L. BA in Acctg., Bus. Adminstrn., Thiel Coll., 1982. Internal auditor Monroe Systems for Bus., Morris Plains, N.J., 1983-85; acct. Am. Airlines, Tulsa, 1985-86, Accountemps, Tulsa, 1986-87; credit investigator Denrich Leasing, Inc., Kansas City, Mo., 1987-89; with accounts receivable dept. Coca Cola Bottling Co. Am., Lenexa, Kans., 1989; with acctg. and accounts payable depts. Wolferman's Fine Breads, 1992-93; tax examining asst. IRS, Kansas City, Mo., 1989-98, customer svc. rep., 1998—2001, collectoin due process/collection appeals case worker, 2001—. Vol., disaster action team mem. ARC, 1996-97; reading tutor Literacy of Kansas City, 2001—. Lutheran. Avocations: reading, movies, singing, counted cross stitch. Home: 8323 W 108th St Apt C Overland Park KS 66210-1625 Office: IRS 2306 E Bannister Rd Kansas City MO 64131-3011

LATZKO, WILLIAM J. management consultant; b. Germany, Oct. 28, 1928; came to U.S., 1939; s. Frederick R. and Wanda K. (Herring) L.; m. Constance Benton, May 22, 1951; children: Victoria Bone, Alexander. BS, Fordham U., 1950; MBA, Rutgers U., 1956, degree in banking, 1978; PhD, Kennedy-Western U., 2000. Cert. quality engr. Chemist, plant mgr. The Joseph Dixon Crucible Co., Jersey City, 1953-57; plant mgr. Alpha Metals, 1957-58; dir. quality Mundet Cork, North Bergen, N.J., 1958-61; dir. mgmt. sci. CBS Columbia, N.Y.C., 1961-70; v.p. quality Irving Trust Co., 1970-83; pres. Latzko Assocs., North Bergen, 1983—; adj. prof. Fordham U., 1984—. Author: Quality and Productivity for Bankers and Financial Managers, 1983, Řízení Jakosti (Managing for Quality), 1996; co-author: Four Days with Dr. Deming, 1995, MICR QC Handbook, 1983; editor Am. Fencing mag., 1961-66. Bd. dirs. U.S. Fencing Assn., 1954-86, mem. exec. com., 1964-86, nat. sec., 1964-72, nat. treas., 1982-86; bd. dirs. U.S. Modern Pentathlon, San Antonio, 1960-65. 1st lt. U.S. Army, 1950-53; Korea. Decorated Bronze Star; recipient W. Edwards Deming medal, 1996; mem. U.S. Olympic Fencing Team, 1968, 72. Fellow Am. Soc. for Quality (regional dir., Ellis R. Ott award 1972, chair Deming medal com. 1997-99, Bd. Dirs. Testimonial award 2001), Royal Philatelic Soc. of London, Am. Statis Assn. (chmn. Q&P 1961—), Am. Soc. Quality; mem. U.S. Fencing Assn. (life, bd. dirs. 1953-70, sec.-treas.), Collectors Club N.Y. (gov. 1965—), Beta Gamma Sigma, Delta Pi Sigma. Avocations: fencing, philately. Home and Office: Latzko Associates 215 79th St North Bergen NJ 07047-5727 E-mail: latzko@att.net.

LAU, ALBERT MAN-FAI, physicist; b. Hong Kong, Aug. 22, 1947; came to U.S., 1966; s. Kwong Ming and Bik Wah Lau; m. Winnie Kwok-Yee Siu, June 16, 1971; children: Scott Bokhay, Winita Vinkay. BS summa cum laude, Yale U., 1970; MA, U. Calif., Berkeley, 1972, PhD, 1975; MS in radiological health physics, San Jose State U., 1995. Postdoctoral physicist SRI Internat., Menlo Park, Calif., 1975-77; staff physicst Exxon Rsch. and Engring. Co., Linden, N.J., 1977-82; sr. mem. tech. staff Sandia Nat. Labs., Livermore, Calif., 1983—. Vis. physicist NYU, N.Y.C., 1983, Princeton (N.J.) U., 1983; prof. invité U. Paris VI, 1979; assoc. prof. U. Paris-S., Orsay, France, 1980, U. Orleans, France, 1982. Contbr. articles to profl. jours., chpts. to books. Bd. dirs. Castro Valley Ednl. Found., 1995. Mem. Am. Phys. Soc., Health Physics Soc., Laser Inst. Am., Phi Beta Kappa. Achievements include pioneering research in laser-induced collisions and reactions, laser-induced predissociation; theoretical prediction and analyses of the photon-as-catalyst effect in laser-matter interaction.

LAU, BOBBY WAI-MAN, marketing professional, investment and financial planner, business startup trainer; b. Hong Kong, Dec. 24, 1944; s. Nelson and Ruby (Choy) L.; m. Sharon Tsai. BS in Math., U. Calif., Davis, 1969, MA in Math., 1971; postgrad. in math., Calif. Inst. Tech.; postgrad. in math and computers, UCLA, 1972-75. Ins. agt. Equitable Life Assurance Soc. of U.S., L.A., 1975-80, sr. dist. mgr., 1980-90; pres. Bobby Lau Seminars for Profls., 1979—. Chmn. bd. dirs. Success Pension & Ins. Svcs. Corp., dir. internat. fin. rsch., 1994—; dir. World Mktg. Power, 1994—. OSJ/BOM, United Securities Alliance, Inc., 2000—. Contbr. articles to mags. and newspapers. Office: PO Box 80223 San Marino CA 91118-8223 E-mail: worldmktgpower@msn.com

LAU, CHARLES KWOK-CHIU, architect, architectural firm executive; b. Hong Kong, Oct. 19, 1954; came to U.S., 1973; s. Oi-Ting and Wai-Han L. BFA in Environ. Design, U. Hawaii Manoa, Honolulu, 1977. Registered architect, Hawaii. Designer CJS Group Architects, Honolulu, 1977-78, Fox Hawaii, Honolulu, 1978-80, Wimberly Allison Tong & Goo, Honolulu, 1980-82, Architects Hawaii, Honolulu, 1982-84; assoc., designer Stringer & Assocs., 1984-85; pres. AM Ptrns., Inc., 1985—. Instr. U. Hawaii, Honolulu,

1987. Principal works include Crystal Fantasy, Hyatt Regency Hotel, Honolulu, 1988 (Merit award Hawaii chpt. AIA 1988), Dole Cannery Sq., Honolulu, 1989 (Merit award Hawaii Renaissance 1989), Danelle Christie's, Ala Moana Hotel, Honolulu, 1989 (Hawaii Region award Illuminating Engring. Soc. N.Am. 1989, Grand and Nat. Grand awards Hawaii Renaissance 1989, Tiger Restaurant, Lahaina, Hawaii, 1990 (Gold Key Excellence in Interior Design award Am. Hotel and Motel Assn. 1990, Nat. and Merit awards Hawaii Renaissance 1990), La Pierre du Roi, ANA Kalakaua Ctr., Honolulu, 1990 (Grand and Nat. Grand awards 1990), Crazy Shirts, Honolulu, 1991 (Grand and Overall awards Hawaii Renaissance 1991), Grand Hyatt Wailea, Maui, Hawaii, 1992 (Merit award Hawaii chpt. AIA 1992), Carrera y Carrera, Ala Moana Ctr., Honolulu, 1992 (Merit award Hawaii chpt. AIA 1992), Danelle Christie's, Outrigger Waikiki Hotel, Honolulu, 1992 (Merit award Hawaii Renaissance 1992), Exec. Ctr. Hotel, Honolulu, 1992 (Merit award Hawaii Renaissance 1992), Centre Ct. Restaurant, Honolulu, 1993 (Merit award Hawaii Renaissance 1993), Lani Huli, Kailua, 1993 (Spl. Recognition award Parade of Homes 1993), 218 Plantation Club Dr., Kapalua, Maui, 1993 (Interior Design award Am. Soc. Interior Design 1993), Royal Garden Restaurant, Alamoana Hotel, Honolulu, 1994 (Brand and Overall award Hawaii Renaissance, 1994, Lani Huli, Kailua, Hawaii (Project of Yr., City and County of Honolulu 1994). Recipient 1994 Best in Am. Living award Profl. Builders, Kapalua Residence in Maui. Mem. AIA (mem. design award jury selection com. Honolulu chpt. 1990), C. of C. Hawaii, Chinese C. of C. Hawaii, Pacific Club. Office: AM Partners Inc 1164 Bishop St Ste 1000 Honolulu HI 96813-2876

LAU, EUGENE WING IU, lawyer; b. Canton, China, Sept. 23, 1931; came to U.S., 1939; s. Eugene K. F. and Ann (Leung) L.; m. Dierdre Florence, July 20, 1962; children: Elyse M., Jennifer M. AB, U. Mich., 1953; LLB, Yale U., 1960. Bar: Hawaii 1960, U.S. Supreme Ct. 1965. Dep. Pros. Attys. Office, Honolulu, 1960-63; pvt. practice, 1963-67, 73—; v.p. Hawaii Corp., 1967-73. Del. People to People Legal Del. to China, 1987; mem. Commn. on Manpower and Full Employment, Honolulu, 1965-67. With U.S. Army, 1954-55. Mem. ABA, Hawaii Bar Assn., Punahou Tennis Club (Honolulu). Home: 3079 La Pietra Cir Honolulu HI 96815-4736 Office: 1188 Bishop St Ste 1912 Honolulu HI 96813-3308 E-mail: EL923@aol.com.

LAU, H. LORRIN, obstetrician/gynecologist, inventor; b. Honolulu, Apr. 21, 1932; s. Henry S. and Helen (Lee) L.; m. Maureen Lau; children: David, Marianne, Mike, Mark, Linda. AB cum laude, Harvard U., 1950-54; MD, Johns Hopkins U., 1954-58, MPH, 1970-71. Asst. prof. Sch. Med. Johns Hopkins U. (Balt.), 1964-82; assoc. prof. U. Hawaii, 1982-84; chief ob-gyn. St. Francis West Hosp., Honolulu, 1990-92, Kuakini Hosp., Honolulu, 1994-95. Fellow AMA; mem. ACOG, Internat. Soc. Biology and Medicine. Inventor pregnancy tests, helped introduce alpha-fetoprotein tests into obstetrics in USA, 1971. Home: 1121 Wilder Ave 1700B Honolulu HI 96822 Office: 1010 S King St Honolulu HI 96814-1701

LAU, HARRY HUNG-KWAN, acoustical and interior designer, consultant; b. Hong Kong, May 8, 1939; s. Kang Hoi and Yuk Jing (Chan) L. BArch, Ohio State U., 1965, M.Arch., 1966; postgrad. in archl. acoustics, MIT, 1967. Acoustical designer Bolt, Beranek & Newman, N.Y.C., 1967-69; archl. designer Marcel Breuer & Asscos., N.Y.C., 1969-70; archl. designer Edward L. Barnes & Asscos., N.Y.C., 1970-74; pres. MKC Design, N.Y.C., 1975-76; pres. Lau & Asscos., N.Y.C., 1977—; instr. of design N.Y. Inst. Tech., 1974. Summer grantee Harvard-Cornell Sardis Expdn., 1966. Mem. Acoustical Soc. Am., Nat. Council Interior Design, Am. Soc. Interior Design. Address: 30 E 95th St New York NY 10128-0718

LAU, HENRY, mechanical engineer, consultant; b. Hong Kong, Feb. 4, 1941; s. Mo Ngok and Julia (Seto) L.; m. Bing Sin, June 6, 1970; 1 child, Ryan Duke. BS, U. Tenn., 1966; MS, Duke U., Durham, N.C., 1969, PhD, 1973. Rsch. assoc. Duke U., Durham, 1973-74; mech. engr. Ayres & Hayakawa Energy Mgrs., L.A., 1974-77; tech. dir. Ayres Assocs., 1977-85; prin. and tech. dir. Ayres, Ezer, Lau Inc., 1985-92; sr. engr. So. Calif. Edison, San Dimas, 1992—. Cons. Lawrence Berkeley (Calif.) Lab., 1978-84, Calif. Energy Commn., Sacramento, 1978-82, Martin Marietta, L.A., 1981; lectr. demand side mgmt., China, 1996. Contbr. articles to profl. jours. Grantee Dow Chem., 1965, ASHRAE, 1974, U.S. Army Rsch., 1969; recipient William R. Gould award So. Calif. Edison, 2000. Mem. ASHRAE, ASME, Sigma Xi. Roman Catholic. Achievements include research in building energy systems, computer energy simulations, energy efficiency standards, indoor air quality, energy conservation, solar energy, thermal storage systems, load management. Home: 1948 S Crest Dr Los Angeles CA 90034-1151 Office: Southern Calif Edison Co 6042 N Irwindale Ave Ste B Azusa CA 91702-3207 E-mail: lauh@sce.com.

LAU, JOANNA T. information technology executive; BS in Computer Sci. and Applied Math., SUNY, Stony Brook; MS in Computer Engring., Old Dominion U., 1985; MBA in Bus. and Ops., Boston U., 1991; PhD (hon.) , Suffolk U., 1999, Bentley Coll., 1998, Bryant Coll., 1997. Software engr. aerospace control systems dept. GE, 1981—83, consumer electronics ops. systems engr., 1983—85, CIM project mgr. aircraft engine bus. group, 1986—89; supr. mfg. engring. Digital Equipment Corp., 1989—90; pres., chmn. bd. LAU Acquisition Corp./LAU Technologies, Littleton, Mass., 1990—. Mem. Army Sci. Bd. Mem. Kennedy Libr. Found., Com. of 200. Named Nat. Turnaround Entrepreneur of the Yr., 1995, 8(a) Small Bus. Person of the Yr. for Mass., 1995; recipient Pinnacle award, Greater Boston C. of C., 1997, Leadership award to Women in Bus., New Eng. Coun., Young Engring. award, GE Aircraft Engine Group. Mem.: Young Pres.'s Orgn., Internat. Women's Forum, Assn. of U.S. Army, Nat. Def. Indsl. Assn. Office: Lau Technologies 30 Porter Rd Littleton MA 01460*

LAU, JOHN HON SHING, electronics scientist; b. China, June 17, 1946; came to U.S., 1973; s. Shui Hong and Mary Au L.; m. Teresa Yu, Sept. 2, 1972; 1 child, Judy M. BS in Civil Engring., Nat. Taiwan U., 1970; MASc in Structural Engring., U. B.C., 1973; MS in Engring. Mechanics, U. Wis., 1974; PhD in Theoretical and Applied Mechanics, U. Ill., 1977; MS in Mgmt., Fairleigh Dickinson U., 1981. Registered profl. engr., N.Y., Calif. Rsch. engr. Exxon Prodn. and Rsch. Co., Houston, 1977; structural specialist Control Data Corp., Sunnyvale, Calif., 1977-78; rsch. assoc. Internat. Paper Co., Tuxedo Park, N.Y., 1978-79; sr. engr. Ebasco Svcs. Inc., N.Y.C., 1979-81, Bechtel Power Corp., San Francisco, 1981-83; MTS Sandia Nat. Lab., N.Mex., 1983-84, Hewlett-Packard Labs., Palo Alto, Calif., 1984-95; pres. Express Packaging Sys., Inc., 1995-2000; sr. scientist Agilent Techs., Inc., San Jose, 2000—. Contbr. articles to profl. jours. and 14 tech. books; assoc. editor: ASME Transaction Jour. Elec. Packaging. Fellow ASME, IEEE; mem. ASM Internat., AAAS, N.Y. Acad. Scis., Sigma Xi. Roman Catholic. Home: 961 Newell Rd Palo Alto CA 94303-2929 Office: 5301 Stevens Creek Blvd Santa Clara CA 95051-7201 E-mail: lau@agilent.com.

LAU, JOSEPH JAMES, investment analyst; b. Bayonne, N.J., Mar. 20, 1975; s. James Michael and Carol Jean (Malack) L. BS in Fin. and Econs., St. Joseph's U., 1997; MBA, Oxford U., 2000. Tax analyst Core States Fin., Phila., 1996-97; performance analytics specialist J.P. Morgan Investment Mgmt., N.Y.C., 1997-98; investment analyst J.P. Morgan Securities, 1998-2000; structured capital markets assoc. Barclays Capital, 2000—. Author: Wander, 1994. Mem. Fin. Mgmt. Assn. (pres. local chpt. 1996-97), Omicron Delta Epsilon. Republican. Roman Catholic. Home: 182 Lighthouse Dr Freehold NJ 07728-1301 Office: Barclays Capital 222 Broadway New York NY 10038 E-mail: joseph.lau@barcap.com.

LAU, LAWRENCE JUEN-YEE, economics educator, consultant; b. Guizhou, China, Dec. 12, 1944; came to U.S., 1961, naturalized, 1974; s. Shai-Tat and Chi-Hing (Yu) Liu. BS with great distinction, Stanford U., 1964; MA, U. Calif., Berkeley, 1966, PhD, 1969; D.Social Sci. honoris causa, Hong Kong U. Sci. and Tech. From acting asst. prof. econs. to assoc. prof. Stanford U., Palo Alto, Calif., 1966-76, prof., 1976—, Kwoh-Ting Li prof. econ. devel., 1992—. Co-dir. Asia/Pacific Rsch. Ctr., Stanford U., 1992-96; dir. Bank of Canton of Calif., San Francisco, 1979-85, Property Resources Equity Trust, Los Gatos, 1987-88, Stanford Inst. Econ. Policy Rsch., 1997-99; cons. The World Bank, Wash., 1976-; vice chmn. Bank of Canton of Calif. Bldg. Corp., San Francisco, 1981-85, Complete Computer Co. Far Eat Ltd., Hong Kong, 1981-89; bd. dirs. Taiwan Fund, Inc., BOC Internat. Holdings Ltd., Hong Kong, Media Partners Internat. Holdings Inc., Hong Kong, Bank of Canton of Calif., San Francisco, 1999-. Co-author: (with D.T. Jamison) Farmer Education and Farm Efficiency, 1982, Models of Devlopment: A Comparative Study of Economic Growth in South Korea and Taiwan, 1986, rev. edit., 1990, Econometrics and the Cost of Capital: Essays in Honor of Dale W. Jorgenson, 2000, (with C.H. Yoon) North Korea in Transition: Prospects for Economic and Social Reform, 2001; contbr. articles to profl. jours. Adv. bd. Self-Help for Elderly, San Francisco, 1982—; bd. dirs. Chiang Ching-Kuo Found. for Internat. Scholarly Exch., 1989—; govs. coun. econ. policy advisors State of Calif., 1993-99; mem. Asian Art Commn., San Francisco, 1998-2001; mem. adv. coun. Innovation and Tech., Hong Kong, 2000-02. John Simon Guggenheim Meml. fellow, 1973; fellow Ctr. for Advanced Study in Behavioral Scis., 1982; Overseas fellow Churchill Coll., Cambridge U., Eng., 1984 Fellow Econometric Soc.; mem. Academia Sinica (academician), Conf. Research in Income and Wealth, Chinese Acad. Social Scis. (hon.), Internat. Eurasian Acad. Scis. (academician). Episcopalian. Office: Stanford U Dept Econs Stanford CA 94305-6072 E-mail: ljlau@stanford.edu.

LAU, MARY APPLEGATE, lawyer; b. Washington, Dec. 17, 1952; d. Robert Lee and Barbara Edith (Pressler) Applegate; m. James Victor Lau, Apr. 1, 1982; 1 child, Chelsea Nicole. BA magna cum laude, Mich. State U., 1974; JD with honors, Fla. State U., 1976. Bar: Fla. 1977, U.S. Dist. Ct. (mid. dist.) Fla. 1977, U.S. Ct. Appeals (11th cir.) 1977. Assoc. atty. Holland and Knight, Tampa, Fla., 1977-82, ptnr., 1982-86; shareholder Lau, Lane, Pieper, Conley & McCreadie, P.A., 1986—. Mem. Fed. Bar Assn., (treas. Tampa Bay chpt. 1993), Hillsborough County Bar Assn. Republican. Roman Catholic. Office: Lau Lane Pieper Conley & McCreadie PA 100 S Ashley Dr Tampa FL 33602-5360

LAU, MICHELE DENISE, advertising consultant, sales trainer, television personality; b. St. Paul, Dec. 6, 1960; d. Dwyane Udell and Patricia Ann (Yri) L. Student, U. Minn., 1979-82. Pub. rels. coord. Stillwater (Minn.) C. of C., 1977-79; asst. mgr. Salkin & Linoff, Mpls., 1982, store merchandiser, sales trainer, 1982-83; rental agt. Sentinel Mgmt. Co., St. Paul, 1983-84; account exec. Community Svc. Publs., Mpls., 1984-85, frwy. news supr., 1985, asst. sales mgr., 1985-86, St. Paul Pioneer Press Dispatch, 1986-91; pres. Promotional Ptnrs., Eden Prairie, Minn., 1991-96; on-air show host Home Shopping Network, 1996—. On-air personality Sta. WCCO II Cable TV Mpls., 1988-89, co-host Afternoon Midwest, 1989-93; co-host Home Shopping Show, host Minn. Voices, Fox 29, 1995; cons. U. Minn. Alumni mag., 1986-89. Author mechandising and sales tng. manuals. Fund-raiser sustaining program YMCA, Mpls., 1986, Jr. Achievement, St. Paul, 1988; cons. Muscular Dystrophy Assn., St. Paul, 1988-89; bd. dirs. St. Paul Jaycees. Mem. NAFE, Nat. Assn. Home Builders, Mpls. Builder Assn. (amb.), Metro-East Profl. Builders Assn. (spl. events com.), Advt. Fedn., The Newspaper Guild, Internat. Platform Assn., Speakeasy Club. Lutheran. Avocations: tennis, golf, aerobics. Home: 4961 Bacopa Ln S Unit 102 Saint Petersburg FL 33715-2621 E-mail: michelelau@aol.com.

LAU, PATRICK HING-LEUNG, radiologist, educator; b. Hong Kong, May 21, 1945; m. Peggy Lau; children: Eric, Chad. BS, St. Louis U., 1970; DO, Midwestern U., 1974. Diplomate Am. Bd. Radiology. Intern Grandview Hosp. Med. Ctr., 1974-75; pvt. practice family medicine, 1975—80; resident Mt. Sinai Med. Ctr., 1981-84; fellow Coll. Medicine U. Ill., 1984-85, radiology instr., 1984-85; asst. prof. radiology Phila. Coll. Osteo. Medicine, 1985-86; chief imaging svcs. VA No. Ind. Healthcare Sys., Marion, 1988—; med. dir. radiology tech. program Ivy Tech. State Coll., 2001—. Adj. faculty Ind. Wesleyan U., 2000—. Contbr. articles to profl. jours. Dep. med. examiner, Monroe County, Mich., 1977-80; police surgeon Am. Law Enforcement Officers Assn., 1979-80. Recipient Abbie Norman Prince award for Outstanding Svc., Mt. Sinai Med. Ctr., 1984, cert. of appreciation, Midwestern U., 1984, 1999, cert. recognition, Am. Osteo. Coll. Radiology, 1985, award of appreciation, SME Boy Scouts Am., 1991, Hands and Heart award VA Affairs, 1995, 2000, Exceptional Svc. award, VFW, 1999. Mem. Am. Coll. Radiology, Radiol. Soc. N.Am. Office: VA No Ind Healthcare Sys 1700 E 38th St Marion IN 46953-4568

LAU, ROY ESME, surgeon; b. Trinidad, Tobago, W.I., July 6, 1924; MD, U. Toronto, 1948, BSc in Medicine, 1950. Diplomate Am. Bd. Surgery. Intern Vancouver Gen. Hosp., 1948-49; fellow in biochemistry U. Toronto, 1949-50; resident N.Y. Hosp. - Cornell Med. Ctr., 1950-52, NYU - Bellevue Med. Ctr., N.Y.C., 1952-54; resident, chief resident in surgery Mt. Sinai Hosp., NY, 1955-57; surgeon Hoag Meml. Hosp., Newport Beach, Calif.; med. dir. Medicare So. Calif., 1993-94; clin. assoc. prof. surgery U. Calif., Irvine. Cons. integrative care oncology and Chinese herbology. Fellow Am. Coll. Surgery; mem. Am. Soc. Clin. Oncology, Soc. Surg. Oncology.

LAUB, CAROLYN MICHELLE, cultural organization administrator; b. Mpls., Aug. 27, 1974; d. Alan John Laub and Margaret Diane Zonana. BA, Stanford U., 1995. Dir. AIDS prevention program YWCA Mid-Peninsula, Palo Alto, Calif., 1995-99; dir., founder Gay-Straight Alliance Network, San Francisco, 1998—. Mem. adv. panel Sta. KQED-AM-FM, San Francisco, 2000-2001. V.p. bd. dirs. Bay Area Young Positives, San Francisco, 1997-2001; mem. adv. bd. Transgender Law Ctr., San Francisco, 2001—. Fellow Echoing Green Found., 1999—, Ashoka, 2000. Mem.: Stanford Gay and Lesbian Alumni Club (bd. dirs. 2001—). Office: GSA Network 160 14th St San Francisco CA 94103-2965

LAUB, DAVID L. music educator; b. North Tonawanda, N.Y., Nov. 8, 1972; s. Robert L. Laub, Linda G. Laub. B in Music Edn., Bowling Green State U., 1994. Cert. profl. tchg. cert. Colo., 1997. Dir. music Battle Mountain H.S., Avon, Colo., 1997—. Dir. regional big band Vail Jazz Found., Vail, Colo., 2001—; pvt. music tchr., Avon, 1997—; musician, Avon, 1996—. Avocations: skiing, kayaking, rock climbing, whitewater rafting, mountain biking. Home: PO Box 2281 Avon CO 81620

LAUB, DORI, psychiatrist; b. Chernovtsy, Romania, June 8, 1937; d. Moshe and Clara (Sattinger) Laub; children: Miri, Avi; m. Johanna Bodenstab. MD, Hebrew U./Hadassah Med. Sch., Jerusalem, Israel, 1961; MA in Clin. Psychology, Bar Ilan U., Ramat Gan, Israel, 1966. Diplomate Am. Bd. Psychiatry and Neurology; cert. in psychoanalysis; lic. Israel, Conn., N.Y., Mass. Intern Rambam Hosp., Haifa, Israel, 1962-63; resident Acre (Israel) Mental Hosp., 1965-66, Boston City Hosp., 1966-67; fellow in psychiatry Austen Riggs Ctr., Inc., Stockbridge, Mass., 1967-69; resident dept. psychiatry Yale U., New Haven, 1969; psychoanalytic tng. We. New Eng. Inst. for Psychoanalysis, 1968-79; psychotherapist, chief group psychotherapy program Conn. Mental Health Ctr., 1970-77; assoc. dir. mental health tng. Connecticut Valley Hosp., 1977-81, dir. residency tng. program, 1981-93, sr. attending physician psychosis and treatment unit Conn. Mental Health Ctr., 1993-95; attending psychiatrist homeless outreach team Access Project, 1995—. Part-time pvt. practice in psychotherapy, 1972—; from instr. to assoc. clin. prof. dept. psychiatry Yale U., 1969—; co-vis. lectr. Yale Law Sch., 1994; acting dir. Genocide Study Program Yale U., 2000, dep. dir. trauma studies, 2001—. Co-author: Testimony-Crisis of Witnessing in Literature, Psychoanalysis and History, 1992; contbr. articles to profl. jours. Recipient Sigmund Freud prize, 1962. Fellow Am. Psychiat. Assn.; mem. AMA, Internat. Psychoanalytic Assn., Soc. for Traumatic Stress Studies. Home: 30 Ranch Rd Woodbridge CT 06525-1912 Office: 315 Whitney Ave Ste 2 New Haven CT 06511-3715 also: 267 William St Middletown CT 06457-3212

LAUB, WILLIAM MURRAY, retired utility executive; b. Ft. Mills, Corregidor, Philippines, July 20, 1924; s. Harold Goodspeed and Marjorie M. (Murray) L.; m. Mary McDonald, July 26, 1947; children: William, Andrew, Mary, David, John. BSBA, U. Calif., Berkeley, 1947, LLB, 1950. Bar: Calif. 1951. Practice law, Los Angeles, 1951-55; with Southwest Gas Corp., Las Vegas, Nev., 1948-88, v.p., gen. counsel, 1958-60, exec. v.p., 1960-64, pres., chief exec. officer, 1964-82, chmn., chief exec. officer, 1982-88. Pres. Boulder Dam Area council Boy Scouts Am., 1967-69, So. Nev. Indsl. Found., 1967-68, So. Nev. Meth. Found., 1967-74; chmn. Nev. Equal Rights Commn., 1966-68; Chmn. Clark County Republican Central Com., 1964-66; nat. committeeman Nev. Rep. Com., 1968-80; trustee Sch. Theology at Claremont, Calif., 1977—; trustee Inst. Gas Tech., 1983-89; nat. bd. advisors, coll. bus. and pub. adminstrn. The U. Ariz., 1985-89; bd. dirs. Alliance for Acid Rain Control, 1985-89. Served to lt. (j.g.) USNR, 1941-45. Mem. ABA, Am. Gas Assn. (bd. dirs., chmn. 1986-87), Pacific Coast Gas Assn. (chmn. 1983), Calif. Bar Assn., Nat. Coal Coun., Jonathan Club, Pauma Valley Country Club, Spanish Trail Golf and Country Club, Las Vegas Country Club. Office: 2810 W Charleston Blvd Ste 53 Las Vegas NV 89102-1906

LAUBACH, ROGER ALVIN, accountant; b. Riegelsville, N.J., July 3, 1922; s. Harry and Daisy (Cyphers) L. Diploma in bus. adminstrn., Churchman Bus. Coll., Easton, Pa., 1941; BS cum laude in Acctg., Rider U., 1949. CPA, N.Y., N.J. Acct. Coopers & Lybrand, CPAs, N.Y.C., 1949-60; asst. to treas. Coca-Cola Bottling Co. N.Y., 1960-63; mgr. audits and systems Atlantic Rsch. Corp., Alexandria, Va., 1964-65; contr. Ely-Cruiskshank Co., Inc., Realtors, N.Y.C., 1965-66, asst. treas., 1966-67, treas., dir., 1967-71; dir. N.Y. Fed. Savs. & Loan Assn., 1970-71; dir. Phila. Acctg. Ctr. Ogden Food Svc. Corp., 1971-72, treas., 1972-77; dir. corp. auditing Ogden Corp., N.Y.C., 1977-79; contr. Burlington County Cmty. Action Program, Burlington, N.J., 1981-84. With U.S. Army, 1942-46; ETO. Decorated Bronze Star, N.J. Disting. Svc. medal, 1998; recipient Cold War cert. recognition, 2000, Burlington County Mil. Svc. medal, 2001, Thank You Am. cert. for participation in liberation of France during World War II, Embassy of France. Mem. AICPA, ARC (vol. bloodmobile 1986—), Inst. Internal Auditors, N.Y. State Soc. CPAs, N.J. Soc. CPAs, Real Estate Bd. N.Y., SAR (registrar, geneal. 1995-2001, War Svc. medal, Liberty medal with 3 bronze oak leaf clusters, cert. of disting. svc.), VFW (life), Am. Legion (life), 100th Inf. Divsn. Assn., Soc. Colonial Wars (life), Laubach Family Assn. (book com. 1989-93), Nat. Trust for Hist. Preservation, Bucks County (Pa.) Hist. Soc., Warren County (N.J.) His. Soc., Delta Sigma Pi (life). Home: 39 Southgate Rd Mount Laurel NJ 08054-2932

LAUBE, ROGER GUSTAV, retired trust officer, financial consultant; b. Chgo., Aug. 11, 1921; s. William C. and Elsie (Drews) L.; m. Irene Mary Chadbourne, Mar. 30, 1946; children: David Roger, Philip Russell, Steven Richard. BA, Roosevelt U., 1942; postgrad., John Marshall Law Sch., 1942, 48-50; LLB, Northwestern U., 1960; postgrad., U. Wash., 1962-64. Cert. fin. cons. With Chgo. Title & Trust Co., Chgo., 1938-42, 48-50, Nat. Bank Alaska, Anchorage, 1950-72, mgr. mortgage dept., 1950-56, v.p., trust officer, mgr. trust dept., 1956-72; v.p., trust officer, mktg. dir., mgr. estate and fin. planning div. Bishop Trust Co., Ltd., Honolulu, 1972-82; instr. estate planning U. Hawaii, 1978-82; exec. v.p. Design Capital Planning Group, Inc., Tucson, 1982-83; pres., sr. trust officer, registered investment adviser Advanced Capital Advisory, Inc. of Ariz., 1983-89; registered rep., pres. Advanced Capital Investments, Inc. of Ariz., Prescott, 1983-89; pres., chief exec. officer Advanced Capital Devel., Inc. of Ariz., 1983-89; mng. exec. Integrated Resources Equity Corp., 1983-89. Pres. Anchorage Estate Planning Coun., 1960-62, Charter mem., 1960-72, Hawaii Estate Planning Coun., 1972-82, v.p., 1979, pres., 1980, bd. dirs., 1981-82; charter mem. Prescott Estate Planning Coun., 1986-90, pres. 1988. Charter mem. Anchorage Community Chorus, 1946, pres., 1950-53, bd. dirs., 1953-72, Alaska Festival of Music, 1960-72; mem. Anchorage camp Gideons Internat., 1947-72, Honolulu camp, 1972-82, mem. Cen. camp, Tucson, 1982-85, Prescott, 1985-90, Port Angeles-Sequim Camp, 1990—; mem. adv. bd. Faith Hosp., Glenallen, Alaska, 1960—, Cen. Alaska Mission of Far Ea. Gospel Crusade, 1960—; sec., treas. Alaska Bapt. Found., 1955-72; bd. dirs. Anchorage Symphony, 1965-72; bd. dirs. Bapt. Found. of Ariz., 1985-90; bd. dirs., mem. investment com. N.W. Bapt. Found., 1991-97; mem. mainland adv. coun. Hawaii Bapt. Acad., Honolulu, 1982—; pres. Sabinovista Townhouse Assn., 1983-85; bd. advisers Salvation Army, Alaska , 1961-72, chmn., Anchorage, 1969-72, bd. advisers, Honolulu, 1972-82, chmn. bd. advisers, 1976-78; asst. staff judge adv. Alaskan Command, 1946-48; exec. com. Alaska Conv., 1959-61, dir. music Chgo., 1938-42, 48-50, Alaska, 1950-72, Hawaii, 1972-82, Tucson, 1982-85, 1st So. Bapt. Ch., Prescott Valley, Ariz., 1985-90; 1st Bapt. of Sequim, Wash., 1990-98; chmn. bd. trustees Hawaii, 1972-81, Prescott Valley, 1986-89, Sequim, Wash., 1991—; worship leader Waikiki Ch., 1979-82. 1st lt., JAGD, U.S. Army, 1942-48. Recipient Others award Salvation Army, 1972 Mem. Am. Inst. Banking (instr. trust div. 1961-72), Am. Bankers Assn. (legis. com., trust div. 1960-72), Nat. Assn. Life Underwriters (nat. com. for Ariz.), Yavapai County-Prescott Life Underwriters Assn. (charter), Anchorage C. of C. (awards com. 1969-71), Internat. Assn. Fin. Planners (treas. Anchorage chpt. 1969-72, exec. com. Honolulu chpt. 1972-82, Ariz. chpt. 1982-90, del. to World Congress Australia and New Zealand 1987), Am. Assn. Handbell Ringers. Baptist. Home: Sunland Country Club 212 Sunset Pl Sequim WA 98382-8515

LAUBENHEIMER, JEFFREY JOHN, civil engineer; b. Westbend, Wis., Aug. 3, 1963; s. Henry Wilbur and Ann Elizabeth (Fassbender) L.; m. Mary Ellen Gebhardt, July 7, 1990; children: Michael John, Bethany Rose. BS in Civil Engring., Marquette U., 1989. Registered profl. engr., Wis., Ill. Civil technician J.C. Zimmerman Engring. Corp., Greenfield, Wis., 1987-89; project engr. Larsen Engrs., Milw., 1989-95; sr. project engr. Raintree Engring., Inc., Pewaukee, 1995-96; sr. engr. Edwards & Kelcey, Inc., Milw., 1997—2000; transp. mgr. Patrick Engring. Inc., 2000—. Mem. Am. Soc. Civil Engrs., Nat. Soc. Profl. Engrs., Wis. Soc. Profl. Engrs. Office: Patrick Engring Inc 330 E Kilbourn Ave Ste 1030 Milwaukee WI 53202

LAUBER, KELLI KATHERINE MARGARET, criminal justice instr. b. Pasadena, Calif., July 31, 1968; d. Dianne Kathleen Johnson. BS in Psychology, Boise State U., 1993, BA in Anthropology, 1995; M in Forensic Sci., Nat. U., San Diego, 1998. Cert. peace officer, Calif. Dep. sheriff Ada County Sheriff's Dept., Boise, Idaho, 1991-96; probation officer juvenile and adult field svcs. San Diego County Probation Dept., 1998-2001; intensive probation officer Maricopa County Probation Dept., Mesa, Ariz., 2001—; criminal justice instr. Education America, Tempe. Mem. San Diego County Juvenile Firesetter's Adv. Coun., San Diego County Sex Offender Mgmt. Program. Mem. Am. Acad. Forensic Scis., Am. Coll. Forensic Examiners. Avocations: seminars, animal rights activist, camping/hiking/outdoor activities, photography. Home: 1325 W Musket Way Chandler AZ 85248 E-mail: kellik31@yahoo.com.

LAUBER, MIGNON DIANE, food processing company executive; b. Detroit, Dec. 21; d. Charles Edmond and Maud Lillian (Foster) Donaker; m. Richard Brian Lauber, Sept. 13, 1963; 1 child Leslie Viane (dec.). Student , Kelsey Jenny U., 1958, Brigham Young U., 1959. Owner, operator Alaska World Travel, Ketchikan, 1964—67; founder, owner, pres. Oosick Soup Co., Juneau, 1969—. Author: Down at the Water Works with Jesus, 1982, Failure Through Prayer, 1983, We All Want to Go to Heaven But Nobody Wants to Die, 1988. Treas. Pioneer Alaska Lobbyists Soc., Pioneer Alaska Lobbyists Soc., Juneau, Juneau, 1977—. Mem.: Bus. and Profl. Women, Alaska C. of C. Libertarian, Washington Athletic Club. Home: 321 Highland Dr Juneau AK 99801-1442

LAUBER, PATRICIA GRACE, writer; b. N.Y.C., Feb. 5, 1924; d. Hubert Crow and Florence (Walker) Lauber. BA, Wellesley Coll., 1945. Rsch., writer Look Mag. Book Dept., N.Y.C., 1945-46; staff writer Scholastic Mags., 1946-48, editor, 1948-54, freelance editor, 1954-56, Challenge Books, Coward-McCann, N.Y.C., 1955-59; founding editor, editor-in-chief Science World, Street & Smith, 1956-59; chief editor Science and Mathematics, The New Book of Knowledge, Grolier, 1961-67; freelance editor Good Earth Books, Garrard, Scarsdale, N.Y., 1973-79. Cons. editor Sci. Am. Books, N.Y.C., 1977—80; cons. Nat. Sci. Resources Ctr., NAS-Smithsonian Instn., 1992—94. Author: (children's book) Volcano: The Eruption and Healing of Mount St. Helens, 1986 (Newbery Honor Book, 1987, N.Y. Acad. Scis. Hon. Mention, 1987), From Flower to Flower: Animals and Pollination, 1986 (N.Y. Acad. Scis. Hon. Mention, 1988), Dinosaurs Walked Here and Other Stories Fossils Tell, 1987, Snakes are Hunters, 1988, Lost Star, the Story of Amelia Earhart, 1988, Meteors and Meteorites: Voyagers from Space, 1989, The News About Dinosaurs, 1989 (N.Y. Acad. Scis. Hon. Mention, 1990), Living with Dinosaurs, 1989 (Orbis Pictus Hon. Mention Nat. Coun. Tchrs. English, 1990), Seeing Earth from Space, 1990 (Orbis Pictus Hon. Mention Nat. Coun. Tchrs. English, 1991), Summer of Fire, 1991, Fur, Feathers, and Flippers, 1994, How Dinosaurs Came To Be, 1996, Hurricanes, 1996, Flood: Wrestling with the Mississippi, 1996, Painters of the Caves, 1998, Purrfectly Purrfect, 2000, Tubs, Toilets and Showers, 2001, others. Recipient award for Overall Contbn. to Children's Lit., Washington Post/Children's Book Guild, 1983, Eva L. Gordon award, Am. Nature Study Soc., 1988, Lit. award, Ctrl. Mo. State U., 1989, Lifetime Achievement commendation, Nat. Forum Children's Sci. Books, Carnegie-Mellon U., 1992, Alumnae Achievement award, Wellesley

Coll., 1998, Kerlan award, 2000. Mem.: PEN, Soc. Children's Book Writers, Authors Guild. Democrat. Congregationalist. Avocations: reading, music, hiking, travel, sailing. Office: care Scholastic Press 555 Broadway New York NY 10012-3919

LAUB-NOVAK, KAREN, artist, writer, sculptor; b. Mpls., Aug. 25, 1937; m. Michael Novak; 3 children. BA, Carleton Coll., 1959; MFA, U. Iowa, 1961. Instr. Carleton Coll., Northfield, Minn., 1961-62, Stanford U., Palo Alto, Calif., 1965-68, SUNY, Old Westbury, 1970, Syracuse (N.Y.) U., 1976-78, Mt. Vernon Coll., Washington, 1979, Georgetown U., Washington, 1980-81; free-lance artist, sculptor, painter, lithographer, 1963—. One-man and group shows include Union Court Gallery, San Francisco, Los Robles Gallery, Palo Alto, Calif., Harvard U., Cambridge, Mass., Yale U., New Haven Conn., Rochester Art Ctr., Des Moines Art Mus., Fox Hall Gallery, Washington, Union Station, Washington, others; sculptures commd. for Empower Am., Becket Fund, Am. Enterprise Inst., Youth for the Third Millennium, Manhattan Inst., others. Studio: Laub-Novak Studio Box 13 Lewes DE 19958

LAUBSCHER, LEEANN, medical and surgical nurse; b. Monticello, N.Y., Apr. 24, 1962; d. Lee Gregory Baumgardt and Carole Ann (Blume) Nicolis; m. Robert Francis Laubscher, Aug. 16, 1986. BSN, Mt. St. Mary Coll., Newburgh, N.Y., 1984; MSN, SUNY, New Paltz, 1996. RN, N.Y. Staff nurse Westchester County Med. Ctr., Valhalla, N.Y., 1984-90, VA Hudson Valley Healthcare Sys., 1990-98, nurse mgr. ICU, 1992, women vets. coord., 1995—2001, patient advocate, 1998—. Breast cancer detection awareness educator Am. Cancer Soc., N.Y., 1995—; cmty. educator LENS (Linking Edn., Nursing and Seniors) Project, 1995. Mem. N.Y. State Nurses Assn. (Dist. 12), Soc. Healthcare Consumer Advocacy, Sigma Theta Tau Internat. Nursing Honor Soc. Avocations: reading, needlework, travel. Office: VA Hudson Valley Healthcare Castle Point NY 12511 E-mail: leeann.laubscher@med.va.gov.

LAUBSCHER, ROBERT JAMES, consumer products company executive; b. Tucson, Mar. 20, 1961; s. James Albert and Geri Lee (Bird) L.; m. Deborah Elaine Fuggles, Apr. 14, 1984; children: Stephanie Claire, Samuel Robert, Jonathan Daniel. BA in Econs., Calif. State U., Northridge, 1985; AS in Fire Tech., Oxnard Coll., 1986; cert. in ind. tax prep., Coll. for Fin. Planning, Denver, 1989. Acctg. mgr. Morning Star Labs., Inc., Moorpark, Calif., 1985-89; acctg. and credit mgr. Am. Tombow, Inc., Westlake Village, 1989-92, v.p. ops. Lawrenceville, Ga., 1992—. Owner Gold Coast Acctg. Svcs., Camarillo, Calif., 1989-92. With USMCR, 1981-87. Mem. Writing Instruments Mfg. Assn. (statis. com.), Bus. Products Credit Assn. (bd. dirs.), Nat. Eagle Scout Assn. Republican. Mem. Full Gospel Ch. Avocation: running. Home: 11390 Donnington Dr Duluth GA 30097-8413 E-mail: rlaubscher@tombowusa.com.

LAUCHENGCO, JOSE YUJUICO, JR. lawyer; b. Manila, Philippines, Dec. 6, 1936; came to U.S., 1962; s. José Celis Sr. Lauchengco and Angeles (Yujuico) Sapota; m. Elisabeth Schindler, Feb. 22, 1968; children: Birthe, Martina, Duane, Lance. AB, U. Philippines, Quezon City, 1959; MBA, U. So. Calif., 1964; JD, Loyola U., L.A., 1971. Bar: Calif. 1972, U.S. Dist. Ct. (cen. dist.) Calif. 1972, U.S. Ct. Appeals (9th cir.) 1972, U.S. Supreme Ct. 1975. Banker First Western Bank/United Calif. Bank, L.A., 1964-71; assoc. Demler, Perona, Langer & Bergkvist, Long Beach, Calif., 1972-73; ptnr. Demler, Perona, Langer, Bergkvist, Lauchengco & Manzella, 1973-77; sole practice Long Beach and L.A., 1977-83; ptnr. Lauchengco & Mendoza, L.A., 1983-92; pvt. practice, 1993—. Mem. commn. on jud. procedures County of L.A., 1979; tchr. Confraternity of Christian Doctrine, 1972-79; counsel Philippine Presdl. Commn. on Good Govt., L.A., 1986. Chmn. Filipino-Am. Bi-Partisan Polit. Action Group, L.A., 1978. Recipient Degree of Distinction, Nat. Forensic League, 1955. Mem. Criminal Cts. Bar Assn., Calif. Attys. Criminal Justice, Calif. Pub. Defenders Assn., Philippine-Am. Bar Assn., U. Philippines Vanguard Assn. (life), Beta Sigma. Lodges: K.C. Roman Catholic. Avocations: classical music, opera, romantic paintings and sculpture, camping, shooting. Office: 3545 Wilshire Blvd Ste 247 Los Angeles CA 90010-2388

LAUCHLE, GERALD CLYDE, acoustics educator; b. Williamsport, Pa., Sept. 20, 1945; s. Clarence Walter and Helen (Borowski) Lauchle; m. Esther E. Smith, July 19, 1996; children: Keith, Paul. BS, Pa. State U., 1968, PhD, 1974. Cert. noise control engr. Am. Bd. Noise Control Engrs. From rsch. asst. to sr. scientist Pa. State U., State College, 1968-90; prof. Pa. State U. Coll. Engring., 1990—. Consult Bell Labs, Murray Hills, NJ, 1991—92, GM, Milford, Mich., 1993, Eastman Kodak, Rochester, NY, 1992, AMETEK Corp, Kent, Ohio, 1993, Fisher Controls, Marshaltown, Iowa, 1994, John Deere, Horicon, Wis., 1995, Knoll Atomic Power Lab, 1996, Nortel Networks, 2000. Co-author: (book) Lecture Notes in Engineering, 1989; contbr. articles to profl jours. Fellow: Acoustical Soc Am Inst Noise Control Eng. Office: Pa State Univ Graduate Program in Acoustics 218-B Applied Sci Bldg University Park PA 16802 E-mail: gcl1@psu.edu.

LAUCHNER, KATHRYN ANN, nursing educator; b. Belleville, Ill., Sept. 20, 1946; d. Ralph R. and Mary Kathryn (Neumann) Conduitt; m. Paul Burris, Aug. 10, 1968 (div. 1982); 1 child, Kelly Lynn Burris. BSN, U. Evansville, 1968, MA, 1973; PhD in Nursing, U. Tex., 1982. Pub. health supr. Commun. Action Program, Evansville, Ind., 1968-69; nurse practitioner Planned Parenthood, 1969-70; asst. prof. nursing U. Ky., Henderson, 1970-73; instr. nursing Anoka (Minn.)-Ramsey C.C., 1973-84; prof. nursing Austin (Tex.) C.C., 1987—. Bd. dirs. Homehealth Agy. Author: Nursing Review for NCLEX-RN; author monographs; presenter in field.; reviewer Delmar Pubs. Recipient Theresa DeVillier Cancer award U. Tex., 1982; Dept. HHS grantee; U. Minn. grantee, 1983. Mem. Nat. Orgn. AD Nursing, Tex. Orgn. AD Nursing, Nat. League for Nursing, Sigma Theta Tau, Alpha Tau Delta, Pi Lambda Theta, Phi Kappa Phi. Home: 2306 W New Hope Dr Cedar Park TX 78613-6060 Office: Austin CC 1020 Grove Blvd Austin TX 78741-3337

LAUCK, A. VICTORIA, small business owner, volunteer; b. Cin., Aug. 31, 1955; d. William Louis and Virginia Elizabeth (Hart) Pohl; m. John William Lauck, Nov. 27, 1982 (div.); 1 child, Christina Maria. BA in English, Trinity Coll., Washington D.C., 1977; MEd in Public Relations, Xavier U., Cin., 1978; attended, Mount Saint Joseph Coll., Cin., 1984. Public relations, advtg. mgr. Eagle Savings Assn., Cin., 1978-83; owner, ptnr. Make A Statement, 1991-93; owner V.P. Typesetting, 1988—. Mem. bd. dirs. ProKids, Cin., 1990-93, 94-95, Jr. League of Cin., 1992-93, exec. bd. mem. 1994-96. Editor: (book) Cincinnati For Kids, 1990. Vol. catalogue writer Cin. Hist. Soc., 1984-86; printing coord. Cmty. Chest, Cin., Ohio, 1985; printing coord. Am. Cancer Soc., 1991-94. Recipient Honor award Assn. of Jr. Leagues, Internat., 1994, 98. Home: 7000 Graves Rd Cincinnati OH 45243-3853

LAUCK, DONNA L. adult psychiatric and mental health nurse; b. Berwick, Pa. d. Earl Andrew and Catherine Arlene Kreiser; m. Ronald Joseph Lauck, Oct. 21, 1966; 1 child, Ronald Joseph Jr. BSN, U. Pa., 1973, MSN, 1982, DNSc, 1991. Diplomate Am. Bd. Forensic Examiners; RN Pa., cert. cert. clin. nurse specialist, ANA, adult psychiat. and mental health nursing, 94, founding certificant, Nat. Registry of Certified Group Psychotherapists, 95, BLS instr., Am. Heart Assn., sexual assault nurse examiner, 96, cognitive behavioral therapist, 01. Oper. room staff nurse Lower Bucks County Hosp., Pa., 1959-60; charge nurse Boron (Pa.) Cmty. Hosp., 1960; part-time staff nurse Barstow (Calif.) Cmty. Hosp., 1960-65; office nurse S.W. French, III, M.D., Barstow, 1960-65; IV team nurse Jefferson Hosp., Pa., 1966; staff nurse critical care unit Presbyn. Hosp., 1966; head nurse ICU/CCU Meth. Hosp., 1966-69; head nurse ICU Frankford (Pa.) Hosp., 1970-76; dir. nursing Geriat. and Med. Ctrs., Inc., 1977-79; staff nurse, asst. sr. nurse, charge nurse Friend's Hosp., Phila., 1971-86, relief 11-7 supr., 1971-86; nursing staff devel. specialist Inst. of Pa. Hosp., 1986-92, clin. nurse specialist, 1992-96; dir. clin. svc. Kirkbride Ctr., 1997; clin. nurse specialist, sr. nurse in-charge admissions Friend's Hosp., 1998-2000, sr. nurse therapist Cognitive Behavioral Unit, 2000, clin. nurse specialist, therapist Adult Svcs., 2000—, advanced practice nurse Adult Svcs., 2000—; therapist Collaborative Practice of Abington, 2002—. Spkr. in fields of violence, AIDS, stress mgmt., nursing rsch. Chmn. U. Pa. Sch. Nursing fundraising telethon, 1981, 82, active mem. to 2001; active mem. liaison program for undergrad. freshman students, U. Pa., 1990—, facilitator comm. workshop sr. student nurses, 1999—; adv. bd. West Phila. Coalition of Neighborhoods and Businesses, Advanced Practice Nurses Coun., Pa. Hosp., 1994-96. Mem. Am. Soc. Clin. Hypnosis, Internat. Assn. for Study of Dissociative Disorders, Psychiat. Advanced Practice Nurses of Pa., Ea. Pa. Assn. Nursing Diagnosis (mem. psychiat.-mental health spl. interest group), Presbyn. Hosp. Alumni Orgn., Internat. Soc. of Hypnosis, Am. Coll. Forensic Examiners. Home and Office: 863 Granite St Philadelphia PA 19124-1728

LAUCKS, THERESE ELAINE, commercial art instructor; b. York, Pa., July 11, 1961; d. Ronald Eugene and Kathleen Elaine (Rosunski) Raffensberger; m. Randall Wayne Laucks, Aug. 11, 1990. AA, Art Inst. of Pitts. Staff artist Envelope Divsn. Boise Cascade, Pitts., 1981; staff artist, designer Strine Printing, Inc., York, Pa.; desktop publ. of art; comml. art instr. York County Area Vo-Tech Sch., 1983—. Chair occupl. adv. bd. Pa. State U., York, State College, Pa. Adv. Student Coun., York, 1989-90, 91, 96-97; 2d v.p. Women Aux., Vol. Fire County, Spry, York, 1997. Avocations: crafts, gardening, family. Home: 390 School St York PA 17402-9536

LAUDA, DONALD PAUL, university dean; b. Leigh, Nebr., Aug. 7, 1937; s. Joe and Libbie L.; m. Sheila H. Henderson, Dec. 28, 1966; children: Daren M., Tanya R. BS, Wayne State Coll., 1963, MS, 1964; PhD, Iowa State U., 1966. Assoc. dir. Communications Center U. Hawaii, 1966-67; assoc. prof. indsl. arts St. Cloud (Minn.) State Coll., 1967-69; asst. dean Ind. State U., 1970-73; chmn. tech. edn. W.Va. U., 1973-75; dean Sch. Tech., Eastern Ill. U., Charleston, 1975-83; dean Coll. Health and Human Svcs. Calif. State U., Long Beach, 1983—. Cons. in field. Author: Advancing Technology: Its Impact on Society, 1971, Technology, Change and Society, 1978, 2d edit., 1985; contbr. articles to profl. jours. Pres. Council on Tech. Tchr. Edn.; dir. Charleston 2000 Futures Project, 1978-81. Served with USAR, 1957-59. EPDA research fellow, 1969-70; Eastern Ill. U. faculty research grantee, 1971 Mem. Future Soc. Internat. Tech. Edn. Assn., Coun. Tech. Tchr. Educators (pres., Tchr. of Yr. award 1978), World Future Soc., Internat. Tech. Edn. Assn. (pres. 1990), World Coun. Assn. Tech. Edn., Am. Vocat. Assn., Phi Kappa Phi (pres. 1993), Epsilon Pi Tau (Laureate citation 1982), Long Beach C. of C. (bd. dirs. 1995—), Japan Am. Soc. (adv. bd.). Office: Calif State U Coll Health & Human Svcs Long Beach CA 90840-0001 *Jobs and careers come through a great deal of effort, education, but, most importantly, through the help of others. It is this input that helps one clarify goals, gain new insights, and synthesize information. The process is reciprocal in that one helps others grow. Reflecting on the past always brings to mind people rather than degrees, positions, salaries, etc. When one loses sight of this, he/she is missing the greatest achievement of life.*

LAUDER, LEONARD ALAN, cosmetic and fragrance company executive; b. N.Y.C., Mar. 19, 1933; s. Joseph H. and Estée (Mentzer) L.; m. Evelyn Hausner, July 5, 1959; children: William Phillip, Gary Mark. BS, Wharton Sch., U. Pa., 1954. With Estée Lauder, Inc., N.Y.C., 1958—, exec. v.p., 1962-72, pres., 1972-82, pres., CEO, from 1982, now chmn., CEO. Vice chmn. bd. CFTA, N.Y.C., 1976-79 Trustee Aspen Inst. for Humanistic Studies, 1978—, U. Pa., Phila., 1977—; pres. Whitney Mus. Am. Art, 1977—; bd. dirs. Adv. Commn. on Trade Negotiations, Washington, 1983-87; bd. govs. Joseph H. Lauder Inst. Mgmt. and Internat. Studies, 1983—. Lt. USNR, 1955-58. Mem. Chief Execs. Orgn., French-Am. C. of C. in U.S. (coun. frn. relations). Office: Estée Lauder Cos Inc 767 5th Ave New York NY 10153-0023

LAUDER, VALARIE ANNE, editor, educator; b. Detroit, Mar. 01; d. William J. and Murza Valerie (Mann) L. AA, Stephens Coll., Columbia, Mo., 1944; postgrad., Northwestern U. With Chgo. Daily News, 1944-52, columnist, 1946-52; lectr. Sch. Assembly Svc., also Redpath lectr., 1952-55; freelance writer for mags. and newspapers including New York Times, Yankee, Ford Times, Travel & Leisure, Am. Heritage, 1955—; editor-in-chief Scholastic Roto, 1962; editor U. N.C., 1975-80, lectr. Sch. Journalism, 1980—. Gen. sec. World Assn. for Pub. Opinion Rsch., 1988-95; nat. chmn. student writing project Ford Times, 1981-86; pub. rels. dir. Am. Dance Festival Duke U., 1982-83, lectr., instr. continuing edn. program, 1984. Contbg. editor So. Accents mag., 1982-86. Mem. nat. fundraising bd. Kennedy Ctr., 1962-63; bd. dirs. Chapel Hill Mus., Inc., 1996-98. Recipient 1st place award Nat. Fedn. Press Women, 1981, 1st place awards Ill. Women's Press Assn., 1950, 51. Mem. Pub. Rels. Soc. Am. (treas. N.C. chpt. 1982, sec. 1983, v.p. 1984, pres.-elect 1985, pres. 1986, chmn. coun. of past pres., chmn. 25th Ann. event 1987, del. Nat. Assembly 1988-94, S.E. dist. officer, nat. nominating com. 1991, 1st pres.'s award 1993), Women in Comms. (v.p. matrix N.C. Triangle chpt. 1984-85), N.C. Pub. Rels. (mem. Hall of Fame com.), DAR, Soc. Mayflower Desc. (bd. dirs. Ill. Soc. 1946-52), Chapel Hill Hist. Soc. (bd. dirs. 1981-85, 94-2001, chmn. pub. com. 1980-85, pres. 1996-2001), Chapel Hill Preservation Soc. (bd. trustees 1993-96, nominating com. 1994), N.C. Press Club (3d v.p. 1981-83, 2d v.p. 1983-85, pres. 1985, 1st pl. awards 1981, 82, 83, 84), Univ. Women's Club (2nd v.p. 1988), The Carolina Club, The Nat. Press Club. Office: U NC Sch Journalism and Mass Comm Cb 3365 Cmn Chapel Hill NC 27599-0001

LAUDERDALE, KATHERINE SUE, lawyer; b. Wright-Patterson AFB, Ohio, May 30, 1954; d. Azo and Helen Ceola (Davis) L. BS in Polit. Sci., Ohio State U., 1975; JD, NYU, 1978. Bar: Ill. 1978, U.S. Dist. Ct. (no. dist.) Ill. 1978, Calif. 1987. Assoc. Schiff, Hardin & Waite, Chgo., 1978-82; dir. bus. and legal affairs Sta. WTTW-TV, 1982-83, gen. counsel, 1983—, also v.p., sr. v.p., gen. counsel legal and bus. affairs, 1993—, acting sr. v.p. Prodn. Ctr., 1994, sr. v.p. new ventures, 1995-99, sr. v.p. network Chgo. implementation, 1999—, sr. v.p. strategic partnerships and gen. counsel, 2000—. Mem. Lawyers Com. for Harold Washington, Chgo. 1983; bd. dirs. Midwest Women's Ctr., Chgo., 1985-94; active Chgo. Coun. Fgn. Rels., 1981—, mem. fgn. affairs com., 1985—; mem. adv. bd. Malcolm X Coll. Sch. Bus., 1996-99. Mem. ABA, Chgo. Bar Assn. (bd. dirs. TV Prodns., Inc. 1986—), Lawyers for Creative Arts (bd. dir. 1984—, v.p. 1998—), ACLU (bd. dirs. 1987-94), Nat. Acad. TV Arts and Scis., NYU Law Alumni Assn. Midwest (mem. exec. bd. 1982—), The Ohio State U. Pres.'s Nat. Adv. Coun. on Pub. Affairs (Chgo. com., 1994—), The U. Chicago Women's Bd., 1996—. Democrat. Office: Sta WTTW-TV 5400 N Saint Louis Ave Chicago IL 60625-4680

LAUDERDALE, VANCE, JR. anesthesiologist; b. N.Y.C., Sept. 11, 1923; MD, Columbia U., 1947. Diplomate Am. Bd. Anesthesiologists. Intern Kings County Hosp., N.Y.C., 1947-49; resident anesthesiology Presbyn. Hosp., 1949-51; cons. emeritus anesthesiology Columbia-Presbyn. Med. Ctr., 1985—; spl. lectr. anesthesiology Columbia U., 1985—. Fellow Am. Coll. Anesthesiologists; mem. AMA, Am. Soc. Anesthesiologists, N.Y. County Med. Soc. (mem. peer review com. bd. censors 1975-85).

LAUDICINA, SALVATORE ANTHONY, film industry executive; b. Bklyn., Sept. 16, 1960; s. Victor Anthony and Anne (Calabrese) L. BS, Pace U. Film inspector United Artists Corp., N.Y.C., 1981-82; print & publicity mgr. MGM/UA Entertainment Co., 1982-84, regional sales coord., 1984-85, east coast sales mgr., 1985-86; coll. sales coord. Films, Inc., 1986, east coast sales mgr., 1986-87; lic. dir. Motion Picture Lic. Corp., Stamford, Conn., 1987-89, v.p. L.A., 1989-96, sr. v.p., 2000—, pres. licensing divsn., 1996-2000. Mem. Calif. Yacht Club. Roman Catholic. Avocations: golf, sailing. Office: Motion Picture Lic Corp 5455 S Centinela Ave Los Angeles CA 90066-6942

LAUDONE, ANITA HELENE, lawyer; b. Boston, Sept. 14, 1948; d. Vincent A. and Wanda L.; m. Colin E. Harley, May 20, 1978; children: Clayton Thomas, Victoria Spencer. AB, Conn. Coll., 1970; JD, Columbia U., 1973. Bar: N.Y. 1974. Law clk. to judge Fed. Dist. Ct., N.Y.C., 1973-74; asso. Davis Polk & Wardwell, 1974-78; assoc. Shearman & Sterling, 1978-79; with Phelps Dodge Corp., 1979-85, corp. sec., 1980-85, v.p., corp. sec., 1984-85. Editor: Columbia Law Rev., 1973. Home: 510 North St Greenwich CT 06830-3439

LAUE, BRANT MITCHELL, lawyer; b. Hanover, Kans., June 24, 1961; s. Lester Clayton and Leanna (Jandera) L. BA summa cum laude, Oral Roberts U., 1983; JD magna cum laude, Cornell U., 1986. Bar: Mo. 1987; U.S. Ct. Appeals (8th cir.) 1988, U.S. Ct. Appeals (9th cir.) 1988, U.S. Ct. Appeals (10th cir.) 1990, U.S. Ct. Appeals (4th cir.) 1992; U.S. Dist. Ct. (we. dist.) Mo. 1989, Kans. 1995, U.S. Ct. Appeals (7th cir.) 1997. Law clk. to judge U.S. Ct. Appeals (8th cir.), Pierre, S.D., 1986-87; assoc. Stinson, Mag & Fizzell, Kansas City, Mo., 1987, 1988-92; spl. asst. to asst. atty. gen. Civil Div. U.S. Dept. Justice, Washington, 1987-88; assoc. Rouse, Hendricks, German, May & Shank, P.C., Kansas City, Mo., 1992-93, shareholder, 1993-97, Shank, Laue & Hamilton, P.C., Kansas City, 1997-2000; of counsel Armstrong Teasdale LLP, 2000—. Mem. ABA, Order of Coif, Phi Kappa Phi. Republican. Lutheran. Avocation: ranching. Office: Armstrong Teasdale LLP 2345 Grand Blvd Ste 2000 Kansas City MO 64108-2617 E-mail: brantlaue@aol.com., blaue@armstrongteasdale.com.

LAUE, BRUCE ANTONIO, financial consultant, writer; b. N.Y.C., July 21, 1953; s. William Rollini and Yolande Violette (Dodelin) L.; m. Sherry Lynn Locher, May 18, 1996. BA, Fairleigh Dickinson U., 1975. Mng. dir. Geneva Capital Resources, Inc., N.Y.C., 1992—. Adv. bd. Soldier's, Sailor's, Marine's and Airman's Club, N.Y.C., 1988—; chmn. scholarship com. The Youth Found., N.Y.C., 1996-2001; mem. St. George's Soc., N.Y.C., 1989—; steward New Eng. Soc., N.Y.C., 1983—; spl. legate to Principality of Seborga, Internat. Federative Alliance of the Sovereign Mil. Order of the Temple of Jerusalem, 1998; Maj., asst. quartermaster Vet. Corps of Artillery, State of N.Y., 1981—; mem. French Am. Friendship Found. Recipient Civic Commendation, Coun. of City of N.Y., 1989, N.Y. State Hist. Mil. Command Commendation, N.Y. Soc. of Mil. and Naval Officers, 1998, N.Y. State Mil. Commendation medal N.Y. State Dept. Mil. and Naval Affairs, 1993. Mem. Nat. Gavel Soc., The Old Guard of the City of N.Y., Sovereign Order of Orthodox Knights, Hospitaller of St. John of Jerusalem (Knight of Grace), Army and Navy Union, USA, Inc., Order of Lafayette (pres.-gen. 1996—), Masons. Roman Catholic. Home and Office: 243 W 70th St New York NY 10023-4318

LAUENSTEIN, ANN GAIL, librarian; b. Milw., Nov. 8, 1949; d. Elmer Lester Herbert and Elizabeth Renatta (Bovee) Zaeske; m. Mark Lauenstein, Aug. 16, 1986; 1 child, Maria. MA, U. Wis., 1972. Asst. libr. U. Wis., Wausau, 1972-73; cataloger, libr. MacMurray Coll., Jacksonville, Ill., 1973-76; corp. libr. Anheuser-Busch Cos. Inc., St. Louis, 1976—. Facilitator Anheuser-Busch Quality Circle, St. Louis, 1984—. Treas. Friends of Kirkwood Libr., 1986-98; mem. adv. coun. Sch. Info. Sci. U. Mo., 1987-95. Mem. AAUW (editor jour. 1981-84, publicity chmn. 1985-87, scholar 1984), Spl. Librs. Assn. (network liaison 1981-83, chmn. employment com. 1983-84, chmn. hospitality com. 1984-85, membership chmn. 1988-89, newsletter editor 1992-94, advt. editor 1995-97, bus. mgr. 1999—), St. Louis Regional Libr. Network (coun. 1981-83), St. Louis Online Users Group, Women in Bus. Network (adv. panel 1980-82, 86-87, programs planner 1987-88, asst. coord. 1988-89), Ohio Coll. Libr. Consortium Acquisitions Users Coun. Avocation: stamp collecting, cooking, cookbook collecting. Office: Anheuser-Busch Co Inc 1 Busch Pl Saint Louis MO 63118-1852

LAUER, ANDREW JAY, lawyer; b. Queens, N.Y., Aug. 2, 1967; s. Elias and Ilse Susan L.; m. Aleeza S. Lauer, Nov. 22, 1989; children: Jennifer Amanda, David Aaron, Ashley Beth, Elias. BA in Acctg. and Econ., CUNY, 1988; JD, Bklyn. Law Sch., 1991; LLM in Labor and Employment Law, NYU, 2002. Bar: N.Y. 1991, N.J. 1991, U.S. Dist. Ct. (eas. and so. dists.) N.Y., U.S. Dist. Ct. N.J., U.S. Supreme Ct. Asst. dist. atty. Kings County, Bklyn., 1991-95; asst. gen. counsel Deloitte & Touche U.S.A., LLP, N.Y.C., 1995—. Primary editor Bklyn. Jour. Internat. Law, 1990-91; editor Queens Coll. Law Jour. Mem. ABA, N.Y. State Bar Assn., Am. Corp. Counsel Assn. Office: Deloitte & Touche USA LLP Office of Gen Counsel 1633 Broadway New York NY 10019 E-mail: alauer@deloitte.com.

LAUER, CLINTON DILLMAN, automotive executive; b. Joliet, Ill., Dec. 8, 1926; s. Thomas Ayscough and Francis (Dillman) L.; m. Lea Merrill, Dec. 9, 1950; children: Joanne L. Buckley, John C. BS, U. Ill., 1948; MBA, U. Pa., 1950. Supply mgr. automotive assembly div. Ford Motor Co., Dearborn, Mich., 1971-76, dir. body and assembly purchasing N.Am. automotive ops., 1976-83, exec. dir. N.Am. Automotive Ops. prodn. purchasing, 1983-87, v.p. purchasing and supply, 1987-92; pres. Lauer and Assocs., LLC, Bloomfield Hills, 1992—. Bd. dirs. Sanderson Industries. Mem. exec. bd. Detroit Area coun. Boy Scouts Am., pres., 1990-92; past bd. dirs. nat. and S.E. Mich. Jr. Achievement, Boys and Girls Club of S.E. Mich. With U.S. Army, 1944-46, 50-52. Mem. Oakland Hills Country Club, Bear Creek Golf Club, S.C. Yacht Club. Republican. Episcopalian. Avocation: golf. Home: 26 Ribaut Dr Hilton Head Island SC 29926-1986

LAUER, ELIOT, lawyer; b. N.Y.C., Aug. 17, 1949; s. George and Doris (Trenk) L.; m. Marilyn Steinberg, June 5, 1977; children: Tamar Rachel, Ilana Jennifer, Michael Jonathan, Samuel Geoffrey. BA, Yeshiva U., 1971; JD cum laude, Fordham U., 1974. Bar: D.C. 1975, N.Y. 1975, U.S. Dist. Ct. (so. and ea. dists.) N.Y. 1975, U.S. Ct. Appeals (2d cir.) 1975, U.S. Supreme Ct. 1984. Assoc. Curtis, Mallet-Prevost, Colt & Mosle, N.Y.C., 1974-82, ptnr., 1982—. Counsel Keren-Or Inc., N.Y.C., 1985—; bd. dirs. Hebrew Acad. Long Beach, N.Y., 1985—, Young Israel Lawrence, Cedarhurst, N.Y., 1984—. Mem.: ABA, N.Y. State Bar Assn., Fed. Bar Coun., Nat. Futures Assn. (arbitrator 1983—), Assn. of Bar of City of N.Y. Republican. Office: Curtis Mallet-Prevost Colt & Mosle 101 Park Ave Fl 34 New York NY 10178-0061 E-mail: elauer@cm-p.com.

LAUER, HARRY CURTIS, civil engineer; b. Jersey City, Jan. 23, 1927; s. Harry Carl and Sarah Cecilia Lauer; divorced; children: Harry Curtis, Pamela Elizabeth, Eric Rivard. BSCE, Ind. Inst. Tech., 1950. Rodman Nickel Plate R.R., Ft. Wayne, Ind., 1950-51; with Lederle Labs/Am. Cynamid, Water Supply, Pearl River, N.Y., 1951-52; engr. DuPont/Atomic Energy Plant Constrn., Aiken, S.C., 1952; resident engr. Western Electric/AT&T, Winston-Salem, N.C., 1952-54; plant and project engr. Universal Atlas Cement div. U.S. Steel, various locations, 1955-70; sr. resident mgr. constrn. GE, Columbia, Md. and Research Triangle Park, N.C., 1970-73; project mgr. J. A. Jones Constrn. Co., Charlotte, 1974-75; project mgr., constrn. mgr. Bendy Engring. Co., Santa Cruz, Calif. and St. Louis, Mo., 1975-85; chief civil engr. Arab Swiss Engring. Co., Cairo, Egypt, 1983; constrn. and plant engr. Fla. Crushed Stone, Brooksville, 1984—. Engr., investigator Bahama Cement Co., Freeport, The Bahamas, 1967. Engr., investigator report Silo Failure Investigation (Commendation award 1967). Chief, founder YMCA Indian Guides, Columbia, Md., 1970; deacon Christian Ch., 1963, 68. With USN, 1944-46. Mem. Am. Inst. Plant Engr. (cert., del. to nat. conv. 1987), Ky. Cols., Am. Legion, Elks, Moose, Hernando Beach Yacht Club. Avocations: sailing, construction projects. Home: 27208 Townsend Blvd Brooksville FL 34601-4369 Office: Fla Crushed Stone/CPL Cement Plant Rd Brooksville FL 34601

LAUER, JAMES LOTHAR, physicist, educator; b. Vienna, Austria, Aug. 2, 1920; came to U.S., 1938, naturalized, 1943; s. Max and Friederike (Rappaport) L.; m. Stefanie Dorothea Blank, Sept. 5, 1955; children: Michael, Ruth. AB, Temple U., 1942, MA, 1944; PhD, U. Pa., 1948; postgrad., U. Calif., San Diego, 1964-65. Scientist Sun Oil Co., Marcus Hook, Pa., 1944-52, spectroscopist, 1952-64, sr. scientist, 1965-77; asst. prof. U. Pa., 1952-55; lectr. U. Del., 1952-58; rsch. fellow mech. engring. U. Calif., San Diego, 1964-65; rsch. prof. mech. engring. Rensselaer Poly. Inst., Troy, N.Y., 1978-85, prof. mech. engring., 1985-93, prof. mech. engring. emeritus, 1993—; rsch. sci. Ctr. Magnetic Recording Rsch. U. Calif., San Diego, 1993-95, vis. scholar applied mechanics and engring. sci., 1995—. Sr. faculty summer rsch. fellow NASA-Lewis Rsch. Ctr., 1986-87; vis. prof. Ctr. for Magnetic Rec. Rsch., U. Calif., San Diego, 1991; cons. Digital Equipment Corp., 1992-94, NASA-Lewis Rsch. Ctr., 1993-95. Author: Infrared Fourier Spectroscopy--Chemical Applications, 1978; co-author: Handbook of Raman Spectroscopy, 2001; contbr. articles to profl. jours.; patentee in field. Active Penn Wynne Civic Assn., 1959-77, Country Knolls Civic Assn., 1978-93. Sun Oil Co. fellow, 1964-65, Air Force Office Sci. Rsch. grantee, 1974-86, NASA Lewis Rsch. Ctr. grantee, 1974-86, Office Naval Rsch. grantee, 1979-82, Army Rsch. Office grantee, 1985-89, NSF grantee, 1987-95, Innovative Rsch. award Soc. Mech. Engrs., 1991, Discovery awards NASA, 1993, 96. Fellow: Inst. Physics (U.K.); mem.: AAAS (life), Optical Soc. Am. (emeritus), Soc. Applied Spectroscopy, Am. Phys. Soc. (emeritus), Am. Chem. Soc. (emeritus), Materials Rsch. Soc., Sigma Chi. Jewish. Home: 7622 Palmilla Dr Apt 78 San Diego CA 92122-4710 Office: U Calif San Diego La Jolla CA 92037 *My advice to those contemplating a career in experimental research is to give much thought to these points: (1) interest, enthusiasm, willingness to work are only basics, (2) a loving and understanding wife is essential, and (3) the knowledge that one can create one's own success at any time is the driving force.*

LAUER, MATT, broadcast journalist; b. Dec. 30, 1957; BA, U. Ohio. Producer WOWK-TV, Huntington, W.Va., 1979-80; program host various locations, 1980-88; substitute host Day's End, ABC-TV, 1989, Esquire Show,

King Prodns./Lifetime, 1988-89, 9 Broadcast Plaza, WWOR-TV, N.Y.C., 1989-91; with WNBC, 1992-96; co-anchor News 4/Live at Five, 1993-96; news anchor NBC News' Today Show, 1994-96, co-anchor, 1997—. Office: NBC News "Today" Show 30 Rockefeller Plz Fl 3D New York NY 10112-0002*

LAUERSEN, NIELS HELTH, physician, educator; b. Denmark, Sept. 10, 1939; came to U.S., 1967, naturalized, 1977; s. Bernhard and Maria L. MD cum laude, U. Copenhagen, 1967, Cornell U., 1968. Diplomate: Am. Bd. Ob-Gyn. Intern, then resident in ob-gyn. N.Y. Hosp.-Cornell U. Med. Center, 1968-72, assoc. prof., 1972-79; assoc. prof. ob-gyn. Mt. Sinai Sch. Medicine, N.Y.C., 1979-83; prof. ob-gyn. N.Y. Med. Coll., 1983—. Author: It's Your Body, A Woman's Guide to Gynecology, 1978, new version, 1993, Clinical Perinatal Biochemical Monitoring, 1981, Principles of Microsurgical Techniques in Infertility, 1982, Listen to your Body, 1982, update, 2000, Childbirth With Love, 1983, Modern Management of High-Risk Pregnancy, 1983, PMS: Premenstrual Syndrome and You, 1984, It's Your Pregnancy, 1987, The Endometriosis Answer Book, 1988, A Woman's Body, 1989, Getting Pregnant, 1990, update, 2000, You're in Charge, 1993, The Complete Book of Breast Care, 1996, update, 1999, You're in Charge, 1997, update, 1997, Getting Pregnant, 2000, Listen To Your Body, 2000; also numerous articles. Served with Danish Air Force, 1958-60. Recipient Profl. Service award AMA, 1979, 80, 82, 84, 86, 88, 92, 94, 96, 98, 2000. Fellow Am. Coll. Obstetricians and Gynecologists (award 1977), Soc. Gynecol. Investigation, Am. Fertility Soc., N.Y. Obstet. Soc., N.Y. Gynecol. Soc., Soc. of Perinatal Medicine; mem. AFTRA, N.Y. Gynecol. Soc., N.Y. Soc. Reproductive Medicine, Soc. for Laparoscopic Surgeons, Hon. Police Surgeons NYC, Author's Guild Am. Home: 750 Park Ave New York NY 10021-4252 Office: 784 Park Ave New York NY 10021-3553 *Through helping others, you will help yourself.*

LAUFER, ALLAN HENRY, chemist; b. N.Y.C., Mar. 27, 1936; s. William and Helen G. (Lipsey) L.; m. Sondra Pallant, June 20, 1959; children: Terri M., Andrea J. BA, NYU, 1956; MS, Lehigh U., 1958, PhD, 1962. Staff chemist Gulf R&D Co., Pitts., 1962-64, Nat. Bur. Standards, Washington, 1964-83, Basic Energy Scis.-Dept. Energy, Washington, 1983-86, supervisory chemist, br. chief fundamental interactions, 1986—. Contbr. more than 55 articles to scholarly and profl. jours. Past pres. local elem. and jr. high sch. PTAs; area v.p. county PTA; active county sch. bd. panels. Recipient Silver Medal award Dept. Commerce, 1983. Achievements include research on vinyl and vinylidene radical absorption spectra. Office: Chem Scis Divsn 19901 Germantown Rd Germantown MD 20874-1207 E-mail: allan.laufer@science.doe.gov.

LAUFER, BEATRICE, composer; b. N.Y.C. m. Theodore Lassoff, Oct. 2, 1940 (dec. 1955); 1 child, Samuel; m. Seymour H. Rinzler, Oct. 19, 1969 (dec. 1970). Student, Julliard Sch. Music, 1944. Composer: Symphony No. 1 (performed by Eastman-Rochester Symphony Orch., 1945-46, performance Germany and Japan under auspices of State Dept., 1948, performed by Nat. Gallery Orch., Washington, 1982), Dance Festival (performed by Eastman-Rochester Symphony, 1946-47); choral compositions include: Under the Pines, Spring Thunder performed Tanglewood, 1949, Song of the Fountain, inter-racial chorus, UN Freedom celebration, 1952; Small Concerto for Chamber Orch. performed McMillan Theatre, Columbia, 1949-50; Ile, opera, world premiere Royal Opera Co., Stockholm, Sweden, 1958, recorded by Yale U. Orch., 1978, Broadcast Nat. Pub. Radio, 1980, 87, performed in Chinese at Nanjing U. World Conf. on O'Neill, Shanghai Opera House, June 1988; Second Symphony performed by Oklahoma City Orch., 1961; premiere concerto at Donnell Library Ctr., 1962; premiere performance Prelude and Fugue for Orch., Brevard Music Ctr., N.C., 1964, Cry! orchestral prelude, Orch. of Am., Town Hall, 1966, Lyric string trio, 1991, Bowdoin Coll. Contemporary Music Festival, 1966, performed with Eastman-Rochester Symphony, 1968, Shreveport Symphony Orch., 1978, Berkshire Symphony Orch., 1981; In the Throes performed Shreveport Symphony, 1980, New Orleans Symphony Orch., 1982, Berkshire Symphony Orch., 1985. Conn. Found. of Arts grantee for performance And Thomas Jefferson Said (symphonic version performed by S.W. Floridan Symphony Orch., 1987), Norwalk Symphony Orch., 1976, 3 excerpts performed by USAF Chamber Players, Washington, 1985, premiere version for concert bank baritone solo performed by The Goldman Meml. Band, 1986, also at the Aspen (Colo.) Music Festival, 1987, orchestral performance We Hold These Truths, S.W. Fla. Symphony, Nov. 1987; master ceremonies Young Am. Artists, radio sta. WNYC; hostess The Conductor Speaks series sta. WNYC. Mem. ASCAP, Am. Symphony Orch. League, Am. Music Ctr. Address: PO Box 3 Lenox Hill Sta New York NY 10021

LAUFER, HANS, developmental biologist, educator; b. Germany, Oct. 18, 1929; s. Sol and Margarete (Freundlich) L.; m. Evelyn Green, Oct. 31, 1953; children: Jessica, Marc, Leonard. BS, CCNY, 1952; MA, Bklyn. Coll., 1953; PhD (James fellow), Cornell U., Ithaca, N.Y., 1957. Research and teaching asst. Cornell U., 1953-57; NRC fellow Carnegie Instn. of Washington, 1957-59; asst. prof. biology Johns Hopkins U., 1959-65; assoc. prof. U. Conn., Storrs, 1965-72, prof., 1972—. Vis. prof. Karolinska Inst., Stockholm, 1972, Charles U., Prague, 1974, Yale U., 1980, Harvard U., 1987-89; participant Nat. Acad. Scis.-Czechoslovak Acad. exchange program, 1974, 77; ad hoc mem. study sect. tropical medicine NIH, 1981, mem., 1982-85; Conklin Meml. fellow Marine Biology Lab., Woods Hole, Mass., 1956, Lalor fellow, 1962, 63, mem. staff, embryology course, 1968-72, mem. corp., 1962— , corp. trustee, 1978-82, mem. exec. com., 1979-80; vis. scholar Case Western Res. U., 1962; mem. NSF-NATO Fellowship Rev. Panel, 1974, 76 Contbg. author numerous books; assoc. editor Jour. Exptl. Zoology, 1969-73, 90-93, Archives Insect Physiology and Biochemistry, 1983-95, Invertebrate Reprodn. and Devel., 1984-86, mng. editor, 1991—; contbr. numerous articles to profl. jours. Recipient Rsch. Svc. award NIH, 1989, Marcus Singer medal for rsch., 1986, 95; NATO sr. fellow, 1973, fellow Lady Davis Trust, Hebrew U., 1988; Japan Soc. Promotion of Sci. Fell., 1980; Rosenstiel scholar Brandeis U., 1973; Dozor vis. prof., Ben Gurion U., 1997. Fellow AAAS (chmn. sect. biology 1975), Royal Entomology Soc. London (fgn. fellow, elected); mem. Internat. Soc. Devel. Biology, Assn. Rsch. Couns. (nat. bd. on grad. edn. of conf. bd. 1971-75), Am. Soc. Zoology (chmn. divsn. developmental biology 1981-82), Soc. Devel. Biology, Am. Soc. Cell Biology, European Soc. Comparative Endocrinology, Am. Assn. Advancement Aging Rsch., Internat. Soc. Differentiation, Tissue Culture Assn. (coun. 1979-82), World Aquaculture Soc., Conn. Acad. Sci. & Engring. Home: 57 Davis Rd Storrs Mansfield CT 06268-2525 Office: U Conn Dept Molecular & Cell Biology U-3125 75 N Eagleville Rd Storrs Mansfield CT 06269-3125 E-mail: laufer@uconnvm.uconn.edu.

LAUFER, IRA JEROME, physician; b. N.Y.C., Mar. 29, 1928; s. Irving and Evelyn (Weisman) L.; m. Barbara Alfandari, July 10, 1955; children: Tina, David. BA, NYU, 1948; MD, NYU Sch. Medicine, 1953. Diplomate Am. Bd. Internal Medicine. Instr. clin. medicine NYU Sch. Medicine, N.Y.C., 1959-69, asst. prof. clin. medicine, 1969-83, clin. assoc. prof. medicine, 1983—; dir. diabetes svc. Cabrini Med. Ctr., 1966-89; dir. medicine N.Y. Eye and Ear Infirmary, 1978-91; med. dir. Diabetes Treatment Ctr., 1985-92; physician-in-charge Diabetes Treatment Program, 1992—; attending physician Cabrini Med. Ctr., 1989—; assoc. attending physician NYU Med. Ctr., 1983—. Lectr. and cons. in field. Co-author: Diabetes Explained, 1976. Capt. USAF, 1955-57, Korea. Recipient Svc. award Am. Diabetes Assn., 1990. Fellow Am. Coll. Clin. Pharmacology, Am. Coll. Endocrinology; mem. ACP. Avocations: tennis. sailing. Office: 247 3rd Ave New York NY 10010-7457

LAUFER, JACOB, lawyer; b. Munich, Feb. 28, 1949; came to the U.S., 1951; s. Moritz and Felicja (Pruszanowska) L.; m. Clara G. Schwabe, Jan. 27, 1983; children: Samara, Aviva, Mia. BS, CUNY, 1971; JD cum laude, Fordham U., 1974. Bar: N.Y. 1975, D.C. 1975, U.S. Ct. Appeals (2d cir.) 1975, U.S. Dist. Ct. (so. and ea. dists.) N.Y. 1976, U.S. Ct. Appeals (5th cir.) 1979, U.S. Supreme Ct. 1980, U.S. Ct. Appeals (3d cir.) 1985, U.S. Ct. Appeals (D.C. cir.) 1994. Spl. atty. Organized Crime and Racketeering Sect., U.S. Dept. Justice, 1974-77; asst. U.S. atty. So. Dist. N.Y., N.Y.C., 1977-79; of counsel Bartels, Pykett & Aronwald, White Plains, N.Y., 1979-81; ptnr. Bornstein & Laufer, N.Y.C., 1981-85, Laufer & ForKash LLP, N.Y.C., 1986—96; with Laufer & Halberstam LLP, 1996—. Mem., contbr. Fordham Law Rev., 1973-74. Mem. D.C. Bar Assn., Bklyn. Bar Assn., Assn. Bar City of N.Y (com. criminal advocacy 1998—). Democrat. Jewish. Notable cases include: Pavelic & LeFlore vs. Marvel Entertainment Group; and Allen vs. National Video, Inc. Avocation: reading. Office: Laufer & Halberstam LLP 39 Broadway Rm 1440 New York NY 10006-3003 E-mail: jlaufer@lauferhalberstam.com.

LAUFER, NATHAN, cardiologist; b. Montreal, Mar. 12, 1953; came to U.S., 1981; s. Jack and Pearl (Brachfeld) L.; m. Judy Franceska Egett, Sept. 2, 1986; 1 child, Andrew. DCS, McGill U., 1972, MD, 1977. Diplomate Nat. Bd. Med. Examiners, Am. Bd. Internal Medicine; cert. Profl. Corp. Physicians Que. Intern, resident U. Toronto, Can., 1977-81; fellow cardiology U. Mich., Ann Arbor, 1981-83, faculty dept. cardiology, 1983-84; cardiologist Affiliated Cardiologists, Phoenix, 1984-2001, mng. cardiologist, 1996-2001; med. dir. Heart & Vascular Ctr. Ariz., 2001—. Dir. coronary care Good Samaritan Hosp., Phoenix, 1986—92, dir. interventional cardiology, 1987—; vis. prof. Chigasaki Tokushi-kai Med. Ctr., Kanagawa-ken, Japan, 1988, Leningrad Postgrad. Med. Inst., St. Petersburg, Russia, 1991; bd. dirs. Integrated Cardiovascular Group. Contbr. articles to profl. jours. Fellow ACP, Am. Coll. Cardiology, Am. Coll. Chest Physicians, Royal Coll. Physicians and Surgeons Can.; mem. AMA, N.Am. Soc. Pacing and Electrophysiology, Soc. Cardiac Angiography and Intervention, Am. Assn. Nuclear Cardiology, Ariz. Med. Assn., Can. Cardiovascular Soc., Maricopa County Med. Assn., Cardiovascular Soc. Ariz. (founder, pres.). Avocations: skiing, tennis, computers, music, films. Home: 9100 N 55th St Paradise Valley AZ 85253-1632 Office: Heart & Vascular Ctr Ariz 1331 N 7th St Ste 375 Phoenix AZ 85006-2712 E-mail: laufer1@cox.net.

LAUFER, WILLIAM HERVEY, artist, printmaker; b. Newark, Apr. 2, 1934; s. Edward Basil and Grace (Krudop) L.; m. Guida Miller Jackson, Feb. 14, 1986. Student, Trinity Coll., Hartford, Conn., 1952-53, New Sch. for Social Rsch., N.Y.C., 1971-73; AA, SUNY, Albany, 1973. Commd. ensign USN, 1960, advanced through grades to lt. comdr., 1968, ret., 1973; exhibition artist-printmaker The Woodlands, Tex., 1973—; founder Third Coast Letter Press, 1993—. Vis. lectr. in art Stephen F. Austin State U., Nacogdoches, Tex., 1998. Author, artist: Indochina Suite, 1994, Author, artist: Surrogates, 1995, Author, artist: Four Sea Interludes, 1996, Author, artist: P: An Excursus Into Liminal Space, 1997, Author, artist: Laughing Woman, 1998, Author, artist: Judith & Bluebeard: A Little Something for the Millennium, 1999, Author, artist: Voice: Some Music in the Sanskrit Mode, 1999, Author, artist: Selected Sanskrit Translations from the Bhagavad Gita and RG Veda, 2000;. Mem. Assn. Difusora obra Grafica Internat. (Barcelona, Spain), Guild Bookworkers.

LAUFF, GEORGE HOWARD, biologist; b. Milan, Mar. 23, 1927; s. George John and Mary Anna (Klein) L. BS, Mich. State U., 1949, MS, 1951; postgrad., U. Mont., 1951, U. Wash., 1952; PhD, Cornell U., 1953. Fisheries research technician Mich. Dept. Conservation, 1950; teaching asst. Cornell U., 1952-53; instr. U. Mich., 1953-57, asst. prof., 1957-61, asso. prof., 1961-62; research asso. Gt. Lakes Research Inst., U. Mich., 1954-59; dir. U. Ga. Marine Inst., 1960-62; asso. prof. U. Ga., 1960-62; research coord. Sapelo Island Research Found., 1962-64; dir. Kellogg Biol. Sta., 1964-90; prof. dept. fisheries and wildlife and zoology Mich. State U., East Lansing, 1964-91, prof. emeritus, 1991—. Mem. cons. and rev. panels for Smithsonian Inst., Nat. Water Commn., NSF, Nat. Acad. Sci., Am. Inst. Biol. Sci., U.S. AEC, Inst. Ecology, others. Editor: Estuaries, 1967, Experimental Ecological Reserves, 1977. Served with inf. U.S. Army, 1944-46. Office of Naval Research grantee; U.S. Dept. Interior grantee; NSF grantee; others. Fellow AAAS; mem. Am. Inst. Biol. Sci., Am. Soc. Limnology and Oceanography (pres. 1972-73), Ecol. Soc. Am., Freshwater Biology Assn., INTECOL, Societas Internationalis Limnologiae, Orgn. Biol. Field Stas., Sigma Xi, Phi Kappa Phi. Home: 3818 Heights Dr Hickory Corners MI 49060-9504 Office: 3700 E Gull Lake Dr Hickory Corners MI 49060-9505

LAUFMAN, HAROLD, surgeon, consultant; b. Milw., Jan. 6, 1912; s. Jacob and Sophia (Peters) L.; m. Marilyn Joselit, 1940 (dec. 1963); children: Dionne Joselit Weigert, Laurien Laufman Kogut; m. June Friend Moses, 1980 (dec. 1999). BS, U. Chgo., 1932; MD, Rush Med. Coll., 1937; MS in Surgery, Northwestern U., Chgo., 1946, PhD, 1948. Diplomate: Am. Bd. Surgery. Intern Michael Reese Hosp., Chgo., 1936-39; resident in gen. surgery St. Marks Hosp., London, Northwestern U. Med. Sch., Cook County Hosp., Hines VA Hosp., 1939-46; attending surgeon Michael Reese Hosp., 1940-53; mem. faculty Northwestern U., 1941-65; from clin. asst. to prof., attending surgeon Passavant Meml. Hosp., Chgo., 1953-65; prof. surgery, history of medicine Albert Einstein Coll. Medicine, N.Y.C., 1965-81, prof. emeritus, 1982—; dir. Inst. Surg. Studies, Montefiore Hosp. and Med. Ctr., Bronx, N.Y., 1965-81; pvt. practice gen. and vascular surgery Chgo., 1941-65, N.Y.C., 1965-82; ret. professorial lectr. surgery Mt. Sinai Sch. Medicine, 1979-83, emeritus, 1983—; attending surgeon Mt. Sinai Hosp., 1979-83. Cons., lectr. in field; chmn. FDA Classification Panel Gen. and Plastic Surgery Devices, 1975-78; pres. Harold Laufman Assocs., Inc., 1977—, sr. ptnr., 1988—. Author: (with S.W. Banks) Surgical Exposures of the Extremities, 1953, 2d edit., 1986, (with R.B. Erichson) Hematologic Problems in Surgery, 1970, Hospital Special Care Facilities, 1981, The Veins, 1986; chmn. editorial bd.: Diagnostica, 1974-79; mem. editl. bd. Surgery, Gynecology and Obstetrics, 1974-92, Infection Control, 1980-88, Med. Instrumentation, 1972-83, Med. Rsch. Engring., 1972-79; contbr. articles to sci. publs. Chmn. bd. dirs. N.Y. Chamber Soloists, 1974-80, Chamber Music Conf. and Composers Forum of the East, 1975-91. Maj. AUS, 1942-46. Recipient James IV Traveling Professorship in Surgery, Israel, Vienna and Moscow, 1963, Disting. Alumnus award, Rush Med. Coll., 1993, U. Chgo. Sch. Medicine, 1999. Fellow: ACS; mem.: Surg. Infection Soc. (councillor 1980—84), Soc. Surgery Alimentary Tract, Internat. Cardiovasc. Soc., Soc. Vascular Surgery, N.Y. Surg. Soc., Ctrl. Surg. Assn., Western Surg. Assn., Societe Internationale de Chirurgie, Am. Surg. Assn., Am. Med. Writers Assn. (pres. 1968—69), Am. Assn. Healthcare Cons., Assn. Advancement Med. Instrumentation (pres. 1974—75, chmn. bd. 1976—77), Willow Ridge Country Club (Harrison, N.Y.), Harmonie Club (N.Y.C.), Phi Sigma Delta, Alpha Omega Alpha, Zeta Beta Tau, Sigma Xi. Home and Office: 31 E 72nd St New York NY 10021-4131

LAUFMAN, HARRINGTON BUTLER, systems programmer; b. Pitts., July 13, 1947; s. Harrington B. and Martha (McCullough) L.; children: Hal, Holly. BA, Washington & Jefferson U., 1969; MAT, U. Pitts., 1972. Tchr. Pitts. Pub. Schs., 1969-71; rsch. specialist Ohio State U. Hosp., Columbus, 1974-81, rsch. asst., 1981-84; rsch. assoc. Ohio State U. Cancer Ctr., 1984-93; mgr. computer ops. Ohio State U. Coop. Extension Svc., 1993—. Actor, dir. Theatre Project, Columbus, 1989—. Contbr. articles to profl. jours. Vol. Riverside Meth. Hosp., Columbus, 1988-90; mem. exec. com. Univ. Community Assn., Columbus, 1990—; docent Columbus Mus. of Art, 1983—. With U.S. Army, 1970-76. Mem. Agrl. Communicators in Edn.

LAUFMAN, LESLIE RODGERS, hematologist, oncologist; b. Pitts., Dec. 13, 1946; d. Marshall Charles and Ruth Rodgers; m. Harry B. Laufman, Apr. 25, 1970 (div. Apr. 1984); children: Hal, Holly; m. Rodger Mitchell, Oct. 9, 1987. BA in Chemistry, Ohio Wesleyan U., 1968; MD, U. Pitts., 1972. Diplomate Am. Bd. Internal Medicine and Hematology. Intern Montefiore Hosp., Pitts., 1972-73, resident in internal medicine, 1973-74; fellow in hemotology and oncology Ohio State Hosp., Columbus, 1974-76; dir. med. oncology Grant Med. Ctr., 1977-92; practice medicine specializing in hematology and oncology, 1977—. Bd. dirs. Columbus Cancer Clinic; prin. investigator Columbus Cmty. Clin. Oncology Program, 1989-98. Contbr. articles to profl. jours. Mem. AMA, Am. Women Med. Assn. (sec./treas. 1985-86, pres. 1986-87), Am. Soc. Clin. Oncology, Southwest Oncology Group, Nat. Surg. Adjuvant Project for Breast and Bowel Cancers. Avocations: tennis, piano, sailing, hiking, travel. also: 8100 Ravines Edge Ct Columbus OH 43235-5426 Office: 8100 Ravines Edge Ct Columbus OH 43235-5426

LAUGHEAD, JAMES MARSHALL, lawyer; b. San Antonio, Oct. 12, 1959; s. George J. and Margaret R. Laughead; m. Lisa Ott Laky, Nov. 7, 1987; children: James Marshall Jr., George Jackson. BA with highest honors, U. Tex., 1981, JD with high honors, 1984. Bar: Tex. 1984. Atty. Graves, Dougherty, Hearon & Moody, Austin, Tex., 1984—. Assoc. editor: Tex. Law Rev. Mem.: ABA, Travis County Bar Assn., State Bar Tex., Order of Coif, Chancellors, Phi Beta Kappa. Office: Graves Dougherty Hearon & Moody 515 Congress Ave Ste 2300 Austin TX 78701-3508 E-mail: jlaughead@gdhm.com.

LAUGHLIN, CHRISTEL RENATE, translator, consultant; b. Berlin, Dec. 18, 1940; came to U.S., 1966; d. Werner Wilhelm and Rosa Ida (Conrad) Friedrich; m. Phillip Edward Laughlin, July 1, 1966; 1 child, Christina Rosa. Cambridge proficiency diploma, Davies's Sch., London, 1960; French lang. diploma, U. Paris, 1961; Italian lang. diploma, Centri Europei Lingua, Florence, Italy, 1961; BA in Translating, U. Geneva, 1964; accredited travel agt., N.Am. Sch. Travel, Newport, Calif., 1976. Mem. touring svc. Swiss Touring Club, Geneva, 1962-63; hostess, interpreter Intercontinental Hotel, 1964, Swiss Nat. Exhbn., Lausanne, 1964; exec. sec. Intercom S.A., Geneva, 1964-65, Soc. Luchard, Paris, 1965-66; outside saleswoman Hunnicutt Travel, Ft. Worth, 1974-76; pres. Simon Stevens Laughlin Travel, 1976-81; cons., translator K.T. Lendt & Co., N.Y.C., 1969-96; tax acct. Tarrant Operators, Inc., Ft. Worth, 1996-98. Market rsch. analyst Power Base, Denver, 1997; cons. Schwartzkopf Cosmetics, Duesseldorf, Germany, 1997; traffic cons. ADAC-Automobil Club Germany, Munich, 1997. Pres. Symphony League Ft. Worth, 1972-74; juror host family, interpreter Van Cliburn Internat. Piano Competition, Ft. Worth, 1973-97; host family interpreter XX World Gymnastics Championships, Ft. Worth, 1979, U.S. Gymnastics Internat., Ft. Worth, 1982. Mem. AAUW, Nat. Assn. Market Rsch. Analysts, Bot. Rsch. Inst. Tex. (sponsor), Arts Coun. Ft. Worth, Modern Art Mus. Fort Worth. Avocations: tennis, skiing, classical music, opera, travel. Home: 6212 Indian Creek Dr Fort Worth TX 76107-3526 E-mail: texasmanlaughlin@hotmail.com.

LAUGHLIN, DAVID EUGENE, materials science educator, metallurgical consultant; b. Phila., July 15, 1947; s. Eugene L. and Myrtle M. (Kramer) L.; m. Diane Rae Seamans, June 13, 1970; children: Jonathan, Elizabeth, Andrew, Daniel BSc, Drexel U., 1969; PhD, MIT, 1973. Asst. prof. materials sci. Carnegie-Mellon U., Pitts., 1974-78, assoc. prof., 1978-82, prof., 1982—, Alcoa prof. phys. metallurgy, 2001—. Rsch. scientist Oxford (Eng.) U., 1985; vis. scientist Alcoa Tech. Ctr., Pa., 1996. Editor: Solid-Solid Phase Transformations, 1982; category editor of copper: Am. Soc. Metals-Nat. Bur. Stds. Phase Diagram Program, 1981-94; assoc. editor: Metall. Trans., 1982-87, editor, 1987—; contbr. more than 280 articles to profl. jours. Mem. sch. bd. Trinity Christian Sch., Pitts., 1976-85, 87-95, pres., 1978-83, sec., 1988-91, pres., 1991-94; ruling elder Covenant Presbyn. Ch., Pitts., 1982-96; foster parent Children's Home of Pitts., 1984-90; bd. dirs. Christian Schs. Internat., 1991-98; vestry mem. Ch. of the Ascension, 1998—, clk., 1999—2000, warden, 2001—. Recipient Ladd Tchg. award Carnegie-Mellon U., 1975, B.R. Teare award for excellence in engring. edn., 1999; postdoctoral fellow Nat. Acad. Scis., 1974. Fellow Am. Soc. Metals; mem. Metall. Soc. AIME, Am. Sci. Affiliation, Materials Rsch. Soc., IEEE Magnetics Soc. Episcopalian. Avocations: sports, books. Home: 2357 Mcnary Blvd Pittsburgh PA 15235-2779 Office: Carnegie-Mellon U Dept Materials Sci Eng Pittsburgh PA 15213 E-mail: dl0p@andrew.cmu.edu.

LAUGHLIN, DREW ALAN, lawyer; b. McKeesport, Pa., Feb. 28, 1952; s. Edward Stanley L. and Delores Easton Weiler. BA, U. Va., 1974; JD, U. S.C., 1977. Bar: S.C., 1977, U.S. Dist. Ct. S.C., 1978, U.S. Ct. Appeals (4th, 1986, 5th, 1983, and 11th cirs.). Atty. Bowen, Cooper, Beard & Smoot, Hilton Head Island, S.C., 1977-84, Bowen, Smoot & Laughlin, Hilton Head Island, 1984-86, Qualey, Laughlin & Qualey, Hilton Head Island, 1986-87, McNair Law Firm, P.A., Hilton Head Island, 1987-90, Laughlin & Bowen, Hilton Head Island, 1990—. Pres. Hilton Head Plantation, Property Owner's Assn, 1996; chmn. Hilton Head Island Planning Commn., 1994-96, Hilton Head Island Corridor Revs. Com., 1992-94; commr. Hilton Head Island Pub. Svc. Dist., 1998—. Avocations: music, golf. Bus. Home: 6 Oyster Reef Cv Hilton Head Island SC 29926-1800 Office: Laughlin & Bowen PO Drawer 21119 Hilton Head Island SC 29925-1119 E-mail: drew@laughlinandbowen.com., drewlaughlin@mindspring.com.

LAUGHLIN, JAMES HAROLD, JR. lawyer; b. Charleston, W.Va., July 18, 1941; s. James Harold and Pearl Ruby L; m. Eleanor Blackford Watson, II, Aug. 3, 1968; children: C. Michelle, Jeanette C., Cheryl Adele. BS in Chem. Engring., W.Va. U., 1964; JD, Am. U., 1968. Bar: D.C. 1968, Va. 1969. Atty. Am. Cyanamid Co., Wayne, N.J., 1968-70, Xerox Corp., Rochester, N.Y., 1971-77; ptnr. Benoit, Smith & Laughlin, Arlington, Va., 1977-93, Lane & Mittendorf, LLP, Washington, 1993-97, Shook, Hardy & Bacon, LLP, Washington, 1997-99, Arter & Hadden, LLP, Washington, 2000-01, Swidler Berlin Shereff Friedman, LLP, 2001—. Mem. ABA, Am. Intellectual Property Law Assn. (bd. dirs. 1976-79, treas. 1982-85, councilman 1993-94), Va. State Bar (chmn. PTC sect. 1982-83), Nat. Coun. Patent Law Assns. (Va. del. 1983—), Nat. Inventors Hall of Fame Found. (bd. dirs. 1988-93, pres. 1991-92). Office: The Washington Harbour 3000 L St NW Ste 300 Washington DC 20007 E-mail: jim.laughlin@jlaughlin.com.

LAUGHLIN, LARRY W. academic administrator, military officer; B, Millikin U., 1967; MD, St. Louis U., 1971; M, U. London, 1979, PhD, 1982. Diplomate Am. Bd. Preventive Medicine, Am. Bd. Internal Medicine, cert. in pub. health, gen. preventive medicine. Dean uniformed svcs. U. Health Scis., 2002—; past commdg. officer Naval Med. Inst., Bethesda, Md.; with Uniformed Svcs. U., 1992—, chmn. dept. preventive medicine and biometrics, 1998—, Sanford chmn. in tropical medicine, dean F. Edward Hebert Sch. Medicine, 2002—. Capt. USN. Office: 4301 Jones Bridge Rd Bethesda MD 20814*

LAUGHLIN, LOUIS GENE, economic analyst, consultant; b. Sept. 20, 1937; s. Eston A. and Cornelia Helen (Snively) L. Student, Pomona Coll., 1955-58; BA, U. Calif., Santa Barbara, 1960; postgrad., Claremont Grad. Sch., 1966-70, 85-86, Sch. Bank Mktg., U. Colo., 1974-75, Grad. Sch. Mgmt., U. Calif., Irvine, 1983. Mgr. Wheeldex-L.A. Co., 1961-62; v.p. Warner/Walker Assocs., Inc., L.A., 1964-65; rep. A.C. Neilsen Co., Chgo., 1962-64; rsch. analyst Security Pacific Nat. Bank, L.A., 1964-67, asst. rsch. mgr., 1967-68, asst. v.p., 1968-72, v.p., mgr. market info. and rsch. divsn., 1972-76, v.p. rsch. adminstrn., pub. affairs/rsch. dept., 1976-82, v.p. govt. rels. dept., 1982-85; dir. R & D Applied Mgmt. Sys., South Pasadena, Calif., 1986; pres. L.G. Laughlin & Assocs., Houston, 1987—. Prin. Courtyard Holdings, Houston, 1988—; pres. CEO, Mastodon Capital Corp., Houston, 1988-89, 94-98; corp. sec. Kestco Co. Inc., Laguna Beach, Calif., 1996-98; mem. Nat. Conf. on Fin. Svcs., 1982-84, mem. policy coun., 1983-84; mem. policy coun. Nat. Conf. on Competition in Banking, 1978-79, 81. Sec. econs. Town Hall of Calif., 1966. Mem. Am. Econs. Assn., Western Econs. Assn., Nat. Assn. Bus. Economists, L.A. C. of C. (food and agr. adv. com. 1981). E-mail: lgl77@compuserve.com.

LAUGHLIN, PATRICIA, university dean; b. Pitts., Nov. 5, 1953; d. William and Dorothy (Diehl) L.; m. Frederick Winston Jones, May 14, 1977; children: Nicholas Laughlin Jones, Benjamin Winston Jones. BA, U. Pitts., 1976, MPA, 1980, PhD, 1993. Asst. dir. Governmental Rels. Office, U. Pitts., 1976-80; asst. dean Coll. Engring., Carnegie Mellon U., Pitts., 1980-87, assoc. dean, 1987—, pres. credit union, 1994—2002. Bd. dirs. Grad. Edn. Minorities, Ind.; lectr. Adminstrv. Mgmt. Inst., Cornell U., 1995—2000. Contbr. articles to profl. publs. Mem. Nat. Coun. Univ. Rsch. Adminstrs. (steering com. 1990-94, publs. com. 1997-99), Soc. Rsch. Adminstrs (program com. 1989-90), Am. Soc. Engring. Edn. (engring. rsch. coun. bd. 2001-04), Women in Engring. Office: Carnegie Mellon U Coll Engring 110 Scaife Hall Pittsburgh PA 15213 E-mail: patl@cmu.edu.

LAUGHLIN, RICK EUGENE, civil engineer; b. Madison, S.D., June 13, 1952; s. Lyle Eugene and Bonnie Jean (Payne) L.; m. Christine Ann Christensen, Oct. 25, 1955; children: Rochelle Ann, Mallory Robin. BS in Civil Engring., S.D. State U., 1984; MBA, U. S.D., 1997. Registered profl. engr., S.D. Precision photo technician EROS Data Ctr., Garretson, S.D., 1978-82; road design engr. S.D. Dept. Transp., Pierre, 1984-86; civil engr. Dept. Def., Fort Leavenworth, Kans., 1986-88; civil engr. transp. City of Sioux Falls (S.D.), 1988-98; sr. transp. engr. HDR Engring., Inc., Wio, Sioux Fals, 1998—. Mem. Sioux Falls Bicycle Planning Com., 1992—; mem. adv. com. advanced traffic analysts ctr. N.D. State U. George Barton scholar Barton-Aschman Inc./Northwestern U., Evanston, Ill., 1992. Mem. NSPE (state sec./treas. 1992—), Am. Pub. Works Assn. (br. sec./treas. 1992—), Inst. Transp. Engrs. Avocations: bicycle-touring, cross-country skiing, photography. Office: HDR Engring Inc 600 S Cliff Ave Sioux Falls SD 57104-5320

LAUGHLIN, ROBERT B. physics educator; b. Visalia, Calif., Nov. 1, 1950; m. Anita Rhona Perry, Apr. 22, 1979; children: Nathaniel David, Todd William. AB in Math, U. Calif., Berkeley, 1972; PhD in Physics, MIT, 1979. Postdoctoral fellow Bell Tel. Labs., 1979—81, Lawrence Livermore Nat. Lab.,

1981—82; research scientist Lawrence Livermore Nat. Lab, 1982—; assoc. prof. physics Stanford (Calif.) U., 1985—89, prof. physics, 1989—, Anne T. and Robert M. Bass prof. Sch. Humanities and Scis., 1992—, prof. applied physics, 1993—. Lectr. in field. Contbr. articles to profl. jours. With U.S. Army, 1972—74. Named Eastman Kodak lectr., 1989, Van Vleck lectr., 1994; recipient E.O. Lawrence award for Physics, 1985, Franklin Inst. medal, 1998, Nobel Prize in Physics, 1998; fellow, IBM, 1976—78. Fellow: Am. Phys. Soc. (Oliver E. Buckley prize 1986); mem.: NAS, AAAS (fellow), Aspen Ctr. Physics, Am. Acad. Arts and Scis. (fellow, 1990). Office: Stanford U Dept Physics LAM Rm 342 476 Lomita Mall Stanford CA 94305*

LAUGHLIN, SARA GAAR, librarian, consultant; b. Richmond, Ind., Apr. 2, 1949; d. James Nicholson and Marcia Gaar (Johnson) Lemon; m. Timothy Ray Laughlin, Sept. 26, 1970; children: Isaac, Hannah. BA, U. Cin., 1971; MLS, Ind. U., 1972, MA, 1985. Cert. libr., Ind. Ref. libr. Pub. Libr. of Cin. and Hamilton County, 1973-76; project rschr. Art Assn. of Richmond, 1978; dir. admissions Ind. Sch. Libr. and Info. Sci., Bloomington, 1978-80; coord. Stone Hills Libr. Network, 1980-95; instnl. advancement and planning specialist Ind. Coop. Libr. Svcs. Authority, 1995-97; cons. Sara Laughlin & Assocs., 1997—. Account exec. Burnison & Martello Assocs., Indpls., 1988. Editor Directory of Indiana Children's Authors and Illustrators, 1996-97, Networks in the New Millennium: Top Ten Trends, 2000, Interface, 2001—; editor spl. issue Ind. Librs.; contbr. articles to profl. jours. Bd. dirs. Monroe County YMCA, Bloomington, 1991-97, mem. gifts and endowment com., 1997-2001; pres. Friends of Ind. Librs., Indpls., 1993-95; sec. PTO, Bloomington, 1995-96; newsletter editor Ind. U. Children's Choir, Bloomington, 1995—; bd.dirs. Monroe County Pub. Libr., 2002—. Mem. ALA, Ind. Libr. Fedn., Assn. Ind. Media Educators. Avocations: swimming, quilting, camping. Home and Office: 1616 Treadwell Ln Bloomington IN 47408-1200 E-mail: laughlin@bluemarble.net.

LAUGHLIN, WILLIAM EUGENE, retired electric power industry executive; b. Sheffield, Ala., May 4, 1936; s. Rawlie Wayne and Nina Louise (Campbell) L.; m. Donna Lynn Blackburn, Jan. 3, 1958; children: Kevin McGregor, Christopher Scott, Laura Shannon, Alison Paige. BS, Auburn U., 1961. Registered profl. and electrical engr., Ala., Tenn., Miss. Elec. engr. Dept. Power, Water and Gas, City of Sheffield, 1961-66; chief engr., asst. mgr. Electric Plant Bd., Bowling Green, Ky., 1966-76; systems mgr. Bowling Green Mcpl. Utilities, 1975-77; gen. mgr. Fayetteville (Tenn.) Electric Systems, 1977-81, Talquin Electric Coop. Inc., Quincy, Fla., 1981—2002. Bd. dirs., v.p. Seminole Electric Coop., Inc., Tampa, Fla.; pres. Fla. Rural Electric Coop. Assn., Tallahassee. Pres. Boys Club, Bowling Green, 1972; v.p. Bowling Green C. of C., 1975, Fayetteville C. of C., 1979; dist. chmn. Boy Scouts Am., Bowling Green, 1972, Fayetteville, 1978; pres. Fayetteville United Way, 1980. Mem. Nat. Rural Elec. Coop. Assn. (mem. regional com., nat. water task force 1995), Am. Water Works Assn., Rotary (bd. dirs. 1986-87, pres. Quincy club 1996-97), Fayetteville 1978-79, Paul Harris fellow), Kiwanis (dir. Bowling Green club 1973-74). Democrat. Mem. Ch. of Christ. Home: 2110 Ellicott Dr Tallahassee FL 32308-0818

LAUGHREY, NANETTE KAY, judge, federal; b. Cheyenne, Wyo., Feb. 11, 1946; m. Christopher Sexton Kelly; children: Hugh, Jessica Katherine. BA, UCLA, 1967; JD, U. Mo. Columbia, 1975. Bar: Mo. 1975, U.S. Dist. Ct. (we. dist.) Mo. 1975, U.S. Ct. Appeals (8th cir.) 1976, U.S. Supreme Ct. 1978. Asst. atty. gen. Mo. Atty. Gen.'s Office, Kansas City, 1975-79; assoc. Craig Van Matre, P.C., Columbia, 1980-83; assoc. prof. law U. Mo. Columbia, 1983-87, prof. law, 1987-89, William H. Pittman prof. law, 1989-96; judge U.S. Dist. Ct. (we. dist.) Mo., Kansas City, 1996—. Mcpl. judge City of Columbia, 1979-83; vis. prof. law U. Iowa, 1990; dep. atty. gen. Mo. Atty. Gen.'s Office, 1992-93. Contbr. articles to profl. jours. Bd. dirs. Columbia Housing Authority. Mem.: ABA, Mo. Bar Assn., Am. Law Inst., U. Mo. Alumni Assn., Am. Whitewater Assn., Mo. Whitewater Assn. Office: US Dist Ct 400 E 9th St Ste 7452 Kansas City MO 64106-2607

LAULICHT, MURRAY JACK, lawyer; b. Bklyn., May 12, 1940; s. Philip and Ernestine (Greenfield) L.; m. Linda Kushner, Apr. 4, 1965; children: Laurie Hasten, Pamela Hirt, Shellie Davis, Abigail Herschmann. BA, Yeshiva U., 1961; LLB summa cum laude, Columbia U., 1964. Bar: N.Y. 1965, N.J. 1968, U.S. Supreme Ct. 1976. Legal staff Warren Commn., Washington, 1964; law clk. Hon. Harold R. Medina U.S. Ct. Appeals, 1964-65; assoc. Kaye, Scholer, Fierman, Hays & Handler, N.Y.C., 1965-68; ptnr. Lowenstein, Sandler, Brochin, Kohl & Fisher, Newark, 1968-79, Pitney, Hardin, Kipp & Szuch, Florham Park, 1979—. Mem. N.J. Consumer Affairs Adv. Com., 1991-93; mem. N.J. Commn. on Holocaust Edn., 1991—, chmn. 1992-95; mem. N.J. Commn. on Character Edn., 2002--; pres. Jewish Edn. Assn., 1981-84, Jewish Fedn. Metro West, 1996-99, Edah, 2001-; chmn. Cmty. Rels. Com., 1988-91, chmn. com. on religious pluralism, 1999—; exec. comm. Coun. of Jewish Fedn., 1996-99; trustee United Jewish Cmtys., 1999—. Recipient Julius Cohn Young Leadership award Jewish Fedn. Metrowest, 1976. Mem. ABA, N.J. State Bar Assn. (dist. X ethics com. 1986-89, bd. editors N.J. Law Jour. 1986-93), N.J. Lawyer Mag. (chmn. 1993-95). Democrat. Avocations: Jewish studies, communal activities. Home: 18 Crestwood Dr West Orange NJ 07052-2004 Office: Pitney Hardin Kipp & Szuch PO Box 1945 200 Campus Dr Florham Park NJ 07932-1007 E-mail: mlaulicht@pkhs.com.

LAUMANN, EDWARD OTTO, sociology educator; b. Youngstown, Ohio, Aug. 31, 1938; m. Anne Elizabeth Solomon, June 21, 1980; children: Christopher, Timothy; children by previous marriage: Eric, Lisa. AB summa cum laude, Oberlin Coll., 1960; MA, Harvard U., 1962, PhD, 1964. Asst. prof. sociology U. Mich., Ann Arbor, 1964-69, assoc. prof., 1969-72; prof. sociology U. Chgo., 1973—, George Herbert Mead Disting. Service prof., 1985—, chmn. dept., 1981—84, dean divsn. of social scis., 1984—92, provost, 1992—93, chmn. dept., 1981—84, 1997—99, 2002—. Bd. govs. Argonne Nat. Lab., 1992-93. Author: Prestige and Associations in an Urban Community, 1966, Bonds of Pluralism, 1973, (with Franz U. Pappi) Networks of Collective Action, 1976, (with John P. Heinz) Chicago Lawyers, 1982, (with David Knoke) The Organizational State, 1987, (with John P. Heinz, Robert Nelson and Robert Salisbury) The Hollow Core, 1993, (with John Gagnon, Robert Michael, Stuart Michaels) The Social Organization of Sexuality, 1994, (with Robert Michael, John Gagnon, Gina Kolata) Sex in America, 1994, (with Robert T. Michael) Sex, Love and Health, 2001, (with Stephen Ellison, Jenna Mahay, Anthony Pain, Yoosik Youm) Sex in the City: The Structure of Sexual Markets and Sexual Relationships in the City; editor Am. Jour. Sociology, 1978-84, 95-97. Mem. sociology panel NSF, Washington, 1972-74; commr. CBASSE, NRC, 1986-91; chair, bd. trustees NORC, 2001--; trustee U. Chgo. Hosps., 1992-93; panel mem. Panel on Elder Mistreatment, 2000-2002. Fellow AAAS (chmn. sect. K 2001—), Soc. Sci. Study of Sexuality; mem. Internat. Acad. Sex Rsch., Sociol. Rsch. Assn., Am. Sociol. Assn., Population Assn. Am. Office: U Chgo 5848 S University Ave Chicago IL 60637-1515 E-mail: ob01@midway.uchicago.edu.

LAUMONT, PHILIPPE EMILE, communications executive; b. Liege, Belgium, June 17, 1944; came to U.S., 1957; s. Gustave J. and Germaine (Cattet-Thellier de Poncheville) L.; m. Anne Colton Adams, July 19, 1978; children: Anne Sophie, Julia Adams, Laura Philippa. BA, U. Louvain, Belgium, 1964, MA, 1965; MBA, Columbia U., 1978. Film producer CBS Inc., N.Y.C., 1969-78; pres. Laumont Labs Inc., 1979—, Laumont Photographics, 1993—, Laumont Editions, 1998—. Mem. Coffee House Club, Ausable Club. Office: Laumont Editions 333 W 52nd St New York NY 10019-6238 E-mail: plaumont@aol.com.

LAUN, LOUIS FREDERICK, government official; b. Battle Creek, Mich., May 19, 1920; s. Louis Frederick and Roena (Graves) L.; m. Margaret West, Jan. 25, 1947; children: Nancy, Kathryn Webb, Margaret. BA, Yale U., 1942. Asst. advt. mgr. Bates Fabrics, Inc., N.Y.C., 1946-48; asst. to pres., indsl. and public relations Bates Mfg. Co., Lewiston, Maine, 1948-55; advt. dir., out-of-town sales mgr. Burlington Industries, N.Y.C., 1955-57; gen. merchandising mgr. Celanese Fibers Co., 1957-60, v.p., dir. mktg., 1960-63, exec. v.p. mktg., 1963-64; pres. Celanese Fibers Mktg. Co. div. Celanese Corp., 1964-71, also v.p. corp., 1964-71; asso. adminstr. ops. SBA, Washington, 1973, dep. adminstr., 1973-77; pres. Am. Paper Inst., N.Y.C., 1977-86; asst. Sec. Commerce for Internat. Econ. Policy Dept. of Commerce, Washington, 1986-89, exec. br. commr., Commn. on Security and Cooperation in Europe, 1988-89; cons. Nat. Exec Svc. Corp, 1989—. U.S. pulp and paper rep. food and agrl. orgns. UN; bd. dirs. Overseas Pvt. Investment Corp., Noranda Aluminum, Inc.; exec. br. mem. Commn. on Security and Cooperation in Europe (Helsinki Commn.); vol. cons. Nat. Exec. Svc. Corps, 1989--. Bd. dirs. N.Y. Bd. Trade, Better Bus. Bur. N.Y., Alliance to Save Energy, Bus. Adv. Com. on Fed. Reports, The Grace Commission on Govt. Waste (exec. committee); indsl. asst. to chmn. Opportunities Industrialization Ctrs. Am.; nat. adv. coun. SBA; chmn. Republican Industry Workshop program; field dir. Com. for Re-election of Pres., 1972; trustee Taft Sch.; mem. exec. com. President's Pvt. Sector Survey on Cost Control; chmn. Kids to Kids Internat., 1999; bd. dirs. New Castle Hist. Soc., 1999—, Edwin Gould Svcs. for Families and Children, 1997—, United Way of No. Westchester, 1998—. Lt col., USMCR, 1942-46. Decorated Bronze Star; recipient Human Rights award Anti-Defamation League, 1968; Achievement award Textile Vets. Assn., 1970; named Young Man of Yr. Lewiston-Auburn C. of C., 1953, Man of Yr. Textile Salesman Assn., 1970, Man of Yr. Fabric Salesmen's Guild, 1971; Gold medal for disting. service SBA, Citation Merit Taft Sch., 1988. Mem. Color Assn. U.S. (sec.), Man-Made Fiber Producers Assn. (chmn. 1967-69), Yale Club (N.Y.C.), Sleepy Hollow Country Club (Scarborough, N.Y.), Met. Club (Washington), Mid-Ocean Club (Bermuda). Home and Office: 25 Spring Ln Chappaqua NY 10514-2607 Fax: 914-238-3023.

LAUNEY, GEORGE VOLNEY, III, economics educator; b. Ft. Worth, Feb. 8, 1942; s. George Volney and Harriet Louise (Pitts) L.; m. Sondra Ann Schwarz, May 29, 1965; children: George Volney IV, David Vincent. BBA, U. N. Tex., Denton, 1965, MBA, 1966; PhD, U. Ark., 1970. Asst. prof. econs. N.E. La. U., Monroe, 1968-70; asst. prof., assoc. prof. econs. Franklin (Ind.) Coll., 1970-83, chmn. econs. and bus. dept., 1971-81, prof. econs., Joyce and E. Don Tull prof. bus. and econs., 1983—, chmn. social sci. div., 1983—. Pres. Econ. Evaluation, Inc., Franklin, 1985—; cons. Von Durpin, Div. Ingersol Rand, Bargersville (Ind.) State Bank, Ind. Dept. Ins., Med. Malpractice Bd., Indpls. Contbr. articles to profl. jours. Recipient Branigin award for teaching excellence Franklin Coll. Bd. Trustees, 1979. Mem. Am. Econ. Assn., Am. Assn. Forensic Economists, Am. Acad. Fin. and Econ. Experts (bd. editors 1988—). Avocation: coin collecting. Home: 1875 Hillside Dr Franklin IN 46131-8542 Office: Franklin Coll Dept Econs Franklin IN 46131

LAUPUS, WILLIAM EDWARD, physician, educator; b. Seymour, Ind., May 25, 1921; s. John George and Laura Kathryne (Hancock) L.; m. Evelyn Estelle Fike, Mar. 6, 1948; children: Patricia, John Richard, Laura (dec.), William Edward. BS, Yale, 1943, MD, 1945. Diplomate Am. Bd. Pediatrics (ofcl. examiner 1966-90, mem. exec. bd. 1972-77, pres. 1976-77). Intern N.Y. Hosp.-Cornell Med. Center, 1945-46; resident, 1948-51; instr. pediatrics Cornell U. Sch. Medicine, 1950-52; asst. prof., then asso. prof., prof. pediatrics Med. Coll. Ga., 1959-63; prof. pediatrics, chmn. dept. Med. Coll. Va., Va. Commonwealth U., Richmond, 1963-75; pediatrician-in-chief Med. Coll. Va. Hosps.; prof. pediatrics Sch. of Medicine East Carolina U., 1975-89, dean Sch. Medicine, 1975-82, dean Sch. Medicine, vice chancellor divsn. Health Scis., 1982-89, dean emeritus, 1989—; prof. preventive medicine and pediatrics East Carolina U. Sch. Medicine, 1989-91. Pres. Am. Bd. Med. Specialists, 1984-86. Contbr. to: Nelson's Textbook of Pediatrics, 1964, 69, 75, Kendig's Respiratory Diseases in Children, 1969, 72, 77, Gellis and Kagen's Current Therapy, 1969-77. Pres. Richmond Area Community Council, 1973-75. Served with AUS, 1946-48. Mem. Am. Acad. Pediatrics (past pres. Va. chpt.), Am. Pediatric Soc., AMA, N.C. Med. Soc., Pitt County Med. Soc., Alpha Omega Alpha, Phi Kappa Phi.

LAUR, WILLIAM EDWARD, retired dermatologist; b. Saginaw, Mich., Nov. 17, 1919; s. Vertner Linton and Ruth Gae (Eyre) L.; m. Mary Elizabeth Kirby, Dec. 31, 1943; children: Eric, Edward, John, J. Michael. BS, Mercer U., Macon, Ga., 1941; MD, U. Mich., 1943; MS in Medicine, Wayne State U., Detroit, 1949. Diplomate Am. Bd. Dermatology. Intern John Sealy Hosp., Galveston, Tex., 1943; resident Wayne State U., Detroit, 1946-49; pvt. practice Amarillo, Tex., 1949-70; pres. High Plains Dermatology Ctr., P.A., 1975-90; ret. Cons. VA, USAF, 1952-90; assoc. prof. Tex. Tech. Health Sci. Ctr., Amarillo, 1965-90. Contbr. articles to profl. jours. including Archives of Dermatology, Internat. Jour. Dermatology, Cutis, So. Med. Jour., Jour. Am. Acad. Dermatology, Panhandle Med. Soc. Bull., Urologic and Cutaneous Rev. Dir. Moon Watch, NASA, Amarillo, 1956. Capt. U.S. Army, 1944-46, ETO. Fellow Am. Acad. Dermatology; mem. AMA, Tex. Med. Assn., Noah Worcester Dermatol. Soc., Potter Randall County Med. Soc. (pres. 1964). Avocations: cooking, duplicate bridge, computer activities. Home: 1607 S Fannin St Amarillo TX 79102-2412 E-mail: blaur@tcac.net.

LAURA, ROBERT ANTHONY, coastal engineer, consultant; b. Syracuse, NY, June 4, 1955; s. John Emil and Rosemary (Ross) L.; m. Susan Ann Sieve, Dec. 30, 1978; children: Carolyn Ruth, Alyson Anne, Katy Marie. BS in Engring. Sci., SUNY, Buffalo, 1977; MS in Ocean Engring., U. Miami, Fla., 1980. Registered profl. engr., Fla. Sr. assoc. Post, Buckley, Schuh & Jernigan, Inc., Miami, Fla., 1979-88; sr. engr. Law Environ. Inc., Ft. Lauderdale, 1988-92; sr. civil engr. South Fla. Water Mgmt. Dist., West Palm Beach, 1992—. Contbr. articles to Jour. of Hydraulic Engring. and proceedings of sci. meetings. Recipient fellowship from Conoco to U. Miami, 1979. Mem. ASCE (control mem. coastal engring. tech. com. 1988—), Am. Water Resources Assn., Am. Shore and Beach Preservation Assn. Democrat. Roman Catholic. Achievements include development of many special computer programs for hydrodynamics and water resources. Home: 2228 Saluda Ln Acworth GA 30101 Office: PBS&J Inc 5665 New Northside Dr Ste 400 Atlanta GA 30328 E-mail: balaura@pbsj.com.

LAURANCE, LEONARD CLARK, marketing researcher, educator and consultant; b. Perth, Australia, Aug. 20, 1932; came to U.S., 1963; s. Thomas Clark and Lorna Ruby (Spencer) L.; m. Lorraine Joan Harwood, June 10, 1954 (div. 1960); 1 child, Beverley Lorraine; m. Judith Ellen Krickan, Sept. 8, 1962; children: Cynthia Ellen, Amanda Lee. Gen. mgr. Ketchikan & No. Terminal Co. Inc., Ketchikan, Alaska, 1963-65; regional mgr. Alaska Steamship Co., 1965-68; pres. Alaska World Travel Inc., 1968-72, Leisure Corp., Ketchikan, 1972-85, AlaskaBound, Inc., Ketchikan, 1985-88, Mariner Inc., Ketchikan, 1988—. Faculty mem. U. Alaska SE, Ketchikan, 1987-97, Juneau, 1995; dir. mktg. Taquan Air, Ketchikan, 1991—; bd. dirs. Hist. Ketchikan, Inc.; mem. Alaska Tourism mktg. coun., 1995—. Mem. AVA Mktg. Coun., Juneau, 1979-84, chair, 1982-84; mem. S.E. Alaska Tourism Coun., Juneau, 1982-86, 96-98, chair., 1982-83; mem. mgmt. com. Sheffield Hotels, Anchorage, 1980-85; chair Alaska Marine Hwy. Task Force, Juneau, 1983-84, UAS Coll. Coun., 1982-83; mem. Ketchikan Gen. Hosp. Adv. Bd., 1973-84, chair, 1979; assemblyperson Ketchikan Gateway Borough, 1976-82. Recipient North Star award Alaska Visitors Assn., 1977, Gov.'s award State of Alaska, 1984, Presdl. award Ketchikan C. of C., 1970. Mem. Alaska Visitors Assn. (bd. dirs. 1969-93, advisor to bd. 1994-97, pres. 1972-73, hon. life 1994), Ketchikan Visitors Bur. (bd. dirs. 1980—, chair 1983-84, 98), UAS Visitor Ind. Program (adv. bd. 1986-97), U. Alaska Statewide Vocational Tech. Edn. coun. Republican. Episcopalian. Avocations: sportfishing, swimming, community service, tourism research. Office: Mariner Inc 5716 S Tongass PO Box 8800 Ketchikan AK 99901-3800

LAURENCE, AMY REBECCA, music educator, composer; b. Florence, Ala., Feb. 14, 1958; MusB, Ohio State U., 1979; MA, Calif. State U., Carson, 1998. Cert. Nat. Piano Guild. Entrepreneur Amy R. Laurence Music, Dublin, 1994—. Liaison Columbus, Ohio and Associated Bd. of the Royal Schs. Music, 1998—. Author, arranger (folios of piano music) The Little Hands Series: Christmas, Classics, Historic Hymns, Hymns, Seasons, 1990-99, (piano rec. and printed folio) Hymns in Black and White, 1990, (piano music series) The Amateur Virtuoso, 1995—; author, composer (musical rec. and printed folio) Songs In The Night, 1990, (piano music series) Amy's Animal Tales, 1999—, Amy's Keyboard Critters, 1999—; author, composer, arranger (printed and recorded music) Music Arch. Series, 1999—; originator, co-author, composer (musical drama) The Adventures of Wallace in Wonderland, 1988; arranger (vocal music) Choral Reef Series, 1994—, (music series) Instrumental Pianist, 1995—, (piano music series) Court Musician Series, 1997—, Gold Medal Series, 2000—; arranger Miss Am. Teen 2000; pub., arranger (operettas) The Parables, 2002, The Prophets, 2002. Active Northwest Chapel, Dublin. Recipient Tchrs. award, Nat. Piano Guild Internat. Composition Contest, 2002. Mem. ASCAP, Music Tchrs. Nat. Assn. (nat. cert. tchr. music), Am. Coll. Musicians, Suzuki Assn. Am., Leschetizky Assn., Ohio Music Tchrs. Assn. (Ohio state composition chmn. 1998-99, sec. exec. bd. ctrl.-east divsn. 1998-2000), Delta Omicron (life). Office: Amy R Laurence Music PO Box 426 Dublin OH 43017-0426 E-mail: Amy@AmyRLaurence.com.

LAURENCE, DAN H. author, literary and dramatic specialist; b. N.Y.C., Mar. 28, 1920; BA, Hofstra U., 1946; MA, NYU, 1950. Performed in profl. theatre, 1932-41; writer, performer Armed Forces Radio, 1942-45; writer for radio, TV U.S. and Australia, 1946-48; grad. asst. NYU, 1950-52, assoc. prof. English, 1962-67, prof., 1967-70; instr. Hofstra U., 1953-58; editor Readex Microprint Corp., 1959-60; lit. and dramatic adv. Estate of George Bernard Shaw, London, 1973-90. Vis. prof. Ind. U., 1969, U. Tex., 1974-75; vis. fellow Inst. Arts and Humanistic Studies, Pa. State U., 1976; spl. cons. Humanities rsch. Ctr., U. Tex., Austin, 1975-77; Andrew W. Mellon prof. humanities Tulane U., New Orleans, 1981; Montgomery fellow Dartmouth Coll., 1982; disting. vis. prof. humanities Guelph U. (Ont., Can.), 1983, U. B.C. (Can.), 1984; adj. prof. drama Guelph U., 1986-91; literary advisor, mem. acting ensemble of Shaw Festival, Ont., 1982-90, assoc. dir., 1987-2000; co-founder Offstage, Inc., San Antonio, 1972. Author: (with Leon Edel) Henry James: A Bibliography, 3d edit., 1981, Robert Nathan: A Bibliography, 1960, Bernard Shaw: A Bibliography, 1983; playwright: The Black Girl in Search of God, 1977; editor: Uncollected Writing of Bernard Shaw: How to Become a Musical Critic, 1961, Platform and Pulpit, 1961, (with David H. Greene) The Matter with Ireland, 1962, rev. edit., 2001, Selected Non-Dramatic Writings of Shaw, 1965, Collected Letters of Bernard Shaw, 4 vols., 1965-88, Bernard Shaw's Collected Plays with Their Prefaces, 7 vols., 1970-74, (with Daniel J. Leary) Flyleaves, 1977, Shaw's Music, 3 vols., 1981, (with James Rambeau) Agitations, 1985, (with Martin Quinn) Shaw on Dickens, 1985, (with Nicholas Grene) Bernard Shaw, Lady Gregory, and the Abbey, 1993, (with Daniel J. Leary) Shaw: Complete Prefaces, 3 vols. 1993-97, Theatrics, 1995, (with Margot Peters) Unpublished Shaw, 1996, (with Fred D. Crawford) Bibliographical Shaw, 2000. Served with USAAF, 1942-45, PTO. John Simon Guggenheim Meml. fellow, 1960, 61, 72, Pres.'s medal Hofstra U., 1990. Mem. Royal Acad. Dramatic Art (assoc.), Phi Beta Kappa, Phi Alpha Theta, Alpha Psi Omega, Phi Gamma Delta. Home: Apt 426 8645 Fredericksburg Rd San Antonio TX 78240-1269

LAURENCE, JEFFREY CONRAD, immunologist, educator; b. N.Y.C., Oct. 21, 1952; s. Harry and Stephanie (Maderic) L.; children: Auden, Galen. BA summa cum laude, Columbia U., 1972; MD, U. Chgo., 1976. Diplomate Am. Bd. Internal Medicine. Rsch. assoc. Inst. for Cancer Rsch., Osaka, Japan, 1974-75; intern, resident, then hematology fellow N.Y.C. Hosp.-Cornell, 1976-82; assoc. physician The Rockefeller U., N.Y.C., 1980-84; asst. prof. Cornell U. Med. Coll., 1982-87, assoc. prof., 1988-2000, prof., 2001—; dir. Lab. AIDS Rsch. Cornell Med. Coll., 1986—. Sr. dir. Immune Tech., Inc., N.Y.C., 1986-95; sr. scientist Am. Found. AIDS Rsch., N.Y.C. and Beverly Hills, Calif., 1986—. Author: (play) Many Happy Returns, 1982; editor-in-chief The AIDS Reader, 1991—; editor AIDS Targeted Info. Newsletter, 1987-92; assoc. editor AIDS Rsch. and Human Retroviruses, AIDS, 1987-95; editor-in-chief AIDS Patient Care and STDs, 1996—; cons. editor Infections in Medicine, 1987—; patentee in field. Recipient Clinician-Scientist award Am. Heart Assn., 1980-85; William S. Paley Found. fellow, 1982-84; Henry Luce Found. scholar, 1974, Rhodes scholar-elect, 1973. Mem. NIH (mem. study sect.), AMA, Fedn. Am. Soc. Exptl. Biology-Medicine, Am. Soc. Microbiology, Am. Soc. Clin. Investigation, Phi Beta Kappa. Presbyterian. Avocations: collecting ancient med. books and sci. instruments, contemporary art, sports, yoga. Home: 86 Brookside Dr Greenwich CT 06831-5345 Office: NY Presbyn Hosp-Cornell Med Ctr Dept Medicine Lab AIDS Rsch 411 E 69th St New York NY 10021-5608 E-mail: jlaurenc@med.cornell.edu.

LAURENCE, MICHAEL MARSHALL, magazine publisher, writer; b. N.Y.C., May 22, 1940; s. Frank Marshall and Edna Ann (Roeder) L.; m. Patricia Ann McDonald, Mar. 1, 1969; children: Elizabeth Sarah, John Marshall. AB cum laude, Harvard U., 1963. From sr. editor to asst. pub. Playboy mag., Chgo., 1967—77, asst. pub., 1977—82; mng. editor Oui mag., 1973-77; editor, pub. Linn's Stamp News, Sidney, Ohio, 1982—2002, also columnist Editor's Choice; sr. v.p., editl. dir. Amos Hobby Pub., 2002—. Co-founder, dir. U.S. 1869 Pictorial Rsch. Assocs., 1975-82. Author: Playboy's Investment Guide, 1971; editor: U.S. Mail and Post Office Assistant, 1975; author articles. Recipient G.M. Loeb award for disting. mag. writing U. Conn., 1968; named to Writers Hall of Fame, Am. Philatelic Soc., 1994. Mem. U.S. Philat. Classics Soc. (life, Elliott Perry award 1975, bd. dir. 1975-81), Harvard Club (N.Y.C.), Collectors Club Chgo. (bd. dires. 1978-82), Collectors Club N.Y.C. Avocations: stamp collecting, gardening. Office: Linn's Stamp News 911 S Vandemark Rd Sidney OH 45365-8974

LAURENCE, ROBERT LIONEL, chemical engineering educator; b. West Warwick, R.I., July 13, 1936; s. Lionel Gerard and Gertrude Sara (Lefebvre) L.; m. Carol Leah Jolicoeur, Sept. 7, 1959; children: Jonathan, Lisa, Andrew. BSChemE, MIT, 1957; MSChemE, U. R.I., 1960; PhDChemE, Northwestern U., 1966; DSc (honoris causa), Inst. Nat. Poly., Toulouse, France, 1989. Rsch. engr. Gen. Dynamics, Groton, Conn., 1957-59, E. I. du Pont de Nemours, Wilmington, Del., 1960-61, field svc. engr. Beaumont, Tex., 1961-63; asst. prof. chem. engring. Johns Hopkins U., Balt., 1965-68; rsch. engr. Monsanto Co., Springfield, Mass., 1968; assoc. prof. U. Mass., Amherst, 1968-73, head dept. chem. engring., 1982-89, prof., 1973-2001, prof. emeritus, 2001—. Vis. prof. Imperial Coll., London, 1974-75, Coll. de France, Paris, 1982-83; invited prof. ENSIGC, Toulouse, France, 1990; vis. rsch. fellow GE, Schenectady, 1989; vis. prof. Rijks U. Gent, 1996; cons. UN Devel. Program, Argentina, 1978, 80, Beijing, 1982; mem. Conseil Technologique Groupe Rhone-Poulenc, Paris, 1988-96. Fellow Am. Inst. Chem. Engrs., Am. Inst. Chemists; mem. Am. Chem. Soc., Soc. Plastics Engrs., Am. Soc. Engring. Edn., Tau Beta Pi. Roman Catholic. Avocation: rugby. Home: 18 Ashley Ter Waterville ME 04901 E-mail: rlaurence@ecs.umass.edu.

LAURENSON, ROBERT MARK, mechanical engineer; b. Pitts., Oct. 25, 1938; s. Robert Mark and Mildred Othelia (Frandsen) L.; m. Alice Ann Scroggins, Aug. 26, 1961; children: Susan Elizabeth Laurenson Matchael, Shari Lynn, Laurenson Lawson. Student, Drury Coll., 1956-58; BS in Mech. Engring., Mo. Sch. Mines, 1961; MS in Mech. Engring., U. Mich., 1962; PhD in Mech. Engring. (NASA tng. grantee), Ga. Inst. Tech., 1968. Registered profl. engr., Mo. Dynamics engr. McDonnell Douglas Corp., St. Louis, 1962-64, sr. dynamics engr., 1968-71, group engr., 1971-74, staff engr., 1974-75, tech. specialist, 1975-78, sr. tech. specialist, 1978-81, sect. chief, 1981-85, prin. tech. specialist, 1985-87, br. chief, 1987-89, prin. mgr. engring., 1989-92; prin. tech. specialist, systems engring. mgr. The Boeing Co., Seabrook, Md., 1992-93, sr. mgr., 1993-95, asst. dir. engring., 1995-97, gen. mgr., 1998-99; ret.; pvt. cons. Crofton, Md., 1999—. Participant 14th Midwestern Mechanics Conf., 1975; lectr. engring. mechanics St. Louis U., part-time 1969-71; adj. assoc. prof. U. Mo.-Rolla Grad. Engring. Ctr., St. Louis, 1980-88; lectr. mech. engring. Johns Hopkins U., 1996—; participant Symposium on Dynamics and Control of Large Flexible Spacecraft, Blacksburg, Va., 1977, In-Space Tech. Experiments Workshop NASA, 1988, Damping, '89 Conf., 1989; mem. panel Am. Astronauticla Soc. Symposium on Dynamics and Control of Nonridig Spacecraft, UCLA, 1974; mem. accreditation bd. engr. and tech. Engring. Accreditation Commn., 1998—, mem. exec. com., 2000—; project coord. ASME/NSF Project Grant, 2000-01. Author: How to Write Winning Proposals, 2001; contbr. articles to profl. jours.; reviewer profl. jours.; author tech. papers Jour. Engring. for Industry, 1972,, Jour. Spacecraft and Rockets, 1973, AIAA Jour., 1976, 78, 80, 85; numerous papers presented at tech. confs. Vestryman Episcopal Ch., 1972-76, sr. warden, 1976, uscher chmn., 1978-80, Sunday sch. tchr., 1980-84, chmn. every mem. canvas, 1983, mem. steering com., 1983-88, chmn. steering com., 1987-88, mem. search com., 1984-85, mem. exec. com., 1991-92, warden, 1991-92; mem. Commn. on Ministry, Diocese of Mo., 1985-91, chmn., 1989-91; mem. standing com. Diocese of Mo., 1990-92; trustee Corp. of Episcopal Diocese of Mo., 1990-92; mem. seminarian com., 1993-98, 2001-, chair, 1994-97, engring. mentor Holy Trinity Episcopal Day Sch., chmn. Parish Commn. on Ministry, 1999-2000, chair parish stratetic planning com., 2001-; pres. Crabtown Square square dance clun, 1998-2000. Fellow ASME (structures materials com. aerospace divsn. 1975-84, com. chmn. 1979-81, session organizer, chmn. ann. meeting 1975, participant ann. meeting 1986, 89, mem. exec. com. aerospace divsn. 1980-85, sec.-treas. 1981-82, vice-chmn. 1982-83, chmn. 1983-84, Flag award aerospace divsn. 1990, mem.

Guggenheim medal bd. 1989-92, mem. conf. organizing com., session chmn. Structures, Structural Dynamics and Materials Conf., 1977, chmn. tech. program 1978, gen. co-chmn. 1979, gen. chmn. 1981, mem. SDM planning com. 1978-82, chmn. 1981-82, session chmn. 1985, 88, adv. com. 1978-82, participant 1979, 83, 86, 90, mech. engrng. evaluator Accreditation Bd. Engrng. and Tech. 1985-91, 94-98, organizer symposium on microgravity fluid mechanics 1986, mem. planning com. edn. conf. 1986, editor Advances in Aerospace Structures 1982, Procs. of 1986 Edn. Conf. The Decade Ahead, bd. engrng. edn. K thru 12 task force 1992-93, bd. pre-coll. edn. 1992-95, 1st alt. nat. nominating com. 1993-94, bd. on engrng. edn. 1998—, engrng. accreditation com. 1998—, exec. com. 1993—, sec. 1995-96, vice chair 1996-97, rep. on Am. Assn. Engrng. Soc.'s Precoll. Edn. Coun. 1993-95, exec. com. 1993-95, Dedicated Svc. award 1995); mem. AIAA (sr., gen. chmn. dynamics specialist conf. 1981, session chmn. 1987), Edison Electric Inst. (adv. com. power engrng. edn. forgivable loan program 1993-94), Sigma Xi, Pi Tau Sigma, Tau Beta Pi, Phi Kappa Phi, Sigma Phi Epsilon. Home: 1104 Jasper Ct Crofton MD 21114-1658

LAURENT, DUANE GILES, memory design engineer; b. New Orleans, Dec. 17, 1952; s. Ewell Joseph and Lorrie Marie (Montz) L.; m. Susan Marie Waguespack, Aug. 2, 1974; 1 child, Sarah Elizabeth. BS, Southeastern La. U., Hammond, 1974; PhD in Physics, La. State U., 1981. Sr. engr. UTC-Mostek Corp., Carrollton, Tex., 1981-85; staff engr. SGS-Thomson Microelectronics, 1985-95; prin. engr. STMicroelects., Tex., 1995—. Contbr. articles to profl. jours. Mem. IEEE, Am. Phys. Soc., Am. Radio Relay League. Home: 905 Brittany Dr Lewisville TX 75067-7493 Office: STMicroelectronics 1310 Electronic Dr # MS2200 Carrollton TX 75006-7005

LAURENT, JEROME KING, economics educator; b. Knoxville, Tenn., Jan. 8, 1940; s. Francis William and Grace Ruth (King) L.; m. Virginia Spencer Huggins, Aug. 20, 1966; children: Katherine Harvie, Thomas King. BA cum laude, U. Wis., Eau Claire, 1961; MA, Ind. U., 1963, PhD, 1973. Grad. asst. Ind. U., Bloomington, 1961-62, teaching assoc., 1962-65; instr. econs. U. Wis., Whitewater, 1965-67, asst. prof., 1967-76, assoc. prof., 1976-81, prof., 1981—. Vis. assoc. prof. U. Wis., Madison, 1980. Contbg. author: International Trade and Finance, 1988, Management Education and Training: An Eastern European Dilemma, 1994; contbr. articles to profl. jours., book revs. to Jour. Econ. History; external reviewer numerous jours. Lay dep. Diocese of Milw. coun. Episcopal Ch., 1968—, trustee of funds, 1983-92, pres., mem. fin. com., 1991-92, combined mut. fund Diocese of Milw.; jr. warden St. Luke's Episcopal Ch., Whitewater, 1981-83, sr. warden, 1984, treas., 1988-90, chmn. fin. com., 1991—; mem. edn. com. Wis. Fed. of Coops., Madison, 1983-99. Faculty fellow Inst. on Latin Am., Hamline U., St. Paul, 1977; recipient Editor's Best Essay on N.Am. Transp. prize Manchester U. Press, 1982. Mem. Am. Econs. Assn., Econ. History Assn., Assn. for Comparative Econ. Studies, Wis. Econs. Assn. (mem. exec. bd. 1977-79, pres. 1983-85), Assn. Great Lakes Maritime History (mem. rsch. and publs. com. 2000—), Lexington Group in Transp. History, Kiwanis (treas. Whitewater Breakfast club 1978-83, mem. audit com. 1996—), Beta Gamma Sigma, Omicron Delta Epsilon. Avocations: reading, hiking, travel. Home: 1268 W Court St Whitewater WI 53190-1625

LAURENT, J(ERRY) SUZANNA, technical communications specialist; b. Oklahoma City, Dec. 28, 1942; d. Harry Austin and M. LaVerne (Barker) Minick; m. Leroy E. Laurent, July 2, 1960; children: Steven, Sandra, David, Debra. AS in Engr. Tech., Okla. State U., 1986. Owner, CEO Technically Write, Mustang, Okla., 1989-95; sr. tech. comms. specialist Applied Intelligence Group, Edmond, 1995-98, DCA Svcs., Oklahoma City, 1998—. Named One of The Top Ten Business Women in Nation Am. Bus. Women's Assn., 1997. Mem.: Am. Bus. Women's Assn. (area coun. pres. 1987—89, v.p. dist. III 1988—89, sec. 1990—91, conf. gen. chair 1992, chmn. bd. dirs. Help Us Grow Spiritually 1993—95, editor Smoke Signals, Bull. award 1977, 1981, 1983, 1984, 1993, 1995, 1997—99, Nat. Newsletter award 1999, Woman of Yr. 1978, 1996, 1997, Bus. Assoc. of Yr. 1983—84), Soc. Tech. Comm. (Superscript editor 1985, v.p. 1985, feature editor 1986, student chpt. pres. 1986, program coord. Okla. chpt. 1992—93, sec. 1993—94, v.p. 1994—95, state pres. 1995—96, state treas. Okla. chpt. 1998—99, dir./sponsor region 5 1999—2002, bylaws com. mgr. 2001—02, Disting. Chpt. Svc. award 1997, Outstanding Achievement award 2001). Democrat. Baptist. Avocations: reading, public speaking, motivating people, volunteer activities. Home: 347 W Forest Dr Mustang OK 73064-3430

LAURENT, LAWRENCE BELL, communications executive, former journalist; b. Monroe, La., Mar. 9, 1925; s. Lewis Emeal and John Ethel (Dawkins) L.; m. Margaret F. Goodwillie, Nov. 1, 1949; children— Richard Sandford, Arthur Halliday, Margaret Funsten, Elizabeth MacLean. Student, U. Va., 1946-49; pvt. study with, Dr. W.Y. Elliott, 1954-56, Dr. Franklin Dunham, 1957-58. With Bluefield (W.Va.) Daily Telegraph, 1949-50, Charlottesville (Va.) Daily Progress, 1950-51; with Washington Post, 1951-82, radio-TV editor, 1953-82, radio-TV editor emeritus, 1982—; cons. Assn. Ind. TV Stas., 1982-85, dir. communication, 1985-86, v.p. communication, 1986-91; congl. cons., 1991—; editor-in-residence Broadcast Pioneers Library, 1985-96; adj. prof. communications Am. U., Washington, 1963-85; chmn. editorial bd. TV Quar., 1963-74, bd. dirs., 1974—. Guest prof. Syracuse U., 1965; vis. prof. U. Detroit, 1967; vis. prof. George Washington U., 1982-95, professorial lectr., 1996—; formerly judge Alfred I. duPont awars, Saturday Rev. Lit. TV awards, Sigma Delt Chi pub. svc. TV awards, Humanitas awards. Editor, author: (with Newton N. Minow) Equal Time, 1964; Contbr. to books, mags. Trustee Human Family Edn. and Cultural Inst.; bd. dirs. Pioneers Edn. Fund, Inc., 1984-94, trustee, 1995—. With USNR, 1943-46. Recipient Front Page award Am. Newspaper Guild, 1964, Disting. Tchr. award Am. U., 1978, TV Acad.'s Silver Circle award, 1988, Pres.'s medal George Washington U., 1999; named to Broadcast Pioneers' Hall of Fame, 1984; du Pont Journalism scholar U. Va., 1947-49. Mem. AAUP, NATAS (life), VFW (life), DAV (life), 593rd Joint Assault Signal Co. Assn., USS Belle Grove Historic Assn., Nat. Press Club, White House Corrs. Assn., Washington Post E-Streeters, Am. Legion (life), Thomas Jefferson Soc. Alumni (U. Va.), Sigma Delta Chi, Pi Delta Epsilon, Theta Chi. Episcopalian. Home: 215 Jefferson St Alexandria VA 22314-4323

LAURENT, PIERRE-HENRI, history educator; b. Fall River, Mass., May 15, 1933; s. Henri and Harriet (Moriarty) L.; m. Virginia Brayton, 1958; children: Paul-Henri, Bradford Webb, Nicole, Alexa. AB, Colgate U., 1956; A.M., Boston U., 1960, PhD, 1964. Instr. polit. economy Boston U., 1961-64; asst. prof. history Sweet Briar Coll., 1964-66; vis. asst. prof. history U. Wis., Madison, 1966-67; asst. prof. history Tulane U., New Orleans, 1967-68, assoc. prof., 1968-70; assoc. prof. history Tufts U., Medford, Mass., 1970-75, prof., 1975—, chmn. dept., 1987-89, adj. prof. diplomatic history/Fletcher Sch. Law and Diplomacy, 1977, 84, chmn. Exptl. Coll., 1973-75, acting dir. internat. relations program, 1979, dir. internat. relations program, 1984-88, co-dir. Internat. Relations Inst. France, 1979-80; acad. dir. Tufts European Ctr., France, 1996. Mem. history devel. bd. Ednl. Testing Svc. of Princeton, 1979-82; instr. JFK Inst. Polit., Harvard U., Cambridge, 1989; mem. nat. screening com. Fulbright-Hays program Inst. Internat. Edn., 1988-91; rsch. assoc. Ctr. for Internat. Affairs, Harvard U. Mem. editorial bd. Jour. Social History, 1966-74; sect. editor Am. Hist. Rev., 1967-77; co-editor: The State of the European Union: Deepening and Widening, 1998, NATO and the European Union: Confronting the Challenges of European Security and Enlargement, 1999; contbr. chpts. to books, articles to profl. jours., mags., encys. Served with USAF, 1956-58. NATO fellow, 1967, NEH fellow, 1969, Paul-Henri Spaak Found. fellow, 1976-77; Sweet Briar Faculty rsch. grantee, 1965, Tufts Faculty rsch. grantee, 1972, 1994, Inst. European Studies-Exxon Ednl. Fund grantee, 1983; Fulbright Rsch. scholar, 1992-93; Fulbright chair Coll. of Europe, Bruges, 1998. Fellow Inst. des Rels. Internationales, Acad. Assoc. Atlantic Coun.; mem. AAUP (exec. com. Mass. State Conf. 1974-76, pres. Tufts U. chpt. 1982-84, 2000-2002), European Cmty. Studies Assn. (exec. com. 1988-92, 95-99, chmn. 1991-92, vice-chmn. 1997-99), Belgian-Am. Edn. Found. (bd. govs. 1986-90). Office: Tufts Univ Dept History Medford MA 02155 E-mail: plaurent@tufts.edu.

LAURENTI, JOSEPH LUCIANO, language educator, writer; b. Hespérange, Luxembourg, Dec. 10, 1931; arrived in U.S., 1949; s. Ernesto Carlo and Angelina Teresa (Dal Canton) Laurenti; m. Luellen W. Watson, June 10, 1967 (dec. June 2000). BA in Spanish, French, Italian, U. Ill., Urbana, 1958; MA in Spanish, French, Italian, U. Ill., 1959; PhD in Spanish, French, U. Mo., 1962. Instr. Spanish U. Ill., Urbana, 1959, U. Mo., Columbia, 1959—62; prof. Spanish, Italian and German Ill. State U., Normal, 1962—2001; ret., 2001. U.S. corres. Quaderni Ibero-Am., Torino, Italy, 1974—93, AZB Revista de Cultura Internacional. Mem. editl. bd. (jour.) Edition Reichenberger, Kassel, Germany, 1983—, reviewer The Modern Lang. Jour., 1978—; author: Bibliografia de la Literatura Picaresca, 1991 (Nicolá Antonio prize, 1994); contbr. ; author: Lazarillo de Tormes: A Critical Study of the Second Part of Juan de Luna, 1965, A Bibliographic Essay of the Spanish Picaresque Novel, 1968, Studies in the Spanish Picaresque Novel, 1970, Critical Prefaces in the Spanish Picaresque Novel, 1971; author: (with Alberto Porqueras Mayo) A Bibliographic Essay of the Prologue in Literature, 1971; author: (with Joseph Siracusa) Literary Relations Between Spain and Italy, 1972; author: A Critical Bibliography of Picaresque Literature, 1973; author: (with Joseph Siracusa) The World of Federico Garl Lorca, 1974; author: The Spanish Golden Age (1472-1700), 1979, A Catalog of Rare Books in the Library of the University of Illinois and in Selected North American Libraries, 1979, A Catalog of Spanish Rare Books (1701-1974) in the Library of the University of Illinois and in Selected North American Libraries, 1984; author: (with A Porqueras Mayo) Estudios bibliográficos sobre la Edad de Oro, 1984; author: Hispanic Rare Books of the Golden Age (1470-1699) in the Newberry Library of Chicago and in Selected North American Libraries, 1989, Catálogo bibliográfico de la literatura picaresca (Siglos VI-XX), 1991; author: (with Mayo) Nuevos estudios bibliograficos sobre la Edad de Oro: Fondos raros y colecciones en la Biblioteca de la Universidad de Illinois, 1994; editor: Antonio de Guevara en la biblioteca de la universidad de Illinois, 1974; editor: (with Vern Williamsen) Varia hispanica . Estudios en los siglos de oro y literatura moderna: Homenaje a Alberto Porqueras Mayo, 1989. Cpl. U.S. Army, 1952—54. Recipient Antonio Nicolas prize, Syracuse U., 1992; fellow, Newberry Libr., Chgo., 1986, Gutenberg Gesellschaft, Mainz, Germany, 1992; grantee Dip. Prov. grantee, Diputacion Provincial, Seville, Spain, 1991—94, Interambios Culturales Hispano-Americanos, Barcelona, Spain, 1984, Program for Cultural Coop. between Spain's Min. of Culture and U.S. Govt., 1989, 1994. Mem.: AAUP, MLA (prize for disting. bibliography 2002), Ill. Assn. Tchrs. of Modern Langs., Midwest Modern Lang. Assn., Am. Assn. Tchrs. of Spanish and Portuguese, Am. Assn. Profs. of Italian, Internat. Assn. Philogists, Internat. Assn. of Hispanists, Assn. de Cervantistas (life), Assn. de Bibliografil Española (life), Sigma Delta Pi (chpt. pres. 1958—59, Medal of Order of Don Quixote). Democrat. Roman Catholic. Home: 2703 Wedgewood Bloomington IL 61704

LAURENZO, VINCENT DENNIS, industrial management company executive; b. Des Moines, May 31, 1939; s. Vincent C. and B.J. (Garver) L.; m. Sherrill S. Mullen, Sept. 10, 1960; children: Lisa, David, Susan, Nancy, James. BBA, U. Notre Dame, 1961; MBA, U. Mich., 1964. With Ford Motor Co., Dearborn, Mich., 1961-66; plant controller Massey Ferguson Inc., 1967-70; with parent co. Massey Ferguson Ltd., Toronto, Ont., Can., 1971-94, dir. fin. Am. div. Can., 1977-78, v.p., comptr. Massey Ferguson Ltd. Can., 1978-80, sr. v.p. planning and adminstrn. Can., 1980-81; pres. Varity Corp. (formerly Massey Ferguson Ltd.), 1981-94, vice chmn. bd. Buffalo, 1988-96, vice chmn., pres., 1988-94; ret., 1994; vice chair bd. dirs. Roman Catholic.

LAURIA, RITA MARIE, media and communications researcher, consultant; children: Carmella, Marcela. BA, U. So. Calif., L.A., 1979; MA, U. N.C., 1987, PhD, 2000. Freelance writer, cons., Chapel Hill, 1982-90; adv. to sec. Dept. Transp. and Comm. Federated States Micronesia, 1990-92; instr. Cape Fear C.C., Wilmington, N.C., 1993-94; dir. global virtual univ. initiative U. N.C., 1998-99; rsch. assoc. Media Interface and Network Design Lab. Mich. State U., Lansing, 1997—. Lectr. N.C. State U., 2000, U. N.C., Wilmington, 2001-02; participant Banff New Media Inst., Banff Ctr. summt on artificial stupidity/artificial intelligence, 2002; me. summer program on legal responses to new comms. tech. Oxford U., 2002. Author: The Law and Regulation of International Space Communications, 1988; contbg. author chpt. book; contbr. articles to profl. jours. and pubs. Recipient endowment Nat. Endowment for Humanities, 1994; Writing and Rsch. grantee Nat. Press Found., 1986. Mem. Assn. U. Women (career devel. fellow, Helen Landers endowment 1996-97). Avocations: skiing, water skiing, weight training, running. E-mail: rlauria@worldnet.att.net.

LAURICH, LAWRENCE ALVIN, company executive; b. Marquette, Mich., Mar. 29, 1943; s. Ludwig B. and Esther Marie (Manners) L.; m. Louise Ann Marley, Oct. 29, 1993; children: Gregory Lawrence, Sandra Marie, Mark David, Marie Susan. BSEE, Mich. Tech., 1965, MSEE, 1966. Sr. engr. IBM, Boulder, Colo., 1967-78; gen. mgr., v.p. sys. divsn. Tandem Computers, Cupertino, Calif., 1978-97; sr. v.p., COO Nex Gen SI, Irvine, 1997-98; pres./CEO N-Light Sys., San Jose, 1998-99; exec. v.p./gen. mgr. Siros Tech., 1999; pres./CEO Vision Solutions, Inc., Irvine, Calif., 1999-2000; pres., CEO Ipmobilenet Inc., Santa Fe Springs, 2000—02. Contbr. articles to profl. jours.; patentee in field. V.p. Optimist Club, Boulder, 1975; bd. dirs. Christian Bros. U., Memphis, 1988-91; mem. adv. bd. San Jose (Calif.) State U., 1990-95; vice chmn. Computer and Comm. Industry Assn., Washington, 1996-97. Mem. IEEE, Tau Beta Pi (Ford fellow 1966). Avocations: airplane instrument and helicopter pilot, golf, biking, scuba. Home: 605 Promontory Dr E Newport Beach CA 92660-7457 Office: 11909 Telegraph Rd Santa Fe Springs CA 90670-3785 E-mail: Larry@Laurich.com.

LAURIE, GERALD TENZER, lawyer; b. St. Paul, Jan. 22, 1942; s. Hyman and Leona (Smith) L.; m. Joellyn Kronick, Mar. 12, 1968; children: Ian, Eben, Joshua. BA, U. Minn., 1964, JD, 1967. Bar: Minn. 1967, U.S. Dist. Ct. Minn. 1967, U.S. Ct. Appeals (fed. cir.) 1987. Spl. asst. atty. gen. Minn. Atty. Gen. Office, St. Paul, 1968-70; ptnr. Laurie & Laurie, P.A., Mpls., 2001—. Contbr. articles in field to legal jours. Mem. City of New Hope Indsl. Commn.; chmn. New Hope Liquor Commn. Fellow Am. Coll. Labor and Employment Lawyers; mem. ABA, Assn. Trial Lawyers Am., Minn. Bar Assn. (cert. civil litigation specialist), Minn. Trial Lawyers Assn. (bd. govs. 1983-89), Hennepin County Bar Assn. Avocations: reading, swimming, biking. Office: Laurie & Laurie PA Parkdale Plz Bldg 1660 S Hwy 100 508 East Minneapolis MN 55416-1534 E-mail: Jerry@laurielaurie.com.

LAURIE, JAMES ANDREW, journalist, broadcaster; b. Eustis, Fla., June 16, 1947; s. Andrew Louis and Geneva Lavina (Pryor) L. BA in History, Am. U., Washington, 1970; postgrad., George Washington U. Free-lance writer Far Eastern Econ. Review, Washington, 1969, 73-74, Phnom Penh, Cambodia and Saigon, Vietnam, 1970-71; reporter NBC News, Saigon, 1971-73, 75, Tokyo, 1976-78; with ABC News, 1978-99, corr., bur. chief, Hong Kong, 1978-81, opened 1st Am. radio-TV bur. in Peking, 1981, bur. chief, Peking, 1981-82, chief Asia corr., Tokyo, 1983-88, corr., bur. chief Moscow, 1989-91, sr. corr., 1991-96, China, 1996—, bur. chief Hong Kong, 1996-99; vice pres. Network News and Current Affairs, Newscorps/Satellite Television, Asia Region, 1999—. Writer, narrator: (ABC Closeup documentaries) Japan: Myths behind the Miracle, 1981, The Unruly Dragon: China's Yellow River, 1988, Soviet segment ABC Spl. "Beyond the Cold War", 1989; covered Mikhail Gorbachev in Cuba, East Germany, Rome, Malta, 1989, Tien An Men Crushing of Democrats Movement, 1989, Gorbachev summit in U.S., 1990, Bush-Gorbachev summit, Moscow, 1991, coup d'etat Moscow, 1991, Somalia Famine, 1992, Iraq Crisis, 1993, Bosnia Crises, 1993, Israeli-Palestinian Negotiations, 1993, Russian Crisis October, 1993, South African elections, 1994, U.S. operation in Haiti, 1994, Crisis in Rwanda, 1995, Human Right Coverage China, 1996, Hong Kong Handover, 1997, Reporting from Tibet, 1997, coup d'etat in Cambodia, 1997. Recipient George Foster Peabody Broadcasting award for reporting fall of Saigon, 1976; Columbia-Dupont award for ABC Closeup documentary Cambodia: This Shattered Land, 1981; award for radio news coverage of assassination of Philippine leader Benigno Aquino, Overseas Press Club, 1983; Emmy award, 1987, N.Y. Festivals award. Office: STAR-TV 8/f One Harbourfront 18 Tak Fung Hong Kong Hong Kong E-mail: lauriej@asiaonline.net, jlaurie@startu.com.

LAURIE, RICH M. federal agency administrator; b. Dallas; Grad., N. Tex. State U. (now U. N. Tex.). Tchr. secondary sch., Dallas; acting adminstrv. asst. to Sen. Kay Bailey Hutchison; dep. dir. coalitions Bush/Quayle '92 campaign; spl. asst. and sr. legis. asst. to Sen. Phil Gramm Tex., 1985—95; exec. dir. Tex. Office State Fed. Regulations; asst. sec. intergovtl. and interagy. affairs Dept. Edn., Washington, 2001—. Office: Dept Edn Intergovtl and Interagy Affairs 400 Maryland Ave SW FOB 6 Washington DC 20202-3500*

LAURIE, ROBIN GARRETT, lawyer; b. Mobile, Ala., June 10, 1956; s. George and Margaret Eloise (Garrett) L.; m. Deborah Dockery; children: Elizabeth Anne, Robin Garrett. AA, Marion (Ala.) Mil. Inst., 1976; BS in Bus., U. Ala., Tuscaloosa, 1978; JD, U.Ala., Tuscaloosa, 1988. Bar: Ala. 1988, U.S. Dist. Ct. (no., mid. and so. dists.) Ala. 1988, U.S. Ct. Appeals (11th cir.) 1988. Ptnr. Balch & Bingham LLP, Montgomery, Ala., 1988—. Lead articles editor Ala. Law Rev., 1986-88. Recipient Outstanding Svc. award Ala. Law Rev., 1988. Mem. ABA, Ala. State Bar, Montgomery County Bar Assn., Montgomery Rotary Club, Order of the Coif. Methodist. Avocations: flying small airplanes, fishing, hunting. Office: Balch & Bingham LLP PO Box 78 Montgomery AL 36101-0078 E-mail: rlaurie@balch.com.

LAURIE, RONALD SHELDON, lawyer; b. San Francisco, June 30, 1942; s. Charles M. and Mimosa (Ezaoui) L.; m. Mina Heshmati, June 1, 1986. BS in Indsl. Engrng., U. Calif., Berkeley, 1964; JD, U. San Francisco, 1968. Bar: Calif. 1969, U.S. Ct. Appeals (9th cir.) 1969, U.S. Patent Office 1969, U.S. Supreme Ct. 1971, U.S. Ct. Appeals (fed. cir.) 1972. Programmer, sys. engr. Lockheed Missiles & Space Co., Sunnyvale, Calif., 1960-64; patent atty. Kaiser Aluminum & Chem. Co., Oakland, 1968-70; ptnr. Townsend and Townsend, San Francisco, 1970-88, Irell & Manella, Menlo Park, Calif., 1988-91, Weil, Gotshal & Manges, Menlo Park, 1991-94, McCutchen, Doyle, Brown & Emersen, San Francisco, 1994-98; chmn. McCutchen Computers and Software Industry Group, 1995-98; ptnr. Skadden, Arps, Meagher & Flom, Palo Alto, Calif., 1998—; co-chair Skadden Arps' Computer and Info. Tech. Group, 1998—. Lectr. computer law Stanford U. Law Sch., 1993-94; advisor NAS, U.S. Copyright Office and U.S. Patent and Trademark Office, Washington, Office Tech. Assessment, U.S. Congress, World Intellectual Property Orgn., Geneva; lectr. patent law U. Calif., Berkeley, 1999—; permanent faculty World Law Inst., 1996—. Co-editor: International Intellectual Property, 1992; contbr. articles to profl. jours. Mem. Internat. Intellectual Property Assn. (exec. com.), State Bar Calif. (past mem. exec. com. intellectual property sect.), Computer Law Assn. (bd. dirs.). Avocation: vintage auto racing. Home: 107 Acacia Ave Belvedere CA 94920-2309 Office: Skadden Arps Meagher & Flom 525 University Ave Palo Alto CA 94301-1903 E-mail: rlaurie@skadden.com., roulaurie@sprintmail.com.

LAURIE, WILLIAM, sports team executive; b. Versailles, Mo. m. Nancy, 1974; 1 child. B in Secondary Edn., Memphis State Coll., 1974. Tchr., basketball coach Christian Bros. Coll. High Sch., Memphis, 1974-78, Rock Bridge High Sch., Columbia, Mo., 1978-83; exec. Crown Ctr. Farms, 1983-99; chmn., owner St. Louis Blues Hockey Team, 1999—; chmn. Savvis Ctr., St. Louis. Booster U. Mo. Tiger Sport. Office: Savvis Ctr 1401 Clark Ave Saint Louis MO 63103-2709*

LAURIN, PIERRE, finance company executive; b. Charlemagne, Que., Can., Aug. 11, 1939; MBA, U. Montreal, 1963; D in Bus. Adminstrn., Harvard U., 1969; PhD (hon.), Concordia U., Montreal, 1983. Dean bus. sch. U. Montreal, 1975-82; v.p. planning and adminstrn. Alcan Co. of Can., 1982-87; vice chmn., pres., Que. Merrill Lynch Can. Inc., Montreal, 1987-98. Exec. in residence, Ecole des Hautes Etudes Commerciales, Montreal, 1999. Author mgmt. textbook. Named officer Order Can. Office: Ecole des Hautes Etudes Commerciales Montreal QC Canada H3T 2A7

LAURISKI, DAVE D. federal agency administrator; Grad., Utah State U., Coll. Ea. Utah. Dir. health, safety, environ. and govt. affairs Interwest Mining Co., 1993—95; gen. mgr. Energy West Mining Co., 1995—99; pres. Lauriski and Assocs. LLC, Price, Utah, 1999—2001; asst. sec. mine safety and health adminstrn. U.S. Dept. Labor, Arlington, Va., 2001—. Office: US Dept Labor 4015 Wilson Blvd Arlington VA 22203*

LAURITSEN, KAJ TORBEN, lawyer, former association executive; b. Selling, Denmark, Dec. 19, 1923; s. Laurits Thomas Thorvald and Thala (Rasmussen-Skovsgaard) L.; grad. Roskilde Katedral Skole, 1943; cand. phil., 1944, cand. jur., 1952, grad. in law, 1952, Degree in Spanish, 1988, Degree in Italian, 1990. m. Jytte Elisabeth Moller, Apr. 24, 1962. Admitted to bar, 1957. Appointments asst. Ministry Housing Denmark, 1948-51; solicitors clk., 1954-57; sole practice, Copenhagen and Kolding, 1957-60; head legal dept. Fedn. Danish Motorists, Odense, 1960-81; legal advisor Welfare Dept., Local Adminstrn., 1982; ret., 1983. Mem. Danish Legal Confedn., Danish Lawyers Community Conservative. Contbr. articles to profl. jours. Home: 10 Billeshave-Vaenget Slukefter 5210 Odense Denmark

LAURSEN, RICHARD ALLAN, science educator; b. Normal, Ill., May 1, 1938; s. Allan Richard and Helen Catherine Laursen; m. Irene Lois Shulman, May 23, 1971; children: Michael, Sarah. BS, U. Calif., Berkeley, 1961; PhD, U. Ill., 1964. Postdoctoral fellow Harvard U., Cambridge, Mass., 1964—66; prof. chemistry Boston U., 1966—. Vis. scientist Max-Planck Inst. Molecular Genetics, Berlin, 1971; specialist in protein chemistry, Chinese Provincial Univs. Devel. Project of the World Bank Hunan Normal U., Changsha, China, 1990; vis. scientist Met. Mus. Art, N.Y.C., 1999. Inventor in field. Recipient Rsch. Career Devel. award, NIH, 1969—74, Pehr Edman award, 1988; fellow predoctoral fellowship, NIH, 1962—64, postdoctoral fellow, 1964—66, Alfred P. Sloan Found., 1972—74. Fellow: AAAS; mem.: Am. Peptide Soc., Protein Soc., Am. Soc. Biochemistry and Molecular Biology, Am. Chem. Soc. Avocations: carpentry, home remodeling. Home: 29 Howard St Newton MA 02458 Office: Boston U Chemistry Dept 590 Commonwealth Ave Boston MA 02215 Office Fax: 617-353-6466. E-mail: laursen@bu.edu.

LAURUS, (LAURUS SKURLA), archbishop; b. Ladomirova, Czechoslovakia, Jan. 1, 1928; s. Michael Ivan and Helen Michael (Martinik) Skurla. BTh, Holy Trinity Sem., 1954. joined Holy Trinity Monastery, 1946; ordained deacon Russian Orthodox Ch. Abroad, 1950, ordained priest, 1954, consecrated bishop, 1967, elevated to archbishop, 1981. Instr. Old Testament Holy Trinity Sem., Jordanville, N.Y., 1960-65, instr. patristics, 1959-93, instr. moral theology, 1973-76, insp., 1958-67, dean, 1973-76, abbot, 1976—, rector, chmn. bd., 1976—; bishop Diocese of Manhattan, 1967-76; bishop, then archbishop Diocese of Syracuse, Jordanville, 1976—2001; 1st hierarch metro., ea. Am. and N.Y. Russian Orthodox Ch., 2001—. Sec. Synod of Bishops, 1967-77, 1986-2001, pres. Synod of Bishops, 2001—; pres. St. John of Kronstadt Meml. Fund, 1976—. Editor Calendar, 1976-96, Orthodox Life, 1991—, Orthodox Russia, 1991—; contbr. articles to ch. publs. and periodicals. Mem. Orthodox Palestine Soc., 1986—. Home: Holy Trinity Monastery PO Box 36 Jordanville NY 13361-0036 Office: Synod of Bishops 75 E 93rd St New York NY 10128-1331

LAUSE, MICHAEL FRANCIS, lawyer; b. Washington, Aug. 3, 1948; s. Walter Francis and Junilla Rose (Marquart) L.; m. Ann G. Hellman, Aug. 29, 1981; children: Andrew Edward, Scott Michael. BA, St. Benedict's Coll., 1970; JD, U. Ill., 1973. Bar: Mo. 1973. Ptnr. Thompson Coburn LLP, St. Louis, 1973—. Mem. mgmt. com. Thompson Coburn LLP, St. Louis, 1988-90. Gen. counsel Mo. Health and Ednl. Facilities Authority, 1986—, St. Louis Zoo, 1992—. Mem. ABA, Mo. Bar Assn., St. Louis Bar Assn., Nat. Assn. Bond Lawyers, Bellerive Country Club. Roman Catholic. Home: 9822 Old Warson Rd Saint Louis MO 63124-1066 Office: Thompson Coburn LLP One US Bank Plz Saint Louis MO 63101

LAUSSEN, PETER CHARLES, pediatric cardiac anesthesiologist, intensive care physician; b. Melbourne, Australia, Nov. 11, 1956; s. Ronald Keith and Joan Margaret Laussen; m. Julia Ann Murphy, Apr. 25, 1981; children: Jacqueline May, Aimee Maree, Jonathan Charles, James Peter. MBBS, Melbourne U., 1980. Cert. anesthesia, intensive care medicine, Australia. Resident, med. officer Austin Hosp., Melbourne, 1981-83, anesthesia registrar, 1984-87; chief registrar ICU Royal Children's Hosp., 1988, staff anesthetist, 1989-92; assoc. in anesthesia Children's Hosp., Boston, 1992-98, asst. in cardiology, 1996—, sr. assoc. anesthesia, 1998—. Asst. prof. Harvard U., Boston, 1997—; co-dir. cardiac anesthesia Children's Hosp., 1996—, asst. dir., cardiac intensive care, 1996—, dir. anesthesia found., 1999—, physician leadership coun., 1998. Fellow Australian and New Zealand Coll. Anesthesists, Intensive Care Faculty; mem. Am. Soc. of Anesthesiologists, Australian Soc. of Anesthesiologist, Soc. Pediatric Anesthesia, Soc. Cardiovascular Anesthesiologist. Office: CUCU Office Children's Hosp 300 Longwood Ave Boston MA 02115-5724

LAUTENBACHER, CONRAD CHARLES, JR. naval officer, management consultant, federal government executive; b. Phila., June 26, 1942; s. Conrad Charles and Dorthea Henrietta (Jensen) L.; m. Susan Elizabeth Scheihing, June 20, 1964; children: Elizabeth Lautenbacher Katz, Conrad John. BS, U.S. Naval Acad., 1964; MS, Harvard U., 1965, PhD, 1968. Commd. ensign USN, 1964, advanced through grades to vice adm., 1994, aide to Vice Chief Naval Ops., Chief Naval Ops., 1974-75, exec. officer USS Benjamin Stoddert Pearl Harbor, Hawaii, 1975-77, program analyst Chief Naval Ops. Washington, 1977-80, comdg. officer USS Hewitt San Diego, 1980-82, dir. program planning Chief Naval Ops. Washington, 1982-86, comdg. officer Naval Sta., Norfolk Va., 1986-88, insp. gen. U.S. Pacific Fleet Hdqrs., 1988-90; comdr. Cruiser-Destroyer Group 5 San Diego, 1990-91; dir. force structure, resources and assessment J-8, Joint Staff, Washington, 1991-94; spl. asst. to asst. sec. navy USN, 1994; commdr. U.S. Third Fleet, 1994-96; dir. office of program appraisal, 1996-97; dep. chief of naval ops. N-8, 1997-2000; ret., 2000; mgmt. cons. Tech., Stategies, and Alliances, Inc., 2000-01; pres., CEO Consortium for Oceanographic Rsch. and Edn., 2001—02; under sec. of commerce , adminstr. NOAA Dept. Commerce, 2002—. Decorated D.S.M. (4), Legion of Merit with 3 gold stars, Meritorious Svc. medal with 2 gold stars, Navy Commendation medal, Navy Achievement medal. Mem. U.S. Naval Inst.. Lutheran. E-mail: cslautenbacher@compuserve.com. *Life is about people and relationships. True happiness begins with sensitivity and responsiveness to the needs of others.*

LAUTENBERG, FRANK R. former U.S. senator; b. Paterson, N.J., Jan. 23, 1924; s. Samuel and Mollie L.; children: Ellen, Nan, Lisa, Joshua. BS, Columbia U., 1949; DHL, Hebrew Union Coll., Cin. and N.Y.C., 1977; PhD (hon.), Hebrew U., Jerusalem, 1978. Founder Automatic Data Processing, Inc., Clifton, N.J., 1952-55, exec. v.p. adminstrn., 1955-69, pres., 1969-75, chief exec. officer, 1975-82, chmn. bd.; mem. U.S. Senate from N.J., 1982-2001, ret., 2001; owner FRL Enterprises, Rochelle Park, NJ, 2001—. Mem. Appropriations Com., Budget Com., Intelligence Com., Environment and Public Works Com., Helsinki Commn.; bd. dirs. The Holocaust Mus., Washington, IDT Corp., Newark, NorCrown Bank, Livingston, N.J., Columbia U., N.Y.C., Cordoza Law Sch. at Yeshiva U., N.Y.C., Alan M. Voorhees Transp. Ctr., Rutgers U., N.J., ADP, Inc., Roseland, N.J; distng. vis. prof. Univ. of Medicine & Dentistry, New Brunswick, N.J. Commr. Port Authority N.Y. and N.J., 1978-82, N.J. econ. devel. coun.; trustee Sch. Bus., Columbia U.; nat. pres. Am. Friends Hebrew U., 1973-74; former hon. gen. chmn., pres. Nat. United Jewish Appeal, 1975-77; mem. bd. overseers N.J. Symphony Orch.; mem. Pres.'s Coun. on the Holocaust; founder Lautenberg Center for Gen. and Tumor Immunology, Med. Sch., Hebrew U., Jerusalem, 1971. Served with Armed Forces, 1943-46, ETO; bd. mem. Montclair Art Mus., mem. adv. bd. Interfaith Hunger Appeal. Recipient Torch of Learning award Am. Friends Hebrew U., 1971, Scopus award, 1975 Mem. Nat. Assn. Data Processing Service Orgns. (pres. 1968-69, dir. from 1974).

LAUTER, JAMES DONALD, retired stockbroker; b. L.A., Sept. 3, 1931; s. Richard Leo and Helen M. (Stern) L.; m. Neima Zwieli, Feb. 24, 1973; children: Walter James (dec.), Gary. BS, UCLA, 1956. Market rsch. mgr. Germain's Inc., L.A., 1961; sr. v.p. investments, former br. mgr. Dean Witter Reynolds, Inc., Pasadena, Calif., 1961-96, ret., 1996. With Armed Forces, 1954-56. Recipient Sammy award L.A. Sales Execs. Club, 1961. Mem. AARP, UCLA Alumni Assn., UCLA Chancellors Assocs., Pasadena Bond Club (pres. 1995-96), Bruin Athletic Club, Coaches Round Table, UCLA Athletics Life Pass Club. Home: 3717 Marfield Ave Tarzana CA 91356 E-mail: jlauter@flash.net.

LAUTER, M. DAVID, family physician; b. Wilmington, Del., Jan. 7, 1951; s. Aaron Mordecai and Anne Marguerite (Scondin) L.; m. Diane Ruel, Oct. 11, 1980; children: Michael, Sara. B in Engring. Scis., Johns Hopkins U., 1973, MA, 1974; MD, Jefferson Med. Coll., 1978. Diplomate Am. Bd. Family Physicians. Resident family practice Ctrl. Maine Med. Ctr., Lewiston, 1978-81; clin. dir. USPHS Indian Hosp., Red Lake, Minn., 1981-84; pvt. practice as family doctor York, Maine, 1984—. With Pub. Health Svc., 1981-84. Office: 12 Hospital Dr York ME 03909-1030 E-mail: dlauter@yorkhospital.com.

LAUTERBACH, EDWARD CHARLES, psychiatric educator; b. Chgo., Mar. 21, 1955; s. Edward G. and Virginia C. (Pochelski) L. AB cum laude, Augustana Coll., Rock Island, Ill., 1977; MD, Wake Forest U., 1982. Lic. psychiatrist, Mo., Pa., N.J., N.C., Ga.; diplomate Nat. Bd. Med. Examiners, Am. Bd. Psychiatry and Neurology with qualifications in geriat. psychiatry. Intern Washington U. Sch. Medicine/Barnes Hosp., St. Louis, 1982-83, resident in psychiatry, 1983-86, clin. asst., 1982-86; instr. neurology movement disorder fellow U. Medicine and Dentistry of N.J., New Brunswick, 1986-87; asst. prof. Mercer U. Sch. Medicine, Macon, Ga., 1988-92, chief div. adult and geriatric psychiatry, dept. psychiatry and behavioral scis., 1988-98, coord. grand rounds dept. psychiatry and behavioral scis., 1989-98, assoc. prof., 1992-96, prof., 1996—, prof. internal medicine/neurology, 1996—, pvt. practice Charlotte, N.C., 1987-88, 1987-88. Chair free comm. IVth World Congress Biol. Psychiatry, Phila., 1985; mem. neurology staff Lyons VA Hosp., 1986; med. staff privileges in neurology Mercy Hosp., Charlotte, 1987, cons., 1987; privileges in psychiatry Med. Ctr. Ctrl. Ga., 1994—, Coliseum Psychiat. Hosp., 1994—, dir. med. staff continuing edn., 1994-96, Middle Ga. Hosp., 1997—; med. dir. geropsychiatry program The Sr. Ctr., Middle Ga. Hosp., 1997—. Editor: Psychiatric Management in Neurological Disease, 2000; guest editor Psychiatric Annals, 2002, editl. reviewer Neuropsychiatry, Neuropsychology and Behavioral Neurology, Biological Psychiatry, Movement Disorders, assoc. editor Jour. Neuropsychiatry and Clin. Neurosci.s., 1999—; contbr. articles. Recipient Med. Dir. of Yr. award S.E. region, Horizon Mental Health Mgmt., Inc., 1999—2001; scholar Rock Sleyster scholar, Wake Forest U., 1981. Fellow: Am. Psychiat. Assn. (course dir. 1990—92, 1994—95, symposium chmn. 1995—97, co-dir. 1998—2001, symposium chmn. 2001), Am. Neuropsychiat. Assn. (rsch. com. 1992—, vice-chair 1998—99, chmn. 1999—2002); mem.: Charlotte Psychiat. Soc., Movement Disorder Soc., Med. Assn. Ga., Mecklenburg County Med. Soc., N.C. Psychiat. Assn., Bibb County Med. Soc., Ga. Psychiat. Physicians Assn. (state com. on contg. med. edn.), Am. Acad. Neurology, AMA.

LAUTERBACH, MICHAEL ALAN, artist; b. Blue Island, Ill., Sept. 6, 1954; s. Harry Lewis and Donna Rae (Jones) L. AA in Art, U. Wis. Ctr., Rice Lake, 1976; BA in Mid. Eastern & S.W. Asian Studies, U. Minn., 1986, BA in Art, 1988; MFA in Visual Arts, U. Ariz., 1992. Material coord. Bell Helicopter Internat., Isfahan, Iran, 1976-78; expediter, material coord. Raymond Internat., Ju'Aymah, Saudi Arabia, 1978-79; storekeeper Air Base Constructors, Ramat-Matred, Negev, Israel, 1980; artist, 1986—. Exhibited in group shows at U. Tex., San Antonio, 1989, U. Ariz. Mus. Art, Tucson, 1992, Pro Arts, Oakland, Calif., 10th Internat. Biennial Print & Drawing Exhbn., Republic of China, 2001. Vol. Bethany Luth. Ch., Mpls., 1997-98. Fellow, Bush Found., 1996, Park Ave. Armory, N.Y., 1996. Avocations: travel, music, cooking, meditation, world cultures. Home: 1401 Portland Ave Apt C201 Minneapolis MN 55404-5560

LAUTERBACH, ROBERT EMIL, steel company executive; b. Erie, Pa., May 31, 1918; s. Emil and Inez (Ricci) L.; m. Jane Stonerod; children: Jeffrey R., Marsha J., Mark S. BBA, Westminster Coll., 1939; postgrad., U. Pitts., 1939-41; LLD (hon.), Wheeling Coll., 1975; DBA (hon.), Westminster Coll., 2000. With Wheeling-Pitts. Steel Corp. and subs., 1939-78; treas. Johnson Steel & Wire Co., 1947-50, asst. sec. parent firm, 1950-52, sec., 1952-58, v.p., 1958-68; exec. v.p. Wheeling Pitts. Steel Corp., 1968-70, pres., 1970—, chmn., 1973-78, also bd. dirs. Bd. dirs. H.H. Robertson Co., Covenant Life Ins. Co. Bd. dirs. United Way of All County, Boy Scouts Am.; treas. local br. Am. Cancer Soc., 1953-62; pres. Mt. Lebanon Libr. Bd., 1962-73; pres. bd. trustees Westminster Coll., 1970-85. With AUS, 1943-46. Recipient George Washington Honor medal Freedoms Found. at Valley Forge. Mem. Am. Petroleum Inst., Am. Iron and Steel Inst., Duquesne Club, Laurel Valley Golf Club, Rolling Rock Club, Fox Chapel Golf Club. Home: 115 Forest Dr Pittsburgh PA 15238-2103

LAUTERBACH, SHIRLEY SUSAN PFIEFFER, principal; b. Louisville, Feb. 8, 1955; d. David Allen and Mary Elaine (Bevins) Pfeiffer; m. Steven Michael Lauterbach, Aug. 21, 1976; children: Christopher Michael, Kara Noelle. BA with high honors, U. Louisville, 1976, MEdn., 1979. Cert. secondary adminstr., Ky. Tchr. Oldham County Mid. Sch., Buckner, Ky., 1976-88, asst. prin., 1988—97; prin. Oldham County Middle Sch., 1997—. Teaching asst. U. Louisville, fall 1978; tchr. Horizons Unltd., fall 1981, SPREE Dimensions, LaGrange, Ky., summers 1982, 83, tchr. Nat. Sch. Excellence, 1984-85, Ky. Career Ladder Project Pilot, Frankfort, 1986-87; supr. tchr. U. Louisville Student Teaching Program, 1980-88; asst. chair Ky. Task Force on Sci. and Tech.-Coun. on Sch. Performance Standards, 1990-91; chair facility planning com. Oldham County Schs., 1991-92; mem. State Performance-Assessment Adv. Task Force, 1991-92, mem. Dist. Local Planning Com., 1998-02. Contbr. articles to profl. jours. Named Oldham County Tchr. of Yr., 1988, Prin. of Excellence, Ky. Dept. Edn., Newark; named to Honorable Order Ky. Cols.; recipient Presdl. award Excellence in Sci. Tchg., Washington, 1984. Mem.: Ky, Acad. Assn. (Gov.'s cup coach 1986—88), Ky. Inst. for Women Sch. Adminstrs., Ky. Sci. Tchrs. Assn. (pres. elect 1989, pres. 1990, past pres. 1991), Ky. Middle Sch. Assn., Ky. Assn. Sch. Administrs., Ky. Assn. Secondary Sch. Prins. (asst. prin. of yr. 1992, middle sch. prin. of yr. 2002), Nat. Sci. Tchrs. Assn., Nat. Assn. Secondary Sch. Prins., Phi Delta Kappa, Chi Omega. Democrat. Baptist. Avocations: tennis, reading, gardening. Office: Oldham County Mid Sch Box 157 4305 Brown Blvd Buckner KY 40010

LAUTERBUR, PAUL C(HRISTIAN), chemistry educator; b. Sidney, Ohio, May 6, 1929; BS, Case Inst. Tech., 1951; PhD, U. Pitts., 1962; PhD (hon.), U. Liege, Belgium, 1984; DSc (hon.), Carnegie Mellon U., 1987; DEng (hon.), Copernicus Med. Acad., Cracow, Poland, 1988; DSc (hon.), Wesleyan U., 1989, SUNY, Stony Brook, 1990; DEng (hon.), Rennselaer Poly. Inst., 1991, U. Mons, Hainaut, Belgium, 1996. Rsch. asst. and assoc. Mellon Inst., Pitts., 1951—54, fellow, 1955—63; 1assoc. prof. chemistry SUNY, Stony Brook, 1963—69, prof. chemistry, 1969—84, rsch. prof. radiology, 1978—85, univ. prof., 1984—85; prof. (4) depts. U. Ill., Urbana, 1985—, Disting. Univ. prof. Coll. Medicine Chgo., 1990—. Mem. sci. couns. Contbr. articles; mem. editl. bds. Cpl. U.S. Army, 1953—55. Recipient Clin. Rsch. award, Lasker Found., 1984, Nat. Medal of Sci., U.S.A., 1987, Fiuggi Internat. prize, Fondazione Fiuggi, 1987, Roentgen medal, 1987, Gold medal, Radiol. Soc. N.Am., 1987, Nat. Medal of Tech., 1988, Gold medal, Soc. Computed Body Tomography, 1989, The Amsterdam (Alfred Heineken) prize in medicine, 1989, Laufman-Greatbatch award, Assn. for Advancement Med. Instrumentation, 1989, Leadership Tech. award, Nat. Elec. Mfrs. Assn., 1990, Bower award and prize for achievement in sci., Benjamin Franklin Nat. Meml. Commn. of the Franklin Inst., 1990, Internat. Soc. Magnetic Resonance award, 1992, Kyoto prize, Inamori Found., 1994. Fellow: Am. Inst. Med. and Biol. Engring., Am. Phys. Soc. (Biol. Physics prize 1983), AAAS; mem.: Internat. Soc. Magnetic Resonance in Medicine (Gold medal 1982), IEEE (sr.), Am. Chem. Soc., NAS. Office: Dept Chemistry U Ill 600 S Mathews 51-6 MC-712 Urbana IL 61801 E-mail: pcl@uiuc.edu.

LAUTERSTEIN, JOSEPH, cardiologist; b. Vienna, Austria, Dec. 1, 1934; came to U.S., 1940; s. Bernard and Hajnalka (Stern) L.; m. Erika Stein, Jan. 24, 1964 (dec. Aug. 1990); children: Deborah Ann Ehret, Brenda Rose Horton; m. Elisabeth Spiegl Lazaroff, Nov. 27, 1994. BA, Syracuse U., 1955; MD, U. Vienna, 1964. Lic. physician, N.Y. Intern, then resident in internal medicine The Bklyn. Cumberland Med. Ctr., 1964-66, 68-69, fellow in cardiology, 1969-70; attending physician, cons. internal medicine and cardiology Hamilton Ave. Hosp., Monticello, N.Y., 1970-78, Catskill Regional Med. Ctr., Harris, NY, 1970—, chief cardiology, 1971—, chief of staff, 1981-82; mem. courtesy staff dept. internal medicine and cardiology The Bklyn. Hosp. Ctr., 1971-95; clin. asst. dept. internal medicine and cardiology St. Vincent's Hosp. and Med. Ctr. N.Y., 1974-80, asst. attending physician, 1981-86, assoc. attending physician, 1987-94, attending physician, 1995—; with Sullivan Internal Medicine Group, P.C., Monticello, 1970—. Mem. pacemaker task force Empire State Med. Sci. and Ednl. Found., 1985-89; med. dir. Sullivan County EMT-D Program, 1989—; police surgeon Village of Monticello, 1974—, Sullivan County, 1972—; med. advisor Monticello Vol. Ambulance Corps, 1970-80, 89—; mem. Sullivan County Emergency Svcs. Coun., 1990, 91; instr. outdoor emergency care, 1991—. Co-contbr. articles to Jour. Cardiovascular Surgery, Annals of Thoracic Surgery, Angiology, Chest. Trustee Cmty. Gen. Hosp. Sullivan County, 1981-82, Catskill Regional Med. Ctr. Found., 1990—; mem. Nat. Ski Patrol, 1979—, med. advisor So. N.Y. region, 1989-94, 97—, med. advisor So. Catskill sect., 1994-97; patroller Holiday Mountain Ski Patrol, 1979—. Capt. M.C., USAF, 1966-68. Named Citizen of Yr., SYDA Found. Sullivan County, 1991. Fellow Am. Coll. Cardiology (N.Y. State chpt., del. to N.Y. Med. Soc. Ho. Dels. 1991—, councilor 1991—, com. mem. 1990—), Am. Coll. Chest Physicians (assoc.), Am. Coll. Angiology, Internat. Coll. Angiology, N.Y. Cardiol. Soc. (exec. bd. dirs. 1982—, mem. various coms.), N.Y. Acad. Medicine; mem. AMA, Am. Geriatrics Soc., ACP/Am. Soc. Internal Medicine, Soc. for Critical Care Medicine, N.Y. Acad. Scis., N.Am. Soc. for Pacing and Electrophysiology, Med. Soc. State of N.Y. (cardiology del. to interspecialty com., cardiology del. to ho. of dels.), others. Office: 370 Broadway Monticello NY 12701-1157 E-mail: jl@catskill.net.

LAUTH, WILLIAM BRIAN, emergency physician, internist, educator; b. Oak Park, Ill., Jan. 31, 1951; BA, U. Iowa, 1973; MD, Loyola U., 1977; M in Med. Mgmt., Tulane U., 2001. Diplomate Am. Bd. Emergency Medicine, Am. Bd. Internal Medicine. Resident internal medicine and emergency medicine Northwestern Meml. Hosp., Chgo., 1977-81; chmn. dept. emergency medicine Ravenswood Hosp. Med. Ctr., 1982-94, Holy Family Med. Ctr., Des Plaines, Ill., 1993-98, Swedish Covenant Hosp. Med. Ctr., Chgo., 1998—. Assoc. clin. prof. medicine Northwestern U. Fellow Am. Acad. Emergency Medicine, Am. Coll. Emergency Physicians, Am. Coll. Forensic Examiners; mem. AMA, ACP, Am. Coll. Emergency Physicians, Am. Coll. Physician Exec. (bd. cert. in med. mgmt.). Avocations: pvt. pilot, triathelete. Office: Swedish Covenant Hosp Med Ctr 5145 N California Ave Chicago IL 60625-3687

LAUTTENBACH, CAROL, artist; b. New Haven, Nov. 26, 1934; d. Gustav Fredrick and Wanda M. (Eshner) Stolze; m. Francis John Lauttenbach; children: Daniel M., William J. Grad. with honors, Washington Sch. Art, Chgo., 1967. One-woman shows include Greene Art Gallery, Guilford, Conn., Carriage House Gallery Ltd., Guilford, Gallery 53, Meriden, Conn., John Slade Ely House Gallery, New Haven, Conn. Recipient Prix de Paris award Musee Des Raymon Duncan, France, 1972, 76, 80, award Salon Des Surindependants, Paris, 1981, Gabriel D. Luchetti award Conn. Classic Arts, 1984, 86, Guilford Savs. Bank award Guilford Art League, 1985, Best in Show award Mt. Carmel Art Assn., Inc., Hamden, 1986, Hon. Mention Arts & Crafts Assn. of Meriden, Inc., 1986, 87, Madison Art soc., 1987, Jean Cowles award Shoreline Alliance for Arts, Guilford, 1987, Elizabeth Greeley Meml. award Mt. Carmel Art Assn., Inc., 1987, 1st prize Conn. classic Arts, Fairfield, 1987, Donald L. Perlroth, Inc. award Mt. Carmel Art Assn., 1988, Koenig Art Emporium prize New Haven Brush & Palette Club, 1990, Henry T. & Stella King Meml. award Arts & Crafts Assn. of Meridan, Inc., 1990, Marc D. Rosenberg Meml. award Mt. Carmel Art Assn., 1990, 3d prize Nat. League Am. Pen Women, Fairfield, 1992, 1st prize Conn. Classic Arts, Fairfield, 1993, Grumbacher Gold Medal award Arts & Crafts Assn. of Meriden, 1993, 3d prize Conn. Classic Arts, Fairfield, 1994, Merriam Motors award Arts & Crafts Assn. of Meriden, 1995, Rosemary Landino Meml. award Conn. Classic Arts, Fairfield, 1995, Hon. Mention New Haven Paint & Clay Club, Inc., New Haven, 1996, Stella King Meml. award Arts & Crafts Assn. of Meridan, Inc., 1997, Jerry's Artarama cert. award Arts & Crafts Assn. of Meridan, 1998, New Haven Savs. Bank award Mt. Carmel Art Assn., Inc. Hamden, 1998, 2d prize in acrylic and oils Conn. Classic Arts, Fairfield, 1998, Beazley Realtors award Mt. Carmel Art Assn., 2000, numerous others. Mem. Conn. Acad. Fine Arts, New Haven Paint and Clay Club, Shoreline Alliance for Arts, Brush and Palette Club, Provincetown Art Assn., Internat. Soc. Artists, Conn. Clasic Arts, Inc., Arts and Crafts Assn. Meriden (Grumbacher silver medal 1983-84, gold medal 1993), Wallingford Hist. Soc. (life), Conn. Acad. Fine Arts. Home: 39 Ridgewood Rd Wallingford CT 06492-2116

LAUTZ, DAVID A. pediatrician; b. Hammond, Ind., Oct. 25, 1955; s. Herbert A. and Jean Lautz; m. Lisa S. Lautz, Dec. 1975; children: Amy, Tim, Matt, Nina. BA, Wabash Coll., Crawfordsville, Ind., 1977; MD, Ind. U., Indpls., 1981. Intern/resident Children's Hosp. Wis., 1981-84; pediatrician Forest View Pediatrics, Hales Corners, Wis., 1984-95, Children's Med. Group, Hales Corners, 1995—. Office: Childrens Med Group 11035 W Forest Home Ave Hales Corners WI 53130-2541

LAUTZENHEISER, MARVIN WENDELL, computer software engineer; b. Maximo, Ohio, Feb. 19, 1929; s. Milton Leander and Mary Lucetta (Keim) L.; m. Jean Bethene Baker, Oct. 26, 1946 (div. Nov. 1986); children: Constance Kay, Thomas Edward, Jan Stephen; m. Paula Ann Keane, Mar. 10, 1990. BS in Math., Mt. Union Coll., 1953. Spl. agt. FBI, Washington, 1953-59; computer analyst Tech. Ops., 1959-64; pres. Anagram Corp., Springfield, Va., 1964-83; computer analyst Onyx Corp., McLean, 1983, Inmark, Springfield, 1983-84, Memory Scis., McLean, 1984-85; software scientist Zitel Corp., San Jose, Calif., 1985-98; cons., 1998—. Inventor, designer in field. Mem. Mensa, Am. Iris Soc., Am. Theater Organ Soc. Avocations: theatre pipe organ, hybrid iris gardening. Home: 7216 Neuman St Springfield VA 22150-4421 E-mail: mlautzenheiser@prodigy.net.

LAUVER, EDITH BARBOUR, nonprofit organization administrator; b. Tarrytown, N.Y., Mar. 2, 1933; d. John Alan and Adelaide Cora (Marden) Barbour; m. Robert Mitchell Lauver, Dec. 16, 1961; children: Alan Jackson, Donald Marden, Robert Barbour. BSN, Skidmore Coll., 1954; MA, Columbia U., 1957; postgrad., U. Ariz., 1980-95. Sch. nurse, tchr. Pub. Schs. of Tarrytowns, North Tarrytown, N.Y., 1956-60; instr. St. Mary's Hosp. Sch. Nursing, Tucson, 1960-62; asst. prof. Coll. Nursing U. Ariz., 1969-73, grad. teaching, rsch. assoc., 1980-85; asst. dir. nursing for pediatrics U. Ariz. Med. Ctr., 1973-74; asst. adminstr. patient care Pima County/Kino Community Hosp., 1974-77; asst. dir. nursing for staff devel. U. Ariz. Health Scis. Ctr., 1978-80; dir. Interfaith Coalition for Homeless, 1987—. Mem. staff Thomas-Davis Clinic, Tucson, 1963-64; staff nurse surg. unit St. Joseph's Hosp., Tucson, 1964-65; adminstrv. asst. Tucson Ecumenical Coun., 1987; weekend relief staff nurse Handmaker Jewish Geriatric Ctr., Tucson, 1988-89. Active Accord Interfaith Soc. Action Group, 1983-94, St. Mark's Prebyn. Presch. and Kindergarten, 1965-87, St. Mark's Presbyn. Ch., 1986—, elder, 1986-92; bd. dirs. Ariz. Coalition for Human Svcs., 1987—; Mobile Meals Tucson, Inc., 1976-87, sec. 1981-83; bd. dirs. Interfaith Coalition for Homeless 1987—; participant Ariz. Women's Town Hall, 1986, 87; mem. adv. bd. Tucson Met. Ministry's Cmty. Closet, 1988-92; bd. dirs. Tucson Met. Ministry, 1989-92; treas. Ariz. Coalition to End Homelessness, 1997-98; mem. oversight com. Gov.'s Homeless Trust Fund, 1999—; active various other civic activities. Recipient Women on the Move award YMCA, 1998. Mem. ANA, Ariz. Nurses' Assn. (fin. com. 1985-87, ANA del. 1986-87, dist. bd. dirs. 1982-84, pres.-elect, pres. dist. 1985-87, various coms.), Soc. Southwestern Authors, Skidmore Coll. Alumni Assn., Sigma Theta Tau (mem. nat. fin. com. 1981-83, treas. local chpt. 1978-81, fin. com. 1974-88, pres.-elect 1990—, pres. 1988-92), Pi Lambda Theta, Phi Delta Kappa, Kappa Delta Pi. Home and Office: 445 S Craycroft Rd Tucson AZ 85711-4549

LAUVER, LYDIA MONSERRAT OLLIS, public relations executive; b. Pitts., May 9, 1958; d. Jay Edwin and Ascension (Romero) Ollis; m. Kevin John Lauver, Jan. 20, 1990; 2 children. AA in Media Tech. with honors, AA in Gen. Studies with honors, Bellevue Community Coll., 1982; BS in Bus., City U., 1983. Graphic illustrator Boeing Co., Seattle, 1978-80; freelance mktg. Kiro Video, City U., 1980-83; dir. pub. rels. Vyzis Devel. Co., Bellevue, Wash., 1983-87; pub. rels. account exec. The Rockey Co., 1987-92; prin. Lauver & Co., 1992—. Trustee Bellevue Schs. Found., 1989-92; bd. dirs. Seattle Seafair, 1989-92; advisor pub. rels. com. YMCA Greater Seattle, 1989—; advisor Wash. State March of Dimes, 1988-91; vol. Spl. Olympics, 1976-80; chair Bellevue Chamber Ann. Dinner, 1990. Seattle Women in Advt. scholar, 1982. Mem. Nat. Pub. Rels. Soc. (APR designation 1987). Roman Catholic. Avocations: traveling, reading, sewing, computers. Office: Lauver & Co 12643 NE 2nd St Bellevue WA 98005-3206

LAUVER, NELSON CHARLES, narrator, voice-over, small business owner; b. McAllisterville, Pa., June 29, 1963; s. Clair Kanode and Thelma Jane (Ward) L. Pres., co-owner Roller Junction Inc., Mifflintown, Pa., 1981-89; owner, mgr. N.C. Lauver Co., venture capitalists, 1981-93; nat. broadcaster Accu-Weather Inc., State College, Pa., 1993-94; voice artist J.D. Xanthopoulus Prodns., Lewistown, 1993—; founder Am. Story-Teller, Mifflintown, 1995—. Owner Nelson Lauver Comm., Mifflintown, 1993—. Author, narrator: (audio book) The American Story-Teller, 1997, Tales From Rural Juniata County and Beyond, 1999; narrator: (audio book) The Destroyer, 1996, If You Thought it was Tough to Sell Try Buying; (film documentaries) Relay for Life, 1996, Camp Can Do, 1996, The History of Kane, 1997, Staying at a Lighthouse, 1998, The History of Mifflin County, 1998, The Last Covered Bridges of Pennsylvania, Host: The American Storyteller Radio Jour., 2001–. Children's rights adv. Pa. Spl. Edn. Task Force, Harrisburg, 1995—; founder Am. Story-Teller's Campaign for Literacy, Mifflintown, 1996—; co-founder, exec. dir. Camp Hope for L.D. Children. Recipient The Dale Carnegie award, 1998, The Communicator award, 1999. Mem. Nat. Story-Telling Assn., Sertoma (charter mem. Susquehanna club). Republican. Lutheran. Avocations: outdoors, fishing, word, name and phrase origins, bungee jumping. Home: 334B Washington Ave Mifflintown PA 17059-1410 Office: 334 Washington Ave Mifflintown PA 17059-1410 E-mail: nelson@acsworld.net.

LAVALLE, JENNIFER SUZETTE, marketing communications specialist, consultant; b. Texas City, Tex., Apr. 15, 1964; d. Peter Joseph and Billie Jo LaValle; m. Kenneth Michael Landgren, May 3, 1997. BS in Human Scis., Tex. Tech. U., 1986; MA in Comm., U. Houston, 1999. Lic. social worker, Tex. Camp/spl. projects coord. U. Tex., M.D. Anderson Cancer Ctr., Houston, 1989-90; child care placement specialist Neighborhood Ctrs., Inc., 1990-91; case mgr. II Tex. Dept. Human Svcs., 1991-94; pub. rels. intern Out There Pub. Rels., 1994-95; advt. and promotions coord. RE/MAX of Tex., Inc., 1994-95; dir. mktg. Williams, Birnberg & Andersen, LLP, 1995-96; pub. rels. cons., 1996-99; mktg. comm. mgr. Compaq Computer Corp., 1999—; now comms. specialist Honeywell IAC, Phoenix. Cons. La Trattoria, Houston; writer Wynn Solutions, Houston. Mem. Internat. Assn. Bus. Communicators, Tex. Assn. Social Workers, Tex. Tech. U. Alumni, U. Houston Alumni. Avocations: jogging, rollerblading, scuba diving. Office: Honeywdll IAC 16404 N Black Canhon Hwy Phoenix AZ 85053 Home: 7613 E Phantom Way Scottsdale AZ 85255-4626 E-mail: jlavalle@hypercon.com., jennifer.lavalle@honeywell.com.

LA VALLEE, ADRIENNE KERNAN, artist, educator; b. Pittsfield, Mass., Feb. 27, 1953; d. Gerard William and Ann Catlin La Vallee. BFA cum laude, U. of Mass., 1975; MFA, Md. Inst. Coll. of Art, Balt., 1977. Visual artist Self Employed, Manchester, NH, 1977—; lectr. St. Anselm Coll., 1986—, New Eng. Coll., Henniker, 1980—; asst. dir. Chapel Art Ctr. St. Anselm Coll., 1988—97; edn. coord. N.H. Inst. of Art, 1983—95. Bd. dirs. N.H. Citizens' Com. for the Arts, Concord, 2002—; co-founder, bd. dirs. N.H. chpt. Women's Caucus for Art, Concord, 1991—95; bd. dirs. Boston chpt. Caucus for the Arts, 1989—90; reviewer Art New Eng., Boston, 1982—87; mng. editor, co-editor OPTIONS: new hampshire's visual arts quar., Henniker, 1979—85. One person exhibition, ; author: (published essay) Carlos Barnas, Painter, Citizen of Ecuador, 2000; paintings, painting, (First Pl. N.H. Art Biennial, 1985), mono-prints, installation with poet rodger martin. Juror N.H. Congl. Dist. One, Manchester, 1996—96, N.H. Found. for the Blind, Concord, 1985. Mem.: AAUP, Coll. Art Assn. Conservative. Avocation: perennial flower garden design, gardening, travel, haiku. Office: Saint Anselm Coll 100 Saint Anselm Dr Manchester NH 03102 Personal E-mail: atelierdelavie@yahoo.com.

LAVALLEE, CHARLES PHILLIP, music educator, musician; b. Williston, Vt., Mar. 23, 1928; s. Arthur Israel and Azilda H. (Roux) L.; m. Rita Poldina Perla; 1 child, Lynn Marie. BA, U. Calif., Los Angeles, 1960; MA, Calif. State U., Los Angeles, 1971; PhD, Columbia Pacific U., 1986. Instr. music I.G. Hook Jr. High Sch., Victorville, Calif., 1960-68, 74-84, Victor Valley High Sch., Victorville, 1968-70, counselor, 1971-73; counselor, instr. music Hesperia (Calif.) Jr. High Sch., 1973-74; instr. music Hesperia (Calif.) High Sch., 1984-92; instr. Victor Valley Coll., Calif., 1991—; dir. jazz Cobalt Mid. Sch., Victorville, 1999—. With U.S. Army, 1950-52. Mem. Music Edn. Nat. Conf., NEA, So. Calif. Sch. Band and Orch. Assn., Am. Fedn. Musicians, Internat. Assn. Jazz Educators. Democrat. Roman Catholic. Avocations: photography, composing and arranging music. Home: 18961 Tamarac Rd Apple Valley CA 92307-4920

LAVALLEE, DAVID KENNETH, chemistry educator, researcher; b. Malone, H.Y., Oct. 1, 1945; s. Bernard Martin and Eleanor Jane (Magoon) Lavallee; m. Eileen Marie Gilmartin; children: Jeffrey Michael, Gregory James, Jocelyn Marie. BS, St. Bonaventure U., 1967; SM, U. Chgo., 1968,

PhD, 1971. Asst. prof. Colo. State U., Ft. Collins, 1972—78; assoc. prof. Hunter Coll., CUNY, 1978—82, prof. chemistry, 1983—94, assoc. provost, 1990—94; provost, v.p. acad. affairs CCNY, 1994—99, SUNY, New Paltz, 1999—. Edn. adv. bd. Chemtech, Washington, 1978—84. Author: The Chemistry and Biochemistry of N-substituted Porphyrins, 1987; author: (with others) Chemistry, 1978. Bd. dirs., v.p. Croton Free Libr., Croton-On-Hudson, NY, 1988—93, pres., 1992—93. Named USPHS fellow, Anatomy Dept. U. Chgo., 1971—72; recipient NATO Rsch. award, Ecole Normale, Superieure, Paris, 1983—85, Fulbright Rsch. Scholar award, oun. Internat. Exch. U. Rene Descartes, Paris, 1985—86, Catalyst award, Chem. Mfrs. Assn., 1986. Mem.: AAAS, Soc. Nuclear Medicine, Am. Chem. Soc. (chair Internat. Chemistry Olympiad 1986—93, soc. com. chem. edn. 1990—96, bd. publs. divsn. chem. edn. 1986—99, chair 1993—97). Democrat. Achievements include patents for for N-substituted metalloporphyrins as Anti-tumor Agents; Synthesis of Radiolabelled metalloporphyrins via N-substituted Precursors. Home: 97 Old Post Rd S Croton On Hudson NY 10520-2401 Office: SUNY 75 S Manheim Blvd Ste 1 New Paltz NY 12561-2499 E-mail: lavallee@newpaltz.edu.

LAVALLEE, DEIRDRE JUSTINE, marketing professional; b. Woonsocket, R.I., June 14, 1962; d. Albert Paul and Margaret Justine (O'Brien) L. BS in Chem. Engring., U. R.I., 1984; MBA, U. Denver, 1995. Sales engr. NGS Assocs. Inc., Canton, Mass., 1985-87; mgr. dist. sales MKS Instruments Inc., Balt., also Boulder, Colo., 1987-96, sales and mktg. mgr. API divsn. Phoenix, 1996, product mktg. mgr. Methuen, Mass., 1996-98, cons., 1998-99; sales mgr. ea. region Applied Sci. and Tech., Inc., Woburn, 1999-2000; staff product mgr. Am. Power Conversion, 2000—01; with MSGI (Boston Ballet), 2001—. Fundraiser MSGI (Boston Ballet), 2001-; v.p., bd. dirs. Nat. Conf. Standards Labs.; mem. adv. bd. Tex. State Tech. Coll.; vol. SCORE, 1999—. Mem. AIChE (sec. chpt.), Am. Soc. Materials, Am. Inst. Physics, Am. Vacuum Soc., Svc. Corps. Ret. Execs. Avocations: piano, sailing, skiing, choir.

LAVALLEE, LAURENT EDMOND, JR. music educator; b. Providence, Dec. 13, 1969; s. Laurent Edmond Lavallee, Sr. and Marie Christine Lavallee, Maria Lambert (Stepmother); m. Melissa Kelley Parker, June 2, 2001. B of Music, Boston Conservatory, 1994; M of Music, U. Mass., 1998. Cert. tchr. N.C., Md. Music dir. Ea. Tech. H.S., Balt., 1998—2001; dir. of bands Spring Creek H.S., Seven Springs, NC, 2002—. Orch. dir. Md. Summer Ctr. of Arts, Salisbury, Sudbrooke Arts Ctr., Pikesville, Md., 1998—2001. Musician (freelance musician). Mem.: Music Educators Nat. Conf., Phi Mu Alpha Sinfonia (pres. 1993—94). Roman Catholic. Avocations: automobiles, landscaping. Home: 1716 Crawford's Pointe Dr Greenville NC 27834 Office: Spring Creek HS 4340 Indian Springs Rd Seven Springs NC 28578 Office Fax: 919-751-7202. Personal E-mail: LarryLav5254@aol.com. Business E-Mail: larry.lavallee@wcps.org.

LAVALLEE, LEO PIERRE, telecommunications executive; b. Providence, Dec. 24, 1959; s. Leo Pierre and Theresa Maria (Correra) L. BA, Ithaca Coll., 1981; MBA, U. New Haven, 1990. Tchr. Eudwell (N.Y.) Sch. Dist., 1981-82, Sch. Dist. #14, Woodbury, Conn., 1982-83; sales rep. Nutmeg Utility Products, Cheshire, 1983-84, sales supr., 1984-85, v.p. mktg. sales and mktg., 1985-90, sr. v.p., chief exec. officer, 1990—; gen. mgr. GSCI Midwest. Religion tchr. St. Bridgetts Roman Cath. Ch., Cheshire, 1984—. Republican. Office: Nutmeg Utility Products 1755 Highland Ave Cheshire CT 06410-1272 Home: 170 Romulus Rd Cheshire CT 06410-3535

LAVALLEE, RAYMOND GEORGE, lawyer; b. Massapequa, N.Y., July 6, 1934; s. George E. and Denise Lavallee; m. Margaretta C. Mullen, June 14, 1960; children: Keith, Denise, Karen. BBA, St. John's U., 1956, LLB, 1959. Spl. agt. FBI, 1960-65; asst. dist. atty. Nassau County, NY, 1965—70; of counsel Officers Assn. Nassau County Police, 1978—, Mineola Custodian Assn., 1998—, Syosett Fire Dist., 1998—. Sgt. U.S. Army, 1954-55, Korea. Mem. N.Y. State Bar Assn., FBI Assn. Republican. Roman Catholic. Avocations: tennis, golf, racquetball. Home: 5 Burrs Ln Massapequa NY 11758

LAVALLEUR, JUNE, obstetrician/gynecologist; b. Ventura, Calif., Aug. 10, 1941; d. John LeRoy LaValleur and Elva Belle Crouch; children: Jon Randall, Stuart Randall, Christopher Randall. MD, U. Minn., 1987. Dir. Mature Women's Ctr., Mpls., 1991—; asst. prof. dept. ob/gyn. U. Minn., 1991—. Office: U Minn Dept ObGyn MMC 395 420 Delaware St SE Minneapolis MN 55455-0348

LAVALLEY, JUDY TUCKER, cardiology critical care nurse; b. Birmingham, Ala., Oct. 6, 1954; d. James Melvin and Clytee (Whitman) Tucker; divorced. Lic. practical nurse, Itawamba Jr. Coll., Tupelo, Miss., 1974, ADN, 1982; BSN, Miss. U. for Women, Tupelo, Miss., 1994. RN, Miss.; cert. in ACLS. Physician's asst. in cardiology Internal Medicine Assocs. Ltd., Tupelo; critical care nurse North Miss. Med. Ctr., staff nurse cardiac catheterization lab., noninvasive cardiol supr. Mem. AACN, Miss. Nursing Assn., Sigma Theta Tau.

LAVALLY, REBECCA JEAN, research editor, journalist; b. Danville, Ill., Dec. 9, 1949; d. Nelson Charles and Mary (Hayes) L.; m. William Warner Kirby, June 7, 1975 (div. 1988); 1 child, Sarah Jean; m. Jeffery Manuel Raimundo, Nov. 16, 1991; stepchildren: Scott, Amy, Todd. BA in Journalism, Calif. State U., 1971. Reporter Lorain (Ohio) Jour., 1972-73; reporter, copy editor Cleve. Plain Dealer, 1973-75; reporter San Jose (Calif.) Mercury News, 1975-77, UPI, Sacto., 1977-85, bur. mgr., 1985-89, Gannett News Svc., Sacto., 1989-90; editor State of Calif., Senate Office of Rsch., 1990—. Co-author newspaper column Stepfamily Tips. Contbr. articles to mags. and newspapers. Vol. parent aide Family Support Programs, Sacto., 1992-95. Mem. Writers Bloc North (founder, treas. 1994-96), Capitol Corrs. Assn. (standing com. 1985-89), Sacto. Press Club, Am. River Natural History Assn. (bd. dirs. 1998-01). Avocations: running, writing, travel. Office: Calif Senate Office of Rsch 1020 N St # 200 Sacramento CA 95814-5624

LAVATELLI, CARLA, sculptor, weaver; b. Rome, Aug. 21, 1928; came to U.S., 1947; U.S. citizen, 1957; Teaching degree, Santa Maria Degli Angeli, Rome, 1946. One-woman shows include Heller Gallery, L.A., 1964, Galleria Carpine, Rome, 1966, Palazzo Cerio, Capri, Italy, 1966, Galleria degli Argenti, Milan, 1967, Galleria La Vernice, Bari, Italy, 1967, Palm Beach (Fla.) Gallery, 1969, 71, 73, 75, Herbert Kende Gallery, N.Y.C., 1969, Galerie Motte, Geneva, 1970, Benjamin Gallery, Chgo., 1970, Galerie Moos, Montreal, 1970, Alexander Iolas, N.Y.C., 1972, Hakone Mus., Tokyo, 1972, Sari Heller Gallery, Beverly Hills, Calif., Phillips Collection, Washington, 1974, Gimpel & Weitzenhoffer, N.Y.C., 1976, A. & J. Rose, N.Y.C., 1978; public commns.: Pinacoteca di Stato, Rome, 1968, Palace of H.S.H. Reinier of Monaco, Principaute de Monaco, 1970, John Upjohn Pharm. Toloverdo, Mich., 1971, Mus. Modern Art Palace Shah of Iran, 1972, Spingold Theater, Brandeis U., Waltham, Mass., Freiburg Bot. Garden, U. Bauamt, Germany, Stanford U., Calif., 1975, Pk. 80 Plz. West, N.J., 1976, Sandoz Pharm., N.J., 1979, Cathedral St. John the Divine, N.Y.C., 1986, 96, 140 Thompson, N.Y.C., 1976-96, Sci. Plz., Brown U., 1985, New Enterprise Assn., San Francisco, 1989, St. Giovanni Battista, Pistoia, Italy, 1991, Vado di Camiore, Lucca, Italy, Sculpture Garden, Picasso Mus. Photography, Mougins, 1993, St. Augustine Cloisters, Pietra Santa, Italy, 1994, Cathedral St. John the Divine, N.Y.C., 1996, UN, 1995, Place du Banc des Amis, France, 1995, Stanford U. Med. Ctr., 1997, The Window of Hope, Vatican City, 1998, Grace Cathedral, San Francisco, 1998, Ferrari-Formula 1, A Ferrari with the Soul, 2001, others; installations: Carla Lavatelli Working Pl. Sculpture Garden, Camaiore Lucca, Italy, 1972—, Woodrow Wilson Bldg. Einstein Inst. Advanced Studies, Princeton U., 1977-79, Ctr. George Pompidou, Paris, 1985, Pecci Mus., Prato, Italy, 1995, Renoir Mus., Cagnes-Sur-Mer, France, 1995, others; author: A Cotton Bag Full of Student Works in Paper, 1982, The Work of Carla Lavatelli, 1970-1984, Our Recipes: A Family Inventory, 1995, 50 Years of Letters: Good Bad & Useless, 2001; inventor Sculpture to Wear, 1968. Recipient Gold medal City of Mougins. Home: Carla Lavatelli Working Pl Sculpture Garden 55041 Camaiore Lucca Italy E-mail: carla@lavatelli.org.

LAVE, JUDITH RICE, economics educator; b. New Brunswick, Can. came to U.S., 1961; d. J.H. Melville and G.A. Pauline (Lister) Rice; m. Lester Bernard Lave, June 21, 1965; children: Tamara Rice, Jonathan Melville. BA in Econs., Queen's U., Kingston, Ont., Can., 1957-61; MA in Econs., Harvard U., 1964, PhD, 1967; LLD, Queen's U., 1994. Lectr., asst. prof. econs. Carnegie Mellon U., Pitts., 1966-73, assoc. prof., 1973-78; dir. econ. analysis Office of Sec., Dep. of Asst. Sec. Planning and Evaluation, Washington, 1978-79; dir. office of rsch. Health Care Fin. Adminstrn., 1980-82; prof. health econs. U. Pitts., 1982—, co-dir. Ctr. for Rsch. on Health Care, 1996—. Cons. Nat. Study Internal Medicine Manpower, Chgo., 1976, Wash. State Hosp. Assn., 1984, Horty, Springer & Mattern, Pitts., 1984, Hogan and Hartson, Washington, 1989, Ont. Hosp. Assn., Conn. Hosp. Assn., 1991; cons. various agys. U.S. HHS (formerly U.S. HEW), 1971-89; mem. adv. panel Robert Wood Johnson Found., Princeton, N.J., 1983-84, 96—, Leonard Davis Inst., Phila., 1984, U.S. Congress, 1977, 82, 83—; com. mem. Inst. Medicine Coms., Washington, 1975-91, Project 2000 Commn. on Future of Podiatry, Washington, 1985-86. Editl. bd. Wiley Series in Health Svcs., 1989-90, Health Svcs. Rsch., 1970-74, Inquiry, 1979-82, AUPHA Press, 1986, Jour. of Health Policy Politics and Law, Health Affairs, 1998—; co-author: Hospital Construction Act - An Evaluation of the Hill Burton Program, 1948-73, 74, Health Status, Medical Care Utilization and Outcome: A Bibliography of Empirical Studies (4 vols.) 1989, Providing Hospital Services, 1989; contbr. numerous articles to profl. jours. Mem. Prospective Payment Assessment Commn., 1993—97, Medicare Payment Adv. Commn., 1997—2000; mem. planning com. ARC, Pitts., 1986—; mem. rev. com. United Way, 1988—90; bd. dirs. Craig House, 1976—77, Presbyn. Sr. Care, Pitts., Jewish Health Care Found., 2002—. Woodrow Wilson fellow, 1961-62. Fellow Assn. Health Svcs. Rsch. (disting., pres. 1977-88, bd. dirs. 1983-93); mem. Found. for Health Svcs. Rsch. (pres. 1988-89, bd. dirs. 1983—), Am. Pub. Health Soc., Am. Econ. Soc. (com. mem.), Inst. Medicine, Nat. Acad. Social Ins., Robert wood Johnson Found. (coun. on econ. impact of health sys. change 1996—). Democrat. Home: 1008 Devonshire Rd Pittsburgh PA 15213-2914 Office: U Pitts A649 Pub Health Pittsburgh PA 15213

LAVEAN, MICHAEL GILBERT, medical device company executive; b. Lansing, Mich., Sept. 17, 1954; s. Gilbert Earl and Barbara Ann (Cowels) LaV.; m. Janet Tlapek, Aug. 21, 1992; 1 child, Madeleine. Student, George Mason U., 1972-76. Polit. staff person various Dem. campaigns, 1972-84; mayor City of Saranac, Mich., 1984-86; polit. cons. Polit. Svcs., Inc., Saranac, 1984—98; pres. Polit. Svcs., Inc. (merger with A.& N. of Phila.), 1985-91; prin. Allan, Drake and LaVean (merger), Mich., 1991-95; chief oper. officer Veos Ltd., St. Helier, Jersey, 1995—, Page Hanes, Saranac, Mich., 1995—. Bd. dir. Page Hanes, Inc., Veos, PLC, Veos, S.A., Conceixgx, Inc. Co-patentee disposable cervical caps, sustained drug delivery, US and Europe; patentee disposal vaginal device, conception cap and conception kit, snap-together vaginal device for multi-drug sustained delivery. Vice-chmn. 5th dist. Dem. Com., Grand Rapids, Mich., 1985-87, chmn., 1987-93, vice-chmn. 3d dist., 1993-99; mem. Dem. Electoral Coll., 1988; bd. dirs. United Way of Ionia (Mich.) County, 1986-92; exec bd. dirs. Ionia County chpt. ARC, 1987-99. Recipient award for patent "Gynecol. Innovation of the Yr.", Quotidion Pharmacien, 1999. Fellow Internat. Napoleonic Soc. (bd. dirs. 1995—); mem. Napoleonic Soc. Am. (bd. dirs. 1991—, sec. 1995—), Masons. Baptist. Avocation: reading. Home: PO Box 31 Saranac MI 48881-0031 also: Le Bois du Gué 35340 La Bouexiere France also: Veos France 203-205 Blvd Jean-Jaures F-92100 Boulougne France E-mail: lavean@veos.com.

LAVECCHIA, JAYNEE, judge; b. Paterson, N.J. m. Michael R. Cole. Grad., Douglass Coll., 1976, Rutgers U., 1979. Bar: N.J. 1980. Pvt. law practice; dep. atty. gen. divsn. of law State of N.J., dir. divsn. of law dept. law anf pub. safety, 1984-98, commr. banking and ins., 1998-99; asst. counsel to Gov. Thomas H. Kean Office of Counsel, dep. chief counsel to Gov. Thomas H. Kean; dir., chief adminstrv. law judge Office of Adminstrv. Law, 1989-94; assoc. justice N.J. Supreme Ct., Trenton, 2000—. Chair various N.J. Supreme Ct. Coms. Fellow ABA; mem. Douglss Coll. Alumnae Assn. Office: North Tower 158 Headquarters Pla Morristown NJ 07960*

LAVEDAN, CHRISTIANE, artist, researcher; b. Toulouse, France, May 10, 1932; came to U.S., 1965; d. Louis Jean and Marguerite Marie (Bourguet) L.; divorced. Student, Lycée Classique Jeunes Filles, Toulouse, France, 1942-49, Marguerite Long/Jorré Sch., Toulouse , 1942-50, Ecole Beaux Arts, 1950-53; Cert., Career Blazers, N.Y.C., 1987-88. Artist verification Dept. Cultural Affairs, N.Y. Designer, builder houses, Ariège-Pyrénées, France, 1954-65; active Naturist Camps, Agde, Ile du Levant, France, 1956-67; street peddler N.Y.C., 1972-73; pvt. practice art therapist, 1974-97. Vis. lectr. Savannah Coll. Arts and Design, 1979, Hunter Coll., N.Y.C., 1988; artist-in-residence Beach H.S., Armstrong Coll., Savannah, 1983. Exhibns. include Salon de l'Art Libre, Paris, 1955-56, Salon Terre Latine, 1957, Galerie Notre Dame, 1957, Barbizon Gallery, N.Y., 1966, Southampton Art Gallery, Long Is., 1969, Arras Gallery, 1971, 74, Artery Gallery, Toronto, 1974, NYU, 1975, Alexander Iolas Gallery, 1977, Historic Savannah Found., 1982, John F. Kennedy Mus., San Francisco, 1982, Columbia U., N.Y.C., 1983, Salon Neo-Classic, N.Y., 1988, Mus. Modern Art, Buenos Aires, 1990, Bronx (N.Y.) Coun. on Arts, 1994; designer tapestries for Tabard Frères, Aubusson, France, 1955-65; permanent collections include Hans Namuth, Chelsea Hotel, Ctr. Integrative Studies, Woodhull Hosp., Ossabaw Is. Found., Hist. Savannah Found., Nicholas Gallery; accordeon concerts at French Youth Am., 1985, L'Alliance Francaise, N.J., 1988; collaborated with Johanne Besserat Selassie, 1973; with sculptor Roderick Ghyka, 1977-78; works included in L'Architecture D'Aujourd'hui, Paris, 1966, Craft of the Modern World, Am. Craft Mus., N.Y., 1968, Craft Horizons, N.Y., 1968, Elle Mag., Paris, 1970, 72, Racorama, Italy, 1973, Columbia U. Daily Spectator, N.Y., 1983. Demonstrator Stop Vietnam March, Washington, 1969, Boycott Lettuce-Cesar Chavez Orgn., Delano, Calif., 1970, Anti-Furs March ASPCA, N.Y.C., 1984, 85, 86; lectr. for Mexican workers Catholic Worker, N.Y., 1970; active Internat. Hostels, France, Italy, Switzerland, Austria, 1951-54, Animal Rights Mobilization, N.Y.C., 1990-95; mem. France-USSR Film Libr., Toulouse, France, 1955-60; guest itinerant lectr. Anti-Vietnam Campaign, Ariz., 1970; guest resident Cesar Chavez Hqrs., Delano, Calif., 1970, Free Tibet, The Milarepa Fund, 1998; govt. census taker, S.C., 1980. Grantee Yaddo, 1968, Ossabaw Is. Project, 1968, 73, 76. Fellow MacDowell Colony (residence grantee 1969, 71, 74, 77); mem. Nat. Mus. Women in the Arts (file in archives, 2000—). Vedanta religion. Avocations: sciences, religion, continuous learning. Office: PO Box 2636 New York NY 10185-2636

LAVEIST, THOMAS ALEXIS, sociologist; b. Bklyn., Feb. 3, 1961; s. William Thomas and Eudora E. (Ramos) LaV.; children: David Thomas Ambee, Naomi Julitte Kai. BA in Sociology, U. Md. Ea. Shore, 1984; PhD in Sociology, U. Mich., 1988, postgrad., 1990. Rsch. assoc. Inst. for Social Rsch. U. Mich., Ann Arbor, 1985-90, teaching asst. Ctr. for Afro-Am. Studies, 1986, instr. dept. sociology, 1987; asst. prof. dept. health policy and mgmt. Johns Hopkins U., Balt., 1990—, asst. prof. dept. sociology, 1992—, faculty assoc. Hopkins Population Ctr., 1993—. Mem. conf. organizing com. Nat. Conf. on Health Status of Black Ams., Johns Hopkins Sch. Hygiene and Pub. Health and Meharry Med. Coll., Balt., 1991; mem. health subcom. gov.'s commn. Status of Black Males, Md., 1990—; participant strategies for improving minority involvement in health svcs. rsch. Agy. for Health Care Policy and Rsch., Washington, 1990; rsch. cons. Walter Reed Army Inst. of Rsch. divsn. Preventive Medicine, 1992; participant Minority Health Careers Acad., Md. Dept. Health and Mental Hygiene, Balt. City Pub. Schs., 1991, 92; participant regional minority health planning meeting Agy. for Health Care Policy and Rsch., Boston, 1992; grant reviewer office adolescent pregnancy prevention U.S. Dept. Health and Human Svcs., 1992; small grant reviewer Agy. for Health Care Policy and Rsch., 1992—; keynote speaker scholarship award banquet Randolph Evans Found., 1993. Mem. editorial bd. Sage Publs., 1991-94; reviewer jours. including Applied Behavioral Sci. Rev., Jours. Gerontology: Social Scis., Am. Sociol. Rev.; contbr. articles to profl. jours. Randolph Evans Meml. scholar, 1979; fellow Com. on Instnl. Coop., 1984-88, Paul B. Cornely sr. fellow U. Mich., 1988-90, Brookdale Nat. fellow, 1991. Mem. APHA (del. to Cuba 1993), Am. Sociol. Assn., Assn. Black Sociologists (session organizer for panel on med. sociology 1991), Population Assn. Am., Gerontol. Soc. Am. Avocations: basketball, golf, music. Office: Johns Hopkins U Sch Hygiene and Pub Health 624 N Broadway Baltimore MD 21205-1900

LAVELLE, ARTHUR, anatomy educator; b. Fargo, N.D., Nov. 29, 1921; s. Frank and Lillie (Hanson) LaV.; m. Faith Evelyn Wilson, 1947; 1 dau., Audrey Anne. BS, U. Wash., 1946; MA, Johns Hopkins, 1948; PhD, U. Pa., 1951. USPHS postdoctoral fellow U. Pa., Phila., 1951-52; mem. faculty dept. anatomy U. Ill. Coll. Medicine, Chgo., 1952—, assoc. prof., 1958-65, prof., 1965-87, prof. emeritus, 1987—. Vis. prof. UCLA, 1968-69; cons. Galesburg (Ill.) State Rsch. Hosp., 1965-68; mem. Biol. Stain Commn., 1953-93, trustee, 1978-93, pres., 1981-86, v.p., 1991-92. Mem. editorial bd. Biotechnic and Histochemistry, 1989-93; contbr. articles to profl. jours. USPHS research grantee, 1953-70; Cerebral Palsy Found. grantee, 1964-68; Guggenheim fellow, 1968-69 Mem. Am. Assn. Anatomists, Am. Soc. Cell Biology, Soc. Developmental Biology, AAAS, Soc. Neurosci., Sigma Xi. Office: 1853 W Polk St Chicago IL 60612-4316

LAVELLE, BETTY SULLIVAN DOUGHERTY, legal professional; b. Omaha, Nov. 12, 1941; d. Marvin D. and Marie C. Sullivan; children from previous marriage: Clayton B. Dougherty, Lance A. Dougherty; m. James S. LaVelle, 1986; 1 child, Lindsay L. A of Pre-Law, U. Nebr., 1960; student, U. Colo., 1964-66; BA in Philosophy, Metro State Coll., 1979; cert. legal assistant, U. San Diego, 1979. Teaching asst. Metro State Coll., Denver, 1978; paralegal Holland and Hart, 1979-85; litigation paralegal Rothgerber, Appel, Powers and Johnson, 1985-88; pres., cons. Vivant, Inc., Boulder, 1987—; owner, adminstr. Homestead Group Home for Elderly, Longmont, 1987-92; ptnr. LaVelle & McMillan, Boulder, 1989-90; water law and litigation paralegal Moses, Wittemyer, Harrison and Woodruff, P.C., 1990-2001, mediation, water rights, real property and litigation contractor, 2001—. Mediator domestic relations 20th Jud. Dist., Boulder, 1984-85. Contbr. articles to profl. jours. Vol. legal aid Thursday Night Bar, Denver Bar Assn., 1979-86, paralegal coordinator, panelist, speaker, 1983-85; sr. paralegal Boulder County Legal Svcs., 1988-89; mediator landlord/tenant project City of Boulder, 1983-87; coach, trainer Ctr. for Dispute Resolution, Denver and Boulder, 1984-86; vol. Shelter for Homeless, Boulder, 1988. Recipient cert. U. Denver Coll. Law, 1981, Hoagland award Colo. Bar Assn., 1984. Mem. Colo. Bar Assn., Soc. Profls. in Dispute Resolution, Rocky Mountain Paralegal Assn. (mem. adv. bd. 1980-81, bd. dirs. 1983-85, 94-96, rep. to Colo. Bar Assn. 1994-96, dir. pro bono svcs. 1984-85). Democrat. Avocations: vol. legal services for the indigent, computer applications. Home: 1660 Bradley Ct Boulder CO 80305-7300

LAVELLE, BRIAN FRANCIS DAVID, lawyer; b. Cleve., Aug. 16, 1941; s. Gerald John and Mary Josephine (O'Callaghan) L.; m. Sara Hill, Sept. 10, 1966; children: S. Elizabeth, B. Francis D. Jr., Catherine H. BA, U. Va., 1963; JD, Vanderbilt U., 1966; LLM in Taxation, NYU, 1969. Bar: N.C. 1966, Ohio 1968. Assoc. VanWinkle Buck, Wall, Starnes & Davis, Asheville, N.C., 1968-74, ptnr., 1974—. Lectr. continuing edn. N.C. Bar Found., Wake Forest U. Estate Planning Inst., Hartford Tax Inst., Duke U. Estate Planning Inst. Contbr. articles on law to profl. jours. Trustee Carolina Day Sch., 1981-92, sec., 1982-85; bd. dirs. The Salvation Army, 1986—; bd. dirs. Western N.C. Cmty. Found., 1986—, sec., 1987-90; bd. advs. U. N.C. Ann. Tax Inst., 1981—. Capt. JAG USAF, 1966-67. Mem. ABA, Am. Coll. Trust and Estate Counsel (state chmn. 1982-85, regent 1984-90, lectr. continuing edn.), N.C. Bar Assn. (bd. govs. 1979-82, councillor tax sect. 1979-83, councillor estate planning law sect. 1982-85, v.p. 1997—), N.C. State Bar (splty. exam. com. on estate planning and probate law 1984-90, chmn. 1990-91, cert. 1987), Rotary. Clubs: Biltmore Forest Country, Asheville Downtown City. Episcopalian. Home: 45 Brookside Rd Asheville NC 28803-3015 Office: 11 N Market St PO Box 7376 Asheville NC 28802-8506 E-mail: glavelle@vwlawfirm.com.

LAVELLE, CHARLES JOSEPH, lawyer; b. Louisville, Aug. 31, 1950; s. James Ronald and Mary Elizabeth (Logan) L.; m. Donna Kay Mulligan, Jan. 21, 1978. BS with high honors, U. Notre Dame, 1972; JD, U. Ky., 1975; LLM in Taxation, NYU, 1977. Bar: Ky. 1975, U.S. Dist. Ct. (wes. dist.) Ky. 1977, U.S. Tax Ct. 1977, U.S. Claims Ct. 1986, U.S. Ct. Appeals (6th and Fed. cirs.) 1986, U.S. Supreme Ct. 1989. Assoc. Greenebaum Doll & McDonald PLLC, Louisville, 1977-82, mem., 1982—. Chmn. bar liaison cen. region IRS, Cin., 1989, sec., 1997, bar liaison southeast region IRS; mem. Regional Counsel Adv. Group, Cin., 1988-89. Contbr. articles to profl. jours. Bd. dirs. Ky. Ctr. Pub. Issues, 1992-94; mem. steering com. Ky. Coalition for Edn., 1993-94; mem. Ky. Ltd. Liability Co. Legislation Drafting Com., 1993-94; mem. planning com. Ky. Conclave on Legal Edn., 1995. Secondary Sci. Tng. grant NSF, U. Ga., 1967, rcsh. grantee NSF, U. Notre Dame, 1969. Mem. ABA (tax sect.), Ky. Bar Assn. (chmn. tax sect. 1992-93), Louisville Bar Assn. (chmn. tax com. 1983, 84, vice chmn., treas. tax com. 1980-82), U. Ky. Law Alumni Assn. (bd. dirs. 1986—, pres. 1989-90, treas. 1987-90, 90—), Ky. C. of C. (bd. dirs. 1991—, exec. com. 1997—, chair pub. policy com. 1997-98, health ins. task force, tax com.), Rotary (bd. dirs. 1991-93, 95-97, treas. 1995-97, dist. conf. chair 1994), Notre Dame Club (pres. 1984-86, chmn. 1986-88, Ky. Man of Yr. 1990), Leadership Ky. (vice chmn. membership svcs. 1995-98, alumni bd. dirs. 1992-92, pres. alumni 1993-94, bd. dirs. 1993-98, exec. com. 1995-98). Office: Greenebaum Doll & McDonald PLLC 3300 National City Tower Louisville KY 40202

LAVELLE, JOSEPH P. lawyer; b. Scranton, Pa., Sept. 7, 1957; s. Patrick Leo and Anne M. (Antal) L.; m. Kathy A. Mlodzienski, Aug. 14, 1982; children: Remy, Joseph, Taylor. BS in Physics, Wilkes Coll., 1979; JD summa cum laude, U. Pitts., 1982. Bar: D.C. 1982, U.S. Ct. Appeals (Fed. cir.) 1982, U.S. Patent and Trademark Office 1982, U.S. Ct. Appeals (3d, 2d and 6th cir.). Assoc. Howrey & Simon, Washington, 1982-90, ptnr., 1991—. Adj. prof. Georgetown U. Law Ctr., 1995—. Editl. bd. ABA Antitrust Law Developments, III, 1992; contbr. articles to profl. jours.; mng. editor U. Pitts. Law Rev., 1981-82. Mem. ABA, AAAS, Am. Phys. Soc., Order of the Coif. Republican. Office: Howrey Simon Arnold & White Ste 1 1299 Pennsylvania Ave Washington DC 20004-2420 E-mail: lavellej@howrey.com.

LAVELLE, MARY LEE DEMETRE, psychiatric nursing educator; b. Charleston, S.C., May 30, 1945; m. John L. Lavelle Jr., Aug. 4, 1973; children: Paul, Rachelle. Diploma nursing with honors, Med. Coll. S.C., 1966, BSN with high honors, 1974, MSN in Psychiat. Nursing with highest honors, 1990. RN, S.C.; cert. BCLS. Staff nurse coronary care unit Med. U. S.C., 1966-68; staff nurse Charleston County Hosp., Charleston, S.C., 1969, head nurse med. fl., supr., 1969-72, supr., 1972-75; coord. alumni affairs Med. U. of S.C., 1974-76; with Family Planning Clinic, Charleston County Health Dept., 1975-76; instr. med. terminology Trident Tech. Coll., Palmer Campus, 1975-79; coord. alumni affairs Med. U. of S.C., Coll. of Nursing, 1982-88; emergency med. system auditor Palmetto Lowcountry Health System, 1986; curator Ruth Chamberlin Hist. Nursing Libr., 1988-92; instr. psychiat. nursing Trident Tech. Coll., 1990—, part-time instr. LPN program, 1991—; mem. nursing pool transitional care unit Med. U. S.C., 1996-98. Asst. intern coord. staff devel. dept., diabetic instr. patient edn. dept. Roper Hosp., Charleston, 1985, clin. instr. psychiat. nursing practical nursing program, 1995—; staff nurse Inst. Psychiatry, Med. U. S.C., 1990-91; instr. psychiat. nursing Med. U. S.C., 1994-95, instr. nursing, 1997—; mem. nursing pool in psychiatry Charleston Meml. Hosp., 1991-96; presenter in field. Mem. S.C. Heart Assn., 1967-78. Recipient Outstanding Alumnus award Med. U. S.C. Coll. of Nursing, 2000; Saul Alexander Ednl. scholar, 1973, scholar Bus. and Profl. Women's Club, 1972, Am. Bus. Women's Assn., 1972. Fellow Nightingale Soc. (hon.); mem. Coll. Nursing Alumni Assn. Med. U. S.C. (v.p. 1967-69, pres. 1969-74, bd. dirs. 1974-75, ex-officio bd. mem. 1982-88, nominating com. 1992-93), Med. U. S.C. Alumni Assn. (councilor 1971-74, sec. 1974-75, v.p. 1977-79, pres. 1979-80, bd. dirs. 1981-88, 92-95), Sigma Theta Tau. Home: 694 Fort Sumter Dr Charleston SC 29412-4336

LAVELLE, WILLIAM AMBROSE, lawyer, judge; b. Athens, Ohio, Jan. 18, 1925; s. Francis Anthony and Belle Elizabeth (Schloss) L.; m. Marion Helen Yanity, Aug. 7, 1954 (dec. Feb. 10, 2002); children: Frank A., John P., Lydia E., Amy M. BBA, Ohio U., 1949; JD, Ohio State U., 1952. Bar: Ohio 1952, U.S. Dist. Ct. (so. dist.) Ohio 1952. Sr. ptnr. Lavelle Law Offices, Athens, Ohio, 1952-91; judge probate/juvenile divsn. Athens County Common Pleas Ct., 1991-94; assigned judge Supreme Ct. of Ohio, 1994; pvt. practice estate planning, trusts, probate, 1994—. Former solicitor City of Nelsonville, Villages of Albany, Chauncey, Coolville, Glouster, Trimble and Zaleski; counsel Margaret Creek Conservancy Dist., L-Ax Water Distbn. Co., Sunday Creek and Hollister Water Assns.; instr. wills, trusts, estate planning Ohio U., Athens, 1991—; mem. commn. on cert. as atty. specialists Supreme Ct. Ohio, 1994. Former chmn. Athens County and Ohio Dem. Party; former mem. Dem. Nat. Com.; chmn. Athens County Bd. Elections, 1967-80; chmn. pers. rev. bd. State of Ohio, 1983-91; trustee, chmn. trustees Ohio U., 1975-81; mem. parish fin. com., parish coun., sch. bd., diocesan bd. lay consultors St. Paul's Cath. Ch., Athens. Served with inf. U.S. Army, 1943-46, ETO, PTO. Mem. ABA, Ohio State Bar Assn. (bd. govs. 1989-92, probate and trust law sect. 1993—, coun. of dels. 1986-89), Athens County Bar Assn. (past pres.), Nat. Acad. Elder Law Attys., Ohio Horse Coun., Tenn. Walking Horse Breeders and

Exhibitors Assn., Walking Horse Owners Assn., Athens Symposiarch Club (past pres., Symposiarch of Yr. 1996), Athens Cotillion Club, Athens Country Club, Athens Rotary Club, VFW, Am. Legion, Am. Vets, Sons of Union Vols., Ohio U. Green and White Club, KC (3d and 4th deg.), St. Francis Soc. Avocation: breeding, raising, riding and driving Tennessee Walking Horses. Home: 39 Cable Ln Athens OH 45701-1304 Office: PO Box 899 Athens OH 45701-0899 Fax: 740-797-1058. E-mail: walavelle@eurekanet.com.

LAVEN, DAVID LAWRENCE, nuclear and radiologic pharmacist, consultant; b. Detroit, Jan. 31, 1953; s. Harold Sanford and Ada Rae (Blumenthal) L.; m. Maxine Frances Miller, May 14, 1977 (divorced); children: Ryan Stuart, Cameron Alexander. BA in History, Biology, Albion Coll., 1975; BS in Pharmacy, U. N.Mex., 1981. Rsch. technologist, biodistbn. specialist U. N.Mex. Coll. Pharmacy, Albuquerque, 1978-81; asst. mgr. Syncor, Inc. (formerly Pharmatopes), Miami, Fla., 1981-84; instr. nuclear pharmacy U. Miami, 1982-85; pres., owner Gammascan Cons., Lenexa, Tex., 1982-98; staff pharmacist Hollywood (Fla.) Med. Ctr., 1983-84; asst. mgr. Nuclear Pharmacy, Inc., Sunrise, Fla., 1984-85; dir. nuc. pharmacy program VA Med. Ctr., Bay Pines, 1985-96; exec. dir. Ala. Pharmacy Assn., 1996-98; poison control splst./mgr. PET Cyclotron/Pharmacy Kans. U. Med. Ctr., Kansas City, Kans., 1998-2001; lead PET nuclear pharmacist Eastern Isotopes/IBA, 2001—02; pharmacist Eckerds Corp., 2002—. Mem. adv. panel in radiopharms. U.S. Pharmacopeial Conv., Inc., Rockville, Md., 1985—96; cons. nuclear pharmacy Nat. Assn. Bds. Pharmacy, Chgo., 1987—2000; adj. asst. clin. prof. U. Fla. Coll. Pharmacy, Gainesville, 1986—98, Nova-Southeastern U. Coll. Pharmacy, North Miami Beach, Fla., 1990—98, Mercer U. Coll. Pharmacy, 1995—98, U. Kans. Coll. Pharmacy, 2000—01; edn. cons. Nuclear Tech. Rev. Series Rev., Inc., 1988—; mem. splty coun. on nuclear pharmacy Bd. Pharm. Specialities, 1988—91; mem. Ala. Coun. Assn. Execs., 1996—98, Nat. Coun. State Pharmacy Execs., 1996—98, Govs. Task Force Prevention Tobacco Use in Ala., 1997—98; chair Smoking Cessation Workgroup. Co-author: Pharmacologic Alterations in the Biorouting/Performance of Select Radiopharmaceuticals Used in Cardiac Imaging, 1990, Pharmacologic Alterations with Biorouting/Performance of Radiopharmaceuticals Used in Nuclear Medicine Abscess, Liver/Spleen, and Tumor/Inflammation Imaging Procedures, 1992, Pharmacologic Alterations in the Biorouting of Radiopharmaceuticals Used in Nuclear Medicine Adrenal, Cerebral, Hepatobiliary, Pulmonary, and Renal Scintigraphic Studies, 1993, International Handbook of Drug-Radiopharmaceutical Interactions and Incompatibilities, 1994; Pharmacologic Alterations in the Biorouting/Performance of Radiopharmaceuticals Used in Cistrnography, Ferrokinetic Studies, Gastrointestinal Imaging, Schillings Testing, Thrombus Localization, Thyroid Uptake/Imaging, and Other Nuclear Medicine Procedures, 1994, A Pharmacist's Guide to Pharmaceuticals Used in Medical Imaging, 2001; editor Ala. Pharmacy Jour., 1996-98, APA Newsletter, 1996-98, Pratique Extrordinaire Newsletter, 1997-98, editor, co-pub. Clini-Scan Monthly, 1982-84; co-guest editor Jour. Pharmacy Practice, Radiologic Pharmacy I, 1989, II, 1989, III, 1994, IV, 2001, mem. editl. bd., 1991—; guest editor Fla. Jour. Hosp. Pharmacy, 1990, cons. editor, 1986-96; guest author In-Svc. Rev. in Nuclear Medicine, 1990—, Poison Control - Part I, 2000, Part II, 2000, Jour. of Pharmacy Practice, Radiologic Pharmacy IV, Parts I and II, 2001; mem. editorial bd. New Perspectives in Cancer Diagnosis and Management, 1992-99; nat. field editor ASHP Signal Newsletter, 1985-87; contbr. chpt. to book. Mem. Henry Morgan chpt. B'nai B'rith, Southfield, Mich., 1975-77; sec. Ala. Pharmacy Assn. Rsch. and Edn. Found., 1996-98. Fellow: Acad. Pharmacy Practice and Mgmt. (nuclear pharmacy sec. ednl. affairs com. 1983—, regulatory affairs com. 1984—, del. 1986—2002, edn. cons. 1987—2001, prof. and sci. affairs com. 1988—, Practitioner Merit award 1990, Presentation award 1990, Poster award 1990, Presentation award 1991, Poster award 1991, Presentation award 1994, Poster award 1994), Am. Soc. Hosp. Pharmacists (edn. program assoc. 1988—95, practice adv. panel 1992—93, chmn. specialized practice group on radiologic pharmacy 1993—95, mem. continuing edn. 1995—98); mem.: Ctrl. Fla. Pharmacy Assn. (sec. 2002—), Ala. Pharmacy Assn. (exec. dir. 1996—98), Polk County Pharmacy Assn., Hillsborough County Pharmacy Assn. (sec. 1991—92, mem. exec. com. 1991—96, pres.-elect 1993—94, pres. 1994—95, newsletter editor 1994—96, pres. 1995—96, Pres. award 1994—95, 1995—96, Pharmacist of Yr. award 1994), Pasco-Hernando Pharmacy Assn. (treas. 1990—93, mem. exec. com. 1990—94, Pharmacist of Yr. award 1995), Pinellas Pharmacists Soc. (mem. exec. com. 1989—97, pres.-elect 1991—92, pres. 1992—93, newsletter editor 1992—96, Pharmacist of Yr. award 1992, Pres' award 1993, FPA Unit Assn. Recognition award 1993, PPS Merit award 1994, Practice Merit award 1994, FPA Unit Assn. Recognition award 1995, Lifetime Merit award 1996), Soc. Nuclear Medicine (mem. S.E. chpt., mem. govt. affairs com. 1985—86, program com. 1988—89, edn. cons. 1989—, mem. Brewster Bill task force 1995, mem. NRC com. 1995—97, chair pharmacy liaison com. 1995—2000), Internat. Pharm. Fedn. (edn. con. Pharmacy World Congress 1992, 1993, editor proceedings spl. session Pharmacy World Congress 1993, vice chmn. nuclear pharmacy subsection 1994—95, chmn. nuclear pharm. group 1994—97, edn. con. Pharmacy World Congress 1995, 1996, chair SIG on radiologic pharmacy bd. of pharm. scis. 1997—2002, edn. con. Pharmacy World Congress 1999, 2001, 2002, editor Radioimmunopharm.: Current and Future Considerations, Sci. Poster award Sect. Hosp. Pharmacists 1992), Fla. Nuclear Medicine Technologists (mem. exec. coun. 1992—97, editor Proceedings 22nd ann. meeting 1993, 24th ann. meeting 1995, 25th ann. meeting 1996), Fla. Soc. Hosp. Pharmacists, Acad. Pharmacy Practice (chmn. nuclear pharmacy sect. 1987—89, chmn. 1988—90, chmn. nuclear pharmacy sect. 1991—93, chmn. 1993—95, Poster Presentation 1st Pl. award 1995), Fla. Pharmacy Assn. (chmn. nuclear pharmacy sect. 1987—89, edn. cons. 1987—96, chmn. acad. pharmacy practice 1988—90, del. 1988—96, chmn. ednl. affairs coun. 1989—90, budget and fin. com. 1989—90, pres. com. 1989—90, mem. task force on mission of pharmacy in Fla. 1989—92, mem. conv. planning com. 1989—93, mem. exec. com. 1989—96, region XII rep. 1989—96, exec. com. 1989—96, chmn. nuclear pharmacy sect. 1991—93, chmn. orgnl. affairs coun. 1992—93, chmn. acad. pharmacy practice 1993—95, editor numerous proceedings for nuclear pharmacy lecture series 1993—96, pres. com. 1994—95, budget and fin. com. 1994—95, mem. conv. planning com. 1995, mem. task force on mission of pharmacy in Fla. 1995, chmn. nuclear pharmacy sect. 2001—02, chmn. nuclear pharmacy section 2001—02, Number 1 Club 1990, Disting. Young Pharmacist award 1990, Acad. Pharmacy Practice Practitioner Merit award 1992, Sidney Simkowitz Pharmacy Involvement award 1992, Disting. Svc. award 1993, Unit Assn. Newsletter awards 1994, 1995, Unit Assn. Newsletter awards (2) 1996), Am. Soc. Pharmacy Law, Ala. Coun. Assn. Execs., Nat. Coun. State Pharmacy Assn. Execs., Am. Assn. Colls. Pharmacy (mem. taskforce on residency programs and support 1990—91, mem. task force on assessment of experimental function 1994—95), Ad Hoc Com. Practice Environ. and Quality of Worklife, Am. Pharm. Assn. (mem. nuclear pharmacy sect., mem. ednl. affairs com. 1983—, mem. regulatory affairs com. 1984—, chmn.-elect 1988—89, edn. adv. com. 1988—89, mem. profl. and sci. affairs com. 1988—, chmn. sect. on specialized pharm. svcs. 1989—90, chmn.-elect 1992—93, edn. adv. com. 1992—94, chmn. sect. on nuclear pharmacy 1993—94, mem.-at-large sect. officer 2000—02, edn. adv. com. 2000—02, chmn.-elect 2002—03), Beta Beta Beta, Phi Alpha Theta, Psi Chi, Kappa Psi. Avocations: art collecting, intramural sports, camping, travel, writing. Office: 633 Sabal Lake Dr # 103 Longwood FL 32779 E-mail: dlavenRx@earthlink.net.

LAVENAS, SUZANNE, writer, editor, consultant; b. Buenos Aires, Dec. 17, 1942; came to U.S., 1955; d. Carlos Fernando and Mary (Sharp) Lavenas; m. Wesley First, Jan. 9, 1982 (dec. Nov. 2001). Student, Antioch Coll., 1960-64, 65-66. Computer programmer N.Y. Telephone, N.Y.C., 1966-68; prodn. editor, then copy editor Travel Weekly, 1968-76, chief copy editor, 1976-79; mng. editor Indsl. Chem. News, 1981-82; editor, writer, cons., 1986-99; pres. Lavenas & Carson, Montauk, N.Y., 1999—. Author numerous articles. Mem. Overseas Press Club, Soc. Silurians. Republican. Episcopalian. Avocations: reading, cooking, computer hacking, walking, cinema. Home: 236 Edgemere St Montauk NY 11954-5249

LAVENDER, ROBERT EUGENE, state supreme court justice; b. Muskogee, Okla., July 19, 1926; s. Harold James and Vergene Irene (Martin) L.; m. Maxine Knight, Dec. 22, 1945; children— Linda (Mrs. Dean Courter), Robert K., Debra (Mrs. Thomas Merrill), William J. LL.B., U. Tulsa, 1953; grad., Appellate Judges Seminar, 1967, Nat. Coll. State Trial Judges, 1970. Bar: Okla. bar 1953. With Mass. Bonding & Ins. Co., Tulsa, 1951-53, U.S. Fidelity & Guaranty Co., Tulsa, 1953-54; asst. city atty., 1954-55; practice, 1955-60, Claremore, Okla., 1960-65; justice Okla. Supreme Ct., 1965—, chief justice, 1979-80. Guest lectr. Okla. U., Oklahoma City U., Tulsa U. law schs. Republican committeeman, Rogers County, 1961-62. Served with USNR, 1944-46. Recipient Disting. Alumnus award U. Tulsa, 1993. Mem. ABA, Okla. Bar Assn., Rogers County Bar Assn., Am. Judicature Soc., Okla. Jud. Conf., Phi Alpha Delta (hon.) Methodist (adminstrv. bd.). Club: Mason (32 deg.). Home: 2910 Kerry Ln Oklahoma City OK 73120-2507 Office: US Supreme Ct Okla Rm 1 State Capitol Oklahoma City OK 73105

LAVENGOOD, LAWRENCE GENE, management educator, historian; b. Tulsa, June 30, 1924; s. Lawrence Wilbur and Elizabeth (Gardner) L.; m. Gloria M. deLeon, Aug. 27, 1947; children: Jessica, Abigail, Timothy, Rachel. MA, U. Chgo., 1947, PhD, 1953. Asst. prof. bus. history Northwestern U., Evanston, Ill., 1953-59, assoc. prof., 1959-69, chmn. dept. policy and environ., 1980-82, prof. bus. history and policy and environ., 1970-94, prof. emeritus, 1994—. Mem. Com. on Ethics in Bus. Edn., 1977-79; cons. on mgmt. devel. edn. U.S. and European corps.; U.S. faculty coord. Sasin Grad. Inst. Bus. Arminstrn., Chulalongkorn U., Bangkok, 1983-95; chmn. bd. dirs. ctr. for ethics Garrett-Evang. Theol. Sem., Evanston, 1995—. Editor, contbr.: Moral Man and Economic Enterprise, 1967. Mem. Bd. Edn. Ill. elem. dist. 65, Evanston, 1967-72, 75-78; bd. dirs. Evanston Comm. Found., 1996—. Recipient Ann. Kellogg Alumni Choice award, 1992. Democrat. Presbyterian.

LAVENSON, SUSAN BARKER, hotel corporate executive, consultant; b. L.A., July 26, 1936; d. Percy Morton and Rosalie Laura (Donner) Barker; m. James H. Lavenson, Apr. 22, 1973; 1 child, Ellen Ruth Stanclift. BA, Stanford U., 1958, MA, 1959; PhD (hon.), Thomas Coll., 1994. Cert. gen. secondary credential tchr., Calif. Tchr. Benjamin Franklin Jr. High Sch., San Francisco, 1960; tchr. French dept. Lowell High Sch., 1960-61; v.p. Monogram Co., 1961-62, creative dir. N.Y.C., 1973-86; pres. SYR Corp., Santa Barbara, Calif., 1976-89; mng. ptnr. Lavenson Ptnrs., Camden, Maine, 1989—. Mem. commn. on co-edn. Wheaton Coll., Norton, Mass., 1985-87; mem. Relais et Chateaux, Paris, 1978-89; cons. World Bank Recruit Divsn., 1993. Author: Greening of San Ysidro, 1977 (Conf. award 1977). Trustee Camden Pub. Libr., 1989—95, v.p., 1991—93; vice chair bd. trustees Thomas Coll., Waterville, Maine, 1990—2001, trustee emerita, 2001—; trustee Atlantic Ave. Trust, 1989—91; founding pres. Maine chpt. Internat. Women's Forum, 1991—; mem. Coun. of Advisors Coll. of the Atlantic, Bar Harbor, Maine, 1996—2001, Ariz. Women's Forum; mem. dean's adv. coun. Ariz. State U., 2002. Recipient Piper award for entrepreneurial excellence, 2002. Mem. Advice Inc., Camden Yacht Club, Stanford Alumni Assn., Com. of 200 (treas. 1985-86), Women's Entrepreneur Corps, Phi Delta Kappa (Stanford U. chpt., founding mem.). Home and Office: 7841 E Shooting Star Way Scottsdale AZ 85262 E-mail: susiebl@earthlink.net. *Three rules to remember: 1) Never take anything personally. 2) Never lose your sense of humor. 3) Keep your eye on the objective - I also like the Apocryphal words: "I am not made or unmade by things that happen to me, but by my reactions to them."*

LAVENTHOL, DAVID ABRAM, newspaper editor; b. Phila., July 15, 1933; s. Jesse and Clare (Horwald) L.; m. Esther Coons, Mar. 8, 1958; children: Peter, Sarah. BA, Yale U., 1957; MA, U. Minn., 1960; LittD (hon.), Dowling Coll., 1979; LLD (hon.), Hofstra U., 1986. Reporter, news editor St. Petersburg (Fla.) Times, 1957-62; asst. editor, city editor N.Y. Herald-Tribune, 1963-66; asst. mng. editor Washington Post, 1966-69; from assoc. editor to pub., CEO Newsday, L.I., N.Y., 1969-86; group v.p. newspapers Times Mirror Co., L.A., 1981-86, sr. v.p., 1987-93, pres., 1987-93; pub., CEO L.A. Times, 1989-93; editor-at-large Times Mirror Co., L.A., 1994-98; editor, pub. Columbia Journalism Rev., 1999—. Mem. Pulitzer Prize Bd., 1982-91, chmn., 1988-89; vice-chmn. Internat. Press Inst., 1985-93, chmn., 1993-95, chmn. com. to protect journalists, 2002—. Bd. dirs. United Negro Coll. Fund, 1988, Mus. Contemporary Art, L.A., 1989—, chmn., 1993-97; bd. dirs. Associated Press, 1993-96, Columbia Journalism Sch., 1995—, Nat. Parkinson Found., 1995—, Saratoga Performing Arts Ctr., 1993—. Recipient Columbia Journalism award for Disting. Svc., 1994. Mem. Am. Soc. Newspaper Editors (chmn. writing awards bd. 1980-83), Council Fgn. Relations. Clubs: Century (N.Y.C.), Regency (L.A.). Office: Columbia Journalism Review Columbia Univ 2950 Broadway New York NY 10027-7004 E-mail: malibunal@aol.com.

LAVERGE, HENDRIK JOHANNES, finance company executive, investor, consultant; b. Jakarta, Java, Indonesia, Apr. 4, 1941; came to US, 1966; s. Albertus and Juliette (Terwindt) L.; m. Regine A. Schade, Dec. 7, 1968 (div. Dec. 1994); children: Albert Johannes, Claire Antoinette. BA, Willibrord Coll., Zeist, The Netherlands, 1959; LLM, Leiden (The Netherlands) U., 1965. Ptnr. Frick Wellington & Laverge, N.Y.C., 1992—, Valenzuela Capital Ptnrs. LLC, N.Y.C., 1992—. Chmn. Devonshire Holding, La Grangeville, N.Y.; bd. dirs. Concordia Agritrading Pte. Ltd., Singapore, 1994—. Dir. Leiden U. Fund., 1995; dir., treas. St. Barnabas Coll., Johannesburg, South Africa, 1990-95; trustee Madison Ave. Presbyn. Ch., N.Y.C., 1975-85. Mem. Union Club N.Y.C. Home: 14 Herb Rd Sharon CT 06069-2326 Office: FW&L 1270 Avenue Of The Americas New York NY 10020-1700 E-mail: HLaverge@valpartners.com.

LAVERY, DANIEL P. management consultant; b. N.Y.C., June 28, 1932; m. Doris E. Guenther, Oct. 23, 1954; children: Daniel, Brian, Kevin, Michael. BS with honors, Manhattan Coll., 1954; MBA, Rutgers U., 1963. Mem. prodn. mgmt. staff, photo products dept. E.I. DuPont de Nemours & Co., Inc., 1954-65; divsn. mgr. Anken Industries, Williamstown, Mass., 1965-71; gen. mgr. Dymo Industries, N.Y.C., 1971-73; dir. cons. studies Quantum Sci. Corps., 1973-79; mgr. strategic mktg. ITT, 1979-80; sr. dir. market rsch. Western Union, 1980-82; v.p. Pactel, Inc., mgmt. cons., N.Y.C., 1982-83; ptnr. Palo Alto Mgmt. Group, Wyckoff, N.J., 1983-98, Matterhorn Group, Wyckoff, 1998—. Served as capt. USAF, 1955-57. Mem. Inst. Mgmt. Cons. (cert. mgmt. cons.), Am. Arbitration Assn. (panel mem. 1985—). Office: Matterhorn Group 458 Sicomac Ave Wyckoff NJ 07481-1120

LAVERY, J. PATRICK, perinatologist; b. N.Y.C., June 24, 1942; s. Joseph F. and Doris Lavery; m. Barbara S. Lavery. BS, Fordham U., 1964; MD, SUNY, Syracuse, 1968. Diplomate Am. Bd. Ob/Gyn. Intern St. Vincents Hosp. and Med. Ctr., N.Y.C., 1968-69, resident, 1969-73; mem. faculty U. Louisville, 1975-87; prof. oby-gyn. Mich. State U., Lansing, 1987—; perinatologist Bronson Hosp., Kalamazoo, 1987—. Editor: The Human Placenta, 1988; co-editor: Pediatric and Adolescent Obstetrics and Gynecology, 1987. Maj. U.S. Army, 1973-75. Fellow Am. Coll. Ob/Gyn. Office: Bronson Hosp 252 E Lovell St Kalamazoo MI 49007-5364

LAVERY, JOHN EDWARD, mathematician; b. Columbus, Ohio, Nov. 23, 1945; s. Thomas Francis and Evelyn Brown Lavery; m. Monica Hauck; children: Kristen, Eileen. BA, Mich State U., 1965; MS, U. Akron, 1968; PhD, U. Md., 1973. Aerospace technologist NASA Goddard Space Flight Ctr., Greenbelt, Md., 1968—73; assoc. prof. Tunghai U., Taichung, Taiwan, 1973—74, Soochow U., Taipei, 1975—77, prof. Taiwan, 1977—79; rschr. Computing Ctr. of Acad. of Scis. of USSR, Novosibirsk, Russia, 1979—80; assoc. prof. Tech. U. Munich, 1980—82, Case Western Res. U., Cleve., 1982—86; aerospace technologist NASA Lewis Rsch. Ctr., 1986—89; program mgr. Office of Naval Rsch., Arlington, Va., 1989—91; dir. Bd. on Math. Scis., Nat. Rsch. Coun., Washington, 1991—94; cons. L1 Assocs., Durham, NC, 1994—; sr. program mgr. Army Rsch. Office, Research Triangle Park, 1995—. Cons. Endocardial Solutions, Inc., St. Paul, 1994—. Medical engring. designer: engring. design and coding Imaging of electrical activity on human endocardium, 1995. Avocations: skydiving, bicycling, skiing, scuba diving, windsurfing. Office: Army Rsch Office PO Box 12211 Durham NC 27709-2211

LAVES, ALAN LEONARD, lawyer; b. Austin, Tex., June 17, 1960; s. Bernard and Cecile Laves; married, 1987; 3 children. BSEE, MIT, 1982; JD with honors, U. Tex., 1985. Bar: Tex. 1985. Assoc. Akin, Gump, Strauss, Hauer & Feld, LLP, Dallas, 1985-94, ptnr., 1994—. Contbr. articles to profl. jours. Office: Akin Gump Strauss Hauer & Feld Ste 2100 300 W 6th St Austin TX 78701 Fax: 512-499-6290. E-mail: alaves@akingump.com.

LAVEZZI, JOHN CHARLES, art history educator, archaeologist; b. Chgo., July 7, 1940; s. Francis M. and Dorothy M. (Kopal) L. AB magna cum laude, Cath. U. Am., 1962; MA, U. Cin., 1965; postgrad., Am. Sch. Classical Studies, Athens, Greece, 1967-70; PhD, U. Chgo., 1973. Sec. of the sch. Am. Sch. Classical Studies at Athens, 1968-70; asst. prof. Sch. Art Bowling Green (Ohio) State U., 1973-80, assoc. prof., 1980—, head divsn. art history, 1998—. Sr. assoc. mem. Am. Sch. Classical Studies at Athens, 1972—, rsch. assoc. Corinth Excavations, 1972—. Contbr. articles to profl. jours. and symposia. Mem. Toledo Mus. Art. Recipient CUA Stratemeier award, 1962, Medici Circle teaching awards, 1986, 94; grantee Am. Philos. Soc., 1973. Mem. Archeol. Inst. Am., Midwest Art History Soc., Soc. for Preservation of Greek Heritage, Nat. Geog. Soc., Smithsonian Instn. Friends, Cyprus Am. Archeol. Rsch. Inst., Cath. Assn. Scientists and Engrs., Blue Key, Phi Beta Kappa (pres. chpt. 1992), Phi Alpha Theta, Delta Epsilon Sigma, Phi Eta Sigma. Roman Catholic. Office: Bowling Green State U Sch Art Bowling Green OH 43403-0211

LAVIDGE, ROBERT JAMES, marketing research executive; b. Chgo., Dec. 27, 1921; s. Arthur Wills and Mary Beatrice (James) L.; m. Margaret Mary Zwigard, June 8, 1946; children: Margaret, Kathleen, William, Lynn Elizabeth. AB, DePauw U., 1943; MBA, U. Chgo., 1947. Analyst Pepsodent div. Lever Bros., Chgo., 1947-48, new products mktg. rsch. mgr. Pepsodent div., 1948-49; asst. dir. mktg. Am. Meat Inst., 1950-51; ptnr. Elrick, Lavidge and Co., 1951-56; pres. Elrick and Lavidge, Inc., 1956-86; pres. emeritus Elrick and Lavidge, Scottsdale, Ariz., 1987—. Lectr. mktg. research, sales adminstrn. Northwestern U., 1950-80; mem. Nat. Mktg. Adv. Com., 1967-71, also exec. com.; bd. govs. Brand Names Edn. Found., 2000—. Trustee Village Western Springs, Ill., 1957-61, pres., 1973-77; trustee McCormick Theol. Sem., 1981-90, 92-96; mem. adv. council U. Chgo. Grad. Sch. Bus. Mem. Am. Mktg. Assn. (v.p. 1963-64, pres. 1966-67, trustee found. 1992—, chmn. 1992-99), Internat. Rels. Soc. (chmn. 1961-65), Internat. Trademark Assn., Econ. Club Phoenix, De Pauw U. Alumni Assn. (pres. 1967-68), Klinger Lake Club (Mich.), Paradise Valley Country Club, Phi Beta Kappa, Beta Gamma Sigma, Sigma Delta Chi. Presbyterian.

LAVIGNE, LAWRENCE NEIL, lawyer; b. Newark, June 30, 1957; s. Daniel S. and Alice M. (Melon) L.; m. Benjie Panesh, Oct. 12, 1980; children: Gabriel A., Derek N. BA, Franklin & Marshall Coll., 1979; JD, Seton Hall U., 1982. Bar: N.J. 1982, U.S. Dist. Ct. N.J. 1982, U.S. Ct. Appeals (3d cir.) 1986, U.S. Supreme Ct. 1986. N.Y. 1989. Assoc. Shanley & Fisher, P.C., Newark, 1982-83; ptnr. Hanlon & Lavigne (and predecessor firm), Edison, N.J., 1983—. Instr. Am. Inst. Paralegal Studies, Mahwah, N.J., 1985-88. Mem.: ABA (litigation sect.), Def. Rsch. Inst., Worrall F. Mountain Inn of Ct. (barrister 1991—93), Nat. Assn. Employment Attys., Somerset County Bar Assn., Somerset Bar Assn., Assn. Trial Lawyers Am., N.J. Def. Assn., Trial Attys. N.J., Middlesex County Bar Assn., N.J. Bar Assn. (product liability com.). Republican. Jewish. Avocations: tennis, music, computers. Office: Hanlon & Lavigne 523 Raritan Center Pkwy PO Box 6146 Edison NJ 08818 Fax: (732) 346-1501. E-mail: larry@hlt-law.com.

LAVIGNE, PETER MARSHALL, environmentalist, lawyer, educator; b. Laconia, N.H., Mar. 25, 1957; s. Richard Byrd and D. Jacquiline (Cobleigh) L.; m. Nancy Gaile Parent, Sept. 20, 1979; 1 child, Rhiannon Genevra Lavigne Parent. BA, Oberlin Coll., 1980; MSEL cum laude, Vt. Law Sch., 1983, JD, 1985. Bar: Mass. 1987. History tchr. Cushing Acad., Ashburnham, Mass., 1983-84; rsch. writer Environ. Law Ctr., Vt., 1985; lobbyist Vt. Natural Resources Coun., Montpelier, 1985; exec. dir. Westport (Mass.) River Watershed Alliance, 1986-88, Merrimack River Watershed Coun., West Newbury, 1988-89; environ. cons. Mass., N.H., Vt., and Oreg., 1990—; N.E. coord. Am. Rivers, Washington, 1990-92; dir. river leadership program River Network, Portland, Oreg., 1992-95, dir. spl. programs, 1995-96; dep. dir. For the Sake of the Salmon, 1996-97; pres. Watershed Cons., 1997-2001; pres., CEO Rivers Found. of the Ams., 2001—. Adj. prof. Antioch New Eng. Grad. Sch., Keene, N.H., 1991-92; mem. Portland Willamette River Task Force, 1997-99; chair adv. bd. Cascadia Times, Portland, 1995-99, Amigos Bravos, Taos, N.Mex., 1993-98; trustee Rivers Coun. Washington, Seattle, 1993-98; bd. dirs. Alaska Clean Water Alliance, 1995-98, acting pres. 1997-98; adv. bd. Glen Canyon Inst., 2000-01, bd. dirs., 2002—; Watershed adv. group Natural Resources Law Ctr. U. Colo., 1995-96; coastal resources adv. bd. Commonwealth of Mass., Boston, 1987-91; adj. assoc. prof. Portland State U., 1997—; Watershed Mgmt. Profl. program dir., Portland State U., 1999-01, sr. fellow exec. leadership inst., 2001—; pres. Cascadia Times Rsch. Fund, 1998-99. Co-author: Vermont Townscape, 1987; contbr. articles to profl. jours. Dir. Mass. League of Environ. Voters, Boston, 1988-92; mem. steering com. N.H. Rivers Campaign, 1988-92; co-founder, co-chair New England Coastal Campaign, 1988-92; EMT South Royalton (Vt.) Vol. Rescue Squad, 1982-86; dir., chairperson Vt. Emergency Med. Svcs. Dist. 8, Randolph, 1984-86; co-founder, v.p. Coalition for Buzzards Bay, Bourne, Mass., 1987; housing renewal commn. City of Oberlin, Ohio, 1980-81; mem. properties com. First Unitarian Ch., 1995. Recipient Environ. Achievement award Coalition for Buzzards Bay, 1988; land use rsch. fellow Environ. Law Ctr., Vt. Law Sch., 1984-85; Mellon found. rsch. grantee Oberlin Coll., 1980. Mem. Natural Resources Def. Coun., River Alliance of Wis., River Network, Idaho River United, League of Conservation Voters, Amigos Bravos, Glen Canyon Inst. Democrat. Unitarian-Universalist. Avocations: sea kayaking, mountaineering, woodwork, reading, photography. Home: 3714 SE 11th Ave Portland OR 97202-3724 Office: Rivers Found of Ams 3619 SE Milwaukie Ave Portland OR 97202-3858 Fax: (503) 232-2887. E-mail: watershed@igc.org.

LAVIN, BERNICE E. cosmetics executive; b. 1925; m. Leonard H. Lavin, Oct. 30, 1947; children: Scott Jay (dec.), Carol Marie, Karen Sue. Student, Northwestern U. Vice chairperson of bd., sec.- treas. Alberto-Culver Co.; dir., v.p., sec.- treas. Alberto-Culver U.S.A., Inc. Sec.-treas., dir. Alberto-Culver Internat., Inc.; sec.-treas. Sally Beauty Co., Inc. Office: Alberto-Culver Co 2525 Armitage Ave Melrose Park IL 60160-1163 E-mail: blavin@alberto.com.

LAVIN, CHARLES BLAISE, JR. association executive; b. Balt., Aug. 13, 1940; s. Charles Blaise and Dorothy (Sturla) L.; m. Eileen Donohue, Sept. 3, 1966; children— Charles, Michael, Kristine, Philip. Student, U. Balt., 1958-62, U.S. Army Sch. Mil. Intelligence, 1962. Exec. dir. New Eng. chpt. Associated Builders and Contractors, Waltham, Mass., 1968-78; exec. v.p. Am. Subcontractors Assn., Washington, 1978-81; exec. asst. to dep. sec. for housing HUD, 1981-82; exec. v.p. Nat. Assn. Plumbing, Heating and Cooling Contractors, 1982-87; exec. dir. and lobbyist Nat. Burglar and Fire Alarm Assn., and Cen. Sta. Alarm Assn., Bethesda, Md., 1987-90; realtor Prudential Preferred Properties, Laurel, 1990-95; exec. dir. Nat. Duckpin Bowling Congress, Balt., 1995-2000. Mng. dir., Spl. Olympics of Md., 1997—; trustee Assoc. Splty. Contractors, Constrn. Jurisdictional Dispute Bd., 1983-85; chmn. County Real Estate Bd., 1993-95. Vice chmn. bd. dirs., chmn. fin. com. Laurel-Beltsville Gen. Hosp. (Md.), 1982-84; mem. Budget Com. Hopkinton, Mass., 1975-77, Planning Commn., 1977-78; bd. dirs. Young Republicans Balt., 1966. Served with CIC U.S. Army, 1962-65. Mem.: Am. Soc. Assn. Execs., Greater Washington Soc. Assn. Execs. (dir.), New Eng. Soc. Assn. Execs. (pres.), West Laurel Recreational Coun. (chmn. 1994—99), Sons of Italy (pres. Laurel, Mo. chpt. 1998—), Washington Dist. Football Ofcls. Assn., D.C. Basketball Ofcls. Assn., U.S. C. of C., Internat. Assn. Basketball Ofcls., Nat. Duckpin Bowling Congress (nat. dir.), Loyal Order of Moose, KC, Am. Legion (Post 60 comdr. 1994—95, exec. com. state of Md. 1998—, comdr. Prince George County coun. 2001—, chmn. legis. com. dept. of Md.). Republican. Roman Catholic. Home: 7006 Redmiles Rd Laurel MD 20707-3244 E-mail: lavdad@erols.com.

LAVIN, DAVID, accountant, educator; b. Chgo., Mar. 28, 1944; s. Bernhard and Esther (Luber) L.; 1 child, Shana. BSc, DePaul U., 1965, MBA, 1969; PhD, U. Ill., 1974. CPA, Ill. Assoc. prof. acctg. Fla. Internat. U., Miami, 1974—. Contbr. articles to profl. jours. Pres. bd. dirs. Hillel Fla. Internat. U., 1980-81, mem. unit bd., 1980-90; mem. cmty. bd. Hillel, 1980-83, 86-89, sec. 1987-88, mem. budget com., 1982-88, v.p. unit bd., 1983-86, bd. coun. treas., 1993-96, Fla. bd. dirs. 1993-97, fin. com. 1993-97, county bd. dirs. 1997-98, personnel com.; chairperson constrn. com. Calusa PTA, 1985-86; co-chairperson Fedn. Appeal, 1985-86. Internat. Exec. Edn. grantee, 1993-94; recipient Tchg. award State of Fla., 1994, 97. Mem. Am. Acctg. Assn., Fla. Internat. U. Acctg. Assn., Beta Alpha Psi, Omicron Delta Kappa. Avocations: traveling, cooking, weightlifting. Office: Fla Internat U Ba 241 A Miami FL 33199-0001

LAVIN, LAURENCE MICHAEL, lawyer; b. Upper Darby, Pa., Apr. 27, 1940; s. Michael Joseph and Helen Clair (McGonigle) L. BS, St. Joseph's U., Phila., 1962; JD, Villanova (Pa.) U., 1965. Bar: Pa., S.C. Vol. U.S. Peace Corps, Thika, Kenya, 1966-67; atty. Community Legal Svcs., Phila., 1968-70, exec. dir., 1971-79, Palmetto Legal Svcs., Columbia, S.C., 1981-85; dir. Law Coordination Ctr., Harrisburg, Pa., 1985-88, Nat. Health Law Program, L.A., 1988—; chmn. bd. dirs. L.A. Poverty Dept. Bd. dirs., chmn. civil com. Nat. Legal Aid and Defender, Washington, 1976-78. Founding mem. Pa. Coun. to Abolish Death Penalty, Harrisburg, 1986; bd. dirs. L.A. Poverty Dept., 1996—. Mem. ABA, Pa. Bar Assn. (chmn. legal svcs. to pub. com. 1985-88). Democrat. Home: 8896 Hubbard St Culver City CA 90232 Office: Nat Health Law Program 2639 S La Cienega Blvd Los Angeles CA 90034-2675 E-mail: lavin@healthlaw.org., llavin@boop.com.

LAVIN, PHILIP TODD, biostatistician executive; b. Rochester, N.Y., Nov. 21, 1946; s. Albert A. and Mary (Rapkin) L.; m. Mary Ellen Saunders, Aug. 23, 1970; children: Andrew, Abby. AB, U. Rochester, 1968; PhD, Brown U., 1972. Rsch. asst. prof. Brown U., Providence, 1972-74, SUNY at Buffalo, Amherst, 1974-77; asst. prof. sch. pub. health Harvard U., Boston, 1977-83, assoc. prof. surgery, 1983—. Pres., founder Boston Biostatistics, Inc., Framingham, Mass., 1983—; dir., founder Boston Biostat Rsch. Found., Framingham, 1988—; mem. editorial bd. Drug Info. Assn., Phila., 1986-88, Anti-microbial Agents and Chemotherapy, Boston, 1987—; cons. FDA, 1983-86, spl. govt. employee, 1992—. Contbr. articles to on medicine and stats. to scholarly jours. Bd. dirs. William Graves Fund, Boston, 1989—. NSF trainee, 1968-72; grantee Nat. Cancer Inst., 1976-80, 87—, Nat. Heart, Lung, Blood Inst., 1985-89. Mem. Biometric Soc., Am. Statis. Assn., Soc. Clin. Trials, Regulatory Affairs Profl. Soc., Phi Beta Kappa. Achievements include development of statistical methods for the analysis of serial biomarker data applicable to the detection of biomarker shifts and trends over time, of natural history models for cancer; organization and management of data coordinating centers for multicenter studies of cancer, hypertension, infertility, obesity, transplantation and cholesterol reduction; research in chronic disease models; founder of leading contract research organization supporting drugs, devices and biologics for FDA approval and not-for-profit research foundation for public health research. Home: 3 Cahill Park Dr Framingham MA 01702-6105 Office: Averion Inc 4 California Ave Framingham MA 01701 E-mail: plavin@averioninc.com.

LAVINDER, GALE JUNE, medical educator, physical therapist, clinician; b. Cheverly, Md., Jan. 16, 1952; d. Pressly and Gertrude (Aderson) L.; 1 child, Marui Sandage. AS, North Va. C.C., Annandale, Va., 1977; BS, George Mason U., 1977, Old Dominion U., 1982; MA, Columbia U., 1994, postgrad., 1995—. Phys. therapy asst. Fairfax (Va.) Hosp., 1977-80; staff phys. therapist Roanoke (Va.) Meml. Hosp., 1982-84, Friendship Manor Nursing Home, 1984-86; sr. supr. phys. therapy Lewis Gale Med. Ctr., 1986-91; staff phys. therapist, trainee The Shield Inst., Bronx, N.Y., 1991-93, JFK Med. Ctr., Edison, N.J., 1993-94, Vols. Am., Bronx, 1994-95; adj. faculty L.I., Bklyn., 1995; asst. prof. phys. therapy U. Medicine and Dentistry of N.J., Newark, 1995—2001; phys. therapist Easter Seals Va., Salem, 2002—. Mem. Am. Phys. Therapy Assn. Democrat. Avocations: hiking, pottery, cooking. Home: 1131 Winona Ave Roanoke VA 24015 Office: Easter Seals Va 201 S Main St Salem VA 24153-3001 E-mail: glavinder@earthlink.net.

LAVINE, ALAN, columnist, writer; b. Sharon, Pa., Feb. 17, 1948; s. Milton and Doris (Helfman) L.; m. Gail Jeanne Liberman, Dec. 20, 1991. BA, Kent State U., 1970; MA, U. Akron, 1973; MBA, Clark U., 1981. Dir. of rsch. Donoghue Orgn., Holliston, Mass., 1981-83; nat. syndicated fin. columnist, 1983—; columnist Am. Online and CNBC.com, 1995. Presenter papers in field ann. meeting AAAS, 1972, ann. meeting Mass. Psychol. Assn., Wellesley, 1978, ann. meeting APA, 1979, Nat. Symposium on Rsch. in Art, U. Ill., 1980; guest lectr. Cornell U., 1990, 91, 92, 93. Author: Diversify: Investor's Guide to Asset Allocation Strategies, 1990 (alt. selection Fortune Book Club), Your Life Insurance Options, 1993 (endorsed Inst. CFPs), Improving Your Credit and Reducing Your Debt, 1994 (endorsed Inst. CFPs), Getting Started in Mutual Funds, 1994, Diversify Your Way to Wealth, 1994 (alt. selection Fortune Book Club), 50 Ways to Mutual Fund Profits, 1995, The Complete Idiot's Guide to Making Money with Mutual Funds, 1996, Love, Marriage and Money, 1998, Rags To Riches: Motivationing Stories of Ordinary People Who Achieved Extraordinary Wealth, 2000, Short and Simple Guide to Life Insurance, 2000, More Rags to Riches: All New Stories of Ordinary People Who Achieved Extraordinary Wealth, 2002; contbr. articles to profl. jours. Mem. Nat. Writers Union, Soc. Am. Bus. Editors and Writers, Inc. Office: Alan Lavine Inc PO Box 14697 North Palm Beach FL 33408 Home: PO Box 14697 North Palm Beach FL 33408-0697 E-mail: mwliblav@aol.com.

LAVINE, HENRY WOLFE, lawyer; b. Phila., Apr. 21, 1936; s. Samuel Phillips and Sarah Pamela (Leese) L.; m. Meta Landreth Doak, Feb. 20, 1960 (div. Feb. 1980); children: Lisa, Lindsay; m. Martha Putnam Cathcart; children: Samuel Putnam, Gwenn Cathcart. BA, U. Pa., 1957, JD, 1961. Assoc. Squire, Sanders & Dempsey L.L.P., Cleve., 1961-70, ptnr. Washington, 1970-85, mng. ptnr. Washington office, 1985-91, sr. mng. ptnr., 1991—. Dir. Greater Washington Bd. of Trade. Mem. The Bretton Woods Com. Mem. Met. Club. Office: Squire Sanders & Dempsey 1201 Pennsylvania Ave NW PO Box 407 Washington DC 20044-0407

LAVINE, LAWRENCE NEAL, investment banker; b. Providence, Sept. 20, 1951; s. Avery B. and Pearl (Burbil) L.; m. Pamela Ferne Selby, Jan. 3, 1981; 1 child, Jason. BS summa cum laude, Northeastern U., 1974; MBA with highest distinction, Harvard U., 1976. V.p. Kidder, Peabody & Co. Inc., N.Y.C., 1976-87; mng. dir. Donaldson, Lufkin & Jenrette, 1987-2000, Credit Suisse First Boston, 2000—. Mem. Harvard Club of N.Y., Harvard Bus. Sch. Club of N.Y., Sunningdale Country Club, Beaver Creek Club, Confrérie des Chevaliers du Tastevin. Avocations: tennis, golf, skiing. Office: Credit Suisse First Boston 11 Madison Ave New York NY 10010 E-mail: larry.lavine@csfb.com.

LAVINE, RICHARD IRA, legislative analyst; b. Worcester, Mass., Nov. 25, 1947; s. Hyman and Dorothy Anne (Poplin) L.; m. Catherine Marie Sims, Jan. 18, 1979; children: Max Sims, Abby Sims. BA magna cum laude, Harvard Coll., 1969; postgrad., Harvard Law Sch., 1971-72; JD cum laude, U. Pa. Law Sch., 1975. Bar: Pa. 1975, Tex. 1980; CFA. Jud. clk. Hon. Paul A. Chalfin, Ct. of Common Pleas, Phila., 1975-76; staff atty. Defender Assn. of Phila., Pa., 1977-79; sr. rschr. House Rsch. Orgn., Austin, 1984-94; fin. analyst Ctr. for Pub. Policy Priorities, 1994—. Author spl. legis. reports, 1984-94; contbr. articles to profl. jours. Founder, bd. dirs. Live Oak Fund for Change, Austin, 1980-92; bd. dirs. Travis County Ctrl. Appraisal Dist., 1996—. Mem. Assn. for Investment Mgmt. and Rsch. Home: 803 Avondale Rd Austin TX 78704-2516 Office: Ctr Pub. Policy Priorities 900 Lydia St Austin TX 78702-2625 E-mail: lavine@cppp.org.

LA VINE, ROBERT L. lawyer; b. San Francisco, Dec. 24, 1929; s. Jack and Fay L.V.; m. Betty Ann La Vine, June 2, 1951; 1 child, Barbra. BS, U. Calif., 1952; JD, U. Calif. (Hastings), 1959. Bar: Calif., 1959; CPA, Calif. Ptnr. La Vine & Shain, San Francisco, 1961—. Capt. U.S. Army, 1952-54. Mem. San Francisco Bar. Assn., San Francisco Lawyers Club. Office: 5 3rd St Ste 415 San Francisco CA 94103-3205 Fax: 415-777-0222. E-mail: sfolaw@earthlink.net.

LAVINE, STEVEN DAVID, academic administrator; b. Sparta, Wis., June 7, 1947; s. Israel Harry and Harriet Hauda (Rosen) L.; m. Janet M. Sternburg, May 29, 1988. BA, Stanford U., 1969; MA, Harvard U., 1970, PhD, 1976. Asst. prof. U. Mich., Ann Arbor, 1974-81; asst. dir. arts and humanities Rockefeller Found., N.Y.C., 1983-86, assoc. dir. arts and humanities, 1986-88; pres. Calif. Inst. Arts, Valencia, 1988—. Cons. Wexner Found., Columbus, Ohio, 1986-87; selection panelist Input TV Screening Conf., Montreal, Can., and Granda, Spain, 1985-86; cons.; faculty chair Salzburg Seminar on Mus., 1989; co-dir. Arts and Govt. Program, The Am. Assembly, 1991; mem. arch. selection jury L.A. Cathedral, 1996, Arch. L.A., 1998-2001; adv. com. The Asia Soc., So. Calif. Ctr., 1998-; co-chair Blue Ribbon Com. on Arts Edn., Los Angeles Unified Sch. Dist., 1997-; vis. com. J. Paul Getty Mus., 1990-1997. Editor: The Hopwood Anthology, 1981, Exhibiting Cultures, 1991, Museums and Communities, 1992. Bd. dirs. Sta. KCRW-FM (NPR), KCET-Pub. TV, L.A. Philharm. Assn., Endowments, Inc.; Cotsen Family Found. Recipient Class of 1923 award, 1979, Faculty Recognition award, 1980 U. Mich.; Charles Dexter traveling fellow Harvard U., 1972, Ford fellow, 1969-74. Jewish. Office: Calif Inst Arts Office Pres 24700 McBean Pkwy Santa Clarita CA 91355-2397

LAVINE, THELMA ZENO, philosophy educator; b. Boston; d. Samuel Alexander and Augusta Ann (Pearlman) L.; m. Jerome J. Sachs, Mar. 31, 1944; 1 child, Margaret Vera. AB, Radcliffe Coll., 1936; A.M., Harvard U., 1937, PhD, 1939. Instr. Wells Coll., 1941-43, asst. prof., 1945-46; asst. prof. philosophy Bklyn. Coll., 1946-51; asst. prof. U. Md., 1955-57, assoc. prof., 1957-62, prof., 1962-65; Elton prof. George Washington U., 1965-85, chmn. dept., 1969-77; Clarence J.Robinson Univ. prof. George Mason U., Fairfax, Va., 1985—. Lectr., seminar cons. Inter-Am. Def. Coll., 1975—; exec. bd. Jour. of Speculative Philosophy, 2000—. Author: From Socrates to Sartre, 1980, From Socrates to Sartre: The Philosophic Quest, 1984; co-author: introduction to Collected Works of John Dewey, Vol. 16, 1990, contbg. author: Rorty and Pragmatism, 1996, contbg. author: Perspectives on Habermas, 2000, contbg. editor: Free Inquiry, 1980—, exec. bd.: Jour. of Speculative Philosophy, 2000—; contbr. ; author: (TV course) From Socrates to Sartre: The Philosophic Quest, 1984; co-author: introduction to Collected Works of John Dewey, Vol. 16, 1990, contbg. author: Rorty and Pragmatism, 1996, contbg. author: Perspectives on Habermas, 2000, mem. exec. bd.: Jour. Speculative Philosophy, 2000—; contbr. articles to profl. jours., revs., chpts. to books. Recipient Outstanding Faculty award U. Md., 1965, Outstanding Faculty award George Washington U., 1968, Alumnae Achievement award Radcliffe Coll., 1991; NEH sr. rsch fellow, 1980; Am. Enterprise Inst. Public Policy Research fellow, 1980-81, Va. Found. Humanities fellow, 1990; Herbert W. Schneider award contbns. to Am. Philosophy, 2000. Mem. Am. Philos. Assn. (5th Ann. Romanell lectr. 1991), Soc. Advancement Am. Philosophy (exec. com. 1979-82, pres. 1992-94), Internat. Soc. Sociology Knowledge, Internat. Soc. Polit. Psychology, Metaphys. Soc. Am., Washington Philosophy Club (pres. 1967-68), Washington Sch. Psychiatry, Forum Psychiatry and Humanities (exec. bd.), Cosmos Club, Harvard Club, SOPHIA, Phi Beta Kappa (pres. chpt. 1978-80). Home: 1625 35th St NW Washington DC 20007-2316 Office: George Mason U Robinsons Profs E 207 Fairfax VA 22030 E-mail: tzlavine@erols.com.

LAVINGTON, MICHAEL RICHARD, venture capital company executive; b. Purley, Surrey, Eng., Feb. 21, 1943; came to U.S., 1972; s. Richard H. and Patricia (Young) L.; m. June Watford, Aug. 13, 1966; children: Susan, Victoria. BA, Cambridge U., 1964; MA, Columbia U., 1965; PhD, Lancaster U., (Eng.), 1968. Dir. Ralli Australia, 1969-71, Bowater America, N.Y.C., 1971-74; pres. Kay Jewelers Inc., Alexandria, Va., 1974-90, Watford Investment Corp., McLean, 1990-97, Fannie Mae, Washington, 1997—. Chmn. St. Stephen's and St. Agnes Sch., Alexandria, 1981-96; trustee Ch. Schs. in Diocese of Va., 1989-96.

LAVIOLETTE, BRUCE EDWARD, industrial manufacturing management executive; b. Dover, N.H., Oct. 19, 1949; s. Henry Joseph and Lucinda Ann (de Rochmont) L.; m. Maryellen Kirkland, Oct. 11, 1981; children: Michelle, Amy. Degree in Elec. Engring., U. N.H., 1967-69; student marine engring, Maine Maritime Acad., 1971-72; BS in Sociology, SUNY, Albany, 1986, BS in Bus., 1987; MS in Mgmt., Golden Gate U., 1987; PhD in Ops. Engring. and Mgmt., Union Inst., 1993. Lic. master electrician, Maine. Lab. leader GE, Somersworth, N.H., 1969-74; nuclear electrician supr. Portsmouth (N.H.) Naval Shipyard, 1974-77; supr. elec. constrn. U.S. Naval Base, Guantanamo Bay, Cuba, 1977-78, elec. estimator and designer Cuba, 1978-82; mgr. indsl. facilities Shore Intermediate Maintenance Activity, Cuba, 1982-88; mgr. maintenance and repair Naval Aviation Depot, Cherry Point, N.C., 1988-90, head tools and property mgmt. br., 1990-91, br. head tools and indsl. planning, 1991-92, head prodn., planning and scheduling, 1993-95, head prodn., 1995-97; head bus. ops. Naval Engine Airfoil Ctr., 1997-98; dir. ISO-9000 implementation Naval Aviation Depot, 1998-99; dir. corp. ISO-9000 Naval Air Command, 1999-2000; dir. Naval Engine Airfoil Ctr., 2000—. Intern to Dr. Edwards Deming. Inventor ionization rsch.; contbr. articles to profl. jours. Dir. fins. Our Lady of Peace Ch., Berwick, Maine, 1970-75, dir. edn., 1972-77; chmn. York County Dem. Com., 1971-75, Berwick Zoning Bd., 1976; mem. Mayor's Com. for Persons with Disabilities; chief game warden U.S. Naval Base, 1977-87; grad. sr. exec. mgmt. devel. program Naval Aviation Exec. Inst.; active Meals on Wheels, Habitat for Humanity. Recipient several Meritorious Civilian Svc. awards U.S. Navy Dept., 1987, Aviation Week award for major contbn. to aviation industry Aviation Week mag., 2000, Laurel award for contbns. to aviation industry Aviation Week, 2001. Mem. Internat. Assn. Elec. Insps., Fedn. Mgrs. Assn., Soc. Am. Mil. Engrs., New Bern. C. of C., Profl. Assn., Diving Instrs. (master scuba trainer), New Bern Hist. Soc., Internat. Assn. Eagle Scouts, Cousteau Soc., East Carolina U. Ednl. Found., Federally Employed Women, Aircraft Owners and Pilots Assn., Masons. Avocations: scuba diving, flying, stamp collecting, Civil War history, college sports, travel. Home: 423 Boros Rd New Bern NC 28560-8424 Office: Naval Aviation Depot C Rm 552 Cherry Point NC 28533 E-mail: Laviotettebe@navair.navy.mil.

LA VISTA, FRANK WILLIAM, author, educator, speaker; b. Bklyn., Nov. 28, 1939; s. Frank William and Constance Edith La Vista; m. Jane Ellen La Vista, 1963 (div. May 1980); 1 child, Kirsten; m. Jacqueline Gable, June 28, 1980. BA in Applied Behavior Sci., Nat. Louis U., 1990; BA in Mgmt., Nat. Coll. of Edn., 1990. With customer svc. United Airlines, N.Y.C., 1960-68, flight ops., 1968-74, faculty mgmt. coll. Chgo., 1974-97; faculty exec. mgmt. program Northwestern U., Evanston, 1985—; pres. La Vista & Assocs. LLC, Scottsdale, Ariz., 1985—. Cons. Wunderlin Co., Louisville, 1998—, E Pluribus Maximus, N.Y., 1999—. Mem. Nat. Spkrs. Assn. Avocations: jogging, travel, reading, the arts, meditation. Home and Office: 7525 E Gainey Ranch Rd 205 Scottsdale AZ 85258-1610

LA VITA, ROBERTO, architect, art director, designer; b. Lecce, Apulia, Italy, July 23, 1950; came to U.S., 1979; s. Ugo and Jolanda (Romano) LaV.; m. Barbara Jameson, Dec. 19, 1988 (div.); children: Ananda, Giacomo; m. Maria Karagevreki. Student, U. Florence, Italy, 1978, Cappiello Acad., Florence, Italy, Ctr. for Media Arts, N.Y.C. Prin. La Vita Products, Florence, Italy, 1975-79; ptnr. Secrest and La Vita, Inc., Bethesda, Md., 1975-79; prin. La Vita Fine Arts, Inc., 1983-87, Unica Design, Bethesda, 1984-87; dir. Washington Gallery of Fine Arts, 1986-88, art dir. and graphic designer, 1987-90, art dir., mktg.-advt. cons. Italy and U.S.A., 1988-90; art dir., designer, prin. La Vita, Inc., N.Y.C., 1990—. Art dir. and graphic designer, 1987-90; art dir., mktg.-advt. cons., Italy and U.S., 1988—. Mem. Am. Inst. Graphic Arts, Am. Assn. Advt. Agys., Art Dirs. Club N.Y., The One Club. Office: 225 Lafayette St Rm 603 New York NY 10012-4015

LAVIZZO-MOUREY, RISA JUANITA, academic administrator, medical association administrator; MD, Harvard U., 1979; MBA, U. Pa., 1986. Sylvan Eismann prof. of medicine U. Pa., Phila., dir. Inst. of Aging, 1995; dep. adminstr. Agy. Healthcare Policy and Rsch., U.S. Dept. Health and Human Svcs., 1991; now sr. v.p., dir., Health Care Group Robert Wood Johnson Found. Mem. Pres.'s Commn. on Consumer Rights and Quality in the Healthcare Industry, 1997-98. Office: The Robert Wood Johnson Foundation PO Box 2316 College Road East and Route 1 Princeton NJ 08543-2316*

LAVOIE, LIONEL A. physician, medical executive; b. St. Brieux, Sask., Can., Aug. 24, 1937; s. Athanase T. and Ella Marie (Mevel) L.; m. Mary Tina Luchewski, Oct. 12, 1964; children: Robert, Michelle, Nicole, Andrea. BA, Ottawa U., Ont., Can., 1958, MD, 1964. Intern, then resident Univ. Hosp., Sask.; assoc. clin. prof. family medicine U. Sask., 1978—; chief of staff Melfort (Sask.) Union Hosp., 1985-90. Commr. Med. Care Ins. Commn., 1984-88. Chmn. Melfort Dist. Minor Sports, 1978-80, Melfort Pks. and Recreation, 1983-86, Sask. Summer Games 1988, 1986-88. Recipient Ramstead award, Jaycees of Province Sask., 1975, Dedication award, Sask. Parks, Recreation and Culture, 1988, Cmty. Recreation award, Melford C. of C., 1989, Commemorative medal, 125th Anniversary Can. Confedn., 1993, award of merit, Faculty of Medicine U. Ottawa Alumni Assn., 2001. Fellow Coll. Family Physicians (Can., cert.), ; mem. Can. Med. Assn. (bd. dirs. 1978-83, pres. elect 1989-90, pres. 1990-91), Sask. Med. Assn. (bd. dirs. 1971-76, v.p. 1974, pres. 1975), Can. Acad. Sports Medicine, Am. Geriatric Soc., Coll. Family Physicians Can. (sec. Sask. province 1967-70), Sask. Acad. Sports Medicine (pres. 1986-88), Coun. Med. Assn. (chmn. 1985-89), Sask. Paraplegic Assn. (bd. dirs. 1978—), Can. Cancer Soc. (adv. com. Sask. div. 1986—), Nat. Aerospace Med. Assn., KC (grand knight 1980-81), Rotary (pres. Melfort club 1987-88). Avocations: golf, curling, horticulture. Home: 402 Stovel E Melfort SK Canada S0E 1A0 Office: Can Med Assn 1867 Alta Vista Dr Ottawa ON Canada K1G 0G8

LAVORATO, LOUIS A. state supreme court chief justice; s. Charles Lavorato; m. Janis M. Lavorato; children: Cindy, Natalie, Anthony, Dominic. BS in Bus. Adminstrn., Drake U., 1959, JD, 1962. Judge Iowa Supreme Ct., Des Moines, 1986—; sole practice, 1962-79; judge Iowa Dist. Ct., 1979-86; justice Iowa Supreme Ct., 1986—2000, chief justice, 2000—. Office: Iowa Supreme Ct St Capitol Bldg Des Moines IA 50319-0001*

LAVORI, NORA, real estate executive, lawyer; b. S.I., N.Y., Aug. 11, 1950; d. William P. and Mary E. Lavori; div. 1990; children: Liana Sterling, Alexander O. Sterling. BA, Bryn Mawr Coll., 1971; JD, Bklyn. Law Sch., 1976. Bar: N.Y. 1977. Atty., N.Y.C., 1977—; ptnr. Orleans Realty, 1978—; officer The Culture Ctr., 1990—. Author: Living Together, Married or Single: Your Legal Rights, 1976. Mem. real estate coun. Metro. Mus. Art, N.Y.C., 1998—; trustee Bryn Mawr (Pa.) Coll., 1999—; vice-chair Columbus Ave. Bus. Improvement Dist., N.Y.C., 2000. Mem. Women's City Club N.Y. (pres. 1995-96; hon. dir.). Home: 100 W 80th St New York NY 10024

LAVU, RANA PRATAP, engineer; b. Pottipadu, India, Mar. 15, 1943; p. Venkateswara Rao and Seeta Ratnam (Pakalapati) L.; m. Nirmala Balusu, Feb. 9, 1966; children: Hemant, Navin. BSME, BVB Coll. Engring. and Tech., Hubli, India, 1962; MMS, U. Poona, Pune, India, 1977; MBA, U. Scranton, 1981; cert. profl. mgmt., James Madison U., 1984. Mfg. supt. Tata Engring. and Locomotive, Pune, 1967-77; tool engring. supr. Chrysler Tank Plant, Eynon, Pa., 1977-83; head engring. sect. Gen. Dynamics, Pomona, Calif., 1983-94; risk mgr., engring. fellow sys. engring. ctr. Raytheon Co., Tucson, 1994—. Avocation: financial and tax management. Home: 5554 E Rio Verde Vista Dr Tucson AZ 85750-6740 E-mail: rlavu@raytheon.com.

LAW, CLARENE ALTA, innkeeper, state legislator; b. Thornton, Idaho, July 22, 1933; d. Clarence Riley and Alta (Simmons) Webb; m. Franklin Kelso Meadows, Dec. 2, 1953 (div.); children: Geresa Meadows Jillson, Charisse Meadows Haws, Steven Riley; m. Creed Law, 1973. Student, Idaho State Coll., 1953. Sec., sub. tchr. Grand County Schs., Cedar City, Utah, 1954-57; UPI rep. newspaper agy. Moab, Utah Regional Papers, Salt Lake City and Denver; auditor Wort Hotel, Jackson, Wyo., 1960-62; innkeeper, CEO Elk Country Motels, Inc., 1962—; rep. Wyo. Ho. of Reps., Cheyenne, 1991—, chmn. house travel com., 1993—, past mem. bank bd. State of Wyo., 1991-98. Bd. dirs. Jackson State Bank, Snow King Resort. Chmn. sch. bd. dirs. Teton County Schs., Jackson, 1983-86; bd. dirs. Wyo. Taxpayers Assn., Bus. Coun., 1998—. Named Citizen of Yr. Jackson C. of C., 1976, 99, Bus. Person of Yr. Jackson Hole Realtors, 1987, Wyo. Small Bus. Person SBA, 1977. Mem. Wyo. Lodging and Restaurant Assn. (pres., chmn. bd. dirs. 1988-89, Big Wyo. award 1987), Soroptimists (charter), Bus. Profl. Womens Orgn. (Woman of Yr. 1975, mem. Heritage steering com. 1996—), Gov.'s 15-Mem. Bus. Coun. Republican. Mem. Lds Ch. Avocations: grandchildren, travel, study, old cars. Address: PO Box 575 Jackson WY 83001-0575 Office: Elk County Motels Inc 43 W Pearl Jackson WY 83001

LAW, DAVID HILLIS, physician; b. Milw., July 24, 1927; s. David Hillis Law III and Hazel Janice (May) Young; m. Patricia Bicking Thornton, Sept. 14, 1949; children: Linda Clark, Wendy, David, Kimberly Rankin, Cassandra. BS, Cornell U., 1950, MD, 1954. Resident in internal medicine Cornell U. Med. Coll., N.Y.C., 1954-57, fellow in gastroenterology, 1957-59; dir. personnel health services N.Y. Hosp., Cornell Med. Ctr., 1959-60; asst. prof. medicine, chief gastroenterology Vanderbilt U. Med. Coll., Nashville, 1960-69; prof., vice chmn. dept. medicine U. New Mex. Sch. Med., Albuquerque, 1969-85; chief med. services Vets. Adminstrn. Med. Ctr., 1969-85; dir. med. services Vets. Adminstrn. Cen. Office, Washington, 1985-86, dep. asst. chief med. dir. for clin. services, 1986-89, asst. chief med. dir. clin. affairs, 1989-91, acting dep. assoc. chief med. dir. for hosp.-based svcs., 1991-95, assoc. dep. chief med. dir. for clin. program, 1993-95, acting chief patient care officer, 1995-96; assoc. chief of staff for edn. Bay Pines (Fla.) Med. Ctr., 1996—2002; prof. internal medicine U. So. Fl., 1998—. Mem. human rsch. com. Los Alamos (N.Mex.) Sci. Lab., 1972-80; sabbatical dept. clin. physiology Karolinska Inst., Stockholm, 1980; bd. dirs., officer N.Mex. Nutrition Improvement Program, 1970-75; sub-com. chmn. U.S. Pharmacopeia Commn. on Revision, 1975-80. Editor, Parenteral Nutrition; mem. editorial bd., Am. Jour. Digestive Diseases, 1968-74; rev. numerous med. jours.; contbr. articles to numerous profl. jours. Bd. dirs., officer Albuquerque Friends of Music, 1975-85; mem. Nat. Digestive Disease Adv. Bd., 1989-95; mem. Interdepartmental Digestive Disease Coordinating Com.; pres. Bay Pines Edn. Found., Inc., 2001. Cpl. U.S. Army, 1945-46. Named Tchr. and Attending Physician of Yr. Dept. Medicine House Staff, 1985. Fellow ACP (gov. 1989-96); mem. AMA (lectr.), Western Assn. Physicians, Western Soc. Clin. Rsch., Am. Gastroenterol. Assn., Am. Inst. Nutrition, Alpha Omega Alpha. Republican. Presbyterian. Avocation: hot air ballooning. Office: Vets Adminstrn Med Ctr 11-B Bay Pines FL 33744 E-mail: david.law@med.va.gov.

LAW, FREDERICK MASOM, engineering educator, structural engineering firm executive; b. Newark, Mar. 8, 1934; s. Frederick T. and Evelyn (Masom) L.; m. Margaret Mary Maus, Oct. 27, 1956; children: Carolyn Jean, Frederick Masom. BS Engring., Princeton U., 1956; MS, N.J. Inst. Tech., 1962; PhD, Rutgers U., 1965. Registered profl. engr., Mass., R.I., N.Y., N.J., Pa., Fla., S.C. Structural engr. H.N.T.& B. Engrs., N.Y.C., 1956-57, 60-61, Austin Co., Roselle, N.J., 1961-63; asst. prof. engring. Newark Coll. Engring., 1963-68; assoc. prof. Pa. State U., Middletown, 1968-70; prof., chmn. dept. civil engring. U. Mass., North Dartmouth, 1970—; prin. Frederick M. Law, P.E., South Dartmouth, 1970—; pres. Timberspan Bridges Inc., 1983—. Vice chmn. Mass. Bd. Registration Profl. Engrs. and Land Surveyors, 1977-82; mem. jury Am. Inst. Steel Constrn. Prize Bridge Competition, 1982 Served to 1st lt. AUS, 1957-60, ETO. Recipient Grand Conceptor Cons. Engrs. Council Am., 1978 Fellow ASCE; mem. Nat. Soc. Profl. Engrs., Mass. Soc. Profl. Engrs. (Outstanding Engring. Achievement 1978), Am. Soc. Engring. Edn., Soaring Soc. Am. Home: 10 Swift Rd South Dartmouth MA 02748-3717 Office: U Mass Dept Civil Engring Old Westport Rd North Dartmouth MA 02747 E-mail: flaw@umassd.edu., frederickmlaw@aol.com.

LAW, GORDON THEODORE, JR. library director; b. Norwood, Mass., Oct. 27, 1945; s. Gordon Theodore and Laura (Andersen) L.; m. Pam Marilyn Baxter, Sept. 29, 1990 BA in History, SUNY, Albany, 1967, MA in Social Scis., 1968, MLS, 1972. Tchr. Mynderse Acad., Seneca Falls, N.Y., 1968-71; dir. Krannert Libr., Purdue U., West Lafayette, Ind., 1983-93; head reference and info. svcs. Catherwood Libr., Cornell U., Ithaca, N.Y., 1972-83, dir. Catherwood Libr., 1993—. Author: A Guide to Information on Closely Held Corporations, 1986; editor Indsl. and Labor Rels. Rev., 1974-83, A Guide to Sources of Information on the National Lbor Relations Board, 2002. Mem. Com. Indsl. Rels. Librs., Spl. Librs. Assn., Indsl. Rels. Rsch. Assn. Office: Cornell U Martin P Catherwood Libr 521D Ives Hall Ithaca NY 14853-3901

LAW, JOHN HAROLD, biochemistry educator; b. Cleve., Feb. 27, 1931; s. John and Katherine (Frampton) L.; m. Jeannette Ward Belcher, Nov. 9, 2000. BS, Case Inst. Tech., Cleve., 1953; PhD, U. Ill., 1957; D (hon.), U. Sofia, 1995. Fellow Harvard U., Cambridge, Mass., 1958-59, from instr. to asst. prof. biochemistry, 1960-65; instr. Northwestern U., Evanston, Ill., 1959-60; prof. U. Chgo., 1965-81, U. Ariz., Tucson, 1981-91, Regents prof., 1991—2001, Regents prof. emeritus, 2001—, chmn. dept. biochemistry, 1981-86, dir. biotech. program, 1986-92; dir. Ctr. Insect Sci., 1993-98; assoc. dean coll. agr. U. Ariz., Tucson, 1988-90. Gov. bd. Internat. Ctr. Insects, Nairobi, Kenya, 1980-87; mem. bd. trust Gordon Rsch. Conf., 1992-98, chmn., 1996; mem. coun. Am. Soc. Biochem. Molecular Biology, 1993-96. Recipient Gregor Mendel medal Czech Acad. Sci., 1992, J.E. Purkinje medal Czech Acad. Sci., 1994. Fellow AAAS, ESA (Recognition award 1999); mem. NAS, Am. Soc. Biochem. Molecula r Biology, Am. Chem. Soc., Entomol. Soc. Am. Home: 2540 E 7th St Tucson AZ 85716-4702 Office: U Ariz Dept Biochemistry Bio Scis W 342A Tucson AZ 85721-0001 E-mail: jhlaw@u.arizona.edu.

LAW, JOHN MANNING, retired lawyer; b. Chgo., Dec. 5, 1927; s. Fred Edward and Elisabeth (Emmons) L.; m. Carol Lufkin Ritter, May 14, 1955; children: John E., Lucy L., Frederick R., Beth K. Student, U. Chgo., 1944-45,

St. Ambrose Coll., 1945; BA, Colo. Coll., 1948; JD, U. Colo., 1951. Bar: Colo. 1951, Ill. 1952, U.S. Ct. Appeals (10th cir.) 1954, U.S. Supreme Ct. 1989. Atty. trust dept. Harris Bank, Chgo., 1951-52; assoc. Dickerson, Morrissey, Zarlengo & Dwyer, Denver, 1952-57; ptnr. Law, Nagel & Clark, 1958-84, Law & Knous, Denver, 1984-93; ret. Mem. law com. Colo. Bd. Law Examiners, 1971-81, Colo. Ofcls. Compensation Commn., 1985-89. Mem. Moffatt Tunnel Commn., Denver, 1966-90. Capt. USNR, 1945-77, ret. Fellow Colo. Bar Found. (charter); mem. ABA (chmn. 1975, mem. com. legal assistance to mil. pers. 1973-77), Colo. Bar Assn. (bd. govs. 1968-71), Denver Bar Assn. (trustee 1971-74), Internat. Soc. Barristers, Denver Country Club. Republican. Presbyterian. Home: 3333 E Florida Ave Unit 35 Denver CO 80210-2541 E-mail: JMLEX2@aol.com.

LAW, MARCIA ELIZABETH, counselor aide; b. Spokane, Wash., Oct. 9, 1950; d. John Glen and Jean Carolyn (Lines) L.; 1 child, Michael Sean. AA, Spokane C.C., 1973. Notary public. Data entry operator, controller CyCare Sys., Spokane, Wash., 1974-78, tape libr., 1978-79; data entry operator Wash. state Dept. Employment Security, 1986-87, Cath. Charities, Spokane, 1987, Cath. Diocese Spokane, 1987-90, Divsn. Vocat. Rehab. Dept. Health & Social Svcs., Seattle, 1990-95, sec. sr., 1994-99, counselor aide, 1999—, regional adv. com.; state internal adv. com. Stakeholders Commn. Avocations: reading, movies, cross stitch, swimming. Home: 3002 S 208th St Apt P3 Seatac WA 98198-5933 Office: 18000 International Blvd Ste 1000 Seattle WA 98188-4251 Fax: 206-439-3753. E-mail: lawm@dshs.wa.gov.

LAW, MARK EDWARD, electrical engineer, educator; b. St. Paul, July 19, 1959; s. Paul Rock and Bernice Edna (Brookshaw) L.; m. Alison Leigh Retz, May 30, 1981; children: Christopher, Heather. BS CprE, Iowa State U., 1981; MSEE, Stanford U., 1982, PhD in Elec. Engring., 1988. Engr. Hewlett Packard, 1982-84; rsch. asst. Stanford (Calif.) U., 1984-87, rsch. assoc., 1988; asst. prof. elec. engring. U. Fla., Gainesville, 1988-93, assoc. prof. elec. engring., 1993-97, prof. elec. engring., 1997—; dir. Nanosci. and Tech. Inst. Presenter, spkr. in field; session chmn. various tech. meetings in field. Author: Floods/Floops User's Manual, 1993; contbr. articles to profl. jours., chpts. to books. Recipient Young Faculty Devel. award IBM, 1988, Tech. Excellence award Semicondr. Rsch. Corp., 1993, Outstanding Young Alumnus award Iowa State U., 1994, Profl. Progress award Iowa State U., 1994; Nat. Merit scholar, 1977-81; grantee NSF, 1992—, SRC, 1989—, 93—, IBM, 1991-93; NSF Presdl. fellow, 1992. Fellow IEEE (guest editor publ. 1991, assoc. editor IEEE Transactions on Semicondr. Mfg. 1996-97, editor Jour. on Tech. Computer Aided Design 1996-02, editor Circuits and Devices Mag. 1996-98), Am. Soc. Engring. Edn., Am. Phys. Soc., Electrochem. Soc., Sigma Xi, Phi Beta Pi, Phi Kappa Phi. Avocations: soccer, golf. Office: U Fla 535 NEB Gainesville FL 32611-6130 E-mail: law@tec.ufl.edu.

LAW, MICHAEL R. lawyer; b. Rochester, N.Y., Nov. 30, 1947; s. George Robert and Elizabeth (Stoddart) L.; m. Cheryl Heller. BS, St. John Fisher Coll., 1969; JD, U. Louisville, 1975. Bar: N.Y. 1976, U.S. Supreme Ct. 1982. Assoc. Wood, P.C., Rochester, N.Y., 1976-77; pvt. practice, 1977-78; assoc. Sullivan, Peters, et al, 1978-80; ptnr., 1980-81, Phillips, Lytle, Hitchcock, Blaine & Huber, Rochester, 1982—. Served with U.S. Army, 1968—74. Mem.: ABA (trial law sect., trial techniques com., editor 1986 Trial Techniques, alternate dispute resolution com. 1995—), Genesee Valley Trial Lawyers Assn. (treas. 1992—93, pres.-elect 1993—95, pres. 1995—98), Monroe County Car Assn. (judiciary com. 1981—88, personal injury com. 1988, chmn. 1999—, profl. responsibility com. 1996—), N.Y. State Trial Lawyers (bd. dirs.), N.Y. State Bar Assn. (trial sect., ins. negligence com.), Am. Bd. Trial Advocates. Republican. Roman Catholic. Home: 3373 Elmwood Ave Rochester NY 14610-3425 Office: Phillips Lytle Et Al 1400 1st Federal Plz Rochester NY 14614-1981 E-mail: mlaw@phillipslytle.com.

LAW, ORLEY THOMAS, retired neuroscientist, poet; b. Clarksburg, W.Va., July 9, 1925; s. Orley T. Law and Genevieve Kate Roberts; m. Reinette Clark, July 15, 1976; children: Daniel Keith, Michael Brian. BA, U. Mich., 1949; MA, U. Mich, 1950, PhD, 1952. Rsch. assoc. U. Mich., Ann Arbor, Mich., 1954—59, sr. rsch. engr. minuteman guidance sys., 1959—60; prof. Claremont Graduate Sch., Claremont, Calif., 1960—75; ret., 1976. Adv. Alzheimers Assn., Grover Beach, Calif., 1998—2001; cons. in field. Author: The Long Good Night, 2001; co-author: Where Poets Gather vol. I, 1999, vol. II, 2000. Candidate Mich. State Senate, Ann Arbor, 1958. With USN, 1943—46, Pearl Harbor. Fellow, NSF, 1953—55; grantee 4 Rsch. grants, NIMH, 1960—65. Avocations: writing, eldercare, motorcycles. Office: Life Systems Development PO Box 7001 Los Osos CA 93402 E-mail: slopoet@aol.com.

LAW, ROBERT, finance executive; b. Glenolden, Pa., July 23, 1968; s. Vincent C. and Agatha M. (Paoletti) L.; m. Jane v. Bull, June 26, 1993; children: Jonathan, Adam. BS in Accountancy, Villanova U., 1990. CPA, N.J. Sr. acct. Bowman & Co. LLP, Voorhees, N.J., 1990-96; fiscal monitor of the City of Camden State N.J. Dept. Cmty. Affairs, Trenton, 1996-97; fin. dir. City of Camden, N.J., 1997-99; CFO City of Woodbury, 2000—. Mem. AICPA, Pa. Inst. CPAs, Greater Woodbury Jaycees-Jr. C. of C. (treas. 1996-97, v.p. external 1997-98, v.p. internal 1999-2000, pres. 2001, 1st Yr. Jaycee award 1995-96). Home: 647 Santa Fe Dr Mantua NJ 08051-1345 Office: City of Woodbury Office Chief Fin Officer PO Box 180 Woodbury NJ 08096-7180

LAW, THOMAS HART, lawyer; b. Austin, Tex., July 6, 1918; s. Robert Adger and Elizabeth (Manigault) L.; m. Terese Tarlton, June 11, 1943 (div. Apr. 1956); m. Jo Ann Nelson, Dec. 17, 1960; children: Thomas Hart Jr., Debra Ann. AB, U. Tex., 1939, JD, 1942. Bar: Tex. 1942, U.S. Supreme Ct. 1950. Assoc. White, Taylor & Chandler, Austin, 1942; assoc. Thompson, Walker, Smith & Shannon, Ft. Worth, 1946-50; ptnr. Tilley, Hyder & Law, 1950-67, Stone, Tilley, Parker, Snakard, Law & Brown, Ft. Worth, 1967-71; pres. Law, Snakard, Brown & Gambill, P.C., 1971-90; of counsel Law, Snakard & Gambill, P.C., 1990—. Gen. counsel Gearhart Industries, Inc., Ft. Worth, 1960-88, Tarrant County Coll. Dist. Chmn. Leadership Ft. Worth, 1974-90; bd. regents U. Tex. System, 1975-81, vice chmn., 1979-81. Lt. USNR, 1942-46. Recipient Nat. Humanitarian award Nat. Jewish Hosp./Nat. Asthma Ctr., 1983; named Outstanding Young Man, City of Ft. Worth, 1950, Outstanding Alumnus, Coll. of Humanities, U. Tex., 1977, Outstanding Citizen, City of Ft. Worth, 1984, Bus. Exec. of Yr., City of Ft. Worth, 1987, Blackstone award for contbns. field of law Ft. Worth Bar Assn., 1990, Disting. Alumnus U. Tex., 1992. Fellow Am. Bar Found., Tex. Bar Found., Am. Coll. Probate Counsel, Tarrant County Bar Found. (founding chmn.); mem. Ft. Worth C. of C. (pres. 1972), Mortar Bd., Phi Beta Kappa, Omicron Delta Kappa, Pi Sigma Alpha, Delta Sigma Rho, Phi Eta Sigma, Delta Tau Delta. Clubs: Ft. Worth (bd. govs. 1984-90), Century II (bd. govs. to 1985), River Crest Country, Exchange (pres. 1972), Steeplechase. Lodges: Rotary (local club pres. 1960). Democrat. Presbyterian. Avocation: numismatics. Home: 6741 Brants Ln Fort Worth TX 76116-7201 Office: Law Snakard & Gambill 1600 W 7th St Ste 500 Fort Worth TX 76102-2598 E-mail: tlaw@lawsnakard.com., jnlent@juno.com.

LAW, THOMAS MELVIN, college president; b. Bristol, Va., Sept. 23, 1925; s. Thomas Keen and Rebecca Ellen (Davis) L; m. Katherine Iris Tillar, Oct. 14, 1954; 1 child, Thomas Fenimore. BS summa cum laude, St. Paul's Coll., 1950, LHD (hon.), 1982; MA, NYU, 1953; EdD, Cornell U., 1962; LHD (hon.), Cuttington U., Liberia, 2001. Dean., prof. St. Paul's Coll., Lawrenceville, Va., 1967-69, pres., trustee, 1989—; v.p. acad. affairs Washington Tech. Inst., 1969-71; pres. Penn Valley Community Coll., Kansas City, Mo., 1971-76, Va. State U., Petersburg, 1976-82; dep. to chancellor spl. programs SUNY, Albany, 1982-86, dep. to chancellor for CC, 1986, assoc. vice chancellor contracts/purchasing, 1986-89, pres., 1989—2001; pres. emeritus St. Paul's Coll. Bd. dirs. Nat. Alumni Assn, Sch. of Human Ecology, Cornell U.; mem. Cornell U. Coun. Bd. dirs. Brunswick County C. of C., Lawrenceville, 1990—, Va. C. of C., Brunswick County Indsl. Devel. Authority, 1994-2002, A.L. Philpott Mfg. Extension Partnership1994-2002; life mem. NAACP; mem. commn. black mins. Union Black Episcs., Inc., by-laws com. United Negro Coll. Fund, Inc. Sgt. U.S. Army, 1942-46. Mem. Am. Assn. for Higher Edn., Nat. Assn. Ind. Colls. and Univs. (commn. campus concerns), Coun. of Ind. Colleges in Va. (exec. com.), Assn. Va. Colleges and Universities (exec com.), Am. Coun. on Edn. (commn. on leadership), Rotary, Phi Delta Kappa. Address: 117 Scrimshaw Dr Chester VA 23836-1200

LAWARE, JOHN PATRICK, retired banker, federal official; b. Columbus, Wis., Feb. 20, 1928; s. John Henry and Ruth (Powles) L.; m. Margery Ann Ninabuck, Dec. 22, 1952; children: John Kevin, Margaret Ann. BA in biology, Harvard U., 1950, grad. Advanced Mgmt. Program, 1975; MA in Polit. Sci., U. Pa., 1951; LHD (hon.), Suffolk U.; D in Polit. Sci. (hon.), Northeastern U. Trainee Chem. Bank & Trust Co., N.Y.C., 1953-54, with credit dept., 1954-56, asst. sec., 1957-60, asst. v.p., 1960-62, v.p., 1962-65, v.p. in charge of mktg. divsn., 1965-68, sr. v.p., 1968-72; sr. v.p. in charge holding co. ops. Chem. N.Y. Corp., 1972-78; pres., dir. Shawmut Corp., 1978-80, Shawmut Bank of Boston N.A., 1978-80, chmn., dir., CEO, 1980-88. Pres., dir. Shawmut Assn. Inc., 1978-80; chmn., CEO Shawmut Bank Boston, 1980-88; mem. bd. govs. FRS, Washington, 1988-95, ret., 1995; pres., dir. Devonshire Fin. Svc. Corp., 1978-88; chmn., treas. Boston Clearing House Assn. Inc., Shawmut Corp. subs.; mem. Internat. Fin. conf.; chmn. Mass. Bankers Assn., 1982-83, Assn. Bank Holding Cos., 1981-88; bd. dirs. Liberty Mut. Ins. Co., mem. compensation com.; adv. dir. Stewart Info. Sys. Corp., 1995-2001, dir., 2001-. Trustee, vice chmn., chmn. fin. com. Northeastern U., 1981-88; trustee, mem. fin. com. Mt. Holyoke Coll., 1984-88; chmn. Children's Hosp. Med. Ctr., 1989-91; past chmn., bd. dirs. Mass. Bus. Roundtable; chmn. coord. com. Boston Bus. Leaders Orgn.; past chmn. bd. trustees Ctr. Blood Rsch., Boston; past chmn. bd. dirs. Alliance for Commonwealth, Boston. Recipient Disting. Citizen award Minuteman Coun. Boy Scouts Am., Chief Exec. Officer of Yr. award Northeastern U. Coll. Bus., Outstanding Citizen award B'nai B'rith-Antidefamation League. Mem. Assn. Bank Holding Cos. (past chmn., dir.). Office: PO Box 30083 Sea Island GA 31561-0083

LAWBER, HAROLD ERNEST, JR. economist, educator; b. Tampa, Fla., Mar. 8, 1950; s. Harold Ernest and Virginia (Gustafson) L.; m. Katherine Margaret Leary, June 9, 1990; children: Matthew Christopher, Christian Philip, Christina. BA, N.C. State U., 1972, M in Econs., 1974; PhD, U. Conn., 1990. Asst. mgr. trainer Liberty Loans, Belmont, N.C., 1974-75; instr. econs. Belmont Abbey Coll., 1975-77, U. Conn., Storrs, 1985-86, Trinity Coll., Hartford, Conn., 1986-87, Salve Regina U., Newport, R.I., 1988-90, asst. prof. econs., 1990-92, assoc. prof. econs., 1993—, dir. MBA in global bus. and fin. program, 1990-94; chair dept. econ., 1994-97. Mem. Am. Econs. Assn., Econ. History Assn., History Econs. Soc., Omicron Delta Epsilon. Methodist. Avocations: numismatics, travel, sports, reading. Home: 150 Atlantic Dr Middletown RI 02842-7206 Office: Salve Regina U Ochre Point Ave Newport RI 02840

LAWER, BETSY, banker; b. Anchorage, July 27, 1949; d. Daniel H. and Betti Jane Cuddy; m. David A. Lawer, June 9, 1972; 1 child. Vice chair bd., COO 1st Nat. Bank Alaska, 1974—. Emeritus bd. dirs. Providence Health Care Found., 2001; shareholder Folie Deux Winery; bd. dirs. Seattle br. 12th Dist. Fed. Res. Bank; bd. dirs. Commonwealth North. Co-chmn. United Way. Selected as one of the Top 25 Most Powerful Alaskans Alaska Jour. of Commerce, 2000; recipient Athena award Anchorage Athena Soc. Mem.: Anchorage Athena Soc. (Athena award).

LAWHON, JOHN E., III, lawyer, former county official; b. Denton, Tex., Dec. 14, 1934; s. John E. and Gladys (Barns) L.; m. Tommie Collins, Aug. 27, 1967; 1 son, David Collins. Student, U. N.Tex., 1951-53; BBA, JD, U. Houston, 1958. Bar: Tex. 1958; cert. specialist in estate and probate law, family law. Asst. dist. and county atty., Denton County, Tex., 1958-61; dist. and county atty., 1961-77; dir. Southridge, Inc., Denton, 1962-72, Lawyers Title Agy. Denton, 1965-74; Legal adviser Denton City-County Day Nursery, 1972-80; tchr. bus. law U. North Tex. (formerly North Tex. State U.), Denton, 1969-71; mem. adv. bd. Tex. Criminal Justice Council, 1973-79; univ. atty. Tex. Woman's U., 1977-83, gen. counsel, 1983—, sec. bd. regents, 1987—. Bd. dirs. Denton County Welfare Coun., 1970-78, Denton Community Coun., 1978-79, 80-82; mem. Denton Forum; chmn. Denton County ARC, 1985-87, Denton County Probation Adv. Bd., 1985-92; mem. City of Denton Land Use Com., 1986-88. Mem. Tex. Bar Assn., Denton Bar Assn. (pres. 1968-69, bd. dirs. 1978-81), Tex. Dist. and County Attys. Assn. (bd. dirs. 1964-66), Denton Jaycees (sec. 1961), Denton C. of C., Tex. Assn. State Univ. Attys. (pres. 1983-84, Denton County crim. justice task force 1992-93, state bar coll. fellow 1995—). Baptist (deacon 1968—). Lodges: KP, Kiwanis (bd. dirs. 1981-86, pres. 1984-85). Home: 2810 Carmel St Denton TX 76205-8310 Office: Tex Woman's U Adminstrn Tower Bldg PO Box 44 Denton TX 76202-0044

LAWHORN, MICHAEL RAY, police administrator, security consultant; b. Cin., Oct. 14, 1945; s. John William and Harriet (Baker) L.; m. Kathleen E. Renner, May 1968 (div. Jan. 1984); 1 child, Lisa; m. Carol Wells, Jan. 19, 1985. Student Middletown Bus. Coll., 1975, Clark Tech. Coll., 1975, Ohio State Patrol Acad., 1976. Chief of police Monroe Div. of Police, Ohio, 1977—; exec. v.p. SCS Security Profsl., Springboro, Ohio, 1986—. Served with USMC, 1965-67, Vietnam. Decorated Meritoris Mast. Mem. Miami Valley Police Assn. (pres. 1972), Internat. Assn. Police Chiefs, Nat. Chiefs of Police Assn., Butler County Chiefs Assn., Am. Soc. Indsl. Security (cert. protection profl.). Avocations: music, racquetball. Home: 7310 Michael Rd Middletown OH 45042-1440

LAWI, DAVID STEVEN, energy, oil and gas, entertainment, agriservice and thermoplastic resins industries executive, merchant banker; b. Baghdad, Iraq, Aug. 3, 1935; came to U.S., 1946, naturalized, 1952; s. Steven David and Marcelle (Masry) L.; m. Anne Shamash, June 9, 1968; children— Nicole, Neil. AA in Sci, N.Y. State Coll., 1955. Registered rep. domestic and fgn. arbitrage Bear, Stearns & Co., N.Y.C., 1956-62; dir. Adobe Brick & Supply, West Palm Beach, Fla., 1962-64; v.p. Molly Corp., Reading, Pa., 1962-64; gen. mgr. United Shoe Machinery Corp., 1964-65; a founder, sec., treas., mem. exec. com., dir. Unimax Group Inc. (formerly Riker-Maxson Corp. ASE), N.Y.C., 1966-80; also dir. all subs., v.p., treas. Telepictures Corp. ASE, 1980-81; chmn. fin. com., sec. Telepictures Corp., 1980-86; exec. v.p., sec. Helm Capital Group, Inc. (ASE), Greenwich, Conn., 1980—; founder, chmn. exec. com., also bd. dirs. Helm Capital Group, Inc. Founder, bd. dirs., sec. Teletrak Advanced Tech. Sys., Inc., 1983—, Continuing Care Assocs., 1982—; sec., bd. dirs., founder, chmn. exec. com. Seitel Inc. (NYSE; formerly Seismic Enterprises, Inc.), 1982-84, now bd. dirs.; advisor Lorimar-Telepictures (acquired by Warner Comm., Inc. 1989/NYSE), 1986, now Time-Warner/NYSE, 1990—; founder, bd. dirs., chmn. exec. com. Intersys., Inc. (ASE; formerly Bamberger Polymers, Inc.), Unipix Entertainment, Inc. (EquiFin, Inc., formerly ASE; formerly Majestic Entertainment, Inc.), Cliff Engle Ltd., Unapix Entertainment Inc. Served with AUS, 1968. Home: Ramapo Trail Harrison NY 10528 Office: Seitel Inc 537 Steamboat Rd Greenwich CT 06830-7153

LAWING, JIM L. attorney; b. Oklahoma City, Feb. 19, 1937; s. Oscar Mitchell and Clara Hattie (Williams) L.; m. Karlin Church, Jan. 24, 1964 (div. Dec. 1979); children: Keith Lawing, Kirsten Spinelli, Chris Lawing; m. Mary Ann, Sept. 2, 1989; children: Jeff Harper, Jennifer Harper, Curry Harper, Gretchen Flatan, Anne Payne, Andy Newlan. BS, Northeastern State U., Okla., 1959; JD, U. Kans., 1965. Bar: Kans. Atty., Wichita, Kans., 1965—. State rep. Kans. House Reps., 1975-76; chmn. Sedgwick County Dem. Party, Kans., 1993-96; lay reader St. Stephen's Episcopal Ch., 1997—. Democrat. Episcopalian. Office: 200 E 1st St N Wichita KS 67202-2111 E-mail: j.lawing@inetmail.att.net.

LAWLER, JAMES EDWARD, physics educator; b. St. Louis, June 29, 1951; s. James Austin and Dolores Catherine Lawler; m. Katherine Ann Moffatt, July 21, 1973; children: Emily Christine, Katie Marie. BS in Physics summa cum laude, U. Mo., Rolla, 1973; MS in Physics, U. Wis., 1974, PhD in Physics, 1978. Rsch. assoc. Stanford (Calif.) U., 1978-80; asst. prof. U. Wis., Madison, 1980-85, assoc. prof., 1985-89, prof., 1989—, Arthur & Aurelia Schawlow prof., 1999—. Product devel. cons. Nat. Rsch. Group, Inc., Madison, 1977-78; cons. GE, Schenectady, N.Y., 1985-96, Teltech, Inc., 1990—; exec. com. Gaseous Electronics Conf., 1987-89, treas., 1992-94, DAMOP program com., 1993-95. Editor: (with R.S. Stewart) Optogalvanic Spectroscopy, 1991; contbr. articles to profl. jours. Recipient Penning award Internat. Conf. on Phenomena in Ionized Gases, 1995; Schumberger scholar U. Mo., 1971-72; grad. fellow U. Wis. Alumni Rsch. Found., 1973-74, NSF, 1974-76, H.I. Romnes faculty fellow U. Wis., 1987. Fellow Am. Phys. Soc. (Will Allis prize 1992), Optical Soc. Am.; mem. Sigma Xi. Achievements include patent for Echelle Sine Bar for dye laser cavity; development of laser diagnostics for glow discharge plasmas, of methods for measuring accurate atomic transition probabilities and radiative lifetimes. Office: U Wis Dept Physics 1150 University Ave Madison WI 53706-1302

LAWLER, JENNIFER L. writer, martial arts instructor; b. Silver Spring, Md., Mar. 2, 1965; d. Yvonne A. (Dixon) Lawler, Thomas J. Lawler; m. Bret D. Kay (div. Jan. 23, 2001); children: Jessica Lawler Kay. PhD, U. Kans., 1996. Black belt Am. Black Belt Assn. Author: (book) The Martial Arts Encyclopedia, 1996, Songs of Life: The Meaning of Country Music, 1996, Martial Arts for Women, 1998, Secrets of Tae Kwon Do, 1999, Coaching Women in the Martial Arts, 1999, Small Business Ownership for Creative People, 2000, Tae Kwon Do for Women, 2001, Encyclopedia of Women in the Middle Ages, 2001, Martial Arts for Dummies, 2002. Mem.: NOW, ACLU, Authors Guild, Korean Martial Arts Instr. Assoc., Assn. Women Martial Arts Instr., Nat. Women's Martial Arts Fedn. Office: PO Box 3724 Lawrence KS 66046 Personal E-mail: jennifer@jenniferlawler.com.

LAWLER, MARITA A. addiction therapist; b. Albany, Calif., July 14, 1947; d. Albert J. and Bonnie Davilla; m. David G. Lawler, June 2, 1990; children: Christopher, Jessica, David Quaschnick II, Trualy Quaschnick, Joshua, Roxann. BS of Human Svcs., Thomas Edison State Coll., 1998; MSc of Human Svcs., Capella U., 2000, postgrad., 1999—. Diplomate Am. Coll. Profl. Mental Health Practitioners; internat. cert. alcohol and drug counselor; nat. cert. master addictions counselor Nat. Bd. Add; nat. cert. criminal justice specialist endorsement; registered addiction specialist Breining Inst.; cert. relapse prevention specialist CENAPS Corp.; cert. chem. dependency counselor II, Alaska; cert. alcohol and drug counselor, Calif. Lead substance abuse counselor and program developer Lassen County, Susanville, Calif., 1988-1990; lead substance abuse counselor MODOC County Alcohol and Drug Dept., Alturas, 1990-91; clin. counselor Youth and Family Svcs., 1991-94; substance abuse counselor Sundown M Ranch, Selah, WAsh., 1994-95; substance abuse counselor, tng. supr. Barth & Assocs. Clinic, Yakima, Wash., 1996; cons.-owner Lawler Consulting, Alturas, 1996-98; clin. chem. dependency counselor MatSu Recovery Ctr., Wasilla, Alaska, 1998-2000; CEO, therapist, cons. Lawler Consulting, Palmer, 2000—. Bd. dirs. Calif. Conf. on Alcohol Problems, Sacramento, Calif., 1989-91; cons. Calif. Dept. Corrections, Susanville, Calif., 1989-91, Modoc County Mental Health, Alcohol & Drug Svcs., Alturas, 1996-98. Actor: (theatrical prodns.) Brigadoon, 1998, A Mid-Summer Nights Dream, 1998; singer: (theatrical prodn.) HMS Pinafore, 1997; contbr. poetry to Anthology of Poetry, 1997. Chair worship com. St. Bartholomew's Episcopal Ch., Palmer, Alaska, 2000—02. Mem. APA, Internat. Assn. Addictions and Offenders Counselors, Am. Counseling Assn., Nat. Bd. Addiction Examiners, Nat. Assn. Alcoholism and Drug Abuse Counselors. Episcopalian. Avocations: reading, camping, rock and fossil hunting, travel, lifelong learning. Home: Ste 3 PMB #352 1150 S Colony Way Palmer AK 99645-6967 Office: Lawler Consulting c/o St Bartholomew's Episcopal Church 323 N Alaska St Palmer AK 99645 Home Fax: (907) 746-2926. E-mail: marita_lawler@hotmail.com., marita.ms@psychotherapist.com.

LAWLER, THOMAS ALBERT, lawyer; b. Eldora, Iowa, June 10, 1946; s. Lewis W. and Mary C. (Schafer) L.; m. Elaine E. Bruch, June 29, 1968; children: Erin Elizabeth, Loretta Mary. BA, St. Ambrose U., 1968; JD, Cath. U. Am., 1971. Bar: Iowa 1972, U.S. Dist. Ct. (no. and so. dists.) Iowa 1974, U.S. Tax Ct. 1985, U.S. Supreme Ct., 1990, U.S. Ct. Appeals (10th cir.) 1998. Pvt. practice, Greene, Iowa, 1972-73; atty., asst. to acct. O's Gold Seed Co., Parkersburg, 1972-73; ptnr. Klinkenborg, Lawler, Hansmann & Mansheim, 1973-85; pvt. practice, 1985-97; mem. Lawler & Swanson, P.L.C., 1997—. Lectr. on taxation and fin. planning for agr. at State Agrl. Acad., Nizhni, Nougorod, Russia, 1995. Author: Iowa Legal Forms, Probate, 1991, Income Tax Consequences of Real Estate Leasing, 1995; contbr. articles to profl. jours. Atty. City of Parkersburg, 1973-91, City of New Hartford, Iowa, 1973—, City of Stout, Iowa, 1973-91, City of Aredale, Iowa, 1981—, Parkersburg Hist. Soc., 1973—; active Parkersburg Econ. Devel. Fellow Iowa State Bar Assn. Found. (v.p.), Am. Coll. Trust and Estate Coun.; mem. ABA, Iowa Bar Assn. (bd. govs., chair agrl. law sect.), Am. Agrl. Law Assn. (past pres.), Butler County Bar Assn., 2A Bar Assn., Parkersburg C. of C. (pres. 1979-80, Citizen of Yr. 1983), Rotary. Democrat. Roman Catholic. Avocations: gardening, reading, woodworking. Office: 601 Coates St Parkersburg IA 50665 Home: PO Box 280 Parkersburg IA 50665-0280 E-mail: tlawler@forbin.com.

LAWLER, THOMAS COMERFORD, protective services official; b. Cumberland, Md., Dec. 19, 1920; DHL(hon.) , St. Joseph's coll., Standish, Maine, 1974; DDiv (hon.) , Notre Dame Pontifical Catechetical Inst., Arlington, Va., 1987. Resigned CIA, 1977. Author: (book) various, including Ancient Christian Writers 15, St. Augustine: Sermons for Christmas and Epiphany, 1952; co-author (and co-editor): The Teaching of Christ: A Catholic Catechism for Adults, 1976, 4th edit., 1995; co-editor: The Catholic Catechism (now The Gift of Faith in reprint edit.), 1986, 2001. Recipient Pro Ecclesia award, Pontifice from Pope John Paul II, 2000.

LAWLER-JOHNSON, DIAN L. singer, instructor of voice, vocal technician; b. Birmingham, Ala., Oct. 29, 1951; d. William Lister Lawler Jr. and Ann Elizabeth Dismukes; m. James Goree Johnson III, July 8, 1989. Student, U. Montevallo, 1970-72; MusB in Vocal Performance, Converse Coll., 1974; MusM in Vocal Performance, U. Ill., 1976. Cert. McClosky vocal technician. Instr. voice Jacksonville (Ala.) State U., 1976-85; instr. U. Ala., Tuscaloosa, 1986-88; instr. voice and theory Carver Creative and Performing Arts Ctr., Montgomery, Ala., 1988-89; instr. voice Dunwoody (Ga.) Sch. Arts, 1989-98; pvt. studio instr. Roswell, Ga., 1989—; instr. Truett-McConnell Coll., Cleve., 1993-95, Shorter Coll., Rome, 1997—. Editor, cons.: Functional Lessons in Singing, 3d edit., 1985; operatic performance Brevard Music Ctr. Opera, 1971-73, 83, So. Regional Opera, 1977-83, Am. Inst. for Musical Studies, Graz, Austria, 1974, Goldovsky Opera Workshop, 1981. Named Outstanding Young Woman of the Yr., 1979, 81. Mem. Nat. Assn. Tchrs. Singing (membership chmn. Ga. 1976-2002), Music Tchrs. Nat. Assn., Atlanta Music Club (chmn. young performers concerts 1994-98), Alpharetta Jr. Woman's Club, Mu Phi Epsilon, Pi Kappa Lambda. Avocations: walking, yoga, Alabama football, coaching pageant contestants, reading mystery books. Home: 1180 Lea Dr Roswell GA 30076-4626

LAWLESS, JOHN JOSEPH, child/adolescent therapist; b. New Hartford, N.Y., Dec. 30, 1964; s. Robert Joseph and Carol Jean Lawless; m. Kathryn M. Ranieri; children: Connor, Aidan. BA, State U. N.Y., Binghamton, 1988—90; MS, State U. N.Y., Albany, 1990—92; PhD, U. Ga., 1993—2000. Cert. AAMFT clin. mem. 1997. Child/adolescent therapist Oneida Indian Nation, Oneida, NY, 1997—2000; faculty MCP Hahnemann U., Philadelphia, 2000—. Mem.: Nat. Coun. Family Rels. Office: MCP Hahnemann U 1505 Race St Philadelphia PA 19102 Office Fax: 215-762-6933. Personal E-mail: jlawless@drexel.edu. Business E-Mail: jlawless@drexel.edu.

LAWLESS, MICHAEL RHODES, pediatrics educator; b. Baytown, Tex., Oct. 13, 1942; s. Wallace Ervin and Amy Ruth (Broussard) L.; m. E. Sandra Johnson, Aug. 27, 1967; children: Melanie Lawless York, Stephanie Lawless Setzer. BA in Zoology, U. Tex., 1964, MD, 1968. Diplomate Am. Bd. Pediat. Intern City Memphis Hosp., 1968-69; resident in pediatrics U. Tex. Med. Br., Galveston, 1969-71; instr. U. Rochester (N.Y.), Sch. Medicine, 1971-72; staff pediatrician Portsmouth (Va.) Naval Hosp., 1972-74; asst. prof. pediatrics Wake Forest U. Sch. Medicine, Winston-Salem, N.C., 1974-80, assoc. prof. pediatrics, 1980-2001, prof. pediatrics, 2001—, dep. assoc. dean student affairs, 1988-96, chief gen. pediatrics and adolescent medicine, 1997—. Lt. comdr. USNR, 1972-74. Fellow U. Rochester, 1971-72. Fellow Am. Acad. Pediatrics (legis. liaison 1980—); mem. Am. Profl. Soc. on Abuse of Children, N.C. Pediatric Soc. (child advocate 1974—), Coun. Med. Student Edn. in Pediatrics (pres. 1998-00), Ambulatory Pediatric Assn. Avocations: tennis, hiking. Office: Wake Forest U Sch Medicine Med Ctr Blvd Winston Salem NC 27157-0001

LAWLESS, ROBERT WILLIAM, academic administrator; b. Baytown, Tex., Feb. 13, 1937; s. James Milton and Belva Ambaline (Mode) Lawless; m. Marcella Jane Emmert; children: Christopher, Cheryl, Diana. BS, U. Houston, 1964; PhD, Tex. A&M U., 1968. Instr., asst. prof. Tex. A&M U., College Station, 1967-69; prof., sr. vice chancellor U. Houston, 1969-82; v.p., CFO S.W. Airlines, Dallas, 1982-85, exec. v.p., COO, 1985-89; cons. Tex. Hosp. Assn., Austin, 1966-82, banks, savs. and loans, 1970-72, NASA, 1970; pres. Tex. Tech U. and Tex. Tech. U. Health Scis. Ctr., Lubbock, 1989-96, Univ.

Tulsa, Okla., 1996—2001. Independent dir Salomon Bros Asset Mgmt Co, 1991—2001, Central and SW Corp, 1991—2000, Williams Communications Group Inc, 2000—; chmn Coun Pub Univ Pres and Chancellors, Tex Higher Educ Sys, 1993—95; mem pres's comn NCAA, 1994—97, mem exec comt, 1998—, chmn., exec. com., 2001—, bd dirs Div I; dir Nat Asn Independent Cols and Univs, Asn Presby Cols and Univs. Contbr. articles to profl jours. Mem formula adv comt Tex State Coordinating Bd, Austin, 1977—89; chmn bd dirs Col Football Asn, 1990—92. Recipient Teaching Excellence Award, Univ Houston, 1972, Disting Alumni Award, 1990, Disting Faculty Award, Col Bus Alumni, 1971, Disting Alumni Award, Lee Col, 1984. Office: Univ of Tulsa 600 S College Ave Tulsa OK 74104-3126 E-mail: robert-lawless@utulsa.edu.

LAWLEY, ALAN, materials engineering educator; b. Birmingham, Eng., Aug. 29, 1933; s. Archibald and Millicent A. (Olorenshaw) L.; m. Nancy A. Kressler, Mar. 26, 1960; children: Carolyn Ann, Elizabeth Ann, Jennifer Ann. BSc, U. Birmingham, 1955, PhD, 1958. Research assoc. U. Pa., 1958-61; mgr. research labs. Franklin Inst. Labs., 1961-66; A.W. Grosvenor prof. materials engring. Drexel U., Phila., 1966—, head dept., 1969-79, 92-98. Cons. to govt., industry. Editor in chief Internat. Jour. Powder Metallurgy; contbr. chpts. to books, articles to profl. jours. Recipient Disting. Svc. award Metal Powder Industries Fedn., 1991. Fellow Am. Soc. Metals (life mem., gold medal recipient), APMI Internat.; mem. AIME (pres. 1987), Minerals, Metals and Materials Soc. (pres. 1982, Educator award 2002), Nat. Acad. Engring., Am. Soc. Engring. Edn., Inst. Materials, Sigma Xi, Phi Kappa Phi, Tau Beta Pi, Alpha Sigma Mu. Home: 336 Hathaway Ln Wynnewood PA 19096-1925 Office: Drexel Univ Dept Materials Engring Philadelphia PA 19104

LAWLEY, ELIZABETH, artist; b. N.Y.C., Apr. 17, 1956; d. Robert K. and Anna (Tino) L.; m. Gary Basaraba, Dec. 17, 1984; 1 child, Cale Basaraba. BFA, Cooper Union U., 1976; MFA, Yale U., 1982. Adj. Cooper Union. One-person show Beitzel & Twining, 1998; two person show at Painting Ctr., 1996, 98; exhibited in group shows Beitzel Gallery, N.Y.C., 1981-85, Twining Gallery, N.Y.C., 1982-86, Nassau County Fine Arts, 1982. Dir. homeless advocacy orgn. Hands in Outreach, Nepal, 1994-96; co-founder non-profit gallery Painting Ctr., N.Y.C., 1992—; bd. dirs. Shire Village, Mass., 1991-97; dir. children's summer cmty. program, Cummington, Mass., 1991-96. Fellow Greenshield Found., Montreal, Can., 1977, Alice Kimball English fellow Yale U., 1982.

LAWLEY, ESTHER GMINDER SMITH, mental health counselor; b. Lima, Ohio, Jan. 29, 1960; d. Albert Borden and Evelyn Maurine (Synan) Gminder; m. Victor Gerald Smith, Oct. 17, 1980 (div. Apr. 1987); 1 child, Joshua Clay; m. Wade Gunter Lawley, May 20, 1989. BS, Elizabeth City State U., 1987; MS, U. N.C., Chapel Hill, 1989. Residential asst. univ. housing U. N.C., Chapel Hill, 1980; file clk. Lipid Rsch., 1981; sec., receptionist, bookkeeper Salvation Army, Statesville, N.C., 1983; checkout cashier, stock person Chappell's Grocery, Winfall, 1984; lic. and title clk. Dept. Motor Vehicle Contracts Perquilnans County C. of C., Hertford, 1985-87; counseling intern Goodwill Industries, Durham, 1988; rehab. counseling intern AIDS case mgmt. team N.C. Meml. Hosp., Chapel Hill, 1988-89; counseling intern adult day treatment OPC Mental Health Ctr., Hillsborough, N.C., 1988-89; outpatient counselor Indian Rivers County Mental Health Ctr., Tuscaloosa, Ala., 1989-90; inpatient counselor chem. dependency/dual diagnosis program DCH Life Mgmt., 1990-98; psychiat/dual-diagnosis counselor North Harbor Psychiatric Svcs., Northport, Ala., 1998—. Vol. Albemarle Hopeline, Shelter Battered Women, Elizabeth City, N.C., 1986-87. Mem. ACA, Am. Rehab. Counseling Assn., Nat. Rehab. Assn., Ala. Alcohol and Drug Abuse Assn. (cert. masters level addiction profl., cert. clin. supr. in addictions, case presentation method examiner). Republican. Methodist. Avocations: mission work, swimming. Home: 11742 Highway 171 S Fayette AL 35555-4503 Office: North Harbor Unit Northport Hosp 2700 Hospital Dr Northport AL 35476-3360

LAWLEY, THOMAS J. dean, medical educator; b. Buffalo; MD, State U. of NY, Buffalo School of Med. Dean sch. medicine Emory U., Atlanta, 1996—, chair., dept. of dermatology, 1994—96; pres. Emory Med. Care Found.; pres. Emory Children's Research Cntr. Office: Emory U Sch Medicine Woodruff Health Scis Ctr Adminstrv Bldg 1440 Clifton Rd NE Atlanta GA 30322-1053*

LAWLIS, PATRICIA KITE, air force officer, computer consultant; b. Greensburg, Pa., May 5, 1945; d. Joseph Powell Jr. and Dorothy Theresa (Allshouse) Kite; m. John Charles Ryan, Feb. 6, 1965 (div. 1973); m. Mark Craig Lawlis, Sept. 17, 1976 (div. 1983); 1 child, Elizabeth Marie. BS in Math., East Carolina U., 1967; MS in Computer Sci., Air Force Inst. Tech., 1982; PhD in Computer Sci., Ariz. State U., 1989. Cert. secondary math. tchr. Employment counselor Pa. State Employment Svc., Washington, 1967-69; math. tchr. Fort Cherry Sch. Dist., McDonald, 1969-74; commd. 2d lt. USAF, 1974, advanced through grades to lt. col., 1994; data base mgr. Air Force Space Command, Colorado Springs, Colo., 1974-77; computer sys. analyst USAF in Europe, Birkenfeld, Germany, 1977-80; prof. computer sci. Air Force Inst. Tech., Wright-Patterson AFB, Ohio, 1982-86, 89-94; ret. USAF, 1994; computer cons., pres. C.J. Kemp Systems, Inc., Fairborn, Ohio, 1983—. Ada cons., Ada Joint Program Office, Washington, 1984-94. State treas. NOW, Pa., 1973-74. Recipient Mervin E. Gross award Air Force Inst. Tech., 1982, Prof. Ezra Kotcher award, 1985. Mem. Computer Soc. of IEEE, Assn. Computing Machinery, Tau Beta Pi (v.p. chpt. 1981-82), Upsilon Pi Epsilon. Office: CJ Kemp Systems Inc PO Box 586 Fairborn OH 45324-0586 E-mail: lawlis@aol.com.

LAWLOR, RICHARD JAMES, analyst; b. Germany, Dec. 7, 1971; s. Richard Whalen and Mary Rose L. BSBA in Acctg., Am. U., 1993, MBA in Internat. Fin., 1995. CPA, Md. Rsch. specialist Securities & Exch. Commn., Office of Inspector Gen., Washington, 1994; acct., auditor Deloitte & Touche, 1995-97; mgmt. cons. Price Waterhouse, 1997-98; analyst World Rsch. Advisory, Reston, Va., 1998—. Vol. high sch. lectr. Jr. Achievement, Washington, 1997. Mem. AICPA, Greater Washington Soc. CPAs, Md. Assn. CPAs. Republican. Roman Catholic. Avocations: skiing, mountain biking, weight-lifting, stock investments, wine tasting. Office: World Rsch Advisory 1807 Michael Faraday Ct Fl 2 Reston VA 20190-5303 E-mail: rick_lawlor@worldresearch.com.

LAWN, RICHARD JOHN, music educator; b. Darby, Pa., May 15, 1949; s. Richard Ludwig and Sara Naomi (Tarr) L.; m. Susan Barbara Yarina, Apr. 13, 1974. MusB, U. Rochester, 1971, MusM, 1976. Instr. saxophone and jazz ensemble Hartwick Coll., Oneonta, N.Y., 1971-73; dir. jazz ensemble U. Rochester, 1974, grad. teaching asst. Eastman Sch. Music, 1975-76; asst. prof., dir. jazz studies U. No. Iowa, Cedar Falls, 1978-80, U. Tex., Austin, 1980-83, assoc. prof., 1983-90, head theory and composition div., 1984-85, assoc. chmn. dept. music, 1985-89, acting chmn., 1989-90, prof., chmn., 1990-94, assoc. dean, 1994-96; dean Coll. Performing Arts The Univ. of the Arts, Phila., 2002—. Author: Jazz Ensemble Directors Manual, 1980; co-author: Jazz Theory and Practice; contbr. numerous articles on jazz to profl. jours.; composer numerous works for jazz ensemble. Recipient Outstanding Svc. to Jazz Edn. award Nat. Assn. Jazz Educators, 1978, 81, 84, 89; Nat. Endowment on Arts grantee, 1973, 88. Mem. ASCAP (Popular Music award 1989), Am. Fedn. Musicians, Phi Kappa Lambda, Phi Mu Alpha Sinfonia. Avocations: amateur radio, fishing. Home: 1021 Owl Ln Cherry Hill NJ 08003- E-mail: r.lawn@uarts.edu.

LAWN, TIMOTHY REGIS, lawyer; b. Phila., Nov. 23, 1962; s. John Joseph and Carolyn Marie (McTamney) L.; m. Arlene Patricia Lawn, Apr. 5, 1991; children: Joshua, Daniel, John, Maureen. BS in Acctg. cum laude, Spring Garden Coll., 1984; JD cum laude, Widener U., 1989. Bar: Pa. 1989, U.S. Dist. Ct. (ea. dist.) Pa. 1990. Assoc. O'Brien & Ryan, Plymouth Meeting, Pa., 1989-96; ptnr. Litvin, Blumberg, Matusow & Young, Phila., 1996—. Adj. faculty Temple Univ. Sch. Law.; instr. Nat. Inst. of Trial Advocacy. Chmn. bd. dirs. Dave Palmer Meml. Found., Phila., 1992—. Recipient Am. Jurisprudence awards (2), 1989. Mem. ATLA, ABA, Pa. Bar Assn., Phila. Bar Assn., Pa. Trial Lawyers Assn., Phila. Trial Lawyers Assn. Office: Litvin Blumberg Matusow & Young 1339 Chestnut St Fl 18 Philadelphia PA 19107-3520 E-mail: tlawn@litvin.com.

LAWNICZAK, JAMES MICHAEL, lawyer; b. Toledo, Sept. 11, 1951; m. Christine Nielsen, Dec. 31, 1979; children: Mara Katharine, Rachel Anne, Amy Elizabeth. BA, U. Mich., 1974, JD, 1977. Bar: Mich. 1977, Ill. 1979, Ohio 1989. Law clk. to the Honorable Robert E. DeMascio U.S. Dist. Ct. (ea. dist.) Mich., Detroit, 1977-79; assoc. Levy and Erens, Chgo., 1979-83; assoc. then ptnr. Mayer, Brown & Platt, 1983-88; ptnr. Calfee, Halter & Griswold, LLP, Cleve., 1988—. Contbg. author: Collier on Bankruptcy, 15th rev. edit., 1997—. Mem. Chgo. Bar Assn. (subcom. on bankruptcy 1983-88), Cleve. Bar Assn. (bankruptcy com.). Home: 14039 Fox Hollow Dr Novelty OH 44072-9773 Office: Calfee Halter & Griswold 800 Superior Ave E Ste 1400 Cleveland OH 44114-2601 E-mail: jlawniczak@calfee.com.

LAWRANCE, CHARLES HOLWAY, retired civil and sanitary engineer; b. Augusta, Maine, Dec. 25, 1920; s. Charles William and Lois Lyford (Holway) L.; m. Mary Jane Hungerford, Nov. 22, 1947; children: Kenneth A., Lois R., Robert J. BS in Pub. Health Engring., MIT, 1942; MPH, Yale U., 1952. Registered profl. engr., Calif. Sr. san. engr. Conn. State Dept. Health, Hartford, 1946-53; assoc. san. engr. Calif. Dept. Pub. Health, L.A., 1953-55; chief san. engr. Koebig & Koebig, Inc., Cons. Engrs., 1955-75; engr. mgr. Santa Barbara County Water Agy., Santa Barbara, Calif., 1975-79; prin. engr. James M. Montgomery Cons. Engrs., Pasadena, 1979-83; v.p. Lawrance, Fisk & McFarland, Inc., Santa Barbara, 1983-96; cons. engr., retired, 1996-99. Author: The Death of the Dam, 1972; co-author: Ocean Outfall Design, 1958; contbr. articles to profl. jours. Bd. dirs. Pacific Unitarian Ch., Palos Verdes Peninsula, Calif., 1956-60, chmn. bd. 1st lt. USMCR, 1942-46, PTO. Fellow ASCE (life, Norman medal 1966); mem. Am. Water Works Assn. (life), Am. Acad. Environ. Engrs. (life diplomate), Water Environment Fedn. (life). Republican. Unitarian Universalist. Home and Office: 1340 Kenwood Rd Santa Barbara CA 93109-1224 E-mail: charleslawrance@earthlink.net.

LAWRENCE, ALICE LAUFFER, artist, educator; b. Cleve., Mar. 2, 1916; d. Erwin Otis and Florence Mary (Menough) Lauffer; m. Walter Ernest Lawrence, Sept. 27, 1941 (dec. Dec. 2001); 1 child, Phillip Lauffer. Diploma in art, Cleve. Inst. Art, 1938; BS in Art Edn., Case Western Res. U., 1938. Grad. asst. in art edn. Kent (Ohio) State U., 1939-40; art tchr. Akron (Ohio) and Cleve. Pub. Schs.; comml. artist B.F. Goodrich Co., Akron, 1942-44; sub. art tchr. Akron Pub. Schs.; sketch artist numerous events Akron, 1945-91. Portrait sketch artist for various cos., including Estée Lauder, O'Neil's Dept. Store, Polsky's, Summit, Rolling Acres, Chapel Hill, Walden Books, K-Mart. Contbr. poetry to anthologies. Mem. Cuyahoga Valley Art Ctr., Women's Art Mus., Akron Art Mus., 1963-94, Rep. Nat. Com., 1998, New Rep. Nat. Fund. Recipient 2d pl. in drawing, Butler Mus. Am. Arts, 1940-41, recipient 1st pl. drawings and prints, Cleve. Mus. Art, 1944. Mem. Woman's Art League Akron (sec. 1962), Ohio Watercolor Soc., Internat. Soc. Poets (life). Republican. Avocation: writing poetry. Home: 1725 Warrington Rd NW Massillon OH 44646-2866

LAWRENCE, BARBARA, information manager; b. N.Y.C., Dec. 16, 1944; d. Seth and Aline (Greenberg) L.; m. Allen I. Laskin, July 1, 1973. BA, U. Vt., 1965; postgrad., Yale U. With Schering, 1967-69, Exxon Rsch. and Engring., 1969-79, Exxon Corp., 1979-82; divsn. dir. tech. infor. AIAA, 1982-94; sr. v.p. rsch. and editl. devel. Peterson's, 1994-98; exec. dir. Newgrange, 1998-99; cons. Laskin Lawrence Assocs., Somerset, N.J., 1999—. Trustee Alice Paul Centennial Found., 2000—, chmn. bd., 2002--; pres. NFAIS, Phila. 1988, dir. 1983-89, pres. Princeton Area NOW, 1982; dir. 51 Jane St Coop, N.Y.C., 1984—, U.S. rep. AGARD NATO, Paris, 1985-91. Mem. Am. Soc. Info. Sci., Spl. Libraries Assn. (divsn. chair). Avocations: photography, gardening. Office: Laskin Lawrence Assocs 383 S Middlebush Rd Somerset NJ 08873-5306 Fax: 732-873-8618. E-mail: barblawrence@aol.com.

LAWRENCE, BETTY TENN, lawyer; b. Memphis, Feb. 3, 1949; d. William Harvey and Margaret Amrhein Lawrence. AB, Rollins Coll., 1971; JD, Duke U., 1983. Bar: N.Y. 1984, N.C. 1986. Curator Pack Meml. Pub. Libr., Asheville, N.C., 1974-80; assoc. Davis Polk and Wardwell, N.Y.C., 1983-86; pvt. practice Asheville, 1986—. Mem. Preservation Soc. Asheville and Buncombe Co., Asheville, 1976—, v.p. 1978-80, pres. 1986-89; Commr. Hist. Resources Commn. of Asheville and Buncombe County, 1978-80, 86-92, 94—, chair, 1999. Mem. N.C. Bar Assn. Home and Office: 142 Hillside St Asheville NC 28801-1206 E-mail: btlawrence@juno.com.

LAWRENCE, BRYAN HUNT, investment banking executive; b. N.Y.C., July 26, 1942; s. Bryan and Suzanne (Walbridge) L.; m. Elizabeth D. Lawrence, Sept. 25, 1965; children: Bryan R., E. Corey. BA, Hamilton Coll., 1964; MBA, Columbia U., 1966. Assoc. Dillon, Read & Co. Inc., N.Y.C., 1966-70, v.p., 1971-74, sr. v.p., 1975-81, mng. dir., 1982-97; mem. Yorktown Ptnrs. LLC, 1997—. Bd. dirs. Vintage Petroleum, Tulsa, D & K Wholesale Drug, St. Louis, Transmontaigne Inc., Denver, Cavell Energy, Calgary, PetroSantander Inc., Houston, Hallador Petroleum, Denver, Savoy Energy L.P., Traverse City, Mich., Oklahoma City, Athanor Resources, Inc., Geneva, Carbon Energy.Denver, Camden Resources, Dallas, Crosstex Energy, Dallas, ESI Energy Svcs. Inc., Calgary. Trustee Hamilton Coll., Clinton, N.Y., 1991-94. Republican. Home: 116 E 63rd St New York NY 10021-7325 Office: Yorktown Ptnrs LLC 410 Park Ave New York NY 10022-4407

LAWRENCE, CARL NICHOLAS, entrepreneur; b. Springfield, Mass., July 26, 1954; s. JOseph Peter and Christine Norma (Provencher) L.; m. Camille O'Grady, May 23, 1980. Student, U. Mass., 1972-75, Inst. Allende, San Miguel de Allende, Guanajuato, Mex., 1974, San Francisco State U., 1997-99. Owner, operator Mobile Munchies, Truro and Foxboro, Mass., 1974-76; ptnr., jeweler Orgon Design, San Francisco, 1978-80; owner, mgr. A-Pri-Originals Design, 1985-92; owner, creative cons. A-Pri-Origins, 1997—. Author short story; reporter New Mission News, San Francisco, 1998-99; jeweler; sculptor. Contbg. writer Peaceful Streets gun-control lobbying orgn. Pell grantee Dept. Edn., 1998-99, Calif. Univ. grantee State of Calif., 1998-99; recipient Balboa Explorers award for solo crossing of Darien Gap Gringo Gap Explorers Club, 1977. Mem. Commonwealth Club Calif. Avocations: sculpture, gourmet, lapidary, camping. Office: A-Pri-Origins Ltd 3288 21st St Ste 95 San Francisco CA 94110 Fax: (415) 648-8079. E-mail: a-pri-origins1@msn.com.

LAWRENCE, CHARLES EDWARD, JR. lawyer, judge; b. Beaumont, Miss., July 29, 1955; s. Charles Edward and Mattie Mae Lawrence; m. Shirley A. Sutton, June 5, 1977; children: Charles E. III (CJ), Chari E. B, U. So. Miss., 1976; JD, Howard U., 1979. Bar: Miss. 1979. Pvt. practice atty., counselor at law, Hattiesburg, Miss., 1979—; mcpl. ct. judge City of Hattiesburg, 1997—. Bd. dirs. BancorpSouth Cmty. Adv. Coun. Contbg. columnist, 1983-85. V.p. Forrest County br. NAACP, Hattiesburg, 1980; councilmember City of Hattiesburg, 1985-97; pres. Hattiesburg City Coun., 1991-97; bd. dirs. Wesley Med. Ctr. Meth. Hosp., Hattiesburg, 1995-97, United Way, Hattiesburg, 1997—. Recipient Svc. award Optimist Internation, 1986, New Medinah Islamic Retreat, 1996. Mem. ATLA, Miss. Bar Assn., Miss. Mcpl. Judge Assn., Magnolia Bar Assn. (so. dist. rep. 1986-87). Baptist. Avocations: camping, reading, bike riding, photography. Home: 606 John St Hattiesburg MS 39401-3948 Office: 606 1/2 John St Hattiesburg MS 39401-3966 Fax: 601-544-9279.

LAWRENCE, CHRISTINE, physician; b. N.Y.C., Oct. 18, 1930; d. Winthrop Stanley and Marybelle Lawrence; m. Milford Fulop, Aug. 3, 1957; children: Michael Alain, Tamara Ann. BS, U. Mich., 1952; MD, Columbia U., 1956. Intern and resident Bronx Mcpl. Hosp. Ctr., 1956-59; fellow in hematology Albert Einstein Coll. Medicine, Bronx, 1959-61, prof. medicine, 1986—2000; dir. hematology Jacobi Med. Ctr., 1972—2000. Contbr. articles to profl. jours. including Blood, New England Jour. of Medicine, Procs. Nat. Acad. Scis., others. Recipient Humanitarian award Harlem Consumer Edn. Coun., 1983. Fellow ACP. Avocations: investing, antiques, photography. Office: Jacobi Med Ctr 1400 Pelham Pkwy S Rm 3N21 Bronx NY 10461-1138 E-mail: chrisL41@hotmail.com.

LAWRENCE, DAVID, JR. journalist, early childhood development advocate; b. N.Y.C., Mar. 5, 1942; s. David Sr. and Nancy Wemple (Bissell) L.; m. Roberta Phyllis Fleischman, Dec. 21, 1963; children: David III, Jennifer Beth, Amanda Katherine, John Benjamin, Dana Victoria BS, U. Fla., 1963; postgrad. advanced mgmt. program, Harvard U., 1983; LHD (hon.), Siena Heights Coll., Adrian, Mich., 1985; HHD (hon.), Lawrence Inst. Tech., Detroit, 1986; LHD (hon.), No. Mich. U., 1987; LD (hon.), Barry U., 1991, Fla. Meml. U., 1992, Northwood U., 1993, U. Fla., 1993, Nova Southeastern U., 1997, Colgate, 1998. Reporter, news editor St. Petersburg (Fla.) Times, 1963-67; news editor Style/Washington Post, 1967-69; mng. editor Palm Beach (Fla.) Post, 1969-71, Phila. Daily News, 1971-75; exec. editor Charlotte (N.C.) Observer, 1975-76, editor, 1976-78; exec. editor Detroit Free Press, 1978-85, pub., chmn., 1985-89, The Miami Herald, 1989-99. Disting. prof. early childhood initiative Fla. Internat. U. Chair Children's Svcs. Coun. Miami-Dade County, Miami-Dade Sch. Readiness Coalition; chair Fla. Partnership for Sch. Readiness; exec. com. Miami Art Mus. Named Disting. Alumnus, U. Fla., 1982; recipient Nat. Human Rights award Am. Jewish Com., 1986, First Amendment Freedoms award Anti-Defamation League, 1988, Ida Wells Nat. award for advancement of minorities Nat. Assn. Black Journalists and Nat. Conf. of Edit. Writers, 1988, John S. Knight Gold medal Knight-Ridder, 1988, Silver Medallion award NCCJ, 1992, Disting. Svc. award Nat. Assn. Schs. Journalism and Mass Comm., 1992, Scripps Howard First Amendment award, 1993, Nat. Assn. of Minority Media Execs. lifetime achievement award. Mem. Am. Soc. Newspaper Editors (pres. 1991-92), Inter Am. Press Assn. (pres. 1995-96), Early Childhood Initiative Found. (pres.). Office: 3250 SW Third Ave 5th Fl Miami FL 33129 E-mail: dlawrence@childreadiness.org.

LAWRENCE, DAVID M. health facility administrator; b. 1940; BA, Amherst (N.Y.) Coll., 1962, DSc (hon.) (hon.), 1994; MD, U. Ky., 1966; MPH, U. Wash., 1973; LittD (hon.) (hon.) , Colgate U., 1995. Cert. gen. preventive medicine. Intern in internal medicine, pediat.; health officer, dir. Multnomah County, Oreg.; v.p., area med. dir. N.W. Permanente Kaiser Found. Health Plan and Hosps., Portland, Maine, 1981—85, v.p., reg. mgr. Colo., 1985—88, sr. v.p., reg. mgr. NC, 1988—89, CEO Calif., 1992—2002, also vice chmn. bd. dirs., 1990—91, also chmn bd. dirs. Mem. various professorships, directorships and fellowships U. Wash., Johns Hopkins U., U. Ky.; bd. dirs. Pacific Gas and Elec. Co., Hewlett Packard, Healthcare Forum, Bay Area Coun., Calif. Coll. Arts and Crafts, Colby Coll.; trustee Rockefeller Found. Named Outstanding Alumnus of the Sch. Pub. Health and Cmty. Medicine, U. Wash., 1980, Outstanding Alumnus of the Coll. Medicine, U. Ky., 1995. Mem.: APHA, Inst. of Medicine of NAS (bd. dirs.), The Conf. Bd. (bd. dirs.), Calif. Bus. Roundtable, Western Consortium for Pub. Health, Group Health Assn. Am., Calif. Assn. Hosps. and Health Sys., Am. Coll. Preventive Medicine, Am. Hosp. Assn., Alpha Omega Alpha.*

LAWRENCE, DAVID LONG, radiologist; b. Jamestown, Ky. s. Marshall Marvin Lawrence and Opal Hilden Long; m. Jeanette Wesley, Jan. 30, 1954 (div. 1990); 1 child, Julia L.; m. Sandra B. Hubbard, Feb. 14, 1992. AB, Centre Coll., Danville, Ky., 1955; MS, U. Ky., 1958; MD, U. Louisville, 1962. Diplomate Am. Bd. Radiology, Nat. Bd. Med. Examiners. Radiologist, v.p. Springfield (Ohio) Radiology, 1971-96; locum tenens cons. Global Med. Staffing, Salt Lake City, 1995—, Vista Med. Staffing, Salt Lake City, 1997—. Med. staff Mercy Med. Ctr.; chmn. bd. Missionary Health Svc., 1991. Lt. comdr., USNR, 1966-68. Mem. Am. Coll. Radiology, Clark County Med. Soc. (pres. 1983), Ohio State Med. Assn. (alternate del.). Episcopalian. Avocations: fly fishing, cosmology, mind/brain interface, etymology. E-mail: sandavidl@hotmail.com.

LAWRENCE, DAVID MICHAEL, lawyer, educator; b. Portland, Oreg., Dec. 26, 1943; s. Robert A. and Maude (Davis) L.; m. Alice Oviatt, June 18, 1966 AB, Princeton U., 1965; JD, Harvard U., 1968. Asst. prof. Inst. Govt., U. N.C., Chapel Hill, 1968-71, assoc. prof., 1971-76, prof. pub. law and govt., 1976-94; Kenan prof. pub. law and govt. U. N.C., 1994—. Counsel N.C. Local Govt. Study Commn., 1972-73, N.C. Open Meetings Study Commn., 1978-79 Author: Local Government Finance in North Carolina, 2d edit., 1991 (award for excellence Rsch. and Publs. Govt. Fin. Officers Assn. U.S. and Can. 1991), numerous other books on local govt. law and fin.; contbr. law articles to profl. jours. Chmn. Durham (N.C.) Hist. Dist. Commn., 1985-89. Recipient Herald prize Princeton U., 1965 Mem. N.C. State Bar, Campus Princeton U. Club, Harvard Club of N.Y. Democrat. Office: University of NC Knapp Bldg Clb # 3330 Chapel Hill NC 27599-0001

LAWRENCE, DEBORAH JEAN, quality assurance professional; b. San Jose, Calif., June 25, 1960; BA in Math., San Jose State U., 1982; MS in Stats., Stanford U., 1985. Math. aide Info. Mgmt. Internat., Moffet Field, Calif., 1980-82; group engr. Lockheed Missiles and Space Co., Sunnyvale, 1982-89; mgr. quality assurance Analog Devices, Inc., Santa Clara, 1989—. Reengring. spl. interest group leader Coun. for Continuous Improvement, 1994-96, QS 9000 spl. interest group leader, 1995-97. Author tech. papers. Mem. Am. Soc. for Quality Control (sr. mem., cert. engr.), Am. Statis. Assn. Office: Analog Devices Inc 1500 Space Park Dr Santa Clara CA 95054-3434

LAWRENCE, DEIRDRE ELIZABETH, librarian, coordinator research services; b. Lawton, Okla., Mar. 15, 1952; d. Herbert Thomas and Joan Roberta (McDonald) L. BA in Art History, Richmond Coll., 1974; MLS, Pratt Inst., 1979; postgrad., Harvard U., 1981-82. Head cataloging and tech. svcs., coord. rsch. svcs. Mus. Fine Arts, Boston, 1980-83; prin. libr., coord. rsch. svcs. mus. and libr. archives Bklyn. Mus., 1983—. Mem. Rsch Libr. Group, bd. nominating com., 1994, adv. com. Getty Projects, 1996—, N.Y. Met. Reference and Rsch. Libr. Agy, conservation preservation adv. coun., 1988-92, bd. trustees, 1995—; grant reviewer fed. and state agys.; cons. in field; lectr. in field. Author: New York and Hollywood Fashion, 1986, Dressing the Part: Costume Sket, 1989, Modern Art--The Production, 1989, Guide to the Culin Archival Collection, 1996, Formation of an Islamic art library collection in an Am. museum, 1996, Culin: Collector and Documentor of the World He Saw, Fashion and How It Was Influenced by Ethnographic Collections in Museums, Native American Art and Culture: Documentary Resources, Access to Visual Images-Past and Present; contbr. articles to profl. jours.; lectr. at internat. and nat. libr. confs.; curator various collections including Bklyn. Mus., 1989, 96, 97, others. Mem. conservation, preservation adv. coun. N.Y. Met. Reference and Rsch. Libr. Agy., 1988-92, bd. trustees, 1995—. Recipient Samuel H. Kress Travel grant, 1993, 95. Mem. Art Librs. Soc. N.Am. (mem. internat. rels. com. 1996-97, other offices), Spl. Librs. Assn., Native Am. Art Studies Assn., Internat. Fedn. Libr. Assns. Office: Brooklyn Mus 200 Eastern Pkwy Brooklyn NY 11238-6099

LAWRENCE, EDWARD JACK, III, lawyer; b. Beaumont, Tex., Sept. 23, 1949; s. Edward Jack and Nelda Rae (McClure) L. BA in Govt., Lamar U., 1971; JD, U. Houston, 1988. Bar: U.S. Dist. Ct. (ea. dist.) Tex. 1993, U.S. Supreme Ct. 1995. Atty. East Tex. Legal Svcs., Beaumont, 1989; pvt. practice, 1990—. Bd. dirs. ACLU, Beaumont, 1978—, Clean Air and Water Orgn., 1996—. Mem. Tex. Bar Assn., Jefferson County Bar Assn. Democrat. Methodist-Unitarian. Avocations: golf, tennis, poetry, astronomy, guitar. Home and Office: 5570 Winfree St Beaumont TX 77705-5939

LAWRENCE, ESTELENE YVONNE, musician, transportation executive; b. Lynch, Ky., Aug. 10, 1933; d. Samuel Coleridge and Florence Estelle (Gardner) Taylor; m. Otto Lee Lawrence, Sept. 14, 1957; children: Stuart, Neil, Adelbert. Student Fenn Coll., 1953-60, Cleve. Inst. Music, 1955-56, John Carroll U., 1977-78, Northeastern U., 1979-80; BA Cleve. State U., 1993. Stenographer Cleve. Transit System/Regional Transit Authority, 1951-76, tng. asst., 1976-78, pers. devel. asst., 1978-82, dist. adminstr., 1983-86; supr./mgmt. skills instr. RTA, 1976-86, dir. tng. and career devel., 1986-88. Dir. music Friendly United Baptist Ch., 1947-95; piano tchr., 1953-73; minister of music Mt. Nebo Baptist Ch., 1995—; pianist/organist Nat. Bapt. Conv., 1971, 80. Publicity chmn. Moses Cleve. Sch. PTA, 1965-75; audit chmn. RTA Main Office Credit Union, 1980-83; dist. sec. Boy Scouts Am., 1982-83; chmn. adv. bd. Baldwin Wallace Coll., 1984-88; mem. adv. bd. Cleve. Mgmt. Devel. Consortium, 1985-88; chief musician RTA Choir; mem. Cleve. Choral Union, 1992-96. Mem. Am. Choral Dirs. Assn., Cleve. Mgmt. Seminars (treas. 1979-81, pres. 1981-83), Conf. Minority Transp. Ofcls., Phi Kappa Gamma (pres. 1966-69), Mu Phi Epsilon (historian 1990-91, chorister 1991-92, pres. 1992-93), Alpha Kappa Alpha. Mem. A.M.E. Ch. Clubs: East 153d St. (v.p. 1980—), East Ky. Social. Home: 4066 E 153rd St Cleveland OH 44128-1926

LAWRENCE, FRANCIS LEO, university president, language educator; b. Woonsocket, R.I., Aug. 25, 1937; BS, St. Louis U., 1959; PhD in French and Italian, Tulane U., 1962. Mem. faculty Tulane U., New Orleans, 1962—90, chmn. dept. French and Italian, 1969—76, acting dean Newcomb Coll., 1976—78, dep. provost, 1978—81, acting provost, grad. dean, 1981—82, prof. French, 1971, acad. v.p., provost, 1982—90; pres. Rutgers U., New Brunswick, 1990—. Author numerous publs. on French 17th century lit;

contbr. articles, revs. and essays to profl. publs. Decorated Chevalier, Palmes Academiques, 1977 Mem. Am. Assn. Tchrs. French, N.Am. Soc. 17th Century French Lit., MLA. Office: Rutgers U, Office of Pres Old Queens Building College Ave Campus, 83 Somerset St. New Brunswick NJ 08901-1281*

LAWRENCE, GERALD GRAHAM, management consultant; b. U.K., June 21, 1947; came to U.S., 1962, naturalized, 1967; s. Raymond Joseph and Barbara Virginia Lawrence; 1 child, Ian Andrew; m. Julie Ann Quiram. BA in Math., Northeastern U., 1970, MA in Econs., 1973; MBA, U. Pa., 1975. Optics rsch. technologist Polaroid Corp., Cambridge, Mass., 1968-70; intern Corning Glass Works, Inc., N.Y.C., 1974; asst. brand mgr. Procter and Gamble, Cin., 1975-76; assoc. Theodore Barry & Assocs., N.Y.C., 1976-79; dir. performance improvement systems Stone & Webster Mgmt. Cons., 1979-84; mgr. utility MAS Deloitte Haskins & Sells, 1984-86; pres. PMC Mgmt. Cons., Inc., Three Bridges, N.J., 1986—. Advisor Commerce & Econ. Devel. Dept. State of N.J.; speaker in field. Designer: auditor system nuclear power plant constrn; innovator; quality assurance for profl. cons. svcs; contbr. articles to profl. jours. Econs. fellow Northeastern U., 1973, adminstrv. fellow Wharton Sch. U. Pa., 1975. Home: 6 Thistle Ln Flemington NJ 08822-7067 Office: PMC Mgmt Cons PO Box 332 Three Bridges NJ 08887-0332 E-mail: pmc@pmc-management.com.

LAWRENCE, GLENN ROBERT, arbitrator, mediator, lawyer; b. N.Y.C., Nov. 8, 1930; m. Nina M. Scaturro; children: David P., Eric A. JD, Bklyn. Law Sch., 1954; BA, U. Louisville, 1968; MA in Psychology, Cath. U., 1977; PhD, Am. U., 1980. Bar: N.Y. 1955, D.C. 1973, U.S. Supreme Ct. 1976, Va. 1997; cert. family mediator, Va., 2002—. Atty. N.Y.C. Legal Aid, 1955-57; ptnr. Lawrence & Lawrence, N.Y.C., 1957-64; agt. N.Y. State, Babylon, N.Y., 1964-66; atty. U.S. Army Engrs., Washington, 1966-69; assoc. chief trial atty. U.S. Dept. Navy, 1969-78; judge adminstrv. law HEW, Camden, N.J., 1978-79, U.S. Dept. Labor, Washington, 1979-93, SEC, Washington, 1993-96; mem. bd. contract appeals U.S. Dept. Labor, 1981-93; arbitrator Nat. Assn. Securities Dealers, Inc., 1996—, Superior Ct., Washington, 1996—; mediator Women's Ctr., Vienna, 1996—. Adj. prof. law George Mason U., Fairfax, Va., 1980-83, Ctrl. Mich. U., Washington, 1981-95, Nat. Jud. Coll. U. Nev., Reno, 1984-88; lectr. Banares Hindu U., Varanasi, India, 1988, Law Coll., Ernakulum, Cochin, India, 1989, Washington Lee U., Lexington, Va., 1990; mem. adv. com. Georgetown U. State Cts. and Toxic Torts, 1991; advisor Judiciary Leadership Devel. Coun. Inc., 1990-99; bd. dirs. Fed. Bar Found., 1994—, v.p., 1996-99, chair profl. ethics com., 1999—, chair sr. lawyers divsn., 1999—. Author: Condemnation Law, 1969. Bd. dirs. Democracy Devel. Initiative. Mem. ABA (chmn. nat. conf. adminstrv. law judges edn. com. 1985-90, chmn. internat. conf. jud. edn. London 1985, pres. fed. adminstrv. law judge conf. 1984-85, chmn. edn. jud. adminstrn. divsn. 1987-91, chmn. confs., chmn. jud. edn. standards program 1991-95, vice chmn. govt. lawyers com. sr. lawyers divsn. 1991-95), Fed Bar Assn. (chmn. adminstrv. judiciary com. 1984-88, continuing edn. bd. 1988-91, chmn. judiciary sect. 1989-91, sect. coord. exec. com. 1992-94, editor Fed. Jurist 1991-96, chair pub. rels. com. 1993-96, chair profl. ethics com. 1996-98), Adminstrv. Trial Lawyers Assn. (pres. 1979-80, chair-elect sr. lawyers divsn. 1998—).

LAWRENCE, HENRY SHERWOOD, retired physician; b. N.Y.C., Sept. 22, 1916; s. Victor John and Agnes (Whalen) Lawrence; m. Dorothea Wetherbee, Nov. 13, 1943; children: Dorothea, Victor, Geoffrey. AB, NYU, 1938, MD, 1943. Diplomate Am. Bd. Internal Medicine. Mem. faculty NYU, N.Y.C., 1949—2001, John Wyckoff fellow in medicine, 1948—49, dir. student health, 1950—57, head infectious disease & immunology div., 1959—2000, prof. medicine, 1961—79, Jeffrey Bergstein prof. medicine, 1979—2000, co-dir. med. svcs., 1964—2000; dir. Cancer Ctr., 1974—79, Ctr. for AIDS Rsch., 1989—94. Vis. physician Tisch Hosp., Bellevue Hosp., 1964—2000; cons. medicine Manhattan VA Hosp., 1964—2000; infectious disease program con. VA Rsch. Svc., 1960—63; cons. allergy and immunology study sect. USPHS, 1960—63, chmn., 1963—65; assoc. mem. commn. on streptococcal and staphylococcal diseases Armed Forces Epidemiol. Bd., Dept. Def., 1956—74; mem. coms. NAS-NRC, 1957—65, chmn. com. transplantation, 1963—65; mem. NRC, 1970—72; mem. allergy and infectious disease panel Health Rsch. Coun., N.Y.C., 1962—75, co-chmn., 1968—75; mem. sci. adv. coun. Am. Cancer Soc., 1973—75. Editor: Medical Clinics of North America, 1957, Cellular and Humoral Aspects of Hypersensitive States, 1959; editor: (with M. Landy) Mediators of Cellular Immunity, 1969; editor: (with Kirkpatrick and Burger) Immunobiology of Transfer Factor, 1983; mem. editl. bd.: Transplantation, Ann. of Internal Medicine, 1965—71, mem. editl. adv. bd.: Transplantation Procs., 1960—, founder, editor in chief: Cellular Immunology, 1970—96. Lt. M.C. USNR, World War II. Recipient Rsch. Career Devel. award, USPHS, 1960—65, prize, Alpha Omega Alpha, 1943, Meritorious Sci. Achievement award, NYU Alumni Assn., 1970, von Pirquet Gold medal, Ann. Forum on Allergy, 1972, award for disting. achievement in sci. of medicine, ACP, 1973, Sci. Achievement award, Am. Coll. Allergists, 1974, Sci. medal, N.Y. Acad. Medicine, 1974, Bristol Sci. award, Infectious Diseases Soc. Am., 1974, Charles V. Chapin medal, 1975, Lila Gruber honor award for cancer rsch., Am. Acad. Dermatology, 1975, Alumni Achievement award, NYU Washington Sq. Coll., 1979; fellow Commonwealth Fund fellow, U. Coll., London, 1959. Fellow: ACP (Bronze medal 1973), Royal Coll. Physicians and Surgeons Glasgow (hon.), Am. Acad. Allergy (hon.); mem.: NAS, Internat. Transplantation Soc. (chmn. constnr. com., councillor), Royal Soc. Medicine (affiliate, Eng.), Infectious Diseases Soc. Am. (charter, councillor 1970—72, Bristol Sci. award 1974), Peripatetic Clin. Soc., Harvey Soc. (sec. 1957—60, lectr. 1973—, councillor 1974—77), Interurban Clin. Club, Soc. for Exptl. Biology and Medicine (editl. bd. procs.), Am. Soc. for Clin. Investigation, Assn. Am. Physicians, Soc. Francaise d'Allergie (corr.), Alpha Omega Alpha. Achievements include discovery of Transfer Factor - a product of lymphocytes (T-cells) which confers and/or augments immunity to mycobacterial, viral and fungal infections when administered to non-immune individuals; research in mechanisms tissue damage and homograft rejection in man. Home: 343 E 30th St New York NY 10016-6417

LAWRENCE, JAMES HUCKABEE, commercial realtor; b. Durham, N.C., Feb. 3, 1953; s. Henry Newman and Margaret (Huckabee) L.; m. Beth Hutt, June 28, 1975; children: Elizabeth, James, John. Student, Gulf Coast Community Coll., Panama City, Fla., 1971-72, Harvard Bus. Sch., 1980, Am. Mgmt. Assn., Washington, 1982. Pub. rels. profl. and sales rep. Sinclair Distbr., Panama City, 1965-69; v.p. new accounts and loans Lawrence Oil Co., Fina, 1970-75; pres., credit factor Sports Emporium, 1976-79; pres., gen. mgr. Lawrence & Sons Oil Co. Inc., 1981-83; adminstr. Sun South Sch. Real Estate, 1984-85; comml. realtor John Davidson Realty/REM Inc., 1985—; exec. v.p., sec. Diamondhead Towers, Inc., Panama City Beach, Fla., 1990—; owner Realty Svcs. Inc. of the South, Panama City, 1993—; ptnr. Assoc. Mortgage Ventures aka AMV Inc., 1994—. Bd. dirs. DHT Inc., DHT Condo Assn., Panama City Beach; mem. Scouting Mag. Readers Panel, 1997—. State lobbyist Nat. Gasohol Commn., Tallahassee, 1977-81; mem. nat. adv. bd. Am. Security Coun., Washington, 1981-82; charter mem. Franklin Mint Assn., 1968—; asst. scoutmaster Boy Scouts Am., 1994—, 2001 Nat. Boy Scout Jamboree coun. com., 1999—. With U.S. Army, 1972-78, Panama Canal. Named Aide de Camp, Ala. Gov., 1989, Ky. Col., 1989, Col. Govs.'s Staff, Tenn., 1990. Mem. Nat. Assn. Realtors, Fla. C. of C., U.S. C. of C. (state dir. 1980), Fla. Jaycees (bd. dirs. 1980-81), U.S. Jaycees (Goodwill Amb. 1974—), Am. Entrepreneurs Assn. Democrat. Episcopalian. Avocations: boating, coin collecting, antique vases, painting, tennis. Office: Realty Svcs of South 801 Jenks Ave Ste D Panama City FL 32401-2569 E-mail: jlawrence-rsi@worldnet.att.net.

LAWRENCE, JAMES KAUFMAN LEBENSBURGER, lawyer; b. New Rochelle, N.Y., Oct. 8, 1940; s. Michael Monet and Edna (Billings) L.; m. George-Ann Adams, Apr. 5, 1969; children: David Michael, Catherine Robin. AB, Ohio State U., 1962, JD, 1965; postgrad., Otterbein Coll., 2002—. Bar: Ohio. 1965, U.S. Dist. Ct. (so. dist.) Ohio 1971, U.S. Ct. Appeals (6th cir.) 1971, U.S. Ct. Appeals (4th cir.) 1978. Field atty. NLRB, Cin., 1965-70; ptnr. Frost Brown Todd LLC, 1970—. Adj. prof. econs. dept. and Coll. Law U. Cin., 1975—, Ohio State U. Coll. Law, 1995—, Xavier U., 1995—, McGregor Sch., Antioch U., 1993—98; adj. prof. MBA program Otterbein Coll., 2002; treas. Potter Stewart Inn of Ct., Cin., 1988—90; tchg. fellow Harvard Negotiation Project, 1991; chmn. adv. panel on appointment of magistrate judges U.S. Dist. Ct. for So. Dist. Ohio, 1993—. Contbr. articles to profl. jours. Mem. nat. coun. Ohio State U. Coll. Law, 1974—; mem. steering com. Leadership Cin., 1985-89; mem. Seven Hills Neighborhood Houses, Cin., 1973-95, pres., 1992-94; bd. dirs. Beechwood Home, Cin., 1973-85; mem. adv. bd. Emerson Behavioral Health Svcs., 1990-95, chmn., 1995; chmn. Labor Dept., 1978-89, Franciscan Hosp. Devel. Coun., 1995-99, chmn., 1996-97; trustee Ctr. for Resolution of Disputes, Inc., 1988-91, treas., 1990-91; mem. Ohio Gov.'s Ops. Improvement Task Force, 1991. Recipient Outstanding Adj. Faculty award, U. Cin., 1998. Fellow Coll. Labor and Employment Lawyers; mem. ABA, Cin. Bar Assn. (chmn. labor law com. 1979-82, comm. adv. com. 1994-96, alternative dispute resolution com. 1996—), Ohio Bar Assn. (vice chmn. labor and employment law sect. 1987-90, chmn. 1990-92), Indsl. Rels. Rsch. Assn. (bd. govs. 1977-80), Alumni Assn. Coll. Law Ohio State U. (pres. 1984-85), Assn. for Conflict Resolution, Cincinnatus Assn. (pres. 1985-86), Collaborative Law Ctr. (steering com. 1996—), Univ. Club; master Potter Stewart Inn of Ct. Avocations: collecting movie posters, biking. Home: 3300 Columbia Pkwy Cincinnati OH 45226-1044 Office: Frost Brown Todd LLC 2500 PNC Ctr 201 E 5th St Cincinnati OH 45202-4182 E-mail: jlawrence@fbtlaw.com.

LAWRENCE, JOHN KIDDER, lawyer; b. Detroit, Nov. 18, 1949; s. Luther Ernest and Mary Anna (Kidder) L.; m. Jeanine Ann DeLay, June 20, 1981. AB, U. Mich., 1971; JD, Harvard U., 1974. Bar: Mich. 1974, U.S. Supreme Ct. 1977, D.C. 1978. Assoc. Dickinson, Wright, McKean & Cudlip, Detroit, 1973-74; staff atty. Office of Judge Adv. Gen., Washington, 1975-78; assoc. Dickinson, Wright, McKean, Cudlip & Moon, Detroit, 1978-81; ptnr. Dickinson, Wright, Moon, VanDusen & Freeman, 1981-98, Dickinson Wright PLLC, Detroit, 1998—. Exec. sec. Detroit Com. on Fgn. Rels., 1988—; trustee Ann Arbor (Mich.) Summer Festival, Inc., 1990—; patron Founders Soc. Detroit Inst. Arts, 1979—. With USN, 1975-78. Mem. AAAS, ABA, Am. Law Inst., State Bar Mich., D.C. Bar Assn., Am. Judicature Soc., Internat. Bar Assn., Am. Hist. Assn., Detroit Athletic Club, Econ. Club Detroit, Phi Eta Sigma, Phi Beta Kappa. Democrat. Episcopalian. Office: Dickinson Wright PLLC 500 Woodward Ave Ste 4000 Detroit MI 48226-3416

LAWRENCE, JOHN RAYNOR MOORE, librarian; b. Greenville, N.C., Mar. 15, 1958; s. Lewis Seller Lawrence and Julia Godwin Moore; m. Rosa Maria Lopez-Canete, Aug. 8, 1983. BA in History, East Carolina U., 1980; MLS, U. N.C., 1985. Ref. librarian Carolina Population Ctr., Chapel Hill, N.C., 1985; ref.-interlibr. loan librarian Univ. Rsch. Libr.-UCLA, 1985-89, E.G. Swem Libr., Coll. of William and Mary, Williamsburg, Va., 1989-2001; assoc. dir. adminstrv. and user svcs. Joyner Lib. East Carolina U., Greenville, N.C., 2001—. Reviewer online book rev. column Lawrence Looks at Books, 2000—. Mem. ALA (vice chair codes com. 2000-01, chair 2001-02), Va. Libr. Assn. (Ill forum chair 1991-92), Coll. William and Mary Librarians Assembly (vice-chair 2000-01). Democrat. Avocation: gardening. Home: 102 Williams St Greenville NC 27858 Office: East Carolina U Joyner Libr 1000 East 5th St Greenville NC 27858-4353 E-mail: lawrencej@mail.ecu.edu.

LAWRENCE, KATHY, medical, surgical, and radiology nurse; b. Searcy, Ark., Dec. 9, 1949; d. S.V. and Pearl (Bolden) Smith; children: Ryan, Damon. ADN, Odessa (Tex.) Coll., 1977; BSN, U. Tex., Galveston, 1992, MSN, 1996. Cert. med. asst., diabetes educator, med.-surg. nurse. Head nurse, acting supr. Med. Ctr. Hosp., Odessa, 1978-80; asst. head nurse Meml. Gen. Hosp., Elkins, W.Va., 1980-81; staff nurse United Hosp. Ctr., Clarksburg, 1981-83; field supr. Upjohn/Healthcare Svcs., Midland, Tex., 1983-85; primary nurse, physician's office Naidu Clinic, Odessa, 1985-88; nursing supr. U. Tex. Med. Br., Galveston, 1988-95, case mgr. outcomes evaluation and nursing rsch., 1995-97; clin. educator II U. Tex. Med. Br. Ednl. Resource Ctr., 1997—. Mem. ANA, Nat. Nursing Staff Devel. Orgn., Am. Assn. Diabetes Educators, Am. Assn. Med. Assts. (sec. local chpt.), Am. Assn. Intravenous Therapists, Am. Radiol. Nurses Assn., Am. Assn. Neurosci. Nurses, Am. Med-Surg. Nurses, Case Mgmt. Soc. Am., Infusion Nurses Soc., Tex. Nurses Assn., U. Tex. Med. Br. Alumni Assn., Galveston Hist. Found., The Grand Opera House, Alpha Nu Chi, Sigma Theta Tau (Alpha Delta chpt. sec., newsletter editor). Home: 5405 Avenue R Galveston TX 77551-5521 E-mail: kalawren@utmb.edu.

LAWRENCE, LAUREN, writer, psychoanalytical theorist, psychoanalyst; b. N.Y.C., June 26, 1950; d. Jack and Elaine (Gaumont) Soefer; m. D. Henry Lawrence, June 24, 1972; 1 child, Graham. MA in Psychology, New Sch. for Social Rsch., 1993. Psychoanalyst, N.Y.C., 1992—. Author: Dream Keys: Unlocking the Power of Your Unconscious Mind, 1999, Dream Keys for Love, 1999, Dream Keys for the Future: Unlocking the Secrets of Your Destiny, 2000, A Quio Revent Les Stars, La Llave De Los Suenos, 2001, Private Dreams of Public People, 2002; contbr. sci. articles; columnist: "Dreams" N.Y. Daily News, columnist: Newport This Week, columnist: Swing Mag., columnist: "Political Dreams" George Mag.; dream analyst (on radio) Joey Reynolds Show, Barry Farber Show, Victoria Jones Show, G. Gordon Liddy Show, MTV Radio, Fox News Network, CBC, CNN, The O'Reilly Factor, Rise, Fox Network, Eng.; contbr. articles; dreams expert Dreamlife.com, Yahoo.com, MSN.com; performer: (TV series) The Dream Zone. Friend N.Y. Psychoanalytic Soc. Achievements include founding of a third person analysis, a new method of analysis in clinical practice, which provides the analysand a narrational objectivity; the covert seduction theory, which expounds the dangers of a non-physical parental seduction, the Actualized Dream, a conscious behavioral manifestation of symbolic material-unconscious desires that manifest themselves during consciousness through extreme behavioral acts, the undisclosed visual cliche, as an attribute or assessment drawn from a visual that leads to a cliche, and the externalized dream as a manifestation of a vision. Avocations: tennis, musical composition, writing poetry, reading, studying Greek. Home and Office: 31 E 72d St New York NY 10021-4146 E-mail: DreamDivaNY@aol.com.

LAWRENCE, MADALENA JOAN VIGNOCCHI, accountant; b. Lake Forest, Ill., July 2, 1952; d. Anthony and Juanita Dolly (Thompson) V.; m. Thomas Stanley Lawrence, Nov. 21, 1981; children: David, Michael. BS in Fin., U. Ill., 1973. CPA, Ill. Staff acct. Ernst & Ernst, Chgo., 1974-75, in-charge acct., 1975-76; semi-sr. internal auditor McGraw-Edison Co., Elgin, 1976-77, tax act., 1977-79; sr. tax analyst Safety Kleen Corp., 1980-84, acctg. supr., 1984-85, mgr. capital budget, property acct., 1985-91; owner Lawrence Enterprises, 1991—. Mem. Am. Inst. CPA's, Women in Mgmt. (pres. No. Fox Valley chpt. 1984-86), Ill. CPA's. Roman Catholic. Avocations: bicycling, photography. Office: Lawrence Enterprises 330 W Morse Ave Bartlett IL 60103-4068 E-mail: tmlaw@quixnet.net.

LAWRENCE, MARGERY H(ULINGS), marketing consultant; b. Harmarville, Pa., June 17, 1934; d. Richard Nuttall and Alva (Burns) Hulings. Student, Bethany Coll., 1951-52; BS in Mktg., Carnegie-Mellon U., 1955. Asst. mdse. buyer Joseph Horne Co., Pitts., 1955-57; home econs. editor Pitts. Group Cos. Columbia Gas Sys., 1957-64, dir. home econs., 1968-72, dist. mktg. mgr. Jennette, 1972-87, divsn. mgr., 1987-91; dir. mktg. Columbia Gas Pa. and Columbia Gas Md., 1991-96; mktg. and bus. cons. M.H. Lawrence Ltd., Beaver Falls, Pa., 1996—. Bd. dirs., sec. Ohio Valley Gen. Hosp. Mem. DAR, Women's Golf Assn. We. Pa., Pa. Med. Soc. (patient adv. bd.).

LAWRENCE, MARJORIE DIANE LONG, computer programming executive, analyst; b. Fullerton, Calif., Sept. 19, 1943; d. Earl Lawrence Whipple and Ruth Juanita (Long) Purcell; children: Stephen, Deborah. Grad. computer programming, LaSalle U., Chgo., 1973; BSBA, U. Phoenix, 1994, MS, 1997. Computer programmer Los Alamos (N.Mex.) Nat. Lab., 1972-81, cons. control data, 1984-89, computer tech., 1989—. Contract programmer Computer Assistance, Inc., Tulsa, 1981-82; profl. svcs. analyst Control Data Corp., Denver, 1982-84, Los Alamos, 1984-89. Mem. Order Ea. Star (past matron). Home: 90 Aspen Grv Jemez Springs NM 87025-9683

LAWRENCE, MARK W. former state legislator, lawyer; b. June 27, 1958; AB, Bowdoin Coll.; JD, U. Maine. Assoc. Dill & Briggs Attys. at Law; mem. from dist. 1 Maine State Ho. of Reps., chmn. legal affairs com., mem. com. to study pub. financing of elec.; mem. from dist. 35 Maine State Senate, 1993-96, pres., 1996—. Mem. Commn. to Study Feasibility of Establishing Piscataqua River Basin Compact; mem. Maine-N.H. Boundary Commn. Bd. dirs. Kittery Land Trust; trustee Kittery Hist. and Navel Mus. Address: PO Box 366 Eliot ME 03903*

LAWRENCE, MARY JOSEPHINE (JOSIE LAWRENCE), artist, retired library official; b. Carbondale, Pa., Mar. 9, 1932; d. Domenick Anthony and Teresa Rose (Zaccone) Gentile; m. John Paul Lawrence, Apr. 25, 1953 (dec. June 1977); children: Mary Josephine, Jane Therese, Susan Michele. BFA, Mass. Coll. Art, 1989; postgrad., Chelsea (Eng.) Sch. Art, 1989, San Pancrazio Art Sch., Tuscany, Italy, 1990, 91, 92; cert. in grad. studies, Guangzhou Acad. Fine Arts, China, 1993; postgrad., Md. Inst. Fine Art, Sorrento, Italy, 1994, Ctrl. Acad. Arts and Design, Beijing, 1997, Skopelos, Greece, 1998, N.Y. Sch. Visual Arts, Barcelona, Spain, 1999, Internat. Sch. Art, Umbria, Italy, 2000. Sales clk. Gorins, 5&10, Jordan Marsh, Boston, 1946-49; clk.-typist, sec. John Hancock Ins. Co., 1950-53; machine operator, quality control supr. Rust Craft Greeting Cards, Dedham, Mass., 1961-69; restaurant hostess Tony's Villa, Waltham, 1972-73; mus. sales clk., artist John F. Kennedy Libr., Boston, 1979-87, mgr. mus. store, supr., 1988-2000; freelance artist, 2000—. Tchr.'s asst. San Pancrazio Art Sch., 1992; guest appearance TAKE TWO cable TV, Channel 11, 1996, Walpole Cmty. TV, 2001, WEZE Family 590 Talk Show, 2001. One woman shows include de Havilland Fine Art Gallery, Boston, 1997, Dr. James McDermott Gallery, Boston, 1996, Cranberry Cafe, Boston, 1997; exhibited in group shows at South Shore Arts Ctr., Cohasset, Mass., 1991, N. River Arts Soc., Marshfield Hills, Mass., 1994 (Best of Show), Boston Visual Artists Union, 1996, de Havilland Fine Art Gallery, Boston, 1997, United South End Open Studios, 1998, Artana Gallery, Framingham, Mass., 2000, Juror Quincy Art Assn., 1996, 98, 2002, Weymouth Art Assn., 1995, 97, Arts Affair, 1999. Recipient Outstanding Achievement awards Nat. Archives and Rsch. Adminstrn., 1989, 94, 96-97, Svc. award, 1990, Hon. Mention award South Shore Arts Ctr., 1991, Best of Show award De Havilland Fine Arts Gallery, 1992, honorium Weymouth Art Assn., 1995, 97, Quincy Art Assn., 1996, 98. Mem. Boston Visual Artist Union, de Havilland Fine Art Gallery, South Shore Art Ctr., North River Arts Soc., Nat. Mus. Women in Arts (charter), Milton Art Mus. (Hon. Mention award 1998), United S. End Artists. Democrat. Roman Catholic. E-mail: josielawrence@attbi.net.

LAWRENCE, MERLOYD LUDINGTON, editor; b. Pasadena, Calif., Aug. 1, 1932; d. Nicholas Saltus and Mary Lloyd (Macy) Ludington; m. Seymour Lawrence, June 21, 1952 (div. 1984); children: Macy, Nicholas; m. John M. Myers, 1985 AB, Radcliffe Coll., 1954, MA, 1957. With Houghton Mifflin Co., 1955-57; free lance translator, 1957-65; editor, treas., v.p. Seymour Lawrence Inc., Boston, 1965-83; pres. Merloyd Lawrence, Inc., 1983—. Translator works of Flaubert and Balzac, modern French fiction, German and Swedish children's books.; contbr. articles to nat. mags. Treas., v.p. Milford House Properties, Ltd., N.S., Can., 1975-80; trustee Milton (Mass.) Acad., 1974-82; mem. com. clin. investigations Beth Israel/Deaconess Hosp. Mem. Am. Translators Assn., New Eng. Forestry Found. (exec. bd. officer 1989—), Mass. Audubon Soc. (dir. 1974-2001, exec. com. 1992-2001, hon. mem. 2001—), Tavern Club, Phi Beta Kappa. Home: 102 Chestnut St Boston MA 02108-1120 Office: 102A Chestnut St Boston MA 02108-1120

LAWRENCE, PAUL ROGER, retired organizational behavior educator; b. Rochelle, Ill., Apr. 26, 1922; s. Howard Cyrus and Clara (Luther) L.; m. Martha G. Stiles, Dec. 14, 1948; children: Anne Talcott, William Stiles. Student, Grand Rapids Jr. Coll., 1939-41; AB, Albion Coll., 1943; MBA, Harvard U., 1947, DCS, 1950. Mem. faculty Harvard U. Bus. Sch., Boston, 1947-91, asst. prof., 1951-56, assoc. prof., 1956-61, prof. organizational behavior, 1961-68, Donham prof. organizational behavior, 1968; retired, 1991. Author (with others): Renewing American Industry, 1983; author: HRM, Trends and Challenges, 1985, Behind the Factory Walls, 1990, Driven, How Human Nature Shapes Our Choices, 2002. Served to lt. USNR, 1943-46. Fellow Acad. Mgmt.; mem. Am. Sociol. Assn. Home: 1010 Memorial Dr Apt 12C Cambridge MA 02138-4856 Office: Cumnock Hall Soldiers Field Boston MA 02163 E-mail: plawrence@hbs.edu.

LAWRENCE, PAULA DENISE, physical therapist; b. Ft. Worth, May 21, 1959; d. Roddy Paul and Kay Frances (Spivey) Gillis; m. Mark Jayson Lawrence, Apr. 20, 1985 (div. 1998). BS, Tex. Women's U., 1982. Lic. phys. therapist, Tex., Calif. Sales mgr. R. and K Camping Ctr., Garland, Tex., 1977-82; staff phys. therapist Longview (Tex.) Regional Hosp., 1982-83, dir. phys. therapy, 1983-87, dir. rehab. svcs., 1987-88; staff phys. therapist MPH Home Health, Longview, Tex., 1983-84; owner, pres. Phys. Rehab. Ctr., Hemet, Calif., 1988—. Mem. adv. com. div. health occupations Kilgore (Tex.) Coll., 1985-88; mem. profl. adv. bd. Hospice Longview, 1985-88. Bd. dirs. V.I.P. Tots; active Valle Vista PTA, sec. 1998-2000, 2001-02, 2002—, v.p. 2000-01. Mem. NAFE, Am. Phys. Therapy Assn., Calif. Phys. Therapy Assn., Am. Bus. Women's Assn. (v.p. 1987, 89, pres. 1990, Woman of Yr. 1988, 91), Assistance League Aux., Soroptomist (corr. sec. 1992, dir. 1993-95, 97-98, sec. 1995-97, v.p. 1998-2000, pres. 2000-2001, bd. dirs. 2991-02), Hemet C. of C. (sec. 1998-99, bd. dirs. 1996-99), Psi Chi, Omega Rho Alpha. Avocation: travel. Home: 43725 Mandarin Dr Hemet CA 92544-8529 Office: 901 S State St Ste 500 Hemet CA 92543-7185 E-mail: prch@koan.com.

LAWRENCE, PERCY LEE, III, health facility administrator; b. Crowley, La., Aug. 2, 1945; s. P.L. Jr. and Elizabeth (Williams) L.; m. Patti (Childress) Lawrence, Dec. 22, 1984; children: Lisa Daniel, John Bradley. BA, Centenary Coll., 1967; MBA, George Washington U., 1970. Adminstrv. staff Meth. Hosp., New Orleans, 1970-81; pres. Meth. Health Sys., 1981-86, VHA of Fla., Inc., Tampa, 1986-99, VHA Southeast, Inc., Tampa, 2000—. Chmn. Met. Hosp. Coun. New Orleans, 1984. Chmn. La. Hosp. Assn., Baton Rouge, 1986, New Orleans East C. of C., Nw Orleans, 1985. Mem. Am. Coll. Health Execs. (diplomate, Regents award 2000), Am. Hosp. Assn., Fla. Hosp. Assn. Republican. United Methodist. Avocations: skiing, boating, golf, music. Office: VHA Southeast Ste 750 3030 N Rocky Pt Dr W Tampa FL 33607

LAWRENCE, RALPH ALAN, minister; b. Wendell, Idaho, Apr. 18, 1931; s. Wayne Harold and Evelyn Frances (McConnell) L.; m. Beverley Jean Miller, (div. 1974); children: Alan, Douglas, Kerry Philpot; m. Audrey Stall Shelden; children: Wayne Shelden, Mark Shelden, Sharon Glover, Laurel Bishop, Scott Shelden. BA, DD (hon.), Albertson Coll. of Idaho; MDiv, Boston U. Ordained minister, 1956. Youth min. Christ Ch., Kennebunk, Maine, 1954-56; min. Oregon-Idaho Conf., United Meth. Ch., 1956-95, dist. supt., 1981-87; ret., 1995; asst. pastor 1st United Meth. Cathedral of Rockies, Boise, Idaho, 1995—. Del. World Meth. Conf., 1986, 91, 96, Jurisdictional Conf., 1984; pres. Classic Journeys Internat., 1979—. Home: 3335 N Bunchberry Way Boise ID 83704-0717

LAWRENCE, RALPH WALDO, manufacturing company executive; b. Mineola, N.Y., Sept. 10, 1941; s. Ralph Waldo and Gertrude (Ingles) L.; m. Judith Alice Frost, June 20, 1964; children: Susan, Carolyn. BA, W.Va. Wesleyan Coll., 1963; M in Pub. Adminstrn., Western Mich. U., 1979. Pres. Lawrence Mfrs., Columbus, Ohio, 1970-85; chief automated info. systems contract svcs. Systems Automation Ctr., 1980-87, chief plans and mgmt. div., 1987-88; chief ops. Constrn. Supply Ctr., 1988-89; chief Info. Ctr. DLA Systems Automation Ctr., Ohio, 1989-92, DISA Office of Tech. Integration, Columbus, 1992-93; dep. of def. integration mgr. CALS, Blacklick, Ohio, 1993-95; prin. info. engr. Boeing Info. Systems, Columbus, 1995; bus. mgr. Computer Scis. Corp., Moorestown, N.J., 1995-97; owner Lawrence Mfrs., Westerville, Ohio, 1997—. Bus. mgr. Computer Scis. Corp., 1995-97; prin., Lawrence Mfrs., 1998—. Served to capt. U.S. Army, 1963-66. Mem. Data Processing Mgmt. Assn. (pres. Columbus chpt. 1987, program dir. Columbus chpt. 1985, bd. dirs. 1987-88), Masons. Republican. Presbyterian. Avocations: golf, sailing. Home: 222 Amherst Ln Crossville TN 38558-8100 E-mail: lawrencedia10@multipro.com.

LAWRENCE, RICHARD DEAN, lawyer; b. Jefferson City, Mo., Sept. 20, 1944; s. Charles Eugene and Edith Lucille (Moore) L.; m. Diana H. McIntyre, Aug. 13, 1967; children: Jennifer, Daniel, Michael, David, Lindsay. AA, U. Cin., 1964, BA, 1967; JD with honors, J.D. Chase Coll. Law, 1971. Bar: Ohio 1971, Ky., 1989, U.S. Dist. Ct. Ohio, U.S. Ct. Appeals. Founder, ptnr., pres. Gustin & Lawrence, 1971—; ptnr., pres. Lawrence, Linder & McGrath, Cin., 1991—; guest lectr. Chase Coll. Law, 1983-87, Ohio Trial Practice Inst., Cin., 1975-77; speaker med. malpractice Ohio Acad. Trial lawyers, Cin. Bar Assn., Ky. Bar Assn. Pres. Washington Hills Assn., Cin., 1977-78; bd. dirs. Hamilton Mut. Ins. Co.; past deacon Pleasant Ridge Presbyn. Ch.; past mem. adminstrv. bd. United Meth. Ch. of Milford. Mem. ABA, Ohio Bar Assn., Cin. Bar Assn., Assn. Trial Lawyers Am., Ky. Bar Assn. , No. Ky. Bar Assn., Hamilton County Trial Lawyers Assn., Ohio Acad. Trial Lawyers, Ky. Acad. Trial Attys. Office: Plz Level Ste 120 50 E Rivercenter Blvd Covington KY 41011-1683

LAWRENCE, ROBERT SWAN, physician, educator; b. Phila., Feb. 6, 1938; s. Thomas George and Catherine (Swan) Lawrence; m. Cynthia Starr Cole, July 1, 1960; children: Job Scott, Matthew Swan, Hannah Starr, Jin Sook,

Sang Bo. AB magna cum laude, Harvard U., 1960, MD, 1964. Intern, resident in internal medicine Mass. Gen. Hosp., 1964—66; surgeon USPHS, 1966—69; resident in internal medicine Mass. Gen. Hosp., 1966—70; asst. prof., then assoc. prof. medicine, chief divsn. cmty. medicine Med. Sch. U. NC, 1970—74; dir. divsn. primary care Harvard U. Med. Sch., 1974—91, assoc. prof. medicine, 1980—81, Charles S. Davidson assoc. prof. medicine, 1981—91. Chmn. dept. medicine Cambridge (Mass.) Hosp., 1980—91; adj. prof. NYU Sch. of Medicine, 1992—95; prof. health policy and mgmt. Johns Hopkins Bloomberg Sch. Pub. health, 1995—, assoc. dean for profl. edn., 1995—, Edyth Schoenrich prof. preventive medicine, 2000—; prof. medicine Johns Hopkins Sch. Medicine, 1996—; mem. com. human rights NAS, 1986—97; chmn. bd. health promotion and disease prevention IOM, 1981—86, chmn. com. health and human rights, 1990—94; chmn. U.S. Preventive Svc. Task Force HHS, 1984—89, active mem., 1990—96; fellow Ctr. for Advanced Study in Behavioral Scis., 1988—89; dir. health scis. Rockefeller Found., 1991—95. Editor Am. Jour. Preventive Medicine, 1990—92; contbr. articles to profl. jours., chapters to books. Bd. trustees Columbia U. Tchrs. Coll., 1992—98; bd. dirs. Physicians for Human Rights, 1986—91, 1997—, pres., 1999—. Recipient Maimonides prize, 1964, John Atkinson Ferrell prize, 1997, Albert Schweitzer Humanitarian prize, 2002. Master: ACP; fellow: Am. Coll. Preventive Medicine (Spl. Recognition award 1988); mem.: APHA, Soc. Tchrs. Preventive Medicine (Spl. Recognition award 1993), Soc. Gen. Internal Medicine (pres. 1978—79, Leadership award 1997), Inst. Medicine NAS, Phi Beta Kappa, Delta Omega. Home: Highfield House 1112 4000 N Charles St Baltimore MD 21218-1760 Office: Johns Hopkins Bloomberg Sch Pub Health 615 N Wolfe St Baltimore MD 21205-2103 E-mail: rlawrence@jhsph.edu.

LAWRENCE, ROBERT EDWARD, electrical engineer; b. Boston, May 29, 1946; s. Jules P. and Gertrude (Lander) L.; m. Marjorie Alberta Holman; 1 child, Andrew Jon. BS, Rensselaer Poly. Inst., 1968, MS, 1969, PhD, 1972. Mem. tech. staff Bell Tel. Labs., Whippany, N.J., 1972-74; engr. Vitro Labs., Silver Spring, Md., 1974-77, sr. staff engr., 1978-80; assoc. Booz Allen & Hamilton, Bethesda, 1977-78; dir. Litton Amecom, College Park, 1980-86; consulting engr. THE MITRE Corp., McLean, Va., 1986-96; corp. dir. advanced tech. BAE Sys. (Marconi/Tracor/Vitro). Founder, bd. dirs. Vitro Fed. Credit Union, 1970; mem. Prince George's County Econ. Devel. Corp., 1985-89; cons. U.S. Army Sci. Bd., 1991, NAS-NRC, 1993-96; tech. chmn. Milcom 1991, bd. dirs., 1993—. Contbr. articles to profl. jours. NSF fellow, 1970. Mem. IEEE (sr.), Nat. Def. Indsl. Assn., Armed Forces Comm. Electronics Assn. (past chpt. v.p., past chpt. treas., bd. dirs. 1993-96, bd. dirs. Washington Nat. chpt.), Assn. Old Crows, Sigma Xi, Tau Beta Pi, Eta Kappa Nu. Home: 9011 Copenhaver Dr Potomac MD 20854-3012 E-mail: r.e.lawrence@ieee.org.

LAWRENCE, RUTH, writer, illustrator; b. Bklyn., Aug. 1, 1926; d. Joseph Katz and Sara Rachel Leibick; m. Martin Robert Lawrence, June 4, 1950 (div. June 1975); children: Sandra, Audrey. AA, Nassau C.C., 1968; BA, C.W. Post Coll., 1975. Artist Merrick (N.Y.) Libr., 1973—75; worker U.S. Govt., 1980—95; artist, poet, tchr., lectr., children's book illustrator, 1995—. Cons. Merrick Art Gallery, 1976. Author: My Famous Grandma, 1996, Mostly Limericks for the Millennium, 1998, Columbus, 1999, Barbara Bubbles, 2000. Recipient 1st in oil award, Nassau C.C., Garden City, N.Y., 1975, Best in Show award, 1975. Mem.: Suburban Art League.

LAWRENCE, RUTH ANDERSON, pediatrician, clinical toxicologist; b. N.Y.C. d. Stephen Hayes and Loretta (Harvey) A.; m. Robert Marshall Lawrence, July 4, 1950; children, Robert Michael, Barbara Asselin, Timothy Lee, Kathleen Ann, David McDonald, Mary Khalil, Joan Margaret, John Charles, Stephen Harvey. BS in Biology summa cum laude, Antioch Coll., 1945; MD, U. Rochester, 1949. Internship and residency in pediatrics Yale New Haven (Conn.) Hosp., 1949-50; asst. resident in Medicine Yale New Haven (Conn.) Community Hosp., 1950-51; postdoctoral fellow Yale New Haven Hosp., 1951, chief resident newborn svc., 1951; cons. in medicine U.S. Army, Ft. Dix, N.J., 1952; from clin. instr. to sr. instr. in pediatrics U. Rochester, N.Y., 1952-64, assoc. resident, 1957-58, asst. prof., 1964-70, assoc. prof., 1970-85, prof. pediatrics, ob.-gyn., 1985—. Rsch. pediatrician, Monroe County Health Dept., Rochester, 1952-58; dir. Finger Lakes Regional Poison Control Ctr., 1958—; chief nursery svc. Strong Meml. Hosp., Rochester, 1960-73, chief dept. pediatrics, The Highland Hosp., Rochester, 1960-91; adj. prof. Sch. Pub. Health, SUNY, Albany, 1996-99; rsch. in field. Author: Breastfeeding: A Guide for the Medical Profession, 5th edit., 1999; editor: various periodicals; contbr. numerous articles to profl. publs. Mem. Safety Coun. Rochester and Monroe County, also past pres.; bd. dirs., past pres. Life Line. Recipient Gold Medal award U. Rochester Alumni Assn., 1979, William Keeler award Rochester Safety Coun., 1982, Civic Contribution citation Rochester Safety Coun., 1984, Career Achievement award Girl Scouts U.S. of Genesee Valley, 1987, Rochester Diocesan award for women, St. Bernard's Inst., 1989, Albert David Kaiser medal, 1991, Chamber Civic Health Care award, 1996, Edward Mott Moore award, Monroe County Med. Soc., 2001, numerous svc. awards; named Woman of Yr. Girl Scouts U.S. of Monroe County, 1968; hon. fellow Am. Sch. Health Assn., 1960, rsch. fellow Jackson Meml. Rsch. Labs., 1945. Fellow Am. Pediatric Soc., Am. Acad. Clin. Toxicology (past trustee); mem. Internat. Soc. for Rsch. in Human Milk and Lactation (exec. com. 1995-98), Human Milk Banking Assn. N.Am. (adv. bd.), NAS (subcom. on nutrition during lactation), Acad. Breastfeeding Medicine (founding bd. dirs. 1994—, pres. 1997-98), Alpha Omega Alpha. Roman Catholic. Office: U Rochester Sch Medicine 601 Elmwood Ave Rochester NY 14620-2945 E-mail: ruth_lawrence@urmc.rochester.edu.

LAWRENCE, SALLY CLARK, academic administrator; b. San Francisco, Dec. 29, 1930; d. George Dickson and Martha Marie Alice (Smith) Clark; m. Henry Clay Judd, July 1, 1950 (div. Dec. 1972); children: Rebecca, David, Nancy; m. John I. Lawrence, Aug. 12, 1976; stepchildren: Maia, Dylan. Docent Portland Art Mus., Oreg., 1958-68; gallery owner, dir. Sally Judd Gallery, Portland, 1968-75; art ins. appraiser, cons., 1975-81; interim dir. Mus. Art Sch. Pacific Northwest Coll. Art, 1981—82, acting dir., 1982-84, dir., 1984—94, pres., 1994—. Bd. dirs. Art Coll. Exch. Nat. Consortium, 1982-91, pres., 1983-84. Bd. dirs. Portland Arts Alliance, 1987—, Assn. Ind. Colls. of Art and Design, 1991—, pres., 1995—96, sec., 1996—2001. Fellow: Nat. Assn. Schs. Art and Design (life; bd. dirs. 1984—91, 1994—2001, pres. 1996—99); mem.: Oreg. Ind. Coll. Assn. (bd. dirs. 1981—, exec. com. 1989—94, pres. 1992—93, v.p. 2001—), Pearl Arts Found. (chair bd. dirs. 2000—). Office: Pacific NW Coll Art 1241 NW Johnson St Portland OR 97209-3023 E-mail: sally@pnca.edu.

LAWRENCE, SANFORD HULL, physician, immunochemist, author; b. Kokomo, Ind., July 10, 1919; s. Walter Scott and Florence Elizabeth (Hull) L. AB, Ind. U., 1941, MD, 1944. Fellow in biochemistry George Washington U., 1941; intern Rochester (N.Y.) Gen. Hosp., 1944-45; resident Halloran Hosp., Staten Island, N.Y., 1946-49; chief med. svce. Ft. Ord Regl. Hosp., 1945-46; dir. biochemistry rsch. lab. San Fernando (Calif.) VA Hosp.; asst. prof. UCLA, 1950—. Cons. internal medicine and cardiology U.S. Govt., Los Angeles County; lectr. Faculte de Medicine, Paris, various colls. Eng., France, Belgium, Sweden, USSR, India, Japan; chief med. svc. Ft. Ord Regional Hosp.; chmn. Titus, Inc., 1982—. Author: Zymogram in Clinical Medicine, 1965, Gyert, 2000; contbr. articles to sci. jours.; author: Threshold of Valhalla, Another Way to Fly, My Last Satyr, and other short stories; traveling editor: Relax Mag. Mem. Whitley Heights Civic Assn., 1952—; pres. Halloran Hosp. Employees Assn., 1947-48. Served to maj. U.S. Army, 1945-46. Recipient Rsch. award TB and Health Assn., 1955-58, Los Angeles County Heart Assn., 1957-59, Pres. award, Queen's Blue Book award, Am. Men of Sci. award; named one of 2000 Men of Achievement, Leaders of Am. Sci., Ky. Col., named Hon. Mayor of West Point, Ky. Mem. AAAS, AMA, N.Y. Acad. Scis., Am. Fedn. Clin. Research, Am. Assn. Clin. Investigation, Am. Assn. Clin. Pathology, Am. Assn. Clin. Chemistry, Los Angeles County Med. Assn. Republican. Methodist. Avocations: bridge, comml. pilot, pianist, organist. Home: Whitley Heights 2014 Whitley Ave Los Angeles CA 90068-3235 also: 160 rue St Martin 75003 Paris France

LAWRENCE, STEPHEN KENT, accountant; b. Greenwich, Conn., Aug. 6, 1961; s. Charles Sealy III and Lilles Ann (Tillinghast) L.; m. Patricia Lynne Downing, May 29, 1993; 1 child, Lindsay Michelle. BBA in Fin. cum laude, Ohio U., 1984; MS in Acctg., Am. U., 1992. Fin. analyst Sherwood Brands Inc., Rockville, Md., 1985-87, mgr. acctg., 1987-89, asst. comptr., 1989-92, comptr., dir. ops., 1992—. Mem. Phi Kappa Phi, Beta Gamma Sigma. Republican. Episcopalian. Avocations: music composition, tennis, golf, skiing. Home: 30 Spring St Gaithersburg MD 20877-1900

LAWRENCE, STEPHEN LEE, secondary school principal, mechanic; b. Salt Lake City, Mar. 11, 1946; s. Don and Helen Lawrence; m. Geraldine Lawrence, July 25, 1969; children: Neil, Nathan, Mark, Miles, Drew. BS, Weber State U., 1971; MEd, Utah State U., 1990; EdD, U. Utah, 1995. Cert. in adminstrn.; cert. master mechanic. Prin. Tooele (Utah) County Schs., 1987—. Bd. dirs. Global Media. Author: Cooperative Learning, 1990; contbr. articles to profl. jours. Founder, dir. Tooele Cmty. Theatre, 1995; mem. Deseret Peak coun. Boy Scouts Am., 1990-92; bd. dirs. Wendover Cmty. Resources; mem. adv. bd. Utah State U. Extension. Recipient Centennial Sch. award Utah State Office Edn., 1995, 99, Svc./Learning award Utah State Office Edn., 1996, Grand Champion Chile award Tooele County Commn., 1996. Mem. Utah Assn. Elem. Sch. Prins. (Region 13 dir. 1996-2000). Avocation: cooking, antique auto restoration, computers.

LAWRENCE, STEVEN THOMAS, lawyer; b. Sacramento, Feb. 28, 1968; s. Thomas Georg and Sharon Lee L.; m. Jodi Lynd Hipps, Aug. 8, 1993. BS, Calif. State U., Sacramento, 1990; JD, U. Pacific, 1994. Fin. cons. Govt. Fin. Strategies, Inc., Sacramento, 1990-91; jud. clk. Ariz. Ct. Appeals, Phoenix, 1994-95; dep. county atty. Maricopa County Atty.'s Office, 1995-96; assoc. atty. Felix & Holohan, 1996-98; assoc. gen. counsel JDA Software Group, Inc., 1998-99; corp. counsel SkyMall, Inc., 1999-2000; assoc. Gallagher & Kennedy, P.A., 2000—. Active First Christian Ch., Phoenix. Mem. ABA, Maricopa County Bar Assn. Republican. Avocations: golf, physical fitness, training hunting dogs. Home: 801 W Glenn Dr Phoenix AZ 85021-8638 Office: Gallagher & Kennedy PA 2575 E Camelback Rd Phoenix AZ 85016 E-mail: stl@gknet.com.

LAWRENCE, THEODORE, physician; b. Phila., Feb. 13, 1921; MD, U. Pa., 1950. Diplomate Am. Bd. Internal Medicine, Am. Bd. Cardiovascular Disease. Intern Bryn Mawr Hosp., 1950-51, resident, 1951-52, Long Beach VA Hosp., 1952-53, Phila. VA Hosp., 1953-54, staff physician, 1965-80, Haverford (Pa.) State Hosp., 1980-97, ret., 1997. Fellow ACP. Home: 808 Galer Dr Newtown Square PA 19073-3503

LAWRENCE, THOMAS EUGENE, judge; b. Dallas, Mar. 2, 1949; s. Thomas Usry and Clara Elizabeth (Peel) L.; m. Mickey Jo Lindgren, Mar. 18, 1978. BA, Chapman U., 1971; JD, South Tex. Coll., Houston, 1980. Bar: U.S. Dist. Ct. (so. dist.) Tex. 1981, U.S. Ct. Appeals (5th cir.) 1981. Gen. mgr. Marine Pollution Control Inc., Houston, 1975-77, Peterson Maritime, Inc., Houston, 1977-79; atty. Texaco, Inc., 1980-82; judge Harris County, 1983—. Chmn. ad hoc coms. Justice of the Peace and Constable Assn. Tex., 1989, justice of the peace sect. State Bar Tex., 1989, State Commn. Jud. Conduct, Austin, Tex., 1996-97; mem. desk rev. com. Tex. Justice Ct. Tng. Ctr., Austin, 1985-87; presiding judge Harris County Justice of the Peace, 1989-90; spkr. in field. Contbr. articles to profl. jours. Adv. bd. mem. Roseate, Inc., Houston, North Harris County Jr. League, Houston, 1994-96; mem. North Harris Montgomery C.C. Found., Houston; trustee Mercer Arboretum Found., Houston, 1991-92; organizer Teen Ct. Program, 1991—; chmn. flaming arrow dist. Sam Houston coun. Boy Scouts Am., Houston, 1995. Lt. USCG, 1971-75. Named Boss of Yr., Am. Bus. Women's Assn., 1989, Vol. of Month, Houston Northwest C. of C., April 1997; recipient Meritorious Svc. award Houston Apt. Assn., 1989, Liberty Bell award North Harris Montgomery C.C. Dist., 1992, Scholars award, 1993; Judge Tom Lawrence Day proclaimed by City of Humble, 1992. Fellow Tex. Bar Found.; mem. Am. Judicature Soc., Tex. Bar Assn., Houston Bar Assn. (alternate dispute resolution com.), Houston Northwest and Northeast Harris County Bar Assns., Tex. Justice Ct. Tng. Ctr. (faculty, legal), Houston Northwest C. of C., Rotary (Paul Harris fellow). Republican. Presbyterian. Avocations: golfing, reading, computers. Office: 7900 Will Clayton Pkwy Humble TX 77338-5849

LAWRENCE, WALTER, JR. surgeon, educator; b. Chgo., May 31, 1925; s. Walter and Violette May (Matthews) L.; m. Susan Grayson Shryock, June 20, 1947; children: Walter Thomas, Elizabeth, William Amos, Edward Gene. Student, Dartmouth Coll., 1943-44; PhB, U. Chgo., 1944, SB, 1945, MD with honors, 1948. Diplomate Am. Bd. Surgery (examiner 1974-78, sr. mem. 1978—). Intern Johns Hopkins, 1948-49, asst. resident, 1949-51; fellow Meml. Sloan-Kettering Cancer Center, 1951-52, 54-56, research fellow, 1956, asst. mem., asst. attending surgeon, 1957-60, asso. mem., asso. attending surgeon, 1960-66; practice medicine specializing in surgery N.Y.C., 1956-66, Richmond, Va., 1966—. Instr. surgery Cornell U., 1957-58, asst. profl. clin. surgery, 1958-63, clin. assoc. prof., 1963-66; vis. investigator Queen Victoria Hosp., East Grinstead, Eng., 1964-65; prof. surgery Med. Coll. Va., Richmond, 1966-90, prof. emeritus, 1990--, chmn. divsn. surg. oncology, 1966-90, exec. vice chmn. dept. surgery, 1966-73, acting chmn., 1973-74, Am. Cancer Soc. prof. clin. oncology, 1972-77; dir. Massery Cancer Ctr., 1974-88, dir. emeritus, 1988—; chmn. surgery test com. Nat. Bd. Med. Examiners, 1973-77; med. dir.-at-large Va. divsn. Am. Cancer Soc., 1967—, med. v.p. Am. Cancer Soc., 1975-77, pres., 1977-79, nat. del., 1972-76, mem. nat. coun. for rsch. and clin. investigation, 1974-78, mem. profl. edn. com., 1982-96, bd. dirs., 1985-98, vice chmn., chmn. M&S com., 1986-88, chmn. M&S exec. com., 1989-90, pres. elect, 1990-91, nat. pres., 1991-92, past office dir., 1993-99, hon. life mem., 1999—; bd. sci. counsellors Nat. Cancer Inst., 1978-82, chmn. surg. oncology rsch. devel. com.; mem. Nat. Cancer Adv. Bd., 1988-94; governing coun. Internat. Union Against Cancer, 1994-2002. Author: (with J.J. Terz) Cancer Management, 1977, (with J.J. Terz, J.P. Neifeld) Manual of Soft Tissue Surgery, 1983; mem. editl. bd. Va. Med., 1977-93, Jour. Surg. Oncology, 1978—, assoc. editor, 1991—; editl. bd. Jour. Cancer Edn., 1986; asst. editor Cancer, 1962-65, assoc. editor, 1991-2000, mem. editl. bd., 2000--; contbr. articles to med. jours. Served with USNR, 1942-46; Served with U.S. Army, 1952-54. Recipient Cancer Rsch. award Alfred P. Sloan Found., 1964; J. Shelton Horsley award Am. Cancer Soc., 1973; Disting. Svc. award U. Chgo., 1976; Va. Commonwealth U. Univ. Award for Excellence, 1988, Disting. Faculty award Med. Coll. Va. Alumni Assn., 1988, Va. Cultural Laureate award, 1992, OBICI award, 1992, Dean's award for Disting. Svc., 1992; named to Humera Soc. (hon.), 1992, Beckstrand Cancer Found. Cancer Fighter of Yr., 1999, Presdl. medallion Va. Commonwealth U., 2000, Lifetime Sci. Achievement award Sci. Mus. Va., 2002. Fellow ACS (commn. on cancer 1973-85, chmn. 1979-81), N.Y. Acad. Scis., Royal Soc. Medicine, Soc. Black Acad. Surgeons (hon.); mem. AAAS, AMA, Am. Assn. Cancer Edn., Am. Assn. Cancer Rsch., Am. Gastroenterol. Assn. (coun. on cancer 1972-76), Am. Surg. Assn., Halsted Soc. (pres. 1975), James Ewing Soc., Soc. Head and Neck Surgeons, Am. Soc. Clin. Oncology, Am. Radium Soc. (exec. coun. 1985-87), Soc. Surgery Alimentary Tract (founder), Soc. Surg. Oncology (exec. com. 1976-77, v.p. 1977-78, pres. 1979-80, chmn. exec. coun. 1980-81, Heritage honoree 2002), Soc. Univ. Surgeons, Surg. Biol. Club III (founding mem.), Transplantation Soc., Collegium Internat. Chirurgiae Digestive, Southeastern Surg. Congress, So. Surg. Assn. (v.p. 1999-2000), Pan Am. Med. Assn., Societè Internationale de Chirurgie, Va. Surg. Soc. (v.p. 1973-74), Richmond Surg. Soc. (pres. 1986-87), Richmond Acad. Medicine (trustee 1986-87, 1st v.p. 1988), So. Surg. Assn. (1st v.p. 1999-2000), Argentine Surg. Assn. (hon.), Sigma Xi, Alpha Omega Alpha. Home: 6501 Three Chopt Rd Richmond VA 23226-3118 Office: Med Coll Va Hosps 1200 E Broad St PO Box 980011 Richmond VA 23298-0011

LAWRENCE, WALTER THOMAS, plastic surgeon; b. Balt., Sept. 5, 1950; s. Walter Jr. and Susan (Shryock) L.; m. Marsha Blake, May 30, 1987. BS, Yale U., 1972; MPH, Harvard U., 1976; MD, U. Va., 1976. Diplomate Am. Bd. Surgery. Diplomate Am. Bd. Plastic Surgery. Intern and resident in gen. surgery U. N.C., Chapel Hill, 1976-78; resident gen. surgery Med. Coll. Va., Richmond, 1978-81; resident plastic surgery U. Chgo., 1981-83; expert NIH, Bethesda, Md., 1983-85; asst. prof. U. N.C., Chapel Hill, 1985-92, assoc. prof., div. chmn., 1992-95; prof., divsn. chmn. U. Mass. Med. Ctr., 1995-99, U. Kans. Med. Ctr., Kansas City, 1999—. Fellow Am. Coll. Surgeons; mem. Am. Assn. Plastic Surgeons, Am. Soc. Plastic and Reconstructive Surgeons, Plastic Surgery Rsch. Coun., Humera Soc., Womack Soc. Avocations: skiing, sailing, tennis. Office: U Kans Med Ctr Sutherland Inst/Pl Surgery 3901 Rainbow Blvd Kansas City KS 66160-0001 E-mail: tlawrence@kumc.edu.

LAWRENCE, WAYNE ALLEN, publisher; b. Cin., Dec. 11, 1938; s. Clarence E. and Edna M. (Newman) L.; m. Carol SueAnn Wisecup, July 28, 1959; children: Jeffrey Thomas, Jon Christopher, Jeremy Wayne. Student public schs., Seaman, Ohio. Advt. salesman Amos Press, Inc., Sidney, Ohio, 1957-61, v.p., 1973-83, sr. v.p., 1983-92, ret., 1992, also bd. dirs. Pub. Stamp World, Linns Stamp News, 1977-82; v.p. advt. Coin World, Sidney, 1973-78; advt. mgr. World Coins, Sidney, 1964-68, advt. dir., 1968-73, v.p., 1973-77; adv. mgr. Numis. Scrapbook, Sidney, 1967-68, advt. dir., 1968-73, v.p. advt., 1973-78; pub. Cars & Parts, Sidney, 1978-85; propr., dir. Sidney Camera, 1981-87; pres. Scott Pub. Co., 1984-92. Contbr. articles and editorials on coins, stamps and cars to Amos publs. Bd. dirs. Shelby County (Ohio) United Way, 1970-76, 1st United Meth. Ch., Sidney, 1982— ; bd. dirs. Sidney-Shelby County C. of C., 1982-85, sec., 1985; mem. U.S. Assay Commn., 1975. Mem. Am. Mgmt. Assn., Am. Numis. Assn., Am. Philatelic Assn., Numis. Lit. Guild, Am. Stamp Dealers Assn., Mag. Pubs. Assn., Am. Motorcycle Assn., Soc. Automotive Historians. Home: 1444 Double D Dr Sevierville TN 37876-0287 Office: 911 S Vandemark Rd Sidney OH 45365-8974

LAWRENCE, WILLIAM CLARENCE, business executive, lawyer; b. Tuskegee, Ala., Dec. 15, 1945; s. James Clarence and Nellie Mae James Lawrence; m. Audrey Rochelle Diggs Rackley, Dec. 30, 1973 (div. Sept. 1979); 1 child, Kimberly Ann; m. Grace Louise McDonald, June 23, 1984; children: Antoinette, Robert David. BS in Polit. Sci., Tuskegee U., 1968; M in Pub. Adminstrn., St. Mary's U., 1976; JD, Ind. U., 1979; M in Mgmt., U. Dallas, 1993. Tax atty. audit divsn. U.S. Treasury Dept., Indpls., 1979-80; commodities mgr. Cummins Engine Co., Columbus, Ind., 1980-82; staff mgr. GTE Network Svcs. Planning, Stamford, Conn., 1982-86; product mgr.-consumer GTE Product Mgmt., Irving, Tex., 1986-89, group product mgr.-wireless, 1989-92, group product mgr.-devel., 1992-96; group mktg. mgr.-systems GTE Bus. Sales Ops., 1996-99; pres., CEO Dakiman Co., Highland Village, Tex., 1999—. Chmn., bd. dirs. GTE Hdqrs. PAC, Irving, 1995-98. Pres., bd. dirs. Boston Home Childrens Found., Dallas, 1988-93; commr. Planning and Zoning Commn., Highland Village, 1996-99; chmn. Irving Sch. Dist. Improvement Com., 1998—; mem. Tex. State Textbook Rev. Adv. Panel, 2000; city coun. and mayor pro tem Highland Village, 1999-2000; mayor City of Highland Village, 2000-02. Col. USAF Res., 1976—. Mem. ABA (assoc., alternate disputes resolution sect.), New Product Devel. Assn., Project Mgmt. Inst., Alpha Phi Alpha, Phi Alpha Delta. Republican. Baptist. Avocations: golf, racquetball, volleyball. Home: 2800 Woodlake Ct Highland Village TX 75077-6496

LAWRENCE, WILLIAM HENRY, JR. neurologist; b. Honolulu, Oct. 24, 1938; s. William Henry Sr. and Marjorie Lawrence (Merritt) L.; m. Mary Esther Tate, June 28, 1969; children: Jennifer Merritt Mark Peter. AB, Princeton (N.J.) U., 1960; MD, Columbia U., 1964. Med. resident SUNY, Bklyn., 1965-66; neurology resident U. Calif., San Francisco, 1967-69; rsch. assoc. Brookhaven Nat. Lab., Upton, N.Y., 1971-72; asst. prof. neurology George Washington U., Washington, 1972-75; chief of neurology VA Med. Ctr., Phoenix, 1975—. Mem. health svcs. Ariz. Mex. Commn., Phoenix, 1991—. Maj. USAF, 1969-71; capt. USNR, 1988—. Fellow Am. Acad. Neurology; mem. Am. Assn. Electro Diagnostics. Republican. Episcopalian. Avocations: Mexican history, naval history, geology. Home: 2119 E Lamar Rd Phoenix AZ 85016-1147

LAWRENCE, WILLIAM JOSEPH, JR. retired corporate executive; b. Kalamazoo, Feb. 1, 1918; s. William J. and Borgia M. (Wheeler) L.; m. Doris Luella Fitzgerald, Aug. 19, 1955; children: Aaron Frances, Cleve Moren, Julie Anne, William III. AB, Kalamazoo Coll., 1941. Engaged in personal investments; dir. emeritus Superior Pine Products Co.; dir. LPI. Trustee emeritus, mem. fin. and adminstrn. com. Kalamazoo Found.; trustee emeritus Kalamazoo Coll., Borgess Med. Ctr. With AUS, 1942-46. Mem. Kalamazoo C. of C., Kiwanis, Com. of Twenty-Five (Palm Springs, Calif.), O'Donnell Golf Club (Palm Springs), Gull Lake Country Club, Park Club. Roman Catholic. Home: PO Box 37 Richland MI 49083-0037 Office: 136 E Michigan Ave Ste 1000 Kalamazoo MI 49007

LAWRENCE-COX, NANCY NELL, retired executive secretary, artist; b. Columbus, Miss., Mar. 4, 1934; d. James Edward and Elizabeth Caplinger (Land) Lawrence. BFA, U. Ark., Little Rock, 1983, postgrad., 1983-84. Office boy Miss. State Hwy. Dept., Columbus, 1952-53; clk.-typist FBI, Washington, 1953-54; sec.-automation Little Rock AFB, Ark., 1984-2000; ret., 2000. Exhibited sculptures at U. Ark., 1982 (Best of Show 1981-82), Centre International D'Art Contemporain, 1984, photography at Les Editions Arts et Images du Monde, 1990, Who's Who Internat. Art, Lausanne, Switzerland, 1993. Civic vol. Yes We Can Team 314th Supply Squadron Care Team, 1989-94. Recipient Cert. of Recognition, Jacksonville C. of C., 1991, other awards.

LAWRENZ, INGRID MARIE HELEN, social worker; b. Algoma, Wis., Jan. 14, 1957; d. Harlow J. and Lucille J. (Johns) Nelson; m. Melvin Edward Lawrenz, June 7, 1975; children: Eva Helen, Christopher Edward. BA in Art and Social Work, Carroll Coll., 1978; MSW, U. Wis., Milw., 1986. Cert. ind. clin. social worker. Social worker Cmty. Based Residential Facility, Milw., 1981-83; clin. social worker New Life Resources, Waukesha, Wis., 1986—. Author: (children's book) The Day Momma Played, 1996, (mag.) Marriage Partnership and Just Between Us, 1994—; editl. advisor: (mag.) Marriage Partnership, 1992—; editor, author: (newsletter) New Life Resources, 1996—. Mem. NASW, Nat. Audubon Soc., Nat. Wildlife Assn., Humane Soc. Am., Nature Conservancy, Ridges Sanctuary, Milw. Zoo, Elmbrook Ch. Evangelical. Avocations: art, nature, hiking, skiing, softball. Home: 21815 Doneswood Dr Waukesha WI 53186-5454 Office: New Life Resources Inc 20700 Watertown Rd Waukesha WI 53186-1800

LAWRIE, MICHAEL J. information technology executive; married; 2 children. BA in History, Ohio U., 1975; MBA in Fin. and Mktg., Drexel U., 1977; grad., Dartmouth Inst.; cert. in fin. planning, U. Pa. Various sales, mktg. and fin. positions IBM, 1977—95, v.p. software Asia Pacific, 1995—97, v.p. industries, 1995—97, gen. mgr. personal software products, head divsn. network computing software, 1997—98, gen. mgr. Europe Mid. E. Africa (EMEA), 1998—2001, sr. v.p., group exec. global sales and distbn., 2001—. Mem.adv. bd. Internet Capital Group. Bd. dirs. Marymount Sch. Office: IBM 1133 Westchester Ave White Plains NY 10604*

LAWROSKI, HARRY, nuclear engineer; b. Dalton, Pa., Oct. 10, 1928; s. Alexander and Nancy (Lutchka) L.; m. Mary Ann DeWoody, Oct. 6, 1962. BS in Chem. Engring, Pa. State U., 1950, MS, 1956, PhD, 1959. Research and devel. work in petroleum refining Pa. State U., 1950-58; instr., thesis advisor Argonne (Ill.) Nat. Lab., 1958-63; supt., asso. project dir. exptl. breeder reactor II power plant Idaho Nat. Engring. Lab., 1968-73; gen. mgr. quality assurance and environmental services Nuclear Services Corp., Campbell, Calif., 1973-76; asst. gen. mgr. nuclear fuel processing and waste mgmt. tech. Idaho chem. programs Allied Chem. Corp., Idaho Falls, 1976-79. Cons., 1979—; lectr. Idaho Acad. Scis.; cons. in field; chmn. sci. and tech. project 1990 Idaho Centennial Celebration. Author; patentee in field. Named Outstanding Engring. Alumnus Pa. State U., 1981 Fellow Am. Nuclear Soc. (treas. 1973-77, dir. 1969-77, pres.-elect 1979-80, pres. 1980-81), Am. Inst. Chem. Engrs. (chmn. nuclear engring. div. 1974), Skull and Bones, Sigma Xi, Tau Beta Pi, Sigma Tau, Phi Lambda Upsilon. Clubs: Rotary, Elks. Home: PO Box 717 Wilson WY 83014-0717

LAWRY, JOHN D. psychologist, educator; b. Pitts., May 26, 1938; s. John Edward and Ruth Elizabeth (Daniels) L.; m. Nancy Fink Early Aug. 27, 1966 (div. 1978); 1 child, Liliana. BA, St. Charles Borromeo Sem., 1960; MA, Duquesne U., 1965; PhD, Fordham U., 1972. Prof. of psychol. Marymount Coll., Tarrytown, N.Y., 1965—. Vis. prof. U. Md., College Park, 1978-79. Author: Guide to History of Psychology, 1991, May You Never Stop Dancing, 1998, College 101, 1999. Mem. AAUP, West Co. Psychol. Assn. Avocations: tennis, concert going, writing. Office: Marymount Coll 100 Marymount Ave Tarrytown NY 10591-3796 E-mail: lawry@mmc.marymt.edu.

LAWRYNOWICZ, WITOLD J. chemist, writer; b. Warsaw, Poland, Jan. 10, 1955; came to U.S., 1983; s. Romuald and Hanna L.; m. Grazyna E. Kmiecik, Aug. 13, 1982; children: Malgorzata J., Maria M. MSChemE, Warsaw Tech. U., 1979; PhD, Rutgers U., 1987. Postdoctoral fellow McMaster U., Hamilton, Ont., Can., 1986-88; rsch. investigator Stelco Tech. Svcs., Burlington, Can.,

1988-90; rsch. asst. Starks Assocs., Inc., Buffalo, 1991-92; scientist Interferon Scis., Inc., New Brunswick, N.J., 1992-98; tech. specialist Xerox-The Document Co., Webster, N.Y., 1998—. Contbr. articles to profl. jours. Mem. Polish Militaria Collectors Assn. Avocation: history. Home: 14 Winding Brook Dr Fairport NY 14450-2541 E-mail: witekjl@aol.com.

LAWS, CAROLYN MARIE RODERICK, medical/surgical nurse, pediatrics nurse; b. Anthony, Kans., Feb. 3, 1949; d. Elbert Eugene and Gwendolyn Marie (Moore) R.; m. Gregory Owen Laws, Aug. 1, 1981; 1 child: Jennifer Marie. Diploma, Wesley Sch. Nursing, 1970; BSN cum laude, Wichita State U., 1985. RN, Kans.. Staff nurse William Newton Meml. Hosp., Winfield, Kans., 1970-72, 87-89, asst. unit supr., head nurse, 1972-87, 89-95, dir. social svcs., discharge planner, patient educator, 1995—. Recipient Soroptimist Tng. award, 1981. Mem. Nat. Nurses Assn., Sigma Theta Tau. Home: 2704 Morningview Ave Winfield KS 67156-8997

LAWS, GORDON DERBY, lawyer; b. Dallas, Feb. 1, 1949; s. Wilford Derby and Ruby (Whiteleather) L.; m. Barbara Ruth Hill, May 9, 1974; children: Gordon Derby Jr., Stephen Richard, Ruthanne. BA in Econs., Brigham Young U., 1973, JD, 1976. Bar: Utah 1976, Tex. 1986, U.S. Supreme Ct. 1981, U.S. Ct. Appeals (5th cir.) 1982, U.S. Dist. Ct. (we. dist.) Tex. 1987, U.S. Dist. Ct. (so. dist.) Tex. 1991. Trial atty. U.S. Justice Dept., Washington, 1976-81; asst. U.S. atty. Western Dist. Tex., San Antonio, 1981-87, asst. chief, civil divsn., U.S. atty., 1985-87; assoc. Gary, Thomasson, Hall & Marks, Corpus Christi, Tex., 1987-89, ptnr./mem., 1989—. Mem. exec. com. Gary, Thomasson, Hall & Marks,1994—. Bishop Ch. of Jesus Christ of Latter Day Saints, Corpus Christi, 1990-95. Avocations: reading, camping. Home: 4158 Eagle Dr Corpus Christi TX 78413-2024 Office: Gary Thomasson Hall & Marks 210 Carancahua Ste 500 PO Box 2888 Corpus Christi TX 78403-2888 E-mail: glaws@gthm.com.

LAWS, KENNETH L. physics educator, author; b. Pasadena, Calif., May 30, 1935; s. Allen L. and Florence (Windsor) L.; m. Priscilla Watson, June 3, 1965; children: Kevin Allen, Virginia. BS, Calif. Inst. Tech., 1956; MS, U. Pa., 1959; PhD, Bryn Mawr Coll., 1962. Instr. physics Hobart and William Smith Colls., Geneva, 1958-59; from asst. prof. to prof. physics Dickinson Coll., Carlisle, Pa., 1962-2000, assoc. dean, dir. summer sch., 1971-77, prof. emeritus, 2000—; adminstrv. dir. summer ballet program Ctrl. Pa. Youth Ballet, 1977-87, pres. bd. dirs., 1988-93. Guest faculty Scientific Aspect of the Art of Dance, U. Washington Med. Sch. and Dance Dept., 1982; bd. reviewers Dance: Current Selected Research, 1985—. Author: The Physics of Dance, 1984; (with Cynthia Harvey) Physics, Dance and the Pas de Deux, 1994, Physics and the Art of Dance, 2002; contbr. articles on dance, physics to profl. jours. Office: Dickinson Coll Dept Physics Carlisle PA 17013 E-mail: laws@dickinson.edu.

LAWSON, A(BRAM) VENABLE, retired librarian; b. South Boston, Va., Jan. 9, 1922; s. Abram Venable and Vivien Strudwick (Moseley) L.; children: Janet Lee, Abram Venable, Mary Vivian. BA, U. Ala., 1946; M.Ln., Emory U., 1950; D Libr. Sci., Columbia U., 1969. Auditor Socony Mobil Oil Co., 1947-48; teller 1st Nat. Bank, Altavista, Va., 1948-49; library asst. Harvard Coll. Library, 1951-54; head reference dept. Atlanta Pub. Libr., 1954-56, coord. pub. svcs., 1956-60; asst. prof. Fla. State U., 1960-65; dir. div. librarianship Emory U., Atlanta, 1965-89. Vis. prof. Clark Atlanta U., 1989-90. Advisor Friends of Librs. U.S.A., 1990-93; bd. dirs. Episcopal Charities Found. With USAF, 1942-46. Recipient George Virgil Fuller award Columbia U., 1964, Nick Davies award Friends of Atlanta Fulton Pub. Libr., 1993, Emory medal, 2002. Mem. ALA, AAUP, Assn. Libr. and Info. Sci. Edn., Southeastern Libr. Assn., Ga. Libr. Assn. (Nix-Jones award for disting. svc. to Ga. librarianship 1989). Home: 1065 Briarcliff Rd NE Atlanta GA 30306-2619 E-mail: avlawso@emory.edu.

LAWSON, BEN F. lawyer, international legal consultant; b. Marietta, Okla., Feb. 7, 1939; s. Woodrow W. and Lennie L. (McKay) L.; m. Diane W. Lawson; children: Nicole, Michael C. BBA, U. Houston, 1965, JD, 1967. Bar: Tex. 1967. Atty. Monsanto/Burmah Oil, Houston, 1967-72; mgr. internat. acquisitions Oxy (formerly Cities Svc. Co.), 1972-78; gen. atty. Damson Oil Corp., 1978-81; gen. counsel, v.p. Newmont Oil Co., 1981-86; pvt. practice internat. law, 1986—. Cons. internat., 1987—. Contbr. numerous articles to profl. jours. Staff sgt. USAF, 1959-65. Fellow Houston Bar Found.; mem. ABA, Am. Corp. Counsel Assn. (chmn. oil and gas com. 1986-87). Republican. Avocations: fishing, antiques. Address: 3027 Bernadette Ln Houston TX 77043-1302 E-mail: customwise@aol.com.

LAWSON, BETH ANN REID, strategic planner; b. N.Y.C., Jan. 9, 1954; d. Raymond Theodore and Jean Elizabeth (Frinks) Reid; m. Michael Berry Lawson, Jan. 29, 1983; children: Rayna, Sydney. BA, Va. Tech., 1976; MPA, Golden Gate U., 1983; postgrad. law, Regent U. From systems analyst I to support ops. asst. City of Virginia Beach, Va., 1977-93, water conservation coord., 1993-94; owner Strategic Planning and Teamwork, Virginia Beach, 1993—; cons. Resort Leadership Coun., 1998-99. Cons., 1996-2000, Lifesaving Mus. Va., 1994, 98, Virginia Beach C.A.R.E. Com., 1995, Virginia Beach Rescue Squad, 1992—, Virginia Beach Mcpl. Employees Fed. Credit Union, 1992—, Virginia Beach Resort Area Adv. Commn., 1993, Virginia Beach Conv. and Visitors Devel. Bur., 1991-93, 98—; customer svc. trainer Virginia Beach Hotel/Motel Superhost, 1995—. Sunday sch. tchr. Wycliffe Presbyn. Ch., Virginia Beach, 1996—, softball coach, 1997. Mem. Virginia Beach Rescue Squad (hon., life), Va. Tech. Alumni Assn. (pres. 1982-83), Rotary (Outstanding Employee award 1993). Avocations: tennis, movies, planning, writing. Home: 701 Earl Of Warwick Ct Virginia Beach VA 23454-2910 Office: Strategic Planning and Teamwork 701 Earl Of Warwick Ct Virginia Beach VA 23454-2910

LAWSON, BEVERLY ELAINE, nursing administrator; b. St. Louis, Mar. 17, 1946; d. Berrie Sr. and Odessa (Wallace) L. BSN, Dillard U., New Orleans, 1968; MPH, Hunter Coll., 1984, cert. Nurse Practitioner, 1981. RN, N.Y. Family nurse practitioner Dr. Martin Luther King Health Ctr., Bronx, N.Y., 1972-88, co-planner health outreach program in maternal child health, 1988-90, tchr. lamaze, 1990—, co-planner adolescent pregnancy program, 1991—, nutrition educator, nursing rep.; dir. nursing svcs., family nurse practitioner Leake and Watts Svcs., 1988-91, clin. computerliaison; part time family nurse practitioner Planned Parenthood, 1991-99; dir. employee health svcs., family nurse practitioner Leake and Watts, 1991—; clin. preceptor Pace U. Lienhard Sch. Nursing, 1998—; family nurse practitioner Woodfield Correctionsl Facility, Vahalla, N.Y., 1995-2000. Part-time women's health nurse practitioner Planned Parenthood, Yonkers Robert Woods Found. grantee. Mem. Assn. Nurse Practitioners, ANA, N.Y. State Nurse's Assn., N.Y. State Cert. FNP, Delta Sigma Theta. Office: Leake & Watts Svcs Inc 463 Hawthorne Ave Yonkers NY 10705-3441 E-mail: blawson@leakeandwatts.org.

LAWSON, CAROLE JEAN, religious educator, author, poet; b. San Antonio, June 18, 1944; d. Albert Joseph and Pearl Nettie (Garner) Fuller; m. James Ray Lawson, Sept. 7, 1962; children: Regina Anne (Lawson) Kacho, Clinton Ray. Founder Love Makes the World Go Around in Peace, Ft. Worth, 1988—; founder, dir. Healing Thru Love Seminars, 1988—; founder Sunshine 'n Rainbows Stress Overcomers, 1985-87; founder, head Omni-Vision Pub. and Prodns., 1990—93, 2002—. Pub. editor Omni Vision newsletter, 1985-93, 2002-; author: To God Be the Glory, poetry collection, 1988-90, My Rocky Mountain High, 1989, The Reflection of God's Smile, 1991. Sec. Lightly Speaking Forum, Ft. Worth, 1987—89; supporter publicity Campaign for the Earth, 1990—91; founder Omni Vision Ministries, 1993—99, 2002—; dir. Chapel of Light Conf. Ctr., Lake Whitney, 2001—02; founder Universal World Investments, Chi Energy Wholeness Ctr., Lake Whitney, Tex., 2001—02. Named Honorary Mayan Centurian. Mem. Internat. Platform Assn. Home and Office: Chi Ctr 1112 Edney St Fort Worth TX 76115-4317 Fax: 254-694-6912. *With the energy shifting at excelerated speed to usher in the new, we must also excelerate our consciousness into the reality of Divine Love with inward harmony and peace. Without this individually expressed by each of us, there will be deterioration and insanity upon the earth resulting in loss of all life as we know it to be as never before experienced. Unconditional love is a must. God is Love!.*

LAWSON, DIANNE JANICE, piano instructor; b. Grand Island, Nebr., Feb. 05; d. Wilbur Bennett and Helen Janice Eby (Gillespie) Olsen; m. Ronald Stephen Lawson, Aug. 18, 1968; children: Ronda, Ryan. BA in Edn., Nebr. Wesleyan U., 1968; MusM, U. Nebr., 1998. Jr. h.s. math instr. Lewis Ctrl. Cmty. Schs., Council Bluffs, Iowa, 1968-69, Carson (Iowa) Macedonia Cmty. Schs., 1969-70; pvt. piano instr. Harlan, Iowa, 1970—; accompanist Harlan Cmty. Schs., 1981—. Piano recitals include Cathedral Arts Concert, Omaha, 1996, Harlan, Iowa, 1997. Christian edn. asst. First United Meth. Ch., Harlan, 1981-87, worship chair, 1994—; cont. edn. scholarship chair P.E.O., Harlan, 1993-97, treas., 1998; scholarship chair used book sale Harlan Fed. Womens Club, 1994-96; musician for benefit Symphony Showhouse, Omaha, 1996. Recipient Layperson Svc. award Harlan Cmty. Schs., 1987, Performance in Keyboard Arts Festival award U. Nebr., Omaha, 1996; grantee Piano Technicians Guild Continuing Edn., 1996, Iowa Fed. Music Clubs, 1996. Mem. Music Tchrs. Nat. Assn. (cert.), Iowa Music Tchrs. Assn. (cert.), S.W. Iowa Music Tchrs. Assn. (pres. 1989-91, rec. sec. 1991-93, festival chmn. 1991—), Iowa Fed. Music Clubs (festival adjudicator 1988—), Nat. Fed. Music Clubs, Tri-County Music Club. United Methodist. Avocations: playing piano for weddings, gardening, reading, church volunteer work. Home: 1210 Durant St Harlan IA 51537-1216

LAWSON, EDWARD EARLE, neonatologist; b. Winston-Salem, N.C., Aug. 6, 1946; s. Robert Barrett and Elsie Chatterton (Earle) L.; m. Rebecca Newhall Fitts, June 21, 1969; children: Katherine Tabor, Robert Barrett II. BA magna cum laude, Harvard U., 1968; MD, Northwestern U., 1972. Diplomate Am. Bd. Pediat. and Neonatal/Perinatal Medicine. Intern then resident pediat. Children's Hosp., Boston, 1972-75, fellow neonatology, 1975-78; from asst. prof. pediat. to prof. pediat. U. N.C., Chapel Hill, 1978-99, chief divsn. neonatal medicine, 1987-95, interim chmn. dept. pediat., 1993-95; vice chmn., dept. pediat., 1995-99; prof. pediat., vice chair dept. pediat. Johns Hopkins U., Balt., 1999—; chief divsn. neonatology, dept. pediat. Johns Hopkins U. Hosp., 1999—. Editor-in-chief Jour. Perinatology, 2001—; assoc. editor Jour. of Pediat., 1985-95; contbr. numerous articles to profl. jours. Recipient Sidney Farber Meml. Rsch. award United Cerbral Palsy, 1982, Rsch. Career Devel. award NIH, 1982-87; fellow E. L. Trudeau, 1978-81, Alexander Von Humboldt, 1985-86; NIH grantee, 1979-2000. Fellow Am. Acad. Pediat.; mem. Am. Lung Assn. (sci. adv. com. 1989-91), Am. Thoracic Soc. (bd. dirs. 1988-90), Am. Bd. Pediat., Am. Pediat. Soc., Perinatal Rsch. Soc. Achievements include research on developmental aspects of respiratory control, particularly physiology and neurobiology. Office: Johns Hopkins Hosp Dept Pediatrics 600 N Wolfe St CMSC 210 Baltimore MD 21287-0001 E-mail: elawson@jhmi.edu.

LAWSON, FRED RAULSTON, banker; b. Sevierville, Tenn., Mar. 26, 1936; s. Arville Raulston and Ila Mary (Lowe) L.; m. Sharon Sheets, Jan. 1, 1982; children: Terry Lawson Akins, Laura Lawson Rathbone, Kristi Watson Newvine. Student, U. Tenn., 1953-59, La. State U. Sch. Banking of South, 1965-68, Harvard Inst. Fin. Mgmt., 1968; D (hon.), Mayrville Coll. From br. mgr. to exec. v.p. Blount Nat. Bank, Maryville, Tenn., 1958-68, pres., 1968-86, also bd. dirs.; pres. Tenn. Nat. Bancshares, Inc., 1971-86, Bank of East Tenn., Knoxville, 1986-92; pres., CEO BankFirst, 1993-2001; commr. dept. fin. instn.s State of Tenn., 2001—. Mem. Covenant Health Fin./Investment Com., 2000—, also bd. dirs. Mem. Blount County Indsl. Devel. bd., 1969—; chancellors assoc. U. Tenn., Knoxville, 1971-78; trustee Carson-Newman Coll., Jefferson City, 1984-94, Harrison-Chilhowee Bapt. Acad., Seymour, Tenn., 1972-85, Pellissippi State Found., 1989-96; adv. bd. U. Tenn. Med. Rsch. Ctr. and Hosp.; bd. regents Mid-South Sch. banking, Memphis, 1982-90; bd. dirs. Thompson Cancer Survival Ctr., Knoxville, 1987-2000, The Downtown Orgn., Tenn. Resource Valley, East Tenn. Hist. Soc., Maryville Coll., 1995—; commr. Dept. of Fin. Instns. of State of Tenn., 2001—. Recipient Tenn. Indsl. Devel. Vol. award, 1977. Mem. Assn. Bank Holding Cos. (bd. dirs. 1978-82), Tenn. Bankers Assn. (chmn. state legis. com. 1980, banking practice com. 1983, bd. dirs. 1990—, pres. 1994-95). Republican. Baptist. Home: 2101 Cochran Rd Maryville TN 37803-2812

LAWSON, GARY B. lawyer; b. N.Y.C., Oct. 5, 1945; s. Dave and Rose Helen (Shapiro) Levy; m. Marcia Krauss, June 19, 1981; 1 child Seth David. AA, Queens Coll., 1966; JD, St. Johns U., 1970; LLM in Taxation, NYU, 1974. Bar: NY, Wis. 73, Ill. 76, Ga. 83, Mass. 83, Tex. 84. Atty. Mut. Life Ins. Co., N.Y.C., 1970—72; assoc. Hoyt, Greene, Meissner and Walsh, Milw., 1972—74, Walsh & Simon, Milw., 1974—76; ptnr. Katten, Muchin, Zavis, Pearl & Galler, Chgo., 1976—81; of counsel Haas, Holland, Lipshutz, Levison & Gilbert, Atlanta, 1981—82, Mintz, Levin, Cohn, Ferris, Glovsky & Popeo, P.C., Boston, 1982—84, Jenkens & Gilchrist, Dallas, 1987—93, Lawson & Fields P.C., 1993—2002, Lawson, Fields, McCue, Lee & Campbell P.C., Addison, Tex., 2002—. Instr. U. Wis.-Milw., 1975. Bd. dirs. Parental Stress Svcs., Chgo., 1980—81, Hope Found., 1989—92, Medisend Internat., 1990—98. Mem.: Boston Estate and Bus. Planning Coun., S.W. Pension Conf. (bd. dirs. 1986—89), New Eng. Employee Benefits Coun. (bd. dirs. 1983—85), ABA (tax sect.). Office: Lawson Fields McCue Lee & Campbell 14135 Midway Rd Addison TX 75001 E-mail: glawson@lfmlc.com.

LAWSON, GARY D. audiology educator; b. Maryville, Tenn., May 19, 1941; s. Silas S. and Geneva M. (Carpenter) Lawson Smith; m. Rebecca S. Epps, Aug. 16, 1970; 1 child, Christopher F. BA, U. Tenn., 1964, MA, 1969; PhD, Mich. State U., 1980. TV prodr.-dir. U. Tenn., Knoxville, 1966-67, rsch. instr., 1969-71, grad. asst., 1971-72; instr. Ohio U., Athens, 1972-75; grad. asst. Mich. State U., East Lansing, 1975-76, 77-78, adj. instr., 1976-77; asst. prof. Western Mich. U., Kalamazoo, 1978-83, assoc. prof., 1983—. Contbr. chpt. to book, articles to profl. jours., including Jour. Auditory Rsch., Jour. Acoustical Soc. Am., Jour. Vestibular Rsch., Jour. Visual Impairment and Blindness. 1st lt. U.S. Army, 1964-66, Korea. Fellow Am. Acad. Audiology; mem. Acoustical Soc. Am. (assoc.), Am. Speech-Lang.-Hearing Assn. (cert. clin. competence in audiology and speech-lang. pathology, legis. councilor 1997-99), Mich. Acad. Audiology, Mich. Speech-Lang.-Hearing Assn. (pres.-elect 1995, pres. 1996, past pres. 1997). Avocations: dancing, camping, hiking. Office: Western Mich U Dept Speech Pathology-Audiology Kalamazoo MI 49008 E-mail: gary.lawson@wmich.edu.

LAWSON, GERALD WILBUR, retired health facility administrator; b. Brunswick, Md., July 4, 1942; s. Harry Clarkson and Pauline Lawson; m. Becky Ann Pounds, Oct. 26, 1985; children: Darwyn, Sherry Hudson, Holly Jo. Grad. H.S., Frederick, Md., car. Animal caretaker NIH, Bethesda, Md., 1964-65, carpenter, 1965-70, cabinet maker, 1970-73, maintenance inspector, 1973-82, contract inspector, 1982-86, project officer, 1986-93, spl. projects mgr., 1993-2000; ret., 2000. Owner home improvement co., Frederick, 1964-78. Pres. Home Owner Assn., Germantown, Md., 1984. Mem. Train Collector's Assn., Elks. Avocation: large scale model railroading. E-mail: lawson4500@aol.com.

LAWSON, HARRY WILBUR, chemist, consultant, writer; b. Chgo., June 22, 1920; s. Harry Wilbur and Maude Lillian (Cleveland) L.; m. Betty Jane Cooper, Mar. 13, 1944; children: Ralph S., Janet Lawson Jenrette, Sally Bailey. BS, U. Ill., 1941; postgrad., U. Cin., 1946-50. Chemist, lab. supr. DuPont, Joliet, Ill., 1941-44; mgr. product devel tech. svc. Procter & Gamble, Cin., 1946-82, founder food svc. rsch. dept., 1947; ret., 1982; chemistry cons., Cin., Florence, Ky., Can., Honduras, 1982—. Hon. mem. faculty Mich. State U., Lansing, 1977; vol. exec. Internat. Exec. Svc., Honduras, 1988; program spkr. Nat. Restaurant Assn., Chgo., 1952-55. Author: Standards for Fats and Oils, 1985, Food Oils and Fats—Technology, Utilization and Nutrition, 1995; contbr. articles to food svc. publs. Mgr. Little League Baseball, Cin., 1954-63; v.p. PTA, Mt. Airy, Ohio, 1957; pres. Aiken H.S. Boosters, Cin., 1966. With USN, 1944-46, PTO. Mem. Am. Chem. Soc., Am. Oil Chemists Soc., Am. Bakers Assn., Am. Assn. Cereal Chemists, Inst. Am. Poultry Industries, Am. Soc. Bakery Engrs. (program chmn.). Republican. Presbyterian. Avocations: travel, reading, walking, volunteering, problem solving. Home and Office: 7152 Cascade Dr Florence KY 41042-2540

LAWSON, H(ERBERT) BLAINE, JR. mathematician, educator; b. Norristown, Pa., Jan. 4, 1942; s. Herbert Blaine and Mary Louise (Corson) L.; m. Carolyn Elaine Pieroni, June 6, 1964 (div. Sept. 1977); children: Christina Corson, Heather Brooke. AB, ScB in Applied Mat. and Russian Lit., Brown U., 1964; MS in Math., Stanford U., 1966, PhD in Math., 1968. Lectr. math. U. Calif., Berkeley, 1968-70, assoc. prof., 1971-74, prof., 1974-80, asst. dean, 1975-77; Disting. prof., chmn. SUNY, Stony Brook, 1978—. Vis. asst. prof. IMPA, Rio de Janeiro, 1970-71; vis. prof. Inst. des Hautes Etudes Scientifiques, Bures-sur-Yvette, France, 1977-78, Ecole Poly., Palaiseau, France, 1983-84; bd. dirs. U.S.-Brazilian Math. Exch., Stony Brook and Rio de Janeiro; trustee Math. Scis. Rsch. Inst., Berkeley; chmn. Nat. Com. Math. NAS, Washington, 1989-91; mem. Inst. Advanced Study, Princeton U., 1973-74; lectr. in minimal submanifolds, 1971. Author: The Theory of Gauge Fields in 4 Dimensions, 1985, Spin Geometry, 1989; editor Jour. Differential Geometry, Topology, The Princeton Mat. Series; contbr. articles to profl. jours. Sloan Found. fellow, 1971, Guggenheim Found. fellow, 1983, Japan Soc. Promotion Sci. fellow, 1985. Mem. Nat. Acad. of Sci., Am. Math. Soc. (coun. 1988-91, v.p. 1997-2000, , editor jour., Steele prize 1975), Brazilian Acad. of Scis. Achievements include construction of minimal surfaces in the 3-dimensional sphere, construction of foliations on higher dimensional spheres; characterization of boundaries of analytic varieties; co-creation of Calibrated Geometries; research on basic results on manifolds on non-positive curvature, on spaces of positive scalar curvature, on stability results for Yang-Mills fields, on relations between algebraic cycles and topology, and on structure of Chow Varieties. Home: 29 North Rd Stony Brook NY 11790-1009 E-mail: blaine@math.synysb.edu.

LAWSON, JACK WAYNE, lawyer; b. Decatur, Ind., Sept. 23, 1935; s. Alva W. and Florence C. (Smitley) L.; m. Sarah J. Hibbard, Dec. 28, 1961; children: Mark, Jeff. BA in Polit. Sci., Valparaiso U., 1958, JD, 1961. Bar: Ind. 1961, U.S. Supreme Ct. 1970, U.S. Dist. Ct. (no., so. dists.) Ind. 1991, Ind. Supreme Ct., Appellate Cts. 1991. Ptnr. Beckman, Lawson LLP, Ft. Wayne, Ind., 1961-84, sr. ptnr., 1984—. Seminar presenter and writer Ind. CLE Forum, Indpls., 1970—. Nat. Health Lawyers Assn., Washington, 1986. Editor-in-chief Indiana Real Estate Transactions; contbr. articles to profl. jours. Mem. Ft. Wayne C. of C., 1975—; small claims ct. judge, Allen County, Ind., 1963-67. Recipient Sagamore Wabash award, Gov. State of Ind., 2001. Mem. Am. Coll. Real Estate Lawyers. Republican. Lutheran. Avocations: sailing, teaching religious seminars, antique consulting. Office: Beckman Lawson LLP 800 Standard Federal Plaza PO Box 800 Fort Wayne IN 46801-0800

LAWSON, JANE ELIZABETH, bank executive; b. Cornwall, Ont., Can. d. Leonard J. and Margaret Lawson. BA, U. N.B., Can., LLB, 1971. With law dept. Royal Bank Can., Montreal, 1974-78, sr. counsel, 1978-84, v.p., corp. sec., 1988-92, sr. v.p., sec., 1992—. Mem.: Am. Soc. Corp. Secs., Inst. Corp. Dirs., Inst. Chartered Secs. and Adminstrs., Que. Bar Assn., N.B. Bar Assn., Can. Bar Assn., Royal Can. Yacht Club, Mt. Royal Tennis Club. Office: Royal Bank Plz PO Box 1 Toronto ON Canada M5J 2J15

LAWSON, J(ENICE) EVELYN, quality assurance professional, pharmacist; b. Ozark, Mo., Jan. 20, 1952; d. Robert Evelyn and Jenice Gemima (Spiess) L. AA, East Cen. Coll., 1972; BS in Pharmacy, U. Mo., Kansas City, 1975; BS in Chemistry, Northwest Mo. State U., 1979; MS in Pharmaceutics and Pharm. Chemistry, Ohio State U., 1985. Registered pharmacist, Mo. Pharmacy intern Federmann Drug Store, Kansas City, 1974; staff pharmacist The Corner Drug, Maryville, Mo., 1975, St. Francis Hosp., Maryville, 1976-78, Easter's Ben Franklin Pharmacy, Maryville, 1979; grad. rsch., teaching assoc. Ohio State U., Columbus, 1980-84; pharmacist Boehringer Ingelheim, Ingelheim, Fed. Rep. Germany, 1985; computer programmer, cons., coll. pharmacy Ohio State U., Columbus, 1986-87; mgr. Lynn Drug Co., 1987-88; regulatory compliance specialist Clorox Tech. Ctr., Pleasanton, Calif., 1989—. Preposition 65 coord., 1989-94, monitor of upcoming legis. pertaining to co., rev. materials for compliance with regulations, submit documents to fed. EPA, Clorox Tech. Ctr., Pleasanton, 1989—. Tutor Laubach Literacy Action, Livermore, Calif., 1989; adult choir, handbell choir, children's choir, pianist, single adult min. worker Trinity Bapt. Ch., Livermore. Mem. Am. Pharm. Assn. Contra Costa German-Am. Club, Soc. Risk Analysis and Exposure Assessment, Diamond Toastmasters (sec. dist. 57 club 4582, 1991, treas. 1991—, pres. 1991, Competent Toastmaster award 1991, Able Toastmaster award 1993), Kappa Epsilon (Nellie Wakeman award 1983). Southern Baptist. Avocations: long distance bicycling, music, German fluency. Office: Clorox Tech Ctr PO Box 493 Pleasanton CA 94566-0803

LAWSON, JENNIFER, broadcast executive; b. Birmingham, Ala., June 8, 1946; d. Willie DeLeon and Velma Theresa (Foster) L.; m. Elbert Sampson, June 1, 1979 (div. Sept. 1980); m. Anthony Gittens, May 29, 1982; children: Kai, Zachary. Student, Tuskegee U., 1963-65; MFA, Columbia U., 1974; LHD (hon.), Teikyo Post U., Hartford, Conn., 1991. Assoc. producer William Greaves Prodns., N.Y.C., 1974-75; asst. prof. film studies Bklyn. Coll., 1975-77; exec. dir. The Film Fund, N.Y.C., 1977-80; TV coord. Program Fund Corp. for Pub. Broadcasting, Washington, 1980-83, assoc. dir. TV Program Fund, 1983-89, dir. TV Program Fund, 1989; exec. v.p. programming PBS, Alexandria, Va., 1989-95; broadcast cons. Md. Pub. TV, 1995—98, exec. cons., 1996—, exec. prodr. Africa, 1998-2001; pres. Magic Box Mediaworks, 1996—. V.p. Internat. Pub. TV, Washington, 1984-88; panelist Fulbright Fellowships, Washington, 1988-90. Author, illustrator: Children of Africa, 1970; illustrator: Our Folktales, 1968, African Folktales: A Calabash of Wisdom, 1973. Coord. Nat. Coun. Negro Women, Washington, 1969. Avocations: painting, reading. Office: 1838 Ontario Pl NW Washington DC 20009-2109

LAWSON, JOHN QUINN, architect; b. Tucumcari, N.Mex., Apr. 11, 1940; s. Tom L. and Mable Marie (Hagglund) L.; m. Elizabeth Jo Waddel, June 4, 1961 (div. 1980); children: Bevan Eugene, Cary Augusta; m. Lorna Miriam Katz, Feb. 20, 1981. BA, Rice U., 1961, BSArch, 1962; MFA in Architecture, Princeton U., 1964. Registered architect, Pa., N.J. Staff architect Doxiadis Assocs., Phila., 1961, Collins, Uhl, Hoisington, Princeton, N.J., 1963, Frank Schlesinger, Doylestown, Pa., 1964, Kneedler Mirick & Zantzinger, Phila., 1964, Mitchell/Giurgola Architects, Phila., 1965-71, assoc., 1972-73, ptnr., 1974-85, John Lawson Architects, Phila., 1986—. Mem. adj. faculty Grad. Sch. Fine Arts U. Pa., 1972-87; chmn. archtl. adv. bd. Spring Garden Coll., Phila., 1986-92. Prin. works include United Way hdqrs. bldg., Phila., 1971, Lang Music Bldg. Swarthmore (Pa.) Coll., 1973, Ind. Nat. Hist. Park maintenance bldg., Phila., 1981, Columbia Ave. Sta. improvements, Phila., 1983, all recipients Pa. Soc. Architects awards, Benjamin Franklin Bridge Lighting Competition, Phila., 1986 (1st runner-up), Diamond Park Competition, Phila., 1987 (winner with Chuck Fahlen), Evancich residence, Phila., 1990 (1st prize Best Residential Renovation), Ctr. for Animal Health and Productivity, Sch. Vet. Medicine, U. Pa., 1990, Comparative Orthop. Rsch. Lab., Sch. Vet. Medicine, U. Pa., 1998, The Vistas at Lake Worth Apts., Ft. Worth, 1998, Coll. Hall Interior Renovations South Central Ground Floor, East Wing, U. Pa., 1999-2000, Smart Classroom, Delaware Valley Coll., Doylestown, Pa., 2001. V.p. Logan Sq. Neighborhood Assn., Phila., 1971-72; mem. Community Leadership Seminar Alumni, Phila., 1982-85; cons. Friends of Starr Garden, Inc., Phila., 1989; vol. exec., Internat. Exec. Svc. Corps, Cairo, 1998. Lowell M. Palmer fellow Princeton U., 1964, NEA Mid-Career fellow Am. Acad. in Rome, 1980. Fellow AIA (mem. architecture for edn. com. 1976-85, chmn. urban design com. Phila. chpt. 1986-98, Fellows steering com. Phila chpt. 1988—); mem. Pa. Soc. Architects, Soc. Hill Civic Assn., City Pks. Assn. (bd. dirs. 1988—), Awbury Arboretum Assn. (bd. dirs. 1989-99), Soc. Hill Towers (coun. 1994-2002). Democrat. Office: John Lawson Architects 812 Chestnut St Apt 2 Philadelphia PA 19107-5115 E-mail: jlawsonarch@earthlink.net.

LAWSON, JONATHAN NEVIN, university official; b. Latrobe, Pa., Mar. 27, 1941; s. Lawrence Winters and Mary Eleanor (Rhea) L.; m. Leigh Farley (div.); children: Paul, Joshua, Jacob; m. Pamela Cross. AA, York Coll. Pa., 1962; BFA, Tex. Christian U., 1964, MA, 1966, PhD, 1970. Dir. composition St. Cloud (Minn.) State U., 1971-77, assoc. dean, 1977-81; asst. vice chancellor Minn. State U. System, St. Paul, 1980-81; dean liberal arts Winona (Minn.) State U., 1981-84; dean arts and scis. U. Hartford, West Hartford, Conn., 1984-86, sr. v.p., dean of faculty, 1986-95; v.p. acad. affairs Idaho State U., Pocatello, 1995—. Mem. S.E. Id. Works Bd., 2000—. Author: Robert Bloomfield, 1980; editor: Collected Works: Robert Bloomfield, 1971; contbr. articles and papers to scholarly publs; assoc. editor Rhetoric Soc. Quar., St. Cloud, 1974-79. Mem. regional adv. bd. Greater Hartford C.C., 1992-94; trustee Hartford Coll. for Women, 1992-94; mem. acad. affairs com. Idaho Bd. Edn., 1995—; bd. dirs. Bannock County Devel. Corp., 1998—, sec., treas., 2001—. Mem. Am. Coun. Edn., Coun. Fellows Alumni, Coun. Liberal Learning, Assn. Gen. and Liberal Studies, Assn. Am. Colls., N.E. Assn. Schs. and Colls. (chmn. commn. on instns. higher edn. 1992-95), Asian Studies Consortium (chmn. bd. 1991-94), Pocatello C. of C. (bd. dirs., v.p.), Lambda

Iota Tau (hon.), Alpha Chi (hon.). Episcopalian. Avocations: fishing, camping, writing, walking. Home: 1401 Juniper Hill Rd Pocatello ID 83204-4921 Office: Idaho State U PO Box 8063 Pocatello ID 83209-0001 E-mail: lawsona@isu.edu.

LAWSON, KENNETH, federal agency administrator; degree, law degree, Fla. State U. Spl. asst. U.S. atty. Ea. Dist. N.C.; asst. U.S. atty. Mid. Dist. Fla., Tampa; mil. prosecutor USMC, 1991—94; asst. sec. for enforcement U.S. Dept. Treasury, Washington, 2001—. Office: US Dept Treasury Under Sec Enforcement 1500 Pennsylvania Ave NW Washington DC 20220*

LAWSON, MELANIE KAY, management administrator, early childhood consultant; b. Fort Valley, Ga., Feb. 8, 1955; d. William C. and Mamie Nell (Brown) Chapman; m. Robert Scott Lawson, Dec. 18, 1975; children: Robert Scott Jr., Joshua Cody, Ashley Jeanell. AA, Cisco Jr. Coll., 1984; BE in Elem./Spl. Edn., Hardin-Simmons U., 1988, MEd in Reading, 1990; MEd in Sch. Adminstrn., Abilene Christian U., 1992; MEd in Higher Edn., Tex. Tech. U., 1996, postdoctoral. Cert. reading specialist, supr., mid-mgmt. tchr. Speech pathology asst. Head Start/Abilene Ind. Sch. Dist., Abilene, Tex., 1983-84; assoc. tchr. Head Start/AISD, 1984-88, cert. tchr., 1988-90; English as second lang. tchr. AISD-Curriculum div., 1990-92; kindergarten tchr. AISD-Long Elem. Sch., 1992-93; asst. dir. Child Devel. Ctr., Dyess AFB, 1993-94; tng. mgr. 7 SVS Squadron, 1994-97; reading specialist North Kansas City Sch. Dist., Kansas City, Mo., 1997-99; 1st grade tchr. Lubbock (Tex.) Ind. Sch. Dist., 1999—. Mem. Youth Task Force, Abilene City Govt., 1994-95, Higher Edn. Working Group, Tex. Head Start Collaboration Project, local conf. corrd., Abilene Work/Family Planning Series Conf. Recipient Key City Reading award Reading Coun., 1988; Pres. Trust Fund scholarship Tex. Assn. for the Edn. of Young Children, 1996. Mem. AAUW, Internat. Reading Assn., Nat. Assn. Edn. of Young Children (Membership Affiliate grant 1994, academy mentor 1995—, validator 1993—), Tex. Assn. Edn. of Young Children (at-large, Tex. Affiliate grant, 1993, 94, exec. bd., chair accreditation, Pres.'s Trust Fund Scholarship 1996), Big Country Assn. for Edn. of Young children (membership chair 1988-90, pres. 1992-94, state repl 1992-94), Tex. Assn. for Gifted/Talented (grant 1991), U.S. Tennis Assn., Coun. Profl. Recognition (rep. 1993—), Golden Key Honor Soc., Kappa Delta Phi, Phi Delta Kappa. Avocations: reading, sewing, walking, ceramics, wood crafts. Home: PO Box 98693 Lubbock TX 79499

LAWSON, NANCY KATHERINE, medical/surgical nurse; b. Greenville, Miss., May 16, 1961; d. Carl Frederick and Nancy Long (Ruscoe) L. AA, U. Cen. Fla., 1984; BSN, U. South Fla., 1991, postgrad., 1991—. Staff nurse Tampa Gen. Hosp., Davis Islands, Fla.; home health nurse Home Health Care, 1992—. 2d lt. USAF, 1984. Named Nurse of Month Maxim Health Care, Tampa, Fla., 3/2000, Nurses Registration award, 2001.

LAWSON, PATRICIA GILLY, secondary education English educator; b. Texarkana, Ark., Aug. 13, 1950; d. Norbert Sidney Jr. and Ora Marie (Chiasson) Gilly; m. James Patrick Lawson Jr., May 4, 1973; children: Ryan Patrick, Christopher Michael, Colin Timothy. BA in English Edn., U. New Orleans, 1972, MEd, 1979, cert. reading cons., 1984; cert. in supervision and adminstrn., Ctrl. Conn. State U., 1993. Cert. 7-12 English tchr., K-12 reading cons., adminstr. and supr., Conn. English tchr. Cohen Sr. H.S., Orleans Parish Sch., New Orleans, 1973; chpt. 1 reading tchr. Toulminville H.S., Mobile County Sch., Mobile, Ala., 1973-74; English and reading tchr. Orleans Parish Sch., 1974-76; 5th-8th grade English and reading tchr. St. Pius X Sch., New Orleans, 1976-77; 7th-8th grade English and reading tchr. St. Rita Sch., Harahan, La., 1978-79; 6th grade reading tchr. Ellender Mid. Sch., Jefferson Parish Schs., Marrero, 1983-84; 9th-12th grade English tchr. RHAM H.S., Region # 8 Schs., Hebron, Conn., 1985—, 7th-12th grade coord reading, English, language arts, 1993—. State assessor State of Conn. Best Program, Hartford, 1993—; mem. com. RHAM Profl. Devel. Com., Hebron, 1991—. Publicity/sports writer Glastonbury (Conn.) H.S., 1992-98, Ctrl. Conn. Youth Hockey Assn., Glastonbury, 1986-92. Mem. ASCD, Conn. ASCD, RHAM Edn. Assn. (rep. coun. mem. 1992—), Nat. Coun. Tchrs. English (mem. conf. on ednl. leadership 1993—), Conn. Coun. Tchrs. English, Conn. Reading Assn., Conn. Heads of English Depts. Roman Catholic. Avocations: reading, landscaping, interior decorating, needlecrafts. Office: RHAM HS 67 Rham Rd Hebron CT 06248-1500

LAWSON, RANDALL CLAYTON, II, financial executive; b. Wabash, Ind., June 20, 1948; s. Randall Clayton and Evelyn Beatrice (Wright) L.; m. Julie Ann Severin, June 30, 1973; children: Randall Clayton III, Erin Elizabeth. BS, Butler U., 1970. CPA, Ind., Ohio. Jr. acct. Price Waterhouse, Indpls., 1970-73, sr. acct. Indpls. and Cin., 1973-76, audit mgr. Cin., 1976-79; unit devel. contr. Ponderosa, Inc., Dayton, Ohio, 1979-81, asst. corp. contr., 1981-82, corp. contr., 1982-84, v.p., corp. contr., 1984-85, sr. v.p., chief acctg. officer, 1985-87, sr. v.p., CFO, 1987; v.p., CFO Tad Tech. Svcs. Corp., Cambridge, Mass., 1988-89; v.p. fin. HydroLogic, Inc., Asheville, N.C., 1993; dir. mgmt. acctg. Rust Indsl. Cleaning Inc., Ashland, Ky., 1994-95; East region contr. Rust Indsl. Svcs., Inc., LaPorte, Tex., 1995, divsn. v.p., contr., 1996-97, v.p., contr., 1997—; group dir. fin. and adminstrn. waste mgmt. indsl. svcs. In Plant Svcs. Group, 1998—. V.p., CFO Onyx Indsl. Svcs., La Porte, 1999—; adj. prof. Wilmington Coll., 1991; bus. cons., 1987—. Mem. agy. audit com. United Way Greater Cin., 1975; mem. fin. and resource allocation com. United Way Greater Dayton, 1985, mem. com. on agy. fins., 1986-87. Mem. AICPA, Ohio Soc. CPAs, Fin. Execs. Internat., Queen City Assn. Club (bd. dirs. 1978), Dayton Racquet Club, Elks, Phi Kappa Psi. Republican. Presbyterian. Avocations: golf, tennis, reading, antiques, crafts. Home: 2810 Countrylake Dr Cincinnati OH 45233-1735

LAWSON, ROBERT BERNARD, psychology educator; b. N.Y.C., June 20, 1940; s. Robert Bernard Sr. and Isabella Theresa (McPeake) L.; children: Christina Megan, Steven Robert, Jennifer Erin. BA in Psychology, Monmouth U., 1961; MA in Psychology, U. Del., 1963, PhD in Psychology, 1965. Mem. faculty U. Vt., Burlington, 1966—, asst. prof. psychology, 1966-69, assoc. prof., 1969-74, prof., 1974—, assoc. v.p. acad. affairs, 1978, assoc. v.p. rsch., dean Grad. Coll., 1978-86, dir. gen. exptl. psychology, 1988-90, chmn. dept. pub. adminstrn., 1990-95, acting dir. MPA program, 1998-99, dir. MPA program, 1999—, chmn. dept. psychiatry, 2002—. Presenter, worker in China, Russia, and Italy; cons. Mgmt. Sys., 1986—; vis. scholar Stanford U., 1986-87; pres. Alliance Mgmt. Cons. Group, Burlington, 1987—, N.E. Assn. Grad. Schs., Princeton, N.J., 1983-86; bd. dirs. Grad. Record Exams-ETS, Princeton, 1984-88. Author: (with S.G. Goldstein and R.E. Musty) Principles and Methods of Psychology, 1975, (with W.L. Gulick) Human Stereopsis: A Psychophysical Approach, 1976, (with Zheng Shen) Organizational Psychology: Foundations and Applications, 1998. Mem. bd. govs. Univ. Press New England, 1978-86, bd. dirs., 1979-80. Recipient numerous grants NIH, NSF, USDA, numerous awards from Nat. Eye Inst. Mem. AAAS, APA, Psychonomic Soc., Coun. Grad. Schs., N.Y. Acad. Scis., Ea. Psychol. Assn. Avocations: international organizational psychology, leadership, motivation, decision making, and organizational culture. Office: U Vt Dept Psychology John Dewey Hl Burlington VT 05405-0001 E-mail: robert.lawson@uvm.edu.

LAWSON, ROBERT DAVIS, theoretical nuclear physicist; b. Sydney, Australia, July 14, 1926; came to U.S., 1949; s. Carl Herman and Angeline Elizabeth (Davis) L.; m. Mary Grace Lunn, Dec. 16, 1950 (div. 1976); children: Dorothy, Katherine, Victoria; m. Sarah Virginia Roney, Mar. 13, 1976 (dec. 1994). BS, U. B.C., Can., 1948; MS, U. B.C., 1949; PhD, Stanford U., 1953. Research assoc. U. Calif., Berkeley, 1953-57; research assoc. Fermi Inst. U. Chgo., 1957-59; assoc. physicist Argonne (Ill.) Nat. Lab., 1959-65; sr. physicist Argonne Nat. Lab., 1965—. Vis. scientist U.K. Atomic Energy Authority, Harwell, Eng., 1962-63, Oxford U., Eng., 1970, 85; vis. prof. SUNY, Stony Brook, 1972-73; vis. fellow Australian Nat. U., Canberra, 1982; vis. prof. U. Groningen, 1973, U. Utrecht, 1974, Technische Hochschule, Darmstadt, 1975, 78, Free U., Amsterdam, 1976, 81, others; TRIUMF, U. B.C., Vancouver, Can., 1984. Author: Theory of the Nuclear Shell Model, 1980. Contbr. articles to sci. jours. Fellow Weizmann Inst. Sci., 1967-68, Niels Bohr Inst., 1976-77; Sir Thomas Lyle fellow U. Melbourne, Australia, 1987. Fellow Am. Phys. Soc. Home: 1590 Raven Hl Wheaton IL 60187-7109 Office: Argonne Nat Lab Bldg 203 Argonne IL 60439

LAWSON, SUSAN COLEMAN, lawyer; b. Covington, Ky., Dec. 4, 1949; d. John Clifford and Louise Carter Coleman; m. William Henry Lawson, June 6, 1980; 1 child, Philip. BA, U. Ky., 1971, JD, 1979. Bar: Ky. 1979. Ptnr. Lawson & Lawson, P.S.C., Harlan, 1995—; atty. Stoll, Keenon & Park, Lexington, Ky., 1979-80; atty., Harbert Constrn. Co., Middlesboro, 1980-81; ptnr. Buttermore, Turner, Lawson & Boggs, P.S.C., Harlan, 1981-94. Mem.: Ky. Bd. Bar Examiners (mem. character and fitness com. 2002—), Harlan County Bar Assn., Ky. Bar Assn., Order of Coif. Democrat. Avocation: golf. Home: 511 W Kentucky Ave Pineville KY 40977-1307 Fax: 606-573-4992. E-mail: susanl@lawson-law.com.

LAWSON, THOMAS CHENEY, fraud examiner; b. Pasadena, Calif., Sept. 21, 1955; s. William McDonald and Joan Bell (Jaffe) L.; m. Susan Sullivan; children: Chri stopher, Brittany, Courtney. Student, Calif. State U., Sacramento, 1973-77. Cert. internat. investigator, fraud examiner. Pres. Tomatron Co., Pasadena, 1970-88, Tom's Tune Up & Detail, Pasadena, 1971-88, Tom's Pool Svc., Sacramento, 1975-78, Tomsupply Co., 1975—; mgmt. trainee Permoid Process Co., L.A., 1970-75; prof. automechanics Calif. State U., Sacramento, 1973-75; regional sales cons. Hoover Co., Burlingame, 1974-76; mktg. exec. River City Prodns., Sacramento, 1977-78; territorial rep. Globe div. Burlington House Furniture Co., 1978; So. Calif. territorial rep. Marge Carson Furniture, Inc., 1978-80; pres. Ted L. Gunderson & Assos., Inc., Westwood, Calif., 1980-81; pres., CEO Apscreen, Newport Beach, 1980—. Founder Creditbase Co., Newport Beach, Calif., 1980-89, Worldata Corp., Newport Beach, 1980-89, Trademark Enforcement Corp., L.A., 1985-86; pres. Carecheck, Inc., Newport Beach, 1990—, CEO Badchex, Inc., Newport Beach, 1992—; expert witness Calif. Superior Ct. Mem. editl. rev. bd. The White Paper. Calif. Rehab. scholar, 1974-77. Mem.: Orange County Employment Mgrs. Assn., Forensic Cons. Assn. of Orange County, World Investigators Network, Soc. Human Resource Mgmt., World Assn. Detectives, Profls. in Human Resources Assn., Nat. Pub. Records Rsch. Assn., Am. Soc. Indsl. Security (cert., chmn. Orange County chpt. 1990), Coun. Internat. Investigators, Christian Businessmen's Com. Internat., Assn. Cert. Fraud Examiners (life; editl. rev. bd. 1995—). Office: 2043 Westcliff Dr Ste 300 Newport Beach CA 92660-5511

LAWSON, THOMAS SEAY, JR. lawyer; b. Montgomery, Ala., Oct. 30, 1935; s. Thomas Seay and Rose Darrington (Gunter) L.; m. Sarah Hunter Clayton, May 27, 1961; children: Rose Gunter, Gladys Robinson, Thomas Seay III. AB, U. Ala., 1957, JD, 1963. Bar: Ala. 1963, U.S. Supreme Ct. 1969. Law clk. to chief judge U.S. Dist. Ct. (no. dist.) Ala., 1963-64; assoc. Steiner, Crum & Baker, Montgomery, 1964-68; ptnr. Capell, Howard, Knabe & Cobbs P.A., 1968-98; asst. dist. atty. 15th jud. cir. of Ala., 1969-70; ptnr. Capell & Howard, P.C., Montgomery, 1999—. Mem. lawyers adv. com. U.S. Ct. Appeals, 5th cir. 1978, 11th cir. 1979-82. Pres. The Lighthouse, 1978-79. Lt. USNR, 1957-60. Fellow Ala. Law Found.; mem. ABA, FBA, Ala. State Bar (pres. young lawyers sect. 1970-71), Montgomery County Bar Assn. (pres. 1980), Am. Judicature Soc., 11th Cir. Hist. Soc. (pres. 1999-2001), Lawyers Adv. Com. U.S. Dist. Ct. (mid. dist.) Ala. (chmn. 2000—), Soc. of Pioneers of Montgomery (pres. 1983), Farrah Law Soc. (pres. 1986-88, Outstanding Alumnus award U. Ala. student chpt. 1989), Montgomery Inn of Ct. (master bencher, bd. dirs. 1989-93, chancellor 1991, pres. 1992-93, emeritus 1994—), Ala. Law Inst. (bd. dirs. 1986—), Ala. Law Sch. Found. (trustee 1985—), Montgomery Country Club. Episcopalian. Home: 1262 Glen Grattan Dr Montgomery AL 36111-1402 Office: Capell & Howard PC PO Box 2069 150 S Perry St Montgomery AL 36102-2069 E-mail: tsl@chlaw.com.

LAWSON, VIRGINIA KING, nutritionist, consultant; b. Pineville, Mo., Oct. 10, 1918; d. Arthur Judson and Blanche Bell (Boyd) King; m. Weston G. Lawson, June 14, 1942 (div. Aug. 1959); children: Victoria, Robert, Weston G. Jr., Melissa; m. H. Scott Grant, Dec. 31, 1983 (dec. Nov. 1996). BS, Kans. State U., 1939; MS, U. Tenn., 1972. Registered dietitian; lic. nutritionist and dietitian. Instr. nutrition St. Joseph Hosp. Sch. Nursing, Memphis, 1957-61, U. Tenn. Coll. Nursing, Memphis, 1957-61, clin. dietitian dept. medicine Diabetic Clinic, 1961-63, clin. dietitian Clin. Rsch. Ctr., 1961-65, head rsch. dietitian, 1965-73, chief rsch. dietitian, 1973-85, asst. prof. medicine, 1973-85; nutrition cons., 1985—. Nutrition cons. Rosewood Convalescent Ctr., Memphis, 1961-65. Food and nutrition columnist Comml. Appeal, Memphis, 1961-65; contbr. articles to profl. jours. Block chmn. Memphis Neighborhood Watch Program, Memphis Police Dept., 1984—. Travel grantee AMA, 1968. Mem. Am. Dietetic Assn. (career guidance com. 1967-68, Lydia J. Roberts fellow 1972-73), Tenn. Dietetic Assn. (pres. 1963, past chmn. numerous coms.), Memphis Dist. Dietetic Assn. (pres. 1961, past chmn. numerous coms., Dietitian of Yr. award 1981), Memphis Area Nutrition Coun. (pres. 1979-80). Republican. United Methodist. Avocations: church work, community service, gardening. Home: 5151 Tarrytown Dr Memphis TN 38117-2125 E-mail: Ginnii80@aol.com.

LAWSON, WILLARD FRANCIS, JR. paper company owner, sales executive; b. Greensboro, N.C., Apr. 28, 1947; s. Willard Francis Sr. and Frances (Lee) L.; m. Katherine Elizabeth Whitlock, Aug. 3, 1947; children: Kevin, Katherine. BSBA, E. Carolina U., 1970; postgrad., N.C. State U., 1973, Fashion Inst. Tech., N.Y.C., 1976-77. Various positions Mt. Hope Finishing Co., Inc., Butner, N.C., 1970-75; with sales Mt. Hope Finishing Co. N.Y., N.Y.C., 1975-79; regional sales mgr. Orchard Corp. Am., St. Louis, 1979-82; product mgr. Häfele, High Point, N.C., 1982-86; pres., owner Lawson Paper Co., Inc., Statesville, 1986—. Chmn., bd. dirs. Young Life. Adminstrv. bd. chmn. New Salem United Meth. Ch., Statesville, 1989—; officer Iredell County (N.C.) Youth Athletic Assn., 1986-89; co-chmn. bd. dirs. Young Life of Statesville/Iredell County. Mem. Color Mktg. Group, Laminating Materials Assn., Commerce Club-East Carolina U. Sch. Bus. Republican. Office: Lawson Paper Co Inc 233 Nottingham Cir Statesville NC 28625-8201

LAWSON, WILLIAM, otolaryngologist, educator; b. N.Y.C., Nov. 23, 1934; s. Alexander and Sophia (Elkind) L.; m. Miriam Patkin, Nov. 7, 1965; 1 child, Vanessa Ann. BA, NYU, 1956, DDS, 1961, MD, 1965. Diplomate Am. Bd. Otolaryngology, Am. Bd. Cosmetic Surgery, Am. Bd. Facial Plastic Surgery. Intern Mt. Sinai Hosp., N.Y.C., 1965-66, rsch. fellow in otolaryngology, 1969-70, resident in otolaryngology, 1970-73; resident in gen. surgery Bronx (N.Y.) VA Hosp., 1966-67, chief otolaryngology, head and neck surgery, 1974—; prof. Mt. Sinai Sch. Medicine, N.Y.C., 1980—; vice chmn., 1996—. Co-dir. Paranasal Sinus Rsch. Lab.; dir. facial plastic surgery clini Mt. Sinai Hosp., N.Y.C.; cons. Nat. Space Biomed. Rsch. Consortium. Author: Paraganglionic Chemoreceptor Systems, 1982, Surgery of the Paranasal Sinuses, 1988, 2nd edit., 1992, External Ear, 1995; contbr. over 200 articles to med. jours., chpts. to books. Capt. M.C., U.S. Army, 1967-69. Fellow ACS, Am. Acad. Facial Plastic and Reconstructive Surgery (svc. awrd), Am. Soc. Head and Neck Surgery, Am. Soc. Maxillofacial Surgeons, Am. Rhinologic Soc., Otologic and Laryngologic Soc., Am. Laryngol. Soc.; mem. Am. Acad. Otolaryngology (svc. award), Am. Bronchoesophagologic Soc. (included in Best Drs. Am., Best Drs. in N.Y.). Avocations: photography, art history, horology. Office: Mt Sinai Med Ctr 1 Gustave L Levy Pl New York NY 10029-6500

LAWSON, WILLIAM DAVID, III, retired cotton company executive; b. Jackson, Miss., Oct. 30, 1924; s. William David Jr. and Elizabeth Vaiden (Barksdale) L.; m. Elizabeth Coppridge Smith, June 9, 1948; children: Margaret Monroe, William David IV, Susan Barksdale, Thomas Nelson. Student, Woodberry Forest Sch., 1940-42; BS, Davidson Coll., 1948; MBA, U. Pa., 1949. Trainee T.J. White and Co., Memphis, 1949-52; v.p. W.D. Lawson and Co., Gastonia, N.C., 1952-70, pres., 1971-81, Lawson, Lewis & Peat, Gastonia, 1981-85, Lawson Cotton Co., Gastonia, 1985-95; v.p. Hohenberg Bros. Co. div. Cargill Inc., Memphis, 1988-95; ret., 1995; pres. Lawson-Harris Cotton, Inc., 1997—. Pres. Covenant Village, 1979-81; hon. dir. 1st Union Nat. Bank, Gastonia. Bd. dirs. Sister Cities Com., Gastonia, pres., 1990-94; del. Sr. Tar Heel Legis.; mem. Gov.'s Adv. Coun. on Aging, 1998-2000; bd. advisors Davidson Coll., 1976-80; mem. bd. mgrs. N.Y. Cotton Exch., 1974-80; elder Presbyn. Ch. 1st lt. inf., U.S. Army, WWII. Named Cotton Man of Year Cotton Digest, 1969, 76; recipient Duke Kimbrell Lifetime Civic Achievement award, 1999, Harry S. Baker Disting. Svc. award Nat. Caxton Coun., 2002. Mem. Nat. Cotton Coun. (advisor 1976—; pres. 1975-76), Am. Cotton Shippers Assn. (pres. 1968-69), Atlantic Cotton Assn. (pres. 1957-58), Cotton Coun. Internat. (pres. 1972-73), Am. Cotton Exporters Assn. (pres. 1979-80), Newcomen Soc., Gaston County C. of C. (pres. 1972-73), Am. Legion, Svc. Corps. Ret. Execs., Rotary Found., Bequest Soc. (pres. 1964-65, dist. gov. 1995-96, pres.' rep. 2000, Major Donor award 1999, citation for Meritorious Svc. 2001), Gaston Country Club, The Point Lake and Golf Club, Kappa Sigma. Avocations: scuba diving, tennis, golf. Home: 1341 Covenant Dr Gastonia NC 28054-3861 Fax: (704)868-3173. E-mail: lawsco@aol.com.

LAWSON, WILLIAM HOGAN, III, electrical motor manufacturing executive; b. Lexington, Ky., Feb. 3, 1937; s. Otto Kirsky and Gladys (McWhorter) L.; div.; children: Elizabeth, Cynthia; m. Ruth Stanat, 1995. BSME, Purdue U., 1959; MBA, Harvard U., 1961. Gen. mgr. svc. divsn. Toledo Scale Corp., 1964-68; exec. v.p., COO Skyline Corp., Elkhart, Ind., 1968-85; chmn. bd. dirs., CEO Franklin Elec. Co., Inc., Bluffton, 1985—, also bd. dirs. Bd. dirs. JSJ Corp., Skyline Corp., Sentry Ins. (a Mut. Ins. Co.); instr. U. Toledo, 1966-67. With U.S. Army, 1961-63. Mem. Harvard U. Bus. Sch. Assn., Ft. Wayne Country Club, Summit Club Ft. Wayne, Bird Key Yacht Club. Republican. Presbyterian. Home: 7126 Blue Creek Dr Fort Wayne IN 46804-1483 also: 232 Bird Key Dr Sarasota FL 34236-1602 Office: Franklin Electric Co Inc 400 E Spring St Bluffton IN 46714-3798

LAWSON-JOHNSTON, PETER ORMAN, foundation executive; b. N.Y.C., Feb. 8, 1927; s. John R. and Barbara (Guggenheim) L.; m. Dorothy Stevenson Hammond, Sept. 30, 1950; children: Wendy, Tania, Peter, Mary. Reporter, yachting editor Balt. Sun Papers, 1951-53; exec. dir. Md. Classified Employees Assn., Balt., 1953-54; pub. info. dir. Md. Civil Def. Agy., Pikesville, 1954-56; sales mgr. Feldspar Corp. subs. Zemex Corp. (formerly Pacific Tin Consol.), N.Y.C., 1956-60; v.p. sales Feldspar Corp. subs. Zemex Corp. (formerly Pacific Tin), 1961-66, v.p., 1966-72, chmn., 1972-81; v.p. Zemex Corp., 1966-72, vice chmn., 1972-75, pres., 1975-76, chmn., 1975—, also bd. dirs. Trustee Solomon R. Guggenheim Found., 1964, v.p. bus. adminstrn., 1965-69, pres., 1969-95, chmn., 1995-98, hon. chmn., 1998—; pres. adv. bd. Peggy Guggenheim Collection; dir. Harry Frank Guggenheim Found., 1968—, chmn., 1971—; ptnr. Guggenheim Bros., 1962-70, sr. ptnr., 1971—; chmn. Anglo Energy, Inc., 1973-86; pres., bd. dirs. Elgerbar Corp.; bd. dirs. Nat. Rev. Inc.; bd. dirs., Jupiter Island Holdings. Trustee The Lawrenceville Sch., 1977-99, trustee emeritus, 1999—, pres., 1990-97; trustee St. Elmo Found., 1996—; mem. adv. bd. U. Va. Art Mus., 1997—, chmn., 1997—. With AUS, 1945-47. Recipient Gertrude Vanderbilt Whitney award Skowhegan Sch. Painting and Sculpture, 1986, Ellis Island Medal of Honor, Nat. Ethnic Coalition Orgns., 1993, Lawrenceville medal Lawrenceville Sch., 1997. Mem. Pilgrims of U.S., Carolina Plantation Soc., U.S. Srs. Golf Assn., Edgartown Yacht Club, Edgartown Reading Room Club, Century Assn., Links, Bedens Brook Club, Pretty Book Tennis Club, Seminole Golf Club, Jupiter Island Club, Brook Club (N.Y.C.), Yeamans Hall Club. Republican. Episcopalian. Home: 215 Carter Rd Princeton NJ 08540-2104 Office: Solomon R Guggenheim Found 527 Madison Ave New York NY 10022-4304

LAWSON-JOWETT, MARY JULIET, lawyer; b. Mobile, Ala., May 26, 1959; d. William Max Lawson and Perina Juliet (Barich) Franc; m. Adam Geoffrey Jowett; 1 child, Caitlin Victoria Jowett. BA, U. Miss., 1981, JD, 1987. Bar: Miss. 1988, U.S. Dist. Ct. (no. and so. dists.) Miss. 1988. Tchr. Ocean Springs (Miss.) Sch. System, 1981-85; atty. Ronald W. Lewis & Assocs., Oxford, Miss., 1988-89; ptnr. occupl. hearing loss and hand-arm vibration syndrome Scruggs, Millette, Lawson, Bozeman & Dent, P.A., Pascagoula, 1989—; gen. practice, civil rights and employment law Juliet Jowett, P.A., 1997—. Cons. Occupational Hearing Loss, P.A., 1989-96. Contbr. articles to profl. jours. Mem. Walter Anderson Players, Ocean Springs, 1973-96. Mem. ABA, ATLA (chmn. occupational hearing loss litigation group 1990-94), Miss. Trial Lawyers Assn. (editor 1990-92), Magnolia Bar Assn. Democrat. Roman Catholic. Avocations: reading, golf, horseback riding, gardening, acting. Office: Juliet Jowett PA PO Office Drawer 1625 1016 La Fontaine St Ocean Springs MS 39564-4934

LAWSON-NDU, OVUNDA A. emergency physician, surgeon; b. Elelenwo, Nigeria, 1951; s. Lawson Ngbachi and Esther Adanma (Nwogbe) N.; m. Elsie Nnenne Jenewari, Dec. 13, 1977 (div. Jan. 1980); children: Jennifer Mboma, Sandra Njimole; m. Donna Marie Grimes, June 27, 1986; 1 child, Anuugo Michelle. BS in Chemistry with honors, U. Wis., 1977; DO, U. Health Sci., 1980. Diplomate Am. Bd. Emergency Medicine. Intern Metro Health Ctr., Erie, Pa., 1981-82; resident in gen. surgery Howard U. Hosp., Washington; mem. staff Lower Bucks Hosp., Bristol, Pa. Mem. hypertension and diabetes screening program Rivers State, Nigeria, 1992—; asst. dir., vice chmn. dept. emergency medicine Temple U. Hosp., Bristol, Pa., 1997—. Active Nat. Exch. Club, Amnesty Internat. Fellow Am. Coll. Emergency Physicians, Am. Acad. Emergency Medicine. Address: PO Box 824 Bensalem PA 19020-0824

LAWTON, CHARLES See HECKELMANN, CHARLES NEWMAN

LAWTON, DEBORAH SIMMONS, educational media specialist; b. Dover, N.J., Sept. 14, 1950; d. Coryden Jerome Simmons and Marjorie Lynd (Jewell) Weber; children: Catherine Randall, Christopher James. BA, Lebanon Valley Coll., 1972; tchr. cert., Coll. St. Elizabeth, 1974; MLS, Rutgers-The State U., 1994. Cert. ednl. media specialist, profl. libr., supr. Confidential ratings analyst Martindale-Hubbell, Summit, N.J., 1972-74; tchr. St. Rose Sch., East Hanover, 1975-77, St. Paul Sch., Princeton, 1977-78; libr. Mary Jacobs Libr., Rocky Hill, 1988-92, South Brunswick H.S., Monmouth Junction, 1994—. Reviewer Infolink, 1995—; chair press rev. com. Am. Assn. Univs. Author: Knowledge Quest, Book Report. Chair Montgomery jointure com., Montgomery Twp., N.J., 1985; coach/dir. Montgomery Girls Softball, 1988-91; v.p., exec. bd. Montgomery Twp. PTSA, 1986-90; pres., treas. Lawrenceville (N.J.) Presbyn. Coop. Nursery Sch., 1981-84; ranking chair jrs. N.J. Tennis Dist.; mem. INFOLINK Book Evaluation Criteria Com., KidsConnect, INFOLINK Youth Svcs. Com.; deacon Blawenburg Reformed Ch., elder. Internet grantee N.J. State Libr., 1994, Instrnl. Coun. grantee South Brunswick Instrnl. Coun., 1995, 96, 97; recipient Pres.'s award N.J. Tennis. Mem. ALA, Am. Assn. Sch. Librs. (assn. Am. univ. presses com. 1996—, legis. com., chair youth svcs. com., intellectual freedom com.), Assn. for Libr. Svc. to Children, Young Adult Libr. Svcs. Assn., Intellectual Freedom Round Table, Ednl. Media Assn. N.J. (legis. chair, intellectual freedom chair), Assn. of Am. Univ. Presses (rev. com.), N.J. Libr. Assn., Beta Phi Mu, Pi Gamma Mu. Avocations: water sports, quilting. Office: South Brunswick HS 750 Ridge Rd Monmouth Junction NJ 08852-0183 E-mail: dlawton@sbschools.org.

LAWTON, FLORIAN KENNETH, artist, educator; b. Cleve., June 20, 1921; m. Lois Mari Ondrey, June 19, 1948; children: Kenneth R., David F., Dawn M., Patricia A. Student, Cleve. Sch. Art, 1941-43, Cleve. Inst. Art, 1948-51, John Huntington Polytech. Inst., 1946-50. Instr. Cooper Sch. Art, Cleve., 1976-80, Cleve. Sch. Art, 1980-82. Cons., instr. Orange Art Ctr., Pepper Pike, Ohio, 1978—; cons. in field, juror, 1968—. Exhbns. include Am. Watercolor Soc., N.Y., Cleve. Mus. Art, Butler Mus., Youngstown, Ohio, Canton (Ohio) Mus., Massillon (Ohio) Mus., Nat. Arts Club, N.Y.C., Pitts. Watercolor Soc., Audubon Artists, N.Y.C., Salmagundi Club, N.Y.C., Parkersburg (W.Va.) Art Ctr., Boston Mills Arts Festival, Peninsula, Ohio, Marietta (Ohio) Coll., Nat. Pks. Assn. Exhbn., 1996, 97, 2000, many others; 25 yrs. retrospective exhbn. Amish paintings, Butler Inst. Am. Art, 1989; represented in collections including Am. Soc. Metals, Ctrl. Nat. Bank, Diamond-Shamrock, Diocese Cleve., Kaiser Found., Ohio Conservation Found., Nat. City Bank Ohio, TRW, Standard Oil Co., Huntington Bank, Nat. Mennonite Mus., Lancaster, Pa., Ohio Bell Telephone Co., Day-Glo Corp., Soc. Bank Corp., The White House Collection, Washington, numerous others U.S. and internat., also pvt. collections; featured mags., calendars; Mill Pond Press; cons., artist (documentary) Amish Romance, 1979; official Coast Guard artist; artist Amish Documentary-PBS, 1996. Cons. Aurora (Ohio) Community Libr., 1990—. Cpl. USAF, 1943-46, PTO. Recipient Disting. Alumni award Garfield Hgts. (Ohio) High Sch., 1990, 1st place award Grand Invitational Exhbn., Akron, Ohio, 1996, numerous others. Mem. Ohio Watercolor Soc. (signature, charter, Grand Buckeye award 1983), Am. Watercolor Soc. (signature, Strathmore award 1977), Nat. Watercolor Soc. (signature), Akron Soc. Artists, Assoc. Audubon Artists, Artists Fellowships Inc. (N.Y.), Ky. Watercolor Soc. (signature), Midwest Watercolor Soc., Pa. Watercolor Soc. (signature), Ga. Watercolor Soc., Whiskey Painters Am., Rotary Club Chagrin Valley (Paul Harris fellow 1989). Office: 410-29 Willow Cir Aurora OH 44202-9131 Fax: 330-562-4102.

LAWTON, JACQUELINE AGNES, retired communications company executive, management consultant; b. Bklyn., June 9, 1933; d. Thomas J. and Agnes R. (McLaughlin) Maguire; m. George W. Lawton, Feb. 14, 1954;

children: George, Victoria, Thomas. With N.Y. Telephone, 1954-82, mktg. mgr. govt., edn. and med. Mid State, 1978-81, mktg. mgr. health care N.Y.C., 1982-82, dist. field market mgr. health care and lodging; with N.E. and Mid Atlantic region AT&T-Am. Bell, N.Y.C., 1982-83; ea. region mgr. pers., mktg. and sales AT&T Info. Sys., Parsippany, N.J., 1983-86; pvt. practice mgmt. and travel cons., Cornish Flat, N.H., 1986-96; diocesan dir. Medjugirje in Am., Manchester, NH, 1992—2000. Republican. Roman Catholic. Home: 27 Fountain Way West Lebanon NH 03784 E-mail: jamjal1@msn.com.

LAWTON, JEAN MARGARET, volunteer; b. Harrow, Middlesex, Eng., June 14, 1930; d. William Arthur and Elsie Mabel (Izzard) Hann; m. David Lloyd Lawton, Mar. 25, 1949 (dec. July 1989); children: Robin Lloyd, Martin Everett. Student, Hiram Coll., 1947-49; BA in Philosophy, Mich. State U., 1960; MA in Adminstrn., Cen. Mich. U., 1979. Libr. Pub. Libr., Mt. Pleasant, Mich., 1968-75; field adminstrv. officer Census Bur., 1979-80; tax-aide Am. Assn. Retired People, Orlando, Fla., 1990; scholarship com. mem. Sorosis, 1990-91; Congl. dist. coord. Am. Assn. Ret. Persons, 1991-93. Bd. dirs. Widowed Persons Svc., Orlando, 1991-93. Pres. LWV-Mt. Pleasant, 1980-82; bd. dirs. LWV of Mich., Lansing, 1982-84; Indian scholarship com. chair Mt. Pleasant Women's Club, 1980-87. Mem.: AARP (cmty. coord. 1997—2001). Avocation: pine needle stitchery. E-mail: jmlawton@worldnet.att.net.

LAWTON, LORILEE ANN, fire sprinkler contractor company owner, accountant; b. Morrisville, Vt., July 17, 1947; d. Philip Wyman Sr. and Margaret Elaine (Ather) Noyes; m. Lee Henry Lawton, Dec. 6, 1969; children: Deborah Ann, Jeffrey Lee. BBA, U. Vt., 1969. Sr. acct., staff asst. IBM, Essex Junction, Vt., 1969-72; owner, pres., chmn. bd. Red-Hed Supply Inc., Colchester, 1972-2001; owner, treas. Firetech Sprinkler Corp., 1992—. Bd. dirs. Merchants Bank, Burlington, Cynosure Corp., Colchester Cmty. Devel. Corp. Mem. Am. Fire Sprinkler Assn., Nat. Fire Protection Assn., Vt. Subcontractors Assn. Republican. Avocations: reading, gardening. Home: 571 Middle Rd Colchester VT 05446-7310 Office: Firetech Sprinkler Corp 1720 Hegeman Ave Colchester VT 05446-3173

LAWTON, MATT, professional baseball player; b. Gulfport, Miss., Nov. 3, 1971; Baseball player Minn. Twins, 1995—2001, Cleveland Indians, 2002—. Office: 34 Kirby Puckett Pl Minneapolis MN 55415 also: Cleveland Indians 2401 Ontario St Cleveland OH 44115*

LAWTON, MICHAEL JAMES, entomologist, pest management specialist; b. Balt., Aug. 6, 1953; s. James William and Mary Eileen (O'Connor) L.; m. Barbara Ann Byron, Dec. 19, 1983. BS, U. Md., 1975. Cert. entomologist. Technician, tech. dir. Atlas Exterminating Co., Towson, Md., 1975-78; asst. tech. dir. Western Exterminator Co., Irvine, Calif., 1978-83, tng. and tech. dir., 1984-95, dir. sales and mktg., 1996, v.p. sales and mktg., 1997—, shareholder, 1999—. Democrat. Office: Western Exterminator Co 305 N Crescent Way Anaheim CA 92801-6709

LAWTON, NANCY, artist; b. Gilroy, Calif., Feb. 28, 1950; d. Edward Henry and Marilyn Kelly (Boyd) L.; m. Richard Enemark, Aug. 4, 1984; children: Faith Lawton, Forrest Lawton. BA in Fine Art, Calif. State U., San Jose, 1971; MFA, Mass. Coll. Art, 1980. Artist-in-residence Villa Montalvo Ctr. Arts, Los Gatos, Calif., 1971, Noble & Greenough Sch., Dedham, Mass., 1990. One-woman shows include The Bklyn. Mus., 1983, Victoria Munroe Gallery, N.Y.C., 1993; group shows include San Francisco Mus. Modern Art, 1973, The Bklyn. Mus., 1980, 83, Staempfli Gallery, N.Y.C., 1984, The Ark. Art Ctr. Mus., Little Rock, 1984, 88, 92, 93, Victoria Munroe Gallery, 1985, 87, 88, 92, Butler Inst. Am. Art, Ohio, 1988, Smith Coll. Mus. Art, Mass., 1988, NAD, N.Y.C., 1988, Reynolds Gallery, Richmond, 1994, Nancy Solomon Gallery, Atlanta, 1995, Arnot Art Mus., Elmira, N.Y., 2001-02, Hunt Inst. for Bot. Documentation, Carnegie Mellon U., Pitts., 2001-02, Hirsch and Adler Galleries, N.Y.C., 2002; public collections include The Ark. Art Ctr. Mus., Art Inst. Chgo., Bklyn. Mus., Smithsonian Am. Art Mus., Washington. Scholar Mellon Found., 1982; N.Y. State Creative Artists grantee, 1983, N.Y. State Arts Devel. Fund grantee, 1989. Home and Office: 78 Willett St Albany NY 12210-1001 E-mail: nancydraws@aol.com.

LAX, KATHLEEN THOMPSON, judge; b. 1945; BA, U. Kans., 1967; JD, U. Calif., L.A., 1980. Law clk. U.S. Bankruptcy Ct., L.A., 1980-82; assoc. Gibson, Dunn & Crutcher, 1982-88; judge ctrl. dist. U.S. Bankruptcy Ct., 1988—. Bd. dirs. L.A. Bankruptcy Forum; bd. govs. Fin. Lawyers Conf., Los Angeles, Calif., 1991—92, Los Angeles, 1994—2000. Bd. editors: Calif. Bankruptcy Jour., 1988—. Office: US Bankruptcy Court 21041 Burbank Blvd Woodland Hills CA 91367-6606

LAX, MELVIN, theoretical physicist; b. Bklyn., Mar. 8, 1922; s. Morris and Rose H. L.; m. Judith Heckelman, June 26, 1949; children: R. Laurie, David A., Jonathan R., Naomi A. BA in Physics (Charles Hayden scholar 1938-42), NYU, 1942; MS in Physics; MS (fellow in applied math. 1942-43), MIT, 1943, PhD (fellow in physics 1943-46, research asso. 1946-47), 1947. Mem. faculty Syracuse (N.Y.) U., 1947-55, Princeton U., 1961, Oxford (Eng.) U., 1961-62; mem. tech. staff AT&T Bell Labs., Murray Hill, N.J., 1955-72; head theoretical physics research dept. Bell Labs., 1962-64, cons., 1972—. Disting. prof. physics CCNY, 1971—; cons. to govt. and industry. Author books and numerous papers in field; bd. editors Phys. Rev., 1958-60, 84-86; editor: Advanced Series in Applied Physics, 1988—; mem. adv. bd. Modern Physics Letters, Internat. Jour. Modern Physics; editorial bd. Quantum Optics, 1992-94. Recipient Willis Lamb medal for laser sci., 1999. Mem. NAS (sec. applied scis., math. engring. class 1989-92, 95-98), AAAS, Am. Phys. Soc.-Chinese Phys. Soc. (telecom. com. 1995-96), Optical Soc. Am. (publs. tech. com. 1991-94, optics letters rev. com. 1995-96). Jewish. Home: 12 High St Summit NJ 07901-2413 Office: CCNY 138th St and Convent Ave New York NY 10031

LAX, PETER DAVID, mathematician, educator; b. Budapest, Hungary, May 1, 1926; arrived in U.s., 1941, naturalized, 1944; s. Henry and Klara (Kornfeld) Lax; m. Anneli Cahn, 1948; 1 child John ;1 child James D. BA, NYU, 1947, PhD, 1949; DSc (hon.) , Kent State U., 1976, Brown U., 1993; DHC (hon.) , U. Paris, 1979; D. Natural Scis. (hon.) , Technische Hochschule Aachen, Germany, 1988; DSc (hon.) , Herriot Walt U., 1990; D. (hon.) , Leningrad State U., 1991; D. (hon.) , U. Md. Baltimore County, 1993; PhD (hon.) , Tel Aviv U., 1992, Beijing U., 1993. Asst. prof. NYU, 1949—57, prof., 1957—99; dir. Courant Inst. Math. Scis., 1972—80. Author (with Ralph Phillips): Scattering Theory, 1967; author: Hyperbolic Systems of Conservation Laws and the Mathematical Theory of Shock Waves, 1973, Scattering Theory for Automorphic Functions, 1976; author: (with A. Lax and S.Z. Burstein) Calculus with Applications and Computing, 1976; author: Linear Algebra, 1997, Functional Analysis, 2002. Mem. Pres.'s Com. on Nat. Medal of Sci., 1976; Nat. Sci. Bd., 1980—86. Served with U.S. Army, 1944—46. Recipient Semmelweis medal, Semmelweis Med. Soc., 1975, Nat. medal Sci., 1986, Wolf prize, Israel, 1987. Mem.: NAS (applied math. and numerical analysis award 1983), AAAS, Russian Acad. Sci. (fgn. assoc.), Acad. des Scis. (fgn. assoc.), Soc. Indsl. and Applied Math., Am. Philos. Soc., Am. Acad. Arts and Scis., Math. Assn. Am. (bd. govs., Chauvenet prize 1974), Am. Math. Soc. (pres. 1979—80, Norbert Wiener prize 1973, Leroy P. Steele prize 1993), London Math. Soc. (hon.), Moscow Math. Soc. (hon.), Hungarian Acad. Sci. (hon.), Acad. Sinica (hon.). Office: Courant Inst Math Scis 251 Mercer St Rm 912 New York NY 10012-1185 E-mail: lax@cims.nyu.edu.

LAX, PHILIP, land developer, space planner; b. Newark, Apr. 22, 1920; s. Nathan and Beckie (Hirschhorn) L.; m. Mildred Baras, Feb. 15, 1948; children: Corinne, Barbara. BS, NYU, 1940, postgrad., 1941-42. With Lax & Co., Newark, 1942-77, v.p., 1950-77; pres. Chathill Mgmt., Inc., 1977—. Cons. World Book of Am. Heritage, 1992. Pres. B'nai Brith Ctr., Rochester, Minn., 1965-70, now hon. pres.; trustee Rutgers U. Hillel; pres. B'nai Brith Rutgers U. Hillel Found. Bldg. Corp., 1969— ; chmn. United Jewish Appeal, Maplewood, N.J., 1966, 76; mem. N.J. region exec. bd. Anti-Defamation League, mem. nat. community rels. bd.; mem. Gov.'s Conf. on Edn., N.J., 1966, mem. bd. trustees Soc. Friends of Touro Synagogue, Newport, R.I., 1996; v.p. Touro Synagogue, 2000—; bd. dirs. Hebrew Immigration Soc. (HIAS); hon. chair B'nai B'rith Ctr. for Pub. Policy. 1999; mem. Mayor's Budget Com., Maplewood, 1958-59; co-chmn. N.J. Opera Ball, 1977; trustee B'nai Brith Found., Washington, 1967— (Philip Lax Gallery of B'nai Brith History and Archives named for him in Philip Klutznick Mus., Room named in his honor Stern Sch. Econs.); co-chmn. B'nai Brith Internat. Coun., 1979, chmn., 1980-85, hon. chmn., apptd. chmn. internat. coun., 1990; voting del. to Jewish Agy., Jerusalem; ECOSOC mem. UN, representing coordinated Bd. Jewish Orgns.; attended UNESCO Conf. in Mex., 1982, with Internat. Coun. B'nai Brith and U.S.; trustee, mem. exec. com. N.J. sect. NCCJ, 1981; trustee Henry Monsky Found., Washington, 1968—; trustee Leo N. Levi Hosp., Hot Springs, Ark., 1968-71, B'nai Brith World Jewish Ctr., Jerusalem, 1982, Nat. Arthritis Hosp., 1976—, N.Y. Statue of Liberty Centennial Found., Touro Synagogue, Newport, R.I., 1996—,; hon. trustee Arts Coun. of Suburban Essex, N.J., 1980, Soc. Friends Touro Synagoague, Newport, 1996; mem. Econ. Devel. Commn., Twp. of Maplewood, 1979—; mem. steering com. to Restore Ellis Island, 1977—; nat. pres. Ellis Island Restoration Commn., 1978—, responsible for planning, funding and operating Family History Ctr. on Ellis Island; appointed to planning team of Statue of Liberty and Ellis Island by Pres. Carter, Dept. of Interior ; mem. Statue of Liberty/Ellis Island Centennial Commn., Com. of Architecture and Restoration of Statue of Liberty-Ellis Island, past chmn.; bd. dirs. Hebrew Immigration Aid Soc. Decorated cavaliere officiale Order of Merit of the Republic of Italy; recipient Found. award B'nai Brith, 1968, Humanitarian award, 1969, Pres.'s Gold medal, 1975; Pro Mundi Beneficio medal Brazilian Acad. Humanities, 1976; Philip Lax chapel at Rutgers U. Hillel named in his honor; named One of 100 Most Influential New Jersey Jews in the 20th Century, Eminent Wisdom fellow Wisdom Hall of Fame, 2000; room named in honor Stern Sch. Econs., NYU; honored by N.J. State Senate. Mem. Am. Soc. Interior Designers, Nat. Soc. Interior Designers (trustee 1970-73), Am. Arbitration Assn., Am. Jewish Hist. Com. (v.p.), Am. Jewish Hist. Soc. (trustee 1984), Am. Soc. Israel Philatelists, Masons (32 deg.), Shriners, B'nai Brith (v.p. Supreme Lodge 1968-71, internat. bd. govs. 1971—, mem. exec. com. of internat. coun.), NYU Club (founding mem. 1956), Nat. Press Club. Home: 35 Claremont Dr Maplewood NJ 07040-2119 Office: Chathill Mgmt 40 Main St Chatham NJ 07928-2402

LAXMINARAYANA, DAMA, geneticist, researcher, educator; b. Hyderabad, India, Apr. 20, 1953; came to U.S., 1990; s. Kishtaiah and Sathyamma; m. Dara Jayalakshmi; children: Dama Bhargavi, Dama Sriharsha, Dama Vishnupriya. BSc, Osmania U., Hyderabad, 1974, MSc, 1976, PhD, 1982. Jr. sci. asst. dept. genetics Osmania U., 1977-78, lectr. dept. zoology, 1985-90; jr. rsch. fellow Indian Dept. Atomic Energy, 1978-81, postdoctoral fellow, 1982-83, rsch. assoc., 1983-85; postdoctoral fellow dept. medicine Case Western Res. U. Sch. Medicine, Cleve., 1990-91; rsch. assoc. dept. internal medicine Wake Forest U. Sch. Medicine, Winston-Salem, N.C., 1991-94, rsch. instr., 1994-98, rsch. asst. prof., 1998—. Conf. presenter in field. Contbr. articles to sci. jours., chpts. to books. Recipient internat. award Tata Meml. Trust, 1985; grantee Univ. Grants Commn. india, 1988-90, Lupus Found. Am., 1993-95, 96-98, NIH, 1999—. Mem. AAAS, Environ. Mutagen Soc. India, India Soc. Cell Biology, Soc. Geneticists and Cytologists India, N.Y. Acad. Scis. Home: 444 Lynn Ave Winston Salem NC 27104 Office: Wake Forest U Sch Medicine Dept Internal Medicine Medical Center Blvd Winston Salem NC 27157 E-mail: dlaxmina@wfubmc.edu.

LAXTON, GREGORY LEE, retired protective services official, Internet company executive; b. Washington, July 23, 1963; s. Walter Leroy and Ella Rae Laxton; m. Cynthia Elaine McCready, Nov. 20, 1997. Grad., So. Md. Police Acad., 1987; postgrad., Coll. So. Md. From patrolman to 1st cmty. police officer St. Mary's Sheriff's Office, Leonardtown, Md., 1987—95, 1st motorcycle officer, 1995—2002, 1st hostage negotiator, 1996—2002, corp., 1997—2002; ret., 2002; owner, v.p. Westgo Enterprises, Inc., Leonardtown, 2000—. Adv. bd. dirs. Marcey House, Leonardtown, St. Mary's Crime Solvers, Leonardtown; freelance photographer and author. Active St. Mary's Hospice, Leonardtown, 2001—. Mem.: Royal GTOs (newsletter editor 1989—2002), St. Mary's Co. Abate (hon.), Masons, Fraternal Order Police, Blue Knights Md. (founding mem., past pres.). Republican. Avocations: antique cars and motorcycles, collecting records, archaeology, music.

LAXTON, JUDY BRINKLEY, social work services administrator; b. Maryville, Tenn., Sept. 14, 1947; d. James Henderson and Alice (Hall) Brinkley; m. Larry Richard Laxton, Dec. 27, 1969; children: Natasha Renea, Maeghan Reanne, Keylan Ross. BS, U. Tenn., 1969, MS in Social Work, 1971. Diplomate Am. Bd. Social Workers; cert. social worker; lic./cert. clin. social worker Ala.; PIP. Psychiat. social worker Searcy Hosp., Mt. Vernon, Ala., 1971-73, unit dir., 1973-75, social work supr., 1975-81, hosp. quality assurance coord., 1981-87, dir. social work svcs., 1981—. Vol. Nat. Alliance for the Mentally Ill, 1988—. Mem. NASW (chmn. continuing edn. com., Social Worker of Yr. 1982), Mental Health Assn. (nominated Ruth P. Brudney award), Acad. Cert. Social Workers. Avocations: reading, mountain climbing, raising children, beaches. Home: 7855 Bardin Dr Semmes AL 36575-6415

LAY, ALFRED ALAN, recording engineer, musician; b. L.A., July 2, 1970; s. Alfred Leroy and Suni Min Lay. BA in Music and Audio Rec. with honors, Calif. State U., Dominguez Hills, 1993. Engr. A&M Studios, Hollywood, Calif., 1993-98; engr., session musician Fox Family Worldwide, L.A., 1998—2002, Funkipeepz Music, Hermosa Beach, Calif., 2001—. Gen. ptnr. Sonnybones Music, Hermosa Beach, Calif., 1997—. Avocations: music, movies, video games, basketball, reading. Home: 621 1st St #2 Hermosa Beach CA 90254

LAY, ANDREW SEAN, secondary school educator, elementary school educator; b. Petersburg, Va., May 20, 1969; s. Michael Jamieson and Marilyn Elizabeth Lay; m. Colleen Scherrie Thompson, July 11, 1999. MusB in Music Edn., Atlantic Union Coll., 1993; MusM in Conducting, Andrews U., 1997. Tchr. music, ESL Pensionado Adventista 'Ciudad de Quito', Ecuador, 1989—90; music tchr. Modesto (Calif.) Adventist Acad., 1994—96; tchr. music, Spanish I Ind. Acad., Cicero, Ind., 1994—. Mem. steering com. Commitment 2002 Capital Campaign Ind. Acad., 2001—. Mem.: ASCD, Assn. Seventh-day Adventist Librs., Internat. Adventists Musicians Assn., Nat. Assn. Music Edn., Am. Choral Dirs. Assn., Am. Guild English Handbell Ringers, Pi Lambda Theta. Republican. Seventh Day Adventist. Avocations: reading, tennis, researching investments, performing music. Office: Ind Acad 24815 State Rd 19 N Cicero IN 46034 Fax: 317-984-5081.

LAY, DONALD POMEROY, federal judge; b. Princeton, Ill., Aug. 24, 1926; s. Hardy W. and Ruth (Cushing) L.; m. Miriam Elaine Gustafson, Aug. 6, 1949; children: Stephen Pomeroy(dec.) , Catherine Sue, Cynthia Lynn, Elizabeth Ann, Deborah Jean, Susan Elaine. Student, U.S. Naval Acad., 1945—46; BA, U. Iowa, 1948, JD, 1951; LLD (hon.) (hon.) , Mitchell Coll. Law, 1985. Bar: Nebr. 1951, Iowa 1951, Wis. 1953. Assoc. Kennedy, Holland, DeLacy & Svoboda, Omaha, 1951—53, Quarles, Spence & Quarles, Milw., 1953—54, Eisenstatt, Lay, Higgins & Miller, 1954—66; judge U.S. Ct. Appeals (8th cir.), 1966—, chief judge, 1980—92, senior judge, 1992—. Faculty mem. on evidence Nat. Coll. Trial Judges, 1964—65, U. Minn. Law Sch., William Mitchell Law Sch.; mem. U.S. Jud. Conf., 1980—92. Mem. editl. bd.: Iowa Law Rev., 1950—51; contbr. With USNR, 1944—46. Recipient Hancher-Finkbine medal, U. Iowa, 1980, Disting. Alumni award, 2000. Mem.: ATLA (bd. govs. 1963—65, Jud. Achievement award), ABA, Am. Judicature Soc., Wis. Bar Assn., Iowa Bar Assn., Nebr. Bar Assn., Internat. Acad. Trial Lawyers, Order of Coif, Sigma Chi, Phi Delta Phi, Delta Sigma Rho (Significant Sig award 1986, Herbert Harley award 1988). Presbyterian. Office: US Ct Appeals 8th Cir 316 Robert St N Ste 560 Saint Paul MN 55101-1461

LAY, KENNETH LEE, former diversified energy company executive; b. Tyrone, Mo., Apr. 15, 1942; s. Omer and Ruth E. (Reese) L.; m. Linda Ann Phillips, July 10, 1982; children: Robyn Anne, Mark Kenneth, Todd David, Elizabeth Ayers, Robert Ray. BA, U. Mo., 1964, MA, 1965; PhD, U. Houston, 1970. Corp. economist Exxon Corp., Houston, 1965-68; asst. prof. and lectr. in econs. George Washington U., 1969-73; tech. asst. to commr. FERC, 1971-72; dep. undersec. for energy Dept. Interior, 1972-74; v.p. Fla. Gas Co. (now Continental Resources Co.), Winter Park, Fla., 1974-76, pres., 1976-79; exec. v.p. The Continental Group, 1979-81; pres., chief operating officer, dir. Transco Energy Co., Houston, 1981-84; chmn., chief exec officer Houston Natural Gas Corp., 1984-85; pres., chief exec. officer, chief operating officer, dir. Enron Corp. (formerly HNG/InterNorth), Houston, 1985—2001, also chmn. bd. dirs., Houston, 2001—02. Asst. prof. George Washington U.; bd. dirs. Eli Lilly & Co., Trust Co. West, Compaq Computer Corp.; past chmn. Greater Houston Partnership. Former chmn. bd. regents U. Houston; bd. trustees The H. John Heinz III Ctr. for Sci., Econs. & the Environment, The Bus. Coun., Am. Enterprise Inst.; Houston Host Com. for 1992 Rep. Nat. Conv.; co-chmn. 1990 Houston Econ. Summit Host. Com.; trustee Howard U.; active Resources for the Future. Decorated Navy Commendation award; recipient Pvt. Sector Coun. Leadership award, 1997, Horatio Alger award, 1998; N.A.M. fellow; State Farm fellow; Guggenheim fellow; named one of 25 Top Mgrs. in the World, Bus. Week., 1999; named to Tex. Bus. Hall of Fame, 1997. Mem. Nat. Petroleum Coun., River Oaks Country Club, Phi Beta Kappa. Republican. Methodist. Office: Enron Corp 1400 Smith St Houston TX 77002*

LAY, NORVIE LEE, law educator; b. Cardwell, Ky., Apr. 17, 1940; s. Arlie H. and Opha (Burns) L.; 1 dau., Lea Anne. BS, U. Ky., 1960; JD, U. Louisville, 1963; LL.M. (Cook fellow), U. Mich., 1964, S.JD, 1967. Bar: Ky. 1963. Asst. prof. law U. Louisville, 1964-67, assoc. prof., 1967-70, prof., 1970—; asst. dean U. Louisville (Sch. Law), 1971-73, assoc. dean, 1973-84, acting dean, 1981-82. Vis. prof. Southwestern U. Sch. Law, summer 1983, N.Y. Law Sch., 1983-84, Coll. of Law U. Iowa, summer 1989. Author: Tax and Estate Planning for Community Property and the Migrant Client, 1970; contbr. articles to profl. jours. Trustee St. Joseph's Infirmary, 1974-78, S.W. Jefferson Community Hosp., 1979-80, Suburban Hosp., 1981-84, Humana-Audubon Hosp., 1985-88, U. Louisville Law Sch. Alumni Found., from 1982-85; bd. dirs. Louisville Ballet, from 1982-88, Louisville Theatrical Assn., 1985-88, Louisville Art Gallery, 1984-87, Watertower Art Assn., 1986-89, Chamber Mus. Soc. of Louisville, 1985-88, Louisville Chorus, 1985-88, Ky. Contemporary Theatre, 1984, Ky. Country Day Sch., 1985-88, Ky. Arts Coun., 1991—; mem. Nat. Conf. Commrs. Uniform State Laws. Recipient Scholarship Key Delta Theta Phi, 1963, Outstanding Graduating Sr. award Omicron Delta Kappa, 1963 Fellow Am. Coll. of Trust and Estate Counsel (acad.), Am. Coll. Tax Counsel; mem. ABA, Ky. Bar Assn., Louisville Bar Assn., Am. Judicature Soc. Republican. Baptist. Office: U Louisville Sch Law Belknap Campus Louisville KY 40292-0001

LAY, THORNE, geosciences educator; b. Casper, Wyo., Apr. 20, 1956; s. Johnny Gordon and Virginia Florence (Lee) L. BS, U. Rochester, 1978; MS, Calif. Inst. Tech., 1980, PhD, 1983. Rsch. assoc. Calif. Inst. Tech., Pasadena, 1983; asst. prof. geosciences U. Mich., Ann Arbor, 1984-88, assoc. prof., 1988-89; prof. U. Calif., Santa Cruz, 1989—. Cons. Woodward Clyde cons., Pasadena, 1982-84; dir. Inst. Tectonics, 1990-94, chmn. earth sci. dept., 1994-2000; dir. Inst. Geophysics and Planetary Physics, 2000—. Author: Structure and Fate of Subducting Slabs, 1997; co-author: (with T.C. Wallace) Modern Global Seismology, 1995; contbr. numerous articles to profl. jours. NSF fellow, 1978-81, Guttenberg fellow Calif. Inst. Tech., 1978, Lilly fellow Eli Lilly Found., 1984, Sloan fellow, 1985-87, Presidential Young Investigator, 1985-90. Fellow Royal Astron. Soc., Am. Geophys. Union (Macelwane medal 1991), Soc. Exploration Geophysicist, Seismol. Soc. Am., AAAS; mem. Nat. Acad. Sci. (life assoc.). Home: 2114 Harborview Ct Santa Cruz CA 95062-1678 Office: U Calif Santa Cruz Earth Sci Bd Santa Cruz CA 95064 E-mail: tlay@es.ucsc.edu.

LAYCOCK, HAROLD DOUGLAS, law educator, writer; b. Alton, Ill., Apr. 15, 1948; s. Harold Francis and Claudia Anita (Garrette) L.; m. Teresa A. Sullivan, June 14, 1971; children: Joseph Peter, John Patrick. BA, Mich. State U., 1970; JD, U. Chgo., 1973. Bar: Ill. 1973, U.S. Dist. Ct. (no. dist.) Ill. 1973, Tex. 1974, U.S. Dist. Ct. (we. dist.) Tex. 1975, U.S. Ct. Appeals (5th and 11th cirs.) 1975, U.S. Supreme Ct. 1976, U.S. Ct. Appeals (6th cir.) 1987, U.S. Ct. Appeals (8th cir.) 1994, U.S. Ct. Appeals (10th cir.) 1997. Law clk. to judge U.S. Ct. Appeals (7th cir.), Chgo., 1973-74; pvt. practice Austin, Tex., 1974-76; asst. prof. U. Chgo., 1976-80, prof., 1980-81, U. Tex., Austin, 1980—, endowed professorships, 1983-88, assoc. dean for acad. affairs, 1985-86, endowed chair, 1988—, assoc. dean for rsch., 1991—. Vis. prof. U. Mich., 1990; reporter com. on motion practice Ill. Jud. Conf., 1977-78. Author: Modern American Remedies, 1985, 2d edit., 1994, 3d edit., 2002, The Death of the Irreparable Injury Rule, 1991; mem. bd. advisors Religious Freedom Reporter, 1990-2001; contbr. articles to law revs. Adv. bd. Consumer Svcs. Orgn., Chgo., 1979-80; exec. bd. Ctr. for Ch./State Studies, DePaul U., Chgo., 1982-87; adv. com. on religious liberty Presbyn. Ch. U.S.A., 1983-88, advisor restatement of restitution, 1984-85, 97—; v.p. St. Francis Sch., 1990-92, bd. dirs., 1990—, pres. 1992-2001; bd. advisors J.M. Dawson Inst. Ch./State Studies, Baylor U., 1990—. Fellow AAAS, Internat. Acad. for Freedom of Religion and Belief; mem. AAUP (mem. com. on status of women in acad. profession 1982-85), Am. Law Inst. (mem. coun. 2001—), Chgo. Coun. Lawyers (v.p. 1977-78), Assn. Am. Law Schs. (chmn., sec. on remedies 1983, 94), chmn., sec. on constitutional law, 2000). Home: 8819 Chalk Knoll Dr Austin TX 78735 Office: U Tex Law Sch 727 E Dean Keeton St Austin TX 78705-3224 E-mail: dlaycock@mail.law.utexas.edu.

LAYCOCK, MARY CHAPPELL, gifted and talented education educator, consultant; b. Jefferson City, Mo., Jan. 11, 1915; d. Alvin E. and Ollie (Harris) Chappell; m. James Charles Laycock, June 22, 1937; children: Charles, Ann, Donald E., Jane. AB, Judson Coll., 1937; MA in Math. Edn., U. Tenn., 1961. Math. tchr. various, 1938-41; math. tchr. Kingsport (Tenn.) Jr. High Sch., 1942; math. coord. Oak Ridge (Tenn.) City Schs., 1956-68, high sch. math. tchr., 1945-68; math. specialist Nueva Ctr. for Learning, Hillsborough, Calif., 1968-98; cons. Hayward, 1990-97. Author many books including Mathematics for Meaning, The Fabric of Mathematics, Algebra in Concrete, Focus on Geometry, Hands On Mathematics for Secondary Teachers, Weaving Your Way from Arithmetic to Mathematics, 1993, The Magician's Castle Fantasy, 1995; developed documentary Don't Bother Me, I'm Learning, 12 videotapes on teaching manipulatives; contbr. articles to profl. jours. Recipient Calif. Educator award, 1989, Elem. Math. Tchr. award Calif. Math. Coun. and State of Calif., 1989, Award of Recognition Calif. Assn. for the Gifted. 1984. Mem. NEA, Nat. Coun. Tchrs. Math., Oreg. Math. Coun., Calif. Math. Coun. (life), Fla. Math. Coun., Greater San Diego Math. Coun., San Mateo County Math. Coun., Calif. Assn. for the Gifted. Avocation: geometric art. Home and Office: 20655 Hathaway Ave Hayward CA 94541-3740 E-mail: info@activityresources.com.

LAYCRAFT, JAMES HERBERT, retired judge; b. Veteran, Alta., Can., Jan. 5, 1924; s. George Edward and Hattie (Cogswell) L.; m. Helen Elizabeth Bradley, May 1, 1948; children: James B., Anne L. BA, U. Alta., Edmonton, 1950; LLB, U. Alta., 1951; LLD (hon.), U. Calgary, Alta., 1986. Bar: Alta. Barrister Nolan Chambers & Co., Calgary, 1952-75; justice trial div. Supreme Ct. of Alta., 1975-79; justice Ct. of Appeal of Alta., 1979-85, chief justice of Alta., 1985-91, ret., 1991. Contbr. articles to law jours. Served to lt. Royal Can. Arty., 1941-46, PTO. Mem. United Ch. of Can. Avocations: amateur radio, fishing.

LAYDE, PETER MARK, epidemiologist, preventive medicine educator; b. Milw., Apr. 16, 1951; s. Durward Charles and Mary Agnes (Lee) L.; m. Angela Jane Carollo, Apr. 30, 1976; children: Michael, Kevin, Molly. MD, U. Wis., 1976; MS, London Sch. Hygiene and Tropical Medicine, 1980. Diplomate Am. Bd. Preventive Medicine and Am. Coll. Epidemiology. Internship McGill U., Montreal, Que., Can., 1976-77; surgeon USPHS, 1977-87; med. epidemiologist Ctrs. Disease Control, Atlanta, 1977-82, chief epidemiology studies br., 1982-83, chief scientist agent orange projects, 1983-85, dir. chronic disease div., 1985-86, chronic disease coord., 1986-87; sr. epidemiologist Marshfield (Wis.) Clinic, 1987—, also bd. dirs. Cons. WHO, Geneva, 1982—, USPHS, Washington, 1987—, Am. Cancer Soc., Atlanta, 1989—. Contbr. numerous articles to profl. jours. Trustee Marshfield Med. Rsch. Found., 1991—. Fellow Am. Coll. Preventive Medicine (rsch. com. 1988—), Am. Coll. Epidemiology; mem. Am. Epidemiol. Soc., Soc. Epidemiologic Rsch. Democrat. Achievements include research in epidemiology of cancer, birth defects and injuries.

LAYDEN, CHARLES MAX, lawyer; b. Lafayette, Ind., Nov. 10, 1941; s. Charles E. and Elnora M. (Parvis) L.; m. Lynn D. McVey, Jan. 28, 1967; children: David Charles, Kathleen Ann, John Michael, Daniel Joseph. BA in Indsl. Mgmt., Purdue U., 1964; JD, Ind. U., 1967. Bar: Ind. 1967, U.S. Dist. Ct. (no. and so. dists.) Ind. 1967, U.S. Ct. Appeals (7th cir.) 1970. U.S. Tax Ct. 1986. Assoc. Vaughan & Vaughan, Lafayette, 1967-70; ptnr. Vaughan, Vaughan & Layden, 1970-86, Layden & Layden, Lafayette, 1986—. Chmn. profl. div. United Way Lafayette, 1986. Mem. ABA, Ind. Bar Assn., Tippecanoe County Bar Assn. (pres. 1994-95), Am. Bd. Trial Advs. (charter mem. Ind.

chpt. 1984—), Ind. Trial Lawyers Assn. (bd. dirs. 1983—). Republican. Roman Catholic. Avocations: photography, classic cars, flying. Home: 2826 Ashland St West Lafayette IN 47906-1510 Office: Layden & Layden PO Box 909 Lafayette IN 47902-0909

LAYDEN, LYNN MCVEY, lawyer; b. Mpls., June 15, 1941; d. David Hugh and Adelyn Martha (Dvorak) McVey; m. Charles Max Layden, Jan. 28, 1967; children: David Charles, Kathleen Ann, John Michael, Daniel Joseph. LBA, Carleton Coll., Northfield, Minn., 1963; JD, Ind. u., 1967. Bar: Ind. 1967, U.S. Dist. Ct. (so. and no. dists.) 1967. Assoc. Vaughan, Vaughan & Layden, Lafayette, Ind., 1967-86; ptnr. Layden & Layden, 1986—. Guardian ad litem Superior Ct. III-Juvenile Ct., Lafayette, 1986-96. Pres. devel. coun. Ivy Tech. State Coll., 1993-99; pres. bd. trustees West Lafayette Sch. Corp., 1988-95; treas. Sycamore Girl Scout Coun., 1999-2002; treas. West Lafayette Parks Found., 2001—. Mem. ABA, Ind. Bar Assn., Tippecanoe County Bar Assn., Order of Coif, Phi Beta Kappa. Home: 2826 Ashland St West Lafayette IN 47906-1510 Office: Layden & Layden Bank 1 Bldg Ste 712 Lafayette IN 47901

LAYDEN, SCOTT, professional sports team executive; With The Jazz; exec. v.p., gen. mgr. N.Y. Knicks, pres., gen .mgr., 2001—. Office: 2 Pennsylvania Ave Plz 14th Fl New York NY 10121*

LAYEGHI, GHOLAM REZA, engineer, researcher, editor; b. Fasa, Fars, Iran, Oct. 11, 1961; s. Ali Reza and Eshrat (Kiani) L. BS, Iran U. Sci. & Tech., Tehran, 1986; MS, Sharif Isnt. Tech., Tehran, 1997. Rschr. Edn. Ministry, Tehran, 1981-83, Iran Ctr. Indsl. Rsch., Tehran, 1986—, Defence Ministry, Tehran, 1990-93; mng. dir. F.S. Computer Ctr., 1988-94; tech. asst. Thought Found., 1995-96; dir. Nat. Press Ctr., 1996-97. Writer for radio and TV orgn., Tehran, 1983—90. Author: 5 books; editor-in-chief Ittela Mo., 1995—; editor: Tehran Q, 1997, Profl. Info. Svcs., 1997; translator: Introduction to Composite Material, 1994, ABC of Copyright, 2001, Copyright in Industrial Developed Countries, 2002, Copyright in Islamic World, 2002, Alt bach International Book Publishing, An Ency., 2001. Recipient citations Def. Ministry, 1992, Culture Ministry, 1994, gold coin Radio and TV. Avocations: swimming, travel, walking, oil and color drawing, graphic design. Fax: 0098-21-8428577.

LAYFIELD, LESTER JAMES, pathologist, educator; BS magna cum laude, U. Calif., Irvine, 1974; MD, UCLA, 1979. Diplomate in anatomic and clin. pathology Am. Bd. Pathology; diplomate Nat. Bd. Med. Examiners; lic. physician, Calif., Utah. Intern U. Wash., Seattle, 1979-80; resident UCLA, 1980-83, chief resident, 1983-84, adj. asst. prof. pathology, 1983-84, asst. prof. dept. pathology, 1984-89, assoc. prof., 1989-90; assoc. prof. dept. pathology U. Iowa Hosps. and Clinics, Iowa City, 1990-92, Duke U. Med. Ctr., Durham, N.C., 1992-96, dir. image analysis lab., 1992-97, chief surg. pathology, 1993-97, prof. dept. pathology, 1996-97; prof. dept. pathology, head surg. pathology dept. U. Utah, Salt Lake City, 1997—. Pathologist Childrens Cancer Study Group UCLA, 1984-90, dir. fine needle aspiration svc., 1984-90; co-dir. cytology U. Iowa Hosps. and Clinics, Iowa City, 1990-92; lectr. cytopathology at local, regional and nat. workshops. Contbr. articles to profl. jours., chpts. to books. Am. Cancer Soc. jr. fellow, 1982. Mem. Arthur Purdy Stout Soc., Papanicolaou Soc. Cytopathology, Internat. Acad. Cytology, Internat. Soc. Breast Pathology (sec.). Office: Health Scis Ctr Dept Pathology U Utah 50 N Medical Dr Dept U Salt Lake City UT 84132-0001

LAYMAN, DALE PIERRE, medical educator, author, researcher; b. Niles, Mich., July 3, 1948; s. Pierre Andre and Delphine Lucille (Lenke) L.; m. Kathleen Ann Jackowiak, Aug. 8, 1970; children: Andrew Michael, Alexis Kathryn, Allison Victoria, Amanda Elizabeth. AS in Life Sci., Lake Mich. Coll., 1968; BS in Anthropology and Zoology with distinction, U. Mich., 1971, MS in Physiology, 1974; EdS in Physiology and Health Sci., Ball State U., 1979; PhD in Health and Safety Studies, U. Ill., 1986. Histological technician in neuropathology U. Mich. Med. Sch., Ann Arbor, 1971-72, tchg. fellow in human physiology, 1972-74; instr. in human anatomy, physiology, and histology Lake Superior State U., Sault Ste. Marie, Mich., 1974-75; prof. med. terminology, human anatomy and physiology Joliet (Ill.) Jr. Coll., 1975—. Author: The Terminology of Anatomy and Physiology, 1983, The Medical Language: A Programmed Body-Systems Approach, 1995; contbr. articles to profl. jours. Founder Robowatch. Named Notable Author, Text and Acad. Authors, Inc., Internat. Intellectual of Yr., Contributions to Medicine, 2001; recipient Presdl. Seal Honor for 2001, 2001. Fellow Soc. of Leading Intellectuals of the World; mem. Human Anatomy and Physiology Soc., Text and Acad. Authors Assn., Inc. (coun. mem.), Ill. Cmty. Coll. Faculty Assn. (campus coord.), Am. Biog. Inst. (continental gov., dep. gov., world laureate, rsch. bd. of advisors, sec. gen. United Cultural Conv.), London Diplomatic Acad. (mem. acad. coun.), Phi Kappa Phi, Kappa Delta Pi. Avocations: running, swimming, reading motivational literature. Home: 509 Westridge Ln Joliet IL 60431-4883 Office: Joliet Jr Coll 1215 Houbolt Rd Joliet IL 60431-8938

LAYMAN, DAVID MICHAEL, lawyer; b. Pensacola, Fla., July 28, 1955; s. James Hugh and Winifred (Smith) L. BA with high honors, U. Fla., 1977, JD with honors, 1979. Bar: Fla. 1980. Assoc. Gunster, Yoakley, Criser & Stewart, West Palm Beach, Fla., 1980-83, Wolf, Block, Schorr & Solis-Cohen, West Palm Beach, 1983-87, ptnr., 1987-88; shareholder Shapiro and Bregman P.A., 1988-91, Greenberg, Traurig, Hoffman, Lipoff, Rosen & Quentel, P.A., West Palm Beach, Fla., 1991-93, Prom, Korn & Zehmer, P.A., Jacksonville, 1993-94, Mahoney Adams & Criser, P.A., Jacksonville, 1994-96, Greenberg, Traurig, P.A., West Palm Beach, 1996—. Mem. Attys. Title Ins. Fund. Contbg. editor U. Fla. Law Rev.; contbr. articles to profl. jours. Del. Statewide Rep. Caucus, Orlando, Fla., 1986; mem. Blue Ribbon Zoning Rev. Com., West Palm Beach, 1986; bd. dirs., pres. Palm Beach County Planning Congress, 1984-89; trustee South Fla. Sci. Mus., 1994-96; bd. dirs., sec., v.p. Ronald McDonald House, Jacksonville, 1994-96, Cultural Coun. of Greater Jacksonville; bd. dirs., v.p. Children's Pl. at Home Safe Inc., 1996—; mem. vestry Holy Trinity Episcopal Ch., West Palm Beach, 2002—. Named one of Outstanding Young Men in Am., 1980. Mem. ABA, Fla. Bar Assn. (bd. govs. young lawyers divsn. 1989-91), Palm Beach County Bar Assn. (pres. young lawyers sect. 1987-88), Fla. Blue Key, Palm Beach County Gator Club (pres., bd. dirs.), Omicron Delta Kappa, Sigma Chi, Phi Kappa Phi. Episcopalian. Bus. Office: 777 S Flagler Dr Ste 300E West Palm Beach FL 33401-6161 E-mail: laymand@gtlaw.com.

LAYMAN, KIM FLORINDA MARIE, pharmacist, writer; b. New Orleans, Oct. 1, 1959; d. Charles Clifton and Audrey Spann Layman. BS in Biochemistry, Xavier U., 1982, BS in Pharmacy, 1985. PharmD, 2000. Lic. pharmacist La., Ind. Staff pharmacist Ochsner Med. Found., New Orleans, 1985—88; pharmacist Deaconess Hosp., Evansville, Ind., 1989—91; clin. pharmacist West Jefferson Med. Ctr., Marrero, La., 1991—. Author: Poems for Everyday People, 1993, I Got Something to Say, 2002. Storyteller Layman's Pre-sch. Acad., New Orleans, 1982—. Mem.: S.E. La. Soc. Health Sys. Pharmacists, La. Soc. Health Sys. Pharmacists, Am. Soc. Health Sys. Pharmacists, Zeta Phi Beta. Roman Catholic. Avocations: French horn, jazz, yoga, reciting poetry, theater . Home: 2710 Pressburg St New Orleans LA 70122

LAYMAN, LAWRENCE, naval officer; b. Laclede County, Mo., Oct. 28, 1930; s. Archibald A. and Zoe Ellen (Hoke) L.; m. Carmen Elizabeth Meyer, Oct. 5, 1953; children: Linda Carmen, Lawrence, Harry Arthur, John Robert. BS, U.S. Naval Acad., 1952; MS in Internat. Affairs, George Washington U., 1972. Commd. ensign U.S. Navy, 1952, advanced through grades to rear adm., 1979; service to Korea and Vietnam; dep. comdr. Naval Telecommunications Command, 1978-79; dir. command, control and communications systems U.S. European Command, 1979-81; vice dir. Def. Communications Agy., Washington, 1981-83; dir. Naval Communications, 1983-86; dir. space command and control Office Chief Naval Ops., 1986-89, ret., 1989. Decorated D.S.M., Def. Superior Svc. medal with oak leaf cluster, Legion of Merit with Gold Star, Bronze Star with combat V, Meritorious Svc. medal. Home: 3429 Silver Maple Pl Falls Church VA 22042-3545

LAYNE, JAMES NATHANIEL, vertebrate biologist; b. Chgo., May 16, 1926; s. Leslie Joy and Harriet (Hausmann) L.; m. Lois Virginia Linderoth, Aug. 26, 1950; children: Linda Carrie, Kimberly, Jamie Linderoth, Susan Nell, Rachel Pratt. BA, Cornell U., 1950, PhD, 1954. Grad. teaching asst. Cornell U., Ithaca, N.Y., 1950-54, assoc. prof. zoology, 1963-67; asst. prof. zoology So. Ill. U., Carbondale, 1954-55; asst. prof., then assoc. prof. biology U. Fla., 1955-63; asst. curator, then assoc. curator mammals Fla. State Mus., Gainesville, 1955-63, research assoc., 1963-65; dir. research, then exec. dir. Archbold Biol. Sta.; Archbold curator mammals Am. Mus. Natural History, 1967-85; sr. rsch. biologist Archbold Biol. Sta., 1985-94, sr. rsch. biologist emeritus, 1994—. Rsch. assoc. Fla. State Collection of Arthropods, Am. Mus. Natural History; vis. scientist primate ecology sect. Nat. Inst. Neurol. Diseases and Blindness, summers 1961-62. Contbr. articles and chpt. to profl. jours. and books. Hon. trustee Fla. Defenders of Environment; bd. dirs. Fla. Audubon Soc.; mem. Fla. Nongame Wildlife Adv. Council, Peace River Basin Bd., Fla. Panther Tech. Adv. Council. Served with USAAF, 1944-46. Fellow AAAS; mem. Am. Soc. Zoologists, Am. Soc. Mammalogists (pres. 1970-72, hon. mem. 1993, C. Hart Merriam award 1976), Ecol. Soc. Am., Soc. for Study of Evolution, Am. Soc. Naturalists, Wildlife Soc., Wildlife Disease Assn., Nature Conservancy (trustee Fla. chpt.), Fla. Acad. Scis. (pres. 1984-85, medalist 1995), Orgn. Biol. Field Stas. (pres. 1986-87), Phi Beta Kappa, Sigma Xi, Phi Kappa Phi, Phi Sigma. E-mail: jlayne@strato.net.

LAYSON, WILLIAM MCINTYRE, retired research consulting company executive; b. Lexington, Ky., Sept. 24, 1934; s. Zed Clark and Louise (McIntyre) L. BS, MIT, 1956, PhD, 1961; postgrad., U. Sydney, Australia, 1957-58. Research scientist European Ctr. Nuclear Research, Geneva, 1960-62; research scientist U. Calif., Berkeley, 1962-64; mem. tech. staff Pan Am World Airways, Patrick AFB, Fla., 1964-67; research scientist Gen. Research Corp., Rosslyn, Va., 1967-70; dir. Sci. Applications Internat. Corp., McLean, 1970-98, sr. v.p., chmn. incentives com., 1975-93, coord. def. nuclear programs, 1975-99, chmn. ethics com., 1994-99; ret., 1999. Dir. Langley Sch., 1992-97, pres., 1995-97; pres. Layson's Buffalo Trace Farms, 1976—. Fulbright scholar U. Sydney, Australia, 1957-58 Democrat. Presbyterian (elder). Avocations: church activities, jogging, swimming, skiing. Home: 8301 Summerwood Dr Mc Lean VA 22102-2213

LAYTON, AMANDA EMIGH, non-profit organization fundraiser; b. Framingham, Mass., July 12, 1971; d. Richard Chapman and Nellie Bunker (Revell) E.; m. William F. Layton, Jr., July 11, 1998; 1 child, William Chapman. BA in Sociology, Villanova U., 1993; postgrad., Rutgers U. Pro bono project adminstr. Delaware County Legal Assistance, Chester, Pa., 1993-94; capital campaign coord. Polisar Cons., Phila., 1994-96, N.J. State Aquarium, Camden, N.J., 1996-97. Guest lectr. Rowan Coll., Glassboro, N.J., 1996; cons. Polisar Cons., 1994—; polit. fin. cons., 1996—. Child advocacy vol. Defenders' Assn., Phila., 1992-93; vol. big sister Rosemont (Pa.) Children's Village, 1993—; ann. giving coord. West Jersey Health & Hosp. Found., Voorhees, 1997—. Mem. Nat. Soc. Fundraising Execs., Assn. Healthcare Philanthropy, Kappa Kappa Gamma Alumnae Assn. Home: 1320 Morgan Ave Cinnaminson NJ 08077-2730 Office: 106 Carnie Blvd Kirkwood Voorhees NJ 08043-4515

LAYTON, DONALD HARVEY, banker; b. May 9, 1950; s. Irving and Charlotte (Bell) L.; m. Sandra Lynn Lazo, June 1, 1974; children: Todd Samuel, Ross Charles. SB in Econs., SM in Econs., MIT, 1972; MBA, Harvard U., 1974. Rsch. asst. Harvard Bus. Sch., Boston, 1974-75; various positions through sr. mng. dir. Mfrs. Hanover Trust Co., N.Y.C., 1975-91; sr. exec. v.p. Chemical Bank, 1992—, vice-chmn., 1995, Chase Manhattan Bank, N.Y.C., 1995-2001, J.P. Morgan Chase & Co., N.Y.C., 2001—. Bd. dirs. Pvt. Export Funding Corp.; dir. Inst. Internat. Fin., 2001—; mem. vis. com. for econs. MIT, 1999—. Gov. Fgn. Policy Assn., 1998—. Baker scholar Harvard U., 1974. Home: 885 Park Ave New York NY 10021-0325 Office: JP Morgan Chase & Co 270 Park Ave Fl 8 New York NY 10017-2089

LAYTON, HARRY CHRISTOPHER, artist, lecturer, consultant; b. Safford, Ariz., Nov. 17, 1938; s. Christopher E. and Eurilda (Welker) L.; m. Karol Barbara Kendall, July 11, 1964 (div. Jan. 1989); children: Deborah, Christopher, Joseph, Elisabeth, Faith, Aaron, Gretchen, Benjamin, Justin, Matthew, Peter. LHD, Sussex Coll., Eng., 1969; RE (hon.), PhD (hon.), DRE (hon.), St. Matthew U., Ohio, 1970; DFA (hon.), DSc (hon.), London Inst. Applied Rsch., Ohio, 1972. Cert. clin. hypnotherapist. Pres., mgr. Poems, Art & Myths; pres., CEO, Layton Studio Graphic Design, L.A. Lectr. ancient art Serra Cath. H.S., Gardena, Calif., 1963-64, L.A. Dept. Parks and Recreation, summers 1962-64; interior decorator Cities of Hawthorne, Lawndale, Compton, Gardena, and Torrance, Calif., 1960-68. One-man shows Nahas Dept. Stores, 1962, 64; group shows include Gt. Western Savs. & Loan, Lawndale, 1962, Gardena Adult Sch., 1965, Serra Cath. H.S., 1963, Salon de Nations, Paris, 1983; represented in permanent collections Sussex Coll., Culver City-Foshey Masonic Lodge, Gt. Western Savs. & Loan; paintings include The Fairy Princess, 1975, Nocturnal Covenant, 1963, Blindas Name, 1962, Creation, 1962; works pub. in Our World's Favorite Gold and Silver Poems, 1991, Our World's Favorite Poems, 1993, World's Best Poems, 1993, Outstanding Poets of 1994, Best Poems of 1995, also others. Elder LDS Ch., Santa Monica, Calif., 1963—. Recipient Editor's Choice award Nat. Libr. Poetry, 1994, 95. Mem. Am. Hypnotherapy Assn., Internat. Soc. Artists, Internat. Platform Assn., Am. Security Coun., Soc. for Early Hist. Archaeology, Am. Councilor's Soc. Psychol. Counselors, Salon des Nation Paris Geneva, Ctr. Internat. Art Contemporain, Internat. Soc. Poets (disting.), Internat. Masonic Poetry Soc., Am. Legion, Masons (32d degre), Shriners, KT, Alpha Psi Omega. Republican. Home and Office: Layton Studio Graphic Design Inc 3654 Centinela Ave Apt 10 Los Angeles CA 90066-3147 E-mail: LSGD@attbi.com, PoetLayton@hotmail.com.

LAYTON, HOWARD MANTON, electrical engineer; b. Bristol, Eng., Nov. 23, 1918; arrived in U.S., 1955; s. Edward Alexander Layton, Edith May George; m. Narcissza Wilhelmina Ludanyi, Sept. 18, 1936; m. Joyce Esther Chalon, Jan. 3, 1925 (div. Nov. 1961). Student, Tech. Coll., Coventry, Eng., Cranwell Coll. Chartered elec. engr.; lic. comml. airplane pilot. Founder, pres., chmn. tech. and chmn. bd. Interlab Inc., Danbury, Conn., 1958—. Owner Sonic Force Inc.; actor Charles Denville o., Liverpool, Scotland, 1947—51, various film cos., 1947—51; dept. mgr. IMHOF Mobile Radio divsn., U.K., London, 1951—55. Author: The Thirteen Club, 2001. With Royal Air Force, 1939—47. Fellow: Instn. of Elec. Engrs. (vice chmn. New Eng. br. 1998—2001); mem.: Aircraft Owners and Pilots Assn. Achievements include patents in field of over 20 in engring. Avocations: flying, writing, crossword puzzles, acting, exercise. Mailing: 11 Falmouth Ct Brookfield CT 06804 Office: Interlab Inc 3 Precision Rd Danbury CT 06810

LAYTON, ROBERT, lawyer; b. N.Y.C., Feb. 19, 1931; s. Benjamin and Ruth (Beck) L.; m. Joan Levy, May 17, 1967 (div. Jan. 1976); children: Elisabeth, Julie; m. Christine Lambert, Dec. 31, 1988. BA, U. Mich., 1951; LLB, Yale U., 1954. Teaching fellow Stanford Law Sch., Palo Alto, Calif., 1957-58; atty. U.S. Dept. Justice, Washington, 1958-62; assoc., ptnr. Gilbert, Segall & Young, N.Y.C., 1962-73; ptnr. Layton and Sherman, 1973-84, Surrey & Morse, N.Y.C., 1984-85, Jones, Day, Reavis & Pogue, N.Y.C., 1986-93. Contbr. articles to internat. profl. jours. Mem. exec. com. Yale Law Sch. Assn., 1992-95. Served to sgt. U.S. Army, 1954-56. Fourth Am. recipient Diploma of The Hague Acad. Law, 1959. Mem.: Yale (N.Y.C.). E-mail: rlayton@laytonbh.com.

LAYTON, ROBERT GLENN, radiologist; b. Bklyn., Oct. 14, 1946; s. Irving and Charlotte (Bell) L.; m. Judith Helene Bohrer, May 31, 1969; children: Andrew, Julia. BS, Union Coll., 1968; MD, Boston U., 1972. Diplomate Am. Bd. Radiology. Resident in radiology Boston City Hosp., 1972-75; jr. attending radiologist L.I. Jewish Hosp., Hillside, N.Y., 1975-76; staff radiologist Cedars Med. Ctr., Miami, Fla., 1978-98, chief of radiology, 1999—. Radiologist Highland Park Gen. Hosp., Miami, 1978-84; clin. asst. prof. U. Miami Sch. Med., 1985-87. Pres. Michael-Ann Russell Jewish Cmty. Ctr., Miami, 1980-82; bd. dirs. Jewish Cmty. Ctrs. South Fla., 1982-86; trustee Temple Sinai of North Dade, North Miami Beach, 1982-01, v.p., 1985-92, pres., 1992-94; nat. bd. dirs. Union Am. Hebrew Congregations, trustee, 1999—. Served to maj. USAF, 1976-78. Mem. AMA, Am. Coll. Radiology, Am. Inst. Ultrasound in Medicine, Miami Radiol. Soc., Begg Soc., Alpha Omega Alpha. Avocations: contemporary art, skiing, golf. Office: Cedars Med Ctr Dept Radiology 1400 NW 12th Ave Miami FL 33136-1003 E-mail: rglmd@bellsouth.net.

LAYTON, RODNEY EUGENE, financial executive, newspaper executive; b. Lusk, Wyo., Feb. 27, 1954; s. Raymond Dwight Layton and Mary Elizabeth (Miller) Spencer; m. Susan Carol Johnson, Jan. 8, 1977 (div.); children: Joshua, Elise, Caleb. Ba in Polit. Sci./Econs., Kearney State, 1977; student, U. Nebr., 1978-80. CPA, Nebr. Auditor State of Nebr., Lincoln, 1979-80; staff auditor Arthur Andersen, Houston, 1980-81; audit sr. McDermott & Miller, Grand Island, Nebr., 1981-82; internal audit sr. Norwest Bank Corp., Omaha, 1982-86; internal audit mgr. Berkshire Hathaway, Inc., 1986-89; treas., controller Buffalo News, 1989—2001, v.p., CEO, 2001—. Treas. Citizens Advocacy, Grand Island, 1981; treas., pres. Crippled Children's Camps, Inc., Buffalo, 1989-93; treas., bd. dirs. Cradle Beach Camp, Buffalo, 1989-94. Mem. AICPAs, Nebr. Soc. CPAs, Internat. Newspaper Fin. Execs. Avocations: tennis, golf, piano. Home: 42 Bywater Ct Amherst NY 14221-1475 Office: Buffalo News PO Box 100 Buffalo NY 14240-0100

LAYTON, WILLIAM GENE, emergency medical service administrator; b. Balt., Aug. 1, 1943; s. William H. and Jean Marie (Diener) L.; m. Suszanna E. Layton, Jan. 1, 1980; 1 child, Chrysanna E. Paramedic, Cen. Fla. Community Coll., Ocala, 1980. Lic. EMT. Paramedic Munroe Regional Med. Ctr., Ocala, 1980, supr. ambulance svc., 1981, mgr. ambulance svc., 1984, dir. ambulance svc., 1989—2001, cmty. health coord., 2001—. Founder, dir., treas. N. Cen. Fla. Trauma Agy., 1990-92, 98—; chmn. emergency med. svcs. adv. coun. Ctrl. Fla. C.C., 1987-99. Vice chmn. Marion County Emergency Mgmt. Coun., 1992-96; mem. Withlacoochee Regional Local Emergency Planning Com., Dist. 5, 1990-2002; bd. dirs. Ocala Civic Theater, 1995-99, also sec.; mem. Fla. State Transformation of Emergency Med. Svcs. Task Force, 1999-2001; mem. Hospice Project Decide, 1999-2001; mem. Cmty. Traffic Safety Team, 1998--. Recipient Brian G. McKay award for outstanding contbns. to Emergency Med. Svc. in North Cen. Fla., 1987. Mem. Coun. on Rural Emergency Med. Svc. (v.p., past pres., sec.), Am. Trauma Soc. (founding dir., sec. Fla. div.), Fla. Assn. County Emergency Med. Svcs. (bd. dirs. 1994-95). Home: 8434 SW 69th Court Rd Ocala FL 34476-8157

LAYTON, WILLIAM GEORGE, retired management consultant, human resources executive, export-import executive; b. Missouri Valley, Iowa, Sept. 11, 1931; s. George Holbert and Margaret (Wilson) L.; m. Caroline R. Tiffany, June 27, 1953; children: Kathleen Layton Medl, Sara Layton Howe, Thomas William. BA, Coe Coll., 1953; MA, U. Ill., 1955. Indsl. rels. trainee Procter & Gamble Co., Cin., 1955-57, pers. specialist, 1957-62, indsl. rels. mgr. France, 1962-66, pers. mgr. European Tech. Ctr., 1966-69, pers. mgr. internat., 1969-72; v.p. human resources Food Svc. div. Heublein, Inc., Louisville, 1972-77; sr. v.p. human resources Holiday Inns, Inc., Memphis, 1977-83; pres. The Layton Group, St. Petersburg, Fla., 1983—2001; sr. ptnr. Johnson-Layton Co. Mgmt. Cons., L.A. and St. Petersburg, 1985-95; pres. CompCom, Inc., 1994-97; chmn., CEO Appliances Internat., Inc., 1997—2002. Bd. dirs., pres. Jr. Achievement of Memphis, 1981-83; mem. Tenn. Jobs Tng. Coordinating Coun., 1982-88; mem. Pvt. Industry Coun. of Memphis and Shelby County, 1982-88; mem. Pres.'s Coun., Rhodes Coll., Memphis, 1983-90. Served with USAF, 1953-55. Mem.: Coun. Mgmt. Cons. (Sr. Examiner Sterling Quality award Fla. 1994), Inst. Mgmt. Cons. (cert. mgmt. cons.), Am. Mgmt. Assn. (human resources coun. 1981-83), Rotary, Phi Beta Kappa. Republican. Presbyterian. E-mail: wglayton@juno.com.

LAZAR, DALE STEVEN, lawyer; b. Cleve., Aug. 16, 1952; s. Donald A. and Mary J. (Zavada) L.; m. Deborah S. Gorecki, Apr. 28, 1979; children: Stephen, Kevin, Vanessa. BS with distinction, Cornell U., 1974, JD, 1977. Bar: D.C. 1977, U.S. Patent and Trademark Office 1978, U.S. Claims Ct. 1979, U.S. Ct. Appeals (D.C. cir.) 1979, U.S. Supreme Ct. 1993, Va. 2001. Assoc. Pillsbury Winthrop LLP, Washington, 1977-82, ptnr., 1982—, mng. ptnr., 1989-93, co-chair Intellectual Property Practice sect., 2000—. Lectr. in field. Mem. Am. Intellectual Property Assn., D.C. Bar Assn., IEEE, Cornell Club Washington (pres. 1989-92), Tau Beta Pi, Eta Kappa Nu. Avocations: swimming, tennis, snow skiing, computers. Office: Pillsbury Winthrop LLP 1600 Tysons Blvd Mc Lean VA 22102

LAZAR, ELIOT JOEL, physician; b. N.Y.C. BS, Bklyn. Coll., 1977; MD, SUNY, Syracuse, 1981; MBA, NYU, 1999. Cert. cardiovascular diseaes 1987, geriatric medicine 1996, Internal Medicine 1984. Intern Bronx Mcpl. Hosp. Ctr., Albert Einstein Coll. Medicine, 1981—82, resident, 1982—84, chief med. resident, 1984—85; cardiology fellow Mt. Sinai Med. Ctr., N.Y., 1985—87; assoc. dir. medicine Einstein Weiler Hosp., Bronx, N.Y., 1987-93; chmn. dept. medicine Bklyn. Hosp. Ctr., 1993-2000; v.p. med. affairs N.Y. Presbyn. Healthcare Sys., N.Y.C., 2000—. Fellow cardiology fellow, Mt. Sinai Med. Ctr., N.Y., 1985—87. Fellow: ACP, Am. Coll. Chest Physicians, Am. Coll. Cardiology; mem.: Alpha Omega Alpha. Office: CPMC AP 1424 161 Fort Washington Ave New York NY 10032-3713

LAZAR, IRVING, psychologist; b. N.Y.C., Feb. 20, 1926; s. Charles and Sylvia L.; m. Jules M. Marquart, Dec. 24, 1981; children: Kathryn S., James Bradford, Richard Alan. BS, CCNY, 1948; MA, Columbia U., 1950, PhD, 1954. Intern The Menninger Clinic, Topeka, 1946-47; instr. clin. psychology U. Rochester (N.Y.), 1948-49; instr. psychology Bard Coll., Amandale-on-Hudson, N.Y., 1949-50; instr. child devel. U. Ill. Coll. Edn., Urbana, 1950-54; assoc. chief mental health sect. Nev. State Dept. Health, Las Vegas, 1954-60; dir. Peterson-Guedel Family Ctr., Beverly Hills, Calif., 1960-64; exec. dir The Neumeyer Found., 1963-68; western mgr. Kirschner Assocs., L.A., 1968-70; assoc. dir. Appalachian Regional Commn., Washington, 1970-72; prof. dept. human svc. studies Cornell U., 1972-91, prof. emeritus, 1991—; external faculty The Santa Fe Inst., 1994-99; rsch. prof. Peabody Coll., Vanderbilt U., Nashville, 1991-99, resident scholar Kennedy Ctr. for Rsch. in Human Devel., 1991—. Cons. in field. Contbr. articles to profl. jours. Trustee Coalition for Quality Children's Media, Santa Fe, 1994—. Rsch. fellow Population Inst., East-West Ctr., Honolulu, 1987. Home: 7425 Somerset Pl Nashville TN 37221-4612 E-mail: i.lazar@comcast.net.

LAZAR, JOHN EDWARD, administrator non-profit organization; b. Bklyn., Mar. 24, 1950; s. John and Elizabeth (Titch) Lazar. BA, St. John's U., Bklyn., 1971; postgrad., Bklyn. Coll., 1972-73; MDiv, Sem. of Immaculate Conception, 1980. Cert. tchr., N.Y.; ordained clergyman Roman Cath. Ch. 1980. English tchr. N.Y.C. Bd. Edn., Bklyn., 1973-79; clergyman Roman Cath. Diocese of Bklyn., 1980-93; pres. POMOC, Inc., N.Y.C., 1981-84; dir. housing Argus Cmty., Inc., Bronx, N.Y., 1993-96; devel. cons. Met. Cmty. Ch., L.A., 1997—; exec. dir. San Fernando Valley Am. Cancer Soc., Sherman Oaks, Calif., 1998—2001; regional v.p. Greater Bay Area Redwood Empire region Am. Cancer Soc., 2001—. Exec. dir. Peregrinatio Ad Petri Sedem-U.S. Office of Pilgrimages, Vatican City, 1985-86. Author: Outpouring the Spirit: Gay and Lesbian Spirituality in the Judeo Christian Tradition, 1996; TV show host Polish Profiles, 1989-93; prodr., host City of West Hollywood Town Hall-Gay Spirituality, 1999, 2000, prodr., moderator, 2001. Commr. City of West Hollywood (Calif.) Lesbian and Gay Adv. Bd., 1998—2001 now co-chair; bd. dirs. City Vol. Corps., N.Y.C. 1990-96, Stonewall Dem. Club, L.A., 1997—; v.p. Polish Am. Congress, N.Y.C., 1989-93; co-prodr. civic celebration Bklyn. Outdoor Mus. of Art, 1993; mem. com. Mayor's Planning Com. L.A. Vol. Festival, 1998, 99; chmn. N.Y.C. Comptr.'s Polish Adv. Com., 1982-89, 94-96; panelist City of West Hollywood Town Hall Election, 2000. Named Hon. Alumnus, Our Lady of the Lake Sem., 1982; recipient Pres.'s award Stonewall Dem. Club, 1998, Commendation award N.Y.C. Comptr., 1995, Citizen of Yr. award Polish Am. World, 1982. Mem. Polish Inst. Arts and Scis. in Am., Inc., So. Calif. Assn. Non Profit Housing, Inc. Democrat. Avocations: bicycling, reading, prestidigitation, downhill skiing. Home: 2790 19th Ave # 21 San Francisco CA 94132 Office: Am Cancer Soc 1700 Webster St Oakland CA 94612 E-mail: JELazer324@aol.com.

LAZAR, JONATHAN KUMIN, computer scientist, educator; b. Columbia, Md., Sept. 24, 1974; s. Martin J. and Libby Kumin Lazar. BBA, Loyola Coll., 1995; MS, PhD, U. Md., Balt., 1999. Asst. prof. Towson U., Md., 1999—; affiliate prof. Ctr. Applied Info. Tech., 1999—. Author: (book) User-Centered Web Development, 2001; editor: Managing IT/Community Partnerships in the 21st Century, 2002; ; mem. editl. rev. bd.: Info. Resources Mgmt. Jour., 2001; contbr. articles to profl. jours. Recipient Fr. Daniel J. McGuire Alumni Assn. award, Loyola Coll., 1995, Bronze medal for nat. Latin exam, Am. Classical League, 1990; grantee, Johns Hopkins U./U.S. Ctrs. for Disease Control, 2001—02, Curriculum grantee, Shriver Ctr./Learn and Serve Am., 2000, Shrivier Ctr./Learn and Serve Am., 2002; scholar Ho. of Dels. scholar, Md. Ho. of Dels., 1991—95. Mem.: Info. Resource Mgmt. Assn., Assn. Computing Machinery (co-chair 2003 conf. workshops 2002—, spl. interest group chair 2001 conf. 2000—01), Green and Grey Soc., Alpha Sigma Nu, Phi Kappa Phi,

Beta Gamma Sigma (v.p. 1994—95), Upsilon Pi Epsilon (faculty advisor 2000—01), Omicron Delta Kappa (faculty advisor 1999—2002, Faculty Advisor of Yr. 2000). Office: Towson U Dept COSC 8000 York Rd Towson MD 21252

LAZAR, KENNETH STUART, architect; b. Bklyn., Jan. 24, 1948; s. Henry Charles and Pauline (Seckular) L.; m. Joan Eleanor Cancelleri, Aug. 16, 1970; children: Jeremy Sean. Marc Johathan. AAAS, N.Y.C. C.C., 1976. Designer David Kraus, AIA, N.Y.C., 1968-73; project mgr. Wm. Barnum Assocs., Greenwich, Conn., 1973-79; sr. assoc. Van Summern & Weingold, Stamford, 1979-84; exec. v.p. Van Summern Group, Inc., Conn., N.Y, 1984-86; ptnr. Design Collaborative Inc., Conn., 1986-88, White Plains, 1986-88, Lake Success, N.Y., 1986-88; prin. Design Ptnrship., Stamford, Conn., 1988, New Rochelle, N.Y.; ptnr., 1988-92; asst. mgr. Eagen Realty Advisors, Tarrytown, NY, 1992-93; pres. Archetype Design, Norwalk, Conn., 1993-96; project mgr. Oracle Corp., Stamford, 1996—. Mem. Internat. Assn. Corp. Real Estate Execs.

LAZAR, LEE ALAN, hospital services company executive; b. Pitts., Dec. 29, 1951; s. Bernard and Ethel L.; m. Karen Laine, Sept. 3, 1978; children: Stephen, Wendy. BA, George Washington U., 1973; JD, Washington U. St. Louis, 1976. Bar: Pa. 1976. Assoc. Kuhn, Engle & Stein, Pitts., 1976-79; labor counsel Leaseway Transp. Corp., Cleve., 1979-80, gen. mgr. personnel leasing div., 1980-86, dir. adminstrn. transp. resource mgmt. group, 1986—; pres. Stendy Corp. and Deliverex of Cleve., 1987—. Contbr. articles to profl. jours. Home: 5265 Fairfield Oval Cleveland OH 44139-1272

LAZAR, LYNN, art association administrator, actress; b. N.Y.C., Jan. 16, 1958; d. John Frank and Dorothy (Baines) Bullough; m. David Henry Lazar, Nov. 1, 1986; children: Morgan, Alexandra. BA in Speech & Theater, Fairleigh Dickinson U., 1981. Dir. philanthropic rsch. N.J. Performing Arts Ctr., Newark, 1993—. Dir. Voices for Life, N.J. Actor (play) Jeffrey, 1999 (Perry award Best Featured Actress in a Play 1999), (musical) The Quilt, A Musical Celebration, 1997 (Perry award Best Actress in a Musical 1997). Mem. Assn. Profl. Rschrs. Advancement (pres. N.J. chpt.). Episcopalian. Avocations: acting, singing, running. Office: NJ Performing Arts Ctr 1 Center St Newark NJ 07102-4501

LAZAR, MAX SEYMOUR, pharmaceutical company executive, retired; b. Bklyn., Dec. 6, 1943; s. Harry and Bessie (Cohen) L.; m. Sherry Dorf, Sept. 5, 1965; children: Lawrence Jay, Lisa Jill. BA in Chemistry, CUNY, 1966. Lab. analyst, supr. Hoffmann-LaRoche Inc., Nutley, N.J., 1966-69; dir. quality control Roche Vitamins & Fine Chems., Belvidere, 1969-86, dir. tech. svcs., 1986-88, divsnl. dir. quality assurance Nutley, 1988-89; asst. v.p., dir. corp. quality assurance Hoffmann-LaRoche Inc., 1989-93, v.p. quality assurance, 1993-94, v.p. FDA and drug enforcement adminstrn. (DEA) compliance, 1994-2001; ret., 2001; FDA compliance cons. Lazar Cons., Surprise, Ariz., 2001—. Vice-chair pharm. waters expert com. U.S. Pharmacopea Mem. editl. bd. Jour. Current Good Mfg. Practices, 1997—; contbr. articles to sci. jours., including Pharm. Tech. Bd. dirs. Parkette Nat. Gymnastics Tng. Ctr., Allentown, Pa., 1980-2001. Mem. AAAS, Am. Chem. Soc., Pharm. Rsch. & Mfrs. Assn. (expert work group topic leader for active pharm. ingredients Internat. Conf. on Harmonization, vice chiar USP pharm. waters expert com. 2000—), Am. Soc. Quality. Avocations: amateur radio operator, photography. Home and Office: 15359 W Sierra Vista Dr Surprise AZ 85374 E-mail: maxslazar@aol.com.

LAZAR, RANDE HARRIS, otolaryngologist; b. N.Y.C., Feb. 27, 1951; s. Irving and Dorothy (Tartasky) L.; m. Linda Zishuk, Aug. 11, 1974; 1 child, Lauren K. BA, Bklyn. Coll., 1973; MD, U. Autonoma de Guadalajara, Mexico, 1978; postgrad., N.Y. Med. Coll., 1978-79. Diplomate Am. Bd. Otolaryngology-Head and Neck Surgery; lic. physician, N.Y., Ohio, Tenn. Gen. surgery resident Cornell-North Shore Community Hosp., Manhasset, N.Y., 1979-80, Cleve. Clinic Found., 1980-81, otolaryngology-head and neck surgery resident, 1980-84, chief resident dept. otolaryngology & communicative disorder, 1983-84; physician Otolaryngology Cons. Memphis, 1984—. Fellow pathology head and neck dept. otolaryngologic pathology Armed Forces Inst. Pathology, Washington, 1983; pediatric otolaryngology fellow Le Bonheur Children's Med. Ctr., Memphis, 1984-85, dir. pediatric otolaryngology fellowship tng., 1989—, chief surgery, 1989, chief staff East Surgery Ctr.; chmn. dept. otolaryngology head and neck surgery Meth. Health Systems, 1990-91; courtesy staff Bapt. Meml. Hosp., Bapt. Meml. Hosp.-East, Eastwood Med. Ctr., Meth. Hosp., Germantown, Tenn.; chief dept. otolaryngology Les Passees Rehab. Ctr., 1988—. Contbr. articles to profl. jours. Bd. dirs. Bklyn. Tech. Found. Recipient award of honor Am. Acad. Otolaryngology-Head and Neck Surgery, 1991. Fellow Internat. Coll. Surgeons; mem. AMA, Am. Acad. Otolaryngology-Head and Neck Surgery, Am. Acad. Facial Plastic and Reconstructive Surgery, Am. Acad. Otolaryngic Allergy, Centurions Deafness Rsch. Found., Am. Auditory Soc., Nat. Hearing Assn., Soc. Ear, Nose Throat Advances in Children, Am. Soc. Laser Medicine and Surgery, So. Med. Assn., N.Y. Acad. Scis., Tenn. Med. Soc., Tenn. Acad. Otolaryngology-Head and Neck Surgery, Memphis and Shelby County Med. Soc., Memphis/Mid South Soc. Pediatrics Office: Otolaryngology Cons Memphis 777 Washington Ave Ste 240P Memphis TN 38105-4550 E-mail: Lazarent@aol.com.

LAZAR, RAYMOND MICHAEL, lawyer, educator; b. Mpls., July 16, 1939; s. Simon and Hessie (Teplin) L.; children: Mark, Deborah. BBA, U. Minn., 1961, JD, 1964. Bar: Minn. 1964, U.S. Dist. Ct. Minn. 1964. Spl. asst. atty. gen. State of Minn., St. Paul, 1964-66; pvt. practice Mpls., 1966-72; ptnr. Lapp, Lazar, Laurie & Smith, 1972-86; ptnr., officer Fredrikson & Byron P.A., 1986—. Lectr. various continuing edn. programs, 1972—; adj. prof. law U. Minn., Mpls., 1983-99. Fellow Am. Acad. Matrimonial Lawyers; mem. ABA (chair divorce laws and procedures com. family law sect. 1993-94), Minn. Bar Assn., Hennepin County Bar Assn. (chair family law sect. 1978-79). Home: 400 River St Minneapolis MN 55401 Office: Fredrikson & Byron PA 4000 Pillsbury Ctr Minneapolis MN 55402-3314 E-mail: rlazar@fredlaw.com.

LAZAR, THEODORE AARON, retired manufacturing company executive, lawyer; b. Chgo., July 16, 1920; s. Philip and Rena (Goodman) L.; m. Betty Jean Papermaster, July 6, 1952; children: Mark D., Paul A., Nancy Paula. JD, John Marshall Law Sch., Chgo., 1951. Bar: Ill. 1951, Wis. 1962, Ohio 1966. Sole practice, Chgo., 1951-62; asst. corp. counsel City of Chgo., 1956-59; atty. NLRB, Chgo. and Los Angeles, 1962-65; corp. counsel Lancaster Colony Corp., Columbus, Ohio, 1965-83, v.p. law, 1983-88, ret., 1988. Sgt. Air Corps U.S. Army, 1942—46. Mem. Columbus Bar Assn. Home: 270 Bryant Ave Columbus OH 43085-3009

LAZARCIK, GREGOR, educator, financial research company executive, economist; b. Horna Streda, Slovakia, Mar. 10, 1923; came to U.S., 1953, naturalized, 1958; s. Gaspar and Maria (Rehak) L.; m. Theresa M. Good, Aug. 14, 1971. BS, State Coll., Slovakia, 1945; MS, Coll. Agr., Brno, Czechoslovakia, 1948; cert., Swiss Inst. Tech., Zurich, 1949; AM, U. Strasbourg, France, 1952; LLM, LLD (fellow), U. Paris, 1953; PhD (fellow), Columbia, 1960. Asst. to mgr. Ctrl. Cutter Dairy, Lucerne, Switzerland, 1948-49; controller dairy products Agrl. Syndicate, Hazebruck, France, 1949-50; with Rsch. Project on Nat. Income Columbia U., N.Y.C., 1956-00, sr. rsch. economist, 1961-70, seminar assoc., 1970—; pres., chmn. bd. L.W. Internat. Financial Rsch., Inc., 1961-00. Lectr. econs. Hunter Coll., CUNY, 1963-64, Columbia U., 1964-68; prof. econs. SUNY, 1968-85, CUNY, 1984—. Author: Le Commerce en Matiere Agricole Entre l'Europe de l'Ouest et l'Europe deL'Est, 1959; co-author: Czechoslovak National Income and Product, 1947-56, 1962, The Performance of Socialist Agriculture, 1963, Scientific Research and its Relation to Earnings and Stock Prices, 1965, Comparison of Agricultural and Nonagricultural Income, 1937, 48-65, 1968, Defense, Education and Health Expenditures and Their Relation to GNP in Eastern Europe, 1978, Economic Growth in Eastern Europe, 1965-82, 1983, Agricultural Output and Productivity in Eastern Europe and Some Comparisons with the USSR and USA, 1985; contbr. to East European Economics Post-Helsinki, 1977, Pressure for Reform in the East European Economics, Joint Econ. Com., U.S. Congress, 1989, The Development of the Private Sector in East Central Europe, 1993, Overview of Transportation Infrastructure in East Central Europe, 1994, The Status of and Prospects for Agriculture in East Central Europe, 1996, Energy in Eastern Europe: Production, Consumption, and Trade, 1970-1987, 1999. Mem. Am. Econ. Assn., Am. Regional Sci. Assn., Assn. Comparative Economic Studies, Am. Assn. Advancement Slavic Studies. Roman Catholic. Address: 100 La Salle St Apt 17-b New York NY 10027-4730 E-mail: gregorlazarcik@aol.com.

LAZARE, AARON, dean, psychiatrist; b. Newark, Feb. 14, 1936; s. H. Benjamin and Anne (Storfer) L.; m. Louise Cannon; children: Robert, Jacqueline, David, Sam, Sarah, Hien, Thomas, Naomi. AB, Oberlin Coll., 1957; MD, Case Western Reserve U., 1961. Intern in medicine Bronx (N.Y.) Mcpl. Hosp. Ctr., 1961-62; resident in psychiatry Mass. Mental Health Ctr., 1962-65; asst. in psychiatry Mass. Gen. Hosp., Boston, 1967-68; chief day hosp. inpatient unit Yale-New Haven Hosp., 1967-68; assoc. dir. adult outpatient psychiatry Mass. Gen. Hosp., Boston, 1968-70, dir. adult outpatient psychiatry, 1970-75, acting dir. residency tng., 1972, dir. outpatient psychiatry, 1975-82, dep. chief psychiatry, 1976-82, clin. dir. psychiatry, 1978-82; prof., chmn. dept. psychiatry U. Mass. Med. Ctr., Worcester, 1982—, interim dean, 1989-90, dean, 1990—, chancellor, 1991—. Prof. Harvard U., 1982. Editor: Outpatient Psychiatry, 1979, 1989, 2nd edit.; contbr. articles to profl. jours.; co-author of books in field. Capt. U.S. Army, 1965-67. Named for Disting. Pub. Svc. Commonwealth of Mass., honorable mention U. Mass., 1987, Commonwealth of Mass., U. Mass., Boston, 1988, Brotherhood award NCCJ, 1992. Mem. AAAS, AMA, Am. Psychiat. Assn. (Benjamin Rush award 1992), Mass. Psychiat. Soc. Office: U Mass Med Ctr Off Chancellor 55 Lake Ave N Worcester MA 01655-0002*

LAZAREFF, JORGE ANTONIO, neurosurgeon, researcher; b. Buenos Aires, Jan. 11, 1953; s. Nicolas and Vera (Budinska) L.; m. Ines Garcia Lloret, May 28, 1982; children: Nicolás, Ana Maria. MD, Nat. Univ. Buenos Aires, 1977. Cert. neurosurgeon Mexican Coun. Neurosurgeons. Resident in neurosurgery Hosp. de Niños, Buenos Aires, 1979-83; chief resident in neurosurgery Hosp. Fernandez, 1983-84; registrar in neurosurgery Groote Schuur Hosp., Red Cross Meml. Children Hosp., Cape Town, 1984-86; rsch. fellow dept. surgery U. Alberta, Edmonton, Can., 1986-88; head dept. exptl. surgery Hosp. Infantil de Mexico, 1988-91, head dept. neurosurgery, 1991—. Mem. rsch. com. Hosp. Infantil de Mexico, 1991. Inventor biopsy probe for sterotactic brain surgery; author papers on neurosurgery and neurophistology. Recipient Rsch. award for spasticity Aaron Saenz Found., 1991. Mem. Soc. for Neurosci. Roman Catholic. Office: Mattel Children's Hosp. UCLA 10833 Le Conte Ave. Los Angeles CA 90095-1752

LAZAREK, JOHN WILLLIAM, music educator, musician; b. Elmhurst, Ny, Feb. 28, 1968; s. John Joseph and Rita Ann Lazarek. BA Music Ed., Five Towns Coll., Dix Hills, NY. 1993. Cert. Music Teacher, K-12 NY State, Adjudicator NY State Sch. Music Assn. Pvt. music educator Musicland, Lindenhurst, NY, 1987—; adj. prof. Five Towns Coll., Dix Hills, 1993—96; band dir. Lindenhurst Pub. Schools, Lindenhurst, 1996—98, Paul Effman Music Svc., Syossett, 1998—99; music dir. North Babylon Pub. Schools, North Babylon, 1999—. Mem.: NY State Sch. Music Assn., Suffolk County Music Educators Assn. Avocations: exercising, writing, arranging, & performing music. Home: 12 Walnut Place Lindenhurst NY 11757-6334 Personal E-mail: nbmusicjl@netscape.net.

LAZARIDIS, MIKE, information technology executive; DEng(hon.) , U. Waterloo. Founder, pres., co-CEO Rsch. in Motion; founder Perimeter Inst., 2000—. Office: Rsch in Motion Ltd 295 Phillip St N2L 3W8 Waterloo ON Canada*

LAZARIS, PAMELA ADRIANE, community planning and development consultant; b. Dixon, Ill., Oct. 13, 1956; d. Michael Christ and Ellen Euridice (Eftax) L.; m. Eugene Dale Monson, Oct. 17, 1987; children: Anthony Edward, Anna Adriane. BFA in Fine Arts, U. Wis., Milw., 1978; MS in Urban and Regional Planning, U. Wis., 1982; MBA, U. St. Thomas, 1992. Analyst planning Wis. Dept. Natural Resources, Madison, 1979-82; asst. city planner City of Albert Lea, Minn., 1982-83; specialist community devel. City of Winona, 1983-85; dir. community devel. City of Waseca, 1985-98; assoc. Real Estate Dynamics, Inc., Madison, Wis., 1998-99; prin. Planning Svc. and Solutions, Lake Mills, 1999—. Vol. spl. events Farmam-Minn. Agrl. Interpretive Ctr., Waseca, 1985-86; mem. Waseca County Econ. Devel. Commn., 1989-98; com. dir. Waseca Area Found., 1989-98; mem. dist. 2 city coun. City of Lake Mills, Wis., 1999—, city plan commn., 1999—; troop 148 advancement coord. Boy Scouts Am., 2002-. Named one of Oustanding Young Women of Am., 1986. Mem. Am. Inst. Cert. Planners (cert.), Am. Planning Assn. (chpt. bd. dirs. 1986-89), Minn. Planning Assn. (v.p. 1989-90, dist. bd. dirs. 1985-89), Toastmasters (chpt. sgt.-at-arms 1987, ednl. v.p. 1988, 91-98), Lake Mills Area C. of C. Avocations: public speaking, travel, art. Home: PO Box 17 Lake Mills WI 53551-0017 Office: 110 E Madison St Lake Mills WI 53551-1644 E-mail: pal@gdinet.com.

LAZARUS, ALLAN MATTHEW, retired newspaper editor; b. New Orleans, Nov. 21, 1927; s. Harry Adolph and Edna Mary (Wodiker) L.; m. Martha Elizabeth Ellis, July 26, 1946; children— Kenneth Wayne, Virginia Lynn BA in History, Centenary Coll., 1951. Copy boy The Times, Shreveport, La., 1944-45, reporter, 1945-46, telegraph editor, 1947-58, news editor, 1958-69, mng. editor, 1969-90. Pulitzer Prize Juror, 1978; pres. La.-Miss. AP Assn., 1977-78. Cpl. USAF, 1946—47. Mem.: Soc. Profl. Journalists (pres. Ar.-La.-Tex. chpt. 1971—72), AP Mng. Editors's Assn. (bd. dirs. 1975—80). Roman Catholic. Home: 7713 Tampa Way Shreveport LA 71105-5701

LAZARUS, ARTHUR, JR. retired lawyer; b. Bklyn., Aug. 30, 1926; s. Arthur and Frieda (Langer) L.; m. Gertrude Chiger, Jan. 8, 1956; children: Andrew Joseph, Edward Peter, Diana Ruth. BA with honors, Columbia U., 1946; JD, Yale U., 1949. Bar: N.Y. 1951, D.C. 1952, U.S. Supreme Ct. 1954. Assoc. Fried, Frank, Harris, Shriver & Jacobson, Washington, 1950-57, ptnr., 1957-91, mng. ptnr. Washington office, 1974-86; of counsel Sonosky, Chambers, Sachse, Endreson & Perry, 1994—. Vis. lectr. Yale Law Sch., 1973-81. Trustee Arena Stage, 1987-98, Georgetown Day Sch., 1963-71. Home: 3201 Fessenden St NW Washington DC 20008-2032 E-mail: ALazarus@Sonosky.com.

LAZARUS, BETTY ROSS, civic activist, retired; b. Chgo., Feb. 22, 1923; d. James Samuel and Ethel Muskogee (Jacobs) Ross; m. David Lazarus, Aug. 15, 1943; children: Barbara, William, Mary Ann, Richard. Student, U. Chgo., 1940-43. Educator Spl. Project Presch. Program U. Ill., Urbana, 1966; adminstrv. asst. Hays Sch., 1967; coordinator suicide prevention svc. Champaign (Ill.) County Mental Health Assn., 1969-70, mental health educator, 1970-72; exec. dir. Champaign County Mental Health Bd., 1972-78. Cons., mem. subcom. Ill. Dept. Mental Health, 1976-77, mental health task force East Cen. Ill. Health Systems Agy., 1976-78. Mem. Coun. Community Integration, 1957-64, Com. of 100, Voices for Ill. Children, 1989—, mem. statewide com., 1991—; bd. dirs. Planned Parenthood, 1955-64, 83-90; adv. com. Family Svc. of Champaign County; mem. adv. com. U.S. Postal Svc., 1998—; bd. dirs. Voices for Illinois Children, 1996—. Recipient Gov.'s Voluntary Action award, 1970, Community Leadership award Assn. Mental Health, 1978. Mem. LWV (bd. dirs. 1958-60, 80-81, 82-92. Home: 502 W Vermont Urbana IL 61801 Home (Summer): 502 W Vermont Ave Urbana IL 61801-4931

LAZARUS, DAVID, physicist, educator; b. Buffalo, Sept. 8, 1921; s. Barney B. and Lillian (Markel) L.; m. Betty Jane Ross, Aug. 15, 1943; children: Barbara, William, Mary Ann, Richard. BS, U. Chgo., 1942, MS, 1947, PhD, 1949. Instr. electronics U. Chgo., 1942-43, electronics engr., 1946-49, instr. physics, 1949; research assoc. radio research lab. Harvard, 1943-45; mem. physics faculty U. Ill., Urbana, 1949—, prof., 1959—. Vis. prof. U. Paris, 1968-69, M.I.T., 1978-79, Harvard U., 1978-79; vis. scientist Am. Inst. Physics, N.Y.C., 1962-69; cons. Phys. Sci. Study Com., 1957-59, Hallicrafters Co., Chgo., 1957-69, Gen. Electric Co., Cin., 1960-68, Gen. Atomic, La Jolla, Calif., 1962-63, Lawrence Radiation Lab., 1967-68, Sandia Lab., 1970-72, Addison-Wesley Pub. Co., Reading, Mass., 1964-80; dir. Council on Materials Sci., U.S. Dept. Energy, 1981-85 Author: (with H. de Waard) Modern Electronics, 1966, (with R.I. Hulsizer) The World of Physics, 1972, (with M. Raether) Practical Physics: How Things Work, 1979; also articles. Guggenheim fellow, 1968-69 Fellow AAAS, Am. Phys. Soc. (coun. 1974-78, 80-91, exec. com. 1980-91, editor-in-chief 1980-91, publs. com. 1980-91, exec. com. div. contensed matter physics 1968-70, 74-78, chmn. New Materials prize com. 1976, chmn. Buckley prize com. 1979); mem. Am. Inst. Physics (governing bd. 1981-92, exec. com. 1981-89, publs. policy com. 1981-92). Home: 502 W Vermont Ave Urbana IL 61801 Home (Summer): 502 W Vermont Ave Urbana IL 61801-4931 E-mail: d-lazars@uiuc.edu.

LAZARUS, FRED, IV, college president; b. N.Y.C., Jan. 1, 1942; s. Fred and Irma (Mendelson) L.; m. Jonna Gane, Nov. 27, 1970; children: Anna Mendelson, Fred Lazarus V. BA, Claremont McKenna Coll., 1964; MBA, Harvard U., 1966. Staff assoc. Nat. Council for Equal Bus. Opportunity, Washington, 1969-71; pres. Washington Council for Equal Bus. Opportunity, 1971-74; exec. asst. to chmn. Nat. Endowment for Arts, Washington, 1975-78; pres. Md. Inst. Coll. Art, Balt., 1978—. Vice chmn. Assn. Ind. Colls. Art and Design, 1992-96; trustee Alliance for Ind. Colls. Art, 1978-91, chmn., 1984-86, 89-91; founding chmn. Nat. Coalition for Edn. in Arts, 1988-90. Trustee St. Paul's Sch., 1988—96, Am. Coun. for Arts, 1980—97, sec., 1991—94; chmn. Ams. for the Arts, 1998—2000; trustee Md. Art Place, 1988—96; trustee emeritus Ptnrs. for Livable Places; bd. dirs. Afro-Am. Newspapers, Balt., Balt. Artists Housing Corp.; chmn. Balt. Coun. for Equal Bus. Opportunity, 1991—2000; vice chmn. Md. Ind. Coll. Assn., 1995—99, chmn., 1999—; mem. Thurgood Marshall Meml. Statue Commn. , 1996—98. Recipient mayor's art award, City of Balt., 1988. Mem. Harvard Club (N.Y.C.) Office: Md Inst Coll Art 1300 W Mount Royal Ave Baltimore MD 21217-4134

LAZARUS, GERALD SYLVAN, physician, university dean; b. N.Y.C., Feb. 16, 1939; s. Joseph W. and Marion (Goldstein) Lazarus; m. Sandra Jacob, Sept. 3, 1961 (dec. 1985); children: Mark, Elyse, Lynne, Laura; m. Audrey Fedyszyn Jakubowski, Apr. 7, 1990. BA, Colby Coll., 1959; MD, George Washington U., 1963. Intern, then resident U. Mich., Ann Arbor, 1963—64, resident in medicine, 1964—65; NIH research ass. NIH, Bethesda, Md., 1965—68; resident in dermatology Harvard U., Cambridge, Mass., 1968—70; research fellow Strangeways Labs., England, 1970—72; assoc. prof. medicine, co-dir. dermatology tng. program Albert Einstein Med. Coll., N.Y.C., 1972—75; J. Lamar Callaway prof. Duke U., Durham, NC, 1977—82, chief dermatology, 1975—82; Milton B. Hartzell prof. U. Pa. Sch. Medicine, Phila., 1982—, chmn. dept. dermatology, 1982—93; dean Sch. Medicine U. Calif., Davis, 1993—97; vis. scholar U. Calif., Inst. Health Policy Rsch., San Francisco, 1997—98; prof. dermatology, biol. chemistry U. Calif. Scholar Inst. for Health Policy, 1998—99; dean, prof. emeritus U. Calif. Davis Sch. Medicine, 1999—; prof. dermatology Johns Hopkins Med. Inst., Balt., 2002—. Sr. investigator Arthritis Found., 1972—77; mem. study sect. NIH, 1976—80; prof. dermatology U. Calif., San Francisco; faculty Inst. of Health Policy; advisor to univ. pres. and hosp. dir. advisor Ministry of Health; vis. prof. Peking Union Med. Coll., Beijing, 1999—2002; advisor to pres. Peking Union Med. Coll. Hosp.; co-dir. China Med. Be. Mgmt. Program. Author (with L. Goldsmith): Diagnosis of Skin Disease, 1980; author: (with Herman Beerman) Tradition of Excellance: History of Dermatology at Univ. Pa. Sch. of Medicine; contbr. Served with USPHS, 1965—68. Fellow John Simon Guggenheim, U. Geneva, 1986; grantee, NIH. Fellow: Am. Soc. Clin. Investigation, Assn. Am. Physicians, ACP; mem.: Am. Acad. Dermatology (Sultzberger award 1986), Biochem. Soc., Soc. Investigative Dermatology (dir., pres. 1996—97, 1997—, Disting Alumnus award George Washington U. 1996), Am. Dermatol. Assn. (Carl Herzog fellow 1970—72). Republican. Jewish. Home: 2010 Bennett Point Rd Queenstown MD 21658 Office: Johns Hopkins Med U 550 N Broadway Ste 1002 Baltimore MD 21205

LAZARUS, KENNETH ANTHONY, lawyer; b. Passaic, N.J., Mar. 10, 1942; s. John Joseph and Margaret (Di Cenzo) L.; m. Marylyn Jane Flemming, Aug. 13, 1966; children: Maggi Ann, John, Joseph. BA, U. Dayton, 1964; JD, U. Notre Dame, 1967; LLM in Taxation, George Washington U., 1971. Bar: N.J. 1967, U.S. Tax Ct. 1970, U.S. Ct. Claims 1970, U.S. Supreme Ct. 1971, D.C. 1976. Trial atty. U.S. Dept. Justice, 1967-71; assoc. counsel and chief counsel to Minority Com. on Judiciary, U.S. Senate, 1971-74; assoc. counsel to Pres. U.S., 1974-77; ptnr. Ward, Lazarus & Grow, Washington, 1977-91; of counsel Dixon & Jessup, 1991-97, Krooth & Atlman, 1997—. Mem. adv. bd. Sch. Law Dayton U., 1975-85; adj. prof. Sch. Law Georgetown U., 1979—; mem. U.S. Adv. Com. on Trade Negotiations, 1983-87; chmn. Sailors and Mchts. Bank and Trust Co., Vienna, Va., 1987-89. Mem. adv. bd. Houston Jour. Internat. Law, 1983-90; contbr. numerous articles to profl. publs. U.S. reporter to UN, 1975-77; mem. adv. coun. Rep. Nat. Com., 1977-80; mem. Presdl. transition team Office of Pres.-Elect, 1980-81; caucus mgr. George Bush Rep. Conv., 1988; bd. trustees Internat. Law Inst., pres., 1990—. Mem.: ABA, Am. Judicature Soc., N.J. Bar Assn., Fed. Bar Assn., Bar Assn. D.C., D.C. Bar Assn., Am. Law Inst. (life). Home: 4501 Connecticut Ave NW Apt 716 Washington DC 20008-3712 Office: Lazarus & Assocs. 1850 M St NW Ste 400 Washington DC 20036-5815

LAZARUS, MAURICE, retired retail executive; b. Columbus, Ohio, June 27, 1915; s. Fred, Jr. and Meta (Marx) L.; m. Nancy Stix, June 7, 1942 (dec. 1985); children: Carol, Jill; m. Nell P. Eurich, Nov. 25, 1988. Student, Ohio State U.; BA, Harvard, 1937; LL.D., Am. Internat. Coll., 1969. Div. mdse. mgr. John Shillito Co., Columbus, 1937-41; head service and control Foley's, Houston, 1945-48, exec. v.p., 1948-58; pres., treas. Filene's, Boston, 1958-64, chmn. bd., 1964-65; vice chmn. Federated Dept. Stores, Inc., Boston, 1965-70, chmn. finance com., 1971-82, also dir. Mem. adv. com. on nat. health ins. issues HEW, 1977-78; bd. dirs. Cambridge Ctr. Adult Edn., 1974-75; mem. adv. Council Pres.'s Commn. on Status of Women, 1963-68; chmn. exec. com. Public Agenda Found., 1987-99; mem. div. health scis. and tech. Harvard U.-M.I.T., 1978-87, Harvard Cmty. Health Plan Found. Bd., 1984—, chmn., 1996-99; mem. adv. bd. Schlesinger Library Women's Archives, Radcliffe Coll., 1972-76; mem. bd. overseers Harvard Coll., 1977-83; mem. ethics adv. bd. HEW, 1978-80; vis. com., chmn. central services, Med. Sch. and Dental Medicine, Sch. Public Health Harvard U., 1978-85, mem. governance com., 1968-71, mem. working group div. health policy research and edn.; chmn. adv. com. Joint Center Urban Studies., 1977-82; trustee Mass. Gen. Hosp., Old Sturbridge Village, 1965-78, Marine Biol. Lab., 1977-84, McLean Hosp., 1980—, Tufts U. Civic Edn. Found. of Lincoln Filene Center for Citizenship and Public Affairs, 1972-80, New Eng. Med. Center Hosp., 1960-78, Beth Israel Hosp., 1958-65, Bennington Coll., 1965-72, Combined Jewish Philanthropy Greater Boston, 1962-65; chmn. exec. com. Pub. Agenda Found., 1977-99; bd. dirs. Boston chpt. ARC, 1962-64; dir. Med. Found., 1987—; chmn. Harvard Cmty. Health Plan, 1984-93; bd. overseers Boston Symphony Orch., 1971-74; bd. dirs. Salzburg Seminars in Am. Studies, Assoc. Harvard Alumni, 1966-73; pres. Assoc. Harvard Alumni, 1972-73; mem. Mass. Higher Edn. Facilities Commn., 1970-74; mem. corp. Northeastern U., Peter Bent Brigham Hosp.; bd. overseers Boston Symphony Orch., 1971-74; mem. M.I.T. Council Arts, 1972-77, Harvard Med. Center, 1977-79; mem. adv. com. hosp. initiatives in long-term care Am. Hosp. Assn.; chmn. bd. dirs. Harvard Cmty. Health Plan, dir. emeritus, 1994—; mem. adv. bd. Brandeis U. Ctr. Social Policy in Middle East, 1978-88. Fellow Am. Acad. Arts and Scis. Clubs: Bay (Boston), Harvard (N.Y.C.); Univ. (N.Y.C.); St. Botolph (Boston), Comml.-Mchts. (Boston). Home and Office: 144 Brattle St 3d Fl Cambridge MA 02138-2202

LAZARUS, MELL, cartoonist; b. N.Y.C, May 3, 1927; s. Sidney and Frances (Mushkin) L.; m. Eileen Hortense Israel, June 19, 1949; children: Marjorie, Suesan, Catherine; m. Sally Elizabeth Mitchell, May 13, 1995. Cartoonist-writer Miss Peach, 1957—, Momma, 1970— ; author anthologies Miss Peach, Miss Peach, Are These Your Children?, Momma, We're Grownups Now!; novels The Boss is Crazy, Too, 1964, The Neighborhood Watch, 1986; plays Everybody into the Lake, Elliman's Fly, Lifetime Eggcreams, 1969-70; juvenile Francine, Your Face Would Stop a Clock, 1975; co-author Miss Peach TV spl. programs Turkey Day Pageant and Annual Heart Throb Ball. Trustee Internat. Mus. Cartoon Art. With USNR, 1945, USAFR, 1951-54. Mem. Nat. Cartoonists Soc. (pres. 1989-93, chmn. membership com. 1965, nat. rep., Humor Strip Cartoonist of Yr. 1973, 79, Reuben award 1981, Silver T-Square award 2000), Writers Guild Am. West, Nat. Press Club, The Century Assn., Newspaper Features Coun. (bd. dirs.), Sigma Delta Chi. Office: Creators Syndicate Inc 5777 W Century Blvd Los Angeles CA 90045-5600

LAZARUS, RICHARD STANLEY, psychology educator; b. N.Y.C., Mar. 3, 1922; s. Abe and Matilda (Marks) L.; m. Bernice H. Newman, Sept. 2, 1945; children: David Alan, Nancy Eve. AB, CCNY, 1942; MS, U. Pitts., 1947, PhD, 1948; Dr. honoris causa, Johannes Gutenberg U., Mainz, Germany, 1988, U. Haifa, Israel, 1995. Diplomate in clin. psychology Am. Bd. Examiners in Profl. Psychology. Asst. prof. Johns Hopkins, 1948-53; psychol. cons. VA,

1952—; assoc. prof. psychology, dir. clin. tng. program Clark U., Worcester, Mass., 1953-57; assoc. prof. psychology U. Calif., Berkeley, 1957-59, prof., 1959-91, prof. emeritus, 1991—. Prin. investigator Air Force contracts dealing with psychol. stress, 1951-53, USPHS grant on personality psychol. stress, 1953-70; NIA, NIDA, and NCI grantee on stress, coping and health, 1977-81, MacArthur Found. research grantee, 1981-84; USPHS spl. fellow Waseda U., Japan, 1963-64 Author 23 books, including (autobiography) The Life and Work of an Eminent Psychologist, 1998; also numerous publs. in sci. jours. 1st lt. AUS, 1943-46. Recipient Disting. Sci. Achievement award Calif. State Psychol. Assn., 1984, Div. 38 Health Psychology, 1989; Guggenheim fellow, 1969-70; Army Rsch. Inst. rsch. grantee, 1973-75 Fellow AAAS, APA (Disting. Sci. Contbn. award 1989); mem. Western Psychol. Assn., Argentina Med. Assn. (hon.). Home: 1824 Stanley Dollar Dr Apt 3B Walnut Creek CA 94595-2833 Office: Univ Calif Dept Psychology Berkeley CA 94720-0001

LAZARUS, ROCHELLE BRAFF, advertising executive; b. N.Y.C., Sept. 1, 1947; d. Lewis L. and Sylvia Ruth (Eisenberg) Braff; m. George M. Lazarus, Mar. 22, 1970; children: Theodore, Samantha, Benjamin. AB, Smith Coll., 1968; MBA, Columbia U., 1970. Product mgr. Clairol, N.Y.C., 1970-71; account exec. Ogilvy & Mather, 1971-73, account supr., 1973-77, mgmt. supr., 1977-84, sr. v.p., 1981—, account group dir., 1984-87; gen. mgr. Ogilvy & Mather Direct, 1987-88, mng. dir., 1988-89, pres., 1989-91, Ogilvy & Mather, N.Y.C., 1991-94, pres. N. Am., 1991-94; pres., COO Ogilvy & Mather Worldwide, 1995-96, CEO, 1996—, chmn., 1997—. Bd. dirs. GE, TIAA-CREF. Mem. The Bus. Coun., Com. of 200; mem. bd. overseers Columbus Bus. Sch.; chair, bd. trustees Smith Coll.; Bd. dirs. Ann Taylor, GE, TIAA-CREF, Advt. Edn. Found., Nat. Women's Law Ctr., World Wildlife Fund, N.Y. Presbyn. Hosp. Recipient YWCA Women Achievers award, 1985, Matrix award, 1995; named Businesswoman of Yr. N.Y.C. Partnership and C. of C., 1996. Mem. Am. Assn. Advt. Agys., Advt. Women N.Y. (Woman of Yr. 1994). Home: 106 E 78th St New York NY 10021-0302 Office: Ogilvy & Mather Worldwide 309 W 49th St New York NY 10019-7316

LAZARUS, SHELLY, advertising executive; m. George Lazarus. BA, Smith Coll.; MBA, Columbia U. Asst. product mgr. Clairol, 1970; supr. hair care accts. Ogilvy & Mathers, N.Y.C., 1971-74, acct. supr., 1976-77, 80-87, Clairol, 1977-80; gen. mgr. direct mktg. br. Ogilvy & Mather, N.Y.C., 1987-94, pres. N.Am. ops., 1994-96, chmn., CEO, 1996—. Mem. Am. Assn. Advt. Agys. (bd. dirs. 1999—, vice chmn. bd.). Office: Ogilvy & Mather Worldwide Plz 1 Soldiers Field Park Apt 413 Boston MA 02163-1702*

LAZARUS, STEVEN S. management consultant, marketing consultant; b. Rochester, N.Y., June 16, 1943; s. Alfred and Ceal H. Lazarus; m. Elissa C. Lazarus, June 19, 1966; children: Michael, Stuart, Jean. BS, Cornell U., 1966; MS, Poly. U. N.Y., 1967; PhD, U. Rochester, 1974. Pres. Mgmt. Systems Analysis Corp., Denver, 1977—; dir. Sci. Application Intern Corp., Englewood, Colo., 1979-84; assoc. prof. Metro State Coll., Denver, 1983-84; sr. v.p. Pal Assocs. Inc., 1984-85; with strategic planning and mktg. McDonnell Douglas, 1985-86; mktg. cons. Clin. Reference Systems, 1986; pres. Mgmt. Sys. Analysis Corp., 1986-89, 95—; assoc. exec. dir. Ctr. Rsch. Ambulatory Health Care Adminstrn., Englewood, 1990-94. Spl. cons. State of Colo., Denver, 1976-81; mktg. cons. IMX, Louisville, 1986-87; speaker Am. Hosp. Assn., Chgo., 1983—; asst. sec. Work Group for Elec. Data Interchange, 1995-96, bd. dirs., 1997—, chmn. bd. elect, 2000, chmn. bd. dirs., 2001—; mng. prin., pres. Boundary Info. Group, 1995—. Contbr. chpts. to books; patentee med. quality assurance. NDEA fellow U. Rochester, 1968-71. Fellow Healthcare Info. and Mgmt. Systems Soc.; mem. Med. GroupMgmt. Assn., Optimists (program chmn. Denver club 1976-78). Home: 7023 E Eastman Ave Denver CO 80224-2845 Office: MSA Corp 4401 S Quebec St Ste 100 Denver CO 80237-2644

LAZEAR, EDWARD PAUL, economics and labor relations educator, researcher; b. N.Y.C., Aug. 17, 1948; s. Abe and Rose (Karp) L.; m. Victoria Ann Allen, July 2, 1977; 1 child, Julia Ann AB, A.M., UCLA, 1971; PhD, Harvard U., 1974; LLD (hon.), Albertson Coll., 1997. Asst. prof. econs. U. Chgo., 1974-78, assoc. prof. indsl. relations, 1978-81, prof. indsl. relations, 1981-85, Isidore and Gladys Brown prof. urban and labor econs., 1985-92; sr. fellow Hoover Instn. Stanford (Calif.) U., 1985—, coord. domestic studies Hoover Instn., 1987-90, prof. econs. and human resource mgmt. Grad. Sch. Bus., 1992-95, Jack Steele Parker prof. econs. and human resource mgmt., 1995—, mem. steering com. Stanford Inst. for Econ. Policy Rsch., 1996—. Econ. advisor to Romania, Czechoslovakia, Russia, Ukraine, Georgia; rsch. assoc. Nat. Bur. Econ. Rsch., Econs. Rsch. Ctr. of Nat. Opinion Rsch. Ctr.; chmn. rsch. adv. bd. World at Work; fellow Inst. Advanced Study, Hebrew U., Jerusalem, 1977-8; lectr. Inst. Advanced Study, Vienna, 1983-84, Nat. Productivity Bd., Singapore, 1982, 85; vis. prof. Inst. des Etudes Politiques, Paris, 1987; Wicksell lectr., Stockholm, 1993; chmn. Am. Compensation Assoc. Adv. Bd., 1999—. Author: (with R. Michael) Allocation of Income Within the Household, 1988; (with J.P. Gould) Microeconomic Theory, 1989, Personnel Economics, 1995, Personnel Economics for Managers, 1998; editor: Economic Transition in Eastern Europe and Russia, 1995; founding editor Jour. Labor Econs., 1982—; assoc. editor Jour. Econ. Perspectives, 1986-89, German Econ. Rev., 2000—; co-editor: Jour. Labor Abstracts, 1996—; contbr. numerous articles to scholarly jours. Recipient Leo Melamed prize for outstanding scholarship, 1998; NSF grad. fellow, 1971-74 Fellow Am. Acad. Arts and Scis., Econometric Soc., Soc. Labor Economists (1st v.p. 1995-96, pres. 1997-98); mem. Am. Econs. Assn. Home: 277 Old Spanish Trl Portola Valley CA 94028-8129 Office: Stanford U Grad Sch Bus Stanford CA 94305-5015 Also: Stanford Univ Hoover Inst Stanford CA 94305-6010

LAZECKO, DAVID JOHN, broadcast executive; b. Dearborn, Mich., Dec. 17, 1956; s. Walter and Rose L.; m. Ellen Wisnieski, June 26, 1993; children: Brian, Bridget. B in Elec. Engring. Tech., Ohio Inst. Tech., 1978. Assoc. engr. ADM Tech., Inc., Troy, Mich., 1979-84; broadcast sys. engr. NBC, Inc., N.Y.C., 1984-89; field tech. mgr. CBS, Inc., 1989-92, dir. studio ops., 1992-95, dir. Olympic ops., 1995—. Recipient Emmy award for Engring. Nat. Acad. Arts and Scis., 1985-86, Emmy award for 1992 Winter Olympics Nat. Acad. Arts and Scis., 1992, Emmy award for 1994 Winter Olympics Nat. Acad. Arts and Scis., 1994. Mem. NATAS, Soc. Motion Pictures and TV Engrs. Office: CBS Inc 524 W 57th St New York NY 10019-2924

LAZERSON, EARL EDWIN, academic administrator emeritus; b. Detroit, Dec. 10, 1930; s. Nathan and Ceil (Stashefsky) L.; m. Ann May Harper, June 11, 1966; children from previous marriage: Joshua, Paul. BS, Wayne State U., Detroit, 1953; postgrad., U. Leiden, Netherlands, 1957-58; MA, U. Mich., 1954, PhD, 1982. Mathematician Inst. Def. Analyses, Princeton, N.J., 1960-62; asst. prof. math. Washington U., St. Louis, 1962-65, 66-69; vis. asso. prof. Brandeis U., 1965-66; mem. faculty So. Ill. U., Edwardsville, 1969—, prof. math., 1973—, chmn. dept. math. studies, 1972-73, dean Sch. Sci. and Tech., 1973-76, univ. v.p., provost, 1977-79, pres., 1980-93; pres. emeritus, 1994—. Chmn. Southwestern Ill. Devel. Authority, City of East St. Louis Fin. Adv. Authority; active Leadership Coun. Southwestern Ill., Gateway Ctr. Met. St. Louis, Inc., St. Louis Symphony Soc.; trustee Jefferson Nat. Expansion Meml. Assn., Ill. Econ. Devel. Bd. Recipient Sr. Teaching Excellence award Standard Oil Found., 1970-71 Mem. Am. Math. Soc., Math. Assn. Am., European Math. Soc., London Math. Soc., Soc. Mathematique France, Fulbright Alumni Assn., Sigma Xi. Home: 122 Forest Grove Dr Glen Carbon IL 62034 E-mail: laze@charter.net.

LAZERUS, GILBERT, lawyer; b. N.Y.C. s. Jacob and Bessie Lazerus; m. Judith Lazerus, Dec. 25, 1940 (dec.); children: Bruce, June. PhB, Yale U., 1931; JD, Columbia U., 1934. Bar: N.Y. 1934, U.S. Dist. Ct. (so. dist.) N.Y. 1940, U.S. Dist. Ct. (ea. dist.) N.Y., U.S. Supreme Ct. 1940. Assoc. Joseph V. McKee, 1938-45; ptnr. Strook & Strook & Lavan, N.Y.C., 1945-83, of counsel, 1983—. Master arbitrator Dept. Ins., State of N.Y.; adminstrv. law judge Trnasit Dept., City of N.Y.; mem. panel of arbitrators Civil Ct. City N.Y., Am. Arbitration Assn., N.Y. Stock Exch., Am. Stock Exch., Nat. Assn. Security Dealers. Mem. Yale Club (N.Y.C.). Home: 1175 York Ave #95 New York NY 10021 Office: 180 Maiden Ln New York NY 10038

LAZICH, DANIEL, aerospace engineer; b. Galjipovci, Yugoslavia, Jan. 1, 1941; came to U.S., 1963; s. Stojan and Ljubica Lazic; m. Spomenka Krkljus, Aug. 11, 1968. BS in Engring., U. Ill., 1974; postgrad., U. Tex., Arlington, 1976-78; MA in Internat. Transactions, George Mason U., 1997. Analytical engr. Pratt & Whitney Aircraft, West Hartford, Conn., 1974-75; aircraft structures engr. Gen. Dynamics Corp., Ft. Worth, 1975-78; aerospace engr. Shrike missile Air Systems Commn. USN, Arlington, Va., 1978-81; sr. propulsion engr. Joint Cruise Missiles Project, Dept. Def., 1981-85; prin. staff engr., tech. advisor kinetic energy weapons Strategic Def. Commn., 1985—. Contbr. articles to profl. jours. Sgt. U.S. Army, 1966-68. Mem. AIAA, Aircraft Owners and Pilots Assn., No. Va. Astronomy Club. Avocations: flying, photography. Home: 43099 Kimberley Ct Leesburg VA 20176-6488

LAZIO, RICK A. former congressman, lawyer; b. Amityville, N.Y., Mar. 13, 1958; s. Anthony and Olive E. (Christensen) L. AB in Polit. Sci., Vassar Coll., 1980; JD, Am. U., 1983. Bar: N.Y. 1984, U.S. Dist. Ct. (ea. and so. dists.) N.Y., 1985. Asst. dist. atty. Suffolk County Rackets Bureau, Hauppauge, N.Y., 1983-88; exec. asst. dist. atty. Suffolk County, 1987-88; village atty. Village of Lindenhurst, 1988-93; mng. ptnr. Glass, Lazio and Glass, Esqs., Babylon, 1988-93; mem. Suffolk County Legislature from 11th Dist., 1989-93, 103rd-106th Congresses from 2nd N.Y. dist., Washington, 1993-2001; dep. majority whip 103d-106th Congresses from 2nd N.Y. dist.; asst. majority leader 106th Congress from 2nd N.Y. dist.; CEO, Pres. Fin. Svcs. Forum, N.Y.C. and Washington, 2001—. Mem. commerce com., banking com., subcom. on health and environ., subcom. on fin. and hazardous materials, chmn. subcom. on housing and cmty. opportunity. Mem. Suffolk County Bar Assn. Roman Catholic. Avocations: numismatics, guitar.*

LAZNICK, HOPE, physical therapist; b. L.I., N.Y., Sept. 9, 1965; d. David Alan Laznick and Nancy Moreno. BS in Phys. Therapy, Hunter Coll., N.Y.C., 1990. Staff phys. therapist New York Presbyn. Hosp., N.Y.C., 1990-92, sr. phys. therapist, 1993-96, asst. chief phys. therapist, 1996—. Guest lectr. Hunter Coll., N.Y.C., 1994-2001, Columbia U., N.Y.C., 1996—, SUNY Health Sci. Ctr., Brooklyn, 2000-. Co-facilitator burn survivor support group, program dir. Children's Burn Camp Mem. Am. Phys. Therapy Assn., Am. Burn Assn. Avocations: acting, volleyball, swimming. Home: 65 E 11th St Apt 5D New York NY 10003-4610 Office: New York Presbyn Hosp 525 E 68th St New York NY 10021-4870 E-mail: hlaznick@nyp.org.

LAZO, CAROLINE EVENSEN, writer; b. Mpls. children: Stephanie, Peter, Mark (Chip). AA, Pine Manor Jr. Coll., Wellesley, Mass., 1949; cert., U. Oslo, 1950; BA, U. Minn., 1978. Author: Wilma Mankiller, 1994 (Tchr.'s choice award, 1995), Arthur Ashe, 1999 (notable children's tradebook award, 1999), Alice Walker: Freedom Writer, 2000 (Honor Book award, 2001), Leonard Bernstein: In Love with Music, 2002, F. Scott Fitzgerald: Voice of the Jazz Age, 2002.

LAZO, JOHN, JR. physician; b. Passaic, N.J., Nov. 29, 1946; s. John and Mary (Beley) Lazo; m. Donnalynn Margaret Materna, July 22, 1972; children: Jonathan Christopher, Ashley Jude. BS, Fairleigh Dickinson U., 1974; MD, Univ. Autonoma de Guadalajara, Mex., 1978. Diplomate Am. Bd. Emergency Medicine, Am. Bd. Forensic Examiners, Am. Bd. Forensic Medicine. Intern Akron (Ohio) City Hosp., 1980-81, resident in emergency medicine, 1981-83, chief resident in emergency medicine, 1982-83; med. dir. emergency svcs. Parma (Ohio) Cmty. Gen. Hosp., 1986-93, chmn. emergency dept., 1994-95, vice-chmn. emergency dept., 1995-99, chmn. emergency dept., 2000—. Dir. Paramedic Edn. Program, Parma, 1986—93; med. dir. Emergeny Medicine Physicians - Cuyahoga County, LLC, 2002—; bd. dirs. Cmty. Emergency Physicians, Inc. Sgt. USAF, 1966—70. Fellow: Am. Coll. Emergency Physicians; mem.: Cleve. Acad. Medicine, Ohio Am. Coll. Emergency. Republican. Russian Orthodox. Avocations: photography, cooking. Home: 545 Eastwood Dr Hinckley OH 44233-9496 Office: Parma Cmty Gen Hosp 7007 Powers Blvd Parma OH 44129-5437

LAZOR, PATRICIA ANN, interior designer; d. Charles A. and Grace E. (Siegrist) LaGattuta; m. E. Alexander Lazor; children: Pamela A., Carolyn L., Charles L., Peter A. BA, Chestnut Hill Coll., 1957; MEd, Rutgers Coll., 1962; cert., N.Y. Sch. Interior Design, 1972. Tchr. Bridgewater (N.J.) Raritan Schs., 1958-60; designer Patricia A. Lazor Interior Design, Bernardsville, N.J., 1975-85; pres. Alexander Abry, Inc., Washington, 1985-87; owner, designer Patricia A. Lazor Interior Design Antiques, Inc., Bernardsville, 1985—. Designer numerous residential interior design projects throughout the U.S.; featured in 100 Designers Favorite Rooms. Rep. com. woman, Somerset County, N.J., 1978; chmn. Family Counseling Svc. Somerset County, 1972-78. Mem. Garden Club Morristown, Morristown Club, Kappa Delta Phi. Office: Patricia A Lazor Inc Roebling Rd Bernardsville NJ 07924

LAZOVIĆ, GAVRILO, internist; b. Sarajevo, Yugoslavia, Aug. 27, 1958; came to U.S., 1992; s. Gordan and Mirjana (Savić) L.; m. Nina Šošić, July 15, 1994; children: Marko, Sonja. MD, U. Sarajevo, 1983; hematologist, U. Zagreb, 1990; internist, U. Sarajevo, 1991; hematologist, U. Zagreb, 1990; internist, McKeesport Hosp., 1997. Diplomate Am. Bd. Internal Medicine. Physician Health Care Inst., Gorazde, Yugoslavia, 1983-87; internist Univ. Hosp., Sarajevo, Yugoslavia, 1987-91; hematologist Univ. Clinic Hematology, 1991-92; rsch. fellow Cancer Immuno Biology Lab., Hilton Head, S.C., 1992-94; resident internal medicine McKeesport (Pa.) Hosp., 1994-97, emergency rm. physician, 1997-98; physician Jefferson Hosp., Pitts., 1997-98; physician critical care and emergency rm. Miami Heart Inst., Miami Beach, Fla., 1998—, med. dir. emergency svcs., 2000—. Adj. prof. Barry U., Miami, Fla., 2001—. Contbr. articles to profl. jours. Fellow ACP; mem. AMA, Pa. Med. Soc., Allegheny County Med. Soc. Avocations: reading bicycle riding, skiing, travel. Home: 6131 La Gorce Dr Miami Beach FL 33140 E-mail: lazovic@pol.net.

LAZUR, JAMES JOSEPH, accounting educator; b. Toledo, Mar. 26, 1946; s. Emery Joseph and Ethel Ann (Kerekgyarto) L. Assoc. Applied Bus., Owens Tech. Coll., Toledo, 1987; BS, U. Toledo, 1988. Cert. tax profl. Store mgr. Gladieux Food Svc., Toledo, 1975-77; exec. and shift mgr. Frisch's Big Boy, 1977-82; asst. office supr. H & R Block, 1982-85; acct., tax preparer, 1985—; computer lab. technician Owens Tech. Coll., 1986-87; instr. Capital U., Dayton, Ohio, 1989-91; instr. various fields Owens Tech. Coll., Toledo, 1987—. Mem. Owens Coll. Alumni Bd., 1988—; tutor acctg. and basic programming, 1987—. Fin. cons., computer operator, team leader, drama minister, youth pastor Found. Stone Christian Ctr., Toledo, 1985—. Mem. Nat. Assn. Accts., Nat. Soc. Tax Profls., Assn. Supervision and Curriculum Devel., Smithsonian Inst., Ohio Soc. Enrolled Agts. Avocations: desktop pub., movie classics, reading. Home: 546 Pleasant Pl Toledo OH 43609-3368

LAZZARA, BERNADETTE See PETERS, BERNADETTE

LAZZARA, DENNIS JOSEPH, orthodontist; b. Chgo., Mar. 14, 1948; s. Joseph James and Jacqueline Joan (Antonini) L.; m. Nancy Ann Pirhofer, Dec. 18, 1971; children: Kristin Lynn, Bryan Matthew, Matthew Dennis, Kathryn Marie, David Brady. BS, U. Dayton, 1970; DDS, Loyola U., 1974, MS in Oral Biology, cert. orthodontics, Loyola U., 1976. Practice dentistry specializing in orthodontics, Geneva, 1976—. Mem. dental staff Delnor Cmty. Hosp., Geneva and St. Charles, Ill., 1976—; sec. dental staff, Geneva, 1978-80, v.p., 1980-82, pres., 1982-84, exec. com., 1982-84. Leader Boy Scouts Am., 1988-90. Recipient award of merit Am. Coll. Dentists, 1974. Mem. ADA, Am. Assn. Orthodontists (presenter ann. meeting 1997, Harry Sicher hon. mention award 1977), Midwestern Soc. Orthodontists, Ill. Soc. Orthodontists, Fox River Valley Dental Soc. (bd. dirs. 1983-86), Blue Key Nat. Honor Soc. Roman Catholic. Avocations: sailing, golf. Office: PO Box 431 Geneva IL 60134-0431

LAZZARO, ANTHONY DEREK, university administrator; b. Utica, N.Y., Jan. 31, 1921; s. Angelo Michael and Philomena (Vanilla) L.; m. Shirley Margaret Jones, Dec. 20, 1941; 1 child, Nancy. BS in Indsl. and Sys. Engring., U. So. Calif., 1948; LL.D. with honors, Pepperdine U., 1974. Registered profl. engr., Calif. Asst. bus. mgr. U. So. Calif., L.A., 1948-60, asst. bus. mgr., dir. campus devel., 1960-65, asso. bus. mgr., dir. campus devel., 1965-71, asso. v.p. bus. affairs, 1971-72, v.p. bus. affairs, 1972-86, sr. v.p. bus. affairs, 1986-88, univ. v.p., 1988-91, v.p. emeritus, 1991—. Cons. HEW. Editorial cons. College and University Business, 1955-58. Mem. nat. adv. coun. United Student Aid Funds, N.Y.C., 1974-77, chmn., 1976-77; dir. Rep. Fed. Savs. & Loan Assn. and subs. corps., L.A., 1961-88; spl. studies cons. div. higher edn. Office Edn. HEW, 1956-59; mem. citizens com. Palos Verdes Bd. Edn., 1955-57; mem. Hoover urban renewal adv. com. Community Redevel. Agy. City of L.A., 1960-88. Lt. USNR, 1941-46. Recipient Pres.'s Outstanding Svc. award U. Redlands, 2000. Mem. Nat. Assn. Coll. and Univ. Bus. Officers (pres. 1978-79, dir. 1972-80, chmn. goals and programs com. 1978, chmn. large inst. com. 1986-87, Disting. Bus. Officer award 1986), Western Assn. Coll. and Univ. Bus. Officers (pres. 1971-72), Soc. Coll. and Univ. Planning, Blue Key, Golden Key, Phi Kappa Phi, Tau Beta Pi. Clubs: Jonathan (Los Angeles). Home: 4012 Via Larga Vis Palos Verdes Estates CA 90274 E-mail: lazzaro@usc.edu., lazzaro@jps.net.

LAZZARO-WEIS, CAROL MARIE, foreign languages educator; b. Dec. 11, 1949; BA in French/Italian, Pa. State U., 1969; MA in French, Villanova U., 1973; MA in Romance Langs., U. Pa., 1974, PhD in Romance Langs., 1978. Instr. in Italian Univ. Saarbrucken, Germany, 1980-84; asst. prof. French U. Md., Europe, 1980-84; asst. prof., dir. Honors Coll. So. Univ., Baton Rouge, 1984-89, assoc. prof., 1989-93, prof., chair fgn. lags., 1993—2002; prof., chair Romance langs. and lit. U. Mo. , Columbia, 2002—. Author: Confused Epiphanies: L'Abbé Prevost and the Romance Tradition, 1991, From Margins to Mainstream: Contemporary Italian Women Writers, 1993, La Signorina and Other Stories by Anna Banti, 2001, 02. Chair Fulbright Tchr. Exch. Interview Com., Baton Rouge, 1991-2002; v.p. Coun. for Devel. of French in La., 2000—. Grantee Fulbright Found., 1990-91, ACLS, 1990-91; scholar-in-residence Bogliasco Found., 1999; NEH summer seminar fellow, 1994. Mem.: MLA (mem. fgn. and lit. lang. adv. bd. 1998—2001), Am. Soc. Eighteenth-Century Studies, South Ctrl. MLA, South Atlantic MLA, Coll. Lang. Assn., Am. Assn. Italian Studies (treas. 2001—), Am. Assn. Tchrs. Italian, Am. Assn. Tchrs. French (pres. La. chpt. 1986—90). Home: 813 Delgado Dr Baton Rouge LA 70808-4733 E-mail: cmarieweis@yahoo.com.

LAZZI, GIANLUCA, electronics engineer, researcher; b. Rome, Apr. 25, 1970; s. Romano and Annamaria (Pastore) L.; m. Dulce Altabella, Mar. 20, 1999. D in Electronics Engring., U. La Sapienza, Rome, 1994; PhD in Elec. Engring., U. Utah, 1998. Registered profl. engr., Rome. Vis. rschr. Nat. Italian Bd. for Nuc. and Alternative Energies, Rome, 1994-95; sci. collaborator U. La Sapienza, 1994-95; rsch. assoc. U. Utah, Salt Lake City, 1995-98, rsch. asst. prof., 1998—; asst. prof. N.C. State U., Raleigh, 1999—. Cons. BCD Sistemi, Rome, 1993-94. Co-author: software packages for the Italian Nat. TV Network, 1988; contbr. articles to profl. jours. Recipient Young Scientist award Internat. Union Radio Sci., 1996, Curtis Carl Johnson Meml. award Bioelectromagnetics Soc., 1996, Career award NSF, 2001. Mem. IEEE (sr.), Italian Elec. and Electronic Soc. Office: NC State U Dept Elec Computer Engring PO Box 7914 Raleigh NC 27695-0001

LE, JO WEISS, artist; b. San Francisco, Dec. 2, 1955; d. Leonard Winchell and Lee Elyse (Crouse) Weiss; m. Anh Hong Le, Mar. 16, 1985; children: Kimberly Anh, Kelvin Anh. BFA, Am. U., 1984, MFA, 1986. Dean Washington Studio Sch., 1985—. Adj. faculty Am. U., Washington, 1995—; guest faculty Georgetown U., Washington, 1995. Mem. Cultural Alliance Greater Washington, Phi Kappa Phi. Avocations: hiking, reading. Office: Washington Studio Sch 3232 P St NW Washington DC 20007-2741

LE, LY NGOC, environmental physicist, educator; b. Hanoi, Vietnam; naturalized, 1988; s. Le Ngoc Can and Phan Thi Chan; m. XuanDung Vu. PhD in Environ. Physics summa cum laude, State Hydromet Inst., St. Petersburg, Russia, 1977. Postdoctoral rsch. assoc. Iowa State U., Ames, 1985-88; scientist III U. Coop. for Atmospheric Rsch. Inst. for Naval Oceanography, Stennis Space Ctr., Miss., 1988-92; sr. rsch. scientist Ctr. for Ocean and Atmospheric Modeling, USM, 1992-93; rsch. prof. Naval Postgrad. Sch., Monterey, Calif., 1993—. Author: Dynamics of the Atmosphere, 1980; contbr. articles to profl. jours. Recipient Rsch. grant Office of Naval Rsch. Mem. N.Y. Acad. Scis., Am. Geophys. Union, Am. Meteorol. Soc., Soc. for Indsl. and Applied Math. Achievements include developments of air-wave-sea coupled model based on a new turbulence concept and of a computer ocean modeling system incorporating a new turbulent closure with a surface wave parameterization and grid generation techniques. Office: Naval Postgrad Sch Dept Oceanography Monterey CA 93943 E-mail: lely@nps.navy.mil., LNLY_99@yahoo.com.

LE, PHUOC HONG, internist, consultant; b. Saigon, Vietnam, July 1963; came to U.S., 1975; s. John Van and Sarah H. Le; m. Lien-Huong H. Le, June 1993; children: Hoang-An T., Vinh Hoang. BA, U. Chgo., 1983; MD, U. Vt., 1990. Diplomate Am. Bd. Internal Medicine. Sr. rsch. asst. Jackson Lab., Bar Harbor, Maine, 1983-86; staff physician Cen. Maine Med. Ctr., Lewiston, 1993—, St. Mary's Med. Assn., Lewiston, 1993—. Physician cons. Novartis Pharm. Co., N.J., 1997—, Merck Pharms., N.J., 1997—. Reviewer: (book) DeGowan's Diagnostic Exam, 6th edit., 1993; contbr. articles to profl. jours. Vol. ARC, Auburn, Maine, 1998—. Mem. ACP, Maine Med. Soc., Androscoggin Med. Soc. Avocations: sailing, classical piano, traveling. Office: St Mary's Med Assocs 99 Campus Ave Ste 201 Lewiston ME 04240-6045

LE, SON MINH, philosophy educator; b. Ninh Binh, Vietnam, Jan. 16, 1945; , U.S., 1964; s. Chuyen Van Le and Tuyet Thi Dinh; m. Mary Kai Ming Cheung, Apr. 6, 1969 (dec. 1977); children: Trang Minh, Dao Minh, Tri Minh; m. Marilyn Jean Matsumura, Aug. 9, 1980; 1 child, Mai Minh. BA, Fordham U., 1967; MA, Antioch Coll., 1968; PhD, Ohio State U., 1971. Philosophy instr. Franconia (N.H.) Coll., 1968, Antioch Coll., Yellow Springs, Ohio, 1968; rssch. assoc. U. So. Calif. Med. Ctr., L.A., 1974-75; prof. philosophy, dept. chair Mission Coll., Santa Clara, 1975—, weekend coll. and evening adminstr., 1986-95. Founding faculty mem. Mission Coll., 1975, chair, faculty com. to draft original Mission Coll. philosophy, 1976. Author: Behavioral Objectives, 1973, Term Deliveryof Primary Care, 1976, Logic Flip Book: A Modular Approach, 1979, Elements of Critical Thinking and Writing, 2000. Vietnam del. World Youth Forum, 1962. Presdl. scholarship Fordham U., 1964. Mem. Nat. Endowment for the Humanities, State of Calif. Coun. for Pvt. Postsecondary and Vocat. Edn., Am. Philos. Assn. Avocation: reading and reflecting. Office: Philosophy Dept Mission Coll 3000 Mission Coll Blvd Santa Clara CA 95054 E-mail: mcphilosopher@yahoo.com.

LE, THUY TRONG, educator, researcher; b. Vietnam, Jan. 20, 1958; came to US, 1980; s. Thich Trong and Le-Phi Thi (Vuong) V.; m. Nhan Thi Le, Aug. 20, 1985; children: Thuy-Nhu Thi, Thi Trong. BS in Nuclear Engring., U. Calif., 1985, MS in Nuclear Engring., 1987, PhD in Engring., 1990. Nuclear reactor operator, health physicist asst. Nuc. Engring. Dept. U. Calif., Berkeley, 1985-88, grad. student instr. Nuc. Engring. and Physics Dept., 1987-90; rsch. asst. physics divsn. Lawrence Berkeley Nat. Lab., 1988-89; physics instr. Calif. Coll. of Alameda, 1989-90; rsch. engr. sci. computation divsn. applied physics group Westinghouse Savannah River Lab., 1990-93; sr. rschr. high performance computing group Fujitsu Am. Incorporation, Calif., 1993-2000. Cons. engr. Sierra Nuclear Corp., Scotts Valley, Calif., 1989—; adj. prof. U. S.C., Aiken, 1991-93; assoc. prof. San Jose State U., 1996—; cons. Fujitsu America Inc. 2001—. Contbr. numerous articles to profl. jours. Mem. IEEE, Am. Nuclear Soc. (math. and computation divsn.). Achievements include authoring GRIMH3 computer code: multi dimensional reactor analysis code, WINDEX System: detailed energy residence treatment code, research in computer architectures, digital design, networking, numerical methods, parallel computing and algorithms, computational physics and engineering, criticality and radiation shielding, nuclear reactor analysis and design. Address: 44291 Pomace St Fremont CA 94539-6537 E-mail: thuytle@email.sjsu.edu.

LE, VINH TU, language educator, translator; b. Quang-Binh, Vietnam, Apr. 25, 1935; arrived in U.S., 1991; s. Oanh Tu Le and Thuan Thi Lam; m. Phuong Thi Ton, Jan. 29, 1958; children: Thuy K., Hai, Grace K., Vance, Tuong K., Trina, Scott, Thomson. Student, U. Hue, Vietnam, 1961—62, U. Saigon, 1963—65, student, 1972—74. Tchr. English Tang Bat Ho HS, Binh Dinh, Vietnam, 1955—58, Cuong De HS, Binh Dinh, 1958—60; instr. English Armed Forces Lang. Sch., Saigon, Vietnam, 1963—68; asst. course dir. Nat. Def. Coll., 1968—70; tchr. English Bode and Chan P. Liem HS, 1970—75, GoVap HS, Saigon, 1979—87; tchr. aide St. Anselm Multicultural Ctr., Garden Grove, Calif., 1991—92. Vice prin. Fgn. Lang. Ctr., Saigon, 1980—87. Translator: The Pride of the Vietnamese, 1992—93, A Vietnamese Girl and An American Soldier, 1997; editor-in-chief Lai Giang Spl. Publ., 1994—. Head steering com. AFLS Assn., 1993—98; sec. gen. Quang Binh Assn., 1997—99; pres. Lai Giang Assn., 1994—. 1st lt. U.S. Army, 1962—70, Vietnam. Recipient 1st class tng. medal, Joint Gen. Staff, 1966, 1st class Honor Staff medal, 1970. Avocations: reading, watching television. Home: 16537 Mt Michaelis Cir Fountain Valley CA 92708

LE, YVONNE DIEMVAN, chemist; b. Vietnam, Nov. 21, 1961; d. Hien Trung and Thanh-Hoa Thi (Luu) L. BA in Chemistry, Math., San Jose State U., 1984. Chem. technician Hewlett Packard Co., Palo Alto, Calif., 1983; assoc. chemist Ampex Corp., Sunnyvale, 1984-86; chemist II Info. Memory Corp., Santa Clara, 1986-88; R&D engring. mgr. Komag, Inc., San Jose, 1988-99; analyst, project mgr. Applied Materials, Santa Clara, 2000—01. Mem. Am. Chem. Soc. Roman Catholic. Avocations: skiing, tennis, piano. E-mail: vyltd@hotmail.com.

LEA, LOLA STENDIG, lawyer; b. N.Y.C., Sept. 20, 1934; d. Hershel and Sophie (Golub) Stendig; m. Robert M. Lea, Sept. 12, 1953 (div. Apr. 1976); 1 child, Jennie. BA cum laude, NYU, 1954; LL.B., Yale U., 1957. Bar: N.Y. 1958, Maine 1989. Law clk. to U.S. dist. judge So. Dist. N.Y., 1957-59, asst. U.S. atty., 1959-61; assoc. C.C. Davis, N.Y.C., 1961-67; mem. firm Davis & Cox, 1967-71, Lea, Goldberg & Spellun PC, N.Y.C., 1971—77, Trubin, Sillcocks, Edelman & Knapp, N.Y.C., 1977-80; counsel Parker & Duryee, 1983-86, mem., 1987-88. Spl. counsel to N.Y. 1st dept. joint interprofl. com. Drs. and Lawyers, 1972-78; lectr. Practising Law Inst., N.Y.C., 1969-70, 74, 79; spl. mediator Med. Malpractice Mediation part Supreme Ct. N.Y., 1971-80; chmn. N.Y. State Commn. Investigation, 1981-83; mem. parole bd. State of Maine, 1999—. Fellow Am. Bar Found., N.Y. Bar Found.; mem. N.Y. Bar Assn. (del. 1972-77, 87-88, mem. exec. com. 1976-77), Assn. Bar City N.Y. (chmn. grievance com. 1978-80, chmn. medicine and law com. 1969-71, chmn. spl. com. on drug laws 1986-88, mem. other coms.), N.Y. County Lawyers Assn. (dir. 1978-81). Home and Office: 22825 Forest Ridge Dr Estero FL 33928 E-mail: lslea@email.msn.com.

LEA, LORENZO BATES, lawyer; b. St. Louis, Apr. 12, 1925; s. Lorenzo Bates and Ursula Agnes (Gibson) L.; m. Marcia Gwendolyn Wood, Mar. 21, 1953; children— Victoria, Jennifer, Christopher. BS, MIT, 1946; JD, U. Mich., 1949; grad. Advanced Mgmt. Program, Harvard U., 1964. Bar: Ill. 1950. With Amoco Corp. (formerly Standard Oil Co. Ind.), Chgo., 1949—, asst. gen. counsel, 1963-71, assoc. gen. counsel, 1971-72, gen. counsel, 1972-78, v.p., gen. counsel, 1978-89. Trustee Village of Glenview (Ill.) Zoning Bd., 1961-63, Cmty. Found. Collier Country; bd. dirs. Chgo. Crime Commn., 1978— , Midwest Council for Internat. Econ. Policy, 1973— , Chgo. Bar Found., 1981— , Chgo. Area Found. for Legal Services, 1981— ; bd. dirs. United Charities of Chgo., 1973—, chmn., 1985—; bd. dirs. Cmty. Foun. of Collier County, 1997—, Naples Bot. Garden, 2000—. Served with USNR, 1943-46. Mem. ABA, Am. Petroleum Inst., Am. Arbitration Assn. (dir. 1980—), Ill. Bar Assn., Chgo. Bar Assn., Assn. Gen. Counsel, Order of Coif, Law Club, Econs. Club, Legal, Mid-Am. (Chgo.), Glen View, Wyndemere, Hole-In-The-Wall, Sigma Xi. Republican. Mem. United Ch. of Christ.

LEA, SCOTT CARTER, retired packaging company executive; b. New Orleans, Nov. 14, 1931; s. Leonard G. and Helen (Stoughton) L.; m. Marilyn Ruth Blair, Oct. 25, 1957; children: Scott, Nancy B., Mark S. BA, Amherst Coll., 1954; MBA, U. Pa., 1959. Sales and mktg. positions Riegel Paper, 1959-66, sales mgr. folding carton dept. southeastern div., 1966-67, gen. sales mgr., 1967-69, v.p. folding carton dept., 1969-71; v.p. bd. conversion div. Rexham Corp., Charlotte, N.C., 1971-73, v.p. packaging group, 1973-74, pres., 1974-90; chmn. bd. Rexham Industries, Inc., 1990-92; bd. dirs. Lance Inc., Charlotte, 1994—, chmn. bd. dirs., 1996-99. Bd. dirs. Speizman Industries, Inc. Trustee Johnson C. Smith U., Charlotte, N.C., 1977—, vice chmn. bd. trustees, 1998—; bd. dirs. Ctrl. Piedmont C.C. Found., Charlotte, 1994—. With U.S. Army, 1954-57. Mem.: N.C. Zool. Soc. (bd. dirs. 1996—2002), Charlotte C. of C. (bd. dirs. 1977—78), Wild Dunes Club (Isle of Palms, S.C.), Quail Hollow Country Club, Carmel Country Club. Home: 3704 Stone Ct Charlotte NC 28226-7343 Office: Lance Inc 8600 South Blvd Charlotte NC 28273-6924

LEA, STANLEY E. artist, educator; b. Joplin, Mo., Apr. 5, 1930; s. Everett G. and Edna F. L.; m. Ruth Lowe, Aug. 19, 1951; children: Kristy Ruth, Kraig, Kelly B. B.F.A., Pitts. State U., 1953; M.F.A., U. Ark., 1961. Prof. art Sam Houston State U., Huntsville, 1961-93, Mexican Field Sch., Puebla, Mexico, 1963-65; vis. artist prof. Mus. Fine Arts, Houston, 1968, 69, 70; prof. art study abroad program London, 1977-78. Juror various art exhibits, 1970-81; workshop demonstrator, E. Tex. State U., Commerce, 1977, 10th ann. color print symposium, Tex. Tech. U., Lubbock, 1983, City of Huntsville mural, 1980; one-man shows paintings and/or prints, Valley House Gallery, Dallas, 1963, Inst. Mex. N. Am. de Rels., Mexico City, 1967, Main Place Gallery, Dallas, 1970-71, U. Tex. Med. Ctr., San Antonio, 1970, Mexico Moody Gallery, Houston, 1976, Sol Del Rio, San Antonio, 1978, 89, Adelle M. Fine Arts, Dallas, 1978, Dubose Gallery, Houston, 1980, Cultural Activities Ctr., Temple, Tex., 1982, Tex. A&M U., College Station, 1986, Mus. at E. Tex., Lufkin, 1989Cultural Ctr., Bryan, Tex., 1993; numerous group shows, latest being Moody Gallery, Houston, 1975, 77, Pecan Square Gallery, Austin, Tex., 1977, Am. Painters In Paris, 1975-76, Waco Art Center, Waco, Tex., 1977, East Tex. State U., Commerce, 1977, Galveston (Tex.) Art Center, 1978, Twenty Five Nat. Printmaker, Lubbock, Tex., 1978, Beaumont (Tex.) Art Mus., 1978, Art League of Houston, 1978, Gates Gallery, Port Arthur, Tex., 1979, Ars Longa, Houston, 1974, Laguna Gloria Mus., Austin, 1979; represented in permanent collections, Library of Congress, Washington, Smithsonian Mus. Am. Art, Washington, Calif. Palace of Legion of Honor, San Francisco, Brit. Mus., London, Mus. Fine Arts, Houston, USIA, N.Y.C., N.Y. Public Library, N.Y.C., Mpls. Inst. Art, Kalamazoo Inst. Art, Boise (Idaho) Gallery of Art, Madison (Wis.) Art Center, Spiva Art Center, Joplin, Mo., Ft. Worth Art Mus., Convention Ctr., The Woodlands, Tex., Cleve. Mus., Inst. Mexicano Norteamericana de Relationes, Mexico City, Smithsonian Inst., Washington, also corp. and pvt. collections. (Recipient numerous awards, latest being, Southwest Graphics Invitational award 1971, Dimensions IX Exhbn. award 1974, 68th Nat. Tex. Fine Arts Exhbn. 1979). Sam Houston State U. grantee, 1970, 74, Lakeside (Mich.) Studio grantee 1972, Casa Argentina grantee, Buenos Aires, 1973, Europe, 1982. Mem. Coll. Art Assn., So. Graphics Council. Home: 3324 Winter Way Huntsville TX 77340-8919

LEAB, DANIEL JOSEPH, history educator; b. Berlin, Aug. 29, 1936; s. Leo and Herta (Marcus) L.; m. Katharine Kyes, Aug. 16, 1964; children: Abigail Elizabeth, Constance Martha, Marcus Rogers. BA, Columbia U., 1957, MA, 1961, PhD, 1969. With Columbia U., N.Y.C., 1966-73, Seton Hall U., 1974—. Co-editor Am. Book Prices Current. Author: A Union of Individuals: The Formation of the American Newspaper Guild, 1970, I Was a Communist for the FBI: the unhappy life and times of Matt Cvetic , 2000; mng. editor: Labor History, 1974—2002, mng. editor: Am. Communist History, 2001—. Bd. of Edn. Region 12 (Washington, Roxbury, Bridgewater), 1997-2002; justice of the peace, 2001—. Recipient Commerford award. N.Y. State Labor History Assn., 1997. Fellow Met. Mus. Art; mem. Historians of Am. Communism (gen. sec.), Century Assn., Grolier Club. Home: PO Box 1216 Washington CT 06793-0216 E-mail: danleab@earthlink.net.

LEABO, DICK A. retired statistics educator; b. Walcott, Iowa, Oct. 30, 1921; s. Albert Thomas and Clara (Beinke) L.; m. Artis M. Van de Voort, June 11, 1955; 1 child, Thomas William (dec. 1977). BS, U. Iowa, 1949, MA, 1950, PhD, 1953. Rsch. asst. U. Iowa, Iowa City, 1950-53, asst. prof., 1953-56; exch. prof. Brookings Instn., 1957—58, Rotterdam Sch. Econs., 1965; asst. prof. Mich. State U., East Lansing, 1956-57, U. Mich., Ann Arbor, 1957-58, assoc. prof., 1959-62, prof., dir. PhD program, 1963-77, Fred M. Taylor Endowed Disting. prof. statistics, 1978-84, Fred M. Taylor Endowed Disting. prof. statistics emeritus, 1984—; mem. North Ctrl. Commn. on Higher Edn., Chgo., 1965—84. Bus. cons., 1957-86; ednl. cons. Toronto (Can.) Dept. Higher Edn., 1973, N.Y. State Dept. Edn., N.Y.C., 1975. Author: Basic Statistics, 5th edit., 1976; contbr. over 25 articles to profl. jours. 1st lt. USAF, 1943—45, 1st lt. USAF, Res. Decorated DFC, Air medal, CBI Theatre Ribbon with 4 Battle Stars. Mem. Disting. Flying Cross Soc. (life), Phi Kappa Phi (life, nat. v.p. 1977). Democrat. Presbyterian. Avocations: writing, golf. Home: 5065 Vivienda Way Sarasota FL 34235-1841 Office: U. Mich 701 Tappan Ave Ann Arbor MI 48109-1234

LEACH, BERTON JOE, science educator; b. Tuscola, Ill., Mar. 30, 1932; s. William Howard Leach and Frances Margaret De Haven; m. Barbara English, June 5, 1955; children: Laura Anne, Berton Franklin. AB, Washington U., 1957; MA, U. Mo., 1960, PhD, 1963. Assoc. prof. George Washington U., Washington, 1963—66; scientist adminstr. NSF, 1966—69; chmn., prof. Ctrl. Meth. Coll., Fayette, Mo., 1969—74; exec. sec. NIH, Bethesda, Md., 1974—76; sr. scientist pvt. industry, Rockville, 1976—89; scientist Omni Rsch., Capital Sys. Group, 1976—89; adj. prof. Georgetown U., Washington, 1989—. Vis. scholar Harvard U., Cambridge, Mass., 1969; gen. reader Marine Biol. Lab., Woods Hole, Mass., 1985—87; guest rschr. NIH/Brain Behavior Lab., Poolesville, Md., 1991—92. Author: Structure and Development of Vertebrates, 1973, Vertebrate Biology Courseware, 1979, Human Neuroanatomy, 1999. Program chmn. Rotary Internat., Bethesda, 1975; vol. swimming instr. Rockville Swim Ctr., 2001; pres. Meth. Men's Club, Columbia, Mo., 1960. Decorated Am. Spirit Honor medal U.S. Army; named F. H. Dearing endowed prof., Ctrl. Meth. Coll., Fayette, 1970—74; fellow USPH rsch. fellow, NIH, Bethesda, 1962—63; grantee, NSF, Washington, 1973—74. Mem.: Am. Soc. Mammalogists (life), Sigma Xi. Republican. Methodist. Achievements include first scientist to ovulate polyovular follicles using exogenous hormones. Avocations: gardening, landscaping. Home: 12707 Weiss St Rockville MD 20853 Office: Georgetown Univ Med Ctr Dept Neurosci 3970 Reservoir Rd NW Washington DC 20007

LEACH, BRENDA LYNNE, conductor, music educator, organist; b. Phila., July 12, 1959; MusB magna cum laude, Susquehanna U., 1981; MusM, Eastman Sch. Music, 1983, DMA, 1988; cert. French, U. Paris Sorbonne, 1987; MEd, Harvard U., 1997; studied conducting with, Alexander Polischuk, Russia, 1998; student, St. Petersburg Conservatory of Music. Instr., asst. univ. organist Susquehanna U., Selinsgrove, Pa., 1978-81; summer study program Oxford U., 1979; student Marie-Claire Alain Conservatoire Nat. de Region, Rueil-Malmaison, France, 1983-85, 1986-87; pvt. study with Daniel Roth St. Sulpice Ch., Paris, 1987-88; harpsichord study with Huguette Dreyfus, 1987-88; instr. music. Wheelock Coll., Boston, 1991-93; instr. Clark U., 1991—; dir. music, lectr. music Harvard U., 1991—, choral dir., organist, 1993—; condr., music dir. Boston Coro di Camera, 1997—; condr. Lowell (Mass.) Philharm. Orch., 1998—. Founding music dir., condr. Boston Chamber Orch.; guest condr. St. Petersburg (Russia) Camerata Orch., Orch. of the Hermitage Mus., Russia, Novgorod (Russia) Philharm., Kaliningrad (Russia) Philharm. Chamber Orch., Pskov Philharm., Norosibirsk Festival Orch., Varna (Bulgaria) State Philharm. Orch., Shumen Philharm. Orch., Bulgaria, Pleven Philharm. Orch., Bulgaria, Madara Music Festival, Bulgaria, Sochi Music Festival, Russia, Boston First Night Festival; conducting fellow with Sir David Willcocks at choral symposium, Ogontz, N.H., 1996; instr. Boston U., summer 1992; lectr. in music Am. U. Paris, 1989; instr. Brookline (Mass.) Pub. Schs. Ctr. for Adult Edn., 1992—; lectr. Boston Ctr. for Adult Edn., 1991; lectr. in music Carnegie Mus. Fine Arts, Pitts., 1990; lectr. Rochester Mus. and Sci. Ctr., 1985; music faculty mem. Parkminster Music Sch., Rochester, 1983-85; pvt. studio Paris, 1985-89; participant Peter the Gt. Internat. Master Class for Condrs., St. Petersburg, Russia, 1997 (prize 1998); music cons. for multimedia project San Francisco Mus. Modern Art, 1997; interim music dir., organist Am. Ch. in Paris, 1986; mem. master class faculty Rimsky-Korsakov Coll. Music, St. Petersburg, 2000; assoc. artistic dir. Peter the Gt. Masterclass Russia, 2000—. Solo organ recitals by invitation in Paris, London, Jerusalem, Tel Aviv, Boston, N.Y.C., St. Petersburg, and other cities; featured artist Detroit Symphony Orch., S.D. Symphony; contbr. articles to profl. jours.; concerts featured on cassette, pub. radio broadcasts. Instr. in music and humanities Dedham County Prison. Recipient Harriet Hale Woolley scholar, 1985-86, Premier Prix de Virtuosite Conservatoire National de Region, Premier Prix d'Excellence Conservatoire National de Region. Mem.: Boston Aria Guild (exec. bd. 1991—), Coll. Music Soc., Am. Guild Organists (spl. projects com. Boston chpt., exec. bd. 1993—94, grant for rsch. in Jerusalem), Condrs. Guild, Am. Symphony Orch. League, Mass. Coun. Chs. (program design team 1992). Avocations: travel, water color painting, yoga, photography. Office: Harvard U 45 Francis Ave Cambridge MA 02138-1911 E-mail: brenda_leach@harvard.edu.

LEACH, DAVE FRANCIS, editor, musician; b. Iowa City, Nov. 12, 1945; s. Joseph Stanley and Thelma Maxine (Strubhar) L.; m. Donna Susan Schoeppner, Dec. 17, 1970 (div. Feb. 1979); children: Arlo Bernard, Cynthia Robin; m. Dorothy Darlene Barnes, Dec. 13, 1986. B Music Edn., Drake U., 1967. Band dir. Melcher (Iowa)/Dallas Schs., 1967-68, Lackland Air Force Band, 1968-70, Coon Rapids (Iowa) Schs., 1970; band instrument repairman Miller Music/Family Music Ctr., Des Moines, 1972—; editor, founder Prayer & Action News, 1989—; producer, host The Uncle Ed Show, 1995—; owner Family Music Ctr., 1999—. Trumpet player Des Moines Mcpl. Band, 1963-78; musician Kingsway, St. Ambrose and St. Augustine Cathedrals, and Simpson United Meth. Ch., 1980-92. Author, composer: (musical comedy) Werld Klas Ejukashun, 1991; author (book) the Gifts of Governments, 1990, God's Cure for Loneliness, 1999. Dem. candidate for state rep., Iowa, 1986, Rep. candidate 1988, 90, 2000, 02; active numerous conservative and grass roots groups; pres., editor Fathers for Equal Rights, Des Moines chpt. 1985-87. Avocations: Bible study, inventing, construction. Office: 4110 SW 9th Ave Des Moines IA 50315-3643 E-mail: Leach@panews.org.

LEACH, DONALD PAUL, small business owner; b. Mount Vernon, N.Y., Mar. 17, 1945; s. Alfred Grahame and Anne Marie (Hantz) L.; m. Nancy Lynne Davis, Jan. 30, 1967; children: Donald Paul, Brian, Deborah. BS, Cedarville Coll., 1968; MBA, U. Dayton, 1974. Acct., mem. corp. staff Top Value Enterprises, Dayton, Ohio, 1969-72; tax analyst, corp. staff Philips Industries, Inc., Dayton, 1972-73; tax mgr. Danis Industries Corp., Dayton, 1973-76, asst. v.p., 1976-78, v.p., treas. constrn. products group, 1978-82; v.p., treas. Moody Bible Inst., Chgo., 1982-88, v.p., spl. asst. to pres. Moody Consumer Ministries, 1988-89; COO Grabill Corp, Oak Forest, Ill.; owner, pres. Advance Refrigeration Co., Bensenville, Ill., 1990—; instr. acctg. Sinclair C.C., Dayton, 1974-82. Mem. fin. com. Dayton Christian Schs., 1981-82; trustee Washington Hts. Bapt. Ch., Dayton, 1981-82, supt., 1977-80; deacon Faith Bapt. Ch., Winfield, Ill., 1984-87; small group leader Cmty. Fellowship Ch., 1996—, elder, 1999—; treas. Alumni Coun. Cedarville (Ohio) Coll., 1981-83, chmn., 1983-87; pres. Dayton Tax Club, 1977-78. Served with U.S. Army, 1967-73. Mem. Nat. Assn. Accts., Inst. Internal Auditors, Christian Ministries Mgmt. Assn. Home: 420 Spring Cress Ln West Chicago IL 60185-1781 Office: Advance Refrigeration Co 1177 Industrial Dr Bensenville IL 60106-1200

LEACH, GORDON L. management consultant; b. Pekin, Ill., Jan. 3, 1931; s. Melvin Dean and Beryl (Potter) L.; m. Cynthia J. Young, Oct. 23, 1954; children: Ginny Mathews, Sara, Andrew. BS, U. Ill., 1954. Cert. assessing officer, Ill. Product safety coord. Stephens-Adamson, Inc., Aurora, Ill., 1957-83; cons., 1983—. Bd. dirs. Sr. Svcs. Assocs., Inc., Elgin, Ill., 1993—, longterm care ombudsman, 1993—. Mem. Am. Soc. Safety Engrs. (profl. mem.), Phi Gamma Delta. Republican. Episcopalian. Avocations: writing, fishing. Home and Office: 1905 Kensington Pl Aurora IL 60506 E-mail: gleach401@aol.com.

LEACH, HAROLD ROBERT, obstetrician/gynecologist; b. Detroit, Sept. 15, 1947; MD, Wayne State U., 1974. Diplomate Am. Bd. Ob-Gyn. Intern, resident Sinai Hosp., Detroit, 1974-78; pvt. practice West Bloomfield, Mich., 1978—. Attending physician Wm. Beaumont Hosp., Royal Oak, Mich., 1978—. Fellow Am. Coll. Ob-Gyn. Office: 6900 Orchard Lake Rd West Bloomfield MI 48322-3405 Fax: (248) 855-7546. E-mail: DRHRL@aol.com.

LEACH, JAMES ALBERT SMITH, congressman; b. Davenport, Iowa, Oct. 15, 1942; s. James Albert and Lois (Hill) L.; m. Elisabeth Foxley, Dec. 6, 1975; 1 child, Gallagher BA, Princeton U., 1964; MA, Johns Hopkins U., 1966; postgrad., London Sch. Econs., 1966-68. Mem. staff Congressman Donald Rumsfeld, 1965-66; U.S. fgn. svc. officer, 1968-69, 70-73; spl. asst. to dir. OEO, 1969-70; mem. U.S. del. Geneva Disarmament Conf., 1971-72, UN Gen. Assembly, 1972, UN Natural Resources Conf., 1975; pres. Flamegas Companies Inc., Bettendorf, Iowa, 1973-76; chmn. bd. Adel Wholesalers, Inc., 1973-76; mem. 95th-106th Congresses from 1st Iowa dist., 1977—; chmn. banking and fin. svcs. com., mem. internat. rels. com.; mem. U.S. Adv. Commn. Internat. Ednl. and Cultural Affairs, 1975-76, mem. com. govt. reform & oversight, transp. & infrastructure. Chmn. Iowa Rep. Directions '76 Com. Episcopalian. Office: 2186 Rayburn Bldg Washington DC 20515-1501*

LEACH, JAMES GLOVER, lawyer; b. Panama City, Fla., Jan. 26, 1948; s. Milledge Glover and Thelma Louise (Hamilton) L.; m. Judith A. Leach, Feb. 26, 1972 (div. 1987); children: Allison, Arica; m. January Parker, Dec. 1997. AS, Gulf Coast Coll., 1968; BA, Duke U., 1970; MBA, Ga. State U., 1974, MI, 1976; JD, Drake U., 1989. Bar: Iowa 1990; CPCU, CLU. Bank officer Bank South, Atlanta, 1972-75; asst. v.p. Johnson & Higgins, 1975-78; pres. Nat. Gen. Ins. Co., St. Louis, 1978-85, AOPA Svc. Corp., St. Louis, 1985-87, Kirke-Van Orsdel Specialty, Des Moines, 1987-89, Gallagher Specialty, St. Louis, 1990-92; prin., dir., counsel Pauli & Co. Inc., 1992-93; sr. v.p., gen. counsel Am. Safety Ins., Atlanta, 1993-98; pres., CEO, gen. counsel, dir. Unistar Fin. Svc. Corp., Dallas, 1998—2001; exec.-in-residence U. Hartford, 2001; sr. v.p., gen. counsel Bldrs. Ins. Group, Atlanta, 2001—. Cons. McDonnell Douglas, St. Louis, 1987; dir. Gateway Ins. Co., St. Louis, 1992; corp. assembly Blue Cross/Blue Shield, St. Louis, 1991-92. Contbr. articles to profl. jours. 1st lt. USAF, 1970-72, Korea. Avocations: pilot, golf. Office: Builders Insurance Group PO Box 723099 Atlanta GA 31139-0099 Office Fax: 678-309-4079. E-mail: jleach@buildersinsurancegroup.com.

LEACH, JANE RILEY, fundraiser; b. Merced, Calif., Dec. 29, 1943; d. Harold Kerns and Vivian (Rimmer) Riley; divorced; 1 child, Carie Lynn Dougherty. Student, Fla. So. Coll., U. Tampa. Dir. lawyer recruitment, tng. and devel. Holland & Knight, Tampa, 1966-85; pres., owner Jane Riley Leach & Co., 1985-95; exec. dir. devel. and law rels. Sch. Law Regent U., Virginia Beach, 1995-2000; dir. major gifts Am. Heart Assn., St. Petersburg, Fla., 2000-01; exec. dir. Fla. Blood Svcs. Found., 2001—. Dir., mem. exec. com. and nat. adv. bd. Nat. Assn. Law Placement, Washington, 1975-85. Campaigner Ken Conner for Gov., Fla., 1994, Jim Gilmore for Gov., Va., 1997; mem. Tampa Ballet, Tampa Mus., Greater Tampa C. of C. CBS superbowl and beautification coms., Nat. Assn. Legal Search Cons., 1985-95. Mem. Assn. Fundraising Profls., Norfolk Hist. Soc., Hillsborough and Pinellas C. of C., Virginia Beach Rep. Women's Club (parliamentarian 1999, pres. 2000), Tampa Club. Republican. Baptist. Avocations: interior design, singing, antiquing, traveling. Home: 3109 W Fielder St Tampa FL 33611 Office: Fla Blood Svcs Found 10100 9th St N Saint Petersburg FL 33716 Fax: 727-568-2230. E-mail: jleach@fbsblood.org.

LEACH, JANET C. publishing executive; Mng. editor The Cin. Enquirer, until 1998; editor Akron Beacon Jour., 1998—. Office: Akron Beacon Jour 44 East Exchange St PO Box 640 Akron OH 44328*

LEACH, JOHN F. editor, journalism educator; b. Montrose, Colo., Aug. 6, 1952; s. Darrell Willis and Marian (Hester) L.; m. Deborah C. Ross, Jan. 2, 1982; children: Allison, Jason. BS in Journalism, U. Colo., 1974, MA in Journalism, 1979; MA in Am. Studies, U. Sussex, Brighton, Eng., 1983. News reporter Boulder (Colo.) Daily Camera, 1974-79, The Ariz. Republic, Phoenix, 1979-85, asst. city editor, 1985-93; news editor The Phoenix Gazette, 1993-94; asst. mng. editor Phoenix Gazette, 1994-95, The Ariz. Republic and The Phoenix Gazette, 1995-97; sr. editor The Ariz. Republic, Phoenix, 1997-99, sr. editor for online news, 1999—2002, editor digital media, 2002—; sr. editor for online news Azcential.com, 1999—2002, editor digital media, 2002—. Faculty assoc. Ariz. State U., Tempe, 1990—; pres., dir. Best of the West, Phoenix. Bd. Regents scholar U. Colo., 1970-74, Rotary Found. scholar, 1982-83. Mem. Ariz. Press Club (treas. 1984-86, pres. 1986-87), Soc. Profl. Journalists, Soc. News Design, Newspaper Assn. Am. New Media Fedn. Office: The Ariz Republic 200 E Van Buren St Phoenix AZ 85004-2238 E-mail: jleach@azcential.com.

LEACH, LUANN MARIE, elementary school educator; b. Grand Rapids, Mich., Oct. 27, 1963; d. Robert Allen and Rose Clare (Williams) L. BS, Western Ky. U., 1989; MS in Health, Leisure & Sports/Phys. Edn, U. West Fla., 2000. Gymnastics instr. Pensacola (Fla.) Jr. Coll., 1989-90; elem. phys. edn. tchr. Ferry Pass and Beulah Elem. Sch., Pensacola, Fla., 1989-90, Myrtle Grove and Beulah Elem. Sch., Pensacola, 1990-92, Myrtle Grove and McArthur Elem. Sch., Pensacola, 1992-93, Myrtle Grove and Lipscomb Elem. Sch., Pensacola, 1993-95; gymnastics instr. Dmitri Bilozertchev Gymnastics Tng., 1995; elem. phys. edn. tchr. Lipscomb and N.B. Cook Magnet Sch. for the Performing Arts, 1995-96; soccer tchr. Lipscomb's After the Bell Program, 1996; elem. phys. edn. tchr. Oakcrest and Warrington Elem. Sch., 1996-97, Oakcrest and Ensley Elem. Sch., Pensacola, 1997-98, O.J. Semmes Montessori Acad., 1998-99, O.J. Semmes Montessori Acad. and Hallmark Elem. Sch., 1999-2000, Spencer Bibbs Elem. Sch., 2000—. Tutor Beyond the Sch. Day program, substitute tchr. Neighborhood Learning program, 1997-98,; presenter in field. Vol. gymnastics tchr. Ferry Pass, Beulah, Myrtle Grove Elem. Schs., Pensacola, 1989-91; vol. coach Fit to Achieve Teams: Beulah and Myrtle Grove Elem. Schs., Pensacola, 1990-92; vol. tennis coach, coord. 10 teams Pensacola Jr. Tennis Assn., Pensacola, 1993-96; vol. coach Jogging Club for Myrtle Grove and Lipscomb Elem. Schs., Pensacola, 1994-95; vol. coach jr. tennis Spencer Bibbs Acad., 2000-02, vol. coach tumbling team, 2000-02; Vacation Bible Sch. and Sunday sch. tchr. First Bapt. Ch., Pensacola, Fla., 1996-98; vol. Habitat for Humanity, 1998; 8th grade cheerleading coach Easthill Christian Sch., Pensacola, 1998-99. Recipient Outstanding Elem. Sch. Team Tennis Coach award Pensacola Jr. Tennis Assn., 1993, cert. of achievement for the Model Phys. Fitness Sch. Program Fla. Govs. Coun. on Phys. Fitness and Sports, 1995, awards for cheerleading teams coached. Mem. ASCD, Fla. Assn. for Health, Phys. Edn., Recreation, Dance and Driver Edn., Escambia County Phys. Edn. Assn. (sec. 1992, pres. 2002--). Republican. Avocations: violin, art, tennis, interior design. Home: 3421 Riverside Dr Pensacola FL 32514-8172

LEACH, LYNNE E. nursing educator; b. Ridley Park, Pa., 1949; d. David J. and Mildred Elizabeth (Wynn) Fleming; m. Joseph P. Leach. RN, Bryn Mawr Hosp. Sch. Nursing, Pa., 1970; BS in Edn., Millersville (Pa.) U., 1975; MS in Nursing, U. Del., Newark, 1983; EdD, Widener U., Chester, Pa., 1994. Staff nurse Queen's Med. Ctr., Honolulu, 1972, Crozer-Chester Med. Ctr., Upland, Pa., 1970-71, 72-76; instr. nursing Bryn Mawr Hosp. Sch. Nursing, 1976-80; asst. prof. nursing Widener U., Chester, 1983-98, assoc. prof. nursing, 1998-2000; assoc. prof., assoc. dean Sch. Nursing, Seattle U., 2001—. Mem.: AWOHNN (edn. coord. Pa. sect. 1985—87, coord. Delco chpt. 1987—88, sec.-treas. Pa. sec. 1988—90, chair Pa. sect. 1991—92, Dist. III adv. coun. 1988—98, chair Dist. III 1993—95, 1996—97, nat. bd. dirs. 1992—98, 2000—01, nat. sec.-treas. 2000—01, chair nat. fin. com. 2000—01), Pi Lambda Theta, Sigma Theta Tau. Office: Seattle U 900 Broadway Seattle WA 98122

LEACH, LYNNETTA JANE, social worker, consultant; b. Cleve., Apr. 10, 1958; d. Leonard Carl and Elsie Jane (Webb) Snuffer; m. Mark Ronald Leach, June 25, 1983; children: Benjamin Leonard, Amelia Rose. BA, Anderson (Ind.) U., 1980; MS and Social Work, U. Louisville, 1981. Lic. clin. social worker, Md.; diplomate Am. Bd. Examiners in Clin. Social Work. Med. social worker Marymount Hosp., Garfield Heights, Ohio, 1982, SW Gen. Hosp., Middleburg Heights, 1982-84; cons. Home Care Co., Washington, 1984; clin. social worker Total Renal Care (formerly Shady Grove Dialysis Ctr.), Rockville, Md., 1984—; dir. social svc. Total Renal Care (now DaVita Dialysis), 1988—. Cons. Md. Home Care, Rockville, 1988-89, Collingswood Nursing Ctr., Rockville, 1988-98. Mem. Acad. Cert. Social Workers, Friendship Star Quilters. Nazarene. Avocations: outdoors, sports, crafts, sewing, camping. Home: 24221 Hailey Dr Damascus MD 20872-2260 Office: DaVita Dialysis 14915 Broschart Rd Ste 100 Rockville MD 20850-3367

LEACH, MICHAEL WILLIAM, research pathologist; b. Darby, Pa., July 14, 1962; s. Frank and Joann (Kurz) L.; m. Lorraine Cheryl Loretz, Nov. 11, 1989; 2 children: Rebecca, Eric. DVM, Purdue U., 1986; PhD, U. Calif., Davis, 1992. Diplomate Am. Coll. Vet. Pathologists. Resident U. Calif., Davis, 1986-92; sr. rsch. pathologist Schering-Plough Rsch. Inst., Lafayette, N.J., 1992—. Contbr. articles to profl. jours. Mem. AVMA, Acad. Pathology, Soc. Toxicology, Soc. Toxicological Pathologists. Avocations: music, racquetball. Office: Schering-Plough Rsch Inst PO Box 32 Rte 94 Lafayette NJ 07848

LEACH, RALPH F. banker; b. Elgin, Ill., June 24, 1917; s. Harry A. and Edith (Sanders) L.; m. Harriet C. Scheuerman, Nov. 18, 1944; children: C. David, H. Randall, Barbara E. AB, U. Chgo., 1938. Investment analyst Harris Trust & Savs. Bank, Chgo., 1940-48, Valley Nat. Bank, Phoenix, 1948-50; chief govt. finance sect. Fed. Res. Bd., Washington, 1950-53; treas. Guaranty Trust Co., N.Y.C., 1953-59, v.p., 1958-59; v.p., treas. Morgan Guaranty Trust Co., N.Y.C., 1959-62, sr. v.p., treas., 1962-64, exec. v.p., treas., 1964-68, vice chmn. bd. dirs., 1968-71, chmn. exec. com., 1971-77. Chmn. emeritus Energy Conversion Devices Inc. Served to capt. USMCR, 1940-45. Mem. Coral Ridge Country Club, Phi Kappa Psi. Home: 4211 NE 25th Ave Fort Lauderdale FL 33308-5706

LEACH, RICHARD MAXWELL, JR. (MAX LEACH JR.), corporate professional; b. Chillicothe, Tex., June 14, 1934; s. Richard Maxwell and Lelia Booth (Page) L.; m. Wanda Gail Groves, Feb. 4, 1956; children: Richard Clifton, John Christopher, Sandra Gail, Kathy Lynn. BS in Acctg. magna cum laude, Abilene Christian U., 1955. Registered Fin. Planner., CLU. Asst. dir. agys. Am. Founders Ins. Co., Austin, Tex., 1960-62; owner A.F. Ins. Planning Assocs., Temple, 1962-65; v.p. sales Christian Fidelity Life Ins. Co., Waxahachie, 1966-67; exec. v.p. Acad. Computer Tech., Inc., Dallas, 1968-69; pres., chief exec. officer Insta-Search Internat., Inc., 1969-71; prin., chief exec. officer, fin. cons. Leach and Assocs., Albuquerque, 1971—; pres. The Wright Edge, Inc., 1988-90; pres., CEO Action Mktg. Programs, Inc., 1989-92; CEO Vacation Premiums Internat., Inc., 1990-92; pres., CEO ITM Corp., Albuquerque, 1993-98; founder, chmn., CEO Health Maximization Rsch. Studies Inst. Internat., 1999—. Chmn. bd. United Quest Inc., Albuquerque, Hosanna Inc., Albuquerque; real estate broker; commodity futures broker; exec. dir., bd. dirs. New Heart, Inc., Albuquerque, 1975-85; owner Insta-Copy, Albuquerque, 1973-76, Radio Sta. KYLE-FM, Temple, 1963-64. Editor, author Hosanna newspaper, 1973-74. Gen. dir. Here's Life, New Mexico, Albuquerque, 1976; exec. dir. Christians for Cambodia, Albuquerque, 1979-80. Served with U.S. Army, 1955-57. Home: 3308 June St NE Albuquerque NM 87111-5029 Office: 10308 Candelaria NE # 345 Albuquerque NM 87112-1505 *Personal philosophy: Success is doing what God wants you to do when and where He would have you do it.*

LEACH, ROBERT ELLIS, physician, educator; b. Sanford, Maine, Nov. 25, 1931; s. Ellis and Estella (Tucker) L.; m. Laurine Seber, Aug. 20, 1955; children: Cathy, Brian, Michael, Craig, Karen, Diane. AB, Princeton U., 1953; MD, Columbia U., 1957. Diplomate Am. Bd. Orthopedic Surgery (treas. 1986-93). Resident orthopedic surgery U. Minn., 1957-62; orthopedic surgeon Lahey Clinic, Boston, 1964-68, chmn. dept., 1968-70; prof., chmn. dept. Boston U. Med. Sch., 1970—. Head physician U.S. Olympic Team, 1984; chmn. sports medicine coun. U.S. Olympic Com., 1984-93; vice chmn. sports medicine coun. U.S. Tennis Assn., 1988—. Editor-in-chief Am. J. Sports Med.; contbr. articles to profl. jours. Served to lt. comdr. USNR, 1962-64. Am., Brit., Can. Orthopedic Travelling fellow, 1971; Sports Medicine Man of the Yr., 1988; recipient Rovere Career Tchg. award, 1995, Ernst Jokl Sports Medicine award, 2000. Mem. Am. Acad. Orthopedic Surgeons, Continental Orthopedic Soc. (sec. 1966), Am. Orthopedic Assn. (pres. 1994), Am. Orthopedic Soc. Sports Medicine (pres. 1983), Longwood Cricket Club. Home: 40 Rockport Rd Weston MA 02493-1428 Office: 230 Calvary St Waltham MA 02453-8366

LEACH, ROBIN, producer, writer, television host; b. London, Aug. 29, 1941; came to U.S., 1963; s. Douglas Thomas and Violet (Phillips) L. Diploma, Nat. Union Journalists, 1961. Reporter Harrow (Eng.) Observer, 1958-61, Daily Mail, London, 1961-63; mag. pub. GO mag., N.Y.C., 1964-67; show bus. editor The Star, 1970-79; show bus. reporter CNN, 1979-80; reporter Entertainment Tonight, 1980-83; exec. producer Leach Entertainment Enterprises, 1983—. Founder SimplyIrresistible.com, 1999; prin. Screenfriends.comm, 2000, Live From Las Vegas, 2000; host, network spokesman Shop NBC. Author: The Go Rock & Roll Manual, 1966, 2d rev. edit., 1967, Lifestyles of the Rich and Famous, 1983, Healthy Lifestyles, 1995; prodr.: (TV shows) Lifestyles of the Rich and Famous, 1983-96 (Emmy nomination), Runaway with the Rich and Famous, The Rich and Famous Worlds Best, Fame, Fortune & Romance; host: KNBC-TV Year in Review, 1986 (Emmy award), Supermodel of the World, 1986, Home Videos of the Stars, 1991, Nitecap, ABC-TV, Talking Food and Gourmet Getaways for TVFN, 1993-98, Most Expensive Videos MTV, 1998, 99, 2000, 2002. Mem. AFTRA, Screen Actors Guild. Avocations: tennis, gourmet cooking. Office: Leach Entertainment Inc 122 East 42d St Ste #1518 New York NY 10168

LEACH, RONALD GEORGE, educational administration educator; b. Monroe, Mich., Feb. 22, 1938; s. Garnet William and Erma (Erbadine) L.; m. Joy Adeline Moore, Dec. 21, 1956; children— Ronald George, Debra Mabel, Catherine Louise, Shane John. BS in Secondary Edn, Central Mich. U., 1966; MA in L.S. (U.S. Office Edn. fellow 1968-69), U. Mich., 1969; PhD in Higher Edn. Adminstrn, Mich. State U., 1980. Head libr. Ohio State U., Mansfield, 1969-70; asst. dir., then acting dir. libr. Lake Superior State Coll., Sault Ste. Marie, Mich., 1970-76; assoc. dir. librs. Central Mich. U., 1976-80; dean libr. svcs. Ind. State U., Terre Haute, 1980-93, assoc. v.p. info. svcs., dean of librs., 1994-97, prof. higher ednl. adminstrn., 1997—. Prof. edn., mem. accreditation teams North Ctrl. Assn. Author articles in field. Served with N.G., 1955-61. Mem. ALA, INFORMA (steering com. 1990—), Assn. Coll. and Rsch. Librs., Libr. Info. and Tech. Assn., Ind. Libr. Assn., Am. Soc. Info. Sci., Libr. Adminstrn. and Mgmt. Assn. (pres. 1985-86), Online Computer Libr. Ctr. User Council (exec. com. 1986, 88). Home: 4815 E Wolf Tree Ave Terre Haute IN 47805-9414 Office: Ind State U Dept Leadership Admin Found Terre Haute IN 47809-0001

LEACH, RUSSELL, judge; b. Columbus, Ohio, Aug. 1, 1922; s. Charles Albert and Hazel Kirk (Thatcher) L.; m. Helen M. Sharpe, Feb. 17, 1945; children: Susan Sharpe Snyder, Terry Donnell, Ann Dunham Samuelson. BA, Ohio State U., 1946, JD, 1949. Bar: Ohio 1949. Clk. U.S. Geol. Survey, Columbus, 1948-49; reference and teaching asst. Coll. Law, Ohio State U., 1949-51; asst. city atty. City of Columbus, 1951, 53-57, city atty., 1957-63, presiding judge mcpl. ct., 1964-66; ptnr. Bricker & Eckler, 1966-88, chmn. exec. com., 1982-87; judge Ohio Ct. Claims, 1988—2002. Commr., Columbus Met. Housing Authority, 1968-74; chmn. Franklin County Republican Com., 1974-78. Served with AUS, 1942-46, 51-53 Named One of 10 Outstanding Young Men of Columbus, Columbus Jaycees, 1956, 57 Mem. ABA, FBA, Ohio Bar Assn. (coun. of dels. 1970-75), Columbus Bar Assn. (pres. 1973-74, Svc. medal 1993), Am. Judicature Soc., Pres.' Club Ohio State U., Am. Legion, Delta Theta Phi, Chi Phi. Presbyterian. Home: Columbus, Ohio. Died June 15, 2002.

LEACH, TERRY RAY, lawyer, judge; b. Ft. Worth, Apr. 6, 1949; s. Herbert W. and Catherine A. (Flanary) L.; m. Dixie Gail Day, Jan 8, 1972; children: Michelle Rene, David Richard, Jennifer Anne. BS in Indsl. Engring., Tex. Tech U., 1971, JD with honors, 1975. Bar: Tex. 1975, U.S. Dist. Ct. (no. dist.) Tex. 1976. Engr. Southwest Bell Telephone, San Antonio, 1970; assoc. Whitley, Boring & Morrison, Bedford, 1975-76; ptnr. Evans, Leach & Ames, Hurst, 1976-82; sr. ptnr. Leach & Ames PC, 1982—. Judge City of Bedford, 1979-93, City of Lakeside, Tex., 1984—, Halton City, Tex., 1986-94; lectr. real estate law Tarrent County Jr. Coll., Hurst, 1980-81; instr. bus. law Tarrent County Jr. Coll., Hurst, 1991-96. Mem. Hurst Zoning Bd. Adjustment, 1985-88, Hurst Planning and Zoning Commn., 1988-93, Hurst Found. Com., 1986; deacon Frist Bapt. Ch., Colleyville, 1997; bd. dirs. N.E. Tarrant County Community Trust, 1987-93, Hurst-Euless-Bedford Ind. Sch. Dist. Edn. Found., 1995—. Mem. ABA, Tex. Bar Assn., N.E. Tarrant County Bar Assn. (pres. 1980-81), Coll. State Bar Tex., Tex. Bd. Specialization (cert., estate planning and probate law 1989—). Office: Leach & Ames PC 460 Harwood Rd Hurst TX 76054-2939

LEACHMAN, RUSSELL DEWITT, lawyer; b. Amarillo, Tex., Aug. 8, 1965; s. William D. and Alexia (Hall) L.; m. Margaret Feuille, July 8, 1989; children: William Benton, Richard Boone. BA in Polit. Sci., Tex. Tech. U., 1986, JD, 1990. Bar: Tex. 1990, U.S. Dist. Ct. (we. dist.) Tex. 1992, U.S. Dist. Ct. (no. dist.) Tex. 1994, U.S. Dist. Ct. (ea. dist.) Tex. 1998, U.S. Ct. Appeals (5th cir.) 1994; Bd. cert. criminal law, 1996. Asst. dist. atty. 34th Judicial Dist. Tex., El Paso, 1990-92; atty. Leachman & Escobar LLP, 1992-94, Diamond Rash Gordon & Jackson, El Paso, 1994—2001, Mounce, Green, Myers, Safi & Galatzan, P.C., El Paso, 2001—. Dir. El Paso Young Lawyers Assn. Mock Trial Competition, El Paso, 1990-95; mem. Ducks Unltd. Area Com., El Paso, 1991—, area chmn., 1999-2000, dist. chmn., 2001—. Mem. Lodge 130 (mason), Phi Gamma Delta, Delta Theta Phi, Delta Phi Epsilon, Phi Rho Pi, Pi Sigma Alpha. Methodist. Office: Mounce Green et al PO Box 1977 El Paso TX 79950-1977 E-mail: Leachman@mgmsg.com.

LEACHTENAUER, JON CLARK, optical scientist; b. Kingston, N.Y., Feb. 25, 1936; s. Clark and Ruby Mae L.; m. Christine Catherine Carr, Aug. 24, 1957 (div. 1975); children: Caroline, Jon, Paul; m. Mary Ellen Kevilly, Jan. 14, 1978; 1 child, Amy. AB in Geology, Syracuse U., 1957, MS in Geology, 1959. Rsch. scientist Aero Svc. Corp., Phila., 1961-65; dept. mgr. Photics Rsch., Montgomeryville, Pa., 1965-68; rsch. scientist Boeing Co., Kent, Wash., 1968-78; rsch. mgr. ERIM Internat., Arlington, Va., 1978-99; pres. J/M Leachtenauer Assoc. Inc., 1999—. Author: (with R. Driggers) Surveillance and Reconnaissance Imaging Systems: Modeling and Performance Prediction, 2001; contbr. chpt. to book: Corona Between the Sun and the Earth, 1997, also articles to sci. jours. Pres. PTA, Annandale, Va., 1989-91, treas., 1995-97; divsn. coord. WAGS Soccer Tournament, Springfield, Va., 1993-95. 1st lt. U.S. Army, 1959-61. Mem. Soc. Info. Display, Human Factors Soc., Am. Soc. Photogrammetry and Remote Sensing, Soc. Motion Picture and TV Engrs., Soc. Photog. Inst. Engring., Soc. Imaging Sci. and Tech., Sigma Xi. Avocations: photography, lutherie, model railroading. E-mail: jcleachtr@aol.com.

LEADBETTER, MARK RENTON, JR. orthopedic surgeon; b. Phila., Nov. 7, 1944; s. Mark Renton and Ruth (Protzeller) L.; m. Letitia Ashby, July 28, 1973 (div. June 1990); m. Jan Saker, 1991. BA, Gettysburg Coll., 1967; MSc in Hygiene, U. Pitts., 1970; MD, Temple U., 1974. Cert. Am. Bd. Ind. Med. Examiners. Surg. intern Univ. Hosps., Boston, 1974-75, resident in surgery, 1975-76; emergency room physician Sturdy Meml. Hosp., Attleboro, Mass., 1976-78; resident in orthopaedics U. Pitts., 1978-81; orthopaedic physician Rockingham Meml. Hosp., Harrisonburg, Va., 1981-82, courtesy staff, 1982—; pvt. practice, Staunton, 1982—; mem. active staff King's Daus. Hosp., 1982—. Active staff Samaritan Hosp., Moses Lake, Wash.; courtesy staff Columbia Basin Hosp., Ephrata, Wash.; med. dir. Ind. Med. Examiners; physician reviewer Physician Rev. Network; orthopaedic surgeon reviewer Physicians Rev. Network. Contbr. articles to med. jours.; patentee safety syringes, safety cannulas, designer of medecal equipment. Fellow: Am. Acad. Disability Evaluating Physicians; mem.: AMA, County Med. Soc., So. Orthopaedic Assn., So. Med. Assn., Am. Bd. Ind. Med. Examiners, Am. Coll. Sports Medicine, Am. Coll. Occupl. and Environ. Medicine, Nat. Futures Assn. (assoc.). Republican. Avocations: flying, skiing, raising bird dogs. Home: 3233 Centralia Alpha Rd Onalaska WA 98570-9610

LEADER, CHRISTOPHER ROBERT, manufacturing executive; b. South Bend, Ind. s. Robert A. and Dorothy R. L.; m. Linda A. Hoyt; three children. BS in Mech. Engring., U. Notre Dame, 1981; MBA, U. Mich., 1991. Lt. USN, navigator, dept. head USS England (CG-22), San Diego (home port), 1981-85; statis. process control analyst GM, Saginaw, Mich., 1985-87, sr. quality engr., 1987-91; prodn. supt. Ford Motor Co., Avon Lake, Ohio, 1991-93, vehicle evaluation mgr., 1993-94, prodn. mgr., area mgr., 1994; v.p. ops., corp. officer Trek USA Bicycle Corp., Waterloo, Wis., 1994-96, Skyline Corp., Elkhart, Ind., 1997—. Co-author: Quality Engineering Jour., 1989. Lt. USN, 1981-85. Mem. Am. Soc. Quality (sr. mem., cert. quality engr.). Office: Skyline Corp 2520 By Pass Rd Elkhart IN 46515 E-mail: cleader@skylinecorp.com.

LEADER, JOYCE E. ambassador; BA, Denison U, 1964; MA, U. Chgo., 1969; MS, Columbia U Sch of Journalism, 1974. Joined U.S. Fgn. Svc., 1982, dep. chief of mission Burkina Faso, Nigeria; political officer U.S. Fgn Svc., Rwanda; prin. officer U.S. Fgn. Svc., Marseille, counselor Sr. Fgn. Svc., U.S. ambassador to Republic of Guinea, 1999-00. E-mail: leaderje@yahoo.com.

LEADER, ROBERT JOHN, lawyer; b. Syracuse, N.Y., Oct. 14, 1933; s. Henry John and Dorothy Alberta (Schad) L.; m. Nancy Bruce, Sept. 23, 1960; children: Henry, William, Catherine, Thomas, Edward. AB, Cornell U., 1956; JD, Syracuse U., 1962. Bar: N.Y. 1963. Assoc. Ferris, Hughes, Dorrance & Groben, Utica, N.Y., 1962-64; ptnr. Cole Leader & Elmer, Gouverneur, 1964-66, Case & Leader, Gouverneur, 1966—. Sec. North Country Hosps. Inc., 1972— ; atty. Village of Hermon (N.Y.), 1968— , Town of Gouverneur, 1967-94, Town of Pitcairn (N.Y.), 1974— , Town of Edwards, 1974— , Town of Rossie, 1985—, Town of Fowler, 1978—; corp. counsel Village of Gouverneur, 1973— ; counsel Gouverneur Ctrl. Sch. Dist., 1980—; bd. dirs. Gouverneur Savs. and Loan. Trustee Edward John Noble Hosp., Gouverneur, 1972—, Gouverneur Libr., 1973-83, Gouverneur Nursing Home Co., Inc., 1972—, past pres., 1979-81, past chmn. bd. trustees, 1979-81; Republican chmn. Town and Village of Gouverneur, 1969-72; del. N.Y. State Jud. conv., 1981—. Served to capt. USAF, 1956-59. Mem. Rotary (pres. 1988-89). Roman Catholic. Home: 27 Howard St Gouverneur NY 13642-1220 Office: 107 E Main St Gouverneur NY 13642-1408

LEAF, ALEXANDER, physician, educator; b. Yokohama, Japan, Apr. 10, 1920; arrived in U.S., 1922, naturalized, 1936; s. Aaron L. and Dora (Hural) Leaf; m. Barbara Louise Kincaid, Oct. 1943; children: Caroline Joan, Rebecca Louise, Tamara Jean. BS, U. Wash., 1940; MD, U. Mich., 1943; MA, Harvard, 1961. Intern Mass. Gen. Hosp., Boston, 1943—44, mem. staff, 1949—, physician-in-chief, 1966—81; resident Mayo Found., Rochester, Minn., 1944—45; rsch. fellow U. Mich., 1947—49; practice internal medicine Boston, 1949—90; faculty Med. Sch., Harvard, 1949—66, Jackson prof. clin. medicine, 1966—81, Ridley Watts prof. preventive medicine, 1980—90, chmn. dept. preventive medicine and clin. epidemiology, 1980—90, Jackson prof. clin. medicine emeritus, 1990—; Disting. physician VA Medical Ctr. Brockton/W. Roxbury Hosps., Boston, 1992—97. Capt. M.C. U.S. Army, 1945—46. Recipient Outstanding Achievement award, U. Minn., 1964; fellow Vis. fellow, Balliol Coll., Eng., 1971—72, Guggenheim, 1971—72. Master: ACP; fellow: Am. Acad. Arts and Scis.; mem.: NAS, Internat. Soc. Nephrology (A.M. Richards award 1997), Assn. Am. Physicians (Kober medal 1995), Biophys. Soc., Am. Physiol. Soc., Am. Soc. Clin. Investigation (past pres.), Inst. Medicine. Home: 5 Sussex Rd Winchester MA 01890-3846 Office: Mass Gen Hosp Bldg 149 13th St Charlestown MA 02129 E-mail: aleaf@parners.org.

LEAF, HOWARD WESTLEY, retired air force officer, military official; b. Menominee, Mich., Sept. 22, 1923; s. Joseph Conrad and Hilda Eugene (Lavoy) L.; m. Madonna Anne; children: Mary Elizabeth, Timothy M., Barbara Anne, Anne Marie Moore, Thomas M., James D. BS, Colo. Sch. Mines, 1950; MS, St. Louis U., 1955; grad., Command and Staff Coll., 1961, Indsl. Coll. Armed Forces, 1969. Commd. 2d lt. U.S. Air Force, 1951, advanced through grades to lt. gen., 1980, ret., 1985; aviation cadet, 1950-51; jet pilot Korea, 1952-53; test pilot, 1955-60; geophysicist, 1961-64; ops. officer (49th Tactical Fighter Wing), Europe, 1965; squadron comdr. S.E. Asia, 1966; staff officer (Hdqrs. USAF), 1966-68, 69-71; wing comdr. 1st and 366th Tactical Fighter Wings, 1971-74; dep. chief staff for requirements Tactical Air Command, 1974-76; comdr. Air Force Test and Evaluation Ctr., Kirtland AFB, N.Mex., 1976-80; insp. gen. U.S. Air Force, Washington, 1980-83, asst. vice chief of staff, 1983-85; sr. v.p. BDM Internat. Corp., McLean, Va., 1984-91; dir. test and evaluation Hdqrs. USAF The Pentagon, Washington, 1992—. Mem. Air Force Sci. Adv. Bd. Decorated D.S.M., Silver Star with one oak leaf cluster, Legion of Merit, D.F.C.; recipient Eugene M. Zuckert Mgmt. Award, 1978, Disting. Achievement award Colo. Sch. Mines, 1982, Exceptional Svc. award USAF, 1997. Mem. Internat. Test and Evaluation Assn. (sr. adv. bd., Allen R. Mattews Award, 1994). Presbyterian. Home: 16002 Dr Bowen Rd Brandywine MD 20613 Office: Hdqs USAF TE 4E-995 The Pentagon Washington DC 20330-0001

LEAF, JOHN BRIAN, art instructor, elementary education educator; b. South Bend, Ind., July 27, 1963; s. William Arthur and Betty Lou (Gannon) L.; m. Ana Teresa Palerm Leaf, Nov. 1m 1985; children: Zane Brien, Eoin Benjamin, Shanah Bernadette. BA in Art Edn., Ctrl. State U., Edmond, Okla., 1986; MEd, U. Ctrl. Okla., Edmond, 1994. Tchr. Victor Schs., Victorville, Calif., 1987-89; art instr. Putnam City Schs., Oklahoma City, 1989-92, Oklahoma City Pub. Schs., 1992-93, Norman (Okla.) Pub. Schs., 1993-1998; edn. instr. Langston U., Tinker AFB Midwest City, Okla., 1994-1995; art instr. Okla. City pub. sch., 1998-2000, Acad. dist. 20, Colorado Springs, Colo., 2000—. Named Most Enthusiastic Tchr. Parkview Elem. Faculty, Victorville, Calif., 1988, Tchr. Who Cares, 1992, Above and Beyond, 1993 U.S. Grant Prin., Okla. Secondary Art Eduacator of the Yr., Okla. Art Edn. Assoc., 1997; grantee Fencing Program Putnam City Found., Oklahoma City, 1991, Advanced Placement Art, Okla. State Dept. Edn., 2000. Mem. Nat. Art Edn. Assn. Republican. Avocations: wrestling, coaching, painting, bridge, basketball. Home: 4116 Tumbleweed Dr Colorado Springs CO 80918 E-mail: leaf-familys@juno.com.

LEAF, PAUL, producer, director, writer; b. N.Y.C., May 2, 1929; s. Manuel and Anna (Dardick) L.; m. Nydia Ellis, Oct. 22, 1955 (div. 1990); children: Jonathan, Alexandra, Ellen; m. Christine Hardy, Dec. 15, 1999. BA in Drama with honors, CCNY, 1952. Pres. Sea Gate Co. Dir., prodr.: 17 Broadway prodns., including The Subject Was Roses, 1964 (Pulitzer prize, 1964), films include: Judge Horton and the Scottsboro Boys, 1976 (Peabody award), Desperate Characters, 1972, Hail to the Chief, 1973, Sister Aimee, 1977, Every Man a King, 1977, Top Secret, 1979, God, Sex and Apple Pie, 1998, TV prodns. include Sgt. Matlovich vs. the U.S. Air Force, 1978 (Best Feature Austin Film Fesival, Audience Favorite Ariz. Internat. Film Festival, Best Comedy Marco Island Film Festival, Best Dir. Ariz. Film Festival); author: Comrades, 1987, Red, Right, Returning, 1989. Founder, chmn. Santa Monica Arts Commn., Santa Monica Arts Found.; founder, cons., bd. dirs. Santa Monica Coll. Art, Design and Architecture, 1990—; mem. grants panel Nat. Endowment for the Arts, 1993, Nat. Endowment for the Humanities, 1994. With U.S. Army, 1952-54. Decorated Meritorious Service medal; recipient 20 internat. festival and profl. awards, including Venice, 1967, London, 1967, 68, 69, 98-99, N.Y., 1967, 68, 69, Berlin, 1972, Austin, Tucson, N.Y., San Diego film festivals. Mem. Dirs. Guild Am., Writers Guild Am. Home: 2800 Neilson Way Santa Monica CA 90405-4025 E-mail: sea.gate@verizon.net.

LEAF, ROBERT JAY, dental insurance consultant; b. Mt. Vernon, N.Y., July 27, 1944; s. Jules William and Evelyn (Schneider) L.; m. Jeanette Ann Benjamin, June 17, 1973; children: Jeremy Robert, David Evan. DMD, Harvard U., 1969. Pres. Universal Profl. Ctrs., N.Y.C., 1971-74; dentist in pvt. practice, 1973-80; pres. Am. Dental Examiners, Inc., 1978—; chmn. Better Benefits, Inc., 1990—. Pres., founder LeafRe Reins. Co., Ariz., 1993—; founder Dental Health Alliance, 1994, pres. 1994-96; cons. Guardian Life Ins. Co., N.Y.C., 1979, Prin. Life Ins. Co., Iowa, 1981, 93, Mass. Mut. Life Ins. Co., 1983, 94, Equitable, N.Y., 1985, Empire Blue Cross, 1986, Prudential, N.J., 1987, Gen. Mills, Minn., 1988, Aetna, Conn., 1989, Am. Airlines, Tex., 1990, Protective Life Ins. Co., Alabama, 1991, 96, 99, Gen. Am. Life Ins. Co., 1992, 94, Blue Cross/Blue Shield, R.I., 1993, Fortis Benefits Ins. Co., Mo., 1988, 93, Chubb Life Ins. Co. Am., N.H., 1993, Jefferson Pilot Life, 1994, Trustmark Life, 1994, Delta Dental Minn., 1994, Healthsource Provident Life Inst. Co., 1996, Delta Dental California, 1997, Shenandoah Life Ins. Co., 1997, WalMart, 1999, Protective Life, 1999, Boston Mut., 2000, Hanover Life Reins., 2000, TransAm. and Delta Dental, 2001, 2002; lectr. at nat. confs. on dental ins., vol. dental ins., and managed dental care, group officers round table, 1985 Author: The Dental Logic System, 1984, The Dental Learning System, 1987; also articles; devel. vol. dental ins. plan. Bd. dirs. Jewish Community Ctr., Harrison, N.Y., 1992. Mem. ADA, Dental Soc. State of N.Y., First Dist. Dental Soc., Acad. Gen. Dentistry, Am. Assn. Dental Cons., Am. Soc. for Preventive Dentistry. Avocations: sailing, skiing, reading. Office: Am Dental Examiners Inc 224 West 35th St 11th Fl New York NY 10001-2507 E-mail: robert@betterbenefits.com.

LEAF, ROBERT STEPHEN, public relations executive; b. N.Y.C., Aug. 9, 1931; s. Nathan and Anne (Feinman) L.; m. Adele Ornstein, June 8, 1958; 1 child, Stuart Nathan. BJ, U. Mo., Columbia, 1952; MA, U. Mo, Columbia, 1954. Account exec. Herbert Kaufman, N.Y.C., 1956-57; various positions Marsteller Orgn., 1957-65; v.p., gen. mgr. Marsteller Internat., Brussels, 1965-68, v.p. Europe, 1968-70; pres. Burson-Marsteller Internat. and Marsteller Internat., London, 1970-81; chmn. Burson-Marsteller Internat., 1985-97, Robert S. Leaf Cons., (Eng.), Eng.; dir. Burson-Marsteller Europe, Burson-Marsteller S.A., (France). Contbr. articles to profl. jours. Mem. Inst. Pub. Relations Eng., Pub. Relations Consultancy Assn. (London), Fgn. Press Assn., Pub. Relations Soc. Am., Hurlingham Club, Alpha Pi Zeta, Kappa Tau Alpha Clubs: Hurlingham (London). Home: 3 Fursecroft George St London W1H 5LF England Office: Robert S Leaf Cons Ltd 44 Grosvener Hill London W1K 3QL England E-mail: bob_leaf@eu.bm.com.

LEAFGREEN, LISA DIANE, education coordinator; b. Cheyenne, Wyo., Nov. 13, 1964; d. Lavern Edward and Errolene Ruth (Clark) L. BS, U. Wyo., 1987. Co-mgr. The Limited, Denver, 1987-89; student svcs. coord. Colo. Free U., 1989-91, tchr. coord., 1991-92; edn. coord. Arvada (Colo.) Cen. for Arts & Humanities, 1992—. Office: Arvada Ctr for Arts & Humanities 6901 Wadsworth Blvd Arvada CO 80003-3448

LEAGUE, VINCENTE CONRAD, management company executive; b. Indpls., June 28, 1947; s. Jonah Bemouth and Thelma Ruth (Pride) L.; student Butler U., 1965-68; B.A. in Pub. Adminstrn., Chgo. State U., 1976. Dir. in charge outreach Soul Ark Youth ministry, Indpls., 1970-71; project dir. Community Orgn. Program, Eastside Indpls., 1971-72; asst. dir. Region 5 Alcohol & Drug Abuse Tng. Center, Chgo., 1972-78; project dir. Western Tng. and Devel. Center, Oakland, 1978— ; pres. A.H. Tng. & Devel. Systems, Inc., Oakland, Calif., 1981— ; prin. Calif. Wine Country, Napa, Calif., 1981-83; dir. A.H. Tng. & Devel., 1983— ; cons. numerous orgns. Bd. dirs. Person Edn.-Devel. Edn., Mpls., 1981— ; chmn. bd. dirs. Grantsmanship Center, Los Angeles, 1974-81. Mem. Am. Soc. Tng. and Devel., Nat. Mgmt. Assn. (bd. dirs. 1983-84), Nat. Assn. Prevention Profls. (pres., co-founder Eugene Oreg., co-conv. coordinator 3d ann. conv. 1980). Co-editor Prevention Action Manual, 1986; author: Developing Successful Programs, 1978, rev. edit., 1983; Funding Handbook, 1981; Management: A Guide for Prevention Programs, 1982; Inside Napa Valley, 1982. Home: 1448 Madison St Apt 404 Oakland CA 94612-4309 Office: 100 Webster St Ste 104 Oakland CA 94607-3724

LEAHEY, ERIN ELIZABETH, sociologist, educator; b. Chgo., Nov. 16, 1969; d. Burke and Barbara Leahey. BA, Wellesley Coll., 1992; MA, U. Mass., 1997; PhD, U. N.C., 2002. Asst. English tchr., Japan, 1992—94; asst. prof. sociology U. Ariz., Tucson, 2002—. Mem.: Am. Sociol. Assn.

LEAHEY, MILES CARY, economist; b. Washington, Sept. 14, 1952; s. Thomas Francis and Eva Smith (Hardy) L.; m. Patricia C. Mosser, Aug. 1, 1987. AB with honors, Clark U., 1974; MA, U. Pa., 1977, PhD, 1978. Fiscal economist Office of Mgmt. and Budget, Washington, 1978-80; sr. economist DRI, Lexington, Mass., 1980-83; sr. v.p., sr. economist Shearson Lehman Bros., N.Y.C., 1983-88; dir. econ. staff GM, 1988-91; chief U.S. fin. markets economist Lehman Bros., 1991-97; chief U.S. economist High Frequency Econ., Valhalla, N.Y., 1997-98; mng. dir., sr. U.S. economist Primark Decision Econs., N.Y.C., 1998-2000; dir., sr. U.S. economist Deutsche Bank, 2000—. Lectr. U. Pa., 1977, Swarthmore (Pa.) Coll., 1978, Boston U., 1983. Author: Government and Capital Formation, 1979; contbr. articles to profl. jours. Mem. Am. Econs. Assn., Nat. Assn. Bus. Economists, Columbia Golf Club, Blue Hill Troupe (N.Y.C.). Democrat. Avocations: theatre, opera, golf. Home: 340 Riverside Dr Apt 7C New York NY 10025-3436 Office: Deutsche Bank 12th Fl 31 W 52d St New York NY 10019

LEAHY, DANIEL F. federal agency administrator; b. Phila., 1947; B Econs., LaSalle U., 1969. With U.S. Internat. Trade Commn., 1974-76, analyst Office of Industries, investigator Office of Investigations, 1977-84, exec. asst. to chair, 1984-88; dep. dir. for policy coordination Office of U.S. Trade Rep., Exec. Office of Pres., 1988-92, dep. dir. Office Exec. and Internat. Liaison, 1992-96; dir. Office of External Rels. U.S. Internat. Trade Commn., Washington, 1996—. With USAF, 1970-74. Office: US Internat Trade Commn Office of External Rels 500 E St SW Washington DC 20436-0001 E-mail: dleahy@usitc.gov.

LEAHY, KEVIN SEAN, energy company strategist; b. Logansport, Ind., Apr. 14, 1958; m. Joyce L. Steiner, 1990. BS in Mech. Engrnig., Purdue U., 1980; MBA, Ind. U., 1987; MPA, Harvard U., 1998. Mech. engr. Commonwealth Edison, Chgo., 1981—82; engr., vol. U.S. Peace Corps, Honduras, 1982—84, assoc. dir. microenterprise devel. Albania, 1993—95; internat. bus. devel. analyst Cummins Engine Co., Columbus, Ind., 1987—89, human rels. mgr., 1989—92; chief strategy officer internat. Cinergy Corp., Cin., 1998—2000, spl. asst. to the CEO, 2000—02, mng. dir. mktg. fundamentals fro energy merchants, 2002—. Cons. World Bank, Washington, 1996. Vocalist Plymouth Music Series Chorus, Mpls., 1996-97. Bd. mem. First Call for Help, Columbus, 1992. Mem. World Affairs Coun. Office: Cinergy Corp 105 E 4th St 30 ATII Cincinnati OH 45202-4015 Fax: 513-287-2037. E-mail: leastein@fuse.net.

LEAHY, LAWRENCE MARSHALL, health care administrator, marketing consultant; b. Astoria, N.Y., Oct. 15, 1949; s. Thomas Joseph and Fannie Marie (Jones) L.; m. Mary Joan Spratt, June 10, 1978; children: Larry, Erin. BS, U. Tenn., 1972; MA, Ball State, 1979; M in Health Care Adminstrn., Baylor U., 1984. Cert. homecare/hospice exec. Med. platoon leader 8th Med. Bn., Mannheim, Germany, 1972-74, co. comdr. Germany, 1974-76; health care adminstr. Walter Reed Army Med. Ctr., Washington, 1976-80; comptroller Dept. of the Army, 1980-82; info. mgr. Darnall Community Hosp., Killeen,

Tex., 1984-86; asst. prof. Acad. Health Scis., San Antonio, 1986-90; exec. officer Seoul (Korea) Community Hosp., 1990-91; fin. analyst Health Svc. Command, San Antonio, 1991-92; exec. dir. Hospice South Tex., 1992-93; adminstr. Hospice New Braunfels, Tex., 1993-94; dir. program integrity Ruth Cons. and Assocs., Victoria, 1994—. Cons. Tex. A&M U., College Station, 1985; assoc. faculty U. Tex., San Antonio, 1987-88; adj. faculty Trinity U., San Antonio, 1989; asst. prof. Baylor U., Waco, Tex., 1989-90. Author: (with others) Health Planning A Primer, 1990. Explorer adv. Boy Scouts of Am., Washington, 1976-79, Killeen, 1984-85; handicapped scouting com. mem. Nat. Capital Area Com. on Handicapped Scouting, Bethesda, Md., 1978-82; bd. mem. Blue Bonnet Home, Yoakum, Tex., 1989-90. Lt. Col. U.S. Army, 1972-92, ret. Names Outstanding Explorer Adv. Boy Scouts of Am., Bethesda, 1979. Mem. Am. Coll. Healthcare Execs (diplomate 1985-97, treas. S. Tex. chpt. 1988-90), Coun. Hospice Profls., Tex. Assn. for Home Care (nominating com. 1996-99), Nat. Assn. for Home Care (cert. home care hospice exec. 1996—, chair cert. com. 1999—, mem. com. 1997—). Republican. Roman Catholic. Avocations: rugby, weight lifting, hash running. Home: 222 Thiele Rd Yoakum TX 77995-2130

LEAHY, MICHAEL JOSEPH, newspaper editor; b. Chgo., Feb. 24, 1939; s. Joseph Michael and Elizabeth Catherine (Keefe) L.; m. Harriet Smith Friday, Sept. 18, 1971; children: Christine Elizabeth, Thomas Joseph, Christopher Michael. AB, Georgetown U., 1961; MS in Journalism, Columbia U., 1966. From copy boy, news clk., copy editor to editor L.I. Weekly N.Y. Times, N.Y.C., 1961-77, editor Conn. Weekly, 1977-81, travel editor, 1982-86, editor arts & leisure sect., 1986-90, dep. editor The Week in Review, 1990-92, real estate editor, 1992—. Editor: If You're Thinking of Living In...All About 115 Great Neighborhoods In & Around New York, (with A.M. Rosenthal, A. Gelb and N. Kerr) The Sophisticated Traveler series. Bd. advisors Georgetown Coll., 1990-96; mem. edn. com. St. David's Sch., 1991-93. 1st lt. U.S. Army, 1961-64. Pulitzer Traveling fellow Columbia U., 1967 Mem. Georgetown Libr. Assocs. (trustee 1981-94, 97—), Columbia Journalism Alumni (pres. 1981-83), Century Assn. Roman Catholic. Office: NY Times Co 229 W 43rd St New York NY 10036-3959

LEAHY, PATRICK JOSEPH, senator; b. Montpelier, Vt., Mar. 31, 1940; s. Howard and Alba (Zambon) L.; m. Marcelle Pomerleau, Aug. 25, 1962; children: Kevin, Alicia, Mark. BA, St. Michael's Coll., Vt., 1961; JD, Georgetown U., 1964. Bar: Vt. 1964, D.C. 1979, U.S. Ct. Appeals (2d cir.) 1966, Vt. Fed. Dist. Ct. 1965, U.S. Supreme Ct. 1968. State's atty., Chittenden County, Vt., 1966-75; U.S. senator from Vt., 1975—; ranking minority mem. com. on the judiciary; mem. com. on agr., nutrition and forestry; mem. appropriations com. Mem. World Hunger bd.; bd. visitors U.S. Mil. Acad. West Point, Gallaudet Coll., Nat. Coll. Deaf, Washington. Recipient 1st Amendment award Soc. Profl. Journalists, John Peter and Anna Catherine Zenger award for outstanding contributions in support of press freedom & the people's right to know, 1999. Mem. Nat. Dist. Attys. Assn. (v.p. 1971-74) Office: US Senate 433 Russell Senate Ofc Washington DC 20510-0001*

LEAHY, T. LIAM, business development, technology investor; b. Camp Legeunne, N.C., Apr. 15, 1952; s. Thomas James and Margaret May (Munnelly) L.; m. Shannon Kelly Brooks, Apr. 21, 1990. BS, St. Louis U., 1974, MA, 1975. V.p. sales Cablecom Inc., Chgo., 1976-80, Kaye Advt., N.Y.C., 1980-82; group pubr. Jour. Graphics Pub., 1983-85; pres., gen. mgr. Generation Dynamics, 1985-86; pres., dir. Hightechbiz.com, 1982—, Los Angeles, Calif., 1982—; assoc. Am Coun. of Execs. Assoc., Glendale, 1991-95; pres. Global Area Network, 2001—. Bd. dirs. Cons. Assn.; dir. RBAC, 1998—2000, Dental Cosmetic Centers of Am., Global Area Network. Contbr. articles to profl. jours. Fellow Success Mgmt. Ctrs. (sr.); mem. Turnaround Mgmt. Assn., L.A. C. of C. Avocations: music, film. Office: Hightechbiz.com 4209 Santa Monica Blvd Ste 201 Los Angeles CA 90029-3027

LEAHY, THOMAS MELVIN, JR. writer; b. Denison, Iowa, Nov. 2, 1923; s. Thomas Melvin and Marie Christiansen Leahy; m. Maudie Lovella Schoolcraft, Oct. 16, 1946; children: Michal Suzanne, Thomas Melvin, Robert Marcus. BA in English and Econs., U. N.Mex., 1960; MA in Journalism and Comm., U. Fla., 1972. Commd. U.S. Army, 1950, advanced through grades to lt. col., ret., 1970; prof. U. Fla., Gainesville, 1973—88. Author: (novels) Sharron's Song, 2000, Blood Red Sand, 2001. Mem.: Ret. Officers Assn., Gator City Kiwanis (pres. 1993—94), Phi Kappa Phi. Lutheran. Avocation: golf. Home: 10 NW 88 Ter Gainesville FL 32607

LEAHY, WILLIAM P. academic administrator, educator; b. Omaha, July 16, 1948; s. Edward and Alice (McGinnis) L. Student, Creighton U., 1966-67, Jesuit Coll., 1967-70; BA in Philosophy, St. Louis U., 1972, MA in U.S. History, 1975; MDiv in Theology, Jesuit Sch. Theology, Berkeley, Calif., 1978, STM in Hist. Theology, 1980; PhD in U.S. History, Stanford U., 1986. Ordained priest Roman Cath. Ch., 1978. Tchr. Campion Jesuit H.S., Prairie du Chien, Wis., 1973-75; tchg. asst. Stanford U., 1981; instr. history Marquette U., Milw., 1985-86, asst. prof., 1986-91, acting asst. chmn., 1988-90, assoc. prof. history, exec. v.p., 1991-96; pres. Boston Coll., Chestnut Hill, Mass., 1996—. Author: Adapting to America: Catholics, Jesuits and Higher Education in the Twentieth Century, 1991; contbr. articles to profl. jours. Bd. trustees Boston Coll., Loyola U., Chgo., Sta. WGBH; bd. dirs. Weston Jesuit Sch. Theology. Mem. Assn. Ind. Colls. and Univs., Univs. Mass. (mem. exec. com.), Am. Cath. Hist. Soc., History Edn. Soc., Orgns. Am. Historians. Office: Boston College Office of the President 18 Old Colony Road Chestnut Hill MA 02467 E-mail: leahy@bc.edu.*

LEAK, BRUCE, information technology executive; BSEE, MSEE, Stanford U. Creator, engrng. team leader, QuickTime Apple Computer; various sr. mgmt. and engrng. pos. Rocket Science Games and Gen. Magic, Inc.; co-founder WebTV Networks, Inc.; pres. WebTV Networks, Inc., of Microsoft, Redmond, Wash., 1997—. Achievements include patents for in tech. field; creator Apple's 32-bit QuickDraw. Office: Microsoft One Microsoft Way Redmond WA 98052-6399*

LEAK, JESSIE ARONOW, anesthesiologist; b. Beaumont, Tex., May 19, 1957; MD, U. Tex. Health Sci. Ctr., 1984. Diplomate Am. Bd. Anesthesiology. Resident in anesthesiology Med. U. S.C., Charleston, 1984-87, fellow in obstet. anesthesiology, pain mgmt., 1987-88; staff anesthesiologist Cape Fear Valley Med. Ctr., Fayetteville, N.C., 1989-98, Highsmith-Rainey Meml. Hosp., Fayetteville, 1988-98; pvt. practice Valley Anesthesia, P.A., 1988-90; founding ptnr., sec. bd. dirs. Cumberland Anesthesia Assocs., P.A., 1990-98; asst. prof. anesthesiology U. N.C., Chapel Hill, 1989-94; assoc. prof. divsn. anesthesia, symptom control and palliative care U. Tex. M.D. Anderson Cancer Ctr., Houston, 1998—. Contbr. articles to profl. jours. Active Fayetteville Area C. of C., 1988-98, Fayetteville Area Econ. Devel. Corp., 1996-98. Recipient 1st prize award Am. Soc. Anesthesiologists Art Exhbn., 1999, 2000. Mem. AMA, Am. Soc. Anesthesiologists, So. Med. Assn., N.C. Med. Soc., N.C. Soc. Anesthesiology (past pres.), Tex. Soc. Anesthesiologists, Tex. Med. Assn. Office: U Tex MD Anderson Cancer Ctr Divsn Anesthesiology 1515 Holcombe Blvd # 42 Houston TX 77030-4009 E-mail: jleak@mdanderson.org.

LEAK, NANCY MARIE, artist; b. Takoma Park, Md., Nov. 24, 1931; d. George Morton and Ella (Oberholtzer) Hinkson; m. Thomas Clayton Leak Jr., Dec. 30, 1950; children: Suzanne M. Street, Sharon Leak-Hayden, Stephen, Scott. Grad. h.s., Washington. Co-illustrator: The Kissing Hand, 1993; exhbns. include Olney Art Assn., Internat. Exhbn. of the Miniature, Fla., Ga., Washington, N.J., Cider Painters Am. Nat. Exhbn., Hunterdon Art Ctr., N.J., Sumner Mus., Washington, Gurmukhs Gallery, Aspen Hill, Md., Nev. Miniature Art Soc., Worldwide Miniature Exhbn., Australia, 2000, Hoffberger Gallery, Balt., Ocean City (Md.) Art League, Rockville (Md.) Art League, Md. Printmakers, Worldwide Miniature Exhbn., London, 1996, Md. Ho. of Dels., Annapolis, NIH, Bethesda, Md., Johns Hopkins Space Telescope Sci. Inst., Balt., Del Bello Gallery, Ont., Can., Rockville Art League, Pinneberg, Germany, Gov's. Mansion, Annapolis, 1999, George Mason U. Art Gallery, Arlington, Va., 2000; participated in numerous juried or invitational exhbns. Recipient numerous awards for art. Mem.: Sr. Artists Alliance, Am. Art League, Rockville ARts Place, Miniature Artists Am., Cider Painters Am., Olney Art Assn., Rockville Art League, Miniature Art Soc. Fla., Sculptors & Gravers Soc. Washington, Miniature Painters, Md. Printmakers Assn., Nat. League Am. Pen Women. Democrat. Methodist. Avocations: crafts, reading, designing notecards, genealogy, photography.

LEAK, ROBERT EDWARDS, economic development consultant; b. Charlotte, N.C., Sept. 15, 1934; s. James Pickett and Cornelia (Edwards) L.; m. Martha Councill, Aug. 25, 1956; children: Robert E., James Councill. BS, Duke U., 1956; MS, U. Tenn., 1957. With Pan Am. Petroleum Co., Lafayette, La., 1957-59, Allied Securities Corp., Raleigh, N.C., 1961-62, Cameron Brown Mortgage Co., Raleigh and Charlotte, 1962-64; with N.C. Dept. Natural and Econ. Resources, Raleigh, 1959-61, 64-76, dir. div. econ. devel., until 1976; dir. S.C. State Devel. Bd., Columbia, 1976-84; pres. Research Triangle Park Found., N.C., 1984-88; prin. Leak-Goforth Co., LLC, Raleigh, 1988—. Mem. U.S. Dept. Commerce Small Bus. Adv. Council, vice-chmn. Dist. Export Council; leader industry organized govt. approved trade and indsl. devel. missions to, Can., Europe, S.Am., Australia, Far East. Bd. dirs. Raleigh YMCA, S.C. Tech. and Comprehensive Edn., N.C. Symphony Fedn., Duke Alumni Assn., Carolina Ballet; chmn. bd. dirs. Wake Tech. C.C. Found.; adv. bd. Duke Hosp.; sr. warden vestry Christ Episcopal Ch. Mem. Am. Indsl. Devel. Coun. (past pres.), Nat. Assn. State Devel. Agys. (past pres.), Raleigh Rotary Club (bd. dirs.). Episcopalian. Home: 3301 Landor Rd Raleigh NC 27609-7012 Office: 4601 Six Forks Rd Ste 500 Raleigh NC 27609

LEAKE, BRENDA GAIL, enterostomal therapist nurse practitioner; b. Harriman, Tenn., Aug. 5, 1950; d. James Frank and Pauline Ruby (McGuffey) Judd; m. Lee Leake, Aug. 1, 1970 (div. Apr. 1974). AS in Nursing, U. Nev., Las Vegas, 1971, BN, 1986; cert. enterostomal therapist, U. Calif., San Diego, 1975. RN, Nev.; cert. enterostomal therapist, urol. nurse. Staff nurse Humana Hosp. Sunrise, Las Vegas, 1971-73, relief charge nurse, 1973-76, enterostomal therapist, 1976—. Speaker Hospice Vol. program, Las Vegas, 1982—, I Can Cope program, Las Vegas, 1984—. Author instructional guide. Vol. Am. Cancer Soc., 1983—, mem. program devel. nurse edn. com. Mem. Internat. Assn. Enterostomal Therapists (cert.), Nat. Assn. Pediatric Pseudobstructure Soc., Am. Nurses Assn., So. Nev. Nurses Assn., World Council Enterostomal Therapists, Am. Urol. Assn. (cert.), So. Nev. Ostomy Assn. (med. advisor 1976—), Crohns & Colitis Assn., Advanced Practitioners Nursing (cert., program chmn. 1986—), Wound Healing Soc., Internat. Assn. Bowel Disfunction, Tourette Syndrome Assn., Inc., Am. Soc. Adults Pseudo Obstruction, Inc., Assn. Advancement of Wound Care, Lupus Found. Republican. Presbyterian. Avocations: hiking, gardening, traveling. Office: Sunrise Hosp 3186 S Maryland Pkwy Las Vegas NV 89109-2306

LEAKE, CHARLES ROBERT, systems analyst, educator; b. N.Y.C., Apr. 23, 1930; m. Rita I. Leake, Feb. 10, 1968; children: Anna M., Charles R. Jr.; 1 child from previous marriage, Robert J. BS in Math., NYU, 1963, MS in Math., 1965, PhD in Math. Edn., 1969. Shipping clk. Gilliams and Rubin, N.Y.C., 1951-63; math instr. Fords (N.J.) Jr. H.S., 1964-65; asst. prof. math. Wagner Coll., N.Y.C., 1965-70; asst. prof. math Bronx (N.Y.) C.C., 1970-73; ops. rsch./sys. analyst Dept. of Def., U.S. Army, 1975—. Adj. faculty Univ. Coll. U. Md., Am. Mil. U., Greenwich U. Author: Linear Algebra, 1970, Pre Algebra Mathematics, 1973. With U.S. Army, 1951. Fellow NYU, 1963-64. Mem. AAAS, Operational Rsch. Soc., Mil. Ops. Rsch. Soc., Washington Evolutionary Sys. Soc., Ancient Mystical Order Rosae Crucis, Mensa. Lutheran. Home: Cmr 420 Box 3133 APO AE 09063-3133 E-mail: cleake@nova.umuc.edu.

LEAKE, DAVID BROWDER, computer scientist, educator; BA in Math., Haverford (Pa.) Coll., 1980; MA in Math., Brown U., Providence, 1984; PhD in Computer Sci., Yale U., 1990. Asst. prof. dept. computer sci. Ind. U., Bloomington, 1990-97, assoc. prof., 1997—. Mem. steering com. Nat. Conf. Cognitive Sci. Soc., 1992; mem. program com. Nat. Conf. Artificial Intelligence, 1994, 96; program co-chair Internat. Conf. on Case-based Reasoning, 1997. Author: Evaluating Explanations, 1992; co-editor: Goal-Driven Learning, 1995; editor: Case-Based Reasoning, 1996; contbr. articles to profl. jours. Recipient Rsch. Initiation award NSF, 1994-97. Mem. Am. Assn. Artificial Intelligence, Cognitive Sci. Soc., Phi Beta Kappa. Achievements include development of artificial intelligence algorithms and computer systems for machine learning, story understanding, planning and introspective reasoning. Office: Ind U Computer Sci Dept Lindley Hall 215 Bloomington IN 47405

LEAKE, JENNIFER LYNN, accountant; b. Mt. Lebanon, Pa., Feb. 28, 1974; d. Walter Lincoln III and Linda Kay (Mount) Smith; m. Michael Allen Leake, July 15, 1995. BA, U. Pitts., 1995. Tax acct. Price Waterhouse, Chgo., 1995; staff acct. Royal Mgmt., 1996-98; asst. controller Tandem Health Care Inc., Coraopolis, Pa., 1998—. Mem. Assembly of God. Avocations: bike riding, camping, waterskiing. Office: Tandem Health Care Inc Cherrington Corp Ctr 200 Corp Ctr Dr Ste 360 Moon Township PA 15108

LEAKE, LARRY BRUCE, lawyer; b. Asheville, N.C., May 19, 1950; s. A.E. and Ann (McDevitt) L. BA, U. N.C., 1971, JD, 1974. Ptnr. Uzzell and Dumont, Asheville, 1974-80, Harrell & Leake, Asheville, 1980—. Chmn. 11th Congl. Dist. YD, 1974-77; nat. committeeman Young Dems. of N.C., 1977-79, pres. 1979-80; gen. counsel Young Dems. of Am., 1981-83; state sen. N.C., 1979-80; mem. State Goals and Policy Bd., N.C., 1978-84, Commn. on the Future, N.C., 1981-83; mem. N.C. State Bd. of Elections, 1993-97, chmn., 1997—, Named 1 of 10 Outstanding Young Dems. N.C., 1977, Mountain Dem. of Yr., 2002; recipient Ella Grasso award, Outstanding Young Dem. in Am., 1983, Order of Long Leaf Pine, Gov. James B. Hunt, 1981, 2000. Mem. Phi Beta Kappa. Presbyterian. Avocations: bowling, spectator sports, tennis. Home: 16 Ridgeway Dr Mars Hill NC 28754-9707 Office: Leake & Scott 501 BB&T Plz Asheville NC 28801

LEAL, GUMERSINDO R. physician; b. Sagua, LV, Cuba, Jan. 6, 1928; came to U.S., 1971; s. Tomas Leal and Aurora Ybanez; widower; children: Rolando, Jorge. MD, Havana U., 1954. Diplomate Am. Bd. Family Practice, Am. Bd. Geriatrics. Physician Delta Med. Ctr., Memphis. Mem. AMA, Am. Family Practice Assn., Am. Geriatric Assn. Republican. Methodist. Home: 734 Eventide Dr Memphis TN 38120-4002 Office: Primary Care 3445 Poplar Ave Ste 1 Memphis TN 38111

LEAL, J. TERRI, academic facility administrator; b. San Antonio, Apr. 20, 1949; d. Antonio Fernando and Maria Teresa (Narvarte) L.; children from previous marriage: Giovanni DeGerolami, Carla DeGerolami; m. Robert K. Young, Nov. 4, 1990. BA, U. Tex., 1971; MS, Trinity U., 1982; PhD, U. Tex., 1988. Lic. profl. counselor, Tex. Test adminstr., counselor San Antonio Coll., 1972-83; from tchg. asst. to dir. instnl. analysis U. Tex., San Antonio, 1982-95, asst. v.p. assessment, dir. instnl. analysis, 1995—. Owner South Tex. Data Cons., San Antonio, 1994—; CEO Fundamental Orientation for Coll. and U. Survival, 1998—. Author: (personality test) Gender Fair Embedded Figures Test, 1988. Mem. Assn. Instnl. Rsch., Tex. Assn. Instnl. Rsch. Roman Catholic. Avocations: sailing, home repair, writing, reading. Office: U Tex 6900 N Loop 1604 W San Antonio TX 78249-1130

LEAL, JOSÉ HENRIQUE, museum director, marine biologist; b. Rio de Janeiro, Feb. 9, 1952; came to U.S., 1984; s. Ayrton Jauffret and Maria Angélica L.; m. Silvia Becker Maciel, Jan. 1982; children: Cecilia Maciel Leal, Julia Maciel Leal. BS in Biology, U. Fed. Rio de Janeiro, 1977, MS in Zoology, 1984; PhD in Marine Biology and Fisheries, U. Miami, 1990. Rsch. asst. Museu Nacional, Rio de Janeiro, 1981-84; vis. prof. Mus. Nat. d'Histoire Naturelle, Paris, 1988; rsch. assoc. div. marine geology and geophysics Rosenstiel Sch. Marine and Atmospheric Scis., U. Miami, Fla., 1991-92; postdoctoral assoc. div. marine geology and geophysics Rosenstiel Sch. Marine and Atmospheric Sci., U. Miami, 1994-95; postdoctoral fellow Nat. Mus. Natural History Smithsonian Instn., Washington, 1992-94; sci. dir. The Bailey-Matthews Shell Mus., Sanibel, Fla., 1996, dir., 1996—. Adj. asst. prof. div. marine biology and fisheries Rosenstiel Sch. Marine and Atmospheric Sci., U. Miami, 1994—; cons. Cognetix, 1998-99; courtesy faculty mem. Coll. Arts and Scis., Fla. Gulf Coast U., Ft. Myers, 1999—; temp. mem. grad. faculty U. Ala., Tuscaloosa, 1999—; rep. for USA Organizing Com. Latin Am. Malacological Congresses, 1999—. Author: Marine Prosobranch Gastropods from Oceanic Islands Off Brazil. Species Composition and Biogeography, 1991; mem. editl. com. Am. Conchologist, 1996—; editor The Nautilus, 1997—; contbr. articles to profl. jours. Bd. dirs. S.W. Fla. Libr. Network, 1999—. Recipient Spl. award Nat. Capital Shell Club, 1989; Lurie scholar for electron microscopy U. Miami, 1989; Bader Meml. Student Rsch. Fund fellow U. Miami, 1987; Sanibel-Captiva Shell Club fellow, 1987; Naples Shell Club fellow, 1986; Reitmeister fellow for conservation studies U. Miami, 1989; Rowlands fellow U. Miami, 1987, 88; Morris Karl Jacobsen scholar for molluscan studies The Astronaut Trail Shell Club, Club of Brevard, Fla., 1988. Mem. Am. Assn. Mus., Fla. Assn. Mus., Calif. Malacozool. Soc., Am. Malacological Soc. (councillor-at-large for biennial 1999-2001, nominating com. 1999-2001, v.p. 2002-), Conchologists of Am. (Grant award 1989, Grantee 1992, 95), Unitas Malacologica, Coun. Sci. Editors. Avocations: diving, running, music, reading. Fax: 941-395-6706.

LEAL, JOSEPH ROGERS, chemist; b. New Bedford, Mass., Sept. 14, 1918; s. Joaquim S. and Mary C. (Rogers) L.; m. Mary Desmond, Apr. 25, 1944; children: Joseph E., Michael J., Patricia M., Victoria A. Diploma, U. Mass., Dartmouth, 1940; BS summa cum laude, U. Mass., 1949; PhD, Ind. U., 1953. Asst. chemist CPC Internat., Edgewater, N.J., 1940-42, Revere Copper & Brass Co., New Bedford, 1942-43, 45-46; rsch. chemist Am. Cyanamid Co., Bound Brook, N.J., 1952-57, tech. rep. Washington, 1957-63, mgr. contract rels. Stamford, Conn., 1963-67; sr. staff assoc. Celanese Rsch. Co., Summit, N.J., 1967-83; pres. Crescent Cons., Maplewood, 1983-97, South Hadley, Mass., 1997-2000. Frederick Gardiner Cottrell fellow, 1950, Corn Industries Rsch. fellow, 1951-52. Mem. AAAS, Am. Chem. Soc., SAMPE, Sigma Xi, Sci. Rsch. Soc. Achievements include research in high temperature resistant polymers, nonflammable fibers, high strength high modulus reinforcement materials, fiber reinforced organic, ceramic and metal composites.

LEALE, OLIVIA MASON, import marketing company executive; b. Boston, May 5, 1944; d. William Mason and Jane Chapin (Prouty) Smith; m. Euan Harvie-Watt, Mar. ll, 1967 (div. Aug. 1979); children: Katrina, Jennifer; m. Douglas Marshall Leale, Aug. 29, 1980. BA, Vassar Coll., 1966. Cert. paralegal, beginning yoga instr. Sec. to dir. Met. Opera Guild, N.Y.C., 1966; sec. to pres. Friesons Printers, London, England, 1974-75; guide, trainer Autoguide, England, 1977-79; ptnr. Inmark Internat. Mktg. Inc., Seattle, 1980—; owner-mgr. Argus Ranch Facility For Dogs, 2001—. Social case worker Inner London Ednl. Authority, 1975-76. Democrat. Presbyterian. Avocations: reading, making doll house furniture, painting, knitting, dog agility. Home and Office: 1233 Shenandoah Dr E Seattle WA 98112-3727

LEALI, SHIRLEY A. mathematician, educator; b. Adel, Ga. d. Rufus and Georgia R. (Hall) Wright; m. Robert M. Leali Jr., June 18, 1971. BA, U. Denver, 1973; MA, U. Colo., Denver, 1984; PhD, U. Denver, 1992. Instr., adminstr. Denver Pub. Schs., 1974-93; assoc. prof. math. Weber State U., Ogden, Utah, 1993—, U. No. Colo., Greeley, Colo., 1995-96. Cons. Ogden Sch. Dist., 1994—; nat. gender equity expert; presenter internat. confs. Contbr. articles to profl. jours. Vol. math. tchr. for incarcerated youth; bd. dirs. State of Utah Black Adv. Coun., 1997—. Ednl. Tech. Initiative grantee Weber State U., 1994, Thiokol, 1994. Fellow Nat. Coun. Tchrs. of Math.; mem. Assn. Math. Tchr. Educators, Internat. Study Group on Ethnomath., Utah Sci. Tchrs. Assn. Achievements include work and recognition for advancing gender equity and awareness. Avocation: playing classical guitar. Office: Weber State U Ogden UT 84403 E-mail: saleali@weber.edu.

LEAMAN, DAVID MARTIN, cardiologist, educator; b. Lancaster, Pa., Apr. 24, 1935; s. Benjamin Denlinger and Elise Mae (Martin) L.; m. Doris Jean Heisey; children: Gretchen Jane, Heidi Jean, Erika Ingrid. Student, Franklin & Marshall Coll., 1956-58; BA, Eastern Mennonite Coll., 1960; MD, Temple U., 1964. Intern Mary Hitchcock Hosp., Hanover, N.H., 1964-66; resident U. Vt., Burlington, 1968-71; asst. prof. medicine Pa. State U., Hershey, 1971-77, assoc. prof., 1977-84, prof., 1984—, chief div. of cardiology, 1984-95, asst. dean for student affairs, 1987-91, asst. dean for admissions, 1991-94. Contbr. articles to med. jours. Sch. dir. Lower Dauphin Sch. Dist., Hummelstown, Pa., 1977-83. Served with USPHS, 1966-68. Named Alumnus of Yr. Eastern Mennonite Coll., 1985. Fellow Am. Coll. Cardiology, Am. Coll. Chest Physicians, ACP, Soc. Cardiac Angiology, Am. Heart Assn. (mem. council on clin. cardiology, Service Recognition award 1981, Disting. Service award 1985, bd. dirs. Pa. affiliate 1975—), Alpha Omega Alpha. Republican. Mennonite. Avocations: reading, photography. Office: Pa State Univ Hershey Med Ctr PO Box 850 Hershey PA 17033-0850 E-mail: dleaman@psu.edu.

LEAMAN, J. RICHARD, JR. paper company executive; b. Lancaster, Pa., Sept. 22, 1934; s. J. Richard and Margaret B. (Leaman); m. Helen Brown, June 15, 1957; children: Lynda B., J. Richard, III. BA, Dartmouth Coll., 1956, MBA, 1957; PhD (hon.), Widener U., 1988. With Scott Paper Co., Phila., 1960-95, v.p. comml. products, 1975-78, exec. v.p. mktg. and sales, 1978—, pres. Packaged Products div., 1983-86, vice chmn., 1991-94, dir., 1986; pres. Scott Worldwide, 1986-91; pres., CEO, S.D. Warren Co., Boston, 1991-95. Bd. dirs. Church & Dwight Co., Inc., Pep Boys, Elwyn Inc., Stonebridge Fin. Corp., GenTerra Corp. Mem. conf. bd.'s coun. Global Bus. Mgmt. Dartmouth Alumni Coun., 1993—96. Recipient Disting. Performance in Mgmt. award Widener U. Mem. Conf. Bd.'s Coun. on Global Bus. Mgmt., Dartmouth Club (Phila.). Republican. Episcopalian. Home: 317 Boot Rd Malvern PA 19355-3317 Office: 225 Franklin St Boston MA 02110-2804

LEAMAN, LEONARD S., JR. science educator; b. N.Y.C., Nov. 30, 1945; s. Leonard S. and Elinore McNamee Leaman. BA, Holy Cross Coll., 1968; MFA, NYU, 1971. Camping and trip leader Camp Winaco, Sebago, Maine, 1970—92; sci. tchr. St. Hilda's and St. Hugh's Sch., N.Y.C., 1976—80, Trinity Sch., N.Y.C., 1980—, dean, 1993—99, 2001—. Writer, dir.: (film) Papa You're Crazy, 1971; writer, dir., photographer: (film) One Year's Spring, 1971; cameraman: (film) Eugene, 1971 (Cine Golden Eagle award 1971). Charles Bluhdorn fellow Trinity Sch., 1983, Earthwatch fellow, 1994. Mem. Assn. Tchrs. in Ind. Schs., Am. Mus. Natural History (assoc.), N.Y. Acad. Scis., Appalachian Mountain Club, Orion Soc., N.Y. Bot. Garden. Roman Catholic. Home: 70 W 95th St New York NY 10025 Office: Trinity Sch 139 W 91st St New York NY 10024 E-mail: lennyleaman@netscape.net.

LEAMAN, THOMAS LEED, medical educator; b. Lancaster, Pa., Aug. 18, 1923; s. Benjamin Moseman and Anna Marie (Leed) L.; m. Jeanne Louise, Mar. 27, 1945; children: Rebecca Susan Pratt, Linda Jeanne Leaman-Kearney, Crystal Louise Leaman-Thomas, Martha Frances. Grad., Gettysburg Coll., 1943, Baylor U., 1944, Southwestern Med. Coll., 1946; MD, George Washington U., 1948. Cert. Am. Bd. Family Practice. Physician pvt. practice, Hershey, Pa., 1949-52, 54-67; prof., chair dept. family & cmty. medicine Pa. State U., Milton S. Hershey Med. Ctr., 1967-87, prof. emeritus, 1987—. Author: Healing the Anxiety Diseases, 1992, New Colleagues, 1998; co-author: Case Studies in Primary Care, 1983, Diagnosis and Treatment of Anxiety Disorders: A Physicians Handbook, 1989, Preventing Malpractice: The Co-Active Solution, 1993, Managed Care Success, 1998. Bd. dirs. Harrisburg Cmty. Check-Up Ctr., 1995-2001, Tri County Planned Parenthood, 1985-91, pres., 1988-91; chair HIV/AIDS Commn. Diocese of Ctrl. Pa., 1997—. Recipient Soc. Tchrs. Family Medicine Recognition award, 1987, Episcopal Diocese Ctrl. Pa. Faith and Hope award, 1995. Mem. Alpha Omega Alpha. Avocation: antiquarian books. Home and Office: 77 Hill Manor Dr Hershey PA 17033-2510

LEAMING, DERYL RAY, dean, emeritus educator; b. Beaver County, Okla., Aug. 10, 1932; s. Willard R. and Clara (Pennington) L.; m. Lila Marie Hoskinson, Nov. 1, 1952; children: Greg, Jeff, Jeremy, Chad. BA, Ft. Hays State Coll., Hays, Kans., 1957; MA, U. Nebr., 1965; PhD, Syracuse (N.Y.) U., 1969. Dept. head Kans. State U., Manhattan, 1967-71; dir. Marshall U., Huntington, W.Va., 1972-88, dean liberal arts, 1988-93; dean Mid. Tenn. State U., Murfreesboro, 1993—2002; pres., CEO Leadearship Tng. Programs, 2001—; co-owner, founder rock Solid Press Pub., Inc. Author: Academic Leadership, 1998, Deans and Chairs. Strategies for Leadership, 2001; pub., editor The Online Jour. of Acad. Leadership, 2000—; bd. advisors The Dept. Chair, 1998—. Staff sgt. USAF, 1950-53. Recipient John Emmens award Ball State U., 1993. Mem. NATAS (bd. govs. 1999-2000), Soc. Profl. Journalists (nat. bd., regional dir. 1988-92, 1st Amendment award 1994). Home: 3594 E Arbor Lakes Dr Hernando FL 34442 E-mail: dleaming@yahoo.com.

LEANDER, ROBERT W. engineer; b. St. Louis, Jan. 2, 1951; s. Edna Washington; m. Vivecca Ann Macon. MusM, So. Ill. U., 1991—91, BSEE, 1995, MEE, 1997; BS in Music Edn., U. of Ill., 1998; PhD, U. Ill., Chgo., 2002. Math tutor Counseling Dept., Southwestern Ill. Coll., Belleville, Ill.; instrumental music specialist Ill. Sch. Dist. 189, East St. Louis, 1976—89; grad. asst. elec. and computer engrng. U. Ill., Chgo., 1999—99; rsch. asst.

bioengrng. U. Ill. , 1999—. Fellow, Ill. Consortium for Ednl. Opportunity, 1995—99; grantee, NSF, 1991; scholar, Nat. Action Counsel for Minorities in Engrng., 1993—95. Mem.: Assn. Rsch. Vision and Ophthalmology, Engrng. Medicine and Biology Soc., Eta Kappa Nu. Avocations: jazz, saxophone, martial arts, writing. Home: 1905 Esic Chicago IL 60625 Business E-Mail: bwashing@eecs.uic.edu.

LEAPHART, ASHLEY REGAN, pharmacist; b. Dec. 10, 1973; BSPharm, U. S.C., 1997, PharmD, 1998. Staff pharmacist Palmetto Health Richland, Columbia, SC, 1997—. Mem. Am. Pharmaceutical Assn., Am. Soc. Health-System Pharmacists. Home: 411 Bernard St Leesville SC 29070-7858 Office: Palmetto Health Richland 5 Richland Medical Park Columbia SC 29203-6897

LEAPHART, W. WILLIAM, state supreme court justice; b. Butte, Mont., Dec. 3, 1946; s. Charles William and Cornelia (Murphy) L.; m. Barbara Berg, Dec. 30, 1977; children: Rebecca, Retta, Ada. Student, Whitman Coll., 1965—66; BA, U. Mont., 1969, JD, 1972. Bar: Mont. 1972, U.S. Dist. Ct., U.S. Ct. Appeals (9th cir.) 1975, U.S. Supreme Ct. 1975. Law clk. to Hon. W.D. Murray U.S. Dist. Ct., Butte, 1972—74; ptnr. Leaphart Law Firm, Helena, Mont., 1974—94; justice Mont. Supreme Ct., 1995—. Office: Mont Supreme Ct Justice Bldg 215 N Sanders St Rm 315 Helena MT 59601-4522 also: PO Box 203001 Helena MT 59620-3001*

LEAR, ERWIN, anesthesiologist, educator; b. Bridgeport, Conn., Jan. 1, 1924; s. Samuel Joseph and Ida (Ruth) L.; m. Arlene Joyce Alexander, Feb. 15, 1953; children: Stephanie, Samuel MD, SUNY, 1952. Diplomate Am. Bd. Anesthesiology, Nat. Bd. Med. Examiners. Intern L.I. Coll. Hosp., Bklyn., 1952-53; asst. resident anesthesiology Jewish Hosp., 1953-54, sr. resident, 1955, asst., 1955-56, adj., 1956-58, assoc. anesthesiologist, 1958-64; attending anesthesiologist Bklyn. VA Hosp., 1958-64, cons., 1977—; assoc. vis. anesthesiologist Kings County Hosp. Ctr., Bklyn., 1957-80, staff anesthesiologist, 1980-81; vis. anesthesiologist Queens Gen. Hosp. Ctr., 1955-67; dir. anesthesiology Queens Hosp. Ctr. Jamaica, 1964-67; chmn. dept. anesthesiology Catholic Med. Ctr., Queens and Bklyn., 1968-80; dir. anesthesiology Beth Israel Med. Ctr., N.Y.C., 1981-98; clin. instr. SUNY Coll. Medicine, Bklyn., 1955-58, from clin. asst. prof. to clin. prof., 1958-80, prof., vice-chmn. clin. anesthesiology, 1980-81; prof. anesthesiology Mt. Sinai Sch. Medicine, 1981-94, Albert Einstein Coll. of Medicine, 1994—. Cons. in field. Author: Chemistry Applied Pharmacology of Tranquilizers; contbr. articles to profl. jours. Served with USNR, 1942-45 Fellow: N.Y. Acad. Medicine (sec. sect. anesthesiology 1985—86, chmn. sect. anesthesiology 1986—87), Am. Coll. Anesthesiologists; mem.: AMA, SUNY Coll. Medicine Alumni Assn. (pres. 1983, trustee alumni fund 1980), N.Y. County Med. Soc., N.Y. State Med. Soc. (chmn. sect. anesthesiology 1966—67, sec. sect. 1977—81), N.Y. State Soc. Anesthesiologists (chmn. pub. rels. 1963—73, assoc. editor Bulletin 1963—77, chmn. com. local arrangements 1968—73, dist. dir. 1972—73, bd. dirs. 1972—94, v.p. 1974—75, pres. 1976, chmn. jud. com. 1977—81, editor Sphere 1978—87, Disting. Svc. award 1996), Am. Soc. Anesthesiologists (ho. of dels. 1973—94, dir. 1981—97, chmn. com. on by-laws 1982—83, editor newsletter 1984—98, chmn. adminstrv. affairs com. 1987—94), Alpha Omega Alpha. Address: 1 Harriman Dr Sands Point NY 11050-1246

LEAR, FLOYD RAYMOND, III, entrepreneur; b. Easton, Pa., June 20, 1942; s. Floyd Raymond Jr. and Mildred M. (Sterner) L.; m. Judith Marie Smith, Dec. 31, 1962 (div. Dec. 1973); children: Eric James, Michael Thomas. Grad., Blair Acad., 1960; attended, Rider Coll., 1961-62. Sales rep. Indsl. Engraving Co. Inc., Easton, 1965-73, v.p. adminstrn. and sales, 1973-82, pres., chief exec. officer, chmn. bd., 1982—; owner, operator Lear Publs., Inc., 1970-74. Co-owner Travel with Carole, Inc., Bethlehem, Pa., 1985—; owner King's Hill Antiques, Easton, 1986—, King's Hill Publs., 1991—; vice chmn. bd. Lafayette Trust Bank, Easton, 1987-89. Mem. Easton Area Jaycees, 1964-79, officer, 1964-69; active Bethlehem, Easton United Way, 1967, ABE Airport Adv. Com., Allentown, Pa., 1983-85; charter mem., bd. dirs. Hist. Easton, 1974-79; mem. exec. com., dir. found. bd. Northampton Area Community Coll., Bethlehem, 1981-88. Named Jaycee of Yr., Easton Area Jaycees, 1965; recipient several pres. awards and honor Easton Area Jaycees, Cornerstone Soc. award Northampton Area Community Coll., 1983. Mem. Allentown Art Mus., Northampton County Hist. Soc., Winterthur Guild, Met. Mus. Art, Rushlight Club (Wethersfield, Conn.). Office: Indsl Engraving Co Inc 1350 Sullivan Trl Easton PA 18040-1144

LEAR, NORMAN MILTON, producer, writer, director; b. New Haven, July 27, 1922; s. Herman and Jeanette (Seicol) L.; children: Ellen, Kate B. Lear LaPook, Maggie B.; m. Lyn Davis; children: Benjamin Davis, Brianna, Madeline. Student, Emerson Coll., 1940-42, HHD, 1968. Engaged in pub. relations, 1945-49; founder Act III Comms., 1987—. Comedy writer for TV, 1950-54; writer, dir. for TV and films, 1954-59; prodr.:(films) Never Too Late, 1965, Start the Revolution Without Me, 1970, (TV) Sanford and Son, 1972, Maude, 1972, Good Times, 1974, Hot L Baltimore, 1975, All That Glitters, 1977, A Year at the Top, 1977, The Baxters, 1979, Sunday Dinner, 1991; exec. prodr.: (films) Fried Green Tomatoes, 1991, Way Past Cool, 2000, (TV), The Andy Williams Show, 1962, One Day at a Time, 1975, The Nancy Walker Show, 1976, Heartsounds, 1984, a.k.a. Pablo, 1984, 704 Hauser, 1994, Channel Umptee-3, 1997; prodr., dir., creator: (TV) All in the Family, 1971 (4 Emmy awards 1970-73, Peabody award 1977), The Powers That Be, 1992; prodr., screenwriter: (films) Come Blow Your Horn, 1963, Divorce American Style, 1967, The Night They Raided Minsky's, 1968; prodr., dir., screenwriter: Cold Turkey, 1971; screenwriter: Scared Stiff, 1953; creator: The Jeffersons, 1975, Fernwood 2-Night, 1977. Pres. Am. Civil Liberties Found. So. Calif., 1973—; trustee Mus. Broadcasting; bd. dirs. People for the American Way; founder Bus. Enterprise Trust. Served with USAAF, 1942-45. Decorated Air medal with 4 oak leaf clusters; named One of Top Ten Motion Picture Producers, Motion Picture Exhibitors, 1963, 67, 68, Showman of Yr., Publicists Guild, 1971-77, Assn. Bus. Mgrs., 1972, Broadcaster of Yr., Internat. Radio and TV Soc., 1973; Man of Yr. Hollywood chpt. Nat. Acad. Television Arts and Scis., 1973; recipient Humanitarian award NCCJ, 1976, Mark Twain award Internat. Platform Assn., 1977, William O. Douglas award Pub. Counsel, 1981, 1st Amendment Lectr. Ford Hall Forum, 1981, Gold medal Internat. Radio and TV Soc., 1981. Disting. Am. award, 1984, Mass Media award Am. Jewish Com. Inst. of Human Relations, 1986, Internat. award of Yr., Nat. Assn. TV Program Execs., 1987, Nat. Arts Medal, 1992; inducted into TV Acad. Hall of Fame, 1984. Mem. Writers Guild Am. (Valentine Davies award 1977), Dirs. Guild Am., AFTRA, Caucus Producers, Writers, and Dirs. Office: Act III Comm 1999 Avenue Of The Stars Los Angeles CA 90067-6022

LEAR, ROBERT WILLIAM, management consultant, retired; b. Canon City, Colo., May 10, 1917; s. Louis and Bertha (May) L.; m. Dorothy Schureman, Sept. 16, 1941; children— William S., Andrew R. BA, U. Colo., 1938; MBA with distinction, Harvard, 1940. Market research analyst U.S. Steel Corp., 1940-43; sales promotion mgr. Duff-Norton Co., 1946-47; corp. dir. marketing services Am. Standard Co., 1947-61; v.p. marketing Carborundum Co., 1961-64, group v.p., 1964-67; pres., dir. Indian Head Inc., 1967-72; pres., chief exec. officer, chmn., dir. F. & M. Schaefer Corp., N.Y.C., 1972-77; exec.-in-residence Columbia Grad. Bus. Sch., 1977-99; prin. Lear, Yavitz & Assocs., LLP, 1996-2001, ret., 2001. Bd. dirs. Newsbank, Ronin Devel., Strang and Hayes, David N. Deutsch, Transition Ptnrs., Six Figure Jobs, Foreview. Author: How to Turn Your MBA into a CEO, 1987, Pressure Points, 1992; chmn. adv. bd. Chief Exec. Mag., 1994—. Bd. dirs. Waveny Care Ctr. Served as lt. USNR, 1943-46. Mem.: Harvard (N.Y.C.); New Canaan Country, Blind Brook, Mill Reef. Home: 45 Prides Crossing New Canaan CT 06840

LEARD, DAVID CARL, lawyer; b. Hartford, Conn., Dec. 9, 1958; BA, Bucknell U., 1981; JD, U. Conn., 1984. Bar: Conn. 1984, U.S. Dist. Ct. Conn. 1985. Assoc. Podorowsky and Wladimer, Hartford, 1985, Manasse, Slaiby & Leard, Torrington, Conn., 1985-88, ptnr., 1989—. Lectr. legal studies Northwestern Conn. Community Coll., Winsted, 1991-92. Contbr. articles to profl. jours. Dir., past pres. Winchester (Conn.) Land Trust, 1988-93; chmn. allocations com. United Way Torrington, 1989—. Mem. Conn. Bar Assn. (workers compensation sect.), Nat. Orgn. Social Security Claimants Reps. Office: Manasse Slaiby & Leard PO Box 1104 Torrington CT 06790-2958

LEARMANN, JUDITH MARILYN, secondary school educator; b. Charleston, Ill., Feb. 1, 1938; d. Charles P. and Estelle M. (DeWitt) Swan; m. Paul C. Learmann, Aug. 29, 1958 (dec.); children: Kevin L., Michael P.(dec.). BS, Wis. State Coll., Oshkosh, 1960; MA, Pacific Western U., 1994. Tchr. Monona (Wis.) Grove H.S., 1960-62, U.S. Army Coll. Program, Denver, 1967, Wood Mid. Sch., Ft. Leonard Wood, Mo., 1983-85, Waynesville (Mo.) H.S., 1985—, chmn. dept. lang. arts, 1987—. Presenter in field; chmn. North Ctrl. Philosophy Com., Waynesville, 1987—88; reviewer textbook Adventures in English Literature Harcourt, Brace, Jovanovich, 1994; reviewer sci. curriculum, 1994—96; reviewer math. curriculum, 1995; reviewer social studies curriculum, 96; reviewer bus. curriculum, 97; reviewer computer sci. curriculum, 97; mem. evaluation steering com. Mo. sch. improvement program, chair instrn. process com. Waynesville R-VI Sch. Dist., 1996—97; mem. strategic planning com. Edn. 2003, 1997—; mem. sch. to work Career Quest com., 1998, Vanguard tech. com., 1999—, Continued Sch. Improvement Plan Learning Environ. com., 2001, PBTE rev. com., 2002. Named Most Influential Tchr. award, U. Mo., 1991; recipient Influential Tchr. Recognition letter, Westminster Coll., 1992, 1995, Tex. A&M U., 1998. Mem.: Cmty. Tchrs. Assn. (chmn. legal svcs. 1991—95, health leave pool com. 1996—), Mo. State Tchrs. Assn., Mo. Tchrs. English (meeting chmn. dist. conv. 1989, 1990, 1998), Mo. Tchrs. Assn., Nat. Coun. Tchrs. English, Phi Delta Kappa (officer nomination, constn. revision coms., tchr. awards). Avocation: reading. Home: 1737 J C St Waynesville MO 65583-2460 Office: Waynesville HS Historic Rt 66 West Waynesville MO 65583 E-mail: jlearmann@waynesville.k12.mo.us.

LEARN, DORIS LYNN, school district purchasing director; b. Long Beach, Calif., May 11, 1949; d. Rowe Francis and Annie Mae (Tunstill) Christopher; m. Thomas Robert Learn, Oct. 17, 1987. Student Foothill Coll., 1966-67, DeAnza Coll., 1969-71, Rider Coll., 1988-90. Cashier Navy Exchange, China Lake, Calif., 1965-66, Navy Exchange, Moffett Field, Calif., 1966-67; exec. sec. Varian Assocs., Palo Alto, Calif., 1967-75; salesperson Jorgensen Steel, Langhorne, Pa., 1976; exec. sec. Pennsbury Sch. Dist., Fallsington, Pa., 1976-82, dir. purchasing, 1982-97. Mem. NAFE, Nat. Assn. Purchasing Mgmt., Pa. Assn. Sch. Bus. Ofcls. (registered sch. bus. specialist, mem. conf. com. 1986, 91, asst. chair conf. com., 1996, bd. dirs. 1994-97, chmn. materials mgmt. com. 1995-97, mem. elections com. 1996, mem. policies com., 1995-97, co-chair self-evaluation task force 1995), Assn. Sch. Bus. Ofcls., Pa. Sch. Bds. Assn., Govt. Fin. Officers Assn., Pennsbury Assn. Suprs. and Adminstrs., Nat. Purchasing Assn., Delaware Valley Assn. Sch. Bus. Officials (pres. 1992-93). Republican. Presbyterian. Avocations: needlecrafts, golf, spectator sports. Home: 19131 Wind Dancer St Lutz FL 33558-9053

LEARN, RICHARD LELAND, corrections classification program manager; b. New Kensington, Pa., Nov. 29, 1955; s. Leland Leroy Learn and Gendolyn Leora (Furman) George; m. Rosamond Amelia Kautz, July 31, 1982; children: Rebecca Amelia, Benjamin Richard. BS in Music Edn., Indiana U. of Pa., 1977, MA in Adult/Community Edn., 1984; PhD in Edn., U. Pitts., 1991. Adult edn. instr. PIC of Westmoreland County, Greensburg, Pa., 1980-82; corrections edn. specialist Pa. State Correctional Instn., 1984-87; acad. support coord. Indiana U. of Pa., 1987-89; sch. prin. Pa. State Correctional Instn., Mercer, 1989-92, Cambridge Springs, 1992-2000; classification and program mgr., 2000—. Chmn. bd. dirs. Young Adult Handicapped, Inc., Apollo, Pa., 1980-82. Mem. Am. Correctional Assn., Corrections Edn. Assn. Democrat. Presbyterian. Avocations: archery, music. Office: State Correctional Instn 451 Fullerton Ave Cambridge Springs PA 16403-1238 E-mail: rilearn@alltel.net.

LEARNARD, JAMES MICHAEL, educator, former finance company executive; b. Worcester, Mass., June 13, 1947; s. James Felix and Katherine M. (Slater) L.; m. Mary Kathryn Douglas, Mar. 16, 1972 (div. June 1974); 1 child, Sean Patrick; m. Joyce Stanek Hogan, June 10, 1989 (div. Nov. 1991); m. Donna Cecile Courtney, Aug. 12, 1993 (div. Aug. 1995). AA, Fla. Jr. Coll., Jacksonville, 1968; BSBA, Century U., Beverly Hills, Calif., 1987, MBA, 1988; BA, Augusta (Ga.) Coll., 1991; PhD (hon.), Century U., 2001. Cert. paralegal, Ga.; cert. nursing asst. Epidemiologist L.A. Dept. Health, 1972-73; credit collector supr. Levy-Wolf, Inc., Jacksonville, 1973-75; correctional officer S.C. Dept. Corrections, Aiken, 1975-76; v.p., office mgr. Nat. Auto Fin. Corp., 1976-81; ins. agt. Security Life Ins. Co. of Ga., Augusta, 1981-82, United Ins. Co. of Am., Aiken, 1982-86, Life Ins. Co. of Ga., Atlanta, 1986-87, The Keller Agy., Aiken, 1992-94; collector ARC, Inc., Augusta, Ga., 1994; owner, collector CSRA Recovery Svcs., Inc., Aiken, 1994-99; collection mgr. Service Loan Co., Augusta, 1999—; tchr. Richmond County (Ga.) Bd. Edn. Collector Apex Fin. Co., Inc., Augusta, 1999; telemarketer So. Ind., Augusta, 1999, Hospitality Mktg. Concepts, Inc., Augusta, 1999, DialAm. Mktg., North Augusta, S.C., 1999; nursing asst. Anna Maria Nursing and Rehab. Ctr., North Augusta, 1999. Author: Words of Love, 1985, Thoughts of Love and Inspiration, 1988, Student Protests at Harvard College, 1766-1780, 1986, Catholic Hospitals in the American Healthcare System, 1988, I Praise Your Name, A Collection of Love Poems, 1998, Recipes from the Heart: Cooking for the One You Love, 1999, How Do I Love Thee? A Collection of Love Poems, 2000, Love Lasts Eternal--Love Poems to a Lovely Lady, 2000, The Not So Famous Quotations and Other Writings of James M. Learnard, 20 vols., 2000; musical compositions include: Tonight (soul ballad), 1982, (pop rock ballad), 1982, Friends (pop rock ballad), 1983, Do You Remember (soul ballad), 1983, Eastern Morn (hymn), 1983, Christmas Day, 1982, Sunset on Tampa Bay (soul ballad), 1982, 83, My Angel (soul ballad), 1983, What Will She Say? (pop rock ballad), 1983, Easter Morn, 1983; prodr. album: Michael Hicks/Love Songs, 1983. Past chmn. Animal Control Adv. Bd., Aiken. Recipient Golden Poet award World of Poetry, 1986, 87, Silver Poet award, 1988, Recognition by the S.C. House of Reps. for accomplishment as an author, poet and lycricist, 1986; commd. admiral S.C. Navy, 1986; recipient Medal of Honor commemorating disting. lifelong achievement Am. Biog. Assn., 1990; Eagle Scout with Bronze Palm, Boy Scouts Am., 1963. Mem. Assn. of MBA Execs., Healthcare Fin. Mgmt. Assn., Fedn. of Am. Health Svcs., Am. Hosp. Assn., Soc. for Hosp. Healthcare and Mktg., K.C. (4th degree). Roman Catholic. Home: 117 Green St Graniteville SC 29829 E-mail: jameslearnard@juno.com.

LEARNARD, WILLIAM EWING, marketing executive; b. Joliet, Ill., July 21, 1935; s. Roy Stevens and Clara (Ewing) L.; m. Susan Douglas-Willan, Oct. 1, 1960; children: Matthew, Roger, Vanessa. BA, Trinity Coll., 1957. With Smith, Kline & French, Phila., 1957-78, v.p. customer affairs, 1976-78; v.p. corp. affairs Smithkline Beckman, 1978-85; pres. Smithkline Consumer Products, 1985-89; vice chmn. Smithkline Beecham Consumer Brands, 1989-91. Chmn. Coun. on Family Health, N.Y.C., 1989-91; bd. dirs. Nelson Comms., DiMark, Inc., Fischer & Porter. Bd. dirs. Chestnut Hill Hosp., Phila., 1982-88, Morris Arboretum, U. Pa., Phila., 1982-92; chmn. Sta. WHYY TV & Radio, Phila., 1990-94. Capt. USAF, 1958-61. Mem. Nonprescription Drug Mfrs. Assn. (chmn. 1989-91), Phila. Cricket Club, George Town Club. Republican. Home: 48 Hillcrest Ave Philadelphia PA 19118-2620 Office: Trident Group Ste 230 Spring House Corp Ctr Ambler PA 19002

LEARNED, VINCENT ROY, electrical engineer, educator; b. San Jose, Calif., Jan. 21, 1917; m. Bernice Evelyn Brown, June 5, 1938; children: Daryl Vincent, Dean Charles, Craig Edwin, Kent Brudeen, Bruce Roy. BSEE, U. Calif., 1938; PhD, Stanford U., 1943. Dir. rsch. and devel. microwave tubes Sperry Rand Corp., 1943-65; prof. elec. and computer engr. San Diego State U., 1968-87, prof. emeritus, 1987—. Fellow Inst. Radio Engrs. Office: 2801 Cohasset Rd Apt 130 Chico CA 95973-0981

LEARS, THOMAS JACKSON, history educator; b. Annapolis, Md., July 26, 1947; s. Walter Lee and Margaret Esther (Baptist) L.; m. Karen Lister Parker, Feb. 1, 1969; children: Rachel, Adin. BA in English, U. Va., 1969; MA in U.S. History, U. N.C., 1973; PhD in Am. Studies, Yale U., 1978. Instr. English Bon Air Sch. for Girls, Richmond, Va., 1970-71; instr. Am. studies Yale U., New Haven, 1977-79; from asst. to assoc. prof. history U. Mo., Columbia, 1979-85; historian Smithsonian Instn., Washington, 1985-86; prof. history Rutgers U., New Brunswick, NJ, 1986—96, Bd. of Govs. prof. history, 1996—. Editor-in-chief Raritan Rev., 2002—. Author: No Place of Grace, 1981, Fables of Abundance, 1994; editor: The Culture of Consumption, 1983, The Power of Cultures, 1993; mem. adv. bd. Wilson Quar., 1990—; mem. editl. bd. Am. Quar., 1982-85, Jour. Am. History, 1986-89. Whiting fellow, 1976-77, Guggenheim fellow, 1984-85, Rockefeller fellow, 1985-86, Davis Ctr. fellow, 1989-90, Winterthur fellow, 1996, NEH fellow, 1997, Smithsonian fellow, 1998. Mem. Am. Hist. Assn., Am. Studies Assn. (nat. coun. 1986-89), Orgn. Am. Historians. Democrat. Avocations: swimming, tennis, gardening. Home: 399 Wertsville Rd Ringoes NJ 08551-1705 Office: Rutgers U History dept PO Box 5059 New Brunswick NJ 08903-5059 E-mail: tjlears@rci.rutgers.edu.

LEARY, CAROL ANN, academic administrator; b. Niagara Falls, N.Y., Mar. 29, 1947; d. Angelo Andrew and Mary Josephine (Pullano) Gigliotti; m. Noel Robert Leary, Dec. 30, 1972. BA, Boston U., 1969; MS, SUNY, Albany, 1970; PhD, Am. Univ., 1988. Asst. to v.p. for student affairs, dir. women's programs Siena Coll., Loudonville, N.Y., 1970-72; asst. dir. housing Boston U., 1972-78; dir. residence Simmons Coll., Boston, 1978-84, assoc. dean, 1984-85; assoc. dir. The Washington Campus, Washington, 1985-86; adminstrv. v.p., asst. to pres. Simmons Coll., Boston, 1988-94; pres. Bay Path Coll., Longmeadow, Mass., 1995—. Past pres., bd. govs. Colony Club; past pres. Cooperating Colls. of Greater Springfield; exec. com., vice-chair Cmty. Found. Western Mass; past pres. WGBY; bd. dirs. Women's Fund of Mass, United Coop. Bank, Women's Coll. Coalition. Mem.: Assn. Ind. Coll. & Univ. Mass. (vice-chair). Avocations: art, traveling overseas, hiking. Office: Bay Path Coll Office of the President 588 Longmeadow St Longmeadow MA 01106-2212

LEARY, DANIEL, artist; b. Glens Falls, N.Y., July 20, 1955; s. John Andrew and Maud Houston (Parkhurst) L. BFA, Antioch Coll., 1979; MFA, Syracuse U., 1996. One person exhbns. include Breedlove Gallery, Westark Cmty. Coll., Fort Smith, Ark., 1984, 85, Comart Gallery, Syracuse U., 1985, 87, The Printspace, U. Ark., Fayetteville, 1985, The Fort Smith Art Ctr., 1986, Printworks Gallery, 1991, 99, 2000, Chgo., 1988, 95, The Hyde Collection, Glens Falls, N.Y., 1990, The Blanden Meml. Art Mus., Fort Dodge, Iowa, 1992, The Bobbit Visual Art Ctr., Albion Coll., Mich., 1993, Sharon Campbell Gallery, Greenville, S.C., 1994, We. Mich. State U., Kalamazoo, 1994, Greenville County Fine Arts Ctr., 2002; group exhbns. include East Tenn. State U., Johnson City, 1985, Gallery Sixty-Eight, Belfast, Maine, 1985, The Fort Smith Arts Ctr., 1985, Syracuse U., 1985, The Ark. Arts Ctr. and the Decorative Arts Mus., Little Rock, 1985, The Soc. Am. Graphic Artists, 1986, Westminster Coll., New Wilmington, Pa., 1986, Joe Fawbush Editions, N.Y., 1986, Cazenovia (N.Y.) Coll., 1987, Jan Turner Gallery, L.A., 1987, The Greenville County Mus. Art, 1988, The Mpls. Inst. Arts., 1988, The Munson-Williams-Proctor Inst. Mus. Art, Utica, N.Y., 1989, The Statesville Arts and Scis. Mus., 1989, The Nat. Exhbn. Ctr. Can., Alma, Quebec, 1989, The Pyramid Arts Ctr., Rochester, N.Y., 1989, The Vero Beach Ctr. For the Arts, Fla., 1989, The Jane Voorhees Zimmerli Art Mus., Rutgers U., New Brunswick, N.J., 1990, Bradford Art Galleries and Mus., England, 1990, The Contemporary Arts Ctr., Cin., 1991, Northwest Art Gallery, Ind. U. Northwest, Gary, 1993, Printworks Gallery, Chgo., 1996, 97, Bibliotèque Nat. Québec, Montréal, Can., 1998, Adirondack C.C., Queensbury, N.Y., 1998, Parkland Coll., Champaign, Ill., 1998, Wayne State U., Detroit, 1999, S.C.'s Gov's. Sch. Arts and Humanities, Greenville, S.C., 1999, 2000; public collections include Adirondack Comty. Coll., Queensbury, Albion (Mich.) Coll., The Ark. Arts Ctr., The Boston Pub. Library, The Blanden Meml. Art Mus., The Carnegie Mus. Art, Pitts., East Tenn. State U., Greenville (S.C.) County Arts Ctr., Greenville County Mus. Art, The Hyde Collection, Glens Falls, The Library of Congress, Washington, D.C., The Metropolitan Mus. Art., N.Y., The Milw. Art Mus., The Mpls. Inst. Arts, The Munson-Williams-Proctor Inst. Mus. Art, The N.Y. Pub. Library, The Spencer Mus. Art, U. Kans., Syracuse U., The Toledo Mus. Art, U. Ariz. Mus. Art, U. Indpls., The Walker Art Ctr., Mpls., We. Mich. U., The Williams Coll. Mus. Art, Williamstown, Mass., Wright State U., Dayton, Ohio, Yale U. Art Gallery, The Jane Voorhees Zimmerli Art Mus., Rutgers U., New Brunswick, N.J. Visual Artists Fellow NEA, 1989, N.Y. Found. for the Arts fellow, 1988. Home: PO Box 136 Hudson Falls NY 12839-0136

LEARY, ROBIN JANELL, administrative secretary, county government official; b. Hudson, Wis., July 9, 1954; d. Edward James and Marlys Marie (Ensign) L. BA in History, U. Wis., Eau Claire, 1976. From stenographer I to program asst. IV U. Wis., 1977—; sec. 3rd Congl. Dist./Dem. Com. Wis., 1993-95, elected vice chmn., 1999-2001; bd. suprs. Dist. 23, Eau Claire County, 1996—. Chair edn. and agr. com. U. Wis. Extension, 2000—. Mem. Eau Claire County Housing Commn., 2002--; chmn. Eau Claire County Dem. Party, 1990-92, 99-2000, sec., 1986-90, ex-officio mem., 2000—, exec. bd., 1993-95, 2000—, 1st vice chmn., 1996-99; elected mem. exec. bd. Eau Claire County Dem. Party, 1995-96; credentials com. Wis. Dem. Com.,1990-95, chair com., 1990-92; elections commn. Wis. Dem. Com., 1990—; alternate platform and resolutions com. Wis. Dem. Com., 2001-02; mem. Chippewa Valley America's Promise steering com., 1998-99, chair publicity and mktg. com. 1998-99; del. Dem. Nat. Conv., Atlanta, 1988, N.Y.C., 1992, Chgo., 1996; mem. appropriations com. United Way of Greater Eau Claire, 1994-96. Recipient Classified Staff Excellence in Svc. award U. Wis.-Eau Clarie, 1995; named Female Dem. Vol. of Yr., Eau Claire County Dem. Party, 1989. Mem. AFL-CIO (Eau Claire area labor coun., treas. 1986-94, trustee 1994-98, 98-99, treas. 1999—, sec. 3d congl. dist. com. on polit. edn. 1993-97, 97—), AAUW, AFSCME Pub. Employees Organized to Promote Legis. Equality (vice chmn. 3d congl. dist. 1992-93, chair com. 1993-95, elected vice-chair 3d congl. dist. P.E.O.P.L.E. 1995-97, coun. 24 family and gender com. 1990-98, 99-2000, tri-coun. state woman's com., coun. 24 contracting out com., exec. bd. liaison, bargaining del. adminstrv. support unit coun. 24 2002--), Internat. Platform Assn., Chippewa Valley-Am.'s Promise (steering Com., chmn. publicity and mktg. com. 1998-99), Wis. State Employees Union (exec. bd. coun. 24 2000-02), Wis. Women's Network. Avocations: reading, bowling. Home: 2104 Providence Ct Eau Claire WI 54703-4103 Office: U Wis 105 Garfield Ave Eau Claire WI 54701-4811 E-mail: learyrj@uwec.edu.

LEARY, THOMAS BARRETT, federal agency administrator; b. Orange, N.J., July 15, 1931; s. Daniel and Margaret (Barrett) L.; m. Stephanie Lynn Abbott, Dec. 18, 1954, June 3, 1991; children: Thomas A., David A., Alison Leary Estep. AB, Princeton U., 1952; JD magna cum laude, Harvard U., 1958. Bar: N.Y. 1959, Mich. 1972, D.C. 1983. Assoc. White & Case, N.Y.C., 1958-68, ptnr., 1968-71; atty.-in-charge antitrust Gen. Motors Corp., Detroit, 1971-77, asst. gen. counsel, 1977-82; ptnr. Hogan & Hartson, Washington, 1983-99; commr. FTC, 1999—. Served to lt. USNR, 1952-55 Mem. ABA (antitrust sect., coun. mem. 1979-83, mem. antitrust adv. bd., BNA antitrust & trade reg. rep., 1981-99. Office: Fed Trade Commn 600 Pennsylvania Ave NW # 520 Washington DC 20580-0002 E-mail: tleary2@ftc.gov.

LEARY, WILLIAM JAMES, educational administrator; b. Boston, Oct. 1, 1935; s. John Gilbert and Josephine Marie (Kelley) L.; m. Joann Linda Parodi, June 25, 1960; children: Lorraine, Lisa, Linda. S.B., Boston Coll.; M.Ed., Boston State Coll.; postgrad. (Fulbright fellow), Sophia U., Tokyo, 1967; cert. advanced study, Harvard U., 1972, Ed.D., 1973, Boston U., 1971. Tchr. pub. schs., Boston, 1957-67; chmn. dept. social studies Dorchester High Sch., 1967-68; dir. curriculum Boston Dist. Pub. Schs., 1969-72, supt. schs., 1972-75; exec. dir. Met. Planning Project, Newton, Mass., 1975-77; supt. schs. Rockville Centre, N.Y., 1977-82, North Babylon, 1982-84, Broward County, Ft. Lauderdale, Fla., 1984-88; supt. Gloucester (Mass.) Pub. Schs., 1989-93; assoc. prof. dept. ednl. leadership, dept. chair U. Miss., Oxford, 1993-98, dir. PhD Program; prof. coll. edn. Lynn U., Boca Raton, Fla., 1998-2000. Assoc. prof. dept. continuing studies Bsoton State Coll., 1970-72; assoc. in edn. Harvard U. Grad. Sch. Edn., 1972-75; adj. prof. edn. Boston U., 1973-75, C.W. Post Ctr., L.I. U., 1979-84, Fla. Internat. U., 1984-88, Salem (Mass.) State Coll., 1990-93; prof. Suffolk U., 1977-82; TV commentator Channel 5, Boston, 1975-76; prodr. edn. programs New Eng. Cablevision, 1989-93; keynote spkr. Harvard U. Grad. Sch. Edn., 1976, NYU, 1980; mem. faculty senate U. Miss., 1994-96, chair subcom. on athletics, 1994-95. Edn. columnist Boston Herald, 1975-78, L.I. News, 1982-84, Gloucester Times; edn. commentator New Eng. Cablevision, 1989-93; contbr. articles to profl. jours. Edn. coord. Boston chpt. United Way, 1974, Rockville Centre United Fund, 1979-80, Broward County chpt., 1985-87; trustee Mus. Fin. Arts, Boston, 1972-77; bd. dirs. Boston Youth Symphony, 1972-77, Edn. Devel. Ctr., 1972-77, Broward Com. of 100, Boys Club Broward County, 1985-88; mem. nat. alumni bd. Boston U., 1975—; mem. vis. com. Suffolk U., 1978-80; adv. bd. Harvard N.Y. Alumni Forums, 1980-84; mem. L.I. Regional Planning Bd., 1983-84, Gov.'s Task Force on Alt. Edn., Fla., 1986-88; mem. Atty. Gen.'s edn. adv. com., Mass., 1991-93; lector, Eucharistic min. Ascension Cath. Ch., Boca Raton. Recipient Friend of Youth award Hayden Goodwill Boys' Home, 1973, Ida M. Johnston Outstanding Alumni award Boston U. Sch. Edn., 1976,

Man of Yr. award Pope's Hill Assn., 1976, Jenkins Meml. award for ednl. leadership N.Y. State Coun., PTA, 1980, Ednl. Leadership award L.I. chpt. NCCJ, 1980, Broward County Med. Aux., 1984, Lifetime Achievement award Matignon H.S. Alumni, 1995, Civil Rights award NAACP Layfayette County, MS, 1996; selected as mem. Exec. Educator 100, Nat. Sch. Bd. Assn., 1987; named to Matignon H.S. Hall of Fame, 1995. Mem. ASCD (nat. commn. on supervision 1984-85), Am. Assn. Sch. Adminstrs. (del. assembly 1991, 92, 93, resolutions com. 1988-89, 93-94, 94-95, 95-96), Am. Hist. Assn., Horace Mann League, Assn. for Asian Studies, Nat. Coun. Social Studies (nat. urban affairs com. 1977-80), Large City Sch. Supts., Mass. Atty. Gen.'s Adv. Group, Harvard Club N.Y.C., Boston Coll.Alumni Club, Varsity Club, KC, Rotary, Harvard Club of Boston, Am. Legion, Phi Delta Kappa. Roman Catholic. Office: Lynn U Grad Sch Edn Boca Raton FL 33431 E-mail: billyjoj@email.msn.com., wleary@lynn.edu. *A person's ability for creative and imaginative thinking is limited only by his/her fear to dream.*

LEASE, ROBERT K. lawyer; b. Cleve., 1948; AB magna cum laude, Dartmouth Coll., 1970; JD cum laude, U. Conn., 1976. Bar: Ohio. Ptnr. Baker & Hostetler LLP, Cleve. Mem. Phi Beta Kappa. Office: Baker & Hostetler LLP 3200 Nat City Ctr 1900 E 9th St Ste 3200 Cleveland OH 44114-3485 E-mail: rlease@bakerlaw.com.

LEASHER, JANET LOUISE, optometric physician; b. Somerville, N.J., Sept. 17, 1961; d. John Willard Jr. and Dorothy Anna Leasher. BS, Pacific U., 1983, OD, 1986; MPH, Tulane U., 1999. Cert. Nat. Bd. Examiners in Optometry; cert. for Diagnostic Pharm. Agt. and Therapeutic Pharm. Agt. use. Optometrist Pearle Vision Ctr., Everett, Wash., 1987-89, Teamsters Med. Ctr., Portland, Oreg., 1989-91, 99—; optometric physician North Portland Optical, 1989-98, Cedar Hills Vision Clinic, Portland, 1989—, Ojos La Ceiba, Honduras, 1996-97; asst. prof. clin. optometry Pacific U. Coll. Optometry, Forest Grove, Oreg., 1991—. Co-founder, v.p., mission leader Vol. Optometric Svc. to Humanity, Oreg., 1991—; faculty advisor, bd. dirs., AMIGOS of Pacific U., Forest Grove, 1991—; presenter in field. Coord. 1st Oreg. Lions in Sight mission Lions Club Internat., Portland, 1995-96; vol. med. team coord. Fundacion Cueroy Salado, La Ceiba, 1996—, Fundacion Parque Nacional Pico Bonito, La Ceiba, 1996—; vol. hurricane disaster relief coord. N.W. Med. Teams, La Ceiba, 1998. Named one of Top 150 Alumni of Pacific U., 2000; recipient Valued Svc. to Humanity award, AMIGOS Club of Pacific U., 1991—92, 1993—94, N.W. Med. Teams, Inc., 1992. Mem. Am. Optometric Assn. (Optometric Recognition award), Oreg. Optometric Assn. (Young Optometrist of Yr. 1993), Portland Met. Optometric Soc. (pres. bd. 1991-94). Democrat. Avocations: gardening, environmental conservation, kayaking, bicycling, hiking. Home: 920 NW Naito Pkwy # J-15 Portland OR 97209 Office: Pacific U Coll Optometry 2043 College Way Forest Grove OR 97116-1797 E-mail: leashejl@pacific.edu.

LEASK, JOHN MCPHEARSON, II, accountant; b. Oct. 21, 1942; s. Haldane Burgess and Laura (Manchester) Leask; m. Phoebe Kamelakis, Aug. 12, 1979; children: John McPhearson III, Peter Rizos(dec.) , Andy Rizos(dec.) , Joanna Rizos Bogardus(dec.). Student, U. Mich., 1961—68; AS in Acctg., Bryant Coll., 1973, BS in Acctg., 1974. CPA Conn. Salesman for Conn. and R.I. Winthrop Lab., N.Y.C., 1969—73; staff acct. Leask & Leask, P.C., Fairfield, Conn., 1973—75, v.p., 1976—80, audit prin., chmn. bd., mng. prin., 1980—2002, prin., 2002—, also dir. Adj. prof. Fairfield U., 1976—91. Contbg. editor: CPA Client Svc., 1991—94, mem. editl. adv. bd.: CPA Firm Profitability, 1994—97. Mem. Libr. Bldg. Com., Fairfield, 1981—83; mem. allocations coun. United Way, Bridgeport, 1991; co-pres. Am. Field Svc. Parents Group, 1983, 1986—91; mem. fin. bd. Bibliomation, 1996—97; mem. bd. Fairfield Rotary Found., 1990—2001, v.p., 1996—2001; vice chmn. East Providence Town Com., 1971—73; chmn. audit com. Congregationalist Ch., 1986—. Recipient Vol. award, United Way, 1983, Score citation, SBA Citations, Dr. Edward J. Kochan Outstanding Citizen award, Bridgeport Dental Assoc., 1998, Pub. Svc. award, CSCPA, 1998. Fellow: Conn. Soc. CPAs (CPE com. 1985—86, mgmt. acctg. practice com. 1985—88, mem. state taxation com. 1987—88, mgmt. acctg. practice com. 1990—94, CPE com. 1993—94); mem.: Fairfield C. of C. (pres. 1983—84, Harold Harris Cmty. Svc. award 1991), AICPA, Rotary Internat. (Fairfield treas. 1983—87, v.p. programs 1987—88, chpt. 1st v.p. 1988—89, dist. treas. 1988—90, pres. 1989—90, various dist. offices 1990—94, gov. R.I. dist. 7980 1995—96, nat. advisor to permanent fund 1999—2002, regional found. coord. 2002—, zone membership devel. coord. 2001—, pres.'s rep. 2002, Citation Meritorious Svc. Found. 1993, Paul Harris Cmty. Svc. award 1988, Paul Harris fellow 1988, 1995, 1997, Disting. Svc. award, Norm Parsells award 1996). Office: Leask & Leask PC CPAs 1100 Kings Hwy East PO Box 320235 Fairfield CT 06432-0235 E-mail: mac@leask.com.

LEASON, JODY JACOBS, newspaper columnist; b. Margarita, Venezuela, June 8, 1926; came to U.S., 1928; d. Jose Cruz Caceres and Graciela Rodriguez; m. Russell L. Jacobs (div.); 1 child, Jessica Jacobs Salet; m. Barney Leason, Dec. 29, 1976. BA, Hunter Coll.-CUNY, 1940's. Assoc. fashion editor Women's Wear Daily, N.Y.C., 1969-70, West Coast fashion editor L.A., 1957-69, London fashion editor, 1970-72; soc. editor L.A. Times, 1972-86. Author: (novel) The Right Circles, 1988. Avocations: needlework, gardening. E-mail: jaclea@lcan.net., jaclea@tcsn.net.

LEASOR, JANE, religion and philosophy educator, musician; b. Portsmouth, Ohio, Aug. 10, 1922; d. Paul Raymond Leasor and Rana Kathryn (Bayer) Leasor-McDonald BA, Wheaton Coll., 1944; MRE, N.Y. Theol. Sem., 1952; PhD, NYU, 1969. Asst. prof. Belhaven Coll., Jackson, Miss., 1952-54; dept. chmn. Beirut Coll. for Women, 1954-59; asst. to pres. Wheaton (Ill.) Coll., 1961-63; dean of women N.Y. Theol. Sem., N.Y.C., 1963-67; counselor CUNY, Bklyn., 1967-74; assoc. prof. Beirut U. Coll., 1978-80; tchr. internat. sch., Les Cayes, Haiti, 1984-85; pvt. tutor, 1985—; tchr. Fayette County (W.Va.) Schs., 1993—; prof. religion dept. U. Charleston, W.Va., 1999—. Author religious text for use in Syria and Lebanon, 1960; editor books by V.R. Edman, 1961-63, Time and Life mags. Mem. Am. Assn. Counselors, Am. Guild Organists. Episcopalian. Avocations: reading, gardening, golf, travel, history Islam religion. Home and Office: 1429 1/2 Quarrier St Charleston WV 25301-3009 *John Cardinal Newman wrote, "I sought to hear the voice of God and climbed the highest steeple. But God declared: 'Go down again; I dwell among the people.'" Words to live by.*

LEASURE, ROBERT ELLIS, writer, photographer; b. Lamar, Colo., Oct. 20, 1921; s. Henry Naley and Pansy Margaret (Leatherman) L.; m. Betty Jean Stulck, July 4, 1945; twins: Mary Margaret and David Lee. Grad. high sch., Lamar, Colo. Cryptographer 15th Air Force Air Def. Command, Colorado Springs, Colo., 1946; staff Colorado Springs (Colo.) Post Office, 1946-76; freelancer photographer, writer, 1976—. Author: Black Mountain, 1975; exhibited at Tex. Fine Art Assn. Mem. Colorado Springs Fine Arts Guild.Sgt. U.S. Army, 1942-45. Mem. VFW. Presbyterian. Avocations: nature, art, history, archaeology, literature. Home: 1210 Milky Way Colorado Springs CO 80906-1715

LEATH, KENNETH THOMAS, research plant pathologist, educator, agricultural consultant; b. Providence, Apr. 29, 1931; s. Thomas and Elizabeth (Wootten) L.; m. Marie Andreozzi, Aug. 1955; children: Kenneth, Steven, Kevin, Maria Beth. BS, U. R.I., 1959; MS, PhD, U. Minn., 1966. Rsch. plant pathologist U.S. Regional Pasture Rsch. Lab. USDA-ARS, 1966-94; prof. Pa. State U., 1966-94; pvt. agrl. cons. Boalsburg, Pa., 1994—. Advisor numerous state and nat. orgns. Contbr. numerous articles to profl. jours. and chpts. to books. With USN, 1951-55. Mem. Elks. Achievements include research on root diseases and systemic wilts of forage species.

LEATH, PAUL LARRY, physicist, educator, former university official; b. Moberly, Mo., Jan. 9, 1941; s. James Lewis and Naomia (Burton) L.; m. Rosemary Rippel, June 2, 1962; children: Steven, Kimberly. Grad., Moberly Jr. Coll., 1960; BS, U. Mo., 1961, MS, 1963, PhD, 1966. Rsch. officer Oxford U., Eng., 1966-67; asst. prof. physics Rutgers U., New Brunswick, 1967-71, assoc. prof., 1971-78, prof., 1978—, assoc. provost for acad. affairs, 1978-87, provost, 1987-92, chair dept. physics and astronomy, 1995—. Sr. vis. fellow Oxford U., 1972-73, 93-94; vis. prof. Mich. State U., 1992-93. Co-author: The Theory and Properties of Randomly Disordered Crystals and Related Physical Systems, 1974. Active Millstone (N.J.) Borough Coun., 1979-84, pres., 1984; bd. dirs. New Brunswick Tomorrow, 1989-92, R&D Coun. N.J., 1980-83. Mem. Am. Phys. Soc., Inst. Physics, AAAS, N.Y. Acad. Sci., Sigma Xi. Achievements include research in theoretical physics, properties of alloys and disordered materials, percolation processes, breakdown phenomena, and vibrational and electronic properties. Office: Rutgers U Dept Physics and Astro 136 Frelinghuysen Rd Piscataway NJ 08854-8019

LEATHER, VICTORIA POTTS, college librarian; b. Chattanooga, June 12, 1947; d. James Elmer Potts and Ruby Lea (Bettis) Potts Wilmoth; m. Jack Edward Leather; children: Stephen, Sean. BA cum laude, U. Chattanooga, 1968; MSLS, U. Tenn., 1978. Libr. asst. East New Orleans Regional Libr., 1969-71; libr. Erlanger Nursing Sch., Chattanooga, 1971-75; chief libr. Erlanger Hosp., 1975-77; dir. Eastgate Br. Libr., 1977-81; dir. libr. svcs. Chattanooga State Tech. Community Coll., 1981-95, dean libr. svcs., 1996—. Mem. Allied Arts, Hunter Mus., High Mus. Art. Mem. ALA, Southeastern Libr. Assn., Tenn. Libr. Assn. (past chair legislation com.), Chattanooga Area Libr. Assn. (pres. 1978-79), Tenn. Bd. Regents Media Consortium (chair 1994-95), Phi Delta Kappa. Episcopalian. Avocations: reading, needlework, traveling.

LEATHERBERRY, ANNE KNOX CLARK, architect; b. Geneva, Jan. 19, 1953; d. Donald William and Margaret Lorraine (Johnson) Clark; m. David Boyd Leatherberry, Aug. 5, 1978; children: Elizabeth Anne, Laura Knox. BS in Bus., Miami U., Oxford, Ohio, 1975. With Carson, Pirie, Scott & Co., Chgo., 1975-77; health care sales specialist Gen. Foods Corp., Northlake, Ill., 1977-78; account mgr. Cin., 1978-79; pres., owner Annie's Originals/Kids Collectables, Ltd., Waukesha, Wis., 1979—; mktg. rep./demonstrator mktg., 1988-91; owner Dreamhouse Designs, 1990—, Creative Enterprises Inc., 1990—. Cons. Lamb's Quarters, Hartford, Wis., 1982-83, Ungerwear, West Alexandria, Ohio, 1982-84, Little Bits, Waukeshaw, 1984-90, Evelyn's Creations, East Troy, Wis., 1986-90, The Queen's Empire, Inc., Pitts., 1989-90, DRC Co., Mukwonago, Wis., 1990—, Don Belman Builders, 1991-92, Millikin Homes, 1992—, Opportunity Homes, 1993—, Affordable Homes, 1993—, Gemini Homes, 1993, Nelson Remodeling, 1993. Active Waukesha Area Symphonic Band, 1979—, 98, 99, sec. bd. dirs., 1987-89, 99-02, v.p.; active Carroll Cllt Cmty. Orch., 1985-86; vol. tchr.'s aide Clarend on Avenue Sch., Mukwonago, 1988-89; asst. leader Girl Scouts U.S.A., 1988, leader, 1988-89; vol. staff aide Jim Thompson for Gov. Campaign, 1975-76; dir. Children's Choir, 1986; summer music dir. Luth. Ch., 1986, 88; events chmn. Edgewood Golf League, 1988-92; vol. Rose Glen Reading Rams, Waukesha, 1990-92, Health Room, 1990-91, tchr.'s aid, 1991-92; pres. archtl. rev. bd. Red Wing Hills Assn., 1993-96; instr. architecture mentor program Waukesha Sch. Dist., 1995—; spirit wear sales chmn., 1998—, Waukesha West H.S. Band Boosters, 1997—, bd. dirs., 1999—. Recipient Ptnrs. for Edn. award, 1998; named Parent Vol. of Yr. Waukesha C. of C., 1998. Mem. NAFE, PEO (officer 1980-82), Direct Mktg. Assn., Soc. Craft Designers, Met. Builders Assn., Nat. Assn. of Remodeling Industry, Kappa Kappa Gamma. Republican. Lutheran. Avocations: painting, sewing, reading, golf, gardening. E-mail address. Home and Office: W241s5910 Autumn Haze Ct Waukesha WI 53189-9512 E-mail: dreamhouse53@cs.com.

LEATHERBURY, GREGORY LUCE, JR. lawyer; b. Mobile, Ala., Feb. 11, 1947; s. Gregory L. and Florence (Greaves) L.; m. Susan Thames, June 13, 1969; children: Gregory L. Leatherbury III, Clifton Thames Leatherbury. BA, U. Ala., Tuscaloosa, 1969, JD, 1972; LLM in Taxation, NYU, 1973. Bar: Ala. 1973, U.S. Dist. Ct. (so. dist.) Ala. 1973. Atty. Hand Arendall, L.L.C., Mobile, 1973-98, Foley, Ala., 1998—. Mem. Mobile Estate Planning Coun., 1986—. Mem. Am. Coll. Mortgage Counsel, Rotary (pres. 1992, Paul Harris fellow 1992). Episcopalian. Avocations: fishing, hunting, scuba diving, skiing. Home: 29512 Canal Rd Orange Beach AL 36561-4407 Office: Hand Arendall LLC PO Box 1231 Foley AL 36536-1231 E-mail: gregl@handarendall.com., gregl2@gulftel.com.

LEATHERMAN, HUGH KENNETH, SR. state legislator, business executive; b. Lincoln County, N.C., Apr. 14, 1931; s. John Bingham and Ada Annis (Gantt) L.; m. Jean Helms, Nov. 11, 1978; children: Sheila Dianne, Hugh Kenneth, Karen Ann, Joyce Lynn, Amy Jean, Sarah Ada. BS in Civil Engring., N.C. State U., 1953; HHD (hon.), Francis Marion Coll., 1987. Engr. then sec. Florence (S.C.) Concrete Products Inc., 1955-72, pres., 1972-93; sec. Hugh-Stan Inc., Myrtle Beach, 1974—. Mem. S.C. Senate, 1980—; commr. S.C. Dept. Consumer Affairs. Deacon 1st Bapt. Ch. Named Legislator of Yr., 1982. Mem. S.C. State Budget & Control Bd.; Majority Leader, S.C. Senate. Home: 1817 Pineland Ave Florence SC 29501-5419 Office: 111 Gressette Bldg Columbia SC 29202

LEATHERMAN, N. DIANE, association executive; b. Kansas City, Mo., Dec. 22, 1937; d. Walter Mann and Nancy Adelia Shawhan Hall; m. Larry Heflin, Aug. 8, 1959 (div. 1972); children: Heidi, Mitchel, Holli, Leland; m. Mark W. Leatherman, June 19, 1982; 1 child, Blythe. AA, William Woods U., 1958; BA, Am. U., 1971. Tchr. Green Acres Sch., Rockville, Md., 1974, 75; park ranger Nat. Park Svc., McLean, Va., 1973-75, Glen Echo, Md., 1976-85; staff dir. Glen Echo Park Found., 1987-90; D.C. coord. Orphan Found., Washington, 1990-94; exec. dir. Friends of the Libr., Rockville, Md., 1994—2001; freelance writer, 2001—. Bd. dirs. Washington Ind. Writers, Beth Davis In Good Co., Glen Echo. Author: (book) Crossing Kansas, 1998; contbr. articles to Village News, Sentinel Newspaper, others. Past pres. Cabin John Citizens Assn., Md., 1993, other offices. Mem. Md. Writers Assn., Nat. Writers Union, Publs. Mktg. Assn., The Writers Ctr., Nat. Campaign to Save Glen Echo Park. Avocations: dance, piano, fabric art. Office: Friends of the Library 99 Maryland Ave Rockville MD 20850-2330 E-mail: diane.leatherman@prodigy.net.

LEATON, MARCELLA KAY, insurance representative, business owner; b. Eugene, Oreg., Oct. 9, 1952; d. Robert A. and Wanda Jo (Garner) Boehm; m. Michael G. Schlegel, Aug. 9, 1975; children: Kaellen June, Krystalynn Michele. Grad. high sch., Springfield, Oreg. Sales rep. The Prudential, Novato, Calif., 1973—; bus. owner Marcella Enterprises, 1983-2000; pvt. practice, 2000—. Owner, operator Meetings Extraordinaire, 1987—; owner Mastermind Escapes, 1990—; ind. travel agt., 1995—. Contbr. articles, poetry to profl. pubs. Mem. Nat. Assn. Life Underwriters (nat. quality award 1978, 80, 84), Marin Life Underwriters, Nat. Assn. Profl. Saleswomen (founder Marin chpt., pres. 1982-85, 91-93, chmn. 1985-87, nat. v.p. 1985-86, awards and recognition chmn. 1985-88, nat. pres. 1987-90, exec. dir. 1988-91, regional v.p. 1991-92, N.W. region conf. chmn. 1993), Leading Life Producers No. Calif., Million Dollar Round Table (qualifying), Marin Rowing Assn. (travel chmn. 1992-93), President's Club, Western Star Club, Leaders Club. Office: Marcella K Leaton Ins Sales and Svc 1929 Benton Ln Novato CA 94945-1747 Fax: 415-897-5347. E-mail: mleaton@aol.com.

LEATTO, RENNE, director, writer; b. Evergreen Park, Ill., Oct. 28, 1952; d. Anthony Gino and Patricia (Bays) L.; m. Matt Ross, June 14, 1974 (div. 1984); m. Lee Sommie, June 27, 1986. Student, L.A. City Coll., 1970-71, So. Oreg. U., 1981-82. Freelance dir., writer, producer, 1982—; pres. i.karumbah Corp., 2001—. Guest lectr. film classes So. Oreg. U., Ashland, 1987. Writer, dir. numerous TV programs, documentaries, dramatic, animated and info. films distributed worldwide and translated into several langs., including Discovery Cove, A Day in Paradise, 2000, Shamu TV: Arctic Animals (series pilot), 1996, The Causes and Effects of Drug Abuse, 1990, Alcohol, Drugs and Kids, 1988, Anger: Handle with Care, 1982; scriptwriter for numerous films and TV programs including Shamu TV (numerous episodes, 2 Emmy awards), 1996-97, Jack Hanna's Animal Adventures, 1998, Company of Animals (several episodes), 1996, Sexual Harassment Awareness, 1992; writer feature film Kelly, 1991, Workplace Violence (series), 1994, AIDS and Kids: A Bridge to Compassion, 1994. Recipient 2 Emmy awards; grantee Oreg. Arts Commn., 1989; Media award Nat. Safety Coun., Silver medal Internat. Film & TV Festival of N.Y., Houston Internat. Film and Video Festival. Mem. Women in Film Cen. Fla. Avocations: bird and wildlife watching, naturalist studies. E-mail: renne@ikarumbah.com.

LEAVELL, JOELLA JOHNSON, small business owner; b. Detroit, Sept. 4, 1948; d. Joseph Johnson, Lessie Mae Palmer; m. Robert L. Leavell, Jan. 10, 1990; children: Breona, Justin, Julian, Jonathane. Med. Transcriptionist Cert., PCI, Mich., 1990; PhD, ULC, Calif., 2001. Adminstrv. asst. Health S.W. Detroit Hosp.; coord. mental health Osteopathic Hosp., Mich.; proprietor ABMIC Propert Mgmt.; dir., owner Legal Expense Plan PPL, Dist. Dental Svcs./AmeriPlan. Minister, Mich., 1999—. Author: poetry in various jours. Recipient award, Nat. Libr. Poetry. Mem.: Internat. Soc. Poetry (Editor's Choice award 1990—). Office: PO Box 2682 Farmington Hills MI 48333

LEAVELL, MICHAEL RAY, computer programmer, analyst; b. Port St. Joe, Fla., Sept. 28, 1955; s. Ray Carl and Willodean (Griggs) L. AS in Electronics Tech., Gulf Coast Jr. Coll., Panama City, Fla., 1975; BS in Systems Sci., U. West Fla., 1979. Engr. Sta. WDTB-TV (now WMBB-TV), Panama City, 1976; radio announcer Sta. WJOE, Port St. Joe, 1979; computer programmer III, Fla. Dept. Labor, Tallahassee, 1979-80, computer programmer, analyst II, 1980-96, systems project analyst, 1996-98, 99—, yr. 2000 specialist, 1998. Office: Fla Dept of Labor Info Mgmt Ctr 264 Howard Bldg Tallahassee FL 32399 E-mail: michael_leavell@fdles.state.fl.us., floridamichael@hotmail.com.

LEAVELL, WILLIAM A. publisher, editor; b. Montgomery, Ala., Apr. 12, 1923; William A. and Myrtle I. (Watson) L.; m. Patty J. Shobe, June 24, 1927; William A. III, Melissa I. BA, U. Ala., 1945; MA, George Washington U., 1947, PhD, 1949. Owner Leavell & Assoc., Belleair, Fla., 1950-62; columnist "Keep Off The Grass" syndicated column, 1963-73; editor, pub. Washington Report, Editor Release Svcs. (Washington Report), St. Petersburg, Fla., 1974-97. Regular guest on several radio and TV stas. Author: (novel) As Honest As Times Permit, 1974. Adminstrv. asst. Congressman Arthur Winstead Washington 1947-49. With USAF 1944-45. Home: 4905 34th St S # 312 Saint Petersburg FL 33711-4511

LEAVENGOOD, VICTOR PRICE, telephone company executive; b. Ocala, Fla., June 2, 1924; s. Hansel Devane and Mildred (Price) L.; m. Elizabeth Lee Bird, Sept. 12, 1950; children: Sally (dec.), Ann, Hansel. BSBA, U. Fla., 1947; MBA, Harvard U., 1949. Bus. mgr. Ocala (Fla.) Star Banner (daily newspaper), 1952-59; circulation dir. Tampa (Fla.) Tribune, 1959-60, dir. community affairs, 1960-64; asst. v.p. Gen. Telephone Co. Fla., Tampa, 1964-70, sec., treas., 1970-87. Bd. dirs. Blue Cross Blue Shield Fla.; chair Hospice of Hillsborough, 1997-2001; mgmt. com. chair Hillsborough County Health Sys. Pres. Hills County Cmty. Coordination Coun., 1964-65, Tampa Econ. Opportunity Coun., 1965-66, Fla. Clergy Econ. Edn. Found., 1964-68, Fla. chpt. United Way, 1969-70; bd. dirs., treas. Fla. Aquarium, 1988-98, Hospice of Hillsborough, Fla.; bd. dirs. West Ctrl. Fla. Area Agy. on Aging, Japan-Am. Soc. Ctrl. Fla., Suncoast coun. Girl Scouts U.S.A.; bd. advisors U. South Fla. Contemporary Art Mus.; trustee Fla. Mental Health Inst.; chmn. Tampa Bay Internat. Super Task Force, Fla. Mcht. Assn., Tampa Commn. on Pub. Art; pres. United Fund Greater Tampa Inc., 1964-68, treas., 1970-75; mem. Fla. Coun. Mental Health Tng. and Rsch., 1967-74, President's Round Table, Eckerd Coll., St. Petersburg, Fla., 1969—; mem. president's coun. U. South Fla., 1974—, Hillsborough County Hosp. Authority; treas. U. South Fla. Found., 1957-80, pres., 1982-83. Comdr. USNR, 1942-47. Mem. Greater Tampa C. of C. (bd. dirs.), Fla. C. of C., edn. com. 1968-71), U.S. C. of C. (edn. com.), Phi Eta Sigma, Phi Delta Theta.; mem. Ye Mystic Krewe of Gasparilla. Democrat. Methodist (ofcl. bd.). Clubs: University (Tampa), Tampa, Tampa Yacht and Country (Tampa). Home: 4516 W Sylvan Ramble St Tampa FL 33609-4214

LEAVEY, JOHN CHRISTOPHER, artist; b. Bronx, N.Y., Mar. 21, 1937; s. Thomas Joseph Leavey and Anastasia Moore; m. Norma Leavey, Jan. 21, 1961. Student, Art Students League, N.Y.C., 1955-61. One-man shows include Columbia U., N.Y.C., 1965, Seamens Ch. Inst., N.Y.C., 1969, Am. Acad. in Rome, 1972, U.S. Info. Svc., Rome, 1972, Agostino Gallery, Rome, 1974, St. Stephens Sch., Rome, 1974, Blue Mountain Gallery, 1980, 83, 87, 89, So. Vt. Art Ctr., 1996, 98, 2001; exhibited in group shows Allied Artists, N.Y.C., 1961, Harbor Gallery, L.I., N.Y., 1965, 66, 67, Gallery Schneider, Rome, 1970, 71, 72, 73, 74, 75, 76, Gallery 88, Rome, 1971, 72, 73, 74, 75, 76, Agostino Gallery, Rome, 1974, 75, 76, Am. Acad. in Rome, 1970-71, Forum Gallery, N.Y.C., 1973, Orgn. Ind. Artists, 1981, Prince St. Invitational, N.Y.C., 1985, Blue Mountain Gallery, 1980, 82, 84, 86, 87, 89, 90, 91, 92, 93, 94, 95, 96, 97, 98, 99, 2000, 2001, Grand Ctrl. Gallery, N.Y.C., 1988-89, Nat. Acad. Design, N.Y.C., 1963, 78, 88, 90, Water Mill Gallery, Bridgehampton, N.Y., 1992, So. Vt. Artists Annual, 1994, 95, 96, 97, 98, 99, 2000, 2001, Audubon Artists, N.Y.C., 1994, 95, 96, 97, 99, 99, 2000, 2001, So. Vt. Art Ctr., 1995, 96, 97, 98, 99, Atelier A/E, N.Y.C., 1994, 95, 96, 97, 98, Spring Studio, N.Y.C., 1995, 97, 99, 2001, 1st St. Gallery, N.Y.C., 1995, Gallery 84, N.Y.C., 1995, Zone 1 Invitational, Asheville, N.C., 1996, Ashwell Gallery, Beverly, Mass., 1996, Staten Island Inst. Arts and Scis., 1997, Roxbury (N.Y.) Arts Group, 1997, Springfield (Mass.) Mus. Art, 1997, Stanford Smith's Works on Paper, N.Y.C., 1997, Western Carolina U., 1997, W.Va. Wesleyan Coll., 1997, Art Internat., N.Y.C., 1998, Beckwith Gallery, Jamacia, Vt., 2000, 01, 02, Harrison Gallery, Williamstown, Mass., 2001, 02; represented in permanent collections Museo della Citta da Roma, Dickinson Coll., Carlisle, Pa., Reader's Digest Collection, Pleasantville, N.Y., Hirschhorn Collection, Nat. Gallery, D.C., Peizer Co., N.Y.C.; executed mural Am. Acad. Rome, N.Y. Louis Comfort Tiffany grantee Tiffany Found., 1965; Edwin Austin Abbey fellow Am. Acad. in Rome, 1969-70, 70-71; recipient B.J. Altman Figure prize Nat. Acad. Design, 1988, McNeely Meml. award Audubon Artists, 1995, Art Students League award Audubon Artists, 2001. Fellow Am. Acad. in Rome; mem. United Scenic Artists Am., Art Students League, Audubon Artists, So. Vt. Artists. Democrat. Avocations: reading, classical music. Home: 289 Lincoln Ln Sandgate VT 05250 Studio: 32 Union Sq New York NY 10003

LEAVEY, TERRANCE CHARLES, historical resources manager; b. Sacramento, Feb. 11, 1947; s. Henry Harold and Harriet T. (Ferguson) L.; m. Frances Elaine Morrone, Nov. 3, 1973; stepchildren: Brena Elaine Richmond, David Benton Richmond. Student, Calif. Inst. of the Arts, 1965-66, Merced (Calif.) Coll., 1974-76; cert. bus. practices, Rio Salado Coll., 1985. Pvt. practice band leader, musician, Calif., 1964-69; computer programmer Williams Turkey Breeding Farms, Oakdale, 1969-70; computer tech. asst. Computer Scis. Corp., L.A., 1970, system programmer Sacramento, 1978-81; computer cons. Am. Info. Devel., San Francisco, 1970-71; cattle man Favier Cattle Co., Merced, 1971-72; computer programmer Merced County, 1973-76; owner Cody Enterprises, Merced, 1976-78; systems programmer Ariz. Pub. Svc., Phoenix, 1981-89. Hist. cons., mem. staff movies Rambo III, 1988, Back to the Future III, 1989, Glory, 1989, Ironclads, 1990, TV Geronimo, 1986, Young Riders, Gathering Clouds, 1989, Geronimo (TNT), 1993, Buffalo Soldiers, 1994, Deadman, 1994, commls. for Hardee's Hamburgers, 1988, Sanyo, 1989. Editor, pub. newsletter AZRA News, 1988—. Chmn. bd. Leavey Found. for Hist. Preservation, Inc., 1988—. Recipient Jefferson Davis medal United Daughters of the Confederacy, 1988, Svc. award City of Phoenix, 1988. Mem. Ariz. Civil War Coun., Inc. (pres. 1984-88, bd. dirs. 1986-88), 602 Ariz., Metro Phoenix Film Bd., Ariz. Reenactors Assn. (pres. 1988—), Electric Horsemen (startup chmn. Phoenix chpt. 1988), SAG, YWCA Camera Club (pres. Phoenix chpt. 1982-84). Republican. Roman Catholic. Office: Leavey Found PO Box 26957 Phoenix AZ 85068-6957 *Personal philosophy: Propaganda the veil over history. History the key to the future.*

LEAVEY, THOMAS EDWARD, international organization administrator; b. Kansas City, Mo., Nov. 10, 1934; BA, Josephinum Coll, 1957; Lic., Cath. Inst., Paris, 1964; MA, Princeton U., 1967, PhD, 1968; cert. in bus. and fin., NYU, U. Tex., U. Va., Duke U., 1969-91. Prof. Tng. and Devel. Inst., Bethesda, Md., 1970-72; dir. Postal Svc. Tng. and Devel. Mgmt. Tng. Ctr., L.A., 1973-75; gen. mgr. employment and placement divsn. USPS Hdqs., 1976-78, 1976-78, dir. postal career exec. svc., 1979; postmaster, sectional ctr. mgr. Charlottesville, Va., 1980; regional dir. human resources cen. region Chgo., 1981; contr. USPS Hdqs., 1982, gen. mgr. internat. mail processing divsn., 1982-87, asst. postmaster gen., sr. dir. internat. postal affairs, 1987-94; dir. gen. internat. bur. Universal Postal Union, Berne, 1995—. Prof. Fairleigh Dickinson U., Teaneck, N.J., George Washington U., Washington, 1968-70. Recipient Heinrich von Stephan medal German Ministry of Post and Telecomm., 1997, ASTD award, 1973. Office: Universal Postal Union Case postale 3000 Bern 15 Switzerland

LEAVITT, DAVID ADAM, writer, English educator; b. Pitts., June 23, 1961; s. Harold Jack and Gloria (Rosenthal) L. BA, Yale U., 1983. Prof. English U. Fla. Author: Family Dancing, 1984 (Nat. Book Critics Cir. award nomination 1984, PEN-Faulkner award nomination 1985), The Lost Language of Cranes, 1986, Equal Affections, 1988, A Place I've Never Been, 1990, While England Sleeps, 1993, (with Mark Mitchell) Italian Pleasures, 1996, Arkansas, 1997, The Page Turner, 1998, Martin Bauman or a Sure Thing, 2000, The Marble

Quilt, 2001, Florence, A Delicate Case, 2002; co-editor: The Penguin Book of Gay Short Fiction, 1994, Pages Passed from Hand to Hand, 1997; contbr. to periodicals including Esquire, Harper's, New Yorker, N.Y. Times Book Rev., Village Voice, others. Recipient Willets prize for fiction Yale U., 1982, O. Henry Award, 1984; Nat. Endowment for Arts grantee, 1985; vis. fgn. writer Inst. Catalan Letters, Barcelona Spain, 1989; Guggenheim fellow, 1990. Mem. PEN, The Author's Guild. Office: U Fla Dept English PO Box 117310 Gainesville FL 32611-7310 E-mail: dleavitt@english.ufl.edu.

LEAVITT, DAVID LIVINGSTONE, architect; b. Omaha, Aug. 26, 1918; s. Frederick William and Mattie Louise Knapp Bennett. BA in Architecture, U. Nebr., 1940; M of Architecture, Princeton (N.J.) U., 1942. Assoc. prof. Princeton (N.J.) U., 1941-42; chief designer Raymond and Rado, N.Y.C., Tokyo, 1951-53; with Firm Leavitt & Henshell, N.Y.C., 1953-60; instr. in design Columbia U., 1956, Pratt Inst., Bklyn., 1957-59; dir. architecture and interior design Hilton Internat., N.Y.C., 1968-76; architectural designer Mr. Bailey Assoc., Athens, 1977-80; hotel design cons. N.Y.C., 1982—. Architectural designer residencies Russel Wright, 1956, Reader's Digest Bldg. Tokyo, 1964, Nanzan U., 1966, U.S. Embassy Housing, Tokyo, 1953. Regents scholarship U. Nebr., 1936; recipient Princeton prize, 1940, Rome prize, 1950. Mem. AIA, Nat. Architects Registration (bd. dirs. 1946-99), Far East Assn. of Architects and Engrs. Avocations: painting, music (piano), reading, swimming, tennis. Home: 118 W 72nd St Apt 903 New York NY 10023-3321 Office: c/o ADA 170 E 61st St New York NY 10021-8551

LEAVITT, JEFFREY STUART, lawyer; b. Cleve., July 13, 1946; s. Sol and Esther (Dolinsky) L.; m. Ellen Fern Sugerman, Dec. 21, 1968; children: Matthew Adam, Joshua Aaron. AB, Cornell U., 1968; JD, Case Western Res. U., 1973. Bar: Ohio 1973. Assoc. Jones, Day, Reavis & Pogue, Cleve., 1973-80, ptnr., 1981—. Contbr. articles to profl. jours. Trustee Bur. Jewish Edn., Cleve., 1981-93, v.p., 1985-87; trustee Fairmount Temple, Cleve., 1982-2002, v.p., 1985-90, pres., 1990-93; trustee Citizens League Greater Cleve., 1982-89, 92-94, pres., 1987-89; trustee Citizens League Rsch. Inst., Cleve., 1989-98, Great Lakes Region of Union Am. Hebrew Congregations, 1990-93; mem. bd. govs. Case Western Res. Law Sch. Alumni Assn., 1989-92; sec. Kulas Found., 1986-88, 93-99, asst. treas., 1989-92. Mem. ABA (employee benefits coms. 1976—), Nat. Assn. Pub. Pension Attys. Jewish. Home: 7935 Sunrise Ln Novelty OH 44072-9404 Office: Jones Day Reavis & Pogue N Point 901 Lakeside Ave E Cleveland OH 44114-1190

LEAVITT, JEROME EDWARD, childhood educator; b. Verona, N.J., Aug. 1, 1916; s. Thomas Edward and Clara Marie (Sonn) L.; m. Florence Elizabeth Wilkins, Aug. 23, 1963. BS, Newark State Coll., 1938; MA, N.Y. U., 1942; Ed.D., Northwestern U., 1952. Tchr. pub. schs., Roslyn Heights, N.Y., 1938-42; instr. Sperry Gyroscope, Bklyn., 1942-45; prin., supr. pub. schs. Los Alamos, N.Mex., 1945-49; prof. edn., exec. asst. to dean Portland (Oreg.) State U., 1952-66; prof. edn. U. Ariz., Tucson, 1966-69; prof. elem. edn., coordinator Child Abuse Project, Calif. State U., Fresno, 1969-81; pres. Jerome Leavitt, Inc., 1981—. Author: Nursery-Kindergarten Edn., 1958, Carpentry for Children, 1959, By Land, By Sea, By Air, 1969, The Beginning Kindergarten Teacher, 1971, America and Its Indians, 1971, The Battered Child, 1974, Herbert Sonn: Yosemite's Birdman, 1975, Child Abuse and Neglect: Research and Innovation, 1983, others; contbr. articles to profl. jours. Mem. ASCD (life), NEA (life), Assn. Childhood Edn. Internat. (life), Soc.Profs. Edn., Calif. Tchrs. Assn., Profs. Curriculum, Phi Delta Kappa, Kappa Delta Pi, Epsilon Pi Tau. Home and Office: Apt 13208 Apt 13208 7500 N Calle Sin Envidia Tucson AZ 85718-7372

LEAVITT, MARTIN JACK, lawyer; b. Detroit, Mar. 30, 1940; s. Benjamin and Annette (Cohen) L.; m. Janice C. McCreary; children: Michael J., Paul J., David A., Dean N., Keleigh R. LLB, Wayne State U., 1964. Bar: Mich. 1965, Fla. 1967. Assoc. Robert A. Sullivan, Detroit, 1968-70; officer, bd. dirs. Law Office Sullivan & Leavitt, Northville, Mich., 1970—, pres., 1979—. Bd. dirs. Tyrone Hills of Mich., Premiere Video, Inc., others. Lt. comdr. USNR, 1965-68. Detroit Edison upper class scholar, 1958-64. Mem. ABA, Mich. Bar Assn., Fla. Bar Assn., Transp. Lawyers Assn., ICC Practitioners, Meadowbrook Country Club, Huron River Hunting and Fishing Club (past pres.), Rolls Royce Owners Club (bd. dirs.). Jewish. Office: Sullivan and Leavitt PC PO Box 5490 Northville MI 48167-5490 E-mail: mjl@sullivanleavitt.com.

LEAVITT, MAURA LYNN, elementary education educator; b. Buffalo, Mar. 7, 1946; d. Joseph Richard and Hermina (Wagner) Takats; m. Henry Clark Leavitt, Jan. 22, 1984. BA, Elmira Coll., 1968; MA, George Wash. U., 1977. Elem. tchr. Candor (N.Y.) Cen. Schs., 1968-72; ednl. dir., coord. Prelude Drug Rehab. Program, Arlington, Va., 1972-76; ednl. coord., tchr. Arlington County Jail - GED program, 1974-77, Argus House - Juv. Detention Home, Arlington, 1977; founder, dir. Ednl. Diagnostic Svcs., 1978-81; adminstrv. asst. Caldwell, Prothro & Wilson, 1981-84; tchr., elem. Flint Hill Prep. Sch., Oakton, Va., 1984-87; tchr., secondary history/govt. Clay/Langston Alt. Schs., Arlington, 1977-81; tchr., elem. Drew Model Sch./Alt. Sch., 1987-91; tchr. Arlington Pub. Schs., 1991-99, curriculum devel. law related edn., 1992-94; tchr. McKinley Elem., Arlington, 1999—. Bd. dirs., v.p. No. Va. Hot Line, Arlington, 1984-86. Mem. Nat. Assn. Children with Learning Disabilities, Va. Assn. Children with Learning Disabilities, Arlington Assn. Children with Learning Disabilities, Greater Wash. Reading Coun., Va. State Reading Assn., Va. Coun. for Social Studies (bd. dirs. 1994-96), Nat. Coun. for Social Studies. Avocations: stained glass design, travel, sports.

LEAVITT, MICHAEL OKERLUND, governor, insurance executive; b. Cedar City, Utah, Feb. 11, 1951; s. Dixie and Anne (Okerlund) L.; m. Jacalyn Smith; children: Michael Smith, Taylor Smith, Anne Marie Smith, Chase Smith, Weston Smith. BA, So. Utah U., 1978. CPCU. Sales rep. Leavitt Group, Cedar City, 1972-74, account exec., 1974-76, mgr. underwriting Salt Lake City, 1976-82, chief operating officer, 1982-84, pres., chief exec. officer, 1984-92; gov. State of Utah, 1993—. Bd. dirs. Pacificorp, Portland, Oreg., Utah Power and Light Co., Salt Lake City, Great Western Thrift and Loan, Salt Lake City. Utah Bd. Regents, chmn. instl. coun. So. Utah State U., Cedar City, 1985-89; campaign chmn. U.S. Sen. Orrin Hatch, 1982, 88, U.S. Sen. Jake Garn, 1980, 86; cons. campaign Gov. Norman Angerter, 1984; mem. staff Reagan-Bush '84. 2d lt. USNG, 1969-77. Named Disting. Alumni So. Utah State Coll. Sch. Bus., 1986. Mem. CPCU. Republican. Mem. Lds Ch. Avocation: golf. Office: Office Gov 210 State Capitol Building Salt Lake City UT 84114-1202 E-mail: governor@utah.gov.*

LEAVITT, SHELDON JOSEPH, civil engineer, architect, consultant; b. Chgo., Oct. 14, 1922; s. Charles Paul and Sadie (Joseph) L.; m. Marian Adele Cogen, Dec. 31, 1951; children: Charles, Jonathan, Shirra. BSCE in Structural Engrng., U. Ill., 1943. Registered architect, Conn., Ill., Ind., Md., Mass., N.C., Ohio, Va.; registered profl. engr., D.C., Md., N.C., Va. Field engr. Va. Engring Co., Norfolk, 1946; archtl. draftsman Bernard Spiegel, AIA, 1946-47; design & field engr. Tidewater Constrn. Co., 1947-50; archtl. & sr. structural designer A. Epstein & Sons, Inc., Chgo., 1950-53; prin. Leavitt Assocs., Architecture and Engring., Norfolk, 1953—. Alternating chmn. Va. State Joint Coop. Com. Architects, Engrs. and Gen. Contractors, 1978-2001; mem. constrn. arbitration panel Am. Arbitration Assn. Author: The Torch Internat. Design of Housing for Elderly, 1988, Archtl. Record Oheb Shalom Temple, Balt., 1960; editor Va. Constrn. Industry Guidelines, 1990-2001. Chmn. Permanent Bldg. Code Comn., Norfolk, 1970-75, City of Norfolk Design Rev. Com., 1973-88; vice chmn. Bldg. Code Bd. Appeals, Norfolk, 1975-97, chmn., 1998—. With USN, 1944-46, PTO, ETO, comdr. CEC, USNR ret. Recipient Ira O. Baker award, Bronze Tablet award. Fellow ASCE (life), Nat. Acad. Forensic Engrs. (nat. rev. com. ASCE proposed manual 1988-89); mem. ASTM (E06 performance of bldg. construction), AIA (bd. dirs. Va. soc. 1977-80, pres. Tidewater sect. 1982, bldg. performance and regs. nat. com. 1989-2000, liason rep. and official testifier to BOCA 1990-2000, Outstanding Svc. to Pub. award 1987, Svc. to Archtl. Profession award 1994), Constrn. Specifications Inst., Soc. Am. Mil. Engrs., Am. Cons. Engrs. Coun. (profl. practice com. 1980—), Nat. Inst. Engring. Ethics, Bldg. Officials and Code Adminstr. Internat (voting rep. Va. prfl. chapt. to BOCA), Tau Beta Pi, Phi Kappa Phi, Sigma Xi, Chi Epsilon, others. Home: 1348 Botetourt Gdns Norfolk VA 23517-2204 Office: Leavitt Assocs 4400 Colley Ave Norfolk VA 23508-2511

LEAVITT, THOMAS WHITTLESEY, retired museum director, educator; b. Boston, Jan. 8, 1930; s. Richard C. and Helen M. (Pratt) L.; m. Jane O. Ayer, June 23, 1951 (div. 1969); children: Katherine, Nancy, Hugh; m. Lloyd B. Carter, Sept. 14, 1978 (div. 1985); m. Michele C. McDonald, Apr. 20, 1991; children: Zachary Leavitt, Collin McDonald. AB, Middlebury (Vt.) Coll., 1951; MA, Boston U., 1952; PhD, Harvard, 1958. Asst. to dir. Fogg Mus., Harvard, 1954-56; exec. dir. fine arts com. People to People Program, 1957; dir. Pasadena (Calif.) Art Mus., 1957-63, dir. Santa Barbara (Calif.) Mus. Art, 1963-68; dir. Andrew Dickson White Mus. Art, Cornell U., Ithaca, N.Y., 1968-73, Herbert F. Johnson Mus. Art, 1973-91; univ. prof. history art Cornell U., 1968-91, prof. emeritus, 1991—; interim dir. RISD Mus. Art, 1993-94, Newport Art Mus., 1994-95, The Menil Collection, Houston, 1999-2000. Dir. mus. program Nat. Endowment for Arts, 1971-72, mem. museum panel, 1972-75; vice chmn. Council on Museums and Edn. in Visual Arts, 1972-76; trustee Gallery Assn. N.Y. State, 1972-78; mem. mus. panel N.Y. State Council Arts, 1975-78, 1980-82; chmn. art adv. com. Nat. Air and Space Mus., 1988—. Author exhbn. catalogs, articles. Trustee Am. Fedn. Arts, 1972-91, Newport Art Mus., 1995-2001; bd. dirs. Am. Arts Alliance, 1976-82, Ind. Sector, 1980-84; bd. govs. N.E. Mus. Conf., 1973-76; trustee Williamstown Regional Art Conservation Lab., 1979-91, pres., 1984-87. Mem. Assn. Art Mus. Dirs. (pres. 1977-78, trustee 1978-80), Am. Assn. Museums (council 1976-79, v.p. 1980-82, pres. 1982-85, Disting. Svc. to Museums award 1997). Home: 25 Waterway Rd Saunderstown RI 02874-3906 Fax: 401-295-5061.

LEAVITT, VICTORIA SEYFERTH, marketing professional; b. Münchweiler, Federal Republic Germany, May 29, 1959; came to U.S., 1960; d. Blaine H. and Barbara (Geyer) S.; m. William E. Leavitt Jr., June 11, 1983. BS in Human Genetics, MA in Communications, U. Mich., 1981. Brand asst. Procter & Gamble Co., Cinn., 1981-82, asst. brand mgr., 1982-84; assoc. product mgr. Gen. Foods Corp., White Plains, N.Y., 1984-85, product mgr., 1985-87, sr. product mgr., team leader, 1987-89; group product mgr. Kraft Gen. Foods, 1988-89; acct. supr. US Comm., 1990-91, Rapp Collins Comm., 1990-91, v.p., 1991-93, sr. v.p., dir. bus. devel. and west coast ops., 1993-97; sr. v.p., dir. bus. devel. Campbell Mithun Esty, Mpls., 1997-98; exec. v.p., dir. bus. devel. Lighthouse Holdings, Chgo., 1998—. Vol. Bruce Mus. Storyhour Jr. League, Greenwich, Conn., 1985—, Jr. League of Mpls., Mentium 100, 1990—. Avocations: tennis, golf. Office: Lighthouse Holdings Inc 676 N Michigan Ave Chicago IL 60611-2883

LEAVY, EDWARD, federal judge; b. 1929; m. Eileen Leavy; children: Thomas, Patrick, Mary Kay, Paul. AB, U. Portland, 1950; LLB, U. Notre Dame, 1953. Dist. judge Lane County, Eugene, Oreg., 1957—61, cir. judge, 1961—76; magistrate U.S. Dist. Ct. Oreg., Portland, 1976—84, judge, 1984—87; cir. judge U.S. Ct. Appeals (9th cir.), 1987—97, sr. judge, 1997—. Office: US Ct Appeals Pioneer Courthouse 555 SW Yamhill St Ste 232 Portland OR 97204-1323

LEAVY, HERBERT THEODORE, publisher; b. Detroit, July 10, 1927; s. Morris and Thelma (Davidson) L.; m. Patricia J. Moran, June 20, 1953; children: Karen, Kathryn, Jill, Jacqueline. BS in Journalism, Ohio U., 1951. Supervisory editor Fawcett Books, N.Y.C., 1951-60; v.p., editorial dir. Davis Publs., 1960-69; founder, pres. Internat. Evaluations, Hauppage, N.Y., 1969-70; pub. dir. Countrywide Publs. Inc., N.Y.C., 1970-75; pres. Communications Devel. Co., 1975-79; editorial dir. Watson-Guptil Publs., 1979-80; pres. Books from Mags., Inc., Smithtown, N.Y., 1980—. Resumes Unltd., Smithtown, 1984—. Author: 101 Fast Track Resumes, The Pleasure, Executive Handbook, Vegetarian Times Cookbook, McCall's Houseplant and Indoor Landscaping Guide, Working Mother Cookbook, Carpentry, Shoe and Leather Repair at Home, The Complete Book of Beards and Moustaches, Air Conditioning-Repair and Maintenance, Designing and Building Beds, Lofts and Sleeping Areas, Wallcovering, Floor Stripping and Refinishing, Packing and Moving, Recreational Vehicles, Appliance Repair, Plumbing Handbook, Successful Small Farms; numerous others; editor-in-chief: The Ohioan Mag. Ohio U., 1950-51. Acting 1st sgt. USAF, 1946—47. Mem. Sales Exec. Club, Am. Soc. Mag. Editors, Nat. Sporting Goods Assn., Am. Mgmt. Assn., Mag. Advts. Sales Club, Electronics Press Club, U.S. Tennis Ct. and Track Builders Assn., Am. Motorcycle Assn., Am. Horse Council, Authors Guild, Motorcycle Industry Council, Nat. Indoor Tennis Assn., Bus./Profl. Advt. Assn., Sigma Delta Chi.

LEB, ARTHUR STERN, lawyer; b. Cleve., June 26, 1930; s. Ernest A. and Bertha (Stern) L.; m. Lois Shafron, Jan. 31, 1954; children: Gerald P., Judith A., Robert B. AB, Columbia Coll., 1952; JD, Case Western Res. U., 1955. Bar: Ohio 1955, U.S. Supreme Ct. 1965. Ptnr. Leb & Halm, Canton, Ohio, 1961-84, Amerman, Bert & Jones, L.P.A., Canton, 1985-90; of counsel Buckingham, Doolittle & Burroughs, L.L.P., 1991—. Founding mem., exec. com. Ohio Coun. Sch. Bd. Attys., 1976-84, pres. 1983. Served to 1st lt. JAGC, USAF, 1955-57. Recipient Merit award Ohio Legal Ctr. Inst., 1964. Fellow Ohio Bar Found.; mem. ABA, Ohio Bar Assn., Stark County Bar Assn. (pres. 1985-86). E-mail: asleb@bdblaw.com.

LEBAMOFF, IVAN ARGIRE, lawyer; b. Ft. Wayne, Ind., July 20, 1932; s. Argire V. and Helen A. (Kachandov) L.; m. Katherine S. Lebamoff, June 9, 1963; children— Damian I., Jordan I., Justin A. AB in History, Ind. U., 1954, JD, 1957. Bar: Ind. 1957, U.S. Dist. Ct. (no. and so. dists.) 1958, U.S. Supreme Ct. 1963. Sole practice, Ft. Wayne, Ind., 1957-68; ptnr. Lebamoff, Ver Wiebe & Snow, 1968-71; mayor City of Ft. Wayne, 1972-75; sole practice Lebamoff Law Offices, Ft. Wayne, 1975—. U.S. commr. No. Dist. Ind., 1957-62; fgn. service officer USIA Dept. Commerce, Bulgaria, 1964; vis. prof. dept. urban affairs Ind. U.-Purdue, Ft. Wayne, 1976-77 Chmn. Allen County Democratic Com., 1968-75, Ft. Wayne Dept. Parks and Recreation, 1984-88; nat. pres. Macedonian Patriotic Orgn. of U.S. and Can., 1983-94. Served with USAF, 1958-64 Mem. ABA, Allen County Bar Assn., Ind. Bar Assn., Am. Trial Lawyers Assn., Ind. Trial Lawyers Assn. Lodges: Kiwanis. Eastern Orthodox. Home: 205 E Packard Ave Fort Wayne IN 46806-1014 Office: Lebamoff Law Offices 918 S Calhoun St Fort Wayne IN 46802-2502

LEBARON, ALICE ANNE, musician; b. Baton Rouge; BA, U. Ala.; MA, SUNY, Stony Brook; PhD, Columbia U. Composer-in-residence New Residencies, Meet The Composer, Washington; asst. prof. composition and music theory U. Pitts., 1997—. Composer: Pope Joan, Traces of Mississippi, Is Money Money, The E. & O. Line, Solar Music, Concerto for Active Frogs, Dish, Blue Harp Studies No. 1 & No. 2, American Icons, Double Harp Concerto, Planxty Bowerbird, Sachamama, Southern Ephemera, Croak, Devil in the Belfry, Sukey, Telluris Theoria Sacra, Nightmare, Strange Attractors; recordings: Sacred Theory of the Earth, Rana, Ritual and Revelations, Bouquet of a Phantom Orchestra, The Musical Railism of Anne LeBaron. Fulbright scholar, Germany, 1980-81; Guggenheim Fellow; recipient CalArts Alpert Award in Arts, 1996. Office: Calif Inst Arts Sch Music 24700 McBean Pkwy Valencia CA 91355-2397 Home: 25315 Via Brasa Valencia CA 91355 E-mail: lebaron@shoko.calarts.edu.

LEBARON, EDWARD WAYNE, JR. retired lawyer; b. San Rafael, Calif., Jan. 7, 1930; s. Edward Wayne and Mabel Butler (Sims) LeB.; m. Doralee M. LeBaron, June 4, 1954; children: Edward Wayne, William Bruce, Richard Wilson. BA, Coll. Pacific, 1950; LLB, George Washington U., 1959. Bar: Calif. bar 1960, Tex. bar 1960, Nev. bar 1967. Football quarterback Washington Redskins, 1952-59; with Dallas Cowboys, 1960-63; exec. v.p. Nevada Cement Co., 1964-65; mem. firm Wynne & Wynne, Dallas, 1960-63, Bible, McDonald & Carano, Reno, 1966-68, Laxalt & Berry, Carson City, Nev., 1969-70; partner firm Jones, Jones, Bell, LeBaron and Brown, Las Vegas, 1970-76; gen. mgr. Atlanta Falcons Football team, 1977-85; ptnr. Powell, Goldstein, Murphy & Frazer, 1986-89, Pillsbury, Madison & Sutro, 1989-94; ret., 1994. Bd. dirs. Tom Brown, Inc.; ptnr LeBaron Ranches. Served with USMC, 1950-52. Decorated Purple Heart, Bronze Star.; named Sportsman of Year in Ga., 1978-79; named to Coll. Football Hall of Fame, 1980. Mem. ABA, Sutter Club, Northridge Country Club. Republican.

LEBARON, FRANCIS NEWTON, biochemistry educator; b. Framingham, Mass., July 26, 1922; s. Paul Burrows and Dorothy (Lamson) LeB.; m. Margaret Lenore Shaw, July 8, 1953; 1 child, Geoffrey Shaw. S.B., MIT, 1944; MA, Boston U., 1948; PhD, Harvard U., 1951. Assoc. biochemist McLean Hosp., Belmont, Mass., 1957-64; asso. biol. chemist Harvard U. Med. Sch., 1959-64; asso. prof. biochemistry U. N.Mex. Med. Sch., 1964-69, prof., 1969-83, chmn. dept., 1971-78, chmn. ad hoc nutrition planning commn., 1969. Vis. scholar Mass. Inst. Tech., 1974-75 Editorial bd.: Jour. Neurochemistry, 1965-74; Contbr. articles to profl. jours. Served with USNR, 1943-46. Mem. Am. Chem. Soc., Biochem. Soc. (London), Am. Soc. Biol. Chemists, AAAS, Internat. Soc. Neurochemistry, Am. Soc. Neurochemistry (pres. 1969-71), Theta Delta Chi Home: 1111 Heatherwood Yarmouth Port MA 02675

LEBARON, JOHN FRANCIS, education educator; b. Montreal, Can., Aug. 15, 1939; came to the U.S., 1974; s. Francis Gordon and Anna Frances (Van Buskirk) LeB.; m. Faith Trumbull McClellan, Nov. 18, 1967; children: Matthew Francis, Jessie McClellan. BA, McGill U., 1963; MEd, U. Mass., 1971, EdD, 1976. Asst. prof. edn. York U., Toronto, 1973-75; dir. non-print media unit Mass. Bd. Libr. Commrs., Boston, 1975-76; dir. planning and devel. Mass. Ednl. TV, 1976-81, exec. dir. Quincy, 1981-87; assoc. prof. U. Mass., Lowell, 1987-95; prof., 1995—; faculty chair edn. U. Mass., Lowell, 1994—. Staff assoc. U. Mass. Sys. Pres., Boston, 1994. Author: Making Television, 1981; editor, author: Innovations in Distance Learning, 1991, Technology in Its Place: Successful Technology Infusion in Schools, 2001. Spl. advisor on tech. Exec. Office of Edn., Boston, 1991-93; adv. coun. mem. Mass. Corp. for Ednl. Tech., Cambridge, 1992—; chair parents fund Amherst (Mass.) Coll., 1993; com. mem. tech. Acton (Mass.) Pub. Schs., 1994—. Recipient Disting. Svc. award Amherst (Mass.) Coll., 1993, Disting. Svc. award Commonwealth Mass., Boston, 1994, Sr. Fulbright scholarship, 1998, Gulbenkian Vis. professorship, 2001. Mem.: NEA, ASCD, Assn. for Advancement of Computing in Edn., Mass. Computer-Using Educators. Avocations: volunteer civic work, photography, antiques. Home: 35 Nashoba Rd Acton MA 01720-2331 Office: Coll Edn U Mass Lowell One University Ave Lowell MA 01854

LEBEAU, BRYAN FRANK, history educator, author; b. July 23, 1947; BA, North Adams State Coll., 1970; MA, Pa. State U., 1971; Phd, NYU, 1982. Dir. Ctr. for Study of Religion and Soc. Creighton U., Omaha, 1988-98, coord. Am. Studies, 1993—, chmn. dept. history, 1996—, John C. Kenefick Chair in Humanities, 1998—. Author: Frederic Henry Hedge: American Transcendentalist, 1985, Jonathan Dickinson and the Formative Years of American Presbyterianism, 1998, The Story of the Salem Witch Trials, 1999, Religion in America to 1865, 2000, Currier and Ives: America Imagined, 2001. Office: Creighton Univ Dept History Omaha NE 68178-0001 E-mail: blbeau@creighton.edu.

LEBEAU, CHARLES PAUL, lawyer; b. Detroit, Dec. 11, 1944; s. Charles Henry Jr. and Mary Barbara (Moran) L.; m. Victoria Joy (Huchin), May 15, l970; children: Jeffrey Kevin, Timothy Paul. AA, Macomb County Community Coll., Warren, Mich., 1967; BA, Wayne State U., 1969; JD, U. Detroit, 1972; grad. tax program, NYU Sch. Law, 1972-73. Bar: Mich. 1973, U.S. Tax Ct. 1973, Calif. 1987, U.S. Ct. Internat. Trade. 1988, U.S. Supreme Ct. 1988, U.S. Dist. Ct. (so. dist.) Calif. 1988. Tax atty. Ford Motor Co., Dearborn, Mich., 1973-75; assoc. Miller, Canfield, Paddock & Stone, Detroit, 1976-78; tax cons. Oceaneering Internat., Santa Barbara, Calif., 1978-79; tax counsel Signal Cos. Inc., Beverly Hills and La Jolla, 1979-83; assoc. Gray, Cary, Ames & Frye, San Diego, 1983-84; of counsel James Watts Esq., La Jolla, 1985, Murfey, Griggs & Frederick, La Jolla, 1986; pvt. practice La Jolla and San Diego, 1987—. Lectr. grad. tax program Golden Gate U., San Diego, 1979-87; adj. prof. law U. San Diego, 1982-85, 88-89; mem. Law Rev., U. Detroit, 1971-72; lectr. in taxation. Contbr. articles on internat. tax to profl. jours.; monthly tax case commentator Taxes Internat., London, 1981-85. Campaign coord. United Way, Santa Barbara, 1979. Recipient Congrl. Medal of Merit, 1999, Presdl. Medal of Honor, 2000, Rep. of Yr., Calif., 2000. Mem. ABA, Mich. Bar Assn., Calif. Bar Assn., San Diego County Bar Assn., Pi Sigma Alpha. Republican. Roman Catholic. Avocations: sailing, tennis, walking. Home: 1999 Via Segovia La Jolla CA 92037-6441 Office: Law Offices Charles LeBeau Hist 1887 Hayward Patterson Bldg 2148 Broadway San Diego CA 92102-1829

LEBEAU, DICK, professional football coach, retired football player; b. , Ohio, Sept. 9, 1937; m. Nancy LeBeau; 1 child Brandon Grant. Attended, Ohio State Univ., 1955—58. Head coach Cin. Bengals, 2000—, asst. head coach & defensive coord., 1997—2000; defensive coord. Pitts. Steelers, 1995—96, asst. coach, 1992—94; defensive coord. Cin. Bengals, 1984—91, asst. coach, Green Bay Packers, 1976—79, Phila. Eagles, 1976—79; cornerback Detroit Linos, 1959—72. Office: Cin Bengels 1 Paul Brown Stadium Cincinnati OH 45202*

LEBEAU, H. ALTON, JR. confectionary company executive; b. Hartford, Conn., July 2, 1931; s. Hector Alton and Gladys (Chester) LeB.; m. Joan Michaelson, May 31, 1955; children: Linda, Jane, Michael, Leslie. BS, U. Tex., 1960; postgrad., Harvard U., 1965. Mktg. dept. staff Gen. Foods, White Plains, N.Y., 1960-73; v.p., gen. mgr. Consol. Brands divsn. Gulf & Western, N.Y.C., 1973-78; sales and mktg. dept. staff Timex, Middlebury, Conn., 1978-80; from v.p. fields ops. to pres. Schweppes U.S.A., Stamford, 1980-84; pres. Rose Holland House, 1984-85, Cadbury U.S.A., 1985-88; sr. v.p. Cadbury Schweppes Inc., Stamford, Conn., 1985-88; pres. The Marcon Group, 1988—; pres., CEO Am. Candy Co., Selma, Ala., 1995-97. Active Stanford Bd. Reps., 1966-69; mem. nat. com. Explorers, Boy Scouts Am., 1970-71; trustee St. Augustine Arts Assn., 1994-97; pres. Marsh Creek Homeowners Assn., 1994-99. Capt. USAF, 1954-58. Elected dean Nat. Candy Wholesalers Assn., 1988. Mem. Union League Club, Marsh Creek Country Club, Beta Gamma Sigma. Republican. Office: 1 10th St Apt 101 Saint Augustine FL 32080-3893

LEBEAU, LAWRENCE R. family practice physician; b. Menominee, Wis., Jan. 30, 1964; s. Merle and Lucille LeB. BS, U. Wis., 1986; DO, Kirksville Coll. Osteo. Med., 1992. Family physician Family Health Care Inc., Mesa, Ariz., 1995-2000, TLC Family Practice, PLLC, Gilbert, 2000—. Mem. Am. Osteopathic Assn., Am. Coll. Osteopathic Family Physicians, Am. Acad. Osteopathy.

LEBEC, ALAIN, investment banker; b. Dunkerque, Nord, France, Apr. 25, 1950; came to U.S., 1971; m. Leah M. Koncelik, June 27, 1981; children: Gabriel, Christina, Xavier. Diplome d'Ingenieur, Ecole Polytechnique, Paris, 1971; MBA, Northwestern U., 1973. Mng. dir. A.G. Becker & Co., N.Y.C., 1973-84; vice chmn., investment banking group Merrill Lynch & Co., 1984—. 2d lt. French Army, 1971. Office: Merrill Lynch & Co North Tower 4 World Fin Ctr Fl 29 New York NY 10080

LEBEDEV, ALEXANDER ALEXANDROVICH, engineering executive, consultant; b. Arkhangelsk, Russia, Oct. 1, 1959; arrived in South Africa, 1992; s. Alexander Glebovich Lebedev and Henrietta Victorovna (Pavlova) Lebedeva; m. Marina Yurievna Zlotnikova, July 30, 1985; 1 child, Maria. MSc in Engring., Inst. Steel & Alloys, Moscow, 1982, PhD in Engring., 1987. Profl. engr., South Africa. Jr. rschr. Inst. Steel and Alloys, Moscow, 1984-88, All Russia Inst. Fire Protection Rsch., Balaskikha, 1988-89, sr. rschr., 1989-90, leading rschr., 1990-91; chief specialist Konkord, Moscow, 1991-92; cons. Protection Projects, Johannesburg, South Africa, 1992-93; sr. cons. Xcel Engring. and Mgmt., Pretoria, South Africa, 1993-99; cons. Lebedev Cons., South Africa, 1999-2001; sr. cons. Fluor Daniel Wright, Vancouver, B.C., Can., 2001—. Contbr. articles to profl. jours. Sr. lt. Russian Def. Force, 1982-84. Mem. Internat. Soc. Computer Simulation, Can. Inst. of Mining, Metallurgy and Petroluem. Avocation: books. Office: 1075 W Georgia St Vancouver BC Canada V6E 4M7 E-mail: alex.lebedev@fluor.com.

LEBEDOFF, DAVID M. lawyer, writer, investment advisor; b. Mpls., Apr. 29, 1938; s. Martin David and Mary Louise (Galanter) L.; m. Randy Louise Miller, Feb. 7, 1981; children: Caroline, Jonathan, Nicholas. BA magna cum laude, U. Minn., 1960; JD, Harvard U., 1963. Bar: Minn. 1963. Spl. asst. atty. gen. Atty. Gen. of Minn., St. Paul, 1963-65; pvt. practice law Mpls., 1967-81; ptnr. Lindquist & Vennum, 1981-91, Briggs & Morgan, Mpls., 1991-95; sr. v.p. Voyageur Asset Mgmt., 1995—; of counsel Gray, Plant, Mooty, Mooty & Bennett, 1995—. Spl. master U.S. Dist. Ct., Mpls., 1974-75. Author: The 21st Ballot, 1969, Ward Number Six, 1972, The New Elite, 1981, Cleaning Up, 1997; contbr. articles to profl. and gen. jours. Bd. regents U. Minn. , Mpls and St. Paul, 1977-89, chmn. bd. 1987-89; chmn. Mpls. Inst. Arts, 1989-91, bd. dirs. 1975—, life trustee, 1997—; bd. dirs. Coun. on Crime and Justice, 1999—; bd. dirs. Ctr. of the Am. Experiment, 1997-2001; former bd. dirs.

Guthrie Theatre U. Minn. Found., The Blake Sch., Mpls. Club. Recipient Outstanding Achievement award U. Minn., 1991, Minn. Book award, 1998. Mem. Mpls. Club, Minikahda Club, Phi Beta Kappa. Home: 1738 Oliver Ave S Minneapolis MN 55405-2222

LEBEDOFF, JONATHAN GALANTER, federal judge; b. Mpls., Apr. 29, 1938; s. Martin David and Mary (Galanter) L.; m. Sarah Sargent Mitchell, June 10, 1979; children: David Shevlin, Ann McNair. BA, U. Minn., 1960, LLB, 1963. Bar: Minn. 1963, U.S. Dist. Ct. Minn. 1964, U.S. Ct. Appeals (8th cir.) 1968. Pvt. practice, Mpls., 1963-71; judge Hennepin County Mcpl. Ct., State Minn., 1971-74; dist. ct. judge State of Minn., 1974-91; U.S. magistrate judge U.S. Dist. Ct., 1991—. Mem. Gov.'s Commn. on Crime Prevention, 1971-75; mem. State Bd. Continuing Legal Edn.; mem. Minn. Supreme Ct. Task Force for Gender Fairness in Cts., mem. implementation com. of gender fairness in cts.. Jewish. Avocations: reading (biographies, history), family, bridge. Office: 300 S 4th St Minneapolis MN 55415-1320

LEBEDOFF, RANDY MILLER, lawyer; b. Washington, Oct. 16, 1949; m. David Lebedoff; children: Caroline, Jonathan, Nicholas. BA, Smith Coll., 1971; JD magna cum laude, Ind. U., 1975. Assoc. Faegre & Benson, Mpls., 1975-82, ptnr., 1983-86; v.p., gen. counsel Star Tribune, 1989—2001; asst. sec. Star Tribune Cowles Media Co., 1990—98; pvt. practice, 2001—. Bd. dirs. Milkweed Editions, 1989-96. Bd. dirs. Minn. Opera, 1986-90, YWCA, 1984-90, Planned Parenthood Minn., 1985-90, Fund for Legal Aid Soc., 1988-96—, Abbott-Northwestern Hosp., 1990-94. Mem. Newspaper Assn. Am. (legal affairs com. 1991—), Minn. Newspapers Assn. (bd. dirs. 1995—, pres. 2002). Home: 1738 Oliver Ave S Minneapolis MN 55405-2222 Office: 3112 Hennepin Ave S Minneapolis MN 55488

LEBEDOW, AARON LOUIS, consulting company executive; b. Chgo., Aug. 19, 1935; s. Isidor and Fannie (Perchikoff) L.; m. Madeleine Hellman; children: Ellen, Francine, Sheri, Sherri Michaels, Tracey Michaels. BS in Indsl. Engring, Ill. Inst. Tech., 1957; MBA, U. Mich., 1958. Cert. mgmt. cons. Asst. marketing mgr. Imperial-Eastman, Chgo., 1960-61; mgr. Corplan Assos., 1961-66; chmn. bd. Technomic, Inc., 1966-87, Technomic Consultants Internat., Deerfield, 1987-93, Global Marketactics Inc., Chgo., 1993—, Global Devel. Network, Inc., 1993—, Hoganson Venture Group Inc., Hinsdale, IL, 1998-2000, Bus. Search Ltd., 2000—. Bd. dirs. Coun. for Jewish Elderly. Served to 1st lt. USAF, 1958-60. Mem. Am. Mgmt. Assn., Am. Mktg. Assn., Tau Epsilon Phi. Mem. B'nai B'rith. Office: Global Devel Network Inc 6540 N Kilbourn Ste A100 Lincolnwood IL 60712-3437 E-mail: lebedowa@aol.com.

LEBEL, GREGORY GALEN, educator, consultant; b. Portsmouth, N.H., Apr. 12, 1950; s. Emile Henry Jr. and Willetta Jane (Vigue) L. BA, U. N.H., 1972, MPA, 1981; MA, U. Md., 1991, postgrad., 1991—. Chief program ops. to program planner N.H. Dept. of Health and Welfare, Concord, 1974-83; nat. staff Americans with Hart, N.H., 1983-84; campaign mgr. Asbury for Congress, Albuquerque, 1984-85; chief ops. officer Ctr. for a New Democracy, Washington, 1985; spl. asst. U.S. Sen. Gary Hart, 1985; exec. dir. The Vol. Com., 1986-87; dir. nat. scheduling Friends of Gary Hart, Denver, 1987; nat. polit. dir. League of Conservation Voters, Washington, 1987; nat. campaign mgr., dep. nat. campaign mgr. Hart for Pres., N.H., 1987-88; rsch. assoc. and adjunct asst. prof. The Grad. Sch. of Polit. Mgmt., 1988-99; asst. dean The Grad. Sch. Polit. Mgmt.; dir. semester in Wash. program George Washington U. Tech. advisor White House Conf. on Aging, Concord, 1981; cons. Global Tomorrow Coalition, Washington, Voter Edn. Project Atlanta, Dem. Congl. Campaign Com., Americans with Hart, N.H. Dept. Health and Human Svcs., The Interfaith Alliance; guest lectr. Williams Coll., U. N.Mex., U. Md., Am. U.; guest scholar John Hopkins U. Ctr. for Study Am. Govt. Co-Author: Sustainable Development: A Guide to Our Common Future, 1989; author: The Advance Manual, 1986. Del. Democratic Nat. Convention, San Francisco, 1984; chair Takoma Park Md. Ethics Comm. Mem. Am. Polit. Sci. Assn., Am. Assn. on Polit. Cons. (ethics com.). Democrat. Episcopalian. Avocation: reading, cooking, sailing. Office: George Washington Semester in Washington 524 Funger Hall 2201 G St NW Washington DC 20052-0001

LEBEL, ROBERT, bishop; b. Trois Pistoles, Que., Can., Aug. 11, 1924; s. Wilfrid and Alexina (Belanger) L. L.Theol., St. Paul U., Ottawa, 1950; D.Theol., Athenee Angelicum, Rome, 1951. Ordained priest Roman Cath. Ch., 1950, consecrated bishop, 1974; tchr. theology Major Sem., Rimouski, Que., 1951-65, rector, 1963-65, Minor Sem., 1965-68; tchr. domatic theology U. Rimouski, 1970-74; aux. bishop St. Jean, Que., 1974-76; bishop Valleyfield, 1976-2000; bishop emeritus, 2000—. Contbr. ch. publs. Mem. Roman Synod on the Christian Family, 1980. Mem. Conf. Can. Cath. Bishops, Soc. Canadienne de Theologie, KC. Address: 183 chemin St Louis Beauharnois QC Canada J6N 2H8 E-mail: robert.lebel@sympatico.ca.

LEBEN, STEVE, judge; b. Eureka, Kans., June 23, 1956; s. Archie R. and Hallie M. Leben; m. Ann E. Warner, Nov. 5, 1994. BS in Journalism, U. Kans., 1978, JD, 1982. Bar: Mo. 1982, Kans. 1983. Atty. Stinson, Mag & Fizzell, Kansas City, Mo., 1982-84, Overland Park, Kans., 1984-88; sole practitioner, 1988-93; dist. judge State of Kans., Olathe, 1993—. Mem. Kans. Justice Commn., 1997-99. Editor: Practitioner's Guide to Kansas Family Law, 1997; contbr. articles to profl. jours., including Kans. Law Rev., Jour. Kans. Bar Assn., Washburn Law Jour., others. Bd. dirs., Clinicare (non-profit home healthcare agy.), Kansas City, Kans., 1987-92; press sec., U.S. Rep. Bob Whittaker, Washington, 1979. Mem. ABA (jud. divsn.), Am. Judges Assn. (editor Ct. Rev. 1998—, bd. govs. 1999—), Kans. Bar Assn. (bd. govs. 1993-2000, bd. editors Jour. 1993—, Outstanding Young Lawyer in Kans. 1993, Outstanding Svc. award 2000), Am. Psychology-Law Soc., U. Kans. Alumni Assn. (bd. dirs. Greater Kansas City chpt. 1987-92). Office: Dist Judge Divsn 8 100 N Kansas Ave Olathe KS 66061 E-mail: sleben@ix.netcom.com.

LEBENSOHN, JEREMY, sculptor; b. Washington, May 20, 1944; s. Zigmond and Mary (Bates) L.; m. Juanita McNeely, 1982. Student, Kenyon Coll., 1962-63, George Washington U., 1968, New Sch. for Social Rsch., N.Y.C., 1969. Prof. of sculpture SUNY, Purchase, 1972-75; theatre set designer Open Theatre Prodns., N.Y.C., 1973-84, Talking Bands Prodns., N.Y.C., 1973-84, Joseph Chaikin Prodns., Princeton, N.J., 1973-84, Jean Claude Van Itallies Prodn., N.Y.C., 1973-84, Am. Theatre Club, N.Y.C., 1973-84, TNC Prodns. Gilles de Rais, N.Y.C., 1973-84; prof. set design NYU, 1985; artist, designer, pres. Studio dell'arte, 1984—. Sculpture fabricator and restorer Mus. Modern Art, Whitney Mus., Guggenheim Mus., Princeton U. Exhibited in group shows at Pelham Art Ctr., N.Y., 1994, Kool-Art Gallery, N.Y.C., 1992, U. We. Ill. Mus., 1990, 1991, Pyramid Gallery, N.Y.C., 1990, Prince St. Gallery, 1977, prin. works include sculptures World Wide Video Festival, Den Haag, Holland, 1996, N.G.B. Kunst, Berlin, 1996, Foro Artistico, Hanover, Germany, 1997, European Media Art Festival, Osnabruck, Germany, 1997, sculpture commns. include, one-man shows include Southampton Gallery, SUNY, 1980, We. Ill. U. Mus., 1991, many others; contbr. Mem. Internat. Platform Assn.

LEBENTHAL, ALEXANDRA, investment firm executive; d. Jim L. Grad., Princeton U. With Kidder Peabody & Co., Lebenthal, N.Y.C., stockbroker, now CEO, pres. Office: Lebenthal 120 Broadway Fl 12 New York NY 10271-0005

LE BERTHON, ADAM, lawyer; b. L.A., June 12, 1962; s. Edward Lynch and Veronica Rose (Franks) Le B; m. Kelly Elizabeth McKee, Mar. 23, 1996; children: John Thomas, Ryan Michael. BA cum laude with dept. honors, U. San Diego, 1985; JD, U. So. Calif., L.A., 1989. Bar: Calif. 1989, U.S. Dist. Ct. (ctrl. dist.) Calif. 1989, U.S. Ct. Appeals (9th cir.) 1989, U.S. Dist. Ct. (so. dist.) Calif. 1990, (no. dist.) Calif. 1990, (ea. dist.) Calif. 1990. Assoc. White & Case, L.A., 1989-91, Straw & Gilmartin, Santa Monica, Calif., 1991-97; ptnr. Gilmartin & Le Berthon LLP, 1997-99; assoc. Arnold & Porter, L.A., 1999—. Editor So. Calif. Law Rev., 1988-89; contbr. articles to profl. jours. Recipient Am. Jurisprudence award U. So. Calif., 1987. Mem. Calif. State Bar Assn., L.A. County Bar Assn., Order of the Coif, Phi Alpha Delta, Omicron Delta Epsilon, Kappa Gamma Pi. Home: 27261 Harwick Pl Valencia CA 91354-1925 Office: Arnold & Porter 44th Fl 777 S Figueroa St Los Angeles CA 90017-5800 E-mail: adam_le_berthon@aporter.com.

LEBHERZ, ANN WEISBURGER, writer, researcher, retired writer; b. N.Y.C., Sept. 3, 1925; d. David Original and Ruth Herman Weisburger; m. Robert Walsh Lebherz; children: Amanda Curley, Robert. BS, Hood Coll., 1948. Founder, pres. Frederick (Md.) County Landmarks, 1971—76; founder, dir. Rose Hill Childrens Mus., 1972—82. Chmn. Md. Hist. Trust, Frederick , 1972—84. Author: (Book) Pre 1800 Houses in Frederik County, 1993 (Delaplaine award Hist. Soc., 1993). Chmn. dir. Social Svcs. Frederick Co., 1991—97. Named Woman of Yr., Frederick Civic Club, 1972. Mem.: Frederick Art Club (pres. 1989—93). Avocations: painting, bridge, writing, reading, cooking. Home: 6733a S Clifton Rd Frederick MD 21703

LE BLANC, ALICE ISABELLE, public health program, academic program administrator; b. New Orleans, Dec. 23, 1949; d. Joseph and Mary Elizabeth (Welsh) Le B.; divorced; 1 child, Matthew. BA in Drama & Comm., U. New Orleans, 1971; MPH, Tulane U., 1996. Sect. editor, feature writer Las Vegas Rev.- Jour., 1972-74; asst. dir. pub. rels. Touro Infirmary, New Orleans, 1980-82; dir. cmty. rels. AMI Riverside Hosp., Corpus Christi, Tex., 1982-84; dir. comm. United Way of the Coastal Bend, 1984-86; dir. pub. rels. & devel. Ada Wilson Hosp. Phys. Medicine and Rehab., 1986-89; mktg. mgr. nat. sexual trauma program River Oaks Psychiat. Hosp., New Orleans, 1989-90; mktg. cons./physician recruitment contract Eye, Ear, Nose & Throat Hosp., 1990; mgr. prog. svcs./exec. MHA recruitment, dept. health sys. Tulane U. Sch. Pub. Health and Tropical Medicine, 1990-96; instr., adminstrv. dir. MPH program La. State U. Health Scis. Ctr., 1996—. Bd. dirs., bd. exec. com., chmn. standing com. United Way of the Coastal Bend, Corpus Christi, 1986, 87; bd. dirs. Early Childhood Devel. Ctr., Corpus Christi, 1988. Recipient Cert. of Appreciation, Gov. of Nev., 1974, Mayor of New Orleans, 1981, First Pl. award La. Hosp. Assn., 1982, Addy award of Excellence, Corpus Christi Advt. Fedn., 1986, 87, Addy First Place awards, 1988, Cert. of Recognition, United Way of the Coastal Bend, 1986, Cert. of Appreciation, Corpus Christi Jr. League, 1987. Mem. APHA. Republican. Roman Catholic. Avocations: gardening, carpentry. Office: La State U Med Ctr Health Sci Ctr 1600 Canal St Ste 800 New Orleans LA 70112-2854

LEBLANC, HANSON PAUL, III, communications educator, researcher; b. Donaldsonville, La., Dec. 18, 1964; s. Hanson Paul and Loretta Ann (Lovett) LeB. BA in Philosophy, St. Mary's U. San Antonio, 1988; MA in Speech Comm., La. State U., 1992; PhD in Speech Comm., So. Ill. U., 2000. Tchg. asst. dept. speech comm. La. State U., Baton Rouge, 1989-92, So. Ill. U., Carbondale, 1992-95, rsch. asst. Ctr. Rural Health and Social Svc. Devel., 1995-96, vis. asst. prof. Coll. Applied Scis. and Arts, 1996-97, rsch. assoc. Ctr. Rural Health and Social Svc. Devel., 1997-98; adj. faculty dept. arts, scis. and humanities Baton Rouge (La.) C.C., 1998; mgr. of ops. La. Acad. of Family Physicians Found., Baton Rouge, 1998-99; instr. dept. comm. studies La. State U., 1999-2001; asst. prof. dept. comm. U. Tex., San Antonio, 2001—. Project coord. Ill./Ind. Nurse Practitioner, Cert. Nurse-Midwife, and Physician Asst. Tng. Consortium, Carbondale, Ill., 1996-97. Author: Plurality and Affirmative Action: The Social Requirement of Diversity, 1996; contbr. articles to profl. jours., chpts. to books. Dep. registrar County of Jackson, Carbondale, Ill., 1996-97. Alumni scholar St. Mary's U. Alumni Assn., 1987. Mem. Nat. Comm. Assn. (new profl. rep. family comm. divsn. 1995-97, electronic informant 1996-98), So. States Comm. Assn., Ctrl. States Comm. Assn., Phi Kappa Phi. Avocations: camping, hiking, travel, photography, music. Office: Dept Comm U Tex San Antonio 6900 North Loop 1604 West San Antonio TX 78249-0643 Home: 14938 Moss Stone San Antonio TX 78232-4644 E-mail: hpl3@hpleblanc.com.

LEBLANC, HUGH LINUS, political science educator, consultant; b. Alexandria, La., Oct. 30, 1927; s. Moreland Paul and Carmen Marie (Haydel) LeB.; m. Shirley Jean Smith, Feb. 28, 1953; children: Leslie Ann, Alexander Hugh. BA, La. State U., 1948; MA, U. Tenn., 1950; PhD, U. Chgo., 1958. Asst. prof. George Washington U., Washington, 1955-58, assoc. prof., 1959-63, prof., 1964-90, prof. emeritus dept. polit. sci., 1991—, chmn. dept., 1963-65, 70-76, 82-88; v.p. Area Inc., Arlington, VA, 1961-63. Author: American Political Parties, 1982, (with D. Trudeau Allensworth) The Politics of States and Urban Communities, 1971; contbr. articles to polit. sci. jours. Served to lt. (j.g.) USNR, 1944-45, 52-55. Named Outstanding Prof. Interfraternity Council, George Washington U., 1963 Mem. Amelia Island Plantation Club (Fla.). E-mail: hllssl@aol.com.

LEBLANC, JAMES LEO, business executive, consultant; b. Ottawa, Ont., Can., May 12, 1955; arrived in U.S., 1993; s. Leo Joseph and Ann (Curry) LeBlanc. BA, Carleton U., 1982, MA in Internat. Affairs, 1984; MPA, Harvard U., 1994. Exec. asst. Amb. for Arms Control, Ottawa, Ont., Can., 1984-89; chief of staff Min. of Sci. and Technol., 1989-92, Min. of Foreign Affairs, Ottawa, 1992-93; pres. J. LeBlanc Internat. LLC, Alexandria, Va., 1994—; mng. ptnr. S&H/Leblanc Internat. Tech. Pub. Affairs; ptnr. The York Group, Internat. Tech. Ptnrs. Bd. dirs., v.p. Can.-Am. Bus. Coun., Washington, 1995—2001, adv. bd. mem., 2001—; U.S. exec. dir. Can. Advanced Tech. Assn., 1994—; mem. Greater Washington Bd. Trade. Adv. bd. InterAm. Econ. Coun.; bd. dirs. pres.'s adv. coun. Carleton U., 1995—, Carleton U. Found., Washington, 1996—; bd. dirs., chmn. internat. com. No. Va. Tech. Coun.; bd. dirs. Trados Corp.; sr. exec. Global Smarts, Inc., 2001—. Mem.: Soc. for Competitive Intelligence Profls. Avocation: Avocations: tennis, music, reading, golf, chess.. Home: 5808 Woodlawn Gren Ct Ste A Alexandria VA 22309-4629

LEBLANC, JANET M. addictions and relationship counselor; b. Altamonte Springs, Fla., Oct. 8, 1947; BA, U. Fla., 1969; MA, Rollins Coll., 1989. Lic. mental health counselor, Fla.; cert. addictions profl.; cert. drug counselor level II; cert. master addictions counselor; cert. alcohol and drug counselor; cert. employee assistance profl.; cert. clin. criminal justice specialist. Dir. Mgmt. Consulting Svcs., Altamonte Springs; dir. outpatient adult alcohol and drug treatment program, substance abuse evaluations, and EAP work; substance abuse provider DOT. Mem. Nat. Alcohol and Drug Assn. for Counselors, Employee Assistance Program Assn. (treas. 1996-99, v.p. 2000—), Mental Health Counselors Ctrl. Fla. (chair cmty. rels. 1999-2002, pres. 2002-), Fla. Alcohol and Drug Assn. for Counselors. Office: Mgmt Cons Svcs PO Box 450 Altamonte Springs FL 32715-0450 E-mail: jmldbamcs@cs.com.

LEBLANC, JEANNE MARIE, psychologist, educator; b. Tallahassee, May 19, 1965; d. Joseph Wilfred Jr. and Annalois (Jackson) LeB.; m. William Robert Hitch, Dec. 17, 1983 (div. Mar. 1992); 1 child, Jessica Elaine; m. Patrick Henry Bogan III, Oct. 8, 1994. AA, Richland Coll., 1987; BA summa cum laude, U. Tex., Dallas, 1989; PhD, U. Tex. Southwestern Med. Ctr., 1997. Lic. psychologist, Tex. Clin. psychology intern Parkland Meml. Hosp., Dallas, 1990-93, Terrell (Tex.) State Hosp., 1990-91, Scottish Rite Hosp., Dallas, 1991-92, So. Meth. U., Dallas, 1992-93; assessment specialist, neurocognitive therapist Pate Rehab., 1993-99, neuropsychol. resident, 1997-99; asst. prof. counseling and human behavior Amber U., Garland, Tex., 1998—; program mgr. Marshall (Tex.) Youth Svcs. Sabine Valley Ctr., 1999—. Test examiner The Psychol. Corp., San Antonio, 1999—. Presenter (symposium) Ecologically Valid Treatment, 1998. Vol. crisis worker The Family Place, Dallas, 1986-88; vol. family facilitator Divert Ct.—Dallas County, 1999. Mem. APA, Tex. Psychol. Assn., MENSA. Avocations: playing clarinet, traveling, attending cultural events, literary discussions. Office: Sabine Valley Ctr 2615 E End Blvd S Marshall TX 75672-7403

LEBLANC, LARRY JOSEPH, management educator; b. New Orleans, July 21, 1947; s. J. Wilfred and Mary (Lachin) LeB.; m. Marguerite Jarreau, Sept. 6, 1969; children: Aimee, Sara. BS, Loyola U., New Orleans, 1969; MS, Northwestern U., 1971, PhD, 1973. Assoc. prof. So. Meth. U., Dallas, 1973-80; assoc. prof. Owen Grad. Sch. Mgmt., Vanderbilt U., Nashville, 1980— ; cons. Dr. Pepper Co., Dallas, 1977, U.S. Army Inventory Research Office, Phila., 1979-82, Trailways, Dallas, 1979, Miss. Chem. Co., Yazoo City, 1980-81, U.S. Dept. Transp., 1981-83; vis. prof. U. Chile, Santiago, 1978, Linkoping Inst. Tech., Sweden, 1980, U. Ulm, Fed. Republic Germany, 1981-82, 84-85, Technion, Haifa, Israel, 1984, Ecole Centrale, Paris, 1987. Author: (with L. Cooper, U. Bhat) Introduction to Operations Research Models, 1977. Contbr. articles to profl. jours. Editorial adv. bd. Transp. Research, 1973— . Served to capt. U.S. Army, 1972-73. Research grantee NSF, 1980-83, U.S. Dept. Transp., 1979-80. Mem. Inst. Mgmt. Scis., Ops. Research Soc. Am. (chmn. transp. sci. sect. 1984-86). Republican. Roman Catholic. Avocations: instrument flying, skin diving, photography, jogging. Home: 424 Manor View Ln Brentwood TN 37027-4334

LEBLANC, LAUREEN ALISON, service company administrator; b. Santa Ana, Calif., Feb. 25, 1964; d. Thomas Albert and Kathleen Mary (Thompson) Cox; m. Mark J. LeBlanc, July 17, 1992; children: Katherine Morgan, (from a previous marriage) Robert Daniel, Alicia Michelle. Grad. high sch., Oakland Park, Fla., 1982. Horse trainer, mgr. various show horse stables, U.S. and Europe, 1975-84; office mgr. Land Title Ins. Co., Ft. Lauderdale, Fla., 1979-82; gen. mgr. Boca Travel Trailer Resort, Boca Raton, 1982-85; asst. mgr. credit Boca Raton Hotel and Country Club, 1985-90; credit and accounts receivable mgr. Callaway Gardens Resort, Pine Mountain, Ga., 1990-94; contr. Holiday Inn Denver Internat. Airport Hotel Trade & Conv. Ctr., 1994—. Mem. NAFE, Internat. Assn. Hospitality Accts., U.S. Dressage Assn., Nat. Assn. Credit Mgrs. Avocations: sailing, fishing, diving, racquetball, tennis.

LEBLANC, LEONARD JOSEPH, electronics company executive; b. Amherst, N.S., Can., Feb. 4, 1941; came to U.S., 1952 naturalized 1959; s. Edgar Marcel and Mary Catherine (Bourgeois) LeB.; m. Janice May Dittrich, Sept. 11, 1965; children: Bryan, Jeffrey, Steven. BS, Coll. of Holy Cross, 1962, MS, 1963, George Washington U., 1966. Fin. analyst to mgr. Philco-Ford Corp., Blue Bell, Pa., 1966-72; asst. corp. controller Centainteed Corp., Valley Forge, 1972-73; sr. v.p. fin. Data Tech. Corp., Costa Mesa, Calif., 1973-76; v.p., controller Memorex Corp., Santa Clara, 1976-82; v.p. fin., treas. Saga Corp., Menlo Park, 1982-87; exec. v.p. fin. and adminstrn. Cadence Design Systems Inc., San Jose, 1987-92; sr. v.p. fin. and adminstrn., CFO GTech Corp., West Greenwich, R.I., 1993-94; exec. v.p., CFO, COO Infoseek Corp., Santa Clara, Calif., 1996-97; exec. v.p., CFO Vantive Corp., 1998-2000. Bd. dirs. OpLink Comms., Inc., EBest Inc. Mem. Monte Sereno Archtl. Com., Calif., 1981-93; bd. dirs. Eastfield Children's Ctr., Campbell, Calif., 1984-87. Served to lt.(j.g.) USN, 1963-66. Recipient commendation U.S. Navy Med. Sch., Bethesda, Md., 1966; fellow Coll. of Holy Cross, 1962 Mem. Fin. Execs. Inst. (pres. Santa Clara chpt. 1986-87).

LEBLANC, RICHARD EDWARD, hospice nurse educator; b. July 27, 1946; BS in Med. Tech., North Adams State Coll., 1971; BSN, U. Mass., Boston, 1983; PhD in Health Care Adminstrn., Pacific Western U., 1994. RN, Nev.; cert. in case mgmt.; cert. ACLS. Clin. lab. scientist, 1963-83; advanced practitioner pediat. nursing, 1983—; asst. dir. patient care svcs. New Beginnings, Lakewood, Calif., 1990-96; program dir. psychiat. svcs. St. Rose Dominican Hosp., Las Vegas, Nev., 1996-97; profl. svcs. mgr. Family Home Hospice, 1997-98; house supervisor Vencor Hosp. of Las Vegas, 1999—; house supr. Integrated Health Svcs., Las Vegas, 2001—; nurse educator Nathan Adelson Hospice, 2001—. Mem. disability adv. com. Nev. State Bd. Nursing, Las Vegas, Nev., 1997-99. Mem. Sigma Theta Tau. Address: 762 Milstead Ct Las Vegas NV 89110-3954 E-mail: rcmrr@aol.com.

LEBLANC, RICHARD PHILIP, lawyer; b. Nashua, N.H., Aug. 5, 1946; s. Ronald Arthur and Jeanette G. (Chomard) LeB.; m. Doris Julie Lavoie, May 25, 1968; children: Justin D., Renée M., Anne-Marie. AB summa cum laude, Coll. of the Holy Cross, 1968; JD cum laude, Harvard U., 1972. Bar: Maine 1972, U.S. Dist. Ct. Maine 1972. Assoc. Bernstein, Shur, Sawyer & Nelson, Portland, Maine, 1972-75, shareholder, 1976-95, LeBlanc & Young, Portland, 1995—. Mem. Probate Law Revision Commn., Augusta, Maine, 1975-80; mem. probate rules and forms adv. com. Maine Supreme Ct. Pres. United Way Greater Portland, 1982-84; trustee Cleverus H.S., Portland, 1982-88; bd. dirs. Habitat for Humanity, Portland, 1984-92, Cumberland County Affordable Housing Venture, Portland, 1987-94, Maine Spl. Olympics, 1988-94, United Way Found. of Greater Portland, 1997—. Fellow Am. Coll. Trust and Estate Counsel; mem. ABA, Maine Bar Assn., Maine Estate Planning Coun. Democrat. Roman Catholic. Home: 142 Longfellow St Portland ME 04103-4027 Office: LeBlanc & Young PO Box 7950 Portland ME 04112-7950

LEBLANC, ROGER MAURICE, chemistry educator; b. Trois Rivières, Que., Can., Jan. 5, 1942; s. Henri and Rita (Moreau) L.; m. Micheline D. Veillette, June 26, 1965; children: Daniel, Hughes, Marie-Jose, Nancy. BSc, U. Laval, 1964, PhD, 1968. NRC postdoctoral fellow Davy Faraday Rsch. Lab. Royal Inst. Great Britain, London, 1968-70; prof. phys. chemistry U. Que., Trois-Rivières, 1970-93, chmn. dept., 1971-75, dir. Biophysics Rsch. Group, 1978-81, chmn. Photobiophysics Rsch. Ctr., 1981-91; prof., chmn. dept. chemistry U. Miami, Coral Gables, Fla., 1994—. Hon. prof. Jilin U., Changchun, China, 1992. Recipient Barringer award Spectroscopy Soc. Can., 1983, Medaille du Merite Universitaire du Que. a Trois-Rivieres, 1987, Commemorative medal for 125th Anniversary of Confedn. Can., 1993, Rsch. award Soc. Cosmetic Chemists Fla. chpt., 1999. Fellow Chem. Inst. Can. (Noranda award 1982, John Labatt Ltd. award 1992); mem. Am. Chem. Soc., Assn. Canadienne Francaise pour l'Avancement des Sciences (Prix Vincent 1978), Am. Soc. Photobiology, Biophys. Soc., European Photochem. Assn. Roman Catholic. Home: 713 Crandon Blvd Apt 203 Key Biscayne FL 33149-2530 Office: U Miami Dept Chemistry Cox Sci Bldg Rm 315 1301 Memorial Dr Coral Gables FL 33124-0431 E-mail: rml@umiami.ir.miami.edu.

LEBLANC, TINA, dancer; b. Erie, Pa. m. Marco Jerkunica, May 1988; 1 child, Marinko James. Trained, Carlisle, Pa. Dancer Joffrey II Dancers, N.Y.C., 1982-83, The Joffrey Ballet, N.Y.C., 1984-92; prin. dancer San Francisco Ballet, 1992—. Guest tchr. Ctrl. Pa. Youth Ballet, 1992, 94—. Work includes roles in (with San Francisco Ballet) Con Brio, Bizet Pas de Deux, Swan Lake, Nanna's Lied, Handel -- A Celebration, La fille mal gardée, Rubies, Tchaikovsky Pas de Deux, Seeing Stars, The Nutcracker, La Pavane Rouge, Company B, Romeo and Juliet, Sleeping Beauty, The Dance House, Terra Firma, Lambarena, Fly by Night, In the Night, Ballo della Regina, The Lesson, The Tuning Game, Quartette, Etudes, Western Symphony, Maelstrom, Pacific, Criss-Cross, Giselle, Theme and Variations, Gala Performance, The Vertiginous Thrill of Exactitude, Taiko, Sandpaper Ballet, La Bayadere, Night, Serenade, Celts, Stars & Stripes, Tarantella; (with other companies) The Green Table, Les Presages, Le sacre du printemps, Les Noces, Light Rain, Romeo and Juliet, Runaway Train, Empyrean Dances, La Vivandière, L'air D'esprit, Corsaire Pas de deux, Don Quixote pas de deux, Lacrymosa, Confetti, Kettentanz Le Beau Danube, Offenbach in the Underworld, Suite Saint Saens, Forgotten Land, Dream Dances, Postcards, Coppelia, Remembrances, Reflections. Recipient Princess Grace Found. award, 1988, Princess Grace Statuette award, 1995, Isadora Duncan award, 1998-99, 2000-01. Office: San Francisco Ballet Assn 455 Franklin St San Francisco CA 94102-4471

LEBLANG, SKIP ALAN, lawyer; b. Phila., Jan. 14, 1953; s. Morton and Leah LeB.; m. Beth Siegel, Nov. 27, 1977; children: Kaitlyn Alexa, Chelsey Jenna. BA magna cum laude, U. Pitts., 1974; JD, U. San Diego, 1977. Bar: Pa. 1977, U.S. Dist. Ct. (we. dist.) Pa. 1977, D.C. 1980, N.Y. 1980, U.S. Dist. Ct. (so. and ea. dists.) N.Y. 1980. Jud. clk. Pa. Ct. Common Pleas, Pitts., 1977-78; atty. FTC, N.Y.C., 1978-81; asst. corp. counsel law dept. City of N.Y., 1981-84; assoc. Kramer, Dillof, N.Y.C., 1984-87; pvt. practice law 1987—, 1987—. Mem. faculty N.E. regional seat Nat. Inst. Trial Advocacy, Hofstra U., Uniondale, N.Y., 1984-2001; mem. faculty advanced trial program Law Sch., Hofstra U., 1984-93, ABA/USTA Trademark Trial Advocacy Inst., 1993; spkr. in field. Author: Police Misconduct, 1981, Emergency Vehicle Liability, 1981, Sidewalks and Roadways, 1981. Co-dir. Coalition to Save Hempstead Harbor, Sea Cliff, N.Y., 1987-2001, pres., 1998—; mem. Environ. Leaders Network, Hicksville, N.Y., 1988; mem. adv. com. Internat. Environ. Conf., Hofstra U., 1990; pres. Coalition, 1998-2000, N. Country Reform Temple, 2002—. Recipient award of merit N.Y. State Gov., 1990. Mem. ATLA, N.Y. State Trial Lawyers Assn., Pa. Bar Assn., Assn. of Bar of City of N.Y., Million Dollar Advocates Forum (elected life mem.). Avocations: family, running, basketball, skiing, fly fishing. Office: 325 Broadway Ste 401 New York NY 10007-1112 Fax: 212-267-5813.

LEBLOND, CHARLES PHILIPPE, anatomy educator, researcher; b. Lille, France, Feb. 5, 1910; s. Oscar and Jeanne (Desmarchelier) L.; m. Gertrude Sternschuss, Oct. 22, 1936 (dec.); children— Philippe L., Paul N., Pierre F., Marie Pascale; m. Odette Lengrand, July 12, 2001. L.Sc., U. Lille, 1932; MD, U. Paris, France, 1934, D. Sc., 1945; PhD, U. Montreal, 1942; DSc Acadia (hon.), McGill U., 1982, York U., 1985. Asst. histology U. Lille and U. Paris, France, 1934-35; Rockefeller fellow anatomy Yale, 1935-37; charge biology div. Lab. Synthese Atom, Paris, 1937-40; research fellow U. Rochester, N.Y.,

1940-41; mem. faculty McGill U., Montreal, Que., Can., 1941—, prof. anatomy, 1948—, chmn. dept., 1957-75. Author: L'Acide Ascorbique dans les Tissues et sa Detection, 1936, Radioautography as a Tool in the Study of Protein Synthesis, 1965, also over 400 articles mainly on cell and tissue dynamics. Decorated companion Nat. Order Can., grand officer Order of Quebec; scholar Fogarty scholar, NIH, 1975. Fellow Royal Soc. London, Royal Soc. Can., Am. Assn. Anatomy, Can. Assn. Anatomists, Am. Acad. ARts and Scis., Prix. Scientifique du Que. Home: 68 Chesterfield St Montreal QC Canada H3Y 2M5 E-mail: cleblond@med.mcgill.ca.

LE BLOND, PATRICIA MORRISON, real estate company executive; b. Columbus, Ohio, June 22, 1933; d. William B. and Elise Hoster (Egle) Morrison; m. Charles J. Le Blond, Dec. 24, 1951; children: Charles J., Jr., William B., Geoffrey T., James Morrison. AB, Smith Coll., 1955. Lic. real estate agent, Ohio, Lic. real estate broker, Ky. Real estate agt. Matt Toebben Builder, Cin., 1972-74; exclusive listing agt. Cliff House Condominiums, 1974-77; agt. Fred A. Schmidt Co., 1978-84; project coord. Granada Royale Hometels, 1979-81; agt. Duffy Better Homes & Gardens, 1985-90, Sibcy, Cline Realtors, Cin., 1991—. Mem. Taste of Cin. Planning Com., United Sustainers of Cin.; vol. Indian Hills Episcopal Ch. fellowship campaign, 1990-92; pres. Maternity Assn. Cin., 1990-92; mem. Cin. Hist. Soc. Mem. Jr. League Cin., Cin. Real Estate Assn. (law and ethics com.), Updowntowners, Univ. Club. Republican. Avocation: tennis. Home: PO Box 43358 Cincinnati OH 45243-0358 Office: Sibcy Cline Realtors 8040 Montgomery Rd Cincinnati OH 45236-2903

LEBLOND, PAUL HENRI, oceanographer, educator; b. Que., Can., Dec. 30, 1938; s. Sylvio and Jeanne (Lacerte) LeB.; m. Josee Michaud (div. 1985); children: Michel, Philippe, Anne. BA, Laval U., Quebec, 1957; BS, McGill U., Montreal, Que., 1961; PhD, U. B.C., Vancouver, Can., 1964; DSc (hon.), Meml. U., Newfoundland, 1992. Prof. depts. oceanography and physics U. B.C., Vancouver, 1965, assoc. dean faculty of sci., 1982-85, head dept. oceanography, 1987-92, dir. program earth and ocean scis., 1992-96, prof. emeritus, 1996—. Chmn. Can. nat. com. World Ocean Circulation Expt., 1987-92; program leader Ocean Prodn. Enhancement Network, Can., 1991-93; pres. Can. Open Frontiers Rsch. Found., 1996-98. Co-author: Waves in the Oceans, 1978, Cadborosaurus, 1995; contbr. articles to profl. jours. Mem. Fisheries Resource Conservation Coun., 1993-98; mem. Pacific Fisheries Resource Conservation Coun., 1998—; chair sci. and industry bd. Inst. Pacific, Ocean Sci. and Tech., 1998—; bd. dirs. Access to Media Edn. Soc., 1998—. Fellow Royal Soc. Can., Can. Meteorol. and Oceanographic Soc. (Pres.'s prize 1981, Tully medal 1991); mem. Am. Geophys. Union, Galiano Conservancy Assn. (bd. dirs. 1996—), Can. Parks & Wilderness Soc. (B.C. chpt. bd. dirs. 2000—). Avocations: hiking, history, science fiction. E-mail: leblond@gulfislands.com.

LEBLOND, RICHARD FOARD, internist, educator; b. Seattle, July 17, 1947; s. Donald E. and Ruth Elizabeth (Foard) LeB.; m. Anita Caraig Garcia, Dec. 28, 1994; children: Sueno Emmeline, Edgardo Alan. AB, Princeton U., 1969; MD, U. Wash., 1972. Diplomate Am. Bd. Internal Medicine (bd. dirs. 1993-98, sec.-treas. 1996-98). Intern Harlem Hosp., N.Y.C., 1972-73; resident in medicine, clin. fellow in oncology U. Wash., Seattle, 1975-78; pvt. practice, Livingston, Mont., 1978-96; dir. Livingston Meml. Hosp., 1979-91, 93-96, chmn. bd. dirs., 1984-91. Clin. asst. prof. medicine Mont. State U., Bozeman, 1979-96, U. Wash., 1991-96, U. Calif., San Francisco, 1991-92; acting instr. Makerere U., Kampala, 1991-92; prof. clin. medicine U. Iowa, Iowa City, 1996—, med. dir. U. Iowa Hosps. and Clinics Family Care Ctr., 1997-2002; bd. dirs. Am. Bd. Family Practice, RRC-1M, Inst. for Clinical Evaluation, treas., 1999-2001. Bd. dir. Park County Friends of the Arts, Livingston, Iowa, 1981—87, Livingston Cmty. Trust, 1986—91. Served in Indian Health Svc. USPHS, 1973—75, Poplar, Mont. Named Regional Trustee of Yr., Am. Hosp. Assn., 1989; recipient med. achievement award Deaconess Found., 1995, Mont. ACP Laureate award, 1996. Fellow ACP; mem. AMA, Am. Soc. for Internal Medicine, Iowa Med. Soc. Avocations: fishing, hunting, hiking, reading, gardening. Home: 2023 Laurence Ct NE Iowa City IA 52240-9150 Office: Univ of Iowa Hosps and Clinics 200 Hawkins Dr Iowa City IA 52242-1009 E-mail: richard-leblond@uiowa.edu.

LEBLOND, RICHARD KNIGHT, II, banker; b. Cin., Nov. 16, 1920; s. Harold R. and Elizabeth (Conroy) LeB..; m. Sara Cordial Chapman, Dec. 11, 1948; children— Mary, Richard, E. Chapman, Elizabeth, David, Virginia, William, Thomas, Sara, Joseph BA, Princeton U.; DCS (hon.), St. John's U., Jamaica, N.Y., 1978. Exec. v.p. Chem. Bank, N.Y.C., 1968-73, vice-chmn. bd., 1973-85, sr. advisor, 1985—. Trustee emeritus Ingersoll Internat., Inc., Rockford, Ill.; sr. advisor Chase Manhattan JP Morgan Chase, Bedford Stuyvestant D&S Corp., Bklyn. Pres. Robert T. Jones Jr. Scholarship Fund; trustee St. Patrick's Cath., N.Y.C. 1st lt. U.S. Army, 1943-46, PTO. Mem. N.Y. State Bankers Assn. (pres. 1979-80), Harvard Bus. Sch. Assn. (pres. 1975-76) Republican. Roman Catholic. Office: Chase Manhattan Bank 11 W 51st St Fl 2 New York NY 10019-6901

LEBLOW, G. HAGNY, artist; b. June 5, 1924; d. Henry Aaron and Mabel Alice (Warn) Hagny; m. Raymond E. Leblow, Mar. 10, 1950; children: Bonnie, Charles, Colin. Grad., h.s., 1942. Formerly sec. with State of Calif., Oakland. Artist, painting country and farm scenes. Republican. Lutheran. Avocations: painting, sewing, reading. Home: 2691 Oakes Dr Hayward CA 94542-1225

LEBMAN, ROBERT RICHARD, social services administrator; b. Amsterdam, N.Y., Sept. 20, 1945; s. Harry and Catherine (Spitzkopf) L. BA cum laude, Harpur Coll., Binghamton, N.Y., 1967; MA, Pa. State U., 1968. With Peace Corps, 1968-72; project dir. AID mission, Afghanistan, 1972-73; cons. Rochester (N.Y.) Sch. Dist., 1973; rsch. assoc. Applied Behavioral Rsch. Assocs., Rochester, 1973-74; from caseworker to clin. dir. Delphi House, 1974-78; dir. N.W. Youth Ctr. of Charles Settlement House, 1978-80; exec. dir. Livingston County Youth Bur., 1981-83, Monroe County Youth Advocacy, Rochester, 1983-86; dir. in-patient svcs. DayBreak Alcoholism Treatment Facility, 1986-89; exec. dir. Huther-Doyle Meml. Inst., N.Y., 1989—; v.p. DePaul, Inc. Author: English Language Teaching in Afghanistan, 1972. Past pres. Helping People with AIDS, Jewish Family Svcs., Region II Consortium on Alcoholism and Substance Abuse Svcs.; mem. profl. adv. HRC, Inc.; mem. behavioral health adv. Excellus Inc.; mem. Monroe County Task Force on Youth and Alcohol, 1976—86; mem. 4-H adv. com. Monroe County Coop. Extension, 1978—80; mem. Black Seeds Scholarship Com., 1981—86, Jewish Chm. Dependency Task Force Com. on Youth and Alcohol; mem. budget adv. com. Rochester City Schs., 1983—85; chmn. Regional Youth Workers Tng. Network; mem. harm reduction adv. bd. AIDS Rochester; v.p. Recovery Net; treas. Coun. Agy. Execs.; bd. dirs. Finger Lakes Health Sys. Agy., Operation U-Turn, Inc.; chair bd. dirs. Rochester Area Task Force on AIDS; bd. dirs. NY State Assn. Alcoholism and Substance Abuse Providers; v.p., bd. dirs. Jewish Family Svcs. NDEA fellow, 1967. Mem.: Arts and Scis. Acad. Rochester (bd. dirs.), Nat. Coun. Crime and Delinquency, Am. Judicature Soc., Acad. Polit. and Social Sci., Am. Polit. Sci. Assn., Acad. Polit. Sci. Democrat. Jewish. Home: 29 Old Winding Ln Fairport NY 14450-1108 Office: 360 East Ave Rochester NY 14604-2612 E-mail: rlebman@depaul.org.

LEBOEUF, RAYMOND WALTER, manufacturing company executive; b. Chgo., Dec. 30, 1946; s. Raymond O'Dillon and Opal Rosalind (Powell) LeB.; m. Loralee Ann Sawyer, Jan. 24, 1968; children— Mandy, Whitney. BA, Northwestern U., 1967; MBA, U. Ill., 1970. Analyst Ford Motor Co., Detroit, 1970-73; asst. comptroller Union Bank, Los Angeles, 1973-74; mgr. banking Ford Motor Co., Detroit, 1974-80; treas. PPG Industries, Inc., Pitts., 1980-84, controller, 1984-86, v.p. purchasing, 1986-88, v.p. finance, 1988-94, exec. v.p., 1994—, pres., COO, 1995-97, pres., CEO, 1997-2000, chmn., CEO, 2000—; trustee Robert Morris Coll.; bd. dirs. PPG Industries, Inc., Magee-Women's Hosp., Praxair, Inc., Extra Mile Edn. Found., Chem. Mfrs. Assn. Office: PPG Industries Inc 1 PPG Pl Pittsburgh PA 15272-0001*

LEBOFF, MERYL SUSAN, physician, medical educator; b. Bklyn., Mar. 14, 1949; married; 2 children. MD, U. Med. and Dentistry of N.J., 1975. Diplomate Am. Bd. Internal Medicine. Fellow in endocrinology Harvard Med. Sch., Boston, 1979-82; intern, resident, chief resident U. So. Calif./L.A. County Hosp., L.A., 1979-82; assoc. physician Brigham and Women's Hosp., Boston, 1982—; instr. in medicine Harvard Med. Sch., 1982-84, asst. prof. medicine, 1984-95, assoc. prof. medicine, 1995—, mem. search com. for asst. prof., 1989; dir. skeletal health and osteo. clin. Brigham and Women's Hosp., 1989-93, dir. housestaff tng. program in endo-hypertension, 1990, dir. skeletal health and osteo. program, 1993—. Mem. editl. bd. Jour. Bone and Mineral Rsch.; contbr. articles to profl. jours. Chmn. bd. dirs. John Winthrop Sch., Boston, 1993. Grantee NIH, 1983-87, 94-97, 95—, Dept. Def., 1999—; named Harvard Sandoz Scholar in Medicine, 1990-93, The Best Drs. Am., 1996-98, One of 50 Most Intriguing Women in Boston, 1997, among Best Physicians in Women's Health, Boston Mag., 2001, Best Physician in Endocrinology, Boston Mag., 2002. Mem. AMWA, ACP, AAAS, NOW, Nat. Osteoporosis Found., Inc. (mem. sci. adv. bd.), Paget's Disease Found., Inc. Avocations: classical music, tennis. Office: Brigham and Womens Hosp 221 Longwood Ave Boston MA 02115-5804

LE BON, DOUGLAS KENT, investment manager; b. Rapid City, S.D., Oct. 27, 1953; s. Stanley and Elodis (Holm) Le B.; m. Eva Marie Dyer; 1 child, Shauna. BSBA, Calif. State U., Dominguez Hills, 1976, MBA, 1979. Valuation cons. Houlihan, Lokey, Howard & Zukin, L.A., 1979-83; v.p., prin. Wilshire Assocs., Inc., Santa Monica, Calif., 1983-90; co-founder, mng. dir. Pathway Capital Mgmt., L.A., 1990—. Vice chmn., chmn. fin. com. L.A. area coun. Boy Scouts Am., 1991-99; mem. corp. bd. Sch. Mgmt. Avocations: scuba diving, skiing. Office: Pathway Capital Mgmt 5 Park Plz Irvine CA 92614-5995

LEBOUITZ, MARTIN FREDERICK, financial services industry executive, consultant; b. Phila., May 16, 1946; s. William and Sylvia (Magen) L.; m. Helene A. Pepe, Oct. 15, 1977; children: Clarke S., Jacqueline B. BS, U.S. Air Force Acad., Colorado Springs, Colo., 1971, MA, 1972; MA, Fletcher Sch. Law and Diplomacy, Tufts U. Asst. v.p. Bankers Trust Co., N.Y.C., 1976-82; v.p. mgr. of planning Barclays Bank of N. Am., N.Y.C., 1982-85; v.p. corp. devel. Chase Manhattan Bank, N.Y.C., 1985-88; v.p. planning and devel. Paine Webber Group Inc., 1988-90; prin. DRI/McGraw-Hill, 1990-91; mng. dir. Fin. Svcs. Cons., 1991-95; v.p. global payments project exec. and industry issues exec. JP Morgan Chase, 1995—. Bd. dirs., chmn. sch. rels. com. N.Y. chpt. Fletcher Sch. Capt. USAF, 1971-76. Mem. Strategic Leadership Forum (dir., chmn. program com. N.Y. chpt.), Assn. for Corp. Growth, Am. Mgmt. Assn., USAF Acad. Alumnae (treas. N.Y. metro area chpt.), Harvard Club, Fletcher Sch. Club N.Y. (chmn. sch. rels. com.), Univ. Club. Office: JP Morgan Chase 140 E 45th St 2d Fl New York NY 10017-1401

LEBOUTILLIER, JANET ELA, writer, real estate investment asset manager; b. Marshfield, Mass., May 10, 1936; d. Preston Carleton and Barbara (Higgins) Ela; m. John Walter McNeill, Oct. 10, 1959 (div. 1970); children: Duncan Davis McNeill, Sarah McNeill Treffry; m. Martin LeBoutillier, May 10, 1986 (dec. Feb. 2001). AA, Briarcliff Jr. Coll., 1956; BA in English Lit., U. Colo., 1958; postgrad. Real Estate/Mortgage Banking, NYU, 1973-78. Lic. N.Y. and Conn. real estate broker; cert. property mgr. Sales, leasing agt. L.B. Kaye Assocs., Ltd., N.Y.C., 1969-74; comml. leasing agt. Kenneth D. Laub & Co., 1975; dir. leasing, asst. bldg. mgr. Douglas Elliman Gibbons & Ives Co., 1975-76; adminstr. REIT adv. unit Chase Manhattan Bank, N.A., 1976-78; asst. dir. real estate investments Mass. Mut. Life Ins. Co., Springfield, Mass., 1978-80; dir. real estate investments Yale U., New Haven, 1980-81; ind. cons. N.Y.C., 1981-83; sr. analyst, equity mgmt., sales and devel. Aetna Realty Investors, Inc., Hartford, Conn., 1983-84, dir. pub. involvement unit, 1984-86; sr. asset mgr. Cigna Investments, Inc., Hartford, 1986-87; v.p. Wm. M. Hotchkiss Co., New Haven, 1987-88; pres., prin. LeBoutillier & LeBoutillier, Inc., Lyme, 1989-93. Author: Mediations on Joy, 1995. Mem. Grace Episcopal Ch., mem. pastoral care and healing commn., coord. prayer team ministry. Mem. Internat. Order of St. Luke the Physician (co-founder, convener Heart of COmpassion Conn. Shoreline, Conn. area chpt. 1993—), Soc. Mayflower Descs., Nat. Soc. Colonial Dames of Am.-Conn. (bd. mgrs., sec.). Democrat. Episcopalian. Avocations: prayer ministry, skiing, fishing, sailing, tennis. Home and Office: 8 Laurel Dr Old Lyme CT 06371-1462 E-mail: jlebout@aol.com.

LEBOUTILLIER, MEGAN, writer; b. N.Y.C., Apr. 5, 1955; d. Charles and Deirdre Jones (Johnson) LeB. BA, Vt. Coll., 1985; PhD, Union Inst., Cin., 1998. Health educator Planned Parenthood, Missoula, Mont., 1977-80, dir. cmty. edn. Atlanta, 1980-85; pres. Seaglass Publs., 1985-88, pres., writer Pawleys Island, S.C., 1988-88; facilitator The Courage to Teach, Free Union, Va., 1998—; freelance writer, 1998—. Vis. author, lectr. Emory U., Atlanta, 1987, 91, Waccamaw Libr., Pawleys Island, 1996, 2000, Coastal Carolina U., Conway, S.C., 1999, 2000; facilitator Leadership Acad., Conway, 1993, 94. Author: Little Miss Perfect, 1990, "No" Is a Complete Sentence, 1995; co-author: Birth Control, The Movie, 1986. Bd. dirs. LWV, Georgetown, S.C., 1989-98, pres., 1993-95; bd. dirs., eductor AIDS Task Force, Georgetown, 1991-96. Avocations: weaving, gardening, hiking, biking, cooking. Office: PO Box 325 Free Union VA 22940 E-mail: mimileb@mindspring.com.

LEBOVITZ, CHARLES NEAL, surgeon; b. Pitts., Jan. 16, 1943; s. Herbert B. and Margaret (Kopelman) L.; m. Rose Linda Benkovitz, Dec. 13, 1975; children: Emily Suzanne, Jeffrey Scott. BS, U. Pitts., 1963, MD, 1966, MBA, 2000. Diplomate Am. Bd. Surgeons. Intern in surgery Hosp. of U. of Pa., Phila., 1966-67; resident in surgery Health Ctr. Hosps. U. of Pitts., Pitts., 1967-68, 70-73; pvt. practice surgery Chetlin & Lebovitz Surg. Assocs., 1973-94, Premier Surg. Assocs., Pitts., 1994-98; pvt. practice White Oak, Pa., 1998—. Clin. asst. prof. surgery U. Pitts., 1973—, med. exec. com., 1993-97; pres. med. staff Braddock Med. Ctr., 1995-97. Lt. comdr. USNR, 1968-70, Vietnam. Fellow Am. Geriatrics Soc; mem. AMA (Pa. and Allegheny County chpts.), Pitts. Surg. Soc., Allegheny County Med. Soc. (med. staff officers group 1993-97), Phi Beta Kappa, Alpha Omega Alpha. Avocations: travel, computers, bicycling. Home: 1046 Lyndhurst Dr Pittsburgh PA 15206-4536 Office: 1220 Lincoln Way Ste 100 White Oak PA 15131-1642

LEBOVITZ, HAROLD PAUL (HAL LEBOVITZ), journalist; b. Cleve., Sept. 11, 1916; s. Isaiah and Celia (Levy) L.; m. Margie Glassman, Feb. 20, 1938; children: Neil Ross, Lynn Gail. BA, Case Western Res. U., 1938, MA, 1942. Sci. tchr., coach Euclid (Ohio) High Sch., 1938-46; reporter, baseball writer, columnist Cleve. News, 1946-60; columnist Cleve. Plain Dealer, 1960-84, sports editor, 1964-84; columnist The Sporting News, 1970-92, Gannett Syndicate, 1979-82; dir. Cleve. Jewish News, 1971-89; baseball umpire, 1937-50; football ofcl., 1940-71; basketball ofcl., 1940-60; Cleve. corr. Sporting News, 1950-64. Author: Pitchin' Man, 1948; (with Phil R. Gilman) Springboards to Science, 1967; contbg. editor: Webster's New World Dictionary, 1983—; syndicated columnist several Ohio newspapers, 1984—; contbr. articles to various periodicals; inventor outdoor playground game Four Sq. Tennis. Mem. recreation com. University Heights, Ohio, 1965-75; bd. dirs. Jewish Community Ctr., Cleve., 1962-63, Alumni Assn. Adelbert Coll. Case-Western Res. U., 1969-83. Named Citizen of Yr. City of University Heights, 1964, Sportsman of Yr. B'rith Emeth Men's Club, 1964, Top Sportswriter Cortron Twelve of Atlantic Fleet, 1961, Sporting News Top Feature Writer, 1963-64; recipient ten best writing awards Cleve. Newspaper Guild, 1948-60, Greater Cleve. Football Coaches Golden Deeds award, 1987, J.G. Taylor Spink award Baseball Hall of Fame, Cooperstown, N.Y., 2000; inducted into Glenville High Sch. Hall of Fame, 1980, JRC-JCC Hall of Fame, 1982, Ohio Baseball Hall of Fame, 1984, Greater Cleve. Softball Hall of Fame, 1989, Sport Media Assn. of Cleve. Hall of Fame, 1990, Cleve. Journalism Hall of Fame, 1991, Euclid (Ohio) Sports Hall of Fame, 1997, Cleve. Sports Stars Hall of Fame, 1998, Glenville C.D. Legends Hall of Fame, 1998, Greater Cleve. Sports Hall of Fame, 1999, Case Western Res. U. Sports Hall of Fame, 2000; recipient Special Tribute award, U. Heights, Ohio, 2000. Mem. Baseball Writers Assn. (pres. 1965-66, bd. dirs. 1966-67), Ohio Sports Editors Assn. (pres. 1965-66), Cleve. Football Ofcls. Assn., Ohio Football Ofcls. Assn., Cleve. Athletic Club (Outstanding Sports Personality award 1984), Cleve. Umpires Assn., Sigma Delta Chi (Disting. Svc. award 1981, Mel Harder Disting. Svc. award 1992). Home: 2380 Edgerton Rd Cleveland OH 44118-3726

LEBOW, IRWIN LEON, communications engineering consultant; b. Boston, Apr. 27, 1926; s. Samuel and Ruth (Tobey) L.; m. Grace H. Hackel, July 8, 1951; children: Judith, William, David. SB, MIT, 1948, PhD, 1951. Staff mem. MIT Lincoln Lab., 1951-60, assoc. leader satellite communications surface techniques group, 1960-65, leader, 1965-70, assoc. head communications divsn., 1970-72, assoc. head data systems divsn., 1972-75, mem. steering com., 1970-75; chief scientist, assoc. dir. tech. Def. Communications Agy., Washington, Dept. Def., Washington, 1975-81; v.p. engring. Am. Satellite Co., Rockville, Md., 1981-84; v.p. Systems Research and Applications Corp., Arlington, Va., 1984-87; ind. cons. Washington, 1987—. Adj. prof. U. Md., Univ. Coll., 1998—. Author: (with others) Theory and Design of Digital Machines, 1962, The Digital Connection, 1991, Information Highways and Byways, 1995, Understanding Digital Transmission and Recording, 1997, (with others) Coping with Your Difficult Older Parent, 1999. With USNR, 1944-46. Awarded rank of Meritorious Sr. Exec., 1980; recipient Meritorious Civilian Service medal Dept. Def., 1981. Fellow Am. Phys. Soc., IEEE; mem. AAAS, Armed Forces Communications and Electronics Assn., Sigma Xi. Home and Office: Apt 909 5600 Wisconsin Ave Chevy Chase MD 20815-4411

LEBOW, MARK DENIS, lawyer; b. Harrisburg, Pa., Apr. 2, 1940; s. Sylvan and Ruth M. (Lebowitz) L.; m. Catherine Maugee, Nov. 22, 1972 (div. 1982); m. Patricia Edith Harris, Jan. 30, 1988; children: Michael, Jeffrey, Alexandra. AB, Yale U., 1961; JD, Harvard U., 1964. Bar: N.Y. 1965, U.S. Ct. Appeals (2d cir.) 1965, U.S. Dist. Ct. (so. and ea. dists.) N.Y. 1966, U.S. Supreme Ct., 1972. Assoc. Coudert Bros., N.Y.C., 1965-71, ptnr., 1972-98; mng. ptnr. Sokolow, Dunaud, Mercadier & Carreras LLP, 1999—. Chmn. N.Y.C. CSC, 1979-92; bd. dirs. Met. Transit Authority of N.Y. State. Chmn. St. Francis Friends of the Poor, Inc., 1991—; trustee St. Bona Venture U., 1997—; pres. Am. Red Magen David for Israel, 2001—. Bus. Home: 1067 5th Ave New York NY 10128-0101 Office: Sokolow Dunaud Mercadier & Carreras LLP 770 Lexington Ave 6th Flr New York NY 10021-8165 E-mail: mlebow@sdmc-law.com.

LEBOW, MICHAEL JEFFREY, lawyer; b. Detroit, Apr. 4, 1956; s. David and Thelma (Shainack) L. BA, Wayne State U., 1978; JD, Detroit Coll. Law, 1981. Bar: Mich. 1982, D.C. 1986, U.S. Dist. Ct. (ea. dist.) Mich. 1982, U.S. Supreme Ct. 2000; diplomate Nat. Bd. Trial Advocacy; cert. civil trial specialist. Litigation assoc. Kemp Klein Endelman & Beer, Birmingham, Mich., 1982-83; sole practice Southfield, 1983-85; ptnr. Lebow & Tobin, Birmingham, 1985-86, Gropman, Lebow & Tobin, Birmingham, 1986-89, Lebow & Tobin, Birmingham, 1989—. State coord. Nat. Bd. Trial Advocacy, 1994—, mem. bd. law examiners, 1993—, bd. dirs. Contbr. articles to profl. jours. Bd. dirs. Mich. Com. Human Rights, Oak Park, 1976—. Mem. ABA (Excellence Nat. Appellate Advocacy award 1981), Mich. Bar Assn., Am. Inns of the Ct. (barrister Oakland County chpt.), Mto Guzzi Nat. Owners Assn., Mich. Handball Assn. Jewish. Avocations: handball, motorcycle collecting, 1950's jazz. Office: Lebow & Tobin PLLC 7001 Orchard Lake Rd Ste 312 West Bloomfield MI 48322-3607 E-mail: mlebow@lebowandtobin.com.

LEBOWITZ, ALBERT, lawyer, writer; b. St. Louis, June 18, 1922; s. Jacob and Lena (Zemmel) L.; m. Naomi Gordon, Nov. 26, 1953; children— Joel Aaron, Judith Leah. AB, Washington U., St. Louis, 1945; LL.B., Harvard U., 1948. Bar: Mo. bar 1948. Assoc. Frank E. Morris, St. Louis, 1948-55; partner firm Morris, Schneider & Lebowitz, 1955-58, Crowe, Schneider, Shanahan & Lebowitz, St. Louis, 1958-66; counsel firm Murphy & Roche, 1966-67, Murphy & Schlapprizzi, St. Louis, 1967-81; partner firm Murphy, Schlapprizzi & Lebowitz, 1981-86; editor lit. quar. Perspective, 1961-80; of counsel Donald L. Schlapprizzi, P.C., 1986—, John T. Murphy, Jr., 1986-88. Author: novel Laban's Will, 1966, The Man Who Wouldn't Say No, 1969, A Matter of Days, 1989; also short stories. Served as combat navigator USAAF, 1943-45, ETO. Decorated Air medal with 3 oak leaf clusters. Mem. ABA, Mo., St. Louis bar assns., Phi Beta Kappa. Home: 743 Yale Ave Saint Louis MO 63130-3120 Office: Gateway One On The Mall 701 Market St Ste 1550 Saint Louis MO 63101-1897

LEBOWITZ, CHARLOTTE MEYERSOHN, social worker; b. Germany, Dec. 22, 1924; came to U.S., 1938, naturalized, 1943; d. Franz and Magda (Wellisch) Meyersohn; m. Marshall Lebowitz, Aug. 7, 1949; children: Wendy, Marian, Mark (dec.). BA, Brown U., 1946; MSW, Simmons Coll., 1948. Psychiat. social worker Jewish Family and Children's Svc., Boston, 1948-49, ARC Home Svc. Dept., Boston, 1949-53, Youth Guidance Ctr., Framingham, Mass., 1962-69, Brandon Sch., Natick, 1969-74, Natick Pub. Schs., Natick, 1975-92. Adj. clin. instr. Boston Coll. Sch. Social Work, 1981-82; mem. exec. bd. Natick Svc. Coun., 1982-95; cons. YWCA, 1970-71. Mem. exec. bd. PTA, 1955-71, chmn. pre-sch. unit, 1955-56, mem. coun., 1956-70; trustee coun. Leonard Morse Hosp., 1976-91. Fellow: Am. Orthopsychiat. Assn.; mem.: NASW, Boston Inst. Devel. Infants and Parents, Social Workers Employed Less than Full Time, Sch. Adjustment Counselors Assn., Acad. Cert. Social Workers, Sisterhood of Temple Israel of Natick, Nonesuch Pond Improvement Assn., Brown U. Alumni Assn., Simmons Coll. Sch. Social Work Alumni Assn. Home: 2 Abbott Rd Natick MA 01760-1913

LEBOWITZ, JOEL LOUIS, mathematical physicist, educator; b. May 10, 1930; came to U.S., 1946, naturalized, 1951; m. Estelle Mandelbaum, June 21, 1953 (dec. Dec. 1996); m. Ann Keay Beneduce, June 3, 1999. BS, Bklyn. Coll., 1952; MS, Syracuse U., 1955, PhD, 1956; hon. doctorate, Ecole Poly. Federale, Lausanne, Switzerland, 1977, Clark U., 1999. NSF postdoctoral fellow Yale U., New Haven, 1956-57; mem. faculty Stevens Inst. Tech., Hoboken, N.J., 1957-59, Yeshiva U., N.Y.C., 1959-77, prof. physics, 1965-77, acting chmn. Belfer Grad. Sch. Sci., 1964-67, chmn. dept., 1967-76; George William Hill prof math. and physics, dir. Ctr. for Math. Scis., Rutgers U., New Brunswick, N.J., 1977—. Co-editor: Phase Transitions and Critical Phenomena, 1980, editor Jour. Statis. Physics, 1975—, Studies in Statis. Mechanics, 1973—, Com. Math. Physics, 1973—; contbr. articles to profl. jours. Recipient Boltzmann medal Internat. Union Pure and Applied Physics, 1992, Max Planck Rsch. award, 1993, Delmar S. Fahrney medal Franklin Inst., 1995, Henri Poincare prize Internat. Assn. of Math. Physics/Daniel Iagolnitzer Found., 2000, Vito Volterra medal Academia Nazionale dei Lincei, 2001; Guggenheim fellow, 1976-77. Fellow AAAS (Sci. Freedom and Responsibility award 1998), Am. Phys. Soc., N.Y. Acad. Scis. (pres. 1979, A. Cressy Morrison award in natural scis. 1986, Heinz R. Pagels Human Rights of Scientists award 1996); mem. NAS, AAUP, Am. Math. Soc., Phi Beta Kappa, Sigma Xi. Office: Rutgers U Ctr Math Sci Rsch 110 Frelinghuysen Rd Piscataway NJ 08854-8019 E-mail: lebowitz@sakharov.rutgers.edu.

LEBRATO, MARY THERESA, lawyer, psychologist; b. Ft. Wayne, Ind., June 13, 1950; d. Joseph James and Veronica (Adamonis) L. BA, U. Dayton, 1971; MA, U. Ala., Tuscaloosa, 1973, PhD, 1975; JD, Lincoln Law Sch., 1986. Bar: Calif. 1986; lic. psychologist, Calif. Psychologist Ala. Dept. Mental Hygiene, Tuscaloosa, 1975, Calif. Dept. Health, Eldridge, Calif., 1975-77, chief statewide evaluation devel. svcs., 1977-79; dir. evaluation Oakland Perinatal Health Project, Calif. Dept. Health, Sacramento, 1979-81; coord. Maternal, Child and Adolescent Health, 1981-82; dir. sexual harassment in employment project Calif. Commn. on Status of Women, 1982-85; chief long range planning Calif. Dept. Devel. Svcs., 1985-88; staff counsel Calif. State Lottery, 1988-91. Co-author (with Marilyn Pearman) Sexual Harassment Investigators Guidebook, 1984; author, editor: Help Yourself: A Manual for Dealing with Sexual Harassment, 1986. Adv. bd. mem. Calif. State Pers. Bd., Appeals Div. Adv. Com., 1987-91; bd. mem. Sacramento Rape Crisis Ctr., 1988. Recipient fellowships in psychology NIMH, U. Ala., Tuscaloosa, 1971, 72, 73, teaching asst. in psychology U. Ala., Tuscaloosa, 1974-75. Mem. APA, ABA, Am. Assn. on Mental Deficiency, Calif. State Bar Assn., Calif. State Psychol. Assn., Calif. Women Lawyers, Sacramento County Bar Assn., Women Laywers Sacramento (bd. mem., chair del. com. 1989, chair scholarship 1990). Avocations: horse breeding, art. Home: 335 Del Wes Ln Rio Linda CA 95673-2031

LEBRECHT, THELMA JANE MOSSMAN, reporter; b. Indpls., Feb. 21, 1946; d. Elmore Somerville and Lois Thelma (Johnson) Mossman; m. Roger Dublon LeBrecht, May 4, 1968. BS in Journalism, U. Fla., 1968. Pub. affairs reporter WBT and WBTV, Charlotte, N.C., 1967-72; freelance reporter Toronto and N.Y.C., 1972-76; reporter KYW Newsradio, Phila., 1976-80; editor ABC Radio Network, N.Y.C., 1980-81; reporter AP Broadcast, Washington, 1981—. Bd. dirs. Washington Press Club Found., 1995—. Mem. Radio and TV Corrs. Assn. in U.S. Capitol (chmn. 1991, AP Oliver S. Gramling Disting. Reporter award 1996). Office: AP Broadcast 1825 K St NW Washington DC 20006-1202

LEBRETON, PAUL M. government official; b. Edmundston, Canada, Mar. 3, 1948; m. Nicole Leger; children: Helene, Luc, Mathieu. BA, U. Moncton, 1968; LLB, U. New Brunswick, 1972. Ptnr. Landry, LeBreton & McIntyre, Moncton, N.B., Can., 1972-81; sec. Law Soc. New Brunswick, 1981-88;

justice, dep. atty. gen. Govt. New Brunswick, 1988-98; dep. min. Dept. Health and Wellness, Fredericton, Can., 1998—. Area dir. Legal Aid New Brunswick, 1975-81; lectr. Ecole de droit U. Moncton, 1979-81. Trustee Sch. Dist. 51, Fredericton, N.B., 1987-88; pres. New Maryland Minor Baseball, Fredericton, 1992-95. Mem. Nat. Com. Practice of Law, Can. Bar Assn., Coun. Law Soc. New Brunswick. Avocations: hockey, baseball. Office: Dept Health and Wellness PO Box 5100 520 King St Fredericton NB Canada E3B 5G8 Fax: 506-453-5243. E-mail: paul.lebreton@gnb.ca.

LEBRUN, GENE N. lawyer; b. Langdon, N.D., July 4, 1939; s. Jules E. and Marie Lebrun; m. Patricia A. Lebrun, Aug. 17, 1963; children: Michael, Kenneth. BA, St. John's U., 1961; JD, U. N.D., 1964. Bar: S.D. 64, 1964. Mem. Lynn, Jackson, Shultz & Lebrun, P.C., Rapid City, S.D., 1964—. Mem. Adv. Commn. on Electronic Commerce, 1999-2000. Mem. Nat. Conf. of Commrs. on Uniform State Laws (pres. 1997-99). Democrat. Office: Lynn Jackson Shultz & Lebrun PC Ste 400 909 St Joseph St Rapid City SD 57701

LEBWOHL, MARK GABRIEL, dermatologist, educator; b. Bklyn., Apr. 27, 1952; married, 1978; 2 children. BA summa cum laude, Columbia Coll., 1974; MD, Harvard Med. Sch., 1978. Diplomate Am. Bd. Internal Medicine, Am. Bd. Dermatology. Intern in internal medicine Mt. Sinai Med. Ctr., N.Y.C., 1978-79, resident in internal medicine, 1979-81, resident in dermatology, 1981-82, NIH fellowship, 1982-83, asst. prof. dermatology, 1983-88, assoc. prof. dermatology, 1988-92, prof. dermatology, 1993—, dir. phototherapy unit, 1982—, clin. dir. dept. dermatology, 1983—, vice chmn. dept. dermatology, 1989—. Dir. divsn. clin. dermatology Mt. Sinai Sch. of Medicine, N.Y.C., 1989—, chmn. dept. dermatology, 1996—; dir. skin cancer screening clinic Mt. Sinai Hosp., 1985-93; chmn. PXE symposium Mt. Sinai Med. Ctr., 1987, chmn. phototherapy symposium, 1992, mem. numerous hosp. and med. sch. coms., 1983—; dir. dermatology course N.Y. Coll. of Podiatric Medicine, 1989—; mem. dermatology test com. Nat. Bd. Podiatric Med. Examiners, 1990-91, med. adv. bd. Nat. Psoriasis Found., 1990—; chmn. Psoriasis Symposium in Istanbul, Turkey, 1993, Ankara, Turkey, 1993, Adana, Turkey, 1993, New Orleans, 1993. Author: Difficult Diagnoses in Dermatology, 1988, Atlas of the Skin and Systemic Disease, 1995, Psoriasis, 1995, Treatment of Skin Disease, 2002; asst. editor The Mount Sinai Jour. of Medicine, 1989—; editorial bd. Nat. Psoriasis Found. Bull., 1990—, Jour. of the Am. Acad. of Dermatology, 1993—; reviewer U.S. Pharmacopeia, 1984-87, 91, Chest, The Cardiopulmonary Jour., 1985, Jour. of the Am. Acad. Dermatology, 1987-89, 91-93, Jour. of Investigative Dermatology, 1987-89, 91-93, Archives of Internal Medicine, 1989, 92-93. Fellow ACP, Am. Acad. Dermatology (faculty genodermatoses symposium 1985, skin cancer campaign coord N.Y. State 1985-93, nat. adv. coun. 1986-89, 89-92, 93—, faculty itch symposium 1993—, psoriasis symposium 1993—, dir. diagnostic update symposium 1993—, cons. editor 1990—); mem. AMA, N.Y. County Med. Soc., Soc. for Investigative Dermatology (chmn. psoriasis symposium 1991), Dermatol. Soc. of Greater N.Y. (pres. 2001-02), Manhattan Dermatol. Soc. (pres. 1985-86), Internat. Dermatology Soc., N.Y. State Soc. for Dermatology (pres. 2001), N.Y. Dermatol. Soc., N.Y. Acad. of Medicine (chmn. dermatology sect. 1996), Phi Beta Kappa. Office: Mt Sinai Sch Medicine 5 E 98th St New York NY 10029-6501

LEBWOHL, PAUL A. physician; b. N.Y.C., Sept. 3, 1942; s. William S. Lebwohl and Mildred Julien; m. Marilyn A., May. 27, 1995; children: Alison, Lauren, Nina, Eliana. BS, Yale U., 1964, MS, 1965, PhD, 1968; MD, U. Miami, 1975. Diplomate Am. Bd. Internal Medicine, Gastroenterology. Pvt. practice, Carmel, N.Y. Mem. AMA, MSSNY, Putnam County Med. Soc. Office: Stoneleigh Ave Carmel NY 10512-2000

LECAPITAINE, JOHN EDWARD, counseling psychology educator, researcher; b. Nov. 21, 1950; s. Vincent Bernard and Evelyn Lucille LeCapitaine; m. Jessica Dale; 1 child, Katherine Briee. BS, U. Wis., 1973, MS, 1975; D, Boston U., 1980, PhD in Metaphysics, 2000. Diplomate forensic psychologist, psychotherapist. Counseling and sch. psychologist Martin Luther King. Jr. Ctr., Boston, 1976-78; adj. prof. Boston U., 1980-90; rsch. cons. Dept. Mental Health, 1985-90; prof. counseling psychology U. Wis., River Falls, 1990—. Contbr. poetry, fiction, and acad. articles to profl. jours. Recipient Disting. award for Schs. as Devel. Clinics, The Edn. Jour., 1999. Mem. APA, ACA, Inst. Noetic Scis., Internat. Biographical Inst., Nat. Assn. Sch. Psychologists, Internat. Coun. Psychologists, Assn. Play Therapy, Assn. Multicultural Counseling and Devel., Assn. Humanistic Devel. and Edn., Internat. Soc. Poets, Phi Delta Kappa. Avocations: fiction writing, poetry. Home: 731 Lumphrey Ct River Falls WI 54022-3426 Office: U Wis Coll Edn and Grad Studies Dept Couns/Sch Psych 410 S 3rd St River Falls WI 54022-5013

LECAVALIER, VINCENT, professional hockey player; b. Ile Bizard, Que., Can., Apr. 21, 1980; Hockey player Rimouski Oceanic, Tampa Bay (Fla.) Lightning, 1998—. Office: Tampa Bay Lightning Ice Palace 401 Channelside Dr Tampa FL 33602*

LECERF, OLIVIER MAURICE MARIE, construction company executive; b. Merville-Franceville, France, Aug. 2, 1929; s. Maurice and Colette (Lainé) L.; m. Annie Bazin de Jessey, Jan. 11, 1958; children: Christophe, Véronique, Nicolas, Patricia. Baccalauréat A in Philosophy, 1946; diploma, Inst. Polit. Studies Paris, 1950; LLM, U. Paris, 1950; diploma Indsl. Studies Ctr., U. Geneva, 1960. Asst. mgr. Omnium pour l'importation et l'exploration, Paris, 1951-56; ast. mgr. Ciments Lafarge, Can., 1956-57, asst. mgr. Brazil, 1958-59, asst. mgr. fgn. dept., 1961, adj. comml. dir., 1962-64; pres., CEO Lafarge Cement N.Am., Vancouver, B.C., Can., 1965; pres. Lafarge Can. Que., Montreal, 1968, Lafarge Can. Ltd., 1969; gen. mgr. Can. Cement Lafarge, Montreal, 1970, exec. gen. mgr. Paris, 1971-73, chmn., CEO (now Lafarge), 1974—, hon. chmn., 1989—, also dir. Dir. L'Oréal. Contbr. articles to profl. jours. With inf. French Army, 1950-51; lt. Res. Decorated officer de la Legion d'Honneur, commandeur Ordre Nat. du Merite. Home: 8 rue Guy de Maupassant 75116 Paris France

LECHAGO, JUAN, pathologist, educator; b. Barcelona, Spain, Aug. 2, 1942; came to U.S., 1973; s. Angel and Dolores (Xicart) L.; m. Lia Virginia Epstein, Feb. 26, 1966 (dec.); children: John Patrick, James Bernard, Sarah Angela; m. Maria Zunilda Nuñez, July 21, 2002; 1 stepchild, Pamela Espino. B of Humanities, Nat. Coll. Monserrat, Cordoba, Argentina, 1959; MD, Nat. U. Cordoba, 1966; PhD in Pathology, Queen's U., Kingston, Ont., Can., 1971. Diplomate Am. Bd. Pathologists. Staff pathologist Harbor UCLA Med. Ctr., Torrance, Calif., 1973-87; asst. prof. pathology UCLA, 1973-79, assoc. prof. pathology, 1979-85, prof. pathology, 1985-87; prof., vice-chmn. dept. pathology U. Tex. So. Med. Sch., Dallas, 1987-90; chief lab. VA Med. Ctr., 1987-90; prof. pathology Baylor Coll. Medicine, Houston, 1990—2002, prof. medicine, 1998—2002; head gastrointestinal pathology Cedars-Sinai Med. Ctr., L.A., 2002—. Dir. morphology Core Ctr. for Study of Inflammatory Bowel Disease, Torrance, 1985-87, Ctr. for Diabetes Rsch., Dallas, 1988-90; dir. surg. pathology svc. The Meth. Hosp., Houston, 1990-2002. Editor: Cellular Basis of Chemical Messengers in the Digestive System, 1981, Endocrine Pathology Update, 1990, Bloodworth's Endocrine Pathology, 3d edit., 1996; contbr. over 120 articles to profl. jours. NIH grantee, 1974-84, 82-86. Mem. U.S. Can. Acad. Pathology (edn. com. 1973—), Gastrointestinal Pathology Soc. (founding mem.; pres. 1987-88), Latin Am. Pathology Found. (pres. 1994-96), Ctrl. Am. Assn. Pathology (hon.), Argentinian Soc. Pathology (hon.). Achievements include work on ultrastructural and histochemical characterization of the digestive endocrine cells in man and animal species, first immunocytochemical cellular localization of the neuropeptides Bombesin and Ranatensin in animals, first immunolocalization of Granuliberin-like peptide in frog brain, molecular biology of Barrett's esophagus-derived cancer. Avocations: gourmet cooking, wine tasting, music and opera listening, martial arts, 2d degree Black Belt Jujitsu. Office: Cedars-Sinai Med Ctr Dept Pathology 8700 Beverly Blvd Los Angeles CA 90048 E-mail: lechagoj@cshs.org.

LECHER, BELVADINE (BELVADINE REEVES), museum curator; b. Plainview, Nebr., Nov. 14, 1921; d. Robert Ancil and Myrtle Ivian (Rodgers) Reeves; m. Raymond Ralph Lecher, June 6, 1943; children: Krissa R. Lecher Randall , Pamela G. Lecher Hersh, Kim N. Lecher. Cert. in Hosp. Adminstrn., St. Louis U., 1967. Sec. Baird Law Office, Gordon, Nebr., 1938-39; cashier, bookkeeper, receptionist Western Pub. Svc. Co., 1939-41, Consumers Pub. Power Co., Chadron, Nebr., 1941-45; cashier, bookkeeper, med. records Luth. Hosp. Homes Soc., Crawford, 1952-62, adminstr., 1962-70; rate auditor, acct. Ross Transfer, Inc., Chadron, 1970-90; curator, dir. Dawes County Hist. Soc. Mus., 1992—. Editor: (newspaper) Golden Age Courier, 1994—, (newsletter) Dawes County Hist. Soc., 1981—; co-editor: (book) Man of Many Frontiers - The Diaries of Billy the Bear Iaeger, 1994. Active Am. Cancer Soc., Dawes County, 1981—2002; tutor adult basic edn., Chadron, 1990—95; bd. dirs. Habitat for Humanity, 1993—95. Recipient Cmty. Svc. award Rotary, Chadron, 1985, Good Neighbor award Ak-Sar-Ben/Omaha World Herald, Omaha, 1994, Woman of the Yr. award Chadron Bus. and Profl. Women's Club, Chadron, 1996, Recognition of Vol. Svc. award Am. Legion Aux., Chadron, 1994. Mem. Nebr. Mus. Assn., Nebr. State Genealogy Soc. (query editor 1982-84), Northwest Genealogy Soc. (county dir. 1992-94), Dawes County Hist. Soc. (pres. 1981-92, mus. curator 1992—), DAR (regent 2000-2002, registrar, treas. 1972-2001), Area C. of C. (vis. com. 1996—). Republican. Methodist. Avocations: historic and lineage research, reading, writing, handcrafts, hiking. Office: Dawes County Hist Soc PO Box 1319 Chadron NE 69337-7329

LECHEVALIER, HUBERT ARTHUR, microbiology educator; b. Tours, Indre et Loire, France, May 12, 1926; came to U.S., 1948; s. Jean Gaston and Marie Emilie L.; m. Mary Pfeil, Apr. 10, 1950; children: Marc, Paul. L ès Sci., Laval U., 1947, MS, 1948, DSc (hon.), 1983; PhD, Rutgers U., 1951. Asst. prof. Rutgers U., New Brunswick, N.J., 1951-56, assoc. prof., 1956-66, prof. microbiology, 1966-91, assoc. dir. Waksman Inst., 1980-88; prof. emeritus, 1991—. Vis. scientist Acad. of Scis. USSR, Moscow, 1958-59, Pasteur Inst., Paris, 1961-62 Author: (with others) A Guide to the Actinomycetes and Their Antibiotics, 1953, Neomycin--Its Nature and Practical Application, 1958, Antibiotics of Actinomycetes, 1962, Three Centuries of Microbiology, 1965, Hungarian transl., 1971, The Microbes, 1971, The Development of Applied Microbiology at Rutgers, 1982; co-editor: CRC Critical Reviews in Microbiology (1970-78), CRC Handbook of Microbiology (1970-89); contbr. numerous articles to profl. jours.; 4 patents. Trustee Am. Type Culture Collection, Rockville, Md., 1973-79. Recipient Lindback award 1976, Bergey award 1989; inducted into N.J. Inventors Hall of Fame, 1990. Mem. Soc. Française de Microbiologie (hon.), Soc. for Indsl. Microbiology (emeritus); Charles Thom award 1982), Soc. for Actinomycetes Japan (hon.) Home: 131 Goddard-Nisbet Rd Morrisville VT 05661-8041 E-mail: mheques@together.net.

LECHEVALIER, MARY PFEIL, retired microbiologist, educator; b. Cleve., Jan. 27, 1928; d. Alfred Leslie Pfeil and Mary Edith Martin; m. Hubert Arthur Lechevalier, Apr. 7, 1950; children: Marc E.M., Paul R. BA in Physiology-Biochemistry, Mt. Holyoke Coll., 1949; MS in Microbiology, Rutgers U., 1951. Rsch. fellow Rutgers U., New Brunswick, N.J., 1949-51, rsch. assoc. inst. microbiology, 1962-74, from asst. to assoc. rsch. prof., 1974-85, rsch. prof. Waksman inst. microbiology, 1985-91, prof. emerita, 1991—; ind. rschr., 1955-59; microbiologist steroid preparative lab. E.R. Squibb and Sons, New Brunswick, 1960-61; vis. investigator Inst. Biology Czechoslovak Acad. Scis., Svc. de Mycologie Pasteur Inst., Prague, Paris, 1961-62. Cons. in field. Contbr. over 100 chpts. to books and articles to rsch. jours.; mem. adv. com. actinomycetes Bergey's Manual of Determinative Bacteriology, 8th edit.; chair adv. com. muriform actinomycetes Bergey's Manual, 9th edit. Assoc. mem. Bergey's Trust, 1989-92. Recipient Charles Thom award Soc. Indsl. Microbiology, 1982, Waksman award Theobald Smith Soc., 1991. Mem. AAAS, Am. Soc. Microbiology (former mem. com. actinomycetales), U.S. Fedn. Culture Collections (exec. com. 1982-85, J. Roger Porter award nominating com. 1983-84, 87-88, chair 1989-90, J. Roger Porter award 1992), N.Am. Mycol. Assn., Soc. for Actinomycetes Japan, Sigma Xi (pres. Rutgers U. chpt. 1977-78). Achievements include patents for immunological adjuvant and process for preparing same, pharmaceutical composition and process, restriction endonuclease Fse I, antibiotic LL-14E605B and O-Methyl LL-14E605B. Home: 131 Goddard-Nisbet Rd Morrisville VT 05661-8041

LECHNER, ALFRED JAMES, JR. judge; b. Elizabeth, N.J., Jan. 7, 1948; s. Alfred J. and Marie G. (McCormack) L.; m. Gayle K. Peterson, Apr. 3, 1976; children: Brendan Patrick, Coleman Thomas, Mary Kathleen. BS, Xavier U., Cin., 1969; JD, U. Notre Dame, 1972. Bar: N.J. 1972, U.S. Dist. Ct. N.J. 1972, N.Y. 1973, U.S. Dist. Ct. (so. and ea. dists.) N.Y. 1974, U.S. Ct. Appeals (2d cir.) 1974, U.S. Supreme Ct. 1975, U.S. Ct. Appeals (3d cir.) 1980. Assoc. Cadwalader, Wickersham & Taft, N.Y.C., 1972-75, MacKenzie, Welt & Duane, Elizabeth, 1975-76, MacKenzie, Welt, Duane & Lechner, Elizabeth, 1976-84; judge Superior Ct. State N.J., 1984-86, U.S. Dist. Ct. N.J., 1986—. Note and comment editor Notre Dame Law Rev., 1972; contbr. articles to profl. jours. Mem. Union County (N.J.) Adv. Bd. Cath. Cmty. Svcs., 1981-83, chmn., 1982. Lt. col. USMCR. Fellow Am. Bar Found.; mem. Assn. Fed. Bar of State N.J., Friendly Sons of St. Patrick (pres. 1982), Union County Club. Office: US Dist Ct Martin Luther King Jr Fed Bldg PO Box 999 Newark NJ 07101-0999

LECHNER, BERNARD JOSEPH, consulting electrical engineer; b. N.Y.C., Jan. 25, 1932; s. Barnard Joseph and Lillian Veronica (Stevens) L.; m. Joan Camp Mathewson, Nov. 21, 1953. BSEE, Columbia U., 1957; postgrad., Princeton U., 1957-60. Mem. tech. staff RCA Labs., Princeton, N.J., 1957-62, project leader, 1962-67, group head, 1967-77, lab. dir., 1977-83, staff v.p., 1983-87; cons., 1987—. Cons. expert on TV matters including high definition TV and flat-panel displays; bd. dirs. Palisades Inst., N.Y.C.; chmn. adv. commn. Mercer County Coll., Trenton, N.J., 1968-85. Contbr. articles to profl. jours.; holder 10 patents. Reader Recording for the Blind, Princeton, 1967-72. Served to cpl. U.S. Army, 1953-55. Recipient David Sarnoff Gold medal RCA Corp., 1962, Outstanding Contributor award Advanced TV Sys. Com., 2000. Fellow: IEEE (chpt. chmn. 1964—66, Best Paper award Solid State Cirs. Conf. 1966), Soc. Motion Picture and TV Engrs. (David Sarnoff Gold Medal award 1996, Progress Medal award 2001), Soc. for Info. Display (pres. 1978—80, Frances Rice Darne award 1971, Beatrice Winner award 1983); mem.: NAB (TV Engring. Achievement award 2002), Am. Relay Radio League, Princeton Sqs. (pres. 1981-87), Eta Kappa Nu, Tau Beta Pi, Sigma Xi. Episcopalian. Avocations: amateur radio, sq. dancing, philately, sailing, swimming. Address: 59 Carson Rd Princeton NJ 08540-2207 E-mail: tvbernie@att.net.

LECHNER, JON ROBERT, nursing administrator, educator; b. Detroit, Nov. 5, 1957; s. Monroe Stanley and Helen Cecelia (Schneider) L. Cert. in practical nursing, Oakland C.C., Southfield, Mich., 1983; ADN, Mercy Coll. Detroit, 1991, BSN, 1992; MSA, Ctrl. Mich. U., 1998. Cert. EMT; RN, ANCC, Mich. Coord. emergency med. svcs., paramedic William Beaumont Hosp., Royal Oak, Mich., 1979-84, nurse, 1986—, asst. nursing mgr., 1992-97, nursing mgr., 1997—; pastoral assoc. St. Mary's Parish & Sch., Toledo, 1984-86; adj. clin. instr. Oakland C.C., Waterford, Mich., 1993—. Cert. BLS instr. Am. Heart Assn., Southfield, 1986—. Vol. Project Health-O-Rama, 1992—, Wellness Networks, Inc., 1992—; voting mem. region I State of Mich. HIV Planning & Prevention Commn., Detroit, 1994—. Mem. Am. Assembly Men Nursing, Am. Assn. Neurosci. Nurses, Acad. Med. Surg. Nurses (charter), Assn. Nurses AIDS Care, Sigma Theta Tau. Democrat. Roman Catholic. Avocations: reading, hiking, walking, cycling, theatre. Home: 28450 Universal Dr Warren MI 48092-2441 Office: William Beaumont Hosp 3601 W 13 Mile Rd Royal Oak MI 48073-6712 E-mail: jlechner@beaumont.edu.

LECHNER, NORBERT MANFRED, architect educator; b. Pahl, Bavaria, Germany, Apr. 19, 1944; came to U.S., 1952; s. Karl and Magdalena Lechner; m. Judith, Mar. 31, 1967; children: A. Walden, Ethan M. BArch, CCNY, 1970; MS in Archtl. Tech., Columbia U., 1972. Registered architect, Ala. Assoc. designer Port of N.Y. and N.J. Authority, N.Y.C., 1971-74; asst. prof., assoc. prof., prof. Auburn (Ala.) U., 1974—. Author: Heating, Cooling, Lighting: Design Methods for Architects, 1991, 2d edit., 2001; inventor in field; prin. works include The Sun Emulator and the Integrating Sun Simulator; contbr. articles to profl. jours. Mem. Soc. Bldg. Sci. Educators, Am. Solar Energy Soc. Avocations: hiking, photography. Home: 719 Mercer Cir Auburn AL 36830-5024 Office: Auburn U Dept Bldg Sci 119 Dudley Hall Auburn AL 36849-5315

LECHOWICZ, LISA MARIE, insurance executive; b. Chgo., Feb. 11, 1954; d. Edmund Lawrence and Gloria Marie (Radtke) L.; m. John F. Hession, Jr. May 26, 1983. BS, MS, Purdue U., 1977. CLU, ChFC; cert. employee benefits specialist, health ins. assoc. Cons. Arthur Andersen & Co., Chgo., 1978-79, sr. cons. Omaha, 1979-81; systems analyst Mutual of Omaha, 1981-82, mgr., 1982-87, asst. v.p., mgr., 1987-89, 2nd v.p., dir., 1989-92, v.p., dir., 1992-95, sr. v.p., 1995-96; pres. Health Data Mgmt. Corp., Omaha, 1996—. Part-time instr. Met. C.C., Omaha, 1988-91, adv. bd., 1989-90, Coll. of St. Mary's, 1990-94. Campaign com. various local candidates, Omaha, 1988—. Mem. CLU Soc., WEDI, Omaha Jaycees (bd. dirs. 1988-89, Bronze Key award 1989). Home: 15611 Burt St Omaha NE 68118-2219 Office: Health Data Mgmt Corp 720 N 129th St Omaha NE 68154-6109 E-mail: ll@hdmcorp.com.

LECHTANSKI, CHERYL LEE, chiropractor; b. Elizabeth, N.J., Dec. 27, 1961; d. Leo Joseph and Barbara Frances (Sullivan) L. BA in Biology and Journalism, NYU, 1985; DC, N.Y. Chiropractic Coll., 1989; AAS in Acctg., Brookdale C.C., 1998; MBA, Monmouth U., 2002. Lic. chiropractor, N.J., N.Y., Pa., Del., Mich. Chiropractic assoc. Chiropractic Arts Ctr., Downingtown, Pa., 1990-91; pvt. practice Newark, 1992-93; with Morganville (N.J.) Family Chiropractic Office, 1993—. Founder Box Turtle Coalition of the N.E. Mem.: BTCNE, Marine Mammal Stranding Ctr., Save the Manatee Club, World Wildlife Fund, Pa. Chiropractic Assn., The Ocean Conservancy, Beta Gamma Sigma, Phi Chi Omega. Buddhism. Buddhist. Avocations: bicycling, hiking, herpetology, softball, ice skating. Home: 1 Kennedy Ct Middletown NJ 07748-3531 Office: Morganville Family Chiropractic Office 52 Tennent Rd Morganville NJ 07751-4153 E-mail: paboxies@hotmail.com.

LECHTENBERG, VICTOR L. agricultural studies educator; b. Butte, Nebr., Apr. 14, 1945; m. Grayce Lechtenberg; 4 children. BS, U. Nebr., 1967; PhD in Agronomy, Purdue U., 1971. Prof. agronomy Purdue U., West Lafayette, Ind., 1971—, assoc. dir. Agrl. Experiment Sta., 1982-89, exec. assoc. dean agr., 1989-93, dean agr., 1994—. Chmn. adv. bd. USDA nat. Agrl. Rsch. Ext., Edn. and Econs., 1996—. Contbr. articles to profl. jours., chpts. to books. Scoutmaster Boy Scouts Am., 1983-85. Recipient Nebr. 4-H Dist. Alumni award, 1981. Fellow Am. Soc. Agronomy (Ciba-Geigy award), Crop Sci. Soc. Am. (past pres.); mem. Crop Sci. Soc. Agrnomy, Coun. Agrl. Sci. and Tech. (past pres., bd. dirs.), USDA (mem., chmn. nat. agrl. rsch., extension, edn. and econs. adv. bd.). Sigma Xi, Alpha Zeta, Gamma Sigma Delta. Roman Catholic. Avocation: woodworking. Office: Purdue Univ 1140 Ag Ad Bldg West Lafayette IN 47907 E-mail: vll@purdue.edu.

LECISTON, DAVID JOHN, computer scientist; b. Passaic, N.J., Dec. 25, 1958; s. Alex and Rose (Kozmoski) L.; m. Diane Carol Hirth, June 19, 1981 (div. Apr. 1985); 1 child, Jennifer Ann; m. Wendie Sue Orr, Feb. 3, 1987 (div. Oct. 1998); children: David Jonathan, Mary Rose; m. Deborah Ann Owens, Dec. 30, 1999. BS in Computer Sci., Seton Hall U., 1982. Computer engr. Software Engring. Ctr. U.S. Army CECOM, Ft. Monmouth, NJ, 2001—. 1st lt. U.S. Army, 1983—87. Mem. IEEE (initiative on software engring. as a profession 1994—), Am. Computing Machinery, Armed Forces Comm. and Electronics Assn. (life). Avocations: fishing, camping, hiking, computers. Home: PO Box 639 Fort Monmouth NJ 07703-0639 Office: US Army Comm Electronics Command Bldg 1210 Rm 223 Rittko Ave Fort Monmouth NJ 07703-5207 E-mail: leciston@ieee.org.

LECKIE, CAROL MAVIS, retired state government administrator; b. Watertown, Wis., Feb. 25, 1929; d. Arthur Walter Bessel and Effie Vada (Squires) Downs; m. Ralph Junior Judd, Sept. 27, 1947 (div. Dec. 1952); Children: Russell Howard, Barbara Rae; m. Leonard John Leckie, Sept. 30, 1977 (dec. May 1990); stepchildren: Leonard John, Gordon Armstrong, Lorna Jean. Grad. h.s., Madison, Wis. Mgr. data processing Dept. Justice, State of Wis., Madison, 1971-79, mgr. Records Mgmt. Program, 1979-83, mgr. Typography Sect., 1983-90; ret. Mem. com. State of Wis. Employees Combined Campaign, Madison, 1986, 88-91, co-chair, 1987; co-chair East 1946 Class Reunion Com. Mem. Assn. Records Mgrs. and Adminstrs. (pres. 1983-84), Assn. Career Employees, Bus. Forms Mgmt. Assn. Lutheran. Avocations: travel, church work. Home: 5555 Tancho Dr Apt 106 Madison WI 53718-1929 E-mail: cmjl106@chorus.net.

LECKMAN, JUDITH ANN, engineering executive; b. Pitts., Aug. 4, 1972; s. Thomas Jay and Patricia Susan (Diederich) L. BS in Mech. Engring., MIT, 1994; MME, Stanford U., 1996. Graduate rotation engr. Intel Corp., Albuquerque, 1994-95, indsl. engr. Santa Clara, Calif., 1995-96, tool install sys. and bus. requirements mgr. Phoenix, 1997, FCT fin. bus. process mgr., 1998—, liaison to Pa. State U. quality and mfg. mgmt. program State Coll., Pa., 1996—, FCT fin. bus. process mgr., 1997—. Presenter in field. Mem. Nat. Soc. Profl. Engrs., Soc. Women Engrs., Toastmasters Internat., Sigma Xi. Avocations: running, hiking. Home: 951 W Saragosa St Chandler AZ 85225-6856

LECLAIR, BETTY JO COGDILL, special education and early childhood educator; b. Oklahoma City, Sept. 25, 1934; d. Mark Loffett and Elma Elizabeth (Wade) Cogdill; m. Charles E. LeClair, Feb. 23, 1957 (div. 1988); children: Rebecca, Joan, Charles III, Laura, Jill. BA, Okla. Bapt. U., 1957; postgrad., Cen. State U., Edmond, Okla., 1970-71, U. S.C., 1974-95; MEd, Columbia (S.C.) Coll., 1988. Cert. elem., spl. edn. tchr., S.C. Spl. edn. tchr. Children's Opportunity Ctr., Ft. Worth, 1960-62; lang. missionary with Indians So. Bapt. Home Mission Bd., Oklahoma City, 1964-67; spl. edn. tchr. Child Study Ctr., Ft. Worth, 1968-69, Midlands Ctr., Columbia, S.C., 1970, Mill Creek Elem. Sch., Richland Dist. No. 1, Columbia, 1970-71; spl. edn. and resource tchr. Ft. Jackson (S.C.) Elem. Schs., 1971-99, tchr., 1993-99, ret., 1999; supr. MAT interns U. S.C., Columbia, 1999—. Former parent advisor for children ages birth-36 months S.C. Sch. for the Deaf and Blind; former mem. Coun. for Exceptional Children, hospitality chmn. chpt. 165, 1988-89, sec., 1989-90, historian, 1990-91. Active North Trenholm Bapt. Ch., Columbia; vol. Help Line of Columbia, 1993-00; mem. Kathwood Bapt. Ch. Avocations: quilting, sewing, baking, piano, walking. Home: 1919 Stanley St Columbia SC 29204-4332

LE CLAIR, CHARLES GEORGE, artist, retired university dean; b. Columbia, Mo., May 23, 1914; s. Carl Amie and Marie (Fess) LeC.; m. Margaret Foster, May 30, 1945 (dec. Nov. 1991). BS, MS, U. Wis., 1935; posgrad., Acad. Ranson, Paris, 1937, Columbia U., 1940-41. Instr. art U. Ala., 1935-36, asst. prof., head dept., 1937-42; asst. prof. art, head dept. Albion Coll., 1942-43; tchr. painting and design Albright Art Sch., Buffalo, 1943-46; assoc. prof., head dept. Chatham Coll., 1946-52, prof., 1952-60; dean Tyler Sch. Art, Temple U., Phila., 1960-74, dean emeritus, 1981—, prof. painting, 1974-81, chmn. painting and sculpture dept., 1979-81. Founder Tyler Sch. Art, Rome, Italy, 1966. Author: The Art of Watercolor, 1985, rev. edit., 1994, expanded edit., 1999, Color in Contemporary Painting, 1991; contbg. author: Everything You Ever Wanted to Know About Oil Painting, 1994; works exhibited Pa. Acad. Met. Mus. Art, Carnegie Inst., Whitney Mus., Corcoran Mus., Chgo. Art Inst., Richmond Mus., Butler Mus. Art, Am. Watercolor Soc., Bklyn. Mus.; one-man shows include Carnegie Inst., 1954, Salpeter Gallery, N.Y.C., 1956, 59, 65, Rochester Inst. Tech., 1958, Phila. Art Alliance, 1962, 73, 2000, Franklin and Marshall Coll., 1969, Galleria 89, Rome, 1970, Left Bank Gallery, Wellfleet, 1983, 87, 96, Temple U., 1978, Visual Images, Wellfleet, 1978-80, Gross-McCleaf Gallery, Phila., 1979, 81, 96, 98, 2002, More Gallery Phila., 1983, 87, 89, Villanova U., 1998, Carspecken-Scott Gallery, Wilmington, Del., 1999. Named Pitts. Artist of Yr., 1957; recipient Pennell medal Pa. Acad. Fine Arts, 1965, achievement award Am. Artist mag., 1995, Lifetime Achievement award Watercolor Honor Soc., 1997; fellow Fund for Advancement Edn. Ford Found., 1952-53. Achievements include being subject of Elizabeth Leonard's book Painting Flowers, 1986, cover story Watercolor mag., 1999. Home: 1810 Rittenhouse Sq Apt 812 Philadelphia PA 19103-5816

LECLAIR, JOHN CLARK, professional hockey player; b. St. Albans, Vt., July 5, 1969; Hockey player Montreal Canadiens, 1987-94, Phila. Flyers, 1995—. Named to ECAC All-Star 2d team, 1990-91, Sporting News All-Star 1st team, 1994-95, NHL All-Star 1st team, 1994-95. Office: Philadelphia Flyers 3601 S Broad St One Core States Complex Philadelphia PA 19148*

LECLAIR, SUSAN JEAN, hematologist, clinical laboratory scientist, educator; b. New Bedford, Mass., Feb. 17, 1947; d. Joseph A. and Beatrice (Perry) L.; m. James T. Griffith; 1 child, Kimberly A. BS in Med. Tech., Stonehill Coll., 1968; MS in Med. Lab. Sci., U. Mass., Dartmouth, 1977; PhD in Clin. Hematology, Walden U., 2001. Cert. clin. lab. scientist; cert. med. technologist. Med. technologist Union Hosp., New Bedford, Mass., 1968-70; supr. hematology Morton Hosp., Taunton, 1970-72; edn. coord., program dir. Sch. Med. Tech. Miriam Hosp., Providence, 1972-79; hematology technologist R.I. Hosp., 1979-80; asst. prof. med. lab. sci. U. Mass., Dartmouth, 1980-84, assoc.

prof. med. lab. sci., 1984-92, prof. med. lab. sci., 1992—. Instr. hematology courses Brown U., Providence, 1978-80; cons. bd. Div. Clin. Hematology, Charlton Meml. Hosp., St. Luke's Hosp., 1984-2000, Nemasket Group, Inc., 1984-87, Gateway Health Alliance, 1985-87, Pawtucket Meml. Hosp., 1999-2001; chair hematology/hemostasis com. Nat. Cert. Agy. for Med. Lab. Pers. Exam. Coun., 1994-98. Editor-in-chief, Clin. Lab. Sci., 2000; contbr. articles to profl. jours.; contbr. articles to jours and chpts. to books; author computer software in hematology. Reviewer Nat. Commn. Clin. Lab. Scis., 1986-89; chairperson Mass. Assn. Health Planning Agys., 1986-87; bd. dirs. Southeastern Mass. Health Planning Devel. Inc., (1975-88, numerous other offices and coms.); planning subcom. AIDS Edn. (presentor Info Series). Mem. Am. Soc. Clin. Lab. Sci. (editor clin. practice sect. CLS jour. 1996-2000, editor-in-chief CLS jour. 2001—), Am. Soc. Med. Tech. Edn. and Rsch. Fund, Inc. (chair 1983-85), Mass. Assn. for Med. Tech. (pres. 1977-78), Southeastern Mass. Soc. Med. Tech. (pres. 1975-76), Alpha Mu Tau (pres. 1993-94). Avocations: choral singing, cooking, reading. Office: U Mass Dept Med Lab Sci Dartmouth MA 02747

LECLERC, LEO GEORGE, guidance counselor; b. Central Falls, R.I., May 27, 1945; s. Joseph A. and Laura (Dube) L.; children: Peter John, Eric James, Jessica Lee. AA, Roger Williams Jr. Coll., 1966; BA, Providence Coll., 1968, MA in Guidance and Counseling, 1972; Cert. Advance Grad. Studies, Bryant Coll., 1976. Counselor Central Falls Sch. Dept., 1976—, dir. elem. guidance. Amb. Cumberland Theatrical Co., Central Falls, R.I. Sec.-treas. Central Falls Crimestoppers; com. mem. Pawtucket Starwalk of Fame; bd. dirs. Central Falls Hist. Soc., Blackstone Valley Tourism Coun., Camp Ruggles, Nat. Youth Sports Camp, R.I. divsn.; chief Explorer Program; chmn. Internat. Steamboat Muster, 1995, Stage A Mgr. of Celebrate R.I. Com., 1995; charter mem. Pawtucket Steamboat Alliance; youth chmn. of 1995 Centennial of City of Central Falls; co-founder Channel 1 Substance Prevention Agy., Central Falls Police Dept.; state chmn. Youth Squire Program, 1995-98; bd. dirs. Blackstone Valley Tourism Coun.; chmn. Channel 1 Screening Com. Mem. Elks, KC (dir. youth program and squire program), R.I. KC (comdr. color corps state marshall R.I. 4th degree). Home: 91 Chestnut St Central Falls RI 02863-2007 Office: Central Falls Sch Dept 21 Hedley Ave Central Falls RI 02863-1900

LECLERC, PAUL, library director; b. Lebanon, N.H., May 28, 1941; s. Louis and M. Juliette (Trottier) LeC; m. Judith Ginsberg, Oct. 26, 1980; 1 child, Adam Louis. BS, Coll. Holy Cross, 1963; student, U. Paris, 1963-64; MA, Columbia U., 1966, PhD with distinction, 1969; LHD (hon.) , L.I. U., 1994, Coll. of the Holy Cross, 1994, Hamilton Coll., 1995, Union Coll., 1997, Hunter Coll., 1997, Fordham U., 1997, U. Paris, 2000. Assoc. prof. French Union Coll., Schenectady, 1969-79, chmn. dept. modern langs. and lit., 1972-77, chmn. humanities div., 1975-77; univ. dean for acad. affairs CUNY, 1979-84; provost and acad. v.p. Baruch Coll., CUNY, 1984-88; pres. Hunter Coll., CUNY, 1988-93; pres., CEO New York Public Library, N.Y.C., 1994—. Bd. dirs. N.Y. Alliance for Pub. Schs., N.Y.C., 1981-84, El Museo del Barrio, The Feminist Press; pres. N.Y. Tchr. Edn. Conf. Bd., Albany, N.Y., 1983-84. Author: Voltaire and Crebillon Pere, 1972, Voltaire's Rome Sauvée, 1992; co-editor: Lettres d'André Moreliet, vol. I, 1991, vol. II, 1994, vol. III, 1996; contbr. articles to profl. jours. Decorated officier Palmes Académiques, chevalier Legion of Honor (France); grantee NEH, 1971, 79, Am. Coun. Learned Socs., 1973, Ford Found., 1979. Mem. MLA, Am. Soc. for 18th Century Studies Office: NY Pub Libr Fifth Ave & 42nd St New York NY 10018

LECLERC, ROBERT L. mining company executive; b. 1944; Chmn., CEO Milner Fenerty, Calgary and Edmonton, Can.; dir. Echo Bay Mines, Englewood, Colo., chmn., 1996—, CEO, chmn. bd., 1997—. Office: Ste 540 6400 S Fiddlers Green Cir Englewood CO 80111-4957

LE COCQ, FRANK, retired obstetrician/gynecologist; b. Aberdeen, S.D., 1915; BS in Chemistry, U. Wash., 1938; MD, U. Oreg., 1941. Diplomate Am. Bd. Ob-Gyn. Intern U. Oreg. Hosps., Portland, 1941-42, resident in ob-gyn., 1946-49; pvt. practice, 1950-96; ret., 1996. Fellow ACS; mem. AMA, ACOG, Pacific Coast Ob-Gyn., Pacific N.W. Ob-Gyn. E-mail: flecocq@prodigy.net.

LECOCQ, KAREN ELIZABETH, artist; b. Santa Rosa, Calif., Nov. 4, 1949; d. Maynard Rodney and Lois May (Lessard) LeC.; m. David Lawrence Medley, Sept. 7, 1995. BA, Calif. State U., Fresno, 1971, MA, 1975; postgrad., Calif. Inst. of the Arts, L.A., 1971-72. Founding mem. Feminist Art Program, Fresno, Calif., 1971, Calif. Inst. of the Arts, L.A., 1972. Vis. artist Merced County Schs., 1977-78, 79-82, 88-91; grad. instr. Calif. State U., Fresno, 1976-78. One-woman shows include Calif. State U. Art Gallery, Fresno, 1970, 76, Merced (Calif.) Coll., 1969, 77, 91, Calif. Inst. of the Arts, L.A., 1972, Womanart Gallery, N.Y.C., 1980, Amos Eno Gallery, N.Y.C., 1994, 97, 750 Gallery, Sacramento, 1995, Meridian Gallery, San Francisco, 1993, Wild Gallery, Sacramento, 1999; group shows include Womanhouse, L.A., 1972, Off Centre Centre, Calgary, Alta., Can., 1985, 86, Ryosuke Gallery, Osaka, Japan, 1986, Gallery Six Oh One, San Francisco, 1989, Fresno Art Mus., 1989, Pro arts Gallery, Oakland, Calif., 1991, Calif. Mus. Art, Santa Rosa, 1991, Harbs Gallery, Lexington, Va., 1992, Russell Sage Gallery, Troy, N.Y., 1992, Amos Eno Gallery, 1994, 97, ARC Gallery, Chgo., 1993, 96, Lengyel Gallery, San Francisco, 1995, 750 Gallery, Sacramento, 1994-96, L.A. Mus. Contemporary Art, 1995, Armand Hammer Mus., L.A., 1996, Whitney Mus. Am. Art, N.Y.C., 1999, numerous others; commns. include Absolut Vodka, 1993. Docent Gallery Guide Art Train, Merced, 1983; artistic dir. Black and White Ball, Merced Regional Arts Coun., 1989-99. Democrat. Home and Office: PO Box 2204 Merced CA 95344-0204 E-mail: lecocq@attitude.com.

LECOMPTE, JANET, historian, writer; b. Phila., May 22, 1923; d. Frederic Barr and Dorothy Price Shaw; m. Oliver Philip Lecompte, Oct. 3, 1944 (div. Feb. 1985); Jenny, Ellen, Louisa, Charles, Thomas, Peter. BA, Wellesley (Mass.) Coll., 1944; LLD, Colo. Coll., Colorado Springs, 1979; postgrad., Washington State U., 1988-91, U. N.Mex., 1990. Bd. dirs. Nat. Rev. Hist. Places, Denver, 1968-86, Colo. Hist. Soc., Denver, 1980-86; trustee Colo. Hist. Found., 1973-78; Colo. adv. bd. Nat. Historic Publs. and Records Commn., Denver, 1977-87. Hist. cons. U.S. Army, Fort Carson, Colorado Springs, 1983-85; cons. exhibits Colo. History Mus., Denver, 1977-78; mem. adv. com. Coll. Letters, Arts and Sci., Colo. U., Colorado Springs, 1971-83. Author: Pueblo Hardscrabble Greenhorn, 1978 (4 awards 1980), Rebellion in Rio Arriba, 1985; editor: Emily: Diary of a Hardworked Woman, 1987, French Fur Traders, 1993; bd. editors N.Mex. Hist. Rev., 1982-93; contbr. articles to profl. jours. Founder, pres. bd. Colorado Springs Sch., 1961-76; mem., subcom. chmn. Com. on Ednl. Endeavors, Legis. Coun., Denver, 1961-64. Recipient Best Non-Fiction Book of Yr., Westerners Internat., 1979, Western Writers Am., 1979 award of merit Am. Assn. State and Local History, 1980. Avocations: tennis, bridge, walking dogs, writing letters. Home: 1606 Pine Cone Rd Moscow ID 83843-9317

LECOMPTE, ROGER BURTON, management consultant; b. Cin., May 22, 1942; s. Joseph Edward and Lefa May (Ayars) LeC.; m. Margaret Morgan, 1969 (div. 1971); m. Helen Lida Smits, Aug. 28, 1976; 1 child, Theodore Edward. BA, U. Cin., 1965; MBA, U. Pa., 1975. Cons. alt. delivery systems Blue Cross Assn., Chgo., 1971-73; asst. to pres. Albert Einstein Med. Ctr., Phila., 1975-77; cons. Lewin & Assocs., Washington, 1977-81; v.p. planning Middlesex Hosp., Middletown, Conn., 1981-92; prin. The Futures Group, Glastonbury, 1993-94; pres. LeCompte & Co. Healthcare Planning, 1992—; dir. network devel. Health Right, Inc., Meriden, Conn., 1995-96. Bd. dirs. Aetna Health Plan of So. New Eng.; vol. US Peace Corps, Kumba, Cameroon, 1965-67; vice-chmn. Vis. Nurses of Lower Valley, Essex, Conn., 1983-86. Author/editor: Prepaid Group Practice Manual, 1973. Mem. bd. edn. Essex Elem. Sch., 1985-91, chmn. sch. bldg. com., 1987-93; vestryman St. John's Episcopal Ch., Essex, 1988-92, chmn. capital fund drive, 1996; bd. dirs. Long Wharf Theater, New Haven, 1998—, mem. nominating com., strategic planning com., 1998—. Mem. Essex Libr. Assn. (treas. 1997-99, bd. dirs. 1996—). Democrat. Home: PO Box 950 Essex CT 06426-0950

LE COMTE, DOUGLAS MUNZER, meteorologist; b. Berkeley, Calif., Jan. 8, 1946; s. Edward Semple and Mia (Munzer) Le C.; m. Adele Cote, Apr. 2, 1983; 1 child, Derek. BA in Meteorology, NYU, 1968; MS in Atmospheric Sci., SUNY, Albany, 1974. Meteorologist, mem. spl. projects staff NOAA Environ. Data and Info. Svc., Washington, 1975-79; meteorologist climate assessment br. NOAA Assessment and Info. Svcs. Ctr., 1979-85, chief climate assessment br., 1985-88; chief agrl. weather sect. Climate Prediction Ctr., Nat. Weather Svc., 1988-98, meteorologist Camp Springs, Md., 1998—. Mem. interagy. task force on African emergency US AID, Washington, 1984-86; mem. nat. emergency mgmt. team Fed. Emergency Mgmt. Agy., Washington, 1981-96; mem. interagy. contact group Nat. Drought Policy Commn., Washington, 1998-00; mem. Interim Nat. Drought Coun., Washington, 2000-. Contbg. editor: Weatherwise mag., 1997—; contbr. articles to sci. jours., including Bull. Am. Meteorol. Soc., Jour. Applied Meteorology, chpt. to book. Capt. USAF, 1968-72. Mem. Am. Meteorol. Soc., Nat. Weather Assn. Office: Climate Prediction Ctr 5200 Auth Rd Camp Springs MD 20746-4304

LE CONGE, MONIQUE ANNE, library director, consultant; b. San Francisco, July 5, 1965; d. Michele Jean Butler; adopted parents: Antoine and Marianne le Conge; m. Jon Benjamin King, June 11, 1988 (div. Nov. 1999); children: Joshua D. King, Marissa R. King, Gregory A. King. BS, U. Calif., Davis, 1987; M of Libr. and Info. Studies, U. Calif., Berkeley, 1988. Libr. Solano County Libr., Fairfield, Calif., 1989-91, children's libr. Vallejo, 1991-94; young adult libr. Benicia (Calif.) Pub. Libr., 1994-98, dir., 1998—. Cons. San Joaquin Valley Libr. Sys., Fresno, Calif., 2001-2002; young adult svcs. cons. North State Coop. Libr. Sys., Willows, Calif., 1997-98; cons. Benicia H.S., 1989. Editor: A Bibliography for Thou Shalt Not Read: Banned and Challenged Books for Children and Young Adults, 1995; contbr. to web site 700 Plus Great Web Sites for Kids, 1995; indexer Librarian's Index to the Internet (Lii.org), 2001—; contbr. articles to profl. jours. Bd. dirs. Benicia Main St. Program, 1999-2001. Mem. ALA, Assn. Children's Librs. of No. Calif. (pres. 1993-94), Bay Area Young Adult Librs., Benicia-Vallejo Am. Assn. Univ. Women, Calif. Libr. Assn., Assn. for Libr. Svc. to Children (com. mem.), Pub. Libr. Assn., Young Adult Libr. Svcs. Assn. (com. chair), Libr. Adminstrn. and Mgmt. Assn., BayNet (v.p., pres.-elect 2001-2003), Rotary Benicia (fundraising chair Benicia 2000-2001, chmn. youth svcs. 2001-02). Roman Catholic. Avocations: travel, hiking, museums. Office: Benicia Pub Libr 150 East L St Benicia CA 94510 Office Fax: 707-747-8122. E-mail: mleconge@ci.benicia.ca.us.

LECOURS, MICHEL, electrical engineering educator; b. Montreal, Que., Can., Aug. 1, 1940; s. Henri and Germaine (L'Archeveque) L.; m. Almut Lange, July 14, 1966; children: Christiane, Mireille, Jean-Yves. BScA, Ecole Poly., Montreal, 1963; PhD, Imperial Coll., London, 1966. Registered profl. engr., Que. Mem. sci. staff Bell-No. Rsch., Ottawa, Ont., Can., 1971-72; prof. elec. engring. U. Laval, Quebec City, 1967—2001, head dept. Que., 1975-77, vice dean, 1977-85. Cons. Lab-Volt (Que.) Ltd., Quebec City, 1981—; vis. researcher Nippon Tel. & Tel., Yokosuka, Japan, 1986. Contbr. numerous articles on electronics and communications to sci. jours.; patentee for short range high resolution radar. Recipient ann. merit award Ecole Poly., 1986, Larry K. Wilson award IEEE, 1997. Fellow IEEE, Engring. Inst. Can. (John B. Stirling medal 1997) Office: Laval Univ Dept Elec Engring Quebec QC Canada G1K 7 P4 E-mail: michel.lecours@gel.ulaval.ca., lcrsm@aol.com.

LECROIX, CHARLES DAVID, research and development company executive, consultant; b. Athens, Ala., June 23, 1947; s. Mahlon Atha and Ruth Swinea LeCroix; m. Setsuko Hayaski LeCroix, May 30, 1982; children: Kenjiro David, Jojiro Jessie. BS, U. Ala., Tuscaloosa, 1968; MA, Rice U., Houston, TX, 1971, PhD, 1972. Staff chemist Proctor & Gamble, Cincinnati, Ohio, 1975—77, sect. head rsch. & devel., 1977—79, Osaka, Japan, 1979—81, Cincinnati, Ohio, 1981—83, assoc. dir. rsch. & devel., 1983—89, Caracas, Venezuela, 1989—91, dir. rsch. & devel. Kobe, Japan, 1991—98, Cincinnati, Ohio, 1998—2001; adj. prof. McGill, MBA, Japan, Tokyo, Japan, 1998—. Co. mem. Am. Chamber Commerce, Kobe, Japan, 1995—98. Contbr. articles to profl. jours. City rep. Cin. Ohio-Gifo Japan, sister city program, Cincinnati, Ohio, 1988—89; pres. & mem. Japanese Am. Citizens League, 1983—2002. Capt. USAF, 1972—75. Mem.: Am. Chem. Soc., Sigma XI, Phi Beta Kappa. Avocations: reading, genealogical research. Office: Charles LeCroix PO Box 32125 Cincinnati OH 45232 E-mail: lecroixcd@aol.com.

LEDBETTER, CALVIN REVILLE, JR. (CAL LEDBETTER), political science educator, university dean, former legislator; b. Little Rock; s. Calvin Reville Sr. and Virginia Mae (Campbell) L.; m. Mary Brown Williams, July 26, 1953; children: Grainger, Jeffrey (dec.), Snow. BA, Princeton U., 1951; LLB, U. Ark., 1954; PhD, Northwestern U., 1960. Bar: Ark., 1954. Pvt. practice, Little Rock, 1954; faculty dept. polit. sci. U. Ark., 1960-97, prof., 1960-97, prof. emeritus, 1997—, dean, 1978-88; cons. law enforcement program, advisor pre-law program; mem. Ark. Ho. of Reps., 1967-76; chmn. spl. legis. com., com. on legis. orgn.; vice chmn. legis. com. state agys. and govt. affairs; com. pub. schs.; mem. Nat. Adv. Com. on Criminal Justice Goals and Standards; mem. adv. com. Nat. Inst. Law Enforcement and Criminal Justice. Dept. head. U. Ark., Little Rock, 1968-78; election night analyst for Ark. congl. and Presdl. elections ABC, 1964-84 Co-author: Politics in Arkansas: The Constitutional Experience, 1972, The Arkansas Plan: A Case Study in Public Policy, 1979, Arkansas Becomes a State, 1985, Carpenter from Conway: George W. Donaghey as Governor of Arkansas 1909-1913, 1993; contbr. articles, book reviews to profl. jours. Mem. Ark. Adv. Coun. on Pub., Elem. and Secondary Edn.; Gov.'s rep. So. Regional Growth Policies Bd.; mem. Ark. Legis. Coun.; del. Ark. Constl. Conv., 1979, v.p., 1979-80; chmn. law enforcement and criminal justice task force Nat. Legis. Conf. Former chmn. coll. and univ. sect. United Fund; del. Dem. Nat. Conv., 1968, 84; mem. exec. com. Ark. Young Dems.; bd. dirs. Health and Welfare Coun. Pulaski County; trustee Philander Smith Coll., chmn. council community advisers; sec. bd. dirs. St. Vincent's Infirmary; bd. dirs. Ark. Humanities Coun., 1989-93, v.p., 1991-93, pres. 1993-94; bd. trustees Ark. Mus. Sci. and History. Served with JAGC AUS, 1955-57. Recipient award for outstanding contbn. to humanities Little Rock Arts and Humanities Commn., 1993; named Educator of Yr., Greater Little Rock Fedn. Women's Clubs, 1968. Mem. ABA, Ark. Bar Assn. (Writing Excellence award 1985-86), Pulaski County Bar Assn., Nat. Conf. State Legislators (exec. com.), Nat. Conf. Acad. Deans (pres. 1987-88), Am. Polit. Sci. Assn., So. Polit. Sci. Assn., Ark. Polit. Sci. Assn. (pres. 1980-81), Ark. Acad. Sci., Am. Acad. Polit. and Social Sci., Ark. Hist. Assn., Ark. Edn. Assn., Pulaski County Hist. Soc. (bd. dirs. 1988-90), Ark. Hist. Commn. (v.p. 1989—, pres. 1990—), Rotary (pres. West Little Rock chpt. 1987-88). Presbyterian. Home: 3416 I St Little Rock AR 72205-4114 Office: Univ Ark Little Rock Polit Sci Dept Little Rock AR 72204

LEDBETTER, DAVID OSCAR, lawyer; b. Santa Rosa, Calif., Mar. 16, 1950; s. Oscar Smith Ledbetter and Nova Nell (Huckaby) Kramer; m. Judith Louise Fischer, Dec. 14, 1976; children: Hannah J., Jordan B. BA, U. Redlands, 1972; JD, Hastings Coll. Law, 1977. Bar: Calif. 1977, Va. 1987. Assoc. Moran, Urich & Evans, San Francisco, 1977-79; trial atty. land and natural resource divsn. U.S. Dept. Justice, Washington, 1979-85; assoc., counsel, ptnr. Hunton & Williams, Richmond, Va., 1985—. Bd. adv. Chem. Waste Litigation Reporter, Washington, 1983—. Co-author: Environmental Law Practice Guide, 1997; co-author, editor: Outline RCRA/CERCLA Enforcement Issues and Holdings, 2001; contbr. articles to profl. jours. Bd. dirs. John Tyler C.C. Found., Chester, Va., 1992—; ednl. adv. coun. Charles City (Va.) County Vocat., 1990—. Mem. ABA, Va. State Bar Assn., Calif. Bar Assn., Environ. Law Inst., Charles City Ruritan Club. Democrat. Methodist. Avocations: gardening, fishing. Home: 16530 The Glebe Ln Charles City VA 23030-3837 Office: Hunton & Williams 951 E Byrd St Ste 200 Richmond VA 23219-4074 E-mail: dledbetter@hunton.com.

LEDBETTER, EUGENE FLOYD ANTONII, JR. vocational education coordinator; b. Charleston, SC, Feb. 5, 1966; s. E. Floyd and Jeannie (Barron) Ledbetter; m. Renee Marie Darch, Mar. 17, 1990; children: Eugene Floyd III, Zachary Tylor, Damia Hinderson. Caterer Barron's Limited, Marietta, Ga., 1982-90; aviation ordinance Security Police USAF, Okinawa/Azores, 1990—95; food svc. U.S. Army, Ft. Leavenworth, Kans., 1995-98, Dept. Justice, Marianna, Fla., 1998—. Bd. dirs. Barrons Ltd., Marietta, Ga., 1988—90; sr. instr. Ga. Hapkido Assn., 1985—90. Contbr. . Asst. scout master Boy Scouts Am., 1984—87, unit commr., 1988—90; altar server Cath. Ch., Marianna, Fla., 1998—2000. Recipient Eagle Scout award, Boys Scouts Am., 1984, Meritorious Svc. medal, USNR, 1988, E award, USN, 1986. Mem.: Nat. Eagle Scout Assn., Theta Chi Alumni. Avocations: painting, reading, law, camping, poetry. Office: Box 7007 11470-045 Marianna FL 32447-7007

LEDBETTER, JOHN STEWART, urologist; b. Bronxville, N.Y., Feb. 27, 1952; s. John Nelson and Rita (Weigl) L.; m. Deborah Swain, June 18, 1974; children: Timothy, Caroline, Hadley. BA, U. Va., 1974; MD, U. Conn., 1980. Diplomate Am. Bd. Urology. Resident in gen. surgery and urology Dartmouth-Hitchcock Med. Ctr., Hanover, N.H., 1980-85; ptnr. North Shore Urol. Assocs., Beverly, Mass., 1985—. Office: North Shore Urol Assocs Parkhurst Medical Bldg Beverly MA 01915-5900

LEDBETTER, KENNETH, federal agency administrator; MS in Aerospace Engring., U. Colo. Mem. Viking Mars landing team NASA, Washington, dep. payload ops mgr. Space Shuttle flight of Space Sextant, 1982, spacecraft ops. mgr. launch and flight of Magellan mission to Venus, 1989, flight programs br. chief OSS astrophysics divsn., 1994—95, dir. mission and payload devel. divsn., 1996—2001, exec. dir. programs Office Space Sci., 2001—. Co-author: Design of Mission Operatiosn Systems for Scientific Remote Sensing, 1991; contbr. articles to profl. publs. Office: NASA Mail Code S 300 E St SW Washington DC 20546

LEDBETTER, LINDA CAROL, pension fund executive, professional organization executive; b. Detroit, Dec. 22, 1948; d. Ray Finley Ledbetter and H. Christine Gore; m. Jerome D. Davis, Jan. 20, 1996. BA, Western Mich. U., Kalamazoo, 1966; MEd, La. State U., New Orleans, 1975; PhD, U. New Orleans, 1978; postgrad., Claremont (Calif.) Coll., 1990-91. Cert. Cert. tchr., prin., supt., parish/county adminstr. La., Mich., Wis. Tchr., Milw., New Orleans, Detroit, 1970-90; assoc. prof., coll. adminstr. U. New Orleans, 1977-82; prof. La. State U. Law Sch., Baton Rouge, 1977-82; pres., CEO The Neron Group, New Orleans, 1993—; exec. dir. Coun. La. Trustees, 1996—. Cons. Nat. Tchr. Ctr., Washington, 1979—83, U.S. Office Edn., Washington, 1979—80, various civic, charitable and polit. groups, 1979—97; spkr. internat. confs., 1989—; provider, sponsor, planner Nat. Pension Fund Conf., 1997—. Contbr. . Mem. exec. coun., v.p. Tchrs. Union New Orleans, 1977—93; trustee pension fund La. Tchrs. Retirement Sys., 1990—94; bd. govs. Coun. La. Trustees, 1995—, nat. conf. planner and sponsor, 1997—; bd. dirs. La. Soc. Prevention of Cruelty to Animals, New Orleans, 1985—90; trustee LA Port Authority Harbor Police Pension Bd., 2002—; del.-at-large Nat. Dem. Conv., Atlanta, 1988. Named Tchr. of Yr., Jr. Achievement La., 1990, Outstanding Young Woman of Am., 1980; recipient Spl. Recognition award, Exec. Dept. State of La., 1993, Cert. of Merit, Mayor's Office City of New Orleans, 1993; fellow Inst. Politics fellow, Loyola U., New Orleans, 1982. Mem.: 100 Club of New Orleans, Freedom Found., Women's Profl. Coun. (membership chair 1997). Avocation: Avocations: travel, horseback riding, sailing. Home and Office: 33 Neron Pl New Orleans LA 70118-4265 E-mail: coltusa@cox.net.

LEDBETTER, MICHAEL RAY, lawyer; b. San Bernardino, Calif., June 13, 1956; s. Raymond Leonard and Anna Laura Ledbetter; m. Diane Elizabeth Burger, Jan. 16, 1987 (div. Aug. 1991); 1 child, Lauren Ann; m. Diane Lorraine Errick, June 30, 1993. BA, U. Calif., Irvine, 1978; JD, U. So. Calif., 1981. Bar: Calif. 1981, U.S. Dist. Ct. (ctrl. dist.) Calif. 1982, U.S. Dist. Ct. (ea. dist.) Calif. 1992, U.S. Ct. Appeals (9th cir.) 1990, U.S. Supreme Ct. Assoc. atty. Roger J. Rosen Law Office, L.A., 1981-83; dep. pub. defender Office of Pub. Defender, Santa Barbara, Calif., 1983-90; sr. dep. counsel Office of County Counsel, 1990—. Bd. dirs. Calif. Joint Powers Ins. Authority, La Palma, 1992-94, 96—. Contbg. editor: California County Counsels Benchbook, 1996, 97, 98. Mem. City Coun., City of Carpinteria, Calif., 1990-94, 96—, mayor, 1991-93. Avocations: music (keyboards), computers, automobiles. Home: 1453 Camellia Cir Carpinteria CA 93013-1608 Office: Office of County Counsel 105 E Anapamu St Rm 201 Santa Barbara CA 93101-6060 E-mail: ldbttr@co.santa-barbara.ca.us., MLdbttr@Netscape.net.

LEDBETTER, PAUL MARK, lawyer, writer; b. San Francisco, Oct. 14, 1947; s. John Paul and Joyce (Mayo) L.; m. Jerald Ann Broyles, Sept. 18, 1971; children: Paul Mark, Sarah Broyles. BA in English, Ouachita Bapt. U., 1970; JD, U. Ark., 1973. Bar: Ark. 1974, Tenn. 1995, U.S. Dist. Ct. (ea. dist.) Ark. 1974, U.S. Ct. Appeals (8th cir.) 1974, U.S. Ct. Appeals (6th cir.) 1991, U.S. Dist. Ct. (mid. dist.) Tenn. 1995. From assoc. to ptnr. Frierson, Walker, Snellgrove & Laser, Jonesboro, Ark., 1974-82; regional def. counsel Sq. D. Co., 1980-82; pres. Mark Ledbetter, P.A., Jonesboro, 1982-86; ptnr. Gerber, Gerber & Agee, Memphis, 1986-89, Taylor, Halliburton, Ledbetter & Caldwell, Memphis, 1989—. Author: The Hearing, 1994, The Thayer Class, 1998, The Wait, 2000. Co-founder St. Mark's Episcopal Day Sch., Jonesboro, 1978; mem. vestry St. Mark's Episcopal Ch., 1979; mem. Forum Commn. City of Jonesboro, 1978-80. Conservation Found. grantee, 1976; Rotary Internat. grantee, Japan, 1979. Mem. ATLA, Am. Bd. Trial Advs. (assoc.), Tenn. Bar Assn., Ark. Bar Assn. (mem. tort reform com. 1980, ho. of dels. 1979-80), Ark. Trial Lawyers Assn. (chmn. amicus curiae com. 1980-81, gov. 1980—), Tenn. Trial Lawyers Assn., Jonesboro C. of C. (bd. dirs. 1978-80), Human Factors and Ergonomics Soc., Rotary. Office: Taylor Halliburton Ledbetter & Caldwell 44 N 2nd St Ste 200 Memphis TN 38103-2270 also: Ledbetter & Caldwell 501 Union St Jonesboro AR 72401-2836 E-mail: mark794@aol.com.

LEDBETTER, SHARON FAYE WELCH, retired educational consultant; b. L.A., Jan. 14, 1941; d. James Herbert and Verdie V. (Mattox) Welch; m. Robert A. Ledbetter, Feb. 15, 1964; children: Kimberly Ann, Scott Allen. BA, U. Tex., Austin, 1963; learning disabilities cert., Southwestern U., Tex., 1974; MEd, Southwest Tex. State U., 1979, prin. cert., 1980, supt. cert., 1984. Speech pathologist Midland (Tex.) Ind. Sch. Dist., Tex., 1963, Austin (Tex.) Ind. Sch. Dist., 1964-72; speech pathologist, asst. prin. Round Rock Ind. Sch. Dist., 1972-84; prin. Hutto Ind. Sch. Dist., 1984-88; asst. dir. divsn. med. sch. edn. Tex. Edn. Agy., 1989-94. Pres. Berkman PTA, 1983-84; v.p. Round Rock Women's Club, 1977, pres., 1978-79; sponsor Jr. Woman's Club, 1980-82; vol. Round Rock Ind. Sch. Dist., 1984; mistress ceremonies Hutto Beauty Pageant, 1986-87. Recipient Meritorious Svc. award St. Judes Children's Rsch. Hosp., 1985, Soc. Disting. Am. H.S. Students, 1984, Disting. Svc. award Tex. Edn. Agy., 1994. Mem. ASCD, Phi Delta Kappa. Home: 43 Woodland Loop Round Rock TX 78664-9776 E-mail: sledbet338@aol.com.

LEDDEN, DENNIS BRUCE, literature educator, writer; b. Sharon, Pa., Dec. 23, 1948; s. Bruce Eastman and Martha Holup Ledden; m. Yong-Hui Kong, Oct. 21, 1972; children: Brian Edward, Alicia Diane. BS, Pa. State U., 1970; MA, U. Pitts., 1980. Cert. secondary English tchr. Pa. Instr. U.S. Army, Columbia, SC, 1970—72; tchg. asst. Edinboro (Pa.) State U., 1972—73; tchr. English Butler (Pa.) Intermediate HS, 1973—; instr. English Youngstown (Ohio) State U., 1984; rschr. U. Pitts., 1985. Contbr. articles to profl. jours. Sgt. U.S. Army, 1970—72, Korea. Mem.: NEA, Butler Edn. Assn., Pa. State Edn. Assn. Avocations: writing, travel, running, weightlifting, reading. Home: 129 Heather Dr Butler PA 16001 Office: Butler Area Sch Dist 110 Campus Ln Butler PA 16001

LEDDON, LEO LEVY, JR. music educator; b. Victoria, Tex., Nov. 13, 1957; s. Leo Levy Leddon, Sr. and Mary Margaret Leddon; m. Sheryl Jean Anderson, June 18, 1994; children: Na Na, Na Na. MusB Edn., U. West Ala., 1980, MA in Tchg., 1982; cert. in ednl. specialist, U. Ala., 2001. Cert. tchr. Ala. Band dir., tchr. Sumter Acad., York, Ala., 1980—81, Jackson Acad., 1981—86; music appreciation tchr. Patrick Henry State Jr. Coll., Clarke County Ext., 1986; band dir., tchr. John Carroll H.S., Birmingham, 1987—90; band dir. Ashford H.S., 1990—91; band dir., tchr. Calera H.S., 1991—92, Millry H.S., 1992—93, So. Choctaw H.S., Silas, 1993—. Mem. sch. improvement team So. Choctaw H.S., 2000—; music leader Millry United Meth. Ch., Ala., 1993—. Chmn. bd. trustees Millry United Meth. Ch., Ala., 2000, lay leader, 1993, mem. pastor/parish rels. com., 1993. Mem.: Ala. Music Educator Assn. (na), Music Educator Nat. Conf. (na), Kappa Delta Pi Internat. (na), Phi Mu Alpha Sinfonia (na). Methodist. Avocations: collecting coins, hunting, fishing. Home: 1021 Ballpark Ave Millry AL 36558 Office: Southern Choctaw High Sch 130 Indian Way Silas AL 36919 Office Fax: 251-542-9650. Personal E-mail: led2edu@millry.net.

LEDDY, JOHN JOSEPH, JR. music educator; b. Bklyn., Sept. 22, 1951; s. John Joseph and Margaret Dolores (Regan) Leddy; m. Diane Alma DeMeo, July 6, 1974; children: James M., Margaret M. BMus, Potsdam Coll., N.Y., 1973; MA, Stony Brook U., N.Y., 1976. Band dir. Connetquot Schs., Bohemia, NY, 1973—. Jazz improvisation tchr. USDAN Summer Camp, Huntington, NY, 2002; guest condr. Suffolk County Music Educators Assn., Hamptons Festival, North Fork Music Festival. Com. chmn. Boy Scouts Am., Oakdale, NY, 1996—2000; life mem. PTA. Fellow Summer fellow, Northwestern U., 1999. Mem.: N.Y. State Sch. Music Assn. (chmn. all-state jazz ensemble

1994—97), Suffolk County Music Educators Assn. (chmn. all-county jazz ensemble 1990—), Percussive Arts Soc., Internat. Assn. Jazz Educators, Music Educators Nat. Conf. Avocations: gardening, sailing, hiking, running. Home: 108 Guilford Ave Oakdale NY 11769 Office: Connetquot High School 190 Seventh St Bohemia NY 11716

LEDDY, SUSAN, nursing educator; b. N.J., Feb. 23, 1939; d. Bert B. and Helen (Neumann) Kun; children: Deborah, Erin. BS, Skidmore Coll., 1960; MS, Boston U., 1965; PhD, NYU, 1973; cert., Harvard U., 1985. Chair dept. nursing Mercy Coll., Debbs Ferry, N.Y.; dean sch. nursing U. Wyo., Laramie, dean coll. health scis.; prof. Widener U. Sch. Nursing, Chester, Pa., 1988—, dean, 1988-93. Author: (with M. Pepper) Conceptual Bases of Professional Nursing, 1985, 4th edit., 1998. Bd. dirs. Springfield Hosp., 1992-94. Postdoctoral fellow U. Pa., 1994-96. Mem. NLN (bd. dirs. and 1st v.p. 1985-87).

LEDE, RICHARD, investment company executive; b. N.Y.C., Mar. 9, 1946; s. Joseph Henry Lede and Anna Mae (O'Donnell) Lede Nichols; m. Maribeth Ann Foster, Nov. 24, 1983; 1 stepchild, Lauren C. Kruta. BA, U. Tampa, 1968; student, Stetson U., 1968. Guest rels. staff Nat. Broadcasting Co., 1968-69; pres. Howle Film Prodns. Ltd., N.Y.C., 1969-73, also bd. dirs.; pres. Delmar Entertainment Corp., N.Y.C., L.A., 1973-83, also bd. dirs.; v.p. Fundamental Brokers U.K., London, 1983-86, MKI Securities Corp., London, 1986-88, Liberty Brokerage, N.Y.C., 1988-92; exec. v.p. S.E. Regional Securities, West Palm Beach, Fla., 1992-93, also bd. dirs.; exec. v.p. Hillman, Lede and Co. Inc., Wets Palm Beach, 1993—, also vice chmn. bd. dirs.; mng. dir. Seaboard Securities Inc., 1994-96; pres. Crown Fin. Assocs., Palm Beach, Fla., 1995—; 5 Crown Capital advisors, 1995—. Non-lawyer mem. Fla. Bar. Griefance Com. Mem. West Palm Beach C. of C., Palm Beach Yacht Club, Mayacoo Lakes Country Club (bd. govs.), Moor Park Gold Club (London), Sigma Phi Epsilon. Avocations: golfing, shooting, big game saltwater fishing. Home: 12735 Newton Pl Wellington FL 33414-6226 Office: Crown Fin Assocs 250 Royal Palm Way Palm Beach FL 33480-4319

LEDEEN, ROBERT WAGNER, neurochemist, educator; b. Denver, Aug. 19, 1928; s. Hyman and Olga (Wagner) L.; m. Lydia Rosen Hailparn, July 2, 1982. BS, U. Calif., Berkeley, 1949; PhD, Oreg. State U., 1953. Postdoctoral fellow in chemistry U. Chgo., 1953-54; rsch. assoc. in chemistry Mt. Sinai Hosp., N.Y.C., 1956-59; rsch. fellow Albert Einstein Coll. Medicine, Bronx, N.Y., 1959, asst. prof., 1963-69, assoc. prof., 1969-75, prof., 1975-91; prof., dir. div. neurochemistry U. Medicine and Dentistry N.J., Newark, 1991—. Contbr. articles to profl. jours.; dep. chief editor Jour. Neurochemistry. Mem. neurol. scis. study sect. NIH; mem. study sect. Nat. Multiple Sclerosis Soc. NIH grantee, 1963—; Nat. Multiple Sclerosis Soc. grantee, 1967-74; recipient Humboldt prize, Javits Neurosci. Investigator award. Mem. Internat. Soc. Neurochemistry, Am. Soc. Neurochemistry, Am. Chem. Soc., Am. Soc. Biol. Chemists, N.Y. Acad. Sci. Jewish. Achievements include discoveries in the biochemistry of brain glycolipids and myelin. Home: 8 Donald Ct Wayne NJ 07470-4608 Office: U Medicine and Dentistry NJ Dept Neuroscis 185 S Orange Ave Dept Newark NJ 07103-2757

LEDER, SANDRA JUANITA, retired elementary school educator; b. Stuttgart, Ark., Apr. 17, 1942; d. Everett Samuel and Lorene (Payer) L. BS, U. Cen. Ark., 1963; MEd, McNeese State U., 1976, EdS, 1979; PhD, Fla. State U., 1984. Cert. elem. tchr., supr., prin., aerospace edn., supr. student tchrs., La.; cert. pvt. pilot. Elem. tchr. DeWitt (Ark.) Pub. Schs., 1963-66, Gillett (Ark.) Pub. Schs., 1966-69; math. tchr. Tulsa County, Tulsa, Okla., 1970; tchr. Calcasieu Parish, Lake Charles, La., 1971-94, Episcopal Day Sch., Lake Charles, 1994-99; asst. prof. McNeese State U., 1999—. Guest instr. McNeese State U., 1995, 96; condr., dir. numerous aerospace camps, 1980—; chmn., judge sci. fairs; com. mem. and chmn. self-study com. So. Assn. Colls. and Schs., 1985-86; presenter, organizer tours and workshops in field. Manuscript rev. panel Sci. Scope, 1988-91, writer, 1992; TV interviews, 1991—; radio and ednl. TV appearances, Tchr. in Space applicant, 1985; contbr. Metric Curriculum Guide for La., 1978; contbr. articles to profl. jours. Vol. reader NEA, 1990; active outreach com. vestry Episcopal Ch. of Good Shepherd, 1994; pres. Lake Charles Regional Airport Authority, 1989, 98, sec., 1990, 93, v.p., 1990, 94, 99, pres., 1991, 95, 2000; mem. gen. adv. coun. Sowela Tech. Inst., 1990-91; active Mayor's Commn. for Women, 1986-91, fall conf. chmn. resource fair, 1988; founder Lake Charles Ninety-Nines, pres., 1993-2000; pres., sec. La. Nat. Airsh Bd., 1993-98. Recipient S.W. Region Frank Brewer Aerospace Edn. award CAP, 1990, Excellence in Aviation Edn. Championship award S.W. region FAA, 1989, Acad. Edn. award Women's History Month, Lake Charles, Great Expectations Tchr. award Sta. KPLC-TV, 1993, Pinnacle award, 1993, NEWMAST award NASA, 1986, STEP award, 1993, Outstanding Young Astronaut Chpt. Leader award, 1993, award State of La. Blue Ribbon Commn. on Tchr. Quality, 2000; grantee Space Acad., 1988, South Ctrl. Bell, 1991, 93, Olin Corp., 1994, 95, 96, 97, 98. Mem. Nat. Sci. Tchrs. Assn., Nat. Space Soc., La. Assn. Educators (del. to convs. 1977-79, 84, 86), Aircraft Owners and Pilots Assn., Delta Kappa Gamma (pres. 1992-94, legis. com. 1985-86, chair social com. 1987-89, comms. com. chair 1990, 94-95), Kappa Kappa Iota (pres. 1975, 86, 99), Phi Delta Kappa. Republican. Episcopalian. Office: McNeese State U Dept Tchr Edn PO Box 92300 Lake Charles LA 70609-0001 E-mail: sleder@mail.mcneese.edu.

LEDERBERG, JOSHUA, geneticist, educator; b. Montclair, N.J., May 23, 1925; s. Zwi Hirsch and Esther (Goldenbaum) Lederberg; m. Marguerite S. Kirsch, Apr. 5, 1968; children: David Kirsch, Anne. BA, Columbia U., 1944; PhD, Yale U., 1947. With U. Wis., 1947-58; prof. genetics Sch. Medicine, Stanford (Calif.) U., 1959-78; pres. Rockefeller U., N.Y.C., 1978-90, univ. prof. Sackler Found. scholar, 1990—. Mem. adv. com. WHO, 1971; chmn. adv. bd. Ellison Med. Found. , 1997—; mem. bd. sci. advisors Antigenics, N.Y.C., Pharmeonics, N.Y.C., Maxygen, Palo Alto, Calif., CombinatoRx, Boston; cons. U.S. Def. Sci. Bd., NSF, NIH, NASA, Arms Control and Disarmament Agy. Trustee Camille and Henry Dreyfus Found. With USN, 1943—45. Named Sr. Scholar, Stanford U. Ctr. Internat. Security and Arms Control, 1998; recipient Nobel prize in physiology and medicine for rsch. in genetics of bacteria, 1958, U.S. Nat. medal of sci., 1989, Alan Newell award, Assn. Computing Machinery, 1996, John Stearns award, N.Y. Acad. Medicine, 1996, Maxwell Finland award, NCIH, 1997, Morris Collen award, Am. Med. Info. Assn., 1999. Fellow: AAAS, Am. Acad. Arts and Scis., Acad. Universelle Cultures (Paris), Am. Philos. Soc. (Benjamin Franklin medal 2002); mem.: NAS, N.Y. Acad. Scis. (hon. life gov.), Royal Soc. London (fgn.), Inst. Medicine (David Roller medal), Ordre des Lettres et des Arts (comdr.), Coun. Fgn. Rels. Office: Rockefeller U 1230 York Ave Stop 174 New York NY 10021-6399 E-mail: lederberg@mail.rockefeller.edu.

LEDERBERG, SEYMOUR SAMUEL, molecular biologist, educator; b. N.Y.C., Oct. 30, 1928; s. Zwi Hirsch and Esther (Goldenbaum) L.; m. Victoria Santopietro, Mar. 15, 1959; children: Tobias Marc, Sarah Lederberg Stone. BA, Cornell U., 1951; PhD, U. Ill., 1955. Asst. prof. Brown U., Providence, 1958-62, assoc. prof., 1962-66, prof., 1966—2001, prof. emeritus, 2001—, chair microbiology and molecular biology, 1970-79, assoc. dean grad. studies, 1985-95, acting co-chair molecular microbiology and immunology, 1997-99, prof. emeritus, 2001—. Vis. asst. prof. U. Calif., Berkeley, 1957-58; vis. lectr. genetics and law Boston U., 1973-82; adj. prof. genetics and law, Boston U., 1982—; sr. genetics cons. NIH, Bethesda, 1970-75; mem. sci. coun. Nat. Cystic Fibrosis Found., Atlanta, 1972-85; sci. adv. to dean, Roger Williams U., Bristol, R.I., 1977-88; mem. Internat. Katzier-Katchalsky Ctr., Weizmann Inst., Rehovoth, Israel, 1972—. Contbr. articles to profl. jours. State Com., Dem. Party, R.I., 1970-84. With USN, 1946-48, Caribbean. Predoctoral fellow Nat. Sci. Found., 1954-55; postdoctoral fellowship Am. Cancer Soc., 1955-57; sr. fellow USPHS, 1965-66. Fellow AAAS, Am. Soc. Microbiology, Genetics Soc. Am., Am. Soc. Human Genetics. Office: Brown U Box G 69 Brown St Providence RI 02912-9091 E-mail: seymour_lederberg@brown.edu.

LEDERBERG, VICTORIA, judge, former state legislator, lawyer; b. Providence, July 7, 1937; d. Frank and Victoria Santopietro; m. Seymour Lederberg, 1959; children: Tobias, Sarah. AB, Pembroke Coll., 1959; AM, Brown U., 1961, PhD, 1966; JD, Suffolk U., 1976, LLD, 1995, Roger Williams U., 2001. Mem. R.I. Ho. of Reps., 1975-82, chmn. subcom. on edn., fin. com., 1975-82; chmn. nat. adv. panel on financing elem. and secondary edn. Washington, 1979-82; mem. R.I. State Senate, 1985-91, chmn. fin. com. subcom. on social svcs., 1985-89, dep. majority leader, 1989-91; prof. psychology R.I. Coll., 1968-93; pvt. practice Providence, 1977-93; justice R.I. Supreme Ct., 1993—, chmn. com. on judicial performance evaluation, 1993—, mem. com. jud. edn., 1993—, chmn. com. on user-friendly cts., 1994-97, chmn. lawday com., 1996-2001; trustee Suffolk U., 2001—. Trustee Brown U., 1983—89, com. on biomed. affairs, 1990—2002; trustee Roger Williams U., 1980—, vice chmn. corp., dir. Sch. Law, Butler Hosp., 1985—93, also sec. of corp., 2000—. USPHS fellow physiol. psychology, 1964-66. Mem. ABA, New Eng. Psychol. Assn., R.I. Bar Assn., Am. Judicature Soc., Nat. Assn. Women Judges, Sigma Xi. Office: 250 Benefit St Providence RI 02903-2719

LEDERER, HERBERT, foreign languages educator; b. Vienna, Austria, June 9, 1921; came to U.S., 1942; s. Hans Lederer and Frida Rosenbaum; m. Eva Marie Hohenberg, June 20, 1948; children: George Kenneth, Barbara Louise. BA, Bklyn. Coll., 1948; MA, U. Chgo., 1949, PhD, 1953. Instr. German U. Chgo., 1949-52; asst. prof. German Wabash Coll., Crawfordsville, Ind., 1952-57; assoc. prof. German Ohio U., Athens, 1957-61, Queens Coll., Flushing, N.Y., 1961-69; prof. German, head dept. Germanic and Slavic langs. U. Conn., Storrs, 1969-89, prof. emeritus, 1989. Chief reader German Ednl. Testing Svc., Princeton, N.J., 1964-68; chmn. German test com. Coll. Entrance Examination Bd., N.Y.C., 1967-71; cons. Nat. Endowment for the Humanities, Washington, 1973-75, 90-91. Author: Reference Grammar of the German Language, 1969, Handbook of East German Drama, 1945-85, 1987, Bilingual Plays, 1997; editor Gedichte von Arthur Schnitzler, 1969; assoc. editor Modern Austrian Lit., 1968-80. Rsch. grantee Am. Coun. of Learned Socs., 1968, Cross of Honor for Arts and Letters Austrian Govt., 1976, Rsch. award Internat. Theatre Inst., 1978, 81, 83, 85, Fed. Cross of Merit German Govt., 1987. Mem. MLA (parliamentarian 1972-88), Am. Assn. of Tchrs. of German (exec. bd. 1970-72, 79-82), Am. Coun. for the Study of Austrian Lit. (pres. 1972-80), Assn. of Depts. of Fgn. Langs. (exec. bd. 1976-79, pres. 1978), Kafka Soc. Am., Nat. Fedn. Modern Lang. Tchrs. Assns. (exec. com. 1970-79, v.p. 1971, pres. 1972). Democrat. Jewish. Avocation: theatre. Home: 143 Separatist Rd Storrs Mansfield CT 06268-2003

LEDERER, JOHN MARTIN, retired aeronautical engineer; b. Solomon, Kans., May 12, 1930; s. George Martin and Angie Belle (Faubion) L.; m. Joan Elizabeth Patrick, June 15, 1963; children: Jeffrey Mark, Carol Elizabeth. BS in Aero. Engring., Kans. State U., 1953; MSEE, Air Force Inst. Tech., 1955; postgrad., U. N.Mex., 1962-65. Registered profl. aero. engr., Ohio. Project engr. Air Force Spl. Weapons Ctr., Albuquerque, 1955-63, chief project engring. div., 1963-67, chief electromagnetics div., 1967-70; tech. adviser Air Force Weapons Lab., 1970-73, 76-87, chief nuclear systems surety div., 1988-91; dir. nuclear systems engring. Nuclear Systems Engring. Directorate/USAF Systems Command, 1991-92; dir. nuclear systems engring. aero. systems ctr. Air Force Materiel Command, 1992-93; tech. dir. 4900th test group, 1973-76, ret. Chmn. Dept. of Def. Design Rev. and Acceptance Group, Albuquerque, 1979-91; flying instr. airplanes, instruments. Co-inventor digital distance measuring instrument. Founder One of Ten Young Am. Football League, Albuquerque, 1964. Served to 1st lt. USAF, 1953-58. Recipient Outstanding Performance award Dept. Air Force, Albuquerque, 1965, 66, 68, 73, 74, 79, Sustained Superior Performance award, 1961, 81, 83-86, 88-93, Air Force Disting. Civilian Svc. award, 1993. Mem. NSPE, FAA (cert. flight instr.), Inst. Aerospace Scis. Republican. Episcopalian. Avocations: archery, flying. Home: 512 El Marta Ct NE Albuquerque NM 87111-5618 E-mail: fishhooks@comcast.net.

LEDERER, KATHERINE GAY, English language educator; b. Trinity, Tex., Mar. 19, 1932; d. Leon MacRae and Katherine Waties (Lipscomb) Gay; divorced; children: Susan, Geoffrey. BA in English, Sam Houston State U., 1952; MA in English, U. Ark., 1958, PhD in English, 1967. Pub. sch. tchr., Houston, 1953-55; grad. asst. U. Ark., Fayetteville, 1956-59, instr., 1959-60; prof. S.W. Mo. State U., Springfield, 1968—. Author: (book) Lillian Hellman, 1979, Many Thousand Gone: Springfield's Lost Black History, 1986; guest editor: Ozarkswatch: African Americans in the Ozarks jour., 1999; prodr. media show on black history, 1983. Bd. dirs. Springfield Little Theater, 1970s; founder, bd. dirs. Springfield Jazz Soc., 1973-79. Recipient Gov.'s Humanities award Mo. Humanities Coun., 1999, award for tchg. S.W. Mo. State U., 1999, Excellence in Cmty. Svc. award, 1999, others; named to Mo. Writers Hall of Fame, 2001. Mem. Midwest Orgn. for Recognition and Recovery of Ethnic History (v.p., exec. com. St. Louis 1997—), Toni Morrison Soc. (charter mem., mem. adv. coun.), Coll. Lang. Assn., MLA, Mo. Folklore Soc. (bd. dirs. 1980s). Democrat. Avocations: reading, writing, Black history rsch., jazz. E-mail: katherinelederer@smsu.edu.

LEDERER, MARION IRVINE, cultural administrator; b. Brampton, Ont., Can., Feb. 10, 1920; d. Oliver Bateman and Eva Jane (MacMurdo) L.; m. Francis Lederer, July 10, 1941. Student, U. Toronto, 1938, UCLA, 1942-45. Owner Canoga Mission Gallery, Canoga Park, Calif., 1967—, cultural heritage monument, 1974—. V.p. Screen Smart Set women's aux. Motion Picture and TV Fund, 1973, pres., 2001—02; founder sister city program Canoga Park-Taxco, Mex., 1963. Mem. Mayor's Cultural Task Force San Fernando Valley, 1973—, L.A. Cultural Affairs Commn., 1980—85; pres. Screen Smart Set, Women's Aux. of Motionn Pictures, TV Fund. Recipient numerous pub. service awards from mayor, city council, C. of C. Mem. Canoga Park C. of C. (cultural chmn. 1973-75, dir. 1973-75) Presbyterian. Home: PO Box 32 Canoga Park CA 91305-0032 Office: Canoga Mission Gallery 23130 Sherman Way Canoga Park CA 91307-1402

LEDERER, MAX DONALD, JR. lawyer; b. Plattsburgh, N.Y., June 21, 1960; s. Max Donald and Mary Lilian (Adie) L. BA magna cum laude, Marshall U., Huntington, W.Va., 1982; JD, U. Richmond, 1985. Bar: Pa. 1986, U.S. Army Ct. Mil. Rev. 1986. Commd. 2d lt. U.S. Army, 1982-86, advanced through grades to capt., 1987—; def. counsel Ft. Sill, Okla., 1986-87; command judge advocate CP Red Cloud, Korea, 1987-88; sr. trial counsel Combined Field Army, 1989; chief adminstrv. law div. Combined Field Army-2d armored div. (forward), 1989-90; command judge adv. Op. Desert Storm 2d armored div. (forward), 1991; officer-in-charge Bremerhaven Legal Ctr., Fed. Republic of Germany, 1991-92; gen. counsel European Stars and Stripes, 1992-96, gen. mgr., 1996-2000; gen. mgr., gen. counsel European and Pacific Stars and Stripes, 2000—. Fellow ABA, Pa. Bar Assn. Avocation: running. Home: 4850 Middleton Dr Lockport NY 14094-1616 Office: 2427 Pondside Ter Silver Spring MD 20906-5752 E-mail: ledererm@stripes.usd.mil.

LEDERER, PAUL EDWARD, landscape architect; b. Paradise, Nova Scotia, Can., Mar. 2, 1942; came to U.S., 1946; s. Emil and Edith (Kann) L. BS, Rutgers U., 1964; B of Land Architecture, U. Mass., 1965, M of Land Architecture, 1969. Registered landscape architect, Mass., N.J., Va., Md., Ala. Landscape architect John Rahenkamp & Assoc, Phila., 1965, Nat. Park Svc., Phila., 1965, 67-69, landscape architect, planner Washington, 1969-97; civil engring. aid Soil Conservation Svc., Northampton, Mass., 1967. Mem. Com. of 100 on Fed. City D.C., 1987. Mem. Am. Soc. Landscape Architects, Am. Planning Assn., Nat. Trust for Hist. Preservation, Nat. Park and Recreation Assn. Jewish. Avocations: fine arts, sculpture, collecting classic cars, photography, swimming.

LEDERER, PETER DAVID, lawyer; b. Frankfurt, Germany, May 2, 1930; came to U.S., 1938; s. Leo and Alice Lederer; m. Midori Shimanouchi, Dec. 16, 1966. BA, U. Chgo., 1949, JD, 1957, M in Comparative Law, 1958. Bar: Ill. 1959, U.S. Supreme Ct. 1966, N.Y. 1967. Law and behavioral sci. rsch. fellow U. Chgo. Law Sch., 1958-59; ptnr. Baker & McKenzie, Zurich, Switzerland, 1960-66, N.Y.C., 1966-94, of counsel, 1994—. Chmn. bd. dirs. Coverage Connect, Inc. Dir. Asian-am. Legal Def. and Edn. Fund, N.Y.C.; chmn. emeritus bd. dirs. The Midori Found.; pres. bd. trustees The Calhoun Sch., N.Y.C., 1980—83; mem. vis. com. U. Miami Law Sch., Coral Gables, Fla., 1974—, U. Chgo. Law Sch., 1988—91, 2000—; mem. adv. coun. Wildlife Trust, Phila., 2000—. With AUS, 1951—53. Mem. ABA, Assn. of Bar of City of N.Y., Internat. Nuc. Law Assn. Office: Baker & McKenzie 805 3rd Ave Fl 29 New York NY 10022-7513 E-mail: peterdlederer@att.net.

LEDERER, RICHARD HENRY, writer, educator, columnist; b. Phila., May 26, 1938; s. Howard Jules and Leah (Perry) L.; m. Rhoda Anne Spangenberg, Aug. 25, 1962 (div. 1986); m. Simone Johanna van Egeren, Nov. 29, 1991; children: Howard Henry, Anne Labarr, Katherine Lee. BA, Haverford Coll., 1959; student, Harvard U., 1959-60, M of Arts and Teaching, 1962; PhD, U. N.H., 1980. Tchr., coach St. Paul's Sch., Concord, N.H., 1962-89. Lectr. in field. Author: Anguished English, 1987, Get Thee to a Punnery, 1988, Crazy English, 1989, The Play of Words, 1990, The Miracle of Language, 1991, More Anguished English, 1993, Building Bridge, 1994, Adventures of a Verbivore, 1994, Literary Trivia, 1994, Nothing Risqué, Nothing Gained, 1995, The Write Way, 1995, Pun and Games, 1996, Fractured English, 1996, The Word Circus, 1998. Sleeping Dogs Don't Lay, 1999 (book of the month club selection), The Bride of Anguished English, 2000, The Circus of Words, 2001, Word Play Crosswords, 2000, 2001; weekly columnist Looking at Lang.; contbr. over 3000 articles to mags. and jours.; broadcaster various radio stas.; numerous TV appearances; host A Way With Words KPBS, San Diego. Recipient Chmns. award, Am. Mensa, Ltd., 2000, Toastmasters Internat. Golden Gavel, 2002, Lifetime Achievement award Columbia Scholastic Press Assn., N.Y.C., 1989, Leadership in Comms. award San Diego Toastmasters; named Internat. Punster of Yr. Internat. Save the Pun Found., Toronto, Can., 1990; Paul Harris Rotary fellow. Mem. Am. Mensa, Phi Beta Kappa, Phi Delta Kappa. Avocations: tennis, cards, film. Office: 9974 Scripps Ranch Blvd San Diego CA 92131-1825 *Whatever you hear about the closing of the American mind and cultural illiteracy, there has never been a more passionate moment in the history of the American love affair with language than right now. I'm exceedingly fortunate to have written books that embrace that passion.*

LEDERER, WILLIAM JULIUS, author; b. N.Y.C., Mar. 31, 1912; s. William J. and Paula (Franken) L.; m. Ethel Hackett, Apr. 21, 1940 (div. Jan. 1965); children: Brian, Jonathan, Bruce; m. Corinne Edwards Lewis, July 1965 (div. May 1976). BS, U.S. Naval Acad., 1936; assoc. Nieman fellow, Harvard U., 1950-51. Enlisted USN, 1930, commd. ensign, 1936, advanced through grades to capt., 1952, ret., 1958; Far East corr. Reader's Digest, 1958-63; lectr. colls. and univs., 1949—. Author in residence, Harvard U., 1966-67; Author: All the Ship's at Sea, 1950, The Last Cruise, 1950, Spare Time Article Writing for Money, 1953, Ensign O'Toole and Me, 1957, A Nation of Sheep, 1961, Timothy's Song, 1965, Pink Jade, 1966, (with Eugene Burdick) The Ugly American, 1958, Sarkhan, 1965, Our Own Worst Enemy, 1967, (with Don D. Jackson) The Mirages of Marriage, 1968, (with Joe Pete Wilson) Complete Cross-Country Skiing and Ski Touring, 1970, (with others) Marriage for and Against, Marital Choices, A Happy Book of Happy Stories, I, Giorghos, 1984, Creating a Good Relationship, 1984. Mem. Signet Soc., Authors Guild, Acad. Orthomolecular Psychiatry, European Acad. Preventive Medicine, Internat. Acad. Preventive Medicine, Internat. Coll. Applied Nutrition, Lotos Club, Trap Door Spiders Club, Harvard Faculty Club, Sigma Delta Chi. Home: 1350 Mayflower Ave Melbourne FL 32940-6723 *If one works at being joyful and physically functional, almost everything else seems to come along on its own. Put energy into the "here and now" and do not distract from it by worrying about either the past or the future.*

LEDERER-ANTONUCCI, YVONNE, management information educator, consultant; b. Phila., May 5, 1958; d. Jay William and Elizabeth (Stratton) Lederer. BSBA in Mgmt. Sci., Shippensburg U., 1980; MS in Mgmt. Sci., Lehigh U., 1983; PhD, Drexel U., 1992. Programmer Shared Med. Systems, Malvern, Pa., 1980-81; prof., dir. Widener U., Chester, 1983—, also bd. dirs. Computer cons., co-owner Simplex Computing Svcs., Chaddsford, Pa., 1984-93; ptnr. Totem Software, Media, 1988-90; lectr., presenter profl. conf. Mem. Data Processing Mgmt. Assn. (edn. coord. 1987-89, coord. student chpt. 1988-91), Assn. Computer Machinery. Lutheran. Home: 44 Sterling Way Chadds Ford PA 19317-9415 Office: Widener U Sch Mgmt Chester PA 19013

LEDERIS, KAROLIS PAUL (KARL LEDERIS), pharmacologist, educator, researcher; b. Noreikoniai, Lithuania, Aug. 1, 1920; arrived in Can., 1969; s. Paul Augustus and Franciska (Danisevicius) L.; m. Hildegard Gallistl, Feb. 28, 1952 (dec. Nov. 2000); children: Aldona Franciska, Edmund Paul. Diploma, Tchrs. Coll., Siauliai, Lithuania, 1939; BSc, U. Bristol, U.K., 1958, PhD, 1961, DSc, 1968. From jr. lectr. to reader U. Bristol, 1961-69; prof. pharmacology and therapeutics U. Calgary, Alta., Can., 1969-89, prof. emeritus Can., 1989—. Vis. prof. univs. in Fed. Republic Germany, Austria, Chile, Argentina, Sri Lanka, Switzerland, Lithuania, France, , USA, USSR, 1963-79, U. Bristol, 1979, U. Kyoto, Japan, 1980; career investigator, mem., chair grants com. Med. Rsch. Coun., Ottawa, Ont., Can., 1970-89, coun. mem., exec., 1983-90; mem. internat. com. Centres Excellence Networks, Ottawa, 1988-89. Author, editor: 5 books on hypothalamic hormones; editor in chief Jour. Exptl. and Clin. Pharmacology, 1977-89; contbr. approximately 350 book chpts. and articles to profl. jours.; patentee hormonal peptides. Recipient Upjohn award in pharmacology, 1990, various fellowships and scholarships in U.K., Fed. Republic of Germany, U.S. Fellow NAS, Royal Soc. Can.; mem. Western Pharmacological Soc. (pres. 1982-83), Lithuanian Club (London), Men's Can. Club, Cabot Yacht and Cruise Club (Bristol). Avocations: music, sailing, golf. Home: 147 Carthew St Comox BC Canada V9M 1T4 Office: U Calgary Health Scis Centre Calgary AB Canada T2N 4N1 E-mail: klederis@shaw.ca.

LEDERMAN, LAWRENCE, lawyer, writer, educator; b. N.Y.C., Sept. 8, 1935; s. Herman Jack and Lillian (Rosenfeld) L.; children: Leandra, Evin. B.A., Bklyn. Coll., 1957; LL.B., N.Y.U., 1966. Bar: N.Y. 1968; Law clk. chief justice Calif. Sup. Ct., 1966-67; assoc. Cravath, Swaine & Moore, N.Y.C., 1968-74; ptnr. Wachtell, Lipton, Rosen & Katz, N.Y.C., 1975-91; ptnr., chmn. corp. practice Milbank, Tweed, Hadley & McCloy, 1991—; adj. prof. law N.Y.U. Sch. Law, 1974—; Chmn. bd. Phoenix House Devel. Corp., mem. Phoenix House Found.; bd. dirs. The Nat. Mentoring Partnership, N.Y. Botanica l Garden. Author: Tombstones: A Lawyer's Tales from the Takeover Decades, 1992; contbr. articles to profl. jours. Served with U.S. Army, 1957-59. Mem. ABA, N.Y. State Bar Assn., Order of the Coif. Office: Milbank Tweed Hadley & McCloy 1 Chase Manhattan Plz Fl 47 New York NY 10005-1413

LEDERMAN, LEON MAX, physicist, educator; b. N.Y.C., July 15, 1922; s. Morris and Minna (Rosenberg) Lederman; m. Florence Gordon, Sept. 19, 1945; children: Rena S., Jesse A., Heidi R.; m. Ellen Carr, Sept. 17, 1981. BS, CCNY, 1943, DSc (hon.) , 1980; AM, Columbia U., 1948, PhD, 1951; DSc (hon.) , No. Ill. U., 1984, U. Chgo., 1985, Ill. Inst. Tech., 1987; 35 additional hon. degrees. Assoc. in physics Columbia U., N.Y.C., 1951, asst. prof., 1952—54, assoc. prof., 1954—58, prof., 1958—89, Eugene Higgins prof. physics, 1972—79; Frank L. Sulzberger prof. physics U. Chgo., 1989—92; dir. Fermi Nat. Accelerator Lab., Batavia, Ill., 1979—89, dir. emeritus, 1989—; Pritzker prof. sci. Ill. Inst. Tech., Chgo., 1992—; resident scholar Ill. Math. and Sci. Acad., 1998—. Dir. Nevis Labs., Irvington, NY, 1962—79; guest scientist Brookhaven Nat. Labs., 1955; cons. Nat. Accelerator Lab., European Orgn. for Nuc. Rsch. (CERN), 1970—; mem. high energy physics adv. panel AEC, 1966—70; mem. adv. com. to divsn. math. and phys. scis. NSF, 1970—72; sci. advisor to gov. State of Ill., 1989—93; chmn. XXIV Internat. Physics Olympiad, 1991—93; co-chair com. on capacity bldg. in sci. Internat. Sci. Unions, 1994—2001; pres. bd. sponsors Bull. Atomic Scientists, 2000—; mem. adv. com. to dean U. Chgo., 2000—; pres.'s coun. The Cooper Union, 2002—. Author: Quarks to the Cosmos, 1989, The God Particle, 1993; editor, contbr.: Portraits of Great American Scientists, 2001; contbr. over 200 articles to profl. jours. Commr. White House Fellows Program, 1997—2000; Univ. Rsch. Assocs., 1967—71, 1992—; mem. sci. adv. bd. Sec. of Energy, 1991—2001; bd. dirs. Mus. Sci. and Industry, Chgo., 1989—, Weizmann Inst. Sci., Israel, 1988—; pres. bd. sponsors Bull. Atomic Scientists, 2001—. Named Hon. Prof., Beijing Normal U.; recipient Nat. medal of Sci., 1965, Townsend Harris medal, CUNY, 1973, Elliot Cresson medal, Franklin Inst., 1976, Wolf prize, 1982, Nobel prize in Physics, 1988, Enrico Fermi prize, 1992, Rosenblith lectr. in Sci. and Tech., NAS, Joseph Priestly award, Dickinson Coll., 1996, Pres.'s medal, CCNY, 1993, Heald prize, Ill. Inst. Tech., 2000, Pupin Med. award, Columbia U., 2000, Faraday award, NSTA, Discover, 2002; fellow Guggenheim, 1958—59, Ford Found., European Ctr. for Nuc. Rsch., Geneva, 1958—59, NSF, 1967, Presdl., World Bank, 1996—99; scholar Great Minds program, Ill. Math. Sci. Acad. Fellow: AAAS (pres. 1990—91, chmn. 1991—92, Abelson award 2001), Am. Phys. Soc. (mem. coun.); mem.: IEEE, NAS (U.S., Argentina, Finland, Mex.), Coun. Advancement of Sci. Writing, Tchrs. Acad. for Math. and Sci. in Chgo. (co-chmn. 1990—), Italian Phys. Soc. (hon.), Ill. Math. Sci. Acad. (vice chmn. 1985—98), Aspen Inst. Physics (pres. 1990—92). E-mail: Lederman@fnal.gov.

LEDERMAN, MICHAEL MARCEL, immunologist; b. Munich, Germany, Aug. 14, 1948; came to U.S., 1949; s. Ezjel and Esther Lederman; m. Mary Sharmon Sollitto, Mar. 1, 1980; children: Myra Claire, Hanna Kate. BA, Brandeis U., 1970; MD, Mt. Sinai Sch. of Medicine, 1974. Diplomate Am. Bd.

Internal Medicine. Intern Case Western Res. U., Cleve., 1974-75, resident, 1975-77, chief resident, 1977-78, fellow in infectious disease, 1978-80, asst. prof. medicine, 1980-88, assoc. prof. medicine, 1988-96, prof. medicine, 1996—. Dir. AIDS clin. trial unit, Cleve., 1987—; dir. spl. immunology unit U. Hosp., Cleve., 1985-89; dir. Ctr. for AIDS Rsch., Case Western Res. U., 1999—. Co-chmn. AIDS Commn. of Greater Cleve., 1988-90. Mem. Infectious Diseases Soc. of Am., Am. Assn. of Immunologists, Clin. Immunology Soc. Office: U Hosp of Cleve 11000 Euclid Ave Cleveland OH 44106-1714

LEDERMAN, SALLY ANN, nutrition researcher; b. N.Y.C., July 8, 1937; d. Joseph Edward and Leanora Rossi; m. Lawrence Lederman, Jan. 26, 1958 (div. Feb. 1991); children: Leandra, Evin. BS in Chemistry, Bklyn. Coll., 1957; MS in Nutrition, Columbia U., 1976, PhD, 1980. Analytical chemist U.S. FDA, N.Y.C., 1957-62; lectr. dept. chemistry Bklyn. Coll., 1962-66, 74; postdoctoral fellow Inst. Human Nutrition Columbia U., N.Y.C., 1980-82, postdoctoral fellow obstetrics and biochemistry, 1983, asst. prof. Sch. Pub. Health, 1983-90, assoc. prof. Sch. Pub. Health, 1990-94, prof. Tchrs. Coll., 1994-97, rschr. Tchrs. Coll., 1997-99; rsch. assoc. divsn. endocrinology, nutrition, diabetes St. Lukes-Roosevelt Hosp. Ctr., 1998—. Editor: Controversial Issues in Public Health Nutrition, 1983; contbr. articles to profl. jours. Mem. APHA, AAAS, Am. Soc. Nutrition Sci., Am. Women in Sci., N.Y. Acad. Scis. Office: St Luke's Hosp Ctr Obesity Rsch Ctr 1090 Amsterdam Ave # 14H New York NY 10025-1737 E-mail: sal1@columbia.edu.

LEDERMAN, SUSAN STURC, public administration educator; b. Bratislava, Slovakia, May 28, 1937; came to U.S., 1948; d. Ludovit and Helen (Reich) Sturc; m. Peter Bernd Lederman, Aug. 25, 1957; children: Stuart, Ellen. AB in Polit. Sci., U. Mich., 1958; MA in Polit. Sci., Rutgers U., 1970, PhD in Polit. Sci., 1978. Vis. instr. Fairleigh Dickinson U., Madison, N.J., 1973-74, Drew U., Madison, 1975-76; from asst. prof. to assoc. prof. pub. adminstrn. Kean U., Union, N.J., 1977-89, prof., dir. MPA program, 1989-97; exec. dir. Gateway Inst. Regional Devel. Kean U., 1997-2000; prof. Kean U., 1990—. Vis. fellow Woodrow Wilson Sch., Princeton (N.J.) U., 1988-89. Co-author: (book) Elections in America—Control and Influence in Democratic Politics, 1980, (monograph) Campaign Watch: A Report on the 1992 Campaign Watch Project, 1993; editor: (book) The SLERP Reforms and Their Impact, 1989; contbr. articles to profl. jours. Mem. nat. gov. bd. Common Cause, Washington, 1994-2000; bd. dirs., sec.-treas. The Jefferson Ctr., Mpls., 1992-2002; dir. Regional Plan Assn., N.Y.C., 1991—; pres. LWV of N.J., 1985-89, program v.p., 1983-85, sec., fiscal policy dir., 1981-83, fiscal policy dir., 1979-81, adminstrn. of justice dir., 1976-79; pres. LWV of U.S., 1990-92, chair edn. fund., 1990-92; mem. bd. trustees exec. com., sec. N.J. Future, 1993—; pub. mem. Supreme Ct. of N.J. Disciplinary Oversight Com., 1994-98, Coun. of Engring. and Sci. Splty. Bds., 1996-2002; mem. Property Tax Commn., 1998; mem. N.J. Legis. Coun. of Acad. Advisors; commr. N.J. State and Local Expenditure Revenue Policy Commn., 1985-88, N.J. Election Law Enforcement Commn., 2000—; pres. Northeastern Polit. Sci. Assn., 1984-85. Recipient Disting. Svc. award N.J. Polit. Sci. Assn., 1984, Pub. Svc. award ASPA, 1993, Eric Neisser Pub. Svc. award Pub. Interest Law Ctr., 2001; rsch. grantee Fund for N.J., 1981, Florence and John Schumann Found., 1988-89. Mem. Internat. Women's Forum (N.J. Forum bd. dirs. 1998—), Phi Kappa Phi, Pi Sigma Alpha, Pi Alpha Alpha. Home: 17 Pittsford Way New Providence NJ 07974-2428 Office: Kean U 1000 Morris Ave Union NJ 07083-7131 E-mail: slederma@kean.edu.

LEDESMA-NICHOLSON, CHARMAINE, psychotherapist; b. L.A., Aug. 29, 1943; d. Louis Edgar Dern and Reba Marie Willis; m. Raymond Cano Ledesma, May 4, 1968 (div. June 1992); 1 child, Michael; m. Steven Nicholson, Aug. 7, 1993. BA, Calif. State U., 1966; MA, Pepperdine U., 1982. Lic. marriage, family, child counselor, Calif.; lic. clin. profl. counselor, Mont. Social worker Dept. Pub. Social Svcs., L.A., 1967-70; child protection svcs. social worker County of Orange (Calif.) Pub. Social Svcs., 1970-88; supr. child protection svcs. Riverside (Calif.) County Pub. Social Svc., 1988-92; psychotherapist for sex offenders Parents United, Beaumont, Calif., 1988-92, Mont. State Prison, Deer Lodge, 1992-96, Crossroads Correctional Ctr., Shelby, Mont., 1999—; pvt. practice Great Falls, 1999—. Self-employed cons., supr., Great Falls, 1999—. 1st responder Avon (Mont.) Quick Response Unit, 1992-99; mem. Lewis & Clark Search & Rescue, Helena, Mont., 1994-99; vol. Eaglemount, Great Falls, 1999— (profl. ski instr. of Am.), ARC, Great Falls, 1990—. Mem. Am. Assn. of Marriage Family Therapists (clin. mem.), Assn. for Treatment of Sex Abusers (clin. mem.), Mont. Sex Offender Treatment Assn. (clin. mem.), Profl. Ski Instrs. Am. Democrat. Roman Catholic. Avocations: horseback riding, sewing, skiing, mountain climbing, canoeing. Home: 5705 62d Ave SW Great Falls MT 59404 E-mail: stevecharm1@juno.com.

LEDET, HENRY JOSEPH, librarian; b. Houston, June 12, 1953; s. Henry Joseph Jr. and Marie (Gaudet) L.; m. Diane Marie Biediger, Nov. 26, 1988; 1 child, Robert Joseph. BS, La. State U., 1976, MLS, 1978. Tchr. English Iberville Parish Schs., Plaquemine, La., 1976-77; asst. dir. Lincoln Lawrence Franklin Regional Libr., Brookhaven, Miss., 1979-81, dir., 1981—. Editor (newsletter) Brookhaven Trust Notes, 1994—; book reviewer Daily Leader Sunday Edition, 1996—. Recipient Pine Hills Culture Program scholar U. So. Miss Ctr. for Oral History and Cultural Heritage, 1996, Leadership in Mgmt. of Info. and Comm. Tech. award Solinet, 1997. Mem. ALA, Miss. Libr. Assn. (treas. 1997-98, pres.-elect 2000, pres. 2001), Brookhaven Trust (pres. 1996), Brookhaven Arts Coun. (sec. 1999). Roman Catholic. Avocations: running, gardening, cooking. Office: Lincoln Lawrence Franklin Regional Libr 100 S Jackson St Brookhaven MS 39601-3347 Fax: 601-833-3381. E-mail: hledet@llf.lib.ms.us.

LEDET, PHYLLIS L. educational administrator; b. Delcambre, La., Apr. 10, 1942; d. John and Claire (Landry) LeBlanc; children: Lonny Ledet, Leah Ledet Terro, Elizabeth Ledet Romero, Laurie. BA in Elem. Edn., U. Southwestern LA, 1963, MEd in Ednl. Counseling, 1989, EdS in Ednl. Adminstrn. and Supervision, 1992. Asst. prin. L. J. Alleman Mid. and Arts Acad., Lafayette, La., 1993—. Bd. dirs. Jr. League Lafayette; mem. Am. Cancer Soc. (Spring Family Fair Chmn.), Govs. Commn. Goals 2000, La. State Dept. Edn. Panel VIII Com., United Way of Acadiana; leader Girl Scouts Am.; pres. Edgar Martin PTC; religious tchr. Holy Cross Cath. Ch. Mem. Assn. Profs. Edn. of La. (state pres. 1996-97), Leadership Lafayette C. of C. (class XI). E-mail: pledet@lft.k12.la.us.

LEDFORD, BRENDA KAY, writer; b. Young Harris, Ga., Apr. 9, 1952; d. James Ronda and Blanche Willie (Lee) L.. BS in Edn., We. Carolina U., Cullowhee, N.C., 1976, MA in Edn., 1979. Cert. tchr. N.C. Clerk, typist FBI, Washington, 1970—71; tchr. Cherokee County Bd. Edn., Murphy, NC, 1976—90; freelance writer Smoky Mountain Sentinel, Hayesville, 1990—2001. Writing instr. John Campbell Folk Sch., Brasstown, NC, 2000; storyteller Clay Revitalization Assn., Hayesville, 1999—2001. Author: poems; editor: Tri-County C.C. newspaper, 1996; contbr. articles. Named winner photo contest, Writers' Jour., 1998; recipient award journalism contest, N.C. Press Assn., 2000. Mem.: DAR, Clay County C. C., Clay County Arts Coun. (bd. dirs. 1999, sec. 1999, poetry contest judge 2000), N.C. Storytelling Guild, N.C. Writer's Network, Order Ea. Star (Clay chpt., Angels Among Us award 1999). Democrat. Baptist. Avocations: travel, piano, drawing, reading, photography.

LEDFORD, DENNIS KEITH, physician; b. Johnson City, Tenn., May 10, 1950; s. Lawrence and Dorothy Ruth (Swatzell) L.; m. Jennifer L. Shelton, June 15, 1974; 3 children. BCE, Ga. Inst. Tech., 1973; MD, U. Tenn., 1976. diplomate Am. Bd. Allergy and Immunology. Med. intern U. Tenn. Hosps., Memphis, 1977, asst. and assoc. resident, 1978-79; chief resident City of Memphis Hosps., 1979-80; fellow in clin. immunology and rheumatology NYU, N.Y.C., 1980-82; fellow in clin. allergy and immunology U. South Fla., Tampa, 1983-85, asst. prof. medicine, 1985-91, assoc. prof. medicine, 1991-99, prof. medicine, 2000—. Instr. dept. medicine U. Tenn. Ctr. Health Scis., Memphis, 1979-80; clin. assoc. internal medicine U. South Fla., 1983-85, dir. tng. program in clin. and lab. immunology, 1992—; mem. AIDS adv. com. James A. Haley VA Hosp., 1987-94; mem. infection control com. Univ. Cmty. Hosp., 1987-96; mem. adv. com. Blue Cross/Blue Shield, 1987-94; med. dir. Asthma and Allergy Clinic of Judeo-Christian Clinic, 1988—; chief allergy, immunology sect. Univ. Cmty. Hosp., 1996—: chmn. med. student selection com. U. South Fla., 1994-98; dir. Am. Bd. Allergy and Immunology. Mem. med. adv. coun. Fla. chpt. Nat. Hemophilia Found., 1990-92; mem. AIDS edn. adv. coun. Hillsborough County Sch. Bd., 1992-95. Recipient Outstanding Spkr. award Marion County Med. Assn., 1987, Vol. of Yr. award Vol. Ctr. Hillsborough County, 1994. Mem. AMA, ACP, Am. Soc. Internal Medicine, Am. Rheumatism Assn. (Fellowship award 1981), Am. Coll. Allergy and Immunology (mem. ann. meeting postgrad. program com. 1996-98), Am. Acad. Allergy and Immunology (mem. continuing med. edn. com. 1987-90, chmn. 1989-90, mem. AIDS com. 1989-98, chmn. 1998-99, postgrad. edn. planning com. 1992-93, mem. core curriculum com. for clin. and diagnostic lab. immunology tng. programs 1993—, co-chair, bd. rev. course 1996-98, co-chmn. clin. lab com. 1999—), Fla. Allergy and Immunology Soc. (sec. 1989-90, v.p. 1990-91, pres. 1991-93, bd. dir. 1993-96). Avocations: gardening, hiking, fishing, music. Office: U South Fla Coll Medicine VA Med Ctr 13000 Bruce B Downs Blvd # 111D Tampa FL 33612-4745

LEDFORD, FRANK FINLEY, JR. surgeon, army officer; b. Jacksonville, Fla., Apr. 22, 1934; s. Frank F. and Hazel H. (Barrette) L.; m. Marilyn Sue Kain, Aug. 23, 1957; 1 child, Cheryl Lynn. BS, U. Dayton, 1955; MD, U. Cin., 1959; postgrad., Indsl. Coll. Armed Forces, 1976—. Diplomate: Am. Bd. Orthopedic Surgery. Commd. 2d lt. U.S. Army, 1958, advanced through grades to lt. gen., 1988; surgeon, 1958-69; intern Brooke Army Hosp., San Antonio, 1959-60; resident in surgery Womack Army Hosp., 1960-61; resident in orthop. surgery Letterman Gen. Hosp., San Francisco, 1961-64; resident in pediat. orthop. surgery Phoenix Crippled Childrens Hosp., 1964-65; chief orthopedic surgery (Army Hosp.), Landstuhl, W.Ger., 1969-71, dep. commr. Heidelberg, W.Ger., 1971-72; asst. chief surg. cons. Office of Surgeon Gen., Washington, 1972-73, chief grad. med. edn., 1973-76; comdr. U.S. Army Hosp., Fort Riley, Kans., 1977-80, Ft. Benning, Ga., 1980; dir. profl. services Office of Surgeon Gen., U.S. Army, Washington, 1980-82; comdr. Letterman Army Med. Ctr. San Francisco, 1982-85; chief surgeon U.S. Army Europe, 1985-88; The Surgeon Gen. Dept. of the Army, Washington, 1988-92; pres. S.W. Found. for Biomedical Rsch., San Antonio, 1992—; clin. prof. Health Sci. Ctr. U. Tex., 1993—. Clin prof. surgery Uniformed Services U. Health Scis. Contbr. articles to med. jours. Fellow ACS, Am. Acad. Orthopedic Surgeons, Am. Coll. Physician Execs.; mem. AMA, Assn. Mil. Surgeons, Soc. Mil. Orthopedic Surgeons, Argyle Club. Methodist. Address: SW Found For Biomedical Research PO Box 760549 San Antonio TX 78245-0549 E-mail: fledford@sfbr.org.

LEDFORD, GARY ALAN, real estate developer; b. San Diego, Dec. 30, 1946; s. Loren Oscar and Madge Francis (Condon) L.; m. Winifred Jess Ledford, Nov. 19, 1994; children: Kelly, Jeanne, Robert. BSCE, U.S. Army Engring. Coll., 1967. Pres. Mastercraft Contractors/Mastercraft Diversified Svcs., Inc./Masterplan, Inc., Colo. Springs, 1969-73; v.p. K.L. Redfern, Inc., Orange, Calif., 1973-75; pres. Ledford Industries, Inc./G.A. Ledford & Assocs., 1975-82, Watt Jess Ranch, Inc., Apple Valley, Calif., 1985-94; chmn. Jess Ranch, 1994—, Jess Ranch Water Co., Apple Valley, 1986—; pres., ceo Jess Ranch Devel. Co., Inc., 1996—; pres. Jess Ranch Security Co., Inc., 1996—; v.p., gen. mgr. Jess Ranch Realty, 1996—. Gen. ptnr. GLBT Assocs., 1978-79; chmn. Watt-Jess/Ledford, Apple Valley, 1992-94; pres. LJ&J Investments, Inc., Apple Valley, Ledford-Schaffer/Rogers, Apple Valley. Designer computer software, 1979. Past pres. Cultural Arts Found., 1991-92, Victorville, Calif; bd. trustees Apple Valley Christian Care Ctr., High Desert Questors, Victorville; past pres. Victor Valley Mus. Assn., Baldy View B.I.A. Capt. C.E., U.S. Army, 1967-69, Vietnam. Mem. Internat. Coun. Shopping Ctrs., Nat. Assn. Home Builders', Nat. Planning Assn., NRA (life), High Desert Constrn. Indsutry Assn. (past v.p.), Bldg. Industry Assn., VFW, Sr. Housing Coun. Republican. Avocations: hunting, chess, equestrian. Home: 11401 Apple Valley Rd Apple Valley CA 92308-7503 Office: Jess Ranch 11401 Apple Valley Rd Apple Valley CA 92308-7599

LEDFORD, JANET MARIE SMALLEY, real estate appraiser, consultant; b. Willimantic, Conn., June 1, 1951; d. Harold Eugene and Elizabeth Louise (Loehr) Smalley; m. Timothy Eugene Ledford, Jan. 23, 1988. AA, Young Harris (Ga.) Coll., 1971; BS, W. Ga. Coll., 1973; MEd, U. Ga., 1978. Math. tchr. secondary schs., Atlanta and, V.I., 1973-82; assoc. appraiser Childers Assoc., Atlanta, 1985-87, Am. Realty Concepts, Atlanta, 1987-88; owner, appraiser, cons. Ledford & Assoc., 1988—. Avocations: travel, golf.

LEDFORD, PATSY SUE SMITH, nursing assistant; b. Boiling Springs, N.C., July 14, 1969; d. Everett Cliffton Smith and Martha Sue Lovelace; m. Derrick Lewis Pursley, Mar. 21, 1988 (div. July 1994); children: James Ray Pursley, Thomas Gordon Pursley; m. Thomas Grover Ledford, Apr. 24, 1999. AAS, Gaston Coll., 1996; cert. nursing asst., Isothermal Coll., Spindale, N.C., 1998. Lead cert. nursing asst. Rutherford Hosp., Rutherfordton, NC, 1998—2000; medication clk. Houston Ho., Union Mills, 2000—01; cert. nursing asst. Carolina Cmty. Care, Forest City, 2001—. Owner Ledford's Cleaning, Bostic, NC, 2000—. Author: Tainted Love, 2001. Cubmaster Boy Scouts Pack 120, Bostic, 1998—2000. Named Vol. of Yr., Sunshine Elem., Bostic, 2000—01. Mem.: Cherry Mountain Ruitans. Republican. Baptist. Home: PO Box 304 195 Ruby Dr Bostic NC 28018

LEDFORD, TANNER O'BRAIN, music educator; b. Houston, Dec. 22, 1975; s. Donald Eugene Ledford and Darlene Ann Isaacks, Michele Ledford (Stepmother); m. Elizabeth Katra, Feb. 14, 1977. BA, Trinity U., 1998, MA in Tchg., 1999. Cert. all level music cert. Strings tchr. 5th grade N. E. Ind. Sch. Dist., San Antonio, 1998—99; orch. dir. Deer Park (Tex.) H.S., 1999—2000; dir. orchs. J. Frank Dobie H.S., Houston, 2000—. Mem.: Tex. Orch. Dirs. Assn., Music Educators Nat. Conf., Am. String Tchrs. Assn., Tex. Music Educators Assn. (region XIX orch. chair 2000—02), Kappa Delta Pi. Avocation: computer programming. Home: 3009 Wildwood St Pearland TX 77581 Office: J Frank Dobie H S 11111 Beamer Rd Houston TX 77089 Home Fax: 954-301-5836. Personal E-mail: tledford@pasadenaisd.org. E-mail: tledford@pasadenaisd.org.

LEDFORD, THOMAS HOWARD, quality assurance professional; b. Macon, Ga., Aug. 24, 1942; s. Howard William Ledford and Evelyn Elizabeth (Tate) Ledford; m. Joan McDaniel; children: Jeffrey, Scott. BS Chemistry, U. Ga., 1964; Ph D, U. Fla., 1973. Staff chemist Exxon Rsch. & Engring., Baton Rouge, 1973—86; chief environ. chemist Rubicon Inc., Geismar, 1987—2001; quality assurance officer La. Dept. of Environ. Quality, Baton Rouge, 2001—02. Mem.: Am. Chem. Soc. Office: Louisiana Dept of Environ Quality 8618 GSRI Rd Baton Rouge LA 70810

LEDGER, HEATH, actor; b. Perth, Australia, Apr. 4, 1979; Actor: (films) Clowning Around, 1992, Blackrock, 1997, Paws, 1997, 10 Things I Hate About You, 1999, The Patriot, 2000, A Knight's Tale, 2001, Monster's Ball, 2001, Four Feathers, 2002, The Sin Eater, 2002, Ned Kelly, 2002; (TV series) Ship to Shore, 1993, Sweat, 1996, Home and Away, 1988, Bush Patrol, 1997, numerous TV guest appearances. Mailing: 2222 N Beachwood Dr Apt 408 Los Angeles CA 90068 also: c/o Shanahans Mgmt PO Box 478 Kings Cross NSW 1340 Australia

LEDGERWOOD, THOMAS L. lawyer; b. Pomeroy, Wash., Oct. 27, 1952; s. William Troy and Ann Marie (Roueche) L.; m. Carlyn Louise Davis, June 16, 1979; children: Troy Allen, Kevin Thomas. BA in Polit. Sci., Wash. State U., 1975; JD, U Puget Sound, 1979. Bar: Wash. 1979, U.S. Dist. Ct. (we. dist.) Wash. 1979, U.S. Dist. Ct. (ea. dist.) Wash. 1981. Assoc. Mann, King, Anderson, Bingham & Scraggin, Tacoma, 1979-80, Irwin, Friel, Myklebust, Clarkston, Wash., 1983-85; ptnr. Anderson, Ledgerwood & Anderson, Tacoma, 1980-83; pvt. practice, Clarkston, 1985—. Mem. Wash. State Bar Assn., Asotin County Bar Assn. (pres. 1985), Wash. State Trial Lawyers Assn., Wash. Assn. Criminal Def. Lawyers. Office: 922 6th St Clarkston WA 99403-2079

LEDGIN, NORMAN MICHAEL, writer; b. Passaic, N.J., July 15, 1928; s. Simon George and Helen (Schlegel) L.; m. Harriet Barbara Levine, Oct. 22, 1951 (div. Aug. 1967); children: Stephanie Paula, David Henry, Allison Grace; m. Marsha Maurice Montague, Mar. 4, 1969; children: Alfred Edward, Nicholas Jerome. BL in Journalism, Rutgers U., 1950, MA in Polit. Sci., 1952. Cert. safety coun. exec. Nat. Safety Coun. Reporter, editor The Morning Call, Paterson, N.J., 1952-56; mgr. Calcasieu Area Safety Coun., Lake Charles, La., 1957-62; gen. mgr. Greater Kansas City (Mo.) Area Safety Coun., 1962-76; editor, pub. The Arthur (Ill.) Graphic Clarion, 1976-77; pvt. practice writer Shawnee and Olathe, Kans., 1977-80; editor, pub. The Blue Valley Gazette, Stanley, 1980-84; freelance writer Oxford Twp., 1984—. Media coord. Red Cross/Civil Def., S.W. La., 1960-62; sec. Kansas City Traffic Coordinating Com., 1962-76; chmn. driver improvement adv. com. Nat. Safety Coun., Chgo., 1967-68, chmn. chpt. conf., 1972-73; touring spkr. on autism topics, 2001-. Author: Diagnosing Jefferson, 2000; editor-in-chief The Targum, Rutgers U., 1949-50, Asperger's and Self-Esteem, 2002. Peace appeal sponsor World Peace Congress, Stockholm, 1950; chmn., tour leader Kansas City Youth Symphony, London, Seville, 1968-69; chmn. Dem. Party Ctrl. Com., Johnson County, Kans., 1974-75; clk. Bd. Oxford Twp., Kans., 1984-85. Recipient Flame of Life, Nat. Safety Coun., Chgo., 1963, Disting. Svc. to Safety award Nat. Safety Coun., 1974, Honor award Assn. Safety Coun. Execs., 1974; named Outstanding Young Man of Yr., Jr. C. of C., Lake Charles, 1962. Avocations: history, music, gardening, painting. Home: 15900 Antioch Rd Stilwell KS 66085-9347 E-mail: normledgin@hotmail.com.

LEDGIN, STEPHANIE P. music journalist, educator; b. N.Y.C., Dec. 23, 1952; d. Norman M. and Barbara H. Ledgin; m. Theodoros Toskos, Mar. 1, 1990. BA in Urban Comm. and Cmty. Devel., Rutgers U., 1974. Asst. editor Pickin' Mag., Denville, N.J., 1975-77; writer, prodn. asst. nat. promotions dept. Hadassah, Women's Zionist Orgn. Am., N.Y.C., 1979-81; editl. asst. Hadassah Mag., 1981-82; assoc. editor Convenience Store Merchandiser, 1982-83; editl. adminstrv. asst. L.F. Kimball Rsch. Inst. N.Y. Blood Ctr., 1984-88; editor, pub. The Traditional MusicLine, New Brunswick, N.J., 1987—. Artist mgr. Beppe Gambetta, New Brunswick, 1989-99; lectr. Am. Studies, Rutgers The State U. N.J., New Brunswick, 1994—; dir. N.J. Folk Festival, New Brunswick, 1994—. Co-editor: Hot Licks for Bluegrass Fiddle, 1984; contbr. articles to profl. jours. Pres. Tenants Assn., N.Y.C., 1985-90; publicity coord. Mine St. Coffeehouse, New Brunswick, 1996-99. Recipient Bill Palius award Folk Music Soc. No. N.J., 1992. Mem. Internat. Bluegrass Music Assn., N.Am. Folk Music and Dance Alliance. Democrat. Jewish. Avocations: languages, travel, clog dancing, ballet, cats, bird watching. Office: PO Box 10598 New Brunswick NJ 08906 E-mail: ledgin@fiddlingwithwords.com.

LEDIN, PATRICIA ANN, nurse, nurse legal consultant; b. Downey, Calif., May 6, 1959; d. Clyde Burdette and Estelle Angelina (Acceturo) Bornhurst; m. Scott Richard Ledin, Sept. 9, 1989. BSN, U. Ariz., 1981; postgrad., U. Phoenix, 2000. Cert. electronic fetal monitoring, inpatient obstetrics, ACLS, PALS, NRP; RN Ariz., cert. instr. PALS. Labor and delivery nurse Tucson Med. Ctr., 1981-86, childbirth instr., 1983-95, nurse, mother-baby unit, 1995-97, clin. educator obstetrics, 1986—95, CPR instr., 1986—, learning and devel. specialist, 2001—, clin. nurse specialist, 2001, clin. educator obstetrics, 1997—2001, nurse recruiting, 2002—. Adj. faculty preceptor U. Ariz., Tucson, 1988—; expert witness for legal cases, 1992—; expert reviewer Lifelines mag., 2002-; faculty, Az. Perinatal Edn. Coalition, 2000—. Contbr. articles to profl. jours. Mem. adv. com. March of Dimes, 1991—95; mentor Nat. Cert. Corp., 2001. Bristol-Meyers fellow, 1994. Mem.: Nat. Nursing Staff Devel. Orgn., Assn. Women's Health, Obstet. and Neonatal Nursing (edn. coord. 1991—98, sec.-treas. 1999—2002, Recognition award for fin. budget submission 2001, 2002, award for outstanding performance in fin. responsibility 2001), Beta mu, Omicron Delta, Sigma Theta Tau (chair nominations 2002—). Avocations: water skiing, NASCAR races, boating, travel, aerobics. Office: Tucson Med Ctr 5301 E Grant Rd Tucson AZ 85712-2805

LEDING, ANNE DIXON, artist, educator; b. Fort Smith, Ark., Jan. 29, 1947; d. Charles Victor Dixon and Elizabeth Johanna (Mitchell) Dixon Roderick; m. Larry Joseph Peters (dec), Jan. 6, 1967; m. John Thomas Leding, June 24, 1978; children: Jonathan Brian (Peters) Leding, Caroline Kristen Leding. Student, Memphis State U., Memphis, 1964-66, Westark C.C., Fort Smith, 1976-78. Cert. custom framer. Art instr. Fort Smith (Ark.) Art Ctr., 1976; pvt. practice art instr. Fort Smith, 1977-78; classical guitar instr. Paul Mendy Guitar Studio, 1978-79; framing merchandise mgr. MJDesigns, 1983-98; sr. cert. framer, framing supr. Michael Arts and Crafts, 1999—2001; cert. art instr. Robert Garden Sch. Art, 2002. Cmty. svc. classical guitar instr. Westmark C.C., 1976. One-woman shows include Ariel Gallery, Fort Smith Art Ctr., Cafe Bliss, La Cima Club; group shows include Del Mar Coll., Ariel Gallery, N.Y.C.; featured in Ency. of Living Artists in Am., 1986-87; listed in N.Y. Art Rev., S.W. Art Rev., 1990-91; critiqued in Artspeak, N.Y., 1990. Mentor Grapevine (Tex.) Mid. Sch. Recipient 1st place Fort Smith Sch. Dist., 1955; letter of recognition Seventeen Mag., 1963; hon. mention Fort Smith Art Ctr. Bicentennial, 1976, Del Mar Coll., 1985, Trinity Arts Competition, 1992, Mid Cities Fine Artists Competition, 1994. Mem. Nat. Mus. Women in the Arts, Nat. Watercolor Soc., Am. Watercolor Soc., Dallas Mus. Art, Kimbel Art Mus., Trinity Arts Guild, Ft. Smith Art Ctr., Toastmasters Internat. (advanced toastmaster, v.p. pub. rels. local chpt., 1998-99, 99-2000), Dallas/Ft. Worth Writer's Workshop. Republican. Anglican. Avocations: photography, music. Home and Office: Anne Leding Illustrations 402 Walden Trl Euless TX 76039-3870

LEDLEY, CHRISTIAN SALVESEN, social worker, researcher; b. Edinburgh, Scotland, Aug. 4, 1925; arrived in U.S., 1956, naturalized, 1967; d. John Stephen and Magda Virginie (Salvesen) Elliot; m. Brian Gunning Ledley, Aug. 9, 1958; 1 child, Jean Elliot Ledley. Cert. in social work, U. Edinburgh, 1948; cert. in child welfare, U. Leeds, Eng., 1949; AM in Social Svc. Adminstrn., U. Chgo., 1958. Child care worker Northumberland County Coun., Newcastle, Eng., 1950-56, Chgo. Child Care Soc., 1958-59; vol. social worker Extended Hand Inc., Silver Spring, 1966-77; researcher Montgomery County, Rockville, Md., 1977-79; tenant liaison, researcher Franklin Assocs./Montgomery Oaks Mgmt., Takoma Park, 1979-91. Co-founder Parent Coop. Nursery Sch. Colesville Presbyn. Ch., Md., 1964—65. Developer, coord. Colesville (Md.) Parent Edn. Program, 1966-77; chmn. Cmty. Credit Fund, Colesville, 1966-69; vol. counselor family aid, fin., sr. health ins. program, U. Md. Extension Svc., 1966—; mem. Takoma Park-East Silver Spring Adv. Commn., 1981-92, chmn., 1986-88, vice chmn., 1991-92; mem. Montgomery County Bd. Social Svcs., 1973-79. Cpl. Brit. Army, 1943-46, ETO. Named Outstanding Vol., Channel 7, Washington, 1972; named to honor roll U. Md. Ext. Svc., 1994; recipient svc. awards. Democrat. Presbyterian. Avocations: swimming, snorkeling, gardening. Home: 13108 Venetian Rd PO Box 4026 Silver Spring MD 20914-4026

LEDLEY, FRED DAVID, physician, business executive; b. Washington, Nov. 27, 1954; s. Robert Steven and Terry (Wachtell) L.; m. Tamara Ann Shapiro, June 6, 1976; children: Miriam Esther, Johanna Sharon. BS, U. Md., 1974; MD, Georgetown U., 1978. Intern, resident Harvard Med. Sch., Boston Children's Hosp., Boston, 1978-81; fellow Harvard Med. Sch., MIT, Am. Cancer Soc., 1981-83; asst. investigator Howard Hughes Med. Inst., Houston, 1986-92; asst. prof. Baylor Coll. of Medicine, 1986-89, assoc. prof. cell biology and pediatrics, 1989—; v.p. medicine and sci. found. GeneMedicine, Inc., 1993-96; pres., CEO Variagenics, Inc., Cambridge, Mass., 1996—. Contbr. over 200 articles to profl. sci. jours. Recipient Upjohn Research award Georgetown U., 1978, Charles Janeway award Harvard Med. Sch./Children's Hosp., 1981. Mem. AAAS, Am. Soc. for Human Genetics, Soc. for Pediatrics Rsch. (coun. 1993-96). Office: Variagenics Inc 60 Hampshire St Cambridge MA 02139-1548

LEDLEY, ROBERT STEVEN, biophysicist; b. N.Y.C., June 28, 1928; DDS, NYU, 1948; MA, Columbia U., 1949. Rsch. physicist Columbia U. Radiation Labs., Columbia, 1948—50; instr. physics Columbia U., 1949—50; vis. scientist Nat. Bur. Standards, 1951—52; physicist, 1953—54; ops. rsch. analyst Johns Hopkins U., 1954—56; assoc. prof. elec. engring George Washington U., 1957—60; instr. pediat. Johns Hopkins U., Sch. Medicine, 1960—63; prof. elec. engring. George Washington U., 1968—70; prof. physiology, biophysics & radiology Georgetown U., 1970—; pres., rsch. dir. Nat. Biomed. Rsch. Found., 1960—; pres. Digital Info. Sci. Corp., 1970—75. Named to Nat. Inventor Hall of Fame, 1990; recipient Nat. medal of Tech., U.S. Dept. Commerce, 1997. Mem.: IEEE, Pattern Recognition Soc., N.Y. Acad. Scis., Biophys. Soc., Soc. Math. Biophysics. Office: Georgetown U Nat Biomed Rsch Found 3900 Reservoir Rd NW Washington DC 20007-2188*

LEDLEY, TAMARA SHAPIRO, earth system scientist, climatologist; b. Washington, May 18, 1954; d. Murray Daniel and Ina Harriet (Gordon) Shapiro; m. Fred David Ledley, June 6, 1976; children: Miriam Esther, Johanna Sharon. BS, U. Md., 1976; PhD, MIT, 1983. Rsch. assoc. Rice U., Houston, 1983-85, asst. rsch. scientist, 1985-90, sr. faculty fellow, 1990-98;

assoc. rsch. scientist Tex. A&M U., College Station, 1995-96; sr. scientist TERC, Cambridge, Mass., 1997—; vis. scientist MIT, 1997-98. Alaska SAR facility archive working team NASA, Pasadena, Calif., 1988, McMurdo SAR faculty sci. working team, 1990; participant workshop of Arctic leads initiative Office Naval Rsch., Seattle, 1988, 1st DeLange Conf. on Human Impact on Environ., Houston, 1991; cons. Houston Mus. Natural Sci., 1989—90, Broader Perspectives, Houston, 1989; dir. weather project for tchr. tng. program George Obs., Rice U., 1990—92; co-dir. Rice Houston Mus. Natural Sci. Summer Solar Inst., 1993; mem. Mus. Tchg. Planet Earth Project, 1998—, GLOBE Program, 1998—; vice chmn. standing com. on cmty. engagement Fedn. Earth Sci. Info. Ptnrs., 2000—02, leader edn. cluster, chair standing com. for edn., 2002—; use case export exploring tchg. methods Digital Libr. Earth Sys. Edn., 2000—01, program chair 3d ann. meeting, 2001—02, chair 4th ann. meeting, 2002—; mem. rev. panels NSF, 1993, 95, NASA, 2002. Contbr. articles to profl. jours. Spl. judge Houston Area Sci. and Engring. Fair, 1985; judge S.W. Tex. Region H.S. Debates, 1986, Houston Area Sci. and Engring. Fair, 1990-92, 95; guest expert Great Decisions '88 Polit. Discussion Group, 1988; participant U.S. Global Change Rsch. Program's Climate Modeling Forum, 1994. Fellow sci. computing Nat. Ctr. for Atmospheric Rsch., 1978, Fed. Jr. fellow, 1972-74; senatorial scholar State of Md., 1972-76; grantee NSF, 1985-87, 89—, Tex. Higher Edn. Coordinating Bd., 1988-92, Univ. Space Rsch. Assn., NASA, 1991-94. Mem. AAAS (electorate nominating com. 1995-98), Am. Geophys. Union (com. global environ. change 1993-2000, chmn., 1996-2000, chair panel on climate change and greenhouse gases, pub. info. com. 2000—, assoc. editor Jour. Geophys. Rsch.-Atmospheres 1993-96), Am. Meteorol. Soc., Oceanography Soc., Sigma Xi, Phi Beta Kappa, Phi Kappa Phi, Alpha Lambda Delta. Avocations: reading, tennis, aerobics, hiking. E-mail: tamara_ledley@terc.edu.

LEDOGAR, ROBERT J. planner, researcher; b. N.Y.C., Aug. 3, 1933; s. Edward J. Ledogar and Margaret C. Meany; m. Eleanor Price, Mar. 4, 1972. M of Sacred Liturgy, DTheol, Cath. Inst. Paris, 1964; M of City Planning, MIT, 1973. Dir. Latin Am. project Consumers' Union of U.S., 1973-75; officer UN Ctr. Bldg. for Housing, Building and Planning, N.Y.C., 1975-76; field dir. American Friends Svc. Com., Lusaka, Zambia, 1976-79; program officer UN Children's Fund, Guatemala, 1979-89, sr. planning officer Guatemala, 1989—95; assoc. exec. dir. CIET Internat., 1995—. Vis. prof. Autonomous U. Guerrero, Mex., 1988—; cons. El Puente, Bklyn., 1995—. Author: Acknowledgement: Praise Verbs in the Early Greek Anaphora, 1968, Hungry for Profits, 1975; contbr. articles to profl. jours., including Internat. Jour. Child Rights, Am. Jour. Pub. Health, others. Loula D. Lasker Found. fellow MIT, 1971-73. Mem. APHA, Am. Planning Assn., Planners' Network. Avocation: choral singing. Office: CIETinternat # 132 511 Ave of the Americas New York NY 10011 Fax: 212-242-5453.

LEDOGAR, STEPHEN J. retired diplomat; b. N.Y.C., Sept. 14, 1929; m. Marcia Hubert, Sept. 16, 1967; children: Lucy, Charles. BS, Fordham U., 1954, LLB, 1958. Bar: N.Y. 1959. Surety claims atty. Chubb & Son, N.Y.C., 1954-59; with Fgn. Svc., 1959-97, ret., 1997; press spokesman, U.S. del. Vietnam Peace Talks, Paris, 1967-72; with U.S. Mission to NATO, 1973-76; spl. asst. to undersec. of state, 1976-77; dir. Office of NATO Affairs, 1977-80; mem. State Dept. Senior Seminar, 1980-81; dep. chief of mission U.S. Mission to NATO, Brussels, 1981-87; amb., U.S. rep. European Conventional Stability Negotiations and Mutual and Balanced Force Reductions Talks, 1987-89; amb. and head U.S. Del. to Negotiations on Conventional Armed Forces in Europe, 1989; amb. and U.S. rep. Conference on Disarmament, 1989-97; prin. U.S. negotiator of chem. weapons conv., 1993; prin. negotiator Comprehensive Nuclear Test Ban Treaty, 1996. Lt. USN, 1949-52, USNR, 1954-60 (Naval Aviator). E-mail: hubert.ledogar@verizon.net.

LEDOUX, HAROLD ANTHONY, cartoonist, painter; b. Port Arthur, Tex., Nov. 7, 1926; s. Antoine Ovide and Pauline Zulma (Bernard) LeD.; m. Jeanne Labbe, 1964 (div. 1979); children: Lorraine Marthe, Noelle Pauline. Grad., Thomas Jefferson High Sch., Port Arthur, Tex., 1944; student, Chgo. Acad. Fine Arts, 1948-49. Cartoonist, illustrator N.Am. Syndicate, 1965—. Cartoonist, Famous Funnies, N.Y.C., 1950-53; asst. cartoonist: syndicated comic strip Judge Parker, 1953-65; represented in permanent collection Mus. of Gulf Coast, Port Arthur, Tex., Internat. Mus. Cartoon Art, Boca Raton, Fla. Advisor Council for Devel. of French in La. Served with U.S. Mcht. Marine, 1944-47. Recipient Atlantic War Zone Bar War Shipping Adminstrn. Mem. Nat. Cartoonists Soc., Comics Council, Southwestern Watercolor Soc. Clubs: Alliance Française. Office: 888 7th Ave New York NY 10106-0001 E-mail: hledoux1@airmail.net.

LEDOUX, JOHN CLARENCE, retired law enforcement official; b. Muskogee, Okla., Oct. 19, 1944; s. Clarence Watson and Nedra Ruth (Dayton) LeD.; m. Anne Marie Sommervold, Aug. 8, 1970; children: Matthew Watson, Justin William Clay. BA, U. Md., 1967; M Criminal Justice, Auburn U., 1977, EdD, 1980. Spl. agt. FBI, Albany, N.Y., 1971, Binghamton, 1972, Opelika, Ala., 1972-80, supervisory spl. agt. Quantico, Va., 1980—. Leadership cons., 1999—; prin. Le Doux Leadership; tng. lt. Aguia Harbour Rescue Squad, 1994—; with tng. inst. lab. Dept. Justice, 1996—; vis. lectr. Bramshill (Eng.) Police Coll., 1998, Internat. Law Enforcement Acad., Hungary, 2000; instr. law enforcement, martial arts. Author: (with others) A Study of Factors Influencing the Continuing Education of Law Enforcement Officers, 1982, The Microcomputer Tutor: A Manager's Guide To Personal Computers, 1991, Every Officer a Leader: Transforming Leadership in Police, Justice and Public Safety, 1999; contbg. author: Critical Issues in First Line Supervision: What Law Enforcement Executives Need to Know; editor Law Enforcement Tng. Network, 1983-89. Mem. Stafford County parks and Recreation Commn., Stafford, Va., 1982—, chmn., 1983,85-89, 90, vice chmn., 1998, 99; co-chmn. Stafford Citizens for Parks and Librs., 1989-93; mem. Stafford County Drug Task Force, 1990-92, Aquia Harbor Rescue Squad, 1992-96; EMT FBI Acad., 1990-99; CPR instr., 1993-96; coun. mem. St. Peter's Ch.; chmn. speakers bur. Stafford Citizens for Parks; reading mentor ESL, Stafford County Pub. Schs., 2000—; advisor Stafford Emergency Relief Through Vol. Effort, 1999-2000. Capt. USMC, 1967-71, Vietnam. Recipient Jeffersonian award U. Va., 1982. Mem. Internat. Police Assn., Acad. Criminal Justice Scis., Law Enforcement Martial Arts Assn. (instr. 1987-2000), Assn. for Devel. of Computer-Based Instructional Systems (editor), Internat. Assn. Computer Investigative Specialists, Nat. Recreation and Park Assn., Stafford Recreational Soccer League (coach 1983-86, commr. 1986-90, chmn. referees 1994-96), Rappanahannock Referees Assn., Spotsylvania Soccer Assn. (coach 1987-91). Lutheran. Avocations: Tae Kwan Do, soccer, tennis, magic, golf. E-mail: ledouxleader@earthlink.net.

LEDUC, JEAN-PIERRE LEON, mathematician, educator; b. Jemappes, Hainaut, Belgium, Apr. 20, 1955; s. Jean Leduc and Emilienne Barigand; m. Nicole Angele Ravalinghien. Student., U. Catholique de Louvain, 1980—82; MS, Columbia U., 1987; PhD in Elec. Engring., U. Catholique de Louvain, 1993, M in Theoretical Physics, 1996. Elect. engr. Faculte Polytech. de Mons, Mons, Belgium, 1973—78, ops. rsch. engr. Belgium, 1978—79, tchg. asst. Belgium, 1979—80; sys. engr. SAIT Electronics, Brussels, 1984—86; rschr. U. Cath. de Louvain, Louvain la Neuve, 1987—93, IRISA-INRIA, Rennes, France, 1993—96; vis. rschr. Ga. Inst. Tech., Atlanta, 1996—97, Wash. U., St. Louis, 1997—2000, U. Md., College Park, 2000—. Rschr. Universite Catholique de Louvain, Louvain-la-Neuve, 1987—93, Irisa-inria, Rennes, France (incl. Monaco), 1993—96; vis. rschr. Ga. Inst. of Tech., Atlanta, 1996—97, Wash. U. in St. Louis, Saint Louis, MO., 1997—2000, U. of Md., College Park, MD., 2000—02. Author: (book) Digital Moving Pictures-Coding Algorithms and Transmission on ATM Networks, 1994; contbr. articles. Grantee, European Commn., 1993—96, Rsch. grant, NATO, Belgian Fgn. Office, 1996—98, USAF, 1998—2001. Avocations: travel, opera, violin, art, swimming. Home: 5401 Columbia Rd Apt 936 Columbia MD 21044 Office: Univ Md Dept Math 1301 Mathematics Bldg College Park MD MD 20-4 Office Fax: 301-314-0827. Business E-Mail: jleduc@math.umd.edu.

LEDUC, KAREN LORAIN LEACU, elementary and middle school education educator; b. Ashland, Mass., July 30, 1956; d. John Michael and Eileen Francis (Hill) Leacu; m. Jacques V. LeDuc, Oct. 27, 1979; children: Laura Marie, Jeanne Michelle. BS in Edn., Framingham State Coll., 1978; MEd, Lesley Coll., 1995; PhD in Ednl. Studies, Lesley U., 2002. Cert. elem. educator (K-8), cons. tchr. reading (K-12), middle sch. (5-9), English (5-9), math curriculum dist. coord. (K-8). 6th grade math./reading tchr. Fuller Mid. Sch., Framingham, Mass., 1994-97; literacy specialist grades 6, 7, 8, 1997-99; mentor program facilitator, 1998-99; math curriculum coord. Framingham (Mass.) Pub. Schs., 1999—. Adj. prof. Framingham State Coll., 1996—, Fitchburg State Coll., Lesley Coll., 2000—; strategic planning co-leader Framingham Pub. Schs., 1996, Fuller sch. coun., 1994-98, facilitator, coord. Fuller Family Night, 1997—, Family Math Night, 1996, coach Math Counts, 1995. Religious edn. tchr. St. Cecilia's Ch., Ashland, 1982-96, eucharistic minister, 1977-96. Mem. ASCD, NEA, Nat. Coun. Tchrs. English, Nat. Coun. Tchrs. Maths., Framingham Tchrs. Assn. Roman Catholic. Office: Walsh Middle Sch 301 Brook St Framingham MA 01701-4371 E-mail: kleduc@framingham.k12.ma.us.

LEDUY, ANH, engineering educator; b. Vietnam, Feb. 6, 1946; s. Thach and Tam (BuiThi) LeD.; m. Suzanne Roger, Sept. 24, 1977; children: Isabelle, Dominic. BS in Mech. Engring., U. Sherbrooke, Que., Can., 1969, MS in Chem. Engring., 1972; PhD in Biochem. Engring., U. Western Ont., Can., 1975. Registered profl. engr., Que. Research asst. CNRC Univ. Sherbrooke, Que., Can., 1975-77; asst. prof. chem. engring. Universite Laval, Sainte-Foy, 1977-81, assoc. prof., 1981-85, prof., 1985—. Mem. grant selection coms.; cons. in field. Presenter symposiums, confs. Contbr. numerous articles to profl. jours. Mem. order of Engrs. of Que., N.Y. Acad. Scis. Office: Universite Laval Dept Chem Engring Sainte-Foy QC Canada G1K 7P4

LEDVOROWSKI, THOMAS EDMUND, secondary education educator; b. Milw., Feb. 11, 1960; s. Richard Joseph and Dorthy (Dymerski) L. BS in Math., Mercy Coll., Detroit, 1982; MS in Math. Edn., Purdue U., West Lafayette, Ind., 1985; postgrad., Cath. Theol. Union, Chgo., 1987-89, U. So. Calif. Grad. asst. Purdue U., West Lafayette, 1983-85; tchr. math. Roger Bacon High Sch., Cin., 1986-87; student mem. Franciscan Friars, 1987-89; tchr. math. Chino (Calif.) Unified Sch. Dist., 1985-86, 89-96, dept. chmn., 1993-96, swimming coach, 1991-93; secondary sch. math. mentor tchr., 1994-96; tchr. math. Roosevelt High Sch. N.E. Ind. Sch. Dist., San Antonio, 1996—, chmn. dept., 1999—. Reader Advanced Placement Calculus Exam., 1995, 96, 97, 98, 99, 2000. Mem. Nat. Coun. Tchrs. Math., Am. Math. Assn. Roman Catholic. Avocations: drawing, computers, swimming, photography, travel. Home: 4943 Timber Farm San Antonio TX 78250-4449 Office: T Roosevelt High Sch 5110 Walzem Rd San Antonio TX 78218-2194 E-mail: tledv004@neisd.net.

LEDWIDGE, PATRICK JOSEPH, lawyer; b. Detroit, Mar. 17, 1928; s. Patrick Liam and Mary Josephine (Hooley) L.; m. Rosemary Lahey Mervenne, Aug. 3, 1974; stepchildren: Anne Marie, Mary Clare, John, David, Sara Mervenne. AB, Coll. Holy Cross, 1949; JD, U. Mich., 1952. Bar: Mich. 1952. Assoc. firm Dickinson, Wright, Moon, Van Dusen & Freeman, Detroit, 1956-63; ptnr. Dickinson Wright PLLC, Bloomfield Hills, Mich., 1964—. Served to lt. j.g. U.S. Navy, 1952-55. Mem. Mich. Bar Assn., Detroit Bar Assn., Am. Law Inst. Clubs: Detroit Athletic, Detroit Golf. Roman Catholic. Office: Dickinson Wright PLLC 38525 Woodward Ave Ste 2000 Bloomfield Hills MI 48304-5092 E-mail: pledwidge@dickinson-wright.com.

LEDWIG, DONALD EUGENE, association executive, former broadcasting executive, former naval officer; b. Lubbock, Tex., Mar. 2, 1937; s. Paul Lawrence and Rose Ledwig; m. Gail Wilcox, Jan. 30, 1965; children: Donald Eugene Jr., David W. BS, Tex. Tech U, 1959; MBA, George Washington U., 1973; disting. grad., Naval War Coll., 1977. Commd. ensign USN, 1959, advanced through grades to capt., 1980; ship's officer U.S. Pacific Fleet, 1959-65, 77-79; mem. staff Adm. H.G. Rickover, Nuclear Propulsion Program, 1966-72; dir. contract policy Naval Materiel Command, Washington, 1979-81; dep. comdr. Naval Electronic Sys. Command, 1981-84; ret., 1984; v.p., treas. Corp. for Pub. Broadcasting, Washington, 1984-86, pres., CEO, 1987-92; exec. dir. Am. Prodn. and Inventory Control Soc., Falls Church, Va., 1992-95; pres. Am. Logistics Assn., Washington, 1995-96; COO, Anchor Mental Health Assn., 1997-98; cons. Assn. Mgmt., 1998—. Sec., Alexandria (Va.) Electoral Bd., 2000—. Decorated Legion of Merit; recipient Barrow Meml. award Hastings Coll. Law, 1989, award Nat. Captioning Inst., 1990, Disting. Alumnus award Tex. Tech U., 1992. Mem. Am. Legion, Nat. Press Club, Army-Navy Country Club.

LEDWITH, JOHN FRANCIS, lawyer; b. Phila., Oct. 3, 1938; s. Francis Joseph and Jane Agnes (White) L.; m. Mary Evans, Aug. 28, 1965; children: Deirdre A., John E. AB, U. Pa., 1960, JD, 1963. Bar: Pa. 1965, N.Y. 1984, U.S. Dist. Ct. (ea. dist.) Pa. 1965, U.S. Ct. Appeals (3d cir.) 1965, U.S. Supreme Ct. 1970. Assoc. Joseph R. Thompson, Phila., 1965-71; mem. Schubert, Mallon, Wallheim & deCindis, 1971-81, LaBrum & Doak, Phila., 1981-95, Marshall, Denchey, Warner, Coleman & Goggins, Phila., 1995—. Author: (with others) Philadelphia CP Trial Manual, 1982. Bd. dirs. Chestnut Hill Cmty. Assn., Pa., 1975-76. With USCG, 1963-71. Mem. ABA, Pa. Bar Assn., Phila. Bar Assn., Def. Rsch. Inst., Fedn. Ins. Corp. Coun., Racquet Club (Phila.), Phila. Cricket Club, Avalon Yacht Club (commodore 1982). Republican. Roman Catholic. Office: Marshall Dennehey Warner Coleman & Goggins 1845 Walnut St Philadelphia PA 19103-4708

LEDYARD, JOHN ODELL, economics educator, consultant; b. Detroit, Apr. 4, 1940; s. William Hendrie and Florence (Odell) L.; m. Bonnie Higginbottom, May 23, 1970; children: Stephen, J. Henry, Meg. BA, Wabash Coll., 1963; PhD, Purdue U., 1967; PhD (hon.), Purdue U./Ind. U., 1993. Asst. prof. Carnegie-Mellon U., Pitts., 1967-70; prof. Northwestern U., Evanston, Ill., 1970-85, Calif. Inst. Tech., Pasadena, 1985—, exec. officer for social sci., 1989-92, chmn. div. humanities and social scis., 1992—2002. Contbr. articles to profl. jours. Fellow Am. Acad. Arts and Scis., Econometric Soc.; mem. Pub. Choice Soc. (pres. 1980-82), Econ. Sci. Assn. (exec. com. 1986-88). Office: Calif Inst Tech Dept HHS Pasadena CA 91125-0001

LEDYARD, ROBINS HEARD, lawyer; b. Nashville, Oct. 14, 1939; s. Quitman Robins and Alma Elizabeth (Stevenson) L.; m. Julia Bordeaux Gambill, Dec. 19, 1962; children: Stevenson Gambill, Quitman Robins II, Margaret Dabney. BA, Vanderbilt U., 1965, JD, 1966. Bar: Tenn. 1966, U.S. Supreme Ct. 1975. Atty. Nat. Life & Accident Ins. Co., Nashville, 1966-68, asst. counsel, 1968-69, assoc. counsel, 1969-70, counsel, 1970-72, assoc. gen. counsel, 1972-75, gen. counsel, 1975-80; partner Bass, Berry & Sims, 1980—. Tchr. C.L.U.s, 1967-75 Asst. editor: Vanderbilt Law Rev., 1965-66; contbr. articles to profl. jours. Active United Way, Nashville, 1967— , Heart Fund, 1970-73; vice chmn. United Diocesan Givers, 1975; bd. dirs. St. Thomas Hosp., 1990—. With USMC, 1958-61. Recipient Bennett Douglas Bell Meml. prize, 1966; Marr scholar, 1965-66 Mem. ABA, Am. Coun. Life Ins. (chmn. tax com. 1978-80), Assn. Life Ins. Counsel (chmn. tax com. 1979-80), Tenn. Bar Assn., Nashville Bar Assn., Internat. Assn. Ins. Counsel, Global Leaders for the South, Order of Coif, Phi Delta Phi, Alpha Tau Omega. Clubs: Belle Meade Country, Capitol of Nashville, KC. Democrat. Roman Catholic. Home: 1215 Chickering Rd Nashville TN 37215-4519 Office: 2700 First American Ctr Nashville TN 37238

LEE, ADRIAN ISELIN, JR. journalist; b. Miami, Fla., Nov. 6, 1920; s. Adrian Iselin and Adriana Lanier (Owen) L.; m. Marie Lainé Santa Maria, Oct. 14, 1950; children: Adrian Iselin III, Catherine Taney, Thomas Sim, William Owen, Anne Marie, Louisa Carrell. BA, Spring Hill Coll., Mobile, Ala., 1943. With The Bulletin, Phila., 1948—, gen. assignment reporter, 1960-82, editorial writer, 1967-72, columnist op-ed page, 1972-82; with Phila. Daily News, 1982-88; speech and op-ed writer U.S. Atty. Gen. Edwin Meese III, 1988-89; writer CBS Radio News, 1989-90. Tchr. editorial writing, dept. journalism Temple U. Active Chestnut Hill Community Assn. Lt. (j.g.) USNR, 1943-46, PTO. Decorated Navy Unit Commendation medal. Mem. Nat. Press Club, Pen and Pencil Club, Phila. Press Assn. (prize for coverage John F. Kennedy assassination 1963), Sigma Delta Chi (prize for column writing 1978) Republican. Roman Catholic. Home and Office: 20 Haws Ln Flourtown PA 19031-2048

LEE, ALDORA G. social psychologist; b. Schenectady, N.Y. d. Alois W. and M. Dorothy (Swigert) Graf. AB, Ind. U.; MA, Stanford U.; PhD, U. Colo. Dir. women studies Wash. State U., Pullman, 1976-78, dir. unit on aging, 1976-81; cons. in market research Syva, Palo Alto, Calif., 1982; staff market rsch. analyst Allstate Rsch. and Planning Ctr., Menlo Park, 1983—. Rep. Wash. Assn. Gerontol. Edn., N.W. region rep. Nat. Women's Studies Assn., 1978-81. Contbr. articles to profl. jours. Mem. Menlo Park Libr. Commn., 1984-92, chmn., 1985-87; instr. Career Action Ctr., Palo Alto, 1984-87; Menlo Park rep. system adv. bd. Peninsula Libr. System, 1992-97; mem. Allstate Found. Com., San Francisco Bay area, 1993-94, No. Calif., 1995-97; libr. reference assoc. vol. Health Libr. Sr. Ctr., Palo Alto, Calif., 1997-98, Health Libr. at Stanford, Palo Alto, 1999—. Recipient Allstate Good Hands award for Cmty. Svc., 1994, 96, 2000. Mem. Am. Mktg. Assn., Am. Psychol. Soc., Am. Sociol. Assn., SRI Organon Toastmasters (Toastmaster of Yr. 1989, Able Toastmaster, Competent Toastmaster, mentor GeoSpeakers 1994, Advanced Toastmaster-Silver, mentor DESperados Toastmasters 2000), Phi Beta Kappa, Sigma Xi.

LEE, ALEXANDRA SAIMOVICI, civil engineer; b. Negrest, Vaslui, Romania, Nov. 6, 1932; came to U.S., 1969; d. Leonidas and Etlea (Schreibman) Saimovici; m. Jack Lee, July 14, 1972. Grad. in constrn. engring., Constrn. Inst., Bucharest, Romania, 1956. Registered profl. engr., S.C. Structural engr. Energo Constructia, Bucharest, 1956-61, Elcora Constrn. Metalicas, Buenos Aires, 1961-69, Walter Kidde, N.Y.C., 1969-70, John Kassner, N.Y.C., 1970-72; civil engr. I, City of Columbia, S.C., 1972-77, design engr., 1977-82, civil engr. II, 1982—. Mem. NSPE, Am. Pub. Works Assn. Home: 45 Longwood Ave Apt 604 Brookline MA 02446-5217 Office: City of Columbia PO Box 147 Columbia SC 29202-0147

LEE, ALFRED THEODORE, research psychologist; b. Port Washington, Wis., June 25, 1946; s. Alfred and Gladys (Loomis) L. BA cum laude Psychology, San Jose State U., 1972, MA in Exptl. Psychology, 1974; PhD in Exptl. Psychology, U. Calif.-Riverside, 1979. Lic. pvt. pilot. Rsch. scientist U. Dayton (Ohio), 1979-82, NASA-Ames Rsch. Ctr., Moffett Field, Calif., 1983-90; pres. Beta Rsch., Inc., Los Gatos, 1990—. Lectr. U. Calif., 1978, teaching asst., 1974-78; rsch. cons. U.S. Dept. Justice, 1978-79, VA, 1978; rsch. asst. San Jose State U., 1972-74. Contbr. articles to profl. jours. Sgt. USAF, 1964-68. Regents fellow U. Calif., 1979. Mem. APA, Human Factors Soc., Assn. of Computing Machinery. Avocations: flying, skiing. Office: 18379 Main Blvd Los Gatos CA 95033-8391 E-mail: info@beta-research.com.

LEE, ALLAN WREN, clergyman; b. Yakima, Wash., June 3, 1924; s. Percy Anson and Agnes May (Wren) L.; m. Mildred Elaine Ferguson, June 16, 1946; 1 dau., Cynthia Ann. BA, Phillips U., Enid, Okla., 1949; MA, Peabody Coll. Tchrs., 1953; B.D., Tex. Christian U., 1955, D.D. (hon.), 1968. Ordained minister Christian Ch. (Disciples of Christ), 1949; pastor chs. in Tex. and Wash., 1955-60, 90—; gen. sec. World Conv. Chs. of Christ, Dallas, 1971-92; mem. gen. bd. Christian Ch., 1971-73; pres. Seattle Christian Ch. Missionary Union, 1964-66, Wash.-No. Idaho Conv. Christian Chs., 1966; pastor Park Ave Christian Ch., N.Y.C., 1999. TV panel mem. Am. Religious Town Hall, 1988-97. Author: Bridges of Benevolence, 1962, Wit and Wisdom, 1963, The Burro and the Bibles, 1968, Under the Shadow of the Nine Dragons, 1969, Reflections Along the Reef, 1970, Disciple Down Under, 1971, Meet My Mexican Amigos, 1972, One Great Fellowship, 1974, Fifty Years of Faith and Fellowship, 1980, Recollections of a Dandy Little Up-to-Date Town, 1985, also articles. Bd. trustees N.W. Christian Coll., Eugene, Oreg., 1985-93; bd. dirs. Melissa Pub. Libr., 1992-94, I.H.S. Hosp., 1998—. With USNR, 1943-46. Recipient Disting. Service citation Children's Home Soc. Wash., 1967, Disting. Service award Bremerton Jaycees, 1959; Jamaica Tourist Bd. citation, 1984 Mem. Disciples of Christ Hist. Soc. (founder, life mem.), Religious Conv. Mgrs. Assn. (v.p. 1972-92), Am. Bible Soc. (nat. adv. coun. 1985-94). Home and Office: 4242 Lomo Alto Dr Apt S37 Dallas TX 75219-1573 *I make every effort to live a life patterned after the life and teachings of the Man of Nazareth, Jesus Christ— that is, to be compassionate, understanding, peaceful and loving.*

LEE, ALVIN A. literary educator, scholar, author; b. Woodville, Ont., Can., Sept. 30, 1930; s. Norman Osborne and Susanna Elizabeth (Found) L.; m. Hope Arnott, Dec. 21, 1957 (dec.); children: Joanna, Monika, Fiona, Alison, Margaret. BA, U. Toronto, Ont., Can., 1953, MA in English, 1958, PhD, 1961; M.Div., Victoria U., Toronto, 1957. Teaching fellow in English U. Toronto, 1957-59; asst. prof. English McMaster U., Hamilton, Ont., 1960-65, assoc. prof., 1966-70, prof., 1970-92, prof. emeritus, 1990—, asst. dean Sch. Grad. Studies, 1968-71, dean Sch. Grad. Studies, 1971-73, acad. v.p., 1974-79, pres., vice-chancellor, 1980-90, pres. emeritus, 1994—; Northrop Frye prof. literary theory U. Toronto, 1992, rsch. assoc. Victoria Coll., 1997—. Mem. Western Ont. coun. Conf. Bd. Can., 1983-90; mem. adv. bd. Medieval and Renaissance History, 1991—. Author: James Reaney, Twayne's World Authors Series, 49, 1968, The Guest-Hall of Eden: Four Essays on the Design of Old English Poetry, 1972, Gold-Hall and Earth-Dragon: 'Beowulf' as Metaphor, 1999; editor: (with Hope Arnott Lee) Wishing and Nightmare, 1972, Circle of Stories: One, 1972, Two, 1972, The Garden and the Wilderness, 1973, The Temple and the Ruin, 1973, The Peaceable Kingdom, 1974; (with Robert D. Denham) The Legacy of Northrop Frye, 1994; gen. editor: McMaster Old English Studies and Texts, 1982-92, Collected Works of Northrop Frye, 1995—; editl. bd. English Studies in Canada, 1982-88; contbr. articles to profl. jours. Trustee, mem. exec. com. Chedoke-McMaster Hosps., 1980-90; mem. Community Edn. Coordinating Com., 1981-90; mem. Council Ont. Univs., 1980-90, vice chmn., 1981-83, chmn., 1983-85, mem. exec. com., 1981-87; mem. Health Scis. Liaison Com., 1980-90; dir. Council Ont. Univ. Holdings Ltd., 1981-90; mem. chancellors coun. Victoria U., U. Toronto, 1983—; hon. bd. dirs. Operation Lifeline, Hamilton, 1980-90; hon. Patron Opera Hamilton, 1982-90; vice chmn. bd., mem. exec. com. Royal Bot. Gardens, Hamilton, 1980-90, chmn. provincial and fed. relations com., 1981-90, vice chmn. sci. and ednl. com., 1981-90, mem. nominating com., 1981-90; vice chmn. bus. adv. conf. Regional Municipality of Hamilton-Wentworth, 1983-90; chmn. fund-raising liaison com. McMaster Hosps. Found/McMaster U., 1983-90; hon. patron Edn. Found. of Fedn. Chinese Can. Profls., Ont., 1984-90; mem., vice chair Can. Merit Scholarship Found., 1990-93; bd. dirs. Art Gallery Hamilton, 1991-94; mem. adminstrn. bd. McMaster Mus. Art. Mem. MLA, Mediaeval Acad. Am., Assn. Univs. and Colls. Can. (coun. univ. pres. 1980-90), Hamilton Assn. Advancement Lit., Sci. and Art (hon. pres. 1980-88), Can. Inst. Advanced Rsch., Internat. Assn. Anglo-Saxonists, Corporate-Higher Edn. Forum, McMaster U. Alumni Coun. (hon. pres. 1980-90), McMaster U. Letterman's Assn. (hon.), Hamilton and Dist. C. of C. (dir., mem. program com. 1982-87, Hamilton Gallery of Distinction 1996—). Office: McMaster U 1280 Main St W Hamilton ON Canada L8S 4L9

LEE, ANN MCKEIGHAN, curriculum specialist; b. Harlan, Iowa, Nov. 18, 1939; d. Earl Edward and Dorothy Elizabeth (Kaufman) McK.; m. Duane Edward Compton, Aug. 13, 1960 (div. 1985); children: Kathleen, David, Anne-Marie, John. Cert. in med. tech., Creighton U., 1960; BA in Art History, Ind. U., 1984; MA, U. South Fla., 1992, PhD, 2002. Cert. secondary tchr., Fla.; cert. med. technologist. Realtor Savage/Landrian Realty, Indpls., 1978-84; lectr. Marian Coll., 1987-88; tchr. Sarasota (Fla.) County Schs., 1989-92, rep. faculty coun., 1991-92; lectr. curriculum & instrn. U. South Fla., 1993—. Vis. prof. U. South Fla., 2001—; docent Historic Spanish Point, Osprey, Fla., 1989—93, Ringling Mus. Art, 1993—; presenter panel Bibliographic Instrn. Art History. Contbr. articles to profl. jours. V.p. fin. LWV, Indpls., 1971-73; v.p. dist. IV aux. ADA, 1976-78, comptroller, 1978-89; coord. Gold Coun. and Ambs. U. South Fla., 1990-92. Recipient Silver Svc. award Crossroads Guild, 1981. Mem.: Sarasota Arts Coun., Gulf Coast Heritage Assn. (ch-chmn. pub. rels.), Soc. Archtl. Historians (tchr. rep. 1990), Coll. Art Assn., Phi Delta Kappa, Phi Kappa Phi. Roman Catholic. Avocations: photography, tennis, landscape architecture, swimming. Home and Office: 3617 Shady Brook Ln Sarasota FL 34243-4840

LEE, ANNE MARIE, endocrinologist; b. Macau, China, Sept. 25, 1963; came to U.S., 1964; BS, U. Fla., 1985; MD, U. South Fla., 1989. Diplomate Am. Bd. Internal Medicine, Am. Bd. Endocrinology, Diabetes and Metabolism. Int., res. int. med. Mercer Univ. Sch. of Med., Macon, GA, 1989-92; fellshp. in endocrinology Cleveland Clin., 1992-94; endocrinologist Health Ptnrs., Mpls., 1994-96, 98—, Asthabula (Ohio) Clinic, 1996-98. Avocation: tennis. Office: Health Ptnrs 2220 Riverside Ave Minneapolis MN 55454-1321 E-mail: Anne.M.Lee@Healthpartners.com.

LEE, ARTHUR VIRGIL, III, biotechnology company executive; b. Detroit, Nov. 24, 1920; s. Arthur Virgil and Emily S. (Burry) L.; m. Elizabeth Hoppin Chafee, Dec. 8, 1945 (div.); children: Arthur C., Sherrill Ann Rosoff, William J., Henry C.; m. Jean Austin LaMothe, Dec. 30, 1967. BA, Williams Coll., 1942; Indsl. Adminstr. (World War II MBA), Harvard Bus. Sch., 1943. With McKesson & Robbins, Inc., Memphis, 1946-47, ops. mgr. Providence div., 1947-63, v.p., mgr. Providence div., 1954-59, with Boston div., 1959-63, with Pitts. div., 1963; asst. dean Harvard U. Bus. Sch., Cambridge, Mass., 1964-65, dir. corp. rels., 1965-72, dir. resources, 1972-73; v.p. Lesley Coll., 1973-77; dir. corp. rels. Tufts U., Medford, Mass., 1977-79; pres. Biotec Internat., Ltd., Williamstown, 1979-95. Bd. dirs. New Eng. Drug Exchange, 1956-63; trustee Am. Coll. Switzerland, 1978-82, Williamstown Theatre Festival, 1984-94, trustee emeritus, 1994—; mem. Weston Town Fin. Com., 1961-66; mem. adv. bd. Coll. Pharmacy, U. R.I., 1957-58. Lt. USNR, 1942-46. Mem. Taconic Golf Club, Yeamans Hall Club (Charleston, S.C.), Alpha Delta Phi. Congregationalist. Home and Office: PO Box 488 Williamstown MA 01267-0488

LEE, B. KYUN, mechanical engineer, educator; b. Taegu, Kyung-Boog, Republic of Korea, Sept. 20, 1952; came to U.S., 1982; s. Jung-Ha and Il-Jin (Kim) L.; m. Misook Park, Oct. 3, 1980; children: Eun-Gi, Nathan. BSME, Young-Nam U., Taegu, 1980; MSME, Oreg. State U., 1984; MA, N.W. Christian Coll., 1988; PhD, Oreg. State U., 1988; MDiv, New Orleans Bapt. Theol. Sem., 1994. Registered profl. engr., Tex. R&D engr. Hyun-Dai Motor Co., Ulsan, Republic of Korea, 1980-82; engr. Evanite Fiber Co., Corvallis, Oreg., 1987-88; assoc. prof. LeTourneau U., Longview, Tex., 1988—; pastor Sae-Nu-Ree Ch., Dae Jeon City, Republic of Korea, 1996-99. Prin. investigator Colt Friction Products, Longview, 1989-90; co-investigator GRACO Children's Products, 1990-91; cons. Stemco Co., Longview, 1990-91; prin. investigator Capacity of Tex., Longview, 1991-94; researcher LeTourneau U., Longview, 1988-96. Author sci. papers. Mem. ASME, Am. Soc. Engring. Edn., Soc. Mfg. Engr., Phi Kappa Phi. Baptist. Avocations: tennis, soccer. Home: 1400 HG Mosley #811 Longview TX 75604 Office: LeTourneau U PO Box 7001 Longview TX 75607-7001

LEE, BARBARA, congresswoman; BA, Mills Coll., 1973; M in Social Welfare, U. Calif. Berkeley, 1976. Rep. Calif. State Assembly, 1990-96; mem. Calif. State Sen., 1996-98, U.S. Congress from 9th Calif. dist., Washington, 1998—; mem. fin. svcs. com., internat. rels. com. Democrat. Office: US Ho Reps 426 Cannon Ho Office Bldg Washington DC 20515-0001*

LEE, BARBARA MAHONEY, career officer, educator; b. Roanoke, Va., July 25, 1942; d. Archer W. and Marie Adeline (Gray) Mahoney; m. Walter Kenneth Lee, Aug. 5, 1956 (div. 1969); children: Kenneth Michael, Alan David. AS, Va. Western C.C., Roanoke, 1970; BA, Hollins (Va.) Coll., 1972; MS, Va. Commonwealth U., Richmond, 1979; postgrad., Am. U. Commd. ed lt. U.S. Army, 1973, advanced through grades to col., 1995; asst. prof. U.S. Mil. Acad., West Point, N.Y., 1979-83; orgnl. effectiveness staff officer Army Materiel Command, Alexandria, Va., 1983-88, Cong. liaison officer, 1988-90; v.p. human resources INTEGRATEC, Inc., Atlanta, 1990-92; orgnl. devel. cons. in pvt. practice, 1992-93; mil. asst. U.S. Army, Pentagon, Washington, 1993—2002; ret. USAR. Decorated Legion of Merit. Mem.: Alliance for Nat. Def., Am. Sociol. Assn., Women in Internat. Security (exec. bd. 1999—), Alpha Kappa Delta. Episcopalian. Home: 11957 Holly View Dr Woodbridge VA 22192-1040

LEE, BETTY REDDING, architect; d. Joseph Alsop and Mary (Byrd) Redding; m. Frank Cayce Lee, Nov. 22, 1940 (dec. Aug. 1978); children: Cayce Redding, Clifton Monroe, Mary Byrd (Mrs. Kent Ray). Student La. State U., 1936-37, 37-38, U. Calif. War Extension Coll., San Diego, 1942-43; sudent Centernary Coll., 1937; attended Roofing Industry Ednl. Inst., 1980-82, 84, 86-88, 89-90, 93, Better Understanding Roofing Sys. Inst., 1989. Sheetmetal worker Consol. Vultee, San Diego, 1942; engring. draftsman, 1943-45; jr. to sr. archtl. draftsman Bodman & Murrell, Baton Rouge, 1954-55; sr. archtl. draftsman to architect Post & Harelson, Baton Rouge, 1955-58; assoc. arch. G. Ross Murrell, Jr., Baton Rouge, 1960-66; staff arch. Charles E. Schwing & Assocs., Baton Rouge, 1966-71, Kenneth C. Landry, Baton Rouge, 1971, 73-74; engring., design draftsman Rayner & McKenzie, Baton Rouge, 1972-73; cons. arch. and planner Office Engring. and Cons. Svcs., La. Dept. Health and Human Resources, Baton Rouge, 1974-82; sr. arch. roofing and waterproofing sect. La. Dept. Facility Planning and Control, 1982-96; pvt. consulting practice, Baton Rouge, 1996—; Betty Redding Lee, Architect, 1996; Author Instructions to Designers for Roofing Systems for Louisiana Public Buildings: co-author: Building Owners Guide for Protecting and Maintaining Built-up Roofing Systems, 1981; designed typical La. country store for La. Arts and Sci. Ctr. Mus. Recipient Honor award Schuller/Johns Manville BURSI Group, 1989, 90, 91, 92, 93. Mem. La. Assn. Children with Learning Disabilities, 1967-69, Multiple Sclerosis Soc., 1963—, CPA Aux., 1960-69, PTA, 1953-66; troop leader Brownies and Girl Scouts U.S.A., 1959-60; asst. den mother Cub Scouts, 1955-57. Licensed architect. Mem. ASTM, Nat. AIA, AIA La., AIA Baton Rouge (first Shreveport & Baton Rouge, La. woman architect), DAR, Roofing Industry Ednl. Inst. Alumni Assn. (charter mem.), Constrn. Specifications Inst.(charter mem. Baton Rouge chpt.), Roof Cons. Inst. (profl. mem.), Roof Cons. Inst. (profl. mem.), Jr. League Baton Rouge, Kappa Delta. Republican. Episcopalian. E-mail: brlee@worldnet.att.net. Home: 881 Kenmore Ave Baton Rouge LA 70806-5521 Office: 225 Kenmore Ave Baton Rouge LA 70806

LEE, BEVERLY ING, educational administrator; b. Honolulu, Oct. 10, 1932; d. Tim Sheu and Helen (Heu) Ing; m. Daniel David Lee, June 21, 1962; children: Helen Ann, Terence Daniel, Scott David. BA, Coll. of the Pacific, Stockton, Calif., 1954; MA, Columbia U., 1957. Policewoman Honolulu Police Dept., 1957-61; counselor Ewa Elem., Highlands Intermediate and Waipahu High Schs., 1961-69; adminstr. Dept. Edn. State of Hawaii, Honolulu, 1969-89; contr., v.p., pres. Classic Travel, 1988—. Bd. dirs. Hawaii State Employees Credit Union, Honolulu, vice chair, 1994, chair, 1995, chairperson, 2000—; bd. dirs. Mahalo Airport Travel Agy.; mem. adv. bd. Travel Univ. Internat. Adv. Bd., 1994—. Mem. Gov.'s Commn. on Child Abuse, Honolulu, 1985-89; bd. dirs. Hawaii Family Stress Ctr., Honolulu, 1983—, Child and Family Svc., 1975-85; mem. Casey Family Program Adv. Com., 1986—, Parents Anonymous, 1988-92, Prevent Child Abuse Hawaii, 1975—. Mem. AAUW (life), Hawaiian Airlines Travel Agy. (adv. bd. 1991-93), Mahalo Airlines Travel Agy. (adv. bd. 1994—), Travel U. Internat. (adv. bd. 1994—), Casey Family (adv. bd. 1986—), Prevent Child Abuse Hawaii (bd. dir. 1975—), Child & Family Svcs. (bd. dir. 1975-85), Delta Kappa Gamma, Tri Delta. Avocations: travel, plants, photography.

LEE, BLAINE NELSON, executive consultant, educator, author; b. Olympia, Wash., Apr. 3, 1946; s. Elwyn Earl and Thelma Marie (Woods) Reeder; m. Shawny Christian Lee; children: Blaine, Benjamin, Adam, Michal, Joseph, Joshua, Casey, Abraham, Eliza, Gabriel, Celeste, Isaac. BS in Psychology, Brigham Young U., Provo, Utah, 1969, MS in Ednl. Psychology, 1972; PhD in Ednl. Psychology, U. Tex., 1982. Cert. ednl. specialist, secondary edn., ednl. adminstrn. Dir. instrnl. sys. USAF, San Antonio, 1972-75; assoc. prof. USAF Acad., Colorado Springs, Colo., 1975-78; edn. dir. Heritage Sch., Provo, Utah, 1978-81; asst. prof. Utah Valley State Coll., Orem, 1981-84; pres. Skills for Living, Salem, 1984-86; v.p. Covey Leadership Ctr., Provo, 1986-97, Franklin Covey Co., Provo, 1997—. Cons. in field. Author: Affective Objectives, 1972, Personal Change, 1982, Stress Strategist, 1986, Principle Centered Leadership, 1990, Power Principle: Influence with Honor, 1997; contbr. articles to profl. jours. High councilman LDS Ch., mem. gen. bd., 1970-72; pres. Provo PTO. Named one of Outstanding Young Men of Am., U.S. C. of C., 1976, 84. Mem. APA, ASTD, Am. Mgmt. Assn., Nat. Spkrs. Assn., Phi Delta Kappa. Avocations: cmty. theatre, choir dir., camping, poetry, soccer coach. Office: Franklin Covey Co 360 W 4800 N Provo UT 84604-5675 Home: 837 S 1700 E Salem UT 84653-8528

LEE, BRANT THOMAS, lawyer, federal official, educator; b. San Francisco, Feb. 17, 1962; s. Ford and Patricia (Leong) L.; m. Marie Bernadette Curry, Sept. 20, 1991. BA in Philosophy, U. Calif., Berkeley, 1985; JD, Harvard U., 1990, M in Pub. Policy, 1994. Bar: Calif. 1992. Counsel subcom. on Constitution, U.S. Senate Judiciary Com., Washington, 1990-92; assoc. Breon, O'Donnell, Miller, Brown & Dannis, San Francisco, 1992-96; dep. staff sec., spl. asst. to Pres. (acting) The White House, Washington, 1993; vis. asst. prof. Syracuse (N.Y.) U. Coll. Law, 1996-97; asst. prof. U. Akron (Ohio) Sch. Law, 1997-2001, assoc. prof., 2001—. Commr. San Francisco Ethics Commn., 1995-96. Bd. dirs., Asian Svcs. in Action, Inc., Akron, 1998—; trustee Chinese for Affirmative Action, San Francisco, 1992-96; bd. dirs. Conf. Asian Pacific Am. Leadership, Washington, 1990-92; staff mem. Dukakis for Pres., Boston, 1988. Mem. ABA, Nat. Asian Pacific Am. Bar Assn. E-mial. Office: U Akron Sch Law Akron OH 44325-0001 E-mail: btlee@uakron.edu.

LEE, BRUCE, editor, writer; b. N.Y.C., Dec. 3, 1930; s. Edward Brooke and Thelma Llewellyn (Lawson) Lee; m. Nancy Faye Hatch, Sept. 28, 1958 (div. Aug. 15, 1980); children: Evalyn Brooke, Bruce Hatch; m. Janetta M MacPherson of Cluny, Mar. 21, 1981. BA, Rollins Coll., Winter Park, Fla., 1954; MFA, Fordham U., 1959. Reporter Adirondack Daily Enterprise, Saranac Lake, NY, 1952—53, N.Y. Daily News, 1954; assoc. editor Newsweek, N.Y.C., 1954—61; Washington corr. Reader's Digest, Washington, 1961—65, assoc. editor N.Y.C., 1965—66, sr. editor, 1966—72; editor-in-chief Reader's Digest Press, 1972—78; sr. editor McGraw Hill Gen. Book Divsn., 1978—82, William Morrow & Co., N.Y.C., 1982—90; author, 1990—. Chmn. bd, Lee Devel. Group, Silver Spring, Md., 1990—95; gen. ptnr. Montgomery Land LLP, Silver Spring, 1981—. Author: (Book) The Boy's Life of John F. Kennedy, 1962, Marching Orders: The Untold Story of World War II, 1995; co-author: Pearl Harbor: Final Judgement, 1992; editor: Bearing The Cross: The Biography of Martin Luther King, Jr., 1997 (Pulitzer prize, 1997). SPE5 NY Nat. Guard USAR, 1954—60. Recipient award for advancing knowledge of cryptogrphic history, Nat. Security Agy., Fort Meade, Md., 1995. Mem.: Royal Northern and Clyde Yacht Club, Royal Yacht Squadron, New York Yacht Club, Seawanhaka Corinthian Yacht Club. Home and Office: 115 E 67th St New York NY 10021

LEE, BURNS WELLS, public relations executive; b. St. Louis, July 21, 1913; s. Channing B. and Rae (Wells) L.; m. Pauline Slocum, Apr. 10, 1939 (div.); m. Kathleen Booth Strutt, July 1, 1960. AB, Occidental Coll., 1935. Publicity dir. Benton & Bowles, Inc., N.Y.C., Hollywood, 1939-42; sr. specialist war savs. staff Treasury Dept., Washington, 1942-43; pub. relations mgr. Rexall Drug Co., Los Angeles, 1946-49; pres. Bergen & Lee/ Pub. Rels., 1949-95. Served as pub. relations officer USMCR, 1943-46. Mem. Pub. Rels. Soc. Am. (bd. dirs. 1949-54, chmn. com. standards of profl. practice 1951, regional v.p. 1952-53, chmn. pub. rels. reference round table 1954-55, chmn. eligibility com. 1962, chmn. grievance bd. 1965-66, chmn. spl. task force on pub. rels. 1975-77, 1st ann. professionalism award L.A. chpt. 1964), Regional Plan Assn. So. Calif. (dir., chmn. pub. rels. com. 1967-70), Central City Assn. (dir. 1971-84), L.A. C. of C. (chmn. pub. rels., bus. outlook conf. 1974, mem. exec. com., internat. commerce coun. 1979-83, 85-89), GrandPeople (L.A., mem. bd. dirs. 1988-92), Exec. Svc. Corps. (cons. L.A. chpt. 1991-98), Publicity Club L.A., Rotary L.A. (editor monthly publ. 1993-99). Home: 1428 S Marengo Ave # 26 Alhambra CA 91803-3001

LEE, CANDIE CHING WAH, retail executive; b. Hong Kong, British Crown Colony, June 17, 1950; came to U.S., 1973:; d. Willard W. and Yuk Ching (Yau) L. Student, Hong Kong Tech. Coll., Kowloon, 1968-70. Office mgr. Crown Enterprises, Ltd., Hong Kong, 1970-73; buyer, mgr. Hawaii Resort Industries, Inc., Honolulu, 1973-76, v.p., 1976-82; pres. Hawaii Resort Shops, Inc., 1983—. Mem. Am. Mgmt. Assn., Oahu Country Club. Republican. Avocation: reading. Office: Hawaii Resort Shops Inc 468 Ena Rd Honolulu HI 96815-1734

LEE, CARL, statistician, educator; b. Chia-I, Taiwan, June 15, 1954; s. Chin-Fei and Yei-Yin Lee; m. Ye-Fu Kao; 1 child Marcia 1 child Grace 1 child Michale. PhD, Iowa State U., 1984. Assoc. prof. Ctrl. Mich. U., 1988—92, prof. stats., 1992—, univ. assessment coord., 1999—2001; vis. assoc. prof. Nat. Ctrl. U., Taiwan, 1990—91. Expert statistician Teltech Resource Network Corp., Mpls., 1990—; sr. rsch. fellow Ctr. for Applied Rsch. in Tech., Mt. Pleasant, 2002—; statis. cons. Ctrl. Mich. U. Contbr. articles to profl. jours. Mem.: Internat. Stats. Inst., Assn. for Advancement of Computing Tech., Biometircs Soc., Internat. Chinese Statis. Assn., Am. Statis. Assn. (pres. 1998—, Outstanding Svc. and Leadership award 2001). Office: PE 206E Dept Math Ctrl Mich U Mount Pleasant MI 48859 E-mail: carl.lee@cmich.edu.

LEE, CAROLYN H. social worker; b. Phila., Aug. 7, 1937; d. Emmett and Marian (Russel) Higgins; m. George Belford, Apr. 6, 1963; children: Geoffrey B., Roslyn. L. BA, Temple U., 1959; MSS, Bryn Mawr Coll., 1961. Lic. social worker, Pa.; cert. social worker. Social worker Children's Unit Ea. Pa. Psychiatric Inst., Phila., 1960-66; social worker Community Mental Health Ctr. Temple U., 1966-68; recruiter, admissions asst. Sch. Social Work Bryn Mawr (Pa.) Coll., 1970-74; counsleor Sch. Social Adminstrn. Temple U., Phila., 1977-79; field liaison Sch. Social Work Bryn Mawr Coll., 1979-84; rsch. asst. outreach coord. Minority Aging Rsch. Project Lincoln (Pa.) U., 1986-89; coord. vols. and support groups The Alzheimers Assn. of Phila., 1990—. Bd. dirs. YWCA, Norristown, Pa., 1972-78; asst. Girls Scouts USA-Valley Forge, Norristown, 1970-76. NIMH fellow. Mem. Twigs Inc. (assoc.) (membership chmn. 1982-84). Democrat.

LEE, CATHERINE, sculptor, painter; b. Pampa, Tex., Apr. 11, 1950; d. Paul Albert and Alice (Fleming) Porter; m. B. R. Mangham, 1967 (div. 1976); 1 child, Monk Parker; m. Sean Scully, 1977. BA, San Jose State U., 1975. Asst. prof. sculpture U. Tex., San Antonio, 2000. Artist-in-residence Mpls. Coll. Art & Design, Minn. Inst. Art, 1982; vis. asst. prof. painting U. Tex., San Antonio, 1983; adj. asst. prof. Columbia U., N.Y.C., 1986-87. Group exhbns. include Albright-Knox Mus., Buffalo, 1987, Mus. Art, Carnegie Inst., Pitts., 1988, Am. Acad. & Inst. Arts & Letters, N.Y.C., 1988, Mus. Folkwang, Essen, Germany, 1992, Stadtische Galerie im Lenbachhaus, Munich, 1992, Neue Galerie Der Stadt Linz, Austria, 1992, Cleve. Mus. of Art, 1993, Galleria Nazionale d'Arte Moderna, San Marino, Italy, 1996, The Tate Gallery, 1994, U. R.I. Art Gallery, 1996, Sonoma State U. Art Gallery, 1997, Bemis Ctr. for Contemporary Art, 1998, Städtische Gallery, Lenbachhaus, Munich, 1999, Lafayette Coll. Art Ctr., Easton, Pa., 1999, San Diego State U. Art Gallery, San Diego, 1999, Grounds for Sculpture, The Johnson Atelier, 2002. Creative Artists Pub. Svc. fellow, 1978; NEA grantee, 1989. Office: 106 Spring St New York NY 10012-3814 also: Galerie Karsten Greve Wallrafplatz 3 5000 Koln Germany also: Galerie Lelong 20 W 57th St New York NY 10019-3917

LEE, CECILIA HAE-JIN, artist, writer; b. Seoul, Nov. 14, 1970; came to U.S., 1977; d. Daniel Pal-Woo and Julia Mi-Ja Lee. BA, U. Calif., San Diego, 1992; postgrad., Inst. Allende, San Miguel de Allende, Mex., 1992, Seoul Nat. U., 1994. Contbg. editor Suite 101, 1999—2002. Freelance writer, artist, and designer; resident Cottages at Hedgebrook, Langley, Wash., 1999. Pub. art, exhibitions include Mus. Death, San Diego, 1992, 1993, Installation Gallery, 1992, Loyola Law Sch. Gallery, L.A., 1993, Artspace Gallery, Woodland Hills, Calif., 1993, SITE Gallery, L.A., 1993, traveling exhibit, exhibitions include L.A. Mcpl. Art Gallery, 1996, Gallery 825, L.A., 1997, Barnsdall Art Ctr. Gallery, 1998, Galeria Asociacion de Bancarios del Urugua , Montevideo, Uruguay, 1998, Cesar Chavez Meml., 1998, Piazza Risorgimento, Sergno, Italy, 1998, Sabina Lee Gallery, 1999, Jr. Arts Gallery, L.A., 1999, Gallery Prince, 1999, Galeria de la Historia de Concepcion, Chile, 1999, UCC Gallery, 2000 (2nd pl. Women in Photography Internat., 2002); contbg. writer: L.A. Times, contbg. writer: Korean Culture Mag., contbg. writer: Minority Engring., contbg. writer: Ency. Sculpture, contbg. writer: Ency. Am. Poetry, contbg. writer: others. Recipient hon. mention Iliad Press, 1995. Mem.: Ind. Writers So. Calif., Archive Korean Am. Artists, Soc. Children's Book Writers and Illustrators. Avocations: travel, building furniture, learning languages, cooking. Address: PO Box 36673 Los Angeles CA 90036-0673

LEE, CHAN-YUN, physicist, process engineer, educator; b. Hwa-Liang, Taiwan, July 19, 1952; came to U.S., 1988; s. Hsiao-Feng and Shu-Yun (Huang) L.; m. Chia-Li Yang, Jan. 13, 1983; children: Yifan E., Ethel Y., Elias Y. BS in Physics, Soochow U., Taipei, Taiwan, 1974; MS, U. So. Calif., 1980; PhD, U. Notre Dame, 1988. Cert. assoc. prof., lectr. Dept. Edn. Asst. prof. physics Tatung Inst. Tech., Taipei, 1982-86, assoc. prof., 1986-88, chmn. physics sect., 1986-88; cons. Tatung Semiconductor Divsn., 1985-88; dir. Tatung Natural Sci. Mus., 1986-88; lab. instr. U. Notre Dame, Notre Dame, Ind., 1988-94; process engr. Lam Rsch. Co., Fremont, Calif., 1994-96, sr. process engr., 1996-99, mgr. metal etch key accounts, 1998-99; assoc. prof. physics San Jose City Coll., 1998-99; reginal chief process technologist Silicon Valley Group, 1999-2000; West Coast press coord., tech. staff Tokyo Electron Am., Santa Clara, Calif., 2000—. Rsch. asst. U. So. Calif., L.A., 1977-79. Contbr. numerous articles to profl. jours. 2d lt. Chinese Artillery, 1974-76. Recipient Excellent Rschrs. prize Chinese Nat. Sci. Coun., Taipei, 1986, 87, 88, Outstanding Acad. Pub. prize Hsieh-Tze Indsl. Revival Com., Taipei, 1987, 88, 27th Ann. Sci. & Tech. Pers. Rsch. & Study award Chinese Nat. Sci. Coun., 1989. Mem. Chinese Physics Assn. Achievements include development of model of relativistic corrections to semiconducting properties of selected materials, simulated and calculated the dynamical sysceptibility of square lattice antiferromagnets; successfully developed the first large size SAC process in the world on high density plasma TCP etcher with satisfactory yields; designed and developed the single chamber dry clean process with AMW downstream and RF plate chamber for metal via applications; designed and constructed a spectrophotometer to measure the absolute photoabsorption cross section of atomic potassium in VUV region. Avocations: moutain hiking, swimming, computer program design, fishing. Home: 471 Via Vera Cruz Fremont CA 94539-5325 Office: Tokyo Electron Am Inc 2953 Bunker Hill Ln Santa Clara CA 95054 E-mail: cylee9334@aol.com.

LEE, CHONG-SIK, political scientist, educator; b. Anju, Korea, July 30, 1931; came to U.S., 1954, naturalized, 1969; s. Bong-Joo and Bong-kye (Moon) Lee; m. Myung-Sook Woo, Mar. 19, 1962; children: Sharon, Gina, Roger(dec.). BA, UCLA, 1956, MA, 1957; PhD, U. Calif., Berkeley, 1961. Instr. polit. sci. U. Colo., Boulder, 1960-61, Dartmouth Coll., Hanover, N.H., 1961-63; asst. prof. polit. sci. U. Pa., Phila., 1963-65, assoc. prof., 1965-73, prof., 1973-99, prof. emeritus, 1999—, dir. Anspach Inst. Diplomacy and Fgn. Affairs, 1980-85, chmn. grad. program internat. rels. Anspach Inst., 1980-85; L. George Paik prof. Yonsei U., Seoul, 2001-02. Chmn. joint com. on Korean Studies Social Sci. Research Council and Am. Council Learned Socs., 1970-77 Author: The Politics of Korean Nationalism, 1963, Counterinsurgency in Manchuria: The Japanese Experience, 1931-40, 1967, (with Robert A. Scalapino) Communism in Korea, 1973, The Life of Kim Kyu-sik, 1974, Materials on Korean Communism, 1945-47, 1977, The Korean Workers' Party: A Short History, 1978, Revolutionary Struggle in Manchuria: Chinese Communism and Soviet Interest, 1922-1945, 1983, Japan and Korea: The Political Dimension, 1985; (with Mike Langford) Korea: Land of Morning Calm, 1988, Recollections of Anti-Japanese Revolutionaries, 1988, Korea Briefing, 1990, 91, North Korea in Transition, 1991, In Search of a New Order in East Asia, 1991, Syngman Rhee: The Prison Years of a Young Radical, 2001; mem. editl. bd. Asian Survey, 1973-97, Jour. N.E. Asian Studies, 1982-97, Orbis, 1980-86, East Asia, 1998—. Mem. Task Force on Equal Ednl. Opportunity and Quality Edn., Pa. Higher Edn. Planning Commn., 1977. Social Sci. Rsch. Coun. grantee, 1963, 66-67, 72, 73-74, Rockefeller Found. grantee, 1965-66, Hoover Inst. grantee, 1980, Yonkang Found. grantee, 1990-93; Ford Found. faculty fellow, 1969-70. Mem. Am. Polit. Sci. Assn. (Woodrow Wilson Found. award for best book in polit. sci. 1974), Assn. Asian Studies. Home: 8 Cypress Ln Berwyn PA 19312-1005 E-mail: cslee@sas.upenn.edu.

LEE, CHRISTOPHER FRANK CARANDINI, actor, author, singer; b. London, May 27, 1922; s. Geoffrey Trollope and Estelle Marie (Carandini) L.; m. Birgit Kroencke, Mar. 17, 1961; 1 child, Christina Erika. Student, Eton Coll., Wellington Coll. With theatrical and film industry, 1946—; actor: (films) Corridor of Mirrors, 1947, The Curse of Frankenstein, 1956, Dracula, 1958, The Three Musketeers, 1974, The Four Musketeers, 1975, The Man with the Golden Gun, 1974, Airport 77, 1977, Caravans, 1978, Return from Witch Mountain, 1978, Circle of Iron, 1979, The Passage, 1979, The Wicker Man, 1973, Jaguar Lives, 1979, 1941, 1980, Bear Island, 1980, The Salamander, 1981, An Eye for an Eye, 1981, Safari 3000, 1982, The Last Unicorn, 1982, The Return of Captain Invisible, 1983, House of the Long Shadows, 1984, Murder Story, 1989, The Return of the Musketeers, 1989, Honeymoon Academy, 1990, Gremlins II: The New Batch, 1990, Police Academy: Mission to Moscow, 1994, Talos the Mummy, 1997, The Stupids, Feast at Midnight, Jinnah, 1997, Sleepy Hollow, 1999; (TV miniseries) The Pirate, 1978, Captain America II, 1979, Goliath Awaits, 1981, The Far Pavillions, 1984, Roadtrip, Mio My Mio, The Girl, The Funny Man, 1993, A Feast at Midnight, 1994; (TV films) Ivanhoe, Poor Devil, 1973, Once Upon a Spy, 1980, Charles and Diana: A Royal Love Story, 1982, The Disputation, Metier du Seigneur, Shaka Zulu, Around the World in Eighty Days, Treasure Island, Young Indy, 1992, Death Train, 1992, Moses, 1996, Im Brunnen der Träume, 1996, The Odyssey, 1997, The Many Faces of Christopher Lee, 1997, Gormenghast, 1999; (TV series) The Lord of the Rings: In The Beginning, 2000; (TV films) Star Wars, Episode II; author: Tall Dark and Gruesome, 1977, rev. edit., 1997, The Great Villains, 1979, Archives of Evil. Served with RAF and Spl. Forces, 1941-46. Decorated Polonia Restituta (Poland); officer Arts, Lettres et Scis. (France); comdr. Order Brit. Empire; Order of St. John of Jerusalem. Mem. Screen Actors Guild, Brit. Actors Equity, Variety, Clubs Internat. Conservative. Clubs: Hon. Company Edinburgh Golfers; Bucks's (London); Travellers (Paris). Mem. Ch. Of Eng.

LEE, CLEMENT WILLIAM KHAN, trade association administrator; b. N.Y.C., Feb. 7, 1938; s. William P. and Helen M. BTh, Concordia Coll., 1958; MDiv, Concordia Theol. Sem., 1962; MA, New Sch. for Social Research, 1976. Asst. exec. dir. Greater Detroit Luth. Ctr., 1962; editor Detroit and Suburban Luth. Newspaper, 1963; assoc. communications dir. Met. Detroit Council of Chs., 1964; dir. media ops. Am. Bible Soc., N.Y.C., 1967; dir. media relations Luth. Council U.S.A., 1971-82, asst. exec. dir. communications and interpretation, 1977-82; dir. dept. telecommunications Luth. Ch. in Am., 1983-87; dir. electronic media Episcopal Ch., 1987-93, program dep. for communication, 1989-93, Episcopal telecomm. dir., 1993-97; dir. Ecusa Media Svc., 1997—. Media cons. Luth. Ch.-Mo. Synod, Spaulding for Children, Metro News of Metro N.Y., Synod of Luth. Ch. Am., archtl. newsletter Window, Luth. Deaconess Assn., Concordia Coll., Bronxville, Physicians for Social Responsibility, Wheatridge Found., Luth. Sch. Theology, Chgo.; chmn. broadcast ops. com. Nat. Council Chs. of Christ U.S.A., 1976-80; vice chmn. bd. mgrs. Communications Commn., 1977-80; chmn. inter-faith Media Data System, 1981; mem. TV awards com. N.Y. Council Chs.; mgr. Lutherans-in-Media Conf. I and II, 1980, Luth. Audio-Visual Conf., 1981; project dir. Lambeth Conf. Inter-Anglican Telecommunication Network, 1988; internat. computer network resource leader Religious Communications Congress 90, 1990; bd. dirs. FACTA TV News, Inc.; pres. N.Y. chpt. Religious Pub. Rels. Coun.; telecommunication cons. World Coun. of Chs., Canberra Assembly, 1990-91, Episc. Bd. Theol. Edn., 1993—. Editor: Media Alert newsletter, 1980-86, Luth. Communication newsletter, 1983-87, Episcopal Media Adv. newsletter, 1989—; creator children's TV series Storyline; producer multi-image sequences, Augustana Jubilee, 1980, multi-image program Proclaim, 1984, multi-image effects, Milw. Conv., 1986, (films) Mission on Six Continents, 1975, Room for a Stranger, 1978, Winter Wheat, 1982; exec. producer, One in Mission, 1985, Gathering of the Family, 1988, Doers of the Word, 1988, The Tully-Freeman Report, 1988, Outpourings of Love, 1989, Faith on a Tightrope, 1989, Fresh Winds Blowing, 1989, Prophecy Fulfilled in Me, 1990, President Carter Center Health Video, 1990, To Walk in Beauty, 1990, Pathways for Peace, 1990, Word in the World, 1991, Executive Council Presents, 1991, Cantenbury in North Carolina, 1992. Mem. Metro N.Y. Synod Evangelical Luth. Ch. in Am. Communication Commn., Religious Pub. Rels. Coun.; mem. communication dept. nat. adv. com. Evang. Luth. Ch. in Am.; chair Telecomm. Task Force Lambeth Anglican Bishops Confs., 1988, Bldg. Restoration com. St. John's Episc. Ch., N.Y.C., 1993-95; gov. Inter-Anglican Info. Network Quest Internat. Mgmt. team, 1992—. Recipient award Detroit Press Club Found., 1963, silver medal Internat. Film and TV Festival, 1975, 79, Creative Excellence award U.S. Indsl. Film Festival, 1986, Brit. Telecommunications award, 1988, Polly Bond award, 1989, 90, 91, 92, N.Y. TV Festival finalist, 1990. Mem. Assn. Edn. Communication Tech., Internat. Assn. Bus. Communicators, Internat. TV Assn., World Assn. Christian Communication (chmn. N.Am. broadcast sect. 1975), Nat. Interfaith Cable Coalition VISN (members' com.), Satellite TV Network (bd. dirs.), Episcopal Cathedral Teleconferencing Network (steering com.). Office: Ecusa Media Svc 815 2nd Ave New York NY 10017-4503

LEE, CORINNE ADAMS, retired educator; b. Cuba, N.Y., Mar. 18, 1910; d. Duston Emery and Florence Eugenia (Butts) Adams; m. Glenn Max Lee, Oct. 30, 1936 (dec. Feb. 1964). BA, Alfred U., 1931. Cert. tchr., N.Y. Tchr. English Lodi (N.Y.) High Sch., 1931-36, Ovid (N.Y.) Cen. Sch., 1936-67. Author: (light verse) A Little Leeway, 1983, (anecedotes, light verse, quips) A Little More Leeway, 1984, (essays, short stories, poems) Still More Leeway, 1986. Trustee Montour Falls Meml. Libr. Mem. life PTA. Mem. Nat. Ret. Tchrs. Assn., N.Y. State Ret. Tchrs. Assn., Schuyler County Ret. Tchrs. Assn., Elmira and Area Ret. Tchrs. Assn., LWV. Avocations: reading, travel, writing.

LEE, CYNTHIA, television producer, playwright, filmmaker; b. Bklyn. BA, San Diego State U. Media analyst Walt Disney Prodns., Burbank, Calif., 1978-80; story analyst NBC, 1980-83; dir. broadcast media May Dept. Stores, L.A., 1980-86; CEO CloverLeaf Prodns., Beverly Hills, Calif., 1986—. Freelance news prodr., photographer various affiliates, 1996—. Author: (book)

Twice Blessed, 1995; (plays) Blavatsky, 1985 (Dramalogue award), Demons and Angels, 1993 (Dramalogue award); prodr: (documentary) The Great Bronze Age of China, 1983, A Hole In The Sky, 1997, A Miracle In Danville, 1997 (winner film grant Am. Film Inst./Nat. Endowment for Arts 1997). Playwriting award Dramalogue, 1986, 93; Recognition award Geisinger Hosp., Danville, Pa., 1997. Mem. Internat. Soc. Panetics, Internat. Documentary Assn., L.A. Playwrights Alliance, Dramatists Guild. E-mail: cleeover@aol.com.

LEE, DAI-KEONG, composer; b. Honolulu; s. Lin Fong and Young Kun (Chang) L.; m. Dorothy Isabelle Moncur, May 16, 1974. Student in pre-medicine, U. Hawaii, 1933-36; scholarship student with Roger Sessions, N.Y.C., 1937-38; fellowship student under Frederick Jacobi, Juilliard Grad. Sch., 1938-41; fellowship student under Aaron Copland, Berkshire Music Ctr., summer 1941; MA under Otto Luening, Columbia U., 1951. Bd. dirs. Am. Music Ctr., N.Y.C., 1960-69. Recorded Prelude, Hula, Symphony No. 1, Polynesian Suite; wrote mus. score for motion picture Letter from Australia, 1945; guest condr., ABC Symphony, Sydney, Australia, 1944-45; composer: orchestral works including Prelude and Hula, 1939, Hawaiian Festival Overture, 1940, Introduction and Allegro for Strings, 1941, Golden Gate Overture for Chamber Orch., 1941, Polynesion Suite, Symphony No. 1, 1941, revised 1947, Symphony No. 2, 1952; chamber works including String Quartet No. 1, 1947, Sonatina for Piano, 1947, Incantation and Dance for Piano and Violin, 1948, Introduction and Allegro for Cello and Piano, 1947; opera Open the Gates, produced by Blackfriars, N.Y.C., 1951; ballet Waltzing Matilda, 1951; mus. score Teahouse of the August Moon, produced by Maurice Evans-George Shaeffer, 1953; Polynesian Suite for Orch., 1958, Violin Concerto, 1947, revised 1955, Mele Olili for Chorus, Solo and Orch., 1960, Canticle of the Pacific, 1968; mus. play Noa-Noa, 1972; Mortal Thoughts of a Buddhist Monk for baritone, chorus and orch., 1976; one-act opera Ballad of Kitty the Barkeep, 1979; mus. plays Jenny Lind, 1981, Gauguin, Maker of Sea and Sky, 1994; Concerto Grosso for string orch., 1952, rev., 1985; contbr. articles to music mags., newspapers. Served with AUS, 1942-45, PTO. Received Albert Metz commn. for violin concerto, 1946; received CBS commn. for Introduction and Allegro for Strings, 1941, Inst. Mus. Art commn. for one-act opera, Poet's Dilemma, 1940; recipient hon. mention Prix de Rome competition Am. Acad. in Rome, 1942; Guggenheim fellow, 1945, 51 Mem. ASCAP, League Composers, Allied MacDowell Club, Dramatists Guild. Achievements include composing orchestral, symphonic, chamber music; 1st orchestral work Valse Pensieroso, performed Honolulu Symphony Orch., 1936; works performed by N.Y. Philharm., Eastman Rochester Philharm., Mpls., San Francisco, Cin., CBS, Nat., Montreal, Manila, N.Y.C. Phila., symphony orchs.; under direction of Kurtz, Monteux, Mitropoulos, Goosens, Barlow, Caston, Dixon, Stokowski, Stoessel, Pelletier, Wallenstein, others. Home: 245 W 104th St New York NY 10025-4249

LEE, DAN M. retired state supreme court chief justice; b. Petal, Miss., Apr. 19, 1926; s. Buford Aaron and Pherbia Ann (Camp) L.; m. Peggy Jo Daniel, Nov. 27, 1947 (dec. 1952); 1 child, Sheron Lee Anderson; m. Mary Alice Gray, Sept. 30, 1956; 1 child, Dan Jr. Attended, U. So. Miss., 1946; LLB, Jackson Sch. Law, 1949; JD, Miss. Coll., 1970. Bar: Miss. 1948. Ptnr. Franklin & Lee, Jackson, Miss., 1948-54, Lee, Moore and Countiss, Jackson, Miss., 1954-71; county judge Hinds County, 1971-77; cir. judge Hinds-Yazoo Counties, 1977-82; assoc. justice Miss. Supreme Ct., Jackson, 1982-87, presiding justice, 1987-95, chief justice, 1995-98; ret., 1998; of counsel Dogan & Wilkinson, PLLC, Jackson, 1999. With U.S. Naval Aviation, 1944-46. Mem. ABA, Hinds County Bar Assn., Miss. State Bar Assn., Aircraft Owners and Pilots Assn., Am. Legion, VFW, Kiwanis Internat. Baptist. E-mail: judgeanddr@aol.com.

LEE, DANA E. student, cabinet maker; b. Bellevue, OH, May 20, 1969; s. Sandi Yvonne Lee, Charles E. Lee; m. Jackie Suzanne Darling; children: Chase, Megan. Biology, University of Houston, Clear Lake, 2001—02. Owner Island Home Care, Galveston, TX, 1996—2002. Certified Vision screener Prevent Blindness Texas, Galveston, TX, 2000—02. Home: 9414 Jamaica Beach Galveston TX 77554 Personal E-mail: Jackychasedana@aol.

LEE, DANIEL KUHN, economist; b. Kyoto, Japan, Dec. 18, 1946; came to U.S., 1977; s. Chu G. and Myung N. (Lee) L.; children: David, Alexander. BS, Kyoto U., Japan, 1970; MA, Seoul Nat. U., Seoul, Republic of Korea, 1973, SUNY, Stony Brook, 1979; PhD, Iowa State U., 1981. Postdoctoral rsch. assoc. Iowa State U., Ames, 1981-82, instr., 1982; sr. economist Miss. Rsch. and Devel. Ctr., Jackson, 1982-88; dir. of econs. Miss. Insts. of Higher Learning, 1988-95; sr. fiscal advisor Barents Group, KPMG Peat Marwick, 1995-97, 99—; pres. Lee Assocs., Olney, Md., 1997-99. Adj. prof. Jackson State U., 1986-88; advisor Gov.'s Econ. Task Force, Jackson, 1982-84. Author: A Study of Mississippi Input-Output Model, 1986; contbr. articles to profl. jours. Exec. dir. So. Regional Assn., Washington, 1992-95; elder Presbyn. Ch. USA, 1991—. Travel grantee UN Indsl. Devel. Orgn., Vienna, Austria, 1986. Mem. So. Regional Sci. Assn., North Am. Regional Sci. Assn., Am. Econ. Assn., So. Econ. Assn., Gamma Sigma Delta. Avocations: jogging, swimming. Office: Barents Group KPMG Tower 1676 International Dr Mc Lean VA 22102-4832 Business E-Mail: dlee@barents-moduva.com., dlee@barents-moldova.com.

LEE, DANIEL YONG-GEUN, economics educator; b. Naju, Korea, May 21, 1954; m. Deborah C. Lee, July 16, 1977; children: Daniel J., Sarah H., Esther G. BS, Chonnam Nat. U., Korea, 1976; MA in Econs., U. Pitts., 1984, PhD in Econs., 1986. Adj. prof. econs. Pa. State U., McKeesport, 1984-85; assoc. prof. econs. Shippensburg (Pa.) U., 1986-91, prof. econs., 1991—. U. Pitts. fellow, 1980-85, 85-86. Mem. Am. Econ. Assn., Western Econ. Assn. Internat., So. Econ. Assn., Pa. Econ. Assn. (bd. dirs 1995—, pres. 1999-2000), Ctrl. Pa. Internat. Bus. Assn. Home: 627 Glenn St Shippensburg PA 17257-2129 Office: Shippensburg U Grove Hall 325 Shippensburg PA 17257 E-mail: DYL@ship.edu.

LEE, DAVID CHANG, physician; b. Seoul, Republic of Korea, Sept. 14, 1940; s. Young C. Lee and Hae W. (Kim) Kim; m. Margaret C. Park, Sept. 10, 1965; children: Edward, Grace, George. MD, Yon-Sei Sch. Med., Seoul, 1965. Diplomate Am. Bd. Otolaryngology. Intern Howard med. Ctr., Washington, 1965-66; resident gen. surgery Roger's Meml. Hosp., 1966-67; resident otolaryngology St. Louis City Hosp., 1967-70, U. Md. Hosp., Balt., 1970-71; staff physician Ft. Howard (Md.) Vets. Hosp., 1971-73; asst. prof. U. Ill., Chgo., 1973—, Chgo. Osteo. Med. Sch., 1999—. Med. staff St. Francis Hosp., Blude Island, Ill., 1973—, Ingall's Meml. Hosp., Harvey, Ill., 1973—. Contbr. articles to profl. jours. Fellow ACS, Am. Acad. Otolaryncology and Head and Neck Surgery; AMA. Presbyterian. Avocations: Tae Kwon Do (3d degree black belt), golf. Office: 5320 159th St Oak Forest IL 60452-4705

LEE, DAVID DEWITT, safety specialist, industrial hygienist; b. Detroit, Feb. 16, 1948; s. Floyd Herbert and Anne Theresa (Damask) L.; m. Lorraine Angeline Wozniak, Sept. 6, 1969; children: Jennifer, Mary, Brian, Jonathan, Sarah. BS Psychology, No. Mich. U., 1975; M Indsl Safety, U. Minn., 1988. Cert. indsl. hygienist, safety profl. Ops. foreman Nat. Steel Pellet Co., Keewatin, Minn., 1976-78, 84-86; safety engr. Hanna Mining Co. Agts., Hibbing, 1978-81, Butler Taconite, Nashwauk, 1981-84; indsl. hygienist Sonora (Calif.) Mining Co., 1988-89, State Indsl. Ins. System, Reno, 1990-92; indsl. hygienist, safety specialist Univ./C.C. System Nev., 1992—. Accredited vis., vis. chmn. Mended Hearts, Inc., Reno, 1993-95. With USN, 1967-70, Vietnam. Scholar Semi-Condr. Safety Assn. Mem. Am. Indsl. Hygiene Assn., Am. Conf. of Govt. Indsl. Hygienist, Am. Acad. Indsl. Hygiene, Am. Bd. Indsl. Hygiene, Am. Soc. Safety Engrs. (chpt. sec. 1994—, chpt. pres.-elect 1995, pres. 1996, area dir. 1997, v.p. region II 1998-2000, Chpt. Safety Profl. of Yr. 2000, Region II Safety Profl. of Yr. 2001), Bd. Cert. Indsl. Hygienist and Safety Profls. Republican. Roman Catholic. Avocations: weightlifting, running, bicycling. Office: U Nev Environ Health & Safety Ms 328 Reno NV 89557-0001 E-mail: david@unr.edu.

LEE, DAVID MORRIS, physics educator; b. Rye, N.Y., Jan. 20, 1931; s. Marvin and Annette (Franks) Lee; m. Dana Thorangkul, Sept. 7, 1960; children: Eric Bertel, James Marvin. AB, Harvard U., 1952; MS, U. Conn., 1955; PhD, Yale U., 1959. Instr. of physics Cornell U., Ithaca, NY, 1959—60, asst. prof. physics, 1960—63, assoc. prof. physics, 1963—68, prof. physics, 1968—97, James Gilbert White disting. prof. phys. scis., 1997—. Vis. scientist Brookhaven Nat. Lab., Upton, NY, 1966—67; vis. prof. U. Fla., Gainesville, 1974—75, Gainesville, 1994, U. Calif., San Diego, 1988, La Jolla, 88; vis. lectr. Peking U., Beijing, 1981; chair mcpl. Joseph Fourier U., Grenoble, France, 1994. Contbr. articles. With U.S. Army, 1952—54. Co-recipient Nobel prize for physics, 1996; recipient Sir Francis Simon Meml. prize, Brit. Inst. Physics, 1976, Wilber Cross medal, Yale U., 1998; fellow John Simon Guggenheim, Guggenheim Found., 1966—67, 1974—75, Japan Soc. Promotion of Scis., 1977. Fellow: AAAS, Am. Acad. Arts and Scis., Brit. Inst. Physics, Am. Phys. Soc. (Oliver Buckley prize 1981); mem.: Nat. Acad. Scis. Achievements include co-discovery of superfluid 3He, of the tricritical point of 3He-4He mixtures; co-observation of spin waves in spin polarized hydrogen gas. Office: Cornell U Physics Dept Clark Hall Ithaca NY 14853-2501

LEE, DAVID OI, engineer; b. Hong Kong, China, Feb. 5, 1940; came to U.S., 1940; s. Quay Fong and Hun Yung (Quan) L.; m. Elizabeth Hon Lang Tan, Aug. 7, 1966 (div.); 1 dau., Andrea. B.S., Tex. A&M U., 1962, M.S., 1964; postgrad. Northwestern U., 1964-67. Registered profl. engr. Sr. mem. tech. staff Sandia Nat. Labs., Albuquerque, 1967— . Co-inventor on 5 U.S. patents; contbr. articles to profl. jours.; patentee in field. Mem. ASME (com. on nuclear quality assurance subcom. on programatic activities working group on R&D quality assurance), Am. Soc. Quality Control (vice chmn. energy & environ. quality assurance divsn. subcom. on environ. R&D), Soc. Petroleum Engrs., Sigma Xi. Methodist. Home: PO Box 14995 Albuquerque NM 87191-4995

LEE, DAVID SACK YEE, internist; b. Jan. 27, 1949; BSE (N.E.), U. Mich., 1972; MD, U. Liege, Belgium, 1984. Diplomate Am. Bd. Internal Medicine. Intern Bridgeport (Conn.) Hosp., 1984-85; resident Sinai Hosp., Balt., 1985-87, attending physician, 1987-88; med. staff Southwood Comty. Hosp., Norfolk, Mass., 1988-93, Charlton Meml. Hosp., Fall River, 1993—, Brockton (Mass.) Hosp., 1994—. Fellow ACP.

LEE, DAVID SEN LIN, executive; b. Beijing, June 23, 1937; came to U.S., 1956; s. Wen-Chi Lee an dLi Ping Wang; m. Cecilia Chi-Ming Wan, Jan. 8, 1965; children: Eric, Gloria, Randy. BSME, Mont. State U., 1960; MSME, N.D. State U., 1962; D of Engring., Mont. State U., 1993. St. engr. tech. staff NCR, Dayton, Ohio, 1962-63; mgr. Friden, San Leandro, Calif., 1963-69; dir. printer engring. Diablo Systems, Hayward, 1970-73; founder, pres. Qume/ITT, San Jose, 1973-85; pres. Data Tech. Corp., 1985-95; chmn. Cortelco, 1995—, eOn Comms. Corp., Cidco Comms., Morgan Hill, Calif., 1999—. Bd. dirs. Linear Tech., Milpitas, Calif., ESS Tech., Fremont, Calif., iBasis, Burlington, Mass. Author: Microcomputer, 1985. Regent U. Calif., Oakland, 1994—; commr. Calif. Post-Secondary Edn. Com., 1997-98; advisor to Pres.'s Bush & Clinton Office of U.S. Trade Rep., 1990, 93; mem. Pres.'s Coun. (Pres. Bush) on the 21st Century Workforce, 2002. Recipient Bus. Entrepreneur award Harvard Bus. Sch., 1979, USA Achievement award Chinese Inst. Engrs., 1983, Outstanding Achievement award Mid-Am. Chinese Sci. & Tech. Assn., 1987, Asian/Pacific Am. Heritage award Pres. George Bush, 1992. Mem. Calif. C. of C. (dir. 1992—).

LEE, DAVID STODDART, retired investment counselor; b. Boston, Jan. 12, 1934; s. George Cabot and Kathleen Bowring (Stoddart) L.; m. Lucinda Hopkins, Apr. 29, 1972; children: Alexander Putnam, Madeline Jackson, Alice Ingalls. AB, Harvard U., 1956, MBA, 1960. V.p., dir. Lee Higginson Corp., N.Y.C., 1960-65; mng. dir., Scudder, Stevens and Clark, Boston, 1965-97; ret., 1997. Dir., pres., asst. treas. Scudder Investor Svcs., Inc. (formerly Scudder Fund Distbrs.); pres., trustee Scudder Calif. Tax Free Trust, Scudder Cash Investment Trust, Scudder U.S. Treas. Money Fund, Scudder Mcpl. Trust, Scudder State Tax Free Trust, Scudder Tax Free Money Fund, Scudder Tax Free Trust; v.p., trustee Scudder Equity Trust, Scudder GNMA Fund, Scudder Portfolio Trust; v.p. Scudder Securities Trust, Scudder Funds Trust, Scudder Mut. Funds, Inc., Scudder Investment Trust, Scudder Variable Life Investment Fund, The Argentina Fund, Inc., The Brazil Fund, Inc., The Korea Fund, Inc., The L.Am. Dollar Income Fund, Inc., Scudder New Asia Fund, Inc., Scudder New Europe Fund, Inc., Scudder World Income Opportunities Fund, Inc.; v.p., asst. treas. Scudder Global Fund, Inc., Scudder Internat. Fund, Inc.; chmn. dir. Scudder Instnl. Fund, Inc., Scudder Fund, Inc.; v.p., asst. treas. AARP Cash Investment Funds, AARP Growth Trust, AARP Income Trust, AARP Tax Free Income Trust, AARP Managed Investment Portfolios Trust; v.p. Scudder Svc. Corp. Trustee Cotting Sch., Boston, 1974—, New Eng. Med. Ctr., 1974—; bd. dirs., chmn. Rogerson Cmtys., 1978—; corporator Mass. Gen. Hosp., 1975—. Lt. (j.g.) USN, 1956-58. Mem. Soc. Chartered Fin. Analysts (chartered investment counsellor), Bald Peak Colony, The Boulders. Clubs: Country, Somerset (Boston). Republican. Episcopalian. Office: 50 Congress St Ste 543 Boston MA 02109-4002

LEE, DAVID Y.S. neurologist; b. Singapore, Feb. 23, 1948; s. Willard Lee and Betty Yue Spector. BS, Washington U., St. Louis, 1972; MD, St. Louis U., 1976. Diplomate in neurology Am. Bd. Psychiatry and Neurology. Intern St. Louis U., 1976-77, resident, 1977-80; fellow Cleve. Clinic, 1980-81; neurologist Neurologic Assocs. of Cape Girardeau, Mo., 1981—. Chmn. multidisciplinary spl. care com. S.E. Mo. Hosp., Cape Girardeau, 1994—; chmn. sect. neurology St. Francis Med. Ctr., Cape Girardeau, 1996—, chmn. dept. neurosciences, 2002--, med. dir. Clin. Neurophysiology Lab., 1996—. Mem. Am. Acad. Neurology, Am. Clin. Neurophysiology Soc., Am. Assn. Electromyography and Electrodiagnosis, Eta Kappa Nu. Avocations: reading, sailing, travel. Office: Neurologic Assocs 3004 Gordonville Rd Cape Girardeau MO 63703-5008

LEE, DENNIS PATRICK, lawyer, judge; b. Omaha, Feb. 12, 1955; s. Donald Warren and Betty Jean (O'Leary) L.; children: Patrick Michael, Katherine Marie, Megan Elizabeth. BA, Creighton U., 1977, JD, 1980. Bar: Nebr. 1980, U.S. Dist. Ct. Nebr. 1980, U.S. Ct. Appeals (8th cir.) 1980, Iowa 1990. Assoc. Thompson Crounse & Pieper, Omaha, 1980-84; ptnr. Lee Law Offices, 1984-87, Silverman, Lee & Crounse Law Offices, 1987-94, Lee Bucchino & Jones Law Offices, P.C., L.L.O., 1994—. Atty. Nebr. State Racing Commn., Lincoln, 1984-87, commr. 1988—, chmn., 1991—; adminstrv. law judge, State of Nebr., 1985-87; lectr. Creighton U., Omaha, 1982-85. Author: Law of Conservatorships, 1981: Legal Aspects of Equine Veterinary Practice, 1984, Planning Opportunities with Living Trusts in Nebraska, 1995; others. Trustee Holy Name Cath. Ch., Omaha, 1980-84; chmn. nat. enforcement officers com. Nat. Assn. State Racing Commrs., Lexington, Ky., 1984-87; commr. Nebr. State Racing Commn., 1988—. Mem. ABA, Nat. Assn. Trial Attys., Comml. Law League Am., Nebr. State Racing Commn. (chmn. 1991), Assn. Racing Commrs. Internat. (treas. 1996-97, v.p. 1997-2000, chmn. and CEO 2000——), Nebr. Bar Assn, Omaha Bar Assn. (chmn. conservatorship com. 1981—), Nebr.-Iowa Referees Assn. (v.p. 1981-88), Omaha C. of C. (Outstanding Young Omahan 1993). Home: 14767 Burt Dr Omaha NE 68154-1944 Office: Lee & Bucchino 12165 W Center Rd Ste 52 Omaha NE 68144-3974

LEE, DENNIS TURNER, civil engineer, construction executive; b. Dallas, Jan. 6, 1941; s. Joseph Thomas and Elizabeth Lee; m. Dianna Christine Ricker, Aug. 8, 1964; children: Christopher Scott, Karen Denise, Suzanne Elizabeth. BSCE, So. Meth. U., 1964; MS in Constrn. Mgmt., Stanford U., 1965. Cert. project mgmt. profl., asbestos contr./supr. Constrn. engr. Kaiser Engrs., Oakland, Calif., 1965—66; project engr. Hoffman Constrn. Co., Portland, Oreg., 1969—76, supt., 1979, project ops. mgr., 1978—84; sr. project mgr. Chanen Constrn. Co., Phoenix, 1985—87, Sundt Corp., Phoenix, 1987—93, Linthicum Constructors, Scottsdale, 1993; account exec. Water Purge Sys., 1994; facilities mgr. InteSys Technologies, Inc., Gilbert, Ariz., 1994—97; project mgr. Motorola New Constrn. Team ICF-Kaiser, Chandler, 1998; project mgr. Target Gen., Inc., Phoenix, 1999—2000, ABACUS Project Mgmt. Inc., Phoenix, 2000—. Mem. lawyer ethics discipline com. Ariz. State Bar, 1990-93. 1st lt. C.E. U.S. Army, 1966-69. Decorated Army Commendation medal. Mem. ASCE, Project Mgmt. Inst. (pres. 1990-93), Environ. Info. Assn. (bd. dirs. 1992-93), Toastmasters (pres. 1992). Achievements include pioneered use of time lapse movie technology in construction operations; designed jobsite concrete precasting and steam curing plants; pioneered use of lasers in construction. Avocations: hiking, camping, skiing, in-line skating. Home: 8019 E Voltaire Ave Scottsdale AZ 85260-4933 E-mail: dennislee0132@msn.com.

LEE, DERREK LEON, baseball player; b. Sacramento, Sept. 6, 1975; m. Christina Lee, 2001. Attended, El Camino HS. Baseball player Fla. Marlins, 1998—. Supporter Cornerstones for Kids programs including Youth Basball Clinics, World of Baseball; co-chmn. Cornerstones for Kids programs. Office: Fla Marlins 2269 Dan Marino Blvd Opa Locka FL 33056*

LEE, DOHYUNG, aeronautics research scientist; b. Seoul, Republic of Korea, Feb. 24, 1964; came to US, 1990; s. Sang Sub and Sookja (Kwak) L.; m. Jeonghoi Jeon, Dec. 27, 1994; children: Daniel Jaewon, Elizabeth Jaeyoung, David Jaeyeon. BS in Aerospace Engring., Seoul Nat. U., 1986, MS in Aerospace Engring., 1988; PhD, U. Mich., 1996. Rsch. scientist Sys. Engring. and Rsch. Inst./Korean Inst. Sci. and Tech., Seoul, 1988-90; postdoct. fellow U. Mich., Ann Arbor, 1996-98; rsch. engr. Ames Rsch. Ctr. NASA, Moffett Field, Calif., 1998—. Editor: Computers and Fluids, 1999, Jour. of Aircraft, 1999; contbr. articles to profl. jours. 2nd lt. The Third Acad. in Korea, 1988-89. The Korean Govt. Oversea fellow Dept. of Edn., 1988; recipient postdoct. awards Nat. Rsch. Coun., 1997. Mem. AIAA. Presbyterian. Avocations: golf, Asian chess. Home: 7229 Via Vico San Jose CA 95129-3545 Office: Hanyang Univ Dept Mechanical Eng Sa 1 Dong KyungKi Do 425 791 An San 94035Republic of Korea

LEE, DON YOON, publisher, academic researcher and writer; b. Seoul, Korea, Apr. 7, 1936; came to U.S., 1957; s. Yoo-ehn and Ch'i-ho (Kim) L. BA, U. Wash., 1963; MA, St. John's U., Jamaica, N.Y., 1967; MS, Georgetown U., 1971; MA, Ind. U., 1975, 90. Founder, pub. Eastern Press, Inc., Bloomington, Ind., 1981—. Author: History of Early Relation Between China and Tibet, 1981, An Introduction to East Asian and Tibetan Linguistics and Culture, 1981, Learning Standard Arabic, 1988, An Annotated Bibliography of Selected Works on China, 1981, Light Literature and Philosophy of East Asia, 1982, An Annotated Bibliography on Inner Asia, 1983, An Annotated Archaeological Bibliography of Selected Works on Northern and Central Asia, 1983, Traditional Chinese Thoughts: The Four Schools, 1990, others. Office: Eastern Press Inc PO Box 881 Bloomington IN 47402-0881

LEE, DONALD YOUNG (DON LEE), publishing executive, editor, writer; b. Tokyo, Dec. 11, 1959; s. Victor Young and Jean Ann (Kim) L. BA in English, UCLA, 1982; MFA in Creative Writing, Emerson Coll., 1986. Writing instr. Emerson Coll., Boston, 1985-89; mng. editor Ploughshares, 1988-92, dir., 1992—. Cons. AGNI, Boston, 1993, Asian Pacific Am. Jour., 1994, New Eng. Review, 1995, Columbia, 1998, Ga. Review, 1999, CLMP, 1999, Salamander, 1999, Lannan Found., 2000. Author: Yellow: Stories, 2001; contbr. short stories, articles to jours. St. Botolph Club Found. fellow, 1990, 91, Mass. Cultural Coun. Fiction fellow, 1998. Mem. PEN Am. New Eng. (bd. dirs.). Democrat. Office: Ploughshares Emerson Coll 120 Boylston St Boston MA 02116-4624

LEE, DONALD JOHN, federal judge; b. 1927; AB, U. Pitts., 1950; LLB, Duquesne U., 1954. Bar: Pa. Supreme Ct. 1955; U.S. Supreme Ct. 1984. Assoc. George Y. Meyer and Assocs., 1954-57; law clk. to Hon. Rabe F. Marsh Jr. U.S. Dist. Ct., Pa., 1957-58; assoc. Wilner, Wilner and Kuhn, 1958-61; ptnr. Dougherty, Larrimer & Lee, Pitts., 1961-84, 86-88; judge Ct. Common Pleas of Allegheny County, Pa., 1984-86, 88-90, U.S. Dist. Ct. (we. dist.) Pa., Pitts., 1990—. Councilman Borough of Green Tree, 1961-63, solicitor, 1963-84, 86-88; spl. asst. atty. gen. Office of Atty. Gen. Commonwealth of Pa., 1963-74; spl. legal counsel Home Rule Study Commn., Municipality of Bethel Park and Borough of Green Tree, 1973-74, City of Pitts., 1978-80, various municipalities, 1970-86; chmn. Home Rule Charter Transition Com. Bethel Park, 1978; bd. dirs. Soldiers' and Sailors' Meml. Hall and Mus. Trust. Mem. ad hoc com. Salvation Army; bd. dirs. Soldiers and Sailors Meml. Hall and Mus. Trust, Inc. With USN, 1945-47. Mem. ABA, Allegheny County Bar Assn., St. Thomas More Legal Soc., Ancient Order of Hibernians, Woodland Hills Swim Club, Gaelic Arts Soc., Tin Can Sailors. Office: US Dist Ct 7th Grant St Rm 916 Pittsburgh PA 15219

LEE, DONALD WILLIAM, mechanical engineer, researcher; b. Buffalo, Nov. 4, 1947; s. Robert Arthur and Elizabeth Anne (Kinkead) L.; m. Veronica Mary Martin, June 15, 1971 (div. 1975); m. Sandra Kaye Stout, Nov. 18, 1979; children: Eric Franklin, Andrew Robert. BSME, Clarkson Coll. Tech., Potsdam, N.Y., 1969, MS in Engring. Sci., 1973; PhD in Applied Mech., U. Mich., 1977. Registered profl. engr., Mich., Tenn. Product design engr. Ford Motor Co., Dearborn, Mich., 1969-70; tchg. asst. Clarkson Coll. Tech., 1970-71; instr. Wayne State U., Detroit, 1975-76; rsch. assoc. Oak Ridge (Tenn.) Nat. Lab., 1977-82, mem. rsch. staff, 1982-89, group leader, 1989-97, program mgr., 1997-99, program leader, 1999—. Adj. assoc. prof. dept. mech. and aerospace engring. N.C. State U.; mem. confs. and program com. Environment and Water Resources Inst., 1999—. Active Boy Scouts Am., 1986—, bd. dirs., 1991—, exec. com., 1997—, lodge advisor, 1998—; mem. London County Task Force on Edn., 1987-88; mem. hydrology com. Town of Farragut, 1988; bd. trustees 1st Farragut United Meth. Ch., 1983-84, 88-90; chmn., 1984. Recipient numerous award Boy Scouts Am., including Silver Beaver award, Vigil Honor award, Founders award, James E. West fellow. Mem. ASME, ASCE (environ. engring. divsn., active air and radiation mgmt. com., profl. activities com.), Am. Acad. Environ. Engrs. (diplomate), East Tenn. Brewers Guild (sec. 1978-80, pres. 1981-83), Sigma Xi. Democrat. Methodist. Avocations: homebrewing, gardening. Office: Oak Ridge Nat Lab PO Box 2008 Oak Ridge TN 37831-2008 E-mail: leedw@ornl.gov., lees@icx.net.

LEE, DONG HOON, mathematician, educator; b. Seoul, Republic of Korea, Nov. 17, 1938; arrived in U.S., 1962; s. Youngki and Junghee Lee; m. Hyosoo Kim, Aug. 3, 1968; children: Michael, Stephen. BS, Seoul Nat. U., 1961; PhD, Tulane U., 1967. Assoc. prof. Case Western Res. U., Cleve., 1973—81, prof., 1981—. Vis. prof. Seoul Nat. U., 1976—77, Tech. U. Darmstadt, Germany, 1997. Author: The Structure of Complex Lie Groups, 2001. Mem.: Am. Math. Soc. Office: Case Western Res U Dept Math Cleveland OH 44106

LEE, DONG HWAN, business administration educator; b. Seoul, Nov. 8, 1952; s. Hee Kwon and Yong Boon (Kim) L.; m. Young Ja Lee, Apr. 16, 1981; 2 children; Hyon Jae and Joan. B of Agr. summa cum laude, Kon-Kuk U., Seoul, 1977; MBA, Okla. State U., 1984; PhD in Bus., Ind. U., Bloomington, 1989. Cert. internat. trade specialist, Ministry of Commerce and Industry/Seoul; cert. tchr. Ministry of Edn., Seoul. Sr. staff mem. overseas bus. Div. Gold Star Telecomm. Co., Inc., Seoul, 1976-80; advisor to comml. counsellor Brit. Embassy in Seoul, 1980-82; lectr. mktg. Sch. of Bus. Ind. U., Bloomington, 1989-90; asst. prof. mktg. SUNY, Albany, 1990-97; assoc. prof. mktg. Manhattan Coll., N.Y.C., 1997—. Mem. editl. rev. bd. Jour. Bus. Rsch., 1997—, Jour. Consumer Satisfaction, Dissatisfaction and Complaining Behavior, 1997—. Recipient Faculty Rsch. awards SUNY, Albany, 1990, 92, 94, 95; Faculty Devel. award, N.Y. State/United U. Profls., 1991, 93, 94; rsch. grantee Manhattan Coll., 1999; Garbriel Hauge Faculty fellow Manhattan Coll., 1999-00. Mem. Am. Mktg. Assn. (Outstanding Doctoral Dissertation award 1990), Assn. Consumer Rsch., Soc. Consumer Psychology, Beta Gamma Sigma. Presbyterian. Home: 9 Old Clave Ct Congers NY 10920-1101 Office: Manhattan College Sch of Business DLS 517 Bronx NY 10471 E-mail: dongh.lee@manhattan.edu.

LEE, DORA FUGH, artist; b. Beijing, China, Aug. 16, 1930; arrived in U.S., 1957; d. Philip and Sarah F.; m. Richard Wen-han Lee; children: April, Sarah, Handel, Helen. Student, Chow Yang Law Sch., Peking, China, 1947; studied Chinese traditional painting, western watercolor, sculpture. Art tchr. Chinese Sch., Tokyo, 1950-53; illustrator CIE Visual sect. U.S. Army, 1953-56. Tchr. Chinese calligraphy George Washington U., 1982; tchr. Chinese traditional painting Smithsonian Instn., 1983. One-person exhbns. in Chinese Cultural Ctr., Washington, 1958, Swan Gallery, Plainfield, N.J., 1963, China Inst., N.Y.C., 1964, Stoneman Gallery, Washington, 1966, 70, 72, 74, Franz Bader Gallery, Washington, 1976, 80, 82, 83, 84, 85, 87, 88, 92, 94, 96, Johns Hopkins, Balt., 1985, Pacific Art Club, Hong Kong, 1989, Courtyard Gallery, Beijing, China, 2000; permanent collections include Smithsonian Inst., Washington, NIH, Bethesda, Md., Nat. Cathedral, Washington, Nat. Portrait Gallery, Washington, Nat. Mus. Women in Arts, Washington, Nat. League Am. PEN Women, Am. Acad. of Arts and Letters (N.Y.C.), numerous others. Mem. Nat. League Am. PEN Women, Am. Watercolor Soc., Washington Watercolor Assn. Home: 6305 Orchid Dr Bethesda MD 20817-5613 E-mail: doraflee@aol.com.

LEE, DOUGLAS A. music educator; b. Carmel, Ind., Nov. 3, 1932; s. Ralph Henley and Flossie Ellen (Chandler) Lee; m. Beverly Ruth Haskell, Sept. 2, 1961. MusB with High Distinction, DePauw U., 1954; MusM, U. Mich., 1958, PhD, 1968; postgrad., U. Md., 1985. Instr. Nat. Mus. Camp, Interlochen, Mich., 1959-62, Mt. Union Coll., Alliance, Ohio, 1959-61, chmn. keyboard instrn., 1959-61; asst. prof. Music Wichita (Kans.) State U., 1964-68, assoc. prof., 1968-74, coord. Music History and Lit., 1968-71, coord. grad. studies in Music, 1969-70, chmn. dept. Musicology, 1971-74, prof. Music, 1974-86, administrv. intern, v.p. bus. affairs, 1983; pvt. practice event coord., 1974-85; prof. Musicology Vanderbilt U., Nashville, 1986—, chmn. Music History and Lit., advisor, 1987—98, prof. of musicology emeritus, 1998. Radio commentator Sta. KMUW-FM, 1969-76; judge various competitions, Mu Phi Epsilon, 1980, Kans. Music Tchrs. Assn., 1975-83, Baldwin Found. awards, 1979, 80; program annotator Nashville Symphony Orch., 1988-2001; cons. U.S. Dept. Edn. Jacob Javits fellowship program, 1988, 89, United Meth. Publishing Ho., 1988, Mayfield Pub. Co., 1990, Prentice-Hall, Inc., 1993, 97. Author: The Instrumental Works of Christoph Nichelmann: The Thematic Index, 1971, Franz Benda: A Thematic Catalogue of His Works, 1984, Franz Benda: A Musician at Court, 1998, Masterworks of 20th-Century Music, 2002; editor: Christoph Nichelmann: Clavier Concertos in E Major and A Minor, 1977, Six Sonatas for Violin and Bass by Franz Benda, with Embellishments, 1981; contbr. articles to The New Grove Dictionary of Music and Musicians, 1980, The New Grove Dictionary of Music in the United States, 1986; contbr. articles to profl. jours., chpts. to books. With U.S. Army, 1955-57, Japan. Rector Scholar Found., 1950-54; Rackham fellow U. Mich., 1961-65, fellow NEH, 1980, 85, Am. Philos. Soc., 1980, Kans. Arts Coun., 1985, Tenn. Arts Coun., 1988, 89. Mem. Am. Musicological Soc. (program chmn. Midwest chpt. 1984, South-Ctrl. chpt. 1989, nat. coun. 1986, pres. South-Ctrl. chpt. 1990-91), Music Tchrs. Nat. Assn. (editor 1971-90), Am. Soc. Eighteenth Century Studies, Coll. Music Soc., Sonneck Soc. Am. Music (program coord. 1987-88, editor The Sonneck Soc. Bull. 1988-90. Episcopalian. Avocation: photography. Office: 6517 Cornwall Dr Nashville TN 37205-3041 E-mail: douglas.lee@vanderbilt.edu.

LEE, DOUGLAS BENNETT, filmmaker, writer; b. Takoma Park, Md., Feb. 3, 1953; s. James Edward and Kathleen Edwards Lee; m. Sigrid Lil, May 20, 2000. BA in German Lang. and Lit., Princeton U., 1975. Staff writer, editor Nat. Geog. Mag., Washington, 1977—91; freelance writer Words and Pictures Prodns., St. Michaels, Md., 1991—, ind. filmmaker, 1996—. Contbg. writer Sports Afield, Beverly Hills, Calif., 2001—02. Author: (TV documentary) Snakes: Africa's Deadly Dozen, 2000; prodr.: (TV documentary) Snakes: Africa's Deadly Dozen, 2000; author: Great Train Journeys, 2002, Sports Afield, 2002. Mem.: Washington Ind. Writers. Avocations: sailing, wilderness travel, photography, diving, outdoor sports. Home: PO Box 121 Bozman MD 21612 Office: Words and Pictures Prodn PO Box 121 Bozman MD 21612

LEE, DOUGLAS OCWAH, medical educator; b. Newark, June 4, 1960; BA, U. Pa., 1982; MD, Temple U., 1987. Gen. psychiat. resident NYU, 1987-91; child and adolescent psychiatry resident Harvard Med. Sch., Boston, 1991-93, clin. instr., 1993-95; asst. prof. Emory U. Sch. of Medicine, Atlanta, 1995—.

LEE, EARL WAYNE, library science educator; b. Rockford, Ill., Nov. 8, 1954; s. Earl Ray and Opal (Sharp) L.; m. Kathleen R. DeGrave, Mar. 10, 1978; children: Nathan, Cambria, Erin. BA, Lyon Coll., 1975; MA, U. Ark., Fayetteville, 1978, U. Wis., 1985. Instr. English No. Ill. U., DeKalb, 1979-80; lectr. English U. Wis., Green Bay, 1983-84; info. specialist Dept. of Transp., Madison, Wis., 1985-86; libr. Phillips U., Enid, Okla., 1986-87, Pittsburg (Kans.) State U., 1987—. Author: Drakulya, 1994, Libraries in the Age of Mediocrity, 1998, Drakulya: The Vampire Play, 2001; contbr. articles to profl. jours. Shrenk scholar U. Wis., 1985, McCain scholar Lyon Coll. Mem. ALA, Kans. Libr. Assn. Unitarian Universalist. Office: Axe Bldg Pittsburg State U Pittsburg KS 66762

LEE, EDNA PRITCHARD, education educator; b. Windsor, N.C., Oct. 6, 1923; d. Peter Bernard and Edna (Smith) Pritchard; m. Mack Lloyd Lee Sr., May 17, 1945 (dec. Nov. 1970); 1 child, Mack Lloyd Jr.; m. Lee Cross, June 1, 1991 (dec. Aug. 1997). BS, State U. N.C., Elizabeth City; MA, NYU, N.Y.C. Cert. N.Y. Adminstr.-Supr. Tchr. elem. schs., Windsor, N.C., 1944-61, Mohegan Lake, N.Y., 1961-68; asst. prin. elem. sch., 1968-82; dir. basic edn. Peekskill (N.Y.) High Sch., 1969-80; adj. prof. Mercy Coll., Peekskill, 1985—. Vice chmn. bd. dirs. Peekskill Area Health Ctr.; bd. dirs. Family Resource Ctr., Montrose Child Care Ctr. Co-author: Syllabus for 4th Grade Social Studies, 1972. Trustee Mt. Olivet Ch., 1993-96l ores, Tee Ettes, 1995—. Named Woman of Yr., NAACP, Peekskill, 1976, Woman Engr. of Yr., Bus. and Profl. Women, Peekskill, 1980; recipient Louis Gregory award Bahai Religion, Peekskill, 1988. Mem. AAUW (v.p. 1970-72), Blacks in Govt., Delta Kappa Gamma, Alpha Kappa Alpha, Tee-Ettes (sec. 1982-88). Avocations: golf, gardening. Home: 101 Dutch St Montrose NY 10548-1517

LEE, EDWARD L. retired bishop; b. Fort Washington, Pa., 1934; m. Kathryn Fligg, 1961; 1 child, Kathryn E. Grad. cum laude, Brown U., 1956; MDiv, Gen. Theol. Seminary, 1959. Ordained diaconate, priesthood Episc. Ch., 1959. Curate Ch. Holy Trinity, Phila., 1959-64; Episc. advisor Univ. Christian Movement Temple Univ., 1964-73; rector St. James Ch., Florence, Italy, 1973-82, St. John's Ch., Washington, 1982-89; bishop Episcopal Diocese We. Mich., 1989—; ret. Sunday, pastoral asst. Ch. Annunciation, Phila.; parish cons. St. Peters Ch., Germantown; lectr. homiletics Phila. Divinity Sch.; nat. chair Episc. Peace Fellowship, 1970-73; with Convocation of Am. Chs. Europe, pres. coun. advice; dep. Gen. Conv., 1976, 79; chair Coun. Coll. Preachers; active Washington Diocesan Coun., chmn. exec. com.; com. inquiry on the nuclear issues Diocesan Peace Commn. Former chair bd. advisors Am. Internat. Sch. Florence. Office: Episcopal Diocese Western Mich 2600 Vincent Ave Portage MI 49024-5600

LEE, ELIZABETH MULLINS, financial analyst; b. Smyrna, Tenn., Aug. 2, 1959; d. Robert Franklin Sr. and Dot (Edmondson) M.; m. Frank Marks Lee Jr., Oct. 2, 1982; children: Hunter Austin, Lindsey Kelton. BS in Acctg., Freed Hardeman Coll., 1981. Staff acct. Capital Air, Smyrna, 1981-83; gen. ledger supr. Health Group, Nashville, 1983-84; sr. fin. analyst Nissan Motor Mfg. Corp. USA, Smyrna, 1984—. Mem. adv. bd. Boys & Girls Club, Smyrna, 1996. Avocations: basketball, children French machine sewing, football, baseball. Home: 113 Oak Hill Dr Smyrna TN 37167-4905 Office: Nissan Motor Mfg Corp USA 307 Nissan Dr Smyrna TN 37167

LEE, ELLEN FAITH, insurance company associate; b. Portland, Oreg., Sept. 30, 1951; d. Ira Lawrence Harris and Doris Louise (Mitchell) Landis; married, July 13, 1983. Cert. med. aide Okla. Bd. Nursing. Aide Williamette Residential, Eugene, Oreg., 1982-84; med. aide Oak Hills Nursing Home, Jones, Okla., 1984-85; group leader, computer problem solver Plaza Alliance, Oklahoma City, 1985-95; computer cons. Jericho Corrections, 1995-96; assoc. Bituminous Ins., 1996—. Avocations: granddaughter, barrell racing. Home: PO Box 922 Jones OK 73049-0922 Office: Bituminous Ins 5400 NW Grand St 545 Oklahoma City OK 73112 Fax: 405-396-2913. E-mail: OKC011@aol.com.

LEE, ELTON R. physician; b. San Francisco, Nov. 2, 1967; s. Paul G.B. and Bo Lee; m. Doris Chan, Aug. 5, 1995. BS in Biomed. Engring. magna cum laude, Boston U., 1989; MD, MPH, Tufts U., 1993. Diplomate Am. Bd. Internal Medicine. Resident Stanford (Calif.) U. Hosp., 1993-96; pvt. practice internal medicine, Seattle, 1996—. Mem. ACP, Tau Beta Pi. Republican. Christian.

LEE, E(UGENE) STANLEY, engineer, mathematician, educator; b. Hopeh, China, Sept. 7, 1930; came to U.S., 1955, naturalized, 1961; s. Ing Yah and Lindy (Hsieng) L.; m. Mayanne Lee, Dec. 21, 1957 (dec. June 1980); children: Linda J., Margaret H.; m. Yuan Lee, Mar. 8, 1983; children— Lynn Hua Lee, Jin Hua Lee, Ming Hua Lee. BS, Chung Cheng Inst. Tech., Taiwan, Republic of China, 1953; MS, N.C. State U., 1957; PhDChemE, Princeton U., 1962. Rsch. engr. Phillips Petroleum Co., Bartlesville, Okla., 1960-66; asst. prof. chem. engring. Kans. State U., Manhattan, 1966-67, assoc. prof. indsl. engring., 1967-69, prof. indsl. engring., 1969—; prof. chem. and elec. engring. U. So. Calif., 1972-76. Hon. prof. Chinese Acad. Sci., 1987—; chaired prof. Yuan-ze Inst. Tech., Taiwan, Republic of China, 1993—; cons. govt. and industry. Author: Quasilinearization and Invariant Imbedding, 1968, Coal Conversion Technnology, 1979, Operations Research, 1981, Fuzzy and Evidence Reasoning, 1996, Fuzzy and Multi-level Decision Making, 2000; editor: Energy Sci. and Tech., 1975; assoc. editor: Jour. Math. Analysis and Applications, 1974—, assoc. editor: Computers and Mathematics with Applications, 1974, editl. bd.: Jour. Engring. Chemistry and Metallurgy, 1989—, editl. bd.: Jour. of Nonlinear Differential Equations, 1992—, editl. bd.: Jour. Chinese Fuzzy Sys. Assn., 1995—, editl. bd.: Fuzzy Optimization and Decision Making, 2000—, editl. bd.: Internat. Jour. Modeling and Optimization, 2001—, editl. bd.: Math. Scis. Rsch. Hot-line, An Internat. Jour. Rapid Publ., 2001—. Grantee Dept. Def., 1967-72, Office Water Resources, 1968-75, EPA, 1969-71, NSF, 1971—, USDA, 1978-90, Dept. Energy, 1979-84, USAF, 1984-88. Mem. Soc. Indsl. and Applied Math., Ops. Rsch. Soc. Am., N. Am. Fuzzy Info. Processing Soc., Internat. Neural Network Soc., Sigma Xi, Tau Beta Pi, Phi Kappa Phi. Office: Kans State U Dept Indsl Engring Manhattan KS 66506 *Nothing can replace hard work and persistence.*

LEE, EVELYN MARIE, elementary and secondary education educator; b. Germantown, Ohio, Dec. 17, 1931; d. Robert Orlandus and Edna Cathern (Durr) Stump; m. John Henry Lee, Dec. 16, 1956; children: Mark Douglas, David Matthew, Lori Ann Lee Delehoy. BS in Edn., Otterbein Coll., 1954; MEd with emphasis in reading, U. Alaska, 1979. Dept. store tng. supr., asst. mdse. mgr. The Home Store, Dayton, Ohio, 1954-55; tchr. Parma (Ohio) Pub. Schs., 1955-56; math aide civil svc. Nat. Adv. Com. for Aeros. Ames Lab., Moffett Field, Calif., 1956-57; substitute tchr. Warren (Ohio) Pub. Schs., 1957-59, tchr., 1959-60, Gwinn (Mich.) Pub. Schs., 1960-64, Anchorage Sch. Dist., 1964-65, 68-87, substitute tchr., 1987-96. Hon. life mem. Alaska PTA; vol. City of Loveland, The Lincoln Ctr., Fort Collins; treas. Rialto Theater Guild. Mem. NEA (ret.; life), NEA-Alaska (ret.; life), Alaska Hist. Soc. (life), Tulpehocken Settlement Hist. Soc., Hist. Soc. Germantown, The Alaskans, Loveland New Friendship Club, Order Eastern Star. United Methodist. Avocations: travel, reading, arts and crafts, genealogy. Home: 1521 Park Dr Loveland CO 80538-4285

LEE, FRANCES HELEN, editor; b. N.Y.C., Jan. 6, 1936; d. Murray and Rose (Rothman) Lee. BA, Queens Coll., 1957; MA, NYU, 1962. Editl. asst. Christian Herald Family Bookshelf, N.Y.C., 1957-62; with Gordon and Breach Sci. Pubs., Inc., 1964-66, Am. Electric Power Svc. Corp. AEP Operating Ideas, N.Y.C., 1966-69, Indsl. Water Engring. Mag., N.Y.C., 1969-71; directory editor photographic divsn. United Bus. Publs., 1971-80; editor Am. Druggist Blue Book Hearst Books/Bus. Publs. Group, 1980-81; spl. projects coord. motor manuels Hearst Book Divsn., 1981-82; editor New Price Report, 1982-84, Am. Druggist Blue Book, 1982-88; freelance editor, cons., 1988—. Supr. Bronx divsn. N.Y. State Civil Defense, 1953-59; mem. com. on N.Y.C. charter revision, Citizens Union, 1975, com. on city mgmt., 1977-92, bd. dirs., co-chmn. com. on N.Y.C. cultural concerns, 1979-97, chmn., 1997-98; vol. N.Y.C. Opera, 1988—, info. project mgr., 2001—. Recipient cert. of honor NYU Alumni Fedn., 1985, Meritorious Svc. award, 1986. Mem. N.Y. Bus. Press Editors (bd. dirs. 1988-90, sec. 1990-91), Women's Equity Action League (chmn. rsch. com.), NYU Alumnae Club (dir. 1976-78, rec. sec. 1978-80, v.p. 1980-82, pres. 1982-84, rep. to bd. dirs. fedn. 1984-86), NYU Alumni Fedn. (dir.-at-large 1986—), Villa-Lobos Music Soc. (sec. 1989-91, treas. 1992-95), NYU Club (bd. govs. 1987-89). Home: 170 2nd Ave New York NY 10003-5754

LEE, FRANCIS CHO-KUEN, aerospace engineering analyst; b. Kwaichow, China, Sept. 20, 1942; s. Leung Lee and Sau Ying Wong; m. Elizabeth Ling-Hing Lee, Mar. 11, 1973; 1 child, Debbie Angela Lee. BSc in Engring., U. Newcastle, Australia, 1969, M in Engring. Sci., 1971; MEng, U. So. Calif., 1986, PhD, 1994. Registered profl. engr., N.J. Field svc. specialist Transam. Delaval Inc., Trenton, N.J., 1976-80; test engr. Boeing Airplane Co., Seattle, 1980-81; mem. tech. staff Rockwell Internat., Canoga Park, Calif., 1981-86, sr. control engr., 1991-95; staff engr. TRW, Redondo Beach, 1986-91; sr. guidance and control engr. Spectrum Astro, Manhatten Beach, 1995-97; prin. lectr. Inst. Vocat. Edn., Hong Kong, 1997—. Contbr. articles to profl. jours. Mem. AIAA. Avocations: squash, guitar, hiking, dancing, bicycling. Home: 22524 Ladeene Ave Torrance CA 90505-2238 E-mail: flee9988@netvigator.com.

LEE, FRANCIS DUANE, consulting engineer; b. Jan. 11, 1940; s. Warren Tingley and Dorothy Lucille (Simmons) L.; m. Marian Marie Peter, June 8, 1965; children: Joseph Duane, Daniel Bryant. MS in Engring., 1968. Registered profl. engr. Oreg., Wash., Idaho. Design engr. Williams and Ellis, Phoenix, 1963-68; project mgr., design engr. Stevens, Thompson and Runyan, Portland, Oreg., 1968-74, Boise, Idaha, 1968-74; office mgr. H.G.E. Inc., Portland, 1974-75; pres. Lee Engring. Inc., Oregon City, Oreg., 1975—. Lectr. in field. Mem. AM. Water Works Assn., Nat. Soc. Profl. Engrs., Am. Cons. Engrs. Coun. Republican. Office: 1300 John Adams St Oregon City OR 97045-1631

LEE, FRED ARTHUR, radiologist, educator; b. Portland, Oreg., Mar. 16, 1929; MD, Oreg. Health Scis. U., 1956. Diplomate Am. Bd. Radiology, Am. Bd. Pediatric Radiology. Intern Temple U. Hosp., Phila., 1956-57; resident U. Pitts. Med. Ctr. Hosps., 1959-62; fellow in pediatric radiology Children's Hosp. Pitts., 1963-64; staff radiologist Children's Hosp., Pitts., 1964-67, asst. prof. radiology, 1964-67, staff radiologist, chief divsn. diagnostic radiology, 1967-82; pvt. practice Pasadena, Calif.; clin. prof. radiology U. So. Calif. Sch. Medicine, L.A.; mem. staff Huntington Meml. Hosp., Pasadena, 1982—. Capt. USAF MC, 1957-59. Office: Huntington Meml Hosp 100 W California Blvd Pasadena CA 91105-3097

LEE, FRED C. electrical engineering educator; b. China, 1946; naturalized Am. citizen; BS, Nat. Cheng Kung U., Taiwan, 1968; MSA, Duke U., 1972, PhD, 1974. Tchg. asst. Duke U., Durham, N.C., 1970-72; rsch. asst. Spacecraft Sys. Rsch. Lab., 1972-74; mem. tech. staff TRW Systems, 1974-77; from asst. prof. to prof. Va. Poly. Inst. and State U., Blacksburg, 1977-83, James S. Tucker prof., 1986-94, Lewis A. Hester engring. chair, 1994-99, univ. disting. prof., 1999—, dir. Va. Power Electronics Ctr., 1985-98; bd. dirs. Zytec, 1986-97; dir. NSFERC Ctr. for Power Electronics Sys., 1998. Bd. dirs. Artesyn Techs., 1997—; mem. adv. bd. Power Integrations Inc., 1988-94; chmn., CEO Va. Power Techs., Inc., 1994—. Recipient, PCIM award for Outstanding Power Electronics Edn., 1990, Arthur Fury award for Outstanding Powere Electronics Innovation, 1998, IEEE Millennium medal, 2000. Fellow IEEE William E. Newell Power Electronics award 1989, IEEE Power Electronics Soc. (chmn. meeting com., mem. advt. com., mem. fellow evaluation com., chmn. power electronics specialists conf. 1987, v.p. 1988, pres. 1993-94), IEEE Engrs. Indsl. Applications Soc., Brit. Inst. Engrs. Office: NSFERC Ctr for Power Electronics Sys 657 Whitemore Blacksburg VA 24061-0111

LEE, FRED STEVEN, telecommunications engineer; b. Wahiawa Oahu, Hawaii, June 7, 1954; s. Michael T. H. and Annette Kimiko (Ozawa) L.; m. Lynn Marie Gray, Aug. 16, 1985; children: Jennifer L. Pearce, Sandra M. Pearce, Christopher M., Nicole M. BSEE, Cornell U., 1975, MSEE, 1976. Head digital task group Watkins-Johnson, Gaithersburg, Md., 1976-78; prin. engr. Fairchild Space and Electronics, Germantown, 1978-82; dir. engring. DAMA Telecom., Rockville, 1982-86, Data Gen. Telecom., Rockville, 1986-87; pres., owner TransDigital Sys., Inc., 1987—. Cons. COMSAT Labs., Germantown, 1987—. Tiger Cub leader Cub Scouts Pack 178, Rockville, 1992-93. Achievements include patents for distributed switching architecture and high speed communication processing system. Avocations: scuba, backpacking, spelunking. Office: TransDigital Sys Inc 7753 Barnstable Pl Rockville MD 20855-2537

LEE, GENE F. accountant; b. Bklyn., July 8, 1960; s. Gam and May Ngon (Tom) L. BBA, Pace U., 1982; MBA, Fordham U., 1988. CPA, N.Y. Bookkeeper part-time McCarthy, Ried, Crisanti & Maffei, Inc., N.Y.C., 1980; account reconciler part-time Paine, Webber, Jackson & Curtis, Inc., 1980-81; project analyst part-time Mfrs. Hanover Trust Co., 1981-82; staff acct. Richard A. Eisner & Co., CPAs, 1982-84; acct. Cometals, Inc., 1984-85; fin. analyst The Hertz Corp., 1985-86; housing analyst, mortgage officer, mgmt. auditor City of N.Y. Dept. Housing Preservation and Devel., 1988-92; acctg. mgr. City of N.Y. Dept. Consumer Affairs, 1993; sr. fin. analyst N.Y. Equity Fund, N.Y.C., 1993-95; corp. acctg. mgr. The Dreyfus Corp., 1995—. Part-time exam grader AICPA, N.Y.C., 1989-91. Vol., chaperone St. Bartholomew Ch. & Sch., Queens, N.Y., 1987—. Scholar N.Y. Regents, 1978-82, United Fedn. Tchrs., Pace U. Mem. Beta Gamma Sigma, Alpha Chi. Roman Catholic. Avocations: gardening, reading, commemorative coins and stamps. Office: Dreyfus Corp 7th Fl 200 Park Ave New York NY 10166-0099

LEE, GENEVIEVE BRUGGEMAN, publishing company executive; b. Mahnomen, Minn., May 23, 1928; d. Joseph William and Mary Martha (Bastain) Bruggeman; m. Joel Kenneth Lee, Aug. 23, 1946; children: Rebecca Marie, Joel Gregory. Clk. Family Svc. Assn., N.Y.C., 1946-47; counselor Cin. Employment Svc., 1968-70; exec. sec. Ch. Bulls. of Buffalo, Inc., 1970-73, v.p., 1973—. Bd. dirs. Woodgate Assn., East Amherst, N.Y.; mem. adv. bd. Schofield Residence, Buffalo, 1983-85, mem. exec. bd., sec., 1985-90, vice chmn./sec., 1991-94, chmn. bd. dirs., 1994-99, treas., 1999—. Mem. Ken-Ton C. of C., Zonta (pres. Kenmore 1984-86, bd. dirs. area 3, 1986-88, 2000—, sec. dist. IV 1988-90), Kenmore C. of C., Printing and Imaging Assn. of We. N.Y. Republican. Roman Catholic. Home: 258 Old Meadow Dr East Amherst NY 14051-2405 Office: Ch Bulls of Buffalo Inc 745 Englewood Ave Buffalo NY 14223-2406 E-mail: RMLEE@pcom.net.

LEE, GILBERT BROOKS, retired ophthalmology engineer; b. Cohasset, Mass., Sept. 10, 1913; s. John Alden and Charlotte Louise (Brooks) L.; m. Marion Corinne Rapp, Mar. 7, 1943 (div. Jan. 1969); children: Thomas Stearns, Jane Stanton, Frederick Cabot, Gilbert Eliot Frazar. BA, Reed Coll., 1937; MA, New Sch. for Social Rsch., 1949. Asst. psychologist U.S. Naval Submarine Base Civil Svc., Psychophysics of Vision, New London, Conn., 1950-53; rsch. assoc. Project Mich., Vision Rsch. Labs., Willow Run, 1954-57; rsch. assoc. dept. ophthalmology U. Mich., Ann Arbor, 1958-72, sr. rsch. assoc., 1972-75, sr. engring. rsch. assoc. ophthalmology, 1975-82, part-time sr. engr. ophthalmology, from 1982. Sec. internat. dept., 23d St. YMCA, N.Y.C.; cons. W.K. Kellogg Eye Ctr., Ann Arbor, 1968—. Local organizer, moderator (TV program) Union of Concerned Scientists' Internat. Satellite Symposium on Nuclear Arms Issues, 1986; producer (TV show) Steps for Peace, 1987; designer, builder portable tristimulus Colorimeter; (videotape) Pomerance Awards, UN.; broken lake ice rescue procedure rsch., by one person in a dry suit, all weather conditions, 1966, 89-93 (videotape). Precinct del. Dem. County Conv., Washtenaw County, 1970, 74; treas. Dem. Club, Ann Arbor, Mich., 1971-72, 74-79; vice chmn. nuclear arms control com., 1979; chmn. Precinct Election Inspectors, 1968-75; scoutmaster Portland (Oreg.) area coun. Boy Scouts Am., 1932-39. Capt. AUS, 1942-46, 61-62. Mem. AAAS, Nat. Resources Def. Coun., Fedn. Am. Scientists, N.Y. Acad. Sci., Nation Assocs., ACLU, Sierra Club, Amnesty Internat. Home: Phoenix, Ariz. Died Jan. 19, 2001.

LEE, GLEN K. dentist; b. Honolulu, Nov. 10, 1950; s. Kenneth Kam Chun Lee and Audrey (Mew Wun) Chun; m. Barbara Lynn Dunnett, Feb. 14, 1981; children: Jayna Christine, Jeffrey Ryan, David Michael. BS, Loyola U., L.A., 1972; DDS, Creighton U., 1976. Pvt. practice, Santa Barbara, Calif., 1976—. Mem. med. staff St. Francis Hosp., Santa Barbara, 1976--, Santa Barbara Cottage Hosp., 1976--, Goleta Valley Hosp., Goleta, Calif., 1976--. Mem. Santa Barbara Trust for Hist. Preservation; bd. dirs. Hope Sch. Dist. Ednl. Found. Mem. ADA, Am. Acad. Implant Dentistry, Am. Acad. Cosmetic Dentistry, Acoustic Neuroma Assn. Am., Calif. Dental Assn., Santa Barbara-Ventura County Dental Soc., Creighton U. Dental Sch. Dental Alumni Adv. Bd., Santa Barbara Hist. Soc. Democrat. Roman Catholic. Avocations: gardening, fishing, cooking. Home: 3641 Tierra Bella Santa Barbara CA 93105-2555 Office: 1919 State St Ste 201 Santa Barbara CA 93101-8452 E-mail: glenkleedds@aol.com.

LEE, GLENN RICHARD, medical administrator, educator; b. Ogden, Utah, May 18, 1932; s. Glenn Edwin and Thelma (Jensen) L.; m. Pamela Marjorie Ridd, July 18, 1969; children— Jennifer, Cynthia. BS, U. Utah, 1953, MD, 1956. Intern Boston City Hosp.-Harvard U., 1956-57, resident, 1957-58; clin. asso. Nat. Cancer Inst., NIH, 1958-60; postdoctoral fellow U. Utah, 1960-63; instr. U. Utah Coll. Medicine, 1963-64, asst. prof. internal medicine, 1964-68, assoc. prof., 1968-73, prof., 1973-96, assoc. dean for acad. affairs, 1973-76, dean, 1978-83, prof. emeritus, 1996—; chief of staff Salt Lake VA Med. Ctr., 1985-95. Author: (with others) Clinical Hematology, 10th edit, 1998; Contbr. (with others) numerous articles to profl. jours.; editorial bd.: (with others) Am. Jour. Hematology, 1976-79. Served with USPHS, 1958-60. Markle Found. scholar, 1965-70; Nat. Inst. Arthritis, Metabolic and Digestive Disease grantee, 1977-82. Mem. A.C.P., Am. Soc. Hematology, Am. Soc. Clin. Investigation, Western Assn. Physicians, Am. Inst. Nutrition. Mem. Lds Ch. Home and Office: 3781 Ruth Dr Salt Lake City UT 84124-2331 E-mail: grichardl@aol.com.

LEE, GLORIA DEANE, artist, educator; b. Council Bluffs, Iowa, Feb. 10, 1937; d. Carroll and Margaret Kathleen (Morse) Hamilton; m. Robert Dean Lee, June 29, 1962. BFA, U. Iowa, 1959; postgrad., Long Beach State U., 1964-68. Tchr. Garden Grove (Calif.) Unified Sch. Dist., 1959-64, Las Vegas (Nev.) Unified Sch. Dist., 1964, Compton Unified Sch. Dist., 1964-72, Manhattan Beach (Calif.) Unified Sch. Dist., 1984-95, L.A. Unified Adult Sch., 1993—; pvt. tutor academics and Positive Parenting, Manhattan Beach, 1978—; tutor Keys to Learning, Redondo Beach, Calif., 1984-96. Tchr. painting Beverly Hills (Calif.) Recreation, 1995-98, Palos Verdes (Calif.) rt Ctr., 1990—, El Segundo (Calif.) Recreation Sr. Ctr., 1996-98; dir. Palos Vedes (Calif.) Artists, 1985-89; mem. edn. com. Palos Verdes Art Ctr., 1986-90; represented by Artist's Studio Galleries, Palos Verdes Peninsula, 1987-99, Gail's Frames Gallery; juried assoc. Watercolor West, 1992, 96—, Women Artists of the West, 1992—, Women Painters West, 1992—, Fine Arts Inst., San Bernardino, Calif., 1995—. One woman shows at Collectors Gallery, Palos Verdes Art Ctr., 1995, Norris Theater, Rolling Hills Estates, Calif., 1995; exhibited in group shows at Malaga Cove Libr., Palos Verdes Estates, 1993, Beckstrand Gallery, Rancho Palos Verdes, 1993, 94, 95, 96, Artists' Studio, Rolling Hills Estates, 1993, 94, 96, Taos (N.Mex.) Convention Ctr., 1993, Stewart Gallery, Rancho Palos Verdes, 1993, 94, 96, 97, Petropavlovsk (Russia) Mus./Gallery, 1993, Gate Gallery, San Pedro, Calif., 1993, Palos Verdes Art Ctr., 1994, 95, 96, 97, 98, Lancaster (Calif.) Art Mus., 1994, Millennium Show, Montrose, CA, 2000, Square One Finegood Gall., West Hills, CA, Village Square Gall., Riverside (Calif.) Art Mus., 1995, 96, Long Beach (Calif.) Arts, 1995, 97, Joslyn Fine Arts Gallery, Torrance, Calif., 1995, 96, 97, 98, San Bernardino County Mus., 1996, Janet Turner Print Gallery, Chico, Calif., 1997, Brand Libr., 1997, Royal Birmingham (Eng.) Soc. Artists Gallery, 1997, Women Artists West, Biloxi, Miss., 1997, Lankersham Art Ctr. Gallery, Calif., 1997, Printmaking Coun. N.J., Cerritos Art Gallery/Cerritos Coll., Calif., 1998, Met. Life, Bridgewater, N.J., 1998, Monoprints and Books, Rancho Palos Verdes, 1998, Gallery 825, L.A., Lankersham Art Gallery, L.A., 1998, 99, NAPA 3d Ann. Exhbn., Covington, La., 1998, 99, Brand XXVIII Works on Paper, Glendale, Calif., 1998, 99, Brand XXIX Works on Paper, 1999-00, WAOW Membership Exhbn., Rancho Capistrano, Calif., 1998, 99, UCLA Med. Ctr., 1998, Lancaster (Calif.) Art Mus., 1999, Finegood Gallery, West Hills, Calif., 2000, Charles Borman Gallery, Montrose, Calif., 2000, Soleil, Manhattan Beach, 2000, others; represented in various pvt. collections; watercolors added to UCLA Med. Ctr. collection, 1998. Mem. South Bay Watercolor Soc. (bd. dirs. 1995-97, pres.), Nat. Acrylic Painters Assn., L.A. Printmaking Soc., Calif. Watercolor Assn., Pacific Art Guild (past officer), Paletteers, Women Artists of the West, Women Painters West. Avocations: singing, playing musical instruments, writing poetry, sailing, gardening. Home: 461 28th St Manhattan Beach CA 90266-2126

LEE, GORDON KENNETH, physician assistant; b. Harlingen, Tex., Jan. 2, 1959; s Ralph Gordon and Enedelia Lee; m. Barbara Jo Lee, Aug. 10, 1985; children: Joseph Randolf, Mark Kenneth. B in Physician Asst. Studies, U. Tex., Galveston, 1985; M in Physician Asst. Studies, U. Nebr., 1997. Physician asst. McGregor Med. Assn., Houston, 1985-87, Tex. Dept. Corrections, Rosharon, Tex., 1987, USAF Regional Hosp., Sheppard AFB, 1987-89, 432d Med. Group, Misawa AB, Japan, 1989-91, Wright-Patterson AFB, Ohio, 1992-93, Parkview Regional Hosp., Mexia, Tex., 1993-97; pres. Paladin Healthcare Assocs., P.C., Wortham, 1997—. Bd. dirs., pres. Eagle Creat Therapeutic Ctr., Inc., 1998-99; bd. dirs. Freestone County Soccer Assn, 1997—; vice chmn. exec. com. Ctr. for Rural Health Initiative, Austin, Tex., 1998-2001. Capt. USAF, 1987-93. Fellow Am. Acad. Physician Assts., Tex. Acad. Physician Assts. (bd. dirs. 1998). Avocations: scuba, motorcycling, parachuting. Home: RR 3 Box 486 Mexia TX 76667-9301 Office: Paladin Healthcare Assocs PC 618 S 3rd St Wortham TX 76693-9722 E-mail: glee@mexia.com.

LEE, GRACE TZE, information services company executive; b. Taipei, Taiwan, Aug. 11, 1953; came to U.S., 1974; d. Tang Chi and Ming (Shu) L. BA, Nat. Taipei U., 1974; BS, U. Nev., 1977; postgrad., UCLA, 1988. Fgn. currency specialist Deak-Perera Co., L.A., 1977-80; asst. mgr. Universal Supply Co., 1980; contr. AJR Electronics Inc., 1981-84; western zone asst. mgr. Samsung Electronics Co., 1984; contr. Gideon Nol Inc., 1985-87, James G. Wiley Co., L.A., 1987-91, Jetset Tours Inc. (N.Am.), L.A., 1991-95, DER Travel Inc., L.A., 1995-96, F&M Sales, Inc., L.A., 1996-98; CFO Entex Info. Svcs., Inc., 1998-99; v.p. fin. Tatsumi USA Inc., Torrance, Calif., 1999—. Home: 23442 Batey Ave Harbor City CA 90710-1204 Office: 19708 Pacific Gateway Dr Torrance CA 90502-1131 E-mail: gracel@tatsumiusa.com., glee811@aol.com.

LEE, GWENDOLIN KUEI, retired ballet educator; b. Shanghai, People's Republic of China, Nov. 17, 1932; came to U.S., 1978; d. Din-Yuan and Ching (Chu) L.; m. C.T. Yu, May 1955 (div. 1965); children: Aldin, Marline. Diplomate, St. Mary's Hall, Shanghai, 1952; cert., Shanghai Inst. Drama, 1955. Instr. ballet Acad. of Shanghai People's Drama, 1954-56; dir. The Lee Sch. Ballet, Shanghai, 1955-66; dir., instr. Champaign, Ill., 1981-99; instr. Shanghai Gymnastic Inst., 1960-63, Shanghai Children's Palace, 1970-78, Parkland Coll., Champaign, 1979-80, McKinley YMCA, Champaign, 1979-81; ret., 1999. Cons. Chgo. City Ballet, 1984-85; artistic dir. Ill. Children's Expo, sponsored by Mercy Hosp., Champaign, 1986-88. Choreographer, artistic dir. numerous ballet recitals including Grandmother's Fairy Tales, 1982, An Evening of Children's Ballet, Cinderella, Faust-The Walpurgis Night Scene, 1984, Magic Key, Swan Lake Act II, 1986, Little Red Riding Hood, The Beautiful Blue Danube, 1988, Persian Market, The Dream Scene from Don Quixote, 1990, It's a Small World, The Nutcracker, 1992, An Enchanting Evening of Children's Ballet, 1994, Grandma's Golden Book, 1996, Don Quixote, 1996; photographer sch. calendars. Mem. Vintage Champaign Coun., 1983-87. Avocations: photography, opera, drama, music.

LEE, HAIGUN, engineer, researcher; b. Chuncheon City, Korea, Sept. 26, 1964; came to U.S., 1988; s. Koo Young and Yoo Kyum (Kim) L.; m. Jeeyae Chei, Sept. 13, 1992; children: Jinjoo Rachel, Hanjoo Richard. BS, Korea U., Seoul, 1987; MS, U. Ill., 1990, PhD, 1995. Rsch., tchg. asst. U. Ill., Chgo., 1988-90, 91-95; student tchr. Korean Sch., 1991-92; postdoctoral rsch. assoc. MIT, Cambridge, Mass., 1995-97, staff rsch. assoc., 1997—. Hon. spot news reporter The Cho-Sun Daily of Am., Chgo., 1993—. Author: Cryogenics, 1997; contbr. articles to profl. jours. 2d lt. Third Mil. Acad., 1990-91. Mem. Materials Rsch. Soc., ASM, Korean-Am. Scientists and Engrs. Assn., U.S. Student Orgn. in Midwest (pres. Chgo. chpt. 1994-95), U. Ill. Chgo. Student Assn. (pres. 1993-94), Sigma Xi. Avocations: golfing, chess, singing, playing guitar. Home: 233 Gerny Rd Chestnut Hill MA 02467 Office: MIT (NW14-3111) 170 Albany St Cambridge MA 02139-4208 E-mail: hlee@jokaku.mit.edu.

LEE, HAMILTON H. education educator; b. Zhouxian, Shandong, China, Oct. 10, 1921; s. Beiyuen and Huaiying Lee; m. Jean Chang, Aug. 14, 1945; children: Wei, Clarence, Karen, Kate. BA, Nat. Beijing Normal U., 1948; MA, U. Minn., 1958; EdD, Wayne State U., 1964. Rsch. assoc. Wayne State U., Detroit, 1958-64; asst. prof. Moorhead (Minn.) State U., 1964-65; assoc. prof. U. Wis., LaCrosse, 1965-66; prof. edn. East Stroudsburg (Pa.) U., 1966—, now prof. emeritus. Vis. prof. Seton Hall U., summer 1964; vis. scholar Harvard U., summer 1965, 66; vis. fellow Princeton U., 1976-78; hon. mem. adv. coun. Internat. Biog. Ctr., Cambridge, Eng., 1995. Author: Readings in Instructional Technology, 1970, (chapbook I) Reflection, 1989, (chapbook II) Revelation, 1991; contbg. editor Edn. Tomorrow, 1972-74; contbr. articles and poetry to profl. jours. and anthologies. Recipient numerous poetry contest awards; fellow World Lit. Acad. Mem. World Future Soc. (profl.), Acad. Am. Poets, Poetry Soc. Am., Pa. Poetry Soc., Internat. Soc. Poets (life mem. adv. panel), Am. Biol. Inst. (rsch. bd.), Phi Delta Kappa. Address: PO Box 980 Los Altos CA 94023-0980 also: 30 Hacienda Dr Woodside CA 94062-2420

LEE, HARRISON HON, naval architecture librarian, consultant; b. Stockton, Calif., Sept. 20, 1943; s. Hon Bo and Lulu Joyce Lee; m. Estelle Toby Wlosko, May 11, 1980. AA, Stockton (Calif.) Coll., 1967; BA, Stanislaus State Coll., Turlock, Calif., 1969; MA, Sonoma State U., Cotati, Calif., 1973; MS in Libr. Sci., Simmons Coll., 1978. Lectr. Ecole d'Humanite, Reuti, Switzerland, 1973-75; libr. M. Rosenblatt & Son, Inc., N.Y.C., 1978-89; libr. cons. SELF, Stockton, 1989—. Mem. Spl. Libr. Assn., Soc. Naval Archs. and Marine Engrs. Unitarian Universalist.

LEE, HARRY ANTONIUS, allergist, immunologist; b. Jakarta, Indonesia, June 27, 1954; came to U.S., 1973; s. Djoe Eng and Jan Nio (Tjan) L.; m. Johanna Francisca Setiawan, Nov. 23, 1977; children: Edwin Christopher, Vanessa Theresa. BS magna cum laude, Fairmont (W.Va.) State Coll., 1977; MD, St. George's U., Grenada, 1982. Cert. in allergy and immunology; cert. in pediats. Resident in pediats. Marshall U. Sch. Medicine, Huntington, W.Va., 1983-86; fellow in allergy and immunology U. South Fla./All Children's Hosp., St. Petersburg, 1989-91; with Air U. Regional Hosp.-Maxwell AFB, Montgomery, Ala., 1991-93, Bapt. Med. Ctr., Montgomery, 1994—, Jackson Hosp., Montgomery, 1994—. Contbr. articles to profl. jours. Fellow Am. Acad. Pediats., Am. Acad. Allergy, Asthma, and Immunology, Am. Coll. Allergy, Asthma, and Immunology; mem. Al. Soc. Allergy and Immunology, Joint Coun. Allergy, Asthma, and Immunology, Med. Assn. State Ala. Republican. Roman Catholic. Office: Allergy Asthma and Immunology of Montgomery 1420 Narrow Lane Pkwy Montgomery AL 36111-2654 Fax: 334-284-4256. E-mail: dochlee@yahoo.com.

LEE, HEI WAI, finance educator, researcher; b. Hong Kong, Jan. 10, 1960; came to U.S., 1982; s. Po On and Yuk Wa (Ching) L.; m. Kamee Angela Lee, May 23, 1988; children: Jonathan Ian, Isabella Jaclyn. B in Social Sci., Chinese U. of Hong Kong, 1982; MBA, U. Okla., 1984; MS in Fin., U. Ill., Champaign, 1986; PhD in Fin., U. Ill., 1989. Cert. cash mgr., CFA. Vis. asst. prof. U. Miami, 1989-90, U. South Fla., Tampa, 1990-94; assoc. prof. corp. fin. and investments U. Mich., Dearborn, 1994—. Contbr. articles to profl. jours. Mem. Am. Fin. Assn., Internat. Fin. Mgmt. Assn., Assn. Investment Mgmt. and Rsch., Inst. CFAs, Midwest Fin. Assn., Ea. Fin. Assn., Investment Analysts Soc. Detroit, Beta Gamma Sigma, Phi Kappa Phi. Home: 44071 Darthmouth St Canton MI 48188-1015 Office: U Mich-Dearborn 4901 Evergreen Rd Dearborn MI 48128-2406

LEE, HENRY, lawyer; b. N.Y.C., Dec. 18, 1952; s. Tong Shong and Toy (Wong) L. BA, Bklyn. Coll., 1973; JD, U. Iowa, 1977. Bar: Calif. 1979, N.Y. 1980, N.J. 1993. Research atty. Calif. Ct. Appeal, San Bernardino, 1977-78; assoc. Mendes & Mount, N.Y.C., 1980-85, ptnr., 1985-91; legal cons. Am. law Peruvian pvt. corps., 1991-92; of counsel Mendes & Mount, N.Y.C., 1992-95, ptnr., 1996-98, L.A., 1998—. Note editor Jour. Corp. Law, U. Iowa Coll. Law, 1976-77. Office: Mendes & Mount LLP 725 S Figueroa St Fl 19 Los Angeles CA 90017-5524 E-mail: henry.lee@mendes.com.

LEE, HEUNG-MAN, surgeon, educator; b. Hong Kong, Jan. 17, 1964; arrived in U.S., 1989; s. Hing Ning Lee and Nam (Yip) Yip. BS, Chinese U. Hong Kong, 1986, MPhil, 1988; PhD, Baylor U., 1997. Tchg. assoc. dept. biochemistry Chinese U. Hong Kong, 1986—88, rsch. assoc. dept. biochemistry, 1988—89; postdoctoral fellow cell biology Baylor Coll. Medicine, Houston, 1997—98; postdoctoral fellow dept. surgery U. Tex. Med. Br., Galveston, 1998—2001, instr. dept. surgery, 2001—. Contbr. articles to profl. jours. Mem.: Am. Chem. Soc., Sigma Xi. Office: U Tex Med Br Dept Surgery Rt 1220 Galveston TX 77555

LEE, HI YOUNG, physician, acupuncturist; b. Seoul, Korea, Oct. 18, 1941; came to U.S., 1965, naturalized, 1976; s. Jung S. and Hwa J. (Kim) L.; m. Sun M. Lee, June 4, 1965; children: Sandra, Grace, David. MD, Yon Sei U., Seoul, 1965. Diplomate Am. Bd. Family Practice. Intern Grasslands Hosp., Valhalla, N.Y., 1965-66; resident VA Hosp., Dayton, Ohio, 1966-70; mem. staff Eastern State Hosp., Medical Lake, Wash., 1970-74; practice family medicine, acupuncturist Empire Med. Office, Spokane, 1974—. Active staff St. Lukes Meml. Hosp., Spokane, 1974—, bd. trustees St. Georges Prep Sch., Wash., 1986—; courtesy staff Deaconess Med. Center, Spokane, 1974—, Sacred Heart Med. Ctr., Spokane, 1974—. Author: Von Recklinghousen's Disease, 1970 (McDermit award); columnist Rainier Forum Korea Post Weekly News, 1996—. Elder First Presbyn. Ch., Spokane, 1975. Fellow Am. Acad. Family Practice; mem. Ctr. for Chinese Medicine, Spokane County Med. Soc., Nat. Acupuncture Rsch. Soc., Christian Med. Soc. Home: 2006 W Liberty Ave Spokane WA 99205-2570 Office: Empire Med Office 17 E Empire Ave Spokane WA 99207-1707 E-mail: acupuncture@u.s.west.net.

LEE, HON CHEUNG, physiology educator; b. Hong Kong, May 7, 1950; came to the U.S., 1967; s. Chai Chong and Yee Chin (Ng) L.; m. Miranda Wong, Aug. 1981; 1 child, Cyrus W. BA, U. Calif., Berkeley, 1971, MA, 1973, PhD, 1978; hon. degree in medicine and surgery, U. Genoa, Italy, 1997. Postdoctoral rschr. U. Calif., Berkeley, 1978-79, Stanford U., Pacific Grove, Calif., 1979-81; asst. prof. U. Minn., Mpls., 1981-86, assoc. prof., 1986-90, full prof., 1990—, Disting. McKnight univ. prof., 1996—. Mem. Reproductive Biology Study Sect., NIH, Bethesda, Md., 1993-97; chmn. Reproductive Biology Spl. Emphasis Panel, NIH, Bethesda, 1994. Contbr. articles to profl. jours. Rsch. grantee NIH, Bethesda, 1983—, 94—, NSF, Washington, 1986-89. Mem. AAAS, Am. Soc. for Cell Biology. Achievements include discovery of Cyclic ADP-ribose and NAADP, messenger molecules for regulating cellular calcium; patents for Cyclic ADP-ribose antagonists and novel caged nucleotides. Office: Univ Minn Dept Pharmacology 321 Church St SE Minneapolis MN 55455-0250 E-mail: leehc@tc.umn.edu.

LEE, HOWARD DOUGLAS, academic administrator; b. Louisville, Mar. 15, 1943; s. Howard W. and Margaret (Davidson) L.; m. Margaret Easley, Nov. 20, 1965; children: Gregory Davidson, Elizabeth Anna. BA in English, U. Richmond, 1964; ThM, Southeastern Seminary, Wake Forest, N.C., 1968; PhD in Religion, U. Iowa, Iowa City, 1971. Prof. religion, devel. dir. Va. Intermont Coll., Bristol, 1971-73; dir. univ. relations Wake Forest (N.C.) U., 1973-78; v.p. devel. Stetson U., DeLand, Fla., 1978-80, v.p. planning and devel., 1980-83, exec. v.p., 1984-86, pres.-elect, 1986-87, pres., 1987—. Contbr. articles to profl. jours. Founding dir. Atlantic Ctr. for Arts, New Smyrna Beach, Fla., 1978—; chmn. DeLand C. of C., 1994; chair Volusia Vision Com., 1994-96. Named Cen. Fla. Fundraiser of Yr. Nat. Assn. Fundraising Execs. 1985. Mem. So. Assn. Colls. and Schs. (exec. coun. 1993-94), Rotary, Deland Country Club, Omicron Delta Kappa. Avocations: running, golf, wood carving, woodworking/antiques, reading. Office: Stetson U Campus Box 8258 421 N Woodland Blvd Deland FL 32720-3761

LEE, HWA-WEI, librarian, educator, consultant; b. Guangdong, China, Dec. 7, 1933; came to U.S., 1957, naturalized, 1962; s. Luther Kan-Chun and Mary Hsiao-Wei (Wang) L.; m. Mary F. Kratochvil, Mar. 14, 1959; children: Shirley, James, Pamela, Edward, Charles, Robert. BEd, Nat. Taiwan Normal U., 1954; MEd, U. Pitts., 1959, PhD, 1964; MLS, Carnegie Mellon U., 1961. Asst. libr. U. Pitts. Librs., 1959-62; head tech. svcs. Duquesne U. Libr., Pitts., 1962-65; head libr. U. Pa., Edinboro, 1965-68; dir. libr. and info. ctr. Asian Inst. Tech., Bangkok, 1968-75; assoc. dir. librs., prof. libr. adminstrn. Colo. State U., Fort Collins, 1975-78; dean librs., prof. Ohio U., Athens, 1978-99, dean emeritus, librs., 1999—; disting. vis. scholar OCLC, 2000—. Fulbright sr. specialist, 2001; cons. FAO, UNESCO, U.S. AID, World Bank, Internat. Devel. Rsch. Ctr., Asia Found., OCLC; del.-at-large White House Conf. Libr. and Info. Svcs., 1991. Author: Librarianship in World Perspectives, 1991, Fundraising for the 1990s: The Challenge Ahead, 1992, Modern Library Management, 1996, Knowledge Management: Theory and Practice, 2002; exec. editor Jour. Ednl. Media and Libr. Sci., 1982—; mem. editl. bd. Internat. Comm. in Libr. Automation, 1975-76, Jour. Libr. and Info. Sci., 1975-78, Libr. Acquisition: Practice and Theory, 1976-83; adv. bd. Jour. Info., Comm. and Libr. Sci., 1994—; contbr. articles to profl. jours. Recipient Disting. Svc. award Libr. Assn. of China (Taiwan), 1989; new bldg. on Ohio U. campus named in his honor: Hwa-wei Lee Libr. Annex, and 1st flr. of the main libr.: Hwa-wei Lee Ctr. for Internat. Collections, 1999. Mem. ALA (councilor 1988-92, 93-97, John Ames Humphry/Forest Press award 1991), Acad. Libr. Assn. Ohio, Am. Soc. Info. Sci., Asian-Pacific Am. Librs. Assn. (Disting. Svc. award 1991), Internat. Fedn. Libr. Assns. and Instns. (standing com. univ. librs. and other gen. rsch. librs. 1989-93), Assn. Coll. and Rsch. Librs. Chinese-Am. Librs. Assn. (Disting. Svc. award 1983), Internat. Assn. Orientalist Librs., Ohio Libr. Coun. (bd. dirs. 1991-92, Libr. of the Yr. 1987, Hall of Fame Libr. 1999), Online Computer Libr. Ctr. (users coun. 1987-91), Ohio Chinese Acad. and Profl. Assn. (founding pres. 1988-90). Home: 19 Mulligan Rd Athens OH 45701-3734 Office: Ohio U Hwa-Wei Lee Libr Annex Athens OH 45701 E-mail: leeh@ohio.edu.

LEE, HYUNYOUNG, computer scientist, educator; b. Seoul, Korea (South), May 29, 1964; d. Yonghee Lee and Bong Chae. BS in Computer Sci., Ewha U., Seoul, Korea (South), 1987; MA in Computer Sci., Boston U., 1997; MS in Computer Sci., Ewha U., Seoul, Korea (South), 1992; PhD in Computer Sci., Tex. A&M U., Coll. Sta., 2001. Instr. Ajou U., Suwon, Republic of Korea, 1992—93; systems programmer Korean Air, Info. Systems Dept., Seoul, Republic of Korea, 1987—90; asst. prof. U. of Denver, Denver, 2001—. Sys. adminstr. Ewha U., Seoul, Republic of Korea, 1991—92; tchg. fellow Boston U., 1995—97; cons. Bellcore (now Telcordia), Morristown, NJ, 1995—96; rsch. and tchg. asst. Tex. A&M U., Coll. Sta., 1997—2001. Avocations: painting, piano, jogging. Office: Univ Denver Dept Comp Sci 2360 S Gaylord Sti Denver CO 80208

LEE, I-MIN, epidemiologist; b. Georgetown, Penang, Malaysia, May 23, 1960; d. Keng Yew and Nguk Huong (Nga) Lee; m. Geoffrey Bernard Kronik, Nov. 27, 1998. M.B.BS, Nat. U. Singapore, 1984; MPH, Harvard U., Boston, 1987, ScD, 1991. Intern Min. of Health, Singapore, 1984—85, med. officer, 1985—86; instr. cmty. health Tufts U., Boston, 1990—92; asst. prof. medicine Harvard Med. Sch., 1993—2000, assoc. prof. medicine, 2001—; asst. prof. epidemiology Harvard Sch. Pub. Health, 1995—2002, assoc. prof. epidemiology, 2002—. Mem. sci. adv. bd. Cooper Inst. for Aerobics Rsch., Dallas, 1995—. Contbr. articles to profl. jours. Recipient Young Epidemiologist award Royal Soc. Medicine, U.K., 1999. Fellow Am. Coll. Sports Medicine (mem. rsch. adv. com. 1996—); mem. Am. Epidemiol. Soc., Soc. for Epidemiologic Rsch. Avocations: running, sports. Office: Harvard Med Sch 900 Commonwealth Ave E Boston MA 02215-1204 E-mail: i-min.lee@channing.harvard.edu.

LEE, INKYU, engineer; MTS Bell Lab, Murray Hill, NJ, 1995—2001, Agere Sys., Murray Hill, 2001—. Mem.: IEEE (editor Transactions on Comms. 2001—02).

LEE, IN-YOUNG, lawyer; b. In-Cheon, Kyonggi-do, Korea, Dec. 5, 1952; came to U.S. 1978; s. In-Seok and Hyun-Bo (Rim) L.; m. Young-Lae Hong, July 1, 1978; children: Casey K., Brian K. LLB, Seoul Nat. U., Korea, 1975; LLM, Harvard U., 1980; JD, UCLA, 1983. Bar: Ill. 1983, N.Y. 1987, D.C. 1989, U.S. Ct. Internat. Trade. Assoc. Baker & McKenzie, Chgo., 1983-86, Marks & Murase, N.Y.C., 1986-87, Baker & McKenzie, N.Y.C., 1987-91; ptnr. Marks & Murase, 1991-96, McDermott, Will & Emory, N.Y.C., 1996—. Gen. counsel Korean C. of C. and Industry in USA, Inc., 1993—, Assn. Korean Fin. Instns. Am., Inc. Articles editor Pacific Basin Law Jour. Presbyterian. Avocations: fishing, golf. Office: McDermott Will & Emery 50 Rockefeller Plz Fl 12 New York NY 10020-1600 E-mail: ilee@mwe.com.

LEE, IVY, JR. public relations consultant; b. N.Y.C., July 31, 1909; s. Ivy and Cornelia (Bigelow) L.; m. Marie F. Devin, Oct. 14, 1988; children: Peter Ivy III (dec.), Jean Downey. BA, Princeton U., 1931; MBA, Harvard U., 1933. Ptnr. Ivy Lee & T.J. Ross, N.Y.C., 1933-45; with Pan Am. World Airways, Miami, Fla. and San Francisco, 1942-45; adminstrv. asst. S.D. Bechtel, Bechtel Cos., San Francisco, 1950-54; pres. Ivy Lee Jr. & Assocs., 1945-85; pres., cons. Ivy Lee Jr. & Assocs., Inc., 1985—. Trustee Princeton (N.J.) U., 1965-69; bd. dirs. San Francisco TB Assn., Bay Area Red Cross, San Francisco, Edgewood Childrens Ctr. Mem. Pub. Relations Soc. Am., Internat. Pub. Relations Assn. (pres. 1976-77). Clubs: Bohemian, Pacific Union. Republican. Presbyterian. Home: 1940 Broadway San Francisco CA 94109-2216

LEE, J. PATRICK, academic administrator; b. Leitchfield, Ky., Nov. 30, 1942; s. Herman G. and Josephine (Pearl) L.; m. Louise Sipple, June 8, 1972. BA, Brescia Coll., 1963; postgrad., U. Paris, 1966-67; PhD, Fordham U., 1971. Asst. prof. French Brescia Coll., Owensboro, Ky., Univ. of Ga., Athens, Ga.; v. p. acad. affairs Belmont N.C. Abbey Coll.; provost Barry Univ., Miami, Fla. Researcher 18th Century French lit., Voltaire works. Woodrow Wilson fellow, 1963, Danforth fellow, 1963-67, Fulbright fellow, 1966-67. Mem. AAUA (exec. bd.), SEASECS (exec. bd., past pres.), Delta Epsilon Sigma (nat. sec./treas.), Phi Beta Kappa. Home: 1341 NE 103rd St Miami FL 33138-2623

LEE, JACK (JIM SANDERS BEASLEY), broadcast executive; b. Buffalo Valley, Tenn., Apr. 14, 1936; s. Jesse McDonald and Nelle Viola (Sanders) Beasley; m. Barbara Sue Looper, Sept. 1, 1961; children: Laura Ann, Elizabeth Jane, Sarah Kathleen. Student, Wayne State U., 1955-57; BA, Albion Coll., 1959. Announcer Sta. WHUB-AM, Cookeville, Tenn., 1956; news dir., program dir. Sta. WALM-AM, Albion, Mich., 1957-59; radio-TV personality WKZO-Radio-TV, Kalamazoo, 1960-62; prodn. dir. Stas. WKMH-WKNR, Detroit, 1962-63; gen. mgr. Sta. WAUK-AM-FM, Waukesha, Wis., 1963-65; asst. program mgr. Sta. WOKY, Milw., 1965-70; program mgr. Sta. WTMJ-WKTI, 1970-76; gen. mgr. Sta. WEMP-WMYX, 1976-88; pres. Jack Lee Enterprises Ltd., 1977—; pres., CEO, Milw. Area Radio Stas., 1989—. Instr. dept. mass comm. U. Wis.-Milw., 1972-81. With U.S. Army, 1959, 61-62; maj. CAP, 1964-01, ret. Decorated Army Commendation medal; cert. radio mktg. cons., Broadcasters Hall of Fame, 1999. Mem. AFTRA, Actors Equity, Milw. Advt. Club, Omicron Delta Kappa, Alpha Epsilon Rho. Home and Office: W277 W N Chicory Ln # 2793 Pewaukee WI 53072 E-mail: jleemars@msn.com. *It is a constant struggle to balance my greatest gift—the ability to express myself—with my biggest failing—the inability to keep my mouth shut.*

LEE, JAE KYUN, biomedical researcher, educator; b. Seoul, Korea (South), June 12, 1962; s. Kongsoon (Kim) and Kongbum Lee; m. Seungwon Jeon, Sept. 7, 1964; 1 child Irene. PhD, U. Wis., Madison, 1994. Rsch. assoc. Unv. So. Calif., L.A., 1995—97; rsch. scientist NIH, Bethesda, Md., 1997—99; asst. prof. U. Va., Charlottesville, Va., 1999—. Author: (scientific article) Nature Genetics, 2000 (Am.Cancer Soc. award, 2002). Fellow Commonwealth Tech. Rsch. Transfer, State of Va., 2001. Mem.: Am. Stats.. Assn. Office: Univ Va Sch Medicine Hosp West Complx Rm 3181 Charlottesville VA 22908 Office Fax: 434-924-8437. Business E-Mail: jaeklee@virginia.edu.

LEE, JAE-WON, journalism educator, political campaign consultant; b. Chinju City, South Korea, Jan. 30, 1940; came to U.S., 1967; s. Song-yol and Pan-son (Choi) L.; m. Jin-won Kim, Nov. 6, 1966 (dec. Aug. 1994); children: Eric S., Gina S.; m. Chae-kyong Moon, Dec. 30, 1997. BA, Seoul Nat. U., 1963, MA, 1966, Marquette U., 1969; PhD, U. Iowa, 1972. Reporter The Korea Times, Seoul, 1963-67; asst. prof. Ill. State U., Normal, 1972-73; from asst. prof. to prof. Cleve. State U., 1973—, asst. to provost, 1993—2001, dir. curricular affairs, 2001—. Vis. prof. Inst. Fgn. Affairs & Nat. Security, Seoul, 1980; Fulbright prof. Yonsei U., Seoul, 1988; vis. fellow East-West Ctr., Honolulu, 1988, 89, 91, 92; fellow Poynter Inst. for Media Studies, St. Petersburg, 1987, 93, Am. Press Inst., Washington, 1993; exec. dir. Olympic Media Awards, Cleve., 1995—. Editor: Seoul Olympics and Global Community, 1992; co-author: Modernization vs. Revolution, 1993; co-editor: Elite Media Amidst Mass Culture, 1994. Pres. Korean Assn. Greater Cleve., 1984; bd. dirs. Internat. Svcs. Ctr., Cleve., 1980-86, Intercultural Cmty. Coun., Cleve., 1998-2000; mem. Nat. Adv. Coun. on Peaceul Unification, Seoul, 1995-2001. Recipient Nat. Tchg. award in journalism Poynter Inst. for Media Studies, 1987; Fulbright scholar, 1967-69. Mem. Assn. for Edn. in Journalism and Mass Comm. (divsn. pres. 1982-83), Korean Am. Comm. Assn. (pres. 1979-81, 90-92), Fulbright Assn. (bd. dirs. N.E. Ohio chpt., pres. 1996-98), Soc. Profl. Journalists (bd. dirs. Cleve. chpt. 1994-2001). Avocation: gardening. Home: 6180 Coldstream Dr Highland Heights OH 44143-3700 Office: Cleve State U Dept Comm Cleveland OH 44115 E-mail: j.lee@csuohio.edu.

LEE, JAMES A. health facility finance executive; b. Red Level, Ala., Dec. 19, 1939; s. H. Alton Lee; m. Charlotte Phillips, Dec. 19, 1963 (div. July 1971); children: Phillip, Michele, Jenifer; m. Melanie Cooper, Dec. 14, 1973; children: Christopher, Amanda. BBA in Acctg., Jacksonville State U., 1964; MS in Hosp. and Health Adminstrn., U. Ala., 1980. CPA, Ala. Sr. acct. Macke, Eldredge, McIntosh, Birmingham, Ala., 1964-67, Touche, Ross, Bailey & Smart, Birmingham, 1967-68; bus. functions mgr. Druid City Hosp., Tuscaloosa, Ala., 1968-71; sr. assoc. adminstr., fin. Univ. Ala. Hosp., Birmingham, 1971-94; CFO Montgomery Cardiovasc. Assocs., PC, 1994—. Asst. prof. health services adminstrn. Univ. Ala. Birmingham, 1980—; asst. prof. Dept. Pub. Health, Univ. Ala. Birmingham, 1984—. Mem. AICPA, Health Care Fin. Mgmt. Assn., Ala. Soc. CPAs. Republican. Baptist. Home: 109 Pemberton Pl Pelham AL 35124-2817 E-mail: jleecpa@aol.com.

LEE, JAMES EDWARD, JR. educational administrator; b. Pitts., Mar. 9, 1939; s. Willard and Gladys Hilda (Jenkins) L.; m. Daisy Mae Tibbs, June 29, 1977; children: Stephen Michael, Monica Michelle, Brian Patrick, Priscilla Demone. BS, Wayne State U., 1962, EdS, 1969; MA, U. Mich., 1964; postgrad., Mich. State U., Wayne State U., U. Minn., U. Colo., 1964-95, Ctrl. Mich. U. Cert. tchr., adminstr., Mich. Tchr. Miller, Durfee and Michael Jr. High Schs., Detroit, 1962-67; team leader Nat. Tchr. Corps, 1967-69; dept. head Noble Jr. High Sch., 1969-74; asst. prin. MacKenzie High Sch., 1974-80, Drew Mid. Sch., Detroit, 1980, prin., 1980-97, Chandler Park Acad., 1997-98; ops. supr. Detroit Mfg. Partnership, 1999-2000; exec. dir. Detroit Pub. Schs., 2000—01; prin. Rivers Mid. Sch., Charleston, SC, 2001—02. Instr. Wayne State U., Detroit, 1967-69, edn. cons., 1970-71; instr. Wayne C.C., 1967-81; prin. adult evening sch., 1974-80, summer gifted program, Detroit, 1986-92; mem. profl. stds. commn. for sch. adminstrs. Mich. Dept. Edn., 1992-96, mem. adminstrv. waiver com., 1992-94. Contbg. author: The Development of Micro Teaching as an Evaluative Instrument in Teacher Training, 1969, (manual) The Principalship, 1990. Co-chair ednl. audit com. Oak Park (Mich.) Sch., 1988-90; bd. dirs. Scott Community Ctr., Detroit, 1988-97; adv. bd. Adrian/Scott program to inspire readiness for ednl. success, Detroit, 1990-97; adv. coun. Christ Child House, Detroit, 1990-92. With USMC, 1956-58. Recipient Prins. and Educators award Booker T. Washington Bus. Assn., Detroit, 1986, 90, Citation for Outstanding Leadership Detroit Bd. Edn., 1986; named finalist Boss of Yr., Detroit chpt. Am. Bus. Women's Assn., 1987. Mem. Nat. Assn. Secondary Sch. Prins., Nat. Mid. Sch. Assn., Mich. Assn. Supervision and Curriculum Devel., Mich. Assn. Secondary Sch. Prins. (exec. bd. 1986-88, Outstanding Mid. Level Prin. of Yr. 1991), Mich. Assn. Mid. Sch. Educators (bd. dirs. 1988-91). Avocation: tennis. Home: 16500 North Park Dr Apt 1117 Southfield MI 48075

LEE, JAMES MATTHEW, Canadian politician; b. Charlottetown, P.E.I., Can., Mar. 26, 1937; s. James Matthew and Catherine (Blanchard) L.; m. Patricia Laurie, July 2, 1960; children: Jason, Laurie Ann, Patti Sue. P.C., St. Dustans U., 1956. Mem. provincial parliament from, 5th Queens Riding, 1975-82; minister Health and Social Service-Province of P.E.I., Charlottetown, from 1979, Tourism, Parks and Conservation, 1980; premier, pres. Exec. Council-Province P.E.I., Charlottetown, 1981-86. Mem. Can. Pension Commn., 1986-97, Privy Council Can., 1982, chmn. workers compensation bd., 1998. Mem. Can. Jaycees (internat. senate 1983), United Comml. Travellers Am. (past sr. councilor), Coun. for Can. Unity (nat. v.p. 1993). Roman Catholic.

LEE, JAMES RICHARD, ophthalmologist, educator; b. San Diego, July 21, 1939; s. Elynor (Maguire) Lee; m. Lynda Karen Johnson; children: James Nicholas, Johanna Maguire. BA, Yale U., 1961; MD, McGill U., Montreal, Que., Can., 1965. Diplomate Am. Bd. Ophthalmology. Surg. intern N.Y. Hosp., N.Y.C., 1965-66, surg. resident, 1966-67; resident in ophthmology Mass. Eye and Ear Infirmary, Boston, 1970-73, corneal fellow, 1973-75; clin. instr. Harvard U. Med. Sch., Cambridge, Mass., 1975—; ophthalmologist Harvard U. Health Svcs., 1980-96. Author: Handbook of Contact Lenses, 1986. Med. officer USN, 1967-69; with Mass. N.G., 1980-99, col., 1990-99. Mem. AMA, Mass. Med. Soc., New Eng. Ophthalmic Soc., Mass. Soc. Eye Physicians and Surgeons. Office: 52 Crest Ave Winthrop MA 02152-1064 E-mail: james.r.lee@gte.net.

LEE, JAMES WADE, humanities educator, writer, actor; b. Lansing, Mich., Mar. 13, 1945; s. James Lester Lee and Thelma Evelyn (Marrison) Lee Parks; m. Erin Gail Taylor (div.); 1 child, Robert Clifford. AA, L.A. City Coll., 1971; BA, Calif. State U., L.A., 1978, MA, 1979; PhD, U. Utah, 1984; LLB, Blackstone Sch. Law, Chgo., 1971. Actor, scriptwriter, L.A., 1968-80; performer, copywriter Salt Lake City, 1980-88; dean acad. affairs Salt Lake City Coll., 1985-87; actor, scriptwriter Las Vegas, Nev., 1988-96; mng. editor Am. Lit. Svc., Las Vegas and Clovis, N.Mex., 1990—; instr. Clovis (N.Mex.)

C.C., 1997—. Part-time lectr. U. Nev., Las Vegas, 1988-89; adj. prof. Nat. U., Las Vegas, 1988-90; adj. asst. prof. Embry-Riddle Aero. U., Clovis, 1996—; founder Sho'Biz Job Finder, L.A., 1973. Author various stage plays, 1971-84, including Will Someone Please Tell me What's Going On Here?, 1974; author: (ednl. video) How to Study, 1988. Mem. MLA, SAG (under profl. name Lee James), Masquer's Club (Hollywood). Avocations: drawing, painting, music, cooking, developing new talented writers, innovation in higher education.

LEE, JANIE C. curator; b. Shreveport, La., Apr. 22, 1937; d. Birch Lee and Joanna (Glassell) Wood; m. David B. Warren, Jan. 2, 1980. Student, Nat. Cathedral Sch., 1951-55; BA, Sarah Lawrence Coll., 1959. Asst. to Cheryl Crawford, Actors Studi o, N.Y.C., 1962-63; co-prodr. Off Broadway Theatre Co., 1963-65; owner, pres. Janie C. Lee Gallery, Dallas, 1967-74, Houston, 1973-96, Janie C. Lee Master Drawings, N.Y.C., 1983-96; curator of drawings Whitney Mus. Am. Art, 1997—. Mem. art appraisal panel IRS, Washington, 1987-94; mem. Menil Found., Inc., 2000—. Prodr. ann. catalogue on 20th Century drawings, 1979-93. Mem. Alumnae Bd. Sarah Lawrence Coll. (1972-74); pres. Nancy Graves Found., 1996—. Mem. Art Dealers Assn. Am. (bd. dirs. 1980-88, 92-94, v.p. 1984-88). Office: 1209 Berthea St Houston TX 77006-6411

LEE, JEAN CLARISSE, editor, writer; b. Eau Claire, Wis., Aug. 15, 1948; d. Richard Roland and Ardythe Ann (Hintermeyer) L; m. Michael Judson Spencer (div.); 1 child, Amber Justine. BA in journalism, Univ. Wis., 1980; MFA, La. State Univ., 1997. Owner Transformations, Eau Claire, 1976-78; editor Univ. Wis., 1980; lifestyle editor Galesburg (Ill.) Register Mail, Galesburg, Ill., 1981; news bureau dir. Knox Coll., 1981-84; owner The Agency, 1984-89; publ. mgr. Knox Coll., 1989-91; dir. publs. unit Ill. State Univ., Normal, 1991-95; mng. editor Exquisite Corp., Baton Rouge, 1995-98; editor La. State U. Press, 1999—2002; program coord. La. Dept. Edn., Divsn. Student Stds. and Assessments, 2002—. Editor Farmer's Market, 1981-95, La. State U. Press, 1999-2002; contbr. articles to profl. jours. and lit. mags. Home: 646 Lucilla Ln Baton Rouge LA 70802-5338 E-mail: jeanclee@aol.com.

LEE, JEANNE KIT YEW, administrative officer; b. N.Y.C., July 31, 1959; d. Tat Yuen and Yow Seum (Chu) Lee. BBA, Baruch Coll., 1982. Clk. typist U.S. Dept. Health and Human Svcs., N.Y.C., 1980-83, U.S. Consumer Product Safety Commn., N.Y.C., 1983-85, adminstrv. asst., 1985-90, sys. adminstr., 1986-93, adminstrv. officer, 1990—. Mem. NAFE, Humane Soc., Nat. Wildlife Fedn. (assoc.), Am. Humane, DAV (Commanders Club 1988—). E-mail: jklee@cpsc.gov.

LEE, JEROME G. lawyer; b. Chgo., Feb. 23, 1924; m. Margo B. Lee, Dec. 23, 1947; children: James A., Kenneth M. BSChemE, U. Wis., 1947; JD, NYU, 1950. Bar: N.Y. 1950, U.S. Supreme Ct. 1964. Assoc. firm Jeffery, Kimball, Eggleston, N.Y.C., 1950-52; assoc. firm Morgan, Finnegan, Durham & Pine, 1952-59; ptnr. Morgan, Finnegan, Pine, Foley & Lee, 1959-86; sr. ptnr. Morgan & Finnegan, 1986-95, of counsel, 1995—. Lectr. in field. Author: (with J. Gould) Intellectual Property Counseling and Litigation, 1988, USPTO Proposals to Change Rule 56 and the Related Rules Regarding a Patent Applicant's Duty of Candour, Patent World, 1992; contbr. articles to legal jours. in patent and trademark litigation splty. Fellow Am. Bar Found.; mem. ATLA, ABA (mem. coun. Intellectual Property Law sect., chmn. com. fed. practice and procedure, chmn. com. Ct. of Appeals Fed. Cir., chmn. com. on ethics and profl. responsibility, stds. com., mem. fed. cir. adv. com. 1992-97), Am. Intellectual Property Law Assn. (bd. dirs. 1984-90, pres. 1991, Am. Judicature Soc., Internat. Fedn. Indsl. Property Attys., Found. for Creative Am. (bd. dirs.), N.Y. Bar Assn., Assn. of Bar of City of N.Y., N.Y. County Bar Assn., N.Y. Patent, Trademark and Copyright Law Assn. (bd. dirs. 1975-80, pres. 1981), others. Home: 3328 Sabal Cove Ln Longboat Key FL 34228-4157 Office: Morgan & Finnegan 345 Park Ave Fl 22 New York NY 10154-0053

LEE, JIAN-MING, biologist; b. Shanghai, China, June 12, 1968; s. Taogen Lee and Shundi He; m. Yan Wei, Nov. 19, 1967; 1 child, Ryan. PhD, U. Ill., 1997. Sr. rsch. scientist Vitamin Inc., Nutley, N.J., 1999—; prin. rsch. biologist Unilever Rsch. U.S., Edgewater, 2001—. Inventor in field. Rsch. grant USDA, 1997. Mem. AAAS, N.Y. Acad. Sci. Office: Unilever Rsch US 45 River Rd Edgewater NJ 07020 E-mail: leejianming@hotmail.com.

LEE, JIM, economics educator; b. Hong Kong, 1960; BA, Wilfrid Laurier U., Waterloo, Ont., 1981; MA, U. Waterloo, 1983; PhD, Pa. State U., 1991. Asst. prof. Ft. Hays State U., Hays, Kans., 1989-99; assoc. prof. econs. Tex. A&M U., Corpus Christi, 1999—. Contbr. articles to profl. jours. Avocations: running, weight training, judo. Office: Tex A&M U 6300 Ocean Dr Corpus Christi TX 78412-5503

LEE, JIMMY CHE-YUNG, city planner; b. Canton, China, May 29, 1946; came to U.S., 1969. s. Che Dui and Fong-Lee (Leung) Lee; m. Annie On-Lin Chan, Nov. 29, 1970 (div. 1987); m. Eileen Oi Ping Cheung, Dec. 16, 1987 (div. 1990); m. Sara Yeuk Siu, June 21, 1994; children: Grace Yeuk Won, Michelle Yeuk Shun. Grad., Sir. Robert Black Coll. Edn., Hong Kong; BA, U. Tex., 1973, MA, 1975. Tchr. English and Chinese Asbury Meth. Primary Sch., Hong Kong, 1966-69; asst. mgr. Trader Vic's Restaurant Dallas Hilton Inn, 1971-75; planner Dallas County Community Action Agy., 1975, dir. projects and resource devel. div., 1975—77; pres. U-Asia Corp., Hong Kong, 1975; owner Dragon Inn Restaurant, 1975; contr. food and beverage div. Plaza of Am. Hotel, 1979-82; comptr. Carlyle Hotels & Restaurants Inc., Harold Farb Cos., 1982; founder, chief exec. officer Lee & Lee Fine Linens, Inc., 1982—; v.p. Asiatex Inc., 1987—, Titan Real Estate Devel. & Investment Group, Inc., 1993—. Bd. dirs. Crown Chpt. Nat. Bank Dallas. Pres. North Tex. Cantonese Assn., 1986-88, hon. pres., 1989—; dir. Dallas chpt. Friends of Hong Kong and Macau; v.p., dir. North Tex. Chinese Culture Divination Soc. Mem. Am. Inst. Planners (assoc.), Tex. Assn. Community Action Agys., Hong Kong Registered Tchrs. Assn., Oakcliff C. of C. Baptist. Home: 629 Killarney Richardson TX 75081-5157

LEE, JINHO, research engineer, consultant; b. Seoul, Korea, Sept. 11, 1963; came to U.S., 1976; s. Sangawan and Junghee (Han) L.; m. Joan E. Carletta, Oct. 3, 1994. BS in Engring., SUNY, Buffalo, 1985, PhD in Engring., 1991. Asst. engr. Calspan Co., Buffalo, 1985-91; rsch. engr. Sverdrup Tech. Inc., Brook Park, Ohio, 1991-94; sr. rsch. engr. NYMA, Inc., 1994-97, NASA Lewis Rsch. Ctr., 1997—. Cons. engr. Waste Minimization Co., Cleveland, 1991-97. Contbr. articles to profl. jours. Mem. AIAA (sr.), ASME, SAE. Republican. Methodist. Achievements include co-development of pollution free cleaning system, co-development of NASA combustor analysis tools. Home: 8026 Twin Oaks Dr Broadview Heights OH 44147-1023 Office: NASA Glenn Rsch Ctr MS-5-10 Cleveland OH 44142

LEE, JOAN ROBERTA, elementary education educator; b. Everett, Mass., Dec. 3, 1939; d. Clifford Waldo and Harriet Alice (Goodridge) Mattsen;m. Robert Edward Lee, Nov. 3, 1962; children: Laura, Scott, Julie. BS in Edn., Bridgewater State U., 1962; MEd in Reading and Language, U. Lowell, 1989. Cert. cons. tchr. of reading, Mass. Tchr. elem. Chelmsford (Mass.) Pub. Schs., 1962-64, Tyngsboro (Mass.) Pub. Schs., 1979-98, reading specialist, 1990-98, Title I dir., 1992-98; retired, 1998. Tchr. rep., reading, writing and acad. coms., Tyngsboro, 1987—, chmn. reading com., 1992—; co-chairperson MA curriculum Frameworks-English-Lang. Study Group, Tyngsboro, 1995-96. Leader Girl Scouts U.S., Chelmsford, 1971-79, Boy Scouts Am., 1973-75; tchr. liaison Parent Vol. Orgn., Tyngsboro, 1988—; Sunday Sch. tchr., Chelmsford, 1970-79; tchr. pub. libr. story hours, Chelmsford, 1973-75. Mem. ASCD, NEA, Internat. Reading Assn., Mass. Reading Assn., Mass. Tchrs. Assn., Merrimack Valley Reading Assn. Avocations: traveling, needlework, crafts, reading. Home: 5 Draycoach Dr Chelmsford MA 01824-1003 Office: Pub Sch 135 Coburn Rd Tyngsboro MA 01879-1703

LEE, JOHN JIN, lawyer; b. Chgo., Oct. 20, 1948; s. Jim Soon and Fay Yown (Young) L.; m. Jamie Pearl Eng, Apr. 30, 1983. BA magna cum laude, Rice U., 1971; JD, MBA, Stanford U., 1975. Bar: Calif. 1976. Assoc. atty. Manatt Phelps & Rothenberg, L.A., 1976-77; asst. counsel Wells Fargo Bank N.A., San Francisco, 1977-79, counsel, 1979-80, v.p., sr. counsel, 1980, v.p., mng. sr. counsel, 1981-98, v.p., asst. gen. counsel, 1998—2001. Mem. governing com. Conf. on Consumer Fin. Law, 1989-93. Bd. dirs. Asian Bus. League San Francisco, 1981—, gen. counsel, 1981. Fellow Am. Coll. Consumer Fin. Svcs. Attys., Inc. (bd. regents 1995-96); mem. ABA (chmn. subcom. housing fin., com. consumer fin. svcs., bus. law sect. 1983-90, vice chmn. subcom. securities products, consumer fin. svcs., bus. law sect. 1995-96, chmn. subcom. elec. banking, com. consumer fin. svcs., bus. law sect. 1996-2000, co-chmn. joint subcom. elec. fin. svcs., bus. law sect. 1997-2000, co-chmn. directory com. minority in-house counsel group 1995-98), Consumer Bankers Assn. (lawyers com.), Soc. Physics Students, Stanford Asian-Pacific Am. Alumni/ae Club (bd. dirs. 1989-93, v.p. 1989-91). Democrat. Baptist. Office: PO Box 1304 San Carlos CA 94070-1304 E-mail: johnjinlee@stanfordalumni.org.

LEE, JOHN MARSHALL, mathematics educator; b. Phila., Sept. 2, 1950; s. Warren W. and Virginia (Hull) L.; m. Pm Weizenbaum, May 26, 1984; children: Nathan Lee Weizenbaum, Jeremy Lee Weizenbaum. AB, Princeton U., 1972; student, Tufts U., 1977-78; PhD, MIT, 1982. Systems programmer Tex. Instruments, Princeton, N.J., 1972-74; Geophys. Fluid Dynamics Lab., GFDL/NOAA, 1974-75; tchr. math. and physics Wooster Sch., Danbury, Conn., 1975-77; programmer and cons. info. processing svcs. MIT, Cambridge, Mass., 1978-82; asst. prof. math. Harvard U., 1982-87, U. Wash., Seattle, 1987-89, assoc. prof. math., 1989-96, prof. math., 1996—. Sr. tutor Harvard U., Cambridge, 1984-87. Author: Riemannian Manifolds: An Introduction to Curvature, 1997, Introduction to Topological Manifolds, 2000, Introduction to Smooth Manifolds, 2002; contbr. articles to profl. jours. Rsch. fellow NSF, 1982. Mem. Am. Math. Soc. (Centennial fellow 1989). Avocations: hiking, wine tasting, music. Office: Univ Wash Math Dept PO Box 354350 Seattle WA 98195-4350 E-mail: lee@math.washington.edu.

LEE, JOHN THOMAS, finance educator, financial planner; b. Cleve., May 31, 1942; s. Harry C. and Lucille B. (Varnell) L.; m. Treasa (Susie) Leming, Dec. 28, 1996; children: Andrea, Joanne. BS in Econs., Tenn. Tech U., 1964; MS in Fin., U. Tenn., 1966; PhD in Fin., U. Ga., 1977. CFP. Instr. fin. Tenn. Tech U., Cookeville, 1966-71, asst. prof., 1973-78, assoc. prof., 1978-84; prof. fin. Mid. Tenn. State U., Murfreesboro, 1984—, Weatherford prof. fin., 1984-91, chmn. dept. econs. and fin., 1991—. Mem. faculty 5th Ann. Cash Mgmt. Inst. Nat. Forum, 1984, Grad. Sch. Banking of South, La. State U., 1986, 88, 89, Tenn. Bankers Sch., Vanderbilt U., 1985; spkr., discussant, moderator, presenter numerous profl. orgns. Contbr. numerous articles to profl. jours. Recipient Outstanding Faculty award Tenn. Tech. U. Coll. Bus. Found.; named Prof. of Yr. Coll. of Bus. Mid. Tenn. State U., 1988, 91; Ayers fellow ABA Stonier Grad. Sch. Banking, summer 1987. Mem. Financial Planning Assn. (Mid. Tenn. chpt. pres., 2001), Internat. Assn. Fin. Planning (pres. greater Tenn. chpt. 1995-96, bd. dirs. 1997-99), Fin. Mgmt. Assn., So. Fin. Assn., Ea. Fin. Assn., Midwest Fin. Assn., Southwestern Fin. Assn., Mid-South Acad. Econs. and Fin. (2d v.p. 1990-91, 1st v.p. 1991-92, pres. 1993-94), Mid. Tenn. Chpt. FPA (bd. dirs. 1996-99, pres. 2001), Civitan (pres. Cookeville 1983-84, Stones River 1990-91, lt. gov. Valley dist. 1984-85, 88-89, 89-90, 94-95), Beta Gamma Sigma (pres. Mid. Tenn. State U. chpt. 1986-87, 92-94), Omicron Delta Epsilon, Sigma Iota Epsilon, Alpha Kappa Psi, Phi Delta Theta. Baptist. Office: Mid Tenn State U E Main St Murfreesboro TN 37132-0001 Home: 2114 Creekwalk Dr Murfreesboro TN 37130-1803

LEE, JOLI FAY EATON, elementary education educator; b. Holdredge, Nebr., Sept. 24, 1951; d. Ray Lee and Lois Illeen (Willoughby) Larkins; m. James Edward Eaton, Aug. 16, 1969 (div. Jan. 1979); children: Threva, James, Beth; m. Chris Lee, Aug. 13, 1991; stepchildren: Michael Lee, Robyn Lee. BS in Elem. Edn., N.Mex. State U., Las Cruces, 1980, MA in Curriculum and Instruction, 1984. Cert. elem. tchr., N.Mex. Tchr. elem. Alamogordo (N.Mex.) Pub. Schs., 1980—. Co-chmn. City Elem. Sci. Fair, Alamogordo, 1989-90, chmn., 1990-92; with Summer Sci. Pilot Program, 1992-94. Contbr. articles to profl. jours. Nat. conv. co-chmn. Nat. Speleological Soc., Tularosa, N.Mex., 1986; joint venturer Cave Rsch. Found., 1983—; person. dir., Guadalupe Area Cave Rsch. Found., N.Mex., 1987-90; del. Cave Exploration Del. to People's Republic of China, 1993. Crimson scholar N.Mex. State U., 1980. Mem. NEA, Nat. Speleological Soc. (sec. Southwestern region 1984, 91-92, 93, Southwestern regional chmn. 1985-86). Republican. Episcopalian. Home: 1405 Saint Frances Dr Tularosa NM 88352-2003 Office: North Elem Sch 1300 Florida Alamogordo NM 88310

LEE, JONG HYUK, accountant; b. Hamheung, Korea, May 6, 1941; s. Jung Bo and Wol Sun Lee; m. Esther Kim, Jan. 24, 1970. BA, Sonoma State U., Rohnert Park, Calif., 1971; MBA in Taxation, Golden Gate U., 1976. CPA, Calif. Cost acct., internal auditor Foremost-McKesson Co., San Francisco, 1971-74; sr. acct. Clark, Wong, Foulkes & Barbieri, CPAs, Oakland, Calif., 1974-77; pres. J.H. Lee Accts. Corp., 1977-97, J. Lee Assocs., Oakland, 1997—. Instr. Armstrong Coll., Berkeley, Calif., 1977-78; lectr. acctg., dir. Sch. Bus., U.S. Korea Bus. Inst., San Francisco State U.; mem. adv. bd. Ctr. for Korean Studies, Insts. East Asian Studies, U. Calif., Berkeley; bd. dirs. United Labor Bank, Oakland. Columnist tax and bus. column Korea Times, 1980. Bd. dirs. Korean Residents Assn., 1974, Multi-Svc. Ctr. for Koreans, 1979, BBB, 1984-87; chmn. caucus Calif.-Nev. Ann. Conf., United Meth. Ch., 1977; commr. Calif. OEO, 1982-86; pres. Korean Am. Dem. Network, Dem. Nat. Fin. Coun.; regional chmn. Adv. Coun. on Peaceful Unificatio Policy, Republic of Korea; commr. Asian Art Mus., San Francisco, 1988-91, Oakland Cmty. and Econ. Devel., 1997; bd. dirs., dir. East Bay Asian Local Devel Corp. With Korean Marine Corp, 1961-64; 1st lt. Calif. Military Res. Mem. AICPA, Nat. Assn. Asian Am. CPAs (bd. dirs.), Am. Acctg. Assn., Nat. Assn. Accts., Internat. Found. Employee Benefit Plans, Calif. Soc. CPAs, Oakland C of C, Korean Am. C. of C. (pres. Pacific North Coast), Rotary. Home: 180 Firestone Dr Walnut Creek CA 94598-3645 Office: 369 13th St Oakland CA 94612-2636 E-mail: jhlee@jhleecpa.com.

LEE, JONG PIL, mathematician, educator; b. Jeonju, Jeonbuk, Korea, Mar. 18, 1937; s. Yun Ki Lee and Bong Sun Choi; m. Myoung Hye Lee, Sept. 16, 1970; children: Lisa, Karen. BS, Jeonbuk Nat. U., Jeonju, Korea, 1961; MA, Bowling Green State U., 1964; PhD , U. Alberta, Edmonton, Canada, 1970. Postdoc. fellow U. B.C., Vancouver, Canada, 1970—71; asst. prof. Ohio State U., Lima, 1971—73; assoc. prof. SUNY , Old Westbury, 1973—85, prof., 1985—90, disting. svc. prof., 1990—. Founder, dir. Inst. Math. Enrichment for Tchrs., Old Westbury, NY, 1986—91, Inst. Math. Enrichment for High Ability Women, Old Westbury, NY, 1988—90; dir. Inst. Creative Problem Solving for HS Tchrs., Old Westbury, NY, 1991—96; founder, dir. Inst. Leadership Devel. Tchrs. of Math. and Tech., Old Westbury, NY, 1996—; dir. Inst. Advanced Placement Math. Tchrs., Old Westbury, NY, 1988—; founder, dir. Inst. Creative Problem Solving for Gifted Students, Old Westbury, NY, 1992—; chmn. Math. Dept. SUNY , Old Westbury, NY, 1983—94. Contbr. articles to profl. jours. Recipient Long Island Math Edn. award, Long Island Math. Conf. Bd., 1989, State of N.Y. and UUP Excellence Prof. award, N.Y. State and United Univ. Professions, 1991, Nat. Partnership award for Math. Edn., The Partnership in Edn. Jour., 1992, Gourdreau award for Ednl. Leadership, Goudreau Mus. Math., 1997, Nassau County Svc. award, Nassau County Exec. Office, 1998; fellow fellowship, Canadian Nat. Rsch. Coun., 1967—70. Mem.: Nat. Coun. of Tchrs. of Math., Am. Math. Soc. Home: 8 Narcissus Dr Syosset NY 11791 Personal E-mail: jplbm@aol.com. Business E-Mail: leejo@oldwestbury.edu.

LEE, JONG-HYEON, computer and communications security researcher, mobile communications researcher; b. Seoul, Dec. 15, 1966; BS in Math., Sogang U., Seoul, 1989; MS in Math., Pohang Inst. Sci. and Tech., Korea, 1991; PhD in Computer Sci., U. Cambridge, Eng., 2000. Teaching asst. dept. math. Pohang (Republic of Korea) Inst. Sci. and Tech., 1989-91; rsch. asst. Computer Lab. U. Cambridge, 1998-99; computer asst. officer Newnham Coll., Cambridge, Eng., 1998-2000; mem. tech. staff mobile com. protocol sect., mobility mgmt. sect. Electronics and Telecom. Rsch. Inst., Taejon, Republic of Korea, 1991-96, sr. mem. tech. staff in mobility mgmt. sect., 1996-97; pres., CEO Filonet Corp., Vancouver, B.C., Can., 2000—. Engring. cons. Mirae Corp., Cheon-an, 1994—99; founder SoftForum, Inc.; mem. supervisory bd. ecom-monitor.com Inc, Czech Republic, 2000—; pres. Filonet Korea, Inc., Seoul, 2000—, Filonet Singapore Pte. Ltd., 2000—. Author: (with Y-H Koo) Modern Cryptology, 1997, (with R.J. Anderson, B. Crispo, C. Manufavas, V. Matyas and F.A.P. Petitcolas) The Global Trust Register, 1998, The Global Internet Trust Register, 1999, (with S. Katzenbeisser and F.A.P. Petitcolas) Information Hiding Techniques for Steganography and Digital Watermarking, 2000; mem. editl. adv. bd. Computer & Communications Security Reviews (pub. by Anbar Electronic Intelligence), 1999-2000; editl. bd. ECommerce Security Monitor, 2000—. Mem. AAAS, IEEE, Am. Math. Soc., Math. Assn. Am., Planetary Soc., Korean Inst. Comm. Scis., Soc. Indsl. and Applied Math, Cambridge Philosophical Soc., Assn. for Computing Machinery. Avocations: racquetball, tennis, mountain climbing, designing software package, swordsmanship (kendo). Office: Filonet Corp 400-1055 W Hastings St Yangchun-gu Vancouver BC Canada V6E 2E9 E-mail: jhlee@filonet.com.

LEE, JOSEPH, musician, educator; b. Bogor, Indonesia, June 6, 1941; arrived in U.S., 1968; s. Njan Fie and Kiun Fong; m. Lois Lee, July 6, 1973; 1 child Jason. Artist diploma, Jakarta (Indonesia) Nat. Conservatory of Music, 1965; performance cert., U. Oreg., 1972; artist diploma, Bklyn. Conservatory of Music, 1982. Performer Ret. Execs. and Profls. Roslyn, NY, 1989—. Named ARTS award, Nat. Found. for Advancement in Arts, 1987. Fellow: Music Tchrs. Nat. Assn.; mem.: Piano Guild. Home: 8544 Homelawn Jamaica Est NY 11432

LEE, JOSEPH WILLIAM, sales executive; b. Florence, S.C., Sept. 19, 1943; s. Warner Lou and Rosalee (Hyman) L.; m. Rita Martin, Sept. 8, 1962; children: Mark Stephen, Allison Lynette. Grad. high sch., Florence. Clk. Atlantic Coast Line R.R., Florence, 1962-69; sales rep. Durham (N.C.) & So. Rwy., 1969-74; dist. sales mgr. Westmoreland Coal Sales Co., Charlotte, N.C., 1974-82, v.p. purchasing Phila., 1982-85, v.p. purchasing distbn., 1985-88, v.p. purchasing and northern sales, 1988-91, sr. v.p., 1991, pres., 1991-95; v.p. sales TECO Coal Corp., 1995. Mem. N.C. Coal Inst., So. Coals Conf., Inc. (trustee 1989-92), Norfolk So. Corp. Adv. Bd., Charlotte C. of C. Republican. E-mail: jwlee@infi.net.

LEE, JOYCE ANN, computer educator; b. Safford, Ariz., Sept. 18, 1942; d. Roy and Minnie R. (Mobley) Brewer; m. Eugene W. Gaddy Jr., Mar. 16, 1970 (div. 1985); children: Carol, Kevin, Aaron; m. Glenn A. Lee, Oct. 16, 1992. AA, Ea. Ariz. Coll., 1980, AAS, 1993; BA in Mgmt., U. Phoenix, 1995, MS in Computer Info. Sci., 2001. Dispatcher Mohave County Sheriff's Office, Kingman, Ariz., 1969-74; sec. Globe (Ariz.) Mobile Home Sales, 1975-83; data entry supr. SMC & Assocs., Globe, 1985-88; tax preparer H&R Block Co., 1992; adminstrv. asst. Am. Pub. Co., 1994—. Instr. computer, bus. classes Ea. Ariz. Coll. Gila Pueblo campus, Globe, 1996-2001, instr. computers Pima Cmty. Coll., 2002. Girls camp dir. LDS Ch., Globe, 1985-90; mem. com. Boy Scouts Am., Globe. Mem. NAFE, Phi Theta Kappa. Democrat. Avocations: hunting, fishing, hiking, archery, camping. Home: 5201 W Bobwhite Way Tucson AZ 85742 Office: Pima Cmty Coll Tucson AZ 85742- E-mail: azgirl1942@yahoo.com.

LEE, JOYCE Y. educational administrator; b. Chgo., Feb. 16, 1973; d. Moses M. and Peggy Y. Lee. BS in Elem. Edn., U. Ill., 1995; postgrad., Northwestern U., 1999-2000. Tchr. Lincolnwood (Ill.) Sch. Dist., 1995-2000; asst. prin. Orchard Sch., San Jose, Calif., 2000-01, Creekside Mid. Sch., Castro Valley, 2001—. Office: Creekside Mid Sch Castro Valley CA 94546 E-mail: rejoice16@hotmail.com.

LEE, JULIET PATRICIA, anthropologist, researcher; b. Fontana, Calif., Apr. 17, 1963; d. Irwin Herbert Lee, Mary Eleanor Coneway. PhD, U. Va., 1998. Lectr. U. Va., Charlottesville, 1997—98; rsch. anthropologist Prevention Rsch. Ctr., Berkeley, Calif., 1999—. Cons. Communitas Cons., Berkeley, Calif., 1999—. Contbr. articles. Bd. dirs. Dolores St. Cmty. Svcs., San Francisco, 1999—2000; mem. Berkeley Cohousing, 2001—; tutor Asian Immigrant Women Advocates, Oakland, 1999—2000. Fellow Fulbright Dissertation fellow, Fulbright Found., 1995. Mem.: Rsch. Soc. on Alcohol, Soc. for Prevention Rsch., Soc. for Applied Anthropology, Am. Anthropol. Assn. Office: Prevention Research Center 2150 Shattuck Ave #900 Berkeley CA 94704

LEE, JUNE WARREN, dentist; b. Boston, Feb. 24, 1952; d. Earl Arnold and Rosemary Regina (Leary) Warren; m. William Lee, July 25, 1976; children: Jaime Michelle, Daniel William. BA, Brandeis U., 1973; DDS, Georgetown U., 1977; student, U.S. Dental Inst., 1985-87. Pvt. practice, Boston, 1977—. Active Pierce Middle Sch. PTO, 1997-2000, Cunningham Sch. PTO, Milton, Mass., 1987-97, Parent-Adv. Coun., Collicot Elem. Sch., Milton, 1986-87; dental instr. Cunningham Sch., 1987-97; dental screening Healthworks, Neponset Health Ctr., Boston, 1981-84; bd. dirs. Delta Dental Plan Mass., 1995-2001, Delta Dental Found. Mass., 1995-2001; vol. Dentist for SmileLine On-Line, Mesas Child Identification Program, 2000—02. Master Acad. Gen. Dentistry (coun. ann. meetings and internat. confs. 1993-98, 2002-, chmn. 1998 local arrangements com., past pres. New Eng. Mastertrack program, pres. Mass. chpt. 1998-2001, past chmn. editl. rev. bd. Audiodent, coun. constitution & bylaws & judicial procedures 2001-02); fellow Am. Coll. Dentists, Internat. Coll. Dentists, Acad. Dentistry Internat.; mem. ADA, Mass. Dental Soc. (allied profl. liaison com. 1998-99, 2000-, amb., 2000), Yankee dental congress steering com. 1997-2000, 2001-02, gen. chmn. 2002-, co-chmn. social and cultural com., 2001, co-chmn. sci. com., 1998, co-chmn. gen. arrangements, 1996, allied sci. co-chmn. 1994), South Shore Dist. Dental Soc. (chmn.-elect 1991, chmn. 1992, chmn. program com. 1995-96), Am. Orthodontic Soc., Am. Assn. for Functional Orthodontics, Am. Assn. Women Dentists (sec. 1987, v.p. 1988, pres.-elect 1989, pres. 1990, A.T. Cross Co. Women of Achievement award 1985, bd. dirs., treas. Gillette Hayden Meml. Found. 1996-2000), Women's Dental Soc. Mass. (sec. 1978, v.p. 1979-81, pres. 1981-83), Mass. Dentists Interested in Legislation, Chestnut Hill Rsch. Study Club. Roman Catholic. Avocations: travel, geneology, reading, writing, celtic music. Office: 383 Neponset Ave Dorchester MA 02122-3104

LEE, JUNG HI, physician; b. Taegu, Korea, Nov. 23, 1945; came to U.S., 1975; s. Jong Bae and Soon Jo (Choi) L.; m. Chung Hee Huh, May 24, 1975; children: Jennifer, Janet, Jason. BS, Kyungpook Nat. U., Taegu, 1968, MD, 1972. Intern St. Clare's Hosp., N.Y.C., 1975-76; resident Trenton (N.J.) Psychiat. Hosp., 1976-79, Trenton Affiliated Hosp., 1982-85; pvt. practice Trenton. Mem. AMa, Med. Soc. N.J. Roman Catholic. Office: 1450 Parkside Ave Ste 5 Trenton NJ 08638-2949

LEE, JUNG-KOO, economist, educator; b. Kwangju, Korea, June 12, 1939; s. Hae Dong Lee and Hyung Ok Choi; m. Soon Ja Ha, Jan. 30, 1969; children: Sungji, Sungmi, Sunghwa, Sangjin. BA in Econs., Chonnam Nat. U., 1962, MA in Econs., 1966, PhD in Econs., 1979. Instr. Chonnam Nat. U., Kwangju, 1966-70, asst. prof., 1970-77, assoc. prof., 1977-83, prof. econs., Coll. Bus. Adminstrn., dir. the Ctr. for Regional Devel., 1983—. Vis. prof. IGS, Stockholm U., Sweden, 1979-80; acting mem. Labor Rels. com. Chonnam Province, 1981—; mem. adv. com. Korea Land Devel. Corp., 1985—. Rsch. fellow SIET Inst. Hyderabad, India. Office: Econs Dept Chonnam Nat U 300 Yong Bong Dong Buk ku Kwangju 500-757 Republic of Korea

LEE, KAMEE ANGELA, financial analyst; b. Hong Kong, Sept. 4, 1961; d. Yick-Kun and Fan-Yuk (Ho) L.; m. Hei-Wai Lee, May 23, 1988; children: Jonathan, Isabella. BA magna cum laude, Whittier Coll., 1984; MS in Fin., U. Ill., 1986, M of Acctg. Sci., 1989; M in Health Svc. Adminstrn., U. Mich., 1997. CPA Fla., cert. mgmt. acct., valuation analyst; fin. mgmt. Tax assoc. Price Waterhouse, Miami, Fla., 1989-90; staff acct. Humana Health Care Plans, Tampa, 1990-92; mgr. finance and accounting Humana Health Care Plan, 1992-94; mgr. data analysis and reporting Access Care, 1994-96; prin. fin. analyst Blue Cross Blue Shield of Mich., 1997—. Recipient Wall Street Journ. Student Achievement award, 1984, Barr scholar, Moss scholarship in acctg., 1987, Whittier Coll. scholarship, 1981-84, Acad. Achievement award, 1983. Mem. AICPA, Fla. Inst. CPA, Inst. of Mgmt. Accts., Phi Kappa Phi. Home: 44071 Darthmouth St Canton MI 48188-1015

LEE, KANG S. artist, educator; b. Seoul, Korea, June 5, 1937; came to U.S., 1967; d. Kee Young and Young Sook (Choy) L.; m. Frank James Sheppard (dec. 1990); m. James C. Brown, Apr. 17, 1999. BFA, Univ. Hong Ik, Seoul, 1963; postgrad., Univ. Colo., 1968-70; MA, Univ. Phoenix, 1989. Cert. tchr. Mgr. advt., presentation J.C. Penney, Colorado Springs, 1970-79, dist. merchandise presentation mgr. Denver, 1980-85; prof. Pikes Peak C.C., Colorado Springs, 1991—. Prof. Univ. Colo., Colorado Springs, 1992—; chairperson bd. dirs. Sheppard Arts Inst. and World Culture Ctr., Colorado Springs, 1998—. Exhibited in group shows Nat. Art Exhibition, Seoul, 1962-66 (Creative Excellence awards); one-woman shows include Ft. Carson Gallery, 1967, Colo. Coll., 1968, J.C. Penney Gallery, 1972, 73, 75. Judge mktg. and distributive edn. Colo. and Nat., 1975-86; v.p. Friendship Force Internat., 1990-98, pres., 1998; coord. Internat. Cultural Celebration, Colorado

Springs, 1993-95; mem. Common Ground Arts and Cultural, Colorado Springs, 1994—, sr. adv. com. Colorado Springs, 1995—; deacon First Presbyn. Ch., Colorado Springs; sr. svcs. adv. com. Colo. Springs Sr. Ctr., Colorado Springs. Recipient 6 Corporation awards, 1974-79. Republican. Avocations: nature, birds, animals, plants, gardening. Home: 4590 Kashmire Dr Colorado Springs CO 80920-7616

LEE, KANG-WON WAYNE, engineer, educator; b. Seoul, Nov. 15, 1947; came to U.S., 1976; s. Chong-Keuk and Jung-Ki (Baik) L.; m. Jee-Bock Hong, July 21, 1979; children: J. Stephen, J. Harold, Grace E. BS, Seoul Nat. U., 1974; MS, Rutgers U., 1978; PhD, U. Tex., Austin, 1982. Civil engr. Lyon Assocs., Inc., Seoul, 1974-76; structural engr. TAMS-Engrs. and Architects, 1976; hwy. constrn. inspector N.J. Dept. Transp., East Brunswick, N.J., 1978; rsch. engring. asst. U. Tex., Austin, 1978-82; asst. prof. King Saud U., Riyadh, Saudi Arabia, 1982-85; from asst. prof. to prof. dept. civil engring. U. R.I., Kingston, 1985—. Vis. rsch. assoc. U. Calif., Berkeley, 1991; vis. prof. Seoul Nat. U., 1991, Korean Advanced Inst. of Sci. and Tech., Daejon, 1992; engring. cons. Lee Engring., Kingston, 1987—; dir. grad. studies, dept. civil engring., U. R.I., Kingston, 1996-99, dir. R & D, Transp. Ctr., 1998—; mem. adv. com. New Eng. Transp. Consortium, Rocky Hill, Conn., 1986—; mem. policy com. Region I Univ. Transp. Ctr., Cambridge, Mass., 1988—; mem. R.I. Transp. Joint Rsch. Coun., Providence, 1994—, NSF Proposal Rev. Panel, 2002--. Contbr. articles to profl. jours. including ASCE Jour. Transp. Engrs., ASCE Jour. of Materials in Civil Engring., Transp. Rsch. Record, ITE Jour., ASTM spl. publ., several others. Recipient Program Devel. award U. R.I., 1987, Murphy Award for faculty excellence, 1990, Meritorious Svc. award RIDOT, 1996, Murphy Rsch. award, 1999. Mem. ASCE (chmn. bituminous materials com. and mem. pavement com.), ASTM, Transp. Rsch. Bd., Assn. of Asphalt Paving Technologists, Inst. Transp. Engrs., Chi Epsilon. Mem. United Ch. of Christ. Achievements include teaching and research in areas of pavement and transportation engineering. Avocations: gardening, hiking, sports. Office: U RI Dept Civil Engring Kingston RI 02881

LEE, KATE LEARY, financial adviser; b. Hastings, Nebr., Dec. 13, 1946; d. Robert Michael and Alyce Rita (Popp) Leary; widowed; children: Modie Alexander Lee, Marni Sue Lee. AA, Mesa Jr. Coll., 1968; BA in Spl. Edn., U. No. Colo., 1970, MA in Learning Disabilities, 1977, MBA, 1982. Lic. tchr., Colo. Speech pathologist, audiologist Unit 13, Scottsbluff, Nebr., 1971-76; tchr. spl. edn. Sch. Dist. 13, Greeley, Colo., 1977-78; master spl. edn. Havern Ctr., Inc., Denver, 1978-80; v.p. R.M. Leary & Co., Inc., 1980-84, pres., 1984—. Sr. arbitrator BBB, 1988—; broker rep. Titan Value Equities Group, Inc., 1983-94. Fin. coun. Notre Dame Cath. Parish, Denver, 1989—; vol. coord. for State of Colo. gubernatorial candidate, 1994. Mem. Western Divsn. Conf. Pensions and Benefits, Colo. Harvard Bus. Sch. Club, Soc. Asset Allocators and Fund Timers, Inc. (dir. 1990-93), Ambassador Club Greater Denver C. of C. Office: PO Box 630 Mead CO 80542-0630

LEE, KATHLEEN MARY, administration and nursing executive; b. Phila., Apr. 12, 1948; d. Daniel Joseph and Mary Ann (Daly) Glackin; m. Gary Douglas MacClay, May 2, 1970 (div. 1980); 1 child, Jeffrey Daniel; m. Glenn Patrick Lee, Feb. 14, 1981. RN diploma, Phila. Gen. Hosp., 1969; BS, St. Joseph Coll., 1985; M Health Svcs. Adminstrn., St. Josephs Coll., 1990; PhD in Health Svcs., Walden U., 1992. RN, Ga., R.I., Pa., Miss.; cert. nursing adminstr. Head nurse, nursery Jeanes Hosp., Phila., 1969-78; administrv. supr. Roger Williams Hosp., Providence, 1981-83; head nurse, nursery svcs. King Fahad Hosp., Rivadh, Saudi Arabia, 1983-85; charge nurse psychiatric N.E. Ga. Med. Ctr., Gainesville, 1986-87; v.p. patient svcs. St. Joseph's Hosp., Dahlonega, Ga., 1987-95, Coffee Regional Med. Ctr., Douglas, 1996-98; assoc. adminstr. Nursing and Profl. Svcs., Ocean Springs, Miss., 1998—. Founder, UNITE, Parent Support Group, Phila., 1976; co-founder, Neonatal Soc. San Antonio, 1979. Capt. USAF, 1978-81. Fellow: Am. Coll. Healthcare Execs.; mem.: ANA, Ga. Nurses Assn. (dist. honoree 1992, Ga. Nurses Make a Difference award 1991), Am. Orgn. Nurse Execs., Miss. Nurses Assn. (Dist. Specialty Nurse of Year award 2000), Sigma Theta Tau. Democrat. Roman Catholic. Home: 1509 Amberjack Dr Gautier MS 39553-7133 Office: Nursing and Profl Svcs 3109 Bienville Blvd Ocean Springs MS 39564-4361

LEE, KENNETH STUART, neurosurgeon, educator; b. Raleigh, N.C., July 23, 1955; s. Kenneth Lloyd and Myrtie Lee (Turner) L.; m. Cynthia Jane Anderson, May 23, 1981; children: Robert Alexander, Evan Anderson. BA, Wake Forest U., 1977; MD, East Carolina U., 1981. Diplomate Nat. Bd. Med. Examiners, Am. Bd. Neurol. Surgeons; med. lic. N.C., Ariz. Intern, then resident in neurosurgery Wake Forest U. Med. Ctr., Winston-Salem, N.C., 1981-88; fellow Barrow Neurol. Inst., Phoenix, 1988-89; clin. asst. prof. neurosurgery East Carolina U., Greenville, N.C., 1989-93, clin. assoc. prof. neurosurgery, 1994—, adj. assoc. prof. health edn., 1997—. Assoc. editor Current Surgery, 1990—; contbr. 30 articles to profl. jours. and 5 chpts. to books. Mem. Ethicon Neurosurgical Adv. Panel, 1989-95. Bucy fellow, 1988. Fellow ACS, Am. Heart Assn. (stroke coun.); mem. AMA, N.C. Med. Soc., Am. Assn. Neurol. Surgeons, Am. Soc. Stereotactic and Functional Neurosurgery, So. Med. Assn., Congress Neurol Surgeons, N.C. Neurosurg. Soc. (sec.-treas. 1991-93, pres. 1994-95), So. Neurosurg. Soc., Alpha Omega Alpha. Republican. Baptist. Achievements include research on the efficacy of certain surgical procedures, particularly carotid endarterectomy, in the prevention of strokes. Home: 3600 Baywood Ln Greenville NC 27834-7630 Office: Ea Carolina Neurosurg 2325 Stantonsburg Rd Greenville NC 27834-7534

LEE, KEUN SOK, business educator, consultant; b. Pusan, Korea, May 12, 1954; came to the U.S., 1981; s. Namho and Okki (Ryo) L.; m. Youn Bin Lee, Apr. 15, 1980; children: Grace, Danny. BA, Hankuk U. of Fgn. Studies, Seoul, 1979; MBA, U. No. Iowa, 1983; DBA, U. Ky., 1987; postgrad., Columbia U. Rsch. cons. U. No. Iowa, Cedar Falls, 1982-83; rsch. asst. U. Ky., Lexington, 1983-84, tchg. asst., 1984-85; instr. Hofstra U., Hempstead, N.Y., 1986-87, asst. prof., 1987-93, assoc. prof., 1998—. Author numerous publs. in mktg. jours. and confs. Recipient best article award Mu Kappa Tau, 1989, Acad. Mktg. Sci., 1991, best paper award AMS, 1991. Mem. Acad. Mktg. Svc., Am. Mktg. Assn. (assoc.). Avocation: Tae Kwon Do (2d degree Black Belt). Home: 1503 John St Fort Lee NJ 07024-2560 Office: Hofstra U 141 Weller Hall Hempstead NY 11550

LEE, KOTIK KAI, physicist; b. Chungking, Peoples Republic of China, May 30, 1941; came to the U.S., 1967; s. Shi-Shan and Wa-J (Hsia) L.; m. Lydia S.M. Rue, Sept. 8, 1967 (div. 1991); children: Jennifer M., Peter H. MS, U. Ottawa, 1967; PhD, Syracuse U., 1972. Asst. prof. Rio Grande (Ohio) Coll., 1973-74; vis. prof. U. Ottawa, Ontario, Canada, 1974-76; scientist U. Rochester, N.Y., 1977-82, TRW, Redondo Beach, Calif., 1982-83; sr. staff scientist Gen. Electric Co., Binghamton, N.Y., 1983-86, Perkin-Elmer Corp., Danbury, Conn., 1986-89; assoc. prof. U. Colo., Colorado Springs, 1989—. Author: Lectures on Dynamical Systems, Structural Stability and Their Applications, 1992; editor: Optical Bistability, Instability and Optical Computers, 1988; contbr. articles to profl. jours. Grad. fellow Nat. Rsch. Coun. Canada, 1966-67. Mem. Am. Phys. Soc. (edn. com. 1992—), Optical Soc. Am. (edn. coun. 1989-91), Am. Math. Soc. (reviewer), N.Y. Acad. Scis. Democrat. Roman Catholic. Achievements include patents and patents pending; research in semiconductor lasers, solid-state lasers, laser phase-locked coupling, non-linear optics. Office: U Colo Dept Elec and Computer Engr Colorado Springs CO 80933-7150

LEE, KUO-HSIUNG, medicinal chemistry educator; b. Kaohsiung, Taiwan, Jan. 4, 1940; came to U.S., 1965; s. Ching-Tsung Lee and Chin-Yeh Yang; m. Lan-Huei Chen; children: Thomas Tung-Ying, Catherine Tung-Ling. BS, Kaohsiung Med. Coll., Taiwan, 1961; MS, Kyoto U., Japan, 1965; PhD, U. Minn., 1968. Postdoctoral scholar dept. chemistry UCLA, 1968-70; asst. prof. Sch. Pharmacy, U. N.C., Chapel Hill, 1970-74, assoc. prof., 1974-77, prof. medicinal chemistry, 1977-91, dir. natural products lab., 1983—, Kenan prof. medicinal chemistry, 1992—, chair divsn. med. chem. and natural products, 1998-99. Adj. prof. Koahsiung Med. Coll., 1977—; mem. devel. therapeutics contract rev. com. Nat. Cancer Inst., NIH, 1984-88, Bio-organic and natural products chemistry study sect., 1990-94, mem. reviewers res., 1994-98; external assessor, res grants coun., Hong Kong, 1994—; cons. natural products program divsn. life scis. NSC, Taiwan, 1986-87, Food and Drug Bur., Dept. Health, Exec. Yuan of Republic of China, Taiwan, 1986-92, Genelabs, Inc., Redwood City, Calif., 1988—, Nat. Rsch. Inst., Chinese Medicine, Taiwan, 1989—, Sphinx Pharms. Corp., Durham, N.C., 1990-94; sci. advisor Nat. Lab. Foods and Drugs, Dept. Health, Exec. Yuan of Republic of China, Taiwan, 1990—; mem. sci. adv. bd. Pharmagenesis, 1992—; mem. acad. adv. com. planning sect. Nat. Health Rsch. Inst., Dept. Health, 1992-95, mem. recruitment and adv. com., 1996—, mem. sci. rev. and sci. coun. com. pharm. and biotech. sect., 1996—; mem. internat. adv. com. Biotechnology Rsch. Inst., Hong Kong U. of Sci. & Tech., 1997—; mem. strategic adv. panel Hong Kong Jockey Club Inst. Chinese Medicine, 2002--; mem. adv. com. Inst. of Botany, Academia Sinica, Taiwan, 2001--, Nat. Sci. Coun.'s Nat. Sci. and Tech. Program in Pharmacy and Tech., Taiwan, 2002--; chair sci. adv. bd. Plantaceutica, Inc., Research Triangle Park, N.C., 2001--; chair com. for promotion of Chinese herbal medicine industry and tech. Ministry of Econ. Affairs, Taiwan, 2000--; hon. advisor Chinese Medicinal Material Rsch. Ctr., Chinese U. of Hong Kong, 1999—, hon. prof. Inst. Med. Plant Devel., Chinese Acad. Med. Scis., 1999. Mem. editl. adv. bd. Abstracts of Chinese Medicines, 1986—, Oriental Healing Arts Internat. Bull., 1987—, Bot. Bull. Academia Sinica, 1988—, The Chinese Pharm. Jour., 1988—, Jour. Pharm. Sci., 1990-92, Jour. Chinese Medicine, 1990—, Internat. Jour. Oriental Medicine, 1989—, Kaohsiung Jour. Med. Sci., 1992—, Internat. Jour. Pharmacognosy, 1991—, Jour. Nat. Prod., 1994—, Jour. Asian Nat. Prod. Rsch., 1998—, Jour. Med. Chem., 1999—, Jour. Biomed. Sci.; contbr. more than 470 articles to profl. jours. Grantee NIH, Am. Cancer Soc., U.S. Army, 1971—; recipient Soine Meml. award U. Minn., 1990, Achievement award Genelabs, 1993, Lifu Acad. award Chinese Medicine, 1994, T.M. Tu Sci. award, 1995, Merit award Nat. Health Rsch. Insts., 1996, Editor's award Japan Oil Chem. Soc., 1997; named Hon. Prof., Shanghai Inst. Materia Medica, 1996--; recipient Outstanding Achievement award U. Minn., 1999. Fellow AAAS, Am. Assn. Pharm. Scientists, Acad. Pharm. Sci.; mem. Am. Chem. Soc., Chem. Soc., Am. Soc. Pharmacognosy, Am. Assn. Pharm. Sci., Am. Assn. Coll. Pharm., Phytochemistry Soc. N.Am., Soc. Syn. Organic Chemistry, Am. Assn. Cancer Rsch., Academia Sinica (academician). Achievements include 40 patents on synthesis of anti-cancer drugs, anti-fungal agts., anti-AIDS compounds, discovery of more than 1,500 novel plant anti-tumor agts. and synthetic analogs; elucidation of structure-activity relationships, mechanisms of action of bioactive products, herbal medicine including Chinese herbal medicine. Office: U NC Sch Pharmacy Chapel Hill NC 27599-0001 E-mail: khlee@unc.edu.

LEE, KWANGJIN, engineer, researcher; s. Jae-Seung and Jeong-Boon Lee; m. Hojeong; children: John, Andrew. BS, Seoul Nat. U., 1985, MS, 1987; PhD, U. Mich., 1993. Rsch. scientist Korea Advanced Inst. Sci. and Tech., Seoul, 1987-88; rsch. asst. U. Mich., Ann Arbor, 1989-91; summer intern GM-Delco Moraine Divsn., Dayton, Ohio, 1990-91; tchg. asst. U. Mich., Ann Arbor, 1991-93; sr. project engr. Delphi Chassis Sys., Milford, Mich., 1994—. Indsl. rep. Automative Rsch. Ctr., Ann Arbor, 1995-96. Contbr. articles to profl. jours. including Jour. Tribology. Recipient scholarship Korean Govt., 1988-90, Korean Sci. and Engring. Found., 1985; Mfg. fellow United Tech. Automotive, 1993-94; Indsl. fellow Oak Ridge Nat. Lab., Dept. Energy, 1998-99. Mem. Engring. Soc. Detroit, Soc. Automotive Engrs., Korean-Am. Profls. in Am. Automotive Industries. Achievements include contributions to the field of thermoelastic instability in automotive brakes; establishment of computer-based methodology for automotive brakes and dampers.

LEE, KYO RAK, radiology educator; b. Seoul, Korea, Aug. 3, 1933; s. Ke Chong and Ok Hi (Um) L.; came to U.S., 1964, naturalized, 1976; MD, Seoul Nat. U., 1959; m. Ke Sook Oh, July 22, 1964; children: Andrew, John. Intern, Franklin Sq. Hosp., Balt., 1964-65; resident U. Mo. Med. Center, Columbia, Mo., 1965-68; instr. dept. radiology U. Mo., Columbia, 1968-69, asst. prof., 1969-71; asst. prof. dept. radiology U. Kans., Kansas City, 1971-76, assoc. prof., 1976-81, prof., 1981—. Served with Republic of Korea Army, 1950-52. Diplomate Am. Bd. Radiology (cert. added qualification in pediat. radiology). Recipient Richard H. Marshak award Am. Coll. Gastroenterology, 1975. Fellow Am. Coll. Radiology; mem. Radiol. Soc. N.Am., Am. Roentgen Ray Soc., Assn. Univ. Radiologists, Kans. Radiol. Soc., Greater Kansas City Radiol. Soc., Wyandotte County Med. Soc., Korean Radiol. Soc. N.Am., Soc., Soc. Pediat. Radiology. Contbr. articles to med. jours. E-mail: klee@kumc.edu. Home: 9800 Glenwood St Shawnee Mission KS 66212-1536 Office: U Kans 39th St and Rainbow Blvd Kansas City KS 66103

LEE, KYU-PIL, electrical engineer, researcher; b. Yeon-gi-goon, Republic of Korea, May 28, 1961; s. Chung-heon Lee and Kyung-ok Ahn; m. Soon-hee Hong, Apr. 26, 1987; children: Ah-Rhem Sol, Ah-Rhem Byeol. BA, Han Yang U., Seoul, 1985; MA, U. Fla., 2000. Jr. engr. Sam Sung Electronics, Ki-heung, Republic of Korea, 1985-89, sr. engr. Republic of Korea, 1989-97, prin. engr. Republic of Korea, 1997-2001; rsch. engr., rsch. asst. U. Fla. Dept. Material Sci. Enring., Gainesville, 1998—. Patentee in field. Avocation: mountain climbing. Home: 5400 NW 39th Ave #S165 Gainesville FL 32606 Office: U Fla Dept Materials Sci Engring 132 Rhines Hall Gainesville FL 32611 E-mail: kplee@ufl.edu.

LEE, LANCE, theater educator, writer; b. N.Y.C., Aug. 25, 1942; s. David and Lucile (Wilds) Levy; m. Jeanne Barbara Hutchings; children: Heather Lee Messner, Alyssa. Student, Boston U., 1960—62; BA, Brandeis U., 1964; MFA, Yale U., 1967. Lectr. English Bridgeport (Conn.) U., 1967—68, So. Conn. State Coll., New Haven, 1968; lectr., asst. prof. drama U. So. Calif., L.A., 1968—71; asst. prof. theater U. Calif., 1971—73. Outside editor engring. MIT, Cambridge, 1986—99, UCLA, 1972—85; freelance editor, 1980—; part-time asst. prof. cinema and TV arts Calif. State U., Northridge, 1981—. Author: (plays) Rasputin, 1966, Gambits, 1971 (Eugene O'Neill Meml. Theatre Ctr. Nat. Playwrights Conf. selection, 1971), Fox, Hound, and Huntress, 1973, Time's Up, 1979; author: (with Ben Brady) (book) The Understructure of Screenwriting for Film and Television, 1988; author: (book of poetry) Wrestling With The Angel, 1990, Becoming Human, 2001, (book) A Poetics for Screenwriters, 2001, (novels) Second Chances, 2001, (book) Time's Up & Other Plays, 2001; contbr. collection of essays; editor: (book) Not Dying, 1977, Youth Rebellion: Pattterns of Interaction, 1980, Keeping Hope Alive, 1986. Pres., chmn. bd. Temescal Canyon Assn., Pacific Palisades, 1971—76, hon. bd. mem., 1976—2002; Environ. del. Cmty. Coun., 1975—76; chmn. coord. coun. Santa Monica Mountains State Pks. Citizens Adv. Coms., Santa Monica, 1975—76; mem. Topanga Canyon State Park Citizens Adv. Com., L.A., 1975—76. Recipient Theron Bamberger award for playwriting, Brandeis U., 1964; fellow, Arts of the Theatre Found., Yale U. Sch. Drama, 1967; grantee creative writing fellow, NEA, 1976, theater devel. grantee, Office for Advanced Drama Rsch., 1971, rsch. and publs. grantee, U. So. Calif., 1970, 1971; scholar F. T. Wells scholar in poetry, Squaw Valley Writers Conf., 1983, scholar in poetry, 1982. Mem.: PEN, Poetry Soc. Am., Am. Acad. Poets. Address: Reece Halse Agy 8733 Sunset Blvd Los Angeles CA 90069

LEE, LANSING BURROWS, JR. lawyer, corporate executive; b. Augusta, Ga., Dec. 27, 1919; s. Lansing Burrows and Bertha (Barrett) L.; s. Natalie Krug, July 4, 1943; children: Melinda Lee Clark, Lansing Burrows III, Bothwell Graves, Richard Hancock. BS, U. Va., 1939; postgrad., U. Ga. Sch. Law, 1939-40; JD, Harvard U., 1947. Bar: Ga. 1947. Corp. officer Ga.-Carolina Warehouse & Compress Co., Augusta, 1957-89, pres., CEO; co-owner Ga.-Carolina Warehouse; pvt. practice, Augusta, 1947—. Bd. dirs. Med. Coll. of Ga. Found. Chmn. bd. trustees James Brice White Found., 1962—; sr. warden Episcopal Ch., also chancellor, lay min.; sr. councillor Atlantic Coun. U.S.; bd. dirs. Med. Coll. Ga. Found. Capt. USAAF, 1942-46. Fellow Am. Coll. Trust and Estate Counsel; mem. Ga. Bar Found., Harvard U. Law Sch. Assn. Ga. (pres. 1966-67), Augusta Bar Assn. (pres. 1966-67), Soc. Colonial Wars Ga., State Bar Ga. (former chmn. fiduciary law sect.), U.S. Supreme Ct. Hist. Soc., U. Va. Thomas Jefferson Soc. Alumni, Internat. Order St. Luke the Physician, Augusta Country Club, Harvard Club Atlanta, President's Club Med. Coll. Ga. Office: First Union Bank Bldg 699 Broad St Ste 904 Augusta GA 30901-1448 Office Fax: 706-722-8902. E-mail: LAWLEE@worldnet.att.net.

LEE, LAURENS CONWAY, judge; b. Fort Valley, Ga., Apr. 11, 1958; s. Milledge Bruce and Valeria Virginia (Brown) L.; m. Kimberly Denise Peeler, May 30, 1986; children: Laurens C. Jr., Kimberly Valeria Virginia, Savannah Rose. BSc, Ga. Coll., 1981; JD, Mercer U., 1984. Bar: Ga., U.S. Dist. Ct. (mid. dist.) Ga. 1984. Assoc. Robert E. Lanyon, Atty., Fort Valley, Ga., 1984-85; asst. dist. atty. Ogeechee Cir. D.A.'s Office, Statesboro, 1985-86; asst. pub. def. Houston County Pub. Defenders Office, Perry, 1986-87; assooc. Hebert L. Wells, Atty., 1987-88; pvt. practice Fort Valley, Ga., 1988—; pub. defender Twiggs County Bd. of Commrs., Jeffersonville, 1988—; chief magistrate Peach County Magistrate Ct., Fort Valley, 1995—; juvenile judge pro-tem Peach & Crawford Counties Juvenile Ct., 1994—. Mem. Downtown Devel. Authority, Fort Valley, 1990-92; atty. Peach Area Habitat for Humanity, Fort Valley, 1990-95, Peach County C. of C., Fort Valley, 1989. Mem. State Bar of Ga., Peach-Crawford Bar Assn., Crawford-Peachs Sons Confederate Vets. Baptist. Avocations: basketball, horseback riding, old cars, reading, politics. Office: 112A S Camellia Blvd Fort Valley GA 31030-3013

LEE, LESLIE ENDERS, artist; b. Washington, Sept. 25, 1946; d. Robert J. and Estelle (Gellard) Enders; m. Dwight E. Lee, Apr. 25, 1970; children: Derek Enders, Dana Rose. BA, Wellesley Coll., 1968. Author: Horseplay, 2000; one-woman shows include Jan Abrams Fine Art, N.Y., 1996, Works Gallery, N.Y.C., 1995, Books & Co., N.Y.C., Brodigan Gallery, Groton Sch., 1993, Almquist Gallery, New Preston, Conn., 1987, Katonah (N.Y.) Gallery, 1982, 100 Pearl Gallery, Hartford, Conn., 2000; group exhibitions include D.C. Moore Gllery, N.Y., 1998, 100 Pearl Gallery, 1997, Gallery Brocken, Tokyo, 1996, Berkeley Square Gallery, London, 1990-96, Glass Gallery, N.Y., 1990-95, Gallery Three Zero, N.Y., 1993, Lintas Worldwide Gallery, N.Y., 1992, Silvermine Guild, New Canaan, Conn., 1989, Mus. of the Nat. Arts Found., N.Y., 1989, U. N.H., Durham, 1988, Nat. Acad. of Design, N.Y., 1988, Lintas Worldwide Gallery, 1987, The Drawings Ctr., N.Y., Washington Square East Galleries, NYU, 1985, Barbara Mathes Gallery, N.Y., Silvermine Guild, 1981, Mus. of Modern Art, N.Y., 1977-81, Katonah Gallery, 1980, Sakai City Mus., Japan, 1998, 100 Pearl Gallery, Hartford, Conn., 2000, Katorak Mus., 2001, Appleton Mus., Ocala, Fla., 2002, Brodigan Gallery, Groton Sch., 2002, Paesaggio Gallery, West Hartford, Conn., 2002; represented in pvt. and corp. collections. Office: Leslie Enders Lee Fine Arts 21 E 87th St New York NY 10128-0506 E-mail: epona925@aol.com.

LEE, LESLIE WARREN, marketing executive, public speaker; b. Mpls., Nov. 21, 1949; s. Adolph Orlando and Eunice Celia (Akerson) L.; m. Kathleen Karen Frie, June 2, 1973; children: Megan Christine, Maren Elisabeth, Matthew Warren. BA in History magna cum laude, Augsburg Coll., Mpls., 1971. CLU, ChFC. Dir. YMCA, Mpls., 1971-73; dist. sales mgr. Chrysler Mtr. Corp., Marshfield, Wis., 1973-75; agt. Northwestern Mut. Life, 1975-81; mgr. advanced underwriting The Rural Cos., Madison, Wis., 1981-83; advanced life mktg. specialist Am. Family Ins., 1983-95; nat. sales dir., v.p. mktg. Flexsystem, 1995-98. Instr. Dept. Bus., U. Wis., Madison, 1981-82, Dept. Econs., U. Wis., Stevens Point, 1978-81; lectr. in field; cons. in litigation involving life ins. Mem. Nat. Assn. Inst. & Fin. Advisors, Madison Assn. Life Underwriters, Nat. Spkrs. Assn., Nat. Assn. Ins. and Fin. Advisors, Wis. Profl. Spkrs. Assn., Soc. Fin. Svc. Profls. Republican. Lutheran. Avocation: philately. Office: Motivation and Tng for Arena Life PO Box 620305 7522 E Hampstead Ct Middleton WI 53562-3609

LEE, LEWIS SWIFT, lawyer; b. Dallas, Nov. 19, 1933; '. Lenoir Valentine and Margaret Louise (Clendon) L.; m. Frances Ann Childress, Mar. 16, 1956; children; Frances Ann Lee Webb, Lewis S. Jr., George Childress, Lenoir Valentine Lee II. AB, U. South, 1955; postgrad., Washington & Lee U., 1954-55; MA, Emory U., 1956, LLB (replaced by JD), 1960. Bar: Fla. 1960, U.S. Dist. Ct. (so. and mid. dists.) Fla., U.S. Ct. Appeals (5th and 11th cirs.). Trainee Citizens & So. Nat. Bank, Atlanta, 1956, 58-59; assoc. Adair, Ulmer, Murchison, Kent & Ashby, Jacksonville, Fla., 1960-63; shareholder Ulmer, Murchison, Ashby & Ball, 1963-95; of counsel LeBoeuf, Lamb, Greene & MacRae, LLP, 1996-99, Martin, Ade, Birchfield & Mickler, PA, Jacksonville, 2000, McGuire Woods LLP, Jacksonville, 2001—. Gen. counsel Fla. Rock Industries, Inc., Jacksonville, 1972—, Patriot Transp. Holdings, Inc., Jacksonville, 1989—; dir. Fla. Sch. Book Depository, Jacksonville, 1990—. 1st lt. AUS, 1956-58. Mem. ABA, Jacksonville Bar Assn., Ponte Vedra Inn & Club, Timuquana Country Club, Fla. Yacht Club, The River Club, Haile Plantation Golf & Country Club (Gainesville). Republican. Episcopalian. Avocations: hiking, skiing, swimming, hunting, travel. Home: 3733 Ortega Blvd Jacksonville FL 32210-4347 Office: McGuire Woods LLP 50 N Laura St Ste 3300 Jacksonville FL 32202

LEE, LINDA M. technical recruiter; b. L.A., Dec. 28, 1972; d. Jack K. C. and Grace K. C. Lee. BA, U. Calif., Berkeley, 1995; cert. in human resource mgmt., cert. in tng. and human resource devel. Tech. recruiter Microsoft Corp., Mountain View, Calif. Vol. Asian Women Shelter, 1998—; mentor Chinatown Leo Club, San Francisco, 1998—, Children and Family Social Svcs., 1999—. E-mail: lindalee00@msn.com.

LEE, LLOYD ENG-MENG, real estate private equity investment; b. Tacoma, Feb. 2, 1971; s. K.J. and Linda (Ho) L. BA, Harvard U., 1992; MS in Hotel Adminstrn., Cornell U., 1995. Sr. cons. Ernst & Young, N.Y.C., 1995-98; v.p. Starwood Capital Group, Greenwich, Conn., 1998—. Asst. cons. to Sultan of Brunei, Juradong, 1994, Longhorn Steaks, N.Y., 1994, Dairy Queen, N.Y.C., 1994. Author, dir.: (corp. video) Interstate Hotel TQM, 1993; writer: TV comml., 1992. Vol. tchr. Montessori Sch., Boston, 1992-93; coord. House and Neighborhood Devel., Cambridge, 1990-92. Mem. Assisted Living Fedn. Am., Asian Real Estate Profls. Assn., Nat. Coun. Sr. Housing, Urban Land Inst., Conn. Venture Assn., N.Y. Venture Roundtable, Cornell Soc. Hotelmen, Cornell Sch. Hotel Adminstrs. Hospitality Global Task Force, Harvard Club N.Y. Avocation: writing educational books for children. Office: Starwood Capital 591 W Putnam Ave Greenwich CT 06830-6005

LEE, LOW KEE, electronics engineer, consultant; b. Oakland, Calif., Feb. 12, 1916; s. Hing Wing and Yan Hai (Louie) L.; m. Alice Jing, Nov. 29, 1953; children: Elliott James, Elizabeth Joanne. BS, U. Calif., Berkeley, 1937, MS, 1939; PhD, Calif. Western U., 1977. Group leader Aerophysics Lab., Los Angeles, 1946-50; lab. mgr. Stanford Research Inst., Menlo Park, Calif., 1950-55; asst. to dir. Gen. Mills, Mpls., 1955-57; dept. mgr. product engring. TRW, Redondo Beach, Calif., 1957-62, asst. dir. product assurance, 1962-78, ret., 1978; cons. Omni Corp., Rancho Santa Fe, Calif., 1983—, Control Data Inc., City of Industry, Calif. Co-author: Design and Construction of Electronic Equipment, 1961; contbr. to books, encys. Fellow IEEE, Chinese Am. Inst. Engrs. and Scientists (pres. San Francisco 1945-46, trustee 1979-81, 89-91, Meritorious award 1985), Masons. Home: 4479 Deerberry Ct Concord CA 94521-4513

LEE, LUNG-FEI, economist, educator; b. Canton, China; came to U.S., 1974; s. Hon-on Lee and Zhiyu Lei; m. Florence S. Y. Lo, July 20, 1973 (div. Apr. 1983); m. Amy J. Chou, June 16, 1987; children: Wesley, Suzanne, Annie, Margaret. BSc, Chinese U. Hong Kong, 1971; M in Math., U. Waterloo, Ont., Can., 1972, MPhil, 1974; PhD, U. Rochester, 1976. From asst. prof. to assoc. prof. U. Minn., Mpls., 1976-84, prof., 1984-91, U. Mich., Ann Arbor, 1991-96, Hong Kong U. Sci. and Tech., 1994-2000; univ. chaired prof. Ohio State U., Columbus, 2000—. Editor, contbr.: econometrics, 1999-2000. Fellow Jour. Econometrics, 1988. Fellow Academia Sinica, Econometric Soc. (mem. exec. com. 2000—). Office: Ohio State U Dept Econs, 410 Arps Hall 1945 N High St Columbus OH 43210-1172 Fax: 614-292-4192. E-mail: lflee@econ.ohio-state.edu.

LEE, MANKOO, device engineer, scientist; b. Kunsan, Republic of Korea, Oct. 23, 1958; came to U.S., 1987, naturalized, 1999; s. Donglee and Ansun Ahn Lee; m. Eunsun Kim, May 21, 1994; children: Jane Junghee and Jean Heejae (twins). BS, Sogang U., Seoul, Republic of Korea, 1981, MS, 1983; PhD, Oreg. Stat U., 1990. Cert. 1st class electronic engr., Govt. Republic of Korea. Sr. rsch. engr. ETRI, Tajon, Republic of Korea, 1982-87; postdoctoral rschr. Oreg. State U., Corvallis, 1990; sr. device engr. Sharp Microelectronics, Camas, Wash., 1990-96; sr IC device physicist Tex. Instruments, Dallas, 1996-98; adv. device engr. IBM Microelectronics, Essex Junction, Vt., 1999—. Cons. Tektronics/TriQuint, Beaverton, Oreg., 1988-89. Contbr. articles to Trans. IEEE Electron Device and Jour. Solid-State Circuit, and other profl. jours. and conf. procs.; patentee in field. Named Best Student with 1st rank in E & CE dept., Oreg. State U., 1990. Mem. IEEE Electron Device Soc. (sr.), IEEE Solid-State Circuit Soc., IEEE Circuit and Sys. Soc. Roman Catholic. Avocations: tennis, bowling, golf, skiing. Home: 37 Sydney Dr Essex Junction VT 05452-3395 Office: IBM 1000 River Rd MS 863 Essex Junction VT 05452-4299

LEE, MARGARET ANNE, psychotherapist, social worker; b. Scribner, Nebr., Nov. 23, 1930; d. William Christian and Caroline Bertha (Benner) Joens; m. Robert Kelly Lee, May 21, 1950 (div. 1972); children: Lawrence

Robert, James Kelly, Daniel Richard. AA, Napa Coll., 1949; student, U. Calif., Berkeley, 1949-50; BA, Calif. State Coll., Sonoma, 1975; MSW, Calif. State U., Sacramento, 1977. Diplomate clin. social worker; lic. clin. social worker, Calif.; lic. marriage and family counselor, Calif.; tchr. Columnist, stringer Napa (Calif.) Register, 1946-50; eligibility worker, supr. Napa County Dept. Social Services, 1968-75; instr. Napa Valley Community Coll., 1978-83; practice psychotherapy Napa, 1977—; oral commr. Calif. Dept. Consumer Affairs, Bd. Behavioral Sci., 1984-90. Bd. dirs. Project Access, 1978-79. Trustee Napa Valley C.C., 1983—, v.p. bd., 1984—85, pres. bd., 1986, 1990, 1995, clk., 1988—89; bd. dirs. Napa County Coun. Econ. Opportunity, 1984—85, Napa chpt. March of Dimes, 1957—71, Mental Health Assn. Napa County, 1983—87; vice chmn. edn. com. Calif. C.C. Trustees, 1987—88, chmn. edn. com., 1988—89, legis. com., 1985—87, bd. dirs., 1989—99, 2nd v.p., 1991, 1st v.p., 1992, pres., 1993; mem. student equity rev. group Calif. C.C. Chancellors, 1992; bd. dirs. C.C. League Calif., 1992—95, 1st v.p., 1992; appointed mem. Napa County Paratransit Coord. Coun., 1999—, coun. chairperson, 2002—; mem. Napa County Transp. Planning Agy. Bd., 2002—; bd. dirs. Napa County Transp. Planning Agy., 2002—. Recipient Fresh Start award Self mag., award Congl. Caucus on Women's Issues, 1984; named Woman of distinction, Soroptimist Internat. and Sunrise Clubs of Napa, 1997. Mem. NASW, Calif. Elected Women's Assn. Edn. and Rsch. Democrat. Lutheran. Office: 1100 Trancas St Napa CA 94558-2908 *Personal philosophy: I believe in treating people as I would like to be treated - with dignity and respect. My attitude toward life has been "Of course you can".*

LEE, MARGARET KENDIG, music educator; b. Williamsport, Pa., Oct. 11, 1942; d. Roscoe Brown and Margaret Bunnell (Creamer) Kendig; m. M. Howard Lee, Feb. 26, 1967; 1 child, Jennifer Katharine. AB in Music, U. Pa., 1964, MEd, 1965; MA in Musicology, U. Ga., 1977. Tchr. Upper Darby (Pa.) Pub. Schs., 1965-67; music tchr. Edmonton (Alta., Can.) Pub. Schs., 1967-69, Newton (Mass.) Pub. Schs., 1969-72; pvt. music instr. Athens, Ga., 1973—. Author: Vihuela Music, 1977. Pres. Parents' Orgn. for Music, Athens, 1984-85. Mem. Music Tchrs. Nat. Assn. (cert.), Ga. Music Tchrs. Assn. (cert.), Athens Music Tchrs. Assn. (v.p. 1981-83, pres. 1983-85, treas. 1987-93). Avocations: gourmet cooking, reading. Home: 275 Sandstone Dr Athens GA 30605-3494

LEE, MARGARET NORMA, artist; b. Kansas City, Mo., July 7, 1928; d. James W. and Margaret W. (Farin) Lee; PhB, U. Chgo., 1948; MA, Art Inst. Chgo., 1952. Lectr., U. Kansas City, 1957-61; cons. Kansas City Bd. Edn., Kansas City, Mo., 1968-86; guest lectr. U.Mo.-Columbia, 1983, 85, 87, 89, 91, 93-95, 97; one-woman shows Univ. Women's Club, Kansas City, 1966, Friends of Art, Kansas City, 1969, Fine Arts Gallery U. Mo. at Columbia, 1972, All Souls Unitarian Ch. Kansas City, Mo., 1978; two-Woman show Rockhurst Coll., Kansas City, Mo., 1981 exhibited in group shows U. Kans., Lawrence, 1958, Chgo. Art Inst., 1963, Nelson Art Gallery, Kansas City, Mo., 1968, 74, Mo. Art Show, 1976, Fine Arts Gallery, Davenport, Iowa, 1977; represented in permanent collections Amarillo (Tex.) Art Center, Kansas City (Mo.) Pub. Library, Park Coll., Parkville, Mo. Mem. Coll. Art Assn. Roman Catholic. Contbr. art to profl. jours.; author booklet. Home: 4109 Holmes St Kansas City MO 64110-1127

LEE, MARILYN MODARELLI (IRMA LEE), lawyer, retired library director; b. Jersey City, Dec. 8, 1934; d. Alfred E. and Florence Olga (Koment) Modarelli; m. Alfred McClung Lee III, June 8, 1957 (div. July 1985); children: Leslie Lee Ekstrand, Alfred McClung IV, Andrew Modarelli. BA, Swarthmore (Pa.) Coll., 1956; JD, Western New Eng. Sch. of Law, 1985. Bar: Mass. 1986. Claims rep., supr. region II Social Security Adminstrn., Jersey City, 1956—59; law libr. County of Franklin, Greenfield, Mass., 1972—78; head law libr. Mass. Trial Ct., 1978—2001. Mem. Franklin County Futures Lab Project (Mass. Cts.), 1994—. Vice chmn. Greenfield Planning Bd., 1987—95; mem. bldg. com. Greenfield Sch., 1995—; mem. Mass. Soc. for Prevention of Cruelty to Children , 2002—, Franklin Regional Planning Bd., 1988—98; moderator All Souls Unitarian Ch., 1996—2000, asst. treas., 1997—98, treas., 1998—2001; chmn. Franklin County (Mass.) Regional Tech., Turners Falls, 1974—76, mem. sch. bldg. com., 1974—76; exec. bd. Franklin Regional Planning Bd., 1992—95; mem. regional bd. Mass. Soc. for Prevention of Cruelty to Children, 2002—; clk. Franklin County Tech. Sch., 1976—81; mem. Greenfield C.C. Found., 1990—, Franklin Regional Transp. Com., 1992—; mem. alumni coun. Swarthmore Coll., 1994—97. Mem. Mass. Bar Assn., Franklin County Bar Assn. (chmn. lawyer referral com. 1992-94, 97-99, vice-chmn. 1994-97, chmn. libr. com. 1992—), Law Librs. of New Eng. (treas. 1993-97), Am. Assn. Law Librs. (mem. state ct. and county law librs. sect. 1972—, bylaws com. 1996-99, chair bylaws com. 1997-98), Greenfield Charter (commn. clk. 1979-83). Avocations: swimming, gardening. Office: Mass Trial Ct Franklin Law Libr 425 Main St Greenfield MA 01301-3304

LEE, MARTHA, artist, writer; b. Chehalis, Wash., Aug. 23, 1946; d. William Robert and Phyllis Ann (Herzog) L.; m. Peter Reynolds Lockwood, Jan. 25, 1974 (div. 1982). BA in English Lit., U. Wash., 1968; student, Factory of Visual Art, 1980-82. Reporter Seattle Post-Intelligencer, 1970; personnel counselor Theresa Snow Employment, 1971-72; receptionist Northwest Kidney Ctr., 1972-73; proprietress The Reliquary, 1974-77; travel agt. Cathay Express, 1977-79; artist, 1980—; represented by Mahler Fine Arts, Seattle, Pacific Rim Gallery, Astoria, Oreg., Pacific Rim Gallery , Cannon Beach. Painter various oil paintings; exhibited in numerous one-woman and group shows throughout Oreg. and Washington; author: To The Beach and Other Poems, 1998. Avocations: horseback riding, beachcombing, reading, music. Home: PO Box 1157 Ocean Park WA 98640-1157

LEE, MARTIN YONGHO (KYUNG-JOO LEE), mechanical engineer; b. Apr. 13, 1937; s. Yee Whan and Myo Ryun (Choi) L.; m. Su Ja Bang, Nov. 29, 1969; children: Mu Young, Tae Young. BSME, Han Yang U., Seoul, Republic of Korea, 1964. Lic. stationary engr., N.Y.; lic. energy mgmt. engrs. 1st class, indsl. power boiler-turbine oper. engrs. 1st class, Korea. Commissioning engr. Sam-Chuch Power Plant, 1963-66; jr. engr. U.S. Army, Camrhan Bay, Vietnam, 1966-69; startup engr. power plant Korea Electric Power Co., Seoul, 1969-75; stationary engr. CUNY, N.Y.C., 1981-92, N.Y. Police Dept., N.Y.C., 1992—. Co-chmn. Lunars Years Festival, Flushing, N.Y., 1999, hon. chmn., 2000; chmn. Flushing Fan-Fare, Queens, N.Y., 1999. Mem. Assn. Energy Engr., Co-Generation Assn., Korean-Am. Assn. Flushing in Queens (v.p. 1996-98, pres. 1998-2000, mem. adv. com. 2000-02). Home and Office: 136-80 41st Ave Flushing NY 11355

LEE, MARY VIRGINIA, artist; b. Clinton, Okla., Nov. 19, 1924; d. Thomas Joseph and Opal Corbin (Sights) Lee; m. Angelo Marelli, June 29, 1959; children: Luciana Powell, Thomas Giuseppe Marelli. Student, Corcoran Art Gallery, Washington, 1940-41; student, Am. U., Phillips Meml. Gallery, Washington, 1943-45, U. N.Mex., 1947; pvt. study, Scuola Beato Angelico, Milan, Italy, 1958-59. V.p. Marelli-Lee, Inc., Italy, N.Mex., Okla., 1961-94. Mem. of fellowship Phillips Meml. Gallery, 1945-46; artist-in-residence Camp Galilee, Lake Tahoe, Nev., 1953, 56; guest instr. Clinton (Okla.) Elem. Sch., 1983. One-man shows include AAUW, Boulder City, Nev., 1950, Okla. Art Ctr., Oklahoma City, 1951, Nev. State Art Gallery, Reno, 1952, N.Mex. State Art Gallery, Santa Fe, 1954; group shows include N.Mex. State Traveling Collection, 1955; painter 2 murals parish ch. Montalto, Parma, Italy, 1980, 4 murals St. Joseph's Ch., Hong Kong, 1993, 15 paintings St. Mary's Ch., Clinton, 1979, 14 paintings Epiphany Ch., Oklahoma City, 1984, double icon, 1984; designer 14 enamels St. Lawrence Cathedral, Amarillo, Tex., 1975, 2 hanging banners St. Mary's Ch., Clinton, 1983, 2 stained glass windows St. Peter's Ch., Guyman, Okla., 1985. Mem. DAR, Nat. Assn. Women Artists, Kappa Pi (hon.). Home: PO Box 132 Clinton OK 73601-0132

LEE, MELVIN JOSEPH, minister; b. New Orleans, Dec. 25, 1929; s. John and Isabelle (Green) L.; m. Dorothy Peterson, June 5, 1971; children: Betty, Barbara, Joseph, Edward. BS in Chemistry, So. U., New Orleans, 1970; MDiv, Union Bapt. Theol. Sem., New Orleans, 1988, ThM, 1989. Ordained to ministry Bapt. Ch., 1984. Assoc. min. 3d Missionary Bapt. Ch., St. Bernard, La., 1984-87, pastor, 1987—, chair deacon bd., 1974-84; coroner's investigator Orleans Parish, New Orleans, 1982—. Bd. dirs. So. Gen. Missionary Bapt. Assn., New Orleans, 1987—, chmn. bldg. com., 1988-92. Author: What Baptists Should Know, 1991; contbr. articles to profl. jours. Chmn. St. Bernard Cmty. Devel. Corp., 1988-93. Sgt. USAF, 1947-52. Democrat. Home: 7514 Dwyer Rd New Orleans LA 70126-4220 Office: Third Missionary Bapt Ch 206 Armstrong Rd PO Box 1012 Saint Bernard LA 70085-1012 *Man's actions are controlled by his beliefs. Therefore, to change a man's actions*change his beliefs.*

LEE, MICHAEL, leasing company executive, real estate company executive; b. Chgo., Nov. 26, 1953; s. Joseph A. and Mildred M. Kathrein; m. Victoria Lee; children: Jane Emily, Joseph Andrew, Theodore Michael, Elizabeth Grace, Fay Golda. BS in Acctg., U. Nebr., 1978; M in Mgmt., Northwestern U., 1985. CPA, Ill.; lic. real estate broker, pilot. Tax mgr. Touche Ross & Co., Chgo., 1978-84; corp. contr., v.p. Lettuce Entertain You Enterprises, 1984-86; pres., CEO Kathrein Leasing Co., 1983—; also bd. dirs.; pres., chief exec. officer Empire Real Estate Investment Co., Chgo., 1986—. Bd. dirs., speaker Nat. Speakers Bur., N.Y.C., 1985-94; cons. Fla. Investor, Inc., Cocoa, 1986—. Author: (how-to book) Real Estate Comparative Analysis, 1986. Bd. dirs. Revenue Crusade of Mercy, United Way, Chgo., 1980. Mem. AICPA, Cert. Mgmt. Accts. Assn. (cert.), Cert. Internal Auditors Assn. (cert.), Nat. Assn. Realtors, Young Pres.'s Orgn., Northwestern U. Alumni Assn., Mensa. Avocations: aviation, lecturing. Home: 7601 N Eastlake Ter Chicago IL 60626-1421

LEE, MICHAEL CALVIN, state agency administrator; b. Brownwood, Tex., Aug. 5, 1968; s. Herbert Calvin and Ronda (Rauhut) L. BBA, U. Tex., 1990, MPA, 1992. Instr. algebra Austin (Tex.) Community Coll., 1990-92; securities investigator Tex. Securities Bd., Austin, 1992-94; compliance investigator III, fin. analyst Nev. Sec. of State, Las Vegas, 1994—. Cmty. chmn. March of Dimes. Mem. Internat. Assn. Corp. Adminstrs., Golden Key, Beta Gamma Sigma. Republican. Presbyterian. Avocations: stock investing, sports. Home: 6205 Shady Brook Ln Apt 153 Dallas TX 75206-1510

LEE, MICHAEL WAYNE, structural engineer, consultant; b. San Antonio, May 1, 1959; s. Gim Chun and May Ying (Chin) L.; m. Grace Andrea Lim, June 16, 1990. BS in Archtl. Engring., U. Tex., 1981, MS with highest honors, 1983. Registered profl. engr., Tex., Okla., Ark. Rsch. asst. dept. civil engring. U. Tex., Austin, 1980-82; project mgr. W.E. Simpson Co., San Antonio, 1982-88; v.p. Gunnin-Campbell Consulting Engrs., Dallas, 1989—94; cons. Wiss, Janney, Elstner Assocs., Inc., 1994—. Recipient Presidential fellowship, U. Tex., 1981. Mem. ASCE, Structural Engrs. Assn. Tex., Am. Concrete Inst., Precast/Prestressed Concrete Inst. Baptist. Office: Wiss Janney Elstner Assocs 3050 Regent Blvd Ste 100 Irving TX 75063

LEE, MIKE, music educator; b. Waco, Tex., Apr. 1, 1954; s. Robert Ernest and Joanne Lee; m. Suzy Schaefer, June 12, 1976; children: Allison Boyd, Randy. MusB in Edn., Hardin-Simmons U., 1977; MusM in Edn., Tex. Tech U., 1984. Cert. Tchr. Tex., 1984, N.Mex., 1984. Contbr. articles to Mags. Mem.: Optimist Club (bd. mem. 2002). Republican. Baptist. Avocations: golf, flying, cigars. Home: 1031 Ivy Dr Roswell NM 88203 Office: Goddard High School 701 E Country Club Rd Roswell NM 88201 E-mail: mlee@risd.k12.nm.us.

LEE, MURLIN E. software company executive; b. Crescent City, Calif., Jan. 4, 1957; s. George Lee and Ida Burl (Wilson) M.; m. Jeanine Marie Metcalfe, Apr. 13, 1985; children: Kimberly, Kristen, Gina. BS in Bus. Adminstrn., Calif. Poly. U., Pomona, 1981; MS in Software Engring., Nat. U., San Jose, Calif., 1988. Mgr. George M. Lee Enterprises Inc., Crescent City, Calif., 1979-80, Wells Aviation, Ontario, 1980-81, Bard Software, San Jose, 1982-84; software engr. Litton Applied Techology, 1984-89; program mgr. Condor Systems, Inc., 1989-95; tech. mktg. mgr., sr. solutions mgr., sr. dir., v.p. I2 Technologies, Inc., Mountain View, Calif., 1995—. Republican. Avocations: computers, gardening, model railroads, bicycling, music. Home: 4081 Will Rogers Dr San Jose CA 95117-2730 Office: I2 Inc 1395 Charleston Rd Mountain View CA 94043-1332

LEE, MYUNG WOO, financial secretary, accountant; b. Korea; came to U.S., 1972, naturalized; s. Sung S. and Sea (Oh) L.; m. Chan Soo Kim, Nov. 15, 1960; children: Francis S., Sang-Gil P., Monica E. BS in Bus. Adminstrn., Chung-Ang U., Seoul, Korea, 1960; MBA in Fin., Oklahoma City U., 1994. CPA; Series 6 stock broker. Chief acct., bd. mem. Hwa Sung Ind. Co. Ltd., Seoul, 1965-72; owner, operator Broadway Texaco, Walters, Okla., 1976-80; support person GM Small Car Divsn., Oklahoma City, 1979—; mgr. Mike's Donut, 1981-83, Lee's Cleaners, Oklahoma City, 1984-92; fin. sec. UAW Local 1999, 1995-98; owner Lee's CPA, Moore, Okla., 1999—. V.p. Chung Ang Econ. Rsch. Club, Seoul, 1958-60; bd. mem. Korean Soc. Oklahoma City, 1996; treas. North Cleve. County Dem. Club, Moore, Okla., 1997; chmn. election com., Korean Soc. of Oklahoma City, 1998; parish council chair Korean Martyrs Cath. Ch., Oklahoma City, 1998-2000. Mem. Okla. Soc. Public Acct., Am. Inst. Cert. Public Acct. Avocations: swimming, table tennis, golf. Home: 801 S Bouziden Dr Moore OK 73160-7324 E-mail: leemoneywiselee@aol.com.

LEE, NANCY RANCK, management consultant; b. Yonkers, N.Y., Oct. 31, 1932; d. William Edward and Marion Edna Ranck; children: John Gregory, Paul Edward. BS, Cornell U., 1953; postgrad., Boston U., 1974-75. Social worker Tompkins County, Ithaca, N.Y., 1953-54; pers. adminstr. GE Advanced Electronics Ctr., 1954-55; fashion publicist Macy's, N.Y.C., 1956-59; mgr. advt. and pub. rels. Josiah Wedgwood & Co., 1959-65; dir. comms. Gregory Fosella Assocs., Boston, 1969-71; dir. mktg. Kuras & Co., 1971-73; internat. sales mgr. Laser Focus Mag., 1973-75; pres. Lee Assocs., 1975-82; exec. v.p. Infotech, 1982-92; pres. Requisite Orgn. Assoc., Sarasota, Fla., 1992—. Lectr. Simmons Coll. Author: Targeting the Top: Everything a Woman Needs to Know to Succeed in Business, 1980. Mem. Cornell Cb, Ivy League Club, Phi Kappa Phi. Avocation: skiing. Home: PO Box 48818 Sarasota FL 34230-5818

LEE, NANCY T. human services administrator, educator; b. Washington, May 19, 1939; d. Robert D. and Marie (Burden) Thompson; m. Orlando W. E. Lee, July 7, 1967; children: Anthony Lester, William Edward. Diploma, Bellevue Sch. Nursing, N.Y.C., 1962; BS summa cum laude, Bowie State U., 1988; MA, Marymount U., 1991; MA in Religious Studies, Howard U., 1999, postgrad., 2002—. Cert. gerontol. nursing. Sch. nurse HHS, Washington; dir. clin. svcs. Staff Builders Temp. Svcs.; instr. U. DC; dir. staff devel. Washington Home; dir. nursing Health Care Inst.; instr. Prince George's CC, Alzheimer's Assn. Instr. divsn. nursing Howard U., Washington, chapel asst. advisor Andrew Rankin Meml. Chapel; cons. in field; clin. educator II Vis. Nurses Assn., Hyattsville, Md. Mem. task force nurse asst. competency exam. Ednl. Testing Svc. Fellow Diversity fellow, Nat. Interfaith Coun. on Aging, 2002—. Mem.: Alzheimer's Assn. (bd. dirs. local chpt.), LPN Assn., Nat. Gerontol. Nurses Assn., DC Nursing Assn., Nat. Black Nurses Assn., Nat. Nurses Staff Devel. Assn., Sigma Theta Tau, Delta Epsilon Sigma.

LEE, NELLIE GREENBERG, social worker, educator, counselor; b. Bereczas, Czechoslovakia, Feb. 9, 1936; came to U.S., 1947; d. Jeno and Honey (Rosenberg) Wiesel; m. George Greenberg, 1954 (div. May, 1975); children: Jeffrey, Leon. BA, Duke U., 1959; MA, Fairleigh Dickinson U., 1974; MSW, Hunter Coll., 1977. Bd. cert. diplomate, ACSW; lic. clin. social worker, Fla., cert. social worker, N.Y. Psychiat. social worker Letchworth Village, Theills, N.Y., 1977-78; sch. social worker Palisades Park (N.J.) Sch. Bd., 1978-80; med. social worker North Beach Dialysis Ctr., Miami, Fla., 1983-84, N. Shore & Parkway Hosp., Miami, 1985; clin. social worker Rape Treatment Ctr., 1985-87; med. social worker Artificial Kidney Ctr., Homestead, Fla., 1986-87; family therapist Here's Help Rehab. Ctr., Opa Locka, 1987; TRUST counselor Dade County Schs., Miami Lakes, 1987—. Clin. social worker pvt. practice, Miami, Fla., 1981—; instr. Miami-Dade County Community Coll., 1982—. Mem. NASW (chmn. Miami-Dade chpt. 1982-85, supr. for clin. social work licensure, 1987—), Assn. Clin. Social Workers. Jewish. Avocations: music, dance, tennis, camping, sailing. Home: 6666 SW 115th Ct Apt 203 Miami FL 33173-4734

LEE, PALI JAE (POLLY JAE STEAD LEE), retired librarian, writer; b. Nov. 26, 1925; d. Jonathan Everett Wheeler and Ona Katherine (Grunder) Stead; m. Richard H.W. Lee, Apr. 7, 1945 (div. 1978); children: Catherine Lani Honcoop, Karin Lee Robinson, Ona G., Laurie Brett, Robin Louise Lee Halbert; m. John K. Willis, 1979 (dec. 1994). Student, U. Hawaii, 1944-46, Mich. State, 1961-64. Cataloguer and processor U.S. Army Air Force, 1945-46; with U.S. Weather Bur. Film Library, New Orleans, 1948-50, FBI, Wright-Patterson AFB, Dayton, Ohio, 1952, Ohio Wholesale Winedealers, Columbus, 1956-58, Coll. Engring., Ohio State U., Columbus, 1959; writer tech. manual Annie Whittenmeyer Home, Davenport, Iowa, 1960; with Grand Rapids (Mich.) Pub. Library, 1961-62; dir. Waterford (Mich.) Twp. Libraries, 1962-64; acquisition librarian Pontiac (Mich.) Pub. Libraries, 1965-71, dir. East Side br., 1971-73; rsch. asst. dept. anthropology Bishop Mus., Honolulu, 1975-83; pub. Night Rainbow Pub., 1984—. Author: Mary Dyer, Child of Light, 1973, Giant: Pictorial History of the Human Colossus, 1973, History of Change: Kaneohe Bay Area, 1976, English edit., 1983, Na Po Makole-Tales of the Night Rainbow, 1981, rev. edit., 1988, Mo'olelo O Na Pohukaina, 1983, Ka Ipu Kukui, 1994, Ho'opono, 1999, The History of a Family, 2001; contbr. articles to profl. jours. Chmn. Oakland County br. Multiple Sclerosis Soc., 1972-73, co-chmn. Pontiac com. of Mich. area bd., 1972-73; sec. Ohana o Kokua, 1979-83, Paia-Willis Ohana, 1982-91, Ohana Kame'ekua, 1988-91; bd. dirs. Detroit Multiple Sclerosis Soc., 1971; mem. Mich. area bd. Am. Friends Svc. com., 1961-69; mem. consumer adv. bd. Libr. for Blind and Physically Handicapped, Honolulu, 1991-96, mem. adv. bd., 1997-98, bd. dirs. 1999; pres. consumer 55 plus bd. Honolulu Ctr. for Ind. Living, 1990-94, pres., 1995-96; pres. Honolulu chpt. Nat. Fedn. of Blind, 1991-93, 1st v.p. #93 state affiliate, 1991-94, editor Na Na Maka Aloha newsletter, 1990-94; 1st v.p. Hawaii chpt. Talking Book Readers Club, 1994-95, pres., 1996. Recipient Mother of the Yr. award Quad City Bus. Mem. 1960, Bowl of Light award Hawaiian Community of Hawaii, 1989. Mem. Internat. Platform Assn., Soc. Friends. Office: PO Box 10706 Honolulu HI 96816-0706 E-mail: palijae@hawii.rr.com.

LEE, PATRICIA, lawyer, diplomat; b. Honolulu; Cert., U. Paris, 1964; BA, U. Hawaii, 1965; MA, Columbia U., 1966; PhD, Northwestern U., 1973; JD, U. Hawaii, 1979. Ptnr. Goodsill Anderson Quinn & Stifel, Honolulu, 1979—; hon. consul of France, 1997—. Mem. bd. regents U. Hawaii , 2000—. Office: France Hon Consulate 1099 Alakea St 1800 Alii Pl Honolulu HI 96813

LEE, PATRICIA ANN, real estate broker; b. Des Moines, Jan. 16, 1939; d. Samuel Ellis and Grace LaNell (Ford) Campfield; m. Wylie Samuel Lee, Dec. 31, 1958; children: Daniel Ellis, Laura Clair (Lee) Anderson, John McKinley. Grad. high sch., Des Moines, 1957. Cert. residential broker. Real estate broker Andrews Realty, Des Moines, 1972-78; real estate broker, owner Lee & Lee, Realtors, 1978-82; real estate broker, ptnr. Hallmark Realty, 1982-85; real estate broker 1st Realty, Better Homes & Gardens, 1985-87, real estate broker, mgr., 1987-2000; real estate agt. First Realty GMAC, 2001—. Chair bldg. com. Windsor United Meth. Ch., 1985-88. Mem. Iowa Assn. Realtors (v.p. 1988-90, chmn. legis. com. 1989-90, pres. 1993, Realtor of Yr. 1993), Greater Des Moines Bd. Realtors (pres. 1988, Realtor of Yr. award 1981), Soc. Cert. Residential Specialists (pres. Iowa chpt. 1989-90), Women Coun. Realtors (pres. Des Moines chpt. 1981, Woman of Yr. award 1982), Nat. Assn. Realtors (bd. dirs. 1991-96). Republican. Methodist. Avocations: family, volunteer work, reading, travel. Office: 1st Realty GMAC 8431 Hickman Rd Des Moines IA 50322-4319 E-mail: patlee@firstrealtyhomes.com.

LEE, PATRICK KEVIN, dermatologist; b. San Francisco, Mar. 23, 1965; BA, U. Calif., Berkeley, 1987; MD, U. So. Calif., 1991. Diplomate Am. Bd. Dermatology. Intern Harbor UCLA Med. Ctr., Torrance, 1991-92; resident in dermatology UCLA, 1992-95, clin. instr., 1996-98; asst. clin. prof., 1998—; mem. clin. staff St. Joseph Hosp., Children's Hosp., Orange, Calif., 1996—2001; pvt. practice Tustin, 1995—. Fellow Am. Acad. Dermatology. Office: 13420 Newport Ave Ste G Tustin CA 92780-3745

LEE, PAUL LAWRENCE, lawyer; b. N.Y.C., 1946; AB, Georgetown U., 1969; JD, U. Mich., 1972. Bar: N.Y. 1974. Editor-in-chief Mich. Law Rev., 1971-72; law clk. to Hon. Walter R. Mansfield U.S. Ct. Appeals (2d cir.), 1973-74; spl. asst. to gen. counsel U.S. Treasury Dept., 1977-78, exec. asst. to dep. sec., 1978-79; dep. supt. and counsel N.Y. State Banking Dept., 1980-81; ptnr. Shearman & Sterling, N.Y.C., 1982-94; exec. v.p., gen. counsel Republic N.Y. Corp., 1994-2000; sr. exec. v.p., gen. counsel HSBC USA Inc., 2000—. Office: HSBC USA Inc 452 5th Ave Fl 7 New York NY 10018-2786 E-mail: paul.l.lee@us.hsbc.com.

LEE, PAUL P. ophthalmologist, educator, consultant, lawyer; b. Taipei, Taiwan, Sept. 8, 1960; s. Pei-Fei and Julia Lee. BA, U. Mich., 1981, MD, 1986; JD, Columbia U., 1986. Bar: Md. 1987, D.C. 1988. Congl. intern U.S. House Select Commn. on Aging, Washington, 1980; biologist NASA, Cape Canaveral, Fla., 1981; med. intern Beth Israel Hosp., Boston, 1986-87; resident in ophthalmology Johns Hopkins Hosp., Balt., 1987-90; fellow glaucoma Mass. Eye & Ear Infirmary, Boston, 1990-91; asst. prof. U. So. Calif., L.A., 1991-95, assoc. prof., 1995-97; prof. Duke U., Durham, N.C., 1997—. Cons. health scis. program Rand Corp., Santa Monica; bd. dirs. Ctr. Partially Sighted, Blind Children's Ctr.; med. dir. Duke Eye Care, LLC. Mem. editl. bd. Archives Ophthalmology, Evidence-Based Ophthalmology, Chinese Jour. Ophthalmology; contbr. articles to profl. jours. Bd. trustees Am. Acad. Ophthalmology, 2000—. Rsch. fellowship Brookdale Inst. on Aging, 1985, sr. fellow Ctr. Aging Duke U.; Stone scholar Columbia U. Law Sch., 1985. Mem. AMA, ABA, APHA, Am. Acad. Ophthalmology (trustee), Assn. Health Svcs. Rsch., Chinese-Am. Ophthalmology Soc., Assn. for Rsch. in Vision and Ophthalmology. Office: Duke U Eye Ctr Dept Ophthalmology Erwin Rd Durham NC 27710-0001 E-mail: lee00106@mc.duke.edu.

LEE, PAUL YUE-YAN, surgeon; b. Hong Kong, Aug. 30, 1938; came to U.S., 1959. MD, U. Oreg., 1967. Intern Wayne County Gen. Hosp., Eloise, Mich., 1967-68; resident Kern Gen. Hosp., Bakersfield, Calif., 1968-72; with Bellflower Kaiser-Permanente Med. Ctr. Mem. Am. Coll. Surgeons. Office: Kaiser Permanente Med Ctr 9400 Rosecrans Ave Bellflower CA 90706-2217 E-mail: mabalee@aol.com.

LEE, PETER, materials scientist; PhD in Metallurgy and Materials, U. Birmingham, Eng., 1983. Project assoc. The Applied Superconductivity Ctr., U. Wis., Madison, 1983—86, asst. scientist, 1986—88, assoc. scientist, 1988—94, sr. scientist, 1994—. Program chair Internat. Cryogenic Engring. Conf., Madison, 2001. Editor: Engineering Superconductivity, 2001; inventor, patentee Artificial and Multiple Phase Micro-Electropolishing, 1994. Mem.: Microscopy Soc. of Am. Office: The Applied Superconductivity Ctr 939 ERB 1500 Engineering Dr Madison WI 53706-1687 Office Fax: 608-263-1087. Business E-Mail: lee@engr.wisc.edu.

LEE, PETER, science educator, dean, computer scientist; BS in Math., BS in Computer & Comm. Sci., MS in Computer & Comm. Sci., U. Mich., 1982, PhD in Computer & Comm. Sci., 1987. Assoc. prof. computer sci. dept. Carnegie Mellon U., Pitts., 1987—; pres. Cedilla Sys. Inc., 1998—99. Grantee Presdl. Young Investigator grant, NSF, 1990. Mem.: Assn. Computing Machinery. Office: Carnegie Mellon Univ Sch Computer Sci 5000 Forbes Ave Pittsburgh PA 15213-3891*

LEE, PETER JAMES, bishop; b. Greenville, Miss., May 11, 1938; s. Erling Norman and Marion (O'Brien) L.; m. Kristina Knapp, Aug. 28, 1965; children: Stewart, Peter James Jr. AB, Washington and Lee U., 1960; LittD, U. of the South, 1999; MDiv, Va. Theol. Sem., 1967; postgrad, Duke U. Law Sch., 1963-64; DD (hon.), Va. Theol. Sem., 1984, St. Paul's Coll., Lawrenceville, Va., 1985, U. of the South, 1993; LittD, Washington and Lee U., 1997. Ordained priest Episc. Ch., 1968, bishop, 1984. Newspaper reporter, editor, Pensacola, Fla., Richmond, Memphis, 1960-63; deacon St. John's Cathedral, Jacksonville, Fla., 1967-68; asst. min. St. John's Ch. LaFayette Sq., Washington, 1968-71; rector Chapel of the Cross, Chapel Hill, N.C., 1971-84; bishop coadjutor Episcopal Diocese of Va., Richmond, 1984-85, bishop, 1985—. Pres. trustees of the funds Diocese of Va., 1985—; dir. Presiding Bishop's Fund for World Relief, 1986-93. Rector bd. trustees Episcopal H.S., Alexandria, Va., 1985—; chmn. Meml. Trustees, Richmond; trustee Wash. Nat. Cathedral, Ch. Pension Fund, 1999—, Berkeley Div. Sch. at Yale, 1999-2002. Recipient duPont Fund Lifetime Achievement award, 1997. Mem. Phi Beta Kappa, Omicron Delta Kappa. Office: Diocese Va 110 W Franklin St Richmond VA 23220-5010 E-mail: pjlee@thediocese.net.

LEE, PHILIP RANDOLPH, medical educator; b. San Francisco, Apr. 17, 1924; divorced; 5 children; 1 stepdaughter. AB, Stanford U., 1945, MD, 1948; MS, U. Minn., 1956; DSc (hon.), MacMurray Coll., 1967; PhD (hon.), Ben Gurion U., Israel, 1995, St. George U., 1998. Diplomate Am. Bd. Internal Medicine. Asst. prof. clin. phys. medicine and rehab. NYU, 1955-56; clin. instr. medicine Stanford (Calif.) U., 1956-59, asst. clin. prof., 1959-67; asst.

sec. health and sci. affairs Dept. HEW, Washington, 1965-69; chancellor U. Calif., San Francisco, 1969-72, prof. social medicine, 1969-93, dir. inst. health policy studies, 1972-93; asst. sec. U.S. Dept. HHS, Washington, 1993-97; prof. emeritus, sr. advisor Inst. Health Policy, San Francisco, 1997—; cons. prof. human biology program Stanford U., 1997—. Mem. dept. internal medicine Palo Alto Med. Clinic, Calif., 1956-65; cons. bur. pub. health svc. USPHS, 1958-63, adv. com., 1978, nat. commn. smoking & pub. policy, 1977-78; dir. health svc. office tech. cooperation & rsch. AID, 1963-65; dep. asst. sec. health & sci. affairs HEW, 1965, mem. nat. coun. health planning & devel., 1978-80; co-dir. inst. health & aging, sch. nursing U. Calif., San Francisco, 1980-93; pres. bd. dirs. World Inst. Disability, 1984-93; mem. population com. Nat. Rsch. Coun.- Nat. Acad. Sci., 1983-86; mem. adv. bd. Scripps Clinic & Rsch. Found., 1980-86. Author of co-author 15 books; contbr. some 100 articles to profl. jours. Chmn. bd. trustees Jenifer Altman Found., 1992-93; trustee Kaiser Family Found., 1991-93, Mayo Found., 1971-75, Carnegie Fedn., 1971-79. Recipient Hugo Schaefer medal Am. Pharm. Assn., 1976. Mem. AAAS, AMA, ACP, Am. Pub. Health Assn., Am. Fedn. Clin. Rsch., Am. Geriatric Soc., Assn. Am. Med. Colls., Inst. Medicine-Nat. Acad. Sci., Alpha Omega Alpha. Achievements include research in arthritis and rheumatism, especially Rubella arthritis, cardiovascular rehabilitation, academic medical administration, health policy. Home: 101 Alma St mt 805 Palo Alto CA 94301 Office: U Calif Inst Health Policy Studies 3333 California St Ste 265 San Francisco CA 94143-0001

LEE, PUI LUEN, civil engineer; b. Hong Kong, Mar. 7, 1952; s. Kon L. and Lai Yu (Wong) L.; came to U.S., 1974. Student Tex. A&M U., 1974-76; BSCE, U. Man. (Can.), 1978; MSCE, Ga. Inst. Tech., 1979. Registered profl. engr., Ga., Tex. Structural engr. Engring. Tech., Atlanta, 1979, Nuclear Structures, Inc., Atlanta, 1980-86; Impell Corp., Norcross, Ga., 1986-88; sr. engr. Simon-Ea. Cons., Inc., 1988-90; with Lee's Design and Assoc. Inc., 1999—. Mem. ASCE, ACI.

LEE, RAPHAEL CARL, plastic surgeon, biomedical engineer; b. Sumter, S.C., Oct. 29, 1949; s. Leonard Powell and Jean Maurice (Langston) L.; m. Kathleen Kelley, Feb. 11, 1983; children: Rachel, Catherine. BS, U. S.C., 1971, ScD (hon.), 1999; MS, Drexel U., 1975; MD, Temple U., 1975; ScD, MIT, 1979. Diplomate Am. Bd. Plastic Surgeons, Am. Bd. Surgery. Chief resident gen. surgery U. Chgo. Hosps., 1980-81; chief resident plastic surgery Mass. Gen. Hosp., 1982-83; assoc. in surgery Brigham and Women's Hosp., 1984-89; assoc. surgeon The Children's Hosp., 1985-89; dir. Electrical Trauma Rsch. Program, 1991—; med. dir. U. Chgo. Burn Unit, 1991-97. Asst. prof. surgery Harvard Med. Sch., 1984—89; VanTassel asst. prof. elec. and bioengring. MIT, 1983—89; asst. prof. bioengring. and surgery Harvard MIT, Divsn. Health Scis. and Tech., 1983—89; prof. surgery, medicine, anatomy and bioengring. U. Chgo., 1992—; chmn. bd. dirs. Avocet Polymers Techs., Inc., 1996—; exec. com. Biomed. Engring. Inst., Ill. Inst. Tech. Author: Electrical Injury, Multidisciplinary Approach, 1994, Occupational Electrical Injury, 1999; editor: Electrical Trauma, Pathophysiology, 1992; assoc. editor Bioelectromagnetics, 1993—; contbr. more than 200 articles to profl. jours. Recipient Alumni Achievement award Class of 1975 Temple Med. Sch., 1995, Searle Scholar award The Searle Found., 1985-88, Disting. Engring. Sch. Alumnus award U. S.C., 1998, award for advancing safety and health Am. Electric Power Assn.; named Ams. 100 Brightest Young Scientists Sci. Digest, 1984; MacArthur Prize fellow John D. and Catherine T. MacArthur Found., 1981-86. Fellow ACS (Schering Scholar in Surgery 1978), Am. Inst. Med. and Biol. Engring.; mem. IEEE, AAAS, Am. Burn Assn. (Lindberg award), Am. Phys. Soc., Am. Soc. for Cell Biology, Am. Assn. Plastic Surgeons (James Barrett Brown award 1988), Biophys. Soc., Nat. Med. Assn. (plastic surgery sect chmn. 1989-91), Soc. for Phys. Regulation in Biology and Medicine (pres. 1995), Soc. of Univ. Surgeons, Surg. Biology Club III, Tau Beta Pi, Alpha Omega Alpha, Sigma Xi. Achievements include 12 patents. Office: U Chgo Hosps Pritzker Sch Medicine-Surgery MC6035 5841 S Maryland Ave Chicago IL 60637-1463 E-mail: rlee@surgery.bsd.uchicago.edu.

LEE, RAYMAN WEI-MIN, critical care physician; b. Taipei, Taiwan, Nov. 22, 1961; s. Sherwin S. and Lily S. Lee. BSEE, Clemson U., 1984; MD, U. N.C., 1988. Diplomate Am. Bd. Internal Medicine. Surg. intern Baylor U., Houston, 1988-90; resident in internal medicine U. Tex. Med. Br./John Sealy Hosp., Galveston, 1990-93, fellow in pulmonary medicine, 1994-96, fellow in critical care medicine, 1996-97. Asst. prof. U. Tex. Med. Br., 1997—. Mem. ACP, Am. Coll. Chest Physicians, Am. Thoracic Soc., Soc. Critical Care Medicine. Office: U Tex Med Br Divsn Pulmonary Medicine 5.112 John Sealy Anx Galveston TX 77555-0561

LEE, RAYMOND WILLIAM, III, institutional stockbroker; b. Atlanta, Feb. 20, 1960; s. William Jr. and Marianne (Hollingsworth) Lee; m. Suzanne Bobbelle Smith, July 7, 1984; children: Virginia Stuart, Catherine Coleman. Student, Furman U., 1978; BBA, U. Ga., 1982; MBA, Ga. State U., 1984. Lic. broker series 7, 63, 4, 24, 27, 55. Sales rep. Harris/Lanier, Atlanta, 1984, maj. account rep., 1985-86; asst. v.p. Donaldson and Co., Inc., 1986, v.p., CFO, 1987-94; pres., founder Paragon Fin. Group, Inc., 1994—, also bd. dirs. Choir mem. St. Martin-in-the-Fields Episc. Ch., 1997—; bd. dirs. Preventive Blindness Ga., 2001—, Ga. Coop. Svcs. Blind, 2001—, Sandy Springs Cmty. Found., 2002—, Bonanza Five, Inc., 2000—. Named one of Outstanding Young Men Am., 1985. Mem.: World Entreprenuers Orgn., Securities Industry Assn. (mem. instnl. com. 2002—), Young Entreprenuers Orgn. (bd. dirs., pres. 2000), Cherokee Town and Country Club, Delta Tau Delta (bd. dirs., v.p. 1992—94, 1998—2000, Karnea chmn. 1994). Republican. Home: 5290 Cross Roads Manor Atlanta GA 30327 Office: Paragon Fin Group Ste 1040 Fifteen Piedmont Ctr Atlanta GA 30305 Business E-Mail: rwl@pfgi.com.

LEE, REBECCA E, psychologist, educator; b. Phoenix, Sept. 17, 1966; d. William P Lee, Margaret E Lee. PhD, U. Md., 1998; MA, San Diego State U., 1994, BA Distinction, 1992. Asst. prof. Sch. Medicine U. Kans. , Kansas City, Kans., 2001—; postdoctoral fellow Sch. Medicine Stanford U., Palo Alto, Md., 1998—2001. Author. Office: Univ Kansas Sch Medicine 3901 Rainbow Blvd Kansas City KS 66160

LEE, RICHARD VAILLE, physician, educator; b. Islip, N.Y., May 26, 1937; s. Louis Emerson and Erma Natalie (Little) L.; m. Susan Bradley, June 25, 1961; children: Matthew, Benjamin. BS, Yale U., 1960, MD cum laude, 1964. Diplomate Am. Bd. Internal Medicine, Am. Bd. Family Practice. Intern Grace-New Haven Hosp., 1964-65, asst. resident in internal medicine, 1965-66, 69-70; fellow in inflammatory disease Yale U., New Haven, 1970-71; practice medicine specializing in internal medicine, 1969-76, Buffalo, 1976—; family practice Poplar, Mont., 1966-68, Chester, 1968-69; asst. prof. medicine Yale U., 1971-74, assoc. prof. clin. medicine, 1974-76; prof. medicine SUNY, Buffalo, 1976—, prof. pediatrics, 1985—, adj. prof. anthropology, 1989—, prof. obstetrics, 1992—, chief div. gen. internal medicine, 1979-82, chief div. maternal and adolescent medicine, 1982—, chief div. geog. medicine, 1991—; dir. primary care ctr. Yale-New Haven Hosp., 1975-76, dir. med. clinics, 1971-75; chief med. svc. Buffalo VA Hosp., 1976-79; head dept. medicine Children's Hosp. Buffalo, 1979-96; chief med. officer WHO Collaborating Ctr. for Health in Housing, 1995—, fellow, 1985—. Cons. internal medicine N.Y. Zool. Soc., 1973—; cons. physician Buffalo Zool. Soc., 1980—2001; aviation med. examiner, 1980—; med. dir. Ecology and Environment, Inc., Lancaster, NY; mem. N.Y. State Bd. for Medicine, 1995—2002; mem. com. Nat. Bd. Med. Examiners, 1999—; mem. N.Y. State Office for Profl. Med. Conduct , 2001—. Sr. editor: Current Obstetric Medicine, 1989—95; corr. editor Jour. Obstetrics and Gynecology, London, 1989—; mem. editl. bd.: Internat. Jour. Environ. Health, 1994—; cons. editor Am. Jour. Medicine, 1976—86, contbr. articles on gen. medicine, infectious diseases, and med. anthropology to med. jours., also articles on med. problems during pregnancy; contbr. chapters to books on obstetrics and toxicology. Served with USPHS, 1966-68. Fellow: ACP (sr. editor Med. Care of the Pregnant Patient 2000), Royal Soc. Asian Affairs, Royal Geog. Soc., Explorers Club N.Y.C.; mem.: AMA, Am. Coll. Occupl. and Environ. Medicine, Internat. Soc. of Travel Medicine, Soc. Obstetric Medicine (pres. 1991—93), Infectious Disease Soc. Am., Am. Soc. Tropical Medicine and Hygiene, Gen. Internal Medicine, Am. Fedn. Clin. Rsch. Soc., N.Y. Acad. Sci., Yale China Assn. (trustee 1992—2001, sec. 1995—2001), Nat. Bd. Med. Examiners, Am. Soc. History of Medicine, Royal Soc. Medicine, Great Lakes Interurban Clin. Club, Alpha Omega Alpha. Home: 7664 East Quaker Rd Orchard Park NY 14127-2015

LEE, RICHARD FRANCIS JAMES, evangelical clergyman, media consultant, lawyer; b. Yakima, Wash., Sept. 13, 1967; s. Richard Francis and Dorothy Aldean (Blackwell). Diploma, Berean Coll., Springfield, Mo., 1989; BA, U. Wash., Seattle, 1990; JD, Gonzaga Sch. Law, 1997; MDiv, Fuller Theol. Seminary, 2001. Ordained Assemblies of God, So. Calif. dist., 1999. Lic. clergyman N.W. dist. Assemblies of God, Seattle, 1989. Author: Tell Me the Story, 1982, The Crimson Detective Motion Picture, 1996. Named Most Likely to be President, Franklin High Sch., Seattle, 1986. Pentecostal. Avocations: collector, writer, itinerant speaker, filmmaker. Office: 2604 E Boone Ave Spokane WA 99202-3718

LEE, RICHARD KENNETH, software company executive; b. Birmingham, Eng., Dec. 10, 1942; came to U.S., 1964; s. Kenneth Jesse Lee and Eleanor Margaret (Bellsham) Dean; m. Melinda Elena Noback, Aug. 20, 1966; children: Sonja Eleanor, Alyssa Claire. BSc with upper 2d class honours, No. Poly. U. London, 1964; MS in Inorganic Chemistry, Northwestern U., 1965; PhD in Inorganic Chemistry, U. London, 1968. Various corp. rsch. positions UOP Inc., Des Plaines, Ill., 1965-74, mgr. catalyst R & D automotive products divsn., 1974-77; v.p., gen. mgr. portable battery div. Gould Inc., St. Paul, 1977-82; v.p., gen. mgr. Elgar Corp., an Onan/McGraw Edison Co., San Diego, 1982-85; v.p. R & D, Pharmaseal div. Baxter Healthcare Corp., Valencia, Calif., 1985-88; v.p. strategic bus. ops. Manville Sales Corp., Denver, 1988-92; pres., chief exec. officer Rocklite Inc., 1992-99; prin. LeeVarage Internat., Castle Rock, 1993-00; chmn., pres., CEO Value Innovations, Inc., Denver, 1999—. Adj. prof. masters tech. program U. Coll., U. Denver, 1993-95; bd. dirs. Q.E.D., Denver; adv. bd. Kodiak, Denver, 1998-99. Author: (videotape) U.S. Competitiveness—A Crisis?, 1992; patentee for vehicle emission control system. Chmn. Summit 91, Denver, 1991, mem. organizing com. Summit 92, Pacoima, Calif., 1992; bd. dirs. Indsl. Rsch. Inst., Inc., Washington, 1991-92, co-chmn. emeriti, 1998-2000. Recipient IR-100 award Indsl. R & D, 1978; Fulbright travel scholar, 1964-65. Mem. Rocky Mountain World Trade Ctr. (vice chmn. 1992-94, exec. com. 1992-94, bd. dirs. 1990-95). E-mail: dick_lee@valueinnovations.net. *The quality of life for U.S. citizens in the early 21st Century will be primarily determined by the results of U.S. industry and government efforts to improve our ability to commercialize technology successfully.*

LEE, RICHARD WILLIAM, city and regional planning educator, consultant; b. Rochester, Minn., Nov. 15, 1955; s. Robert Eugene and Anna Junkerman Lee; m. Mary Kuehn, July 4, 1987; children: Jack, Kent. MSCE, U. Calif., Berkeley, 1984, PhD in City and Regional Planning, 1994. Sr. lectr. Massey U., Palmerston North, New Zealand, 1995-98; sr. transp. planner TJKM Transp. Cons., Pleasanton, Calif., 1988-93; project dir., prof. Calif. Poly. State U., San Luis Obispo. Commr. various transp. coms. San Luis Obispo City and regional govts., 1999-2001. Mineta Transp. Rsch. grantee, 2001. Mem. Am. Inst. City Planners, Inst. Transp. Engrs. Office: Calif Poly State U 1 Grand Ave San Luis Obispo CA 93407 Office Fax: 805-756-1340. E-mail: rwlee@calpoly.edu.

LEE, ROBERT ANDREW, librarian; b. Washington, Dec. 7, 1923; s. Frederic Edward and Edna (Stewart) L. BA in English, Oberlin Coll., 1947; MLS, U. So. Calif., 1966. Jr. cataloger Columbia U. Law Library, 1950-51; reference librarian N.Y. Daily Mirror, 1952-54; researcher for Dore Schary MGM, Culver City, Calif., 1955; with Universal City Studios, 1955—, research librarian, 1960-69, head research dept., 1969-89. Contbr. articles to profl. jours. Served with AUS, 1943-46. Decorated Bronze Star with oak leaf cluster. Mem. Acad. Motion Picture Arts and Scis. (gov. 1973-75), Acad. TV Arts and Scis., Am. Film Inst., Am. Cinematheque. Home: 400 Hauser Blvd Apt 11A Los Angeles CA 90036-5522

LEE, ROBERT DORWIN, public affairs educator, administrator; b. Detroit, Jan. 14, 1939; s. Robert Dorwin Sr. and Virginia (Stanow) L.; children: Robert, Craig, Cameron. BA, Wayne State U., 1960; MA, Syracuse (N.Y.) U., 1963, PhD, 1967. From asst. to prof. Pa. State U., University Park, 1966—, head pub. adminstrn. dept., 1988-94, prof. hotel, restaurant, and recreation mgmt., 1994—, interim dir. sch. hotel restaurant and recreation mgmt., 1999-2000, assoc. dir. sch. hotel restaurant and recreation mgmt., 2000—. Author: Public Personnel Systems, 3d edit., 1993; lead author: Public Budgeting Systems, 6th edit., 1998. Avocations: backpacking, swimming, bicycling. Home: 304 Sawmill Rd Port Matilda PA 16870-9026 Office: Pa State U Sch Hotel Restaurant & Rec 201 Mateer Bldg University Park PA 16802-1307 E-mail: rdl@psu.edu.

LEE, ROBERT EARL, retired physician; b. North Sydney, N.S., Can., Sept. 26, 1928; came to U.S., 1928, naturalized, 1942; s. Matthew and Amy Roberts (Moulton) L.; m. Sally Gosling, June 23, 1953 (annulled 1967); children: Diane, Cynthia, Susan, Robert; m. Elaine Katherine Chapleau, Dec. 15, 1967. AB, Colgate U., 1948; MD, Cornell U., 1952. Diplomate Am. Bd. Internal Medicine. Intern N.Y. Hosp., Cornell Med. Ctr., N.Y.C., 1952-53, resident, 1955-56; asst. clin. prof. internal medicine Med. Coll.; fellow Manhattan VA Hosp., 1956-57; cons. internal medicine N.Y. Hosp., Cornell Westchester Divsn., 1958, dir. med svcs., 1967-80; attending physician Burke Rehab., White Plains, N.Y., 1957-71, cons., 1971-93; attending physician White Plains Hosp., 1957-93, St. Agnes Hosp., White Plains, 1971-93; ret., 1993. Cons. in medicine Dobbs Ferry Hosp., N.Y., 1968-90; pres. White Plains Hosp. Med. Staff, 1975-76; mem. Westchester County Bd. Mgrs., Divsn. Lab. and Rsch, 1970, chmn. 1984—. Bd.dirs. Westchester Coun. Social Agys., 1972-77; sr. warden, Ch. of St. James the Less, Scarsdale, N.Y., 1988; vol. vol. advisor, Scarsdale Ambulance Corps, 1977—; v.p., Greenburgh Nature Ctr., Scarsdale, 1982-84. Served to 1st lt., U.S. Army, 1953-55. Named to Am. Soc. Most Venerable Order of St. John of Jerusalem, 1984 (comdr.). Mem. ACP, N.Y. State Med. Soc., Westchester County Med. Soc. (bd. dirs. 1970-72), Fox Meadow Tennis Club (Scarsdale, pres. 1980-81), Union League. Home: 9 Old Windy Bush Rd New Hope PA 18938-1133

LEE, ROBERT ERICH, information technology consultant; b. Spokane, Wash., Dec. 26, 1955; s. Robert Edward Lee and Edith Freida (Klasen) Moore; m. Vicky Ann Rowland, Jan. 31, 1981 (div. June 1998); children: Erich Rowland, Christopher Michael; m. Heidi LaVerne Christensen, Sept. 13, 1998. Student, Vanderbilt U., 1973-77, Corpus Christi (Tex.) State U., 1977, U. Tex., El Paso, 1980. Mgr., instr. Neptune Equipment Co., Nashville, 1976-77; customer engr. Hewlett-Packard Co., Los Angeles, 1977-82, dist. service mgr., 1982-85, region service adminstrn. mgr. North Hollywood, Calif., 1985-86; dir. mgmt. info. Tova Corp., Beverly Hills, 1986-87; dir. info. tech. PrimeSource/Sequoia Supply, Inc., Irvine, 1987-92; pres. Results From Tech.!, 1992—; v.p. info. tech. Triton Found., 1998—. Spkr. in field. Author: The ISDN Consultant, 1996; columnist Interex Press, 1995-97; writer Interact, 1995-97, Sun World Online, 1996-99. Honors Eagle Scout, Cub Scout Woodbadge. Republican. Avocations: skiing, scuba diving, travel, hiking, cycling. Home and Office: Results From Tech! 30127 Centro Vista Highland CA 92346-5928 E-mail: rob@roblee.com.

LEE, ROBERT HUGH, management executive; b. Honolulu, Jan. 3, 1950; s. Hugh Sebastian and Margaret Carol (Bennett) L.; m. Lois Ann Brown, Jan. 31, 1981. BA in Communications, Coll. St. Francis, 1972; MBA, No. Ill. U., 1977. Pres., owner Robert Hugh Lee Pub., Lockport, Ill., 1973-76; pres. Robert Hugh Lee, MBA and Assocs., DeKalb, 1978—; pres., chmn. bd. dirs., treas. Lee, Williams, Rogers & Assocs., Inc., Freeport, 1988—. Lectr. , tchr. bus. strategy, mktg. and fin. at several univs. in Midwest. Author: King of Laoise's Crusade, A Board Game of War and Strategy, 2002; creator: board game King of Laoise's Crusade, 2002. Dem. candidate Clk. of Cir. Ct., McLean County, Ill., 1980, Treas. DeKalb County, Ill., 1986, DeKalb County bd., 1988, Ill. Gen. Assembly, 1988; Dem. ward capt. cen. com., Blackhawk County, Iowa, 1982-85; trustee DeKalb County Regional Sch. Bd., 1987-95. Mem. Lions Club Internat. Avocations: carpentry, touch football, golf. Home and Office: 530 Woodlyn Dr Aurora IL 60504-9759

LEE, ROBERT LEYNE, conglomerate advisor, consultant; b. Penang, Malaysia, Apr. 17, 1942; arrived in U.S., 1990; s. Hock Seng and Aivy (Leyne) L.; m. Mavis Margaret Soars Lee, Apr. 20, 1963; children: Robert Ernest Lee Jr., Ralph Edward Lee. Diploma in plantation mgmt., Inc. Soc. Planters, Kuala Lumpur, Malaysia. Asst. mgr. Malaysian Estates Agencies, Malaysia, 1962-65; sr. asst. mgr. Kumpulan Guthrie, Malaysia, 1966-69; mgr., group mgr. Rubber Trust Plantations, Malaysia, 1969-73; planting adv., vis. agt. Plantation Agencies, Penong, Malaysia, Indonesia, 1974-81; dir., sr. planting adv. Taiko Plantations, Ipoh, Perak, Malaysia, 1981-89; pres., owner Texacrop Agri Mgmt., Houston, 1990-93; pres., dir. Genesis Capital Corp., 1993-94; pres., CEO, part owner Texacorp Consulting, 1995—; pres., owner Graceleyne Fin., 1996—. Registered cons. The U.S. Agy. for Internat. Devel., Washington, 1992—, The World Bank, Washington, 1991—, The Inter-Am. Devel. Bank, Washington, 1993—, The African Devel. Bank, Adidjan, The Ivory Coast, 1994—, The Islamic Devel. Bank, Jeddah, Saudi Arabia, 1995—. Mem. New Republican Majority Fund, Rep. nat. Com., Rep. Presdl. Task Force. Republican. Avocations: writing, music, nature activities, golf. Office: Graceleyne Fin Inc 2537 S Gessner Rd Ste 114 Houston TX 77063-2026

LEE, ROBERT W(ILLIAM), journalist, researcher; b. Salt Lake City, June 19, 1937; s. William Orme Jr. and Golda Alice (Anderson) L.; m. Karen Brinkerhoff, Nov. 24, 1958; children: Michael Don, Gary Dean, William Reed, Robert Bruce, Lawrence Alan. BS, U. Utah, 1960. Pres. Thermotech, Inc., Salt Lake City, 1960-65; adminstrv. asst. John Birch Soc., Washington, 1965-72, Washington rep., 1972-77; adminstrv. asst. Salt Lake County Commn., 1979-81; contbg. editor Am. Opinion Mag., Belmont, Mass., 1981-85, Rev. of the News Mag., Belmont, 1969-85, Conservative Digest Mg., Ft. Collins, Colo., 1985-89; talk-show host Radio Sta. KTKK, Salt Lake City, 1989-94; contbg. editor The New Am. Mag., Appleton, Wis., 1985—. Author: The United Nations Conspiracy, 1981; co-author: A Taxpayer Survey of the Grace Commission Report, 1984, Flight 007: Were There Survivors?, 1986; editor/pub. newsletter Comments and Corrections, 1981—. Mem. Lds Ch. Avocations: golf, chess, bowling, sport shooting, books. E-mail: rwlee@xmission.com.

LEE, ROBERT WILLIAM, organic chemist; b. Honolulu, July 16, 1960; s. Robert Son Hak and Fumiye (Yoshida) Lee; m. Susan Drummond, Oct. 2000; children: Brian, Ellen, Kevin. BS in Biology and Chemistry, U. Washington, 1982; PhD in Phys. Bioorganic Chemistry, U. Calif., Santa Barbara, 1990. Rsch. investigator Sterling Winthrop, Inc., Rensselaer, N.Y., 1990-92, sr. rsch. investigator Collegeville, Pa., 1992-94, NanoSystems, Collegeville, 1994-96, prin. rsch. investigator, 1996-97, mgr. King of Prussia, 1997-2000, élan Pharm. Techs., King of Prussia, 2000—01, sr. mgr., 2001—. Adj. asst. prof. U. Kans., Lawrence, 1992—. Contbr. articles to profl. jours. Robert H. DeWolfe Teaching fellow U. Calif., 1988. Mem. Am. Chem. Soc., Am. Assn. Pharm. Scientists, PDA. Achievements include patents in field; co-invention of robotics-based system to perform particle size reduction and automated particle size measurements in support of NanoCrystal projects. Home: 1335 Roberts Rd Gilbertsville PA 19525-8804 Office: 3500 Horizon Dr King Of Prussia PA 19406 E-mail: robert.lee@elan.com.

LEE, ROLAND ROBERT, radiologist, educator; b. Cleve., July 18, 1954; s. Chia Huan and Ellen Lee. BS in Physics, Calif. Inst. Tech., 1975; MA in Physics, U. Calif., Berkeley, 1977; MD, UCLA, 1985. Diplomate Am. Bd. Radiology (added qualifications in neuroradiology). Physicist Lawrence Livermore Nat. Lab., Livermore, Calif., 1975-77; intern Harbor-UCLA Med. Ctr., Torrance, 1985-86; resident in radiology Brigham & Women's Hosp.-Harvard U., Boston, 1986-90; fellow MRI Meml. Magnetic Resonance Ctr., Long Beach, Calif., 1990-91; fellow neuroradiology U. Calif., San Francisco, 1991-92; asst. prof. radiology Johns Hopkins Hosp., Balt., 1992-97; assoc. prof. radiology U. N.Mex. and VA Med. Ctr., Albuquerque, 1997—; dir. magnetic source imaging U. N.Mex., 1997—. Cons. radiology, neuroradiology, and magnetic source imaging, functional neuroimaging Balt., 1992-97, Albuquerque, 1997—. Author, editor: Spinal Imaging, 1995; contbr. book chpts.: Magnetic Resonance Imaging, 1992, The Adult Spine: Principles and Practice, 1996; contbr. articles to sci. jours. Mem. AMA, Am. Soc. Neuroradiology (sr.), Am. Coll. Radiology, Radiolog. Soc. N.Am. Avocations: tennis, classical music. Office: Dept Radiology Univ Nmex Sch Medicine Albuquerque NM 87131-0001 E-mail: rrlee@unm.edu.

LEE, RONALD DEMOS, demographer, economist, educator; b. Sept. 5, 1941; s. Otis Hamilton and Dorothy (Demetracopoulou) L.; m. Melissa Lee Nelken, July 6, 1968; children: Sophia, Isabel, Rebecca. BA, Reed Coll., 1963; MA, U. Calif., Berkeley, 1967; PhD, Harvard U., 1971. Postdoctoral fellow Nat. Demographic Inst., Paris, 1970-71; asst. prof. to prof. U. Mich., Ann Arbor, 1971-79; prof. demography and econs. U. Calif., Berkeley, 1979—. Dir. Berkeley Ctr. on Econs. and Demography of Aging; chair com. on population, NAS, 1993-97; cons. in field. Author, editor: Econometric Studies of Topics in Demographic History, 1978, Population Patterns in the Past, 1977, Population, Food, and Rural Development, 1988, Economics of Changing Age Distributions in Developed Countries, 1988, others; editor: Population Change in Asia: Transition, Development, and Aging, 2000, Demographic Change and Fiscal Policy, 2000, United States Fertility: New Patterns, New Theories, 1996; contbr. over 130 articles to profl. jours. Peace Corps. vol., Ethiopia, 1963-65. Recipient Mindel C. Sheps award Population Assn. of Am. and U. N.C. Sch. Pub. Health, 1984, MERIT award Nat. Inst. Aging, 1994-03, Taeuber award Population Assn. of Am. and Princeton U., 1999; NIH fellow, 1965-67; NSF fellow, 1968-69, fellow Social Sci. Rsch. Council, 1970-71; NIH grantee, 1973—; Guggenheim fellow, 1984-85. Fellow Brit. Acad. (corr.); mem. NAS, Population Assn. Am. (pres. 1987), Am. Econ. Assn., Internat. Union Sci. Study of Population. Democrat. Home: 2933 Russell St Berkeley CA 94705-2333 Office: U Calif Dept Demography 2232 Piedmont Ave Berkeley CA 94720-2120 E-mail: rlee@demog.berkeley.edu.

LEE, RUBY BEI-LOH, multimedia and computer systems architect; b. Singapore; came to the U.S., 1970, naturalized, 1996; m. Howard F. Lee, July 27, 1974; children: Patrick, Josephine. AB in Computer Sci. and Comparative Lit. with distinction, Cornell U., 1973; MS in Computer Sci., Stanford U., 1975, PhDEE, 1980. Asst. prof. elec. engring. Stanford (Calif.) U., 1980-81; lead architect Hewlett Packard Co., Palo Alto, Calif., 1982-84, lead designer microprocessors, 1984-86, project mgr. Cupertino, 1987-90, chief arch. computer sys. architecture, multimedia, security, 1991-97; chief arch. Security Architecture, 1997-98; Forrest G. Hamrick prof. elec. engring. Princeton (N.J.) U., 1998—. Cons. assoc. prof. elec. engring. Stanford U., 1990-95, cons. prof., 1995-98. Designer PA-RISC (Precision Architecture Reduced Instrn. Set Computer) architecture, Multimedia Acceleration EXtensions (MAX) architecture; contbr. articles to profl. jours.; inventor, patentee in field, including 20 U.S. patents and more than 63 foreign ones. Fellow Assn. for Computing Machinery; mem. IEEE (sr.; mem. exec. com., mem. tech. com. on microprocessors, mem. program com. Compcon conf. San Francisco 1991-97, program chairperson Hot-Chips Symposium, Stanford 1992-93, assoc. editor-in-chief IEEE Micro Spectrum, mem. editl. bd. IEEE Spectrum, guest editor spl. issues IEEE MICRO 1994, 96), Phi Beta Kappa, Alpha Lambda Delta. Methodist. Office: Princeton U Dept Elec Engring Princeton NJ 08544-0001 E-mail: rblee@princeton.edu.

LEE, SALLY A. editor-in-chief; m. Rob Niosi. Grad., Durham U., Eng., Clark U., Mass. Reporter Worcester (Mass.) Telegram; mng. editor Worcester (Mass.) Monthly; spl. features editor Woman's World mag., N.Y.C.; articles editor Woman's Day mag.; sr. editor Redbook mag.; editor-in-chief YM/Young & Modern mag., 1994-96, Fitness Mag., N.Y.C., 1996-98, Parents Mag., N.Y.C., 1998—. Corr. E! Entertainment Network. Office: Parents Mag 375 Lexington Ave Fl 10 New York NY 10017-5514

LEE, SANG M. management educator; b. Seoul, Republic of Korea, Apr. 1, 1939; came to U.S., 1961; s. Chang Woo Lee and Duck Soon Bahng; m. Joyce A. Sturm, Mar. 16, 1991; children: Tosca Lee Phillips, Amy L. BA in Econs., Seoul Nat. U., 1961; MBA, Miami U., Oxford, Ohio, 1963; PhD, U. Ga., 1969, U. Tirana, Albania, 1998, Cheongju U., Korea, 2001, Bangkok U., 2002. Prof. Va. Poly. Inst., Blacksburg, 1968-76; disting. prof., chair U. Nebr., Lincoln, 1976—. Cons. Omaha Pub. Power, 1983-86, Ssang Yong Corp., Seoul, 1984-97; project dir. U.S. Agy. Internat. Devel., 1991—; sr. scientist Gallup, 2001-. Author: Operations Management, 1995, Management Science, 4th edit., 1995, World-Class Organization, 1996 and many others. Recipient Valley Forge Leavy award Freedoms Found., 1995. Fellow Acad. Mgmt., Pan Pacific Bus. Assn. (pres. 1985—), Decision Scis. Inst. (pres. 1984-85). Republican. Office: U Nebr 209 CBA Lincoln NE 68588 E-mail: slee1@unl.edu.

LEE, SANGDON, transportation engineer; b. Seoul, Aug. 12, 1962; s. Siwoo and Hyunsoon Lee; m. Seung-Lye Kim. BS, Seung Kyun Kwan University, Seoul, South Korea, 81—87; MS, Wayne State U., 1993, PhD, 1996. Cert.

quality engr., reliability engr. Bus. planner Lucky Goldstar Info. and Telecomm.; sr. contact engr. GM, Warren, Mich., 1996—2002. Contbr. Mem.: Am. Soc. Quality. Home: #108 1930 Golfview Dr Troy MI 48084 Personal E-mail: sangdonlee@yahoo.com.

LEE, SCOTT SHIH SHIA, obstetrician and gynecologist; b. Tokyo, June 26, 1956; m. Cheryl Ann Lee, Sept. 11, 1993; 1 child, Matthew. BA, U. Calif., San Diego, 1978; MD, U. Calif., Irvine, 1983. Diplomate Am. Bd. Family Physicians, Am. Bd. Ob-Gyn. Intern and resident San Bernardino County Med. Ctr., 1983-86; resident ob-gyn. Loma Linda U. Med. Ctr., 1986-89; pvt. practice Women's Health Ctr., Mission Viejo, Calif., 1989-90; staff physician FHP Inc., Fountain Valley, 1990-95, County of Riverside, 1995-96; pvt. practice Doctors of Women, Orange, 1996, Bristol Park Med., Mission Viejo, 1996—. Vol. Ams. for Free Choice in Medicine, Newport Beach, Calif., 1995; supporter Citizens Against Govt. Waste, 1993. Fellow ACOG. Republican. Avocations: sailing, music, running. Office: Bristol Park Medical 23512 Madero Ste 110 Mission Viejo CA 92691-2743

LEE, SEONG-JAE, researcher; b. Kwangyang, Chunnam, South Korea, Apr. 30, 1963; s. Yong-Dae Lee and Il-Lim Suh; m. Sung-Hye Yoon; children: Sharon, Amy. BS, Yonsei U., Seoul, 1986, MS, 1988; PhD, Iowa State U., 1998. Rsch. asst. Iowa State U., Ames, 1993—98, rsch. assoc., 1998—2002. Contbr. Mem.: Sigma Xi (2000 2000—01). Home: Apt 4 240 Raphael Ames IA 50014 Office: Iowa State U Ames Lab 258H Metals Devel Bldg Ames IA 50011 Personal E-mail: sjlee430@yahoo.com. Business E-Mail: sjlee@ameslab.gov.

LEE, SEUNG JAI, lawyer, legal administrator; b. Seoul, Korea, Nov. 19, 1947; came to U.S. 1976; s. Joong Gi and Eun Jung (Chung) L.; m. In Ai Kim Lee, July 4, 1975; children: Nancy, Janice. LLB, Seoul Nat. U., 1971, postgrad., 1973-75; JD, Temple U., 1984. Bar: Pa. 1984, U.S. Dist. Ct. (ea. dist.) Pa. 1985. Atty. Malcolm P. Rosenberg & Assocs., Phila., 1985; law clk. Ct. Common Pleas of Berks County, Reading, Pa., 1985-90; adminstrv. law clk. Commonwealth Ct. of Pa., Harrisburg, 1990—. Recipient Am. Jurisprudence award Lawyers Coop Pub. Co., 1984. Mem. Pa. Bar Assn. (judicial adminstrv. com. 1991—, minority bar assn. com. 1991—, civil rights and responsibilities com. 1993—). Home: 425 Nottingham Ave Lancaster PA 17601-3017 Office: Commonwealth Ct of Pa 608 S Office Building Harrisburg PA 17120-0023 E-mail: slee0425@aol.com.

LEE, SHEPARD, automobile dealership owner; b. Lewiston, Maine, Nov. 13, 1926; s. Joseph and Ethel (Richelson) Lifshitz; m. Nancy Margolis (div.); children: Jonathan, Catherine, Adam, Beth; m. Candice Thornton Lee, Feb. 24, 1995. AB magna cum laude, Bowdoin Coll., 1947. Owner Lee Auto Malls, Cape Elizabeth, Maine, 1947—. Spkr. Nat. Can. Auto Dealers Assn.; cons. French Bank, Credit Gen. Indsl.; lectr. in China on free enterprise Brandeis U.; bd. dirs. Fin. Authority of Maine. Mem. New Eng. adv. coun. Fed. Res. Bank, Boston; bd. dirs. Cumberland Club, Portland, Maine, George J. Mitchell Scholarship Rsch. Inst.; mem. adv. bd. U. Maine Inst. Family Owned Bus.; mem. bd. givs. U. Maine Law Sch., Edmund S. Muskie Sch. Pub. Affairs, adv. bd. Sch. Bus. Recipient Dealer of Distinction award AIADA Sports Illustrated, 1985; named one of eight Outstanding Dealers in Country Time Mag., 1982. Mem. ACLU (bd. dirs., Roger Baldwin award), Nat. Auto Dealers Assn. (mem. project 2000 Commn.), Phi Beta Kappa. Democrat. Avocations. Office: Lee Auto Malls 200 MAin St Westbrook ME 04092 E-mail: slee@leeauto.com.

LEE, SHERMAN EMERY, art historian, curator; b. Seattle, Apr. 19, 1918; s. Emery H. and Adelia (Baker) L.; m. Ruth A. Ward, Sept. 3, 1938; children: Katharine C. (Mrs. Bryan Reid), Margaret A. (Mrs. Stephen Bachenheimer), Elizabeth K. (Mrs. William Chiego), Thomas W. BA, MA, Am. U.; PhD, Western Res. U. Curator, Far Eastern art Detroit Inst. Art, 1941-46; with dept. arts and monuments, div. civil info. and edn. sect. Gen. Hdqrs. SCAP, Tokyo, 1946-48; asst. dir., then asso. dir. Seattle Mus. Art, 1948-52; curator Oriental art Cleve. Mus. Art, 1952-83, dir., 1958-83; prof. art Western Res. U., 1983-97. Adj. prof. U. N.C., Chapel Hill, 1984-97. Author: Chinese Landscape Painting, rev. edit., 1962, (with Wen Fong) Streams and Mountains Without End, 1955, Japanese Decorative Style, 1961, History of Far Eastern Art, 5th edit., 1994, (with W.K. Ho) Chinese Art under the Mongols, 1968, Reflections of Reality in Japanese Art, 1983, Past, Present, East and West, 1983; editor: On Understanding Art Museums, 1977. Trustee Amon Carter Mus. Western Art. Served from ensign to lt. (j.g.) USNR, 1944-46. Decorated Legion of Honor; Order North Star; Order of Sacred Treasure 3d class. Mem. Am. Acad. Arts and Scis., Asia Soc. (hon. trustee), Century Assn (N.Y.C.). Home: 5 Carolina Mdws Apt 103 Chapel Hill NC 27517-8522

LEE, SHEW KUHN, retired optometrist; b. Balt., Apr. 24, 1923; s. Mong Har and Gum Tuey (Wong) L.; m. Florence Gin Toy, Oct. 29, 1949; children: Wayson Perry, Davin Jeffrey. OD, Ill. Coll. Optometry, 1949; postgrad., Cath. U. Am., 1957, Md. U., 1959. Pvt. practice optometry, Washington, 1949-88; ret., 1988. Lectr. D.C. Traffic Safety Sch.; v.p. D.C. Bd. Optometry, 1959-65; mem. D.C. Bd. Examiners in Optometry, 1973-84, sec., 1974; mem. Eye Bank Coun.; vision rsch. cons. HEW, 1973. Rsch. publs. in field. Bd. dirs. Eye Bank and Rsch. Found., Washington Hosp. Ctr. With U.S. Army, 1943—45, 2d lt. USAR, 1949—52. Decorated Purple Heart, Bronze Star medal with oak leaf cluster; recipient France's Thank You America cert. for WWII Vets, 2001, Italy's Anzio Cert. of Honor for WWII Vets, 2001, Meritorious Pub. Svc. award, Govt. of DC, 1965. Mem.: Flying Optometrist Assn. Am. (bd. dirs. 1974—), Chinese Consol. Benevolent Assn. (founder), Lees Assn. (trustee), D.C. Optometric Soc. (sec. 1956—57), Am. Legion (life; post comdr. D.C. 1960, citation of merit 1954), Am. Optometric Assn. (life; pres. joggers 1968—, Disting. Svc. award 1974), Lions (charter pres. Chi-Am. 1960, zone chmn. 1961, dep. dist. gov. 1963, hon. mem. Capitol Hill, Washington Host, Extension award 1960, 1975, Key award 1966, Presdl. Banner award 1975), Beta Sigma Kappa. Home: 2939 McKinley St NW Washington DC 20015-1217

LEE, SHUISHIH SAGE, pathologist; b. Soo-chow, Kiang su, China, Jan. 5, 1948; came to U.S., 1972, naturalized, 1979; m. Chung Seng Lee; children: Yvonne Claire, Michael Chung. MD, Nat. Taiwan U., 1972; PhD, U. Rochester, 1976. Resident in pathology Strong Meml. Hosp., Rochester, N.Y., 1976-78, Northwestern Meml. Hosp., Chgo., 1978-79; dir. cytology and electron microscopy Parkview Meml. Hosp., Ft. Wayne, Ind., 1979—. Clin. prof. Ind. U. Med. Sch. Contbr. articles to profl. jours. Fellow: Am. Soc. Clin. Pathologists, Coll. Am. Pathologists; mem.: AMA, Internat. Assn. Chinese Pathologists (pres. 1999—2001, 1999—2001), Ft. Wayne Acad. Physicians and Surgeons (pres. 1990), Ft. Wayne Med. Soc. (pres. 2001—02), Electron Microscopy Soc. Am., Internat. Acad. Cytology, Internat. Acad. Pathology, Am. Soc. Cytology, Am. Assn. Pathologists, N.Y. Acad. Scis., Ind. Assn. Pathologists, N.E. Ind. Pathologists Assn. (sec. 1984), Ind. Med. Assn. Home: 5728 The Prophets Pass Fort Wayne IN 46845-9659 Office: Parkview Meml Hosp 2200 Randallia Dr Fort Wayne IN 46805-4699

LEE, SHUNG-MAN, nephrologist; b. Canton, Peoples Republic of China, Feb. 22, 1949; arrived in U.S., 1968; s. Ning-Woo and Shui-Fong Lee; m. Ellen Poon, Aug. 4, 1976; 1 child Andrew. BS, U. Toronto, 1972, MD, 1976. Diplomate Am. Bd. Nephrology, Am. Bd. Internal Medicine, Am. Bd. Med. Examiners. Intern Sunnybrook Med. Ctr. U. Toronto, 1976-77, resident, 1977-78, Jewish Gen. Hosp. McGill U., Montreal, 1978-79; clin. fellow in nephrology Billings Hosp. U. Chgo., 1979-81, rsch. fellow, 1981-82; pres., med. dir. Biotronics Kidney Ctr., Beaumont, Tex., 1990—. Orange, 1999—. Cons. nephrologist, mem. med. staff St. Elizabeth Hosp., Beaumont, Bapt. Hosp. S.E. Tex., Beaumont, Beaumont Med. Surg. Hosp., 1982—90; med. dir. Cmty. Dialysis Svcs., Beaumont, 1986—90; cons. nephrologist, mem. courtesy staff Dr.'s Hosp., Groves, Tex., Bapt. Hosp., Orange, Tex., Park Place Hosp., Port Arthur, Tex.; clin. asst. prof. U. Tex. Med. Br. at Galveston, 1991—; founder, owner Biotronics Kidney Ctr. Beaumont, Inc.; founder Lake Charles Dialysis Ctr., Lake Charles, La. Contbr. Organizer, founding mem. Adult Indigent Clinic for S.E. Tex., Beaumont, 1992—. Fellow, Chgo. Heart Assn., 1991; scholar, Ont. Cancer Soc., 1974, Ann Shepard Meml. scholar in biology, 1970. Fellow: ACP; mem.: AMA, New Century Health Care Internat. (pres.), Tex. Med. Assn., Am. Soc. Internal Medicine, So. Med. Assn., Jefferson County Med. Soc., Am. Soc. Nephrology, Internat. Soc. Peritoneal Dialysis, Internat. Soc. Nephrology. Office: Biotronics Kidney Ctr 2755 Liberty Ave Beaumont TX 77702-1917 also: 2965 Harrison St Ste 116 Beaumont TX 77702-1148

LEE, SILAS, III, sociologist, public opinion research consultant; b. New Orleans, July 24, 1954; s. Silas Hilton Jr. and Henrietta (Johnson) L. BA, Loyola U., 1976; MS, U. New Orleans, 1979, PhD in Urban Studies, 1999. Cert. expert in social and econ. status of blacks, La. Prof. Sociology Xavier U., New Orleans, 1978—; pres. Silas Lee and Assocs., Pub. Opinion Research Co., 1983—. Instr. sociology Xavier U., New Orleans. Methodist. Avocation: photography. Office: Silas Lee and Assocs 1750 Saint Charles Ave New Orleans LA 70130-5252

LEE, SIN HANG, pathologist, educator; b. Hong Kong, Nov. 17, 1932; came to U.S., 1963, naturalized, 1976; s. Yat Sun and Siu Tsing (Wong) L.; m. Kee Hung Hau, Dec. 31, 1958; children: Emil, Karen. MD, Wuhan Med. Coll., China, 1956. Diplomate Am. Bd. Pathology. Intern South Balt. Gen. Hosp., 1963-64; resident N.Y. Hosp., 1964-66; bacteriologist Sichuan Med. Coll., Chengdu, China, 1956-61; demonstrator in pathology U. Hong Kong, 1961-63; instr. pathology Cornell-N.Y. Hosp., 1966-67; fellow in pathology Meml. Hosp. for Cancer, N.Y.C., 1967-68; asst. prof. McGill U., Montreal, 1968-71; assoc. prof. Yale U., New Haven, 1971-73, assoc. clin. prof., 1973—. Guest prof. Wuhan Med. Coll. (China), 1984— ; attending pathologist Hosp. St. Raphael, New Haven, Conn., 1973— . Contbr. articles in field to profl. jours.; patentee in field. Mem. AAAS, Royal Coll. Physicians and Surgeons of Can., Internat. Acad. Pathology, Am. Assn. Pathologists, Pathol. Soc. Great Britain and Ireland, N.Y. Acad. Scis. Office: 1450 Chapel St New Haven CT 06511-4405

LEE, STEPHEN W. lawyer; b. New Castle, Ind., Oct. 25, 1949; s. Delmer W. Lee and Loma F. (Thurston) McCall; m. Pamela A. Summers, Aug. 2, 1969; children: Erin E., Stephanie M. BS, Ball State U., 1971; JD summa cum laude, Ind. U., 1977. Bar: Ind. 1977, U.S. Dist. Ct. (so. dist.) Ind. 1977, U.S. Ct. Appeals (7th cir.) 1977, U.S. Supreme Ct. 1982. Officer, lt.(j.g.) USNR, Phila., 1971-74; law clk. U.S. Dist. Ct. (no. dist.) Ind., Ft. Wayne, 1977-78; assoc. Barnes, Hickam, Pantzer & Boyd, Indpls., 1978-82, Barnes & Thornburg, Indpls., 1982-83, ptnr., 1984—. Dir. The Julian Ctr., Indpls., 1999—; mem. Ind. U. Sch. of Law Bd. of Visitors, 1999—. Editor-in-chief: Indiana Law Jour., 1976-77. Dir. Ind. Repertory Theatre, Indpls., 1986-91; exec. coun. Ind. U. Alumni Assn., Bloomington, 1989; dir. Ind. U. Sch. of Law Alumni Assn., Bloomington, 1984-90, pres., 1991-92; mem. Ball State U. Coll. Bus. Alumni Bd., 1991-2000, Ball State U. Entrepreneurship Adv. Bd., 1994—. Mem. Ind. State Bar Assn., Indpls. Bar Assn. (chmn. bus. sect. 1985), Highland Golf & Country Club. Republican. Avocation: golf. Office: Barnes & Thornburg 11 S Meridian St Ste 1313 Indianapolis IN 46204-3535 E-mail: slee@btlaw.com.

LEE, STEVEN PEYTON, philosophy educator; b. Schenectady, N.Y., May 19, 1948; s. Robert Edward and Marguerite VanVliet (Wood) L.; m. Janice Levin, June 12, 1970 (dec. Jan. 1977); m. Cherry Myers Rahn, Dec. 15, 1981; children: Amanda McLaughlin (stepchild), Charlotte Rahn-Lee, Lilah Rahn-Lee. BA, U. Del., 1970, MA, 1973; PhD, York U., 1978. Asst. prof. philosophy Bowling Green State U., 1978-80, Hobart and William Smith Coll.s, Geneva, 1981-85, assoc. prof., 1985-91, prof., 1991—. Author: Morality, Prudence, and Nuclear Weapons, 1993; co-author: The Nuclear Predicament: Nuclear Weapons in the Cold War and Beyong, 2d edit., 1992; editor: (with Avner Cohen) Nuclear Weapons and the Future of Humanity, 1986; contbr. articles to profl. jours. Mem. ethics com. Huntington Nursing Home, Waterloo, N.Y., 1992—. Am. Coun. Learned Socs. grantee, 1985, MacArthur Found. grantee, 1988-89; NEH fellow, 1980-81, 88, Harvard fellow, 1994-95, Rockefeller fellow, 1986-87. Mem. AAUP, Internat. Assn. for Philosophy Law and Social Philosophy, Am. Philos. Assn., Concerned Philosophers for Peace, Creighton Club. Democrat. Office: Hobart and Wm Smith Colls Dept Philosophy Geneva NY 14456

LEE, SUN MYUNG, physician; b. Seoul, Korea, July 9, 1940; d. Jong Suk and Soo Nam Lee; m. Hi Young; children: Sandra Shon, Grace, David. BS, Yonsei U., Seoul, 1961, MD, 1965; cert. in lay ministry, Whitworth Coll., 2001. Diplomate Am. Acad. Family Practice; ordained elder Korean Presbyn. Ch., 1999. Intern Riverside Methodist Hosp., Columbus, Oh., 1967-68; resident Veteran's Adminstrn. Hosp., Dayton, 1968-69; intern Riverside Meth. Hosp., Columbus, Ohio, 1966-67; resident Ohio State VA Hosp., Dayton, 1967-70; pvt. practice family medicine Drs. Lee & Lee PS, Spokane, Wash., 1974—. Mem. med. staff Ea. State Hosp., Medical Lake, Wash., 1972-74; pres. Drs. Lee & Lee P.S., 1974—. Author: Best Poetry of 1997, 1997; columnist Rainier Forum, Korea Post, 1995-96. Pres. Korean Lang. Sch., Spokane, 1974; Guwonsa, Korean Presbyn. Ch. Spokane, 1989-99; trustee Korean Assn. Inland Empire, Spokane, 1995; elder Korean Presbyn. Ch., Spokane, 1999, chair music ministry team, 2001. Recipient Editors Choice award Nat. Libr. Poetry, 1996. Fellow Am. Acad. Family Physicians. Avocations: choral music, poetry, gardening. Office: Drs Lee and Lee PS 17 E Empire Ave Spokane WA 99207-1707 E-mail: drsunleemd@yahoo.com.

LEE, SUNG HO, psychiatrist; b. Seoul, June 28, 1934; s. Suk K. Lee and Chung Won Kim; m. Myung H. Lee, Nov. 17, 1959; children: Benjamin, May. Student, Yonsei U., 1953-55, MD, 1959; MSc, Ohio State U., 1967; postgrad. med. cert., UCLA, 1968. Diplomate Am. Bd. Psychiatry and Neurology, Korean Bd. of Psychiatry and Neurology. Psychiat. resident Brentwood Psychiat. Hosp., VAMC, L.A., 1967-68, Ohio State U. Hosp., Columbus, 1965-67; neurology resident Cin. Gen. Hosp., 1964-65; psychiat. resident Yonsei U. Hosp., Seoul, 1960-62, staff psychiatrist, 1968-69; chief psychiatrist Ewha U. Hosp., 1969-70; clin. dir. unit B Broughton State Hosp., Morganton, N.C., 1970-71; chief psychiatrist VA Med. Ctr., Dayton, Ohio, 1971-79; staff psychiatrist Eastway Cmty. Mental Health Ctr., 1975-95; med. dir. South Cmty. Inc., Centerville, Ohio, 1990-95; pvt. practice Dayton, 1975-95; chief psychiatrist Kyung Hee Pundang CHA Gen. Hosp., Seoul, 1995-96; staff psychiatrist Accord Behavioral Healthcare, Dayton, 1996—; staff psychiatrist, dep. med. dir. Eastway Corp., 1996—. Cons. psychiatrist South Cmty Inc., Centerville, 1980-90, Dayton Mental Health Ctr., 1975-95, Eastway Cmty. Mental Health Ctr., 1975-79; assoc. clin. prof. Wright State U., Dayton, 1979—, asst. clin. prof., 1975-79; prof. Kyung Hee U., 1975-76; asst. clin. prof. Ohio State U., Columbus, 1971-75; asst. prof. Ewha U. Coll. of Medicine, 1969-70; instr. Yonsei U. Coll. of Medicine, 1968-69, 1961-64. Home: 7706 Normandy Ln Dayton OH 45459-4118 Office: Eastway Behavioral Health 600 Wayne Ave Dayton OH 45410-1122

LEE, SUNGHO H. education educator, consultant, dean; b. Kyonggi-do, Rep. of Korea, Nov. 3, 1946; s. Kiwon and Imae (Song) L.; m. Hwadong Kim, Feb. 17, 1973; children: Haichung, Haiseok. BA, Yonsei U., Seoul, Rep. of Korea, 1970, MA, 1975; student, Ruhr U., Bochum, Germany, 1976-77; EdD, George Washington U., 1980. Instr. Yonsei U., 1975-76, asst. prof., 1981-85, assoc. prof., 1986-90, prof., 1991—, dean Coll. Edn., 1998-2000, dean Grad. Sch., 2000—02, v.p., 2002—. Asst. min. Ministry of Edn., Rep. of Korea, 1993; dir. univ. evaluation Korean Coun. for Univ. Edn., Korea, 1983-90; mem. Presdl. Commn. 21st Century, 1989-93. Author: Shaking Parents and Straying Children, 1997 (award Chosun Daily Newspaper Co. 1997); co-author: Scientific Development and Higher Education, 1989 (award NSF 1986), Academic Profession in the World, 1995, Teaching Methods in Schools, 1999; contbr. chpts. to books. Cons. New Cmty. Devel. Movement Assn., Korea, 1996-99; mem. Nat. Commn. UNESCO, Korea, 1993-95; bd. trustees Nat. Inst. Curriculum Devel., 1998-99; mem. nat. adv. com. for edn. policy, Korea, 1996-99; mem. standing com. Presdl. Com. for Rebuilding Korea, 1998-2000; mem. adv. com. Korean Air Force, 2001—; chmn. Nat. Edn. Policy Adv. Com. Sgt. US I Corps., 1970-73. Decorated U.S. Army Commendation medal, Order of Svc. Merit Pres. of Korea; recipient award, Nat. Carnegie Found., 1992; grantee, Nat. Assn. Trade and Tech. Schs., 1980, Ford Found., 2001. Mem. Korean Soc. for Study Edn. (bd. trustees 1981-83, 86-90, 98-2000), Korean Higher Edn. Assn. (bd. trustees 1994—). Evangelical. Avocation: golf. Office: Yonsei U Dept Edn Shinchon-dong 134 Sodaemoon-ku Seoul 120-749 Republic of Korea E-mail: leesh@yonsei.ac.kr.

LEE, SUSAN ANN, social worker, therapist; b. Beaver Falls, Pa., Apr. 16, 1952; d. Robert Lester Lee and Dolores Ilene (Brashears) Zajac. BA in behavioral sci., Hardin Simmons U., 1979; MSW, Rutgers U., 1994. Social worker N.Y. Cath. Guardian Soc., N.Y.C., 1986-89, Mt. Carmel Guild MHC, Jersey City, 1994-96. In retail bus., 1996—. With USAF, 1972-76. Mem. Nat. Assn. Social Workers. Avocations: reading, camping, bowling, water skiing.

LEE, TAY BONG, surgeon, otolaryngologist; b. Sangju, Korea, 1939; MD, Seoul Nat. U., 1962. Diplomate Am. Bd. Surgery, Am. Bd. Otolaryngology. Intern Springfield Hosp. Med. Ctr., 1965-66, resident in surgery, 1966-70; resident N.Y. Meml. Hosp.-Allied Diseases, N.Y.C., 1970-71; resident in otolaryngology Roosevelt Hosp., N.Y.C., 1971-74; sr. attending in otorhinolaryngology St. Lukes-Roosevelt Hosp., 1980—; asst. clin. prof. otorhinolaryngology Columbia Phys. and Surg. Fellow ACS; mem. AMA, Am. Acad. Otolaryngology and Head and Neck Surgery. Office: 30 Central Park S New York NY 10019-1628

LEE, TERRY, real estate broker, martial artist; b. Blufton, Ind., Jan. 6, 1979; s. Lee Will and Jo Irwin Pamela. Cert. real estate broker, R.E.C.P., Indpls., Goldcoast Sch. Real Estate, Palm Beach, Fla. Lic. real estate broker Fla., Ind. Profl. fighter U.S. Tae Kwon Do Union, 1993—; broker, v.p. Red Cow Real Estate Co., Fla., 1998—2000, Ind., 2000—. Author: The Truth and Reason of Fighting, 1998; author, inventor: math. Theory of Broken Chain, 2001. Support runner, guardian Olympic Torch Relay, Ft. Wayne, Ind., 2002; vol. martial arts instr. Peacemaker II Orgn., Armory, 2000—01. Named 3-time Gold medalist, 1 time Silver, 1 time Bronze, Tae Kwon Do, 3-time Fla. State Champion, 2-time champion, Choi's Open Tae Kwon Do Championship, Miami, Fla. Mem.: KuKKiwon/WTF, U.S. Tae Kwon Do Union, Realtor Assn. Avocations: music, athletics, travel. Office: Red Cow Real Estate Co 126 S High St Hartford City IN 47348 Fax: 765-348-3771. E-mail: redcow@skyenet.net.

LEE, THEODORE BO, real estate developer; b. Stockton, Calif., Dec. 28, 1932; s. Wong Bo and Daisy (Lum) L.; m. Doris Shoong, June 14, 1969; children: Gregory T.H., Ernest T.H. BA, Harvard Coll., 1954; JD, U. Calif., Berkeley, 1959, MBA, 1966. Bar: Hawaii 1962, Calif. 1960. Jr. lectr. U. Singapore, 1960-61; legal assoc. Fong, Miho, etal, Honolulu, 1961-62; assoc. dir. East West Ctr., 1962-64; real estate atty. Urban Cons., San Francisco, 1964-82; chmn. Urban Group, 1971—. Dir. Ind. Nev. Casino Operators, Las Vegas, Nihonmachi Cmty. Devel. Corp., San Francisco. Author: Laws of the Commonwealth (Singapore), 1961. Pres. St. Pauls Parents Assn., Concord, N.H., 1980-88; trustee, vice chair Berkeley Found., 1984-97. Recipient internat. legal fellowship U. Calif., Berkeley, 1959, Wheeler Oak award Berkeley Found., 1985. Mem. Harvard Alumni Assn. (trustee, dir. 1982-85, overseeer 1994-2000, alumni award), Boalt Hall Alumni Assn. (pres.). Avocations: foreign travel. Office: Urban Land Nev 3271 S Highland Dr Ste 704 Las Vegas NV 89109-1051

LEE, THOMAS ALEXANDER, accountant, educator; b. Edinburgh, Scotland, May 18, 1941; s. Thomas Henderson and Dorothy Jane (Norman) L.; m. Ann Margaret Brown, Sept. 14, 1963; children: Sarah Ann, Richard Thomas. Chartered acct., Inst. Chartered Accts.Scotland, Edinburgh, 1964; tax acct., Inst. Tax, Glasgow, Scotland, 1965; MS, U. Strathclyde, Glasgow, Scotland, 1969, DLitt, 1984. Audit asst., Edinburgh, 1959-64, Glasgow, 1964-66; lectr. U. Strathclyde, 1966-69, U. Edinburgh, 1969-73, prof. Eng., 1976-90, U. Liverpool, Eng., 1973-76; dir. rsch. Inst. Chartered Accts. Scotland, 1983-84; prof. U. Ala., 1990—2001, dir. PhD program, 1991—2001, emeritus prof., 2001—. Vis. prof. U. Md., 1986, U. Utah, 1987-88, U. Edinburgh, 1991-94, Deakin U., 1994—; hon. prof. U. Dundee, Scotland, 1995—. Editor: Internat. Jour. Auditing; mem. editl. bd. various jours., 1971—. Acad. Acctg. Historians, pres., 1999, past pres., 2000. Recipient Burnum award U. Ala., 1997. Mem. Fellow Royal Soc. Arts; mem. Inst. Chartered Accts. Scotland (coun. 1989-90), Inst. Taxation. Presbyterian. Avocations: church, road running, cricket history. Home: IF2 48 Marchmont Rd Edinburgh EH9 1HX Scotland Office: Dept Accountancy U Dundee Nethergate Dundee DD1 4HN Scotland

LEE, THOMAS TEHWEN, neurosurgeon; b. Tainan, Taiwan, Dec. 27, 1967; s. Chang Kuei and Shiu-Hoa Shu L.; m. Margaret Yu, Aug. 31, 1993. BA, U. Calif., Berkeley, 1989; MD, UCLA, 1993. Diplomate Am. Bd. Neurol. Surgery, Nat. Bd. Med. Examiners. Resident neurosurgeon U. Miami - Jackson Meml. Med. Ctr., 1993-99; attending neurosurgeon Westchester Medical Ctr., N.Y., 1999—. Med. edn. liaison Congress of Neurol. Surgeons, Park Ridge, Ill.; com. mem. edn., sci. program com. of Congress of Neurol. Surgeons, Park Ridge; mem. editl. rev. bd. The Spine, 1999—. Contbr. articles to profl. jours., chpt. to books in field. Mem. med. response team Championship Auto Racing Team, 1995-99. Mem. AMA, N.Am. Spine Soc., Am. Assn. Neurol. Surgeons, Golden Key, Phi Beta Kappa. Avocations: movie poster collection, swimming, tennis, target shooting. E-mail: ThomasTLeemd@aol.com.

LEE, TIMOTHY EARL, international agency executive, paralegal; b. Seattle, May 23, 1947; s. Charles Augusta and Esther Letty (Young) L.; m. Marcia Lea Wulff, July 6, 1968 (div. May 1976); children: Vincent Dean, Dante' Claude; 1 stepson, Kevin Paul McCorkle; m. Jayne Elizabeth Ashley, Apr. 28, 1984 (div. Apr. 1995). Cert., Ivy Tech., 1981, Am. Inst. Paralegal Studies, 1988. Mgr. Gen. Fin. Corp., Evanston, Ill., 1970-74, FBT Capital Corp., South Bend, Ind., 1974-76; owner Lee's Internat. Investigative Rsch. Agy., Ft. Wayne, 1978—. Mem. Heritage Foun., Citizens Against Govt. Waste; spl. adv. Allen Superior Ct. With U.S. Army, 1966-68, Vietnam. Recipient Cert. of Appreciation, DAV, 1968. Mem. VFW, Ind. Assn. Pvt. Detectives (v.p. N.E. region Ind. 1984—), Ind. Sheriff's Assn., Ft. Wayne Allen County Security Assn., Coun. for Inter-Am. Security, Nat. Security Ctr., Nat. Def. Inst., 27th Field Artillery Assn. (v.p., founding father), Am. Legion, Vietnam Vets, Internat. Platform Assn., Concord Coalition. Home: 8516 River Canyon Dr Fort Wayne IN 46835-1015 E-mail: Liira@gte.net.

LEE, TOM STEWART, judge; b. 1941; m. Norma Ruth Robbins; children: Elizabeth Robbins, Tom Stewart Jr. BA, Miss. Coll., 1963; JD cum laude, U. Miss., 1965. Ptnr. Lee & Lee, Forest, Miss., 1965-84; pros. atty. Scott County, 1968-71; judge Scott County Youth Ct., Forest, 1979-82, U.S. Dist. Ct. (so. dist.) Miss., Jackson, 1984-96, chief judge, 1996—. Asst. editor: Miss. Law Jour. Pres. Forest Pub. Sch. Bd., Scott County Heart Assn.; bd. trustees Miss. Coll. Named one of Outstanding Young Men Am. Mem. Miss. Bar Assn., Scott County Bar Assn., Hinds County Bar Assn., Fed. Bar Assn., Fed. Judge's Assn., 5th Cir. Jud. Coun., CACM com. Jud. Conf., Disting. Svc. award), Ole Miss. Alumni Assn. (pres.), Miss. Coll. Alumni Assn. (bd. dirs.) Am. Legion. Office: US Dist Ct 245 E Capitol St Ste 110 Jackson MS 39201-2414 E-mail: JoyceWorrell@mssd.uscourts.gov-SCA-I.

LEE, TONG HUN, economics educator; b. Seoul, Nov. 20, 1931; came to U.S., 1955, naturalized, 1968; s. Chong Su and Yun (Lee) L.; m. Yul Jah Ahn, June 11, 1960; children: Bruce Keebeck, James Keewon. BS, Yonsei U., 1955; PhD, U. Wis., 1961. Asst. prof. econs. U. Tenn., Knoxville, 1962-64, assoc. prof., 1964-67; prof. econs. U. Wis., Milw., 1967-96, chmn. dept. econs., 1978-82; disting. prof. econs. Ajou U., Suwon, Korea, 1997—. Author: Interregional Intersectoral Flow Analysis, 1973; contbr. articles to profl. jours. NSF grantee, 1965-67, 73-75 Mem. Am. Econ. Assn., Am. Fin. Assn., Am. Statis. Assn., Econometric Soc. Home: 55 W Delaware Pl Apt 1021 Chicago IL 60610-6073 Office: Ajou U Sch Bus Adminstrn 5 Wonchon-Dong Paldal-Gu Suwon 442-749 Republic of Korea *Success comes from determination, persistence and hard work, but the ultimate measure of success is derived from the inner life of a person.*

LEE, TSOUNG-CHAO, education educator; b. Taipei, Taiwan, Oct. 25, 1935; came to U.S., 1963; s. Chiou-Chin and Yu-Ing (Chen) L.; m. Chung-lien Shih, Jan. 25, 1964; children: Tony Jay, Jean May. BS, Nat. Taiwan U., 1958; MS, U. Ill., 1965, PhD, 1967. Teaching asst. Nat. Taiwan U., 1960-63; rsch. asst. U. Ill., Urbana-Champaign, 1963-65, Wright fellow, 1965-67; vis. scholar U. Wis., Madison, 1966; asst. prof. U. Conn., Storrs, 1967-71, assoc. prof., 1971-75, prof., 1975—. Rsch. scientist U. Ga., Athens, 1977-78; vis. prof. Nat. Taiwan U., 1989; vis. rsch. full prof. Nat. Sci. Coun., Taipei, 1989. Author: Estimating the Parameters of the Markov Probability Model from Aggregate Time Series Data, 1970, 2d edit., 1977, Theory and Practice of Econometrics, 1980, 2d edit., 1985, Introduction to the Theory and Practice of Econometrics, 1982, 2d edit., 1988; reviewer articles for profl. jours. 2nd lt. Army, 1958-60, Taiwan. Recipient scholarship Cooperative Bank of Taiwan, Taipei, 1958, Book award Nat. Taiwan U., 1958, Cert. of Statistician Nat. Civil Svc. Gen. Exam, 1960, Travel fellowship Agr. Devel. Coun., N.Y., 1963-67, Cert. Gamma Sigma Delta, Storrs, 1972, sr. award Gamma Sigma Delta, 1996,

Excellence in Teaching award Alumni Assn. Coll. Agr. and Natural Resources U. Conn., 1997, Outstanding Educators of Am. Award cert. (A divsn. of Fuller & Dees), 1975. Mem. Am. Agr. Econ. Assn., Econometric Soc., Northeastern Agr. and Resource Econs. Assn., Am. Stat. Assn. (editorial collaborator 1969-76). Avocations: photography, music, computer programming. Home: 127 Beech Mountain Rd Mansfield Center CT 06250 Office: U Conn U 21 1376 Storrs Rd Storrs Mansfield CT 06269-4021 E-mail: tsoung@uconnvm.uconn.edu.

LEE, VERNON ROY, minister; b. Jackson, Miss., Feb. 1, 1952; s. Samuel Rayford and Evie Mae (Abel) L.; m. Rhonda Sue Parker, Nov. 6, 1970; 1 child, Shannon Grant. Pastor Mt. Moriah Bapt. Ch., Junction City, Ark., 1971-72, Pleasant Grove Bapt. Ch., El Dorado, 1972-74, Pilgrims Rest Bapt. Ch., Spearsville, La., 1974-76, Bethany Bapt. Ch., Bastrop, 1976-78, 1st Bapt. Ch., Taylor, Ark., 1978-83, Farmington Bapt. Ch., Corinth, Miss., 1983-86, Wyatt Bapt. Ch., El Dorado, 1986—. Trustee Southeastern Bapt. Coll., Laurel, Miss., 1983-86, Ctrl. Bapt. Coll., Conway, Ark., 1992-96, 99—, asst. chmn. bd. trustees, 1993-95, chmn., 1995-96; vol. Boy's Clubs, El Dorado, 1986-91, YMCA, Corinth, 1983-86. Mem. Bapt. Missionary Assn. Am. (v.p. 1986-88, pres. 1990-92, clk. missionary com. 1989-91, asst. ch. adv. com. 1992-95, v.p. pastor's & laymen's conf. 1996-98, pres. pastor's & laymen;s conf. 1998-2000, chmn. adv. com. 2000—), Miss. Bapt. Assn. (pres. 1984-86). Avocations: golf, fishing, basketball, softball. Home: 625 Royal Oak El Dorado AR 71730 Office: Wyatt Bapt Ch 4621 W Hillsboro El Dorado AR 71730-6768

LEE, VIRGINIA DIANE, lay worker; b. Hackensack, N.J., Sept. 3, 1939; d. Harold Ehler and Marion Estelle (Pierrez) True; m. Jerald Dana Lee, June 7, 1962; children: Diana, Tara, James. BS, Albright Coll., 1961; MS, Ohio U., 1963. Deacon Presbyn. Ch. of Kennett Square, Pa., 1981-84, elder, 1988-91, asst. clk. of session, 1989-91, co-chmn. personnel com., 1989-90, chmn. personnel com., 1990-91. V.p. Presbyn. Women's Assn., Kennett Square, 1983-85; dressmaker, Mendenhall, Pa., 1984-94. Mem. Winterthur (Del.) Guild, 1990-91; alumna rep. for student recruitment Albright Coll., Reading, Pa., 1990-91; membership com. Westminster Presbyn. Ch., Wilmington, Del., 1991-92, food svc. chmn., 1993, Communion com., 1994, 95, 96, co-chmn. Circle, 1994, stewardship com., 1995, sec. Women of Westminster, 1997, 98, 99; examiner New Castle Presbytery, 1998; deacon Westminster Presbyn. Ch., 1999-2001, Cluster convener Westminster Presbyn. Ch., 1999, 2000, 01. Mem. AAUW (mem. scholarship com. Wilmington, Del. chpt. 1980, 81), Phi Upsilon Omicron. Republican. Home: PO Box 4 Mendenhall PA 19357-0004 E-mail: jlee@kennett.net.

LEE, VIRGINIA FERN, community volunteer; b. Mar. 14, 1921; BA, Coll. of St. Scholastica, 1943; postgrad., Stanford U., 1970. Dir. med. info. Hosp. Dept. Universitario for Rockefeller Found., Cali, Colombia, 1956-58, VA Med. Ctr., Palo Alto, Calif., 1962-82; chief coord. VA Registrar Svc. Workshop, Boulder, 1965. Bd. dirs., sec. Children's Health Coun. Aux., Palo Alto, 1997—99; bd. dirs., v.p., sec., chmn. fin. com. Palo Alto Aux. to Packard Children's Hosp., 1987—93. Mem. Am. Health Info. Mgmt. Assn. (hon.), Calif. Health Info. Mgmt. Assn. (hon., pres., treas. 1968-70), Ctrl. Calif. Health Info. Mgmt. Assn., (v.p., then pres. 1965-68), Minn. Health Info. Mgmt. Assn. (pres., chmn. pub. rels. com. 1953-59). Avocations: collecting teddy bears, public speaking. Address: 433 Guinda St Palo Alto CA 94301-2110

LEE, W. BRUCE, management consultant; b. Sacramento, Jan. 23, 1953; s. Wade Bruce and Marguerite (Stogner) L.; m. Nell Jeanette Alford, Aug. 13, 1977; children: Jessica, Amanda. BA in Adminstrn., U. Calif., Davis, 1971-75; MPA in Adminstrn., MA in Internat. Affairs, Calif. State U., 1977. Cert. in bus. and industry mgmt., mktg. and distbn., govt., pub. adminstrn. Adminstr./cons. State of Calif., Sacramento, 1973-76; mng. dir. Horizon Rsch. and Managerial Cons., 1978-87; exec. dir. Calif. Bus. League, 1987-90, Calif. Refuse Removal Coun., Sacramento, 1990-94; pres. Horizon Mgmt. and Assn. Svcs., Roseville, Calif., 1995—. Commentator internat. affairs KXPR Pub. Radio, Sacramento, 1977-78; newspaper columnist Sacramento Union, 1990-94. Author: Beyond Accounting, 1985; contbr. articles to profl. jours. Mayor, City of Loomis, Calif., 1991-96; chmn. Placer County Flood Control Dist., Auburn, Calif., 1993-96; treas. Sierra Econ. Devel. Dist., Auburn, 1994; founder South Placer Cmty. Prayer Breakfast, Rocklin, 1993—; mem. Local Agy. Formation Commn., Auburn, 1991-92; mem. Placer County Water Agy., Auburn, 1996—; co-chmn. fin. com. Billy Graham Crusade, Sacramento, 1995-96. Recipient Calif. Senate Rules Com. Resolution of Commendation, Calif. Assembly Resolution of Commendation. Mem. Calif. Soc. Assn. Execs., Am. Soc. Assn. Execs., Sacramento Jaycees (state dir. 1978, Outstanding Lt. Gov. 1971), Calif. Jaycees (Presdl. Award of Merit, mem. legis. coun. 1977). Avocations: photography, travel, cross country skiing, flying, scuba.

LEE, WEI-CHIN, political scientist; b. Su-Ao, I-lan, Taiwan, Nov. 1, 1956; came to U.S., 1981; m. Cristina Yu, 1983; children: Rae-yao, Rae-ling. BA, Nat. Taiwan U., Taipei, 1978; MA, U. Oreg., 1983, PhD, 1986. Instr. U. Oreg., Eugene, 1985-86; asst. prof. Wake Forest U., Winston-Salem, N.C., 1987-92, assoc. prof., 1993—. Book rev. editor Jour. Asian and African Studies, 1993-2000; coord. Conf. Group on Taiwan Studies, 1997-99; mem. editl. bd. Jour. Chinese Polit. Sci., 1995—. Author: Taiwan, 1990; editor: Taiwan in Perspective, 2000; contbr. articles to profl. jours. Fellow Pew Found., 1990, Carnegie Coun. on Ethics and Internat. Affairs, 1990, Inst. on Global Conflict and Cooperation, 1990; grantee Ministry of Fgn. Affairs, Taiwan, 1998, 99, 2001. Mem.: Internat. Studies Assn., Assn. for Asian Studies (mem. regional exec. coun. 1999—2002), Am. Polit. Sci. Assn. Office: Wake Forest U Dept Polit Sci PO Box 7568 Winston Salem NC 27109-7568 E-mail: leewei@wfu.edu.

LEE, WILLIAM JOHNSON, lawyer; b. Jan. 13, 1924; s. William J. and Ara (Anderson) L. Student, Akron U., 1941-43, Denison U., 1943-44, Harvard U., 1944-45; JD, Ohio State U., 1948. Bar: Ohio 1948, Fla. 1962, U.S. Dist. Ct. (no. dist.) Ohio 1960, U.S. Dist. Ct. (so. dist.) Fla. 1965, U.S. Dist. Ct. (so. dist.) Ohio 1970. Research asst. Ohio State U. Law Sch., 1948-49; asst. dir. Ohio Dept. Liquor Control, chief purchases, 1956-57, atty. examiner, 1951-53, asst. state permit chief, 1953-55, state permit chief, 1955-56; asst. counsel, staff Hupp Corp., 1957-58; spl. counsel City Attys. Office, Ft. Lauderdale, Fla., 1963-65; asst. atty. gen. Office Atty. Gen. State of Ohio, 1966-70; administr. State Med. Bd. Ohio, Columbus, 1970-85. Mem. Federated State Bd.'s Nat. Commn. for Evaluation of Fgn. Med. Schs., 1981-83; mem. Flex 1/Flex 2 Transitional Task Force, 1983-84; pvt. practice law, Ft. Lauderdale, 1965-66; acting municipal judge, Ravenna, Ohio, 1960; instr. Coll. Bus. Adminstrn., Kent State U., 1961-62. chmn. legal aid com. Portage County, Ohio, 1960. Mem. Editl. bd. Ohio State Law Jour., 1947-48; contbr. articles to profl. jours. Mem. pastoral relations com. Epworth United Meth. Ch., 1976; troop awards chmn. Boy Scouts Am., 1965; mem. ch. bd. Melrose Park (Fla.) Meth. Ch., 1966. Served with USAAF, 1943-46. Mem. ATLA, Exptl. Aviation Assn. S.W. Fla., Franklin County Trial Lawyers Assn., Am. Legion, Fla., Columbus, Akron, Broward County (Fla.) bar assns., Delta Theta Phi, Phi Kappa Tau, Pi Kappa Delta. Home: Apple Valley 704 Country Club Dr Howard OH 43028-9530

LEE, WILLIAM BRADLEY, education educator; b. Flint, Mich., June 29, 1924; s. Walter Henry and Gladys Rosiland Lee; m. Dagmar Pauls Lee, June 21, 1968; children: Bradley Thomas, Jefferson William. BA in Social Studies & English, Mich. State U., 1948, PhD in Edn., 1967; MA in Philosophy, U. So. Calif., 1953; cert., Alliance Française, Paris, 1959, diploma, 1960, Inst. Phonétique, 1960. Tchr., Delano, Calif., 1951-52, Long Beach, 1952-53, U.S. Dependents Sch., 1953-62; dir. host nation rels. USAF Dependent Schs., Wiesbaden, Germany, 1963-64, various, 1964-65, Europe, 1967-68; instr. Johns Hopkins U., Bologna, Italy, 1968; assoc. prof. U. So. Calif., L.A., 1968—. Rsch. cons. U.S. Dependent Schs., Euorpe, 1978; chief-of-party U.S. Agy. Internat. Devel., Yaounde, Cameroon, 1987-89, cons., Benin, West Africa, 1992. Co-author: Philosophy of Education in Cultural Perspective, 1977, Social Studies in West German Schools: Firsthand Perspectives for Educators, 1978, Alternative Classrooms in Canada and Abroad, 1994, John Dewey and Celestin Freinet: Freinet Pedagogy Theory and Practice, 1995, French Elementary Education and the Ecole Moderne, 2000; contbr. articles to profl. jours. With USMC, 1942-46, PTO. Decorated Palmes Academiques (France); recipient medal recognizing svcs. to Franco-Am. cmty. Mil. Order Fgn. Wars/U.S. Embassy, France, 1962; Inter-Univ. fellow Mott Found., 1965-66; Rsch. grantee Spencer Found., 1976. Mem. AAUP, NEA, Assn. Francophone Edn. Comparée, Comparative and Internat. Edn. Soc. (gen. sec. 1981-83, editor newsletter 1982-83), Phi Delta Kappa, Phi Kappa Phi. Avocations: hiking, traveling. Office: U So Calif Los Angeles CA 90089-0031

LEE, WILLIAM CHARLES, judge; b. Ft. Wayne, Ind., Feb. 2, 1938; s. Russell and Catherine (Zwick) L.; m. Judith Anne Bash, Sept. 19, 1959; children: Catherine L., Mark R., Richard R. AB, Yale U., 1959; JD, U. Chgo., 1962; LLD (hon.), Huntington Coll., 1999. Bar: Ind. 1962. Ptnr. Parry, Krueckeberg & Lee, Ft. Wayne, 1963-69, chief dep., 1966-69; U.S. atty. No. Dist. Ind., 1970-73; ptnr. Hunt, Suedhoff, Borror, Eilbacher & Lee, 1973-81; U.S. dist. judge U.S. Dist. Ct. (no. dist.) Ind., 1981—. Instr. Nat. Inst. Trial Advocacy; lectr. in field. Co-author: Business and Commercial Litigation in Federal Courts, 1998; author: Volume I Federal Jury Practice and Instructions, 1999; contbr. to numerous publs. in field. Co-chmn. Fort Wayne Fine Arts Operating Fund Drive, 1978; past bd. dirs., v.p., pres. Fort Wayne Philharm. Orch.; past bd. dirs., v.p. Hospice of Fort Wayne, inc.; past bd. dirs. Fort Wayne Fine Arts Found., Fort Wayne Civic Theatre, Neighbors, Inc., Embassy Theatre Found.; past bd. dirs., pres. Legal Aid of fort Wayne, Inc.; past mem. chm. coun., v.p. Trinity English Lutheran Ch. Coun.; past trustee, pres. Fort Wayne Cmty. Schs., 1978-81, pres., 1980-81; trustee Fort Wayne Mus. Art, 1984-90; past bd. dirs., pres. Fort Wayne-Allen County Hist. Soc. Griffin Scholar, 1955-59; chmn. Fort Wayne Cmty. Schs. Scholarship Com.; bd. dirs. Arts United of Greater Fort Wayne, Fort Wayne Ballet. Weymouth Kirkland scholar, 1959-62; named Ind. Trial Judge of Yr., 1988. Fellow Am. Coll. Trial Lawyers, Ind. Bar Found.; mem. ABA, Allen County Bar Assn., Ind. State Bar Assn., Fed. Bar Assn., Seventh Cir. Bar Assn., Benjamin Harrison Am. Inn of Ct., North Side High Alumni Assn. (bd. dris., pres.), Fort Wayne Rotary Club (bd. dirs.), Phi Delta Phi (past bd. dirs., 1st pres.). Republican. Lutheran. Office: US Dist Ct 2145 Fed Bldg 1300 S Harrison St Fort Wayne IN 46802-3495

LEE, WILLIAM FRANKLIN, III, association administrator, musician, composer; b. Galveston, Tex., Feb. 20, 1929; s. William Franklin Jr. and Anna Lena (Keis) L.; m. Jacqueline Tyler; children: William Franklin IV, Robert Terry, Patricia Lynn, Peggy Ann. MusB, N. Tex. State U., 1949, MS, 1950; MusM, PhD, U. Tex., 1956. Prof. music St. Mary's U., San Antonio, 1952-55; asst. to dean fine arts U. Tex., 1955-56; chmn. dept. music Sam Houston State Coll., 1956-64; dean Sch. Music U. Miami (Fla.), 1964-82, provost, exec. v.p., 1982-86, disting. prof., composer in residence, 1986-88; dir. arts Fla. Internat. U., Miami, 1988-90; dean coll. fine arts and humanities U. Tex., San Antonio, 1990-94; exec. dir. Internat. Assn. Jazz Educators, 1994-98, ret., 1998. Performances with Houston, Dallas symphony orchs., performances with Gene Krupa and Artie Shaw, guest clinician, condr., composer, 1952— ; composer, author, arranger more than 100 published works.; author: Music Theory Dictionary, 1962; also articles, music publs.; biographer, discographer of Stan Kenton, 1981, Maynard Ferguson, 1997, Bill Evans, 2000; editor, co-founder: Southwestern Brass Jour., 1958, Belwin New Dictionary of Music and Musicians, 1988. Mem. AAUP, ASCAP (recipient 33 awards 1968—including Deems Taylor awards 1981, 85), Nat. Assn. Am. Composers and Condrs., Music Educators Nat. Conf., Am. Fedn. Musicians, Music Tchrs. Nat. Assn., Pi Kappa Lambda, Kappa Kappa Psi, Phi Mu Alpha. E-mail: Blee3rd@aol.com.

LEE, WILLIAM JOHN, petroleum engineering educator, consultant; b. Lubbock, Tex., Jan. 16, 1936; s. William Preston and Bonnie Lee (Cook) L.; m. Phyllis Ann Bass, June 10, 1961; children: Anne Preston, Mary Denise. B in Chem. Engring., Ga. Inst. Tech., 1959, MSChemE, 1961, PhD in Chem. Engring., 1963, NAE, 1993; Disting. Engring. Alumni, Ga. Tech. Acad., 1994. Registered profl. engr., Tex. Sr. rsch. specialist Exxon Prodn. Rsch. Co., Houston, 1962-68; assoc. prof. petroleum engring. Miss. State U., Starkville, 1968-71; tech. advisor Exxon Co., Houston, 1971-77; prof. petroleum engring. Tex. A&M U., College Station, 1977—, holder Noble chair in petroleum engring., 1985-93, Peterson chair in petroleum engring., 1993—. Dir. Crisman Inst. for Petroleum Reservoir Mgmt. at Tex. A&M U., 1987-93; exec. v.p. S.A. Holditch & Assocs., Inc., College Station, 1979-99. Author: Well Testing, 1982, Gas Reservoir Engineering, 1996. Recipient award of excellence Halliburton Edn. Found., 1982, Meritorious Engring. Tchg. award Tenneco, Inc., 1982, 2000, Disting. Tchg. award Assn. Former Students Tex. A&M U., 1983, Continuing Edn. award, 2001, Mineral Industries Edn. award AIME, 2002, Mineral Industries Edn. Award, 2002; Tex. Engring. Experiment Sta. fellow, 1987-88, sr. fellow, 1990; named to Dream Team, Tex. Soc. Profl. Engrs., 2001. Mem. NAE, AIME (hon.), Soc. Petroleum Engrs. (hon.; disting., chmn. edn. and accreditation com. 1985-86, disting. lectr. 1980, Disting. Faculty Achievement award 1982, Reservoir Engring. award 1986, Regional Service award 1987, Disting. Svc. award, 1992, Carll award 1995, dir. 1996-99, hon. 2001), Am. Inst. Mining Metallurgical and Petroleum Engrs. (hon.). Presbyterian. Avocation: travel. Home: 9310 Lake Forest Ct S College Station TX 77845-8758 Office: Tex A&M U Dept Petroleum Engring 3116 Tamu College Station TX 77843-3116 E-mail: johnlee@tca.net., lee@spindletop.tamu.edu.

LEE, WILLIAM MARSHALL, lawyer; b. N.Y.C., Feb. 23, 1922; s. Marshall McLean and Marguerite (Letts) L.; m. Lois Kathryn Plain, Oct. 10, 1942; children: Marsha (Mrs. Stephen Deryck), William Marshall Jr., Victoria C. (Mrs. Larry Nelson). Student, U. Wis., 1939-40; BS, Aero. U., Chgo., 1942; postgrad., UCLA, 1946-48, Loyola U. Law Sch., L.A., 1948-49; JD, Loyola U., Chgo., 1952. Bar: Ill. 1952, U.S. Supreme Ct., 1972. Thermodynamicist Northrop Aircraft Co., Hawthorne, Calif., 1947-49; patent agt. Hill, Sherman, Meroni, Gross & Simpson, Chgo., 1949-51, Borg-Warner Corp., Chgo., 1951-53; ptnr. Hume, Clement, Hume & Lee, 1953-72; pvt. practice, 1973-74; ptnr. Lee and Smith (and predecessors), 1974-89, Lee, Mann, Smith, McWilliams, Sweeney & Ohlson, Chgo., 1989—; ind. expert intellectual property Barrington, Ill., 1999—. Cons. Power Packaging, Inc. Speaker and contbr. articles on legal topics. Pres. Glenview (Ill.) Citizens Sch. Com., 1953-57; v.p. Glenbrook High Sch. Bd., 1957-63. Lt. USNR, 1942-46, CBI. Recipient Pub. Svc. award Glenbrook High Sch. Bd., 1963 Mem. ABA (chmn. sect. intellectual property law 1986-87, sect. fin. officer 1976-77, sect. sec. 1977-80, sect. governing coun. 1980-84, 87-88), Ill. Bar Assn., Chgo. Bar Assn., 7th Fed. Cir. Bar Assn., Am. Intellectual Property Law Assn., Intellectual Property Law Assn. Chgo., Licensing Execs. Soc. (pres. 1981-82, treas. 1977-80, trustee 1974-77, 80-81, 82-83, internat. del. 1980—), Phi Delta Theta, Phi Alpha Delta. Republican. Office: 84 Otis Rd Barrington IL 60010-5128

LEE, WON JAY, radiologist; b. Seoul, Korea, Feb. 2, 1938; came to U.S., 1965; s. Kang Sei and Choon Ja (Park) L.; m. Moon Jung, Feb. 24, 1968; children: Julie, Lisa, Jennifer. MD, Yonsei U., Seoul, 1962. Diplomate Am. Bd. Radiology, Am. Bd. Nuclear Medicine. Intern Wyckoff Heights Hosp., Bklyn., 1965-66; resident in radiology NYU Med. Ctr., N.Y.C., 1966-69; fellow, asst. radiologist L.I. Jewish Med. Ctr., New Hyde Park, N.Y., 1969-71, staff radiologist, 1975-82, chief uroradiology, 1983—; assoc. radiologist Binghamton (N.Y.) Gen. Hosp., 1971-75. Asst. prof. SUNY, Stony Brook, 1975-86, assoc. prof. radiology, 1987-89; prof. radiology Albert Einstein Coll. Medicine, 1989—; clin. prof. diagnostic radiology Yonsei U. Coll. Medicine, Seoul, 1996—; cons. in field. Asst. editor: Jour. Endourology, 1987-96; assoc. editor: Jour. Korean-Am. Med. Assn., 1995-98, editor-in-chief, 1999-2000; contbr. chpts. to books and articles to profl. jours. First lt. Republic of Korea Army M.C., 1962-65. Recipient Sci. Paper award Soc. Uroradiology, 1994, Clin. award Can. Assoc. Radiologists, 1979, Disting. Svc. award Yonsei U. Col. Med. Alumni Assn., 1998. Fellow Am. Coll. Radiology, Cardiovasc. and Interventional Radiology (emeritus), Soc. Uroradiology; mem. Assn. Univ. Radiologists, Am. Roentgen Ray Soc. (Merit award 1983), Radiol. Soc. N.Am., Korean-Am. Med. Assn. (chmn. sci. and edn. divsn. 1996), Korean Radiol. Soc. N.Am., Severance Alumni Assn. Am. (pres. 1997). Democratic. Methodist. Avocations: gardening, golf, travel. Home: 15 Lucille Ln Huntington Station NY 11746-5848 Office: LI Jewish Med Ctr 270-05 76th Ave New Hyde Park NY 11040-1433 E-mail: wlee@lij.edu.

LEE, WOONG MAN, pathologist; b. Seoul, Korea, Dec. 3, 1938; came to U.S., 1967; s. Jay Hyuck and Sung Yong Lee; m. Young Sook Kim, 1968; children: Danny Eugene, Francis Eusun, Peggy Eurie. BS, Seoul Nat. U., 1960, MD, 1964. Asst. resident Albany (N.Y.) Med. Ctr. Hosp., 1967-70, resident, 1970-72, asst. attending pathologist, 1974-79; instr. Albany Med. Coll., 1970-74, asst. prof., 1974-79; attending pathologist Albany VA Hosp., 1974-79; pathologist Glens Falls (N.Y.) Hosp., 1979—. Roman Catholic. Office: Glens Falls Hosp 100 Park St Glens Falls NY 12801-4447

LEE, XIAOYANG, scientist; b. Beijing, July 23, 1956; came to the U.S., 1985; s. Yi-Minn and Shu-Zhi (Zhang) L.; m. Amy Lee; children: James, Joan. BSEE, Beijing U. Post and Telecom., 1982; MSEE, Columbia U., 1987. Design engr. Berkeley Varitronics Sys., Metuchen, N.J., 1987-91; engr. Rsch. Inst. Telecom. Transmission, MPT, Beijing, 1982-85; sr. scientist Panasonic Techs., Inc., Princeton, N.J., 1991-2000; disting. mem. tech. staff Siemens ICM-N, San Diego, 2000—. Mem.: IEEE (sr.). Achievements include patents for frequency measuring system, asynchronous data transmitting and receiving systems, combination brouter and cluster controller, audio/video distribution systems, asynchronous data transmitting and receiving systems, method and apparatus for increasing system efficiency of TDMA system by reducing time slos guard time. Home: 12 Essex Dr Monmouth Junction NJ 08852-2502 Office: Siemens ICM-N 16745 W Bernardo Dr San Diego CA 92127 E-mail: xiaoyang_lee@yahoo.com.

LEE, YANG-CHIH, cell biologist, researcher; b. Yuanlee, Taiwan, Dec. 12, 1944; came to U.S., 1979; s. Shie-Chan and Chuan-Chee C. Lee; m. Bi-Zu Huang, Nov. 1, 1971; children: Catherine, Jennifer. BS, Tamkang U., Tan-Swei, Taiwan, 1968; MS, Nat. Tsing Hua U., Shin-Chu, Taiwan, 1970; PhD, Mich. State U., 1983. Sr. chemist Inst. Nuclear Energy Rsch., Taipei, Taiwan, 1971-79; postdoctoral fellow U. Utah, Salt Lake City, 1983-84; NMR mgr. Hahnemann U., Phila., 1984-86; co-dir. Thomas Jefferson U., 1986—. Assoc. prof. Taipei Inst. Tech., 1975-79; cons.Hong Yang INdustries, Taipei, 1974-78. Contbr. articles to profl. jours. Recipient 2 awards Inst. Nuclear Energy Rsch., Taiwan, 1974, 78; NIH/NIAAA grantee, 1987—. Mem. Soc. Magnetic Resonance in Medicine, Biophys. Soc. Avocations: badminton, tennis, photography, camping. Office: Thomas Jefferson U 1020 Locust St Philadelphia PA 19107-6731

LEE, YEU-TSU MARGARET, surgeon, educator; b. Xian, Shensi, China, Mar. 18, 1936; m. Thomas V. Lee, Dec. 29, 1962 (div. 1987); 1 child, Maxwell M. AB in Microbiology, U. S.D., 1957; MD, Harvard U., 1961. Diplomate Am. Bd. Surgery. Assoc. prof. surgery Med. Sch., U. So. Calif., L.A., 1973-83; commd. lt. col. U.S. Army Med. Corps, 1983, advanced through grades to col., 1989; chief surg. oncology Tripler Army Med. Ctr., Honolulu, 1983-98; ret. U.S. Army, 1999; assoc. clin. prof. surgery Med. Sch., U. Hawaii, Honolulu, 1984-92, clin. prof. surgery, 1992—. Author: Malignant Lymphoma, 1974; author chpts to books; contbr. articles to profl. jours. Pres. Orgn. Chinese-Am. Women, L.A., 1981, Hawaii chpt., 1988; active U.S.-China Friendship Assn., 1991—. Decorated Nat. Def. Svc. medal, Army Commendation medal, Army Meritorious Svc. medal, Army Humanitarian Svc. medal; recipient Chinese-Am. Engrs. and Scis. Assn., 1987; named Sci. Woman Warrior, Asian-Pacific Womens Network, 1983. Mem. ACS, Soc. Surg. Oncology, Assn. Women Surgeons. Avocations: classical music, movies, hiking, ballroom dancing. Address: PO Box 6486 Honolulu HI 96818-0486 E-mail: ytm_lee@hotmail.com.

LEE, YONG JIN, electrical engineer; b. Seoul, Korea, Nov. 27, 1964; came to U.S., 1983; s. Chul Choo and Sung Sook (Hong) L.; m. Soenkyung Pak, Dec. 27, 1992. BSEE, Stanford U., 1987, MSEE, 1990, MS in Engring. Mgmt., 1992, AB in Econs., 1990, PhD in Elec. Engring., 1994. Engr. Daewoo Electronics, Seoul, Korea, 1986; mem. tech. staff Tex. Instruments, Dallas, 1992-94; chief scientist CVC Products, Fremont, Calif., 1994, dir., chief scientist, 1994—. Senator Associated Students of Stanford (Calif.) U., 1988. Recipient F.E. Terman award Stanford U., 1987, Korean Honor scholarship South Korean Govt., 1990. Mem. IEEE, Tau Beta Pi, Phi Beta Kappa. Achievements include invention of Acoustic Temperature and Film Thickness Monitor, Sensor for Measuring the Temperature of Ambient over Silicon Wafer, Photoacoustic Oscillator Sensor for Temperature and Film Thickness Measurements, Multizone Real-Time Emissivity Correction System for semi-conductor processing, advanced illuminator for rapid thermal processing, gas delivery system for chemical vapor deposition, advanced physical vapor deposition systems. Home: 781 Rosewood Dr Palo Alto CA 94303-3638 Office: CVC Products 3100 Laurelview Ct Fremont CA 94538-6535

LEE, YOUNG HO (JINWOL), Buddhist monk, educator; b. Uiwang, Kyonggi, Korea, Apr. 28, 1950; came to U.S., 1986; s. Chong Taek and Kyong Bok (Kim) L. BA, Dongguk U., Seoul, 1984, Sogang U., Seoul, Korea, 1986; MA, U. Hawaii, 1990; PhD, U. Calif., Berkeley, 1998; Diploma, Haein Sangha Coll., Korea. Buddhist monk. Pres. Soc. Zen Studies, Seoul, 1982-83; Dharma tchr. Kiwonjong-sa Temple, 1984-86; Dharma and Zen tchr. Daewonsa Temple, Honolulu, 1986-92; v.p. Hawaii Assn. Internat. Buddhists, 1992-94; internat. advisor Soc. Buddhist Christian Studies, Pitts., 1994-96; Zen and Dharma tchr. Group in Buddhist Studies U. Calif., Berkeley, 1996—. Cons. United Religion, San Francisco, 1996. Contbr. articles to profl. jours. Mem. Am. Acad. Religion, Soc. Buddhist-Christian Studies, Calif. buddhist Assn. (founder, pres., advisor 1992-96). Home: 2810 Lavender Dr Walnut Creek CA 94596-6420 Office: Univ of Calif-Berkeley Group in Buddhist Studies Berkeley CA 94704

LEE, YUAN TSEH, chemistry educator; b. Hsinchu, Taiwan, China, Nov. 29, 1936; arrived in U.S., 1962, naturalized, 1974; s. Tsefan and Pei (Tasi) Lee; m. Bernice Wu, June 28, 1963; children: Ted, Sidney, Charlotte. BS, Nat. Taiwan U., 1959; MS, Nat. Tsinghua U., Taiwan, 1961; PhD, U. Calif., Berkeley, 1965. From asst. prof. to prof. chemistry U. Chgo., 1968—74; prof. emeritus U. Calif., Berkeley, 1974—, also former prin. investigator Lawrence Berkeley Lab., 1974—97; pres. Academia Sinica, Taiwan, 1994—. Contbr. articles. Recipient Nobel Prize in chemistry, 1986, Ernest O. Lawrence award, Dept. Energy, 1981, Nat. Medal of Sci., 1986, 1990, Peter Debye award for phys. chemistry, 1986, Harrison Howe award, 1983; fellow, Alfred P. Sloan, 1969—71, John Simon Guggenheim Found., 1976—77; scholar Tchr. scholar, Camille and Henry Dreyfus Found., 1971—74. Fellow: Am. Phys. Soc.; mem.: Am. Chem. Soc., Am. Acad. Arts and Scis., AAAS, NAS. Office: Acad Sinica Pres Office 128 Academia Rd Sec 2 Nankang Taipei 11529 Taiwan

LEE, YUEN SAN, chemist; b. Taipei, Taiwan, Oct. 13, 1939; m. Helen Fung-Ping; children: James, May. PhD, U. Md., 1969; MS, Utah State U., 1965; BS, Nat. Taiwan U., 1962. Prof. U.D.C., Washington, 1977—; chemist D.C. Pub. Health Lab., 1971—77; food technologist Wei-Shin Food, Inc., 1969—71, prodn. supr. Taiwan, 1963—64. Mem.: Inst. Food Technologists. Home: 5 Maplewood CT Greenbelt MD 20770 Office: U DC 4200 CT Ave NW Washington DC 20008- E-mail: ylee@udc.edu.

LEE, YUNG-KEUN, physicist, educator; b. Seoul, Korea, Sept. 26, 1929; came to U.S., 1953, naturalized, 1968; s. Kwang-Soo and Young-Sook (Hur) L.; m. Ock-Kyung Pai, Oct. 25, 1958; children: Ann, Arnold, Sara, Sylvia, Clara. BA, Johns Hopkins, 1956; MS, U. Chgo., 1957; PhD, Columbia, 1961. Research scientist Columbia U., N.Y.C., 1961-64; prof. physics Johns Hopkins U., Balt., 1964—. Vis. mem. staff Los Alamos Sci. Lab., 1971; vis. researcher Institut Scis. Nucléaires, Grenoble, France, 1975; cons. Idaho Nat. Engring. Lab., 1988-91; mem. Brahms collaboration Brookhaven Nat. Lab., 1996—. Contbr. articles to profl. jours. Mem. Am. Phys. Soc. Clubs: Johns Hopkins. Democrat. Methodist. Home: 1318 Denby Rd Baltimore MD 21286-1627 Office: Johns Hopkins U 34th and Charles Sts Baltimore MD 21218 E-mail: yklee@jhu.edu.

LEEB, CHARLES SAMUEL, clinical psychologist; b. San Francisco, July 18, 1945; s. Sidney Herbert and Dorothy Barbara (Fishstrom) L.; m. Storme Lynn Gilkey, Apr. 28, 1984; children: Morgan Evan, Spencer Douglas. BA in Psychology, U. Calif.-Davis, 1967; MS in Counseling and Guidance, San Diego State U., 1970; PhD in Edn. and Psychology, Claremont Grad. Sch., 1973. Assoc. So. Regional Dir. Mental Retardation Ctr., Las Vegas, Nev., 1976-79; pvt. practice, Las Vegas, 1978-79; dir. biofeedback and athletics Menninger Found., Topeka, 1979-82, dir. children's div. biofeedback and psychophysiology ctr. The Menninger Found., 1979-82; pvt. practice, Claremont, Calif., 1982—; dir. of psychol. svcs. Horizon Hosp., 1986-88; dir. adolescent chem. dependency and children's program Charter Oak Hosp., Covina, Calif., 1989-91; founder, chief exec. officer Rsch. and Treatment Inst.,

Claremont, 1991-2002; co-founder and dir. Live Aok Campus Sch., 1992—; lectr. in field. Contbr. articles to profl. jours. Mem. Am. Psychol. Assn., Calif. State Psychol. Assn. Office: 1420 N Claremont Blvd #102-A Claremont CA 91711-3358

LEECH, CHARLES RUSSELL, JR. lawyer; b. Coshocton, Ohio, July 29, 1930; s. Charles Russell and Edna (Henry) L.; m. Patricia Ann Tubaugh, June 20, 1953; children— Charles Russell III, Timothy David (dec.), Wendy Ann. AB cum laude, Kenyon Coll., 1952; JD, Ohio State U., 1955; MA, U. Toledo, 1969. Bar: Ohio 1955. Assoc. Fuller & Henry Ltd. and predecessors, Toledo, 1957-64, ptnr., 1964-97, counsel, 1997-99. Mng. editor: Ohio State Law Jour, 1955. Mem. exec. com. alumni council Kenyon Coll., 1967-72, trustee coll., 1974-80. Served with USNR, 1955-57. Fellow Ohio State Bar Found.; mem. ABA, Ohio Bar Assn., Kenyon Coll. Alumni Assn. Maumee Valley (past pres.), Beta Theta Pi, Phi Delta Phi. Republican. Home: 20285 Zion Rd Gambier OH 43022-9643

LEECH, JAMES WILLIAM, investment company executive; b. St. Boniface, Man., Can., June 12, 1947; s. George Clarence and Mary Elizabeth (Gibson) L.; m. Deborah Barrett; children: Jennifer Hilton, Joanna Marjorie Thiessen, James Andrew Douglas. BS in Math. and Physics with hons., Royal Mil. Coll. Can., 1964; MBA, Queen's U., Can., 1973. Exec. asst. to pres. Commerce Capital Corp., Ltd., Montreal, Que., Can., 1973-74, v.p. Can., 1974-75; exec. v.p. Commerce Capital Trust Co., Calgary, Alta., Can., 1976-78; sr. v.p. Eaton/Bay Fin. Services Ltd., Toronto, Ont., Can., 1979; pres., bd. dirs. Unicorp Canada Corp., 1979-88; pres., CEO, bd. dirs. Union Energy, Inc., 1985-93, Disys Corp., Toronto, 1993-96; vice-chmn., bd. dirs. Kasten Chase Applied Rsch. Ltd., Mississauga, Ont., 1996-99; pres., CEO, bd. dirs. InfoCast Corp., Toronto, 1999-2001; sr. v.p., Tchrs. Mcht. Bank, Ont. Tchrs. Pension Plan, 2001—. Bd. dirs. Harris Steel Group, Inc., Chemtrade Logistics Income Fund. Vice-chmn. adv. coun. sch. bus. Queens U., 1979-83, chmn. 1998-2001, mem. gen. coun., 1978-97, mem. investment com. bd. trustees, 1980-97, trustee, 1984-96, mem. fund coun., 1988-97; bd. dirs., chmn., pres., mem. exec com. Can. Stage Co., 1989-94; v.p., bd. dirs. Toronto Arts Coun., 1994-2000, Toronto Gen. and Western Hosp. Found., 1996—. D.I. McLeod scholar, 1971-73; Seagram rsch. fellow, 1983, Samuel Bronfman Found. fellow, 1973, Transp. Devel. Agy. fellow, 1972, Gold Medalist, Canadian Securities Course, 1974. Mem. World Pres. Orgn., The Nat. Club, Muskoka Lakes Golf and Country Club. United Ch. Can. Home: 51 Mathersfield Dr Toronto ON Canada M4W 3W4 E-mail: jim_leech@otpp.com.

LEECH, SALLY See KEMP, SARAH

LEED, ROGER MELVIN, lawyer; b. Green Bay, Wis., July 15, 1939; s. Melvin John and Veronica Sarah (Flaherty) L.; m. Jean Ann Burg, Mar. 1967; children: Craig, Maren, Jennifer. AB, Harvard U., 1961; JD cum laude, U. Mich., 1967. Bar: Wash. 1967, U.S. Dist. Ct. (we. dist.) Wash. 1968, U.S. Ct. Appeals (9th cir.) 1969, U.S. Supreme Ct. 1973. Law clk. Wash. Supreme Ct., Olympia, 1967-68; assoc. Perkins, Coie et al, Seattle, 1968-70; ptnr. Schroeter, Goldmark et al, 1970-76; sole practice, 1976—. Adj. prof. law U. Puget Sound, Tacoma, 1974-77. Editor Shorelines Mgmt., the Wash. Experience, 1972. Pres. Cen. Seattle Community Council Fedn., 1972, Wash. Environ. Council, 1980-82; bd. dirs. Allied Arts, Seattle, 1971-72, Downtown Human Services Council, Seattle, 1985-92. Mem. ABA (standing com. on environtl. law 1980-84), Wash. State Bar Assn., King County Bar Assn., Assn. Trial Lawyers Am., Montlake Cmty. Club (v.p., bd. dirs. 1994-98), Seattle Tilth (bd. dirs. 1990-2001). Clubs: Met. Dem., Washington Athletic. Office: 2003 Western Ave Ste 600 Seattle WA 98121-3126 E-mail: leedlaw@pipeline.com.

LEEDER, ROBERT JOHN, broadcast executive; b. Providence, Mar. 20, 1939; s. Urban Ambrose and Doris Anabel (Parker) L.; m. Nancyann Pachco, Sept. 24, 1960 (div. 1964); children: Robert John Jr., Scott David, Kevin Charles; m. Esther Jean Drew, Sept. 17, 1965; children: Susan Marie Lynch Rodier, Paul Drew, Drew, Glenn. BA, Amherst Coll., 1961. Dir. of news WPAT AM & FM, Paterson, N.J., 1972-74, prgram mgr., 1974-76; dist dir. affiliate relations CBS Radio Network, N.Y.C., 1976—. Mem. Planning Bd., Montville, N.J., 1978-88. Republican. Office: CBS Inc 51 W 52nd St New York NY 10019-6119

LEEDOM, E. PAUL, banker; b. Havre de Grace, Md., June 11, 1925; s. Elridge L. and Beatrice L. (Brown) L.; m. Mildred E. Both, Oct. 21, 1978. BS, U. Md., 1951; MBA, Adelphi U., 1967. Civilian tech. cons. Aberdeen Proving Ground, Md., 1953-57; various mgmt. positions Ambac Industries, Inc., Carle Place, N.Y., 1957-68; pres. Digimatics Inc., Garden City, 1968-74; 1st v.p. Anchor Savs. Bank, Northport, 1974-90; bd. dirs. Spencer Savings Bank, Garfield, N.J., 1992-95; pres. Applied Solutions Corp., Miller Place, N.Y., 1996—. Life mem. Rep. Nat. Com. Served with USN, 1943-46, with Signal Corps, U.S. Army, 1951-52. Named to corridor of disting. alumni Sch. Bus. Adminstrn., Adelphi U. Mem. Am. Mgmt. Assn., Internat. Assn. for Fin. Planning, Delta Mu Delta. Presbyterian. Home and Office: 27 Dogwood Hollow Ln Miller Place NY 11764-1709

LEEDOM, JOHN NESBETT, distribution company executive, state senator; b. Dallas, July 27, 1921; BSEE, Rice U., 1943. Engr. Naval Rsch. Lab., Washington, 1943-45; asst. sales mgr. Sprague Products Co., North Adams, Mass., 1945-50; founder, CEO Wholesales Electronic Suply Inc., Dallas, 1950—. Pres. Levco, Inc., 1973—; mem. Tex. Senate, 1980-96. Author: The Group and You, Whose Water. Chmn. Dallas County Republican Com., 1962-66, mem. state exec. com., 1966-68; mem. Dallas City Coun., 1975-80. Served to lt. (j.g.) USNR, 1943-45. Mem.: IEEE, Nat. Assn. Wholesale Distbrs. (pres. 1972—73), Nat. Electronic Distbrs. Assn. (pres. 1971—72), Weather Modification Assn. (chmn. legis. com. 2001—), Mil. Order World Wars, Navy League, Tau Beta Pi. Office: 2809 Ross Ave Dallas TX 75201-2519 E-mail: jleedom@altinet.net.

LEEDOM-ACKERMAN, JOANNE, writer, educator; b. Washington, Feb. 7, 1947; d. John Nesbit and Joanne (Shriver) Leedom; m. Peter Ackerman, June 3, 1972; children: Nathanael Leedom Ackerman, Elliot Leedom Ackerman. BA, Principia Coll., Elsah, Ill., 1968; MA in Creative Writing, Johns Hopkins U., 1969; MA in English, Brown U., 1974. Reporter The Christian Sci. Monitor, Boston, 1969-72; asst. prof. NYU, N.Y.C., 1976-77; lectr. CUNY, 1974-76, Occidental Coll., L.A., 1978-81, UCLA Extension, 1985-87. Author: No Marble Angels, 1985, The Dark Path to the River, 1988. Bd. dirs. Save the Children, Conn., 1994-2000, Human Rights Watch, N.Y.C., 1999—, Internat. Crisis Group, Brussels and Washington, 1996—, Albert Einstein Inst., Boston, 1984-2001; trustee Brown U., 1996-2002 Johns Hopkins U., 1996—; mem. nat. adv. bd. Woodrow Wilson Nat. Fellowship Found., 1999-2002. Mem. PEN Am. Ctr. PEN USA West (pres. 1988-89), Authors Guild, English PEN, Internat. PEN (v.p. 1997—), PEN Faulkner Found. (v.p., bd. dirs. 1998—), Poets and Writers (bd. dirs. 1985—). E-mail: jlaajoanne@aol.com.

LEEDS, BARRY HOWARD, English language educator; b. N.Y.C., Dec. 6, 1940; s. Andrew Samuel and Paula (Stark) Leeds; m. Robin Leigh Flowers, Apr. 20, 1968 (div. Dec. 2000); children: Brett Ashley, Leslie Lion(dec.). BA, Columbia U., 1962, MA, 1963; PhD, Ohio U., 1967. Lectr. CUNY, 1963-64; instr. U. Tex., El Paso, 1964-65; asst. prof. Cen. Conn. State U., New Britain, 1968-71, assoc. prof., 1971-76, prof., 1976-91; disting. prof., 1991—. Cons. Am. lit. Choice mag., Middletown, Conn., 1968—; vis. mem. faculty Yale U., 1984-85. Author: The Structured Vision of Norman Mailer, 1969, Ken Kesey, 1981, The Enduring Vision of Norman Mailer, 2002; editor: Conn. Rev., 1989-92, mem. editl. bd., 1986-95; contbg. editor D.C. Health Anthology Am. Lit., 1986—; contbr. articles to profl. jours. incl. Saturday Rev., Modern Fiction Studies, Jour. Modern Lit. Alumni interviewer Columbia Coll., N.Y.C., 1982-95. Conn. State U. grantee, 1986—; recipient Disting. Svc. award Cen. Conn. State U., 1982. Mem. Conn. Acad. Arts and Scis. (elected). Avocations: scuba diving, weight lifting, ballroom dancing, competition target shooting. Home: 200 Blakeslee St Apt 121 Bristol CT 06010-8800 Office: Cen Conn State U Dept English 1615 Stanley St New Britain CT 06053-2439 E-mail: bhleeds01@snet.net.

LEEDS, CHARLES ALAN, publishing executive; b. Mpls., Aug. 20, 1951; s. Charles Phillips and Irene (Pollard) L.; m. Karen Sue Biggs, Aug. 2, 1986; children: Charles Austin, Tyler Dixon. BA, Drake U., 1973, MPA, 1978. Mktg. coord. Register and Tribune Syndicate Inc., Des Moines, 1973-79; sales mgr. Washington Post Writers Group, Washington, 1979-89; pres. and editorial dir. L.A. Times Washington Post News Svc., 1989—. Asst. professorial lectr. George Washington U., Washington, 1986, 88. Mem. nat. adv. bd. Sch. Journalism and Mass Comm. Drake U., 1996-2001, chmn. Bus. Basics, 1999—2001. Recipient Best in Bus. award Am. Journalism Rev., 1995. Mem. Internat. Press Inst. (assoc.), Soc. Profl. Journalists, Sigma Delta Chi, Kappa Tau Alpha. Presbyterian. Avocations: jogging, tennis, golf. Home: 4714 17th St N Arlington VA 22207-2031 Office: LA Times-WA Post News Svc 1150 15th St NW Washington DC 20071-0001

LEEDS, DOUGLAS BRECKER, advertising agency executive, theatre producer; b. N.Y.C., Mar. 15, 1947; s. Richard Henry and Nancy Ann (Brecker) L.; m. Christine (Anki) Castler, Jan. 14, 1980; 1 child, Victoria Brecker. BS, Babson Coll., 1970. V.p., dir. Auto Data Systems, Inc., Natick, Mass., 1970-72; dir. leasing Beacon Cos., Inc., Boston, 1972-77; account exec. Thomson-Leeds Co., Inc. div. The WPP Group, N.Y.C., 1977-84, exec. v.p., 1985-88, pres., 1988-97, chmn., CEO, 1989—. Chmn. ednl. rels. com. Point of Purchase Advt. Inst., 1986—, elected bd. dirs., 1989, vice chmn., 1994—; bd. dirs. Checker Board Found. Co-producer: (Broadway musical) Streetheat, 1985; assoc. producer: (Broadway play) Sleight of Hand, 1986; patentee in field. Chmn., founder Lobby Gallery Assocs. Whitney Mus. Am. Art, N.Y.C., 1983-90; trustee Guild Hall of East Hampton (Mus. and Theatre), 1990-92, John Drew Theatre; chmn. men's com. Boys Club N.Y., 1989; bd. dirs. chmn. Friends Henry Street Settlement House, N.Y.C., 1977-80; trustee Whitney Mus. Am. Art, 1992—, co-chmn. membership com., 1993—, Worcester Acad., 1982-85; also trustee emeritus; trustee Babson Coll., 1979-86, also co-chmn. devel. and pub. affairs com.; mem. dream team Meml. Sloan-Kettering Cancer Ctr.; bd. dirs. Am. Theatre Wing, 1991—, treas., sec. bd. dirs., 1998—, mem. adminstrn. com. Tony Awards; mem. coun. Frick Collection, 2000—. Mem. Babson Coll. Alumni Assn. (bd. dirs., v.p. 1975-79), Union Club, Doubles Club, Royal Tennis Court Club (Middlesex, Eng.).

LEEDS, ELIZABETH LOUISE, miniature collectibles executive; b. L.A., July 24, 1925; d. Charles Furnival and Etta Louise (Jackson) Mayes; m. Walter Albert Leeds, Jan. 20, 1973 (dec.); children: Pam Ravey Lewis, Linda Ravey McCallam, Diane Ravey Lathrop, Tom Ravey. Student pub. sch., Prescott, Ariz. Lic. real estate agt., Ariz., cert. motel mgr. Real estate agt., Prescott, Ariz., 1962-64; sec. to mgr. Kon Tiki Hotel, Phoenix, 1964-65; draftsman Goleta Water Dist., Calif., 1965-68; asst. to v.p. rsch. and design House of Mosaics, Santa Barbara, Calif., 1968-69; exec. chmn. poster design, dept. music U. Calif.-Santa Barbara, 1969-74; v.p. Colorform West, Inc., Santa Barbara, 1974-75; pres. Leeds Miniatures, Inc., Lincoln City, Oreg., 1975-86, Leed's Co., Inc., 1989—; cert. instr. Technologies for Creating, DMA, Inc., 1986—; lamp and silk screen designer Colorform West, Inc.; ind. assoc. The Environ. Network. Illustrator: Just A Story by Gustav Coenod, 1964. Active Global Vols., 1993, Oceanic Soc. Expeditions, 1993. Mem. Hobby Industry Am., Miniatures Industry Assn. Am., Nat. Assn. Female Execs., Eugene C. of C., Eugene Bus. and Profl. Women (cert. practitioner neuro-linguistic programming, trainer values realization). Clubs: Assn. Humanistic Psychology, Internat. New Thought Alliance, Assn. Transpersonal Psychology. Home: 2290 Arthur Ct Eugene OR 97405-1525

LEEDS, NANCY BRECKER, sculptor, lyricist; b. N.Y.C., Dec. 22, 1924; d. Louis Julius and Dorothy (Faggen) Brecker; m. Richard Henry Leeds, May 9, 1945; children: Douglas Becker, Constance Leeds Bennett. BA, Pine Manor Coll., 1944. Pres. Roseland Ballroom, N.Y.C., 1977-81. One-woman shows include Andrew Crispo Gallery, N.Y.C., 1979, Jeannette McIntyre Gallery Fine Arts, Palm Springs, Calif., 1987-88; exhibited in group shows at Bond St. Gallery, Great Neck, N.Y., Gallery Ranieri, N.Y.C., 1978, Country Art Gallery, 1984, Nature Conservatory Show, Country Art Gallery, 1985, Bonwit Teller, Manhasset, N.Y., 1985, Jeanette C. McIntyre Gallery, Palm Springs, Calif., 1987, The Empire Collection, N.Y.C., 1988, 89, Nassau County Mus. of Art, 1992, Chrysalis, East Hampton, 1998, Christmas Miniature Art Show at Chelsea, Nassau County Mus. of Art "Dance Dance", 2000; represented in permanent collections at New Orleans Mus. Art; writer lyrics for musical Great Scot, 1965, score for Scrooge Musical Theatre of Ariz., 1989; lyricist for popular music. Trustee Floating Hosp., N.Y.C., 1975—, v.p.; mem. Upper Brookville (L.I., N.Y.) Planning Bd., 2000-01. Mem. ASCAP, Dramatist Guild, Songwriters Guild.

LEEDS, NORMA STERNE, chemistry educator; b. N.Y.C. d. Harry Archer and Teenie Sterne; m. Morton W. Leeds, Feb. 4, 1945; 1 child, Valerie Ann. PhD, Rutgers U., 1950. Rsch. assoc. Sloan Kettering Inst. Cancer Rsch., N.Y.C., 1950-55; supr. Gen. Aniline & Film, Linden, N.J., 1955-58; asst. prof. Fairleigh Dickinson U., Florham Park, 1959-62; assoc. prof. Caldwell (N.J.) Coll. for Women, 1962-64; from assoc. prof. to prof. chemistry Kean Univ., Union, N.J., 1964-91, chair dept. chemistry, 1970-72, prof. emeritus, 1991—. Contbr. articles to profl.jours.; editor: Opera at Florham Assn., 1992—97. Cottrell grantee Rutgers U., 1946-48; Univ. Rsch. Coun. fellow Rutgers U., 1946-48. Mem. Fortnightly Club (chair membership 1993-95), Sigma Xi. Unitarian Universalist. Home: 6 Sunningdale Ct Maplewood NJ 07040-2420 E-mail: normaleeds@yahoo.com.

LEEDS, ROBIN LEIGH, transportation executive; b. Athens, Ohio, Jan. 4, 1942; d. Clarence Thomas and Jean B. (Foster) Flowers; m. John A Cornwell, Oct. 28, 1957 (div. Jan. 1968); children: Michael John, Brian Arthur; m. Barry H. Leeds, Apr. 20, 1968; children: Brett Ashley, Leslie Robin. BS in Edn., Ohio U., 1967. Cultural arts dir. Regional Sch. Dist. # 10, Burlington, Conn., 1978-81; exec. dir. Conn. Sch. Transp. Assn., Newington, 1982—. Exec. sec. N.E. Sch. Transp. Safety Inst., West Hartford, 1987—; regulatory liaison Nat. Sch. Transp. Assn., Alexandria, Va., 2000-; columnist Sch. Transp. News, Redondo Beach, Calif., 2002—; chmn. Conn. Sch. Transp. Safety Commn., 1990—; state del. Nat. Standards Congress, Warrensburg, 1990, 95, 2000; mem. Gov.'s Motor Carrier Adv. Com., Conn., 1989—, Dept. Motor Vehicles Safety Task Force, Conn., 1991-96. Contbr. articles to profl. jours.; mem. adv. bd. Sch. Transp. News, 1994—. Chmn. gifted edn. task force, Regional Sch. Dist., 1976-78; arbitrator Dept. Consumer Protection, Conn., 2002—. Named Contractor of Yr., Sch. Bus Fleet Mag., 1990, Exec. of Yr., Conn. Soc. Assn. Execs., 1993. Mem. Nat. Sch. Transp. Assn., Nat. Assn. Pupil Transp., Nat. Safety Coun., Conn. Soc. Assn. Execs. (Assn. Exec. of Yr. award). Avocation: ballroom dancing. Home: 133 Jerome Ave Burlington CT 06013-2433 Office: Conn Sch Transp Assn 135 Day St Newington CT 06111-1244 E-mail: leeds@costa.necoxmail.com.

LEEDS, SANFORD J., III, financial executive, educator; b. N.Y.C., May 4, 1964; s. Sanford J. and Marion J. Leeds; m. Jennifer E. Leeds, May 18, 1996. BS in Corp. Fin./Investment Analysis, U. Ala., 1986; JD, U. Va., 1989; MBA in Fin., U. Tex., 1995. Bar: Tex.; CFA. Assoc. Jackson & Walker, Dallas, 1989-90; asst. dist. atty. Dallas County Dist. Atty.'s Office, 1990-93; cons. Webb & Shirley, Tulsa, Okla., 1995-96; sr. atty. NASD Regulation, Washington, 1997-98; v.p., portfolio mgr. Trust Co. Okla., Tulsa, 1999-2001; lectr. U. Tex., Austin, 2001—. Adj. instr. fin. U. Tulsa, 1998-2001. Office: U Tex Fin Dept B6600 Austin TX 78712 E-mail: sjleeds@aol.com.

LEEDS, VALERIE ANN, museum curator; b. Summit, N.J., Jan. 22, 1958; d. Morton W. and Norma Leeds. BA in Art History, U. Rochester, 1979; MA in Art History, Syracuse U., 1981; PhD in Am. Art, CUNY, 2000. Curatorial asst. Whitney Mus. Am. Art, N.Y.C., 1982-84; rschr., gallery asst. Spanierman Gallery, 1984-86; curator exhbns. Tampa (Fla.) Mus. Art, 1987-90; cur. 19th and 20th century Am. art Orlando (Fla.) Mus. Art, 1990-96; curatorial cons., 1996—. Adj. curator Am. Art Flint Inst. Arts, Mich., 2000. Author, curator exhbn. and book: My People: The Portraits of Robert Henri, 1994; author exhbn. catalogues: Robert Henri and Santa Fe, 1998, Leon Kroll Revisited, 1998; author, co-curator exhbn.: In The American Spirit: Realism and Impressionism from the Lawrence Collection, 1999; author: Ernest Lawson, 2000, Works from the John and Dolores Beck Collection, 2000. CUNY grantee, 2000; CUNY Am. art fellow, 1999—. Home: 728 Sergeantsville Rd Stockton NJ 08559

LEEDS-HORWITZ, SUSAN BETH, school system administrator, speech-language pathology educator; b. L.A., Mar. 14, 1950; d. Robert Herbert and Lee (Weiss) Leeds; m. Stanley Martin Horwitz, Nov. 28, 1975; 1 child, Brian David. BA, Calif. State U., Northridge, 1971; MEd, U. S.C., 1973; adminstrv. credential, U. LaVerne, 1984. Itinerant speech pathologist L.A. City Schs., 1973-74; severe lang. disorders tchr. L.A. County Bd. Edn., Downey, Calif., 1974-88; tchr. on spl. assignment Santa Clarita Valley Spl. Edn. Local Plan Area, Newhall, 1986-88; coord. spl. programs, testing, evaluation and migrant edn. Castaic (Calif.) Union Sch. Dist., 1988-94, adminstr., 1988-1994; ednl. cons. Richmond, Calif., 1994-95; coord. grants and project devel. Glendale (Calif.) Unified Sch. Dist., 1995-2000; dir. spl. projects, grants and tech. Beverly Hills (Calif.) Unified Sch. Dist., 2000—. Adj. prof. Nat. U., 1998—. Author: Project Próspero: A Traditional Bilingual Education Program for Grades 2-8, 1991, Project TEAM: Together Everyone Achieves More Comprehensive School Program, 1995, Hoover-Keppel-Keppel Healthy Start Family Resource Center, 1996, Volunteers for Youth: From the Community for the Community, 1996, FRANKLIN: Focusing on Educational Restructuring and Needs of Kids and Their Families Through Upgraded Learning and Instruction with a Neighborhood Learning Center, 1996, SB1510 School-Based Educational Technology Program, Daily High School, 1996, Project Y.E.S. (Youth Enrichment Services), 1997, Pathway to Teaching, 1997, Glendale High School Healthy Start Family Resource Center, 1998, Opening New Doors to Careers, After School Learning and Safe Neighborhoods Partnership, 2000. Grantee student enhancement program Kaiser-Permanente Community Svcs., 1992, Opening Need Doors to Careers, School-to-Career grantee Burbank, Glendale and La Cañada Sch. Dists., 1997, Tobacco Use Prevention Edn. grantee, 1998, 2002. Mem. ASCD, Am. Speech Lang and Hearing Assn. (cert.), So. Calif. Assn. Alumnae Panhellenic (pres. 1993-94), Down Syndrome Congress, Assn. Calif. Sch. Adminstrs., San Fernando Valley Panhellenic Assn. (rep. 1976-96, pres. 1993-95), Glendale Schs. Mgmt. Assn., Santa Clarita Valley C. of C. (edn. com., anti-gang com., tchr. tribute com.), Delta Kappa Gamma, Alpha Xi Delta (Edna Epperson Brinkman award 1985), Phi Delta Kappa, Delta Rho Bldg. Corp. of Alpha Xi Delta (pres. 1996—). Office: 255 S Lasky Dr Beverly Hills CA 90212-3644 Fax: 310-551-5163. E-mail: shorwitz@bhusd.k12.ca.us.

LEEDY, DANIEL LONEY, retired ecologist; b. Butler, Ohio, Feb. 17, 1912; s. Charles Monroe and Bernice Camilla (Loney) L.; m. Barbara E. Sturges, Nov. 25, 1945 (dec. Mar. 12, 1988); children: Robert Raymond, Kathleen Eleanor; m. Virginia Lee Bittenbender, Sept. 22, 1989. AB with honors, Miami U., Oxford, Ohio, 1934, B.Sc., 1935; M.Sc., Ohio State U., 1938, PhD, 1940. Asst. geology and zoology depts. Miami U., 1933-35; instr. wildlife mgmt. Ohio State U., 1940-42; leader Ohio Coop. Wildlife Research Unit, 1945-48; biologist charge coop. wildlife research units U.S. Fish and Wildlife Service, Washington, 1949-57; mem. biol. sci. com. Dept. Agr. Grad. Sch., 1950-75; pres. Wildlife Soc., 1952, exec. sec., 1953-57; chief br. wildlife research U.S. Fish and Wildlife Service, 1957-63; chief div. research Bur. Outdoor Recreation, Dept. Interior, 1963-65; water resources research scientist Office Water Resources Research, 1965-74; ret., 1974; sr. scientist Nat. Inst. Urban Wildlife, Columbia, Md., 1975-95. Contbr. over 100 articles to profl. publs. Served to capt. USAAF, 1942-45. Decorated Bronze medal; recipient cert. of merit Nash Conservation awards program, 1953, Am. Motors Conservation award, 1958, U.S. Dept. Interior Disting. Svc. award, 1972, Disting. Alumni award Ohio State U., 1975, Daniel L. Leedy Urban Wildlife Conservation award established in his honor Nat. Inst. Urban Wildlife, 1985. Fellow AAAS; mem. Wildlife Soc. (hon., Aldo Leopold award for disting. service to wildlife conservation 1983), Am. Ornithologists Union (elective mem.), Wilson Ornithol. Soc., Am. Fisheries Soc., Sigma Xi. Clubs: Field Biologists, Cosmos (Washington). Home: 12401 Ellen Ct Silver Spring MD 20904-2905

LEEDY, EMILY L. FOSTER (MRS. WILLIAM N. LEEDY), retired education educator, consultant; b. Jackson, Ohio, Sept. 24, 1921; d. Raymond S. and Grace (Garrett) Foster; MEd, Ohio U., 1957; postgrad. Ohio State U., 1956, Mich. State U., 1958-59, Case Western Res. U., 1963-65; m. William N. Leedy, Jan. 1, 1943; 1 son, Dwight A. tchr. Frankfort (Ohio) schs., 1941-46, Ross County Schs., Chillicothe, Ohio, 1948-53; elem. and supervising tchr. Chillicothe City Schs., 1953-56; dean of girls, secondary tchr. Berea City Schs., 1956-57; vis. tchr. Parma City Schs., 1957-59; counselor Homewood-Flossmoor High Sch., Flossmoor, Ill., 1959-60; teaching fellow Ohio U., 1960-62; asst. prof. edn., 1962-64; assoc. prof., counselor Cuyahoga Community Coll., 1964-66; dean of women Cleve. State U., 1966-67, assoc. dean student affairs, 1967-69; guidance dir. Cathedral Latin Sch., 1969-71; dir. women's service div. Ohio Bur. Employment Svcs., 1971-83; cons. in edn., 1983-87. Mem. adv. com. S.W. Community Info. Svc., 1959-60; youth com. S.W. YWCA, 1963-70, chmn., 1964-70, bd. mgmt., 1964-70; group svcs. coun. Cleve. Welfare Fedn., 1964-66; chmn. Met. YWCA Youth Program study com., 1966, bd. dirs., 1966-72, v.p., 1967-68; chmn. adv. coun. Ohio State U. Sch. Home Econs., 1977-80, chmn., 1978-80. Named Cleve. area Woman of Achievement, 1969; named to Ohio Women's Hall of Fame, 1979, Chillicothe Ross Women's Hall of Fame, 1988; recipient Outstanding Contbn. special award Nat. Assn. Commns. for Women, 1983, Meritorious Svc. award Nat. Assn. Women Deans, Adminstrs. and Counselors, 1984. Mem. AAUW (Berea-Parma br. v.p. 1995-97), Am., Northeastern Ohio (sec. 1958-59, exec. com. 1963-64, pub. rel. chmn. 1962-64, newsletter chmn., editor 1963-64, del. nat. assembly 1959-63) personnel and guidance assns., LWV, Am. Assn. Retired Persons (Ohio women's initiative spokesperson 1987-89, state legis. com. 1989-90, AARP/VOTE state coord. Ohio 1990-94), Nat. Assn. Women Deans and Counselors (publs. com. 1967-69, profl. employment practices com. 1980-82, Meritorious Svc. award 1984), Ohio (program chmn. 1967, editor Newsletter 1968-71), Cleve. Counselors Assn. (pres. 1966), Zonta Internat. (exec. bd. 1968-70, treas. 1970-72, chmn. dist. V Status of Women 1980-81), Nat. Assn. Commns. for Women (dir. 1980-81, sec. 1981-83), Rio Grande Coll. Alumni Assn. (Atwood Achievement award 1975), Bus. and Profl. Women's Club (Nike award 1973, Berea treas. 1996-97), Ohio Retired Tchrs. Assn., Svc. Corps of Retired Execs. Delta Kappa Gamma, Women's City Club (Cleve.). Home: 580 Lindberg Blvd Berea OH 44017-1418 Office: 699 Rocky Rd Chillicothe OH 45601-9469

LEEGE, DAVID CALHOUN, political scientist, educator; b. Elkhart, Ind., May 18, 1937; s. Harold Martin and Nellie Josephine (Bliss) L.; m. Patricia Ann Schad, June 8, 1963; children— David McChesney, Lissa Maria, Kurt Johannes BA, Valparaiso U., 1959; postgrad., U. Chgo., 1959-60; PhD, Ind. U., 1965. Instr. social sci. Concordia Coll., River Forest, Ill., 1962-64; asst. prof. polit. sci., dir. pub. opinion survey unit U. Mo., Columbia, 1964-68; assoc. prof., dir. survey research center SUNY, Buffalo, 1968-70; assoc. prof. U. Ill., Chgo., 1970-72, prof., 1972-76, head dept., 1972-73; prof. govt. and internat. studies U. Notre Dame, Ind., 1976—, dir. center for study of contemporary society, 1976-85, dir. London program, 1982, dir. program for research on religion, church and society, 1984—; dir. Hesburgh Program in Pub. Service, 1987-92. Program dir. for polit. sci. NSF, 1974-76; mem. vis. faculty York U., Toronto, Ont., Can., 1970, U. Mich., 1971, 73, U. Leuven, Belgium, 1980, Cath. U. Am., 1985-86, U. Ariz., 2001, 02. Author: (with Wayne Francis) Political Research, 1974, (with Lyman Kellstedt) Rediscovering the Religious Factor in American Politics, 1993, (with K. Wald, B. Krueger and P. Mueller) The Politics of Cultural Differences, 2002; editor: The Missouri Poll, 1965-68, (with Joseph Gremillion) The Notre Dame Study of Catholic Parish Life Report Series, 1984-89; contbr. articles to profl. jours. Mem. bd. overseers Am. Nat. Election Studies, 1991-99, chair, 1994-97; mem. coun. ICPSR, 1966-69; bd. dirs. Luth. Music Program, Inc. Recipient numerous profl. prizes. Mem.: Midwest Polit. Sci. Assn. (chair nominating com., coun., program co-chair), Am. Polit. Sci. Assn. (sect. officer, program com., chmn. task force). Lutheran. Office: U Notre Dame Dept Govt Notre Dame IN 46556-0368 Home: 2155 W Via Nuevo Leon Green Valley AZ 85614

LEEK, JAY WILBUR, management consultant; b. Albany, Ind., Apr. 24, 1928; s. Cecil and Hazel (Lindley) Leek; m. Lauravne M. DelaHunt, Sept. 22, 2001; children from previous marriage: Roderick Jay, Stacy LeAnn, Scott Lee, Timothy Lane, Debra Jan, Marilynn Sue, James Jay. BS in Indsl. Engring., Pacific Western, 1969, MS in Mgmt., 1976, D in Bus. Adminstrn., 1980. Registered profl. engr., Calif. Mgr. Nutone, Inc., Cin., 1951-53, Bulova Watch Co., N.Y.C., 1953-59, Martin Marietta Corp., Orlando, Fla., 1959-75; v.p. Northrop Corp., L.A., 1975-80; pres., COO Philip Crosby Assocs., Winter Park, Fla., 1980-87, also bd. dirs.; mgmt. cons., Ft. Myers, 1987-91; pres., CEO Carchi-Resources, Inc., Ocala, Fla. Bd. dirs. So. Bank, Longwood, Fla., Electro-World, Orlando. Author: Workmanship Standards, 1974; co-author: (with others) AMA Management Handbook, 1986, Quality Management Handbook, 1986. Trustee Orlando Sports Inc., 1985-87, Fla. State Univ. Found., Tallahassee, 1986-96; bd. dirs. Fla. Citrus Sports Assn., Orlando,

1984-90. With USN, 1944-46. Recipient Academician award Internat. Acad. for Quality, Grobenzell, Fed. Republic Germany, 1985; named to Wall of Fame, Am. Mgmt. Assn., 1979. Fellow: Am. Soc. Quality Control (pres. 1980—81); mem.: Sapphire Lakes Country Club, Sawgrass Country Club, Ponte Vedra Beach Country Club, Shriners, Masons. Republican. Home: 951 Spinnakers Reach Dr Ponte Vedra Beach FL 32082 E-mail: bearj824@aol.com.

LEEKLEY, JOHN ROBERT, lawyer; b. Phila., Aug. 27, 1943; s. Thomas Briggs and Dorothy (O'Hora) L.; m. Karen Kristin Myers, Aug. 28, 1965 (dec. Mar. 1997); children: John Thomas, Michael Dennis; m. Gerry Lee Gildner, June 5, 1999. BA, Boston Coll., 1965; LLB, Columbia U., 1968. Bar: N.Y. 1968, Mich. 1976. Assoc. Curtis, Mallet-Prevost, Colt & Mosle, N.Y.C., 1968-69, Davis Polk & Wardwell, N.Y.C., 1969-76; asst. corp. counsel Masco Corp., Taylor, Mich., 1976-77, corp. counsel, 1977-79, v.p., corp. counsel, 1979-88, v.p., gen. counsel, 1988-96, sr. v.p., gen. counsel, 1996—. Bd. visitors Columbia U. Law Sch., N.Y.C., 1994-96; mem. Freedom Twp. Bd. Tax Appeals, 1984-85. Mem. ABA (com. long range issues affecting bus. practice 1976-96), Mich. State Bar Assn. Democrat. Roman Catholic. Avocations: Percheron horse breeding, hunting, fishing, outdoor activities. Office: Masco Corp 21001 Van Born Rd Taylor MI 48180-1300

LEELAND, STEVEN BRIAN, electronics engineer; b. Tampa, Fla., Dec. 27, 1951; s. N. Stanford and Shirley Mae (Bahner) L.; m. Karen Frances Hayes, Dec. 20, 1980; children: Crystal Mary, April Marie. BSEE, MSEE magna cum laude, U. South Fla., 1976. Registered profl. engr., Ariz. Engr. Bendix Avionics, Ft. Lauderdale, Fla., 1976-77; prin. engr., instr. Sperry Avionics, Phoenix, 1977-84; prin. staff engr. Motorola Govt. Electronics Group, Scottsdale, Ariz., 1984-88; engring. fellow, mgr. dept. software engring. Fairchild Data Corp., 1988-98; prin. staff engr. Teledesic Sys. Arch., Motorola Space Sys. Tech. Group, 1998-99; contractor Dantel, Fresno, Calif., 1999—. Cons. Motorola Govt. Electronics Group, 1991. Patentee systolic array, 1990; contbr. articles to profl. jours. Mem. IEEE (Phoenix chpt. Computer Soc. treas. 1978-79, sec. 1979-80, chmn. 1980-81, 81-82), Tau Beta Pi, Pi Mu Epsilon, Phi Kappa Phi, Omicron Delta Kappa, Themis. Adventist. Avocations: chess, computers, bible study, exercise, health. Home: 10351 E Sharon Dr Scottsdale AZ 85260-9000 Office: Dantel PO Box 55013 2991 N Argyle Ave Fresno CA 93747-5013 E-mail: steven.leeland@worldnet.att.net.

LEEMAN, SUSAN EPSTEIN, neuroscientist, educator; b. Chgo., May 9, 1930; d. Samuel and Dora (Gubernikoff) Epstein; m. Cavin Leeman (div.); children: Eve, Raphael, Jennifer. BA, Goucher Coll., 1951; MA, Radcliffe Coll., 1954, PhD, 1958; DS (hon.), SUNY, Utica, 1992; hon. degree, Goucher Coll., 1993. Instr. Harvard Med. Sch., Boston, 1958-59; postdoctoral fellow Brandeis U., Waltham, Mass., 1959-62, 62-66; rsch. assoc., adj. ast. prof., asst. rsch. prof. Brandeis U., 1966-68, 68-71; asst. prof. Harvard Med. Sch., 1972-73, assoc. prof., 1973-80; prof. U. Mass. Med. Ctr., Worcester, 1980-92, dir. interdept. neurosci. program, 1984-92; prof. dept. pharmacology Boston U. Sch. Medicine, 1992—. Burroughs Wellcome vis. prof. U.Ky., 1992. Fogarty scholar NAS, 1994; recipient Women in Sci. award N.Y. Acad., 1995. Mem. NAS (197th Lilly lectr. 1994, Fred Conrad Koch award 1994, Women in Sci. award 1995), Am. Acad. Arts and Scis. (Isadore Rosenberg lectr. 1999). Office: Boston U Sch Medicine Dept Pharmacology 715 Albany St # R-616 Boston MA 02118-2526

LEE-MCCARTER, JEANETTE, social services administrator; b. Terrell, Tex., Mar. 9, 1968; d. Louise and Garfield Lee; m. James Earl McCarter; children: Joshua Nixon, Jordan McCarter. AA, Ranger Jr. Coll., 1988; BA, Lamar U., 1991. Electronic documentation leader Alcatel, Richardson, Tex., 1996—99; project mgr. Allegiance telecom, Dallas, 2000—02. Big sister Big Bros. and Sisters of Dallas, 1998—2002; foster parent. Democrat. Avocation: dance, running. Office: Allegiance Telecom Dallas United States

LEEPA, ALLEN, artist, educator; b. N.Y.C., Jan. 9, 1919; s. Harvey and Esther (Gentle) L. Student (scholar), The New Bauhaus Sch., 1937-38; scholar, Hans Hofmann Sch., 1938-39; BS, Columbia U., 1942, MA (scholar), 1948, Ed.D., 1960. Art instr. Hull Sch., Chgo., 1937-38, Bklyn. Art Ctr., 1939-40, 99, Met. Mus., N.Y.C., 1940-41, St. Marks Center, N.Y.C., 1941-42; draftsman Acrotorque Co., Conn., 1942, Glen Martin Aircraft, N.Y.C., 1942-44; prof. art Mich. State U., 1945-84, ret. prof. emeritus. Mem. Leepa Gallery of Fine Art, Tarpon Springs, Fla., 1987-90. Author: The Challenge of Modern Art, 1949, 95, Abraham Rattner, 1974; contbr.: (anthologies) The New Art, 1966, 68, The Humanitites in Contemporary Life, 1960, Minimal Art; art editor: The Centennial Rev. Arts and Scis. Jour., 1959-62; one man shows Artists Gallery, N.Y.C., 1953, La Cours D'Ingres, Paris, 1961, Artists Mart, Detroit, 1969, Duke U., 1981; group shows include Mus. Modern Art, N.Y.C., 1953, VII Bienal, São Paulo, Brazil, 1963, Prado Mus., Madrid, Spain, 1956, Detroit Inst. Arts, 1948, 50, 56, 80, Pa. Acad. Fine Arts, 1951, 63; represented in permanent collections Mich. State U., Grand Rapids (Mich.) Mus., South Bend (Ind.) Mus.; lifetime work Tampa Mus. Fine Art, Leepa/Rattner Mus. Fine Arts St. Petersburg (Fla.) Jr. Coll. Fulbright award to Paris, 1950-51; Ford Found. grantee Brazil, 1970; recipient numerous prizes for paintings including: 1st prize statewide mural competition, Mich., 1983; 1st prize abstract painting Guild Hall Mus., East Hampton, N.Y., 1985 Mem. Mich. Acad. Arts, Scis., Letters. E-mail: lpwac@aol.com.

LEEPER, HAROLD HARRIS, arbitrator; b. Kansas City, Mo., July 29, 1916; s. Truman Elmer and Bess Mayburn (Harris) L.; m. Maribelle Potts, Sept. 21, 1941; children: Robert Chester, Marilyn Anne. BSBA, U. Mo., 1937; JD, Oklahoma City U., 1956. Bar: Okla. 1957, U.S. Supreme Ct. 1969. Regional pers. officer VA, Oklahoma City, 1946-52; state adminstrv. officer IRS, 1952-56; pers. officer FAA, 1956-63, from hearing officer to chief hearing officer Washington, 1963-71; adminstrv. law judge Social Security Adminstrn., Dallas, 1971-73; freelance labor mgmt. arbitrator, 1974—. Chmn. pers. com. Wesley Rankin Cmty. Ctr., Dallas, 1989—95; pres. Way Back House, Inc., 1975—77, bd. dirs., 1977—80; scoutmaster Boy Scouts Am., S.D., Okla., Va. 1st lt. U.S. Army, 1943—46, lt. col. USAR. Mem. Fed. Bar Assn. (pres. D.C. chpt. 1982-83), Nat. Acad. Arbitrators (regional chmn. 1990-92), Mil. Order World Wars (comdr. D.C. chpt. 1969-70), Mason, Shriner. Democrat. Methodist. Avocations: golf, sailing, flying, church activities.

LEEPER, RAMON JOE, physicist; b. Princeton, Mo., Apr. 1, 1948; s. Joe Edd and Jeanne (Gaul) Leeper; m. Sumiko Yasuda, Dec. 21, 1976; 1 child Joe Eric. BS, MIT, 1970; PhD, Iowa State U., 1975. Rsch. assoc. Ames (Iowa) Lab. U.S. Dept. Energy, 1975-76; mem. tech. staff Sandia Nat. Labs., Albuquerque, 1976-86, dept. mgr. diagnostics and target physics dept., 1986—. Guest scientist Argonne Nat. Lab., Ill., 1971—76; invited lectr. NATO Advanced Study Inst., Italy, 1983, Internat. Sch. Plasma Physics, Italy, 2001. Contbr. articles to profl. jours. Recipient Outstanding Tchg. award, Iowa State U., 1973; fellow NDEA, 1971—73. Mem.: IEEE (session chmn. 1984), Am. Phys. Soc. (chmn. high temperature plasma diagnostics conf. 1992), Sigma Xi. Republican. Achievements include patents in field. Home: 6905 Rosewood Rd NE Albuquerque NM 87111-1021 Office: Diagnostics & Target Physics Dept 1677 Sandia Nat Labs Albuquerque NM 87185

LEERABHANDH, MARJORIE BRAVO, chemist, educator; b. Negros Occidental, Philippines; came to U.S., 1982. d. Rustico Ginese and Monica Tolosa (Tolosa) Bravo; m. Sunai Leerabhandh, Oct. 2, 1986. BS in chemistry cum laude, U. Santo Tomas, 1979; PhD in chemistry, U. So. Calif., 1990; MBA in Fin., Calif. Luth. U., 2000. Rsch. teaching asst. chem. dept. U. So. Calif., L.A., 1984-89; faculty mem. chem. dept. Moorpark (Calif.) Coll., 1992—; project mgr. Med. Analysis Sys., Inc., Camarillo, Calif., 1989-93, rsch. team leader, 1993-94, mgr. rsch. and devel., 1994-2000, dir. tech. product support, interim dir. logistics, 2000—. Author: Nitrogen Tixation Research Progress, 1985, Nitrogen Fixation: 100 Years After, 1988; contbr. articles to profl. jours. Mem. Am. Chem. Soc., Am. Assn. for Clinical Chem., Chem. Soc. U. Santo Tomas Manila (pres., 1979). Achievements include patents for Fructosamine Reagent and Calibrator Systems, Stabilization of Functional Proteins. Office: Med Analysis Sys Inc 5300 Adolfo Rd Camarillo CA 93012-8661

LEES, ALFRED WILLIAM, writer, former magazine editor; b. Kansas City, Kans., June 12, 1926; s. Alfred Whitaker and Blanche (Pontius) L. BA, Stanford U., 1950. Editor, writer Home Craftsman, N.Y.C., 1953-59, Family Handyman, 1960, Popular Sci., N.Y.C., 1960-62, sr. editor, writer, 1967-71, group editor, reader activities, 1972-88; editor, writer Popular Mechanics, 1962-66; home care columnist Cosmopolitan, 1965-67; dir., judge nat. ann. design competition Am. Plywood Assn., Tacoma, 1976-86; pres. Nat. Assn. Home and Workshop Writers, 1990-92. Author: Leisure Homes, 1980, 67 Prizewinning Plywood Projects, 1984; co-author: Wood Finishing and Painting, 1955, DIY Projects for Your Own Backyard, 1978, 2d edit., 1984, What's Wrong with My Car?, 1990, Decks and Sunspaces, 1991, Longtime Companions, 1999. With USAAF, 1944-45. Mem. Delaware Valley Arts Alliance, Dutch Treat Club, Traveler's Century Club. Avocations: world travel, photography. Home: 140 Nassau St Apt 9B New York NY 10038-1526

LEES, ANDREW, information technology executive; married; 2 children. BS in Computer Sci., Bradford U., Eng. Leader tech. consulting group, dir. mktg. offices systems Hewlett-Packard Co. U.K. subs.; product mgr. Microsoft U.K. subs., 1990, various pos., to dir. emerging mkts. group, 1990—2000; corp. v.p., U.S. mktg., sales and ptnrs. Microsoft, Redmond, Wash., 2000—. Avocation: travel. Office: Microsoft One Microsoft Way Redmond WA 98052-6399*

LEES, FRANCIS ANTHONY, economics educator; b. Bklyn., Jan. 19, 1931; s. Roy A. and Mary (Ozustowicz) L.; m. Kathryn V. Murphy, June 6, 1959; children— Veronica Ann, Francis, Daniel, Jeannette Marie. BA, Bklyn. Coll., 1952; MA, St. Louis U., 1953; PhD, NYU, 1961. Instr. Fordham U., N.Y.C., 1956-60; asst. prof. St. Johns U., Jamaica, N.Y., 1960-61; fin. analyst Dominick & Dominick, N.Y.C., 1961-62; assoc. prof. St. John's U., 1962-68, prof., 1968—. Cons. Conf. Bd., 1979-86, U.S. Govt., 1985 financial analyst, econ. cons. Dominick & Dominick, N.Y.C., 1961-62, Internat. Report, 1982-84, CIA, 1985-86. Author: Capital Controls and the US Balance of Payments, 1968, International Banking and Finance, 1974, International Financial Markets, 1975, Foreign Banking and Investment in the United States, 1976, Economic and Political Development of the Sudan, 1977, International Lending, Risk, and the Euromarkets, 1979, Foreign Multinational Investment in the U.S., 1986, Banking and Financial Deepening in Brazil, 1990, Global Finance, 1995, 98, Foreign Participation in China's Banking and Securities Markets, 1996, China Superpower, 1997; founder, co-editor Jour. Emerging Markets, 1996—; contbr. articles to profl. jours. Served with AUS, 1953-56. Am. Bankers Assn. Summer Research fellow, 1969; Fulbright research scholar, 1987-88. Home: 14 Hunting Hill Rd Woodbury NY 11797-1404 Office: St Johns U Grand Central And Utopia Pkwy Jamaica NY 11439-0001

LEES, MARJORIE BERMAN, biochemist, neuroscientist; b. N.Y.C., Mar. 17, 1923; d. Isadore I. and Ruth (Rogalsky) Berman; m. Sidney Lees, Sept. 17, 1946; children: David E., Andrew, Eliot. BA, Hunter Coll., 1943; MS, U. Chgo., 1945; PhD, Harvard U., Radcliffe Coll., 1951. Assoc. biochemist, asst. biochemist McLean Hosp., Belmont, Mass., 1953-62; rsch. assoc. Darmouth Med. Sch., Hanover, N.H., 1962-66; assoc. biochemist McLean Hosp., Belmont, 1966-76; prin. and sr. rsch. assoc. Harvard Med. Sch., Boston, 1966-85; biomed. scientist E.K. Shriver Ctr., Waltham, Mass., 1976-98; prof. biochemistry (neurology) Harvard Med. Sch., Boston, 1985-94, prof. emerita, 1994—; biochemist Mass. Gen. Hosp., 1976-98; assoc. dir. biochemistry E.K. Shriver Ctr., Waltham, 1982-90, dir. biochemistry, 1990-93, assoc. dir. mental retardation rsch. ctr., 1994-97, sr. biomed. sci., 1998—; sr. scientist U. Mass. Med. Sch., 1999. Mem. adv. com. biomed. and behavioral rsch. NASA/NIH, 1993—; mem. sci. adv. com. Nat. Multiple Sclerosis Soc., 1988-93. Chief editor Jour. of Neurochemistry, 1986-90; author (with others) books; contbr. articles to profl. jours. Mem. adv. coun. Nat. Inst. Neurological Disorders, Bethesda, Md., 1979-82; chmn. Radcliffe Grad. Soc., Cambridge, Mass., 1978-80. Predoctoral fellow USPHS, 1947-50, postdoctoral fellow Am. Cancer Soc., 1951-53; Javits Neurosci. grantee NIH, 1983-90, 91-97, prin. grantee NIH, 1962-98; named to Hunter Coll. Hall of Fame, 1982. Mem. Am. Soc. Biochemistry and Molecular Biology, Internat. Soc. Neurochemistry, Am. Soc. Neurochemistry (treas. 1975-81, pres. 1983-85), Soc. for Neurosci., Am. Assn. Neuropathology (assoc.), Internat. Soc. Neuroimmunology, N.Y. Acad. Scis., Am. Women in Sci., Phi Beta Kappa. Office: Shriver Ctr U Mass Med Sch Biomed Sci Dept 200 Trapelo Rd Waltham MA 02452-6332 E-mail: marjorie.lees@umassmed.edu.

LEES, WILLIAM GLENWOOD, finance executive, retail executive; b. Flat River, Mo., Nov. 18, 1916; m. Mary Louise Meier, Aug. 22, 1937; children: Graham (dec.), Van P.G. Grad. high sch., Flat River, 1934. Office clk. Schramm Grocery Co., Flat River, 1934-36; asst. mgr. Wetterau Grocery Co., Desloge, Mo., 1936-39; owner Lees Food Market, Flat River, 1939-48, Lees Tom Boy Store, Farmington, Mo., 1948-55; pres. Lees Shopping Ctr. Inc., 1955-80, So. Acceptance Corp., Inc., Farmington, 1961-98; ret., 1998; pres. Lees Home Furnishings Inc., Farmington, 1980—. Pres. Presbyn. Home for Children, Farmington, 1958-70; v.p. Camp Penuel, Inc., Ironton, Mo., 1977—; elder Presbyn. Ch., Farmington, 1958-70, Penuel Fellowship,Ironton, 1977—. With U.S. Army, 1943-46. Mem. C. of C. (bd. dirs. 1956-58), Masons, Shriners (pres. 1963). Republican. Avocations: golf, travel. Home: 18 Airline Dr Farmington MO 63640-1106

LEE-SMITH, HUGHIE, artist, educator; b. Eustis, Fla., Sept. 20, 1915; s. Luther and Alice (Williams) Smith; m. Mabel Louise Everett, 1940 (div. 1953); 1 child, Christina; m. Helen Nebraska, 1965 (div. 1974); m. Patricia Thomas-Ferry, 1978. Student, Art Sch. of Detroit Soc. Arts and Crafts, 1934-35; grad., Cleve. Inst. Art, 1938; BS, Wayne State U., 1953; DFA (hon.), Md. Inst. Coll. Art, 1995. Instr. painting Grosse Pointe War Meml., Mich., 1956-66, Studio-on-the-Canal, Princeton, N.J., 1959-64; art tchr. Princeton Country Day Sch., 1964-65; artist-in-residence Howard U., 1969-71; instr. painting Art Students League, N.Y.C., 1972-87, ret., 1987. Adj. prof. Trenton State Coll., 1972-73 One-man shows include Detroit Artists Market, Howard U. Gallery, Washington, Grand Central Art Galleries, N.Y.C., Janet Nessler Gallery, N.Y.C., U. Chgo., June Kelly Gallery, N.Y.C., Butler Inst. Am. Art, Youngstown, Ohio, Chgo. Cultural Ctr., Greenville (S.C.) Mus. Art, Ogunquit (Maine) Mus. Am. Art, Pensacola (Fla.) Mus., Appleton Mus., Ocala, Fla., others; exhibited group shows Cleve. Mus. Art, Detroit Inst. Arts, Butler Inst. Am. Art, Youngstown, Bklyn. Mus., Wadsworth Atheneum, Boston Mus., San Francisco Mus., Mus. Modern Art, Whitney Mus., Am. Acad, and Inst. Arts and Letters, N.Y.; represented in permanent collections Met. Mus., Phila. Mus., Detroit Inst. Arts, Parrish Mus., Southampton, L.I., N.J. State Mus., Standard Oil of Ohio, AT&T, Wadsworth Atheneum, U. Mich., Wayne State U., Schomburg Coll., N.Y.C., Howard U., Nat. Mus. Am Art, U.S. Navy Art Ctr., Chase Manhattan Bank, N.Y.C., Forbes Mag. Collection, N.Y.C., Kidder & Peabody Co., N.Y.C., Mus. Internat. Art, Sofia, Bulgaria, Century Assn., N.Y.C., Lagos (Nigeria) Mus. With USN, 1944-45. Recipient Thomas B. Clark prize NAD, 1959, prize Allied Artists Am., 1958, Emily Lowe award, 1957, Founders prize Detroit Inst. Arts, 1953, cert. of commendation USN, 1974, Art Achievement award Wayne State U., Key to the City of Hartford (Conn.) award, Ranger Fund purchase award NAD, 1977, Audubon Artist prizes, 1982, 83, 85, 86, Medal of Merit Lotos Club, 1996, Benjamin West Clinedinst Meml. medal Artists Fellowship Inc., 1996, Key to City of Eustis, Fla., 1998, others; named Mich. Painter of Yr. Detroit News, 1953. Mem. Artists Equity Assn. (bd. dirs.), Allied Artists Am., Princeton Art Assn., Mich. Acad. Sci., Arts and Letters, NAD (mem. coun., awards juries), Audubon Artists (pres. 1980-82, exhbn. coord.), Artists Fellowship (trustee, v.p. 1985-88), Century Assn., Lotos Club (N.Y.C.) Home: 11508 Pine Top Ln NE Albuquerque NM 87111-6585

LEESON, JANET CAROLINE TOLLEFSON, cake specialties company executive; b. L'anse, Mich., May 23, 1933; d. Harold Arnold and Sylvia Aino (Makikangas) Tollfeson; children by previous marriage: Warren Scott, Debra Delores; m. Raymond Harry Leeson, May 20, 1961; 1 child, Barry Raymond. Student, Prairie State Coll., 1970-76; master decorator degree, Wilton Sch. Cake Decorating, 1974; grad., Cosmopolitan Sch. Bus., 1980. Mgr. Peak Svc. Cleaners, Chgo., 1959; co-owner Ra-Ja-Lee TV, Harvey, Ill., 1961-66; founder, head fgn. trade dept. Wilton Enterprises, Chgo., 1969-75; tchr. cake decorating J.C. Penney Co., Matteson, Ill., 1975; office mgr. Pat Carpenter Assocs., Highland, Ind., 1975; pres. cake supplies and cake sculpture and decorating co. Leeson's Party Cakes, Inc., Tinley Park, Ill., 1975—. Lectr. and demonstrator cake sculpture and decorating; lectr. small bus. and govt. Sec., Luth. Ch. Women. Active Boy Scouts Am. and Girl Scouts U.S., 1957-63; bd. dirs. Whittier PTA, 1962-70, South Suburban Parkinson's Support Group, 1984-2001; adv. bd. Suburban Parkinson's Support Group, 1993—; active Bremen Twp. Rep. Com. Recipient numerous awards for cake sculpture and decorating, 1970—. Mem. Internat. Cake Exploration Soc. (charter, Outstanding Mem. Ill. 1984), Retail Bakers Am., Chgo. Area Retail Bakers Assn. (1st pl. in regional midwest wedding cake competition 1978, 80, 1st pl. nat. 1982, others), Am. Bus. Women's Assn. (chpt. publicity chmn., hospitality chmn. 1982-83, membership chmn. 1988-90, Woman of Yr. 1986), Ingalls Meml. Hosp. Aux., Lupus Found. Am. Lutheran. Home and Office: 6713 163rd Pl Tinley Park IL 60477-1717

LEESON, LEWIS JOSEPH, research pharmacist, scientist; b. Paterson, N.J., Apr. 26, 1927; s. Alfred Elias and Rose (Sandow) L.; m. Barbara Rothstein, Dec. 20, 1953; children: Suzanne, Erica, Alex. BS in Pharmacy, Rutgers U., Newark, 1950, MS in Pharm. Chemistry, 1954; PhD in Pharm. Chemistry, U. Mich., 1957. Registered pharmacist, N.J., N.Y., Mich. Pharmacist Mack Drug Co., Paterson, N.J., 1950-52, Fried's Drugs, Paterson, 1952-54; lab. asst. Rutgers U. Coll. Pharmacy, Newark, 1952-54, U. Mich., Ann Arbor, 1954-57; rsch. pharmacist, project leader Lederle Labs., Pearl River, N.Y., 1955-67; dir. product R & D, Union Carbide Co., Greenburgh, 1967-69; asst. dir. product R & D, Geigy Pharm., Suffern, 1969-71; dir., sr. dir., sr. rsch. fellow Ciba-Geigy Pharm., Summit, N.J., 1971-84; disting. rsch. fellow Ciba-Geigy Corp., 1984-93, ret., 1993; pres. LJL Assocs. Inc, Pharm. R&D Cons., Montville, N.J., 1993—. Dean Louis W. Busse lectr. U. Wis., 1993; mem. exec. com. USP, 1990—95, N.J. DURC, 1984—89; founder, chief sci. officer Cogent Pharm., 1997—. Editor: Dissolution Technology, 1971; contbr. over 40 articles to profl. jours; patentee in field. Recipient Disting. Alumnus award U. Mich., 1990. Fellow Acad. Pharm. Sci., Am. Assn. Pharm. Scientists; mem. Am. Pharm. Assn., Sigma Xi, Rho Chi, Phi Lambda Upsilon. Jewish. Achievements include 14 patents in field. Home and Office: LJL Assocs Inc 134 Ridge Dr Montville NJ 07045-9473 E-mail: lewisleeson@erols.com.

LEESON, SUSAN M. state supreme court judge; Law clerk U.S. 9th Cir. Ct. of Appeals; Tom. C. Clark judicial fellow U.S. Supreme Ct.; prof. polit. sci., assoc. prof. law Willamette U., Salem, Oreg.; judge Oreg. Ct. Appeals, 1993—98; justice Oreg. Supreme Ct., 1998—. Former mem. Oreg. Criminal Justice Coun., Marion-Polk Local Govt. Boundary Commn. Office: Supreme Ct Bldg 1163 State St Salem OR 97310-1331*

LEESTMA, ROBERT, federal agency administrator, educator; b. Detroit, Oct. 15, 1927; s. Richard and Jeanne (Nivarre) L.; m. Margaret Elizabeth Bell, Aug. 13, 1955 (dec. 1982). AB, U. Mich., 1949, AM, 1951, PhD, 1956. Rsch. teaching asst., cmty. adult edn. program U. Mich., Ann Arbor, 1949-50; tchr. English and social studies Ann Arbor pub. schs., 1950-51; asst. dir. Audio-Visual Edn. Ctr., lectr. sch. edn. U. Mich., 1951-55, assoc. prof., dir. Peace Corps tng. program, 1961-64; ICA edn. and mass. comm. advisor Govt. of Vietnam, Vietnam, 1955-58; edn. adviser Govt. of Thailand, 1958-61; dep. chief edn. div. Bur. Africa, AID, 1964-65; dir. Office Multilateral Policy and Programs, Multilateral Policy Planning Staff, Bur. Ednl. and Cultural Affairs, Dept. State, 1965-67; asst. to asst. sec. edn. for internat. edn. HEW, 1967-68; dir. Inst. Internat. Studies, assoc. commr. internat. edn. U.S. Office Edn., 1968-74, assoc. commr. instl. devel. and internat. edn., 1974-79; dep. dir. planning and implementation Office Edn. for Overseas Dependents, U.S. Dept. Edn., 1980-82; assoc. dir. dissemination and improvement of practice Nat. Inst. Edn., 1982-83, assoc. dir. field initiated and internal studies, 1984-85; dir. U.S. study edn. in Japan, Office Ednl. Rsch. and Improvement Dept. Edn., 1986-89; v.p. internat. programs Am. Assn. State Colls. and Univs., Washington, 1989-91; dir. spl. studies staff U.S. Dept. Edn. Office Ednl. Rsch. and Improvement, 1991-94; also policy advisor Edn. Rsch. and Devel. Bur. AID, 1992-94; interim dir. Nat. Libr. Edn., 1994; edn. cons., 1995—. Mem., chmn. and/or adviser U.S. dels. internat. confs.; U.S. rep., chmn. edn. com. OECD; U.S. rep. governing coun. Internat. Bur. Edn., UNESCO; mem. Indo-U.S. Subcommn. on Edn. and Culture, U.S.-Egyptian Joint Working Group on Edn. and Culture, U.S.-Japan Culcon Edn. Com., U.S. Nat. Commn. for UNESCO; alt. mem. U.S.-Japan Friendship Commn., also Am. panel Joint Culcon Com.; mem. adv. com. Hanna Collection, Hoover Instn., Com. on Edn. and Successor Generation of Atlantic Coun. U.S.; bd. dirs. Pericles Inst., Abraham A. Low Inst. Author, co-author and/or editor books, chpts. and articles in profl. jours., including Japanese Education Today, 1987, Japanese Educational Productivity, 1992. With AUS, 1946-47. Payne scholar U. Mich., 1951-52, Hinsdale scholar, 1953-54. Mem. Am. Ednl. Rsch. Assn., Comparative and Internat. Edn. Soc., Assn. Asian Studies, Phi Delta Kappa. Home: 2712 George Mason Pl Alexandria VA 22305-1620

LEET, MILDRED ROBBINS, corporate executive, consultant; b. N.Y.C., Aug. 9, 1922; d. Samuel Milton and Isabella (Zeitz) Elowsky; m. Louis J. Robbins, Feb. 23, 1941 (dec. 1970); children: Jane, Aileen; m. Glen Leet, Aug. 9, 1974 (dec. 1998). BA, NYU, 1942; LHD (hon.), Coll. Human Svcs., 1988; LLD honoris causa, Marymount Coll., Tarrytown, N.Y., 1991; HHD, Lynn U., 1993; D Humanitarian Svc. (hon.), Norwich U., 1994; DHL, Conn. Coll., 1996. Pres. women's div. United Cerebral Palsy, N.Y.C., 1951-52, bd. dirs., 1953-55; rep. Nat. Coun. Women U.S. at UN, 1957-64, 1st v.p., 1959-64, pres., 1964-68, hon. pres., 1968-70; sec., v.p. conf. group U.S. Nat. Orgns. at UN, 1961-64, 76-78, vice chmn., sec., 1962-64, mem. exec. com., 1961-65, chmn. hospitality info. svc., 1960-66; vice chmn. exec. com. NGO's UN Office Public Info., 1976-78, chmn. ann. conf., 1977; chmn. com. on water, desertification, habitat and environment Conf. NGO's with consultative status with UN/ECOSOC, 1976-77; mem. exec. com. Internat. Coun. Women, 1960-73, v.p., 1970-73; chmn. program planning com., women's com. OEO, 1967-72; chmn. com. on natural disasters N.Am. Com. on Environment, 1973-77; N.Y. State chmn. UN Day, 1975; ptnr. Leet & Leet (cons. women in devel.), 1979—98. Co-founder Trickle Up Program, 1979—, pres., 1991—2000, chair, 2001—02; mem. task force on Africa UN, 1995—. Contbr. articles to profl. jours.; editor UN Calendar & Digest, 1959-64, Measure of Mankind, 1963; editorial bd.: Peace & Change. Co-chmn. Vols. for Stevenson, N.Y.C., 1956; vice chmn. task force Nat. Dem. Com., 1969-72; commr. N.Y. State Commn. on Powers Local Govt., 1970-73; chmn. Coll. for Human Svcs. Audrey Cohen Coll., 1985-2000; former mem. bd. dirs. Am. Arbitration Assn., New Directions, Inst. for Mediation and Conflict Resolution, Spirit of Stockholm; bd. dirs. Hotline Internat.; v.p. Save the Children Fedn., 1986-93 rep. Internat. Peace Acad. at UN, 1974-77, Internat. Soc. Cmty. Devel., 1977-98, del. at large 1st Nat. Women's Conf., Houston, 1977; chmn. task force on internat. interdependence N.Y. State Women's Meeting, 1977; mem. Task Force on Poverty, 1977; chmn. Task Force on Women, Sci. and Tech. for Devel., 1978; U.S. del. UN Status of Women Commn., 1978, UN Conf. Sci. and Tech. for Devel., 1979, Brazzaville Centennial Celebration, 1980; mem. global adv. bd. Internat. Expn. Rural Devel., 1981—; mem. Coun. Internat. Fellows U. Bridgeport, 1982-88; trustee overseas edn. fund LWV, 1983-91; v.p. U.S. Com. UN Devel. Fund for Women, 1983-94, trustee, 1998-2000; mem. Nat. Consultative Com. Planning for Nairobi, 1984-85; co-chmn. women in devel. com. Interaction, 1985-91; mem. com. of cooperation Interam. Commn. of Women, 1986; bd. dirs. Internat. Devel. Conf., 1991-2001; mem. UN task force informal sector devel. Africa, 1995—. Recipient Crystal award Coll. Human Svcs., 1983, Ann. award Inst. Mediation and Conflict Resloution, 1985, Woman of Conscience award Nat. Coun. Women, 1996, Temple award Inst. Noetic Scis., 1987, Presdl. End Hunger award, 1987, Giraffe award Giraffe Project, 1987, Woman of the World award Eng.'s Women Aid, 1989, Mildred Robbins Leet award Interaction, 1995; co-recipient Rose award World Media Inst., 1987, Human Rights award UN Devel. Fund for Women, 1987, Leadership award U.S. Peace Corps, Woman of Vision award N.Y.C. NOW, 1990, Matrix award Women in Comm., Inc., Spirit of Enterprise award Rolex Industries, 1990, Ann. Bush's Ann. Points of Light award, 1992, Internat. Humanity award ARC Overseas Assn., 1992, Excellence award U.S. Com. for UNIFEM, 1992, Champion of Enterprise award Avon, 1994, Achievement award NYU-Washington Sq. Coll. Alumni. Assn., 1995, Lizette H. Sarnoff Vol. Svc. award Yeshiva U., 1996, Disting. Svc. award N.Y. African Studies Assn., 1996, Disting. Svc. award 50th Anniversary United Cerebral Palsy, 1997, Eleanor Schnurr award UN Assn./USA, Women of Distinction honoree Birmingham So. Coll., Spirit award Nat. Assn. Women Bus. Owners, 1998, Nat. Caring Inst. award, 2001. Mem. AAAS, Women's Forum, Coun. on Fgn. Rels., Cosmopolitan Club, Princeton Club. Home and Office: 54 Riverside Dr New York NY 10024-6509 E-mail: info@trickleup.org.

LEET, RICHARD HALE, oil company executive; b. Maryville, Mo., Oct. 11, 1926; s. Theron Hale and Helen Eloise (Rutledge) L.; m. Phyllis Jean Combs, June 14, 1949; children: Richard Hale II, Alan Combs, Dana Ellen. BS in Chemistry, N.W. Mo. State Coll., 1948; PhD in Phys. Chemistry, Ohio State U., 1952. Rsch. chemist Standard Oil Co., Whiting, Ind., 1953-64; dir. long-range and capital planning, mktg. dept. Am. Oil Co., Chgo., 1964-68, mgr. ops. planning, mfg. dept., 1968-70, regional v.p., 1970-71, v.p. supply Chgo., 1971-74; v.p. planning and adminstrn. Amoco Chems. Corp., 1974-75, v.p. mktg., 1975-77, exec. v.p., 1977-78, pres., 1978-83; dir. Amoco Corp., Chgo., 1983-91, vice chmn., 1991-92; retired, 1992. Bd. dirs. emeritus Gt. Lakes Chem., Vulcan Materials Corp., ITW, Landauer, Inc. Former chmn. bd. mgrs. Met. YMCA, Chgo.; former pres. Boy Scouts Am.; former chmn. bd. Am. Indsl. Health Coun.; former bd. visitors Emory U., 1970-71; hon. v.p. found. bd. Ohio State U; trustee Brenau U. With USNR, 1944-46. Mem. Am. Chem. Soc., Soc. Chem. Industry (exec. com.), Am. Petroleum Inst. (bd. dirs.), Société Industrielle de Chemie, Chem. Mfrs. Assn. (dir.), Phi Sigma Epsilon, Gamma Alpha. Office: Lighthouse Acres 3631 Lantern Dr Gainesville GA 30504-5420

LEETCH, BRIAN JOSEPH, hockey player; b. Corpus Christi, Tex., Mar. 3, 1968; Student, Boston Coll. With N.Y. Rangers, 1986—. Mem. U.S. Olympic hockey team, 1988, Team USA for 1991 Can. Cup Tournament, Stanley Cup championship team, 1994. Named mem. U.S. Coll. first-team All-Am. team, 1987, Sporting News NHL Rookie of Yr., 1989, Player of the Year, Hockey East, 1986-87, Rookie of the Year, 1986-87, Sporting News All-Star team, 1991-92; recipient Calder Meml. trophy for NHL Rookie of Yr.,1988, 1989, James Norris Meml. trophy for best defenseman, 1991, 92, Conn Smythe trophy, 1993-94. Office: NY Rangers Madison Sq Garden 2 Penn Plz New York NY 10121-0101*

LEETE, WILLIAM WHITE, artist; b. Portsmouth, Ohio, June 12, 1929; s. Bernard Emerson and Lois Trowbridge (Denison) L.; m. Doris Louise Knight, Sept. 19, 1952; children: Amy MacDonald, Robin Schodt. BA, Yale U., 1951, BFA, 1955, MFA, 1957. Mem. faculty dept. art U. R.I., Kingston, 1957-95, prof. emeritus, 1995, acting dept. chmn., 1968, 69-70, 76. Represented in permanent collections, De Cordova Mus., Lincoln, Mass., Cleve. Mus., Worcester Mus., Fleet Bank, also various pvt. collections. Served with USMC, 1951-53. Mem. Coll. Art Assn., Siggraph. Home: 202 Silver Lake Ave Wakefield RI 02879-4231

LEETS, PETER J. consulting firm executive; b. London, Mar. 12, 1946; came to U.S., 1948; s. Earl Edward and Doris Eileen L.; m. Anne E. Shahinian, May 15, 1982. BS in Mktg., Ind. U., 1969. Salesman Ortho Pharm. Corp., Raritan, N.J., 1969-74; account mgr. Revlon Inc., Indpls., 1974-76, regional dir. Cleve., 1976-79, field sales mgr. Bay Village, 1979-83; N.Am. field sales mgr. Binney & Smith, Bethlehem, Pa., 1983-85; v.p., dir. sales Dell Pub. Co., Inc., N.Y.C., 1985-87; exec. v.p. Geneva Corp., Irvine, Calif., 1987-88; pres. Geneva Cos., Costa Mesa, 1988-90; exec. v.p. Exec. Assets Corp., Irvine, 1990-91, pres., 1992-94; reg. mng. prin. Right Mgmt. Cons., Irvine, Calif., 1994—. Bd. dirs. Career Beginnings, Career Transition Ptnrs., Constl. Rights Found., Prof. Coaches Mentors Assn. Chairperson Orange County Econ. Outlook Conf.; bd. dirs. Forum for Corp. Dirs., PIHRA Found., Chapman U. Fellow Outplacement Inst.; mem. Internat. Assn. Career Mgmt. Profls. (bd. dirs.), Ind. U. Alumni (life), Delta Chi. Office: Ste 650 18111 Von Karman Ave Irvine CA 92612-7123

LEEVES, JANE, actress; b. London, Apr. 18, 1961; Appearances include (TV series) The Benny Hill Show, Throb, Frasier 1993-, Murphy Brown, Seinfeld, Hercules, 1998 (films) Miracle on 34th Street, 1994, To Live and Die in L.A., The Meaning of Life, The Hunger, Mr. Wright, James and the Giant Peach, The Great War, 1996, Pandora's Clock, 1996, Us Begins With You, 1998, Just Deserts, 1999, Music of the Heart, 1999, Adventures of Tom Thumb and Thumbelina (voice), 2000; TV guest appearances include Murder, She Wrote, 1984, Hooperman, 1987, Who's the Boss, 1984, Caroline and the Bad Back, 1995, Caroline in the City, 1995. Recipient Q award, 1995, SAG award, 2000. Avocations: reading, cooking, sports, dance.*

LEEVY, CARROLL MOTON, medical educator, hepatology researcher; b. Columbia, S.C., Oct. 13, 1920; s. Isaac S. and Mary (Kirkl) L.; m. Ruth S. Barboza, Feb. 4, 1956; children: Carroll Barboza, Maria Secora. AB, Fisk U., 1941; MD, U. Mich., 1944; ScD (hon.), N.J. Inst. Tech., 1973, U. Nebr., 1989; HHD (hon.), Fisk U., 1981. Intern Jersey City Med. Ctr., 1944-45, resident, 1945-48, dir. clin. investigation, 1947-57; fellow Banting-Best Inst., U. Toronto, Ont., Can., 1953; research assoc. Harvard U. Med. Sch., Cambridge, Mass., 1959; assoc. prof. U. Medicine and Dentistry of N.J., 1960-64, prof., 1964, Disting. prof., 1990—; physician in chief Univ. Hosp., 1975-91; dir. Liver Ctr. U. Medicine and Dentistry N.J., 1983-85; dir. div. hepatology and nutrition N.J. Med. Sch., 1959-75, acting chmn. dept. medicine, 1966-68, chief of medicine, 1968-71, chmn. dept. medicine, 1975-91; disting. prof. medicine Univ. Hosp., physician in chief, 1975-91; acting chmn. Sammy Davis Jr. Nat. Liver Inst., 1984-86, pres., sci. dir., 1989—, dir., 1991—, N.J. Med. Sch. Liver Ctr., 1991—. Chief medicine VA Hosp., East Orange, N.J., 1966-71; cons. NIH, 1965—, FDA, 1970-80, VA, 1971—, Alcohol and Nutrition Found., 1970-80, Am. Liver Found., 1979-84; cons. Health Care Fin. Adminstrn., 1990—, mem. adv. com. on liver transplantation, 1991—; mem. Nat. Commn. on Digestive Disease, 1975-78; mem. expert com. on chronic liver disease WHO, 1978; mem. nat. adv. com. digestive disease HHS, 1989-93; chmn. monitoring com. VA Coop. Study on Alcoholic Hepatitis, 1989-94—, VA Rsch. Study on Colchicine Alcoholic Cirrhosis, 1994—; med. dir. Univ. Hosp. Liver Transplant Program, 1989—; disting. prof. U. Medicine and Dentistry N.J., 1991—; chmn. Newark Hepatitis C Study Group, 2000—. Author: Practical Diagnosis and Treatment of Liver Disease, 1957, Evaluation of Liver Function in Clinical Practice, 1965, 2d edit., 1974, Liver Regeneration in Man, 1973, The Liver and Its Diseases, 1973, Diseases of the Liver and Biliary Tract, 1977, Guidelines for Detection of Drug and Chemical-Induced Hepatotoxicity, 1979, Alcohol and the Digestive Tract, 1981, Standardization of Nomenclature, Diagnostic Criteria and Prognosis for Diseases of the Liver and Biliary Tract, 1994; contbr. numerous articles to med., sci. jours.; patentee in field. Bd. dirs. U. Cape Town, South Africa Fund, 1984-2001; active Pilgrim Congl. Ch. Cmdr. USNR, 1954-59. E.V. Gabriel scholar, 1938, Kellog Med. scholar, 1942; recipient Modern Med. award, 1972, Edward Ill award, 1973, United Negro Coll. Fund award, 1980, Key to City of Newark, 1981, Key to City of Columbia, S.C., 1987, Key to City of Secaucus, N.J., 1981, 50th N.J. Achievement award U. Medicine and Dentistry N.J., 1995, Honor and Commendation for viral hepatitis rsch. N.J. State Senate and Gen. Assembly, 1999, Disting. Achievement award U. Mich. Med. Ctr. Alumni Soc., 1999; 40th Anniversary Faculty Honoree, U. Medicine and Dentistry N.J., 1995. Mem. AAAS, ACP (publs. com. 1969-74, master), AMA (vice-chmn., chmn. program com. sect. on gastroenterology 1971-74), NAACP, Am. Assn. for Study Liver Diseases (pres. 1967-68, chmn. steering com. 1968-74, Disting. Svc. award 1991), Internat. Assn. for Study Liver (pres. 1970-74, chmn. criteria com. 1972—), Am. Gastroenterol. Assn. (edn. and tng. com. 1967-71), Assn. Profs. Medicine (Robert Williams Disting. Chmn. award 1991), Assn. Am. Physicians, Soc. Exptl. Biology and Medicine, Am. Soc. Clin. Nutrition, Am. Inst. Nutrition, Nat. Med. Assn. (award 1987, Centenial award 1995), Am. Fedn. Clin. Rsch., Assn. Acad. Minority Physicians (pres. 1986-88, chmn. bd. trustees 1988—, Disting. Achievement award 1995), Internat. Com. on Informatics in Hepatology (chmn. 1986—), Internal Hepatology Informatics Group (chmn. 1984-01, UNOS cert. transplant hepatologist med. dir. 1989—), N.J. Acad. Medicine, N.J. Liver Study Group (chmn. 1996—), Detection Counseling on Treatment Hepatitus Cir. Inner City Residents (chmn., 1986-2001, chmn. exec. com.), Phi Beta Kappa, Alpha Omega Alpha, Sigma Pi Phi. Home: 35 Robert Dr Short Hills NJ 07078-1525 Office: UMDNJ Med School 100 Bergen St Newark NJ 07103-2484 E-mail: Leevyc.m.@umdng.edu. *My goal has been to help improve quality of life of all people, the disadvantaged and advantaged. Efforts have been made through medical education and research to decrease the incidence and untoward effects of disease, as well as improve communication and the social environment.*

LE FAUVE, RICHARD ALLEN, investment company executive, marketing consultant; b. Buffalo, Nov. 19, 1950; s. George Julien and Edith Elenor (Gowan) Le F.; m. Lynn Carol Rosenzweig, Oct. 7, 1978; children: Ari Julien, Justin Charles. BS in Edn., SUNY, Brockport, 1973; master's cert. in edn., SUNY, Buffalo, 1975. Cert. permanent tchr., in phys. edn. and health sci., N.Y. Tchr., coach Sweet Home Ctrl. Schs., Amherst, N.Y., 1973-77; stock broker, br. mgr. 1st Jersey Securities, Buffalo, 1977-84; v.p., bd. dirs. Anodyne Energy Corp., 1984-86, mem. adv. bd., 1986-87; regional mgr., dir. tng. and broker devel. Thomas-James Assocs., 1986—, mktg. cons., 1993—. Recruitment cons. Reliance Fin. Group, Williamsville, N.Y., 1990. Author, editor: (manuals) New Broker Training, 1991, Recruitment, 1993; editor: (manuals) Merit Advisors—Asset Allocation, 1992, Marketing, 1993. Scholarship fundraiser Sweet Home Ctrl. Schs., 1988—, mem. adv. bd. scholarship investment com., 1988—. Named Vol. of Yr., Sweet Home Ctrl. Schs., 1994. Mem. Securities Industry Assn., Nat. Assn. Securities Dealers (registered rep. series 7, prin. series series 24), N.Y. State Life Ins. Agts., Albright-Knox Art Gallery, Loch Lee Homeowners Assn. Avocations: weight training, cycling, martial arts. Home: 214 Harrogate Sq Buffalo NY 14221-4046

LEFEBVRE, ALAN J. lawyer; b. Akron, Colo., Mar. 17, 1953; s. Vern L. and Adeline V. (Molacek) L.; m. Eileen Helen Buhmann, Feb. 26, 1987; 1 child, Rachel Elisabeth. BA in Polit. Sci. with high honors and departmental distinction, U. Calif., Santa Barbara, 1975; JD, U. San Francisco, 1978. Bar: Calif. 1978, Nev. 1979, U.S. Dist. Ct. Nev. 1979, U.S. Ct. Appeals (9th cir.) 1979, U.S. Supreme Ct. 1992, U.S. Dist. Ct. (cen. dist.) Calif. 1994. Law clk. 8th Jud. Dist. Ct., Las Vegas, Nev., 1978-79; assoc. Jolly, Urga & Wirth, 1979-80; assoc., ptnr. Beckley, Singleton, DeLanoy Jemison & List, 1980-89; sr. ptnr. Lefebvre & Barron, 1989—. Mem. Nev. Commn. on Jud. Discipline, Carson City, 1991—. Mem. Internat. Assn. Def. Counsel. Republican. Roman Catholic. Avocations: boating, French horn, classical music. Office: 1404 S Jones Blvd Las Vegas NV 89146-1231

LEFER, ALLAN MARK, physiologist; b. N.Y.C., Feb. 1, 1936; s. I. Judah and Lillian G. (Gastwirth) L.; m. Mary E. Indoe, Aug. 23, 1959; children: Debra Lynn, David Joseph, Barry Lee and Leslie Ann (twins). BA, Adelphi Coll., 1957, Western Res. U., 1959; PhD (NSF fellow), U. Ill., Urbana, 1962. Instr. physiology, USPHS-NIH fellow Western Res. U., 1962-64; asst. prof. physiology U. Va., 1964-69, assoc. prof., 1969-71, prof., 1972-74; vis. prof. Hadassah Med. Sch., Jerusalem, 1971-72; prof., chmn. dept. physiology Jefferson Med. Coll., Thomas Jefferson U., Phila., 1974—; dir. Ischemia-Shock Rsch. Inst., 1980-95. Cons. Merck & Co., Upjohn Co., Genentech Inc., Syntex, Inc., Ciba-Geigy, NIH, Nitromed, IBEX Technologies, Bristol-Myers Squibb, Cytel Corp., Wellcome Found.; vis. prof. 1985-86, Pfizer vis. prof. cardiovascular medicine, 1995; Nat. Bd. of Med. Examiners, Step 1, 1993-95; vis. prof. U. Calif., San Diego, 1995-96. Author: Pathophysiology and Therapeutics of Myocardial Ischemia, 1977, Prostaglandins in Cardiovascular and Renal Function, 1979, Cellular and Molecular Aspects of Shock and Trauma, 1983; Leukotrienes in Cardiovascular and Pulmonary Function, 1985; mng. editor: Eicosanoids, 1988-93; cons. editor Circulatory Shock, 1973-80; field editor Jour. of Pharmacology and Exptl. Therapeutics Cardiovascular, 1994—; mem. editl. bd. Critical Care Medicine, Shock Am. Jour. Physiology, Endothelium, Cardiovasc. Pathology, Drug News and Perspectives; contbr. to World Book Ency. Sci. Yearbook, 1979, Cardiovasc. Drug Reviews, Circulation Rsch. Drugs Today; contbr. over 600 articles to profl. jours. Active Acad. Com. on Soviet Jewry, 1970-95; chmn. United Jewish Appeal, 1973-74; coach basketball and baseball Huntingdon Valley Athletic Assn., 1975-78. Recipient Pres. and Visitor's prize in rsch. U. Va., 1970, Disting. Alumnus award U. Ill., 1996, Disting. Svc. award Coll. Grad. Studies, Thomas Jefferson U., 1999. Fellow Am. Coll. Cardiology; mem. AAAS, Am. Physiol. Soc., Am. Soc. Pharmacology and Exptl. Therapeutics, Internat. Heart Rsch. Soc., Am. Heart Assn. (established investigator 1968-73, fellow circulation coun., nat. grant rev. com. 1993-95), Pa. Heart Assn. (rsch. com.), Shock Soc. (chmn. membership com., pres. 1983-84, chmn. devel. com. 1985-89, chmn. internat. rels. com. 1993), Internat. Fed. Shock Scs. (coun. 1994—, pres. 4th internat. shock congress 1996-99), Soc. Exptl. Biology and Medicine, Soc. Leukocyte Biology, Israel Soc. Physiology and Pharmacology, Phila. Physiol. Soc. (pres. 1978-79), Sierra Club, B'nai B'rith (Charlottesville chpt., v.p. 1967-68, chmn. Va. Hillel 1970-71), Sigma Xi. Democrat. Home: 3590 Walsh Ln Huntingdon Valley PA 19006-3226 Office: Thomas Jefferson Univ 1020 Locust St Philadelphia PA 19107-6799 E-mail: AlLefer@aol.com.

LEFER, DIANE, writer; b. N.Y.C. d. Henry and Sylvia (Ladner) L. Student, Radcliffe Coll., 1968-70. Mem. faculty MFA in Writing program Vt. Coll., Montpelier, Vt., 1987—; mem. faculty MFA in Creative Writing program Antioch U., L.A. and Marina del Rey, Calif., 2000. Co-founder, artistic dir. Triumvirate Pi theatre co., L.A., 2000—; mem. adv. bd. Nat. Writers Voice, 1997—98. Author: (short stories) The Circles I Move In, 1994, Very Much Like Desire, 2000, (play with music)) American Buggery, 2001, (novels) Radiant Hunger, 2001; contbr. ; author: (plays) Tell Me Which Way a Hanged Man's Feet Will Hang, 2001. Primate behavior observation team rsch. dept. L.A. Zoo, 1998—; Spanish-English interpreter Ctrl. Am. Resource Ctr., L.A., 1999-2000. Creative writing fellow NEA, 1983, N.Y. Found. Arts, 1986. Mem.: PEN (USA W.) (judge Literary Award in Fiction 2000, Syndicated Fiction prize 1983, 1985, 1987), Dramatists Guild, Assoc. Writing Programs, Alliance L.A. Playwrights (vice chair 2000—). E-mail: desilef@cs.com.

LEFEVER, HOLLIS K. family practice; b. Wichita, Kans., Jan. 16, 1931; s. Edward and Ruth (Hancock) L.; m. Ruth Anne, June 11, 1954; four children. BA, Ottawa U., 1953; MD, U. Kans., 1957. Pvt. practice, Glendive, Mont., 1958-61, Lewistown, 1961-96, Townsend, 1996—. Fellow Am. Acad. Family Physicians; mem. AMA, Mont. Med. Assn. (pres. 1972-73). Republican. Baptist. Home: 249 Goosebay Ln Townsend MT 59644

LEFEVER, MAXINE LANE, music educator; b. Elmhurst, Ill., May 30, 1931; d. Thomas Clinton and Georgia Marie (Hampton) Lane; m. Orville Joseph Lefever, Aug. 18, 1951 (div.); m. Geoffrey Ashe, Dec. 8, 1992. Student, Ill. Wesleyan U., 1949-51; BA, Western State Coll., 1958; MS, Purdue U., 1964, postgrad., 1965. Elem. sch. tchr. Leaf River (Ill.) Pub. Schs., 1953-54, Mancos (Colo.) Pub. Schs., 1954-56; elem./jr. h.s. tchr. Cortez (Colo.) Pub. Schs., 1956-60; instr. bands Purdue U., Lafayette, Ind., 1965-79, asst. prof., 1980-88, prof. emerita, 1989. Cons. numerous festivals and contests; pres., dir. Am. Mus. Ambassadors, 1967—. Contbr. articles to profl. jours.; composer percussion ensembles. Hon. mem. U.S. Navy Band. Mem. Inc. Music Educators Assn., Music Educators Nat. Conf., Nat. Band Assn. (exec. sec., citation of excellence), Coll. Band Dirs. Nat. Assn., Percussion Ats Soc., John Philip Sousa Found. (v.p., exec. sec., Star of Order of Merit), Big Ten Band Dirs. Assn., Alpha Lambda Delta, Delta Omicron, Tau Beta Sigma, Kappa Kappa Psi (hon.), Phi Sigma Kappa (hon.). Office: 225 Tamiami Trl West Lafayette IN 47906-1207 E-mail: mlefever@gte.net.

LEFEVOUR, MARY KAY CATHERINE, foundation director; b. Chgo., Dec. 3, 1955; d. Charles F. and Rosella L. (Green) LeF. MusB, Alverno Coll., 1977; MA, George Wash. U., 1986. Sales tng. coord. Blunt, Ellis, Loewi, Milw., 1977-78; office mgr. U. Wis., 1978-80; program coord. George Washington U., Washington, 1980-84; adminstrv. dir. Pub. Voice Food and Health Policy, 1985-87; dir. Trial Lawyers for Pub. Justice, 1987-89, 1989—. Contbr. articles to profl. jours. Dir. DCAFC Chorus. Recipient Citizen award Milw. County Bd., 1979. Mem. NAFE, Am. Mgmt. Assn., Nat. Women Studies Assn., Nat. Soc. Fund Raising Execs., Greater Washington Soc. Assn. Execs., Nat. Stained Glass Guild, Nat. Com. for Responsive Philanthropy, Fred Appel Fencing Club. Democrat. Office: TLPJ Found Ste 800 1717 Massachusetts Ave NW Washington DC 20036-2006

LEFEVRE, ADAM, actor, writer; b. Albany, N.Y., Aug. 11, 1950; s. Ira Deyo and Helen Tate (Rhodes) LeF.; m. Cora Ann Bennett, Nov. 3, 1979; children: Tate Augusta, Isaac Bennett. BA, Williams Coll., 1972; MFA, U. Iowa, 1976; student, Nat. Theatre Inst. English Northeastern U., 1979-80, CUNY, N.Y.C., 1981. Actor: (plays) Buried Child, Turnbuckle, Romeo and Juliet, 1981, The Wake of Jamey Foster, 1982, Goose & Tom Tom, 1982, (Broadway plays) Devil's Disciple, 1989, Our Country's Good, 1991, Summer and Smoke, 1995, Footloose, 1999, (films) Return of the Secaucus 7, 1978, Reckless, 1983, Second Sight, 1989, Bonfire of the Vanities, 1990, The Ref, 1994, You Can Count on Me, 2000, Hearts in Atlantis, 2001; playwright: Yucca Flats, 1973, The Crashing of Moses Flying By, 1983, Americansaint, 1989, Waterbabies, 1997.

LEFEVRE, DONALD KEITH, electrical engineer; b. Casper, Wyo., Feb. 12, 1956; s. Lorin Durward and Margery Phyllis (Green) L.; m. Susan Lesley Nichols, May 31, 1975; children: Justin, Michelle, Mark, Kristen, Gregory, Sean, Brendan. BS in Physics, Elec. Engring., S.D. Sch. Mines and Technology, 1978; MS in Elec. Engring., U. Utah, 1985. Sr. engr. Sperry Def. Systems, Salt Lake City, 1978-84; chief engr. Anderson Scientific, Rapid City, S.D., 1984-86; asst. prof. elec. engring. S.D. Sch. Mines and Technology, 1986-90; pres. Wesha Technologies, Inc., 1987; pres., founder Cynetics Corp., 1988—, Wireless Control Sys., Inc., 1990-94, dir., 1990—. Leader of team for world's first multiple-channel compressed digital video broadcast sys.; founder, pres. African TV Investors, LLC; bd. dirs. Tepco. Patentee in field. Mem. bd. advisors Black Hills Bus. Innovation Ctr., Rapid City, 1986-90; founding mem. Black Hills Entrepreneur Network, 1988, dir., 1991-95; chmn. Ptnrs. in Entrepreneurship Com. Rapid City, 1993-95; mem. audit com. S.D. Sch. Mines and Tech. Found. Recipient Nat. Merit scholar; named Outstanding Recent Grad. in Elec. Engring. award S.D Sch. Mines and Tech., 1989. Mem. IEEE, Soc. Photo-Optical Instrumentation Engrs., Planetary Soc., Soc. Physics Students (chpt. pres. 1977), Eta Kappa Nu, Tau Beta Pi, Sigma Pi Sigma, Pi Mu Epsilon. Lodges: KC. Republican. Roman Catholic. Home: 4911 S Canyon Rd Rapid City SD 57702-1876 Office: Cynetics Corp PO Box 2422 Rapid City SD 57709-2422

LEFEVRE, EDMUND ARTHUR, JR. scenic designer; b. Wilmington, Del., July 8, 1964; s. Edmund A. and Nancy Keith LeFevre; life ptnr. Keith L. Wiggs; children: Connor, Taylor. BA, Brown U., 1986; MFA, Carnegie Mellon U., 1990. 1st asst. Paul De Pass, Inc., N.Y.C., 1990-92; resident resigner Miranda Theatre Co., 1991-93; asst. scenic designer Met. Opera, 1993-95, 97; prin. asst. designer on Beauty and the Beast, Disney Theatrical, 1994-96; resident designer Surflight Theatre, Beach Haven, N.J., 1998-99; assoc. designer on Aida, Disney Theatrical, N.Y.C., 1999—2002. Recipient Tony award, 2000. Mem. Alpha Delta Phi. E-mail: ted.lefevre@disney.com.

LEFEVRE, ELBERT WALTER, JR. civil engineering educator; b. Eden, Tex., July 29, 1932; s. Elbert Walter Sr. and Hazie (Davis) LeF.; m. Joyce Ann Terry, Nov. 28, 1957; children: Terry Ann, Charmaine Rene, George Walter, John Philip. BS in Civil Engring, Tex. A&M U., 1957, MS in Civil Engring, 1961; PhD, Okla. State U., 1966. Registered profl. engr., Ark., Tex. Faculty Tex. A&M U., Bryan, 1958, Tex. Technol. Coll., Lubbock, 1959-63, Okla. State U., Stillwater, 1963-66, U. Ark., Fayetteville, 1966—, head dept. civil engring., 1971-82, dean engring., 1982-83; sr. v.p. Engring. Svcs., Inc., Springdale, Ark., 1973—; dir. Nat. Rural Transp. Study Ctr., 1992-96, dir. emeritus, 1996—. Mem. Ark. State Bd. Registration for Profl. Engrs. and Land Surveyors, 1984-96, pres., 1989, 94; mem. Nat. Coun. Examiners for Engring. and Surveying, 1984-96, v.p. So. zone, 1991-93, mem. accreditation bd. engring. and tech., 1985-91. Served to 1st lt. AUS, 1953-56. Fellow ASCE (pres. Mid-South sect. 1972, chmn. dist. 14 1977-80, dir. dist. 14 1983-86, v.p. zone II 1996—), NSPE (v.p. profl. engrs. in edn. 1982, v.p. S.W. region 1984-86, pres. 1989-90), Inst. Engrs. of Ireland, Am. Soc. Engring. Edn. (pres. midwest sect. 1976-77); mem. Transp. Rsch. Bd., Ark. Soc. Profl. Engrs. (pres. 1979-80, Outstanding Ark. Engr. 1980) Masons, Rotary (pres. 1973), Sigma Xi, Chi Epsilon, Tau Beta Pi, Phi Beta Delta. Home: 300 Paradise Ln Springdale AR 72762-3832 Office: Univ Ark Dept Civil Engring Fayetteville AR 72701 E-mail: ewl@engr.uark.edu. *I owe a great debt to those whose efforts have provided me the opportunity to accomplish these things. Personal relationships dwarf the honors I have received.*

LEFEVRE, JOHN FREDERICK, figure skating association administrator, lawyer; b. Troy, Ohio, Jan. 16, 1942; s. Frederick Campbell and Virginia (Forward) L.; m. Linda Joan Palmer, Oct. 20, 1973; 1 child, Sarah Pace. BA, Williams Coll., 1964; JD, George Washington U., 1967. Bar: D.C. 1971. Atty. FTC, WAshington, 1971-98; exec. dir. U.S. Figure Skating Assn., Colorado Springs, Colo., 1998—, bd. dirs., 1980-98. Judge World singles, pairs and ice dancing, 1987-98. Mem. choir Nat. Presbyn. Ch. Lt. USNR, 1967-71. Mem. FBA, D.C. Bar Assn. Avocations: music, figure skating, piano. Home: 3107-A Broadmoor Valley Rd Colorado Springs CO 80906 Office: US Figure Skating Assn 20 1st St Colorado Springs CO 80906 E-mail: jlefevre@usfsa.org.

LEFEVRE, PERRY DEYO, minister, theology educator; b. Kingston, N.Y., July 12, 1921; s. Johannes and Faye (McFerran) LeF.; m. Carol Baumann, Sept. 14, 1946; children: Susan Faye, Judith Ann, Peter Gerret. AB, Harvard U., 1943; BD, Chgo. Theol. Sem., 1946, DD, 1992; PhD, U. Chgo., 1951. Ordained to ministry Congl. Ch., 1946. Instr. religion Franklin and Marshall Coll., 1948-49; asst., then assoc. prof. religion Knox Coll., 1949-53, Fed. Theol. Sem., U. Chgo., 1953-61; prof. constructive theology Chgo. Theol. Sem., 1961-92, dean of faculty, 1961-81, acting dean, 1990-91. Author: The Prayers of Kierkegaard, 1956, The Christian Teacher, 1958, Introduction to Religious Existentialism, 1963, Understandings of Man, 1966, Philosophical Resources for Christian Thought, 1968, Conflict in a Voluntary Association, 1975, Understandings of Prayer, 1981, Aging and the Human Spirit, 1981, Radical Prayer, 1982; editor: Paul Tillich: The Meaning of Health, 1984, Spiritual Nurture and Congregational Development, 1984, Daniel Day Williams Essays in Process Theology, 1985, Pastoral Care and Liberation Praxis, 1986, Bernard Meland Essays in Constructive Theology, 1988, Creative Ministries in Contemporary Christianity, 1991, Modern Theologies of Prayer, 1995, Challenge and Response, 1999. Mem. Phi Beta Kappa. Address: 1613 Foulkeways Gwynedd PA 19436-1033

LEFEVRE, THOMAS VERNON, retired utility company executive, lawyer; b. Dallas, Dec. 5, 1918; s. Eugene H. and Callie E. (Powell) L.; m. Lillian Herndon Bourne, Oct. 12, 1946; children: Eugene B., Nicholas R., Sharon A., Margot P. BA, U. Fla., 1939, LLB, 1942; LLM, Harvard U., 1946. Bar: Fla. 1945, N.Y. 1947, D.C. 1951, Pa. 1955, U.S. Supreme Ct. 1953. Atty. IRS and various firms, N.Y.C., Washington, and Phila., 1946-55; ptnr. Morgan, Lewis & Bockius, Phila., 1956-79; pres., chief exec. officer UGI Corp., Valley Forge, Pa., 1979-85, chmn., 1983-89. Chmn. G.P. Hospitality, Inc., 1981—; mem. Commr.'s Adv. Group IRS, 1976-77. Bd. dirs. Zool. Soc. Phila., 1982-91, WHYY Inc., 1982-96; chmn. U. Arts, 1986-89; trustee Franklin Inst., 1980-89, Fox Chase Cancer Ctr., 1979-88. With USMC, 1942-46. Fellow ABA (vice chmn. govt. rels. sect. of taxation 1976-79), Am. Bar Found.; mem. Pa. Bar Assn., Merion Cricket Club, Merion Golf Club, Sankaty Head Golf Club, Nantucket Yacht Club. Episcopalian. Office: 5 Radnor Corp Ctr Wayne PA 19087-4526

LEFF, ALAN RICHARD, medical educator, researcher; b. May 23, 1945; s. Maurice D. and Grace Ruth (Schwarz) Leff, Maurice D. and Grace Ruth (Schwarz) Leff; m. Donna Rae Rosene, Feb. 14, 1975; children: Marni, Karen, Alison; m. Donna Rae Rosene, Feb. 14, 1975. AB cum laude, Oberlin Coll., 1967; MD, U. Rochester, 1971. Diplomate Am. Bd. Internal Medicine, Am. Bd. Pulmonary Disease. Intern U. Mich. Hosp., Ann Arbor, 1971-72, resident, 1974-76; fellow U. Calif., San Francisco, 1976-77, postdoctoral fellow, 1977-79; asst. prof. medicine U. Chgo., 1979-85, assoc. prof. medicine and clin. pharm., 1985-89, prof. medicine, anesthesia, critical care and clin. pharm., 1989—, prof. cell physiology, 1992—, prof. pediats., pharm. and phys. scis., 1993—, dir. pulmonary medicine svc., 1984-87, dir. Pulmonary Function Lab., 1979-87, chief sect. pulmonary and critical care medicine, 1987-2000, sr. dir. R&D biol. scis., 2000—02. Dir. NIAID Asthma and Allergic Disease Coop. Rsch. Ctr., Chgo., 1993—97; co-chair asthma sect. NIAID Task Force on Immunology, 1996—98; advisor San Francisco Dept. Pub. Health, 1977—79, Chgo Dept. Health, 1979—; dir. Ctr. of Excellence in Asthma Glaxo Smith Kline, 2000—. Editor: Am. Jour. Respiratory Critical Care Medicine, 1994—99; contbr. Bd. dirs. Chgo. Lung Assn., 1984—93. With USPHS, 1972—74. Recipient Citation of Merit, Chgo. Lung Assn., 1974, Am. Lung Assn., 1998; fellow, Leopold Schepp Found., 1967—69. Fellow: Am. Coll. Chest Physicians; mem.: Am. Assn. Immunologists, Ctrl. Soc. for Clin. Investigation, Am. Thoracic Soc. (Spl. Citation 1999), Assn. Am. Physicians, Am. Physiol. Soc., Am. Soc. Clin. Investigation, Am. Fedn. Clin. Rsch. (councilor 1983—86), Sigma Xi. Avocation: music. Home: 5730 S Kimbark Ave Chicago IL 60637-1615 Office: U Chgo Pritzker Sch Medicine Div Biological Scis MC 6076 5841 S Maryland Ave Chicago IL 60637-1463 E-mail: aleff@medicine.bsd.uchicago.edu.

LEFF, DEBORAH, government executive; b. Washington, Oct. 25, 1951; d. Sam and Melitta Leff. AB, Princeton (N.J.) U., 1973; JD, U. Chgo., 1977. Trial atty. Civil Rights divsn. U.S. Dept. Justice, Washington, 1977-79; dir. office of pub. affairs Fed. Trade Commn., 1980-81; sr. producer Nightline-ABC News, Washington and London, 1983-89, World News Tonight-ABC News, N.Y.C., 1990-91; pres. The Joyce Found., Chgo., 1992-99, also bd. dirs.; pres., CEO Am.'s Second Harvest, 1999-2001; dir. John F. Kennedy Presdl. Libr., Boston,

2001—. Bd. dirs. CARE, Inc., Children's Def. Fund; chmn. Midwest Rhodes Scholars Selection Com., Chgo., 1992. Office: John F Kennedy Libr Columbia Point Boston MA 02125 E-mail: deborah.leff@nara.gov.

LEFF, ILENE J(AFNEL), management consultant, corporate and government executive; b. N.Y.C., Mar. 29, 1942; d. Abraham and Rose (Levy) L. BA cum laude, U. Pa., 1964; MA with honors, Columbia U., 1969. Statis. and computer analyst McKinsey & Co., N.Y.C., 1969-70, rsch. cons., 1971-74; mgmt. cons., N.Y.C. and Europe, 1974-78; dir. exec. resources Revlon, Inc., N.Y.C., 1978-81, dir. human resources, 1981-83, dir. pers., 1983-86; cons. APM Inc., 1986-88; mgmt. cons. The Estee Lauder Cos., 1988-92; dep. asst. sec. for mgmt. HUD, Washington, 1993-94; pres. Leff Mgmt. Cons., N.Y.C., 1995-97; mng. dir. Eisner LLP, 1997-2000; pres. Leff Mgmt., 2000—. Rsch. asst. U. Pa., Phila., 1964-65; employment counselor State of N.J., Newark, 1965-66; tchr., Newark, 1966-69; lectr. Grad. Program in Pub. Policy, New Sch. for Social Rsch., Wharton Sch., Duke U.; chmn. com. on employment and unemployment, mem. exec. com. Bus. Rsch. Adv. Coun., U.S. Bur. Labor Stats., 1980; sr. del. econ. rels. and trade Sino-U.S. Conf., 1986. Contbr. issues papers and program recommendations to candidates for U.S. Pres., U.S. Senate and Congress, N.Y. State gov., mayor N.Y.C. Mem. ops. coun. Jr. Achievement Greater N.Y., 1975-78; cons. Com. for Econ. Devel., N.Y. Hosp., Regional Plan Assn., Am. Cancer Soc.; mem. adv. bd. First Book; vol. for dep. mayor for ops. N.Y.C., 1977-78. Mem. N.Y. Human Resource Planners (treas. 1984), Fin. Women's Assn. N.Y. (exec. bd. 1977-78, 83-84), Fashion Group (treas. 1989). Office: 767 Fifth Ave New York NY 10153-0023

LEFF, JOSEPH NORMAN, yarn manufacturing company executive; b. N.Y.C., Dec. 17, 1923; s. Phillip and Lillian (Wiesen) L.; m. Joyce Hochberg, June 12, 1954 (div. 1958); 1 child, Julie; m. Juanita Hughey, Dec. 17, 1967; 1 child, Valerie. BS, Columbia U., 1944, AB, 1946. Treas. Nat. Spinning Co. Inc., N.Y.C., 1949-63, pres., CEO, 1963-83, chmn., CEO, 1983-97, chmn. bd. dirs. Mem. bd. visitors Columbia Coll., N.Y.C., 1987-92; trustee Park Ave. Synagogue, N.Y.C., 1987-95; bd. dirs., pres. 92d St. YM/YWHA, N.Y.C., 1994-97, chmn., 1997—; bd. dirs. Inst. Textile Tech., Va., 1982-97; mem. Purchase Coll. Found., 1999—. With U.S. Army, 1944-45. Mem. Harmonie Club (pres. 1974-75) (N.Y.C.), Quaker Ridge Golf Club (Scarsdale, N.Y.), Boca Rio Country Club (Boca Raton, Fla.). Jewish.

LEFF, SANDRA H. gallery director, consultant; b. N.Y.C., Dec. 24, 1939; d. I. Bernard and Rose (Kupfer) L. BA, Cornell U., 1960; MA, Inst. Fine Arts, N.Y.C., 1969. Editorial asst. Indsl. Design Mag., N.Y.C., 1960-61; instr., asst. Mus. of City of N.Y., 1962-65; assoc. print dept. Sotheby Parke Bernet, N.Y.C., 1969-73; rsch. asst. Daniel Chester French Exhibit, Washington, 1975-77; dir. Am. painting Graham Gallery, N.Y.C., 1977-93. Author: (exhbn. catalogs) Thomas Anshutz: Paintings, Watercolors and Pastels, 1979, Guy Pène du Bois: Painter, Draftsman and Critic, 1979, Helen Torr, 1980, John White Alexander: Fin-de-Siècle American, 1980, Jan Matulka & Vaclav Vytlacil, 1992. Ford Found. fellow, 1967. Mem. Phi Beta Kappa. Avocations: reading, traveling, jogging, film, photography. Office: 11 W 17th St Apt 10 New York NY 10011-5500 E-mail: michsan@juno.com.

LEFFALL, LASALLE D(OHENY), JR. surgeon; b. Tallahassee, May 22, 1930; s. LaSalle Doheny Sr. and Martha (Jordan) L.; m. Ruth McWilliams; 1 child, LaSalle Doheny III. BS, Fla. A&M U., 1948; MD, Howard U., 1952. Intern Homer G. Phillips Hosp., St. Louis, 1952-53; resident Freedmen's Hosp., Washington, 1953-57; fellow Meml. Sloan Kettering Cancer Ctr., N.Y.C., 1957-70; chmn. dept. surgery Howard U. Coll. Medicine, Washington, 1970-95, acting dean, 1970, Charles R. Drew prof. surgery, 1992—. Contbr. articles on cancer to profl. publs. Pres. Soc. Surg. Oncology, 1978-79, Am. Cancer Soc., 1978-79, ACS, 1995-96; chmn. Pres.'s Cancer Panel, 2002, Susan G. Komen Breast Cancer Found., 2002. Capt. U.S. Army, 1960-61. Recipient St. George medal and citation Am. Cancer Soc., 1977, Nat. Achievement award Black Caucus Dem. Nat. Com., 1982, Exceptional Black Scientist award CIBA-Geigy, 1984. Mem. Internat. Fedn. Surg. Colls. (assoc.), Med. Edn. for South African Blacks (bd. dirs. 1988—). Avocations: tennis, modern jazz, fgn. langs. Office: Howard Univ Coll Med Surgery Office 2041 Georgia Ave NW Ofc Washington DC 20059-0001

LEFFEK, KENNETH THOMAS, chemist, educator; b. Nottingham, Eng., Oct. 15, 1934; emigrated to Can., 1959, naturalized, 1966; s. Thomas and Ivy Louise (Pye) L.; m. Janet Marilyn Wallace, Sept. 26, 1958; children: Katharine, Geoffrey. BS, Univ. Coll., London, 1956, PhD, 1959. Asst. prof. chemistry Dalhousie U., Halifax, N.S., 1961-67, assoc. prof., 1967-72, prof., 1972-94, dean grad. studies, 1972-90, prof. chemistry, 1990-94, ret., 1994. Chmn. Atlantic Provinces Interuniv. Com. on Scis., 1975-77. Author: Sir Christopher Ingold, a Biography; contbr. articles on phys.-organic chemistry to profl. jours. Leverhulme fellow U. Kent (Eng.), 1967-68 Fellow Chem. Inst. Can., Royal Soc. Arts (London; chmn. Atlantic Can. chpt. 1987-91); mem. Chem. Soc. London, Chem. Inst. Can. (nat. dir. tech. and sci. affairs 1980-83, nat. v.p. 1985-86, pres. 1986-87) Home: 980 Kentwood Ter Victoria BC Canada V8Y 1A6 E-mail: kleffek@vanisle.net.

LEFFELL, DAVID JOEL, dermatologist, surgeon, health facility administrator, educator, writer; b. Montreal, Feb. 28, 1956; came to U.S., 1973; s. Allen Bernard and Freda (Deckelbaum) L. BS, Yale U., 1977; MD, McGill U., Montreal, 1981. Diplomate Am. Bd. Dermatology, Am. Bd. Internal Medicine. Resident in internal medicine Meml. Sloan-Kettering Cancer Ctr., N.Y.C., 1981-84; instr. medicine Cornell U. Sch. Medicine, 1983-84; lectr., fellow dermatologic surgery U. Mich., Ann Arbor, 1987-88; resident in dermatology Yale U. Sch. Medicine, New Haven, 1984-86, chief Mohs micrographic surgery and laser surgery, 1988—, dir. Yale skin cancer detection program, 1988—, med. dir. faculty practice plan, 1996-98, prof. dermatology, plastic surgery and otolaryngology, 1998—, assoc. dean clin. affairs, 1999-2000, sr. assoc. dean clin. affairs, 2001—; dir. Yale Med. Group, 1999—. Sci. advisor Nat. Hereditary Hemorrhagic Telangiectasia Found., New Haven, 1991—; bd. dirs. Am. Coll. Mohs Micrographic Surgery and Cutaneous Oncology. Author: Manual of Skin Surgery, 1996, Total Skin: The Definitive Guide to Whole Skin Care for Life, 2000; contbg. editor Jour. Dermatologic Surgery and Oncology, 1992-97; assoc. editor Med. and Surg. Dermatology; mem. editl. bd. Archives of Dermatology, Jour. Aesthetic Dermatology and Cosmetic Surgery, 1999—; assoc. editor Skin and Aging, 1996-98; inventor laser fluorescence device to measure photoaging. Bd. dirs., Conn. Pub. TV, 2001—. Recipient Frederic Mohs award Skin Cancer Found., 1988, 91. Mem. Conn. Dermatology Soc. (pres.). Home: 40 St Ronan St New Haven CT 06511-2251 Office: Yale Sch Medicine PO Box 208059 New Haven CT 06520-8059

LEFFERTS, GEORGE, producer, writer, director; b. Paterson, N.J. BA in Engring., Drew U., 1940; BA in English, U. Mich., 1942. Exec. prodr., writer, dir. NBC, 1947-57; pres. George Lefferts Assocs., 1968—; exec. prodr. ABC, 1966-67, Time-Life Films, 1980-81; tchr. John Hopkins U., Balt., 1989-90, Rutgers U., 1992—; prodr., writer, dir. Network for Continuing Med. Edn., 1990—. Program cons. ABC, 1981. Exhibited sculpture, Sculpture Gallery, N.Y.C., 1960; producer: series Report from America, U.S. Dept. State, Tactic, Am. Cancer Soc., others; (Recipient Nat. Media award 1961, Fame award 1962, Fgn. Press award 1963, Golden Globe award 1967, Plaudit award Producers Guild 1968, 69, Cine Golden Eagle award 1974, Peabody award 1970, 75, 1st prize San Francisco Film Festival 1970; nominee Humanitas Prize 1988); author: plays Nantucket Legend, 1960, The Boat, 1968, Hey Everybody, 1969; columnist N.Y. Observer, Litchfield County Times, 1984-87 (1st prize New England Journalism award, 1984, 85); also author mag. articles, works on piano method, syndicated columns, others; prodns. include Biographies in Sound (Peabody award 1956), NBC Theatre, (Ohio State award 1955), Kraft Theatre, Armstrong Circle Theatre, Studio One, Lights Out, Frank Sinatra Show; spl. program Pain, 1971, Bravo Picasso!, 1972, What Price Health; program NBC Investigative Reports, 1972 (Albert Lasker award), CBS, Ben Franklin Series (Peabody award 1975, Emmy award 1975), Ryan's Hope, 1977 (Emmy award 1977), Purex Specials, 1966 (Emmy award 1966), The People vs. Jean Harris, 1981; exec. prodr., writer, dir., NBC, Spls. for Women (2 Emmy awards 1965); series (Emmy award 1962), 1961 (Golden Globe award 1961); exec. prodr.: series Breaking Point, 1962-64 (Prodrs. Guild Plaudit award 1963), CBS, Smithsonian Spls., 1974-75, ABC, Wide World of Entertainment, 1973-74, Bing Crosby Prodns., 1962-64; exec. prodr.: Wolper Prodns., 1974-75, Time/Life Films, 1978-79; original films produced include: The Living End, 1959, The Stake, 1960, The Teenager, 1965, The Harness, 1972, The Night They Took Miss Beautiful, 1977, Bud & Lou, 1978, Mean Dog Blues, 1979, The Search for Alexander the Great, 1981, Dressed to Kill, 1980; prodr.: series Hallmark Hall of Fame, 1969-70, Never Say Goodbye, 1987 (Emmy award 1988, Humanitas award nomination 1988), TV play Teacher, Teacher, 1974 (Emmy award 1974). With AUS, 1942-45. William Rose scholar Drew U., 1940. Mem. NATAS, Am. Acad. Motion Picture Arts and Scis., Christopher Morley Knothole Assn. Clubs: South Bay Cruising (Babylon, (N.Y.).

LEFFERTS, GILLET, JR. architect; b. N.Y.C., May 6, 1923; s. Gillet and Helen Willets (Lambert) L.; m. Lucia Beverly Hollerith, Apr. 21, 1951; children: Helena Gillet (dec.), Robert Beverly, John Willets, Sarah Fox, David Hollerith. AB, Williams Coll., 1947; MFA, Princeton, 1950. Apprentice Moore & Hutchins, N.Y.C., 1947-48, 50-55, assoc., 1955-66, ptnr., 1967-72, Hutchins, Evans & Lefferts, N.Y.C., 1972-89; mem. The Hall Partnership, Archs., LLP, 1990—. Instr. Mechanics Inst., N.Y.C., 1955-58. Prin. works include SUNY-Binghampton, Buffalo, master plan Coll. Agr., Malaya, St. Johnland Nursing Home, L.I., N.Y., Clark Gymnasium, Cooperstown, N.Y., Nat. Baseball Hall of Fame and Mus. Expansion, Cooperstown, Scholes Libr. Coll. Ceramics, Alfred U. Zoning bd. appeals Town of Darien, Conn., 1961-69, mem. planning and zoning commn., 1969-77, chmn., 1973-77, mem. bd. selectmen, 1983-89; bd. dirs. Darien Hist. Soc., 1978-83, pres., 1982-83; trustee Darien Pub. Libr., 1991-97; bd. dirs. Darien Nature Ctr., 1997—, pres., chmn. 1999-2001. With USAAF, 1943-46. Decorated Air medal with oak leaf cluster. Fellow AIA; mem. Fairfield County Alumni Assn. Williams Coll. (v.p. 1965-67), Nat. Inst. Archtl. Edn. (chmn. bd. trustees 1963-65, treas. 1970-73), Williams Club of N.Y.C., Delta Psi. Episcopalian. Office: 42 E 21st St New York NY 10010-7216 E-mail: glefferts@hallarchitech.com.

LEFFERTS, SYBIL, social worker; b. Chgo., Feb. 21, 1930; d. Anatol Frikin and Ruth (Fleischman) Hagy-Brod; m. Robert B. Lefferts, Oct. 9, 1964; 1 child, Edward Buffman. AB, Sarah Lawrence Coll., 1971; EdM, Harvard U., 1971; MSW, SUNY, Stony Brook, 1982. Cert. social worker, N.Y. Spl. asst. to pres. Greenleigh Assocs., N.Y.C., 1964-69; cons., 1971-72; lectr. SUNY, Stony Brook, 1972-77, 81; asst. provost acad. affairs Antioch U. East, 1977-78; assoc. dean Antioch U., Balt., 1978; pvt. psychotherapy practice N.Y., 1978-81, 82—; social work supr. div. community mental health Suffolk County Dept. Health Svcs., Hauppauge, 1983-89, sr. psychiat. social worker div. community mental health, 1989-95. Editor: Suffolk County People's Guide to Health Care, 1982, 73, 76, Practitioner's Guide to Complementary Therapies, 1982. Mem. Cen. and North Brookhaven Health Coun. (founder), Women's Health Alliance Long Island Inc., Concern for Mental Health, Inc. (bd. dirs.), NASW. Avocations: gardening, playing guitar, singing, rowing. Home and Office: 33 Old Coach Rd East Setauket NY 11733-3818

LEFFERTS, WILLIAM GEOFFREY, physician, educator; b. Towanda, Pa., Mar. 24, 1943; s. William LeRoy and Beatrice (Smith) L.; m. Susan Lynn Hiles, Oct. 31, 1970. BA, Hamilton Coll., 1965; MD, Hahnemann Med. Coll., 1969. Intern Hahnemann Hosp., 1969-70; resident in internal medicine Cleve. Clinic Hosp., 1970-73, chief med. resident, 1972-73; asst. prof. internal medicine Hahnemann Med. Coll., 1973-77; assoc. prof. Med. Coll. Pa., 1978-82, dir. primary care unit, 1978-82, dir. div. gen. internal medicine, 1979-82; staff physician Cleve. Clinic Found., 1982—. Fellow ACP. Office: 9500 Euclid Ave Cleveland OH 44195-0001

LEFFLER, CAROLE ELIZABETH, mental health nurse, women's health nurse; b. Sidney, Ohio, Feb. 18, 1942; d. August B. and Delores K. Aselage; children: Veronica, Christopher. ADN, Sinclair Community Coll., Dayton, Ohio, 1975. Cert. psychiat. nurse supr. Nurse Grandview Hosp, Dayton, 1961-76; substitute sch. nurse Fairborn (Ohio) City Schs., 1981-82; dir. nursing Fairborn Nursing Home, 1983; psychiat. nurse supr. Twin Valley Behavioral Health Ctr., 1984—. Mem. exec. bd. 1199; chmn. disaster mental health com. ARC Ohio. Vol., instr., disaster health nurse ARC, chmn. State of Ohio disaster mental health com.; officer, leader, camp nurse for Girl Scouts, Boy Scouts; Ch. Parish Coun. Recipient Fleur de Lis award Girl and Boy Scouts, Svc. award ARC, Fairborn Mayor's Cert. of Merit for Civic Pride, State of Ohio Govs. award Innovation Ohio. Mem. ANA, Ohio Nurses Assn. Home: 3020 N Dayton Lakeview Rd New Carlisle OH 45344-8505

LEFKO, JEFFREY JAY, hospital administrator; b. St. Paul, July 15, 1945; s. Morris and Dorothy (Mindell) L.; m. Philomena M. Corno, Mar. 6, 1970 (div. Dec. 1984); children: Melissa Ann, Benjamin Scott, Ellen Rachael; m. Mary Wilson, Jan. 10, 1986 (div. June 1989); m. Susan H. Shockley, Jan. 5, 1990. BSBA with distinction, U. Nebr., 1967; M in Hosp. Adminstrn., Washington U., St. Louis, 1969. Adminstrv. resident St. John's Mercy Hosp., St. Louis, 1968-69; nat. fellow Health Services Adminstrn. Am. Hosp. Assn.-Blue Cross Assn., Chgo., 1969-70; v.p. planning/ops. Meth. Hosp. of Ind., Indpls., 1970-75; v.p. Jewish Hosp., St. Louis, 1975-78; v.p. planning Greenville (S.C.) Hosp. System, 1979-88; exec. cons. The Lash Group, Greenville, 1988-90; v.p. planning Union Meml. Hosp., Balt., 1990-93; v.p. planning and mktg. St. Joseph Med. Ctr., 1993-98; exec. v.p. Am.'s Dr., Inc., 1998—, Americasdoctor.com, 1998-2000; v.p. e-bus. HCIASachs, Inc., 2000—, Greystonenet, 2001—. Adj. instr. Washington U., 1976-78; guest lectr. Duke U., Univ. S.C., Clemson U., Ind. U.; instr. Furman U., Greenville, 1982-84, Med. Univ. of S.C. 1989. Contbr. articles to profl. jours.; contbr. to (book) Guide to Strategic Planning for Hosps., 1981; mem. edit. bd. Health Care Strategic Mgmt., 1984—. Mem. Am. Hosp. Ass. (pres. Soc. for Hosp. Planning and Mktg. 1984-85), Am. Coll. of Health Care Execs., Carolinas Soc. of Hosp. Planning (founding mem.), Innocents Soc., Beta Gamma Sigma. Lodges: Rotary. Avocations: coaching boys' baseball, basketball clubs, reading, tennis, baseball card collecting. Office: 7004 Wardman Rd Baltimore MD 21212 E-mail: jlefko@greystonenet.com.

LEFKOVITS, ALBERT MEYER, dermatologist; b. N.Y.C., June 30, 1937; s. Aaron Melchoir and Muriel (Mark) L.; A.B., Cornell U., 1958; M.D. (Lederle research fellow), N.Y. Med. Coll., 1962; m. Cheryl Beth Kornberg, Apr. 25, 1971; children— Ari Nathan, Lauren Blair. Intern, Newark Beth Israel Hosp., 1962-63; resident in dermatology Kings County Hosp. Center, SUNY, Downstate Med. Center, Bklyn., 1963-65; chief resident dermatology Mt. Sinai Hosp., N.Y.C., 1965-66, research fellow in dermatology, 1966-67, asst. attending physician, 1966— ; practice medicine specializing in dermatology, N.Y.C., 1966— ; asst. attending physician Beekman-Downtown Hosp., N.Y.C., 1966-75; instr. dermatology Mt. Sinai Sch. Medicine, 1966-68, clin. asso. dermatology, 1968-73, asst. prof., 1974, acad. council, 1973-78, 1886—; instr. dermatology N.Y. Med. Coll., 1966-69. Alumni fund-raising chmn. Horace Mann Sch., 1976-78; treas. Mt. Sinai Alumni, 1988-90, sec., 1991-93, v.p., 1993-95, pres. 1995-97. Served to maj. M.C., AUS, 1969-71. Recipient Fredrick Wise Dermatology award N.Y. Acad. Medicine, 1965, Torch of Liberty award Anti-Defamation League, 1987, Maimonides award Keren Or Found. for Handicapped Blind Children, 1994; mem. med. adv. bd. Skin Cancer Found. Mem. Harvey Soc., Soc. Investigative Dermatology, Dermatology Found., Soc. Tropical Dermatology, Am. Acad. Dermatology (task force on therapeutics and FDA liaison com., comm. coun., physicians practice com.), Am. Acad. Dermatology (comm. coun., physicians practice com.), AMA, Internat. Soc. Human and Animal Mycology, Mycology Soc. Ams., N.Y. Acad. Sci., Am. Physicians Fedn. (trustee, exec. com.), Jewish Chautauqua Soc. (life), Dermatology Soc. Greater N.Y. (pres., chmn. physicians advocacy com.), N.Y. State Med. Soc., Cornell Alumni Assn. N.Y. (bd. govs. 1974-76) Med. Adv. Bd. Skin Cancer Found., 1986—. Jewish (dir. congregation Emanu-El men's club). Clubs: Harmonie, Town, Cornell (N.Y.C.), Friar's, Lawrence Yacht (fleet surgeon 1982-83, sec. 1984, treas. 1985, commodore 1987). Address: 1040 Park Ave New York NY 10028-1032

LEFKOW, MICHAEL FRANCIS, lawyer; b. Dec. 9, 1940; s. Frederick Lord and Marjorie Claiborne (Freeman) L.; 1 child, Duschia; m. Joan Marilyn Humphrey, June 21, 1975; children: Maria, Helena, Laura, Margaret. BA, North Cen. Coll., Naperville, Ill., 1962; JD, Northwestern U., 1966. Bar: Ill. 1966, U.S. Dist. Ct. (no. dist.) Ill. 1967, Colo. 1969, U.S. Ct. Appeals (7th cir.) 1971, U.S. Supreme Ct. 1971, Fla. 1982, U.S. Ct. Appeals (fed. cir.) 1986. Gen. counsel Chgo. Welfare Rights Orgn., 1969-72, Ill. Welfare Rights Orgn., Chgo., 1972-76; pvt. practice, 1977-78, 85—; mng. atty. Prairie State Legal Svcs., Inc., Wheaton, Ill., 1978-79; supervisory trial atty. EEOC, Miami, Fla., 1979-82; asst. regional labor counsel U.S. Postal Svc., Chgo., 1982-85. Spl. commr. U.S. Dist. Ct. (no. dist.) Ill., 1985-87; atty. U.S. Fed. Defender Panel, 1991—. Chpt. v.p. League United Latin-Am. Citizens, Miami, 1979; mem. Social Concerns Com., Episcopal Diocese South Fla., Miami, 1981; mem. vestry St. Luke's Episcopal Ch., Evanston, Ill., 1992-95; mem. Episcopal Vol. Lawyers Network, Diocese Chgo., 1996—; area chair 48th ward Dem. Party and Dem. Coalition, 1996, 48th ward Dem. party, 1996—. Mem. ABA, Chgo. Coun. Lawyers (bd. dirs. 1972-74, 87-89), Plaintiffs Employment Lawyers Assn., Chgo. Bar Assn., (past bd. dirs., vice chair lawyers referral svc. com., 2000-01, chair, 2001-02, mem. fin. com.), Nat. Clearinghouse for Legal Svcs., Lake County Bar Assn. Democrat. Episcopalian. Office: 53 W Jackson Blvd Ste 918 Chicago IL 60604-3607 Fax: (312) 427-6053. E-mail: lefkowmf@att.net.

LEFKOWITZ, ALAN ZOEL, lawyer; b. Pitts., Dec. 1, 1932; s. Curtis and Lily Rose Lefkowitz; m. Francine Marcia Kaplan, Feb. 5, 1956; children: Curtis Robert, Gail Ann, David Edward. AB, U. Pitts., 1953; JD, U. Mich., 1955. Bar: Pa. 1956, U.S. Supreme Ct. 1959, U.S. Ct. Appeals (3d cir.), U.S. Dist. Ct. (we. dist.) Pa., U.S. Tax Ct. Assoc. Kaplan, Finkel & Roth, Pitts., 1955-72; mng. ptnr. Kaplan, Finkel, Lefkowitz, Roth & Ostrow, 1972-82, Finkel Lefkowitz Ostrow & Woolridge, Pitts., 1982-88; ptnr., head corp. sect. Tucker Arenberg, P.C., 1988-93; dir. Kabala & Geeseman, 1993-99. Adj. prof. arts and law Heinz Sch. Pub. Policy and Adminstrn./Carnegie Mellon Un.; sec. TPC Comm., Inc., Pitts., 1970-91, Computer Rsch., Inc., Pitts., 1969-92, Star-Tron Tech., Inc., Pitts., 1986-92. Mem. Pitts. Coun. Internat. Visitors; trustee United Jewish Fedn. Pitts., 1964-68, Rodef Shalom Congregation, Pitts., 1962-64, 90-98; bd. dirs., treas., v.p. Jewish Family and Childrens Svcs., Pitts., 1967-68; bd. dirs. Family Resources, 1986X, U.S. Counter-Intelligence Corp. With U.S. Army, 1956-59. Mem. ABA, Internat. Assn. Fin. Planners (Pitts. chpt. v.p. ethics regulation), Internat. Assn. Jewish Lawyers, Pa. Bar Assn., Allegheny County Bar Assn. (former chair arts law sect., former chair, coun. corp. sec., chair securities regulation com., former chair internat. com.), Photoimagers Guild, Acad. Arts and Scis. (photography sect., bd. dirs. 1994X), Silver Eye Ctr. for Photography (trustee, sec.). Avocations: photography, theatre.

LEFKOWITZ, HOWARD N. lawyer; b. Utica, N.Y., Oct. 28, 1936; s. Samuel I. and Sarah Lefkowitz; m. Martha Yelon, June 16, 1958; children: Sarah, David. BA, Cornell U., 1958; LLB, Columbia U., 1963. Bar: N.Y. 1963. Ptnr. Proskauer Rose LLP, N.Y.C., 1963—. Tri-bar opinion com. Author: New York LLC and LLP Forms and Practice Manual, Data Trace, 3d edit. 2001; co-author: Transactional Lawyers Deskbook: Advising Business Entities West, 2001; editor Columbia Law Rev., 1963. Lt. (j.g.) USN, 1958-61. Kent scholar Columbia U. Law Sch. Fellow: Am. Coll. Investment Counsel; mem.: Pvt. Investment Fund Forum (treas.), N.Y. County Lawyers Assn. (chmn. com. on comm. entertainment and arts-related law 1983—86), Assn. of Bar of City of N.Y. (chmn. com. on corp. law 1990—93, com. on corp. law 1997—2000), ABA (mem. ltd. liability entity subcom. of bus. sect. 1993—). Office: Proskauer Rose LLP 1585 Broadway Fl 23 New York NY 10036-8299

LEFKOWITZ, JEROME, lawyer; b. N.Y.C., Mar. 24, 1931; s. Jack and Sue (Horowitz) L.; m. Myrna Judith Weishaut, Aug. 12, 1956; children: Jay, Mark, Miriam, Alan. Student, Jewish Theol. Sem., N.Y.C., 1948-51; BA, NYU, 1952; JD, Columbia U., 1955. Bar: N.Y. 1955, U.S. Dist. Ct. (so. and ea. dists.) N.Y. 1990. Asst. atty. gen. N.Y. State Dept. of Law, Albany, 1958-60; counsel, dep. commissioner N.Y. State Dept. of Labor, N.Y.C., Albany, 1960-67; dep. chmn., mem. N.Y. Pub. Rels. Bd., Albany, 1967-87; adj. faculty Albany Law Sch. Columbia U., N.Y.C., Albany, 1968-89; dep. counsel Civil Svc. Employment Assn., Albany, 1987—. Cons. State of Mich., 1969, State of Hawaii, 1970, State of Pa., 1976, State of Mass., 1978. Author: Public Employee Unionism In Israel, 1971; editor: Public Sector Labor & Employment Law, 1988, 2d edit., 1998, The Evolving Process--Collective Negotiations In Public Employment, 1985. Chmn. community rels. com. Albany Jewish Fedn., 1980-84, 86-87; pres. Massad Hebrew Speaking Camps. Mem. N.Y. State Bar Assn. (chmn. com. on pub. sector labor rels. 1975-79, chmn. com. on legis. 1980-83, chmn. labor law sect. 1991-92). Republican. Avocations: tennis, skiing, reading, history. Home: 54 Maxwell St Albany NY 12208-1639 Office: Civil Svc Employment Assn 143 Washington Ave Albany NY 12210-2303 E-mail: lefkowitz@cseains.org.

LEFKOWITZ, JOEL M. psychologist, educator; b. N.Y.C., Oct. 17, 1940; s. Frank Morris and Charlotte (Van Dam) L.; m. Merle Ellen Goldner, Sept. 12, 1965 (div. May 1982); children: Jared, Melanie; m. Setha M. Low, June 26, 1994. BBA, CCNY, 1961; MS, Case Western Res. U., Cleve., 1963, PhD, 1965. Lic. psychologist, N.Y.; diplomate Am. Bd. Profl. Psychology. Asst. prof. to prof. psychology Baruch Coll., CUNY, N.Y.C., 1965—. Ind. cons., N.Y.C., 1965—; mem. nat. bd. mem. Am. Bd. Profl. Psychology, 1995—. Contbr. articles to profl. jours. Mem. APA, Am. Psychol. Soc. Avocations: tennis, photography. Office: Baruch Coll Box B8-215 1 Bernard Baruch Way New York NY 10010 E-mail: Joel_Lefkowitz@Baruch.CUNY.edu.

LEFKOWITZ, LOUIS HIRSCH, obstetrician-gynecologist; b. Bklyn., Oct. 20, 1937; s. Paul Howard and Bertha (Schulman) L.; m. Patricia Smith; 1 child, Andrew, Philip. BA, U. N.C., 1959; postgrad., U. bologna, 1959-62; MD, N.Y. Med. Coll., 1964. Diplomate Am. Bd. Ob-gyn. Intern Beth Israel Med. Ctr., N.Y.C., 1964-65; resident in ob-gyn N.Y. Med. Coll., Flower Fifth Avenue and Met. Hosp. Ctr., 1965-69; dir. ob-gyn. dept. Good Samaritan Hosp., Suffern, N.Y., 1988-92. Maj. U.S. Army, 1969-71. Fellow ACOG, ACS, Am. Assn. Reproductive Medicine; mem. Am. Assn. Gynecologic Laparoscopy, Rockland County Med. Soc., N.Y. State Med. Soc. Jewish. Office: Tallman Ob-Gyn PC 134 Route 59 Suffern NY 10901-4917 also: 673 Route 17M Monroe NY 10950-3318 E-mail: mdlou@aol.com.

LEFKOWITZ, MARY ROSENTHAL, Greek literature educator; b. N.Y.C., Apr. 30, 1935; d. Harold L. and Mena (Weil) Rosenthal; m. Alan L. Lefkowitz, July 1, 1956 (div.); children: Rachel, Hannah; m. Hugh Lloyd-Jones, Mar. 26, 1982. BA, Wellesley Coll., 1957; AM, Radcliffe Coll., 1959, PhD, 1961; LHD (hon.), Trinity Coll., Hartford, Conn., 1996, Grinnell Coll., 2000; PhD (hon.), U. Patras, Greece, 1999. Instr. Greek Wellesley (Mass.) Coll., 1960-63, asst. prof. Greek and Latin, 1964-69, assoc. prof. Greek and Latin, 1969-75, prof. Greek and Latin, 1975-79; Andrew W. Mellon prof. in the humanities Wellesley (Mass.) Coll, 1979—. Vis. prof. U. Calif., Berkeley, 1978; vis. fellow St. Hilda's Coll., 1979-80, Corpus Christi Coll., 1991. Author: Heroines and Hysterics, 1981, Lives of the Greek Poets, 1981, Women in Greek Myth, 1986, First Person Fictions, 1991, Not Out of Africa, 1996, 2d edit., 1997; co-editor: Women's Life in Greece and Rome, 1982, 2d edit., 1992, Black Athena Revisited, 1996. Fellow NEH, 1979-80, 91, ACLS, 1972-73, Hon. fellow St. Hilda's Coll., Oxford, 1994—. Mem. Am. Philol. Assn. (bd. dirs. 1974-77), Class Assn. New Eng. (pres. 1972-73). Home: 15 W Riding St Wellesley MA 02482-6914 Office: Wellesley Coll 106 Central St Wellesley MA 02481-8268 E-mail: mlefkowitz@wellesley.edu.

LEFLAND, RENEE RACHEL, internist; b. N.Y.C., June 28, 1962; m. Mitchell Lefland, Nov. 30, 1985; 3 children. BS, Cornell U., 1984; MD, U. Vt., 1988. Diplomate Am. Bd. Internal Medicine. Pvt. practice, Garden City, N.Y., 1991—. Office: 877 Stewart Ave Garden City NY 11530-4803

LEFLER, WADE HAMPTON, JR. ophthalmologist; b. Statesville, N.C., Feb. 27, 1937; s. Wade Hampton and Eunice Trudye (Chilcoat) L.; m. Katherine Webb Davis, Apr. 1, 1961; children: Elizabeth Ashley Wilson, Rosemary Kirsten, Ririe. AB, U. N.C., 1959; MD, Bowman Gray Sch. Medicine, 1963. Diplomate Am. Bd. Ophthalmology. Intern N.Y. Hosp./Cornell Med. Ctr., 1963-64; resident in ophthalmology Duke U. Med. Ctr., Durham, N.C., 1966-69; practice medicine specializing in ophthalmology, Hickory, 1969—; ptnr. Graystone Eye, Ear, Nose and Throat Ctr., 1974—; clin. assoc. prof. ophthalmology Duke Med. Ctr., 1969—. Mem. staff Catawba Meml. Hosp., Hickory, Frye Regional Med. Ctr., Hickory, Western Carolina Center, Morganton, N.C., Duke Eye Center, Durham, N.C., Oteen VA Hosp., Asheville, N.C. Trustee Catawba Meml. Hosp., 1990-94. Served to capt. M.C., U.S. Army, 1964-66. Duke U. Med. Ctr. grantee, 1968-70. Mem. AMA, N.C. Med. Soc., Catawba County Med. Soc., Med. Alumni Assn. Bowman Gray Sch. Medicine (pres. 1993, Disting. Svc. award 1995), Lake Hickory Country Club, Phi Beta Kappa, Alpha Omega Alpha. Presbyterian. Home: 1260 6th St NW Hickory NC 28601-2408 Office: PO Box 2588 Hickory NC 28603-2588 E-mail: khlefler@twave.net.

LEFLORE, JOHN LAUZINE, artist, historian; b. L.A., Mar. 10, 1952; s. John Lauzine Jr. and Mattie Frazier LeFlore. BA in Painting and Art History, San Francisco State U., 1981, postgrad., 1981—87; cert. in computer studies, Control Data Inst., San Francisco, 1986. Painter, artist, San Francisco, 1988—. Lectr. San Francisco State U., 1977—89, Laney Coll., Oakland, Calif., 1977—89. Roman Catholic. Home: PO Box 425406 San Francisco CA 94142-5406

LEFLY, DIANNE LOUISE, research psychologist; b. Denver, July 17, 1946; d. Gordon Eugene Boen and Elizabeth (Welsh) Tuveson. AB, U. No. Colo., 1968; MA, U. Colo., 1980; PhD, U. Denver, 1994. Classroom tchr. Adam County Sch. Dist. 12, Thornton, Colo., 1968-77; rschr. John F. Kennedy Child Devel. Ctr., Denver, 1979-81, U. Colo. Health Scis. Ctr., 1981-89, U. Denver, 1989-98; rschr. mgr. Denver Pub Schs., 1998—. Cons. Colo. Dept. Edn., 1997—, Colo. Dept. Pub. Health and Environ., 1997—, Piton Found., 2002—. Contbr. articles to profl. jours. Mem. Colo. Rep. Party, Denver, 1968—. Scholarship U. No. Colo., 1964-68; fellowship U. Denver, 1989. Mem. Mensa, Am. Ednl. Rsch. Assn., Nat. Coun. on Measurement in Edn. Republican. Avocations: computer activities, dancing, hiking, reading. Home: 6215 Secrest St Arvada CO 80403 Office: Denver Pub Schs 900 Grant St Denver CO 80203-2907

LEFORTE, JOHN STEWART ARCHIBALD, retreat house manager; b. Glace Bay, N.S., Can., Aug. 15, 1951; s. George Peter Lafargue-L. and Helen Louise Bradley-MacIsaac. BS in Geology, St. Francis Xavier U., Antigonish, N.S., 1973; Diploma in Ministry, St. Francis Xavier U., 1998. Cert. Canadian Mgmt. Profl. Cert. (CMP), 2002. Geol. field asst. N.S. Dept. Mines, Stellarton, 1971—72, Noranda Exploration, Bathurst, 1973; mgr. W.E.L.L. Woodworkers, Glace Bay, N.S., 1973-75; reporter, photographer Coastal Courier, 1977-81; bd. dirs. Family Svcs. Ea. N.S., Sydney, 1982-83; mgr. retreat house Episcopal Corp. Antigonish, 1985—. Chair adv. bd. Glace Bay Family Svcs., 1979-84; mem. comms. com. Diocese of Antigonish, 1998—, editor, web coord., 1998—. Editor, webmaster: Heraldry Soc. Can., 1999—2002. With pub. rels., press releases, ads Cape Breton East Richmond Liberal Campaign, Glace Bay, 1984; vice chair St. Anthony Parish Coun., Glace Bay, 1982-83; Nova Scotia coord. Engaged Encounter Movement, 1995—; vol. St. John Ambulance Brigade, 1999—; citizen appointee Cape Breton Regional Municipality. Decorated Knight Sacred and Mil. Constantinian Order St. George, 1994, granted Coat of Arms Can. Heraldic Authority, 1996; recipient certificates of appreciation U. Coll. Cape Breton. Mem. Cath. Communicators Can., Heraldry Soc. Can., Heraldry Soc. Eng., Ctr. Genealogique des Landes, Equestrian Knightly Order of Holy Sepulchre of Jerusalem (apptd. Megistral Del. for Can.-Atlantic 2001, Cross of Merit 2001, named Knight Comdr. 2002, mem. Internat. Commn. Orders of Chivalry 2001--), Equestrian Order Atlantic Provinces (webmaster, editor, writer 1999, pres. Atlantic Can. sect. Toronto Lieutenancy 1999-2001, Knight). Roman Catholic. Avocations: heraldry, orders of chivalry, genealogy, photography. Office: Villa Madonna Retreat House 12 Villa Dr Little Bras d'Or NS Canada B1Y 2X1 Fax: (902) 736-1421. E-mail: j.stewart@canada.com.

LEFRAK, EDWARD ARTHUR, cardiovascular and thoracic surgeon; b. Newark, Apr. 21, 1943; s. Bernard David and Lillian (Hollander) L.; m. Trudy Glaser, Aug. 8, 1973; children: Lisa, Allison, Shayna, Ashley, Mikaela. BA cum laude, SUNY, Buffalo, 1965; MD, Ind. U., 1969. Diplomate Am. Bd. Surgery, Am. Bd. Thoracic Surgery. Intern in gen. surgery Baylor Coll. Medicine Affiliated Hosps., Houston, 1969-70, resident in gen. surgery, 1970-75; resident cardiopulmonary surgery U. Oreg. Med. Sch., 1975-77; chief cardiac surgery Inova Heart Ctr. at Fairfax Hosp., Falls Church, Va., 1977—, dir. cardiac surgery rsch.; pres. Cardiovascular and Thoracic Surgery Assocs., P.C., Annandale; clin. assoc. prof. surgery Uniformed Svcs. U. Health Scis., Bethesda, Md.; asst. clin. prof. surgery Georgetown U. Sch. Medicine, Washington; active staff Cardio-Thoracic Surgery Svc. Nat. Naval Med. Ctr., Bethesda. Asst. prof. surgery U. Oreg. Med. Sch., 1977; mem. courtesy staff Alexandria (Va.) Hosp.; active staff Arlington (Va.) Hosp., Alexandria (Va.) Hosp.; cons. Clin. Ctr. NIH, Bethesda; mem. med. adv. com. Washington Regional Transplant Consortium; dir. heart and lung transplantation Va. Heart Ctr. Fairfax, 1986-86; mem. critical care com. Fairfax Hosp., 1978-93; mem. com. for clin. investigation involving human beings Baylor Coll. Medicine, 1974; jour. cons. Chest, Cancer Chemotherapy Reports. Author: Cardiac Valve Prostheses, 1979; prodr. films in field; contbr. articles to profl. publs. Fellow ACS, Am. Coll. Cardiology, Am. Coll. Chest Physicians, Internat. Coll. Surgeons; mem. AMA, Am. Heart Assn. (bd. dirs. No. Va. chpt. 1978), Albert Starr Surg. Soc., Fairfax County Med. Soc., Med. Soc. Va., Met. Washington Soc. Thoracic and Cardiovascular Surgeons, Michael E. DeBakey Internat. Cardiovascular Soc., So. Thoracic Surgeons, Internat. Soc. for Heart and Lung Transplantation, So. thoracic Surg. Assn., Washington Area Transplant Soc., Am. Assn. Thoracic Surgery, Colegio Interamericano de Médicos y Cirujanos. Address: 3301 Woodburn Rd Annandale VA 22003-1229

LEFRAK, SAMUEL JAYSON, housing and building corporation executive; b. N.Y.C., Feb. 12, 1918; s. Harry and Sarah (Schwarz) LeF.; m. Ethel Stone, May 14, 1941; children: Denise, Richard, Francine, Jacqueline. Grad., U. Md., 1940; postgrad., Columbia U., Harvard U.; LLD (hon.), U. of Studies, Rome, 1971, N.Y. Law Sch., 1974, Colgate U., 1979; HHD (hon.), Pratt Inst., 1988, U. Md., 1990, Queens Coll., 1994, Mich. State U., 1995, St. John's U., 1996. Pres. Lefrak Orgn., 1948—, chmn. bd., 1975—; creator, sponsor, builder Lefrak City, Battery Park City, Gateway Pla., Newport Complex. Mem. adv. bd. Sta. WHLI, 1955; commr. Landmarks Preservation Commn., N.Y.C., 1966; commr. pub. works Borough Manhattan, 1956-58; commr. Interstate Sanitation Commn., 1958; Saratoga Springs Commn., 1962—; mem. adv. bd. Chem Bank.; guest lectr. Harvard Grad. Sch. Bus. Adminstrn., 1971, Yale, 1975, NYU, 1977; guest speaker Fin. Women's Assn., N.Y., 1975; guest lectr. Princeton U., U. Haifa, 1983, Oxford U., 1984, Pratt Inst., 1987, Harvard U., 1987, Columbia Sch. Bus., 1988, Wharton Sch. Bus., 1989, Sch. Bus. NYU, 1989; speaker UN, 1988; featured speaker Instl. Investment Real Estate Conf., 1975, Fed. Home Loan Bank Conf., 1990; guest lectr. Japanese Govt., Finnish Govt., Switzerland, 1967; U.S. del. Internat. Conf. Housing and Urban Devel., Switzerland, 1967; dir. N.Y. World's Fair Corp., 1964-65, N.Y. Indsl. Devel. Corp., 1975—, chmn. bd. L.I. Post; pres. N.Y.C. Comml. Devel. Corp., 1967-71, chmn., 1971—; founding mem. World Business Coun., Inc., 1970; mem. Pres.'s Com. Employment Handicapped; spl. cons. urban affairs State Dept., 1969; mem. adv. coun. Real Estate Inst., N.Y. U., 1970—; mem. gov. fin. Pres.'s Club U. Md., 1971, com. N.Y. State Traffic Safety Council, 1966; bd. visitors Sch. Law, Columbia U., 1983; commr. Saratoga-Capital dist. N.Y. State Park and Recreation Commn., 1973; mem. real estate coun. exec. com. Met. Mus. Art, 1982; mem. N.Y.C. Pub. Devel. Corp., Nat. Energy Coun., U.S. Dept. Commerce, Mayor's Com. on Housing Devel., N.Y.C., 1974—; mem. exec. com. Citizen's Budget Com. for N.Y.C., Inc., 1975—; mem. Gov. Cuomo's Adv. Coun., 1983, N.Y. State Gov.'s Task Force on Housing, 1974; establish Lefrak Lecture Series, U. Md., 1982; creator, developer residential and business property. Vice chmn.-at-large ARC, N.Y.; mem. U.S. com. UN Orgn., 1957; chmn. nat. bd. Histadrut, 1967—; mem. Israel Bonds Prime Minister Com., 1980; dir. Ronald McDonald House, 1986; chmn. bldg. com. Saratoga Performing Arts Ctr.; mem. Fifth Ave. Assn.; dir., chmn. real estate div. Greater N.Y. Fund; hon. com. AAU; Queens chmn. United Greek Orthodox Charities, 1973; chmn. Celebrity Sports Night-Human Resources Ctr., 1973-74, Sports Assn. Hebrew U. of Jerusalem, 1979; patron Met. Mus. Art; sponsor Israel Philharm. Orch., Jan Groth Exhibit, Guggenheim Mus.; trustee, dir. Beth-El Hosp.; bd. dirs. USO, Citizens Housing and Planning Council, N.Y., 1957—, Interfaith Movement, Diabetics Found., Queens Cultural Assn., Consumer Credit Counseling Svc. Greater N.Y., Astoria Motion Picture and TV Ctr. Found.; trustee N.Y. Law Sch., Queens Art and Cultural Ctr., Jewish Hosp. at Denver, N.Y Civic Budget Com.; trustee, med. adv. bd. Brookdale Hosp. Med. Ctr., Pace U.; mem. exec. bd. Greater N.Y. couns. Boy Scouts Am.; founder Albert Einstein Sch. Medicine; mem. Bretton Woods Com.; bd. govs. Invest-in-Am. Nat. Coun.; mem. task force on energy conservation Div. Community Housing, 1981—; mem. com. N.Y. State Traffic Safety Coun., 1966; chmn. Scandinavia Today, 1981—; bd. visitors Sch. Law Columbia U., 1983; mem. adv. bd. The Explorer's Club, 1984; mem. Nat. Com. on U.S.-China Rels. Inc.; bd. dirs. Inst. Nautical Archaeology; trustee Queens Coll., 1989; adv. dir. Met. Opera, 1990; conf. bd. Keynote Address-Annual Fin. Seminar, 1987; mem. Lambda Alpha Internat. bd. trustees Guggenheim Mus., 1993; mem. bd. trustees Dana Farber Cancer Inst. Harvard Med. Sch., 1992. Decorated officer Order of Lion of Finland, 1980, Medal of Parliament, 1988; officer Order St. John of Jerusalem Knights of Malta, 1982; Order of the North Star of Sweden, 1982; comdr. Royal Norwegian Order of Merit, 1987; Chevalier des Artes et des Lettres medal, France, 1996, Commendatore Order of Merit, Italy, 1997; recipient Mayor N.Y.C. award outstanding citizenship, 1960; Nat. Boys Club award, 1960; Citizen of Year award B'nai Brith, 1963; Am. Achievement award, 1984; Disting. Achievement award Pratt Inst., 1967; Man of Year award VFW, 1963; Brotherhood award NCCJ, 1964; Chief Rabbi Herzog gold medal; Torah Fellowship citation Religious Zionist Am., 1966; John F. Kennedy Peace award, 1966; Man of Year award Bklyn. Community Hosp., 1967; Builder of Excellence award Brandeis U., 1968; Master Builder award N.Y. Cardiac Ctr., 1968; Disting. Citizen award M Club Found. U. Md., 1970; Disting. Alumnus award U. Md. Alumni Assn., 1970; Disting. Citizen and Outstanding Community Svc. award United Way, 1986; Am. Achievement award Ency. Britannica, 1984; Am. Eagle award nat. coun. Invest-in Am., 1972; Exec. Sportsman award Human Resources Ctr., 1973; Archtl. award Fifth Av. Assn., 1974; Excellence in Design award Queens C. of C., 1974; Flame Truth award Fund Higher Edn., 1986; LeFrak Forum Mich. State U., 1997; elected hon. citizen Md., 1970; Citizen of Yr. award Bklyn. Philharm. Orch., 1983; dedication of Samuel J. LeFrak Hall U. Md., 1982, LeFrak Gymnasium, Amherst Coll., 1986, LeFrak Terrace Explorers Club, 1996, LeFrak Moot Ct., N.Y. Law Sch., 1990, LeFrak Meadow, N.Y.C., 1991, LeFrak Concert Hall, Queens Coll., LeFrak Gallery and Sculpture Terrace, Guggenheim Mus.; LeFrak Lecture Series at U. Md. established, 1982, LeFrak Learning Ctr. Temple Emanuel, 1995; LeFrak Gymnasium and Scholarship Barnard Coll., 1997; LeFrak IMAX Theatre in Am. Mus. Natural History; Comdr. of the Royal Norwegian Order of Merit, presented by King Olav V, 1987; Rough Riders award Boy Scouts Am., 1987; Torch of Progress Assoc. Builders and Owners Greater N.Y.; award Soc. Fgn. Consuls, 1988, Gold medal and Man of Yr. award Israel Bonds Found., 1990, Developer of the Yr. Associated Builders and Owners of Greater N.Y., 1990; award Assn. Graphics Arts, 1990, Disting. Citizen of World award UN, 1994, Alumni Hall of Fame award U. Md., 1995, award N.J. Hist. Soc., 1999, hon. N.Y. Ear and Ear Infirmary, 1999; named to Nat. Sales Club Hall of Fame, 1990, Songwriter's Hall of Fame, 1997, Samuel J. LeFrak Day named in hon. gov. N.Y., N.Y. State license plate deicated in hon., 1998, Man of Yr. gov. Philippines, 1999, 100 most important New Yorkers during past 400 yrs. whose work contributed to city's cultural and econ. success Crain Mag., 1999. Mem. Sales Execs. Club N.Y. (dir.), United Hunts Racing Assn., Philharm. Symphony Soc. N.Y., Explorers Club (dir.), Newcomen Soc. U.S., Phi Kappa Phi, Tau Epsilon Phi (established Samuel J. LeFrak scholarship award 1975). Clubs: U. Md. Pres.'s (mem. Gov. N.Y. fin.), Lotos (bd. dirs. 1975—, Merit award 1973), Grand Street Boys, Friars (dir. Found.), Advertising, Economic, Downtown Athletic (N.Y.C.); Town, Turf and Field; Cat Cay (Nassau, Bahamas); Xanadu Yacht (Freeport, Grand Bahamas); Palm Bay (Miami Beach, Fla.); Seawane; Ocean Reef (Key Largo); Sag Harbor Yacht (L.I.). Lodges: Masons (32d degree), Shriners. Office: Lefrak Orgn Inc 97-77 Queens Blvd Rego Park NY 11374-3317

LEFRANC, MARGARET (MARGARET SCHOONOVER), artist, illustrator, editor, writer; b. N.Y.C., Mar. 15, 1907; d. Abraham and Sophie (Teplitz) Frankel; m. Raymond E. Schoonover, 1942 (div. 1945). Student, Art Students League, N.Y.C., Kunstschule des Westerns, Berlin, NYU Grad. Sch., Andre L'Hote, Paris, Acad. Grande Chaumiere, Paris. Tchr. art Adult Edn., Los Alamos, 1946, Miami (Fla.) Mus. Modern Art, 1975-76. Mem. Art in the Embassies Program, Paris, 1998—2001. Exhibitions include one-person show Mus. N.Mex., Santa Fe, 1948, 1951, 1953, Philbrook Art Ctr., Tulsa, Okla., 1949, 1951, Okla. Art Ctr., 1950, Recorder Workshop, Miami, Fla., 1958, St. John's Coll., Santa Fe, N.Mex., 1993, 1997, A Lifetime of Imaging (works on paper), 1921—95, Figurative Works, 1920—30, Cline Fine Art Gallery, 1997, exhibitions include group shows Salon de Tuileries, Paris, 1928, 1929, 1930, Art Inst. Chgo., 1936, El Paso Mus. Art, 1964, Mus. Modern Art, 1974, North Miami Mus. Contemporary Art, 1984, Miami Collects, 1989, Women's Caucus Invitational, 1990, Gov.'s Gallery, Santa Fe, 1992, Gene Autry Western Heritage Mus., 1995, Gilcrease Mus., Tulsa, 1996, Mus. N.Mex., Santa Fe, 1996, Brigham Young U., Provo, Utah, 1996, Art in the Embassies Program, Paris, 1998—2001, Purdue U. Women Artists of the Am. West: Past and Present, 1998, Art Trends: Miami's Trek 1: The Decades of Art in Miami, 1940s-1960s, 1999—2000, Gerald Peters Gallery, Modernistic Peaks, Santa Fe, N. Mex, 1999, Ind. State Univ. and Swope Art Mus. Women Artists, Terre Haute, Ind., 1999, Represented in permanent collections Belles Artes, Mex. City, Mus. Fine Arts, Santa Fe, N.Mex., exhibitions include On the Mark: Twentieth Century Prints and Drawings, Gerald Peters Gallery, Santa Fe, 2001—02. Bd. dirs., pres. Artist Equity of Fla., 1964-68; v.p. Miami Art Assn., 1958-60; founder, bd. dirs. Guild Art Gallery, N.Y.C., 1935-37. Recipient Illustration award Fifty Best Books of Yr., Libr. of Congress, 1948, Hon. Mention award Rodeo Santa Fe, Mus. N.Mex., 1949, others, Gov.'s award for Excellence and Achievement in the Arts, 1996. E-mail: McKenzieHi@aol.com.

LEFTON, HARVEY BENNETT, gastroenterologist, educator, author; b. Cleve., May 17, 1944; s. Nat L. and Edith (Waintrup) L.; m. Paulette Lipkowitz, Aug. 24, 1968; children: Allison Rachel, Daniel Adam. BS, U. Pitts., 1966; MD, Jefferson Med. Coll., Phila., 1970. Cert. Nat. Bd. Med. Examiners, Am. Bd. Internal Medicine, Am. Bd. Gastroenterology. Intern medicine Cleve. Clinic, 1970-71, resident internal medicine, 1971-72, fellow gastroenterology, 1972-74; chief gastroenterology Scott AFB, Belleville, Ill., 1974-76; asst. clin. prof. medicine Med. Coll. Pa., Phila., 1976-78, assoc. clin. prof. medicine, 1978-81, clin. prof. medicine, 1981—; chief gastroenterology Frankford Hosps., 1997—, pres. med. staff, 1998-2000. Cons. gastroenterology Friends Hosp., Belmont Psychiat. Hosp., Pa., 1980—. Contbr. articles to profl. jours. Maj. USAF, 1974-76. Named Outstanding Vol. Physician, Med. Coll. Pa., 1994. Fellow ACP, Am. Coll. Gastroenterology, Coll. Physicians Phila.; mem. Am. Soc. Gastroenterol. Endoscopy, Pa. Soc. Gastroenterology (sec. 1999-2001, program chmn. 1999, 2002), Omicron Delta Kappa. Home: 559 Long Ln Huntingdon Valley PA 19006-2935 Office: 2 Bala Plz Ste Il 22 Bala Cynwyd PA 19004-1501

LEFTON, NORMAN BARRY, economist, metals company executive; b. St. Louis, Apr. 25, 1934; s. Samuel Israel and Sarah (Offstein) L.; m. Margaret Clare Bennetto Banks, Nov. 1, 1962 (div. Oct. 1992); children: Simon J., Sarah J. BS in Indsl. Engring., U. Ill., 1955; AM in Econs., U. Chgo., 1963, PhD in Econs., 1972. Indsl. engr. Caterpillar Tractor Co., Peoria, Ill., 1955-56; asst. prof. econs. U. Hawaii, Honolulu, 1965-70; cons. economist Rsch. Corp., U. Hawaii, 1972-74; chmn. bd. Lefton Iron & Metal Co., East St. Louis, Ill., 1976—; pres. Lefton Enterprises, Inc., 1984—. Adj. assoc. prof. econs. So. Ill. U., Edwardsville, 1985-2001, Central Mich. U., Inst. of Personal and Career Devel., 1972-85, Washington U., St. Louis, 2001—; vis. lectr. Hawaii Loa Coll., Kaneohe, 1975; bd. govs. Ill. Coun. on Econ. Edn., 1985-94; trustee Ea. St. Louis State C.C., 1990-95. Served with C.E., USNR, 1956-59. Woodrow Wilson fellow, 1962-63; U. Chgo. fellow, 1963-64. Mem. Navy League of U.S., Ret. Officers Assn., Nat. Assn. Bus. Econs. (pres. St. Louis Gateway chpt. 1993-94), Am. Econ. Assn., Southwestern Ill. Indsl. Assn. (exec. com. 1986-92), Res. Officers Assn. U.S., Greater East St. Louis C. of C. (bd. dirs. 1988-99), Media Club, Zeta Beta Tau. Republican. Office: 327 Missouri Ave Ste 516 East Saint Louis IL 62201-3088

LEFTWICH, CYNTHIA SHELTON, commercial interior designer; b. Childress, Tex., Sept. 12, 1951; d. Thomas Lee and Joann (Goff) Shelton; m. Jack Wilson Leftwich, July 27, 1974 (div. Aug. 1986); children: Jack Wilson II, Charles Shelton, Nancy Kristina. Student, U. Tex., Arlington, 1970-71, Clarendon Jr. Coll., Clarendon, Tex., summers 1970-73, Tex. Tech U., 1971-74, 1989—. Registered interior designer, Tex. Designer/drafts person Lubbock Ind. Sch. Dist., Tex., 1975-80; project mgr. M. Verner Interiors, Lubbock, 1975-79; pres. Shelton-Leftwich, Inc. dba Leftwich & Assocs., Lubbock dba, 1980—; prin. Shelton-Leftwich, Inc. Prin. design works include: (renovation) Lubbock Cotton Exch., First Nat. Bank of Lubbock; (new contrn.) McInturff Conf. Ctr. at Univ. Med. Ctr., Med. Office Plz. at Univ. Med. Ctr., Leadership Bank of Oklahoma City, United Bank of Midland, ER & radiology expansion Univ. Med. Ctr., Lexus Dealership of Lubbock, Butler Ob-gyn. Clinic; pub.: 100 Designers Favorite Rooms, Vol. I, 1992, II, 1994. Bd. dirs. Lubbock Symphony Guild, Lubbock Mcpl. Arts Com.; mem. Lubbock Cultural Affairs Coun. Recipient Achievement award Lubbock Historical Soc., 1986. Mem. Internat. Interior Design Assn., Am. Soc. Interior Designers (state bd.), Nat. Coun. for Interior Design Qualifications, Tex. Assn. Interior Designers, Lubbock C. of C. Republican. Methodist. Avocations: scuba diving, skiing, biking, sculpting, golf. Office: Leftwich & Assocs 1711 Avenue S Ste 108 Lubbock TX 79401-4816

LEFTWICH, JAMES STEPHEN, management consultant; b. Stevenage, Eng., Nov. 30, 1956; came to U.S., 1957; s. James Wright and Del Maureen (Thomson) L.; m. Carol Petersen, Nov. 7, 1980 (div. Jan. 1982). AA in Criminal Justice, Butte Coll., Oroville, Calif., 1981; BA, S.W. U., 1993. Lic. internat. accredited safety auditor; cert. hazardous material specialist. Prodn. mgr. Artistic Dyers Inc., El Monte, Calif., 1976-80; mgr. loss control and risk mgmt. Mervyn's Dept. Stores, Hawyard, 1982-91; dir. risk mgmt. Save Mart Corp., Modesto, 1991-93; v.p. ops. I.C.S. Corp., San Ramon, 1993-94, pres. Irvine, 1994-95; v.p. Health Systems of Am. Internat., 1995-96; CEO Corp. Health Systems Internat., Walnut Creek, Calif., 1996-99, CHSI of Nev., Las Vegas, 1996—. Cons. R.I.M. Assocs., Walnut Creek, Calif., 1989-96; instr. Claims Mgmt. Inst., 1993; bd. dirs. Am. Real Estate Bur., San Ramon, 1996-98. Scriptwriter, tech. advisor 12 safety videos; contbr. articles on safety and risk mgmt. to profl. publs. Res. police officer Cotati (Calif.) Police Dept., 1983-85; fundraiser United Way, Hayward, 1986, Am. Found. for AIDS Rsch., L.A., 1990; bd. dirs. Bay Area Safety Coun., Oakland, Calif., 1987-88; trustee Calif. Safety Ctr., Sacramento, 1990-91, dir., 1991-97. Mem. Am. Soc. for Safety Engrs., Nat. Safety Mgmt. Soc., Nat. Fire Protection Assn., Risk and Ins. Mgmt. Soc., Nat. Assn. Chiefs Police, Nat. Environ. Tng. Assn. Avocations: snow skiing, swimming, running, biking, jet skiing. Office: CHSI of Nevada Internat 1771 E Flamingo Rd Ste 223B Las Vegas NV 89119 E-mail: jleftwich@chsi-nv.com.

LEFTWICH, ROBERT EUGENE, oncological and adult nursing educator; b. Lubbock, Tex., July 2, 1940; s. Eugene L. and Georgia (Kirkpatrick) L. BSN, Baylor U., 1963; MS, Northern Ill. U., 1970; PhD, Clayton U., 1977. Head nurse Baylor U. Med. Ctr., Dallas, 1963-64; supr. U.S. Air Force Nurse Corps, Fla., Tex., 1964-67; instr. nursing Cameron State Coll., Lawton, Okla., 1967-68, Rock Valley Coll., Rockford, Ill., 1968-70; dir. ADN program Kankakee (Ill.) Community Coll., 1970-71, dean health edn., 1971-72; chmn. dept. adult nursing Med. Coll. Ga., Augusta, 1972-75; asst. prof. U. Louisville, 1975-77; prof. nursing Governors State U., University Park, Ill., 1977—. Bd. mem. Community Health Planning Bd., Kankakee, 1970-72; curriculum cons. Purdue U., Westville, Ind., 1983; oncology nursing cons. Ingalls Hosp., Harvey, Ill., 1979-85; grievance chairperson Univ. Profls. of Ill., University Park, 1981-83. Author: Nursing, Nutrition and the Adult Client, 1974, Humanistic Teaching Strategies and Nursing Students' Attitudes about Death and Dying, 1977, Self-Care Guide for the Cancer Patient, 1989; primary rschr.: Acuity Levels in an Adult Oncology Unit, 1981, Sexual Harrassment in Nursing Education, 1995; contbr. articles to profl. jours. Organist Trinity United Meth. Ch., Chgo., 1985—87; organist, choirmaster Bethel Covenant Ch., Flossmoor, 1987—96; organist Immanuel Ch., Evergreen Park, 1996—99, 1st Presbyn. Ch., Homewood, 1999—2001; mus. dir., organist Presbyn. Ch., Orland Park, 2001—. 1st lt. U.S. Air Force, 1963-67. Mem. Univ. Profls. Ill., Am. Guild Organists, Sigma Theta Tau. Avocations: ch. organist, choirmaster, concert organist, pianist, tenor soloist. Office: Governors State U Dept Nursing University Park IL 60466 E-mail: r-leftwich@govst.edu.

LEFTWICH, RUSSELL BRYANT, allergist, immunologist, consultant; b. Glasgow, Ky., Nov. 1, 1951; married; 2 children. BSChemE, Arizona State U., 1974; MD, Vanderbilt U., 1978. Diplomate Am. Bd. Allergy and Immunology, Am. Bd. Internal Medicine, Nat. Bd. Med. Examiners. Resident dept. internal medicine Vanderbilt U., Nashville, 1978-81, clin. asst. prof. medicine, 1984—; staff physician Green Hosp., La Jolla, Calif., 1981-83; dir. allergy ctr. Bapt. Hosp.; mem. group practice in allergy and clin. immunology, 1983-84; pvt. practice, 1985—; chief divsn. allergy U. Tenn.-Bapt. Hosp. Internal Medicine Residency, 1989—. Mem. editl. bd. Annals of Allergy, Asthma and Immunology, 1998—; contbr. articles to profl. jours. Chmn. Comm. & Public Svc. Com., 1997—; dir. Bapt. Hosp. Allergy Ctr. Summer Rsch. grantee Ariz. Heart Assn., 1974; fellow Scripps Clinic and Rsch. Found., 1981-83, chief clin. fellow, 1982-83. Fellow Am. Acad. Allergy and Immunology (sinusitis com., chmn. computers and tech. com.); mem. AMA, Am. Acad. Pediat., Am. Coll. Allergy and Immunology (mem. pub. rels. com., regional coord. pub. rels. network, chmn. computers and tech. com. 1994—), Tenn. Med. Assn. (del. ho. dels. 1990—), Tenn. Soc. Allergy and Immunology (pres. 1989-92), Nashville Acad. Medicine (chmn. young physicians com. 1990-91, mem. comm. and pub. svc. com., chmn. 1997-98, bd. dirs. 1999—), Nashville Soc. Internal Medicine, Southea. Soc. Allergy and Immunology, So. Med. Assn., Alpha Omega Alpha, Tau Beta Pi. Office: Allergy & Asthma Assocs 2010 Church St Ste 307 Nashville TN 37203-2097

LEGA, MARK, internist, pulmonologist; b. Jersey City, Jan. 11, 1954; s. Elizabeth L. BA in Biology, Springfield (Mass.) Coll., 1976; postgrad., U. Rome, 1977-81; MD, Northwestern U., 1983. Residency internal medicine U. Wis., Madison, 1983-86; pulmonary-critical care medicine U. Pitts., 1986-90; attending, asst. prof. medicine Med. Coll. of Pa., Pitts., 1991—; med. dir. Vencor Hosp., 2000—. Dir. lung transplant program Allegheny Gen. Hosp., Allegheny U. of Health Scis., Pitts., 1991—. Vol. Rainbow Med. Clinic, Homestead, Pa., 1990—. Office: Allegheny Gen Hosp Pulmonary Unit Pittsburgh PA 15201

LEGACÉ, BERNARD, performing company executive; b. Montreal, Que., Can. Designer sets and props PPS Danse, 1984—; founder En Orbite, Montreal, 1998—2002; exec. dir. O Vertigo, 2002—. Recipient Bessie Ward award, 2002; grantee, Can. Coun. Arts, 1995. Office: O Vertigo Danse Inc 4455 rue de Rouen Montreal Qu H1V 1H1 Canada

LEGAL, KENNETH JOSEPH, control systems engineer; b. Summit, N.J., Mar. 2, 1955; m. Myriam L. Jaramillo, Dec. 4, 1992; children: Diana, Cesar. B of Engring., Stevens Inst. Tech., Hoboken, N.J., 1977. Project engr., Linden, N.J., 1977-82; supr. pilot plant ops. group, 1982-85; site planner Exxon Rsch. and Engring. Co., Annandale, N.J., 1985-86; engring. mgr. N.E. region Siemens Indsl. Automation and Tex. Instruments, Inc., Cranford, 1987-89, master application engr. North Jersey, 1989-95, project mgr. ea. region for Cascade controls, 1995-97; owner, pres. KenMyr Controls, Jackson, 1997—. Author: (computer program) Automated Loop Tuning in a TI 565 Controller, 1989 (Best Value Report of Month award). Mem. AIChE (author papers on process modelling and control 1987), Internat. Soc. of Measurement and Controls (course instr. 1991—), Tau Beta Pi. Avocations: ice hockey, baseball, astronomy, music, spending time with family.

LEGANT, PATRICIA, internist, oncologist; b. N.Y.C., 1946; BA, Stanford U., 1968; PhD, Yale U., 1972; MD, Columbia U., 1977. Diplomate Am. Bd. Internal Medicine with subspecialty in oncology. Intern U. Utah Affiliated Hosp., Salt Lake City, 1977-80, fellow in hematology/oncology, 1981-83; pvt. practice, 1983—. Active med. staff Pioneer Valley Hosp., Salt Lake City; pres. med. staff Cottonwood Hosp., Salt Lake City, 1994. Mem. AMA, Am. Soc. Internal Medicine, Am. Soc. Clin. Oncology (bd. dirs. 1998), S.W. Oncology Group. Office: 164 E 5900 S Ste A106 Salt Lake City UT 84107-7268

LEGANZA, LEONARD F. business executive; b. 1930; Bd. dirs. The Eastern Co., Naugatuck, Conn., 1980—, pres., CEO, 1997—. Office: The Eastern Co 112 Bridge St PO Box 460 Naugatuck CT 06770-0460

LEGARRETA, GEORGE ISRAEL, civil engineer; b. Chgo., May 31, 1950; s. Jorge and Eva L.; m. Carol Ann Cook, June 28, 1975; children: Benjamin James, Samuel Troy. AA, St. Petersburg Jr. Coll., 1971; BA in Math., U. South Fla., 1973, MA in Math. Edn., 1977; BS in Civil Engring., U. Md., 1984. Tchr. high sch. math. Hillsborough County Pub. Schs., Tampa, Fla., 1974-82; civil engr. Fed. Aviation Adminstrn., Washington, 1984—. Co-chmn. aircraft deicing facilities Fed. Aviation Adminstrn., Washington, 1991—; rep. airport design study group UN, Montreal, Can., 1995—; U.S. rep. Internat. Civil Aviation Orgn. Coach Montgomery (Md.) Youth Soccer, 1991-97. Mem. Soc. Automotive Engrs. (vis. mem.), Tau Beta Pi, Chi Epsilon. Avocations: stamp collecting, soccer, football. Office: Fed Aviation Adminstrn 800 Independence Ave SW Washington DC 20591-0001 E-mail: george.legarreta@faa.gov.

LEGASPI, JESUSA CRISOSTOMO, agricultural scientist, entomologist; b. Pasay, Manila, Philippines; m. Benjamin Antonio Legaspi Jr.; children: Michelle Elaine, Jon Kyle. BS, U. Philippines, Los Banos, 1978; MSc, U. Newcastle-Upon-Tyne, Eng., 1984; PhD, Purdue U., 1991. Rsch. asst. Philippine Coun. for Agr., Los Banos, 1980-82, Internat. Rice Rsch. Inst., Los Banos, 1985-86; grad. rsch. asst. Purdue U., West Lafayette, Ind., 1987-91; rsch. assoc. USDA, Weslaco, Tex., 1992-95; asst. prof. Tex. Agrl. Experiment Sta., 1995-2001; rsch. entomologist USDA-Agrl. Rsch. Svc., Tallahassee, 2001—. Contbr. articles to profl. jours. Sci. judge Jackson Elem. Sch., McAllen, Tex., 1992; vol. Ind. State Fair, Indpls., 1990; mem. Fil-Am Assn., Rio Grande Valley, Tex., 1993. David Ross fellow Purdue U., 1987; Colombo Plan scholar Brit. Coun., 1982. Mem. Entomol. Soc. Am., Philippine Assn. of Entomologists, Sigma Xi, Gamma Sigma Delta. Roman Catholic. Avocations: swimming, bowling, reading, travel. Office: USDA-ARS South Fla A&M U 310 Perry-Paige Bldg Tallahassee FL 32307 E-mail: jlegaspi@nettally.com.

LEGATES, JOHN CREWS BOULTON, information scientist; b. Boston, Nov. 19, 1940; s. Eber Thomson and Sybil Rowe (Crews) LeGates; m. Nancy Elizabeth Boulton, Apr. 28, 1993. BA in Math., Harvard U., 1962. Edn. svcs. mgr. Telcomp Dept. Bolt Beranek & Newman, Cambridge, Mass., 1966-67; v.p. Washington Engring. Svcs., 1967-69; v.p., co-founder Cambridge Info. Systems, 1968-69; v.p., founder Computer Adv. Svc. to Edn., Wayland, Mass., 1966-72; exec. dir. Educom Interuniversity Communications Coun., Boston, 1969-72; founder, mng. dir. Program on Info. Resources Policy Harvard U., 1973—, founder, pres. Ctr. Info. Policy Rsch., 1978—. Mem. Arpanet NWG, core Arpanet/Internet design team, 1970-72; U.S. del. First World Conf. on Computer Comms., Amsterdam, 1970; cons. in field; pioneer ednl. computing. Contbr. articles to profl. jours. Bd. dirs. Nat. Telecommunications Conf., Washington, 1979. Kent fellow, 1964. Mem. NAS/NRC (telecommunications privacy, reliability and integrity panel), IEEE, Nat. Sci. Found., Soc. for Values in Higher Edn., Nashoba Valley Hunt Club (pres. 1974-80). Unitarian Universalist. Achievements include pioneering educational computers, building world's first hospital integrated information system at Mass. Gen. Hosp. Corp. Bds. Avocations: sailing, fox-hunting, mountaineering, classical music. Home: PO Box 6331 Lincoln MA 01773-6331

LEGENDRE, LOUIS, oceanographer, educator, research scientist; b. Montreal, Que., Can., Feb. 16, 1945; s. Vianney and Marguerite (Venne) Legendre. BA, U. Montreal, 1964, BSc, 1967; PhD, Dalhousie U., Halifax, 1971; Doctorat honoris causa, U. Liege, 1997. Postdoctoral fellow U. Paris VI, Villefranche-sur-Mer, France, 1971-73; rsch. assoc. U. Laval, Quebec City, Canada, 1973, asst. prof. Canada, 1974-77, assoc. prof. Canada, 1977-81, prof. Canada, 1981-2000, emeritus prof. Canada, 2001—; rsch. prof. CNRS, France, 2000—; dir. Villefranche-sur-Mer Oceanography Lab., 2001—. V.p. Groupe Interuniversitaire de Recherches Océanographiques du Que., 1989—2000; group chmn. Natural Scis. and Engring. Rsch. Coun. Can., Ottawa, 1989—92. Author (with P. Legendre): (book) Numerical Ecology, 1983, 1998; contbr. articles to profl. jours. V.p. Model Environ., Liege, Belgium, 1993—. Decorated Knight of Malta; recipient Léo-Pariseau award, Assn. Canadienne-Française pour l'Avancement des Scis., 1985, Michel-Jurdant award, 1986, Que. Sci. prize, Pure and Applied Scis., 1997, Excellence in Ecology prize, Interant. Ecology Inst., 2001; fellow Killam Rsch., Can. Coun., 1996—98. Fellow: Royal Soc. Can.; mem.: Am. Geophys. Union, Am. Soc. Limnology and Oceanography (G. Evelyn Hutchinson award 2002). Office: LOV BP 28 06234 Villefranche-sur-Mer Cedex France E-mail: legendre@obs.vlfr.fr.

LEGER, PHILIPPE, legal administrator; b. 1938; Mem. judiciary Min. of Justice, 1966-70; head of and subsequently tech. advisor Pvt. office of Min. for Living Stds., 1976; tech. advisor Pvt. Office of Garde des Sceaux, 1976-78; dep. dir. criminal affairs and reprieves Min. Justice, 1978-83; sr. mem. Ct. of Appeal, Paris, 1983-86; dep. dir. Pvt. Office of Garde des Sceaux, Min. for Justice, 1986; pres. Regional Ct. Bobigny, 1986-93; head pvt. office Ministre d'État, the Garde des Sceaux, Min. for Justice, 1993-94; advocate gen. Ct. Appeal, Paris, 1993-94; assoc. prof. René Descartes U., 1988-93; advocate gen. Ct. Justice, Luxembourg, 1994—. Office: European Ct of Justice Blvd Konrad Adenauer L-2925 Kirchberg Luxembourg

LEGERE, KATHY ANN, artist, poet; b. Lakenhealth, Suffolk, Eng., Feb. 24, 1967; d. Richard William and Eleanor Ruth Doucet; m. James John Legere, June 3, 1989. BFA in Painting, Maine Coll. Art, 1990. One-woman shows include Cheyenne (Wyo.) Civic Ctr., 1999, La Petite Galerie, Gallery Ten, Rockford, Ill., 1996; exhibited in group shows at Maine Coll. Art, Portland, 1994, Gallery Ten, Rockford, Ill., 1995, 96, Peoria (Ill.) Art Guild, 1996, Ctrl. Wyo. Coll. Open Exhbn., Riverton, 1999; publ. (art calendar) Getting the Word Out, 1995, The Best of Pastel, 1996, Nature's Echoes, 2000, Web of Memories, 2001, The Sound of Poetry, 2001, Treasures to Discover, 2001, Under a Quicksilver Moon, 2002, Mysterious Motions, 2002, The Best Poems and Poets of 2002, 2002. Recipient Crabbie award for Art Calendar, 1994. Avocations: skiing, hiking, genealogy, travel. E-mail: kathylegere@email.com., jlegere@wyoming.com.

LEGERE, PHOEBE HEMENWAY, composer, artist; b. Lexington, Mass., July 4, 1961; d. John Philip Legere and Winifred Hemenway. Crw, Vassar Coll., 1981; studied with John Lewis, Modern Jazz Quartet; studied painting with Larry Rivers. Artist CBS, N.Y.C., 1983-86, Dead Dog Records, N.Y.C., 1990-92, FunTone Records, N.Y.C., 1993-97, Random Records, 1997-98. Resident composer The Wooster Group, N.Y.C., 1980-81; multimedia educator and lectr. Author/composer: (musical) Hello Mrs. President, 1990 (Jerome Found. award 1993), (musical) The Lingerie Killers, 1989, (movie) Marquis De Slime, 1998; author text: The Waterclown, 2000; composer (full length CD) Last Tango in "Bubbleland", 1998, Swingalicious, 1999, Boobopolis, 1999, Blue Curtain, Magically Fourteenth St., 2000; commd. for new opera by Roulette Found. "The Queen of New England", 2001; artist in residence, Ragdale Found.; host Roulette TV; host, prodr. Sirius Radio. Active in ednl. and polit. affairs; nat. dir. MP3.All Stars; East Coast spokesman Mp3.com. Grantee N.Y. State Coun. of Arts, 2000. Mem. Am. Assn. Accordionists (nat. spokesperson), Vassar Club. Episcopalian. Avocations: poetry, hiking, distance bicycling, painting, photography.

LEGG, BENSON EVERETT, federal judge; b. Balt., June 8, 1947; s. William Mercer Legg and Beverly Mason; m. Kyle Prechtl Legg; children: Jennifer, Charles, Matthew. AB magna cum laude, Princeton U., 1970; JD, U. Va., 1973. Bar: Md. 1973. Law clk. to Hon. Frank A. Kaufman, Balt., 1973-74; assoc. Venable, Baetjer & Howard, 1975-81, ptnr., 1982-91; judge U.S. Dist. Ct., Dist. Md., 1991—. Spl. reporter appeals com. and standing com. on rules of practice and procedure Ct. Appeals Md., 1983-85; faculty mem. nine day intensive trial advocacy program Md. Inst. Continuing Profl. Edn. for Lawyers, Inc., 1987, program on appellate advocacy, 1988; lectr. and panelist in field. Mem. editl. bd. Va. Law Rev., 1973-74; contbr. articles to profl. jours. Bd. dirs. Ctrl. Md. chpt. ARC, 1979-88, past chpt. gen. counsel; mem. adv. bd. Nat. Aquarium in Balt., 1987—; trustee Balt. Zoo. Mem. ABA (bus. torts litigation com. 1987), Md. State Bar Assn., Inc. (chmn. econs. of litigation com. 1981-82), Bar Assn. Balt. City (vice chmn. CLE com. 1986-87, chmn. 1987-88, exec. coun. 1987-88, judiciary com. 1989-90), The Serjeant's Inn Law Club, Order of Coif. Office: US Dist Ct 101 W Lombard St Ste 340 Baltimore MD 21201-2605

LEGG, HILDA GAY, federal agency administrator; BS in Sociology, Campbellville Coll.; MEd, We. Ky. U. Tchr. social sci. jr. and sr. hs, Adair County, Ky., 1974—81; acting exec. dir. nat. coun. on handicapped U.D. Dept. of Edn., Washington, 1981—83; field rep. Senator Mitch McConnell, Bowling Green, Ky., 1985—87; dir. admissions Lindsey Wilson Coll., Columbia, 1987—90; alt. fed. co-chmn. Appalachian Regional Commn., Washington, 1990—93; exec. dir., CEO Ctr. for Rural Develop., Somerset, Ky., 1994—2001; adminstr. rural utilities svcs. USDA, Washington, 2001—. Office: USDA Rural Utilities Svcs 1400 Independence Ave SW Washington DC 20250*

LEGG, WILLIAM JEFFERSON, lawyer; b. Enid, Okla., Aug. 20, 1925; s. Garl Paul and Mabel (Genson) L.; m. Eva Imogene Hill, Dec. 16, 1950; children: Melissa Lou, Eva Diane, Janet Sue. Grad., Enid Bus. Coll., 1943; student, Pittsburg State U., 1944; BBA, U. Tex., Austin, 1946; JD, U. Tulsa, 1954. Bar: Okla. 1954, U.S. Supreme Ct., U.S. Ct. Appeals (10th cir.), U.S. Dist. Ct. (we. dist.) Okla. With aviation sales Phillips Petroleum Co., 1946-48; atty. Marathon Oil Co., 1954-61; pvt. practice Oklahoma City, 1962—; with Andrews Davis Legg Bixler Milsten & Price, Inc. and predecessor firms, 1962—2002, pres., 83-86, also dir., 1973-77, 80-81, 83-86, 90, sec., 1975-80, 82-83, 90; sr. counsel, 1991—2002. Adj. prof. law Oklahoma City U., 1975-80; lectr. Okla. U. Law Sch., 1986; bd. dirs., v.p. internat. oil cos., Turkey, Australia, Brunei, 1967-82; bd. dirs., gen. counsel N.J. Natural Resources Co., Wall, N.J., 1986-91; bd. dirs. Skillpath Seminars, Inc., Kansas City, Mo., 1994-98; lectr. energy seminars; rsch. fellow The Ctr. for Am. and Internat. Law (formerly Southwestern Legal Found)., Dallas, 1989—, mem. CLE adv. bd., 1998—. Contbr. articles to profl. jours. Mem. legal com. Okla. Gov.'s Energy Adv. Coun., 1973, Okla. Blue Ribbon Com. on Natural Gas Well Allowables, 1983; ordained Community of Christ (formerly Reorganized Ch. of Jesus Christ of Latter Day Saints), 1964; dist. pres. Community of Christ formerly Reorganized Ch. of Jesus Christ of Latter Day Saints, 1975—80, br. pres., 1986—91, evangelist, 1993—; trustee Am. Inst. Discussion, 1962—88, chmn., 1969—72; trustee Jenkins Found. Rsch., sec., 1975—81; trustee Restoration Trails Found., 1975, Graceland U., Lamoni, Iowa, 1986—2000, mem. exec. com., chmn. bus. affairs com., 1988—98, mem. investment com., 1998—2000; trustee Met. Lib. Endowment Trust, 1986—99, treas., 1988—99, chmn. investment com. With USN, 1943—46, lt. (j.g.) USNR, 1946—66. Mem. ABA, Okla. Bar Assn. (past com. chmn.), Oklahoma County Bar Assn. (past com. chmn.), Internat. Bar Assn., Internat. Assn. Energy Econs., Econ. Club Okla., Men's Dinner Club, Petroleum Club. Home: 3017 Brush Creek Rd Oklahoma City OK 73120-1855

LEGGETT, DONALD YATES, academic administrator; b. Windsor, N.C., Oct. 31, 1935; s. Turner Carter Leggett and Ruby (Harden) Lanier; m. Nancy Lou Porter, Aug. 17, 1980; 1 stepson, Clayton Porter Johnston. BS in Phys. Edn., Social Studies, East Carolina U., 1958, MA in Edn., 1962; postgrad., N.C. State U., 1966-67. Tchr., coach Benhaven (N.C.) High Sch., 1958-59, Buies Creek (N.C.) High Sch., 1959-64; coach, tchr., Needham B. Broughton High Sch., Raleigh, N.C., 1964-66, asst. prin., 1966-70; dir. alumni affairs East Carolina U., Greenville, N.C., 1970-73, dir. alumni affairs and founds., 1973-79, dir. alumni rels., 1979-85, asst. to vice chancellor for instl. advancement, 1985-92, assoc. vice chancellor for alumni rels., 1992-97, acting dir. Regional Devel. Inst., 1993, spl. asst. to v. chancellor for planned giving, 1998—, interim assoc. vice chancellor for instnl. advancement, 2000-01, interim dir. found. and corp. rels., 2001—. Driver tng. coord. Raleigh City Sch. System, 1964-66; mem. numerous coms. at East Carolina U., 1970—. Editor East Carolina U. Alumni pubs. 1979-85; contbr. articles to alumni pubs. Past mem. bd. dirs. Pitt County Boys Club, Pitt-Greenville Arts Coun. (past mem. steering com.); former bd. dirs. Ea. N.C. village of Yesteryear; former vice chmn. Pitt-Greenville Conv. and Visitors Authority. Named Boss of Yr. Greenville Jaycees, 1976. Mem. Coun. for Advancement and Support of Edn., East Carolina U. Pirate Club, Pitt-Greenville C. of C., Kiwanis Club (charter mem., past bd. dirs. Univ. City), Greenville Golf and Country Club, Phi Kappa Phi, Phi Delta Kappa. Baptist. Avocations: wood working, gardening. Home: 113 Bells St Greenville NC 27858-8498

LEGGETT, JAMES DANIEL, bishop; b. Williamston, N.C., Oct. 21, 1939; s. James S. and Hazel Louise (Wynn) L.; m. Clara Faye Watts, June 25, 1961; children: James Jr., Joseph Talmadge, Cynthia Faye, John David. BA, Pembroke State U.; ThB, Holmes Coll. of the Bible, hon. doctorate, 1988. Ordained to ministry Pentecostal Holiness Ch., 1960. Pastor Swan Quarter Pentecostal Holiness Ch., 1962-64, Pinetown Pentecostal Holiness Ch., 1962-64, Mt. Olive Pentecostal Holiness Ch., Pembroke, 1964-70, Culbreth Meml. Pentecostal Holiness Ch., Falcon, 1970-86; supr. N.C. Conf. Pentecostal Holiness Ch., 1986-89; asst. gen. supt. Internat. Pentecostal Holiness Ch., Bethany, Okla., 1989-93, vice chmn., 1993-97. Exec. dir. Evangelism USA, 1989-97; pres. Extension Loan Fund, 1989-97; gen. supt. (bishop) Internat. Pentecostal Holiness Ch., 1997—; co-chmn. exec. com. Pentecostal/Charismatic Chs. N.A.; bd. dirs. Nat. Assn. Evangs.; mem. adv. com. Pentecostal World Fellowship; mem. adv. coun. Internat. Charismatic Consultation on World Evangelisation; mem. N.Am. Renewal Svc. Com.; mem. Mission Am.; former mem. Evang. Curriculum Commn., writer Sunday Sch. lit., instr. extension classes Holmes Coll. of Bible, Emmanuel Coll. Sec. bd. trustees Holmes Coll. of the Bible, past bd. dirs. Office: Pentecostal Holiness Ch 7300 NW 39th Expy Bethany OK 73008-2340

LEGGETT, JOHN WARD, writer; b. N.Y.C., Nov. 11, 1917; s. Bleecker Noel and Dorothy (Mahar) L.; m. Mary Lee Fahnestock, Oct. 2, 1948 (div. 1986); children: Timothy, John, Anthony; m. Edwina Benington, Oct. 26, 1986. BA, Yale U., 1942. Editor Houghton Mifflin Co., Boston, 1951-60, Harper & Row, N.Y.C., 1960-69; dir. writers' workshop U. Iowa, Iowa City, 1969-87. Dir. Napa Valley Writers' Conf., Napa, Calif., 1987—. Author: Ross and Tom, 1974, A Daring Young Man, 2002, others; editor: (textbook series) Elements of Literature, 1988. Lt. USN, 1943-45. Mem. Century Assn. Home: 1781 Partrick Rd Napa CA 94558

LEGGETT, NANCY PORTER, university administrator; b. Greenville, N.C., Aug. 14, 1952; d. Earl Lindeburgh and Louise (Adams) Porter; m. Ted Clayton Johnston, Nov. 19, 1971 (div. Dec. 1979); 1 child, Clayton Porter; m. Donald Yates Leggett, Aug. 17, 1980. Student, East Carolina U., 1971-73, Pitt C.C., Greenville, 1975-76. Sec./coord. grad. ext. and tchr. edn. programs Divsn. Continuing Edn., East Carolina U., Greenville, 1971-80; sect. sec. ambulatory pediatrics Sch. Medicine, East Carolina U., 1981-83; adminstrv. sec. to chmn. dept. pediatrics East Carolina U., 1983-94; resource person dept. pediatrics Sch. Medicine, East Carolina U., 1984-94, exec. asst. to chmn. dept. pediatrics, 1994—. Mem. traffic appeals com., E Carolina U., Greenville, 1995-96, chair benefits com., 1995-97, parking and traffic com., 1996—, staff forum, 1999-2000. Mem. Greenville Cmty. Appearance Commn., 1990-94, Greenville Mus. Art, 1980-82; com. mem. N.C. Symphony, Greenville, 1988-89; mem., mem. steering com. Children's Miracle Network Telethon, Greenville, 1986-90; vol. Friends of Children's Hosp. Greenville, 1986-88; mem. Nat. Scleroderma Found., 1987-88, Hist. Hope Found., Windsor, N.C., 1990-96; bd. dirs. Rose H.S. Acad. Boosters, 1994-95. Mem. Greenville Country Club, Kiwanis (charter mem., bd. dirs. 1990-91). Baptist. Avocations: gardening, reading, walking, birdwatching. Home: 113 Bells St Greenville NC 27858-8498 Office: East Carolina Univ Sch of Medicine Dept Pediatrics Greenville NC 27858 E-mail: leggettn@mail.ecu.edu.

LEGGETT, PAUL ARTHUR, minister; b. Montclair, N.J., July 3, 1946; s. Joseph Hoyt and Jane (Stenstrom) L.; m. Beth Petrie, Nov. 28, 1981; children: Elisabeth, Gwendolyn, James. BS in Speech and Drama cum laude, Syracuse U., 1968; MDiv, Princeton Theol. Sem., 1971, ThM, 1973; PhD, Union Theol. Sem., N.Y.C., 1982. Ordained to ministry Presbyn. Ch. (U.S.A.), 1971. Interim pastor Disston Meml. Presbyn. Ch., Phila., 1971-72; asst. pastor Huntingdon Valley (Pa.) Presbyn. Ch., 1972-73; prof. theology Latin Am. Bibl. Sem., San Jose, Costa Rica, 1974-80; pastor Grace Presbyn. Ch., Montclair, 1981—. Vis. lectr. Vassar Coll., Poughkeepsie, N.Y., 1979-80, 82-83; spl. cons. Gen. Assembly Mission Coun., 1980-81; chmn. Hispanic com. Newark Presbytery, 1982, 97-99, ch. and soc. com., 1983-85, moderator, 1989, 1993; vice moderator spl. com. 15 Brief Statement of Faith, Presbyn. Ch. U.S.A., 1990-91. Author: Torence Fisher: Human, Myth and Religion, 2001; co-editor: Lectura Teologica del Tiempo Latino Americano, 1979; contbr. articles to profl. jours. Pres. Montclair Rotary Club, 1991-92. Recipient Margot M. Studer award Montclair State Coll., 1984; Paul Harris fellow Rotary, 1995. Mem. Montclair Clergy Assn. (pres. 1994-95). Home: 63 Tuxedo Rd Montclair NJ 07042-5043 Office: Grace Presbyn Ch 153 Tuxedo Rd Montclair NJ 07042 *The grace and mercy of God surround us in more ways than we can imagine.*

LEGGETT, ROBERTA JEAN (BOBBI LEGGETT), retired social services administrator; b. Kankakee, Ill., Nov. 30, 1926; d. Clyde H. and Sybil D. (Billings) Karns; m. George T. Leggett, Aug. 25, 1956. Sec. Cardov div. Chemetron Corp., Chgo., 1951-60; sec., asst. mgr. Ravisloe Country Club, Homewood, Ill., 1961-65; sec. Nationwide Paper Co., Chgo., 1966-68; exec. dir. Am. Bd. Oral and Maxillofacial Surgery, 1969-87. Mem. Chgo. Soc. Assn. Execs., Conf. Med. Soc. Execs. of Greater Chgo., Profl. Secs. Internat. Methodist.

LEGGETT, WILLIAM C. biology educator, academic administrator; b. Orangeville, Ont., Can., June 25, 1939; s. Frank William and Edna Irene (Wheeler) L.; m. Claire Holman, May 9, 1964; children: David, John. BA, Waterloo U. Coll., 1962; MSc, U. Waterloo, 1965; PhD, McGill U., 1969, DSc, 2001, U. Waterloo, 1992; LLD, Wilfred Laurier U., 1994; DSc, Laval U., 1996. From rsch. scientist to rsch. assoc. Essex (Conn.) Marine Lab., 1965-73; asst. prof. McGill U., Montreal, Que., Can., 1970-72, assoc. prof. Can., 1972-79, prof. Can., 1979—, chmn. dept. biology Can., 1981-85, dean of sci. Can., 1986-91, acad. v.p. Can., 1991-94; prin., vice chancellor Queen's U., Kingston, Ont., Can., 1994—; chmn. bd. Huntsman Marine Lab., 1980-89; pres. Groupe Interuniversitaire de Recherche Oceanographique du Que., 1986-91. Chmn. grant selection com. for population biology Natural Scis. and Engring. Research Council Can., 1980-81, chmn. grant selection com. for oceans, 1986-87; exec. com. Coun. Ontario Univs., 1996—; mem. exec. com. internationalization Assn. Univ. Colls. Can. Mem. editl. bd.: Can. Jour. Fisheries and Aquatic Sciences, 1980-85, steering com. global oceans experiment, Le Naturaliste Canadien, 1980-91, Can. Jour. Zoology, 1982-86; contbr. articles in field. Recipient Dwight D. Webster award Am. Fisheries Soc., 1989, Award for Excellence for Fisheries Edn., 1990, Fry medal Can. Soc. Zoologists, 1990, Outstanding Biologist award Can. Coun. Biol. Chmn., 1993; grantee in field. Fellow Rawson Acad., Royal Soc. Can., Order of Can.; mem. Am. Fisheries Soc. (pres. North-East divsn. 1977-78, EO Sette award 1996, Excellence award 1997), Can. Com. for Fishery Rsch., Can. Soc. Zoologists, Am. Soc. Limnology and Oceanography, Am. Soc. Naturalists. Office: Queen's U Office of the Prin Kingston ON Canada K7L 3N6

LEGGIERE, PHILIP GUY, publicist, writer, consultant; b. Teaneck, N.J., July 6, 1955; s. Philip Samuel and Maureen Catherine (Ives) L.; m. Beth Jennings, May 26, 1991. BA, U. Pa., 1979. Pres., editor Marshall Comms., Hoboken, N.J., 1995-97, Further States of the Arts, Hoboken, 1997—; reporter, reviewer Upside Mag., 1998—; high tech industry analyst Bus. Comm. Co., Norwalk, Conn., 1997—; market analyst Frontline Tech. Rsch., San Francisco, 2000—; reporter PRWeek, 2000—, Media Mag. , 2002. Contbg. editor: Continental Airlines mag. Mem. publicity and fundraising coms. Hoboken Friends of the Libr., 1992—; mem. Electronic Frontier Found., Washington, 1995; sustaining mem. Librs. for the Future, N.Y.C., 1995. Mem. Penn Alumni Club (charter). Roman Catholic. Avocations: rare book collecting, computers, hiking. Office: 741 Park Ave Fl 3D Hoboken NJ 07030-4005

LEGLER, APRIL ARINGTON, librarian, educator; b. Gary, Ind., Apr. 20, 1946; d. James Berry Arington and Charlotte Bushong Arington Canine; m. Theodore Rex Legler II, Aug. 26, 1967; children: Melinda, Sara, Tad. AB in Comparative Lit., Ind. U., 1968, MLS, 1971. Various capacities in pub. and acad. librs., 1961-70; head librarian Math., Physics and Astronomy Libr. Ind. U. Librs., Bloomington, 1970-71; instr. Big Bend C.C., Berlin, Germany, 1986-88, Midlands Tech. Coll., Columbia, S.C., 1988-91, U. Md., Heidelberg, Germany, 1992, Schiller Internat. U., Heidelberg, 1991-92, head libr., 1992-95; career counselor Ind. U. Kelley Sch. of Bus., 1997-99; course mgr. I.U. Kelley Sch. of Bus., 1999-2000, career edn. assoc., 2000—. Author monograph. Life mem. Girl Scouts U.S., 1979—, instr. adult leader devel., 1983-85, bd. dirs. Congaree coun., Columbia, 1989-91, bd. dirs. North Atlantic, Europe, 1992-95; adult mem. Boy Scouts Am., 1973-99, instr. adult leader devel., 1973-92; instr. outdoor living skills Am. Camping Assn., 1985-87; vol. ARC. Recipient Silver Beaver award Boy Scouts Am., 1987, Congaree award Girl Scouts U.S., 1991. Mem. German-Am. Women's Club (v.p. 1992-93), Am. Found. for Visual Awareness (Ind. state trustee 1996-98, Ind. state sec. 1998-2000), Ind. U. Alumni Assn. (life), Ind. U. Women's Club (2nd v.p. 1999-00, program chair 2000-2001), Beta Phi Mu, Psi Iota Xi (treas. 1999—). Avocations: needlework, gourmet cooking. Office: Kelly Sch Bus P100 Ind U 1309 E 10th St Bloomington IN 47405-1701 Home: 4630 Chatham Dr Bloomington IN 47404-1319

LEGLER, MITCHELL WOOTEN, lawyer; b. Alexandria, Va., June 3, 1942; s. John Clarke and Doris (Wooten) L.; m. Harriette Dodson; children: John Clarke, Dorothy Trumbull, Harriette Holland. BA in Polit. Sci. with honors, U. N.C., 1964; JD, U. Va., 1967. Bar: Va. 1967, Fla. 1967. Pres. Commander, Legler, Werber, Dawes, Sadler & Howell, Jacksonville, Fla., 1976-91; ptnr. Foley & Lardner, 1995—2000; pres. Mitchell W. Legler, P.A., 2001—, Kirschner & Legler, P.A., 2001—. Chmn. Fla. Bar Consumer Protection Law Com. Editorial bd. Va. Law Rev., 1966-67. Mem. Va. Bar Assn., Fla. Bar Assn. (lectr. continuing legal edn.), Order of Coif, Phi Beta Kappa, Phi Eta Sigma, Delta Upsilon, Delta Theta Phi. Office: 300A Wharfside Way Jacksonville FL 32207-8153

LE GOC, MICHEL JEAN-LOUIS, business educator; b. Toul, France, May 12, 1921; s. Yves and Suzanne (Badie) Le G.; m. Jacqueline Grapin, Apr. 6, 1971; children: Yves, Isabelle, Jean, Brigitte, Claire, Julien. Engring. degree, French Air Force Acad.; Sup. Educ. of Polit. Econ. and Pub. Law, PhD in Mgmt. Sci. summa cum laude. Surveyor European Defense Community, 1951-55; with fin. div. then procurements div. French Nat. Aeronautic Bd., 1955-57; gen. sec. European econ. issues Elec. Mfrs. Assn., 1957-60; co-founder, cons. Eurofinex, 1960-65; sr. v.p. devel. Cegos, 1965-71; founder, cons. Interfinexa, Geneva, 1971-86; prof. econs. U. Geneva, 1973-85; prof. internat. bus. Am. U. Washington, 1997—. Ptnr. Air Cons., Geneva; spl. advisor H.H. Shamarpa Rinpoche, Delhi, India. Author: The Concentration of Enterprises, The Imperatives of Success, Development Techniques for International Technology Transfer; contbr. articles to profl. jours. Res. mem. supervisory agy. French Armed Forces. Served to gen. Free French Air Force, World War II. Named to Pres. Swiss br. Légion d'Honneur, Commandeur; decorated Croix de Guerre, Médaille de la Résistance, Médaille des Evadés, others. Mem. USAF Assn., Assn. Free French Air Force, Assn. Profs. Univ. Geneva, PEN Club, Club Alpin, Cosmos Club Washington, Lions Club. Office: 4745 Massachusetts Ave NW Washington DC 20016-2345 E-mail: mlegoc@aol.com.

LEGORRETA, GERARDO A. bank executive; b. Mexico City, Mex., Nov. 16, 1967; s. Pablo Chauvet Legorreta, Concepcion Carrera Creel; m. Mariana Campero. M.Fin., London Bus. Sch., 1995. Assoc. CIBC World Mkts., N.Y.C., 1995—97; exec. dir. UBS Warburg, Stamford, Conn., 1997—. Mem. Brit. Airport Group, England, 2000—. Author: (book) Legal Framework of Financial Institutions, 1992 (Honors, 1992). Recipient Productivity award, Creel, Garcia-Cuellar y Muggenburg, 1989, 1990. Mem.: London Bus. Sch. Alumni Assn. Roman Catholic. Avocation: tennis, travel, skiing. Office: UBS Warburg LLC 677 Washington Blvd Stamford CT 06901 Office Fax: 203-719-1620. Personal E-mail: gerardo.legorreta@ubsw.com. Business E-Mail: gerardo.legorreta@ubsw.com.

LE GRAND, CLAY, lawyer, former state justice; b. St. Louis, Feb. 26, 1911; s. Nicholas and Mary Margaret (Leifeld) Le G.; m. Suzanne Wilcox, Dec. 30, 1935, (wid.); children: Mary Suzanne Le Grand Murray, Julie A. Le Grand Ekstrand, Nicholas W.; m. Margaret Morris Burrows, Dec. 11, 1993. Student, St. Ambrose Coll., Davenport, Iowa, 1928-31; LL.B., Catholic U. Am., 1934. Bar: Iowa 1934. Practice law, Davenport, 1934-57; judge Dist. Ct., 1957-67; justice Supreme Ct. Iowa, Davenport, 1967-83; of counsel Stanley, Rehling, Lande & Van Der Kamp, 1983-92, Noyes, O'Brien, Gosma and Brooke, Davenport, 1992-95, Noyes & Gosma, Davenport, 1995-98, Gosma & Gallagher, Davenport, 1998—. Lectr. St. Ambrose Coll., 1957-67 Recipient award for outstanding achievement in field of law and the cts. Cath. U. Am., 1969; award of merit for profl. achievement St. Ambrose Coll., 1976 Mem. Am., Iowa, Scott County bar assns., Am. Judicature Soc., Inst. Jud. Adminstrn. Home: 4130 Northwest Blvd Apt 32 Davenport IA 52806-4234 Office: Gosma & Gallagher 4301 E 53rd St # 300 Davenport IA 52807-3040

LEGRAND, MICHEL JEAN, composer; b. Paris, Feb. 24, 1932; came to U.S., 1955; s. Raymond and Marcelle Legrand; children: Hervé, Benjamin, Eugénie, Dominique. Diploma, Conservatoire Nationale Superieur de Musique, Paris, 1951. Composer, condr., pianist, 1965—. Composer: (score, song, adaptation) I Will Wait for You, 1965 (3 Acad. award nominations), Windmills of Your Mind, 1968 (Acad. award 1968), film scores include Summer of 42, 1970 (Acad. award 1970), Brian's Song, 1971, Lady Sings the Blues, 1972, The Three Muscateers, 1973, Ode to Billy Joe, 1975, The Other Side of Midnight, 1977, Atlantic City, 1980, The Mountain Men, 1980, Never Say Never Again, 1983, Yentl, 1984 (Acad. award 1984), The Pickle, 1993, Ready to Wear, 1994, Madeline, 1998, also over 100 albums; arranger (album) I Love Paris, 1954; contbr. jazz pianist with numerous orchs. including Pitts. Symphony, Minn. Orch., Buffalo Philharm.; collaborated with various artists including Barbra Streisand, Sarah Vaughan, Jack Jones, Lena Horne, Dame Kiri Te Kanawa, Ray Charles, Miles Davis, Neil Diamond, Johnny Mathis, Jessye Norman; dir. (film) 5 Days in June, 1989. Mem. Dramatists Guild, Songwriters Guild of Am., Am. Fedn. Musicians, AFTRA, ASCAP, Acad. Motion Picture Arts and Scis. (Oscar award 1967, 70, 83). Avocations: boating, airplane pilot, tennis, horseback riding. Office: care Jim DiGiovanni PO Box 2040 New York NY 10101-2040 E-mail: jjosie157@aol.com.

LEGRAND, SHAWN PIERRE, computer systems programmer; b. San Diego, Nov. 27, 1960; s. Roger and Violet Louise (Howe) L. Grad. high sch., El Cajon, Calif.; student, U. Calif., San Diego, 1992-95. Cert. computer programmer; cert. in neural networks. Computer operator Grossmont CCD, El Cajon, 1978-79; computer systems programmer ICW, San Diego, 1979—. Recipient Math. Achievement award Bank of Am., 1978. Mem.: Am. Math. Soc., Soc. Indsl. & Applied Mathematicians, Assn. Computing Machinery, IEEE computer Soc. Republican. Office: ICW 11455 El Camino Real San Diego CA 92130-2088 E-mail: splegrand@yahoo.com.

LEGUEY-FEILLEUX, JEAN-ROBERT, political scientist, educator; b. Marseilles, France, Mar. 28, 1928; came to U.S., Aug. 1949; s. E. Feilleux and Jeanne (Leguey) Feilleux Levassort; m. Virginia Louise Hartwell, Sept. 19, 1953; children— Michele, Monique, Suzanne, Christiane. M.A., Ecole Superieure de Commerce, France, 1949; Diplome Superieur d'Etudes Coloniales, U. d'Aix-Marseille, France, 1949; M.A., U. Fla., 1951; Ph.D., Georgetown U., 1965. Lectr. Sch. Foreign Service Georgetown U., Washington, 1957-66; dir. research Inst. World Polit. Georgetown U., 1960-66; asst. prof. St. Louis U., 1966-70, assoc. prof., 1970— , chmn. polit. sci. dept., 1983-96; vis. scholar Harvard Law Sch., Cambridge, Mass., 1974-75; chmn. Fulbright Commn. for France Inst. Internat. Edn., N.Y.C., 1974-76; vis. researcher UN, N.Y.C., 1981; mem. academic delegation, Jordan, 1988, Israel, 1990, Syria, Bahrain, Kuwait, 1991, Kuwait, Syria, 1992, Syria, 1993—, Yemen, 1995, Morocco, Tunisia, Spain, 1996, Tunisia, 1997, Yemen, 1998. Author (with others): Law of Limited International Conflict, 1965. Contbr. chpt. to books Implications of Disarmament, 1977, Democracy in a High-technology Society, 1988, The External Environment, 1991, Proceedings of First Gobal Village Conference, 1992, Great Events from History II: Human Rights, 1992, Science and Politics of Food, 1995. Contbr. articles to profl. jours. Author testimony Pres.'s Commn. on 25th Anniversary of UN, 1970. Recipient Medaille d'Or Institut Comml., France, 1949, Fulbright award U.S. State Dept., 1950, Cert. Disting. Service Inst. Internat. Edn., 1976; named Outstanding Educator Nutshell Mag., 1982; Malone fellow in Jordan, 1988. Mem. UN Assn. (mem. nat. coun. chpt. and div. pres. 1972-73, steering com. 1973-75), Am. Biog. Inst. (named to Hall of Fame, 1986), Internat. Human Rights Task Force (chmn. 1975-81), Character Research Assn. (pres. 1980-83, 89-90), Acad. Coun. on UN System, Am. Coun. for UN Univ., Georgetown U. Gold Key Soc., Alpha Sigma Nu, Phi Alpha Theta, Pi Sigma Alpha, Delta Phi Epsilon, Pi Delta Phi. Roman Catholic. Home: 6139 Kingsbury Ave Saint Louis MO 63112-1101 Office: Saint Louis U Dept Polit Sci 221 N Grand Blvd Saint Louis MO 63103-2006

LE GUIN, URSULA KROEBER, writer; b. Berkeley, Calif., Oct. 21, 1929; d. Alfred Louis and Theodora (Kracaw) Kroeber; m. Charles A. Le Guin, Dec. 22, 1953; children: Elisabeth, Caroline, Theodore. BA, Radcliffe Coll., 1951; MA, Columbia, 1952; 9 hon. degrees. Vis. lectr. or writer in residence numerous workshops and univs., U.S. and abroad. Author: Rocannon's World, 1966, Planet of Exile, 1966, City of Illusion, 1967, A Wizard of Earthsea, 1968, The Left Hand of Darkness, 1969, The Tombs of Atuan, 1970, The Lathe of Heaven, 1971, The Farthest Shore, 1972, The Dispossessed, 1974, The Wind's Twelve Quarters, 1975, A Very Long Way from Anywhere Else, 1976, Orsinian Tales, 1976, The Word For World is Forest, 1976, The Language of the Night, 1979, rev. edit., 1992, Leese Webster, 1979, Malafrena, 1979, The Beginning Place, 1980, Hard Words, 1981, The Eye of the Heron, 1983, The Compass Rose, 1982, King Dog, 1985, Always Coming Home, 1985, Buffalo Gals, 1987, Wild Oats and Fireweed, 1988, A Visit from Dr. Katz, 1988, Catwings, 1988, Solomon Leviathan, 1988, Fire and Stone, 1989, Catwings Return, 1989, Dancing at the Edge of the World, 1989, Tehanu, 1990, Searoad, 1991, Fish Soup, 1992, A Ride on the Red Mare's Back, 1992, Blue Moon Over Thurman Street, 1993, Wonderful Alexander and the Catwings, 1994, Going Out With Peacocks, 1994, A Fisherman of the Inland Sea, 1994, Four Ways to Forgiveness, 1995, Unlocking the Air, 1996, (with Diana Bellessi) The Twins, The Dream, 1997, Lao Tzu: Tao Te Ching: A Book About the Way and the Power of the Way, 1997, Steering the Craft, 1998, Jane on Her Own, 1999, Sixty Odd, 1999, The Telling, 2000, The Other Wind, 2001, Tales From Earthsea, 2001, The Birthday of the World, 2002; also numerous short stories, poems, criticism, screenplays. Recipient Jupiter award 1975, 76, Lewis Caroll Shelf award 1979, Internat. Fantasy award 1988, Howard D. Vursell award Am. Acad. Arts and Letters, 1991, Pushcart prize, 1991, Boston Globe-Hornbook award for excellence in juvenile fiction, 1968, Newbery Honor medal, 1972, Nebula award (novel) 1969, 75, 90, (story) 1975, 96, Hugo award (novel) 1969, 75, (story) 1974, 88, Gandalf award, 1979, Kafka award, 1986, Nat. Book award, 1972, H.L. Davis award Oreg. Inst. Literary Arts, 1992, Hubbub annual poetry award, 1995, Asimov's Reader's award, 1995, James Tiptree Jr. award, 1995, 97, Retrospective award, 1996, Theodore Sturgeon award (story), 1995, Locus Readers award (novel), 1973, (story) 1984, 95, 2002, (collection) 1996, (novel and story) 2001, Prix Lectures-Jeunesse award, 1987, Bumbershoot Arts award, Seattle, 1998, Lifetime Achievement award Robert Kirsch/L.A. Times, 2000, Lifetime Achievement award Pacific NW Booksellers Assn., 2001, Endeavor award, 2001, Willamette Writers Lifetime Achievement award, 2002, PEN/Malamud award for short fiction, 2002. Mem. NARAL, Amnesty Internet. USA, Environ. Def. Fund, Nat. Resources Def. CTEE, Planned Parenthood Fedn. of Amer., Oreg. Nature Conservancy, Sci. Fiction Research Assn., Sci. Fiction Writers Assn., Authors League, PEN, Writers Guild West, Phi Beta Kappa. Office: care Virginia Kidd Lit Agy PO Box 278 Milford PA 18337-0278 also: care Eric Zohn William Morris Agy 1350 Avenue Of The Americas New York NY 10019-4702

LEGUIZAMÓ, JOHN, actor; b. Bogota, Columbia, July 22, 1964; Movies include Casualties of War, 1989, Whispers in the Dark, 1992, Super Mario Bros., 1993, Carlito's Way, 1993, A Pyromaniac's Love Story, 1995, To Wong Foo, Thanks for Everything, Julie Newmar, 1995, Executive Decision, 1996, The Fan, 1996, The Pest, 1996, Spawn, 1997, Doctor Doolittle (voice), 1998, Summer of Sam, 1999, Titan A.E. (voice), 2000. Recipient Tony award for his play Freak. Office: William Morris Agy 151 S El Camino Dr Beverly Hills CA 90212-2775

LEGUM, JEFFREY ALFRED, automobile company executive; b. Balt., Dec. 16, 1941; s. Leslie and Naomi (Hendler) L.; m. Harriet Cohn, Nov. 10, 1968; children: Laurie Hope, Michael Neil. Student, The Park Sch., 1959; BS in Econs., Wharton Sch. U. Pa., 1963; grad., Chevrolet Sch. Merchandising and Mgmt., 1966. With Park Circle Motor Co., Balt., 1963—, exec. v.p., 1966-77, pres., 1977—; pres., dir. Legum Chevrolet-Nissan, 1977-89; ptnr. Pkwy. Indsl. Ctr., Dorsey, Md., 1965-91; ltd. ptnr. Circle Ltd. Partnership, Glen Burnie, 1991; v.p., dir. P.C. Parts Co., 1967—, pres., 1995—, One Forty Corp., Westminster, Md., 1972-97. Dir., exec. com. United Consol. Industries, 1970-73; dist. chmn. Chevrolet Dealers Coun., 1975-77; chmn. Washington zone, 1982-83. Chmn. transp. div. Associated Jewish Charities, Balt., 1966-69; bd. dirs. Assoc. Placement Bur. (Jewish Vocat. Svc.), Balt., 1964-76, v.p., 1972-76, Preakness Celebration, Inc., 1988-89; mem. adv. bd. The Competitive Edge, Albuquerque, 1977-81; mem. investment com. Balt. Hebrew Congregation, 1980-99, bd. electors, 1990-93, Md. Svc. Acad. Review Bd., 1975-77, bus. adv. bd. to Atty. Genl., 1985-87, Balt. Mus. Art, 1992—, fine arts accessions com., 1992—, chaired legal panel, 1996-99, investment com., 1992—, chmn., 1995-96, exec. com., 1993, fin. com., 1995—, contbr., 1994-96, sec., treas., 1996—, pres.'s com. U. Toronto, 1983—; trustee The Park Sch. Balt., 1979-94, chmn. investment com., 1980-96, mem. exec. com., chmn. fin. com., treas., 1981-91, mem. sr. adv. bd., 1994—, The Legum Found., 1967—; trustee, mem. fin. com. Johns Hopkins Med. Insts., 1997—; sponsor endowment for Jeffrey and Harriet Legum professorship in acute neurol. medicine Johns Hopkins U.; adv. coun. Wilmer Eye Inst., The Johns Hopkins Hosp., 1991—; mem. inst. rev. bd. for human subjects rsch. Johns Hopkins Bayview Med. Ctr., 1992-98; mem. steering com. Govt. House Trust, 1996—. Recipient award of honor Assn. Jewish Charities of Balt., 1967, 68, Cadillac Master Dealer award, 1980-88, 91, Cadillac Pinnacle of Excellence award, 1986, Young Pres.'s Orgn. Cert. Appreciation, 1984, Nissan Nat. Merit Master award, annually 1979-89, Sales Giant award Automotive News, 1987, Minute of Gratitude The Park Sch. Bd. Trustees, 1994. Mem. Young Pres. Orgn. (pres.'s forum 1977-92), World Pres.' Orgn., Benjamin Franklin Assocs., Johns Hopkins Assocs., Md. Hist. Soc. (exec. com. Library of Md. History 1981-90), Chesapeake Pres.' Orgn., Suburban Club (Balt. County), U. Pa., Center Club, U. Toronto Faculty Club (hon.). Home: 10 Stone Hollow Ct Baltimore MD 21208-1860 Office: 1829 Reisterstown Rd Baltimore MD 21208-6320

LEGWAND, DAVID, hockey player; b. Detroit, Aug. 17, 1980; Ctr. Nashville Predators, 1998—; named CHL Rookie of the Yr., 1997—98; winner Red Tilson Trophy, 1997—98. Office: Nashville Predators 501 Broadway Nashville TN 37203*

LEH, AMY S.C. educational technology educator; MA, Ariz. State U., 1994, MED, 1992, PhD, 1997. Asst. prof. Okla. State U., Stillwater, 1997-98, Calif. State U., San Bernardino, 1998-2000, assoc. prof., 2000—. Tech. std. reviewer Calif. Commn. on Tchr. Credentialing, Sacramento, 2000—. Contbr. articles to profl. jours. Mem. Assn. Ednl. Comm. and Tech. (internat. divsn. bd.), Assn. for Advancement of Computing in Edn., Am. Ednl. Rsch. Assn., Computer-Using Educators, Honor Soc. for Internat. Scholars (treas. 1998), Internat. Coun. Ednl. Media.

LEHAN, JONATHAN MICHAEL, judge; b. Los Angeles, Apr. 25, 1947; s. Bert Leon and Frances (Shapiro) L.; m. Annett Jean Garrett, Aug. 1, 1970; children: Joshua Michael, Melanie Janine. BA, Calif. State U., Fullerton, 1968; JD, Calif. Western Sch. Law, 1971; grad., Nat. Drug Ct. Inst., 2000, Nat. Ctr. for State Cts., Williamsburg, Va. Bar: Calif. 1972, U.S. Dist. Ct. (no. dist.) Calif. 1973, U.S. Supreme Ct. 1975. Law clk. to presiding and assoc. justice Calif. Dist. Ct. Appeals, San Bernardino, 1971-73; dep. dist. atty. Mendocino County, Ukiah, Calif., 1973-76, coast asst. dist. atty. Fort Bragg, 1976-83; pvt. practice, 1983-84; ptnr. Lehan & Kronfeld, 1984-90; judge Mendocino County Superior Ct., Ft. Bragg, 1990—. Instr. Barstow C.C., Calif., 1972, Mendocino C.C., Ukiah, 1974-75, Coll. Redwoods, Ft. Bragg, 1981-82; seminar faculty Calif. Jud. Coll., U. Calif., Berkeley, 1993; faculty Calif. Judges Assn. Mid-Year Conf., 1998, ann. conf., 1999; contbr. Calif. Drunk Driving Law, Kuwatch, 1995. Bd. dirs. Salmon Restoration Assn., Fort Bragg, Gloriana Opera Co., Mendocino, Mendocino Art Ctr. Editor Calif. Western Sch. Law Law Rev., 1971. Mem. ABA, Mendocino County Bar Assn. (pres. 1989), Phi Delta Phi, Mendocino C. of C. (bd. dirs.). Democrat. Avocations: violist Mendocino string quartet, violinist Osprey string quartet. Office: Mendocino Superior Ct 700 S Franklin St Fort Bragg CA 95437-5464 E-mail: judgejon@judgejon.com.

LEHAR, STEVEN M. research scientist; b. N.Y.C., Jan. 22, 1953; s. Francis Paphazay and Sophie Lehar; m. Ginny Mullen; children: Sophie, Maggie, Alex. PhD, Boston U, 1994. Prof. psychology Salem (Mass.) State Coll., 1996—97; ind. rschr. Schepens Eye Rsch. Inst., Boston, 1997—. Author: (book) The World In Your Head: A Gestalt View of the Mechanism of Conscious Experience, 2002. Home: 14 Crooked Ln Manchester MA 01944 Office: Peli Lab / Schepens Eye Rsch Inst 20 Staniford St Boston MA 02114-2500 Personal E-mail: slehar@cns.bu.edu.

LEHFELDT, MARTIN CHRISTOPHER, nonprofit association executive; b. N.Y.C., Aug. 18, 1940; s. Martin Rudolf and Amanda Hermine (Schneider) L.; m. Anne Russell, 1963 (div. 1970); children: Elizabeth Anne, Conrad Peter; m. Ann Ashford, 1972 (dec. 1988); m. Linda Graham, 1989. BA, Haverford Coll., 1961; M Div., Union Theol. Sem., 1965. Program dir. Woodrow Wilson Nat. Fellowship Found., Princeton, N.J., 1965-69; v.p. devel. Clark Coll., Atlanta, 1969-76; dir. devel. Atlanta Univ. Ctr., 1976-79; pres. Lehfeldt and Assocs., Inc., Atlanta, 1979-90, The Lehfeldt Co., Atlanta, 1990-97, Southeastern Coun. Founds., Atlanta, 1998—. Co-author: (biography) The Sacred Call: A Tribute to Donald L. Hollowell—Civil Rights Champion, 1997; author: (play) Can You Hear Me in the Back Pew, 1981, (play) Back to Bethlehem, 1973. Mem., past chmn., bd. dirs. Acad. Theatre, Atlanta, 1972-86, Lit. Action, Inc., Atlanta, 1972-82; chair Ctr. for Positive Aging, 1995-97; trustee Johnson C. Smith Theol. Sem., 1991-2000, 2002—. Presbyterian. Avocations: playwriting, fiction writing. Office: Southeastern Coun Founds 50 Hurt Plz SE # 350 Atlanta GA 30303-2914 E-mail: martin@secf.org.

LEHMAN, ARNOLD LESTER, museum official, art historian; b. N.Y.C., July 18, 1944; s. Sidney and Henrietta F. L.; m. Pamela Gimbel, June 21, 1969; children— Nicholas Richard, Zachary Gimbel. BA, Johns Hopkins, 1965, MA, 1966, Yale U., 1968, PhD, 1973. Chester Dale fellow Met. Mus. Art, N.Y.C., 1969-70; lectr. art history Cooper Union and Hunter Coll., 1969-72; dir. Urban Improvements Program, N.Y.C., 1970-72, Parks Council of N.Y.C., 1972-74, Met. Mus. and Art Centers, Miami, Fla., 1974-79, Balt. Mus. Art, 1979-97, Bklyn. Mus. Art, 1997—. Adj. prof. dept. art history Johns Hopkins U., 1986-97; dir. or trustee several corps. and non-profit orgns. Author: The Architecture of Worlds Fairs 1900-1939, 1972, The New York Skyscraper: A History of its Development 1870-1939, 1974; editor: Oskar Schlemmer, 1986; also various mus. catalogs. Trustee Acad. Arts, Easton, Md., Am. Fedn. Arts, N.Y., several non-profit orgns.; mem. exec. planning com. The Bard Grad. Ctr. for Studies in the Decorative Arts; mem. Bklyn Arts Coun. Mem. Assn. Art Mus. Dirs. (trustee 1987-93, pres. 1990-91), Harmonie Club (N.Y.C.). Office: Bklyn Mus Art 200 Eastern Pkwy Brooklyn NY 11238-6052

LEHMAN, CHRISTOPHER M. international business consultant; b. Phila., Dec. 15, 1948; s. John F. and Constance (Cruice) L.; m. Maureen Daly, Oct. 1971; children: Brian Thomas, Robert Francis, Christopher M. BA, St. Joseph's Coll., 1971; MA in Law and Diplomacy, MA in Internat. Rels., Fletcher Sch., 1974, PhD in Internat. Rels., 1993. Research assoc. Fgn. Policy Research Inst., Phila., 1974-76; legis. asst. Senator Harry Byrd, Washington, 1976-78, Senator John Warner, Washington, 1979-81; office dir. Dept. State, 1981-83; spl. asst. to Pres. The White House, 1983-85; sr. v.p. Black, Manafort, Stone & Kelly, Alexandria, Va., 1985-87; pres. Commonwealth Cons. Corp., Washington, 1987—. Bd. advisors KIDS Found.; chmn. bd. Northern Va. Scholarship Trust. Served with USNR, 1969-71. H.B. Earhart fellow, 1971, 72, 73. Mem.: Great Falls Lacrosse Assn. (pres.).

LEHMAN, DAVID, poet, writer; b. N.Y.C., June 11, 1948; BA magna cum laude, Columbia U., 1970, PhD in English, 1978; BA, MA, Cambridge (Eng.) U., 1972. Asst. prof. English Hamilton Coll., 1976-80; fellow Soc. Humanities Cornell U., Ithaca, N.Y., 1980-81; lectr. Wells Coll., 1981-82; free-lance writer, 1982—; book critic, writer Newsweek, 1982-89; prof. Columbia U., N.Y.C., 1995—97; prof. MFA progam New Sch. for Social Rsch., 1996—; prof. N.Y.U., 1997. V.p. Nat. Book Critics Cir., 1987-92; vis. prof. English Hamilton Coll., 1992; prof. MFA program Bennington Coll., 1994—. Author: An Alternative to Speech, 1986, Operation Memory, 1990, Valentine Place, 1996, The Daily Mirror, 2000, The Evening Sun, 2002; author poems which appeared in numerous magazines including The New Yorker, The New York Rev. of Books, The New Republic, The Paris Rev.; editor: Beyond Amazement: New Essays on John Ashbery, 1980, (with Charles Berger) James Merrill: Essays in Criticism, 1983, Ecstatic Occasions, Expedient Forms, 1987, rev. edit., 1996, The Perfect Murder: A Study in Detection, 1989 (Edgar Allan Poe award nominee 1990), The Line Forms Here, 1992, Signs of the Times: Deconstruction and the Fall of Paul de Man, 1991 (N.Y. Times Notable Book of Yr. 1991); contbg. editor Partisan Rev., 1986-95, The Big Question, 1995; series editor The Best American Poetry, 1988—; gen. editor Poets on Poetry series, 1994—; contbr. articles, essays, revs. to profl. jours. NEA fellow in poetry, 1987, Guggenheim fellow in poetry, 1989; recipient Consuelo Ford award The Poetry Soc. Am., 1988, Bernard F. Conners prize The Paris Rev., 1988, Literature award Am. Acad. and Inst. Arts and Letters, 1990, Lila Wallace-Reader's Digest Writer's award, 1992-94, Ingram Merrill Found. award in poetry, 1993.

LEHMAN, DENNIS DALE, chemistry educator; b. Youngstown, Ohio, July 15, 1945; s. Dale Vern and Coryn Eleanor (Neff) L.; m. Maureen Victoria Tierney, July 19, 1959 (div. Mar. 1981); children: Chris, Hillary; m. Kathleen Kim Kuchta, May 15, 1983. BS, Ohio State U., 1967; MS, Northwestern U., 1968, PhD, 1972. Prof. chemistry, chmn. dept. Chgo. City Colls., 1968—, chmn. dept. phys. sci., 2000—. Prof. chemistry Northwestern U., Evanston, Ill., 1974-98, dir. Rsch. Experience for Tchrs., 2002--, lectr. biochemistry Med. Sch., Chgo., 1979-90, lectr. chemistry, 1998; cons. Chgo. Bd. Edn. Author: Chemistry for the Health Sciences, 1981, 8th edit., 1998, Laboratory Chemistry for the Health Sciences, 1981, 8th edit., 1998. Mem. AAAS, Am. Chem. Soc., Sigma Xi. Home: 5918 Tomlinson Dr Mchenry IL 60050-1715 Office: Chgo City Colls 30 E Lake St Chicago IL 60601-2403 E-mail: dlehman@ccc.edu.

LEHMAN, DONALD RICHARD, physicist, educator; b. York, Pa., Dec. 13, 1940; s. Frederick Hinkle and Wilhelmina Emma (Ruesskamp) Lehman; m. Elyse Joan Brauch, Aug. 24, 1962. BA in Physics, Rutgers U., 1962; PhD in Theoretical Physics, George Washington U., 1970. NAS NRC postdoctoral rsch. assoc. Nat. Bur. Stds., Gaithersburg, Md., 1970-72; from asst. to assoc. prof. physics George Washington U., Washington, 1972-82, prof. physics, 1982—, dep. chair physics, 1986-87, chair physics, 1987-93, dir. ctr. nuclear studies, 1990-93, assoc. v.p. rsch. and grad. studies, 1993-96, v.p. for acad. affairs, 1996—. Guest worker Nat. Bur. Stds., Gaithersburg, 1972—89, program analyst, 1974; vis. staff mem., collaborator Los Alamos (N.Mex.) Nat. Lab., 1973—2001; spkr. internat. confs. Contbr. articles to profl. jours. Grantee, Rsch. Corp., N.Y., 1974—76, Dept. Energy, Germantown, Md., 1979—98, NATO, Belgium, 1987—91. Fellow: Am. Phys. Soc.; mem.: Southeastern Univs. Rsch. Assn. (chair bd. trustees 2002—). Achievements include include elucidation of the physics of the 3 body structure of 6Li; unraveling of the physics underlying the role of exact three body continuum states in the photodisintegration of 3He. Office: George Washington U Academic Affairs 2121 I St NW Washington DC 20037-2353

LEHMAN, EDWARD WILLIAM, sociology educator, researcher; b. Regensburg, Germany, Feb. 7, 1936; arrived in US, 1939; s. William and Kate (Hoffman) Lehman; m. Ethna V O'Flannery, May 26, 1962; 1 child Robert. BS, Fordham U., 1956, MA, 1959; PhD, Columbia U., 1966. Lectr. Fordham U., 1958-59; vis. research sociologist dept. psychiatry Montefiore Hosp., Bronx, N.Y., 1959-61; lectr. Sch. Nursing, Columbia U., N.Y.C., 1964-67; research sociologist Cornell U. Med. Coll., 1961-67; asst. prof., then assoc. prof. sociology NYU, 1967-78; prof., 1978—; chmn. dept., 1978-84, 93-96. Assoc dir Ctr Policy Research, New York, NY, 1976—85, sr research assoc, NY, 1969—89; mem minority adv comt NY State Dept Mental Hygiene, 1981—90. Author: (book) Coordinating Health Care: Explorations in Interorganizational Relations, 1975, Political Society: A Macrosociology of Politics, 1977, The Viable Polity, 1992; editor (with others): A Sociological Reader in Complex Organizations, 1980, Autonomy and Order: A Communitarian Anthology, 2000. Served to capt U.S. Army, 1957. Mem.: Am Polit Sci Asn, Am Sociological Asn. Democrat. Roman Catholic. Home: Apt 8B 1 Washington Square Village New York NY 10012-1632

LEHMAN, ELYSE BRAUCH, psychology educator; b. Apr. 5, 1942; BA with honors, Rutgers U., 1962; MA, George Washington U., 1967, PhD, 1970. Rsc. assoc. in psychology George Washington U., 1970-72; cons. clin. investigations svc. devel. metabol. neurol. br. Nat. Inst. Neurol. Diseases and Stroke, 1972-75; asst. prof., assoc. prof. psychology George Mason U., Fairfax, Va., 1976-97, prof., 1997—. Adj. asst. prof. psychology George Washington U., 1972-76; vis. scholar U. N.C., Chapel Hill, 1993. Office: George Mason U Dept Psychology (MSN-3F5) Fairfax VA 22030-4444 E-mail: elehman@gmu.edu.

LEHMAN, GEORGE MORGAN, food sales executive; b. Chgo., Apr. 28, 1938; s. George Daniel and Margaret Marie (Cunningham) L.; m. Kathleen Marie Loftus, June 30, 1962; children: Robert Patrick, Daniel Joseph, Kathleen Marie, Michael Francis, William Terrance, Marilyn Elizabeth. BS, Marquette U., 1960; postgrad., Marquette Law Sch., 1962. Salesman, area mgr., city mgr. Am. Dist. Telegram Co., Chgo., 1964-79; security cons. A.I.C. Security Systesm, 1981-83; exec. acct. mgr. Murphy Butter & Egg Co., 1984-90; acct. exec. Badger/Murphy Food Svc., 1990—. Assoc. mem. Chef's De Cuisine, Chgo., 1985-97. V.p. Sch. Dist. 126, Oak Lawn, Ill.; coach, umpire, v.p. Oak Lawn Little League; coach YMCA Basketball, Oak Lawn Pk. Dist. Basketball. Recipient Those Who Excell in Edn. award Ill. Assn. Sch. Bds., 1991, Cert. of Achievement, 1992. Mem. Roosevelt Stamp Club, Beverly Stamp Club, Delta Sigma Pi. Roman Catholic. Avocations: stamps, basketball, darts. Home: 10733 Lawler Ave Oak Lawn IL 60453-5113 Office: Badger/Murphy Food Svc 700 N Western Ave Chicago IL 60612-1218 also: PO Box 228 Oak Lawn IL 60454-0228

LEHMAN, HARRY JAC, lawyer; b. Dayton, Ohio, Aug. 29, 1935; s. H. Jacques and Mildred (Benas) L.; m. Linda L. Rocker, June 7, 1964 (div. Mar. 1977); children: Sara Beth, Adam Henry, Matthew Daniel; m. Patricia L. Steele, Aug. 30, 1980; 1 child, Alexandra Steele. BA, Amherst Coll., 1957; JD, Harvard U., 1960. Bar: Ohio 1960. Assoc. Burke, Haber & Berick, Cleve., 1960-61, Falsgraf, Kundtz, Reidy & Shoup, Cleve., 1961-66, ptnr., 1967-70; of counsel Benesch, Friedlander, Coplan & Aronoff, 1971-80; ptnr. Jones, Day, Reavis & Pogue, Columbus, 1980-99. Adj. prof. law Ohio State U., Columbus, 1980-84, 86-87; mem. Bd. Bar Examiners, State of Ohio, Columbus, 1983-85. Contbr. articles to profl. jours. Mem. Ohio Ho. of Reps., Columbus, 1971-80; chmn. House Judiciary Com., 1975-80; mem. Ohio Elections Com., Columbus, 1983-88, State Underground Parking Com., Columbus, 1983-87, chmn., 1984-86. Served with USAR, 1960-66. Named one of Ten Outstanding Young Men, Cleve. Jaycees, 1968-69; recipient Disting. Service award NAACP, 1968, Outstanding Freshman Legislator award Ohio Legis. Correspondents Assn., 1971-72, Disting. Service award Ohio Edn. Assn., 1972, Most Effective Legislator award Ohio Legis. Correspondents Assn., 1973-74, Pub. Service award Ohio Pub. Defender Assn., 1974, Outstanding Pub. Service award Ohio Pub. Transit Assn., 1978, Disting. Service award ACLU Ohio Found., 1978, Most Effective Legislator 112th Gen. Assembly Ohio award Columbus Monthly Mag., 1980, Most Effective Legislator 113th Gen. Assembly Ohio award Columbus Monthly Mag. Mem. Ohio Bar Assn., Columbus Bar Assn., Cleve. Bar Assn., Columbus Athletic Club, New Albany Country Club. Democrat. Jewish. Avocations: reading, golf, family. Home: 2642 Charing Rd Columbus OH 43221-3628 Office: Jones Day Reavis & Pogue 41 S High St Ste 1900 Columbus OH 43215-6196

LEHMAN, ISRAEL ROBERT, biochemist, educator; b. Tauroggen, Lithuania, Oct. 5, 1924; arrived in U.S., 1927; s. Herman Bernard Lehman and Anne Kahn; m. Sandra Lee Lehman, July 5, 1959; children: Ellen, Deborah, Samuel. BA, Johns Hopkins U., 1950, PhD, 1954; MD (hon.) , U. Gothenberg, Sweden, 1987; DSc, U. Paris, 1992. Asst. prof. Stanford (Calif.) U., 1959-62, assoc. prof., 1962-67, prof. biochemistry, 1967—, chmn. dept. biochemistry, 1974—79. Mem. sci. adv. bd. U.S. Biochem., Cleve., 1984-98, RPI Pharms., Boulder, Colo., 1991-96, Genetrol, Oakland, Calif., 1998—; cons. Abbott Labs, Chgo., 1990-94. Author: Principles of Biochemistry, 7th edit., 1984. Sgt. U.S. Army, 1943-46, ETO. Recipient Merck award Am. Soc. Biochemistry and Molecular Biology, 1994. Fellow: Am. Acad. Arts and Scis.; mem.: Am. Soc. Biochemistry and Molecular Biology (pres. 1995), Nat. Acad. Scis. Democrat. Jewish. Office: Sch of Medicine Stanford U Stanford CA 94305

LEHMAN, JAMES ORTEN, library director; b. Apple Creek, Ohio, Dec. 22, 1932; s. Willis Albert and Sarean Aldula (Amstutz) L.; m. Dorothy Anna Amstutz, Sept. 5, 1953; children: Lynn, Orval, Gerald, Beverly, Alan. BA, Ea. Mennonite Coll., Harrisonburg, Va., 1959; MLS, Kent State U., 1965, cert. advanced studies in libr. sci., 1969. Prin., tchr. Sonnenberg Mennonite Sch., Kidron, Ohio, 1955-57, 59-60; libr., tchr. Cen. Christian High Sch., 1961-68; asst. libr. Ea. Mennonite Coll. and Sem., 1969-73, dir. librs., 1973—. Mem. hist. com. Mennonite Ch., Goshen, Ind., 1973-77, 87-93; chmn. hist. com. Va. Mennonite Conf., Harrisonburg, Va., 1975—; chmn. Ea. Mennonite Assoc. Librs. and Archives, Lancaster, Pa., 1977-89; various positions Sonnenberg Mennonite Ch., Lindale Mennonite Ch., 1955—. Author congl. and community histories in Ohio, 1969, 74, 75, 78, 80, 86, 90; contbr. numerous articles to religious jours. Served at mil. duty Univ. Hosp., Cleve., 1953-55. Mem. ALA, Va. Libr. Assn., Am. Assn. for State and Local History, Ohio Hist. Soc., Mennonite Ch. Hist. Assn., Lancaster Mennonite Hist. Soc., Mennonite Historians Ea. Pa., Kidron Community Hist. Soc., Shenandoah Valley Mennonite Historians. Office: Ea Mennonite Univ Libr 1200 Park Rd Harrisonburg VA 22802-2404

LEHMAN, JEFFREY SEAN, dean, law educator; b. Bronxville, N.Y., Aug. 1, 1956; s. Leonard and Imogene (McAuliffe) L.; children: Rebecca Colleen, Jacob Keegan, Benjamin Emil. AB, Cornell U., 1977; M of Pub. Policy, U. M of Pub. Policy, JD, U. Mich., 1981. Bar: D.C. 1983, U.S. Ct. Appeals (fed. cir.) 1984, U.S. Ct. Appeals (D.C. cir.) 1987, U.S. Supreme Ct. 1987. Law clk. to chief judge U.S. Ct. Appeals (1st cir.), Portland, Maine, 1981-82; law clk. to assoc. justice U.S. Supreme Ct., Washington, 1982-83; assoc. Caplin & Drysdale, Chartered, 1983-87; asst. prof. U. Mich. Law Sch., Ann Arbor, 1987-92, prof., 1992-93, prof. law and pub. policy, 1993—, dean, 1994—. Vis. prof. Yale U., 1993, U. Paris II, 1994. Co-author: Corporate Income Taxation, 1994; editor-in-chief: Mich. Law Rev., 1979-80. Foster parent Arlington County Dept. Human Svcs., 1983-87; trustee Skadden Fellowship Found., 1995—. Henry Bates fellow, 1981. Mem. ABA, Am. Law Inst., Order of Coif. Democrat. Jewish. Office: U Mich Law Sch 324 Hutchins Hall 625 S State St Ann Arbor MI 48109-1215 E-mail: jlehman@umich.edu.

LEHMAN, JOAN ALICE, real estate executive; b. Jamaica Queens, N.Y., May 8, 1938; d. Hans Newman and Margot (Deutsch) Senen; m. Eugene Lehman, June 17, 1956 (div. Mar. 1990); children: Joel, Peter, Alan, Ira, Helen Ann, Helen Beth, Robert, Jacqueline, John, Steven, Robin, Elizabeth, Jody, Lisa, David, Andy, Jeremy, Jay. AA, Nassau C.C., East Meadow, N.Y., 1971; BS, Nova U., 1982. Lic. real estate broker, Fla. Owner Joan Lehman Real Estate Mgmt. Co., Old Bethpage, N.Y., 1961-82; tchr. Broward County Schs., Ft. Lauderdale, Fla., 1982-86; owner Joan Lehman Real Estate, Plantation, 1986—; pres. Jo Al 1 Inc. Mem. Sunset Sch. Adv. Bd., Ft. Lauderdale, 1994-96; pres. The Pointe Condo Assn., 2001—; bd. dirs. Property Owners Ctrl. Lauderhill, Fla., 1996; den mother Boy Scouts Am., Old Bethpage, N.Y.; leader Girl Scouts U.S., Old Bethpage. Avocations: bowling, travel, theater. Office: 2880 NE 14th Street Cswy Pompano Beach FL 33062-3651

LEHMAN, JOHN F., JR. industrialist; b. Phila., Sept. 14, 1942; s. John F. and Constance (Cruice) L.; m. Barbara Wieland, 1975; children: John F., Alexandra, Grace. BS in Internat. Relations, St. Joseph's Coll., 1964; BA in Law with honors, MA in Internat. Law and Diplomacy, Cambridge U., 1967; PhD in Internat. Relations, U. Pa., 1974. Sr. staff mem. Nat. Security Council, 1969-74; dep. dir. U.S. Arms Control and Disarmament Agy., 1975-77; pres. Abingdon Corp., 1977-81; sec. of navy Washington, 1981-87; mng. dir. Paine Webber, 1988-91; chmn. J.F. Lehman & Co., N.Y.C., 1991—, Sperry Marine Inc., N.Y.C., 1993-96, OAOT Corp., 2001—. Bd. dirs. Ball Corp., ISO, Inc. Author: Command of the Seas, 1989, Making War, 1992, On Seas of Glory, 2001. Capt. USNR, 1968— . E-mail: jfl@jflpartners.com.

LEHMAN, JOHN MICHAEL, experimental pathologist-virologist; b. Abington, Pa., June 19, 1942; s. John Holland and Emily (Doliney) L.; m. Elizabeth Bowen; children: Deborah, Eric. BS, Phila. Coll. Pharmacy, 1964; PhD, U. Pa., 1970. Asst. prof. Sch. Medicine U. Colo., Denver, 1972-76, assoc. prof. Sch. Medicine, 1976-80, prof. Sch. Medicine, 1980-85; Theobald Smith Alumni chmn., prof. Albany (N.Y.) Med. Coll., 1985—. Cellular physiology NIH, Bethesda, Md., 1978-82; cons. Los Alamos (N.Mex.) Sci. Lab., 1972-92; bd. dirs. Toolan Inst., Benington, Vt., 1988-91. Grantee Nat. Cancer Inst., 1976—, NSF, 1978-80. Mem. Am. Assn. Cancer Rsch., Cell Biology, Am. Soc. Microbiology, Tissue Culture Assn., Analytical Cytology Soc. Home: 22 Southwood Dr Slingerlands NY 12159-9752 Office: Albany Med Coll 47 New Scotland Ave Albany NY 12208-3412

LEHMAN, KENNETH WILLIAM, lawyer; b. N.Y.C., Dec. 4, 1956; AB summa cum laude, Hamilton Coll., 1978; JD, U. Va., 1981. Bar: N.Y. 1982, U.S. Dist. Ct. (we. dist.) N.Y. 1982, Maine 1986, U.S. Dist. Ct. Maine 1986. Assoc. Nixon, Hargrave, Devans & Doyle (now Nixon, Peabody), Rochester, N.Y., 1981-85; asst. atty. gen. Maine Dept. of Atty. Gen., Augusta, Maine, 1986-92; pntr. Bernstein, Shur, Sawyer & Nelson, Portland, 1992—. Adj. instr. U. New England Coll. Osteopathic Med., Biddeford, Maine, 1991—. Bd. dir. Congregation Bet Ha'am, Portland, 1987-01, Cerebral Palsy Assn. Greater Portland, 1992-94, Am. Lung Assn. of Maine, Augusta, 1993-99. Recipient Cert. of Award Maine Citizens Against Sexual Abuse, 1990. Mem. Maine State Bar Assn., Maine Bar Found. (fellow, dir. 1990—), Maine Vol. Lawyer's Project (chair 1990-01), Phi Beta Kappa. Home: 28 Newell Ridge Rd Cumberland Center ME 04021-9349 Office: Bernstein Shur Sawyer & Nelson PO Box 9729 Portland ME 04104-5029 E-mail: klehman@mainelaw.com.

LEHMAN, LARRY L. state supreme court justice; Judge Wyo. County Ct., 1985-88, Wyo. Dist. Ct. (2nd dist.), 1988-94; chief justice Wyo. Supreme Ct., Cheyenne, 1998—2002, justice, 1994—. Office: Supreme Court Bldg 2301 Capitol Ave Cheyenne WY 82002-0001*

LEHMAN, LAWRENCE HERBERT, consulting engineering executive; b. N.Y.C., Apr. 30, 1929; s. Samuel and Shirley (Freiberg) L.; m. Susan E. Green, June 29, 1957; children: Scott Jeffrey, Christopher Adam. BCE, NYU, 1949; MBA, Iona Coll., 1978. Registered profl. engr., N.Y., N.J., Ky., Ill., Mass., Conn., Ind., Pa., Md., Fla., Tenn. Project engr. Andrews & Clark (Cons. Engrs.), N.Y.C., 1951-57; project mgr. Barstow, Mulligan & Vollmer (Cons. Engrs.), 1957-59; chief engr., ptnr. Vollmer Assos. (Cons. Engrs.), 1959-67; chief exec. officer, dir. Berger, Lehman Assos. (P.C.), Rye, N.Y., 1967—. Mem. City of Rye Planning Commn. Recipient Third award U.S. Steel Corp., 1966, Bridge award Pre-stressed Concrete Inst., 1975, Honor award Nat. ACEC, 1995, nat. awards USDOT, 2000, Am. Cons. Engrs. Coun., 2000, others. Fellow ASCE (life); mem. NSPE, Am. Cons. Engrs. Coun., Soc. Am. Mil. Engrs., Transp. Rsch. Bd., Am. Ry. Engring. Assn., Internat. Assn. Bridge and Structural Engrs., Inst. Transp. Engrs., Am. Arbitration Assn. (nat. panel arbitrators), N.Y. Assn. Cons. Engrs. (Engring. Excellence awards 1975, 79, 90, 95), Conn. Engrs. in Pvt. Practice, West County Profl. Engrs. Soc. (Engr. of Yr. award 1991), The Moles, High Speed Rail Assn. Home: 10 Chester Dr Rye NY 10580-2204 Office: 411 Theodore Fremd Ave Rye NY 10580-1410 E-mail: blalehman@aol.com.

LEHMAN, LEONARD, lawyer, consultant; b. Bklyn, July 5, 1927; s. Samuel and Marcy (Dolgenas) L.; m. Imogene McAuliffe, June 11, 1954; children—Jeffrey, Toby, Amy, Zachary. B.A., Cornell U., 1949; J.D., Yale U., 1952. Bar: N.Y. 1953, U.S. Supreme Ct. 1969, D.C. 1979, U.S. Ct. Internat. Trade 1981, U.S. Ct. Appeals (fed. cir.) 1982. Atty.-advisor U.S. Tax Ct., Washington, 1952-55; sole practice, N.Y.C., 1955-63; sr. counsel Office Tax Legis. Counsel, U.S. Dept. Treasury, Washington, 1963-65; asst. to chief counsel U.S. Customs Service, 1965-67, dep. chief counsel, 1968-71, asst. commr. 1971-79; ptnr. Barnes, Richardson and Colburn, N.Y.C., Washington and Chgo., 1979-89, counsel, 1989-95; mem. industry functional adv. com. on customs/trade policy U.S. Dept. Commerce, 1989-95. Recipient U.S. Treasury Meritorious Service award, 1971, Exceptional Service award, 1979; U.S. Customs Honor award, 1977. Mem. ABA (standing com. on customs law 1974-80, chmn. 1980, customs and tariff com., adminstrv. law sect. 1971-88, vice chmn. 1981-83, chmn. 1984-88), Phi Beta Kappa, Phi Kappa Phi. Contbr. articles to profl. jours. Home and Office: 18 Rich Branch Ct North Potomac MD 20878-2461

LEHMAN, MYRA HARRIET, sculptor, dental hygienist; b. Far Rockaway, N.Y., Apr. 30, 1936; d. Aaron David and Frances Zipporah (Slobodkin) Wisan; m. Richard Emil Lehman, Jan. 27, 1963 (dec. 1979); children: Lisa L. Gordon, Renee L. Condon, Rosalind, Richard Emil Jr. Registered dental hygienist, U. Pa., 1956; BA, Sarah Lawrence Coll., 1983. Dental hygienist various offices, various cities, N.Y., 1960—. Juror Rowayton Arts Coun., 2000. Three-woman shows Our World Gallery at Stone Studio, Stamford, Conn., 2001; exhibited in group shows, including Putnam Arts Coun., Rye (N.Y.) Free Reading Rm., Mari Gallery, Mamaroneck, N.Y., Sarah Lawrence Coll., Bronxville, N.Y., Hammond Mus., North Salem, Beaux Arts Finale, Bronxville, Cooperstown (N.Y.) Ann. Nat. Art Exhibit, Lever House, Mamaroneck, Art 54 Gallery, Portfolio Gallery, Stamford, Conn., Ferncliff Wildlife Ctr., Mamaroneck, Salmagundi Club, Pen and Brush Club, SONO Arts Festival, Hurlbutt Gallery, Lehman Coll., Catharine Lorillard Wolfe Art Club, Greenwich Art Soc., Farmington Art Soc., 1997, Cabrini Art Gallery, 1997, White Plains (N.Y.) Libr., 1997, Art Life Studio, 1999, Art Soc. Old Greenwich, 1999 (hon. mention sculpture); prin. works include Westchester Fedn. Women's Clubs, Inc. (1st place for sculpture 1998). Recipient 1st prize sculpture Art Soc. Old Greenwich, 2001, 1st prize Rye Woman's Club, 1997, Mamaroneck Artists Guild, 1995, Salmagundi Club award, 1993, 2d place Art Soc. Old Greenwich, 1992, Mari Galleries Nat. Juried Fine Arts, 1992, Mamaroneck Woman's Club, 1991, Argos Foundry award Putnam Arts Coun., 1st prize Rye Woman's Club, 1988, 90, 1st place sculpture Mamaroneck Artists Guild, 2002. Mem. Am. Acad. Dental Hygiene. Home: 13 Eve Ln Rye NY 10580-4113 E-mail: myrah@sprynet.com.

LEHMAN, ORIN, retired state official; b. N.Y.C., Jan. 14, 1922; s. Allan S. and Evelyn (Schiffer) L.; children: Susan, Brooke, Sage. BA, Princeton U., 1942; MA, NYU, 1956, PhD, 1961; LHD (hon.), Hartwick Coll., 1962, Marist Coll., 1993; LLD (hon.), Manhattan Coll., 1985. Economist Lehman Bros., N.Y.C., 1947-52; pub. and chmn. Colgreene Pub., Inc., Hudson, N.Y., 1951-59; chmn. Colgreene Broadcasting Co., Catskill, 1958-75, Picket Prodn., Inc., N.Y.C., 1968-75; commr. N.Y. State Office of Parks, Recreation and Hist. Preservation, Albany, 1975-94; chmn. N.Y. State Commn. for Restoration of the Capitol, 1979. Adv. U.S. del. UN Conf. Trade and Devel., 1964-68; chmn. N.Y. State Gov.'s Com. on Employment of Handicapped, 1956-65; mem. public adv. bd. Econ. Cooperation Adminstrn., 1950-52; mem. U.S. Nat. Commn. for UNESCO, 1968-71; chmn. N.Y.C. Bd. Corrections, 1974-75; mem. exec. com. N.Y.C. Criminal Justice Coordinating Com., 1974-75 Trustee, past chmn. New Sch. Social Research, N.Y.C., Parsons Sch. Design; trustee, chmn. Just-One-Break, Inc.; trustee, past exec. dir. Eleanor Roosevelt Meml. Found.; bd. dirs. Ednl. Broadcasting Corp., 1965-74; pres. N.Y. Citizens Com. Public Higher Edn., 1964-68. Served to capt. U.S. Army, 1942-47. Decorated D.F.C., Bronze Star, Purple Heart; recipient Disting. Svc. award Nat. Govs. Assn, 1992, citations Anti-Defamation League, citations N.Y.C. Jaycees, citations N.Y. State Jaycees, citations Pres.'s Com. on Employment of Handicapped, citations CSC U.S., citations CCNY, citations Marist Coll., citations Taft Sch., Pres.'s Pub. Svc. award Nature Conservancy, Pugsley medal Nat. Park Found., 1989. Office: Orin Lehman Found Inc c/o Wallace 20 E 69th St New York NY 10021-4922

LEHMAN, PAUL ROBERT, retired music educator; b. Athens, Ohio, Apr. 20, 1931; s. Harvey C. and Vera Marjorie (Simmons) L.; m. V. Ruth Wickline, June 27, 1953; children: David Alan, Laura Ann. BS in Edn. with honors, Ohio U., 1953; MusM, U. Mich., 1959, PhD in Music, 1962. Tchr. Jackson Twp. Sch. Dist., Massillon, Ohio, 1953-55; from instr. to asst. prof. U. Colo., Boulder, 1962-65; from assoc. prof. to prof. U. Ky., Lexington, 1965-70; music specialist U.S. Dept. Edn., Washington, 1967-68; prof. Eastman Sch. Music, Rochester, N.Y., 1970-75, U. Mich., Ann Arbor, 1975-96, assoc. dean sch. music, 1977-89, sr. assoc. dean, 1989-96. Cons. NEA, U.S. Dept. Edn., Coun. of Chief State Sch. Officers, Nat. Assessment of Ednl. Progress, various univs., sch. systems, state depts. of edn., corps. Author: The Class of 2001, 1985, Music in Today's Schools: Rationale and Commentary, 1987; contbr. articles to profl. jours. Served to 1st lt. USAF, 1955-57. Recipient Cert. Merit Found. Advancement Edn. in Music, 1986, Nat. Fedn. of Music Club, 1993, Phi Mu Alpha, 1996, Music Industry Conf., 1997. Mem. Music Educators Nat. Conf. (pres. 1984-86), Coll. Music Soc. (exec. bd. 1981-83), Internat. Soc. Music Edn. (bd. dirs. 1988-92). Office: U Mich 602 Burton Meml Tower Ann Arbor MI 48109

LEHMAN, RICHARD LEROY, lawyer; b. Johnstown, Pa., Feb. 4, 1930; s. John S. and Deliah E. (Chase) L.; m. Lucia M. Ragnone; children: Ann Laurie, Leslie Ann, Lucia Marie. AB in Social Work, U. Ky., 1957; LLB, U. Detroit, 1960. Bar: Mich. 1961, U.S. Dist. Ct. (ea. dist.) Mich. 1961, U.S. Ct. Appeals (6th cir.) 1961. Pvt. practice, Detroit; ptnr. Garan, Lucow, Miller, Lehman, Seward & Cooper, 1961-79; pres. Home Bldg. Plan Svc., Inc., Portland, Oreg., 1979-82; pres., gen. counsel Matvest Inc., Farmington Hills, Mich., 1980-86; pres. Xi Industries, Flint, 1982-86; ptnr. Lehman & Valentino, P.C., Bloomfield Hills, 1986—; pres. Premiere Packaging, Inc., Flint, 1987-91, chmn., CEO, 1990-98. Vis. lectr. U. Detroit Law Sch., 1970-74, also Inst. Continuing Legal Edn. Mem. exec. com. pres.'s cabinet U. Detroit, 1975-79; mem. Old Newsboys Goodfellow Fund Detroit, 1966—, bd. dirs., 1975-78. 1st lt. AUS, 1947-53. Recipient Algernon Sydney Sullivan Medallion U. Ky., 1957; fellow U. Ky. Mem. SAR, Mich. Bar Assn., Genesee County Bar Assn. (mem. bench and bar com. 1975-78), U. Ky. Alumni Assn., U. Detroit Law Sch. Alumni Assn. (dir. 1970-77, pres. 1974-75), U. Detroit Alumni Assn., 6th Cir. Jud. Conf. (life), Pine Lake Country Club (bd. dirs. 1991-96, pres. 1994-95), K.C., Am. Legion, VFW. Roman Catholic. Avocations: golf, downhill skiing, carpentry. Home: 6790 Telegraph Rd Bloomfield Township MI 48301 Office: Lehman & Valentino PC 43996 S Woodward Ave Bloomfield Hills MI 48302-0546

LEHMAN, TODD WILSON, artist; b. Harrisburg, Pa., Apr. 30, 1941; s. Ralph Emanuel and Eleanor Elizabeth (Wilson) L. BS, Okla. State U., 1965; student, Pratt Inst., Bklyn., summer 1974, Art Students League, N.Y.C., 1972-75. One-man shows include Lancaster (Pa.) Mus. Art, 1993, DTW Gallery, N.Y., 1996, Otto-Galerie, Munich, Germany, 2000; exhibited in group shows at Gardiner Art Gallery, Okla. State U., Stillwater, 1993, Broadway Mall Gallery, N.Y., 1994, Pleiades Gallery, N.Y., 1995, Lancaster Mus. Art, 1997, Caelum Gallery, N.Y.C., 1998, Ralls Collection, Washington, 2002; theater designer. Ludwig Vogelstein Found. grantee, 1995. Mem. Art Students League of N.Y. (life), N.Y. Artists Equity Assn. Avocation: pianist.

LEHMANN, A SPENCER, retired chemist, retired chemical engineer; b. Los Angeles, Calif., Sept. 23, 1916; s. Aldo Mayer and Elsie Thompson Lehmann; m. Rosalie Belle Lowther, Dec. 18, 1943; children: Lawrence Spencer, Bruce Aldo. AB, Stanford U., Stanford, CA, 1938; PhD, Brown U., Providence, RI, 1941. Rsch. chemist, engr. Naval Rsch. Lab, Washington, 1941—42, Tenn. Eastman Co., Oak Ridge, Tenn., 1942—46; rsch. chemist, gen. mgr. Shell Oil, Houston, 1946—76. Exec. bd., dir. Joint Powers Ins. Agy., Sacramento, 1986—96. Chair-water supply & distbn. Houston Chamber Commerce, Houston, 1972—75; dir. Houston/Galveston Subsidence Dist, 1973—76; dir., bd. pres. San Diego Blood Bank Found., San Diego, 1986—98. Recipient Cert. Of Appreciation, Am. Petroleum Inst., 1967; scholar Phi Beta Kappa, Sigma Xi, Brown Chapter-Brown U., 1941. Mem.: Am. Chem. Soc., Rotary Club of Fallbrook.

LEHMANN, CHRISTOPH ULRICH, pediatrician, neonatologist, medical informatician; b. Kiel, Germany, Sept. 4, 1964; s. Fritz Max Karl and Erna Klothilde (Hofmann) Lehmann; children: Jenna Sue, Lukas Karl. MD, U. Munster, Germany, 1990. Intern Marshall U., 1992-93, resident pediat., 1993-95; fellow neonatology Johns Hopkins U., 1995-98, instr. neonatology, 1998—, asst. prof. pediat., 2000—, asst. prof. health info. scis., 2001—. Med. webmaster, 1995—. Applied Informatics fellow Nat. Libr. Medicine, 1998-00. Fellow Am. Acad. Pediat.; mem. Am. Med. Informatics Assn., Soc. for the Internet in Medicine, Alpha Omega Alpha. Office: Johns Hopkins U 600 N Wolfe St Cmsc 210 Baltimore MD 21287-0001

LEHMANN, DORIS ELIZABETH, elementary education educator; b. Ramsey, N.J., Aug. 17, 1933; d. Alfred Harrison and Anna Elizabeth (Gerhold) Rockefeller; m. Victor S. Lehmann, June 25, 1955; children: Joanne E. Cathy Lynn, Victor A., Kristie Sue. BS in Edn. magna cum laude, Wagner Coll., 1955; student in edn., Columbia U., summers 1988-91, Jersey City State, 1990—, William Paterson, 1971. Elem. tchr. Sch. St. Sch., Ramsey, 1955-56; bedside instr. N. Bergen County schs., N.J., 1966-71; elem. tchr. Edith A. Bogert Sch., Upper Saddle River, 1971-2000. Author numerous poems; author: (with others) Curriculum for Values Education in New Jersey, 1991. Indian cons. Bergen County Mus. of Art and Sci., Paramus, N.J., 1983—. Recipient Fellowship of Life award Luth. Layman's Movement, 1955. Fellow Upper Saddle River Edn. Assn. (social sec. 1972-73, v.p. 1974-75, 84-85, liaison to USR hist. soc. 1986—) N.J. Edn. Assn., N.J. North Edn. Assn., Alpha Omicron Pi (life, treas. 1954, v.p. 1955). Republican. Lutheran. Office: Edith A Bogert Sch 395 W Saddle River Rd Saddle River NJ 07458-1622 E-mail: vlcco@aol.com.

LEHMANN, ERICH LEO, statistics educator; b. Strasbourg, France, Nov. 20, 1917; came to U.S., 1940, naturalized, 1945; s. Julius and Alma Rosa (Schuster) L.; m. Juliet Popper Shaffer; children: Stephen, Barbara, Fia. MA, U. Calif., Berkeley, 1943, PhD, 1946; DSc (hon.), U. Leiden, 1985, U. Chgo., 1991. From asst. dept. math. to prof. U. Calif., Berkeley, 1942-55, prof. dept. stats., 1955-88, emeritus, 1988—, chmn. dept. stats., 1973-76. Vis. assoc. prof. Columbia, 1950-51, Stanford, 1951-52; vis. lectr. Princeton, 1951 Author: Testing Statistical Hypotheses, 1959, 2d edit., 1986; (with J.L. Hodges, Jr.) Basic Concepts of Probability and Statistics, 1964, 2d edit, 1970, Nonparametrics: Statistical Methods Based on Ranks, 1975, Theory of Point Estimation, 1983, (with Casella) 2nd edit., 1998, Elements of Large Sample Theory, 1998. Recipient Fisher award Coms. of Pres. Stats. Socs. in N.Am., 1988; Guggenheim fellow, 1955, 66, 79; Miller research prof., 1962-63, 72-73; recipient Samuel S. Wilks Meml. medal Am. Statis. Assn., 1996, Gottfried Noether award Am. Statis. Assn., 2000. Fellow Inst. Math. Stats., Am. Statis. Assn., Royal Statis. Soc. (hon.); mem. Internat. Statis. Inst., Am. Acad. Arts and Scis., Nat. Acad. Scis. Office: U Calif Dept Statistics Berkeley CA 94720-0001

LEHMANN, ERNEST KARL, consulting company executive, geologist; b. Heidelberg, Fed. Republic of Germany, June 8, 1929; came to U.S., 1935; s. Karl and Elwine (Hartleben) L.; m. Sarah Anne Willius, July 24, 1953; children: Frederick C., Kathrine, Charlotte, Walter G. BA, Williams Coll., 1951; postgrad., Brown U., 1952-53, Harvard U. Bus. Sch., 1982-84. Cert. profl. geologist. Geologist Signal Mining Co., Bannack, Mont., 1950; asst. dist. geologist Bear Creek Mining Co., Mpls., 1951-58; pvt. practice cons., 1958-59; v.p., treas. Lindgren and Lehmann, Wayzata, 1959-66; pres. E. K. Lehmann and Assocs., Mpls., 1967—, N. Ctrl. Mineral Ventures Inc., 1985—. Chair bd. dirs. Franconia Minerals Corp., 1999. Pres., bd. dirs. Lowry Hill Residents, Inc., Mpls., 1969-75; mem. Mpls. Housing Appeals Bd.; chmn. Calhoun Isle Planning Commn., Mpls.; vice-chmn. planning com. Plymouth Village, Minn., 1962-66. Sgt. U.S. Army, 1953-55. Mem. Am. Inst. Profl. Geologists (pres. 1985, Ben H. Parker medal 1987, chair 1985—), Soc. Econ. Geologists (life), Soc. Mining Engrs., Northwest Mining Assn., Mining and Metall. Soc. Am., Minn. Exploration Assn. (pres. and dir. 1992—). Republican. Office: E K Lehmann & Assoc Inc Plymouth Bldg 12 S 6th St Ste 622 Minneapolis MN 55402-1506

LEHMANN, ESTHER STRAUSS, investment company executive; b. Binghamton, N.Y., Apr. 19, 1944; d. Julius and Betty (Lind) Strauss; m. Aaron Lehmann, Feb. 27, 1966; children: Shanna, Shira, Marc, David. BS, Cornell U., 1966; cert. in vol. and non-profit orgn. mgmt., U. Conn., 1976; cert. employee benefits specialist, U. Pa., 1983. V.p. Fairway Mgmt., West Hartford, Conn., 1976-80; investment exec. Herzfeld & Stern, Paramus, N.J., 1980-86; assoc. v.p. Gruntal & Co., Inc., Ft. Lee, 1988—. Home: 1632 Dover Ct Teaneck NJ 07666-2965

LEHMANN, MICHAEL STEPHEN, film director; b. San Francisco, Mar. 30, 1957; s. Herbert and Minette L.; m. Holland Sutton; children: Alexander, Natalie. BA, Columbia U., 1978; MFA, U. So. Calif., 1985. Mgr. electronic cinema div. Zoetrope, Hollywood, Calif., 1981-83. Dir. (films) Heathers, 1989 (Best First Feature award Ind. Feature Project 1990), Meet the Applegates, 1991, Hudson Hawk, 1991, Airheads, 1994, The Truth About Cats and Dogs, 1996, My Giant, 1998, 40 Days and 40 Nights, 2002, The West Wing (TV series), 1999; exec. prodr. (film) Ed Wood, 1994. Office: Creative Artists Agy 9830 Wilshire Blvd Beverly Hills CA 90212-1825*

LEHMANN, PHYLLIS WILLIAMS, archaeologist, educator; b. Bklyn., Nov. 30, 1912; d. James Barnes and Florence Lourene (Richmond) Williams; m. Karl Lehmann, Sept. 14, 1944 (dec. Dec. 1960). BA, Wellesley Coll., 1934, L.H.D., 1976; PhD, NYU, 1943; Litt.D., Mt. Holyoke Coll., 1971; D.F.A., Coll. Holy Cross, 1973. Asst. charge classical collection Bklyn. Museum, 1934-36; part-time instr. history art Bennett Jr. Coll., 1936-39; mem. faculty Smith Coll., 1946—, prof. art, 1955-67, Jessie Wells Post prof. art, 1967-72, William R. Kenan, Jr. prof. art, 1972-78, prof. emeritus, 1978—, dean, 1965-70; asst. field dir. excavations conducted by Archaeol. Research Fund of NYU at Samothrace, 1948-60, acting dir., 1960-62, adv. dir., 1962—; research prof. Inst. Fine Arts, NYU, 1961-62; adj. prof. Inst. Fine Arts, N.Y. U., 1965—. Flexner lectr. Bryn Mawr Coll., 1977; Baldwin lectr. Oberlin Coll., 1982 Author: Statues on Coins of Southern Italy and Sicily in the Classical Period, 1946, Roman Wall Paintings from Boscoreale in the Metropolitan Museum of Art, 1953, The Pedimental Sculptures of the Hieron in Samothrace, 1962, Samothrace, vol. 3, 1969, (with Karl Lehmann) Samothracian Reflections. Aspects of the Revival of the Antique, 1973, Skopas in Samothrace, 1973, Cyriacus of Ancona's Egyptian Visit and Its Reflections in Gentile Bellini and Hieronymus Bosch, 1977, Samothrace, Vol. 5, 1982, contbr. Vol. 7, 1992; also articles in profl. jours.; Editor: (with Karl Lehmann) Samothrace, 1961—; asst. editor: Art Bull., 1945-47; book rev. editor, 1949-52. Named hon. citizen of Samothrace, 1968; recipient Wellesley Coll. Alumnae Assn. Achievement award, 1976; Gold medal Pan Samothracian Hearth of Athens, 1981; hon. mem. Pan Samothracian Hearth of Athens, 1979; Fulbright research grantee Italy, 1952-53; Guggenheim fellow, 1952-53; Bollingen fellow, 1960 Fellow Am. Acad. Arts and Scis.; mem. Archaeol. Inst. Am. (trustee 1970-73), Coll. Art Assn. Am., Am. Numis. Soc., Soc. Archtl. Historians (Alice D. Hitchcock award 1969), AAUW, Renaissance Soc. Am., Am. Sch. Classical Studies in Athens (research fellow fall 1970, 76, exec. com. 1970-75, publ. com. 1975-80, chmn. 1977-80), Williamsburg Hist. Soc., Phi Beta Kappa. Clubs: Cosmopolitan. Home: 127 Main St Haydenville MA 01039-9713 Office: Smith Coll Hillyer Hall Northampton MA 01063

LEHMANN, WILLIAM LEONARDO, electrical engineer, educator; b. Milw., Dec. 17, 1924; s. William Christian and Johanna Alma (Schrumpf) L.; m. Barbara Taylor, June 29, 1948; children: Johanna, William, Katherine, Wendy, Christianne. AB, Haverford (Pa.) Coll., 1944; MS, Syracuse (N.Y.) U., 1948, PhD, 1953. Registered profl. engr., Ohio. Prof. physics acting dean Air Force Inst. Tech., 1951-66; lectr. Ohio State U., 1957-60; dep. for labs. Office Asst. Sec. Air Force Research and Devel., 1966-74; dir. Air Force Office Sci. Research, 1974-78, Air Force Weapons Lab., Kirtland AFB, N.Mex., 1978-81; chief scientist Combat Devel. Experimentation Ctr. U.S. Army Sci. Support Lab, Ft. Ord, Calif., 1982-85; sr. sci. analyst N.Mex. Engring. Research Inst., 1985-93; prof. elec. engring. U. N.Mex., Albuquerque, 1988-93; sr. assoc. Ctr. for Occupational R & D, 1993—. Vis. prof. U. N.Mex., 1981-82, also adv. bd. Coll. Engring.; Past mem. Gov. N.Mex. Tech. Excellence Com.; mem. USAF Scientific Adv. Bd., 1985-92. Patentee solar orientation device. Mem. Beaver Creek (Ohio) Sch. Dist. Bd., 1965-66; trustee Lovelace Med. Found. Served with AUS, 1944-45. Recipient Air Force Exceptional Civilian Service medal with three oak leaf cluster, 1981, Ohio Engr.'s award, 1966, award Ohio Soc. Profl. Engrs., 1965 Fellow AAAS; mem. Air Force Assn. (citation honor 1978), Am. Soc. Engring. Edn., AIAA, Am. Def. Preparedness Assn., Sigma Xi, Sigma Pi Sigma, Tau Beta Pi. Lodges: Rotary. Republican. Episcopalian. Home: 700 Island Retreat Rd Port Aransas TX 78373-6012 Office: Port Aransas High Sch PO Box 1297 Port Aransas TX 78373-1297 E-mail: bblehmann@aol.com.

LEHMANN-CARSSOW, NANCY BETH, secondary school educator, coach; b. Kingsville, Tex., Sept. 9, 1949; d. Valgene William and Ella Mae (Zajicek) Lehmann; m. William Benton Carssow, Jr., Aug. 1, 1981. BS, U. Tex., 1971, MA, 1979. Freelance photographer, Austin, Tex., 1971-99; geography tchr., tennis coach Austin Ind. Sch. Dist., 1974-98, geography tchr., instrnl. specialist, girls' wrestling coach, 1999—. Founder Custom Pet Wheels, 1997; salesperson, mgr. What's Going On-Clothing, Austin, 1972-78; area adminstr. Am. Inst. Fgn. Study, Austin, 1974-81; area rep. World Encounters, Austin, 1981—, tour guide, Egypt, Kenya, 1977, 79, 81, 87, 92, 97, 98, 99, 2000; participant 1st summer inst. Nat. Geog. Soc., Washington, 1986; tchr., cons. Nat. Geog., 1986—; tchr. Leader for People in Soviet Union, 1989, 90; vol. First Internat. Environ. Expedition to Antarctica, 1995; presenter for Zero Population Growth, 1995—. Author curriculum materials; photographer (book) Bobwhites, 1984. Co-chair PeaceWorks. Recipient Merit award Nat. Coun. Geog. Edn., 1975, Creative Tchg. award Austin Assn. Tchrs., 1978, study grant to Malaysia and Indonesia, 1990, Excellence award for outstanding H.S. tchr. U. Tex., 1997, Edn.'s Unsung Hereos award No. Life, 1998, Outstanding Tchg. of the Humanities award, 1998, Excellence award Tex. State Bd. Edn., 1995, Peacemaker award Austin Dispute Resolution Ctr., 1998; Fulbright scholar, Israel, 1983. Mem. NEA, Nat. Coun. Geog. Edn., Earthwatch (participant archaeol. dig in Swaziland 1984), World Wildlife Fund, Rotary, Delta Kappa Gamma (pres. 1986-88), Phi Kappa Phi. Democrat. Roman Catholic. Avocations: stained glass, photography, tennis, gardening, needlepoint. Home: 1025 Quail Park Dr Austin TX 78758-6749 Office: Lanier High Sch 1201 Payton Gin Rd Austin TX 78758-6699 E-mail: nlehmann@ev1.net.

LEHMANN-HAUPT, CHRISTOPHER CHARLES HERBERT, book reviewer; b. Edinburgh, Scotland, June 14, 1934; came to U.S., 1934; s. Hellmut Otto Emil and Letitia Jane H. (Grierson) Lehmann-H.; m. Natalie Robins, Oct. 3, 1965; children: Rachel Louise, Noah Christopher. BA, Swarthmore Coll., 1956; M.F.A., Yale U., 1959. Editor A.S. Barnes & Co., Inc., N.Y.C., 1961-62, Holt, Rinehart & Winston, 1962-63; sr. editor Dial Press, 1963-65; mem. staff N.Y. Times Book Review, 1965-69; sr. daily book reviewer N.Y. Times,

1969-95, daily book reviewer, 1995-2000, chief obituary writer, 2000—. Asst. prof. lit. CUNY, 1973-75 Author: Me and Di Maggio, 1986, A Crooked Man, 1995. Mem.: Century. Office: New York Times 229 W 43rd St New York NY 10036-3959 E-mail: clhaupt@nytimes.com.

LEHMBERG, ROBERT HENRY, research physicist; b. Phila., Dec. 4, 1937; s. Henry and Marguerite Elenore (Schock) L.; m. Norma Geder, Dec. 29, 1966; 1 child, Karl Robert. BSc, Pa. State U., 1959; MSc, U. Ariz., 1961; PhD, Brandeis U., 1968. Rsch. physicist Naval Air Devel. Ctr., Warminster, Pa., 1966-72, Naval Rsch. Lab., Washington, 1972—. Chmn. program com. Conf. on Lasers and Electro-Optics, Washington, 1991. Contbr. articles to profl. jours.; patentee in field. Recipient E.O. Hulbert Ann. Sci. award Naval Rsch. Lab., 1997. Fellow Am. Phys. Soc. (Excellence in Plasma Physics Rsch. award 1993); mem. AAAS, IEEE, Sigma Xi. Achievements include development of optical beam smoothing techniques for laser fusion, optical design of the Naval Research Laboratory's Nike laser facility, and research in nonlinear optics, excimer laser physics and laser-plasma interaction physics. Office: Naval Rsch Lab Plasma Divsn 4555 Overlook Ave SW Washington DC 20375-0001 E-mail: lehmberg@this.nrl.navy.mil.

LEHMBERG, STANFORD EUGENE, historian, educator; b. McPherson, Kans., Sept. 23, 1931; s. Willard Eugene and Helen (Stanford) L.; m. Phyllis Barton, July 23, 1962; 1 son, Derek Grantham. BA, U. Kans., 1953, MA, 1954; PhD, Cambridge (Eng.) U., 1956, DLitt, 1990. Mem. faculty U. Tex., Austin, 1956-69; mem. faculty U. Minn., 1969-98, prof. history, 1967-98, chmn. dept., 1979-85. Author: Sir Thomas Elyot, Tudor Humanist, 1960, Sir Walter Mildmay and Tudor Government, 1966, The Reformation Parliament, 1970, The Later Parliaments of Henry VIII, 1977, The Reformation of Cathedrals, 1988, The People of the British Isles to 1688, 1991, 2d edit., 2001, Cathedrals Under Siege, 1996, (with Ann M. Pflaum) The University of Minnesota, 1945-2000, 2001; also articles, revs. Fulbright scholar, 1954-56; Guggenheim fellow, 1965-66, 85-86 Fellow Royal Hist. Soc., Soc. of Antiquaries; mem. Am. Hist. Assn., Midwest Conf. Brit. Studies (pres. 1982-84), Renaissance Soc. Am., Am. Soc. Reformation Research. Episcopalian. Home: 1005 Calle Largo Santa Fe NM 87501-1068 E-mail: lehmberg@earthlink.net.

LEHMKUHL, MARGIE MAE, occupational health nurse; b. Falls City, Nebr., Aug. 21, 1950; d. Arthur E. and Dora W. (Harper) Jimeson; m. Ronald Joseph Lehmkuhl, June 1, 1968; children: Darcie G., Joseph B. AA with honors, Johnson County C.C., Overland Park, Kans., 1977; BSN with highest distinction, U. Kans., Kansas City, 1979. RN, Kans., Mo. Pediatric and float nurse Humana Hosp., Overland Park, 1979-81, unit mgr., 1981-85; utilization rev. coord. Blue Cross/Blue Shield, Kansas City, Mo., 1985-86; joint venture liaison Blue Cross/Blue Shield and Managed Healthcare Resources, 1986-87; continuing care provider Managed Healthcare Resources, Overland Park, 1987-88; nursing supr. Hickman Mills Clinic, Kansas City, Mo., 1988-91, asst. adminstr., clin. Kans. City, 1991-92; mgr. occupational health Vis. Nurse Assn. Greater Kansas City, 1993—. V.p. Kans. State Sigma Phi Epsilon Mothers Club, 1992-94; mem. ways and means com. Shawnee Mission West Booster Club, 1983-91; coord. Holy Trinity Religious Edn. Pre-sch., Lenexa, Kans., 1975, 76, instr., 1973-75, bd. dirs., 1975-76. Arthur S. and Leora J. Peck scholar, 1977; Allstate Found. nursing scholar, 1977. Mem. ANA, Kans. State Nurses Assn., U. Kans. Nursing Alumni Assn. (Alumni award 1979), Occupational Health Nurses Assn. (chair social and hospitality com. 1995-97, bd. dirs. 1995-97), Assn. for Profls. in Infection Control & Epidemiology, Sigma Theta Tau, Phi Kappa Phi. Avocations: swimming, refinishing furniture, aerobics, gardening. Home: 14912 W 89th St Lenexa KS 66215-2908 Office: Vis Nurse Assn Corp 2801 Wyandotte St Fl 5 Kansas City MO 64108-3345 E-mail: mlehmkuhl@vnakc.com.

LEHN, JEAN-MARIE PIERRE, chemistry educator; b. Rosheim, Bas-Rhin, France, Sept. 30, 1939; s. Pierre and Marie (Salomon) Lehn; m. Sylvie Lederer, 1965; 2 children. Grad., U. Strasbourg, France, 1960, PhD, 1963; PhD (hon.), U. Jerusalem, 1984, U. Autonoma, Madrid, 1985, U. Göttingen, 1987, U. Brussels, 1987, U. Herakliou, Greece, 1989, U. Bologna, 1989, Charles U., Prague, 1990, U. Twente, 1991, U. Sheffield, 1991, U. Athens, 1992, U. Polytech. Athens, 1992, Poly. U. Bucharest, 1994, Ill. Wesleyan U., 1995, U. Montreal, 1995, Bielefeld U., 1998, USTC, Hefei, 1998, Southeast U., Nanjing, 1998, Weizmann Inst., Rehovoth, 1998; applied Scis., U. Brussels, 1999, U. Nagoya, 2000, U. Sherbrooke, 2000, U. Trieste, 2001. Various positions Nat. Ctr. Sci. Rsch., France, 1960—66; postdoctoral rsch. assoc. Harvard U., Cambridge, Mass., 1963—64; asst. prof. U. Strasbourg, France, 1966—69; assoc. prof. U. Louis Pasteur of Strasbourg, 1970, prof. of chemistry, 1970—79; prof. Coll. France, Paris, 1979—. Vis. prof. chemistry Harvard U., 1972—74, E.T.H., Zurich, Switzerland, Cambridge (Eng.) U., 1984, Barcelona (Spain) U., 1985, Fankfurt (Germany) U., 1985—86; Heinrich-Hertz Gast prof. Karlsruhe U., 1989; Woodward vis. prof. Harvard U., Cambridge, Mass., 1997; Newton-Abraham vis. prof. Oxford U., 1999—2000. Contbr. articles. Decorated commandeur Légion d'Honneur, officer Order Nat. du Mérite, Ordre pour le Mérite for Scis. and Arts; recipient Bronze, Silver and Gold medals, Ctr. Nat. Sci. Rsch. (CNRS), Pontifical Acad. Sci., 1981, Swiss Chem. Soc., 1982, von Humboldt prize, 1983, Nobel prize for chemistry, 1987, Karl-Ziegler prize, 1989, Bonner Chemiepreis, 1993, Ettore Majorana-Erice-Sci. for Peace prize, 1994, Gold medal, Soc. Acad. Arts, Scis., Lettres, 1995, Davy medal, Royal Soc., 1997, Lavoisier medal, SFC, 1997, A.R. Day award, 1998, others. Mem.: Russian Acad. Scis., Royal Irish Acad., Acad. Scis. Torino, Pontifical Acad. Scis., Third World Acad. Scis., The Czech Learned Soc., Korean Acad. Sci. and Tech., Royal Soc., Acad. Roumaine, Inst. Grand Ducal (Luxembourg), Acad. Scis. Ukraine, Acad. Arts and Scis. P.R., Royal Acad. Scis., Letters and Fine Arts (Belgium), Polish Acad. Scis., Indian Acad. Scis., Yugoslav Acad. Arts and Scis. Zagreb, Acad. Wissenschaften, Acad. Wissenschaften Literalur-Mainz, Acad. Europaea, Am. Philos. Soc. (Phila., fgn. mem.), Royal Netherlands Acad., Acad. Nazionale dei Lincei, Deutsche Acad. der Naturforscher Leopoldina, Inst. de France, AAAS (fgn.) (hon.), NAS (fgn.) (assoc.). Home: 6 rue des Pontonniers 67000 Strasbourg France Office: Coll France 11 pl Marcelin Berthelot 75005 Paris France also: U Louis Pasteur 4 rue Blaise Pascal 67000 Strasbourg France

LEHNE, PASCAL HORST, chemistry educator, consultant; b. Hamburg, Germany, Apr. 17, 1915; s. Richard Wilhelm and Clarita (Voigt) L.; m. Julita Tapang Dawat, Aug. 4, 1972; 1 child, Rowena. Diploma in chemistry, U. Heidelberg, Germany, 1944. Asst. master Gewerbeschule Hansestadt Hamburg, 1956-65, sr. asst. master, 1966-80, ret., 1980, temporary appointed tutor, 1981-83; hon. co-worker Mus. für Hamburgische Geschichte, Hamburg, 1994—. Vice dir. evening sch. English Inst., Heidelberg, 1950-52; subdir., tutor Inst. für Lernsysteme, Hamburg, 1980-86. Author: The Normal Gauge Electric Light Railway Altrahlstedt-Volksdorf-Wohldorf, 4 edits., 1954-86; co-author: Lead and Silver, 1966, 2nd edit., 1975, About the Mariana Islands, 1972; calculator of orbital elements of comet Paraskevopoulos (1941c) from pvt. observations; author numerous edits. Periodic Chart of Elements, 1938-52; contbr. articles to profl. jours. Mem. Gesellschaft Deutscher Chemiker, Bund für Deutsche Schrift, The Planetary Soc., Wöhler-Vereinigung für Anorg.Chemie. Avocations: preparing Tagalog-German dictionary, compilation of comprehensive collections of elements and inorganic compounds; completion of a gear drive for presenting mean sidereal movements of the major planets. Home: Hamburger Strasse 110b 22949 Ammersbek Germany Office: Staatliche Gewerbeschule für Chemie Billwerder Billdeich 614 21033 Hamburg Germany

LEHNEN, JOSEPH E. pharmaceutical executive; BS in Physics, Santa Clara U.; MS in Physics, Yale U.; M Public Policy, Harvard U. V.p. investment banking JP Morgan & Co.; CFO MaxCyte. Office: MaxCyte 9640 Med Ctr Dr Rockville MD 20850*

LEHNER-QUAM, ALISON LYNN, library administrator; b. Oak Harbor, Wash., Apr. 25, 1960; d. Paul Elias and Johanna Marie (Vinson) Q.; m. Matthias Karl-Eugen Lehner, Oct. 3, 1997; 1 child, Peter Elias Bernhard Lehner. BA, U. Wash., 1983; cert. tech. theater, Yale U., 1985; MS in Libr. Sci., Columbia U., 1991. Freelance costumer various prodns., N.Y.C., 1984-90; cataloging asst. Fashion Inst. of Tech., 1986-91; intern Bank St. Sch., 1991; asst. dir. Columbia Children's Lit. Inst., 1990; libr. dir. Lincoln Ctr. Inst., 1991—, mgr. website, 2000—. Project dir. Arts Edn. Reference Window on the Work, 1992—. Pub. mgr.: (periodical) The Institute View, 1996—, Lincoln Ctr. Inst., 1999, website mgr., 2000—. Vol. mgr. Lincon Ctr. Inst., N.Y.C., 1995—. Recipient Dirs.' Emeriti award Lincoln Ctr. for Performing Arts, 1997; scholar Sch. Libr. Svcs., Columbia U., 1989, 90. Mem. ALA, N.Y. Arts in Edn. Roundtable (steering com. 1995-98), Theater Libr. Assn., Beta Phi Mu (bd. dirs. Theta chpt. 1997—, v.p. 1994-96). Avocations: reading, the arts. E-mail: alquam@lincolncenter.org.

LEHNHOFF, TERRY FRANKLIN, mechanical engineering; b. St. Louis, July 7, 1939; s. Chester Franklin and Gladys Victorene (Terry) L.; m. Donna Louise Hoecker, Aug. 27, 1960; children: Mark, Lori, Stephen, Hope. BS, U. Mo., Rolla, 1961, MS, 1962; PhD, U. Ill., 1968. Profl. engr., Mo. Instr. U. Ill., Champaign, 1965-68; from asst. prof. to prof. mech. and aerospace engring. U. Mo.-Rolla, 1968—. Rsch. engr. Caterpillar Tractor Co., Peoria, Ill., 1962-65; cons. in field; pres. Enmeco, Inc., Rolla, 1983—. Grantee Ford Found. Mem. ASME, Pi Mu Epsilon, Pi Tau Sigma, Sigma Gamma Tau, Sigma Xi, Tau Beta Pi. Republican. Avocations: photography, furniture restoration. Office: U Mo Rolla Rolla MO 65401

LEHOCZKY, JOHN PAUL, statistics educator; b. Columbus, Ohio, June 29, 1943; s. Paul Nicholas and Thelma Marie (Heisterkamp) L.; m. Mary Louise Zimmerman, Sept. 10, 1966; children: Jennifer Lynne, Jessica Augusta. BA, Oberlin Coll., 1965; MS, Stanford U., 1967, PhD, 1969. Asst. prof. stats. Carnegie Mellon U., Pitts., 1969-73, assoc. prof., 1973-81, prof., 1981-96, head dept., 1984-95, Thomas Lord prof. stats., 1997—, dean humanities & social scis., 2000—; assoc. editor IEEE Transactions on Computers, 1995-98. Cons. in legal stats., statis. anlysis, math. fin. and real-time computing. Dept. editor Mgmt. Sci., 1981-86; assoc. editor Jour. Real-Time Systems, 1989—; contbr. over 100 rsch. papers in various diciplines. Fellow Am. Statis. Assn. (statistician of yr. Pitts. chpt. 1987), Inst. Math. Stats.; mem. IEEE, AAAS, Assn. for Computing Machinery, Internat. Statis. Inst., Informs. Office: Carnegie Mellon Univ Dept Stats Pittsburgh PA 15213 E-mail: jpl@stat.cmu.edu.

LEHR, DENNIS JAMES, lawyer; b. N.Y.C., Feb. 7, 1932; s. Irwin Allen and Teeny (Scofield) L.; m. Enid J. Auerbach, June 10, 1956; children— Austin Windsor, Bryant Paul, Amy Lynn BA, NYU, 1954, LLM, 1961; LLB, Yale U., 1957. Bar: N.Y. 1959, D.C. 1967. Atty. Allstate Ins. Co., N.Y.C., 1958-59; atty. Regional Office SEC, 1959-61; assoc. Borden and Ball, 1961-63; atty. Office Spl Counsel Investment Co. Act Matters SEC, Washington, 1963-64; assoc. chief counsel Office Comptroller Currency U.S. Treasury Dept., 1964-67; assoc. Hogan & Hartson, 1967-69, ptnr., 1969-94, of counsel, 1994—. Bd. advs. So. Meth. U. Grad. Sch. Banking; adj. prof. Georgetown Law Sch., 1964-68; legal adv. com. Nat. Ctr. on Fin. Svcs., U. Calif.; lectr. Practicing Law Inst.; adv. coun. Banking Law Inst.; pub. mem. Adminstrv. Conf. of the U.S. Bd. contbrs. Fin. Services Law Report. Contbr. articles to profl. jours. Mem. ABA (coun. mem. sect. bus. law, former chmn. com. on Long Range Issues Affecting Bus. Law Practice, former chmn., com. on devels. in investment svcs, chmn. steering com. on Gavel Awards.). Office: Hogan and Hartson 555 13th St NW Ste 800E Washington DC 20004-1161

LEHR, FRANK HENRY, engineer; b. Easton, Pa., Apr. 2, 1925; s. Francis H. and Sadie (Fulse) L.; m. Veronica Shevock, June 24, 1950; children: Diane C., Frank F., Janice S. BS in Engring, Pa. State U., 1950; MS, N.J. Inst. Tech. (name formerly Newark Coll. Engring.), 1956. Registered profl. engr., N.J., N.Y., Pa., Mass., Conn., Ohio. Field engr. C.R.R. of N.J., Jersey City, 1950-51; structural designer Arthur G. McKee & Co., Union, N.J., 1951, 53-54; constrn. engr. Jersey Testing Lab., Inc., Newark, 1954-57; pres. Frank H. Lehr Assocs. (cons. civil engrs.), East Orange, N.J., 1957—. Chmn. Joint Meeting Sewer Commn. Union and Essex Counties, N.J., 1969-76; mem. Summit (N.J.) Bd. Appeals, 1958-75; mem. City Council, Summit, 1962-76, pres., 1970-76; mem. Summit Bd. Sch. Estimates, 1964-69; mayor City of Summit, 1976-80; freeholder Union County (N.J.), 1981-83, chmn., 1983; chmn. N.J. Natural Resources Com. Served to capt. USMCR, 1943-47, 51-53. Fellow Am. Cons. Engrs. Council, ASCE; mem. Union County Soc. Profl. Engrs. (past pres.), Marine Corps Res. Officers Assn., ASTM, Bldg. Ofcls. N.J. Clubs: Kiwanis (dir. East Orange chpt.). Home: 16 Myrtle Ave Summit NJ 07901-3409 Office: Frank H Lehr Assocs 101 S Harrison St East Orange NJ 07018-1702

LEHR, GARY FULTON, computer scientist, consultant; b. Rockville Centre, NY, July 16, 1952; s. Eugene Jacob Lehr and Aileen Marie Fulton; m. Suzanne Trueblood, July 4, 1981; children: Jacob, J. Tyson, Aaron. BA, Manhattanville Coll., 1975; PhD, Brown U., 1980. Cons. E.I. duPont de Nemours & Co., Wilmington, Del., 1981—97; sr. computer scientist Computer Sciences Corp., Newark, 1997—. Contbr. articles to profl. jours. Home: 122 Chatham Pl Wilmington DE 19810 Office: Computer Sciences Corp 400 Commerce Dr Newark DE 19718

LEHR, JANE MARIE, research scientist; b. N.Y.C., Aug. 25, 1963; d. Robert Joseph and Helen Therese (Brider) Messerschmitt; m. F. Mark Lehr, Nov. 1, 1994; 1 child, Lucius Joseph. B in Engring., Stevens Inst. Tech., 1985; MSEE, Poly. U., 1988, PhD in Elec. Engring., 1996. Rsch. engr. Tetra Corp., Albuquerque, 1993-95; rsch. scientist Fiore Industries, 1995-97, USAF, Phillips Lab, Kirtland AFB, 1997—2002; power group Sandia Nat. Labs., Albuquerque, 2002—. Contbr. articles to IEEE. Recipient rsch. award Westinghouse, 1985, 86, IEEE Region 6 Cmty. Svc. award, 2001, N.Mex. Outstanding Woman award, 2001; inductee N.Mex. Hall of Fame, 2001; grantee Air Force Office Sci. Rsch., 1992, 93; scholar N.Y. State, 1981. Mem. Am. Phys. Soc., Electromagnetic Compatibility (local chpt.). Achievements include research in measurement of ultrafast breakdown in liquids; development of 20GW ultra-wideband electromagnetic source. Office: Sandia Nat Labs PO Box 5800 MS 1193 Albuquerque NM 87185-1193 Business E-Mail: jmlehr@sandia.gov.

LEHR, LEWIS WYLIE, diversified manufacturing company executive; b. Elgin, Nebr., Feb. 21, 1921; s. Lewis H. and Nancy (Wylie) L.; m. Doris Stauder, Oct. 13, 1944; children— Mary A. Lehr Makin, William L., Donald D., John M. BSChemE, U. Nebr., 1947, ScD (hon.), 1977. From mem. staff to chmn. 3M Co., St. Paul, 1947—80, chmn., chief exec. officer, 1980—86. Mem. adv. bd. Clarke-Bardes, Pasadena, Calif. Trustee U. Nebr. Found. Served with AUS, 1943-46, ETO. Recipient Alumni Achievement award U. Nebr. Alumni Assn., 1976, State of Nebr. Wagon Master award, 1995. Mem. Am. Chem. Soc. Clubs: North Oaks Golf, White Bear Yacht, Minnesota. Address: Minn World Trade Ctr 30 7th St E Ste 3050 Saint Paul MN 55101-4901

LEHRER, JAMES CHARLES, television journalist; b. Wichita, Kans., May 19, 1934; s. Harry Frederick and Lois Catherine (Chapman) L.; m. Kate Staples, June 4, 1960; children: Jamie, Lucy, Amanda. AA, Victoria Coll., 1954; B.J., U. Mo., 1956. Reporter Dallas Morning News, 1959-61; reporter, columnist, city editor Dallas Times Herald, 1961-70; exec. producer, corr. Sta. KERA-TV, Dallas, 1970-72; pub. affairs coordinator Public Broadcasting Service, Washington, 1972-73; corr. NPACT-WETA-TV, 1973—; exec. editor, anchor The NewsHour with Jim Lehrer, 1995—; instr. creative writing Dallas Coll., So. Meth. U., 1967-68. Author: (fiction) Viva Max, 1966, We Were Dreamers, 1975, Kick the Can, 1988, Crown Oklahoma, 1980, The Sooner Spy, 1990, Lost and Found, 1991, Short List, 1992, A Bus of My Own, 1992, Blue Hearts, 1993, Fine Lines, 1994, The Last Debate, 1995, White Widow, 1997, Purple Dots, 1998, The Special Prisoner, 2000, No Certain Rest, 2002, (plays) Chili Queen, 1986, Church Key Charlies Blue, 1987, The Will and Bart Show, 1992. Served with USMC, 1956-59. Recipient Columbia-Dupont award, George Polk award, Peabody award, Emmy award; inducted into Acad. TV Arts Scis. Hall of Fame, 1999, Nat. Humanities medal, 1999. Mem. Am. Acad. Arts and Scis., Dramatists Guild, Authors Guild, Tex. Inst. Letters, Coun. on Fgn. Rels. Office: Sta WETA-TV 3620 27th St S Arlington VA 22206-2302

LEHRER, KENNETH EUGENE, real estate advisor, economic consultant; b. N.Y.C., Apr. 17, 1946; s. Charles Carlton and Evelyn Estelle (Rosenfeld) L.; m. Myrna Sue Newman, Apr. 4, 1981 (div. 1988); m. Geraldine Trudy Fishman, Mar. 18, 1994. BS, NYU, 1967, MBA, 1969, MA, 1972, D in Pub. Adminstrn., 1980. Registered investment advisor; cert. real estate appraiser; lic. real estate broker. Asst. treas. Banker's Trust Co., N.Y.C., 1970-73; dir. devel. Coventry Devel. Corp., 1974-77; asst. v.p. Affiliated Capital Corp., Houston, 1977-80; dir. fin. Allison/Walker Interests, 1980-82; mng. dir. Lehrer Fin. and Econ. Adv. Svcs., 1982—. Prof. real estate fin. U. Houston Grad. Sch. Bus. Adminstrn., 1985-2002; chmn., bd. dirs. Acadia Savings and Loan Assn., Crowley, La., French Market Homestead Savs. Assn., Metairie, La., Twin City Savs. Bank, West Monroe, La., 1st Savs. La., LaPlace, 1988-89, Integrated Resource Techs., Inc., 1992-95. Pres. Cornerstone Mcpl. Utilities Dist. 1978-85; bd. dirs. Ft. Bend County Mcpl. Utility Dist #106, 1987-98, Houston Caliber Fin. Group chmn. 1994-96; Tex. Rep. Assn., Rep. Senatorial Inner Cir. (life, Medal of Freedom 1994). Mem. Am. Horse Show Assn. (life), Nat. Steeplechase and Hunt Assn. (life), U.S. Tennis Assn. (life), Am. Real Estate and Urban Econs. Assn., Am. Real Estate Soc., Nat. Assn. Bus. Economists, NYU Money Marketeers, Nat. Forensic Ctr., Nat. Assn. Corp. Dirs., Am. Acad. Econ. and Fin. Experts, Internat. Coll. Real Estate Cons. Profls., Internat. Assn. Corp. Real Estate Execs., Nat. Assn. Forensic Economists, Am. Arbitration Assn., Houston Bus. Economists, Western Econ. Assn., Fin. Club N.Y.C., Real Estate Educators Assn., Am. Econ. Assn., N. Am. Econs. and Fin. Assn., So. Econ. Assn., NYU Alumni Fedn. (bd. dirs. 1974-77), Houston C. of C. (mem. govtl. rels. com.), Princeton Club (N.Y.), St. James's Club (London), Capitol Hill Club (Washington), Royal Oaks Country Club (Houston). Episcopalian. Home: 5555 Del Monte Dr Unit 802 Houston TX 77056-4117 Office: Lehrer Fin & Econ Adv Svcs 1775 Saint James Pl Ste 110 Houston TX 77056-3403 E-mail: drken@lehecoserv.com.

LEHRER, LEONARD, artist, educator; b. Phila., Mar. 23, 1935; s. Abraham and Bessie Lehrer; m. Marilyn Bigard, May 29, 1977; 1 child, Anna-Katrina Picard (dec.); stepchildren: Tracy Peel, Janna Peel, John Peel, Jamye Peel. BFA, Phila. Coll. Art, 1956; MFA, U. Pa., 1960. Faculty Phila. Coll. Art, 1956-70, co-dir. found. program, 1965-70; prof. art U. N.Mex., 1970-74, chmn. dept., 1970-73; prof. U. Tex., San Antonio, 1974-77, dir. divsn. art and design, 1974-75; prof., dir. Sch. Art, Ariz. State U., Tempe, 1977-90; dir. Visual Art Rsch. Studios, 1984-91; prof. art NYU, 1991-99, chair dept. art and art professions, 1991-96, prof. emeritus, 1999; dean Sch. Fine and Performing Arts Columbia Coll., Chgo., 2001. One-man shows include Utah Mus. Fine Arts, Salt Lake City, 1973, 82, Marian Locks Gallery, Phila., 1974, 77, 84, McNay Art Mus., San Antonio, 1975, Galerie Kühl, Hannover, Germany, 1976, 79, 82, 91, Bomann Mus., Celle, Germany, 1980, Marilyn Butler Fine Art, Scottsdale, Ariz., 1980, Assoc. Am. Artists, Phila., 1984, Am. Cultural Affairs Ctr., Madrid, 1984, MyungSook Lee Gallery, N.Y.C., 1997, others; exhibited in group shows at Ljubljana Internat. Print Biennial, 1981, Graphic Arts Biennial of Ams., Cali, Colombia, 1981, Brit. Internat. Print Biennial, Bradford, Eng., 1982, Internat. Printmaking Invitational, San Bernardino, Calif., 1983, XXXV Art Fair, Munich, 1992, XXIV Art Fair, Hannover, 1993, 2000, Contemporary Korean and Am. Art, Seoul, 1999; represented in permanent collections Met. Mus. Art, N.Y.C., Mus. Modern Art, N.Y.C., Phila. Mus. Art, Nat. Gallery Art, Fed. Res. Bd., Corcoran Gallery, Libr. of Congress, Washington, Albright-Knox Art Mus., Buffalo, Sprengel Mus. Art, Hannover; curator Large Scale Am. Prints in Art Multiple Dusseldorf, Germany, 1992; author: (introductory essay) The Art of the Book; works featured in The Art of Leonard Lehrer, 1986; contbr. articles to profl. jours. Bd. trustees Internat. Print Ctr. N.Y., Inc.; chair Arts Acad. Adv. Com., The College Bd., 1996—; bd. dirs. Apex Art Curator Program, N.Y. Recipient 1st prize Miami Internat. Print Biennial, 1980, Western States Art Found. Printmaking Fellowship award, 1979, Heitland Found. prize, Celle, 1980, XX Yrs. Heitland Prize Winner, Konstalle, Darmstadt, Germany, 2000, Gold Medal award Ariz. chpt. Nat. Soc. Arts and Letters, 1981; Acad. Specialist grant USIA to Colombia, 1997; Fulbright scholar to Greece, 2001—.

LEHRER, MERRILL CLARK, retail sales consultant; b. Queens, N.Y., May 24, 1955; s. Stanley and Laurel Lehrer; m. Elisabeth Pine, Oct. 24, 1984. BA in Communications magna cum laude, Adelphi U., 1976. Asst. buyer Lafayette Electronics, Syosset, N.Y., 1976-78; dept. mgr. Abraham & Straus, Massapequa, 1978-80; dept. mgr., assoc. buyer, buyer Rich's, Atlanta, 1980-84, sr. buyer, 1984-88; mng. editor USA Today mag., Valley Stream, N.Y., 1988-89; buyer Burdine's, Miami, Fla., 1989; sr. buyer, v.p., gen. mdse. mgr. Office Depot, Delray Beach, 1989-97; divsnl. mdse. mgr. Petco, San Diego, 1997—2001; pres. Retail Samurai Sales, 2001—. Contbr. articles to USA Today; contbg. editor, columnist: Pet Age Mag., Office Products Internat., Kitchenware News, Pets Internat., 2002; ; author: Retail Detailed: Secrets to Selling Retail Chain Stores, 2002. E-mail: mlehrer@san.rr.com.

LEHRER, ROBERT NATHANIEL, retired educator, executive, consultant; b. Sandusky, Ohio, Jan. 17, 1922; s. Henry William and Margaret (Boyd) L.; m. Patricia Lee Martin, July 7, 1945; children— Joan Elizabeth. BS in Mech. Engring. with distinction, Purdue U., 1945, MS, 1947, PhD, 1949; student engring., Midshipman Sch., 1945. Registered profl. engr., Ga. Research asst., instr. Purdue U., 1946-49; asst. prof. indsl. engring. Oreg. State Coll., 1949-50; assoc. prof. indsl. engring., research assoc. Ga. Inst. Tech., 1950-54, prof. indsl. engring., research assoc., 1954-58; prof. indsl. engring., chmn. dept. Technol. Inst., Northwestern U., 1958-63; prof., assoc. dir. Sch. Indsl. Engring., Ga. Inst. Tech., Atlanta, 1963-66; dir. Sch. Indsl. and Systems Engring., 1966-78, prof., 1978-81, prof. emeritus, dir. emeritus, 1981—. Assoc., vis. sr. adv. Am. Productivity Ctr., 1978-79; cons., 1950—; mem. Nat. Acad. Scis. panel to Indonesia, 1971. Author: Work Simplification: Creative Thinking About Work Problems, 1957, The Management of Improvement: Concepts, Organization and Strategy, 1965, Participative Productivity and Quality of Work Life, 1982, White Collar Productivity, 1983; editor-in-chief: Jour. Indsl. Engring, 1953-61, exec. editor, 1961-62; cons. editor textbook series Reinhold Pub. Corp., 1960-67; contbr. articles to tech. jours. Adv. bd. mil. personnel supplies NRC, 1965-68; mem. nat. research council Am. Acad. Scis., 1965-68; expert indsl. engring. UNESCO, Mexico, 1962-63; mem. adv. bd. dept. indsl. engring. Coll. Engring., Clemson U., 1984-90. Served with USNR, 1943-46. Designated Disting. Alumnus, Purdue U., 1964; recipient Frank and Lillian Gilbreath Indsl. Engring. award Inst. Indsl. Engrs., 1987. Fellow Am. Inst. Indsl. Engrs. (Outstanding Indsl. engr. in Southeast 1957, v.p. publs. 1960-62), AAAS; mem. Sigma Xi, Tau Beta Pi, Phi Kappa Phi, Alpha Pi Mu, Pi Tau Sigma, Phi Delta Theta. Episcopalian. Home: PO Box 19996 Atlanta GA 30325-0996

LEHRER, RUTH JEANNETTE, social work supervisor; b. N.Y.C., Apr. 17, 1923; d. Samuel and Mollie (Berman) Kinbar; widowed. BS, Hunter Coll., 1944; MSW, Columbia U., 1946. Med. social worker Jewish Hosp. of Bklyn., 1946; social worker N.Y. Assn. for New Ams., N.Y.C., 1946-50; med. social worker Maimonides Hosp., Bklyn., 1950-51; social worker Jewish Family Svc. Assn., Essex County, N.J., 1951-58; med. social worker Mt. Sinai Hosp., N.Y.C., 1958-59; social worker N.Y. Guild for Jewish Blind, 1959-61, Wiltwyck Sch. for Boys, N.Y.C., 1961-64; sr. social worker Lincoln Hosp. Cmty. Mental Health Ctr., Bronx, N.Y., 1964-67; instr. Albert Einstein Sch. Medicine, 1964-67; sr. social work supr. Maimonides Hosp. Cmty. Mental Health Ctr., Bklyn., 1967-97. Mem. NASW. Avocations: folk dancing, sketching, Scrabble, reading, ping-pong. Home: 129 W 89th St New York NY 10024-1908

LEHRER, STANLEY, magazine publisher, editorial director, corporate executive; b. Bklyn., Mar. 18, 1929; s. Martin and Rose L.; m. Laurel Francine Zang, June 8, 1952; children: Merrill Clark, Randee Hope. BS in Journalism, N.Y. U., 1950; postgrad. in edn, San Antonio Coll., 1952. Editor and pub. Crossroads mag., Valley Stream, N.Y., 1949-50; youth svc. editor Open Road mag., N.Y.C., 1950—51; mng. editor School & Society, 1953-68, v.p., 1956-68; pub. School & Society Books, 1963-86; pres., pub. School & Society mag., 1968-72; founder, pres., pub. Intellect mag., 1972-78, editl. dir., 1974-78; founder, pres., pub., editl. dir. USA Today, Valley Stream, NY, 1978—99, Newsview newsletter, 1979—99; pres., pub., editorial dir. Your Health newsletter, 1980-99, The World of Sci. newsletter, 1980-99. Cons. Child Care Publs., N.Y.C., 1955. Prodr., commentator: (WBAI-FM radio program) Report on Eucation, N.Y.C., 1960-61; guest spkr. Midwestern Writers' Conf., Chgo., 1950, Writers and Artists Group Nat. Music Camp, Interlochen, Mich., 1950, World of the Little Magazine, WNYC-AM, N.Y.C., 1977, Titanic Symposium Mariners' Mus., Newport News, Va., 1998, Steamboats on the Hudson River, PBS-TV, 2002; author: John Dewey: Master Educator, 1959, Countdown on Segregated Education, 1960, Religion, Government, and Education, 1961, A Century of Higher Education: Classical Citadel to Collegiate Colossus, 1962, Automation, Education, and Human Values, 1966, Conflict and Change on the Campus: The Response to Student Hyperactivism, 1970, Leaders, Teachers, and Learners in Academe: Partners in the Educational Process, 1970, Education and the Many Faces of the

Disadvantaged: Cultural and Historical Perspectives, 1972, Titanic: Fortune & Fate, 1998; contbr. articles to nat. mags., newspapers and profl. jours.; exhibited Stanley Lehrer maritime collection on transatlantic ships at N.Y. Yacht Club, 1983, on Cunard Line's 150th anniversary at Forbes Mag. Galleries, N.Y.C., 1989-90, on French Line's Normandie at French Embassy, N.Y.C., 1992, and Bass Mus. Art, Miami, Fla., 1993, on Ships of State: The Great Transatlantic Liners, PaineWebber Art Gallery, N.Y.C., 1994-95, on the Wreck of the Titanic, Nat. Maritime Mus., London, 1994-95, on S.O.S. Safety on Ships: Learning from New York's Maritime Tragedies, Water Street Gallery, Seamen's Church Institute, N.Y.C., 1996, on Titanic: Fortune & Fate at the Mariners' Mus., Newport News, Va., 1998; on Titanic: The Artifact Exhibition at World Trade Center, Boston, 1998; on Titanic: the Exhibition, Union Depot, St. Paul, 1998-99, on Blue Ribband: Quest for Speed Across the Atlantic, U.S. Courthouse, N.Y.C., 1999, on Titanic: The Experience, Tropicana, Atlantic City, NJ, 1999, on Titanic, Better Living Ctr., Toronto, Can., 1999-2000; on Titanic: The Artifact Exhibit, Fair Park, Dallas, 2000; on Titanic: The Exhbn., Mus. Sci. & Industry, Chgo., 2000, on Titanic, Tropicana, Atlantic City, 2000, on Titanic, Mus. Ctr., Cin., 2000, on Titanic, Opryland Hotel, Nashville, 2001, on Titanic, Kans. City Mus., Union Station, 2001, on Dazzle & Drab: Ocean Liners at War, Water Street Gallery, Seamen's Church Inst., N.Y.C., 2001-02; life jackets for Broadway musical Titanic, Lunt-Fontanne Theatre, N.Y.C., 1997 (based on Stanley Lehrer Titanic Collection); photographs and artifacts from Stanley Lehrer maritime collection featured in books and videos: On Board The Titanic, 1996, Lost Liners, 1997, Titanic: Legacy of the World's Greatest Ocean Liner, 1997, Titanic: Fortune & Fate, 1998; Nat. Geog. Soc. booklet on Titanic, 1998, Eyewitness: Titanic, 1999, Molly Brown: Unraveling the Myth, 1999, Titanica (video), 1998. V.p. Garden City Park (N.Y.) Civic Assn., 1961-63; treas. Citizens' Com. Edn., Garden City Park, 1962; mem. nat. jr. book awards com. Boys' Clubs Am., 1954; mem. nat. hon. com. for Richard H. Heindel Meml. Fund, Pa. State U., 1979-80. With Signal Corps, U.S. Army, 1951-53. Recipient non-fiction awards Midwestern Writers Conf., Chgo., 1948 Mem. New Hyde Park (N.Y.) C. of C. (dir. 1961-62), Titanic Hist. Soc., S.S. Hist. Soc. Am., Titanic Internat., Soc. Advancement of Edn. (treas. 1953-99, trustee 1963-99, pres. 1968-99), Ocean Liner Mus. (N.Y.C.), Psi Chi Omega. Home: 82 Shelbourne Ln New Hyde Park NY 11040-1044

LEHRLING, TERRY JAMES, real estate broker; b. Feb. 23, 1950; s. Phillip James and Phyllis Cecele (Capps) L.; m. Virginia Lucille Bogart, Feb. 27, 1971; children: Eric Terry, Adam James, Nicholas Justin. Student, U. Ariz., 1969-70, Pima C.C., 1970-71. Sales exec. San Xavier Realty & Trust Co., 1972; residential sales mgr. 1st Realty & Investment Co., Inc., Tucson, 1973; founder, broker Terry J. Lehrling & Assocs., 1974—. Founder Teleco Product Devel. and Mkg., Tucson, 1976— ; broker Red Carpet Realtors, Tucson, 1976— ; founder Teleco Realty & Devel., 1978; founder, pres. Number One Mktg. Group, Tucson, 1978—; asst. mgr. Shadron Bus. Brokerage, 1983— ; v.p. Am. Bus. Enterprises, 1983— ; founder, chief exec. officer Legal Research Assocs., 1983— . Mem. Pima County Parks and Recreation Commn., 1973—, chmn., 1976—; mem. Democratic Precinct Com., 1972— , Ariz. Com., 1972— ; bd. dirs. Pima Community Coll., 1970; del. Dem. Regional Conv., 1976; bd. dirs. Met. Youth Council, 1977, chmn. bd., 1978-79; pres. bd. dirs. Hudlow Kindergarten, 1977; chmn. Ariz. Supreme Ct. Foster Care Rev. Bd. No. 5, 1979-83, mem. state bd., 1980— , mem. C.A.T.S. com. Central Ariz. Project; bd. dirs., active mem. Tucson Boys' Chorus, 1985—; pres. Dietz. PTA, 1983-84; mem. Autocap Bd. for Pima County Atty. and Ariz. Automobile Assn., 1996; vice chmn. noise reduction task force Mayor and Coun., City of Tucson, 1996. Recipient copper letter for cmty. svc. Mayor of Tucson, 1980, Copper Plaque Pima County Bd. Suprs., 1991. Mem. Ariz. Parks and Recreation Assn., DeMolay Club. Home: PO Box 30304 Tucson AZ 85751-0304 Office: PO Box 18536 Tucson AZ 85731-8536 E-mail: terrylehrling@earthlink.net., teleco@theriver.com., teleco@earthlink.net.

LEHRMAN, IRVING, rabbi; b. Tiktin, Poland, June 15, 1911; came to U.S. 1916; s. Abraham and Rachel Minnie (Dinowitz) L.; m. Bella Goldfarb, May 21, 1935; children: David Lehrman, Rosalind Lehrman. DHL, Jewish Theol. Sem. of Am., N.Y.C., 1948, DD, 1969; DHL, St. Thomas U., Miami, Fla., 1989; DL, Barry U., Miami, 1992; DHL, Fla. Internat. U., 1992. Ordained rabbi, 1943. Student rabbi Temple Shomrei Emunah, Montclair, N.J., 1939-43; rabbi Temple Emanu-El of Greater Miami, Miami Beach, Fla., 1943-93; founding rabbi, dean Lehrman Day Sch., 1993—. Vis. prof. Homiletics Jewish Theol. Sem. Am.; nat. pres. Synagogue Coun. Am.; chmn. United Jewish Appeal Nat. Rabbinic Cabinet; chmn. Greater Miami Combined Jewish Appeal; chmn. bd. govs. Greater Miami State of Israel Bonds; found. chmn. Jewish Nat. Fund; hon. pres. S.E. region Rabbinical Assembly of Am. Author: In the Name of God, collection of sermons, articles, 1979, L'Chaim, thoughts for Jewish living, 1985, Portraits in Charcoal, 1980. Mem. White House Commn. on Obscenity and Pornography, Aging, and Food, Nutrition and Health (co-chmn. religious task force); bd. dirs. Miami Jewish Home and Hosp. for Aged, Internat. Synagogue at JFK Airport, N.Y.C.; nat. v.p. Zionist Orgn. Am.; adv. bd. St. Thomas U., Nat. Conf. Christians and Jews; former mem. exec. com. UNESCO, Greater Miami Community Rels. Bd. Recipient silver medal NCCJ, Prime Min.'s medal State of Israel, Albert Einstein Brotherhood award Technion U., Golda Meir Leadership award State of Israel Bonds, Spirit of Excellence award Miami Herald, 1993, Pontifical medal Benemerenti Pope John Paul II, 2000, also others; Lehrman Dr. named in his honor, Miami Beach, 1986; Rabbi Irving Lehrman Park established in his honor by Miami Friends of Tel Aviv Found., Tel Aviv, 1988; Rabbi Irving & Belle Lehrman Recreation and Picnic Area established Jabotinsky Park, Shuni, Israel, 1992. Mem. Rabbinical Assn. Greater Miami (past pres.). Office: Temple Emanu-El 1701 Washington Ave Miami Beach FL 33139-7513 *There is one principle that has guided my life and I always share it with others: "No matter how difficult it may seem, you will never be sorry for doing the right thing.".*

LEHRMAN, NAT, magazine editor; b. Bklyn., Aug. 5, 1929; s. Louis and Lena (Goldfarb) L.; m. Kazuko Miyajima, Nov. 13, 1956; children: Jerome M., Cynthia H. BA, Bklyn. Coll., 1953; MA, NYU, 1961. Travel editor internat. travel dept. Am. Automobile Assn., 1955-57; editor Relax mag., 1958, Dude, also Gent mags., 1959-61; assoc. to sr. editor Playboy mag., Chgo., 1966-71; editor new publs. Playboy Enterprises, 1972; editor, then assoc. pub. Oui mag., 1973-75; sr. v.p., assoc. pub. Playboy mag., 1976-85, dir. mag. divsn., 1980-85, pres. pub. div., 1982-85; pub.'s cons., 1985-87; dir. Essence mag.; tchr. fiction Columbia Coll., Chgo., 1967, chmn. journalism dept., 1987-96; ret., 1996. Author: Masters and Johnson Explained, 1970. Bd. dirs. Chgo. Chamber Musicians. With U.S. Army, 1953-55. Mem. Chgo. Classical Guitar Soc. (bd. dirs.). Clubs: Lincoln Park Tennis (pres.). E-mail: mrnat@aol.com.

LEHTIHALME, LARRY K. (LAURI LEHTIHALME), financial planner; b. Montreal, Que., Can., Feb. 26, 1937; came to U.S., 1964; s. Lauri Johann and Selma Maire (Piispanen) L.; m. Elizabeth Speed Smith, Sept. 9, 1961; children: Tina Beth, Shauna Lyn. Student, Sir George Williams U., Montreal, 1960-64, Mission Coll., San Fernando, Calif., 1978-80, Pierce Coll., Woodland Hills, Calif., 1990-92. Lic. in variable annuity, life and disability ins., Calif.; lic. securities series 7 SEC, series 63. Acct., customer svc. cons. No. Electric, Montreal, 1957-64; salesman Remington Rand Systems, Wilmington, Del., 1964-67; account exec., comm. cons. Pacific Tel. & Telegraph Co., L.A., 1968-84; tech. customer support specialist AT&T, 1984-85; fin. adv., registered rep. Am. Express Fin. Advisors, 1987—. Mem. L.A. World Affairs Coun., 1998—. Mem. ctrl. com. Calif. 39th Assembly Dist. Rep. Com., 1976-81, City of L.A., 12th dist. adv. com.; pres. North Hills Jaycees, 1969-70; sec.-treas. Com. Ind. Valley City and County Govt., 1978-82; subchmn. allocations United Way, Van Nuys, Calif., 1990; fundraiser North Valley YMCA, 1986-98; formerly active numerous comty. and polit. orgns. in San Fernando Valley. Named Jaycee of Yr., Newark (Del.) Jaycees, 1966, Granada Hills Jaycees, 1971; recipient cert. of merit U.S. Ho. of Reps., 1973, cert. appreciation City of L.A., 1980, 84, State of Calif., 20th senate dist., 1983, Comty. Spirit award, 1990. Mem. L.A. Olympic Organizing Com. Alumni Assn., Jr. Chamber Internat. (life, senator 1973), U.S. Jaycees (life, Jaycee of Yr. 1965, Outstanding Local Jaycee 1965-66, Presdl. award Honor 1967, Jaycee of Month 1966-67, asst. gen. chmn. 1970-71, state dir. N. Hollywood chpt. 1970-71, Cert. Merit 1971, state gen. chmn., 1971-72, 72-73, Outstanding State Chmn. Calif. dist. 22 1973-74), L.A. World Affairs Coun., Granada Hills C. of C. (bd. dirs. 1976-83, Man of Yr. award 1973), Granada Hills Jr. C. of C. Episcopalian. Avocation: community service. Home: 11408 Haskell Ave Granada Hills CA 91344-3959 Office: Am Express Fin Advisors 17050 Chatsworth St Ste 235 Granada Hills CA 91344-5898 E-mail: lauri.k.lehtihalme@aexp.com.

LEHTINEN, JANNE TAPANI, orthopedist; MD, PhD, U. Tampere, Finland, 1999. Rschr. Rheumatism Found. Hosp., Heinola, Finland, 1997-99; orthopedic resident Vammala (Finland) Dist. Hosp., Finland, 1999-2000; vis. fellow Harvard Shoulder Svc., Mass. Gen. Hosp., Boston, 2000—. Team physician Ilkon Ryhti, Pirkanmaa, 1995—. Contbr. articles to profl. jours., chpt. to book. With Finnish armed forces, 1992-93. Mem. Finnish Soc. Orthopedic Rheumatology, Finnish Soc. Rheumatology. Avocations: sports, food, wine. Home: 265 Clarendon St Boston MA 02116 Also: Kiuruntie 21 36200 Kangasala Finland E-mail: jlehtinen@partners.org.

LEHTINEN, SEPPO ILMARI, retired management consultant, educator; b. Helsinki, July 10, 1937; s. Toivo Ilmari and Helmi Amanda (Hällström) L.; m. Kaija Annikki Kärki, Nov. 3, 1962; children: Vesa Ilmari, Pia Katriina. Grad., Tekninen Opisto, Helsinki, 1965. Chief engr. Suomen Kaapelitehdas, Helsinki, 1965-67; project chief Nokia Cableworks, Tampere, Finland, 1967-68; product mgr. Nokia Kondencer, 1968-70, mgr. product rsch., 1970-73, product devel. mgr., 1973-77; regional exec. Coll. Leadership, Helsinki-Tampere, 1977-78; mgr. edn. Oy Nokia AB, Helsinki, 1978-87; prin. Indsl. Acad. Nokia, 1979-87; mng. dir. PVKS Palvelut Ky., Tampere, 1987-98, ret., 1998. Instr. orgnl. psychology Tampere U., 1972-2000; mem. tech. com. Internat. Elec. Com., Europe, 1974-86; civil-judge on ct., 1997-2001 Co-author: Management and Leadership, 1972, 2d edit., 1980; contbr. articles to profl. jours. Pres. various community orgns., Tampere, 1970—; mem. Finnish Red Cross, Tampere, 1980—. Lt., now capt. Finnish Army Res., 1958—. Decorated knight Order of White Rose (Finland), 1989; recipient gold medal Finnish Ministry Def., 1980, silver badge C. of C. Cen. Helsinki, 1985, Blue Cross by Veterans, 1990, Silver medal of Chief Engr., 1994, Pres. of Hon., Kokoomus Party in Tampere, 1994, Golden Mannerheim Badge by Scout Union, Golden badge Finnish Adult Edn. Assn., 1992-2000, Golden medalist of South Chief Officer and Underofficer, 2001. Mem. League Elec. Engrs., Cen. League Entrepreneurs, Assn. Finnish Chief Educators, Tampere C. of C., Mil. Def. Res. Officers and Noncommd. Officers Assn. (regional leader 1986-2001), Engrs. Club, J Club, Finnish Small Bus. Union. Mem. Kokoomus Party. Lutheran. Avocation: scientific essays (minor). Home and Office: Pahkinamaenkatu 5 C 16 SF-33840 Tampere Finland

LEI, ZHENMIN, endocrinologist, researcher; b. Fuzhou, Fujian, China, May 15, 1956; s. Gongzhao Lei and Xiufeng Dai; m. Xian Li; 1 child, Peng. MD, Fujian Med. Coll., 1980; MS, Tianjin (China) Med. Coll., 1984; PhD, U. Louisville, 1995. Instr. Fujian Med. Coll., Fuzhou, 1984-87; postdoctoral fellow U. Louisville, 1987-90, asst. prof., 1995-2000, assoc. prof., 2001—. Vis. prof. Fujian Med. Coll., 2000— Author: Principles and Practice of Endocrinology and Metabolism, 2000; contbr. articles to profl. jours. NIH rsch. grantee, 1995, 99—. Mem. AAAS, Am. Endocrine Soc., Soc. for Study of Reprodn. Buddhist. Avocations: running, travel, reading, philately. Fax: (502) 852-0881. Office: U Louisville Med Sch 511 S Floyd St Louisville KY 40292 E-mail: zhenminleizl@netscape.net.

LEIBACH, DALE WILLIAM, government relations and public affairs executive; b. St. Louis, Sept. 23, 1951; Reporter Kansas City Star; mgr. pub. affairs Ford Motor Co., Washington; asst. press sec. White House, 1977-81; press sec. to U.S. senator Tom Harkin; sr. v.p., mng. dir. Powell Adams & Rinehart (Ogilvy & Mather), Washington; COO Powell Tate & Weber Shandwick, mng. dir., COO, 1999; mng. dir. global pub. affairs Shandwick Internat.; exec. v.p. Cassidy & Assocs. Office: Powell Tate & Weber Shandwick 700 13th St NW Ste 400 Washington DC 20005-6618 E-mail: dleibach@cassidy.com.

LEIBEL, STEVEN K. lawyer; b. N.Y.C., Sept. 21, 1956; s. Bernard and Sylvia Leibel; m. Julie Oberdorfer, May 16, 1987; children: Lauren Molly, Michelle, Jonathan. BA, Queens Coll., 1977; JD, Emory Law Sch., 1980. Bar: Ga., D.C., U.S. Ct. Appeals (4th, 5th and 11th cirs.), U.S. Supreme Ct.; Police Officers Standards and Tng. certification, 1985. Trial atty. Nat. Labor Rels. Bd., Atlanta, 1980-86; pvt. practice, 1987—; assoc. judge Duluth Mcpl. Ct., 2000—. Host WGST Radio, Atlanta, 1988-90. V.p. B'nai B'rith Gate City Lodge, Atlanta, 1985-90, North Ga. Edn. Found.; police officer Gwinnett County Sheriff's Dept., Atlanta, 1986-89; pres. Home Pk. Bus. Assn., Atlanta, 1989-90; mem. Leadership Sandy Springs, Atlanta, 1989-90; reserve police officer Duluth Police Dept., 1990-99. Mem. Ga. Trial Lawyers Assn., Police Benevolent Assn. (outside counsel 1987-2002). Republican. Avocations: skiing, swimming. Office: PO Box 93506 Atlanta GA 30377-0506

LEIBER, ANNETTE PERONE, artist, art association administrator; b. Chgo., June 1, 1941; d. Vincent James and Micheline Frances (Przewrocki) Perone; m. Donald C. Leiber, Sept. 21, 1963; children: Michael Donald, Lynne M. BA, No. Ill. U., 1963. Chmn., dir. Addison (Ill.) Cultural Arts Commn., 1975—; grants writer A.C.A.D.C., 1982—; art tchr., lectr. Addison Pk. Dist., 1985—. Exhibited throughout Chgo. Bd. dirs., treas. Addison Cmty. Theatre, 1990-98; bd. dirs., dir., treas. Addison Children's Theatre, 1993-98; pres., dir. Addison Ctr. Arts, 1994—. Named Citizen of the Month Lerner-Voice Newspapers, 1980, Outstanding Women Leader in Arts & Culture YWCA, 1989, Studs Terkel Ill. Humanities Svc. award, 1999; numerous art awards, 1970—. Mem. Ill. Arts Alliance (Yates Arts Advocacy award 1993), Addison Art Guild (founder, pres.), Elmhurst Artists' Guild (pres., sec. edn. 1985-90), DuPage Art League (jury chmn. 1989-92). Avocations: art, music, theater. Home: 1245 White Fence Ln Addison IL 60101-1149 Office: Addison Ctr Arts 28 W Lake St Addison IL 60101-2764

LEIBER, JUDITH MARIA, designer, manufacturer; b. Budapest, Hungary, Jan. 11, 1921; came to U.S., 1947, naturalized, 1949; d. Emil and Helen (Spitzer) Peto; m. Gerson Leiber, Feb. 6, 1946. Student pvt. schs., Hungary and Eng.; DFA (hon.), Internat. Fine Arts Coll., 1993; PhD (hon.), Bar Ilan U., Israel, 1993, Internat. Fine Arts Coll., Miami, Fla., 1993. Master handbag maker, Hungary, 1942; pattern maker, designer Nettie Rosenstein, N.Y.C., 1947-60, Koret, N.Y.C., 1960-61; owner, mgr. Judith Leiber, Inc., 1963—. Author: Judith Leiber, The Artful Handbag, 1995; designs represented in 30-yr. retrospective F.I.T. Mus., N.Y., 1993-94; exhbn. of handbags at Corcoran Mus., 2002. Recipient Swarovski award and Am. Handbag Designer award, Leather Industries Am., 1970, Hall of Fame award, Accessory Coun., 2001, George Washington award, Am. Hungarian Found., 2001, Coty award, Am. Fashion Critics, 1973, Neiman-Marcus award, 1980, Women Who Made a Difference award Fashion Group, 1986, Lifetime Achievement award, Dallas Mart, 1991, Am. Acad. Achievement award, 1992, FAAB Lifetime Achievement award, 1992, Ellis Island Medal Honor, 1993, Lifetime Achievement award, Coun. Fashion Designers Am., 1993, Fashion Hall of Fame award, Shannon Rodgers & Jerry Silverman Sch. Fashion Design and Merchandising, Kent State U., 1995, featured Retrospective of Work New Orleans Mus. Mem. Nat. Handbag Authority (dir. 1972—) Achievements include pioneering woman master handbag maker, Hungary; first woman patternmaker Am. handbag industry.

LEIBER, JUSTIN, philosopher, writer; b. Chgo., July 8, 1938; s. Fritz and Jonquil Leiber; m. Barbara Foorman; 1 child Casey ; m. Aleta Misal (div. Jan. 16, 1963); 1 child Arlynn Presser. BA, U. Chgo., 1959, MA, 1961, PhD, 1962; PhilB, Oxford (Eng.) U., 1972. Asst. prof. Lehman Coll., CUNY, N.Y.C.; prof. U. Houston, 1978—. Author: (book) Noam Chomsky: A Philosophic Overview, 1975, Structuralism, 1978, Beyond Rejection, 1980, Can Animals and Machines Be Persons?, 1986, Beyond Humanity, 1987, Beyond Gravity, 1988, Invitation to Cognitive Science, 1991, Paradoxes, 1992. Office: U Houston Philosophy Dept 1600 Calhoun Rd Houston TX 77004 Business E-Mail: jleiber@uh.edu.

LEIBERT, RICHARD WILLIAM, special events producer; b. N.Y.C., Nov. 11, 1948; s. Richard William and Rosemarie Martha (Bruns) L. BS, Boston U., 1966-70; student, Northwestern U., 1971. Producer Sta. WBZ AM/FM, Boston, 1968-70; prodn. dir. Sta. WMMR-FM, Phila., 1970; exec. producer Sta. WIND-AM, Chgo., 1970-72; program dir. Sta. KGB AM-FM, San Diego, 1972-80; pres. Events Mktg., Inc., L.A., 1980—. Dir. Nat. Fireworks Ensemble, Los Angeles, Calif., 1985—. Creator (mascot, publicity stunts) Sta. KGB Chicken, 1974; creator, producer (radio fireworks show) Sta. KGB Sky Show, 1976; writer, producer (network radio show) New Music News, 1983; creator, dir. (touring co.) Nat. Fireworks Ensemble, 1985. Recipient Emmy award, 1978; named Program Dir. of Yr. Billboard Mag., 1976, Radio Program of Yr. Billboard Mag., 1976. Avocations: sailing, baseball. Office: Events Mktg Inc PO Box 65694 Los Angeles CA 90065-0694

LEIBIN, HARVEY BRUCE, architect; b. Waterbury, Conn., May 7, 1947; s. Samuel and Helen (Blumenfeld) L.; m. Florence Epstein, June 28, 1970; children: Bradford A., Kate E., Kara B. BA, Cornell U., 1969; BS, U. Mich., 1971, MArch, 1973. Registered profl. architect, Conn., Mass., N.Y., N.J., R.I. Draftsman, designer Daniel Schwartzman & Assocs., N.Y.C., 1973-75; designer, job capt. Van Summern and Weigold, 1975-77; designer, project architect Russell Gibson von Dohlen, Farmington, Conn., 1977-87; prin., owner Leibin Assocs., Hartford, 1987-90; prin., ptnr. DuBose Assocs., Inc., 1990—. Bd. dirs. Constrn. Inst. Prin. projects include The North Dormitory Complex Renovation at Conn. Coll., Hartford Pub. H.S., The Univ. Conn. at Stamford, The Sci. Ctr. of Conn., Harman & Kravis Halls The Loomis Chaffee Sch., Southern Conn. State U., Swing Space Bldg., Security Ins. Corp. Interiors, The Hartford Courant Hdqrs., UTC Rsch. Labs., Otis Elevator Rsch. Bldg., single family residences. Mem. East Hartford (Conn.) Design Rev. Bd., 1987-90, Beth El Bd. and House Com., West Hartford, Conn., 1990-92; chmn. Pond Place Assn. Design Rev., Avon, Conn.; mem. program com. The Constrn. Inst. Mem. U.S. Army Res., 1969-75. Recipient Downtown Workplace award for Aetna Cityplace and Landmark Bank/Cityplace, Hartford Archtl. Conservancy, 1986; Security Ins. Hdqs. named Readers Poll/Best Interior, Interior Design Mag., 1980; Rogow Found. Scholar, Hartford. Mem. Conn. Soc. Architects, AIA, NCARB, Bldg. Owners and Mgrs. Assn., Cornell Club of Hartford, Mich. Club of Hartford. Jewish. Home: 65 Buttonwood Hill Rd Avon CT 06001-3241 Office: DuBose Assocs Inc 49 Woodland St Hartford CT 06105-2337

LEIBOLD, ARTHUR WILLIAM, JR. lawyer; b. Ottawa, Ill., June 13, 1931; s. Arthur William and Helen (Cull) L.; m. Nora Collins, Nov. 30, 1957; children: Arthur William III, Alison Aubry, Peter Collins. AB, Haverford Coll., 1953; JD, U. Pa., 1956. Bar: Pa. 1957. With Dechert, Price & Rhoads, Phila., 1956-69, ptnr., 1965-69, Washington, 1972-97. Gen. counsel Fed. Home Loan Bank Bd. and Fed. Savs. & Loan Ins. Corp., Washington, 1969-72, Fed. Home Loan Mortgage Corp., 1970-72; lectr. English St. Joseph's Coll., Phila., 1957-59 Contbr. articles to profl. publs. Mem. Pres. Kennedy's Lawyers Com. Civil Rights, 1963, Adminstrv. Conf. U.S., 1969-72; bd. dirs. Marymount Coll. Va., 1974-75; Mem. Phila. Com. 70, 1965-74, Fellowship Commn. Mem. ABA (mem. ho. dels. 1967-69, 79-88, treas. 1979-83, mem. fin. com., mem. bd. govs. 1977-83), Fed. Bar Assn. (mem. nat. coun. 1971-80), D.C. Bar Assn., Phila. Bar Assn., Am. Bar Found. (treas. 1979-83), Am. Bar Ret. Assn. (dir. 1978-83), Am. Bar Endowment (bd. dirs. 1984-97, pres. 1995-97), Am. Bar Ins. (bd. dirs. 1999—), Phila. Country Club (Gladwyne, Pa.), Chester River Yacht and Country Club (Chestertown, Md.), Skating Club Phila., Orpheus Club (Phila.), Order of Coif, Phi Beta Kappa. Republican. Roman Catholic. Home: 200 River Shore Rd Chestertown MD 21620 Office: Dechert 1775 Eye St NW Ste 1100 Washington DC 20006-2424 E-mail: leibold1@aol.com., aleibold@dechert.com.

LEIBOLD, PETER MCCLOSKEY, professional association executive; b. Bryn Mawr, Pa., June 19, 1963; s. Arthur W. Jr. and Nora C. Leibold; m. Elizabeth McCloskey, May 30, 1987; children: Brian M., Collin M., Nora L. BA, Haverford Coll., 1985; JD, Yale U., 1988. Bar: Pa. 1989, D.C. 1991. Clk. to hon. Wilfred Feinberg, N.Y.C., 1988-89; counsellor, legis. dir., chief of staff Senator John C. Danforth, Washington, 1989—94; of counsel Bryan Cave, St. Louis, Washington, 1995-96; gen. counsel Cath. Health Assn., Washington, 1996-99; exec. v.p., CEO Am. Health Lawyers Assn., 1999—. Office: Am Health Lawyers Assn 1025 Connecticut Ave NW Ste 600 Washington DC 20036-5428 E-mail: pleibold@healthlawyers.org.

LEIBOVICH, SIDNEY, engineering educator; b. Memphis, Apr. 2, 1939; s. Harry and Rebecca (Palant) L.; m. Gail Barbara Colin, Nov. 24, 1962; children: Bradley Colin, Adam Keith. BS, Calif. Inst. Tech., Pasadena, 1961; PhD in Theoretical Math., Cornell U., 1965. NATO postdoctoral fellow U. Coll., London, 1965-66; asst. prof. thermal engring. Cornell U., Ithaca, N.Y., 1966-70, assoc. prof. thermal engring., 1970-78, prof. mech. and aerospace engring., 1978-89, Samuel B. Eckert prof. mech. and aerospace engring., 1989—, S.C. Thomas Sze dir. Sibley Sch. Mech. and Aerospace Engring Ithaca , 1998—. Editor: Nonlinear Waves, 1974; assoc. editor: Jour. Fluid Mechanics, 1982-93; co-editor: Acta Mechanica, 1986-92; mem. editorial bd. Ann. Revs. of Fluid Mechanics, 1989-93; gen. editor Cambridge U. Press Monographs on Mechanics, 1994—. Disting. lectr. Naval Ocean Rsch. Devel. Activity, 1983. Recipient MacPherson prize Calif. Inst. Tech., 1961. Fellow ASME (chmn. applied mechanics div. 1987-88), Am. Phys. Soc. (chmn. div. fluid dynamics 1987-88), Am. Acad. Arts and Scis., U.S. Nat. Com. for Theoretical and Applied Mechanics (chair 1990-92.), Nat. Acad. Engring., Am. Geophys. Union, Soc. Indsl. and Applied Math. E-mial. Office: Cornell U Upson Hall Ithaca NY 14853 E-mail: sl23@cornell.edu.

LEIBOVIT, ARNOLD L. film producer, director; b. Miami Beach, Fla., June 18, 1950; s. Meyer and Geraldine L.; m. Barbara Schimpf. AA, U. Fla., 1971; BA cum laude, UCLA, 1973. Dir. Sedona (Ariz.) Spirit Theatre, 1989-92; pres., dir. Talking Rings Entertainment, Beverly Hills Calif., 1988-96, Arnold Leibovit Entertainment, 1996—. Dir., editor (shorts) The Fatherland, 1973, Judgement: An Essay on War, 1974, Penny Lane, 1975; assoc. dir., editor: Rascal Dazzle, 1980; prodr., dir., writer (film/documentary) The Fantasy Film Worlds of George Pal, 1986; prodr., writer (motion picture) The Puppetoon Movie, 1987; exec. prodr. (motion picture) The Time Machine, 2001; prodr. (record, CD) The Time Machine, 1987; dir. (motion picture) Time Being, 2001. Recipient Saturn award Acad. Sci. Fiction & Fantasy, 1986, Golden Eagle award CINE, 1974, 86. Avocations: toy collecting, movie memorabilia, music. Office: Arnold Leibovit Entertainment PO Box 261 Cedar City UT 84721 E-mail: director@scifistation.com.

LEIBOW, RONALD LOUIS, lawyer; b. Santa Monica, Calif., Oct. 4, 1939; s. Norman and Jessica (Kellner) L.; m. Linda Bengelsdorf, June 11, 1961 (div. Dec. 1974); children: Jocelyn Elise, Jeffrey David, Joshua Aaron; m. Jacqueline Blatt, Apr. 6, 1986. AB, Calif. State U., Northridge, 1962; JD, UCLA, 1965. Bar: Calif. 1966, U.S. Dist. Ct. (cen. dist.) Calif. 1966, U.S. Dist. Ct. (no., so. and ea. dists.) Calif. 1971. Spl. asst. city atty. City of Burbank, Calif., 1966-67; from assoc. to ptnr. Meyers, Stevens & Walters, L.A., 1967-71; ptnr. Karpf, Leibow & Warner, Beverly Hills, Calif., 1971-74, Volk, Newman Gralla & Karp, L.A., L.A., 1979-81, Spector & Leibow, L.A., 1982-84, Stroock & Stroock & Lavan, L.A., 1984-94, Kaye Scholer LLP, L.A., 1994—, mng. ptnr., 1996-97. Lectr. law UCLA, 1968-69; asst. prof. Calif. State U., Northridge, 1969-71. Contbr. articles to profl. jours. Pres. Jewish Cmty. Ctr., Greater L.A., 1983-86; vice chair Jewish Cmty. Ctr. Assn. N.Am., N.Y.C., 1988—; vice chair Jewish Fedn. Greater L.A., 1988—, chair planning and allocations com., 1998-2001; internat. bd., exec. com. Starlight Childrens Found., 1997—. Mem. ABA (bus. bankruptcy com.), Phi Alpha Delta. Avocations: writing, tennis, skiing, travel. Office: Kaye Scholer LLP 1999 Avenue Of The Stars Fl 16 Los Angeles CA 90067-6022 E-mail: rleibow@kaye.scholar.com.

LEIBOWITT, SOL DAVID, lawyer; b. Bklyn., Feb. 18, 1912; s. Morris and Bella (Small) Leibowitt; m. Ethel Leibowitt, June 18, 1950 (dec. Aug. 1985); m. Babs Lee, Dec. 28, 1986 (dec. June 2000). BA, Lehigh U., 1933; JD, Harvard U., 1936. Bar: N.Y. 1937, Conn. 1970. Pvt. practice, N.Y.C., 1937-84, Stamford, Conn., 1970-78, Milford, 1978-79; gen. counsel New Haven Clock and Watch Co., 1955-59, pres., 1958-59, Diagnon Corp., 1981-83, vice chmn., 1983-86. Chmn. Card Tech. Corp., 1983-85; dir. Data Card Internat. Corp., Hevant, Eng., 1977-79. Pres. Ethel and David Leibowitt Found.; dir. Am. Com. for Weizmann Inst. Sci.; mediator family law Supreme Ct. State Fla. 15th Jud. Ct., 1990—; arbitrator Am. Arbitration Assn., Fla.; chmn. Israel Cancer Assn. USA; dir. Am. Assocs., Ben-Gurion U., 1999. Recipient Human Rels. award Anti-Defamation League, 1969, Ethel Leibowitt Fund Johns Hopkins U. Sch. Medcine Meml. award Anti-Defamation League, 1971, Tikvah award Israel Cancer Assn., 1995. Mem.: ABA, Am. Soc. for Technion

U. (bd. dirs., v.p., Conn. pres., life trustee), Anti-Defamation League (commr.), NY State Bar Assn., Assn. Bar N.Y.C., Banyon Country Club (West Palm Beach, Fla.), Harvard Club (N.Y.C.), Lotos Club.

LEIBOWITZ, DAVID PERRY, lawyer; b. Bronx, N.Y., Jan. 21, 1950; s. Bernard B. and Annette (Friedman) L.; children: Rachel, Saryn. BA in Econs., Northwestern U., 1970; JD cum laude, Loyola U., 1974. Bar: Ill. 1974, U.S. Dist. Ct. (no. dist) Ill. 1974, U.S. Ct. Appeals (7th cir.) 1974, U.S. Supreme Ct. 1982, U.S. Ct. Appeals (11th cir.) 1985. Assoc. Goebel & Kal, Chgo., 1974-75; judicial clerk Ill. Appellate Ct., 1975-76; ptnr. Schwartz, Cooper, Kolb & Gaynor, 1976-91, Freeborn & Peters, Chgo., 1992-99; pvt. practice Waukegon, 1999—. Adj. prof. John Marshall Law Sch., 1997—. Mem. bd. edn. Highland Park (Ill.) Sch. Dist., 1987-92; pres. bd. edn. North Shore Sch. Dist. 112, Highland Park, 1992-98; pres. bd. trustees Highland Park Pub. Libr., 1991-92. Mem. Am. Bankruptcy Inst., Ill. Bar Assn., Chgo. Bar Assn., Lake County Bar Assn. Office: Law Offices David P Leibowitz 222 Washington St Waukegan IL 60085-5618 E-mail: dpl@lakelaw.com.

LEIBOWITZ, DEBORAH GOLUB, early childhood, gifted and parent education consultant; b. N.Y.C., July 4, 1934; d. Jay and Sarah (Simon) Golub; children from previous marriage: David, Gary, Paula Lynn Leibowitz Sayag. BS, Cornell U., 1955; MA, Western Md. U., 1976. Cert. elem. tchr., adminstrn. and supervision Md. Elem. grade tchr. Montgomery County (Md.) Pub. Schs., 1968-73, tchr. gifted, 1982-85; early childhood specialist Cen. and Area Office, 1973-77; tchr. 2nd grade Burning Tree Elem. Sch., 1977-78; tchr., coord. Cluster Classes Ctr. for Gifted, 1978-82; prin. trainee William Tyler Page Elem. Sch., 1985; acting dir. interrelated arts and gifted artists program, 1986; asst. prin. various elem. schs., Md., 1986-89; gifted and talented specialist Cen. Office of Montgomery County Pub. Schs., Rockville, 1989-90; program dir., early childhood model program Montgomery Knolls Elem. Sch., 1990-92, early childhood specialist, 1992-97; ret., 1997. Coord., editor, writer curriculum and program devel./design for gifted/early childhood/reading lang. arts, 1974—89; alumni interviewer Cornell U., 1961—; spkr. in field. Grantee Javits, U.S. Dept. Edn. Avocations: theater , poetry, writing. Home: 5225 Pooks Hill Rd Apt 1010S Bethesda MD 20814-2019 E-mail: dleibowitz3@home.com.

LEIBOWITZ, HERBERT AKIBA, English language educator, author; b. Staten Island, N.Y., Apr. 26, 1935; s. Morris and Rose (Rabinowitz) L.; m. Susan Yankowitz, May 3, 1978; 1 son, Gabriel. BA, Bklyn. Coll., 1956; MA, Brown U., 1958; PhD, Columbia U., 1966. Asst. prof. English Columbia U., 1967-70; asst. prof. humanities Richmond Coll., Staten Island, N.Y., 1971-73, assoc. prof., 1973-76; assoc. prof. English Coll. S.I., 1976-81; prof. English Coll. Staten Island, CUNY and Grad. Ctr., CUNY, 1981—; prof. English emeritus, 1991—. Fannie Hurst vis. prof. Washington U., St. Louis, 1995; Fulbright prof. U. Barcelona, 1999, U. Autonoma, 1999. Author: Hart Crane: An Introduction to the Poetry, 1968, Fabricating Lives, 1989; editor: Selected Music Criticism of Paul Rosenfeld, 1970, Parnassus: Poetry in Review, 1972, Parnassus: Twenty Years of Poetry in Review, 1994, Asphodel, That Greeny Flower and Other William Carlos Williams Love Poems, 1994. Recipient Fels award for edil. distinction Coordinating Coun. Lit. Mags., 1975, Elizabeth Kray award Poets House, 2002; postdoctoral fellow U. Ill. Ctr. Advanced Study, 1968-69, Chamberlain fellow Columbia U., 1970, fellow N.Y. Inst. Humanities, 1987—, Mellon Seminar fellow NYU, 1988, Guggenheim fellow, 1991-92. Mem. PEN (Nora Magid award for disting. editing of lit. mag. 1995), Nat. Book Critics Circle (bd. dirs. 1988-94, pres. 1992-94). Jewish. Home: 205 W 89th St New York NY 10024-1828 Office: Poetry Rev Found 205 W 89th St Apt 8F New York NY 10024-1835 E-mail: Parnew@aol.com.

LEIBOWITZ, JACK RICHARD, physicist, educator; b. Bridgeport, Conn., July 21, 1929; BA, NYU, MS, 1955; PhD in Physics, Brown U., 1962. Rsch. physicist MIT Lincoln Lab., 1956—61, Westinghouse Rsch. Labs., Pitts., 1961—64; asst. prof. U. Md., College Park, 1964—69; assoc. prof. physics Cath. U. Am., Washington, 1969—73, prof. physics, 1974—95, prof. physics emeritus, 1995—, assoc. dean for grad. studies, 1988—93, chmn. art dept., 1982—86, acad. senate. Sci. cons. govt. agys., NBC-TV. Contbr. Fellow: Wash. Acad. Scis., Am. Phys. Soc.; mem.: Sigma Xi. Achievements include research in condensed matter physics; superconductivity, electron-phonon interaction, band structure. Address: PO Box 31761 Santa Fe NM 87594-1761 E-mail: jrleib@earthlink.net.

LEIBOWITZ, LEONARD D. retired pediatrician; b. Bklyn., May 7, 1932; s. David M. and Celia H. (Hershcovici) L.; m. Sharon A. Bloom, Feb. 7, 1957; children: Michael, Jeffrey, Paul, Dena. AB, NYU, 1953; MD, Boston U., 1957. Diplomate Am. Bd. Pediatrics. Intern Maimonides Hosp., Bklyn., 1957-58, resident, 1958-60; pediatrician West Penn Hosp., Pitts., 1963; pvt. practice Monroeville, Pa., 1963-96; ret. Capt. USAF, 1960-62. Fellow Am. Acad. Pediatrics; mem. Pa. Med. Soc., Allegheny County Med. Soc., Pitts. Pediatric Soc. Republican. Jewish. Avocation: civil war buff.

LEIBSLA, MELVIN DONALD, audit executive; b. Cleve., Mar. 27, 1953; s. Melvin Donald and Marguerite (Scribbner) L.; m. Barbara A. Stasko, July 4, 1981; children: Michael, Jason. BS in Applied Sci., Miami U., 1975; grad., Sch. Bank Mgmt., Madison, Wis., 1990. Programmer/analyst Fed. Res. Bank Cleve., 1975-80; system analyst Olympia Brewing, Tumwater, Wash., 1980-82; system analyst/auditor N.W. Pipeline, Salt Lake City, 1982-84; EDP audit mgr., dir. internal audit svcs. Zions Bancorp, 1984—, v.p., dir. internat. audit svcs., 2000—. Speaker in field. Contbr. articles to profl. jours. Active in developing digital signatures on internet for the State of Utah. Active local ch. parish coun., Salt Lake City, 1989—. Mem. EDP Auditors Assn. (pres., v.p. 1989-91, bd. dirs. 1989-94), Data Processing Mgmt. Assn. Republican. Roman Catholic. Avocations: marathons, coaching and refereeing soccer, church activities. Office: Zions Bancorp Audit Dept Office 1162 Salt Lake City UT 84111 E-mail: mleibsla@msn.com.

LEIBSON, IRVING, retired industrial executive; b. Wilkes Barre, Pa., Sept. 28, 1926; s. Henry and Sonia (Rose) L.; m. Lola Pavalow, Feb. 16, 1950; children: Russell, Sandra Eve. B.Chem. Engring. cum laude, U. Fla., 1945, MS, 1947; MS Carnegie Inst. Tech., 1949; D.Sc., Carnegie Inst. Tech., 1952. Registered profl. engr. emeritus, Calif., Tex. Chem. engr. to supr. Humble Oil and Refining Co., Baytown, Tex., 1952-61, mgr. process engring., 1961-63, tech. mgr., 1963-65, dir. R & D, 1965-67; gen. mgr. ABS div., 1967-68; v.p. Dart Industries Chem. Group, Paramus, N.J., 1969-74; asst. to sr. v.p., investment dept. Bechtel Corp., San Francisco, 1974-75; mgr. process and environment, v.p. C & I/Girdler Inc. (a Bechtel Co.), 1976-78; v.p., mgr. rsch. and engring. Bechtel Nat. Inc., 1978-79; sr. v.p. Bechtel Inc., 1979-81; sr. v.p., mgr. mktg. Bechtel Group Inc., 1981-85, sr. v.p., sr. tech. officer, 1985-87, exec. cons., 1987-94; founder, pres. Bold Techs., 1987-97; ret., 1997. Part-time prof. Rice U., 1957, U. Md., 1954 Contbr. articles to profl. jours.; patentee in field. Dist. commr. E. Harris County dist. Boy Scouts Am., 1958-61; vice-chmn. Intersoc. Task Force Energy, 1973; assoc. World Coal Study, 1979-80; assoc. coal industry adv. bd. Internat. Energy Agy., 1980-95; treas., vice chmn., chmn. mem. exec. com. Coun. Alternate Fuels, 1982-87; mem. Nat. Coal Coun., 1985-94, chmn. Coal Policy Commn., 1987-91; mem. exec. com., 1987-95; mem. adv. bd. Ctr. Chem. Process Safety Tech., 1985-88; mem. liquid fuels com. NRC, 1989-90. With AUS, 1953-54. Recipient Disting. Alumnus award U. Fla., 1988. Fellow Am. Inst. Chem. Engrs. (dir. 1967-69, v.p. 1973, pres. 1974, Publ. award S. Tex. chpt. 1957, Founders award 1976, Disting. Svc. award 1996); mem. Am. Chem. Soc., Engrs. Joint Coun. (dir. 1969-78), Engrs. Manpower Commn., Coal and Slurry Tech Assn. (chmn. 1986-89), Round Hill Golf and Country Club (San Francisco), World Trade Club (San Francisco), Sailfish Point Golf Club (Stuart, Fla.). Home: 2920 SE Dune Dr Stuart FL 34996-4949

LEIBY, ARTHUR PAUL, music educator, musician, composer; b. Phila., Mar. 6, 1956; s. Charles Fredrick and Louisa Georgie Leiby; m. Cynthia Lynn Stroup, July 3, 1999. MusB, U. of the Arts, Phila., 1979; MusM, U. Miami, 1987. Tchr. cert. music K-12 N.J. Instrumental music instr. Mardon , Phila., 1980—82, Instrumental Music Programs, Wilmington , Del., 1983—85; music editor, arranger Musicians Publs., West Trenton, NJ, 1987—88; instrumental music instr. Waterford (N.J.) Twp. Pub. Schs., 1988—. Jazz band dir. U. Pa., Phila., 1990—92. Composer: (brass quintet) Bound for Glory, 1988, Scott Joplin: A Portrait in Brass, 1988, (trombone duet accompaniments) Rochut for Two, 2002. Recipient Tchr. Recognition award, State of N.J., 1992. Mem.: International Trombone Assn., Am. Fedn. Musicians, Music Educators Nat. Conf. Avocations: bicycling, canoeing, fishing, travel. Home: 36 Bowker Rd Medford Lakes NJ 08055 Personal E-mail: twobones@net-gate.com.

LEIBY, BRUCE RICHARD, secondary education educator, writer; b. Media, Pa., Aug. 30, 1947; s. Edward Charles and Margaret Ellen (Strawbridge) L.; m. Linda Pauline Flounders, June 26, 1971. BSBA, Tusculum Coll., Greeneville, 1969; postgrad. West Chester U., 1970, 72. Tchr. Interboro Sch. Dist., Prospect Park, Pa., 1969-70, Delaware County C.C., Media, 1974; acct., tchr. info. processing Upper Darby (Pa.) Adult Sch., 1970-88, Upper Darby Sch. Dist., 1970—. Staff asst. Upper Darby H.S., 1987—, mem. bus. edn. adv. bd., co-sponsor Bus. Club, 1987-88; mem. bus. edn. curriculum com., 1992—. Author for Greenwood Press, Westport, Conn., 1988—; author: Gordon Macrae--A Bio-Bibliography, 1991, Howard Keel--A Bio-Bibliography, 1995; co-author: A Reference Guide to Television's Bonanza, 2001. Co-lay leader Meth. ch.; mem. Voices of Praise Choir. Mem. NEA, Pa. Edn. Assn., Upper Darby Edn. Assn. (past membership chmn.), Am. Film Inst., Suburban Phila. Bus. Edn. Assn., Internat. Friends of Gordon Macrae, Internat. Doris Day Soc., Shirley Jones Fan Club, Michael Ball Fan Club. Republican. Avocations: music, reading, collecting performing arts memorabilia, acting. Home: 13 E 6th St Media PA 19063-2501 Office: Upper Darby HS Lansdowne Ave Upper Darby PA 19082-5410

LEIBY, ROBERT E. county agricultural agent; b. Allentown, Pa., Sept. 25, 1953; s. Earl R. and Gladys M. Leiby; m. Christina A. Leiby, Apr. 24, 1980 (div. Sept. 1997); 1 child, David; m. Jan Marie Allen, July 15, 2000. BS, Delaware Valley Coll., Doylestown, Pa., 1975; MEd, Pa. State U., 1982. County agrl. agt. Pa. Stat U. Lehigh County, Allentown, 1981—, county extension dir., 1986—. Cons. U.S. AID, Swaziland, 1990, 91; treas. Spanish Ctr., Allentown, 1998-2002; cons., vol. Agrl. Coop. Develop. Internat./Vol. in Overseas Coop. Assistance, Moscow, 1999. Weekly columnist The Morning Call, 1981-2002. Mem. Nat. Assn. County Agrl. Agts. (Disting. Svc. award 1993), Potato Assa. Am., Pa. Assn. County Agrl. Agts., Pa. Plant Food and Protectant Edn. Soc. (bd. dirs. 1995-97). Mem. United Ch. of Christ. Avocation: outdoors. Office: Pa State U 4184 Dorney Park Rd Allentown PA 18104-5728 E-mail: rleiby@psu.edu.

LEICH, JOHN FOSTER, political scientist, European languages educator; b. Evansville, Ind., June 27, 1920; s. Clarence and Josephine (Foster) L.; m. Jean Elizabeth Ferriss, June 24, 1950; children: Ellen Leich Moon, Christopher Martin. BA, Swarthmore Coll., 1942; MA, Yale U., 1947; PhD, U. Mass., 1976. Fgn. svc. officer U.S. Dept. State, Gdansk, Warsaw, Munich, Bremen, 1947-50; dep. divisional dir. Free Europe, Inc., N.Y.C. and London, 1950-65; rsch. scientist, cons. George Washington U., Washington, 1965-67; prof. polit. sci. and fgn. langs. La. Tech. U., Ruston, 1967-90; mem. faculty Taconic Learning Ctr. Inst. World Affairs, Salisbury, Conn., 1990—, Swiss Hospitality Inst., Washington, 1990-96. Author: The Communist Parties in the European Parliament, 1976; contbr. articles to profl. jours. Pres. Greenwich Village Brotherhood Com., N.Y.C., 1959-60; dist. capt. Rep. Party, N.Y.C., 1956; treas. A Conn. Party, Cornwall, 1994-99; founder Ruston (La.) Community Theatre, 1977; mem. alumni coun. Swarthmore Coll., 1995-2000; justice of the peace, Cornwall, 1997—. Decorated Cavalier's Cross of Order of Merit Republic of Poland, 1996. Mem. Coun. on Fgn. Rels., Conf. Group on Italian Politics, Am. Coun. on Germany, Polish Inst. Arts and Scis. in Am., Salisbury Rotary Club (pres. 1996-97), UN Assn. (N.W. Conn. chpt. 1998—, sec. 1998-2000), Phi Beta Kappa. Episcopalian. Avocations: languages, choral music, swimming. Home: 34 Bald Mountain Rd Cornwall Bridge CT 06754-1313 also: PO Box 1701 Sharon CT 06069-1701

LEICHMAN, KENNETH WILLIAM, investment executive; b. Bklyn., June 12, 1937; s. Joseph and Ruth (Kaplow) L.; m. Leslee Evelyn Seidenfrau, June 20, 1959; children: Michael, Robin. BBA, U. Miami, Coral Gables, Fla., 1959. Cert. fin. planner. Cost acct. 3M, Schenectady, N.Y., 1959-60; office mgr. Kennett Sales Corp., Albany, 1960-64; office mgr., contbr. Hobart Sales & Svc., 1964-69; stockbroker CBWL-Hayden Stone, 1969-73; sr. v.p. First Albany Corp., 1973-2000; also bd. dirs. 1st Albany Corp.; mng. dir. First Union Securities, Albany, NY, 2000—01; sr. v.p. Janney Montgomery Scott, 2001—. Bd. dirs. Albany Patroons, 1985-91, Jewish Fedn. Endowment Com.; mem. fin. com. Temple Gates of Heaven. Mem. Internat. Assn. Fin. Planning (bd. dirs. 1984-98), Colonie Country Club, Eastpointe Country Club. Avocations: golf, tennis. Home: 712 Waldens Pond Rd Albany NY 12203-6005 Office: Janney Montgomery Scott 8 Southwoods Blvd Albany NY 12211 E-mail: kleichman@jmsonline.com.

LEICHT, SUSAN DALE, occupational therapist; b. Sydney, NSW, Australia, June 27, 1961; came to U.S., 1993; d. William David and Esmae Leonette (Francis) McBay; m. Leslie Robert John Leicht, June 28, 1981 (div. Dec. 2001); children: Nathan John, Ruth Ann. B Occupl. Therapy, U. Queensland, Brisbane, Australia, 1981; MS in Advanced Occupl. Therapy, East Carolina U., 1998. Lic. occupl. therapist, N.C., Tenn.; bd. cert. in neurorehab. Occupl. therapist Rockhampton (Queensland) Base Hosp., 1982, occupl. therapist in-charge, 1980; pvt. practice state and fed. govt. contracts, Australia, 1983-89; sr. occupl. therapist Gracemere (Australia) Gardens Retirement Village, 1988-89, Lenoir Meml. Hosp., Kinston, N.C., 1994-95; travelling occupl. therapist JWS Health Cons., Houston, 1993-94; occupl. therapist III, Pitt County Meml. Hosp., Greenville, NC, 1995—99; asst. prof. occupl. therapy Ithaca (N.Y.) Coll., 1999—. Mem. Am. Occupl. Therapy Assn., Neuro Devel. Treatment Assn. (rsch. com. 1998), N.C. Occupl. Therapy Assn., Phi Kappa Phi. Avocations: family, church, hiking, camping, travel. Home: PO Box 69 Union Springs NY 13160-0069

LEICHTER, FRANZ S. federal agency administrator; b. Vienna, Austria, Aug. 19, 1930; s. Otto and Kathe (Pick) L.; m. Nina Williams, July 3, 1958 (dec. Feb. 1995); children: Katherine, Joshua. BA, Swarthmore Coll., 1952; JD, Harvard U., 1957. Bar: N.Y. 1957, U.S. Dist. Ct. (so. and ea. dists.) N.Y. 1959, U.S. Ct. Appeals (2d cir.) 1961. Mem. N.Y. State Assembly, Albany, 1969-74, N.Y. State Senate, Albany, 1975-98, ranking mem. environ. conservation com., 1986-90, ranking mem. judiciary com., 1991-98; ptnr. Wachtell, Manheim & Grouf, N.Y.C., 1974-88; of counsel Walter, Conston, Alexander & Green, 1988-2000; dir. Fed. Housing Fin. Bd., Washington, 2000—. Chair N.Y. State Senate Dem. Policy Com., 1983-90. Author various reports, 1979—. Del. Dem. Nat. Convention, 1964, 84, 88, 96. Cpl. U.s. Army, 1953-55. Recipient award Austrian Govt., 1984. Mem. ACLU, Assn. of Bar of City of N.Y., N.Y. State Bar Assn., Am. Jewish Congress. Democrat. Jewish. Avocations: hiking, skiing, tennis, reading history works. Home: 216 E 47th St New York NY 10017-2102

LEICHTLING, MICHAEL ALFRED, lawyer; b. N.Y.C., Mar. 30, 1943; s. Stanley Arthur and Roslyn Priscilla (Fuhr) L.; m. Arlene Dorf, July 30, 1966; children: Julie Karen Nacos, Nina Anastasia, Noah James. BA, SUNY, Binghamton, 1963; JD, Northwestern U., 1966; postgrad., Columbia U., 1968. Bar: N.Y. 1969, U.S. Ct. Appeals (2d cir.) 1969. Assoc. Aranow Brodsky Bohlinger Einhorn & Dann, N.Y.C., 1966, Parker Chapin & Flattau, N.Y.C., 1969-77; ptnr. Parker Chapin Flattau & Klimpl, LLP, 1977-2001; mem. exec. com. Parker Chapin Flattau & Klimpl, 1987-92; ptnr. Jenkens & Gilchrist Parker Chapin LLP, 2001—. Bd. dirs. H. Warshow & Sons Inc., N.Y.C. Editor Northwestern U. Law Rev., 1965-66, Equipment Leasing Jour., 1986—; co-editor Commercial Finance Guide, 1997—, Commercial Loan Documentation Guide, 1997—. Bd. dirs. Friends of Israel Disabled Vets., N.Y.C., 1986—, Equipment Leasing and Fin. Found., Arlington, Va., 1998—. With U.S. Army, 1966-68; Vietnam. Decorated Bronze Star; Regents scholar, 1963, Newman scholar, 1963-66. Mem. N.Y. State Bar Assn. (corp. law sect.), N.Y. County Lawyers Assn. (banking law com., secured lending com.), Equipment Leasing Assn. Am. (bd. dirs., industry future coun., 2001), Ea. Assn. Equipment Lessors (gen. counsel 1986—). Avocations: reading, painting, swimming, golf. Home: 148 Quinn Rd Briarcliff Manor NY 10510-2133 Office: 405 Lexington Ave New York NY 10174-0002 E-mail: mleichtling@jenkens.com.

LEIDER, CHARLES L. landscape architect, planner; b. Howard, S.D., Oct. 12, 1932; s. Louis Isadore and Ardath Ruth (Willoughby) L.; m. Yuvone Fleming, Sept. 9, 1963; children: Charles W., Stephen F. BSLA, Mich. State U., 1957; MCP, Yale U., 1964; PhD, Okla. State U., 1989. Assoc. prof. U. Nebr., Lincoln, 1965-70; dir. planning Clark & Enersen, 1965-72, HNTB, Kansas City, Mo., 1972-81, The SP Group, Irvine, Calif., 1981-82; mng. dir. Pereira Assocs., Doha, Qatar, 1982—; owner Leider & Assocs., Stillwater, 1985—; prof., dir. landscape arch. program Okla. State U., 1985—. Pres. Univ. Estate Homeowners Assn., Stillwater, 1996-97; mem. Downtown Planning Com., Stillwater, 1988-90. Recipient Citation of Merit for pub. Okla. Hist. Preservation Office, 1992, Silver medal U. Nac. Federico Villarreal, Lima, 1996. Fellow Am. Soc. Landscape Architects (Award Recognition 1995, pres. Prairie Gateway chpt. 1975-77, pres. Okla. chpt. 2001—); mem. Am. Inst. Cert. Planners, Am. Planning Assn. (chmn. environ. planning divsn. 1979-81), U.S./Internat. Commn. on Monuments and Sites, Phi Kappa Phi. Avocations: sailing, gardening, swimming, tennis. Office: Okla State Univ Landscape Arch Program 360 AGH Stillwater OK 74078-6027 E-mail: cll1032@okstate.edu.

LEIDHEISER, HENRY, JR. retired chemistry educator, consultant; b. Union City, N.J., Apr. 18, 1920; s. Henry and Margaret Marie (Steinel) L.; m. Virginia Townsend, Feb. 21, 1944; children: Margaret Frances, Henry III. BS in Chemistry, U. Va., 1941, MS in Phys. Chemistry, 1943, PhD in Phys. Chemistry, 1946. Research associate U. Va., Charlottesville, 1946-49; research chemist, dir. Va. Inst. for Sci. Research, Richmond, 1949-68; prof. chemistry Lehigh U., Bethlehem, Pa., 1968-90, prof. emeritus, 1990—. Cons. space science NASA, 1972-84; cons. numerous indsl. orgns. Author or editor of 8 books; 275 publs. in tech. lit.; 7 patents on crystal growth and metal surface treatment. NATO fellow to Cambridge U., England, 1969; recipient J. Shelton Horsley Rsch. award Va. Acad. Sci., 1948, Oak Ridge Inst. Nuclear Studies Rsch. award, 1949, Westinghouse Signal and Brake Award of Inst. Metal Finishing, 1954, Silver medal Am. Electroplaters' Soc., 1978, Arch T. Colwell award Soc. Automotive Engrs., 1979, Humboldt Sr. Scientist award, 1985, Tambour award 11th Congress Metal Finishing, 1984, Silver medal South African Corrosion Inst., 1986, Libsch Rsch. award Lehigh U., 1987, Mattiello Rsch. award Fedn. Soc. Coatings Tech., 1990 Fellow AAAS; mem. Am. Chem. Soc., Electrochem. Soc. (Young Author's award 1948, Rsch. award 1986, 91), Nat. Assn. Corrosion Engrs. (Whitney award 1983), Rotary. Republican. Presbyterian. Avocations: bridge, golf, collecting ceramics. Home: 822 Carnoustie Dr Venice FL 34293-4343 E-mail: hleid@worldnet.att.net.

LEIDINGER, WILLIAM JOHN, clinic administrator; b. Chgo., Feb. 1, 1940; s. Arthur George and Anna (Choisek) L.; m. Karen Aldinger, Sept. 1, 1962; children: Michael, Steven. BA, Loras Coll., Dubuque, Iowa, 1962; MA, State U. Iowa, 1963. Adminstrv. asst. to city mgr., Park Forest, Ill., 1963-65; asst. to city mgr. Alexandria, Va., 1965-71; asst. city mgr. Richmond, 1971-72; city mgr., 1972-78; v.p. Rolm/Atlantic Corp., 1979-81; exec. dir. McGuire Clinic, Richmond, 1981-86; exec.v.p., chief lending officer Security Federal Savings, Va., 1986-91; county executive Fairfax County, Fairfax, 1992—; instr. Purdue U., No. Va. Community Coll. Guest lectr. U. Richmond, mem. bd. assos., Va. Commonwealth U. Bd. dirs., pres. Greater Richmond Transit Co., 1973-78; mem. Richmond City Planning Commn., 1971-78; bd. dirs. Richmond Eye Hosp., 1979— , St. Luke's Hosp, Richmond Cerebral Palsy Ctr; mem. Richmond City Council, 1980— ; bd. dirs. Port of Richmond. Mem. Internat. City Mgmt. Assn. (chmn. labor/mgmt. relations com. 1974-75), Nat. League Cities, Va. Municipal League, Am. Soc. Pub. Adminstrn. Roman Catholic. Office: Office of the County Exec 12000 Government Center Pky Fairfax VA 22035-0001*

LEIDY, CAROL MAXINE, real estate broker; b. Marysville, Calif., May 21, 1949; d. Donald Max and Gladys Irene (Bruner) L.; m. William Ray Bohannon, Aug. 6, 1976 (div. July 1985); children: Alison, Candice. BA, Calif. State U., Sacramento, 1971, MS, 1973. Lic. real estate broker, Calif. Asst. tchr. Nev. Union H.S., Grass Valley, Calif., 1964-67; sec., clk. Calif. State U., Sacramento, 1967-68; sec. Lincoln U. Law Sch., 1969-70; rschr., sec. Ralph Nader, 1970; govt. tchr. McClatchy H.S. Adult Edn., 1971-72; counselor El Camino H.S. and Bella Vista H.S., 1973-79; real estate broker Bertrando & Assoc., Auburn, 1981-90, mgr., 1987-89; real estate agt. Re/Max of Auburn, 1990-96, owner, broker, 1997—. Author: Free...To A Good Home, 1970; contbr. articles to various mags. Bd. dirs. Mother Lode Youth and Family Svcs., Applegate, Calif., 1979-82. Mem. Nat. Assn. Realtors, Calif. Assn. Realtors. Democrat. Avocations: writing, reading, travel. Office: Re/Max of Auburn 13555 Bowman Rd Ste 600 Auburn CA 95603-3194

LEIDY, JOHN WILLIAM, JR. endocrinologist, educator; b. Woodbury, N.J., July 1, 1950; s. John William and Margaret (Redfield) L.; m. Joan C. Finno, Apr. 7, 1979; children: William James, Jennifer Margaret, Allison Elizabeth. BS, Brown U., 1972; MD, PhD, U. Wash., Seattle, 1979. Diplomate Am. Bd. Med. Examiners, Am. Bd. Internal Medicine, Am. Bd. Endocrinology and Metabolism. Intern Albert Einstein Med. Ctr., Phila., 1979-80; resident in internal medicine Med. Coll. Pa., 1980-82; fellow in endocrinology and metabolism U. Colo. Health Scis. Ctr., Denver, 1982-85, instr., 1985-86; staff physician Huntington (W.Va.) VA Med. Ctr., 1986—; asst. prof. medicine Marshall U. Sch. Medicine, Huntington, 1986-90, assoc. prof. medicine, 1990—, prof. medicine, physiology and pharmacology, 1995—. Recipient Nat. Rsch. Svc. award NIH, 1984-86, VA Merit Rev. grant, 1989—. Mem. ACP, Am. Fedn. Clin. Rsch., Endocrine Soc., Soc. for Neurosciences, Am. Diabetes Assn., Tristate Diabetes Assn. (pres.). Avocations: outdoors, wine, cooking, computers, gardening.

LEIER, CARL VICTOR, internist, cardiologist; b. Bismarck, N.D., Oct. 20, 1944; married; 3 children. Grad., Creighton U., 1965, MD cum laude, 1969. Diplomate Am. Bd. Internal Medicine, Cardiovascular Medicine, Critical Care Medicine, Geriatric Medicine, Electrocardiography, Nat. Bd. Med. Examiners; lic. med., surgical Nebr., med. Ohio. Intern Ohio State U. Coll. Medicine, Columbus, 1969-70, med. resident (instr.) dept. medicine, 1971-73, chief resident (instr.), 1973-74, fellowship divsn. cardiology, 1974-76; pathology resident dept. pathology St. Vincent Hosp., Worcester, Mass., 1970-71; trainee NIH Tng. Grant, 1974-75; asst. prof. medicine cardiology dept., Ohio State U. Coll. Medicine, Columbus, 1976-80, asst. prof. pharmacology, 1976-80, assoc. prof., 1980-84, faculty mem. grad. sch., 1980—, dir. rsch. divsn. cardiology, 1980-83, James W. Overstreet prof. of medicine, 1983—, prof. of medicine divsn. cardiology, 1984—, prof. pharmacology, dept. pharmacology, 1984—, dir. divsn. cardiology, 1986-98. Hosp. procedures com. Ohio State U. Hosps., 1973-74; mem. pharmacology and therapeutics com. Ohio State U. Hosps., 1976-80; mem. rsch. com. ctrl. Ohio chpt. Am. Heart Assn., 1977-84, bd. trustees, 1979-88, exec. rsch. com., 1979-84, vice chmn. rsch. com., 1980-82, chmn. rsch. peer rev. com., 1982-84, v.p., 1984-86, pres. elect, 1986-88; numerous other coms.; cons. cardiorenal adv. bd. Smith-Kline Labs., 1982-85, com. on cardio-vascular rsch. and devel., 1982-85, AMA on Drugs and Tech., 1985—, FDA Cardiorenal adv. com. 1986-92, Lilly-Elanco devel. ractopamine, 1989; mem. ad hoc adv. com. on carvedilol in congestive heart failure, Smith, Kline and Beacham Pharms., 1991, ad hoc adv. com. on PDEI devel., McNeil Pharms., 1991, ad hoc adv. com. for clin. trials on Ibopamine, Zambon Pharms., 1993, sci. adv. com. Ohio State Univ. Brain Tumor Rsch. Ctr., 1993—, data safety monitoring bd., Otsuka Vesnarinone Trials, 1993— mem. chmn. Annual Sci. Sessions of the Am. Coll. of Cardiolog, 1996-97; vis. prof., lectr. and presenter at numerous sci. confs., insts. in U.S. and internationally. Editor: (book) Cardiotonic Drugs, 1986, 2d rev. edit., 1991; co-author: (with H. Boudoulas) CardioRenal Disorders and Diseases, 1986, 2d edit., 1992 (with J. Vincent) Critical Care Medicine: Recent Advances in Cardiovascular Medicine, 1990; contbr. more than 40 chpts. to other medical books and almost 200 articles to peer reviewed jours. including: Vascular Surgery, Archives of Internal Medicine, Circulation, Brit. Heart Jour., Jour. Electrocardiology, Clinical Pharmacologic Therapy, Chest, Am. Jour. Medicine, Jour. Cardiovascular Pharmacology, Am. Heart Jour., Geriatrics, Annals of Internal Medicine and others; editor in chief Congestive Heart Failure: Index and Revs., 1988—; mem. editorial bds. of ten medical jours. concerned with heart diseases, the review bds. of others including New Eng. Jour. Medicine, Internat. Jour. Cardiology, Jour. of Lab. and Clin. Medicine. Recipient Upjohn award, 1969, Lange Scholar award, 1969, Golden Apple Student Tchg. award, 1973, 75, Young Investigator award Ctrl. Ohio Heart Chpt., Am. Heart Assn., 1976-78, Rsch. Recognition award, 1978. Fellow Am. Coll. Clin. Pharmacology, Coun. on Clin. Pharmacology, Am. Heart Assn., Am. Coll. Cardiology, Am. Coll. Physicians, Coun. on Geriatric Cardiology; mem. AAAS, Ohio State Med. Assn., Am. Fedn. for Clin. Rsch., Ctrl. Soc. for Clin. Rsch., Am. Soc. Clin. Investigation, Assn. Univ. Cardiologists, Internat. Soc. for Heart Rsch., Internat. Soc. Cardiovascular Pharmacotherapy, Assn. Profs. of Cardiology. Office: Ohio State U Med Ctr Divsn Cardiology 473 W 12th Ave Columbus OH 43210-1250

LEIES, JOHN ALEX, theology educator, clergyman; b. Chgo., Apr. 24, 1926; cre; BS in Edn., U. Dayton, 1948; STB, U. Friborg, Switzerland, 1954, STL, 1956, STD, 1958. Asst. to provincial Soc. of Mary, St. Louis, 1961-64; regional superior Marianist Missions, Peru, 1964-68; prof. theology, dir. campus ministry St. Mary's U., San Antonio, 1974-81, chmn. grad. theology dept., 1980-81, acad. v.p., 1981-85, pres., 1985-88, grad. advisor theology dept., 1977-81, chmn. dept., 1996—, dir. Ctr. for Profl. Ethics, 1991—. Dir. Cath. Charismatic Bible Inst., 1977-86, 91—; theologian mem. ethics com. Santa Rosa Hosp., 1978-81, 89-94; mem. gen. chpt. Soc. of Mary, 1966-67, 71, 76, 81, 86, 91; rsch. fellow cons. The Nat. Cath. Bioethics Ctr., Boston, Mass., 1988—; trustee Tex. Ctr. for Legal Ethics and Professionalism, 1994-95. Mem. Lambda Chi Alpha, Univ. Faculty for Life, Fellowship of Cath. Scholars. Avocation: reading. Address: St Mary's Univ of San Antonio 1 Camino Santa Maria St San Antonio TX 78228-5433 E-mail: theojohn@stmarytx.edu.

LEIFER, ANDREW GENE, emergency physician; b. N.Y.C., 1954; MD, Albert Einstein Coll. Medicine, 1980. Diplomate Am. Bd. Emergency Medicine, Am. Bd. Internal Medicine. Resident in medicine Hartford Hosp., 1981-83; assoc. attending emergency medicine St. Luke's Roosevelt Hosp., N.Y.C.; asst. prof. clin. medicine Columbia U. P&S. Fellow Am. Coll. Emergency Physicians.

LEIFER, JACK, engineering educator, mechanical engineer; b. N.Y.C., Aug. 10, 1965; s. Morton and Felice L. BS, MIT, 1987; MS, U. Tex., 1989, PhD, 1995. Engr. in tng., Tex. Instr. part-time Austin C.C., 1992-94; instr. U. S.C., Aiken, 1994-95, asst. prof. engring., 1996-2000; asst. prof. mech. engring. U. Ky. Extended Campus Program, Paducah, 2000—. Author: Introduction to Powerpoint, 2002; contbr. articles to profl. jours. Recipient Joint Faculty Appt. Dept. of Energy, 1994, 95, 99; NASA summer faculty fellow, 2002. Mem.: AIAA, ASME, Am. Soc. Engring. Edn. Jewish. Avocations: choral singing, weight training. Office: PO Box 7380 Crounse Hall Paducah KY 42002

LEIGH, GLORIA LORRAINE, retired religious studies educator; b. Columbus, Ohio, May 6, 1939; d. William Franklin and Catherine Aileen Leigh; children: Anthonia Mcdaniel. AA, Monterey Peninsula Coll., 1961; cert. in black cath. studies, Xavier U., 1990; MA in Religion, Athenaeum Of Ohio, 1996. Dir. religious edn. Resurrection Cath. Ch., Dayton, Ohio, 1988—96, Mary, Help of Christians Cath. Ch., Fairborn, 1996—2001; coord. christian initiation for adults St. Martin De Porres Cath. Ch., Lincoln Heights, 2001—. Adv. Tribunal Archdiocese Cinn., 1990; catechetical leader Archdiocese Cinn., 1996, Fedn. Christian Ministries, 2000; cons. St. Anthony Messenger Press, Cinn., 1997—; coord. Nguzo Saba, Cinn., 2002—. President Greater Dayton Christian Coun., 1992—94; bd. dirs. Greater Dayton Christian Connection, 1998—2002; pres. Interfaith Ministers for Reconciliation, 2001; rep. Southwest Priority Bd., Dayton, 1988—91; steering com. Dayton Dialogue on Race Rels., 1998—2002. Grantee, Epiphany Found., 1994; scholar, Benjamin E. Mays, 1992, Gabrielle Bouscaren, 1994—96. Mem.: Dayton Area Religious Edn. Assn. (co-chair 1999—2001), Fedn. Christian Ministries, Delta Sigma Theta (life; chaplain 1999—2001). Roman Catholic. Avocations: travel, reading, weaving, yoga, gardening. Home: 148 N Ardmore Avenue Dayton OH 45417 Home Fax: 937-268-0521. Personal E-mail: GloriaLeigh300@CS.com.

LEIGH, HOYLE, psychiatrist, educator, writer; b. Seoul, Korea, Mar. 25, 1942; came to U.S., 1965; m. Vincenta Masciandaro, Sept. 16, 1967; 1 child, Alexander Hoyle. MA, Yale U., 1982; MD, Yonsei U., Seoul, 1965. Diplomate Am. Bd. Psychiatry and Neurology. Asst. prof. Yale U., New Haven, 1971-75, assoc. prof., 1975-80, prof., 1980-89, lectr. in psychiatry, 1989—. Dir. Behavioral Medicine Clinic, Yale U., 1980-89; dir. psychiat. cons. svc. Yale-New Haven Hosp., 1971-89; chief psychiatry VA Med Ctr., Fresno, Calif., 1989—; prof., vice chmn. dept. psychiatry U. Calif., San Francisco, 1989—, head dept. psychiatry, 1989—; cons. Am. Jour. Psychiatry, Archives Internal Medicine, Psychosomatic Medicine. Author: The Patient, 1980, 2d edit., 1985, 3d edit., 1992; editor: Psychiatry in the Practice of Medicine, 1983, Consultation-Liaison Psychiatry: 1990's & Beyond, 1994, Biopsychosocial Approaches in Primary Care: State of the Art and Challenges for the 21st Century, 1997. Fellow ACP, Internat. Coll. Psychosomatic Medicine (v.p.), Am. Acad. Psychosomatic Medicine; mem. AMA, AAUP, World Psychiat. Assn. Avocations: reading, music, skiing. Office: U Calif Dept Psychiat 2615 E Clinton Ave Fresno CA 93703-2223

LEIGH, MARGIE, mortgage company administrator; b. Campbellsville, Ky., June 6, 1946; d. Bennie Lawrence and Evelyn Garnetta (Seay) DeWitt; children: Susan Leigh, Tracy Lynne. Grad. in elem. edn., Western Ky. U., 1968; postgrad., U. Ky., Lexington, 1986, U. Ky., Elizabethtown, 1988. Real estate agt. Nat. Realtors Assn., Elizabethtown, Ky., 1986-92; mortgage originator Nat. Bankers Assn., McLean, Va., 1993—; br. mgr. Old Kent Mortgage Co. Mem. adv. bd. Hardin County Sch., Elizabethtown, 1985-87. Recipient Apple award Elizabethtown Sch. Sys., 1985; named to Order of Ky. Cols. Mem. Order Ea. Star. Republican. Baptist. Avocations: golf, tennis, writing.

LEIGH, STEPHEN, industrial designer; b. N.Y.C., May 21, 1931; s. Herman Lerner and Rhea (Drinkhouse) L.; children: Harvey Alan, Madeleine Beth; m. Wendy Horton, June 6, 1999. BFA, Cooper Union, 1951. Interior designer Robert Gruen Assocs., N.Y.C., 1951-55; designer, project dir. Michael Saphier Assocs., 1955-59; pres. Stephen Leigh & Assocs. Inc., 1959—. Interior designers, cons. specializing in comml. usage, United Jewish Appeal, 1963, U.S. Pavilion, Venezuelan Pavilion, N.Y. World's Fair, 1964-65, Random House, 1969, Mitsubishi Internat. Corp., 1980, Rapid Am. Corp., 1982, Bowery Savs. Bank, 1986; lectr. NYU. Columnist Real Estate Weekly, 1963-65, The Office Mag., 1985—; one-man shows of sculpture at Cartier and East River Savings Bank; recent prin. works include Union Chelsea Nat. Bank, Faberge, Fino Restaurant, Il Menestrello Restaurant, Schenley, redesign of landmark facade at 111 8th Ave., 1989; sculpted permanent team trophy for Eisenhower Golf Tournament. Recipient AIA design award for Venezuelan Pavilion N.Y. World's Fair, 1964-65, Excellence award The Archtl. Woodwork Inst., 1988. Mem. Am. Soc. of Interior Designers (N.Y. chpt.), Charge des Missions of the Confrerie de la Chaine des Rotisseurs (Bronze Star of Excellence), Brotherhood of the Knights of the Vine Avocations: sculpture, painting, cooking, travel, collecting Americana and American flags. Office: 157 E 57th St New York NY 10022-2104

LEIGH, VINCENTA M. health administrator; b. N.Y.C., June 27, 1947; d. Emanuel and Ines Masciandara; m. Hoyle Leigh, Sept. 16, 1967; 1 child, Alexander. BA, Lehman Coll., 1968; MSN, Yale U., 1973. Psychiat. clinician Jacobi Hosp., Bronx, N.Y., 1971; pediatric nurse Conn. Mental Health Ctr., New Haven, 1971-73; instr. in psychiat. nursing Yale U., 1973-77; asst. dir. mental health nursing edn. Conn. Valley Hosp., Middletown, 1980-81; nurse coord. Inst. of Living, Hartford, Conn., 1981-85, asst. dir. nursing, 1985-89; asst. clin. profl. psychiatry U. Calif., San Francisco, 1989—; coord. Intensive outpatient program Kaiser Permanente, Fresno, Calif., 1996—. Contbr. articles to profl. jours. Mem. ANA, Am. Psychosomatic Soc., Internat. Coll. Psychosomatic Medicine, Am. Orthopedic Assn., Jr. League. Avocations: piano, reading, trombone, skiing.

LEIGHLY, HOLLIS PHILIP, JR. metallurgical engineering educator, researcher; b. St. Joseph, Ill., May 28, 1923; s. Hollis Philip and Bessie (Haworth) L.; m. Elizabeth Marie Petersen, Aug. 31, 1951; children: Karen, David. BS, U. Ill., 1948, MS, 1950, PhD, 1952. Registered profl. engr., Calif.; chartered engr. U.K. Rsch. metall. Bendix Corp. Rsch. Labs., Detroit, 1952-54, Denver Rsch. Inst., 1954-60; chmn. metall. dept. U. Denver, 1957-60; assoc. prof. to prof. U. Mo., Rolla, 1960—. Referee 13th Internat. Symposium on Influence of Radiation on Material Properties, 1987; vis. prof. Benjamin Meaker Found., U. Bristol, 1991. Contbr. articles to profl. jours. With U.S. Army, 1943-46, ETO. Olin Industries fellow Univ. Ill., 1951-52, NATO fellow Univ. Guelph, Ont., Can., 1974, British Sci. & Engring. Rsch. Coun. fellow Univ. East Anglia, 1979-80. Mem. Sigma Xi (chp. pres. 1959, 64). Achievements include research in defects in metals and alloys using positron annihilation. Home: 29 Sydney Ct Rolla MO 65401-3820 E-mail: hpl@umr.edu.

LEIGHTON, ALBERT CHESTER, history educator; b. Chester, N.H., Sept. 6, 1919; s. Arthur Edmund and Sarah Elizabeth (Edwards) L.; m. Estella Ruth Dietel, Jan. 17, 1958; children: Cedric Edmund George. AB, U. Calif., Berkeley, 1960, MA, 1961, PhD, 1964. Enlisted U.S. Army, 1937, commd. 2d lt., 1946, advanced through grades to capt., 1953, ret., 1957; ops. officer, Germany, 1947-50, staff officer Hdqrs., Washington, 1950-53, 55-57, ops. officer, Korea, Japan, Taiwan, 1954-55; assoc. prof. history SUNY-Oswego, 1964-69, prof., 1969-85, prof. emeritus, 1985—; adj. prof., lectr. U. Tex. at San Antonio, 1987—; Fulbright Rsch. prof. U. Munich, 1978-79; faculty exchange scholar SUNY, 1981-85; coordinator internat. rsch. in hist. cryptanalysis, 1969—; speaker Internat. Congress, St. Petersburg formerly Leningrad, 1970, Moscow, 1971, Tokyo, 1974, Edinburgh, 1977. Author: Transport and Communication in Early Medieval Europe, 1972; contbr. Ency. Americana; contbr. articles to profl. jours. Rsch. fellow Ctr. Medieval and Renaissance Studies UCLA, 1984, Medieval Insts. fellow Duke U., 1976, SUNY Binghamton fellow, 1985. Mem. Am. Hist. Assn., Medieval Acad. Am., Am. Cryptogram Assn., Beale Cypher Soc., Ancient and Honorable Arty. Co. Mass., New Eng. Hist. and Genealogical Soc., Ret. Officers Assn. Home: 8406 Burwell San Antonio TX 78254-2538

LEIGHTON, CHARLES MILTON, retired specialty consumer products executive; b. Portland, Maine, June 4, 1935; s. Wilbur F. and Elizabeth (Loveland) L.; children: Julia Loveland, Anne Throop; m. Roxanne Brooks McCormick, May 23, 1992. AB, Bowdoin Coll., 1957, LLD (hon.), 1989; MBA, Harvard U., 1960. Product lines mgr. Mine Safety Appliances Co., Pitts., 1960-64; instr. Harvard Bus. Sch., 1964-65; group v.p. Bangor Punta Corp., Boston, 1965-69; chmn., CEO CML Group, Inc., Acton, Mass., 1969-97; pvt. investor, cons. mergers and acquisitions Bolton, 1997—. Bd. dirs. Met. Life Ins. Co., N.Y.; trustee Lahey Clinic. Past pres. Alumni Coun. Harvard Bus. Sch., Cambridge, Mass.; past pres. trustees Concord (Mass.) Acad. Mem. N.Y. Yacht Club (commodore 1993-94, chmn. trustees Am.'s Cup 2000 Challenge), Chatham (Mass.) Yacht Club (vice commodore 1957), Harvard of N.Y.C., Harvard Faculty Club, Tarratine Club, Carnegie Abby Golf Club. Republican. Episcopalian. Home: PO Box 247 Bolton MA 01740-0247 E-mail: whitecap20@aol.com.

LEIGHTON, FRANCES SPATZ, writer, journalist; b. Geauga County, Ohio; m. Kendall King Hoyt, Feb. 1, 1984 (dec. Aug., 2001). Student, Ohio State U. Washington corr. Am. Weekly, Internat. News Svc.; corr. and Washington editor This Week Mag.; Washington corr. Met. Group Sunday Mags.; contbg. editor Family Weekly; free-lance journalist Metro Sunday Group, Washington. Lectr. summer confs. Dellbrook-Shenandoah Coll., Georgetown U., Washington Author over 30 books on hist. figures, celebrities, Hollywood, psychiatry, the White House and Capitol Hill, 1957—; (with Louise Pfister) I Married a Psychiatrist, 1961, (with Francois Rysovy) A Treasury of White House Cooking, 1968, (with Frank S. Caprio) How to Avoid a Nervous Breakdown, 1969, (with Mary B. Gallagher) My Life with Jacqueline Kennedy, 1969, (with Traphes Bryant) Dog Days at the White House, 1975, (with William Fishbait Miller) Fishbait—The Memoirs of the Congressional Doorkeeper, 1977, (with Lillian Rogers Parks) My 30 Years Backstairs at the White House (made into TV mini-series), 1979, (with Hugh Carter) Cousin Beedie, Cousin Hot--, My Life with the Carter Family of Plains, Georgia, 1978, (with Jerry Cammarata) The Fun Book of Fatherhood-or How the Animal Kingdom is Helping to Raise the Wild Kids at Our House, 1978, (with Natalie Golos) Coping with Your Allergies, 1979, (with Ken Hoyt) Drunk Before Noon— The Behind the Scenes Story of the Washington Press Corps, 1979, (with Louis Hurst) The Sweetest Little Club in the World, The Memoirs of the Senate Restaurateur, 1980, (with John M. Szostak) In the Footsteps of Pope John Paul II, 1980, (with Lillian Rogers Parks) The Roosevelts, a Family in Turmoil, 1981, (with June Allyson) June Allyson, 1982, (with Beverly Slater) Stranger in My Bed, 1985 (made into TV movie, 1987), The Search for the Real Nancy Reagan, 1987, (with Oscar Collier) How To Write and Sell Your First Nonfiction Book, 1990, How to Write and Sell Your First Novel, 1986, rev. edit., 1998, (with Stephen M. Bauer) At Ease at the White House, 1991; contbr. numerous feature stories on polit., social and govtl. personalities to various publs. Bd. dirs. Nat. Found., from 1963. Recipient Edgar award, 1961 Mem. Senate Periodical Corr. Assn., White House Corr. Assn., Am. News Women's Club, The Writers Club, Nat. Press Club, Writers League of Washington (pres.), Washington League Am. Pen Women (pres.), Washington Ind. Writers, Smithsonian Assocs., Nat. Trust Historic Preservation, Lake Barcroft Women's Club, Delta Phi Delta, Sigma Delta Chi. Unitarian Universalist. Office: Lake Barcroft 6336 Lakeview Dr Falls Church VA 22041-1331

LEIGHTON, GEORGE NEVES, retired federal judge; b. New Bedford, Mass., Oct. 22, 1912; s. Antonio N. and Anna Sylvia (Garcia) Leitao; m. Virginia Berry Quivers, June 21, 1942; children: Virginia Anne, Barbara Elaine. AB, Howard U., 1940; LLB, Harvard U., 1946; LLD, Elmhurst Coll., 1964; LLD., John Marshall Law Sch., 1973; LLD, Southeastern Mass. U., 1975, New Eng. U. Sch. Law, 1978, R.I. Coll., 1992, So. New Eng. Sch. Law, 2000; LLD (hon.), Loyola U., Chgo., 1989. Bar: Mass. 1946, Ill. 1947, U.S. Supreme Ct. 1958. Ptnr. Moore, Ming & Leighton, Chgo., 1951-59, McCoy, Ming & Leighton, Chgo., 1959-64; judge Cook County Circuit Ct., 1964-69, Ill. Appeals Ct. (1st cir.), 1969-76; U.S. dist. judge U.S. Dist. Ct. (no. dist.) Ill., 1976-86, sr. dist. judge, 1986-87; ret.; of counsel Earl L. Neal & Assocs., 1987—. Adj. prof. John Marshall Law Sch., Chgo., 1965—; commr., mem. character and fitness com. for 1st Appellate Dist., Supreme Ct. Ill., 1955-63, chmn. character and fitness com., 1961-62; joint com. for revision Ill. Criminal Code, 1959-63; chmn. Ill. adv. com. U.S. Commn. on Civil Rights, 1964; mem. pub. rev. bd. UAW, AFL-CIO, 1961-70; Asst. atty. gen. State of Ill., 1950-51; pres. 3d Ward Regular Democratic Orgn., Cook County, Ill., 1951-53; v.p. 21st Ward, 1964; spl. counsel to chmn. bd. Chgo. Transit Authority, 1988. Contbr. articles to legal jours. Bd. dirs. United Ch. Bd. for Homeland Ministries, United Ch. of Christ, Grant Hosp., Chgo.; trustee U. Notre Dame, 1979-83, trustee emeritus, 1983—; bd. overseers Harvard Coll., 1983-89. Capt., inf. AUS, 1942-45. Decorated Bronze Star; recipient Civil Liberties award Ill. div. ACLU, 1961, U.S. Supreme Ct. Justice John Paul Stevens award, 2000, Father Agustus Tolton awardCath. Archdioceses Chgo., 2000; named Chicagoan of Year in Law and Judiciary Jr. Assn. Commerce and Industry, 1964, Laureate, Acad. Ill. Lawyers, 2000. Fellow ABA (chmn. coun. 1976, mem. coun. sect. legal edn. and admissions to bar), Am. Coll. Trial Lawyers; mem. NAACP (chmn. legal redress com. Chgo. br.), John Howard Assn. (bd. dirs.), Chgo. Bar Assn., Ill. Bar Assn. (joint com. mem. for revision jud. article 1959-62, sr. counselor 1996), Nat. Harvard Law Sch. Assn. (mem. coun.), Howard U. Chgo. Alumni Club (chmn. bd. dirs.), Phi Beta Kappa. Office: Earl L Neal & Assocs Ste 2300 203 N LaSalle St Chicago IL 60601-1213

LEIGHTON, JACK RICHARD, small business owner, former educator; b. Boise, Idaho, May 10, 1918; s. Ralph Waldo and Lucia Marie (Strub) L.; m. Helen Louise Wirtenberger, July 24, 1942; 1 child, James Carl. Student, U. Wash., 1938-39; BS, U. Oreg., 1941, MS, 1942, PhD, 1954; postgrad., U. Iowa, 1950. Dir. phys. edn. and athletics Montpelier (Idaho) H.S., 1941-42; exec. asst. phys. medicine rehab. svc. Vancouver (Wash.) VA Hosp., 1946-50; assoc. prof. phys. edn. Pa. State U., State College, 1952-53; assoc. prof. Ea. Wash. U., Cheney, 1953-56, prof., 1956-81, dir. divsn. health, phys. edn., recreation and athletics, 1953-81; pres. Leighton Flexometer Co. Inc., Spokane, Wash., 1985—. Mem. com. on secondary sch. health and phys. edn. Idaho Dept. Edn., Boise, 1942; cons. state adv. com. on sch. activity and phys. edn. Wash. Dept. Pub. Instrn., Olympia, 1954-55, mem. com. on phys. edn. curriculum guide, 1957-58. Author: Physical Education for Boys, 1942, Objective Physical Education, 1946, Progressive Weight Training, 1961, Fitness, Body Development & Sports Conditioning Through Weight Training, 1983; assoc. editor Rsch. Quar. AAHPERD, 1960-63, Jour. Health, Phys. Edn. and Recreation, 1967-68; editor Jour. Assn. for Phys. and Mental Rehab., 1963-67; mem. editl. bd. Am. Corrective Therapy Jour., 1972-79; contbr. articles to profl. jours., chpts. to books; patentee instrument to measure range of joint motion. Mem. Ea. Wash. U. Retirees Bd., 1996-99; mem. Spokane County Cmty. Svcs. Devel. Disabilities Adv. Bd., 2000—. With AUS, 1942-46. Fellow Am. Coll. Sports Medicine; mem. AAHPERD (necrology com. 1955-58, chmn. fitness sect. 1960-61, mem. rsch. coun., com. to study purpose and propose revisions of structure and procedures gen. divsn. 1960-61; mem. N.W. dist. honor awards com. 1955-57, 76-79, chmn. 1976-77, mem. constn. com. 1957-60, chmn. rsch. sect. 1957-58, v.p. phys. edn. 1957-58, chmn. fitness sect. 1963-64, pres. 1971-72), Wash. Assn. Health, Phys. Edn. and Recreation (phys. fitness steering com. 1955-57, constn. com. 1957-58, chmn. tchr. tng. sect. 1956-57, phys. fitness steering com. 1957-59, v.p. ea. dist. 1957-58, pres. 1959-60), Spokane United Sch. Groups (Ea. Wash. U. rep. 1957-60), Spokane Area C. of C. (small bus. coun. 1993—), Phi Delta Kappa, Phi Epsilon Kappa. Home and Office: 1321 E 55th Ave Spokane WA 99223-6311

LEIGHTON, KIM GREGORY, information systems specialist; b. St. Louis, May 13, 1952; s. James Leland and Rosemary Dolores (Schroll) L. BA in Biology, U. Mo., 1974, MBA, 1976, MS in Mgmt. Info. Systems, 1986. CPA, Mo. Auditor Ernst & Whinney, St. Louis, 1976-79; sr. auditor Anheuser-Busch Cos., 1979-81; fin. analyst Seven-Up Co., 1981-82, mgmt. info. systems field coordinator, 1982-85; asst. controller Amedco, Inc., Chesterfield, Mo., 1985-86, dir. acctg. and adminstrn., 1986-87, dir. infosystems and tech., 1987-88; MIS dir. York Products, Inc., Houston, 1988-90, The York Group Inc., Houston, 1990-97, cons., 1998; v.p. Sapphire Sys., Ltd., St. Louis, 1998—. Cons. Cen. Med. Ctr., St. Louis, 1979-80, Seven-Up Co., 1985-86. Mem. Backers of St. Louis Repertory Theatre, Friends of St. Louis Art Mus., Friends of St. Louis Zoo, Mo. Bot. Garden, Laumeier Sculpture Park. Mem. AICPA, Inst. Econometric Rsch., Mensa, U. Mo. at St. Louis Alumni Assn., Beta Gamma Sigma, Beta Alpha Psi. Roman Catholic. Avocations: tennis, music, movies, reading, jogging. Home: 535 Fee Fee Hills Dr Hazelwood MO 63042-2812 Office: Sapphire Sys Ltd 8747 Big Bend Blvd Saint Louis MO 63119-3729 E-mail: kimleighton@netzero.net.

LEIGHTON, LAWRENCE WARD, investment banker; b. N.Y.C., July 1, 1934; s. Sidney and Florence (Ward) L.; m. Mariana Stroock, June 21, 1959; children: Sandra L. Galvin, Michelle S. Wykoff. BSE, Princeton U., 1956; MBA, Harvard U., 1962. V.p. Kuhn Loeb & Co., N.Y.C., 1962-69, Clark, Dodge & Co., Inc., 1970-74; dir. Norton-Simon, Inc., 1974-78; ltd. ptnr. Bear, Stearns & Co., 1978-82; mng. dir. Chase Investment Bank, 1983-88; pres., CEO Union d'Etudes et d'Investissements Mcht. Bank of Credit Agricole, 1989-93; vice-chmn. 2I, Inc., 1993-94; mng. dir. LM Capital Corp., 1994-96; sr. advisor Bentley Assocs., LP, 1997—. Dir. Corp. Renaissance Group, 1994-2000; chmn. Princeton Schs. Com. of N.Y., 1965-85. Mem. exec. com. Princeton U. Alumni Coun., 1975-80; mem. exec. com. alumni coun. The Lawrenceville Sch., 1999—; vice-chmn. nat. schs. com. Princeton U., 1980—; chmn. Harvard Bus. Sch. Fund of N.Y., 1964-65; mem. nat. fin. com. Pete DuPont for Pres., 1986-88; trustee Waterford Inst., 1985—. Lt. (j.g.) USN, 1957-60. Mem. Stanwich Club (Greenwich, Conn.), Princeton Club of N.Y. (scholarship com. 1970—, bd. govs. 1989-96), Coral Beach and Tennis Club (Bermuda). Avocations: flying, golf, photography. Home: 1088 Park Ave New York NY 10128-1132 Office: Bentley Assocs Rm 2200 101 Park Ave New York NY 10178-2101 E-mail: lwleighton@bentleylp.com.

LEIGHTON, LESLIE STEVEN, gastroenterologist; b. N.Y.C., Jan. 18, 1952; s. Fred Victor and Sitty (Hess) L.; m. Deborah Gilda Perl, Apr. 25, 1982; children: Andrew David, Lauren Sophia, Jennifer Ellen, Rachel Johanna. BA with high distinction, U. Va., 1974; MD, Johns Hopkins U., 1978. Diplomate Am. Bd. Internal Medicine, Am. Bd. Gastroenterology. Intern, then resident in medicine NYU-Bellevue Hosp., N.Y.C., 1978-81; gastroenterology fellow Brigham and Women's Hosp., Boston, 1981-84; teaching asst. NYU Sch. Medicine, N.Y.C., 1980-81; clin. fellow Harvard Med. Sch., Boston, 1981-83, rsch. fellow, 1983-84; pvt. practice Peachtree Gastroenterology, P.C., Atlanta, 1984—; clin. instr. Emory U. Sch. Medicine, 1986-90, clin. asst. prof. medicine, 1990—. Chmn. dept. internal medicine Ga. Bapt. Med. Ctr., 1991-94; asst. clin. prof. medicine Med. Coll. Ga., 1992—; staff physician Piedmont Hosp., Atlanta, 1984—. Vice chmn. Nat. Found. Ileitis and Colitis, Atlanta, 1989-91, chmn., 1991-93. Mem. AMA, Med. Assn. Atlanta, Am. Gastroenterol. Assn., Am. Coll. Physicians, Am. Coll. Gastroenterology, Druid Hills Golf Club, Buckhead Club. Avocation: golf. Fax: 404-352-3256. E-mail: leslieleighton@jhu.edu.

LEIGHTON, RICHARD FREDERICK, retired dean; BA, Western Md. Coll., 1951; MD, U. Md., 1955; ScD (hon.), Med. Coll. Ohio, Toledo, 2000. Diplomate Am. Bd. Internal Medicine (Specialty Cardiovascular Disease). Intern U. Hosp., Balt., 1955—56; flight surgeon USN, 1956—58; resident Ohio State U. Hosp., 1959—61, resident, cardiology fellow, 1961—64; from asst. prof. to assoc. prof. medicine Coll. Medicine Ohio State U., 1965—74, dir. coronary care unit, 1968—69, dir. cardiac catheterization labs., 1970—74; prof. medicine, chief cardiology Med. Coll. Ohio, 1974—90, acting chmn. dept. medicine, 1988, vice chmn., 1988—90, v.p. acad. affairs, dean Sch. Medicine, 1990—95, sr. v.p. acad. affairs, dean Sch. Medicine, 1995—96, emeritus, ret., 1997; prof. medicine Mercer U. Med. Sch., 1998—; chmn. instnl. rev. bd. Meml. Health U. Med. Ctr., 1998—. Editl. bd. La Lettre du Cardiologue, 1985—; contbr. numerous articles to profl. jours. Fellow ACP, Am. Coll. Cardiology (gov. Ohio chpt. 1985-88), Am. Heart Assn (coun. circulation, epidemiology, clinical cardiology, coun. rep. Ohio 1977-80), Royal Soc. Medicine; mem. Ctrl. Soc. Clin. Rsch., Societe Francaise Cardiologie (corr.), Alpha Omega Alpha. Office: Meml Health U Med Ctr Dept Internal Med Edn PO Box 23089 Savannah GA 31403-3089 E-mail: rflfsl@bellsouth.net., leighril@memorialmed.com.

LEIGHTON, ROBERT BRUCE, investment company executive; b. London, Feb. 28, 1956; s. David Straun Robertson and Helen Margaret (House) L.; m. Doreen Bernadette Jones, Dec. 6, 1991. BA with honors, U. Calgary, Can., 1977; MA in African Politics, U. London, 1980; MBA, Harvard Bus. Sch., 1984. Analyst Credit Lyonnais, Calgary, 1980-82; from officer trade fin. to asst. supr. The Bank of Nova Scotia, Toronto, Can., 1984-88; sr. fin. officer Export Devel. Corp., Ottawa, Can., 1988-90; investment officer Internat. Fin. Corp., Washington, 1990-96, resident rep. Brazil, 1996—. Bd. dirs. PISA, Jaguarive, CRP Caderi, Porto Alegre. Rep. Can. Crossroads Internat., Calgary, 1981-83; sponsor Foster Parents Plan, Toronto, 1979-91. Recipient Prix d'Honneur Banff Ctr., Alberta, Can., 1978. Mem. Inst. Fin. Execs., Harvard Bus. Sch. Club Brazil, Commonwealth Inst. Avocations: running, scuba, hiking, clarinet. Home: 1818 H St NW # Ifc-res Washington DC 20433-0001 Office: Internat Fin Corp Rua Guararapes 2064 04561004 Sao Paolo Brazil also: Leighton and World Bank 1818 H St NW # Ifc Washington DC 20433-0001 E-mail: BLeighton@IFC.org.

LEIGHTON, ROBERT JOSEPH, state legislator; b. Austin, Minn., July 7, 1965; s. Robert Joseph Sr. and JoAnn (Mulvihill) L. BA, U. Minn., 1988; JD, U. Calif., Berkeley, 1991. Minn. state rep. Dist. 27B, 1995—. Presdl. and Waller scholar U. Minn., 1988. Mem. ABA, Minn. Bar Assn., Minn. Trial Lawyers Assn., Phi Beta Kappa. Home: 900 4th St NW Austin MN 55912-2001 Office: Leighton Meany Cotter & Enger 601 N Main St Austin MN 55912-3319

LEIGHTON, WILLIAM D. plastic and reconstructive surgeon; b. Battle Creek, Mich., Sept. 27, 1952; m. Judith Peltier, July 2, 1976; children: Joshua, Jason. BA, U. Colo., 1974; MD, U. Ill., 1978. Diplomate Am. Bd. Plastic Surgery. Intern Phoenix Integrated Surg. Residency, 1978, gen. surgery resident, 1979-83, resident in plastic surgery, 1983-85; micro-surgery fellow So. Ill. U., 1985; chief plastic surgery Good Samaritan Hosp., Phoenix, 1988-93, Phoenix Children's Hosp., 1989-92, Maricopa Med. Ctr., 1987-91, Scottsalde (Ariz.) Meml. North, 1994—. Mem. Ariz. Soc. Plastic and Reconstructive Surgeons (pres.), Am. Soc. Plastic Surgeons, Am. Soc. Aesthetic Plastic Surgery. Office: 10210 N 92d St # 200 Scottsdale AZ 85258

LEIGHTTY, SHARON HOWERTON, artist, fine arts educator; b. Springfield, Mo., Sept. 29, 1954; d. Jerry Lee and Doris Laverne (Mallard) H.; m. Michael Wayne Wooden, Mar. 21, 1974 (div.); children: Kenton, Kelly; m. David Lindsay Leightty, June 22, 1991; stepchildren: April, Paul. BA with honors, U. Louisville, 1989; MFA, Ind. U., 1993. Art glass designer, pub. rels. specialist Fenestra Art Glass Studio, Louisville, 1986-88; asst. dept. edn. U. Louisville, 1989-90; grad. asst. fine arts Ind. U., 1990-92, tchg. asst., 1992-93; instr. Ind. U. Southeast, New Albany, 1995-96; instr. fine arts U. Louisville, 1993—, vis. asst. prof., 2000—01. Juror scholastic art awards Jefferson County Schs., Louisville, 1996, 97. Artist drawings (Purchase award 1991, Merit award 1995, Siegfried Weng Purchase award, 1998). Presentation cons. Jefferson County Office for Women, Louisville, 1997; contbr. art auction Louisville Visual Art Assn., 1990—; co-leader Louisville Women's Issues Group, 1990-95; organizer workshop First Unitarian Ch., Louisville, 1994.

Fellow artist fellow, Ky. Arts Coun., 2002; grantee, Ky. Found. Women, 1996, U. Louisville, 1996, rsch. on women grantee, 1998, women's ctr. cmty. bldg. grantee, 1999; scholar Della Fricke scholar for Art Educators, Ind. U., 1992. Mem. reg. coord. Foundations in Art Theory and Edn. (presenter conf. 1996), Women's Caucus for Art, Women's Drawing Group, panel mem. women's history conf., Ky. State U. Democrat. Office: Allen R Hite Art Inst U Louisville Louisville KY 40292-0001

LEIJONHUFVUD, AXEL STIG BENGT, economics educator; b. Stockholm, Sweden, Sept. 6, 1933; came to U.S., 1960; s. Erik Gabriel and Helene Adelheid (Neovius) L.; m. Marta Elisabeth Ising, June 10, 1955 (div. 1977); m. Earlene Joyce Craver, June 18, 1977; children— Carl Axel, Gabriella Helene, Christina Elisabeth Fil. kand., U. Lund, Sweden, 1960; MA, U. Pitts., Pa., 1961; PhD, Northwestern U., 1967; Fil. Dr. (hon.), U. Lund, Sweden, 1983; Dr. (hon.), U. Nice, Sophia-Antipolis, France, 1995. Acting asst. prof. econs. UCLA, 1964-67, assoc. prof. econs., 1967-71, prof. econs., 1971—, chair dept. econs., 1980-83, 90-92; dir. Ctr. for Computable Econs., 1992-97; prof. monetary theory and policy U. Trento, Italy, 1995—. Co-dir. summer workshops Siena Internat. Sch. Econ. Rsch., 1987-91; participant numerous profl. confs.; cons., lectr., vis. prof. econs. various colls. and univs.; cons. Republic of Tatarstan, 1994. Author: On Keynesian Economics and the Economics of Keynes: A Study in Monetary Theory, 1968, Keynes and the Classics: Two Lectures, 1969, Information and Coordination: Essays in Macroeconomic Theory, 1981; co-author (with D. Heymann): High Inflation, 1995, Macroeconomic Instability and Coordination, Selected Essays, 2000; editor: Monetary Theory as a Basis for Monetary Policy, 2001, Monetary Theory and Policy Experience, 2001. Mem. econ. expert com. of pres. Kazakhstan, 1991-92. Brookings Instn. fellow, 1963-64; Marshall lectr. Cambridge U., Eng., 1974; Overseas fellow Churchill Coll., Cambridge, 1974; Inst. Advanced Study fellow, 1983-84 Mem. Am. Econ. Assn., Western Econ. Assn., History of Econs. Soc. Office: UCLA Dept Econs Los Angeles CA 90024 E-mail: axel@ucla.edu.

LEIKEN, EARL MURRAY, lawyer; b. Cleve., Jan. 19, 1942; s. Manny and Betty G. L.; m. Ellen Kay Miner, Mar. 26, 1970; children: Jonathan, Brian. BA magna cum laude, Harvard U., 1964, JD cum laude, 1967. Asst. dean, assoc. prof. law Case Western Res. U., Cleve., 1967-71; ptnr. Hahn, Loeser, Freedheim, Dean & Wellman, 1971-86, Baker & Hostetler, Cleve., 1986—. Adj. faculty, lectr. law Case Western Res. U., 1971-86. Pres. Shaker Heights (Ohio) Bd. Edn., 1986-88, Jewish Community Ctr., Cleve., 1988-91, Shaker Heights Family Ctr., 1994-97; mem. Shaker Heights City Coun., 2000—. Named one of Greater Cleve.'s 10 Outstanding Young Leaders, Cleve. Jaycees, 1972; recipient Kane award Cleve. Jewish Community Fedn., 1982. Mem. ABA, Greater Cleve. Bar Assn. (chmn. labor law sect. 1978). Home: 20815 Colby Rd Cleveland OH 44122-1903 Office: Baker & Hostetler 3200 Nat City Ctr 1900 E 9th St Ste 3200 Cleveland OH 44114-3475

LEIKHIM, NANCE, artist; b. Indpls., Mar. 23, 1949; d. Joseph Henry and Elizabeth Elaine (Kreider) L.; m. Dennis Craig Dunn, June 2, 1984 (div. July 1995); m. C. Philip Crampton, June 2002. AAS in Textile Design cum laude, Fashion Inst. Tech., N.Y.C., 1969; student, Truckee Meadows C.C., Sparks, Nev., 1977, Sierra Coll., 1990, 93. Colorist Cranston Print Works, Co., N.Y.C., 1968; freelance needlepoint designer Chgo., Colorado Springs, 1970-74; art dir./graphic designer Denver and Reno, Nev., 1975-95; computer artist Tahoe Software Prodns., Truckee, Calif., 1993-94; art cons. Gallery at Squaw Creek, Olympic Valley, 1994-95; artist-in-residence Sierra Arts Found., Reno, 1996—2001; tchr. painting Nev. Mus. of Art, 1998—2000. Artist: (paintings) Big Bang: Life:Inspiration:Art, 1992, Image: Imagine:Reflection:Reflect, 1996, The River, 2000; solo shows at No. Calif. Ctr. for the Arts, Grass Valley, North Tahoe Art Ctr., Tahoe City, Calif., Sierra Arts, Reno, Nev., 2001. Grantee Nev. County Arts Coun. and NEA, Truckee, Calif., 1993-94, awards Calif. Discovery Art of Calif. mag., 1993, 94, Northstar's 15th Ann. Fine Arts Show, 1993. Mem. Sierra Artists' Network, Nev. Arts Coun. Avocations: gardening, hiking, skiing. Home: 15257 Icknield Way Truckee CA 96161-1320

LEIKIN, MITCHELL, retired judge; b. Chgo., July 31, 1921; s. Irving and Fannie Leikin; m. Evelyn Leikin, Aug. 10, 1952; children: Jerrold Blair, Robin Cheryl Pomeroy. BS, U. Ill., 1943; JD, DePaul U., 1949. Pvt. practice law, 1950; judge Cir. Ct. of Cook County, Chgo., 1980—2000; ret. Comdr. USNR, 1943—81. Mem.: Decalogue Soc. Lawyers (bd. dirs.), N.W. Suburban Bar Assn., North Suburban Bar Assn. (pres. 1968), Ill. Judges Assn. Home: 8909 Kolmar Ave Skokie IL 60076-1835

LEIMAN, JOAN MAISEL, hospital and university administrator, hospital administrator; b. Rochester, Minn., Apr. 26, 1934; d. John Josiah and Ida (Rubenstein)Maisel; m. Leonard M. Leiman June 26, 1955; children: Elizabeth, Alan. BA, Wellesley (Mass.) Coll., 1955; MA, Columbia U., 1958, MPhil, 1976, PhD, 1977. Prog. analyst N.Y.C. Bur. Budget, 1966-68, sr. budget examiner, 1968-69, asst. budget dir., 1969-71; advisor to Mayor N.Y.C. Govt., Office of Mayor, 1972-74; v.p. prog. devel. and budget Manpower Demonstration Research Corp., N.Y.C., 1977-81; v.p. planning Interfaith Med. Ctr., 1982-84; exec. dep. v.p. Columbia U. Health Scis., 1984-2001; chief of staff to the pres. and CEO, N.Y. Presbyn. Hosp. and Healthcare Sys., 2001—. Clin. prof. pub. health Columbia U., 1991—; pres. past. pres. Grad. Facules, Alumni of Columbia U., 1985-91; dir., vice chair N.Y. Found., 1985-93; del. White House Conf. on Aging, 1995; exec. dir. Commonwealth Fund Commn. on Women's Health, 1993-99; cons. in field. Durant scholar, 1954-55. Fellow: N.Y. Acad. Medicine (chair sect. health care delivery); mem.: Women's Health Forum, Am. Med. Women's Assn. Found. (bd. dirs. 1999—2001), Am. Assn. Med. Colls., Health Care Exec. Forum (v.p. 1986—87), YMCA Acad. Women Achievers, Women's City Club, Phi Beta Kappa. Office: NY Presbyn Hosp AP-1466 161 Ft Washington Ave New York NY 10032-3795

LEIMAS, CAROL ANN, women's association consultant; b. N.Y.C., Sept. 12, 1931; d. Reuben and Lillian (Segall) Chauls; m. Irwin Leimas, Oct. 18, 1963; 1 child, Stacie. AB, Syracuse U., 1952; Certificat D'etudes Politiques, L'Inst. D'etudes Politiques, Paris, 1953. Researcher Anti-Defamation League, N.Y.C., 1953-55; inquiry specialist World Affairs Ctr., 1955-58; dir. info. reference dept. Fgn. Policy Assn., 1958-67; U.N. rep. AAUW, Washington, 1969-84. Cons. AAUW, 1984-86, N.Y.C. Commn. on the Status of Women, 1985, Assn. for Women in Devel., N.Y.C., 1988; bd. dirs. Conf. of U.N. Reps., 1975-85, pres., 1977-80. Mem. U.N. Assn. of the U.S. (bd. dirs. 1975-85), Women's City Club of N.Y. (bd. dirs. 1987-2002, program chair 1988-97, v.p. 1997-98, bd. dirs. Metro N.Y. chpt., U.S. com. for Unifem 1981—), Phi Beta Kappa.

LEIMKUHLER, FERDINAND FRANCIS, industrial engineering educator; b. Balt., Dec. 31, 1928; s. Ferdinand Frank and Louise (Kimmel) L.; m. Natalie Therese Morin, July 4, 1956; children: Kristin, Margaret, Jeanne, Benedict, Thomas, Ernest. BS cum laude, Loyola Coll., Balt., 1950; B.Engring., Johns Hopkins U., 1952, D.Engring. with distinction, 1962. Mgmt. engr. E.I. DuPont de Nemours & Co., Inc., 1950-57; research engr. Johns Hopkins U., 1957-61; prof. indsl. engring. Purdue U., 1961-99, head Sch. Indsl. Engring., 1969-74, 81-93, dir. tech. assistance program, 1993-96; ret., 1999. Vis. prof. U. Calif., Berkeley, 1968-69, 90; vis. prof. (Fulbright-Hayes sr. lectr.), U. Ljubljana, Slovenia, 1974-75; cons. in field. Served with AUS, 1952-54. Fellow Inst. Indsl. Engrs.; mem. Ops. Rsch. Soc. Am., Inst. Mgmt. Scis., Am. Soc. Engring. Edn., Sigma Xi, Alpha Sigma Nu, Tau Beta Pi.

LEIMKUHLER, GERARD JOSEPH, JR. financial holding company executive; b. Phila., June 13, 1948; s. Gerard Joseph and Dorothy Joan (Gaffney) L.; m. Karen Roberta Hall, Oct. 13, 1973; 1 child, Courtney Hall BBA, Temple U., 1970. Mem. Phila. Stock Exch., 1971-75; v.p. Oxford First Corp., Phila., 1975-82, sr. v.p., 1982-87, exec. v.p., 1987-93, vice chmn., 1993—; sr. v.p., sec. Oxford Communities, Inc., Oxford Fin. Cos. Inc., 1985-87, exec. v.p., sec., 1987-93, vice chmn., 1993-95; pres. Gen. Acquistions Corp., Phila., 1977-95; chmn., pres. chief officer Eagle Capital Corp. and Eagle Capital Mortgage, Ltd., 1997—; mng. dir. Barwyn Capital Group, 1995—. Vice-chmn. Newtown Twp. Planning Commn., Delaware County, Pa., 1976-77, 84—, chmn., 1995-98; chmn. investment adv. bd. Newtown Twp. Investment, 1987—. With U.S. Army, 1970-71. Mem. Internat. Found. for Timesharing (chmn. investment com.) 1990, Turnaround Mgmt. Assn. Phila. (bd. dirs., treas.), Urban Land Inst., Am. Resort Devel. Assn., Mensa, Aronimink Golf Club. Republican. Roman Catholic. Office: 170 Hunt Valley Circle Berwyn PA 19312

LEINEN, MARGARET SANDRA, oceanographic researcher; b. Chgo., Sept. 20, 1946; d. Earl John and Ester (Louis) Leinen; 1 child, Daniel Glenn Whaley. BS, U. Ill., 1969; MS, Oreg. State U., 1975; PhD, U. R.I., Kingston, 1980. Marine scientist U. R.I., Kingston, 1980-82, asst. rsch. prof., 1982-86, assoc. prof., 1986-88, prof., 1988—, assoc. dean, 1988-92, dean and vice provost, 1992—; asst. dir. geoscis. NSF, Alexandria, Va. Office: NSF 4201 Wilson Blvd Rm 705N Arlington VA 22230-0001 E-mail: mleinen@nsf.gov.

LEINENWEBER, HARRY D. federal judge; b. Joliet, Ill., June 3, 1937; s. Harry Dean and Emily (Lennon) L.; m. Lynn Morley Martin, Jan. 7, 1987; 5 children; 2 stepchildren. AB cum laude, U. Notre Dame, 1959; JD, U. Chgo., 1962. Bar: Ill. 1962, U.S. Dist. Ct. (no. dist.) Ill. 1967. Assoc. Dunn, Stefanich, McGarry & Kennedy, Joliet, Ill., 1962-65, ptnr., 1965-79; city atty. City of Joliet, 1963-67; spl. counsel Village of Park Forest, Ill., 1967-74; spl. prosecutor County of Will, 1968-70; spl. counsel Village of Bolingbrook, 1975-77, Will County Forest Preserve, 1977; mem. Ill. Ho. of Reps., Springfield, 1973-83, chmn. judiciary I com., 1981-83; ptnr. Dunn, Leinenweber & Dunn, Joliet, 1979-86; fed. judge U.S. Dist. Ct. (no. dist.) Ill., Chgo., 1986—. Bd. dirs. Will County Bar Assn., 1984-86, State Jud. Adv. Coun., 1973-85, sec. 1975-76; tchr. legis. process seminar U. Ill., Chgo., 1988-2001; coord. U. Ill. Disting. Lecture Series, 2002--; mem. U. Ill. Inst. Govt. and Pub. Affairs Nat. Adv. Com., 1998-2001. Bd. dirs. Will County Legal Assistance Found., 1982-86, Good Shepard Manor, 1981—, Am. Cancer Soc., 1981-85, Joliet (Ill.) Montessori Sch., 1966-74; del. Rep. Nat. Conv., 1980; precinct committeeman, 1966-86; mem. nat. adv. com. U. Ill. Inst. Govt. and Pub. Affairs, 1998-2001. Recipient Environ. Legislator Golden award. Mem. Will County Bar Assn. (mem. jud. adv. coun., 1973-85, sec. 1975-76, bd. dirs. 1984-86), Nat. Conf. Commrs. on Uniform State Laws (exec. com. 1991-93, elected life mem. 1996), The Law Club of Chgo. (bd. dirs. 1996-98). Roman Catholic. Office: US Dist Ct 219 S Dearborn St Ste 1946 Chicago IL 60604-1801

LEINEWEBER, PETER ANTHONY, forest products company executive; b. Portland, Oreg., Sept. 28, 1944; s. Peter Cornelius and Isabel (Brown) L.; m. Heidi Milly Baxter, July 14, 1978; children: John James, Joseph Stephen, Thomas Gregory. BS, Portland State U., 1968; MBA, U. Wash., 1970. Loan officer U.S. Nat. Bank Oreg., Portland, 1962-69; mgr. Pacific N.W. Bell, 1970-76; sr. v.p. Market Transport, Ltd., 1976-90; v.p. Crown Pacific, 1990—; pres. Yellowstone Trucking, L.P., Coeur d'Alene, Idaho, 1998-2000. Dir. TOC Mgmt. Svcs., Tigard, Oreg. Bd. dirs. SOLV. Mem. Multnomah Athletic Club, University Club, Arlington Club. Republican. Roman Catholic. Avocations: youth activities, volunteer work. Office: Crown Pacific 121 SW Morrison St Ste 1500 Portland OR 97204-3160

LEINIEKS, VALDIS, classicist, educator; b. Liepaja, Latvia, Apr. 15, 1932; came to U.S., 1949, naturalized, 1954; s. Arvid Ansis and Valia Leontine (Brunaus) L. BA, Cornell U., 1955, MA, 1956; PhD, Princeton U., 1962. Instr. classics Cornell Coll., Mount Vernon, Iowa, 1959-62, asst. prof. classics, 1962-64; assoc. prof. classics Ohio State U., 1964-66, U. Nebr., Lincoln, 1966-71, prof. classics, 1971—, chmn. dept. classics, 1967-95, chmn. program comparative lit., 1970-86, interim chmn. dept. modern langs., 1982-83. Author: Morphosyntax of the Homeric Greek Verb, 1964, The Structure of Latin, 1975, Index Nepotianus, 1976, The Plays of Sophokles, 1982, The City of Dionysos, 1996; contbr. articles to profl. jours. Mem. AAUP, Am. Classical League, Classical Assn. Middle West and South, Am. Philol. Assn. Home: 2505 A St Lincoln NE 68502-1841 Office: U Nebr Dept Classics Lincoln NE 68588-0337

LEININGER, MADELEINE MONICA, nursing educator, editor, writer; b. Sutton, Nebr., July 13, 1925; d. George M. S. and D. Irene (Sheedy) L. BS in Biology, Scholastic Coll., 1950, LHD, 1976; MS in Nursing, Cath. U. Am., 1953; PhD in Anthropology, U. Wash., 1965; DSc (hon.), U. Indpls., 1990; PhDN (hon.), 1990, U. Kuopio, Finland, 1991. RN; cert. transcultural nurse FAAN/Am. Acad. Nursing. Instr., mem. staff, head nurse med.-surg. unit, supr. psychiat. unit St. Joseph's Hosp., Omaha, 1950-54; assoc. prof. nursing, dir. grad. program in psychiat. nursing U. Cin. Coll. Nursing, 1954-60; research fellow Nat. League Nursing, Eastern Highlands of New Guinea, 1960-62, 78, 92; research assoc. U. Wash. Dept. Anthropology, Seattle, 1964-65; prof. nursing and anthropology, dir. nurse-scientist PhD program U. Colo., Boulder and Denver, 1966-69; dean sch. nursing, prof. nursing, lectr. anthropology U. Wash., Seattle, 1969-74; dean coll. nursing, prof. nursing and anthropology U. Utah, Salt Lake City, 1974-80; Anise J. Sorell prof. nursing Troy (Ala.) State U., 1981; prof. nursing, adj. prof. anthropology, dir. Ctr. for Health Research, dir. transcultural nursing offerings Wayne State U., Detroit, 1981-95, prof. emeritus, 1995—; prof. Coll. Nursing U. Nebr. Med. Ctr., 1997—2001; ret., 2001—. Adj. prof. anthropology U. Utah, 1974-81; adj. prof. nursing U. Nebr., 1997—; disting. vis. prof. over 85 univs., U.S. and overseas, 1970—; transcultural nursing cons. Saudi Arabia, Brazil, Europe, Japan, China, Burnei, Indonesia, South Africa, Sweden, The Netherlands, New Guinea, Australia, Jordan, Thailand, Russia, Iran, Africa, Taiwan, Portugal, Switzerland, Puerto Rico, Norway, Phuket, 60 health instns. in U.S., numerous others. Author: 28 books including Nursing and Anthropology: Two Worlds to Blend, 1970, Contemporary Issues in Mental Health Nursing, 1973, Caring: An Essential Human Need, 1981, Reference Sources for Transcultural Health and Nursing, 1984, Basic Psychiatric Concepts in Nursing, 1960, Care: The Essence of Nursing and Health, 1984, Qualitative Research Methods in Nursing, 1985, Care: Discovery and Clinical-Community Uses, 1988, Ethical and Moral Dimensions of Caring, 1990, Culture Care, Diversity and Universality: A Theory of Nursing, 1991, 2002, Care: The Compassionate Healer, 1991, Caring Imperative for Nursing Education, 1991, Transcultural Nursing 2d edit., 1995, Transcultural Nursing Concepts, Theories, Research and Practice, 3d edit., 2002; editor, founder Jour. of Transcultural Nursing, 1988-2000; contbr. over 210 articles to profl. jours., chpts. to books. Recipient Outstanding Alumni award Cath. U. Am., 1969, hon. award Am. Assn. Colls. of Nursing, 1976, 96, Nurse of Yr. award Dist. 1 Utah Nurses Assn., 1976, Lit. award Utah Nurses Assn., 1978, Trotter Disting. Pub. Lectr. award U. Tex., 1985, Disting. Faculty Tchg. Recognition award Wayne State U., 1985, Outstanding Faculty Rsch. scholar award Wayne State U. and Gerontology Inst., 1985, Gershenson Rsch. award Wayne State U., 1985, Pace Inst. Rsch. award, 1992, Hewlett Packard Rsch. award, 1992, award for Acad. Excellence AAUW-Detroit, 1986, Disting. award Bd. Govs., 1987, Pres. Excellence in Tchg. award, 1988, Women of Sci. award U. Calif. at Fullerton, 1990, Outstanding Univ. Grad. Mentor award Wayne State U., 1995, Nightingale Rsch. award Oakland U., 1995, outstanding nursing leader Russell Sage Coll, Sigma Theta Tau Intl. Disting. scholar award Russell Sage Coll., 1995, Nobel prize nominee, 1999; Leininger Learning and Transcultural Nursing Collection libr. and reading sects. at Madonna U., Livonia, Mich. named in her honor, 1996; Leininger Archival Room at Trinity Coll., Moline, Ill. named in her honor, 2002; Mary Boynton Disting. lectr., 1998; Disting. vis. scholar Jimmy Crockett Lectr. Series, Disting. Vis. scholar U. Nebr., 1999; named Disting. scholar U. Wis., 2001, 2002; Worldwide Transcultural Nursing Ctr. named in her honor, 2001. Fellow ANA, Am. Anthropol. Soc. for Applied Anthropology (exec. com. 1980-84), Am. Acad. Nursing (Living Legend award 1998), Royal Coll. Nursing Australia (First Internat. Achievement award 2000); mem. Am. Assn. Humanities, Am. Applied Anthropol. Soc., Royal Coll. Nursing Australia, Mich. Nurses Assn. (Bertha Culp Human Rights award 1994), Ctrl. States Anthropology, Amnesty Internat., Transcultural Nursing Soc. (founder, bd. dirs., pres. 1974-80), Cultural Cmty. Group Assn. (ethics, humanities heritage study group), Nat. Rsch. Care Confs. (leader human care rsch.), Internat. Assn. Human Caring (founder, pres., bd. dirs.), Nordic Caring Soc. Sweden (hon.), Sigma Xi, Pi Gamma Mu, Sigma Theta Tau (Lectr. of Yr. 1987—), Delta Kappa Gamma, Alpha Tau Delta. Office: 11211 Woolworth Plz Omaha NE 68144-1875

LEINO, DEANNA ROSE, business educator; b. Leadville, Colo., Dec. 15, 1937; d. Arvo Ensio Leino and Edith Mary (Bonan) Leino Maleck; 1 adopted child, Michael Charles Bolan. BSBA, U. Denver, 1959, MS in Bus. Adminstrn., 1967; postgrad., C.C. Denver, U. No. Colo., Colo. State U., U. Colo., Met. State Coll. Cert. tchr., vocat. tchr., Colo. Tchr. Jefferson County Adult Edn., Lakewood, Colo., 1963-67; tchr. bus., coord. coop. office edn. Jefferson H.S., Edgewater, 1959-93, ret., 1993; sales assoc. Joslins Dept. Store, Denver, 1978—; mem. ea. team. clk. office automation Denver Svc. Ctr., Nat. Park Svc., 1993-94; wage hour technician U.S. Dept. Labor, 1994—. Instr. C.C. Denver, Red Rocks, 1967-81, U. Colo., Denver, 1976-79, Parks. Coll. Bus., (now Parks Coll.), 1983—, Front Range C.C., 1998-2000; dist. advisor Future Bus. Leaders Am. Author short story. Active City of Edgewater Sister City Project Student Exch. Com.; pres. Career Women's Symphony Guild; treas. Phantoms of Opera, 1982—; active Opera Colo. Assocs. and Guild, I Pagliacci; ex-officio trustee Denver Symphony Assn., 1980-82. Recipient Disting. Svc. award Jefferson County Sch. Bd., 1980, Tchr. Who Makes a Difference award Sta. KCNC/Rocky Mountain News, 1990, Youth Leader award Lakewood Optimist Club, 1993; inducted into Jefferson H.S. Wall of Fame, 1981; named to Jefferson County Hist. Commn. Hall of Fame, 2000, countess of the Wheat Ridge Carnation Festival, 2001. Mem. NEA (life), Colo. Edn. Assn., Jefferson County Edn. Assn., Colo. Vocat. Assn., Am. Vocat. Assn., Colo. Educators for and about Bus., Profl. Secs. Internat., Career Women's Symphony Guild, Profl. Panhellenic Assn., Colo. Congress Fgn. Lang. Tchrs., Wheat Ridge C. of C. (edn. and scholarship com.), Federally Employed Women, Tyrolean Soc. Denver, Delta Pi Epsilon, Phi Chi Theta, Beta Gamma Sigma, Alpha Lambda Delta. Republican. Roman Catholic. Avocations: decorating wedding cakes, crocheting, sewing, music, world travel. Home: 3712 Allison St Wheat Ridge CO 80033-6124 E-mail: dleino@dal.dol-esa.gov.

LEINWAND, FREDA, photographer; b. Toronto, Jan. 25, 1932; came to U.S., 1937; d. Nathan and Clara L.. Student, Columbia U., 1965-67, Rutgers U., Newark, 1951-53, New Sch., N.Y.C., 1960-62, Art Students League, 1957-58. Staff photographer, picture editor Med. Opinion and Rev., N.Y.C., 1966-68; freelance photographer, 1965—. Guest instr. Marymount Manhattan Coll., N.Y.C., 1979, 95; guest lectr. and juror. Exhibited photographs in solo shows at Harcourt, Brace, Jovanovich, N.Y.C., 1975, Radcliffe Coll., Cambridge, Mass., 1981; group shows include U. Toronto, 1972, Soho Photo Gallery, N.Y.C., 1972, Am. Inst. Graphic Arts, N.Y.C., 1976, Lowe Art Gallery/Syracuse U., 1982, Salmagundi Club, N.Y.C., 1988, Audart Gallery, 1997, Westbeth Gallery, N.Y., 1972—; represented in collections at Calif. Inst. Arts, Valencia, Taiwan Provincial Mus., Schlesinger Libr./Radcliffe Coll., Visitor Ctr. of Women's Rights Nat. Hist. Park, Seneca Falls, others; contbr. to publs. including N.Y. Times, Le Devoir, Popular Photography, Ms, Forbes, Family Health, Woman's World, Med. Econs., Scholastic Mags., Image Nation; contbr. photographs to books. Recipient Medal of Honor, Vet. Feminists of Am., 2001, Susan B. Anthony award, NOW-N.Y.C., 2002. Mem.: Profl. Women Photographers, Am. Soc. Picture Profls. Office: 463 West St New York NY 10014-2010

LEINWAND, HARRIS DONALD, lawyer; b. Mt. Vernon, N.Y., Dec. 5, 1944; s. Isidor E. and Florence M. Leinwand; 1 child, Joseph Gabriel. BA, U. Pitts., 1965; JD, Cornell U., 1968. Bar: N.Y. 1969, U.S. Dist. Ct. (so. and ea. dists.) N.Y. 1970, U.S. Ct. Appeals (2d cir.) 1982. Ptnr. Leinwand Maron Hendler & Krause, N.Y.C., 1973-80; pvt. practice, 1980—. Office: 9 E 40th St New York NY 10016-0402 E-mail: hleinwand@aol.com.

LEINWEBER, BRUCE KORNBLATT, obstetrician, gynecologist; b. Phila., Sept. 11, 1935; s. Arthur Richter and Florence (Kornblatt) L.; m. Nancy Schwartz, 1960 (dec. 1971); children: Cynthia Beth, Melanie Joy; m. Joan Halperin Glick, 1976; stepchildren: Suzanne Lynn Glick, Jennifer Beth Glick, Adam Brett Glick; 1 child, Dara Hope. BA in Biology, Lafayette Coll., 1955; DDS, Temple U., 1959; MD, Jefferson Med. Coll., 1963. Lic. dentist, N.Y., Pa.; lic. MD, Pa.; diplomate Nat. Bd. Dental Examiners, Nat. Bd. Med. Examiners, Am. Bd. Ob-gyn. Rotating intern, then resident in ob-gyn. Albert Einstein Med. Ctr., Phila., 1963-67, mem. active staff, 1967—, Rolling Hill Hosp. divsn. United Hosps. of Phila., Elkins Park, Pa., 1967-91, Frankford Hosp., Phila., 1967-91; pvt. practice ob-gyn., 1967-78, 86-00, Bensalem, Pa., 1978-91; founder Bensalem Premenstrual Syndrome Ctr., 1984; clin. asst. prof. ob-gyn. Med. Coll. Pa., Phila., 1976-91; clin. asst. prof. ob-gyn. Sch. Medicine Temple U., 1976-99; clin. asst. prof. ob-gyn. Jefferson Med. Coll., 2000—. Panelist Med. Malpractice of southeastern Pa. Contbr. articles to profl. jours. Capt. USAR, 1957-65. Ford scholar, 1951-55. Mem. AAAS, AARP, AMA, Acad. Natural Scis. Phila., Am. Assn. Gynecol. Laparascopists, Am. Assn. Sex Educators, Counselors and Therapists, Am. Coll. Ob-Gyn., Am. Fertility Soc., Fedn. State Med. Bds., Obstet. Soc. Phila., Pa. Med. Soc., Philadelphia County Med. Soc., World Med. Assn., World Affairs Coun. Phila., Zool. Soc. Phila., Assn. Vol. Sterlization, Soc. Laparoendoscopic Surgeons, Am. Soc. Colposcopy and Cervical Pathology, Phi Lambda Kappa. Democrat. Jewish. Home: 169 Fernbrook Ave Wyncote PA 19095-1506

LEIPER, ROBERT DUNCAN, local government official; b. Houston, July 22, 1953; s. William Harper Leiper and Frances Ann (Wright) Freeman; m. Glynna Dell Wilson, May 18, 1985; children: Kelsey Allison, Chad Wilson. AAS in Fire Protection, San Jacinto Coll., 1983; BA in Pub. Mgmt., U. Houston, 1988. Master fire fighter, Tex.; cert. fire protection specialist. Lt. Spring Br. Fire Dept., Houston, 1973-75; asst. svc. mgr. Archer Motor Sales, 1975-77; fire fighter Baytown (Tex.) Fire & Rescue, 1977-80, driver, 1980-83, lt., 1983-88, capt., 1988-92, fire chief, 1992—2002; asst. city mgr. City of Baytown, 2002—. Instr. Tex. A & M U., College Station, 1988-92, Lamar U., Beaumont, Tex., 1990-92. Chmn. bd. Baycoast Med. Ctr., Baytown, Tex., 1994-95. Named Exec. Fire Officer, Nat. Fire Acad.; recipient Fire Fighter of Yr. award VFW, 1987, 90. Mem. Nat. Fire Protection Assn., Tex. Fire Chief's Assn. (dir.), Baytown Profl. Fire Fighters (v.p. 1982), Hispanic C. of C., Baytown C. of C., Kiwanis Club (pres. 1994, Rookie of Yr. award 1989). Avocations: wood working, camping, photography. Office: City of Baytown PO Box 424 Baytown TX 77522-0424 E-mail: bleiper@baytown.org.

LEIPOLD, WILLIAM CHARLES, JR. plastics company executive, consultant; b. West Reading, Pa., Mar. 30, 1949; s. William Charles Sr. and Patricia (Feehan) L. BS in Chem. Engring., Ohio State U., 1972; MBA, U. Chgo., 1973. Asst. to mfg. mgr. W.R. Grace & Co., Burlington, Mass., 1973, process engr. polyfibron div. Owensboro, Ky., 1974, gen. supr. polyfibron div., 1975; mgr. dept. electronics div. Raychem Corp., Menlo Park, Calif., 1976, engring. mgr., 1977-78, U.S. product mgr. pipe protection div. Redwood City, 1978-79; plant mgr., mgr. rsch. and devel. solar div. Sealed Air Corp., Hayward, 1981; mgr. ops. Custom Coating & Laminating, Worchester, Mass., 1980; pres., chmn. Columbine Plastics Corp., Boulder, Colo., 1982—. Cons. Medac, Inc., Bethesda, Md., 1987-89, Earthcare Techs., Inc., Springfield, Va., 1997—. Pres. Waterford Homeowners Assn. Mem. AIChE (pres. 1970-72, Disting. Svc. award 1972), Soc. Plastic Engrs. (sr. mem.), Texnikoi. Clubs: Boulder Country, Lagniappe, Enology. Libertarian. Avocations: tennis, skiing, astronomy, photography. Office: Columbine Plastics Corp 3195 Bluff St Boulder CO 80301-2103

LEIPPER, DALE FREDERICK, physical oceanographer, meteorologist, educator; b. Salem, Ohio, Sept. 8, 1914; s. Robert and Myrtle (Cost) L.; m. Virginia Alma Harrison, May 14, 1942; children: Diane Louise, Janet Elizabeth, Bryan Robert, Anita Dale. BS in Edn., Wittenberg Coll., 1937, DSc (hon.), 1968; MA, Ohio State U., 1939; postgrad., UCLA, 1939-40; PhD, Scripps Instn. Oceanography, 1950. Tchr. city schs., San Diego, 1940-41; research oceanographer, tchr. Scripps Instn. Oceanography, U. Calif., 1945-49; mem. faculty dept. oceanography and meteorology Tex. A&M U., 1949-68, head dept., 1949-64, prof., 1964-68; prof., chmn. dept. oceanography Naval Postgrad. Sch., 1968-79; rsch. prof. U. Nev., 1996-97. Supr. rsch. program NSF, FAA, Internat. Geophys. Year, Office Naval Rsch.; mem. tech. panel oceanography, exec. vice chmn. meteorology panel U.S. Nat. Com. Internat. Geophys. Year; chmn. com. marine scis. So. Regional Edn. Bd., 1952-56; assoc. dir. Tex. A&M Rsch. Found., 1953-54. Contbr. articles on West Coast fog, oceanography, hurricane-ocean interaction, ocean currents to jours. in field. Served as maj. USAAF, 1941-45; weather officer, oceanographer. Mem. Am. Meteorol. Soc., Am. Geophys. Union, Am. Soc. Limnology and Oceanography (pres. 1957-58), Tex. Acad. Sci. (pres. 1955), Nat. Acad. Sci. (panel chmn. 1959-64), Marine Tech. Soc., Am. Soc. Oceanography (pres. 1967-68), U. Corp. for Atmospheric Rsch. (founding mem., bd. dirs.), The Oceanography Soc., Sigma Xi, Phi Kappa Phi. Clubs: Rotary (pres. Bryan, Tex. 1965-66). Home and Office: 716 Terra Ct Reno NV 89506-9606 E-mail: dalelr@attglobal.net.

LEIPZIG, ARTHUR, photographer, educator emeritus; b. Bklyn., Oct. 25, 1918; s. Julius M. and Esther Pearl (Rubin) L.; m. Mildred Levin, Mar. 21, 1942; children: Joel Myron, Judith Anne. Student, Photo League, 1942-43, Paul Strand Photo Workshop, 1946. Staff photographer PM newspaper, N.Y.C., 1942-46, Internat. News Photos, N.Y.C., 1946; freelance photographer, Sea Cliff, N.Y., 1946-68; prof. art, dir. photography C.W. Post Sch. of Arts, L.I. U., Greenvale, 1968-90, prof. emeritus, 1990—. Contbr. photographs to Fortune, Look, Parade, Life, Natural History, Sunday Times, also indsl. mags.; guest editor Infinity Mag., N.Y.C., 1970, mem. editorial bd., 1973-75; interview and photographs included Life Documentary Photo Book, N.Y.C., 1972, 83; exhibited works Mus. Modern Art, 1946-51, 55-58, Met. Mus. Art, 1961, 62, Nassau Mus. Art, 1975, Queens Mus. Art, 1982, Transco Gallery, Houston, 1985, Daniel Wolf Gallery, N.Y.C., Houston Foto Fest, 1986, Photo Find Gallery, Woodstock, Coll. Art Gallery, New Paltz, N.Y., Smithsonian Mus., Washington, 1987, Mus. of the City of N.Y., Children's Games, 1988, Photofind Gallery, N.Y.C., 1990, ICP, Bklyn., 1992; one-man shows include Midtown Y Gallery, 1978, Henry St. Settlement, Arts for Living Ctr., 1986, Frumkin Adams Gallery, N.Y.C., 1990, 92, Photofind Gallery, 1990, Howard Greenberg Gallery, 1991, 98, Salena Gallery, Bklyn., 1992, Port Washington Libr., 1994, Mus. of the City of N.Y., 1995, 96, Albin O. Kuhn Gallery, Balt., Md., Milw. Inst. Art & Design, 1998, Balt. Mus. Art, 1998, Whitney Mus. Am. Art, 1999, Am. Embassy, Copenhagen Artin Embassies, 1999, The Jewish Mus., The Changing Face of Family, 1999, Firehouse Gallery, Nassau C.C., 2001, Arthur Leipzig: A Tribute to Influence; represented in permanent collections Mus. Modern Art, Bklyn. Mus., Eastman House, Nat. Gallery Art, Nassau Mus. Art, Houston Mus. Fine Arts, Midtown Y Gallery, Visual Studies Workshop, Pablo Casals Mus., Internat. Ctr. Photography, Nat. Mus. Am. Art, Washington, Consol. Freightways, San Francisco, Bank of Am. Art Program, San Francisco, Bibliotheque Nationale, Paris, The Jewish Mus., N.Y.C., Mus. Folkwang, Essen, Germany, The Nat. Portrait Gallery, Washington, The Gilman Paper Co., Queens Coll., N.Y., Dreyfus, N.Y.C., Soho Grand Hotel, Columbus Mus. Art, Nassau C.C.; retrospective exhbn. Hillwood Gallery, Brookville, N.Y., 1989, Musée De La Civilisation, Quebec City, 1990; featured on World of Photography, Sta. WABC-TV; pub. Classic Photographs from the Brooklyn Museum Collection, 1987, Sarah's Daughters, 1988, Master Photographs Photography in Fine Arts Exhbt. Internat. Ctr. Photography, 1988, 92, The Nat. Portrait Gallery, 1992, High Mus., Altlanta, 1992, Growing up in N.Y., 1995. Adv. bd. Midtown Y Gallery, 1983; bd. dirs. Nassau Mus. Fine Art, 1973-75. Recipient Nat. Urban League award, 1962, ORT award, 1976, Nassau County Office Cultural Devel. award, 1982, David Newton Excellence in Teaching award, 1989, Award for Scholarly Achievement, L.I. U. Trustees, 1983, 89. Mem. Am. Soc. Mag. Photographers (bd. govs., trustee 1960-65, treas. 1965). Office: LI Univ CW Post Coll Art Dept Northern Blvd Greenvale NY 11548-1207 *My photogrpahy is very personal, my focus the human condition, exploring people, their humanity and inhumanity. I am not a cerebral photographer. My Images come as intuitive responses and they deal with my deepest feelings about life. Through my work I have learned about myself and the world.*

LEIS, HENRY PATRICK, JR. surgeon, educator; b. Saranac Lake, N.Y., Aug. 12, 1914; s. Henry P. and Mary A. (Disco) L.; m. Winogene Barnette, Jan. 8, 1944; children: Henry Patrick III, Thomas Frederick BS cum laude, Fordham U., 1936; MD, N.Y. Med. Coll., 1941. Diplomate Am. Bd. Surgery. Intern Flower and Fifth Ave Hosps., N.Y.C., 1941-42, resident, 1943-44, 46-49, attending surgeon, chief breast service, 1960-81; resident in surgery Kanawa Valley Hosp., Charleston, W.Va., 1942-43; attending surgeon, chief breast svc. Met. Hosp., N.Y.C., 1960-81, emeritus chief breast svc., 1982—; attending surgeon Coler Meml. Hosp., 1960-76; chief breast surgery Cabrini Hosp. Med. Ctr., 1978-85, cons. breast surgery, 1985—; emeritus surgeon Lenox Hill Hosp., N.Y.C., 1980-83; hon. mem. surg. staff Lenox Hill Hosp., 1984—, Drs. Hosp., N.Y.C.; hon. mem. surg. staff, cons. breast surgery Breast Ctr. Grand Strand Regional Med. Ctr., Myrtle Beach, S.C., 1985—; attending surgeon Westchester County Med. Ctr., 1977-81, emeritus surgeon, 1982—; clin. prof. surgery U. S.C. Sch. Medicine, Breast Surg. Oncology, Columbia, 1985-2000, prof. emeritus, 2000—; hon. dir. breast cancer ctr., cons. in breast surgery Winthrop Univ. Hosp., Mineola, 1971—; cons. in breast surgery VA Hosp., Columbia, S.C., 1985—; breast surg. oncologist Carolina Cancer Ctr., 1997—. Cons. in breast surgery St. Claires Hosp., N.Y.C., 1979; attending surg. staff Richland Meml. Hosp., Columbia, 1986-90; clin. prof. surgery, 1960-81, prof. emeritus, 1982—, co-dir. Inst. Breast Diseases, 1978-82, emeritus, 1982—, chief breast svc. N.Y. Med. Coll., 1960-81, emeritus, 1982—; cons. in breast surgery SUNY Div. Rehab., 1965—. Med. and Surg. Specialists Plan N.Y.; mem. Am. Joint Com. on Breast Cancer Staging and End Results; v.p. N.Y. Met. Breast Cancer Group, 1975-76, pres., 1977-79; cons. Med. Advs. Selective Svc. System, N.Y.C. Alumni trustee N.Y. Med. Coll., 1971-76; adv. coun. Fordham Coll. Pharmacy, 1968; bd. dirs. Hall Fame and Mus. Surg. History and Related Scis. Author: Diagnosis and Treatment of Breast Lesions: The Breast, 1970, Management of Breast Lesions, 1978, Breast Cancer: Conservative and Reconstructive Surgery, 1989, Breast Lesions: Diagnosis and Treatment, 1988; co-editor: Breast; hon. editor Internat. Surgery Jour.; mem. editorial bd. jour. Senolgia, 1982—, Breast: An Internat. Jour.; contbr. articles to profl. jours. Mem. Women's Cancer Task Force of S.C. Capt. M.C., AUS, 1944-46, PTO. Decorated knight Grand Cross Equestrian Order Holy Sepulchre Jerusalem, knight Mil., Order of Malta, Knight Noble Co. of the Rose; recipient award of Merit Am. Cancer Soc., 1969, 87, cert. and award for outstanding and devoted services to indigent sick City N.Y., 1965, Dr. George Hohman Meml. medal, 1936, N.Y. Apothecaries medal, 1936, Internat. cert. merit for disting. service to surgery, 1970, award of merit N.Y. Met. Breast Cancer Group, 1976, medal of Ambrogino (Italy), 1977, Service award of Honor N.Y. Med. Coll., 1969, medaille d'Honneur (France), medal of City of Paris, 1979, Silver Palm Jerusalem award 1996, citation for svcs. to indigent sick in S.C.; Henry P. Leis, Jr. Breast and Women's Ctr. named in his honor, Grand Strand Reg. Med. Ctr., Myrtle Beach, S.C., 1999. Fellow ACS (cancer liaison physician Surgeons commn. on Cancer 1988-98, emeritus cancer liaison physician commn. on Cancer 1999—, Cancer Liaison Physician Merit award Grand Strand Regional Med. Ctr., 1988-98), Peruvian Acad. Surgery (hon.), Am. Acad. Compensation Medicine, Am. Soc. Clin. Oncology, Am. Assn. Cancer Rsch., Am. Geriats. Soc., Indsl. Med. Assn., Internat. Coll. Surgeons (1st v.p. 1974-75, pres. 1977-78, v.p., chmn. coun. examiners U.S. sect. 1962-68, pres. 1971, Svc. award of honor 1971), Internat. Paleopathology Assn. (founder), N.Y. Acad. Medicine, N.Y. Coun. Surgeons, Royal Soc. Health (Eng.); mem. AMA, AAAS, AAUP, Am. Cancer Soc. (com. breast cancer), Am. Med. Writers Assn., Am. Soc. Breast Diseases and Breast Surgeons, S. Carolina Women's Cancer Coalition, Breast Surgical Cons. of Carolina Cancer Ctrs. (mem. profl. edn. and risk factors coms.), Am. Profl. Practice Assn., Assn. Am. Med. Colls., Am. Coll. Radiology (com. mammography and breast cancer), Assn. Mil. Surgeons U.S., Am. Soc. Breast Diseases, Am. Soc. Breast Surgeons, Cath. Physicians Guild (pres. N.Y. 1970-78), Gerontol. Soc., Internat. Platform Assn., N.Y. Cancer Soc., N.Y. County Med. Soc., N.Y. Surg. Soc., Pan Am Med. Assn. (v.p. N.Am. sect. on cancer 1967—), Pan Pacific Surg. Assn. (v.p. 1980, Res. Officers Assn. U.S., Soc. Acad. Achievement (mem. editl. bd. 1969—), Nat. Consortium Breast Ctrs. (bd. dirs. 1991-96), Soc. Med. Jurisprudence, Soc. Nuc. Medicine Surg. Soc. N.Y. Med. Coll., WHO, World Med. Assn., Alumni Assn. N.Y. Med. Coll. (gov. 1960—, pres. 1971), Assn. Mil. Surgeons U.S., Catholic War Vets. Assn., VFW, Hollywood Acad. Medicine (hon.), Alpha Omega Alpha, Phi Chi; hon. mem. Argentine Soc. Mammary Pathology, Argentina Cardiac and Thoracic Surg. Soc., Ecuador Med. Assn., Mo. Surg. Soc., Venezuela Surg. Soc., Italian Surg. Soc., S.C. Oncology Soc., So. Med. Assn. Clubs: Surf, Rotary. Lodges: K.C. (4th deg.).

LEISER, BURTON MYRON, philosophy and law educator; b. Denver, Dec. 12, 1930; s. Nathan and Eva Mae (Newman) L.; m. Janet A. Johnson, Aug. 12, 1984; children: Shoshana, Illana, Phillip, stepdaughter Sheri Johnson. BA, U. Chgo., 1951; MHL, Yeshiva U., 1956; PhD, Brown U., 1968; JD, Drake U., 1981. Bar: Iowa 1982, N.Y. 1985, U.S. Dist. Ct. (so. dist.) N.Y. 1986, U.S. Supreme Ct. 1986. Instr. Fort Lewis Coll., Durango, Colo., 1963-65; asst. prof. SUNY, Buffalo, 1965-68, assoc. prof., 1968-70, Sir George Williams U., Montreal, Can., 1969-72; prof., chmn. Drake U., Des Moines, 1972-83; E.J. Mortola prof. philosophy, adj. prof. law Pace U., N.Y.C., 1983-88, disting. prof. philosophy, 1988—. Del. UN for Am. Profs. for Peace in the Middle East, 1988-91; chair orgn. com. 19th World Congress on Philosophy of Law and Social Philosophy; exec. com. Internat. Assn. Philosophy Law and Social Philosophy, 1999—. Author: Custom, Law and Morality, 1969, Values in Conflict, 1981, Liberty, Justice and Morals, 1986. Chmn. bd. trustees Congregation Bet Am Shalom, White Plains, N.Y., 1990-92; chmn. regional bd. Anti-Defamation League, Westchester-Putnam-Rockland Counties, 1995-97, nat. commr., 1995—; vice-chmn. N.Y. Regional Bd., 1999—. Brown U. fellow 1959-62, NYU fellow 1955-57; grantee NEH, Exxon Ednl. Found. Mem. Am. Profs. for Peace in the Middle East (nat. sec. 1983-89), Am. Soc. Value Inquiry (pres. 1978-80). Republican. Jewish. Avocations: bird watching, music. Office: Pace Univ 11 Meadow Pl Briarcliff Manor NY 10510 E-mail: bleiser77@aol.com., bleiser@pace.edu. *If God hadn't wanted us to stick our necks out, he wouldn't have given us necks.*

LEISER, ERNEST STERN, journalist; b. Phila., Feb. 26, 1921; s. Monroe Felsenthal and Gertrude (Stern) L.; m. Caroline Thomas Camp, Oct. 26, 1946; children: Nancy, Shelley, Nicholas. AB, U. Chgo., 1941. Reporter City News Bur. Chgo., 1941; asst. picture editor Chgo. Herald-Am., 1941-42, 46; corr. Overseas News Agy., 1947-52; successively corr., producer, dir. TV news, exec. producer CBS News, N.Y.C., 1953-72, sr. producer, producer bicentennial coverage, spl. reports, 1975-79, v.p. spl. events and polit. coverage, 1979-81, v.p., dep. dir. news, 1981-85; exec. producer ABC News, N.Y.C., 1972-75; sr. fellow Gannett Ctr. for Media Studies, 1987-88. Author: This is Germany, 1950; contbr. articles to mags. Served with AUS, 1942-46. Decorated Bronze Star, Croix de Guerre; recipient Sigma Delta Chi award for TV reporting, 1956, Peabody awards for TV reporting and producing, 1956, 77, Ohio State awards, 1969, 77, Nat. Acad. TV Arts and Scis. award, 1968-71. Home: 15 College Ave South Nyack NY 10960-4207

LEISEY, DONALD EUGENE, educational materials company executive, educator; b. Pa., Sept. 23, 1937; s. Alvin L. and E. Marie L.; m. Patricia M. Leisey; children: Kristen, Kendra. BS in Edn., West Chester (Pa.) U., 1959; MA in Adminstrn., Villanova U., 1962; cert. in bus. adminstrn., U. So. Calif., 1970, EdD in Adminstrn., 1973. Cert. gen. adminstrv., gen. secondary, gen. elem., Calif. Tchr., Coatesville, Pa., 1959-62; prin. Downingtown, 1962-64, Dept. Def. Dependent Schs., Japan, 1964-67; asst. sup. Lennox Schs., Inglewood, Calif., 1967-71; dir. adminstrv. svcs. San Rafael (Calif.) City Sch. Dist., 1971-73; sup. schs., 1973-79; instr. Dominican Coll., 1973-79; v.p., regional mgr. Am. Learning Corp., Huntington Beach, Calif., 1979-80; v.p., treas. Kittredge Sch. Corp., San Francisco, 1980-83; instr. Calif. State U., Hayward, 1981; chmn., CEO Merryhill Schs., Inc., Sacramento, 1981-89; pres., chmn. bd., CEO The Report Card, Citrus Heights, 1990—; co-dir. Internat. Acad. Ednl. Entrepreneurship, 2000—. Apptd. bd. councilors U. So. Calif., Rossier Sch. Edn., 1999; apptd. bd. trustees Fund West Chester U., 2000. Co-author: The Educational Entrepreneur: Making a Difference, 2000. Apptd. to Gov.'s Child Care Task Force, Calif., 1984, Gov.'s Child Devel. Program Adv. Com., Calif., 1985—. Recipient Disting. Alumnus award West Chester State U., 1983, Disting. Svc. award L.A. County Sheriff, 1969, Hon. Svc. award PTA, 1970. Home and Office: 21 Silk Oak Cir San Rafael CA 94901-8301 Office: 6366 Tupelo Dr Citrus Heights CA 95621-1700 E-mail: DELAPLUS@aol.com.

LEISH, KENNETH WILLIAM, publishing company executive; b. Cambridge, Mass., Dec. 31, 1936; s. Frank and Lillian (Kargir) L.; m. Barbara Lynn Ackerman, Nov. 27, 1966; children: Matthew, Emily, Adam. AB magna cum laude, Harvard U., 1958; MS in Journalism, Columbia U., 1959. Interviewer Oral History Office, Columbia, 1960; free lance drama reviewer Variety, 1961-66; editor Am. Heritage Pub. Co., Inc., N.Y.C., 1961-69, v.p., gen. mgr. book div., 1971-77; editor-in-chief Am. Heritage Press, 1970-71; mgr. large-format paperbacks Bantam Books Inc., N.Y.C., 1977-81; editor-in-chief Grolier Inc. Project Editorial Group, 1981-87; v.p., dir. product devel. Grolier Internat., Inc., Danbury, Conn., 1988-91; v.p. new product devel. Grolier Inc., 1992-95; v.p., mng. editor Grolier Ednl., 1996—2002. Author: The White House, 1972, A History of the Cinema, 1974. Served with U.S Army, 1959-60. Home: PO Box 1681 White Plains NY 10602-1681 E-mail: leishbk@aol.com.

LEISING, DAVID MICHAEL, industrial engineer; b. Buffalo, Jan. 18, 1950; s. Lawrence Valentine and Patricia (Masterson) L.; m. Mary Kathleen Coyle, July 19, 1969; 1 child, Michelle. AAS, Jamestown (N.Y.) C.C., 1977; BS, Rochester Inst. Tech., 1992. Indsl. engr. Weber Knapp Co., Jamestown, N.Y., 1977-99; steam engr. Chautauqua Belle, Mayville, NY, 1999—; mfg. engr. Blackstone Bus. Enterprises, Jamestown, 2000—. With USN, 1969-73. Mem. ASME, Am. Assn. Indsl. Engrs., Waltonians (bd. dirs. 1993-94). Roman Catholic. Avocations: hunting, fishing, carpentry, camping, sailing. Home: 94 Lister St Jamestown NY 14701-2742

LEISING, MARY KATHLEEN, manufacturing executive; b. Corry, Pa., Mar. 15, 1950; d. Francis Morgan and Florence Marie (McEvoy) Coyle; m. David Michael Leising, July 19, 1969; 1 child, Michelle Anne. AS, Regents Coll., 1972, BS, 1975; MBA, St. Bonaventure U., 1990. Tchr.'s aide Lauderdale County Schs., Meridian, Miss., 1972-73; from shipping clk. to coord. synchronous mfg. Valeo Engine Cooling (formerly Blackstone Corp.), Jamestown, N.Y., 1975-90; mgr. inventory control Valeo Engine Cooling, 1991, mgr. logistics, 1991-98, program mgr., 1998—. Mem. Program Mgmt. Inst. Roman Catholic. Avocations: reading, camping, sailing. Office: Valeo Engine Cooling 2258 Allen Street Ext Jamestown NY 14701-2396

LEISNER, ANTHONY BAKER, publishing company executive; b. Evanston, Ill., Sept. 13, 1941; s. A. Paul and Ruth (Solms) L.; children: Justina, William, Sarah; m. Patricia Anne Leisner, 1996. BS, Northwestern U., 1964, MBA, 1983. Salesman Pitney Bowes Co., 1976-77; with Quality Books Inc., Lake Bluff, Ill., 1968—, v.p., 1972—, gen. mgr., 1979—91. Adj. faculty Lake Forest (Ill.) Sch. Mgmt., 1983—, Kellogg Grad. Sch. Mgmt. Northwestern U., Evanston, Ill.; assoc. prof. internat. mktg. Schiller Internat. U., Dunedin, Fla., 1995—; head global strategic planning, spl. asst., CEO Dawson Group, Folkestone, Eng. pres. Watersedge Properties Inc., Tarpon Springs, Fla.; ptnr. Wikle Properties Mgmt., Palm Harbor, Fla.; bd. dirs. Highland Properties, Inc., Palm Harbor, Fla. Bank of Commerce, Palm Harbor; mem. Pinellas Workforce Bd., Pinellas County, Fla. Author: Official Guide to Country Dance Steps, 1980; contbr. articles to jours. Pres. bd. dirs. Lake Villa Pub. Libr., 1972-78; bd. dirs. No. Ill. Libr. Sys., 1973-78, St. Petersburg (Fla.) Coll. Found., Leepa-Rattner Mus.; chmn. Libertarian Party Lake County (Ill.), 1980-81, 2002; probation officer Lake County CAP, 1981; chmn. Econ. Devel. Tarpon Springs, Fla. Mem. ALA (councilor, del. pub. com., White House conf. on librs. and info. svcs.), Ill. Libr. Assn. (Gerald L. Campbell award 1980), Acad. Mgmt., Am. Mktg. Assn., World Future Soc., World Isshin Ryu Karate Assn., Tarpon Springs C. of C. (chmn. econ. devel.). Home and Office: 1350 Riverside Ave Tarpon Springs FL 34689-6614

LEISSA, ARTHUR WILLIAM, mechanical engineering educator; b. Wilmington, Del., Nov. 16, 1931; s. Arthur Max and Marcella E. (Smith) L.; m. Gertrud E. Achenbach, Apr. 11, 1974; children: Celia Lynn, Bradley Glenn. BME, MS, Ohio State U., 1954, PhD, 1958. Engr., Sperry Gyroscope Co., Great Neck, N.Y., 1954-55; rsch. assoc. Ohio State U., 1955-56, instr. engring. mechanics, 1956-58, asst. prof. engring. mechanics, 1958-61, assoc. prof. engring. mechanics, 1961-64, prof. engring. mechanics, 1964-99, prof. mech. engring., 1999-2001, prof. emeritus, 2001—. Vis. prof. Eidgenossische Technische Hochschule, Zurich, Switzerland, 1972-73, USAF Acad., Colorado Springs, Colo., 1985-86, U. Canterbury, Christchurch, N.Z., 1997; Plenary lectr. 2nd Internat. Conf. Recent Advances in Structural Dynamics, Southampton, Eng., 1984, 4th Internat. Conf. on Composite Structures, Paisley, Scotland, 1987, Dynamics and Design Conf., Japan Soc. Mech. Engrs., Kawasaki, 1990, Energy Sources and Tech. Conf., ASME, Houston, 1992, Symposium on Mechs. of Continuous Sys., Sapporo, Japan, 1996 ; gen. chmn. Pan Am. Congress Applied Mechs. , Rio de Janeiro, 1989; hon. chmn. 1st Internat. Symposium on Vibrations of Continuous Sys., Estes Park, Colo., 1997 ; gen. chmn. 2nd Internat. Symposium on Vibrations of Continuous Sys. , Grindelwald, Switzerland, 1999, 3d Internat. Symposium on Vibrations of Continuous Sys., Grand Teton Nat. Park, 2001 ; cons. in field. Author: Vibration of Plates, 1969, Vibration of Shells, 1973, Buckling of Laminated Composite Plates and Shell Panels, 1985; assoc. editor Applied Mechanics Revs., 1985-93, editor-in-chief, 1993—; assoc. editor Jour. Vibration and Acoustics, 1990-93; mem. editl. bd. Jour. Sound and Vibration, 1971—, Internat. Jour. Mech. Sci., 1972—, Composite Structures, 1982—, Applied Mechanics Revs., 1988-93, Jour. Vibration and Control, 1994—, Internat. Jour. Structural Stability and Dynamics, 2000—; contbr. over 150 articles to profl. jours. Performer Columbus Symphony Orch. Operas, 1971-79; leader Ohio State U. Mt. McKinley Expdn., 1978. Recipient Recognition plaque Inst. de Mecanica Applicada, Argentina, 1977, Centennial cert., Am. Soc. Engring. Edn., 1993. Fellow: ASME, Japan Soc. Promotion Sci., Am. Acad. Mechs. (pres. 1987—88, Disting. Svc. medal 2001); mem.: Am. Soc. Engring. Edn., Am. Alpine Club. Home: 1294 Fountaine Dr Columbus OH 43221-1520 Office: 206 W 18th Ave Columbus OH 43210-1189 E-mail: awleissa@mindspring.com.

LEISURE, GEORGE STANLEY, JR. retired lawyer; b. N.Y.C., Sept. 16, 1924; s. George S. and Lucille E. (Pelouze) L.; m. Joan Casey, June 22, 1949; children: Constance, Timothy, Matthew, George III. BA, Yale U., 1948; LLB, Harvard U., 1951. Bar: N.Y. 1953, U.S. Supreme Ct. 1966. Asst. U.S. atty. So. Dist. N.Y., 1954-56; trial atty. antitrust divsn. Dept. Justice, N.Y.C., 1956-57; ptnr. Donovan Leisure Newton & Irvine, 1957-93. Spl. counsel to Gen. William Westmoreland in Westmoreland vs. CBS, 1984-85. With USN, 1943-46, lt. USNR, 1951-53. Fellow Am. Coll. Trial Lawyers (chmn. N.Y. downstate com. 1975-77); mem. Fed. Bar Council (pres. 1976-78), Assn. Bar City N.Y. (exec. com. 1962-66), Fed. Bar Assn., ABA, N.Y. State Bar Assn., N.Y. County Lawyers Assn. Home: Cottage 467 PO Box 30221 Sea Island GA 31561-0221

LEISURE, PETER KEETON, federal judge; b. N.Y.C., Mar. 21, 1929; s. George S. and Lucille E. (Pelouze) L.; m. Kathleen Blair; Feb. 27, 1960; children: Lucille K. (dec.), Mary Blair, Kathleen K. BA, Yale U., 1952; LL.B., U. Va., 1958. Bar: N.Y. 1959, U.S. Supreme Ct. 1966, D.C. 1979, U.S. Dist. Ct. Conn. 1981. Assoc. Breed, Abbott & Morgan, 1958-61; asst. U.S. atty. So. Dist. N.Y., 1962-66; partner firm Curtis, Mallet-Prevost, Colt & Mosle, 1967-78; ptnr. Whitman & Ransom, N.Y.C., 1978-84; judge U.S. Dist. Ct. So. N.Y., New York, NY, 1984—. Bd. dirs. Retarded Infants Svcs., 1968-78, pres., 1971-75; bd. dirs. Community Coun. of Greater N.Y., 1972-79, Youth Consultation Svcs., 1971-78; trustee Ch. Club of N.Y., 1973-81, 87-90; mem. jud. ethics com. Jud. Conf., 1990-93, fin disclosure com. 1st lt. USAR, 1953-55. Recipient Ellis Island medal of honor, 2000. Fellow Am. Bar Found., Am. Coll. Trial Lawyers; mem. ABA, Am. Law Inst., Fed. Judges Assn., Am. Judges Assn., D.C. Bar Assn., Fed. Bar Coun. (trustee, v.p. 1973-78), Bar Assn. City of N.Y., Nat. Lawyers Club (hon.). Office: US Dist Ct 1910 US Courthouse 500 Pearl St New York NY 10007-1316

LEITCH, RICHARD, political science educator; b. Nov. 23, 1962; m. Kaeko Saruhashi (Saruhashi), Jan. 25, 1986; children: William, Abilene. MA in Asian Studies, U. Ill., 1990, PhD in Polit. Sci., 1995. Asst. prof. polit. sci. Gustavus Adolphus Coll., St. Peter, Minn., 1996—. Home: 229 Long St Mankato MN 56001-5243 Office: Gustavus Adolphus Coll Polit Sci Dept Saint Peter MN 56082 E-mail: rleitch@gac.edu.

LEITCH, VINCENT BARRY, literary and cultural studies educator; b. Hempstead, N.Y., Sept. 18, 1944; s. Eugene Vincent and Lucile Jean (Amplo) L.; m. Jill Robin Berman, May 20, 1970 (div. May 1987); children: Kristin M., Rory G. BA, Hofstra U., 1966; MA, Villanova U., 1967; PhD, U. Fla., 1972. Postdoctoral fellow Sch. Criticism and Theory, U. Calif., Irvine, 1978; interim asst. prof. U. Fla., Gainesville, 1972-73; from asst. prof. to prof. English Mercer U., Macon, Ga., 1973-86; prof. English Purdue U., West Lafayette, Ind., 1986-97, co-dir. English and philosophy doctoral program, 1986-93; Paul and Carol Daube Sutton chair English U. Okla., Norman, 1997—. Mem. adv. bd. Modern Fiction Studies, 1992—97, Symploke, 1995—; reviewer NEH, 1985—88; Moss chair of excellence U. Memphis, 1991; sr. Fulbright lectr. U. Tampere, Finland, 1979; vis. prof. U. Debrecen, Hungary, 2002. Author: Deconstructive Criticism, 1983, American Literary Criticism from the 1930s to the 1980s, 1988, Cultural Criticism, Literary Theory, Poststructuralism, 1992, Postmodernism: Local Effects, Global Flows, 1996; mem. editl. bd. lit. and film series Fla. State U. Press, 1983—, Purdue Univ. Press, 1988—90, South Atlantic Rev., 1985—87, Genre, 1997, Project for Discourse and Theory U. Okla. Press, 1998—, The Norton Anthology of Theory and Criticism, 2001—, mem. adv. bd. Minn. Review, 1996—, South Crtl. Review, 1999—2002; gen. editor: The Norton Anthology of Theory and Criticism, 2001. Recipient Outstanding Acad. Book award Assn. Coll. and Rsch. Librs., 1988; Am. Philos. Soc. grantee, 1974; fellow NEH, 1980, Mellon Found., 1981, Am. Coun. Learned Socs., 1985-86, Ctr. for Humanistic Studies, Purdue U., 1989, 96, Okla. Humanities Coun., 2002. Mem. MLA (publs. com. 1990-93, assembly del. 1990-92, 93-95, chair organizing com. 1995, chair ad hoc com. on governance issues 1995, mem. 1996, exec. com. lit. criticism divsn. 1994-98), Soc. for Critical Exch. (bd. dirs. 1978-83), PEN Am. Ctr., Internat. Assn. for Philosophy and Lit., Am. Comparative Lit. Assn., South Ctrl. Modern Lang. Assn. Office: U Oklahoma Dept English Norman OK 73019 E-mail: vbleitch@ou.edu.

LEITE DE FARIA, HERNANI J. investment analyst; b. Porto, Portugal, July 10, 1955; arrived in Switzerland, 1988; s. Hernani and Gertrude Ann (Schwinghammer) L. Diploma in engring, Technische Hochschule, Karlsruhe, Fed. Republic Germany, 1980; diploma in wirtsch engring., Technische U., Munich, 1983. Sci. asst. Technische U., Munich, 1981—84; asst. to dirs. EKATO Rühr-und Mischtechnik GmbH, Schopfheim, Fed. Republic Germany, 1984-88; dir. corp. devel. Lonza AG, Basel, Switzerland, 1988-96; dir., investment analyst UBS AG, Zurich, Switzerland, 1996—. Adv. bd. IKO-Erbslöh, Germany, 1994—2000, Erbslöh Geisenheim, Germany, 1990—. Mem. Verein der Münchner AWA Absolventen, Schweizerische Vereinigung fur Finanzanalyse und Vermegensverwaltung. Avocations: horses, golf, yachting, painting. Bus. Home: Hohle Gasse 589 4323 Wallbach Aargau Switzerland Office: UBS Asset Mgmt HO BQQL DFH Gessnerallee 3 CH-8098 Zurich Switzerland E-mail: hernani.de-faria@ubs.com., hernani.de.faria@bluewin.ch.

LEITER, EDWARD HENRY, cell biologist; b. Columbus, Ga., Apr. 17, 1942; m. Susan Shaw, Sept. 5, 1964. BS, Princeton U., 1964; MS, PhD in Cell Biology, Emory U., 1968. Fellow U. Tex., Austin, 1968-71; asst. prof. CUNY, Bkyn., 1971-74; assoc. staff scientist Jackson Lab., Bar Harbor, Maine, 1974-75, staff scientist, 1975-90, sr. staff scientist, 1990—. Recipient rsch. award, Juvenile Diabetes Found., 1994. Achievements include research in include research in genetics and immunology of diabetes. Office: Jackson Lab 600 Main St Bar Harbor ME 04609-1500

LEITER, JEFFREY CARL, sociologist, educator; b. Cin., Apr. 7, 1948; s. Steven Max and Charlotte Michal Leiter; m. Janice Hope Heilbrunn, June 30, 1970 (div. 1977); m. Carrie Jane Knowles, June 28, 1979; children: Neil, Hedy, Cole. BA, Williams Coll., 1970; PhD, U. Mich., 1977. Vis. asst. prof. U. Ill., Chgo., 1977-78; asst. prof. N.C. State U., Raleigh, 1978-84, assoc. prof., 1984-95, prof. sociology, 1995—, dir. grad. programs dept. sociology and anthropology, 1998-2000. Author: Hanging By a Thread, 1991; contbr. articles to profl. jours. Avocation: gardening. Office: NC State U Dept Sociology Anthropology Raleigh NC 27695-0001 E-mail: jeff@server.sasw.ncsu.edu.

LEITER, JOHN M. lawyer; b. Marietta, Ga., July 14, 1951; s. Hans David and Lilo (Schwartzchild) L.; m. Mary Clayton, May 8, 1976; children: Jonathan, Elizabeth, Kristin. BA, Emory U., 1973; JD, U. S.C., 1978. Bar: S.C. 1978, Ga. 1978, U.S. Dist. Ct. S.C. 1978, U.S. Dist. Ct. (no. dist.) Ga. 1978, U.S. Ct. Appeals (4th and 5th cirs.), U.S. Supreme Ct. Assoc. Harmon, Smith & Bridges, Atlanta, 1978-82, Lawn & Leiter, Myrtle Beach, S.C., 1982-87; ptnr. Leiter & Tall, 1988-92; pvt. practice, 1992-94; prin. Leiter and Snook, P.A., 1994—. Intern World Peace Through Law Conf., Manila, 1977. Bd. dirs. Myrtle Beach Housing Authority, 1987—. David Means scholar, 1977. Mem. ABA, S.C. State Bar Assn., Ga. State Bar Assn., Horry County Bar Assn. (pres. 1995). Office: PO Box 7516 Myrtle Beach SC 29572-0013 E-mail: mbbw@sccoast.net.

LEITER, RICHARD ALLEN, law librarian, law educator; b. Sacramento, Mar. 21, 1952; s. Lionel and Lois Rose Leiter; m. Wendy Ellin Werges, Dec. 30, 1978; children: Emily Grace, Madeline Rose, Anna Joy, Rebecca Hope. BA in Anthropology and Religious Studies with honors, U. Calif., Santa Cruz, 1976; JD, Southwestern U., 1981; M of Libr. and Info. Sci., U. Tex., 1986. Libr. asst. Irell & Manella, L.A., 1977-78; libr. Hopkins, Mitchell & Carley, San Jose, Calif., 1982-84; head of reference Law Sch., U. Tex., Austin, 1984-86; pub. svcs. libr. Law Sch., U. Nebr., Lincoln, 1986-88; head libr.

Littler, Mendelson, Fastiff & Tichy, San Francisco, 1988-91; dir. law libr., assoc. prof. law Regent U. Sch. Law, Virginia Beach, Va., 1991-94; assoc. prof. law Howard U. Sch. Law, A.M. Daniels Law Libr., Washington, 1994-98, dir. law libr., 1994—2000; assoc. dean, prof. Howard U., 1998-2000; dir. Schmid Law Libr., prof. law U. Nebr., Lincoln, 2000—. Mem. Westlaw Acad. Adv. Bd., 1990-93; sec. bd. dirs. StoneBridge Sch., 1993-94; mem. adv. bd. Oceana Publs., Inc., 1994—. Editor: (book sect.) Yellow Pads to Computers, 1986, 91; author: (bibliography) New Frontiers of Forensic & Demonstrative Evidence, 1985; editor: Automatome, 1987-89, The Spirit of Law Librarianship, 1991, National Survey of State Laws, 1993, 3d edit., 1999; (with A. White) Concordance of Federal Legislation, 1999; editor Southwestern U. Law Review; contbr. articles to profl. jours. Mem. adv. com. StoneBridge Ednl. Found. Mem. ABA, Assn. Computing Machinery, Am. Soc. Info. Sci., Am. Assn. Law Librs. (so. chpt., automation and sci. devel. spl. interest sect. 1986—, chair 1989-90, indexing of periodical lit. adv. com. 1990-91, 2001—, chair 1990-91, mem. spl. com. to promote development of resources for legal info. cmty. 1994-96, recruitment com. 1995-97, chair rsch. com. 1998-99), San Francisco Pvt. Law Librs. (steering com. 1989), Consortium Southeast Law Librs. (vice chair), Scribes. Avocations: bicycling, reading, backpacking. Home: 1301 N 37th St Lincoln NE 68503-2015 Office: U Nebr Schmid Law Libr Coll Law Lincoln NE 68583-0902 E-mail: rleiter@unl.edu.

LEITER, ROBERT ALLEN, journalist, magazine editor; b. Phila., Apr. 21, 1949; s. Samuel Simon and Beverly (Agins) L.; m. Barbara Ann Field, May 6, 1973; children: Lauren, James, Rebecca. BA in English and Creative Writing with honors, U. Iowa, 1970. Freelance writer short stories, book revs., feature articles The Nation, The New Republic, Redbook, Am. Scholar, N.Y. Times, Partisan Rev., The Forward, others, 1973—; mng. editor, book columnist Inside mag., Phila., 1983-87; gen. reporter, book editor Jewish Exponent, 1987-98. Co-editor Friday, lit. supplement newspaper Jewish Exponent, Phila., 1983-87, mgn. editor Jewish Exponent 100th Anniversary edit., 1987, editor Extra Extra, weekly mag. sect., 1987-94; news editor Jewish Exponent, 1994-95, literary supplement editor, 1995-98, interim editor-in-chief, 1998-99, literary editor, 1999—; editor-in-chief, Inside Mag., 2000—; contbr. editor Am. Poetry Rev., Phila., 1987—; instr. writing, Am. lit., theater Cheltenham (Pa.) Adult Sch., 1983-87; instr. Jewish Am. lit., Jews in politics Daroff Campus Adult Studies, Pa., 1984, 99-2001. Author: (with others) Jewish Profiles, 1992. Asst. to vice chmn. U.S. Commn. on Civil Rights, Washington, 1987-88. Recipient Smolar award for excellence in N.Am. Jewish journalism for article series, 1989, Simon Rockower award, 1990, (2) 93, 96, 98, Keystone Press award, 1994, Soc. Profl. Journalists award 1996, 2001. Mem. Phi Beta Kappa. Jewish. Avocation: collecting books, antique furniture and paintings. Home: 1002 Prospect Ave Elkins Park PA 19027-3058 Office: Phila Jewish Exponent 2100 Arch St Philadelphia PA 19103-1300 E-mail: bleiter@jewishexponent.com.

LEITES, BARBARA L. (ARA LEITES), artist, educator; b. Hamilton, Ohio, June 3, 1942; d. Wilbur Frank and Alice Marie (Butts) Mayer; m. William Michael Whitley, Oct. 29, 1972 (div. Nov. 1977); 1 child, Rachel; m. Andre Leo Leites, Dec. 15, 1981 (div. Mar. 2000); chldren: David, Bevin; 1 stepchild, Daniella. BFA, Miami U., Oxford, Ohio, 1964, MFA, 1967. Tchr. Madison Elem. Sch., Hamilton, 1964-65; tchr. art and humanities Key West (Fla.) H.S., 1967-70, tchr. adult edn. in art, 1968-70; isntr. Fla. Keys Jr. Coll., Key West, 1969-70; co-dir. Kleinert Gallery, Woodstock, N.Y., 1977-80; self employed artist under the name Ara Leites, 1981—. Bd. dirs. Woodstock Guild of Craftsmen, 1978—79; instr. drawing and painting, divsn. head visual arts Georgiana Bruce Kirby Preparatory Sch., Santa Cruz, Calif., 1998—2001, ret., Calif., 2001. Exhibited at Gallery El Ciruello, Tepoztlan, Mex., Club 209 Gallery, Cuernavaca, Mex., Black Sheep Art Gallery, Eng., Westminster Gallery, London, Cin. Art Mus., Dayton Art Inst., Springfield (Mo.) Art Mus., Miami U.; U.S. nat. exhbns. of over 175 shows and 65 awards including Rocky Mountain Nat., Watercolor USA, Adirondacks Nat., Nat. Watercolor Soc., Am. Watercolor Soc., Audubon Artists, Phila. Watercolor Club, Allied Artists, N.Y.C., Calif. Nat. Watercolor Soc.; subject of articles in publs. Mem. AAUW, Internat. Soc. Exptl. Artists (signature), Am. Artists Profl. League (signature), Nat. Watercolor Soc. (signature), Nat. Soc. Painters in Casein and Acrylic (signature), Nat. Acrylic Painters Assn. (signature), Watercolor USA Honor Soc. (signature), Ky. Watercolor Soc. (signature), Tex. Watercolor Soc. (signature), Ga. Watercolor Soc. (signature), Mo. Watercolor Soc. (signature), Miss. Watercolor Soc. (signature), Phila. Watercolor Club Soc. (signature), Audubon Artists (signature), Mont. Watercolor Soc. (signature), Rocky Mountain Nat. Watercolor Soc. (signature), Fedn. of Can. Artists (signature), Soc. Layerists in Mixed Media (signature), Watercolor Soc. Ala. (signature), Pa. Watercolor Soc. (signature), Taos Nat. Watercolor Soc. (signature), Delta Delta Delta Alumnae Assn. Democrat. Avocations: gardening, carpentry, skiing, snowboarding, surfing. Home: 168 Oxford Way Santa Cruz CA 95060-6447 E-mail: araleites@sbcglobal.net.

LEITH, CECIL ELDON, JR. retired physicist; b. Boston, Jan. 31, 1923; s. Cecil Eldon and Elizabeth (Benedict) L.; m. Mary Louise Henry, July 18, 1942; children: Ann, John, Paul. AB, U. Calif. at, Berkeley, 1943, PhD, 1957. Exptl. physicist Lawrence Radiation Lab., Berkeley, 1946-52, theoretical physicist Livermore, Calif., 1952-68; sr. scientist Nat. Center for Atmospheric Research, Boulder, Colo., 1968-83, div. dir., 1977-81; physicist Lawrence Livermore Nat. Lab. (Calif.), 1983-90. Symons Meml. lectr. Royal Meteorol. Soc., London, 1978; chmn. com. on atmospheric scis. NRC, 1978-80, sci. program evaluation com. Univ. Corp. for Atmospheric Rsch., 1991-96; mem. joint sci. com. world climate research program World Meteorol. Organ. and Internat. Council Sci. Unions, 1976-83; mem. program adv. com. Office Advanced Sci. Computing, NSF, 1984-85. Served with AUS, 1944-46. Fellow Am. Phys. Soc., Am. Meteorol. Soc. (Meisinger award 1967, Rossby research medal 1982) Home: 627 Carla St Livermore CA 94550-2316 Office: Lawrence Livermore Nat Lab PO Box 808 Livermore CA 94551-0808

LEITH, EMMETT NORMAN, b. Detroit, Mar. 12, 1927; s. Albert Donald and Dorothy Marie (Emmett) Leith; m. Lois June Neswold, Feb. 17, 1956; children: Kim Ellen, Pam Elizabeth. BS, Wayne State U., 1950, MS, 1952, PhD, 1978; DSc (hon.) , U. Aberdeen, Scotland, 1996. Mem. rsch. staff U. Mich., 1952—, prof. elec. engring., 1968—. Cons. several indsl. corps. Contbr. articles to profl. jours. With USNR, 1945—46. Named Man of Yr., Indsl. Rsch. mag., 1966; recipient Gordon Meml. award, SPIE, 1965, citation, Am. Soc. Mag. Photographers, 1966, Achievement award, U.S. Camera and Travel mag., 1967, Excellence of Paper award, Soc. Motion Picture and TV Engrs., 1967, Daedalion award, 1968, Stuart Ballantine medal, Franklin Inst., 1969, Alumni award, Wayne State U., 1974, cited by Nobel Prize Commn. for contbns. to holography, 1971, Holley medal, ASME, 1976, Nat. medal of Sci., 1979, Russel lecture award, U. Mich., 1981, Denins Gabor medal, Soc. Photo-Instrumentation Engrs., 1983, Gold medal, 1990, Mich. Trailblazer award, 1986. Fellow: IEEE (Liebmann award 1967, Inventor of Yr. award 1976), Optical Soc. Am. (Wood medal 1975, Herbert Ives medal 1985), The Royal Photographic Soc. of Great Britain (hon.), Engring. Soc. Detroit (hon.); mem.: NAE, Sigma Pi Sigma, Sigma Xi. Achievements include patents in field; first demonstrating (with colleague) capability of holography to form high-quality 3-dimensional image. Home: 51325 Murray Hill Dr Canton MI 48187-1030 Office: Univ Mich Inst Sci and Tech PO Box 618 Ann Arbor MI 48106-0618 E-mail: leith@umich.edu.

LEITH, JOHN HADDON, clergyman, theology educator; b. Due West, S.C., Sept. 10, 1919; s. William H. and Lucy Ann (Haddon) L.; m. Ann Caroline White, Sept. 2, 1943; children— Henry White, Caroline Haddon. AB, Erskine Coll., 1940, DD (hon.), 1972; BD, Columbia Theol. Sem., 1943; MA, Vanderbilt U., 1946; PhD, Yale U., 1949; DD (hon.), Davidson Coll., 1978; DLitt (hon.), Presbyn. Coll., 1990. Ordained to ministry Presbyn. Ch. 1943. Pastor chs. in, Nashville and Auburn, Ala., 1944-59; Pemberton prof. theology Union Theol. Sem., Richmond, Va., 1959-90. Vis. prof. Columbia Theol. Sem., Eckerd Coll., New Coll. at U. Edinburgh; adj. prof. Va. Commonwealth U.; mem. ad interim com. to revise book of ch. order Presbyn. Ch. U.S., 1955-61, mem. com. to write brief statement of faith, 1960-62, mem. com. to prepare brief statement of reformed faith, 1984-91; chmn. com. revision of chpt. 3 of Confession of Faith, 1959-60, mem. permanent nominating com. gen. assembly, 1972-75; chmn. bd. Presbyn. Survey, 1961-70; bd. dirs. Presbyn. Outlook Mag., 1962-99; moderator Presbyn. Synod N.C., 1977-78; mem. Gov.'s Commn. on Seasonal and Migrant Farm Workers, 1982-94; mem. adv. coun. Ctr. of Theol. Inquiry, Princeton, N.J., 1989-94. Author: Creeds of the Churches, 1963, 3d. rev. edit., 1982, The Church, A Believing Fellowship, 1965, rev., 1980, Assembly at Westminster, 1973, Greenville Church, The Story of a People, 1973, rev. edit. 1997, The Reformed Tradition, A Way of Being the Christian Community, 2d edit., 1981, John Calvin, the Christian Life, 1984, The Reformed Imperative, 1988, John Calvin's Doctrine of the Christian Life, 1989; editor: Guides to Reformed Theology, The Reformed Imperative, 1988, From Generation to Generation, 1990, Basic Christian Doctrine, 1993; editor (with Stacy Johnson) A Reformed Reader, A Source Book for Christian Theology, 1993, Crisis in the Church, the Plight of Theological Education, 1997, The Pilgrimage of a Presbyterian, 2000. Trustee Erskine Coll.; bd. dirs. Inst. Religion and Democracy, 1985-93; mem. Richmond City com. Dem. Party, 1973-93. Kent fellow, 1946-48; Folger Library fellow, 1964; grantee Advanced Religious Studies Found., 1974 Mem. Calvin Studies Soc. (pres. 1980-83) Home: Presbyn Home of SC 205 Bud Nalley Dr # 46 Easley SC 29642-3570

LEITINGER, CHRISTIANE, educator; b. Jacksonville, Fla., Apr. 13, 1962; d. Johann and Ilse Abshagen L.; m. Charles Stuart Shimanski, May 30, 1992; children: Isabel Claire, Eva Sophia. BA, Grinnell (Iowa) Coll., 1986; MEd, Loyola Coll., Balt., 1998. Montessori tchr. Family Star, Denver, 1993-94, The Montessori Inst. Children's House, Denver, 1994-96; Montessori mentor Family Star, 1997-98, 2000—, The Montessori Inst. Children's House, Denver, 1998-99, The Montessori Internat. Children's Ho., Denver, 1999-2000. Cons. in field. Mem. Assn. Montessori Internat., N.Am. Montessori Tchrs. Assn. Avocations: mountain climbing, reading. Home: 67 Paul's Rd Evergreen CO 80439 Office: Family Star 2246 Federal Blvd Denver CO 80211

LEITMAN, BARRY STEVEN, radiologist, educator; b. N.Y.C., July 21, 1950; BS, CUNY, 1971; MD, N.Y. Med. Coll., 1975. Diplomate Am. Bd. Radiology. Surg. intern L.I. Jewish-Hillside Med. Ctr., New Hyde Park, N.Y., 1975-76; radiology resident N.Y. Med. Coll., Valhalla, 1976-79, instr. radiology, 1979-80; asst. prof. radiology NYU Sch. Med., N.Y.C., 1980-87, clin. assoc. prof. radiology, 1987—; asst. attending Westchester County Med. Ctr., 1979-80, Met. Hosp., 1979-80, Tisch Hosp., 1980-87, assoc. attending, 1987—; asst. attending Bellevue Med. Ctr, 1980-87; assoc. attending Bellevue Med. Ctr., 1987—; attending and chmn. dept. radiology Bklyn. Hosp. Ctr., 1995-98; assoc. dir. Tisch Hosp. Radiology, 1998—2001, Bellevue Hosp. Radiology, N.Y.C., 2001—. Contbr. articles to profl. jours. Mem. Am. Coll. Radiology, Am. Roentgen Ray Soc., Radiol. Soc. N.Am., Phi Beta Kappa, Alpha Omega Alpha. Office: Bellevue Hosp Dept Radiology 550 First Ave NBV-3W40 New York NY 10016 E-mail: barry.leitman@med.nyu.edu.

LEITMANN, GEORGE, mechanical engineering educator; b. Vienna, Austria, May 24, 1925; s. Josef and Stella (Fischer) L.; m. Nancy Lloyd, Jan. 28, 1955; children: Josef Lloyd, Elaine Michèle. BS, Columbia U., 1949, MA, 1950; PhD, U. Calif., Berkeley, 1956; D Engring. honoris causa, Tech. U. Vienna, 1988; D honoris causa, U. Paris, 1989, Tech. U. Darmstadt, 1990. Physicist, head aeroballistics sect. U.S. Naval Ordnance Sta., China Lake, 1950-57; mem. faculty U. Calif., Berkeley, 1957—, prof. engring. sci., 1963—, prof. grad. sch., 1995—, assoc. dean acad. affairs, 1981-90, assoc. dean rsch., 1990-94, acting dean, 1988, chair of the faculty, 1994-98. Cons. to aerospace industry and govt. Author: An Introduction to Optimal Control, 1966, Quantitative and Qualitative Games, 1969, The Calculus of Variations and Optimal Control, 1981, others; contbr. articles to profl. jours. Served with AUS, 1944-46, ETO. Decorated Croix de Guerre France, Fourragere Belgium, Comdr.'s Cross, Order of Merit Germany, Commendatore, Order of Merit Italy; named Miller Rsch. prof., 1966; recipient Pendray Aerospace Lit. award, AIAA, 1979, Von Humboldt U.S. Sr. Scientist award, Von Humboldt Found., 1980, Levy medal, Franklin Inst., 1981, Mechanics and Control of Flight award, AIAA, 1984, Berkeley citation, U. Calif.-Berkeley, 1991, Von Humboldt medal, Von Humboldt Found., 1991, Rufus Oldenburger medal, ASME, 0995; fellow Berkeley, 2002. Mem. NAE, Acad. Sci. Bologna, Internat. Acad. Astronautics, Argentine Nat. Acad. Engring., Russian Acad. Natural Sci., Georgian Acad. Engring., Bavarian Acad. Sci., A.V. Humboldt Assn. Am. (pres. 1994-97), Georgian Acad. Sci. Office: U Calif Coll Engring Berkeley CA 94720-0001 E-mail: gleit@uclink4.berkeley.edu.

LEITNER, ALFRED, mathematical physicist, educator, educational film producer; b. Vienna, Austria, Nov. 3, 1921; came to U.S., 1938, naturalized, 1944; s. Philipp and Lona (Machlup) L.; m. Marzia O'Neil, Nov. 24, 1948; children: Kathleen, Deborah Jones, David. BA, U. Buffalo, 1944; MS, Yale U., 1945, PhD, 1948. Research assoc. Courant Inst. Math. Scis., N.Y. U., 1947-51; from asst. prof. to prof. physics Mich. State U., 1951-67; prof. physics Rensselaer Poly. Inst., 1967-88, prof. emeritus, 1988—; research assoc. Harvard U., 1965-66. Cons. Harvard project physics, 1966-68; vis. prof. U.S. Mil. Acad., West Point, 1983-85. Author papers on theory spl. functions, boundary value problems, antennas, history of sci., teaching.; Films Liquid Helium, 1963, Superconductivity, 1966, Project Physics, 1965-68; Dispersion, 1973, Fraunhofer (2 films), 1974, A Story of Research, 1981; (videotapes) Our Favorite Physics Demonstrations, 1987. Guggenheim fellow, 1958-59; Deutscher Akademischer Austauschdienst fellow, 1977 Fellow Am. Phys. Soc.; mem. Am. Assn. Univ. Profs., Phi Beta Kappa, Sigma Xi. Home: 1201 8th Ter N Naples FL 34102-5411 E-mail: ltnr@aol.com.

LEITNER, PAUL REVERE, lawyer; b. Winnsboro, S.C., Nov. 11, 1928; s. W. Walker and Irene (Lewis) L.; m. Jeannette C. Card, Mar. 16, 1985; children by previous marriage: David, Douglas, Gregory, Reid, Cheryl. AB, Duke U., 1950; LLB, McKenzie Coll., 1954. Bar: Tenn. 1954; cert. civil trial specialist Nat. Bd. Trial Advocacy and Tenn. Commn. on CLE and Specialization. Pvt. practice law, Chattanooga, 1954; assoc. Leitner, Williams, Dooley & Napolitan and predecessor firms, 1952-57; ptnr. Leitner, Warner, Moffitt, Williams, Dooley, Carpenter & Napolitan and predecessor firms, 1957—. Tenn. chmn. Def. Rsch. Inst., 1978-89. Bd. dirs. Family Service Agy., 1957-63, Chattanooga Symphony and Opera Assn., 1986-89, sec., 1987-89; mem. Chattanooga-Hamilton County Community Action Bd.; mem. Juvenile Ct. Commn., Hamilton County, 1955-61, chmn., 1958-59; chmn. Citizens Com. for Better Schs.; mem. Met. Govt. Charter Commn. Served with U.S. Army, 1946-47. Named Young Man of Yr. Chattanooga Area, 1957 Fellow Am. Coll. Trial Lawyers, Tenn. Bar. Found, Chattanooga Bar Found. (founding); mem. ABA, Tenn. Bar Assn., Jaycees (Chattanooga, pres. 1956-57), Fed. Ins. Corp. Counsel, Internat. Assn. Def. Coun., Trial Attys. Am., Tenn. Def. Lawyers Assn. (pres. 1975-76), Am. Bd. Trial Advs. (advocate), U.S. Sixth Cir. Jud. Conf. (life), Am. Inss of Ct. Methodist. Home: 3926 Windward Ln Soddy Daisy TN 37379 E-mail: pleitner@leitnerfirm.com.

LEITZEL, JOAN RUTH, university president; BA in Math., Hanover Coll., 1958; MA in Math., Brown U., 1961; PhD in Math., Ind. U., 1965. Instr. math. Oberlin (Ohio) Coll., 1961-62; asst. prof. math. Ohio State U., Columbus, 1965-70, assoc. prof., 1970-84, prof., 1984-92, vice-chmn. dept., 1973-79, acting chmn., 1978, assoc. provost, 1985-90; prof. dept. math. and stats. U. Nebr., Lincoln, 1992-96, sr. vice chancellor for acad. affairs, 1992-96, interim chancellor, 1995-96; pres. U. N.H., Durham, 1996—2002. Adv. com. Griffith Ins. Found., 1979-82; cons. Ohio Dept. Edn., 1980-83; participant Am. Coun. on Edn., 1980, 82; cons. Nat. Commn. on Excellence in Edn., U.S. Dept. Edn., 1982; univ. math. edn. del. to China, 1983; dir. divsn. materials devel., rsch. and info. sci. edn. NSF, 1990-92; presenter in field, 1980—; bd. dirs. Am. Assn. Higher Edn., chmn.-elect, 1996-97, chmn., 1997-98; mem. interpretive reports adv. bd. Nat. ssessment Ednl. Progress, 1995-98; trustee Consortium on Math. and Its Applications, 1994-95; mem. exec. coun. com. on acad. affairs Nat. Assn. State Univs. and Land-Grant Colls., 1994-96, bd. dirs., 1997-99, chmn. com. on faculty, 1994-96; coord. coun. for edn. NRC, 1993-95, mem. bd. on math. scis. edn., 1985-87, math. scis. edn. bd., chmn. 2000—. Bd. dirs. United Way Lincoln, 1995-96, 1st Plymouth Ch., 1996, Lincoln Partnership for Econ. Devel., 1996, N.H. Charitable Found., 1998-02, Durham Cmty. Ch., 1996-02. Recipient Disting. Alumni award Hanover Coll., 1986, dir.'s award for mgmt. excellence NSF, 1991; grantee NSF, 1976-79, 84-88, Battelle Found., 1981-83, SOHIO, 1983-85. Mem. AAAS (edn. com. 1981-84), Am. Math. Soc. (com. on excellence in scholarship 1993-95), Assn. for Women in Math., Math. Assn. Am. (nominating com. 1978-79, com. on tchr. tng. and accreditation Ohio sect. 1976-79, nat. com. on undergrad programs 1982-85, chmn. joint task force on curriculum for grades 11-13 with Nat. Coun. Tchrs. Math. 1986-88), Nat. Coun. Tchrs. Math., Mortar Bd., Sigma Xi, Phi Kappa Phi. Home: 912 Linworth Village Dr Columbus OH 43235

LEITZELL, TERRY LEE, lawyer; b. Williamsport, Pa., Apr. 15, 1942; s. Ernest Richard and Inez Mae (Taylor) L.; m. Lucy Acker Emmerich, June 18, 1966; children: Thomas Addison, Charles Taylor, Robert Davies. AB, Cornell U., 1964; JD, U. Pa., 1967. Bar: D.C. bar 1967. Consular officer Dept. State, Bombay, India, 1968-70, atty.-adv. for oceans affairs Washington, 1970-77, chief U.S. negotiator UN law of sea negotiations Geneva, also N.Y.C., 1974-77; asst. adminstr. for fisheries and dir. Nat. Marine Fisheries Service, NOAA, Dept. Commerce, Washington, 1978-81; practice law, 1981-92, Seattle, 1992—; gen. counsel Icicle Seafoods. Mem.: Wash. Bar Assn. Democrat. Home: 3150 W Laurelhurst Dr NE Seattle WA 98105-5346 Office: Icicle Seafoods 4019 21st Ave W Ste 300 Seattle WA 98199-1299 E-mail: terryl@icicleseafoods.com.

LEIZEAR, CHARLES WILLIAM, retired information services executive; b. Balt., Dec. 15, 1922; s. Charles R. and Nellie Beyer L.; m. Jean Smith, Nov. 26, 1947; children: Robin DeBarry, Kathy King. Charles R. II BS cum laude, Loyola Coll., Balt., 1949. With Burroughs Co., 1949-71; v.p. mktg. data systems Singer Co., N.Y.C., 1972-76; group v.p. cash mgmt. services Nat. Data Corp., Atlanta, 1976-81, exec. v.p. fin. service and systems, 1981-83, exec. v.p. ops., 1983-85, exec. v.p. retail systems, 1984, sr. v.p., 1985-88; mktg. and quality process cons. Charles Assocs., 1989-98; ret., 1998. Bd. dirs. Lupus Specialists, Inc., Atlanta. With U.S. Army, 1942-45. Recipient Susan Anthony award for highest acad. achievement Loyola U., 1947 Home: Fairhaven Unit C111 7200 3d Ave Sykesville MD 21784-5231 E-mail: buckl@prodigy.net.

LEJEUNE, J. KENNETH, respiratory therapist; b. Port Neaches, Tex., Sept. 25, 1954; s. Felton Joseph and Wavy (Miller) LeJ.; divorced; m. Lorie A. LeJeune, May 25, 1979; children: Kristi Ann, Aaron Joseph. AS, Texarkana Coll., 1980; BSE, U. Ark., 1993; MSIS, Tex. A&M U., Texarkana, 1997. Lic. respiratory therapist Ark., Tex., cert. health instr. Ark., respiratory therapy technician, registered therapist Nat. Bd. Respiratory Care, cert. pulmonary function technologist Nat. Bd. REapiratory Care. Staff technician Brackenridge Hosp., Austin, 1977-78; asst. dir. respiratory care Cmty. Hosp., Tyler, Tex., 1978-79, Newburn Meml. Hosp., Jacksonville, 1980-84; dir. cardiopulmonary Nevada County Hosp., Prescott, Ark., 1984-87; clin. coord./ednl. coord. St. Michael Hosp., Texarkana, 1987-89; dir. clin. respiratory edn. U. Ark. Cmty. Coll., Hope, 1989, program dir. respiratory edn., 1989-97, chmn. divsn. allied health, 1997—. Owner, prin. Respiratory Care Cons., 1989-91; cons. State of Va., 1995; item writer Applied Measurement Profls., 1992—; manuscript reviewer F.A. Davis, J.B. Lippincott, Simon & Koltz, and Delmar Pubs., 1990-99; mem. home health adv. bd. Hempstead County, 1985-87. Judge Ark. Odyssey of the Mind, 1994-95. Mem.: Am. Lung Assn. (dist. chmn. 1984—88), Am. Cancer Soc. (dist. chmn. 1984—88), Am. Heart Assn. (cmty. tng. ctr. coord. 1998), Ark. Soc. Respiratory Care (southwest dist. chmn. 1988, 1989, summer symposium coord. 1989, fall symposium coord. 1989, scholar com. 1980), Am. Assn. Reapiratory Care (edn. sect. 1991—98, Blue ribbon panel 1991, abstract and poster reviewer 1993—94), Nat. Soc. Collegiate Scholars, Lambda Beta, Golden Key Honor Soc. Democrat. Roman Catholic. Avocations: camping, woodworking. Home: 286 County Road 23 Hope AR 71801-8819 Office: U Ark Cmty Coll 2500 S Main St Hope AR 71802 E-mail: KLejeune@mail.uacch.cc.ar.us.

LEKSON, STEPHEN HENRY, archaeologist; b. West Point, N.Y., May 18, 1950; s. John S. and Gladys M. (Pecsok) K.; m. Catherine M. Cameron, Jan. 12, 1979. BA, Case Western Res. U., 1972; MA, Ea. N.Mex. U., 1978; PhD, U. N.Mex., 1988. Archaeologist, project dir. U. Tenn., Knoxville, 1973; archaeologist Ea. N.Mex. U., Portales, 1974-75, Nat. Park Svc., Albuquerque, 1976-86; rsch. assoc. Ariz. State Mus., Tucson, 1987-90; curator archaeology Mus. of N.Mex., Santa Fe, 1991-92; pres., CEO Crow Canyon Archaeol. Ctr., Cortez, Colo., 1992—. Author: Great Pueblo Architecture of Chaco Canyon, N.Mex., 1986, Nana's Raid, 1987, Mimbres Archaeology, 1990, Ancient Land, Ancestral Places, 1993. Mem. Am. Anthropol. Assn., Soc. Am. Archaeology, Am. Assn. Mus., World Archaeol. Congress. Home: 92 Benthaven Pl Boulder CO 80305-6200 Office: Crow Canyon Archaeol Ctr 23390 County Road K Cortez CO 81321-9408

LELAND, CHRISTOPHER TOWNE, writer, English educator; b. Tulsa, Oct. 17, 1951; s. Benjamin Towne L. and Julia Elizabeth Sanford; m. Osvaldo R. Sabino, June 13, 1979. BA, Pomona Coll., 1973; MA, U. Calif., San Diego, 1980, PhD, 1982. Briggs Copeland asst. prof. Harvard U., Cambridge, Mass., 1983-88; faculty mem. Bennington (Vt.) Coll., 1988-90; prof. English Wayne State U., Detroit, 1990—. Author: Mean Time, 1982, The Last Happy Men: The Generation of 1922, Fiction, and the Argentine Reality, 1986, Mrs. Randall, 1987, The Book of Marvels, 1990, The Professor of Aesthetics, 1994, Letting Loose, 1996, The Art of Compelling Fiction, 1998, The Creative Writers Style Guide, 2002. Fulbright grantee, 1979, 89, 96. Office: Wayne State U Dept English 51 W Warren Ave Detroit MI 48201-1305

LELAND, DAVID CHARLES, lawyer, record producer, talent agent; b. Berkeley, Calif., Mar. 26, 1953; s. Richard William and Carol Arlene (Plumly) L.; m. Jo-Ann Charak, Nov. 23, 1982; 1 child, Benjamin Nathan; m. Loretta A. Smith, Aug. 12, 1989 (div. Dec. 1991); m. Penelope Irene Barsley Challans, Aug. 26, 1996. Student, New Coll. Calif., 1974-75; BA, U. Calif., Berkeley, 1978; postgrad., Paris, summer 1979; JD, Golden Gate U., 1981. Bar: Mass. 1986, U.S. Dist. Ct. (no. dist.) Calif. 1987, U.S. Dist. Ct. Mass. 1994, U.S. Supreme Ct. 1994, U.S. Ct. Appeals (1st cir.) 1994, U.S. Tax Ct. 1996. Hearing officer San Francisco Residential Rent Bd., 1981-82; pvt. investigtor Pat Kohn Detective Agy., San Francisco, 1980-83; pres. Wilbur & Son, Boston and San Francisco, 1982-84; mktg. mgr. Nat. Bus. Cons., Santa Monica, Calif., 1984-85; sales cons. Entre Computer Corp., San Francisco, 1985; legal asst. Kuvara Law Firm, San Jose, Calif., 1986-87; assoc. Parrish & Assocs., San Francisco, 1987-88; cons. atty. Goshkin, Pollatsek, Meredith & Lee, 1988; cons. Compulaw, Inc., Culver City, Calif., 1987-90, Law Office of David Leland, 1992-98; markup lang. expert Xerox Lang. Svcs., 1998-99; markup analyst FT.com, 1999—. Legal counsel, bd. dirs. Friends of Newton Free Libr., 1993-95; bd. mem. Boston Music Fest, 1994; bd. dirs. Boston Music Fest, 1994; presenter XML 2000 AsiaPacific. Mem. ABA (lt. gov. law student div. 1980-81, Silver Key award 1981), Assn. Trial Lawyers Am., Phi Alpha Delta. Democrat. Avocations: painting, photography, writing, cooking. Office: 15 Saint James Ct Orinda CA 94563-1113

LELAND, HENRY, psychology educator; b. N.Y.C., Feb. 13, 1923; s. Ida (Miller) L.; m. Helen D. Faitos (div. 1979); children: Colombe, David Jean, Daniel Louis; m. Sherrie Lynn Ireland, Dec. 7, 1980. AB, San Jose State Coll., 1948; PhD, Université de Paris, Paris, 1952. Lic. psychologist, Ohio. Clin. psychologist with Dr. Jean Biro, Paris, 1949-52; sr. clin. psychologist N.Y. State Mental Health Commn., Syracuse, 1952-54; dir. dept. psychol. svc. Muscatatuck State Sch., Butlerville, Ind., 1954-57; chief clin. psychologist Parsons (Kans.) State Hosp. and Tng. Ctr., 1957-63, coord. profl. tng., edn. and demonstration, 1963-70; assoc. in child rsch. Kansas U. Bur. child Rsch., Lawrence, 1963-70; assoc. prof. psychology Ohio State U., Columbus, 1970-72, prof., 1972-93, prof. emeritus, 1993—, mem. senate, 1985-88; chief psychology Herschel W. Nisonger Ctr., 1970-93. Tchg. asst. Ind. U. Extension Svc., 1956-57; assoc. prof. Kansas State Coll., 1958-70; dist. vis. lectr. U. So. Calif., L.A., 1969; prin. investigator Adaptive Behavior Project, Ohio Dept. Mental Health and Mental Retardation, 1972-75, cons., 1972-76; examiner State Bd. Psychology Ohio, 1987-88, 92-94, sec., 1988-89, pres., 1989-90, 94-95, active, 1986-95; cons. Cen. Ohio Psychiat. Hosp., 1986-93; com. on acad. misconduct Ohio State U., 1990-93. Author: (with D. Smith) Play Therapy with Mentally Subnormal Children, 1965, (with others) Brain Damage and Mental Retardation, 1967, (with others) Handbuch der Kinderpsychotherapie, Vol. II, Germany, 1968, (with others) Social Perceptual Training Kit for Community Living, 1968, Impairment in Adaptive Behavior: A Community Dimension, Tracks, Vols. II, 12, 1960-67, (with others) Social Inference Training of Retarded Adolescents at the Pre-Vocational Level, 1968, (with others) Mental Health Services for the Mentally Retarded, 1972, (with others) Sociobehavioral Studies in Mental Retardation, 1973, (with D. Smith) Mental Retardation: Current and Future Perspectives, 1974, (with others) Research to Practice in Mental Retardation and Education and Training, II, 1977, (with others) International Encyclopedia of Psychiatry, Psychology, Psychoanalysis and Neurology, II, 1977, (with others) Psychological Management of Pediatric Problems, 1978, (with Deutsch)Abnormal Behavior, 1980, (with others) Psychoeducational Assessment of Preschool and Primary Age

Children, 1982, (with others) Comprehensive Handbook of Mental Retardation, 1983, (with others) The Foundations of Clinical Neuropsychology, 1983, (with others) Institutions for the Mentally Retarded: A Changing Role in Changing Times, 1986, (with others) Encyclopedia of Human Intelligence Vol. I, 1994, AAMR Adaptive Behavior Scale-Residential and Community, 1995, AAMR Adaptive Behavior Scale-School, 1993; cons. editor Am. Jour. Mental Deficiency, 1965-70, Profl. Psychology, 1977-95, Mental Retardation, 1980-84; contbr. articles to profl. jours. Mem. Franklin County Bd. Mental Retardation/Devel. Disabilities, 1980—82; trustee Goodwill Rehab. Ctr., 1975—, mem. exec. com., 1985—; trustee, treas. Shalom House, Inc., 2000—. Recipient Disting. Svc. in Mental Deficiency award, Am. Assn. on Mental Deficiency, 1985. Fellow AAAS, APA (councilor 1986-90 , Edgar A. Doll Meml. award div. 33 1990), Am. Assn. on Mental Retardation (councilor 1964-68), Ohio Psychol. Assn., Soc. for Pediatric Psychology, Kans. Psychol. Assn. (pres. 1966), Ctrl. Ohio Psychol. Assn. (pres. 1996). Democrat. Jewish. Avocations: stamp collecting, gourmet cooking. Home: 2120 Iuka Ave Columbus OH 43201-1322 E-mail: irelandleland@columbus.rr.com.

LELAND, JOY HANSON, anthropologist, alcohol research specialist; b. Glendale, Calif., July 29, 1927; d. David Emmett and Florence (Sockerson) Hanson; m. David A. Riegert, Nov. 14, 1993. BA in English Lit., Pomona Coll., Claremont, Calif., 1949; MBA, Stanford U., 1960; MA in Anthropology, U. Nev., 1972; PhD in Anthropology, U. Calif., Irvine, 1975. With Desert Research Inst., U. Nev., 1961—, asst. research prof., 1975-77, assoc. research prof., 1977-79, rsch. prof., 1979-89, rsch. prof. emerita, 1990—. Author: monograph Firewater Myths, Frederick West Lander-A Biographical Sketch; contbg. author: Smithsonian Handbook of North American Indians; also articles, book chpts. Trustee Robert and Joy Leland Charitable Trust, 1992—. NIMH grantee, 1972-73; Nat. Inst. Alcohol Abuse and Alcoholism grantee, 1974-75, 79-81 Mem. Am. Anthrop. Assn., Southwestern Anthrop. Assn., Soc. Applied Anthropology, Soc. Med. Anthropology, Gt. Basin Anthrop. Conf., Phi Kappa Phi. Address: 6126 Carriage House Way Reno NV 89509-7326

LELAND, MARC ERNEST, trust advisor, lawyer; b. San Francisco, Apr. 20, 1938; s. Herbert and Sarah Betty (Robinson) L.; m. Elisabeth Gustava De Rothschild, July 7, 1970 (div. Sept. 1980); children: Natasha Hanna, Olivia Mitzi; m. Jacqueline de Botton, 1989. AB in Govt., Harvard U., 1959; MA in Law, St. John's Coll.-Oxford U., Eng., 1961; JD, U. Calif.-Berkeley, 1963. Ford Found. fellow Inst. Comparative Law-U., Paris, 1963-64; assoc. Cerf Robinson & Leland, San Francisco, 1964-68, ptnr., 1972-76; faculty fellow Harvard U. Law Sch., Boston, 1968-70; gen. counsel Peace Corps, Washington, 1970-71, ACTION, Washington, 1971-72; ACDA rep. Force Reduction Talks, Vienna, Austria, 1976-78; resident ptnr. Proskauer Rose Goetz & Mendelsohn, London, 1978-81; asst. sec. internat. affairs Dept. Treasury, Washington, 1981-84; pres. Marc E. Leland & Assocs., 1984—. Republican. Jewish. Office: 1001 19th St N Ste 1700 Arlington VA 22209-1725

LELAND, RICHARD G. lawyer; b. Oceanside, N.Y., Jan. 25, 1949; s. Arnold Joseph and Eunice (Himlyn) L.; m. Jane E. Schwartz; children: Jennifer Schultz, David Jarett. BS, Cornell U., 1971; JD with distinction, Hofstra U., 1974. Bar: N.Y. 1975, U.S. CT. Appeals (2nd cir.) 1975, U.S. Dist. Ct. (so. and ea. dists.) N.Y. 1976, U.S. Supreme Ct. 1979. Assoc. Winer, Neuburger & Sive, N.Y.C., 1974-76; law sec. to Justice Douglas F. Young Supreme Ct. N.Y. Nassau County, Mineola, 1976-79; assoc. Ruskin, Schlissel, Moscou & Evans, P.C., 1979-82, ptnr., 1982-89, Rosenman & Colin LLP, N.Y.C., 1989—. Spl. prof. Hofstra U., Hempstead, N.Y., 1991—; mem. Real Estate Bd. of N.Y., Inc.; chair Commn. on Environ. Law. Contbr. articles to profl. jours. Mem. N.Y. State Bar Assn., Hofsta Law Sch. Alumni Assn. (pres. 1995-99). Office: Rosenman & Colin LLP 575 Madison Ave Fl 15 New York NY 10022-2511 E-mail: rgleland@rosenman.com.

LELAND, TIMOTHY, retired newspaper executive; b. Boston, Sept. 24, 1937; s. Oliver Stevens and Frances Chamberlain (Ayres) L.; m. Natasha Bourso, Sept. 26, 1964 (div. 1981); children: Christian Bourso, London Chamberlain; m. Julie S. Hatfield, Nov. 23, 1984. AB cum laude, Harvard U., 1960; MS with honors, Columbia Sch. Journalism, 1961. Med. editor Boston Herald, 1963-64; sci. editor Boston Globe, 1965-66, State House bur. chief, 1966-67, asst. city editor, 1968-69, investigative reporter, 1970-71, asst. mng. editor, 1972, mng. editor (Sunday), 1976-81, mng. editor (daily), 1981-82, asst. to pub., 1984-97, asst. to chmn., 1997-98, v.p., 1990-98. Bd. dirs. Boys and Girls Clubs of Boston, World Affairs Coun. of Boston. Recipient Am. Polit. Sci. award, 1968; Pulitzer Prize for investigative reporting, 1972; Sigma Delta Chi award for civic service (reporting), 1972; award for pub. service A.P. Mng. Editors, 1974; Sevellon Brown award, 1974; U.S.-South African Leader Exchange Program traveling grantee, 1969; Internat. fellow Columbia, 1961. Mem. Harvard Club. Office: Boston Globe 3 School St Boston MA 02108

LELI, DANO ANTHONY, neuropsychologist, educator; b. S.I., N.Y., July 22, 1947; s. Peter and Viola (Troisi) L.; m. Patricia Gaile Percy, June 1, 1972; children— David Anthony, Shannon Marguerite. B.A., U. Central Fla., 1972, M.S., 1974; Ph.D., U. South Fla., 1978. Postdoctoral fellow in clin. neuropsychology U. Ala.-Birmingham Med. Sch., 1978-79, asst. prof. dept. psychology, 1980-87 , clin. assoc. prof. dept. psychology, 1987—, asst. prof. dept. psychiatry, 1981-87 , research asst. prof. dept. neurology, 1979— , adj. asst. prof. dept. neurology, 1987—, dir. clin. neuropsychology lab., 1979— , assoc. scholar Ctr. for Aging, 1984— ; adv. cons. NIH-NINCDS; ad hoc reviewer Jour. Cons. and Clin. Psychology, dir. clin. Neuropsychology Lab., 1979-87; assoc. scholar Ctr. fog Aging, 1984-87; Contbr. articles to profl. publs. Served with USAF, 1968-70. Grantee U. Ala., 1982-83, Cerebrovascular Disease Research Ctr., 1983-86, Nat. Inst. of Aging, 1987— . Mem. N.Y. Acad. Scis., Internat. Neuropsychol. Soc., Am. Psychol. Assn., Southeastern Psychol. Assn., Psi Chi. Democrat. Office: Florida Medical Pla 2501 N Orange Ave Ste 509 Orlando FL 32804-4674

LELLIG, CYNTHIA, public library director; b. Ogden, Iowa, June 29, 1951; d. Robert Emery and Doris Esther (Wiener) M.; m. Donald Leo Lellig, Nov. 30, 1974; children: Matthew Robert, Melanie Ann Lellig. BA in Libr. Sci. and Math., U. No. Iowa, 1973. Cert. pub. libr. level V, State Libr. of Iowa. Jr. sr. h.s. instructional materials ctr. dir. Grundy Ctr. (Iowa) Comty. Schs., 1973-75; elem. and jr. h.s. libr. Jesup (Iowa) Comty. Schs., 1975-80; libr. dir. City of Jesup, 1987—. Mem. media adv. coun. Area Edn. Agy. 7, Cedar Falls, Iowa, 1975-77; advisor for design, fund raising, etc. for a new libr. bldg., Jesup, 1990-93; mem. grant rev. com. State Libr. Iowa, Des Moines, 1993. Bd. dirs. ARC, Buchanan County, Iowa, 1995-96; mem. Jesup Middle Sch. Adv. Coun., 1995-96. Mem. Iowa Libr. Assn., Iowa Small Libr. Assn., Cath. Daughters of Am., Jesup C. of C. (bd. dirs. 1994-96). Avocations: reading, camping. Office: Jesup Pub Libr PO Box 585 Jesup IA 50648-0585

LELONEK, DAVID, optometrist; b. Bklyn., Aug. 24, 1959; s. Charles and Sylvia (Haskel) L.; m. Laura Friedman, Nov. 15, 1992; children: Rachel, Jessica, Anna. BS, CUNY, 1981; OD, SUNY, N.Y.C., 1986. Diplomate Nat. Bd. Med. Examiners. Optometrist Wizard of Eyes, Bklyn. and S.I., N.Y., 1986-88, Pearl Express, Bellrose, 1991-93, Eye Supply Optical, 1993-95; chief optometrist Eye Inst. S.I., 1988-91; pvt. practice, Baldwin, N.Y., 1991-94, Costco, Westbury, 1995—. Spring tng. optometrist N.Y. Mets Major League Baseball Team, 1999. Scoutmaster Boy Scouts Am., Bklyn., 1980-82, 85-98; vol. United Cerebral Palsy, 1982-98, Multiple Sclerosis Soc., 1985-98. Recipient various awards for vol. svcs. Mem. Am. Optometric Assn. (Presdl. award 1995). Democrat. Jewish. Avocations: camping, photography, baseball. Home: 486 Spruce Ln East Meadow NY 11554-3704 Office: 1250 Old Country Rd Westbury NY 11590-5624 E-mail: dlelonek@optonline.net.

LELYVELD, DAVID SIMON, university administrator, historian; b. Cin., June 22, 1941; s. Arthur Joseph and Toby (Bookholtz) L.; m. Meena Alexander, May 1, 1979; children: Adam Kuruvilla, Svati Mariam. AB magna cum laude, Harvard U., 1963; MA, U. Chgo., 1967, PhD, 1975. Tutor Madras Christian Coll., Tambaram, India, 1963-64; asst. prof., assoc. prof. U. Minn., Mpls., 1970-76, 77-85; field dir. Berkeley Urdu Lang. Program, Lahore, Pakistan, 1976; program officer Asia Soc., N.Y.C., 1985-86; dean of students Columbia U. Sch. Gen. Studies, 1986-95; program officer Social Sci. Rsch. Coun., 1995-96; exec. dir. Mario Einaudi Ctr. for Internat. Studies Cornell U., Ithaca, NY, 1997—2002; prof. history, assoc. dean humanities and social sci. William Peterson U., Wayne, NJ, 2002—. Vis. lectr. U. Wash., Seattle, 1991; rsch. assoc. Fairbank Ctr., Harvard U., Cambridge, Mass., 1985-86. Author: Aligarh's First Generation, 1978; book rev. editor: Jour. Asian Studies, 1984-87; contbr. articles to profl. jours. Trustee Tarakhnath Das Found., N.Y.C., 1988—. Fulbright fellow, India, 1963-64; Fgn. Area fellow, India, 1967-69; fellow Am. Inst. Indian Studies, India, 1979, 82; NEH fellow, 1996-97. Mem. Assn. Asian Studies (South Asia coun. 1988-91), Phi Beta Kappa. Jewish. Office: 170 Uris Hall Cornell U Ithaca NY 14853

LELYVELD, GAIL ANNICK, actress; b. Boston, May 22, 1948; d. Edward I. and Beatrice Elizabeth (Hewitt) L. BA in Polit. Sci., Boston U., 1970; MA in Polit. Sci., Goddard Coll., 1974; studies with Paul Barry, Peter Donat, Ray Reinhardt, Darrell Lauer, others. Actress, 1970—; tech. staff USA Prodns. and Midseason, Hempstead, N.Y., 1986-87, prodn. stage mgr., 1987—. Tech. staff Gray Wig, Hempstead, 1986, 87; cons. Talking With prodn. M.A., C.W. Post. Appeared in numerous films including Frances, Halloween III, Children On Their Birthdays, Project 1917, Rocky II, Happy Endings, Seeds of Innocence, Bonfire of the Vanities, The Music of the Heart, The Bird's Eye View, Insomnia, Monster Math, The Lesson, I'm Not Rappaport, City Hall, The House of the Venus Flytrap (ind. film), Believe for Hofstra University (film); (TV shows): Archie Bunker's Place, Mister Clown Says, White Noise, The Gentle Creature, (ABC Afterschool Spl.) Summer Stories: The Mall, Mathnet, Bill Cosby Murder Mystery, Cosby: You're OK, I'm Hilton, Upright Citizen Brigade; actor: Alice in Wonderland, Not So Grimm Fairytale Players; actress (Littletop Theater Co.) Toby Tyler, Marmalade Gumdrops, Bohemian Lights, King Lear - Tenant, Doctor & Knight Plainedge Playhouse, The Hostage, USA Prodns., The Cherry Orchard, Broadhollow Theater Bay Way Art Ctr., The House of Blue Leaves, The Lady of Larkspur Lotion, Broadhollow Theatre Bay Way Arts Ctr., Sarah Good and the Voice of Martha Corey, BDR Repertory Co., also The Worst Play in the World, Women's Theatrical Collective, The Man Who Came to Dinner, U.S.A. Prodns., Holocaust Survivor-Columbia Univ.; reader Yom Kippur Svcs., Temple Emanuel San Francisco; Singer: Gospel Oedipus at Colonus evangelist, townsperson, choir, Musicum Collegium Hofstra U., Pala Opera Assn., St. Patrick's Cathedral Choir, Temple Emanuel New Hyde Park Choir; singer and leader Christmas Carols Garden City Group Christmas Party, Garden City Group Chorus Holiday Songs and Soloist; soloist piano recital, solo singer Ecumenical Thanksgiving Svc.; one-person performance, Dona Gracia Nasi, Memoirs of Glüchel of Hameln, Temple Emanuel of New Hyde Park; theater tech. involvement includes stage mgr., sound asst. Wings; sound asst. Danton's Death; asst. stage mgr. props, fx, dresser Accomplice; cons. on reading The Sisters Rosenweig. Mem. AFTRA Jewish. Avocations: reading, knitting, walking. Home: 291 Saville Rd Mineola NY 11501-1345 E-mail: Gail_Lelyveld@gardencitygroup.com.

LELYVELD, JOSEPH SALEM, retired newspaper editor, correspondent; b. Cin., Apr. 5, 1937; s. Arthur Joseph and Toby (Bookholz) L.; m. Carolyn Fox, June 14, 1959; children: Amy, Nita. BA summa cum laude, Harvard U., 1958, MA, 1959; MS in Journalism, Columbia U., 1960. Reporter, editor N.Y. Times, 1963—, fgn. corr., Johannesburg, New Delhi, Hong Kong, London, 1965-86, columnist mag., staff writer, 1977, 84-85, fgn. editor, 1987-89, mng. editor, 1990-94, exec. editor, 1994—2001. Author: Move Your Shadow, 1985 (Pulitzer prize, L.A. Times Book prize, Sidney Hillman award, all 1986). Recipient George Polk Meml. award, 1972, 84; Guggenheim fellow, 1984. Mem. The Century Assn.*

LELYVELD, STEVEN, pediatric emergency physician; b. South Weymouth, Mass., Aug. 25, 1948; MD, Albany Med. Coll., 1974. Diplomate Am. Bd. Emergency Medicine, Am. Bd. Pediat., Am. Bd. Pediatric Emergency Medicine. Intern Children's Meml. Hosp. - Northwestern, 1974-75, resident in pediat., 1975-77; resident in emergency medicine Evanston Hosp. - Northwestern, 1977; assoc. prof. pediats., emergency medicine U. Chgo. Sch. Medicine. Chmn. Emergency Med. Sys. for Children adv. bd. Ill. Dept. Pub. Health, 1995—. Mem. Am. Acad. Pediat. (pres. Ill. chpt.). Office: M/C0810 5839 S Maryland Ave Chicago IL 60637-1463 E-mail: ktfrogge@uchicago.edu.

LEM, RICHARD DOUGLAS, painter; b. Nov. 24, 1933; s. Walter Wing and Betty (Wong) L.; m. Patricia Ann Soohoo, May 10, 1958; 1 child, Stephen Vincent. BA, UCLA, 1958. One-person shows include Gallery 818, L.A., 1965; exhibited in group shows Lynn Kottler Galleries, N.Y.C., 1973, Palos Verdes Art Gallery, 1968, Galerie Mouffe, Paris, 1976, Le Salon des Nations, Paris, 1984, numerous others; represented in permanent collections; writer, illustrator: Mile's Journey, 1983, 2d edit., 1995, I'm Dying, but I'm Not Sick. The Final Journey, 1999, Searching for The Soul, 2002; cover illustrator: The Hermit, 1990, The Hermit's Journey, 1993. With AUS, 1958-60. Address: 1861 Webster Ave Los Angeles CA 90026-1229 *Personal philosophy: It requires a great deal of inner strength to pursue your personal vision with single mindedness-it's a challenge that justifies my existence.*

LEMAIRE, JACQUES, professional hockey coach; b. Lasalle, Que., Can., Sept. 7, 1945; Player Montreal Canadiens, 1967-79, head coach, 1983-85; head coach, player Sierre Hockey Club, Switzerland, 1979-81; asst. coach SUNY Coll., Plattsburgh, 1981-82; coach Longueuil Chevaliers, maj. jr. league, Que., 1982-83; dir. of hockey pers. Montreal Canadiens, 1985-87, asst. to mng. dir., 1987-93; head coach N.J. Devils, 1993-98; cons. to gen. mgr. Montreal Canadiens, 1998-00; head coach Minnesota Wild, Saint Paul, 2000—. Mem. Stanley Cup Championship teams, 1968, 69, 71, 73, 76-79. Named NHL Coach of Yr., Sporting News, 1993, 94; inducted into Hockey Hall of Fame, 1984 Address: Minn Wild Piper Jaffray Tower 444 Cedar St Ste 900 Saint Paul MN 55101-2126*

LE MAISTRE, CHARLES AUBREY, internist, epidemiologist, educator; b. Lockhart, Ala., Feb. 10, 1924; s. John Wesley and Edith (McLeod) LeM.; m. Joyce Trapp, June 3, 1952; children: Charles Frederick, William Sidney, Joyce Anne, Helen Jean. BA, U. Ala., 1943, LLD (hon.), 1971; MD, Cornell U., 1947; LLD (hon.), Austin Coll., 1970; DSc (hon.), U. Dallas, 1978, Southwestern U., 1981; D honoris causa, U. Guadalajara (Mex.), 1989. Intern, then resident medicine N.Y. Hosp., 1947-49; rsch. fellow infectious diseases Cornell U. Med. Coll., 1949-51, mem. faculty, 1951-54, asst. prof. medicine, 1953-54; mem. faculty Emory U. Sch. Medicine, 1954-59, prof. preventive medicine, chmn. dept., 1957-59; prof. medicine U. Tex. Southwestern Med. Sch., 1959-78, assoc. dean, 1965-66; vice chancellor health affairs U. Tex. System, Austin, 1966-68, exec. vice chancellor, 1968-69, dep. chancellor, 1969-70, chancellor, 1971-78, prof. medicine, 1978-96; pres., internist, prof. medicine U. Tex. M.D. Anderson Cancer Ctr., 1978-96. Cons. epidemiology Communicable Disease Center, USPHS, 1953-69; cons. medicine VA, 1954-59; area med. cons. VA (Atlanta area), 1958-59; vis. staff physician Grady Meml. Hosp., Atlanta, 1954-59, Emory U. Hosp., 1954-59; sr. attending staff mem. Parkland Meml. Hosp., Dallas, 1959-66; med. dir. chest div. Woodlawn Hosp., Dallas, 1959-65; mem. Surgeon Gen.'s Adv. Com. Smoking and Health, 1963-64, AMA-Edn. Research Found. com. research tobacco and health, 1964-66; chmn. Gov. Tex. Com. Tb Eradication, 1963-64; cons. internal medicine Baylor U. Med. Center, Dallas, 1962-66, St. Paul Hosp., Dallas, 1966; cons. div. hosp. and med. facilities USPHS, 1966; mem. N.Y.C. Task Force on Tb, 1967; cons. Bur. Physician, HEW, 1967-70; mem. grad. med. edn. nat. adv. com. Health Resources Adminstrn., 1977-80; mem. Tex. Legislature Dept. Health, Edn. and Welfare, 1967, Tex. Legislature Com. on Organ Transplantation, 1968, Carnegie Commn. on Non-Traditional Study, 1971-73; mem. bd. commrs. Nat. Commn. on Accrediting, 1973-76; mem. joint task force on continuing competence in pharmacy Am. Pharm. Assn.-Am. Assn. Coll. in Pharmacy, 1973-74; mem. exec. com. Legis. Task Force on Cancer in Tex., 1984-86; adv. bd. 6th World Conf. on Smoking and Health. Contbr. articles to med. jours.; contbg. author: A Textbook of Medicine, 10 and 11th edits, 1963, Pharmacology in Medicine, 1958; translating author: The Tubercle Bacillus, 1955; mem. editorial bd. Am. Rev. Respiratory Diseases, 1955-58. Mem. President's Commn. White House Fellows, 1971; chmn. subcom. on diversity and pluralism Nat. Council on Ednl. Research, 1973-75; bd. dirs. Assn. Tex. Colls. and Univs., 1974-75; mem. devel. council United Negro Coll. Fund, 1974-78; mem. nat. adv. council Inst. for Services to Edn., 1974-78; mem. exec. com. Assn. Am. Univs., 1975-77; mem. Project HOPE com. on Health Policy, 1977; chmn. steering com. Presbyn. Physicians for Fgn. Missions, 1960-62; mem. Ministers Cons. Clinic, Dallas, 1960-62; trustee Austin Coll., 1979-83, Stillman Coll., 1978-84; bd. dirs. Ga. Tb Assn., 1955-59; bd. dirs. Damon Runyon-Walter Winchell Cancer Fund, 1976-85, chmn. exec. com., v.p., 1978, pres., 1979-83; trustee Biol. Humanics Found., Dallas, 1973-82; chmn. health manpower com. Assn. Am. Univs., 1975-78; sec. Council So. Univs., Inc., 1976-78, pres., 1977-78; hon. life trustee Menninger Found.; host com. Houston Econ. Summit, 1990. Recipient Cornell Univ. Alumni of Distinction award, 1978, Disting. Alumnus award U. Alabama Sch. Medicine, 1982, Pres.' award Am. Lung Assn., 1987, Gibson D. Lewis award for Excellence in Cancer Control Tex. Cancer Coun., 1988, award of Honor Am. Soc. Hosp. Pharmacists, 1988, Svc. to Mankind award Leukemia Soc. Am. Tex. Gulf Coast chpt., 1991, People of Vision award Tex. Soc. to Prevent Blindness, 1991, Outstanding Tex. Leader award 7th Ann. John Ben Sheppard Pub. Leadership Forum, 1991; Inst. Religion's Caring Spirit Tribute, 1993, AMA Disting. Svc. award, 1995, Disting. Pub. Svc. medal NASA, 1995, Ala. Acad. of Honor, 1998, Disting. Svc. award NASA, 1998, Charles A. LeMaiste Clinic Bldg. U. Tex. M.D. Anderson Cancer Ctr., Houston, 1997; named Houstonian of Yr., Houston Sch. for Deaf Children, 1987, Lamar award Assn. Tex. Colls. and Univs., 2000; named to Ala. Healthcare Hall of Fame, 1999. Mem. AMA, (Disting. Svc. award 1995), NASA, NIH (chair joint adv. com. behavioral rsch. 1992), Am. Thoracic Soc. (past v.p.), So. Thoracic Soc. (past pres.), Nat. TB Assn., Tex. Med. Assn., Ga. Med. Assn., Soc. Assn. Oncology (bd. dirs.), Am. Cancer Soc. (Tex. bd. dirs. 1977-89, med. and sci. com. 1974, chmn. study com. on tobacco and cancer 1976, pub. edn. com. 1976-87, chmn., mem. various nat. coms., v.p., pres. 1986, med. dir.-at-large 1977-89, Ted C. Mars award 1998, medal of Honor 1998), Houston C. of C. (dir. 1979-89), Philos. Soc. Tex. (pres. 1980-81), Greater Houston Partnership (bd. dirs. 1989-96), Alpha Omega Alpha. Presbyterian. Home: 7 Bristol Grn San Antonio TX 78209-1846

LEMAL, DAVID MARKHAM, chemistry educator; b. Plainfield, N.J., Feb. 20, 1934; s. Richard Francis and Margaret Irene (Markham) L.; m. Helen Theresa Moran, Jan. 26, 1963 (div. June 1991); children: Anne-Marie, Marielle, Richard James, Corinne; m. Lee Ann Gabriel, Mar. 11, 1994. AB, Amherst Coll., 1955; PhD in Chemistry, Harvard U., 1959. Instr. chemistry U. Wis., Madison, 1958-60, asst. prof., 1960-65; assoc. prof. Dartmouth Coll., Hanover, N.H., 1965-69, prof., 1969-81, dept. chair chemistry, 1976-79, Albert W. Smith prof., 1981—. Chair hydrocarbon chemistry Gordon Rsch. Conf., Andover, N.H., 1970, chair heterocyclic compounds, New Hampton, N.H., 1970, bd. trustees, 1973-79, chair, 1977-78. Contbr. articles to profl. jours. NSF fellow, 1955-58, A.P. Sloan Found. Rsch. fellow, 1968-70; recipient Catalyst award Chem. Mfrs. Assn., 1987; named New Hampshire Prof. of Yr., Coun. for Advancement and Support of Edn., 1989. Mem. Am. Chem. Soc. (co-chair Winter Fluorine Conf. 1987, 89, chair fluorine divsn. 1990, Creative Work on Fluorine Chemistry award 2002), Phi Beta Kappa, Alpha Chi Sigma, Phi Lambda Upsilon. Democrat. Avocations: tennis, skiing. Office: Dartmouth Coll Burke Laboratory Hanover NH 03755 E-mail: david.m.lemal@dartmouth.edu.

LEMAN, CRAIG BILLINGS, surgeon; b. Chgo., Mar. 12, 1923; MD, Harvard U., Boston, 1952. Intern Presby. Hosp., Chgo., 1952-53; surgical resident Peter Bent Brigham Hosp., Boston, 1954-57; fellow in surgery Harvard U., 1953-54; pvt. practice, Corvallis, Oreg.; ret. Courtesy staff Good Samaritan Hosp., Corvallis, from 1990. Fellow ACS. E-mail: lemann@ucs.orst.edu.

LEMANN, THOMAS BERTHELOT, lawyer; b. New Orleans, Jan. 3, 1926; s. Monte M. and Nettie E. (Hyman) L.; m. Barbara M. London, Apr. 14, 1951 (dec. 1999); children: Nicholas B., Nancy E.; m. Sheila Bosworth Bell, June 1, 2000. AB summa cum laude, Harvard U., 1949, LL.B., 1952; M.C.L., Tulane U., 1953. Bar: La. 1953. Assoc. Monroe & Lemann, New Orleans, 1953-58, ptnr., 1958-98; of counsel Liskow & Lewis, 1998—. Bd. dirs. B. Lemann & Bro., Mermentau Mineral and Land Co., So. States Land & Timber Corp., Avrico Inc.; advisory bd. dirs. Riviana Foods. Contbr. articles to profl. publs. Mem. council La. State Law Inst., sec. trust adv. com.; chmn. Mayor's Cultural Resources Com., 1970-75; pres. Arts Coun. Greater New Orleans, 1975-80, bd. dirs.; mem. vis. com. art museums Harvard U., 1974-80; trustee Metairie Park Country Day Sch., 1956-71, pres., 1967-70, New Orleans Philharmonic Symphony Soc., 1956-78, Flint-Goodridge Hosp., 1960-70, La. Civil Service League, pres., 1974-76, New Orleans Mus. Art, 1986-92; bd. dirs. Zemurray Found., Hever Found., Parkside Found., Azby Fund, Azby Art Fund, Greater New Orleans Found., Arts Coun. New Orleans, Musica da Camera. Served with AUS, 1944-46, PTO. Mem. ABA, La. Bar Assn. (bd. govs. 1977-78), New Orleans Bar Assn., Assn. Bar City N.Y., Am. Law Inst., Soc. Bartolus, Phi Beta Kappa. Clubs: New Orleans Country, Wyvern (New Orleans). Jewish. Home: 6020 Garfield St New Orleans LA 70118-6039 Office: Liskow & Lewis 701 Poydras St Ste 5000 New Orleans LA 70139-5099 E-mail: tblemann@liskow.com.

LEMANSKE, ROBERT F., JR. allergist, immunologist; b. Milw., 1948; MD, U. Wis., 1975. Diplomate Am. Bd. Pediats., Am. Bd. Allergy and Immunology. Intern U. Wis. Hosp., Madison, 1975-76, resident in pediats., 1976-78, prof. pediats. medicine, divsn. head pediat. allergy, immunology & rheumatology. Fellow: Am. Acad. Allergy and Immunology, Am. Acad. Pediat. Office: Clin Sci Ctr Rm K4/916 600 Highland Ave Madison WI 53792-0001

LEMANSKI, LARRY FREDRICK, medical educator, university administrator; b. Madison, Wis., June 5, 1943; s. Fredrick Everett and Marjery Ulila (Hill) L.; m. Sharon Lee Wulf, Aug. 6, 1966; children: Scott Fredrick, Jennifer Lee. BS, U. Wis., Platteville, 1966; MS, Ariz. State U., 1968, PhD, 1971. Asst. prof. U. Calif., San Francisco, 1975-77; assoc. prof. U. Wis., Madison, 1977-79, prof., 1979-83; prof., chmn. dept. anatomy and cell biology SUNY, Syracuse, 1983-97, cell & molecular biology doctoral tng. program & consortium, 1987-97; rsch. prof. biology Syracuse U., 1988-97; assoc. v.p. for rsch. Tex. A&M. U., College Station, 1997—. Mem. ad hoc rev. panel NIH, mem. cardiovasc. study sect., 1993-97. Bd. dirs. Oak Ridge Assoc. Univs., 1999—; adult leader for Boy Scouts Am., mem. nat. staff Boy Scout Jamboree 1989, coun. tng. chmn., 1992—. Officer USAR, 1965-69. Recipient Pres'. award Rsch. SUNY HSC, 1987, Disting. Alumnus award U. Wis., 1990, Profl. Excellence award N.Y. State/United Univ. Professions, 1990, 95, Pres.'s award for affirmative action, 1995, Outstanding Rschr. award SUNY Coll. of Medicine, 1997; NIH fellow, 1968-71, 71-73, Muscular Dystrophy fellow, 1973-75; grantee NIH, 1975—. Mem. AAAS, Am. Heart Assn. (Wis. affiliate rsch. com. 1982-83, Louis N. Katz Rsch. prize 1978, Outstanding Rsch. award 1982, Established Investigator award 1976-81), Electron Microscopy Soc. Am., Tex. Soc. for Biomed. Rsch. (bd. dirs. 1999—), Am. Assn. Anatomy, Cell Biology, and Neurobiology (chairperson nat. coun. 1997—), Am. Assn. Anatomists, Am. Soc. Cell Biology (congrl. liaison com. 1993—), Soc. Devel. Biology, Am. Assn. Anatomy Chmn., N.Y. Acad. Scis., Masons (3d degree master), Sigma Xi, Beta Beta Beta, Phi Beta Delta. Methodist. Avocations: gardening, fishing, boating, camping, music. Office: Tex A&M U 312 Administration Bldg College Station TX 77843-0001 Fax: 409-845-1855. E-mail: l-lemanski@tamu.edu.

LEMARBE, EDWARD S. marketing executive, engineering manager, engineer; b. Chicago Heights, Ill., June 30, 1952; s. Gerald Joseph and Irene Helen (Jelen) LeM.; m. Patricia Ann Czyz, May 28, 1977; children: Kyle Bradford, Randall Jered. BS in Mech. Tech., Purdue U., 1976; MBA, Lewis U., 1984. Field engr. Morrison Constrn. & Engring., Hammond, Ind., 1976-78; sr. engr. Miner Enterprises, Inc., Geneva, 1978-85; mgr. product devel. Alco Dispensing Systems div. Alco Standard, Torrington, Conn., 1985-88; v.p. engring. Jet Spray Corp., Norwood, Mass., 1988-92; sr. dir. Engring. Multiplex Co., Ballwin, Mo., 1992-95; sr. dir. key accounts mktg., R&D Multiplex Co., 1995-97, v.p. nat. accounts, 1997—, dir. bus. devel., 2000—; product line dir. Manitowoc Beverage divsn. Manitowoc Food Svc. Group, 2002—. Mem. pres.' staff Alco Dispensing/Selmix-Alco, Torrington, 1986-88; mem. exec. com. Jet Spray Corp., Norwood, 1988-92; mem. resource allocation com. Multiplex Co. Inc., 1992-96, mem. strategic planning, 1996—. Mem. ASTM (subcom. 1988—), Am. Mgmt. Assn. (assoc.), Internat. Food Svc. Mfrs. Assn. (corp. mem.), Hickory Bend Condo Assn. (bd. dirs. 1984-85). Republican. Roman Catholic. Avocations: golf, tennis, scuba diving. E-mail: elemarbe@earthlink.net., lemarbee@servend.com.

LE MASTER, DENNIS CLYDE, natural resource economics and policy educator; b. Startup, Wash., Apr. 22, 1939; s. Franklin Clyde and Delores Ilene (Schwartz) Le M.; m. Kathleen Ruth Dennis, Apr. 4, 1961; children: Paul, Matthew. BA, Wash. State U., 1961, MA, 1970, PhD, 1974. Asst. prof. dept. forestry and range mgmt. Wash. State U., Pullman, 1972-74, assoc. prof., 1978-80, prof., chair dept., 1980-88; prof., head dept. forestry and natural resources Purdue U., West Lafayette, Ind., 1988—; dir. resource policy Soc. Am. Foresters, Bethesda, Md., 1974-76; staff counsel subcom. on forests Ho. of Reps., Washington, 1977-78. Cons. USDA Forest Svc., Washington, 1978, Com. on Agr., Ho. of Reps., 1979-80, Forest History Soc., Durham, N.C., 1979-83, The Conservation Found., 1989-90, Office Tech. Assessment, Washington, 1989-91, Consultative Group on Biol. Diversity, 1991. Author: Decade of Change, 1984; co-editor 8 books; contbr. articles to profl. jours. Bd. dirs. Pinchot Inst. for Conservation, treas., 1996-97, vice-chair, 1998-99, chair, 2000-01. Mem. AAAS, Soc. Am. Foresters (coun. 1988, chair house of soc. dels. 1982), Inland Empire Soc. of Soc. Am. Foresters (chair 1980-81, Forester of Yr. award 1982, fellow 2000), Soc. for Range Mgmt., Forest Products Soc., Omicron Delta Epsilon, Beta Gamma Sigma, Epsilon Sigma Phi, Xi Sigma Pi. Democrat. Episcopalian. Avocation: fishing. Home: 824 Lazy Ln Lafayette IN 47904-2722 Office: Purdue U Dept Forestry and Natural Resources West Lafayette IN 47907

LEMASTER, SHERRY RENEE, fundraising administrator; b. Lexington, Ky., June 25, 1953; d. John William and Mary Charles (Thompson) LeM.; BS, U. Ky., 1975, MS in Higher Edn. Adminstrn., Bryn Mawr Coll. Inst. for Women, 1984. Cert. fund raising exec. Lab. technician in Cen. Ky. Animal Disease Diagnostic Lab., Lexington, 1975-76; grant coord., environ. specialist Commonwealth Ky. Dept. for Natural Resources and Environ. Protection, Frankfurt, 1976-78; coord. residence hall program Murray (Ky.) State U., 1978-80; dean students Midway (Ky.) Coll., 1980-81, v.p. devel., alumnae affairs, 1981-86; dir. devel. Wilderness Road Coun. Girl Scouts U.S., Lexington, 1986-88, Coll. of Agr. and Life Scis. Va. Tech., Blacksburg, Va. 1988-94; sr. major gifts officer Sch. Medicine Wake Forest U. and N.C. Baptist Hosp., Inc., Winston-Salem, N.C., 1994-98; exec. dir. U. Oklahoma City, Okla., 1998-2000; owner, cons. LeMaitre fund raising, 2001-; amb. U. Ky. Coll. Agr.; cons. U.S. Dept. Edn., 1987—; chmn. Midway chpt. Am. Heart Assn., 1981; mem. adminstrv. bd. First United Meth. Ch., Lexington, 1982-84, 87; mem. Coun. for Advancement and Support Edn., 1981—, chmn. Ky. conf., 1982; planning com. charter mem. Nat. Disciples Devel. Execs. Conf., 1984; mem. East Ky. First Quality of Life Com., 1987-88. Recipient Young Career Woman award Bus. and Profl. Women's Club, Frankfort, 1981; named to Hon. Order of Ky. col., 1977, hon. sec. state, 1984. Mem. Nat. Soc. Fund Raising Execs. (bd. dirs. Lexington chpt. 1986), Advancement Women in Higher Edn. Adminstrn. (former state planning com. Ky.), U. Ky. Alumni Assn. (life), P.E.O. (charter, chpt. X-Ky., sec. chpt. AU-Va. 1991-93, Va. state chpt., amendments and accommendation com. 1990-92), Ninety-Nines Internat. Assn. Women Pilots (vice chmn. Ky. Bluegrass chpt. 1986-87, chmn. and chmn. bd. 1987-88, dir. South Ctrl. sect. 2000-2002), Kentuckians N.Y., Jr. League, Pi Beta Phi Nat. Alumnae Assn. (alumnae province pres. 1980-81, sec. bd. dirs. Ky. Beta chpt. 1982-84, pres. Va. Zeta chpt. house corp. 1991-94). Avocations: needlepoint, swimming, equitation. Office: 396 Hwy DD Defiance MO 63341

LEMASTER, SUSAN M. marketing executive, writer; b. Cody, Wyo., May 9, 1953; d. Floyd Morris and Virginia Kristena (Renner) LeM. AA, Casper Coll., 1977; BA, U. Wyo., Casper, 1979. Reporter, night editor Casper Star Tribune, 1972-76; copy editor, editor In Wyo. mag., Casper, 1979; info. dir. Wyo. Rural Electric Assn., 1980-81; story editor Wyo. Horizons mag., 1981-82; asst., instr. English lab. Casper Coll., 1982-84; mktg. mgr. Chen & Assocs., Inc., 1984-87; mktg. cons., 1987-90; dir. mktg. KaWES and Assocs., Inc., 1990-91, pub. rels. and mktg. cons., 1992-95; comm. mgr. Arthur Andersen, L.A., 1995-97, assoc. dir. sales and mktg., 1997-99, mktg. dir., 1999-2000, Pacific Region Bus. Consulting, 2000—01, mktg. mgr. healthcare, 2001—02; dir. PacifiCare Dental & Vision, Santa Ana, Calif., 2002—. Freelance writer and editor, 1982—; night sch. instr. Casper Coll., 1983-84, summer sch. instr., 1984. Editor Casper Jour., 1983-84. Recipient 1st Place News Story award Wyo. Press Assn., 1973, 1st Place Editing award Wyo. Press Women, 1980. Mem. L.A. Press Club, Phi Theta Kappa, Phi Kappa Phi, Alpha Mu Gamma. Democrat. Home: 1059 E Cypress Ave Burbank CA 91501-1309 Office: PacifiCare Dental & Vision 3110 Lake Center Dr Santa Ana CA 92704

LEMAY, JACQUES, lawyer; b. Quebec City, Can., July 10, 1940; s. Gerard and Jacqueline (Lachance) LeM. BA, Que. Sem., 1959; LL.L., Laval U., 1962; postgrad., U. Toronto, 1964; D.E.S., 1965. Bar: Que. 1963. Practice in Quebec City, 1964—; mem. firm Prevost, Gagne, Flynn, Chouinard & Jacques, 1964-67; ptnr. Flynn, Rivard, Jacques, Cimon, Lessard & LeMay, 1968-86, Flynn, Rivard, 1986—; legal adviser Societe des Ajusteurs d'Assurance, 1969. Bd. dirs. Can. 88 Energy Corp., 1991—2000. Mem. Societe des Etudes Juridiques (pres. 1969) Clubs: Cercle de la Garnison (Que.). Home: 2342 Marie-Victorin Sillery QC Canada G1T 2W5 Office: 70 Dalhousie Bureau 500 Quebec QC Canada G1K 7A6 E-mail: jlemay@flynn.qc.ca.

LEMAY, J(OSEPH) A(LBERIC) LEO, American literature educator; b. Bristow, Va., Jan. 17, 1935; s. Joseph Albert and Valencia Lee (Winslow) L.; m. Muriel Ann Clarke, Aug. 11, 1965; children: John Clarke, Lee Clarke, Kate Clarke. AB, U. Md., 1957, AM, 1962; PhD, U. Pa., 1964. From instr. to asst. prof. English George Washington U., Washington, 1963-65; asst. prof. English UCLA, 1965-70, assoc. prof., 1970-75, prof. English, 1975-77; H.F. du Pont Winterthur prof. English U. Del., Newark, 1977—. Author: Men of Letters in Colonial Maryland, 1972, The Canon of Benjamin Franklin New Attributions, 1986, The American Dream of Captain John Smith, 1991, Did Pocahontas Save Captain John Smith?, 1992; (internet book) A Documentary History of Benjamin Franklin, 1997—; editor Robert Bolling Woos Anne Miller, 1990. Adv. com. Ctr. Editions of Am. Authors, 1974-76; mem. Inst. Early Am. History and Culture, 1978-81, Cosmos Club, 1984—. With U.S. Army, 1957-59. Fellow Inst. Advanced Study, U. Del., 1980-81, 98-99, Guggenheim Found., 1974-75. Mem. MLA (Hon. Scholar award 1999), Am. Humor Studies Assn. (pres. 1981), Am. Antiquarian Soc., Soc. for Study of So. Lit. Office: Univ Del Memorial Hall Newark DE 19716-2595 Home: 55 Sunset Rd Newark DE 19711-5237 E-mail: lemay@udel.edu.

LEMBARK, CONNIE WERTHEIMER, art consultant; b. Omaha, Mar. 8, 1934; d. Sam Wertheimer and Elinor (Livingston) Wertheimer-Dombrowsky; m. Daniel Lembark, July 10, 1955; 1 child, Steven. Student, U. Ariz. Docent UCLA, 1964-71; owner, art cons. Connie W. Lembark, Nashville, L.A.; owner, founding ptnr. Art Posters Ltd., 1971-82; art cons., 1983—. Lectr. L.A. County Mus. Art, 1994; founder Mus. Contemporary Art L.A. Author: The Prints of Sam Francis, 1992.

LEMBERG, FREDERIC GARY, lawyer; b. Los Angeles, Sept. 25, 1944; s. Jack and Rose (Zuckerman) L.; m. Ellen S. Lemberg; children: Carren Lynn, Serena Melody, Jamie Leigh. BS, Ariz. State U., 1966, JD, 1971. Bar: Ariz. 1971, U.S. Dist. Ct. Ariz. 1971, U.S. Ct. Appeals (9th cir.) 1977. Ptnr. Pollock & Lemberg, Phoenix, 1971-73, Lemberg, Green, Lester & Walsh, Phoenix, 1973-76, Mallin & Lemberg, Phoenix, 1980-83, Fannin, Terry & Lemberg, P.A., Phoenix, 1983-88, Quarles & Brady & Fannin, Phoenix, 1988—90, Logan & Geotas, 1999—. Mem. ABA, Ariz. Bar Assn., Maricopa County Bar Assn., Assn. Trial Lawyers Am.

LEMBERG, LOUIS, cardiologist, educator; b. Chgo., Dec. 27, 1916; s. Morris and Frances Lemberg; m. Dorothy Feinstein, 1940 (dec. 1969); children: Gerald, Laura Bott, Paula Saltzman; m. Miriam Mayer, Jan. 29, 1971. BS, U. Ill., Chgo., 1938; MD, U. Ill., 1940. Intern Mt. Sinai Hosp., Chgo., 1940-41, resident, 1945-48; asst. prof. med., 1955-58; assoc. prof. med., 1958-70; prof. clin. cardiology U. Miami Sch. Medicine, Fla., 1970—, dir. coronary care unit, 1965-75. Chief cardiology Mercy Hosp., 1974-79; chief staff Nat. Children's Cardiac Hosp., 1959-66; cons. cardiology VA Hosp., Miami, 1953-64; dir. cardiology Dade County Hosp., 1953-64, dir. Heart Sta. and Electrocardiography, U. Miami Jackson Meml. Med. Ctr., 1952-75, program dir. Courses in Coronary Care for Practicing Physician, 1970—, Master Approach to Cardiovascular Problems, 1972-82, Cardiology Update for Intensive Care Nurses, 1978-92, Cardiology Update, 1987—. Author: Vectorcardiography, 1969, 2d edit., 1975, Electrophysiology of Pacing and Conversion, 1969; editor-in-chief Current Concepts in Cardiovascular Disorders, 1984-86; contbr. to med. publs. Served to maj. AUS, 1941-55, ETO. Recipient U. St. Torres (Phillippines) Luis Guerrero hon. lectr. award, 1977, Recognition award U. Miami Sch. Medicine, Lifetime Achievement award Jackson Meml. Med. Ctr. U. Miami, 1997, Key to City of Miami Beach, Fla., Nurses Pioneering Spirit award Am. Assn. Critical Care, 2000, Physicians Recognition awards AMA. Fellow ACP, Am. Coll. Cardiology (editl. bd. jour.); mem. Heart Assn. Greater Miami (pres.), Fla. Heart Assn. (pres.), Am. Heart Assn. (fellow coun. clin. cardiology), Palm Bay Club (Miami), Williams Island Club. Democrat. Jewish. Achievements include pioneer in development Demand Pacemaker, 1964, a chair in cardiology established at the U. Miami Sch. of Medicine entitled The Louis Lemberg Professor of Cardiology, 1990. Home: 720 NE 69th St Apt 18 South Miami FL 33138-5738 Office: U Miami Sch Medicine Divsn Cardiology PO Box 016960 Miami FL 33101

LEMBERGER, LOUIS, pharmacologist, physician; b. Monticello, N.Y., May 8, 1937; s. Max and Ida (Siegel) L.; m. Myrna Sue Diamond, 1959; children: Harriet Felice Schor, Margo Beth. BS magna cum laude, Bklyn. Coll. Pharmacy, L.I. U., 1960; PhD in Pharmacology, Albert Einstein Coll. Medicine, 1964, MD, 1968; Doctorate (hon.), L.I. U., 1994. Pharmacy intern VA Regional Office, Newark, summer 1960; postdoctoral fellow Albert Einstein Coll. Medicine, 1964-68; intern in medicine Met. Hosp. Center, N.Y. Med. Coll., N.Y.C., 1968-69; rsch. assoc. NIH, Bethesda, Md., 1969-71; clin. pharmacologist Lilly Lab. for Clin. Rsch., Eli Lilly & Co., Indpls., 1971-75, chief clin. pharmacology, 1975-78, dir. clin. pharmacology, 1978-89, clin. rsch. fellow, 1982-93; asst. prof. pharmacology Ind. U., 1972-73, asst. prof. medicine, 1972-73, assoc. prof. pharmacology, 1973-77, assoc. prof. medicine, 1973-77, prof. pharmacology, 1977—, prof. medicine, prof. psychiatry, 1977—, mem. grad. faculty, 1975—; adj. prof. clin. pharmacology Ohio State U., 1975-86; physician Wishard Meml. Hosp., 1976-98. Cons. U.S. Nat. Commn. on Marijuana and Drug Abuse, 1971-73, Can. Commn. Inquiry into Non-Med. Use of Drugs, 1971-73; mem. Pharm. Mfrs. Assn. Commn. on Medicines for Drug Dependence and Abuse, 1990-93, Ind. Optometric Legend Drug Adv. Com., 1991-96; guest lectr. various univs., 1968—; lectr. U. Minn., 1993—; mem. adv. com. Faseb Life Scis. Rsch. Office, 1993-96. Author: (with A. Rubin) Physiologic Disposition of Drugs of Abuse, 1976; contbr. numerous articles on biochemistry and pharmacology to sci. jours.; editorial bd.; Excerpta Medica, 1972-96, Clin. Pharmacology and Therapeutics, 1976-96, Communications in Psychopharmacology, 1975-91, Pharmacology, Interant. Jour. Exptl. and Clin. Pharmacology, 1978-94, Drug and Alcohol Abuse Rsch., 1979-86, Drug Devel. Rsch., 1980-87, Trends in Pharmcol. Scis., 1980-85. Post adviser Crossroads of Am. coun. Boy Scouts Am., 1972-77. With USPHS, 1969-71. Recipient Disting. Alumnus award Albert Einstein Coll. Medicine, 1989, Disting. Alumnus award L.I. U., 1990, Pres. award L.I. U., 1998, Cornerstone award for Oustanding Lifetime Achievement in Health Scis., Am. Drugstore Mus., 2000. Fellow ACP, AAAS, Am. Coll. Neuropsychopharmacology (chmn. credentials com. 1993) , Am. Coll. Clin. Pharmacology; mem. Am. Soc. Pharmacology and Exptl. Therapeutics (com. div. clin. pharmacology 1972-78, chmn. com. 1978-83, coun. 1980-83, chmn. long-range planning com. 1984-86, pres. 1987-88, ASPET award in Therapeutics, 1985, Harry Gold award for rsch. and teaching excellence in clin. pharmacology 1993), Am. Soc. Clin. Pharmacology and Therapeutics (chmn. sect. neuropsychopharmacology 1973-80, chmn. fin. com. 1976-83, 89-92, v.p. 1981-82, pres. 1983-84, dir. 1975-81, 84-87, Rawls-Palmer award 1986, Henry Elliot Disting. Svc. award 1992), Am. Soc. Clin. Investigation, Collegium Internat. Neuro-Psychopharmacologicum, Am. Fedn. Clin. Rsch. Ctrl. Soc. Clin. Rsch., Soc. Neuroscis., Sigma Xi, Alpha Omega Alpha, Rho Chi. Jewish. Achievements include being first person to administer and study the actions in humans of the antidepressant drug Prozac (fluoxetine), Permax (pergolide) the drug used to treat Parkinson's disease, and the cannabinoid drug Cesamet (nabilone) utilized for the treatment of nausea and vomiting secondary to cancer chemotherapy and Zyprexa (Olanzepine) the drug utilized in schizophrenia; responsible for directing and spearheading the clinical development of Prozac, Permax and Cesamet through clinical trials, regulatory approval and eventually into the marketplace. Home: 3315 Walnut Creek Dr N Carmel IN 46032-9038 Office: Ind Univ Sch Medicine Dept Pharmacology and Medicine Indianapolis IN 46202

LEMENS, WILLIAM VERNON, JR. banker, finance company executive, lawyer; b. Austin, Tex., Oct. 26, 1935; s. William Vernon and Lylia (Engberg) L.; m. Jean Lemens, May 31, 1959; children: William Vernon III, Shandra Christine. BA, U. Tex., 1958, LLB, JD, U. Tex., 1962. Bar: Tex. 1962; lic. real estate broker, Tex. Pvt. practice, Austin, 1962—; pres. Standard Fin. Co., 1963-67, First State Loan, Austin, 1967—; chief exec. officer Southwest Computer Svcs., Inc., 1965—. Pres., chief instr., mgmt. cons. Decision Dynamics, Inc., Austin, 1965-75; exec. v.p., atty. Northwest Savs. Assn., Austin, 1975-78; chmn. bd. First State Bank, Jarrell, Tex., 1975-87; pres., chief exec. officer First Am. Fin. Co., Ft. Worth, 1982—, Eagle Bank, Jarrell, 1987—. Author: Elements of Objective Orientation, 1971, SSAM-The Power of Perfect Decisions, 1972, Successful Financial Institution Operation, 1978, National Standard Financial Company Operations, 1981. Pres. Ballet Austin, 1967, Southwest Regional Ballet Assn., 1968; deacon Univ. Bapt. Ch., Austin, 1979—. Mem. State Bar Tex., Austin Bd. Realtors, Tex. Fin. Inst. (bd. dirs. 1975—), Tex. Consumer Fin. Assns. (bd. dirs. 1995—). Office: 1509 Guadalupe St Ste 200 Austin TX 78701-1608

LEMENSE, FAY ANN, special education educator; b. Kewaunee, Wis., Apr. 17, 1965; d. Leon Ernest and Ruth H. (Sternard) S.; m. Patrick S. LeMense. BS in Elem. Edn. and Spl. Learning Disabilities, Silver Lake Coll., 1987; MA in elem. principalship, U. Wis., 1995. Headmistress, tchr. John Hutter Emily Steward Found., Sturgeon Bay, Wis., 1987-88; tchr. learning disabled Oneida (Wis.) Tribal Sch., 1988-94, coord., supr. spl. edn. program, 1988-95; prin. Oneida Nation Elem. Sch., 1995; spl. edn. coord. K-12 Oneida Nation Sch., 2000—. Tutor, Green Bay, Wis., 1989—. Mem. Coun. for Exceptional Children. Lutheran. Office: Oneida Nation Sch Sch N7125 PO Box 365 Oneida WI 54155

LEMER, ANDREW CHARLES, engineer, economist; b. Maxwell Field, Ala., Dec. 25, 1944; s. Samuel Theodore and Carol (Oppenheimer) L.; m. Patricia Spear, Aug. 1967 (div. Dec. 1981); m. Jane Felsten, Aug. 1992; children: Elizabeth Catherine, Daniel Evan, Rebekah Simone. SB, MIT, 1967, SM, 1968, PhD, 1971. Assoc. Alan M. Voorhees & Assoc., Inc., McLean, Va., 1971-76; sr. assoc. PRC Planning & Econs., Inc., 1976-80; chief planner PRC (Nigeria) Ltd., Lagos, 1980-82; div. v.p. PRC Engring., Inc., McLean, 1982-85; pres. Matrix Group, LLC, Balt., 1985—; dir. bldg. rsch. bd. Nat. Acad. Scis., 1988—93. Cons. Fed. Rail Adminstrn., Washington, 1975, FAA, Washington, 1986—, World Bank, Washington, 1980—, Abell Found., Balt., 1993—, Transp. Rsch. Bd., Washington, 1993—; vis. prof. civil engring. Purdue U., West Lafayette, Ind., 1995-96; adj. faculty environ. earth scis. and policy Johns Hopkins U., Balt., 1994—. Prin. author: In Our Own Back Yard: Principles for Improving the Nation's Infrastructure, 1993, Toward Infrastructure Improvement: A Research Agenda, 1994, Solving the Innovation Puzzle: Challenges Facing the U.S. Design and Construction Industry, 1996; contbr. articles to profl. jours.; editl. adv. bd. Jour. Infrastructure Sys., Constrn. Bus. Rev., Constrn. Mgmt. and Econs., Pub. Works Mgmt. and Policy. Mem. ednl. coun. MIT, Washington, 1974—. Loeb fellow Harvard U., 1992-93. Mem. ASCE, Am. Inst. Cert. Planners, The Am. Soc. Macroengring. (bd. dirs. 1997—, pres. 2000—), Lambda Alpha Internat. Office: 4701 Keswick Rd Baltimore MD 21210-2322

LEMESIS, GUNTIS VICTOR, retired telecommunications company executive; b. Jekabpils, Latvia, May 17, 1943; came to U.S., 1950; s. Alberts and Alma Lemesis; m. Mara Kalva, Aug. 2, 1979 (div. 1988); m. Susan Durden, Aug. 26, 1989. BA, Wesleyan U., 1966. Compensation specialist Honeywell, Inc., Phoenix, 1978-79, human resources planning specialist, 1979-80, mgr. benefits planning Mpls., 1980-82; dir. compensation & benefits United Airlines, Elk Grove Village, Ill., 1982-86; dir. compensation & mgmt. resources Contel Corp., Atlanta, 1986-91; v.p. compensation GTE Corp., Stamford, Conn., 1991-93; dir. compensation & human resources planning Sci.-Atlanta, Inc., Norcross, Ga., 1993-2000. Instr. World at Work (formerly Am. Compensation Assn.), Scottsdale, Ariz., 1985—; mem. exec. adv. panel Acad. Mgmt., Boston, 1997—. Co-author: Determining Compensation Costs, 1992, Compensation Guide, 1993; mem. editl. bd. Executive Compensation Reports, 1999—. Mem. employee benefits com. U.S. C. of C., Washington, 1981-86. Recipient 1st pl. Pub. Utilities Advt. Assn., 1972, 1st pl. Ariz. Assn. Bus. Communicators, 1974. Mem.: Soc. Human Resources Mgmt., World at Work. Republican. Methodist. Avocations: music, wine collecting, amateur photography, chess.

LEMIEUX, CLAUDE, professional hockey player; b. Buckingham, Que., July 16, 1965; Right wing Montreal Canadiens, 1983-90, N.J. Devils, 1990-95, 1999—2000, Colo. Avalanche, 1995-99, Phoenix Coyotes, 2000—. Mem. Stanley Cup Championship teams, 1986, 95, 96. Named to Que. Major Jr. Hockey League All-Star second team, 1983-83, first team, 1984-85; recipient Guy Lafleur trophy, 1985, Conn Smythe trophy for most valuable player in playoffs, 1995. Office: Pheonix Coyotes America West Center 9375 E. Bell Road Scottsdale AZ 85260*

LEMIEUX, JEROME ANTHONY, JR. electrical and computer engineer; b. Fond du Lac, Wis., July 9, 1957; s. Jerome Anthony and Janet Ann (Lehman) L.; children: Angela Kay, Jerome Anthony III. BSEE, U. Wis., 1980; MSEE, Miss. State U., 1984, PhD in Elec. Engring., 1987; postgrad., Air Command and Staff Coll., 1998, Air War Coll., 2000. Commd. 2d lt. USAF, 1980, advanced through grades to lt. col., squadron officer sch. residence program Ala., 1985, T-38 instr. pilot 50th Flying Tng. Squadron Columbus AFB, Miss., 1982-86, fighter lead in tng. capt. 434th Tactical Fighter Squadron Hollomon AFB, N.Mex., 1986, fighter pilot capt. 21st and 562nd Tactical Fighter Squadron George AFB, Calif., 1986-87, F-16C/F-46 combat ready fighter pilot, flight comdr., instr. pilot, capt. Spangdahlem Air Base, Germany, 1987-90, devel. engr., 1994—; ret.; tech. staff mem., sys. and signal processing engr. MIT Lincoln Lab., Lexington, Mass., 1990-94, cons. engr., 1994—; airline pilot Delta Air Lines/J.F.K. Internat. Airport, N.Y.C., N.Y., 1991—. Adj. prof. elec. engring. Boston U., 1988-91, U. Md., 1987-88; cons. engr. USAF, Electronic Systems Ctr., Hanscom AFB, Mass., 1994—; chmn. 1997 IEEE Internat. Radar Conf., Washington, com. mem., 1993-97; pres. Bus. Ads Online, Internet Consulting and Design Co.; pres. Bus. Ads Online, 1996—; pres., CEO Am. Aviation Inc. Flight Test & Engring. Svcs. Co., 1991—, Am. Aviation, Inc.-Engring., Internet and Aviation Svcs. Editor: Fourier Analysis Textbook, 1994; contbr. numerous articles to profl. jours. Lt. col. USAFR, 1999—. Decorated Air Force Commendation medal with oak leaf cluster. Mem. IEEE, IEEE Aerospace and Electronics Sys. Soc., IEEE Signal Processing Soc., IEEE Computer Soc., Air Line Pilots Assn. Internat. (safety chmn. New Eng. region), Alpha Delta Phi, Tau Beta Pi, Eta Kappa Nu, Kappa Mu Epsilon. Avocations: running, weightlifting, reading, computer programming, flying. Office: ESC/SR 11 Barksdale St Hanscom AFB MA 01731-1700 Home: 3 Osprey Ln Dover NH 03820

LEMIEUX, JOSEPH HENRY, manufacturing company executive; b. Providence, Mar. 2, 1931; s. Mildred L. Lemieux; m. Frances Joanne Schmidt, Aug. 11, 1956; children: Gerald Joseph, Craig Joseph, Kimberly Mae Lemieux Wolff, Allison Jo Smith. Student, Stonehill Coll., 1949-50, U. R.I., 1950-51; BBA summa cum laude, Bryant Coll., 1957. With Owens-Ill., Toledo, 1957—, various positions with glass container div. and closure and metal container group; exec. v.p. Owens-Ill. Owens-Ill., Inc., 1984, pres. pkg. ops., 1984, pres., COO, 1986-90, pres., CEO, 1990-91, chmn. bd., CEO, 1991—, also bd. dirs. Bd. dirs. Nat. City Bank Northwest, Toledo, Nat. City Corp., Cleve. Trustee Bryant Coll. Staff sgt. USAF, 1951-55. Named one of Outstanding Young Men Am., Jaycees, 1965, Recipient glass industry's Phoenix award, 1997. Mem. Glass Packaging Inst. (chmn. 1984-86), Inverness Club (Toledo). Roman Catholic. Avocations: golf, tennis. Office: Owens-Illinois Inc 1 Seagate Toledo OH 43666-0001

LEMIEUX, LINDA DAILEY, museum director; b. Cleve., Sept. 6, 1953; d. Leslie Leo LeMieux Jr. and Mildred Edna (Dailey) Tutt. BA, Beloit Coll., 1975; MA, U. Mich., 1979; assoc. cert., Mus. Mgmt. Program, Boulder, Colo., 1987. Asst. curator Old Salem, Inc., Winston-Salem, N.C., 1979-82; curator Clarke House, Chgo., 1982-84, Western Mus. Mining and Industry, Colorado Springs, Colo., 1985-86, dir., 1987—. Author: Prairie Avenue Guidebook, 1985; editor: The Golden Years--Mines in the Cripple Creek District, 1987; contbr. articles to mags. and newspapers. Fellow Hist. Deerfield, Mass., 1974—. Research grantee Early Am. Industries Assn., 1978. Mem. Am. Assn. Mus., Am. Assn. State and Local History, Colo.-Wyo. Mus. Assn., Colo. Mining Assn., Nev. Mining Assn., Mountain Plains Assn. Mus., Women in Mining. Congregationalist. Home: 1337 Hermosa Way Colorado Springs CO 80906-3050 Office: Western Mus Mining & Industry 1025 N Gate Rd Colorado Springs CO 80921-3018 E-mail: wmmidirector@aol.com., lindalemieux1@aol.com.

LEMIEUX, MARIO, professional sports team executive, professional hockey player; b. Montreal, P.Q., Can., Oct. 5, 1965; m. Nathalie Asselin, June 26, 1993; 4 children. With Pitts. Penguins, 1984-97, owner, 1998-, with, 2000—. Mem. NHL All-Star team, 1987-88, 88-89, 92-93, Stanley Cup Championship team, 1991, 92; player NHL All-Star game, 1992-93. Recipient Hart Meml. trophy for most valuable player, 1988, 89, 96, Conn Smythe trophy for most valuable player in playoff, 1991, Art Ross Meml. trophy, 1987-88, 88-89, 91-92, 92-93, 96, Dodge Performance of the Year award, 1987-88, 88-89, Dodge Ram Tough award, 1988-89, Michel Briere trophy, 1983-84, Jean Beliveau trophy, 1983-84, Michael Bossy trophy, 1983-84, Guy LaFleur trophy, 1983-84, Calder Meml. trophy, 1984-85, Lester B. Pearson award, 1985-86, 87-88, 92-93, Pro Set NHL Player of the Year, 1991-92, Bill Masterson Meml. trophy, 1992-93; named Sporting News All-Star team, 1987-88, 88-89, 92-93, Player of the Year Canadian Hockey League, 1983-84, All-Star game MVP, 1985, 88, 90, Player of the Year NHL, 1992-93, inducted Hockey Hall of Fame, 1997. Office: Pittsburgh Penguins Mellon Arena 66 Mario Lemieux Drive Pittsburgh PA 15219*

LEMING, W(ILLIAM) VAUGHN, electronics engineer; b. Pawhuska, Okla., Dec. 11, 1945; s. William Dalton Leming and Mattie Cornelia (Hatfield) Kafer; m. Janis Diana Lee (div.); children: Heather Lynne, Hilary Ann; m. Donna Faye Sartor, May 18, 1975 (div.); 1 child, Chandra Paige. Student, U. Okla., 1964-67. 68-70, U. Tulsa, 1967-68; cert., diploma, DeVry Inst. Tech., Chgo, 1977; cert., diploma with highest honors, Nat. Radio Inst., Washington, 1981. FCC Gen. Radio telephone, Naber Cert., IHF Consumer Audio Assoc. Spl. instr. Tri County Vocat.-Tech. Sch., Bartlesville, Okla., 1975-76; pres., chief exec. officer Fantasia Sound Systems, Inc., Jenks, 1976-77; announcer KWON Radio, Bartlesville, 1980-81; chief electronics technician The Sound Centre, 1978-81; electronic technician 1A Burlington No. R.R. Co., Tulsa, 1981-92; founder, CEO FeS2 Pictures, 1991—. Musician, actor, entertainer, 1966—; bassist The New Orleans Jazz Band, Jenks, Okla., 1979—; actor: (films) The Outsiders, 1982, Rumble Fish, 1983, Fandango, 1984, Schizophrenia, 1989; dir., editor: (documentary) Adjuvant Nutrition in Cancer Treatment Symposium; photographer (campaign exhibit) Picture What Women Do, Lifetime TV, 1994. Tribal mem. Choctaw Nation of Okla. Recipient Gold medal in electronics U.S. Skill Olympics, Lawton, Okla., 1976. Avocations: pet cat, collecting Disney artifacts, genealogy, Native American interests. Home: 523 E E St Jenks OK 74037-3326 Office: 523 E E St Jenks OK 74037-3326 E-mail: fes263457@aol.com.

LEMIRE, ANDRE, investment company executive; b. Quebec City, Que., Can., Mar. 15, 1943; s. Adrien and Gabrielle (Martel) L.; m. Ann C. Chisholm, Sept. 6, 1969. BS, U. Ottawa, 1967. Tax analyst Bell Can., Montreal, 1968-69; investment analyst Jones Heward Co., Ltd., 1969-72; asst. dir. rsch. Levesque, Beaubien Inc., 1972-74, dir. investment rsch., 1974-78, v.p. internat., chmn. investment com., 1978—, sr. v.p., 1979-85, exec. v.p., 1985-88; pres., CEO Lemvest Capital Inc., 1999—. Pres., bd. dirs. Marleau Lemire Inc., 1990-98; past gov. Montreal Exch. Contbr. articles to profl. jours. Bd. dirs., chmn. investment com. Montreal Children's Hosp. Found. Mem. Montreal Soc. Fin. Analysts, Montreal Mus. Arts, Mt. Royal Club, Mt. Bruno Country Club, Turnberry Golf Club. Roman Catholic. Home: 2 Westmount Sq PH C Westmount QC Canada H3Z 2S4 Office: Lemvest Capital Inc 2 Westmount Sq Montreal QC Canada H3Z 2S4

LEMIRE, DAVID STEPHEN, school psychologist, educator; b. Roswell, N.Mex., May 23, 1949; s. Joseph Armand and Jeanne (Longwill) Lemire. BA, Linfield Coll., 1972, MEd, 1974; EdS, Idaho State U., 1978; postgrad., U. Wyo., EdS in Ednl. Adminstrn. and Instrnl. Leadership, 1988, postgrad.; PhD in Curriculum and Instrn., Kansas State U. Cert. sch. counselor, sch. psychologist, psychotherapist. Student pers. worker, psychology instr., Calif. Sch. counselor, psychol. technician and tchr. Goshen County Sch. Dist. 1, Torrington, Wyo.; counselor Aspen (Colo.) HS; sch. counselor Unita County Sch. Dist., Evanston, Wyo., coord. R&D Lifelong Learning Ctr., 1986—87; dir. spl. svcs. and sch. psychologist Bighorn County Sch. Dist. #4, Basin, 1989—90; sch. psychologist Sweetwater County Sch. Dist. #2, Green River,

1990—91; dir. housing, residence supr. Pratt (Kans.) CC, 1991—92; tchr. Highland CC and Cloud County CC; pres. David Lemire Software Enterprises, Evanston; dir. Inst. for Advanced Study of Thinkology. Author (with Richard Mueller): Instructional Psychology, Fifty or More Ethical Dilemas: Reading/Writing Activities for the Secondary and College Classroom; author: Twenty Simple and Inexpensive Learning Style/Personal Style/Self Concept Instruments for Professionals and Educators with Rsearch and Supporting Documentation; editor (former): WACD Jour.; editor: (former mng.) Jour. Humanistic Edn.; contbr. articles to profl. jours. Mem.: APA, ASCD, Nat. Assn. Sch. Psychologists (cert.). Office: Creative Therapeutics Adminstrv Offices 2390 Riviera St Reno NV 89509-1144 *Personal philosophy: Teaching is the most important function of higher education. All education should focus on what students are successful at, then help students (young or old) to shape their own skills and learn more effectively. In general, my concern is with the quality of instruction more than with the quantity of instruction.*

LEMIRE, JEROME ALBERT, lawyer, geologist; b. Cleve., June 4, 1947; s. George A. and Matilda (Simon) Lemire; m. Sandra Marsick, Oct. 1, 1976; children: Laura, Lesley, Thomas. BS in Geology, Ohio State U., 1969, MS in Geology, 1973, JD, 1976. Bar: Ohio 1976; cert. fin. planner. Geologist United Petroleum Co., Columbus, Ohio, 1976—77; assoc. Brownfield, Bowen & Bally, 1977—79; land mgr. POI Energy Inc., Cleve., 1979—81; cons. Jefferson, 1981—83; v.p. Carey Resources Inc., 1984—86; pres. Lemire & Assocs Inc., 1986—. Cons. in field. Vice chmn. Tech. Adv. Coun., Columbus, 1984—94; solicitor Village of Jefferson. Served to 1st lt. U.S. Army, 1970—72. Mem.: VFW, Astabula County Bar Assn. (pres. 2002—), Ohio Bar Assn., Rotary. Home: 838 N State Route 46 Jefferson OH 44047-9785

LEMISCH, JESSE, history educator, writer; b. N.Y.C., Sept. 27, 1936; s. Tobias Brown and Beatrice (Cohen) L.; m. Naomi Weisstein, June 14, 1965 BA with high honors, Yale U., 1957; AM in History, Columbia U., 1958; PhD in Am. Studies, Yale U., 1963. Instr. history Yale U., New Haven, 1962-63; asst. prof. history U. Chgo., 1963-68; vis. asst. prof. history Northwestern U., Evanston, Ill., 1968-69; asst. prof. history Roosevelt U., Chgo., 1969-71, assoc. prof. history, 1971-73; assoc. prof. history and Am. studies SUNY, Buffalo, 1973-88; vis. assoc. prof. history CUNY, Baruch Coll., N.Y.C., 1985-88; assoc. prof. history CUNY, John Jay Coll. Criminal Justice, 1988—2000, emeritus prof. history, 2000—. Participant, chair numerous confs.; internat. lectr. in field, including Yale U., 1994, Meml. for E.P. Thompson, N.Y.C., 1993, Tikkun Mag. conf., N.Y.C., 1988, USSR Acad. Scis., Internat. Conf. Americanists, Moscow, 1991, others. Author: Jack Tar vs. John Bull, 1997, On Active Service in War and Peace: Politics and Ideology in the American Historical Profession, 1975; editor: Benjamin Franklin: Autobiography and Other Writings, 1961; contbr. and revs. to profl. jours. and newsletters, chpts. to books; contbr. articles to profl. jours. including The Nation, The New Republic, N.Y. Times, Chronicle of Higher Edn., Radical Hist. Rev., others. Advisor and cons. to numerous Am. Revolution Bicentennial activities and orgns., 1976. NEH rsch. grantee 1970-71, Am. Coun. Learned Socs. fellow 1965-66, U. Chgo. Willett Faculty fellow 1965. Mem. Am. Hist. Assn. (com. on commemoration of Am. Revolution Bicentennial 1971-76), Orgn. Am. Historians (nominating bd. 1976-78). Avocation: participation in N.Y.C. street life. E-mail: utopia1@attglobal.net.

LEMKE, ALAN JAMES, environmental specialist; b. Appleton, Wis., May 22, 1945; s. Edwin R. and Ethel Mae (Noe) L.; m. Joyce Eileen Kruse, May 24, 1975; 1 child, David Edwin. BS in chemistry, Coll. Idaho, 1968. Rsch. chemist Am. Med. Ctr., Denver, 1972-74; chemist U.S. Geol. Survey, 1975-77; chemist II Occupl. Health Lab., Portland, Oreg., 1977-80, State Hygienic Labs., Des Moines, 1980-82; indsl. hygienist Iowa Divsn. Labor, 1982-88; environ. specialist Iowa Dept. Natural Resources, Spencer, 1988—. Small bus. owner Al's Stamps and Collectables. Author: The Noe Family's Involvement in the Civil War: A History of Wisconsin's 19th Volunteer Infantry Regiment, 1994. Republican. Evangelical. Avocations: camping, hiking, fishing, history, reading. Home: 1110 15th Ave W Spencer IA 51301-2943 Office: Iowa Dept Natural Resources 1900 N Grand Ave Spencer IA 51301-2200

LEMKE, HENRY ROBERT, physician assistant; b. Alamogordo, N.Mex., Oct. 4, 1954; s. Henry John and Adelina Roberta (Castro) Lemke; m. Gayle Evelyn Egerton, Sept. 5, 1975; children: Jason Phillip, Laura Beth, Stephanie Renee. BS, U. Okla., 1982; M Med. Sci., St. Francis Coll., 1995. Cert. physical asst. Enlisted USAF, 1974, advanced through grades to maj.; mem. staff primary care clinic USAF Med. Ctr., Wright-Patterson AFB, Ohio, 1982-88, exec. officer to comdr., 1989-90; mem. staff family practice clinic 20 Med. Group Hosp., RAF Upper Heyford, Eng., 1990-93; dir. clin. tng. physician asst. program USAF, Sheppard AFB, Tex., 1993-95, program dir., 1995-96, ret., 1996; program dir. physician asst. studies, asst. prof. U. North Tex., Ft. Worth, 1996—. Risk mgr USAF Med Ctr, 1987—88, health consumer adv coun, 1987—90; total quality mgt course coord 20 Med Group Hosp, 1992—93; Seven Habits of Highly Effective People facilitator 882 Training Group, 1994—96. Contbr. . Fellow: Tex Acad Physician Assts (treas 1999—), Soc Air Force Physicians Assts (pres 1995—96, dir at large 1990—94), Am Acad Physicians Assts (chmn elections comt 1994—97). Republican. Avocations: sailing, golf. Office: U North Tex Health Sci Ctr 3500 Camp Bowie Blvd Fort Worth TX 76107-2644 E-mail: hlemke@hsc.unt.edu.

LEMKE, HERMAN ERNEST FREDERICK, JR. retired elementary education educator, consultant; b. Argo, Ill., July 13, 1919; s. Herman and Augusta Victoria (Statt) L.; m. Geneva Octavene Davidson, Sept. 5, 1942; children: Patricia, Herman E.F. III, Gloria, John, Elizabeth. BA, George Peabody Coll., 1949, MA, 1952. Cert. social sci. tchr., Tenn., elem. tchr., Calif. Tchr. Cadd Parish Sch., Shreveport, La., 1950-55, Pacific Sch. Dist., Sacramento, 1956-58, Sacramento Sch. Dist., 1958-89; part-time tchr. Sacramento County Sch., 1974-84. Substitute tchr., 1989—. Co-author: Natural History Guide, 1963, (field guide) Outdoor World of Sacramento Region, 1975; contbr. articles to profl. jours. Asst. dist. Commn. Boys Scouts Am., Shreveport, 1954, cubmaster, 1954; leader 4-H Club, Shreveport, 1950-54; elder Faith Luth. Ch., Fair Oaks, Calif., 1981-88. Recipient Scouter award, Boy Scouts Am., Shreveport, 1954, Honorary Svc. award Am. Winn Sch. PTA, 1982, Calif. Life Diploma Elem. Schs., 1961. Mem. Calif. Congress Parents Tchrs. Inc. (life). Democrat. Avocations: backpacking, coin collecting, stamp collecting, antiques, fishing. Home: 7720 Magnolia Ave Fair Oaks CA 95628-7316

LEMKE, JILL, city planner; b. Buffalo, Jan. 17, 1967; d. James Paul and Lynne Marie Lemke. BS in Comm., SUNY, Brockport, 1989; M of Regional Planning, Cornell U., 1997. Legis. intern Monroe County Legislature, Rochester, N.Y., 1989-90; comm. coord. N.Y. State Asembly, 1991-94; rsch. and tchg. asst. Cornell U., Ithaca, N.Y., 1994-96; govt. rels. officer Greater Buffalo Partnership, 1997; planning specialist Buffalo Gen. Health Sys., 1997-98; outreach coord. Heart of the City Neighborhoods, Buffalo, 1998-99; dir. cmty. planning City of Buffalo, 2001—. Rsch. asst. Neighborhood Reinvestment Corp., Buffalo, 1996. Contbr. chpt. to book. Sec. 23d Legislature Dem. Com., Rochester, 1993-94; polit. organizer Dem. Com. and campaigns, Rochester and Buffalo, 1989—; mem., vol. Western N.Y. Hispanics and Friends Civic Assn., Buffalo, 1997—; vol. Habitat for Humanity, 1992-96; mem. housing com. Allentown Assn., Buffalo, 1996-99. Acad. All-Am. scholar, 1985-86; Dem. Women of the Legislature grantee, 1994. Mem. Am. Planning Assn., Am. Inst. Cert. Planners. Avocations: music, politics, painting, rollerblading. Office: City of Buffalo Mayors Office Planning Rm 920 City Hall Buffalo NY 14202 E-mail: jlemke@ch.ci.buffalo.ny.us.

LEMKE, JUDITH A. lawyer; b. New Rochelle, N.Y., Sept. 28, 1952; d. Thomas Francis and Sara Jane (Blish) Fanelli; m. W. Frederick Lemke, Apr. 1, 1980; 1 child, Morgan Frederick. Student, Manhattanville Coll., Purchase, N.Y., 1970-72; BA, Case Western Res. U., Cleve., 1974, MA, 1975, JD, 1978. Sr. cert. pub. acct. Price Waterhouse, Cleve., 1978-81; assoc. Benesch Friedlander Coplan & Aronoff, 1981-85; adjunct faculty Cleve. Marshall Coll. Law, 1982-86; ptnr. Benesch Friedlander Coplan & Aronoff, Cleve., 1986-94; prin. Kahn Kleinman Yanowitz & Arnson Co., 1994-95; tax mgr. N.Am./L.Am. tax planning and compliance Chiquita Brands Internat., Cin., 1995-97, tax mgr. Europe, Colombia, Panama, 1998—, asst. v.p. taxation, 1998-99; v.p. tax Pepsi Bottling Group, Somers, N.Y., 1999—. Adj. faculty Case Western Res. U. Sch. of Law, 1993-95. Recipient Elijah Watt Sells award for highest distinction AICPA, N.Y.C. 1979. Mem. ABA, Ohio State Bar Assn., Cleve. Tax Club, Internat. Fiscal Assn., Case Western Res. U. Undergrad. Alumni Assn. (exec. com. 1987-95, trustee 1987-95, chmn. spl. events com. 1989-90, pres. 1990-92, v.p. 1993-94). Avocations: kayaking, wilderness canoe camping, guitar. Home: 39 Brundige Dr Goldens Bridge NY 10526-1413 Office: Pepsi Bottling Group 1 Pepsi Way Ste 4 Somers NY 10589-2204

LEMKE, LAURA ANN, foreign language educator, assistant principal; b. Hollis, L.I., N.Y., May 4, 1964; d. Ronald Louis Zarobinski and Donna Jean (Strayer) Williams; m. David Michael Lemke, Aug. 25, 1984; children: Kelsey Marie, Kayla Nicole. BA in French and Bus. with honors, Mich. State U., 1987, M in Edn. Adminstrn., 1993. Cert. secondary tchr., vocat. and adminstrn. Teaching asst. East Lansing (Mich.) Pub. Schs., 1985-87, French and bus. tchr. comty. edn., 1985-87; tchr. French and bus. Grand Blanc (Mich.) Comty. Schs., 1987&, coord. elem. fgn. lang., 1990-91, coord. K-12 fgn. lang., 1991-94. Chair North Cen. accreditation Grand Blanc Mid. Sch., 1990-96. Vol. Flint Internat. Inst., 1987-91, United Way, Flint, 1992. Mem. Nat. Bus. Edn. Assn. (Award of Merit 1987), Am. Assn. of Tchrs. of French, Mich. Fgn. Lang. Assn. (presider's chair 1994-95), Mich. Bus. Edn. Assn. (Outstanding Bus. Educator award 1986-87), Phi Kappa Phi. Avocations: reading mysteries, camping, traveling. Home: 2128 Perlin Ct Grand Blanc MI 48439-7312 Office: Grand Blanc Comty Schs 11920 S Saginaw St Grand Blanc MI 48439-1402 E-mail: llemke@central-office.grand-blanc.k12.mi.us.

LEMKE, MICHAEL JOSEPH, science educator, researcher; b. Shawano, Wis., June 23, 1958; s. Fred William Lemke and Janice Marie Stoehr; m. Amy Maria Miller, Jan. 14, 1997. BS, U. Wis., 1980; MS, U. B.C., Vancouver, Canada, 1985; PhD, Mich. Tech. U., 1992; postgrad., Kent State U., 1992—94, U. Ala., 1995—97. Vis. asst. prof. U. West Ala., Livingston, Ala., 1994—95; asst. prof. Pace U., Pleasantville, NY, 1997—99, U. Ill., Springfield, 1999—. Vis. scientist Am. Mus. Natural History, N.Y.C., 2001—; mem. Emiquon Sci. Adv. Coun. for Nature Conservancy, 2000—02; sci. adv., co-acad. dir. Woodrow Wilson Nat. Fellowship Found., 1999—2001. Contbr. articles to profl. jours. Fellow fellowship, Mich. Tech. U., 1988—92; grantee grant-in-aid of rsch., Sigma Xi, 1992, Ohio Sea Grant, 1996, Scholarly Rsch. grant, Pace U., 1998. Mem.: NAm. Benthological Soc., Internat. Soc. Microbial Ecology (mem. editl. bd. Microbial Ecology Jour. 2000—), Ecological Soc. Am., Am. Soc. Microbiology. Avocations: fishing, hiking, woodworking. Office: U Ill Biol Dept PO 19243 Springfield IL 62794 Business E-Mail: lemke.michael@uis.edu.

LEMLE, ROBERT SPENCER, lawyer; b. N.Y.C., Mar. 6, 1953; s. Leo Karl and Gertrude (Bander) L.; m. Roni Sue Kohen, Sept. 5, 1976; children: Zachary, Joanna. AB, Oberlin Coll., 1975; JD, NYU, 1978. Bar: N.Y. 1979. Assoc. Cravath, Swaine & Moore, N.Y.C., 1978-82; assoc. gen. counsel Cablevision Sys. Corp., Woodbury, N.Y., 1982-84, v.p., gen. counsel, 1984-86, sr. v.p., gen. counsel, sec., 1986-94, exec. v.p., gen. counsel, sec., 1994-2001, vice chmn., gen. counsel, sec., 2001—; vice chmn. Madison Sq. Garden, 1999—. Bd. editors Cable TV and New Media Law and Fin., N.Y.C., 1983-99, bd. dirs. Cablevision Systems Corp., 1988—. Trustee L.I. Children's Mus., 1990—, pres., 1996—; trustee Oberlin Coll., 1996—, vice chair, 2001--. Mem. ABA, N.Y. State Bar Assn. Avocation: real estate. Office: Cablevision Systems Corp 1111 Stewart Ave Bethpage NY 11714-3581 E-mail: rlemle@cablevision.com.

LEMLEY, DIANE CLAIRE BEERS, principal; b. Hollywood, Calif., Sept. 24; d. LaVerne and Claire Beers; married, 1966; children: Tina Slankas, Lea Devine, Chad Lemley. BA, U. Ariz., 1965, MEd, 1972; EdD, U. San Francisco, 1988. Tchr. Laguna Beach (Calif.) Pub. Schs., 1965-68, Territory Guam Schs., Dededo, Guam, 1969-71; counselor Window Rock high Sch., Ft. Defiance, Ariz., 1976; counselor, instr. Cochise Coll., Sierra Vista, 1981-84; tchr. gifted Sierra Vista Pub. Schs., 1989-94; instr. Chapman U., Sierra Vista, 1990-93; prin. Mammoth (Ariz.) Elem. Sch., 1994-2000; dir. curriculum and fed. projects San Carlos (Ariz.) Unified Sch. Dist., 2000—01; prin. Agua Caliente Elem. Sch. Tanque Verde USD, Tucson, 2001—. Cons. Advanced Tech. Systems, McLean, Va., 1985-87; pres. Student NEA, Tucson, 1960-61; speaker and presenter in field. Chmn., vice chmn. Sci. & Tech. Commn., Sierra Vista, 1990-94; mem. tech. adv. com. Ariz. Dept. Edn., 1997-99; Ariz. Sch. Support team, 1997-99. Named Regional Toastmaster of Yr., San Francisco, 1987, Disting. Elem. Adminstr. Ariz. Sch. Adminstrs., 1998. Mem. ASCD, Nat. Assn. Elem. Prins., Ariz. Sch. Adminstrs., Ariz. Educators fot. Gifted & Talented (pres. 1993-94), Rotary (pres. San Manuel 1998-99, nominee Tchr. of Yr. 1993), Phi Delta Kappa. Home: 4120 E Megan Tucson AZ 85712 Office: Agua Caliente Elem Sch 11420 E Linberlast San Carlos AZ 85550

LEMLICH, ROBERT, chemical engineer, educator; b. Bklyn., Aug. 22, 1926; s. Marcus S. and Mary (Marcus) L.; m. Elizabeth Ann Murphy, Jan. 31, 1976. B.Chem. Engring. summa cum laude, N.Y. U., 1948; M.Chem. Engring., Poly. Inst. Bklyn., 1951; PhD, U. Cin., 1954. Registered profl. engr., N.Y., Ohio. Research chem. engr. Allied Chem. & Dye Corp., 1948-49; mem. faculty U. Cin., 1952—, prof. chem. engring., 1962-85, prof. emeritus, 1985—; fellow U. Cin. Grad. Sch., 1971—, chmn. fellows, 1976-78. Fulbright lectr., Israel, 1958-59, Argentina, 1966, USSR, 1991, researcher, cons. in field. Rsch. Corp. grantee, 1954-55, NSF grantee, 1956-59, 73, 77-81, 85-88, NIH grantee, 1959-69, P & G grantee, 1976-77. Editor: Adsorptive Bubble Separation Techniques, 1972; editor, originator: Jour. Chem. Engring. Edn, 1962-65. Served in USN, 1944-46. Recipient Sigma Xi award distinguished research U. Cin., 1969 Fellow AAAS, Am. Inst. Chem. Engrs. (named Chem. Engr. of Yr. Ohio Valley sect. 1979). mem. Am. Chem. Soc., Am. Soc. Engring. Edn., Sigma Xi, Tau Beta Pi, Phi Lambda Upsilon. Home: 346 Bonnie Leslie Ave Bellevue KY 41073-1718 E-mail: Robert.Lemlich@UC.edu.

LEMMO, ROBERTA JUNE, financial advisor; b. Cleve., Jan. 25, 1954; d. Herbert J. and Mildred A. (Krizan) Wolf; m. Michael P. Lemmo, Dec. 1, 1973; 1 child, Stephanie A. BS in Acctg., Dyke Coll., 1975; M of Taxation, U. Akron, 1983; M of Fin. Planning, Coll. Fin. Planning, Denver, 1991. CPA, CFP; cert. personal fin. specialist. Acct. Lewandowski, Veres Co., Cleve., 1973-76; tax analyst TRW, Inc., Euclid, Ohio, 1976-79; tax acct. Internat. Merch Co., Cleve., 1979-80; fin. planner Investment Advisors Internat., 1980-83, v.p., 1983-85, sr. v.p., 1985—. Trustee David N. Myers Coll., Cleve., 1997—. Mem. AICPA, Ohio Soc. CPAs. Home: IMG Ctr Ste 100 1360 E 9th St Cleveland OH 44114-1782 Office: Investment Advisors Internat Ste 100 IMG Ctr 1360 E 9th St Cleveland OH 44114-1782

LEMMON, HARRY THOMAS, retired state supreme court justice; b. Morgan City, La., Dec. 11, 1930; s. Earl and Gertrude (Blum) L.; m. Mary Ann Vial; children: Andrew, Lauren, Roslyn, Carla, Jake, Patrick. BS, Southwestern La. Inst., 1952; LLB cum laude, Loyola U., New Orleans, 1963. Atty. firm Vial, Vial & Lemmon, Hahnville, La., 1963-70; judge Court Appeals 4th Cir., 1970-80; justice Supreme Ct. La., New Orleans, 1980—2001. Vis. prof. law La. State U. Law Ctr., Tulane U. Sch. Law,; adj. faculty Loyola U. Sch. Law, New Orleans. Chmn. La. Jud. Coll. With U.S. Army.*

LEMMON, JEAN MARIE, editor-in-chief; b. Duluth, Minn., Nov. 11, 1932; d. Lawrence Howard and Marie Julien (Gunderson) H.; m. Richard LuVerne LemMon, Apr. 17, 1965 (div. 1976); 1 child, Rebecca Jean. BA, U. Minn., 1954. Editor Better Homes and Gardens Mag., Des Moines, 1961-63, dept. head crafts, 1985-86, editor-in-chief, 1993—2001; women's editor Successful Farming, 1963-68; pres. Jean LemMon & Assocs., 1968-84; project editor Meredith Pub. Svcs., 1984-85; editor-in-chief Country Home Mag., 1986-93. Adv. bd. Drake U. Journalism Sch., 1991—. Mem. ASCAP, Mensa Internat., Am. Soc. Interior Designers.*

LEMMON, MARILYN SUE, retired advertising and human resources executive; b. Avon, Ill., Nov. 2, 1939; d. Morrison Huffman and Rose Ellen Eslinger; m. James Marcus Lemmon, Aug. 31, 1957; children: J. Craig, Stephanie S. Lemmon DeVrieze, JoEllyn R. Lemmon Larrison. Student, U. Houston, 1958-59, So. Ill. U., 1965-66; AA in Bus. Adminstrn., Black Hawk Coll., 1978; BA in Bus. Adminstrn., Western Ill. U., 1983. Cert. profl. sec. Sec. H.J. Porter & James W. Porter Ind. Oil Operators, Houston, 1957-61; office mgr. Joseph A. Holland, DDS, Oral Surgeon, Godfrey, Ill., 1967-68; counseling sec. guidance dept. United Twp. High Sch., East Moline, 1969-74; word processing sec. IBM, Moline, 1974-75; adminstrv. sec. Deere & Co. Corp. Hdqrs., 1975-84, mgr. advt. adminstrn., 1984-92, instr., 1992-97; ret., 1997. Career speaker pers. dept. Deere & Co., Moline, 1979-95; mem. Quad City Addy Club, Am. Advt. Fedn., 1991-92; loaned exec. United Way of Quad Cities, 1992, mem. planning bd., 1993-95; mem., sec., bd. dirs. Midwest Writing Ctr. Author: Naked Came the Plow Man; Getting Published, How the Pros Do It, 1999. Adminstrv. asst. to chmn. Quad City Unification Project, Moline, 1988; chmn. Career Speakers, Rock River chpt. Profl. Sec.'s Internat., 1976-85; mem. exec. bd. Midwest Writing Ctr., 2000, sec., 2000. Recipient Short Fiction award Miss. Valley Writers Conf., 1990, 91, Romance Writer award, 1990. Mem. Romance Writers Am. (pres. Quad City chpt. 1990-92, 97-99, literacy chair 1994-96, Synopsis award Ont. chpt. 1990). Democrat.

LEMMONS, GREGORY BERTRAM, SR. accountant; b. Oakland, Calif., July 19, 1950; s. Toy Sr. and Lela (Witt) L.; m. Sandra G. Wesley, Aug. 17, 1974; children: Gregory, Rashanya, Jacobian. BS, U. Calif., Berkeley, 1974; MBA, John F. Kennedy U., 1995. Cost engr. Kaiser Engrs., Oakland, 1968-76; acct. Safeway Stores, Walnut Creek, Calif., 1978-80; gen. acct. Hunt Wesson Foods, Fullerton, 1980-81; acct. Kaiser Health Plan, Oakland, 1981—; sys. adminstr. Blue Shield Calif., 2000—02. Cons. treasury Kaiser Found. Health Plan, 1999—2000. Asst. program dir. Eastlake YMCA, Oakland, 1968; athletic coach's asst. St. Augustine Sch., Oakland, 1985-93; fundraiser Cate Sch., Carpinteria, Calif., 1992-96; basketball coach Castilleja Sch., Palo Alto, Calif., 1993-94; adv. bd. mem. A Better Chance Program, Boston, 1993—; bus. libr. asst. John F. Kennedy U., Orinda, Calif., 1995—; CFO, vol. Oakland Conciliation Bd. Democrat. Baptist. Avocations: bicycling, walking, writing poetry, coaching children, college planning. Home: 743 Stonebridge Way Pleasant Hill CA 94523-4851 Office: Kaiser Permanente Med Program 1950 Franklin St Ste 16 Oakland CA 94612-5103

LEMNIOS, ANDREW ZACHERY, aerospace engineer, educator, researcher; b. Newburyport, Mass., Nov. 23, 1931; s. Zaharias Vasilios and Evangelia (Malamoglou) L.; m. Aspasia Soula Hanos, Sept. 26, 1954; children: Karen Eve, Keith Harold. SB, MIT, 1953, SM, 1954; PhD, U. Conn., 1967; grad. advanced mgmt. program, Harvard U., 1983. Rsch. engr. United Techs. Rsch., East Hartford, Conn., 1954-60; sr. analytical engr. Kaman Aerospace Corp., Bloomfield, 1961-63, chief fluid mechanics, 1963-68, chief rsch. engr., 1969-76, dir. rsch. and tech., 1976-89, asst. v.p. rsch. and tech. programs, 1989-93; mem. rotorcraft adv. com. Rensselaer Poly. Inst., Troy, N.Y., 1985-92, clin. prof., dir. Rotorcraft Tech. Ctr. NY, 1993—99; v.p. Rensselaer at Hartford, Conn., 1999—. Adj. prof. Western New Eng. Coll., Springfield, Mass., 1956-76, U. Mass., Amherst, 1976-78; mem. aeronautics adv. com. NASA, Washington, 1979-84; mem. rotorcraft adv. com. U. Md., College Park, 1985-92, Ga. Inst. Tech., Atlanta, 1985-92. Patentee controllable twist rotor, rotor trim tab. Fellow AIAA (assoc.), Am. Helicopter Soc. (hon.). Republican. Greek Orthodox. Avocations: carpentry, gardening, music, reading. Home: 144 Primrose Dr Longmeadow MA 01106-2534 Office: Rensselaer Polytechnic Inst at Hartford 275 Windsor St Hartford CT 06120-2910

LEMOLE, GERALD MICHAEL, surgeon; b. S.I., N.Y., Dec. 17, 1936; s. Joseph Michael and Mary (Boylan) L.; m. Emily Jane Asplundh, Dec. 8, 1962; children: Lisa Jane, Laura Leigh, Emily Anne, Gerald Michael Samantha Mary, Christopher Robin. BS in Biology, Villanova U., 1958; MD, Temple U., 1962. Diplomate Am. Bd. surgery, Am. Bd. Thoracic Surgery. Intern S.I. Hosp., 1962-63; resident Temple U., Phila., 1963-67, Baylor Affiliated Hosps., Houston, 1967-69; practice medicine specializing in throacic surgery Phila., 1969—, Browns Mills, N.J., 1972-84. Chief sect. cardiac and thoracic surgery Temple U. Hosp., Phila., 1970-77; prof. surgery Temple U. Health Scis. Ctr., 1975-77; chmn. dept. surgery Deborah Heart and Lung Ctr., Phila., 1972-84; chief sect. cardiovascular surgery Med. Ctr. Del.; vis. prof. cardiac surgery U. Dublin, Ireland, 1974, u. Istanbul, Turkey, 1982, Mil. Med. Coll., Ankara, Turkey, 1985, Beijing Heart Inst., 1991; clin. prof. surgery U. Pa., 1979, Rutgers Med. Sch., Thomas Jefferson U., 1999—; rschr. in field. Contbr. numerous articles on cradiovascular surgery and disease to med. jours. Recipient Disting Alumnus award Villanova U., 1987. Fellow ACS, Coll. Cardiology, Am. Coll. Chest Physicians (cardiovascular com. 1974—); mem. AMA, Am. Assn. Thoracic Surgery, Am. Fedn. Clin. Rsch., Pan Am. Thoracic Soc., Am. Heart Assn. (cardiovascular coun. 1973—, pres. Del. chpt. 1991, chmn. bd. dirs. 1992), Pa. Med. Soc., Pa. Assn. Thoracic Surgery (program chaor 1975—), , Pa. Assn. Thoracic Surgeons, Phila. County Med. Soc., Phila. Acad. Surgery, Phila. Acad. Cardioloby (pres. 1976-79, chmn. exec. com. 1976—), Phila. Coll. Physicians, Internat. Cardiovascular Soc., Assn. Acad. Surgeons, Soc. Casvular Surgery, Denton A. Cooley Cardiovascular Surg. Soc. Home: 404 Tomlinson Rd Huntingdon Valley PA 19006-4818 Office: Med Ctr Del 4745 Ogletown Stanton Rd # 20 Newark DE 19713-2067

LEMON, LESLIE GENE, retired diversified services company executive; b. Davenport, Iowa, June 14, 1940; BS, U. Ill., 1962, LLB, 1964. Bar: Ill. 1964, Ariz. 1972. Asst. gen. counsel Am. Farm Bur. Fedn., Chgo., 1964-69; sr. atty. Armour and Co., 1969-71; with Viad Corp (formerly The Dial Corp and Greyhound Corp.), Phoenix, 1971-99; gen. counsel The Dial Corp (formerly Greyhound Corp.), 1977-96, v.p., 1979-99; ret., 1999; chmn. State of Ariz. Citizens Clean Elections Commn. Vestryman All Saints Episcopal Ch., Phoenix, 1975-81; trustee Phoenix Art Mus., 1985-98; bd. dirs. Phoenix Children's Hosp., 1985-98; bd. visitors U. Calif. Med. Sch., Davis, 1983—. Mem. ABA, Nat. Conf. Uniform Law Commrs., Assn. Gen. Counsel, Maricopa County Bar Assn., State Bar Ariz., Phoenix C. of C. (bd. dirs. 1989-95), Am. Arbitration Assn. (bd. dirs. 1996—). Home: 1136 W Butler Dr Phoenix AZ 85021-4428 E-mail: l.lemon@azbar.org.

LEMON, STANLEY M. hospital administrator; BS, Princeton U.; MD, U. Rochester Sch. Medicine and Dentistry. Cert. Am. Bd. Internal Medicine, diplomate in infectious diseases. Resident in internal medicine N.C. Meml. Hosp., Chapel Hill; postdoctoral fellow, divsn. infectious diseases U. N.C., 1983—89, prof. medicine, microbiology and immunology, 1989—97; Samuel Baron Disting. prof. dept. microbiology and immunology U. Tex. Med. Branch, 1997—, chmn. dept. microbiology and immunology, 1997—99, interim dean of medicine, 1999—2000, dean of medicine, 2000—. Contbr. articles to profl. jours. With U.S. Army Med. Corps, 1977—83, lt. col. USAR. Office: Office of the Dean of Medicine 301 Univ Blvd 5 106 Adminstrn Bldg Galveston TX 77555-0133*

LEMON, WILLIAM JACOB, lawyer; b. Covington, Va., Oct. 25, 1932; s. James Gordon and Elizabeth (Wilson) L.; m. Barbara Inez Boyle, Aug. 17, 1957; children: Sarah E. Lemon Ludwig, William Tucker, Stephen Weldon. BA, Washington & Lee U., 1957, JD, 1959. Bar: Va. 1959. Assoc. Martin, Martin & Hopkins, Roanoke, Va., 1959-61; ptnr. Martin, Hopkins & Lemon, 1962—. Trustee Washington and Lee U., Lexington, Va., 1988-97, North Cross Sch., Roanoke, 1995—; pres. Specific Reading and Learning Difficulties Assn. Shedd Early Learning Ctr., 1985-86, George C. Marshall Found., Lexington, Va., 1997—. With U.S. Army, 1952-54. Mem. Va. Bar Assn., Roanoke Bar Assn. (pres. 1982-83), Va. State Bar, Shenandoah Club. Presbyterian. Avocations: farming, hunting, travel. Office: Martin Hopkins Lemon First Union Tower 10 S Jefferson St Ste 1000 Roanoke VA 24011-1314 also: PO Box 13366 Roanoke VA 24033-3366

LEMONCELLI, LORINE BARBARA, counselor; b. Pittston, Pa., Sept. 28, 1958; d. Lawrence and Valerie (Mislevy) Dalessandro; m. Peter Jerome Lemoncelli, Oct. 24, 1987; 1 child, Violetta Enrica. BA in Tchg., Coll. Misiercordia, 1981; MA in Counseling, Marywood Coll., 1996; Phebotomy Cert., Allied Med. Career, Scranton, Pa., 1986. Tchr. Montessori Sch., Scranton, 1990-92; counselor Act 1, Wilkes-Barre, Pa., 1995, Friendship House, Scranton, 1995, Keystone City Residence, Scranton, 1996-97, Scranton Counseling, 1997-2000. Mem. PTA Riverside H.S., Taylor, Pa., 1995—. Mem. Am. Counseling Assn., Marywood Counseling Assn. (pres. 1995-96), Wyoming Valley Mental Health Assn., Chi Sigma Iota. Democrat. Roman Catholic. Avocations: walking, music, travel, reading. Home: PO Box 3061 Scranton PA 18505-0061

LEMONE, MARGARET ANNE, atmospheric scientist; b. Columbia, Mo., Feb. 21, 1946; d. David Vandenberg and Margaret Ann (Meyer) LeMone; m. Peter Augustus Gilman; children: Patrick Cyrus, Sarah Margaret. BA in Math., U. Mo., 1967; PhD in Atmospheric Scis., U. Wash., 1972. Postdoctoral fellow Nat. Ctr. for Atmospheric Rsch., Boulder, Colo., 1972-73, scientist, 1973-92, sr. scientist, 1992—. Mem. bd. on atmospheric sci. and climate NRC, 1993-97, 2001—; mem. sci. adv. com. U.S. Weather Rsch. Program, 1997-99. Contbr. articles to profl. jours.; contbg. author: D.C. Heath Earth Science, 1983-93; editor Jour. Atmospheric Scis., 1991-95. Woodrow Wilson fellow, NSF fellow,

NDEA fellow, 1967. Fellow AAAS, Am. Meteorol. Soc. (councillor, mem. exec. com. 1992-96, Editor's award); mem. Am. Geophys. Union, Nat. Acad. Engring. Achievements include research in dynamics of linear convection (roll vortices) in daytime atmospheric boundary layer and its relationship to clouds; demonstrating that bands of deep convection (like squall lines) can increase the vertical shear of horizontal wind (contrary to conventional wisdom at that time); developing technique to estimate small fluctuations in air pressure from aircraft flying over land, used to estimate pressure field around clouds and storms. Avocations: paleontology (invertebrate), reading, hiking, drawing. Home: 2048 Balsam Dr Boulder CO 80304-3618 Office: Nat Ctr Atmospheric Rsch PO Box 3000 Boulder CO 80307-3000 E-mail: lemone@ucar.edu.

LEMONS, DONALD W. state supreme court justice; b. Feb. 22, 1949; Justice Supreme Ct. Va., 2000—. Office: Supreme Ct Bldg 100 N Ninth St, 5th Floor Richmond VA 23219 also: PO Box 1315 Richmond VA 23218-1315*

LEMONS, JAMES STANLEY, history educator; b. Louisville, June 14, 1938; s. Leland Carol and Lena May (Lusk) L.; m. Nancy Jane Simmons, Sept. 3, 1960; m.Linda L. Bausserman, Jan. 13, 2001. AB summa cum laude, William Jewell Coll., 1960; MA, U. Rochester, 1962; PhD, U. Mo., 1967. Hons. instr. U. Mo., 1963-65; instr. Ohio State U., 1965-67; asst. prof. R.I. Coll., 1967-71, assoc. prof., 1971-76, prof., 1976—; Mary Tucker Thorp disting. prof., 1988. Vis. prof. Southwest Tex. State U., 1979-80 (Paul Maixner Tchg. award Tex. State U. and R.I. Coll. 1998); project cons., program developer for A Lively Experiment, statewide program of the Providence Pub. Libr. funded by the Nat. Endowment for the Humanities, 1981-83. Author: The Woman Citizen: Social Feminism in the 1920s, 1973 (paperback 1975, reissued 1990), Aspects of the Black Experience, 1975, (with George Kellner) Rhode Island: the Independent State, 1982, The First Baptist Church in America, 1988, (with Emily Stier Adler) The Elect: Rhode Island's Women Legislators, 1922-90, 1990;First: The History of The First Baptist Church in America, 2001; contbr. articles to profl. jours. Mem. Gov.'s Task Force on Records and Archives, 1978-79; hist. cons. to R.I. Com. for the Humanities Coun. project Rhode Island Legacy, 1984-88, 90-91, 93-94; moderator Gender and Politics forum R.I. state capitol, 1985; cons. Newport Hist. Soc. in planning of exhibits for 350th anniversary of city's founding, 1988; mem. Citizens Adv. Com. Town of North Providence, 1973-74, Mental Health Svcs. of Northwestern R.I., 1986-87, R.I. Bapt. Edn. Soc., 1988-94 (recording sec. 1989-90); bd. dirs. R.I. Com. for the Humanities, 1993-99; mem. steering com. Newell D. Goff Ingenuity & Enterprise Ctr., 1993-97, fellowship awards com. John Nicholas Brown Ctr. for Study Am. Civilization, Brown U., 1996—. Recipient Am. Philos. Soc. rsch. grant, 1974, R.I. Coll. faculty rsch. grants, 1968, 74, 85, 86, 87, R.I. Historic Preservation Commn. rsch. and publ. grants, 1986, 87, 88, 89. Mem. Am. Hist. Assn., Orgn. Am. Historians (R.I. mem. on com. on the Status of History in Schs., 1974-79), Am. Studies Assn., New Eng. Hist. Assn., New Eng. Am. Studies Assn., R.I. Hist. Soc. (edn. com. 1991-95), Providence Preservation Soc., Phi Alpha Theta. Baptist. Avocations: collecting antiques, travel, singing. Home: 12 Pleasant Ave Greenville RI 02828-1906 Office: R I Coll Dept History Providence RI 02908 E-mail: jlemons@ric.edu.

LE MONS, KATHLEEN ANN, investment officer, portfolio manager; b. Trenton, N.J., Apr. 6, 1952; d. Albert Martin and Veronica Grace (Kerr) LeM.; m. Walter Everett Faircloth, Apr. 15, 1978 (div. Dec. 1988); m. Jeffery West Benedict, June 29, 1991. Student, Rollins Coll., 1970-71, Fla. State U., 1971-76; BSBA magna cum laude, Christopher Newport U., 1995; MBA in Fin., Coll. William and Mary, 1998. Registered rep. NASD/NYSE; registered investment advisor; cert. portfolio mgr.; accredited asset mgmt. specialist. Sci. rsch. assoc. NASA, Hampton, Va., 1973-76; fin. cons. Merrill Lynch Pierce Fenner Smith, 1985-88; v.p., investment officer, portfolio mgr. Wheat First Butcher Singer (now Wachovia Securities), Newport News, Va., 1988—; v.p., investment officer Wachovia Securities (formerly First Union Securities). Life mem. Capital Dist. Found., 1992; mem. exec. panel fund distbn. Va. Peninsula United Way, 1996-97; Hampton Rds. chair March of Dimes Walk Am., 1996-98; bd. dirs. Greater Hampton Rds. March of Dimes Found., 1997—. George F. Hixson fellow Kiwanis Internat., 1996. Mem. Am. Mktg. Assn., Va. Peninsula C. of C. (transp. task force 1993-97, govtl. affairs task force 1993-99), Rotary, Oyster Point Kiwanis (charter, pres. 1991-92, 98-99), Coll. of William and Mary Part-Time MBA Assn. (charter, curriculum com. chair 1995-97, v.p. 1996-97, bd. dir. 2001-), Christopher Newport U. Pres.' Coun., Christopher Newport Univ. Alumni Soc. (bd. dirs. 1996—, v.p. bd. dirs. 1998—), Mensa, James River Country Club (9-hole golf group), Smithfield Women's Club, Smithfield Rotary Club, Kiwanis Internat. (life), Alpha Chi. Republican. Avocations: golf, snowskiing. Home: 20454 Gatling Pointe Pkwy S Smithfield VA 23430-5756 also: 20454 Gatling Pointe Pkwy S Smithfield VA 23430-5756 Office: Wheat First Butcher Singer 11817 Canon Blvd Newport News VA 23606-2569

LEMOYNE, TERRI LYNNE, sociologist; b. Washington, May 3, 1958; d. Joseph Bate LeMoyne and Reba Campbell. BA, U. Md., 1983, BA, 1987, MA with honors, 1989, PhD, 1996. Instr. U. Md., College Park, 1990—94; asst. prof. U. Tenn., Chattanooga, 1997—. Cons. Erlanger Hosp., Chattanooga, 2002; conf. coord. U. Md., College Park, 1988—89, rsch. asst.; vis. asst. prof. Mt. St. Mary's Coll., Emmitsburg, Md. Author: (book chpt.) Explorations in Social Theory by George Ritzer, 2001, Sociological Beginnings by George Ritzer, 1993, Metatheorizing in Sociology by George Ritzer, 1991, (book) Resource Book for Teaching Sociological Theory, 2001; contbr. articles to profl. jours. Vol. Nat. and Lesbian Gay Task Force, Washington, 1984—86; advisor Women's Action Coun., Chattanooga, 1999—2000, Erlanger Hosp., Chattanooga, 2002. Named Prof. of Month, Chi Omega, 2002, Outstanding Prof. of Yr., U. of Tenn. Alumni Assn., 2001. Mem.: So. Sociol. Assn., Ea. Sociol. Soc., Am. Sociol. Assn. Home: 4514 Sherry Ln Hixson TN 37343 Office: U Tenn 615 McCallie Ave Chattanooga TN 37403 Personal E-mail: terri-lemoyne@utc.edu. E-mail: terri-lemoyne@utc.edu.

LEMP, JOHN, JR. telecommunications engineer; b. Trenton, N.J., Dec. 10, 1936; s. John and Helena M. (Braddock) L.; m. Susan N. Rose, 1955; children: John, Thomas K., Carl A., Adam F.H. BSEE, Princeton U., 1959; MSEE, Poly. Inst. Bklyn., 1968; MBA, Colo. State U., 1973; grad., Air Command and Staff Coll., 1974, Indsl. Coll. Armed Forces, 1981. Cert. instrument flight instr., FAA. Project engr. Gen. Devices, Inc., Princeton, N.J., 1959-60; with USAF, 1960-89; supr. Bell Telephone Labs., N.J. and Colo., 1962-74; mgr. bus. planning Aeronautic Ford Corp., Willow Grove, Pa., 1974-76; mgr. R & D ITT, Corinth, Miss., 1976-78; lectr. sch. bus. Temple U., Phila., 1976; project leader Nat. Telecomm. & Info Adminstrn. U.S. Dept. Commerce, Boulder, Colo., 1978-82; dir. Info. Access Systems, Inc., 1981-84, Lemp Devel. Co., Inc., Boulder, 1975—; mgr. Swinerton & Walberg Property Svcs., Inc., 1995, McGuckin Hardware, Boulder, 1996—, dept. head, 1998—. Lectr. U. Colo., Sch. Bus., Boulder, 1982-94; adj. prof. U. Denver, 1999—. Contbr. articles to profl. jours.; patentee in field. Mem. CAP, 1970—; pres. Carolym Heights Civic Assn., 1972-73; treas. Frazier Woods Civic Assn., 1975-76, Light Fantastic, 1990-91, pres., 1991-92, treas., 1990=91. Col. USAFR. Decorated Air Force Commendation medal, Meritorious Svc. medal, Legion of Merit. Mem. IEEE (sr.), Inst. Ops. Rsch. & Mgmt. Sci., Am. Armed Forces Comm. & Elecs. Assn. (Outstanding Elec. Engr. 1959), Assn. Computing Machinery. Home: 3745 23rd St Boulder CO 80304-1611 Office: McGuckin Hardware 2525 Arapahoe Ave Boulder CO 80302-6795 also: Denver U 2101 S University Blvd Rm 580 Denver CO 80208-0001 E-mail: lempj@mcguckin.com., jlemp@du.edu.

LEMPERT, JOSEPH, retired physicist; b. North Adams, Mass., July 3, 1913; s. Samuel and Fannie Lempert; m. Jean Handler; children: Eugene, Judith, Larry. BS, MIT, 1935; MS, Stevens Inst. Tech., Hoboken, N.J., 1943. Engr., Westinghouse Electronic Divsn., NJ, 1937—53; sect. mgr. Elmira, NY, 1953—58; fellow scientist Westinghouse Rsch. Labs., Churchill, Pa., 1958—78, cons., 1978—83; ret., 1983. Fellow: IEEE; mem.: Am. Phys. Soc. Achievements include patents for 23 patents in field.

LEMPERT, PHILIP, advertising executive, author, syndicated columnist, television correspondent; b. East Orange, N.J., Apr. 17, 1953; s. Sol and Lillian E. L.; m. Laura Gray; 1 son. BS in Mktg., Drexel U., 1974; degree in Package Design, Pratt Inst., 1978. With Lempert Co., Belleville, N.J., 1974-89; pres. Consumer Insight, Inc., 1990—; sr. v.p., sr. ptnr. AGE Wave Inc., 1991-93; pres., CEO Supermarketguru.com. Founder, CEO Supermarket Alliance, 1993—; adj. prof. Fairleigh Dickinson U., Seton Hall U. Pub., editor newsletter The Lempert Report; also TV corr., lectr. Author: Phil Lempert's Supermarket Shopping and Value Guide, 1996, Top Ten Trends for Baby Boomers for Business, 1997, Being the Shopper: Understanding Consumer Choices for the Second Millenium, 2002; columnist Chgo. Tribune, 1993-98, Knight-Ridder/Tribune Syndicate, Supermarket News, L.A. Times, 2000-02; food editor, corr. Today Show, BBC Radio 5; talk show host WOR Radio Network; news corr. Discovery Health Network. Chmn. Tribune Food Task Force, 1996-98; bd. dirs. Powerhouse Theatre, 2001—. Mem. Am. Assn. Advt. Agys. (bd. govs. 1986-88, legis. liason 1988-90, legis. coord. 1987-90), Nat. Food Brokers Assn. (chmn. food svcs. com.). Office: Consumer Insight Inc 3015 Main St Ste 320 Santa Monica CA 90405-6401 E-mail: Plempert@lempertreport.com.

LEMPERT, RICHARD OWEN, lawyer, educator; b. Hartford, Conn., June 2, 1942; s. Philip Leonard and Mary (Steinberg) L.; m. Cynthia Ruth Willey, Sept. 10, 1967 (div.); 1 child, Leah Rose; m. Lisa Ann Kahn, May 26, 2002. AB, Oberlin Coll., 1964; JD, U. Mich., 1968, PhD in Sociology, 1971. Bar: Mich. 1978. Asst. prof. law U. Mich., Ann Arbor, 1968-72, assoc. prof., 1972-74, prof. law, 1974—, prof. sociology, 1985—, Francis A. Allen collegiate prof. law, 1990—2001, acting chair dept. sociology, 1993-94, chair dept. sociology, 1995-98, dir. life scis., values and soc. program, 2000—, Eric Stein Disting. Univ. prof. law and sociology, 2001—; dir. divsn. social and econ. scis. NSF, 2002—. Mason Ladd disting. vis. prof. U. Iowa Law Sch., 1981; vis. fellow Centre for Socio-Legal Rsch., Wolfson Coll., Oxford (Eng.) U., 1982; mem. adv. panel for law and social sci. div. NSF, 1976-79, mem. exec. com. adv. com. for social sci., 1979; mem. com. law enforcement and adminstrn. of justice NRC, vice chmn., 1984-87, chmn., 1987-89; mem. adv. panel NSF program on Human Dimensions of Global Change, 1989, 92-94; mem. com. on DNA technology in forensic sci. NRC, 1989-92, com. on drug testing in workplace, 1991-93; vis. scholar Russell Sage Found., 1998-99; vis. scholar Russell Sage Found., 1998-99. Author: (with Stephen Saltzburg) A Modern Approach to Evidence, 1977, 2d edit., 1983, 3d edit. (with Sam Gross and James Liebman), 2000; (with Joseph Sanders) An Invitation to Law and Social Science, 1986, Under the Influence, 1993; editor: (with Jacques Normand and Charles O'Brien) Under the Influence? Drugs and the American Work Force, 1994; editorial bd. Law and Soc. Rev., 1972-77, 89-92, 98—, editor, 1982-85; mem. editl. bd. Evaluation Rev., 1979-82, Violence and Victims, 1985—, Jour. Law and Human Behavior, 1980-82; contbr. articles to profl. jours. Fellow Ctr. for Advanced Study in Behavioral Scis., 1994-95; vis. scholar Russell Sage Found., 1998-99. Fellow Am. Acad. Arts and Scis.; mem. Am. Sociol. Assn. (chair sect. sociology of law 1995-96), Law and Society Assn. (trustee 1977-80, 90-93, exec. com. 1979-80, 82-87), Order of Coif, Phi Beta Kappa, Phi Kappa Phi. Office: U Mich Law Sch 625 S State St Ann Arbor MI 48109-1215 E-mail: rol25@hotmail.com.

LEMPERT, SUSAN G. mayor; b. N.Y.C., Aug. 2, 1931; d. Louis and Evelyn (Hamburger) Goodstein; m. Arthur Lempert, July 1, 1955; children: Robert, Edward Tad, Elizabeth. AB in Journalism, Stanford U., 1952; MA in Pub. Law & Govt., Columbia U., 1955; MPA, San Francisco State U., 1983. Pub. rels. GE, San Francisco, 1952-54; rschr. Coun. on Fgn. Rel., N.Y.C., 1954-56; editl. staff U.S. News & World Report, San Francisco, 1956-57; housing dir. Human Investment Program, San Mateo, 1983-88; exec. dir. Age Ctr. Alliance, Inc., Menlo Park, 1989-95; mayor City of San Mateo, 1993—. Mem. Met. Transp. Commn., San Mateo County Congestion Mgmt. Agy. Bd. dirs. San Mateo Union H.S. Dist., 1983-93; San Mateo City Elem. Sch. Dist., 1973-83. Mem. LWV (pres. 1968). Avocations: tennis, skiing, bicycling. Office: City Hall 330 W 20th San Mateo CA 94403

LEMR, SANDRA J. geriatrics nurse, administrator; b. Painesville, Ohio, Aug. 31, 1951; d. Charles J. and Dorothy J. (Vasinosky) Nagy; m. James C. Lemr, May 10, 1974; children: Melissa Ann, James Robert. AAS, Lakeland Community Coll., Mentor, Ohio, 1971; student, Lake Erie Coll., Painesville, Ohio. Nursing supr. Lake Hosp. Systems, Painesville, 1971-86, Heartland of Mentor, 1986-91; asst. dir. nursing Madison (Ohio) Health Care, 1991—97, Continuum Home Health Care, 1997—. Home: 26 W High St Apt 4 Painesville OH 44077-3347

LENAGHAN, DONNA DISMUKE, educational and management consultant; b. Atlanta, Nov. 28, 1954; d. William Thomas Dismuke and Elizabeth (Taylor) Dismuke Fraser; m. Michael J. Lenaghan, Sept. 18, 1982. BA in Psychology, Salem Coll., Winston-Salem, N.C., 1976; BS in Mgmt. and Cmty. Devel., U. Md., 1983; EdD in Adult and Continuing Edn., Va. Poly. Inst., 1990; EdS in Endl. Computing and Tech., Barry U., 1999. Dir. leadership project Nat. Hemophilia Found., N.Y.C., 1983-85; dir. project ARC, Washington, 1985-88; pres. Lenaghan Group, Chevy Chase, Md., 1988-92; v.p., curricula and devel. svcs. Ctr. for Profl. Devel., Shawnee, Kans., 1993-94; pres. Multigogy, Miami, Fla., 1994—. Vis. prof. U. Coll. Galway, Ireland, 1985; strategic planner Campfire Nat. Hdqrs., Kansas City, Mo., 1989-92; prof. edn. and psychology Miami-Dade C.C., 1993-99; dir. ednl. computing and tech., Barry U., Miami Shores; curriculum and tng. specialist nat. sems., 1992-93; cons. in field. Contbr. articles to profl. jours. Deacon, educator Presbyn. Chs., N.C., Md., Kans. and Fla., 1976—; adv. bd., New Horizons Meth. Ch., 1999; leadership vol. Girl Scouts U.S.A., 1976—; bd. dirs. Campfire Coun., Washington, 1983-87; vol. Laubach Literacy Coun., Lee's Summit, Mo., 1992-94. Named to Young Profls. Hall of Fame, Am. Hist. Archives, 1987. Mem. Midwest Leadership Inst. Presbyterian. Avocations: volunteering, teaching, community service, water sports. Office: Multigogy 8900 NW 194th Ter Hialeah FL 33018-6218

LENAHAN, WALTER CLAIR, retired foreign service officer; b. Everett, Wash., Apr. 20, 1934; s. James Harold and Doris Anne (Larson) L.; m. Patricia Anne Casey, July 6, 1957; children— Karen Diane, Desiree, Lorelei, Casey James BA, U. Oreg., 1960. Commd. fgn. service officer Dept. State, 1961, officer, 1961-72, U.S. Embassy, Beijing, People's Republic of China, 1979-81, Dept. Commerce, Washington, 1981-86, dep. asst. sec. for textiles and apparel, 1982-86; v.p. Am.-Philippine Fiber Industry, Inc., Manila, 1972-76; pres. Internat. Bus. and Econ. Research Corp., Washington, 1986-95; retired, 1995. Served to sgt. U.S. Army, 1953-56 Recipient Sr. Fgn. Service Presdl. award Dept. State, 1984 Lutheran. Avocations: tennis; contract bridge.

LENARD, GEORGE DEAN, lawyer; b. Joliet, Ill., Aug. 26, 1957; s. Louis George and Jennie (Helopoulos) L.; m. Nancy Ilene Sundquist, Nov. 11, 1989. BS, Ill. State U., 1979; JD, Thomas Cooley Law Sch., 1984. Bar: Ill. 1984, U.S. Dist. Ct. (no. dist.) Ill. 1984, U.S. Ct. Appeals (6th cir.) 1998, U.S. Supreme Ct. 1990, Mich. 1998, Ariz. 1999, Calif. 2001. Asst. states atty. Will County States Attys. Office, Joliet, 1984-88; pvt. practice law, 1988—. Mem. ABA (mem. Ill. capital litigation trial bar, lead counsel), ATLA, Nat. Assn. Criminal Def. Lawyers, State Bar Ariz., State Bar Mich., State Bar Calif., Phi Alpha Delta (Isaac P. Christiancy chpt.). Avocation: golf. Office: 81 N Chicago St Ste 206 Joliet IL 60432-4383

LENARD, LLOYD EDGAR, financial consultant; b. West Monroe, La., July 29, 1922; s. James Edward and Doshie (Boyette) L.; m. Betty-Jo Sawyer, Dec. 23, 1947; children: Carla Dawn, Brian Drury, Lloyd E. BA in Journalism, La. State U., 1943; MA in Advt. and Mktg., U. Mo., 1947. CLU, ChFC. News reporter Shreveport (La.) Times, 1946; exec. trainee Neiman-Marcus, Dallas, 1947-48; advt. mgr. Sta. KNOE, Monroe, La., 1948-52; life ins. agt. Aetna Life, 1952-53, asst. agy. mgr. Shreveport, 1953-56; agy. mgr., owner Pan Am. Life, 1956-80; freelance fin. cons., 1980-96; county commr. Caddo Parish Commn., 1983-94, pres., 1988-89, 89-90. Radio talk show host Sta. KWKH, Shreveport; TV talk show host Sta. KSLI, Shreveport. Author fiction and non-fiction books; contbr. articles to profl. jours. Chmn. Reps., Caddo Parish, La., 1975; chmn. Reps. five parish area; treas. La. Rep. Party; mem. Rep. State Ctrl. Com., Heart Assn. Named Young Man of Yr. Jr. Chamber, 1956, Gen. Agt. of Yr. Pan Am. Life, 1963; recipient various speech trophies. Mem. Nat. Assn. County Govts. (taxation and fin. steering com.), Kiwanis, Mid-City Kiwanis Club Sport (dist. lt. gov. 1978). Republican. Baptist. Avocations: writing, speaking, physical fitness, walking, golf. Home and Office: Ind Fin Cons 6122 River Rd Shreveport LA 71105-4834 E-mail: LLenard@aol.com.

LENARD, MARY JANE, accounting and information systems educator; b. York, Pa., July 8, 1955; d. Martin and Anne Ruth (Zimmerman) Kondor; m. Robert Louis Lenard, July 9, 1977; children: Kevin, Kelsey. BS in Econ. and Adminstrv. Sci., Carnegie Mellon U., 1977; MBA in Fin., U. Akron, 1982; PhD in Bus. Adminstrn., Kent State U., 1995. Cert. mgmt. acct. Mgmt. trainee Equibank, NA, Pitts., 1977-78; acct., auditor Goodyear Tire and Rubber Co., Akron, Ohio, 1978-86; instr. U. Akron, 1986-93; mem. adj. faculty Cleve. State U., 1994-97; assoc. prof. Barton Coll., Wilson, NC, 1997—2001; asst. prof. U. N.C., Greensboro, 2001—. Author procs.; contbr. articles to profl. jours. Pres. Hillcrest Elem. PTA, Richfield, Ohio, 1992—93; v.p. Summit County PTA, Akron, 1994—96; mem., newsletter dir. Wakefield Mid. Sch. PTSA, 2000—02; coord. Vol. Income Tax Assistance, Barton Coll., Wilson, 1998—2001; active Revere Schs. Computer Curriculum Com., 1994—95; mem. Wakefield H.S. PTSA, 2002—. Grantee Faculty Devel. grant, Barton Coll., 1997, 1999. Mem.: Decision Scis. Inst., Akron Women's Network, Assn. for Info. Systems, Inst. Mgmt. Accts. (dir. mem. retention 1994—96), Am. Acctg. Assn. (Best Paper award 1998), Beta Gamma Sigma. Office: U NC Bryan Sch Bus & Econ Greensboro NC 26165 E-mail: mjlenard@uncg.edu.

LENARD, MICHAEL BARRY, merchant banker, lawyer; b. Chgo., May 20, 1955; s. Henry Madart and Jacqueline Jo Anne (Silver) L.; m. Amy Jeanne Rifenbergh, Oct. 10, 1987; children: Madeline Michael, Nicholas Xavier. BBA, U. Wis., 1977; postgrad., NYU, 1981-82; JD, U. So. Calif., 1982. From assoc. to ptnr. Latham & Watkins, L.A., 1984-93; mng. dir., counsellor William E. Simon & Sons, 1993—; mng. dir. Indsl. Sport, 2001—. Bd. dir. William E. Simon & Sons, Hong Kong; spl. adv. bus. affairs V.P. U.S., Washington, 2000—. With So. Calif. Law Rev. mag., 1980-81. V.p. U.S. Olympic Com., 1989-96, mem. exec. com., bd. dirs., 1985-96, mem. athletes' adv. coun., 1981-89, vice chmn. athletes' adv. coun., 1985-89; named to Internat. Coun. for Arbitration of Sport, 1994—; bd. dirs. L.A. Sports Coun., 1988—, Atlanta Com. for Olympic Games, 1990-98. Named semi-finalist Outstanding Undergrad. Achievement award, 1977, USA Team Handball Athlete of Yr., 1985, USOC Olympian Mag. Team Handball SportsMan of Yr., 1985, Nat. Champion in Team Handball, 1975, 77, 79-80, 82, 87, 95; recipient Harry A. Bullis scholarship, 1977, Disting. Svc. award U.S. Sports Acad., 1996; mem. 1984 Olympic Team, U.S. Nat. Team, 1977-85 (capt. 1985). Mem. Order of the Coif, Phi Kappa Phi, Beta Gamma Sigma, Beta Alpha Psi, Phi Eta Sigma. Achievements include development of A.C. Sushi Master, 1985. Office: William E Simon & Sons 10990 Wilshire Blvd Ste 500 Los Angeles CA 90024-3917 E-mail: mlenard@wesandsons.com.

LENARDIC, KENNETH RALPH, systems architect, consultant; b. Cleve., May 18, 1945; s. Ralph and Dolores (Klish) L.; m. Karen Lynn Pierce, Sept. 21, 1968; children: Janis, Kerri. Student, Internat. Data Processing Inst, Cleve., 1966, Kent State U., Euclid, Ohio, 1969. Ops. supr. Towmotor Corp., Cleve., 1969-70; sr. systems analyst Caterpillar Indsl. Inc., Mentor, Ohio, 1978-83, mktg. systems engr., 1983-92; instr. Lakeland C.C., 1988-89; systems architect Mitsubishi-Caterpillar Forklift, 1992-94; info. systems mgr. Webb Supply, Cleve., 1994—. Computer cons., Concord, Ohio, 1988-92; pres. Micro Systems Architects, Mentor, 1994—; guest speaker in field. Contbr. articles to profl. jours. Republican. Roman Catholic. Avocations: music, photography, physical fitness. Home and Office: Micro Systems Architects 10265 Cherry Hill Dr Concord OH 44077-1515

LENCEK, RADO LUDOVIK, Slavic languages educator; b. Mirna, Slovenia, Oct. 3, 1921; came to U.S., 1956; s. Ludovik Ivan and Kati (Jaksa) L.; m. Nina A. Lovrencic, May 4, 1946; children: Bibi-Alice, Lena-Maria Student, U. Ljubljana, Slovenia, 1940-45, U. Padova, Italy, 1946-47; tchg. diploma, Inst. Magistrale, Gorizia, Italy, 1947; MA in Linguistics, U. Chgo., 1959; PhD in Slavic Langs., Harvard U., 1962. Asst. prof. Inst. Magistrale Sloveno, Gorizia-Trieste, Italy, 1944-55; editor USIS, Trieste, Italy, 1951-54; asst. prof. U. Ill., Urbana, 1962-65; from asst. prof. to prof. Slavic langs. Columbia U., N.Y.C., 1965-92, prof. of langs. emeritus, 1992—. Assoc. Averell Harrinan Inst. for Advanced Study of the Soviet Union and of the Inst. on East Cen. Europe, 1966—; vis. assoc. prof. NYU, 1969-72; vis. prof. Yale U., 1974, U. Ill., Urbana, 1977; coord. Nat. Com. Serbo-Croatian Teaching Materials, 1982-94; U.S. coord. for Cooperation Project on Slavistics, 1983—; active U.S.-USSR Commn. on the Humanities and Social Scis., Inst. East Ctrl. Europe; participant Internat. Congs. of Slavists Prague, 1968, Warsaw, 1973, Zagreb-Ljubljana, 1978, Kiev, 1983, Sofia, 1988, Bratislava, 1993; coord. Columbia U. Program in Slavic Cultures, organized symposia Columbia U., 1974, 84, Prato di Resia, Italy, 1979, Northwestern U., 1980, U. Chgo., 1984, Acad. of Scis. USSR, Moscow, 1987, Am. Assn. Tchrs. of Slavic and East European Langs. Annual Convention, San Francisco, 1991, Toronto, Can., 1993; mem. adv. bd. Slovenski jezik-Slovene Linguistic Studies, 1994—; mem. faculty Sch. of Internat. Affairs, 1966—. Author: Ob Jadranu, Ethnographic Studies, 1947, The Verb Pattern of Contemporary Slovene, 1966, A Bibliographical Guide to Slavic Civilizations, 1966, An Outline of the Course on Slavic Civilizations, 1970, 2d edit., 1978, The Structure and History of Slovene Language, 1982, Slovenes, The Eastern Alpine Slavs, and Their Cultural Heritage, 1989, The Correspondence Between Jan Baudouin de Courtenay (1845-1929) and Vatroslav Oblak (1864-96), 1992, Izbrane Razprave in Eseji (selected papers and essays), 1996; editor: (with others): Xenia Slavica, Gojko Ruzicic Festschrift, 1975, The Dilemma of the Melting Pot: The Case of the South Slavic Languages, 1976, To Honor Jernej Kopitar, 1780-1980, 1982, A Bibliography of Recent Literature on Macedonian, Serbo-Croatian and Slovene Languages, 1990; co-editor: Who's Who of Slovene Descent in the United States, 1992, 2d rev. edit., 1995, 3d edit., 1998; editor U.S. Info. Svcs. Bull., Trieste, Italy, 1951-54, others; editor (series) Papers in Slovene Studies, 1975-76, editl. com., editor book revs. Slovene Studies, 1979—; editl. com. Folia Slavica, 1976-89, Nationalities Papers, 1979-98, Geschichte, Kultur und Geisteswelt der Slowenen, Munich, 1982-91, Beiträge zur Kenntnis Südosteuropas, Munich, 1983-91, Münchner Zeitschrift für Balkankunde, 1983-91, Geschichte, Kultur und Geisteswelt der Südslaven, Munich, 1990; mem. coun. jours. Slavistična revija, 1991—; contbr. numerous articles in field of Slavic linguistics and cultures to scholarly jours. and proceedings of internat. confs., symposiums: "Kopitar's Understanding of Historical Evolutionary Trends of Older Slovene Written Texts," 1996, (selected papers) Izbrane razprave in eseji, 1996, "Sociolinguistic Components of Adam Bohoric's Concept of his Literacy Standard of Written Slovene," 1996, "An Attempt of Stratification of Early Slovene Christian Terminology of the Oldest Eastern Alpine Slavic Texts," 1996, "Matija Murko's Letters in Baudouin's Manuscript Collectanea of the Archives of the Russian Academy of Sciences in St. Petersburg," 1997, "Jan Baudouin de Courtenay-Vatroslav Oblak's Master and Teacher," 1997; contbr. papers and essays to profl. jours. Fulbright fellow, 1986; named Amb. of Rep. of Slovenia for Sci. by Ministry for Sci. and Tech. of Rep. of Slovenia, 1995; grantee NSF, 1974, 79, Japan Soc. for Promotion Sci., 1989, Internat. Rsch. Exchs. Bd., 1971, 72, 83, 85, 94; recipient Lit. prize for publ. of Who's Who of Slovene Descent in U.S. 1995 Soc. Slovene Intellectuals of Trieste (Italy), 1996. Fellow Am. Coun. Learned Socs., Bulgarian Acad. Scis.; mem. Slovenska Kulturna Akcija (Buenos Aires), Slavists' Assn. Slovenia (hon. Ljubljana chpt. 1989—), Linguistic Soc. Am., Linguistic Circle N.Y., Am. Assn. Advancement Slavic Studies, Am. Assn. Tchrs. Slavic and East European Langs. (Disting. Scholarly Career award 1994), Soc. Slovene Studies (founder, pres. 1973-83, editor SS Newsletter 1973-77, editor Letter 1978-83, dir. Rsch. and Documentation Ctr., Columbia U., Inst. East Ctrl. Europe 1988—); corresponding mem. Slovene Acad. Scis. and Arts in Ljubljana, European Acad. Scis. and Arts in Salzburg, Acad. Scis. and Arts in Belgrade, Prague, Cracow, and Moscow, Fulbright Assn.; mem. Am. Slovene Cong. (orgnl. com. 1993-94, acad. advisor to its coun. on acad. activities 1994—, award for contbn. to knowledge and recognition of Slovene culture in U.S. Am. by Pres. Republic Slovenia). Home: 560 Riverside Dr New York NY 10027-3202 Office: Columbia U 420 W 118th St New York NY 10027-7213

LENDERMAN, JOANIE, elementary education educator; b. Medford, Oreg., Jan. 20, 1946; d. Jay Lenderman and Vivian Spencer. BS in Edn., So. Oreg. Coll., Ashland, 1969; MS in Edn., Portland State U., 1972; postgrad., U. Va., 1985. Elem. tchr. Beaverton (Oreg.) Schs., 1972-76, Internat. Sch. Svcs., Isfahan, Iran, 1976-78; ESL instr. Lang. Svcs., Tucker, Ga., 1983-84; tchr. Fairfax (Va.) Schs., 1985-86; elem. tchr. Beaverton (Oreg.) Schs., 1990-96. Home: 4105 Jefferson Pkwy Lake Oswego OR 97035-1479

LENEHAN, JAMES T. pharmaceutical executive; Mktg. positions Johnson & Johnson, 1976—90, pres., 1990—, worldwide chmn., med. devices and diagnostics group, 1994—, mem. exec. com., 1994—, vice chmn., 2001—. Office: Johnson and Johnson 1 Johnson and Johnson Plza New Brunswick NJ 08933*

LENEHAN, MICHAEL DANIEL, editor, writer; b. Passaic, N.J., Feb. 3, 1949; s. Daniel Joseph and Eva Ruth (Cavallini) L.; m. Mary Margaret Williams, Oct. 29, 1983; children: John Francis (Jack), Rose Elizabeth. BA in Comm. Arts, U. Notre Dame, 1971. Editorial intern Cue Mag., NYC, 1971; style editor, scriptwriter Ency. Britannica, Chgo., 1971-73; assoc. editor Chgo. Reader, 1975-81, sr. editor, 1982-87, mng. editor, 1987-90, editor, 1990-95, exec. editor, 1995—; contbg. editor Atlantic Monthly, 1984-93; founder Acad. for Altrnative Journalism, 2000. Contbr. articles to mags. and newspapers. Mem. bd. visitors Northwestern U. Medill Sch. Journalism, 2001—. Recipient Westinghouse Sci. Writing award AAAS, 1978. Office: Chgo Reader 11 E Illinois St Chicago IL 60611-5652

LENEY, GEORGE WILLARD, consulting engineer; b. Nov. 13, 1927; s. Bert and Iva Irene (Skoog) L.; m. Arax G. Tefankjian, June 25, 1955 (dec. Aug. 1983); children: Sara Ann, Janet Ellen, John Alan, Ruth Alison. BS, U. Mich., 1950, MS, 1952, MA, 1955. Tchg. fellow U. Mich., 1951-53, 53-55; geophysicist Gulf Oil Co., Harmarville, Pa., 1955-56; chief geophysicist Hanna Mining Co., Cleve., 1956-64; staff geophysicist Shell Oil Co., Houston, 1964-66; chief geologist H.K. Porter Co., Inc., Pitts., 1966-76; cons., 1976-77, 81-86; regional geologist U.S. Dept. Energy, 1977-81; air pollution adminstr. Allegheny County Health Dept., Pa., 1986-97. V.p., bd. dirs. Pacific Asbestos Corp., 1970-75. With USN, 1946-48. Recipient Robert Peele Meml. award AIME, 1965 for pioneering work in geophysical exploration of iron ore. Mem. Soc. Econ. Geologists, Am. Inst. Mining Engrs., Soc. Exploration Geophysicists, Geologic Soc. Am., Pa. Acad. Sci., Air and Waste Mgmt. Assn. Achievements include being principally noted for technical achievements in mineral exploration and mining geophysics, including discovery of the Pilot Knob iron ore body in Missouri. Career included work with the Geological Survey of Canada on canoe reconnaissance in Labrador and the Northwest Territories. Organized and carried out minerals exploration programs for asbestos, iron ore, base metals, gold, oil and gas, and uranium in the U.S., Canada, Brazil and Cameroon; established a second career in air pollution, becoming recognized in the fields of emissions inventory and ozone planning. Address: 5335 Tomfran Dr Pittsburgh PA 15236-2217

LENFANT, CLAUDE JEAN-MARIE, physician; b. Paris, Oct. 12, 1928; arrived in U.S., 1960, naturalized, 1965; s. Robert and Jeanine (Leclerc) Lenfant; children: Philipe, Bernard, Martine Lenfant Wayman, Brigitte Lenfant Martin, Christine. BS, U. Rennes, France, 1948; MD, U. Paris, 1956; DSc (hon.) , SUNY, 1988. Asst. prof. physiology U. Lille, France, 1959—60; from clin. instr. to prof. medicine physiology and biophysics U. Wash. Med. Sch., 1961—72; assoc. dir. lung programs Nat. Heart, Lung and Blood Inst. NIH, Bethesda, Md., 1970—72, dir. divsn. lung diseases, 1972—80; dir. Fogarty Internat. Ctr. NIH, 1980—82, assoc. dir. internat. rsch., 1980—82; dir. Nat. Heart, Lung and Blood Inst., 1982—. Mem. editl. bd.: Undersea Biomed. Rsch., 1973—75, mem. editl. bd.: Respiration Physiology, 1971—78, mem. editl. bd.: Am. Jour. Physiology and Jour. Applied Physiology, 1970—76, mem. editl. bd.: Am. Rev. Respiratory Disease, 1973—79, mem. editl. bd.: Jour. Applied Physiology, 1976—82, mem. editl. bd.: Am. Jour. Medicine, 1979—82; editor: Lung Biology in Health and Disease. Recipient Nathan Davis award, AMA, 1998, Gold Heart award, Am. Heart Assn., 2002. Fellow: Royal Soc. Medicine, Royal Coll. Physicians; mem.: French Nat. Acad. Medicine, USSR Acad. Med. Scis., Inst. Medicine of Nat. Acad. Sci., Undersea Med. Soc., N.Y. Acad. Scis., Am. Physiol. Soc., French Physiol. Soc., Am. Soc. Clin. Investigation, Assn. Am. Physicians, Alpha Omega Alpha. Home: PO Box 83027 Gaithersburg MD 20883-0027 Office: Nat Heart Lung & Blood Inst Bldg 31A Rm 5A52 Bethesda MD 20892 E-mail: lenfantc@nih.gov.

LENFEST, HAROLD FITZ GERALD, former cable television executive, lawyer; b. Jacksonville, Fla., May 29, 1930; s. Harold Churchill and Herrena (FitzGerald) L.; m. Marguerite Brooks, July 9, 1955; children: Diane, H. Chase, Brook. AB, Washington and Lee U., 1953; LLB, Columbia U., 1958; DHL, Ursinus Coll., 1999, Temple U., 2002. Bar: N.Y. 1959. Assoc. Davis Polk & Wardwell, N.Y.C., 1958-65; assoc. counsel Triangle Publs., Phila., 1965-70, mng. dir. comm. divsn. N.Y.C., 1970-74; editorial dir., pub. Seventeen mag., 1970-74; pres. Suburban Cable TV Co., 1970-2000, Empire State Cable TV Co., 1970-74, Lenfest Comm., Inc., 1974-2000. Bd. dirs. TCI West, Inc., Seattle, Liberty Media Corp., Cable Advt. Bur., Videopole, France, Australis Media Ltd., Australia, Voice FX, Inc.; chmn. Video JukeBox, Inc.; CEO Cable AdNet, Inc., 1981—92, StarNet, Inc., 1989—, TelVue, Inc., 1990—, CAM Sys., 1995—. Trustee Walter Kaitz Found., Oakland, Calif., 1986—88; trustee, nat. campaign chmn. Washington and Lee U., 1990—98, hon. chair campaign, 2000—; mem. bd. regents Mercersburg Acad., 1989—97, pres., 1994—97; trustee Columbia U., 2000—; mem. James Madison Coun. Libr. of Congress, 1989—; trustee, exec. com. Chesapeake Bay Found., 1995—; bd. dirs., v.p. Columbia U. Sch. Law, N.Y.C., 1960—65, 1974—78, mem. bd. visitors, 1992—; bd. dirs., exec. com. Phila. Mus. Art, 1993—, chair, 2001—; bd. dirs. C-SPAN, 1995—2000. Capt. USNR, 1953—76, active duty USNR, 1953—56, active duty USNR, 1962. Named Man of Yr., Phila. Area Easter Seal Soc., 1992; recipient Disting. Achievement award, Columbia U. Sch. Law, 1997, Individual Leadership award, Phila. Arts and Bus. Coun., 2002, Patron of Yr. award, Gov. of Pa., 2002. Mem. Pa. Cable TV Assn. (bd. dirs., officer 1976-79), Mayflower Soc., Soc. Colonial Wars, Order of the Coif. Office: The Lenfest Group 1332 Enterprise Dr West Chester PA 19380-5970 E-mail: glenfest@lenfest.com.

LENG, DOUGLAS ELLIS, chemical engineer, scientist; b. Kitchener, Ontario, Can., May 28, 1928; came to U.S., 1955; s. Douglas Harry and Blanche (Ellis) L.; m. Marguerite Lambert, June 18, 1955; children: Ronald Bruce, Janet Elaine, Douglas Lambert. BSc, Queen's U., Kingston, Ontario, Can., 1951, MSc, 1953; PhD, Purdue U., 1956. Sr. rsch. scientist Dow Chem., Midland, Mich., 1986-96; mixing cons. Leng Assoc., 1996—. Adv. bd. Queen's U., Kingston, 1985-87; adv. panel Nat. Inst. Stds. & Tech., NRC, Washington, 1985-98. Patentee (8) in field; contbr. articles to profl. jours. Pres. Midland (Mich.) Curling Club, 1963-64, Midland Hockey, 1965. Recipient Dow Gold medal Dow Chem., 1993, Proctor & Gamble award N. Am. Mixing Forum, Miami, 1995. Fellow AIChE; mem. Am. Chem. Soc. Avocations: sailing, curling, photography, computers. Home: 1714 Sylvan Ln Midland MI 48640-2538 Office: Leng Assoc 1714 Sylvan Ln Midland MI 48640-2538 E-mail: deleng@chartermi.net.

LENG, MARGUERITE LAMBERT, b. Edmonton, Alta., Can., Sept. 25, 1926; came to the U.S., 1950; d. Joseph Edouard and Marie (Kiwit) Lambert; m. Douglas Ellis Leng, June 18, 1955; children: Ronald Bruce, Janet Leng Dumas, Douglas Lambert. BSc in Honours Chemistry, U. Alta., 1947; MSc, U. Sask., 1950; PhD, Purdue U., 1956. Rsch. asst. U. Mich. Med. Rsch. Inst., Ann Arbor, 1950-53; with agrl. dept. Dow Chem. Co., Midland, Mich., 1956-59, 66-76, with health and environ. scis. dept., 1976-86, mgr. internat. regulatory affairs, 1986-90; ret., 2002. Editor: Pesticide Chemist and Modern Toxicology, 1981, Agrochemical Environmental Fate Studies: State of the Art, 1995; contbr. articles to profl. jours., chpts. in books and encys. Life ins. med. rsch. fellow Equitable Life Assurance Co., 1949-50. Fellow: Am. Inst. Chemists (bd. dirs. 1991—97); mem.: Internat. Soc. for Study Xenobiotics, Am. Chem. Soc. (agrochem. divsn. fellow 1976, chmn. 1981, program chmn. 1980.). Avocations: international travel, family activities, foreign languages, sailing. Home: 1714 Sylvan Ln Midland MI 48640-2538 E-mail: mlleng1@chartermi.net.

LENGA, J. THOMAS, lawyer; b. Toledo, Dec. 16, 1942; s. Casimir M. and Rose C. (Sturniolo) L.; children by previous marriage: Christina M., John Thomas Jr., Peter M. BA, U. Toledo, 1965, JD, 1968. Bar: Mich. 1968, Ohio 1968. Capt. JAGC U.S. Army, 1968—72; mem. Dykema Gossett PLLC, Detroit, 1972-96, Clark Hill P.L.C., Detroit, from 1996, CEO, from 2001. Mem. com. on std. jury instrns. Mich. Supreme Ct.; advocate Am. Bd. of Trial Advocates. Named Disting. Alumnus, Coll. Law, U. Toledo, 1987. Fellow: Am. Coll. Trial Lawyers, Internat. Acad. Trial Lawyers; mem.: Internat. Assn. Def. Counsel, State Bar Mich. (bd. commrs. from 1992, treas. 1995—96, v.p. 1996—97, pres.-elect 1997—98, pres. 1998—99), Detroit Bar Assn. (pres. 1989—90). Home: Plymouth, Mich. Died 2002.

LENGEMANN, FREDERICK WILLIAM, physiology educator, scientist; b. N.Y.C., Apr. 8, 1925; s. Peter and Dorathea Johanna (Wolter) L.; m. J. Joan Doremus, Dec. 23, 1950; children— Frederick William Jr., David Munson. Student, N.Y. State Sch. Agr., Farmingdale, 1942-43; BS with distinction, Cornell U., 1950, MNutrition Sci., 1951; PhD, U. Wis., 1954. Research asso. U. Tenn.-AEC Agrl. Research Program, Oak Ridge, 1954-55; asst. prof. dept. chemistry U. Tenn. Med. Sch., Memphis, 1955-59; prof. dept. physiology N.Y. State Coll. Vet. Medicine, Cornell U., 1959-88, prof. physiology emeritus, 1988—; biochemist div. biology and medicine AEC, 1962-63. Cons. FAO-IAEA, Vienna, Austria, 1966-67, 76-77, Fed. Radiation Council, 1964-65, NRC, 1970-73, Nat. Com. on Radiation Protection, 1970-73, 79, 82; IAEA expert U. Nacional Agraria, Peru, 1978; lectr., dir. tng. courses Contbr. articles to profl. jours. Mem. planning bd. Town of Dryden, N.Y., 1963-68; treas. Rome (Pa.) Presbyn. Ch. Served with USNR, 1943-46. Decorated Air medal with 3 stars. Fellow AAAS; mem. Council Agrl. Sci. and Tech., Am. Dairy Sci. Assn., Am. Nutrition Soc., Fed. Am. Socs. for Exptl. Biology, Nat., N.Y. State Christmas tree growers assns., Sigma Xi, Phi Kappa Phi. Home: PO Box 217 Rome PA 18837-0217 Office: Cornell U NY State Coll Vet Medicine Dept Physiology Ithaca NY 14853

LENGER, JOHN RICHARD, journalism educator; b. Washington, Mo., Jan. 26, 1964; s. Richard Lenger and Bev (stepmother) and Joan and Craig Hart (stepfather); m. Maria Cristina Caballero, Aug. 5, 2000. B of Journalism, BA in Polit. Sci., U. Mo., 1986; MEd, Harvard U., 2002. Editor The LaBelle (Mo.) Star, 1986, Suburban Newspapers Greater St. Louis, 1986-90; Sunday editor The Post-Star, Glens Falls, N.Y., 1990-92; copy editor Gazette Newspapers, Schenectady, 1992-93; freelance editor, writer Foxboro, Mass., 1993-94; asst. editor Harvard U. Gazette, Cambridge, 1994-95, editor in chief, 1995-98; publs. dir. Harvard U. Office News & Pub. Affairs, 1998—; instr. journalism Harvard U., 1997—. Bd. dirs. Learning Success Network, Acton, Mass., 2000—01. Co-author: (chpt.) The Writer's Handbook, 2001, Living Ethics: Developing Values in Mass Communication, 1996; editor: The Harvard Guide, 2000, 2002; contbr. articles to profl. jours. Mentor Graham & Parks Alternative Pub. Sch., Cambridge, 1995—2002. Mem. Soc. Profl. Journalists, New England Press Assn. (vol. coord. 1999—). Office: Harvard U News & Pub Affairs 1060 Holyoke Ctr Cambridge MA 02138 E-mail: john_lenger@harvard.edu.

L'ENGLE, MADELEINE (MRS. HUGH FRANKLIN), writer; b. N.Y.C., Nov. 29, 1918; d. Charles Wadsworth and Madeleine (Barnett) Camp; m. Hugh Franklin, Jan. 26, 1946; children: Josephine Franklin Jones, Maria Franklin Rooney, Bion. AB, Smith Coll., 1941; postgrad., New Sch., 1941-42, Columbia U., 1960-61; holder 19 hon. degrees. Tchr. St. Hilda's and St. Hugh's Sch., 1960—; mem. faculty U. Ind., 1965-66, 71; writer-in-residence Ohio State U., 1970, U. Rochester, 1972, Wheaton Coll., 1976—, Cathedral St. John the Divine, N.Y.C., 1965—. Author: The Small Rain, 1945, Ilsa, 1946, Camilla Dickinson, 1951, A Winter's Love, 1957, And Both Were Young, 1949, Meet the Austins, 1960, A Wrinkle in Time, 1962, The Moon by Night, 1963, The 24 Days Before Christmas, 1964, The Arm of the Starfish, 1965, The Love Letters, 1966, The Journey with Jonah, 1968, The Young Unicorns, 1968, Dance in the Desert, 1969, Lines Scribbled on an Envelope, 1969, The Other Side of the Sun, 1971, A Circle of Quiet, 1972, A Wind in the Door, 1973, The Summer of the Great-Grandmother, 1974, Dragons in the Waters, 1976, The Irrational Season, 1977, A Swiftly Tilting Planet, 1978, The Weather of the Heart, 1978, Ladder of Angels, 1980, A Ring of Endless Light, 1980, Walking on Water, 1980, A Severed Wasp, 1982, And It Was Good, 1983, A House Like a Lotus, 1984, Trailing Clouds of Glory, 1985, A Stone for a Pillow, 1986, Many Waters, 1986, Two-Part Invention, 1988, A Cry Like a Bell, 1987, Sole Into Egypt, 1989, From This Day Forward, 1988, An Acceptable Time, 1989, The Glorious Impossible, 1990, Certain Women, 1992, The Rock That Is Higher: Story As Truth, 1993, Anytime Prayers, 1994, Troubling a Star, 1994, Penguins and Golden Calves, 1996, A Live Coal in the Sea, 1996, Glimpses of Grace, 1996, Wintersong, 1996, Mothers and Daughters, 1997, Friends for the Journey, 1997, Bright Evening Star: Mystery of the Incarnation, 1997. Pres. Crosswicks Found. Recipient Newbery medal, 1963, Sequoyah award, 1965, runner-up Hans Christian Andersen Internat. award, 1964, Lewis Carroll Shelf award, 1965, Austrian State Lit. award, 1969, Bishop's Cross, 1970, U. South Miss. medal, 1978, Regina medal, 1985, Alan award Nat. Coun. Tchrs. English, 1986, Kerlan award, 1990, Margaret Edwards award, 1998; collection of papers at Wheaton Coll. Mem. Authors Guild (mem. council), Authors League (mem. council), Writers Guild Am. Episcopalian. Home: 924 W End Ave Apt 95 New York NY 10025-3544 Office: Cathedral Libr St John the Divine 1047 Amsterdam Ave New York NY 10025-1747 also: care Random House Children's Media 1540 Broadway New York NY 10036-4039 *Over the years I've worked out a philosophy of failure which I find extraordinarily liberating. If I'm not free to fail, I'm not free to take risks, and everything in life that's worth doing involves a willingness to take a risk and involves the risk of failure. Each time I start a new book I am risking failure. Although I have had over 60 books published, there are at least 6 full unpublished books which have failed, but which have been necessary for the book which then gets published. The same thing is true in all human relationships. Unless I'm willing to open myself up to risk and to being hurt, then I'm closing myself off to love and friendship.**

LENGYEL, ALFONZ, art history, archeology and museology educator; b. Godollo, Hungary, Oct. 21, 1921; came to U.S., 1957; s. Aurel and Margit (Furedy) L.; m. Hongying Liu. Terminal degree in law and polit. sci., Miskolc Law Acad., Budapest, 1944; MA, San Jose State Coll., 1959; PhD, U. Paris, 1964; LLD (hon.), London Inst. Applied Rsch., 1973. Asst. prof. San Jose State Coll., Calif., 1961-63; faculty U. Md. European Div., Paris and Heidelberg, Germany, 1963-68; intern museology Ecole du Louvre, Paris, 1965-66; prof. Wayne State U., Detroit, 1968-72, No. Ky. U., Highland Heights, 1972-77; dean, prof. Inst. Mediterranean Art and Archaeology, Cin., 1977-82; coord. art history Rosemont Coll., Pa., 1982-86; rsch. prof. art history, dir. Goebel's Print Collection, 1986-88; pres. Fudan Mus. Found., China, 1988—. Adj. curator Detroit Inst. Arts, 1968-72; cons. Paris Am. Acad., 1963—; dir. UPAO, Washington, 1983—; adv. prof. Fudan U., Shanghai, People's Republic of China; cons. prof. Xian Jiaotong U., Xian, People's Republic of China, founder Sino-Am. Summer Field Sch. Archaeology; mem. governing bd. Mus. Asian Art, Sarasota, Fla. Author: Pub. Rels. for Mus., 1992, Archaeology for Museologists, 1993, Chinese Chronological History, 1993; co-author: The Archaeology of Roman Pannonia, 1983; contbr. numerous articles to profl. jours. Bd. dirs. Hungarian-Am. Fedn., Cleve., 1983-91, exec. v.p., Ft. Lauderdale, Fla., 1951—; mem. Rep. Presdl. Task Force, Washington, 1982—; mem. adv. bd. U.S. Dept. Interior Nat. Pk. Svc., 1987-91; bd. dirs. Mus. Asian Art, Sarasota, Fla., 2001—. Rockefeller Found. grantee U. Vienna, 1957; Govt. of France grantee U. Paris, 1962-63; S.H. Kress Found. lectureship Denison U. (Ohio), 1967-68; Smithsonian Instn. grantee, 1968; NEH grantee, 1971, 76. Fellow Internat. Acad. Sci. and Lettres, Arpad Acad. (pres. 1982—), Szechenyi Acad., Am. Assn. Swiss, German, Austrian Profs.; mem. Internat. Coun. Mus., Renaissance Soc. Am., Coll. Art Assn. Am., Archaeol. Inst. Am., Nat. Fedn. Hungarian-Ams., Soc. Architectural Historians, N.Y. Acad. Scis., Mich. Acad. Scis. and Letters, Soc. Profl. Archaeologists, Christopher Giest Hist. Soc., Detroit Classical Assn. Republican. Roman Catholic. Home: 4206 73d Terrace E Sarasota FL 34243 Office: Sino-Am Field Sch Archaeology Fudan Mus Found Sarasota FL 34243 E-mail: fmfsafsa@juno.com.

LENGYEL, DAVID, federal agency administrator; BS, U.S. Naval Acad.; MBA, U. Mo.; MA in Internat. Affairs, Washington U., St. Louis. Sr. aircrew tng. instr. McDonnell-Douglas, St. Louis; exec. officer to adminstr. NASA, Houston, 1993, mgr. Moscow Tech. Liaison Office, Internat. Space Sta., exec. dir. Aerospace Safety Adv. Panel, 2000—. Lt. col. USMC, Res. Achievements include logged over 2,000 flight hours. Office: Aerospace Safety Adv Panel NASA Hqrs 300 E St SW Washington DC 20546*

LENGYEL, ISTVÁN, chemist, educator; b. Kaposvar, Hungary, July 12, 1931; came to the U.S., 1958; s. István and Margit (Palásthy) L. Diploma in chemistry, Eotvos Lorand U., Budapest, 1955; PhD in Organic Chemistry, MIT, 1964. Rsch. chemist G. Richter Pharm. Works, Inc., Budapest, 1953-55; chemist State Geophys. Inst., 1955-56; rsch. chemist Biochemie GmbH, Kundl, Austria, 1957-58; rsch. asst. Johns Hopkins Med. Sch., Balt., 1958-59; predoctoral fellow MIT, Cambridge, 1959-63, postdoctoral fellow, 1964; NIH postdoctoral fellow Techn. U., Munich, 1964-65; rsch. assoc. MIT, Cambridge, 1965-67; prof. chemistry St. John's U., Jamaica, N.Y., 1967-98, chmn. dept. chemistry, 1985-91, prof. emeritus, 1999—. Vis. scholar U.S. Nat. Acad. Sci. and Hungarian Acad. Scis., 1973. Sr. Recipient award Alexander von Humboldt Found., 1973-74. Avocations: swimming, travel. Home: 84-01 169th St Jamaica NY 11439-0001 Office: Saint Johns U 8000 Utopia Pkwy Jamaica NY 11432-1335 Fax: (718) 990-1876.

LENHARDT, BENJAMIN F., JR. investment company executive; b. Asheville, N.C., June 18, 1940; s. Benjamin F. and Virginia Allie Lenhardt; m. Lucinda Kingery; children: David, Brian. BA, U. N.C., 1962. V.p. 1st Nat. Bank Chgo., 1974—81, sr. v.p., 1981—92; mng. dir. Brinson Ptnrs., Inc., Chgo., 1992—99; chmn., CEO Brinson Partners, Inc., 1999—. Trustee John G. Shedd Aquarium, Chgo., 1989—2002; life trustee Chgo. Acad. Scis., 1991—2002; mem. adv. bd. Northwestern U., Kellogg Sch. Mgmt., Evanston, Ill., 2001—02; bd. dirs. Midwest Adv. Bd. Inst. of Internat. Edn., Chgo., 1990—2002. Lt. (j.g.) USN, 1962—64. Mem.: Indian Hill Club. Avocations: gardening, travel. Home: 777 Bryant Ave Winnetka IL 60093 Office: Brinson Ptnrs, Inc 209 S LaSalle St Chicago IL

LENHART, CYNTHIA RAE, conservation organization executive; b. Cheverly, Md., Nov. 3, 1957; d. Donald Edward and Vesta Jean (Morris) L. BS in Environ. Studies, Coll. William & Mary, 1979; MS in Environ. Sci., SUNY, Syracuse, 1983. Asst. to pres. Environ. Policy Inst., Washington, 1979-81; wildlife policy analyst Nat. Audubon Soc., 1984-90; exec. dir. Hawk Mountain Sanctuary, Kempton, Pa., 1990—. Bd. dirs. Am. Bird Conservancy, Washington, Pa. Environ. Coun., Phila. Contbr. chpts. to Audubon Wildlife Report, 1985, 87, 88, 89. Chair Everglades Coalition, Washington, 1986-88. Office: Hawk Mountain Sanctuary 1700 Hawk Mountain Rd Kempton PA 19529-9379 E-mail: lenhart@hawkmountain.org.

LENHART, GARY ALAN, poet; b. Newark, Oct. 15, 1947; s. Forrest and Margaret Anne (Garrow) L.; m. Louise Elizabeth Hamlin, Aug. 19, 1980; 1 child, Katherine Marie. BA, Siena Coll., Loudonville, N.Y., 1969; MA, U. Wis., 1973. Lit. agt. Curtis Brown, N.Y.C., 1982-84; adminstrv. asst. Poetry Project, 1979-82; assoc. dir. Tchrs. & Writers Collaborative, 1984-94. Tchr. various colls. and univs. Author: (poetry books) One at a Time, 1983, Light Heart, 1991, Father and Son Night, 1999; editor: The T& W Guide to William Carlos Williams, 1998, Selected Poems of Michael Scholnick, 1998, The T & W Guide to Classic American Literature, 2001; contbr. articles to profl. jours., poetry various lit. pubs.

LENHART, SUZANNE MARIE, mathematician, educator; b. Louisville, Nov. 19, 1954; d. Louis William and Louise Theresa (Metz) Lenhart; m. Peter Volkman Andreae, Mar. 16, 1985; 1 child Phillip Volkman Andreae. BA, Bellarmine Coll., Louisville, 1976; MS, U. Ky., 1978, PhD, 1981. Cert. secondary tchr. Prof. math. U. Tenn., Knoxville, 1981—; rschr. Oak Ridge Nat. Lab., Tenn., 1987—. Editor: Jour. Computational and Applied Math, 2000, Math. Models and Methods in Applied Sci., 1998; contbr. V.p. Green Elem. Sch. PTA, Knoxville, 1996—98. Named Mentor of the Yr., So. Regional Edn. Bd., 1998. Mem.: Math. Assn. Am. (S.E. sect. Lectr. of the Yr. 1999), Assn. for Women in Math. (pres. 2001—), Assn. for Women in Sci. (pres. 1997—99), Soc. Indsl. and Applied Math. (mem. coun. 1994—2000, program chmn. control activity group 1996—98), Soc. of Math. Biology (bd. dirs. 2000—). Roman Catholic. Avocations: tennis, soccer. Home: 9609 Highlander Way Knoxville TN 37922 Office: Univ of Tenn Dept Math Knoxville TN 37996-7300

LENHOFF, HOWARD MAER, biological sciences educator, academic administrator, activist; b. North Adams, Mass., Jan. 27, 1929; s. Charles and G. Sarah Lenhoff; m. Sylvia Grossman, June 20, 1954; children: Gloria, Bernard. BA, Coe Coll., 1950, D.Sc. (hon.), 1976; PhD, Johns Hopkins U., 1955. USPHS fellow Loomis Lab., Greenwich, Conn., 1954-56; vis. lectr. Howard U., Washington, 1957-58; rsch. assoc. George Washington U., 1957-58; postdoctoral fellow Carnegie Instn., 1958; investigator Howard Hughes Med. Inst., Miami, 1958-63; prof. biology, dir. Lab. for Quantitative Biology U. Miami, Coral Gables, 1963-69; prof. biol. scis. U. Calif., Irvine, 1969-92, prof. polit. sci., 1986-92, assoc. dean biol. scis., 1969-71, dean grad. div., 1971-73, faculty asst. to vice chancellor of student affairs, 1986-88, 90-96, chair faculty senate, 1988-90, prof. emeritus, rsch. prof., 1993—; adj. prof. psychology U. Mass., Amherst, 2001—. Adj. prof. biology U. Miss., Oxford, 2001—; vis. scientist, Louis Lipsky fellow Weizmann Inst. Sci., Rehovot, Israel, 1968-69; vis. prof. chem. engring., Rothschild fellow Israel Inst. Tech., 1973-74; vis. prof. Hebrew U., Jerusalem, spring 1970, fall 1971, 77-78; Hubert Humphrey Inst. fellow Ben Gurion U., Beersheva, Israel, 1981; sr. rsch. fellow Jesus Coll., U. Oxford, 1988; dir. Nelson Rsch. & Devel. Co., Irvine, 1971-73; bd. dirs. BioProbe Internat., Inc., Tustin, Calif., 1983-89, chmn. bd., 1983-86. Editor/author: Biology of Hydra, 1961, Hydra, 1969, Experimental Coelenterate Biology, 1972, Coelenterate Biology— Review and Perspectives, 1974, Hydra: Research Methods, 1983, Enzyme Immunoassay, 1985, From Trembley's Polyps to New Directions in Research on Hydra, 1985, Hydra and the Birth of Experimental Biology, 1986, Biology of Nematocysts, Conception to Birth, 1988; mem. editorial bd. Jour. Solid Phase Biochemistry, 1976-80. Vice chmn. So. Calif. div. Am. Assn. Profs. for Peace in Middle East, 1972-80; bd. dirs. Am. Assn. for Ethiopian Jews, 1974-93, pres., 1978-82; bd. govs. Israel Bonds Orange County, Calif., 1974-80, Dade County Heart Assn., Miami, 1958-61, So. Calif. Technion Soc., 1976; pres. Hillel Coun. of Orange County, 1976-78; nat. chmn. faculty div. State of Israel Bonds, 1976; mem. sci. adv. bd. Am. Friends of Weizman Inst. Sci., 1980-84; bd. dirs. Hi Hopes Identity Discovery Found., Anaheim, Calif., 1982-87, pres. bd. govs., 1983-85, William Syndrome Found., trustee, 1992, 99—, pres., bd. dirs., 1993-95, exec. v.p., 1995-99; v.p. edn. Williams Syndrome Assn., 1994, bd. dirs., 1993-94, mem. adv. bd., 2001; mem. adv. bd. Berkshire Hills Music Acad., 2000—. 1st lt. USAF, 1956-58. Recipient Career Development award USPHS, 1965-69; Disting. fellow Iowa Acad. Sci., 1986. Fellow AAAS; mem. Soc. Physics and Natural History of Swiss Acad. Scis. Geneva (hon.), Am. Chem. Soc., Am. Biophys. Soc., Am. Soc. Zoologists, History of Sci. Soc., Am. Soc. Cell Biologists, Am. Soc. Biol. Chemists, Biophysics Soc., Soc. Gen. Physiologists, Soc. Growth and Devel. Home: 1739 University Ave Pmb 344 Oxford MS 38655 Office: U Calif Sch Biol Scis Irvine CA 92697-2300 E-mail: hmlenhof@uci.edu.

LENIART, DANIEL S, science educator, researcher; s. Stanley and Anna Leniart; m. Elizabeth Carmern Leniart, June 26, 1971; children: Keith Daniel, Kristiana Elizabeth. Bachelor Sci., The Citadel, Charleston, South Carolina, 1960—64; PhD, Cornell U., Ithica, New York, 1964—71. Rsch. devel. Vartan Associates, Palo Alto, Calif., 1969—81, Hewlett Packard Co., Palo Alto, 1981—84, Technicon, Tarrytown, NY, 1985—92; cons. Leniart Associates, Broolfield, Conn., 1993—2000; tchr. Bristol Sch. Sys., Bristol, 2001—02. Contbr. scientific papers to numerous journal publications. Fellow Sage Teeple, Cornell U., 1964-1968, NIH, 1969. Achievements include patents for Immunology Methods. Home: 6 Guernsey Road Brookfield CT 06804-3915 Personal E-mail: danleniart@aol.com.

LENIHAN, ROBERT JOSEPH, II, lawyer; b. Detroit, Jan. 16, 1947; s. Robert J. and Rita M. (O'Rourke) L.; m. Ann Carolyn Kelly, July 3, 1971; children: Robert J. III, James K. BS, Xavier U., 1969; JD cum laude, Wayne State U., 1972. Bar: Mich. 1972, U.S. Dist. Ct. (ea. dist.) Mich. 1972, U.S. Dist. Ct. (we. dist.) Mich. 1974, U.S. Ct. Appeals (6th cir.) 1986. Ptnr. Lenihan & Plese, Birmingham, Mich., 1972-85; sr. ptnr., prin. Colombo & Colombo, Bloomfield Hills, 1986-96; prin., ptnr. Harness, Dickey & Pierce, P.L.C., Troy, 1997—. Served to lt. col. USAR, 1973-93. Mem. ABA, Mich. Bar Assn., Oakland County Bar Assn., Fed. Bar Assn., Order of Barristers, Detroit Boat Club (pres. 1985-86), Renaissance Club. Avocations: golf, carpentry, reading, boating. Office: Harness Dickey & Pierce PLC 5445 Corporate Dr Ste 400 Troy MI 48098-2683

LENK, RICHARD WILLIAM, JR. history educator; b. Hackensack, N.J., Aug. 29, 1936; s. Richard William and Eleanor Marion (Haenschen) L.; BA cum laude, Fairleigh Dickinson U., 1959; PhD, NYU, 1969. Lectr., L.I. U., 1964-65, Bklyn. Coll., 1965-67; instr. N.Y. U., summer 1968; lectr. Hunter Coll., N.Y.C., 1969; asst. prof. Bergen C.C., Paramus, N.J., 1969-73, assoc. prof., 1973-80, prof. history, 1980-98, prof. emeritus, 1998 . Trustee, Bergen County Hist. Soc., 1977-80, pres., 1980-83; mem. Hackensack Tercentenary Com. for N.J., 1962-64; historian City of Hackensack, 1999—. Mem. Am. Hist. Soc., Orgn. Am. Historians, Archaeol. Inst. Am., N.Y. Hist. Soc., N.J. Hist. Soc., Assn. Ancient Historians. Contbr. articles to profl. jours. Office: Dept Social Scis Bergen Community Coll 400 Paramus Rd Paramus NJ 07652-1508

LENKE, JOANNE MARIE, publishing executive; b. Chgo., Aug. 27, 1938; d. August Julian and Dorothy Anna (Gold) L. BS, Purdue U., 1960; MS, Syracuse U., 1964, PhD, 1968. Tchr. pub. schs., Evanston, Ill., 1960-63; editor Test Dept. Harcourt, Brace & World, Inc., N.Y.C., 1967-70; rsch. psychologist Harcourt Brace Jovanovich, Inc., 1970-73, exec. editor, 1973-75; asst. dir. ednl. measurment divsn. The Psychol. Corp., 1975-83, dir. ednl. measurement and psychometrics Cleve., 1983-85, San Antonio, 1986, v.p. dir. measurement divsn., 1986-88, sr. v.p., 1988-91, exec. v.p., 1991-97, pres., 1997-99; cons., 1999—. Field reader U.S. Office Edn., 1972. Adv. editor Jour. Ednl. Measurement, 1974-78. NSF grantee, 1963-64. Mem. APA, Nat. Coun. Measurement in Edn., Am. Ednl. Rsch. Assn. Home: 1311 Vista Del Monte San Antonio TX 78216-2229 E-mail: jlenke@usa.net.

LENKER, SUSAN S. mathematician, educator, consultant; b. Bridgeport, Conn., Nov. 13, 1945; d. William and Helen Bodnar Stamm; m. James Lush, Jan. 1966 (div. 1967); m. Terry D. Lenker; children: Scott Davidson, Carl Witmer. BS, Western Conn. State U., 1969; MA, U. Colo., 1970; PhD, U. Mont., 1975. CPA Va. Tchr. Maguk H.S., Monroe, Conn., 1967; asst. prof. U. Louisville, 1975—76; from asst. to assoc. prof. Ctrl. Mich. U., Mt. Pleasant, 1976—. Editor: INPUT: Innovative Programs Using Technology in Mathematics Education, 1998. Bd. mem. Shepherd (Mich) Sch. Bd., 1992—95. Recipient Tech. in Edn. award, The Annenberg/CPB Project, Ctrl. Mich. U., 1996—. Mem.: MAA, ASA (treas. Mid-Mich. chpt.). Methodist. Avocations: tennis, bridge, tai chi, gardening, choir. Office: Ctrl Mich Univ Mount Pleasant MI 48859-0001

LENKOSKI, LEO DOUGLAS, psychiatrist, educator; b. Northampton, Mass., May 13, 1925; s. Leo L. and Mary Agnes (Lee) L.; m. Jeannette Teare, July 12, 1952; children— Jan Ellen, Mark Teare, Lisa Marie, Joanne Lee. AB, Harvard, 1948, spl. student, 1948-49; MD, Western Res. U., 1953; grad., Cleve. Psychoanalytic Inst., 1964. Intern Univ. Hosps., Cleve., 1953-54, resident in psychiatry, 1956-57, dir. psychiatry, 1970-86, chief of staff, 1982-90; dir. profl. services Horizon Ctr. Hosp., 1980; asst. resident in psychiatry Yale U., New Haven, 1954-56; teaching fellow Case Western Res. U., Cleve., 1957-60, from instr. to prof. psychiatry, 1960-93; prof. emeritus, 1993—; assoc. dean Sch. Medicine Case Western Res. U., Cleve., 1982-93, dir. Substance Abuse Ctr., 1990-93. Cons. Cleve. Ctr. on Alcoholism, DePaul Maternity and Infant Home, St. Ann's Hosp., Def. Dept., Cleve. VA Hosp., Psychiat. Edn. br. NIMH; mem. Cuyahoga County Mental Health and Retardation Bd., 1967-73, 94—, Health Planning and Devel. Commn., 1967-73, Ohio Mental Health and Retardation Commn., 1976-78. Contbr. articles to profl. jours. Bd. dirs. Hough-Norwood Health Ctr., Hitchcock Ctr., Hopewell Inn, Woodruff Found, 2001—. 1st lt. USAAF, 1943-46. Decorated D.F.C., Air medal with oak leaf cluster.; Career Tchr. grantee NIMH, 1958-60 Fellow Am. Psychiat. Assn. (life), Am. Coll. Psychiatrists, Am. Coll. Psychoanalysts (pres. 1988-89); mem. AMA, AAAS, Ohio Psychiat. Assn. (pres. 1974—), Am. Psychoanalytic Assn., Assn. Am. Med. Colls., Cleve. Acad. Medicine (bd. dirs. 1987-90), Ohio Med. Assn., Pasteur Club, Am. Assn. Chairmen Depts. Psychiatry (pres. 1978-79), Alpha Omega Alpha. Home: 1 Bratenahl Pl Apt 1010 Cleveland OH 44108-1155 Office: 11000 Euclid Ave Cleveland OH 44106-1714

LENKOWSKY, LESLIE, federal agency administrator; b. N.Y.C., Mar. 30, 1946; s. Mandel and Toby Lenkowsky; m. Kathleen Mary Dougherty, Aug. 29, 1968; children: Adam, Matthew. AB, Franklin and Marshall Coll., 1968; postgrad., U. Strathclyde, Glasgow, Scotland, 1973-74; PhD, Harvard U., 1982. Rsch. asst. Harvard U., Cambridge, Mass., 1971-73; asst. to sec. Pa. Dept. Pub. Welfare, Harrisburg, 1975-76; dir. rsch. Smith Richardson Found., N.Y.C., 1976-83, cons., 1984-85; dep. dir. USIA, Washington, 1983-84; resident fellow Am. Enterprise Inst., 1985; pres. Inst. for Ednl. Affairs, 1985-90, Hudson Inst., Indpls., 1990—; chief executive off. Corp. for Nat. and Comm. Serv., Washington, 2001—. Adj. prof. Georgetown U., Washington, 1985-90; mem. adv. bd. Ind. U. Ctr. on Philanthropy, Indpls., 1989—; chmn. exec. com. Madison Ctr. for Ednl. Affairs, Washington, 1990—. Author: Politics, Economics and Welfare Reform, 1986; co-author: The New Consensus on Family and Welfare, 1987; contbr. articles to mag. Trustee Fgn. Policy Rsch. Inst., Phila., 1987—, Bodman Found., 1991—, Achelis Found., 1991—; mem. Nat. Coun. on Disability, Washington, 1987-90, Commn. on Nat. and Community Svc., Washington, 1991—; bd. dirs. Park Tudor Sch., Indpls., 1991—, Greater Indpls. Progress Commn., 1992—. Capt. USAR. Grad. fellow Danforth Found., Harvard U., 1968-72, Frank Know Meml. fellow, 1973-74. Mem. Nat. Assn. Scholars (bd. advisors 1987—), Econs. Club (bd. dirs. 1992), Univ. Club, Phi Beta Kappa. Jewish. Office: Corp for Nat and Comm Serv Off of the Chief Exec Off 1201 New York Ave NW Washington DC 20525-0001*

LENMAN, BRUCE PHILIP, historian, educator; b. Aberdeen, Scotland, Apr. 9, 1938; s. Jacob Philip and May (Wishart) L. MA in History with 1st class honors, Aberdeen U., 1960; MLitt, U. Cambridge, 1965, LittD, 1986. Asst. prof. U. Victoria, Canada, 1963; lectr. Queen's Coll., Dundee, Scotland, 1963—67, U. Dundee, 1967—72, U. St. Andrews, Scotland, 1972—78, sr. lectr., 1978—83, reader, 1983—92, prof. of modern history, 1992—. James Pinckney Harrison prof. history Coll. William and Mary, Williamsburg, Va., 1988-89; Bird prof. history Emory U., Atlanta, 1998; mem. humanities com. Coun. for Nat. Acad. Awards, London, 1985-87. Author: From Esk to Tweed, 1975, Economic History of Modern Scotland, 1977 (Scottish Arts Coun. award 1977), The Jacobite Risings 1689-1746, 1980 (Scottish Arts Coun. award 1980), Scotland 1746-1832, 1981, The Jacobite Clans of the Great Glen, 1984, The Jacobite Cause, 1986, The Eclipse of Parliament, 1992, England's Colonial Wars, 2000, Britain's Colonial Wars, 2001; co-author: (with John S. Gibson) The Jacobite Threat, 1990; editor: Chambers Dictionary of World History, 1993, rev. edit., 2000. Brit. Acad.-Newberry Library fellow, 1982, John Carter Brown Library fellow, 1984, Mellon fellow Va. Hist. Soc., 1990, Mayers fellow Huntington Libr., 1996, Folger Libr. fellow, 1997. Fellow Royal Hist. Soc.; mem. Am. Soc. for 18th Century Scottish Studies, Am. Soc. for 18th Century Studies, Soc. for History of Discoveries, Hakluyt Soc. Clubs: Royal Commonwealth (London); New Golf (St. Andrews). Avocations: golf, hill walking, swimming, Scottish country dancing, badminton. Office: U St Andrews Dept Modern History St Katharine's Lodge Saint Andrews KY16 9AL Scotland E-mail: bl@st-andrews.ac.uk.

LENN, MARJORIE PEACE, education association administrator, consultant; b. Bowling Green, Ohio, Jan. 17, 1946; d. Frederick Elwynn and Nelvia P. Peace; m. D. Jeffrey Lenn; 1 child, Rebecca. BA, Transylvania Coll., 1968; M in Arts and Religion, Yale U., 1970; MEd, U. Mass., 1973, EdD, 1978. Dir. student svcs. U. Mass., Amherst, 1970-79, dir. residential life, 1979-82; dir. profl. svcs. Coun. on Postsecondary Accreditation, Washington, 1982-89, v.p., 1989-92; exec. dir. Ctr. for Quality Assurance in Internat. Edn., 1992—, Global Alliance for Transnat. Edn., Washington, 1996—2000. Cons. govts. China, India, Indonesia, South Africa, Mex., Belize, Argentina, Chile, Mauritius, Romania, Hungary and others in higher edn. reform, 1991—; spl. adviser on trade in edn. svcs. U.S. Govt., 2000—. Author: International Developments in Assuring Quality in Higher Education, 1994, Ambassadors of U.S. Higher Education: Quality Credit Bearing Programs Abroad, 1997, Globalization of the Professions and the Quality Imperative, 1997, Multinational Discourse on Professional Accreditation, Certification, and Licensure: Bridges for the Globalizing Professions, 1998, The Foundations of Globalization of Higher Education and the Professions, 1999, The Globalization of the Professions in the United States and Canada: A Survey and Analysis, 2000, Higher Education and Training in the Global Marketplace: Exporting Issues and the Trade Agreements, 2002; author: (with others) Ethics in Higher Education, 1990; editor: New England Consultation Network, 1978, Site Visitors in the Accreditation Process: A Guide to Issues and Practical Concerns, 1988, International Education and Accreditation: Uncharted Waters, 1990, Conflicts of Interest in the Accreditation Process, 1991, Distance Learning and Accreditation, 1991, Diversity, Accessibility, and Quality: An Introduction to Education in the United States for Educators for Other Countries, 1995; editor, contbr. Globalization of Higher Education and the Professions: The Mobility of Students, Scholars, and Professionals, 1993, Globalization of Education and the Professions: The Case of North America, 1994, (series) Studying in the United States, 1994; contbr. articles to profl. jours. Bd. dirs. Regents Coll., 1996-98, Hong Kong Coun. Acad. Accreditation, 1989-92; v.p. adminstrv. Women's Nat. Dem. Club, Washington, 1990-91; elder Old Presbyn. Meeting House, Alexandria, Va., 1983—. Recipient Outstanding Alumni award Transylvania U., 1998, Outstanding Contbn. to Global Higher Edn. award Assn. Christian Colls. and Univs., Internat. Ecumenical Forum, 1998. Fellow Soc. for Values in Higher Edn. (bd. dirs. 1994-95); mem. Women Adminstrs. in Higher Edn. (bd. dirs. 1984-90), Internat. Network Quality Assurance Agys. in Higher Edn. (bd. dirs. 1994—), Sigma Kappa (Colby award for outstanding svc. 2000). Democrat. Presbyterian. Avocations: choral music, travel. Office: Ctr for Quality Assurance in Int Edn Nat Ctr for Higher Edn 1 Dupont Cir NW Ste 515 Washington DC 20036-1135 E-mail: cqaie@aacrao.org.

LENN, STEPHEN ANDREW, investment banker; b. Ft. Lauderdale, Fla., Jan. 6, 1946; s. Joseph A. and Ruth (Kreis) L.; 1 child, Daniel Lenn. BA, Tufts U., 1967; JD, Columbia U., 1970. Assoc. Kronish, Lieb, Shainswit, Weiner & Hellman, N.Y.C., 1970-72, Shereff, Friedman, Hoffman & Goodman, N.Y.C., 1972-75; exec. v.p., gen. counsel Union Commerce Bank, Union Commerce Corp., Cleve., 1975-83; ptnr., mng. ptnr. Porter, Wright, Morris & Arthur, 1983-88; ptnr. Baker & Hostetler, 1988-97; CEO Capital Strategies Inc., 1997—. Trustee Gt. Lakes Sci. Ctr. Mem. ABA, Oakwood Club. Office: Capital Strategies Inc 1801 E 9th St 1350 Cleveland OH 44114

LENNARZ, WILLIAM JOSEPH, research biologist, educator; b. N.Y.C., Sept. 28, 1934; s. William and Louise (Richter) L.; m. Roberta S. Lozensky, June 16, 1956 (div. June 1973); children: William, Matthew, David; m. Sheila Jackson, July 13, 1973. BS, Pa. State U., 1956; PhD, U. Ill., 1959; research fellow, Harvard, 1959-62. Mem. faculty Johns Hopkins Sch. Medicine, 1962-83, assoc. prof. biochemistry, 1966-70, prof., 1971-83; R.A. Welch prof. and chmn. dept. biochemistry and molecular biology U. Tex. Cancer Ctr., M.D. Anderson Hosp., Houston, 1983-89; disting. prof., chmn. dept. biochemistry and cell biology SUNY, Stony Brook, 1989—; dir. Inst. for Cell and Devel. Biology, 1990—. Cons. NIH, seminars in cell and developmental biology, growth and differentiation. Mem. editl. bd.: Biochem. Biophys. Rsch. Commn., mem. editl. bd.: Jour. Biochemistry. Clayton Found. scholar, 1962-64; Lederle Faculty awardee, 1965-67; recipient Distinguished Young Scientist award Md., 1967 Mem. NAS, Am. Chem. Soc., Am. Soc. Biol. Chemists and Molecular Biologists (pres. 1989-90), Am. Soc. Microbiology, Am. Soc. Cell Biology (pub. affairs com.), Assn. Med. Grad. Sch. Dept. Biochemistry (pres. 1993), Internat. Union Biochemistry and Molecular Biology (exec. com.), Worcester Found. (mem. scientific adv. bd.), Soc. Glycobiology (pres. 1993), Sigma Xi, Phi Kappa Phi, Alpha Chi Sigma. Rsch. biochemistry of cell surface molecules and of fertilization. Home: 43 Erland Rd Stony Brook NY 11790-1124 Office: SUNY at Stony Brook 450 Life Scis Stony Brook NY 11790 E-mail: wlennarz@notes.cc.sunysb.edu.

LENNES, GREGORY, manufacturing and financing company executive; b. Chgo., Aug. 5, 1947; s. Lawrence Dominic and Genevieve (Karoll) L.; m. Kathie Lennes; children: Robert, Sandra, Ryan, Bonnie. BA, U. Ill., 1969, MA, 1971, postgrad., 1971-73. Corp. archivist Navistar Internat. Corp. (formerly Internat. Harvester Co.), Chgo., 1973-80, records mgr., 1980—, asst. sec., 1980—; dir. document mgmt., 1997—; sec. Navistar Fin. Corp., Schaumburg, Ill., 1980—, Internat. Truck and Engine Corp., 1987—. Editor: Historical Records in the Farm Equipment Industry, 1977. Mem. Am. Soc. Corp Secs., Assn. Records Mgrs. and Adminstrs., Soc. Am. Archivists, Midwest Archives Conf., Assn. Info. and Image Mgmt., Nat. Assn. Stock Plan Profls. Home: 6412 S Knox Ave Chicago IL 60629-5522 Office: Internat Truck and Engine Corp 4201 Winfield Rd Warrenville IL 60555

LENNON, JOSEPH LUKE, college official, priest; b. Providence, Sept. 21, 1919; s. John Joseph and Marjorie (McCabe) L. AB, Providence Coll., 1940; STB, Immaculate Conception Coll., 1946; MA, U. Notre Dame, 1950, PhD, 1953; LLD, Bradford Durfee Coll. Tech., 1963; LittD (hon.), U. Southeastern Mass., 1975; DHL (hon.), Roger Williams Coll., 1980. Ordained priest Roman Cath. Ch., 1947; instr. U. Notre Dame, 1948-50; mem. edn. dept. Providence Coll., 1950-51, 53-56, asst. dean men, 1953, dean of men, 1954-56, dean of coll., 1956-68, v.p. community affairs, 1968-88, ret., 1988. Dir. Tchrs. Guild of Thomistic Inst., 1953-56, Pennywise Shop; bd. trustees So. New Eng. Sch. of Law, 1994—. Author: The Role of Experience in the Acquisition of Scientific Knowledge, 1952, The Dean Speaks, 1958, College is for Knowledge, 1959; rev. as 30 Ways to Get Ahead at College, 1964. Mem. adv. council Citizens Ednl. Freedom; adv. bd. Perceptional Edn. and Research Center; co-chmn. Easter Seals, 1968; arbitrator R.I. Bd. Labor; adv. com. Mental Retardation, R.I.; chmn. Nat. Library Week, 1962; mem. R.I. Adv. Com. Vocational Edn.; ann. lectr. Psychology and Everyday Life, WJAR-TV, 1960-75; mem. Gov. R.I. Com. to Study R.I. State Inst. at, Howard; chmn. speaker's bur. United Fund Campaign, 1971; coordinator Civil Rights Affirmative Action Program, 1970-78; mem. Com. Future Jurisprudence in, R.I; com. clergy renewal Diocese Providence; mem. Com. for CROP-Community Hunger Appeal of Ch. World Service, 1974-75; mem. subcom. on family law Gov.'s Commn. on Jurisprudence of Future; mem. membership com. Cancer Control Bd., R.I., 1977; mem. Gov.'s Commn. on Consumer's Council, 1977, Gov.'s Leadership Conf. on Citizen Participation.; bd. dirs. Blue Cross and Blue Shield, Progress for Providence, R.I. Legal Services, Fed. Hill House, Pawtucket YMCA, The Samaritans, Handgun Alert, Vols. in R.I. Schs., Meeting St. Sch., Big Sisters, Big Bros. Assn. R.I., R.I. Easter Seal, Blackstone Valley Surgicare, R.I. Heart Assn.; chmn. 1975 Heart Fund campaign; trustee R.I. chpt. Leukemia Soc. Am.; adv. bd. Parents Without Partners; bd. govs. John E. Fogarty Found., Irish Scholarship Found.; bd. dirs., trustee Big Sisters Assn., R.I.; bd. dirs. Diabetes Assn.; adv. bd. St. Joseph's Merged Hosps.; mem. corp. R.I. Hosp.; trustee Emma Pendleton Bradley Hosp., 1984—, Southern New Eng. Sch. Law, 1994—; chmn. Laborer's Internat. Union North Am. Scholarship Program, 1995—; mem. adv. council Quirk Inst.; mem. Spl. Legis. Commn. Created on Catastrophic Health Ins., 1979-82, Gov.'s Screening Com. for the Judiciary, 1980-89; mem. Save the Bay, 1986-88; bd. dirs. John Burke Scholarship Found., 1973— Scholarship Funds of the Laborers' International Union of North America. Recipient Seal of Approval R.I. Automobile Dealers Assn., 1978; Father Lenon O.P. Park established in his honor, City of Providence, 1998; inducted into R.I. Heritage Hall of Fame, 1999. Mem. Nat. Cath. Edn. Assn., Am. Cath. Sociol. Soc., Nat. Soc. Study Edn., Am. Philosophers Edn. Assn., New Eng. Ednl. Assn., New Eng. Guidance and Personnel Assn., Greater Providence Epilepsy Assn., Nat. Soc. Study Edn., Am. Arbitration Assn., Alpha Epsilon Delta, Delta Epsilon Sigma (pres. 1966-69)

LENNOX, DONALD D(UANE), automotive and housing components company executive; b. Pitts., Dec. 3, 1918; s. Edward George and Sarah B. (Knight) L.; m. Jane Armstrong, June 11, 1949; children: Donald D., J. Gordon. BS with honors, U. Pitts., 1947. CPA, Pa. With Ford Motor Co., 1950-69, Xerox Corp., 1969-80, corp. v.p. and sr. v.p. info. tech. group N.Y., 1969-73, group v.p. and pres. info. tech. group, 1973-75, group v.p., pres. info. systems group, 1975-80, sr. v.p., sr. staff officer Stamford, Conn., 1973-74; sr. v.p. ops. staff Navistar Internat. Corp., Chgo., 1980-81, exec. v.p., 1981-82, pres., chief operating officer, 1982, chmn., chief exec. officer, 1983-87, also bd. dirs.; chmn., chief exec. officer Schlegel Corp., Rochester, N.Y., 1987-89; chmn. Internat. Imaging Materials, Inc., Amherst, 1990-97; ret., 1997. Bd. dirs. Prudential-Securities Mut. Funds, Gleason Corp. Served with AC USN, 1942-45. Decorated D.F.C. with 2 gold stars, Air medal with 4 gold stars. Mem. Rochester Area C. of C. (pres. 1979), Country Club of Rochester, Genesee Valley Econ. Club, Chgo. Club, Order of Artus, Beta Gamma Sigma. Republican. *What modest success I have enjoyed is the result of hard work and dedication to the success of the organization public or private. Rarely is one's contribution to the success of the organization not recognized or rewarded.*

LENNOX, EDWARD NEWMAN, holding company executive; b. New Orleans, July 27, 1925; s. Joseph Andrew and Alice (Newman) L.; m. Joan Mary Landry, Sept. 3, 1949; children: Katherine Sarah, Anne Victoria, May Elizabeth, Laura Joan. BBA, Tulane U., 1949. Mktg. svc. clk. Shell Oil Co., New Orleans, 1949; with W.M. Chambers Truck Line, Inc., 1950-60, exec. v.p., 1954-60; v.p., gen. mgr. Radcliff Materials, Inc., 1961-71; v.p. Office Pub. Affairs, So. Industries Co., 1971-88; v.p. Dravo Natural Resources Co., 1982-91; ret., 1992. Pres. Tidelands Industries, Inc., 1982-85; bd. dirs. Home Savs. & Loan Assn., 1979-89, pres., 1982-88, chmn., 1984-89; cons. Martin-Marietta Aggregates, 1995—. Pres. La. Tank Truck Carriers, 1954-55; mem. La. Bd. Hwys., 1965-67; chmn. New Orleans Aviation Bd., 1965-66; bd. dirs. Travelers Aid Soc., 1966-68, Met. Area Com., 1967-80, Constrn. Industry Legis. Coun., 1968-85, Miss. Valley Assn., 1969-72; pres. bd. levee commrs. Orleans Levee Dist., 1969-72; pres. Met. New Orleans Safety Coun., 1969-71; vice chmn. transp. task force Goals for La., 1969-72; mem. New Orleans Bd. Trade, 1971-89; mem. Ala. Gov.'s Adv. Coun. on Econs., 1971-72, Gov.'s Adv. Com. River Area Transp. and Planning Study, 1971-72; area v.p. Pub. Affairs Rsch. Coun. La., 1972-73; mem. exec. com. La. Good Roads Assn., 1972-74; industry del. La. Constl. Conv., 1973; mem. exec. com. Miss. Valley World Trade Coun., 1973-74; bd. dirs., mem. exec. com. Pendleton Meml. Meth. Hosp., 1963-81, dir. emeritus, 1981—; bd. dirs. Boys' Clubs Greater New Orleans, 1973-79; bd. dirs., mem. exec. bd. Goodwill Industries Greater New Orleans, Inc., 1975-79, 81—, treas., 1984-85, 1st v.p., 1987-88, chmn., 1989-90; bd. dirs. Tragedy Fund, Inc., 1976—; bd. govs. La. Civil Svc. League, 1974—, pres., 1977-78; dir. chmn. bd. trustees La. Found. Pvt. Colls., 1980-83. Capt. AUS, 1943-46. Recipient industry svc. award Assn. Gen. Contractors Am., 1967, cert. of appreciation Constrn. Industry Assn. New Orleans, 1972, New Orleans Jaycees award, 1960, cert. of merit Mayoralty of New Orleans, 1964, 67, Monte M. Lemann award La. Civil Svc. League, 1976, Goodwill Achiever award Goodwill Industries Vol. Svcs., 2001; named Hon. Life Chmn., 1980, Hon. Citizen and Amb. at Large, City of Jacksonville, 1966. Mem. La. Motor Transport Assn. (pres. 1963-64), Ala. Trucking Assn. (v.p. 1956-60), So. Concrete Masonry Assn. (pres. 1963-68), Greater New Orleans Ready Mixed Concrete Assn. (pres. 1966-68), La. Shell Prodrs. Assn. (pres. 1966-68), C. of C. New Orleans Area (bd. dirs. 1968-73, 75-77, pres.-elect 1973), Traffic Club New Orleans, Lakeshore Property Owners Assn. (bd. dirs. 1974-86, pres. 1976-77, 79-80), Tulane U. Alumni Assn., Mobile Area C. of C., Metairie Country Club (bd. govs. 1976-82, 89-92, pres. 1980-81). Home: 862 Topaz St New Orleans LA 70124-3626 Office: 160 James Dr E Ste 200 Saint Rose LA 70087-4038

LENNOX, GLORIA (GLORIA DEMEREE), real estate executive; b. Baden, Pa., Feb. 14, 1931; d. Gilbert and Marion (Slosson) Whetson; m; William Lennox, June 19, 1954 (div. 1985); children: Cheryl Lennox Watson, Lynda Lennox Huerta, Jim; m. Philip Demeree, July 4, 1985. BS in Edn., Kent State U., 1954; MA in Spl. Edn., Ariz. State U., 1968; grad., Realtor's Inst. Cert. residential specialist, residential broker state and nat. Tchr. Maple Leaf Sch., Garfield Heights, Ohio, 1954-55, Madison (Ind.) Dist. Elem. Sch., 1958, Scottsdale (Ariz.) Schs., 1961-68, Devereux Sch., 1968-70, Tri-City Mental Health Sch., Mesa, Ariz., 1970-71; br. mgr. M. Leslie Hansen, Scottsdale, 1972-74; v.p., gen. mgr. John D. Noble and Assocs., 1974-83; pres., broker Gloria Lennox & Assocs., Inc., 1983-96; sales mgr., v.p. Coldwell Banker Success, 1996—. Chmn. bd. Interfaith Counseling Svc., 1988, 89; trustee Scottsdale Congl. United Ch. of Christ, 1986-88, 92, 96-2000. Kent State U. scholar, 1950-54; disting. honoree Women's Impact Group, 1998. Mem. Nat. Assn. Realtors, Ariz. Assn. Realtors (Realtor Assoc. of Yr. 1975), Scottsdale Assn. Realtors (life, Hall of Fame award 1992, Disting. Career award 1994), Women's Coun. Realtors, Realtor Nat. Mktg. Inst., Scottsdale Bd. Realtors (pres. 1981-82, Realtor of Yr. 1982), Ariz. Town Halls, Ariz. Country Club. Republican. Avocations: bridge, golf, traveling. Home: 7561 N Via Camello Del Sur Scottsdale AZ 85258-3098 Office: Coldwell Banker Success Office VP 10605 N Hayden Rd # 6102 Scottsdale AZ 85260-5594

LENNOX, JO STEWART, college relations and external affairs director; b. Northampton, Mass., Aug. 28, 1955; d. Richard Henry and Patricia Ann (Maynard) S.; m. Daniel Robert Lennox, May 19, 1979; children: Adelyn, Page. BA, U. Mass., 1978. Dir. pub. rels. Montserat Coll., Beverly, Mass., 1989-96; dir. coll. rels. Montserat Coll. Art, 1996-2000, dir. coll. advancement, 2001—02, dir. coll. rels. and external affairs, 2002—. Co-founder, past pres. North Shore Press Club, Salem, Mass., 1979-81. Bd. dirs. North Shore Coun. for Children, Danvers, Mass., 1987-90; co-leader Girl Scouts U.S., Middleton, Mass., 1991-94; chmn. Trinity Episcopal Ch. Parish Life Commn., 1994-99; mem. membership com. Beverly C. of C., 1996-97, bd. dirs., 2000—. Mem.: Coun. for Advancement and Support Edn., Beverly Rotary. Office: 23 Essex St Beverly MA 01915-4508

LENNOX, R. IAN, health products executive; Former pres., CEO Monsanto Can. Inc., Drug Royalty Corp., Inc.; former CEO Phoenix Internat. Life Sci.; pres., CEO MDS Drug Discovery & Develop. Sector, Drug Royalty, Toronto, Canada, 2000—. Bd. dirs. Hemosol Inc. Office: Drug Royalty Corp 8 King St E Ste 202 Toronto ON M5C 1B5 Canada Office Fax: 416-863-5161. E-mail: petrad@drugroyalty.com.*

LENOFF, MICHELE MALKA, lawyer; b. Balt., Apr. 10, 1961; d. Israel and Dina (Munz) Drazin; m. Steven Lenoff, Sept. 23, 1984; children: Michael Monroe, Jonathan David, Joseph Nathan, Rachel Lauren. BA cum laude, Bar-Ilan U., Ramat Gan, Israel, 1979; MA in Clin. Psychology, U. Md., 1981; JD cum laude, Nova U., 1986. Bar: Fla. 1987, U.S. Dist. Ct. (so. dist.) Fla. 1991. Therapist Rosewood Hosp., Balt., 1981-82; psycologist Young Adult Inst., N.Y., 1982-83; law clk. Md. Pub. Defender's Office, Balt., 1984; law clk. to presiding justice Fla. Cir. Ct., Ft. Lauderdale, 1985; assoc. McCune & Hiaasen, 1985-88; ptnr. Lenoff & Lenoff P.A., Deerfield Beach, Fla., 1988—; of counsel Law Office of Robert T. Carlilie, 1988-91, G. Ware Cornell Jr., Ft. Lauderdale, Fla., 1988-90. Adj. prof. Howard Community Coll., Columbia, Md., 1981-82; legal rsch. and writing instr. Nova U. Ctr. for the Study of Law, Ft. Lauderdale, 1988-89. Mem. Nova Law Rev., 1985-86. Goodwin fellow Nova U., 1986. Mem. ABA, Fla. Bar Assn. Republican. Jewish. Office: Lenoff & Lenoff 1761 W Hillsboro Blvd Ste 405 Deerfield Beach FL 33442-1563

LENOIR, GLORIA CISNEROS, consultant, educator; b. Monterrey, Nuevo Leon, Mex., Aug. 18, 1951; came to U.S., 1956, naturalized; d. Juan Antonio and Maria Gloria (Flores) Cisneros; m. Walter Frank Lenoir, June 6, 1975; children: Lucy Gloria, Katherine Judith, Walter Frank IV. Student, Inst. Am. Univs., 1971-72; BA in French Art, Austin Coll., 1973, MA in French Art, 1974; MBA in Fin., U. Tex., 1979, postgrad. doctoral program in ednl. policy and planning, 2001—. French tchr. Sherman (Tex.) H.S., 1973-74; French/Spanish tchr, dept. chmn. Lyndon Baines Johnson H.S., Austin, 1974-77; legis. aide Tex. State Capitol, Tex., 1977-81; stock broker Merrill Lynch, 1981-83, Schneider, Bernet and Hickman, Austin, 1983-84; bus. mgr. Holleman Photographic Labs., Inc., 1984-87, 88-90; account exec., stock broker Eppler, Guerin & Turner, 1987-88; ind. distbr. Austin, 1990-93; owner, cons. Profl. Cons. Svcs., 1991—2001; adj. faculty Spanish for internat. trade St. Edwards U., 1991-99; bilingual interviewer The Gallup Orgn., 1997-98; Spanish tchr., club sponsor Hyde Park Bapt. Schs., 1997-99; tchr. computer applications Travis H.S. Comm. Acad., 1999-2000, 9th grade coord., 2000-01, tchr. French and English, club sponsor, 2001—02. Group counselor, organizer Inst. Fgn. Studies, U. Strasbourg, France, summer 1976; mktg. intern IBM, Austin, summer 1978; mktg. cons. Creative Ednl. Enterprises, Austin, 1980-81; hon. speaker Mex.-Am. U. of Tex., Austin, 1984; speaker various orgns., bus. classes, Austin, 1981-84; spkr., coord. small bus. workshops, 1985; group sponsor, advisor Travel Selections, 1997—; mem. Travis H.S. Campus Adv. Coun., 1999-2002; Southwest area rep. Travel Selections from Campbell, Calif., 2000—. Photographs pub. in Women in Space, 1979, Review, 1988; exhibited in group shows throughout Tex., 1979, 88-89, 99. Neighborhood capt. Am. Cancer Soc., Austin, 1982-86, 90, Am. Heart Assn., 1989; active PTA, 1989—, Advantage Austin, 1988; mem. Bryker Woods Elem. PTA Bd., 1990-92, pres., 1990-91, mem. Austin City coun. PTA Bd., 1991-96, Kealing Jr. H.S. PTA Bd., 1992-94, chair 50th anniversary celebration com., 1990, hospitality chmn., 1st grade coord., Austin, 1986, mem. legis. com. Tex. State, 1990-92; vol. liaison leads program Austin Coll., 1983-2000; peer panelist Maj. Art Insts., Austin; elder Ctrl. Presbyn. Ch., 1988-90, 2000-02, renovation and implementation com., 2002—; Megaskills leader Austin Ind. Sch. Dist., 1991-96; bd. dirs. Magnet Parents Coalition, 1995-98; cultural arts chair Dist. 13 PTA Bd., 1996-97; participant NASA Urban and Rural Cmty. Enrichment Program. Recipient Night on the Town award IBM, 1978. Mem.: NEA, Edn. Austin, Tex. Fgn. Lang. Assn., Am. Assn. French Tchrs., Pi Lambda Theta. Republican. Home and Office: 1801 Lavaca St Apt 11E Austin TX 78701-1331 E-mail: mrs_lenoir@hotmail.com.

LENOX, ANGELA COUSINEAU, healthcare consultant; b. Vergennes, Vt., Dec. 12, 1946; d. Romeo Joseph and Colombe Mary (Gevry) C.; m. Donald Allen Lenox, Oct. 5, 1969 (div.); 1 child, Tiffanie Jae. RN diploma, Albany Med. Ctr. Sch. Nursing, 1969; BS, Barry U., 1982; M of Health Mgmt., St. Thomas U., 1990. Cert. in profl. healthcare quality. Intravenous therapist Holy Cross Hosp., Ft. Lauderdale, Fla., 1979-91; utilization review coord. North Broward Hosp., Pompano Beach, 1984-89; med. staff quality mgr. Humana Bennett, Plantation, 1990-91; med. resource analyst Hermann Hosp., Houston, 1991-93; assoc. mgr. quality improvement The Prudential, Sugar Land,

1993-95; quality dir. United Healthcare of Tex., 1999—. Contbr. articles to profl. jours. Capt. U.S. Army res., 1991—. Mem. Tex. Gold Coast Assn. Healthcare Quality, Tex. Soc. Quality Assurance, Nat. Assn. Healthcare Quality. Avocations: skiing, running, reading, writing. Home: 8523 Dawnridge Dr Houston TX 77071-2441 E-mail: alenox9590@cs.com.

LENSKI, RICHARD EIMER, evolutionary biologist, educator; b. Ann Arbor, Mich., Aug. 13, 1956; AB in Biology, Oberlin Coll., 1977; PhD in Zoology, U. N.C., 1982. Postdoctoral rsch. assoc. dept. zoology U. Mass., Amherst, 1982-85; asst. prof. dept. ecology and evolutionary biology U. Calif., Irvine, 1984-88, assoc. prof., 1988-91; Hannah prof. Ctr. for Microbial Ecology Mich. State U., East Lansing, 1991—. Vis. asst. prof. dept. biol. scis. Dartmouth Coll., Hanover, N.H., 1984; mem. NRC Commn. on Life Scis., 1990-96, NRC Bd. Biology, 1990-96. Assoc. editor Evolution, 1990-93; editorial bd. Microbial Ecology, 1991-93; contbg. author: Coevolution, 1983; contbr. articles to Sci., Nature, Ecology, Am. Naturalist. NSF fellow, 1977-81; Presdl. Young Investigator NSF, 1988-93; rsch. fellow Guggenheim Found., 1992-93; vis. fellow All Souls Coll., Oxford U., 1992-93; McArthur fellow, 1996. Fellow Am. Acad. Arts Sci.; mem. Am. Soc. Microbiology, Am. Soc. Naturalists, Ecol. Soc. Am.(com. on environ. applications genetically engineered organisms 1988), Genetics Soc. Am., Soc. Study Evolution, Sigma Xi. Achievements include research on ecology, genetics and evolution of microbial populations including studies on coevolution of bacteria, viruses and plasmids, causes of mutation. Office: Ctr Microbial Ecology Mich State U 288 Plant And Soil Science East Lansing MI 48824-1325

LENT, JAMES DOUGLAS, musician, music educator; b. Houston, Jan. 26, 1973; s. William Scott and Robin Kler Lent. MusB, U. Houston, 1998; MusM, M in Musical Arts; D of Musical Arts, Yale U., 2001. Tchr. S.C. Govs. Sch. for the Arts and Humanities, Greenville, 1997—; artist Concert Artists Guild, N.Y.C., 1999—. Performer ednl. concerts nationally Cmty. Concerts, N.Y.C., 1999—. Recipient Mgmt. award, Concert Artists Guild, 1999, Scholarship prize, Nat. Chopin Found., 2000. Home: 108 Oak Grove Lake Rd Greenville SC 29615 E-mail: drjameslent@aol.com.

LENT, JOHN ANTHONY, journalist, educator; b. East Millsboro, Pa., Sept. 8, 1936; s. John and Rose (Marano) L.; children: Laura, Andrea, John, Lisa, Shahnon. BS, Ohio U., 1958, MS, 1960; PhD, U. Iowa, 1972; cert., Press Inst. of India, Sophia U., Tokyo, Japan, U. Oslo, Guadalajara, Mex., Summer Sch. Dir. public relations, instr. English W.Va. Tech., Montgomery, 1960-62; Newhouse research asst. and asst. to dir. communications research Syracuse (N.Y.) U., 1962-64; lectr. De La Salle Coll., Manila, 1964-65; asst. prof. W.Va. Tech., 1965-66; asst. prof. journalism U. Wis., Eau Claire, 1966-67; asst. prof. journalism, head tchrs.' journalism sequence Marshall U., Huntington, W.Va., 1967-69. Vis. assoc. prof. U. Wyo., Laramie, 1969—70; asst. editor Internat. Comm. Bull., Iowa City, 1970—72; coord. mass comm. U. Sains Malaysia, Penang, 1972—74; assoc. prof. comm. Temple U., Phila., 1974—76, prof. comm. journalism, 1976—95, prof. comm. broadcasting, telecomm. and mass media, 1995—, Benedum vis. disting. prof., 1987; Rogers disting. prof. U. Western Ont., Canada, 2000; guest prof. Shanghai U., 2002—. Author: Asian Newspapers Reluctant Revolution, 1971, Asian Mass Communications: A Comprehensive Bibliography, 1975, Asian Mass Communications: A Comprehensive Bibliography, 2d edit., 1978, Third World Mass Media and Their Search for Modernity, 1977, Broadcasting in Asia and Pacific, 1978, Topics in Third World Mass Media, 1979, Caribbean Mass Communications: A Comprehensive Bibliography, 1981, Asian Newspapers: Contemporary Trends and Problems, 1982, Videocassettes in the Third World, 1989, Asian Film Industry, 1990, Caribbean Popular Culture, 1990, Caribbean Mass Communications, 1990, Transnational Communications, 1991, Women and Mass Communications: An International Annotated Bibliography, 1991, Bibliographic Guide to Caribbean Mass Communications, 1992, Bibliography of Cuban Mass Communications, 1992, Cartoonometer, 1994, Animation, Caricature, and Gag and Political Cartoons in the U.S. and Canada: An International Bibliography, 1994, Comic Art of Europe: An International, Comprehensive Bibliography, 1994, Comic Books and Comic Strips in the United States: An International Bibliography, 1994, Asian Popular Culture, 1995, A Different Road Taken, 1995, Comic Art in Africa, Asia, Australia and Latin America: A Comprehensive, International Bibliography, 1996, Global Productions, 1998, Themes and Issues in Asian Cartooning, 1999, Pulp Demons, 1999, Women and Mass Communications in the 1990's, 1999, Illustrating Asia, 2001, Animation in Asia and the Pacific, 2001, others; editor: Westview Press Internat. Comm. series, 1992—95, Asian Cinema, 1994—, Hampton Books Popular Culture series, —. Anchor Hocking scholar, 1954-59, U. Oslo scholar, 1962, Fulbright scholar, The Philippines, 1964-65; recipient Benedum award, 1968, Broadcast Preceptor award (2), 1979, Paul Eberman Outstanding Rsch. award, 1988, Ray and Pat Browne Nat. Book award, 1995, Temple U. Exceptional award, 1995; decorated Chapel of Four Chaplains' Legion of Honor. Mem. Malaysia/Singapore/Brunei Studies Group (founding chmn. 1975-82), Caribbean Studies Assn., Assn. Asian Studies, Internat. Assn. Mass Comm. Rsch. (visual and comic art organizer, chair 1984—), Asian Cinema Studies Soc. (chmn. 1994—), Popular Culture Assn. (founding chmn. Asian popular culture group 1996—), Sigma Delta Chi, Sigma Tau Delta, Kappa Tau Alpha, Phi Alpha Theta. Home: 669 Ferne Blvd Drexel Hill PA 19026-3110 Office: Temple Univ Broadcasting/Telecomm Dept Philadelphia PA 19122 *I have cherished the principles of hard work over long hours, accuracy, comprehensiveness, and honesty in my intellectual and scholarly endeavors. I have considered it important to set and meet goals, to share my work with others, to remain untainted by organizations or individuals who, I feel, are not working for the good of humankind. I also cherish, and protect and use, my right to speak out on those issues which I feel are offensive to the public; the result has been that my writings have incurred the wrath of government ministers in at least two countries.*

LENT, NORMAN FREDERICK, JR. former congressman; b. Oceanside, N.Y., Mar. 23, 1931; s. Norman Frederick and Ellen (Bain) L.; m. Barbara Ann Morris, Aug. 4, 1979; children from previous marriage: Norman Frederick III, Barbara Anne, Thomas Benjamin (dec.). BA, Hofstra U., 1952; JD, Cornell U., 1957; LLD (hon.), Kyung Hee U., Seoul, Republic of Korea, 1975, Molloy Coll., 1985, Hofstra Coll., 1988. Bar: N.Y. 1957, Fla. 1976. Assoc. police judge, East Rockaway, N.Y., 1958-60; confidential law sec. to N.Y. State Supreme Ct., 1960-62; mem. N.Y. State Senate, 1963-70, chmn. joint legislative com. public health, 1966-70; mem. 92nd Congress 5th Dist. N.Y., 1971-73; mem. 93rd-102d Congresses 4th Dist. N.Y., 1973-93; vice chmn. Energy and Commerce com. 100th-102nd Congresses U.S. Ho. Reps., 1986-93, vice chmn. Mcht. Marine subcom., 1987-93; cons. Lent Scrivner & Roth, Washington, 1993—. Cons. Lent Scrivner & Roth, Washington, 1993—. With USNR, 1952—54. Recipient George Estabrook Disting. Service award Hofstra U., 1967, Israeli Prime Minister's medal, 1977, Disting. Achievement medal N.Y.C. Holland Soc., 1987, Tree of Life award Jewish Nat. Fund, 1987, Anatoly Sharansky Freedom award L.I. Com. for Soviet Jewry, 1983. Office: Lent Scrivner & Roth 1240 New York Ave NW Washington DC 20005-2302 E-mail: nlent@lentde.com.

LENTIN, DENNIS HENRY, communications executive; b. Port Jefferson, N.Y., Aug. 21, 1940; s. Hillman Isreal and Betty (Davidson) L.; m. Carole Solnet, Jan. 15, 1967 (div. Apr. 1992); m. Dolores Kansa, Aug. 20, 1992; children: Steven Hillman, Tami Beth; 1 stepchild, Robert Kennedy Busher. BBA, U. Miami, 1962. Exec. v.p. Art Originals, Inc., Hialeah, Fla., 1966-70; pres. Flamingo Lampshade Corp., 1968-71; exec. v.p. V.L. Industries, Inc., 1968-71; v.p., dir. Eco Electric Mfg. Co., Inc., 1969-71; pres., CEO Paladin Lampshade Corp., Miami, Fla., 1971-87; v.p. S.O.I. Ind., Inc., Hialeah, 1987-89; pres. Contract Furnishings Cons., Inc., Miami, Boynton Beach, Fla., 1989—; sales mgr. Bostom and Assocs. Co., Inc., Aurora, Ind., 1991-93; pres. D.L. Fin. Cons., Inc., Boynton Beach, 1991—. Sr. long term care specialist G.E. Fin. Assurance Co. Mem. BBB. Republican. Avocations: fishing, scuba diving. Home and Office: 3852 Black Forest Cir Boynton Beach FL 33436-3151

LENTINI, JOSEPH CHARLES, government agency management analyst; b. Washington, Oct. 2, 1943; s. Joseph and Pearl (Crosman) L.; m. Colleen Gail Sargent, Dec. 5, 1983; children: Randolph, Lois, Steven, Suzanne, Richard. AA cum laude, Prince Georges C.C., Largo, Md., 1977; BS cum laude, U. Md., 1982; MS in Pub. Adminstrn., Am. U., 1991; CIO cert., Info. Resources Mgmt. Coll., 1997. Owner, operator N.Am. Van Lines, Ft. Wayne, Ind., 1974-79; materiel bus. adminstr. E-Systems, Inc., Falls Church, Va., 1979-81; adminstrv. mgr. MA/COM, Inc., Rockville, Md., 1981-83; computer specialist VA, Washington, 1983-89; web master, mgmt. analyst, IRM expert EPA, 1989—. Mem. adv. com. Nat. Multiple Sclerosis Soc., Washington, 1993-95. Served with USN, 1961-69. Decorated Purple Heart, Presdl. Unit citation, 1967. Mem. ASPA, DAV, Assn. Fed. Info. Resources Mgrs., Armed Forces Comm. and Electronics Assn., Am. Legion, Fleet Res. Democrat. Avocations: biking, camping, reading, judo, music. Home: 12632 Maryland Rte 216 Highland MD 20777-9731 Office: EPA # 3615M 1200 Pennsylvania Ave NW # 3615M Washington DC 20460-0001

LENTNER, HOWARD HENRY, political scientist; b. Detroit, Sept. 8, 1931; s. Frank Richard and Millicent Marie (Kelley) L.; m. Margaret Nancy Taylor, Aug. 23, 1958 (div. 1983); children: Tarah (dec.), J Talar, Leseh. BS, Miami U., 1958; MA, Syracuse U., 1959, PhD, 1964. Instr. polit. sci. Western Res. U., 1962-63, asst. prof., 1963-68; assoc. prof., chmn. dept. polit. sci. McMaster U., Hamilton, Ont., Can., 1968-72; assoc. prof. CUNY Baruch Coll. and Grad. Sch., N.Y.C., 1973-76, prof., 1977—, exec. officer PhD program polit. sci., 1979-82. Author: Foreign Policy Analysis: A Comparative and Conceptual Approach, 1974, State Formation in Central America: The Struggle for Autonomy, Development, and Democracy, 1993, International Politics: Theory and Practice, 1997; co-editor: Power in Contemporary Politics: Theories, Practices, Globalizations, 2000. Served with U.S. Army, 1953-55. Mem. Am. Polit. Sci. Assn., Internat. Studies Assn., Northeastern Polit. Sci. Assn., Internat. Polit. Sci. Assn. Office: 17 Lexington Ave New York NY 10010-5518 E-mail: HowardH.Lentner@att.net.

LENTON, ROBERTO LEONARDO, research facility and environmental administrator; b. Buenos Aires, Feb. 28, 1947; s. Leonard Gersham and Katie (McCulloch) L.; m. Julia Anne Frend, June 11, 1971; children: Alexandra, James, Christopher, Jessica. Civil Engr., U. Buenos Aires, 1971; SM in Civil Engring., MIT, 1973, PhD in Water Resources Systems, 1974. Planning asst. Ministry Pub. Works, Buenos Aires, 1970-71; vis. rsch. engr. MIT, Cambridge, 1971-72, rsch. asst., 1972-74, asst. prof., 1974-77; project specialist Ford Found., New Delhi, 1977-80, program officer, 1980-83, N.Y.C., 1983-86; dep. dir. gen. Internat. Irrigation Mgmt. Inst., Kandy, Sri Lanka, 1986-87, dir. gen. Colombo, Sri Lanka, 1987-94; dir. sustainable energy and environ. divsn. UN Devel. Programme, N.Y.C., 1995-2000; exec. dir., secretariat internat. affairs and devel. Internat. Rsch. Inst. for Climate Prediction, Columbia U., 2001—. Co-author: Applied Water Resources Systems Planning, 1979. Bd. dirs., treas. Am. Embassy Sch., New Delhi, 1981-83; bd. dirs. Overseas Children's Sch., Colombo, 1989-93; trustee Iwokrama Internat. Ctr. for Rain Forest Conservation and Devel., Georgetown, Guyana, 1998—. Mem. ASCE, Am. Geophys. Union, Centro Argentino Ingenieros. Avocations: windsurfing, tennis, running. Home: 48 Rye Rd Rye NY 10580-2231 Office: IRI Lamont-Doherty Earth Observatory Columbia U 124 Monell Palisades NY 10964-8000 E-mail: rlenton@iri.ldeo.columbia.edu.

LENTS, PEGGY IGLAUER, marketing executive; b. St. Louis, Apr. 14, 1950; d. Hank S. and Elizabeth Ruth (Metzger) Iglauer; m. Don G. Lents, Aug. 27, 1972; children: Stacie Lee, Kelsey Lynn. BA magna cum laude, Tufts U., 1971; MPA, Harvard U., 1974. Legis. aide Congressman Symington, Washington, 1971; adminstrv. mgr. May Co., London, 1974; buyer Famous Barr subs. May Co., St. Louis, 1976-78; gen. mdse. mgr. Roman Co., 1978-80, mktg. dir., 1981-82, v.p., 1982; mktg. cons., 1983-86; ptnr. Andrew & Lents, St. Louis, 1987-89; pres. Lents & Assocs., 1990—. Cons. Human Resources Adminstrn., N.Y.C.; teaching fellow Tufts U., 1971-72. Bd. dirs. Lucky Lane Sch., 1980-81, Springboard to Learning, 1987—, UN Assn., 1987-88, Mo. Bot. Garden, 1988-92, Ctr. Contemporary Arts, 1989—; chmn. adv. bd. Alzheimer's Assn., 1993—; bd. dirs. St. Louis Conservatory and Sch. for the Arts, 1992-93; bd. dirs. Jewish Family and Children's Svcs., 1998—; v.p. planning and devel. NCJW, 1986-90; adv. bd. Metro Link Arts in Transit, Internat. Ctr. for Tropical Ecology, 2000-2001; counsel Direct Mktg. ASsn., 2001-; chmn. NCD Nat. Leadership Program, 1974; cons., Washington, 1972, polit. campaigns N.D., Iowa; mem. Adv. bd. Synchronia Mus. Soc., 1993-95; mem. Chancellor's Com. Arts, U. Mo. St. Louis, 1999—, mem. devel. bd. Univ. fellow Tufts U., 1971; fellow Harvard U., 1974. Mem. Am. Mgmt. Assn., Fashion Group, Jewish Hosp Sch. Nursing Alumni Assn. (hon. life), Pioneers, Direct Mail Club St. Louis, Direct Mktg. Assn. (sr. cons. 2000—), Women in Bus., Directory Group (U.K.), Westwood Country Club. Address: 1750 S Brentwood Blvd Ste 552 Saint Louis MO 63144-1302

LENTZ, CORLISS C. political scientist, educator; b. Hartford, Conn., Nov. 17, 1946; d. William L. and Kathryn (McCowen) Carter; m. Gordon J. Lentz, July 22, 1967; children: Jennifer, Rebecca, Christopher. BA, Morris Harvey Coll., 1969; MA in Pub. Adminstrn., No. Ill. U., 1987, PhD, 1995. Instr. St. Xavier U., Chgo., 1992—94, No. Ill. U., DeKalb, 1994—; assoc. prof. Sam Houston State U., Huntsville, Tex., 1995—. Dir. grad. studies dept. polit. sci. Sam Houston State U., 1997—; internship advisor dept. polit. sci., 2000—. Contbr. articles. Bd. dirs. Minooka (Ill.) Grade Sch. Bd. Edn., 1983—85; elder Woodlands (Tex.) Cmty. Presbyn. Ch., 2000—. Mem.: Pi Alpha Alpha, Pi Sigma Alpha. Office: Sam Houston State Univ PO Box 2149 Dept Polit Sci Huntsville TX 77341

LENTZ, EDWARD ALLEN, consultant, retired health administrator; b. Superior, Wis., May 30, 1926; s. Otto Albert and Martha Mary Ann (Gruhel) L.; m. Margaret Ann Denier, May 30, 1952; 1 child, Elizabeth Ann Clark. BS, U. Cin., 1951; MHA, Wayne State U., Detroit, 1957. Asst. dir. Pub. Health Fedn., Cin., 1954-57; dir. health planning United Cmty. Coun., Columbus, Ohio, 1957-62; asst. dir. Columbus Hosp. Fedn., 1962-65; assoc. exec. dir. Ohio Hosp. Assn., Columbus, 1965-69; exec. dir. Health Planning Assn. of Ohio River Valley, Cin., 1969-70; asst. prof. grad. program in health svcs. adminstrn. Coll. of Medicine, Ohio State U., Columbus, 1970-72, adj. assoc. prof. preventive medicine, 1957—; dep. dir. med. care adminstrn. Ohio Dept. Health, 1972-75; pres., CEO Med. Advances Inst., 1975-79; v.p. corp. devel. Mt. Carmel Health System, 1979-95, cons., 1995-97. Cons. cmty. health planning USPHS; bd. dirs. Scioto Valley Health Sys. Agy. Contbr. articles to profl. jours. Mem., chair Ohio Dept. Human Svcs./Ohio Med. Care Adv. Com., Columbus, 1975—; bd. dirs., vice chair Netcare Corp., Columbus, 1989—. Served with USN, 1944-46; 1st lt. U.S. Army, 1951-53, Korea. Recipient Spl. Citation for hosp. planning and mktg. in Ohio and Delbert L. Pugh Conf., Ohio State U. Coll. Medicine and Ohio Hosp. Assn., 1991. Fellow Am. Pub. Health Assn. (bd. dirs., vice chmn. bd. trustees 1979-83); mem. Ohio Pub. Health Assn. (pres. 1969-70), Am. Assn. Areawide Planning Agencies (pres. 1969-70), Ohio Hosp. Assn. Soc. for Hosp. Planning and Mktg. (pres. 1987-88), Columbus Rotary (com. chair). Presbyterian. Avocations: fishing, photography, tennis. Home: 585 Keyes Ln Worthington OH 43085-3503

LENTZ, EDWIN LAMAR, art historian; b. Houston, Mar. 31, 1951; s. Edwin Lonzo and Gerald Dwain (Flack) L. BA, U. Tex., 1973, MA, 1991. Spl. asst. to Harry H. Ransom Harry Ransom Humanities Rsch. Ctr., U. Tex., Austin, 1971-73, curator Coral Maud Oneal Rm., 1975—; mus. registrar Lyndon Baines Johnson Libr. and Mus., 1974-75; asst. to registrar Mus. Fine Arts, Houston, 1975-76; dir. libr. and mus. collections Festival-Inst. at Round Top, Tex., 1976—. Author (catalog): Cora Maud Oneal Room, 1979, 85; contbr. articles to profl. jours. Ransom Ctr. rsch. grantee, 1985, 86, 88; Victorian Soc. Am. scholar, 1992. Mem. Coll. Art Assn. (mem. mus. com. 1993-99), Am. Friends of Attingham, Victorian Soc. Am., Phi Kappa Phi. Avocations: rare books, theatre. Office: Festival-Inst at Round Top PO Box 89 Round Top TX 78954-0089 E-mail: lamarl@festivalhill.org.

LENTZ, LUTHER EUGENE, graphic arts technical specialist; b. Harrisburg, Pa., June 24, 1937; s. Luther Levi and Leola Mae L.; m. Joanne Marie Rohland, June 30, 1962; children: Mark Eugene, Kenneth Andrew. BS, Rochester Inst. Tech., 1959. Sr. tech. svc. rep. E.I. duPont de Nemours & Co., Wilmington, Del., 1965-85; supr. color dept. Dixie Graphics, Nashville, 1985-87; regional tech. mgr. AGFA divsn. Bayer Corp., Irving, Tex., 1987-96; ret., 1996. Capt. USMC, 1961-64. Avocations: woodworking, photography, cycling, physical fitness. Home: 6117 Seven Lakes W West End NC 27376-9320 E-mail: holeinone6117@earthlink.net.

LENTZ, MARY A. lawyer, educator; b. Cleve., May 17, 1942; BA, Ursuline Coll., Cleve., 1964; MA, Georgetown U., 1968; JD, Cleve. State U., 1973. Bar: Ohio 1973, Pa. 1984, U.S. Dist. Ct. (no. and ea. divsns.) Ohio 1974, U.S. Ct. Appeals (6th dist.) 1975, U.S. Ct. Appeals (D.C. cir.) 1986, U.S. Supreme Ct. 1977; cert. secondary tchr., Ohio. Tchr. Cleve. Pub. Schs., 1965-74; legal counsel Ohio State Dept. Edn., Columbus, 1974-76; asst. pros. atty. criminal divsn. Cuyahoga County, Cleve., 1976-78; atty., ptnr. Weston, Hurd, Fallon, Paisley & Howley, 1978-92; atty. in pvt. practice, 1992-95; police prosecutor City of Westlake (Ohio), 1994—96; ptnr. Walter & Haverfield, Cleve., 1995-99; pvt. practice Chagrin Falls, 1999—. Lectr. and presenter in field. Editor Ohio Sch. Jour., 1977—; author quar. periodical Pvt. Sch. Law Digest, 1982-89. Recipient FBI Dir.'s Cmty. Leadership award, 1999. Mem. ABA, Ohio State Bar Assn., Greater Cleve. Bar Assn., Geauga (Ohio) Bar Assn., Pa. Bar Assn., D.C. Bar ASsn.

LENTZ, RICHARD DAVID, psychiatrist, educator; b. Passaic, N.J., Jan. 27, 1942; s. Harold Arthur and Ruth (Bitterman) L.; m. Joan Ellen Sacks, June 25, 1983; children: Daniel Keith, Andrew Simon. Student, John Hopkins U., 1959-61; AB cum laude, NYU, 1964; MS in Pathology, MD with distinction, U. Rochester, 1969. Diplomate Am. Bd. Psychiatry and Neurology, Am. Bd. of Pediatrics, Am. Bd. of Pediatric Nephrology. Intern U. Minn. Hosps., Mpls., 1969-70, resident in pediatrics, 1970-71, fellow in pediatric nephrology, 1972-74; resident in neurology and pediatrics Washington U., St. Louis, 1971-72; resident in psychiatry, fellow consultation-liaison U. Minn. Hosps., Mpls., 1979-81; chief pediatric nephrology Walter Reed Army Med. Ctr., Washington, 1974-76; instr. dept. of pediatrics Georgetown Med. Ctr., 1975; asst. prof. U. Md., Balt., 1978; cons. psychiatrist Park Nicollet Clinic/HSM, St. Louis Park, Minn., 1981—, vice chmn. dept. psychiatry, 1981-85, chmn. patient rels., 1983-95, risk mgmt. com., ops. com., dir. Medctr. Health Plan, 1985-90; chmn. risk mgmt. Health Sys. Minn., 1995-99; from clin. asst. prof. to assoc. prof. U. Minn., Mpls., 1981-90, clin. prof., 1990—. Chmn. psychiatry Abbott-Northwestern Hosp., Mpls., 1991-92; assoc. dir. profl. assessment program Abbott-Northwestern Hosp., 1993; cons. Courage Ctr., Mpls., Comprehensive Epilepsy Ctr., Bill Kelly House, numerous others. Contbr. articles to profl. jours. Maj. U.S. Army, 1974-76. Mem. Am. Psychiat. Assn., Minn. Med. Assn., Hennepin County Med. Soc. Office: Park Nicollet Med Ctr 2001 Blaisdell Ave Minneapolis MN 55404-2414 E-mail: lentzr@hsmnet.com.

LENTZ, SANDRA M. family nurse practitioner; b. Williamsport, Pa., May 11, 1962; d. Wesley Bruce and Marian Elizabeth (Avery) Lentz; m. Steven F. Kuni, Feb. 14, 1987 (div. Feb. 1988); 1 child Avery Christopher Kuni ; m. Roderick C. Strother, June 19, 1999; 1 child Ethan Campbell Lentz Strother. AA magna cum laude, Williamsport Area C.C., 1982; BS, York Coll. Pa., 1985; MS, U. S.C., 1993. RN; cert. family nurse practitioner. Nurse Humana Hosp., Augusta, Ga., 1990-93; family nurse practitioner Pee Dee Cmty. Health. Svcs., Society Hill, S.C., 1993-94; dir. Chambersburg (Pa.) Hosp. Maternity Clinic, 1994-96; family nurse practitioner Rappahannock Family Physicians, Fredericksburg, Va., 1996-98, Pa. State U. Health Svcs., 1999—2000; nurse practitioner Women's Health Care Assocs., 2000—. Bd. dirs. March of Dimes, 1994—96. With Nurse Corps U.S. Army, 1986—91. Decorated Army Commendation medal. Mem.: Am. Coll. Nurse Practitioners, Am. Acad. Nurse Practitioners. Independent. Lutheran. Avocations: outdoor activities, jazz, tennis, walking, sewing.

LENTZ, THOMAS LAWRENCE, biomedical educator, dean, researcher; b. Toledo, Mar. 25, 1939; s. Lawrence Raymond and Kathryn (Heath) L.; m. Judith Ellen Pernaa, June 17, 1961; children: Stephen, Christopher, Sarah. Student, Cornell U., 1957-60; MD, Yale U., 1964. Instr. in anatomy Yale U. Sch. Medicine, New Haven, 1964-66, asst. prof. anatomy, 1966-69, assoc. prof. cytology, 1969-74, assoc. prof. cell biology, 1974-85, prof. cell biology, 1985—, asst. dean for admissions, 1976-2000, assoc. dean for admissions, 2000—, vice chmn. cell biology, 1992—. Mem. cellular and molecular neurobiology panel NSF, 1987-88, mem. cellular neurosci. panel, 1988-90; mem. neurology B-1 study sect. Nat. Inst. Neurol. Disorders and Stroke, NIH, 1996, 98; mem. exptl. virology study sect. Nat. Inst. Allergy and Infectious Disease, NIH, 1997, 98. Author: The Cell Biology of Hydra, 1966, Primitive Nervous Systems, 1968, Cell Fine Structure, 1971; contbr. over 100 articles to sci. publs. Vice chmn., chmn. Planning and Zoning Commn., Killingworth, Conn., 1979—; active Killingworth Hist. Soc. Recipient Conn. Fedn. Planning and Zoning Agys. award, 1995, Citizen of Yr. award Killingworth Lions Club, 1993; fellow Trumbull Coll., Yale U.; grantee NSF, 1968-92, Dept. Army, 1986, NIH, 1987-2000. Mem. AAAS, Am. Soc. Cell Biology, Soc. for Neurosci., N.Y. Acad. Scis., Appalachian Mountain Club (trails com., Warren Hart award, Pychowska award, White Mountain Four Thousand Footer Club), Fla. Trail Assn., Appalachian Trail Conf., Mt. Washington Obs., Wonalancet Out Door Club, Alpha Omega Alpha. Republican. Mem. United Ch. of Christ. Achievements include study of primitive nervous systems, identification of neurotoxin binding site on the acetylcholine receptor, identification of cellular receptor for rabies virus. Office: Yale U Sch Medicine Dept Cell Biol 333 Cedar St PO Box 208002 New Haven CT 06520-8002

LENZ, CARL OTTO, European advocate general; b. Berlin, June 5, 1930; s. Otto and Marieliese (Pohl) L.; 5 children. Dr.iur., Univ. Bonn, Germany, 1961. Sec. gen. Christian Dem. Group EP-Lux, 1959-66; mem. German Bundestag, 1965-84; advocate gen. European Ct. Justice, Luxembourg, 1984—. Chmn. legal com. German Bundestag, 1969-80; coord. Franco-German Cooperation, 1982-84; mem. North Atlantic Assembly, 1981-84. Author: Notstandsverfassung des Grundgesetzes Kommentator, 1971; editor: Recht im Binnenmarkt, 1994, EG-Vertrag Kommentar, 1994; contbr. articles to profl. jours. Recipient Grosses Verdienstkreuz Bundes Pres. Germany. 1976, Offizier der Ehrenlegion Président de la République Française, 1980, Grossoffizier des Nationalen Verdienstordens, 1983. Mem. Arbeitskreis Europäische Integration, Internat. Juristenkommission, Kuratoriums Europaische Rechtsakademie, Lions Club Internat. Office: Baker & McKenzie 149 av. Louise B-1050 Brussels Luxembourg

LENZ, CRAIG, academic administrator; married; 3 children. BS in aerospace engring., Princeton U.; postgrad., U. Pa.; DOM, Phila. Coll. Osteo. Medicine. Cert. Am. Bd. Emergency Medicine, Am. Bd. Osteo. Family Practitioners. Emergency dept. physician Redington-Fairview Hosp., Maine; clin. clerkship coord., area health edn. program U. New England Coll. Osteo. Medicine; osteo. dir. med. edn. for family practice residency program Ea. Maine Med. Ctr.; dean Coll. Osteo. Medicine of the Pacific Western U. Health Scis., 2000—. Fellow: Acad. Osteo. Dirs. and Med. Educators; mem.: Am. Osteo. Assn. Office: Western Univ Health Scis 309 E Second St Coll Plza Pomona CA 91766-1854*

LENZ, DEBRA LYNN, financial analyst; b. Watertown, Wis., June 8, 1973; d. Ron Floyd and Sandy Jean Lenz. BS in Acctg., Marquette U., Milw., 1996, postgrad. CPA, Wis. Sr. auditor Deloitte & Touche LLP, Milw., 1996-99; sr. fin. analyst Rockwell Automation, 1999-2000, Harley-Davidson, Milw., 2000—. Mem. AICPA, Bus. Profl. Women, Wis. Inst. CPAs, Alpha Sigma Nu, Beta Gamma Sigma. Home: 8472 Northview Dr Pleasant Prairie WI 53158 Office: Harley-Davidson 3700 W Juneau Ave Milwaukee WI 53208 E-mail: debra.lenz@harley-davidson.com.

LENZ, EDWARD ARNOLD, trade association executive, lawyer; b. White Plains, N.Y., Sept. 28, 1942; s. Fritz and Hildegarde (Bunzel) L.; m. Anna Maria Bartusiak, Mar. 21, 1987; children: Scott, Eric. BA, Bucknell U., 1964; JD, Boston Coll., 1967; LLM, NYU, 1968. Bar: N.Y. 1968, D.C. 1973, Mich. 1982. Trial atty. U.S. Dept. Justice, Washington, 1970-72; assoc. gen. counsel U.S. Cost of Living Coun., 1973; assoc. Miller & Chevalier, 1973-80; counsel Health Ins. Assn. Am., 1980-82; v.p., asst. gen. counsel Kelly Svcs. Inc., Troy, Mich., 1982-89; chmn. legis. com. Am. Staffing Assn., Alexandria, Va., 1985-89, sr. v.p., gen. counsel, 1989-93, sr. v.p. legal and govt. affairs, 1993-99, sr. v.p. pub. affairs, gen. counsel, 1999—. Author: Co-employment--Employer Liability Third-Party Issues in Staffing, 1994, 4th edit., 2000. Capt. U.S. Army, 1968-70, Vietnam. Decorated Bronze Star. Fellow Coll. Labor and Employment Lawyers; mem. ABA, N.Y. Bar Assn., D.C. Bar Assn., Am. Corp. Counsel Assn., Pi Sigma Alpha, Sigma Alpha Epsilon. Home: 818 S Lee St Alexandria VA 22314-4334 Office: Am Staffing Assn 277 S Washington St Ste 200 Alexandria VA 22314-3675

LENZ, HENRY PAUL, management consultant; b. N.Y.C., Nov. 24, 1925; s. Ernest and Margaret (Schick) L.; m. Norma M. Kull, Jan. 25, 1958; children: Susan, Scott, Theresa. AB, U. N.C., 1946; MBA, Coll. Ins., 1974. Underwriter U.S. Casualty Co., N.Y.C., 1948-55; underwriting mgr. Mass. Bonding & Ins. Co., 1955-60; with Home Ins. Co., 1960-85, sr. v.p., 1972-75, exec. v.p., dir.,

1975-85; chmn. bd. Lenz Enterprises Ltd., Chatham, NJ, 1985—. Former pres., dir. Home Indemnity Co.; pres., dir. Home Ins. Co. Ind., Home Ins. Co. Ill., City Ins. Co., Home Group Risk Mgmt.; chmn. bd. Home Reins. Co., Scott Wetzel Services Inc.; chmn., pres. Cityvest Reins. Ltd., City Ins. Co. (U.K.) Ltd.; trustee Am. Inst. Property and Liability Underwriters, Ins. Inst. Am. Served with USNR, 1944-47, 52-53. Decorated Army Commendation medal. Mem. Soc. CPCU's, Phi Beta Kappa, Sigma Nu. Office: Lenz Enterprises Ltd 42 Edgehill Ave Chatham NJ 07928-1937

LENZ, JEANNE ANN, security professional; b. Frankfort, Mich., Feb. 22, 1954; d. Joy Richard and Mary Louise (Johnson) L. AA in acctg., Muskegon (Mich.) Bus. Coll., 1974; AA in data processing, West Shore C.C., Scottville, Mich., 1981; cert. EMT, West Shore C.C., 1982; cert. security officer, CPP/Pinkerton, Van Nuys, Calif., 1988; diploma PC repair, ICS, Scranton, Pa., 1995; diploma PC specialist, ICS, 1997; diploma computer-assisted bookkeeping, Harcourt Learning Direct, 2000. Mgr., acct., sec. Joy R. Lenz Farm, Kaleva, Mich., 1969-81; acctg. clk. City of Manistee (Mich.), 1974-77; salesperson Hydrotex, 1978; scaler, acct., sec. (seasonal) Howes Co., Copemish, Mich., 1979-90; crewleader, office clk. Bur. of the Cenus, Mt. Pleasant, 1980; security guard Burns Internat. Security Svcs., Inc., Portage, 1982-83; cashier Woodland Oil Co., Kaleva, 1984-85; security officer CPP/Pinkerton, Van Nuys, Calif., 1988-89; auditor RGIS Inventory Specialists, Rochester, Mich., 1989-90; enumerator U.S. Bur. Census, Traverse City, 1990; cashier Meijer, 1992-96; security officer Per Mar Security, Davenport, Iowa, 1996-97; Reman technician Nabco, Kaleva, Mich., 1998—2001; ward clk. West Shore Ctr., 2001; asst. acct., stocker and cashier Kaleva Country Market, 2001. Instr. ARC, 1982-97, disaster rep., 1996; asst. treas. Maple Grove Twp., 1966-77; mem. fin. and altar coms. Bethany Luth. Ch. of Kaleva, 1981-87, Manistee County Sheriff's rescue squad dept., 1979-86, 97. Mem. Venerable Order of St. Francis of Assisi, 1991—. Mem.: NAFE, Safe Driver Assn., Am. Fedn. Police, Nat. Soc. EMS Adminstrs., Mich. Assn. EMTs (treas. 1982—83, alt. rep. region 7 1983—94), Nat. Assn. EMTs, Geneal. Soc. Manistee County (v.p. 1976—), U.S. CB Radio Assn., Lions. Home: 7680 Lenz Rd Kaleva MI 49645-9767

LENZ, LOIS MARTIN ELSER, psychiatric and mental health nurse; b. Waynesboro, Pa., Oct. 26, 1932; d. Abram Paul and Sarah Catherine (Etter) Martin; m. Theodore Edwin Elser, Sept. 24, 1953 (div. Mar. 1978); children: Linda Sue, Jeanne Lynn, Theodore Jr.; m. Edward P. Lenz, Sr., July 21, 2002. Diploma, Washington County Hosp. Sch. of Nursing, 1953; BA in Psychology, U. Balt., 1980; postgrad., Salisbury State U., 1984-86. RN, Md. Various health positions, 1953-68; community health nurse Washington County Health Dept., Hagerstown, Md., 1968-70; community health nurse supr. Howard County Health Dept., Ellicott City, 1970-73; community mental health nurse Anne Arundel County Health Dept., Annapolis, 1973-77; community mental health nurse supr. Walter P. Carter Ctr., Balt., 1977-80; staff nurse psychiat. in-patient mental health unit Greater Laurel (Md.)-Beltsville Hosp., 1980-81; psychiat. nurse team leader day hosp. U.S. Pub. Health Hosp., Balt., 1981-82; head nurse Springfield Hosp. Ctr., Sykesville, 1982-83, backup to nursing div. chief, 1983-84; nursing div. chief Ea. Shore Hosp. Ctr., Cambridge, 1984-87; nursing supr. Great Oaks Ctr., Silver Spring, 1987; community mental health nurse day treatment program Prince George's County Health Dept., Cheverly, 1987-88, community mental health nurse outpatient clinic, 1988-93; ret., 1993; agy. nurse Sheppard Pratt Hosp., 1993—94; various agy. assignments in psychiatric hosps. and clinics, 1994—; agy. nurse Sheppard Pratt Hosp., 1998—2001; cert. nursing asst. instr. Howard C.C., 2001; PRN staff psychiat. unit Howard County Gen. Hosp., 2001. Home: 7355 Hickory Log Cir Columbia MD 21045-5030

LENZER, IRMINGARD ISOLDE, psychology educator; b. 1938; arrived in Can., 1979; d. Johann and Maria (Pfaffinger) L.; children: Alexander Lemond, Anna Lemond. BA in Psychology, UCLA, 1964; PhD in Psychology, Ind. U., 1969. Diplomate Am. Bd. Forensic Examiners. Asst. prof. psychology St. Mary's U., Halifax, N.S., Can., 19698-73; assoc. prof., 1973-81; prof., 1981—. Mem. Internat. Neuropsychol. Soc., Assn. for Treatment of Sexual Abusers, Can. Psychol. Assn. Home: 1232 Edward St Halifax NS Canada B3H 3H4 Office: St Mary's U Dept Psychology Robie St Halifax NS Canada B3H 3C3

LENZI, ALBERT JAMES, JR. lawyer; b. Chgo., Feb. 15, 1955; s. Albert Joseph Sr. and Helen Lenzi; adopted children: April Lynn Sorensen, Sean Patrick Sorensen. Student, U.S. Naval Acad., 1972-74; BA, Loyola U., Chgo., 1976; JD, U. of the Pacific, 1979. Bar: Calif. 1979, U.S. Dist. Ct. (ea. dist.) Calif. 1982, U.S. Supreme Ct. 1990. Asst. prof. law Wilamette U., Salem, Oreg., 1979-80; assoc. Thompson Mayhew & Michel, Sacramento, 1980-81, Goldstein, Barceloux & Goldstein, Chico, Calif., 1981-82, Brislain & Zink, Chico, 1982-84; ptnr. Brislain, Zink & Lenzi, 1984-94, Zink & Lenzi, Chico, 1994—. Served with USN, 1972-74. Mem. ABA, Calif. Trial Lawyers, Consumer Attys. Calif. (bd. mem. 1997-98), Calif. Bar Assn., Chico Kiwanis Club (pres. 1998-99). Democrat. Roman Catholic. Avocations: bowling, reading. Office: Zink & Lenzi 250 Vallombrosa Ave Ste 175 Chico CA 95926-3973

LEO, MARGARET ELEANOR, social worker; b. San Bernardino, Calif., Aug. 15, 1937; d. James Buell and Frances Clara (Stone) Chessington; m. Arnold Leo, Apr. 14, 1958 (div. 1973); children: Erik, Melissa. BA in Art and Edn., Hunter Coll., 1970; MEd in Elem. Edn. and Counseling, Antioch U., 1973; MSW, Smith Coll., 1985. Lic. social worker, Mass., Vt. Clin. social worker N.Y. State Edn., 1986-94; family therapist Fordham Tremont Cmty. Mental Health Ctr., Bronx, 1990-93; therapist Human Resource Ctr., Athol, Mass., 1993-94; dir. Putney (Vt.) Family Svcs., 1994—. Union del. Local 1199, N.Y.C., 1990-93. Avocations: art, sewing, skiing, traveling, theatre. Home: RR 3 Box 108 Putney VT 05346-9311

LEO, MICHAEL CHARLES, emergency physician, surgeon, educator; b. Wilkes-Barre, Pa., Sept. 20, 1948; MD, Jefferson Med. Coll., 1974. Cert. emergency medicine, cert. surgery. Resident in gen. surgery Berkshire Med. Ctr.-U. Mass. Sch. Medicine, 1974-78; chief resident Berkshire Med. Ctr., 1977-78; fellow Berkshire Med. Ctr.-U. Mass. Sch. Medicine, 1978-79; chief surgery USPHS, Ft. Defiance, Ariz., 1979-82; attending emergency dept. staff Berkshire Med. Ctr., Pittsfield, Mass., 1983-87, dir. emergency dept., 1987-92; attending emergency dept. VA Med. Ctr., Albuquerque, 1992-95, chief emergency med. svc., 1995—; dir. emergency dept. N.Mex. VA Health Care Sys., 1995—. Asst. prof. emergency medicine and surgery U. Mass. Sch. Medicine, 1983-92; assoc. prof. emergency medicine and surgery U. N.Mex. Sch. Medicine. Fellow Am. Coll. Emergency Physicians, ACS; mem. Commd. Officers Assn. of USPHS.

LEO, PETER ANDREW, newspaper columnist, writing educator; b. Aug. 3, 1943; s. Maurice Matthew and Mary (Trincellita) L.; m. Sylvia Weed, July 26, 1970; children: Steven, Jane. AB, U. Toronto, 1966; MA, NYU, 1967. Tchr. H.S. Peace Corps, Nairobi, Kenya, 1968-69; reporter AP, N.Y.C., 1970, Greenboro (N.C.) Record, 1971-72, Wilmington (Del.) News Jour., 1973-78; reporter, asst. city editor, columnist, assoc. editor Pitts. Post-Gazette, 1978—. Instr. U. Pitts., 1999—. Recipient Healiners award Atlantic City Press Club, 1972, Golden Quill award Pitts. Press Club, 1980, Keystone award Pa. Newspaper Pubs. and Editors Assn., 1984. Home: 5266 Beelermont Pl Pittsburgh PA 15217-1010 Office: PG Pub Co 34 Blvd Of The Allies Pittsburgh PA 15222-1200

LEOGRANDE, WILLIAM MARK, political science educator, writer; b. Utica, N.Y., July 1, 1949; s. John James and Patricia Ann (Ryan) LeoG; m. Martha J. Langelan AB, Syracuse U., 1971, MA, 1973, PhD, 1976. Asst. prof. Hamilton Coll., Clinton, NY, 1976-78; dir. polit. sci. Am. U., Washington, 1980-82, asst. prof. polit. sci., 1978-83, assoc. prof., 1984-89, prof., 1989—, chair dept. govt., 1992-96, dean Sch. Pub. Affairs, 1997-99, 2002—. Mem. profl. staff U.S. Senate, 1982-83, cons., 1984-85 Author: Cuba's Policy in Africa, 1980; editor: (with Morris Blachman) Confronting Revolution: Security Through Diplomacy in Central America, 1986, (with Louis Goodman) Political Parties and Democracy in Central America, Our Own Backyard: The United States in Central America, 1998; dir. Latin Am. Rsch. Rev., 1982-86, World Policy Jour., 1983-93. Dir. svc. com. Unitarian-Universalist Ch., Boston, 1983-86; mem. staff Michael Dukakis Presdl. Campaign, 1988. Council Fgn. Relation Internat. Affairs fellow, 1982-83, Pew Faculty fellow, 1994-95. Mem. Coun. Fgn. Rels., Am. Polit. Sci. Assn., Latin Am. Studies Assn. (exec. council 1984-87) Democrat. Home: 7215 Chestnut St Bethesda MD 20815-4051 Office: Am U Sch Pub Affairs Ward Cir Washington DC 20016 E-mail: wleogra@AMERICAN.edu.

LEON, ARTHUR SOL, research cardiologist, exercise physiologist; b. Bklyn., Apr. 26, 1931; s. Alex and Anne (Schrek) L.; m. Gloria Rakita, Dec. 23, 1956; children: Denise, Harmon, Michelle. BS in Chemistry with high honors, U. Fla., 1952; MS in Biochemistry, U. Wis., 1954, MD, 1957. Intern Henry Ford Hosp., Detroit, 1957-58; fellow in internal medicine Lahey Clinic, Boston, 1958-60; fellow in cardiology Jackson Meml. Hosp.-U. Miami (Fla.) Med. Sch., 1960-61; dir. clin. pharmacology research unit Hoffmann-La Roche Inc.-Newark Beth Israel Med. Ctr., 1969-73; from instr. to assoc. prof. medicine Coll. Medicine and Dentistry N.J., Newark, 1967-73; from assoc. prof. to prof. div. epidemiology U. Minn., Mpls., 1973—, H.L. Taylor prof. exercise sci. and health enhancement, dir. lab. physiol. hygiene and exercise sci., div. kinesiology, Coll. Edn., 1991—, dir. applied physiology and nutrition, 1973-91. Mem. med. eval. team Gemini and Apollo projects NASA, 1964-67. Editor Procs. of the NIH Consensus Conf. on Phys. Activity and Cardiovasc. Health, 1997; assoc. editor Surgeon Gen.'s Report on Health Benefits of Exercise, 1996; contbr. numerous articles to profl. pubs. Trustee Vinland Nat. Sports Health Ctr. for Disabled, 1978—; mem. gov.'s coun. physical fitness sports, 1979—. Served as officer M.C. U.S. Army, 1961-67, 90-91, col. Res. 1978-92, ret. Recipient Anderson award AAHPER, 1981, Presdl. award for exercise sci. rsch. Internat. Olympic Com., 1999; Am. Heart Assn. fellow, 1960-61 Fellow Am. Coll. Cardiology, Am. Coll. Chest Physicians, Am. Coll. Clin. Pharmacology, N.Y. Acad. Scis., Am. Coll. Sports Medicine (trustee 1976-78, 82-83, v.p. 1977-79, pres. Northland chpt. 1975-76, Citation award 1995), Am. Assn. Cardiovasc. and Pulmonary Rehab. (trustee 1989-90), Am. Acad. Kinesiology and Phys. Edn.; mem. Am. Physiol. Soc., Am. Soc. Pharmacology and Exptl. Therapeutics, Am. Inst. Nutrition, Am. Heart Assn. (v.p. Hennepin County divsn. 1980-81, pres. 1982-83), Am. Coll. Nutrition, Am. Fedn. Clin. Rsch., Minn. Lung Assn. (trustee 1978-81), Phi Beta Kappa, Phi Kappa Phi. Jewish. Home: 5628 Glen Ave Minnetonka MN 55345-6610 Office: U Minn Sch Kinesiology & Leisure Studies 202 Cooke Hall Minneapolis MN 55455-0136 E-mail: leonx002@tc.umn.edu.

LEON, BRUCE FREDERICK, environmental scientist; b. L.A., Nov. 6, 1952; s. Herman I. and Carol (Waterstone) L.; m. Linda Gail Gross, Jan. 7, 1990. BS, U. Mich., 1974; MA, Princeton U., 1976, PhD, 1979. Cert. sr. ecologist; profl. wetland scientist. Environ. scientist Ecol Scis., Inc., Milw., 1978-80; asst. prof. landscape architecture and planning U. Ill., Urbana, 1981-85; mgr. environ. planning Quadrant Cons. Inc., Houston, 1985-90; mgr. environ. studies Brown & Root, 1990—. Contbr. articles in field to ecol. jours. NSF postgrad. fellow, 1975-78; U. Ill. rsch. grantee, 1983. Mem. Ecol. Soc. Am., Soc. Wetland Scientists. Office: Brown & Root 9900 Westpark Dr Houston TX 77063- E-mail: bruce.leon@halliburton.com.

LEON, BRUNO, architect, architecture educator; b. Van Houten, N.Mex., Feb. 18, 1924; s. Giovanni and Rosina (Cunico) L.; m. Louise Dal-Bo, Sept. 4, 1948 (dec. 1974); m. Bonnie Bertram, Sept. 12, 1976; children: Mark Jon, John Anthony, Lisa Rose. Student, Wayne State U., 1942, U. Detroit, 1945-48, LHD (hon.), 1984; BArch, N.C. State U., 1953. Registered architect, Mich., N.C., Mass., N.Y., N.Mex., Fla. Head design staff Fuller Research Found., Raleigh, N.C., 1954-55; archtl. designer I.M. Pei & Assos., N.Y.C., 1955-56; instr. Mass. Inst. Tech., 1956-59; designer Catalano & Belluschi (architects), Cambridge, Mass., 1958-59; asst. prof. U. Ill., Urbana, 1959-61; dean Sch. Architecture, U. Detroit, 1961-93, dean emeritus, 1993; pvt. practice architecture, 1956—. With USAAF, 1942-45. Fellow AIA (dir. Detroit 1963-64); mem. Alpha Sigma Nu (hon.), Phi Kappa Phi. Home: 9 Redondo Ct Santa Fe NM 87508-8308 E-mail: volterra@newmexico.com. *I believe the integral quality of the human spirit to be the ability to dream rather than to rationalize.*

LEON, EDWARD, investor; b. Benton, Ill., May 2, 1925; s. John and Mary (Letukas) L.; m. Mary Ellen Cooper, Aug. 29, 1953; children: Ellen, Edward, Carol. BS in Chemistry, U. Ill., 1949; MS in Chemistry, U. Mich., 1950, PhD in Chemistry, 1956. Rsch. supr. Occidental Petroleum, Grand Island, N.Y., 1954-68; rsch. mgr. Borg-Warner Chems., Parkersburg, W.Va., 1968-77, dir. cen. rsch. lab. Des Plaines, Ill., 1977-88; owner, pres. Cooper-Leon Fin. Svcs., Inc., Barrington, 1988-92. Contbr. articles to profl. jours.; holder 12 U.S. patents, numerous fgn. patents. With U.S. Army, 1944-46, ETO. Decorated Purple Heart. Mem. Am. Chem. Soc. (chmn. Mid-Ohio Valley sect. 1972, nat. counselor 1973-75), Internat. Assn. for Fin. Planning (bd. dirs. Greater O'Hare chpt. 1990). Avocations: foreign languages, music, gardening. Office: 224 Old Barn Rd Barrington IL 60010-1655

LEON, KAREN RENÉE, elementary education educator; b. Sept. 3, 1963; BS in Elem. Edn., Fla. A&M U., Tallahassee, 1988, MEd, 1998. 3d grade tchr. Leon County Sch. Dist., Tallahassee, 1988, 2d grade tchr., 1988—. Mem. NEA, Internat. Reading Assn., Leon County Tchrs. Union, Pi Lambda Theta, Alpha Delta Kappa. Office: 2465 Atlas Rd Tallahassee FL 32303-3703 E-mail: kleon@nettally.com.

LEON, ROBERT LEONARD, psychiatrist, educator; b. Denver, Jan. 18, 1925; s. Louis and Rae (Brown) L.; m. Willena Lee, Sept. 14, 1947; children: Alexis Kay, Mark Robert, Jeffrey Clayton, Stacy Lee. MD, U. Colo., 1948. Diplomate Am. Bd. Psychiatry and Neurology. Intern U. Mich. Hosp., Ann Arbor, 1948-49; resident in psychiatry U. Colo. Med. Ctr., Denver, 1949-52, child psychiatry fellow, 1951-52, Bur. Mental Hygiene, New Haven, Conn. Dept. Health/Student Health Svc., Yale U., 1952-53; asst. dir., acting dir. child psychiatry Greater Kansas City Mental Health Found., 1953-54; instr. psychiatry U. Kans. Sch. Medicine, Kansas City, 1956-57; asst. prof. psychiatry U. Tex. Health Sci. Ctr. at Dallas, Southwestern Med. Sch., 1957-61, assoc. prof., 1961-65, prof., 1965-67; prof., chmn. dept. psychiatry Sch. Medicine U. Tex. Health Sci. Ctr., San Antonio, 1967-95, interim chmn., 1995-96; Ashbel Smith prof. U. Tex. Health Sci. Ctr., 1990—. Chief psychiatry U. Health Sys., Bexar County, San Antonio, 1967-96; cons. psychiatry Audie Murphy Vet.'s Hosp., 1973—; cons. Mental Health Orgn., region IV, HEW, 1957-73; mem. Psychiat. Tng. Rev. NIMH, Rockville, Md., 1970-74; hon. cons. World Health Orgn., Geneva, 1996. Author: Psychiatric Interviewing: A Primer, 1982, 2d edit., 1989; contbr. articles to profl. jours. Sr. surgeon USPHS, 1954-57. Fellow ACP (pres. 1987-88), Am. Psychiat. Assn. (life), Am. Orthopsychiat. Assn. (life), Am. Acad. Child and Adolescent Psychiatry (life), Am. Assn. Social Psychiatry (pres. 1990-92); mem. Am. Assn. Chmn. Depts. Psychiatry (pres. 1982-83), Benjamin Rush Soc., World Assn. for Social Psychiatry. Home: 6866 Stonykirk St San Antonio TX 78240-2743 Office: U Tex Health Sci Ctr 7703 Floyd Curl Dr MS 7792 San Antonio TX 78229-3900 E-mail: leon@uthscsa.edu., leon@uthsesa.dcci.com.

LEON, ROLANDO LUIS, lawyer; b. Ponce, P.R., Oct. 18, 1952; s. Luis Manuel and Patricia (Cruz) L.; m. Janet Williams, May 20, 1994; children: Brandon Alexandre, Bryan Christopher, Lauren Patricia. BA in Govt., U. Tex., Arlington, 1972; JD, Tex. Tech. U., 1975; MS in Pub. Adminstrn., Golden Gate U., 1979. Bar: Tex. 1976, U.S. Ct. Mil. Appeals 1977, U.S Dist. Ct. (we., so. dists) Tex. 1981, U.S. Ct. Appeals (5th cir.) 1985; cert. in personal injury and civil trial law Tex. Bd. Legal Specialization, 1985; cert. civil trial advocacy Nat. Bd. Trial Advocacy, 1990. Ptnr. Thornton, Summers, Biechlin, Dunham & Brown LC, Corpus Christi, Tex., 1980-99; mng. ptnr. Barker, Leon, Fancher & Matthys, LLP, 2000—. Editor: Tex. Tech. U. Law Rev., 1974-75. Lt. USN, 1976-80. Mem. ABA, Tex. Bar Assn., Assn. Trial Lawyers Am. Office: Barker Leon Fancher & Matthys LLP Ste 1200 555 N Carancahua St Corpus Christi TX 78478 E-mail: rleon@blfmlaw.com.

LEONARD, ANGELA MICHELE, educator, librarian; b. Washington, June 26, 1954; d. Walter Jewell and Betty (Singleton) L. AB, Harvard U., 1976; MLS, Vanderbilt U., 1982; MPhil, George Washington U., 1987, PhD, 1994; postgrad., Dartmouth Sch. Criticism and Theory, 1996, NEH Inst., 1998, Chesapeake Regional Scholars Inst., 1999. Cons. Seigenthaler Assocs., Nashville, 1979-81; instr. Trevecca Nazarene Coll., 1979, Nashville State Tech. Inst., 1980-81; rschr., learning libr. program Fisk U. Libr., 1981-82; cataloguer Howard U. Librs., 1983; reference libr. Founders Grad. Libr., 1983-89; tchg. asst. George Washington U., 1986-90; lectr. Bowdoin Coll., 1990-91; instr. St. Cloud State U., 1991; asst. prof. Dickinson Coll., 1992-94, Bucknell U., 1994-95; lectr. UMCP, 1995; asst. prof. Loyola Coll., Md., 1996—. Vis. prof. Johns Hopkins U., 1998; corp. and spl. ref. libr., 1988-90, 95-97. Copy editor Am. Quarterly, 1988-90; editor: Boorstin Bibliography, Antislavery Materials; contbr. articles to books, profl. jours. Mem. ALA, NAACP, AAUW, Am. Hist. Assn., Orgn. Am. History, Semiotics Soc. Am., Nat. Soc. Exptl. Edn., Nat. Urban League, Ga. Hist. Soc., Mo. Hist. Soc., Alpha Kappa Alpha, Beta Phi Mu. Roman Catholic. Office: Loyola Coll Dept Hist 4501 N Charles St Baltimore MD 21210-2601 E-mail: aleonard@loyola.edu.

LEONARD, SISTER ANNE C. superintendent, education director; b. N.Y.C., Dec. 22, 1936; d. Patrick A. and Mary T. (McAlpin) L. BS in Edn. and Social Sci., Fordham U., 1962, MA, 1965; CAGS, Boston U., 1972; postgrad., Hunter Coll., U. San Francisco, U. Northern Ill., Notre Dame U. Cert. tchr. K-12, adminstr. N.Y. Tchr., asst. prin., prin. Notre Dame Acad., Staten Island, N.Y., 1957-68; prin. Maternity B.V.M. Sch., Bourbonnais, Ill., 1968-69, St. Jude the Apostle Sch., South Holland, 1969-78; dir. Cath. Elem. Schs. Archdiocese of Chgo., 1978-83, dir. ednl. svcs., mem. Cardinal Bernadin's cabinet, 1983-90, exec. officer commn. ednl. svcs., 1983-90; supt. schs., dir. edn. Archdiocese of Okla. City, 1990-96; U.S. province leader Congregation of Notre Dame, Ridgefield, Conn., 1996—. Chair edn. divsn. Cath. Conf. Ill., 1988-90; del. gen. chpt. Congregation Notre Dame, mem. provincial coun.; mem. edn. com. U.S. Cath. Conf. Bishops, Washington, 1985-88; mem. Nat. Cath. Bishops' Millennium Com.; speaker in field; lectr., presenter workshops; mem. Fortune 500 panel edn. and bus.; devel. mission statement, just principles compensation, new models compensation for prins., 1987-91; initiated, organized Dirs. Edn. Wis., Ill., Ind., Ohio, Mich.; attended symposia in field; mem. com. prep. Office of Cath. Edn. Conciliation Process; exec. officer local sch. bds.; initiated individually guided edn. program St. Jude Sch. Cons. textbooks William H. Sadlier, Inc.; contbr. articles to profl. jours. Trustee DePaul U., 1986—; trustee Midwestern U., 1999—, bd. dirs., vice chair acad. affairs com.; bd. dirs. Jr. Achievement, Chgo., 1984-90, Oklahoma City, 1991-96; mem. NCCJ, 1992-96, Gov. Ill. adv. com. on non-pub. schs., Springfield, 1978-82, planning com. Big Shoulders Project, officer Leadership Conf. of Women Religious (Region I), 1997—; active Congregation of Notre Dame Mem. ASCD, Nat. Cath. Ednl. Assn. (pres. chief adminstrs. Cath. edn. 1991-94, v.p. 1989-91, vice chair bd. 1991-94, task force 1990-91, centennial com. 1997—, supervision, pers., curriculum, Educator of Yr. award 1990), Archdiocesan Prins. Assn. (pres. 1973-78), Nat. Religious Retirement Bd. (grant com.), Chgo. Coun. Fgn. Rels., Phi Delta Kappa (Educator of Yr. 1984). Avocations: reading, swimming, travel. Home and Office: 223 W Mountain Rd Ridgefield CT 06877-3627 Fax: 203-894-9686. E-mail: provsec@juno.com.

LEONARD, ARTHUR, retired physician; b. Phila., Apr. 20, 1939; s. Charles and Estelle (Block) L.; m. Beatriz V.; children: Kimberly E., Christopher C. BA, Temple U., 1960; MD, Jefferson Med. Coll., 1964. Diplomate Am. Bd. Internal Medicine, Am. Bd. Nephrology. Straight med. intern, 1964-65; resident in internal medicine, 1965-67; renal resident Michael Reese Hosp. and Med. Ctr., 1967-68; mem. faculty, clin. coord. U. Minn. Sch. Medicine/Hennepin County Med. Ctr., Mpls., 1970-78; med. dir. David Herman Nursing Home, 1973-78; assoc. dean, chair internal medicine U. Ill. Sch. Medicine, Urbana-Champaign, 1978-81; chair internal medicine Franklin Sq. Hosp., Balt., 1981-85; pvt. practice Sarasota, Fla., 1985-88; med. dir. Humana, Boynton Beach, 1988-90; vice chair U. Nev. Sch. Medicine, Las Vegas, 1991-92; pvt. practice Southwest Med. Assn., 1993-94, Ocean Beach Clinic, Ilwaco, Wash., 1994-95, Summerlin Med. Group, Las Vegas, 1995-97; ret., 1997. Contbr. articles to profl. jours. Planning commnr., Golden Valley, Minn., 1973-76. Lt. comdr. USN, 1968-70. Fellow ACP. Home: 203 Poplar Ridge Ct Apt 24 Owings Mills MD 21117-5707 E-mail: AandB@aol.com.

LEONARD, BOBBI BOWERS RANGE, educator, librarian; b. Elizabethton, Tenn., Nov. 30, 1940; d. Samuel Murray Bowers Sr. and Eunice Martisha (Parlier) Bowers-Carr; m. Ronald Stephen Range, Sr., Mar. 26, 1960 (dec. May 1980); children: Ronald Stephen Jr., Richard Edward; m. Alan Palmer Leonard, Sr., Mar. 26, 1988 (dec. Oct. 1992). BS in English and Libr. Sci., East Tenn. State Coll., 1962; MA in English, East Tenn. State U., 1977. Cert. tchr., Tenn. Libr. Cloudland H.S., Roan Mountain, Tenn., 1962-63, Lincoln Elem. Sch., Kingsport, 1963-69; English tchr. Dobyns-Bennett H.S., 1974-87, head libr., 1987-93; dir. pub. rels. Kingsport City Schs., 1984-87; retired. Chairperson English sect. East Tenn. Edn. Assn., 1993-. Writer, editor, prodr. (sch. sys. newsletter) Intercom, 1984-88. Active Am. WWII Orphans Network, 1993—; founding mem. Nat. Campaign for Tolerance, 1993-; regional coord. Dem. Nat. Com., 1999—. Recipient award of merit for brochure Nat. Sch. Pub. Rels. Assn., 1984, award of excellence, 1987. Democrat. Avocations: reading, crossword puzzles, cooking, hiking. E-mail. Home: 532 Fleetwood St Apt D Kingsport TN 37660-3491 E-mail: Roberta@Chartertn.net.

LEONARD, BRIAN FRANCIS, lawyer; b. Rolla, N.D., Jan. 27, 1948; s. Howard Francis and Millie Mae (Olson) L.; m. Martha Ellen Ziff, May 11, 1945;children: Sarah, Emily, Brian. BA, U. N.D., 1970; JD, U. Minn., 1973. Bar: Minn. 1973, U.S. Dist. Ct. Minn. 1973, U.S. Ct. Appeals (8th cir.) 1976, U.S. Supreme 1981. Assoc. O'Neill, Burke, O'Neill, Leonard and O'Brien, Ltd., St. Paul, 1973-78, ptnr., 1978-94, Leonard, O'Brien, Wilford Spencer and Gale, Ltd., Mpls., 1994—. Bus. law instr. adult extension St. Paul TV I, 1978—; adj. prof. U. Minn. Law Sch., 1989—. Bd. dirs. Minn. Literacy Coun., 1993-2000. Mem. ABA, Minn. Bar Assn. (bankruptcy sect.), Ramsey County Bar Assn., St. Paul Jaycees (bd. dirs. 1975-79), Rotary club (chmn. com. St. Paul chpt.1985). Roman Catholic. Home: 1532 Tamberwood Trl Saint Paul MN 55125-3362 Office: 100 S 5th St Ste 1200 Minneapolis MN 55402-1216 E-mail: bleonard@lowsg.com.

LEONARD, CAROLYN BRANCH, publisher, editor, writer; b. Buffalo, Aug. 21, 1937; d. Ernest S. and Imogene (Parsons) Branch; m. John C. Leonard, Apr. 15, 1956 (div. June 1984); children: Judith G., James C.; m. Jon Heavener, Feb. 14, 1993. BA, Oklahoma City U., 1991. Pub. SAGEst PRESS, Oklahoma City, 1990—. Pub. affairs asst. U.S. Treas., Oklahoma City, 1988-94. Asst. editor: Woodward County Jour. Newspaper, 1982-83; editor: Harper Co. Jour., Buffalo, Okla., 1983-88, News U Can Use, Nat. Treas. Employees Union, Oklahom a City, 1994-96. Senate encoder Okla. State Capitol, 1996-99; area rep., bd. dirs. Briarcreek Neighborhood Assn.; treas. Profit Ptnrs. Investment Club, 1997—; mem. Meth. Ch. of the Servant, Okla. Hist. Soc. Recipient numerous awards. Mem. DAR, Writers of the Purple Sage (past pres.), Oklahoma City Writers (past pres.), Okla. Writers Fedn., Mayflower Descendants Soc., Okla. Hist. Soc., Mo. Hist. Soc., Ohio Hist. Soc., Ill. Hist. Soc., Bentonville Anti-Horse Thief Soc., Servants Dinner Club.

LEONARD, DAVID KING, political science educator; b. Orange, N.J., Nov. 11, 1941; s. Rowland K. and Mary Jane (Kerr) L.; m. Leslie Leggett Leonard, Aug. 23, 1965; children: Kenneth L., Joanna E., Christopher K., James K. BA with honors, Haverford Coll., 1963; MA, U. Chgo., 1967, PhD, 1974. Programme sec. YMCA, Harare, Zimbabwe, 1963-64, dist. sec. Kitwe, Zambia, 1965; lectr. U. Nairobi, Kenya, 1969-73; sr. lectr. U. Dar es Salaam, Tanzania, 1974-76; vis. lectr. U. Calif., Berkeley, 1973-74, prof., 1976—, dean internat. and area studies, 1999—. Prin. investigator U.S. Agy. for Internat. Devel. Project on Mng. Decentralization, 1979-81; mgmt. advisor Kenya Ministries of Agr. and Livestock Devel., Nairobi, 1980-82; mem. adv. panel Office of Tech. Assessment, U.S. Congress, Washington, 1985-86; chair African Studies Ctr., Berkeley, 1986-92, chair Peace and Conflict Studies, Berkeley, 1996-99. Author: Reaching the Peasant Farmer, 1977, African Successes, 1991; author, editor: Institutions of Rural Development for the Poor, 1982, Africa's Changing Markets for Health and Veterinary Services, 2000; co-author: Africa's Stalled Development, 2002. Pres. Coun. of U. Calif. Faculty Assns., 1995-97; chair Berkeley Faculty Assn., 1994-96. Fellow Danforth Found., 1965-68, Fulbright fellow U.S. Dept. Edn., Kenya, 1985-86; recipient 1st prize Rsch. for 3d World award Govt. Netherlands, 1992. Democrat. Mem. Soc. Of Friends. Home: 1309 Ordway St Berkeley CA 94702-1123 Office: Univ Calif IAS 360 Stephens Hall Berkeley CA 94720-2300

LEONARD, DAVID MORSE, lawyer; b. Akron, Ohio, Dec. 4, 1949; s. Frank O. and Barbara J. Leonard. BS in Chem. Engring., Purdue U., 1972; JD, Emory U., 1975. Bar: Ga. 1975, U.S. Ct. Appeals (4th, 5th and 11th cirs.), U.S. Dist. Ct. (no., mid. and so. dists.) Ga., U.S. Dist. Ct. (so. dist.) Ala., U.S. Dist. Ct. (we. dist.) La.; cert. mediator, cert. mediation tng. Assoc. Montet & Smith, Atlanta, 1975-79, Hurt, Richardson, Garner, Todd & Cadenhead, Atlanta, 1979-83, ptnr., 1983-85; of counsel Lord, Bissell & Brook, 1985-87, ptnr., 1987—. Mem. panel of arbitrators Am. Arbitration Assn., 1995—. Mem. ABA (litigation sect., tort and ins. practice sect.), Profl. Liability Underwriting Soc., Atlanta Lawyers Club, Atlanta C. of C., Am. Arbitration Assn. (panel of arbitrators). Home: 4152 Club Dr NE Atlanta GA 30319-1116 Office: Lord Bissell & Brook Ste 1900 1170 Peachtree St NE Atlanta GA 30309-7675

LEONARD, EDWIN DEANE, lawyer; b. Oakland, Calif., Apr. 22, 1929; s. Edwin Stanley and Gladys Eugenia (Lee) L.; m. Judith Swatland, July 10, 1954; children: Garrick Hillman, Susanna Leonard Hill, Rebecca Leonard McCauley, Ethan York. BA, The Principia, 1950; LLB, Harvard U., 1953; LLM, George Washington U., 1956. Bar: D.C. 1953, Ill. 1953, N.Y. 1957. Assoc. Davis Polk Wardwell Sunderland & Kiendl, N.Y.C., 1956-61; ptnr. Davis Polk & Wardwell, 1961-97, sr. counsel, 1998—. Trustee the Brearley Sch., N.Y.C., 1980-90. Served to 1st lt. JAGC, 1953-56. Mem. ABA, N.Y. Bar Assn., N.Y. County Bar Assn., Assn. of Bar of City of N.Y. (chmn. various coms.). Home: 157 Conklin Hill Rd Stanfordville NY 12581-5639 Office: Davis Polk & Wardwell 450 Lexington Ave Fl 31 New York NY 10017-3982 E-mail: deaneleonard@worldnet.att.net.

LEONARD, ELIZABETH ADNEY, social worker; b. Lebanon, Ind., Apr. 27, 1917; d. Frank Brown and Ethel Fern (Coons) Adney; m. Alan J. Leonard, Aug. 4, 1949; children: Arthur Alan, Jean Elizabeth. BA, Ind. U., 1939, MSW, 1947; postgrad., Columbia U., N.Y.C., 1948. Lic. clin. social worker, Calif. With Psychiat. Clinic for Youth, Long Beach, Calif., 1958-74, chief social worker, 1974-82, ret., 1982. Mem. AAUW, NASW, Am. Orthopsychiat. Assn., Zeta Tau Alpha. Home: 2339 Avenida Sevilla Apt A Laguna Beach CA 92653-0836

LEONARD, GEORGE EDMUND, real estate, bank, high tech and consulting executive; b. Phoenix, Nov. 20, 1940; s. George Edmund and Marion Elizabeth (Fink) L.; m. Gloria Jean Henry, Mar. 26, 1965 (div. Feb. 1981); children: Tracy Lynn McKinney, Amy Theresa Blanchard, Kristin Jean Steel; m. Mary C. Short, Sept. 22, 1990. Student, Ariz. State U., 1958-60; BS, U.S. Naval Acad., 1964; postgrad., Pa. State U., 1969-70; MBA, U. Chgo., 1973. Commd. ensign USN, 1964, advanced through grades to lt. comdr., 1975; v.p. 1st Nat. Bank Chgo., 1970-75; exec. v.p., chief banking, CFO, chief lending officer Mera Bank, Phoenix, 1975-90, also bd. dirs., 1982-90; pres., CEO Ctrl. Savs., San Diego, 1985-87; chmn., CEO AmBank Holding Co. of Colo., Scottsdale, Ariz., 1990-91, Consumer Guarantee Corp., Phoenix, 1996; pres., CEO Diversified Mgmt. Svcs., Inc., 1991-96, GEL Mgmt. Inc., Phoenix, 1991—; CFO Western Pacific Airlines, Colorado Springs, 1996-98, bd. dirs., 1996-98; exec. v.p., CFO, treas., sec., dir. fin. Radi Sys. Microwave Sys. Corp., Des Moines, 1998—. COO, bd. dirs., 2000—01. Active Phoenix Thunderbirds, 1979—; bd. dirs. Maricopa C.C.s Found., treas., 2nd v.p., 1991-93, 1st v.p., 1993-94, pres., 1994-95, past pres., 1995-96, Camelback Charitable Trust, 1991-92, The Samaritan Found., 1993-96, chmn. fin. com., 1994-96, vice chmn., 1996. Mem. Phoenix Met. C. of C. (bd. dirs. 1975-82), Inst. Fin. Edn. (bd. dirs. 1980-87, nat. chmn. 1985-86), Ariz. State U. Coll. of Bus. Deans Coun. of 100, Paradise Valley Country Club (bd. dirs. 1991-98, treas. 1992-95, pres. 1995-97), White Mountain Country Club, Glen Oaks Country Club, Kiwanis. Republican. Roman Catholic. Home: 409 Silverado Pt Waukee IA 50263-8150 Office: Radi Sys Microware Sys Corp 1500 NW 118th St Des Moines IA 50325-8242

LEONARD, GLEN MILTON, museum administrator; b. Salt Lake City, Nov. 12, 1938; s. Burnham J. and Allene (Green) L.; m. Karen Wright, Mar. 15, 1968; children: Cory, Kyle, Keith. BA, U. Utah, 1964, MA, 1966, PhD, 1970. Mng. editor Utah State Hist. Soc., Salt Lake City, 1970-73; sr. rsch. assoc. history divsn. Ch. of Jesus Christ of LDS, 1973-78; dir. Mus. Ch. History and Art, 1979—. Mem. adv. bd. editors Utah Hist. Quarterly, Salt Lake City, 1973-88; assoc. editor Jour. Mormon History, Provo, Utah, 1974-80; bd. dirs. Western Studies Ctr., Brigham Young U., Provo. Co-author: The Story of the Latter-day Saints, 1976; Author: A History of Davis County, 1999, Nauvoo: A Place of Peace, A People of Plenty, 2002. Mem. Hist. Preservation Commn., Farmington, Utah, 1986-92; mem. adv. coun. Mormon Pioneer Nat. Hist. Trail, Nat. Pk. Svc., 1980-86; mem. Utah Pioneer Sesquicentennial Celebration Coordinating Coun., 1995-97. Recipient Dale Morgan Article award Utah State Hist. Soc., 1973, Mormon History Assn. Article awards, 1990, 96. Mem. Orgn. Am. Historians, Western History Assn., Am. Assn. Mus. (mus. assessment program cons.), Western Mus. Assn., Utah Mus. Assn. (bd. dirs. 1980-83), Am. Assn. State and Local History. Avocations: photography, music, gardening. Office: Mus Ch Hist & Art 45 N West Temple Salt Lake City UT 84150

LEONARD, GUY MEYERS, JR. international holding company executive; b. Bluefield, W.Va., Sept. 22, 1926; s. Guy Meyers and Mabel (Bonham) L.; m. Pat Kirby, June 28, 1949; children: Calvin David, Dinah Lynn. AB, BS, Morris Harvey Coll., 1949; BDiv, Southwestern Bapt. Sem., 1952; STM, Harvard U., 1957. Commd. ensign USN, 1952, advanced through grades to capt., 1968, ret., 1972; dir. R&D Ency. Britannica Ednl. Corp., Chgo., 1972-76; pres. Communication Programming Svcs., inc., Charleston, S.C., 1976—; pres., CEO First Don Trading Co., 1982—; chmn., CEO Transocean Ltd., Internat. Holding Co., 1982-86; pres. GHL, Inc., Pacific Rim, Africa, 1991—. Cons. drug control programs for schs., cons. Ency. Britannica, Home Mission Bd. and Brotherhood Commn. So. Bapt. Conv. Sec., U.S. Power Squadron, Charleston, 1969; chmn. Spl. Commn. on Drug Abuse for Armed Forces, 1970-72; active Conn. coun. Boy Scouts Am., 1959-62; chmn. stewardship com. Episc. Diocese of S.C., 1994-95; bd. dirs. CWA Found. Ch. Adv. Bd. CWA. Bd. dirs. CWA Found. Served with USN, 1943-72. Decorated Legion of Merit, Meritorious Svc. medal, Navy Commendation medal, Disting. Svc. medal; recipient Disting. Svc. award City of Louisville, 1963. Mem. Harvard Club S.C., C. of C., Trident Chamber (Charleston), Navy League U.S., Ret. Officers Assn., Kiwanis (spl. projects chmn. 1964-65). Achievements include the design and prodn. with Harvard U. and sta. WGBH, Boston, mediated coll. curriculum leading to BS degree for use by naval personnel.

LEONARD, HERMAN BEUKEMA (DUTCH LEONARD), public finance and management educator; b. Carlisle Barracks, Pa., Dec. 26, 1952; s. Charles Frederick and Margery Alden (Beukema) L.; m. Kathryn Anne Angell, Oct. 9, 1983; children: Whitney Angell, Dana Angell. AB summa cum laude, Harvard U., 1974, AM, 1976, PhD, 1979. Asst. prof. pub. policy John F. Kennedy Sch. Govt., Harvard U., Cambridge, Mass., 1979-83, assoc. prof., 1983-86, George F. Baker prof. pub. mgmt., 1986—, acad. dean for teaching programs, 1992-2000. Bd. dirs., Harvard Pilgrim Health Care, 2000—; mem. Gov.'s Coun. Econ. Policy, Alaska, 1980-82; chmn. Gov.'s Task Force on Coll. Opportunity , Mass., 1987-88; bd. dirs. Mass. Health and Ednl. Facilities Authority, 1988-99; mem. adv. bd. N.Y.C. Debt Mgmt., 1990-94; mem. Mass Performance Enchancement Commn., 1997-98. Co-author: Discrimination in Rural Housing, 1976, The Federal Budget and the States, 1993-99; author: Checks Unbalanced: The Quiet Side of Public Spending, 1986, By Choice or By Chance? Tracking the Values in Massachusetts Public Spending, 1992; contbr. numerous articles on pub. fin. and mgmt. to jours. in field. Recipient grad. fellowship NSF, 1974; jr. fellow Soc. Fellows, Harvard U., 1976-79; Presdl. scholar, 1970. Mem. Phi Beta Kappa. Office: Harvard U John F Kennedy Sch Govt 79 JFK St Cambridge MA 02138-5801

LEONARD, J. RICH, federal judge, educator; b. 1949; AB, U. N.C., 1971, MEd, 1973; JD, Yale U., 1976. Bar: N.C. 1976. Law clk. to Hon. Franklin T. Dupree, Jr., U.S. Dist. Ct., 1976-78; assoc. Sanford, Adams, McCullough & Beard, 1978-79; magistrate judge for ea. dist. N.C., U.S. Magistrate Ct., 1981-92; bankruptcy judge for ea. dist. N.C., U.S. Bankruptcy Ct., Wilson, 1992-99, chief U.S. bankruptcy judge ea. dist. N.C., 1999—. Adj. prof. civil procedure N.C. Ctrl. U. Sch. Law, 1985-86, adj. prof. bankruptcy law, 1995-97; adj. profl. U. N.C., Law Sch., Chapel Hill, 1995; dir., sec.-treas. Nat. Inst. for Dispute Resolution. Mem. ABA, FBA (N.C. adv. coun.), N.C. Bar Assn. (v.p. 1995), Wake County Bar Assn., 4th Circuit Jud. Conf. (com. on case mgmt. and ct. adminstrn.), N.C.-Fed. Jud. Coun. Office: 1760 Parkwood Blvd W Wilson NC 27893-3564

LEONARD, J. WAYNE, energy company executive; BA in Acctg., Ball State U., 1973; MBA, Ind. U., 1987. CPA, Ind. Various positions PSI Energy, sr. v.p., CFO, 1989-94; group v.p., CFO, Cinergy, 1994-96, pres. energy commodities strategic bus. unit, 1996-98; pres. Cinergy Capital and Trading, 1996-98; pres., COO domestic bus. units, in-charge for internat. ops. Entergy Corp., New Orleans, 1998, CEO, 1999—. Leader BusinessLINC, Mississippi River Delta bus.-to-bus. mentoring. Mem. AICPA. Office: Entergy Corp 639 Loyola Ave New Orleans LA 70113-3125*

LEONARD, JAMES EDWARD, accountant; b. Binghamton, N.Y., Oct. 14, 1951; s. Ray Monty and Beatrice Mary (Williams) L.; m. Michelle Louise Montgomery, Aug. 3, 1985; 1 child, Celeste. Student, U. Hawaii, 1971-72, U. Md., Okinawa, Japan, 1973-74; AS in Bus., Broome C.C., Binghamton, N.Y., 1976; BS in Acctg. magna cum laude, U. Albany, 1978. CPA, N.Y. Staff acct. Peat, Marwick, Mitchell, White Plains, N.Y., 1978-80; exec. v.p. Richardson & Co., PC, Endicott, 1980-85; owner James E. Leonard, CPA, 1986—. Founder, chmn. Chugnut Riverwalk Com., Endicott, 1992—; dir., treas. Broome County Pub. Libr., Binghamton, N.Y., 1993-99; dir., officer Boys & Girls Club Western Broome, Endicott, 1993-99; mem. Broome County Econ. Devel. Zone Bd., 1995-99. Petty officer 2d class USN, 1970-74. Mem. AICPA, N.Y. State Soc. CPA's, United Health Svcs. Found. (dir. 1994—, trustee 1998—), Ideal Sr. Living Ctr. (dir. 1994—, chmn. 1998—), Endicott Rotary Club (past pres. 1982—), Endicott Rotary Found. (dir. 1992—). Avocations: reading, live steam engines, home winemaking, cooking. Office: James E Leonard CPA 515 East Main St Endicott NY 13760

LEONARD, JAMES JOSEPH, physician, educator; b. Schenectady, June 17, 1924; s. James Joseph and Helena (Flood) L.; m. Helen Louise Mitchell, Oct. 24, 1953; children: James Joseph, W. Jeffrey, Paul Mitchell, Kathleen Marie. MD, Georgetown U., 1950. Intern medicine Georgetown U. Hosp., 1950-51, jr. asst. resident, 1951-52, fellow cardiology, 1953-54; asst. resident medicine Boston City Hosp., 1952-53; resident pulmonary diseases D.C. Gen. Hosp., 1954-55, med. officer, 1955-56; instr. medicine Georgetown U. Med. Sch., 1955-56, Duke Med. Center, 1956-57; asst. prof. medicine, dir. div. cardiology Georgetown U. service D.C. Gen. Hosp., 1957-59; asst. prof. medicine U. Tex. Med. Br., Galveston, 1959-62; asso. prof. medicine Ohio State U. Med. Sch., 1962-63; dir. div. cardiology U. Pitts. Med. Sch., 1963-70, asso. prof. medicine, 1963-67, prof. medicine, 1967-77, acting chmn. dept., 1970, chmn. dept., 1971-77; prof., chmn. dept. medicine Uniformed Services U. of Health Scis., 1977—. Master ACP; mem. So. Soc. Clin. Investigation, Am. Clin. and Climatol. Assn., Central Soc. Clin. Research, Assn. Am. Physicians, Assn. Profs. Medicine, Assn. U. Cardiologists. Home: 3200 Farmington Dr Chevy Chase MD 20815-4827 Office: 4301 Jones Bridge Rd Bethesda MD 20814-4712

LEONARD, JAMES KEVIN, mechanical engineer; b. Bklyn., Oct. 7, 1950; s. James Joseph and Virginia Isabel (Curtin) L. Student, Marquette U., 1969-73; AAS, N.Y.C. Cmty. Coll., 1975; postgrad., Fordham U., 1976. V.p. Lencon, Bklyn., 1978, 1986—; technician Bd. of Higher Edn., 1979-81; safety engr. Dept. Housing, Preservation & Devel., 1982-83; asst. rschr. Bklyn. Hist. Soc., 1985. Author: (plays) Pictures, 1979, Siblings, 1985. Mem. Alpha Delta Gamma. Republican. Roman Catholic. Avocations: literature, N.Y. Times, tennis, swimming. Home: 2101 Bedford Ave Apt 6H Brooklyn NY 11226

LEONARD, JAMES PATRICK, writer, editor, communications consultant, instructor; b. Boston, July 6, 1968; s. James Joseph and Kathleen Helen Leonard; m. Elizabeth Anne Kearns, June 5, 1999; 1 child Audrey Elizabeth. Student, Nat. U. Ireland, Galway, 1989; BA, Boston College, 1990, MA, 1998. Sr. editor/writer Cahners Publ., Reed-Elsevier, Inc., Newton, Mass., 1990—95; freelance writer, editor, media consultant, project mgr., 1995—; tech. editor, mng. editor, dir. Aberdeen Group, Inc., Boston, 1998—2002; comml. mgr. Pub. Products Group Mgmt. Ventures, Inc., Cambridge, 2002—. Freelance instr., ESL tutor, 1995-98; adj. instr. and lectr. Boston College, 1996-98, Aquinas Coll., Newton, Mass., 1999, Suffolk U., Boston, 1999; instr., publ. cons. Pine Manor Coll., Chestnut Hill, Mass., 1997—. Asst. editor: Eire-Ireland, 1996—; contbr: Encyclopedia of the Irish in America, 1999, secondary sch. textbooks, 1999, contbr. to profl. jours. Mem.: Internat. Assn. for Study of Irish Lits. (ann. conf. presenter 1996, 1997), Boston Coll. Alumni Assn. (career adv. network vol.). Roman Catholic. Avocations: internat. travel, hiking, music. Office: Management Ventures Inc 20 University Rd Cambridge MA 02138

LEONARD, JOHN FRANCIS, psychiatrist; b. L.A., May 11, 1931; s. Albert and Jean Taylor Leonard; m. Barbara Jean Ferris, June 15, 1957; children: Deborah Ann, Elaine Marie, Meredith Lynn, Cara Lee. BA, UCLA, 1953, MD, 1957. Diplomate Am. Bd. Psychiatry and Neurology, Child and Adolescent Psychiatry. Gen. rotating intern U.S. VA Gen. Med. and Surg. Hosp.; resident in psychiatry UCLA/U.S. VA Neuropsychiat. Hosp., Brentwood, Calif.; pvt. practice L.A., 1963—; clin. assoc. prof. of psychiatry U. Calif. Med. dir. Culver City (Calif.) Clinic, 1965-71, Westwood Hosp. Cmty. Psychiat. Ctrs., Inc., L.A., 1971-74; clin. dir. child/adolescent psychiatry Harbor/UCLA Med. Ctr., Torrance, Calif., 1990—. Capt. USAF, 1961-63. Mem. Phi Beta Kappa. Avocations: High Sierra pack trips, fishing, skiing, trekking. Office: 14229 W Sunset Blvd Pacific Palisades CA 90272-3916 E-mail: leonardj@ucla.edu.

LEONARD, JOHN HARRY, advertising executive; b. N.Y.C., June 28, 1922; s. Frederick H. and Florence (Kiechlin) L.; m. Marjorie Jane Haslun, Oct. 19, 1946; children— John Kiechlin, Janet Ann. BS, N.Y. U., 1942, MBA, 1951. Advt. mgr. Autographic Register Co., 1946-47; promotion mgr. Macfadden Pub. Co., 1947-50; successively copywriter, account exec., v.p. and account supr. Batten, Barton, Durstine & Osborn, 1950-64; with DDB Needham Worldwide (formerly Doyle Dane Bernbach, Inc.), N.Y.C., 1964-87, group sr. v.p., 1972-87. Lectr. Grad. Sch. Bus., N.Y. U., 1959-61 Bd. dirs., past exec. com. Am. Bible Soc.; past chmn. bd. dirs. Wartburg Home, Mt. Vernon, N.Y.; trustee NYU, 1978-84. With USAAF, 1943—46. Recipient Alumni Meritorious Service award N.Y. U., 1969 Mem. NYU Grad. Sch. Bus. Alumni Assn. (pres.), NYU Commerce Alumni Assn. (pres. 1979-80), Alpha Delta Sigma. Home: 310A Heritage Vlg Southbury CT 06488-1752 E-mail: margejohn46@aol.com.

LEONARD, JOSEPH HOWARD, association organization executive; b. Cambridge, Md., Oct. 20, 1952; s. Joseph Francis and Catherine (Hill) L.; m. Jacquelyn Lee McCall, June 7, 1975 (div. Dec. 1981); m. Margaret Ann Shenton, June 26, 1982; children: Stephanie Kristina, Jacquelyn Margaret. BA in Psychology, Salisbury State U., 1976; MA in Rehab. Counseling, Gallaudet U., 1979; postgrad., Washington Coll., Chestertown, Md., 1984, 88, U. Md., 1986-87, San Diego State U., 1996, Johns Hopkins U., 1998. Cert. profl. counselor, Md. Staff electrician John W. Tieder, Inc., Cambridge, Md., summers 1973-74; prodn. supr. W.H. Leonard & Sons, Inc., Seward, summers 1968-70, 75; instr., program coord. Dorchester Devel. Unit, Inc., Cambridge, 1976-77; rehab. counselor Tex. Rehab. Commn., Austin, 1979; instr. Am. Sign Lang., developmental disabilities Chesapeake Coll., Wye Mills, Md., 1979—; case mgr., coord. spl. programs Dorchester County Health Dept., Cambridge, 1979-90; ind. interpreter Am. Sign Lang. Md., 1979—; exec. dir. Deaf Ind. Living Assn., Inc., Salisbury, Md., 1990—; adj.faculty, interpreter tng. program Catonsville (Md.) C.C., 1995—. V.p. bd. dirs. Deaf Ind. Living Assn., Inc., Md., 1984-90; trustee Md. Sch. for the Deaf, 1985—, pres., 1996—; mem. adv. bd. Devel. Disabilities program Chesapeake Coll., 1986-90; mem. Gov.'s Commn. on the Hearing Impaired, Md., 1984-90; surveyor Applied Rsch. and Evaluation U., U. Md., 1988-89; bd. dirs. Md. Assn. Cmty. Svcs.; mem. mental health adv. com. for deaf and hearing impaired, Md., 1990—. Contbr. articles to profl. jours. Asst. scoutmaster Boy Scouts Am., Cambridge, 1973-78; v.p. bd. dirs. Dorchester County Family YWCA, 1985; pres. bd. dirs. Dorchester Assn. for Devel. Disabled, 1979-88; bd. dirs. Eastern Shore Ctr. Ind. Living, 1998—; pres. Trappe Little League Baseball and Softball Assn., 2000—. With USN, 1970-73, with USCGR, 1975-86. Recipient Founder's award Gallaudet U., 1993, Disting. Svc. award Md. Assn. of the Deaf, 1995. Mem. Am. Deafness and Rehab. Assn., Am. Assn. Mental Retardation, Nat. Assn. Deaf, Registry of Interpreters for the Deaf (bd. dirs. Potomac chpt. 1996—), Md. Assn. for Retarded Citizens, Chi Sigma Iota, Psi Chi, Rho Sigma Chi. Roman Catholic. Avocations: woodcarving, backpacking, canoeing, sailing, scuba diving. Home: 29972 Holly Acres Rd Trappe MD 21673-1612 Office: Deaf Ind Living Assn Inc PO Box 4038 Salisbury MD 21803-4038 E-mail: JHLDILA@aol.com.

LEONARD, JUDITH PRICE, educational advisor; b. Milw., July 10, 1941; d. Ralph H. and Sylvia (Shames) Price; m. Richard Black Leonard Jr., Dec. 15, 1962 (dec. Dec. 1978); m. Norman Crasilneck, Aug. 31, 1991. BS in Math., Antioch U., 1963; MS in Math., St. Louis U., 1970. Tchr. math. Ferguson Florissant (Mo.) Schs., 1963-94, coord., 1971-73; mentor, co-dir., faculty advisor Engelmann Math. & Sci. Inst., U. Mo., St. Louis, 1988-96; supr. student tchrs. U. Mo., 1995, 96; coord. Regional Inst. Sci. Edn., 1996-2000; cons., evaluator math. programs St. Louis Pub. Schs., 1994—2002; faculty advisor NSF Young Scholars, U. Mo., St. Louis, 1997, NSF Students & Tchrs. as Rsch. Scientists, U. Mo., St. Louis, 1998—99. Co-dir. Post Dispatch and Monsanto Greater St. Louis Sci. Fair, 1998—99; mem. adv. bd. Post Dispatch and Monsanto Greater St. Louis Sci. Fair, 1997—2002, Intel Internat. Sci. and Edn. Fair, 1996—99, adults in charge, 1997—99, fair dir., 1999; chair Discovery Young Scientist Challenge, St. Louis, 1999—2002; presenter, judge, chmn. judges for computer sci., physics and engring. Jr. Sci., Engring. and Humanities Symposium , 1995—2001; sec. exec. bd. Math Educators Greater St. Louis, 2001—02; mem. Math. Sci. Network of Greater St. Louis (Expanding Your Horizons), 1995—2002. Author: Word Problems, Basic Skills Instructional Fair, 1996; author, editor: (brochure) Teacher Linking Collaborative, 1997. Hon. Engelmann scholar Engelmann Math. and Sci. Inst., St. Louis, 1993, NSF Young Scholar award U. Mo., St. Louis, 1997, NSF STARS award U. Mo., St. Louis, 2000. Mem. NEA, Nat. Coun. Tchrs. Math., Mo. Coun. Tchrs. Math. (life), Math. Educators Greater St. Louis (Math. Edn. award 1994), Ferguson Florissant NEA (life). Avocations: tennis, biking, walking. Home: 22 Bellerive Acres Saint Louis MO 63121-4321 E-mail: judy@judyleonard.net.

LEONARD, KURT JOHN, plant pathologist, retired university program director; b. Holstein, Iowa, Dec. 6, 1939; s. Elvin Elsworth and Irene Marie (Helkenn) L.; m. Maren Jane Simonsen, May 28, 1961; children: Maria Catherine, Mary Alice, Benjamin Andrew. BS, Iowa State U., 1962; PhD, Cornell U., 1968. Plant pathologist Agrl. Rsch. Svc. USDA, Raleigh, N.C., 1968-88, dir. Cereal Disease Lab. U. Minn. St. Paul, 1988—2001. Author: (with others) Annual Review of Phytopathology, 1980; co-editor: Plant Disease Epidemiology, vol. 1, 1986, vol. 2, 1989; editor-in-chief: Phytopathology, 1981-84, Am. Phytopathol. Soc. Press, 1994-97; contbr. numerous articles to profl. jours. Fellow Am. Phytopathol. Soc. (coun. 1981-84, 94-97); mem. Am. Mycol. Soc., Internat. Soc. Plant Pathology (councilor 1982-93), Brit. Soc. Plant Pathology, Phi Kappa Phi, Sigma Xi, Gamma Sigma Delta. Achievements include description of new species and genera of plant pathogenic fungi; research on spread of disease through crop mixtures, on relationships between virulence and fitness in plant pathogenic fungi. Office: U Minn USDA ARS Cereal Disease Lab Saint Paul MN 55108

LEONARD, LINDA FAYE, secondary education educator; b. Crowley, La., Nov. 3, 1948; d. Grady and Beulah (Melancon) Lapearous; m. Russell Lynn Leonard, Dec. 26, 1947; four children. BA, McNeese State U., 1974, MEd, 1975. Tchr. Sam Houston H.S., Lake Charles, La., 1975-76, Welsh (La.) H.S., 1976-77, Washington-Marion H.S., Lake Charles, 1983-95; tchr., speech coach Iowa (La.) H.S., 1995—. Yearbook adviser Iowa (La.) H.S., 1997—. Mem. Nat. Assn. Parliamentarians, Nat. Forensic League, Nat. Coun. Tchrs. English, Nat. Debate Coaches Assn., La. High Sch. Speech League, La. Scholastic Pres Assn., Columbia Scholastic Press Assn., Nat. Scholastic Press Assn., Quill and Scroll. Avocations: drawing, painting, theatre, quilting, camping. Home: 711 Hardy St Iowa LA 70647-3929 Office: Iowa HS 401 W Miller Ave Iowa LA 70647-3922 E-mail: linda.leonard@cpsb.org.

LEONARD, MARKUS DAYLE, systems support specialist; b. Florence, AZ, Apr. 12, 1964; s. Harold Lee and Lynda Mae L.; m. Shauna Morgan, Nov. 7, 1998. BS, Ariz. State U., 1987. Programmer analyst Motorola Semiconductor Products Sector, Phoenix, 1988-90, info. sys. engring. analyst Tempe, 1990-92; sr. engr. computer integrated mfg. SEMATECH, Austin, Tex., 1992-94, Motorola, Tempe, 1994-96; tech. cons. Transarc, Pitts., 1996-98; mgr. Andersen Consulting, Overland Park, Kans., 1998-2000; tech. specialist Sprint PCS, 2000—. Cons. Goldman Sachs, N.Y.C., 1997, Circadence, Boulder, Colo., 2000, SBC Comm., St. Louis, 2000. Contbg. author, editor reports in profl. jours. Campaign fin. mgr. Kathryn Bailey for Ariz. State Legislature, 1996. Mem.: IEEE. Republican. Assembly of God. Avocations: photography, golf. Office: Sprint PCS 6420 Sprint Pky Overland Park KS 66210

LEONARD, MARY EILEEN, retired medical technologist, educator; b. Charleston, S.c., Jan. 9, 1925; d. Edward Andrew and Honora Elizabeth (Price) L. Attended, Barry U., Miami, Fla., 2 yrs.; BS, Coll. of Charleston, 1945; postgrad. in Med. Tech., Med. U. S.C., 1947. Med. technologist Med. U. S.C., Charleston, 1946-79, Roper Hosp., Charleston, 1979—2001; ret., 2001. Chmn. adv. com. Trident Tech. Coll., Charleston, 1992-02. Named Alumnae of Yr., Coll. Charleston, 2001; recipient Highest Achievement award, Am. Soc. Clin. Pathology, 2000. Mem. West Ashley Civitan (bd. dirs. 1998-00). Roman Catholic. Home: 1538 Dunnes Ln Charleston SC 29407-5013

LEONARD, MICHAEL A. automotive executive; b. Cadillac, Mich., Aug. 3, 1937; s. Hugel A. and Mildred (Johnson) L.; m. Frances Erickson, June 18, 1960; children: Kristin, Anne. MA, Alma Coll., 1959; MBA, Wayne State U., 1964; MS, MIT, 1971. Exec. Chrysler Corp., Highland Park, Mich., 1959-75; group v.p. Bendix Corp., Southfield, 1975-83; v.p., group exec. Allied Signal Automotive, Bloomfield Hills, 1983-91; pres. Harman, Inc., Southfield, 1991-94; mng. ptnr. Exec. Resources Inc., Bloomfield Hills, 1994—2002. Bd. dirs. Kalyani Brake Co., Pune, India, Bendix France, Paris, Bendix Italy, and fgn. subs. Trustee Alma (Mich.) Coll.; chmn. Presbyn. Villages of Mich. Sloan fellow, MIT. Mem. Soc. Automotive Engrs., Delta Sigma Phi (pres. 1958-59). Presbyterian. Avocations: swimming, golf, boating. Home: 4375 Barchester Dr Bloomfield Hills MI 48302-2116 Office: Executive Resources Inc PO Box 625 Bloomfield Hills MI 48303-0625

LEONARD, MICHAEL STEVEN, industrial engineering educator; b. Salisbury, N.C., Feb. 2, 1947; s. Charles Thomas and Dorothy Francis (Loflin) L.; m. Mary Elizabeth Stewart, June 21, 1969; children: Dorothy Elizabeth, Amanda Brooke, Gabrielle Francis. B in Engring., U. Fla., 1970, M in Engring., 1972, PhD, 1973. Registered profl. engr., Mo., S.C. Asst. prof. health systems rsch. ctr. Georgia Tech, Atlanta, 1973-75; asst. prof. indsl. engring. U. Mo., Columbia, 1975-79, assoc. prof. indsl. engring., 1979-82, prof. indsl. engring., 1982-90, dept. chmn. indsl. engring., 1985-90; chmn. dept. indsl. engring. Clemson (S.C.) U., 1990-95, 2001—. Bd. dirs. Accreditation Bd. Engring. and Tech., Balt., 1999—. Editor Jour. Soc. for Health Systems, 1989-91; contbr. articles to profl. jours. Evaluation adv. com. Am. Blood Commn., Washington, 1977-80; bd. dirs. Am. Cancer Soc. Boone County Mo. unit, Columbia, 1978-90. Mem. Soc. Health Systems (bd. dirs. 1989-94, pres. elect 1991-92, pres. 1992-93), Inst. Indsl. Engrs. (nat. dir. career guidance 1987-95, v.p. acad. affairs 1997), Mo. Soc. Profl. Engrs. (cen. chpt. treas. 1988-89, v.p. 1989-90). Office: Clemson U Dept Indsl Engring Clemson SC 29634-0001

LEONARD, NELSON JORDAN, chemistry educator; b. Newark, Sept. 1, 1916; s. Harvey Nelson and Olga Pauline (Jordan) L.; m. Louise Cornelie Vermey, May 10, 1947 (dec. 1987); children: Kenneth Jan, Marcia Louise, James Nelson, David Anthony; m. Margaret Taylor Phelps, Nov. 14, 1992. BS in Chemistry, Lehigh U., 1937, Sc.D., 1963; B.Sc., Oxford (Eng.) U., 1940, D.Sc., 1983; PhD, Columbia U., 1942; D. (hon.), Adam Mickiewicz U., Poland, 1980; D.Sc. (hon.), U. Ill., 1988. Fellow and rsch. asst. chemistry U. Ill., Urbana, 1942-43, instr., 1943-44, assoc., 1944-45, 46-47, asst. prof., 1947-49, assoc. prof., 1949-52, prof. organic chemistry, 1952-73, head div. organic chemistry, 1954-63, prof. chemistry and biochemistry, 1973-86, R.C. Fuson prof. chemistry, mem. Ctr. for Advanced Study, 1981-86, R.C. Fuson prof. emeritus, 1986—. Investigator antimalarial program Com. Med. Research, OSRD, 1944-46; sci. cons. and spl. investigator Field Intelligence Agy. Tech., U.S. Army and Dept. Commerce, 1945-46; mem. Can. NRC, summer 1950; Swiss-Am. Found. lectr., 1953, 70; vis. lectr. UCLA, summer 1953; Reilly lectr. U. Notre Dame, 1962; Stieglitz lectr. Chgo. sect. Am. Chem. Soc., 1962; Robert A. Welch Found. lectr., 1964, 83; Disting. vis. lectr. U. Calif.-Davis, 1975; vis. lectr. Polish Acad. Scis., 1976; B.R. Baker Meml. lectr. U. Calif., Santa Barbara, 1976; Ritter Meml. lectr. Miami U., Oxford, Ohio; Werner E. Bachman Meml. lectr. U. Mich., Ann Arbor, 1977; vis. prof. Japan Soc. Promotion of Sci., 1978; Arapahoe lectr. U. Colo., 1979; Tanabe rsch. lectr. Scripps Rsch. Inst., La Jolla, Calif., 1993; mem. program com. in basic scis. Arthur P. Sloan, Jr. Found., 1961-66; Philips lectr. Haverford Coll., 1971; Backer lectr., Groningen, Netherlands, 1972; FMC lectr. Princeton U., 1973; plenary lectr. Laaxer Chemistry Conf., Laax, Switzerland, 1980, 82, 84, 88, 90, 92; Calbiochem-Behring Corp. U. Calif.-San Diego Found. lectr., 1981; Watkins vis. prof. Wichita State U. (Kans.), 1982; Ida Beam Disting. vis.

prof. U. Iowa, 1983; Fogarty scholar-in-residence NIH, Bethesda, Md., 1989-90; Sherman Fairchild Disting. scholar Calif. Inst. Tech., 1991; Syntex. disting. lectr. U. Colo., 1992; faculty assoc. Calif. Inst. Tech., 1992—; mem. adv. com. Searle Scholars program Chgo. Community Trust, 1982-85; ednl. adv. bd. Guggenheim Found., 1969-88, mem. com. of selection, 1977-88. Editor: Organic Syntheses, 1951-58, mem. adv. bd., 1959—, bd. dirs., 1969—, v.p., 1976-80, pres., 1980-88; editorial bd. Jour. Organic Chemistry, 1957-61, Jour. Am. Chem. Soc., 1960-72; adv. bd. Biochemistry, 1973-78, Chemistry International, 1984-91, Pure and Applied Chemistry, 1984-91; contbr. articles to profl. jours. Recipient medal Synthetic Organic Chem. Mfrs., 1970, Wheland award U. Chgo., 1991, creativity award U. Oreg., 1994, Arthur C. Cope Scholar award Am. Chem Soc., 1995; named to Mt. Vernon (N.Y.) H.S. Hall of Fame, 1985; fellow Rockefeller Found., 1950, Guggenheim fellow, 1959, 67. Fellow Am. Acad. Arts and Scis. (v.p. 1991-93); mem. NAS, AAAS, Polish Acad. Scis. (fgn.), Ill. Acad. Sci. (hon.), Am. Chem. Soc. (award for creative work in synthetic organic chemistry 1963, Edgar Fahs Smith award and lectureship Phila. sect. 1975, Centennial lectr. 1976, Roger Adams award 1981, Paul G. Gassman Disting. Svc. award divsn. organic chemistry 1994, A.C. Cope rsch. scholar award 1995), Am. Soc. for Biochemistry and Molecular Biology, Chem. Soc. London, New Swiss Chem. Soc., Internat. Union Pure and Applied Chemistry (sec. organic chemistry divsn. 1989, v.p. 1989-91, pres. 1991-93), Pharm. Soc. Japan (hon.), Am. Philos. Soc., Phi Beta Kappa, Phi Lambda Upsilon (hon.), Tau Beta Pi, Alpha Chi Sigma. Achievements include patents on synthesis of sparteine; esters of pyridine dicarboxylic acid as insect repellents; fluorescent derivatives of adenine- and cytosine-containing compounds. Home: 389 California Ter Pasadena CA 91105-2463

LEONARD, PATRICIA LOUISE, education educator, consultant; b. Wales Township, Mich., Aug. 26, 1940; d. Leo James and Laurelda Rose (Lashbrook) L. BS, Ea. Mich. U., 1963; MA, Ctrl. Mich. U., 1969; Ednl. Specialist, Mich. State U., 1978; PhD, U. Tenn., 1982. Cert. tchr., Mich.; cert. coop. edn. coord. Tchr. Millington (Mich.) Cmty. H. S., 1963-68, Bullock Creek Schs., Midland, Mich., 1968-69; asst. prof. Ctrl. Mich. U., Mt. Pleasant, 1969-80, 82-83; grad. tchg., rsch. asst. U. Tenn., Knoxville, 1980-82; assoc. prof. Rider U., Lawrenceville, N.J., 1983—. Mem. vocat. adv. coun. Mercer County Spl. Svcs. Sch. Dist., Trenton, N.J., 1992—; cons. in edn. and bus., 1982—. Contbr. articles to profl. jours. Mem. Nat. Bus. Edn. Assn., Am. Vocat. Assn., N.J. Bus. Edn. Assn. (bd. dirs. 1992-99, observer, editor 1994-96), Ea. Bus. Edn. Assn. (gen. co-chair 1988-89), Pi Omega Pi (nat. coun. 1991-95, 97—), Delta Pi Epsilon, Phi Kappa Phi, Phi Delta Kappa, Omicron Tau Theta. Avocations: swimming, reading, needlework, drawing. Home: RR 3 Box 3346 Browns Mills NJ 08015-9803 Office: Rider U 2083 Lawrenceville Rd Lawrenceville NJ 08648-3099

LEONARD, PAUL HARALSON, retired lawyer; b. Houston, Mar. 4, 1925; s. Paul Haralson and Dovie Lore (Shuler) L.; m. Barbara Ann Underwood, Nov. 26, 1948; children: Leslie Ann, Scott Paul. BA, Rice U., 1948; JD, South Tex. Coll. of Law, 1957. Bar: Tex. 1957, U.S. Patent and Trademark Office 1960, U.S. Ct. Appeals (10th cir.) 1963, U.S. Ct. Mil. Appeals 1965, U.S. Supreme Ct. 1965, U.S. Ct. Appeals (5th cir.) 1981, U.S. Ct. Appeals (Fed. cir.) 1982. Acct. Highland Oil Co., Houston, 1948-50; statis. acct. Union Oil and Gas Corp. of La., 1953-59; assoc. Hayden & Pravel, 1959-61; patent atty. Halliburton Co., Duncan, Okla., 1961-69; div. patent atty. Ethyl Corp., Baton Rouge, 1969-87; v.p. Cen. Foods, Inc., 1979-90, bd. dirs. V.p. Plato Dependent Sch. Dist., Duncan, Okla., 1966-67, pres., 1968. Served to lt. comdr., USNR, 1942-67. Me. Tex. Bar Assn, Masons. Republican. Avocations: U.S. coins, stamp collecting. Home and Office: 10639 Rondo Ave Baton Rouge LA 70815-4847

LEONARD, R. MICHAEL, lawyer; b. Atlanta, Feb. 27, 1953; s. Charles C. and Catherine (Martin) L.; m. Margaret Ellen Mead, June 29, 1985 (div. 1993); 1 child, Sarah Marie; m. Michelle Merritt, May 27, 2001. AB, U. N.C., 1975, JD with honors, 1978. Bar: Ala. 1978, N.C. 1987. Assoc. Cabaniss, Johnston, Gardner, Dumas & O'Neal, Birmingham, Ala., 1978-85, ptnr., 1985-86; assoc. Womble Carlyle Sandridge & Rice, Winston-Salem, N.C., 1986-88, ptnr., 1988—. Author: Trail and Naturalist's Guide to Oak Mountain State Park, Alabama, 1982. Bd. dirs. Ala. Conservancy, Birmingham, 1981-85, Ruffner Mountain Nature Ctr., Birmingham, 1982-86, pres. 1985-86, Nature Sci. Ctr., Winston-Salem, N.C., 1987-91, Piedmont Land Conservancy, Greensboro, N.C., 1989-91; bd. dirs. Ala. Trails Assn., Birmingham, 1985—, founder, pres., 1985-87; trustee N.C. Nat. Heritage Found., Raleigh, 1989-92; gov.'s appointee bd. trustees N.C. Natural Heritage Trust Fund, 1994—, Ala. scenic Byways Program Adv. Coun., 2000—; nat. adv. coun. Trust for Pub. Land, San Francisco, 1991—; mem. adv. coun. N.C. Yr. of the Mtns., 1995-96; mem. Nat. Coun. Conservation Fund, Arlington, Va., 1997—; pres. Bethania (N.C.) Hist. Property Owners Assn., Inc., 1996—; founding chmn. Ga. Pinhoti Trail Assn., Rome, 1996—; bd. dirs. Bethania Historical Assn., 1996—, Coalition for the Blue Ridge Pkwy, Asheville, N.C., 1997—, Bethabara Hist. Park, Winston-Salem, 2001—; adv. coun. Blue Ridge Pkwy. Found., Winston-Salem, 1998—, High Country Conservancy, Boone, N.C., 1999—; bd. visitors Warren Wilson Coll., Black Mtn., N.C., 1999—, U. N.C., Chapel Hill, 1999—. Recipient Chevron Conservation award, San Francisco, 1998, Leon E. Rice Cmty. Svc. award, Winston-Salem, 1998, E-Town E-chievement award, Boulder, Colo., 1997, Pres.'s Conservationist of Yr. award Conservation Fund, Arlington, 1996, Oak Leaf award Nature Conservancy, Washington, 1991, Sol Feinstone Environ. award Coll. Environ. Sci. & Forestry, SUNY, Rochester, 1991, Chpt. Svc. award N.C. Chpt. Sierra Club, 1990, Malcolm Stewart Conservationist of Yr. award Ala. Conservancy, Birmingham, 1983, N.C. Wildlife Fedn. Environ. Essay award, 1970. Mem. Ala. Bar Assn., N.C. Bar Assn., Birmingham Bar Assn., Forsyth County Bar Assn., Winston-Salem Rotary Club, Carolina Club, Black Bear Club, Order of Coif, Phi Beta Kappa, Phi Eta Sigma. Democrat. Avocations: writing, hiking, mountain climbing, camping, turkey hunting. Office: Womble Carlyle Sandridge & Rice 200 W 2nd St Winston Salem NC 27101-4019

LEONARD, RICHARD HART, journalist, educator; b. N.Y.C., May 23, 1921; s. Richard Barstow and Stella Burnham (Hart) L.; m. Barbara Klausner, July 11, 1948; children: Laurie, Lisa. BA, U. Wis., 1947. Reporter Milw. Jour., 1947, picture editor, 1948, with Madison (Wis.) bur., 1949-50, state desk, 1951-52, state editor, 1953-62, mng. editor, 1962-66; editor, v.p. Milw. Jour. Co., 1967-85; ret., 1986; editor-in-residence East-West Ctr., Honolulu, 1987. Sr. fellow East-West Ctr., 1988-89; mem. Pulitzer Prize Bd., 1976-86; Nieman prof. journalism Marquette U., 1989-99, emeritus, 1999—. With AUS, 1942-46. Recipient Carr Van Anda award Ohio U., 1972, East-West Ctr. Disting. Svc. award, Disting. Svc. award U. Wis. Mem. Am. Soc. Newspaper Editors, Internat. Press Inst. (chmn. 1984-86), Milw. Press Club (pres. 1965, elected Hall of Fame), Sigma Delta Chi (nat. pres. 1976), Phi Kappa Phi. Presbyterian. Home: 330 E Beaumont Ave Milwaukee WI 53217-4867

LEONARD, ROBERT DOUGHERTY, communications company executive; b. Chgo., Apr. 15, 1942; s. Robert D. and Ruth Janet (Tankersley) L.; m. Janet Catherine Link, May 10, 1969; children: James Richard, John Banks, Anne Catherine. BS in Gen. Engring., U. Ill., 1964, BS in Communications, 1965. Engr. Teletype Corp., Skokie, Ill., 1965-68, tech. pubs. engr., 1968-72, planning engr., 1972-77; engring. staff mgr. AT&T Network Svcs., Basking Ridge, N.J., 1977-80; staff mgr. AT&T Bus. Svcs., 1980-82; dep. chief AT&T Teletype Corp., Skokie, 1982-85; dist. mgr. printers AT&T Computer Systems, 1985-87; regional mgr. gateways Mitek Systems Corp., Northfield, Ill., 1987-88; product mgr. broadcast transmission line products Andrew Corp., Orland Park, 1988—. Contbr. to profl. publs. Mem. Am. Mktg. Assn. (exec.), Numismatic Lit. Guild (life), Am. Numismatic Assn., Am. Numismatic Soc., Am. Israel Numismatic Assn., Token and Medal Soc. (treas. 1993—). Republican. Methodist. Avocations: numismatic research, writing, speaking. Home: 1065 Spruce St Winnetka IL 60093-2169 Office: Andrew Corp 10500 153rd St Orland Park IL 60462-3071

LEONARD, SAMUEL WALLACE, oil company and bank executive; b. Cumberland, R.I., Sept. 29, 1922; s. Samuel James and Hazel Della (Flagg) L.; m. Dorothy Wilma Carpenter, Oct. 15, 1949. BS in Acctg. and Fin., Bryant Coll., 1941; BA in Econs., Brown U., 1948; AMP, Harvard Bus. Sch., Soldiers Field, Mass., 1968. Internal auditor Conoco Inc., Ponca City, Okla., 1948-51, asst. dir. employee benefits Houston, 1952-54; pres., gen. mgr. Sahara Petroleum Co., Alexandria, Egypt, 1954-60; v.p., treas. Pasa Petroquimica Argentina, Buenos Aires, 1961-66; pres. Conoco Libya, Tripoli, 1966-71, Conoco Española, Madrid, Spain, 1971-72; exec. asst. pres. Conoco Inc., Stamford, Conn., 1972-76; v.p., gen. mgr. Dubai (United Arab Emirates) Petroleum, 1976-82; ret.; chmn. bd. dirs. Security Bank & Trust Co. (merger 4th Fin. Corp. 1993), Ponca city, 1992-93. Bd. dirs. Bank IV Okla., Ponca City. Chmn. Little League, Tripoli, Libya, 1966-71; bd. dirs. Ponca City Libr., 1988-94. Staff sgt. U.S. Army, 1942-45, U.S. and Europe. Decorated Purple Heart, Bronze Star Valor. Mem. VFW, Am. Legion, Ponca City Country Club (bd. dirs., treas. 1995-98), Elks. Republican. Episcopal. Avocations: hunting, fishing, travel, gardening. Home and Office: PO Box 667 Ponca City OK 74602-0667

LEONARD, STEVEN K. orchestra director, educator; b. Pitts., May 12, 1959; s. Stanley S. and Margaret H. Leonard; m. Kathleen A. Whelan, Oct. 28, 1952; children: Keith Patrick. BMus with distinction, Eastman Sch. of Music, 1981; MA in Music Edn., Truman State U., 1985. Cert. masters level music educator, Ga. Strings tchr. Ala. Symphony Strings Acad., Birmingham, 1982—94; orch. dir., elem. strings tchr. DeKalb County Sch. Sys., Atlanta, 1998—, strings coach youth orch., 1998—, dept. chmn. elem. orch., 2000—01. Asst. concertmaster Ala. Symphony Orch., Birmingham, 1982—94; violin performer, instr. Symphony Sch. Am., LaCrosse, Wis., 1984—85, U. Ala., Birhamington, 1986—91, Birhamington So. Coll., 1986—91; instr. applied music and music end. Truman State U., Kirksville, Mo., 1984—85; violin instr. Huntingdon Coll., Montgomery, Ala., 1986—93; string orch. dir., chamber ensemble dir. Met. Youth Symphony Orch. Atlanta, 2001—. Musician: Georgia Sinfonia, Atlanta Symphony Orch., Colo. Philharmonic, Augusta Symphony Orch., 2000. Vol. DeKalb County Cmty. Svc. Bd., Cobb County Cmty. Svc. Bd., Atlanta, 1995—98, Meals on Wheels, Birmingham, 1986—89; vol, piano tchr. VA Hosp., 1982—84; vol. South Highlands Hosp., 1982—83; musician, vol. Corpus Christi Cath. Ch., Atlanta, 1999; dir. of bell choir St. Paul's Cath. Ch., Birmingham, 1983—88. Mem.: Autism Soc. Am., Music Tchrs. Nat. Assn. (fedn. judge 1998—99), PA of Ga. Educators, Am. Fedn. Musicians, Am. String Teacher's Assn. (grantee 2002), Music Educators Nat. Conf. (chmn. HS orch. festival 1999—2001, chmn. elementary orch. workshop 1999—2001). Roman Catholic. Avocation: collector of flow blue pottery and hummel figurines, advocate for special needs children. Office: MYSO of Atlanta PO Box 680033 Marietta GA 30068-0001 E-mail: spectacularstrings@yahoo.com.

LEONARD, THOMAS, lawyer; b. Phila., Sept. 5, 1946; s. Thomas Aloysius and Mary Teresa (Kelly) L.; m. Kathleen Mary Duffy; children: Sarah, Mary Kate, Tom. BS, Drexel U., 1968; JD, Temple U., 1971. Bar: Pa., U.S. Supreme Ct., U.S. Ct. Appeals (3d cir.), U.S. Dist. Ct. (ea., mid., we. dists.) Pa., U.S. Dist. Ct. (so. dist.) N.J., U.S. Dist. Ct. Utah, U.S. Dist. Ct. (so. dist.) N.Y. Assoc. Dilworth, Paxson, Kalish & Kauffman, Phila., 1972-76, ptnr., 1976—79, 1983—91, sr. ptnr., mem. exec. com., 1979—83; controller City of Phila., 1991—; chmn. litigation dept., sr. ptnr., permanent mem. mgmt. com. Obermayer, Rebmann, Maxwell and Hippel, Phila., 1991—. Bd. dirs. Fed. Nat. Mortgage Assn., Independence Blue Cross, World Affair Coun. Phila., Cora Social Svcs., Pa. Bus. Bank, U.S. Facilities; vice chmn. Phila. Gas Commn., 1979-83; register of wills City of Phila., 1976-79; mem. disciplinary bd. Supreme Ct., Pa., 1991-95, vice chmn., 1995-96, chmn., 1996—; chmn. Delaware Valley Real Estate Investment Fund, 1999—; chmn. Permalith Plastics. Mem. editorial bd. Amran's Pa. Practice, 1972; contbr. articles to profl. publs. Mem. Dem. Nat. Com., Washington, 1976-83, mem. fin. com., 1988, vice chair fin., 1993—, Pa. fin. chair, 1993—, bd. dirs.; del. Dem. Nat. Conv., 1976, 80, 92, 96; chmn. Pa. fin. com. Clinton for Pres., 1992, 96; co-chair Rendell for Mayor, 1991, 95; mem. coun. Phila. Orch., 1981-86; bd. dirs. Acad. Scis., Phila., 1981-85; pres. Pa. chpt. Irish Am. Partnership. Capt. U.S. Army, 1971-77. Recipient Man of Yr. award Emerald Soc., 1979, Korean-Am. Friendship Soc., 1982, Carmel Humanitarian award Haifa U., 1981, Merit award Chapel of Four Chaplains, 1983. Mem. ABA, Pa. Bar Assn., Phila. Bar Assn. (bd. govs. 1979-82), Union League, Phila. Racquet Club, Serra Club (past pres.). Roman Catholic. Office: Obermayer Rebmann Maxwell and Hippel 1617 John F Kennedy Blvd Fl 19 Philadelphia PA 19103-1821 E-mail: thomas.leonard@obermayer.com.

LEONARD, THOMAS, dean, educator, librarian; BA (hon.), Univ. Mich., 1966; PhD, Univ. Calif., 1973. Librarian Univ. Calif., Berkeley. Speaker and cons. in field. Author: Above the Battle: War-Making in America from Appomattox to Versailles, 1978, The Power of the Press: The Birth of American Political Reporting, 1986, News for All: America's Coming of Age with the Press, 1995; contbr. numerous articles to profl. jours. Office: U Calif Berkeley Libr 245 Doe Library MC 6000 Berkeley CA 94720-6000

LEONARD, THOMAS MICHAEL, university program director, educator; b. Elizabeth, N.J., Nov. 8, 1937; s. Edward Carroll and Amelia Teckla (Chap) L.; m. Yvonne Ann-Marie Clements, Aug. 13, 1960; children: Thomas Jr., Robert, Randall, Edward, David, Stacy. BS, Mt. St. Mary's Coll., Emmitsburg, Md., 1959; MA, Georgetown U., 1963; PhD, The Am. U., Washington, 1968. Sales exec. Weston Instruments, Newark, 1959-60; tchr. social studies Balt. County Bd. Edn., Towson, Md., 1960-62; instr. to assoc. prof. history St. Joseph Coll., Emmitsburg, 1962-73; assoc. prof. to prof., dir. internat. studies U. North Fla., Jacksonville, 1973—. Bd. dirs. N.E. Fla. Export Trading Co.; vis. prof. Inst. Advanced Studies, Guadalajara, Mex., 1978, Mt. St. Mary's Coll., Emmitsburg, 1979-84, U. San Diego, Guadalajara, 1992, U. Warsaw, Poland, 2002; Fulbright lectr. Inst. Juan XXIII, Bahía Blanca, Argentina, 1984; adj. instr. U. Fla., 1980—; cons. U.S. Dept. Edn., 1996-97. Author: Day By Day: The Forties, 1977, United States and Central America, 1944-49: Perceptions of Political Dynamics, 1984, Central America and United States Policies: Guide to Issues and Sources, 1985; author: (with others) Day By Day: The Seventies, 1988; author: Central America and the United States: The Search for Stability, 1991, Panama and the United States: Guide to Issues and Sources, 1993, Guide to Archival Material in the United States on Central America, 1994, The United States and Latin America, 1850-1903: Establishing a Relationship, 1998; : Castro and the Cuban Revolution, 1999, James K. Polk: Clear and Unquestionable Destiny , 2001; contbr. chapters to books, articles to profl. jours. Grantee Franklin D. Roosevel Presdl. Libr., 1991, U. North Fla., 1993, Andrew W. Mellon Found., 1994, U.S. Dept. Edn., 1998—2000, John F. Kennedy Libr., 2000, Lyndon Baines Johnson Found., 2001. Avocations: travel, reading, sports. Home: 1104 Pond View Ct Jacksonville FL 32259-2950 Office: U North Fla St John's Bluff Rd Jacksonville FL 32224 E-mail: tleonard@unf.edu.

LEONARD, TIMOTHY DWIGHT, judge; b. Beaver, Okla., Jan. 22, 1940; s. Dwight and Mary Evelyn Leonard; m. Nancy Louise Laughlin, July 15, 1967; children: Kirstin Dione, Ryan Timothy, Tyler Dwight. BA, U. Okla., 1962, JD, 1965; student, Mil. Naval Justice Sch., 1966. Bar: Okla. 1965, U.S. Dist. Ct. (no. and we. dists.) Okla. 1969, U.S. Ct. Appeals (10th cir.) 1969, U.S. Supreme Ct. 1970. Asst. atty. gen. State of Okla., 1968-70; mem. Okla. Senate, 1979-88; ptnr. Blankenship, Herrold, Russell et al, Oklahoma City, 1970-71, Trippet, Leonard & Kee, Beaver, 1971-88; of counsel Huckaby, Fleming et al, Oklahoma City, 1988-89; U.S. atty. Western Dist. Okla., 1988-92; judge U.S. Dist. Ct. (we. dist.) Okla., 1992—. Guest lectr. Oklahoma City U., 1988—89; mem. U.S. Atty. Gen.'s Adv. Com., 1990—92, chmn. office mgmt. and budget subcom., 1990—92, mem. jud. conf. com. on fin. dosclosure, 1998—2001, 2001—, jud. coun. of 10th cir., 1999—2001, 10th cir. adv. coun., 2002—. Co-author: 4 Days, 40 Hours, 1970. Rep. Party candidate for lt. gov. of Okla.; minority leader Okla. State Senate, 1985-86; White House mil. aide, Washington, 1966-67; ex officio mem. Okla. State Fair Bd., Oklahoma City, 1987-90; mem. Gov.'s Coun. on Sports and Phys. Edn., Oklahoma City, 1987-89; mem. Donna Nigh Found., Edmond, Okla., 1987-9. Lt. USN, 1965-68. Named Outstanding Legislator, Okla. Sch. Bd. Assn., 1988. Fellow ABA; mem. Okla. Bar Assn., Okla. County Bar, Phi Alpha Delta, Beta Theta Pi. Republican. Presbyterian. Avocations: basketball, running, reading. Office: US Courthouse 200 NW 4th St Ste 5012 Oklahoma City OK 73102-3031

LEONARD, WALTER RAYMOND, retired biology educator; b. Scott County, Va., July 5, 1923; s. Homer Stanley and Minnie Eunice (Neal) L.; m. Alice Ann McCaskill, Sept. 1, 1951; children— Leslie Ann, Walter Raymond. BA, Tusculum Coll., Greeneville, Tenn., 1946; MA, Vanderbilt U., 1947, PhD, 1949. Mem. faculty Wofford Coll., Spartanburg, S.C., 1949-93, John M. Reeves prof. biology, 1954-87, William R. Kenan Jr. prof. biology, 1987-93, William R. Kenan Jr. prof. emeritus, 1993—. Instl. rev. bd. mem. Spartanburg Regional Med. Ctr., 1994-98; faculty athletic rep. NCAA. Served with USAAF, 1942-43. Named to Sports Hall of Fame, Tusculum Coll., 1983; Walter Raymond Leonard scholarship created Wofford Coll., 1973; W. Ray Leonard award established Beta Beta Beta, 1993; W. Ray Leonard Retirement Fund established Former Students Wofford Coll., 1993, disting. citizen award Wofford Coll. Nat. Alumni Assn., 1999. Mem. AAAS, S.C. Acad. Sci., Scabbard and Blade (hon.), Lamda Chi Alpha (named to Hall of Fame 1996), Letterman's Club (hon.). Methodist. Achievements include rsch. on cell metabolism. Home: 110 Pinetree Cir Spartanburg SC 29307-2938 Office: Wofford Coll N Church St Spartanburg SC 29301 E-mail: wrleonard11@msn.com.

LEONARD, WILLIAM NORRIS, economist, educator; b. Pitts., Dec. 13, 1912; s. Burt Hayes and Mabel Etta (Norris) L.; m. Elizabeth Flora Waugh, Aug. 24, 1939; children: Virginia Leonard Ewing, John Waugh. AB, U. Va., 1936; MA, U. Tex., 1938; PhD (fellow), Columbia U., 1945. Oil field worker Devonian Oil Co., Tulsa, 1930-32; instr., later asst. prof. econ. U. Conn., 1939-42; indsl. analyst, transp. officer WPB, 1942-45; asst. coordinator planning Trans-World Airlines, Kansas City, Mo., 1945-46; asso. prof., chmn. dept. econ. Rutgers U., 1946-49; prof. econ., head dept. econ. and commerce Pa. State Coll., 1949-53; chmn. dept. econ. and div. social sci. Hofstra U., Hempstead, N.Y., 1953-59, asst. pres., 1965-66; Fulbright prof. Haiti, 1974; prof., chmn. dept. econs. H. Lehman Coll., CCNY, 1974-78; Disting. lectr. econs. U. South Fla., Tampa, 1978-79; vis. prof. U. Tampa, 1980—. Cons. FTC, 1968, Senate Antitrust and Monopoly Subcom., 1969-74; pres. Fed. R.R. Progress, 1953-56 Author: Business Size, Market Power and Public Policy, 1969; also articles. Planning commr. Nassau County, 1962, chmn., 1963-65; mem. Hillsborough Area Regional Transit, 1979-90; bd. dirs. So. Scholarship Found., 1990—. Mem. AAUP, Am. Econ. Assn., N.Y. State Econ. Assn. (pres. 1972-73), Eastern Econ. Assn. (pres. 1984-85), Raven Soc., Phi Beta Kappa. Home: 713 Mccallister Ave Sun City Center FL 33573-7019

LEONARDOS, GREGORY, chemist, odor consultant, educator; b. Cambridge, Mass., Dec. 30, 1935; s. Nicholas C. and Evangeline (Niarchos) L.; m. Virginia Shinopoulos, May 23, 1965; children: Nicholas, Charles. AB in Biochem. Sci., Harvard U., 1957; MS in Chemistry, Northeastern U., 1964, MBA, 1969. Rsch. assoc. Protein Found., Boston, 1960-63; sr. project leader Arthur D. Little Inc., Cambridge, Mass., 1963-80; prin. G. Leonardos Cons., Arlington, 1980—. Vis. lectr. U. Mass., Dartmouth, 1992-94; adj. asst. prof. Bentley Coll., 1994—. Contbr. articles to profl. jours. Mem. Am. Chem. Soc., Air and Waste Mgmt. Assn. (chmn. TT-4 com. 1975-78). Greek Orthodox. Avocations: coaching youth soccer, golf. Home and Office: 43 Ronald Rd Arlington MA 02474-1421 E-mail: gleonardos@bentley.edu.

LEONE, FRANK HARRISON, health care educator, consultant; b. Bklyn., Sept. 5, 1944; s. Frank Anthony and Dorothy Alice (Harrison) L.; m. Diane Marcy Mainini, July 5, 1980; 1 child, Ryan Harrison. BA, Vanderbilt U., 1966; MBA, Babson Coll., 1972; MPH, UCLA, 1981. Systems analyst Amicon Corp., Lexington, Mass., 1969-72; survey specialist Rsch. Triangle Inst., Research Triangle Park, N.C., 1972-75; social scientist Rand Corp., Santa Monica, Calif., 1975-82; exec. dir. New Eng. Life Flight-U. Mass. Med. Ctr., Worcester, 1982-87; pres. Ryan Assocs., Santa Barbara, Calif., 1985—. Contbr. articles to various jours. Dir. polling, Sen. Frank Church presdl. campaign, Washington, 1976; vol. VISTA, Pitts., 1966-67. Mem. Am. Pub. Health Assn., Nat. Assn. Occupational Health Profls. (exec. dir. 1990—), Physicians for Social Responsibility (pres. Cen. Mass. chpt. 1985-87). Democrat. Roman Catholic. Avocations: running, golf, movies, travel, tennis. Home: 1726 Lasuen Rd Santa Barbara CA 93103-1820 Office: Ryan Assocs 1525 State St Santa Barbara CA 93101-2500 E-mail: fleone@naohp.com.

LEONE, GEORGE FRANK, pharmaceutical executive; b. Astoria, N.Y., Aug. 1, 1926; s. George and Fannie K. (Teano) L.); m. Mary Louise Potts, Dec. 14, 1945; children: Pamela Ann, George Frank. BS, Wesleyan U., 1949; postgrad., NYU, 1951; grad. Advanced Mgmt. Program, Harvard Bus. Sch., 1959; postgrad., U. Tex., 1977; DSc (hon.), Tex. Wesleyan U., 1990. Chemist, Lederle Labs., Pearl River, N.Y., 1949-50; with Alcon Labs., Inc., Ft. Worth, 1950-91, med. sales rep., 1950-54, dist. sales mgr., 1954-58, regional sales mgr., 1958-63, nat. sales mgr., 1963-66, dir. mktg., 1966-69, gen. mgr. domestic, 1969-70, v.p. sci., tech., 1971-81, sr. v.p., 1981-91, also dir.; Pres. Laksmi Corp., Fort Worth, 1989-97. Pres. Avicon, Inc., 1972-79; exec. com. trustee Alcon Rsch. Inst., 1980-98; trustee C.V. Whitney Lab., U. Fla., St. Augustine, 1996-2002; mem. bd. govs. Harris Methodist Health Found., 1997—; trustee & COO George F. & Mary L. Leone Found., Ft. Worth, Tex., 1979—. Pres., commr. Earth County Water Control and Improvement, Dist. 1, 1976-80; trustee Tex. Wesleyan U., fin. com., exec. com., 1985-91, audit and fin. com., 1993-2002; bd. dirs. Tex. Christian U. Rsch. Found., 1976-82; chmn. athletic com. Dan Danciger Jewish Community Ctr.; pres. Peninsula Pecan Growers Assn., 1980-85; mem. fin. com. Fort Worth Acad., 1984-88, bd. dirs., 1986-88. With USN, 1944-46. Named Disting. Alumnus, Tex. Wesleyan U., 1979. Mem. Yoga Soc. N.Y. (pres. 1978-94, bd. dirs. 1978—), Am. Radio Relay League, Alpha Chi. Clubs: Fort Worth. Home: 4100 Hildring Dr E Fort Worth TX 76109-4714 also: 321 Monika Pl Saint Augustine FL 32080-6441

LEONE, JEANNE, marketing, advertising, and public relations consultant, artist; b. Revere, Mass., June 8, 1946; d. Gerard Leone and Jeanne Irene DeSimone. BA Polit. Sci. with highest honors, Adelphi U., 1968. Lic. real estate broker, Mass. Dir. advt., mktg., publ. rels. Keydata Corp., Watertown, MA, 1970-74; founding and managing editor The Jour. Technol. Horizons in Edn., Acton, 1974-76; pres. M & M Constrn., Chestnut Hill, 1978-82; cons. F.L. Putnam Brokerage Hse., Boston, 1981; dir. advtg., mktg., publ. rels. Gould Computer Sys., Plantation, FL, 1983; cons. Northern Telecom, Toronto, Canada, 1984-85; closing and title officer Malibu Escrow Corp., Malibu, CA, 1986-87; cons. Wespac Investors Trusts, Santa Monica, 1988-90, The Marquardt Co., Van Nuys, 1990-95, Philip R. Gustlin, Esq., 1994-95, Technol. Renaissance Corp., Atlanta, 1996, Microtrends, Inc., Pasadena, CA, 1996-97, Bklyn., 1999—. Founder Greenpoint Riverfront Artists, 1999. One-woman shows include Univ. Pl. Gallery, Harvard U., Cambridge, Mass., 1991, Wilshire Landmark Bldg,. L.A., 1993-94, Margaret Crow Gallery, Pasadena, Calif., 1995-96; commn. to create art book on the Earl Gales Jr. Collection of West African Art, Art on the Loose, 1998. Bd. dirs. Cmty. Champions, San Francisco. Mem. MENSA. Fax: 718-383-9658. E-mail: leonejean@aol.com.

LEONE, JUDITH GIBSON, educational media specialist, video production company executive; b. Toms River, N.J., Sept. 27, 1945; d. James Delaney and Louise Gertrude (Eberhardt) Gibson; m. Stephan Robert Leone, Nov. 27, 1971; stepchildren: Cheryl, Debra. BA, Kean Coll., 1970; MLS, Rutgers U., 1980. Cert. edn. media specialist. Tchr. Toms River Schs., 1970-84, media specialist, 1984-89; v.p., owner Prodn. House, Toms River, 1985-94; libr. coord. Amb. Christian Acad., 1989-95; exec. dir. Designer Showcase, 1995-96. Mem. region 5 book evaluation com. N.J. State Libr. System, 1986-90. Sec., bd. dirs. The Shelter, Inc., Bricktown, N.J., 1979—; past pres. Open Arms, Inc.; past pres., bd. dirs. Harbor House; v.p., bd. dirs. Ocean County chpt. United Way, 1992-2000; pres. Garden State Philharm.; bd. dirs., past pres. Italian-Am. Cultural and Heritage Soc.; candidate N.J. State Senate, 1997; co-founder Dem. POWER, 1999; mem. WWFM Adv. Commn., 1999—; mem. Ocean County Dem. Fin. Com., 2001—. Honoree for cmty. svc. Italian Am. Cultural Soc., 1995; named Vol. of Yr., United Way of Ocean County, 1996, Humanitarian of Yr., Nat. Conf. Christians Jews, 1998. Mem.: Toms River Country Club. Democrat. Avocations: sailing, skiing, handbell choir, golf. Home: 143 Cranmoor Dr Toms River NJ 08753-6805

LEONE, ROSE MARIE, psychotherapist; b. N.Y.C., June 3, 1930; d. Pietro and Maria (Marinelli) L. BA in Religious Edn., Philathea Coll., London, Ont., Can., 1967; MA in Rehab. Counseling, NYU, 1973; MSW, Hunter Coll., 1976. Counselor Lincoln Hosp. Dept. Psychology, Bronx, 1970-74; sr. counselor, dir. N.Y. Med. Coll., N.Y.C., 1974-77; project dir. Addiction Svcs., 1977-78; dir. women's program Project Return Found., 1978-80; project dir. N.Y. State Office of Alchohol and Substance Abuse Svcs., 1980-81; asst. administr. Misericordia Hosp. MMTP, Bronx, N.Y., 1983-84; sr. drug rehab. counselor N.Y. State DSAS, 1981-83, clin. supr. criminal justice unit, 1984-92, tech. assistance specialist, 1992-97; clin. dir. Reality House, Inc., N.Y.C., 1997-98; asst. dir. Roosevelt Hos. Substance Abuse Program, 1998—. Trainer, public spkr. N.Y. State Office of Alcoholism and Substance Abuse Series, N.Y.C., 1980-97; adj. prof. Lehman Coll., Bronx, 1997; evening group facilitator

United Bronx Parents, 1997—; part-time pvt. practice, N.Y.C., 1974—. Contbr. articles to profl. jours. Fellow N.Y. State Clin. Social Work Psychotherapists, Inc.; mem. NASW. Avocation: public speaking. Home and Office: 249 W 101st St New York NY 10025-4991

LEONE, STEPHAN ROBERT, lawyer; b. Patterson, N.J., Aug. 24, 1939; s. Esterino Brando and Hilda (DeRose) L.; m. Diane Buzzard, June 1959 (div. June 1969); children: Cheryl Alice, Debra Grace; m. Judith Gibson, Nov. 27, 1971. BA, Columbia U., 1961; JD, Yeshiva U., 1988. Bar: N.J. 1989, U.S. Dist. Ct. N.J. 1989, N.Y. 1989, U.S. Dist. Ct. (so. dist.) N.Y. 1989, D.C. 1989. Ptnr. Bathgate, Wegener, Dugan & Wolf, Newark and Lakewood, N.J., 1988-97; mng. mem. Carluccio, Leone, Dimon, Doyle & Sacks, LLC, Toms River, 1997—. Mem. Ocean County Dem. Fin. Com., 1991—, chmn.; trustee Ocean County Coll. Found., 1973—; trustee Nature Conservancy of NJ, 2002-; chmn. Ocean City Dem. Fin. Com. Recipient Disting. Svc. award Brick Jaycees, 1962; named Man of Yr. Brick Twp. C. of C. 1976, Humanitarian of Yr., Italian Am. Cultural Soc., 1999. Mem. N.J. Bar Assn., Ocean County Bar Assn., Toms River Country Club. Avocations: skiing, sailing, tennis. Office: Carluccio Leone Dimon Doyle & Sacks LLC 9 Robbins St Toms River NJ 08753-7628 E-mail: sleone1054@aol.com.

LEONE, STEPHEN JOSEPH, English language educator, computer technology consultant; b. Nyack, N.Y., Sept. 24, 1953; s. Anthony John and Anne Helen (Renella) L.; m. Dee Ann Hammond, July 15, 1989; children: Stephanie Kara, Rebecca Dawn. BA in English and Edn., LaSalle U., Phila., 1975; MA in English, Villanova U., 1982; postgrad., St. John's U., Queens, N.Y., 1994—. Cert. educator N.Y., Pa. Tchr. Bishop Egan H.S. Cath. Schs. of Phila., Fairless Hills, Pa., 1975-82; tchr. Sewanhaka H.S. Ctrl. H.S. Dist., Elmont, N.Y., 1982-85; tchr. Farmingdale (N.Y.) H.S., 1985-88; tchr. Manhattanville Coll., Purchase, N.Y., 1990-94, Westchester C.C., Valhalla, 1989—, Rockland C.C., Suffern, 1993—; program adminstr. Westchester County Coll., 2001—. Computer cons. Nyack Fire Dept., 1993—; adv. lit. mag. Bishop Egan H.S., 1978-80; adv. drama club Sewanhaka H.S. Ctrl. H.S. Dist., Elmont, N.Y., 1982-85; English curriculum coord. Verizon Next Step Program, 2001—. Editor D.A. Report, 1996-98. Founding mem. Rockland County YMCA Youth Svcs., Nyack, 1985-88; chmn. Nyack YMCA Bd. Mgrs., 1986-88; chair Mazeppa Planning Com., Nyack, 1985-95; sec. Mazeppa Engine Co. #2, Nyack, 1982-91, pres., 1991-97. Named Am. Legion Good Citizen, Nyack. Mem. MLA, Nat. Coun. Tchrs. of English, Conf. on Coll. Composition, Alliance Computers and Writing, LaSalle Edn. Alumni Assn. Home: 118 Helene Rd Valley Cottage NY 10989-2623 Office: Westchester CC 75 Grasslands Rd Valhalla NY 10595

LEONE, WILLIAM CHARLES, retired manufacturing executive; b. Pitts., May 3, 1924; s. Joseph and Fortuna (Sammarco) L.; m. Sara Jane Hollenback, Aug. 26, 1950; children: William Charles, David M., Patricia Ann, Mary Jane. BS, Carnegie Inst. Tech., 1944, MS, 1948, DSc, 1952. Asst. prof. engring. Carnegie Inst. Tech., Pitts., 1946-53; mgr. Indsl. Sys. divsn. Hughes Aircraft, L.A., 1953-59; v.p., gen. mgr., dir. Rheem Califone, 1960, Rheem Electronics, L.A., 1960-68; group v.p. Rheem Mfg. Co., 1968-71, exec. v.p., 1971-72, pres., 1972-76, also dir.; pres. City Investing Co. Internat., Inc., 1972-76; pres., dir. Farah Mfg. Co., El Paso, Tex., 1976-77; bus. cons., 1977-79; acting vice chmn. McCulloch Oil Corp. (MCO), L.A., 1979-80, also bd. dirs.; pres., dir. MAXXAM Inc. (formerly MCO Holdings, Inc.), 1980-90; vice chmn. MAXXAM Inc., 1990-92. Chmn., CEO, dir. Pacific Lumber Co., 1986-90, Horizon Corp., 1984-89. Author: Production Automation and Numerical Control; contbr. articles to tech. jours.; patentee in field. Trustee Carnegie Mellon U., 1986-92. Mem. ASME, IEEE, Am. Inst. Aerospace and Aeronautics, Sigma Xi, Tau Beta Pi, Pi Tau Sigma, Theta Tau, Pi Mu Epsilon. Home: 2209 Chelsea Rd Palos Verdes Peninsula CA 90274-2603

LEONETT, ANTHONY ARTHUR, banker; b. Summit, N.J., Jan. 4, 1929; s. Joseph J. and Margaret (DiGuglielmo) L.; m. Ann Marino, Oct. 6, 1974; 1 son by previous marriage, Anthony Arthur. BS, Seton Hall U., 1950; cert., Am. Inst. Banking, 1956; postgrad., U. Wis., 1962. Mgr. First Nat. Bank & Trust Co., Summit, 1950-56; sr. v.p., auditor Nat. State Bank, Elizabeth, N.J., 1956-91; ret., 1991. Instr. principles of auditing and bank ops. Am. Inst. Banking; mem. faculty N.J. Data Processing Sch., Princeton, Bank Adminstrn. Sch. of U. Wis. Bd. dirs. N.J. affiliate Am. Heart Assn. With U.S. Army, 1951-53. Recipient Irving Grabiel award for outstanding leadership in banking, 1979 Mem. Am. Inst. Banking (dir. chpt.), Bank Adminstrn. Inst. (N.J. state dir. 1977-79, pres. N.J. chpt., dist. dir. 1979-81) Clubs: K.C., Minisink (Chatham). Republican. Roman Catholic. Home: 102 N Hillside Ave Chatham NJ 07928-2825

LEONETTI, EVANGELINE PHILLIPS, retired nursing educator; b. Judith Gap, Mont., Sept. 29, 1924; d. Henry Harrison and Florence Elizabeth (Bascom) Phillips; m. Joseph Leonetti, Aug. 5, 1955 (dec. July 1989); 1 stepchild, Doris Leonetti Dwork. BSN, Loma Linda (Calif.) U., 1955, postgrad., 1985-93; MEd, UCLA, 1968; postgrad., U. So. Calif., L.A., 1971-83. Nursing instr. East L.A. Coll., 1959-64; DON Golden Age Convalescent, Covina, Calif., 1985, Mission Convalescent, San Gabriel, 1985; supr. Med. Home Care, Alhambra, Calif., 1985-87; nursing instr. med. and dental careers Concord Career Coll., North Hollywood, 1987-90; nursing instr. Pacific Coast Coll., Encino, 1992-94, St. Clare's Home Health, 1994, ret., 1994. House mother to oriental boys Exchange Students, 2000—. Contbr. articles to profl. jours. Vol. ARC, 1997-98; mem. Tabitha Henken's and Robert Gates Julliard Sch. of Mus. SDA Choir, Alhambra; house mother Internat. Students Am. English Sch. Mem. U. Calif. Alumni Assn., Loma Linda U. Alumni Assn., UCLA Grad. Alumni Assn.

LEONETTI, MICHAEL EDWARD, financial planner; b. Oak Park, Ill., Aug. 23, 1955; s. Michael Louis and Dolores Mary (DiOrio) L. BA, St. Marys Coll., 1977. Cert. fin. planner, fund specialist; registered investment advisor. Sales rep. Metropolitan Life, Des Plaines and Rosemont, Ill., 1977-80; fin. planner Money Masters Inc., Buffalo Grove, 1980-82, Leonetti & Assocs., Buffalo Grove, 1982—. Instr. fin. planning Harper Coll., 1982-84. Author: Retire Worry Free: Financial Strategies for Tomorrow's Independence; adv. bd. Practical Fin. Planning; contbr. articles to profl. jours. Named one of Best Fin. Planners in U.S., Money Mag., 1987, One of Top Balanced Style Money Managers in U.S., 1992. Mem. Nat. Assn. Personal Fin. Advisors (pres. 1986-87), United Shareholders Assn., Internat. Assn. Fin. Planning (bd. dirs.), Inst. Cert. Fin. Planners (bd. dirs. 1986—), Registry Fin. Planning Practitioners, Investment Rsch. Inst. (cert. fund specialist), St. Mary Coll. Weight Lifting Club (pres., founder 1973-77). Republican. Roman Catholic. Avocations: golf, weight training, bodybuilding. Home: 4468 Kettering Dr Long Grove IL 60047 Office: Leonetti & Assocs 1130 W Lake Cook Rd Ste 300 Buffalo Grove IL 60089-1976

LEONG, CAROL JEAN, electrologist; b. Sacramento, Jan. 9, 1942; d. Walter Richard and Edith (Bond) Bloss; m. Oliver Arthur Fisk III, Apr. 12, 1964 (div. 1973); 1 child, Victoria Kay. BA in Sociology, San Jose (Calif.) State Coll., 1963; degree, Western Bus. Coll., 1964; cert. in electrolysis, Bay Area Coll. Electrolysis, 1978; degree in esthetics, Zenzi's Coll., 1998. Registered and cert. clin. profl. electrologist, Calif. Model various orgns., Calif., 1951-64; employment counselor Businessmen's Clearinghouse, Cin., 1966-67; dir. personnel Kroger Food Corp., 1967-68; prin. Carol Leong Electrolysis, San Mateo, Calif., 1978—. Prin. Designs by Carol, San Mateo, 1987—; mem. Profl. Women's Forum, 1988—. Contbr. articles to profl. publs. Pres. Peninsula Aux. Lighthouse for the Blind, 1984-85, 95-2002, 1st v.p., 1993-95, pres., 1999, 2000, 2001, 2002; mem. Civic Garden Club, 1995—, Best Friends Animal Orgn., 1992—, The Nature Conservancy, 1995—, Nat. Fedn. Rep. Women, 1996; vol. Nat. Kidney Found. No. Calif., 1995—. Recipient Cert. of Appreciation San Francisco Lighthouse for the Blind, 1981-82, 83. Mem. Internat. Guild Profl. Electrologists (mem. continuing edn. com.), NAFE, Profl. Women's Forum, Peninsula Humane Soc., San Francisco Zool. Soc., Friends of Filoli, Am. Electrologists Assn., Electrologists Assn. Calif., Internat. Platform Assn, Order of Eastern Star, Chi Omega. Republican. Presbyterian. Avocations: golf, tennis, ballet, theater, photography. Home: 1447 Woodberry Ave San Mateo CA 94403-3712 Office: Carol Leong Electrolysis 359 N San Mateo Dr Ste 4 San Mateo CA 94401-2584 E-mail: jeanssk8@aol.com.

LEONG, HELEN VANESSA, systems programmer; b. Chgo., Dec. 14, 1949; d. Linton and Sue Lin (Hong) L.; m. Stephen Occhiuzzo, Aug. 28, 1993. BS in Liberal Arts/Math., Ill. Inst. Tech., 1971. Computer sys. analyst Ill. Bell Tel., Chgo., 1971-76; commd. ensign USN, 1977, advanced through grades to lt. comdr., 1992; pers. officer NAS Glenview, Ill., 1977-78, pub. affairs officer, 1979-80; computer sys. analyst Space and Naval Warfare Sys. Command, Washington Navy Yard, Washington, 1980-83; program mgr. asst. Dept. of Navy (OP-942) Pentagon, 1983-86; joint action officer Office Joint Chiefs of Staff (J-6), Pentagon, 1986-87; exec. officer Naval Regional Data Automation Ctr., Newport, R.I., 1987-89; sys. programmer Stanford (Calif.) Health Svcs., 1989-97, PKS Info. Svcs., 1997—99, (i)structure, Inc., Omaha, 1999—. Mem. Svc. Acad. Adv. Bd. Frank Wolf, Tenth Dist., Va., 1985-87; chairperson energy com. Skyline Condo Assn., Falls Church, Va., 1986. Decorated Navy Achievement medal, 1982, Joint Commendation medal, 1987, Navy Commendation medal, 1989, Nat. Def. medal, 1992. Mem. NAFE, Nat. Sys. Programmers Assn. Avocations: downhill skiing, ice skating, roller blading, knitting, reading. Office: (i)structure Inc 11707 Miracle Hills Dr Omaha NE 68154-4457

LEONG, LAMPO (LANBO LIANG), artist, educator; b. Guangzhou, Guangdong, China, July 3, 1961; came to U.S., 1983; BFA in Chinese Brush Painting, Guangzhou Fine Arts Inst., 1983; MFA in Painting with high distinction, Calif. Coll. Arts & Crafts, 1988. Instr. art Calif. Coll. Arts and Crafts, Oakland, 1986-87, U. Calif. Ext. and ASUC, Berkeley, 1989, 90-99, San Jose (Calif.) State U. Ext., 1989-91, Chabot Coll., Hayward, Calif., 1989-94; lectr. San Francisco State U., 1988-95, asst. prof., 1996—2001, U. Mo., Columbia, Mo., 2001—. Guest spkr. Asian Art Mus. San Francisco, San Francisco, 1985, 90, 92, 92, 94, 1996—2001; guest spkr. inst. internat. studies Stanford U., Palo Alto, Calif., 1999—2000; guest spkr. dept. art history U. Calif., Berkeley, Calif., 1997—98, 2001. One-man shows include Markings Gallery, Berkeley, 1984, Calif. Coll. Arts & Crafts, 1985, Rosicrucian Egyptian Mus., San Jose, 1986, U. Utah, Salt Lake City, 1986, Patrick Gallery, Regina, Sask., Can., 1986, Mus. Macao Luis De Camoes, Macao, 1986, Kai Ping County Mus., Guangdong, 1987, Guangzhou (China) Fine Arts Mus., 1988, Moy Ying Ming Gallery, Chgo., 1990, Chinese Culture Ctr., San Francisco, 1991, Stanwood Gallery, San Francisco, 1992, Sanuk Fine Asian Collectables, San Francisco, 1992, The Univ. Gallery, San Francisco, 1994, Michael Thompson Gallery, San Francisco, 1995, China Art Expo '95, Guangzhou, China, 1995, Galerie du Monde, Hong Kong, 1997, d.p. Fong Galleries, San Jose, Calif., 1997, 2000, Instituto Cultural de Macau, 1998, Santa Catalina Gallery, Monterey, Calif., 1999, Legacy Art, Columbia, Mo., 2002, We. Ill. U., Macomb, Ill., 2002; exhibited in group shows at Hong Kong Arts Ctr., 1980, Chinese Painting Exhibit Guangdong Province, 1981 (3d Prize award 1981), Macao Artists Assn. Exhbn., 1982-96, Mus. Guangzhou Fine Arts Inst., 1983, Nat. Mus. Art, Beijing, 1985, Macao Young Artist Exhbn. (Excellence award, 1st prize), Pacific Art Ctr., Seattle, 1985, Chinese Culture Ctr., 1986, Faculty & MFA Show Calif. Coll. Arts & Crafts, San Francisco Campus, 1986, Chinese-Am. Artist Exhbn., Taipei, Taizhong, Taiwan, 1986, Sullivan Galleries, Salt Lake City, 1987, Oriental Gallery, N.Y., 1987, Santa Cruz Art League (Spl. award 1988, 1st prize 1990), Asian Resource Gallery, Oakland, 1988, Nat. Mus. Fine Arts, Beijing, 1988, 90, Chinese Art Gallery, San Leandro, Calif., 1989, Stanwood Gallery, 1989, Gallery Imago, San Francisco, 1990, Sun Gallery, Hayward, 1990, N.Y. Art Expo, N.Y.C., 1991, Gallery 5, Santa Monica, Calif., 1991, Butterfield & Butterfield Auction, San Francisco, 1992, 95-96, Asian Art Mus., San Francisco, 1992, Ke Shan Art Gallery, Taipei, 1993, Wan Fung Art Gallery, Hong Kong, 1993, Gallery On The Rim, San Francisco, 1994, Resource for Art, 1995, Ginsberg Collection, 1995, Macao Art Expo, 1988-96, Acad. Art Coll., San Francisco, 1996, Shanghai Arts Mus., 1997, Pacific Heritage Mus., San Francisco, 1998, Ethan Cohen Fine Art, N.Y., 1998, 99, Chinese Culture Ctr., San Francisco, 2000, Zhuhai Mus., Guaungdong, China, 2000, Am. Inst. Taiwan, , 2001, U. Mo., Columbia, Mo., 2001, U. Wis.- Parkside, Kenosha, Wis., 2002, Bismarck Art & Galleries Assn., N.Dak., 2002, Columbia Coll., Columbia, Mo., 2002, New City Gallery, Taipei, Taiwan, 2002, Legacy Art, Columbia & Capitol Rotunda, Jefferson City, Mo., 2002, Columbia Art League, Columbia, Mo., 2002, Rosenthal Gallery, Fayetteville State U., N.C., 2002, Fredericksburg Ctr. Creative Arts, Fredericksburg, Va., 2002, Watercolor Art Soc., Houston, Tex., 2002, La. State U. Union Art Gallery, Baton Rouge, La., 2002, SUNY, Stony Brook, N.Y., 2002, Period Gallery Internat., Omaha, Nebr., 2002; work represented in various mus., corp. and pvt. collections including Guangzhou Arts Mus., Macao Camoes Mus., Mus. Guangzhou Fine Arts Inst., Asian Art Mus., Macao Mus. Art, San Francisco, United Savs. Bank, Calif., Hotel East 21, Tokyo, The Tokyo Westin Hotel, Comml. Bank, San Francisco, Westin Surabaya, Indonesia; author: Brush Paintings of Lam-Po Leong, 1986, Journey of the Heart, 1994, Lampo Leong: Contemplation.Forces, 1997, The Common Ground of Light and Gravity: Lampo Leong's Contemplation/Forces, 1998; illustrator: Brushstrokes-Styles and Techniques of Chinese Painting, 1993, The Tao of Power, 1986; designer (granite medallion) Woh Hei Yueh Chinatown Pk., San Francisco, 1993; designer (multi-image projection) Ctr. Arts Yerba Buena Gardens, San Francisco, 1996. Recipient Outstanding Merit award Young Art Now Competition, 1980, Decade of Achievement award Asian/Pacific Heritage Week, 1988, 2d prize Zunyi Internat. Brush Painting Competition, 1989, Gold Medal award 15th Macao Painting and Calligraphy Exhbn., 1998, Bronze Medal Forte Cup 20th Century Asian Pacific Art Competition, Washington, 1999; inductee Pan-Pacific Asian Hall of Fame at San Francisco Internat. Expo., 1987; grantee City of Oakland Cultural Arts Divsn., 1994-96. Mem. Asian Artists Assn. Am., Oriental Art Assn., U.S.A. (v.p.), Macao Soc. Social Scis., Hai-Ri Artists Assn. (China), Nat. Modern Meticulous Painting Soc. (China), Chinese Am. Culture Exch. Assn. (co-founder, dir. 1992—). Avocations: film, ballroom dance, travel, photography. Office: Univ Mo Columbia A126 Fine Arts Columbia MO 65211-6090 Fax: 573-884-6807. E-mail: L@lampoleong.com.

LEONG, STEPHANIE MEI, financial planner; b. Stockton, Calif., July 21, 1947; d. Edward G. and Ly H. (Ng) L.; m. Truman D. Wong, Aug. 24, 1969 (div. Mar. 1995); 1 child, Alexandra G.; m. Raymond Tom, June 17, 1995. BA, Mills Coll., 1970. Software cons. ComputerLand, San Francisco, 1983-86; trainer acctg. software Data Integrity, 1986-88; fin. cons. Shearson Lehman Bros., San Francisco, Larkspur, Calif., 1988-92, FN Investment Ctr., San Francisco, 1992-95; registered prin. Assoc. Securities Corp., Santa Rosa, Calif., 1995-99, Investment Architects, Inc., 1999—. Vol. Donaldina Cameron House, San Francisco, 1962-83; mem. fin. com. Santa Rosa Symphony Assn., 1996—, bd. dirs., 1998—; bd. dirs. Jr. League Napa-Sonoma, Santa Rosa, 1996—, San Francisco Opera Guild, 1998—; docent Asian Art Mus., San Francisco, 2000—; alumnae admissions rep. Mills Coll., 2000—. Named to Golden Scale Coun., Putnam Investments, Boston, 1993. Mem. Internat. Assn. Fin. Planning, Kiwanis (bd. dirs. Santa Rosa, suburban chmn. interclub 1996-98, Outstanding Achievement award 1998). Presbyterian. Avocations: classical music, dance, art, travel, sailing. Office: Investment Architects Inc 2513 Saddleback Ct Santa Rosa CA 95401-0805 E-mail: stephanieleong@yahoo.com.

LEONG, SUE, retired community health and pediatrics nurse; b. Alameda, Calif., Feb. 15, 1930; d. Leong Dai Sun and Leong San See. BS, U. Calif., San Francisco, 1953; MPH, U. Mich., 1963; MA, San Francisco Theol. Sem., 1958. Cert. sch. nurse, sch. nurse practitioner, nurse specialist. Head nurse Lafayette Clinic, Detroit; pub. health nurse San Francisco Health Dept.; assoc. dir. Ecumenical Campus Ctr., Ann Arbor, Mich.; sch. nurse practitioner Ann Arbor Pub. Schs. Adj. asst. prof. U. Mich. Contbr. articles to profl. jours. Parish nurse cons., 1996—. Mem. NEA, Mich. Assn. Sch. Nurses (Disting. Svc. award 1990, Dorothy Christy award 1993). Home: 1506 Golden Ave Ann Arbor MI 48104-4327

LEONHARDT, CLIFTON ANDREW, lawyer, public official; b. New Orleans, Dec. 27, 1947; s. Robert Crawford and Mary Gay (Labrot) L.; m. Mary Alice Leonhardt, Dec. 18, 1988; children: Theodore Lawrence, Christine Alexandra. AB with honors, Cornell U., 1969; JD cum laude, Harvard U., 1972; postgrad., Oxford (Eng.) U., 1972-73. Assoc. Robinson & Cole, Hartford, Conn., 1973-74; legis. counsel Commn. on Govt. Ops., U.S. Senate, Washington, 1974-75; dep. sec. State of Conn., Hartford, Conn., 1975-78, senator, 1979—83; dir. Atlantic Wood Industries, Savannah, Ga., 1978-85; assoc. Wiggin & Dana, New Haven, 1984-89; chairperson Dept. Pub. Utility Control, State of Conn., 1991-93; prin. de Fontenay, Savin & Kiss, Greenwich, Conn., 1994-95; chief counsel Freedom of Info. Commn., State of Conn., 1996—; law lectr. U. Conn., Hartford, 1983-85. Law lectr. U. Conn., Hartford, 1983—85. Contbr. articles to profl. jours. Del. Dem. Nat. Conv., San Francisco, 1984; bd. dirs. Conn. Trust for Hist. Preservation, New Haven, 1995—2001, Conn.Correctional Ombudsman, Hartford, 1994—; treas., bd. dirs. Neighborhood Music Sch., New Haven, 1985—90. Mem. N.Y. Yacht Club, Hartford Tennis Club, Fishers Island Yacht Club, Phi Beta Kappa. Democrat. Episcopalian. Avocations: tennis, sailing. Home: 46 Mountain Spring Rd Farmington CT 06032 Office: Freedom of Info Commn 18-20 Trinity St Hartford CT 06106 E-mail: clifton.leonhardt@po.state.ct.us.

LEONHARDT, DARRIN, atomic physicist; b. Cleve., Sept. 23, 1965; s. David Alan and Anita Doris (D'Ercole) L.; m. Judith Lea Rider, May 28, 1988. BS in Chem., Physics, Kent State U., 1988; postgrad., U. Md., 1988—. Rsch. chemist Liquid Crystal Inst., Kent., Ohio, 1984-88; teaching asst. U. Md., College Park, 1988-90, rsch. asst., 1990—. Named Hon. Mem. Soc. Physics Students, Kent State, Ohio, 1986. Mem. Am. Physical Soc.

LEONHARDT, DEBBIE ANN, counselor, writer, minister; b. Valdese, N.C., June 11, 1953; d. Douglas Franklin and Jettie Arcena (Stilwell) L. BA, Lenoir-Rhyne Coll., 1975, MA, 1986; MDiv, Southeastern Bapt. Theol. Sem., 1977. Cert. Nat. Bd. Cert. Conselors, N.C. Bd. Licensed Profl. Counselors; ordained to ministry Bapt. Ch., 1983. Min. edn. Front St. Bapt. Ch., Statesville, N.C., 1978-80; assoc. min. First Bapt. Ch., Taylorsville, 1980-85; sch. counselor Alexander County Pub. Schs., 1985—; pres. Alexander Counseling and Consulting Svcs., Inc., 1994—. Instr. cont. edn. Catawba Valley C.C., Hickory, N.C., 1993—; cons., seminar leader Catawba County Family Support Network, Hickory, N.C., 1996. Author: Survival Kit: A Guide for Brain Injured Patients, 1995; contbr. article to profl. jour., poems to collection. Vol. chaplain Catawba Meml. Hosp., Hickory, N.C., 1994-95; mem. Smart Start Partnership Task Force, Alexander County, N.C., 1995-96; mem., cons. Catawba County Traumatic Brain Injury Resource Com., Hickory, N.C., 1996. Name Young Career Woman Bus. and Profl. Women's Club, 1984. Mem. Nat. Brain Injury Assn., Nat. Bd. Cert. Counselors (test item writer Master Addictions Counselor, test item review com. 1996), N.C. Bd. Licensed Profl. Counselors, N.C. Sch. Counslors Assn., N.C. Brain Injury Assn. Democrat. Avocations: public speaking, coaching basketball, swimming. Home: RR 2 Box 443 Hiddenite NC 28636-9454 Office: Alexander Counseling & Cons Svcs 125 Wilkesboro Rd NW Taylorsville NC 28681-2321

LEONHARDT, FREDERICK WAYNE, lawyer; b. Daytona Beach, Fla., Oct. 26, 1949; s. Frederick Walter and Gaetane Laura Leonhardt; m. Victoria Ann Cook, Dec. 27, 1975; children: Ashley Victoria, Frederick Whitaker. BA, U. Fla., 1971, JD, 1974. Bar: Fla. 1974, N.C. 1984, D.C. 1985; cert. real estate lawyer, Fla. Gen. cousnel Fla. Ho. of Reps., 1974-75; ptnr. Cobb, Cole and Bell, Daytona Beach, 1975-79; pres. Leonhardt & Upchurch, 1979-87; ptnr. Holland & Knight, Orlando, Fla., 1987-93, Gray, Harris & Robinson, Orlando, Melbourne, Tallahassee, Clermont, Tampa, Lakeland, 1993—. Chmn. bd. dirs. Orlando/Orange County Compact, 1989-90, Orlando/Orange County Civic Facilities Authority, 1998-2000; founder Leadership Daytona Beach; grad. Leadership Fla., mem. bd. regents, 1995—; chmn. state program, 1997-98, chair-elect 1999, chair, 2000-2001; active Leadership Ctrl. Fla., Leadership Orlando; past chmn. Ctrl. Fla. Sports Commn., bd. dirs., 1992-98; mem. Orange County Civic Facilities Authority, 1998-2001; bd. dirs. Orlando/Orange County Conv. and Visitors Bur.; founder VCARD; past gen. campaign mgr. Volusia County United Way; bd. dirs. Celebration Health Found., Ctr. for Drug Free Living, Prevent Blindness Fla.; mem. Gov.'s Growth Mgmt. Study Commn.; exec. com. Floridians for Better Transp., 2000—; treas. U. Ctrl. Fla. Found., 2000—; bd. dirs. Econ. Devel. Commn. Mid-Fla., 2001—; mem. adv. bd. Ronald McDonald House. Mem. ABA (chmn. stae and local govt. law sect. 1997-98, editor sect. newsletter 1991-94), Orange and Volusia Counties Bar Assn., Greater Orlando C. of C. (chmn. 1991-92), Daytona Beach Area C. of C. (pres. 1985), Fla. C. of C. (bd. dirs. 1984-90, 93—), Phi Alpha Delta, Delta Chi. Office: Gray Harris & Robinson PA PO Box 3068 301 E Pine St Ste 1400 Orlando FL 32801-2731 E-mail: fleonhardt@grayharris.com.

LEONHARDT, THOMAS WILBURN, librarian, library director; b. Wilmington, N.C., Feb. 7, 1943; s. Thomas Beauregard and Rachel Virginia (Callicutt) L.; m. Margaret Ann Pullen, Sept. 19, 1966; children: Hilary, Thomas, Rebecca, Benjamin. AA, Pasadena (Calif.) City Coll., 1968; AB, U. Calif., Berkeley, 1970, MLS, 1973. Head gift and exch. div. Stanford (Calif.) U. Librs., 1973-76; head acquisition dept. Boise (Idaho) State U. Libr., 1976-79, Duke U. Librs., Durham, N.C., 1980-82; asst. univ. libr. U. Oreg., Eugene, 1982-87; dean librs. U. of the Pacific, Stockton, Calif., 1987-92; dir. tech. svcs. U. Okla. Librs., Norman, 1992-97; libr. dir. Oreg. Inst. Tech., Klamath Falls, 1997—2001; founding libr. Internat. U., Bremen, Germany, 2001; cons., 2002—. Editor RTSD Newsletter, Chgo., 1986-89, Info. Tech. & Librs., Chgo., 1990-95. Editor Advances in Collection Development and Resource Management, JAI Press, 1994-97; publisher, editor Callicutt Family Chronicle; contbr. articles to profl. jours. Bd. dirs. No. Regional Libr. Facility, Richmond, Calif., 1988-92, Feather River Inst. for Libr. Acquisitions, Blairsden, Calif.; del. Online Computer Libr. Ctr. AMIGOS Bibliog. Coun., Inc., 1996-97; chair Orbis Coun., 1999-2001; mem. Klamath Symphony, 1997-2001. Mem. ALA, Assn. Coll. Rsch. Librs., Libr. and Info. Tech. Assn. (pres. 1997-98), Assn. for Libr. Collections and Tech. Svcs., Ctrl. Assn. Librs. (bd. dirs. Stockton chpt. 1987-92). Democrat. Avocations: trumpet, guitar. Home and Office: 985 Lewis Ave Apt 9 Eugene OR 97402 E-mail: twleonhardt@earthlink.net.

LEONI, TEA (ELIZABETH TEA PANTALEONI), actress; b. N.Y.C, Feb. 25, 1966; m. David Duchovny, 1997. Actress Television: Santa Barbara, 1984, Flying Blind, 1992, The Counterfeit Contessa, 1994, The Naked Truth, 1995; Films: Switch, 1991, A League of Their Own, 1992, Wyatt Earp, 1994, Bad Boys, 1995, Flirting with Disaster, 1996, Deep Impact, 1998, There's No Fish Food in Heaven, 1999, The Family Man, 2000, Jurassic Park 3, 2001, Hollywood Ending, 2002. Recipient Saturn Award, best actress for "The Family Man", 2001.*

LEONIDAS, JEAN-ROBERT, endocrinologist, educator; b. Jeremie, Haiti, June 11; came to U.S., 1973; s. Barthold Themistocle and Lucienne (Jean-Francois) Leonidas; m. Wilhelmine Dupiton, May 23, 1973; children: Sidney, Melissa. MD, Faculty Medicine Haiti, Port-au-Prince, 1971. Diplomate Am. Bd. Internal Medicine, Am. Bd. Endocrinology. Intern Mineola (N.Y.) Hosp., 1973-74; med. resident Misericordia Hosp., Bronx, N.Y., 1974-76, chief resident, 1976-77; fellow in endocrinology Downstate Hosp., Bklyn., 1977-79; attending physician Kings County Hosp., 1979—; asst. prof. SUNY Health Sci. Ctr., 1981—. Author books in French; contbr. articles to profl. jours. Fellow ACP; mem. AAAS, Endocrine Soc., Assn. Haitian Physicians Abroad (v.p. N.Y. chpt. 1979-81). Office: 1016 Ditmas Ave Brooklyn NY 11218-6034

LEONIE, ANDREW DRAKE, III, judge, lawyer; b. Loma Linda, Calif., Dec. 13, 1952; s. Andrew and Norma Lou Leonie; m. Jamie Lorraine Chism, June 16, 1995; children: Andrew, Aaron, Rachel. BS, Western Ill. U., 1972; MA, U. Ill., 1974; JD, St. Mary's U., 1977; postgrad., Andrews U., 19985. Bar: Tex., U.S. Dist. Ct. (so. dist.) Tex., U.S. Dist. Ct. (no. dist.) Tex., U.S. Supreme Ct. Assoc. Smith, McIlheran, Lauderdale & Jones, Weslaco, Tex., 1977-79; ptnr. Jones, Marsh, Rodriguez, Welch & Leonie, McAllen, 1980-85; asst. atty. gen. Atty. Gen. Tex., Dallas, 1987-94; pvt. practice, 1994-95; judge, family law ct. master 1st Jud. Region Tex., 1995—. Presiding judge City of Lavon, Tex.; mediator Christian Conciliation Svc., McAllen, Tex., 1984—; advisor Tex. Senate Com. on Family Law Issues, 1996; bd. advisors Iverson Inst. Ct. Reporting; mem. transition com. Tex. Atty. Gen. John Cornyn, 1998-99; mem. child support legis. com. Tex. Sunset Commn., 1999. Contbr. article to profl. jour., chpt. to book. Mem. exec. com. Rockwall (Tex.) Rep. Party, 1989-98; commr. planning and zoning commn. City of Rockwall, 1990-92; bd. dirs. Tex. Rural Legal Aid, 1985. Recipient Pro Bono award Rockwall County Bar Assn., 1995. Mem. Am. Jud. Assn., Tex. Bar Assn. (chair mcpl. judges sect.), Dallas Bar Assn. (mem. judiciary com., ethics com. 19945), Hidalgo County Bar Assn. (sec. bd. dirs. 1977-82), Christian Legal Soc., Rotary (pres. Rockwall (Tex., Rotarian of Yr. 1991, Breakfast Club). Republican. Episcopalian. Avocations: running, gardening, religious history.

Home: 4617 Lakepointe Ave Rowlett TX 75088-6862 Office: First Jud Region Tex George Allen Civil Cts Bldg 600 Commerce St 7th Fl Dallas TX 75202-4616 E-mail: judgeleonie@airmail.net.

LEON-PORTILLA, MIGUEL, historian, educator; b. Mexico City, Mex., Feb. 22, 1926; s. Miguel and Luisa (Portilla) L.; m. Ascension Hernandez Treviño, May 2, 1965; 1 child, Marisa. BA, Loyola U., L.A., 1948, MA, 1951; PhD, Nat. U. Mex., 1956, So. Meth. U., 1980; DHL (hon.) , U. Tel Aviv, 1987, So. Calif. U., 1989, Toulouse U., France, 1990, Colima U., San Andres, 1994, U. La Paz, Bolivia, 1994, Brown U., 1996; PhD (hon.) , U. Carolina, Prague, 2000, Calif. State U., San Diego, 2002, U. Iberoamericana, Mexico City, 2002. Sec. Interam. Indian Inst., Mexico City, 1955-58, asst. dir., 1958-60, dir., 1960-66; prof. faculty philosophy Nat. U. Mex., 1957—, dir. Inst. Hist. Rsch., 1966-76; researcher emeritus Inst. Hist. Rsch. Nat. Univ. Mexico, Mexico City. Sec.-gen. Internat. Congress Americanists, Mexico City, 1962; disting. lectr. Am. Anthrop. Assn., 1974. Author: La Filosofia Nahuatl estudiada en sus fuentes, 9th edit., 1997, Vision de las Vencidos, 18th edit., 2001, Broken Spears-Aztec Account of Conquest of Mexico, 10th edit., 1994, Aztec Thought and Culture, 1964, 12th edit., 1996, Le Crepuscule des Azteques, 1965, Trece Poetas del Mundo Azteca, 1967, Pre-Columbian Literatures of Mexico, 1969, Testimonios Sudcalifornianos, 1970, Religion de los Nicaraos, 1972, Time and Reality in the Thought of the Maya, 1972, The Voyages of Francisco de Ortega to California, 1932-36, 1972, Historia Natural y Cronica de la Antiqua California, 1973, Il Rovescio della Conquista, Testimoniaze Asteche Maya e Inca, 1974, Anthropology and the Endangered Cultures, 1976, New Light on the Sources of Torquemada's Monarchia Indiana, 1979, Native Mesoamerican Spirituality, ·1980, Toltecayotl, Aspectos de la Cultura Nahuatl, 1980, The Natural History of Baja California, 1980, The Testaments of Culhuacan, 1984, La Pensèe Azteque, 1985, Time and Reality in the Thought of the Maya, 1988; editor: Monarquia Indiana (Father Juan de Torquenada), 1975, Hamnotzejim Jazon, 1976, Culturas en peligro, 1976, Indian Place Names in Baja California, 1977, Los manifiestos en nahuatl de Emilian Zapata, 1978, Native Mesoamerican Spirituality, Ancient Myths, Discourses, Stories, Doctrines, Hymns, Poems from the Aztec, Yucatec, Quichè-Maya, and Other Sacred Traditions, 1980, The Natural History of Baja California, 1980, Place Names in Nahuatl: Their Morphology, 1981, Fifteen Poets of the Aztec World, 1992, Aztec Image of Self and the Others, 1994, Tonantzin Guadalupe, 2000, El Retorno de Quetzalcoatl, 2002, (with Earl Shorris) In the Language of Kings, 2002. Bd. regents Nat. U. Mex., 1976-86; amb. of Mex. to UNESCO, 1987-92, permanent del., Paris, 1987-92. Decorated Order of Great Cross, Alfonso X the Wise (Spain), Palmes Academiques (France); recipient Elias Sourasky prize in Humanistic Rsch. Mex. Sec. Edn., 1966; recipient Serra award of the Ams., 1978, Nat. prize in Social Scis. Govt. of Mex., 1981, Gamio award, 1983, Raphael Heliodoro Valle prize in History, 1984, Nat. U. Mex. prize, 1994, Bartolomé de las Casas prize, Madrid, 2000, Alfonso Reyes Internat. prize, Mex., 2000, Menédez Pelayo Internat. prize, Santander, 2001, B. de las Casas prize, 2001; Guggenheim fellow, 1969; Fulbright fellow, 1975. Mem. NAS (fgn.), Mex. Acad. History (pres. 1996), Royal Spanish Acad. Lang., Smithsonian Coun., Am. Hist. Assn. (hon.), Societè des Americanistes de PAris, Inst. Different Civilizations, Sociedad Mexicana de Antropologia, Am. Anthrop. Assn., El Colegio Nacional Mex., Royal Acad. Letters of Extremadura. Home: Coyoacán 103 Alberto Zamora 04000 Mexico City Mexico Office: Ciudad U Inst de Investig Históricas 04510 Mexico City Mexico Fax: (52) 56 65 00 70. E-mail: portilla@servidor.uman.mx.

LEONSIS, TED, media executive; b. Bklyn., Jan. 8, 1956; BA magna cum laude, Georgetown U., 1976; postgrad., Suffolk U. Law Sch., 1980. Copywriter, advt. mgr. Wang Labs., Inc., 1976-78, corp. publicity/pub. rels. dir., 1978-81; dir. mktg. comm. Harris Corp., Melbourne, Fla., 1981-83; founder, CEO Redgate Pub. Co., Vero Beach, 1983—, also dir.; founder, CEO Redgate Comm. Corp., 1986-94; pres. Am. Online Svcs. Co., Vienna, 1994-96; pres., CEO AOL Studios, 1996—; co-owner Washington Capitals. Founder Collegiate Entrepreneurs Fund; dir. Preview Travel Inc., Thrive, Interzine, The Hub, Digital City, Planet Out, Tribune Interactive, Best Buddies, Georgetown U. Internat. TV & Radio Soc., Brevard Venture Fund. Chmn. Author: Software Master for the IBM Pc, Mastering the IBM Assistant Series, Software Master for PFS, Blue Magic; pub. The Macintosh Buyer's Guide, App[001b]le II Rev., The Apple IIGS Buyer's Guide, COMPAQ, FYI, The Harris Mag. ofr INfo. Mgmt.; contbr. articles to profl. jours. Chmn. United Fund campaign, Wang Labs. Inc., 1980; bd. dirs. Big Bros. Brevard County, 1981, Brevard Art Ctr. and Mus., Brevard Coun. of Arts, 1981, Juvenile Employment Project, Lowell, Mass., Merrimack Regional Theatre. Named one of entrepreneurs of yr. Chivas Regal, 1989, one of 200 global leaders of tomorrow World Econ. Forum, 1993. Mem. Pub. Rels. Soc. Am. (cert.), Publicity Club Boston, Bus. Profl. Advt. Adminstrs., Am. Mktg. Assn. Office: AOL Studios 490 Sea Oak Dr Vero Beach FL 32963-3245 Address: c/o Washington Capitals 401 9th St NW Ste 750 Washington DC 20004-2132*

LEONTSINIS, GEORGE JOHN, lawyer; b. St. Louis, Feb. 23, 1937; s. John Peter and Lula (Lorandos) L.; m. Patricia Marie Demetrulias, July 9, 1967; children: Anne Marie, Michelle Lynne. BSBA, Washington U., St. Louis, 1958, JD, 1961; LLM, NYU, 1964. Bar: Mo. 1961. Ptnr. Greensfelder, Hemker & Gale, P.C., St. Louis, 1964—. Bd. dirs. Ahepa Apts., St. Louis, 1985-95, Citizens for Modern Transit, St. Louis, 1988-96, Citizen's com. high speed rail Chgo.-St. Louis Corridor, Springfield, Ill., 1992-96. Capt. U.S. Army, 1961-63. Mem. Am. Hellenic Ednl. and Profl. Assn., Racquet Club. Avocation: tennis. Office: Greensfelder Hemker & Gale P C 10 S Broadway Saint Louis MO 63102-1712

LEOPOLD, LUNA BERGERE, geology educator; b. Albuquerque, Oct. 8, 1915; BS, U. Wis., 1936, DSc (hon.), 1985; MS, UCLA, 1944; PhD, Harvard, 1950; D Geography (hon.), U. Ottawa, 1969; DSc (hon.), Iowa Wesleyan Coll., 1971, St. Andrews U., 1981, U. Murcia, Spain, 1988. With Soil Conservation Service, 1938-41, U.S. Engrs. Office, 1941-42, U.S. Bur. Reclamation, 1946; head meteorologist Pineapple Research Inst. of Hawaii, 1946-49; hydraulic engr. U.S. Geol. Survey, 1950-71, chief hydrologist, 1957-66, sr. research hydrologist, 1966-71; prof. geology U. Calif. at Berkeley, 1973—. Author (with Thomas Maddock, Jr.): The Flood Control Controversy, 1954; author: Fluvial Processes in Geomorphology, 1964, Water, 1974; author: (with Thomas Dunne) Water in Environmental Planning, 1978; author: A View of the River, 1994, Water, Rivers and Creeks, 1997, also tech. papers. Capt. air weather svc. USAAF, 1942—46. Recipient Disting. Svc. award, Dept. of Interior, 1958, Veth medal, Royal Netherlands Geog. Soc., 1963, Cullum Geog. medal, Am. Geog. Soc., 1968, Rockefeller Pub. Svc. award, 1971, Busk medal, Royal Geog. Soc., 1983, Berkeley citation, U. Calif., David Linton award, Brit. Geomorphol. Rsch. Group, 1986, Linsley award, Am. Inst. Hydrology, 1989, Caulfield medal, Am. Water Resources Assn., 1991, Nat. Medal Sci., NSF, 1991, Palladium medal, Nat. Audubon Soc., 1994, Joan Hodges Queneau Palladium medal, Am. Assn. Engring. Socs., 1994. Mem.: Am. Philos. Soc., Am. Acad. ARts and Scis., Am. Geol. Inst. (Ian Campbell medal), Am. Geophys. Union (Robert E. Horton medal 1993), Geol. Soc. Am. (pres. 1972, Kirk Bryan award 1958, Disting. Career award geomorphological group 1991, Penrose medal 1994), ASCE (Julian Hinds award), NAS (Warren prize), Cosmos Club (Washington), Phi Kappa Phi, Sigma Xi, Chi Epsilon, Tau Beta Pi. Home: PO Box 1040 Pinedale WY 82941-1040 Office: U Calif Dept Geology Berkeley CA 94720-0001

LEOPOLD, MARK F. lawyer; b. 1950; s. Paul F. and Corinne (S.) L.; m. Jacqueline Rood, June 9, 1974; children: Jonathan, David. BA, Am. U., Washington, 1972; JD, Loyola U., 1975. Bar: Ill. 1975, U.S. Dist. Ct. (no. dist.) Ill. 1975, Fla. 1976, U.S. Ct. Appeals (7th cir.) 1976, U.S. Ct. Appeals (8th cir.) 1979. Assoc. McConnell & Campbell, Chgo., 1975-79; atty. U.S. Gypsum Co., 1979-82, sr. litigation atty., 1982-84, USG Corp., Chgo., 1985-87, corp. counsel, 1987, sr. corp. counsel, 1987-89; asst. gen. counsel G.D. Searle & Co., 1989-93, Household Internat., Inc., Prospect Heights, Ill., 1993—. Mem. adv. bd. Roosevelt U. Legal Asst. Program, 1994-2000; legal writing instr. Loyola U. Sch. Law, Chgo., 1978-79. Pres., bd. dirs. Internat. Policyholders Assn., 1992-93; del. candidate Rep. Nat. Conv., 1996; mem. Lake County Study Commn. II, Waukegan, Ill., 1989-90; commr. Lake County, Waukegan, 1982-84, Forest Preserve, Libertyville, Ill., 1982-84, Pub. Bldg. Commn., Waukegan, 1980-82; chmn. Deerfield Twp. Rep. Cen. Com., Highland Park, Ill., 1984-86, officer, 1981-89; vice chmn. Lake County Rep. Cen. Com., Waukegan, 1982-84; bd. dirs. Am. Jewish Com., Chgo., 1988-91, A Safe Place, Lake County, Ill., 2001—. Recipient Disting. Svc. award Jaycees, Highland Park, 1983. Mem. ABA, (antitrust com. 1976—, litigation com. 1980—, torts and ins. practice com. 1989—), Pi Sigma Alpha, Omicron Delta Kappa. Republican. Office: Household Internat 2700 Sanders Rd Prospect Heights IL 60070-2701

LEOPOLD, MARTIN ROBIN, ophthalmologist; b. Bklyn., Apr. 3, 1952; s. Robert Wallace and Phila (Banner) L.; m. Karen Kravarik, Apr. 13, 1975; children: Yona Ruth, David Karol, Daniel Robert. BA summa cum laude honors in Physics, Hofstra U., 1974; MD, Cornell U., 1978. Diplomate Am. Bd. Ophthalmology; lic. MD, N.Y. Intern Northport (N.Y.) VA Hosp., 1979; resident in ophthalmology Mt. Sinai Hosp., N.Y.C., 1980-82; med. retina fellow NYU/Belleview Hosp., 1983; pvt. practice Fishkill, N.Y., 1983—; dir. ophthalmology Vassar Bros. Hosp., 2000—. Instr./lectr. Mt. Sinai Med. Ctr., N.Y.C., 1992—; investigator Wyeth-Ayerst for Tolrestat, Nat. Eye Inst.-HEDS Study. Author: Ultrasound in Medicine, 1979, AIDS: The Epidemic of Kaposis Sarcoma and Opportunistic Infections, 1984; contbr. articles to profl. jours. Mem. Dutchess County Traffic Safety Bd., Poughkeepsie, N.Y., 1985-88. Citibank Med. scholar, 1975-78. Fellow ACS, Am. Acad. Ophthalmology; mem. AMA, N.Y. State Med. Soc., Dutchess County Med. Soc., Phi Beta Kappa. Avocations: skiing, scuba diving, golf. Office: Hudson Valley Eye Surgeons 200 Westage Business Center Dr Fishkill NY 12524 E-mail: eyes@hves.com.

LEPAGE, CANDYCE RUTH, school psychologist; b. Springfield, Mass., Aug. 5, 1951; d. Stephen Edward and Ina Ruth (Melenek) LeP. BS in Edn., Am. Internat. Coll., 1973; MEd, CAGS, Springfield Coll., 1974. Cert. sch. psychologist; NCSP., lic. ednl. psychologist. Home tchr. Springfield (Mass.) Pub. Schs., 1975; substitute tchr. Springfield and Chicopee (Mass.) Pub. Schs., 1975-77; substitute sch. psychologist Chicopee Pub. Schs., 1975, counselor-examiner, 1977-78, counselor, examiner, chair chpt. 766, 1978-80; sch. psychologist Ralph C. Mahar Regional Sch., Orange, Mass., 1980—. Bd. dirs. membership Human Resource Ctr. for Rural Communities, Athol, Mass., 1985-86. Mem. Nat. Sch. Psychologists Assn., Mass. Sch. Psychologists Assn., We. Mass. Sch. Psychologists Assn., Franklin/Hampshire Guidance Assn., Athol-Orange Health and Human Svcs. Coalition, Athol-Orange Community Devel. Corp., Psi Chi. Avocation: reading.

LEPAGE, GERARD PETER, physics educator; b. Montreal, Que., Can., Apr. 13, 1952; s. Gerard L. and Kathleen T. (Walsh) L.; m. Deborah J. O'Connor, June 20, 1985; children: Michael, Daniel, Matthew. BS, McGill U., 1972; postgrad., Cambridge U., 1973; PhD, Stanford U., 1978. Rsch. assoc. Stanford Linear Accelerator Ctr., Palo Alto, Calif., 1978; rsch. assoc. in physics Cornell U., Ithaca, N.Y., 1978-80, asst. prof., 1980-84, assoc. prof., 1984-89, prof., 1990—, chair dept. physics, 1999—. Alfred P. Sloan fellow, 1983-85, John Simon Guggenheim fellow, 1996-97. Fellow Am. Phys. Soc. Office: Physics Dept/Cornell U 109 Clark Hall Ithaca NY 14853-2501 E-mail: gpl@mail.lns.cornell.edu.

LEPAGE, ROBERT, actor, director, playwright; b. Quebec City, Canada, 1957; Degree in drama, Conservatoire d'Art Dramatique, Quebec, 1978. Actor Ligue Nationale d'Improvisation, 1984-88; actor, dir. Le Theatre Repere, 1982-89; artistic dir. French theatre Nat. Arts Ctr., Ottawa, Can, 1989-93; founder, artistic dir. Ex Machina, Que., 1994—. Prodsn. include (TV) Needles and Opium, 1991, Tectonic Plates, 1990, A Midsummer Night's Dream, 1992, Coriolanus, 1992, Seven Streams of the River Ota, 1994, The Dragon's Trilogy, 1985; in theatre: dir., co-writer Circulations, 1984; dir., writer, actor Vinci, 1986; dir.: (play) Le Polygraphe, 1987, (movie), 1996; dir. Echo, 1989, Macbeth, 1993, The Tempest, 1992, 93, 98; actor (films) Jesus of Montreal, 1988, Ding et Dong le Film, 1992, Montreal vu par, 1992; dir. (films) Confessional, 1995, Polygraph, 1996, No, 1998, Possible Worlds, 2000. Recipient Gov. Gen.'s Performing Arts award, 1994; decorated Ordre du Quebec, 1999. E-mail: roleinc@attglobal.net.

LEPELSTAT, MARTIN L. lawyer; b. Bklyn., Apr. 10, 1947; s. Larry and Nana (Citrin) L.; m.. Audrey A. Fireman, Jan. 18, 1975; children: Rachel M., Michael H. BBA, CCNY, 1968; JD, Cornell U., 1971; MBA, U. Mich., 1970; LLM, NYU, 1976. Bar: N.J. 1978, N.Y. 1972, Fla. 1972. Tax cons. Touche Ross, N.Y.C., 1971-73; assoc. Weil, Gotshal & Manges, 1973-78, Greenbaum, Rowe, Smith, Woodbridge, N.J., 1978—. Bd. dirs. Winston Towers 300 Assn., Inc., Cliffside Park, N.J., 1978-86. Fellow Am. Coll. of Trust and Estate Counsel, 1991—; mem. ABA (tax and real estate probate com.), N.J. State Bar Assn., Middlesex County Bar Assn. (pres. tax com. 1987-88, pres. probate com. 1986-87, trustee 1988-92), Fla. Bar Assn. Home: 20 Snoden Ln Watchung NJ 07069-6253 Office: Greenbaum Rowe Smith PO Box 5600 Woodbridge NJ 07095-0988 E-mail: mlepelstat@greenbaumlaw.com.

LEPIDI-CARINO, MADELINE JOANNE, clinical social worker, therapist; b. Greensburg, Pa., Sept. 23, 1944; d. Massimo and America Mary (Vittori) Lepidi; m. Fernando Jaico Carino, Sept. 11, 1971; children— Carla Celeste, Claudette Marie, Christopher Felipe. B. Elem. Edn., U. Pitts., 1967; M. Social Adminstrn., Case Western Res. U., 1970; post-masters certificate, Gestalt Inst. Cleve., 1986. Cert. social worker. Social worker, Catholic Service League, Akron, 1973-75; psychiat. social worker Akron Child Guidance, 1980-82; psychiat. social worker St. Joseph Hosp., Warren, Ohio, 1984-86; clin. social worker, Twinsburg, Ohio, 1986— . Mem. Nat. Assn. Female Execs., Nat. Assn. Social Workers, Nat. Orgn. Italian-Am. Women. Roman Catholic. Avocations: horseback riding; exercise; reading. Home: 2843 Middleton Rd Hudson OH 44236-1907

LEPKE, CHARMA DAVIES, musician, educator; b. Delavan, Wis., Oct. 1, 1919; d. Ithel B. and Florence Mary (Jones) Davies; m. John Richard Lepke, Dec. 22, 1949 (div. July 1974). BA, Wellesley Coll., 1941, MA, 1942; MMusic, Am. Conservatory of Music, Chgo., 1946. Piano tchr., organist Fairfax Hall Jr. Coll., Waynesboro, Va., 1942-44; piano tchr. U. Nebr., Lincoln, 1946-50; ch. organist Trinity Methodist, Unitarian, 1946-50; missionary Am. Bd. Congl. Ch., Durban, Johannesburg, South Africa, 1950-56; ch. organist, choir dir. Congl. United Ch. of Christ, Oconomowoc/Sheboygan, Wis., 1957-70; organist Coloma, Mich., 1970-73; ch. organist Brick Bapt. Ch., Walworth, Wis., 1974, United Meth. Ch., Delavan, 1974-77, Congl. United Ch. of Christ, Delavan, 1977—. Music editor revised Zulu hymnal Amagama Okuhlabelela, South Africa, 1951-56; composer preludes for organ, piano pieces, song and anthem. Recipient 1st prize for song Wis. Fedn. Music Clubs, 1960, others. Mem. Am. Guild of Organists, Music Tchrs. Nat. Assn., Wis. Alliance for Composers, Delavan Musical Arts Soc. (founder, pres.), Phi Beta Kappa. Congregationalist. Home: 223 W Geneva St Delavan WI 53115-1626

LEPKOWSKI, WIL (WILBERT CHARLES LEPKOWSKI), journalist; b. Salem, Mass., Sept. 3, 1934; s. Charles J. and Alice (Bartnicki) L.; m. Jane Littlefield, Oct. 28, 1961 (div. May 1975); children: David E., Rebecca A., Thomas M.C.; m. Helene Kay Hollander, Feb. 4, 1984; 1 child, Katherine Angela. BS in Chemistry, U. Mass., 1956; MS in Biochemistry, Ohio State U., 1961. Asst. chemist Doeskin Products Inc., Easthampton, Mass., 1956; asst. editor Chem. Abstracts Svcs., Columbus, Ohio, 1956-58; reporter UP Internat., 1960, Providence Jour.-Bull., Westerly, R.I., 1961; sci. writer Johns Hopkins Med. Instns., Balt., 1961-63, Newhouse Newspapers, Washington, 1963-65; bur. head, S.E. Chem. & Engring. News, 1965-69, sr. corr., 1977-99, contbg. editor; sci. corr. Bus. Week, 1969-75; free-lance writer, cons., 1975-77. Adj. prof. sci. and tech. studies Va. Poly. and State U., 2002—; journalist in residence Columbia U. Ctr. for Sci., Policy and Outcomes, 1999—. Contbr. articles to jours. in field. Sloan/Rockefeller fellow Advanced Sci. Writing Prgram, Columbia U. Grad. Sch. Journalism, 1959-60. Mem. Nat. Press Club, Nat. Assn. Sci. Writers, Am. Sci. Affiliation, Latin Am. Parents Assn. Roman Catholic. Avocations: natural history, geography, poetry, spiritual reading. E-mail: willep@erols.com. *Tell the truth.*

L'EPLATTENIER, NORA SWEENY HICKEY, nursing educator; b. N.Y.C., Mar. 16, 1945; 1 child, Brendan Sweeny Hickey. Diploma, Bellevue Mills Sch. Nursing, 1965; BS in Health Sci. summa cum laude, Bklyn. Coll., 1978; MS in Psychiat.-Mental Health Nursing, Adelphi U., 1982, PhD, 1988. RN N.Y., N.J., cert. clin. specialist in adult psychiat. mental health, in group psychotherapy, lic. nurse practitioner in psychiatry, N.Y., Reiki therapist, cert. holistic nurse. Dir. psychiat. staff devel. Bellevue Hosp. Ctr., N.Y.C., 1980-82; group psychotherapist Jewish Inst. Geriatric Care, New Hyde Park, N.Y., 1983; staff psychotherapist New Hope Guild, N.Y.C., 1984; assoc. prof. undergrad. L.I. U. Bklyn., 1986—; nurse rschr. Englewood (N.J.) Hosp. and Med. Ctr., N.Y., 1994-97; pvt. practice, 1982—; psychiat. nurse practitioner Alternatives Counseling Project, Riverhead, 2000—. Maj. USAR, 1977—. Isabel McIsaac scholar, 1983, Am. Legion scholar, 1962. Mem. Nurse Practioner Assn. N.Y. State, Sigma Theta Tau.

LEPLEY, CHARMAINE GUNNOE, special education educator; b. Charleston, W.Va., Dec. 20, 1939; d. Arnold Leo and Ruth Louise (Fleck) Thomas; m. William Delano Lepley; children: Timothy, Pamela. BA, Glenville State Coll., 1961; MA, W.Va. U., 1970, EdD, 1993. Cert. spl. edn., reading, coop. learning tchr. Educator Kanawha County Schs., Charleston, 1961-92; adj. instr. Coll. of Grad. Studies U. W.Va., Institute, 1985-92; prof., head tchr. edn. U. Rio Grande, Ohio, 1992—. Curriculum cons. W.Va. Dept. Edn., Charleston, summer 1985-87; session speaker W.Va. Reading Assn., White Sulphur Springs, 1988-92; workshop cons., speaker U. W.Va. Coll. of Grad. Studies, Institute, 1989-92, U. Rio Grande, 1992—. Co-author (class text) Ideophobia, 1990; guest editor newspaper articles, 1991; contbr. articles to newsletters and jours. Pres. Pilot Club, St. Albans, W.Va., 1994. Mem. ASCD, Internat. Reading Assn. (session speaker 1988, 94), Coun. for Exceptional Children (co-founder student chpt. 1994), Ohio Assn. Tchr. Edn., Ohio Assn. Pvt. Colls. for Tchr. Edn. (trustee), Phi Delta Kappa. Democrat. Avocations: reading, volunteer work, cooking, gardening. Home: 105 Cedar Ln Saint Albans WV 25177-3401 Office: Univ Rio Grande 210 N College Rio Grande OH 45674

LEPOFF, RONALD BART, physician; b. Phila., Aug. 19, 1941; s. Nathan Stuart and Rose (Badian) L.; m. Dorothy Halstead, Mar. 12, 1967; children: Naomi, Rebecca. BA, Wesleyan U., Middletown, Conn., 1962; MD, U. Rochester, N.Y., 1967. Cert. in anat. and clin. pathology Am. Bd. Pathology. Intern Univ. Hosps. of Cleve., 1967-68, resident in gen. surgery, 1968-69; resident in anat. and clin. pathology U. Colo. Health Scis. Ctr., Denver, 1972-74; dir. labs. Denver Health and Hosps., 1976-89, Colo. Health Scis. Ctr., 1989—; prof. pathology and medicine U. Colo., 1995—. Pres. Colo. Physician Health Program, Denver, 1995. Maj. USAF, 1969-71. Fellow Coll. Am. Pathologists (gov. 1999—). Office: U Colo 4200 E 9th Ave # A022 Denver CO 80220-3706

LEPOME, PENELOPE MARIE, rehabilitation counselor, educator; b. Buffalo, Dec. 17, 1945; d. Raymond Arthur and Mildred Evelyn (Johnson) Kramer; m. Robert Charles LePome, May 26, 1966 (div. Jan. 1982); children: Lisa Anne, Kathryn Jane, Robert Charles II. BA in Biology, SUNY, Buffalo, 1967; MS in Vocat. Rehab., U. Nev., Las Vegas, 1984; postgrad., U. Nev., Reno, 1993-2000. Cert. rehab. counselor, substance abuse counselor, disability mgmt. specialist; lic. substitute tchr. and sch. counselor, Nev.; lic. alcohol and drug abuse counselor, Nev.; pupil personnel credential (sch. counselor), Calif. Co-owner, salesman Flamingo Realty, Las Vegas, Nev., 1974-76; substitute tchr. Clark County Sch. Dist., 1969-74, 82-84; adj. faculty Clark County C.C., 1984-86, Truckee Meadows C.C., Reno, 1987; bus. and industry field specialist Tng. Inst. Clark County C.C., 1985-86; probation officer on call Clark County Juvenile Svcs., Las Vegas, 1984; counselor Nike House, 1984; mental health technician III State of Nev., 1984-86; rehab. coord. I Nev. Bur. Vocat. Rehab., Reno, 1986-92; pvt. practice rehab. counseling, 1984-86; rehab. counselor GENEX Svcs. Inc., Reno, 1992-95; quality assurance specialist Divsn. Mental Health & Mental Hygiene, State of Nev., 1995-96; substance abuse counselor Divsn. Parole & Probation, 1996-2000; spl. svcs. coord., counselor Cerro Coso C.C., Ridgecrest, Calif., 2000—; social worker Aspira Foster Family Agy., 2000—; spl. edn. tchr. Total Edn. Solutions, Inc., 2002—. Active Nev. Womens Polit. Caucus, Las Vegas, 1983-85; carnival chmn. Rex Bell PTA, Las Vegas, 1974-75, treas., 1975-76; leader Frontier Area Girl Scouts U.S., Las Vegas, 1975-76, cookie sale chmn., 1980; treas., bd. dirs. Young Audiences, Las Vegas, 1979-80; mem. Reno City Coun. Adv. Com. Persons With Disabilities, 1991-93. N.Y. State Regents scholar, 1963. Mem. Am. Counseling Assn., AAUW (divsn. officer Nev. 1983-85, pres. 1982-83, v.p. programming 1981-82, v.p. membership 1980-81, life mem.), Assn. Part-time Profls. (bd. dirs.). Republican.

LEPORIERE, RALPH DENNIS, retired quality engineer; b. Elizabeth, N.J., Nov. 8, 1932; s. Maximo and Christian (Lello) L.; m. Judith Louise Crowhurst, Nov. 19, 1960; children: Bonnie Ann, David Anthony. BS in Chemistry, Rutgers U., 1954. Registered profl. engr., Calif. Chemist N.Y. Quinine & Chemical Works, Newark, 1954-55; asst. to chief quality control C.D. Smith Pharmacal Co., New Brunswick, N.J., 1955-56; asst. supr. quality control White Labs., Kenilworth, 1958-60; statistician Calif. and Hawaiian Sugar Co., Crockett, Calif., 1960-2000; ret., 2000. Instr., chmn. quality control dept. Laney C.C., Oakland, Calif., 1967-87; asst. prof., chmn. quality control dept. John F. Kennedy U., Martinez, Calif., 1967-72; instr., mem. adv. com. ann. statis. short course U. Calif., Davis, 1969-94 Pres. PTA Napa Junction Elem. Sch., Napa County, Calif., 1971-73; mem. early childhood com., program adv. com. Napa Valley Unified Sch. Dist., Napa County, 1972-76; v.p. Am. Canyon County Water Dist., American Canyon, Calif., 1971-73, pres., 1973-83, gen. mgr., 1981. Recipient Hon. Service award Calif. State PTA, 1973. Fellow Am. Soc. Quality Control (cert. quality engr., chmn. San Francisco sect., founder East Bay Subsect. 1970-71); mem. Soc. Mfg. Engrs. (sr.), Am. Statis. Soc., Am. Chem. Soc. Republican. Roman Catholic. Home: 618 Kilpatrick St American Canyon CA 94503-1305 Office: Calif & Hawaiian Sugar Co 830 Loring Ave Crockett CA 94525-1104 E-mail: umpralph@aol.com.

LEPOW, MARTHA LIPSON, pediatric educator; b. Cleve., Mar. 28, 1927; d. Harry A. and Anna (Miller) L.; m. Irwin H. Lepow, Feb. 7, 1958 (dec. 1984); children— Lauren, David, Daniel. B.A., Oberlin Coll., 1948; M.D., Case Western Res. U., 1952. Intern, resident in pediatrics Case Western Res. U., Cleve., 1952-56, fellow, asst. prof. pediatrics, 1958-67; assoc. prof. to prof. pediatrics U. Conn., Farmington, 1967-78; prof. pediatrics Albany Med. Coll., N.Y., 1978— , vice chmn. pediatrics, 1981— , dir. Clin. Studies Ctr., 1979-87; attending physician Albany Med. Ctr. Hosp.; cons. pediatric infectious disease St. Peter's Hosp.; spl. fellow Oxford, Eng., USPHS, 1961-62; bd. dirs. Albany Coll. Pharmacy, 1987—. Contbr. articles to profl. jours. Editorial bd. Pediatrics, 1976-81. Sec. HEW Task Force on Immunization Practices, 1977-78; mem. Conn. Acad. Sci. and Engring., 1977; adv. council Inst. Allergy and Infectious Disease, NIH, 1978-82; bd. dirs. Whitney Young Health Ctr., Albany; mem. profl. adv. com. Ctr. for Disabled, Albany. Mem. Am. Acad. Pediatrics (com. infectious diseases 1985—, assoc. editor report), Capital Dist. Pediatric Soc., Inst. Medicine, Com. on Vaccines, Am. Soc. Immunology (com. on status of women 1982-85), Am. Soc. Pediatric Research, Am. Pediatric Soc., Am. Soc. for Microbiology, Infectious Diseases Soc. Am., Sigma Xi, Alpha Omega Alpha. Home: 73 Bentwood Ct E Albany NY 12203-4809

LEPOW, RONALD S. podiatrist; BS in Psychology, U. Houston , 1967; DPM, Ill. Coll. Podiatric Medicine , 1971. Cert. diplomat Am. Bd. Podiatric Surgery , 1978, Am. Bd. Podiatric Public Health, 1987. Surg. tng. Oak Cliff Cmty. Hosp., Dallas, 1971—72; pvt. practice Houston, 1972—. Pres. Am. Podiatric Med. Assoc. , 1999—2000. Office: Lepow Foot Spec 6624 Fannin St Ste 1690 Houston TX 77030-2340*

LEPOWSKY, JAMES, mathematician, educator; b. N.Y.C., July 5, 1944; s. Edward and Frances (Rice) L.; m. Lael Leslie. AB, Harvard U., 1965; PhD, Mass. Inst. Tech., 1970. Lectr., rsch assoc. Brandeis U., 1970-72; asst. prof. Yale U., 1972-77; assoc. prof. Rutgers U., 1977-80, prof., 1980—. Mem. Inst. Advanced Study, 1975-76, fall 1980, spring 1985, 87-88, fall 1992, Math. Scis. Rsch. Inst., 1983-84. Co-author: (with I. Frenkel and A. Meurman) Vertex Operator Algebras and the Monster, 1988, (with C. Dong) Generalized Vertex Algebras and Relative Vertex Operators; contbr. articles to profl. jours. Sloan Fellow, 1976-78, Guggenheim Fellow, 1987-88. Mem. Am. Math. Soc. (coun. mem.-at-large 1993, com. on sci. policy 1993—), Math Assn. Am., Am. Phys. Soc. Office: Rutgers U Dept Math New Brunswick NJ 08903

LEPOWSKY, WILLIAM LEONARD, mathematics and statistics educator; BA summa cum laude, Harvard U., 1967; MA, U. Calif., Berkeley, 1968, 76, postgrad., 1981. Instr. Laney Coll., Oakland, Calif., 1969—, chair dept. math., 1979—80, 2000—02, supr. math. lab., 1987-99. Statis. cons. Panel on Skin Cancer, NAS, Washington, 1976-77; curriculum cons. Vista Coll., Berkeley, 1989; statis. cons. and expert witness, Berkeley, 1989—. Author: (textbook) Statistics in Action, 1994; contbr. articles to profl. jours. Scholar Nat. Honor Soc., Harvard Coll., Cambridge, 1963; Nat. Merit scholar, Harvard Coll., 1963-67; Harvard Coll. scholar, 1964-67; NSF grad. fellow U. Calif.,

Berkeley, 1967-68; Profl. Devel. grantee Laney Coll., Oakland, Calif., 1989; recipient tchg. excellence award Calif. Math. Coun. for C.C., 2000. Mem. Am. Statis. Assn., Calif. Math. Coun. for C.C. (bd. dirs. 1974-75), Phi Beta Kappa. Office: Laney Coll 900 Fallon St Oakland CA 94607-4808

LEPP, GERALD PETER, lawyer; b. Milw., Sept. 26, 1932; s. William Harris and Ida (Mendelson) L.; m. Sept. 8, 1963; children: Rebecca Anne, Michael Niels. BA, U. Wis., 1954; JD, Harvard U., 1959; LLM, NYU, 1973. Bar: Wis. 1959, D.C. 1962, N.Y. 1963, U.S. Supreme Ct. Assoc. counsel Continental Grain Co., N.Y.C., 1969-78, dir. of arbitration, 1987—92. Gen. counsel Cobec (USA) Brazilian Trading Co., Inc., N.Y.C., 1978-80; mng. atty. Gerald P. Lepp, N.Y.C., 1980-86; counsel to Nourse & Bowles, N.Y.C., 1986-87; ADR adminstr., U.S. Dist. Ct. (ea. dist.) N.Y., Bklyn., 1992—. Contbr. articles to profl. jours. 1st Lt. USAR, 1954-56. Mem. ABA, Inter-Pacific Bar Assn. Avocation: squash. E-mail: gerald_p._lepp@nyed.uscourts.gov.

LEPPARD, RAYMOND JOHN, conductor, harpsichordist; b. London, Aug. 11, 1927; came to U.S., 1976; s. Albert Victor and Bertha May (Beck) L. MA, U. Cambridge, Eng., 1955; DLitt (hon.), U. Bath, Eng., 1973; PhD (hon.), U. Indpls., 1991, Purdue U., 1992, Butler U., 1994, Wabash Coll., 1995; DMusic (hon.), Ind. U., 2001. Fellow Trinity Coll., Cambridge; lectr. music U. Cambridge, 1958-68; condr. Indpls. Symphony Orch., 1987-2001, condr. laureate, 2001—. Mus. dir. English Chamber Orch., London, 1959-77; prin. condr. BBC Philharm., Manchester, Eng., 1972-80; condr. symphony orchs. in Am. and Europe, Met. Opera, N.Y.C., Santa Fe Opera, San Francisco Opera, Covent Garden, Glyndebourne, Paris Opera; prin. guest condr. St. Louis Symphony Orch., 1984-90, music dir. Indpls. Symphony Orch., 1987-2001, European tours, 1993, 97; rec. artist, composer numerous film scores; author: Authenticity in Music, 1989, Raymond Leppard on Music/An Anthology of Critical and Personal Writings, 1993. Decorated Commendatore Della Repub-lica Italiana; comdr. Order Brit. Empire Office: c/o Clarion/Seven Muses 47 Whitehall Park London N19 3TW England also: Indianapolis Symphony Orch 45 Monument Circle Indianapolis IN 46204-2919

LEPPERT, PHYLLIS CAROLYN, obstetrician, gynecologist; b. Phila., July 7, 1938; 1. Walter Jennings and Alice (Brubach) L. BS, Columbia U., 1961, MS, 1964; MD, Duke U., 1973; PhD, Columbia U., 1986; DSc (hon.), DePauw U., Greencastle, Ind., 2000. Diplomate Nat. Bd. Med. Examiners, Am. Bd. Obstetrics and Gynecology. Clin. scholar Duke U., Durham, N.C., 1973-74; resident in pediatrics Duke U. Med. Ctr., 1974-76; resident in ob-gyn. Yale U. Med. Sch., New Haven, 1976-79; assoc. in ob-gyn. Columbia U., N.Y.C., 1979-81, asst. prof. ob-gyn., 1981-88; vis. prof. Tokyo (Japan) Coll. of Pharmacy, Hachioji, 1989; chmn. dept. ob-gyn. Rochester (N.Y.) Gen. Hosp., 1989-95; from assoc. prof. to prof. U. Rochester Sch. of Medicine and Dentistry, 1989-95; prof. SUNY, Buffalo, 1996-98, chmn. ob-gyn., 1996-98; chief reproductive scis. br. Nat. Inst. Child Health and Devel./NIH, Bethesda, Md., 1999—. Mem. adv. com. women's health initiative program NIH, 1993-97, mem. ad hoc study sect.; mem. N.Y. State Coun. on Grad. Med. Edn., 1994-99, mem. subcom. on health care reform and financing, mem. subcom. on med. edn. consortium; mem. Bd. Profl. Med. Conduct, N.Y., 1990-99; mem. Buffalo Vanguard Ctr. Women's Initiative NIH, 1996-98; founder Internat. Confs. on Extra Cellular Matrix of the Reproductive Tract; program dir. Western N.Y. Perinatal Database, 1997-98; vis. prof. St. Louis U., 1999—; adj. prof. ob-gyn., Uniform Svcs. U., Bethesda, 2000—. Co-editor: The Extracellular Matrix of the Reproductive Tract, 1991; sr. editor Primary Care for Women, 1996; contbr. numerous articles to profl. jours. Mem. Monroe County Bd. Health, 1992-96; bd. dirs. Maternity Ctr. Assn., N.Y.C., 1988-96, Preferred Care, Rochester, 1990-94, Riverdale Mental Health Assn., 1986-89, St. Luke/Roosevelt Hosp., N.Y.C., 1986-88; mem. vestry Christ Ch. Riverdale, Bronx, N.Y., 1984-86; mem. adv. com. Office of Tech., U.S. Congress, 1984; mem. stewardship com. All Saints Ch., Chevy Chase, Md. Berlex Found. Internat. rsch. fellow, 1989. Fellow ACOG; mem. AAAS, Am. Gynecol. Obstet. Soc., Am. Coll. of Ob-Gyn (past mem. com. on the underserved, mem. com. on acad. rsch. fellowship, past mem. gynecol. practice com., obstetrics practice com., mem. genetics com.), Coun. on Resident Edn. in Ob-gyn. (rep. region I 1999—, residency rev. com. for ob-gyn.), Soc. for Exptl. Biology and Medicine, N.Y. Obstet. Soc., Soc. for Gynecol. Investigation, Am. Soc. Profs. of Ob-Gyn. (region 1 rep. to coun. on grad. med. edn. in ob-gyn 1999), Soc. for Study of Reproduction, Am. Soc. Reproductive Medicine, Alpha Omega Alpha. Avocations: gardening, reading, singing, music. Office: NIH 6100 Executive Blvd Bethesda MD 20892-0001

LEPPIK, ILO E. neurologist, educator; b. Tartu, Estonia, Aug. 18, 1942; s. Elmar Emil and Lilly (Hanson) L.; m. Margaret Ann White, June 18, 1967; children: Peter, David, Karina. BS, Haverford (Pa.) Coll., 1964; MD, U. Pa., 1968. Diplomate Am. Bd. Neurology and Psychiatry, Am. Bd. Clin. Neuro-physiology. Rsch. fellow Montreal (Que.) Neurol. Inst., McGill U., 1974-76; asst. prof. neurology U. Minn., Mpls., 1976-80, assoc. prof. neurology, 1980-87, prof. neurology, 1987-89, clin. prof. neurology, 1989—, clin. assoc. prof. pharmacy, 1986-89, clin. prof. pharmacy, 1987—; dir. rsch. MINCEP Epilepsy Care, 1990—. Author: Contemporary Diagnosis and Management of the Patient with Epilepsy, 1993, 5th edit., 2000; editor books in field; contbr. articles to profl. jours.; founding editor Jour. Epilepsy Rsch., 1987—. Bd. dirs. Am. Bd. Clin. Neurophysiology, 1992-94. Maj. USAF, 1969-71. Fellow Am. Acad. Neurology; mem. Am. Epilepsy Soc. (pres. 1992-94, treas. 1983-86), Ctrl. Soc. Neurol. Rsch. (pres. 1991-92), Assn. Neurologists of Minn. (pres. 1983-89), Epilepsy Found. Am. (chmn., profl. adv. bd. 1989-91, bd. dirs. 1982-92). Republican. Unitarian Universalist. Achievements include devel. of new drugs for treatment of epilepsy. Avocation: cross country skiing. Office: MINCEP Epilepsy Care 5775 Wayzata Blvd Minneapolis MN 55416-1222

LEPPIK, MARGARET WHITE, state legislator; b. Newark, June 5, 1943; d. John Underhill and Laura Schaefer White; m. Ilo Elmar Leppik, June 18, 1967; children: Peter, David, Karina. BA, Smith Coll., 1965. Rsch. asst. Wistar Inst., U. Pa., Phila., 1967-68, U. Wis., Madison, 1968-69; mem. Minn. Ho. Reps., St. Paul, 1990—, chair higher edn. fin. com. Active Golden Valley (Minn.) Planning Commn., 1982—90, Golden Valley Bd. Zoning Appeals, 1985—87, sec., 2002—; commr. Midwest Higher Edn. Commn., 1999—; bd. dirs. Partnership for Action Against Tobacco, 1998—. Named Citizen of Distinction, Hennepin County Human Svcs. Planning Bd. 1992, Legislator of Yr., U. Minn. Alumni Assn., 1995, 98-2001, Minn. State U. Student Assn., 1999. Mem. LWV (v.p., dir. 1984-90), Minn. Opera Assn. (pres. 1986-88), Rotary Internat., Optimists Internat. Republican. Avocations: gardening, biking, canoeing. Home: 7500 Western Ave Golden Valley MN 55427-4849 Office: 485 State Office Bldg Saint Paul MN 55155-0001 E-mail: rep.peggy.leppik@house.leg.state.mn.us.

LEPPLA, DAVID CHARLES, pathology educator; b. Denver, July 22, 1953; s. Charles Frederick and Lucille Josephine (Schneider) L. BS, Seattle U., 1975; MD, Colo. U., 1979. Diplomate Am. Bd. Pathology. Intern in internal medicine U. Tex. Health Sci. Ctr., Dallas, 1979-80, fellow in mineral metabolism and endocrinology, 1980-82, rsch. assoc., 1982-83; resident in pathology Marshall U. Sch. Medicine, Huntington, W.Va., 1984-87, chief resident in pathology, 1987-88, asst. prof., 1988-99, assoc. prof., 1999—. Fellow Am. Soc. Clin. Pathology (alt. to adv. com. 1990), Assn. Clin. Scientists; mem. Alpha Omega Alpha. Office: Marshall U Sch Medicine 1542 Spring Valley Dr Huntington WV 25704-9588

LEPPO, JEFFREY ALLEN, cardiologist; b. Bklyn., Nov. 17, 1947; s. Seymour and Shirley (Gordon) L.; m. Marjorie Sue Safran, Aug. 27, 1970; children: Maura S., Maia S. AB, U. Rochester, N.Y., 1969; MD, SUNY, Bklyn., 1973. Intern State U., Kings County Hosp. Ctr., Bklyn., 1973-74, jr. and sr. resident, 1974-76; fellow in cardiology Montefiore Hosp. and Med. Ctr., Bronx, N.Y., 1976-78; NIH postdoctoral rsch. fellow in cardiology Montefiore Hosp. and Med. Ctr., Albert Einstein Coll. Medicine, 1978-79; NIH postdoctoral rsch. fellow in cardiovascular nuclear medicine Mass. Gen. Hosp., Boston, 1979-80; asst. prof. medicine Boston U. Sch. Medicine, 1980-83, adj. asst. prof. medicine, 1983—; dir. exercise lab. Boston City Hosp., 1981-83; assoc. prof. medicine and nuclear medicine U. Mass. Med. Ctr., Worcester, 1983-90, clin. dir. nuclear medicine, 1990—, prof. medicine and nuclear medicine, 1991-98, prof. radiology, divsn. chief nuclear medicine, 1998—, interim chair dept. radiology, 2001—. Cons. Vanqwish Trial Nuclear Cardiology, VA Multicenter Trial, 1992-96; cons. IV dipyridamole Boehringer-Ingelheim, 1985-91, isonitriles dipyridamole DuPont Pharma, North Billerica, Mass., 1987-94. Contbr. articles to profl. jours., chpts. to books. Bd. dirs. Am. Heart Assn., Worcester, 1995—, Internat. Artists Series, Worcester, 1985-96; mem. allocations com. Worcester Jewish Fedn., 1986-89. Recipient Med. Found. fellowship Am. Heart Assn., Mass., 1980-82, New investigator award NIH, 1982-85; grantee NIH, Washington, 1986-94. Fellow ACP, Am. Coll. Cardiology, Am. Heart Assn. (clin. coun.); mem. Soc. Nuclear Medicine (cardiovascular pres. 1989), Am. Fedn. Clin. Rsch., Am. Soc. Nuclear Cardiology (bd., pres. 1993-94, disting. svc. award 1997). Office: U Mass Med Ctr/Nuclear Medicine 55 Lake Ave N Worcester MA 01655-0002 E-mail: jeffrey.leppo@umassmed.edu.

LEPS, THOMAS MACMASTER, civil engineer, consultant; b. Keyser, W.Va., Dec. 3, 1914; s. Thomas Davis and Grace (King) L.; m. Catherine Mary Sacksteder, June 22, 1940; 1 son, Timothy. BA, Stanford U., 1936; MS, MIT, 1939. Jr. and asst. civil engr. Calif. Divsn. Hwys., U.S. C.E. & Bur. of Reclamation, 1936-41; chief civil engr. So. Calif. Edison Co., L.A., 1946-61; chief engr. Shannon & Wilson Co., Seattle, 1961-63; cons. civil engr. U.S. and abroad, Dinuba, Calif., 1963—. Mem. over 90 bds. of cons. on hydro, steam and nuclear power projects. Contbr. articles to profl. jours., chpts. to engring books. Served to comdr. USNR, 1943-46, 46-60. Recipient certificate of Appreciation Calif. Dept. Water Resources, 1971 Mem. NAE (life mem., nominations com. for officers 1981), ASCE (life mem., cert. of appreciation 1961), U.S. Com. on Large Dams (life mem. vice-chmn. exec. com. 1980-81), Phi Beta Kappa, Tau Beta Pi. Presbyterian. Address: PO Box 217 Dinuba CA 93618-0217

LEPUCKI, RICHARD JOHN, engineer; b. Aug. 28, 1949; B in Engring., Stevens Inst. Tech., 1971; post grad., U. Akron, 1975-76. Prin. engr. Babcock and Wilcox, R & D, Alliance, Ohio, 1971-97; project mgr. Seifert Tech., Massillon, 1997—. Home: 2326 Rutgers St NW North Canton OH 44720-5757

LE QUÉRÉ, JEAN FRANÇOIS MARIE, scientific instrumentation re-searcher; b. Pabu, France, Apr. 7, 1933; s. Yves Marie and Yvonne Marie Rose (Ollivier) Le Q.; m. Jacqueline Marie Le Colas, Mar. 26, 1964; children: Anne Marie, Isabelle Marie, Jean-Yves Marie, Blandine Marie. Upper tech. diploma, Nat. Conservatory Arts-Trade, Paris, 1965, engr. physicist grad., 1968; DEng, U. Pierre and Marie Curie, Paris, 1983. Electrician Regie Renault, Paris, 1950-61; lab. technician, 1961-65; lab. upper rsch. technician, 1965-68; engr. physicist U. Paris 6, 1968-72, engr. rschr., 1972-96; mem. faculty U. Paris 7, 1972-94, engr. rschr., 1972—. Contbr. articles to profl. jours. With French Army, 1953. Mem. Assn. Tchg. (pres. 1996). Home: 22 rue Pierre Brossolette 93160 Noisy le Grand France E-mail: jean_lequere@laposte.net.

LE QUESNE, PHILIP WILLIAM, chemistry educator, researcher; b. Auckland, New Zealand, Jan. 6, 1939; came to U.S., 1967; s. Ernest W. B. and Bettie A. (Colwill) Le Q.; m. Mary E. Kinloch, 1965 (dec. 1988); children: Elizabeth Ruth, Martin James. BS, U. Auckland, 1960, MS, 1961, PhD, 1964, D.Sc. (hon.), 1979. Asst. prof. U. Mich., Ann Arbor, 1967-72; assoc. prof. Northeastern U., Boston, 1973-78, prof., 1978—, chmn. dept. chemistry, 1979-87, vice provost for rsch. and grad. edn., 1991-93. Assoc. dir. Barnett Inst. for Chem. analysis and Materials Sci., 1993-97. Contbr. articles on chemistry to profl. jours. Sr. warden Ch. of the Advent, Boston, 1990-96. Home: 17 Stafford Rd Newton Center MA 02459-1818 Office: Northeastern U Chemistry Dept 360 Huntington Ave Boston MA 02115-5000 E-mail: p.lequesne@neu.edu.

LERAAEN, ALLEN KEITH, financial executive; b. Mason City, Iowa, Dec. 4, 1951; s. Myron O. and Clarice A. (Handeland) L.; m. Mary Elena Partheymuller, Apr. 14, 1978. BBA in Data Processing and Acctg., No. Ariz. U., 1975. CFA. Data processing supr. Stephenson & Co., Denver, 1978-81, contr., 1981-85, arbitrageur, trader, 1985-88, v.p., 1985-90, exec. v.p., portfo-lio mgr., 1990—. V.p., sec. bd. dirs. Circle Corp., Denver, 1985—; v.p. StarTek, Inc., Denver, 1997—. Mem. Assn. Investment Mgmt. and Rsch., Denver Soc. Security Analysts. Avocation: flying. Home: 5692 S Robb St Littleton CO 80127-1942 Office: 100 Garfield St Fl 4 Denver CO 80206-5597 E-mail: al@great.net.

LERACH, RICHARD FLEMING, lawyer; b. Pitts., Oct. 26, 1940; s. Richard E. and Evelyn (Fleming) L.; m. Judith Ifft, June 29, 1963; children: Mollie Lerach Gannon, Richard I. BBA, U. Pitts., 1962, LLB, 1965. Bar: N.Y. 1966, Pa. 1969. Atty. US Steel Corp., Pitts., 1968—76, gen. atty., 1976—85, sr. gen. atty., 1985—98, asst. gen. counsel, 1998—. Bd. dirs. Bank Pitts. Home: 796 Flint Ridge Rd Pittsburgh PA 15243-1101 Office: US Steel Corp 600 Grant St Ste 1500 Pittsburgh PA 15219-2800

LERANGIS, PETER D. writer; b. Bklyn., Aug. 19, 1955; s. Nicholas Peter and Mary Condos Lerangis; m. Cristina L. de Varon; children: Nicholas James de Varon Lerangis, Joseph Alexander de Varon Lerangis. AB in Biochem. Scis., Harvard Coll., 1977. Author: (young adult book) The Yearbook, 1994, (children's book) It Came From the Cafeteria, 1996, Spring Fever, 1997, Attack of the Killer Potatoes, 1998, Antarctica, 2000, (children's book series) Watchers, 1998—99, Abracadabra, 2001. Mem.: SAG, PEN, Actors Equity, Authors Guild, Soc. Children's Book Writers/Illustrators. Avocations: photog-raphy, running, singing. Home: 7 W 96 St New York NY 10025

LERER, NEAL M. lawyer; b. Chelmsford, Mass., June 20, 1954; m. Rose P. Meegan, July 28, 1991; children: Scott Harold, Benjamin Joseph. BA, Brown U., 1976; JD, Duke Law Sch., 1979. Bar: Mass. 1979, U.S. Dist. Ct. Mass. 1980, U.S. Ct. Appeals (1st cir.) 1991. Ptnr. Martin, Magnuson, McCarthy & Kenney, Boston, 1980-96; mng. atty., pvt. practice Chelmsford, Mass., 1996—. Corporator Lowell (Mass.) 5 Cents Savings Bank, 1985—. Co-author: Personal Injury and Death, 1980, Damages in Massachusetts, 1990, Personal Injury Litigation in Massachusetts, 1991, Premises Liability, 1994. Reader Recording for the Blind, Cambridge, Mass., 1987-94; bd. dirs. Goodwin Fund; dir. Town of Chelmsford Scholarship Com. Mem. Mass. Bar Assn., Mass. Bar Found., Greater Lowell Bar Assn., Brown Club of Boston (bd. dirs., co-pres. 1998-2000). Home: 4 Manahan St Chelmsford MA 01824-2844 E-mail: neallerer@aol.com.

LEREW, LLOYD EUGENE, consultant; b. Carlisle, Pa., Sept. 27, 1949; s. Lloyd Miller and Kathryn Maxine (Karns) L.; m. Jane E. Myers, Aug. 18, 1994; 1 child, Ryan Kyle. BS, Mich. State U., 1971, MS, 1972, PhD, 1978. Engring. trainee USDA, Soil Conservation Svc., Harrisburg, Pa., 1968-69; undergrad. rsch. assoc. dept. agrl. engring. Mich. State U., East Lansing, 1970, grad. asst., 1971-73, 75-76, instr., 1977-78, asst. prof., 1979-80; gen. mgr., bus. mgr. Lerew's Farm Market, Inc., Dillsburg, Pa., 1974-80, v.p., 1981-86, pres., 1986—; cons., 1990—. Chmn. York County Solid Waste and Refuse Authority, York, Pa., 1983-89, vice-chmn., 1990-91; mem. No. York County Sch. Dist. Vocat. Agrl. Adv. Bd., Dillsburg, Pa., 1985-87. Author: Primer for the Michigan State University CDC 6500, 1973; contbr. articles to profl. jours. Mem. Am. Soc. Agrl. Engrs., Alpha Epsilon. Republican. Avocations: com-puters, antique toys, nature, gardening. Home: 2130 Old York Rd Dillsburg PA 17019-8911 E-mail: lelerew@earthlink.net.

LERITTE, JENNIFER JONES, social worker, mental health administrator; b. Ville Platte, La., Feb. 26, 1953; d. John Clifton and Marie Clamie (Richard) Jones; m. John Downs Hutchins, Dec. 18, 1971 (div. Apr. 1977); m. George Alan Leritte, Nov. 22, 1980; children: Jonathan Christopher, Jeremy Wilton. BA in Sociology, N.E. La. State U., 1975; MSW, La. State U., 1981. Cert. social worker, La., social work clin. practitioner, Tex. Food stamp eligibility worker I Bossier Parish Office of Family Security, Benton, La., 1978-79; food stamp eligibility worker II Caddo Parish Office of Family Security, Shreve-port, 1979; student intern Family Counseling and Children's Svcs., 1979-80; housing insp. I Shreveport Dept. Urban Devel., 1980; social worker supr. I Ellisville (Miss.) State Sch., 1982; program coord. Sabine Valley Regional Mental Health/Mental Retardation Ctr., Longview, Tex., 1982-84; residential coord., social worker supr. Normal Life La., Layfayette, 1984-86; svc. coord. supr. ACCESS, Shreveport, 1986-90; mental health spl. svcs. dir. I, La. dept. health/hosps. Office Human Svcs., Div. Mental Health, 1990-94; exec. dir. Cmty. Interaction Svc., Inc., Bossier City, La., 1994-96; group co-therapist Sexual Behavior Modification Program, 1994—; owner, clin. soc. worker JJL Consultinf & Triple J Mgmt., Inc., Shreveport, La., 1996—. Active parent, tchr. Family Counseling and Children Svcs., Shreveport., 1989-91. Field Day coord. St. Joseph Sch. Home-Sch. Assn., Shreveport, 1990; mem. Mayor's Citizens Adv. Group on Disabilities, City of Shreveport. Mem. NASW (bd. sec. 1989-91, treas. 1990-92, sec. La. state chpt. 1992-94, Shreveport region rep. 1995—, registered, qualified clin.social worker, diplomate in clin. social work, Dorothy Schenthal Leadership award La.-Shreveport region 1996), Acad. Cert. Social Workers, Civitan Internat. (Shreveport club). Republican. Roman Catholic. Avocations: reading, walking, darts, backgammon. Office: JJL Consulting & Triple J Mgmt Inc 2800 Youree Dr Ste B422 Shreveport LA 71104-3661

LERITZ, DANIEL RAYMOND, pharmaceutical company executive, con-sultant; b. St. Louis, Jan. 24, 1945; s. Joseph D. and Agnes (Lyons) L.; m. Retta J. Schoen, Nov. 9, 1974; children: Daniel, Retta. BS in Chem., St. Louis U., 1966; MBA, Washington U., 1971. Loss control cons. The Hartford Ins. Group, St. Louis, 1970-71; mgr. new products Carboline Co., 1971-78; acct. exec./dir. mktg. BHN Advt., 1978-80; mgr. sales Carnegie div. Rexall Corp., 1980-81; mgr. western sales The Vitarine Co., Inc., Springfield Gardens, N.Y., 1981-82; mgr. sales Pvt. Formulations, Inc., Edison, N.J., 1982-87; pres. The Leritz Co., Inc., St. Louis, 1985—. Bd. dirs. Nutri-Pac Corp., Interstate Foods Mktg., Ltd. Co-authored numerous articles. Bd. dirs. Am. Cancer Soc., Mo., 1980; chmn. bd. trustees York Woods, Mo., 1984; mem. alumni bd. St. Louis U. High. Mem. Am. Chem. Soc., Assn. Drug & Chem. Industry of Mo., Norwood Hills Country Club, Delta Sigma Phi. Roman Catholic. Avocations: golf, travel, fishing. Home: 1 Cricket Ln Saint Louis MO 63144-1021 Office: The Leritz Co Inc 2652 Melvin Ave Saint Louis MO 63144-2551

LERITZ, LAWRENCE R. choreographer, singer, actor, dancer, producer; b. Alton, Ill., Sept. 26, 1952; s. Leonard Henry and Marcella Rose (Fravle) L. Student, Harkness Ballet Sch., 1973-74, Sch. Am. Ballet, 1975-76. Debut: State Fair, St. Louis Muny Opera, 1969, appeared in Can Can, 1983; TV appearances include Capitol, 1982, All My Children, 1981-85, Home Sweet, Homeless; Rodney Dangerfield: It's Lonely at the Top, HBO, 1992, various comms.; guest expert on various talk shows including Rolonda, Charles Perez, Maury Povich, Show Biz Today, Am. Muscle Mag., Rosie O'Donnell Show; film debut: Stardust Memories, 1979; appeared in Easy Money, 1982, Stag, 1997; star Leritz and His Girls, 1983-85; Broadway appearances include: Fiddler on the Roof, 1981, Fonteyn and Nureyev on Broadway, 1975; prodr. and choreographer off-Broadway musical, Boobs!, 2000; appeared Met. Opera telecast of Manon Lescaut, 1980; choreographer feature film musical The Last Dragon, 1984; choreographer, co-star home video Treehouse Trolls Birthday Day, 1993; dancer with Harkness Ballet, Paris Opera, Hamburg Ballet, Chgo. Ballet, world wide guest star; dir., choreographer own co. Dance Celebration which represented U.S. at Internat. Choreographic Competitions, Paris, 1979; dir. mus. numbers for Shields and Yarnell; creator mus. indsls. for Lily of France, Bausch & Lomb, Christian Dior; pres. Leritz Prodns., Ltd., N.Y.C. and L.A., 1983—; star exercise cruise on Queen Elizabeth II, 1995; rec. artist: It Takes Two to Tango, 1984, Crank It Up, 1989, Bright Light, 1992; song lyricist, composer; East coast prodr. Day of Compassion, 1995-97; choreog-rapher, guest dancer Placido Domingo's L.A. Music Ctr. Opera, 1987. Writer Muscular Devel. mag., Ironman mag., Men's Fitness mag., Muscle & Fitness mag.; creator, star of video Total Stretch! with Lawrence Leritz, 1992. Full scholar Sch. Am. Ballet, Harkness Ballet Sch.; Lawrence R. Leritz Day declared; recipient Key to City, Wood River, Ill., 1983, Alton, Ill., 1987; appeared on cover Dance Pages mag., fall 1987, spring 1989 Time Mag.'s Local Hero, 1996. Mem. AFTRA, ASCAP (Pop Music awards for songwriting 1985—), SAG (film nominating com. 1996), Actors Equity Assn., Am. Guild Musical Artists (bd. govs. 1979-92, 94—, prodn. supr./choreographer 50th Ann. Gala 1986, Life Membership award for disting. svc. 1991). Office: 250 W 19th St Apt 10M New York NY 10011-4054 E-mail: lleritz@aol.com.

LERMAN, ALLEN H. economist; b. N.Y.C., Mar. 21, 1943; s. Louis and Elizabeth L. (Solomon) L.; m. Barbara I. Cohen, Aug. 25, 1968; children: Jeffrey C., Melissa A., Ari R. AB, Columbia U., 1964; MA, Yale U., 1965, MPhil, 1967. Cons. Pres.'s Council of Econ. Advisors, Washington, 1965-68; teaching assoc. Dept. Econs., Yale U., New Haven, 1966-67, asst. in instruction, 1968-70; research fellow The Brookings Instn., Washington, 1967-68; economist Office of Tax Analysis, U.S. Treasury Dept., 1971—. Author: High Income Tax Returns 1974 and 1975, 1977, High Income Tax Returns, 1975 and 1976, 1978; contbr. articles to profl. jours.; editor: Kennedy and the Press, 1965. NSF fellow, 1964-68, The Brookings Instn. fellow, 1967-68. Mem. Am. Econ. Assn., Nat. Tax Assn. Jewish. Home: 14905 Waterway Dr Rockville MD 20853-3618 Office: Office of Tax Analysis 5408 Main Treasury Washington DC 20220-0002

LERMAN, EILEEN R. lawyer; b. N.Y.C., May 6, 1947; d. Alex and Beatrice (Kline) L. BA, Syracuse U., 1969; JD, Rutgers U., 1972; MBA, U. Denver, 1983. Bar: N.Y. 1973, Colo. 1976. Atty. FTC, N.Y.C., 1972-74; corp. atty. Samsonite Corp. and consumer products divsn. Beatrice Foods, Denver, 1976-78, assoc. gen. counsel, 1978-85, asst. sec., 1979-85; ptnr. Davis, Lerman & Weinstein, 1985-92, Eileen R. Lerman & Assocs., Denver, 1993—. Bd. dirs. Legal Aid Soc. of Met. Denver, 1979-80. Bd. dirs., vice chmn. Colo. Postsecondary Ednl. Facilities Authority, 1981-89; bd. dirs., pres. Am. Jewish Com., 1989-92; mem. Leadership Denver, 1983. Mem. ABA, Colo. Women's Bar Assn. (bd. dirs. 1980-81), Colo. Bar Assn. (mem. bd. govs.), Denver Bar Assn. (trustee), N.Y. State Bar Assn., Rhone Brackett Inn (pres. 1997-98), Denver Law Club, Rutgers U. Alumni Assn., Univ. Club. Home: 1018 Fillmore St Denver CO 80206-3332 Office: Lerman & Assocs PC 50 S Steele St Ste 820 Denver CO 80209-2813

LERMAN, KENNETH BARRY, marketing professional, consultant; b. Bklyn., Apr. 15, 1947; s. Albert J. and Dorithee (Goldman) L.; m. Geri Anne Appel, Apr. 24, 1976. BA, Coll. of Emporia, 1972; MBA, Emporia State U., 1976. Product mgr. H. J. Heinz, Pitts., 1976-77; sr. product dir. Johnson & Johnson, New Brunswick, N.J., 1977-81; mktg. dir. Pizza Hut/Pepsico, Inc., Wichita, Kans., 1981-83, Taco Tico, Inc., Wichita, 1983-85; owner Kenneth B. Lerman, Cons., 1985—; pres., owner North Am. Mktg., 1989—. Presenter in field. Contbr. articles to pubs. Bd. dirs. Botanica, The Wichita Gardens, 1994—, Nat. Found. for Tchg. Entrepreneurship, 1994-95, Crime Stoppers, Wichita, 1987-88, Wichita River Festival, 1985-88, Huntingdon's Disease Found., Wichita, 1987-88; bd. dirs., founder Music Theatre for Young People, Wichita, 1985-88; founder, pres. Wichita chpt. Planning Forum, Inc., 1985-88; elected del. pres. White House Conf. on Small Bus., 1995. Decorated Navy Combat Action medal, Navy Unit Commendation medal. Mem. Downtown Rotary Club Wichita. Christian Scientist. Avocations: cooking, travelling. Address: North American Marketing 1668 N Sagebrush St Wichita KS 67230-7010 E-mail: kbl@kenlerman.com.

LERMAN, KENNETH BRIAN, lawyer; b. N.Y.C., Mar. 3, 1961; s. Robert Allan and Ellen Lerman. BA in Bus. Mgmt. and Govt., Clark U., 1983; JD, Emory U., 1986. Bar: Conn. 1987, U.S. Dist. Ct. Conn. 1987, Fla. 1997. Assoc. Siegel, O'Connor, Schiff, Zangari & Kainen, Hartford, Conn., 1986-88; pvt. practice Kenneth B. Lerman, P.C., Windsor, 1988—. Counsel Conn. chpt. Sickle Cell Disease Assn. of Am., 1991—. Co-founder, v.p. Wadsworth Atheneum Art Club, Hartford, 1990-93; mem. exec. com. Hartford chpt. Anti-Defamation League, 1993—; founder, coach, pres. Lacrosse team Clark U., 1981-83; bd. dirs. Sonia Plumb Dance Co., Hartford, 1999-2001; dir. amb. recruitment Hugh O'Brian Youth Leadership Found. of Conn., 1999-2000. Mem. ABA, Fla. Bar Assn., Conn. Bar Assn., Hartford County Bar Assn., New Eng. Intercollegiate Lacrosse Assn. (v.p., dir. club divsn. 1983). Office: 651 Day Hill Rd Windsor CT 06095-1719

LERNER, ABRAM, retired museum director, artist; b. N.Y.C., Apr. 11, 1913; s. Hyman and Sarah (Becker) L.; m. Pauline Hanenberg, Oct. 7, 1940; 1 child, Aline. BA, NYU, 1935; student, Ednl. Alliance, Art Students League, Bklyn. Mus.; pvt. studies, Florence, Italy. Asso. dir. A.C.A. Gallery and Artist's Gallery, N.Y.C., 1945-57; curator Joseph H. Hirshhorn Collection, 1957-66; dir. Hirshhorn Mus. and Sculpture Garden, Washington, 1967-85; founding dir. emeritus, ret. Hirshhorn Mus. and Sculpture Garden, Smithsonian Instn., 1985. Adv. bd. Archives Am. Art, 1970— Author: Hirshhorn Museum and Sculpture Garden - Inaugural Book, 1974, Gregory Gillespie, 1977; contbr. to mags., mus. catalogues.; one man show, Davis Gallery, N.Y.C., 1958, group shows include, A.C.A. Gallery, Peridot Gallery, Bklyn.-Mus., Pa. Acad., Davis

Gallery; represented in pvt. collections. Decorated commandeur in de Orde Van Oranje-Nassau (The Netherlands); chevalier dans L'Ordre des Arts et des Lettres (France). Home: 98 Lewis St Southampton NY 11968-5006

LERNER, ALAN CHARLES, financial market economist, educator; b. Bklyn., July 24, 1944; s. Isidore and Florence (Leschinski) L.; m. Bonnie Marilyn Taub, Jan. 28, 1967 (div. Apr. 1980); children: Lisa, Jennifer; m. Linda Joy Hunter, Feb. 1, 1981 (dec. Sept. 1982); 1 child, Kali; m. Wendy Watson, Aug. 20, 1985. BA, Bklyn. Coll., 1966; MBA, NYU, 1968. Instr. econs. NYU, 1969-72; economist Salomon Bros., N.Y.C., 1972-74; economist, sr. v.p. Banker Trust Co., 1974—93; pres. Lerner Cons., 1993—. Adj. prof. econs. and fin. NYU, 1974— Author: weekly market letter Prospects for the Credit Markets, 1976—93. NDEA fellow, 1967-69 Mem. Am. Fin. Assn., Money Marketeers (v.p. 1981—, past pres.). Jewish.

LERNER, ALAN JAY, lawyer; b. Scranton, Pa., July 29, 1949; s. Jack and Dorothy Rene (Golob) L.; m. Mary Alicia Kincaid, Nov. 9, 1979; children—Hailey, Joan; m. Estelle Fields, Dec. 21, 1970 (div. Apr. 1978); children—Sonia, Bernadette. B.A. in Polit. Sci. cum laude, San Fernando Valley Coll., 1971; J.D. magna cum laude, U. Toledo, 1974. Bar: Mont. 1974, U.S. Dist. Ct. Mont. 1975, U.S. Ct. Appeals (9th cir.) 1975, U.S. Supreme Ct. 1984. Assoc. Crowley Law Firm, Billings, Mont., 1974-75, Hartelius & Lewin, Great Falls, Mont., 1975-76; ptnr. Richter & Lerner, 1976-81; sole practice, Bigfork, Mont., 1981-88; sole practice Kalispell, Mont., 1988—. Author U. Toledo Law Rev., 1973, editor, 1974. Author: (novel) Spare Parts, 1980. Teaching fellow U. Toledo, 1973; Ohio State Bar scholar, 1972, PAD Nat. scholar, 1973. Mem. Assn. Trial Lawyers Am., Mont. Trial Lawyers Assn., Mont. Bar Assn., N.W. Mont. Bar Assn. Democrat. Jewish. Home: 88 Stafford St Kalispell MT 59901-2729 Office: 2450 Us Hwy 93 S Kalispell MT 59901-7532

LERNER, ALEXANDER ROBERT, association executive; b. Chicago, Ill., June 26, 1946; s. Peter Lerner and Lillian Orlinsky Joseph; m. Marianne Ryan, Apr. 21, 1979; 1 child, Lindsey Anne. BS, No. Ill. U., 1970. Adminstrv. asst. Gov. of Ill., 1970-72; adminstrv. asst. speaker Ill. Ho. of Reps., Springfield, 1973-74; asst. dir. pub. affairs div. AMA, Chgo., 1974-75; dir. Ill. State Med. Soc., 1975-78; pres. Govtl. Affairs, Inc., 1978-81; chief exec. officer Ill. State Med. Soc. and Ins. Svcs. Inc., Ill. State Med. Inter Ins. Exch., 1981—. Adv. com. to dir. Ctrs. Disease Control and Prevention; bd. dirs. Lincoln Park Zoo. Chmn. Ill. Sports Facilities Authority, 1992—. Mem. Am. Assn. Med. Soc. Execs., Am. Soc. Assn. Execs., Chgo. Soc. Assn. Execs., Assn. Forum Chgo., Union League Club, Chgo. Yacht Club, Michigan Shores Club, Execs. Club of Chgo., Conway Farms Golf Club. Avocations: nautical antiques, presidential history, travel, golf. Office: Ill State Med Soc 20 N Michigan Ave Chicago IL 60602-4811

LERNER, ALFRED, professional sports team executive, real estate and financial executive; b. Brooklyn, New York, May 8, 1933; s. Abraham and Clara (Abrahmson) Lerner; m. Norma Wokloff, Aug. 7, 1955; children: Nancy Faith, Randolph David. BA, Columbia U., 1955. Chmn. bd., chief exec. officer Multi-Amp Corp., Dallas, 1970—80, Realty Refund Trust, Cleve., 1971—90; pres., chief exec. officer Refund Advisers, Inc., 1971—, Town & Country Mgmt. Corp., 1979—93; chmn., dir. Equitable Bancorp., Balt., 1981—90; chmn., bd. dirs. Prog. Corp., Cleve., 1988—93; chmn., CEO, pres. MBNA Corp., Newark, 1991—; chmn., CEO Town & Country Trust, 1993—; co-owner, chair Cleveland Browns, 1998—. Chmn., bd. dirs. MNC Corp., Balt., 1991—93. Trustee Columbia U., Case Western Res. U.; pres. Cleve. Clin. 1st lt. Res. USMC, 1955—57. Mem.: Young Pres. Orgn., Harmonie Club (N.Y.C.), Beechmont Club (Cleve.). Jewish. Home: 19000 S Park Blvd Cleveland OH 44122-1853 Office: MBNA Corporation 1100 N King St Wilmington DE 19884-0001 also: Cleveland Browns 76 Lou Groza Blvd Berea OH 44017*

LERNER, BARBARA, public policy consultant, researcher, writer; b. Chgo., Mar. 31, 1935; d. Jacob Israel and Mary (Turen) L. BA with honors, U. Ill., 1956; MA, U. Chgo., 1961, PhD, 1965, JD, 1977. Bar: Ill. 1977. Intern U. Chgo. Hosp. and Clinic, 1962-63; instr. Coll. Medicine U. Ill., 1963-64; clin. psychologist Ill. Mental Health Ctr., Chgo., 1965-68; assoc. prof. Ohio U., Athens, 1968-70; pvt. practice clin. psychologist Chgo., 1970-78; assoc. prof. Roosevelt U., 1972-74; study dir. Nat. Acad. Scis., Washington, 1977-78; pres. Lerner Assocs., Princeton, N.J., 1981-96, Chgo., 1997—. Vis. scholar Ednl. Testing Svc., Princeton, 1978-79, sr. rsch. scientist, 1980-81; expert witness fed. cts. Debra P. vs. Turlington, Tampa, Fla., Marshall vs. Ga., 1983; vis. prof. U. Tex., Austin, 1989. *Dr. Barbara Lerner's research (Public Interest, fall 1982), uncovered the fact that our students scored far below their foreign peers, and was the basis for A Nation at Risk, the report that launched the education reform movement that began in the 1980's and continues today. Her testimony in Debra P. v. Turlington, 730 F.2d 1405 (1984) and NAACP v. Georgia, 775 F.2d 1403 (1985) convinced the federal courts that making minimum competence testing and / or achievement grouping unconstitutional would be a burden, not a benefit for minority students.* Author: Therapy in the Ghetto, 1972, Minimum Competence, Maximum Choice, 1980; assoc. editor U. Chgo. Law Rev., 1975-77; columnist Phila. Inquirer, 1992-93; contbr. articles to profl. jours., newspapers and mags. Pres. nominee U.S. Dept. Edn., Washington, 1986; mem. adv. com. U.S. Commn. Civil Rights, N.J., 1985-87. Recipient Cert. of Appreciation award for outstanding service U.S. Dept. Edn., 1985. Mem. Phi Beta Kappa, Sigma Xi. Avocation: gardening. Office: 5050 S East End Ave Chicago IL 60615-5901 E-mail: xlerner@mindspring.com.

LERNER, CAROL MENZEL, social worker; b. Neptune, N.J., June 26, 1945; d. William J. and Margaret (Anderson) Menzel; m. Eric John Lerner, Oct. 28, 1973 (div. Apr. 2000); children: Kristin G., Erin K. BA, Coll. N.J., 1967; MSW, U. Pa., 1969. Cert. sch. social worker, N.J.; supr. cert. Rider U. Social worker Germantown Settlement House, Phila., 1969-70, Associated Day Care Svcs., Phila., 1970-72; program developer div. youth and family svc. Youth and Family Svc. State of N.J., Trenton, 1972-73; dir. group home div. Riverdale Children's Assn., N.Y.C., 1975-76; social worker, supr. Project Child, Trenton, 1986—; coord. N.J. At Risk Info. Network, 1987—; field instr. Sch. Social Work Rutgers U., New Brunswick, N.J., 1988-92; coord. Project Adults, Trenton, 1993—. Cons. Bd. Edn. N.Y.C., 1979; writer, researcher Bus. Communications Co., Stamford, Conn., 1979-82. Author: Transition from School to Adult Life, 1999. Chair, founder Cranford (N.J.) Com. for a Nuclear Weapons Freeze, 1981-83; state ex-steering com. N.J. Commn. for a Nuclear Weapons Freeze, Montclair, 1982-86; trustee, v.p. Pine Knoll Neighborhood Assn., Lawrenceville, N.J., 1985-88; gen. coord., founder Ben Franklin Community Playground Constrn., Lawrenceville, 1986-88; chair Mercer Area Partnership, 1994-2002; mem. Coalition for Peace Action, 2001-02. Recipient cert. Bd. Edn. Lawrence Twp., Lawrenceville, 1986, 87, Lawrence Twp. Coun., Lawrenceville, 1987, Outstanding Improvement award Mercer County Bd. Realtors, Trenton, 1987; fellow NIMH, Washington, 1967-69. Mem. NEA, N.J. Early Intervention Coalition (program com. chair 1989), Family Resource Coalition, Assn. for Persons in Supported Employment. Avocations: writing, camping. Home: 20 Pine Knoll Dr Lawrenceville NJ 08648-3144 Office: Project Adults 1050 Old Trenton Rd Trenton NJ 08690-1230

LERNER, FREDERIC HOWARD, finance executive, educator; b. Bklyn., Feb. 10, 1957; s. Irving and Judith (Zarchin) L.; m. Sheryl Ann Gorman, June 5, 1983; children: Jacklyn Michele, Allison Genna. BS in Acct., SUNY, Albany, 1979. Staff acct. Kipnis & Karchmer, N.Y.C., 1979-81; fin. analyst Bank Leumi Trust Co., 1981-84; asst. sec. N.J. Trust Co., Jersey City, 1984-91; asst. v.p. The CIT Group/Bus. Credit Inc., N.Y.C., 1991-94, v.p., 1994-96, Congress Fin. Corp., N.Y.C., 1996-97; sr. mgr. Deloitte and Touche LLP, 1997-98; audit mgr. Transam. Bus. Credit Corp., Rye, N.Y., 1998-99; CPAs sr. mgr. Marden, Harrison & Kreuter, CPAs, White Plains, 1999-2001; v.p. Wells Fargo Bus. Credit, N.Y.C., 2001—. Prof. NYU, 1983—; pvt. practice, N.Y.C., 1984—; cons. in field. Contbr. articles to profl. jours. Recipient Teaching award for excellence, 1987, Svc. to Univ. award NYU, 1987. Mem. Nat. Comml. Fin. Assn. Home: 22 River Terrace 12J New York NY 10282 Office: Wells Fargo Business Credit Fl 2 119 W 40th Street New York NY 10018

LERNER, HAROLD S. apparel executive; b. N.Y.C., Mar. 27, 1928; s. David Lerner, Edith Lerner; m. Jean Pulsky, June 4, 1954 (div. Nov. 1980); children: Todd, Mitchell, Abbe; m. Janina Bieganska, Apr. 11, 1980; 1 child Marian. Student, CCNY. Owner, pres. Hal Jean Corp., Inwood, NY; v.p. Gordon of Phila, Conhuttocken, Pa.; dir. Liz Claiborne, North Bergen, NJ; sr. mgr. Victoria Secret Catalogue, Columbus, Ohio. Tech. sgt. U.S. Army, 1945—47, ETO. Mem.: Jewish War Vets Am. Post 122. Jewish. Achievements include invention of HL Ballmark; HL Golf Towel; HL Shoe Bar. Home: 335 Harrogate Loop N Westerville OH 43082

LERNER, HARRY JONAS, publishing company executive; b. Mpls., Mar. 5, 1932; s. Morris and Lena (Liederschneider) L.; m. Sharon Ruth Goldman, June 25, 1961 (dec. 1982); children: Adam Morris, Mia Carol, Daniel Aryeh, Leah Anne; m. Sandra Karon Davis, Aug. 24, 1996. Student, U. Mich., 1952, Hebrew U., Jerusalem, 1953-54; BA, U. Minn., 1957. Founder Lerner Publs. Co., Mpls., 1959, chief exec. officer, 1959—; founder Muscle Bound Bindery, Inc., 1967, chief exec. officer, 1967—; founder Carolrhoda Books, Inc., 1969; gen. mgr. Interface Graphics Inc., 1969—, CEO, 1993—. Bd. visitors U. Minn. Press; del. White House Conf. on Libr. and Info. Svcs., 1979; chmn. North Loop Bus. Assn., Mpls., 1972-79, Minn. Book Pubs. Roundtable, 1974; bd. overseers Hill Monastic Manuscript Libr., St. John's U., Collegeville, Minn., 1986-89; bd. dirs., libr. dir. Jewish Community Ctr. Pres. Twin City chpt. Am. Jewish Com., 1980-85; bd. dirs. Fgn. Policy Assn. Minn., 1970-71, bd. dirs. Children's Book Coun., N.Y.C., 1991-94, Minn. Libr. Assn. Found., 1997; bd. advisors Books for Africa, 1996. Recipient Brotherhood award, NCCJ, 1961, Kay Sexton award, 2002, numerous graphic arts awards. Mem. ACLU, Mpls. Inst. Art, Walker Art Ctr, St. Paul-Mpls. Com. on Fgn. Affairs, Jewish Hist. Soc. Upper Midwest, Ampersand Club, Daybreakers Breakfast Club (Mpls.). E-mail: lernerbooks.com. Home: 2215 Willow Ln N Minneapolis MN 55416-3862 Office: Lerner Pub Group 241 1st Ave N Minneapolis MN 55401-1676

LERNER, HERBERT J. retired accountant; b. Newark, Aug. 19, 1938; s. Morris David Lerner and Evelyn L. (Shapiro) Kaplan; m. Dianne Joan Prag, Aug. 23, 1959; children— Joy Ellen, Mark Allen BS, Rutgers U., 1959; LL.B., Georgetown U., 1963. Bar: D.C. 1964; C.P.A., D.C. With Ernst & Young, Washington, 1963-96, ptnr., 1970-83, 83-89, vice chmn. tax, 1990—, nat. dir. tax policy and standards; ret. Mem. IRS Commrs. Adv. Group, 1982-83, 96-98; treas., trustee Am. Tax Policy Inst., 1990-97. Author: (with others) Federal Income Taxation of Corporations Filing Consolidated Returns, 4 vols., 1975, with ann. supplement thru 1997; contbr., editor pvt. letter rulings column Jour. Taxation. Mem. AICPA (exec. com. tax divsn. 1979-82, 85, 89, past chmn., bd. dirs., co-chmn. nat. conf. lawyers and CPAs), ABA, George Town Club. E-mail: Herblerner@aol.com.

LERNER, ILYA, artist; b. Moscow, 1966; came to U.S., 1990; Student, Perovo Art Sch., Moscow, 1979-82, CUNY, 1991, Pratt Inst., 1992; student private studios, Moscow, 1981-84. Resident Vt. Studio Ctr., 2000, Buffalo River Nat. Park, 2001, Mill Atelier Gallery, Santa Fe. One-man shows include Perovo Youth Ctr., Moscow, 1983, Tsvetaeva House, Sommerville, Mass., 1994, Naz Art Gallery, Newton, Mass., 1996, Eclipse Gallery, Boston, 1998, Lee Coll., Baytown, Tex., 2000, Maturango Mus., Ridgecrest, Calif., 2002, Blair Carnahan Fine Art, Santa Fe, N.Mex., 2002, Hensley Galleries, Taos, N.Mex.; exhibited in group shows Internat. Mus. Art, El Paso, Tex., Fuller Art Mus., Brockton, Mass., Crane Collection Gallery, Wellesley, Mass., Millioud Gallery, Houston, Expo Arts, Montreal, Que. Can., 1984—; represented in permanent collections Pres. George W. Bush, Nat. Park Svc., Harrison, Ark., Internat. Mus Art, El Paso, others. Recipient Purchase award El Paso Art Mus., 2000; Cultural Connections grantee Tex. Commn. Art, 2001. E-mail: ilerner@hotmail.com.

LERNER, JAMES PETER, software engineer; b. N.Y.C., Aug. 7, 1956; s. Arnold Aaron and Rita (Guggenheim) L.; m. Anita Elisabeth Springer, Sept. 12, 1987. BS in Biology/Computer Sci. with honors, Union Coll., Schenectady, N.Y., 1978. Engr. Raytheon Co., Sudbury, Mass., 1978-81; cons. Paramin, Inc., Wellesley, 1981-83; engr. Kurzweil Applied Intelligence, Waltham, 1983-87; mgr. Sun Microsystems, Chelmsford, 1987-94; dir. prod. devel. Vectis Corp., Waltham, 1994—96; software cons., 1996—. Author: (software) Portable Mail, 1989. Mem. IEEE, Sigma Xi. Achievements include software patents for linguistic expert system, mouse emulation, fast I/O. Home: 17 Tamarac Rd Newton MA 02464-1220

LERNER, JOSHUA, finance educator; b. Chgo., May 26, 1960; s. Ralph Lerner, Carol Lerner; m. Wendy Wood. BA, Yale U., 1982. Jacob H. Schiff prof. investment banking Harvard Bus. Sch., Boston, 1991—. Organizer Innovation Policy and the Economy Group, Nat. Bur. Econ. Rsch., Boston, 1999—2002. Author: The Venture Capital Cycle, 1999, Venture Capital and Private Equity, 2000, 2d edit., 2002, The Money of Invention, 2001. Office: Harvard Bus Sch Morgan Hall Rm 395 Boston MA 02163 Office Fax: 617-496-7357. Business E-Mail: jlerner@hbs.edu.

LERNER, LAUREN LIPSHUTZ, physician; b. Balt., Dec. 4, 1956; d. Marvin L. and Tala M. (Lipshutz) L.; m. Keith J. Lerner; children: Rachel, Mark. BA, MD, Boston U., 1980. Cert. Am. Bd. Phys. Medicine and Rehab., Am. Bd. Electrodiagnostic Medicine. Med. dir. rehab. svcs. Wright Patterson AFB, Dayton, Ohio, 1983-87; asst. clin. prof. Wright State U. Sch. Medicine, 1983-87; med. dir. head trauma program Health South Sunrise Rehab. Hosp., Ft. Lauderdale, Fla., 1987—, med. dir. spinal cord injury program, 1988—; med. dir. Sunrise Rehab. Hosp., 1993-95. Maj. USAF, 1983-87. Fellow Am. Acad. Phys. Medicine and Rehab. Avocations: piano, writing. Office: Health South Sunrise Rehab Hosp 4399 N Nob Hill Rd Fort Lauderdale FL 33351-5813

LERNER, LAURENCE M. college administrator; b. N.Y.C., Aug. 21, 1939; s. Meyer Philip and Rose (Goss) L.; m. Susan Goodstein, sept. 8, 1963; children: Elisabeth, Marc. BA, NYU, 1961; MA, U. Wis., 1963, PhD, 1970. Asst. adminstr. history U. Wis., Madison, 1964-66; instr. Hofstra U., Hempstead, N.Y., 1967-68; sr. assoc. Drummond Assocs., Inc., N.Y.C., 1968-71; lectr. Am. history Barnard Coll., 1971; asst. editor Bus. Internat., Inc., 1972-73, asst. editor mgmt. practices, 1972-73; dir. rsch. United Jewish Appeal, 1973-79; dir. devel. Am. Jewish Congress, 1979-80; exec. v.p. Alumni Fedn. of NYU, Inc., 1980-89; sr. v.p., spl. asst. to the pres. Manhattan Coll., Riverdale, 2000—, v.p. coll. advancement, 1989-95, sr. v.p. capital campaign, 1996—2000. Bd. dirs. Hamilton-Madison House, N.Y.C., 1985-91, U.S. Com./Sports for Israel, N.Y.C., 1979-81; mem. historian's com. Am. Mus. Immigration, N.Y.C., 1982—; bd. advisors Coun. of Mcpl. Performance, N.Y.C., 1977-84; bd. trustees Horace Mann-Barnard Sch., Riverdale, 1979-82. Mem. NYU Alumni Assn. (bd. dirs. 1996—), Alumni Fedn. NYU (bd. dirs. 1982-96), NYU Club (ex-officio bd. govs. 1983-89), Univ. Club of Washington, Princeton club of N.Y., Univ. Glee Club of N.Y.C. Democrat. Jewish. Avocation: singing. Office: Manhattan College Lavelle Hall Manhattan Coll Pkwy Bronx NY 10471 E-mail: llerner@manhattan.edu.

LERNER, LISA SUE, special education educator; b. Newark, Nov. 11, 1951; d. Harold Joseph and Tobie Charlotte (Kincus) Castelbaum; children: Daniel Scott, Rebecca Kirsh. BS in Edn., Ohio U., 1974; MA, Kean Coll., 1989. Cert. tchr. of handicapped, Ohio, Mich., Ga., N.J.; cert. tchr. cons. for learning disabled, N.J.; cert. in supervision, N.J. Tchr. spl. edn. Cleve. Bd. Edn., 1974-76, Birmingham (Mich.) Bd. Edn., 1976, Cobb County Bd. Edn., Marietta, Ga., 1977-78, 81-83, Somerville (N.J.) Bd. Edn., 1983—. Recipient Gov's.Tchr. Recognition award, 1999. Mem. Assn. Children with Learning Disabilities, Coun. for Exceptional Children (presenter N.J. conf. 1995, chair local profl. devel. com. 2000—).

LERNER, MARTIN, museum curator; b. N.Y.C., Nov. 14, 1936; s. Joseph and Rose (Kolberg) L.; m. Roberta M. Rubenstein, Feb. 26, 1968; children: Benjamin Louis, Seth Laurence, Jocelyn Ann. BA, Bklyn. Coll., 1959; postgrad., Inst. Fine Arts, NYU, 1961-65. Asst. prof. U. Calif., Santa Barbara, 1965-66; asst. curator Oriental art Cleve. Mus. Art, 1966-72; asst. prof. Case Western Res. U., 1968-72; vice chmn. charge Far Eastern art Met. Mus. Art, N.Y.C., 1972-75, curator Indian and S.E. Asian art, 1978—. Cons. in field; internat. lectr. Author: Bronze Sculptures from Asia, 1975, Blue and White: Early Japanese Export Ware, 1978, The Flame and the Lotus, 1984, (with W. Felten) Cambodian and Thai Sculpture: From the 6th to the 14th Century, 1989, Entdeckungen: Skulpturen der Khmer und Thai, 1989, (with S. Kossak), The Lotus Transcendent, 1991, Ancient Khmer Sculpture, 1994; contbr. articles to profl. jours. Served with U.S. Army, 1959-61. Mem.: East India; Devonshire (London). Home: Giglio Ct Croton On Hudson NY 10520 Office: Met Mus Art 82nd & Fifth Ave New York NY 10028

LERNER, MAX KASNER, lawyer; b. N.Y.C., Dec. 27, 1916; s. Louis Lerner and Beckie Kasner; m. Lila Schachner, Oct. 5, 1943; children: Helene, Beth. LLB, Bklyn. Law Sch., 1939. Bar: N.Y. 1940, U.S. Supreme Ct. 1952. Author: ABA Journal of Limitations Imposed on Radio and TV, 1949. Home: 350 1st Ave New York NY 10010-4902

LERNER, RENÉE, artist; b. N.Y.C., Mar. 30, 1936; d. Joseph and Helen (Kahn) Orlan; m. Henry R. Lerner, Mar. 15, 1959; children: Stephen, Claire, Alan. BA, Vassar Coll., 1957; postgrad., Art Ctr. Northern N.J., 1981-85, Art Students League, N.Y.C., 1981-82, Sch. Visual Arts, 1983-84, New Sch. Social Rsch., 1984-85. One woman shows include William Carlos Williams Ctr. Gallery, Rutherford, N.J., 1987, Maurice M. Pine Free Pub. Libr., Fair Lawn, N.J., 1993, Ceres, Soho, 1995, 98; exhibited in group shows at Pindar Gallery, N.Y.C., 1989, White Gallery, Franklin Lakes, N.J., 1989, Silvermine Galleries, New Canaan, Conn., 1989, 91, Butler Inst. Am. Art, Youngstown, Ohio, 1989, 94, Paterson Mus., N.J., 1991, William Paterson Coll., Wayne, N.J., 1992, City Without Walls, Newark, 1993, Lever House, N.Y.C., 1993, Stedman Gallery Rutgers U., Camden, N.J., 1993, Ceres, Soho, 1994, 96, 97, Lobby Gallery, N.Y.C., 1995, Viridian Gallery, N.Y.C., 1995, 96, John Harms Intermission Gallery, Englewood, N.J., 1997, Frauen Mus., Bonn, Germany, 1998; numerous pvt. collections. Past pres., past acting dir. Art Ctr. No. N.J., New Milford, trustee, 1987—. Fellow N.J. State Coun. on Arts/Dept. State, 1991-92; recipient Outstanding Achievement award Long Beach Island Found., 1993. Mem. Painting Affiliates of Art Ctr. of Northern N.J., Salute to Women in the Arts. Democrat. Jewish. Home: 25 Stephen Dr Englewood Cliffs NJ 07632-2230 Studio: 40 W Palisade Ave Englewood NJ 07631-2700

LERNER, STEPHEN ALEXANDER, microbiologist, physician, educator; b. Chgo., Oct. 4, 1938; s. David G. and Florence (Trace) L.; m. June 6, 1963 (div. 1990); children: Deborah, Daniel, Susan; m. Aug. 18, 1991. AB magna cum laude, Harvard U., 1959, MD magna cum laude, 1963. Intern, then resident Peter Bent Brigham Hosp., 1963-65; rsch. assoc. NIH, 1965-68; postdoctoral fellow Stanford (Calif.) U., 1968-71; asst. prof. then assoc. prof. U. Chgo., 1971-86; prof. of medicine Wayne State U., Detroit, 1986—2002, assoc. dean faculty affairs, 2002—. Convenor Soviet-Am. Symposium Antibiotics and Chemotherapy, Moscow, 1988; mem. merit rev. subcom. on infectious disease VA, 1998-2001; co-chair exec. com. Mich. Antibiotic Resistance Reduction Coalition, 1999—. Editor: Aminoglycoside Ototoxicity, 1981; mem. editl. bd. Antimicrobial Agts. and Chemotherapy, 1981—, European Jour. Clin. Microbiology and Infectious Diseases, 1992—, Antibiotic Resistance Updates, 1997—; contbr. articles to profl. jours. With USPHS, 1965-67. Recipient Borden Rsch. award, 1963. Fellow Infectious Disease Soc. Am., Am. Acad. Microbiology (com. on awards 1993-96); mem. Am. Soc. Microbiology (chmn. antimicrobial chemotherapy 1987-88, divsn. group rep. 1990-92, councillor 1990-92, chmn. confs. com. 1993-96, internat.com. 1993—, chmn. 1996—), Inter-Am. Soc. for Chemotherapy (pres. 1986-88, bd. dirs., chmn. 1988-93), Internat. Union Microbiol. Socs. (U.S. nat. com. 2001—), Internat. Soc. Chemotherapy (exec. com. 1987-93), Phi Beta Kappa, Sigma Xi, Alpha Omega Alpha. Democrat. Jewish. Avocations: travel photography, Russian language, collecting antique maps. Office: Harper Hosp Div Infectious Diseases 3990 John R St Detroit MI 48201-2097 E-mail: slerner@intmed.wayne.edu.

LERNER, THEODORE RAPHAEL, dentist; b. Bklyn., Sept. 28, 1932; s. Meyer and Tillie (Brimberg) L.; m. Barbara Ellen Bernstein, June 29, 1974; children by previous marriage: Andrea Holly, Evan Andrew. DDS, U. Pa., 1957. Diplomate Am. Bd. Endodontics. Dentist, endodontist pvt. practice, Bklyn., 1957-93, Forest Hills, 1968-93, Boca Raton, Fla., 1992—. Fellow Internat. Coll. Dentists, Am. Coll. Dentists; mem. ADA, 2d Dist. Dental Soc. (pres. 1971), Dental Soc. State of N.Y. (pres. 1983), Fla. Dental Assn. Home: 7040 Lions Head Ln Boca Raton FL 33496-5931 Office: 2499 Glades Rd Ste 204 Boca Raton FL 33431-7201 E-mail: trlray@netzero.net.

LERNER, VLADIMIR SEMION, computer scientist, educator; b. Odessa, Ukraine, Sept. 12, 1931; came to U.S., 1990; s. Semion N. and Manya G. (Grosman) L.; m. Sanna K. Gleyzer, Sept. 28, 1954; children: Alex, Tatyana, Olga. BSEE, Odessa Poly. Inst., 1954; MEE, Inst. Problem's Controls, Moscow, 1959; PhD in Elec. Engring., Moscow Power Inst., 1961; D Sci. in Systems Analysis, Leningrad State U., 1974. Prof. elec. engring. Kishinev (Moldova) State U., 1962-64; prof. elec. engring. and control systems Kishinev Poly. Inst., 1964-79; sr. scientist in applied math. Acad. Sci., Kishinev, 1964-79; dir. math. modeling and computer sci. lab. Rsch. Inst., Odessa, 1979-89; sr. lectr. UCLA, 1991-93, rschr., 1993—; chmn. computer sci. dept. West Coast U., L.A., 1993-97, Nat. U., L.A., 1997-99. Mem. adv. bds. Acad. Sci., Kishinev, 1964—79, Poly. Inst. Kishinev, 1964—79; vis. prof. Leningrad State U., 1971—73; cons., mem. adv. bd. Poly. Inst. Odessa, 1979—89. Author: Physical Approach to Control Systems, 1969, Superimposing Processes in Control Problems, 1973, Dynamic Models in Decision Making, 1974, Special Course in Optimal and Self Control Systems, 1977, Lectures in Mathematical Modelling and Optimization, 1995, Mathematical Foundations of Informational Macrodynamics, 1996, Lectures in Informational Macrodynamics, 1996, Information Systems Analysis and Modelling: An Informational Microdynamics Approach, 1999; mem. editl. adv. bd. (hon.): Ency. Life Support Sys. Recipient Silver medal for rsch. achievements, Moscow, 1961, outstanding achievements in edn., Kishinev, 1975. Avocations: bicycling, travel. E-mail: vslerner@yahoo.com.

LERNER, WARREN, historian, educator; b. Boston, July 16, 1929; s. Max and Rebecca (Rudnick) L.; m. Francine Sandra Pickow, Aug. 16, 1959; children: Suzanne Rachel Knuiman, Amy Florence Coyle, Daniel Joseph. BS, Boston U., 1952; MA and cert. of Russian, Inst. Columbia U., 1954, PhD, 1961. Asst. prof. history Roosevelt U., 1959-61; asst. prof. Duke U., 1961-65, assoc. prof., 1965-72, prof., 1972—2002, chmn. dept., 1985-90, prof. emeritus, 2002—. Cons. NEH, 1974-80 Author: Karl Radek: The Last Internationalist, 1970, A History of Socialism and Communism in Modern Times, 1982, rev. edit., 1993; editor: The Development of Soviet Foreign Policy, 1973, (with Clifford M. Foust) The Soviet World in Flux, 1967; contbr. articles to profl. jours.; mem. internat. editorial bd. Studies in Comparative Communism, 1973-91. Served with U.S. Army, 1954-56. Am. Philos. Soc. fellow, 1972, 82; NEH, 1974-75; Am. Council Learned Socs.-Social Svc. Rsch. Coun. fgn. area fellow. Mem. Conf. Slavic and East European History (exec. council 1978-80, pres. 1986-87), Am. Assn. Advancement Slavic Studies, Am. Hist. Assn., So. Conf. Slavic Studies. Jewish. Office: Duke U Dept History PO Box 90719 Durham NC 27708-0719 E-mail: wlerner@duke.edu.

LERNER, WILLIAM C. lawyer; b. Phila., July 17, 1933; s. Al and Tillie (Goodman) L.; BA, Cornell U., 1955; LLB, NYU, 1960; m. G. Billie Campbell, Aug. 15, 1957; children: Bonnie, Edwina. Bar: N.Y. 1961, Pa. 1992. Atty. SEC, 1960-64; asst. v.p. Am. Stock Exch., 1965-68; sr. v.p., sec. Carter, Berlind & Weill, Inc. (predecessor to Smith Barney, Inc.), N.Y.C., 1968-71; practicing atty, Buffalo, 1971-85, Snow, Becker & Krauss, P.C., N.Y.C., Washington, Pa., 1990—; v.p., gen. counsel The Geneva Cos., Irvine, Calif., 1986-89, Hon. Devel. Co., Laguna Hills, Calif., 1990-91; bd. dir. Helm Resources, Inc., Seitel, Inc., Rent-Way, Inc., Micros-to-Mainframes, Inc., Chmn. Erie County Pub. Utilities Task Force, 1974-75; mem. Art Coll. Coun. Cornell U. , 1977-85, N.Y. Gov.'s Hazardous Waste Facilities Task Force, 1983-85. 1st lt. Q.M.C., U.S. Army, 1955-57. Mem. ABA, N.Y. State Bar Assn., Phi Alpha Delta. Office: 423 E Beau St Washington PA 15301-3605 also: 5905 La Rosa Ln Apollo Beach FL 33572-2908

LERNER-LAM, EVA I-HWA, transportation executive; b. N.Y.C., Dec. 27, 1954; d. Sau-Wing and Jean (Lu) Lam; m. Arthur Lawrence Lerner-Lam, Sept. 4, 1977; children: Timothy Chi-Wen, Matthew Ta-Wen, Katherine I-Wen. AB, Princeton U., 1976; MS, MIT, 1978. Asst. planner County of San Diego, San Diego, 1977-78; dir. transp. planning group PRC Toups/Voorhies, La Jolla, Calif., 1978-79; assoc. planner Orange County Transit Dist., Garden Grove, 1979-80, San Diego Met. Transit Devel. Bd., 1980, sr. planner, 1981, dir. planning and ops., 1982-84; gen. mgr. Regency Motors, Montclair, N.J., 1984-85; asst. v.p., dir. planning and adminstrn. The Dah Chong Hong Trading Corp., N.Y.C., 1985-88; prin., cons. The Palisades Cons. Group Inc., Tenafly, N.J., 1988—; transport sys. advisor Economist Confs. Group, 1994—; co-founder ChinaTransport.net, 2000—. Mem. coun. on Fgn. Rels., 1996—, bd. adv. ENO Transp. Found., 1997—; chair Transit Cooperative Rsch. Program Transit-IDEA, Transp. Rsch. Bd., 1998—; bd. dirs. Transit Stds.

Consortium, Inc. Founder, coord. Asian-Am. Admissions Vols. Group, Princeton, N.J., 1985—; chmn. bd. dirs. Si-Yo Music Soc. Found., N.Y.C., 1988—; bd. dirs. Princeton U., 1984-88, founder, bus. mgr. and condr. Princeton U. Jazz Ensemble, 1973-76; mem. Coun. on Fgn. REls., 1996—; bd. advisors Eno Transp. Found., 1997—. Outstanding student fellow State Farm Cos., Princeton, 1974; recipient Outstanding Achievement award Tribute to Women in Industry, San Diego, 1983; named Auto Dealer of Yr., N.J. Living Mag., 1985. Mem. NSF (transp. rsch. bd.), ASCE (vice chmn. planning com. urban transp. divsn. 1987-91, vice chairperson exec. com. 1991-92, chmn. exec. com. 1992-93, Frank M. Masters Transp. Engrng. award 1998), Am. Planning Assn., Inst. Transp. Engrs. (best paper award 61st ann. meeting 1991, Innovative Intermodal Solutions for Urban Transp. award 1993, Ivor S. Wisepart Engr. award 1995), IVHS Am. (founding mem.), Asian Alumni of Princeton (mem. exec. com. Beijing 2000—, Outstanding Achievement award 1988), Campus Club (bd. dirs. 1984-94), San Diego Princeton Club (pres. 1983-84). Avocations: piano, swimming, running, bicycling, hiking. E-mail: elernerlam@palisadesgroup.com.

LERNER-SEXTON, MARIE ALMA, choral music educator, musician, writer; b. Louisville, Mar. 19, 1946; d. Frank Joseph and Norma Emily (Tewes) Kraus; m. Paul Sexton, Mar. 20, 1982. AB, Washington U., St. Louis, 1968; MA in Musicology, U. Kans., 1975. Registered music educator, Music Educator's Nat. Conf.; cert. tchr., Kans. Choral music tchr. Shawnee Mission (Kans.) South H.S., 1970-93, Olathe (Kans.) South H.S., 1993—. Music cons. The Coll. Bd., N.Y.C., 1981-90; com. mem. Advanced Placement Music Exam., Ednl. Testing Svc., Princeton, 19977-81; conductor Kans. Youth Chorale, Shawnee Mission, European choir tours 1984, 87, 95; singer Choral Arts Ensemble, Kansas City, Mo., 1982-91; singer Robert Show Inst. Singers, Souillac, France, N.Y.C., and Phoenix, 1992-93. Editor: Teacher's Guide to the Advanced Placement Course in Music Theory, 1997; singer Carnegie Hall Profl. Workshops, 1989, 91, 92, 93; conductor choral/orch. performances Kans. Music Educators Assn. Profl. Workshops, 1974, 78, 85, 87, 90; contbr. articles to Kans. Music Rev., 1980—. Vol. KCPT Channel 19 (PBS), Kansas City, 1992-95; guest spkr., choral artist, Johnson County Bar Assn. Naturalization Ceremonies, Fed. Ct., Kansas City, 1974—; vol. Alumni Ptnrs. Program, Washington U., 1994—. Recipient Liberty Bell award Johnson County Bar Assn., 1994. Mem. Am. Choral Dirs. Assn. (Repertoire and Stds. Women's Choir chair, 1992-97), MENC, Kans. Music Educators Assn. (choral chair Dist. I 1980-82, 93-95), Mu Phi Epsilon, others. Avocations: travel, reading, writing letters, crosswords, hiking, cooking.

LE ROUX, PETER DAVID, neurosurgeon; b. Durban, Republic of South Africa, May 14, 1960; came to U.S., 1985; s. Petrus Andries Jacobs and Sally Ann LeRoux; m. Eleanor Merle LeRoux, Nov. 6, 1993; children: Peter Donlon, James Patrick. MB ChB, U. Cape Town, Republic South Africa, 1983, MD, 1995. Diplomate Am. Bd. Neurological Surgery. Resident in neurosurgery U. Wash., Seattle, 1985-93; fellow neurosci. Ecole Normale Superieure, Paris, 1993-94; asst. prof. neurosurgery NYU, 1994-2000; assoc. prof. neurosurgery U. Pa., Phila., 2000—01, vice chmn. dept. neurosurgery, 2001—. Coord. NYU Neurosurgery Residency Program, 1998-2000. Editor: Current Management of Cerebral Aneurysms, 1998; ad hoc reviewer Jour. of Neurosurgery, Neurosurgery, Jour. of Neurology, Neurosurgery and Psychiatry; contbr. articles to profl. jours. Named Young Neurosurgeon World Fedn. of Neurosurg. Socs., 1993; faculty rsch. fellowship ACS, 1996, Charles Elsberg Neurosurgery fellowship N.Y. Acad. of Medicine, 1993, Whitehead fellowship NYU, 1999; recipient Clin. Investigator Devel. award NIH, 1997. Fellow ACS, Am. Heart Assn. (Stroke fellowship); mem. Am. Assn. of Neurologic Surgeons, Am. Congress of Neurologic Surgeons, Soc. for Neurosci., AANS/CNS (joint sect. on cerebrovascular surgery). Office: U Pa Dept Neurosurgery 330 S 9th St Philadelphia PA 19107 E-mail: lerouxp@uphs.upenn.edu.

LEROY, BETH SEPERACK, jazz musician, piano teacher; b. Bridgeport, Conn., Feb. 18, 1964; d. Reinhold Joseph and Marjorie Louise (Lundahl) Seperack; m. Jonathan Paul LeRoy, Feb. 8, 1994; 1 child: Jessica Michelle. BMusic in Jazz Studies, Ind. U., 1989. Lic. kindermusik educator. Piano instr. DeSantis Music Schoolhouse, Syracuse, N.Y., 1986-91, Carondelet Music Ctr., Latham, 1994-96; pianist Nelson Riddle Orch., Watertown, 1999; keyboardist Nat. Touring Co. of Annie, Schenectady, 1997; owner, instr. Creative Keyboard Studio, Latham, 1996—; owner, artist Keyboard Occasions, 1996—. Piano accompanist Syracuse Opera Co., 1989. Mem.: Albany Music Tchrs. Assn., Music Tchrs. Nat. Assn. (auditions asst. 1999, chmn. fall recital 1999, 2000, 2001), Am. Fedn. Musicians. Avocations: running, making hand-hooked rugs, baking, weight training. Office: Keyboard Occasions PO Box 962 Latham NY 12110-0962

LEROY, CLAUDE, physics educator, researcher; b. Charleroi, Hainaut, Belgium, Sept. 30, 1947; s. Bernard and Rénee (Jacobeus) L. Mathématique Spéciale, Faculté St. Louis, Brussels, 1967; Lic. en Sci., U. Louvain, Belgium, 1971, D in Scis., 1976. Rsch. assoc. McGill U., Montréal, 1977-80; attaché de rsch U. Montréal, 1978-80; rsch. assoc. Northwestern U., Evanston, Ill., 1980-81; chercheur du fonds du devel. scis. U. Louvain, 1981-83; rsch. scientist Inst. Particle Physics, Montréal, 1983-90; assoc. prof. physics McGill U., 1983-90; titular prof. physics U. Montréal, 1990—, dir. nuclear physics lab., 1991-94, 2000—. Vis. rsch. fellow U. Southampton, Eng., 1976-77; sci. assoc. Ctr. European Rsch. Nuclear physics, Geneva, Switzerland, 1980—, dept. energy U. Florence; hon. prof. Nat. U. Peru, 1994—. Contbr. more than 300 papers to sci. jours. Killam Rsch. fellow The Can. Coun., 1993-95; recipient prize for Achievements in Physics Sci. Coun. Joint Inst. Nuclear Rsch., Moscow, 2000. Fellow Royal Soc. Can. (Rutherford Prize for Physics, 1988, mem. Acad. Scis.); mem. Inst. Particle Physics Can., Can. Assn. Physicists. Roman Catholic. Avocations: Egyptian Hieroglyphics, Chinese, history, fishing. Home: 4464 Rue Cartier Montréal QC Canada H2H 1W5 Office: U Montréal Nuclear Physics Lab CP 6128 succursale Centre-ville Montreal QC Canada H3C 3J7 E-mail: leroy@lps.umontreal.ca., claude.leroy@CERN.ch.

LEROY, DAVID HENRY, lawyer, state and federal official; b. Seattle, Aug. 16, 1947; s. Harold David and Lela Fay (Palmer) L.; 2 children. BS, U. Idaho, 1969, JD, 1971; LL.M., NYU, 1972; JD (hon.), Lincoln Coll., 1993. Bar: Idaho 1971, N.Y. State 1973, U.S. Supreme Ct. 1976. Law clk. Idaho 4th Dist. Ct., Boise, 1969; legal asst. Boise Cascade Corp., 1970; asso. firm Rothblatt, Rothblatt, Seijas & Peskin, N.Y.C., 1971-73; dep. prosecutor Ada County Prosecutor's Office, Boise, 1973-74, pros. atty., 1974-78; atty. gen. State of Idaho, Boise, 1978-82, lt. gov., 1983-87; ptnr. Runft, Leroy Coffin & Matthews, 1983-88, Leroy Law Offices, 1988—. Candidate for Gov. of Idaho, 1986, U.S. Congress, 1994; U.S. nuclear waste negotiator, 1990-93; U.S. Presdl. elector, 1992; lectr., cons. in field. Mem. State Task Force on Child Abuse, 1975; mem. Ada County Coun. on Alcoholism, 1976; del. Rep. Nat. Conv., 1976, 80, 84; chmn. Nat. Rep. Lt. Gov.'s Caucus, 1983-86; bd. dirs. United Fund, 1975-81; del. Am. Coun. Young Polit. Leaders, USSR, 1979, Am. Coun. for Free Asia, Taiwan, 1980, U.S./Taiwan Investment Forum, 1983; del. leader Friendship Force Tour USSR, 1984; legal counsel Young Reps., 1974-81; candidate for Gov. Idaho, 1986; presdl. elector, 1992; candidate U.S. Ho. Reps. 1st Dist, Idaho, 1994. Mem. Nat. Dist. Attys. Assn., Idaho Prosecutors Assn., Am. Trial Lawyers Assn., Idaho Trial Lawyers Assn., Nat. Assn. Attys. Gen. (chmn. energy subcom., exec. com., del to China 1981), Western Attys. Gen. Assn. (vice chmn. 1980-83, chmn. 1981), Nat. Lt. Govs. Assn. (exec. bd. 1983), Idaho Bar Assn., Ada County Lincoln Day Assn. (pres. 2000), Found. for Idaho History (pres. 2001--), Sigma Alpha Epsilon. Presbyterian. Office: The Leroy Offices PO Box 193 Boise ID 83701-0193 E-mail: dave@dleroy.com.

LEROY, EDWARD CARWILE, rheumatologist; b. Elizabeth City, N.C., Jan. 19, 1933; s. J. Henry and Grace Brown (Carwile) LeR.; m. Garnette DeFord Hughes, June 11, 1960; children: Garnette DeFord, Edward Carwile. BS summa cum laude, Wake Forest Coll., 1955; MS in Pathology, U. N.C., 1958, MD with honors, 1960. Med. intern Presbyn. Hosp., N.Y.C., 1960-61, resident, 1961-62; clin. asso. Nat. Heart Inst., Bethesda, Md., 1962-65; fellow in rheumatology Columbia U., 1965-67; dir. Edward Daniels Faulkner Arthritis Clinic; asso. attending physician Presbyn. Hosp., N.Y.C., 1970-75; asso. prof. Columbia U. Coll. Phys. and Surg., 1970-75; prof. medicine, dir. div. rheumatology and immunology Med. U. S.C., Charleston, 1975-95, prof., chmn. dept. microbiology and immunology, 1995-2000, disting. univ. prof. Bd. dirs. Arthritis Found. Contbr. articles med. jours. Recipient Alexander von Humboldt prize U. Cologne (Germany), 1995-96. Master: ACR, ACP; fellow: Am. Coll. Rheumatology, Am. Coll. Physicians; mem.: AAAS, Usher First Scots Presbyn., Orthopedic Rsch. Soc., Assn. Am.Physicians, So. Soc. Clin. Investigation, N.Y. Acad. Scis., Microvascular Soc., Am. Soc. Clin. Investigation, Soc. Exptl. Biology and Medicine, Am. Assn. Immunologists, Harvey Soc., Am. Fedn. Clin. Rsch., Carolina Yacht, Yeamans Hall. First Scots Presbyterian. Clubs: Yeamans Hall, Carolina Yacht. Office: 173 Ashley Ave # 25054 Charleston SC 29425-0001 E-mail: leroyc@musc.edu.

LEROY, G. PALMER, art dealer; b. N.Y.C., July 15, 1929; s. John Minturn and Georgiana Kip (Palmer) LeR.; m. Kyra Hawkins, June 18, 1955; children: Kyra, Nina, Pamela. BA, Harvard U., 1951. With N.Y. Times, 1951-52, Frank Best & Co., N.Y.C., 1952-53, Kenyon & Eckhardt, Inc., N.Y.C., 1953-55, Inmont Corp., U.S. and Europe, 1955-83; v.p. sales Inmont Internat., Inc., N.Y.C., 1974-83; ptnr. Clinton R. Howell, Inc. Antiques, Pound Ridge, N.Y., 1984-85; mng. dir. Met. Opera Guild, Inc., N.Y.C., 1985-94; pub. Opera News, 1985-94; dealer 19th and 20th Century Am. Art Palmer LeRoy Fine Art, Nantucket, Mass., 1994—. Mem. industry sector adv. com. chem. industry U.S. Commerce Dept., 1976-83. Pres. Friends of John Jay Homestead, Inc., Katonah, N.Y., 1977-95, chmn., 1995-98, chmn. emeritus, 1998—; bd. dirs. The Bedford Assn., 1972-85, pres., 1975-80, bd. dirs. emeritus, 1986-97; bd. dirs. Wildlife Preservation Trust Internat., Inc., Phila., 1983-94, pres., 1990-93, emeritus coun., 1994—; bd. dirs. N.Y. br. English Speaking Union, 1993-98, chmn., 1994-97; sr. warden St. Matthew's Ch., Bedford, 1985-89.

LEROY, KAREN LESLIE, English language educator; b. Detroit, Apr. 11, 1954; d. Garrett and Thelma Ethel (Hawkins) LeR.; m. Reuven Resch, June 17, 1982 (div. Oct. 1988); 1 child, Shera Elana. AB in English and Anthropology, Mount Holyoke Coll., 1976; MA in Anthropology, Columbia U., 1978. Instrnl. staff Coll. New Rochelle, N.Y., 1980-88; acad. coord. support svcs. Fordham U., N.Y.C., 1989-90; adj. instr. CUNY, 1990-93; asst. prof. Mercy Coll., Dobbs Ferry, N.Y., 1993—. Adj. lectr. Columbia U., N.Y.C., 1979-81; adj. asst. prof. Iona Coll., New Rochelle, 1988-90; adj. instr. NYU, N.Y.C., 1991-92, Marist Coll., Poughkeepsie, N.Y., 1991-93; coord. Mercy Coll. Bronx Campus Honors Program, 2000—. Ford Found. fellow, 1976-79, Minority Grants fellow Mercy Coll., 1995-96; faculty devel. rsch. grantee Mercy Coll., 1994. Mem.: MLA, Nat. Collegiate Honors Coun., Am. Anthropology Assn., Nat. Coun. Tchrs. English, Alpha Kappa Alpha. Avocations: reading, travel, film. Office: Mercy Coll English Dept 555 Broadway Dobbs Ferry NY 10522-1134

LEROY, MISS JOY, model, designer; b. Riverdale, Ill., Sept. 8, 1927; d. Gerald and Dorothea (Wingebach) Reasor. BS, Purdue U., 1949. Model, sales rep. Jacques, Lafayette, Ind., 1950; book dept. sales rep. Loebs, 1951-52; window trimmer Marshall Field's and Co., Evanston, Ill., 1952-53; sales and display rep. Emerald Ho., 1954-55. Model, narrator, designer J.L. Hudson Co., GM Corp., Coca Cola Co., Hoover Vacuum Co., Jam Handy Orgn., Am. Motors Corp., Speedway Petroleum Corp., Ford Motor Co. Auto, Tractor & Implement Divsn.-The Sykes Co., Detroit, 1956-61; tour guide, model The Christian Sci. Publ. Soc., spl. events coord. Prudential Ins. Co., model Copley 7, Boston, 1962-70. Author: Puzz-its, 1986-2002; contbr. articles to profl. jours. Founding angel Asolo Theatre, Sarasota, 1960; mem. Ft. Lauderdale Internat. Film Festival, 1990, Mus. of Art, 1978, Fla. Conservation Assn., Rep. Senatorial Com. Inner Cir., 1990, Rep. Nat. Hall of Honor, 1992, Congl. Com., 1990, Nat. Trust for Hist. Preservation, 1986, Fla. Trust for Hist. Preservation, 1987, Nat. Park Trust; one of founding friends 1000 Friends of Fla., 1991; mem. Rep. Presdl. Legion of Honor, 1993, Rep. Medal of Freedom and Wall of Honor, 1994, Rep. Presdl. Task Force, 1993, Grand Club Rep. Party Fla., 1996. Recipient disting. 20th Century Rep. Leader, 1998, Hallmark medal of honor, Founder's Wall award, Rep. Presdl. Roundtable, 2001, Internat. Order of Merit, Am. Order of Excellence, 2000, Order of Internat. Ambs., 2000, World Laureate of Eng., Rep. Senatorial Millennium Medal of Freedom. Fellow Order of Internat. Fellowship (Internat. Woman of Yr. 1996-99, Woman of Yr. 1998-99, 2001-02), Internat. Honor Soc.; mem. Nat. Parks and Conservation Assn., Ellis Island Found. (charter), Duke of Gloucester Soc., Am. Queen Inaugural Soc., Stratford Shakespearean Festival of Can., USS Constn. Mus. (charter mem. 1993), Libr. of Congress (nat. mem), Purdue U. Alumni Assn. (pres.'s coun.), Wilderness Soc., Magic Kingdom Entertainment Club, Maupintour Travelers Club, Heritage Found., Soc. Honorary Mariners, Heralds of Nature Soc., Ducks Unltd., Paddlewheel Steamboatin' Soc. Am., Cunard World Club, Skald Club, Seabourn Club, The Crystal Soc., The Cousteau Soc., Nat. Corvette Owners Assn., Corvette Club, Coastal Conservation Assn., Captain's Cir., Intravler Club, Zeta Tau Alpha. Avocation: travel, art, education, design. Home: 2100 S Ocean Ln Apt 2104 Fort Lauderdale FL 33316-3827

LERSCH, ARTHUR DAVID, director, educator; b. Ravenna, Ohio, Apr. 19, 1962; s. Arthur Charles and Jeny Lersch. BA, Kent State U., Ohio, 1984; MA, Kent State U., 1988, MPA, 1998. Asst. mgr. DuBois Bookstore, Kent, Ohio, 1992—2000; mgr. virtual bus. incubator Kean U. COPC, Union, NJ, 2000—. Adj. prof. pub. adminstrn. Kean U., Union, NJ, 2000—. Vol. Habitat for Humanity, Ravenna, 1997—98. Mem.: ASPA (Kent State student rep. 1997—). Democrat. Roman Catholic. Avocation: reading, hiking, volunteering. Home: 181 Stiles Street Apartment A3 Elizabeth NJ 07208-1834 Office: Kean University COPC 1000 Morris Avenue Union NJ 07283 Fax: 908-737-5885.

LERSCH, DELYNDEN RIFE, computer engineering executive; b. Grundy, Va., Mar. 22, 1949; d. Woodrow and Eunice Louise (Atwell) Rife; m. John Robert Lersch, May 9, 1976; children: Desmond, Kristofor. BSEE, Va. Poly. Inst. & State U., 1970; postgrad., Boston U., 1975—. With Stone & Webster Engrng. Corp., 1970-91, elec. engr., supr. computer applications, 1978-80, mgr. computer graphics, 1984-87, mgr. engrng. sys. and computer graphics, 1984-87, divsn. chief info. techs., 1987-90, v.p., 1990-91; chief ADP officer Univ. Rsch. Assocs., 1991-94, 97-99, also bd. dirs., 1997-99; dir. Global Elec. Security & Bus. Continuity, CARE Pvt. Mortgage Ins. Sys. Corp.; acct. mgr. Perot Sys. Corp., Dallas, 1994—. Author: Cable Schedule Information Systems As Used in Power Plant Construction, 1973, 2d edit., 1975, Information Systems Available for Use By Electrical Engineers, 1976; contbr. articles in field of computer-aided design and engineering. Grantee Mass. Solar Energy Rsch., 1978; honored for contbns. to constrn. industry Engrng. News Record Mag., 1983. Mem. IEEE (sr.), Assn. Women in Sci., Soc. Women Engrs. (sr.), Women in Sci. and Engrng., Energy Communicators, Nat. Computer Graphics Assn., Profl. Coun. New England, Women in Energy (dir. Mass. chpt. 1978, New Eng. region 1979), LWV, Rotary (Rotarian of yr. 1993-94). Clubs: Boston Bus. and Profl. Women's. Congregationalist. Home: Seis Lagos 503 Riva Rdg Wylie TX 75098-8264 Office: Perot Sys Corp 12377 Merit Dr Ste 1100 Dallas TX 75251-2200

LERT, RANDALL P. trust company executive; Degree in History, U. Calif., Riverside; degree in Bus. Adminstrn., U. Calif., Berkeley. Chief investment officer Frank Russell Co., 1985—. Mem. exec. com. Frank Russell Co., mem. op. com. Office: Frank Russell Company 909 A Street Tacoma WA 98402*

LESACK, BEATRIZ DIAZ, secondary education educator; b. Arequipa, Peru, Dec. 2, 1948; came to U.S., 1977; d. Jésus Heradio Díaz Vargas and Elisa (Huamán) Díaz Peralta; m. Federico Vera Ponce de León, May 22, 1965 (div. 1977); 1 child, Edson Giovanni; m. Leo Pap Dorn, Oct. 27, 1977. BS in Spanish, San Agustin U., 1974; MS in Gen. Edn., SUNY, New Paltz, 1978-81, postgrad. Cert. elementary and secontary tchr., French and Spanish lang. tchr., N.Y. Tchr. Spanish Huguenot Nursery Sch., New Paltz, N.Y., 1983; tchr. elem. bilingual Ellenville (N.Y.) Sch. Dist., 1984-85; tchr. Spanish Poughkeepsie (N.Y.) Sch. Dist., 1985-86, Liberty (N.Y.) Sch. Dist., 1986-88, Fla. Unified Sch. Dist., Fla., N.Y., 1988-89; tchr. Spanish-French Hyde Park (N.Y.) Sch. Dist., 1989-91; tchr. Spanish Greenburgh Eleven Unified Sch. Dist., Dobbs Ferry, N.Y., 1991—, Copake-Taconic Hills Sch., Hillsdale, 1995-96, FDR Sch., Bristol Twp., Pa., 1996-97; tax examiner U.S. Treasury, 1998-99, rschr., 1999—. Substitute tchr. Newburgh, Wallkill, Onteora Sch. Dists., Poughkeepsie, N.Y., 1982-83; exec. sec. Hotels and Restaurants Assn., Arequipa, 1972-73; mem. asst. Radio Club Dr. Oscar Guillen, Arequipa, 1971; tax examiner U.S. Treasury, 1998-99, rsch., 1999-2000. Fund chairman Dem. Com., New Paltz, 1991-92; mem. fundraising com. Multicultural Edn., New Paltz, 1992; mem. Mid. Sch. Steering Com., 1989-91, Multicultural Edn. Com., 1991—, steering com. Maurice Hinchey Nat. Bilingual Edn., 1980—; candidate for Phila. Bd. Edn., 2000. Fulbright Hays fellow to Dominican Rep., 1991; faculty grantee SUNY, 1978, 83-84. Mem. NAFE, Am. Assn. Tchrs. Spanish, N.Y. Fgn. Lang. Tchrs. Assn. (pres.), N.Y. Union Tchrs., Faculty Wives and Women (pres. 1989-92). Avocations: photography, video production, handicrafts, reading, golf. Home: 5411 Vicaris St Philadelphia PA 19128-2823 Office: Greenburgh Eleven Unified Sch Dist PO Box 501 Dobbs Ferry NY 10522-0501

LESAK, DAVID MICHAEL, safety engineer, educator, consultant; b. Phila., July 5, 1952; s. Joseph Michael and Charlotte (Rockel) L.; m. Lora Jean Schmoyer, June 12, 1976; children: Jana Bryn, Scott David. BS, Kutztown U., 1976. Lab. technician Air Products and Chems. Inc., Trexlertown, Pa., 1976-78; sci. tchr. Parkland Sch. Dist., Orefield, 1978-79, Quakertown (Pa.) Sch. Dist., 1980; owner, pres. Hazard Mgmt. Assocs., Allentown, Pa., 1981—. Adj. prof. Nat. Fire Acad., Allentown, Pa., 1981—, devel. team mgr. Hazmat courses, Pa., course developer for emergency response to terrorism, Pa., Dept. of Justice; adj. prof. Emergency Mgmt. Inst., Emmitsburg, 1985—; contract instr., course developer FBI Hazmat Programs; contract instr. U.S. Dept. State Diplomatic Security Svc.; mem. Hazardous Materials Transp. Uniform Safety Act, Nat. Hazardous Materials Curriculum Devel. Com. Nat. Response Team; chief Lehigh County Hazmat Team, 1990—2001; mem. state and local adv. group U.S. Dept. Justice Nat. Domestic Preparedness Office. Author: Chemistry of Hazardous Materials, 1983, (study guide) Fire Chemistry I and II, 1991; author, prodr., narrator: (videotape) Fire Fighter Safety, 1984, (text) Hazardous Materials Strategies and Tactics, 1998; author, presenter: (videotape) Oxidizers, 1991; author GEDAPER emergency ops. decision-making process Nat. Fire Acad.; prodr.: (videos) Container Damage Assessment, 1993, Spill Control, Stop It, Confine It, 1993, Flammable Liquids and Gases, 1993, Flammable Solids and Dusts, 1993, Explosives and Other Unstable Substances, 1993, Alkali and Alkali Earth Metals, 1993. Chmn. Lehigh County Hazardous Materials Adv. Commn., Allentown, 1990-93; fire chief Lower Macangie Twp., Pa., 1984-86. Mem. Am. Soc. Safety Engrs., Pa. Assn. Hazardous Material Techs. (sec. 1994-97, 2d v.p. 1998-2000). Home and Office: Hazard Mgmt Assocs PO Box 3004 Allentown PA 18106-0004

LESAR, DAVID J. oil industry executive; Ptnr. in charge of energy mfg. and retail practices Arthur Andersen & Co., Dallas; exec. v.p. fin. and adminstrn. Halliburton Energy Svcs. bus. segment, 1993-95; exec. v.p., CFO Halliburton Co., 1995—97, pres., 1997—2000, chmn., pres., CEO, 2000—. Office: 3600 Lincoln Plz 500 N Akard St Dallas TX 75201-3320*

LESAR, JAMES HIRAM, lawyer; b. Lawrence, Kans., May 23, 1940; s. Hiram Henry and Rosa Lee (Berry) L.; m. May Siang Lim, Aug. 31, 1968; 1 child, Jennifer Claire. BA, U. Ill., 1962, postgrad., 1962-64; JD, U. Wis., 1969. Bar: U.S. Ct. Appeals (D.C. cir.) 1971, D.C. 1972, U.S. Dist. Ct. D.C. 1972, U.S. Ct. Appeals (6th cir.) 1973, U.S. Supreme Ct. 1974, U.S. Ct. Appeals (5th and 11th cirs.) 1981, U.S. Ct. Claims 1986, U.S. Ct. Appeals (1st cir.) 1987, U.S. Dist. Ct. Md. 1990, U.S. Ct. Appeals (4th cir.) 1990. Atty. Com. to Investigate Assassinations, Washington, 1970-74; pvt. practice, 1976—; part-time atty. Fensterwald & Assocs., 1980-85. V.p. Assassination Archives and Rsch. Ctr., Washington, 1985-91, pres., 1991—. Mem. Am. Soc. Access Profls. Avocations: reading, basketball, bowling. Office: Assassination Archives and Rsch Ctr 1003 K St NW Ste 204 Washington DC 20001-4425 E-mail: jlesar@mindspring.com.

LESCH, MICHAEL OSCAR, lawyer; b. Berlin, May 28, 1938; came to U.S., 1940, naturalized, 1946; s. Adolf F. and Maria E. Leschnitzer; m. Judith Willis, Aug. 31, 1965; children— Sara, Benjamin AB, Columbia U., 1958; LLB, Harvard U., 1961. Bar: N.Y. 1961, U.S. Dist. Ct. (so. dist.) N.Y. 1963, U.S. Dist. Ct (ea. dist.) N.Y. 1965, U.S. Ct. Appeals (2d cir.) 1968, U.S. Supreme Ct. 1975, U.S. Ct. Appeals (3d cir.) 1979, U.S. Ct. Appeals (7th cir.) 1979, U.S. Ct. Appeals (9th cir.) 2001. Assoc. Shea & Gould and predecessors, N.Y.C., 1961-69, ptnr., 1970-94, LeBoeuf, Lamb, Greene & MacRae, N.Y.C., 1994—. Contbr. articles to profl. jours. Mem. ABA, N.Y. State Bar Assn., Assn. Bar City N.Y., Fed. Bar Council, Am. Arbitration Assn. (panel of arbitrators). Office: LeBoeuf Lamb Greene & MacRae 125 W 55th St New York NY 10019-5369

LESCINSKI, JOAN, higher education administrator, English educator; b. Albany, N.Y., June 27, 1947; BA, Coll. St. Rose, 1970, MA, 1974; PhD, Brown U., 1981. Cert. secondary tchr., N.Y. Prof. Coll. St. Rose, Albany, N.Y., 1974-91; assoc. academic dean Avila Coll., Kansas City, Mo., 1991-93; dean, v.p. Fontbonne Coll., St. Louis, 1993-98; pres. St. Mary-of-the-Woods (Ind.) Coll., 1998—. Avocation: organic vegetable gardening. Office: St-Mary-of-the-Woods Coll St-Mary-of-the-Woods Coll Saint Mary Of The Woods IN 47876 E-mail: presofc@smwc.edu.

LE SHANA, DAVID CHARLES, retired academic administrator; b. Lucknow, India, Nov. 15, 1932; came to U.S., 1949; naturalized, 1958; s. Newman John and Gwendolyn Beatrice (White) Le S.; m. Rebecca Ann Swander, June 8, 1951; children: Deborah Lynn, James David, Catherine Ann, Christine Joy. AB, Taylor U., Upland, Ind., 1953; AM in Edn, Ball State U., 1959; PhD, U. So. Calif., 1967; LHD (hon.), George Fox Coll., 1982; EdD (hon.), Taylor U., 1996; DD (hon.), Western Evang. Sem., 1996. Ordained to ministry Friends Ch., 1953; pastor Ypsilanti (Mich.) Friends Ch., 1953-54; dir. pub. relations, chaplain Taylor U., 1954-61; pastor 1st Friends Ch., Long Beach, Calif., 1961-67; mem. staff George Fox Coll., Newberg, Oreg., from 1967, pres., 1969-82, pres. emeritus, 1996—; pres. Seattle Pacific U., 1982-91, pres. emeritus, 1991—; pres. Western Evang. Sem., Portland, Oreg., 1992-96, pres. emeritus, 1996—. Min. Pacific N.W. Conf. of Free Meth. Ch.; bd. dirs. Coun. Ind. Colls., 1971-80, chmn., 1976-78; chmn. commn. higher edn. Nat. Assn. Evangelicals, 1973-75; chmn. Oreg. Ind. Colls. Assn., 1971-72, 81-82; mem. So. Calif. Radio and TV Commn., 1963-67; bd. dirs. Christian Coll. Consortium, chmn., 1984-86; mem. fact-finding group to Bangladesh, 1972; mem. adv. bd. Oriental Missionary Soc.; bd. advs. Latin Am. Mission, Friends Ctr., Azusa Pacific U.; mem. capital campaign com. Taylor U., 1995—; bd. dirs. N.W. Christian Cmty. Found., Westlake Home Owners Assn., KWI Found. Author: Quakers in California, 1969; Rec.: album Songs of Discipleship, 1965. Bd. dirs. Oreg. Ind. Coll. Found., 1969-82, 92—, George Fox Coll. Found., 1971-82, Herbert Hoover Found., Oreg., 1975-82, Ind. Colls. of Wash., 1982-91, Wash. Friends of Higher Edn., 1982-91; bd. assocs. Pacific Sci. Ctr.; mem. Wash. Gives Leadership Coun., 1989-92, mem. edn. commn. States Task Force on State Policy and Ind. Higher Edn., 1986-89; trustee CRISTA Ministries, 1982-88, 90-96, bd. dirs., 1982—; chmn. bd. Christian Coll. Coalition, 1991. Recipient Alumni Service award Taylor U., 1961, Chamber of Achievement award, 1978; Tchr. of Yr. award Ball State U., 1978 Mem. Nat. Assn. Evangs. (bd. dirs. 1980-99, chmn. theology com. 1992-94).

LESHEM, OSNAT ALICE, healthcare administrator; b. Israel, Oct. 2, 1944; came to U.S., 1968; d. Shlomo and Menoha (Newman) Rabinovitz; m. Adam Leshem, Aug. 13, 1964; children: Jerry, Eddie, Steven. Student in Nursing, Kaplan Hosp., Rehovot, Israel, 1964; Nurse Practitioner, Israel, 1966; BA in Psychology, Hartford U., 1978; MS in Counseling for Agys., Cen. Conn. State U., 1982. Cert. geriatric nurse, ANA. Staff nurse Kaplan Hosp., Rehovot, 1964-65; nurse practitioner Ministry of Health, Tel-Aviv, 1966-68; staff nurse St. Francis Hosp., Hartford, Conn., 1968-69; staff nurse, head charge nurse, supr., resource clinician, instnl. rsch. coord. Hebrew Health Care , West Hartford, 1969—, acting dir. home health care agy.; dir. rsch., evalutions and outcome Hebrew Home and Hosp. Cons. standard policies and procedures, geriat. and related rsch. Co-author: (book) Long Term Care Nursing Standards, Policies and Procedures, 1992, also yearly supplements; contbr. numerous articles to profl. jours. Past pres. Assn. Jewish RNs; mem. C.H.A. ethics group, Hadassah, NEON, Conn. Rsch. Task Force. Home: 14 Hammick Rd West Hartford CT 06107-1221 Office: Hebrew Home and Hosp 1 Abrahms Blvd West Hartford CT 06117-1525 E-mail: aleshem@hebrew-home-hospital.com.

LESHER, STEPHEN HARRISON, lawyer; b. Tucson, Dec. 31, 1953; s. Robert Overton and June Ruth (Huffer) L. BA, U. Vt., 1975; JD, U. Ariz., 1978. Bar: Ariz. 1978, U.S. Dist. Ct. Ariz. 1978, U.S. Ct. Appeals (9th cir.) 1991. Assoc. Lesher & Kimble PC, Tucson, 1978-79; ptnr. Lesher, Clausen & Borodkin PC, 1980-83, Lesher & Borodkin PC, Tucson, 1983-91, Lesher & Williams, Tucson, 1991-93, Lesher & Lesher, Tucson, 1993-99, Kimble,

Lesher, Corradini & Toone, Tucson, 1999—. Mem. Am. Bd. Trial Advocates, Def. Rsch. Inst. Republican. Avocation: computers. Home: 5667 N Via Salerosa Tucson AZ 85750-1154 also: 777 N Thomas Rd Ste 210 Phoenix AZ 85014 E-mail: shl@klctlaw.com.

LESHER, WILLIAM RICHARD, retired academic administrator; b. Carlisle, Pa., Nov. 14, 1924; s. David Luther and Carrie LaVerne (Adams) L.; m. Veda E. Van Etten, June 16, 1946; children— Eileen Fern, Martha Zoe Lesher Keough Th.B., Atlantic Union Coll., South Lancaster, Mass., 1946; MA, Andrews U., 1964; PhD, NYU, 1970. Ordained to ministry Seventh-day Adventist Ch., 1951. Pastor No. New Eng. Conf. Seventh-day Adventists, 1946-56; pastor, mission dir. Delta sect. Nile Union Seventh-day Adventists, Alexandria, Egypt, 1957-58; prin. Nile Union Acad., Cairo, Egypt, 1959-61; sec. Middle East Div. Seventh-day Adventists Beirut, Lebanon, 1962-64; assoc. prof. religion, dir. summer sch., asst. to pres. Atlantic Union Coll., 1964-71; assoc. dir. Sabbath sch. dept. Gen. Conf. Seventh-day Adventists, Washington, 1971-79; dir. Bibl. Research Inst., Gen. Conf. Seventh-day Adventists, 1979-84; gen. v.p. Gen. Conf. Seventh-day Adventists, 1981-84; pres. Andrews U., Berrien Springs, Mich., 1984-94; ret., 1994. Author: Tips for Teachers, 1979; editor adult Sabbath Sch. lessons, 1971-79, studies in sanctuary and atonement, 1980-81; contbr. articles to religious jours. Recipient Founders Day award NYU, 1970 Home: 4703 Greenfield Dr Berrien Springs MI 49103-9566 E-mail: richardlesher@earthlink.net.

LESH-LAURIE, GEORGIA ELIZABETH, university administrator, biology educator, researcher; b. Cleve., July 28, 1938; d. Howard Frees and Josephine Elizabeth (Taylor) Lesh; m. William Francis Laurie, Aug. 16, 1969. BS, Marietta Coll., 1960; MS, U. Wis., 1961; PhD, Case Western Reserve U., 1966. Asst. prof. SUNY, Albany, 1966-69; asst., then assoc. prof. Case Western Reserve U., 1969-77, asst. dean, 1973-76; interim dir. Cleve. State U., Ohio, 1980, prof., chairperson, 1977-81, dean grad. studies, 1981-86, dean arts and scis., 1986-91, interim provost, v.p. academic and student affairs, 1989-90; vice chancellor acad. and student affairs U. Colo., Denver, 1991-95, interim chancellor, 1995-97, chancellor, 1997—. Cons. in field; reviewer numerous granting agencies, profl. jours., 1968—; advanced placement exam. Edn. Testing Service, Princeton, N.J., 1982-83. Contbr. sci. articles to profl. pubs. Trustee Marietta Coll., Ohio, 1980-84, 85-95; mem. city/univ. interchange com., Cleve., 1983-91. Fellow NSF, NIH; grantee NIH, Am. Cancer Soc., Am. Heart Assn., Research Corp., 1968—; recipient Wright fellowship Bermuda Biol. Station; named among AAUW Women of Distinction; named to Girl Scouts Women's Leadership Cir. Fellow AAAS; mem. Am. Soc. Zoologists, Soc. Devel. Biology, Am. Soc. Cell Biology, Phi Beta Kappa. Home: 1761 E Phillips Ave Littleton CO 80122-3260 E-mail: georgia.lesh-laurie@cudenver.edu.

LESHNER, ALAN IRVIN, science foundation administrator; b. Lewisburg, Pa., Feb. 11, 1944; s. Saul S. and Martha (Schmidt) L.; m. Agnes Farkas, May 18, 1969; children: Sarah, Michael. AB, Franklin and Marshall Coll., 1965; MS, Rutgers U., 1967, PhD, 1969. Asst. prof. psychology Bucknell U., 1969-73, assoc. prof., 1973-78, prof., 1978-82; program assoc. divsn. behavioral and neural scis. NSF, Washington, 1979-80, dep. dir. divsn. behavioral and neural scis., 1983-85, dir. divsn. precoll. materials devel. and rsch., 1984-85, exec. officer biol., behavioral and social scis., 1985-87; project mgr. Office Dir., 1980-82; dep. exec. dir. Commn. on Precoll. Edn., Nat. Sci. Bd., 1982-83; dep. dir. NIMH, 1988-90, acting dir., 1990-92; dir. Nat. Inst. Drug Abuse NIH, Wash., DC, 1994—2001; CEO AAAS, 2002—. Vis. scientist U. Wis., 1976-77, dir. Natl. Inst. on Drug Abuse, HHS, Washington, 1994—; Fulbright lectr. Weizmann Inst. Sci., Rehovoth, Israel, 1977-78; Am.-Hungarian Acads. Sci. exchange scientist Postgrad Med. Sch., Budapest, 1974. Author: An Introduction to Behavioral Endocrinology, 1978; contbr. chpts., numerous articles on roles of hormones in behavior, sci. and tech. policy, higher edn. to profl. publs. Recipient Nat. Rsch. Svc. award, 1976, Pres. Merit Exec. Rank award, 1990, Pres. Dist. Exec. Rank award, 1996. Fellow AAAS, APA, Am. Psychological Soc., N.Y. Acad. Scis., Internat. Soc. Rsch. on Aggression; mem. I.O.M., Phi Beta Kappa. Democrat. Jewish. Office: AAAS 1200 New York Ave NW Washington DC 20005*

LESHY, JOHN DAVID, lawyer, legal educator, government official; b. Winchester, Ohio, Oct. 7, 1944; s. John and Dolores (King) L.; m. Helen M. Sandalls, Dec. 15, 1973; 1 child, David Alexander. AB cum laude, Harvard U., 1966, JD magna cum laude, 1969. Trial atty. Civil Rights Divsn. Dept. Justice, Washington, 1969-72; atty. Natural Resources Def. Coun., Palo Alto, Calif., 1972-77; assoc. solicitor energy and resources Dept. Interior, Washington, 1977-80; prof. law Ariz. State U., Tempe, 1980—2002; spl. counsel to chair Natural Resources Com. U.S. Ho. Reps., Washington, 1992-93; solicitor (gen. counsel) Dept. Interior, 1993-2001. Cons. Calif. State Land Commn., N.Mex. Atty. Gen., Western Govs. Assn., Congl. Rsch. Svc., Ford Found., Hewlett Found., Pew Charitable Trusts, Wyss Found.; mem. com. Onshore Oil & Gas Leasing, NAS Nat. Rsch. Coun., 1989-90; vis. prof. Sch. Law U. San Diego, 1990; disting. vis. prof. law U. Calif. Hastings Coll. Law, 2001-02; disting. prof. law, U. Calif. Hastings, 2002-. Author: The Mining Law: A Study in Perpetual Motion, 1987, The Arizona State Constitution, 1993; co-author Federal Public Land and Resources Law, 5th edit., 2002, Legal Control of Water Resources, 3rd edit., 2000; contbr. articles, book chpts. to profl. jours., environ. jours. Bd. dirs. Ariz. Ctr. Law in Pub. Interest, 1981-86, Grand Canyon Trust, 1987-1992, 2002-, Natural Heritage Inst., 2002-, Ariz. Raft Adventures, 1982-92, 2002--; mem. Gov.'s Task Force Recreation on Fed. Lands, 1985-86, Gov.'s Task Force Environ. Impact Assessment, 1990, City of Phoenix Environ. Quality Commn., 1987-90. Robinson Cox vis. fellow U. Western Australia Law Sch., Perth, 1985, rsch. fellow U. Southampton, Eng., 1986; Ford Found. grantee, Resources for the Future grantee. Democrat. Avocations: piano, hiking, whitewater rafting, photography. Office: Calif Hastings Coll Law 200 McAllister St San Francisco CA 94102-4978 E-mail: leshyj@uchastings.edu.

LESIKAR, JAMES DANIEL, II, physicist, engineer; b. Houston, Feb. 24, 1954; s. James Daniel and Ludine Luella (Kosel) L.; m. Sara Goeller, Dec. 9, 1995. BSME cum laude, Rice U., 1976, MME, 1978, MA, 1981, PhD in Physics, 1982. Registered profl. engr., Va., Md., Tex. Rsch. asst. T.W. Bonner Nuc. Labs. Rice U., Houston, 1976-81; asst. prof. physics U.S. Naval Acad., Annapolis, Md., 1984-85; sr. analyst fed. sector civil group Computer Scis. Corp., Lanham, 1986—. Mem. Md. State Bd. for Profl. Engrs., 1996-2001, vice-chmn., 1998-2001; chair Md. Profl. Engr. Complaints Com., 1996-2001; spkr. in field; adj. faculty Anne Arundel C.C., Arnold, Md., 2001—. Author (with others) NASA reports, 1987—; author of scope of practice for the design professions bill which was signed into law in Md., 2001; contbr. articles to Physics Letters, Phys. Rev., Phys. Rev. Letters. Co-moderator Math Counts Program, Annapolis, Md., 1991, 95, 96, 98, 99, 2000, 01, 02; judge Hubble Space Telescope Engrng. Competition, 1998, Solar and Heliospheric Observatory Engrng. Competition, 1999; spkr. Nat. Engrs.' Week, Duval H.S., Lanham, Md., 1999; proctor Md. Mathcounts, 1996, 99, 2002; sci. fair judge St. John the Evangelist Sch., Severna Park, Md., 2000-02. Capt. U.S. Army, 1981-85; lt. col. USAR, 1988—. Decorated Bronze Cross for Achievement Legion of Valor, Nat. Def. Svc. medal, Army Parachutist Badge; recipient Outstanding Teamwork award Goddard Space Flight Ctr., 2000; grad. fellow Rice U., Houston, 1976-77, Nettie S. Autrey Meml. fellow in sci., 1978-79, Order of the Engr., 1998. Fellow AIAA (life assoc., guidance navigation and control tech. com. 2001—); mem. ASME (chair profl. practice and ethics com. Balt. sect. 1998—), AAAS, NSPE (sec.-treas. Annapolis chpt. 1994-97), Nat. Coun. Examiners for Engrng. and Surveying (mem. com. on examination audit 1998-99, com. on uniform procedures and legis. guidelines 2000-02, mech. exam group 2000-01), Am. Phys. Soc. (life), Soc. of Am. Mil. Engrs. (sec. Houston chpt. 1978), Md. State Soc. (v.p. 2001-2, pres.-elect 2002-), Nat. Def. Indsl. Assn. (life), Optimists (bd. dirs. East Lawton Okla. chpt. 1983-84), Sigma Xi (life), Sigma Pi Sigma (pres. Rice U. chpt. 1976-77). Achievements include supervision and participation with flight dynamics support team for the Cosmic Background Explorer, POLAR and Fast Auroral Snapshot Telescope Scientific Satellites, GOES-10 and GOES-12 Weather Satellites, Earth Observing System AM-1/Terra and PM-1/Aqua Environmental Monitoring Satellites; research in high energy spin-dependence of hadron interactions. Home: 463 Yorkshire Dr Severna Park MD 21146-1650 Office: Computer Scis Corp 7700 Hubble Dr Lanham Seabrook MD 20706-2295 E-mail: jlesikar@asme.org.

LESKES, ANDREA, literature educator; b. Washington, Sept. 9, 1943; d. Theodore and Florence Mildred L.; m. Tommy Olof Elder, June 27, 1981; 1 child, Ambjörn Olaf. BA magna cum laude in Zoology, Vassar Coll., 1964; MA in Zoology, U. Mass., 1986; PhD in Life Scis., The Rockefeller U., 1969. Asst. dean faculty of arts and scis. Dartmouth Coll., Hanover, N.H., 1986-90; assoc. dean for humanities, arts and social scis. Brandeis U., Waltham, Mass., 1990-91; vice provost for undergrad. edn. Northeastern U., Boston, 1991-96; v.p. for acad. affairs, dean of faculty, prof. comparative lit. The Am. U. of Paris, 1996-99, prof. comparative lit., 1996-99, interim pres., 1997-98; v.p. for edn. and quality initiatives The Assn. of Am. Colls. and Univs., Washington, 1999—; dir. Greater Expectations; co-dir. Asheville Inst. on Gen. Edn. Co dir. Asheville Inst. gen. edn., 1990; dir. Greater Expectations; adj. asst. prof. compartive lit. Dartmouth Coll., 1989-90; adj. assoc. prof. French Brandeis U., Waltham, Mass., 1990-91; adj. assoc. prof. modern langs. Northeastern U., Boston, 1991-96; cons. new England Resource Ctr. for Higher Edn., Boston, 1994-96, New Eng. Assn. of Schs. and Colls., 1995-99, many colls. and univs., NSF, 1990—. Translator: Leonora: The Buried Story of Guadeloupe, 1995, Tribaliks, 1987; editor: Grants for Graduate Students, 1986-88, 1986. Mem. Internat. Sch. for Theory in the Humanities (faculty assoc.), Assn. U. Adminstrs. (exemplary model adminstrv. leadership award 1996), Phi Beta Kappa, Sigma Xi. Office: Assn of Am Colls and Univs 1818 R St NW Washington DC 20009 Home: 4701 Willard Ave Apt 836 Chevy Chase MD 20815

LESKIEN, HERMANN ADALBERT, library director; b. Koenigsberg, Germany, Dec. 23, 1939; s. Bruno and Maria (Rikowski) L.; m. Marga Schmidt, June 19, 1965 (div.); children: Cosima, Titus; m. Elisabeth Heinrich, May 24, 1993. PhD, U. Wuerzburg, Germany, 1966. Lic. libr. Acquisition dept. head U. Libr., Wuerzburg, 1967-73, dir. Bamberg, Germany, 1973-79, U. Libr. Munich, 1979-92, Bavarian State Libr., Munich, 1992—, dir. gen., 1999—. Avocations: classical music, hiking, cycling. Home: Graubuendener Str 55 D-81475 Munich Germany Office: Bayerische Staatsbibliothek D-80328 Munich Germany E-mail: leskien@bsb-muenchen.de.

LESKO, HARRY JOSEPH, transportation company executive; b. Cleve., Dec. 6, 1920; s. Theodore Prokop and Bertha Barbara (Trojack) L.; m. Evelyn Martha Culley, Feb. 3, 1945; children— Harry Richard, Larry J., Garry E., Mark J., John M., Joseph. BBA, Cleve. State U., 1956. Schedule analyst Cleve. Ry. System, 1938-40; pres., dir. Greyhound Lines, Inc., Phoenix, 1940—; pres. Atlantic Greyhound Lines of Va., Inc.; v.p. Gelco Bus Leasing Co., 1979—; pres. Trailways Lines Inc., Dallas, 1979—. Pres., dir. The Trailways Corp., Trailways, Inc.; dir. Trailways Lines Inc. (25 subs.), Southeastern Stages, Inc., Atlanta, N.Mex. Transp. Co., Roswell, KG Lines, Tulsa, Okla. Transp. Co., Lubbock, Tex., Jefferson Lines Inc., Mpls., Kerrville Bus. Co., Tex., Continental Lines, Amarillo, Tex., Service Coach Co., Jacksonville, Fla., Gen. Fire and Casualty Co. Served to capt. USMC, 1942-46. Mem. Am. Bus. Assn. (dir.) Roman Catholic.

LESKO, LEONARD HENRY, Egyptologist, educator, publisher; b. Chgo., Aug. 14, 1938; s. Matthew Edward and Josephine Bernice (Jaszczak) L.; m. Barbara Jadwiga Switalski, Dec. 29, 1966. BA, Loyola U., Chgo., 1961, MA, 1964; PhD, U. Chgo., 1969; MA ad eundem, Brown U., 1983. Tchr. Quigley Prep. Sem. South, Chgo., 1961-64; Egyptologist, epigrapher, epigraphic survey Oriental Inst., U. Chgo., Luxor, Egypt, 1964-65; acting instr. U. Calif. at Berkeley, 1966-67, acting asst. prof., 1967-68, asst. prof., 1968-72, asso. prof., 1972-77, prof. Egyptology, 1977-82, dir. Center Nr. Eastern Studies, 1973-75, chmn. dept., 1975-77, 79-81, chmn. grad. program in ancient history and Mediterranean archeology, 1978-79, chmn. humanities council, 1980-81; dir. Seila project, 1981; C.E. Wilbour prof. Egyptology, chmn. dept. Brown U., 1982—; chmn. faculty, faculty exec. com., 1992-93. Author: The Ancient Egyptian Book of Two Ways, 1972, Glossary of the Late Ramesside Letters, 1975, King Tut's Wine Cellar, 1977, Index of the Spells on Egyptian Middle Kingdom Coffins and Related Documents, 1979; co-author: Religion in Ancient Egypt, 1991, Pharoah's Workers: The Villagers of Deir el-Medina, 1994; editor: A Dictionary of Late Egyptian, vol. I, 1982, vol. II, 1984, vol. III, 1987, vol. IV, 1989, vol. V, 1990, 2d edit., Vol. I, 2002, Egyptological Studies in Honor of Richard A. Parker, 1986, Exodus: The Egyptian Evidence, 1997, Ancient Egyptian and Mediterranean Studies in Memory of William A Ward, 1998; co-editor: Joseph Lindon Smith: Paintings from Egypt, 1998; contbr. articles to profl. publs. and encys. Active Friends of Libr., Brown U.; assoc. John Carter Brown Libr. Recipient award computer oriented rsch. in humanities Am. Coun. Learned Socs., 1973; NEH fellow, 1970-71, grantee, 1975-79, co-dir. Summer Inst., 1995; FIAT faculty fellow U. Torino, 1990; grantee R.I. Com. for the Humanities, 1998. Mem.: Soc. Francaise d' Egyptologie, Found. Egyptologique Reine Elizabeth, Egypt Exploration Soc., Internat. Assn. Egyptologists., Archeol. Inst. Am. (pres. San Francisco chpt. 1976—78, pres. Narragansett chpt. 1994—95), Am. Oriental Soc., Am. Rsch. Ctr. in Egypt (gov. 1973—75), Maserati Owners Club, U.S. Lighthouse Soc., R.I. Acad. of Wine, John Russell Bartlett Soc. (pres. 1997—98), Chevalier de Confrèrie de la Chaine des Rotisseurs (vice chargè de presse 1999), Chevalier de Ordre Mondial des Gourmets Dègustateurs, Lighthouse Preservation Soc., Miserati Club Internat., Ferrari Club Am., Ferrari Owners Club, The Club of Odd Vols. (Boston), Univ. Club (Providence), Explorers' Club (N.Y.). Office: Brown U Dept Egyptology PO Box 1899 Providence RI 02912-1899

LESKO, RONALD MICHAEL, osteopathic physician; b. Homestead, Pa., Mar. 25, 1948; s. Andrew Paul and Elizabeth Ann (Tarasovic) L.; m. Helena Alexandra Shalayeva, July 29, 1990. BS, U. Pitts., 1970; DO, Coll. Osteo. Medicine & Surgery, Des Moines, 1973; MPH, Loma Linda U., 1985. Diplomate Am. Osteo. Bd. Family Physicians, Am. Osteo. Bd. Preventive Medicine (bd. dirs., chmn. pub. health rep., chmn. bd. exam. com. 1991-97). Family physician pvt. practice, Port Richey, Fla., 1974-80; flight surgeon USN, NAS Chase Field Beeville, Tex., 1981-83; resident gen. preventive medicine Loma Linda (Calif.) U. Med. Ctr., 1983-85; pvt. practice family and preventive medicine, pvt. practice, Del Mar, Calif., 1988—; flight surgeon, capt. USNR, NAS Miramar, San Diego, 1988-95, ret. Loma Linda, Calif., 1996; attending physician ambulatory care svc. J.L. Pettis Meml. VA Hosp., 1986-88; staff physician Scripps Meml. Hosp., La Jolla, 1990—. Lectr., 1995—; cons. Jour. Am. Osteo. Assn., Chgo., 1987, phys. rediness div. USN, Washington, 1988; med. advisor blue ribbon adv. com. Nutrition Screening Initiative, Washington, 1991. Contbr. articles to med. jours.; rschr. in nutrition and metabolism in human physiology. Med. adviser March of Dimes Suncoast chpt., New Port Richey, 1977-79; bd. dirs. Fla. Gulf Health Systems Agy., Region IV, 1977-79, Price-Pottenger Nutrition Found., San Diego, 1988—. Fellow Am. Osteo. Coll. Occupational and Preventive Medicine (trustee 1989-91, chmn. pub. health divisional com. 1989-91), Am. Coll. Preventive Medicine; mem. APHA, Am. Osteo. Assn., San Diego Osteo. Med. Assn., Osteo. Physicians and Surgeons Calif., Am. Coll. Family Physicians-Osteo., U.S. Naval Flight Surgeons. Avocations: scuba diving, photography, marksmanship, art, music. Office: 13983 Mango Dr Ste 103 Del Mar CA 92014-3146

LESKO-BISHOP, JULIA, editor; b. Casablanca, Morocco, July 17, 1956; d. Stephen Howard Lesko and Sonja E Kneer; children: Kaleigh Marie Bishop, Brooke Alison Bishop. BA communication, Okla. City U., Oklahoma, OK, 1974—78, Masters Edn., 1988—90. Publications advisor tchr. Del City H.S., Del City, Okla., 1978—2001; asst. editor Mattison Ave. West Publications, Oklahoma City, 1999; coord., student publications Rose State Coll., Midwest City, 2001—. Mem., cons. Okla. Writing Project, Norman, Okla., 1997—. Author: (book) Writing Up a Storm, (article) Community College Times. Avocations: golf, reading, quilting, quilting. Home: 114 Orchard Drive Midwest City OK 73110 Office: Rose State College 6420 Southeast 15th Midwest City OK 73110 Office Fax: 405-733-7931. E-mail: jlesko-bishop@rose.edu.

LESLEY, MELLINEE K. literature educator; b. Fresno, Calif., Nov. 11, 1956; d. Patrick K. and Marlys N. Lesley; m. Stephen P. Koutrelakos, Aug. 12, 2000; m. Ron D. Lile, June 1, 1991 (div. July 1997); 1 child Mireille Lile. BA, U. Iowa, 1988; MA, N.Mex. State U., 1990; PhD, U. Pa., 1998. Grad. tchg. asst. dept. English N.Mex. State U., 1988—90; fellow West Tex. writing project U. Tex., El Paso, 1992; tchr. Loretto Acad. H.S., 1991—93; rsch. asst. Grad. Sch. Edn. U. Pa., Phila., 1993—95, grad. asst. Penn Literacy Network, 1995—96; asst. prof. reading Ea. N.Mex. U., Portales, 1997—, coord. devel. reading, 1998—. Lectr. Phila. Coll. Textiles, 1993—94; instr. dept. English El Paso (Tex.) C.C., 1990—93; presenter in field. Contbr. articles to profl. jours. Mem. tchr. quality task force N.Mex. State Dept. Edn., 2000—; vol. Rocking Read a Thon Portales Pub. Libr., 2002; ptnr. Strengthening Quality Schs. program Portales Sch. Dist., 1998—2000; mem. content adv. com. N.Mex. Assessment of Tchr. Competency, 1998; organizer book drive N.Mex. Christian Children's Home, Portales, 1998; tutor Broad Horizons Alternative H.S., 1997—98; bd. drs. Roosevelt County Literacy Coun., 1998—2001. Recipient GOALS 2000 grant, Ea. N.Mex. U., 1999; grantee, Ctr. for Tchg. Excellence, 1999, Ranchvale Elem. Sch., Clovis, N.Mex., 1999—2001, Pew Charitable Trust, 1999—2000, Portales Sch. Dist., 1998—99. Mem.: Coll. Reading Assn., Nat. Assn. Devel. Edn., N.Mex. Reading Educators, N.Mex. Coun. Tchrs. English, Pedagogy of the Oppressed, Internat. Reading Assn., Nat. Coun. Tchrs. English, Am. Ednl. Rsch. Assn. Avocations: violin, gardening.

LESLIE, BEN, race car driver; Mechanic and rear tire changer Roush Racing, Concord, NC, 1994—97, crew chief, 1997—. Office: Roush Racing 7020 Aviation Blvd Concord NC 28027-8196

LESLIE, HENRY ARTHUR, lawyer, retired banker; b. Troy, Ala., Oct. 15, 1921; s. James B. and Alice (Minchener) L.; m. Anita Doyle, Apr. 5, 1943; children: Anita Lucinda Leslie Bagby, Henry Arthur Jr. BS, U. Ala., 1942, JD, 1948; JSD, Yale U., 1959; grad., Rutgers U., 1964. Bar: Ala. 1948. Asst. prof. bus. law U. Ala., 1948-50, 52-54; prof., asst. dean U. Ala. Sch. Law, 1954-59; v.p. trust officer Birmingham Trust Nat. Bank, Ala., 1959-64; sr. v.p., trust officer Union Bank & Trust Co., Montgomery, 1964-73, sr. v.p., sr. loan officer, 1973-76, exec. v.p., 1976-78, pres. CEO, 1978-91, also bd. dirs.; ret., 1991; pvt. practice Montgomery, Ala., 1991—. Mem. Ala. Oil and Gas Bd., 1984-85. Pres. Downtown Unltd., 1983-84; mem. Ala. Bd. Bar Examiners, 1973-78, bd. dirs. YMCA, 1992—; mem., vice-chmn. Ala. Jud. Campaign Oversight Com., 1999-2001. Decorated Bronze Star. Mem. ABA, Ala. Bar Assn., Montgomery Bar Assn. (Liberty Bell award 1989), Ala. Ind. Bankers (chmn. 1983-84), Ala. Bankers Assn. (trust div. pres. 1963-65), Ind. Bankers Assn. Am. (dir. 1983-90), Farrah Order Jurisprudence (pres. 1973), Order of Coif Alumni, Newcomen Soc. N.Am., Montgomery C. of C. (dir. 1983-84, pres. 1987-88), Maxwell Officers Club, Montgomery Country Club, Kiwanis, Delta Sigma Pi, Phi Delta Phi, Omicron Delta Kappa, Pi Kappa Phi. Episcopalian (past sr. warden). Home: 3332 Boxwood Dr Montgomery AL 36111-1702

LESLIE , JACK See LESLIE, JOHN WEBSTER JR.

LESLIE, JACQUES ROBERT, JR. journalist; b. L.A., Mar. 12, 1947; s. Jacques Robert and Aleen (Wetstein) L.; m. Leslie Wernick, June 21, 1980; 1 child, Sarah Alexandra. BA, Yale U., 1968. Tchr. New Asia Coll., Chinese U., Hong Kong, 1968-70; free-lance journalist Washington, 1970-71; fgn. corr. L.A. Times, Saigon, 1972-73, Phnom Penh, 1973, Washington, 1974, chief New Delhi (India) bur., 1974-75, Madrid, 1975-76, chief Hong Kong bur., 1976-77; freelance journalist, 1977—; contbg. writer Wired Mag., 1993—. Contbg. writer Wired mag., 1993—. Author: The Mark: A War Correspondent's Memoir of Vietnam and Cambodia Recipient Best Fgn. Corr. award Sigma Delta Chi, 1973, citation for reporting Overseas Press Club, 1973, J. Anthony Lukas Book-in-Progress award, 2002; Individual Artist grantee Marin Arts Coun., 1999; grantee, William and Flora Hewlett Found., 2001, Fred Gellert Family Found., 2001. Home: 124 Reed St Mill Valley CA 94941-3448 E-mail: jacques@well.com.

LESLIE, JOHN, artist, designer, fine art photographer, sculptor; b. Phila., July 11, 1923; s. John Joseph and Mary Kathryn (Bauermees) L.; m. Kathryn Elizabeth Frame, Feb. 4, 1946 (div. 1948); m. Mary Frances Huggins, Apr. 2, 1950; children: Karol Ann, John Joseph III, Mary Lee. Grad. comml. art, Murrell Dobbins Tech., Phila., 1941; postgrad., Fleisher Art Meml., Phila., 1939-42; postgrad, Phila. Museum Sch. Indsl. Art, 1944; postgrad., Phila. Music Acad., 1965-67, Pa. State U., 1982—. Staff artist Phila. Daily News, 1942; founder, creative dir. Graphic Ad Displays, Inc., Phila., 1944; artist/muralist Bonwit Teller, 1944-46; collaborative designer fashion show stage sets and Gimbel Bros. Thanksgiving Day Parade, 1945; pres., art dir. Duplex Display and Mfg. Co., Inc., 1947-54; pres., designer Leslie Creations, Inc., Lafayette Hill, Pa., 1954-65; pres., founder Mail Order Methods, Inc., 1954-67; pres. World Treasures, Seven Seas House, Inc., 1960-65; founder, creative dir. Kopy Kat Inc. with 150 franchised instant printing ctrs., Fort Washington, Pa., 1968-77; art dir. designer Jesse Jones Industries, Inc., Phila., 1978-79; co-founder, art dir. Galerie Marjolé, Inc., Sanatoga, Pa., 1987-89, lectr. ltd. edition prints, 1987—. Fine art spokesman radio, TV, 1989—; guest spkr. Hundred Million Club, N.Y.C., 1963; stage set designer Bessie V. Hicks Sch., Dramatic Arts, Phila., 1944-46. Patentee U.S. Kopy Kat, Inc. and Fla. Military Heritage Mus. trademark; prin. works include site selection Jeanes Meml. Libr., Lafayette Hill, Pa., 1967; executed murals Phila. Savs. Fund Soc., Phila. Eagles Football Team, E.F. Houghton Co., 1945-53; originator of 3-Ds (3-dimensional collages of paper-sculpture, painted artwork and layered composition bd.), 1940s; originator/designer first giant 3-D Dioramic Collages in U.S., 1940's; created wrought iron and chromed steel functional metal sculptures, 1954-79; designer the Crystal Mall concept (a climate-controlled atrium enclosing entire existing downtown shopping dists.), 1990; designer U.S. WWII Vets. Meml. Hall of Honor, 1996; designer official emblem and proposed interior, Fla. Mil. Heritage Mus., Punta Gorda, 2001; artworks in U.S. Embassy, Paris, J.F.K. Libr., Boston, Woodmere Art Mus., Pa. Acad. Fine Arts, Phila., Mus. Art, and 20 other U.S. museums; first artist to use tissue paper as papier maché sculptural medium, 1940s; released 3 ltd. edit. lithographic prints and many fine art photographs, 1988—; designer homes and avant garde furniture including first ocean front A-Frame home on Atlantic coast, first lakeside French Provencial motif home Port Charlotte, Fla., the Slab Chair, made of interlocking leather-covered foam rubber panels; designer Mannequettes for dept. store windows; creator Plasti-Coils, 1940-50; inventor Showoff cabinet and Room Divider Record Screen, a 3-way folding screen, to file, store, and display LP record albums and video discs, 1954-63; designer the Skyscraper, welded chromed steel functional metal sculpture, 1978; exhibited in shows at Art Expo N.Y.C., 1988, Ursinus Coll., Collegeville, Pa., 1983, Phila. Sketch Club, 1987, Englewood Art Guild Fine Art Photo Expos, Fla., 1996—, United Passtelists of Am., Upper Nyack On-the-Hudson, N.Y., 1997, Woodmere Art Mus., Philadelphia, Pa., 1967, 68, 79, 80, 85, 89, 90, First Annual Galeria Exhib., N.Y., 1988; author: weekly column on fine art photography, "Lasting Impressions," Englewood Herald, Fla., 2000—. Pres., founder Ctrl. Citizens Com., Inc. (limiting strip mining in residential areas), Whitemarsh Twp., Pa., 1960-75; active Big Bros. Am., Phila., 1957-65, YMCA Indian Guides, Montgomery County, Pa., 1965-68; conservationist, animal rights activist Am. Anti-Vivisection Soc., 1959—; mem. Arts and Humanities Coun. of Charlotte County, Fla.; pres. Lions, Lafayette Hill, Pa., 1960-70. With 8th Armored Divsn. Tank Corps., U.S. Army, 1943. Named Citizen of Week Montgomery Newspapers, 1978; recipient Direct Mail Leaders award Direct Mail Advt. Assn., 1957, 60, Artistic Merit award Playboy Mag., 1958, Japanese Graphic Arts Industry award, 1975, King of Prussia Fine Arts award Upper Merion Cultural Ctr., 1966, Disting. Svc. award Citizens Com. on Pub. Edn., Phila., 1981, Walter Emerson Baum Award for An American Impressionist Painting, Sellers Mus., Bucks County, Pa., 1995, The Sellers Mus. award for Impressionism in Fine Art Photography, Bucks County, Pa., 2001; inducted into Artist's Hall of Fame Murrell Dobbins Tech., Phila., 1988; presented artist's proof to French World Cup Soccer Champions, Paris, 1998. Mem. Woodmere Art Mus. (Phila.), Boca Grande Fla. Art Alliance, Englewood (Fla.) Photographers Assn., Les Amis de Veterans Francais, N.Y. Oil Pastel Assn., Nat. Amvets., 8th Armored Divsn. Assn., Fla. Mil. Heritage Mus., Oil Pastel Assn. N.Y. Roman Catholic. Avocations: collecting antique photographs, pottery, opera, jazz. Studio: Blueberry Hill 6318 Zeno Cir Port Charlotte FL 33981

LESLIE, JOHN WEBSTER, JR. (JACK LESLIE), communications company executive; b. Milw., July 20, 1954; s. John and Joanne Marie (Chamberlain) L.; m. Laura Elizabeth Bafford, June 7, 1986; children: Finn Elizabeth, John Webster III. BS in Fgn. Service, Georgetown U., 1976. Legis. asst. Senator Edward Kennedy, Washington, 1976-80; campaign dir. northeast region Kennedy for Pres., 1980-81; polit. dir. Senator Edward Kennedy for U.S. Senate, 1981-82; exec. dir. Fund for Dem. Majority, 1982-83; pres. Sawyer/Miller Group, N.Y.C., 1983-93; ptnr. Robinson Lerer Sawyer Miller, 1993-96; pres. BSMG Worldwide, 1997; chmn. Weber Shandwick. Bd. dirs. Internat. Policy Research, Inc., N.Y.C., Creative Media, Inc., N.Y.C. Contbr. articles to profl. jours.; speaker in field. Bd. dirs. Nat. Student Edn. Fund,

Washington, 1977-79, USA for UNHCR, 1997—. Fellow Circumnavigators Found., Am. Assn. Polit. Cons, Coun. on Fgn. Rels, bd. of the Found. for Accountability. Roman Catholic. Office: 640 5th Ave New York NY 10019-6102*

LESLIE, JOHN WILLIAM, public relations and advertising executive; b. Indpls., Nov. 22, 1923; s. John Edward and Catherine (Harris) L.; m. Joan Williams, Dec. 26, 1970; 1 dau. by previous marriage, Catherine Alexandra. Student, U.S. Naval Acad., 1943-44, George Washington U., 1949, Indsl. Coll. Armed Forces, 1956. Dep. excise adminstr., Ind., 1946-47; pvt. pub. relations bus., 1947-49; dir. pub. relations Ind. Democratic State Central Com., 1948-49, Ind. Dept. Vets. Affairs, 1949; press officer Dept. Labor, 1949-51, acting asst. dir. info., 1951-52, asst. dir., 1952-56, dep. dir., 1956-59, dir., 1959-81; sr. assoc. Kamber Group, Washington, 1981-84, counselor, 1984-88, exec. v.p., COO, 1988-96, vice chmn., sec., 1997-98, pub. rels. cons., 1998—, also bd. dirs. Mem., dir. pub. D.C. Com. Employment Physically Handicapped, 1952-53; charter mem. U.S. Sr. Exec. Svc., 1979—. Author numerous articles in field. Advt. cons. Pres.'s Com. on Youth Employment, 1964-80; U.S. del Internat. Graphic Design Coun., Japan, 1973; trustee Washington chpt. Leukemia Soc. Am., 1976-82; chmn. Pub. Printers Adv. Com. on Printing and Publs, 1977-79. Served with USN and USNR, 1941-46. Recipient commendation President's Com. Employment Physically Handicapped, 1954; Disting. Service award Dept. Labor, 1962; citation outstanding service Navy Dept., 1964; Presdl. citation, 1966; Merit award Internat. Labor Press Assn., 1969; Disting. Career Service award Dept. Labor, 1973; Communications award Ga. chpt. Pub. Relations Soc. Am., 1972; Sec. Labor's Recognition award, 1974; Communicator of Yr. award Nat. Assn. Govt. Communicators, 1981 Mem. Am. Assn. Polit. Cons., Am. League Lobbyists, Nat. Press Club, English Speaking Union, Univ. Club (Winter Park, Fla.), Stag Club of Winter Park. Episcopalian. Home and Office: Sweetwater Country Club 2433 Orchard Dr Apopka FL 32712-2562 E-mail: TwoLeslies@aol.com.

LESLIE, LISA DESHAUN, professional basketball player; b. Gardena, Calif., July 7, 1972; Grad., U. So. Calif., 1994. Basketball player USA Women's Nat. Team, 1996, L.A. Sparks WNBA, 1997—. Mem. gold medal winning 1994 Goodwill Games Team. Named 1993 USA Basketball Female Athlete of Yr.; recipient gold medal Atlanta Olympics, 1996, Sydney Olympics 2000; named MVP 1st WNBA All-Star Game, 1999 names MVP of season, WNBA Championship & All-Star Game, 2001. Office: Los Angeles Sparks 555 N Nash St El Segundo CA 90245 Office Fax: 310-330-2437.*

LESLIE, LYNN MARIE, secondary education educator; b. Lake City, Fla., Nov. 17, 1948; d. Billy Verlyn Spooner and Dorothy Marie (Odom) Loomis; m. Roy Hamner Leslie, Nov. 25, 1967; children: Kim Ball, Billy Leslie, Dodi Leslie. BS in Edn., Trevecca U., 1970; ME in Spl. Edn., Tenn. State U., 1987, postgrad. in adminstrn./supervision, 1998; postgrad. in Edn., Cumberland U., 1996; cetr. in supervision and adminstrn., Tenn. State U., 1998. Cert. career ladder III, Tenn. Tchr. Leesburg (Fla.) Elem. Sch., 1970-71, Wessington Pl. Elem. Sch., Hendersonville, Tenn., 1974-87, Knox Doss Mid. Sch., Hendersonville, 1987—2000, Spring Run Elem. Sch., Midlothian, Va., 2000—. Mem. Sumner County Ins. Trust, Gallatin, Tenn., 1991-96; tchr, Hall of Fame Jr. Achievement, 1993. Mem. 5 year goal planning com. Sumner County, extended contract procedures com., 1992. Mem. NEA (del.), Va. Edn. Assn., Chesterfield Edn. Assn., Sumner County Edn. Assn. (pres. 1991-92, 95-96, sec. 1992-95, sec./treas. 1996—, calendar com. 1992, 96, 98, numerous coms. chair, tchr. welfare com. 1990-91). Mem. Ch. of Nazarene. Avocations: reading, travel. Home: 15825 Fox Marsh Drive Moseley VA 23120

LESLIE, MAE SUE, writer; b. Forrester, Ark., Dec. 22, 1940; d. Doyle Joseph and Ruby Estelle (Stewart) Davis; m. Gerald Robert Leslie, Sept. 2, 1967; children: Neal R., Denise. Student, Instituto Allende, San Miguel Allende, Mex., 1960-61; BA in Journalism, Sam Houston State U., 1966. Cert. nursing home social worker, Tex. Sec. Am. Gen. Ins. Co., Houston, 1966-67; social worker Harris County, 1968; sec. temp. agys., 1977-81; freelance writer, 1981—. Author: (novel) Canadian Capers, 1998; author of three childrens books and screenplay; freelance cartoonist. Pianist, Sunday sch. tchr. Riverside (Tex.) Bapt. Ch., 1963-65. Recipient 3d pl. for article Fla. State Writing Competition, 1994, 2d pl. for short story Manuscripts Guild, 1994, 3d pl. for nonfiction, 1994. Mem. Nat. Writer's Union, Houston Screenwriters, Nat. Honor Soc. for Journalism Students. Democrat. Baptist. Home: 5326 De Lange Ln Houston TX 77092-4208

LESLIE, MAUREEN HEELAN, university director; b. Bronx, N.Y. d. James Joseph, Sr. and Evelyn (McDonald) H.; m. Bruce Allan Leslie; children: James Christopher, Michael Patrick. BA in Bus. Mgmt. cum laude, Molloy Coll., 1997. Adminstrv. asst. Berkeley Coll., N.Y.C., 1965-68; A placement dir., counselor, 1968-71; entrepreneur The Silk Floral Gallery, Huntington, N.Y., 1984-86; gen. orgn. treas. South Huntington (N.Y.) Sch. Dist., 1984-98; devel. assoc. Molloy Coll., Rockville Ctr., 1998-99; dir. alumni rels., 1999—. Mem. industry adv. bd. South Huntington Sch. Dist., 1998—, Mt. Sinai (N.Y.) Sch. Dist., 1999—. V.p. St. Hugh of Lincoln Sch. Bd., Huntington Sta., N.Y., 1983; mem. LIA/Long Isalnd Works Coalition, Commack and Melville, N.Y., 1998—. Mem. AAUW, Exec. Women's Golf Assn., Long Island Women's Agenda, Long Island Ctr. Bus. and Profl. Women, Huntington C. of C. (mem. industry adv. bd. 2001—), South Huntington Jr. C. of C. (mem. industry adv. bd. 1998—), Delta Epsilon Sigma, Delta Epsilon Pi, Lambda Pi Eta. Roman Catholic. Avocations: tennis, golf, swimming, dancing, reading. Office: 1000 Hempstead Ave Rockville Centre NY 11570-1100 E-mail: mleslie@molloy.edu.

LESLIE, RICHARD MCLAUGHLIN, lawyer, educator; b. Chgo., Oct. 31, 1936; s. Richard S. and Belle (McLaughlin) L.; m. Nancy Elizabeth Lomax; children: Saralynn, Richard W., Lance T. BA, U. Fla., 1958; JD, U. Mich., 1961. Bar: Ill. 1961, Fla. 1962, U.S. Dist. Ct. (no. dist.) Ill., U.S. Dist. Ct. (so. and mid. dists.) Fla., U.S. Ct. Appeals (5th cir.), U.S. Ct. Appeals (11th cir.), U.S. Supreme Ct. 1970. Assoc. Jacobs & McKenna, Chgo., 1961-63, Louis G. Davidson, Chgo., 1963; assoc., then ptnr. Shutts & Bowen, Miami, Fla., 1964—. Adj. prof. trial advocacy program U. Miami Law Sch., 1979-89. Chmn. bd. trustees Plymouth Congl. Ch., Miami, 1978. Capt. USAR, 1961-67. Mem. ABA (com. chmn. torts and ins. practice sect. 1980, 88, 93, elect. to council 1998—, mem. House Delegates 1999—), Fla. Def. Lawyers Assn. (pres. 1987), Fedn. Ins. and Corp. Counsel (v.p. 1987, bd. dirs. 1988-93), Dade County Bar Assn. (bd. dirs. 1987-90, 94-97, 99—), Maritime Law Assn. U.S., Fla. Bar Assn. (trial lawyers com.), Ill. Bar Assn., Average Adjustors Assn., Phi Delta Theta, Delta Theta Phi, Miami City Club, Riviera Country Club, Fisher Island Club. Avocations: tennis, skiing, travel. Home: 4116 Pinta Ct Coral Gables FL 33146-1119 Office: Shutts & Bowen Miami Ctr 201 S Biscayne Blvd Ste 1500 Miami FL 33131-4308 E-mail: rleslie@shutts-law.com.

LESLIE, ROBERT FREMONT, mobile testing executive, non-destructive testing inspector; b. St. Louis, July 8, 1952; s. Robert Day and Dena (Lange) L. BA in Bus., Psychology, North Cen. Coll., 1975. Salesman Fairmount Hydraulics, Chgo., 1975-77; salesman, technician Torco Equip. Co., Louisville, 1978-81; pres., insp. Delta Mobile Testing, Inc., LaGrange, Ky., 1981—. Mem. ASTM (F18 com. 1988—), Nat. Fire Protection Assn. (stds. writing com. 1988—), Am. Welding Soc. Achievements include development of intensified fluoroscopic X-ray. Home and Office: Delta Mobile Testing Inc 2306 Running Brk La Grange KY 40031-9395

LESLIE, ROBERT LORNE, lawyer; b. Adak, Ala., Feb. 24, 1947; s. J. Lornie and L. Jean (Conelly) L.; children: Lorna Jean, Elizabeth Allen. BS, U.S. Mil. Acad., 1969; JD, U. Calif., San Francisco, 1974. Bar: Calif. 1974, D.C. 1979, U.S. Dist. Ct. (no. dist.) Calif. 1974, U.S. Ct. Claims 1975, U.S. Tax Ct. 1975, U.S. Ct. Appeals (9th and D.C. cirs.) 1974, U.S. Ct. Mil. Appeals 1980, U.S. Supreme Ct. 1980. Commd. 2d lt. U.S. Army, 1969, advanced through grades to maj., 1980; govt. trial atty. West Coast Field Office, Contract Appeals, Litigation and Regulatory Law divsns., Office JAG, Dept. Army, San Francisco, 1974-77; sr. trial atty., team chief Office of Chief Trial Atty., Dept. of Amry, Washington, 1977-80; ptnr. McInerney & Dillon, Oakland, Calif., 1980—, 1980—. Lectr. on govt. contracts CSC, Continuing Legal Edn. Program; lectr. in govt. procurement U.S. Army Material Command. Served to col. USAR, ret. Decorated Purple Heart, Silver Star. Mem. ABA, Fed. Bar Assn., Associated Gen. Contractors, The Beavers. Office: McInerney & Dillon Ordway Bldg Fl 18 Oakland CA 94612-3610

LESLIE, SEAVER, artist; b. Boston, Aug. 22, 1946; s. John Frederick and Joan (Warland) L.; m. Anne Cleland Rogers; children: Genevieve, Marion, Frances. BFA, RISD, 1969, MEd, 1970. Instr. painting RISD, Providence, 1971-81, 97-2000, Parsons sch. Design, N.Y.C., 1980-82, Wellesley (Mass.) Coll., 1983-84; artist-in-residence U Calif., San Diego, 1984-85,1987-88. Exhibited in shows at Hirschl & Adler Gallery, N.Y.C., 1981, Tatistcheff Gallery, N.Y.C., 1982, DeCordova Mus., Lincoln, Mass., 1989, Maine Coast Artists, Rockport, 1993, 2000, Portland (Maine) Mus. Art, 1993, 2000; author: 12 Points: Putting the Case for Customary Measure, 1979, Why America Should Not Go Metric, 1993. Founder Ams. for Customary Weight and Measure, N.Y.C., The Morris Farm Trust; co-founder Maine Trans. Coalition, Wicasset. Studio: PO Box 248 Old Stone Farm Wiscasset ME 04578

LESLIE, SEYMOUR MARVIN, communications executive, director; b. N.Y.C., Dec. 16, 1922; s. Harry and Fay (Goldstein) L.; m. Barbara Miller, Mar. 30, 1947; children: Ellen, Jane, Carol. EE, Syracuse U., 1945; grad., Advanced Mgmt. Program, Harvard U., 1971; DHL, Hofstra U., 1974. Sales mgr. Voco, Inc., N.Y.C., 1946-52; founder Pickwick Internat., Inc., Woodbury, N.Y., 1953, chmn. bd., pres., 1953-77; chmn. Leslie Group, Inc., 1977—; pres. CBS Video Enterprises div. CBS, Inc., N.Y.C., 1980-82; chmn., pres., chief exec. officer MGM/UA Home Entertainment Group, Inc., 1982-87; co-chmn. Leslie/Linton Entertainment Corp., 1993—. Bd. dirs. Cen. Park Video; vice chair Songwriters Hall of Fame; vis. disting. prof. Syracuse U. Sch. Music, 1984. Active Boy Scouts Am., 1947-50; mem. corp. adv. coun. Syracuse U.; mem. coun. Hofstra U.; bd. govs. Anti Defamation League, 1960—; v.p., dir. T.J. Martell Found.; pres. Friars Found.; v.p., bd. dirs. Songwriter's Hall of Fame. Sgt. U.S. Army, 1942-46, PTO. Recipient Presdl. award Nat. Assn. Record Merchandisers, 1976, Disting. Svc. award, 1977, Outstanding Arendts Alumnus award Syracuse U., 1978; named Man of Yr. Time Mag., 1987; named to Video Hall of Fame, 1987. Mem. ASCAP, N.Y. Coun. for Humanities (dir.), Record Industry Assn. Am. (profl. group), B'nai B'rith, Friars Club, Harvard Club, Harvard Bus. Club. Office: Leslie Group Inc Ste 2602 1370 Avenue Of The Americas New York NY 10019-4651

LESLIE, WILLIAM BRUCE, history educator; b. Orange, N.J., July 21, 1944; s. William and Annette (Riedell) L.; stepmother, Dorothy Kaul; children: William Andrew, Sarah Acton. BA, Princeton U., 1966; PhD, Johns Hopkins U., 1971. Asst. prof. history SUNY, Brockport, 1970-79, assoc. prof., 1979-96, prof., 1996—; vis. prof. Jordanhill Coll., Scotland, 1972, dir. grad. studies in history Scotland, 1984-90, 97-99. Co-dir. SUNY Social Sci. Program, London, 1978-79, 82-83, 89; cons. Regents Coll., ETS, AP Exams., Fulbright, Scandinavian Selection. Author: Gentlemen and Scholars, 1993; mem. editl. bd. History of Higher Edn. Ann., 1991—; contbr. articles and revs. to profl jours. Fulbright scholar, Denmark, 1996-97. Mem. Orgn. Am. Historians, Am. Hist. Assn., History of Edn. Soc., Adirondack Mountain Club, Western Monroe Hist. Soc., Princeton Club N.Y. Democrat. Avocations: camping, travel, gardening. Office: SUNY History Dept Brockport NY 14420-2956

LESLY STEVENS, ELIZABETH, journalist; b. Evanston, Ill., Nov. 4, 1966; m. Mitchell J. Stevens, Oct. 9, 1993. BA, U. Calif., 1988; MS, Northwestern U., 1990. Media columnist New York mag., 1997-98; assoc. editor media entertainment Business Week Mag., N.Y.C., 1992-98; exec. editor Brill's Content mag., 1998-99, 1998-2000; sr. editor Talk mag., 2000—02. E-mail: eleslystevens@hotmail.com.

LESMAN, MICHAEL STEVEN, lawyer; b. N.Y.C., May 26, 1953; s. Herman and Estelle (Levy) L.; m. Gail R. Grossman, May 26, 1980; children: Adam, Laura. BA magna cum laude, CUNY, 1975; JD, Bklyn. Law Sch., 1982. Bar: N.Y. 1983. From assoc. to supervising atty. Jacobowitz & Lysaght, N.Y.C., 1983-88; atty. of record, mng. atty. Jacobowitz, Garfinkel & Lesman, 1989—. Staff counsel Am. Internat. Cos., N.Y.C., 1989—. Mem. ABA, N.Y. State Bar Assn., N.Y. County Lawyers Assn., Def. Rsch. Inst., N.Y. State Trial Lawyers Assn. Office: Jacobowitz Garfinkel & Lesman 110 William St Fl 17 New York NY 10038-3914 E-mail: michael.lesman@aig.com.

LESNER, SHARON A. audiologist, educator; b. Lorain, Ohio, Apr. 1, 1951; d. Donald A. and Sylvia A. Lesner. BA, Hiram Coll., 1975; MA, Kent State U., 1975, Wayne State U., 1976; PhD, Ohio State U., 1979. Cert. clin. competency Am. Speech, Lang. and Hearing Assn., lic. audiologist Ohio. Prof. U. Akron, Ohio, 1979—, fellow Inst. Life Span Learning and Gerontology, 1985—. Co-author: Hearing Care for Older Adults, 1995. Bd. dirs. Quota Club, Akron, 1983—89. Recipient Ace award, Am. Speech and Hearing Assn., 1989, 1993, 1995, Golden Apple award, 1995. Fellow: Am. Acad. Audiology; mem.: Ohio Acad. Audiology (pres. 1996), Acad. Rehabilitative Audiology (pres. 1973). Office: Sch Speech Pathology and Audiology Univ Akron Akron OH 44325-3001

LESNICK, JOHN RICHARD, lawyer, consultant, retired lawyer; b. Homestead, Pa., June 11, 1917; s. Michael Joseph Lesick and Mary Teresa Gavalek; m. Mary Eleanor Gillespie, May 29, 1942; children: John Richard II, Lawrence Thomas. BA, Ohio Wesleyan U., 1941; grad., U.S. Naval Sch., Port Hueneme, Calif., 1946; LLB, U. Cin., 1948. Bar: Ohio 1949. Lawyer, Cin., 1949—; ins. salesman W.E. Lord Co., 1952—56; assoc. C.L. Scroggins Assocs., 1957—62; pres. Profl. Mgmt. Assn. Inc., 1963—90; ret. Contbr. articles to profl. jours. Co-founder Village of Forest Park; vol., chmn. bd. Forest Park Hist. Soc.; mem. Forest Park Hall of Fame Commn.; pres. pro-tem City of Forest Park, Ohio, coun. mem. Maj. USMC, 1941—46, PTO. Republican. Avocations: writing, sports, public speaking. Home: 509 Curly Maple Sq Cincinnati OH 45246-4170

LESNIEWSKI-LAAS, MAREK, lawyer; b. Warsaw, Poland, July 2, 1950; came to U.S., 1965; s. Jerzy and Maria Jadwiga (Czerski) Lesniewski; m. Elizabeth Trechsel, July 3, 1979; children: Christopher, Alicia, Nicholas, Alexandra. AB, Bowdoin Coll., Brunswick, Maine, 1973; JD, Boston U., 1976. Self employed lawyer, prin., Boston, 1977; asst. atty. gen. Office of Atty. Gen. Mass., 1985-91; dep. commr., gen. counsel Commonwealth of Mass. Dept. Med. Security, 1991-96; v.p. legal affairs The Stanton Group, 1996—2000; pvt. practice, 2000—. Lectr. legal continuing edn. seminars and health care confs., Boston, 1987-92. Hon. consul Republic of Poland, 1994—. Mem. Consular Corps Boston, Union Club Boston, Ancient and Hon. Artilery Co. Mass., Am. Assn. Polish-Jewish Studies (dir.), Polish Am. Congress. Avocations: sailing, photography, travel, shooting sports. E-mail: marek@shore.net.

LESONSKY, RIEVA, editor; b. N.Y.C., June 20, 1952; d. Gerald and Muriel (Cash) L. BJ, U. Mo., 1974. Rschr. Doubleday & Co., N.Y.C., 1975-78, Entrepreneur Mag., L.A., 1978-80, rsch. dir., 1983-84, mng. editor, 1985-86, exec. editor, 1986-87, editor Irvine, Calif., 1987-90; sr. v.p., editor dir. Entrepreneur Media, Inc., 1990—; rsch. dir. LFP Inc., L.A., 1980-82; editor in chief Entrepreneur mag., Irvine, CA. Spkr., lect. in field. Author: Start Your Own Business, 1998, 2d edit., 2001, Young Millionaires, 1998, Get Smart!, 1999, 303 Marketing Tips, 1999; editor: Complete Guide to Owning a Home-based Business, 1990, 168 More Businesses Anyone Can Start, 1991, 111 Businesses You Can Start for Under $10,000, 1991; contbr. articles to mags. Bd. disting. counselors Johnson & Wales U.; mem. nat. adv. coun. SBA, 1994—96, 1996—2000; bd. dirs. Students in Free Enterprise, Johnson & Wales U. Named Dist. Media Advocate of Yr., Small Bus. Adminstrn., 1993, Dist. Women in Bus. Advocate, Small Bus. Adminstrn., 1995. Mem. Women's Network for Entrepreneurial Tng. (bd. dirs., advisor, nat. steering com.). Avocations: books, magazines, baseball. Office: Entrepreneur Media Inc 2445 Mccabe Way Irvine CA 92614-6244 E-mail: rieva@entrepreneur.com.

LESOURD, NANCY SUSAN OLIVER, lawyer, writer; b. Atlanta, Aug. 22, 1953; d. Carl Samuel and Jane (Meadows) Oliver; m. Jeffrey Alan LeSourd, Oct. 18, 1986; children: Jeffrey Luke, Catherine Victoria. BA in Polit. Sci., Agnes Scott Coll., 1975; MA in History, Edn., Tufts U., 1977; JD, Georgetown U., 1984. Bar: Pa. 1985, D.C. 1986, Va. 1992, Fed. Cir. Ct. Appeals., 1988, U.S. Claims Ct., 1988, U.S. Supreme Ct. Instr. Newton (Mass.) High Sch., 1976-78, The Stony Brook (N.Y.) Sch., 1978-81; assoc. Gammon and Grange, Washington, 1984-88; shareholder Gammon and Grange, P.C., 1988—; mgr. Marshall-LeSourd L.L.C., 1996—. Legal commentator (radio shows) UPI News, Washington, 1985-91, Focus on the Family (Washington corr.), Colorado Springs, Colo., 1987-94; legal columnist Christian Mgmt. Rev., Downers Grove, Ill., 1987-90; spkr. numerous confs. Author: No Longer The Hero, 1992; editor: Georgetown Law Jour., 1982-84; contbr. articles to profl. jours.; cons./prodr. three tv movies based on "Christy", 2000—. Founder, vice-chmn. bd. trustees Ambleside Sch., 1998—2001; Bd. dirs. Arlington County Equal Employment Opportunity Commn., 1985. William Robertson Coe fellow SUNY, Stony Brook, 1978. Mem. D.C. Bar Assn., Va. Bar Assn., Christian Legal Society (bd. dirs. 1990-93). Republican. Home: 2624 New Banner Ln Herndon VA 20171-2659 Office: Gammon and Grange PC 8280 Greensboro Dr Fl 7 Mc Lean VA 22102-3807 E-mail: nol@gandglaw.com.

LESS, ANTHONY ALBERT, retired naval officer; b. Salem, Ohio, Aug. 31, 1937; s. Joseph Anthony and Mildred Gertrude (Bair) L.; m. Leanne Carol Kuhl, Mar. 3, 1962; children: Robyn, Pamela, Theresa, Christina. BS in Chemistry, Heidelberg Coll., 1959. Designated naval aviator. Commd. ensign USN, 1960, advanced through grades to vice adm., 1991, ret., 1994; comdg. officer USS Wichita (AOR-1), 1979-81, USS Ranger (CV-61), 1982-83; chief of staff Comdr. 7th Fleet, Yokosuka, Japan, 1983-84; dir. Polit. Mil Br. JCS, Washington, 1985-87; comdr. Carrier Group One, Pacific, 1987-88, Mid. East Force, Manama, Bahrain, 1988-89; dir. Plans and Policy Navy Staff, Washington, 1989-91; comdr. Naval Air Force Atlantic Fleet, Norfolk, Va., 1991-94; pres. Assn. Naval Aviation, Washington, 1995. Cons. Kaman Aerospace, Bloomfield, Conn., 1994—; v.p. govt. programs Kaman Aerospace, Arlington, Va. Mem. Assn. Naval Aviation (pres. 1994), Soc. Naval Engrs. Roman Catholic. Avocations: racquetball, farming, reading. Office: Kaman Aerospace Ste 810 1421 Jefferson Davis Hwy Arlington VA 22202

LESSARD, ARNOLD FRED, international business executive; b. Newburyport, Mass., Oct. 9, 1923; s. Fred Soloman and Azilda Mary (Goodreau) L.; m. Francine Colette Treutenaere, June 30, 1975; 1 son, Arnaud Alfred. Diploma in acctg., Burdett Coll., 1943; BS with honors, Boston U., 1949; MA with honors, Columbia U., 1951; postgrad., Georgetown U., 1953-56, George Washington U., 1953-56. Head pers. devel. divsn. Nat. Security Agy., 1951-56; cons. Booz, Allen & Hamilton, Inc., N.Y.C., 1956-59, assoc., 1959-61, v.p., 1961-69, regional v.p., 1969-71; chmn. bd. Resources Engring. & Mgmt. Internat., London and Denver, 1971-78; v.p., dir. Chase World Info. Corp., Chase Trade Banking Group (Chase Manhattan Bank), N.Y.C., 1978—79; with Sears Roebuck & Co., 1983—; founder Lessard Assocs. Dir. for Europe, Middle East and Africa, Sears World Trade, Washington, 1983-84, sr. v.p. Internat. Planning and Analysis Ctr., 1984-85; founder Lessert Assocs., 1983-; founding chmn. Internat. Coal Exploration Symposium, London, 1975; pvt. sector and banking advisor West and Ctrl. Africa, U.S. Agy. for Internat. Devel., Abidjan, Ivory Coast and Paris, 1985-89; nat. banking and pvt. sector advisor U.S. Agy. for Internat. Devel., Kinshasa, Zaire, 1989-92; dep. exec. dir. Uganda Investment Authority, Kampala, Uganda, 1992-95; sr. internat. project cons. UN Devel. Program, U.S. Agy. Internat. Devel., UN Com. Trade and Industry, The World Bank, 1995—. Served with USAAF, 1943-46; served to capt. USAF, 1951-53. Mem. World Assn. Investment Promotion Agys., Inst. Mgmt. Consultants (founding mem., cert. mgmt. cons., regional v.p. Europe 1971-78), Soc. for Pers. Adminstrn., Acad. Mgmt., Export Fin. Group, U.S. C. of C., Phi Delta Kappa, Pi Gamma Mu, Kappa Delta Pi, Reform Club (London). Office: 14 Unicorn St Newburyport MA 01950-2622 E-mail: arnles@aol.com.

LESSARD, MICHEL M. finance company executive; b. Quebec City, Can., Aug. 31, 1939; s. Maurice and Jacqueline (Lacasse) L.; children: Eric, Christine. BA, Laval U., Quebec, 1958, B in Commerce, 1961, M in Commerce, 1962; MBA, Harvard U., 1967. With Can. Ingersoll Rand, Allied Chem. Can., DomGlass Ltd., Montreal, Que., Can.; with Credit Foncier, 1970-86, asst. gen. mgr., treas., 1978-79, sr. asst. gen. mgr., 1979-80, exec. v.p., 1980-81, pres., dir., mem. exec. com., 1981-86, pres., chief exec. officer, 1984-86; pres. Sogexfi Inc., 1986—; pres. and CEO Immobiliere Natgen Inc., 1993-95; gen. mgr. Hippodrome De Montreal Inc., 1997-99; pres. Domaine de L'isle aus oyes Inc., 2000—. Bd. dirs. Kree Tech., Inc., Montreal, Fonds de Solidarite, FTQ Groupe Redressement. Fellow Trust Cos. Inst., Winchester Club, Club de Golf de la Vallee du Richelieu. Home: 11 O'Reilly Apt 1503 Verdun QC Canada H3E 1T6

LESSENCO, GILBERT BARRY, lawyer; b. Balt., June 19, 1929; s. Jacob David and Sarah (Bank) L.; m. Elaine Beitler, Sept. 3, 1952; children: Susan Donna, Amy Gail, Robert Howard. BS, Johns Hopkins U.; LLB, Harvard U. Bar: D.C. 1953, Md. 1955. Atty. Wilner and Bergson, Washington, 1955-60; ptnr. Wilner & Scheiner, 1960-90, Semmes, Bowen & Semmes, Washington, 1990-95, mng. ptnr., 1992-95; of counsel Thompson & Hine , 1995—. Prof. bus. law and mktg. law Johns Hopkins U. Sch. Profl. Studies in Bus. and Edn., 1997—. Chmn. Internat. Visitors Svc. Coun., 1962; bd. dirs. Mental Health Assn. Montgomery County, 1996, pres., 1981—82; mem. Johns Hopkins U. Com. for Washington, 1996; trustee Meridian Ho. Found.; commr. Washington Suburban San. Commn., 1987—93, chmn., 1989—90; co-chmn., fundraiser St. Luke's Ho., 1989; mem., treas. Dem. Ctrl. Com., Montgomery County, Md., 1970—74; bd. dirs. Jewish Social Svc. Agy. Greater Washington, 1978—, pres., 1984—86. Lt. USAF, 1953—55. Named Outstanding Young Lawyer of Yr., D.C. Jr. Bar, 1965. Mem. Phi Sigma Delta (v.p.). Home: 10731 Gloxinia Dr Rockville MD 20852-3442 Office: 1920 N St NW Washington DC 20036-1601 E-mail: gil.lessenco@thompsonhine.com.

LESSER, CAROLYN S. educator, writer, consultant; b. Oshkosh, Wis., Mar. 21, 1939; d. Karl Arthur and Anita Mildred Schmidt; m. Peter William Lesser (div.); children: Anne Adams Marshall, Christopher Chase Marshall, Michael Edison, Peter William. BS Elem. Edn., The U. of Wisconsin-Oshkosh. State of Missouri Public School Life Certificate, Grades 3-7. Author: (children's books and articles) various. Recipient First Pl. in ceramic sculpture, North County Artist's Guild, 1969, Award for lit. merit, The Friends Of Am. Writers, 1984. Home: 8 Brown Court Falmouth MA 02540 Home Fax: 508-540-6819. Personal E-mail: clesser@aol.com.

LESSER, DEBORAH LYNN, broadcasting educator; b. Chgo., Nov. 18, 1961; d. Ronald S. and Sara L. (Fatka) Rozak; m. Ron Lesser, Sept. 2, 1990; children: Charles, Margaret. BS, Ill. State U., 1983, MS, 1984. Mgr. Cox Cable, Maywood, Ill., 1984; dir. radio Ill. State U., Normal, 1985—. Bd. dirs. Ill. State U. Child Care Ctr., Normal; host Midwest Regional Conf. Nat. Assn. Coll. Broadcasters, Bloomington, Ill., 1996; voice and talent Insight Comm., AT&T, TCI and Telecable, Bloomington, 1989—; program host Cityvision Page One, Page One Extra; mem. faculty adv. com. Mus. Broadcasting, Chgo., 1992—. Host Child Care Forum, Bloomington, 1993; co-host Ill. Spl. Olympics, Bloomington, 1994-96, Walk for Child, Bloomington, 1995-97, Christmas Parade, 1998-99. Mem. Assn. for Women in Comm., Coll. Media Advisors. Roman Catholic. Office: Ill State U Sta WZND PO Box 4481 Normal IL 61790-0001

LESSER, EVE GERTRUDE, investment banker; b. July 14, 1955; AB, Princeton U., 1977; MBA, Harvard U., 1980. V.p. Lehman Bros. Kuhn Loeb, N.Y.C., 1980-85, Goldman Sachs, N.Y.C., 1985—2001.

LESSER, FELICE A. choreographer, dancer, playwright, screenwriter, filmmaker; b. Norwalk, Conn., May 28; d. Laurence Martin and Ethel Lesser; m. Joel Richard Blatt. BA in Music , MA in Dance, Dance Edn., Columbia U. Artistic dir., choreographer, dancer Dance 2000: The Felice Lesser Dance Theater Found., Inc., N.Y.C., 1975—. Adj. instr. U. Conn., Stamford, 1981—; artist-in-residence Nev. State Coun. of the Arts, 1983—, Idaho Commn. for the Arts, 1987—, Mont. State Coun. for the Arts, 1988-89, 91—. Choreographer over 40 dance works; plays and screenplays: Running Backwards on the Treadmill, Infernal Love, Funding The Arts; filmmaker: Grand Central, Dancing on the Keyboard, New York, N.Y. Recipient Lawrence S. Epstein prize for choreography, 1988. Mem. Am. Guild Variety Artists.

LESSER, IAN O. foreign affairs expert; b. Oct. 22, 1957; Ba in Internat. Politics, U. Pa., 1979; MSc in Internat. Rels., The London Sch. Econs., 1980; MA in Law, Diplomacy, Tufts U., 1982; PhD in Internat. Politics, Oxford U., 1988. Sr. fellow The Atlantic Coun. of U.S., Washington, 1980-81; staff cons. Internat. Energy Assocs. Ltd., 1982-83; sr. fellow Ctr. Strategic and Internat. Studies, 1985-88; sr. analyst Nat. Security Rsch. Divsn. RAND, Santa Monica, Calif., 1989-94; assoc. dir. strategy and doctrine program Project Air Force RAND, 1996-98; sr. internat. policy analyst RAND, Washington, 1996—; mem. policy planning staff U.S. Dept. State, 1994-95. Author: Mediterranean Security, 1992, Security in North Africa: Internal and External Challenges, 1993, Turkey's New Geopolitics, 1993, A Sense of Siege: The Geopolitics of

Islam and the West, 1994, Strategic Exposure: Proliferation Around the Mediterranean, 1996, Sources of Conflict in the 21st Century, 1998. Mem. Coun. Foreign Rels., Pacific Coun. Internat. Policy, Internat. Inst. Strategic Studies, Atlantic Coun. (councillor). Office: Rand Corp 1200 S Hayes St Arlington VA 22202

LESSER, JOAN L. lawyer; b. L.A. BA, Brandeis U., 1969; JD, U. So. Calif., 1973. Bar: Calif. 1973, U.S. Dist. Ct. (cen. dist.) Calif. 1974. Assoc. Irell and Manella LLP, L.A., 1973-80, ptnr., 1980—. Mem. planning com. Ann. Real Property Inst., Continuing Edn. of Bar, Berkeley, 1990-96; speaker at profl. confs. Trustee Windward Sch.; grad. Leadership L.A., 1992; bd. dirs. L.A. chpt. Legion Lex. Mem. Orgn. Women Execs. (past pres., bd. dirs.), Order of Coif. Office: Irell & Manella LLP 1800 Avenue Of The Stars Los Angeles CA 90067-4276 E-mail: jlesser@irell.com.

LESSER, LAURENCE, musician, educator; b. Los Angeles, Oct. 28, 1938; s. Moses Aaron and Rosalyne Anne (Asner) L.; m. Masuko Ushioda, Dec. 23, 1971; children— Erika, Adam AB, Harvard U., 1961; student of Gaspar Cassadó, Germany, 1961-62; student of Gregor Piatigorsky, 1963-66. Mem. faculty U. So. Calif., Los Angeles, 1963-70, Peabody Inst., Balt., 1970-74, New Eng. Conservatory Music, Boston, 1974—, pres., 1983-96, pres. emeritus, 1997—. Former vis. prof. Eastman Sch. Music, Rochester, N.Y.; vis. prof. Toho Gakuen Sch. Music, Tokyo, 1973-95; performed with New Japan Philharm., Boston Symphony, London Philharm., L.A. Philharm. and Marlboro, Spoleto, Casals, Santa Fe and Banff festivals; rec. artist; overseer emeritus Boston Symphony Orch. Trustee emeritus WGBH Ednl. Found.; mem. adv. coun. Chamber Music Am. Recipient prize Tchaikovsky Competition, Moscow, 1966; Fulbright scholar, 1961-62; Ford Found. grantee, 1972. Mem. Am. Acad. Arts and Scis., Harvard Mus. Assn., Phi Beta Kappa, Pi Kappa Lambda, Sigma Alpha Iota. Jewish. Home: 65 Bellevue St Newton MA 02458-1918 Office: New Eng Conservatory Music 290 Huntington Ave Boston MA 02115-5018 E-mail: llesser@rcn.com.

LESSER, LORYN SARI, director; d. Bertram Britwar and Roslyn Vivian (Ment) L.; m. Wallace Kleid, July 1, 1979; children: Micah Saul, Matthew Brett. BA with honors, Richmond Coll. CUNY, 1971; MA with honors, Montclair State Coll., 1973; Montessori tng. cert., Fairleigh Dickinson U., 1975; MS in Instrnl. Tech., Towson U., 1997, PhD, 1984. Cert. clin. mental health counselor, Nat. Bd. Cert. Counselors; lic. clin. profl. counselor, Md.l cert. sch. counselor, Md.; cert. sch. libr. media specialist, Md.; lic. tchr., N.Y. Founder, dir. Mountaineer Montessori Sch., Charleston, W.Va., 1975-76; founding dir. counseling Women's Health Ctr., 1976-77; family planning clinic asst., counselor dept. ob-gyn. George Washington U., 1978-79; counselor Suburban Mental Health Assn., Balt., 1979-81; mem. faculty psychology Catonsville Coll., 1979-91; psychologist Rosewood Ctr., 1989-90; founder, counselor Womancare, Balt., 1982—; mem. faculty Beth Tfiloh Cmty. Sch., 1997—2001, dir. psycho-ednl. testing svc., 2002—. Supr. Jewish Vocat. Svc., 1990-93; program dir. dept. edn. Dundalk C.C., 1982-83; mem. exec. planning com. Md. Conf. on Families, 1979-80; mem. adj. faculty Towson U., 1996—. Bd. dirs. Coalition for Optional Parenthood Edn., Washington, 1978-79; exec. dir. Balt. City Commn. Women, 1984-86. Mem. ACA, Nat. Acad. Cert. Clin. Mental Health Counselors (bd. dirs. 19-85), Am. Mental Health Counselors Assn. (bd. dirs. 1978-79), Am. Assn. State Counseling Bds. (exec. dir. 1995—), Md. Assn. Counseling and Devel., Md. Mental Health Counselors (mem. exec. bd., pres. 1985-86), Md. Examiners Profl. Counselors (chairperson 1986-94), State of Md. Israel Bonds (chair women's divsn.).

LESSER, MARGO ROGERS, legal consultant; b. Oklahoma City, Aug. 30, 1950; d. William Wright and Velma June (Clark) Rogers; m. George Robert Lesser, Apr. 25, 1982; children: Scott Robert, Kira Michelle. AB, Cornell U., 1972; JD, Georgetown U., 1975. Bar: D.C. 1975, Mich. 1990, U.S. Ct. Claims 1976, U.S. Tax Ct. 1979, U.S. Ct. Appeals (fed. cir.) 1982, U.S. Supreme Ct. 1979. Law clk. to Hon. judge Oscar Davis U.S. Appellate Ct. Claims, Washington, 1975-76; assoc. Covington & Burling, 1976-81; asst. prof. Wayne State U. Law Sch., Detroit, 1981-88; legal cons. Birmingham, Mich., 1988—. Exec. dir. Ind. Dir. Found., Detroit, 1990-2000. Co-author: Michigan Corporation Law and Practice, 1990, supplements through, 2002; assoc. editor: Internat. Soc. Barristers Quar., 1988—; contbr. Mem. ABA, Mich. Bar (co-reporter Bus. Corp. Act subcom., law sect. 1986-97, reporter ad hoc limited liability co. rev. com. 1991—). Avocations: family, tennis, sailing. Home and Office: 1044 N Glenhurst Dr Birmingham MI 48009-1111 E-mail: MRLesser@aol.com.

LESSER, MARTIN L. statistician; b. Far Rockaway, Ny, Feb. 2, 1953; s. Marc Lesser and Selma Weil; m. Jane Emily King, July 4, 1974; children: Lenard, Lori. BA, Cornell U., Ithaca, NY, 1970—74; MS, Rutgers U., New Brunswick, 1974—76, PhD, 1976—78. Emt-Cc NY State Dept. Health / EMS. Rsch. assoc. Meml. Sloan-Kettering, New York, NY, 1978—82; dir. Biostatistics Dept., Montefiore Med. Ctr., Bronx, 1982—85; asst. prof. Albert Einstein Coll. Medicine, 1982—85; dir. Biostatistics Unit, North Shore LIJ Rsch. Inst., Manhasset, 1985—; assoc. prof. (adj.) Cornell U. Med. Coll., New York, 1985—; assoc. prof. NYU Sch. Medicine, 1997—. Chmn. irb North Shore U., Manhasset, NY, 2000—; pres. Assn. GCRC Statisticians, 1994—95. Vol. emt East Rockaway, Fire Department Rescue, NY; v.p. Hewlett E. Rockaway Jewish Ctr., East Rockaway, 1994—2002. Recipient Chief's Award, East Rockaway Fire Dept., 2000. Mem.: Soc. for Clin. Trials, Internat. Biometrics Soc., Am. Statis. Assn. Home: 1A Howland Rd East Rockaway NY 11518 Office: North Shore LIJ Research Inst Biostat 1129 Northern Blvd #302 Manhasset NY 11030

LESSER, STEVEN JOHN, organizational development consultant; b. Sydney, NSW, Australia, May 20, 1950; s. Hans Georg and Louise (Kranz) L.; m. Hilary Josie Edge, Sept. 27, 1977 (div.); children: Stefanie Jane, Michael William. B Bus., Charles Sturt U., Bathurst, NSW, Australia, 1981; M Applied Fin., Macquarie U., Sydney, 1985. Sr. mgr. Commonwealth Bank, Sydney, 1968-84; dep. state mgr. Challenge Bank Ltd., 1985; gen. mgr. corp. banking Nippon Credit Bank, 1986-88; sr. dir. comml., lending and credit quality Omega Performance Corp., 1989-95; CEO Infoworks Internat., Killara, Australia, 1996—. Vis. lectr. U. Tech., Sydney, Macquarie U., Charles Stuart U., Bathurst; dir. 3 cos.; guest lectr.fin. svcs. confs. in Australia and S.E. Asia. Dist. gov. Rotaract, Sydney, 1970. Fellow Australian Inst. Bankers, Australian Inst. Co. Dirs., Instrnl. Sys. Assn. (bd. dirs.); mem. Australian Credit Mgmt. Assn. (assoc.), New Zealand Bankers Inst., Australian Inst. Tng. and Devel. (assoc.). Office: Infoworks Internat 22 Churchill Rd Killara 2071 Australia

LESSER, WENDY, literary magazine editor, writer, consultant; b. Santa Monica, Calif., Mar. 20, 1952; d. Murray Leon Lesser and Millicent (Gerson) Dillon; m. Richard Rizzo, Jan. 18, 1985; 1 stepchild, Dov Antonio; 1 child, Nicholas. BA, Harvard U., 1973; MA, Cambridge (Eng.) U., 1975; PhD, U. Calif., Berkeley, 1982. Founding ptnr. Lesser & Ogden Assocs., Berkeley, 1977-81; founding editor The Threepenny Rev., 1980—. Bellagio resident Rockefeller Found, Italy, 1984. Author: The Life Below the Ground, 1987, His Other Half, 1991, Pictures at an Execution, 1994, A Director Calls, 1997, The Amateur, 1999, Nothing Remains the Same, 2002; editor: Hiding in Plain Sight, 1993. Fellow NEH, 1983, 92, Guggenheim fellow, 1988, ACLS, 1996, Open Soc. Inst. fellow, 1998, Columbia U. Nat. Arts Journalism Program sr. fellow, 2000-01. Democrat. Office: The Threepenny Rev PO Box 9131 Berkeley CA 94709-0131

LESSER, WILLIAM HENRI, marketing educator; b. N.Y.C., Dec. 19, 1946; s. Arthur and Ethel (Boissevain) L.; m. Susan Elizabeth Bailey, Dec. 27, 1975; children: Andrew, Jordan. BA in Geography, U. Wash., 1968; MS in Resource Econs., U. R.I., 1974; PhD in Agrl. Econ., U. Wis., 1978. , 1993-94; from asst. to assoc. prof. mktg. Cornell U., Ithaca, N.Y., 1978-91, prof., 1991—, dir. undergrad. program NY, 1998—99. With Internat. Acad. Environ., Geneva, 1993-94, FAO vis. scientist, 2002; grad. field rep. Dept. Agrl. Econs., Ithaca, 1985-88; dir. Cornell Western Socs. Program, 1991-93; cons. World Bank, Washington, US/AID, Winrock Internat., Morrilton, Ark. Editor: Animal Patents: The Legal Economic and Social Issues, 1990; author: Equitable Patent Protection in the Developing World, 1991, Marketing Livestock and Meat, 1993, Sustainable Use of Genetic Resources under the Convention on Biological Diversity, 1998. Zone capt. Dem. com. Town of Ithaca, 1985-90, mem. planning bd., 1987-93, councilman, 1999—. Nat. fellow Kellogg Found., 1988-91. Mem. Am. Agrl. Econ. Assn., Patent & Trademark Office Soc. Avocations: gardening, painting, antique cars. Home: 406 Coddington Rd Ithaca NY 14850-6012 Office: Cornell U Dept Argl Econs 405 Warren Hall Ithaca NY 14853-7801 E-mail: whl1@cornell.edu.

LESSEY, SAMUEL KENRIC, JR. foundation administrator; b. Newark, Oct. 9, 1923; s. Samuel Kenric and Ruth (Turner) Lessey. BS, U.S. Mil. Acad., 1945; student, Vanderbilt U., 1945; LLB, Harvard U., 1951; postgrad., Washington U. Law Sch., 1951-52, U. Md., 1951-53; MBA, Harvard U., 1956; postgrad., Air War Coll., 1974-75. Bar: N.Y., U.S. Dist. Ct. D.C., U.S. Ct. Claims, U.S. Tax Ct., U.S. Ct. Mil. Appeals, U.S. Ct. Appeals (D.C. cir.), U.S. Supreme Ct. Commd. USAF, 1945, advanced through grades to brig. gen., active duty, 1942-54, 76-78; with USAFR, 1954-83; v.p., bd. dirs. Nat. Aviation Corp. Investment Trust, 1957-68; v.p. Shearson Hammill and Co., Inc., 1968-74; moblzn. asst. to dir. Fed. Emergency Mgmt. Agy., 1979-82; insp. gen. U.S. Synthetic Fuels Corp., 1982-86; dir. Selective Svc. System, 1987-91. Civilian aide to Sec. of Army, 1992. Bd. dirs. Nat. Stroke Assn., 1991—, chmn. bd., 1994—2000, chmn. emeritus, 2001—. Decorated Legion of Merit with Oak Leaf Cluster, Army Outstanding Civil Svc. award, Selective Svc. Disting. Svc. medal, WWII Victory medal, Occupation medal, Nat. Def. Svc. medal, Am. Campaign medal, UN Svc. medal, Air Force Outstanding Unit award; Korean Svc. medal. Mem. AIAA, IEEE, Aerospace Analysts Soc. (past pres.), Am. Fighter Pilots Assn., Air Force Assn. (past v.p. Iron Gate chpt.), Am. Astronautical Soc., Am. Def. Preparedness Assn., Am. Helicopter Soc., Assn. U.S. Army (N.H. pres.) , Aviation Space Writers Assn., Elec. and Electronic Analysts Group, Fin. Analysts Fedn., N.Y. Soc. Security Analysts, Mil. Order of World Wars, Res. Officers Assn., Am. Assoc. Royal Acad. Arts, Def. Orientation Conf. Assn. (dir.), Wings Club (past bd. dirs.), Ctr. for Mil. Readiness (adv. bd.), Nat. Aviation Club, N.Y. Athletic Club, Lincoln's Inn Soc., Harvard Club (N.Y.C.), Capitol Hill Club, Army & Navy Club. Avocations: skiing, tennis, swimming, traditional jazz, antiques. Home: Brimstone Corner PO Box 57 Hancock NH 03449-0057 Office: Nat Stroke Assn 9707 E Easter Ln Englewood CO 80112-3754

LESSICK, MIRA LEE, nursing educator; b. Hazleton, Pa., Jan. 25, 1949; d. Jack H. and Shirley E. (Frumkin) Lessick. Diploma in nursing, Albany (N.Y.) Med. Ctr., 1969; BSN, Boston U., 1972; MS, U. Colo., 1973; PhD, U. Tex., 1986. Staff nurse Boston City Hosp. and Mass. Gen. Hosp., 1969-72; instr. to asst. prof. nursing, genetics clinician U. Rochester, N.Y., 1973-79; asst. prof. nursing, practitioner Rush U. Coll. Nursing, Chgo., 1986-91, assoc. prof. nursing, 1992—2001, project dir. genetic health nursing program, 1993—2001; assoc. prof. U. Toledo, 2001—. Mem. human genome rsch. initial rev. group, ethical, legal, and social implications subcom. Nat. Human Genome Rsch. Inst., NIH, 1996-99; peer reviewer Bur. Health Professions, HHS, 2001—. Mem. editl. adv. bd. AWHONN Lifelines, 1999—; genetics column editor Medsurg Nursing: The Jour. of Adult Health; contbr. articles to profl. jours. Recipient Bd. of Govs. award, Excellence in Pediatric Nursing award Albany Med. Ctr., 1969, Outstanding Nurse Recognition award March of Dimes Birth Defects Found., 1991, Recognition award for Individual Contbn. to Maternal-Child Health Nat. Perinatal Assn., 1993, Founders Award in Edn., Internat. Soc. Nurses in Genetics, 1997. Mem. AAAS, ANA, APHA, Internat. Soc. Nurses in Genetics (chair rsch. com. 1993—, Founders award in Edn. 1997), Assn. Women's Health, Obstetric, and Neonatal Nurses, Am. Soc. Human Genetics, Chgo. Nurses Assn. (legis. com. 1990-91), N.Y. Acad. Scis., Midwest Nursing Rsch. Soc., Sigma Theta Tau (Luther Christman award for excellence in published writing 1993, Luther Christmas award Excellence Pub. Writing, 1998), Phi Kappa Phi. Achievements include development of a genetic health area of concentration within a graduate level nursing program. Office: U Toledo Coll Health and Human Svcs Scott Park Campus Toledo OH 43606-3390 E-mail: mlessic@utnet.utoledo.edu.

LESSIN, LAWRENCE STEPHEN, hematologist, oncologist, educator; b. Washington, Oct. 14, 1937; s. Maurice and Anna (Brodsky) L.; m. Judith Ann Lustok, Dec. 23, 1961; children: Jennifer Lynn, Jonathan Lustok, Martine Rose. Student, U. Mich., 1955-58; MD, U. Chgo., 1962. Diplomate Am. Bd. Internal Medicine (assoc. mem. 1976-82). Intern, resident in internal medicine, chief resident, fellow in hematology Hosp. U. Pa., 1962-67; spl. fellow Nat. Heart Inst., Inst. for Cell Pathology, Paris, 1967-68; assoc. prof. medicine Duke U., 1968-70; assoc. prof. medicine and pathology George Washington U., 1970-74, prof. medicine and pathology, dir. div. hematology and oncology, 1974—; dir. George Washington U. Cancer Ctr., Washington, 1991-93; med. dir. Washington Cancer Inst. Washington Hosp. Ctr., 1993—. Vis. physician medicine br. Nat. Cancer Inst., 1971-74; cons. hematology Washington VA Hosp., 1971—; cons. ARC Blood Bank, 1972—, Nat. Naval Med. Ctr., Bethesda, Md., 1974—, Nat. Heart, Lung and Blood Inst., 1974; Walter Reed Army Med. Ctr., 1978—; ad hoc cons. Nat. Heart, Lung and Blood Inst., Study Sect. Program-Project Grants, 1977; mem. NASA Biomed. Rev. Panel, 1981-88; chmn. div. blood diseases and resources adv. com. Nat. Heart, Blood and Lung Inst., NIH, 1985-86, mem. inst. sci. rev. com., 1997-99; mem. data safety monotoring bd. NHLBI, NIH, 2000—; chmn., program dir. Assn. Hematology-Oncology, 1983-87; vol. spl. emphasis panel Comprehensive Sickle Cell SCOR Applications, 1997-99; mem. FDA panel on spongiform encephalopaties, cons. panel on oncology drugs, ODAC. Editorial reviewer: Annals of Internal Medicine, 1969— , Nouvelle Revue de Hematologie, 1970— , Blood, Jour. Hematology, 1971— , Archives of Internal Medicine, 1972— , Nature, 1973, Jour. Clin. Investigation, 1973— , New Eng. Jour. Medicine; mem. editorial Blood Cells, 1979—, Hematologic Pathology, 1985—; contbr. articles to profl. jours., chpts. to books. Served to capt. M.C. USAR, 1963-69. Named Intern of Year U. Pa. Hosp., 1963; nominee for Golden Apple award, 1975; Nat. Heart Inst. spl. fellow Paris, 1967-68 Master ACP (chair Hematology Med. Knowledge Self-Assessment program 1992—); fellow Internat. Soc. Hematology; mem. Am. Soc. Hematology, Am. Fedn. Clin. Research, Am. Soc. Clin. Oncology, Am. Blood Commn., Am. Soc. Internal Medicine, D.C. Med. Soc., Internat. Blood Cells Club, Am. Soc. Clin. Oncology, Sigma Xi, Alpha Omega Alpha. Clubs: Cosmos (Washington). Office: Washington Cancer Inst 110 Irving St NW Washington DC 20010-2976

LESSIN, MICHAEL EDWARD, oral-maxillofacial surgeon; b. Chgo., Jan. 24, 1944; m. Cathy Irene Wilkinson, June 22, 1968; children: Amy Suzanne, Beth Michele. BDS, U. Ill., 1965; DDS, Ill. Coll. Dentistry, 1969. Diplomate Am. Bd. Oral Maxillofacial Surgery. Commd. 1st lt. U.S. Army, 1969, advanced through grades to col., 1983, ret., 1989; resident in oral and maxillofacial surgery Letterman Army Med. Ctr., San Francisco, 1974-77; clin. assoc. prof. dept. oral and maxillofacial surgery U. Tex., San Antonio, 1985-89; clin. prof. surgery W.Va. U., Morgantown, 1990—; assoc. dept. dental medicine and surgery Geisinger Med. Ctr., Danville, Pa., 1990—, dir. dept. dental medicine and surgery, 1998—; clin. assoc. prof. surgery Med. Coll. Pa., Hahnemann, 1995—. Cons. ROK Ctrl. Army Hosp., Seoul, Korea, 1977-79, U.S. Army Dental Activity Gen. Practice Residency Program, Ft. Sill, Okla., 1985-86, 87, to surgeon gen., 1987-89, William Beaumont Army Med. Ctr., El Paso, Tex., 1990-91, Dwight D. Eisenhower Med. Ctr., Augusta, Ga., 1990, residency program, Ft. Campbell, Ky., 1992-93; lectr. in field; mem. exam. com. Am. Bd. Oral Maxillofacial Surgery, 1992-98. Contbr. articles to profl. jours. Fellow Am. Coll. Oral Maxillofacial Surgeons; mem. ADA (program site evaluation commn. 2000—), Am. Trauma Soc., Pa. Dental Assn., Tri-county Dental Assn., 38th Parallel Dental Soc. Avocations: travel, golf. Office: Geisinger Med Ctr Academy Ave Danville PA 17822-0001 E-mail: mlessin@geisinger.edu.

LESSING, BRIAN REID, actuary; b. Miami, Fla., Feb. 2, 1954; s. Kenneth Oliver Ralph and Margaret (Takash) L. AB magna cum laude, Princeton (N.J.) U., 1976; MS, N.Y.U., 1979. Cert. FSA, Soc. Actuaries, 1989, CLU, Am. Coll., 1992. Tech. asst. Mutual of N.Y., 1980-84; actuarial asst. Equitable Life Assurance, N.Y.C., 1984-87; asst. actuary, 1987-89; assoc. actuary, 1989-91; actuary, 1991-93; asst. v.p., 1993-98; v.p., 1998—. Adj. instr. N.Y. Inst. Tech., 1979, Pace U., N.Y.C., 1979, 80; adj. asst. prof. The Coll. of Ins., N.Y.C., 1989-91. Mem. ch. coun. exec. com. Community Ch. of N.Y., 1984-87, fin. com., 1989-99. Recipient Rsch. assistantship N.Y.U., 1976-80. Fellow Soc. of Actuaries; mem. Soc. Fin. Svc. Profls., Am. Acad. Actuaries, Phi Beta Kappa. Unitarian Universalist. Office: Equitable Life Assurance 14th Flr Location 14 093 1290 Avenue Of The Americas New York NY 10104-0101

LESSING, DORIS (DORIS MAY), writer; b. Kermanshah, Persia, Oct. 22, 1919; d. Alfred Cook Tayler and Emily Maude McVeagh; m. Frank Charles Wisdom, 1939 (div. 1943); m. Gottfried Anton Nicholas Lessing, 1945 (div. 1949); children: John W. (dec.), Jean W., Peter L. Educated in, So. Rhodesia; DLitt (hon.), Princeton U., 1989, Durham U., 1990; D Fellow in Lit., Sch., Eng. Am. Studies, U. East Anglia, 1991; DLitt (hon.), Warwick U., 1994; LittD (hon.), Bard Coll., 1994, Harvard U., 1995, Open Univ., 1999, Univ. London, 1999. Author: (novels) The Grass is Singing, 1950, Five Short Novels, 1953, Retreat to Innocence, 1959, The Golden Notebook, 1962 (Prix Medicis award , 1976), Children of Violence, 5 vols., 1964—69, Briefing For a Descent Into Hell, 1971, The Summer Before the Dark, 1973, The Memoirs of a Survivor, 1975, Shikasta, 1979, Marriages Between Zones Three, Four and Five, 1980, The Sirian Experiments, 1981, The Making of the Representative for Planet 8, 1982, Documents Relating to the Sentimental Agents in the Volyen Empire, 1983, The Good Terrorist, 1985 (W.H. Smith Lit. award, 1986, Palermo prize, 1987, Premio Internazionale Monello, 1987), The Libretto of the Making of the Representative for Planet 8, 1988, The Fifth Child, 1988, Playing the Game, 1995, Love, Again, 1996, Mara and Dann, 1999, Ben, In The World, 2000, The Old Age of El Magnifico, 2001, The Sweetest Dream, 2001, (nonfiction) In Pursuit of the English, 1961, Particularly Cats, 1967, Going Home, 1968, Prisons We Choose to Live Inside, 1987, The Wind Blows Away Our Words...and Other Documents Relating to the Afghan Resistance, 1987, Particularly Cats and More Cats...And Rufus, 1991, African Laughter: Four Visits to Zimbabwe, 1992, Under My Skin: Volume One of My Autobiography, to 1949, 1994, Walking in the Shade: Volume Two of My Autobiography, 1949-62, 1994; author: (under pseudonym Jane Somers) Diary of a Good Neighbour, 1983, and If the Old Could... , 1984; author: (short stories) This Was the Old Chief's Country, 1952, The Habit of Loving, 1957, A Man and Two Women, 1963, African Stories, 1965, The Temptation of Jack Orkney and Other Stories, 1978, The Story of a Non-Marrying Man, 1972, Collected African Stories, 1978, The Sun Between Their Feet, 1981, London Observed: Stories and Sketches (U.K.)/The Real Thing (U.S.), 1992, (collections) To Room 19 , vols. 1 and 2, 1978, The Doris Lessing Reader, 1990, (plays) Each in His Own Wilderness, 1958, Play with a Tiger, 1973, The Singing Door, 1973, (essays) A Small Personal Voice, 1974, (poetry) Fourteen Poems, 1959, (Operas) (music by Philip Glass) The Making of the Representative for Planet 8, 1988; contbr. columns in newspapers. Recipient Somerset Maugham award Soc. of Authors, 1954, Austrian State prize for European Lit., 1981, Shakespeare prize, Hamburg, 1982, Grinzane Cavour award, Italy, 1989, David Cohen prize, 2001; named Woman of Yr. Norway, 1995, awarded Premi Internatl. Catalunya, 1999, Principe de Asturias, Spain, 2001. Fellow MLA (hon.); mem. Nat. Inst. Arts and Letters., Am. Acad. Arts & Letters (assoc. mem. 1974), Inst. Cultural Rsch. (Companion of Honor 2000). Office: care Jonathan Clowes Ltd 10 Iron Bridge House London NW1 8BD England

LESSOFF, ALAN H. history educator; b. Boston, Feb. 24, 1959; s. Stanley Lessoff and Carole Halterman; m. Mineke Reinders, April 25, 1987; 1 child, Audrey. BA, Columbia U., 1981, Cambridge U., England, 1983; MA, Johns Hopkins U., 1985, PhD, 1990. Asst. prof. Dickinson Coll., Carlisle, Pa., 1990-92; asst. to assoc. prof. Tex. A&M U., Corpus Christi, 1992-2000; Fulbright prof. U. Kassel, Kassel, Germany, 1996-97; assoc. prof. history Ill. State U., Normal, 2000—. Author: The Nation and Its City, 1994, Legacy: A History of the Art Museum of South Texas, 1997; mem. editl. bd. Jour. Urban History, 2002--; contbr. articles to profl. jours. Active McLean County Hist. Soc., Bloomington, Ill., 2000—. Recipient Fulbright jr. lectr. 1996-97, Kellett fellow to Clare Coll., Cambridge, Columbia U., 1981-83. Mem. Soc. Historians of the Gilded Age and Progressive Era (newsletter editor 1999—), Urban History Assn. (prize com. chair 1999, program com. 2002), Soc. for Area, City, and Regional Planning History (program com. 1998-2001), Orgn. Am. Historians, Am. Hist. Assn. Democrat. Jewish. Avocations: travel, bicycling. Home: 1415 N Clinton Blvd Bloomington IL 61701 Office: Ill State U Dept History Campus Box 4420 Normal IL 61790-4420 Fax: 309-438-5607. E-mail: ahlesso@ilstu.edu.

LESSTRANG, DAVID MATTHEW, public relations executive; b. Ann Arbor, Mich., Feb. 22, 1963; s. Jacques Earle LesStrang and Jean Audrey Mentzer Paul; m. Elaine Marie Dalpiaz, July 31, 1993; 1 child, Matthew Jacques. BA with honors, Hillsdale (Mich.) Coll., 1985. Editorial asst. Harbor House Pub., Inc., Boyne City, Mich., 1981-85; press sec. U.S. Congressman Jerry Lewis, Washington, 1985-95, dep. chief of staff, 1997—, legis. dir., 1999—2002; govt. affairs mgr. EMC Corp., 2002—. Staff asst. U.S. Congressman Carl D. Pursell, Washington, spring 1984; rsch. asst. Edn. and Rsch. Inst., Washington, summer 1984; lectr. The Am. U.; sr. policy advisor, press sec. subcom. House Va.-HUD Appropriations, 1995—. Capitol Hill host Meridian Internat. Ctr., 1993-96; mem. adv. bd. Meridian Internat. Ctr., Washington, 1993-97; vol. Habitat for Humanity; developer House that Congress Build campaign. Mem. Alliance Francaise. Republican. Avocations: international travel, writing, investments, politics, athletics.

LESTAGE, DANIEL BARFIELD, retired naval officer, physician; b. Jennings, La., July 7, 1939; s. Henry Oscar Jr. and Juliet Xavier (Barfield) L.; m. Helen Newcomer, Mar. 9, 1963; children: Juliet Lestage Hirsch, Diane Lestage Davis, Daniel B. Jr. Grad., La. State U., 1959, MD, 1963; grad., Naval Sch. Aviation, 1964; MPH, Tulane U., 1969; diploma, Indsl. Coll. Armed Forces, 1978. Diplomate Am. Bd. Preventive Medicine, 1971, Am. Bd. Family Practice, 1978. Commd. ensign USN, 1960, advanced through grades to rear adm., 1986; rotating intern Charity Hosp., New Orleans, 1963-64; resident in family practice Lafayette (La.) Charity Hosp., 1964; student flight surgeon Naval Sch. Aviation Medicine, Pensacola, Fla., 1964; staff flight surgeon/med. officer Carrier Air Wing 16 USS Oriskany, NAS Lemoore, Calif., 1965-67; sr. med. officer Naval Med. Clinic, NAS New Orleans, 1967-68, USS John F. Kennedy, Norfolk, Va., 1971-73; resident in aerospace medicine Naval Aerospace Med. Inst., Pensacola, 1969-71; sr. med. officer Br. Clinic, Jacksonville NAS, 1973-77; chief preventive medicine dept. Naval Regional Med. Ctrs., Jacksonville, 1973-77; spl. asst. to surgeon gen. Navy Bur. Medicine and Surgery Dept. Navy, Washington, 1978-81; head operational medicine br., aeromed. advisor Office of Chief Naval Ops., 1978-81; dir. clin. svcs., dir. med. edn., exec. officer Naval Regional Med. Ctr., Portsmouth, Va., 1981-83; commanding officer Naval Hosp., Millington, Tenn., 1983-84; comdr. U.S. Naval Med. Command, London, 1984-86; fleet med. officer U.S. Naval Forces Europe, 1984-86; fleet surgeon U.S. Atlantic Fleet, Norfolk, 1986-88; command surgeon U.S. Atlantic Command U.S. Atlantic Command/Supreme Allied Comdr., 1986-89; asst. dir. naval medicine Office of Chief Naval Ops., 1989; insp. gen. Navy Bur. of Medicine and Surgery, 1989-90; comdr. Naval Med. Ctr., Portsmouth, Va., 1990-92; from corp. med. dir. to v.p. healthcare svc. Blue Cross/Blue Shield of Fla., Jacksonville, 1992—99, v.p. healthcare programs Jacksonville , 1999—2001. Asst. dean Ea. Va. Med. Sch., Norfolk, 1981-83, assoc. dean, 1990-92; del. AMA ho. of dels from Aerospace Med. Assn., 1993—; del. Fla. Med. Assn. ho. of dels. from Duval County Med. Soc., 1995—; bd. trustee Am. Bd. Preventive Medicine, 1988-94. Bd. dirs. Blood Bank, Jacksonville, 1973-77, Cath. Family Svcs., Portsmouth, 1981-83, Fraser-Millington Mental Health Ctr., Memphis, 1983-84, Fla. Assn. HMOs, 1999—2001, USO N.E. Fla., 1999—, We Care Jacksonville, 1999-; mem. Gov.'s Diabetes Adv. Coun., 1998-2000, Fla. Commn. Mental Health and Substance Abuse, 1999-2000, Gov. Strategic Panel on Tobacco, 2002.. Decorated Legion of Merit with four oak leaf clusters, Meritorious Svc. medal, Air medal with oak leaf cluster, Navy Commendation medal; recipient Physician's Recognition award AMA, 1972, 75, 78, 81, 85, 88, 91, 94, 97, 2000. Fellow ACP, Am. Coll. Preventive Medicine, Am. Acad. Family Physicians, Aerospace Med. Assn. (pres. 1988-89, chair fellows group 1997—); mem. AMA (del. 1993—), Fla. Acad. Family Physicians (bd. dirs. 1995-2001, Found. bd. dirs. 2001—), Fla. Soc. for Preventive Medicine (pres. 1995-96), Fla. Med. Assn. (del. 1995—), VFW, Am. Legion, Internat. Acad. Aviation and Space Medicine (bd. dirs. 2000—), Assn. Mil. Surgeons U.S., Soc. Med. Cons. to Armed Forces, Rotary, Elks. Roman Catholic. Avocations: travel, cooking. Home: 1782 Long Slough Walk Orange Park FL 32003-7033 Office: Blue Cross/Blue Shield Fla 4800 Deerwood Campus Pkwy Jacksonville FL 32246-8273 E-mail: daniel.lestage@bcbsfl.com.

LESTELLE, TERRENCE J. lawyer; b. New Orleans, May 31, 1949; s. August Jr. and June Rose (Pays) L.; m. Andrea Sucherman, Sept. 21, 1975; children: Evan Pays, Nicole Jessica. BA, Tulane U., 1971; JD, Loyola U.,

1974; LLM, U. London, 1976. Bar: La. 1974, U.S. Dist. Ct. (ea. dist.) La. 1974, U.S. Ct. Appeals (5th cir.) 1975, U.S. Dist. ct. (we. dist.) La. 1977, U.S. Dist. Ct. (mid. dist.) La. 1979, U.S. Ct. Appeals (11th cir.) 1981, U.S. Supreme Ct. 1983, Miss. 1990, Colo. 1990, U.S. Dist. Ct. (so. and no. dist.) Miss. 1990. Law clk. to Hon. James A. Comiskey U.S. Dist. Ct. (ea. dist.) La., New Orleans, 1974-75; law clk. to Hon. Frank Summers La. Supreme Ct., 1975; assoc. Deutsch, Kerrigan & Stiles, 1975, Lemle, Kelleher, Kohlmeyer, Dennery, Hunley, Moss & Frilot, New Orleans, 1976-78, Law Firm of Amato & Creely, Gretna, 1978-81; prin. Law Office of Terrence J. Lestelle, New Orleans, 1981-84; ptnr. Lestelle & Lestelle, 1984—. E-mail: lestelle@lestellelaw.com.

LESTER, ALICIA L. financial analyst; b. Niagara Falls, N.Y., Aug. 28, 1955; d. Belmira Hinto Harris and James Lester; children: Deláno Thompson, Michael, Jr. Thompson. BS, Commerce, Niagara Falls, NY, 1977. Underwriting cert. 1997. Mktg., acctg. analyst Carborundum Abrasives Co., Niagara Falls, NY, 1978—87; self employed contractor - analytical various corps., Buffalo, 1990—96; comml. fin. analyst Fleet Boston Financial - Corp. Banking, 1996—2000; fin. analyst Motorola Inc., Elma, 2000—01. Cons. Thunder - Fin., Programming and Mktg. Solutions Orgn., Buffalo, 1997—2002. Chair, arts facet Niagara Falls Chpt. The Links, Inc., 2000—02, co-chair, tech. Niagara Falls Chpt.; chair Clark Acad. Performing Arts, 1990—2002. Mem.: Fin. Women Internat. (comm. chair 1997—99). Personal E-mail: A.Lester@Verizon.net.*

LESTER, ANDREW WILLIAM, lawyer; b. Mpls., Feb. 17, 1956; s. Richard G. and Marion Louise (Kurtz) L.; m. Barbara Regina Schmitt, Nov. 22, 1978; 1 child, Susan Erika. Student, Ludwig-Maximilians Univ., Munich, 1975-76; BA, Duke U., 1977; MS in Fgn. Service, JD, Georgetown U., 1981. Bar: Okla. 1981, D.C. 1985, Tex. 1990, U.S. Supreme Ct. 1992, Colo. 1995. Cons. Dresser Industries, Inc., Washington, 1979-81; assoc. Conner & Winters, Tulsa, 1981-82; asst. atty. City of Enid, Okla., 1982-84; ptnr. various law firms Enid, Oklahoma City, 1984-96; ptnr. Lester, Loving & Davies P.C., Edmond, 1996—. Adj. prof. Okla. City Univ. Sch. of Law; lectr. in field; U.S. magistrate judge Western Dist. Okla., 1988-96; constl. law specialist Ctrl. and East European Law Initiative, ABA, Ukraine, Belarus and Moldova, 1993; adj. scholar Okla. Coun. Pub. Affairs; bd. dirs. St. Mary's Episcopal Sch. Author: Constitutional Law and Democracy, 1994; contbr. book revs. and articles to profl. jours. Intern Office of Senator Bob Dole, Washington, 1977-78; mem. transition team EEOC Office Pres.-Elect Reagan, Washington, 1980-81; chmn. Enid Police Civil Service Commn., 1985-87; bd. dirs. Enid Habitat for Humanity, 1986-88, Booker T. Washington Community Ctr., Enid, 1987-90, St. Mary's Episcopal Sch. of Edmond, 1999-2001; mem. Martin Luther King, Jr. Holiday Commn. of Enid, 1988-91; deacon First Bapt. Ch. of Oklahoma City. Fellow Okla. Bar Found.; mem. Okla. Bar Assn., Colo. Bar Assn., Okla. Assn. Mcpl. Attys. (bd. dirs. 1987-91, 94-98, 2000—, gen. counsel 1987-88, pres. 1988-90), Oklahoma County Bar Assn., Def. Rsch. Inst. (govt. liability com.), Federalist Soc. (vice chmn. civil rights practice group 1996—, pres. Ctrl. Okla. chpt. 1996-99). Republican. Avocations: German language, cartography. Office: Lester Loving & Davies PC 1505 S Renaissance Blvd Edmond OK 73013-3018 E-mail: alester@lldlaw.com.

LESTER, BARNETT BENJAMIN, editor, retired foreign affairs officer; b. Toronto, Can., Aug. 7, 1912; came to U.S., 1917; s. Louis and Lena (Rubenstein) L.; m. Rita Constance Hatcher, May 31, 1943 (dec.); m. Claudette Yvonne Gionet, Apr. 19, 1970. Student, Cleve. Coll., Western Res. U., 1933; AB (Miller Scholar), Oberlin Coll., 1934, grad. scholar, 1934-35, Nat. Inst. Pub. Affairs, Washington, 1935-36; scholar, Syracuse U., 1935-36, Acad. Internat. Law, The Hague, 1936; student, fellow, Fletcher Sch. Law and Diplomacy, 1935-36; student, Fgn. Service Inst., 1952, 56, Dep. Chiefs Mission Seminar, Dept. State, 1981. Mem. staff, corr. Cleve. Plain Dealer and Cleve. News, 1928-33; feature writer Boston Sunday Post, 1935-38; mng. editor, later editor Exclusive Features Syndicate, Boston, 1936-38; asso. editor The Writer mag., 1936-38; info. officer Dept. Justice, 1938-41; asst. dir. feature div. Office Inter-Am. Affairs, 1941-45; info. publicist Dept. State, 1945; pub. relations exec. Al Paul Lefton Co., Inc., Phila., 1945-46; info. specialist, chief motion pictures, acting chief audio-visual sect. USPHS, Office Surgeon Gen., 1947-48; info. specialist Fed. Security Agy., 1948-49; chief editorial and prodn. sect. Nat. Heart Inst. (info. specialist, sci. reports br. NIH), 1949-52; pub. info. chief NIH, 1950; review officer Dept. State, 1952-61, supervisory publs. editor, 1961-63, editor-writer, 1963-73, pub. info. officer, 1973-85; assoc. editor Newsletter, 1977-81, State Mag., 1981-86, sr. editor, 1986-89, on contract, 1989; pub. affairs specialist, 1985-89. Fgn. svc. res. officer, 1965-73, assigned to policy and pub. info. affairs program, 1962-67; assigned to policy and pub. info affairs program Newsletter and Info. Office, Office Dir. Gen. Fgn. Svc., 1967-81, Office Pub. Affairs and State Mag., Office Dir. Gen. Fgn. Svc., 1981-89, Career counselor Oberlin Coll., 1940—, pub. affairs officer Inter-Am. Air Pilot Program, sponsored by War Dept. and Office of Inter-Am. Affairs, 1942-44; rep. Office Surg. Gen., USPHS, on Interdepartmental com. med. tng. aids, 1947-48; invited participant U.S. Commr. Edn. Conf. Audio-Visual Aids to Edn., 1948; mem. info. staff Pres.'s Midcentury White House Conf. on Children and Youth, 1950; mem. spl. survey audio-visual tchg. and tng. aids Nat. Heart Inst., USPHS and Assn. Am. Med. Colls., 1951; invited participant symposium The White House: The First 200 Yrs., White House Hist. Assn., 1992;invited participant, symposium Two Hundred Years at the White House: Actors and Observers, White House Histo. Assn., 2000. Author: (with others) The Writer's Handbook, 1936. Recipient War Service award Coord. Inter-Am. Affairs, 1945, Meritorious Honor Group award Dept. State, 1967, 40 Year Service award, 1979, Spl. Achievement award, 1979, Superior Honor award, 1983, Superior Honor Group award, 1984; Loy W. Henderson—Joseph C. Satterthwaite award for pub. service, 1987; Bicentennial award Am. Revolution Bicentennial Adminstrn., 1977; award for excellence Soc. Tech. Communications, 1982; award for achievement Soc. Tech. Communication, 1985; 50 Yr. Pin, Fletcher Sch. Law and Diplomacy, 1986; 50 Yr. Svc. award, bronze plaque for 51 yrs. U.S. Govt. Svc., 1989; John Jacob Rogers award for outstanding career achievement, Dept. State, 1989; cert. commendation Dept. State, 1989. Mem. Am. Fgn. Svc. Assn., Am. Polit. Sci. Assn., Acad. Polit. Sci., Diplomatic and Consular Officers Ret., Fed. Editors Assn. (Blue Pencil award 1975), Nat. Assn. Govt. Communicators (Blue Pencil Publs. award 1983), Marquis Libr. Assn. (adv. mem.), U.S. Diplomatic Courier Assn. (hon., Silver Diplomatic Courier medal and cert. appreciation 1990), Nat. Press Found. (charter), Nat. Trust for Hist. Preservation, U.S. Capitol Hist. Soc., Assn. for Diplomatic Studies and Tng., Fgn. Affairs Retirees of No. Va., Internat. Club (charter, honored as founding mem.), Nat. Press Club, Silver Owls Club, Am. Fgn. Svc. Achievements include having two suggestions adopted by U.S. Postal Service resulted in issuing Treaty of Paris stamp and Great Seal of U.S. embossed stamped envelope. Home: 2507 N Lincoln St Arlington VA 22207-5023

LESTER, BIJOU YANG, economist, educator; b. Sinchu Hsien, Taiwan, Republic of China, Apr. 2, 1950; d. Gwei-Far and Yuei-Mey (Chou) Y.; m. Shi-Tao Yeh, (div. Oct. 1986); children: Andrew C. Yeh, Cynthia Yeh; m. David Lester, Oct. 22, 1987. BA in Econs., Nat. Taiwan U., Taipei, 1971, MA in Econs., 1974; AM in Econs., U. Pa., 1975, PhD in Econs., 1981. Economist Wharton Econometric Forecasting Assocs., Phila., 1981-83; asst. prof. Villanova (Pa.) U., 1983-85, Stockton State Coll., Pomona, N.J., 1985-86, Trenton (N.J.) State Coll., 1986-87, Drexel U., Phila., 1987—. Author: Economic Perspectives in Suicide, 1997, Suicide and Homicide in the 20th Century, 1998; contbr. articles to profl. jours. Pres. Chinese Student Club at U. Pa., Phila., 1978-79. Mem. Am. Econ. Assn. (mem. com. on status of women in econ. profession), Eastern Econ. Assn., Pa. Econ. Assn. (bd. dirs. 1993—), Soc. Advancement Behavioral Econ. (treas. 1992-94). Avocations: movies, plays, bowling, traveling. Home: 5 Stonegate Ct Blackwood NJ 08012-5356 Office: Drexel U Dept Econ and Internat Bus 32nd and Market St 11-501 Philadelphia PA 19104-2875

LESTER, CHARLES TURNER, JR. lawyer; b. Plainfield, N.J., Jan. 31, 1942; s. Charles Turner and Marlyn Elizabeth (Tate) L.; m. Nancy Hudmon Simmons, Aug. 19, 1967; children: Susan Hopson, Mary Elizabeth. BA, Emory U., 1964, JD, 1967. Bar: Ga. 1966, U.S. Dist. Ct. (no. dist.) Ga. 1967, D.C. 1970, U.S. Ct. Appeals (5th cir.) 1967, U.S. Ct. Appeals (11th cir.) 1982, U.S. Ct. Appeals (10th cir.) 1984, U.S. Supreme Ct. 2001. Assoc. Sutherland, Asbill & Brennan, Atlanta, 1970-77, ptnr., 1977—. Mem. Leadership Atlanta, 1980-81; pres. Atlanta Legal Aid Soc., 1979-80. Lt. JAGC, USNR, 1967-70. Fellow Am. Bar Found; mem. ABA, State Bar of Ga. (pres. young lawyers sect. 1977-78, bd. govs. 1977-78, 80-93, chmn. formal adv. opinion bd. 1987-90, exec. com. 1977-78, 1987-93, pres. 1991-92), Atlanta Bar Assn., Am. Judicature Soc., Lawyers Club Atlanta (treas. 1982-83, exec. com. 1982-90, 2d v.p. 1986-87, 1st v.p. 1987-88, pres. 1988-89), D.C. Bar Assn., Ga. C. of C. (bd. dirs. 1994-2000), Lawyers Com. for Civil Rights Law (bd. dirs., vice-chmn. S.E. region, co-chair 1999-2001). Democrat. Methodist. Home: 1955 Musket Ct Stone Mountain GA 30087-1703 Office: Sutherland Asbill & Brennan 999 Peachtree St NE Ste 2300 Atlanta GA 30309-3996

LESTER, JOHN JAMES NATHANIEL, II (SEAN LESTER), engineer, environmental analyst, human rights activist; b. Houston, May 7, 1952; s. John James Nathaniel Lester and Margaret Louise (Tisdale) Sharp. Student, U. Tex., 1970, Lee Coll., 1971; AS, Grossmont Coll., 1979; BA in Behavioral Sci., Nat. U., 1987, y. Registered profl. stationary engr., Tex.; cert. peramaculture specialist. Nuclear power specialist USN, various, 1971-77; microbiology lab. technician VA, San Diego, 1978; prin. engring. asst. San Diego Gas & Electric, 1979-85, engring. environ. analyst, 1985-88. Owner Calif. Triad Gem & Mineral Co.; founder Ctr. for Creative Healing. Dir. logistics, mem. regional bd. Gary Hart Presdl. Campaign, San Diego, 1984; founding mem. Inlet Drug Crisis Ctr., Houston, 1970; vol. dir. Aid for Guatemalan Refugees and Orphans, 1988; vol. for Dali Lama, Tibetan Refugee Rights and Ceremonies, 1989; mem. bldg. com. Tibetan Sch. Medicine, Crestone, Colo.; mem. San Luis Valley Tibetan Project, Crestone; active Clinton Presdl. Campaign, 1992; founder Pema Tashi Ling Found. for Tibetan Studies, 1992—; mem. com. on alt. energy and energy conservation Maui County Coun., 1999; mem. Maui Arts and Cultural Ctr.; bd. dirs. Maui Tomorrow. Mem. ASME, IEEE (interim pres., founding mem. San Diego region Ocean Engring. Soc. 1984-85), Mensa, Assn. Humanistic Psychology, Amnesty Internat., Hunger Project, Earth Stewards, Human Rights Watch, Tibet Watch, Sierra Club, Hawaiian Organic Farmers Assn., Orion Soc. Buddhist. Avocations: scuba diving, freelance photography, photojournalism, back-packing, Tibetan Buddhist ceremonial rites and practice. Home and Office: PO Box 880520 Pukalani HI 96788

LESTER, JULIUS B. author; b. St. Louis, Jan. 27, 1939; s. W.D. and Julia (Smith) L.; m. Milan Sabatini; children: Jody Simone, Malcolm Coltrane, Elena Milad, David Julius, Lian Brennan. BA, Fisk U., 1960. Prof. Judaic studies U. Mass., Amherst, 1971—. Profl. musician and singer, recording for Vanguard Records, folklorist and writer, dir., Newport Folk Festival, 1966-68; author: (with Pete Seeger) The 12-String Guitar as Played by Leadbelly, 1965, Look Out, Whitey, Black Power's Gon' Get Your Mama, 1968, To Be a Slave, 1968 (Newberry Honor book 1968), Black Folktales, 1969, Revolutionary Notes, 1969, Search for the New Land, 1970, The Knee-High Man and Other Tales, 1972, Long Journey Home: Stories from Black History, 1972, Two Love Stories, 1972, Who I Am, 1974, All Is Well, 1976, This Strange New Feeling, 1982, Do Lord Remember Me, 1985, The Tales of Uncle Remus: The Adventures of Brer Rabbit, 1987, The Tales of Uncle Remus, The Further Adventures of Brer Rabbit, 1988, Lovesong: Becoming a Jew, 1988, How Many Spots Does A Leopard Have?, 1989, Further Tales of Uncle Remus, 1990, Falling Pieces of the Broken Sky, 1990, Last Tales of Uncle Remus, 1994, And All Our Wounds Forgiven, 1994, The Man Who Knew Too Much, 1994, John Henry, 1994 (Boston Globe-Horn Book award 1995), Othello: A Novel, 1995, Sam and the Tigers, 1996, From Slave Ship to Freedom Road, 1998, Black Cowboy, Wild Horses, 1998, What A Truly Cool World, 1999, When the Beginning Began, 1999, Pharaoh's Daughter, 2000, Albidaro and the Mischievous Dream, 2000, The Blues Singers: Ten Who Shook the World, 2001, Ackamarackus: Julius Lester's Sumptuosly Silly Fantastically Funny Fables, 2001, When Dad Killed Mom, 2001; editor: Seventh Son: The Thoughts and Writings of W.E.B. DuBois, vol. 1 and 2, 1971; assoc. editor: Sing Out, 1964-69; contbg. editor: Broadside of New York, 1964-70. Office: U Mass Judaic Studies Herter Hall Amherst MA 01003 E-mail: jbles@charter.net. *The older I become, the greater the mystery of my life. I think I see my life as journey into mystery, in awe and fear, with joy and apprehension. Whatever my accomplishments, my life is more than and other than, and finally, best expressed by the silence of winter snow, prairie skies, or a feathered serpent. To be as true and eloquent as a drop of water hanging from a twig— that is my ideal.*

LESTER, JUNE, library information studies educator; b. Sandersville, Ga., Aug. 25, 1942; d. Charles DuBose and Frances Irene (Cheney) L.; 1 child, Anna Elisabeth Engle. BA, Emory U., 1963, M in Librarianship, 1971; D in Libr. Sci., Columbia U., 1987, cert. in advanced librarianship, 1982. Asst. prof., cataloger U. Tenn. Libr., Knoxville, 1971-73; libr. divsn. libr. and info. mgmt. Emory U., Atlanta, 1973-81, asst. prof. div. libr. and info. mgmt., 1976-80, assoc. prof., 1980-87; accreditation officer Am. Libr. Assn., 1987-91, assoc. dean, assoc. prof., 1991-93; dir. Sch. Libr. and Info. Scis., U. North Tex., Denton, 1993-2000; prof. Sch. Libr. and Info. Studies, U. Okla. , Norman, 1993—. UCLA sr. fellow, 1987. Mem. ALA (coun. mem. 1987), Assn. for Libr. and Info. Sci. Edn. (bd. dirs. 1985-87, 94-97, pres. 1995-96), Am. Soc. Info. Sci. and Tech., Okla. Libr. Assn., Phi Beta Kappa, Beta Phi Mu. Unitarian Universalist. Home: 2006 Trailview Ct Norman OK 73072-6654 Office: U Okla Sch Libr and Info Studies 401 W Brooks St Norman OK 73019-6030 E-mail: jlester@ou.edu.

LESTER, KEN HARRISON, lawyer; b. Wilson, N.C., Apr. 4, 1941; s. Lonnie H. and Polly Lester; m. Rose Nell Bruorton, Nov. 26, 1964; children: Kris, Ken Jr., Kelli. BA, U. S.C., 1964, JD, 1966. Bar: S.C. 1966. Ptnr. Lester & Jones, Columbia, S.C. Fellow Acad. Matrimonial Lawyers; mem. Am. Coll. Family Trial Lawyers, S.C. Trial Lawyers Assn. (bd. govs., mem. various coms.), Richland Co. Bar Assn. (family law com), Lexington Co. Bar Assn., Beaufort Co. Bar Assn.. Office: Lester & Jones 1716 Main St Columbia SC 29201-2820 also: 1 Professional Dr Port Royal Beaufort SC 29935 E-mail: KLester33@aol.com.

LESTER, MARK CHARLES, neurosurgeon; b. Pitts., Sept. 23, 1952; AB, Cornell U., 1973; MD, U. Pitts., 1977; MBA, U. Pa., 2002. Diplomate Am. Bd. Neurol. Surgery. Intern gen. surgery U. Health Ctr. Hosps., Pitts., 1977—78, resident in neurological surgery, 1978—83; neurosurgeon Allentown, 1983—; chief, Divsn. Neurol. Surgery Lehigh Valley Hosp., 1992—2001, co-med. dir. trauma/neuro ICU, 1998—2001, vice-chmn. for opers., dept. surgery, 1999—, med. dir. oper. rm., 1999—; clin. assoc. prof. Pa. State Coll. of Medicine, Hershey, Pa., 1995—; head sect. neurotrauma Lehigh Valley Hosp., Allentown, 1991-95. Adj. clin. asst. prof. Hahnemann U., Phila., 1988— Fellow Am. Coll. Surgeons; mem. Am. Assn. Neurolog. Surgeons, AAAS. Office: Neurosurg Assocs of Lehigh Valley Physician Group Ste 1100 1210 S Cedar Crest Blvd Allentown PA 18103

LESTER, NOEL K. music educator, concert pianist; b. Gasport, N.Y., June 26, 1951; s. William Harold and Jeanne (Jessup) L.; m. Roseann Markow, June 28, 1975; children: Marie, David. MusB, Peabody Conservatory, Balt., 1973, MusM, 1975, D Musical Arts, 1984. Nat. cert. in piano, Mus. Tchrs. Nat. Assn. Instr. music Hood Coll., Frederick, Md., 1974-78, asst. prof. music, 1978-85, assoc. prof. music, 1985-94, prof. music, 1994—. Participant ann. European study trips for Hood Coll., 1992—; organist, choir dir., Woodbrook Bapt. Ch., Balt., 1971-85, dir. music Grace United Ch. Christ Ch., Frederick, 1986-90. Performances include Carnegie Recital Hall debut, 1982, Kennedy Ctr. debut, 1988, European debut, Hamburg, Germany, 1992, Lincoln Ctr. debut, 1998, ann. European tours, 1992—, Japanese tour, 2000; recorded performances (CD rec.) include Music of the Americas, 1993, Piano Portraits from 19th Century America, 1995, Rags to Riches, 1997, Charles Martin Loeffler: Forgotten Songs, 1998, Charles Martin Loeffler: A Dream Within a Dream, 1999, Syncopated Sensations, 2000, Purrfectly Classical, 2001, A Christmas Fantasy, 2001. Bd. dirs., Md. Lyric Opera, Frederick, 1990-95. Winner Profl. Recital debut, Balt. Music Club, 1976, Balt. Chamber Music award, 1998. Mem. Music Tchrs. Nat. Assn. (cert. in piano), Coll. Music Soc., Md. State Music Tchrs. Assn. Avocations: reading, cooking, travel. Office: Hood Coll 401 Rosemont Frederick MD 21701 E-mail: nlester@hood.edu.

LESTER, RICHARD GARRISON, radiologist, educator; b. N.Y.C., Oct. 24, 1925; s. L. I. and Pauline (Smolan) L.; m. Marion Louise Kurtz, Jan. 17, 1949; children: Elizabeth P., Andrew W. AB, Princeton U., 1946; MD, Columbia U., 1948. Intern N.Y.C. Hosp., 1948-49; asst. resident radiology Stanford Hosp., 1950-51, 53-54; from instr. to asso. prof. radiology U. Minn., 1954-61; prof. radiology, chmn. dept. Med. Coll. Va., 1961-65, Duke Sch. Medicine, 1965-76; prof. radiology U. Tex. Med. Sch., Houston, 1976-84, chmn. dept., 1977-81; interim pres. Meharry Med. Coll., Nashville, 1981-82; dean Eastern Va. Med. Sch., Norfolk, 1984-89, prof. radiology, 1984-93, chmn. dept., 1989-91; prof. emeritus, 1993—; v.p. acad. affairs Med. Coll. of Hampton Roads, formerly Eastern Va. Med. Authority, Norfolk, 1984-89. Trustee Meharry Med. Coll., 1975— Author: (with others) Congenital Heart Disease, 1965, Exposure of the Pregnant Patient to Diagnostic Radiations, 1985, 2d edit., 1997; also numerous articles. Deacon Freemason St. Bapt. Ch. Capt. USAF, 1951-53. Fellow Am. Coll. Radiology, Am. Coll. Chest Physicians; mem. Assn. Univ. Radiologists, Am. Roentgen Ray Soc., Soc. Pediatric Radiology, Radiol. Soc. N.Am. (dir. 1976— , chmn. bd. 1981, pres. 1983). Home: 1362 De Bree Ave Norfolk VA 23517-2131 Office: Ea Va Med Sch PO Box 1980 Norfolk VA 23501-1980 E-mail: rglester@aol.com.

LESTER, ROBIN DALE, educator, author, former headmaster; b. Holdrege, Nebr., Mar. 1, 1939; s. Earl L. and Evelyn Grace (Robinson) L.; m. Helen Sargent Doughty, Aug. 26, 1967; children: Robin Debevoise, James Robinson. Student, St. Andrews U., Scotland, 1958-61; BA, Pepperdine U., 1962, MA, 1963; MAT, U. Chgo., 1966, PhD, 1971. Resident head, dean students office U. Chgo., 1964-72, Ferdinand Schevill fellow dept. history, 1966-68; asst. prof. history Columbia Coll., Chgo., 1966-70, chmn. social scis. dept., 1970-72; chmn. history dept. Collegiate Sch., N.Y.C., 1972-75; headmaster Trinity Sch., 1975-86, San Francisco U. Sch., 1986-88, Latin Sch. of Chgo., 1989-92; tchr. Francis W. Parker Sch., Chgo., 1994-97. Adj. prof. Columbia Coll., Chgo., 1992-95; interim head Blake Sch., Mpls., 1997-98. Author: Stagg's University, 1995, Wuzzy Takes Off, 1995, Roy Foy, 1996, Going to School and Awww!, 1997; contbg. author: Problems in American Sports History, 1997; contbr. to N.Y. Times, Jour. Am. History, Chgo. Tribune, Jour. Sports History, History Edn. Quar., U. Chgo. mag. Mem. Manhattan Borough Dem. Com., N.Y.C., 1977-86; commr. Commn. on Ednl. Issues, 1980-84; mem. edn. com. Chgo. Hist. Soc., 1991-95; mem. Chgo.-Prague Sister Cities Com., 1991-97; trustee, treas. St. Andrews U. Am. Found., 1985—; precinct capt. Dem. Party, Chgo., 1964. Lauder fellow Aspen Inst., 1985. Mem. Am. Hist. Assn., Am. Studies Assn., N.Am. Soc. Sport Historians (Book of the Yr. award 1995), Orgn. Am. Historians, Headmaster's Assn., University Club (N.Y.C.), Quadrangle Club (Chgo.). Episcopalian. E-mail: rl1709@att.net.

LESTER, VIRGINIA LAUDANO, education administrator; b. Phila., Jan. 5, 1931; d. Edmund Francis and Emily Beatrice (Downes) Laudano; children: Pamela Lester Golde, Valerie Lester. BA, Pa. State U., 1952; MEd, Temple U., 1955; PhD, Union Grad. Sch., 1972; JD, Stanford U. Law Sch., 1988. Tchr. pub. schs., Abington, Pa., 1952-55, Greenfield Center, N.Y., 1956; instr. edn. dept. Skidmore Coll., Saratoga Springs, 1962-64, dir. ednl. research, 1967-72, asst. to the pres., 1968-72; asst. dir. Capitol Dist. Regional Supplementary Edn. Center, Albany, N.Y., 1966-67; assoc. dean, asst. prof. state-wide programs Empire State Coll., State U. N.Y., Saratoga Springs, 1973-75, sr. assoc. dean, assoc. prof., 1975-76, acting dean state-wide programs, 1976; pres., prof. interdisciplinary studies Mary Baldwin Coll., Staunton, Va., 1976-85, cons. to bd. trustees, 1985-88; assoc. Hunton & Williams, Richmond, Va., 1988-90; interim pres. Friends World Coll., Huntington, N.Y., 1990-91; dir. presdl. search consultation svc. Assn. of Governing Bds. of Univs. and Colls., 1991-94; of counsel spl. projects office of exec. dir. Am. Assn. Retired Persons, 1994—2001. Mem. cons. core faculty Union Grad. Sch., Union for Experimenting Colls. and Univs., Cin., 1975—82; vis. faculty fellow Harvard U. Grad. Sch. Edn., 1976; bd. dirs. So. Bankshares, So. Bank, Coun. Advancement of Small Colls., 1977—81, Am. Council Edn., 1983-85; adj. faculty mem. Grad. Sch. George Washington U., 1996, 2002—; cons. Nat. Exec. Svc. Corp., 1991—. Mem. com. on criminal sexual assault Va. State Crime Commn., 1976; v.p. Costume Collection, Inc., 1971-73; v.p. Warren, Washington, Saratoga Counties Planned Parenthood, 1972-74, bd. dirs., 1970-74; mem. Saratoga Springs Housing Bd. Appeals, 1966-76, Commn. on Future of Va., 1982-84; bd. dirs. Nat. Urban League, 1979-86; pres. commn. NCAA, 1984-85. Mem. Am. Acad. Polit. and Social Scis., Va. Found. Ind. Colls. (trustee, exec. com.), Va. Council Ind. Colls., Am. Council on Edn. (commn. on women in higher edn. 1977-80, bd. dirs. 1981-85), Nat. Assn. Ind. Colls. and Univs. (dir.), Assn. Va. Colls. (sec.-treas. 1978-79, pres. 1980-81, dir.), Assn. Ch. Related Colls. and Univs. of South (pres. 1983), Pi Lambda Theta, Pi Gamma Mu, Chimes. Mem. Soc. Of Friends. E-mail: vlester55@msn.com.

LESTER, WILLIAM ALEXANDER, JR. chemist, educator; b. Chgo., Apr. 24, 1937; s. William Alexander and Elizabeth Frances (Clark) L.; m. Rochelle Diane Reed, Dec. 27, 1959; children: William Alexander III, Allison Kimberleigh. BS, U. Chgo., 1958, MS, 1959; postgrad., Washington U., St. Louis, 1959-60; PhD, Cath. U. Am., 1964. Phys. chemist Nat. Bur. Stds., Washington, 1961-64; asst. dir. Theoretical Chemistry Inst./U. Wis., Madison, 1965-68; rsch. staff IBM Rsch. Lab., San Jose, Calif., 1968-75, mgr., 1976-78; tech. planning staff IBM T.J. Watson Rsch. Ctr., Yorktown Heights, N.Y., 1975-76; dir. Nat. Resource for Computation in Chemistry, Lawrence Berkeley (Calif.) Lab., 1978-81, also assoc. dir., staff sr. scientist, 1978-81, faculty sr. scientist, 1981—; prof. chemistry U. Calif., Berkeley, 1981—, assoc. dean Coll. Chemistry, 1991-95. Lectr. chemistry U. Wis., 1966-68; cons. NSF, 1976-77, mem. chem. divsn. adv. panel, 1981-83, adv. com. Office Advanced Sci. Computing program, 1985-87, chmn., 1987, sr. fellow for sci. and engring., asst. to dir. for human resource devel., 1995-96; mem. U.S. nat. com. Internat. Union Pure and Applied Chemistry, 1976-79; mem. com. on recommendations for U.S. Army Basic Sci. Rsch. NRC, 1984-87, mem. steering com., 1987-88; chemistry rsch. evaluation panel AF Office Sci. Rsch., 1974-78; chmn. Gordon Conf. Atomic and Molecular Interactions, 1978; mem. NRC panel on chem. physics Nat. Bur. Stds., 1980-83; mem. com. to survey chem. scis. NRC, 1982-84, Fed. Networking Coun. Adv. Com., 1991-95; mem. blue ribbon panel on high performance computing NSF, 1993; mem. com. on high performance computing and comm.: status of a major initiative NRC, 1994-95, mem. com. on math. challenges from theoretical computational chemistry, NRC, 1994-95; mem. tech. assessment bd. Army Rsch. Lab., NRC, 1996-99; coun. mem. Gordon Rsch. Conf., 1997-2000, selection and scheduling com., 2000-; mem. adv. bd. Model Instns. Excellence Spelman Coll., 1997—; mem. external vis. com. Nat. Partnership Advanced Computational Infrastructure, 1999—; mem. pres. com. Nat. Medal Sci., 2000-; mem. dept. energy adv. com. on advanced sci. computing, 2000-. Editor: Procs. of Conf. on Potential Energy Surfaces in Chemistry, 1971, Recent Advances in Quantum Monte Carlo Methods, 1997; co-editor (with J. Govaerts and M.N. Houkonnou): Contemporary Problems in Mathematical Physics, 2000; co-editor: (with S.M. Rothstein and S. Tanaka) Recent Advances in Quantum Monte Carlo Methods, Part II, 2002; co-author (with Brian L. Hammond and Peter J. Reynolds): Monte Carlo Methods in Ab Initio Quantum Chemistry, 1994; mem. editl. bd. Jour. Phys. Chemistry, 1979—81, Jour. Computational Chemistry, 1980—87, Computer Physics Comm., 1981—86, mem. adv. bd. Sci. Yr., 1989—93, Comms. on Analysis, Geometry and Physics, 1997—. Recipient Alumni award in sci. Cath. U. Am., 1983 Fellow AAAS (com. on nominations 1988-91, nat. bd. dirs. 1993-97), Calif. Acad. Scis., Am. Phys. Soc. (chmn. div. chem. physics 1986); mem. Am. Chem. Soc. (sec.-treas. Wis. sect. 1967-68, chmn. div. phys. chemistry 1979, treas. div. computers in chemistry 1974-77), Nat. Orgn. Black Chemists and Chem. Engrs. (Percy L. Julian award 1979, Outstanding Tchr. award 1986, exec. bd. 1984-87). Home: 4433 Briar Cliff Rd Oakland CA 94605-4624 Office: U Calif Dept Chemistry Berkeley CA 94720-1460 E-mail: walester@lbl.gov. *Perseverance is the watchword-the will to hold on.*

LESTER, WILLIAM LEON, political science educator, researcher; b. Grants, N.Mex., Apr. 26, 1963; s. Sharon Marie Howard, July 7, 1990; children: Bethany, William, Daniel. BA, U. Tex., 1990; MPA, Tex. Tech U., 1996, PhD, 2000. Asst. prof. Howard Payne U., Brownwood, Tex., 1999—, Othal Brand prof. free enterprise and pub. policy, 2000—, brand chmn. free enterprise and pub. policy. Othal brand chair of free enterprise and pub. policy Howard Payne U., 2000—. Civitas scholar Ctr. for Pub. Justice and the Pew Charitable Trusts, 1999. Mem. Am. Polit. Sci. Assn., Am. Soc. of Pub. Adminstrn., Christians in Polit. Sci., Golden Key Nat. Honor Soc. Office: Howard Payne U 1000 Fisk Ave Brownwood TX 76801 Home: 1806 14th St Brownwood TX 76801-5318

LESTINA, ROGER HENRY, English language educator; b. Yosemite Nat. Pk., Calif., Apr. 7, 1940; s. Henry Francis and Mary Roselyn (O'Brien) L.; m. Linda Jeanne Fish, Aug. 24, 1963; children: Deanna, Joseph, Nicholas, Daniel. BA in English, Loyola U., L.A., 1962; MA in English, U. Alaska, 1974. Cert. secondary education tchr., Calif. Commd. 2d lt. USAF, 1962, advanced through grades to maj., 1974, ret., 1984; instr. USAF Acad., Colorado Springs, Colo., 1975-79; parish adminstr. St. John the Bapt. Cath. Ch., Edmond, Okla., 1984-90; lead instr. freshman composition Okla. State U., Oklahoma City, 1990—. Co-author: (textbook) The Freshman Writer: Finding, Organizing, and Supporting Ideas, 1999; author, editor: Oklahoma State University, Oklahoma City Self-Study for the North Central Association (NCA) of Colleges and Schools, 1999; editor: (handbook) The Conservation Officer's Guide to Collection and Preservation of Evidence, 1995. Ch. cantor/choir mem. St. John the Bapt. Cath. Ch., Edmond, Okla., 1979-91, 98—, St. Francis of Assisi Parish, Tinker AFB, Okla., 1991-98; sec. faculty coun. Okla. State U.-Oklahoma City, 1997-98. Mem. Ret. Officers Assn. Republican. Roman Catholic. Avocation: singing. Home: 708 Concord Cir Edmond OK 73003-6123 Office: Okla State U 900 N Portland Ave Oklahoma City OK 73107-6195 E-mail: lestina@osuoke.edu.

LESTON, GERD, research chemist, retired; b. Bielefeld, Wstphalia, Germany; s. Leo Leopold and Johanna Leston; m. Gloria Kohnterg Leston; children: Laura, Jeffry. Bachelor Sci., CCNY, New York, New York, 1941—48; Masters Sci., Purdue U., Lafayette, Indiana, 1948—49, PhD, 1949—52. Various chemist positions Kopper Co. Inc., Pittsburgh, Pa., 1952—85. Chmn. Am. Chem. Soc., Pittsburgh, Pa., Chemists Club, Pittsburgh, Pa., 1996. Contbr. articles to journal publications. Sch. dir. Charities Valley, Pittsburgh, Pa.; trustee Scot Twp. Libr. Masters Ceremony. Staff sgt. US Army, 1943—46, Europe. Recipient Sigma xi, Rsch. Hon. Soc. US, Beta Gamma Sigma, Nat. C Burns Academic Honor Soc. Mem.: Spl. Pros Copy Soc. Pittsburg, Soc. Analytical Chemists Pitts., Chem. Soc. (chmn.). Achievements include inventor 38 US patents. Avocations: skiing, tennis, golf, swimming, travel.

LESTON, PATRICK JOHN, judge; b. Maywood, Ill., May 2, 1948; s. John R. and Lorraine (McQueen) L.; m. Kristine Brzezinski; children: Alison, Adam. BS in Communications, U. Ill., 1970; JD cum laude, Northwestern U., Chgo., 1973. Bar: Ill. 1973, U.S. Dist. Ct. (no. dist.) Ill. 1973, U.S. Ct. Appeals (7th cir.) 1973. Ptnr. Jacobs & Leston, Villa Park, Ill., 1973-79; pvt. practice Glen Ellyn, 1979-89; ptnr. Keck, Mahin & Cate, Oakbrook Terrace, 1989-95; judge 18th Cir. Ct., DuPage County, 1995—. Presenter at profl. confs. Editor Ill. State Bar Assn./Young Lawyers Divsn. Jour., 1983-85. Class rep. Northwestern U. Law Sch. Fund, 1982-88; organizer DuPage County (Ill.) Law Explorers. Fellow ABA (Ill. del. to ABA/Young Lawyers divsn. assembly 1982-85), Ill. Bar Assn. (chmn. fellows 1991-92, mem. bd. govs. 1990-97, chmn. young lawyers divsn. 1985, chmn. agenda com. 1986, del. to 18th jud. cir. assembly 1982-88), Ill. Judges Assn. (bd. dirs. 1997—), Ill. Bar Found. (charter), Am. Bar Found.; mem. DuPage County Bar Assn. (pres. 1987, bd. dirs. 1979-84, chmn. judiciary com. 1988, gen. counsel 1989), Lions, Chi Psi. Avocations: volleyball, skiing, scuba diving, travel, golf. Office: 18th Jud Cir Ct 505 N County Farm Rd Wheaton IL 60187-3907

LESZCZYNSKI, JERZY RYSZARD, chemistry educator, researcher; b. Tomaszow, Poland, May 26, 1949; came to U.S., 1986; s. Leslaw and Hanna (Kaptur) L.; m. Danuta, June 25, 1972; children: Rafal, Magda. MS, Tech. U. Wroclaw (Poland), 1972, PhD, 1975. Lectr. chemistry Tech. U. Wroclaw, 1976-86; vis. sci. U. Fla., Gainesville, 1986-88; rsch. assoc. U. Ala., Birmingham, 1988-90; from asst. to assoc. prof. Jackson (Miss.) State U., 1990-95, prof., 1995—, Pres.'s Disting. fellow, 2001. Conf. chmn. organizing com. Current Trends in Computational Chemistry, 1992-2002, So. Schs. on Computational Chemistry, 2001-02; dir. Computational Ctr. for Molecular Structure and Interactions, NSF, 1998—; presenter in field. Author chpts. to books; editor: Computational Chemistry, Reviews of Current Trends, 1995, 96, 97, 98, 99, 00, Computational Molecular Biology, 1999; co-author: Computational Quantum Chemistry, 1988, Combustion Efficiency and Air Quality, 1995, Interaction of DNA Bases and the Structure of DNA, 1996, Molecular Structure and Infrared Spectra of DNA Bases and Their Derivatives: Theory and Experiment, 1997, Tautomeric Properties of Nucleic Acid Bases: Abvinitio Study, 1998, Chemistry of the Liquid State: Current Trends in Quantum-Chemical Modeling, 1999, Computational Approaches to the Studies of the Interactions of Nucleic Acid Bases, 1999, Current Trends in Modeling Interactions of DNA Fragments with Polar Solvents, 1999; editor-in-chief Internat. Jour. Molecular Sci.; editor Electronic Jour. of Theoretical Chemistry; sr. editor Asian Jour. Spectroscopy; guest editor: Structural Chemistry, 1995, Jour. Molecular Structure Theochem., 1996, 97, 98, 99, 2000, 01; guest ed. Biopolymers Nucleic Acid Sci., 2001-02, Parallel Computing, 2000; ref.: Jour. Am. Chem. Soc., Internat. JourQuantum Chemistry, Chem. Physics Letters, Structural Chemistry, Jour. Organic Chemistry, Jour. Phys. Chemistry, Jour. Molecular Structure, Jour. Computational Chemistry, Jour. Biomolecular Structure and Dynamics, Chem. Physics, Computers Chemistry, Jour. Phys. Organic Chemistry, Vibrational Spectroscopy, Inorganic Chemistry, Jour. Chem. Soc. Perkin Transaction 2, Jour. Computer-Aided Design, Theoretical Chemistry Accounts, Jour. Organic Chemistry, Collection Czechoslovak Chem. Comm.; mem. editl. bd. Structural Chemistry; contbr. articles profl. jours. Recipient Outstanding Faculty award, AT&T, 1992, White Ho. Millennium HBCU award for Sci. and Tech., 2001. Mem. Am. Chem. Soc., Internat. Soc. Quantum Biology and Pharmacology (exec. com. 1995-98), Miss. Acad. Sci. Office: Jackson State U Dept Chemistry 1400 Lynch St Jackson MS 39217-0001 E-mail: jerzy@ccnsi.jsums.edu.

LET, FRED VAN, technical director; b. The Hague, The Netherlands, Sept. 3, 1949; m. Ank Barendse, Sept. 13, 1974; children: Bart, Sanne. MS, Tech. U., Delft, The Netherlands, 1975. Sr. cons. ATEL, Almere, The Netherlands, 1975-80; group mgr. CASEMA, Rijswijk, The Netherlands, 1980-85, tech. dir. The Netherlands, 1985-98, dir. Competence Ctr. on Broadband Tech. The Hague, 1999—. Office: NV CASEMA PO Box 2500 BD The Hague Netherlands E-mail: fvlet@office.casema.nl.

LETBETTER, R. STEVE, energy company executive; BA in Acctg., Tex. A&M U. CPA, Tex. Acct. Haskins & Sells, Houston, H, until 1977; asst. sec., asst. treas. HL&P, 1974-77, asst. comptr., 1977-78, comptr., 1978-83, v.p., 1981-83, v.p. regulatory rels., 1983-88, group v.p. fin. and regulatory rels., 1988-93, pres., COO, 1993-97; pres., CEO Reliant Energy Inc., 1999-2000, chmn., pres., CEO, 2000—. Bd. dirs. Chase Bank-Houston. Mem. devel. coun. Lowry Mays Coll. and Grad. Sch. Bus., Tex. A&M U., also mem. task force com. Vision 2020; bd. dirs. Ctrl. Houston, Houston Internat. Festival; bd. dirs., mem. exec. com. Greater Houston Partnership;mem. Tex. Gov.'s Bus. Coun.; mem. coun. overseers Rice U. Jesse H. Jones Grad. Sch. Mgmt. Recipient Outstanding Alumnus award Tex. A&M U., 1998. Mem. AICPA, Edison Electric Inst. (bd. dirs.), Electric Power Rsch. Inst. (bd. dirs.), Assn. Electric Cos. Tex. (bd. dirs.), Am. Gas Assn. (bd. dirs.), Tex. Soc. CPAs, Houston Soc. CPAs, Office: Reliant Energy Inc 1111 Louisiana St Houston TX 77002-5200*

LETENDRE, SCOTT LEE, physician, scientist; b. Saratoga Springs, N.Y., Dec. 15, 1960; s. Victor Edmund and Irene Gertrude Letendre. BS, U. Notre Dame, 1982; MD, Georgetown U., 1986. Diplomate Am. Bd. Internal Medicine. Internal medicine intern Naval Hosp., Oakland, Calif., 1986-87; flight surgeon trainee Naval Aerospace Med. Inst., Pensacola, Fla., 1987-88, Second Marine Aircraft Wing, Cherry Point, N.C., 1988-90; resident in internal medicine Naval Med. Ctr., San Diego, 1990-92, gen. internist, 1992-94; fellow in infectious disease Duke U., Durham, N.C., 1994-97; rsch. fellow U. Calif., San Diego, 1997-99, asst. prof. medicine, 1999—. Contbr. articles to profl. jours. Recipient Career Devel. award NIMH, 1999. Mem. ACP/Am. Soc. Internal Medicine, Infectious Disease Soc. Am., Am. Soc. for Microbiology, Am Fedn. Med. Rsch., Internat. Soc. Neurovirology. Office: HNRC UCSD 150 W Washington St Ste 200 San Diego CA 92103-2005 E-mail: sletendre@ucsd.edu.

LETHBRIDGE, FRANCIS DONALD, retired architect; b. Hackensack, N.J., Oct. 5, 1920; s. Berry B. and Florence A. (Lapham) L.; m. Mary Jane Christopher, June 21, 1947; children: Catherine B. (Mrs. Robert A. Grove), Mary P. (Mrs. Christopher G. Cromwell), Christopher B., Margaret F. (Mrs. Arsim Cejku). Student, Stevens Inst. Tech., 1937-40, Yale Sch. Architecture, 1945-46. Ptnr. archtl. firm Keyes, Smith, Satterlee & Lethbridge, Washington, 1951-55, Keyes, Lethbridge & Condon, Washington, 1956-75, Francis D. Lethbridge & Assocs., Washington, 1975-90. Mem. fgn. bldgs. archtl. rev. panel U.S. State Dept., 1977-80; mem. archtl. adv. panel Fed. Res. Bd., 1979-83; mem. Potomac Planning Task Force, 1965-67; bd. advisers Nat. Trust for Hist. Preservation, 1969-71; mem. Joint Com. Landmarks Nat. Capital, 1964-79, chmn., 1964-73 Co-author: Guide to the Architecture of Washington, D.C; prin. works include Pine Spring Community, Fairfax County, Va., 1951-54, Potomac Overlook, 1955-58, U.S. Chancery, Lima, Peru, 1957, Forest Industries Bldg., Washington, 1961, Carderock Springs Community, Montgomery County, Md., 1963-65, Unitarian Ch, River Road, Md., 1964, master plan Arlington Nat. Cemetery, 1966-68, Ft. Lincoln New Town, 1968, Visitors Ctr., Arlington Nat. Cemetery, 1988. Trustee Nantucket Atheneum; advisor Nantucket Hist. Assn. Officer, pilot USNR, 1942-45. Decorated D.F.C., Air medal; recipient Design Merit award AIA, 1955, 66, 1st honor award, 1966, Potomac Valley Chpt. archtl. award, 1956, 58, 60, 62, 64, 66, 68, 70, 72, 74, 76, joint award of honor AIA-Nat. Assn. Home Builders, 1960; award in architecture Washington Bd. Trade, 1953, 55, 61, 63, 65, 67, 69, 71, 73; Renchard prize for historic preservation, 1983 Fellow AIA (pres. Washington Met. chpt. 1964, v.p. 1969-70, pres. AIA found. 1971-73); mem. Cosmos Club (Washington). Home and Office: 48 Orange St Nantucket MA 02554-3937

LETICHE, JOHN MARION, economist, educator; b. Uman, Kiev, Russia, Nov. 11, 1918; came to U.S., 1941, naturalized, 1949; s. Leon and Mary (Grossman) L.; m. Emily Kuyper, Nov. 17, 1945; 1 son, Hugo K. BA, McGill U., 1940, MA, 1941; PhD in Econs, U. Chgo., 1951. Rockefeller fellow Council Fgn. Relations, N.Y.C., 1945-46; Smith-Mundt vis. prof. U. Aarhus and U. Copenhagen, Denmark, 1951-52; spl. tech. econ. adv. UN ECA, Africa, 1961-62; prof. U. Calif. at Berkeley, 1960—. Cons. AID, U.S. Depts. State, Labor, HUD and Treasury, 1962—; emissary to Japan and Korea, Dept. State, 1971; cons. Econ. Coun. Can., 1972—, World Bank, 1981—, Bank of Eng., London, Bundesbank, Frankfurt, Germany; lectr. Stockholm, Paris, Uppsala, Hamburg, Kiel, Oxford (Eng.), 1973—, Vancouver, Toronto, Montreal, Zagreb, 1983, Frankfurt, Bonn, Moscow and Nakhodka Acad. Scis. USSR, 1986, Hong Kong, Shanghai, Wuhan, Beijing, London, Bonn, Frankfurt, De Hague, 1987, Bundesbank, 1992, 93, 99, China, Beijing, Shanghai, 1988, 90, 94, New Delhi, Addis Ababa, Kuala Lumpur and Seoul, 1996, 99, U.S. War Coll., Quintico, Va., 1997, Acad. Scis., Taipei, 1989, Moscow, 2001, joint session Calif. legis., 1975; ext. examiner adv. degrees U. Hong Kong, U. Calcutta, India. Author: Reciprocal Trade Agreements in the World Economy, 1948, in Japanese, 1951, System or Theory of the Trade of the World, 2d edit., 1957, Balance of Payments and Economic Growth, 2d edit., 1976, A History of Russian Economic Thought, 2d edit., 1977, The Key Problems of Economic Reconstruction and Development in Nigeria, 1970, Dependent Monetary Systems and Economic Development, 1974, Lessons of the Oil Crisis, 1977, Gains from Trade, 1979, Controlling Inflation, Recession, Federal Deficits and the Balance of Payments, 1980, The New Inflation and Its Urban Impact, 1980, Monetary Systems of Africa in the 1980s, 1981, International Economic Policies and Their Theoretical Foundations, 1982, 2d edit., 1992; Russian Statecraft: An Analysis and Translation of Iuril Krizhanich's Politika, 1985, Economics of the Pacific Rim, 1989; editor Royer Lectures, 1980-90, Toward a Market Economy in China, 1992, China's Emerging Monetary and Financial Markets, 1995, India's Economic Reforms, 1996, Causes of the Financial and Economic Crisis in Southeast Asia, 1998, Lessons from the Euro Zone for the East Asian Economies, 2000; contbr. articles to encys., congl. coms. and profl. jours. Supervisory bd. Sch. Econs., St. Petersburg, Russia, 1994—. Recipient certificate merit Ency. Brit., certificate merit Inst. World Affairs, certificate merit Internat. Legal Center, U. Mich., U.S. Office Personnel Mgmt. Sr. Fed. Govt. Execs. and Mgrs., U. Calif.-Berkeley, Adam Smith medal U. Verona, 1977, Medal, Ioffe Inst. Physics and Tech., 1998; Guggenheim fellow, 1956-57 Mem. Am. Econ. Assn. (nominating com. 1968-69), Econometric Soc., Royal Econ. Soc., U.S.-Asian Econ. Com. (bd. dirs. 1983—), African Studies Assn., Am. Soc. Internat. Law (bd. 1969-72). Home: 968 Grizzly Peak Blvd Berkeley CA 94708-1549 E-mail: letiche@econ.berkeley.edu.

LETIZIA, DOROTHY, nursing educator; b. Dover, N.J., Dec. 20, 1938; d. Max and D. Marie (McManus) Meichsner; m. Carl Letizia, July 2, 1960; children: Karen, Janie. BSN, U. Pa., 1960, MSN, 1970; EdD, Rutgers U., 1989. RN, N.J. Clin. adj. faculty mem. Gloucester County Coll., Sewell, N.J., 1982-88; clin. assoc. prof. Camden County Coll., Blackwood, 1990—; assoc. dean, curriculum coord. Our Lady of Lourdes Sch. Nursing, Camden, 1990-2000, dean, 2000—. Mem. adv. bd. coop. programs in nursing Camden County Coll., 1990—, med.-surg. nursing coord., 1970-90; mem. Colleagues in Caring Project, 1996—. Mem. AACN, AAUW, Acad. Med. Surg. Nurses, Fedn. for Accessible Nursing Edn. and Licensure, Nat. League Nursing, Am. Assn. Adult and Continuing Edn., Assn. Diploma Schs. Profls. Nursing, Sigma Theta Tau. Home: 209 Crest Rd Marlton NJ 08053-7133

LETOURNEAU, JEAN-PAUL, business association executive and consultant; b. St.-Hyacinthe, Que., Can., May 4, 1930; s. Eugene and Annette (Deslandes) L.; m. Claire Paquin, Sept. 26, 1956. Counsellor in Indsl. Relations, U. Montreal, Que., 1953; cert. c. of c. adminstrn., U. Syracuse, 1962; cert. advanced mgmt. U.S. C. of C, 1965. Mcpl. sec. Mont St.-Hilaire, Que., 1950-53; personnel mgr. Dupuis Freres (mail order house), 1953; editor Jeune Commerce, weekly tabloid Fedn. Que. Jr. C's. of C., 1953. Sec. gen. Montreal Jr. C. of C., 1953-56; asst. gen. mgr. Province Que. C. of C., Montreal, 1956-59, gen. mgr., 1959-71, exec. v.p., 1971-90. Author: Quebec, The Price of Independence, 1969, Report on Corporate Social Responsibilities, 1982. Mem. C. of C. Execs. Can. (pres. 1982-83, mem. coun. excellence 1986), Corp. Consellors in Indsl Rels. of Que., Am. C. of C. Execs. (bd. dirs. 1982-83), Can. Exec. Svc. Orgns. (bd. dirs. 1991-95, vice chair 1993-95), Office Persons Handicapped of Que. (bd. dirs. 1992-98, exec. com. 1994-98). Roman Catholic. Office: 165 Cote Ste-Catherine #202 Outremont QC Canada H2V 2A7 *Liberty is priceless; but liberty imposes responsibility, and if one is not responsible he will lose his liberty.*

LETOURNEAU, RICHARD HOWARD, retired college president; b. Stockton, Calif., Jan. 3, 1925; s. Robert G. and Evelyn (Peterson) LeT.; m. Louise Marion Jensen, Feb. 8, 1947; children: Robert Gilmore, Caleb Roy, Linda Louise, Liela Lynn. Student, Wheaton Coll., 1946, LeTourneau Coll., 1956; BS, Tex. A&M U., 1958, MS, 1961; PhD, Okla. State U., 1970. Gen. mgr. Miss. divsn. R.G. LeTourneau, Inc., Longview, Tex., 1949-52, v.p. prodn., 1952-57, exec. v.p., 1966, pres., 1966-71; sr. v.p. Marathon Mfg. Co., Houston, 1971-72, dir., 1971-76; pres. Mosley Machinery Co., Waco, Tex., 1972-73; v.p. LeTourneau Found., 1973-75; prof. bus. mgmt. Belhaven Coll., Jackson, Miss., 1993-99; pvt. practice Longview, 1999—. Mem. Tex. Indsl. Commn., 1959-66; adminstrv. v.p. LeTourneau Coll., 1958-62, pres., 1962-68, 75-85, chancellor, 1985-86, pres. emeritus, 1986—, chmn. bd. trustees, 1968-75; cons. to higher edn., 1986-93. Author: Management Plus, 1973, Keeping Your Cool in a World of Tension, 1975, Success Without Succeeding, 1976, Success Without Compromise, 1977, Democracy in Trouble, 1985, More Than Knowledge, 1985, Laws of Success for Christians, 1985, Finding Your Niche in Life, 1985, The Earthensteel Report, 2000, Leadership with Truth and Ethics, 2000. Past pres. LeTourneau Found. Served with C.E. AUS, 1944-46, PTO. Mem. Sigma Xi, Phi Kappa Phi, Tau Beta Pi, Alpha Pi Mu. Home and Office: 1205 Amherst Ln Longview TX 75601 E-mail: rhlet@juno.com. *As a successful industrialist, educator and author, I have found that life is more than mind and body. Everyone, to have a joyous and truly successful life must also trust Jesus Christ as Lord for a spiritual dimension and overall balance in life. With this element missing, regardless of the profession followed, life will be hollow and meaningless, and an eternity of regret is certain.*

LETSINGER, ROBERT LEWIS, chemistry educator; b. Bloomfield, Ind., July 31, 1921; s. Reed A. and Etna (Phillips) L.; m. Dorothy C. Thompson, Feb. 6, 1943; children: Louise, Reed, Sue. Student, Ind. U., 1939-41; BS, Mass. Inst. Tech., 1943, PhD, 1945; DSc (hon.), Acadia U., Can., 1993. Research assoc. MIT, 1945-46; research chemist Tenn. Eastman Corp., 1946; faculty Northwestern U., 1946—, prof. chemistry, 1959—, chmn. dept., 1972-75, joint prof. biochemistry and molecular biology, 1974—, Clare Hamilton Hall prof. chemistry, 1986-92, Clare Hamilton Hall prof. emeritus chemistry, 1992—; founder Nanosphere Inc., 2000—. Mem. med. and organic chemistry fellowship panel NIH, 1966-69, medicinal chem. A study sect., 1971-75; bd. on chem. scis. and tech. NRC, 1987-90. Mem. bd. editors Nucleic Acids Research, 1974-80; contbr. articles to profl. jours. Guggenheim fellow, 1956; JSPS fellow Japan, 1978; recipient Rosenstiel Medallion, 1985, Humboldt Sr. US Scientist award, 1988, NIH merit award, 1988, Arthur C. Cope scholar award, 1993, B.F. Goodrich Collegiate Inventors award, 1997. Fellow Am. Acad. Arts and Scis., Nat. Acad. Scis., Am. Assn. Arts and Scis.; mem. Am. Chem. Soc. (bd. editors 1969-72, bioconjugate chemistry 1992—), Internat. Union Pure and Applied Chemistry, Sigma Xi, Phi Lambda Upsilon (hon. mem.). Home: 1034 Sassafras Cir Bloomington IN 47408 Office: Northwestern U Chemistry Dept 2145 Sheridan Rd Evanston IL 60208-0834 E-mail: r-letsinger@chem.northwestern.edu.

LETSON, WILLIAM NORMAND, lawyer; b. N.Y.C., Mar. 24, 1930; s. Benjamin Hugle and Ellen (Skon) L.; m. Barbara C. Briggs, Jan. 22, 1956 (div. May 1980); children: Benjamin B., Katherine L., William C.; m. Brenda Powell, Oct. 10, 1981 (div. Oct. 1995); m. Linda White, Nov. 20, 1999. AB cum laude, Harvard U., 1952, JD magna cum laude, 1955. Bar: Ohio 1955, N.Y. 1956, D.C. 1973, Pa. 1975. Assoc. Shearman & Sterling, N.Y.C., 1955-62; ptnr. Letson, Letson & Kightlinger, Warren, Ohio, 1962-71; gen. counsel U.S. Dept. Commerce, Washington, 1971-73; v.p. gen. counsel, sec. Westinghouse Electric, Pitts., 1973-76; ptnr. Schiff, Hardin & Waite, Washington, 1977-79, Letson, Griffith, Woodall & Lavelle, Warren, Ohio, 1979-86, Letson & Jarrett, Warren, 1986-95, Letson, Griffith, Woodall Lavelle & Rosenberg, L.P.A., 1995—. Dir. HON Industries, Muscatine, Iowa, 1977-94; mem. Pres. Commn. on Personnel Interchange, Washington, 1976-80; mem. U.S.-USSR Sci. and Tech. Commn., Washington, 1972-73; mem. Harvard Law Review, 1953-55. Mem. State Com. to elect Clarence Brown Gov., 1982; mem. law sch. adv. com. U. Akron, 1981—. Mem. ABA, Ohio State Bar Assn., Warren Area C. of C. (dir. 1984-87), Duquesne Club, Fox Chapel Club (Pitts.), Trumbull Country Club, Buckeye Club (Warren). Republican. Avocations: skiing, sailing, fly fishing, tennis, golf. Home: 930 Fairway Dr NE Warren OH 44483-5640 Office: Letson Griffith Wooddall Lavelle & Rosenberg LPA PO Box 151 155 S Park Ave Warren OH 44482 E-mail: lawfirm@lgwlr.com.

LETSOU, GEORGE VASILIOS, cardiothoracic surgeon; b. Boston, 1958; s. Vasilios George and Helen (Valacellis) L.; m. Jane Elizabeth Carter, June 1, 1985; children: Christopher George, Philip Taylor, John Carter. AB magna cum laude, Harvard U., 1979; MD, Columbia U., 1983. Diplomate Am. Bd. Surgery, Am. Bd. Thoracic Surgery. Resident in gen. surgery Yale-New Haven Hosp., 1983—88, chief resident and instr. surgery, 1987—88, clin. fellow in cardiothoracic surgery, 1988—89, Cystic Fibrosis Found. fellow cardiopulm. transplantation, 1988—89, Winchester scholar in cardiothoracic surg. rsch., 1989—90, resident in cardiothoracic surgery, 1990—91, chief resident in cardiothoracic surgery, 1991—92; attending surgeon Yale U., 1992—95, instr. surgery, 1987-88, 91-92, asst. prof. surgery, 1992—95; attending surgeon Yale-New Haven Med. Ctr., 1992—95, Meth. Hosp., Ben Taub Hosp., Houston, 1995—; assoc. prof. surgery Baylor Coll. Medicine, 1995—99; attending surgeon Meml.-Hermann Hosp., 1998—; assoc. prof. surgery U. Tex., 1999—. Mem. AMA, ACS, Am. Coll. Cardiology, Am. Coll. Chest Physicians, Soc. Thoracic Surgeons. Office: Univ Tex-Houston Cardiothoracic Surgery 6431 Fannin St # 1214 Houston TX 77030-1501 Fax: 713-500-0650. E-mail: George.V.Letsou@uth.tmc.edu.

LETT, CYNTHIA ELLEN WEIN, speaker, trainer, coach; b. Takoma Park, Md., Dec. 24, 1957; d. Arthur Benjamin and Mary Louise (Barker) Wein; m. Gerald Lee Lett, June 1, 1991; 1 child, Cameron Barker Wein. BS, Purdue U., 1979; M, Antioch Sch. Law, 1982-83. Mktg. researcher Sheraton, Washington, 1979-80; sales mgr. Sea Pines Plantation Co., Hilton Head Island, S.C., 1980-81; dir. sales Sheraton Potomac Hotel, Rockville, Md., 1981-82, Ritz Carlton Hotel, Washington, 1982-83; pres. Creative Planning Internat., 1983—; dir. The Lett Group, 1996—. Dir. mem. Great Inns Am., Annapolis, 1987-89; etiquette cons., 1989—; dir. meetings Am. Healthcare Inst., 1991-92; corp. affairs mgr. MCI Telecom Corp., 1992-95; pres. The Lett Group, 1996—. Author: Getaway Innstyle, America's Fifty Best Inns, 1990; editor Travel Inn Style Newsletter, 1990-91, Apropos!, 1996—. Mem. ASTD, Profl. Conv. Mgmt. Assn., Found. for Internat. Meetings (bd. govs. 1985-86), Internat. Soc. Protocol and Etiquette Profls. (exec. dir.), Nat. Spkrs. Assn., Washington Conv. Visitors Assn., Purdue Club, Univ. Club. Avocations: classical music, amateur photography, country inns, foreign travel, gardening. Office: Lett Group 13116 Hutchinson Way Ste 100 Silver Spring MD 20906-5947 E-mail: clett@lettgroup.com.

LETT, JAMES CHANCEY, surgeon, retired; b. Knoxville, Aug. 3, 1931; MD, U. Tenn. Health Sci. Ctr., Memphis, 1955. Diplomate Am. Bd. Surgery. Intern Tenn. Hosp.-Rsch. Ctr., Knoxville, 1955-56; resident Harlan Appalachian Hosp., 1960-64; pvt. practice, Greencastle, Ind., 1964-74; chief surgery Trinity Hosp., Erin, Tenn., 1978-92, ret., 1992. Fellow ACS; mem. AMA, Tenn. Med. Assn., Knoxville Acad. Medicine, So. Med. Assn. Home: 652 Sedgley Dr Knoxville TN 37922-4362

LETT, MARK, editor; b. Detroit; m. Carole Lett; 1 child, Brent; 1 child from previous marriage, Courtney. Student, Ctrl. Mich. U.; BA in Journalism, Wayne State U. City editor The Detroit News, 1973-85, The Pitts. Press, 1985; dep. city editor Detroit Free Press, 1986-87; asst. mng. editor The Detroit News, 1986-87; editor Post-Tribune, Gary, Ind., 1996-98; exec. editor, responsible for newsgathering and presentation State of S.C., 1998—. Office: PO Box 1333 1401 Shop Rd Columbia SC 29202*

LETT, PHILIP WOOD, JR. defense consultant; b. Newton, Ala., May 4, 1922; s. Philip Wood Sr. and Lily Octavia (Kennedy) L.; m. Katy Lee Howell, June 26, 1948; children: Kathy, Warren, Lisa. B MechE, Ala. Poly. Inst., 1943; MS in Engring., U. Ala., 1947; PhD MechE, U. Mich., 1950; MS in Indsl. Mgmt., MIT, 1960. Registered profl. engr., Mich. Lab. engr., engring. div. Chrysler Corp., 1950-52, project engr., def. engring. div., 1952-54, chief engr., def. engring. div., 1954-61, operating mgr., def. engring. div., 1961-73, head XM1 Tank task force Mich., 1973-76; gen. mgr. Sterling Def. div. Chrysler Corp., 1976-79; v.p. engring. Chrysler Def. Inc., Center Line, Mich., 1980-82; v.p. research & engring. Gen. Dynamics Land Systems Div., 1982-86, v.p., asst. to gen. mgr., 1986-87; pres. PWL Inc., 1987—. Mem. U.S. delegation to NATO Indsl. Adv. Group. Contbr. articles to tech. jours. and to Internat. Def. Rev. Trustee Judson Ctr., 1989—. Capt. U.S. Army, 1943-46. Decorated Cheonsu medal Republic of Korea; awarded membership U.S. Nat. Acad. Engring., 1984; recipient Outstanding Engr. award Auburn U., 1984, Ben S. Gilmer award, 1991, Gold medal Am. Def. Preparedness Assn., 1997; named Disting. Engring. fellow U. Ala. Coll. Engring., 1992; elected to Ala. Engring. Hall of Fame, 1992; Sloan fellow MIT, 1960-61. Mem. Orchard Lake Country Club. Baptist. Home: 1330 Oxford Rd Bloomfield Hills MI 48304-3952 Office: PO Box 2074 Warren MI 48090-2074

LETTICH, SHELDON BERNARD, director, screenwriter; b. N.Y.C., Jan. 14, 1951; s. Max and Sonja (Shapelska) L.; m. Toni Dorthera Williams, Mar. 5, 1954; children: Micheline, Jessica, Angelique. Student, Brooks Inst., Santa Barbara, Calif., 1974; AA, Santa Monica Coll., 1974-76; student, Am. Film Inst., Beverly Hills, 1977-78. Author: (with others) play Tracers, 1980 (Los Angeles Drama Critics award, 1981), film Russkies, 1987, Rambo III, 1988; author: film Bloodsport, 1988; dir., writer films Lionheart, 1990, Only the Strong, 1993; dir., writer, co-prodr. film Double Impact, 1991; dir. films Perfect Target, 1996, The Last Patrol, 2000, The Order, 2001; writer, exec. prodr. film Legionnaire, 1999. Served to cpl. U.S.M.C., 1969-72, Vietnam. Mem. Dirs. Guild Am., Writers Guild Am. Office: Hard Corps Prodns Inc Ste 1060 10100 Santa Monica Blvd Los Angeles CA 90067-4100

LETTIERI, RICHARD J(OSEPH), lawyer; b. Chelsea, Mass., May 29, 1947; s. Rosario and Genevieve Helen (Sokoloski) L. AB in History, Villanova U., 1969; JD, Boston Coll., 1974. Bar: Mass. 1975, U.S. Dist. Ct. Mass. 1975, U.S. Ct. Appeals (1st cir.) 1979, U.S. Ct. Appeals (D.C. cir.) 1985. Pvt. practice, Boston, 1975-77; staff atty. Mass. Port Authority, 1977-81, chief legal counsel, 1981-86; assoc. Ropes & Gray, 1987-90, ptnr., 1990—. Mem. Boston Bar Assn., Justinian Law Soc. Office: Ropes & Gray 1 International Pl Fl 4 Boston MA 02110-2624

LETTON, ALVA HAMBLIN, surgeon, educator; b. Tampa, Fla., May 23, 1916; s. James Hervey and Minerva (Hamblin) L.; m. Roberta Rogers, Oct. 7, 1938; children: Robert Hamblin (dec.), Alice Roberta Zachodski. Student, U. Tampa, 1933-35, U. Fla., 1935-37; MD, Emory U., 1941. Diplomate Am. Bd. Surgery. Intern Ga. Baptist Hosp., Atlanta, 1941-42, resident, 1942-43; pvt. practice medicine specializing gen. surgery (oncology) Atlanta, 1946—; chief staff, attending surgeon Ga. Bapt. Hosp., 1965-73; sr. mem. Letton and Mason Surgery, Atlanta, 1980-95; dir. breast cancer demonstration project Bapt. Med. Ctr., 1972-78, chmn. exec. com. oncology dept. 1972-78; clin. prof. surgery Med. Coll. Ga.; A. Hamblin Letton chair surg. oncology Ga. Bapt. Med. Ctr., 1990—; founder Atlanta Cancer Ctr. Vis. prof. Egypt Cancer Inst., 1985, Med. and Dental Sch. N.J., 1986, Coll. Medicine U. Ill., Peoria, 1990; cons. Cobb. Gen. Grady Meml., Scottish Rite hosps.; chmn. cancer task force a. Regional Med. Program, 1966—71; mem. Ga. Sci. and Tech. Com., 1969—70; active Am. Cancer Soc., 1947—, nat. chmn. pub. edn., 1965—68, nat. chmn. svc. com., 1968—69, nat. chmn. med. and sci. com., 1969—70, v.p., nat. pres. elect, 1970—71, nat. pres., 1971—72, hon. bd. dirs. life, 1979—; pres. Atlanta Med. Ctr., 1965—90, Atlanta Health Evaluation Ctr., 1973—82; mem. Gov.'s Sci. Adv. Coun., 1972—75, U.S. nat. com. NAS, 1976—79; Roswell Park Meml. lectr., 1983; A. Hamblin Letton ann. lectr. Southeastern Surg. Congress, 1985—; bd. judges Criss Award; mem. Ethicon Gen. Surg. Adv. Panel, 1975—85; mem. cancer control adv. com. Nat. Cancer Inst., 1975—79; chmn. first cancer postgrad. course USA/USSR/ Union Internat. Contre Cancer, Leningrad, Former Soviet Union, 1999; mem. profl. edn. com. Union Internat. Contre Cancer, 1966—78; cons., Budapest, Hungary, 1986; cons. to exec. sec., Budapest, Hungary, 72; cons. to forming Russian Cancer Soc., 1991—93; vis. prof. Pacific N.W. Cancer Found., 1998; mem. adv. bd. Ga. U. Sys., 1999—. Mem. editorial bd. Internat. Advances in Surg. Oncology, Jour. Cancer Prevention and Detection, 1985—; chmn. editorial bd. Oncology Times, 1979-90; guest editor Seminars in Surg. Oncology; contbr. articles to profl. jours., films. Deacon Bapt. ch. With M.C. USNR, 1943-46. Recipient Presdl. citation, 1944, Aven Citizenship award Fulton County Med. Soc., 1960, Honor Alumnus award Emory U., 1973, Hardman award Med. Assn. Ga., 1973, highest award John Muir Med. Film Festival, 1978; Disting. Svc. award Am. Cancer Soc., 1980, Nat. divsn. award, 1986, Vaughn award Ga. divsn., 1987; Atlanta Cmty. Svc. award, 2000. Fellow: ACS, Southeastern Surg. Congress (hon.; sec.-dir 1960—86, Disting. Svc. award 1982); mem.: Letton Cancer Found. (pres. 1999), Soc. Internat. de Chirugie, Am. Thyroid Assn., Soc. Nuclear Medicine, So. Surg. Assn., Soc. Surg. Oncology, Univ. Yacht Club (Flowery Branch, Ga.), Capital City Club (Atlanta). Baptist. Home: 3747 Peachtree Rd NE Apt 1508 Atlanta GA 30319-1374 Office: 315 Boulevard NE Atlanta GA 30312-1200

LETTOW, CHARLES FREDERICK, lawyer; b. Iowa Falls, Iowa, Feb. 10, 1941; s. Carl Frederick and Catherine (Reisinger) L.; m. Sue Lettow, Apr. 20, 1963; children: Renee, Carl II, John, Paul. BS in Chem. Engring., Iowa State U., 1962; LLB, Stanford U., 1968; MA, Brown U., 2001. Bar: Calif. 1969, Iowa 1969, D.C. 1972, Md. 1991. Law clk. to Hon. Ben C. Duniway U.S. Ct. Appeals (9th cir.), San Francisco, 1968-69; law clk. to Hon. Warren E. Burger U.S. Supreme Ct., Washington, 1969-70; counsel Council on Environ. Quality, 1970-73; assoc. Cleary, Gottlieb, Steen & Hamilton, 1973-76, ptnr., 1976—. Pres. Busy Way Farms, Inc., 1989—. Contbr. articles to profl. jours. Trustee Potomac Sch., McLean, Va., 1983-90, chmn. bd. trustees, 1985-88. 1st lt. U.S. Army, 1963-65. Mem. ABA, Am. Law Inst., D.C. Bar, Iowa Bar Assn., Order of Coif. Clubs: University. Office: 2000 Pennsylvania Ave NW Washington DC 20006-1801 E-mail: clettow@cgsh.com.

LETTS, LINDSAY GORDON, pharmacologist, educator; b. Warragul, Victoria, Australia, Jan. 9, 1948; came to U.S., 1987; m. Barbara Dawn Hawkey, Sept. 13, 1969; children: Michelle Maree, Kathryn Jane, David Gordon. BS, Monash U., Australia, 1971; PhD, Sydney U., 1980. Tutor Sydney (Australia) U., 1976-80; rsch. scientist Royal Coll. Surgeons Eng., London, 1980-82; sr. rsch. fellow Merck Frosst Can. Inc., 1982-87; dir. pharmacology Boehringer Ingelheim Pharms., Inc., Ridgefield, Conn., 1987-93; v.p. rsch. NitroMed Inc., Cambridge, Mass., 1993-96, chief sci. officer, sr. v.p. R&D, 1997—. Adj. assoc. prof. Yale U. Sch. Medicine, New Haven, 1991-94. Editor Mediators of Inflammation, 1992-98, Pulmonary Pharmacology and Therapeutics, 1992—; sect. editor Prostaglandins, 1986—; editor Inflammation Rsch., 1994—. Bd. dirs. Nat. Inst. for Community Health Edn., Quinnipiac Coll., Hamden, Conn., 1990-94, Conn. United Rsch. Excellence, Wallingford, 1991-94. Mem.: Internat. Assn. Inflammation Socs. (v.p. 2001—), Inflammation Rsch. Assn. (bd. dirs. 1992—, pres. 1996—98). Office: NitroMed Inc 12 Oak Park Dr Ste 2 Bedford MA 01730-1426 E-mail: gletts@nitromed.com.

LETTVIN, THEODORE, concert pianist; b. Chgo., Oct. 29, 1926; s. Solomon and Fannie (Naktin) L.; m. Joan Rorimer; children: Rory, Ellen, David. Mus. B., Curtis Inst. Music, 1949; postgrad., U. Pa., U. N.H., U. Calif., San Jose, Fla. State U. Head piano dept. Cleve. Music Sch. Settlement, 1957-68; prof. piano New Eng. Conservatory Music, Boston, 1968-77; prof., dir., doctoral program in piano performance U. Mich. Sch. Music, Ann Arbor, 1977-87; disting. prof. dept. music Rutgers U., New Brunswick, N.J., 1987-98, dir. doctor of mus. arts and artist's diploma program, 1987-92, studio tchr., coach chamber music, 1992-98. Vis. lectr. U. Colo., 1956-57; tchr. master classes U. S.E. Mass., summer 1973, U. Calif., San Jose, 1992, 93; mem. faculty Chamber Music Sch., U. Maine, Orono. First appeared as concert pianist, 1931, solo debut with Chgo. Symphony Orch., 1939, solo, orchestral appearances include Boston Symphony Orch., N.Y. Philharm., Phila. Orch., Cleve. Orch., Chgo. Orch., Washington Nat. Symphony, Pitts. Symphony, Seattle Symphony, Mpls. Symphony, Atlanta Symphony, other Am. and European orchs.; radio appearance Bell Telephone Hour, 1948, debut Ravinia Festival, 1951, apprentice condr. William Steinberg, Buffalo Symphony Orch., 1950-51, concertized throughout U.S., Can., Europe, Africa, 1952-85; concert appearances Pitts., Cin., Atlanta, Boston, N.Y.C., Phila., Chgo., Cleve., Mpls. and Chautauqua, Ravinia, Interlochen and New Coll., Town Hall, Alice Tully Hall concerts, in N.Y.C., Boston Symphony Orch.; performances in concert with Bernard Greenhouse, cellist; concert tours, Europe, 1952, 55, 58, 60, 62-85, Israel, 1973, Africa and Japan, 1974; also numerous performances with European orchs., summer festivals, TV; asst. artist: Africa and Japan, Marlboro Music Festival, 1963. Recipient award Soc. Am. Musicians, 1933, Naumberg award, 1948, Michaels Meml. award, 1949, Laureate internat. piano competition Queen Elisabeth of Belgium. Mem. Am. Fedn. Musicians, Am. Guild Mus. Artists, AAUP (exec. com.), Music Tchrs. Nat. Assn., Am. Liszt Soc., Curtis Inst. Music Alumnae Assn. (bd. dirs.). Home: 463 Rowe Mountain Rd Bradford NH 03221-3408 E-mail: tjlettvin@juno.com.

LETWIN, JEFFREY WILLIAM, lawyer; b. Pitts., Nov. 26, 1953; s. Myron Harvey and Phyllis Harriet (Unatin) L.; m. Roberta Lee Rosenbloom, July 24, 1983; 1 child, S. Ari; stepchildren: Andrew B. Filipek, Amanda H. Filipek. BA in History and Lit., U. Pitts., 1975; JD, Am. U., 1979. Bar: Pa. 1980, D.C. 1980. Staff atty. Dept. Justice, Washington, 1979-80; assoc. Gilloti, Goldberg & Capristi, Pitts., 1980-83, Finkel, Lefkowitz & Ostrow, Pitts., 1983-85, Rosenberg & Kirshner, Pitts., 1986-94; assoc., v.p. Doepken Keevican & Weiss, 1994—, also bd. dirs. Lectr. Pa. Bar Inst., 1983, 87, 88; mem. Pitts. High Tech. Council, 19855, Enterprise Group, Pitts., 19855; arbitrator N.Y. Stock Exch; solicitor Allegheny County Airport Authority, 19995. Bd. dirs. Holocaust Commn., Pitts., 19835, Jewish Family and Children's Svc., Pitts., 1983-86, Cmty. Coll. Allegheny County Found., Allegheny County Sanitary Authority, 20005; bd. dirs. United Jewish Fedn., Pitts., 1984-86, 985, chmn. young bus. and profl. divsn., 1985-87, chmn. exec. and profl. divsn. 1987-88; mem. Young Leadership Cabinet USA, 1984-87; participant Leadership Pitts., 19895; chmn. Holocaust Commn. of Greater Pitts., 1991-94, Pitts. Israel C. of C. 1991-97; commr. City of Pitts. Planning Commn., 19965; bd. dirs. Pitts. Film Office, 19965, Leadership Pitts., Jewish Assn. on Aging, 19975 ; v.p. C.C. of Allegheny County Edn. Found., 19965; mem. exec. com. United Jewish Fedn., 19975; solicitor Allegheny County Airport Authority, 1999—; bd. dirs. Allegheny County Sanitary Authority, 2000—. Named one of Outstanding Young Men in Am., 1985; recipient Stark Young Leadership award, 1989. Mem. ABA, Pa. Bar Assn., D.C. Bar Assn., Alleghany County Bar Assn. (bus., banking, and comml. sect., continuing legal edn. com.), Nat. Assn. Securities Dealers (arbitrator). Democrat. Jewish. Avocations: golf, tennis, films. Office: Doepken Keevican 5800 USX Tower Pittsburgh PA 15219

LETWIN, LEON, law educator; b. Milw., Dec. 29, 1929; s. Lazar and Bessie (Rosenthal) L.; m. Alita Zurav, July 11, 1952; children— Michael, Daniel, David Ph.B., U. Chgo., 1950; LL.B., U. Wis., 1952; LL.M., Harvard U., 1964. Bar: Wis. 1952, Calif. 1969. Teaching fellow Harvard Law Sch., Boston, 1963-64; faculty Law Sch. UCLA, 1964—, prof., 1968-92, prof. emeritus, 1993—. Coord. Native-Am. Grave Protection and Repatriation Act, UCLA, 1998—2002. Contbr. articles to profl. jours. Active ACLU. Mem. Lawyers Guild, State Bar Calif. Home: 2226 Manning Ave Los Angeles CA 90064-2002 Office: UCLA Law Sch 405 Hilgard Ave Los Angeles CA 90095-9000

LETZ, EILEEN KORBER, retired community health nurse; b. Custer, Mont., Dec. 31, 1916; d. Louis Charles and Gertrude Helen (Jackman) Korber; m. Arthur P. Letz, May 17, 1941 (dec.); children: Philip, Richard, Nancy. RN, Bozeman Deaconess Hosp., 1939; BSN, Mont. State U., 1964; MPH, U. Hawaii, 1968. RN, Mont. Supr. surg. fl. Billings (Mont.) Deaconess Hosp., 1952-56; community health nurse Yellowstone County, Billings, 1964-67, 68-70; community health nurse Ft. Peck reservation Indian Health Svc., Poplar, Mont., 1970-72, community health nurse Crow reservation Crow Agency, 1972-75, nursing cons., program mgr. cmty. health nursing Billings, 1975-82, ret., 1982. Mem. Mont. league for Nursing (bd. dirs. 1980-84, 91-92, v.p. 1984-91), Am. Assn. Ret. Persons. Democrat. Seventh Day Adventist. Avocations: bowling, hiking, history, card playing. Home: 2820 Oakland Dr Apt 19 Billings MT 59102-3766

LEUBERT, ALFRED OTTO PAUL, international business consultant, investor; b. N.Y.C., Dec. 7, 1922; s. Paul T. and Josephine (Haaga) L.; m. Celestine Capka, July 22, 1944 (div. 1977); children: Eloise Ann Cronin, Susan Beth; m. Hope Sherman Drapkin, June 4, 1978 (div. 1982). Student, Dartmouth Coll., 1943; BS, Fordham U., 1946; MBA, NYU, 1950. Account mgr. J.K. Lasser & Co., N.Y.C., 1948-52; controller Vision, Inc., 1952-53, Old Town Corp., 1953-54, sec., controller, 1954-56, sec.-treas., 1956-57, v.p., treas., 1957-58; dir. subsidiaries Old Town Corp. (Old Town Internat. Corp., Old Town Ribbon & Carbon Co., Inc.), Mass. and Calif., 1955-58; v.p., controller Willcox & Gibbs, Inc., N.Y.C., 1958-59, v.p., treas., 1959-65, pres., dir., CEO, 1966-76; founder, pub., pres. Leubert's Compendium of Bus. (Fin. and Econ. Barometers), 1978-82; pres. Alfred O.P. Leubert Ltd., 1981-82, chmn. CEO, 1993—; chmn., CEO Solidyne, Inc., 1982; chmn. bd., pres., CEO, dir. Chyron Corp., 1983-91; dir. K & E Real Estate Ltd., China, 1994-96; chmn. bd. CEO Leubert & Co. (H.K.) Ltd., 1994-98; dir. Laser-Pacific Media Corp., 1995-96; chmn. bd., CEO, bd. dirs. Chyron Group (U.K.) Ltd., 1985-89; dir. Isis Interactive Inc., 1996—; dir., vice chrmn. Advanced Definition Systems, Inc., 1996-97; chmn. bd., CEO, bd. dirs. CMX Corp., 1983-91; bd. dirs. Aurora Sys., 1988-91; dir. Avid Nordic AB, 1997-2000; strategic advisor PlasmaNet, Inc., 1999—, Tru-You.Com, Inc., 2000—01, Dir. Media, Inc., 2000-2001. CEO, dir. CGS Units, Inc., 1988-90, chmn. bd., 1989-90; bd. dirs. Digital Svcs. Corp.; vice chmn. bd. dirs. CMX Laser Sys., Inc., 1988-93; instr. accountancy Pace Coll., 1955-57. Bd. dirs. United Fund of Manhasset, 1963-69, pres., 1964-65; bd. dirs. Actor's Studio, 1972-76; adv. bd. St. Anthony's Guidance Clinic, 1967-69. Served to capt. USMCR, 1943-46. Decorated Bronze Star; recipient Humanitarian award Hebrew Acad., N.Y.C., 1971 Mem. AICPA, N.Y. State Soc. CPAs, Fordham U. Alumni Assn., N.Y. Athletic Club. Roman Catholic. Home and Office: 1 Lincoln Plz New York NY 10023-7129

LEUBSDORF, CARL PHILIPP, publishing executive; b. N.Y.C., Mar. 17, 1938; s. Carl Philipp and Bertha (Boschwitz) Leubsdorf; m. Carolyn Cleveland Stockmeyer, Mar. 26, 1963 (div. 1978); children: Carl Philipp Jr., E. William Jr. Stockmeyer, C. Cleveland Stockmeyer, Claire C. Goodwin1 stepchild Loma Stockmeyer ; m. Susan Page, May 23, 1982; children: Benjamin Page, William Page. BA in Govt., Cornell U., 1959; MS in Jour., Columbia U., 1960. Staff writer AP, New Orleans, 1960-63, Washington, 1963-75; corr. Balt. Sun, 1976-81; Washington bur. chief Dallas Morning News, 1981—. Recipient Columbia Journalism Sch. Alumni award, 1999. Mem.: Nat. Press Club (Washington), White Ho. Corrs. Assn. (pres. 1995—96), Gridiron Club. Office: Dallas Morning News 1325 G St NW Ste 250 Washington DC 20005-3115

LEUCHTMAN, STEPHEN NATHAN, lawyer; b. Detroit, Oct. 14, 1945; s. Alexis C. and Frances J. (Boucher) L.; m. Jacque Ward, Nov. 29, 1991; children: Stephen, John II, Lucinda. BA, U. Mich., 1967, JD, 1970. Bar: Mich. 1970, Calif. 1993, U.S. Dist. Ct. (ea. and so. dists.) Mich. 1970, U.S. Ct. Appeals (6th cir.) 1982. Assoc. Eggenberger, Eggenberger, McKinney & Weber, Detroit, 1970-75, Tyler & Canham, Detroit, 1975-80; ptnr. Sommers, Schwartz, Silver & Schwartz, Southfield, 1980-97; founding ptnr. Trowbridge Law Firm, P.C., Detroit, 1997-2001; atty. Stephen N. Leuchtman, P.C., 2001—. Contbr. articles to profl. jours. Mem. ABA, ATLA, Am. Bd. Trial Advocates, Million Dollar Advocates Forum, Consumer Attys. of Calif., Mich. Bar Assn., Calif. Bar Assn. Democrat. Avocations: writing, golf, travel. Home: 241 Strathmore Rd Bloomfield Hills MI 48304-3667 Office: 1380 E Jefferson Ave Detroit MI 48207 E-mail: snl2@mediaone.net.

LEUCK, MARK JOSEPH, lawyer; b. Kenosha, Wis., Mar. 8, 1953; s. Donald and Jeanette Leuck; m. Rosanne M. Stella, Aug. 3, 1974; children: Vanessa, Matthew. BA, U. Wis., Kenosha, 1974; JD, Harvard U., 1977. Bar: Wis. 1977. Assoc. Heide, Hartley, Tom, Wilk & Guttormsen, Kenosha, 1977-83; ptnr. Schoone, Leuck, Kelley, Pitts & Knurr, S.C., Racine, Wis., 1983—. Mem. Urban League, Racine, 1992-94; trustee St. Joseph H.S., Kenosha, 1999-2001. Mem. ABA, ATLA, State Bar Wis., Wis. Acad. Trial Lawyers. Home: 3615 13th St Kenosha WI 53144 Office: 6800 Washington Ave Racine WI 53406-3928

LEUKEFELD, CARL GEORGE, researcher, educator; b. Lake Forest, Ill., May 14, 1943; s. Karl Frederick (Stepmother) and Berta (Link) Leukefeld. BS, Mo. Valley Coll., 1965; MSW, U. Mich., 1967; DSW, Cath. U. Am., 1975; cert., Harvard Sch. Pub. Health, 1980. Program dir. Boys Club, Pontiac, Mich., 1966; commd. lt. USPHS, 1967, advanced through grades to capt., 1980, mental health officer, 1967-71, mental health adv. Rockville, Md., 1971-73, staff asst., then spl. asst. Nat. Inst. on Drug Abuse, 1975-77, dep. dir., acting dir. divsn. of resource devel., 1978-81, dep. dir., then dir. divsn. prevention and treatment devel., 1981-82, acting dir., dep. dir. divsn. clin. rsch., 1982-90; prof. psychiatry and behavioral sci., dir. Ctr. Drug and Alcohol Rsch. U. Ky., Lexington, 1990—; chair dept. behavior sci.U. Ky. Coll. Medicine, 2001. Prin. investigator AIDS Rsch. NIH, 1993; prin. investigator Inst. for Women Substance Abuse Treatment, 1993, Ky. State Substance Abuse Needs Assessment, Drug Addictions Treatment, 1995, 98, Structured Behavior Therapy, 1996, Health Svcs. Used by Chronic Drug Users, 1997, Enhancing Drug Count Employment, 1999, HIV Reduction for Rural Probationers, 2000; detailed to Naval Mil. Pers. Command, 1983; chief health svcs. officer USPHS, 1984—89, chair social work career devel. com., 1982, chair social work profl. adv. subcom., 83; mem. Intra-Agy. Task Force Emergency Preparedness, 1987—90; adj. faculty Va. Commonwealth U., 1986—90. Decorated Commendation medal, , Outstanding Svc. medal, Meritorious Svc. medal; named Hon. Order Ky. Cols., State Ky., 1990; recipient Pub. Health Svc. citation, 1988, 1990, Torch award, Am. Humanics Found., 1978, Disting. Alumni award, Cath. U. Am., 1994. Mem.: APHA, AAAS, NASW (chmn. health and mental health commn. 1985—87, co-chair fund devel. Whitham/Knee awards), Am. Probation and Parole Assn., Family Counseling Svc. (bd. dirs. 1997—99), Prevention Rsch. Inst. (bd. dirs.), Soc. Clin. Social Workers (bd. dirs. Bluegrass chpt. 1990—92), Am. Correctional Assn., Social Work Coun., Commd. Officers Assn. USPHS (bd. dirs. 1984—90), Assn. Mil. Surgeons (chmn. med. svc. corp. sect. 1987), Nat. Acads. Practice, Acad. Cert. Social Workers, Pi Gamma Mu, Alpha Phi Omega, Tau Kappa Epsilon. Presbyterian. Home: 1121 Sheffield Pl Lexington KY 40509-2018 Office: U Ky Coll Medicine 643 Maxwelton Ct Lexington KY 40508-4012 E-mail: cleukef@pop.uky.edu.

LEUNG, ALEXANDER KWOK-CHU, pediatrician; b. Hong Kong, Oct. 1, 1948; s. Ping and Wai (Tai) Leung; children: Albert, Alex Jr., Amy, Alan, Andrew. MB BS, U. Hong Kong, 1973; DCH, Royal Coll. Physicians London, 1977, Royal Coll. Physicians Ireland, 1979. Intern U. Hong Kong, 1973-74; lectr. in child health U. Queensland, Brisbane, Australia, 1977; resident in pediat. U. Calgary, Alta., Can., 1974-77, fellow in pediat. endocrinology, 1978-80, clin. asst. prof. pediat., 1980-90, cons. Univ. Med. Info. Svc., 1988—, clin. assoc. prof. pediat., 1990—; med. dir. Asian Med. Ctr. in affiliation with U. Calgary Med. Clin., 1994—; cons. pediat. Alta. Children's Hosp., Calgary, 1980—. Hon. advisor Am. Biog. Inst. Rsch., Raleigh, NC, 1987—, Internat. Biog. Ctr., Cambridge, England, 1988—; examiner Med. Coun. Can. Qualifying Examination. : mem. editl. bd. Advances in Therapy, 1995—, : mem. editl. bd. Can. Clin. Jour. Medicine, Med. Scope Monthly, 1996—2000; contbr. articles to profl. jours, chapters to books. Recipient Physician Recognition award, AMA, 1985, 1988, 1990, 1993, 1996, Gold Medal award, Am. Biog. Inst., 1992. Fellow: Can. Pediat. Soc., Am. Acad. Pediat. (PREP fellow award 1987, 1990, 1996), Royal Coll. Physicians (London), Royal Coll. Physicians and Surgeons Glasgow, Royal Coll. Physicians Ireland, Royal Coll. Physicians Can., Royal Coll. Pediats. and Child Health, Royal Coll. Physicians Edinburgh, Royal Acad. Medicine, Royal Soc. Health (Eng.); mem.: Royal Soc. New Zealand. Office: # 200 233-16th Ave NW Calgary AB Canada T2M OH5

LEUNG, BETTY BRIGID, nursing administrator; b. Shanghai, People's Rep. China, Oct. 28, 1949; d. Chek Sang and Si Iun (Vong) L. Diploma, St. James Sch. Nursing, 1974; BSN, Hunter-Bellevue Sch. Nursing, 1985; MS in Nursing, CUNY, 1989. Nurse ICU St. James Mercy Hosp., Hornell, N.Y., 1974-80; sr. staff ICU NYU Med. Ctr., N.Y.C., 1980-81, nurse clinician, 1981-85, asst. clin. coord., 1985-88, clin. coord., 1988-91, nursing supr., 1991-97, organ transplant coord., 1997-98; clin. coord. White Plains (N.Y.) Hosp. Ctr., 1998-2001, nurse mgr., 2001—. St. James Sch. Nursing scholar, 1972-74; recipient Women's Bd. award, 1974, Therese Cornell Meehan Nursing Rsch. award 1990. Mem. AACN, Am. Orgn. Nurse Execs. Roman Catholic. Avocations: photography, travel, collecting coins and stamps. Office: White Plains Hosp Ctr Davis Ave at E Post Rd White Plains NY 10601 E-mail: bleung@stellarishealth.org.

LEUNG, CHARLES CHEUNG-WAN, technological company executive; b. Hong Kong, June 27, 1946; came to U.S., 1969; s. Mo-Fan and Lai-Ping (Tam) L.; m. Jessica Lan Lee, Sept. 1, 1972; children: Jennifer W., Cheryl E., Albert H. BS with spl. honors, U. Hong Kong, 1969; PhD, U. Chgo., 1976. Sr. staff scientist Corning (N.Y.) Glass Ctrl. Lab., 1975-79; sr. mem. tech. staff Motorola, Mesa, Ariz., 1979-81; engring. mgr. Avantek, Santa Clara, Calif., 1981-88; chmn., pres. Bipolarics Inc., Los Gatos, 1981—. Mem. IEEE, Am. Phys. Soc., Am. Vacuum Soc., Asian Am. Mfrs. Assn. Achievements include patent on wafer planarization technology; developed fastest silicon transistor, widest bandwidth microwave oscillator 2-20 GHz; inventor of silicon microwave monolithic integrated circuit technology for communication. Office: Bipolarics Inc 46766 Lakeview Blvd Fremont CA 94538-6529

LEUNG, FIRMAN, investment bank executive; b. N.Y.C., Nov. 15, 1957; s. Kwok Choy and Moo-Kit (Tsui) L.; m. Mary Elizabeth Gose, July 23, 1988; children: Anthony, Philip. BS, The Wharton Sch., 1979; MBA, Amos Tuck Sch., 1985. Product mgr. Citibank, N.A., N.Y.C., 1979-80; assoc. Morgan Stanley & Co. Inc., 1980-83; v.p. Merrill Lynch & Co., 1985-91; mng. dir. Serfin Securities, 1991-94; dir. Salomon Bros. Inc., 1994—. Mem. N.Y. Athletic Club. Republican. Home: 28 Meadow Rd Scarsdale NY 10583-7640 Office: Salomon Smith Barney 390 Greenwich St New York NY 10013-2375

LEUNG, FRANKIE FOOK-LUN, lawyer; b. Guangzhou, China, 1949; married; 1 child. BA in Psychology with honors, Hong Kong U., 1972; MS in Psychology, Birmingham U., Eng., 1974; BA, MA in Jurisprudence, Oxford U., Eng., 1976; JD, Coll. of Law, London, 1977. Bar: Calif. 1987. Barrister, Eng. and Hong Kong, 1977—. Lectr. Chinese law for businessmen Hong Kong U., 1984-85, 85-86; vis. scholar Harvard U. Law Sch., 1983; barrister, solicitor Supreme Ct. of Victoria, Australia, 1983—, Calif. Bar, 1987—; cons. prof. Chinese Law Diploma Program, U. East Asia, 1986-87; adj. prof. Loyola Law Sch., L.A., 1988-2000, Pepperdine U. Law Sch., 1989-90; lectr. Stanford U. Law Sch., 1995-96, U. So. Calif. Law Sch., 1998—. Author books on Chinese and Hong Kong law, Asian politics, Asian trade and bus. mgmt.; contbr. numerous articles to profl. jours., and 6 books. Bd. advisors Hong Kong Archives Hoover Inst.-Stanford U., 1988—; adv., Central Policy Unit, Hong Kong govt., 1997-99, dir. YMCA, Pasadena, Calif., 1997-99. Mem. Am. Arbitration Assn. (bd. dirs.), Calif. State Bar (mem. exec. coun. internat. sect. 1989-92, Wiley W. Manuel award 1993), Hong Kong Bar Assn., European Assn. for Chinese Law (mem. exec. coun. 1986—, country corr. 1985—), Am. C. of C. (chmn. subcom. on Chinese intellectual property law 1985-86), Am. Soc. Internat. Law (judge moot ct. 1984-96). Office: 444 S Flower St Fl 31 Los Angeles CA 90071-2901 Fax: 213-228-8923. E-mail: frankieleunglaw@aol.com.

LEUNG, JACKSON YI-SHUN, music educator; b. Hong Kong, Dec. 27, 1959; arrived in U.S., 1981; s. Pui-Yan Leung and Chi-Tak Tse; m. Benita Wan-Quan Tse, Aug. 11, 1984; 1 child Benjamin. BMus, Hong Kong Bapt. U., 1981; MMus, Temple U., 1984; DMA, U. Cin., 1990. Performer's diploma Associated Bd. Royal Schs. Music, Eng., 1979. Lectr. preparatory dept. U. Cin., 1986—91, lectr., Evening Coll., 1989—91; asst. prof. music Wright State U., Dayton, Ohio, 1991—97, assoc. prof. music, coord. keyboard studies, dir. chamber orch., 1997—. Co-dir. Leung Piano Studios, West Chester, Ohio, 1991—; music dir. Cin. Chinese Ch., Mt. Healthy, Ohio, 1984—95. Performer (CD): Danzas, 2001; contbr. articles to profl. jours. Recipient Grand prize, Mo. So. Internat. Piano Competition, Joplin, 1988, 2d prize, Young Keyboard Artist Assn. Internat. Competition, Ann Arbor, Mich., 1988; grantee Profl. Devel. grant, Wright State U. Rsch. Coun., 1994—2002. Mem.: Nat. Fedn. Music Clubs (nat. cert.), Music Educators Nat. Conf. (nat. cert.), Music Tchrs. Nat. Assn. (nat. cert.). Avocations: reading, collecting CDs, travel. Home: 8377 Meadowlark Dr West Chester OH 45069 Office: Wright State U Dept Music 3640 Colonel Glenn Hwy Dayton OH 45435

LEUNG, KASON KAI CHING, computer specialist; b. Hong Kong, July 2, 1962; came to U.S., 1963; s. Patrick Kin Man and Esther Mo Chee (Shum) L. BA in Computer Sci., U. Calif., 1984. Microcomputer specialist Coopers & Lybrand, San Francisco, 1985-87; freelance computer specialist, 1988-90; computer applications specialist T.Y. Lin Internat., 1990-92; tech. specialist Ziff-Davis Labs., Foster City, Calif., 1993-94; tech. analyst PC Mag., 1995; sr. tech. analyst Ziff-Davis Benchmark Operation, 1996; sr. tech. specialist Ziff-Davis Labs., 1997-98; sys. adminstr. TurboLinux, Inc., Brisbane, 1999; sys. programmer II Office of the Pres., U. Calif., Oakland, 2000—. Mem. Assn. for Computing Machinery. Avocations: computers, sports, music, reading. Home: 90 Stanford Heights Ave San Francisco CA 94127-2318 E-mail: kason.leung@ucop.edu., kasonleung@earthlink.net.

LEUNG, LAWRENCE LIT-KING, physician; b. Hong Kong, Mar. 21, 1949; m. Jean D. Leung; children: Thomas H., Rita K. BS with honors, McGill U., Que., Can., 1971; MD, Columbia U., 1975. Diplomate Am. Bd. Internal Medicine, Am. Bd. Hematology, Am. Bd. Med. Oncology. Intern, resident N.Y. Hosp.-Cornell Med. Ctr., 1975-78; asst. prof. medicine Stanford U. Med. Sch., Palo Alto, Calif., 1985-91, assoc. prof., 1991—2002, chief divsn. hematology, 1995—, prof., 2002—. Dir. vascular biology Gilead Scis., Inc., Foster City, Calif., 1992-94, mem. sci. adv. bd., 1995—. Mem. Am. Soc. Clin. Investigation, Am. Soc. Hematology. Office: Stanford U Sch Med Divsn Hem CCSR 1155 269 Campus Dr Stanford CA 94305-5156 E-mail: lawrence.leung@stanford.edu.

LEUNG, PAUL, psychologist, rehabilitation educator; b. Jackson, Mich., Dec. 1, 1941; s. Chiu Sang and Rose (Chan) L.; m. Wendy Lee Ong, Sept. 5, 1965. BS, Calif. Bapt. Coll., Riverside, 1963; MA, Ariz. State U., 1967, PhD, 1970. Cert. rehab. counselor. Asst. prof. U. Ariz., Tucson, 1970-82; rehab. psychologist St. Mary's Hosp./Health Ctr., 1975-82; assoc. prof./prof. U. N.C., Chapel Hill, 1982-90; prof. rehab. U. Ill., Champaign/Urbana, 1990—96; prof., head of sch. Deakin U., Melbourne, Australia, 1996—99; prof. U. North Tex., Denton, 1999—. Editor Jour. Rehab., 1987—; contbr. articles to profl. jours. Mem. Pres.'s Com. on Employment of People with Disabilities, Washington, 1990—. Recipient Outstanding Svc. award Nat. Coun. on Disability, 1993. Mem. APA (pres. divsn. 22 rehab. psychology 1993-94), ACA, AAAS, Am. Rehab. Assn., Nat. Acad. Neuropsychology, Internat. Neuropsychol. Soc., Nat. Coun. on Rehab. Edn. (pres. 1995—, Rehab. Educator of the Yr. 1988). Democrat. Avocation: jogging. Office: Univ of N Tex PO Box 311456 Denton TX 76203-1456

LEUNG, PINGSUN, economist; b. Hong Kong, Mar. 27, 1952; m. Juo Miao Leung; children: Shelton, Lorina. PhD, U. Hawaii, Manoa, 1977. Prof., rschr. U. Hawaii at Manoa, Honolulu, 1981—. Hon. guest prof. Jilin U., China, 1992. Co-editor: Internat. Jour. Aquaculture Economics and Mgmt., 1987—. Scholar Fulbright scholar, USIA, 1987—88. Mem.: Am. Agrl. Econ. Assn., World Aquaculture Soc., Internat. Assn. Aquaculture Econ. and Mgmt. (sec. 1993—99), Internat. Inst. Fisheries Econ. and Trade, Internat. Soc. Multiple

Criteria Decision Making. Office: Univ Hawaii at Manoa MBBE/CTAHR 3050 Maile Way Gilmore 123 Honolulu HI 96822 Office Fax: 808-956-9269. Business E-Mail: psleung@hawaii.edu.

LEUNG, RODERICK CHI-TAK, architect; b. Kumming, Peoples Republic of China, Aug. 12, 1949; s. Pe Ban and Kit Chong (Fung) L.; m. Julia Dexter Clark, Sept. 5, 1982; children: Emily, Rebecca. BArch, U. Minn., 1975; MArch, MIT, 1978. Architect Skidmore, Owing & Merrill, Chgo., 1975-83, John Portman & Assocs., Atlanta, 1983-84, Cooper Carry & Assocs., Atlanta, 1984-91, Seattle Pacific Industries, 1991—. Mem. AIA Seattle, MIT Alumni Assn., So. Ctr. for Internat. Studies, Nat. Coun. Architectural Registration Bd., Wash. State Internat. Trade Coun., Wash. China Coun.

LEUPP, EDYTHE PETERSON, retired education educator, administrator; b. Mpls., Nov. 27, 1921; d. Reynold H. and Lillian (Aldridge) Peterson; m. Thomas A. Leupp, Jan. 29, 1944 (dec.); children: DeEtte (dec.), Patrice, Stacia, Roderick, Braden. BS, U. Oreg., 1947, MS, 1951, EdD, 1972. Tchr. various pub. schs., Idaho, 1941-45, Portland, Oreg., 1945-55; dir. tchr. edn. Northwest Nazarene Coll., Nampa, Idaho, 1955-61; sch. adminstr. Portland Pub. Schs., 1963-84; dir. tchr. edn. George Fox Coll., Newberg, Oreg., 1984-87; ret., 1987. Vis. prof. So. Nazarene U., Bethany, Okla., 1988-95; vis. prof. Asia Pacific Nazarene Theol. Sem., 1996, prof., 2000; adj. prof. Warner Pacific Coll., Portland, 1996-97; pres. Portland Assn. Pub. Sch. Adminstrs., 1973-75; dir.-at-large Nat. Coun. Adminstrv. Women in Edn., Washington, 1973-76; state chmn. Oreg. Sch. Prins. Spl. Project, 1978-79; chair Confdn. Oreg. Sch. Adminstrs. Ann. Conf.; rschr. 40 tchr. edn. programs in colls. and univs.; designer tchr. edn. program George Fox Coll. Author tchr. edn. materials. Pres. Idaho State Aux. Mcpl. League, 1957, Nampa PTA, 1958, Nampa unit AAUW, 1956; bd. dirs. Portland Fedn. Women's Clubs, 1963. Recipient Golden Gift award, 1982; named Honored Tchr. of Okla., 1993, Hazel Fishwood scholar, 1970; Idea fellow Charles Kettering Found., 1978, 80, 87, 91, 92, 93, 94. Mem. Am. Assn. Colls. Tchr. Edn., Delta Kappa Gamma (pres. Alpha Rho State 1986-88), Phi Delta Kappa, Pi Lambda Theta. Republican. Nazarene. Avocations: travel, crafts, photography. Home: 8100 SW 2nd Ave Portland OR 97219-4602

LEUS MCFARLEN, PATRICIA CHERYL, water chemist; b. San Antonio, Mar. 12, 1954; d. Norman W. and Jacqueline S. (Deason) Leus; (div.); 1 child, Kevin Bryant. AA, Highline Community Coll., 1974; BS in Chemistry, Eastern Wash. U., 1980. Cert. operator grade II water treatment and distbn., grade I wastewater and collection operator Ariz. Dept. Environ. Quality; cert. in asbestos identification through microscopy, McCrone Group; cert. CPR and first aid. Lab. technician, oil analyst D.A. Lubricant, Vancouver, Wash., 1982-83; plant chemist Navajo Generating Sta., Page, Ariz., 1983-92, chemist, 1992—. Sci. judge Page Schs. Sci. Project Fair, 1985, 91; chemist Navajo Generating Sta./Page Sch. Career Day, 1986, 89, 90; life mem. Girl Scouts Am.; vol., leader AWANA Clubs Internat., 1992-98. Mem. Am. Chem. Soc., Cousteau Soc., Menninger Soc., Sigma Kappa (life, treas. 1976-78). Baptist. Avocations: rifle/pistol marksmanship and safety, aviation, sewing, crafts, flower gardening. *Personal philosophy: I strive to do the best I can at all tasks, whether they are pleasant or not. The sense of accomplishment is rewarding to me.*

LEUTHOLD, RAYMOND MARTIN, agricultural economics educator; b. Billings, Mont., Oct. 13, 1940; s. John Henry and Grace Irene L.; m. Jane Hornaday, Aug. 20, 1966; children— Kevin, Gregory. Student, Colo. U., 1958-59; BS, Mont. State U., 1962; MS, U. Wis., 1966, PhD, 1968. Faculty U. Ill., Urbana-Champaign, 1967—, now prof. emeritus dept. agrl. econs., T.A. Hieronymus disting. prof. Vis. scholar Stanford U., 1974, Chgo. Mercantile Exch., 1990, 91. Co-author: The Theory and Practice of Futures Markets, 1989; editor: Commodity Markets and Futures Prices, 1979; co-editor: Livestock Futures Research Symposium, 1980. Served with U.S. Army, 1962-64. Fulbright research scholar Institute de Gestion Internationale Agro-Alimentaire, Cergy, France, 1981 Mem. Am. Econ. Assn., Am. Agrl. Econs. Assn. (Disting. Policy award 1980, Outstanding Instr. award 1986, 88, 90, 92, College Funk award 1993). Office: 305 Mumford Hall 1301 W Gregory Dr Urbana IL 61801-9015

LEUTY, GERALD JOHNSTON, osteopathic physician and surgeon; b. Knoxville, Iowa, July 23, 1919; s. John William and Mable Reichard (Johnston) L.; m. Martha L. Weymouth, Jan. 24, 1940 (div. 1957); children: Maxine Joanne, Robert James, Gerald Johnston Jr., Karl Joseph; m. Norma Jean Hindman, Dec. 30, 1969; children: Barbara Jayne, Patrick Jack. AB, Kemper Mil. Sch., Boonville, Mo., 1939; postgrad., Drake U., Des Moines, 1944-45; DO, Des Moines Coll. Osteopathy, 1949; embalmer, Coll. Mortuary Sci., St. Louis, 1941. Mortician/embalmer Coalwell-McJihon Funeral Home, Des Moines, 1939-40; aero. engr. Boeing Aircraft Co., Wichita, Kans., 1941-42; osteopathic physician and surgeon Knoxville (Iowa) Ostepathic Clinic, 1949-56; dir. Leuty Osteopathic Clinic, Earlham, Iowa, 1957-77; osteopathic physician and surgeon in pvt. practice Santa Rosa, Calif., 1977—; prof. clin. med. Western U. Health Svcs., Pomona, 1985—. Mem. Iowa's Gov. Blue Med. Adv. Bd., 1972-77. With U.S. Army, 1942-46. Named Physician of the Yr., 6th Dist. Iowa Ostepathic Soc., 1975, Disting. Leadership award, Am. Biog. Inst., 1988, others. Fellow Internat. Co. Angiologists; mem. Am. Ostepathic Assn. (ho. of dels., life mem. 1989), Iowa Osteopathic Soc. (pres. 6th dist. 1974), Soc. Osteopathic Physicians, No. Calif. Osteopathic Med. Soc. (pres. 1981), Osteopathic Physicians and Surgeons of Calif. (pres. 1982), Am. Acad. Osteopathy (chmn. component socs. com. 1988, pres. Calif. divsn. 1987, pres. No. Calif. divsn. 1989, 91-93, 95), North Coast Osteopathic Med. Assn. (pres. 1992), Am. Med. Soc. Vienna (life mem.), Am. Legion (6th dist. comdr. 1974-75), Lions (pres. 1946). Republican. Presbyterian. Avocations: photography, travel. Home: 5835 La Cuesta Dr Santa Rosa CA 95409-3914

LEV, TAL, venture capitalist; b. Haifa, Israel, Sept. 7, 1965; s. Paul Lev. MBA(hon.) , Wharton School, U of Penn, Philadelphia, PA, 1999—2001; B.Sc. EE (hon.) , Tel Aviv University, Tel Aviv, Israel, 1983—87, M.Sc. (hon.) Computer Science, 1995; MA International Studies, University of Pennsylvania, Philaelphia, PA, 1999—2001. Major Israel Defense Forces, n/a, Israel, 1987—92; Sr. Design Engineer ECI Telecom Ltd., Petach Tikva, Israel, 1992—96; R&D Director Ceragon Networks, Tel Aviv, Israel, 1996—99; Associate Apax (Patricof & Co. Ventures), New York, NY, 2000—00; Sr. Associate Jerusalem Venture Partners, 2001—. Major n/a, 1987—92, Israel. Office: Jerusalem Venture Partners 41 Madison Avenue, 25th Floor New York NY 10010

LEVA, JAMES ROBERT, retired electric utility company executive; b. Boonton, N.J., May 10, 1932; s. James and Rose (Cocci) L.; m. Marie Marinaro, Dec. 19, 1950; children: James, Daniel, Linda, Michael, Christopher. BSEE magna cum laude, Fairleigh Dickinson U., 1960; JD, Seton Hall Law Sch., 1980. Lineman Jersey Ctrl. Power and Light Co., Morristown, N.J., 1952-60, elec. engring. and oper. depts., 1960-62, pers. rep., 1962-68, mgr. employee rels., 1968-69, v.p. pers. and svcs., 1969-79, v.p. consumer affairs, 1979-82, dir., 1976-82; pres., COO, dir. Pa. Electric Co., Johnstown, 1982-86; pres., COO Jersey Ctrl. Power & Light Co., Morristown, 1986-92; chmn., CEO, bd. dirs. Gen. Pub. Utilities, 1992-97, ret., 1997. Chmn., pres., CEO, bd. dirs. GPU Svc. Corp., Parsippany, N.J.; chmn. bd. dirs. GPU Nuc. Corp., Parsippany, N.J.; chmn. CEO, bd. dirs. Met. Edison Co., Reading, Pa., Pa. Electric Co., Johnstown, Pa., Utilities Mut. Ins. Co., N.J. Utilities Assn.; chmn. St. Clares Health Care Found.; trustee Tri-County Scholarship Fund, Fairleigh Dickinson U.; chmn. Sch. Planning & Pub. Policy Rutgers U. Served with USMC, 1949-51, Korea. Mem. N.J. Bar Assn., Mendham Golf and Tennis Club, Naples Nat. Golf Club. Roman Catholic.

LEVA, NEIL IRWIN, psychotherapist, hypnotherapist; b. N.Y.C., Sept. 18, 1929; s. Charles and Alice Lee (Peirce) L.; m. Jean Kathryn Walters, Dec. 4, 1952 (div. May, 1988); children: Steven L., Michael N., Scott A.; m. Susan Mary Callagy, Aug. 12, 1988. BA in Govt., U. Tex., 1963; MA in Systems Mgmt., U. So. Calif., 1973; MA in Psychology, Cath. U. Am., 1976; MSW, U. Md., 1990. Diplomate in clin. social work. Commd. 2nd. lt. U.S. Army, 1953, advanced through grades to col., 1976, retired, 1976; with psych. factors divsn. Quadraennial Bd. for Rev. of Mil. Compensation, Washington, 1974-76; psychotherapist Village Counselling Ctr., Potomac, Md., 1978-86, Met. Psychotherapist Group, Bethesda, 1986-90, Village Counseling Ctr., Potomac, Md., 1990—. Human factors cons. The Artery Orgn., Washington, 1978-83, Montgomery County Schs., Rockville, Md., 1979-81. Decorated D.F.C., Bronze Star with V device and 4 oak leaf clusters, Air medal with V device and 10 oak leaf clusters, Purple Heart, Legion of Merit. Mem. NASW, DAV, Am. Assn. Marriage and Family Therapists, Am. Assn. Profl. Hypnotherapists, Internat. Transactional Analysis Assn., Mil. Order of Purple Heart, Am. Legion. Democrat. Avocations: musician, outdoors, fishing. Office: Village Counseling Ctr 10011 Counselman Rd Potomac MD 20854-5019

LEVA, SUSAN MARY, social worker; b. Bronx, N.Y., Apr. 7, 1956; d. Joseph Vincent and Ruth Patricia (Van Nuis) Callagy; m. Neil Irwin Leva, Aug. 12, 1988. AA, Montgomery Coll., 1989; BA magna cum laude, U. Md., 1991, MSW, 1992. Dental asst. Dis Apton & Fine, Stonybrook, N.Y., 1975-76; sales clk. Magic Shoppe, Waukegan, Ill., 1976; dental asst. Dr. Mildred Romans, Olney, Md., 1976-80; sec. Wang Labs., Inc., Rockville, 1980-86; word processing instr. Bell Sch. Bus, Balt. and Washington, 1986-88; case mgr. Boys and Girls Homes of Md., Silver Spring, 1992-94; program dir. Bridges to Pals Mental Health Assoc., Rockville, 1994-97; psychotherapist Village Counseling Ctr., Potomac, Md., 1993—. Big sister mentor Mental Health Assn., Rockville, 1996—. Mem. NASW, Nat. Assn. for Play Therapy, Phi Theta Kappa, Phi Kappa Phi. Home and Office: 10011 Counselman Rd Potomac MD 20854-5019 E-mail: vcco@starpower.com., vcco@erols.com.

LEVAI, PIERRE ALEXANDRE, art gallery executive; b. Paris, Mar. 6, 1937; came to U.S., 1967; s. Paul Victor and Jeanne (Illa) L.; m. Rosemary Hare, Aug. 22, 1969; children: Paula, Max. Degree in bus. and polit. sci., Inst. d'Etudes Politiques, 1959. With Marlborough Gallery, London, 1964-67, pres., dir. N.Y.C., 1967—. Mem. Chelsea Arts Club (London). Roman Catholic. Office: Marlborough Gallery 40 W 57th St Fl 2 New York NY 10019-4069

LEVAL, PIERRE NELSON, federal judge; b. N.Y.C., Sept. 4, 1936; s. Fernand and Beatrice (Reiter) L.. BA cum laude, Harvard U., 1959, JD magna cum laude, 1963. Bar: N.Y. 1964, U.S. Ct. Appeals 2d Circuit 1964, U.S. Dist. Ct. So. Dist. N.Y 1966. Law clk. to Hon. Henry J. Friendly, U.S. Ct. Appeals, 1963—64; asst. U.S. atty. So. Dist. N.Y., 1964—68, chief appellate atty., 1967—68; assoc. firm Cleary, Gottlieb, Steen & Hamilton, N.Y.C., 1969—74; ptnr. firm, 1973—75; 1st asst. dist. atty. Office of Dist. Atty., N.Y. County, 1975—76, chief asst. dist. atty., 1976—77; U.S. dist. judge So. Dist. N.Y., N.Y.C., 1977—93; judge U.S. Ct. of Appeals (2d cir.), 1993—2002; sr judge, 2002—. Contbr. With U.S. Army, 1959. Mem.: N.Y. County Lawyers Assn., Assn. Bar City N.Y., Am. Law Inst. (coun.). Office: US Courthouse 40 Foley Sq New York NY 10007-1502*

LEVALLEY, JOAN CATHERINE, accountant; b. Decatur, Ill., Nov. 27, 1931; d. Clarence and Pearl Mae (McClure) Krall; m. Charles R. LeValley, Apr. 13, 1958 (div.); children: Curtis Ray, Cara Marie. BA in Bus., Manchester Coll., 1957. Accredited tax advisor, Ill. Acct. with various firms, 1960-76; pvt. practice acctg., Park Ridge, Ill., 1964-79; pres., dir. LeValley & Assocs., Inc., Park Ridge, 1979—; mem. tax adv. com. Chgo. IRS Dirs.; mem. com. United Way of Park Ridge, 1991, co-chmn., 1992. Mem. Nat. Assn. Pub. Accts., Ind. Acct. Assn. Ill. (2d woman pres. 1987-88, Person of Yr. award 1990), Bus. and Profl. Women Park Ridge (pres. 1974-75, Bus. Woman of Yr. 1983), Park Ridge C. of C. (treas. 1985-87). Baptist. Avocations: baking; sewing; gardening. Home: 2200 Bouterse St Apt 101 Park Ridge IL 60068-2367 Office: LeValley & Assocs Inc 6215 S 44th St Lincoln NE 68516-5506

LEVALLIANT, DEBBIE, information technology executive; Stockbroker; pres., CEO Amirix Systems, Halifax, Canada, 1990—. Office: Amirix Systems 77 Chain Lake Dr Halifax NS B3S 1E1 Canada*

LEVAN, DEBORAH JO, internist; b. Louisville, Dec. 10, 1949; d. James Walter LeVan and Martha Koenig; m. Ross Gail Parker, May 5, 1984; children: Sarah LeVan Parker, Alexander LeVan Parker. BA, Chatham Coll., 1971; MPH, U. Pitts., 1973; DO, Mich. State U., 1976. Diplomate Am. Bd. Internal Medicine. Intern Detroit Osteo. Hosp., Highland Park, Mich., 1976-77, resident in internal medicine, 1977-80, internist, 1980-92; program mgr. internal medicine Bi-County County Hosp., Warren, 1988-94, Detroit Riverview Hosp., 1994—, dir. med. edn., 1996—, internist, 1992—. Clin. prof. Mich. State U., East Lansing, 1984-98; prof. medicine Kirksville Coll. Osteopathic Medicine, 1994-99. Bd. dirs. Night to Care Charity, Detroit, 1997—. Fellow Am. Coll. Osteopathic Internists; mem. ACP. Presbyterian. Avocations: running, reading. Home: 54 Merriweather Rd Grosse Pointe Farms MI 48236-3623 Office: Motor City Internists 11447 Joseph Campau Hamtramck MI 48212

LE VAN, NOLAN GERALD, lawyer, consultant; b. Tulsa, July 10, 1934; s. Nolan Guinn Le Van and Mary Bell La Van; m. Sara Nell Ashworth, Jan. 5, 1957; children: Mary Elizabeth Le Van Riley, Nolan Guy, Marthe Nell. BA, So. Meth. U., 1956; JD, La. State U., 1962. Bar: La. 1962, U.S. Ct. Appeals (5th cir.) 1963. Ptnr. Smitherman, Lunn, Shreveport, La., 1962—71, Breazeale Sachse, Baton Rouge, 1982—84; prof. law La. State U., 1971—82; spl. counsel Kean, Miller, 1989—2000; mng. dir. The Le Van Co., Black Mtn., NC, 1986—. Author: Louisiana Wills & Trusts, 1982, Lawyers Lives Out of Control, 1993, Survival Guide for Business Families, 1998; editor-in-chief La. Law Rev., 1962. Pres. Baton Rouge Symphony, 1978; bd. trustees Presbyn. Found., Louisville, 1996—2002. Lt. USCGR, 1956—73. Fellow: Family Firm Inst., Am. Coll. Trust and Estate Counsel (former regent); mem.: La. Bar Assn., Internat. Acad. Estate and Trust Law (academician 1978—). Democrat. Avocations: golf, hiking, travel, music, literature. Office: The Le Van Co 101 West St Black Mountain NC 28711-3166

LEVANDER, ANDREW JOSHUA, lawyer; b. N.Y.C., Aug. 15, 1953; s. Seymour S. and Ellenore B. L.; m. Carol A. Loewenson, Sept. 18, 1983; children: Samuel, Benjamin. BA summa cum laude, Tufts U., 1973; JD, Columbia U., 1977. Bar: N.Y. 1978, D.C. 1978, U.S. Supreme Ct., U.S. Ct. Appeals (2d, 3d, 5th, 7th and D.C. cirs.), U.S. Dist. Ct. (so. and ea. dists.) N.Y. Law clk. Judge Wilfred Feinberg, U.S. Ct. Appeals, N.Y.C., 1977-78; asst. Solicitor Gen.'s Office, U.S. Dept. Justice, Washington, 1978-81; asst. U.S. atty. U.S. Attys. Office, N.Y.C., 1981-85; ptnr. Shereff, Friedman, Hoffman & Goodman, 1985-98; assoc. ind. counsel Washington, 1987; ptnr. Swidler Berlin Shereff Friedman LLP, N.Y.C., 1998—. Bd. dirs. Swidler, Berlin, Shereff Friedman, mem. exec. com., 1990. Co-author: The Prosecution and Prevention of Computer and High Technology Crime, 1986, Settling Commercial Litigation, 1999; contbr. articles to profl. jours. Chmn. scholar com. Westside Youth Soccer League, N.Y.C., 1996—. Mem. ABA (litig. com. 1997—), Bar Assn. City of N.Y. (securities regulation com. 1997—). Avocations: tennis, travel, coaching. E-mail. Office: Swidler Berlin Shereff Friedman 405 Lexington Ave New York NY 10174-0002 E-mail: ajlevander@swidlaw.com.

LEVANDER, HAROLD POWRIE, JR. lawyer; b. St. Paul, Aug. 28, 1940; s. Harold and Iantha (Powrle) L.; m. Carla Ann Augst, Nov. 15, 1969; children: Eric, Wade, Laura. BA in Polit. Sci., Gustavus Adolphus Coll., 1962; JD, Harvard U., 1965. Bar: Minn. 1965. Ptnr. LeVander Gillen Miller Anderson & Kuntz, St. Paul, 1965-88, Maun & Simon, St. Paul, 1989-2000, Felhaber, Larson, Fenlon & Vogt, St. Paul, 2000—. Chmn., pres. Ford Commn., Minn. Del. Nat. Rep. Conv., Kansas City, 1976; chmn. St. Paul Area ARC, 1985-87, bd. govs., 1988-94; mem. Gov.'s Coun. Red River Valley Flood Control, 1997. Named one of Outstanding Young Men of Am., U.S. Jaycees, 1972. Mem. ABA, Dakota County Bar Assn. (pres. 1983-86), Nat. Rural Electric Coop. Assn. (region 6 rep. lawyer's com. 1986-88, 1993-96). Lutheran. Avocations: public speaking, tennis, squash, hunting, politics. Home: 8086 Somerset Knls Saint Paul MN 55125-2362 Office: Felhaber Larson Fenlon & Vogt #2100 30 7th St E # 2100 Saint Paul MN 55101-4914

LEVANDOWSKI, BARBARA SUE, educational administrator; b. Mar. 16, 1948; d. Earl F. and Ann (Klee) L. BA in Edn. and Spanish, North Park Coll., 1970; MS in Elem. Edn., No. Ill. U., 1975, degree in curriculum and supervision/, 1977, EdD, 1979. cert. elem. tchr.; cert. secondary tchr.; cert. in administrv. with supt. endorsement; cert. sr. reviewer, Ill. Tchr. Round Lake (Ill.) Sch. Dist., 1970-75, Schaumburg (Ill.) Sch. Dist., 1975-87, asst. prin., 1977-87; prin., staff devel. dir. Dist. 200 Northwood Elem. Sch., Woodstock, Ill., 1987-94, dir. curriculum and instrn., 1994—. Curriculum cons. Spring Grove (Ill.) Sch. Dist., 1980-81; instr. various courses, Schaumburg, 1984-86; dir. Einstein Sch. Writing Project, 1986-87; dir. Dist. 200 Thinking Thinking Skills, 1988—; co-instr. Dist. 200 Tchg. Thinking Skills Across the Curriculum, 1992—, dir. curriculum and instrn.; chair north ctrl. assn. visitation team Huntley Sch. Dist, 1989; co-developer 4 yr. tchr. mentor program, 1994—. Mem. editorial bd. Ill. Sch. R & D Jour., 1981—; contbr. articles to profl. jours. Chair Computer/Tech. Strategic Action Team, Woodstock, 1988-89. Recipient numerous awards for excellence in teaching, Those Who Excel award State of Ill., 1979; fed. grantee. Mem. NAESP, NAFE, ASCD (insvc. presenter 1984—, presenter state and nat. conv. 1989—), Am. Biog. Rsch. Assn. (bd. dirs. 1985—, publs. com. 1983), Nat. Staff Devel. Coun., Nat. Coun. of States for Insvc., Ill. Staff Devel. Coun., Ill. Assn. for Supervision and Curriculum Devel. (chair rsch. com. 1982), Ill. Computer Educators, Inst. Ednl. Rsch. (editorial bd. advisors, co-chair effective teaching characteristics observation 1990—, Omega award), Ill. Prin. Assn. Phi Delta Kappa, Delta Kappa Gamma. Home: 426 Normandie Ln Round Lake IL 60073-3711 Office: Woodstock Sch Dist 200 227 W Judd St Woodstock IL 60098-3126 E-mail: levandbs@netscape.net.

LEVANDOWSKY, MICHAEL, marine biologist; b. Knoxville, Tenn., Aug. 15, 1935; s. Daniel and Evelyn (Mooney) L.; m. Jane Adams, 1959 (div. 1962). BA in Math., Antioch Coll., 1961; MA in Zoology, Columbia U., 1965, PhD in Biol. Scis., 1970; MS in Math., NYU, 1975. Instr. biology Bard Coll., Annandale-on-Hudson, N.Y., 1967-69; asst. prof. biology York Coll., CUNY, Jamaica, 1973-74; rsch. sci. Haskins Lab., Pace U., N.Y.C., 1970—; faculty mem. Sch. Visual Arts, 1979—. Visiting sci. math. dept. U. British Columbia, Vancouver, BC, Can., 1980, 81, U. Heidelberg, West Germany, 1983, 85, 86; trustee The River Project, N.Y.C., 1986—. Editorial adv. bd. The Jour. of Protozoology, 1981-84, Marine Ecology Progress Series, 1979-95; mem. editl. bd. Art & Academe, 1988—, The Jour. Eukaryotic Microbiology, 1999—; editor: (with S.H. Hutner) (4 vols.) Biochemistry and Physiology of Protozoa, 1978, 81. Mem. steering com. Citizens Adv. Com. Resource Recovery, Bklyn.; sec. Environ. Scis. for Global Survival, N.Y.C., 1982-91. Named Disting. Lectr. N.E. Algal Symposium, Woods Hole, Mass., 1986, co-convenor, 1992; recipient Sci. Faculty Fellowship NSF, Washington, 1971-72, award Ctr. for Theology and Natural Scis.; grantee Hudson River Found., N.Y.C., 1989-91, 2002—, Sea Grant Inst. N.Y., Stony Brook, 1989-91, NSF, 2001-02. Mem. Am. Soc. Microbiology, AAAS, Soc. of Protozoologists, N.Y. Acad. Scis., Phycol. Soc. Am., Am. Soc. Limnol. Oceanography, Torrey Botanical Soc., Internat. Soc. Ecol. Econ. Office: Pace U Haskins Labs 41 Park Row New York NY 10038-1508 E-mail: mlevandowsky@pace.edu.

LEVANT, RONALD F. psychologist, educator; b. L.A., Oct. 26, 1942; s. Harry G. and Wilma I. Levant; m. Carol L. Slatter, Jan. 17, 1995; 1 child, Caren E. BA, U. Calif., Berkeley, 1964, BA in Psychology with honors, 1969; postgrad., U. Calif., San Francisco, 1965-67; EdD in Clin. Psychology & Pub. Practice, Harvard U., 1973; MBA in Gen. Mgmt., Boston U., 1987. Grad. asst. in psychiatry Harvard U. Sch. Medicine, Mass. Gen. Hosp., Boston, 1970-71; psychology asst. Boston State Hosp., 1971; intern in psychology Cambridge (Mass.) Guidance Ctr., 1971-72; psychology trainee VA Outpatient Clinic, Boston, 1972; clin. team leader, then clin. psychologist Human Resource Inst., 1974-75, 75-83; cons. clin. psychologist Mass. Rehab. Commn., 1975-77; pvt. practice, 1983-97; assoc. prof. dept. psychology Boston State Coll., 1974-75; assoc. in Edn. Harvard U., 1974-75; asst. prof. counseling psychology, then clin. assoc. prof. Boston U., 1975-88; assoc. prof. Rutgers U., 1989-90; lectr. psychology Harvard U. Sch. Medicine, Dept. Psychiatry, 1990-95, assoc. clin. prof. psychology, 1995—; dean and prof., Ctr. for Psychol. Studies Nova Southeastern U., Ft. Lauderdale, Fla., 1997—. Asst. dir. Robert W. White Sch., Erich Lindemann Mental Health Ctr., 1972-73, dir., 1973-74; dire. The Fatherhood Project, Boston U., 1983-88; clin. supr. The Couples and Family Ctr., Cambridge Hosp., 1990-97; courtesy staff Allied Health Profl., Dept. Psychiatry, Choate Health sys., 1993-97; mental health educator Commonwealth of Mass., Dept. Mental Health, 1970; cons. tng. in family therapy, Boston City Hosp., 1977, foster parent tng., Mass. Bd. Regional Cmty. Colls., 1978, Roxbury children's Svc. Inc., 1978-80, Family cohesion and Evaluation Rsch., Boston U., 1984-87; trustee Robert W. White Sch., 1973-74, Mass. Sch. Profl. Psychology, 1987-89. Author: Family Therapy: a comprehensive overview, 1984; co-author: Between Father and Child, 1989, Masculinity Reconstructed, 1995; editor: Family Systems and Family Therapy: A Book of Readings, 1978, Psychoeducational Approaches to Family Therapy and Counseling, 1986; co-editor: Mothering and Fathering: Dispelling Myths, Creating Alternatives, 1979, Client-Centered Therapy and the Person-Centered Approach: New Directions in Theory, Research and Practice, 1984, Integrating Research and Clinical Practice, 1985, others; mem. editl bd. Am. Jour. Family Therapy, 1981—, Jour. Marriage and Family therapy, 1982-99, Family Rels., 1983-86, Jour. Family Psychology, 1985-92, 98—, Masculinities, 1994-97, Jour. of Gender, Culture and Health, 1996-99, Men and Masculinities, 1998—, Jour. African Am. Men, 1998—, Jour. Trauma Practice, 2000—, In Session: Psychotherapy in Practice, 2000—; guest editor The Counseling Psychologist, 1983, Psychotherapy, 1987, 90, Jour. of African Am. Men, 1997, Jour. of Clin. Psychology in Med. Settings, 1999; contbg. editor Washington Update Column, The Independent Practitioner, 1995—, Practitioner Report Column, Psychotherapy Bull., 1995—, Relationship column, Modern Dad Mag., 1995-96; contbr. articles to profl. jours., chpts. to books. Fellow APA (holder various offices including chair com. for advancement of profl. practice 1993-95, recording sec. 1998-2000, 2001—, chair bd. dirs. finance subcom. 1999-2000, coord. nominations subcom. 1998—, chair bd. dirs. task force on coun. representation, bd. dirs. 1995-97, others, Disting. Profl. Svc. award 1996, Family Psychologist of Yr. award 1996, Outstanding Psychologist of Yr. award 1997), Am. Orthopsychiat. Assn., Mass. Psychol. Assn. (bd. profl. affairs, chair 1978-80, mem. ins. and awards com. 1981-82, mem. legis. com. 1982-83, sec. 1983-85, pres.-1987-89, chair long range planning com. 1988-89, rep. to APA coun. 1990-93, 93-95, Ezra Saul Psychol. Svc. award 1995); mem. Acad. Psychologists in Marital and Family Therapy, Am. Assn. for Marriage and Family Therapy, Ea. Psychol. Assn., New Eng. Psychol. Assn. (steering com. 1984-85, 86-88, 89-91, 92-94), Fla. Psychol. Assn. (chair com. on psychology of men 1999—), Nat. Coun. Family Rels., Am. Family Therapy Assn., Internat. Acad. Family Psychology. Avocations: bicycling, backpacking. Office: Nova Southeastern U Ctr for Psychol Studies 3301 College Ave Fort Lauderdale FL 33314 E-mail: Rlevant@aol.com.

LEVASSEUR, LEE ALLAN, fine artist; b. Hartford, Conn., Apr. 8, 1950; s. Euclid Roland and Beatrice Marie (Daigle) LeV.; m. Evelyn M. Tucker, June 30, 1973 (div. Mar. 1986); 1 child, Robert Aaron. BS in Art Edn., So. Conn. State U., 1973. Cert. art tchr. K-12. Artist Organic Surrealism, Branford, Conn., 1989—, prodr., dir., 1991; custom picture framer APN Gallery, Conn., 1990-92, Off the Wall Gallery, Madison, 1992-93; archival picture framer Northlight Gallery, Branford, 1995—. Co-prodr., dir. "America 500" Quintcentennial, Buenos Aires, New Haven, Boston, N.Y.C., 1992; lectr. Rotary, Guilford, Conn., 1990. Exhibited Internat. Festival of Arts and Ideas, New Haven, 1999, Brandon Gallery, Madison, Conn., 2001. Recipient Cert. of Excellence Artitudes Internat. Art Competition, N.Y.C., 1989, Blue Ribbon Branford (Conn.) Festival, 1991, Prize E SoHo Internat. Art Competition, 1992, First Pl. Mixed Media, Cheshire Art League, 2000. Mem. Shoreline Alliance of Artists, Art Coun. New Haven (Conn.), Branford C. of C. Democrat. Roman Catholic. Avocations: hiking, herbalism, camping, gardening, environmental conservator. Office: Organic Surrealism 525 E Main St Trlr 40 Branford CT 06405-2930 Fax: (203) 483-0121.

LEVAUX, HUGH PIERRE, pharmaceutical executive, consultant; b. Lubumbashi, Congo, Jan. 23, 1965; s. Rene Alfonse Levaux and Mireille Marie-Rose Lambrechts; life ptnr.; children: Eric, Roger. MA in Internat. Rels., U. Libre de Bruxelles, Brussels, Belgium, 1989; MA in Internat. Econ. & Internat. Rels., Johns Hopkins U., 1991; PhD in Policy Analysis, RAND U., 1999. Coord. sales promotions Matsushita Electric Co., Osaka, Japan, 1991—94; analyst The RAND Corp., Santa Monica, Calif., 1994—99; from v.p. health economics to sr. v.p. Quintiles Inc. d/b/a Lewin-TAG, San Francisco, 1999—2001; sr. v.p. Quintiles Inc d/b/a Quintiles Late Phase, 2001—. Dir. BelCM, Brussels, 1988. Author: The Cutting Edge-A Half Century of US Fighter R&D, 1998. Fellow Rsch. fellowship, NATO, Brussels, Belgium, 1988. Mem.: Drug Info. Assn., Coun. on Fgn. Rels. Avocations: running, languages, travel.

LEVAY, SIMON, neuroscientist, writer, educator; b. Oxford, England, Aug. 28, 1943; BA in Natural Scis., Cambridge U., 1966; PhD in Neuroanatomy, U. Gottingen, 1971. Postodoctoral fellow Harvard U., 1972-74, from instr. to assoc. prof. neurobiology, 1974-84; assoc. prof. Salk Inst. for Biol. Scis., La

Jolla, Calif., 1984-92. Author: The Sexual Brain, 1993, Queer Science, 1996, Albrick's Gold, 1997; contbr. articles to profl. jours.; co-author: (with Elisabeth Nonas) City of Friends: A Portrait of the Gay and Lesbian Community in America, 1996, (with Kerry Sieh) The Earth in Turmoil, 1998, (with David Koerner) Here Be Dragons, 2000, (with Curt Freed) Healing the Brain, 2002, (with Sharon Valente) Human Sexuality, 2002. Achievements include research demonstrating that the brains of heterosexual and homosexual men are anatomically different. Avocation: bicycling. E-mail: slevay@aol.com.

LEVCHIK, SERGEI V. research chemist; b. Minsk, Belarus, Apr. 2, 1957; came to U.S., 1996; s. Vladimir N. and Maria A. Levchik; m. Galina F. Ivanovich, Apr. 16, 1957; children: Andrei, Anton. MS in Inorganic Chemistry, Belarussian U., 1979; PhD in Phys. Chemistry, Belarussian U., Minsk, 1985. Jr. rsch. chemist, rsch. chemist, sr. rsch chemist Belarussian U., Minsk, 1979-89, sr. rsch. chemist, 1991-92, prin. rsch. chemist, 1994-95, head rsch. lab., 1997; postdoctoral fellow U. Turin, Italy, 1990, vis. rsch. fellow, 1992-94; vis. scientist Poly. U., Bklyn., 1996, Akzo Nobel Chems., Dobbs Ferry, N.Y., 1997-99; prin. rsch. chemist Akzo Nobel Functional LLC, 2000-01, application mgr., 2001—. Author: Correlations in the Modern Chemistry, 1989; contbr. chpts. to books and articles to profl. jours. Rsch. fellow Italian Ministry Fgn. Affairs, 1990. Mem. Am. Chem. Soc., Soc. Plastics Engring. Achievements include 7 patents in field. Avocations: traveling, hiking. Home: 51 Harrison St Croton On Hudson NY 10520 Office: Akzo Nobel Functional Chems LLC 1 Livingstone Ave Dobbs Ferry NY 10522 Office Fax: 914-693-1782. E-mail: Sergei.Levchik@akzo-nobel.com.

LEVE, ALAN DONALD, electronic materials manufacturing company owner, executive; b. Los Angeles, Dec. 15, 1927; s. Milton Lewis and Etta L.; m. Annette Einhorn, Sept. 3, 1962; children— Laura Michelle, Elise Deanne. BS, UCLA, 1951. CPA, Calif. Staff acct., mgr. Joseph S. Herbert & Co. (C.P.A.s), Los Angeles, 1951-57, ptnr., 1957-63; fin. and adminstrv. v.p., sec./treas. Mica Corp., Culver City, Calif., 1963-82, also bd. dirs., 1963-82, chmn. bd., chief exec. officer, 1982-83; v.p., bd. dirs. Micaply Internat. Inc., 1968-1982; v.p. Micaply AG, Switzerland, 1972-83, also bd. dirs. Switzerland, chief exec. officer, also bd. dirs. Switzerland, 1982-83; v.p., bd. dirs. Micaply Internat., Ltd., U.K., 1971-82; chmn. bd., mng. dir., chief exec. officer Micaply Internat. Ltd., U.K., 1982-83; v.p., bd. dirs. Titan Chem. Corp., Edgecraft Corp., Culver Hydro-Press, Inc., L.A., 1963-75; chmn. bd., pres., chief exec. officer Ohmega Techs., Inc., Culver City, Calif., 1983—, Ohmega Electronics, Inc., Culver City, 1986—. Served with USAAF, 1946-47. Home: 16430 Dorado Dr Encino CA 91436-4118 Office: 4031 Elenda St Culver City CA 90232-3723

LEVEE, JOHN HARRISON, artist, designer; b. Los Angeles, Apr. 10, 1924; s. Michael Charles and Roze L.; m. Claude Marie, Dec. 19, 1964. BA, UCLA, 1948; postgrad., New Sch. Social Research, N.Y.C., 1949, Acad. Julian, 1950. Vis. prof. art U. Ill., 1965, N.Y. U., 1967-68, U. So. Calif., 1971 One-man shows include Konig Galerie, Geneva, 1971, Andre Emmerich Gallery, N.Y.C., 1957-59, 62, 66, Gimpel Fils, London, 1958, 60, 66, Galerie de France, 1961, 62, 64, 69, Nora Gallery, Jerusalem, Haira (Israel) Mus. Art, Moose Gallery, Toronto, 1963, Phoenix Mus. Art, 1964, U. Ill. Krannert Art Mus., 1965, Tel Aviv (Israel) Mus., 1969, Margo Leavin Gallery, L.A., 1970, Galerie la Toabis, Paris, 1975, Palm Springs (Calif.) Mus., 1978, Mus. Nice, France, 1980, Galerie La Closerie des Lilacs, Paris, 1983, 86, Galerie 1900-2000, Paris, Galerie de Poche, Paris, 1990, Galerie Patrick Renolds, 2001; one-man retrospective Galerie Le Gall, Paris, 1986, retrospective of the 1950's, Gallerie Callu, Paris, 1989, retrospective of the 1960's, 1989, retrospective 1953-93 Toulouse Mus., France, retrospective 1990-1997 Gallerie Roquefeuil-Pallade, Paris; group shows, Salon de Mai, Paris, 1954-2001, Salon des Realités Nouvelles, 1954-96, Salon Comparison, 1978-97, Paris, Carnegie Internat., 1955-58, Washington's Corcoran Gallery of Art, 1956, 58, Mus. Modern Art N.Y.C., 1957, Whitney Mus., 1957-59, 65, Arts Club Chgo., 1958, Guggenheim Mus., 1966, Salon des grands et jeunes d'aujourd'huis 1996, 1978-2001, Musee du Grand Palais, L'ecole de Paris, 1945-57, Hqrs. UNESCO, 50th anniversary, Paris, 1996, Salon Grands et Jeunes d'aufourd hurs, Paris, 1978-92, competition Salon Grands et Jeunes Mus. Modern Art, Paris, others, many archtl. projects, France, U.S.A. Served with USAAF, 1944-46. Recipient prizes including Watercolor Assn. Ann. 1955, 56, Commonwealth of Va. Biann. Purchase award 1966, grand prix Woolmark Found. 1974-75, gran prix Biennale de Paris 1969; Ford grantee, 1969; Tamarind fellow Los Angeles, 1969 Jewish. Home and Office: 119 rue Notre Dame des Champs 6 Paris France *Most thinkers and artists are not historical geniuses who have broken with previous tradition, perceived relationships hitherto unnoticed, or even invented new relationships or had new visions thus transforming the categories in terms of which human beings think of their place in the universe. But for each historical period there are these men of genius and it is the moral imperative of us all to strive, to reach out in our own way and within our own limits, toward this end.*

LEVEEN, ROBERT FREDERICK, radiologist; b. Jersey City, July 24, 1946; s. Harry Henry and Jeanette Lois (Rubricius) LeV.; m. Sandra Sue Hickstein, May 28, 1974; children: Emily, Rob. BA, Grinnell Coll., Iowa, 1968; MD, U. Nebr., Omaha, 1974. Diplomate Am. Bd. Radiology. Intern dept. surgery U. Washington, 1974-75; resident in radiology Coll. Medicine U. Nebr., 1975-78; asst. prof. radiology U. Nebr. Med. Ctr., Omaha, 1978-80; from asst. prof. radiology to assoc. prof. U. Pa., Phila., 1980-90; research assoc. VA Med. Ctr., 1980-83, clin. investigator, 1985-90; coordinator, angiography research U. Pa., Dept. Radiology, 1985-90; assoc. prof. radiology U. Nebr. Med. Ctr., 1991-99; chief radiology svc. VA Med. Ctr., Omaha, 1991-99; assoc. prof. U. Fla., Gainesville, 1999—. Recipient Career Devel. award, VA, 1985; Stauffer award, Assn. U. Radiologists, 1986. Fellow Am. Coll. Radiology; mem. Soc. Cardiovascular and Interventional Radiology, Radiologic Soc. N.Am., Assn. U. Radiologists, Nebr. Radiolog. Soc. (pres. 1998-99), Fla. Radiolog. Soc. Presbyterian. Office: U Fla Coll Medicine Dept Radiology PO Box 100374 Gainesville FL 32610-0374 E-mail: leveer@radiology.ufl.edu.

LEVEILLE, GILBERT ANTONIO, food products executive; b. Fall River, Mass., June 3, 1934; s. Isidore and Rose (Caron) L.; divorced; children: Michael, Kathleen, Edward; m. Carol A. Phillips, Aug. 7, 1981. B in Vocat. Agr., U. Mass, 1956; MS, Rutgers U., 1958, PhD in Nutrition and Biochemistry, 1960. Prof. nutritional biochemistry U. Ill., Urbana, 1965-71; chmn. dept. food sci. and human nutrition Mich. State U., East Lansing, 1971-80; dir. nutrition and health sci. Gen. Foods Corp., Tarrytown, N.Y., 1980-86; v.p. for rsch. and tech. svcs. Nabisco Inc., East Hanover, N.J., 1986-96; pres. Leveille Assocs., Denville, 1996-99; v.p. worldwide, sci. and regulatory affairs McNeil Consumer Healthcare, Fort Washington, Pa., 1999—2001; v.p. tech., food sys. design Cargill, Inc., 2000—. Author: The Set Point Diet, 1985 (N.Y. Times nonfiction bestseller); also over 300 articles. Served to 1st lt. U.S. Army, 1960-62. Recipient rsch. award Poultry Sci. Assn., 1965, Disting. Faculty award Mich. State U., 1980, Carl Fellers award IFT, Chancellor's Medal, U. Mass., 2000. Mem. AAAS, Am. Chem. Soc., Am. Soc. Nutritional Sci. (pres. 1988-89, Mead Johnson rsch. award 1971, Elvehjem award 2002), Am. Soc. for Clin. Nutrition, Inst. Food Technologists (pres. 1983-84, fellow 1983, Carl Fellers award 1992). E-mail: gilbert_leveille@Cargill.com.

LEVELL, EDWARD, JR. retired aiport executive; b. Jacksonville, Ala., Apr. 2, 1931; m. Rosa M. (Casellas) L, Aug. 3, 1951 (dec.); children: Edward III (dec.), Ruben C., Kenneth W., Randy C., Raymond C. (dec.), Cheryl D. Levell Rivera, Michael K. BS, Tuskegee Inst., 1953; MA in Urban Sociology, U. No. Colo., 1972; M in Mgmt., Indsl. Coll./Air War Coll., 1974. Commd. 2d lt. USAF, 1953, advanced through grades to col., 1978, various flight tng., air ops. and command positions, 1953-69; comdr. cadet group, then dep. commandant cadet wing USAF Acad., 1969-73; dep. comdr., wing comdr., vice comdr. 1st spl. ops. wing USAF, 1973-77, wing comdr. 58th tactical air command tng. wing, 1977-78, col., vice comdr., comdr. 20th air divsn., 1978-83, ret., 1983; dep. commr. aviation City of Chgo. Dept. Aviation, 1983-89; dep. dir. aviation, fin. and adminstrn. City of New Orleans Dept. Aviation, 1989-90, dep. dir. aviation, ops. and maintenance, 1990-92, dir. aviation, 1992—99; ret., 2000. Bd. dirs. Tourist & Conv. Commn., New Orleans; trustee Dryades YMCA, New Orleans; mem. transp. com. World Trade Ctr. Decorated Legion of Merit, D.F.C. (2), Meritorious Svc. Medal (2), Air Medal (8), Air Force Commendation Medal; recipient Disting. Svc. award Jacksonville, Ala., 1974, State of Fla. Commn. Human Rels. award for spl. recognition, 1977, Air Force Assn. Spl. Citation of Merit, 1977, Disting. Svc. award City of Chgo. Dept. Aviation, 1986, 87, 88; inducted in Tuskegee Univ. Hall of Fame, 1991. Mem. Airport Ops. Coun. Internat. (task force chmn. ann. conf. New Orleans 1991), Am. Assn. Airport Execs., Gulf Coast Internat. Hispanic C. of C. Home: 13881 Cinch Ln Gainesville VA 20155

LEVEN, ANN RUTH, financial planner, consultant; b. Canton, Ohio, Nov. 1, 1940; d. Joseph J. and Bessie (Scharff) L. AB, Brown U., 1962; cert. with distinction in program in bus. adminstrn., Harvard-Radcliffe Univs., 1963; MBA, Harvard U., 1964. Product mgr. household products div. Colgate-Palmolive, N.Y.C., 1964-66; account exec. Grey Advt., 1966-67; fin. asst. Met. Mus. Art, 1967-69, asst. treas., 1970-72, treas., 1972-79; v.p., sr. corp. planning officer Chase Manhattan Bank, N.Y.C., 1979-83; pres. ARL Assocs., 1983—; treas. Smithsonian Instn., 1984-90; dep. treas. Nat. Gallery Art, Washington, 1990-94, treas. and CFO, 1994-99. Adj. asst. prof. Grad. Sch. Bus., Columbia U., 1975—77, adj. assoc. prof., 1977—79, adj. prof., 1980—93; exec.-in-residence Amos Tuck Sch., Dartmouth Coll., 1976, 84; bd. dirs. Del. Group, Recoton, Systemax; bd. govs. Investment Co. Inst., 1997—. Artist (awarded prizes for painting and graphic arts); author articles on grad. bus. edn., mgmt. studies on the arts. Exec. bd. new leadership divsn. Fedn. Jewish Philanthropies, 1968-70; coun. mem. N.Y. Public Library, exec. com., 1976-79; mus. adv. panel N.Y. State Council on Arts, 1977-79; bd. dirs. Camp Rainbow, 1970-84, v.p., 1976-78, treas., 1982-84; bd. overseers Amos Tuck Sch., 1978-84, chmn. ednl. affairs com., 1979-84; trustee Brown U., 1976—, fin. and budget com., student life com., devel. com., adv. and exec. coms.; bd. dirs. Ctr. for Fgn. Policy Devel., 1989-94, 2002-, Am. Arts Alliance, 1990-92; bd. dirs. Twyla Tharp Dance Found., 1982-87, Reading Is Fundamental, 1987-91, adv. coun., 1991-94; trustee Artists' Choice Mus., 1979-87; vis. com. Harvard U. Bus. Sch., 1979-84; bd. overseers Hood Mus.-Hopkins Ctr. Dartmouth Coll., 1984-91, chmn., 1988-91; trustee ARC Endowment Fund, 1985-90, N.Y. Sch. Interior Design, 1996—, Andy Warhol Found., 1999—; staff Presdl. Task Force on Arts and Humanities, 1981. Recipient Young Leadership award Council Jewish Fedns. and Welfare Funds, 1968; named N.Y. State's Outstanding Young Woman, 1976 Mem. Harvard Bus. Sch. Alumni Assn. (exec. coun. 1976-79, v.p. 1978-79), Women's Fin. Assn., Women's Forum, Econ. Club of N.Y., Cosmopolitan Club, Harvard Bus. Sch. Club, Radcliffe Club, Brown Club, Art Table, Century Assn. Home: 785 Park Ave New York NY 10021-3552

LEVEN, CHARLES LOUIS, economics educator; b. Chgo., May 2, 1928; s. Elie H. and Ruth (Reinach) R.; m. Judith Danoff, 1950 (div. 1970); m. Dorothy Wish, 1970 (div. 1999); children: Ronald L., Robert M., Carol E., Philip W., Alice S. Student, Ill. Inst. Tech., 1945-46, U. Ill., 1947; BS, Northwestern U., 1950, MA, 1957, PhD, 1958. Economist Fed. Res. Bank of Chgo., 1950-56; asst. prof. Iowa State U., 1957-59, U. Pa., 1959-62; asso. prof. U. Pitts., 1962-65; prof. econs. Washington U., St. Louis, 1965-91, chmn. dept. econs., 1975-80, prof. emeritus, 1991—; dir. Inst. Urban and Regional Studies, 1965-85. Disting. prof. U. Mo., St. Louis, 1991-99; cons. EEC, Ill. Auditor Gen., Polish Ministry of Planning and Constrn., St. Louis Sch. Bd., Ukrainian Ctr. for Markets and Entrepreneurship, Joel Popkin & Co. Author: Theory and Method of Income and Product Accounts for Metropolitan Areas, 1963, Development Benefits of Water Resource Investment, 1969, An Analytical Framework for Regional Development Policy, 1970, Neighborhood Change, 1976, The Mature Metropolis, 1978. Served with USNR, 1945-46. Ford Found. fellow, 1956; grantee Social Sci. Rsch. Coun., 1960; grantee Com. Urban Econ., 1965; grantee NSF, 1968, 73, Merc. Bancorp., 1976, HUD, 1978, NIH, 1985, 2001. Mem. Am. Econ. Assn., Regional Sci. Assn. (pres. 1964-65, Walter Isard award for distig. scholarship 1995), Western Regional Sci. Assn. (pres. 1974-75, Disting. fellow 1999), So. Regional Sci. Assn. (disting. fellow 1991). Home: 151 Marigold Ln Milford PA 18337-7322 Office: Washington U Box 1208 1 Brookings Dr Saint Louis MO 63130-4899 *Achievement is satisfying, but especially so when one can win without others losing. At the same time, it appears unnecessary to be a failure to prove one's sincerity.*

LEVEN, STEPHEN H. human resources professional; BS, Cornell U.; MBA, So. Meth. U. Adminstr. Tex. Instruments, Dallas, 1973-80, employee rels. profl., 1980-82, mgr. human resources, 1982-92, sr. v.p. human resources semiconductor group, 1992-98, sr. v.p. and mgr. worldwide human resources, 1998—. Office: Texas Instruments Inc 12500 TI Blvd Dallas TX 75243 E-mail: s-leven@ti.com.

LEVENBACK, KAREN L. educator, writer, editor; b. N.Y.C., Nov. 11, 1951; d. Gerald and Gloria Adele (Levin) Levenback; m. Michael John Neufeld, June 14, 1994. BA, SUNY, Stony Brook, 1972; MA, Georgetown U., 1974; postgrad., Cornell U., 1974-75; PhD, U. Md., 1981. Instr. Anatolia Coll., Thessaloniki, Greece, 1981-83; prof. Sch. Bus. Adminstrn. and Liberal Arts, 1981-83; lectr. George Washington U., Washington, 1984-2000. Author: Annual Bibliography of Woolf Scholarship, 1987-90, Virginia Woolf and the Great War, 1999; mem. editl. bd. GW Forum, 1998-99; book rev. editor Virginia Woolf Miscellany, 1999—; assoc. editor Woolf Studies Ann., 1994-99; contbr. essays to Anne Tyler as Novelist, 1994, Virginia Woolf and War, 1991; contbr. articles and revs. to profl. jours. Ombudsman, bd. dirs. Thessaloniki Players, 1981-83. Mem. MLA, N.E. MLA, Internat. Virginia Woolf Soc. (sec.-treas. 1988-90, pres. 1991-93).

LEVENDOGLU, HULYA, gastroenterologist, educator; b. Samsun, Turkey, Nov. 20, 1948; came to U.S., 1973; d. Ali Riza and Hidayet (Acar) L.; m. Mustafa Orhan Kaymakcalan, June 21, 1974 (div. 1981). MD, Hacettepe U., 1972. Diplomate Am. Bd. Internal Medicine, Am. Bd. Gastroenterology. Intern and resident in internal medicine Cook County Hosp., Chgo., 1973-76, fellow, 1976-78, attending physician, 1978-80; acting chief divsn. gastroenterology Bklyn. VA Hosp., 1981-83; chmn. divsn. gastroenterology Cook County Hosp., Chgo., 1983-89; assoc. prof. SUNY Health Sci. Ctr., Bklyn., 1989—; chmn. divsn. gastroenterology Brookdale U. Hosp. Med. Ctr., 1989—. Contbr. articles to med. jours. Named One of Best Doctors in N.Y.C., N.Y. mag., 1998; rsch. grantee SUNY, 1981, Elli Lilly & Co., 1984, UpJohn Co., 1985, Ortho Pharm. Co., 1985, Schering Plough, 1998, Amgen, 1999. Fellow ACP, Am. Coll. Gastroenterology; mem. AAAS, Am. Gastroent. Assn., Am. Soc. for Gastrointestinal Endoscopy, Am. Soc. for Study Liver Diseases, Bklyn. Gastroenterol. Assn. (pres. 1995-99). Moslem. Office: Brookdale U Hosp Med Ctr 1 Brookdale Plz Brooklyn NY 11212-3139

LEVENDUSKY, PHILIP GEORGE, psychologist, science administrator; b. Lowell, Mass., Oct. 21, 1946; s. Harry George and Phyllis Mary (Cowgill) Levendusky; m. Cynthia Ann Becton; children: Jason Philip, Anya Prentiss, Katya Sprague. BA magna cum laude, U. Mass, 1968; MS, Wash. State U., 1971, PhD, 1973. Diplomate Am. Bd. Profl. Psychology. Asst. to dir. Human Rels. Ctr., Wash. State U., Pullman, 1971-73; asst. psychologist McLean Hosp., Belmont, Mass., 1974-82, assoc. psychologist, 1982-92, psychologist, 1992—, dir. cognitive behavior therapy unit, 1974-94, dir. ambulatory care, 1991-95, asst. gen. dir., 1993-95, v.p. network devel., 1995—, dir. dept. psychology, dir. clin. tng., 1996—; instr. psychiatry Harvard Med. Sch., Boston, 1974-88, asst. prof., 1988-97, assoc. prof., 1997—; dir. Levendusky and Assocs., Arlington, 1980—. Cons. VA Hosp., Boston, 1977—85, Boston Cardiovasc. Health, 1983—85, Mass. Dept. Mental Health, 1987—, Mass. Dept. Mental Retardation, 1997—; dir. Bain & Co., Employee Consultation, Boston, 1987—; mem. Mass. Bd. Psychology, 1988—93. Contbr. articles to profl. jours., mags., newspapers, chapters to books; guest numerous TV and Radio programs, Boston. Mem. Sch. Bd., Manchester, Mass.; bd. dirs. Feeding Ourselves, 1980, Anorexia Bulemia Care, 1991—93. Mem.: APA, New Eng. Soc. Behavior Analysis and Therapy (bd. dirs. 1991), Assn. Advancement Behaviour Therapy, Blue Hill Country Club, Phi Beta Kappa. Republican. Roman Catholic. Avocations: skiing, jogging. Office: McLean Hosp 115 Mill St Belmont MA 02478-1048

LEVENE, SHIRLEY SCHECHTER, psychotherapist; b. N.Y.C., Oct. 10, 1917; d. William and Edith (Herman) Goldsmith; m. Alfred Schechter, July 1938; m. Jack Levene, Nov. 1983; children: Judith Schechter Lasko, Ruth Schechter Rubinow. BA, Vassar Coll., 1938; MS, Columbia U., 1942; cert. analytic group psychotherapy, Postgrad. Ctr. Mental Health, 1968, cert. supervision of individual and group therapy, 1971. Psychotherapist Family Consultation Svc., Eastchester, N.Y.; pvt. practice psychotherapist White Plains. Contbr. articles to profl. jours. Fellow AGPA; mem. NASW (diplomate), Eastern Group Psychotherapy Soc. (past pres.), N.Y. Soc. Clin. Social Work Psychotherapists (diplomate N.Y. State cert. social worker). Home and Office: 111 Miles Ave White Plains NY 10606-3816

LEVENFELD, MILTON ARTHUR, lawyer; b. Chgo., Mar. 18, 1927; s. Mitchell A. and Florence B. (Berman) L.; m. Iona R. Wishner, Dec. 18, 1949; children— Barry, David, Judith Ph.B., U. Chgo., 1947, JD, 1950. Bar: Ill. 1950. Ptnr. Altman, Levenfeld & Kanter, Chgo., 1961-64, Levenfeld and Kanter, Chgo., 1964-80, Levenfeld, Eisenberg, Janger & Glassberg, Chgo., 1980-99; of counsel Levenfeld Pearlstein, 1999—. Former dir. Bank of Chgo., Garfield Ridge Trust & Savs. Bank; lectr. in fed. taxation Contbr. articles to profl. jours. Bd. dirs. Spertus Coll. Judaica, Jewish Fedn. Chgo., 1975-84, Am. Israel C. of C., 1st nat. v.p.; chmn. legacies and endowments com., 1982-84; co-gen. chmn. Chgo. Jewish United Fund, 1977, vice chmn. campaign, 1979; gov. mem. Orchestral Assn. Chgo. Symphony Orch.; vis. com. U. Chgo. Law Sch., 1989-91; pres. Am. Israel C. of C. of Met. Chgo., 1993-95, 96-98. With USNR, 1944-45. Recipient Keter Shem Tov award Jewish Nat. Fund, 1978 Mem. ABA, Ill. Bar Assn., Chgo. Bar Assn., Am.-Israel C. of C. (past pres.). Home: 866 Stonegate Dr Highland Park IL 60035-5145 Office: 33 W Monroe St Chicago IL 60603-5300 E-mail: mlevenfeld@lplegal.com.

LEVENS, DORSEY (HERBERT LEVENS), professional football player; b. Syracuse, N.Y., May 21, 1970; Student, U. Notre Dame, Ga. Poly. U. Running back Green Bay (Wis.) Packers, 1994—2001; mem. Super Bowl 31 Championship team, 1996; lost Super Bowl 32 to New Eng. Patriots, 1997; mem. Pro Bowl team, 1997; running back Phila. Eagles, 2002—. Office: Phila Eagles One NovaCare Way Philadelphia PA 19145*

LEVENS, JOSEPH DAVID, investment company executive; b. Boston, July 13, 1957; s. Frederick M. and Ruth R. (Raphael) L.; m. Beth Anne Wolfson, July 27, 1986; 1 child, Samuel L. BA Polit. Sci., U. Mass., 1979; MPA, Syracuse U., 1981. Adminstrv. asst. UN, Geneva, 1977, 78; grad. asst. Syracuse U., N.Y., 1979-81; cons. Info. Bus., Cambridge, Mass., 1980; rsch. asst. Operation Drake, Sulawesi, Indonesia, 1980; sr. cons. Booz Allen & Hamilton, Washington, 1981-84; sr. mgmt. analyst Gen. Electric, Lynn, Mass., 1984-86; prin. Am. Mgmt. Sys. Inc., Cambridge, 1986-94; dir. Fidelity Investments, Boston, 1994—. Author: (with others) Personnel Management in Government, 1981. Bd. dirs. U. Mass. Alumni Bd., Amherst, 1985-87; mem. troop 182 com. coun. Boy Scouts Am., 1985—. Avocations: cross country skiing, scuba diving, photography, hiking, gardening.

LEVENSON, ALAN BRADLEY, lawyer; b. Long Beach, N.Y., Dec. 13, 1935; s. Cyrus O. and Jean (Kotler) L.; m. Joan Marlene Levenson, Aug. 19, 1956; children: Scott Keith, Julie Jo. AB, Dartmouth Coll., 1956; BA, Oxford U., Eng., 1958, MA, 1962; LLB, Yale U., 1961. Bar: N.Y. 1962, U.S. Dist. Ct. D.C. 1964, U.S. Ct. Appeals (D.C. cir.) 1965, U.S. Supreme Ct. 1965. Law clk., trainee div. corp. fin. SEC, Washington, 1961-62, gen. atty., 1962, trial atty., 1963, br. chief, 1963-65, asst. dir., 1965-68, exec. asst. dir., 1968, dir., 1970-76; v.p. Shareholders Mgmt. Co., L.A., 1969, sr. v.p., 1969-70, exec. v.p., 1970; ptnr. Fulbright & Jaworski, Washington, 1976—. Lectr. Cath. U. Am., 1964-68, Columbia U., 1973; adj. prof. Georgetown U., 1964, 77, 79-81, U.S. rep. working party OECD, Paris, 1974-75; adv. com. SEC, 1976-77; mem. adv. bd. Securities Regulation Inst., U. Calif., San Diego, 1973—, vice chmn. exec. com., 1979-83, chmn., 1983-87, emeritus chmn., 1988—; mem. adv. coun. SEC Inst., U. So. Calif., L.A., Sch. Acctg., 1981-85; mem. adv. com. Nat. Ctr. Fin. Svcs,. U. Calif.-Berkeley, 1985-89; mem. planning com. Ray Garrett Ann. Securities Regulation Inst. Northwestern U. Law Sch.; mem. adv. panel to U.S. compt.-gen. on stock market decline, 1987, panel of cons., 1989-98; mem. audit adv. com. GAO, 1992—. Mem. bd. editl. advisors U. Iowa Jour. Corp. Law, 1978—; Bur. Nat. Affairs adv. bd. Securities Regulation and Law Report, 1976—; bd. editors N.Y. Law Jour., 1976—; bd. advisors, corp. and securities law advisor Prentice Hall Law & Bus., 1991-95; contbr. articles to profl. jours.; mem. adv. bd. Banking Policy Report. Trustee, chair audit com., chair oral history com. SEC Hist. Soc. Recipient Disting. Service award SEC, 1972; James B. Richardson fellow Oxford U., 1956 Mem. ABA (adv. com., fed. regulation securities com., task force rev. fed. securities laws, former chair subcom. on securities activities banks), Fed. Bar Assn. (emeritus mem. exec. com. securities law com.), Am. Law Inst., Practicing Law Inst. (nat. adv. com. 1974, adv. com. ann. securities reg. inst.), AICPA (pub. dir., bd. dirs. 1984-91, fin. com. 1984-91, chmn. adv. coun. auditing standards bd. 1979-80, future issues com. 1982-85), Nat. Assn. Securities Dealers (corp. fin. com. 1981-87, nat. arbitration com. 1983-87, gov.-at-large, bd. govs. 1984-87, exec. com. 1986-87, long range planning com. 1987-90, chmn. legal adv. bd. 1988-93, spl. com. governance and structure 1989-90, numerous adv. coms.), Transparency Internat. USA (bd. dirs.). Home: 12512 Exchange Ct S Potomac MD 20854-2431 Office: Fulbright & Jaworski LLP 801 Pennsylvania Ave NW Washington DC 20004-2615 E-mail: alevenson@fulbright.com.

LEVENSON, ALAN IRA, psychiatrist, physician, educator; b. Boston, July 25, 1935; s. Jacob Maurice and Frances Ethel (Biller) L.; m. Myra Beatrice Katzen, June 12, 1960 (div. 1993); children: Jonathan, Nancy; m. Linda Ann Nadell, Jan. 30, 1994. AB, Harvard U., 1957, MD, 1961, MPH, 1965. Diplomate: Am. Bd. Psychiatry and Neurology. Intern U. Hosp., Ann Arbor, Mich., 1961-62; resident psychiatry Mass. Mental Health Center, Boston, 1962-65; staff psychiatrist NIMH, Chevy Chase, Md., 1965-66, dir. div. mental health service programs, 1967-69; prof. psychiatry U. Ariz. Coll. Medicine, Tucson, 1969-2000, prof. emeritus, 2000—, head dept. psychiatry, 1969-89; chief exec. officer Palo Verde Mental Health Svcs., 1971-91, chief med. officer, med. dir., 1991-93; chmn. bd. dirs., CEO Psychiatrists' Purchasing Group, 1991—; chmn. bd. dirs. Psychiatrists' Risk Retention Group, 1991-2000. Mem. staff Tucson Med. Ctr., U. Med. Ctr., Tucson. Author: The Community Mental Health Center: Strategies and Programs, 1972; Contbr. papers and articles to psychiat. jours. Bd. dirs. Tucson Urban League, 1971-78, Pima Council on Aging, 1976-83. Served with USPHS, 1965-69. Fellow Am. Psychiat. Assn. (treas. 1986-90), Am. Coll. Psychiatrists (regent 1980-83, v.p. 1983-85, pres.-elect 1985-86, pres. 1986-87), Am. Coll. Mental Health Adminstrn. (v.p. 1980-82, pres. 1982-83); mem. Group for Advancement Psychiatry, Harvard Alumni Assn. (bd. dirs. 1988-91). Office: 75 N Calle Resplendor Tucson AZ 85716-4937

LEVENSON, DAVID IRWIN, endocrinologist; b. Bronx, N.Y., Oct. 8, 1965; s. Harold Edward and Mildred (Pallas) L.; m. Marissa Julie Goldberg, Jan. 14, 1990; children: Jonathan Nachum, Jacob Meir, Michael Aryeh, Larry Ezra. BA, BS, Univ. Miami, 1985; MD (hons.), N.Y. Univ. Sch. Medicine, 1989. Intern L.I. Jewish Medical Ctr., New Hyde Park, N.Y., 1990-91, resident internal medicine, 1991-93; fellow endocrinology Cornell U., 1992-94; fellow geriatrics U. Miami, Fla., 1994-95; pvt. practice Physicians Specialty Group, Boca Raton, 1995-97, East Coast Med. Assn., Inc., Boca Raton, 1997—. Contbr. articles to profl. jours. Dir. Young Israel of Boca Raton, 1995-97, Hillel Cmty. Day Sch., Boca Raton, 1996—. Fellow Am. Coll. Endocrinology; mem. Am. Assn. of Clinical Endocrinologists, Am. Coll. Physicians, The Endocrine Soc. Office: East Coast Med. Assocs Inc # 301A 7301A W Palmetto Park Rd Boca Raton FL 33433

LEVENSON, JACOB CLAVNER, English language educator; b. Boston, Oct. 1, 1922; s. Joseph Mayer and Frances (Hahn) L.; m. Charlotte Elizabeth Getz, June 6, 1946; children: Anne, Jill L. Eisenberg, Paul Getz L. Brown. AB, Harvard U., 1943, PhD, 1951. Tutor in history and lit. Harvard, 1946-50, vis. lectr. English and gen. edn., 1951-52; instr. English U. Conn., 1950-54; asst. prof. to prof. English U. Minn., 1954-67; Edgar Allan Poe prof. English U. Va., Charlottesville, 1967-99, chmn. dept., 1971-74, prof. emeritus, 1999—; faculty Salzburg (Austria) Seminar in Am. Studies, 1947, 49. Mem. Com. of Cons., Notable Am. Women, 1607-1950, 63-72. Author: The Mind and Art of Henry Adams, 1957, Hist. and Critical Introductions The Works of Stephen Crane, II-V, VII, 1969-76; editor: Stephen Crane: Prose and Poetry, 1984, Mark Twain Life on the Mississippi, 1967, Discussions of Hamlet, 1960, The Letters of Henry Adams I-III, 1982, IV-VI, 1988; mem. editorial bd.; Am. Quar., 1964-70, Va. Quar. Rev., 1968-99, New Literary History, 1969-2000, Am. Lit., 1988-91; contbr. articles to profl. jours. Served with AUS, 1943-45. Decorated Bronze Star; Guggenheim fellow, 1958-59; Am. Council Learned Socs. fellow, 1961-62; Am. Philos. Soc. Penrose grantee, 1956; recipient E.

Harris Harbison award for disting. teaching Danforth Found., 1966 Fellow U. Va. Soc. Fellows (hon.); mem. MLA, Am. Studies Assn., Signet Soc., Phi Beta Kappa. Home: 1581 Belvedere Dr Charlottesville VA 22901-1862 E-mail: jcl3g@virginia.edu.

LEVENSON, MARC DAVID, optics and lasers specialist, scientist, editor; b. Phila., May 28, 1945; s. Donald William and Ethyl Jean Levenson; m. Naomi Francis Matsuda, Oct. 24, 1971. SB, MIT, 1967; MS, Stanford U., 1968, PhD, 1971. Rsch. fellow Harvard U., Cambridge, Mass., 1971-74; asst. prof. physics U. So. Calif., L.A., 1974-77, assoc. prof., 1977-79; mem. rsch. staff IBM Rsch. div., San Jose, Calif., 1979-93, head mgr. OSC, 1987, mgr. quantum metrology, 1990; v.p. Focused Rsch., Inc., Sunnyvale, 1993-95; propr., cons. Marc D. Levenson Optics, Saratoga, 1993—. Vis. fellow Joint Inst. for Lab. Astrophysics, U. Colo., Boulder, 1995-96; vis. prof. Rice U., Houston, 1996. Author: Introduction to Nonlinear Laser Spectroscopy, 1988; editor: Lasers, Spectroscopy, New Ideas, 1987, Resonances, 1991; West Coast editor Solid State Tech. mag., 1993—; editor-in-chief Microlithography World Mag., 1995—; contbr. articles to profl. jours. Alfred Sloan rsch. fellow, 1975. Fellow IEEE, Optical Soc. Am. (Adolph Lomb medal 1976), Am. Phys. Soc., Bay Area Chrome Users Soc./Soc. Photog. and Instrumentation Engrs. (award 1991). Avocations: gardening, reading. E-mail: marcl@pennwell.com.

LEVENSON, MARIA NIJOLE, retired medical technologist; b. Kaunas, Lithuania, Mar. 24, 1940; came to U.S., 1948; d. Zigmas and Monika (Galbuogis) Sabataitis; m. Coleman Levenson, Nov. 21, 1975. BA, Annhurst Coll., 1962. Sr. rsch. technician Case Western Res. U., Cleve., 1962-69; phys. sci. technician Nat. Oceanographic Data Ctr., Washington, 1969-70; biologist NIH, Bethesda, Md., 1970-76; nuclear medicine technologist VA Med. Ctr., New Orleans, 1977-79; paramed. examiner Hooper Industries, 1980-82; assoc. chemist Computer Scis. Corp., Stennis Space Ctr., Miss., 1982-83; med. technologist VA Med. Ctr., New Orleans, 1984-96. Sec. Lithuanian Cath. Youth Assn., Putnam, Conn., 1960-62, Lithuanian Club, Annhurst Coll., South Woodstock, Conn., 1960-62. Participant Freedom Movement for Baltic Independence, Slidell, La., 1990-91; counselor Life with Cancer, Slidell, 1989—; vol. docent Dauphin Island Estuarium, 1997—. La. State Nursing Sch. scholar, 1989. Mem. Daus. of Lithuania, Internat. Platform Assn., Forever Dauphin Island. Avocations: reading, traveling, cooking, flying, family. Home: PO Box 593 Dauphin Island AL 36528-0593 E-mail: Cole323@juno.com.

LEVENSON, MARK JOSEPH, otolaryngologist; b. Boston, 1946; MD, N.Y. Med. Coll., 1972. Cert. otolaryngologist, 1983. Intern Jackson Meml. Hosp., 1972-73; residency Manhattan Eye Ear Hosp., 1980-83, fellow otology, 1983-84, surgeon dir., 1996, chief of otology, 1997; clin. asst. prof. Cornell U. Med. Coll., 1996. Mem. AMA, Am. Acad. Otolaryngology Head and Neck Surgery, Am. Coll. Surgeons, Triological Soc. Office: 3 E 71st St New York NY 10021-4154 E-mail: earsurgeon@psinet.com.

LEVENSON, STANLEY RICHARD, public relations and advertising executive; b. Cin., Dec. 28, 1933; s. Irven Philip and Dorothy (Aftel) L.; m. Barbara Lind, July 23, 1962; children: Laura, Amy. BA, U. Mich., 1956; postgrad., Am. U. S.W. sales and promotion mgr. DOT Records, Hollywood, Calif., 1959-62; S.W. sales and mktg. rep. Pickwick Internat. Co., 1963-65; pres., chmn. bd. Stan Levenson Assos., Dallas, 1966-76; exec. v.p., gen. mgr. public relations div. S.W., Bozell & Jacobs, 1976-81; pres., CEO Levenson & Levenson, 1981-83; CEO Levenson Pub. Rels., 1984—; dir. Fidelity Nat. Bank, Dallas. Adj. prof. in pub. relations mgmt. So. Meth. U., 1987-88, mem. adv. bd. Pub. Rels. sequence studies. Group leader comm. task force Dallas Police Dept.; assoc. mem. Dallas Assembly; bd. dirs. Dallas Arboretum, Vis. Nurses Assn., Family Place, Dallas Coun. World Affairs, Dallas Urban League, 2001; mem. adv. bd. Crystal Charity Ball; co-chmn. Dallas Mayor's Task Force on Mktg.; mem. exec. com., bd. dirs. Ctrl. Downtown Assn., Dallas, 1993-94, Dallas Urban League; bd. dir. Dallas chpt. Am. Heart Assn.; mem. Dallas Citizens Coun., 1997—; arts adminstrn. and corp. comm. adv. bd. So. Meth. U., 2000—; trustee TACA, 1980, bd. dirs., 2000; trustee Dallias Alliance, 1988; mem. exec. com. Ctrl. Dallas Assn.; state com. chmn. March of Dimes, 2002; Dallas bd. dirs. Am. Heart Assn., comm. chmn. 2002—. With U.S. Army, 1956-58. Mem. Pub. Rels. Soc. Am. (accredited, North Tex. Teich award), Soc. Profl. Journalists, Greater Dallas Chamber (mktg. and comm. adv. coun. 2000—). Home: 4545 Mill Run Rd Dallas TX 75244-6432 Office: Plz Ams S Tower 600 N Pearl St Ste 910 Dallas TX 75201-7484

LEVENTHAL, BENNETT LEE, psychiatry and pediatrics educator, administrator; b. Chgo., July 6, 1949; s. Howard Leonard and Florence Ruth (Albert) L.; m. Celia G. Goodman, June 11, 1972; children: Matthew G., Andrew G., Julia G. Student, Emory U., 1967-68, La. State U., 1968-70, BS, 1972, postgrad., 1970-74, MD, 1974. Diplomate Am. Bd. Psychiatry and Neurology in Psychiatry, Am. Bd. Psychiatry and Neurology, Child Psychiatry; lic. physician N.C., La., Ill., Va. Undergrad. rsch. assoc. Lab. Prof. William A. Pryor dept. chemistry, La. State U., 1968-70; house officer I Charity Hosp. at New Orleans, 1974; resident in psychiatry Duke U. Med. Ctr., Durham, N.C., 1974-78, chief fellow divsn. dept. psychiatry, 1976-77, chief resident dept. psychiatry, 1977-78, clin. assoc. dept. psychiatry, 1978-80; staff psychiatrist, head psychiatry dept. Joel T. Boone Clinic, Virginia Beach, Va., 1978-80; staff psychiatrist, faculty mem. dept. psychiatry Naval Regional Med. Ctr., Portsmouth, 1978-80; asst. prof. psychiatry and pediats. U. Chgo., 1978-85, dir. Child Psychiatry Clinic, 1978-85, dir. Child and Adolescent Psychiatry Fellowship tng. program, 1979-88; Irving B. Harris prof. child and adolescent psychiatry Irving B. Harris, 1998—; dir. Sonia Shankman Orthogenic Sch., 2002—. Psychiat. cons. Caledonia State Prision/Halifax Mental Health Ctr., Tillery, N.C., 1976-77, Fed. Correctional Inst., Butner, N.C., 1977-78; cons. Norfolk Cmty. Mental health Ctr., 1978-80; adj. prof. psychology, biopsychology, and devel. psychology U. Chgo., 1990, adj. assoc. prof. dept. psychology and com. on biopsychology, 1987-90; meed. dir. Child Life and Family Edn. program Wyler Children's Hosp. of U. Chgo., 1983-95; dir. child and adolescent programs Chgo. Lakeshore Hosp., 1986—; Pfizer vis. prof. dept. psychiatry U. P.R., 1992; examiner Am. Bd. Psychiatry and Neurology in Gen. Psychiatry and Child Psychiatry, 1982—; mem. steering com. Harris Ctr. for Devel. Studies, U. Chgo., 1983—; mem. com. on evaluation of GAPS project AMA, 1993—; treas. Chgo. Consortium for Psychiat. Rsch., 1994; pres. Ill. Coun. Child and Adolescent Psychiatry, 1992-94; vis. scholar Hunter Inst. Mental Health and U. New Castle, NSW, Australia, 1995; mem. Gov.'s Panel on Health Svcs., 1993-94; prof. psychiatry & pediats. U. Chgo., 1990—, chmn. dept. psychiatry, 1991-98, Irving B. Harris prof. child & adolescent psychiatry, 1998—; presenter in field. Mem. editl. bd. Univ. Chgo. Better Health Letter, 1994-96; cons. editor: Jour. Emo tional and Behavioral Disorders, 1992-96; reviewer: Archives of Gen. Psychiatry, 1983—, Biol. Psychiatry, 1983—, Am. Jour. Psychiatry, 1983—, Jour. AMA, 1983—, Jour. Am. Acad. Child and Adolescent Psychiatry, 1983—, Sci., 1983—; book rev. editor Jour. Neuropsychiatry and Clin. Neuroscis., 1989-92, mem. editl. bd., 1989-92; contbr. articles to profl. jours. Lt. comdr. M.C., USNR, 1978-80. Recipient Crystal Plate award Little Friends, 1994, Individual Achievement award Autism Soc. Am., 1991, Merit award Duke U. Psychiat. Resident's Assn., 1976, Bick award La. Psychiat. Assn., 1974; Andrew W. Mellon Found. faculty fellow U. Chgo., 1983-84; John Dewey lectr. U. Chgo., 1982. Fellow Am. Acad. Child and Adolescent Psychiatry (Outstanding Mentor 1988, dep. chmn. program com. 1979—, chmn. arrangements com. 1979—, new rsch. subcom. for ann. meeting 1986—, mem. work group on rsch. 1989—), Am. Psychiat. Assn. (Falk fellow, mem. Ittleson Award Bd. 1994-97, mem. Am. Psychiat. Assn./Wisniewski Young Psychiatrists Rsch. Award Panel 1994—), Am. Acad. Pediats., Am. Orthopsychiat. Assn.; mem. AAAS, Am. Coll. Psychiatrists, Brain Rsch. Inst., Ill. Coun. Child and Adolescent Psychiatry, Ill. Psychiat. Soc., Soc. for Rsch. in Child Devel., Soc. of Profs. of Child and Adolescent Psychiatry, Soc. Biol. Psychiatry, Nat. Bd. Med. Examiners, Mental Health Assn. Ill. (profl. adv. bd. 1991—), Sigma Xi. Office: U of Chgo Pritzker Sch of Medicine 5841 S Maryland Ave Chicago IL 60637-1463 E-mail: b-leventhal@uchicago.edu.

LEVENTHAL, ELLEN IRIS, portfolio manager, financial services executive; b. N.Y.C. d. Harry and Laura (Schapira) L. BA, Barnard Coll., N.Y.C., 1971; MA, Columbia U., 1973; MBA, NYU, 1978; student, Harvard U., 1968. Registered rep. NASD. Sr. investment analyst Comptrollers Office, City of N.Y., 1978-79; asst. investment officer Chem. Bank, N.Y.C., 1980-81; v.p., portfolio mgr. E.F. Hutton, 1981-87, Shearson Lehman Bros., N.Y.C., 1987-89, Ellaure Corp., N.Y.C., 1989—. Portfolio mgr. Delta Capital Mgmt., 1993—. Mem. Investment Tech. Assn., N.Y. Soc. Security Analysts, NYU Bus. Forum, NYU Fin. Club, Money Marketeers of NYU, Princeton Club of N.Y., Barnard Coll. Club of N.Y., City Club of N.Y., Women's City Club of N.Y., Kappa Delta Pi. Avocations: golf, piano, ballet, tennis.

LEVENTHAL, LAWRENCE JAY, rheumatologist, educator; b. N.Y.C., June 5, 1958; s. Samuel and Anne Leventhal; m. Linda Currao, May 15, 1988; 2 children. BA in Biology magna cum laude, Brandeis U., 1980; MD, Hahnemann U., 1984. Resident in internal medicine Albert Einstein Med. Ctr., Phila., 1984-87; fellow in rheumatology U. Pa., 1987-90, clin. assoc. in medicine, 1989-91, clin. asst. prof. medicine, 1989-97; clin. asst. prof. Med. Coll. Pa., Phila., 1990—; assoc. prof. medicine Hahnemann U., 1997—. Dir. arthritis rsch. edn. Presbyn. Hosp., Phila., 1990—93; assoc. chief rheumatology Grad. Hosp., Phila., 1993—98, chief rheumatology, 1998—, vice chair dept. medicine, 2001—. Author: Primer of Rheumatic Disease, 1994; editor: Jour. Clin. Rheumatology; contbr. articles to profl. jours. Named one of Best Drs. in Am., Ctr. for the Study Svcs., 1996—2001. Fellow ACP, Am. Coll. Rheumatology, Phila. Coll. Physicians; mem. AMA (physicians recognition award 1987—), Am. Soc. Internal Medicine, Phila. Rheumatism Soc. (pres. 1996), Arthritis Found. (exec. bd.). Office: Grad Hosp 1800 Lombard St Philadelphia PA 19146-1497

LEVENTHAL, NATHAN, performing company executive, lawyer, municipal official; b. N.Y.C., Feb. 19, 1943; s. Harry and Fay (Bronstein) L.; m. Gretchen Dykstra, Feb. 12, 1993. BA in Pub. Affairs, Queens Coll., 1963; JD cum laude, Columbia U., 1966. Bar: N.Y. 1967. Commr. Rent and Housing Maintenance, N.Y.C., 1972-73; chief counsel U.S. Senate Subcom. Adminstrv. Practice and Procedure, Washington, 1973-74; assoc. and ptnr. Poletti, Freidin, Prashker, Feldman & Gartner, N.Y.C., 1974-78; commr. Housing Preservation and Devel., 1978-79; dep. mayor ops. City of N.Y., 1979-84; pres. Lincoln Ctr. for Performing Arts, 1984—2000; dir. Dreyfus Mutual Funds, 1987—; chmn. N.Y.C. Mayor's Com. on Appointments, 2002—. Lectr. govt. housing policy New Sch. Social Rsch., N.Y.C., 1979; lectr. health care and pub. policy Columbia Law Sch., N.Y.C., 1971. Editor-in-chief: Columbia Law Rev., 1965-66. Bd. visitors City Univ. Law Sch., N.Y.C., 1983—, Columbia Law Sch., 1989—, The New Sch., N.Y.C., 1992—; chmn. Citizens Union, 1994—; active Coun. on Jud. Adminstrn., Bar Assn. N.Y.C., 1983-90; dir. Nat. Youth Svc. Corp. for N.Y.C., 1983-85; commr. N.Y.C. Charter Revision Commn., 1986-89, N.Y. State Commn. on Constl. Revision, 1993-95; dir. Queen's Coll. Found., 1988—; chair David M. Dinkins Mayoral Transition Com., 1989-90; chair Michael Bloomberg's Mayoral Transition Com., 2001-2002. Harlan Fiske Stone scholar Columbia Law Sch., 1963-65, Jerome Michael scholar, 1965-66; Disting. Svc. award Citizens Housing and Planning Coun., N.Y.C., 1984, Am. Soc. Pub. Adminstrn. Outstanding Pub. Adminstr. award, 1982, Columbia Univ. Medal for Excellence, 1985, Austrian Grand Decoration of Honor, 1992, Theodore L. Kesselman award San Arts Edn., 1998.

LEVENTHAL, RUTH, retired parasitology educator, university official; b. Phila., May 23, 1940; d. Harry Louis Mongin and Bertha (Rosenberg) Mongin Blai; children: Sheryl Anne, David Alan. BS, U. Pa., 1961, PhD, 1973, MBA, 1981; HHD (hon.), Thomas Jefferson U., 1995; student, Pa. Acad. Fine Arts, 2000—. Cert. med. technologist, clin. lab. scientist. Trainee NSF, 1971, USPHS, 1969-70, 73; asst. prof. med. tech. U. Pa., Phila., 1974-77, acting dean, 1977-81; dean Hunter Coll., CUNY, 1981-84; provost, dean, prof. biology Capital Coll., Pa. State U., Middletown, 1984-95; prof. biology Pa. State U. Hershey Med. Ctr., 1996—2002; ret., 2002. Site visitor Mid. State Assn. Colls. and Secondary Schs., Phila., 1983—98. Author (with Creadle): Medical Parasitology: A Self Instructional Text, 1979; author: 5th edit., 2002. Chmn. founds. Tri-County United Way, South Central Pa., 1996, 97; mem. health found. bd. Harrisburg Hosp., Pa., 1984-92; pres. bd. dirs. Open Stage Harrisburg, 1996-97, bd. dirs. 1996-2000; bd. dirs. Tri-County Planned Parenthood, 1984-87, Harrisburg Acad., Wormleysburg, Pa., 1984-88, Metro Arts of Harrisburg, 1984-87, Tech. Coun. Ctrl. Pa., 1996-99; founding chmn. Coun. Pub. Edn., 1984-99. Recipient Alice Paul award Women's Faculty Club, U. Pa., 1981; Recognition award NE Deans of Schs. of Allied Health, 1984, Athena award Capital Region C. of C., 1992, John Baum Humanitarian award Am. Cancer Soc., 1992, Lifetime Achievement award Family and Children's Svcs., 1996, Coll. and Cmty. Svc. award Harrisburg Area C.C., 1993; named Disting. Dau. Pa. by Gov. of Pa., 1995. Avocations: painting, sculpture.

LEVENTIS, GEORGE CHRIS, lawyer; b. Columbia, S.C., June 26, 1949; s. Chris P. and Kathryn (Kapsalis) L.; m. Anne-Marie Catherine Noe, Aug. 4, 1973 (div. Nov. 1990); children: Kristianna, George Jr., Renee, Gabriel. BA, U. Va., 1971; JD, U. S.C., Columbia, 1974, MPA, 1984. Bar: U.S. Dist. Ct. S.C., U.S. Ct. Appeals (4th cir.). Legis. aide U.S. Senator J. Strom Thurmond, Washington, 1968; dir. rsch. and adminstrn. House Edn. and Pub. Works Com., Columbia, S.C., 1974-78, 80-81; ptnr. Leventis, Scott and Dickson, 1978-79; dir. legal, legis. and policy svcs. S.C. Sch. Bds. Assn., 1981-87; atty. Childs and Duff PA, 1987-89; dir. legal, legis. and policy svcs. Va. Sch. Bds. Assn., Charlottesville, 1989-90; adj. prof. U. S.C. Coll. Edn., Columbia, 1990-92; sr. gen. counsel S.C. Dept. Edn., 1990—. Mem. S.C. Procurement Rev. Panel, Columbia, 1994-99, S.C. Dept Youth Svcs. Governing Bd., 1992-93. Mem. Leadership Charlottesville, 1989. Mem. Nat. Coun. State Edn. Attys. (chair 1998), Nat. Coun. Sch. Attys. (bd. dirs. 1988-92), S.C. Bar Assn. (chair-elect gov. law sect. 1988-89), Columbia Rotary Club (bd. dirs., Paul Harris fellow 1987). Office: SC Dept Edn 1429 Senate St Columbia SC 29201-3730 Fax: 803-734-4384. E-mail: gleventi@sde.state.sc.us.

LEVENTIS, NICHOLAS, chemistry educator, consultant; b. Athens, Greece, Nov. 12, 1957; came to U.S., 1980; s. Spyro and Ephrosine (Nenou) L.; m. Chariklia Sotiriou, Nov. 12, 1988; 1 child, Theodora E. BS in Chemistry, U. Athens, Greece, 1980; PhD in Chemistry, Mich. State U., 1985; grad. cert. in adminstrn. and mgmt., Harvard U., 1992. Grad. asst. Mich. State Univ., East Lansing, 1980-85; rsch. assoc. MIT, Cambridge, Mass., 1985-88; project dir. Molecular Displays, Inc., 1988-90, v.p. R & D, 1990-93; prof. chemistry U. Mo., Rolla, 1994—. Cons. Igen, Inc., Rockville, Md., 1987—94, Hyperion Catalysis Internat., Cambridge, 1988—94, Delta F Corp., Woburn, Mass., 1992—94, Moonwatch Inc., N.Y.C., 1995—2001, Pleotint LLP, 1998—2001. Contbr. articles on electrochromic phenomena and devices to Yearbook of Ency. of Sci. & Tech., Jour. Mat. Chem., Chem. of Materials, Jour. Electrochem. Soc., Polymer News, Jour. Phys. Chemistry, Analytical Chemistry. Recipient Greek Inst. State Scholarships awards Greek Govt. Dept. Edn., 1976-79, Katie Y. F. Yang prize Harvard U., Cambridge, 1992; named Ethyl Corp. fellow Mich. State U., East Lansing, 1983, Yates Meml. fellow Mich. State U., East Lansing, 1984, U.S. Naval Rsch. Lab. Summer Faculty fellow, 1998. Mem. Am. Chem. Soc. (Arthur K. Doolittle award 1993), Electrochemical Soc., Internat. Union Pure & Applied Chemistry (affiliate mem.), Soc. for Info. Display. Greek Orthodox. Achievements include patents for electrochromic, electroluminescent and electrochemiluminescent displays, apparatus for detecting moisture in garments; electrically conductive polymer composition, method of making same and device incorporating same; apparatus for conducting a plurality of simultaneous measurements of electrochemiluminescent phenomena; apparatus for detecting moisture in garments. Home: 1604 McCutchen Dr Rolla MO 65401-2651 Office: U Mo Dept Chemistry Rolla MO 65401 E-mail: leventis@umr.edu.

LEVER, ALVIN, health science association administrator; b. St. Louis, Jan. 27, 1939; s. Jack I. and Sabina (Vogel) L.; m. Norine Sue Schwedt, Jan. 27, 1963; children: Daniel Jay, Michael Leonard. BS in Archtl. Scis., Washington U., St. Louis, 1961, BArch, 1963; MA in Applied Psychology, U. Santa Monica, 1992. Registered architect, Mo., Ill. Project designer Sir Basil Spence, Architects, Edinburgh, Scotland, 1963-65; sr. project designer Hellmuth, Obata & Kassabaum, St. Louis, 1965-68, v.p., project mgr., 1968-72; v.p. facility devel. Michael Reese Med. Ctr., Chgo., 1972-74; v.p., gen. mgr. Apelco Internat., Ltd., Northbrook, Ill., 1974-90; dir. membership and fin. Am. Coll. Chest Physicians, 1990-92, exec. dir., 1992-95, exec. v.p., CEO, 1995—. Pub. jour. Chest. Pub. Chest. Bd. dirs. Chest Found., 1997; v.p. Congregation B'nai Tikvah, 1987-91, pres., 1993-95. Mem. Profl. Conv. Mgmt. Assn., Am. Soc. Med. Soc. Execs., Am. Soc. Assn. Execs., Chgo. Soc. Assn. Execs., Chgo. Assn. Healthcare Execs., Alliance for Continuing Med. Edn., Mission Hills Country Club. Avocations: scuba diving, bicycling, travel., golf. Office: Am Coll Chest Physicians 3300 Dundee Rd Northbrook IL 60062-2303

LEVER, O. WILLIAM, JR. chemist; b. Greenville, S.C., Sept. 11, 1944; s. Oscar William and Dorothy (Smith) L.; m. Andrea Maria Lance, July 31, 1993; 1 child, O. William III. BS, MS, U. S.C., 1969; PhD, MIT, 1974. Sr. medicinal chemist Burroughs Wellcome Co., Research Triangle Park, N.C., 1974-84; group leader drug discovery Ortho Pharm. Corp., Raritan, N.J., 1984-88; dir. rsch. Bausch & Lomb, Rochester, N.Y., 1988-95, dir. clin. affairs, 1995-96, dir. global bus. devel., 1996-98, dir. global bus. devel. and solution program, 1999—. Mem. Commn. on MIT Edn., 1970. Contbr. 35 articles to profl. jours.; reviewer for profl. jours. Mem. Am. Chem. Soc., Assn. for Rsch. in Vision and Ophthalmology, Contact Lens Assn. Ophthalmologists, Indsl. Rsch. Inst., N.Y. Acad. Sci., AAAS, Soc. Biomaterials, Sigma Xi. Democrat. Methodist. Achievements include 6 U.S. patents and 20 foreign patents for antiallergic, cardiovascular and antitumor agent potentiation; research in analgesics, antiinflammatories, allergy, cardiovascular; development of OTC health care products. Home: 14 Fenimore Dr Pittsford NY 14534-3252 Office: Bausch & Lomb 1400 Goodman St N Rochester NY 14609-3596

LEVERE, RICHARD DAVID, internist, educator; b. Bklyn., Dec. 13, 1931; s. Samuel and Mae (Fain) L.; m. Diane L. Gonchar, Jan. 15, 1978; children: Elyssa C., Corinne G., Scott M. Student, NYU, 1949-52; MD, SUNY, N.Y.C., 1956. Intern Bellevue Hosp., N.Y.C., 1956-57, resident, 1957-58, Kings County Hosp., 1960-61; asst. prof. medicine SUNY Downstate Med. Center, 1965-69, assoc. prof., 1969-73, prof., 1973-77, vice-chmn. dept. medicine, 1975-77, chief hematology/oncology div., 1970-77; asst. prof. Rockefeller U., 1964-65; prof., chmn. dept. medicine N.Y. Med. Coll., 1977-93, vice dean, 1991-93; med. dir. Westchester County Med. Ctr., 1991-92; v.p. med. affairs St. Agnes Hosp., 1991-93; sr. v.p. Bklyn. Hosp. Ctr., 1994-98; assoc. dean NYU Sch. Medicine, 1994-99, prof. medicine, 1994-2000, adj. prof., 2000—. Adj. prof. Rockefeller U., 1973—98, vis. prof., 1998—2000; dep. dir. Lang Rsch. Ctr., N.Y. Hosp., Queens, 1999—2001; clin. prof. medicine Weill Cornell Sch. Medicine, N.Y.C., 2001—. Contbr. articles to profl. jours. Bd. dirs. Leukemia Soc. Am., 1970-85, Am. Heart Assn., 1978-94; trustee Our Lady of Mercy Med. Ctr., 1993-96. NIH grantee, 1971-76, 65-86. Master ACP (gov. N.Y. State 1990-94, pres. N.Y. State chpt. 1992-93, Physician Recognition award 1986); fellow N.Y. Acad. Medicine; mem. Harvey Soc., Am. Soc. Clin. Investigation, Soc. Study of Blood (pres. 1973-74), Soc. Devel. Biology, Am. Soc. Pharm. Exptl. Therapeutics (William Dock Teaching award, Tinsley Harrison Rsch. award), Den Tiroler Adler-Ordern of Austria, Alpha Omega Alpha. Home: 5 Seymour Pl W Armonk NY 10504-2516 Office: Rockefeller U 1230 York Ave New York NY 10021-6399

LEVERENZ, HUMBOLDT WALTER, retired chemical research engineer; b. Chgo., July 11, 1909; s. Paul Frederick and Lydia (Humboldt) L.; m. Edith Ruggles Langmuir, Nov. 30, 1940; children: David, Edith, Julia, Ellen. BA in Chemistry, Stanford U., 1930; postgrad., U. Muenster, 1930-31. Rsch. engr. RCA Mfg. Co., Camden, Harrison, N.J., 1931-42, RCA Labs., Princeton, 1942-54, dir. physics and chem. rsch. lab., 1954-57, asst. dir. rsch., 1957-59, dir. rsch., 1959-61, assoc. dir., 1961-68; staff v.p. RCA Corp., 1968-74. Mem. Materials Adv. Bd., Washington, 1964-68. Author: Luminescence of Solids, 1950, 70; contbr. articles to profl. publs. Named Modern Pioneer Nat. Assn. Manufacturers, 1940; recipient Frank P. Brown medal Franklin Inst., 1954. Fellow Am. Phys. Soc., Optical Soc. Am., IEEE; mem. Nat. Acad. Engring., Am. Chem. Soc., Sigma Xi. Achievements include 67 patents; devel. of phosphors and luminescent screens used in fluorescent lamps and picture tubes, ferrites for TV receivers. Home: 2240 Gulf Shore Blvd N Apt K4 Naples FL 34102-1613

LEVERETT, BRIAN STUART, music educator; b. Detroit, Apr. 12, 1959; m. Rita Leverett; children: Jason, Arielle. M Music Edn., Wayne State U., 1996. Tchr. music Detroit Bd. Edn., 1982—. Composer: (songs) Send 'Em Down Yo-Ho!, 1999 (John Lennon Song Writing Contest, 1999). Resident composer, asst. youth chour dir. St. Timothy United Meth. Ch., Detroit, 2001—. Office: Detroit Open School 24601 Frisbee Detroit MI 48219 Personal E-mail: Timbila@aol.com.

LEVERETT, MARGARET ANN, women's health nurse practitioner; b. Tallahassee, Feb. 18, 1951; d. Harold and Elizabeth (Cogswell) Brown; children: Anne Michelle, Amy Kayleen, Allison Elizabeth. BSN, U. Wyo., 1976; cert., Women's Health Care Nurse Practitioner Prog., 1990. Cert. Nurses Assn. Am. Coll. Ob-Gyn., NCC, nurse practitioner, RN first asst. Pub. health nurse Sedgwick County, Wichita, Kans.; recovery rm. nurse, childbirth educator Ea. Idaho Regional Med. Ctr., Idaho Falls; childbirth educator Powell (Wyo.) Hosp. & Powell Women's Clinic; nurse practitioner Powell Womens Clinic and Nowcap, Cody, Wyo., Teton Womens Health Ctr., Idaho Falls, Idaho. Named Profl. Woman of the Yr., Idaho Falls C. of C., 1998. Mem. ACOG, Idaho Med. Assn. Office: 3585 Sun Cir Idaho Falls ID 83404 E-mail: lavert50@aol.com.

LEVERICH, KATHLEEN, writer; b. Greenwich, Conn., Feb. 2, 1948; d. Robert Cameron and Constance (Valadon) Leverich; m. Walter Henry Lorraine, Jan. 23, 1988. Student, U. So. Calif., L.A., 1966-67; BA, Regents' Coll., Albany, N.Y., 1982. Ops. supr. visitor's svcs. Lincoln Ctr., N.Y.C., 1968-70; editor internat. newsletter Diner's Club, 1971-73; editor Cricket mag. Carus Group, Chgo., 1974-75; editor-in-chief children's books Addison Wesley Pub. Co., Reading, Mass., 1975-78. Author: Best Enemies, 1989, Best Enemies Again, 1991, Hilary and the Troublemakers, 1993, Brigid Bewitched, 1994, Best Enemies Forever, 1995, Brigid Beware, 1996, Brigid the Bad, 1997, The New You, 1998. Yaddo fellow, 1984. Mem. The Authors Guild, Soc. of Children's Book Writers and Illustrators. Avocation: dogs. Home and Office: 40 Rogers Ave Somerville MA 02144 E-mail: katlev@attbi.com.

LEVERMORE, CHARLES DAVID, mathematics educator; b. Teaneck, N.J., Nov. 19, 1951; s. Charles Herbert and Helen (Henze) L. BS in Math., BS in Math., BS in Physics, MS in Math., Clarkson Coll., Potsdam, N.Y., 1974; PhD in Math., Courant Inst./NYU, 1982. Math. physicist O-Group, Lawrence Livermore (Calif.) Nat. Lab., 1979; asst. prof. math. U. Pitts., 1979-82; mathematician A-Div., Lawrence Livermore (Calif.) Nat. Lab., 1982-88; assoc. prof. math. U. Ariz., Tucson, 1988-92, prof. math., 1992—. Cons. Livermore Nat. Lab., 1979—, Los Alamos (N.Mex.) Nat. Lab., 1988—. Editor: Singular Limits of Dispersive Waves, 1993; contbr. numerous articles to profl. jours. Hertz fellow Fannie & John Hertz Found., 1975. Mem. Am. Math. Soc., Math. Assn. Am., Soc. of Indsl. and Applied Math., Phi Kappa Phi, Pi Mu Epsilon, Sigma Pi Sigma. Office: Univ of Ariz Dept Of Math Tucson AZ 85721-0001

LEVERT, FRANCIS EDWARD, nuclear engineer, researcher; b. Tusculoosa, Ala., Mar. 28, 1940; s. John Clemins and Bessie Leona (Williams) LeV.; m. Faye Burnett, June 5, 1965; children: Francis Edward, Gerald Clemins, Lisa Ann. BSME, Tuskegee Inst., 1964; MS in Nuclear Engring., U. Mich., 1966; PhD in Nuclear Engring., Pa. State U., 1971. Registered profl. engr, Tenn. Assoc. prof., head mech. engring. dept. Tuskegee (Ala.) Inst., 1972-73; nuclear engr. Commonwealth Edison, Chgo., 1973-74, Argonne (Ill.) Nat. Lab., 1974-79; sr. scientist Tech. for Energy Corp., Knoxville, Tenn., 1979-85; v.p. K.E.M.P. Corp., 1985—2002, Shoe Spring, Inc., 2002—. Author: (book) Literature Review and Commercial Source Evaluation of AM.-261 (AEC-ORO-4333), 1973, (book) A Guide to Patent Applications, (Van Nostrand Reinhold 1993); contbr. over 65 articles to tech. publs. AEC fellow, 1964-66, Def. Nat. Edn. Act fellow, 1968-70, Am. Soc. Engring. Edn. Ford Found. fellow, 1973-74. Mem. Am. Soc. Mech. Engrs. (exec. com. Plant Main div. 1989—). Achievements include 20 patents for Heat Flux Monitor, Slag Depositor Monitor, Level Gages, Solid State Neutron Sensor, Directional Sensitive Self-power Gamma Detectors, self-power hair curlers, upwardly deployed venetian blinds, spring cushioned shoe. Home: 1909 Matthew Ln Knoxville TN 37923-1340 Office: KEMP Corp Knoxville TN 37917 E-mail: fel@levertco.com.

LEVESON, IRVING FREDERICK, economist; b. N.Y.C., June 28, 1939; s. Hyman Wolf and Minnie L.; m. Barbara Diane Wurtzelman, Jan. 28, 1961; children: Stephen Martin, Scott Owen. BA (N.Y. State Regents scholar), CCNY, 1960, MBA, 1963; PhD, Columbia U., 1968. Rsch. analyst, rsch. asst. Nat. Bur. Econ. Rsch., 1963-67; rsch. economist N.Y.C. Health Svcs. Adminstrn., 1967-68; economist RAND Corp., 1968-69; dir. rsch. Office Comprehensive Planning, N.Y.C., Planning Commn., 1969-71; asst. adminstr. health systems planning N.Y.C. Health Services Adminstrn., 1971-74; sr. profl. staff, dir. econ. studies Hudson Inst., Croton-on-Hudson, N.Y., 1974-84; sr.

v.p., dir. rsch. Hudson Strategy Group, N.Y.C., 1984-90; pres. Leveson Cons., Marlboro, N.J., 1990—, ForecastCenter.com, LLC, Marlboro, 1999—. Adj. sr. fellow Hudson Inst.; lectr., cons. in field. Author: The Future of the Financial Services Industry, 1982, American Challenges, 1991; editor: Quantitative Explorations in Drug Abuse Policy, 1980; co-editor: Western Economies in Transition, 1980, Analysis of Urban Health Problems, 1976. Mem. Am. Econ. Assn., Nat. Assn. Bus. Economists. Jewish. Home and Office: 10 Inverness Ln Jackson NJ 08527-

LEVESQUE, RENE JULES ALBERT, retired physicist; b. St. Alexis, Que., Can., Oct. 30, 1926; s. Albert and Elmina Louisa (Veuilleux) L.; m. Alice Farnsworth, Apr. 6, 1956 (div.); children: Marc, Michel, Andre; m. Michèle Robert, Feb., 1992. B.Sc., Sir George Williams U., 1952; PhD, Northwestern U., 1957. Research assoc. U. Md., 1957-59; asst. prof. U. Montreal, 1959-64, assoc. prof., 1964-67, prof., 1967-87, dir. nuclear physics lab., 1965-69, chmn. dept. physics, 1968-73, vice dean arts and scis., 1973-75, dean, 1975-78, v.p. research, 1978-85, v.p. research and planning, 1985-87, prof. emeritus, 1987; mem. Atomic Energy Control Bd., Ottawa, Can., 1985-87, pres. Can., 1987-93; ret., 1993. Mem. adv. com. ING project Atomic Energy of Can. Ltd., 1966-69; mem. adv. bd. physics NRC Can., 1972-74, pres. nuclear physics grant selection, 1973; mem. adv. bd. on TRIUMF, 1979-87; v.p. Commn. Higher Studies Que. Ministry Edn., 1976-77, Natural Scis. and Engring. Research Council Can., 1981-87; v.p. bd. dirs. Can.-France-Hawaii Telescope Corp., 1979-80, pres., 1980-81; pres. permanent research com. Conf. Rectors and Prins. Que. Univs., 1979-80; pres. Mouvement Laïc de Langue française, 1961. Named Officer Order of Can., 1997. Mem. Can. Assn. Physicists (pres. 1976-77), U. Montreal Faculty Assn. (pres. 1971), Fedn. Que. Faculty Assn. (pres. 1971-72), Interciencia Assn. (v.p. bd. dirs. 1979-80), Assn. Scis., Engring. and Tech. Comty. Can. (v.p. 1979-80, pres. 1980-81), Order of Can. (officer 1997). Home: 190 Willowdale PH 1 Outremont QC Canada H3T 1G2

LEVETON, IAN SINCLAIR, civil engineer; b. Birmingham, Eng., Nov. 27, 1942; came to U.S., 1953; s. Eric Karl and Zena (Altman) L. BA in Physics and Econs., NYU, 1965; cert. of achievement, Orange Coast Coll., Costa Mesa, Calif., 1990. Computer programmer trainee Bklyn. Union Gas Co., 1969; computer programmer Elizabeth Arden Sales Corp., N.Y.C., 1970; electronics expeditor Bendix Navigation & Controls, Teterboro, N.J., 1971; inventory control supr. Roman Products Inc., South Hackensack, 1972; nuclear mech. engr. Pub. Svc. N.J., Newark, 1973; mech. engr. Chemplant Designs divsn. DuPont, N.Y.C., 1974-78, Holmes and Narver, Inc., Orange, Calif., 1978-82; tech. writer nuclear safety So. Calif. Edison, Rosemead, 1983-85; civil engr. tech. City of Santa Ana, 1985—. Cons. Islian Assocs., Teaneck, N.J., 1970-71. Mem. Teaneck Bicentennial Com., 1976; coord. United Way, City Pub. Works Agy., Santa Ana, 1992. Mem. KP (sec. 1974-76). Avocations: tennis, boating, reading, music, traveling. Home: 19302 Steven Ln Huntington Beach CA 92646-2711

LEVEY, GERALD SAUL, dean, internist, educator; b. Jersey City, Jan. 9, 1937; s. Jacob and Gertrude (Kantoff) Levey; m. Barbara Ann Cohen, June 4, 1961; children: John, Robin. AB, Cornell U., 1957; MD, N.J. Coll. Medicine, 1961. Diplomate Am. Bd. Internal Medicine. Med. intern Jersey City Med. Ctr., 1961—62, asst. med. resident, 1962—63; postdoctoral fellow dept. biol. chemistry Harvard U. Med. Sch., 1963—65; med. resident Mass. Gen. Hosp., Boston, 1965—66; clin. assoc. clin. endocrinology br. Nat. Inst. Arthritis and Metabolic Diseases NIH, Bethesda, Md., 1966—68, clin. assoc. Nat. Heart and Lung Inst., 1968—69, sr. investigator Nat. heart and Lung Inst., 1969—70; assoc. prof. medicine U. Miami Sch. Medicine, Fla., 1970—73, prof. medicine, 1973—79; prof., chmn. dept. medicine U. Pitts. Sch. Medicine, 1979—91; physician-in-chief Presbyn.-Univ. Hosp., Pitts., 1979—91; sr. v.p. for med. and sci. affairs Merck and Co., Inc., Whitehouse Sta., NJ, 1991—94; provost med. scis., dean Sch. of Medicine UCLA, 1994—. Harold Jeghers lectr. N.J. Coll. Medicine, 1977; Marian Blankenhorn lectr. Cin. Soc. Internal Medicine, 1982—; co-prin. investigator Nat. Study of Internal Medicine Manpower, 1984—. Mem. editl. bd.: Endocrinology, 1972—76, mem. editl. bd.: Am. Jour. Physiology, 1972—76, mem. editl. bd.: Jour. Applied Physiology, 1972—76, mem. editl. bd.: Annals of Internal Medicine, 1981—84, cons. editor: Hosp. Medicine, 1981—91; contbr. articles to profl. jours. Mem. United Jewish Fedn. Pitts. Leadership Devel., 1981—82; bd. dirs. Jewish Family and Children's Svcs., 1982—83, Am. Jewish Com., Miami, 1975—79. Grantee, NIH, 1971—91, Fla. Heart Assn., 1971—74. Fellow: ACP; mem.: AMA, Assn. Am. Physicians, Soc. Gen. Internal Medicine, So. Soc. Clin. Investigation, Assn. Profs. Medicine (chmn. ad hoc com. for use of animals in rsch. 1982—85, chmn. task force on internal medicine manpower 1983—90, nat. pres. 1990—91), Endocrine Soc., Am. Soc. Clin. Investigation, Am. Fedn. Clin. Rsch. (councillor so. sect. 1973—76, pres. so. sect. 1977—78), Am. Thyroid Assn. (mem. membership com. 1977—80), Alpha Omega Alpha. Home: 1132 Laurel Way Beverly Hills CA 90210-2221 Office: UCLA Deans Office Sch Medicine 10833 Le Conte Ave Los Angeles CA 90095-3075*

LEVEY, ROBERT FRANK, newspaper columnist; b. N.Y.C., June 2, 1945; s. Stanley Victor and Sylvia Rose (Frank) L.; m. Jane Ellen Freundel, May 17, 1980; children: Emily Susanna, Alexander Freundel. BA, U. Chgo., 1966. Reporter Albuquerque Tribune, 1966-67; reporter, editor Washington Post, 1967-81, columnist, 1981—. Vis lectr. Duke U., Durham, N.C., 1979—; adviser journalism Cath. U. Am., Washington, 1979-81. Co-author: Washington Album, 2000; talk show host Sta. WRC, 1981—83, Sta. WBAL, 1988—92, Sta. WJLA-TV, 1984—86, Sta. WETA-FM, 1985—90, Sta. WTOP, 1997—2001, Newschannel 8, 2000—. Woodrow Wilson fellow. Mem. Reporters Com. for Freedom of the Press, Newspaper Guild (chmn. Washington Post unit 1972-75), AFTRA, U. Chgo. Alumni Assn. (bd. govs. 1992-2000, pres. 1998-2000), Sigma Delta Chi. Jewish. Office: Washington Post 1150 15th St NW Washington DC 20071-0002 E-mail: leveyb@washpost.com.

LEVI, BARBARA GOSS, physicist, editor; b. Washington, May 5, 1943; d. Wilbur H. and Mildred C. (Wallin) Goss; m. Ilan M. Levi, Sept. 10, 1966; children: Daniel S., Sharon R. BA, Carleton Coll., 1965; MS, Stanford U., 1967, PhD, 1971. Assoc. editor Physics Today Am. Inst. Physics, N.Y.C., 1969-70, cons. editor Physics Today, 1970-89, assoc. editor Physics Today, 1987-88; sr. assoc. editor Physics Today, 1989-93, sr. editor, 1993—; mem. tech. staff Bell Labs, Holmdel, N.J., 1982-83; mem. rsch. staff Ctr. for Energy and Environ. Studies Princeton (N.J.) U., 1981-82, 83-87. Lectr. Fairleigh Dickinson U., Madison, NJ, 1970—75, Ga. Tech., Atlanta, 1976—80; cons. U.S. Office Tech. Assessment, Washington, 1976—93; vis. prof. Rutgers U., Piscataway, NJ, 1988—89; adj. assoc. prof. physics U. Calif., Santa Barbara, 1998—. Editor (with others): (book) Energy Sources: Conservation and Renewables, 1985, The Future of Land-Based Strategic Missiles, 1989, Global Warming: Physics and Facts, 1992. Treas. LWV, Holmdel and Colts Neck, NJ, 1983—94. Fellow: AAAS (mem. steering com. physics group 1997—), Am. Phys. Soc. (edn. com. 1989—91, chmn. forum on physics and soc. 1988—89, forum councilor 1992—95, mem. exec. bd. 1994—95, Lilienfeld prize com. 1993—95, chair 1995, com. on coms. 1994—96, chair 1996, mem. exec. com. forum edn. 1997—98, mem. Nicholson medal com. 1998—99, chair 1999); mem.: AAUW (mem. nuc. energy task force 1975—77), Am. Assn. Physics Tchrs., Fedn. Am. Scientists (gov. bd. 1985—89). Avocations: tennis, travel, hiking, skiing.

LEVI, DAVID F. federal judge; b. 1951; BA, Harvard U., MA, 1973; JD, Stanford U. Bar: Calif. 1983. U.S. atty. ea. dist. State of Calif., Sacramento, 1986-90; judge U.S. Dist. Ct. (ea. dist.) Calif., 1990—. Chmn. task force on race, religious and ethnic fairness U.S. Ct. Appeals (9th cir.), 1994-97, mem. jury com., 1993-95. Adv. com. on Civil Rules, 1994—, chair, 2000—; vis. com. U. Chgo. Law Sch., 1995-98. Mem. Am. Law Inst., Milton L. Schwartz Inn of Ct. (pres. 1992-95). Office: 501 I St Rm 14-230 Sacramento CA 95814-7300

LEVI, HERBERT WALTER, biologist, educator; b. Frankfurt, Germany, Jan. 3, 1921; came to U.S., 1938, naturalized, 1945; s. Ludwig and Irma (Hochschild) L.; m. Lorna Rose, June 13, 1949; 1 child, Frances. Student, Art Students League, N.Y.C., 1938-39; BS, U. Conn., 1946; MS, U. Wis., 1947, PhD, 1949; MA (hon.), Harvard U., 1970. Instr., then asst. prof. to asso. prof. zoology, extension div. U. Wis., 1949-56; asst. curator arachnology Mus. Comparative Zoology Harvard U., 1956-57, assoc. curator, 1957-66, curator, 1966-91, prof. biology, 1970-91, Agassiz prof. zoology, 1972-91, prof. emeritus, 1991—. Sec. Rocky Mountain Biol. Lab., 1959-65; vis. prof. Hebrew U., Jerusalem, 1975; bd. govs. Nature Conservancy, 1956-62; taxonomic cons. Smithsonian project, 1979; cons. Syntax, Cambridge, Mass., 1986. Author: (with L.R. Levi) Spiders and Their Kin, 1968, 69, Aranas y especies afines, 1971; also numerous articles; translator, editor: Invertebrate Zoology (Kaestner), 3 vols.; bd. reviewers Pacific Insects, 1980-85; bd. editors Psyche, 1957-92, Zoomorphology, 1980-85, Sci. Bull. de Mus., Paris, 1980—, (internat.) Annales Zoologici Warszawa Poland, 1993—, Memorias do Instituto Butantan, São Paulo, Brazil, 1994—. Fellow AAAS; mem. Am. Soc. Zoologists, Soc. Study Evolution, Soc. Systematic Zoology (councillor 1967-69), Am. Micros. Soc. (bd. reviewers 1973-94), Am. Arachnol. Soc. (hon. mem., bd. editors 1974— , dir. 1975-83, pres. 1979-81), Am. Ecol. Soc., Am. Inst. Biological Scis., Wildlife Soc., Am. Ornithol. Union, Assn. Systematics Collections (council nat. systematic collections and resources 1975), British Arachnological Soc., Cambridge Entomology Club, Internat. Soc. Arachnology (v.p. 1965-68, pres. 1980-83, hon. mem. 1995—), Japanese Arachnological Soc. (hon.), Soc. Systematic Biologists, Spider Club So. Africa (hon.), Wilson Ornithological Soc., Wilderness Soc. Home: 45 Wheeler St Pepperell MA 01463-1025 Office: Harvard U Mus Comparative Zoolog Cambridge MA 02138-2902

LEVI, JAMES HARRY, real estate executive, investment banker; b. Boston, Oct. 28, 1939; s. Robert Emmett and Doris (Cohen) L.; m. Constance Jo Adler, Dec. 30, 1967; children: James H. II, Andrew R., Deanne D., Constance Jo. AB, Harvard U., 1961, MBA, 1964. Past pres. Value Properties Inc., N.Y.C.; now pres. Levi Co., Larchmont, N.Y. Chmn. bd. dirs. New Millenium Energies, Inc., St. Louis; pres. Gt. Train Store co., Dallas, others; prof. Bus. Sch. Columbia U., N.Y.C.; past pres. Oppenheimer Properties, Inc., N.Y.C.; exec. v.p., mem. exec. com. Oppenheimer & Co., Inc.; pres., chmn. bd. dirs. numerous affiliated cos. Mem. Bus. Sch. coun. Tulane U., N.Y.; mem. bd. govs. Hebrew Union Coll./Jewish Inst. Religion; mem. bd. overseers Sch. Architecture, Ill. Inst. Tech.; mem. exec. bd. Westchester Putnam coun. Boy Scouts Am.; mem. traffic commn. Village of Larchmont, N.Y.; mem. joint planning commn. Villages of Larchmont and Mamaroneck; trustee Larchmont Hist. Soc. Ensign USN, 1961-62. Named Man of Yr., St. Louis Rabbinical Coll., 1986. Mem. Real Estate Securities and Syndication Inst. (former gov.), Nat. Assn. Realtors, Nat. Assn. Rev. Appraisers (cert.), Soc. for Indsl. Archeology, Soc. Archtl. Historians, Nat. Assn. Security Dealers (registered prin.), Sheldrake Yacht Club (past treas.). Avocations: boating and sailing, collecting antiques, travelling, opera, kinetic sculpture. Home: 85 Larchmont Ave Larchmont NY 10538-3748 Office: Levi Co 85 Larchmont Ave Larchmont NY 10538-3748

LEVI, JANICE LAWAN, counselor; b. Refugio, Tex., July 4, 1946; d. Guy Nolen and Lillian Lorene (Whitten) Weeks; m. Thomas Jack Levi, Jan. 18, 1968; children: Kimberly D. , Marcel N. BS, Tex. A&I U., 1964; MS, U. Houston, 1988. Lic. profl. counselor Tex., chem. dependency counselor Tex. Journalism tchr. Sinton (Tex.) Ind. Sch. Dist., 1968—70; drama tchr. Pasadena (Tex.) Ind. Sch. Dist., 1970—88; lead counselor Pasadena (Tex.) Ind. Sch. Dist. Alternative Sch., 1988—96; sch. coord. Clear Creek Ind. Sch. Dist. Harris County Youth Village, Houston, 1996—97; counselor LaPorte (Tex.) Ind. Sch. Dist. Alternative Sch., 1997—. Facilitator family support groups Pasadena Ind. Sch. Dist., 1989—94. Active C. of C. Leadership Pasadena Group, 1994—95. Grantee Alcoa Found. grantee, Alcoa Aluminum, Pasadena, 1995, Edn. Found. grantee, LaPorte Edn. Found., 2001. Mem.: ACA, Tex. Counseling Assn. Methodist. Avocations: woodturning, motorcycle riding, stained glass, sewing, arts and crafts. Office: DeWalt Alternative Sch 301 E Fairmont Pkwy La Porte TX 77571

LEVI, JOHN G. lawyer; b. Chgo., Oct. 9, 1948; s. Edward H. and Kate (Sulzberger) L.; m. Jill Felsenthal, Oct. 7, 1979; children: Benjamin E., Daniel F., Sarah K.H. AB, U. Rochester, 1969; JD, Harvard U., 1972, LLM, 1973. Bar: Ill. 1973. Ptnr. Sidley & Austin, Chgo. Vice chmn. bd. Weiss Mem. Hosp., Chgo.; pres. bd. Francis W. Parker Sch., Chgo.; bd. dirs. Chgo. Child Care Sco.; vis. com. U. Chgo. Coll.; mem. Citizens Com. Juvenile Ct., Chgo. Mem. ABA, Ill. Bar Assn., Chgo. Bar Assn., Law Club Chgo. Office: Sidley & Austin Bank One Plz 425 W Surf St Apt 605 Chicago IL 60657-6139

LEVI, JOSEF ALAN, artist; b. New York, Feb. 17, 1938; s. Jacob and Evelyn D. (Speizer) L. BA, U. Conn., 1959; postgrad., Columbia U., 1960. Artist in residence Appalachian State U., N.C., 1969, vis. prof. art, Pa. State U., 1976 One-man shows of paintings include Stable include N.Y.C., 1966, 67, 68, 69, 70, Arts Club of Chgo., 1967, J.B. Speed Art Mus., Louisville, Ky., 1968, Appalachian State U., Boone, N.C., 1969, Lambert Gallery, Los Angeles, 1971, Gertrude Kasle Gallery, Detroit, 1971, Jacobs Ladder Gallery, Washington, 1972, Images Gallery, Toledo, Ohio, 1972, A.M. Sachs Gallery, N.Y.C., 1975, 76, 78, O.K. Harris Gallery, N.Y.C., 1983, 85, 87, 90, 92, 94, 96, 99, Adams-Middleton Gallery, Dallas, 1986, Harmon Meek Gallery, Naples, Fla., 1996, 2001; numerous group shows, 1965—, latest being, Balt. Mus. Art, 1975, Mus. Art, R.I. Sch. Design, 1976, Art Mus., U. N.C., Greensboro, 1977, Russell Sage Coll., Troy, N.Y., 1977, Washington U., St. Louis, 1977, Whitney Mus., N.Y.C., 1978-79, Meml. Art Gallery, U. Rochester, N.Y., 1979, Aldrich Mus. Contemporary Art, Ridgefield, Conn., 1980, Western Assn. Art Museums, 1981, Worcester (Mass.) Art Mus., 1981, Palace Theatre of Arts Gallery, Stamford, Conn., 1984, Randolph Macon Coll., Ashland, Va., 1985, Robert I. Kidd Galleries, Birmingham, Mich., 1985, Elaine Benson Gallery, Bridgehampton, N.Y., 1985; others; represented in numerous permanent collections including, Aldrich Mus. Contemporary Art, Albright-Knox Gallery, Buffalo, N.Y., Mus. Modern Art, N.Y.C., Krannert Art Mus., U. Ill., Urbana, Va. Mus. Fine Arts, Richmond, AT&T, N.Y.C., Corcoran Gallery, Washington, U. Md., College City, Chrysler Corp., Detroit., Spellman Coll., Atlanta, Exxon Corp., N.Y.C., Minolta Corp., N.Y.C., Des Moines Art Ctr., Newark Mus., Dartmouth Coll., Hanover, N.H., Storm King Art Ctr., Mountainville, N.Y., U. Notre Dame Art Gallery, South Bend, Ind., J. B. Speed Art Mus., Louisville, Bank of N.Y., N.Y.C., Lewis and Clark Coll., Portland, Oreg., Technimetrics Inc., N.Y.C., Best Products Corp., Ashland, Va., Southland Corp., Dallas, TRW Corp., Cleve., Bklyn. Mus. Art, Worcester (Mass.) Art. Mus., Nat. Gallery of Art, Washington, Albion (Mich.) Coll., Prudential Ins. Co. Am., Newark. Served to 1st. lt. Adj. Gen. Corps U.S. Army, 1959-60. Mem. N.Y. Artist Equity Assn.

LEVI, LOUISE LANDES, poet, translator, musician; b. N.Y.C., July 20, 1944; d. Nathaniel H. and Betty (Landes) L. Student, U. Calif., 1962-69. Music tchr. Jivamukti Yoga Ctr., N.Y.C., 1989-97, Manhatten Sch. Music, N.Y.C., 1991; poetry tchr. Naropa Inst., Boulder, Colo., 1991, Sullivan County Correctional Facility, South Fallsburg, 1997. Author: RASA (transl. by René Daumal), 1982, The Water Mirror, 1982, Vers La Complétude (transl. by Henri Michaux), 1984, Amiata, 1984, Departure, 1985, Concerto, 1988, Extinction, 1988, The Tower, 1993, The Highway Queens, 1994, Sweet on my Lips: The Love Poems of Mira Bai, 1997, The House Lamps Have Been Lit, but, 1996, Makara/A Karma, 2002, Guru Punk, 1999, Chorma, 2000, Michaux's Michaux, 2001. Mem. Guru Punk. Home: 508 E 5th St Rm 10 New York NY 10009 E-mail: llevi32@hotmail.com.

LEVI, MARGARET, humanities educator; b. Balt., Mar. 5, 1947; d. Beatrice Looban and Joseph Meyer Levi; m. Robert David Kaplan. BA, Bryn Mawr Coll., 1968; PhD, Harvard U., 1974. Harry Bridges chair in labor studies U. Wash., 1996—2000, Jere I. Bacharach prof. internat. studies, 2000—. Dir., WTO history project U. Wash. Author: Of Rule and Revenue, 1988, Consent, Dissent and Patriotism, 1997; editor: Trust and Governance, 1998, Competition and Cooperation, 1998; gen. editor: Cambridge Studies in Comparative Politics. Mem. exec. bd. Ctr. for a Changing Workforce, Seattle, 1999; mem. coordinating com. Scholars, Artists and Writers for Social Justice, Washington, 1997—99; chairperson task force on pers. law Seattle Mayor's Office, 1978; lender (with Robert D. Kaplan) Seattle Art Mus., 1995; mem. nat. exec. coun. Students for a Dem. Soc., 1964—66. Recipient Allan Sharlin Meml. prize hon. mention, Social Sci. History Assn., 1998. Mem.: Am. Acad. Arts and Scis., Am. Polit. Sci. Assn. (exec. bd., v.p., chair ann. program, task force on civic edn. 1997—2001). Democrat. Jewish. Avocation: collecting Australian Aboriginal art. Office: U Wash Dept Polit Sci Box 353530 Seattle WA 98195 Office Fax: 206-685-2146.

LEVI, MAURICE DAVID, economics educator; b. London, Sept. 28, 1945; came to U.S., 1967; s. Karl and Louisa Hannah (Magson) L.; m. Kathleen Birkinshaw, Jan. 14, 1979; children— Adam Julian, Naomi Anne, Jonathan Karl. BA in Econs. with 1st class honors, U. Manchester, Eng., 1967; MA, U. Chgo., 1968, PhD, 1972. Vis. prof. Hebrew U., Jerusalem, 1978; vis. assoc. prof. U. Calif.-Berkeley, 1979; vis. scholar MIT, Cambridge, 1980; prof. business U. B.C., Vancouver, Can., 1972—. Vis. prof. London Bus. Sch., 1985, U. Exeter, 1990, U. New S. Wales, 1997. Author: Economics Deciphered, 1981, Thinking Economically, 1985, International Finance, 3rd edit., 1996, Economics and the Modern World, 1994; contbr. articles to profl. jours. Mem. Vancouver Mayor's Econ. Adv. Commn., 1983-84, Fed. Provincial Initiative, 1987-90. Recipient Seagram award, 1978; grantee Ford Found., 1969-70, Can. Coun., 1978, 80, 85; Nomura fellow U. Exeter, 1990. Jewish. Avocations: astronomy; salmon fishing.

LEVI, VICKI GOLD, picture editor, historical consultant, actress, author; b. Atlantic City, Sept. 16, 1941; d. Albert and Beverly Valentine Gold; m. Alexander Hecht Levi, May 31, 1970; 1 child, Adam Hecht Levi. Student, Montclair State Coll., 1959-60, New Sch. Social Rsch., N.Y.C., 1970-73, Sch. Visual Arts, 1972, Lee Strass Berg Sch. Acting, 1961. Actress, Atlantic City, N.Y.C and L.A., 1945—; asst. to pres. Family Fare, Inc., N.Y.C., 1966; advt. rep. Cosmopolitan Mag., 1967; publicity dir. Misty Harbor, Ltd., 1968; freelance picture researcher, 1972—; contbg. picture editor Esquire Mag., N.Y.C., 1980—, Mirabella Mag., N.Y.C., 1991-93, Atlantic City Mag., 1988-2000, New Woman Mag., 1995—, Family Cir., 2000—. Story cons. Alvin Cooperman Prodns., N.Y.C., 1985—; hist. cons. various Atlantic City, N.Y.C., 1994—; lectr. on Atlantic City, 1979—; guest exhibitor Internat. Ctr. Photography, N.Y.C., 1979; guest exhibitor and lectr. Cooper Hewitt, N.Y.C., 1980; guest curator Songwriters Hall of Fame, N.Y.C., 1979; guest lectr. Mcpl. Art Soc., N.Y.C., 1979; co-founder Atlantic City Hist. Mus., 1985—, bd. dirs., exhibit dir., 1995—; hist. cons. Toast to Times Square Com., N.Y.C., 1988—; curator Atlantic City Playground of the Nation, Atlantic City Hist. Mus., 1994; co-curator Charles K. Doble's Atlantic City, 1994, Images of African Americans in Atlantic City, 1995, Seventy-Five Years of Miss America in Pictures, 1995, The Al Gold Years, 1996, Bettmann on the Boardwalk, 1997, 360 Degrees of Atlantic City, 1998, Stompin' at the Shore, 1999, Star Shine, 2001, Atlantic City Hist. Mus., 1996, Noyes Mus. Through the Lens, 1998, Up From the Boardwalk, Down by the Sea, 1998, The Illustrated World of Atlantic City, Atlantic City Art Ctr., 1999; bd. dirs. Hecht-Levi Found.; preliminary judge Miss America, 1997. Co-author: Atlantic City: 125 Years of Ocean Madness, 1979, rev. edit., 1994, Live and Be Well: A Celebration of Yiddish Culture in America, 1982, rev. edit., 2000, You Must Have Been a Beautiful Baby, 1992, Cuba Style, 2002; columnist Phila. Bull., The Way It Was, 1980, The Shore Thing, Talk of the Boardwalk, 1997-99, AC Insider's Guide, Then and Now, 1997; prodr., dir. (hist. video) Boardwalk Ballyhoo, 1992 (Am. Assn. State and Local History award 1995, Atlantic City Tourism Coun. Resolution award 1995, Tourism Advocacy award Greater Atlantic City Region Tourism Coun. 1996); rschr.: Miss America, The Dream Lives On, 1995; hist. cons. (prodn.) Atlantic City Experience, 1995, (Broadway prodn.) Having Our Say, 1995, Time and Again; hist. image cons. (PBS prodn.) I Hear America Singing, 1996; hist. rschr. (Disney World prodn.) BoardWalk Resort, 1996, (Broadway prodn.) Steel Pier (hist. cons.), 1998, (Broadway prodn.) The Civil-War, 1999 (hist. pictorial editor); preliminary judge Miss Am., 1997; commentator PBS, There She Is: The History of Miss America, 2002. Preliminary judge Miss Am., 1997; appeared There She is: The History of Miss Am. 2002. Recipient Author's Citation, N.J. Inst. Tech., Divsn. Continuing Edn., 1980, Senate Resolution, N.J. State Senate, 1979, Outstanding Achievement award, Atlantic City Women's C. of C., 1981, Proclamation from mayor of Atlantic City, 1981, Encore award, 2000; named An Atlantic City Treasure, Atlantic City Women's C. of C., 1989; named to Atlantic County Woman's Hall of Fame, 1997. Mem. NATAS (Emmy judge 1987-89, spl. events com. 1989-90), SAG, Am. Fedn. TV and Radio Artists, Am. Soc. Picture Profls. (bd. dirs. 1984). Democrat. Jewish. Avocations: world travel, memorabilia collecting. Home and Office: 211 Central Park W New York NY 10024-6020 E-mail: AC08401@aol.com.

LEVI, VICTOR H. retired electrical engineer; b. N.Y.C., July 23, 1932; s. Aris H. and Nina Levi; m. Norma M. Willer (dec. Jan. 20, 1980); children: Nina DeGracia, Kenneth. BEE, The Cooper Union, N.Y.C., 1953. Jr. engr. Norden Ketay Corp., N.Y.C., 1953—55; elec. engr. Sperry Gyroscope Co., Great Neck, 1955—58; supervisory elect. engr. gs-14 U.S. Army Sig. R&D Labs, Ft. Monmouth, NJ, 1958—63; prin. engr. Sperry Phoenix Co., Phoenix, 1964—65; project engr. Teledyne Ryan Co., San Diego, 1965—82; sr. sys. engr. Pacific Aerosystem Inc., 1982—89. Author: (book) And the Tongue of the Dumb Shall Sing, 1998. Jewish. Avocation: classical music. Home: 17621 Corte Potosi San Diego CA 92128 Personal E-mail: verdi@san.rr.com.

LEVIE, HOWARD S(IDNEY), lawyer, educator, writer; b. Wolverine, Mich., Dec. 19, 1907; s. J. Walter and Mina (Goldfarb) L.; m. S. Blanche Krim, July 24, 1934 AB, Cornell U., 1928, JD, 1930; LL.M., George Washington U., 1957. Bar: N.Y. 1931, Mo. 1965, U.S. Dist. Ct. (ea. dist.) N.Y. 1934, U.S. Dist. Ct. (so. dist.) N.Y. 1935, U.S. Supreme Ct. 1947, U.S. Ct. Appeals (D.C. cir.) 1949, U.S. Ct. Mil. Appeals 1953. Assoc. Weit & Goldman, N.Y.C., 1931-42; with JAGC, U.S. Army, 1942, advanced through grades to col., 1954; staff officer UN Command Armistice Del., Korea, 1951-52; chief internat. affairs div. Office of JAG, 1954-58; legal adviser U.S. European Command, Paris, 1959-61; ret. 1963; prof. law St. Louis U., 1963-77, prof. emeritus, 1977—; prof. U.S. Naval War Coll., Newport, R.I., 1971-72, Charles H. Stockton prof. internat. law, 1971-72; instr. internat. law Salve Regina Coll., 1984-88. Adj. prof. Naval War Coll., 1991—. Author: Prisoners of War in International Armed Conflict (Internat. Soc. for Mil. Law and the Law of War Ciardi prize 1982), 1979, Documents on Prisoners of War, 1980, Protection of War Victims, 4 vols., 1979-81, The Status of Gibraltar, 1983, The Code of International Armed Conflict, 1986, The Law of Non-International Armed Conflict, 1987, The Law of War and Neutrality: A Selected English-Language Bibliography, 1988, Mine Warfare at Sea, 1992, Terrorism in War: The Law of War Crimes, 1993; editor vols. 7-12: Terrorism: Documents of International and Local Control, 1997, Levie on the Law of War, 1998. Decorated Legion of Merit, Bronze Star; grantee Ctr. for Advanced Rsch., Naval War Coll., 1980-82, U.S. Inst. Peace, 1991; Howard S. Levie Mil. Chair of Operational Law established by U.S. Naval War Coll., 1994; recipient Outstanding Civilian Svc. medal Dept. of the Army, 1995; named Disting. Mem. of Judge Advocate Gen.'s Corps Regiment, 1995, The Col. Howard S. Levie Libr., established at the Army Judge Advocate's School is named in his honor. Mem. ABA, Am. Soc. Internat. Law (exec. coun. 1969-70), Internat. Law Assn., Ret. Army Judge Advs. Assn., Internat. Soc. for Mil. Law and Law of War, Phi Beta Kappa. Home and Office: 41 Sherman St Newport RI 02840-2959 E-mail: hlevie41@aol.com.

LEVIE, JOSEPH HENRY, lawyer, banker; b. N.Y.C. s. Mortimer Joseph and Pearl (Seelig) L.; m. Hallie Ratzkin, Jan. 26, 1963; children: Matthew Benjamin, Jessica Ruth. AB, Columbia U., 1949, LLB, 1951. Bar: N.Y. 1952, U.S. Supreme Ct. 1954. Assoc. Laporte & Meyers, N.Y.C., 1955-59; asst. gen. counsel Loew Theatres Inc., 1959-63; from assoc. to ptnr. Rathheim, Hoffman, Kassel & Levie, 1964-81; ptnr. Rogers & Wells, 1982-94, ret., 1994, sr. counsel, 1995—. Dir. Chinese Am. Bank, 1998—; arbitrator N.Y. Stock Exch., NASD. Contbr. articles to profl. jours. With JAGC, U.S. Army, 1952-55. Fellow Am. Coll. Comml. Fin. Attys.; mem. Columbia Coll. Alumni (pres. class of 1949). Home: 131 Riverside Dr New York NY 10024-3713 Office: Clifford Chance Rogers & Wells 200 Park Ave New York NY 10166-0800 E-mail: leviej@aol.com.

LEVIEN, ROGER ELI, strategy and innovation consultant; b. Bklyn., Apr. 16, 1935; s. Abraham Mark and Rosalind (Horowitz) L.; m. Carla Johanna Sherow, Oct. 9, 1960; children: Royce Adam, Alisa Tova. BS, Swarthmore Coll., 1956, MS, 1958; PhD, Harvard U., 1962. Mem. rsch. staff RAND Corp., Santa Monica, Calif., 1960-67, head sys. scis. dept., 1968-71, dir. Washington domestic program Washington, 1971-74; program leader Internat. Inst. Applied Sys. Analysis, Laxenburg, Austria, 1974-75, gen. dir. Austria, 1975-81; dir. strategic sys. analysis Xerox Corp., Stamford, Conn., 1981-85, corp. v.p. strategy office, 1985-92, corp. v.p. strategy and innovation, 1992-97. Adj. prof. UCLA, 1970-81; mem. adv. bd. Carnegie-Bosch Inst., Pitts., 1995-2002, Poly. U., Bklyn., 1995-97; bd. dirs. BNS Co., Warwick, R.I.; chmn. com. on internet addressing and the domain name sys. NRC, 2000--. Author: The Emerging

Technology, 1972, Research and Development Management, 1975, Taking Technology to Market, 1997; contbr. chpts. to books. Bd. dirs. Nat. Corp. Theatre Fund, N.Y.C., 1985—, Conn. Grand Opera and Orch., Stamford, 1994—. Recipient Ehrenkreuz First Class in Arts and Sci. award Austrian Govt., 1982. Mem. Mfrs. Alliance Coun. on Strategy (chmn. 1990-91), Coun. Planning Execs. (conf. bd.), Coun. on Mgmt. of Innovation and Tech. (chmn. conf. bd. 1996-97), Phi Beta Kappa, Sigma Xi, Tau Beta Pi. Avocations: skiing, photography, collecting North American Indian art, musical theater. Office: Strategy and Innovation Cons 2 River Ln Westport CT 06880-1925 E-mail: rlevien@aol.com.

LEVI-MONTALCINI, RITA, neurobiologist, researcher; b. Turin, Italy, Apr. 22, 1909; came to U.S., 1947; naturalized, 1956; d. Adamo Levi and Adele Montalcini. MD, U. Turin, 1936. Asst. in neurology Inst. Anatomy, Neurology Clinic, Turin Sch. Medicine, 1936—37; researcher Neurol. Inst. Brussels, 1939; with Allied Health Svc., Italy, 1944—45; resident, assoc. zoologist Washington U., 1947—51, assoc. prof., 1951—58, prof., 1958—81, prof. emeritus, 1977; dir. neurobiology rsch. program CNR (Nat. Rsch. Coun.), Rome, 1961—69, dir. cellular biology lab., 1969—79, guest prof. cellular biology lab., 1979—89; guest prof. inst. neurobiology CNR (Italian Nat. Rsch. Coun.), 1969—; pres. Inst. della Enciclopedia Italiana Treccani. Pres. Ency. Italiana, 1993, Italian Nat. Commn. of United World Colls., 1993. Author: In Praise of Imperfection: My Life and Work, 1988. Recipient Albert Lasker Med. Rsch. award, 1986, Nobel prize Physiology-Medicine, (with Stanley Cohen) for work on chem. growth factors which control growth and devel. in humans and animals, 1986, Lewis S. Rosenstiel award, U.S. Nat. Medal of Sci.; named Sen. for Life, Italian Parliament, 2001. Mem. AAAS, Soc. Devel. Biology, Am. Assn. Anatomists, Tissue Culture Assn., NAS, Pontifical Acad., Nat. Acad. dei Lincei, Harvey Soc., Am. NAS, Belgian Royal Acad. Medicine, NAS of Italy, European Acad. Scis., Arts and Letters, Acad. Arts and Scis. of Florence. Office: CNR Piazzale Aldo Moro, 7 00185 Rome Italy*

LEVIN, A. THOMAS, lawyer; b. Rockville Centre, N.Y., Dec. 27, 1942; s. Irving and Belle Levin; m. Iris Saletsky, Aug. 13, 1967; children: Amy Beth, Karen Jill. AB in Philosophy, Brown U., Providence, 1964; JD, NYU, 1967, LLM, 1968. Bar: N.Y. 1967, U.S. Dist. Ct. (ea. and so. dists.) N.Y. 1969, U.S. Ct. Appeals (2d cir.) 1970, U.S. Supreme Ct. 1971, Fla. 1980, U.S. V.I. 1991. Sr. dep. county atty. Nassau County Atty.'s Office, Mineola, N.Y., 1968-70; law sec. N.Y. State Supreme Ct., 1970-72; ptnr. Jaspan, Ginsberg, Ehrlich & Levin, Garden City, N.Y., 1972-88, Blodnick, Schultz & Abramowitz, Lake Success, 1988-89, Meyer, Suozzi, English & Klein, Mineola, 1989—. Reporter to pubs. com. N.Y. State Assn. Supreme Ct. Justices, 1970—; counsel N.Y. State Assembly Jud. Com., Joint Legis. Com. on State's Economy; lectr. in field. Editor: Bench Book for Trial Judges, 1971—; contbr. Village atty. Village of Great Neck Estates, Hewlett Neck, North Hills, Saddle Rock, Thomaston, Woodsburgh; spl. counsel Great Neck Cable Commn., Pub. Access TV Corp., Inc., Nassau County, City of Long Beach, Village of East Hills, Village of Freeport, Village of Great Neck Plaza, Village of Kensington, Village of Kings Point, Village of Lake Success, Village of Laurel Hollow, Village of Munsey Park, Village of Plandome, Village of Plandome Heights, Village of Plandome Manor, Village of Rockville Centre, Village of Russell Gardens, Village of Sea Cliff, We. Suffolk Bd. Coop. Ednl. Svcs., Town of North Hempstead, Town of Brookhaven, Hempstead Sch. Dist.; gen. counsel Child Care Coun. Nassau County, 1972—, Rosa Lee Young Childhood Ctr., Inc., 1972—; mem. Land Use Law Ctr. Conf. Bd., Pace U. Sch. Law; bd. trustees L.I. Cmty. Found., 1995—2000; past counsel Nassau County Planning Commn.; bd. dirs. Nassau Symphony Orch.; trustee Ctrl. Synagogue Nassau County; Village atty. Oyster Bay Cove. Fellow: N.Y. Bar Found., Am. Bar Found.; mem.: ABA, Nat. Inst. Mcpl. Law Officers, Nassau Bar Tech. Ctr. Inc. (founding dir. 1994—96, v.p. 1995—96), Suffolk County Bar Assn. (mcpl. law com.), Fla. Bar Assn. (out-of-state practitioners divsn.), V.I. Bar Assn., Nassau Acad. Law (assoc. dean, counsel, lectr.), Nassau County Bar Assn. (1st v.p. 1989—90, pres. 1991—92, chmn. exec. com. 1991—92, bd. dirs., life), N.Y. State Conf. Bar Leaders (exec. coun. 1990—95, chair 1992—93), N.Y. State Bar Assn. (ho. of dels. 1984—87, 1990—, exec. com. 1995—, mcpl. law sect. exec. com. 1995—, v.p. 1998—2001, sec. 2001—02, pres-elect 2002—), Brown U. Club L.I. (pres. 1972—80, sec.-treas. 1980—88, pres. 1988—98, sec.-treas. 1998—, pres. 1999—, bd. dirs.). Office: Meyer Suozzi English Klein 1505 Kellum Pl Mineola NY 11501-4824 E-mail: atlevin@msek.com.

LEVIN, ALAN M. television journalist; b. Bklyn., Feb. 28, 1926; s. Herman and Shirley (Levinstein) L.; m. Hannah Alexander, Oct. 30, 1948; children: Marc, Nicole, Danielle, Juliet. BA, Wesleyan U., Middletown, Conn., 1946. Reporter, columnist Plainfield (N.J.) Courier News, 1957-60; statehouse corr. AP, Trenton, N.J., 1960-61; writer N.Y. Post, 1961-63; press sec. Sen. Harrison Williams, Washington, 1963-64; news producer, writer WABC-TV, N.Y.C., 1965-67; owner Levin Mediaworks Inc., producers documentaries for comml. and pub. TV; sr. prodr. Blowback Prodns. Documentary film maker, NET, N.Y.C., 1968-69, documentary film maker, pub. affairs, news writer, dir., producer, WNET-TV, N.Y.C., 1969-82 Served with AUS, 1944-46. Recipient numerous awards including George Polk Meml. award, Dupont Columbia award, Emmy awards. Home: 88 Claremont Ave Maplewood NJ 07040-2024 Office: Levin Prodns 601 W 26th St Fl 17 New York NY 10001-1101 E-mail: avanti11@comsat.net.

LEVIN, ALAN SCOTT, pathologist, allergist, immunologist, lawyer; b. Chgo., Jan. 12, 1938; s. John Bernhard and Betty Ruth (Margulis) L.; m. Vera S. Byers, June 15, 1971. BS in Chemistry, U. Ill., Champaign-Urbana, 1960; MS in Biochemistry, U. Ill., Chgo., 1963, MD, 1964; JD, Golden Gate U., 1995. Diplomate Am. Bd. Allergy and Immunology, Am. Bd. Pathology; bar: Calif. 1995, Tex. 1996, Nev. 1999. Intern Children's Hosp. Med. Ctr., Boston, 1964-65; postdoctoral fellow Harvard U., 1965-66; adj. instr. pediatrics U. Calif., San Francisco, 1971-72, asst. prof. immunology dept. dermatology, 1972-78, adj. assoc. prof., 1978-88; dir. lab. immunology U. Calif. & Kaiser Found. Rsch. Inst. Joint Program Project, 1971-74; attending physician dept. medicine Mt. Zion/U. Calif. San Francisco Hosps., 1971—; dir. div. immunology Western Labs., Oakland, Calif., 1974-77; med. dir. MML/Solano Labs. Div. Chemed-W.R. Grace, Inc., Berkeley, 1977-79; med. dir. Levin Clin. Labs., Inc., San Francisco, 1979-81; pvt. practice, 1981—. Contbr. articles to profl. jours., chpts. to books. Lt. USN, 1966-69, Vietnam. Decorated Silver Star medal, Bronze Star medal with Combat V, 4 Air medals; Harvard Med. Sch. traineeship grantee, 1964, USPHS hematology tng. grantee U. Calif., San Francisco Med. Ctr., 1969-71; recipient Faculty Rsch. award Am. Cancer Soc., 1970-74. Fellow Coll. Am. Pathologists, Am. Coll. Emergency Physicians, Am. Soc. Clin. Pathologists; mem. AMA, Am. Acad. Allergy and Immunology, Am. Coll. Allergy and Immunology, Am. Assn. Clin. Chemists, Am. Acad. Environ. Medicine, Calif. Med. Assn., San Francisco Med. Soc. Jewish.

LEVIN, ALEXANDER B. mathematics educator, researcher; b. Moscow, Sept. 25, 1952; came to U.S., 1993; s. Boris I. Levin and Mariam S. Yanskaya; m. Tatyana I. Fedorova, Aug. 8, 1986. MS in Math., Moscow State U., 1974, PhD in Math., 1984. Cert. acad. status of assoc. prof. higher math., Ministry Higher Edn., USSR, 1987; cert. good work in field of math edn., Russia, 1989. Assoc. prof. math. Moscow Metall. Inst., 1974-86, 1986-92; math. instr. Montgomery Coll., Rockville, Md., 1993-95; asst. prof. math. Cath. U. Am., Washington, 1995-99, assoc. prof. math, 1999—. Author: 12 textbooks in fourier series, math. programming, difference and differential algebra, other topics; contbr. articles. Mem. Am. Math. Soc., Math. Assn. Am. Avocation: chess. Home: 10619 Pine Haven Ter Rockville MD 20852-3434

LEVIN, ALLEN JAY, lawyer; b. Bridgeport, Conn., May 27, 1932; s. Simon H. and Adele Miriam (Rossinoff) L.; m. Judith Ann Rubinstein, Aug. 18, 1957 (div. 1987); children: Jennifer Suzanne, Miriam Adele, David Newmark, Michael Aaron; m. Gabrielle Hasson-Azar, Feb. 24, 1995. BA, NYU, 1954; postgrad., Boston U., 1954-55; JD, U. Miami, 1957. Bar: Fla. 1957, Conn. 1958, U.S. Dist. Ct. Conn. 1960, U.S. Dist. Ct. (so. dist.) Fla. 1962, U.S. Dist. Ct. (mid. dist.) Fla. 1969, U.S. Ct. Appeals (11th cir.) 1981, U.S. Supreme Ct. 1972. Small claims ct. judge County of Charlotte, Punta Gorda, Fla., 1962-72; legal counsel Port Charlotte-Charlotte Harbor (Fla.) Fire Control Dist., 1965-86; mcpl. judge City of North Port, Fla., 1973-76, city atty., 1977-87; pvt. practice Charlotte. Legal counsel Charlotte County Habitat for Humanity, Inc. Of counsel Charlotte County Habitat for Humanity Inc. Mem.: ABA, Port Charlotte-Charlotte County C. of C., Charlotte County Bar Assn., Fla. Bar Assn. (probate law com., real property probate and trust laws sect.), Port Charlotte-Charlotte County Bd. of Realtors (assoc.), Kiwanis (pres. 1984—85, youth svcs. chmn. Port Charlotte Club 1986—, pres. 1998—99, lt. gov.- elect divsn.18 so. Fla. dist. 1999—2000, lt. gov. 2000—01, trustee Fla. dist. found. 2002—, dist. chair com. on bylaws, practice & procedure, protocol Fla. Dist. 2002—), Elks. Avocation: stamp collecting. Home: 125 Graham St SE Port Charlotte FL 33952 Office: 3440 Conway Blvd Ste 1A Port Charlotte FL 33952 E-mail: ajlgal@juno.com.

LEVIN, ARNOLD MURRAY, social worker, psychotherapist; b. Bklyn., Dec. 26, 1924; s. William and Pauline Levin; m. Elaine M. Zimmerman, Dec. 19, 1946 (dec. Aug. 1971); children: Michael, Nancy Jo Noteman, Amy Louise. BA, U. Mass., 1948; MA, U. Chgo., 1950, PhD, 1975; Cert., Chgo. Inst. Psychoanalysis, 1955. ACSW, LCSW, BCD. Case worker Jewish Family Svcs., Chgo., 1950-53; group therapist Portal House Clinic Alcoholism, 1952-55; exec. dir. Family Svc., Mental Health Ctr. So. Cook County, Park Forest, Ill., 1953-60; pvt. practice in social work Chgo., 1960—. Founder, pres. Inst. Clin. Social Work, Chgo., 1979—; bd. dirs. Jewish Childrens Bur., Chgo., 1987—; founder, pres., Ill. Soc. Clin. Social Workers, Chgo., 1971-76; mem. 90 for the 90's, Ill. Author: Private Practice of Psychotherapy, 1983. Sgt. U.S. Army, 1943-46. NIMH grantee, 1971; recipient Gov.'s award, Chgo., 1975, Alumnus of Yr. award U. Chgo., 1976. Mem. Nat. Registry of Health Care Providers in Clin. Social Wk. (bd. dirs. 1985-88), Nat. Fedn. Socs. for Clin. Social Work (founder 1971-75), Am. Acad. of Practice (diplomate, disting. practitioner). Avocations: acting, theatre, biking. Home: 3180 N Lake Shore Dr Apt 11G Chicago IL 60657-4865 Office: 151 N Michigan Ave Apt 809 Chicago IL 60601-7543 E-mail: arnielev@aol.com.

LEVIN, BURTON, diplomat; b. N.Y.C., Sept. 28, 1930; s. Benjamin and Ida (Geller) L.; m. Lily Lee, Jan. 4, 1960; children: Clifton, Alicia. BA, CUNY, 1952; M Internat. Affairs, Columbia U., 1954; postgrad., Harvard U., 1964; LLD (hon.), Carleton Coll., 1993. Commd. fgn. service officer Dept. State, 1954; counselor/econ. officer Am. Embassy, Taipei, Taiwan, 1954-56, polit. officer Taiwan, 1969-74; intelligence research specialist Dept. State, Washington, 1956-58, dir. Republic China affairs, 1974-77; polit. officer Am. Embassy, Jakarta, Indonesia, 1959-63, Am. Consulate Gen. Hong Kong, 1965-69, dep. chief mission, 1977-78, consul gen., 1981-86; dep. chief mission Am. Embassy, Bangkok, Thailand, 1978-81; amb. to Burma, 1987-90; dir. Asia Soc. Hong Kong Ctr., 1990-95. Vis. prof. Carleton Coll., 1995; vis. fellow Stanford U., 1974; vis. lectr. Harvard U., 1986, Carleton Coll., 1994; bd. dirs. Mansfield Found., China Fund; mem. coun., co-chmn. Hopkins-Nanjing U. Ctr. for Chinese and Am. Studies Johns Hopkins U. Mem. Am. Fgn. Service Assn. Clubs: Am., Hong Kong Country. Home: 314 2nd St E Northfield MN 55057-2204

LEVIN, CARL, public and government relations consultant, inventor; b. Ringgold, La. m. Doris Wechsler; m. Sonia Atlas, Oct. 13, 1958; children: Judith Friedman, Richard (dec.), Virginia Levin Vinik, Alan Schwartzbach. Student, CCNY, 1930-33. Corr. CCNY N.Y. Herald Tribune, 1930-34, staff reporter, 1934-43, Washington corr., 1943-45, 46-50, war and fgn. corr. Europe, 1945-46; free lance mag. writer, 1942-50; Washington mgr. William H. Weintraub & Co. (advt. and pub. rels.), 1950-52; charge Washington activities Schenley Industries, Inc., 1952-62, v.p. Washington activities, 1952-62; dir. pub. support Trade Expansion Act, White House, 1962; pres. Carl Levin Assos., Inc., 1962-68; v.p., gen. mgr. Burson-Marsteller, Washington, 1968-72, v.p., sr. cons., 1972-83, sr. v.p., 1983-87; pub. affairs cons., writer, 1987—. Mem. Nat. Small Bus. Adv. Coun., 1964-68. Collaborator books on journalism, postwar security investigations; contbr. to nat. mags. Active in founding Am.-Israel Pub. Affairs Soc.; bd. dirs. Interracial Coun. Bus. Opportunity, 1972-75; mem. bd. Com. Accuracy on Middle East Reporting in Am., 1985-91, Am. Gas Index Fund, 1990-2000; trustee Opera Soc. Washington, 1963-70, Ford's Theater, Washington, 1975-81; co-chmn. Citizens Com. Opera, 1963. Mem. Soc. Profl. Journalists, Lotos Club (N.Y.C.). Home: 5450 Whitley Park Ter Apt 809 Bethesda MD 20814-2061

LEVIN, CARL, senator; b. Detroit, June 28, 1934; m. Barbara Halpern, 1961; children: Kate, Laura, Erica. BA, Swarthmore Coll., 1956; JD, Harvard U., 1959. Ptnr. Grossman, Hyman & Grossman, Detroit, 1959-64; asst. atty. gen., gen. counsel Mich. CRC, 1964-67; chief appellate defender City of Detroit, 1968-69, mem. coun., 1970-73, pres. coun., 1974-77; ptnr. Schlussel, Lifton, Simon, Rands & Kaufman, 1971—73, Jaffe, Snider, Raitt, Garratt & Heuer, 1978—79; U.S. senator from Mich., 1979—. Past instr. Wayne State U., U. Detroit; chmn. Armed Svcs. Com., Govtl. Affairs Com., Com. on Small Bus., Senate Dem. Steering & Coordination Com., Senate Select Com. on Intelligence. Mem. Mich. Bar Assn., D.C. Bar. Democrat. Office: US Senate 269 Russell Senate Ofc Bldg Washington DC 20510-2202 E-mail: senator@levin.senate.gov.

LEVIN, CAROLYN MELINDA, media educator, documentary filmmaker; b. Houston, Apr. 25, 1965; d. William Brooks and Carolyn (Weaver) Matney; m. Ben Levin, May 20, 1989. BS, Mont. State U., 1988; MS, U. North Tex., 1992; MFA, U. Okla., 1995. Media rschr., cons., co-editor Justus Liebig U., Giessen, Germany, 1988; dir. media svcs. Cambridge (Mass.) Ctr. for Behavioral Studies, 1989-90; dir. vis. artists program U. North Tex., Denton, 1992-96, prof. dept. radio, TV and film, 1995—; grad. program dir., 1999—2002. Juror Tex. Commn. on Arts, Austin, 1995-97, 99, 2000, USA Film Festival, Dallas, 1997; legal cons. Vinson and Elkins, Dallas, 1997—; trustee Univ. Film and Video Found., 1997—, sec., 1999—; faculty del. NATAS, 1997. Mem. editl. rev. bd. Jour. Film and Video; contbr. articles to Internat. Documentary Mag., Jour. of Film and Video; co-prodr. sculptural video installation Tag Rag: Heartland, 1996; dir. documentary film Standing on the Edge Watching, 1997 (shown at numerous festivals, mus., and TV broadcast). Media dir. Tex. Spl. Olympics, 1994. Recipient Professing Women award Women's Studies Roundtable, U.. North Tex., 1996, 99; ethnographic film grantee Apple Computer, Inc., 1992. Mem. Broadcast Edn. Assn. (divsn. membership co-chmn. 1996-98), Univ. Film and Video Assn. (bd. dirs. 1995-97, conf. v.p. 1999-2001), Internat. Documentary Assn. (columnist 1993-98), Assn. Ind. Video and Filmmakers, Cilect, Phi Kappa Phi. Avocations: snow skiing, running, travel, films. Office: U North Tex Dept Radio TV and Film 2d Fl Media & Performing Arts Bldg Denton TX 76203

LEVIN, CHARLES EDWARD, lawyer; b. Chgo., Oct. 6, 1946; m. Barbara Serwer, Dec. 28, 1975. BA with high honor, DePaul U., 1968; JD cum laude, Northwestern U., Chgo., 1971. Bar: Ill. 1971. Asst. instr. legal writing and rsch. Northwestern U. Law Sch., 1970-71; assoc. D'Ancona & Pflaum, Chgo., 1971-76, ptnr., 1977-90, Jenner & Block, Chgo., 1990-2000, McDermott, Will & Emery, Chgo., 2000—. Mem. governing bd. Comml. Fin. Assn. Edn. Found., 1990—; asst. instr. legal writing, rsch. Northwestern U., 1970-71. Mem. bd. editors Northwestern U. Law Rev., 1970-71. Mem. aux. bd. Chgo. Architecture Found., 1989-99; mem. founders leadership coun. C omml. Fin. Assn. Edn. Found., N.Y. Mem. ABA (bus. sect. 1992—), Chgo. Bar Assn. (vice chmn. architecture and law com. 1974-75, vice chmn. divsn. D, mem. exec. com. fed. tax com. 1983-84, comml. fin. and trans. com. 1990—, Article 9 drafting subcom.), East Bank Club Chgo., Met. Club. Avocations: acquisition fine arts, support arts organizations, jogging. Office: McDermott Will & Emery 227 W Monroe St Ste 4400 Chicago IL 60606-5016

LEVIN, CHARLES LEONARD, state supreme court justice; b. Detroit, Apr. 28, 1926; s. Theodore and Rhoda (Katzin) L.; children: Arthur, Amy, Fredrick. BA, U. Mich., 1946, LL.B., 1947; LL.D. (hon.), Detroit Coll. of Law, 1980. Bar: Mich. 1947, N.Y. 1949, U.S. Supreme Ct. 1953, D.C. 1954. Pvt. practice law, N.Y.C., 1948-50, Detroit, 1950-66; ptnr. Levin, Levin, Garvett & Dill, 1951-66; judge Mich. Ct. Appeals, 1966-73; assoc. justice Mich. Supreme Ct., 1973-96. Mem. Mich. Law Revision Commn., 1966 Trustee Marygrove Coll., 1971-77, chmn., 1971-74; mem. vis. coms. to Law Schs., U. Mich., U. Chgo., 1977-80, Wayne State U. Mem. Am. Law Inst. Office: Mich Supreme Ct 500 Woodward Ave Fl 20 Detroit MI 48226-5498

LEVIN, DEBBE ANN, lawyer; b. Cin., Mar. 11, 1954; d. Abram Asher and Selma Ruth (Herlands) L. BA, Washington U., St. Louis, 1976; JD, U. Cin., 1979; LLM, NYU, 1983. Bar: Ohio 1979. Staff atty. U.S. Ct. Appeals (6th cir.), Cin., 1979-82; shareholder Schwartz, Manes & Ruby, Cin., 1983-2002; of counsel Drew & Ward Co., LPA, Cin., 2002—. Editor: U. Cin. Law Rev., 1972-79. Trustee Cin. Estate Planning Coun. Mem. ABA, Ohio Bar Assn., Cin. Bar Assn. (chair advanced estate planning inst. 2001), Nat. Acad. Elder Law Attys., Greater Cin. Planned Giving Coun., Order of Coif. Jewish. Office: Drew & Ward Co LPA One W Fourth St Ste 2400 Cincinnati OH 45202 E-mail: dlevin@drewlaw.com.

LEVIN, DONALD ROBERT, business and finance executive, motion picture producer, professional sports team owner; b. Chgo., Oct. 17, 1947; s. Jack Levin and Henrietta (Wolf) Berman; m. Kathleen Ann Fitzsimmons; 1 child, Robert James. Student pub. schs., Chgo. Pres. Adams Apple Distbg. Co., Chgo., 1969-82, Republic Tobacco, Inc., Chgo., 1982—, D.R.L. Mgmt. Svcs., Chgo., 1982—; CEO Adams Apple Film Co., 1982—, Republic Techs., Perpignan, France. Pres. Top Tobacco Co.; chmn., CEO Chgo. Wolves hockey team; bd. dirs. Republic Entertainment Internat., Chgo., Dr. Levin Family Found.; chmn. D.D.M. Film Co. With USMCR, 1965-71. Mem. Nat. Assn. Tobacco Distbrs., Nat. Candy Wholesalers Assn., So. Candy and Tobacco Assn. Jewish. Office: DRL Mgmt Svcs Inc 2301 Ravine Way Glenview IL 60025-7627

LEVIN, EDWARD JESSE, lawyer; b. Balt., Oct. 31, 1951; s. Cyril and Virginia Lee (Kremer) L.; m. Cheri Wyron, Feb. 18, 1973; children: Paul Clifford, Benjamin Lawrence. BA, Johns Hopkins U., 1973; JD, U. Va., 1976. Bar: Md. 1976, U.S. Supreme Ct. 1980. Assoc. Piper & Marbury, Balt., 1976-84; ptnr. Piper Rudnick LLP (formerly Piper & Marbury LLP), 1984—. Co-author: Maryland Real Estate Leasing Forms and Practice, 1988. 1st v.p. Balt. Bd. of Jewish Edn., 1987-89, pres., 1989-91; trustee Balt. Hebrew U., 1999-2000. Fellow Am. Coll. Real Estate Lawyers (chmn. attys.' opinions com. 1992-99); mem. Md. State Bar Assn. (chmn. sect. real property, planning and zoning 1988-90. co-chmn. spl. joint com. lawyers' opinions comml. transactions 1989-90), Balt. City Bar Assn. (co-chmn. spl. joint com. lawyers' opinions comml. transactions 1989-90). Democrat. Jewish. Office: Piper Rudnick LLP 6225 Smith Ave Baltimore MD 21209

LEVIN, EDWARD M. retired lawyer, retired government administrator; b. Chgo., Oct. 16, 1934; s. Edward M. and Anne Meriam (Fantl) L.; children from previous marriage: Daniel Andrew, John Davis; m. Margot Aronson, Apr. 4, 1993. BS, U. Ill., 1955; LLB, Harvard U., 1958. Bar: Ill. 1958, U.S. Supreme Ct. 1968. Mem. firm Ancel, Stonesifer, Glink & Levin and predecessors, Chgo., 1958, 61-68; draftsman Ill. Legis. Reference Bur., Springfield, 1961; spl. asst. to regional adminstr. HUD, Chgo., 1968-71, asst. regional adminstr. community planning and mgmt., 1971-72; asst. dir. Ill. Dept. Local Govt. Affairs, 1973-77; of counsel Holleb, Gerstein & Glass, Ltd., 1977-79; chief counsel Econ. Devel. Adminstrn., U.S. Dept. Commerce, Washington, 1979—85, 1997—2001; sr. fellow Nat. Gov's. Assn., 1985-86; sr. counsel U.S. Dept. Commerce, Washington, 1987-96. Lectr. U. Ill., 1972—73, adj. assoc. prof. urban scis., 1973—79; lectr. Loyola U., 1976—79, No. Va. Law Sch., 1988; instr. Mgmt. Concepts, Inc., Vienna, 2001—. Assoc. editor Assistance Mgmt. Jour., 1990-95; contbr. articles to profl. jours. Mem. Ill. Nature Preserves Com., 1963-68, Northea. Ill. Planning Commn., 1974-77, Ill.-Ind. Bi-State Commn., 1974-77; bd. dirs. Cook County Legal Assistance Found., 1978-79, D.C. Appleseed Ctr., 1994—; mem. Ill. divsn. ACLU, 1965-68, 77-79, v.p., 1977-78; chmn. ABA fed. assistance com., 1995-96. With AUS, 1958-60. Recipient Lincoln award Ill. Bar Assn., 1977, Gold medal U.S. Dept. Commerce, 2000, Corrigan award Econ. Devel. Adminstrn., 2000. Mem. FBA (chmn. fed. grants com. 1991-95), Nat. Grants Mgmt. Assn. (bd. dirs. 1988-92, Pres.'s award 1994), Appleseed Found. (bd. dirs., mem. exec. com. 1994—). Home: 3201 Porter St NW Washington DC 20008-3212 E-mail: elevin111@erols.com.

LEVIN, EVANNE LYNN, lawyer; b. L.A., Nov. 6, 1949; d. Marshall Levin and Rose (Tolchin) Levin Albert; m. Jeffrey Neal Oliver, Sept. 5, 1992 (div. Dec. 1996). BA in Polit. Sci. cum laude, UCLA, 1971; JD, Loyola Law Sch., L.A., 1974. Bar: Calif. 1995; lic. real estate broker, Calif. Assoc. Ervin, Cohen & Jessup, Beverly Hills, Calif., 1977-78, Mason & Sloane, L.A., 1978-82; atty. Orion Pictures Corp., 1982-84; sr. dir. TV prodn. legal affairs Twentieth Century Fox Film Corp., Beverly Hills, 1986-89; of counsel Weinberg, Zipser, Arbiter & Heller, L.A., 1990; v.p., gen. counsel Zodiac Entertainment, Studio City, Calif., 1991-95; prin., owner Law Offices of Evanne L. Levin, L.A., 1995—; inst. entertainment law UCLA, 1999-01. Instr. personal mgmt. pub. and music career courses The Learning Network, 1985-86, instr. entertainment law, asst. atty. tng. program, 1999—. Contbr. articles to profl. publs.; columnist L.A. Women in Music Newsletter,1 986-88. Bd. dirs. Hollywood Women's Coalition, 1985-86, arts festival, 1985; exec. bd. mem. Wellness Guild. Mem. L.A. County Bar Assn. (vols. in parole, exec. bd. Intellectual Property sect.), Beverly Hills Bar Assn. (former bd. govs., barristers bd. govs., founding mem./co-chair com. for arts, entertainment law com., del. to state bar and ABA convs.), Women in Entertainment Law, L.A. Women in Music (bd. dirs. 1986-88, adv. com.), Calif. Copyright Conf. Avocations: scuba diving, personal weight training, collecting kaleidoscopes, travel. Office: Apt 111 4958 Woodman Ave Sherman Oaks CA 91423-1381 Fax: 310 589-5039. E-mail: el@tvfilmmusiclaw.com., evlevin@charter.net.

LEVIN, EZRA GURION, lawyer; b. Bklyn., Feb. 10, 1934; s. Harry and Bertha Levin; m. Batya Ann Schaefer, June 19, 1960; children: Zachary Abraham, Ayala Deborah Levin-Kruss. AB, Columbia U., 1955; postgrad., U. Chgo., 1955-56; LLB, Columbia U., 1959. Bar: N.Y. 1961. Assoc., then ptnr. Marshall, Bratter, Greene, Allison & Tucker, N.Y.C., 1961-79; ptnr. Kramer Levin Naftalis & Frankel LLP, 1979—. Bd. dirs. Kaiser Aluminum Corp., MAXXAM, Inc., Houston; adj. prof. sociology Columbia U., 1973-77, 87, 93; adj. faculty U. Conn. Law Sch., 1970-73; vis. prof. U. Wis. Law Sch., 1967, 98. Contbr. articles to profl. jours. Mem.-at-large Jewish Cmty. Rels. Coun., N.Y.C., 1983—, pres., 2001—; vice chmn. Coalition for Soviet Jewry, 1984—93, co-chair, 1994—2001; counsel Am. Friends Sarah Herzog Meml. Hosp.-Jerusalem, Inc., 1975—; sec., bd. dirs. Scholarship, Edn. and Def. Fund for Racial Equality, 1961—70; founding chair Solomon Schechter High Sch. N.Y., 1992—96. Mem.: Hebrew Free Loan Soc. (bd. dirs.), Law and Soc. Assn., ABA. Avocation: tennis. Office: Kramer Levin Naftalis & Frankel LLP 919 3rd Ave New York NY 10022-3902 E-mail: elevin@kramerlevin.com.

LEVIN, FRANK S. physicist, educator; b. N.Y.C., Apr. 14, 1933; s. James J. and Celia (Aronovitch) L.; m. Madeline Carol McMurrough, Apr. 1973; 4 children. BA, Johns Hopkins U., 1955; PhD, U. Md., 1961. Rsch. assoc. Rice U., Houston, 1961-63, Brookhaven Nat. Lab., Upton, N.Y., 1963-66, U.K. Atomic Energy Authority, Harwell, Eng., 1965-67; mem. faculty Brown U., Providence, 1967—, prof. physics, 1977-98, emeritus prof., 1998—. Co-organizer 9th Internat. Conf. on Few-Body Problems, 1980. Author: An Introduction to Quantum Theory, 2002; co-editor (series): Finite Systems and Multiparticle Dynamics. Recipent Sr. U.S. Scientist award Alexander von Humboldt Stiftung, 1979. Fellow Am. Phys. Soc. (founder, 1st chmn. topical group on few body systems and multiparticle dynamics) Office: Brown U Physics Dept PO Box 1843 Providence RI 02912-1843

LEVIN, FREDRIC GERSON, lawyer; b. Pensacola, Fla., Mar. 29, 1937; s. Abraham I. and Rose (Lefkowitz) L.; m. Marilyn Kapner, June 14, 1959; children: Marci Levin Goodman, Debra Levin Dreyer, Martin, Kimberly Levin Brielmayer. BSBA, U. Fla., 1958, JD, 1961. Bar: Fla. 1961, U.S. Dist. Ct. (no. dist.) Fla., U.S. Ct. Appeals (5th cir.). Assoc. Levin, Middlebrooks, Thomas & Mitchell PA, Pensacola, 1961—. Counsel Fla. Senate, 1981-82. *Mr. Levin was named the top Civil Litigator in Florida in 1999 by the National Law Journal. In 1999 he was honored at the United Nations by being installed as a Chief in the Republic of Ghana. In1998, the University of Florida's Law School name was officially changed to the University of Florida Fredric G. Levin College of Law. Mr. Levin's outside activities are primarily concerned with the business of boxing and in 1995 the Boxing Writers Association of America named him National Manager of the year.* Author: Effective Opening Statements, 1983; contbr. articles to profl. jours. Fellow Acad. Fla. Trial Lawyers (dir. 1977-84), mem. Inner Circle of Advocates, Ala. Trial Lawyers Assn., Tex. Trial Lawyers Assn., Pa. Trial Lawyers Assn. Democrat. Jewish. Home: 533 Deer Point Dr Gulf Breeze FL 32561-4543 Office: Levin Middlebrooks Thomas & Mitchell PA 316 S Baylen St Pensacola FL 32501-5900

LEVIN, GEOFFREY ARTHUR, botanist; b. Los Alamos, N.Mex., Dec. 7, 1955; s. Jules Samuel and Jane Walden (Settle) L.; children: Tobias, Madeline; m. Lori E. Davis, 2001. BA, Pomona Coll., 1977; MS, U. Calif., Davis, 1980, PhD, 1984. Asst. prof. Ripon (Wis.) Coll., 1982-84; curator, chmn. botany dept. San Diego Natural History Mus., 1984-93; lectr. U. San Diego, 1984-90; asst. profl. scientist Ill. Natural History Survey, Champaign, 1994-96, assoc. profl. scientist, dir. Ctr. for Biodiversity, 1996—. Adj. asst. prof. dept. plant biology U. Ill., 1995—; rsch. assoc. Mo. Bot. Garden, 1994—. Contbr. articles to jours. in field. Bd. dirs. Fond du Lac Audubon Soc., 1983-84, San Diego Audubon Soc., 1986-87; pres. Summit Unitarian Universalist Fellowship, El Cajon, Calif., 1989-91; treas. Unitarian Universalist Ch., Urbana, Ill., 1996-98, moderator, 1998-2000. Recipient Jesse M. Greenman award. Mo. Bot. Garden, 1987; NSF grad. fellow, 1977-81. Mem. Am. Inst. Biol. Scis., Am. Soc. Plant Taxonomists, Bot. Soc. Am., Soc. Systematic Biologists, Calif. Bot. Soc. (bd. editors 1992-95), Phi Beta Kappa, Sigma Xi. Democrat. Office: Ill Natural History Survey Ctr for Biodiversity 607 E Peabody Dr Champaign IL 61820-6970

LEVIN, GEORGE, association and organization administrator; Dir. Aero. and Space Engring. Bd. Nat. Acad. Scis., Washington, 1997—; engr. Goddard Space Flight Ctr. NASA, 1962—72, mgr. devel. Hubble Space Telescope, 1972—81, mgr. devel. Space Shuttle and Delta II rockets, 1981—97. Office: Nat Acad Science 2001 Wisconsin Ave NW Washington DC 20007*

LEVIN, GILBERT VICTOR, health information, services and products; b. Balt., Apr. 23, 1924; s. Henry I. and Lillian R. (Richman) L.; m. Karen Bloomquist, Oct. 25, 1953; children: Ron L., Henry L., Carol Y. BE, Johns Hopkins U., 1947, MS, 1948, PhD, 1963. Registered profl. engr., D.C., Md. With Md. State Dept. Health, 1948-50, Calif. Dept. Health, 1950-51, D.C. Dept. Pub. Health, 1951-55; v.p. Resources Research, Inc., Washington, 1955-63; dir. life systems div. Hazleton Labs., Inc., Reston, Va., 1963-67; CEO, chmn. bd. Spherix Inc. (formerly Biospherics, Inc.), Beltsville, Md., 1967—. Contbr. 120 articles to profl. jours.; mem. editorial bd. BioScience, 1960-63; over 100 patents in field. Trustee John Hopkins U., 1982-85. Merchant Marine USCG, 1944-46. Recipient Pub. Svc. medal NASA, 1977; Whiting medal Johns Hopkins U., 1987, Disting. Alumnus award, 1995. Fellow Am. Pub. Health Assn.; mem. ASCE, AAAS (Newcomb Cleveland prize 1977), Am. Water Works Assn., Water Pollution Control Fedn., Am. Soc. Microbiology, N.Y. Acad. Scis. Clubs: Cosmos. Achievements include being NASA experimenter Mariner 9 mission, 1971; Viking Mission Labeled Release Life Detection experiment producing evidence of extant microbial life in Martian soil, 1976; mem. team Mars oxidant expt. for Russian Mars lander, 1996; inventor PhoStrip process for wastewater nutrient removal, microbial radiorespirometry, nonfattening sweeteners, use of D-tagatose as antihyperglycemic agent and in diabetes treatment; applications of chiral chemistry to foods and environmental products; application of firefly bioluminescent assay for adenosine triphosphate to biomass determination and to microbial enumeration. Home: 3180 Harness Creek Rd Annapolis MD 21403-1614 Office: Spherix Inc 12051 Indian Creek Ct Beltsville MD 20705-1200 E-mail: glevin@spherix.com. *Man's ability to accumulate information through learning and to pass it on to his descendents frees his generations from endless repetition. He may hope to understand the universe and his place in it.*

LEVIN, HARVEY JAY, financial institution design and construction specialist, developer, auctioneer; b. Fitchburg, Mass., Apr. 27, 1936; s. Abe and Ila L.; children: Kimberly, Tara, Robin, Vanessa. Student, Brandeis U., Boston U., U. Md., Ind. U.; BBA in Fin., U. Mass., 1960; MA in Econs., U. N.H., 1970; PhD, LaSalle U.; PhD in Philosophy Bus. Mgmt., 1996. Lic. real estate broker, Mass., N.H., R.I.; lic. comml. pilot; lic. auctioneer, Maine, Mass., N.H., Vt., Fla. Accredited Auctioneer Real Estate, CAI. Pres. Central Tool Warehouse, Leominster, Mass., 1959-66; dir. mktg. and sales Spacemakers, Canton, 1970-72, New Eng. Homes, Biddeford, 1973-74; gen. mgr. Great No. Homes, Boston, 1966-70; cons. svc. mgr. Bank Bldg. Corp., St. Louis, 1974-80; v.p. Shelter Resources, Birmingham, Ala., 1972-73, Fin. Concepts, Natick, Mass., 1980-85; pres. Am. Bank Design, Inc., and Credit Union Bldg. Corp., Portsmouth, N.H., Harv Levin, Inc., Auctioneers, 1986—. Cons. Republic Homes, Truro, Can., 1974. Author, lectr. personal and profl. seminars. Chmn. sch. bldg. com. Kensington, N.H., 1985; pres. Pheasant Run Condominium Assn., 1993-95; chairperson Parents Fund, U. N.H., 1993-95, pres.-elect Parents Coun., 1995. Served with U.S. Army, 1955-57. Recipient Award of Honor, Bank Bldg. Corp. of Am., 1976, 1st Place Design award Bank Bldg. Corp. of Am., 1977, Best Mktg. and Sales Plan award Automation in Housing Assn., 1972, FMHA award for Best Elderly Housing Project (Hazel Dell Apts., Alfred, Maine); named Hon. Lt. Col. Aide-de-Camp by Gov. of Ala., 1978. Mem. Aircraft Owners and Pilots Assn., Phi Sigma Kappa. Clubs: The River (Kennebunkport, Maine); Hampton River Boat, Portsmouth Power Squadron, Wentworth By the Sea Country Club. Lodges: Masons. Office: Hazel Dell Mgmt PO Box 2114 New Castle NH 03854-2114 E-mail: info@auctionsnewengland.com.

LEVIN, HENRY STUART, ophthalmologist; b. Bklyn., Mar. 30, 1954; m. Susan A. Hodgson, June 24, 1990. BS, SUNY, Stony Brook, 1975; MD, Mt. Sinai Sch. Medicine, 1980. Diplomate Am. Bd. Ophthalmology. Med. intern Westchester County Med. Ctr., 1980-82; resident in ophthalmology N.Y. Med. Coll., 1982-85; pvt. practice New Rochelle, NY, 1988—. Office: 421 Huguenot St New Rochelle NY 10801-7004 E-mail: eyedok@aol.com.

LEVIN, HERBERT, retired diplomat, retired foundation executive; b. N.Y.C., Jan. 14, 1931; s. Sol and Kate (Gottlieb) L.; m. Cornelia Rose, Feb. 21, 1954; children: Martha, Jonathan C. BA, Harvard U., 1952; MA, Fletcher Sch. Law Diplomacy, 1956. Internat. economist Dept. of State, 1956-58; Chinese lang. and area tng. Taichung, Taiwan, 1959-61; econ. officer Am. Consulate Gen., Hong Kong, 1961-64; polit. officer Am. Embassy, Taipei, 1964-67, Tokyo, 1967-70; staff mem. East Asia Nat. Security Coun., 1970-71; deputy dir. Japanese affairs Dept. of State, 1971-74; deputy chief mission Am. Embassy, Dar-es-Salaam, 1975-77, Colombo, 1977-79, New Delhi, 1979-81; asst. nat. intelligence officer East Asia East and South Asia Nat. Intelligence Coun., 1981-83; staff mem. policy planning coun. Dept. State, 1983-85; staff dir. subcom. Asian and Pacific Affairs Ho. Reps., 1985; diplomat-in-residence, dir. studies Asia Found., San Francisco, 1986-88; spl. asst. Office of Sr. Rep. for Strategic Tech. Policy Dept. State, 1988-90, exec. asst. to amb.-at-large and spl. asst. to sec. of state for non-proliferation and nuclear energy affairs, 1990-91; spl. advisor to UN under-sec. gen. Ji Chaozhu N.Y.C., 1991-94; exec. dir.-Am.-China Soc., 1994-99. Adviser U.S. Del. to 14th Gen. Assembly of UN, 1985. With U.S. Army, 1953-55, Far East Command; U.S. Fgn. Svc. 1956-91. Fellow Ctr. Internat. Affairs, Harvard U., 1974-75. Fellow: Am.-China Forum (nat. com. U.S.-China rels.), Atlantic Coun. (assoc.); mem.: UN Assn. N.Y. (bd. dirs.), Fairbank Ctr. East Asian Rsch. Harvard U. (assoc. in rsch.), Assn. Asian Studies (life), Am. Fgn. Svc. Assn. (life), Diplomatic & Consular Officers Ret. (life), Coun. Fgn. Rels., Asia Soc., Cosmos Club, Harvard Club N.Y., Lake Mansfield Trout Club (life), Hong Kong Cricket Club (life), Sri Lanka Hill Club (life), Dar-es-Salaam Yacht Club (life). Home: Box 93 675 Long Meadow Hill Calais VT 05648-0093

LEVIN, HERVEY PHILLIP, lawyer, director; b. Oct. 22, 1942; s. Julius L. and Gertrude (Cohen) L.; m. Madeleine J. Raskin, Sept. 22, 1970; children: Arianne, Nicole, David. BBA, U. Mich., 1964, MBA, 1968; JD, DePaul U., 1969. Bar: Ill. 1969, Tex. 1979, U.S. Dist. Ct. (no. dist.) Ill. 1970, U.S. Ct. Appeals (5th cir.) 1981, U.S. Ct. Appeals (7th cir.) 1971, U.S. Supreme Ct. 1972. Assoc. Potts Randall & Horn, Chgo., 1970-71; assoc., jr. ptnr. Mehlman, Ticho, Addis, Susman, Spitzer, Randall, Horn & Pyes, 1971-75; pvt. practice, 1975-78, Dallas, 1979—. Dir. Leedal Inc., Chgo.; cons. in workers' compensation, occupational disease and gen. practice. Bd. dirs. Solomon Schecter Acad. of Dallas, 1979—, Cong. Shearith Israel, Dallas, 1981-88, Am. Jewish Congress, Dallas, 1980-85, Nat. Assn. Mortgage Planners, 1995—. Named Ky. Col. Mem. ABA (workers compensation com. torts and ins. practices sect., chmn. 1989-90, sr. vice-chair 1990—, coun. mem. torts and ins. practices sect. 1995-98, 99—, ho. of dels. 1999—, various adminstrv. coms., torts and ins. practices sect. 1990—, liaison to Internat. Assn. Indsl. Accident Bds. and Comms. 1989—, cons. labor stds. subcom., house edn. and labor com., U.S. Congress, chmn. solo and small firm practices com. 1994-95), Ill. Bar Assn., Tex. Bar Assn., Dallas Bar Assn., Chgo. Bar Assn. Office: 6918 Blue Mesa Dr Ste 115 Dallas TX 75252-6140 Fax: 972-733-3269. E-mail: hervey@airmail.net.

LEVIN, JACK S. lawyer; b. Chgo., May 1, 1936; s. Frank J. and Judy G. (Skerball) L.; m. Sandra Sternberg, Aug. 24, 1958; children: Lisa, Laura, Leslie, Linda. BS summa cum laude, Northwestern U., 1958; LL.B. summa cum laude, Harvard U., 1961. Bar: Ill. 1961; C.P.A. (gold medalist), Ill., 1958. Law clk. to chief judge U.S. Ct. of Appeals 2d Circuit, N.Y.C., 1961-62; asst. for tax matters to Solicitor Gen. of U.S., Washington, 1965-67; assoc. law firm Kirkland & Ellis, Chgo., 1962-65, ptnr., 1967—. Frequent lectr. on legal aspects of venture capital transactions, mergers, acquisitions, buyouts, workouts, fed. income tax matters; vis. com. Harvard Law Sch., 1987-93, lectr., 1997—; lectr. Law Sch. U. Chgo., 1988—. Author book on structuring venture capital, pvt. equity and entrepreneurial transactions; co-author multi-volume treatise on mergers, acquisitions and buyouts; case editor Harvard Law Rev., 1959-61; contbr. numerous articles to legal jours. and chpts. to law books. Parliamentarian Winnetka (Ill.) Town Meetings, 1974-83, 89, 93-96; chmn. nat. fundraising drives Harvard Law Sch., 1985-86, 90-91, 95-96, 2001, chmn. lawyer's divsn. Jewish United Fund Chgo., 1993-95. Mem. ABA (chmn. subcom. 1968-79), Fed. Bar Assn., Chgo. Bar Assn. (exec. com. 1985—), Am. Coll. Tax Counsel. Clubs: Mid-Am. (bd. dirs. 1985-88), Birchwood (Highland Park, Ill.) (pres. 1980-82). Home: 985 Sheridan Rd Winnetka IL 60093-1558 Office: Kirkland & Ellis 200 E Randolph St 57th Fl Chicago IL 60601-6608 Business E-Mail: jack.levin@kirkland.com.

LEVIN, JEFFREY L. lawyer; b. Bklyn., Aug. 10, 1950; s. Lester E. and Evelyn S. L.; m. Diane S. Levin, Apr. 4, 1976; children: Michael, Allison. BS in Acctg., SUNY, Buffalo, 1972; JD, St. John's U., 1975. Bar: N.Y.; U.S. Dist. Ct. (no., so. and ea. dists.) N.Y. Asst. corp. counsel City of Mt. Vernon, N.Y., 1977-78, City of Long Beach, 1978-79; assoc. Bruckman Bernstone & Goldman, N.Y.C., 1980-82; ptnr. Law Offices of Jeffrey L. Levin, N.Y.C. and Port Chester, N.Y., 1982—. Bd. dirs. Temple Israel Cmty. Hebrew H.S., White Plains, N.Y., 1997—, Scarsdale Little League, N.Y., 1997—. Home: 16 Ridgedale Rd Scarsdale NY 10583-7313 Office: Law Offices Jeffrey L Levin 10 Midland Ave Port Chester NY 10573-4927 E-mail: jdmalevin@aol.com.

LEVIN, JUDITH MARIA, health science association administrator, consultant; b. July 23, 1953; BS, George Mason U., 1990; M in Social Sci., Syracuse U., 1999. Cons. to internat. not-for-profit orgns., Washington, 1981-99; program specialist Fogarty Internat. Ctr. NIH, Bethesda, Md., 2000—.

LEVIN, LEONARD IRVING, newspaper editor; b. Providence, Mar. 4, 1931; s. Samuel and Beckie (Nozick) L.; m. Linda Lee Lotridge, Apr. 1, 1967; children: Sara, Rachel. BA in History, Providence Coll., 1952; MS in Journalism, Boston U., 1953. Reporter, copy editor Pawtucket (R.I.) Times, 1953-63; copy editor Providence Jour., 1963-66, copy desk chief, 1966-88, night metro editor, 1988-96; spl. instr. journalism U. R.I., Kingston, 1969—; copy editor Quincy (Mass.) Patriot Ledger, 1996—. Presenter writing and editing workshops, 1990—. Mem. Soc. Profl. Journalists (New Eng. chpt. pres. 1982-83, Yankee Quill award N.E. chpt. 1995), New Eng. Soc. Newspaper Editors (pres. 1993-94), Soc. for Am. Baseball Rsch. (sec. 1988, Bob Davids award 1997, treas. 2000). Avocations: reading, sports, travel. Home: 282 Doyle Ave Providence RI 02906-3355 E-mail: lenlevin5@hotmail.com.

LEVIN, LEONID A. computer science educator; b. Dnepropetrousk, Ukraine, Nov. 2, 1948; s. Anatoly A. and Anna Levin; m. Larissa V. Lastovetskaya, Sept. 3, 1977; children: Rebecca A., Naomi T., Andrei J. MA in Math., Moscow U., 1970, postgrad., 1972; PhD, MIT, 1979. Rschr. MIT, Cambridge, Mass., 1978-80; prof. Boston U., 1980—. Vis. prof. U. Calif., Berkeley, 1986, Calif. Inst. Tech., Pasadena, 1987, Hebrew U., Jerusalem, 1993-94; math. lab. asst. NAS, Inst. Info. Transmission, Moscow, 1972-73; rsch. scientist Moscow U., 1970-72. Guggenheim Found. fellow, 1993-94; NSF rsch. grantee, 1980—. Jewish. Home: 460 Commonwealth Ave Newton MA 02459-1333 Office: Boston U Computer Sci Dept 111 Cummington St Boston MA 02215-2411

LEVIN, LEWIS, information technology executive; BA in Bus. Adminstrn., Quantitative Analysis & Fin., U. Cin.; MA, MIT. Sr. product mgr. Micropro Internat.; from mem. staff to corp. v.p. Microsoft, Redmond, Wash., 1986, corp. v.p. platforms tech. strategy. Office: One Microsoft Way Redmond WA 98052-6399*

LEVIN, LYNN ELLEN, poet; b. St. Louis, Jan. 10, 1953; d. Marvin Edgar and Gloria May L.; m. Steven Weitman, Nov. 29, 1980; children: Lauren, Benjamin. BA, Northwestern U., 1975; MFA, Vt. Coll., 2000. Copywriter Little, Brown and Co., Boston, 1978-80; pvt practice Southampton, Pa., 1980—. Adj. asst. prof. English Drexel U. Author: A Few Questions About Paradise, 2000; translator: The Forest: Poems by Besnik Mustafaj, 2001. Campaign mgr., press sec. various local and county candidates, Southampton, 1989-95. Home: 1850 Dover Rd Southampton PA 18966-4550 E-mail: iamblel@aol.com.

LEVIN, MARLENE, human resources executive, educator; b. Detroit, Oct. 7, 1934; d. Louis and Cele (Drapkin) Bertman; m. Jerome J. Goodman, Apr. 4, 1954 (dec. Mar. 1962); children: Bennett J., Marc R.; m. Herbert R. Levin, June 7, 1967. Student, U. Miami, 1952-53; BA, Coll. of New Rochelle, 1975; MPA, NYU, 1978. Cert. human resource mgr. Asst. adminstr. Richmond Children Ctr., Yonkers, N.Y., 1973-74; research assoc. Westchester Country Dept. Mental Health, 1975-80, clinic adminstr., 1980-82; founder, pres. The Phoenix Group, Armonk, N.Y., 1982-88; v.p. human resources and adminstrn. Ensign Bank, N.Y.C., 1988-92. Adj. prof. Iona Coll. , New Rochelle, NY, 1978—88; cons. Social Area Rsch., Scarsdale, NY, 1983—84; lectr., trainer Volvo of Am., Inc., Rockleigh, NJ, 1983—84, Lederle Labs., Spring Valley, NY, 1984—88; docent trainer Mus. Art, Ft. Lauderdale, Fla., 1993—; art consulting and adv. svcs., event and program planning:lectr. staff tng. for art edn, South Fla., 1989—. Contbr. articles to profl. jours. Mem legis. adv. com. N.Y. State 37th Dist., 1991. Mem. Nat. Staff Devel. Council, NOW (v.p. White Plains 1978-80). Democrat. Jewish. Home: 2576 NW 63rd St Boca Raton FL 33496-2029

LEVIN, MARTIN P. publishing executive, lawyer; b. Phila., Dec. 20, 1918; s. Harry and Sarah (Haimovitz) L.; m. Marcia Obrasky, Apr. 2, 1939; children: Jeremy, Wendy, Hugh Lauter. BS, Temple U., postgrad. (personnel Council fellow), , 1950; JD, N.Y. Law Sch., 1983. Adminstrv. officer U.S. War Dept., 1940-44, VA, 1945-50; sr. v.p. Grosset & Dunlap, Inc., N.Y.C., 1950-66; pres. book pub. div. Times Mirror Co., 1966-83; cons. Times Mirror; counsel Cowan, Leibowitz and Latman, P.C., 1984—. Adj. prof. N.Y. Law Sch.; resident fellow pub. course Stanford U.; cons. Ford Found., India, 1957-58; mem. Pres.'s Working Com. on Books and Pubs. Abroad; mem. exec. com. Ctr. for the Book, Libr. of Congress; trustee Harvard U. Press; mem. Assn. Am. Pubs. delegation to USSR, 1976, to People Republic of China, 1979; former chmn. Franklin Book Programs. Author: Be Your Own Literary Agent, ed edit., 2002; contbr. articles to profl. jours. Trustee William Alanson White Inst.; chmn. Assn. Am. Book Pubs., 1982. With AUS, 1944-45. Recipient Pub. of Yr. award ADL, 1980, Friend of Jerusalem award, 1985, Curtis Benjamin award for Lifetime Achievement in Publ., 1999. Mem. Assn. Am. Pubs. (chmn., dir. exec. com.), Pubs. Lunch Club (past pres.), Friars Club. Home: 221 Kirby Ln Rye NY 10580-4321 also: 9150 Blind Pass Rd Sarasota FL 34242-2978 Office: Cowan Leibowitz & Latman Ste 36000 1133 Avenue Of The Americas New York NY 10036-6799 E-mail: mlevin7276@aol.com, mpl@cll.com.

LEVIN, MARVIN EDGAR, physician; b. Terre Haute, Ind., Aug. 11, 1924; s. Benjamin A. and Bertha Levin; m. Barbara Yvonne Symes; 3 children. BA, Washington U., St. Louis, 1947, MD, 1951. Diplomate Am. Bd. Internal Medicine. Intern Barnes Hosp., St. Louis, 1951-52, asst. resident in internal medicine, 1952-53; Nat. Polio Found. fellow in metabolism and endocrinology Sch. Medicine, Washington U., 1953-55; prof. clin. medicine, assoc. dir. Endocrine, Diabetes and Metabolism Clinic, Washington U. Vis. prof. endocrinology and diabetes People's Republic of China, 1982, Jakarta, Indonesia, Cairo, 92, Taipei, 94, Malvern, England, 96; med. dir. Harry and Flora D. Freund Meml. Found. Author: Levin and O'Neal's The Diabetic Foot, 6th edit., 2001; contbr. numerous articles to profl. jours., book chpts. Recipient Disting. Alumni award, Washington U., 1989, Arts and Scis. Disting. award, 1998. Fellow ACP, Soc. Vascular Medicine and Biology; mem. AMA, Am. Diabetes Assn. (nat. bd. dirs. 1984-86, chmn. publ. com. 1986-87, bd. dirs. Mo. chpt. 1987-93, editor in chief Clin. Diabetes 1988-93, co-editor Diabetes Spectrum 1988-93, Outstanding Clinician award 1979, Outstanding Physician Educator award 1991), Am. Dietetic Assn. (hon., Marvin E. Levin, MD Scholarship Program for rsch. in diabetic lower extremity disease named in his honor), St. Louis Clin. Diabetes Assn. (pres. 1965-66), Am. Thyroid Assn., Endocrine Soc., St. Louis Soc. Internal Medicine, St. Louis Internist Club (pres. 1972), Sigma Xi, Alpha Omega Alpha. Avocations: golf, collecting Belle Epoque French prints. Office: 732 Fairfield Lake Dr Town And Country MO 63017-5928 E-mail: blevin0001@aol.com.

LEVIN, MICHAEL DAVID, musician, educator; b. Syracuse, N.Y., May 29, 1954; s. Jacob Joseph and Doris Levin. BA summa cum laude, U. Ill., 1975; MA, U. Chgo., 1976; PhD in Comm., U. Ill., 1985. Performed and/or recorded with The Alternatives, The Temptations, The Four Tops, The Supremes, Night on Earth, Barrett Deems, Johnny Frigo, Clark Terry, Cerqua Rivera Art Experience, The Chgo. Jazz Allstars, Sueños, D-Section, Mothra, Sumo, Henry Johnson, Charlie Musselwhite, Ben Vereen, Nash Kato, Bobby Vinton, David Amram, Lovo Thoughts, Ivan Neville, Nell Carter, Jim Post, Claudia Schmidt, Ethos Chamber Orch., Ill. Philharm. Orch., The Revolution Ensemble, Diane Schuur, Hamid Drake, Oscar Brown, Jr.; performed music for theatrical prodns., including works at Northlight Theatre, Drury Lane, The Royal George Theatre, and Steppenwolf Theatre; solos featured in recordings including Terry Hunter, Jere McAllister, Glen Underground, Paul Johnson. Edmund James scholar, 1972-75. Mem. Chgo. Fedn. Musicians, Phi Beta Kappa, Sigma Delta Chi, Phi Kappa Phi. Home and Office: 1528 Elmwood Ave Berwyn IL 60402-1304 E-mail: MichaelLevin11@aol.com.

LEVIN, MICHAEL HENRY, lawyer; b. Phila., Nov. 24, 1942; s. Benjamin and Beatrice G. (Jackson) L.; m. Nora Jean Bieler, Jan. 5, 1966; children: Jeremy Ben, Daniel Hirsch. BA summa cum laude, U. Pa., 1964; MLitt, Oxford U., 1970; JD cum laude, Harvard U., 1969. Bar: D.C. 1970, U.S. Ct. Appeals (8 cirs.) 1970-77, U.S. Supreme Ct. 1973. Atty. appellate ct. br. NLRB, Washington, 1969-71; spl. asst. Office of Solicitor U.S. Dept. Labor, 1971-72; counsel for appellate litigation OSHA, U.S. Dept. Labor, 1972-77; dep. dir. Task Force on Workplace Safety and Health, The White House, 1977-78; legis. aide U.S. House, Senate, 1978-79; dir. regulatory reform staff U.S. EPA, 1979-88; counsel Nixon, Hargrave, Devans & Doyle, 1988-95; ptnr. McGuire, Woods, Battle & Boothe, LLP, 1995-99; shareholder Leonard Hurt Frost Lilly & Levin PC, 2000—; co-founder Nat. Landfill Gas Consortium LLC, 1996—. Vis. lectr. on regulation Harvard, Columbia, Va. univs., 1976-89; chair task force on market approaches Clean Air Working Group, Washington, 1989-90; mem. nat. adv. panel U.S. Office Tech. Assessment, Washington, 1990-92. Contbr. articles to profl. jours. Thouron fellow to Oxford, U. Pa., Phila., 1964-66, Congl. fellow U.S. Civil Svc. Commn., Washington, 1978-79; recipient Gold medal EPA, 1982. Mem. ABA (vice-chmn. environ. values com. 1988-90), Air and Waste Mgmt. Assn. (govt. affairs com. 1989-96, co-chmn. strategic environ. planning subcom. 1991-92, sec. legal com. 1993-94, vice-chmn. legal-liability com. 1994-96, chmn. 1996-99), D.C. Bar Assn., Phi Beta Kappa. Office: Leonard Hurt Frost Lilly & Levin Ste 300 1701 K St NW Washington DC 20006-1522

LEVIN, MICHAEL JOSEPH, lawyer; b. Detroit, Feb. 1, 1943; s. Bayre and Lydia Ruth (Kahn) L.; m. Adah Hanson, Aug. 3, 1974; children: Andrew, Stephen. BA, Johns Hopkins U., 1964; JD, U. Mich., 1967. Bar: Mich. 1968, N.Y. 1973. Assoc. Milbank, Tweed, Hadley & McCloy, N.Y.C., 1971-86; ptnr. Boyle, Vogeler & Haimes, 1986-93, Sutherland, Asbill & Brennan, N.Y.C. and Washington D.C., 1993-97; of counsel Menaker & Herrmann LLP, N.Y.C., 1997-2000, Barger & Wolen LLP, N.Y.C., 2000—. Served to lt. col. USMCR, 1963-90. Mem. Mich. Bar Assn., N.Y. State Bar Assn., Assn. of Bar of City of N.Y. Office: Barger & Wolen LLP 500 5th Ave New York NY 10110

LEVIN, MORTON D(AVID), artist, printmaker, educator; b. N.Y.C., Oct. 7, 1923; s. Louis and Martha (Berusch) L. BS in Art Edn, CCNY, 1948; student in painting, Andre LHote, Paris, 1950; in sculpture, Ossip Zadkine, 1950; etching and engraving, Federico Castellon, N.Y.C., 1948, Stanley W. Hayter, Paris, 1951; student in lithography, Pratt Graphic Art Center, N.Y.C., 1966. Founder, dir., instr. printmaking, painting Morton Levin Graphics Workshop, San Francisco, 1972-91. One-man shows include Galerie Breteau, Paris, 1952, Winston Gallery, San Francisco, 1972, 80, 83, 85-97, 98-2002; exhibited in group shows at Seattle Art Mus., 1946-49, Libr. of Congress, Washington, 1946, 49, Pa. Acad. Fine Arts, 1948, Mus. Modern Art, Paris, 1951, Pallazzo del Academia, Genoa, Italy, 1951; represented in permanent collections at N.Y. Pub. Libr., Libr. of Congress, History of Medicine Divsn. Nat. Libr. Medicine; work featured in Jour. Erotic Arts, Yellow Silk #34, 1990. Served with inf. U.S. Army, 1943-45. Recipient Bryan Meml. prize Villager Travel Exhbn., N.Y.C., 1964, prize Washington Sq. Art Exhbn., 1964 *My goal has been to define our world and the primal forces of desire, love, procreation, death, and rebirth. To this end, I have created a universe in my art inhabited by the natural and fantastic. Humans, birds, and beasts, male and female, interact and strive on an elemental level. In a romantic expressionistic style, I have attempted to illuminate the human condition.*

LEVIN, MURRAY NEWMAN, retired surgeon; b. Burlington, Vt., Jan. 14, 1918; s. Charles and Sophie (Newman) L.; m. Patricia Etta de Young, June 6, 1948; children: Susan Ella Fisher, Carol Betsy Levin Adelman. BS, U. Vt., 1939, MD, 1943. Diplomate Am. Bd. Surgery, Nat. Bd. Med. Examiners. Intern New Rochelle (N.Y.) Hosp., 1943-44; resident in surgery Mt. Sinai Hosp., N.Y.C., 1947-48; ward surgeon Vet. Adminstrn. Hosp., Hampton, Va., 1948-50, Manchester, N.H., 1950-56, asst. chief surg. svc., 1956-58, chief surg. svc., 1958-62, acting chief surg. svc. Dayton, Ohio, 1963, chief surg. svc. Rutland, Mass., 1963-65; active staff mem. Holden (Mass.) Dist. Hosp., 1965-81, chief of staff, 1976-77, chief of surgery, 1976-77, emergency rm. physician, 1977-78; physician, indsl. medicine Indsl. Med. Ctr., Lawrence, 1978-81. Courtesy staff Hahnemann Hosp., Worcester, 1965-72; cons. in surgery Rutland Heights State Hosp., 1963-65; asst. clin. prof. surgery Boston U. Sch. of Medicine, Boston, 1959-61. Contbr. articles to profl. jours. Trustee Nesmith Libr., Windham, N.H., 1983-93, 99-2002, bldg. com., 1995-97, fundraising com., 1995-98; vol. Golden Brook Sch., Windham, 1981-2001, Elliot Hosp., Manchester, 1990-97. Capt. Med. Corps, U.S. Army, 1944-46. Recipient Carl Heidenblad award Friends of Libr., 1993, You've Made the Difference award N.H. Sch. Adminstrv. Unit #28, 1995, N.H. Vol. Tchr. award N.H. Ptnrs. in Edn., Pub. Svc. Co. of N.H. and N.H. Dept. of Edn., 1999. Fellow ACS; mem. AMA, N.H. Med. Soc., Mass. Med. Soc., Rockingham County Med. Soc. Jewish. Avocations: stamp collecting, golf. Home: 2 Rolling Ridge Rd Windham NH 03087-2120 E-mail: murraylevin@msn.com.

LEVIN, MURRAY SIMON, lawyer; b. Phila., Feb. 8, 1943; s. Sidney Michael and Eva (Goldstein) L.; m. Jalond Marie Robinson, June 9, 1968; children— Adrianne Lesley, Alexandra Amber-Rose. BA, Haverford Coll., 1964; MA, LLB, Harvard U., 1968; cert., Hague Internat. Acad. Law, 1967. Bar: Pa. 1968, U.S. Dist. Ct. (ea. dist.) Pa. 1970, U.S. Ct. Appeals (3d cir.) 1970, U.S. Supreme Ct. 1979. Instr. English Harvard U., 1965-68; law clk. to U.S. Dist. Ct. Judge, 1968-70; instr. govt. Haverford Coll., 1970-71; litigation ptnr. Pepper, Hamilton LLP, Phila., 1970—, mem. firm exec. com., 1993-95. Overseas lectr., U.K., Sweden, Germany, Senegal, Kenya, Cameroon, Morocco, Israel, Vietnam, Italy, 1988—; law seminar speaker. Weekly commentator radio Sta. WCAU Dick Clayton Show, TV program Morningside, 1973-76; weekly host, interviewer Sta. WHYY, 1974-79; TV commentator O.J. Simpson trial, 1995; contbr. articles to profl. jours. Chmn. Phila. Coun. Expt. in Internat. Living, 1968-70; mem. Phila. Urban Coalition Housing Task Force, 1968-80; chmn. coll. divsn. Allied Jewish Appeal, 1968-70; pres. Ctrl. Phila. Reform Dems., 1973-74; bd. dirs. Grad. Hosp. Phila., 1976-96, Friends Ctrl. Sch., 1988-96, divsn. Fgn. Policy Rsch. Com. Mid. East Coun., 1992-94, Mid. East Forum, 1994—; candidate for Dem. Party nomination for U.S. Senate from Pa., 2000. Root-Tilden fellow, 1964. Mem. ABA, Pa. Bar Assn. (ho. of dels.), Phila. Bar Assn. (young lawyers exec. bd. 1973, bd. govs. 1985-88, zone del. 1988—, chmn. profl. guidance com. 1989-92, co-chmn. internat. human rights com. 1990-91), Phila. Trial Lawyers Assn., Assn. Internat. des Jeunes Avocats Brussels (bd. dirs. 1981-85, 1st Am. pres. 1985-88), Union Internationale des Avocats Paris (advisor to pres., mem. exec. com. 1993—, pres. Am. chpt. 1995-97, congress pres. 1997), Am. Law Inst., Am. Judicature Soc., Phi Beta Kappa. Office: Pepper Hamilton LLP 3000 2 Logan Sq 18th & Arch Sts Philadelphia PA 19103-2799 E-mail: levinm@pepperlaw.com.

LEVIN, PETER J. hospital administrator, public health educator; b. N.Y.C., Apr. 25, 1939; s. Sol and Kate (Gottlieb) L.; m. Judith S. Bolton, June 3, 1967; children: Edward, Gael, Karen. BA, Harvard U., 1961; M.P.H., Yale U., 1965;

Sc.D., Johns Hopkins U., 1969. Asso. exec. dir. Bronx (N.Y.) Municipal Hosp. Center, 1970-72; exec. dir. New Haven Health Care, Inc., 1972-74; assoc. commr. Dept. Health, N.Y.C., 1974-77; assoc. v.p. med. affairs, exec. dir. Stanford U. Hosp., 1977-81; asst. clin. prof. dept. epidemiology and pub. health Yale Med. Sch., 1973-75; assoc. clin. prof. dept. community health Albert Einstein Coll. Medicine, 1976-77; clin. assoc. prof. dept. family, community and preventive medicine Stanford U., 1978-81; dean Coll. Pub. Health, prof. health adminstrn. U. Okla., Oklahoma City, 1982-84; dean Coll. Pub. Health U. South Fla., Tampa, 1984-94, prof. pub. health, 1984-97. Vis. scholar Hoover Inst., Stanford U., 1994-95; health policy counsel to Senator Connie Mack U.S. Senate, 1997-2001; dean Sch. Pub. Health, SUNY, Albany, 2001—. Chmn. Hosp. Cost Containment Bd., State of Fla., 1985-88, Fla. HMO Quality Care Interagy. Task Force, 1987, Hillsborough County Health Care Adv. Bd., 1990-92. Served with U.S. Army, 1961-65, USPHS, 1965-67.

LEVIN, RICHARD ALLEN, government finance consultant; b. N.Y.C., Mar. 18, 1945; s. Louis and Beatrice Levin; m. Ann Abramson; children: Julia, Amy; 1 stepson, Ronnie Freud. BS in Econs., Ohio State U., 1967, MA in Econs., 1970. Rsch. dir. Ohio Dept. Taxation, Columbus, 1973-83, dep. state tax commr., 1983-91; govt. fin. cons. Levin & Driscoll, Columbus, 1991—; city auditor City of Bexley, Ohio, 1997—2001. Instr. Ohio State U. Sch. Pub. Policy, Columbus, 1989-95, Franklin U. Coll. Bus., Columbus, 1979-91. Ohio corr. State Tax Notes, 1993—; columnist The Hannah Report, 1995—. Richard A. Levin Rsch. Libr. dedicated in his name, Ohio Dept. Taxation, Columbus, 1994. Mem. Nat. Tax Assn., Am. Soc. Pub. Adminstrn., Fedn. Tax Adminstrs. Democrat. Jewish. Avocations: running, tennis, travel, reading. Office: Levin & Driscoll 60 E Broad St Ste 350 Columbus OH 43215-3549 E-mail: rlevin@netwalk.com.

LEVIN, RICHARD C. lawyer; b. Dallas, June 15, 1945; s. Paul Michael and Yetta Gail (Caplan) L.; m. Kay Robins, June 18, 1982; children: Edward C., Henry A. BA, Tulane U., 1967; JD, Georgetown U., 1970. Bar: Tex. 1975. Law clerk 5th cir. U.S. Ct. Appeals, 1970-71; assoc. Sulivan & Cromwell, N.Y.C., 1971-74, Akin, Gump, Strauss, Hauer & Feld L.L.P., Dallas, 1974-77, ptnr., 1978—. With Dallas Mgmt. com., 1989—; co-head litigation sect. Akin, Gump, Strauss, Hauer & Feld, head antitrust sect., internat. litigation sect.; spkr. in field. Contbr. articles to profl. jours. Former mem. exec. bd. Dallas Opera; former mem. bd. govs. Dallas Symphony; corp. com. Dallas Mus. Fine Arts; former mem., v.p. bd. trustees Hist. Preservation League; former mem. Landmark Com. City Dallas, bd. trustees Arts Magnet Sch.; former mem., dep. vice chmn., mgmt. com. Arts Dist. in Dallas; former chmn. Task Force Multi-Purpose Performing Arts Hall Dallas Opera, Dallas Ballet; bd. dirs. Dallas Opera, Salzburg Music Festival. Mem. Dallas Bar Assn. (coun. mem. Antitrust, Trade Regulation sect. 1987—, internat. law sect. 1990—). Jewish. Avocations: classical music, art, sports. Home: 4408 Saint Johns Dr Dallas TX 75205-3825 Office: Akin Gump Strauss Hauer & Feld 1700 Pacific Ave Ste 4100 Dallas TX 75201-4675

LEVIN, RICHARD CHARLES, university president, economist; b. San Francisco, Apr. 7, 1947; s. D. Derek and Phylys M. (Goldstein) L.; m. Jane Ellen Aries, June 24, 1968; children: Jon, Daniel, Sarah, Rebecca. BA, Stanford (Calif.) U., 1968; LittB, Oxford (Eng.) U., 1971; PhD, Yale U., 1974; LLD (hon.), Princeton U., 1993, Harvard U., 1994; D in Civil Law (hon.), Oxford U., 1998. With Yale U., New Haven, 1974—, pres., 1993—, chmn. econs. dept., 1987-92, Frederick William Beinecke prof. econs., 1992—, dean Grad. Sch., 1992-93. Rsch. assoc. Nat. Bur. Econ. Rsch., Cambridge, Mass., 1985-90; program dir. Internat. Inst. Applied Sys. Analysis, Vienna, 1990-92; trustee Tanner Lectures on Human Values; cons. numerous law and bus. firms. Trustee Hopkins Sch., New Haven, 1988-95. Yale-New Haven Hosp., 1993—, Univs. Rsch. Assn., 1994-99; bd. dirs. Yale-New Haven Health Svcs. Corp., Inc., 1993—; mem. bd. on sci., tech. and econ. policy Nat. Rsch. Coun.; mem. The William and Flora Hewlett Found. Fellow Merton Coll. Oxford U., 1996. Fellow Am. Acad. Arts and Scis.; mem. Am. Econ. Assn., Econometric Soc., Sutmetrix. Democrat. Jewish. Office: Yale U Office of Pres 105 Wall St New Haven CT 06511-6608 also: Yale University Office of Public Affairs 265 Church Street, Suite 901 New Haven CT 06511*

LEVIN, RICHARD LOUIS, English language educator; b. Buffalo, Aug. 31, 1922; s. Bernard and Meta (Block) L.; m. Muriel Abrams, June 22, 1952; children: David, Daniel. BA, U. Chgo., 1943, MA, 1947, PhD, 1957. Mem. faculty U. Chgo., 1949-57, asst. prof. English, 1953-57; prof. English, SUNY at Stony Brook, 1957—, acting chmn. English dept., 1960-63, 65-66. Mem. adv. bd. World Center for Shakespeare Studies.; mem. acad. adv. council Shakespeare Globe Ctr.; Fulbright lectr., 1984-85 Author, cons. in field.; Editor: Tragedy: Plays, Theory and Criticism, 1960, The Question of Socrates, 1961, Tragedy Alternate, 1965, (by Thomas Middleton) Michaelmas Term, 1966, The Multiple Plot in English Renaissance Drama, 1971, New Readings vs. Old Plays: Recent Trends in the Reinterpretation of English Renaissance Drama, 1979. Served to lt. (j.g.) USNR, 1943-46, ETO. Recipient Explicator award, 1971; Am. Council Learned Socs. fellow, 1963-64; research fellow State U. N.Y., 1961, 65-68, 71, 73; NEH sr. fellow, 1974; Guggenheim fellow, 1978-79, Nat. Humanities Ctr. fellow, 1987-88; SUNY faculty exchange scholar. Mem. MLA (mem. adv. com. publs., mem. del. assembly), Internat. Shakespeare Assn., Shakespeare Assn. Am. (trustee), Joseph Crabtree Found., Marlowe Soc. Am., Medieval and Renaissance Drama Soc. (mem. council), Columbia Shakespeare Seminar. Democrat. Jewish. Home: 26 Sparks St Melville NY 11747-1727 Office: SUNY English Dept Stony Brook NY 11794-5350 E-mail: rlevin@ms.cc.sunysb.edu.

LEVIN, ROBERT ALAN, glass artist; b. Balt., Sept. 25, 1948; s. Benjamin and Bette Clair (Sandler) L.; m. Wanda Solez, Dec. 4, 1971; children: Molly, Hannah. BFA, Denison U., 1971; MFA, So. Ill. U., 1974. Tchg. asst. Pilchuck Glass Sch., Stanwood, Wash., 1974-75; glass instr. Penland (N.C.) Sch., 1975-76, artist-in-residence, 1976-80, Artpark, Lewiston, N.Y., 1987. Vis. asst. prof. Rochester (N.Y.) Inst. Tech., 1988; vis. glass instr. Wanganui (N.Z.) Coll., 1990; lectr. in field; condr. workshops in field. Exhbns. include N.C. Mus. Art, Raleigh, 1976, 77, Huntington (W.Va.) Galleries, 1976, Habatat Gallery, Dearborn, Mich., 1976, 78-85, Mint Mus. Art, Charlotte, 1976, 78, Xerox Gallery, 1976, Fairtree Gallery, 1976, Woodson Art Mus., Wausau, Wis., 1978, Tucson Mus. Art, 1978, Fine Arts Mus. San Francisco, 1979, Corning Mus. Glass, 1979, Chrysler Mus., Norfolk, Va., 1979, Greenville County Mus. Art, 1980, Lakeview Mus. Arts and Scis., Peoria, Ill., 1980, Fine Arts Gallery, Lake Placid, N.Y., 1980, Mus. Contemporary Crafts, N.Y.C., 1980, Naples (Fla.) Art Gallery, 1981, Dan Klein Gallery, London, 1982, Broadfield House Glass Mus., Stourbridge, Eng., 1982, Worcester Mus., Eng., 1982, J. Barrett Galleries, Toledo, 1982, Morris Mus. Arts and Scis., Morristown, N.J., 1982, Sarah Lawrence Gallery, Bronxville, N.Y., 1983, Human Arts Gallery, Dallas, 1985, Heller Gallery, 1985, Gibbs Gallery, 1986, B'nai B'rith Mus., Washington, 1987, U. Fla. Gallery, 1989, Nat. Mus. Jewish History, Phila., Folk Art Museum, Moscow and The Heritage, Leningrad, 1990, Asheville Art Mus., 1992, , Wellington B. Gray Gallery, Greenville, 1993, Goldman Art Gallery, Washington, 1994, The Glasmuseum, Ebeltoft, Denmark, 1995, Huntsville (Ala.) Mus. Art, 1996, Kunstindustrimuseum, Copenhagen, 1997, Plotkin Mus., Phoenix, 1998, Steninge Castle, Stockholm, 1999, many others; collections include Corning Mus. Glas, Ebeltoft Glasmuseum, Denmark, Glasmuseum Frauenau, Bavaria, Contemporary Glas Mus., Madrid, Mint Mus., New Orleans Mus. Art, Huntsville Mus. Art, Mus. Am. Glass, Millville, N.J., Asheville Art Mus., J.B. Speed Art Mus., Louisville, numerous companies, foundations and pvt. collections U.S., Can., Europe and Japan. Bd. dirs. Penland Sch., 1991-95; vis. panelist N.C. Arts Coun., Raleigh, 1992-93; reading tutor Blue Ridge Reading Team, Burnsville, N.C., 1990-96; chmn. Edn. Task Force, Burnsville, 1990-91. Recipient Steuben Glass/G.A.S. Project award, 1991; N.C. Arts Coun. grantee, 1980, 89-90, 96; So. Arts Fedn./NEA fellow, 1995. Mem. Am. Crafts Coun., Glass Art Soc. (bd. dirs. 1991-94), Piedmont Craftsmen (bd. dirs. 1984-88), Tri-State Sculptors, So. Highlands Craft Guild. Avocations: music, hiking, reading.

LEVIN, ROBERT BARRY, motion picture company executive; b. Chgo., May 31, 1943; s. Albert Harold and Sally Ethel (Bloom) L.; children: Jordan, Leigh; m. Pamela Knussmann, Dec. 2, 1990; 1 stepchild, Taylor Thompson; 1 child, Spencer. BS in Journalism and Comm, U. Ill., 1965. Copywriter Sears Roebuck and Co., Chgo., 1965-66; pub. relations Natural Gas Pipeline Co. Am., 1966-69; accounts exect. Hurvis Binzer and Churchill, 1969-70; with McCann-Erickson, Chgo., 1975-82, acct. supr., 1975-79; mgmt. supr. Needham Harper Worldwide, Chgo., 1982-85; pres. mktg. Walt Disney Co., Burbank, Calif., 1985-94, chief corp. mktg. and comm., 1994-95; pres. worldwide mktg. Savoy Pictures, Santa Monica, 1995-96, Sony Pictures Entertainment, Culver City, 1996—2001, MGM Studios, 2001—.

LEVIN, ROBERT EARL, clinical rheumatologist; b. Providence, Apr. 26, 1953; s. Julius Meyer and Ruth Zelda (Paige) L.; m. Mona Joan Gastfreund, June 27, 1976; children: Jonathan, Kenneth, Adam. ScB magna cum laude, Brown U., 1975, MD, 1978. Diplomate Am. Bd. Internal Medicine and Subspecialty Bd. in Rheumatology, Nat. Bd. Med. Examiners. Med. intern and resident Med. Coll. Pa., Phila., 1978-81; fellow in rheumatology U. Conn. Health Ctr., Farmington, 1981-83; assoc. in group practice in rheumatology Neptune, N.J., 1983-84; clin. asst. prof. medicine dept. medicine Tufts U., Boston, 1989—; pvt. group practice in rheumatology New London, East Lyme, Norwich, 1984—. Vis. cons. in rheumatology William W. Backus Hosp., Norwich, Conn., 1985—, Day-Kimball Hosp., Putnam, Conn., 1988-91, Lawrence and Meml. Hosp., New London, Conn., 1984—, Jersey Shore Med. Ctr., Neptune, 1983-84, Point Pleasant Hosp., 1983-84. Contbr. articles to profl. jours. Mem. med. and sci. com. Arthritis Found. Conn., 1986-88; bd. dirs. Congregation Beth El, New London, 1990-2002, dir.-at-large Jewish Fedn. Eastern Conn., 1986-91, Jewish Com. Rels. Coun., 1991-95, Lupus Found. Am., 1985—. William Cherry Meml. scholar, 1974. Fellow ACP, Am. Coll. Rheumatology; mem. Conn. State Med. Soc., New London County Med. Assn. (legis. com. 1989—, trustee, bd. dirs. 1997-99, sec. 1999-2001, v.p. 2001092, pres.-elect 2002—), Am. Coll. Rheumatology, Brown Med. Alumni Assn., Touro Assn., Sigma Xi. Avocations: skiing, hiking, family genealogy, Talmud study, medico-legal writing. Office: PO Box 490 131 Boston Post Rd East Lyme CT 06333-0490

LEVIN, ROBERT JOSEPH, retail grocery chain store executive; b. Everett, Mass., Mar. 19, 1928; s. Edward A. and Rose E. L.; m. Carrol Silverman, June 21, 1948; children: Richard J., Cathy Levin Shuman. BA cum laude, U. Wis., 1948. From dir. store ops. and purchasing to pres., treas. C.B. Perkins Tobacco Co., Boston, 1948-73; from dir. store ops. and purchasing to pres., treas. C.B. Perkins Tobacco Co. (co. merged with Stop & Shop), 1970; v.p., then pres. Medi Mart div. Stop & Shop, 1971-75; group v.p. Stop & Shop Cos., Inc., Boston, 1975-79, sr. v.p., 1979-82, vice. chmn., 1982—, also dir. Bd. dirs. S.A.Y. Industries, Sterling Inc.; chmn. bd. S.A.Y. Packaging, 1988—. Bd. dirs. U. Wis. Found. Mem. Nat. Mass Retailing Inst. (dir.) Jewish. Home: 4762 Exeter Estate Ln Lake Worth FL 33467-8105 Office: 1776 Heritage Dr Quincy MA 02171-2119 also: PO Box 369 Boston MA 02101-0369

LEVIN, ROGER MICHAEL, lawyer; b. N.Y.C., Oct. 20, 1942; s. Harold F. and Blanche M. (Tarr) L. BA in Polit. Sci., U. Chgo., 1964; MA with distinction in polit. sci., U. Calif.-Berkeley, 1966; JD, NYU, 1969. Bar: N.Y. 1970, D.C. 1982, U.S. Dist. Ct. (so. and ea. dists.) N.Y., 1971, U.S. Ct. Appeals (2d cir.) 1971, U.S. Ct. Appeals (D.C. cir.) 1979, U.S. Customs Ct. 1974, U.S. Tax Ct. 1981, U.S. Ct. Customs and Patent Appeals 1974, U.S. Supreme Ct. 1974. Personal asst. to U.S. rep. Dept. State, Quang Nam Province, South Vietnam, 1966; asst. to dir. Nr. East/South Asia Bur. Office Internat. Security Affairs, Office Sec. of Def., Washington, 1967. Rsch. editor NYU Jour. Internat. Law and Politics. Fulbright scholar U. Sri Lanka, 1964-65; Woodrow Wilson fellow U. Calif.-Berkeley, 1966; named Best Oralist, Jessup Internat., Law Moot Ct. Regional Competition, NYU, 1969. Office: 15 E 90th St New York NY 10125-0001 E-mail: rmlevin@hotmail.com.

LEVIN, RONALD MARK, law educator; b. St. Louis, May 11, 1950; s. Marvin S. and Lois (Cohn) L.; m. Anne Carol Goldberg, July 29, 1989. BA magna cum laude, Yale U., 1972; JD, U. Chgo., 1975. Bar: Mo. 1975, D.C. 1977. Law clk. to Hon. John C. Godbold U.S. Ct. Appeals, 5th cir., 1975-76; assoc. Sutherland, Asbill & Brennan, Washington, 1976-79; asst. prof. law Washington U., St. Louis, 1979-80, assoc. prof. law, 1980-85, prof. law, 1985-2000, assoc. dean, 1990-93, Henry Hitchcock prof. law, 2000—. Cons. Adminstrv. Conf. U.S., 1979-81, 93-95. Co-author: Administrative Law and Process, 4th edit., 1997, State and Federal Administrative Law, 2d edit., 1998. Chair senate coun. Washington U., 1988-90. Mem.: ABA (chair sect. adminstrv. law and regulatory practice 2000—01), Assn. Am. Law Sch. (chair sect. adminstrv. law 1993, chair sect. legis. 1995). Home: 7352 Kingsbury Blvd Saint Louis MO 63130-4142 Office: PO Box 1120 Saint Louis MO 63188-1120

LEVIN, RONALD MITCHELL, geriatrician; b. Phila., July 29, 1958; s. Herbert A. and Marlene (Axelrod) L.; m. Carol Lynn Most, June 17, 1979; children: Jay Samuel, Marc Andrew, Eric Brian. BA cum laude, LaSalle U., 1980; MD in Internal Medicine and Geriatrics with distinction, Hahnemann U., 1984. Diplomate Am. Bd. Internal Medicine, Nat. Bd. Med. Examiners. Intern, resident internal medicine Bryn Mawr Hosp., Phila., 1984-87; physician Lawndale Family Practice, 1987-88; pvt. practice, 1988-95, 2001—; clin. instr. medicine Hahnemann MCP Sch. Medicine, 1993—, Allegheny U. Health Scis., 1993—; internist Abington Meml. Hosp., 1995-2001; med. dir. U.S. Homecare, Phila., 1991-94. Interviewer med. sch. admissions com. Hahnemann Med. Coll. Pa. Sch. Medicine, 1995-97. Fellow ACP; mem. AMA (Physician's Recognition award 1991, 94, 97, 2000), Am. Geriatric Soc., Pa. Med. Soc., Phila. County Med. Soc., Delaware Valley Geriatrics Soc. Office: Levin & Most-Levin Med Assocs LLC 6921 Frankford Ave Ste B Philadelphia PA 19135-1623 E-mail: rmlmdfacp@aol.com.

LEVIN, SANDER M. congressman; b. Detroit, Sept. 6, 1931; s. Saul R. and Bess (Levinson) L.; m. Victoria Schlafer, 1957 BA, U. Chgo., 1952; MA, Columbia U., 1954; LL.B., Harvard U., 1957. Supr. Oakland County Bd. Suprs., Mich., 1961-64; mem. Mich. Senate, 1965-70; fellow Kennedy Sch. Govt., Inst. Politics, Harvard U., Cambridge, Mass., 1975; asst. adminstr. AID, Washington, 1977-81; mem. U.S. Congresses from 12th (formerly 17th) Mich dist., 1983—; mem. ways and means com. Adj. prof. law Wayne State U., Detroit, 1971-74 Chmn. Mich. Dem. Com., 1968-69; Dem. Candidate for Gov., 1970, 74. Office: US Ho of Reps 2300 Rayburn House Office Bldg Washington DC 20515-0001*

LEVIN, SIMON ASHER A. mathematician, ecologist, educator; b. Balt., Apr. 22, 1941; s. Theodore S. and Clara G. L.; m. Carole Lotte Leiffer, Aug. 4, 1964; children: Jacob, Rachel. BA in Math., Johns Hopkins U., 1961; PhD in Math. (NSF fellow), U. Md., 1964; DSc (hon.), Ea. Mich. U., 1990. Teaching asst. U. Md., 1961-62, research assoc., 1964, visitor, 1968; NSF fellow U. Calif., Berkeley, 1964-65; asst. prof. math. Cornell U., 1965-70, assoc. prof. applied math., ecology, theoretical and applied math., 1971-77, prof. applied math. and ecology, 1977-92, Charles A. Alexander prof. biology, 1985-92, adj. prof., 1992—, chmn. sect. ecology and systematics div. biol. scis., 1974-79, dir. Ecosystems Rsch. Ctr., 1980-87, dir. Ctr. for Environ. Rsch., 1987-90; George Moffett prof. biology Princeton U., 1992—, associated faculty applied math., 1992—; dir. Princeton Environ. Inst., 1993-98. Vis. scholar U. Wash., 1973-74; vis. scientist Weizmann Inst., Rehovot, Israel, 1977, 80; hon. prof. U. B.C., 1979-80; Lansdowne lectr. U. Victoria, 1981; disting. vis. scientist SUNY, Stony Brook, 1984; vis. fellow All Souls Coll., U. Oxford, 1988; vis. scientist, Woods Hole Oceanographic Instn., Geophysical Fluid Dynamics Summer Prog., 1994; Ostrom lectr. Wash. State U., Pullman, 1994; lectr. Third Annual Stanislaw Ulam Meml., Santa Fe Inst., 1996; The Per Brinck Lecture, U. Lund, Sweden, 1999; co-chmn. Gordon Conf. on Theoretical Biology, 1970, chmn. Gordon Conf. on Theoretical Biology and Biomath., 1971; chmn. Am. Math. Soc./ Soc. Indsl. and Applied Maths. Com. on Maths. in Life Scis., 1973-79; mem. core panel on math. in biol. scis., program com. Internat. Congress Mathematicians, 1977-78; co-convenor Biomath. Conf., Oberwolfach, West Germany, 1978; co-dir. Internat. Ctr. for Theoretical Physics Autumn Course on Math. Ecology, Trieste, Italy, 1988, 92, 96, 2000; mem. adv. com. divsn. environ. scis. Oak Ridge Nat. Lab., 1978-81; vice chmn. math. Com. Concerned Scientists, N.Y.C., 1979—; mem. sci. panel Hudson River Found., 1982-86, chmn., 1985-86, bd. dirs., 1986-96; mem. Commn. on Life Scis., NRC, 1983-89, mem. com. ecosys. mgmt. of sustainable marine fisheries ocean studies bd., 1995-98; mem. Health and Environ. Rsch. Adv. Com. Dept. of Energy, 1986-90; prin. lectr. Conf. Bd. on Math. Scis. course on math. ecology, 1985; mem. oversight rev. bd. U.S. Nat. Acid Precipitation Assessment Program; spkr. commencement address Ea. Mich. U., 1990; sci. bd. Santa Fe Inst., 1991—, Inst. Med. Bio Math., Bene Ataroth, Israel, 1999—; bd. dirs. Beijer Inst., 1994-99, chmn. 1997-99; The H. John Heinz III Ctr. for Sci., Econs. and the Environment, 1994-99. Author: Fragile Dominion: Complexity and the Commons, 1999; editor: Lectures on Mathematics in Life Sciences, vols. 7-12, 1974-79, Ecosystem Analysis and Prediction, 1974, (with R.H. Whittaker) Niche: Theory and Application, 1975, Studies in Mathematical Biology, 2, vols., 1978, New Perspectives in Ecotoxicology, 1983, Mathematical Population Biology, 1984, Mathematical Ecology, 1984, Math Ecology: An Introduction, 1986, (with others) Mathematical Ecology, 1988, Ecotoxicology: Problems and Approaches, 1989, Perspectives in Theoretical Ecology, 1989, (with T. Hallam and L. Gross) Applied Mathematical Ecology, 1989, (with T. Powell and J.H. Steele) Patch Dynamics, 1993, Frontiers in Mathematical Biology, 1994, (with Abe and Higashi) Biodiversity: An Ecological Perspective, 1997; editor-in-chief Ecological Applications, 1988-95, Ency. of Biodiversity, 1997—; Mathematical and Computational Biology Book Series, 1997—; editor: Ecology and Ecol. Monographs, 1975-77; editor Jour. Math. Biology, 1976-79, mng. editor, 1979-95; mng. editor Biomath., 1976-95, Lecture Notes in Biomath., 1973-95; mng. editor Princeton U. Press, Monographs in Population Biology, 1992—; assoc. editor Theoretical Population Biology, 1976-84; mem. editl. bd. Evolution Theory, 1976—, Ecol. Issues, 1995—, Conservation Ecology, 1995—, Discrete Applied Math., 1978-87, Internat. Jour. Math. and computer Modelling, 1979—, SIAM Rev., 1997—, Santa Fe Inst., 1998—, Philosophical Transactions of the Royal Soc., Series B, 1998—, Jour. Biomath., 1999; mem. editl. bd. Princeton U. Press, Complexity series, 1992—; mem. adv. bd. Jour. Theoretical Biology, 1977—, Ecological Rsch., 1996—, Ecosystems, 1996—; also various other editl. positions. Bd. dirs. N.J. chpt. Nature Conservancy, 1995-97. Guggenheim fellow, 1979-80, Japanese Soc. for Promotion of Sci. fellow, 1983-84; recipient Disting. Statis. Ecologist award Internat. Assn. Ecology, 1994. Fellow AAAS (bd. dirs. 1994-98), Am. Acad. Arts and Scis.; mem. Ecol. Soc. Am. (chmn. Mercer awards subcom. 1976, mem. coun. 1975-77, ad hoc com. to evaluate ecol. consequences of nuclear war 1982-83, pres. 1990-91, MacArthur award 1988, Disting. Svc. citation 1998, chmn. MacArthur award com. 1999-2000), Soc. and Indsl. and Applied Math. (mem. coun. 1977-79, coun. exec. com. 1978-79, coun. rep. to bd. trustees 1978-79, chmn. human rights com. 1980-83, mng. editor Jour. Applied Math. 1975-79), Am. Inst. Biol. Scis., Am. Soc. Naturalists, Soc. Math. Biology (pres. 1987-89), Soc. for Conservation Biology, Brit. Ecol. Soc., Soc. Study Evolution, U.S. Com. for Israel Environ., Sigma Xi. Jewish. Home: 11 Beechtree Ln Princeton NJ 08540-7428 Office: Princeton U Dept Ecology & Evolutionary Biology Eno Hall Princeton NJ 08544-1003*

LEVIN, STEVEN JAMES, artist; b. Mpls., May 3, 1964; s. Donald David and Mary Lynn (Blasena) L. Student, Mpls. Coll. Art and Design, 1982-83, Atelier Lesueur, Mpls., 1983-89. Instr. drawing and painting Atelier Lesueur, Mpls., 1988-95. Asst. editor, writer: Classical Realism Jour., 1993—96;one-man shows include John Pence Gallery, San Francisco, 1997, 1999, 2001, White Oak Gallery, Edina, Minn., 1998, 1999, 2000, 2002, exhibited in group shows at Cannon Bldg., Washington, 1988, Mpls. Inst. Arts, 1990, N.Mex. Art League, Juan Tabo, 1991, Akron Soc. Artists, Cuyahoga Falls, Ohio, 1993, 1994, 1996, Salmagundi Club, N.Y.C., 1991, 1992, 1993, 1994, 1995, 1999, 2000, Oil Painters of Am., Chgo., 1995, San Antonio, 1996, John Pence Gallery, San Francisco, 1996, 1997, 1998, 1999, 2000, 2001, Am. Soc. Classical Realism Exhbn., Boston, Milw., 1996, Hastings-on-Hudson, N.Y., 2001, Royal Portrait Soc., London, 1997, Am. Soc. Portrait Artists, N.Y.C., 2000 (Pres. award and People's Choice award, 2000). Recipient 2d prize Masters divsn. N.Mex. Art League, 1991, 3d prize Akron Soc. Artists, 1993, Lelia Gardin Sawyer award and John R. Grabach award Am. Artists Profl. League, N.Y.C., 1993, 2000, Outstanding Merit award The Portrait Inst., N.Y.C., 1996, Allied Artists of Am. award Am. Artists Profl. League, N.Y.C., 1999, 2nd prize The Artist's Mag., Cin., 1996, 99. Mem. Am. Soc. Classical Realism, Allied Artists Am. (assoc.), Oil Painters Am. (assoc., gold medal 1995), Am. Soc. Portrait Artists. Avocations: travel, reading, golf.

LEVIN, SUSAN BASS, lawyer; b. Wilmington, Del., July 18, 1952; d. Max S. and Harriet C. (Rubin) Bass; children: Lisa, Amy. BA, U. of Rochester, 1972; JD, George Washington U., 1975. Bar: D.C. 1975, U.S. Ct. Claims 1975, N.J. 1976, Pa. 1981, U.S. Ct. Appeals (3rd cir.) 1983, U.S. Supreme Ct. 1984. Law clk. to assoc. justice U.S. Ct. Claims, Washington, 1975-76; assoc. Covington & Burling, 1976-79; pvt. practice Cherry Hill, N.J., 1979-87; counsel Ballard, Spahr, Andrews & Ingersoll, Phila., Camden (N.J.), 1993-96, Pepper Hamilton LLP, Phila. and Cherry Hill, Pa., 1996-2000; spl. counsel Fox Rothschild OBren Frankel, 2001—02; commr. NJ Dept. Cmty. Affairs, 2002—. Pres. Cherry Hill (N.J.) Twp. Coun., 1986—88; mayor City of Cherry Hill, 1988—2002; trustee N.J. Coalition of Small Bus. Orgns., 1985—87; del. to President's Summit on Am.'s Future, chair Pam's List; commr. N.J. Dept. Cmty. Affairs, 2002—; del. Dem. Presdl. Conv., 1992, 1996; bd. dirs. N.J. Alliance for Action, South Jersey Devel. Coun., U.S. Holocaust Coun., Big Bros./Big Sisters, Boys and Girls Club, trustee; bd. dirs. N.J. League Municipalities. Recipient Woman of Achievement award Camden County Girl Scouts, 1986, Barbara Boggs Sigmuno award N.J. Women Polit. Caucus, 1996, Gov.'s award on volunteerism, 1998. Mem. Tri County Women Lawyers (pres. 1984-85), N.J. Assn. Women Bus. Owners (state pres. 1984-85 named Woman of Yr. 1985), Phi Beta Kappa, Order of Coif. Office: 1001 Broad St Trenton NJ 08002

LEVIN, SUSAN R. RAVITZ, interior designer; b. Phila., Feb. 7, 1949; d. Ben and Esther (Miller) Klein; m. Steven Jay Ravitz, May 10, 1970 (div.); children— Jason Allen, Shawn Darren, Brett Justin; m. Harvey Levin, Dec. 26, 1985. B.A. in Art Edn., Tyler Sch. Art, Temple U., 1971. Art tchr. Cherry Hill High Sch., N.J., 1971-72; profl. artist Designs by Susan, Cherry Hill, 1971-76; owner, instr. South Jersey Acad. of Art, Cherry Hill, 1974-76; interior designer Touch of Class Interior Designs, Cherry Hill, 1977-86, Phila., 1985— ; designer Show House Phila. Vassar Club. Bd. trustees Jewish Community Ctr., Cherry Hill, 1980-81; co-chmn. First Annual Cultural Arts Program, Cherry Hill, 1981; com. officer Women's Inst. for Self Enrichment, Cherry Hill, 1976-81, chmn., 1979-80; bd. dirs. Phila. Make a Wish Found., 1986-87. Mem. Nat. Home Fashions League Inc., Am. Soc. Interior Designers, Cherry Hill C. of C., N.J. Assn. Women Bus. Owners. Jewish. Avocations: Painting; reading. Home: PO Box 778 Cherry Hill NJ 08003-0778

LEVIN, WILLIAM COHN, hematologist, former university president; b. Waco, Tex., Mar. 2, 1917; s. Samuel P. and Jeanette (Cohn) L.; m. Edna Seinsheimer, June 23, 1941; children: Gerry Lee Levin Hornstein, Carol Lynn Levin Cantini BA, U. Tex., 1938, MD, 1941; MD (hon.), U. Montpellier, 1980. Diplomate: Am. Bd. Internal Medicine. Intern Michael Reese Hosp., Chgo., 1941-42; resident John Sealy Hosp., Galveston, Tex., 1942-44; mem. staff U. Tex. Med. Br. Hosps., 1944—, assoc. prof. internal medicine, 1948-65, prof., 1965—; Warmoth prof. hematology U. Tex. Med. Br., 1968-86, Ashbel Smith prof., 1986—, pres., 1974-87, pres. emeritus, 1987. Past chmn., past mem. cancer clin. investigation rev. com. Nat. Cancer Inst., past. mem. Bd. Sci. Counselors. Exec. com., mem. nat. bd. Union Am. Hebrew Congregations; trustee Houston-Galveston Psychoanalytic Found., 1975-78, Menil Found., 1976-83. Recipient Nicholas and Katherine Leone award for adminstrv. excellence, 1977; decorated Palmes Académiques France. Fellow ACP, Internat. Soc. Hematology; mem. Am. Fedn. Clin. Research, Central Soc. Clin. Research, Am. Soc. Hematology, Phi Beta Kappa, Sigma Xi, Alpha Omega Alpha. Office: Univ Tex Med Br Galveston TX 77555-0001

LEVIN, WILLIAM EDWARD, lawyer; b. Miami, Fla., June 13, 1954; s. Harold A. and Phyllis (Wolfson) L.; m. Mary Catherine Egan, June 25, 1994; 1 child: Sean Alexander. Student, Conn. Coll., 1972-74; BA, Emory U., Atlanta, 1976; JD, U. Miami, 1979. Bar: Fla. 1979, Calif. 1982; lic. real estate broker, Calif. Distbr. N.Y. Times, Atlanta, 1975-76; legis. intern Congressman William Lehman, Washington, 1974; law clk. Superior Ct. Hillsborough County, Tampa, Fla., 1974; legal asst./law clk. U. Miami Sch. Law, 1977-78; law clk. Shevin, Shapo & Shevin, Miami, 1977-79; assoc. Law Offices of John Cyril Malloy, 1979-82; assoc./ptnr. Flehr, Hohbach, Test, Albritton & Herbert, San Francisco, 1982-87; ptnr. Cooper, White & Cooper, 1987-88; pvt. practice trademark and copyright law, 1988-92, Irvine, 1993-96; broker/sole proprietor Levin Realty, San Francisco, 1987-92; of counsel Goldstein & Phillips, 1988-91, Hawes & Fischer, Newport Beach, 1992-93, Gauntlett & Assocs., Irvine, 1995-96; mng. partner Levin & Gluck, Laguna Beach, 1996-97; founding ptnr. Levin & Hawes, 1997—. Co-chmn. trademark com. San Francisco Patent & Trademark Assn., 1985-86; moot ct. judge Giles Rich Moot Ct. Competition, San Francisco, 1986; ofcl. arbitrator Am. Arbitration

Assn., 1987-96; mem. exec. com. L.A. Complex Inns of Ct., 1994-96; lectr. in field. Author: Trade Press Protection, 1996; mem. editorial bd. Trademark World, London, 1987-90, Trademark Reporter, 1987-89, 93-2000, Trademark Reporter Task Force, 1994-97, San Francisco Atty., 1986-89; mem. adv. bd. United States Patents Quarterly, 2000—; contbr. articles to profl. jours. Mem. adminstrv. bd. Californians for Missing Children, San Francisco, 1989-92, Hebrew Inst. Law, San Francisco, 1986-88; atty's. steering com. Jewish Cmty. Fedn., San Francisco, 1987-88; fin. com. Temple Emanu-el, San Francisco, 1985-86; bd. dirs. Ctr. 500, Orange County Performing Arts Ctr. Support Group, 1996, Anti-Defamation League Orange County and Long Beach Region, 1998—; trustee Shir Ha Ma'lot Temple, 1997-2002; mem. intellectual property adv. bd. Whittier Law Sch., 2002—. Named Rep. of Yr., Nat. Rep. Congl. Com., 2001. Mem. ABA, Internat. Trademark Assn., Orange County Bar Assn., Orange County Patent Law Assn. Jewish. Lead trial counsel in case resulting in $143 million trademark infringement jury verdict, largest award of this type in the world, Oct. 1999. Avocations: biking, skiing, gardening. E-mail: william.levin@levinhawes.com.

LEVINE, AARON, executive; b. Boston, Aug. 5, 1918; s. Isaac William and Sybil (Mannis) L.; m. Estelle Malloy, Sept. 7, 1941 (dec. Mar. 1988); children: Joseph, Deborah, Jonathan (deceased); m. Nancy Goldstein, Nov. 16, 1991; children: Larry, Blaine, Jeffrey. AB, Harvard U., 1940, MA, 1941; DHL (hon.), U. Cin., 1996. With Fed. Dept. Stores, Cin., 1956-82; fin. officer Hebrew U. Coll., 1982-88; co-dir., founder Inst. for Learning in Retirement, U. Cin., 1989-96, emeritus, 1996—. Named to Ohio State Sr. Citizens Hall of Fame, 1996. Home: 3012 Burning Tree Ln Cincinnati OH 45237-1716 E-mail: amannis1@worldnet.att.net.

LEVINE, ALAN, lawyer; b. Middletown, N.Y., Jan. 17, 1948; s. Jacques and Florence (Tananbaum) L.; children: Emily Jane, Malcolm Andrew. BS in Econs., U. Pa., 1970; JD, NYU, 1973. Bar: N.Y. 1974, U.S. Dist. Ct. (so. dist.) N.Y. 1974, U.S. Dist. Ct. (ea. dist.) N.Y. 1980, U.S. Tax Ct. 1980, U.S. Ct. Appeals (2d cir.) 1975. Law clk. U.S. Dist. Ct. (so. dist.) N.Y., N.Y.C., 1973-75; asst. U.S. atty. U.S. Attys. Office, so. dist. N.Y., Dept. Justice, 1975-80; assoc. Kronish, Lieb, Weiner & Hellman, 1980-82, mem., 1982—, mng. ptnr., 1998—. Chmn. bd. dirs. Park Ave. Synagogue, N.Y.C., 1993-98; bd. dirs. Jewish Theol. Sem., 1998, MYF Legal Svcs. Inc., 1990-93; law chmn. N.Y. County Rep. Com., 1991-93. Recipient Atty. Gen. Dirs. award U.S. Dept. Justice, 1980, Torch of Learning award Am. Friends Hebrew U., 1995, Human Rels. award ADL, 2001. Fellow Am. Bar Found., Am. Coll. Trial Lawyers; mem. ABA (ho. of dels. 1983-84, chmn. spl. com. for youth edn. for citizenship, 1988-91, vice chmn. white collar crime com. 1996—), N.Y. State Bar Assn. (chmn. com. on citizenship edn. 1979-84, ho. of dels. 1982-84, award of achievement 1984), Sunningdale Country Club (bd. trustees 1988-90 Scarsdale, N.Y.), Mask and Wig Club (Phila.). Republican. Jewish. Home: 1185 Park Ave New York NY 10128-1308 Office: Kronish Lieb Weiner & Hellman 1114 Avenue Of The Americas New York NY 10036-7703

LEVINE, ALAN JAY, physician; b. Bronx, N.Y., July 3, 1949; s. George and Harriet (Pine) L.; m. Jana Helene Heller, Aug. 18, 1949; children: Meredith Brooke, Matthew Lawrence. MD, Medizinische Fakultat Univ., Graz, Austria, 1978. Intern Baystate Medical Ctr., Springfield, Mass., 1978-79, resident, 1979-80; sr. resident North Shore Univ. Hosp., Manhasset, N.Y., 1980-81; fellow in pediatric hemology oncology Long Island Jewish Hosp., New Hyde Park, 1981-82; pvt. practice Levittown, 1982—. Fellow Am. Acad. Pediatrics; mem. Nassau County Pediatric Soc. Office: 3601 Hempstead Tpke Levittown NY 11756-1375

LEVINE, ANN MEBANE, university administrator; b. Reidsville, N.C., Oct. 14, 1943; d. Clark Cornelius and Nantce (Weaver) Mebane; m. Arnold Jules Levine, June 17, 1967 (dec. Dec. 1990); children: Cynthia Levine Crouch, Melissa F. BA, Mary Baldwin Coll., 1965; MA, Emory U., 1967. Instr. Morris Brown Coll., Atlanta, 1967-68; adminstv. asst. Faculty & Course Devel. Internat. Studies W.Va. U., Morgantown, 1980-93, asst. dir. Faculty & Course Devel. Internat. Studies, 1993—. Mem. Svc. League Morgantown, W.Va. Univ. Club, Campus Club W.Va. U. Democrat. Unitarian Universalist. Office: WVa U Dept Polit Sci Morgantown WV 26506-6317

LEVINE, ARTHUR SAMUEL, dean, physician, scientist; b. Cleve., Nov. 1, 1936; s. David Alvin and Sarah Ethel (Rubinstein) L.; m. Ruth Eleanor Rubin, Oct. 14, 1959; children: Amy Elizabeth, Raleigh Hannah, Jennifer Leah. AB, Columbia U., 1958; MD, Chgo. Med. Sch., 1964. Diplomate Am. Bd. Pediatrics, Am. Bd. Pediatric Hematology-Oncology. Intern in pediatrics U. Minn., Mpls., 1964-65, resident in pediatrics, 1965-66, USPHS fellow in hematology and genetics, 1966-67; capt. USPHS, 1967-92, rear adm., asst. surgeon gen., 1992-98; clin. assoc. div. cancer treatment Nat. Cancer Inst., Bethesda, Md., 1967-69, sr. staff fellow, 1969-70, sr. investigator, 1970-73, head sect. infectious disease, pediatric oncology br., 1973-75, chief pediatric oncology br., 1975-82; sci. dir. Nat. Inst. Child Health and Human Devel., 1982-98; sr. vice chancellor for health scis., dean Sch. Medicine, U. Pitts., 1998—, prof. medicine and molecular genetics and biochemistry, 1998—. Clin. prof. medicine and pediatrics Georgetown U., Washington, 1975-98; clin. prof. pediatrics Uniformed Svcs. U. Health Scis., Bethesda, 1983-98; vis. prof. Cold Harbor Spring Lab., N.Y., 1973, Benares Hindu U., India, 1975, U. Minn., 1974, Hebrew U., Israel, 1981, U. Bologna, 1989, Northwestern U., 1992, Moscow State U., 1996; Karon meml. lectr. U. So. Calif., 1983; Seham lectr. U. Minn., 1983; Harris lectr. Va. Commonwealth U., 1995; Markey lectr. Wash. U., 1996; Green lectr. European Molecular Biology Lab. Heidelberg, 1997. Author: Cancer in the Young, 1982; editor-in-chief The New Biologist, 1989-92; contbr. articles to profl. jours. Recipient Disting. Alumnus award Chgo. Med. Sch., 1972, NIH Dir.'s award, 1984, Meritorious Svc. award USPHS, 1987, Disting. Svc. award, 1991, Surgeon Gen.'s Exemplary Svc. award, 1993. Mem. AAAS, Am. Soc. Clin. Investigation, Soc. Pediatric Research, Am. Assn. Cancer Research, Am. Soc. Hematology, Am. Soc. Clin. Oncology, Am. Fedn. Clin. Research, Am. Soc. Microbiology, Am. Soc. Pediatric Hematology/Oncology, Alpha Omega Alpha. Office: U Pittsburgh 3550 Terrace St Pittsburgh PA 15261-0001

LEVINE, BARRY WILLIAM, internist, pulmonologist; b. Everett, Mass., Mar. 21, 1940; s. Irving and Betty (Nemon) L.; m. Ellen S. Haas, June 30, 1963; children: Susan, Rachel. BA, Dartmouth Coll., 1962, BS in Medicine, 1963; MD, Harvard U., Boston, 1965. Diplomate Am. Bd. Internal Medicine, Am. Bd. Pulmonary Disease. Intern Presbyn. St. Lukes Hosp., Chgo., 1965-66; resident Harvard Svc./Boston City Hosp., 1966-68; fellow in pulmonary disease Mass. Gen. Hosp., Boston, 196870; intern Presbyn.-St. Lukes Hosp., Chgo., 1965-66, resident in medicine, 1966-67, Boston City Hosp.-Harvard U., 1967-68; fellow Mass. Gen. Hosp., Boston, 1968-70; asst. in medicine Mass. Gen Hosp., 1970-80, assoc. physician, 1980—. Bd. dirs. North Haven Devel. Corp., 1984—; trustee Mus. Transp. Fellow ACP; mem. Union Club Boston, Masons, Shriners. Avocations: sailing, jogging, collecting art, gardening, model building. Home: 14 Manor House Rd Newton MA 02459-1520

LEVINE, BENJAMIN, lawyer; b. May 22, 1931; s. George and Frances (Levovsky) L.; m. Arleen Ella Rosenblatt, Jan. 14, 1962; children: Joshua, Sarah. BA, U. Conn., 1953; JD, Rutgers U., 1963. Bar: N.Mex. 1964, N.Y. 1965, N.J. 1967, U.S. Supreme Ct. 1980; cert. trial atty., 1986; diplomate Nat. Bd. Trial Advocacy, 1989. Law clk. N.Mex. Sup. Ct., 1963-64; spl. asst. N.J. Commr. Conservation and Econ. Devel., 1965-67; dep. atty. gen. State of N.J., 1967-70; pvt. practice Newark and N.Y.C., 1970—. Adj. prof. law Ramapo Coll., Mahwah, N.J., 1978-80; arbitrator U.S. Dist. Ct. N.J., 1989. Author: Medical Malpractice; Zoning Guide for Local Officals; contbr. articles to profl. jours. Pres. Environ. Action Inst. N.J., 1977-80; chmn. North Plainfield (N.J.) Environ. Commn., 1974-76; trustee South Branch Watershed Assn., 1976-80, Rabbinical Coll. Am., 1994—. Lt. (j.g.) USN, 1956-60. Mem.: ATLA, Million Dollar Advocates Forum, NY County Lawyers Assn. (chmn. state legis. com. 1976—80, mem. com. on constn., com. on civil cts. 1980—82), Am. Arbitration Assn. (nat. panel arbitrators 1973—), NJ Bar Assn. (bd. dirs. med.mal.com., cert. trial lawyers sect.). Office: 1 Gateway Ctr Ste 2500 Newark NJ 07102-5315 E-mail: levine@ix.netcom.com.

LEVINE, DANIEL BLANK, classical studies educator; b. Cin., July 22, 1953; s. Joseph and Elizabeth (Blank) L.; m. Judith Robinson, Aug. 14, 1984; children: Sarah Ruth, Amy Elizabeth. Student, Am. Sch. Classical Studies, Athens, 1974, 78-89; BA in Greek and Latin magna cum laude, U. Minn., 1975; PhD in Classics, U. Cin., 1980. Seymour fellow Am. Sch. Classical Studies, 1978-79; asst. prof. U. Ark., 1980-84, assoc. prof., 1984-98, prof., 1998—. Dir. Summer Session Am. Sch. Classical Studies, Athens, 1987, 95; dir. study tour in Greece Vergilian Soc., 1990, Greece Univ. Ark., 2000, 01; referee Classical Jour., 1984-88, Helios, 1984-88, Cornell U. Press, 1988-89, 91—, Classical Outlook, 1988-89; panelist NEH, Washington, 1986; co-dir., instr. gifted and talented H.S. students summer program State of Ark. Dept. Edn. Grant, 1988; mem. mng. com. Am. Sch. Classical Studies Athens, 1991—. Contbr. articles to profl. jours. Grantee NEH 1981, 82, 83, 84, 92; recipient Outstanding Tchr. award Mortar Bd. Sr. Honor Soc., U. Ark., 1991, Master Tchr. award Fulbright Coll., 1995. Mem. Am. Philological Assn. (Excellence in Teaching Classics award 1992), Am. Classical League, Classical Assn. Mid. West and South (Ovatio 1996, v.p. com. promotion Latin in Ark. 1980-86, 91-95, chmn. regional rep. com. for promotion Latin, Outstanding State V.P. for 1982-83), U. Ark. Teaching Acad., Phi Beta Kappa. Home: 904 Park Ave Fayetteville AR 72701-2027 Office: U Ark Dept Fgn Langs 425 Kimpel Hall Fayetteville AR 72701

LEVINE, DAVID, artist; b. Bklyn., Dec. 20, 1926; s. Harry L.; children: Matthew, Eve. B.F.A., BS in Edn, Temple U., 1949; postgrad., Hans Hoffman Sch. Paintings, 1950. One-man shows Forum Gallery, N.Y.C., 1966—, Ga. Mus. Art, 1968, Calif. Palace Legion of Honor, 1968-69, 71-72, 83, Wesleyan U., 1970, Bklyn. Mus., 1971, Princeton U., 1972, Galerie Yves Lambert, Paris, 1972, Yale U., 1973, Hirshhorn Mus. and Sculpture Garden, Washington, 1976, Galerie Claude Bernard, 1979, Phillips Gallery, 1980, Pierpont Morgan Library, 1981, Santa Fe East Gallery, 1983, Ash Molean Mus., Meredith Long, Houston, 1984; represented by Forum Gallery; author: The Man From M.A.L.I.C.E., 1966, Pens and Needles, 1969, No Known Survivors, 1970, The Arts of David Levine, 1978, Aesop's Fables. Served with U.S. Army, 1945-46. Recipient Tiffany award, 1955, Isaac N. Maynard prize, 1958, Julius Halligarten prize, 1960, Thomas B. Clark prize, 1962, George Polk award, 1965, Childe Hassam Purchase prize 1972, Benjamin Altman prize, 1973, Gold medal for Graphic Work, Am. Acad. Inst. Arts and Letters, 1992, Thomas Nast award, 1995; Guggenheim fellow, 1967. Mem. AAAL, Century Assn. Address: care Forum Gallery 745 5th Ave New York NY 10151-0099

LEVINE, DAVID ETHAN, lawyer; b. Niagara Falls, N.Y., Feb. 28, 1955; s. Morree Morell Levine and Marbud Juel (Gagen) Prozeller; m. Ann Lee Ruhlin, May 23, 1981. BS in Bus., Miami U., 1977; JD, Capital U., 1981. Bar: N.Y. 1982, U.S. Dist. Ct. (we. dist.) N.Y. 1982. Assoc. Grossman, Levine and Civiletto, Niagara Falls, 1981-89, Cummings and Levine, Niagara Falls, 1989-92; pvt. practice, 1992—. V.p. Buffalo Area Recreational Cyclists, Inc., 1995; bd. dirs. Niagara County Legal Aid Soc. Mem. N.Y. State Bar Assn., Erie County Bar Assn., Niagara Falls Bar Assn., Niagara County Sportsman's Assn. Unitarian Universalist. Avocations: skiing, photography, bicycling, camping. Home: 22 Hemlock Dr Grand Island NY 14072-3315 Office: PO Box 922 669 Main St Niagara Falls NY 14302 E-mail: del/4072@aol.com.

LEVINE, DAVID LAWRENCE, software engineer; b. Albany, N.Y., June 22, 1957; s. Leonard S. and Mildred Hoffman (Cohen) L.; m. Janice Leslie Glasser, Sept. 9, 1990; children: Julia Stephanie, Benjamin Samuel. BSME, Cornell U., 1978; MS in Computer Sci., George Washington U., 1987; PhD in Computer Sci., U. Calif., Irvine, 1993. Registered profl. engr., D.C. Staff engr. Chrysler Corp., Highland Park, Mich., 1978-79; mem. tech. staff The Aerospace Corp., Washington, 1980-87, Sci. Applications Internat. Corp., Newport Beach, Calif., 1987-91; sr. mem. tech. staff Ascom Nexion Inc., St. Louis, 1993-96; rsch. assoc. Washington U., 1996—99, dir. Distributed Object Computing Ctr., 1999—2000; v.p. engring. CombineNet, Pitts., 2000—. Cons. Electric and Hybrid Vehicle Devel. Project, U. Calif., Irvine, 1991-93. Mem. IEEE, Assn. for Computing Machinery, Soc. Automotive Engrs. Avocations: amateur radio, antique and spl. interest automobiles. Office: CombineNet 311 S Craig St Pittsburgh PA 15213-

LEVINE, DAVID M. newspaper editor; b. Newark, Oct. 2, 1949; s. Seymour I. and Fay D. Levine; m. Arleen Weintraub, Apr. 5, 1987. BA, Montclair State Coll., 1971; MS, Columbia U., 1973. Reporter, state house corr. Herald-News, Passaic, N.J., 1971-74; editorial writer Phila. Bull., 1974-79; night mng. editor Trenton (N.J.) Times, 1979-83; exec. fin. editor Washington Times, 1983-85; exec. editor Lebhar-Friedman Co., N.Y.C., 1985-86; editor Daily Jour., Elizabeth, N.J., 1986-87, Hudson Dispatch, Union City, 1987-91, The Daily Jour., Elizabeth, 1990-92; editor, v.p. The Herald-News, Passaic, 1992-94; editor-in-chief, v.p. Tribune-Democrat Pub. Co., Johnstown, Pa., 1997—; journalist-in-residence Pa. State U., 2001—. Adj. instr. English dept. Rutgers U., Newark, 1987-93; adj. instr. journalism Cambria County Area C.C., Johnstown, Pa., 1997—; prin. Jour. Publs., Trenton, 1971—, Levine Publs., Trenton, 1974—; bd. dirs. The Phoenix Corp. Author: Editorial Style, 1974. Mem. Pa. Soc. Newspaper Editors (bd. dirs.), Am. Soc. of Newspaper Editors. E-mail: newsboy@post.com.

LEVINE, DONALD ARTHUR, anesthesiologist; b. N.Y.C., 1938; BA in Chem., U. Buffalo, 1959; MD, SUNY, Buffalo, 1963; MPH, UCLA, 1973. Diplomate Am. Bd. Anesthesiology. Intern Cedars-Lebanon Hosp., L.A., 1963-64; resident in anesthesiology Stanford U. Hosp., Palo Alto, Calif., 1964-67; resident in preventive medicine UCLA Ctr. Health Scis., 1974-76; fellow in anesthesiology Stanford U., 1966-67; pvt. practice Westlake Village, Calif. Mem. AMA, Am. Soc. Anesthesiologists, Internat. Anesthesia Rsch. Soc. Office: 945 Ranch House Rd Westlake Village CA 91361-2073 E-mail: levineteam@earthlink.net.

LEVINE, DONALD NATHAN, sociologist, educator; b. New Castle, Pa., June 16, 1931; s. Abe and Rose (Gusky) L.; m. Joanna Bull, Nov. 6, 1955 (div. 1967); children: Theodore, William; m. Ruth Weinstein, Aug. 26, 1967; 1 child, Rachel. AB, U. Chgo., 1950, MA, 1954, PhD, 1957; postgrad., U. Frankfurt, Germany, 1952-53. Asst. prof. sociology U. Chgo., 1962-65, assoc. prof., 1965-73, prof., 1973-86, dean of Coll., 1982-87, Peter B. Ritzma prof., 1986—. Founder, pres. Aiki Exts., Inc., 1998—. Author: Wax and Gold: Tradition and Innovation in Ethiopian Culture, 1965, Georg Simmel on Individuality and Social Forms, 1971, Greater Ethiopia: The Evolution of a Multiethnic Society, 1974, Simmel and Parsons: Two Approaches to the Study of Society, 1980, The Flight from Ambiguity: Essays in Social and Cultural Theory, 1985, Visions of the Sociological Tradition, 1995; editor: The Heritage of Sociology series, 1988—. Mem. adv. bd. Ethiopian Cmty. Assn. Chgo., 1993—. Recipient Quantrell award U. Chgo., 1971, Cert. of award Ethiopian Rsch. Coun., 1993, Amoco Found. award for disting. contbn. to undergrad. tchg., 1996, Outstanding Cmty. Support award Ethiopian Cmty. Assn. of Chgo., 2000; Guggenheim fellow, 1980; fellow Ctr. for Advanced Study in Behavioral Scis., 1980-81. Mem. Internat. Soc. Comparative Study Civilization, Am. Sociol. Assn. (chair theory sect. 1996-97). Jewish. Office: U Chgo 1126 E 59th St Chicago IL 60637-1580 E-mail: dlok@midway.uchicago.edu.

LEVINE, EDWARD A. surgeon, educator; b. Chgo., May 2, 1959; s. Franklin and Joan L.; m. Joan, 1981. BS magna cum laude, No. Ill. U., 1981; MD, Chgo. Med. Sch., 1985. Resident in surgery Michael Reese Hosp., Chgo., 1985-90; fellow in oncology U. Ill., 1990-92; asst. prof. surgery La. State U., New Orleans, 1992-97, assoc. prof. surgery, 1997-98, chief surg. oncology, 1994-98; assoc. prof., chief surg. oncology Bowman Gray Sch. Medicine Wake Forest U., Winston Salem, N.C. Contbr. articles to profl. jours., chpts. to books. Office: Wake Forest U Sect Surg Oncology Medicial Center Blvd Winston Salem NC 27157-0001

LEVINE, ELAINE PRADO, school psychologist, musician, artist; b. Inglewood, Calif., Feb. 16, 1962; d. John Franklin, Jr. and Carolyn Mae (Cable) Watler; m. Paul David Prado, Mar. 2, 1985 (div. 1994); children: Paul David, Lauren Mae; m. Leonard Ralph Levine, Jan. 8, 2000 (dec. May 2001). BA in Music Composition and Theory/Flute, UCLA, 1986; MA in Edn.-Counseling, Calif. State U., 1999. Tchr. multiple subjects Torrance (Calif.) Unified Sch. Dist., 1994-96, tchr. music, dir. band and choir, 1996-99, counselor, 1999-00; sch. psychologist Hemet (Calif.) Unified Sch. Dist., 2000—02, Palm Springs (Calif.) Unified Sch. Dist., 2002—. Part-time asst. prof. Calif. State U., Dominguez Hills, 1999-00; prodr., dir., pub. Prado Prodn. and Publ., Hemet, 2000—. Author: He Always Goes First!, 1998; prodr., dir. CD Dreams of the Jaguar, 1999. Sec., faculty rep. Jefferson Sch. Site Coun., Torrance, 1998-99. Mem. Nat. Assn. Sch. Psychologists, Calif. Assn. Sch. Psychologists, Calif. Tchrs. Assn., So. Calif. Vocal Assn., Screen Actors Guild, Wiseburn Fac. Assn. (scholarship 1985), Phi Kappa Phi. Avocations: tennis, snow skiing, swimming, travel, gardening. Home and Office: Prado Prodns & Publ 26208 Avenida Hortensia Hemet CA 92544-6548 E-mail: musesmaker@aol.com.

LEVINE, GAIL CARSON, writer; b. New York, Ny, Sept. 17, 1947; d. David and Sylvia Carson; m. David Matthew Levine, Sept. 2, 1967. BA, City Coll. NY, New York, NY, 1969. Author: (children's novel) Ella Enchanted (Newbery Honor Book, 1998), For Biddle's Sake, (children's picture book) Betsy Who Cried Wolf, (children's novel) Dave at Night, The Fairy's Mistake, The Princess Test, Princess Sonora and the Long Sleep, The Wish, Cinderellis and the Glass Hill, The Two Princesses of Bamarre, The Fairy's Return. Mem.: Soc. Children's Book Writers and Illustrators, PEN, Author's Guild.

LEVINE, GEORGE RICHARD, English language educator; b. Boston, Aug. 5, 1929; s. Jacob U. and Rose Lillian (Margolis) L.; m. Joan Adler, June 8, 1958 (div. 1977); children— David, Michael; m. Linda Rashman, Apr. 17, 1977. BA, Tufts Coll., Medford, Mass., 1951; MA, Columbia, 1952, PhD, 1961. Lectr. English Columbia, 1956-58; instr. Northwestern U., 1959-63; mem. faculty SUNY, Buffalo, 1963—2001, prof. emeritus, 2001—; prof. English State U. N.Y., 1970—, dean faculty arts and letters, 1975-81. Author: Henry Fielding and The Dry Mock, 1967; editor: Harp on the Shore: Thoreau and the Sea, 1985, Jonathan Swift: A Modest Proposal and Other Satires, 1995; contbr. articles to profl. jours. Chmn. bd. dirs. Youth Orch. Found., Buffalo, 1974-75; trustee Buffalo Chamber Music Soc., Arts Devel. Svcs.; bd. dirs. Buffalo Philharm. Orch., 1992-97; pres. Arts in Edn. Inst. Western N.Y. With AUS, 1952-54. Univ. fellow Columbia U., 1958-59, Faculty Research fellow SUNY, 1966-67; Fulbright lectr. W. Ger., 1969-70; recipient Chancellor's award excellence in teaching SUNY, Buffalo, 1973-74. Mem. MLA, Am. Soc. 18th Century Studies, Internat. Assn. Univ. Profs. English, Adirondack Mountain Club. Jewish. Home: 18 Saint Andrews Walk Buffalo NY 14222-2010 Office: SUNY Dept English 306 Clemens Hall Buffalo NY 14260-4600 E-mail: grlevine@acsu.buffalo.edu.

LEVINE, GEORGE LEWIS, English language educator, literature critic; b. N.Y.C., Aug. 27, 1931; s. Harris Julius and Dorothy Sara (Podolsky) L.; m. Margaret Bloom, Aug. 19, 1956; children: David Michael, Rachel Susan. BA, NYU, 1952; MA, U. Minn., 1953, PhD, 1958. Instr. Ind. U., Bloomington, 1959-62, asst. prof., 1962-65, assoc. prof., 1965-68; prof. English Rutgers U., New Brunswick, N.J., 1968—, chmn. dept., 1979-83, Kenneth Burke prof., 1985—. Vis. prof. U. Calif.-Berkeley, 1968, Stanford U., Calif., 1974-75; vis. rsch. fellow Girton Coll., Cambridge U., Eng., 1983; Avalon prof. lit. Northwestern U., 1998; dir. Ctr. for Critical Analysis of Contemp. Culture. Author: Boundaries of Fiction, 1968, The Endurance of Frankenstein, 1975, The Realistic Imagination, 1981, One Culture, 1987, Darwin and the Novelists, 1988, Lifebirds, 1995, Dying to Know, 2002; author, editor: The Art of Victorian Prose, 1968, Mindful Pleasures, 1975, Constructions of the Self, 1992, Realism and Representation, 1993, Aesthetics and Ideology, The Politics of Research, 1994; editor: Victorian Studies, 1959-68, Cambridge Companion to George Eliot. Served with U.S. Army, 1953-55. Guggenheim Found. fellow, 1971-72; NEH fellow, 1978-79; Rockefeller Found. fellow, 1983; Rockefeller Found. Bellagio fellow, 1996, Bogliasco Found. fellow, 1999. Mem. MLA, AAUP Democrat. Jewish. Home: 108 Wesley Ave Atlantic Highlands NJ 07716 Office: Rutgers U Ctr Critical Cont Culture New Brunswick NJ 08903

LEVINE, HAROLD, lawyer; b. Newark, Apr. 30, 1931; s. Rubin and Gussie (Lifshitz) L.; children: Brenda Sue, Linda Ellen Levine Gersen, Louise Abby, Jill Anne Levine Lipari, Charles A., Cristina Gussie, Harold Rubin II; m. Cristina Cervera, Aug. 29, 1980. BS in Engring., Purdue U., 1954; JD with distinction, George Washington U., 1958. Bar: D.C. 1958, Va. 1958, Mass. 1960, Tex. 1972, U.S. Patent Office 1958. Naval arch., marine engr. U.S. Navy Dept., 1954-55; patent examiner U.S. Patent Office, 1955-58; with Tex. Instruments, Inc., Attleboro, Mass., 1959-77, asst. sec. Dallas, 1969-72, asst. v.p. and gen. patent counsel, 1972-77; ptnr. Sigalos & Levine, 1977-93; prin. Levine & Majorie LLP, 1994-2000, Levine & Starr LLP, 2001—. Chmn. bd. Vanguard Security, Inc., Houston, 1977—; chmn. Tex. Am. Realty, Dallas, 1977—; lectr. assns., socs.; del. Geneva and Lausanne (Switzerland) Intergovtl. Conf. on Revision, Paris Pat. Conv., 1975-76. Editor George Washington U. Law Rev., 1956-57; mem. adv. bd. editors Bur. Nat. Affairs, Pat., Trdmk. and Copyright Jour.; contbr. chpt. to book and articles to profl. jours. Mem. U.S. State Dept. Adv. Panel on Internat. Tech. Transfer, 1977. Mem. ABA (chmn. com. 407 taxation pats. and trdmks. 1971-72), Am. Patent Law Assn., Dallas Bar Assn., Assn. Corp. Pat. Csl. (sec.-treas. 1971-73), Dallas-Ft. Worth Patent Law Assn., Pacific Indsl. Property Assn. (pres. 1975-77), Electronic Industries Assn. (pres. pat. com. 1972), NAM, Southwestern Legal Inst. on Patent Law (planning com. 1971-74), U.S. C. of C., Dallas C. of C., Kiwanis, Alpha Epsilon Pi, Phi Alpha Delta. Republican. Jewish. Office: Levine & Starr LLP Bank Am Pl Tower 101 E Park Blvd Ste 755 Plano TX 75074 Fax: 972-398-6095.

LEVINE, HARRY BRUCE, stockbroker; b. Bklyn., Oct. 24, 1935; s. William and Thelma (Goodman) L.; m. Frances Ellen Kavesh, Dec. 4, 1963; children: Sandra Lyn Levine Charlap, David Jay. BS in Bus. Adminstrn., Lehigh U., 1956. Registered rep. N.Y. Inst. Fin. Registered rep. Hill, Darlington & Grimm, N.Y.C., 1960-61; ptnr. Percy Friedlander & Co., 1962-71; v.p. Fred Alger & Co., 1971-74; asst. v.p. Shearson Hayden Stone, 1974-76; sole proprietor N.Y. Stock Exch., 1976-80; pres. Levine Securities, Inc., 1980—. Mem. N.Y. Stock Exch., 1961-96. Lt. (j.g.) USN, 1957-60. Mem. Cedar Hill Country Club (dir. 1995-96). Jewish. Avocations: golf, travel. Home: 3 Drummond Ter Livingston NJ 07039-1103 E-mail: www.hlvsec@aol.com.

LEVINE, HENRY DAVID, lawyer; b. N.Y.C., June 7, 1951; s. Harold Abraham and Joan Sarah (Price) L.; m. Barbara Wolgel, Aug. 28, 1976; children: David, Rachel, Daniel. AB, Yale U., 1972; JD, M in Pub. Policy, Harvard U., 1976. Bar: N.Y. 1977, D.C. 1978, U.S. Supreme Ct. 1980. Assoc. Wilmer, Cutler & Pickering, Washington, 1976-80, Morrison & Foerster, Washington, 1981-83, ptnr., 1983-92, Levine, Blaszak, Block & Boothby LLP, Washington, 1993—. Cons. to GSA on FTS2001, 1994—; chmn. bd. Tech-Caliber, LLC, 1999—. Editor Telematics, 1984-89. Mem. Nat. Rsch. Coun. Com on High Tech. Bldgs., 1985-88; bd. dirs. Washington Hebrew Congregation, 1996—, treas. 2002—, Appleseed Found., 2001—. Named one of the twenty-five most powerful people in networking Network World, 1996. Mem. ABA, Fed. Communication Bar Assn., Forum Com. on Comm. Law. Home: 5208 Edgemoor Ln Bethesda MD 20814-2342 Office: Levine Blaszak Block & Boothby 2001 L St NW Ste 900 Washington DC 20036-4940 E-mail: hlevine@lb3law.com.

LEVINE, HOWARD ALLEN, mathematician, educator; b. St. Paul, Jan. 15, 1942; s. Morris Levine; m. Elyse M. Levine, June 16, 1974; children: Joseph, Margo. BA, U. Minn., 1964; MA, Cornell U., 1967, PhD, 1969. Asst. prof. U. Minn., Mpls., 1969-73, U. R.I., Kingston, 1973-75, assoc. prof., 1975-78, Iowa State U., Ames, 1978-79, prof., 1979-98, disting. prof. math., 1998—. Cons. Naval Underwater Sys. Ctr., 1976-78, Lawrence Livermore Nat. Lab., Calif., 1984-87. Assoc. editor Jour. Math. Analysis Application, 1996—, Math. Application Sci., 1990—. NSF Rsch. grantee, 1998-2001, NATO Collaborative Rsch. grantee, 1995-97. Mem. Am. Math. Soc., Soc. Indsl. and Applied Math. Office: Iowa State Univ Dept Math Ames IA 50011 E-mail: halevine@iastate.edu.

LEVINE, HOWARD ARNOLD, state supreme court justice; b. Mar. 4, 1932; m. Barbara Joan Segall, July 25, 1954; children: Neil Louis, Ruth Ellen, James Robert. BA, Yale U., 1953, LLB, 1956; LLD (hon.), Union U., 1994. Bar: N.Y. 1956. Asst. in instrn., research assoc. in criminal law Yale Law Sch., 1956-57; assoc. firm Hughes, Hubbard, Blair, Reed, N.Y.C., 1957-59; practiced in Schenectady, 1959-70; asst. dist. atty. Schenectady County, N.Y., 1961-66, dist. atty., 1967-70; judge Schenectady County Family Ct., 1971-80; acting judge Schenectady County Ct., 1971-80; adminstrv. judge family cts. N.Y. State 4th Jud. Dist., 1974-80; assoc. justice appellate div. 3d dept. N.Y. State Supreme Ct., 1982-93; assoc. judge N.Y. Ct. of Appeals, 1993—. Vis. lectr. Albany Law Sch., 1972-81; mem. N.Y. Gov.'s Panel on Juvenile Violence, N.Y. State Temp. Commn. on Child Welfare, N.Y. State Temp. Commn. on Recodification of Family Ct. Act, N.Y. State Juvenile Justice Adv. Bd., 1974-80; mem. ind. rev. bd. N.Y. State Div. for Youth, 1974-80; mem. rules and adv. com. on family ct. N.Y. State Jud. Conf., 1974-80 Contbr. articles to law revs. Bd. dirs. Schnecatady County Child Guildance Ctr., Carver Community Ctr., Freedom Forum of Schnectady. Mem. ABA, Am. Law Inst., N.Y. State Bar Assn. (chmn. spl. com. juvenile justice), Assn. Family Ct. Judges State N.Y. (pres. 1979-80) Home: 2701 Rosendale Rd Niskayuna NY 12309-1300 Office: County Jud Bldg 612 State St Schenectady NY 12305-2113*

LEVINE, HOWARD MARVIN, obstetrician, gynecologist; b. N.Y.C., Apr. 24, 1933; s. Benjamin and Esther (Brody) L.; m. Alice Esta Edelman, June 12, 1954; children: Linda Krause, Steven Brody, Douglas Becker. AB, NYU, 1953; MD, U. Louisville, 1957. Diplomate Am. Bd. Ob-Gyn. Intern Mt. Sinai Hosp., N.Y.C., 1957-58; resident in ob-gyn Albert Einstein Coll. Medicine, Bronx Mcpl. Hosp. Ctr., 1958-62; practice medicine specializing in ob-gyn Mpls., 1964—. Assoc. clin. prof. U. Minn., 1985—. Served as capt. USAF, 1962-64. Fellow Am. Coll. Ob-Gyn, ACS, Am. Geriatrics Soc., Internat. Coll. Surgeons, Am. Soc. Colpolscopy and Cervical Neoplasia. Home: 11215 57th Ave N Minneapolis MN 55442-1565

LEVINE, I. ROBERT, business executive; b. Albany, N.Y., Oct. 17, 1932; s. Louis and Golda (Baer) L.; m. Barbara Seff Rosen, June 12, 1955; children: Marc, Gary. AB, Dartmouth Coll., 1954; MBA, Amos Tuck Grad. Sch. Bus., 1955. CPA. Ptnr. Ernst & Young, N.Y.C., 1959-81; sr. v.p. UST, Inc., Greenwich, Conn., 1981-97; chmn. Montshire Assocs., LLC, 1997—. Dir. Saga Holidays, Boston, 1982-89; adv. dir. Conn. Nat. Bank, Stamford, 1982-88. Author: Handbook of Mergers and Acquisitions, 1981. Pres. Vol. Assn. for Sr. Citizen Activities, N.Y.C., 1988-91; dir. Am. Classical Orch., Norwalk, Conn., 1995—, Bennington (Vt.) Mus., 1990—, VASCA, N.Y.C., 1987— Mem.: Innis Arden Golf Club. Republican. Jewish. Avocations: travel, golf, computer. Office: Montshire Assocs LLC 21 West Way Old Greenwich CT 06870-2429 Fax: 203-698-2498. E-mail: vtnh@optonline.net.

LEVINE, IRVING RASKIN, news commentator, university dean, author, lecturer; b. Pawtucket, R.I. s. Joseph and Emma (Raskin) L.; m. Nancy Cartmell Jones, July 12, 1957; children— Jeffrey Claybourne Bond, Daniel Rome, Jennifer Jones. BS, Brown U., 1944, LHD (hon.), 1969; MS, Columbia, 1947; LHD (hon.), Bryant Coll., 1974; D.Journalism (hon.), Roger Williams Coll., 1985; LLD (hon.), U. R.I., 1988; LHD (hon.), Lynn U., 1992; LLD (hon.), Northeastern U., 1993; D in Journalism (hon.), R.I. Coll., 1996. Writer obits. Providence Jour., 1940-43; fgn. news editor Internat. News Service, 1947-48; chief Vienna (Austria) bur., 1948-50; with NBC, 1950-95, war corr. Korea, 1950-52; radio anchor World News Roundup, N.Y.C., 1953-54; chief corr. NBC, Moscow, 1955-59, Rome, 1959-71, London, 1967-68, chief econs. corr. Washington, 1971-95; dean Coll. Internat. Comms., Lynn U., Boca Raton, Fla., 1995—. Commentator Consumer News and Bus. Channel Cable TV affiliate svc. NBC TV News, 1990-96; commentator Pub. Broadcasting Sys. TV, Nightly Bus. Report, 1997—; spl. writer London Times, 1955-59; covered assignments in Can., China, Czechoslovakia, Bulgaria, Poland, Japan, Vietnam, Formosa, Thailand, Eng., France, Germany, Switzerland, Algeria, Congo, Israel, Turkey, Tunisia, Greece, Yugoslavia, Union of South Africa, Denmark, Sweden, Ireland; press group with pres. Ford, Carter, Reagan, Bush, Clinton; attended G-7 Econ. Summits, 1975-95; world affairs lectr. Holland Am. Cruise Line. 1995-97, Cunard Cruise Line, 1998-2001, Radisson Seven Seas Cruise Line, 2000—; lectr. univs., bus. groups, cruise ships; writer Internet World Traveler Column, 1997-99; moderator Bus. Update TV Program, Fla. TV programs, 1998-99; nat. spokesperson First Penn-Pacific Life Ins. Co., 1997-99; anchor Bus. Trends TV program, 2000. Author: Main Street, USSR, 1959, Travel Guide to Russia, 1960, Main Street, Italy, 1963, The New Worker in Soviet Russia, 1973; contbr. articles to nat. mags.; guest on numerous TV shows including Murphy Brown, 1989, David Letterman Show, 1990, Jay Leno Show, 1990. 2d lt. Signal Corps, U.S. Army, 1943-46, Philippines, Japan. Recipient award for best radio-TV reporting from abroad Overseas Press Club, 1956, award for outstanding radio network broadcasting Nat. Headliners Club, 1957, 50th Anniversary award Columbia Sch. Journalism, 1963, Emmy citation 1966, Martin R. Gainsbrugh award for best econ. reporting, 1978, William Rogers award Brown U., 1988, Silver Circle award Nat. Acad. TV Arts and Scis., 1990; named one of 10 Outstanding Young Men, U.S. Jaycees, 1956; named to R.I. Hall of Fame, 1972, Pawtucket Hall of Fame, 1986, Nat. Broadcasters Hall of Fame Lifetime Achievement award, 1995, TJFR and Master Card award as one of 100 top bus. news luminaries, 2000; named Among 100 Most accomplished Grads. 20th Century Brown Alumni mag., 2000; honoree Loyola Coll.'s Beta Gamma Sigma, 1994, Mem. Coun. on Fgn. Rels. (fellowship 1952-53), Cosmos, Phi Beta Kappa, Beta Gamma Sigma. Office: Lynn U 3601 N Military Trail Boca Raton FL 33431-5598

LEVINE, ISRAEL E. writer, public relations company executive; b. N.Y.C., Aug. 30, 1923; s. Albert Ely and Sonia (Silver) L.; m. Joy Elaine Michael, June 23, 1946; children: David, Carol. BS, CCNY, 1946. Asst. dir. pub. rels. CCNY, 1946-54, dir., 1954-77, editor Alumnus Mag., 1952-74, 87-89; editor Health Care Week, 1977-79, William H. White Publs., 1979-81; dir. comm. Am. Jewish Congress, 1981-87; COO, Richard Cohen Assocs., N.Y.C., 1987-99; pres. I.E. Levine Pub. Rels., 2000—. Author: (with A. Lateiner) The Techniques of Supervision, 1954; The Discoverer of Insulin: Dr. Frederick G. Banting, 1959, Conqueror of Smallpox: Dr. Edward Jenner, 1960, Behind the Silken Curtain: The Story of Townsend Harris, 1961, Inventive Wizard: George Westinghouse, 1962, Champion of World Peace: Dag Hammarskjold, 1962, Miracle Man of Printing: Ottmar Mergenthaler, 1963, Electronics Pioneer: Lee DeForest, 1964, Young Man in the White House: John Fitzgerald Kennedy, 1964, 91, Oliver Cromwell, 1966, Spokesman for the Free World: Adlai Stevenson, 1967, Lenin: The Man Who Made a Revolution, 1969, The Many Faces of Slavery, 1975; contbr. over 200 articles to mags. Mem. exec. com. Com. for Pub. Higher Edn., N.Y.C., 1987—. 2d lt., navigator USAAF, 1943-45, ETO. Decorated Air medal with 3 oak leaf clusters, 3 battle stars USAAF; recipient 125th Anniversary medal; CCNY, 1972, Svc. medal CCNY Alumni Assn., 1974. Mem. The Authors Guild, Authors' League Am., Soc. of Silurians, 2d Air Divsn. Assn. Jewish. Avocation: gardening. Office: # S10 2001 Marcus Ave New Hyde Park NY 11042

LEVINE, JACK, artist; b. Boston, Jan. 3, 1915; s. Samuel Mayer and Mary (Grinker) L.; widowed; 1 child, Susanna Levine Fisher. AFD, Colby Coll., Waterville, Maine, 1956. One-man shows include Downtown Gallery, N.Y.C., 1938, Artists, 1942, Mus. Modern Art, N.Y.C., 1943; exhibited in group shows at Jeu de Paume, Paris, 1938, Carnegie Internat. exhbns., 1938-40, Artists for Victory, Met. Mus., N.Y.C., 1942, retrospective at Jewish Mus., N.Y.C., 1978-79, Bklyn. Mus., 1999; represented in permanent collections Mus. Modern Art, Met. Mus. Art, N.Y.C., William Hayes Foggs Mus., Harvard U., Addison Gallery, Andover, Mass., Mus. Vatican, D.C. Moore Gallery, N.Y. With AUS, 1942-45. Mem. Am. Acad. Arts and Letters (pres., chancellor), Inst. Arts and Letters (pres. 1993), Nat. Acad. Design, Century Club.

LEVINE, JACK ANTON, lawyer; b. Monticello, N.Y., Dec. 23, 1946; s. Milton and Sara (Sacks) L.; m. Eileen A. Garsh, Sept. 7, 1974; children: Matthew Aaron, Dara Esther. BS with honors, SUNY, Binghamton, 1968; JD with honors, U. Fla., 1975, LLM in Taxation, 1976. Bar: Fla. 1975, U.S. Ct. Appeals (11th cir.) 1981, U.S. Tax Ct., 1982. Tax atty. legis. and regulations divsn. Office chief counsel IRS, Washington, 1977-81; assoc. Holland & Knight, Tampa, Fla., 1981-83, ptnr., 1984—. Lectr. in field. Contbr. articles to profl. jours. Mem. ABA, Fla. Bar Assn. (sect. taxation exec. coun. 1984—, chmn. ptnrship. com. 1985-88, chmn. taxation regulated public utilities com. 1988-92, co-chmn. corps. and tax-exempt orgns. com. 1992-2001, bd. cert. in tax law 1984—). Democrat. Jewish. Avocations: golf, reading, traveling. Home: 10905 Carrollwood Dr Tampa FL 33618-3903 Office: Holland & Knight 400 N Ashley Dr Ste 2300 Tampa FL 33602-4322

LEVINE, JAMES, conductor, pianist, artistic director; b. Cin., June 23, 1943; s. Lawrence M. and Helen (Goldstein) L. Studied piano with Rosina Lhevinne and Rudolf Serkin, studied conducting with Jean Morel, Fausto Cleva and Max Rudolf, studied theory and interpretation with Walter Levin; student, Juilliard Sch. Music; hon. degree, U. Cin., New Eng. Cons., Northwestern U., SUNY, Potsdam, Juilliard Sch. Music dir. Ravinia Festival, 1973-93; artistic dir. Met. Opera Assn., 1986—; guest lectr. Sarah Lawrence Coll., Harvard U., Yale U. Piano debut with Cin. Symphony, 1953; conducting debut at Aspen Music Festival, 1961; Met. Opera debut, 1971; Chgo. Symphony debut at Ravinia Festival, 1971; regularly appears throughout U.S. and Europe as condr. and pianist, including Vienna Philharm., Berlin Philharm., Chgo. Symphony, Phila. Orch., Boston Symphony, N.Y. Philharm., Dresden Staatskapelle, Philharmonia Orch., Israel Philharm., Munich Philharm., Wagner Festival at Bayreuth; made Bayreuth debut in new prodn. Parsifal, 1982; condr. Salzburg Festival, 1975-93; Salzburg premieres include Schönberg's Moses und Aron, 1987, Offenbach's Tales of Hoffmann, 1980, Mahler's Seventh Symphony, Mendelssohn's Elijah; condr. Met. premiere prodns. of Verdi's I Vespri Siciliani, Stiffelio, I Lombardi, Weill's The Rise and Fall of the City of Mahagonny, Stravinsky's Oedipus Rex, Berg's Lulu, Mozart's Idomeneo and La Clemenza di Tito, Gershwin's Porgy and Bess, Schönberg's Erwartung and Moses und Aron, Rossini's La Cenerentola, world premieres Corigliano/Hoffman The Ghosts of Versailles, 1991, Harbison The Great Gatsby, 1999; subject of documentary for PBS; artistic dir. Met. Opera. Chief condr. Munich Philharm., 1999—. Recipient Smetana medal, 1987, 8 Grammy awards. Office: Munchner Philharmoniker Kellerstr 4 Munich D-81667 Germany

LEVINE, JANE SHEILA, nurse, health insurance consultant; b. Bklyn., Jan. 2, 1946; d. Irvine Richard and Ann (Odell) L.; m. Robert Nevin Stewart, Sept. 1, 1988. Grad., Bellevue Sch. Nursing, 1966; student, Am. U., 1966-67, Marymont Manhattan Coll., 1967, Fla. Internat. U., 1976-78. Staff nurse Washington Hosp. Ctr., 1966; nurse N.Y. Office Paramount Pictures, 1967-68; oper. room nurse Beth Israel Hosp., N.Y.C., 1968-70; pub. health nurse Bellevue Hosp., 1970-74; regional rep. N.Y. State Nurses Assn., 1974-75; asst. dir. nursing Parkway Gen. Hosp., Miami, Fla., 1975-77; dir. Staff Builders, 1977-78; v.p. for nursing Westchester Gen. Hosp., 1978-80; dir. nursing svcs. Med. Pers. Pool Am., 1981-82; founder Elder Designs Inc., 1982-91; health, life and fin. counsel Equitable Life Assurance, Miami, 1983-86; brokerage cons. Springfield/Monarch Ins. Brokers, 1986; founder, employee benefits counselor Fin. Designs, 1987-94; founder, pres. World Impact Now, Inc., 1988-90, Home Health HiTech Nursing and Woundcare Specailists, 1991—2001; dops New Heart Home Health, 2001—. Dir. nursing Atlantic Allcare, 1999; mktg. cons. World Mktg. Alliance, 1999—. Mem. ANA, Fla. Nurses Assn., Nat. Assn. Life Underwriters, Nat. Assn. Health Underwriters, Fla. Assn. Health Underwriters. Home: Regency Lakes 5220 Eagle Cay Way Coconut Creek FL 33073-2605

LEVINE, JEROME, psychiatrist, educator; b. N.Y.C., July 10, 1934; s. Abraham and Sadie (Glowatz) L.; children: Ross W., Lynn R., Andrew R. BA, U. Buffalo, 1954, MD, 1958. Intern, then psychiat. resident E.J. Meyer Meml. Hosp., Buffalo, 1958-61; sr. psychiat. resident St. Elizabeth's Hosp., Washington, 1961-62; staff psychiatrist USPHS Hosp., Lexington, Ky., 1962-64; research psychiatrist, asst. chief psychopharmacology research br. NIMH, 1964-67, chief of br., 1967-81, chief pharmacologic and somatic treatments research br., 1981-84; research prof. psychiatry U. Md. Sch. Medicine, Balt., 1985-94; dep. dir. Nathan Kline Inst. for Psychiat. Rsch., Orangeburg, N.Y., 1994—; rsch. prof. psychiatry NYU, 1994—. Instr. psychiatry Johns Hopkins Med. Sch., 1964-72; vis. prof. U. Pisa, Italy, 1977 Author books and papers on psychopharmacology, clin. trial methodology, somatic treatment assessment for psychiat. disorders. Mem. Soc. Clin. Trials, Am. Psychiat. Assn. (Hofheimer Research prize 1970), Am. Coll. Neuropsychopharmacology, Collegium Internationale Neuropsychopharmacologicum, Am. Soc. Clin. Pharmacology and Therapeutics. Home: 15 Stony Hollow Chappaqua NY 10514-2014 Office: Nathan Kline Inst Bldg 35 140 Old Orangeburg Rd Ste 35 Orangeburg NY 10962-1159 E-mail: levine@nki.rfmh.org.

LEVINE, JEROME LESTER, lawyer; b. L.A., July 20, 1940; m. Maryanne Shields, Sept. 13, 1966; children: Aron Michael, Sara Michelle. BA, San Francisco State U., 1962; JD, U. Calif., 1965. Bar: Calif. 1966, U.S. Supreme Ct. 1986. Dir. operational svcs., assoc. dir. Western Ctr. on Law and Poverty, L.A., 1968-72; assoc. Swerdlow, Glikbarg & Shimer, Beverly Hills, Calif., 1972-77; ptnr. Lans Feinberg & Cohen, L.A., 1977-79, Albala & Levine, L.A., 1980-83, Neiman, Billet, Albala & Levine, L.A., 1983-90, Levine & Assocs., L.A., 1991-2000, Holland & Knight LLP, L.A., 2000—. Lectr. U. So. Calif. Law Ctr., Loyola U. Sch. Law. Mem. ABA, L.A. County Bar Assn., Fed. Bar Assn., Internat. Assn. Gaming Lawyers. Office: 633 W 5th St Ste 2100 Los Angeles CA 90071-2017 E-mail: jllevine@hklaw.com.

LE VINE, JEROME EDWARD, retired ophthalmologist; b. Pitts., Mar. 23, 1923; s. Harry Robert and Marian Dorothy (Finesilver) L.; m. Marilyn Tobey Hiedovitz, Apr. 14, 1957; children: Loren Robert, Beau Jay, Janice Lynn. BS, U. Pitts., 1944; MD, Hahnemann Med. Sch., Phila., 1949; postgrad. in ophthalmology, U. Pa., 1951-52. Diplomate Am. Bd. Disability Cons., Am. Bd. Quality Assurance & Utilization Rev. Intern St. Francis Hosp., Pitts., 1949-50; resident in ophthalmology Jefferson U. Med. Sch. Hosp., Phila., 1952-54; ophthalmologist Leech Farm VA Hosp., Pitts., 1955-59; chief eye dept. Stanocola Clinic, Baton Rouge, 1959-64; sole practice medicine specializing in ophthalmology, 1959-86; ret., 1986. Cons. La. State U., East La. State Hosp. Infirmary, Villa Feliciana Geriatric Hosp., disability dept. Social Security Adminstrn., div. blind La. State Pub. Welfare dept.; mem. staff Our Lady of the Lake Hosp., Baton Rouge Gen. Hosp., Women's Hosp.; instr. spl. edn. U. Southeastern La., 1971. Mem. Am. Bd. Quality Assurance and Utilization Rev., 1990. With MC, AUS, 1942-44. Fellow Am. Geriatric Soc., Royal Soc. Health; mem. AMA, La. State Med. Soc., East Baton Rouge Parish Med. Soc., 6th Dist. Med. Soc., New Orleans Acad. Ophthalmology, So. Med. Assn., La. Med. Soc., Baton Rouge Parish Med. Soc., Pi Lambda Phi, Phi Delta Epsilon. Democrat. Jewish. Office: PO Box 66787 Baton Rouge LA 70896-6787 Fax: 225-924-6801.

LEVINE, JOEL, music director, conductor; Grad. with honors, Eastman Sch. Music. Music dir. Oklala. City Philharmonic Orch., Okla., 1988—. Mus. dir. Symphony Orch. of Portugal, Lisbon, Czech Nat. Symphony Orch., Prague, St. Louis Symphony, Detroit Symphony, Denver Symphony, others. CD released on Warner-Reprise label. Recipient Gov.'s Arts award, 1989; named Okla. Musician of Yr., 1991, Okla. Fedn. Music Clubs. Office: Civic Ctr Music Hall 428 W California Ste 210 Oklahoma City OK 73102-2454*

LEVINE, JOEL SETH, medical school administrator, educator; b. Key West, Fla., Feb. 22, 1947; s. Carl Michael and Sophie Barbara (Halpern) L.; m. Frieda Zylberberg, Aug. 1, 1970; children: Daniel Ian, Steven Neal, Karyn Ann. BS, Bklyn. Coll., 1967; MD, SUNY, Bklyn., 1971. Asst. prof. medicine U. Colo., Denver, 1978-84, vice chmn. dept. medicine, 1984-92, assoc. prof. medicine, 1984-92, assoc. dean clin. affairs, 1989-92, prof. medicine, 1992—, sr. assoc. dean clin. affairs, 1992—; dir. gastroenterology unit Univ. Hosp., Denver, 1989—, pres. med. staff, 1989-92. Editor: Decision Making in Gastroenterology, 1985, 92; contbr. articles to profl. jours. Trustee Kern Rsch. Found., Denver, 1982—, Total Long Term Care, Denver, 1989-2000, Univ. Hosp., Denver, 1989-92. Lt. comdr. USN, 1973-75. NIH grantee, 1977-78, Clin. Investigator awardee, 1978-81; Robert Wood Johnson Found. fellow, 1988-89. Fellow ACP (gov. Colo. chpt. 1996-2001, regent 2001—); mem. Am. Gastroenterological Assn. (chair, pub. policy comm. 1997-00), Am. Fedn. Clin. Rsch., Western Soc. Clin. Rsch. Jewish. Avocations: tennis, history, education. Office: Univ of Colo Health Sci Ctr B-158 4200 E 9th 9th Ave Denver CO 80262-0001

LEVINE, JOHN ROBERT, author, lecturer; b. N.Y.C., May 10, 1954; s. Robert J. and Virginia W. (Arnold) L. BA, Yale U., 1975, PhD, 1984. Propr. IECC, Trumansburg, N.Y., 1981—; trustee, commr. Water and Sewer Commn., Village of Trumansburg, 1997—. Sr. mem. tech. staff Segue Software, Inc., Newton, Mass., 1989-93, dir., 1992—. Author: The Internet for Dummies, 1993, 8th edit., 2002, Internet Secrets, 1995, 2d edit., 2000, Windows XP: The Complete Reference, 2001, 20 other books; co-host (pub. tv show) The Internet Show, 1994, The Internet for Grownups, 1999. Trustee First Unitarian Soc. Ithaca, N.Y., 2000—. Mem. Assn. for Computing Machinery, Authors' Guild. Unitarian Universalist. Office: IECC PO Box 727 Trumansburg NY 14886-0727 E-mail: mww@johnlevine.com.

LEVINE, LAURENCE BRANDT, investment banker; b. N.Y.C., Dec. 17, 1941; s. Martin and Beulah (Brandt) Levine; m. Laura Lynn Vitale; 1 child Blair Brandt. BA (Francis Biddle prize 1961), Princeton U., 1964; LLB, Stanford U., 1967. V.p., voting shareholder Drexel Burnham Lambert, N.Y.C., 1968-73; corp. planning officer, Office of Chmn. Ogden Corp., 1973-75; pres. Investment Rsch. Assocs., West Chester, Pa., 1975-80; sr. v.p., dir. investment banking Kramer Capital Corp., 1980-82; exec. v.p., dir. corp. fin. Henry Ansbacher Inc., N.Y. and London, 1982-84; sr. v.p. Rothschild Inc., N.Y., 1984-86; exec. v.p. and dir. corp. fin. Smith New Ct. Inc., N.Y. and London, 1986-89; chmn. Blair Holdings Corp., 1989—. Dir. First Internat. Fin. Group, Hamburg, London and Bermuda, Landmark Funds Svcs., Inc., N.Y.C.; dir., vice chmn. Signature Fin. Group, Boston, chmn. EdVerifY, Inc., Palm Beach, Fla.,1998—. Bd. vis. Stanford U. Law Sch., 1968-71, exec. com., 1970; dir. Musica Sacra, N.Y., 1981-86, Concert Artists Guild, N.Y., 1989-92, Ballet Fla., 1992—; pres. Palm Beach Sch. Arts Found., 1993—; adv. bd. Kravis Ctr., 1991—. With USMCR, 1961-65. Mem.: St. James (London) Club, Old Oak Country Club (Purchase), Harmonie (N.Y.C.) Club, Princeton Club, City Athletic Club. Mailing: PO Box 2244 Palm Beach FL 33480 E-mail: brandt41@aol.com.

LEVINE, LAWRENCE STEVEN, lawyer; b. Bklyn., Mar. 30, 1934; s. Harry and Bess (Feiner) L.; m. Linda Robbins, June 16, 1957; children: Lauren Victoria, Audrey Elizabeth, Hilary Anne. AB, Colgate U., 1955; LLB, Yale U., 1958. Bar: N.Y. 1958, U.S. Supreme Ct. 1973. Asst. U.S. atty. for ea. dist. N.Y. U.S. Dept. Justice, N.Y.C., 1958-62; assoc. Kronish & Lieb, 1962-63; ptnr. Beldock Levine & Hoffman LLP, 1964—2001, counsel, 2002—. Vis. instr. Harvard Law Sch., 1991—. Bd. dirs. Jewish Fund for Justice, 1984—, chair, 1988-96; mem. nat. bd. New Jewish Agenda, 1980-89, New Outlook Mag., 1982-90; trustee YM-YWHA's Greater N.Y., Harry Levine Meml. Found., 1965—, Riverdale Coutnry Sch., 1979-89. Mem. Fed. Bar Assn., N.Y. County Lawyers Assn., N.Y. Civil Liberties Union (cooperating counsel), Yale Club. Democrat. Home: 122 E 76th St New York NY 10021-2833 Office: Beldock Levine & Hoffman 99 Park Ave Fl 16 New York NY 10016-1508 E-mail: llevine@blhny.com.

LEVINE, LOUIS DAVID, museum director, archaeologist; b. N.Y.C., June 4, 1940; s. Moe Wolf and Jeanne (Greenwald) L.; m. Dorothy Abrams, Dec. 30, 1962 (div. 1991); children: Sarra L., Samuel E.; m. Pat Molholt, May 25, 1997. Student, Brandeis U., 1960; BA with honours, U. Pa., 1962, PhD with distinction, 1969. Instr. of Hebrew U. Pa., 1966-69; asst. curator Royal Ont. Mus., Toronto, Can., 1969-75, assoc. curator Can., 1975-80, curator Can., 1981, assoc. dir. Can., 1987-90; asst. commr., dir. N.Y. State Mus., Albany, 1990-98; dir. collections & exhbns. Mus. Jewish Heritage, N.Y.C., 1998—. Vis. sr. lectr. Hebrew U., Jerusalem, 1975-76; vis. prof. U. Copenhagen, 1985; asst. prof. U. Toronto, 1969-74, assoc. prof. U. Toronto, 1974-81, prof., 1981-90; dir. Seh Gabi Expdn., western Iran, 1971-73, dir. Mahidasht Project, western Iran, 1975-79. Author: The Neo-Assyrian Zagros, 1974; editor: Scream the Truth at the World, 2001, Lives Remembered, 2002; contbr. articles to profl. jours. NDEA fellow U. Pa., 1962-65, Fulbright fellow, 1965, W.F. Albright fellow, Am. Schs. of Oriental Rsch., 1966, fellow Inst. for Advanced Studies, Hebrew U. Mem. Brit. Inst. of Persian Studies, Brit. Sch. of Archaeology in Iraq, Am. Assn. Mus., Am. Oriental Soc. Jewish. Avocations: woodworking, music. Office: Mus Jewish Heritage 1 Battery Park Plz Fl 25 New York NY 10004-1484 E-mail: Llevine@mjhnyc.org.

LEVINE, MACY IRVING, physician; b. Johnstown, Pa., May 19, 1920; s. Elliott B. and Ida (Leuin) L.; m. Evelyn B. Levine, June 28, 1948 (dec. July 1996); children: Alan, Amy, Paul, Robert. BS, U. Pitts., 1940, MD, 1943. Diplomate Am. Bd. Internal Medicine, Am. Bd. Internal Medicine and Allergy. Intern U. Pitts. Med. Ctr., 1944; resident in allergy VA Hosp., Aspinwall, Pa., 1947-48, resident in medicine, 1948-49; fellow in medicine Lahey Clinic, Boston, 1950-51; USPHS postdoctoral fellow in medicine Peter Bent Brigham Hosp.-Harvard Med. Sch., 1951-52; pvt. practice Pitts., 1952—. Clin. prof. medicine U. Pitts. Sch. Medicine. Editor: Monograph on Insect Allergy, 1995; editor Bull. of the Allegheny County MEd. Soc., 1975-86, Pitt Medicine Med. Alumni Assn., U. Pitts., 1987-99; contbr. more than 70 articles to profl. jours. Bd. dirs. Self Help Group Network, 1989-95, B'nai Israel Congregation, Pitts., 1965-71, Hebrew Free Loan Assn. Pitts., 1980—. Capt. U.S. Army, 1944-46, PTO. Recipient Disting. Svc. award Am. Acad. Allergy and Immunology, 1987, Frederick M. Jacob, M.D. Physician Merit award for Outstanding Svc. Allegheny County Med. Soc., 1988. Fellow Am. Acad. Allergy, Asthma and Immunology (v.p. 1982-83, Outstanding Vol. Clin. Faculty award 1996), Pa. Allergy Assn. (pres. 1970-71, Spl. Recognition award 1989), fellow, ACP; mem. Pitts. Allergy Soc. (pres. 1959-61), U. Pitts. Med. Alumni Assn. (pres. 1976-77), U. Pitts. Alumni Assn. (pres. 1984-85). Avocations: tennis, bridge. Home: 220 N Dithridge St Apt 400 Pittsburgh PA 15213-1421

LEVINE, MADELINE GELTMAN, Slavic literatures educator, translator; b. N.Y.C., Feb. 23, 1942; d. Herman and Nettie (Kritman) Geltman; m. Steven I. Levine; children: Elaine, Daniel. BA, Brandeis U., 1962; MA, Harvard U., 1964, PhD, 1971. Asst. prof. Grad Sch. CUNY, N.Y.C., 1971-74; assoc. prof. U. N.C., Chapel Hill, 1974-80, prof., 1980-94, Kenan prof. Slavic lits., 1994—, chmn. dept. Slavic langs., 1979-87, 94-99. Chmn. joint com. on Ea. Europe, Am. Coun. Learned Socs.-Social Sci. Rsch. Coun., 1989-92; chmn. bd. govs. U. N.C. Press, 1999-. Translator: A Memoir of the Warsaw Uprising (Miron Bialoszewski), 1977, 2d edit. 1991, The Poetry of Osip Mandelstam: God's Grateful Guest (Ryszard Przybylski), 1987, Beginning With My Streets: Essays and Recollections (Czeslaw Milosz), 1992, A Year of the Hunter (Czeslaw Milosz), 1994, Bread for the Departed (Bogdan Wojdowski), 1997, Lost Landscapes: In Search of Isaac Bashevis Singer and the Jews of Poland (Agata Tuszynska), 1998, Milosz's ABCs (Czeslaw Milosz), 2001; translator with Francine Prose: A Scrap of Time and Other Stories (Ida Fink), 1986, 2d edit., 1995; author: Contemporary Polish Poetry, 1925-75, 1981; co-editor (with Bogdana Carpenter): To Begin Where I Am: Selected Essays (Czeslaw Milosz), 2001. NEH fellow, 1984, 2000; recipient (with Francine Prose) award for lit. translation PEN-America, 1988. Mem. Am. Assn. for Advancement of Slavic Studies, Polish Inst. of Arts and Scis. Am., Am. Assn. Tchrs. of Slavic and East European Langs., Am. Literary Translators Assn., Pen-Am. Home: 5001 Whitehorse Rd Hillsborough NC 27278-9399 Office: U NC CB # 3165 425 Dey Hall Chapel Hill NC 27599-3165 E-mail: mglevine@email.unc.edu.

LEVINE, MAITA FAYE, mathematics educator; b. Cin., Oct. 17, 1930; d. Aaron and Jessie (Byer) L. BA, U. Cin., 1952, BE, 1953, MA in Tchg., 1966; PhD, Ohio State U., 1970. Tchr. Woodward H.S., Cin., 1953-63; instr. math. U. Cin., 1963-70, asst. prof., 1970-76, assoc. prof. math edn., 1976-86, prof. math. sci., 1986-96, prof. emeritus, 1996—. Lectr. NSF Inst., 1962-94, Ohio Bd. Regents Insts., 1988-93. Writer Nat. Longitudinal Study Math. Abilities, 1963, Am. Coll. Testing Program, 1973, 81, 88-89; contbr. articles to profl. jours. Fellow NSF. Mem. AAUP (mem. coun., 1st v.p., chair com. W), Math. Assn. Am., Sch. Sci. and Math. Assn., Assn. Women in Math., Nat. Coun. Tchrs. Math., Ohio Coun. Tchrs. Math., Phi Beta Kappa, Sigma Xi, Delta Kappa Gamma. Democrat. Jewish. E-mail: maita.levine@uc.edu.

LEVINE, MARILYN ANNE, artist; b. Alta., Can., Dec. 22, 1935; came to the U.S., 1973; d. Herman Rutherford and Annie Louise Hayes; m. Sidney Levine, Sept. 30, 1959 (div. 1977). BSc, U. Alta., Edmonton, 1957; MSc, U. Alta., 1959; MA, U. Calif., Berkeley, 1970, MFA, 1971. Tchg. fellow dept. chemistry U. Alta., Edmonton, 1957-59; chemist I Geology Survey Can., Ottawa, 1959-61; chemistry instr. Campion Coll., U. Sask., Regina, Can., 1962-64; ceramics instr. dept. ext. U. Regina, Sask., 1966-69, ceramics instr., 1971-73. Vis. art instr. U. Calgary, Alta., summers 1968, 71; lectr. in art U. Calif., Davis, 1972; visual arts lectr. U. Regina, 1972-73; asst. prof. art U. Utah, Salt Lake City, 1973-76; vis. asst. prof. art-sculpture U. Calif., Berkeley, 1975-80; vis. art lectr. Calif. State Coll., Hayward, 1981. One-woman shows include Hansen Fuller Gallery, San Francisco, 1971, 75, 80, 83, Norman Mackenzie Art Gallery, Regina, 1974, O.K. Harris Works of Art, N.Y.C., 1974, 76, 79, 81, 84, 85, 91, Inst. Contemporary Art, Boston, 1981, Galerie Alain Blondel, Paris, 1981, Rena Bransten Gallery, San Francisco, 1990. Mackenzie Art Gallery, Regina, also traveling, 1998—; group exhibits include Nat. Mus. Modern Art, Kyoto, 1971, Sidney Janis Gallery, N.Y., 1972, Musee d'Art de la Ville de Paris, 1973, Whitney Mus. Am. Art Downtown Br., N.Y., 1974, Mus. Contemporary Crafts, N.Y., 1975, Australian Nat. Gallery, Canberra, 1977, Everson Mus. Art, Syracuse, N.Y., 1979, Denver Art Mus., 1979, Pa. Acad. Fine Arts, Phila., 1981-83, Mackenzie Art Gallery, U. Regina, 1980, Abbaye Saint-Andre, Meymac, Correze, France, 1983, Am. Craft Mus., N.Y., 1986-92, Philbrook Mus. Art, Tulsa, 1987-89, Scripps Coll., Claremont, Calif., 1994-96; represented in permanent collections U. Art Mus., Berkeley, Can. Coun. Art Bank, Australian Nat. Gallery, Canberra, Mus. Contemporary Art, Chgo., Nelson-Atkins Mus. Art, Kansas City, Mo., Nat. Mus. Modern Art, Kyoto, Montreal Mus. Fine Art, Va. Mus. Fine Arts, Richmond, San Francisco Mus. Modern Art, Everson Mus. Art, Syracuse, Philbrook Mus. Art, Tulsa, Mus. Contemporary Ceramic Art, Shigaraki, Japan, Mint Mus. Craft and Design, Charlotte, N.C. Recipient David P. Gardner Faculty Rsch. grantee U.

Utah, Salt Lake City, 1975, Sr. Arts Grant award Can. Coun., Ottawa, Ont., Can., 1976; Visual Artists Fellowship grantee Nat. Endowment for the Arts, Washington, 1976, 80. Home: 950 Sixty First St Oakland CA 94608 E-mail: info@marilynlevine.com.

LEVINE, MARILYN MARKOVICH, lawyer, arbitrator; b. Bklyn., Aug. 9, 1930; d. Harry P and Fannie L (Hymowitz) Markovich; m. Louis L Levine, June 24, 1950; children: Steven R, Ronald J, Linda J Morgenstern. BS summa cum laude, Columbia U., 1950; MA, Adelphi U., 1967; JD, Hofstra U., 1977. Bar: NY 1978, US Dist Ct (no and ea dists) NY 1978, DC 1979, US Supreme Ct 1982. Sole practice, Valley Stream, N.Y., 1978—. Panel arbitrator retail food indust, New York, NY, 1980—; arbitrator NY Dist Cts, Nassau County, 1981—; contract arbitrator bldg serv indust, New York, NY, 1982—; mem Nat Acad Arbitrators, 1992—. Panel arbitrator Suffolk County Pub Employee Relations Bd, 1979—, Nassau County Pub Employee Relations Bd, 1980—, Nat Mediation Bd, 1986—; mem adv coun Ctr Labor and Indust Relationa, NY Inst Technology, 1985—; counsel Nassau Civic Club, 1978—. Mem.: ABA, Fed Mediation Bd (arbitrator 1980—), Am Arbit Asn (arbitrator 1979—), NJ Bd Mediation (panel arbitrator), Nassau County Bar Asn, DC Bar Asn, NY State Bar Asn. Home and Office: 1057 Linden St Valley Stream NY 11580-2135 E-mail: mmllevine@yahoo.com., ml-levine@worldnet.att.net.

LEVINE, MARK DAVID, research laboratory administrator; b. Cleve., May 26, 1944; s. Hyman and Rebecca (Spector) L.; m. Irma Herrera, June, 1990. AB summa cum laude, Princeton U., 1966; PhD, U. Calif., Berkeley, 1975. Staff scientist Ford Found. Energy Policy Project, Washington, 1972-73; sr. energy policy analyst SRI Internat., Menlo Park, Calif., 1974-78; staff scientist Lawrence Berkeley Lab., Berkeley, 1978-84, dept. program leader, 1984-86, leader energy analysis program, 1986-96, dir. environ. energy techs. divsn., 1996—. Cons. Ford Found., TEM, Inc., Pacific Gas & Electric Co., QED Research, Inc., Energy Found., 1978—. Contbr. articles to profl. jours. Bd. dirs. Am. Coun. Energy Efficient Economy, Ctr. Clean Air Policy, Ctr. Resource Solutions, Beijing Energy Efficient Ctr. Woodrow Wilson fellow, 1966; Fulbright scholar, 1966. Fellow Calif. Coun. on Sci. and Tech. Jewish. Home: 5701 Barrett Ave El Cerrito CA 94530-1408 Office: Lawrence Berkeley Lab Bldg 90 Room 3125 Berkeley CA 94720 E-mail: mdlevine@lbl.gov.

LEVINE, MELDON EDISES, lawyer, former congressman; b. Los Angeles, June 7, 1943; s. Sid B. and Shirley B. (Blum) L.; children: Adam Paul, Jacob Caplan, Cara Emily. AB, U. Calif., Berkeley, 1964; MPA, Princeton U., 1966; JD, Harvard U., 1969. Bar: Calif. 1970, D.C. 1972. Assoc. Wyman, Bautzer, Rothman & Kuchel, 1969-71; legis. asst. U.S. Senate, Washington, 1971-73; ptnr. Levine Krom & Unger, Beverly Hills, Calif., 1973-77; mem. Calif. Assembly, Sacramento, 1977-82, 98th-102d Congresses from 27th Calif. dist., Washington, 1983-93; ptnr. Gibson, Dunn & Crutcher, L.A., 1993—. Author: The Private Sector and the Common Market, 1968; contbr. articles to various publs. Mem. governing bd. U.S.-Israel Sci. and Tech. Commn., U.S. Holocaust Meml. Mus.; mem. amateur baseball team Hollywood Stars, 1971—. Mem. Calif. Bar Assn., Los Angeles Bar Assn. Office: Gibson Dunn & Crutcher 2029 Century Park E Ste 4000 Los Angeles CA 90067-3032 E-mail: mlevine@gibsondunn.com.

LEVINE, MELVIN CHARLES, lawyer; b. Bklyn., Nov. 12, 1930; s. Barnet and Jennie (Iser) L. BCS, NYU, 1952; LLB, Harvard U., 1955. Bar: N.Y. 1956, U.S. Supreme Ct. 1964. Assoc. Kriger & Haber, Bklyn., 1956-58, Black, Varian & Simons, N.Y.C., 1959; sole practice, 1959—. Devel. multiple dwelling housing; dir. Am. ORT; mem. Am. ORT Nat. Campaign Com.; trustee Bramson ORT Coll.; mem. housing ct. adv. coun. N.Y. State Unified Ct. Sys.; mem. ind. dem. jud. screening panel N.Y.C civil ct. judges; mem. Character and Fitness Com., First Jud. Dept. Trustee Jewish Ctr. of the Hamptons. Recipient N.Y. Ort Scholarship Fund Cmty. Achievement award. Mem. N.Y. County Lawyers Assn. (dir., co-chair civil ct. practice sect., civil ct. com., housing ct. com., uniform housing ct. rules com., liaison to Assn. Bar City of N.Y. on selection of housing, civil and criminal ct. judges, com. on jud., task force on tort reform, Civil Ct. Practice Sect. Disting. Svc. award), Assn. Bar of City of N.Y. (adj. mem. jud. com.) Democrat. Jewish. Home: 146 Waverly Pl New York NY 10014-3848 Office: 271 Madison Ave Ste 1404 New York NY 10016-1001

LEVINE, MICHAEL, public relations executive, writer, announcer; b. N.Y.C., Apr. 17, 1954; s. Arthur and Virginia (Gaylor) L. Student, Rutgers U., 1978. Owner, operator TV News Mag., Los Angeles, 1977-83; owner Levine/Schnieder Pub. Rels., now Levine Comms. Office, 1982—. Mem. Gov.'s adv. bd. State Calif., Sacramento, 1980-82; pres., owner Aurora Pub., L.A., 1986—; moderator Thought Forum; lectr. in field; founder, moderator L.A. Media Roundtable; media expert KFWB Radio; host Access L.A. Radio Show. Author: The Address Book: How to Reach Anyone Who's Anyone, 1984, The New Address Book, 1986, The Corporate Address Book, 1987, The Music Address Book, 1989, Environmental Address Book, 1991, Kid's Address Book, 1991, Guerrilla P.R., Lessons at Halfway Point, 1995, Take It From Me, Selling Goodness, 1998; : The Princess & The Package, 1998, Guerrilla PR Wired; pub., writer: For Consideration newsletter; host Spiritual Seeker KRLA 1110 AM, Spiritual Seeker Radio Show KRLA, nat. syndicated via Talk Am. Radio Network, talk show host Inside/Out Radio Show, KRLA. Mem. Ronald Reagan Pres.'s Libr.; founder The Actor's Conf., Aurora Charity, 1987; bd. dirs. Felice Found., Micah Ctr.; adv. bd. Dare America; founder, moderator L.A. Media Roundtable; moderator U. Judaism Thought Forum. Mem. TV Acad. Arts and Scis., Entertainment Industries Coun., Musician's Assistance Program, West Hollywood C. of C. (bd. dirs. 1980-82). Jewish. Office: 10333 Ahston Ave Los Angeles CA 90024 E-mail: levinepr@earthlink.net.

LEVINE, MICHAEL, corporate real estate manager; b. Washington, Sept. 14, 1947; s. Bernard Levine and Erma Nadel; m. Jane Levine, Sept. 20, 1981; children: Zachary, Sabrina. BS in Commerce and Engrng. cum laude, Drexel U., 1970; MS, U. Hartford, 1974; MBA summa cum laude, Rutgers U., 1975. CPA; cert. comml. investment mem.; master corp. real estate. Student intern IBM, Phila., 1967-70; mem. auditor/contr. staff United Techs. Corp., Hartford, Conn., 1970-74; auditor/cons. Arthur Andersen & Co., Washington, 1975-77; sr. internal auditor Martin Marrietta Corp., Bethesda, Md., 1977-79; mgr.-packaged software Am. Mgmt. Systems, Arlington, Va., 1979-81; mgr. fin. support AT&T Long Lines, Oakton, 1981-83; mgr. cash planning AT&T Comms., Morristown, N.J., 1983-86; mgr. fin. products AT&T Capital Corp., Whippany, 1986-91; mgr. econ. analysis and maj. transactions AT&T Global Real Estate, Pleasanton, Calif., 1991—. Contbr. articles to profl. jours. Mem. U.S. Army Res., 1970-76. Mem. AICPA, Inst. Comml. Real Estate, Phi Kappa Phi, Beta Gamma Sigma, Sigma Alpha Mu. Avocations: tennis, hiking, biking, travel. Home: 108 Margone Ct Danville CA 94526-1958 Office: AT&T Global Real Estate 4480 Willow Rd Pleasanton CA 94588-3050 E-mail: mlevine@att.com.

LEVINE, MICHAEL ELIAS, law educator, executive; b. N.Y.C., Apr. 8, 1941; s. Morris and Sara (Meltzer) L.; m. Carol June Stover, June 2, 1967; children: Sara Rebecca, Anna Rachel. BA in Philosophy, Reed Coll., 1962; JD, Yale U., 1965. Atty. CAB, Washington, 1965-66; spl. asst. C.C. U.S. Task Force Econ. Growth and Opportunity, 1966-67; law and econs. fellow U. Chgo. Law Sch., 1967-68; asst. prof. law U. So. Calif. Law Ctr., 1968-70, assoc. prof. law, 1970-72, prof. law, 1972-84, Dalessi prof. law, 1985-87; Gen. George Rogers Clark prof. mgmt. studies Sch. Mgmt. Yale U., New Haven, 1987-90, William S. Beinecke prof. mgmt. studies, 1988-92, dean Sch. Mgmt., 1990-92; Henry R. Luce prof. law and social change in tech. soc. Calif. Inst. Tech., Pasadena, 1973-83; on leave Calif. Inst. Tech., U. So. Calif., 1977-79, 81-83; dir. Bur. Pricing and Domestic Aviation, CAB, 1978, gen. dir. internat. and domestic aviation, 1979; exec. v.p. mktg. Continental Airlines, 1981-82; pres., CEO N.Y. Air, 1982-84; exec. v.p. mktg. Northwest Airlines, St. Paul, 1992-94, exec. v.p. mktg. and internat., 1994-99; adj. prof. law Harvard Law Sch., 1999—; chmn. Rohn Industries, Inc., 1999—. Mgmt. intern Def. and Fgn. Affairs Orgn. exec. office Pres. Bur. Budget, 1964; vis. prof. Duke U., 1972-73; acad. visitor London Sch. Econs. and Polit. Sci., 1977; vis. lectr. Inst. Air and Space Law, McGill U., 1978; mem. U.S. Aviation Safety Commn., 1987-88; mem. adv. panel airport and air traffic ctrl. sys. office tech. assessment, 1980-81; cons. subcom. administrv. practice and procedure U.S. Senate, 1974-75, Commonwealth PR, 1974, Nat. Sci. Found., 1975-77, Calif. Air Resources bd., 1976, Energy Resources Conservation and Devel. Commn., Calif., 1976, U.S. Interstate Commerce Commn., 1980, U.S. Civil Aeronautics Bd., 1977, 1980, Port Authority N.Y. and NJ, 1984-85, Nat. Coun. Pub. Works Improvement, 1987-88, Corp. and Consumer Affairs Canada, 1988-89, U.S. Dept. State, 1989-91, OECD, 1991-92. Contbr. articles on air transp. regulation, theories of legal process and regulatory behavior; referee Jourbal Law and Economics, Journal of Law, Economic and Organization, others. Bd. trustees Ctr. Law Pub. Interest, L.A., 1971-76; trustee Wenner-Gren Found. for Anthrop. Research, 1983-89, Reed Coll., 1984—; bd. dirs. Institut du Transport Aerien, Paris, 1984—, UNR Personal Injury Plaintiffs Trust asbestos bankruptcy, 1989—. Recipient award for excellence and disting. public service CAB, 1979, Transp. Rsch. Group Disting. Lifetime Rschr. award, 2000; vis. scholar Inst. Advanced Legal Studies, London, 1977. Fellow Nat. Acad. Pub. Adminstrn., 1997—; U.S. Aviation Safety Commn., 1987-88, Nat. Acad. Scis. Com. on airline svc. and saftey deregulation, 1989-91.

LEVINE, MICHAEL JOSEPH, economic development executive; b. Boston; s. Sam and Helen Alice (Michelman) L.; children: Samuel Jacob, Rebecca Lynn. BA, Boston U.; MBA, N.Mex. State U. ChFC, CLU, CPCU; cert. ins. counselor. Dir. Small Bus. Devel. Ctr. Sul Ross State U., Alpine, Tex., 1992-2000, N.Mex. State U., Las Cruces, 2000—. Instr. fin. and ins., N.Mex. State U., Las Cruces; pres., dir. Small Bus. Devel. Ctr., Sul Ross State U., Alpine, Tex., 1992—. V.p. Border Area Mental Health Svcs., So. N.Mex., 1978—; pres. Deming Arts Council, 1979-81; treas. Luna County (N.Mex.) Crimestoppers, Inc., 1979—; dir. Big Bend Econ. Forum, 1993—. Mem. Mensa, Soc. CPCU's (cert.), Soc. Cert. Ins. Counselors (cert.), Ins. Mktg. Assocs., Luna County C. of C. (v.p. 1981-84), Ind. Ins. Agts. N.Mex. (state dir. 1985—), Southwest N.Mex. Ind. Ins. Agts. (treas. 1981-83, pres. 1983-85), Alpine C. of C. (bd. dirs. 1993-98). E-mail: michaellevine@zianet.com.

LEVINE, MICHAEL STEVEN, science educator; b. L.A., Mar. 5, 1955; married; 2 children. BA, U. Calif., Berkeley, 1976; PhD, Yale U., 1981. Postdoctoral staff U. Basel, 1982—83, U. Calif., Berkeley, 1983—84; asst. prof. dept. biol. scis. Columbia U., 1984—86, assoc. prof. dept. biol. scis., 1986—88, prof. dept. biol. scis., 1988—90; prof. dept. biology U. Calif., San Diego, 1991—96, prof. divsn. genetics Berkeley, 1996—, Frances Williams profl. genetics, 2002—. Mem. devel. biology study sect. NSF, 1988—90, genetics study sect. NIH, 1990—94; co-dir. MBL Embryology, Woods Hole, Mass., 1991—96; vis. prof. Zoology Inst., U. Zürich, 1999—2000. Editor: (jours.) Mech. Devel., 1990—95, Devel., 1995—; mem. editl. bd. (jours.) Cell, Genes & Devel., —, Current Opinion Cell Biology, —, Procs. Nat. Acad. Sci., —; contbr. Recipient award in molecular biology, NAS, 1996; fellow Jane Coffin Childs postdoctoral, 1982—84, Alfred P. Sloan Rsch., 1985—87. Searle Scholars, 1985—88. Fellow: Am. Acad. Arts and Sci.; mem.: Nat. Acad. Scis. Office: Univ Calif Dept MCB Divsn Genetics 401 Barker Hall Dept Mcb Berkeley CA 94720-3208

LEVINE, MONROE I. orthopedic surgeon, educator; b. Bklyn., June 6, 1936; s. David and Eva Levine; m. Celinda Miltenberger, Oct. 16, 1968; children: Scott Arthur, Emily Debra, SaraBeth, David Richard. BA, Va. Mil. Inst., 1957; MD, NYU, 1961. Diplomate Am. Bd. Surgery. Intern Balt. City Hosp., 1961-62; commd. gen. med. officer U.S. Army, 1962; resident gen. surgery U.S. Army Hosp., Ft. Hood, Tex., 1964-65, Walter Reed Med. Ctr., Washington, 1964-68, fellow, 1972, asst. chief orthopaedic surgery, 1976-82; chief orthopaedic surgery 2d Surg. Hosp., Vietnam, 1968-69, Kimbrough Army Hosp., Ft. Meade, Md., 1969-71, Womack Army Hosp., Ft. Bragg, N.C., 1972-75; asst. prof. surgery Uniformed Svcs. U. Health Scis., Bethesda, Md., 1976-91, clin. prof., 1992—; ret. active duty U.S. Army, 1982; assoc. prof. orthopaedic surgery U. Mo., Kansas City, 1982-85; prof. surgery, chief orthopaedic surgery Med. Coll. Ga., 1985—, ret. prof. emeritus, 2002—. Instr. Georgetown U. Hosp., Washington, 1975-85; instr. Walter Reed Army Med. Ctr., 1980-81, lectr., 1983; co-dir., lectr. George Washington Hosp., 1980-82; lectr. Armed Forces Inst. Pathology, Washington, 1983, 84, 86, Greater S.E. Cmty. Hosp., 1983, Mo. State Med. Assn., Kansas City, 1985; vis. prof. Chgo. Med. Sch. N. Chgo. VA, 1983, Dwight D. Eisenhower Army Med. Ctr., Ft. Gordon, Ga., 1983, 84, Guthrie Clinic, Sayre, Pa., 1987, Savannah (Ga.) Meml. Hosp. Contbr. articles to profl. jours. Bd. dirs. Congl. Children Israel, Augusta, Ga., 1990—, v.p., 1991-93, pres., 1993-96; mem. Soup Kitchen Team, Augusta, 1992—. Fellow ACS, Am. Acad. Orthopaedic Surgeons; mem. AMA, Soc. Mil. Orthopaedic Surgeons, Soc. Mil. Surgeons, Am. Congress Rehabilitative Medicine, Am. Soc. Surgery Hand, Am. Orthopaedic Assn., Acad. Orthopaedic Soc., Soc. Med. Cons. Armed Forces, Ga. Med. Soc., Ga. Orthopaedic Soc., Richmond County Med. Soc. Home: 2717 Wellington Dr Augusta GA 30909-3762 Office: Med Coll Ga Surgery Dept 1120 15th St Augusta GA 30912-0006 Fax: 706-721-1794.

LEVINE, MURRAY, psychology educator; b. Bklyn., Feb. 24, 1928; s. Israel and Birdie Levine; m. Adeline Gordon, June 15, 1952; children: David Israel, Zachary Howard. BS, CCNY, 1949; MA in Psychology, U. Pa., 1951, PhD in Psychology, 1954; JD, SUNY, Buffalo, 1983. Bar: N.Y. 1984; lic. psychologist, N.Y.; diplomate in clin. psychology Am. Bd. Profl. Psychology. Psychologist VA, Phila., 1949-57, Devereux Schs., Devon, Pa., 1957-63; from asst. to assoc. prof. psychology Yale U., New Haven, 1963-68; prof. SUNY, Buffalo, 1968—, disting. svc. prof., 1995-2000, prof. emeritus, 2000—. Author: Community Psychology, 1987, 2d edit., 1997, Helping Children, 1992, Psychological Problems, Social Issues and Law, 2002; contbr. articles to profl. jours. Chmn. bd. dirs. Ctr. for Health, Environment and Justice, Falls Church, Va., 1983—; U.S. adv. bd. Child Abuse and Neglect. Recipient Seymour Sarason award Soc. for Cmty. Rsch. and Action, 1997, Kurt Lewin award N.Y. State Psychol. Assn., 1997. Mem. APA (fellow sects. 12, 27, 41, disting. contbns. award 1987, teaching and mentoring award 1992), Am. Psychology and Law Soc. (pres. 1999-2000). Home: 74 Colonial Cir Buffalo NY 14213-1467 E-mail: psylevin@acsu.buffalo.edu.

LEVINE, NAOMI BRONHEIM, university administrator; b. N.Y.C., Apr. 15, 1923; d. Nathan and Malvina (Mermelstein) Bronheim; m. Leonard Levine, Apr. 11, 1948; 1 dau., Joan. BA, Hunter Coll., 1944; LLB, Columbia, 1946, JD, 1970. Bar: N.Y. 1946. With Scaadrett, Tuttle & Chalaire, N.Y.C., 1946-48, Charles Gottleib, N.Y.C., 1948-50, Am. Jewish Congress, 1950-78, exec. dir., 1972-78; v.p. to sr. v.p. external affairs NYU, 1978—2002, spl. adv. to pres., 2002—. Asst. prof. law and police sci. John Jay Coll., N.Y.C., 1969—73, L.I. Univ., L.I., NY, 1965—69. Author: Schools in Crisis, 1969, The Jewish Poor-an American Awakening, 1974, Politics, Religion and Love, 1990; mem. editl. bd. Columbia Law Rev., 1945-46. Bd. dirs. Jewish Cmty. Rels. Coun., Am. Women's Econ. Devel. Council; trustee N.Y. UJA-Fedn. Named to Hunter Coll. Hall of Fame, 1972. Office: NYU 29 Washington Square West New York NY 10011

LEVINE, NORMAN, physician; b. Detroit, May 18, 1945; BA, U. Mich., 1966, MD, 1970. Cert. Dermatologist. Intern internal medicine Montefiore Hosp., Bronx, 1970-71; gen. med. officer U.S.A.F., Wright-Patterson AFB, OH, 1971-73; rsch. fellow Einstein Coll. Medicine, Bronx, 1973-75, resident dermatology, 1975-77, asst. prof. medicine, 1977-78; asst. prof. dermatology U. Ariz., 1978-83, assoc. prof. dermatology, 1983-86, prof./chief dermatology, 1986—. Editorial advisory bd. Dermatology Times, Cleve., 1988—, exam writing com. Am. Bd. Dermatology, Detroit, 1992-96. Editor: Pigmentation and Pigmentary Disorders, 1993; author: Skin Healthy, 1995. Capt. USAF, 1971-73. Fellow Am. Acad. Dermatology; mem. Soc. Investigative Dermatology. Avocations: sports, computers, reading. Office: Univ Ariz Sec Dermatology 1605 N Campbell Ave Tucson AZ 85724-5038 E-mail: nlevine@u.arizona.edu.

LEVINE, NORMAN GENE, insurance company executive; b. N.Y.C., Sept. 14, 1926; s. Harris J. and Dorothy S. (Podolsky) L.; m. Sandra Leibow, Dec. 11, 1969; children— Linda, Daniel, Donald. Student, U. Wis.-Madison, 1943-48. Agt. Aetna Life Ins. Co., N.Y.C., 1948-56, supr., 1956-59, gen. agt., 1959-75; mng. gen. agt. Mut. Benefit Life Ins. Co. in No. Calif., San Francisco, 1975-91; br. mgr. Sun Life of Can., 1991-97; pres. Levine Enterprises, Palm Springs, Calif., 1994—. Internat. speaker in field; past div. v.p. Million Dollar Round Table; nat. chmn. Life Underwriters Tng. Council, 1983-84; nat. pres. Gen. Agts. and Mgrs. Conf., 1986-87. Author: How to Build a $100,000,000 Agency in Five Years or Less, Yes You can, Life Insurance to Diversification, Selling with Silk Gloves Not Brass Knuckles, The Norman Levine Reader, High Trust Leadership, A Passion for Compassion; editor: bi-weekly news report Probe; contbr. numerous articles to profl. jours.; author tapes on ins., mgmt., photography, Americanism. Past mem. bd. dirs. Calif. Law Enforcement Needs Com.; chmn. Gama Found.; chmn. Million Dollar Round Table Mentoring Coun. Served with AUS, 1944-46, ETO. Recipient Julian Myrick award, 1969, John Newton Russell Meml. award, 1986; named to Hall of Fame Gen. Agts. and Mgrs. Conf., 1982 Mem. N.Y.C. Assn. Life Underwriters (pres. 1967-68), N.Y. State Assn. Life Underwriters (pres. 1968-69), Nat. Assn. Life Underwriters (pres. 1974-75, dir. polit. action com. 1967-69), N.Y.C. Life Mgrs. Assn. (pres. 1974-75), Assn. Advanced Life Underwriters, Am. Soc. C.L.U.s, San Francisco Gen. Agts. and Mgrs. Assn. (pres. 1983), Golden Key Soc., Linnaean Soc., San Francisco C. of C., Audubon Soc., Am. Israel Friendship League (trustee) Mem. Order B'nai Zion (pres. 1964-67). Home: 2162 Silverado Cir Palm Springs CA 92264-9209 Office: Levine Enterprises 555 S Sunrise Way Ste 219 Palm Springs CA 92264-7869 E-mail: norman@levineenterpise.com., levineente@aol.com. *Profit and concern for people are not mutually exclusive and, in fact, people working in a synergistic relationship produce greater profit and general well-being. Democracy with all its problems is still clearly the best of all available methods of government; capitalism and free enterprise create the competition and reward that best challenge the human mind and body; and freedom to "stand tall" with faith, integrity and dignity are the basis for one's conscience and a guide for society's morality.*

LEVINE, NORMAN M. academic administrator; b. Chgo., 1943; BS Engring., Ill. Inst. Tech., 1964; MBA, Marquette U., 1969. Sr. v.p., CFO DeVry Inc., Oakbrook Terrace, 2001—. Mem. Fin. Execs. Internat. Office: DeVry Inc Ste 1000 One Tower Ln Oakbrook Terrace IL 60181 Fax: 630-571-0317.

LEVINE, PAMELA GAIL, business owner; b. Alameda, Calif., Nov. 20, 1942; d. Carl B. and Lucille N. (Lua) Leverenz; m. George David Barth (div. 1974); children, Claudia Anne, Shanette Michelle; m. Leonard Stuart Levine; children: Leslie, Julie, Susan, Stuart Carl. BA in Archtl. Design/Fine Arts, U. Calif., Berkeley, 1965. Designer Trude of Calif., San Francisco, 1965-66; tchr. TWA, Kansas City, Mo., 1966-69; ptnr., owner, archtl. designer Leverenz of N.Y., 1970—; owner, designer Ressco, Katonah, N.Y., 1974—. Cons. archtl. design and real estate devel.; founder, owner Sintec-Internat. Bus. Opportunities, 1989—; founder, co-owner TheArtsMarket.com, I-The Arts Market. Designer of Sets/Costumes, Chappaqua Drama Group, 1973—. Devel. com. Mount Holyoke Coll., S. Hadley, Mass., 1987—; co-founder Looking Glass Players, Mt. Kisco, N.Y., 1985—; active Jr. League, Caramoor, Katonah Mus. Mem. No. Westchester Ctr. for the Arts (exec. com., v.p. bd. dirs., bd. dirs. devel. com., co-chmn. bldg. com.), Chappaqua Drama Group (bd. dirs.). Republican. Avocations: painter, costume design, set design, doll design, artist. Home: RR 6 Katonah NY 10536-9806 Office: Real Estate Support Svcs PO Box 574 Katonah NY 10536-0574

LEVINE, PAUL MICHAEL, paper industry executive, consultant; b. Bklyn., Apr. 15, 1934; s. Isaac Bert and Jessie Sue (Palevsky) L.; m. Lois Jaffin, June 11, 1954 (div.); children: Daniella Sarah, Julie Ann, Carl Joseph; m. 2d Noelle Tenedou, July 14, 1974; children: Simone Allana, Alexander Owen. AB in Econs., Harvard Coll., 1954; A.M. in Internat. Econs., Fletcher Sch. Internat. Law and Diplomacy, 1955. Sales mgr. U.S. Industries, Stamford, Conn., 1956-61; chief exec. officer subs. cos. Parsons and Whittemore-Black Clawson, N.Y.C., 1962-69; dep. adminstr. City of N.Y., 1970-72; v.p. S&S Corrugated Paper Machinery Co., Bklyn., 1973-76, Continental Group, Stamford, Conn., 1977-83; chmn. New Lehigh Corrugated Products, Farmingdale, N.Y., United Container Corp., Phila. Lectr., fellow Yale U., U. Conn., Fordham U., 1979-90; Neeltran Inc., New Milford, Conn., Shulz Electric Corp., New Haven, Conn., Gulf Copper Mfg. Co., Port Arthur, Tex., Gas Tech Engring., Tulsa, Okla. Author: Proceedings 6th World Forestry Congress, 1966; editor: Study of Peoria County Model Program, 1970, Practical Exporting, 1962, The Role of Venture Capital in Europe and the World Trustee Hartman Regional Theatre, Stamford, 1981-82; bd. dirs. Ridgefield Orch., 1978-83, Bklyn. Arts and Culture Assn., 1973-92. Mem. Turnaround Mgmt. Assn., Explorers Club. Democrat. Jewish. Office: Paul M Levine & Assocs 466 Ridgebury Rd Ridgefield CT 06877-1228 E-mail: levassoc@aol.com. *Creativity, innovation and laughter are the glories of the world.*

LEVINE, PETER ARTHUR, medical society executive; b. Balt., Jan. 12, 1953; s. Myron and Barbara Levine; m. Marion V. Day, May 19, 1984; 1 child, Evan. BA, U. Mich., 1975, MPH, 1980. Program dir. Greater Flint (Mich.) Hosp. Assy., 1980-86; dir. Cmty. Hospice, Flint, 1980-84; exec. dir. Physicians Programs, Inc., 1989—, Med. Soc. Found., Flint, 1989—, Emergency Med. Ctr., Flint, 1989—, Genesee County Med. Soc., Flint, 1986—. Assoc. adj. prof. Coll. Human Medicine, Mich. State U., East Lansing, 1992—; bd. dirs. Health Edn. Sys., Palo Alto, Calif., 1989-96. Contbr. articles to profl. jours. Trustee Urban Coalition, Flint, 1989—, Durand-Vernon Ambulance Assn., 1987-96; trustee, exec. com. Flint Jewish Fedn., 1990-98; charter trustee Mich. Hospice Orgn., 1981-88, also v.p. Named Health Advocate of Yr., Am. Lung Assn., 2000; recipient Outstanding Svc. award, Mich. Hosp. Assn., 1990, Mich. Dept. Cmty. Health, 1996, Alfred Humanitarian award, 1999. Mem.: APHA, Mich. Coun. Med. Soc. Execs. (chair 1996—), Am. Assn. Med. Soc. Execs., Am. Soc. Assn. Execs. Avocations: music, travel, fishing. Office: Genesee County Med Soc 4438 Oakbridge Dr Ste B Flint MI 48532-5467

LEVINE, PHILIP, classics educator; b. Lawrence, Mass., Sept. 8, 1922; s. Samuel and Jennie (Derdak) L.; m. Dinnie Moseson, June 19, 1955; children— Jared Elliott, Harlan Alcon. AB, Harvard, 1946, A.M., 1948, PhD, 1952; DHL (hon.), U. Judaism, 1986. Instr., asst. prof. classics Harvard, 1952-59; assoc. prof. classical langs. U. Tex. at Austin, 1959-61; assoc prof., prof. classics UCLA, 1961-91, prof. emeritus, 1991—; dean div. humanities U. Calif. at Los Angeles, 1965-83; Biggs resident lectr. Washington U., 1993. Info. officer Coun. U. Calif. Emeriti Assn. Author: Lo Scriptorium Vercellese da S. Eusueblo ad Attone, 1958, St. Augustine, City of God, Books 12-15, 1966; editor: Latin lt. sect. Twayne World Author Series, 1964—; adv. editor, U. Calif. Publs. in Classical Studies, 1963-72; assoc. editor, contbr. to U. Calif. Studies in Classical Antiquity, 1967-75, sr. co-editor, 1975-78; mem. editorial bd. Classical Antiquity, 1986-93. Mem. rev. com., sr. fellowship program Nat. Endowment for Humanities, 1966-70; bd. govs. U. Judaism, 1968-90, coun. visitors, 1990-94, acad. adv. coun., 1994—. With AUS, 1943-46. Sheldon fellow Italy; Guggenheim fellow; Fulbright Research grantee; recipient Bromberg Humanities award; decorated Cavaliere dell' Ordine al Merito della Repubblica Italiana. Mem. Am. Philol. Assn. (dir. 1968-70), Mediaeval Acad. Am. (exec. council 1969-72), Renaissance Soc., Am. Philol. Assn., Pacific Coast (chmn. gen. lit. 1964-65), Phi Beta Kappa. Home: 224 S Almont Dr Beverly Hills CA 90211-2507 Office: U Calif Dept Classics Los Angeles CA 90095-0001 E-mail: levine@ucla.edu.

LEVINE, PHILIP, poet, retired educator; b. Detroit, Jan. 10, 1928; s. A. Harry and Esther Gertrude (Priscol) L.; m. Frances Artley, July 12, 1954; children: Mark, John, Teddy. BA, Wayne State U., 1950, A.M., 1955; M.F.A., U. Iowa, 1957, studied with John Berryman, 1954. Instr. U. Iowa, 1955-57; instr. Calif. State U., Fresno, prof. English, 1969-92, Tufts U.; tchr. Princeton U., Columbia U., U. Calif., Berkeley.; ret., 1992; Elliston lectr. poetry U. Cin.; poet-in-residence Vassar Coll., Nat. U. Australia; instr. Am. Acad. Art and Letters, 1997, Am. Acad. Arts and Scis., 2002. Chmn. lit. panel Nat. Endowment Arts, 1985; adj. prof. NYU, Spring, 1984, Univ. prof. Brown U., spring 1985; tchr. NYU, U. Iowa, Vanderbilt U., U. Houston; part-time vis. prof. various univs. Author: On the Edge, 1961, Silent in America: Vivas for Those Who Have Failed, 1965, Not This Pig, 1968, 5 Detroits, 1970, Thistles, 1970, Pili's Wall, 1971, Red Dust, 1971, They Feed They Lion, 1972, 1933, 1974, On The Edge & Over, 1976, The Names of the Lost, 1976 (Lenore Marshall award Best Am. Book Poems 1976), 7 Years from Somewhere, 1979 (Nat. Book Critics Circle prize 1979, Notable Book award Am. Libr. Assn. 1979), Ashes, 1979 (Nat. Book Critics Circle prize 1979, Nat. Book award 1979), Don't Ask, 1979, One for the Rose, 1981, Selected Poems, 1984, Sweet Will, 1985, A Walk with Tom Jefferson, 1988 (Bay Area Book Reviewers award), What Work Is, 1991 (L.A. Times Book Prize 1991, Nat. Book award for poetry, 1991), New Selected Poems, 1991, Earth, Stars, and Writers, 1992, The Bread of Time: Toward an Autobiography, 1994, Simple Truth, 1994 (Pulitzer Prize for poetry 1995), The Mercy, 1999; editor: (with Henri Coulette) Character and Crisis, 1966, (with E. Trejo) The Selected Poems of Jaime Sabines, (with Ada Long) Off the Map, The Selected Poems of Gloria

Fuertes, 1984, (with D. Wojahn and B. Henderson) The Pushcart Prize XI, 1986, The Essential Keats, 1987, Poetry, 1998, Unselected Poems, 2000, So Ask, 2002. Active anti-Vietnam war movement. Recipient Joseph Henry Jackson award San Francisco Found., 1961, The Chaplebrook Found. award, 1968, Frank O'Hara Meml. prize, 1973; Amer. Academy of Arts and Letters Award of Merit, 1974; Levinson Prize, 1974; Harriet Monroe Meml. prize for poetry, 1976; Golden Rose award New Eng. Poetry Soc., 1985, Ruth Lilly Poetry Prize, Modern Poetry Assn. and Am. Council Arts, 1987, Elmer Bobst award NYU, 1990, Lit. Lion New York Public Library 1993; named outstanding lectr. Calif. State U., Fresno, 1971, outstanding prof. Calif. State U. System, 1972; Stanford U. poetry fellow, 1957, Nat. Inst. Arts and Letters grantee, 1973, Guggenheim fellow, 1973-74, 80; Nat. Endowment for Arts grantee, 1969, 70 (refused), 76, 81, 87. Mem. AAAL, Acad. Am. Poets (chancellor 2000). Address: 4549 N Van Ness Blvd Fresno CA 93704-3727 also: 106 Willow St Brooklyn NY 11201-2202 *My hope is to write poetry for people for whom there are no poems.*

LEVINE, RAPHAEL DAVID, chemistry educator; b. Alexandria, Egypt, Mar. 29, 1938; brought to U.S., 1939; s. Chaim S. and Sofia (Greenberg) L.; m. Gillah T. Ephraty, June 13, 1962; 1 child, Ornah T. MSc, Hebrew U., Jerusalem, 1959; PhD, Nottingham (Eng.) U., 1964; DPhil, Oxford (Eng.) U., 1966; PhD honoris causa, U. Liege, Belgium, 1991, Tech. U., Munich, Germany, 1996. Vis. asst. prof. U. Wis., 1966-68; prof. theoretical chemistry Hebrew U., Jerusalem, 1969—, chmn. research ctr. molecular dynamics, 1981—, Max Born prof. natural philosophy, 1985—; faculty Dept. Chemistry and Biochemistry UCLA, L.A. Battelle prof. chemistry and math. Ohio State U., Columbus, 1970-74; Brittingham vis. prof. U. Wis., 1973; adj. prof. U. Tex., Austin, 1974-80, MIT, 1980-88, UCLA, 1989—; Arthur D. Little lectr. MIT, 1978; Miller rsch. prof. U. Calif., Berkeley, 1989, A.D. White prof. at large Cornell U., 1989-95. Author: Quantum Mechanics of Molecular Rate Processes, 1969, Molecular Reaction Dynamics, 1974, Lasers and Chemical Change, 1981, Molecular Reaction Dynamics and Chemical Reactivity, 1986, Algebraic Theory of Molecules, 1995; mem. editorial bds. several well known scientific jours.; contbr. articles to profl. jours. Served with AUS, 1960-62. Recipient Ann. award Internat. Acad. Quantum Molecular Sci., 1968, Landau prize, 1972, Israel prize in Exact Scis., 1974, Weizman prize, 1979, Rothschild prize, 1992, Max Planck prize for Internat. Cooperation, 1996; co-recipient Chemistry prize Wolf Found., 1988; Ramsay Meml. fellow, 1964-66, Alfred P. Sloan fellow, 1970-72. Fellow Am. Phys. Soc.; mem. Israel Chem. Soc., Israel Acad. Scis., Max Planck Soc. (fgn. mem.), Academia Europaea (fgn.), Am. Acad. Arts and Scis. (fgn. hon. mem.), Am. Philos. Soc. (fgn.), Royal Danish Acad. Scis. and Letters (fgn.), Natl. Acad. of Sci., US, (fgn.). Office: UCLA Dept Chemistry & Biochemistry 607 Charles E Young E Dr Los Angeles CA 90095-1569 also: Hebrew U Jerusalem Fritz Haber Rsch Ctr Molecular Dynamics Jerusalem 91904 Israel Business E-Mail: rafi@fh.huji.ac.il.

LEVINE, RICHARD A. physician; b. Miami Beach, Fla., July 6, 1953; s. Morris Joseph and Sybil R. (Panossian) L.; m. Lidia Foffo; children: Mitchell, Kimberly, David. BS cum laude in zoology, U. Fla., 1975; MD, Universita di Roma, Italy, 1982. Diplomate Am. Bd. Internal Medicine, Am. Bd. Geriatric Medicine; cert. med. examiner FAA. Resident in internal medicine U. Va. Affiliated Hosps., Roanoke-Salem, Va., 1983-86; pvt. practice Boca Raton, Fla., 1987—. Bd. dirs. South Fla. Health Care Assocs., Boca Raton, 1994; lectr. in field. Dir. med. edn. com. Am. Cancer Soc., Boca Raton, 1990; local coord. 1st pilot program of Put Prevention Into Practice (partnership with ACP and Office of Disease Prevention and Health Promotion, Washington), 1994. Fellow ACP; mem. AMA, Fla. Med. Assn., Palm Beach County Med. Soc. (bd. dirs. 1994), Va. Med. Soc. Avocations: marine biology, biking, music, travel. Office: 880 NW 13th St Boca Raton FL 33486-2342 Fax: 561-368-0151.

LEVINE, RICHARD E. lawyer; b. Flushing, N.Y., Aug. 6, 1950; s. Sol and Betty Levine; m. Lori A. Balter, Oct. 28, 1979; 1 child, Jamie Balter. BS in Mech. Engring., Bucknell U., 1972; JD, U. Md., 1975; LL.M. in Taxation, Georgetown U., 1978. Bar: Md. 1975, U.S. Tax Ct. 1979, D.C. 1980, U.S. Supreme Ct. 1983, U.S. Ct. Appeals (4th cir.) 1984. Assoc. Miles & Stockbridge, Balt., 1978-83, prin., 1983—2001; ptnr. Piper Rudnick, 2002—. Adj. prof. U. Md. Law Sch., Balt., 1988. Contbr. articles to profl. jours. Bd. dirs. Har Sinai West Sr. Citizens Housing, Balt., 1983-92. Fellow Am. Coll. Tax Counsel; mem. ABA (tax sect., chair partnerships 1990-92), Md. State Bar Assn. (tax sect. coun. 1983-86), The Center Club (house com. 1990—, bd. govs. 1996—). Avocations: golf, music. Office: Piper Rudnick 6225 Smith Ave Baltimore MD 21209-3600

LEVINE, RICHARD JAMES, publishing executive; b. N.Y.C., Jan. 24, 1942; s. Irving Joseph and Dorothy Joyce (Thome) L.; m. Neil Ann Stuckey, June 1, 1963; children: Jonathan Donald, Russell Neilan. BS, Cornell U., 1962; MS with high honors, Columbia U., 1963. Gen. assignment reporter Wall St. Jour., Washington, 1966-67, labor corr., 1967-70, mil. writer, 1970-75, chief econ. writer, outlook columnist, 1976—80; editl. dir., data base pub. Dow Jones & Co., Princeton, N.J., 1980-87, v.p. info. svcs. group, 1987-89, v.p. and editl. dir. info. svcs. group, mem. mgmt. com., 1989-92, v.p., mng. editor info svcs. segment, mem. mgmt. com. N.Y.C., 1992-95; v.p. fin. info. svcs. group, mng. editor Dow Jones News Svcs., Dow Jones & Co., 1995-97; v.p., mng. editor Dow Jones Newswires, Dow Jones & Co., Jersey City, 1997—2001, v.p., exec. editor Jersey City and Princeton, 2001—. Dep. chmn. VWD GmbH. Author: (with others) The Wall Street Journal Views America Tomorrow, 1977. Vice chmn. bd. trustees Opera Festival N.J.; trustee McCarter Theatre Ctr., Princeton, N.J. 1st lt. U.S. Army, 1964-66. Recipient Pulitzer Travelling fellowship, 1963—64. Mem. Cornell U. Tower Club, Cornell U. Coun. (adminstrv. bd.), Soc. Profl. Journalists, Cornell Club (N.Y.C.), Princeton Indoor Tennis Ctr. Home: 108 Parkside Dr Princeton NJ 08540-4815 Office: Harborside Fin Ctr 800 Plaza Two Jersey City NJ 07311-1199

LEVINE, ROBERT A. cardiologist; b. N.Y.C., Jan. 29, 1953; s. Jules and Shirley (Krupnick) L. AB summa cum laude, Harvard Coll., 1974; MD, Harvard Med. Sch., 1978. Diplomate Am. Bd. Internal Medicine. Intern, resident in medicine Beth Israel Hosp., Boston, 1978-81; fellow in cardiology Mt. Sinai Hosp., N.Y.C., 1981-83; clinical & rsch. fellow Mass. Gen. Hosp., Boston, 1983-85; instr. in medicine Harvard Med. Sch., 1985-87, from asst. prof. to assoc. prof. medicine, 1987-2000, prof., 2000—. Staff physician cardiac unit Mass. Gen. Hosp., Boston, 1985—, dir. cardiac ultrasound labs., 1995—; sci. session abstract chmn. Am. Soc. Echocardiography, 1993-95, program chmn., 1996-98, bd. dirs.; adj. prof. bioengring. Ga. Inst. Tech., Atlanta, 1995—. Editl. bd. Jour. Am. Coll. Cardiology, 1991-95, 99-2001, Circulation, 1996—, Jour. Amer. Soc. Ech., 1998-2002. Recipient awards NIH, 1985, 87, 95, 98, 2001, Israel Heart Soc., 1999, Doris Duke Charitable Found. Innovations Med. Rsch. award, 2000; clinician-scientist, established investigator Am. Heart Assn., 1986, 91, Atna Found. Quality Care Rsch. Fund, 2001, Richard Popp award for mentoring Am. Soc. Echocardiography, 2002. Office: Mass Gen Hosp Cardiac Ultrasound VBK523 Boston MA 02114 E-mail: rlevine@partners.org.

LEVINE, ROBERT ALAN, anthropology educator, researcher; b. N.Y.C., Mar. 27, 1932; s. Aaron and Emily (Fried) LeV.; m. Barbara Bloom, Aug. 31, 1953 (div. May 1963); m. 2d Sarah Eleanor Friedberger, Dec. 8, 1968; children— Anna Louisa, Alexander John. A.B., U. Chgo., 1951, M.A., 1953; Ph.D., Harvard U., 1958. Instr., then asst. prof. anthropology Northwestern U., Evanston, Ill., 1958-60; asst. prof. U. Chgo., 1960-63, assoc. prof., 1963-67, prof., 1967-76; Roy E. Larsen prof. edn. and human devel. Harvard U., 1976— , prof. anthropology, 1983— ; dir. Ctr. for Psychosocial Studies, Chgo., 1972-74; Author: Nyansongo: A Gusil Community in Kenya, 1966; Ethnocentrism, 1972; Culture, Behavior and Personality, 1973, Human Conditions, 1986; Parental Behavior in Diverse Societies, 1988, Child Care and Culture: Lessons from Africa, 1994; contbr. articles to profl. jours. Bd. dirs. Social Sci. Research Council, N.Y.C., 1978-84, chmn., 1980-83; bd. overseers Shady Hill Sch., Cambridge, Mass., 1981-83; bd. dirs. Spencer Found., 1991—. Recipient Research Career Devel. award NIMH, 1962-72, Research Scientist award, 1972-76; fellow Found.'s Fund for Research in Psychiatry, 1962-65, Ctr. for Advanced Study in Behavioral Scis., 1971-72. Fellow Am. Acad. Arts & Scis., Am. Anthrop. Assn., Swedish Collegium Advanced Study in Social Scis., 1992-93; mem. Nat. Acad. Edn. (sec.-treas. 1989-92). Office: Harvard Univ Grad Sch Edn Larsen Hall Appian Way Cambridge MA 02138

LEVINE, ROBERT ARTHUR, economist, policy writer; b. Bklyn., July 7, 1930; s. Isaac Bert and Jessie Sue (Palevsky) L.; m. Esther Carol Knudsen, Mar. 2, 1953; children: David Knudsen, Peter Kemmerer, Joseph Karl. BA, Harvard U., 1950, MA, 1951; PhD, Yale U., 1957. Economist Rand Corp., 1957-61, sr. economist, 1962-65, 69-73, 87—, sr. economist emeritus, cons., 1994-98, 98—; research assoc. Harvard U. Center Internat. Affairs, 1961-62; asst. dir. for research, plans, programs and evaluation OEO, Washington, 1966-69; pres. N.Y.C.-Rand Inst., 1973-75; dep. dir. Congl. Budget Office, Washington, 1975-79; v.p. System Devel. Corp., Santa Monica, Calif., 1979-85; pres. Canyon Analysts, 1985—. Sr. fellow Nat. Security Studies Program, UCLA, 1964-65; vis. prof. public policy Stanford U. Grad. Sch. Bus., 1972; adj. prof. econs. Pepperdine U. Sch. Bus. and Mgmt., 1984 Author: The Arms Debate, 1963, The Poor Ye Need Not Have With You, 1971, Public Planning: Failure and Redirection, 1972, Evaluation Research and Practice, 1981, Still the Arms Debate, 1990, Turmoil and Transition in the Atlantic Alliance, 1991. With USN, 1951-54. Ford Found. grantee, 1969, 85; German Marshall Fund grantee, 1979; Carnegie Corp. grantee, 1986. Mem. Inst. Strategic Studies. Clubs: Beverly Glen Democratic. Home and Office: 10321 Chrysanthemum Ln Los Angeles CA 90077-2812 E-mail: ral@rand.org.

LEVINE, ROBERT JAY, lawyer; b. Hackensack, N.J., Aug. 7, 1950; s. Nathan R. and Naomi (Bendel) L.; m. Joan Beth Mirviss, Aug. 10, 1975. AB, Brown U., 1972; JD, U. Pa., 1975. Bar: N.Y. 1976, U.S. Dist. (so. and ea. dist.) N.Y. 1976. Assoc. Davis Polk & Wardwell, N.Y.C., 1975-82, ptnr., 1983—. Pres. and dir. Sylvan Winds, Inc. Mem. ABA, N.Y. State Bar Assn., Assn. of Bar of City of N.Y., Phi Beta Kappa. Clubs: Brown of N.Y.C. Democrat. Jewish. Avocations: golf, travel, cooking, film. Home: 115 Central Park W New York NY 10023-4153 Office: Davis Polk & Wardwell 450 Lexington Ave Fl 31 New York NY 10017-3982

LEVINE, ROBERT JEFFREY, lawyer; b. Miami Beach, Fla., Nov. 27, 1956; s. I. Stanely and Elaine (Martz) L. BSBA magna cum laude, U. Fla., 1978; JD, George Washington U., 1981. Bar: Fla. 1981, U.S. Dist. Ct. (so. dist.) Fla. 1981, U.S. Ct. Appeals (5th and 11th cirs.) 1981, U.S. Supreme Ct. 1986. Assoc. Barron, Lehman & Cardenas, Miami, 1981-82; ptnr. Haves & Levine, 1982-83; pvt. practice law, 1983-85; ptnr. Toland & Levine, 1985-90, Levine & Geiger, P.A., Miami, 1990-94, Levine & Ptnrs., P.A., Miami, 1994—. Mem. Fla. Bar Assn., Assn. Trial Lawyers Am., Acad. Fla. Trial Lawyers. Avocations: diving, fishing, skiing, golf, tennis. Home: 136 Rosales Ct Coral Gables FL 33143-6547 Office: Levine & Ptnrs PA 1110 Brickell Ave 7th Fl Miami FL 33131-3132 E-mail: RJL@levinelawfirm.com.

LEVINE, ROBERT JOHN, physician, educator; b. N.Y.C., Dec. 29, 1934; s. Benjamin Bernard and Ruth Florence (Schwartz) L.; m. Jeralea Fooshee Hesse, Nov. 28, 1987; children from previous marriage: John Graham, Elizabeth Hurt Braun; stepchildren: Stephen B. Hesse, Katherine H. Cerrone. Student, Duke U., 1951-54; MD with distinction, George Washington U., 1958. Diplomate Am. Bd. Internal Medicine. Med. house officer Peter Bent Brigham Hosp., Boston, 1958-59, asst. resident in medicine, 1959-60; clin. assoc. Nat. Heart Inst., Bethesda, Md., 1960-62, investigator, 1963-64; chief med. resident VA Hosp., West Haven, Conn., 1962-63; mem. faculty depts. medicine and pharmacology Yale U., New Haven, 1964-73, chief sect. clin. pharmacology, 1966-74, prof. medicine, lectr. pharmacology, 1973—, co-chair exec. com. interdisciplinary program bioethics, 1999—; mem. med. staff Yale-New Haven Med. Ctr., 1964-68, attending physician, 1968—, co-dir. Ctr. Interdisciplinary Rsch. on AIDS, Law, Policy and Ethics Core, 1997-2000, dir., 2000—. Mem. Conn. Adv. Com. on Foods and Drugs, 1967-82, sec. 1969-71, chmn., 1971-73; mem. adv. com. AIDS program U.S. HHS, 1989-95; cons. Nat. Commn. Protection of Human Subjects of Biomed. and Behavioral Rsch., 1974-78; bd. dirs. Medicine in the Pub. Interest, Inc., 1976—, sec., 1983—; mem. ethics subcom. of dir.'s adv. com. Ctrs. for Disease Control and Prevention, 1997-2001; HIV prevention scis. working group Nat. Insts. of Health: Office of AIDS Rsch., 1998—; mem. adv. com. Nat. Human Rsch. Protections, 2000—. Author: Ethics and Regulation of Clinical Research, 1981, 2d edit., 1986; editor Clin. Rsch., 1971-76, IRB: Rev. Human Subjects Rsch., 1978-2000, chairperson editl. bd., 2000—; contbr. numerous articles to profl. jours. Mem. Conn. Humanities Coun., 1983-89, chmn. 1988-89, Coun. Internat. Orgn. Med. Scis., co-chmn. steering com. revision internat. ethical guidelines for biomed. rsch. involving human subjects, 1991-93, chmn., 1998—; chairperson working group for revision of Declaration of Helsinki, World Med. Assn., 1998-99. Multiple rsch. grantee. Fellow ACP, The Hastings Ctr., AAAS (coun. del. 1987-91); mem. Am. Soc. Clin. Investigation, Am. Soc. Clin. Pharmacology and Therapeutics (bd. dirs. 1981-85), Am. Fedn. Clin. Rsch. (nat. coun. 1967-76, exec. com. 1971-76), Am. Soc. Pharmacology and Exptl. Therapeutics (exec. com. 1974-77), Am. Soc. Law, Medicine and Ethics (bd. dirs., pres. 1989-90, 94-95), Pan Am. Health Orgn. (internat. bioethics adv. bd. 2000—), Pub. Responsibility in Medicine and Rsch. (bd. dirs.), Soc. for Bioethics Consultation (bd. dirs. 1988-94), Nat. Inst. Mental Health (human subjects rsch. coun. working group 1999—), Sigma Xi, Alpha Omega Alpha. Office: Yale U Sch Medicine 367 Cedar St Rm 309 New Haven CT 06510-3209

LEVINE, ROBERT SIDNEY, chemical engineer, consultant; b. Des Moines, June 4, 1921; s. George Julius and Betty (Dennen) L.; m. Sharon Lorraine White; children: George, Gail, Tamara, Michelle, James. BS in Chem. Engring, Iowa State U., 1943; S.M. (Std. Oil Co. Ohio fellow 1947-48), M.I.T., 1946, Sc.D., 1949. With Rocketdyne div. Rockwell Internat. Co., 1948-66; assoc. research dir. NASA, 1966-74; chief liquid rocket tech. Nat. Bur. Stds., Washington, 1974-97; chief fire dynamics Nat. Bur. Stds. (now Nat. Inst. Stds. and Tech.), 1975-97. Mem. faculty UCLA, 1962-64, George Washington U., 1977; pres. Combustion Inst., 1974-78; chmn. Am. and Soviet Com. on Fire Rsch. in Housing, 1977-82. Author papers in field; mem. Washington editl. rev. bd. NIST, 1976-97. Named Engr. of Year Los Angeles sect. Am. Inst. Chem. Engrs., 1961 Mem. Am. Chem. Soc., AIAA, Nat. Fire Prevention Assn. Home: 19017 Threshing Pl Gaithersburg MD 20886-3143 E-mail: rslevine@erols.com.

LEVINE, RONALD JAY, lawyer; b. Bklyn., June 23, 1953; s. Louis Leon and Marilyn Priscilla (Markovich) L.; m. Cindy Beth Israel, Nov. 18, 1979; children: Merisa, Alisha. BA summa cum laude, Princeton U., 1974; JD cum laude, Harvard U., 1977. Bar: N.Y. 1978, U.S. Dist. Ct. (so. and ea. dists.) N.Y. 1978, D.C. 1980, N.J. 1987, U.S. Supreme Ct. 1982, U.S. Ct. Apeals (2d cir.) 1983, N.J. 1987, U.S. Dist. Ct. N.J. 1987, U.S. Dist. Ct. (we. dist.) N.Y. 1991, U.S. Ct. Appeals (3d cir.) 1991, Pa. 1995. Assoc. Phillips, Nizer, Benjamin, Krim & Ballon, N.Y.C., 1977-80, Debevoise & Plimpton, N.Y.C., 1980-84, Herrick, Feinstein, N.Y.C., 1984-85, ptnr., 1985—. Gen. counsel Greater N.Y. Safety Council, N.Y.C., 1979-81; arbitrator Small Claims Ct. of Civil Ct. of City of N.Y., 1983-85; chmn. fee arbitration com. Mercer County, N.J. Mem. Site Plan Rev. Adv. Bd., West Windsor, N.J., 1986, planning bd., 1987. Mem. ABA (litigation sect.), N.Y. State Bar Assn. (chmn. com. on legal edn. and bar admission 1982-92, com. on profl. discipline 1989-90), N.J. State Bar Assn. (product liability com. 1991—, profl. responsibility com. 1992-96), Assn. of Bar of City of N.Y. (coun. jud. adminstrn. 1994-95, com. on profl. responsibility 1980-83, com. on legal assistance 1983-86, product liability com. 1987-91, trustee career devel. awards 1989-90), Phi Beta Kappa. Home: 6 Arnold Dr Princeton Junction NJ 08550-1521 Office: Herrick Feinstein 2 Park Ave Fl 20 New York NY 10016-9302

LEVINE, RUTH ROTHENBERG, biomedical science educator; b. N.Y.C. d. Jacob and Jeannette (Bandel) Rothenberg; m. Martin J. Levine, June 21, 1953. BA magna cum laude, Hunter Coll., 1938; MA, Columbia U., 1939; PhD, Tufts U., 1955. Asst. prof. sch. medicine Tufts U., 1955-58; asst. prof. pharmacology sch. medicine Boston U., 1958-61, assoc. prof. sch. medicine, 1961-65, prof. sch. medicine, 1965—, univ. prof., 1972—; chmn. grad. div. med. and dental scis. Boston U. Sch. Medicine, 1964-89, assoc. dean grad. biomed. scis., 1981-89, assoc. dean emeritus, 1989—. Mem. sci. adv. bd. U.S. EPA, 1976-82, Internat. Joint Commn., State Dept., 1983-89. Author: Pharmacology, Drug Actions and Reactions, 1973, 6th edit., 2000; coord. internat. symposia of subtypes of muscarinic receptors. Named to Hall of Fame, Hunter Coll. of City of N.Y. Fellow AAAS; mem. Am. Soc. Pharmacology and Exptl. Therapeutics (sec.-treas. 1975-76), Biophys. Soc., Am. Chem. Soc., Am. Pharm. Assn., Acad. Scis., Phi Beta Kappa, Sigma Xi. Office: Boston U Sch Medicine Div Med and Dental Scis Boston MA 02118

LEVINE, SAMUEL MILTON, lawyer, retired judge, mediator, arbitrator; b. Syracuse, N.Y., Feb. 24, 1929; s. Joseph and Sophie Levine; m. Leona Miller, Sept. 9, 1950; children: Judith, Donald, Gary. BBA, Syracuse U., 1950; JD, Bklyn. Law Sch., 1953. Bar: N.Y. 1953, U.S. Supreme Ct. 1960, U.S. Dist. Ct. (ea. and so. dists.) N.Y. 1962; cert. mediator, arbitrator. Assoc. Law Office of William S. Miller, Esq., N.Y.C., 1954-62, Law Office of Ferdinand I. Haber, Esq., Mineola, N.Y., 1958-62; pvt. practice Nassau County, 1962-65; counsel English, Cianciulli, Reisman & Peirez, 1962-65; supt. of real estate Nassau County, 1965-84; pvt. practice Garden City, N.Y., 1984—. Lobbyist for handicapped; pres. bd. of judges Dist. Ct. Nassau County; lectr. in field. Contbr. articles to profl. jours. Past chmn. Sch. Aid Coun. L.I., Citizens Com. for Elmont Schs., N.Y.; former counsel, trustee Temple Bnai Israel, Elmont; former bd. visitors Pilgrim State Hosp.; treas., counsel N.Y. State Coun. Orgns. for Handicapped; past pres. Nassau County Epilepscy Found.; former chmn. Health and Welfare Coun. Nassau County; former mem. Nassau-Suffolk Health Sys. Agy.; del. White House Conf. on Children and Youth, 1960; candidate N.Y. State Senate, 1964; Dem. candidate Dist. Ct. Judge, 1985; candidate N.Y. State Supreme Ct., 1990; counsel Health Advs., Voice for Handicapped, Fedn. Parent Orgns., League of Voters for Handicapped; del. White House Conf. on Disabilities, 1970; del. White House Conf. on Mental Health, 1999. With U.S. Army, 1948. Recipient Adv. of Yr. award L.I. Coun. Fedn. Parents Orgns., 1978. Mem. Nat. Acad. Elder Law Attys., N.Y. State Bar Assn., Nassau County Bar Assn. (former chmn. social svc. and health law com., legis. com.), Syracuse U. Alumni Club, Kiwanis, Knights of Pythias, B'nai B'rith. Home: 711 Shore Rd Apt 2E Long Beach NY 11561-4707

LEVINE, SANFORD HAROLD, lawyer; b. Troy, N.Y., Mar. 13, 1938; s. Louis and Reba (Semegren) L.; m. Margaret R. Appelbaum, Oct. 29, 1967; children: Jessica Sara, Abby Miriam. AB, Syracuse U., 1959, JD, 1961. Bar: N.Y. 1961, U.S. Dist. Ct. (no. dist.) N.Y. 1961, U.S. Dist. Ct. (we. dist.) N.Y. 1979, U.S. Dist. Ct. (ea. and so. dists.) N.Y. 1980, U.S. Ct. Appeals (2d cir.) 1962, U.S. Supreme Ct. 1967. Law asst. to assoc. judge N.Y. Ct. Appeals, Albany and to justice N.Y. Supreme Ct., 1962-66, N.Y. Ct. Appeals, Albany, 1964; asst. counsel N.Y. State Temporary commn. on Constl. Conv., N.Y.C., 1966-67; assoc. counsel SUNY System, Albany, 1967-70, dep. univ. counsel, 1970-78, acting counsel, 1970-71, acting univ. counsel, 1978-79, univ. counsel and vice chancellor legal affairs, 1979-97, prof. Sch. of Edn., dir. program in edn. and law, 1997—. Adj. prof. Sch. of Edn. State U. N.Y., Albany, 1992-97; mem. paralegal curriculum adv. com. Schenectady County Community Coll., 1975— . Editl. bd. Syracuse U. Law Rev., 1960-61; editl. adv. bd. Jour. Coll. and Univ. Law, 1977-81. Fellow Am. Bar Found., N.Y. Bar Found., State Acad. for Pub. Adminstrn.; mem. ABA (ho. dels. 1987-89), N.Y. State Bar Assn., Albany County Bar Assn., Nat. Assn. Coll. and Univ. Attys. (exec. bd. 1979-82, bd. dirs. 1982-89, pres. 1986-87), Am. Soc. Pub. Adminstrn. Home: 1106 Godfrey Ln Schenectady NY 12309-2712

LEVINE, SOLOMON BERNARD, business and economics educator; b. Boston, Aug. 10, 1920; s. Isaac William and Sybil (Mannis) l.; m. Elizabeth Jane Billett, Dec. 24, 1943; children: Janet Ruth Levine Thal, Michael Alan, Samuel Billett, Elliott Mannis. AB magna cum laude, Harvard Coll., 1942; cert. Japanese Lang., U. Colo., 1944; MBA with honors, Sch. Bus. Adminstrn., Harvard U., 1947; postgrad., MIT, 1947-49, PhD in Indsl. Econs., 1951. Teaching asst. dept. econs. and social sci. MIT, 1947-49; faculty U. Ill., 1949-69, prof. labor and indsl. relations and Asian studies, 1964-69; prof. bus. and econs. U. Wis.-Madison, 1969-89, prof. emeritus, 1989—, mem. East Asian Studies Program, chmn., 1968-77, co-chmn., 1982-88, dir. Nat. Resource Ctr. for East Asian Studies, 1985-87, participating faculty mem. Indsl. Relations Research Inst. Fulbright prof. Keio U., Tokyo, 1959; vis. prof. dept. econs. Pa. State U., 1960; vis. prof. labor relations dept. econs. MIT, 1962-63; vis. prof. econs. U. Singapore, 1968; vis. lectr. and research scholar various univs., Indonesia, 1973, Australia, 1973, N.Z., 1973, vis. scholar univs., Japan, 1978, Australia, 1978, N.Z., 1978, Singapore, 1978, South Korea, 1978; vis. prof., sr. scholar Monash U., Australia and Japan, 1981-82, vis. research scholar Macquarie U., Australia, 1985; vis. prof. Internat. U. Japan, 1984; vis. prof. Nanzan U., Nagoya, Japan, 1989-91, U. Hawaii, Manoa, 1991; vis. fellow Swinburne Inst. Tech., Australia, 1992; vis. scholar Japan Ctr. for Mich. Univ., Japan, 1994. labor arbitrator. Author: Industrial Relations in Postwar Japan, 1958, Japanese transl., 1959, (with Hishashi Kawada) Human Resources in Japanese Industrial Development, 1980; co-editor, co-author: chpts. and preface Workers and Employers in Japan: The Japanese Employment Relations System, 1973, (with Koji Taira) Japan's External Economic Relations: Japanese Perspectives, 1991; contbr. to sect. Ency. Americana; chpts. to books, articles to publs. Treas. Stevenson for Pres. Campaign, Champaign-Urbana, Ill., 1952; mem. Community Integration Council, 1965-69. Sheldon traveling fellow Harvard U., Mex., 1942; Social Sci. Rsch. Coun. tng. fellow, 1948-49; Fulbright rsch. scholar and Ford Found. rsch. fellow Hitotsubashi U., Tokyo, 1953-54; Social Sci. rsch. Coun. fellow Carnegie Inst. Tech., 1957; life fellow Found. Keio U., 1961; Fulbright-Hays faculty rsch. scholar Japan, 1968, 73, 78, Singapore, 1968, 78, Australia, 1978; Fulbright-Hays faculty scholar N.Z., 1978; Japan Found. scholar, 1978; hon. Fulbright sr. scholar Australia, 1981. Mem. Indsl. Rels. Rsch. Assn., Assn. for Asian Studies, Midwest Conf. of Asian Affairs (pres. 1961), Japan Soc., Internat. House of Japan, Internat. Indls. Rels. Assn., Japan Illini Club (hon. life), Wis. Alumni Assn. Japan (pres. 1990), Phi Beta Kappa, Beta Gamma Sigma. Home: 88 Oak Creek Trl Madison WI 53717-1510

LEVINE, STANLEY WALTER, chemical company executive; b. Boston, Dec. 13, 1929; s. Bernard T. and Sonia (Spector) L.; m. Tochia Levine; children: Robert, Douglas, Elizabeth. BS in Journalism, Butler U., 1952; postgrad., Boston Coll., 1967; grad., FBI Citizens Acad. Nat. mktg. dir. Bates Mfg. Co., N.Y.C., 1965-68; mgmt. cons. Frederick Chusid Co., 1971-76, Fashioncade, N.Y.C., 1968-71; pres., CEO Internat. Coating & Chem. Co. Inc., Fairfield, Conn., 1976—. Contbr. articles to Nat. Chem. Weekly, Harpers. Mem. Nat. Republican Congl. Com., Rep. Com. Fairfield County (Conn.); bd. dirs. Butler U., So. Poverty Law Ctr.; bd. dirs. Ariz. and Nat. regional rep., pres. Am. Jewish Com. Served to capt. USAF, 1952-55. Decorated Korean Honor medal. Mem. Am. Mgmt. Assn., Chem. Week Contbrs., Pres.'s Club N.Y., Nat. Chem. Club, N.Y. Acad. Scis., Internat. Platform Assn., Harmonie Club, Paradise Valley Country Club, Plaza Club (bd. dirs.), Rolls Royce Club (chmn. pres. S.W. region), Coddington Landing Assn. (bd. dirs.), Camelback Estates I (bd. dirs.), Gainey Ranch Country Club (bd. dirs.), Alexis de Tocqueville Soc., Sigma Delta Chi, Sigma Alpha Mu, Alpha Phi Omega. Office: care Intern Coating & Chem Co 1226 Post Rd Fairfield CT 06430-6008 also: PO Box 6345 Scottsdale AZ 85261-6345

LEVINE, STEVEN ALAN, real estate appraiser, association executive; b. Cin., Aug. 28, 1951; s. E. Pike and Beverly Rae (Friedman) L. BA with honors, U. Cin., 1975; postgrad., George Washington U., 1975-77. Appraiser Real Estate Evaluators and Cons., Cin., 1969-75; program asst. U.S. Renegotiation Bd., Washington, 1975; assessor D.C. Govt., 1976-77; emergency mgmt. specialist Fed. Emergency Mgmt. Agy., 1977-80; v.p. Am. Res. and Appraisal Ctr., Cin., 1980-82; pres. Steven A. Levine & Assocs., Inc., 1982—; v.p., exec. v.p. Nat. Assn. Environ. Risk Auditors, 1995—. Cons. U.S. Army, 1982—, U.S. Dept. Interior. Author: Environmental Challenges Can Create Work for Real Estate Appraisers, Environmental Liabilities Affecting Real Estate, Kuwait: An Environmental Nightmare, The Renegotiation of Defense Contracts, Military Installation Real Property Management, Property Tax Relief Measures for the Elderly. Mem. Forum for Urban Studies, Washington, 1977; mem. adv. coun. The Appraisal Found., 1997—. Sgt. USAF, 1969-75. Named to Hon. Order Ky. Cols., Louisville, 1979; named lt. col. aide-de-camp Staff of Gov. of Ga., Atlanta, 1979, lt. col. aide-de-camp Staff of Gov. of Ala., Montgomery, 1983. Mem. Nat. Assn. Environ. Risk Auditors (v.p., exec. dir., cert. environ. risk assessor, rep. Appraisal Found. Adv. Coun.). Avocations: running, classical music, golf, reading, interior design. Home: 3073 Buell Rd Cincinnati OH 45251-4505 Office: 6645 Colerain Ave Cincinnati OH 45239-5539 Office Fax: 513-674-0680. E-mail: kalevine@fuse.net.

LEVINE, STEVEN JON, lawyer; b. N.Y.C., Sept. 27, 1942; s. Irving I. and Freda S. (Silverman) Levine; m. Linda Jane Silberman, Apr. 23, 1967; 1 child Lawrence Alan. BS, Syracuse U., 1964; JD, St. John's U., 1966; MA, CCNY, 1973; LLM, NYU, 1978. Bar: NY 1967. Assoc. Augustin J. San Filippo & Steven Jon Levine, PC, predecessor, N.Y.C., 1968-78; mem. Vittoria & Forsythe and predecessor, 1978-93, Levine & Zelman, 1993—. Arbitrator N.Y. County Civil Ct. Panel, 1980-93; asst. csl. N.Y. State Senate Judiciary Com.,

1977. *Steven Jon Levine has been a practicing attorney for over 25 years. Mr. Levine's firm, Levine & Zelman, provides representation in the areas of matrimonial/family law, real estate, trusts and estates and civil litigation. He is also an experienced arbitrator and mediator.* Author: of legal column Tomorrow newspapers, 1991-2000; co-author: Divorce Q & A: Answers to Questions about Divorce, Equitable Distribution, Maintenance, Custody and Child Support; host weekly radio law program Sta. WVOX, 1990-91; creator, narrator: (audio cassette program) Coping with Separation and Divorce. Committeeman, Bronx County, 1970-76; bd. dirs. Jewish Conciliation Bd. Am., 1973-93. Mem. ABA, N.Y. State Bar Assn., Westchester County Bar Assn., Assn. Bar City N.Y. (sect. vice chmn. matrimonial com. 1977-80), Am. Arbitration Assn. (no-fault, comml. panels 1975-88). Office: 50 Main St Ph White Plains NY 10606-1901 also: Levine & Zelman 630 5th Ave New York NY 10111-0100

LEVINE, STEVEN MARK, lawyer; b. N.Y.C., Feb. 1, 1956; s. Arthur Morton and Selma (Aber) L.; m. Patricia Mary Petersilia, Sept. 2, 1990; children: Caitlin, Ryan. BA, Clark U., 1978; JD, George Washington U., 1981. Bar: D.C. 1981, Md. 1987, Va. 1994, U.S. Dist. Ct. D.C. 1982, U.S. Dist. Ct. Md. 1985, U.S. Dist. Ct. (ea. dist.) Va. 1995, U.S. Ct. Appeals (D.C. cir.) 1982, U.S. Ct. Appeals (1st cir.) 1991, U.S. Ct. Appeals (2d cir.) 1986, U.S. Ct. Appeals (3d cir.) 1987, U.S. Ct. Appeals (4th cir.) 1983, U.S. Supreme Ct. 2000. Atty. Wilson, Elser, Moskowitz, Edelman & Dicker, Washington, 1981-93; prin. The Law Office of Steven M. Levine, 1993—. Bd. dirs. SOC Enterprises, Inc., Arlington, Va., 1994-2000. Contbr. chpt. to book. Officer of Election, Arlington County Bd. Elections, Arlington, Va., 1990-97. Democrat. Jewish. Home: 2631 S Grant St Arlington VA 22202-2519 Office: 2000 L St NW Ste 803 Washington DC 20036-4913 E-mail: slevinelaw@aol.com.

LEVINE, STEVEN NEIL, endocrinologist; b. N.Y.C., June 10, 1946; s. Milton and Miriam (Gerofsky) L.; m. Laurie Rita Winkler, July 27, 1969; children: Amy, Karen, Jonathan. BA in Gen. Sci. with distinction, U. Rochester, 1968; MD, NYU, 1971. Diplomate Am. Bd. Internal Medicine. Intern N.C. Meml. Hosp., Chapel Hill, 1971-72, resident in medicine, 1972-74; fellow in endocrinology U. N.C. Sch. Medicine, 1976-79, clin. instr. medicine, 1976-79; asst. prof. medicine La. State U. Med. Ctr., Shreveport, 1979-84, assoc. prof. medicine, chief sect. endocrinology, 1984-91, prof. medicine, chief sect. endocrinology, 1991—. Instr. dept. medicine N.C. Meml. Hosp., Chapel Hill, 1976-79; staff physician La. State U. Med. Ctr., 1979, Shreveport VA, 1979; courtesy staff Schumpert Med. Ctr., Shreveport, 1980, Highland Hosp., Shreveport, 1981. Reviewer Archives of Internal Medicine, 1981—, Jour. Clin. Endocrinology and Metabolism, 1985—, Obstetrics and Gynecology, 1985—, Clin. Toxicology, 1985—, Biochem. Pharmacology, 1991—; contbr. numerous articles to profl. jours.; also abstracts. Recipient 1st ann. Outstanding Attending award House Staff of Dept. Internal Medicine, La. State U. Med. Ctr., 1990; grantee Am. Heart Assn.-La. Inc., 1981-82, 83-84, 84-85, 85-88,, 89-91, NIH, 1976-79, 81-82, 82-83, Edward P. Stiles Trust Fund, 1979-80, 82-83, 85-87, La. State Bd. Regents, 1984-85, VA Rsch. Adv. Group, 1987-89, Am. Diabetes Assn, 1988-89. Fellow ACP; mem. Shreveport Med. Soc., La. State Med. Soc., Am. Fedn. Clin. Rsch., Am. Diabetes assn. (N.W. La. chpt. bd. dirs. 1980-83, pres. 1983-84), Endocrine Soc. (program dirs. com. 1988—), Am. Heart Assn. (basic sci. coun. 1984—), Alpha Omega Alpha. Office: La State U Med Ctr PO Box 33932 1501 Kings Hwy Shreveport LA 71103-4228

LEVINE, SUMNER NORTON, industrial engineer, educator, editor, author, financial consultant; b. Boston, Sept. 5, 1923; s. Frank and Lillian (Gold) L.; m. Caroline Gassner, Nov. 27, 1952; 1 dau., Joanne. BS, Brown U., 1946; PhD, U. Wis., 1949; postgrad., M.I.T., 1956. Instr. U. Chgo., 1949-50; sr. research fellow Columbia, 1950-54; dir. research labs. VA, East Orange, N.J., 1954-56; adv. scientist comml. atom power div. Westinghouse Electric Co., Pitts., 1956; dir. chemistry Metallurgy and Materials Labs.; also staff adv. engr. Gen. Engring. Labs., Am. Machine & Foundry Co., Greenwich, Conn., 1956-58; sect. head, materials and advanced electronic devices RCA, 1958-61; chmn. materials scis. dept., prof. engring., also prof., dir. grad. program in indsl. adminstrn. SUNY, Stony Brook, 1961-91; dir. urban research, vis. prof. CUNY Grad. Center, 1967-68; Danforth vis. lectr., 1968-69; vis. prof. Yale Sch. Orgn. and Mgmt., 1976; prof. fin. Coll. Urban and Policy Scis., SUNY, Stony Brook, 1978—. Cons. to industry; bd. dirs. Norteck Assocs.; editorial adviser Ocean Engring. Author textbooks, profl. articles; editor: Financial Analysts Handbook, 1975, 2d edit., 1987, Investment Manager's Handbook, Dow Jones-Irwin Bus.and Investment Almanac, 1976—, Acquisition Manual, 1990, Turnaround and Bankruptcy Investing, 1991, Handbook of Global Investing, 1992, Internat. Bus. and Investment Almanac, 1992—; editor-in-chief Jour. Biomed. Materials Rsch., 1966-78, Jour. Socio-Econ. Planning Scis., 1966, Advances in Biomed. Engring. and Med. Physics, 1966. Recipient award for distinguished contbn. to biomed. materials research, 1973 Mem. IEEE, World Conf. Planning Scis., Am. Chem. Soc., Am. Soc. Metals, Electrochem. Soc., Ops. Research Soc. Am., Inst. Mgmt. Scis., Fgn. Policy Assn., N.Y. Acad. Scis. (chmn. conf. materials in biomed. engring. 1966, chmn. colloquia socioecon. planning 1966-68), Soc. for Biomaterials (dir. 1974-76), N.Y. Soc. Security Analysts (chmn. edn. and seminar com., Vols. award 1984), Mus. Modern Art, Met. Mus. of Art, Princeton Club N.Y., Brown U. Club, Sigma Xi. Office: 29 Brandywine Dr Setauket NY 11733-0883

LEVINE, SUSAN MICHELLE, social worker; b. Bklyn., July 29, 1963; d. Norman and Barbara Ellen (Fishman) L.; life ptnr. Karen J. Docherty. BA in Psychology, SUNY, Stony Brook, 1986, MSW, 1990; MPA, Ga. State U., 1993; postgrad., So. Poly. State U., 1998—. Lic. clin. social worker, Ga. Foster care worker Angel Guardian Home, Bklyn., 1986-87; child protective svcs. worker N.Y.C. Dept. Human Resources, 1987-88; cmty. asst. Chapin Apt. Complex, Stony Brook, 1989-90; sr. caseworker Fulton County Family and Children's Svcs., Atlanta, 1991-92; clin. social worker Ga. Mental Health Inst., 1992-98; long term care facility surveyor Office of Regulatory Svcs., 1998—. Guest lectr. Ga. State U. Dept. Mental Health, 1994; clinician mobile crisis psychiat. assessment team Brawner Hosp., 1995, Charter Peachford, 1996. Disaster mental health counselor ARC, Atlanta, 1996. Mem. NASW (continued edn. com. 1991—, legis. com. 1992, panel mem. com. on inquiry Ga. chpt. 1995—, counselor for depression hotline 1992), Am. Soc. Pub. Adminstrs., Pi Alpha Alpha. Avocations: travel, hiking, bicycling, attending concerts and plays.

LEVINE, THOMAS JEFFREY PELLO, lawyer; b. Santa Monica, Calif., Mar. 6, 1952; s. Allan Lester and Shirley Elaine (Pello) L.; children: Marissa, Matthew, Molly. Student, U. Denver, 1970-71, Calif. State U., Northridge, 1971-73, Uppsala U., Sweden; BA, Calif. State U., Sacramento, 1974; JD, Southwestern U., 1977; postgrad., Yale U., 1999. Bar: Calif. 1977, U.S. Dist. Ct. (cen. dist.) Calif. 1978. Ptnr. Levine & Levine, L.A., 1977-83; staff atty. Fed. Deposit Ins. Corp., Newport Beach, Calif., 1983-85; v.p., assoc. counsel Imperial Bank, Inglewood, 1985-88; v.p., counsel Community Bank, Pasadena, 1988; gen. counsel, sr. v.p., sec. Calif. Commerce Bank, Banamex USA Bancorp, L.A., 1988-2001; gen. counsel, sr. v.p. Banamex-Citibank, 2001; spl. counsel, office of the gen. counsel L.A. Unified Sch. Dist., 2002—. Legal affairs com. mem. Calif. Bankers Assn., San Francisco, 1990—; chmn. Am. Bankers Assn. Bank Counsel Com. 1993-97. Dir. Angelino Heights Historic Preservation Assn., L.A., 1985-95; sec., dir. Carroll Ave. Restoration Found., L.A., 1979-87; dir. Wilshire C. of C., L.A., 1982. Mem. L.A. County Bar Assn., Braemar Country Club (bd. govs. 1979-83). Jewish. Avocations: running, golf, Aztec history, historic preservation. Office: Levine & Levine 5460 White Oak Ave Ste A330 Encino CA 91316

LE VINE, VICTOR THEODORE, political science educator; b. Berlin, Dec. 6, 1928; came to U.S., 1938; s. Maurice and Hildegard (Hirschberg) LeV.; m. Nathalie Jeanne Christian, July 19, 1958; children: Theodore, Nicole. BA, UCLA, 1950, MA, 1958, PhD, 1961. Research assoc. UCLA, 1958-60; prof., head dept. polit. sci. U. Ghana, Legon, 1969-71; vis. prof. Hebrew U., Jerusalem, 1978, U. Yaounde, 1980; Fulbright prof. U. Yaounde, Cameroon, 1981-82; prof. polit. sci. Washington U., St. Louis, 1961—. Cons. U.S. Dept. State, Dept. Def., 1971—; lectr. USIA, 1981—; mem. U.S. Nat. Commn. UNESCO, 1964; dir. Office Internat. Studies, Washington U., 1975-76; vis. lectr. Fudan U., U. Nanjing (China), 1987, Ibn Saud and King Abdulazziz Univs., Saudi Arabia, 1990; mem. Carter Ctr. Internat. monitoring team to Ghana nat. elections, 1992. Author: Cameroons: Mandate to Independence, 1964, 70, Cameroon Federal Republic, 1971, Political Corruption: Ghana, 1975, (with Timothy Luke) Arab-African Connection, 1979; (with Heidenheimer and Johnston) Political Corruption: A Handbook, 1990; Conceptualizing Ethnicity and Ethnic Conflict: A Controversy Revisited, 1997Parapolitics: Mapping The Terrain of Informal Politics, 2002. Mem., dir. UN Assn., St. Louis, 1964-74; mem. Coun. on World Affairs, 1969-2000; pres. Ctr. for Internat. Understanding, 1988-2000. With U.S. Army, 1951-54. Ford. Found. fellow Cameroon, 1960-61; Hoover Instn. fellow, 1974; Lester Martin fellow Truman Instn., Jerusalem, 1978; Fulbright lectr. U.S. Fulbright Commn., Yaounde, Cameroon, 1981-82 Mem. Am. Polit. Sci. Assn., African Studies Assn., Mideast Studies Assn., Midwest Polit. Sci. Assn., Mo. Polit. Sci. Assn. Office: Washington U Dept Polit Sci Saint Louis MO 63130 E-mail: vlevine@artsci.wustl.edu.

LEVINE, WALTER DANIEL, lawyer, accountant; b. Paterson, N.J., July 19, 1941; s. Samuel M. and May (Zaretzky) LeV.; m. Joy Herman, Dec. 24, 1964 (div. 1972); children: Lee Jason, Stephen Ian; m. Ellen R. Ignatoff, Feb. 12, 1976 (div. 2000); children: Elissa Whitney, Evan Harris. BA, Rutgers U., 1962; JD, Temple U., 1965; BS, Fairleigh Dickinson U., 1967. Bar: N.J. 1965. Assoc. Gutkin & Miller, Newark, 1965-72; ptnr. firm Gutkin Miller Shapiro Berson, Millburn, N.J., 1972-78; sole practice Fairfield, 1978-88; sr. ptnr. Friedman LeVine & Brooks, Florham Park, 1988-91; sole practice, 1991—. Sec., dir. Tekimage Inc., Florham Park, 1986-97; pres., dir. Macet Corp., Florham Park, 1988-97. Author: Prentice Hall Tax Reports, 1971. Bd. dirs., v.p. Men's Club, Congregation B'nai Jeshurun, 1991, pres., 1993-95; coach, mgr. Livingston (N.J.) Am. Little League, 1988-95. Mem. N.J. Bar Assn. (mem. taxation com. 2000), Passaic County Bar Assn. (chmn. tax com. 1989), K.P. (chancellor-comdr. Passaic chpt. 1987), Mensa. Democrat. Jewish. Avocations: sports autographs, sports memorabilia. Home: 345 Walnut St Livingston NJ 07039 Office: 23 Vreeland Rd Florham Park NJ 07932-1510 E-mail: taxlaw1@aol.com.

LEVINE, WILLIAM SILVER, electrical engineering educator; b. Bklyn., Nov. 19, 1941; s. Louis Nathan and Gertrude (Silver) L.; m. Shirley Johannesen, Feb. 14, 1963; children: Bruce Jonathan, Eleanor Joan. BEE, MIT, 1962, MEE, 1965, PhD in Elec. Engring., 1969. Project engr. Data Tech. Inc., Cambridge, Mass., 1962-64; grad. asst. MIT, 1964-69; asst. prof. U. Md., College Park, 1969-73, assoc. prof., 1973-81, prof., 1981—. Cons. IBM Fed. System Div., Gaithersburg, Md., 1972-75, Computational Engring. Inc., Laurel, Md., 1980-90. Co-author: Using MATLAB to Analyze and Design Control Systems, 1992, 2d edit., 1995; editor: The Control Handbook, 1996; editor: Control Engineering Series, 1996-; contbr. articles to profl. jours. Recipiet numerous rsch. grants, 1969—. Fellow IEEE, IEEE Control Systems Soc. (pres. 1990, disting. mem. 1990); mem. IEEE Engring. in Medicine and Biology Soc. (disting. lectr. 1991), Soc. for Indsl. and Applied Math. Office: U Md Dept Elect & Computer Engring College Park MD 20742-0001

LEVINGER, JOSEPH SOLOMON, physicist, educator; b. N.Y.C., Nov. 14, 1921; s. Lee J. and Elma (Ehrlich) L.; m. Gloria Edwards, Aug. 14, 1943; children— Sam, Laurie, Louis, Joe; m. Hedi McKinley, Sept. 4, 1998. BS, U. Chgo., 1941, MS, 1944; PhD, Cornell U., 1948. Physicist Metall. Lab., U. Chgo., 1942-44, Franklin Inst., Phila., 1945; instr. Cornell U., 1948-51, vis. prof., 1961-64; from asst. prof. to prof. La. State U., 1951-61; prof. physics Rensselaer Poly. Inst., 1964-92, prof. emeritus, 1992—; Fulbright fellow, asso. prof. U. Paris— Sud, 1972-73. Author: Nuclear Photo-disintegration, 1961, Secrets of the Nucleus, 1967, The Two and Three Body Problem, 1974. Guggenheim fellow, 1957-58 Fellow Am. Phys. Soc. Home: PO Box 411 Altamont NY 12009-0411 Office: Rensselaer Poly Inst Dept Physics Troy NY 12180 E-mail: levinj@rpi.edu .

LEVINGSTON, ERNEST LEE, engineering company executive; b. Pineville, La., Nov. 7, 1921; s. Vernon Lee and Adele (Miller) L.; m. Kathleen Bernice Bordelon, June 23, 1944; children: David Lewis, Jeanne Evelyn, James Lee. BME, La. State U., 1960. Registered profl. engr., La., Tex., Miss., Ark., Tenn., Pa., Md., Del., N.J., D.C., Okla., Colo. Gen. forman T. Miller & Sons, Lake Charles, La., 1939-42; sr. engr., sect. head Cities Svc. Refining Corp., 1946-57; group leader Bovay Engrs., Baton Rouge, 1957-59; chief engr. Augenstein Constrn. Co., Lake Charles, 1959-60; pres. Levingston Engrs., Inc., 1961-85; gen. mgr. SW La. Austin Indsl., 1985-88; pres. Levingston Engrs., Lake Charles, 1989-96, chmn. bd., 1996-2000, pres., chmn. bd., 2000—. Mem. Lake Charles Planning and Zoning Commn., 1965-70; adv. bd. Sowela Tech. Inst., 1969—; mem. Regional Export Expansion Coun., 1969-70, chmn. code com., 1966—; mem. La. Bd. Commerce and Industry, 1978—; bd. dirs. Lake Charles Meml. Hosp.; bd. dirs., regional chmn. La. Chem. Industry Alliance, 1990—. With USNR, 1942-46. Named Jaycee Boss of Yr., 1972. Mem. La. Engring. Soc. (pres. 1967-68, state bd. dirs. 1967-68, 90-91), Nat. Inst. Cert. Engring. Technologists (past trustee, mem. exam. com.), La. Assn. Bus. and Industry, Lake Area Industries/McNeese Engring., Lake Charles C. of C. (dir. 1969-73). Baptist (deacon 1955—). Office: PO Box 1865 Lake Charles LA 70602-1865 Fax: 337-474-3789.

LEVINGSTON, JOHN COLVILLE BOWRING, telecommunications executive; b. Rawalpindi, Punjab, Pakistan, Apr. 10, 1929; came to U.S., 1961; s. Thomas Clarke and Kathleen Patricia (Farley) L.; m. Elizabeth Ann Baumer, June 6, 1958 (div. Apr. 1968); m. Paula Angela Eriksen, Feb. 29, 1980 (div. Jan. 2000); children: Thomas Arthur, Alexandra Jane. Grad., Harrow Sch., Eng., Royal Mil. Acad., Sandhurst, Eng. Sales mgr. British-Am. Tobacco Co., East Africa, 1952-55, W.L. Mackenzie Co., Vancouver, B.C., Can., 1957-61; v.p. Precipitator Inc., Santa Fe Springs, Calif., 1973-78; cons. Calif. Inst. Tech., Pasadena, 1979; v.p. Kingmont Oil, Pine Knot, Ky., 1980; cons. Sta. KCET-TV, Hollywood, Calif., 1981; founder, chmn. Straightley Films, 1982-86; founder, chmn., chief exec. officer Interactive Telemedia, Sherman Oaks, Calif., 1986-89; chmn. Levingston & Assocs., Beverly Hills, 1989—; founder, CEO, Home Savings Trust Ltd., 1994—. Inventor Straightley automobile, 1969. Lt. Parachute Regt., 1950-52. Mem. NATAS, SAG, Internat. Platform Assn., Masons. Avocations: music, writing, racquetball, golf. Office: Levingston & Assocs PO Box 1951 Beverly Hills CA 90213-1951 E-mail: straightley@hotmail.com.

LEVINO-JONES, ALISON, interior designer; b. Schenectady, N.Y., May 26, 1956; d. Theodore Prussing and Anne (Laycock) LeVino; m. R. Scott Jones, May 2, 1981. Student in sociology, Lynchburg Coll., 1977; BA in Interior Design, U. Conn., 1979. Project designer Gresham, Smith & Ptnrs., Nashville, 1979-81; project dir. Quantrell Mullins, Atlanta, 1981-83; prin. Godwin & Assocs./Atlanta, 1983-88; pres. Godwin Procurement Corp., Atlanta, 1985-88; owner LeVino-Jones Health Facility Design Interiors, 1988—. Lectr. in field. Contbr. design work to profl. mags. Vol. Children's Wish Found., Atlanta, 1986—; fundraiser Am. Heart Assn., Atlanta, 1984-86; mem. vol. fundraising program Ga. Alliance for Children, Atlanta, 1985-86; mem. Peachtree Hills Civic Assn., Atlanta, 1983—. Mem. Am. Soc. Interior Designers (bd. dirs. 1985-87, chmn. programs com. 1985-86, chmn. awards com. 1987, chmn. community services spl. project 1986-87), Inst. Bus. Designers, Atlanta Women's Network, Buckhead Bus. Assn. Republican. Episcopalian. Avocations: travel, equestrian, photography. Home: 2335 Virginia Pl NE Atlanta GA 30305-4236

LEVINS, JOHN RAYMOND, investment advisor, management consultant, educator; b. Jersey City, Aug. 4, 1944; s. Raymond Thomas and Catherine (Kelly) L. BS in Acctg., U. N.H., 1973; MBA, U. N.H., Plymouth, 1976. Registered investment advisor; cert. mgmt. cons., enrolled to practice IRS; cert. licensing instr., real estate and multiple lines ins. broker, comml. arbitration panelist; accredited tax advisor; cert. mediator; registered securities prin. Office Supervisory Jurisdiction. Mgmt. risk analyst Express Treaty Mgmt. Corp., N.Y.C., 1962-67; asst. risk mgr. Bigelow-Sanford, Inc., 1967-71; cons., broker BYSE, Inc., Laconia, N.Y., 1971-74; asst. prof. Nathaniel Hawthorne Coll., Antrim, N.H., 1975-82, Keene (N.H.) State Coll., 1982—; prin. Levins & Assocs., Concord, N.H., 1986—; investment advisor Reality Techs., Internat. Fin., Concord, 1991—. Dir. Small Bus. Inst. Keene State Coll., 1982-86; exec. seminar leader Strategic Mgmt. Group, Inc., 1986—, Boston U., 1976—; mem. bd. advisors Am. Biog. Inst.; pvt. practice real estate, ins. cons., Concord, 1981; panelist securities arbitration Nat. Assn. Security Dealers, Am. Stock Exch., N.Y. Stock Exch., Gen. Securities Prin.; consumer affair mediator Dept. Justice, Office of Atty. Gen., N.H.; mortgage banker; comml. financing broker; mem. SEC, spkr., seminar leader in field; fin. faculty grad. programs Boston U., 1996 fin. and investment provider Dun & Bradstreet, 1997. Author: Finance and Accounting, 1979 (Excellence award 1980), Financial Analysis, 1981 (Excellence award 1980), Managing Cash Flow, 1988 (Excellence award 1988), Finance and Management, 1989. Incorporator Spaulding Youth Ctr., Tilton, N.H., 1990; colleague Found. for Acctg. Edn., assoc., profl. standing, 1988; mem. Nat. Consortium Edn. and Tng., Madison, Wis., 1989. With USN, 1969-71, S.E. Asia. Named Outstanding Support Leader U.S. Small Bus. Adminstrn., Concord, 1985, Oustanding Svc. Leader Community Leaders Am., N.H., 1990, One of Outstanding Young Men Am. U.S. Jaycees Bd. Adv.'s, 1983. Mem. AICPA (mem. Profl. Devel. Inst., sponsor trainer 1988-89), Found. Acctg. Acctg., Investment Co. Inst. (assoc., nat. standing 1987), Inst. Mgmt. Cons. (assoc., nat. standing 1985, cert. profl. cons. to mgmt.), Nat. Soc. Pub. Accts. (del., profl. standing 1985), Nat. Soc. Non-Profit Orgns. (svc. provider 1989, colleague), Accreditation Coun. for Accountancy (fed. taxation accreditation 1987, colleague). Avocations: boating, teaching, community service, athletics. Home and Office: Levins & Associates 490 N River Rd Manchester NH 03104 Fax: 603-629-9333. E-mail: Levinsjohn@attbi.com.

LEVINSKY, NORMAN GEORGE, physician, educator; b. Boston, Apr. 27, 1929; s. Harry and Gertrude (Kipperman) Levinsky; m. Elena Sartori, June 17, 1956; children: Harold, Andrew, Nancy. AB summa cum laude, Harvard U., 1950, MD cum laude, 1954. Diplomate Am. Bd. Internal Medicine. Intern Beth Israel Hosp., Boston, 1954—55, resident, 1955—56; commd. med. officer USPHS., 1956; clin. assoc. Nat. Heart Inst., Bethesda, Md., 1956—58; NIH fellow Boston U. Med. Center, 1958—60; practice medicine, specializing in internal medicine and nephrology Boston, 1960—; chief of medicine Boston City Hosp., 1968—72, 1993—97; physician-in-chief, dir. Boston U. Med. Ctr. Hosp., Boston, 1972—97; asst. prof., then assoc. prof. medicine Boston U., 1960—68, Wesselhoeft prof., 1968—72, Wade prof. medicine, 1972—97, chmn. medicine, 1972—97, prof. medicine, assoc. provost, 1997—. Mem. drug efficacy panelNRC; mem. nephrology test com. AM. Bd. Internal Medicine, 1971—76; mem. gen. medicine B rev. group NIH; mem. comprehensive test com. Nat. Bd. Med. Examiners, 1986—89; chmn. com. to study end-stage renal disease program NAS/Inst. Medicine, 1988—90, chmn. com. on Xenografts, 1995. Editor (with R.W. Wilkins): Medicine: Essentials of Clinical Practice, 3d edit., 1983; editor: (with R. Rettig) Kidney Disease and the Federal Government, 1991; editor: Ethics and the Kidney, 2001; contbr. chapters to books, sci. articles to med. jours. Master: ACP (Disting. Tchr. award 1992); mem.: AAAS, Interurban Clin. Club (pres. 1985—86), Inst. Medicine NAS, Am. Soc. Nephrology, Assn. Profs. Medicine (sec., treas. 1984—87, pres.-elect 1987—88, pres. 1988—89), Am. Physiol. Soc., Assn. Am. Physicians, Am. Heart Assn., Am. Soc. Clin. Investigation, Am. Fedn. Clin. Rsch., Alpha Omega Alpha, Phi Beta Kappa. Home: 20 Kenwood Ave Newton MA 02459-1439 Office: Boston U Med Ctr 75 E Newton St Boston MA 02118-2340 E-mail: nlevinsk@bu.edu.

LEVINSON, ARNOLD IRVING, allergist, immunologist; b. Balt., 1944; MD, U. Md. Sch. Medicine, 1969. Diplomate Am. Bd. Internal Medicine, Am. Bd. Allergy and Immunology. Intern Balt. City Hosps., 1969-70, resident internal medicine, 1970-71; prof. medicine and neurology U. Pa., Phila., 1987—. Fellow, U. Pa., Phila., 1971—72, U. Calif., San Francisco, 1972—73. Fellow Am. Acad. Allergy, Asthma and Immunology, Am. Assn. Immunologists, Am. Fedn. for Clin. Rsch., Am. Soc. for Clin. Investigation; mem. Clin. Immunology Soc. Office: U Pa Hospital 3400 Spruce St Philadelphia PA 19104-4206

LEVINSON, BARRY L. film director; b. Balt., Apr. 6, 1942; Ed., Am. U., Washington. Film writer, actor: Silent Movie, 1976, High Anxiety, 1978; writer: ...And Justice for All, 1979, Inside Moves, 1980, Best Friends, 1982, Unfaithfully Yours, 1984; dir.: The Natural, 1984, Young Sherlock Holmes, 1985, Good Morning Vietnam, 1987, Rain Man, 1988 (Academy award 1989, Dirs. Guild Am. award 1989); screenwriter, dir.: Diner, 1982, Tin Men, 1987, Avalon, 1990 (Writers Guild Am. award 1990); co-prodr., dir. Bugsy, 1991, Disclosure, 1994, Wag the Dog, 1997, Sphere, 1998, An Everlasting Piece, 2000, Bandits, 2001; co-writer, dir., prodr. Toys, 1992; prodr. Donnie Brasco, 1997; writer, dir., prodr. Jimmy Hollywood, 1994 (also actor), Sleepers, 1996, Liberty Heights, 1999; actor: Quiz Show, 1994; dir., exec. prodr. (TV) Homicide: Life on the Street, 1993 (Emmy award, Outstanding Individual Achievement in Directing in a Drama Series, 1993, Peabody award 1993); exec. prodr. (TV) Oz, 1997; dir, and prodr., The Beat, 2000 (TV). Recipient ACE Golden Eddie Filmmaker of Yr. award, 2002. Mem. Dirs. Guild Am., Writers Guild Am. Address: c/o Baltimore Pictures 4000 Warner Blvd Bldg 133 Burbank CA 91522-0208

LEVINSON, BETTY ZITMAN, artist; b. Chgo., May 14, 1908; d. Samuel and Ella (Block) Z.; m. Julius Yale Levinson, Aug. 19, 1928 (dec. Dec., 1981); children: Lila Scher, Joyce Levinson, Robin Boushie. Student, U. Chgo., 1966, Art Inst. Chgo., 1972. Exhibitions include N. Shore Art League, Chgo., Spertus Mus., 57th St. Art Festival, Old Town Chamber Art Festival, Oak Park Art Festival, Faulkner Gallery (3d prize award), Santa Barbara, Calif., 1999; represented in collections at Deer Path Gallery, Lake Forest, Camino Real Gallery, Boca Raton, Fla., Prism Gallery, Evanston, Ill., Fort Wayne (Ind.) Mus. Art Alliance; juried group shows include Palm Springs (Calif.) Mus., Faulkner Libr. Gallery, 1998. Founder, mem. United Cerebral Palsy Assn. N.Y.C., 1949, pres. Stamford, Conn., 1954-58, v.p. Chgo., 1968—; patron Mus. Contemporary Art, Chgo. Historic Soc.; trustee Spertus Mus., Chgo.; active supporter print and drawing club Art Inst. Chgo. Recipient Honor Mother of Yr. Conn. Mother of Yr. Am. Mother's Com., N.Y., 1954, Award of Excellence Chgo. Soc. Artists, 1980, 1st prize David Adler Cultural Ctr., Libertyville, Ill., 1986, award of excellence, 1988, 2d prize Am. Jewish Art Club, Chgo., 1990, award of excellence Deer Path Gallery, Lake Forest, Ill., 1994, award for excellence, Cultural Ctr. for Abstract Painting, 1995, 96, award United Cerebral Palsy Chgo., 1996, award excellence Karpeles Manuscript Mus., Santa Barbara, 1997, 98, 3d prize Faulkner Gallery, Santa Barbara, 1999. Mem. English Speaking Union, Shakespeare Globe Ctr., Chgo. Soc. Artists, United Cerebral Palsy Chgo. (life v.p.), Master Santa Barbara Mus. Avocations: golf, walking, swimming, art. Home: Casa Dorinda 300 Hot Springs Rd Apt 89 Montecito CA 93108-2053

LEVINSON, DANIEL RONALD, federal agency administrator, lawyer; b. Bklyn., Mar. 24, 1949; s. Gerald Sam and Risha Rose (Waxer) L.; m. Luna Frances Lambert, Sept. 13, 1980; children: Luna Claire, Hannah Louise. AB, U. So. Calif., 1971; JD, Georgetown U., 1974; LLM, George Washington U., 1977. Bar: N.Y. 1975, Calif. 1976, D.C. 1976, U.S. Supreme Ct. 1978. Law clk. appellate divsn. N.Y. Supreme Ct., Bklyn., 1974-76; assoc. McGuiness & Williams, Washington, 1977-81, ptnr., 1982-83; dep. gen. counsel U.S. Office Personnel Mgmt., 1983-85; gen. counsel U.S. Consumer Product Safety Commn., 1985-86; chmn. U.S. Merit Sys. Protection Bd., 1986-93; of counsel Shaw Bransford & O'Rourke, 1993-94; chief of staff U.S. Rep. from Ga. Bob Barr, 1995-98; labor and employment advisor Koch Industries, Inc., 1998-2000; insp. gen. General Serv. Admin., 2001—. Adj. lectr. Am. U., Washington, 1981-82, Cath. U. Am., Washington, 1982. Notes and comments editor Am. Criminal Law Rev., 1973-74; contbr. articles to profl. jours. Bd. dirs. Washington Hebrew Congregation, 1993-96; prin. Coun. for Excellence in Govt., 1993-94. Mem. ABA, Adminstrv. Conf. U.S. (govt. mem. 1984-93), Phi Beta Kappa. Republican. Office: GSA Insp Gen 1800 F St NW Washington DC 20405 Office Fax: 202-501-4119. E-mail: Daniel.Levinson@gsa.gov.*

LEVINSON, DENNIS JOEL, internist, rheumatologist, educator; b. Chgo., Feb. 16, 1941; s. Harold and Esther L.; m. Phyllis Brody; children: Robin, Marc, Adam. BS, U. Ill., 1962; MD, Chgo. Med. Sch., 1967. Diplomate Am. Bd. Internal Medicine. Intern Michael Reese Hosp. and Med. Ctr., Chgo., 1967-68, resident, 1968-69, 71-72, assoc. attending physician, 1975-77, assoc. dir. divsn. rheumatology, 1975—, attending physician, 1977—, chmn., dept. head, program dir. internal medicine, residency, 1999—; USPHS postdoctoral fellow in rheumatology U. Chgo., 1972-74, asst. prof., 1975-82, assoc. prof., 1982-87, 87-90; clin. assoc. prof. U. Ill. at Chgo., 1991—; v.p., med. dir. Michael Reese Dr.'s Group, IPA, Inc., 1985—. Pres. Chgo. Rheumatism Soc., 1983-85; vice chmn. med. and scientific com. Arthritis Found. Ill. chpt., 1983-85; mem. instnl. and med. staff quality improvement coms., Michael Reese Hosp. and Med. Ctr., 1990—; chair med. records adv. bd., Michael Reese Hosp. and Med. Ctr., 1991-95; bd. dirs. Michael Reese Hosp., 1998—. Contbr. articles to profl. jours. Recipient Rsch. grant Ill. chpt. Arthritis Found.,

1975-85, NIH grant, 1979-84, McCormick Trust Ednl. grant, 1985-86. Fellow Am. Coll. Rheumatology; mem. AMA, ACP, Ill. Med. Soc., Chgo. Med. Soc., Am. Coll. Physican Execs., Chgo. Rheumatism Soc., Am. Assn. Med. Dirs. Office: Florsheim Profl Bldg 2800 S Vernon Chicago IL 60616

LEVINSON, FRANK H. information technology executive; BS in Maths. and Physics, Butler U.; MS, PhD in Astronomy, U. Va. Mem. tech. staff AT&T Bell Labs., Bellcore, 1984; prin. optical scientist Raychem Corp., 1985; mgr. optical dept. Raynet, Inc., 1986—88; founder Finisar, Sunnyvale, Calif., 1987, CEO, 1988—99, chief tech. officer, 1999—, chmn. bd. Office: Finisar 1308 Moffett Park Dr Sunnyvale CA 94089*

LEVINSON, HARLAN SHAW, investment banker; b. N.Y.C., July 21, 1961; s. Theodore H. and Doris (Shaw) L. AB, Lafayette Coll., 1983. Asst. treas. The Bank of N.Y., 1983-86, asst. v.p., 1986-89; asst. mgr. Morgan Grenfell Fin., Inc., N.Y.C., 1989-91; pres. Tandem Group, 1991-93; v.p. UNET 2 Corp., 1993-98; exec. v.p. Kenmare Capital Corp., 1998—. Mem. Union Club (N.Y.C.), The Leash (N.Y.C.). Avocations: ice hockey, squash. Office: Kenmare Capital Corp 134 Spring St New York NY 10012-3827

LEVINSON, HARRY, psychologist, educator; b. Port Jervis, N.Y., Jan. 16, 1922; s. David and Gussie (Nudell) L.; m. Roberta Freiman, Jan. 11, 1946 (div. June 1972); children— Marc Richard, Kathy, Anne, Brian Thomas; m. Miriam Lewis, Nov. 23, 1990. BS, Emporia (Kans.) State U., 1943, MS, 1946; PhD, U. Kans., 1952. Coordinator profl. edn. Topeka State Hosp., 1950-53, psychologist, 1954-55; dir. div. indsl. mental health Menninger Found., Topeka, 1955-68; visiting prof. MIT, 1961-62, U. Kans. Bus. Sch., 1967, Texas A&M U., 1976; Thomas Henry Carroll-Ford Found. distinguished vis. prof. Harvard Grad. Sch. Bus., Boston, 1968-72; adj. prof. Coll. Bus. Administrn., Boston U., 1972-74; lectr. Harvard Med. Sch., 1972-85; adj. prof. Pace U., 1972-83; clin. prof. psychology Harvard Med. Sch., 1985-92, emeritus prof., 1992—; head sect. orgnl. mental health Mass. Mental Health Ctr., 1983-92; pres. The Levinson Inst., 1968-91, chmn. bd., 1991—. Mem. Am. Bd. Profl. Psychology, 1972-80, chmn., 1978-80; Ford Found. prof. Mathur Inst., Jaipur India, 1974; conducted internat. course on social psychiatry Finnish Govt. Inst., 1979. Author: Emotional Health In the World of Work, 1964, Executive Stress, 1970, The Exceptional Executive (McKinsey Found. and Acad. Mgmt. awards), 1968 (James A. Hamilton Hosp. Adminstrs. Book award), Organizational Diagnosis, 1971, The Great Jackass Fallacy, 1973, Psychological Man, 1976, Casebook for Psychological Man; (with S. Rosenthal) CEO: Corporate Leadership in Action (Am. Coll. Health Care Adminstrs. Book award 1986), 1984, Ready, Fire, Aim, 1986, Designing and Managing Your Career, 1989, Career Mastery, 1992, Organizational Assessment, 2002. Chmn. Kans. adv. com. U.S. Civil Rights Commn., 1962-68; chmn. Topeka Human Relations Commn., 1967-68. Served with F.A. AUS, 1944-46. Recipient Perry Rohrer Cons. Psychology Practice award, 1984, Career award Mass. Psychol. Assn., 1985, First award Soc. Psychologists in Mgmt.; Eminent scholar in bus. Fla. Atlantic U., 1995. Fellow APA (award for disting. profl. contbn. to knowledge 1992), Am. Psychol. Found.; mem. Acad. Mgmt., Authors Guild. Home: 4889 Pineview Cir Delray Beach FL 33445-4318 E-mail: handmlevinson@earthlink.net.

LEVINSON, HERBERT SHERMAN, civil and transportation engineer; b. Chgo., Sept. 25, 1924; s. Israel and Tillie (Gash) L.; m. Sally Farver, July 3, 1977. BSCE, Ill. Inst. Tech., 1949; cert. in hwy. traffic, Yale U., 1952. Jr. traffic engr. Chgo. Park Dist., 1949-51; from assoc. to sr. v.p. Wilbur Smith & Assocs., New Haven, 1952-80; prin. Herbert S. Levinson Transp. Cons., 1980—; prof. civil engring. U. Conn., Storrs, 1980-86; prof. transp. Poly. Inst. of N.Y., N.Y.C., 1986-88, rsch. prof., 1988—. UTRC mentor CCNY, 1999—; vis. lectr. Yale U., New Haven, 1961-80; transp. cons. Author: Future Highways and Urban Growth, 1961, Transportation and Parking for Tomorrow's Cities, 1966, (with D. Votaw) Elementary Sampling for Traffic Engrs., 1961, (with R. Weant) Urban Transportation Perspectives and Prospects, 1983, Parking, 1990; contbr. numerous articles to profl. jours. Served as cpl. USAF, 1943-46. Recipient Presdl. Design award Nat. Endowment for the Arts, 1988. Fellow ASCE (Benjamin Wright award 1993, Wilbur S. Smith award 1997), Inst. Transp. Engrs. (hon., Transp. Engr. of Yr. 1976, Tech. Coun. award 1982, Theodore M. Matson award 1997); mem. NAE, Transp. Rsch. Bd. (Roy W. Crum award 1997), Am. Planning Assn., Conn. Acad. Sci. and Engring. E-mail: hslevinson@aol.com.

LEVINSON, JAY HARRY, protective services official; b. Newark, June 24, 1949; arrived in Israel, 1981; s. Philip and Nettie (Schwarzman) L.; m. Beverly Weitzner, Sept., 1970; children: Philip, Shoshana, Shimon, Chana Leah, Yitzchak, Chaim, Mordechai, Rivkah. BA, NYU, 1969, MA, 1971, PhD, 1974. Questioned document examiner U.S. CIA, Washington, 1972-81, Israel Police, Jerusalem, 1981-85; head disaster victim identification unit Israeli Police, 1985-97. Bd. dirs. Air Disaster Mgmt. Inst., Washington, 1993—; chmn. disaster victim identification standing com. Interpol, Lyons, 1993-98. Author: Questioned Documents: A Lawyer's Handbook, 2000, Urban Terrorism, 2001; contbr. articles to profl. jours., chpts. to books; mem. editorial bd. Disaster Prevention and Mgmt., 1990—, Jour. Forensic Document Examination, 1994—. Mem. Am. Soc. Questioned Document Examiners, Israel Soc. for Disaster Mgmt., Forensic Sci. Soc. India. Jewish. Avocation: philately. Home: PO Box 23067 Jerusalem 91230 Israel

LEVINSON, JERROLD, humanities educator; b. Bklyn., July 11, 1948; s. Max and Paula (Forster) L.; m. Alicia Janet Greene, Aug. 2, 1970 (div. June 1981); m. Karla Ruth Hoff, July 14, 1985; 1 child, Melanie Augusta Hoff. BS in Philosophy and Chemistry, MIT, 1969; PhD in Philosophy, U. Mich., 1974. Vis. prof. State U. N.Y., Albany, 1974-75; prof. U. Md., College Park, 1976—. Vis. prof. U. London, 1991, Johns Hopkins U., 1993, U. de Rennes, France, 1998, U. Canterbury, New Zealand, 1999, Columbia U., 2000; dir. NEH Summer Inst., 2002. Editor: Aesthetics and Ethics, 1998, Aesthetic Concepts, 2001, Oxford handbook of Aesthetics, 2002; author: Music, Art and Metaphysics, 1990, Pleasures of Aesthetics, 1996, Music in the Moment, 1998, L'Art la Musique, et l'Histoire, 1998; contbr. articles to profl. jours. Fellow NEH, 1980. Mem. Am. Soc. Aesthetics (v.p./pres. 1999-02), British Soc. Aesthetics, Am. Philos. Assn. Democrat. Jewish. Avocations: racket sports, baroque recorder, jazz, francophonie. Office: Univ Md Dept Philosophy Skinner Bldg College Park MD 20742-0001 E-mail: JL32@umail.umd.edu.

LEVINSON, JOHN MILTON, obstetrician, gynecologist; b. Atlantic City, Aug. 17, 1927; m. Elizabeth Carl Bell; children: Patricia Anne, John Carl, Mark Jay. BA, Lafayette Coll., Easton, Pa., 1949; MD, Thomas Jefferson U., 1953. Diplomate Am. Bd. Ob-Gyn. Intern Atlantic City Hosp., 1953-54; Am. Cancer Soc. clin. fellow Jefferson Med. Coll. Hosp., Phila., 1954-55; resident in ob-gyn. Del. Hosp., Wilmington, 1955-57; pvt. practice ob-gyn., 1957-85; prof. dept. ob-gyn. Jefferson Med. Coll., Thomas Jefferson U., Phila., hon. clin. prof., 1990—; sr. attending physician emeritus Med. Ctr. Del., Wilmington, 1986—; attending chief dept. ob-gyn. St. Francis Hosp., chief emeritus, 1986-92. Founder, pres. Aid for Internat. Medicine, Inc., 1966—; med. dir., chief surgeon Quark Expeditions, 1991-95; cons. Riverside Hosp., 1972-86, Wilmington Pa. Blue Shield, 1982—; cons. gynecology U.S. VA, 1974-85; founding mem., treas., bd. dirs. Physicians Health Svcs., Del., Ltd., 1985-87; vis. prof., cons., ship's surgeons, practicing physician various orgns. in Africa, Antarctica, Arctic regions, Ctrl. Am., Europe, S.E. Asia,, S.W. Asia, 1963—; lectr. in field; internat. med. cons. to Sen. Edward M. Kennedy, 1967—; chmn. Antarctic expdns. study group to advise NSF, 1992-93; co-chmn. Com. for Safety in Arctic and Antarctic Frontier Expeditions, 1992-93. Author: Shorebirds: The Birds, the Hunters, the Decoys, 1991, Safe Passage Questioned: Medical Care and Safety for the Polar Tourist, 1998, Advanced First Aid Afloat, 2000; assoc. prodr. 3 films on explorer Ernest Shackleton; contbr. articles to profl. jours., chpts. to books. Bd. dirs. Del. com. Project H.O.P.E., 1965-75, ARC, 1968-70, Charles A. Lindbergh Fund, Inc., 1985-90; trustee Blue Cross/ Blue Shield Del., Inc., 1968-86, Brandywine Coll., 1972-77; bd. dirs. Nat. Assn. Blue Shield Plans, 1971-77; mem adv. com. Trinity Alcohol and Drug Program, 1978-85; mem. Del. Gov.'s Commn. on Health Care Cost Mgmt., 1985-87; bd. dirs. founding mem. World Affairs Coun. Wilmington Inc, v.p., 1981-86; pres. Rockland Mills Cmty. Assn., 1992-94; mem. bd. advisors World Sportsmen Ctr., Orlando, 1997—, With USN, 1945-47; col. M.C., USAFR, 1984-87. Recipient Brandywine award Brandywine Coll., 1968, cert. of appreciation for med. svcs. Ministry of Health, Republic of Vietnam, 1963-66, commendation Pres. of U.S., 1971, The Eisenhower award People to People Internat., 1986, Commemorative medal Charles A. Lindbergh Fund, 1987, Phila. Explorers award 1987, Citation for Outstanding Contbn. to People of Del., Med. Soc. Del., 1992. Fellow Am. Coll. Ob.-Gyn., Royal Geog. Soc. London; mem. AMA, Am. Assn. Gyn. Laporoscopists (founding, bd. dirs.), Del. Obstetric Soc. (pres. 1980-82), Phila. Obstetric Soc., Med. Soc. Del. (Citation of Merit award 1992), New Castle County Med. Soc., Soc. Ob-Gyn. Vietnam (hon.), Ducks Unltd. (sponsor, mem. Del. com. 1980-92), Explorers Club (fellow 1966—, chmn. Phila. chpt. 1983-85, bd. dirs. 1981-88, pres. N.Y.C. 1985-87), Univ. and Whist Club Wilmington (life, bd. govs. 1961-64), Rotary (bd. dirs. local club 1991-93), Theta Chi (pres. 1945) Phi Beta Pi (pres. 1952), Kappa Beta Phi (pres. 1952). Avocations: hunting, polar history, sailing, carving bird decoys. Home: 55 Millstone Ln Rockland DE 19732

LEVINSON, JOSEPH E. physician, emeritus educator; b. Cin., Apr. 7, 1920; s. Samuel W. and Rebecca (Lewin) L.; m. Mimi Freiberg, Mar. 21, 1945 (dec. Apr. 1992); children: Steven Henry, Henry Samuel, Richard Peter; m. Carol Weihl, Oct. 10, 1993 (dec. Mar. 1999); m. Sophia Ralson, Nov. 10, 2001. Student, Columbia U., 1937-40; BA, Stanford U., 1941; MD, U. Cin., 1944. Clin. and rsch. fellow in medicine Harvard U./Mass. Gen. Hosp., Boston, 1950-52; instr. medicine U. Cin., 1953-61, assoc. prof. medicine, 1961-73, prof. medicine and pediatrics, 1973-85, dir. divsn. pediatric rheumatology, 1975-86, assoc. dir. Multipurpose Arthritis Ctr., 1978-82, prof. emeritus medicine and pediatrics, 1985—. Dir. arthritis tchg. svc. Cin. Gen. Hosp., 1960-64. Contbr. articles to profl. jours. Bd. dirs. Seven Hills Sch., Cin., 1993-2001, Cancer Family Care, Cin., Anthem Found., Cin., 1999—, Friends of the Spl. Treatment Ctr.; bd. dirs. Planned Parenthood of the Cin. Region, 2000—. Mem. Am. Coll. Rheumatology (master). Avocations: tennis, horse and mule wilderness pack trips, travel. Office: Children's Hosp Med Ctr 3333 Burnet Ave Cincinnati OH 45229-3026 Home: Apt 802 2121 Alpine Pl Cincinnati OH 45206-3697 Fax: 513-221-7091. E-mail: jelevinson@fuse.net.

LEVINSON, KENNETH S. lawyer, corporate executive; b. Mineola, N.Y., Oct. 27, 1947; s. Max Leonard and Eva (Klamen) L.; m. Laura R. Levinson, Sept. 14, 1969 (div. 1981); 1 child, Barbara Ann Schmidt; m. Jerelyn E. Jarmacz, Feb. 6, 1982; children: Alexander T., Brianna F., Joshua K. BA in Polit. Sci. with distinction, U. Wis., 1969; JD with honors, George Washington U., 1975; LLM in Taxation, Georgetown U., 1978. Bar: D.C. 1975, Va. 1975, U.S. Ct. Claims 1976, U.S. Dist. Ct. (D.C. dist.) 1976, U.S. Tax Ct. 1976, U.S. Ct. Appeals (D.C. cir.) 1976, U.S. Supreme Ct. 1979. Atty., advisor Office Chief Counsel Interpretative div. IRS, Washington, 1975-78, reviewer, asst. br. chief Office Chief Counsel, 1978-79; sr. tax atty. Pepper, Hamilton & Scheetz, 1979-81; v.p., mng. tax dir. Marriott Corp., Bethesda, Md., 1981-85, v.p. internat. project fin., 1985-90; from v.p. tax to v.p. tax, risk mgmt. & ins. Northwest Airlines, Inc., Eagan, Minn., 1990—96, v.p. tax, risk mgmt. and ins., 1996—2001; mng. dir. structurl risk fin. practice KPMG, 2002—. Adj. prof. Georgetown U. Law Ctr., Washington, 1978-86; asst. sec., v.p. various Marriott Corp. subs., Bethesda, 1981-90; v.p. Wings Holdings, Inc./N.W. Airlines Corp., 1990—; v.p. tax N.W. Airlines, Inc., 1990—, v.p. various subs.; cons. The Chechhi Group, Beverly Hills, Calif., 1989-90; bd. dirs. City Harbour Hotel, Ltd., London. Contbr. articles to profl. jours. Bd. dirs. Minn. Taxpayers Assn., Mpls. Lt. USN, 1969-72. Mem.: ABA (subcom. chair 1978—84), Minn. Taxpayers Assn. (bd. dir. 1998—, exec. com. 1998—), Nat. Taxpayers Assn. (bd. dir. 1999—), Internat. Air Transport Assn. (chair taxation com. 1991—92, 1999—2000, v.chmn. 1999, chmn. ins. com. 1994, 1997—99, chair internat. risk mgrs. forum 1995, 1998—2001, conf. chair 2001, chmn. air 2002), Air Transport Assn., Washington Tax Group, Tax Execs. Inst. (bd. dir. Minn. chpt. 1999—), Va. State Bar, D.C. Bar. Avocations: golf, art appreciation/collection, boating, equestrian show jumping, skiing.

LEVINSON, LAWRENCE EDWARD, lawyer, corporation executive; b. N.Y.C., Aug. 25, 1930; s. Samuel Keever and Sara Lee (Tarvin) L.; m. Margaret Anne Bishop, Aug. 20, 1989; children: Elizabeth, Suzanne, Lucia. BA magna cum laude, Syracuse U., 1952; LLB, Harvard U., 1955. Bar: N.Y. 1957, U.S. Supreme Ct. 1958. Atty. Office Sec. Air Force, Washington, 1957-63; spl. assignments Office Sec. Def., 1963-65; dep. counsel to Pres. U.S., 1965-69; sr. v.p. Paramount Communications, Inc., N.Y.C., 1969-94; sr. Washington counsel VIACOM Internat., 1994-95; ptnr. Verner, Liipfert, Bernhard, McPherson and Hand, Washington, 1995—. Mem. Nat. Council on Health Planning and Devel., Washington, 1978-84; host pub. affairs TV program Capital Notebook, 1991—. Mem. bd. visitors Syracuse U. Coll. Arts and Scis., 1981—. Served with Judge Adv. div. U.S. Army, 1955-57. Mem. N.Y. State Bar Assn., Assn. Am. Pubs. (bd. dirs. 1989-95), Army-Navy Country Club (Washington). Home: 5715 Little Falls Rd Arlington VA 22207-1554 E-mail: lelvinson@verner.com.

LEVINSON, NANETTE SEGAL, international relations educator, administrator; b. Boston, Nov. 8, 1946; d. Oscar and Rose (Menicks) Segal; m. Peter Joseph Levinson, Mar. 30, 1968; children: Sharman Risa, Justin David. AB cum laude, Harvard U., 1968, EdM, 1969, EdD, 1979. Asst. prof. Am. U., Washington, 1980-86, dir. advanced tech. mgmt. program, 1983-88, assoc. prof., 1986—, assoc. dean sch. internat. svc., 1988—; visiting prof. Inst. Etudes Politiques, Paris, 2001. Cons. David Taylor Naval Ship Rsch. and Devel. Ctr., 1984-86, Xerox Corp., Leesburg, Va., 1986-91; chair bd. dirs. Nat. Conf. on Advancement of Rsch., 1992-93, bd. dirs., 1996-2000—; bd. dirs. Women's Fgn. Policy Group, 1997-2000, mem. adv. cou., 2000—; bd. dirs. Transatlantic Info. Exch. Svcs., sec.-gen., 1997-99; vis. scholar Ritsumeikan U., Kyoto, Japan, 1993; bd. dirs. Internat. Adv. Bd. Transatlantic Internet Seminars, 2000—; vis. prof. Fondation Nationale des Sciences Politiques/Inst. d'Etudes Politiques de Paris, 2001. Contbr. numerous articles to profl. jours. Bd. dirs. Joint Bd. on Sci. and Engring. Edn., Washington, 1982-85; co-chair The Rsch. Project on Women Leaders in Internat. Affairs, 1995-99. Mem. Internat. Studies Assn., Am. Polit. Sci. Assn., Internat. Assn. for Media and Comm. Rsch. Office: Am U Office of Dean 4400 Massachusetts Ave NW Washington DC 20016-8071 E-mail: nlevins@american.edu.

LEVINSON, PETER JOSEPH, retired lawyer; b. Washington, June 11, 1943; s. Bernard Hirsh and Carlyn Virginia (Krupp) L.; m. Nanette Susan Segal, Mar. 30, 1968; children: Sharman Risa, Justin David. AB in History cum laude, Brandeis U., Waltham, Mass., 1965; JD, Harvard U., 1968. Bar: U.S. Supreme Ct. 1975. Summer supr. Harvard Legal Aid Bur., Cambridge, Mass., 1968; rsch. asst. Harvard Law Sch., 1968-69; tchg. fellow Osgoode Hall Law Sch. York (Can.) U., 1969-70, rsch. assoc., 1969-70, asst. prof., 1970-71; dep. atty. gen. State of Hawaii, 1971-75; vis. fellow Harvard U., 1976-77; ptnr. Levinson and Levinson, Honolulu, 1977-79; spl. asst. to dir. office program support Legal Svcs. Corp., Washington, 1979; cons. Select Commn. on Immigration and Refugee Policy, 1980-81; minority counsel subcom. on immigration, refugees and internat. law com. on judiciary U.S. Ho. of Reps., 1981-85, minority counsel subcom. monopolies and comml. law, 1985-89, minority counsel subcom. econ. and comml. law, 1989-95, counsel com. on judiciary, 1995-2001, ret., 2001. Lawyer; b. Washington, June 11, 1943; s. Bernard Hirsh and Carlyn Virginia (Krupp) L.; m. Nanette Susan Segal, Mar. 30, 1968; children: Sharman Risa, Justin David. AB in History cum laude, Brandeis U., Waltham, Mass., 1965; JD, Harvard U., 1968. Bar: Hawaii 1971, U.S. Supreme Ct. 1975. Summer supr. Harvard Legal Aid Bur., Cambridge, Mass., 1968; research asst. Harvard Law Sch., 1968-69; teaching fellow Osgoode Hall Law Sch., York U. (Can.), 1969-70, research assoc., 1969-70, asst. prof., 1970-71; dep. atty. gen. State of Hawaii, 1971-75; vis. fellow Harvard U., 1976-77; ptnr. Levinson and Levinson, Honolulu, 1977-79; spl. asst. to dir. Office Program Support, Legal Services Corp., Washington, 1979; cons. Select Commn. on Immigration and Refugee Policy, Washington, 1980-81; minority counsel subcom. on immigration, refugees and internat. law com. on judiciary, U.S. Ho. of Reps., Washington, 1981-85, minority counsel subcom. monopolies and comml. law, 1985-89, minority counsel subcom. econ. and comml. law, 1989-95, counsel com. on judiciary, 1995—. Trustee, Hawaii Jewish Welfare Fund, 1972-75, chmn. fund drive, 1972; trustee Temple Emanu-El, Honolulu, 1973-75; mem. alumni admissions council Brandeis U., 1978-82. Recipient award of merit United Jewish Appeal, 1974. Mem. Hawaii State Bar Assn. (chmn. standing com. on continuing legal edn. 1972, chmn. standing com. on jud. adminstrn. 1979), ABA, Am. Judicature Soc. Contbr. articles to profl. jours. Contbr. articles to profl. jours. Trustee Hawaii Jewish Welfare Fund, 1972-75, chmn. fund drive, 1972; trustee Temple Emanu-El, Honolulu, 1973-75; alumni admissions coun. Brandeis U., 1978-82. Recipient Merit award United Jewish Appeal, 1974. Mem. ABA, Am. Judicature Soc. Home: PO Box 5690 Washington DC 20016

LEVINSON, ROBERT ALAN, textile company executive; b. Balt., July 26, 1925; s. Louis and Frieda (Kellert) L.; m. Patricia S. Schulte, Apr. 23, 1954; children: Margot, Andrew, John. AB, Dartmouth Coll., 1946; postgrad., London Sch. Econs., 1946-47. With Burlington Industries, N.Y.C., 1949-51; v.p., dir. Bangor Punta, Inc., 1964-68; chmn. bd. Duplan Corp., 1968-79; chmn. Andrex Industries Corp. Cons. Dillon Yarn Corp.; chmn., pres. Levcor Internat.; dir., chmn., pres., CEO, mem. exec. com. Carlyle Industries, Inc. Bd. dirs. World Policy Inst.; vice-chmn. Nat. Acad. Mus., Harlem Sch. Arts; trustee Bklyn. Mus., chmn., 1972-84; chmn. Harlem Sch. of Arts, Nat. Dance Inst.; bd. dirs., exec. com., vice chmn. Nat. Commn. on U.S.-China Rels.. With USNR, 1943-45, 52-54. Home: 1035 5th Ave New York NY 10028-0135 Office: Levcor Internat Inc 462 7th Ave New York NY 10018-7606

LEVINSON, ROBERT ARLEN, computer science educator, consultant; b. Mpls., Oct. 30, 1958; s. Morton William and Chernie Rae (Braufman) L. BS in Math., BS in Computer Sci., U. Minn., 1981; PhD, U. Tex., 1984. Tech. support analyst Minn. Gas Co., Mpls., 1975-79; tchg. asst. U. Minn., 1980-81; grad. rsch. fellow dept. chemistry U. Tex., Austin, 1983-85; asst. prof. U. Calif., Santa Cruz, 1986-93, assoc. prof., 1993—. Contract programmer U. Minn. Computing Ctr., Mpls., 1979-81; vis. prof. FMC Corp., Santa Clara, Calif., 1989-90; cons. Textwise, Syracuse, N.Y., 1995-97, Stock Sci., 1999-2000; gen. chair 9th Internat. Conf. on Conceptual Structures, 2001. Editor: Conceptual Structures, Applications, Implementation and Theory, 1995, procs. 3d Internat. Conf. on Conceptual Structures, 1995, ICCS-2001 Procs. Stanford U., 2001; editl. bd.: Multi-Senser Info. Fusion jour., 2000-2001; pubs. chair Second Internat. Conf. on Multisource-Multisensor Info. Fusion, 1999. Grantee NSF, Washington, 1989-94, grad. fellow, 1979-83; grantee NASA, Ames, Calif., 1986-87. Avocations: chess, sports, stock market investments. Home: 41 Grandview St Apt 1507 Santa Cruz CA 95060-6800 Office: U Calif 225 Applied Scis Santa Cruz CA 95064 Fax: (831) 459-4829. E-mail: levinson@cse.ucsc.edu.

LEVINSON, SHAUNA T. financial services executive; b. Denver, Aug. 1, 1954; d. Charles and Geraldine D. Titus; m. Kenneth L. Levinson, Dec. 21, 1986. BA cum laude, U. Puget Sound, 1976; M Bank Mktg. with honors, U. Colo., 1986. Cert. fin. planner. Fin. planning analyst Swift and Co., Chgo., 1977-79; from credit analyst to asst. v.p. Ctrl. Bank of Denver, 1979-84; v.p. fin. svcs. First Nat. Bank S.E. Denver, 1984-94; dir. mktg. First Nat. Banks, 1991-94; pres., CEO Fin. Directions, Inc., Denver, 1994—; CEO Levinson Resources, Inc., 1994—. Mem. bankers edn. com. Colo. Bankers Assn., Denver, 1992-94. Contbr. articles to profl. jours. Chmn. human resources com., mem. adminstrv. coun. Jr. League Denver, 1983—, mem. cmty. assistance fund, placement adv. com.; fundraiser Women's Libr. Assn., U. Denver, 1990—94, 1996—98, Good Shepherd Cath. Sch., 1986—95, Jewish Cmty. Ctr., Denver, 1990—95, St. Mary's Acad., 1995—99; active Denver Campus for Jewish Edn., 2000—, Allied Jewish Fedn. Colo., 2000—. Recipient Gold Peak award Am. Bankers Assn.-Bank Mktg. Assn., 1987; named Businessperson of Week Denver Bus. Jour., 1995. Mem.: Jr. League Denver (sustaining), U. Denver Pioneer Hockey, St. Andrews Soc. (life), Betty Lambert Soc. (life), Crestmoor Gardeners (treas. 1994—2000), Phi Chi Theta, Phi Kappa Phi, Kappa Alpha Theta (Chgo. NW alumnae 1977—79, Denver alumnae 1980—, rush adv. com. 2000—). Office: 1624 Market St Ste 475 Denver CO 80202-1518

LEVINSON, STEPHEN ELIOT, engineering educator, electrical engineer; b. N.Y.C., Sept. 27, 1944; s. Benjamin Adler and Doris Ruth (Goldstein) L.; m. Diana Elaine Sheets, June 6, 1976. AB, Harvard U., 1966; MS, U. R.I., 1972, PhD, 1974. J.W. Gibbs instr. Yale U., New Haven, 1974-76; Disting. mem. tech. staff Bell Labs., Murray Hill, N.J., 1976—, head linguistics rsch. dept., 1990-97; prof. elec. computer engring. Beckman Inst. U. Ill., Urbana, 1997—. Vis. researcher NTT Labs., Tokyo, 1979; vis. fellow Cambridge U., U.K., 1984. Editor Computer Speech and Language jour., 1986—; patentee in speech recognition field. Fellow IEEE, Acoustical Soc. Am.; mem. AAAS, Assn. for Computing Machinery, N.Y. Acad. Sci., Sigma Xi (rsch. award U. R.I. chpt. 1973). Avocations: violin, sailing, skiing.

LEVINSON, STEPHEN RONALD, otolaryngologist; b. Balt., Mar. 4, 1946; MD, Johns Hopkins U., 1971. Diplomate Am. Bd. Otolaryngology. Intern U. Calif., San Diego, 1971-72; resident in surgery Wadsworth Va Hosp.-UCLA, 1972-73; resident in head and neck surgery UCLA, 1973-76; pvt. practice Fairfield, Conn. Mem. staff Bridgeport (Conn.) Hosp.; mem. acad. staff Mt. Sinai Sch. Medicine. Fellow ACS; mem. AMA, Am. Acad. Otolaryngology, Am. Acad. Facial Plastic and Reconstructive Surgery. Address: 52 Beach Rd Fairfield CT 06430-6017 E-mail: ASALLC@aol.com.

LEVINSON, STEVEN HENRY, state supreme court justice; b. Cincinnati, OH, June 8, 1946; BA with distinction, Stanford U., 1968; JD, U. Mich., 1971. Bar: Hawaii 1972, U.S. Dist. Ct. Hawaii 1972, U.S. Ct. Appeals (9th cir.) 1972. Law clk. to Hon. Bernard H. Levinson Hawaii Supreme Ct., 1971-72; pvt. practice Honolulu, 1972-89; judge Hawaii Cir. Ct. (1st cir.), 1989-92; assoc. justice Hawaii Supreme Ct., Honolulu, 1992—2002. Staff mem. U. Mich. Jour. Law Reform, 1970-71. Active Temple Emanu-El. Mem. ABA (jud. adminstrn. divsn. 1989—), Hawaii State Bar Assn (dir. young lawyers divsn. 1975-76, dir. 1982-84), Nat. Jud. Coll., Am. Judges Assn., Am. Judicature Soc. Jewish. Office: Supreme Ct Hawaii Aliiolani Hale 417 S King St Honolulu HI 96813-2912

LEVINSON, WARREN MITCHELL, broadcast journalist; b. Bklyn., Feb. 23, 1953; s. Abraham and Roslyn Anne (Bell) L.; m. Debra Lynn Galant, Sept. 1, 1985; children: Margot, Noah. BA, Duke U., 1975. Reporter Sta. WCHL Radio, Chapel Hill, N.C., 1974-77; news dir. Sta. WBLG/WKQQ Radio, Lexington, Ky., 1977-78; newswriter AP, N.Y.C., 1979-82; corr. AP Radio, 1982—. Co-host (radio talk program) Newsweek on Air, 1985—. Recipient Silver medal for News Mag. Internat. Radio T.V. Soc., 1989, Crystal award of Excellence, Nat. Communicator Awards, 2000. Avocations: bicycling, poetry. Office: Associated Press 50 Rockefeller Plz Fl 5 New York NY 10020-1666 E-mail: wlevinson@ap.org.

LEVINSON-MILLER, CAROLYN, mental health services professional, researcher; b. Norwalk, Conn., Aug. 18, 1968; d. Doris Jalkow Levinson, Daniel Richard Levinson; m. Edward Charles Miller. BA, Johns Hopkins U., 1990; MPH, Yale U., 1999. Rsch. assoc. dept. psychiatry Yale U., New Haven, 1999—. Mem.: Nat. Alliance for the Mentally Ill. Home: 193 Seymour Rd Woodbridge CT 06525 Office: Yale U Dept Psychiatry 950 Campbell Ave/182 West Haven CT 06516 Business E-Mail: levinscm@biomed.med.yale.edu.

LEVINTHAL, BETH ELLEN (KUBY LEVINTHAL), educator; b. Oceanside, N.Y., Nov. 21, 1951; d. Milton and Selma Florence (Miller) Kuby; m. Charles Frederick Levinthal, Dec. 16, 1973; children: David, Brian. BA in Graphic Design, Hofstra U., 1973, MS in Elem. Edn., 1975. Cert. elem. education N-6, art K-12, N.Y. Art instr. Huntington (N.Y.) Twp. Art League, 1987-94; art tchr. Jefferson Elem., Huntington, 1991-92; coord. of sch., youth and family programs Heckscher Mus. of Art, 1994-96, coord. of edn., 1996-97, dir. edn. and pub. programs, 1997-2000, exec. dir., 2001—. Adj. instr. C.W. Post Coll., Brookville, N.Y., 1998-2000. Editor: Huntington Twp. Art League newsletter, 1989-94. Fellow Mid-Atlantic Assn. of Mus. (Malcolm Arth fellow 1996); mem. NYSATA, Am. Assn. Mus., L.I. Mus. Assn. Jewish. Home: 9 Royal Oak Dr Huntington NY 11743-4427 Office: Heckscher Mus of Art 2 Prime Ave Huntington NY 11743-7702

LEVINTHAL, CHARLES FREDERICK, psychologist, psychology educator, writer; b. Cin., July 6, 1945; s. Sam and Mildred (Greenburg) L.; m. Beth Ellen Kuby, Dec. 16, 1973; children: David Justin, Brian Ross. AB, U. Cin., 1967; MA, U. Mich., 1968, PhD, 1971. Asst. prof. Hofstra U., Hempstead, N.Y., 1971-78, assoc. prof., 1978-87, prof., 1987—. Author: (books) Messengers of Paradise: Opiates and the Brain, 1988, Introduction to Physiological Psychology, 3d edit., 1990, Drugs, Behavior and Modern Society, 3d edit., 2002. With USAR, 1968-74. Fellow Woodrow Wilson Found., 1967, NSF, 1967-71. Mem. APA, Soc. for Neurosci. Jewish. Avocations: piano, composition. Home: 9 Royal Oak Dr Huntington NY 11743-4427 Office: Hofstra U 1000 Fulton Ave Hempstead NY 11549-0001

LEVINTHAL, ELLIOTT CHARLES, physicist, educator; b. Bklyn., Apr. 13, 1922; s. Fred and Rose (Raiben) L.; m. Rhoda Arons, June 4, 1944; children— David, Judith, Michael, Daniel. BA, Columbia Coll., 1942; MS, Mass. Inst. Tech., 1943; PhD, Stanford U., 1949. Project engr. Sperry Gyroscope Co., N.Y.C., 1943-46; research assoc. nuclear physics Stanford (Calif.) U., 1946-48, sr. scientist dept. genetics Sch. Medicine, 1961-74, dir. Instrumentation Research Lab., 1961-80, assoc. dean for research affairs, 1970-73, adj. prof. genetics Sch. Medicine, 1974-80, research prof. mech. engring., dir. Inst. Mfg. and Automation Sch. Engring., 1983-90, assoc. dean for research Sch. Engring., 1986-90, assoc. dean spl. programs, 1990-91, prof. emeritus, 1991—; research physicist Varian Assocs., Palo Alto, Calif., 1949-50, dir. research, 1950-52; chief engr. Century Electronics, 1952-53; pres. Levinthal Electronics, 1953-61; dir. def. scis. office Def. Advanced Projects Agy., Dept. Def., Arlington, Va., 1980-83. Mem. NASA Adv. Coun., 1980-84, space studies bd., NRC, 1989-91, mem. human exploration, 1991-92, army sci. bd., 1989-91; cons. HEW; chmn. bd. dirs. Euroe, Inc. Recipient NASA Public Service medal, 1977 Mem. AAAS, IEEE, Am. Phys. Soc., Optical Soc. Am., Biomed. Engring. Soc., Sigma Xi. Democrat. Jewish. Home: 59 Sutherland Dr Atherton CA 94027-6471 Office: Stanford U Sch Engring 530 Duena St Rm 104 Stanford CA 94305-2209 E-mail: levinthal@stanford.edu.

LEVINTON, JEFFREY S. biology educator, oceanographer; b. N.Y.C., Mar. 20, 1946; s. Nathan and Lillian (Moshman) L.; m. Joan Miyeko Miyazaki, Mar. 30, 1979; children: Nathan Toshi, Andrew Koji. BS, CCNY, 1966; MPhil, Yale U., 1969, PhD, 1971. Asst. prof. biology SUNY, Stony Brook, 1970-75, assoc. prof., 1975-83, prof., 1983—, head dept., 1984-90, 91-93. Vis. prof. U. Arhus, Denmark, 1966-67, Uppsala (Sweden) U., 1981, U. Cambridge, England, 1983, U. Sydney, Australia, 1999; chmn. panel Hudson River Found, 1986-90. Author: Marine Ecology, 1982, Genetics, Paleontology, and Macro-evolution, 1988, 2d ed., 2001, Marine Biology, 1995, 2d ed., 2001; reviewer, contbr. over 100 articles to profl. jours. Mem. Environ. Policy Com. Conn., 1969. NSF fellow, 1969, Sterling hon. fellow, 1969, John Simon Guggenheim fellow, 1983, Sir Kirby Lang fellow U. Wales, 1998; Fulbright sr. fellow, 1999. Mem. Ecol. Soc. Am. (editor 1986-93), Am. Soc. Naturalists (editor 1974-79). Democrat. Office: SUNY Dept Ecology And Evolution Stony Brook NY 11794-0001

LEVIS, ALEXANDER HENRY, systems engineer, educator, consultant; b. Yannina, Greece, Oct. 3, 1940; came to U.S., 1959; s. Henry N. and Jeannette (Matathia) L.; m. Ilze E. Sedriks, Mar. 26, 1970 (dec. 1994); children: Livia, Philip; m. Margaret C. Miller, May 13, 2001. AB, Ripon Coll., 1963; BS, MS, MIT, 1965, ME, 1967, ScD, 1968. Asst. prof. Poly. Inst. Bklyn., 1968-73, assoc. prof., 1973-74; mgr. sys. rsch. dept. Systems Control, Inc., Palo Alto, Calif., 1973-79; sr. rsch. scientist MIT, Cambridge, 1979-90, univ. prof., 1996—; prof. George Mason U., Fairfax, Va., 1990—96, chair sys. engring. dept., 1992—95, 1996—98. Mem. Air Force Sci. Adv. Bd., 1990-94, 98—. Editor five books; assoc. editor IEEE Transactions on Automatic Control, 1975-77, Automatica Jour., 1980-85; contbr. articles to sci. jours. Recipient Exceptional Civilian Svc. medal Air Force, 1994, Disting. Svc. Edn. award AFCEA, 1996. Fellow AAAS, IEEE Control Systems Soc. (v.p. 1984-85, pres. 1987, Disting. Mem. award 1987); mem. AIAA (sr.). Home: 10607 Springvale Ct Great Falls VA 22066-1740 Office: George Mason U C3I Ctr Fairfax VA 22030 E-mail: alevis@gmu.edu.

LEVIS, DONALD JAMES, psychologist, educator; b. Cleve., Sept. 19, 1936; s. William and Antoinette (Stejskal) L.; children: Brian, Katie. PhD, Emory U., 1964. Postdoctoral fellow clin. psychology Lafayette Clinic, Detroit, 1964-65; asst. prof. psychology U. Iowa, Iowa City, 1966-70, assoc. prof., dir. research and tng. clinic, 1970-72; prof. SUNY-Binghamton, 1972—. Author: Learning Approaches to Therapeutic Behavior Modification, 1970, Implosive Therapy, 1973; cons. editor: Jour. Abnormal Psychology, 1974-80, Jour. Exptl. Psychology, 1976-77, Behavior Moedifications, 1977-81, Behavior Therapy, 1974-76, Clin. Behavior Therapy Rev., 1978— ; contbr. articles to profl. jours. Served to capt. AUSR, 1958-66. Fellow Behavior and Therapy Research Soc. (charter, clin.), Am. Psychol. Assn.; mem. Assn. Advancement Behavior Therapy (publ. bd. 1979-82), AAAS, Psychonomic Soc., N.Y. State Psychol. Assn., Sigma Xi Home: 48 Riverside Dr Binghamton NY 13905-4402 Office: SUNY at Binghamton Dept Psychology Binghamton NY 13901

LEVIS, RICHARD GEORGE, secondary school educator; b. Kenosha, Wis., Nov. 20, 1946; s. Elso R. and Valentina (Maraccini) L.; m. Diane Rose Christie, June 12, 1971; 1 child, Maureen R. BS, U. Wis., 1968, MS, 1973. Tchr. social studies Parker Jr. H.S., Janesville, Wis., 1969, Washington Jr. H.S., Kenosha, 1969-98, Mary D. Bradford H.S., Kenosha, 1998—2002. Mem. com. on vandalism and mid. schs. Kenosha Unified Schs., social studies benchmarks and stds. com.; jr. h.s. rep. Kenosha Ednl. Found., 1994; KABA bowl coach Bradford H.S., 1999—. Co-author: (with James Hansen) United Nations Resource Materials and Bibliographies, 1974. V.p. Kenosha Tchrs. Union, 1971-73; exec. bd. Kenosha Dem. Party, 1969-86; mem. canvass bd., Kenosha; rep. United Fund, 1985—. Mem. NEA, Nat. Coun. Social Studies, Wis. Social Studies Coun., Wis. Edn. Assn., Kenosha Edn. Assn. (bd. dirs. 1975-77), Phi Delta Kappa. Democrat. Roman Catholic. Avocations: golf, reading, watching sports, politics, travel. Home: 3520 14th Pl Kenosha WI 53144-2939 Office: Mary D Bradford HS 3700 Washington Rd Kenosha WI 53144-1641

LEVISON, STEVEN WILLIAM, scientist, educator; b. Bklyn., Aug. 6, 1961; s. Fredric Eliot and Carol Furgatch Levison; m. Teresa Lynne Wood, July 26, 1996 BS, U. Rochester, 1983; PhD, U. N.C., 1990. Postdoctoral fellow Columbia U., N.Y.C., 1990-93; asst. prof. Pa. State U., Hershey, 1993-99, assoc. prof. neurosci. and anatomy, 1999—. Sr. editor Devel. Neurosci., 1999; contbr. articles to profl. jours. Rsch. grantee NIH, Bethesda, Md., 1994, 98, 98, Nat. Multiple Sclerosis Soc., N.Y., 1998. Mem. Am. Soc. for Neurochemistry, Soc. for Neurosci. (pres. Ctrl. Pa. chpt. 1999). Democrat. Home: 835 Verden Dr Hummelstown PA 17036-9700 Office: Pa State Coll Medicine PO Box 850 Hershey PA 17033-0850 Fax: 717-531-0714. E-mail: slevison@psu.edu.

LEVISS, STEPHEN R. gynecologist; b. Newark, July 30, 1941; s. Louis A. and Alice (Karelitz) L.; m. Shari Lynn Weinberg, Oct. 25, 1963; children: Stewart, Jonathan, David. AB in English, Tufts U., 1963; MD, Albert Einstein Coll. Medicine, 1967. Diplomate Am. Bd. Ob-Gyn. Intern Albert Einstein Coll. Medicine, Bronx, N.Y., 1967-68, resident in ob-gyn., 1968-69, 71-73; pvt. practice Parsippany, N.J., 1973—. Instr. ob-gyn. Albert Einstein Coll. Medicine, Bronx, 1973-75; clin. asst. prof. ob-gyn. U. Medicine and Dentistry N.J., Newark, 1975—. Maj. M.C., USAF, 1969-71. Fellow Am. Coll. Ob-Gyn. Democrat. Avocations: running, walking, fitness. Office: 50 Cherry Hill Rd Parsippany NJ 07054-1101

LEVIT, EDITHE JUDITH, physician, medical association administrator; b. Wilkes-Barre, Pa., Nov. 29, 1926; m. Samuel M. Levit, Mar. 2, 1952; children: Harry M., David B. BS in Biology, Bucknell U., 1946; MD, Med. Coll. Pa., 1951, DMS (hon.) , 1978; DSc (hon.) , Wilkes U., 1990. Grad. asst. in psychology Bucknell U., 1946—47; intern Phila. Gen. Hosp., 1951—52, fellow in endocrinology, 1952—53, clin. instr., assoc. in endocrinology, 1953—57, dir. med. edn., 1957—61, cons. med. edn., 1961—65; asst. dir. Nat. Bd. Med. Examiners, Phila., 1961-67, assoc. dir., sec. bd., 1967—75, v.p., sec. bd., 1975—77, pres., CEO, 1977—86, pres. emeritus, life mem., bd. dirs., 1987—. Adv. coun. Inst. for Nuclear Power Ops., Atlanta, 1988—93; cons. in field. Contbr. articles to profl. jours. Bd. sci. counselors Nat. Libr. Medicine, 1981—85; bd. dirs. Phila. Gen. Hosp. Found., 1964—70, Phila. Council for Internat. Visitors, 1966—72. Recipient award for outstanding contbns. in field of med. edn., Commonwealth Com. of Woman's Med. Coll., 1970, Alumni award, Bucknell U., 1978, Disting. Dau. of Pa. award, 1981, Spl. Recognition award, Assn. Am. Med. Colls., 1986, Disting. Svc. award, Fedn. State Med. Bds., 1987. Master: ACP; fellow: Coll. Physicians of Phila.; mem.: AMA, Phila. County Med. Soc., Pa. Med. Soc., Inst. Medicine Nat. Acad. Scis., Phi Sigma, Alpha Omega Alpha, Phi Beta Kappa. Home: The Rittenhouse #2305 210 W Rittenhouse Sq Philadelphia PA 19103-5726

LEVIT, HÉLOÏSE B. (GINGER LEVIT), art historian, art dealer, art consultant; b. Phila., Apr. 2, 1937; d. Elmer and Claire Frances (Schwartz) Bertman; m. Jay Joseph Levit, July 14, 1962; children: Richard Bertman, Robert Edward, Darcy Francine Honker. BA in French Literature, U. Pa., 1959; MA in French Literature, U. Richmond, 1975; MA Art History, Va. Commonwealth U., Richmond, 1998; Cert., Alliance Française, Paris, 1991, Chambre de Commerce et d'Industrie de Paris, 1991, La Sorbonne, Paris, 1994, Istituto Lorenzo di Medici Firenze, Italy, 1996. Arts broadcaster, Richmond, Va., 1976-82; dir. Fine Arts Am., Inc., 1982-84; tchr. Henrico County Pub. Schs., 1984-88; dir. devel. Sta. WVST-FM Va. State U., Petersburg, 1987-88; mgr., dir. devel. Richmond Philharm. Orch., 1988-99; fine arts and media cons. Art-I-Facts, Richmond, 1988—; cons., 1997-98. Author: Moments, Monuments & Monarchs, 1986 (Star award, 1986); arts writer: Richmond Rev., 1989—90, arts writer: Mid-Atlantic Antiques monthly column Washington Jewish Week; anchor, prodr. (syndicated radio series) Va. Arts Report, 1978—83, Va. Women, 1984 (Va. Press Women award, 1986, Va. Press Women award, 2001, Press Women award, 2000). V.p. Va. Mus. Collector's Cir., Richmond, 1986-91, mem. steering com.; pres. Richmond Area Dem. Women's Club, 1992-93; mem. Va. Mus. Coun., Richmond; rec. sec. Richmond Symphony Orch. League, 1998-2000, dir. pub. rels., 2000—, guest condr., 2000. Mem. Am. Assn. Tchrs. of French, Va. Capitol Corrs. Assn., Va. Press Women (2d pl. award 2001), U. Pa. Alumni Club (v.p. 1980-90, Ben Franklin award 1990), Am. Symphony Orch. League, Amicale Francaise, Alliance Francaise (cert. 1989, 91), La Table Francaise (chmn. 1996—), Va. Writers Club. Avocations: tennis, art collecting, classical music, foreign travel. Home and Office: Art-I-Facts 419 Dellbrooks Pl Richmond VA 23233-5559

LEVIT, JAY J(OSEPH), lawyer; b. Phila., Feb. 20, 1934; s. Albert and Mary Levit; m. Heloise Bertman, July 14, 1962; children: Richard Bertman, Robert Edward, Darcy Francine. AB, Case Western Res. U., 1955; JD, U. Richmond, 1958; LLM, Harvard U., 1959. Bar: Va. 1958, D.C. Ct. Appeals 1961, U.S. Supreme Ct. 1961. Trial atty. U.S. Dept. Justice, Washington, 1960-64; sr. atty. Gen. Dynamics Corp., Rochester, N.Y., 1965-67; ptnr. Stallard & Levit, Richmond, Va., 1968-77, Levit Mann Halligan Warren, Richmond, 1978—. Instr. U. Mich. Law Sch., Ann Arbor, 1964-65; adj. assoc. prof. U. Richmond Law Sch., 1974-77; adj. lectr. Va. Commonwealth U., Richmond, 1970-85; lectr. in field. Contbg. editor The Developing Labor Law-Bur. Nat. Affairs, 1974—. Recipient ABA and Bur. Nat. Affairs Books Cert. of Appreciation for significant contbns. to advancement of the law, 1999, 2000, 2001. Mem. ABA (labor com.), Va. Bar Assn. (labor and employment com., Chair's award for extraordinary contbns. to labor and employment law sect. 1999), Fed. Bar Assn. (labor and employment com.). Avocations: art collecting, jogging, swimming, travel. Home: 419 Dellbrooks Pl Richmond VA 23233-5559 Office: Levit Mann Halligan Warren 1301 N Hamilton St Richmond VA 23230-3959 also: Levit Mann Halligan Warren 127 Thompson St Ashland VA 23005-1511 E-mail: levmanhal@mindspring.com.

LEVIT, MARK SHELDON, advertising executive; b. Cleve., Mar. 9, 1949; s. Irwin and Gertrude Helene (Berk) L.; m. Kathy Gray Levit, Aug. 28, 1970 (div. 1973); 1 child, Efrem. BS, Kent State (Ohio) U., 1971. Acct. exec. Griswold Eshleman Co., Cleve., 1972-75; sr. acct. exec. N.W. Ayer, N.Y.C., 1975-76; acct. supv. KSW&G Advt., 1976-80; pres. Levit & Sherman Advt., 1980-95, Partners & Levit Inc., N.Y.C., 1995—; prof. mktg. NYU. Dir. League of Advt. Agencies, N.Y.C. Recipient Andy award Advt. Club of N.Y., AIAA Gold award Am. Indsl. Advt. Assn. Republican. Avocations: skiing, photography, computers, music. Office: Partners & Levit Inc 8 W 38th St Rm 1213 New York NY 10018-6259 Fax: 212-683-7689. E-mail: markl@partnerslevit.com.

LEVIT, WILLIAM HAROLD, JR. lawyer; b. San Francisco, Feb. 8, 1938; s. William Harold and Barbara Janis Kaiser L.; m. Mary Elizabeth Webster, Feb. 13, 1971; children: Alison Jones Baumler, Alexandra Bradley Kovacevich, Laura Elizabeth Fletcher, Amalia Elizabeth Webster Todryk, William Harold, III. BA magna cum laude, Yale U., 1960; MA Internat. Rels., U. Calif., Berkeley, 1962; LLB, Harvard U., 1967. Bar: N.Y. 1968, Calif. 1974, Wis. 1979. Fgn. service officer Dept. State, 1962-64; assoc. Davis Polk & Wardwell, N.Y.C., 1967-73; assoc. ptnr. Hughes Hubbard & Reed, N.Y.C., L.A., 1973-79; sec. and gen. counsel Rexnord Inc., Milw., 1979-83; ptnr., dir., chair internat. practice group Godfrey & Kahn, 1983—. Substitute arbitrator Iran-U.S. Claims Tribunal, The Hague, 1984-88; lectr. Practicing Law Inst., ABA, Calif. Continuing Edn. of Bar, State Bar of Wis. Contbr. to: Mergers and the Private Antitrust Suit: The Private Enforcement of Section 7 of the Clayton Act, 1977. Bd. dirs. Wis. Humane Soc., 1980-90, pres., 1986-88; bd. dirs. Vis. Nurse Corp., Milw., 1980-90, chmn., 1985-87; bd. dirs. Vis. Nurse Found., 1986-95, chmn., 1989-91; bd. dirs. Aurora Health Care Inc., 1988-93, Wis. Soc. to Prevent Blindness, 1981-91, Aurora Health Care Ventures, 1993—, chair, 1998-2000, 2002-; bd. trustees Columbia Coll. Nursing, 1992—, chair, 2002—; trustee Mt. Mary. Coll. 2002-, dir.; adv. bd. Med. Coll. Wis. Cardiovasc. Ctr., 1994—, chmn., 1999-2002, chmn. Bd. Ad Oversight Supreme Ct. Wis. Office Lawyer Regulation, 2000—; rep. Assn. Yale Alumni, 1976-79, 81-84, 90-93; pres. Yale Club So. Calif., 1977-79; mem. neutral advisor panel and franchise, and ins. panels CPR Inst. for Dispute Resolution. Ford Found. fellow U. Pa., 1960-61, NDEA fellow U. Calif., Berkeley, 1961-62. Mem.: ABA, Am. Arbitration Assn. (comml. panel 1977—, internat. panel 1997—), Inst. Jud. Adminstrn., Am. Soc. Internat. Law, N.Am. Coun. London Ct. of Internat. Arbitration, N.Y. Stock Exch. (panel arbitrators 1988—), Chartered Inst. Arbitrators (London), Nat. Assn. Security Dealers (panel arbitrators 1988—), Am. Br. Internat. Law Assn., Bar Assn. 7th Cir. (pres. 2002—), State Bar Wis. (dir. internat. bus. transactions sect. 1985—92, dist. 2 Wis. Supreme Ct. bd. attys. profl. responsbility com. 1985—94, chmn. 1993—94), L.A. County Bar Assn. (ethics com. 1976—79), State Bar Calif. (com. on continuing edn. of bar 1977—79), Assn. Bar City N.Y., Am. Soc. Corp. Secs. (dir. 1981—92, pres. Wis. chpt. 1982—83), Am. Law Inst., Town Club, Milw. Athletic Club, Milw. Club, Phi Beta Kappa. Office: 780 N Water St Ste 1500 Milwaukee WI 53202-3512 E-mail: walevit@gklaw.com.

LEVITAN, DAVID M(AURICE), lawyer, educator; b. Tver, Lithuania, Dec. 25, 1915; (parents Am. citizens); m. Judith Morley; children: Barbara Lane Levitan, Stuart Dean Levitan. BS, Northwestern U., 1936, MA, 1937; PhD, U. Chgo., 1940; JD, Columbia U., 1948. Bar: N.Y. 1948, U.S. Dist. Ct. (so. dist.) N.Y. 1948, U.S. Supreme Ct. 1953. Various U.S. Govt. adminstrv. and advisory positions with Nat. Youth Adminstrn., Office Price Adminstrn., War Prodn. Bd., Fgn. Econ. Adminstrn. Supreme Hdqrs. Allied Expeditionary Force, and Cen. European div. Dept. State, 1940-46; cons., sec. joint-com. of 5th and 6th coms., 2d Gen. Assembly, dir. com. of experts for establishing adminstrv. tribunal UN, 1946-47; cons. pub. affairs dept., producer series of pub. affairs programs on TV and radio ABC, 1946-53; pvt. practice N.Y.C., 1948-66; counsel Hahn & Hessen, 1966-68, ptnr., 1968-86, counsel, 1986-96; instr. U. Chgo., 1938-41; adj. prof. public law Columbia U., 1946-65; adj. prof. John Jay Coll. Criminal Justice, CUNY, 1966-75; adj. prof. polit. sci. Post Coll., 1964-66; adj. prof. law Cardozo Sch. Law, 1978-82; pvt. practice, N.Y.C., 1996—. Asst. to Ill. state adminstr. Nat. Youth Adminstrn., chief budget sect., Washington, 1940-41; mgmt. analyst Office of Price Adminstrn., 1941; spl. asst. to chmn. War Prodn. Bd., 1942-43; chief property control divsn. Fgn. Econ. Adminstrn., Washington, 1944-45; with U.S. Group of Control Coun. for Germany at SHAEF, London, 1944; advisor Ctrl. European divsn. U.S. Dept. State, 1945; cons. UN, 1946-47, Sect. Joint Com. 5th and 6th Coms., 1946-47, 2d session of 1st Gen. Assembly, 1946-47; dir. Com. of Experts on Establishment of Adminstrn. Tribunal, 1946-47; cons. pub. affairs dept. ABC, 1946-53. Contbr. articles to legal jours. Mem. Nassau County (N.Y.) Welfare Bd., 1965-69; chmn. Planning Bd., Village of Roslyn Harbor, N.Y., 1965-66; chmn. Bd. of Zoning Appeals, Village Roslyn Harbor, 1967-86. Recipient Demobilization award Social Sci. Rsch. Coun., 1946-48. Fellow Am. Coll. Trust and Estate Counsel; mem. ABA, Am. Polit. Sci. Assn., Am. Soc. Internat. Law, Am. Law Inst., Assn. Bar City N.Y. Home: 103 NE 19th Ave Deerfield Beach FL 33441-6106 Office: Ste 704 455 North End Ave New York NY 10282

LEVITAN, JAMES A. lawyer; b. N.Y.C., Mar. 24, 1925; s. Leo and Della (Brody) L.; m. Ruth Terry White, Jan. 30, 1951; children— Deborah A., Judith T., Susan J. BS in Chem. Engring, M.I.T., 1948; LL.B. (mem. bd. Law Rev. 1950-51), Columbia U., 1951. Bar: N.Y. bar 1951. Since practiced in, N.Y.C.; ptnr. Skadden, Arps, Slate, Meagher & Flom, 1965-95, of counsel, 1995—. Life mem. MIT Corp., Cambridge, Mass., 1995-99, emeritus, 2000, chmn. audit com., 1994-2000; regional chmn. N.Y.C. MIT Ednl. Coun., 1974-90; lectr. in field of tax. Served with USNR, 1944-46. Stone scholar, 1948-51; Kent scholar, 1950 Mem. N.Y. State Bar Assn., Assn. Bar City N.Y., Tau Beta Pi. Home: 26 Wake Robin Ln Stamford CT 06903-4611 Office: Skadden Arps Slate Meagher & Flom 4 Times Sq Fl 33 New York NY 10036-6522 E-mail: jlevitan@optonline.net., jlevitan@skadden.com.

LEVITAN, KATHERINE D. lawyer; b. Vienna, Austria, July 8, 1933; came to U.S. 1938, naturalized 1942; d. Otto and Hedweega (Saltzer) Lenz; m. Leonard Levitan, Sept. 12, 1952; children— Joel, Jeffrey, Debbie, Diane. B.A. cum laude, N.Y.U. 1952, J.D. cum laude, 1955, LL.M. in Criminal and Family Law, 1977. Bar: N.Y. 1956, U.S. Dist. Ct. (ea. dist.) N.Y. 1972, U.S. Supreme Ct. 1974. Tchr. bus. law N.Y. Inst. Tech., Old Westbury, 1968-69; assoc. Bennett Reiss, Great Neck, N.Y., 1969-70, Malone and Dorfman, Freeport, N.Y., 1970-71; sole practice, Jericho, N.Y., 1971-80; practice with assocs., Mineola, N.Y., 1980— ; also lectr.; assoc. prof. Hofstra Law Sch. Bd. dirs., legal counsel For Our Children and Us, Inc., Nassau chpt. ACLU, 1975— ; mem. Nassau County Democratic Com., 1969— , law guardian adv. panel 2d dept. Human Rights Adv. Commn. Nassau County; past pres. Nassau chpt. N.Y. Civil Liberties Union. Mem. Nassau Bar Assn. (grievance com., martim com.), Nassau/Suffolk Women's Bar Assn. (past pres., legal counsel), Nassau Civil Liberties Union, L.I. Women's Network, Acad. Matrimonial Lawyers, Contbr. articles to profl. publs. Home: PO Box 846 New Lebanon NY 12125-0846 Office: 83 Prospect St Huntington NY 11743-3306

LEVITAN, LAURENCE, lawyer, former state senator; b. Oct. 22, 1933; s. Maurice and Nathlie (Rosenthal) L.; m. Barbara E. Levin, 1957; children: Jennifer, Michelle, Lisa. BS, Washington and Lee U., 1955; JD, George Washington U., 1958. Bar: Md. 1964. With Levitan, Cramer & Weinstein, 1959-72, Levitan Ezrin, West & Kenxton, 1973-85, Beckett Cromwell & Goldman, 1990-92; of counsel Baker & Hostetler, 1992-95; ptnr. Rifkin, Livingston, Levitan and Silver, LLC, Annapolis, Md., 1995—. Mem. Md. Ho. of Dels., 1971-74; mem. Md. Senate, 1975-94, chmn. budget and taxation com., policy com., spending affordability com, mem. joint com. on mgmt. pub. funds, legis. com. on budget and audit, gov.'s commn. to rev. state taxes and taxes structure, joint legis. com. on tax refrm, govtl. commn. to revise annotated code of Md., joint subcom. on program open space, chmn. drunk and drugged driving task force, chmn. joint com. on ins. tax reform; mem. Montgomery County Exec.'s Commn. for Higher Edn. in High Tech.; past mem. Gov.'s Commn. to Study Unification of Cir. Ct., Gov.'s Commn. to Study Condominium Laws, Gov.'s Commn. Law Enforcement and Adminstrn. Justice, Gov.'s Subcom. on Revenue Structure of Task Force to Study State-Local Rels.; mem. Gov.'s Commn. to Study Feasability of Biennial Budget, Gov.'s Task Force on Real Property Closing Costs, Task Force to Study Md. Tax Ct., Gov.'s Commn. Sch. Funding, Joint Task Force on Md.'s Procurement Law; apptd. co-chmn. transition team on budget rev. Gov. Glendening; chmn. Gov.'s Jud. Compensation Commn., 1998—; mem. Commn. on Md.'s Fiscal Structure, 2002-03. Mem. ABA, D.C. Bar Assn., Md. Bar Assn., Nat. Conf. State Legislatures (mem. subcom. on fed. budget and taxation com., fiscal affairs govt. oversight com.), So. Legis. Conf. (chmn. fiscal affairs and govt. ops. steering com. 1992-93), Am. Legis. Exch. Coun. (tax task force). Democrat. Jewish. Office: 225 Duke Of Gloucester St Annapolis MD 21401-2506 also: 11426 Georgetowne Dr Potomac MD 20854-3722 E-mail: checkoffLL@aol.com.

LEVITAN, MAX FISHEL, geneticist, anatomy educator; b. Tverai, Telsiu Aps, Lithuania, Mar. 1, 1921; came to U.S., 1928; s. Solomon Leib and Hannah (Siev) Levitan; m. Beth Sheva German, Oct. 25, 1947; children: Eve Leah Gerber, Sara Anne, Marjorie Ruth Gross. AB, U. Chgo., 1944; MA, U. Mich., 1946; PhD, Colmubia U., 1951. Asst. in zoology Columbia U., N.Y.C., 1946-49; assoc. prof. biology Va. Poly. Inst., Blacksburg, 1949-55; asst. prof. anatomy Woman's Med. Coll. Pa., Phila., 1955-58, assoc. prof., 1958-60, prof. anatomy and med. genetics, 1960-66, acting chmn. anatomy dept., 1964-66; prof. biology, chmn. dept. George Mason U., Fairfax, Va., 1966-68; assoc. prof. anatomy Mt. Sinai Sch. Medicine, N.Y.C., 1968-70; prof. anatomy Mt. Sinai Sch. Medicine, CUNY, 1970—, prof. human genetics, 1995—. Author: Textbook of Human Genetics, 1971, 3rd edit. 1988; contbng. author: Clinical Genetics, 1973, Genetics and Biology of Drosophila, 1982, Drosophila Inversion Polymorphism, 1992, Encyclopedia of Human Biology, 1992, 1997, Encyclopedia of Science and Technology, 1992, 1997, Genetics of Natural Populations, 1995; assoc. editor Evolution, 1977-79; contbr. articles to profl. jours. Named Edward Everett Just Meml. lectr. Howard U., Washington, 1968; recipient Rsch. Career Devel. award NIH, 1963. Fellow AAAS; mem. Genetics Soc. Am., Soc. for Study of Evolution, Am. Soc. Naturalists, Sigma Xi (sec. VPI chpt. 1954-55, sec.-treas. Mt. Sinai chpt. 1975—). Jewish. Achievements include rsch. in linkage disquilibria in inversion systems, unique chromosomal breakage factor, suppressor systems in evolution. Home: 1212 5th Ave New York NY 10029-5210 Office: Mt Sinai Sch Medicine CUNY 1 Gustave L Levy Pl New York NY 10029-6500 E-mail: max.levitan@mssm.edu.

LEVITAN, STEPHAN J. psychiatrist; b. N.Y.C., Jan. 15, 1941; s. Eli Benjamin and Felice Bianca (Solomon) L.; m. Judith Levitan; children: Elizabeth, Peter. BA, NYU, 1961; MD, U. Buffalo, 1965. Diplomate in psychiatry Am. Bd. Psychiatry and Neurology; cert. in psychoanalytic medicine. Intern Brookdale Hosp. Ctr., N.Y.C., 1965-66; resident psychiatry Hillside Hosp., Glen Oaks, N.Y., 1966-69; pvt. practice psychiatry and psychoanalysis, N.Y.C.; mem. staff Columbia-Presbyn. Med. Ctr., 1969—. Clin. prof. psychiatry Columbia-Presbyn. Med. Ctr., 1980—. Fellow Am. Psychiat. Assn.; mem. AMA, Am. Psychoanalytic Assn., Am. Psychosomatic Soc., Am. Soc. Clin. Psychopharmacology, Assn. for Psychoanalytic Medicine (past pres.), Soc. for Liaison Psychiatry (past pres.). Office: 185 E 85th St Apt 29J New York NY 10028-2143

LEVITAS, MIRIAM C. STRICKMAN, documentary filmmaker, designer, consultant intergenerational relationships; b. Aug. 3, 1936; d. Morris and Bella (Barsky) Cherrin; m. Bernard Strickman, June 3, 1956 (dec. Jan. 1975); children: Andrew Strickman, Brian Strickman, Craig Strickman, Deron Strickman; m. Theodore Clinton Levitas, Apr. 25, 1976; children: Steven, Leslie, Anthony. Student, Temple U., 1953-56; accelerated student, LaSalle U., Chgo., 1968; cert. in gerontology/cmty. svc., Ga. State U., 1988. Intergenerational Connections Contact State of Ga., 1989—. V.p. programming interior design Nat. Home Fashions League, Atlanta, 1974—75, Ga. Bd. Realtors, 1971—; founding adminstr. Stanley H. Kaplan Ednl. Ctr., Atlanta, 1974—84; owner, pres. Levitas Svcs. Inc. (Internat. Destinations), Atlanta, 1984—85; owner, v.p. Nat. Travel Svcs. and Internat. Destinations, Atlanta, 1984—85; realtor Philip White Properties Inc./Sotheby's Internat. Realty, 1985—91, Coldwell Banker Previews, 1991—; intergenerational programs and events cons.; creative designer for loft living. Prodr.(host cmty. svc. videos TV cable broadcast): , 1988—91. Pres. Ahavath Achim Sisterhood, Atlanta, 1977—79, 1996—98; bd. dirs. Jewish Family Svcs., 1993—96; bd. dirs. Atlanta chpt. Nat. Osteoporosis Found., 1990—91, Outings in the Park, 1989—91; chmn., coord. Tea at the Ritz Scottish Rite Children's Med. Ctr., 1987—90; chmn. women's divsn. Israel Bond, Atlanta, 1987, 1988, 1989, mem. aux.; chmn., coord. Who's Bringing in the Great Chefs Scottish Rige Children's Med. Ctr., 1990, 1991, 1992; mem. Atlanta Symphony, High Mus. Art, Nat. Mus. of Women in Arts, William Bremen Jewish Heritage Mus., Alliance Theater Atlanta, Atlanta Hist. Ctr.-Atlanta Hist. Soc., Alliance No. Dist. Dental Soc.; charter mem. U.S. Holocaust Mus.; bd. dirs. Jewish Ednl. Loan Fund; nat. bd. advisors Brevard Mus. Ctr., 1993—. Named Woman of Achievement, Atlanta Jewish Fedn., 1993; scholar, Phila. Bd. Edn., 1952. Mem.: NAFE, Image Film and Video Ctr., Am. Women in Radio and TV, Women in Film (Atlanta chpt.), Internat. Furnishings and Design Assn., Spl. Children of the South (chmn. 1991—93), Atlanta Bd. Realtors, Ga. Gerontology Soc., Scots (life), B'nai Brith (life), Nat. Coun. Jewish Women (life), Hadassah (life), Brandeis Nat. Women (life), Ga. Dental Assn. Aux., Children's Med. Ctr. Aux. E-mail: mslprod1@aol.com.

LEVITAS, VALERY, mechanics and materials educator, researcher; b. Kiev, Ukraine, Apr. 3, 1956; arrived in Germany, 1993, U.S., 1999; s. Ilya and Shanna (Beresina) L.; m. Ludmila Borodyanskaya, Aug. 25, 1978 (div. 1992); 1 child, Oleg; m. Natasha Danekina, Jan. 20, 1993; 1 child, Roman. MSc with honors, Kiev Poly. Inst., 1978; PhD, Inst. Superhard Materials, Kiev, 1981; DSc, Inst. Elect. Machine Bldg., Moscow, 1988; D of Engring. Habilitation, U. Hannover, Germany, 1995. Registered profl. engr., Tex. Jr. rschr. Inst. for Superhard Materials, Kiev, 1978-84, leader rsch. group, 1982-95, sr. rschr., 1984-89, leading rschr., 1985-95; vis. rschr. Inst. Problems of Mechanics,

Moscow, 1985; vis. and rsch. prof. U. Hannover, Germany, 1992, 93-99; assoc. prof. mech. engring. Tex. Tech U., Lubbock, 1999—2002, prof. mechanics and materials, 2002—; pres. Material Modelling, 2002—. Cons. Inst. for Superhard Materials, Kiev, 1995—; dir. Firm Strength, Kiev, 199 -92; cons. Los Alamos Nat. Lab., 2001—; spkr. in field. Author: Large Elastoplastic Deformations of Materials at High Pressure, 1987, Thermomechanics of Phase Transformations and Inelastic Deformations in Microinhomogeneous Materials, 1992, Large Deformations of Materials with Complex Rheological Properties at Normal and High Pressure, 1996; bd. editors High Pressure Physics and Tech., 1996—; mem. editl. adv. bd. Superhard Materials, 1990—. Recipient medal Ukrainian Acad. Scis., 1984, Disting. Paper award Internat. Jour. Engring. Sci., 1995, Richard von Mises award Soc. Applied Math. and Mechanics, 1998; Humboldt Rsch. fellow, 1993-95. Mem. ASME, Internat. Assn. for Advancement of High Pressure Sci. (exec. com. 1993-99), Soc. Engring. Sci. Office: Tex Tech U Dept Mech Engring Lubbock TX 79409 E-mail: valery.levitas@coe.ttu.edu.

LEVITCH, JOSEPH See **LEWIS, JERRY**

LEVITEN, RIVA SHAMRAY, artist; b. L.A., Oct. 26, 1928; d. Peter Leo and Edythe (Smith) Shamray; m. Paul Leviten, Oct. 15, 1950 (dec. Oct. 19, 1988); children: Priscilla Leviten Warner, Marcia Leviten, Peter Leviten. BS in Apparel Design, UCLA, 1950; postgrad., Cal Arts, L.A., 1949-50, Exptl. Etching Studio, Boston, 1980-90. 1st v.p. R.I. chpt. Nat. Mus. Women in the Arts, 1997-99. Visual Rev. Bd. Newport Rev., 1997-98, R.I. Women Speak, Nat. Mus. Women in the Arts, Crone elderwoman, 1997, Monotype Printmaking and Painting Travel Show, 1998—; represented in collections at R.I. Sch. Design Mus., Danforth Mus., Slater Mus., El Paso Mus., Midwest Mus. Am. Art, Mass. Coll. Art, R.I. Coll., Tougaloo Coll., U. Ark., Marist Coll., Muscatine Art Ctr., Laura Musser Mus. Dickenson State U., Art in Embassies U.S. Dept. State, Saginaw Art Mus.; exhibited Russia, Australia, Mex., Can. Founding mem. Gallery of Social and Polit. Justice, Boston, 1996—. Recipient Herbert Cross prize South County Art Assn., Kingston, R.I., 1979. Founding mem. Showcase for Collage; elected artist mem. Mystic Art Assn.; mem. Providence Art Club, Monotype Guild of New Eng., Providence Art Club (Providence Art Club award 1998, J. Bannigan Sullivan award 1995, Bradford Swan award 1987), Nat. Assn. Women Artists (Martha Reed award 1994). Avocations: urban gardening, interior design, writing poetry, innkeeping, public speaking at art symposiums. Home and Office: 425 Benefit St Providence RI 02903-2933

LEVITIN, DANIEL JOSEPH, cognitive science researcher, journalist; b. San Francisco, Dec. 27, 1957; s. Lloyd Alan and Sonia (Wolff) L. m. Caroline A. Traube, 1999. AB with distinction in Cognitive Sci., Stanford U., 1992; MS in Cognitive Psychology, U. Oreg., 1993, PhD in Cognitive Psychology, 1996. cons. Booz-Allen Hamilton, San Francisco, 1984, C.B.S. Records, L.A., 1988-90. Editor Palos Verdes View (Calif.) Newspaper, 1975-78; fin. analysis mgr. Pacific Tel., San Francisco, 1982-84; A&R dir., staff prodr. 415/CBS Records, 1984-88; ind. rec. engr., prodr., 1988-90; music prodn. editor REP mag., 1989-1993; instr. depts. music, anthropology Stanford U., 1992-93; instr. dept. psychology, rsch. asst. U. Oreg., Eugene, 1993-96; mem. rsch. staff Interval Rsch. Corp., Palo Alto, Calif., 1996-1998; vis. asst. prof. psychology U. Calif., Berkeley, 1999; asst. prof. psychology McGill Univ., Montreal, PQ, Can., 2000—, assoc. prof. music theory Can., 2000—, FCAR strategic prof. Can., 2000—. Lectr. dept. music Stanford U., 1996—. Contbr. over 300 articles to Audio, Billboard, Mix, Grammy, Perception and Psychophysics mags., 1990—; music editor Rec., Engring. and Prodn., 1990-92. Bd. dirs. U. Oreg. Hillel, 1994-96, Halachic Minyan, Eugene, Oreg., 1993-96. Recipient NSF Young Psychologists Program award U.S. Nat. Acad. Sci., 1996, Dept. Def. Office Naval Rsch. grad. fellowship, 1992-95. Mem. NARAS, APA (Guilford award for undergrad. rsch. 1992), Acoustical Soc. Am., Am. Psychol. Soc., Audio Engring. Soc., Am. Statis. Assn. Achievements include producing and engineering popular music recordings; research in visual and auditory psychophysics, memory, statistical methods for periodic data.

LEVITIN, LEV BEROVICH, engineering educator; b. Moscow, Sept. 25, 1935; came to U.S., 1981; s. Ber L. and Tzetzilia (Gushansky) L.; m. Yulia Shmukler, 1959 (div. 1970); 1 child, Boris. MSc, Moscow U., 1960; PhD, Acad. Scis. USSR, 1969. Sr. rsch. scientist Inst. Info. Transmission Problems/USSR Acad. Scis., 1961-73; sr. lectr. Tel-Aviv U., 1974-80; vis. prof. Bielefeld U., W.Ger., 1980-81, Syracuse (N.Y.) U., 1981-82; prof. engring. Boston U., 1982-86, disting. prof. engring. sci., 1986—. Vis. scientist Heinrich-Hertz Inst., Berlin, 1980, Inst. for Optoelektronik, Oberpfaffenhofen, W.Ger., 1981; cons. Vishay Israel, Ltd., Tel-Aviv, 1979, SEL Forschungszentrum, Stuttgart, Germany, 1987, Humboldt U., Berlin, 1997—. Editor: Principles of Cybernetics (in Russian), 1967; contbr. articles to profl. jours. Fellow IEEE; mem. AAUP, AAAS, Am. Math. Soc., Assn. Computing Machinery, Soc. Indsl. and Applied Math., N.Y. Acad. Scis., Am. Soc. for Engring. Edn., Math. Assn. Am., Memento, Resistance Internat., Amnesty Internat. E-mial. Office: Boston U Coll Engring 8 Saint Marys St Boston MA 02215-2421 E-mail: levitin@bu.edu.

LEVITIN, MICHAEL JAY, lawyer; b. Norfolk, Va., July 26, 1960; s. Jordan S. and Carol A. (Hyman) L.; m. Caryn F. Ginsberg, Oct. 7, 1990. AB, Harvard U., 1982, JD, 1986; MA in Law and Diplomacy, Fletcher Sch. Law & Diplomacy, 1990. Bar: N.Y. 1987, D.C. 1988. Atty.-advisor Office of Gen. Counsel, U.S. Dept. Treas., Washington, 1986-88; assoc. Sidley & Austin, 1988-94, Winthrop, Stimson, Putnam & Roberts, Washington, 1994-2000; adj. prof. Georgetown U. Law Ctr., 1999—; sr. ptnr. Hale and Dorr LLP, Washington, 2000—. Co-author: Export and Trade Finance, 2d edit., 2000.

LEVITON, ALAN EDWARD, curator; b. N.Y.C., Jan. 11, 1930; s. David and Charlotte (Weber) L.; m. Gladys Ann Robertson, June 30, 1952; children: David A., Charlotte A. Student, NYU, 1948; AB, Stanford U., 1949, MA, 1953, PhD, 1960; postgrad., U. Nebr., 1954, Columbia U., 1948; student, U. Nebr., 1954. Asst. curator herpetology Calif. Acad. Scis., San Francisco, 1957—60, assoc. curator, 1960—61, chmn., curator, 1962—82, 1989—92, 2001—, curator, 1983—88, 1993—2000, chmn. computer svcs., 1983—92, editor sci. publs., 1994—; assoc. curator zool. collections Stanford U., 1962—63, lectr. biol. sci., 1963—70; professorial lectr. Golden Gate U., 1953—63; adj. prof. biol. sci. San Francisco State U., 1967—2000, rsch. prof., 2000—. Author: North American Amphibians, 1970, Reptiles of the Middle East, 1992, T.H. Hittel's California Academy of Sciences, 1997; contbr. articles to profl. jours. Grantee Am. Philos. Soc., 1960, NSF, 1960-61, 77-79, 80, 83-89, 91-93, 2002—, Belvedere Sci. Fund, 1958-59, 62; recipient Fellows' medal Calif. Acad. Scis., 1999. Fellow AAAS (coun. 1976-97, com. coun. affairs 1983-85, sec.-treas. Pacific divsn. 1975-79, exec. dir. 1980-98, 2000-2001, pres.-elect 1998, pres. 1999-2000), Calif. Acad. Scis., Geol. Soc. Am. (vice-chmn. history geology divsn. 1989-90, chmn. 1990-91); mem. Am. Soc. Ichthyologists and Herpetologists (mem. bd. govs. 1960-84), Soc. Systematic Zoology (sec.-treas. Pacific sect. 1970-72), Forum Historians of Sci. Am. (coord. com. 1986-88, sec.-treas. 1988-90), Herpetologists League (pres. 1961-62), History of Sci. Soc. Home: 571 Kingsley Ave Palo Alto CA 94301-3225 Office: Calif Acad Scis Golden Gate Park San Francisco CA 94118

LEVITT, B. BLAKE, medical and science writer; b. Bridgeport, Conn., Mar. 25, 1948; d. John Joseph and Beatrice Blake; m. Andrew Levitt, Dec. 20, 1968 (div. May 1977); m. Jon P. Garvey, Nov. 19, 1983. BA in English magna cum laude, BA in History summa cum laude, Quinnipiac Coll., 1972; postgrad., Yale U., 1988. Instr. English as fgn. lang. U. Khon Kaen, Thailand, 1968-69; market researcher Lyons Bakeries Ltd., London, summer 1971; traffic mgr., copywriter Provocatives Advt. Agy., Danbury, Conn., 1976-78; tech. writer tng. divsn. Jack Morton Prodns., N.Y.C., 1978-82; freelance feature and med. writer Litchfield County Times, New Milford, Conn., 1982-85, N.Y. Times, N.Y.C., 1985-89; freelance writer med. and sci. books, 1989—. Author: Electromagnetic Fields: A Consumer's Guide to the Issues and How to Protect Ourselves, 1995 (Will Solimene Book Award of Excellence 1996), 50 Essential Things to Do When the Doctor Says It's Infertiltiy, 1995; co-author: (with John R. Sussman M.D.) Before You Conceive, The Complete Pre-Pregnancy Guide, 1989 (Will Solimene Book Award of Excellence 1991); editor: Cell Towers-Wireless Convenience? or Environmental Hazard? Proceedings of the Cell Towers Forum, State of the Sci./State of the Law, 2001; contbr. articles to N.W. Hills Mag., New Eng. Monthly, Con. Mag. Founding mem., bd. dirs. Warren (Conn.) Land Trust, 1989-91, Lake Watch, Inc., Lake Watch Ednl. Inst., 1996—; trustee Berkshire-Litchfield Environ. Coun., 1999—; mem. Dem. Town Com., Warren, 1993—; vice chmn. zoning bd. appeals Town of Warren, 1993-95. Mem. Nat. Assn. Sci. Writers, Bioelectromagnetics Soc., N.Y. Acad. Scis., Am. Med. Writers Assn., Author's Guild, Author's League. Avocations: architectural design and renovation, reading, hiking, gardening.

LEVITT, GEORGE, retired chemist; b. Newburg, N.Y., Feb. 19, 1925; m. Julie Zeto; children: Barbara Klein, Jeffrey, David, Gregory. BS, Duquesne U., 1950, MS, 1952; PhD, Mich. State U., 1957. Rsch. chemist Exptl. Sta. E.I. du Pont de Nemours & Co., Inc., 1956—63, rsch. chemist Stine Lab., 1963—66, rsch. chemist Exptl. Sta., 1966—68, sr. rsch. chemist, 1968—80, rsch. assoc., 1981—86. Instr, Del. Tech. and C.C., 1975—80. Pres. Ronald McDonald House of Del, 1986—87, bd. dirs., 1986—94. Recipient Internat. pesticide rsch. award, Swiss Soc. Chem. Industries, 1982, award, Chesapeake chpt. Nat. Agrl. Mktg. Assn., 1987, disting. alumni award, Duquesne U. Coll. Arts and Sci., 1988, Nat. Medal of Tech., 1993, Disting. Inventor award, Intellectual Property Owners Am., 1983. Mem.: AAAS, Internat. Union Pure & Applied Chemistry, Am. Chem. Soc. (Creative Invention award 1989, Kenneth Spencer award 1991, internat. award for rsch. in agrochems. 1998, Hero of Chem. award 1999), Sigma Xi. Achievements include research in research in organic syntheses, herbicides, fungicides, medicinals, pesticides; synthesis of heterocyclic compounds; characterization and identification of novel organic compounds for biological evaluation; defined and optimized chemical structure-biological activity relationships and sulfonylurea herbicides. Home: 110 Downs Dr Greenville DE 19807-2556 E-mail: gleanr@msn.com.

LEVITT, GERALD STEVEN, engineering services executive; b. Bronx, N.Y., Mar. 21, 1944; s. Charles and Beatrice (Janet) L.; m. Natalie Lillian Hoppen; children: Mark, Roy. B in Mgmt. Engring., Rensselaer Poly. Inst., 1965; MBA, DePaul U., 1972. Registered profl. engr., Ill. Tech. rep. Worthington Air Conditioning Co., Ampere, N.J., 1965-67; indsl. sales engr. Peoples Gas Light & Coke Co., Chgo., 1967-71; planning specialist Peoples Gas Co., 1971-72; v.p. Stone & Webster Mgmt. Cons., Inc., N.Y.C., 1972-82; exec. v.p., chief staff officer South Jersey Gas Co., Folsom, N.J., 1982-98; v.p., CFO South Jersey Industries, Inc., 1987-98; sr. v.p., treas., CFO Greenhorne & O'Mara, Inc., Greenbelt, Md., 1998—. Past bd. dirs. Camden County coun. Boy Scouts Am., West Collingswood, N.J., Rowan Coll. Found. Mem. Greater Atlantic City C. of C. (past bd. dirs.), N.J. State C. of C. (past bd. dirs.). Office: Greenhorne & O'Mara Inc 9001 Edmonston Rd Greenbelt MD 20770-1083 E-mail: glevitt@g-and-o.com.

LEVITT, HARRY, speech and hearing scientist; b. Johannesburg, South Africa, May 19, 1937; came to U.S., 1964; s. Boris and Thelma (Kagan) L.; m. Eleanor Claire Sosnow, June 15, 1969 (dec. Sept. 2000); 1 child, David Avrum. BSc, U. Witwatersrand, Johannesburg, 1958; PhD, Imperial Coll. Sci. and Tech., London, 1964. Tech. staff mem. AT&T Bell Labs., Murray Hill, N.J., 1964-69; assoc. prof., prof., disting. prof. CUNY, 1969-2000. Cons. AT&T Bell Labs., 1980—, BBN, 1970—, Audimax, 1970—, various univs.; reviewer NIH, NSF, Office Edn., VA, 1970—. Sr. editor: Sensory Aids for Hearing Impaired, 1989; invited editor: Jour. Comm. Disorders, Jour. Rehab., Rsch. and Devel., 1980—; patentee in field; contbr. numerous articles to profl. jours. Beit fellow, 1960-63; fellow Acoustical Soc. Am., 1970, Am. Speech and Hearing Assn., 1980; recipient Nat. Winner for Computing to Aid the Handicapped Johns Hopkins, 1981, N.Y.C. Mayor's award for contbns. to sci. and tech., 1999, Lifetime Achievement award Am. Auditory Soc., 2001. Achievements include introducing computer assisted adaptive testing to the field of audiology; developed first digital hearing aid. Home: 998 Sea Eagle Loop Bodega Bay CA 94923-0610 Office: CUNY Grad Sch 365 5th Ave New York NY 10016-4334 E-mail: hlevitt@pon.net.

LEVITT, IRVING FRANCIS, investment company executive; b. Braddock, Pa., July 3, 1915; s. Charles and Frances (Goretsky) L.; m. Florence Chaikin, Oct. 10, 1937; children: Robert Bruce, Linda Ann (Mrs. Stanley L. Ehrenpreis). BS (hon.) in journalism, U. Mich., 1936. Advt. mgr. feature writer Braddock (Pa.) Free Press, 1936-37; advt. mgr. Levitt Bros. Furniture Stores, 1936-38, partner, exec. adminstr. stores in Pa., 1938-55; exec. asst., v.p. Levinson Steel Co., Pitts., 1942-44; real estate, indsl. devel., 1938-82; pres. Lepar, Inc., 1950-80; pres., chmn. bd. Union Screw & Mfg. Co., Pitts.; chmn. bd. Investment Capital Corp., 1955—, Radix Orgn., Inc., N.Y., Radix Real Estate, Inc., RRE Enterprises, Inc.; pres. Kirwan Heights Land Co., King Land Co., Ind., Blawnox Realty Co.; chmn. bd. Apollo Industries, Inc., 1959-68; chmn. bd., dir. Apollo Internat. Corp.; pres., dir. Apollo-Peru S.A., Oakland Investment Corp., Pitts.; v.p., dir. Apollo Indsl., Inc., Apollo Investment Co., Pitts.; sr. v.p. Parker-Levitt Corp., Sarasota, Fla., Marble Island, Inc., Vt.; ptnr. Oliver-Smithfield Venture, Pitts., Nineteen Hundred Group Ltd., Sarasota, Fla. Bd. dirs. Comml. Bank & Trust Co., Pitts., Nuclear Materials & Equipment Corp., Ednl. Audio Visual, Inc., N.Y., London, Radix Ventures, N.C., N.Y.; chmn. bd., dir. Lido Beach Devel. Co., Inc., Sarasota, Fla.; partner One Hundred Kennedy Ltd., Tampa, Fla., SMP, Ltd., Pine Run Devel., Inc., Sarasota; mem. Pitts. Bd. Realtors, New Kensington Indsl. Devel. Corp., Smaller Mfrs. Coun. Bd. dirs. Massanutten Mil. Acad., Woodstock, Va., United Jewish Fedn. Finance, Pitts., Irene Kaufman Settlement Bd.; trustee Levitt Found. Pitts., Rodef Shalom Temple, Pitts. Mem. Nat. Sales Execs. Club (dir. 1952-82), Am. Jewish Com. (nat. coun., nat. bd. govs.), Chautauqua Soc., Am. Arbitration Assn. (panel of arbitrators), Nat. Assn. Securities Dealers (bd. arbitration). Clubs: Westmoreland Country (Export, Pa.) (v.p. 1948-83); Metropolis Country (White Plains, N.Y.); Longboat Key Country; Marco Polo (N.Y.C.); Standard (Pitts.) (dir.), Pitts. Athletic Assn. (Pitts.); Belfry New Century (London); Univ. (Sarasota). Office: Investment Capital Corp 595 Bay Isles Rd Ste 120G Longboat Key FL 34228-3199 Fax: 941-387-9377.

LEVITT, ISRAEL MONROE, retired astronomer; b. Phila., Dec. 19, 1908; s. Joseph and Jennie (Marriner) L.; m. Alice Gross, July 3, 1937; children: Peter Leighton, Nancy Bambino. BSME, Drexel U., 1932, DSc, 1958; MA, U. Pa., 1937, PhD, 1948; DSc, Temple U., 1958, Phila. Coll. Pharmacy and Sci., 1963. Astronomer, Fels Planetarium of The Franklin Inst., Phila., 1934-39, asst. asso. dir., 1939-49, dir., 1949-72, v.p. inst., 1970-72; exec. dir. Phila. Mayor's Sci. and Tech. Adv. Council, 1972-93; ret., 1994. Sr. lectr. astronomy U. Pa., 1977; astronomer The Flower Obs., 1946-48; dir. (Sci. Council), 1953—; sci. cons. to City of Phila., 1956-2001; chmn. Air Pollution Control Bd. Phila., 1965-2001. Author: Precision Laboratory Manual, 1932, (with Roy K. Marshall) Star Maps for Beginners, 1942, Space Traveler's Guide to Mars, 1956, Target for Tomorrow, 1959, Exploring The Secrets of Space, 1963, (with Dandridge M. Cole) Beyond the Known Universe, 1974; developer NASA Spacemobile; inventor oxygen mask, pulse counting photoelectric photometer (with William Blitzstein); contbr. articles to profl. jours., mags.; columnist: internationally syndicated space & sci. column for Gen. Features. Recipient USN Ordnance Devel. award, 1945; Henry Grier Bryant gold medal Geog. Soc. Phila., 1962; Joseph Priestley award Spring Garden Inst., Phila., 1963; Writing award Aviation/Space Writers Assn., 1965; Samuel S. Fels Medal award, 1970; cert. of recognition and cash award NASA, 1977, Obermeyer cash award, 1992. Fellow AAAS (life), Am. Astronautical Soc., Brit. Interplanetary Soc.; mem. AIAA, Am. Astron. Soc., Rittenhouse Astron. Soc. (past pres.), Acad. Scis. Phila. (v.p. 1993), Nat. Assn. Sci. Writers, Aviation Writers Assn., Explorers Club, Pi Tau Sigma. Home: 3900 Ford Rd Apt 19D Philadelphia PA 19131-2036

LEVITT, JAREN, real estate corporation officer; b. N.Y.C., Mar. 19, 1946; s. Seymour and Harriet (Finorsky) L.; children: Jaden, Janna; m. Theresa Julyun Kim, Oct. 16, 1995. BS in Psychology and Biology, Syracuse U., 1965; MS in Clin. Psychology, U. Tex., 1967; PhD in Clin. Psychology, UCLA, 1974. Spl. asst Mayor's Office, N.Y.C., 1968-71, Pres. U.S., Washington, 1971; pres. Med. Cons. Internat., Woodland Hills, Calif., 1973-78; mktg. dir. vacation planning Playboy Internat., McAffe, N.J., 1978-80; regional mktg. dir. Gen. Devel. Co., Miami, Fla., 1981-88, asst. v.p., 1988, v.p. Cen. Region and Far East Norridge, Ill., 1988-90, pres. Am. Real Estate Devel. Corp. Fla.; pres. Global Acquisition and Devel. Corp., 1990-95, Stone Trend Internat., Inc., Sarasota, 1995—, owner, RoadWarriorTrading.com. Cons. substance abuse projects to bus. and fgn. govts., 1968-78. Contbr. articles to profl. jours. Mem. Heritage Found. Republican. Jewish. Avocations: scuba, skiing, sky-diving, tennis, flying. Office: 6244 Clark Center Ave Bldg 3 Sarasota FL 34238-2752 E-mail: thinkpad@msn.com., stonetrend@aol.com., jaren@roadwarriortrading.com.

LEVITT, JERRY DAVID, medical educator; b. Phila., Apr. 11, 1941; s. Abraham and Nettie (Dash) L.; m. Julie Meranze, June 2, 1967; children: Rachel, Daniel, Gabriel. BA, U. Pa., 1962, MD, 1966. Diplomate Am. Bd. Anesthesiology, Pain Mgmt.; lic. physician, Pa., Maine. Intern Mt. Sinai Hosp., N.Y.C., 1966—67; resident in anesthesia U. Pa. Hosp., Phila., 1967—69, rsch. fellow, 1971—72; instr. anesthesia U. Pa., 1972—73, asst. prof. anesthesia, 1973—82; assoc. prof. anesthesiology Med. Coll. Pa. Hahnemann Sch. Medicine, 1982—2002, Drexel U. Coll. of Medicine, Phila., 2002—. Author: (with others) Basic Pharmacology in Medicine, 1990; contbr. articles to profl. jours. With USPHS, 1969-71. Avocations: photography, sailing, music, motorcycles. Office: Hahnemann Univ Hosp Broad & Vine Sts Philadelphia PA 19102

LEVITT, JESSE, retired foreign language educator; b. N.Y.C., June 15, 1919; s. Louis and Mollie (Goldstein) L.; m. Selma Kojan, May 9, 1958; children: Vera Louise, Lorraine Elizabeth Levitt Katz. BA magna cum laude, CCNY, 1938; MA in French, Columbia U., 1940, PhD in Romance Philology, 1963. Translator, news wire editor U.S. Fgn. Broadcast Info. Svc., Washington, 1941-54; tchr. high sch. Balt., 1955-56; tchr. jr. high sch. Greenlawn, N.Y., 1956-57; tchr. French, Spanish, Latin Rye Neck High Sch., Mamaroneck, 1957-59; asst. prof. Wash. State U., Pullman, 1960-65; prof. fgn. langs. U. Bridgeport, Conn., 1965-89; ret., 1989. Tchr. French history, lit. and current worls history in sr. learning program, Bridgeport, Conn., 1999—. Author: The Grammaire des Grammaires of Girault Divivier, A Study of 19th Century French, 1968; co-editor: Geolinguistic Perspectives, 1987, Justice: Interdisciplinary and Global Perspectives, 1988, Language in Contemporary Soc., 1993, Constructed Languages and Language Construction, 1996, Language and Communication in the New Century, 1998; contbr. articles in linguistics, onomastics and French lit. to scholarly publs. Mem. MLA, Soc. Internat. de dialectologie et geolinguistique, Am. Soc. Geolinguistics (editor 1973-98, sec., editor internat. conf. 1992), Am. Name Soc., Simon Wiesenthal Ctr., Handgun Control Inc., Phi Beta Kappa. Democrat. Home: 485 Brooklawn Ave Fairfield CT 06432-1805

LEVITT, LEON, business administration educator; b. N.Y.C. s. Abraham and Anna (Kubit) L.; m. Esther Mayo, Mar. 7, 1943 (div. 1978); children: Daniel Mark, David Shelby, Alan Joel; m. Kathryn Mary Anderson, Apr. 22, 1978; children: Noah Abraham, Anna Martine. BA, NYU, 1947, MA, 1948, U. So. Calif., 1965, EdD, 1970. Cert. marriage, family and child counselor, Calif. Prof. English, psychology counselor L.A. Community Coll., 1963-65; asst. prof. edn. U. So. Calif., L.A., 1965-72; dean. continuing edn., prof. edn. and bus. adminstrn. Loyola Marymount U., 1972-84; prof. Madonna U., Livonia, Mich., 1984—, chmn. dept., 1984-91, sr. rsch. prof., 1991—98, prof. bus. ethics, 1998—. Contbr. articles to profl. jours. Mem. Ctr. for Volunteerism, Detroit; adv. com. United Community Svcs., Detroit, 1986-89. With USAF, 1942-45. Mem. Soc. Bus. Ethics, Acad. Mgmt., Phi Delta Kappa. Office: Madonna Coll 36600 Schoolcraft Rd Livonia MI 48150-1176

LEVITT, MARTIN LEE, library administrator, historian; b. Toms River, N.J., Nov. 2, 1953; s. Ben B. and Geraldine (Blumburg) L.; m. Cynthia J. Navarre, July 1, 1977 (div. 1996); children: Allison P., Rachael J. BA, Fla. State U., 1975; MA, Fla. Atlantic U., 1982; MLS, Fla. State U., 1986; PhD, Temple U., 1990. Cert. archivist. Assoc. libr. for adminstrn. Am. Philos. Soc., Phila., 1986—; prof. history Temple U., 1992—. Trustee David Library of Am. Revolution, Washington's Crossing, Pa., 2000-01, Balch Inst. for Ethnic Studies, Phila., 1995-2002, libr. oversight com., Historical Soc. of Pa.; mng. editor The Mendel Newsletter, Phila., 1992—; mem. selection com. Fulbright Found., 1996-98; mem. exam. devel. com. Acad. Cert. Archivists, 1997—, chmn. ACA Task Force on Archive Edn., 1999—, regent for exam. adminstrn., 2001—; mem. editl. adv. bd. Digital Image Archive of Eugenics; regent Acad. Cert. Archivists, 2001—. Contbr. articles to profl. jours. Fulbright fellow Fulbright/USIA, Eng., 1991-92, fellow David and Mary Eccles Ctr. for Am. Studies, 1992, Andrew W. Mellon sr. staff fellow Am. Philos. Assn., 2001. Mem. ALA, Soc. Am. Archivists (chair Archival Educator's Roundtable 1996-97), Nat. Coun. on Pub. History, Fulbright Assn., Orgn. of Am. Historians, Beta Phi Mu, Phi Alpha Theta. Office: Am Philos Soc 105 S Fifth St Philadelphia PA 19106-3386

LEVITT, MIRIAM, pediatrician; b. Lampertheim, Germany, June 10, 1946; came to U.S., 1948; d. Eli and Esther (Kingston) L.; m. Harvey Flisser, June 25, 1967; children: Adam, Elizabeth, Eric. AB, NYU, 1967; MD, Albert Einstein Coll. Medicine, Yeshiva U., 1971. Diplomate Am. Bd. Pediatrics. Intern Montefiore Med. Ctr., Bronx, N.Y., 1970-71, resident in pediatrics, 1971-73, attending pediatrician, 1975—; dir. outpatient svcs. pediatrics Bronx-Lebanon Hosp., N.Y.C., 1973-77; instr. pediatrics Albert Einstein Coll. Medicine, 1973-76, asst. prof. clin., 1976—; med. staff Lawrence Hosp., Bronxville, NY, 1978—, dir. pediatrics, 1988—, pres. med. staff, 2002—, mem. bd. govs., 2002—. Sch. physician Bronxville Bd. Edn., 1983—. Expert office profl. med. conduct N.Y. State Dept. Health, 1996—. Named Hon. Founder, Albert Einstein Coll. Medicine, 1995, hon. founder, 1995—. Fellow Am. Acad. Pediatrics; mem. Westchester County Med. Soc., Albert Einstein Coll. Medicine Alumni Assn. (nat. bd. govs. 1999—). Office: 1 Pondfield Rd Bronxville NY 10708-3706

LEVITT, MIRIAM, research scientist, educator; b. Milw., Jan. 16, 1949; d. Hiram and Ruth Levitt. BS, No. Ill. U., 1990, MA, 1992, PhD, 1996. Registered med. technologist. Med. technologist Reddy Meml. Hosp., Montreal, Que., Can., 1970-76, Miami Heart Inst., Miami Beach, Fla., 1976-80; rsch. specialist Yale U. Sch. Medicine, New Haven, 1981-83; med. technologist Camberra Labs., New Britain, 1983-85; rsch. specialist U. Ill. Coll. Medicine, Rockford, Ill., 1986-88; instr./rsch. assoc. No. Ill. U., DeKalb, 1991-96; prof. Ga. So. U., Statesboro, 1997-98, U. Cin., 1999—. Contbr. articles to profl. jours. Recipient NSF travel grant Am. Polit. Sci. Assn., 1994, German Marshall travel grant German Marshall Fund of U.S., 1994, Cmty. Svc. award Mid. Ga. divsn. March of Dimes Birth Defects Found., 1997, Cmty. Svc. award Greater Cin./No. Ky. divsn. March of Dimes Birth Defects Found., 2000. Mem. ASPA, Assn. Politics and Life Scis., Pi Alpha Alpha. Avocations: swimming, tennis. Home: 4343 Green Arbors Ln Cincinnati OH 45249 Office: Univ Cin PO Box 210375 Cincinnati OH 45221-0375 Fax: 513-556-2314. E-mail: Miriam.Levitt@uc.edu.

LEVITT, RAYMOND ELLIOT, civil engineering educator; b. Johannesburg, Republic of South Africa, Aug. 7, 1949; came to U.S., 1972; s. Barnard and Riva Eleanor (Lazarus) L.; m. Kathleen Adele Sullivan, Nov. 26, 1976; children: Benjamin John, Joanna Maurine, Zoë Ellen. BSCE, U. Witwatersrand, Johannesburg, 1971; MSCE, Stanford U., 1973, PhDCE, 1975. Project engr. Christiani & Neilsen, Cape Town, Republic of South Africa, 1971-72; asst. prof. civil engring. MIT, Cambridge, 1975-79, assoc. prof., 1979-80, Stanford (Calif.) U., 1980-88, prof., 1988—. Dir. Ctr. for Integrated Facility Engring.; mem. adv. bd. USBuild.com, Project Kiosk.com; dir. Design Power, Inc., Cupertino, Calif.; chmn. bd. Vite, Palo Alto, Calif.; advisor U.S. Dept. Labor, Washington, 1976-77, Calif. Pub. Utilities Commn., San Francisco, 1982-84. Co-author: Union and Open-Shop Construction, 1978, Construction Safety Management, 1987, 2d edit., 1993, Knowledge-Based Systems in Engineering, 1990. Pres. Stanford Homeowners Assn., 1981-83. Recipient Marksman award Engring. News Record, N.Y.C., 1985, Commitment to Life award Nat. Safe Workplace Inst., 1987. Mem. ASCE (Huber Prize award 1982, Computing Civil Engring. award 2000), INFORMS, Am. Assn. Artificial Intelligence, Project Mgmt. Inst. Unitarian Universalist. Avocations: swimming, trout fishing, music, surfing. Office: Stanford U Dept Civil Engring # 4020 Stanford CA 94305

LEVITT, ROBERT E. gastroenterologist; b. Phila., Oct. 22, 1948; s. Martin E. and Miriam G. (Elson) L.; m. Linda Levitt, Mar. 13, 1976; children: Adam, Ashley. BA summa cum laude, Temple U., 1970, MD, 1974. Diplomate Am. Bd. Internal Medicine, Am. Bd. Gastroenterology. Chief hepatology and gastrointestinal rsch. Presbyn. U. of Pa. Med. Ctr., Phila., 1979-88, staff gastroenterologist, 1979—, assoc. dir. Inst. Gastroenterology, 1981-89; chief svc. gastroenterology Bryn Mawr (Pa.) Hosp., 1985—, chief gastrointestinal sect. dept. medicine, 1988—, dir. endoscopy ste., 1988—; asst. prof. medicine

U. Pa. Sch. Medicine, 1979—; dir. endoscopy suite Bryn Mawr Hosp., 1988—. Clin. assoc. prof. medicine, Jefferson Med. Coll., Thomas Jefferson U., Phila. Contbr. articles to med. jours., chpts. to med. books; mem. editorial adv. bd. Post-Grad. Medicine. Fellow ACP; mem. AMA (Physicians Recognition award 1978, others), Am. Gastroenterol. Assn., Am. Coll. Gastroenterology, Am. Soc. for Gastrointestinal Endoscopy, Pa. Soc. Gastroenterology, Med. Club Phila., Phi Eta Sigma, Alpha Omega Alpha. Office: 933 E Haverford Rd Bryn Mawr PA 19010-3819

LEVITT, RONALD LARRY, public relations consulting executive, freelance writer/journalist; b. Mar. 23, 1931; s. Maurice and Pearl (Altman) L.; m. Geraldine Rita Wortsman, June 20, 1954; children: Lynn Barbara, Howard Jay. AB, U. Miami, 1956. Staff corr. UP, 1956-59; news dir., accounts supr. Mandell/Newman, 1959-60; pres. Ronald Levitt Assocs., Inc.; pub. rels. cons. Coral Gables, Fla., 1961-95; chmn. Levitt Pub. Rels. Group, 1996—. Asst. sec. of state State of Fla., 1978-81; lectr. pub. rels. colls. throughout U.S.; guest lectr. in field. Contbr. articles to mags. V.p. Miami Symphony; vice-chmn. Dade Cultural Affairs Coun., 1995-96; v.p. Lowe Art Mus., U. Miami; mem. exec. com. U. Miami Citizens Bd., 1994—; chmn. Coral Gables Internat. Affairs Commn., 1995—; chmn. Dade Cultural Alliance, 1998-99; pres. Coral Gables Sister Cities Program, 1997-2000; gubernatorial appointee Fla.-France Linkage Com., 1996—; exec. dir. Law Enforcement Officers Charitable Found., 2000-01. With USN, 1950-54. Recipient Dept. Def. award, 1953, svc. awards Pub. Rels. Soc. Am., 1966, 67, 68, 69. Mem.: Soc. Profl. Journalists (Fla. sec. 2001—02), U. Miami Citizens Bd. (exec. com. 1986—), Miami Internat. Press Club (sec. 1998, pres. 1999—2002), Internat. Pub. Rels. Assn., Internat. Assn. Bus. Communicators, Fla. Pub. Rels. Assn., Am. Assn. Polit. Cons., Internat. Platform Assn., Pub. Rels. Soc. Am. (pres. Fla. 1966, chmn. S.E. dist. 1968—70, Royal Palm award for pub. svc. 1997), U. Miami Alumni Assn. (Maxie award for cmty. svc. 1999), European-Am. C. of C. (pres. 1996—), French-Am. C. of C. (sec.-treas. 1986—88, pres. 1988—96), Cascade Club (Vail, Colo.), Weston Hills Country Club, Bankers Club, Progress Club of Miami (pres. 1988), U. Miami Hurricane Club. E-mail: ron@levittgroup.com.

LEVITT, SEYMOUR HERBERT, physician, radiology educator; b. Chgo., July 18, 1928; s. Nathan E. Levitt and Margaret (Chizever) D.; m. Phillis Jeanne Martin, Oct. 31, 1952 (div. Oct. 1981); children: Mary Jeanne, Jennifer Gaye, Scott Hayden; m. Solveig I. Ostberg, Feb. 6, 1983. BA, U. Colo., 1950, MD, 1954, DSc (hon.), 1997. Diplomate Am. Bd. Radiology. Intern Phila. Gen. Hosp., 1954-55; resident in radiology U. Calif. at San Francisco Med. Center, 1957-61; instr. radiation therapy U. Mich., Ann Arbor, 1961-62, U. Rochester, N.Y., 1962-63; asso. prof. radiology U. Okla., Oklahoma City, 1963-66; prof. radiology, chmn. div. radiotherapy Med. Coll. Va., Richmond, 1966-70; prof., head dept. therapeutic radiology U. Minn., Mpls., 1970—. Cons. in field. Exec. bd. Am. Joint Com. for End Result Reporting and Cancer Staging; com. radiation oncology studies Nat. Cancer Inst.; trustee Am. Bd. Radiology, 1977-89; bd. dirs. Found. for Rsch. and Edn.; fgn. adj. prof. Karolinska Inst., Stockholm, 2002. Bd. dirs., mem. exec. com. Am. Cancer Soc., 1990-95. With M.C., AUS, 1955-57. Recipient Disting. Svc. award U. Colo., 1988. Fellow: Am. Coll. Radiology (bd. chancellors, Gold medal 1995); mem.: Am. Soc. Therapeutic Radiologists (exec. bd. 1974—78, pres. 1978—79, chmn. bd. 1979—80, Gold medal 1991), Am. Soc. Clin. Oncology, Soc. Nuclear Medicine, Internat. Soc. Radiation Oncology (pres. 1981—85), Soc. Chmn. Acad. Radiation Oncology Programs (pres. 1974—76), German Soc. Radiation Oncology (hon.), European Cong. Radiology (hon.), German Soc. Radiology (hon.), Am. Roentgen Ray Soc., Am. Cancer Soc. (pres. Minn. divsn. 1979—80, nat. bd., exec. com.), Am. Assn. Cancer Rsch., Radiol. Soc. N.Am. (bd. dirs. 1991—2000, chmn. bd. dirs. 1997—98, pres.-elect 1998, pres. 1999—), Am. Radium Soc. (sec. 1981—83, pres. 1983—84, Janeway medal 1989), Alpha Omega Alpha, Sigma Xi, Phi Beta Kappa. Home: 7233 Lewis Ridge Pkwy Minneapolis MN 55439-1933 Office: U Minn Med Sch PO MMC 436 Minneapolis MN 55455

LEVITT, SIDNEY BERNARD, lawyer; b. Bklyn., Mar. 23, 1920; s. Abraham and Becky (Turetsky) L.; m. Lillian Cohen, June 18, 1950; children: Kenneth Ross, Jeffrey Alan. BA, Bklyn. Coll., 1942; LLB, Bklyn. Law Sch., 1948, JD, 1967; LLM in Labor Law, NYU, 1953. Bar: N.Y. 1949, U.S. Dist. Ct. (ea. and so. dists.) N.Y., U.S. Tax Ct., U.S. Supreme Ct. Pvt. practice law, Seagate, N.Y. Small claims arbitrator N.Y. Civil Ct. Active Boy Scouts Am., Planning Bd.; instr. ARC. Capt. U.S. Army, 1942-46. Mem. Bklyn. Bar Assn., Jewish War Vets. USA, Knights Pythias. Republican. Jewish. Office: 4310 Beach 43d St Seagate NY 11224-1032

LEVITT, STEPHAN HILLYER, indologist; b. Bklyn., Feb. 9, 1943; s. Abraham and Ida (Harlick) L. BA in Anthropology, Columbia U., 1964; PhD in Oriental Studies, U. Pa., 1973. Cataloguer of Indic MSS U. Pa. Libr., Phila., 1971-72; rsch. asst. U. Pa., 1972-74; vis. asst. prof. anthropology U. Denver, 1974-76; tutor English dept. Queensborough C.C., N.Y.C., 1977-78; cons. U. Pa. Libr., 1978—, Ctr. Judaic Studies, U. Pa. (formerly Annenberg Rsch. Inst.), Phila., 1978—, Burke Libr. Union Theol. Seminary, N.Y.C. Contbr. articles to profl. jours. Recipient Am. Coun. Learned Socs. fellowship, 1967, Am. Inst. Indian Studies Travel-Study award, 1974, U. Denver Faculty Rsch. grant, 1975. Mem. Am. Oriental Soc., The Asiatic Soc., Bhandarkar Oriental Rsch. Inst., Friends of the Libr. U. Pa. Jewish. Avocation: stamp collecting. Home: 144-30 78th Rd Apt 1H Flushing NY 11367-3572

LEVITZ, I. S. artist, educator, curator; b. Bklyn., Aug. 24, 1943; d. Irving Jacob and Mary (Matts) Steiner; m. Martin N. Levitz, June 19, 1965; children: Robin, David, Jodi. Student, Vesper George Sch. Art, Boston, Hartford Art Sch., Trinity Coll., Hartford, Wesleyan U., Middletown, Conn. Artist-in-residence Brandeis U. Women's Commn.,1994. Juried exhibits include Mattatuck Mus. "Conn. Vision", 1992, Silvermine Guild, Norwalk, Conn., 1983, New Britain Mus. Am. Art, 1982, 85, 87, 90, Conn. Acad. Fine Arts, 1988-91, 95, 96, Three Women Artists - Chase Freedom Gallery, Hartford Jewish Ctr., 1994, Women in the Arts, Wave Gallery, New Haven, 1995, Yale-New Haven Hosp. The Arts in Health Care, 1995. Vol. Toys for Tots, Bloomfield, 1989-92; active Hartford Arts Coun., 1976; chmn. Ann Randall Arts Com., 1978-80. Recipient Purchase award Town of Bloomfield, 1991. Mem. West Hartford Art League (chmn. selection com. for exhbns. 1983-84), Conn. Watercolor Soc.(mem.), Conn. Acad. Fine Arts (bd. dirs. 1995-96), New Britain Mus. Am. Art. Avocations: hiking, skiing, ice skating, travel, family. Home: 1328 Asylum Ave Hartford CT 06105-6001

LEVITZ, JOHN BLASE, investment management consultant; b. Miami, Fla., June 4, 1956; s. John Robert and Barbara Jean (Schwab) L.; m. Mayra Aleida Lopez, Mar. 31, 1990. BA, Fla. State U., 1978; MBA with honors, Barry U., 1993. Cert. fund specialist; cert. investment mgmt. analyst. V.p., investment cons. Levitz Electric Co., Inc., Miami, 1979-86; v.p., retirement plan investment cons. S.E. Fla. Electric, Inc., 1986-90; pres., chief investment officer Levitz Investment Mgmt., Inc., 1991-94; investment cons. Smith Barney, Coral Springs, Fla., 1994—. Mem. Investment Mgmt. Cons. Assn., Inst. Cert. Fund Specialists, Barry Univ. Alumni Assn. (bd. dirs.). Office: 3111 N University Dr Ste 900 Coral Springs FL 33065-5061

LEVITZ, PAUL ELLIOT, publishing executive; b. Bklyn., Oct. 21, 1956; s. Alfred Lazarus and Hannah (Brenner) L.; m. Jeanette Francine Cusimano, Nov. 2, 1980; children: Nicole, Philip, Garret. Student, N.Y. U., 1973-76. Editor, pub. The Comic Reader, Bklyn., 1971-73; writer, asst. editor Nat. Periodical Publs., Inc., N.Y.C., 1973-76; editor, editorial coordinator, writer DC Comics, 1976-80, mgr. bus. affairs, 1980-82, v.p. ops., 1982-84, exec. v.p., 1984-89, exec. v.p., pub., 1989—2002, MAD mag., 1993—; pres. & publ. DC Comics, 2002—. Jewish. Home: 23 Stony Hollow Rd Chappaqua NY 10514-2014 Office: DC Comics 1700 Broadway New York NY 10019-5905 E-mail: paul.levitz@warnerbros.com.

LEVITZKY, MICHAEL GORDON, physiology educator, researcher; b. Elizabeth, N.J., Jan. 3, 1947; s. Edward and Shirley (Worfman) L.; m. Ellen Marie De Roxtro, June 27, 1969 (div. Dec. 18, 1984); m. Elizabeth Gouaux, Mar. 13, 1985; children: Edward Benjamin, Sarah Elizabeth. BA, U. Pa., 1969; PhD, Albany Med. Coll., 1975. Physiology instr. Albany (N.Y.) Med. Coll., 1974-75; asst. prof. physiology La. State U. Health Scis. Ctr., New Orleans, 1975-80, assoc. prof. physiology, 1980-85, prof. physiology, 1985—, prof. anesthesiology, 1991—. Adj. prof. pediats. Tulane U. Sch. Medicine, New Orleans, 1990—, adj. prof. physiology, 1991—; dir. basic sci. curriculum La. State U. Med. Sch., 1998—. Author: Pulmonary Physiology, 5th edit., 1999; co-author: Cardiopulmonary Physiology in Anesthesiology, 1997, Introduction to Respiratory Care, 1990. Grantee NIH, 1976-78, 78-86. Mem. Am. Physiol. Soc. (edn. com. 1988-91, Arthur C. Guyton Tchr. of Yr. 1998), Am. Thoracic Soc., Coun. Sci. Editors, N.Y. Acad. Scis., Soc. for Exptl. Biology and Medicine, Sigma Xi. Office: La State U Health Scis Ctr 1901 Perdido St New Orleans LA 70112-1393 E-mail: mlevit@lsuhsc.edu.

LEVNER, LOUIS JULES, contract administrator; b. N.Y.C., Feb. 10, 1951; s. Carl and Hilda (Moses) L.; m. Efrat Zohar. BS in Aero. Adminstrn., Parks Coll., 1973; MS in Contract and Acquisition Mgmt., Fla. Inst. Tech., 1993. Sales engr. Israel Aircraft Industries, Ltd., Tel Aviv, Israel, 1979-82; contract adminstr. Tadiran, Ltd., Holon, Israel, 1982-85; aircraft specification engr. Lockheed Ga. Co., Marietta, Ga., 1985-87; sr. subcontract adminstr. AAI Corp., Hunt Valley, Md., 1987-90; sr. contracts adminstr. Diversified Internat. Scis. Corp., Lanham, 1990-93; cons. Comsys, 1994-95; dir. contracts Comm. Systems Tech., Inc., Columbia, Md., 1995-2000; mgr. contract adminstrn. InfoEdge Tech., Inc., Arlington, Va., 2000—. Mem. Nat. Contract Mgmt. Assn. (cert.), Alpha Eta Rho. Avocations: flying, restoring antique aircraft. Home: 14 Windy Meadow Ct Randallstown MD 21133-4346 Office: Ste 1450 1101 Wilson Bvld Arlington VA 22209

LEVOVITZ, PESACH ZECHARIAH, rabbi; b. Poland, Sept. 15, 1922; came to U.S., 1923; s. Reuben and Leah Zlate (Kustanowitz) L.; m. Bluma D. Feder, Feb. 5, 1945 (dec. 1970); children: Sivya, Yaakov; m. Eleanore Herman Klugmann, 1972 (dec. Nov. 1980); children: Maurice, Danny, Renee, Jackie; m. Frayde Twersky Perlow, Dec. 18, 1989; stepchildren: Yitzchok, Faige, Joseph. BA, Yeshivah U., 1942. Rabbi Mesivtha Tifereth Jerusalem Rabbinical Sem., 1943, Congregation Sons of Israel, Lakewood, N.J., 1944—; founder, 1945; since dean Bezalel Day Sch.; Pres. Rabbinical Council Am., 1966-68, chmn. commn. on internat. affairs, 1972; asso. chmn. Soviet Jewry commn., 1980. Mem. exec. com. Synagogue Council Am., 1953— ; standing com. Conf. European Rabbis and Asso. Rabbis, 1964— ; steering com. World Conf. Ashkenazi and Sephardi Synagogues; Co chmn. rabbinic cabinet Bonds for Israel, 1972; chaplain Lakewood Police Dept., 1950— ; vis. chaplain Naval Air Sta., Lakehurst, N.J., 1945— ; nat. chmn. ann. conv. Rabbinical Council of Am., 1971; v.p. Religious Zionists Am., 1974; nat. chmn. Vaad Haroshi Religious Zionists Am., 1975; pres. Beth Din of Am., 1986; chmn. internat. conf. Rabinnical Coun. Am., 1966. Mem. adv. bd. Lakewood Housing Council, Nat. Community Relations Adv. Council, United Jewish Appeal; chmn. bd. Sons of Israel Sr. Citizens Housing Inc., 1980; mem. N.J. Drug Utilization Council.; chmn. adv. council on protection kosher legislation to Atty. Gen., State of N.J.; mem. exec. Ocean County Jewish Fedn., 1988, chmn. Jewish Family and Children Svc., 1997; co-chmn. Blue Ribbon Panel Lakewood Twp., 1992—; apptd. Jewish chaplain Vis. Nurses Assn. Ctrl. N.J. Hospice Program, 2000. Recipient Revel Meml. award in religion and religious edn. Yeshivah Coll. Alumni Assn., 1967; award for outstanding rabbinic leadership Union of Orthodox Jewish Congregations Am., 1969; Nat. Assn. Hebrew Day Schs., 1980; chief Rabbi Issas Halevi Herzog Torah Fellowship award Religious Zionists Am., 1972; chmn. nat. conv., 1974; named Rabbi of Yr., Israel Bond Orgn., 1991. Mem. Conf. Presidents Nat. Jewish Orgns., Am. Conf. Soviet Jewry, Vis. Nurses Assn. (spiritual counselor 2000). Home: 403 6th St Lakewood NJ 08701-2705 Office: Congregation Sons of Israel Madison Ave Lakewood NJ 08701

LEVOW, JUDITH L(EE) HOLTZ (JUDI LEVOW), interior designer; b. Boston, Sept. 27, 1933; d. Morris and Bertha Holtz; m. Barry Levow, Feb. 22, 1955 (dec. Aug. 1988); children: Faye Elizabeth, Lawrence Nathan. Student, Colby Coll., 1951-53, various colls., 1967-73; BSW, Regis Coll., 1977; MSW, Boston U., 1978; postgrad., Chamberlayne Coll., 1983-84. Social worker Madonna Hall, Marlboro, Mass., 1980-82; interior designer Levow Interiors, Weston, 1983—2001; CEO Levow Inc., 1988-98; interior designer Judi Design, Lake Worth, Fla., 2001—. (featured in Boston Globe Sunday Home sect., photographed by Better Homes & Gardens). Formerly active Mass. Assn. Children with Learning Disabilities, founder, pres., 1962—72; active numerous C.C. and ch. orgns., 1985—. Mem.: NASW, Internat. Furnishings and Design Assn. Avocations: golf, swimming, cooking, bridge. Home and Office: 9666 Thormina St Lake Worth FL 33467

LEVOY, MYRON, author; b. N.Y.C., Jan. 30, 1930; s. Bernard and Elsie (Schwartz) L.; m. Beatrice Fleischer, Jan. 27, 1952; children: David, Deborah. BS in Chem. Engring., CCNY, 1952; MS in Chem. Engring., Purdue U., 1953. Engr. Pratt & Whitney Aircraft Co., East Hartford, Conn., 1953-56; project engr. Reaction Motors Inc., Rockaway, N.J., 1956-67; engr. specialist Polytech. Design, Livingston, 1973-81; writer, 1955—. Author: (novel) A Necktie in Greenwich Village, 1968, Penny Tunes and Princesses, 1972, The Witch of Fourth Street and Other Stories, 1972 (Book World Honor Book, 1972, Children's Book Showcase award, 1973), Alan and Naomi, 1977 (Boston Globe-Horn Book award, Honor Book, 1978, Jane Addams Honor Book award, 1978, Nat. Book award finalist, 1980, Silver Pencil award The Netherlands, 1981, Austrian State prize for children's lit, 1981, German State prize for young adult lit., 1982, Buxtenhuder Bulle award Fed. Republic Germany, 1982), A Shadow Like a Leopard, 1981 (ALA Best Book for Young Adults, 1981), Three Friends, 1984, The Hanukkah of Great-Uncle Otto, 1984, Pictures of Adam, 1986 (ALA Best Book for young adults, 1986, Internat. Reading Assn. young adult choice, 1986), The Magic Hat of Mortimer Wintergreen, 1988 (Jr. Lit. Guild selection, 1988), Kelly 'N' Me, 1992, poetry and plays; contbr. Mem. PEN, The Authors Guild, The Dramatists Guild. Jewish. Avocations: tennis, cross-country skiing, swimming, museums, films. Office: Writers House Inc 21 W 26th St New York NY 10010-1003

LEVY, ALAN JOSEPH, editor, journalist, writer; b. N.Y.C., Feb. 10, 1932; s. Meyer and Frances (Shield) L.; m. Valerie Wladaver, Aug. 7, 1956; children: Monica, Erika AB, Brown U., 1952; MS in Journalism, Columbia U., 1953. Reporter Louisville Courier-Jour., 1953-60; free-lance writer Life, Sat. Eve. Post, N.Y. Times, others, 1960-91; investigator Carnegie Commn. Ednl. TV, Boston, 1966-67; fgn. corr. Life, N.Y. Times mags., Prague, Czechoslovakia, 1967-71; freelance author, dramatist, corr. Vienna, 1971-90; dramaturg Vienna's English Theatre, 1977-82; founding editor in chief The Prague Post (Eng. language weekly newspaper), 1991—. Lectr. on theatre Salzburg Seminar in Am. Studies, Austria, 1981; adj. prof. lit. and journalism Webster U., Vienna, 1983-95; lectr.-in-residence Gritti Palace, Venice, Italy, 1987; prof. non-fiction Ctrl. European U. Summer Seminars, Prague, 1994, Charles U. Summer Writers' Workshop, Prague, 1996—; internat. juror, Slow Food Award, Bra, Italy, 2001. Author: Draftee's Confidential Guide, 1957, 2d edit., 1966, Operation Elvis, 1960, The Elizabeth Taylor Story, 1961, Wanted: Nazi Criminals at Large, 1962, Interpret Your Dreams, 1962, 2d edit., 1975, Kind-Hearted Tiger, 1964, The Culture Vultures, 1968, God Bless You Real Good, 1969, Rowboat to Prague, 1972, 2d edit. titled So Many Heroes, 1980, Good Men Still Live, 1974 (Czech publ. 2001), The Bluebird of Happiness, 1976, Forever, Sophia, 1979, 2d edit., 1986, Treasures of the Vatican Collections, 1983, Ezra Pound: the Voice of Silence, 1983, W.H. Auden: In the Autumn of the Age of Anxiety, 1983, Vladimir Nabokov: The Velvet Butterfly, 1984, Ezra Pound: A Jewish View, 1988, The Wiesenthal File, U.K. edit. 1993, U.S. edit. 1994 (U.S. Author of the Year Am. Soc. of Journ. and Authors, 1995), An American Jew in Vienna, 2000; dramatist The World of Ruth Draper, 1982; librettist Just an Accident?, 1983 (Ernst Krenek prize City of Vienna, 1986). Trustee Thomas Nast Found., Landau, Germany, 1978—, Saving Our Heritage Assn., Oberdorf, Switzerland, 1994—. With U.S. Army, 1953-55. Recipient New Republic Younger Writer award, 1958, Best Enterprise Reporting award Sigma Delta Chi, 1959, Golden Johann Strauss medal City of Vienna, 1981, travel writing awards Pacific Area Travel Assn., 1978, Govt. of Malta, 1985, Franz Kafka medal European Franz Kafka Circle, Prague, 1996, T.G. Masaryk medal Masaryk Acad. of the Arts, Prague, 1996, Jan Masaryk Gratias Agit prize Czech Republic Fgn. Ministry, 1999; Bernard De Voto fellow Middlebury Coll., 1963. Mem. PEN, Am. Soc. Journalists and Authors, Authors Guild and Dramatists Guild of Authors League of Am., Overseas Press Club Am., Austrian Soc. Authors, Composers and Music Pubs., Czech Union Journalists. Democrat. Jewish. Office: Alicka Pistek Nicholas Ellison Lit Agy 55 Fifth Ave 15th Fl New York NY 10003 Address: The Prague Post Stepanska 20 CZ-11000 Prague 1 Czech Republic E-mail: alevy@praguepost.cz.

LEVY, ALAN RICHARD, television executive; b. Miami, Fla., Sept. 26, 1957; s. Samuel and Helen Barbara (Kurtz) L. BS, Fla. State U., 1979. Freelance cameraman, Miami, 1979-80; staff cameraman Sta. WPBT-TV, 1980-84, producer, dir., 1984-87; ind. producer, dir., 1987—. Lighting cons. Bar Shabatai Prodns., Miami, 1986—; dir. numerous commls., music videos and indsl. films. Prodr.(dir., writer): (TV films) Ovation: The Rythym of Brick, Mortar and Stone; author (screenwriter, dir): (TV films) The Great Voice, 1985, The Bee That Stung Comtel, 1991; dir.: (TV series) Front Row Center, 1986; (TV films, Spl.) Sneakers, 1987 (3 Emmy awards, Fla. Emmy Best Dir. award, 1988); (TV films) Andrew: A Movie in the Making, 1993 (Emmy award, 1993); prodr.: Songs for Fun, 1994 (Emmy award, 1994), Family Aids Quiz, 1994 (Emmy award, 1994), (dir.) Shopping the Net, 1996 (Emmy award, 1996); author: (TV films) Two Pianos: One Passion, 1996 (Emmy award, Telly award, 1996); prodr.(dir): (TV films) World Bus. Rev. with Caspar Weinberger and Gen. Alexander Haig (4 Telly awards, 2 Aegis awards), Ordinary People: Extraordinary Deeds (2 Telly awards), Making Memoirs (Telly award). Named Eagle Scout Boy Scouts Am., Miami, 1974. Mem. NATAS, Am. Film Inst. Jewish. Avocations: bicycling, backpaking, playing music. E-mail: bshabata1@aol.com.

LEVY, ALAN DAVID, real estate executive; b. St. Louis, July 19, 1938; s. I. Jack and Natalie (Yawitz) L.; m. Abby Jane Markowitz, May 12, 1968; children: Jennifer Lynn, Jacqueline Claire. Grad., Sch. Real Estate Washington U., 1960. Property mgr. Solon Gershman Inc. Realtors, Clayton, Mo., 1958-61; gen. mgr. Kodner Constrn. Co., St. Louis, 1961-63; regional mgr. Tishman Realty & Constrn. Co., Inc., N.Y.C., 1963-69; v.p. L.A., 1969-77; exec. v.p., dir. Tishman West Mgmt. Corp., 1977—88; pres. Tishman West Cos., 1988-92; chmn. Tishman Internat. Cos., 1993—. Guest lectr. on real estate mgmt. to various forums. Contbr. articles on property mgmt. to trade jours. Mem. L.A. County Mus. Art; former chmn. Am. Art Coun.; trustee Archives Am. Art, Harvard-Westlake Sch.; bd. govs. W.L.A. coun. Boy Scouts Am., Cedars-Sinai Med. Ctr.; bd. councillors USC Sch. of Social Work. Bryant fellow Met. Mus. of Art. Mem. Bldg. Owners and Mgrs. Assn., L.A. (bd. dirs.), N.J. (co-founder, hon. dir.), Inst. Real Estate Mgmt. (cert. property mgr.), Urban Land Inst., Internat. Coun. Shopping Ctrs. Office: 10900 Wilshire Blvd Ste 510 Los Angeles CA 90024-6533

LEVY, ALAN JOSEPH, mechanical engineering educator, researcher; b. N.Y.C., Oct. 30, 1955; s. Marvin Joshua and Nettie (Freund) L.; m. Janice Salpeter, June 23, 1991. BS, SUNY-Buffalo, 1977; MS, Columbia U., 1979, MPhil, 1981, PhD, 1982. Computer aide Kingsborough C.C., Bklyn., 1977-78; teaching asst. Columbia U., N.Y.C., 1978-81; assoc. prof. Syracuse U., 1982—; rsch. fellow U.S. Army Summer Faculty, 1987, 88. Recipient Outstanding Young Man of Am. award, 1983. Mem. ASME (svc. cert. 1985, 86), Soc. Indsl. and Applied Math., Am. Acad. Mechanics, Sigma Xi, Pi Tau Sigma (Outstanding Mech. Engr. Prof. award 1990). Jewish. Avocations: basketball, camping, reading. Office: Syracuse U Dept Mech Engring 127 Link Hl Syracuse NY 13244-0001

LEVY, ALAN M. lawyer; b. Milw., Nov. 10, 1940; s. Sam and Emma (Gold) L.; m. Tee Gee Azine, Mar. 3, 1964; children: Shawn, Joshua, Pamela, Jonathan. AB, U. Chgo., 1963, JD, 1965. Bar: Wis. 1965, Ill. 1982, U.S. Ct. Appeals (2d, 5th, 6th, 7th, 8th, 9th and 10th cirs.) 1968, U.S. Dist. Ct. (ea. dist.) Wis. 1965, (no. dist.) Ill. 1982, (so. dist.) Ill. 1969, U.S. Supreme Ct. 1980, U.S. Dist. Ct. (we. dist.) Mich. 2001. Ptnr. Goldberg, Previant, Uelman, Gratz, Miller et al, Milw., 1965-82; sr. legal counsel, dir. plan devel./compliance Central States, S.E. and S.W. Areas Pension Fund, Chgo., 1982-85; assoc. O'Neil, Cannon & Hollman, S.C., Milw., 1985-91, Lindner & Marsack, S.C., Milw., 1991—. Bd. incorporators Commonwealth Mutual Savs. Bank, Milw., 1977-82; adj. prof. labor law U. Wis., Milw., 1974—. Contbr. articles to profl. jours. Chmn. U. Chgo. Alumni Schs. Com., Milw., 1987—; trustee Congregation Emanu-El B'Ne Jeshurun, Milw., 1978-82, 86-92; campaign co-chmn. Urban Day Sch., Milw., 1988; active ACLU, Milw., 1966-82. Named Page scholar, U. Chgo., 1961, Iron Mask, 1961-64. Mem. ABA (labor law sect. 1967—), Wis. Bar Assn. (labor law sect. chmn. 1979-80), Ill. Bar Assn., Iron Mask Soc., U. Chgo. Alumni Assn. of Milw. (chmn. 1996-98), U. Chgo. Alumni Assn. (bd. govs. 1998—, v.p. 2002--). Office: Lindner & Marsack SC 411 E Wisconsin Ave Ste 1000 Milwaukee WI 53202-4416 E-mail: alan.levy2@gte.net., alevy@lindner-marsack.com. *Notable cases include: Phillips vs. Alaska HERE Pension Fund, 11 EBC 1929 W.D. Wash., 1989, which involved class action regarding eligibility criteria as structural defect in a multiemployer pension fund; I-Mark Industries, Inc., et al vs. Arthur Young & Co., et al, 148 Wis. 2d 605, 436 N.W. 2d 311, 1989, which involved third party borrower's liability to plaintiff lender for malpractice by defendant acct.; Teamster's Local 348 Health and Welfare Fund, et al vs. Kohn Beverage Co., 749 F. 2d 315 6th Cir., 1984, which involved the enforcement of benefit fund contribution obligations regardless of union activity; Loran W. Robbins, et al vs. The Pepsi-Cola Met. Bottling Co., et al, 7 EBC 2033 N.D. Ill, 1986, which involved the withdrawal liability obligations to multiemployer pension fund; Wardle vs. Cen. States, S.E. and S.W. Areas Pension Fund, 627 F. 2d 820 7th Cir., 1980, which involved the right to jury trial and standard of rev. in pension benefit claim; Inland Trucking Co. vs. NLRB, 440 F. 2d 562 7th Cir., 1971, which involved the use of replacement employees during a single employer lock-out.*

LEVY, ALBERT, family physician; b. Stanleyville, Congo, Nov. 8, 1948; came to U.S., 1977; s. Moise and Eugenie J. (Menache) L.; children: Antonia G., Eric M. MD, Fed. U. Brazil, Rio de Janeiro, 1973, MS in Field Medicine, 1976. Diplomate Am. Bd. Family Physicians, Am. Bd. Family Practice, Am. Bd. Geriatric Medicine. Chief family medicine sect. Our Lady of Mercy Hosp., Bronx, N.Y., 1989-96; pvt. practice family medicine Manhattan Family Practice, N.Y.C., 1990—; physician Montefiore Med. Ctr., Bronx, 1994—; asst. clin. prof. dept. family medicine Albert Einstein Coll. Medicine, N.Y., 1994—; asst. prof. N.Y. Med. Coll., Valhalla, 1994—; asst. prof. medicine Mt. Sinai Sch. Medicine, 1999—. With Beth Israel Med. Ctr., 1986, St. Luke's/Roosevelt Med. Ctr., 1986, Lenox Hill Hosp., 1995, Mt. Sinai Med. Ctr., 1999. Fellow Am. Acad. Family Physicians, Royal Soc. Medicine, (Eng.), N.Y. Acad. Medicine; mem. AMA, Am. Geriatric Soc., World Orgn. Nat. Colls./Acads. Family Physicians, N.Y. Acad. Scis., Med. Soc. State of N.Y., N.Y. County Acad. Family Physicians (v.p. 1992), Soc. Tchrs. Family Medicine. Jewish. Avocations: tennis, opera, travel, wind surfing. Home: 311 Wilton Rd Westport CT 06880-1426 also: 25 Sutton Pl S New York NY 10022-2441 Office: Manhattan Family Practice 911 Park Ave New York NY 10021-0337

LEVY, ARNOLD S(TUART), real estate company executive; b. Chgo., Mar. 15, 1941; s. Roy and Esther (Scheff) L.; m. Eva Cichosz, Aug. 8, 1976; children: Adam, Rachel, Deborah. BS, U. Wis., 1963; MPA, Roosevelt U., 1970. Dir. Neighborhood Youth Corps, Chgo., 1966-68; v.p. Social Planning Assn., 1968-70; planning dir. Office of Mayor, 1970-74; dep. dir. Mayor's Office Manpower, 1974-75; sr. v.p. Urban Investment & Devel. Co., 1975-93; pres., CEO Stone-Levy, LLC, 1994—. Mem. S-L Hospitality Group, LLC, 1995—; pres. JMB/Urban Hotels, Hotel and Resort Devel. Group, JMB/Urban Devel. Co., 1985-93; bd. dirs. Hostmark Mgmt. Group, Inc.; mem. Urban Land Inst. Pres. Ark, Chgo., 1970-72, Parental Stress Svcs., Chgo., 1978-79; past lectr. DePaul U., Roosevelt U., Loyola U.; v.p. Inst. Urban Life, Chgo., 1983—. Co-editor: The Professionals' Guide to Commercial Property Development, 1988. Bd. dirs. Mus. Broadcast Comms., Am. Shalom; pres. Ill. Humane Soc.; steering com. Radio Hall of Fame; chmn. Spertus Inst. Jewish Studies, Glencoe Plan Commn.; v.p. Inst. of Urban Life. Mem.: Twin Orchard Club, Glen Club, Carlton Club (Chgo.). Home: 535 Park Ave Glencoe IL 60022-1501 Office: Stone-Levy LLC 630 Dundee Rd Ste 220 Northbrook IL 60062-2750 E-mail: alevy@stonelevy.com.

LEVY, ARTHUR JAMES, public relations executive, writer; b. Bklyn., Dec. 23, 1947; s. Bernard and Bernice (Lipner) L.; m. Andrea Susan Hall, May 11, 1980; children: Zoe Jess, Jake Benjamin. BA, Brandeis U., 1969. Account exec., disc jockey Sta. WBUS-FM, Miami Beach, Fla., 1971; pop music critic Magic Bus Newspaper, 1971; sr. editor, writer Zoo World mag., Ft. Lauderdale, Fla., 1971-74; chief writer Atlantic Records, N.Y.C., 1975-78; assoc. dir. Press and Pub. Info. dept. Columbia Records, 1978-88, nat. dir. media services, publicity dept., 1988-93; v.p. Sony Music Entertainment Comms. Dept., 1993-95. So. regional v.p. Rock Writers of the World, 1973-74; seminar panelist United Jazz Coalition, N.Y.C., 1983—, CMJ Folk, 1987—, New

Music Seminar Folk, 1989—; ind. music publicity cons., writer, 1995—; prodr. (ann. concert series) A Klezmer Rave, 1997-98. Writer, rschr. album and video liner notes for Sammy Davis, Jr., Rolling Stones, Eric Andersen, Johnny Cash, Herbie Mann, Taj Mahal, Al Kooper, Robert Johnson, Jan Hammer, Julio Iglesias, Joan Baez, Manfred Mann, Jimmy Webb, Pete Seeger, Burl Ives, Montreux Festival '77, Elvis Presley: Golden Celebration, 1985 (Grammy nomination), Songs of the Civil War, Iggy Pop; appeared on album session (Finnadar Records) Idil Biret's New Line Piano, 1978, (Columbia) Jaroslav Jakubovic's Checkin' In, 1978, Sony Music 100 Years: Soundtrack For A Century (Folk, Gospel and Blues) (Grammy nomination), 1999. Named Publicist of Yr. Columbia Records, 1982, 87, Media Man of Yr. Record World mag., N.Y.C., 1981. Mem. NARAS (gov. N.Y. chpt., Grammy voting com., Liner Notes com.), Rock and Roll Hall of Fame (nominating com., mus. experts com.), Nat. Acad. Popular Music. Avocation: record collecting. Fax: 718-601-1399. E-mail: mortedart@aol.com.

LEVY, BERN, communications executive, optical applications consultant; b. Oct. 28, 1929; m. Anne Marilyn King, June 22, 1958; children: Leah, Janna, Matthew. AA, Fairleigh Dickinson U., 1950. Cinematographer Sta. WKNY-TV, Kingston, N.Y., 1953-56, Sta. WNBC-TV, West Hartford, Conn., 1956-59, United Aircraft Rsch. Lab., East Hartford, 1959-65; mktg. mgr. Radiant-Pathé, Morton Grove, Ill., 1965-68, Angenieux Corp. Am., Bohemia, N.Y., 1968-84; cons. Bern Levy Assocs., Northport, 1984—. Cons. Insight Vision Systems, Gt. Britain, 1985-86, Tamron Optics, Port Washington, N.Y., 1985-86, Cinema Products Corp., L.A., 1984—, Century Precision Optics, L.A., 1984—. Author: (indsl. photography) Cine Lens Glossary, 1973, A Guide to Depth-of-Field/Field-of-View for 16mm Cine Lenses, 1974, Getting Closer with Diopter Lens Attachments, 1987, (video systems) Lens Reality, 1987, (broadcast mgmt., engring.) Lenses: Maintaining Your Image, 1987; co-author: American Cine Manual. Home and Office: 21 Whippoorwill Ln Palmyra VA 22963-2252

LEVY, DANIEL, economics educator; b. Tschakaia, Georgian Republic, Georgia, Nov. 13, 1957; came to U.S., 1983; s. Shabtai and Simha (Leviashvili) L.; m. M. Sarit Adler, Spet. 10, 1981; children: Avihai, Eliav. BA, Ben-Gurion U., Beer-Sheva, Israel, 1982; MA, U. Calif., Irvine, 1989, PhD, 1990. Lectr. U. Minn., Mpls., 1983-88, St. Olaf Coll., Northfield, Minn., 1986-88, The Coll. St. Catherine, St. Paul, 1987-88; prof. Pepperdine U., Irvine, 1989-90, U. Calif., Irvine, 1990-91, Union Coll., Schenectady, N.Y., 1991-92, Emory U., Atlanta, 1992—, Bar-Ilan U., 1999—. Computer software programmer Mac Cartuli, 1989. Contbr. articles to profl. jours. Treas. Minn. Student Orgn., 1984-85. Mem. Am. Econ. Assn., Soc. Econ. Dynamics and Control, Econometric Soc., Western Econ. Assn., Mensa. Avocations: basketball, tennis, chess, computers, piano. Office: Emory U Dept Economics Atlanta GA 30322-0001 E-mail: econdl@emory.edu., levyda@mail.biu.ac.il.

LEVY, DAVID, retired lawyer, insurance company executive; b. Bridgeport, Conn., Aug. 3, 1932; s. Aaron and Rachel (Goldman) L. BS in Econs., U. Pa., 1954; JD, Yale U., 1957. Bar: Conn. 1958, U.S. Supreme Ct. 1963, D.C. 1964, Mass. 1965, N.Y. 1971, Pa. 1972; CPA, Conn. Acct. Arthur Andersen & Co., N.Y.C., 1957-59; sole practice Bridgeport, 1959-60; specialist tax law IRS, Washington, 1960-64; counsel State Mut. Life Ins. Co., Worcester, Mass., 1964-70; assoc. gen. counsel taxation Penn Mut. Life Ins. Co., Phila., 1971-81; sole practice Washington, 1982-87; v.p., tax counsel Pacific Life Ins. Co., Newport Beach, Calif., 1987-2001; ret., 2001. Author: (with others) Life Insurance Company Tax Series, Bureau National Affairs Tax Management Income Tax, 1970-71. Mem. adv. bd. Tax Mgmt., Washington, 1975-90, Hartford Inst. on Ins. Taxation, 1990-97; bd. dirs. Citizens Plan E Orgn., Worcester, 1966-70. With AUS, 1957. Mem. ABA (vice-chmn. employee benefits com. 1980-86, ins. cos. com. 1984-86, torts and ins. practice sect., subcom. chair ins. cos. com. tax sect. 1994—), Assn. Life Ins. Counsel, AICPA, Beta Alpha Psi. Jewish.

LEVY, DAVID ALFRED, immunology educator, physician, scientist; b. Washington, Aug. 27, 1930; s. Stanley A. and Blanche B. (Berman) L.; m. Annette Levy-Badoux; children: Jill, William, Stanley. BS, U. Md., 1952, MD, 1954. Diplomate Am. Bd. Internal Medicine, Am. Bd. Allergy and Immunology. Intern, resident in medicine U. Hosp., Balt., 1954-59; physician VA Hosp., 1961-62; fellow dept. microbiology Sch. Medicine Johns Hopkins U., 1962-66, asst. prof. radiol. sci. Sch. Hygiene and Pub. Health, 1966-68, assoc. prof., 1968-71, prof. radiol. sci. and epidemiology, 1972-73, prof. biochemistry, 1973-82, with joint appointments in epidemiology and medicine, 1973-82, in pathobiology, 1980-82, prof. immunology and infectious diseases, 1982-86. Mem. FDA Panel on Rev. of Allergenic Extracts, 1975-83; mem. allergy and immunology rev. com. Nat. Inst. Allergy and Infectious Diseases, 1975-77; adj. dir. Centre d'Immunologie et de Biologie, Pierre Fabre, S.A., 1985-90; cons. to pharm. industry, 1990—. Editorial bd. Clin. Immunology and Immunopathology, 1971-76, Revue d'Allergologie Française; clin. reviews in Allergy and Immunology. contbr. articles to med. jours. and books. Clin. rsch. Centre d'Allergie, Hopital Tenon, Paris, 1991—. With U.S. Army, 1959-61. Fellow Am. Acad. Allergy and Immunology; mem. Internat. Union Immunol. Socs. (vice chmn. allergen standardization subcom. 1980-83), Am. Assn. Immunologists, French Soc. Allergology, European Acad. Allergology and Clin. Immunology, Sigma Xi. Home and Office: 11 Quai St Michel 75005 Paris France E-mail: dalevy@wanadoo.fr.

LEVY, DAVID CORCOS, museum director; b. N.Y.C., Apr. 10, 1938; s. Edgar Wolf and Lucille (Corcos) L.; m. Janet Meyer, June 7, 1959 (div.); children: Jessica Anne, Thomas William; m. Carole L. Feld, May 19, 1992; 1 child, Alexander Wolf. BA, Columbia U., 1960; MA, NYU, 1969, PhD, 1979; DFA (hon.), New Sch. for Social Rsch., 1989, Cedar Crest Coll., 1998. Asst. dir. admissions Parson Sch. Design, N.Y.C., 1961-62, dir. admissions, 1962-67, v.p., 1967-70, dean, chief adminstrv. officer, 1970-79, exec. dean, chief adminstrv. officer, 1979-89; chancellor New Sch. for Social Rsch., 1989-90; pres., dir. The Corcoran Gallery of Art, Washington, 1991—. Photographer of works exhibited in Guggenheim Mus., Mus. Modern Art; art dir. jours., books, posters; contbr. articles to jours. and newspapers. Decorated Chevalier des Arts et des Lettres (France). Home: 2556 Massachusetts Ave NW Washington DC 20008-2822 Office: Corcoran Gallery of Art 500 17th St NW Washington DC 20006-4804*

LEVY, DAVID LAWRENCE, lawyer, legal association administrator; b. N.Y.C., Nov. 7, 1936; s. Arthur Morgan and Shirley (Lanz) L.; 1 child from previous marriage, Justin; m. Virginia Carey, May, 1974 (div. 1980); m. Ellen Dublin, Dec., 1984; 1 child, Diana. BA, U. Fla., 1958, JD, 1961. Bar: D.C. 1968, U.S. Supreme Ct. 1983. Lawyer U.S. Copyright Office, Libr. Congress, Washington, 1962-69, 77-97, ret., 1997; co-founder, pres., CEO Children's Rights Coun., 1985—. Author: Potomac Conspiracy, 1976; editor: The Best Parent Is Both Parents, 1993; editor-in-chief student newspaper, U. Fla., 1957-58 (recipient awards). Chmn. Students for Kennedy for Pres., 1959, 60. Recipient Civic award Prince George's County (Md.) Civic Fedn., 1989, Disting. Svc. to Children award Parents Without Ptnrs. Internat., 1996, Lifelong Achievement award for untiring efforts on behalf of children U.S. Fed. Child Support Office, 2000, Svc. to Children award N.J. Coun. for Children's Rights, 2000. Mem.: Stepfamily Assn. Am. (bd. dirs.), U.S. Supreme Ct. Bar, D.C. Bar Assn. Jewish. Office: Children's Rights Coun 6200 Editors Park Drive Ste 103 Hyattsville MD 20782

LEVY, DAVID WALTON, music educator; b. Orlando, Fla., Aug. 18, 1972; s. David Walton Cramp, Coleen Victoria Fallarino; m. Heather Leanne Leverence, Nov. 28, 1998. BMus in Jazz Studies, U. North Fla., 1994; MA in Music Edn., U. Ctrl. Fla., 2000. Cert. music K-12 Fla. Dept. Edn. Tchr. elem. music Ridgewood Park Sch., Orlando, Fla., 1996—98, Chickasaw Sch., Orlando, 1998—. East area elem. music team leader Orange County Pub. Schs., Orlando, 2000—; pvt. woodwinds instr., Orlando, 1994—. Chmn. bd. edn. Zion Luth. Ch., Gotha, Fla., 1999—. Named Elem. Tchr. of the Yr., Chickasaw Elem. Sch., 2001, Disney Teacherrific, Walt Disney World Co., 2001; scholar Am. Music scholar, U. N. Fla., 1990—94. Mem.: NEA, Fla. Elem. Music Educators Assn., Music Educators Nat. Conf. Lutheran. Avocations: puzzles, reading, jazz performance and composition. Home: 633 Harbor Villa Ct Clermont FL 34711

LEVY, DELORES JANE, artist; b. Superior, Wis., Nov. 15, 1928; d. Henry George and Emma (Guthmiller) Gross; m. Donald Jerome Levy, Apr. 14, 1953; children: Jane, Nancy, Kenneth, Laura. BS, Wis. State U., 1949; postgrad., Art Inst. Chgo., 1950. Tchr. Abner Baker Elem. Sch., Ft. Morgan, Colo., 1949-50; teller Bank Am., L.A., 1950-51; tchr. Lodi (Calif.) High Sch., 1951-54, 77-82, chmn. creative arts dept., 1978-79; instr. art San Joaquin Delta Evening Coll., Stockton, Calif., 1972-78. Art reviewer Stockton Record, 1980-82; portrait artist state and county fairs, festivals, cruise ships Island Princess and Stardancer. Represented in permanent collections San Joaquin County Mus., Lodi Meml. Hosp.; continuous group exhibitions include Lodi (Calif.) Art Ctr.; commd. portraits include Comdr. Dorance Ochs, USN; numerous pvt. collections. Past pres. Lodi Art Ctr. Mem. Nat. League Am. Pen Women, Nat. Mus. Women in Arts (charter), San Joaquin County Hist. Mus. Home: 93 Madera Dr Lodi CA 95240-0713

LEVY, DENA CHRISTINE, television producer, director; b. Woodland Hills, Calif., Sept. 28, 1965; d. Stanley Gerald and Deanna Marie (Coury) L.; children: Lonna Weber, Dena Levy. BA in Journalism, U. So. Calif., 1986. Profl. tennis player Women's Tennis Assn., USTA, 1986-88; prodr., dir. Two-D Prodns., Hollywood, Calif., 1989—. Recipient Best Documercial award Nat. Infomercial Mktg. Assn., 1994. Avocations: tennis, golf, skiing, softball. Office: 4714 Park Olivo Calabasas CA 91302-1733 Fax: 818 222 0589.

LEVY, DONALD HARRIS, chemistry educator; b. Youngstown, Ohio, June 30, 1939; s. Gabriel and Minnie (Lerner) L.; m. Susan Louise Miller, June 14, 1964; children— Jonathan G., Michael A., Alexander B. BA, Harvard U., 1961; PhD, U. Calif.-Berkeley, 1965. Asst. prof. chemistry U. Chgo., 1967-74, assoc. prof., 1974-78, prof., 1978—, chmn. dept. chemistry, 1983-85, Ralph and Mary Otis Isham prof., 1994-97, Albert A. Michelson Dist. Svc. prof., 1997—. Mem. chemistry adv. com. NSF; Lady Davis vis. prof. The Technion, Haifa, Israel, 1998. Assoc. editor Jour. Chem. Physics, 1983-98; editor Jour. Chem. Physics, 1998—. Fellow AAAS, Am. Phys. Soc. (Plyler prize 1987), Optical Soc. Am. (Ellis A. Lippencott award 2000—); mem. Am. Chem. Soc., Am. Acad. Arts and Scis., Nat. Acad. Scis. Office: U Chgo Dept Chemistry 5640 S Ellis Ave Chicago IL 60637-1433 E-mail: levy@silly.uchicago.edu.

LEVY, EDWARD CHARLES, JR. manufacturing company executive; b. Detroit, Nov. 14, 1931; s. Edward Charles and Pauline (Birndorf) Levy; 2 children. SB, MIT, 1952. From staff to exec. v.p. Edward C. Levy Co., Detroit, 1952-70, pres., 1970—. Bd. dirs. Edward C. Levy Found., Karmanos Cancer Inst., Detroit, Round Table of Christians and Jews, Mackinac Ctr. for Pub. Policy; trustee Children's Hosp. of Mich., Citizens Rsch. Coun. Mich., Washington Inst. for Near East Policy; officer Am. Israel Pub. Affairs Com. Mem. ASTM, Am. Concrete Inst., Engring. Soc. Detroit, Detroit Club, Renaissance Club, Franklin Hills Country Club. Jewish. Office: Edward C Levy Co Inc 8800 Dix St Detroit MI 48209-1096

LEVY, EZRA CESAR, aerospace scientist, real estate broker; b. Habana, Cuba, Sept. 22, 1924; s. Mayer D and Rachel Levy; m. Margot Webb, 2000; children from previous marriage: Daniel M, Diana M Levy Friedman, Linda R Levy Brenden. MS, UCLA, 1951. Sect. head Douglas Aircraft Co., Santa Monica, Calif., 1951—54; dept. head Lockheed Aircraft Co., Van Nuys, 1954—56, Librascope, Glendale, 1956—57, Radioplane, Van Nuys, 1957—58; asst. dept. mgr. Space Tech. Labs., Redondo Beach, Calif., 1958—60; asst. divsn. dir. TRW, 1960—74; now real estate broker, owner Jaunty Real Estate, Valencia, 1984—. Researcher EKG analysis Heart Research Found, 1953—68; spec traffic consult South Bay Cities, 1960—65. Author: (book) Laplace Transform Tables, 1958, Selling Your Property?, 1995, Sample Contractual (Real Estate) Terms, 1996, A Glossary of Real Estate Terms, 1998, A Glossary of Real Estate Terms, 2d ed, 2000, Masonry in Los Angeles Silver Trowel Lodge, 2001; contbr. articles to profl jours. With U.S. Army, 1944—46. Mem.: Temple City C. of C. (bd. dirs. 1992—97, pres. 2000—01), Eastern Star (past patron), Masons (past master and sec.). Democrat. Jewish. Avocations: art, music, philately. Home and Office: 24688-A Brighton Dr Valencia CA 91355

LEVY, GERALD DUN, nonprofit organization administrator; b. N.Y.C., May 11, 1924; s. Robert Louis and Beatrice (Straus) L.; m. Marion Fennelly, Dec. 27, 1952; children: Alison, Elizabeth, Robert. BS, Harvard U., 1945, MBA, 1947. From asst. buyer to mdse. v.p. R.H. Macy & Co. Inc., N.Y.C., 1947-73; v.p. Roosevelt Hosp., 1973-77; assoc. exec. dir. Vis. Nurse Svc., 1977-81; various mgmt. positions to pres. edn. group, bd. dirs. Nat. Exec. Svc. Corps, 1981—. Chmn. bd. World Edn., Inc., Boston, 1980-95; vice chmn. bd. U.S Com. for UNICEF, N.Y.C., 1975-85; v.p. bd. dirs. N.Y. Heart Assn., N.Y.C., 1975-85; vice chmn. bd. Fund for Peace, 1990—. 1st lt. field arty. U.S. Army, 1943-46, ETO. Avocations: fly fishing, gardening, reading, tennis. Home: 333 E 68th St New York NY 10021-5693 Office: Nat Exec Svc Corps 120 Wall St New York NY 10005

LEVY, H. RICHARD, biochemistry educator; b. Leipzig, Germany, Oct. 22, 1929; came to U.S., 1946; s. Berthold and Charlotte Agnes Hedwig (Frank) L.; m. Betty Louise Samuels, June 12, 1960; 1 child, Karen. BSc in Chemistry, Rutgers U., 1950; PhD in Biochemistry, U. Chgo., 1956. Instr. Ben May Lab. for Cancer Rsch., U. Chgo., 1959-61, asst. prof., 1961-63; asst. prof. dept. bacteriology and botany Syracuse (N.Y.) U., 1963-66, assoc. prof. dept. bacteriology and botany, 1966-70, assoc. prof. dept. biology, 1970-71, prof. of biochemistry, 1971-2000, chmn. dept. biology, 1993-99, prof. emeritus, 2000—. Contbr. articles and revs. to profl. publs. Grantee NIH, NSF, 1963-99. Mem. AAAS, AAUP, Am. Chem. Soc., Am. Soc. for Biochemistry and Molecular Biology, Protein Soc. Home: 604 Scott Ave Syracuse NY 13224-2132 Personal E-mail: rlevy1@twcny.rr.com. Business E-Mail: hrlevy@syr.edu.

LEVY, HAROLD DAVID, psycholinguist; b. Rochester, N.Y., Aug. 25, 1938; s. Barnet Lewis and Ada Sylvia (Zimmerman) L.; m. Jan Patricia Schwartz, Mar. 3, 1959 (div. 1961); 1 child; m. Natalie Miller, Nov. 27, 1969 (div. 1982); 1 child; m. Judy Weiner, Sept. 9, 1987. BS in Gen. Studies, U. Rochester, 1969, MA in Edn., 1971. Permanent cert. to teach French, grades 7-12. Sociotherapist Convalescent Hosp. for Children, Rochester, 1971-72; tutor spl. edn. City Sch. Dist., 1973-83; editor, ednl. dir. Operaton Friendship, 1983-88; pvt. tutor home and social agencies, 1982-91; vol. and activities asst. therapist Genesee Hosp., 1983-93. Dramatics instr. Hochstein Music Sch., Rochester, 1972; lang. tchr. Harley Sch. and Talmudical Inst. Upstate N.Y., 1974-75. Author: Forced Categories: A Taxonomy for Languages, 1971, Languages: Their Common Elements, 1990, Language Learning by Slices, 1990, Linguistics: The Binary System, 1990, Psycholinguistic Interpretation of Names as Language Field Universals, 1995, Lexical Transformations: The Brain's Code, 1996, The Psycholinguistic Development of Terminal Information Systems, 1997; contbr. articles to sci. jours. Avocations: jazz piano, mental health education, nutrition. Home: 111 East Ave Apt 719 Rochester NY 14604-2542

LEVY, HAROLD JAMES, physician, psychiatrist; b. Buffalo, Feb. 15, 1925; s. Sidney Harold and Evelyn (Sperling) L.; m. Arlyne Adelstein, July 3, 1958; children: Sanford Harvey, Richard Alan, Kenneth Lee. MD, U. Buffalo, 1946. Diplomate in psychiatry Am. Bd. Neurology and Psychiatry. Intern Erie County Med. Ctr., Buffalo, 1946-47, asst. resident in psychiatry, 1947-48, asst. chief psychiatry, 1953-58, attending psychiatrist, 1957-90, cons. psychiatrist, 1990—; fellow in psychosomatic medicine Med. Sch. U. Buffalo, Erie County Med. Ctr., 1950-53; psychiatrist Buffalo, 1950—; mem. courtesy staff Millard Fillmore Hosp., 1957, clin. asst., 1958, asst. attending physician, 1959-63, assoc. attending physician, 1963-64, attending physician, 1964-90, chmn. dept. psychiatry, 1968-90, cons., 1990—. Attending psychiatrist BryLin Psychiat. Hosp. (formerly Linwood Bryant Hosp.), Buffalo, 1955—, clin. dir. psychiatry, 1966-91; staff psychiatrist Psychiat. Clinic, Family Ct. Erie County, N.Y., 1959-63, psychiat. dir. clinic, 1963-80; mem. courtesy staff in psychiatry St. Joseph's Intercommunity Hosp., Buffalo, 1969-71, cons. in psychiatry, 1971—; cons. in psychiatry St. Francis Hosp., 1972-91, Sisters of Charity Hosp., 1985—; asst. in psychiatry Med. Sch. SUNY, Buffalo, 1950-52, instr. 1952-55, assoc. 1955-70, clin. asst. prof. 1970-86, clin. assoc. prof., 1986—; mem. psychiat. staff Rosa Coplon Jewish Home and Infirmary, 1957-72, chmn. dept. psychiatry, 1969-72; staff psychiatrist Chronic Disease Rsch. Inst., sect. on alcoholism Med. Sch. SUNY, Buffalo, 1950-53; psychiat. cons. Dent Clinic Found. Millard Fillmore Hosp., 1967—, Lafayette Gen. Hosp., Buffalo, 1973-85. Pres. Lemezo Enterprises Inc., Buffalo, 1970, Sanricken Enterprises Inc., Buffalo, 1970—; mem. exec. com. Blue Shield Western N.Y.; treas. LKLWL Properties., 1998—. Served to capt. M.C., AUS, 1948-50, Korea. Fellow Am. Psychiat. Assn. (life, pres. Western N.Y. dist. br. 1969-70), Am. Soc. Psychoanalytic Physicians, Am. Soc. Advancement Electrotherapy; mem. AMA, Israel Med. Assn., N.Y. State Med. Soc., Erie County Med. Soc. (chmn. com. on mental health, econs. com., publ. com. for bull. 1959-78), Buffalo Acad. Medicine, Maimonides Med. Soc. (pres. 1968-69), N.Y. State Soc. Med. Rsch., Western N.Y. Neuropsychiat. Soc. (pres.-elect 1965-66), Western N.Y. Psychiat. Assn. (pres. 1974-75), Gen. Alumni Assn. SUNY, Buffalo (treas. exec. bd. 1967-69, numerous offices), SUNY-Buffalo Sch. Medicine Alumni Assn. (past pres., numerous offices), Med. Students' Aid Soc. (past nat. pres., chmn. bd. dirs. 1990-92), B'nai B'rith (exec. com. Anti Defamation League), Cherry Hill Colf and Country Club, Alpha Omega Alpha, Phi Lambda Kappa (nat. dir., past nat. v.p., past nat. pres., chmn. bd. dirs. 1990-92), Beta Sigma Rho. Home: 47 Longleat Dr Buffalo NY 14226-4114 Office: Psychiat Assocs of Western NY 2740 Main St Buffalo NY 14214-1702

LEVY, IRA HOWARD, marketing professional, real estate investor; b. N.Y.C., Dec. 28, 1937; s. Samuel B. and Ada Levy. Student, UCLA, 1956-58. Sr. v.p. corp. creative mktg. Esteé Lauder Cos., 1961-91; co-owner Sta. WKZE-AM-FM, Conn.; co-founder Conifer Ptnrs., Salisbury. Cons. Origins divsn. Estee Lauder, C.F. Hathaway and Co., Gen. Cigar Co., Inc., others. Former chmn. Contemporary Arts Coun., Mus. Modern Art, N.Y.C.; bd. dirs. emeritus Pilobolus Dance Col.; mem. Coun. Advisors, Coll. of the Atlantic, Maine; mem. exec. com. bd. trustees Sharon Hosp., Conn.; mem. coun. design excellence Coll. Arch., Ariz. State U. Avocations: sailing, cross country skiing. Home: Deer Run Salisbury CT 06068 Office: Conifer Ptnrs 2A Main St Salisbury CT 06068-1800

LEVY, JEROME, dermatologist, retired naval officer; b. Bklyn., Aug. 17, 1926; s. Alexander and Pauline (Wollkof) L.; m. Leona Elsie Eligator, June 6, 1948; children: Andrew B., Eric J., Peter C., David J. Student, Wesleyan U., 1944-45, postgrad., 1952-54; AB, Yale U., 1947, MD, Albany Med. Coll., 1958. Diplomate Am. Bd. Dermatology. Commd. ensign USN, M.C., 1957, advanced through grades to capt., 1972; intern U.S. Naval Hosp., Newport, R.I., 1958-59, resident Phila., 1960-62, U. Pa. Grad. Sch. Medicine, Phila., 1962-63, chief dept. dermatology Memphis, 1963-67, Yokosuka, Japan, 1967-70, Long Beach, Calif., 1974-75; head outpatient dermatology clinic San Diego Naval Hosp., 1970-72; sr. med. officer Keflavik, Iceland, 1972-74; ret., 1975; med. dir. dermatology Westwood Pharm. Co., Buffalo, 1975-82; acting chief dermatology dept. Buffalo Gen. Hosp., 1981-82; practice medicine specializing in dermatology Coronado, Calif., 1982-90. Cons. Erie County Health Dept., 1979-82; clin. assoc. prof. SUNY, Buffalo Med. Sch., 1980-82. Contbr. articles to med. jours. and popular mags. Decorated Navy Commendation medal Joint Svc. Commendation medal; Knight's Cross of the Order of Falcon (Iceland). Fellow ACP, Am. Acad. Dermatology; mem. AMA, So. Med. Assn., Assn. Mil. Surgeons, U.S. Navy League, City Club San Diego, Alpha Omega Alpha. Democrat. Jewish. Home: 3352 Lucinda St San Diego CA 92106-2932 E-mail: zitzapper@aya.yale.edu.

LEVY, JOSEPH, lawyer; b. N.Y.C., June 9, 1928; s. Morris Joseph and Dora (Cohen) L.; m. Gertrud C. Roeder, Jan. 20, 1967; children— Diana N., Susan R. BBA cum laude, CCNY, 1950; JD cum laude, NYU, 1954. Bar: N.Y. 1955, D.C. 1968. Assoc. Parker, Chapin and Flattau, N.Y.C., 1954-62; ptnr. firm Rivkin, Sherman & Levy (and predecessors), 1962-84, Schnader, Harrison, Segal & Lewis, 1984-93; v.p., sec., dir. Trecom Bus. Sys., Inc., Edison, N.J., 1993-97. Sec., dir. Horizons Comms. Corp., 1970-78, Quad Typographers, Inc., 1965-79; sec. Savin Bus. Machines Corp., 1959-84, On-Line Systems, Inc., 1968-78, Lambda Tech., Inc., 1970-78, Programming Methods, Inc., 1969-72, Kreisler Mfg. Cor., 1969-72, Peck & Peck, 1970-73, v.p., sec., dir. Trecom Bus. Systems, Inc., 1985-97, Business Edge Solutions, Inc., Edison, N.J., 1999—. Served to capt. AUS, 1951-53. Home: 254 University Way Paramus NJ 07652-5516

LEVY, JOSEPH BRUNO, foundation administrator, educator; b. Milan, Nov. 8, 1930; arrived in Argentina, 1957; s. Moise Joseph and Alice Levy; m. Suzanne Eskenazi, June 12, 1956 (div. 1965); children: Andrew David, Alexandra Alice. BSc, Manchester (Eng.) U., 1950, 51, 52; MS, U. Mass., 1954; MA, Princeton (N.J.) U., 1956, PhD, 1957; fellow, Textile Inst., Manchester, 1958. Chartered textile technologist. Dir. Du Pont Argentina, Buenos Aires, 1957-75, 81-87; gen. dir. Du Pont Italiana, Milan, 1976-78; group dir. Du Pont Mex., Mexico City, 1979-80; pres. Internat. Human Ecology Found., Buenos Aires, 1990—. Contbr. articles to profl. jours. Mem. N.Y. Acad. Sci., Sci. and Med. Network, Soc. for Sci. Exploration, Sigma Xi. Jewish. Avocations: trout fishing, golf, travel, physics, cooking. Home: Libertador 356 (1001) Buenos Aires Argentina Office: Triar SA Cordoba 950 (1054) Buenos Aires Argentina

LEVY, JOSEPH WILLIAM, department stores executive; b. Fresno, Calif., 1932; m. Sharon Sorokin; children: Felicia, Jody, Bret. BS, U. So. Calif., 1954. Asst. merchandising mgr., then mgr. Gottschalks, Inc., Fresno, 1956-72, exec. v.p., 1972-82, chmn., chief exec. officer, 1982—. Chmn. exec. com. Frederick Atkins Inc., N.Y.C., 1992—, also bd. dirs. Chmn. Fresno Econ. Devel. Corp., 1982-83; mem. Calif. Transp. Commn., 1983-91, chmn., 1986-87; sec. City of Fresno Equipment Corp.; mem. bus. adv. coun. Sch. Bus. and Adminstrv. Scis., Calif. State U., Fresno; trustee Community Hosps. Cen. Calif. With USNR, 1950-58. Mem. Calif. C. of C. (bd. dirs.), Fresno County and City C. of C. (transp. com.), U. So. Calif. Sch. Bus. Alumni Assn., San Joaquin Country Club, U. Sequoia-Sunnyside Country Club, Downtown Club (Fresno). Home: 6475 N Sequoia Dr Fresno CA 93711-1232 Office: Gottschalks Inc PO Box 28920 Fresno CA 93729-8920

LEVY, KENNETH, music educator; b. N.Y.C., Feb. 26, 1927; s. Meyer and Sylvia Levy; m. Clara Brooks Emmons, Jan. 25, 1956; children: Robert Brooks, Helen Gardner. AB, Queens Coll., 1947; M.F.A., Princeton U., 1949, PhD, 1956. Instr. music Princeton (N.J.) U., 1952-54; from asst. prof. to Fredrick R. Mann. prof. Brandeis U., Waltham, Mass., 1954-66; prof. music Princeton U., 1966—, chmn. dept. music., 1967-70, 88, Scheide prof. music history, 1988-95. Author: Music: A Listener's Introduction, 1983, Gregorian Chant and the Carolingians, 1998; assoc. editor: Anthologie de la Chanson Parisienne au Seizieme Siecle, 1953; Festschrift: The Study of Medieval Chant: In Honor of Kenneth Levy, 2001; mem. editl. bd. Monumenta Musicae Byzantinae, 1968—, Grove's Dictionary, 6th edit, Early Music History, 1980—; contbr. articles to profl. jours. With USNR, 1945-46. Recipient Fulbright award Italy, 1962-63, Howard T. Behrman award for disting. achievements in humanities, 1983, Deems Taylor award ASCAP, 1989, Pres.'s Disting. Teaching award Princeton U., 1995; Guggenheim fellow, 1955-56, Am. Coun. Learned Socs. fellow, 1970-71, sr. fellow Dumbarton Oaks, Harvard U., 1992-96; vis. fellow Cambridge U., 1995. Fellow Medieval Acad. Am.; mem. Am. Philos. Soc. Office: Princeton U Dept Music Woolworth Ctr Mus Studies Princeton NJ 08544-0001

LEVY, KENNETH JAMES, advertising executive; b. Cleve., June 15, 1949; s. Morton Leonard and Joan (Beitman) L.; m. Carol Wallisa, Sept. 7, 1974; children: Michael, Allison. BSBA, Ohio State U., 1971, MBA, 1973. Asst. account exec. Ketchum Advt., Pitts., 1973-75, account exec., 1975-77, account supr., 1977-78; account exec. Grey Advt., N.Y.C., 1978-79, account supr., 1979-80, v.p., mgmt. supr., 1980-84, v.p., group mgmt. supr., 1984-87, sr. v.p., 1987-94; exec. v.p. Grey Worldwide, 1994-2001, exec. v.p., mng. ptnr., 2001—. Advisor Jr. Achievement Pitts., 1979; bd. dirs. Give Kids the World Village. Mem. Ohio State U. Alumni Assn., Whippoorwill Country Club (Armonk, N.Y.). Avocations: golf, physical fitness, biographical reading. Home: 3 Carolyn Pl Armonk NY 10504-1101 E-mail: klevy@grey.com.

LEVY, KENNETH JAY, psychology educator, academic administrator; b. Dallas, Sept. 18, 1946; s. Reuben and Ruth (Okon) L.; children: Ryan S., Scott D. BA, U. Tex., 1968, MA, 1969; PhD, Purdue, 1972. Asst. prof. psychology SUNY, Buffalo, 1972-75, assoc. prof., 1976-78, prof., 1979—, chmn. dept. psychology, 1976-78, dean social scis., 1978-82, various adminstrv. positions, 1985—, assoc. provost, 1987—. Contbr. numerous articles to profl. jours.; editorial cons. Psychometrika. Home: 39 Shire Dr S East Amherst NY 14051-1816 Office: SUNY at Buffalo Capen Hall Buffalo NY 14260

LEVY, LEAH GARRIGAN, federal official; b. Miami, Fla., Apr. 29, 1947; d. Thomas Leo and Mary (Flaherty) Garrigan; m. Roger N. Levy, May 2, 1977; children: Philip, Aaron. BA in Polit. Sci., George Mason U., 1998, postgrad., 2001—. Mem. legis. staff U.S. Ho. Reps., 1973-75; mem. scheduling staff U.S. Senate, 1975-77, mem. administrv. scheduling staff, 1977-81; staff asst. pub. liaison The White House, 1982-84; spl. asst. U.S Dept. Transport, Washington, 1984-89, U.S. Dept. Housing, Washington, 1989—; scheduling asst. Empower Am., 1993-94; scheduler majority leader Dick Armey U.S. Ho. of Reps., 1995-2001; dir. scheduling and advance Sec. of Labor, 2001—. Contbr. to Rep. Nat. Com., Washington. Contbr. Rep. Nat. Conv. Va. Rep. Party, Washington; del. Va. State GOP Conv., Richmond, 1994. Mem. Alpha Chi. Roman Catholic. Avocations: tennis, golf, reading (non-fiction). E-mail: thelevys@aol.com., levy-leah@dol.gov.

LEVY, LEONARD WILLIAMS, history educator, author; b. Toronto, Ont., Can., Apr. 9, 1923; s. Albert and Rae (Williams) L.; m. Elyse Gitlow, Oct. 21, 1944; children: Wendy Ellen, Leslie Anne. BS, Columbia U., 1947, MA, 1948, PhD (Univ. fellow), 1951; LHD, Brandeis U., 1987; DHL (hon.), Claremont Grad. Sch., 1991, Ripon Coll., 1996. Research asst. Columbia U., 1950-51; instr., asst. prof., assoc. prof., prof. Brandeis U., Waltham, Mass., 1951-70, first incumbent Earl Warren chair constl. history, 1957-70, dean Grad. Sch. Arts and Scis., 1958-63, dean faculty arts and scis., 1963-66; Andrew W. Mellon prof. humanities, history, chmn. grad. faculty history Claremont (Calif.) Grad. Sch., 1970-90, prof. emeritus, 1990—; Disting. scholar in residence So. Oreg. State Coll., 1990—. Reiser lectr. U. Chgo. Law Sch., 1964; Gaspar Bacon lectr. Boston U., 1972; Elliott lectr. U. So. Calif. Law Sch., 1972; Hugo Black lectr. U. Ala., 1976; Bicentennial lectr., City of St. Louis, 1976; disting. lectr. U. Cin., 1978. Author: The Law of the Commonwealth and Chief Justice Shaw, 1957, Legacy of Suppression; Freedom of Speech and Press in Early American History, 1960, Jefferson and Civil Liberties; The Darker Side, 1963, Origins of the Fifth Amendment, 1968 (Pulitzer Prize in history 1969), Judgments: Essays on American Constitutional History, 1972, Against The Law: The Nixon Court and Criminal Justice, 1974, Treason Against God: History of the Offense of Blasphemy, 1981, Emergence of a Free Press, 1985, Constitutional Opinions, 1986, The Establishment Clause, 1986, Original Intent and the Framers' Constitution, 1988, Blasphemy: Verbal Offense Against the Sacred, 1993, Seasoned Judgments, 1994, A License to Steal: The Forfeiture of Property, 1996, Origins of the Bill of Rights, 1999, The Palladium of Justice, 1999, Ranters Run Amok, 1999, Two Rights, 2002, Facets of Freedom, 2002; editor: Major Crises in American History, 1962, The American Political Process, 1963, The Presidency, 1964, The Congress, 1964, The Judiciary, 1964, Parties and Pressure Groups, 1964, Freedom of the Press from Zenger to Jefferson, 1966, American Constitutional Law, 1966, Judicial Review and the Supreme Court, 1967, Freedom and Reform, 1967, Essays on The Making of the Constitution, 1969, rev. edit. 1987, The Fourteenth Amendment and the Bill of Rights, 1970, The Supreme Court Under Earl Warren, 1972, Jim Crow in Boston, 1974, Essays on the Early Republic, 1974, Blasphemy in Massachusetts, 1974, The Framing and Ratification of the Constitution, 1987, The American Founding, 1988, American Constitutional History, 1989; co-editor: Ency. Am. Presidency, 4 vols., 1993; gen. editor: Am. Heritage Series, 60 vols., Harper Documentary History of Western Civilization, 40 vols.; editor-in-chief Ency. Am. Constn., 4 vols., 1986, supplement, 1991; gen. editor: Bicentennial History of the American Revolution; adv. bd.: Revs. in Am. History, John Marshall Papers, Salmon P. Chase Papers; contbr. articles to profl. jours. Mem. nat. bd. Commn. on Law and Social Action, Am. Jewish Congress; mem. U.S. Bicentennial Commn. Am. Revolution, 1966-68; mem. exec. council Inst. for Early Am. History and Culture; mem. nat. adv. council ACLU, Pulitzer prize juror, chmn. biog. jury, 1974, history jury, 1976. With AUS, 1943-46. Recipient Sigma Delta Chi prize for journalism history, 1961, 86; Frank Luther Mott prize Kappa Tau Alpha, 1961; Pulitzer prize for history, 1969; Commonwealth Club prize for non-fiction, 1975; Oboler Meml. Prize of Am. Library Assn. for Intellectual Freedom, 1986; Cert. Merit ABA, 1986; Henry L. Mencken award Free Press Assn., 1986; Dartmouth Medal Am. Library Assn., 1987, 95; Guggenheim fellow, 1957-58; Center For Study Liberty in Am. fellow Harvard, 1961-62; Am. Bar Found. sr. merit fellow, 1973-74; Am. Coun. Learned Socs. fellow, 1973; NEH sr. fellow, 1974. Mem. Am. Hist. Assn. (Littleton-Griswold com. legal history), Orgn. Am. Historians, Am. Soc. Legal History (dir.), Am. Antiquarian Soc., Soc. Am. Historians, Inst. Early Am. History and Culture (exec. coun.), Mass. Hist. Soc., Kappa Delta Pi. Democrat. Home: 1025 Timberline Ter Ashland OR 97520-3436

LEVY, LESLIE ANN, management consultant, educator, application developer; b. N.Y.C., N.Y., Dec. 25, 1941; d. Paul and Ruth Candace (Tachna) Bauman; m. Marc Gersan Gerard Levy, Oct. 1962 (div.); children: Benjamin Gerard, Remy Marcel Gerard. BA summa cum laude in philosophy and history, Smith Coll., 1962; MBA, Harvard U., Boston, 1976, DBA, 1980. Cert. French Fashion Acad., 1964. Tchg. asst. in philosophy UCLA, 1962-63; pres. Commonwealth Collaborative, Inc., Cambridge and Sarasota, Fla., 1976—99; sr. rsch. assoc. Harvard Sch. Bus. Adminstrn., Boston, 1979-81; asst. prof. mgmt. policy, industry analysis, bd. dirs. Case Western Res. U., Cleve., 1981-84; pres., CEO Acad. for Corp. Governance, Fordham U. Grad. Sch. Bus., 1990-91; pres., dir., treas., sec. Directors, Data, Inc., 1999—; pres., sec. Life Choices and Death Wishes, 2000—. Sr. adv. Inst. Rsch. on Bd. Dirs., 1998-; engring., fin., mktg. and mgmt. staff Honeywell Info. Sys., Boston, 1971-75; cons. and lectr. in field. Author: Director Motivation: Incentives and Disincentives to Board Service, 1996, Separate Chairmen of the Board: Their Roles, Legal Liabilities, and Compensation; editor, co-author: Boards of Directors Part II; columnist: Directors and Boards, 1996-97; contbr. aricles to profl. jours. Mem. Boston and Tampa Bay Com. on Fgn. Rels. Acad. Corp. Governance rsch. fellow; Fulbright scholar. Mem. Am. Soc. Corp. Secs., Nat. Assn. Corp. Dirs., Acad. Mgmt. (article reviewer), Nat. Investor Rels. Inst., Inst. of Dirs., Federalist Soc., Women in Pensions, So. Fin. Assn., Harvard Club of Sarasota, Am. Jewish Com., Am. Jewish Congress, Nat. Coun. Jewish Women. Avocations: hiking, art history, construction, whitewater canoeing. E-mail: llirbd@comcast.com., dirsdata@home.com., dirsdata@comcast.net.

LEVY, LOUIS EDWARD, retired accounting firm executive; b. Cleve., Nov. 16, 1932; s. Jerome and Bessie (Goldberg) L.; m. Sandra Harris, Mar. 4, 1956; children: Jerold, Richard, Lawrence. BBA, Case Western Res. U., 1956. CPA, N.Y. Agt. IRS, Cleve., 1956; ptnr., vice chmn. KPMG Peat Marwick, N.Y.C., 1958-90. Bd. dirs. Household Internat. Inc., ISI Mut. Funds, Scudder mut. Funds; former mem. emerging issues task force Fin. Acctg. Standards Bd.; former adj. prof. Columbia U. Grad. Sch. Bus. Trustee, chmn. Nat. Multiple Sclerosis Soc., N.Y.C., 1978-2000. Recipient Braden award Weatherhead Sch. Mgmt. Case Western Res. U., 1984, Community Svc. award Brandeis U., 1980; fellow Brandeis U., Boston, 1981—. Mem. AICPA (former chmn. quality control inquiry com.), Maplewood Country Club (N.J.), Sky Club, Longboat Key Country Club. Republican. Jewish. Avocations: tennis, boating, golf. E-mail: loulevy@msn.com.

LEVY, MARK ALLAN, lawyer; b. Cambridge, Mass., May 31, 1939; s. Robert A. and Muriel (Goldman) L.; m. Ellen Grob, Oct. 2, 1966; children: Abigail R., Eric V.R. AB, Harvard U., 1961; LLB, Columbia U., 1964, MBA, 1965. Bar: N.Y. 1964, Mass. 1965. Assoc. Parker, Chapin, Flattau & Klimpl, N.Y.C., 1965-68; sr. ptnr. Stroock & Stroock & Lavan, 1968—. Contbr. articles to profl. jours. Former mem. Planning Bd. Town of Greenburgh, N.Y.; trustee Jewish Bd. Family and Childrens Svcs. Mem. N.Y. State Bar Assn., Columbia Law Sch. Alumni Assn. (former dir.). Home: 60 Highridge Rd Hartsdale NY 10530-3605 Office: Stroock & Stroock & Lavan 180 Maiden Ln Fl 17 New York NY 10038-4937 E-mail: mlevy@stroock.com.

LEVY, MARK HIRSCH, internist, medical educator, researcher; b. Birmingham, Ala., Nov. 13, 1964; s. Irving Hirsch and Marcie Seligman L.; m. Susan May Levy, Apr. 26, 1992; 1 child, Robert. BS in Chemistry, U. Mich., 1986; MD, 1990. Diplomate Am. Bd. Internal Medicine. Intern U. Cin. Hosp., 1990—92; resident Jewish Hosp. Cin., 1992—93; med. dir. Manor Care Rehab. Ctr., Highland Park, Ill., 1997—; asst. prof. medicine Rush Presbyn. St. Lukes Med. Ctr., Chgo., 1998—. Profl. spkr. in field. Contbr. articles to profl. jours. Mem. AMA, ACP, CMS, AMDA, ASC. Office: Rush North Shore Med Ctr 9600 Gross Point Rd Skokie IL 60076

LEVY, MARK IRVING, lawyer; b. Chgo., June 28, 1949; s. Kenneth Warren and Arleen (Langhaus) L.; m. Judith Jarrell Levy, Sept. 8, 1979; children: Elizabeth Sara, Mitchell Bennett. BA summa cum laude with exceptional dist., Yale U., 1971, JD, 1975. Bar: D.C. 1976, U.S. Dist. Ct. D.C. 1977, U.S. Supreme Ct. 1980, Ill. 1986, U.S. Ct. Appeals (D.C. cir.) 1990, U.S. Ct. Appeals (6th, 7th and 8th cirs.) 1990, U.S. Tax Ct. 1990, U.S. Ct. Appeals (9th cir.) 1993, U.S. Ct. Appeals (2d, 4th and 10th cirs.) 1994, U.S. Ct. Appeals (3d, 5th, 11th and Fed. cirs.) 1996, U.S. Ct. Appeals (1st cir.) 2000. Law clk. Judge Gerhard A. Gesell, Washington, 1975-76; assoc. Covington & Burling, 1976-79, 81-83; asst. to solicitor gen. U.S. Dept. Justice, 1979-81, 83-86; ptnr. Mayer, Brown & Platt, Chgo., 1987-93; dep. asst. atty. gen. (Appellate) Civil Divsn. U.S. Dept. Justice, Washington, 1993-95; ptnr. Howrey & Simon, 1995—. Adj. faculty, appellate sem. U. Va. Sch. Law, 1999-2000, 01-02. Exec. editor Yale Law Jour., 1974-75. Recipient Israel H. Peres prize Yale Law Sch., 1975. Mem. Am. Acad. Appellate Lawyers, D.C. Cir. adv. com. on procedures, Lawyers Club of Chgo., Yale Law Sch. Alumni Assn. (former treas., exec. com. mem. 1987-90), Edward Coke Appellate Am. Inn of Ct. (master), Phi Beta Kappa (fellow). Home: 7609 Winterberry Pl Bethesda MD 20817-4847 Office: Howrey Simon Arnold & White LLP 1299 Pennsylvania Ave NW Washington DC 20004-2402 E-mail: levym@howrey.com.

LEVY, MARLENE LOIS, clinical social worker; b. Queens, N.Y., Aug. 23, 1946; m. Ronald Levy (div. 1991); children: Susan Igel, Elizabeth Igel. BA, L.I. U., 1979; MSW, Adelphia U., 1981; PhD, Newport U., Calif., 1984. Diplomate in clin. social work Am. Assn. Clin. Hypnosis, in pain mgmt. Am. Acad. Pain Mgmt.; lic. clin. social worker. Pvt. practice, N.Y.C., 1990—; founder, exec. dir. N.Y. Ctr. for Co-Dependent Therapy, 1989—. Pres. bd. dirs. Pvt. Counseling Ctr., N.Y.C., 1976-86. Author: N.Y. Society of Clinical Hypnosis Workbook, 1989-93. Fellow Am. Orthopsychiat. Assn., N.Y. Soc. of Clin. Hypnosis (exec. bd. dirs. 1987—). Avocations: gardening, reading. Office: 7 Oak Tree Ln Port Washington NY 11050-1119

LEVY, MATTHEW DEGEN, investment banking technology and operations company executive, consumer products business development and planning executive, management consultant; b. N.Y.C., Dec. 5, 1958; s. Herbert Monte and Marilyn (Wohl) L.; m. Laura Ann Goldin, Aug. 20, 1989; children: Ely Samuel, Philip Benjamin. BA magna cum laude and spl. honors, Tufts U., 1980; MBA, Yale U., 1983. Rsch. assoc. State St. Cons., Boston, 1980-81; cons. to vice chmn. Yankelovich, Skelly & White, Inc., Stamford, Conn., 1982; staff fin. analyst IBM Corp., White Plains, N.Y., 1983-86; co-founder, COO White, Skelly, Yankelovich Cons. Group, Inc., Greenwich, Conn., 1986-93; area dir. and mng. cons. Renaissance Strategy Group, N.Y.C., 1993-95; dir. bus. planning and devel. Sara Lee Corp., 1995-97; v.p. global ops. Salomon Bros. Inc., 1997; v.p. tech. and ops. Salomon Smith Barney Inc., 1997-98; v.p. info. tech. Goldman Sachs, 1999—. Cons. Yale Sch. Mgmt. Alumni Assn., 1989; bus. mgr., anchorman WMFO Radio, Medford, Mass., 1977-80; co-instr. course on decision-making Tufts U., 1977. Contbr. articles to mags. Bd. dirs. DOROT, N.Y.C., 1986-97, pres. bd., 1991-94; mem. allocations com. United Way of Greenwich, 1984-86; bd. dirs. Am. Jewish World Svc., N.Y.C., 1997—. Home: 160 Riverside Dr Apt 8C New York NY 10024-2111 Office: Goldman Sachs 180 Maiden Ln 13th Fl New York NY 10038-4958 E-mail: mdlnyc@aol.com.

LEVY, MICHAEL B. business educator; b. Balt., July 12, 1947; m. Bonny B. Wolf; 1 child. BA, Brown U., 1969; PhD, Rutgers U., 1979. Tchr. social studies, coach Loyola High Sch., Balt., 1969—72; teaching asst. Rutgers U., New Brunswick, NJ, 1973—76, instr., 1978; asst. prof. Tex. A&M Univ., College Sta., 1978-84, assoc. prof. polit. sci., 1984-85; economist joint econ. com. U.S. Congress, Washington, 1985-87; adminstrv. asst. to Sen. Lloyd Bentsen U.S. Senate, 1987-93; asst. sec. legis. affairs U.S. Dept. Treasury, 1993-95; adj. instr. Georgetown U., 1986-93, disting. prof., 1995—; sr. advisor to U.S. Treas. Sec. Robert Rubin U.S. Dept Treas., 1995. Legis. cons. Brownstein, Hyatt & Farber, Denver and Washington, 1995—. Editor: Political Thought in America, 1981, 87, (with Philip Abbot) The Liberal Future in America: Essays in Renewal, 1985, (with Edward Portis) Handbook of Political Theory and Policy Sciences, 1989; contbr. articles to profl. jours. Bevier fellow Rutgers U., 1979; R.J. Reynolds fellow for So. High Sch. Tchrs. Office: Georgetown U Sch Bus 411 Ol North Washington DC 20057-0001

LEVY, MICHAEL HOWARD, environmental management professional; b. Newburgh, N.Y., Oct. 2, 1947; s. Max and Helen (Rankell) L.; m. Judith Linenbroker, Aug. 28, 1971; children: Matthew, Andrew. BS in Civil Engring., Rensselaer Polytech. Inst., 1969, ME in Environ. Engring., 1972; postgrad., Fairleigh Dickinson U., 1977-78. Registered profl. engr., N.Y.; cert. environ. auditor. Jr. civil engr. N.Y. State Dept. Transp., Albany, 1969-72; asst. sanitary engr. N.Y. State Dept. Environ. Conservation, 1972-73, sr. air pollution engr., 1973-76; environ. engr. Allied Chem. Co. div. Semet Solvay, Morristown, N.J., 1976-78; supt. environ. and quality control div. Allied Chem. Co., Detroit, 1979; with Mobil Chem. Co./Mobil Corp., 1979-83, mgr. environ. affairs, 1984-87, mgr. legis. and regulatory affairs Fairfax, Va., 1987-89; v.p. Franklin Assocs., Ltd., McLean, 1990-92; pres. Environ. Strategies & Solutions, 1993—; dir. energy and materials policy Am. Forest & Paper Assn., Washington, 1993-94; exec. dir. Polystyrene Packaging Coun., Arlington, Va., 1994—. Expandable Polystyrene Resin Suppliers Coun., 1994—. Sports vol. McLean (Va.) Youth, Inc., 1988-89; registrar troop 128, Boy Scouts Am., 1985-99. Sgt. USAR, 1970-76. Mem. ASCE, Am. Soc. Assn. Execs., Air Pollution Control Assn., Profl. Engring. Soc., Phi Sigma Kappa (alumni pres. 1969-71). Avocations: basketball, tennis, travel. Home: 744 Ridge Dr Mc Lean VA 22101-1623 Fax: 703-253-0651. E-mail: Mike_Levy@plastics.org.

LEVY, MICHAEL LEE, neurosurgeon; b. San Diego, Sept. 20, 1960; s. Lee Issaac and Sharline Sheridan (Day) Levy; m. Karen Marie Lorman, Jan. 7, 1989; children: Danielle Montana, Dillon Michael. BA, U. Calif. San Diego, 1981; MD, U. Calif. San Francisco, 1986, PhD, 2001. Resident U. So. Calif. Sch. Medicine, L.A., 1986-93; sr. resident Divsn. Neurol. Surgery Children's Hosp. of L.A., 1989, Huntington Meml. Hosp., Pasadena, Calif., 1989, Kenneth E. Norris Cancer Hosp., L.A., 1990; resident supr. U. So. Calif. Sch. Medicine, 1992; fellow in pediatric neurol. surgery Dept. Neurol. Surgery, 1993; dir. surg. epilepsy team, dir. neurotrauma Children's Hosp. L.A. Mem. cons. in field; chmn./sgt.-at-arms com. Congress of Neurol. Surgeons Ann. Meeting, San Francisco, 1995; mem. ann. meeting com. Congress of Neurol. Surgeons , 1999, chmn. pub. rels., 99; dir. surg. epilepsy team, dir. neurotrauma Children's Hosp. L.A. Editor (newsletter): Congress of Neurol. Surgeons, 1996—99; editor: Neurosurgery News, 2000—02; contbr. Recipient Rudolph Taussig scholarship, U. Calif. San Francisco, 1982—84, CHOMP scholarship, 1983—86, Tucker scholarship, 1984—86, numerous awards in field. Mem.: L.A. Acad. Medicine, L.A. County Med. Assn., Calif. House Officer Med. Soc., Calif. Med. Assn., Am. Assn. Neurol. Surgeons, Congress of Neurol. Surgeons (exec. com. 1996—), Alpha Omega Alpha. Achievements include development of an endoscopic system for the treatment of hydrocephalus, heads-up virtual displays for microneurosurgery, three dimensional anatomic image reconstruction and stereolithography; specialization in pediat. vascular and midline tumor surgery. Avocation: Avocations: surfing, diving. Office: Childrens Hosp of LA 1300 N Vermont Ave Ste 906 Los Angeles CA 90027-6005 Home: 3306 Coy Dr Sherman Oaks CA 91423 E-mail: mlevy@hsc.usc.edu.

LEVY, MOISE L. dermatologist, pediatrician, educator; b. Houston, Mar. 28, 1951; s. Moise Dreyfus Levy and Lois Ellen (Edel) Grenader; m. Joan L. Levy, Aug. 15, 1971; children: Michael, Andrew. BA, U. Tex., 1973, MD, 1979. Diplomate Am. Bd. Pediatrics, Am. Bd. Dermatology. Pediat. intern, resident U. Tex. Med. Sch., Houston, 1979-82, pediat. chief resident, 1982-83; dermatology resident Baylor Coll. Medicine, 1983-86, asst. prof. pediatrics, dermatology, 1989-94, assoc. prof., 1994-98, prof., 1998—; chief dermatology svc. Tex. Children's Hosp., 1988—, pres. med. staff, 2002—. Med. staff Tex. Children's Hosp., Meth. Hosp., Harris County Hosp. Dist., St. Luke's Episcopal Hosp., Shriner's Hosp. for Crippled Children, VA Hosp., Women's Hosp.; rschr. in field; vis. prof. U. Louisville, 1992. Contbr. articles to profl. jours., chpts. to books; presenter in field. Mem. Am. Acad. Pediatrics (exec. bd.), Am. Acad. Dermatology (mem. recert. com.), Tex. Med. Assn., Soc. Pediat. Dermatology (bd. dirs.), Soc. for Investigative Dermatology, Harris County Med. Soc., Alpha Omega Alpha. Office: Tex Childrens Hosp Dermatology Svc 6621 Fannin St # Mc33315 Houston TX 77030-2303

LEVY, NELSON LOUIS, physician, scientist, corporate executive; b. Somerville, N.J., June 19, 1941; s. Myron L. and Sylvia (Cohen) L.; m. Joanne Barnett, Dec. 21, 1963 (div. 1972); children: Scott, Erik, Jonathan; m. Louisa Douglas Stiles, Dec. 21, 1974; children: Michael, Andrew, David. BA/BS summa cum laude, Yale U., 1963; MD, Columbia U., 1967; PhD, Duke U., 1972. Diplomate Am. Bd. Allergy and Immunology. Intern U. Colo. Med. Ctr., Denver, 1967-68; resident Duke U. Med. Ctr., Durham, N.C., 1970-73; rsch. assoc. NIH, Bethesda, Md., 1968-70; asst. prof. immunology Duke U. Med. Ctr., Durham, 1972-75, assoc. prof. immunology and neurology, 1975-80, prof., 1980-81; dir. biol. rsch. Abbott Labs., Abbott Park, Ill., 1981, v.p. rsch., 1981-84; pres. Nelson L. Levy Assocs. Inc., 984-87; CEO The CoreTechs Corp., Lake Forest, Ill., 1987-92; pres. Fujisawa Pharm., Deerfield, 1992-93; CEO Ill. Tech. Devel. Corp., 1993-95; chmn. bd. dirs., CEO The Core Techs Corp, Lake Forest, Ill., 1995-99. Chmn. bd. dirs. Horizon Quest Inc., Laguna Hills, Calif., 1996-97, ColesCraft Corp., 1997—, IMM UVA Corp., New Orleans, 1997—; bd. dirs. ChemBridge Corp., San Diego, Targeted Genetics Corp., Seattle, Biona PTY Ltd., Laguna Beach, Internat. Med. Rsch/, Inc., Brea, Calif., Cary Pharm. Co., Bethesda, Md.; chmn. sci. adv. bd. Neoprobe Corp.; mem. sci. adv. bd. Ligand Pharms. Inc., First Horizon Pharmaceuticals, Inc.; cons. Upjohn Co. Inc., Kalamazoo, 1976-77, G.D. Searle Inc., Skokie, Ill., 1984-87, Erbamont Inc., Stamford, Conn., 1984-90, Eastman Kodak, Rochester, N.Y., LyphoMed Inc., Rosemont, Ill., 1985-89, The Nutrasweet Co., Skokie, 1985-88, Bayer AG, 1987-89, Fujisawa Pharm. Co., 1988-92, Alcide Corp., 1991—, Ameritech, 1993—, several venture cos., U.S. Dept. treasury, 1999—. Editor several books; contbr. articles to profl. publs., chpts. to books. Coach Little League, Am. Youth Soccer Orgn.; corp. adv. bd. Family Svc. of South Lake County, 1991—. Surgeon USPHS, 1968-70. Grantee Am. Cancer Soc., 1970-75, NIH, 1971-81, Nat. Multiple Sclerosis Soc., 1974-81, Ill. Dept. Commerce and Cmty. Affairs, 1993—. Mem. Am. Assn. Immunologists, Am. Assn. Cancer Rsch., Licensing Execs. Soc., Rotary, Phi Beta Kappa, Sigma Xi, Alpha Omega Alpha, Phi Gamma Delta. Avocations: triathlons, biking, rock 'n roll. Office: 1391 Concord Rd Lake Forest IL 60045-1506

LEVY, NORMAN, motion picture company executive; b. Bronx, N.Y., Jan. 3, 1935; s. Irving and Helen (Saunders) L.; m. Hirsch, Nov. 11, 1962; children— Jordan, Brian, Matthew. BA, CCNY. Salesman Universal Pictures, 1957-67, Nat. Gen. Pictures, 1967-74; gen. sales mgr. Columbia Pictures, Burbank, Calif., 1974-75, exec. v.p. in charge domestic sales, 1975-77, exec. v.p. mktg., 1977-78, pres. domestic distbn., 1978-80, pres. Twentieth Century Fox Entertainment Group, 1980-81, vice chmn., 1981-85; mktg., distbn. cons., 1985—; chmn. New Century/Vista Film Co. L.A., 1985-91; chmn., chief exec. officer Domino Entertainment, 1991-92; pres., CEO Creative Film Enterprises, 1992—. Served with U.S. Army, 1955-57. Office: Creative Film Enterprises 4965 Queen Florence Ln Woodland Hills CA 91364-4745

LEVY, NORMAN B. psychiatrist, educator; b. N.Y.C., 1931; s. Barnett Theodore and Lena (Gulnick) L.; m. Lya Weiss (dec.); children: Karen, Susan, Joanne; m. Carol Lois Spiegel, 1 son, Robert Barnett. BA cum laude, NYU, 1952; MD, SUNY. Diplomate Am. Bd. Psychiatry and Neurology (examiner). Intern Maimonides Med. Center, Bklyn.; resident physician in medicine U. Pitts.-Presbyn. Hosp.; resident in psychiatry Kings County Hosp. Center, Bklyn.; instr. psychiatry SUNY Downstate Med. Ctr. Coll. Medicine, asst. prof., assoc. prof.; prof. State U. N.Y. Downstate Med. Center Coll. Medicine, 1980-95; presiding officer faculty SUNY Downstate Med. Ctr. Coll. Medicine, assoc. dir. med-psychiat. liaison service, 1965-80; prof. psychiatry, medicine, surgery and coordinator psychiat. liaison services N.Y. Med. Coll., 1980-95; clin. prof. psychiatry, adj. prof. of medicine Health Science Ctr. SUNY, Bklyn., 1996—; dir. psychiatry Kingsboro (Bklyn.) Psychiat. Hosp., 2000—. Dir. liaison svcs. psychiatry divsn. Westchester County Med. Ctr., 1980-95, mem. exec. com. med. staff, 1981-85, 89-92, N.Y. Med. Coll., 1980-95; clin. prof. psychiatry, adj. prof. medicine health sci. ctr. SUNY, Bklyn., 1996—; dir., consultation-liaison and emergency psychiatry Coney Island Hosp., Bklyn., 1996-2000; vis. prof. psychiatry and medicine So. Ill. U. Sch. Medicine; vis. prof. psychiatry John A. Burns Sch. Medicine, U. Hawaii, 1981; coord. 1st Internat. Conf. Psychol. Factors in Hemodialysis and Transplantation, 1978, 2d-9th Internat. Confs. on Psychonephrology; cons. NIMH; chief med. svcs. USAF Hosp., Ashiya, Japan; clin. prof. psychiatry, adj. prof. medicine SUNY Health Sci. Ctr., Bklyn., 1996. Author: (with others), editor: Living or Dying: Adaptation to Hemodialysis, 1974, Psychonephrology I: Psychological Factors in Hemodialysis and Transplantation, 1981, Men in Transition: Theory and Therapy, 1982, Psychonephrology II: Psychological Problems in Kidney Failure and their Treatment, 1983; contbr. articles to jours., chpts. to textbooks in field.; assoc. editor: Gen. Hosp. Psychiatry, 1978-82, sect. editor, 1982—; sect. editor: Internat. Jour. Psychiatry in Medicine, 1977-78; mem. editl. bd., book rev. editor Jour. Dialysis and Transplantation, 1979-97, Facta Universitatis, 1997—; mem. editl. bd. Resident and Staff Physician, 1981-91, Internat. Jour. Artificial Internal. Organs, 1983-93, Geriatric Nephrology and Urology, 1990—, Kidney: A Current Survey of World Literature, 1990—, Dialysis and Transplantation, 1979--. Served to capt. M.C., USAF. Served to capt. M.C. USAF. Recipient William A. Console Master Tchr. award, SUNY, Bklyn., 1991. Fellow ACP, Am. Coll. Psychiatrists, Am. Psychiat. Assn. (pres. Kings County dist. br. 1981-82), Acad. Psychosomatic Medicine (Thomas P. Hackett award 1993); mem. AAAS, Am. Psychosomatic Soc. (coun. 1994-97), N.Y. Acad. Scis., Psychonephrology Found. (pres. 1978—), Internat. Soc. Nephrology, Am. Soc. Nephrology, Soc. Liaison Psychiatry (bd. dirs. 1979-80, sec. 1980-81, pres.-elect 1991-92, pres. 1992-94, bd. dirs. 1995-98, award 1998), Serbian Acad. Medicine, Phi Beta Kappa, Sigma Xi. Home: 169 Westminster Rd Brooklyn NY 11218-3445 Office: Kingsboro Psychiat Hosp 681 Clarkson Ave Brooklyn NY 11203

LEVY, NORMAN JAY, investment banker, financial consultant; b. N.Y.C., Aug. 14, 1942; s. Benjamin and Sophie (London) L.; m. Rene S. Cohen; children— Ellen, David BBA, U. Cin., 1964; MBA, Columbia U., 1966. Assoc., v.p. Salomon Bros., N.Y.C., 1966-77, spl. ptnr., 1977-79, gen. ptnr., 1979-81; sr. v.p. Wertheim & Co., 1982; mng. dir. L.F. Rothschild, Unterberg, Towbin, 1983-84; private practice investment cons. Tenafly, N.J., 1985—. Mem. Securities Industry Assn. (com. on acctg. 1977-79) Home: 40 Mayflower Dr Tenafly NJ 07670-3130

LEVY, PHYLLIS CHARLOTTE, interior designer, trade showroom executive, product designer; b. Bklyn., Aug. 14, 1929; d. Irving George and Norma Sarah (Tucker) Gross; m. Gilbert Levy, June 25, 1950; children— Jill Levy Brooks Esquire, Fran Enid Levy Katz. A.A., Wilsey Ints., Hempstead, N.Y., 1970. Underwriter Continental Ins. Co., N.Y.C., 1948; legal asst. Consol. Tax Payers, Bklyn., 1949-50; jewelry salesperson Fortunoff's, Westbury, N.Y., 1967-69; owner, designer Phyllis Levy Interiors, Dix Hills, N.Y., 1970-79, Fact & Fantasy Ltd., West Palm Beach, Fla., 1979— . Fund raiser City of Hope, East Meadow, N.Y., 1953-63, del. to pilot ctr., Duarte, Calif., 1965. Jewish. Avocations: collecting art and antiques; watercolor, oil and pastel painting. Office: Fact & Fantasy Ltd D & D Centre 401 Clematis St West Palm Beach FL 33401

LEVY, RALPH, engineering executive, consultant; b. London, Apr. 12, 1932; came to U.S., 1967, naturalized, 1978; s. Alfred and Esther L.; m. Barbara Dent, Dec. 12, 1959; children: Sharon E., Mark S. BA, Cambridge U., 1953, MA, 1957; PhD, Queen Mary Coll. U. London, 1966. Mem. sci. staff GEC, Stanmore, Middlesex, Eng., 1953-59; mem. sci. staff Mullard Research Labs., Redhill, Eng., 1959-64; lectr. dept. elec. and electronic engring. U. Leeds, 1964-67; v.p. research Microwave Devel. Labs., Inc., Natick, Mass., 1967-84; v.p. engring. KW Engring., San Diego, 1984-88; v.p. research Remec Inc., 1988-89; R. Levy Assocs., 1989—. Author: (with J.O. Scanlan) Circuit Theory, 1970, 2d vol., 1973; contbr. articles in field; patentee in field. Fellow IEEE (editor Transactions on Microwave Theory and Techniques 1986-88, Career award IEEE Microwave Theory and Techniques Soc. 1997); mem. Instn. Elec. Engrs. (London). Office: 1897 Caminito Velasco La Jolla CA 92037-5725 E-mail: r.levy@ieee.org.

LEVY, RALPH DAVID, theology educator; b. London, Aug. 3, 1951; came to U.S., 1975; s. Jack and Lucy L. BA in Linguistics and Modern Langs. with honors, U. York, Eng., 1974; MA in Edn., Calif. State U., L.A., 1987; PhD in Bibl. Studies, Union Inst. & U., Cin., 1995. Cert. secondary tchr., Tex., Spanish, ESL; cert. Spanish lang. ct. interpreter. Instr. Spanish, ESL and theology Ambassador U., Pasadena, Calif., 1981-90, Big Sandy, Tex., 1990-96; tchr. Spanish, Longview (Tex.) Ind. Sch. Dist., 1996-97; tchr. ESL, Carrolton (Tex.)-Farmer's Branch Ind. Sch. Dist., 1997-98; tchr. Amb. Bible Ctr., United Ch. of God, Cin., 1999—. Author: The Symbolism of the Azazel Goat, 1998. Elder United Ch. of God. Mem. World Affairs Coun. of Greater

Cin. Avocations: aerobics, foreign languages, travel, reading. Home: 250H Postoak Ln Milford OH 45150-8737 Office: Ambassador Bible Ctr PO Box 54992 Cincinnati OH 45254-0992 E-mail: drrdl@man.com.

LEVY, RICH, advertising executive; BS in Mktg. and Fin., Syracuse U. Pharm. sales rep. Merrell Dow Pharms.; v.p., acct. group supr. TRL Advt.; sr. v.p., mng. dir. Adair-Greene Healthcare Comms., 1995; now pres., COO Adair-Greene Healthcare Comms., Atlanta. Office: Adair-Greene 200 Tech Ctr 1575 Northside Dr NW Atlanta GA 30318-4235 Fax: (404) 351-1495. E-mail: info@adair-greene.com.*

LEVY, RICHARD A. statistician; b. Flushing, N.Y. s. Walter M. and Judith R. Levy. BS, Cornell U., 1991; MPA, NYU, 1998. Program coord. Hosp. for Spl. Surgery, N.Y.C., 1992-98; program analyst U.S. Census Bur., Washington, 1998-2000, statistician, 2000—. Mem. Nat. Assn. Hist. Preservation. Democrat. Avocations: piano, exercise. Office: US Census Bur US Dept Commerce Rm 1433-3 Washington DC 20233

LEVY, RICHARD C. television production executive, author, producer, inventor; b. Wilkes-Barre, Pa., Jan. 7, 1947; s. Sidney Z. and Bettie (Abrahamson) L.; m. Sheryl G. Slate; 1 child, Bettie. Diploma, U. Madrid, 1965, U. Paris, 1966; BA in Communications, Emerson Coll., 1968. Spl. asst. to pres. Paramount Films of Spain, Madrid, 1967, Paramount Internat. Pictures, N.Y.C., 1968; dir. Cen. Am. advt., publicity Paramount Films of Panama, Panama City, 1968-69; dir. fgn. advt., publicity Avco Embassy Pictures, Inc., N.Y.C., 1970-71; pres. Ricsher Prodns. Ltd., 1971-82; dep. dir. USIA TV and Film Service/Worldnet, Washington, 1982-85; pres. Richard C. Levy Assocs., 1986—. Author: Wife Beating: The Silent Crisis, 1976, How to Use the Freedom of Information Act, 1978, Plane Talk: The Consumer's Air Travel Guide, 1980, Secrets of Selling Inventions, 1984, Desperately Seeking: Romance in the Want Ads, 1986, Inventing and Patenting Sourcebook: How to Sell and Protect Your Ideas, 1989, Inside Santa's Workshop, 1990, Inventor's Desktop Companion, 1990, 2d edit., 1995, From Workshop to Toy Store, 1992, The Complete Idiot's Guide to Cashing in on Your Inventions, 2002; producer: (documentaries) Hal David: Expressing a Feeling, We the People, (UN Presentation video) KAL-007; co-producer numerous TV documentaries; contbr. articles to profl. jours.; inventor Adverteasing, Adverteasing Junior 1988, Noteability, 1990, Screen Challenge, 1991, Adverteasing II, 1992, Oops and Downs, 1992, Blirds, 1992, Wayne's World: Party On Video Game, 1992; producer (video) Speed Force, 1996, Family Reunion, 2002, Route 66: The Great American Road Trip Game, 2002, Men Are From Mars, Women Are From Venus: The Game, 2002 . Bd. dirs. Intellectual Property Owners, Inc. Recipient Best Game award Inventors Clubs of Am., 1989, Innovation award SBA D.C., 1987. Mem. NATAS. Republican. Avocations: scuba diving, hiking, oil painting. Office: PO Box 34828 Bethesda MD 20827-0828

LEVY, ROBERT EDWARD, management consultant; b. Cin., May 23, 1939; s. Aaron F. and Elizabeth W. (Hirsch) L.; m. Candace Ann Wolfe, June 20, 1970; children: Brian D., Jessica A. BChemE, Cornell U., 1962; PhD-ChemE, U. Calif. at Berkeley, 1967. Various positions, including mgr. synthetic fuels devel., rsch. and enging. Exxon Co., Florham Park, N.J., 1967-80, 84-86; mgr. tech. dept. Lago Oil & Transport Co., Esso Interam. divsn. Exxon Co., Aruba, Netherlands Antilles, 1980-84; v.p., dir. tech. devel. M.W. Kellogg Co., Houston, 1987-93; v.p. govt. and regulatory affairs Energy Biosystems Corp., The Woodlands, Tex., 1993-97; mgmt. cons. Houston, 1997-99; sr. v.p. Allan F. Dow & Assocs., 1998-99, UniPure Corp., Houston, 2000—. Cons. in field. Patentee in field. Indsl. mem. Comm. for Prevention of Shoreline Pollution by Oil, Aruba, 1982-84. Mem. AIChE, Indsl. Rsch. Inst. (bd. editors 1992-95, pre-coll. edn. com. 1995-2000, chmn., 1996-97), Sigma Xi (pres. Kellogg chpt. 1991-92). Avocations: tennis, jogging, sailing. Office: 12 E Greenway Plz Ste 1380 Houston TX 77046-1294 E-mail: bob@unipurecorp.com.

LEVY, ROBERT MORRIS, judge; BA, Harvard Coll., 1971; JD, NYU, 1975. Bar: N.Y., U.S. Dist. Ct. (so. and ea. dists.) N.Y., U.S. Ct. Appeals (D.C. and 2nd cirs.), U.S. Supreme Ct. Staff atty. juvenile rights divsn. Legal Aid Soc., N.Y.C., 1976-77; staff atty. mental health law project N.Y. Civil Liberties Union, 1977-80, dir. mental health law project, 1980-85, sr. staff atty., 1985-93; gen. counsel N.Y. Lawyers for the Pub. Interest, 1993-94; U.S. magistrate judge Ea. Dist. N.Y., Bklyn., 1995—. Advisor on jud. reform in the Republic of Georgia, Ctrl. and East European Law Initiative ABA, 1998; adj. prof. Bklyn. Law Sch., 1989—, NYU Law Sch., 1991—, Columbia U. Law Sch., 1993—. Author: (with V. Rosenthal) Rights of Nursing Home Residents in New York, 1984, (with L. Rubenstein) Rights of People with Mental Disabilities, 1996. Bd. dirs. NYU Pub. Interest Law Found., N.Y.C., 1980-82; mem. Gov.'s Task Force on Advocacy, N.Y., 1988-91; mem. adv. bd. Protection and Advocacy Svcs. for the Mentally Ill, N.Y.C., 1991-93; vol. factfinding missions Human Rights Watch, No. Ireland and Romania, 1990, 91, 92, 93. Mem. Fed. Bar Coun. (2nd cir. cts. com. 1998—, com. on pub. svc. 2001—), Assn. Bar of the City of N.Y. (com. on internat. human rights 1995-98). Office: 225 Cadman Plz E # 621 Brooklyn NY 11201-1818 Fax: 718-260-2647. E-mail: RobertM.Levy@nyed.uscourts.gov.

LEVY, ROBIN CAROLE, elementary guidance counselor; b. Berlin, Apr. 13, 1964; , parents Am. citizens; d. Kenneth and Henrietta Nan (Weithorn) Kaplan; m. Guy Glickson Levy, July 27, 1986; children: Clare Sydney, Frankie Hannah. BS, Fla. State U., 1986; MEd, Coll. William and Mary, 1991. Cert. tchr. Va. Presch. tchr. Talent House Pvt. Sch., Fairfax, Va., 1986-87; 4th grade tchr. Mt. Vernon Elem. Sch., Tabb, 1987-92; elem. counselor Bethel Manor Elem. Sch., LAFB, 1992-95. Family mediator Dispute Settlement Ctr., Norfolk, Va., 1993—2000, Richmond, Va., 1994—95; contract mediator EEOC, 2001—. Past pres., v.p. Denbigh Jaycees (Project Mgr. of Yr. 1991, 93, Outstanding Local Pres. 1994), Va., 1987—94; sec., treas. Denbigh Jaycees. Democrat. Jewish. Avocation: Avocations: jogging, swimming, reading. Home: 463 Cheshire Ct Newport News VA 23602-6404

LEVY, ROCHELLE FELDMAN, artist; b. N.Y.C., Aug. 4, 1937; d. Harry and Eva (Krause) Feldman. M. Robert Paley Levey, June 4, 1955; children: Kathryn Tracey, Wendy Paige, Robert Paley, Angela Brooke, Michael Tyler. Student, Barnard Coll., 1954-55, U. Pa., 1955-56; BFA, Moore Coll. Art, 1979. Mgmt. cons. Woodlyn Sch., Rosemont, Pa., 1983-84; sr. ptnr. DRT Interiors, Phila., 1983—; ptnr. Phila. Phillies, 1981-94. One-woman Shows: Watson Gallery Wheaton Coll. Norton, Mass., 1977, U. Pa., 1977, Med. Coll. Pa. Phila., 1982, Aquaduct Race Track, 1982, Phila. Art Alliance, 1983, Paley Gallery, Moore Coll. Art and Design, 1984, Art Alliance, 1994, Frost & Reed Gallery, Saratoga, N.Y., 2000, 01. Pres. League of Children's Hosp. Phila., 1969-70; bd. overseers Ctr. for Judaic Studies U. Pa., 1993-96; bd. mgrs. Moore Coll. Art and Design, 1970—, chmn. exec. com., 1982-99, trustees 1979, chmn. emerita bd. trustees, 1999. Recipient G. Allen Smith Prize Woodmere ARt Gallery, Chestnut Hill, Pa., 1979; woman honoree Samuel Paley Day Care Ctr., Phila., 1990; Jefferson Bank Declaration award, 1991, Nat. Philanthropy honoree The Nat. Soc. of Fund Raising Execs. Greater Phila. chpt., 1994; trustee Moore Coll. Art 1979—, Honorary Doctorate of Humanities, 1998 (chmn. bd. trustees, 1988-99). Mem. Pa. Acad. Fine Arts (selections and acquisitions com. 1970—, bd. mgrs. 1975—, chmn. exec. com. 1982—, trustee 1990—), Artist's Equity, Phila. Art Alliance, Phila. Mus. Art (assoc), Phila. Print Club. Office: 2 Logan Sq Ste 2450 Philadelphia PA 19103-2724

LEVY, RUTH J. clinical psychologist, consultant; b. N.Y.C., Apr. 5, 1915; d. Edward and Rose (Gell) Jacobs; m. Wolfgang E. Levy, Feb. 11, 1934; children: Reuben E., Edna L. Lowe, Ralph D. BA, NYU, 1935; MA, Columbia U., 1937, PhD, 1940; JD, Lincoln U., San Jose, Calif., 1965. Diplomate Am. Bd. Examiners in Profl. Psychology. Clin. psychologist Ednl. Clinic/CCNY, N.Y.C., 1935-41, Washington Children's Home Soc., Seattle, 1943-56, VA Mental Hygiene Clinic, Seattle, 1947-51; prof. psychology Seattle U., 1953-56; clin. psychologist Santa Clara County Hosp., San Jose, 1956-58; dir. peace officers project San Jose City Health Dept., 1958-68; pvt. practice clin. psychology, San Jose, 1968—. Author: Reductions in Recidivism through Therapy, 1941; contbr. articles to profl. jours. Mem. Sigma Xi. Avocations: archaeology, amateur radio. Home: PO Box 813 Saratoga CA 95071-0813 E-mail: robin246@webtv.net.

LEVY, S. WILLIAM, dermatologist, educator; b. San Francisco, Sept. 28, 1920; s. Joseph and Dora (Taylor) L.; m. Elisabeth Rellstab, Mar. 17, 1974; children: David Lewis, Ann Louise. BS, U. Calif., San Francisco, 1943, MD, 1949. Practice medicine specializing in dermatology, San Francisco; research dermatologist Biomechanics Lab., U. Calif.; mem. staff Children's Hosp. of the Calif.-Pacific Med. Ctr., Mt. Zion Hosp. and Med. Center. Cons. to Letterman Army Hosp.; central med. adv. Calif. Blue Shield, San Francisco; clin. prof. dermatology U. Calif.; cons. in field. Author: Skin Problems of the Amputee, 1983; co-author: The Skin in Diabetes, 1986, Dermatology, 3rd edit., 1992, Dermatology in General Medicine, 5th edit., 1998, Atlas of Limb Prosthetics, 2d edit., 1992, 3rd edit., 2002, Cutis, 1995, Biomechanics, 1999, In Motion-Amputee Coalition of America, 2000; lectr. on skin problems of amputees, skin problems of diabectics, landmines and effects on soc., 2001-02. Served with USN, 1943-46. Recipient Lehn and Fink Gold Medal award. Fellow Am. Acad. Dermatology (life, Gold medal); mem. San Francisco Dermatol. Soc. (pres.), Pacific Dermatologic Assn. (v.p.), AMA, Calif. Med. Assn. (sci. council 1977-84), San Francisco Med. Soc. Office: Ste 305 599 Sir Francis Drake Blvd Greenbrae CA 94904-1732

LEVY, SALOMON, mechanical engineer; b. Jerusalem, Apr. 4, 1926; came to U.S., 1945; s. Abraham Isaac and Sultana Claire (Elyachar) L.; m. Eileen Dolores Jaques, Oct. 14, 1951; children: Marshall Douglas, Linda C. BSME, U. Calif., Berkeley, 1949, MME, 1951, PhD in Mech. Engring., 1953. Engr. Gen. Electric Co., Schenectady, N.Y. and San Jose, Calif., 1953-59, mgr. heat transfer San Jose, 1959-66, mgr. systems engring., 1966-68, mgr. design engring., 1968-71, gen. mgr., 1971-75, gen. mgr. boiling water reactor ops., 1975-77; chmn. S. Levy Inc., Campbell, Calif., 1977-98; owner Levy & Assocs., 1998—. Adj. prof. UCLA, 1986-87; Springer prof. U. Calif., Berkeley, 1979-80; bd. dirs. IES Industries, Inc., Cedar Rapids. Author: Two-Phase Flow in Complex Systems, 1999; patentee in field. Fellow ASME (hon., chmn. heat transfer divsn. 1964-65, heat transfer meml. award 1966, heat transfer conf. award 1963, 50th Ann. Heat Transfer Divsn. award 1988), Am. Nuclear Soc. (chmn. thermal hydraulics divsn. 1985-86, Thermal Hydraulics Divsn. Achievement award 1987, Power Divsn. Walter H. Zinn award 1989); mem. NAE, AIChE (Donald Kern award 1993), Inst. Nuclear Power Ops. (adv. coun.). Democrat. Mem. Unitarian Ch. Avocations: racquetball, golf. Home: 1829 Dry Creek Rd San Jose CA 95124-1002 Office: Levy and Assocs Ste 225 3425 S Bascom Ave Campbell CA 95008

LEVY, SAMUEL ROBERT, lawyer; b. Bklyn., Nov. 25, 1931; s. Martin and Bertha (Freeman) L.; m. Gloria Waldman, Oct. 12, 1963; children: Robin C., Marlene F. AB, NYU, 1952, LLB, 1954. Bar: N.Y. 1954, U.S. Supreme Ct. 1961, U.S. Dist. Ct. (ea. dist.) N.Y. 1957, U.S. Dist. Ct. (so. dist.) N.Y. 1957, U.S. Tax Ct. 1961, U.S. Ct. Claims 1961. Jr. ptnr. Levy-Levy, Bklyn., 1957-58; pvt. practice, 1959—. Notary pub., Kings County, N.Y., 1956—. Mem. Channel Thirteen, Jewish Nat. Fund, Partnership for Caring; capt. Clarendon Dem. Club, Bklyn., 1960-62. With U.S. Army, 1954-56. Mem. AARP, N.Y. State Bar Assn., NYU Alumni Assn., NYU Law Alumni Assn., Automobile Assn. Am., Nat. Geog. Soc., World Jewish Congress, Choice in Dying Orgn., Am. Assn. Kidney Patients, Inc., Simon Wiesenthal Ctr. Jewish. Home and Office: 1845 Ocean Ave Brooklyn NY 11230-7711

LEVY, STANLEY HERBERT, lawyer; b. Phila., Apr. 11, 1922; s. Max and Rose (Cohen) L.; m. Gloria Kamber, Dec. 20, 1953; children: Steven M., Peter B. BA, Cornell U., 1943; LL.B., Harvard U., 1949, JD, 1968. Bar: N.Y. 1949, U.S. Dist. Ct. (ea. and so. dists.) N.Y., U.S. Treasury 1949, U.S. Supreme Ct. 1961. Practiced in N.Y.C., 1949—. Mem. Republican Town Com., Scarsdale, 1963-65, Temple Emanu-el, Westchester, N.Y. Served to 1st lt. F.A., AUS, 1943-47. Mem. Assn. Bar City N.Y., Confrérie des Chevaliers du Tastevin (officier commandeur), Commanderie de Bordeaux (comdr.), Harvard Club, Yale Club, Century Country Club (Purchase, N.Y.), Mashomack Fish and Game Preserve (Pine Plains, N.Y.). Home: 3 Richbell Rd Scarsdale NY 10583-4421 Office: 521 5th Ave New York NY 10175-0003 E-mail: stanley@kamberinc.com.

LEVY, STEPHEN RAYMOND, high technology company executive; b. Everett, Mass., May 4, 1940; s. Robert George and Lillian (Berfield) L.; m. Sandra Helen Rosen, Aug. 26, 1961; children: Phillip, Susan. BBA, U. Mass., 1962, LLD (hon.) , 2001. Chmn. emeritus, dir. Bolt Beranek and Newman Inc., Cambridge, Mass., CEO, 1976—94; gen. ptnr. Levy Venture Ptnrs. LP. Chmn. bd. dirs. Kaon Interactive Corp. Chmn. Mass. Telecomms. Coun., 1996 Decorated Army Commendation medal. Mem. Am. Electronics Assn. (chmn. 1986), Mass. High Tech. Coun. (chmn. 1987-89), Mass. Telecommn. Coun. (chmn 1996). Home: 300 Boylston St Apt 1204 Boston MA 02116-3940 Office: Levy Venture Ptnrs LP 150 Cambridgepark Dr Cambridge MA 02140-2322

LEVY, STEVEN, lawyer; b. Chgo., Sept. 3, 1954; BA, U. Ill., 1975; JD, IIT, 1978. Bar: Ill. 1979, Fla. 1980, U.S. Dist. Ct. (no. dist.) Ill. 1979, U.S. Ct. Appeals (7th cir.) 1979, U.S. Dist. Ct. (so. and mid. dists.) Fla. 1980, U.S. Ct. Appeals (10th and 11th cirs.) 1980, U.S. Supreme Ct. 1993. Pvt. practice, Chgo., 1983—. Lectr. in field; apptd. to com. on profl. responsibility Ill. Supreme Ct., 1996—98, apptd. rules com., 1998—2001. Contbr. articles to profl. publs. Founding mem. DuPage County chpt. Am. Inns of Ct. Mem. Ill. State Bar Assn. (mem. editl. bd. Bar Jour. 1996—, standing CLE 1997—), Fla. Bar Assn., DuPage County Bar Assn. (editor-in-chief Bar Jour. 1995-99, recipient 20th ann. Lawyer of Yr. award, 2d ann. Professionalism award). Office: 40 Shuman Blvd Ste 151 Naperville IL 60563-8224

LEVY, SUSAN (ALEXANDRA LEVY), construction company executive; b. Rockville Centre, N.Y., Apr. 26, 1949; d. Alexander Stanley and Anna Charlotte (Galasieski) Jankoski; m. William Mack Levy, Aug. 12, 1977. Student, Suffolk Community Coll., Brentwood, N.Y., 1976. Cert. constrn. assoc. Supr. N.Y. Telephone Co., Babylon, 1970-74; v.p. Aabbacco Equipment Leasing Corp., Lindenhurst, N.Y., 1974-81; pres., owner Femi-9 Contracting Corp., Lindenhurst, 1981—. Bd. dirs. Brighter Tomorrows Shelter, 1997; mem. affirmative action adv. coun. N.Y. State Dept. Transp., Albany, 1984-88, human resources adv. panel Long Island Project 2000; mem. Presdl. Task Force, Washington, 1982—; mem. Leadership Am., 1994-95; bd. dirs. Brighter Tomorrows Shelter, 1997—. With U.S. Army, 1967-69. Recipient Henri Dunant Corp. award ARC Suffolk County, 1986, Race to the Top award Bridgestone Tire Corp., 1992, Nawbo award Nat. Assn. Women Bus. Owners, 1993; named honoree Women on the Job, 1989. Mem. Nat. Assn. Women in Constrn. (founder L.I. chpt., pres. 1983-85, regional chmn. woman-owned bus. enterprise com., nat. chmn. pub. rels. and mktg. com., nat. dir. Region 1 1988-89, Mem. of Yr. L.I. chpt. 1987, Exec. of Yr. L.I. chpt., nat. dir., 1988-89, nat. treas. 1991-93, nat. v.p. 1993-94, nat. pres.- elect 1994-95, pres. 1995-96), Nassau Suffolk Contractors Assn. (sec. 1984-87, sec.-treas. 1987-96, bd. dirs.), Nat. Assn. Women Bus. Owners (charter, Top Woman Bus. Owner award 1993), Am. Platform Assn. Republican. Roman Catholic. Avocations: reading, writing, golf. Home: 133 Hollins Ln East Islip NY 11730-3006 Office: Femi-9 Contracting Corp 305 E Sunrise Hwy Lindenhurst NY 11757-2521

LEVY, VALERY, publisher; b. Khartoum, Sudan, Feb. 16, 1946; came to U.S., 1959; d. Robert and Victorine (Malka) Braunstein; m. Joseph Levy, Aug. 24, 1968; children: Nomi, Berti. BA in political sci., Fairleigh Dickinson U., 1976, MA in internat. studies, 1978. Eng. tchr. Am. Inst. Cultural Affairs, Barcelona, Spain, 1965-66; Montessori tchr. Ft. Lee (N.J.) Community Ctr., 1974-81; project coord. Friends of Hebrew U., N.Y.C., 1981-83; devel. cons. Ft. Lee, 1983-85; editor, sr. editor Holt, Rinehart & Winston, N.Y.C., 1986-88; sr. editor, exec. editor Simon & Schuster Edn. Co., Morristown, Englewood, N.J., 1988-90; pres. Wonder Well Publishers, Ft. Lee, 1990-98; mng. editor Sch. divsn. McGraw-Hill, 1999—. Author: Alphabet Connections, 1990; editor: Room Of Mirrors, 1991. Address: 2100 Linwood Ave Fort Lee NJ 07024-3186

LEVY, WILLIAM JOEL, endocrinologist; b. Pitts., Mar. 7, 1949; s. Millard Levy and Shirley (Lubovsky) L.; m. Tammey J. Naab; children: Nicole, Natalie, Adam, Alaina. BA, Case Western Res. U., 1971; MD, U. Pitts., 1975. Intern Cleve. Clinic, 1975-76, resident, 1976-78, fellow in endocrinology, 1978-90; chief endocrinology St. Thomas Hosp., Akron, Ohio, 1980-84; endocrinologist in pvt. practice, 1980-84, No. Va., 1985, Prince George County, Md., 1986-93; endocrinologist Silver Spring, 1993—. Contbr. articles to profl. jours. Fellow ACP; mem. Am. Diabetes Assn., Am. Thyroid Assn. Office: 344 University Blvd W Ste 328 Silver Spring MD 20901-1948 E-mail: wjlevy@aol.com.

LEVY, JR. RALPH JACOB, retired theater educator; b. Northampton, Mass., Dec. 1, 1927; s. Ralph Jacob and Dorothy Levy. MA Theater, Western Res. U., Cleveland, OH, 1952; BA Speech and Dramatic Art, State U. of Iowa, Iowa City, IA, 1951. Teacher Certification MA, 1952. Adminstr. aide Commonwealth of Mass., Boston, 1989—2002; speech and theater educator Northampton H.S., Northampton, 1976—87, Duquesne U., Pittsburgh, Pa., 1952—54; pres. and mgr. Harry Daniel's Inc., Northampton, Mass., 1956—76; fin. clk. US Army, Fort Dix, NJ, 1946—48. Author: (magazine column) Hampshire Magazine, (book) The Career of Milton Aborne, Biography of Morris J. Raphall. Bd. mem. and campaign chair Hampshire Cmty. United Way, Northampton, Mass., 1956—76; chairperson Downtown Merchants Assn., 1956—76; ex-officio mem. Chamber of Commerce Bd. of Directors, 1956—76; founder and dir. Dollors for Scholars, 1971—2002; program chair and host WHMP Radio AM, 1971—2000. Cpl. t-5 US Army, 1946—48, New Jersey. Recipient Citizen of the Yr., Northampton Chamber of Commerce, 1973, Jaycee of the Yr., Mass. Jaycees, 1961, Disting. Svc. Award, Hampshire Cmty. United Way, 1960. Democrat-Npl. Jewish. Avocations: walking, acting, reading, research. Home: 19 Carpenter Avenue Northampton MA 01060

LEW, D(UKHEE) BETTY, physician; b. Seoul, Korea, June 1, 1952; came to U.S., 1972; d. H.S. and M.S. Lew. BS, Temple U., 1976, MD, 1980. Intern, resident Shands Med. Ctr., Gainesville, Fla., 1980-83; fellow Nat. Jewish Ctr. for Immunology and Respiratory Medicine, Denver, 1983-86; asst. then assoc. prof. U. Tenn., Memphis, 1986—99, prof., 1999—. Grantee Am. Lung Assn., 1991—, Am. Lung Assn. Tenn., 1990-91; recipient 1st award NIH, 1991-96, 1998—. Mem. Am. Acad. Allergy & Immunology, Am. Coll. Allergy & Immunology, Ten. Soc. Allergy & Immunology, Tenn. Thoracic Soc., Soc. Pediat. Rsch., Soc. Leukocyte Biology. Methodist. Avocations: organ, photography. Home: 2490 Ayrshire Cv Memphis TN 38119-7506 Office: LeBonheur Children's Med Ctr 1 Children's Plz Memphis TN 38105

LEW, JOYCELYNE MAE, actress; b. Santa Monica, Calif., Feb. 25, 1962; d. George and Mabel Florence (Lum) L. BA in Theatre Arts, UCLA, 1981, teaching credential, 1982; MA in Urban Edn., Pepperdine U., 1984; bilingual cert., U. So. Calif., 1983; postgrad., Stella Adler Acad., 1988; studied with, The Groundlings Improv Group, 1987. Exec. com. Acad. T.V. Arts & Scis., 2000-01. Appeared in films Tai-Pan, 1987, Fatal Beauty, 1989, The Royal Affair, 1993, Shattered Image, 1993, Dr. Boris and Mrs. Duluth, 1994, Hindsight, 1996, Fire in My Heart, 1996, Ginseng Power, 1998; TV programs The Young and the Restless, 1990, Phil Donahue Show, 1993, Hard Copy, 1994, Current Affair, 1995, Gordon Elliott, 1995, Married With Children, 1997, True Hollywood Stories, 1997, Nat. Enquirer TV, 2000, Arrest & Trial, 2000, Extra, 2001, Men are from Mars, Women are from Venus, 2001, Sins of Hollywood, 2002; (theater) Mary Tape, 2000; voice over artist, mag. model, body double, dancer; appeared in comml. Good Seasons, 1996, Pillsbury Doughboy, 1996, Pacific Bell, 1996, Beefsteak Rye Bread, 1998, Miller Beer, 1998; co-writer film script They Still Call Me Bruce, 1986 (award); song lyricist Nighttime Blues (award Allure Mag., 2002). Mem. judging com. for film grants Nat. Endowment for Arts, 1986; mem. L.A. Beautiful, 1993. Mem. AFTRA, SAG, AEA, ATAS (exec. com. performer's branch, 2000, blue ribbon com. for Emmy awards 1986-96), Assn. Asian Pacific Am. Artists (treas. 1983-89), Nat. Asian Am. Telecomms. Assn., Am. Film Inst. Conservatory Workshop, Calif. PTA (life). Avocations: calligraphy, makeup art and hair, charcoals, fashion and interior design. Home and Office: 1952 N Van Ness Ave Los Angeles CA 90068-3625 E-mail: Joycelyne@finalprint.com.

LEW, LESLIE, artist; b. N.Y.C., Jan. 3, 1953; BFA, The Sch. of the Art Inst. of Chgo., 1981, postgrad., 1981—82. One-woman shows include Sensory Evolution Gallery, N.Y.C., 1985—86, Bernice Steinbaum Gallery, 1987, Margulies Taplin Gallery, Bay Harbor Island, Fla., 1990, OK Harris Gallery, N.Y.C., 1992, Vered Gallery, East Hampton, N.Y., 1992, Margulies Taplin Gallery, Miami, 1995, Light Gallery, L.A., 1996, Chappaqua Libr. Gallery, Chappaqua, N.Y., others, 2001, exhibited in group shows at numerous, including Westchester Arts Coun., White Plains, N.Y., 2001, Represented in permanent collections various, including Bellevue Hosp., N.Y., Bank of Sicily, N.Y., Elektra Asylum Records, N.Y., Mayo Clinic, Minn., MCA Records, N.Y.; contbr. book. Grantee Pollack Krasner grant, N.Y., 1991, Rauchenberg grant, 1991. Studio: 628 Chappaqua Rd Briarcliff Manor NY 10510

LEW, ROGER ALAN, manufacturing company executive; b. N.Y.C., Mar. 16, 1941; s. Louis Arthur and Estelle Bebe (Marcus) L.; m. Marilyn Drourr, May 29, 1962; children— William, Jeffrey, Richard. BS in Fin, NYU, 1963. With Franklin Nat. Bank, N.Y.C., 1963-66; sr. v.p. Security Nat. Bank, 1966-75; v.p. NVF Co., 1975-78, sr. v.p., 1978-81, treas., 1979-81; pres., dir. Wormuth Bros. Foundry, Inc., Athens, N.Y., 1981—. Pres., bd. dirs. Mirage Fin., Inc., 1985—, transmission Gear Sales, Inc., 1985—, Hudson Valley Buyers, Inc., 1985—; former sr. v.p., treas. Sharon Steel Corp., Pa. Engring. Corp., DWG Co., Southeastern Pub. Svc. Co.; former sr. v.p., treas., bd. dirs. Wilson Bros.; former mem. small bus. and agr. adv. coun. to N.Y. Fed. Res. Bank. Trustee, former exec. v.p. Universal Housing & Devel. Co.; former v.p. Security Mgmt. Corp. Served with U.S. Army, 1959-60. Mem. Am. Iron and Steel Inst. Clubs: Colonie Country (Voorhees, N.Y.); Sag Harbor (N.Y.) Yacht. Office: Howard Hall Rd PO Box 171 Athens NY 12015-0171 E-mail: ralew@wormuth.com.

LEW, SALVADOR, radio station executive; b. Camajuani, Las Villas, Cuba, Mar. 6, 1929; s. Berko and Clara (Lewinowicz) Lew; 1 child Esther Maria. JD magna cum laude, U. Havana, 1952. Editor Sch. Mural Newspaper, Camajuani, Cuba, 1941-43; pres. youth sect., nat. sect. Cuban People's Party, 1948-53; Lat. Am. cons. Waltes, Moore & Costanzo, Miami, 1961-72; news dir. Sta. WMIE and Sta. WQBA, 1961-70; gen. mgr., news dir. Sta. WRHC, 1973-89; host talk show, 1989—2001. Pres. adv. bd. Cuba Broadcasting, 1992—2001; dir. Office of Cuba Broadcasting, Radio & TV Marti, appointed by President Geroge W. Bush, 2001; sr. cons. Everet Clay Assocs., 1989—2001. Trustee, dir. United Way, 1985—; sr. cons. Everet Clay Assoc. Everet Clay Assoc., 1989. Recipient Lincoln Marti award, Sec. HEW, 1964, FBI award for cmty. svcs., 1983, cmty. svc. awards, various orgns. Mem.: Cuban Lawyers Assn., Exile. Jewish. Home: 2863 SW 23rd St Miami FL 33145-3309

LEWALLEN, ELINOR KIRBY, religious organization executive, lay church worker; b. Miltonvale, Kans., May 17, 1919; d. Osbourn Eddy and Grace Dale (Gorrell) Kirby; m. Thomas Monroe Lewallen, Jr., Aug. 14, 1948 (dec. July 2001); children: Janet, Dean, Gary, Kent, Bonnie. AA, Coffeyville Jr. Coll., 1939; BA, Baker U., 1943; postgrad., U. Colo., 1969-70, Iliff Sch. Theology, Denver, 1986, 90, 94. Youth pres. Kans. Conf. United Meth. Youth, Baldwin, Kans., 1940-41; program dir. for young adults YWCA, Rockford, Ill., 1943-46; program dir. Bus. and Profl. Girls Club of YWCA, Denver, 1946-48; nat. pres. Fedn. Parents and Friends of Lesbians and Gays, 1987-88, chmn. Fedn. Parents-FLAG Religious Issues Task Force, 1988-91. Rsch. sec. values study The Iliff Sch. of Theology, 1977-84; numerous leadership roles Park Hill United Meth. Ch., Denver, 1953—; del. to Rocky Mtn. ann. conf. Colo., 1979-88; mem. conf. task force on AIDS, 1986-92, com. on sexuality ministries, 1981-99; mem. steering com. John Wesley Iliff Group; presenter United Meth. Gen. Conf. Com. to Study Homosexuality, St. Louis, 1991; mem. adminstrv. coun. Park Hill United Meth. Ch., 1993-96, ch. staff parish com., 1998-2002. Author: Viewpoint. Chmn. impact neighborhood task force Denver Anti-Crime Coun., 1972-80; election judge, Denver 1981-97; mem. Colo. Gov.'s Adv. Coun. on AIDS, 1987-88. Recipient award of recognition Denver Anti-Crime Coun., 1980, Outstanding Leadership award Nat. Parents, Families, and Friends of Lesbians and Gays, 1988, 92, Hall of Honor and Swan award Denver Parents, Families and Friends of Lesbians and Gays, 1994, Civil Rights Awd. A.A.U.W. Trailblazers event (Denver), 1998, Pres. award for distinction to ch. and soc. ILIFF Sch. Theology, Denver, 2000, Family Tree award Lift Every Voice, 2000. Mem. LWV, A.A.U.W., Assn. Group Workers (charter Colo. chpt.). Democrat. Home: 2258 Krameria St Denver CO 80207-3931 *The images I have gathered through many years of growing and sharing in the world of so many beautiful gay/lesbian people* *would by now create a rose window in a cathedral. I stand in awe that our children are finding their strength without role models, their direction without roadmaps for their remarkable journeys. They are discovering their power through the testing of their spirits. They are walking through deep waters as many with AIDS daily face their mortality. They are leaving legacies of creativity, courage, and caring. How can I as parent, a friend and a committed Christian do less?.*

LEWALLEN, WILLIAM MARVIN, JR. ophthalmologist; b. McGregor, Tex., Aug. 31, 1927; s. William M. and Lois Pauline (Sherrill) L.; m. Katherine Louise Mosley, June 12, 1947 (div. Nov. 1985); children: Margaret Anne, William Michael, Susan, Cynthia. BS, Southern Meth. Univ., 1944; MD, Southwestern Med. Coll. Tex., 1947. Diplomate Am. Bd. Otolaryngology, Am. Bd. Ophthalmology. Internship Baylor Univ., Dallas, 1947-48; residency otolarygology Southwestern Medical Coll., 1948-50; residency ophthalmology Jefferson Davis Hosp., Houston, 1953-54; pvt. practice Pueblo, Colo., 1955—. Asst. clin. prof. Univ. Colo. Medical Sch., Denver, 1956—; cons. Colo. State Hosp., Pueblo, 1956—, U.S. VA Hosp., Ft. Lyon, Colo., 1956—; chief ophthalmology St. Mary-Corwin Hosp., 1970-72, exec. com., 1970-74; bd. dirs. Republic Nat. Bank, Centenial Banks Pueblo & Blende. Contbr. articles to profl. jours. Bd. dirs. YMCA, Pueblo, 1958-60; pres. bd. dirs. Rocky Mountain Coun. Boy Scout Am., 1960-72; mem. sch. bd. Pueblo Sch. Bd. Dist. 60, 1959-71, pres. sch. bd., 1967-69; chmn. bd. dirs. Pueblo Blvd. Bank, 1979-93; pres. Rotary Club, 1975-76, dir., 1974-77. Lt. comdr. U.S. Navy, 1950-52. Fellow Am. Acad. Ophthalmology. Republican. Protestant. Avocations: bicycling, fishing, hiking, skiing. Home and Office: 205 Dunsmere Ave Pueblo CO 81004-1026 Fax: (719) 545 1951.

LEWAND, F. THOMAS, lawyer; b. San Diego, July 24, 1946; s. Barbara (Boening) L.; m. Kathleen Sullivan, Aug. 3, 1968; children: Thomas, Kevin, Kristen, Carrie. BA, U. Detroit, 1968; JD, Wayne State U., 1970. Bar: Mich. 1970, U.S. Dist. Ct. (ea. dist.) 1970. Law clk. to judge U.S. Ct. Appeals (6th cir.), Detroit, 1970; commr. Oakland County, Pontiac, 1978-80; chief of staff to Gov. J. Blanchard Lansing, 1982-83; ptnr. Jaffe, Raitt & Heuer, Detroit, 1970-92, Bodman, Longley & Dahling, Detroit, 1992—. Trustee Gov. Blanchard Found., Lansing, 1982—; dir. Wayne County Econ. Devel. Corp., 1997—, Nat. Conf. on Cmty. and Justice, 1999—; trustee U. Detroit Mercy., 1996—, chmn., 2001—. Campaign mgr. Gov. James J. Blanchard, MIch., 1978; chmn. Mich. Dems., 1989-91. Mem. State Bar Mich., Nat. Assn. Bond Lawyers. Office: Bodman Longley & Dahling 100 Renaissance Ctr Fl 34 Detroit MI 48243-1001

LEWANDO, ALFRED GERARD, JR. oceanographer; b. Boston, Apr. 17, 1945; s. Alfred Gerard and Marie Helen (Coughlin) L.; m. Carol Ann Kologe, Nov. 8, 1969; children: Jennifer Ann, Christina Marie. BS in Earth Sci., State Coll. Boston, 1967; MBA, U. So. Miss., 1986, MS in Polit. Sci., 1989, MS in Pub. Rels., 1990, MEd in Adult Edn., 1991. Lic. real estate broker and notary pub., Miss. Staff oceanographer Naval Oceanographic Office, Washington, 1967-76, head fleet support br., 1976-80, dir. tactical analysis div. Bay St. Louis, Miss., 1980-86, dir. oceanographic programs div., 1986-88; dep. asst. chief of staff for ops. Naval Oceanography Command, Stennis Space Ctr., Miss., 1988-94; asst. chief staff for command mgmt. and inspector gen. Naval Meteorology and Oceanography Command, Stennis Space Center, 1994-98; dir. ocean surveys dept. Naval Oceanographic Office, Stennis Space Ctr., 1998—; mem. policy bd. Ctr. of Higher Learning, Stennis Space Ctr., Miss., 1990—; sr. exec. fellow John F. Kennedy Sch. Govt. Harvard U., 1996. Mem. adv. com. Cape Fear Jr. Coll., Wilmington, N.C., 1974—, Miss. State U. Rsch. Ctr., 1988—; mem. steering com. Summer Indsl. fellowships for Gulf Coast Tchrs., 1990—; mem. organizing com. 44th Internat. Sci. and Engring. Fair, 1993. Contbr. articles to profl. publs. Commr., City of Long Beach (Miss.) Port Authority, 1986-88. Sr. Exec. fellow Harvard U., 1996. Mem. Miss. Acad. Scis., Gamma Theta Upsilon. Home: 553 Mockingbird Dr Long Beach MS 39560-3134 Office: Naval Oceanographic Office Bay Saint Louis MS 39529 E-mail: aglewando@aol.com.

LEWANDOWSKI, ANDREW ANTHONY, utilities executive, consultant; b. Kiel, Germany, Nov. 29, 1946; came to U.S., 1949; s. Kazimierz and Emily (Lewandowski) L.; m. Mary Ann Zuza; 1 child, Adam Christopher. Student, Rutgers U., 1964-66; BS in Mech. Engring., N.J. Inst. Tech., 1969; postgrad., Pa. State U., 1969-70; MS in Mech. Engring., N.J. Inst. Tech., 1973. Registered profl. engr., N.J.; cert. profl. planner, N.J. NSF trainee N.J. Inst. Tech., 1970-72; Engr. I DeLeuw, Cather & Co., Newark, 1970; gas utilities engr. DeLeuw, Cather & Co. of N.Y., Inc., N.Y.C., 1972, specifications writer, 1972-74, chief specifications, 1974-75; supv. engr. Elizabethtown Gas Co., Iselin, N.J., 1976-79, mgr. planning, system improvement, 1979-81, mgr. planning, budgets, 1981-86, internal cons., computer mgmt. Elizabeth, N.J., 1986-87, internal cons. ops., engring. Iselin, 1987-89, internal cons. engring., budgets Union, 1989-95, sr. planning engr., 1995-98; sys. adminstr. NUI/Utility Bus. Svcs., 1998-99, mgr. applications, 2000—. Editor Jaycee newsletter, 1979-80, local Rep. newsletter, 1986; monthly contbr. Film Score Monthly, 1993-97. Den leader, asst. cubmaster Cub Scouts Boy Scouts Am., sec. troop com., merit badge counselor; active various local govt. religious, polit. and charitable orgns. Recipient Dir. of Yr. award South Plainfield Jaycees, 1972, Disting. Svc. award, 1975, Outstanding Young Man of Yr. award N.J. Jaycees. 1975, South Plainfield Jaycees, 1976, den leader award Boy Scouts Am. 1994; inducted into South Plainfield H.S. Hall of Fame, 1997. Mem. NSPE, ASME, KC, Internat. Platform Assn., South Plainfield Polish Nat. Home, The Film Music Soc. Republican. Roman Catholic. Home: 1910 Murray Ave South Plainfield NJ 07080-4713 Office: NUI/Utility Bus Svcs 1085 Morris Ave Union NJ 07083-7136 E-mail: alewandowski@nui.com., el_cid@att.net.

LEWANDOWSKI, THEODORE CHARLES, psychology educator; b. Phila., Apr. 26, 1945; s. Theodore A. and Teresa M. Lewandowski; m. Regina F. Blake, Sept. 21, 1968; children: Michael T., Joan T. BA, Villanova U., 1967, MS, 1969; CAGS, Temple U., 1979. Lic. psychologist, Pa. Lectr. Villanova (Pa.) U., 1974-79; prof. Delaware County Coll., Media, Pa., 1969—. Lectr. Thomas Jefferson U., Phila., 1981—; credential evaluator Pa. State Bd. Psychology, Harrisburg, 1987-97, vice-chairperson, 1980-86; mem. Pa. Drug, Device and Cosmetic Bd., Harrisburg, 1987-92. Author: Abnormal Psychology Case Interviews, 1971; co-author: Instructor's Manual to accompany Understanding Abnormal Behavior, 1971. Emergency coord. for Ea. Pa. Am. Radio Relay League, Newington, Conn., 1989-92. Mem. APA (state liaison 1970-72), Am. Ednl. Rsch. Assn., Am. Psychol. Soc., Ea. Psychol. Assn., Pa. Psychol. Assn. (stds. com. 1973-74), Pa. Ednl. Rsch. Assn. Office: Delaware County Coll 901 S Media Line Rd Media PA 19063-1094 E-mail: tlewand@dccc.edu.

LEWCOCK, RONALD BENTLEY, architect, educator; b. Brisbane, Australia, Sept. 27, 1929; s. Harry Kingsley and Ena (Orrock) L.; m. Barbara Sansoni, Aug. 8, 1981. Student, U. Queensland, 1947-49; BArch, Cape Town U., South Africa, 1951; PhD, U. Cape Town, South Africa, 1961; MA, Cambridge U., Eng., 1970; DArch (hon.), Natal U., South Africa, 1999. Pvt. practice architecture, 1951—; Whitehead research fellow Clare Hall, Cambridge U., Eng., 1970-72, ofcl. fellow Eng., 1976-84; research officer Middle East Centre, Cambridge U., Cambridge, 1973-80; Aga Khan prof. architecture for Islamic culture, dir. program in architecture for Islamic socs. MIT, 1984-91; chmn. Aga Khan program for Islamic architecture MIT and Harvard U., 1985-87; prof. architecture Ga. Inst. Tech., Atlanta, 1991—. Cons. UNESCO, Habitat, World Bank, British Coun., Am. Rsch. Cen., Egypt, 1976-83; lectr. U. Natal, 1952-57, sr. lectr., 1958-69; lectr., examiner Cambridge U., 1973-85; unit leader design in developing world Archtl. Assn., London, 1977-81; lectr. Archtl. Assocs. Sch., London, 1971-82; vis. prof. grad. sch. architecture Ga. Inst. Tech., 1979-84, Harvard, 1984, Louvain U., 1984; vis. Aga Khan prof., MIT, 1991-93, UQT, Australia, 1996. Author: Early 19th Century Architecture in South Africa, 1963, Traditional Architecture in Kuwait and the Northern Gulf, 1978, 2d edit. 81, Wadi Hadramawt and the Walled City of Shibam, 1986, The Old World City of San'a', 1986, The Architecture of an Island—Sri Lanka, 1998; editor: (with R.B. Serjeant) San'a' an Arabian Islamic City, 1983; contbr. articles to profl. jours., Architecture in the Islamic World, 1976, New Grove Dictionary of Music and Musicians, 1980, 97. Mem. coun. Inst. History and Archaeology East Africa, London, 1976-86, Middle East Centre, Cambridge, Eng., 1981-88, British Sch. Archaeology in Jerusalem, London, 1981-98; tech. coord. Internat. Campaign for the Conservation of Sana'a in Yemen Arab Rep. and Shibam and Wadi Hadramaut in Peoples Dem. Rep. of Yemen, 1978-93, UNESCO/UNDP Campaign for Conservation of Monuments and Cities in Uzbekistan, 1994-97; steering com. mem. Aga Khan award, 1990-93, Aga Khan Trust for Culture, Geneva, 1993—. Howard vis. fellowship Columbia U., 1963. Mem. Royal Inst. British Architects (assoc.). Office: Georgia Inst of Technology 225 North Ave NW Atlanta GA 30332-0002 also: 13 Norwich St Cambridge CB2 1ND England

LEWE, DIANE ADELE, social worker; b. Cin., June 9, 1947; d. Harry T. and Adele A. (Richter) L.; m. Joseph J. Pauls, June 28, 1975. AA with honors, U. Cin., 1967, BA with honors, 1970; MSW, U. Chgo., 1973. Crisis worker Virginia Beach (Va.) Social Svcs., 1973-74, tng. specialist, 1974-75; social worker Cath. Charities, New Orleans, 1975-77; partial hosp. supr. Scioto Paint Valley YMHC, Chillicothe, Ohio, 1977-78, dir. adminstrv. svcs., 1978-80, clin. dir., 1980-89, exec. dir., 1989—. Treas. Pub.-Pvt. Solutions, 1997. Bd. dirs. Inter-Ag. Childcare, Chillicothe, 1992—, treas., 1996—; mem. Ross County Dem. Women, Chillicothe, 1993—. Mem. Ohio Coun. Behavioral Healthcare (bd. dirs. 1990—, treas. 1996-98, v.p. 1998-99). Roman Catholic. Avocations: gardening, cooking, photography, horses. Home: 321 Woodview Dr Chillicothe OH 45601-9722 Office: Scioto Paint Valley Mental Health Ctr PO Box 6179 Chillicothe OH 45601-6179

LEWELL, PETER A. international technology executive, researcher; b. St. John, N.B., Can. Exec. dir. N.B. Rsch. and Productivity Coun., Fredericton, N.B., Can. Bd. dirs. Incutech, Ctr. Nuclear Energy Rsch. Office: NB Rsch & Productivity Coun 921 ch College Hill Rd Fredericton NB Canada E3B 6Z9

LEWELLEN, ROBERT THOMAS, research geneticist; b. Nyssa, Oreg., Apr. 27, 1940; s. John and Frances M. (Klinkenberg) L.; m. Priscilla Ellen Stark, Sept. 15, 1962. BS, Oreg. State U., 1962; PhD, Mont. State U., 1966. Agronomist Mont. Agr. Experiment Sta., Bozeman, 1965-66; geneticist rsch. div. USDA-Agrl. Rsch. Svc., Salinas, Calif., 1966—. Fellow Am. Soc. Agronomy; mem. Am. Soc. Sugar Beet Tech. (bd. dirs. 1989-91, Meritorious award 1991), Am. Phytopathol. Soc. Achievements include development of unique sugarbeet varieties, parental lines, breeding lines, and germplasm; identification and development of sources of resistance to plant diseases, e.g. rhizomania, virus diseases, powdery mildew, etc.; research in genetics of sugarbeets. Home: 1186 San Angelo Dr Salinas CA 93901-3903 Office: US Agrl Rsch Sta 1636 E Alisal St Salinas CA 93905-3018

LEWELLEN, WILBUR GARRETT, management educator, consultant; b. Charleroi, Pa., Jan. 21, 1938; s. Anthony Garrett and Cozie Harriett (Watson) L.; m. Jean Carolyn Vanderlip, Dec. 8, 1962 (div. 1982); children— Stephen G., Jocelyn A., Jonathan W., Robyn E.; m. Eloise Evelyn Vincent, Mar. 5, 1983 BS, Pa. State U., University Park, 1959; MS, MIT, Cambridge, 1961, PhD, 1967; LhD (hon.), Budapest U. of Econ. Scis., 1996. Asst. prof. mgmt. Purdue U., West Lafayette, Ind., 1964-68, assoc. prof. mgmt., 1968-72, prof., 1972-83, Loeb prof. mgmt., 1983-88, Krannert disting. prof. mgmt., 1988—, dir. exec. edn. programs, 1985—. Cons. Bank Am., San Francisco, 1975—90, Ind. Bell Tel. Co., Indpls., 1976—90, Am. Water Works Co., Wilmington, Del., 1978—94, Indpls. Power and Light Co., 1993—99, NiSource, Inc., 2000—; bd. dirs. Indsl. Dielectrics, Inc. Author: Executive Compensation in Large Industrial Corporations, 1968, Ownership Income of Management, 1971, The Cost of Capital, 1981, Financial Management: An Introduction to Principles and Practice, 2000. Recipient Salgo-Noren award as Outstanding Tchr. in Grad. Profl. Programs, Salgo-Noren Found., 1973, 77, 79, 84. Mem. Fin. Mgmt. Assn. (v.p. 1973-74), Am. Fin. Assn., Strategic Mgmt. Soc., AAUP, Western Fin. Assn., Lafayette Country Club. Methodist. Office: Purdue Univ Grad Sch Mgmt West Lafayette IN 47907

LEWENT, JUDY CAROL, pharmaceutical executive; b. Jan. 13, 1949; BA, Goucher Coll., 1970; MS in Mgmt., MIT, 1972. With corp. fin. dept. E.F. Hutton & Co., Inc., 1972-74; asst. v.p. for strategic planning Bankers Trust Co., 1974-75; sr. fin. analyst corp. planning Norton Simon, 1975-76; div. contr. Pfizer, Inc., 1976-80; dir. acquisitions and capital analysis Merck & Co., Inc., Whitehouse Station, N.J., 1980-83, asst. contr., 1983-85, exec. dir. fin. evaluation and analysis, 1985-87, v.p., treas., 1987-90, v.p. fin., CFO, 1990-92, sr. v.p., CFO, 1993-2001, exec. v.p., CFO, 2001—. Bd. dirs. Dell Computer Corp., Motorola Inc., Nat. Bur. Econ. Rsch.; life mem. MIT Corp.; trustee Rockefeller Family Trust. Mem. exec. com. Penn Medicine. Office: Merck & Co Inc PO Box 100 One Merck Dr Whitehouse Station NJ 08889-0100

LEWERT, ROBERT MURDOCH, microbiologist, educator; b. Scranton, Pa., Sept. 30, 1919; s. Philip John and Nell (Bertholf) L.; m. Evelyn P. Allen, Feb. 19, 1948; children— Philip Allen, Barbara Joan. BS, U. Mich., 1941; MS, Lehigh U., 1943; Sc.D., Johns Hopkins, 1948. Diplomate: in parasitology Am. Bd. Microbiologists. Instr. biology Lehigh U., 1941-43, Hobart and William Smith Colls., Geneva, 1943-44; instr. dept. bacteriology and parasitology U. Chgo., 1948-52, asst. prof., 1952-56, assoc. prof. microbiology, 1957-61, prof., 1961-85, prof. emeritus dept. molecular genetics and cell biology, 1985—. Vis. prof. parasitology U. Philippines Inst. Hygiene, 1961, 63-66; mem. com. on parasitic diseases Armed Forces Epidemiological Bd., 1955-73; cons. to surgeon gen. Dept. Army, 1956-75; cons. on parasitic diseases Hines (Ill.) VA Hosp., 1975-82; mem. tropical medicine and parasitology study sect. USPHS, 1965-69, allergy and infectious diseases tng. grant com., 1969-73 Mem. editorial bd.: Jour. Parasitology, 1958-64, Abstracts of Bioanalytic Tech, 1959-63, Jour. Infectious Disease, Am. Jour. Epidemiology, Am. Jour. Tropical Medicine and Hygiene. Served with USNR, 1944-46. Fulbright fellow, 1961; Guggenheim fellow, 1961; recipient U. Chgo. Med. Alumni Gold Key award, 1997. Fellow Am. Acad. Microbiology; mem. Am. Soc. Tropical Medicine and Hygiene, Nippon Bijitsu Token Hozon Kyokai (life), Japanese Sword Soc. of U.S. (chmn. 1977-83), Nihontoken Hozon Kai, Kunzan-Sensei Ni Manabu-Kai, Token Soc. Gt. Britian, Sigma Xi. Achievements include research on immunity to schistosomiasis, histochem. and cytochem. studies on invasiveness of parasites, biochemistry of host-parasite relationships. Home: 37 Henry Mountain Rd Brevard NC 28712-9705 E-mail: kaneyama@webtv.net.

LEWES, ULLE ERIKA, English educator; b. Tallinn, Estonia, Europe, Mar. 22, 1942; d. Karl Erik Allik and Ella (Vaher) Laaman; m. Kenneth Lewes, June 1967 (div. June 1975); m. Allen Dunlap, Jr., June 17, 1988 (dec. Sept. 1997). BA, Cornell U., 1964; MA, Harvard U., 1965, PhD, 1972. Asst. prof. Temple U., Phila., 1971-78; assoc. prof. Ohio Wesleyan U., Delaware, Ohio, 1978-83, full prof., 1983—. Cons. Ohio Bd. Regents, 1995-97, Mellon Found., Ohio Wesleyan Grant, 1979-82, Jefferson County Schs., Ohio, 1989-97, numerous writing projects in Ohio, 1982-98. Author: (books) Life in Forest, 1979, Writing as Learning, 1990; contbr. articles to Tristania jour. Life supporter So. Poverty Law Ctr., Montgomery, Ala. Mem. NOW, MLA, Amnesty Internat., Nat. Coun. Tchrs. English, Conf. on Coll. Composition and Comms., Medieval Acad. Am., Coun. of Writing Program Adminstrs., Tristan Soc., Shakespeare Soc. Avocations: photography, travel, ethnic cuisines, prisoners' rights struggle. Office: Ohio Wesleyan Univ Sturges 211 Delaware OH 43015-1937

LEWICKY, ROMAN TARAS, orthopedic surgeon; b. Sambir, Ukraine, Jan. 1, 1942; arrived in U.S., 1949; s. Witold G. and Irene (Antonowych) Lewicky; m. Puka Therese Gizinski, June 26, 1965; children: Andrey, Yuri. BS, Holy Cross Coll., Mass., 1964; MD, Northwestern U., 1968. Diplomate Am. Bd. Orthop. Surgery. Intern Denver Gen. Hosp., 1968-69; resident in orthopedic surgery Northwestern U., Chgo., 1971-75; orthopedic surgeon No. Ariz. Orthopedics, Flagstaff, 1975—. Med. dir. Flagstaff Outpatient Surgery Ctr., 1991—2001; cons. athletics No. Ariz. U., 1975. Mem. pres. adv. coun. U. No. Ariz., 1982—84. Fellow: ACS, Am. Acad. Orthop. Surgeons; mem.: AMA, Ariz. Med. Assn. (Sports Medicine Physician of Yr. 1983), We. Orthop. Assn., Arthroscopy Assn. N.Am., Am. Orthop. Sports Medicine Soc. Greek Catholic. Avocation: breeding Arabian horses. Home: RR 4 Box 711 Flagstaff AZ 86001-9301 Office: No Ariz Orthopedics 1485 Turquoise Dr Ste 200 Flagstaff AZ 86001-1481 E-mail: veselkartl@aol.com.

LEWIN, DAN'L, information technology executive; Exec. leading sales and mktg. divsns. various cos., including Apple Computer Corp., NeXT Software, Inc., Go Corp.; cons. emerging cos. such as Kaleida and Taligent, venture capital firms, such as Kleiner Perkins Caufield & Byers, and SOFTBANK Venture Capital; CEO Aurigin Systems Inc.; corp. v.p., Microsoft.NET Bus. Devel. Microsoft, Redmond, Wash. Office: One Microsoft Way Redmond WA 98052-6399*

LEWIN, JEFFREY DAVID, lawyer; b. Mpls., Feb. 11, 1945; s. Harry Davidson and Leota Rose (Seitz) L.; m. Eva Gertrud Sonnenberg, Dec. 21, 1971; children: Eric, Peter. BA with honors, Stanford U., 1967; JD, Calif. Western U., 1975. Bar: Calif. 1976, U.S. Supreme Ct. 1979. Trial atty. antitrust div. U.S. Dept. Justice, Chgo., 1975-76; assoc., then ptnr. Sullivan, Jones & Archer, San Diego, 1976-82; ptnr. Sullivan, Hill, Lewin Rez & Engel, 1983—. Lectr., instr. continuing edn. of bar NITA, San Diego, 1985—. Contbr. articles to profl. publs. Trustee Calif. Western Sch. Law, San Diego, 1981—; lawyer del. 9th Cir. Jud. Conf., San Diego, 1982-84. Mem. ABA, San Diego County Bar Assn., Harvard Club San Diego (bd. dirs. 1990-93). Office: Sullivan Hill Lewin Rez & Engel 550 W C St Ste 1500 San Diego CA 92101-3570

LEWIN, KLAUS JONATHAN, pathologist, educator; b. Jerusalem, Israel, Aug. 10, 1936; came to U.S., 1968; s. Bruno and Charlotte (Nawratzki L.; m. Patricia Coutts Milne, Sept. 25, 1964; children: David, Nicola, Bruno. Attended, King's Coll. U. London, 1954-55; MB, BS, Westminster Med. Sch. London, Eng., 1959; MD, U. London, 1966. Diplomate Am. Bd. Pathology, Royal Coll. Pathologists (London), lic. Calif. Casualty officer Westminster Med. Hosp., 1960; resident Westminster Hosp. Med. Sch., London, 1960-68; pediatric house physician Westminster Hosp. Med. Sch., Westminster Children's Hosp., 1961; house physician St. James Hosp., Balham, London, 1961; asst. prof. pathology Stanford (Calif.) U., 1979-86; assoc. prof. pathology UCLA, L.A., 1977-80, vice chmn. dept. pathology, 1970-86; attending physician Dept. Medicine Gastroenterology divsn. UCLA-Wadsworth VA Hosp., 1978—; prof. pathology UCLA Med. Sch., 1980—, prof. dept. medicine divsn. gastroenterology, 1986—; dir. divsn. surg. pathology UCLA Ctr. Health Scis., 1986-95, mem. diagnostic surg. pathology svc., dir. divsn. liver, pancreas and gastrointestinal pathology, 1996—2002. Resident pathologist clinical chemistry, bacteriology, hematology, blood transfusion, serology, Westminster Hosp. Med. Sch., 1961-62, registrar dept. morbid anatomy, 1962-64, rotating sr. registrar morbid anatomy, Royal Devon, Exeter Hosp., 1964-68; vis. asst. prof. pathology, Stanford U. Med. Sch., 1968-70; vice chmn. pathology UCLA, L.A., 1979-86; pres. L.A. Soc. Pathologists Inc., 1985-86; mem. curriculum com. U. Calif. Riverside, 1977-84; cons. Wadsworth VA Hosp., L.A., carcinoma of esophagus intervention study, Polyp Prevention study, Nat. Cancer Inst., Cancer Preservation Studies br., Bethesda, Md.; chief gastrointestinal liver/pancreas sect. surg. pathology; rschr. structure, function, pathologic disorders of gastrointestinal tract and liver; vis. prof. U. Leeds, Eng., Porto Alegre, Brazil, Nat. Cancer Inst., Washington, 1999. Co-author (Riddel R., Weinstein W.): Gastrointestinal Pathology and Its Clinical Implications, 1992; co-author: (Henry Appelman) Atlas of Tumor Pathology: Tumors of the Esophagus and Stomach, 1997; editl. bd. Human Pathology, 1986—, Am. Jour. Surg. Pathology, 1990—, reviewer Gastroenterology and Archives of Pathology; contbr. . Recipient Chesterfield medal Inst. Dermatology, London, 1966; named Arris and Gale lectr. Royal Coll. Surgeons, London, 1968; Welcome Trust Rsch. grantee, 1968; fellow Found. Promotion Cancer Rsch., Tokyo, 1992. Fellow Royal Coll. Pathologists (Eng.); mem. Pathological Soc. Great Britain, Am. Gastroenterology Soc., Gastrointestinal Pathology Soc. (founder, pres. 1985-86, exec. com., edn. com. 1990-99), U.S. Acad. Pathology, Can. Acad. Pathology, Assn. Clin. Pathologists, Pathological and Bacteriological Soc. Great Britain, Internat. Acad. Pathology, L.A. Pathology Soc. (bd. dirs.), Calif. Soc. Pathology (edn. com. 1983—), So. Calif. Soc. Gastrointestinal Endoscopy, Arthur Purdy Stout Soc., Gastrointestinal Pathology Soc. (pres., by-laws com., chmn. edn. com., exec. com.). Avocations: internat. travel, geographic pathology, hiking, swimming. Home: 333 Las Casas Ave Pacific Palisades CA 90272-3307 Office: UCLA Sch Medicine Dept Pathology 10833 Le Conte Ave Los Angeles CA 90095-3075

LEWIN, MARION EIN, consultant, physician, former medical association administrator; grad., MD, Columbia U. Dir. Ctr. for Health Policy Rsch. Am. Enterprise Inst. for Pub. Policy Rsch.; dep. dir. Nat. Health Policy Forum; sr. staff officer, dir. Office Health Policy Programs Inst. of Medicine, Washington. Sr. cons. Grantmakers in Health; dir. project Assn. for Health Svcs. Rsch. Co-editor: Information Trading: How Information Influences the Health Policy Process; contbr. Jour. Med. Practice Mgmt., JAMA, among others. Bd. dirs. Providence Hosp., Washington, chair planning com.*

LEWIN, PEARL GOLDMAN, psychologist; b. Bklyn., Apr. 25, 1923; d. Frank and Anna Goldman; m. Seymour Z. Lewin, Oct. 17, 1943; children: David, Jonathan. BA, Hunter Coll., 1943; MS, U. Mich., 1947; PhD, NYU, 1980. Lic. psychologist, N.Y. Insp. chemist quarter master corps U.S. Army, 1943-45, chemist chem. warfare Md., 1945; asst. psychologist Bur. Psychol. Svcs., U. Mich., Ann Arbor, 1947-48; freelance rsch. asst. chemistry N.Y.C., 1955-71; adj. lectr. CUNY, Bklyn., 1973-74, instr., 1974-79, asst. prof., 1979-80; psychologist Creedmore Psychiat. Ctr., N.Y.C., 1980-82; sr. psychologist Manhattan Family Ct., 1982-87; cons., 1987—. Mentor Peer Counseling Orgn., Bklyn. Coll., 1976-80, coord. student svcs. New Sch. Liberal Arts, 1974-76, adminstr. acad. regulations, 1974-76. Author: Sexist Humor, 1979. Mem. APA, Pi Lambda Theta, Phi Kappa Phi. Avocations: management, reading, woodworking. Home and Office: 4231 N Walnut Ave Arlington Heights IL 60004-1302

LEWIN, PETER ANDREW, electrical engineer, educator; b. Oct. 27, 1945; BSc and MSc, U. Denmark, 1969, PhD, 1979. Project leader Bruel & Kjaer Naerum, Copenhagen, Denmark, 1969-78; project mgr. Danish Inst. Biomed. Engring., 1978-80; rsch. fellow U. Denmark, 1980-83; prof. dept. elec. and computer engr. Drexel U., 1983—, Richard B. Beard disting. prof. Fellow IEEE (mem. tech. com. IEEE Ultrasonics Symposium 1985, mem. stds. subcom. on ultrasonics, sensors, session chmn. IEEE Ultrasonics Symposia, session chmn./organizer, Lithotripsy, Engring. in Medicine and Biology conf. 1990, co-chmn. med. ultrasound track EMBS conf. 1990, co-chmn. indsl. exhibits com. EMBS conf. 1990, co-editor IEEE Med. Ultrasound Parameter Measurement Guide 1984-88, reviewer IEEE Transactions, co-editor spl. issue IEEE Transactions on Ultrasonics, Frequency and Frequency Control 1988), Acoustical Soc. Am., Am. Inst. Ultrasound in Medicine. Office: Drexel University Dept Electrical & Computer Eng Philadelphia PA 19104

LEWIN, RALPH ARNOLD, biologist; b. London, Apr. 30, 1921; came to U.S., 1947; s. Maurice and Ethel Lewin; m. Joyce Mary Chismore, June, 1950 (div. 1965); m. Cheng Lanna, June 3, 1969. BA, Cambridge U., Eng., 1942, MA, 1946; PhD, Yale U., 1950; ScD, Cambridge U., Eng., 1973. Instr. Yale U., New Haven, 1951-52; sci. officer Nat. Rsch. Coun., Halifax, N.S., Can., 1952-55; ind. investigator NIH, Woods Hole, Mass., 1956-59; from assoc. prof. to prof. U. Calif., La Jolla, 1960—. Editor: Physiology and Biochemistry of Algae, 1962, Genetics of Algae, 1976, Biology of Algae, 1979, Biology of Women, 1981, Origins of Plastids, 1993, Internacia Vortaro de Mikroba Genetiko, 1994; co-editor: Prochloron, a microbial enigma, 1989; transl. Winnie-La-Pu (Esperanto), 1972, La Dektri Horlogoj, 1993, Merde, 1999, Abacus & Swallows, 2000. Served with British Army, 1943-46. Mem. Phycological Soc. Am. (pres. 1970-71, Darbaker prize 1963). Avocations: Esperanto, recorders, badminton. Home: 8481 Paseo Del Ocaso La Jolla CA 92037-3024 Office: U Calif San Diego Scripps Inst Oceanogra # 0202 La Jolla CA 92093 E-mail: rlewin@ucsd.edu.

LEWIN, RHODA GREENE, editor, historian, columnist; b. Mpls., Apr. 6, 1929; d. Louis and Florence (Glick) G.; m. David J. Jacobs, July 23, 1950; m. Thomas M. Lewin, Sept. 19, 1963; children: Ellen, Susan, Kate, Jeffrey. BA in Journalism, U. Minn., 1949, MA in Journalism, 1961, PhD in Am. Studies, 1978. Free lance writer, editor, Mpls., 1956—; instr. journalism U. Wis., Superior, 1961-63; instr. communications U. Minn., Mpls., 1963-65, instr. creative writing extension div., 1977-83. Elected mem. Acad. Coun. Am. Jewish Hist. Soc., 1990—; chair archives com. Temple Israel, Mpls., 1986-98; cons., interviewer Mpls. Pub. Libr. Oral History Project, 1983-87; lectr. in field. Author: Images of America: The Jewish Community of North Minneapolis, 2001; editor: Witnesses to the Holocaust: An Oral History , 1989, Security, 1982, Those Were Days of Yesteryear, 1978, (magazine) Identity mag., 1980—88, Soviet Jewry Action News, 1985—90, Hill and Lake Press, 1978—82; contbg. editor: Mpls. Star, 1981—83; author: (booklet) Temple Israel: A Brief History, 1987; contbr. chapters to books; columnist: Am. Jewish World. Mem. exec. bd. Oral History Assn. of Minn., 1991—; bd. dirs., chair capital campaign Theatre in the Round Players, 1983—86; assoc. chair Kenwood Park Planning Com., 1979—84; mem. Human Devel. Task Force Capital Long-Range Improvement Com., City of Mpls., 1980—82; mem. lake levels adv. com. Mpls. Park and Recreation Bd., 1979—84; bd. dirs. B'nai B'rith Chaplaincy at Mayo Clinic, Rochester, Minn., 1987—92; mem. exec. bd. Twin Cities chpt. Am. Jewish Com., 1980—98. Mem. Minn. Independent Scholars Forum (pres. 1983-84), Oral History Assn., Oral History Assn. Minn., Nat. Coalition Ind. Scholars. Democrat. Avocations: reading, travel, family, friends, community service. E-mail: TRLewin@aol.com.

LEWIN, ROSS ALLEN, lawyer; b. Chgo., Apr. 2, 1955; s. Herbert Martin and Gertrude Anne (Gordon) L.; m. Nancy Deborah Feldman, May 18, 1986; children: Gina, Gabriel. BA, Trinity Coll., 1977; JD, Yale Law Sch., 1982. Bar: N.J. 1983, U.S. Dist. Ct. N.J. 1983, U.S. Ct. Appeals, U.S. Supreme Ct. Law clerk Justice Alan Handler N.J. Supreme Ct., Trenton, N.J., 1982-83; deputy atty. gen. Atty. Gen. N.J., 1983-89; deputy chief counsel Gov. of N.J., 1989-90; assoc. Jamieson Moore Peskin & Spicer, Princeton, 1990-93, ptnr., 1993-2000, Windels, Marx Lane & Mittendorf, LLP, Princeton, 2001—. Dir. Legal Svcs. of N.J., Iselin, 1996—, Mercer County Legal Aid Soc., Trenton, 1992-96. Contbr. articles to profl. jours. Mem. Yale Law Sch. Assn. of N.J. (pres. 1996-97, v.p. 1995-96). Office: Windels Marx Lane & Mittendorf LLP Ste 201 104 Carnegie Ctr Princeton NJ 08540 E-mail: rlewin@windelsmarx.com.

LEWIN, SEYMOUR ZALMAN, chemistry educator, consultant; b. N.Y.C., Aug. 16, 1921; s. Charles and Ida (Lazaroff) L.; m. Pearl Goldman, Oct. 17, 1943; children: David, Jonathan. BS, CCNY, 1941; MS, U. Mich., 1942, PhD, 1950; Prof. (hon.), Instituto Químico de Sarria, Spain, 1961. Lectr. U. Mich., Ann Arbor, 1947-48, rsch. fellow, 1948-50; instr. NYU, N.Y.C., 1950-51, asst. prof., 1951-54, assoc. prof., 1954-59, prof. chemistry, 1959-91, emeritus, 1991—; cons. in field; vis. prof. Internat. Ctr. Conservation, Venice, Italy, 1974-88. Author: Earth, Air, Fire, Water and DNA, 1970; Editor: Chemists' Dictionary, 1963; Funk & Wagnall Ency., 1972-77. Patentee in field. With U.S. Army, 1943-45. Recipient K. Fajans prize U. Mich., 1954, Golden Dozen Teaching Excellence awards NYU, 1960, 89, Oscar Foster prize N.Y. Chemistry Tchrs. Soc., 1973; Belgian-Am. Found. fellow, 1962. Fellow N.Y. Acad. Scis. (Cressy Morisson prize 1958), Am. Inst. Chemists; mem. Am. Chem. Soc. (chmn. analytical group N.Y. sect. 1973-74, tour speaker of yr. 1970-71), Am. Assn. Cereal Chemists, Sigma Xi (pres. NYU chpt. 1965-66), Inst. Food Technologists. Home: 4231 N Walnut Ave Arlington Heights IL 60004-1302

LEWIN, WERNER SIEGFRIED, JR. lawyer; b. San Francisco, Apr. 13, 1954; s. Werner Siegfried and Libby (Lewis) L.; married. BS, Cornell U., 1975; JD, U. Calif., Hastings, 1980. Bar: Calif. 1980. Assoc. Lynch, Loofburrow et al, San Francisco, 1980-82, Rudy Rapoport & Holden, San Francisco, 1982-86, Hanson, Bridgett, Marcus, Vlahos & Rudy, San Francisco, 1986-87; prin. Werner S Lewin Jr., Esq., Novato, 1987—. Founder, pres. Attorney Assistance, San Francisco Bay Area, 1986—. Office: Atty Assistance Co Hdqs 55 Cavalla Cay Novato CA 94949-5341

LEWINGER, JEAN ELIZABETH, pediatrics nurse, neonatal intensive care nurse; b. Bklyn., Oct. 30, 1946; d. Donald and Grace W. (Mowat) Gordon; m. Arnold A. Lewinger, Nov. 4, 1967; children: William Anthony, Andrea Jean. Diploma in nursing, Kings County Hosp. Ctr., Bklyn., 1967; BSN, Cedar Crest Coll., 1986; MSN, U. Pa., 1988. Med. surg. staff nurse Terrace Heights Hosp., Hollis, N.Y., 1967-72; staff nurse neonatal ICU Southside Hosp., Bayshore, 1973-76; staff nurse, charge nurse pediatric spl. care unit Ea. Maine Med. Ctr., Bangor, 1976-81, transport nurse, 1977-81; neonatal transport nurse Allentown (Pa.) Hosp., 1981-88, neonatal ICU, 1981-88; neonatal nurse practitioner Pa. Hosp., Phila., 1988-89, Episc. Hosp., Phila., 1989-95, Thomas Jefferson U. Hosp., Phila., 1995-97; with N.C. Baptist Hosps. Inc., 1997—. CPR instr.; nurse laision for neonatal support group, Phila.; regional instr. neonatal resuscitation program. Contbr. articles to profl. publs. Mem. ANA, NAACOG (cert. neonatal intensive care practitioner, cert. neonatal intensive care nurse), AHWONN, Am. Assn. Nurse Practitioners, Nat. Assn. Neonatal Nurses, Am. Bd. Examiners, Ob-Gyn. Nurses, Nat. Perinatal Assn., Am. Acad. Nurse Practitioners, N.C. Nurses Assn., Pa. Perinatal Assn., Phila. Perinatal Assn., Delaware Valley Assn. Neonatal Nurses (Pa.), Triad Assn. Neonatal Nurses (N.C., sec., pres.), N.C. Assn. Nurses. E-mail: jlewinger@triad.rr.com.

LEWINS, STEVEN, security analyst, investment advisor, corporate executive, diplomatic advisor; b. N.Y.C., Jan. 22, 1943; s. Bruno and Kaethe (Czhoeck) L.; m. Rayna Lee Kornreich, July 4, 1968 (div. 1991); children: Shani Nicole, Scott Asher. BA, Queens Coll., CUNY, 1964, MA in Diplomatic-Econ. History, 1966; postgrad. in bus. adminstrn., NYCSC, SUNY, 1967. Park ranger, historian Nat. Park Svc., Statue of Liberty, N.Y.C., 1964-66; traffic asst. AT&T, White Plains, N.Y., 1966; adminstrv. intern N.Y. State, Albany, 1966-67; asst. to commr. N.Y. State Narcotic Addiction Control Commn., N.Y.C., 1967-69; security analyst Value Line Investment Survey, 1969-71, assoc. rsch. dir., 1971-74, rsch. dir., directing editor, 1975-80; creator Value Line Fin. Database, 1974; v.p. Arnold Bernhard & Co., 1975-80, dir., 1976-80, mem. exec. com., 1977-80; ptnr. Ray-Lux Products, 1978-80; pres. RayLux Assocs., 1980-81, dir., 1980-86. Founder RayLux Fin. Svc., 1980 (1st SEC-registered electronic investment adv. svc.); v.p. unit head investment divsn. Citibank N.A., 1981-86, v.p. Citicorp Investment Mgmt., Inc., 1986-88; v.p. transp. and aerospace investment mgmt; chancellor Capital Mgmt., 1988-92; mng. dir., rsch. dir., head of equity First Capital Advisers/F.C. Fin. Svcs., N.Y.C., 1992-93; v.p. Investment Rsch. Gruntal & Co., Inc., 1994-2000; adv. corp. disclosure com. SEC, 1977-78, ICC, 1982-92, Dept. Transp., 1982-92, 95-2000, interval funds investment cons., 1997-2000, Dept. Justice, 1982-92, 95-96, Dept. State, 1986-92, Surface Transp. Bd. Legal Panel, 1996-97; advisor Sir Transport Assn., 1965-2000, Fed. Res. Bd., 1996-2000, infrastructure com. U.S. Ho. of Reps., 1997-2000, Summit Bank, 1998-2000; spkr. security analysis, econs., transp., aerospace, def., corp. disclosure, deregulation, air traffic control and safety, fin. data svcs., U.S. megatrends, USSR Glastnost and Perestroika, C.I.S., resurgent economy. Author: Fashoda Crisis of 1898, 1966, Knowing Your Common Stocks, 1979, The Social Overhaul of the USSR, 1986, Economic Reform in the U.S.S.R., 1990, USA: 21st Century World Transportation Crossroads, 1994, U.S. Needs World-Class Transportation System, 1994, Transports as Economic Indicators, 1995, The New Union Pacific, 1996, Transportation Trends into the 21st Century, 1996, The Global Terrorist Threat, 1996, The Boeing Company: Firing on All Cylinders, 1997, U.S. Transportation "Consolidations" and "Surprise," 1997, Secular Trends in Global Transportation, 1997; co-author: (with Parkanskii) US-USSR Summit Agenda, 1995, (with Bogdanov and Bobrakov) US-USSR Anti-International Terrorist Protocol, 1989, Rights of Terrorist, 1990, US-USSR Space Cooperation, 1990; editor: Megatrends, 1980, Witch Doctor of Wall Street, 1990; creator Global Transportation and Orbital Space Transport Investment Trust, Gruntal & Co., L.L.C., 1998-2000. Participant U.S.-USSR Emigration/Jackson Vanek, 1984-91, U.S.-USSR Pan Am.-Aeroflot Aviation Agreement, 1985, USSR Student Exch., 1985-86, U.S.-USSR Anti-Internat. Terrorism, 1985-91, U.S.-USSR Rights of Terrorists, 1985, U.S.-USSR Trans-Siberian-CSX Corp. Initiative, 1989, TRW, Inc-Energia N.P.O. Look Down Satellite Agreement, 1989-90, U.S.-USSR Orbital Space Coop. Agreement, 1989-90, U.S.-USSR Def. Conv. Projects, 1990-93, Reagan-Gorbachev Summit Preparations, 1986, 87, 88, Bush-Gorbachev Summit Preparation, 1990, U.S.-USSR AMR Corp.-Aeroflot Bilateral Discussion, 1989, U.S.-USSR Spl. Mission/Secure Info. Negotiation, 1983-92, U.S.-Japan airline bilateral negotiation, 1996, CSX Corp./CIS indsl. negotiation, 1996-97; sponsor U.S.-USSR Pace U., rsch. exch., 1990; Citicorp liaison USSR mission to UN, 1982-88, Inst. U.S. and Can., Acad. Scis. USSR, 1985-88, econs. dept. Acad. Scis. USSR, 1988; liaison Chancellor Capital Mgmt., USSR, 1988-92; overseasr fact-finding visits include Saudi Arabia, Egypt, Jordan, Israel, 1979, Peoples Republic of China, Japan, Hong Kong, 1981, USSR, 1985, 86, 89, 90, Georgia SSR, 1985, 90, Uzbekistan SSR, 1986, Baykhal, Irkutsk, Olha, Siberia, 1989, Kazakhstan SSR, Republic of Georgia, Baykonour-Soyuz Launch Ctr., 1990, Bangkok, Thailand, 1988, Rio de Janeiro, Brazil, 1990; mem. Croton-on-Hudson Narcotics Guidance Coun., 1972-75, Cortland Indsl. Com., 1975-77; dist. leader Dem. Party, 1979-83; founding mem. Challenger Found., 1987, Nat. Space Mus., Dulles, Tex., 1998. Acting col. Secure Information Negotiation, USAF, Military Airlift Command, Baikonour, Kazakhstan, 1990, brigadier, 1999—. Recipient Commendation citation for Gulf War, 1992, USSR Supreme Soviet election for 50th birthday award in svc. to USSR for peace, 1990. Fellow Fin. Analyst Fedn.; mem. N.Y. Soc. Security Analysts (sr. security analyst, membership com., computer applications symposium, airline splinter group, motor carrier splinter group, aerospace splinter group), Bus. Economists Coun., Washington Transp. Roundtable, Assn. Computer Users, Internat. Platform Assn., N.Y. Assn. Bus. Economists, Nat. Assn. Bus. Economists, Nat. Planetary Soc., Nat. Space Soc., Nat. Air and Space Mus., Nat. Air and Space Soc. (founding mem. 1998—), Tau Delta Phi (pres. 1963, 64, Undergrad. of Yr. 1963, Spl. Student Senate Recognition 1964, Coll. Distinction medal French 1964). Democrat. Home: 66 Grand St Croton On Hudson NY 10520-2519 E-mail: sniwelist@aol.com.

LEWINSOHN, HILTON CECIL, physician; b. Wolmaransstad, Transvaal, South Africa, Nov. 7, 1928; came to U.S., 1976; s. Arthur and Ella (Paradise) L.; m. Anne M. Young, Feb. 21, 1961; children: Emma Jane, Charles Arthur. MB B.Ch., Witwatersand U., Johannesburg, South Africa, 1952; Diploma in Indsl. Health, Soc. of Apothecaries, London, 1968. Fellow Faculty of Occupl. Medicine, London, lic. physician Conn., N.H., Mass. Physician, surgeon and med. officer Springkell Johannesburg Sanitorium and Addington Hosp., Durban, Johannesburg, South Africa, 1953-56; physician, resident asst. physician London Chest Hosp., Pinewood Hosp., Farnborough Hosp., U.K., 1956-61; resident, rsch fellow Bronx Mcpl. Hosp. Ctr. and Albert Einstein Coll. Medicine, N.Y., 1961-63; Pneumoconiosis med. officer Ministry of Pensions and Nat. Insur. Albert Bridge House W., Manchester, U.K., 1963-66; med. officer Turner Bros. Asbestos Co., Ltd., Rochdale, U.K., 1966-69; chief med. officer T.B.A. Limited, Manchester, U.K., 1969-76; group med. advisor T&NLH; corp. med. dir. Raybestos-Manhattan, Inc., Trumbull, Conn., 1976-81, The Perkin-Elmer Corp., Norwalk, 1981-82; asst. corp. med. dir. (eastern region) Union Carbide Corp., Danbury, 1982-86; med. dir. Chem. and Plastics Co. Inc., Union Carbide Corp., 1986-91; assoc. corp. med. dir. Union Carbide Corp., 1991—92; assoc. med. dir. Ctr. for Occupl. and Environ. Health, Exeter (N.H.) Hosp., 1992—94, dir. Ctr. for Asthma, Allergy and Respiratory Disease, 1994—99; med. cons. AGFA Corp., Wilmington, Mass., 1994—2000; cons. occupl. health physician, 1994—2001. Cons. Norwalk (Conn.) Hosp. , 1981—92; lectr. dept. epidemiology Yale Med. Sch., New Haven, 1977—; clin. assoc. dept. lab. medicine U. Conn., Farmington, 1977—92. Contbr. numerous articles to British and Am. profl. jours. Fellow: Royal Soc. Medicine, Am. Coll. Chest Physicians, Am. Coll. Occupl. Medicine (liaison com. internat. sect., chmn. com. on occupl.lung disorders 1983—85, 1988, co-chmn. coun. on sci. affairs 1984, chmn. 1986—87). E-mail: hclewinsohn@prodigy.net.

LEWIS, ALEXANDER INGERSOLL, III, lawyer; b. Detroit, Apr. 10, 1946; s. Alexander Ingersoll Jr. and Marie T. (Fuger) L.; m. Gretchen Elsa Lundgren, Aug. 8, 1970; children: Jennifer L., Katherine F., Elisabeth M., Alexander Ingersoll IV. BA with honors, Johns Hopkins U., 1968; JD cum laude, U. Pa., 1971. Bar: Md. 1972, U.S. Dist. Ct. Md. 1972, U.S. Ct. Appeals (4th cir.) 1975, U.S. Supreme Ct. 1976, D.C. 1982. Assoc. Venable, Baetjer & Howard, LLP, Balt., 1972-75, 78-80, ptnr., 1981—, head estate and trust practice group, 1993-99, sr. ptnr. estate and trust practice group, 1993—; asst. atty. gen. State of Md., 1975-77. Cons. subcom. on probate rules, standing com. on rules and procedures Md. Ct. Appeals, 1976—; mem. Md. Gov.'s Task Force to Study Revision of Inheritance and Estate Tax Laws, 1987—88; lectr. Md. Inst. Continuing Profl. Edn. Lawyers, 1978—2001, Nat. Bus. Inst., 1986—87, 1992—99, Cambridge Inst., 1986—90, Nat. Law Found., 1988—99. Contbr. articles to legal jours. Vice chmn. Md. Gov.'s Task Force on Long-Term Fin. Planning for Disabled Individuals, 1990-94. 1st lt. U.S. Army, 1972. Fellow Am. Coll. Trust and Estate Counsel (state laws coord. for Md. 1991-2001); mem. ABA, Md. Bar Assn. (chmn. probate reform and simplification com. estates and trusts coun. 1984-86, sec. 1987-88, chmn. 1989-90, com. on laws 1994-98), D.C. Bar Assn., Bar Assn. City Balt., Balt. Estate Planning Coun., Johns Hopkins Club. Republican. Roman Catholic. Avocations: canoeing, camping, tennis. Home: 922 Army Rd Ruxton MD 21204-6703 Office: Venable Baetjer & Howard LLP 1800 Two Hopkins Plz Baltimore MD 21201

LEWIS, ALFRED BAKER, psychiatrist; b. Cambridge, Mass., Mar. 22, 1928; s. Alfred Baker and Lena Helen (Greenspan) L.; m. Mary Elizabeth Sullivan, Nov. 6, 1954 (div. Jan. 1976); children: Alfred B. III, Anne H., Katherine R.; m. Ellen Peterson, Feb. 3, 1991. BA, Harvard U., 1949; MD, U. Pa., 1953. Lic. Am. Psychiatry Bd., 1960. Intern Roosevelt Hosp., N.Y.C., 1953-54; resident N.Y. Hosp., 1954-57; capt. U.S. Army Med. Corps, 1957-59; asst. prof. psychiatry Cornell Med. Coll., N.Y.C., 1961-69, assoc. prof. clin. psychiatry, 1969-93, prof. clin. psychiatry, 1993—. Attending psychiatrist N.Y. Hosp., N.Y.C., 1962—. Contbr. articles to profl. jours. Fellow Am. Psychiat. Assn. (life). Home: 60 Sutton Pl S New York NY 10022

LEWIS, ALVIN EDWARD, pathology educator; b. N.Y.C., Nov. 21, 1916; s. Herman and Libbie (Levy) L.; m. Oct. 23, 1943, (widowed 1974); children: Joan, Elizabeth; m. July, 1, 1976. BA, U. Calif. L.A., 1938; MA, Stanford U., 1939, MD, 1944. Chief, pathology sect, atomic energy project UCLA, 1949-53; dir. clin. labs. Mount Zion Hosp., San Francisco, 1953-66; pathology prof. Mich. State U., East Lansing, 1966-72; pathology prof., chmn. U. S. Ala., Mobile, 1972-74; pathology prof. U. Calif., Davis, 1974-87, prof. emeritus, 1987—. Rev. com. mem. Nat. Libr. Medicine, Bethesda, Md., 1972-75, med. quality rev. com. Dist. 3, Sonoma, Calif., 1989-94. Author: Biostatistics, 1966, 1984 (2d ed.), Principles of Hematology, 1970. Lt. (j.g.) USNR, 1945-46. Fellow Coll. Am. Pathologists; mem. Am. Physiol. Soc. Republican. Jewish. Avocations: sailing, photography, music (recorder ensemble). Home: 21 Woodgreen St Santa Rosa CA 95409-5921

LEWIS, ANDRÉ LEON, artistic director; b. Hull, Que., Can., Jan. 16, 1955; s. Raymond Lincoln and Theresa L. Student, Classical Ballet Studio, Ottawa, Royal Winnipeg (Man.) Ballet Sch., 1975; studies with David Moroni, Arnold Spohr, Rudi van Dantzig, Jiri Kylian, Peter Wright, Hans van Manen, and Alicia Markova, among others. Mem. corps de ballet Royal Winnipeg (Man.) Ballet, 1979-82, soloist, artistic coord., 1984-89, interim artistic dir., 1989-90, assoc. artistic dir., 1990-96, artistic dir., 1996—. Staged Danzig's Romeo and Juliet, Teatro Comunale, Florence, Italy, Greek Nat. Opera, Athens. Dancer, soloist (ballets) Song of a Wayfarer, Fall River Legend, Nuages Pas de Deux, Lento A Tempo E Appassionatto, Nutcracker, Four Last Songs, Romeo and Juliet, Belong Pas de Deux, Ecstasy of Rita Joe, (TV and films) Fall River Legend, Giselle, Heartland, Romeo and Juliet, The Big Top, Firebird; performed at many events including the opening Gala performance of the Internat. Ballet competition in Jackson, Miss., Le Don Des Etoiles, Montreal, a spl. gala honoring Queen Beatrix of Holland and at a Gala performance in Tchaikovsky Hall, Moscow; appeared as a guest artist throughout N.Am., the Orient and USSR. Avocation: listening to opera. Office: Can Royal Winnipeg Ballet 380 Graham Ave Winnipeg MB Canada R3C 4K2 E-mail: ballet@rwb.org.

LEWIS, ANDREA ELEN, editor; b. Detroit, June 4, 1957; d. Frank Joe and Mae (Shaw) L. BS, Ea. Mich. U., 1982. Arts and entertainment editor Plexus: West Coast Women's Press, Oakland, Calif., 1984-88; rsch. editor Mother Jones mag., San Francisco, 1990-92; editl. asst. Harper Collins Pubs., 1992-94; sr. editor Third Force mag., Oakland, 1992—; assoc. editor Pacific News Svc., San Francisco, 1996—2000; writer NBCi.com, 1997—. Mem. adv. bd. Nat. Radio Project, 1996—. Contbg. writer: The Black Women's Health Book, 1990, Beyond Identity Politics, 1996; contbg. artist (CD rec. project) Bob Ostertag's Fear No Love, 1995; commentator (radio broadcasting) Pacifica Radio, 1995, 96, 97; co-host/prodr. The Morning Show KPFA Radio, Berkeley, Calif., 2000-. Chorus mem. San Francisco Symphony Chorus, 1987—, sect. leader, alto, 1991, 92, 93, 95, 99, mem. artistic adv. com., 1995, 96, 98, 99; mem. planning com., panelist, spkr. Media and Democracy Congress, San Francisco, 1996; fellow Vallecitos Mountain Refuge, N.Mex., 1998. Recipient Merit award Local Music Series, 2001, Nat. Fedn. Comty. Broadcasters Golden Reel awards, 2001. Mem. NARAS (Grammy awards for best choral recording 1992, 95). Avocations: massage therapist, musician, golfer, outdoor activities. Office: KPFA Radio 1929 Martin Luther King Jr Way Berkeley CA 94704

LEWIS, ANDREW LINDSAY, JR. (DREW LEWIS), former transportation and natural resources executive; b. Phila., Nov. 3, 1931; s. Andrew Lindsay and Lucille (Bricker) L.; m. Marilyn S. Stoughton, June 1, 1950; children: Karen Lewis Sacks, Russell Shepherd, Andrew Lindsay IV. BS, Haverford (Pa.) Coll., 1953; MBA, Harvard U., 1955; postgrad., MIT, 1968. With Henkels & McCoy, Inc., Blue Bell, Pa., 1955-60, Am. Olean Tile Co., Inc., Lansdale, 1960-68, Nat. Gypsum Co., Buffalo, 1960-70; chmn. Simplex Wire & Cable Co., Boston, 1970-74, chief exec. officer, 1972-74; pres., chief exec. officer Snelling & Snelling, Inc., 1972-74; fin. and mgmt. cons. Lewis & Assocs., Plymouth Meeting, Pa., 1974-81; sec. U.S. Dept. Transp., Washington, 1981-83; chmn. Warner Amex Cable Communications Inc., N.Y.C., 1983-86; chmn., chief exec. officer Union Pacific R.R., Omaha, 1986; pres. Union Pacific Corp., N.Y.C., 1986-87, chmn., CEO Bethlehem, Pa., 1987-97. Bd. dirs. Am. Express, Millenium Bank, FPL Group Inc., Gannett Co., Inc., Union Pacific Resources, Inc.; trustee Com. for Econ. Devel. Rep. candidate for gov., Pa., 1974; mem. Rep. Nat. Com., 1976-90, dep. chmn., 1980; dep. polit. dir. Reagan-Bush Campaign Com., 1980; co-chmn. Nat. Econ. Commn., 1988-89; chmn. The Bus. Roundtable, 1990-99; mem. nat. exec. bd. Boy Scouts of Am. Mem. Phila. Club, Sunnybrook Golf Club (Plymouth Meeting, Pa.), Saucon Valley Country Club (Bethlehem, Pa.), Bohemian Club (San Francisco), Loblolly Pines Golf Club (HobeSound, Fla.). E-mail: lilliputfarm2msn.com.

LEWIS, ANTHONY, newspaper columnist; b. N.Y.C., Mar. 27, 1927; s. Kassel and Sylvia (Surut) L.; m. Linda Rannells, July 8, 1951 (div.); children: Eliza, David, Mia; m. Margaret H. Marshall, Sept. 23, 1984 AB, Harvard U., 1948. Deskman Sunday dept. N.Y. Times, 1948-52; staff Democratic Nat. Com., 1952; reporter Washington Daily News, 1952-55, Washington bur. N.Y. Times, 1955-64; chief London bur. N.Y. Times, 1965-72, editorial columnist, 1969—2001. Lectr. on law Harvard U., 1974-89; James Madison vis. prof. Columbia U., 1983—. Author: Gideon's Trumpet, 1964 (award as best fact-crime book Mystery Writers Am.), Portrait of a Decade: The Second American Revolution, 1964, Make No Law: The Sullivan Case and the First Amendment, 1991; contbr. articles to profl. jours. Recipient Heywood Broun award, 1955, Pulitzer prize for nat. reporting, 1955, 63; Nieman fellow, 1956-57 Mem. Am. Acad. Arts and Scis., Tavern Club. E-mail: tlewis@galaxy.net.

LEWIS, ARTHUR DEE, corporation executive; b. Greenville, Tex., Sept. 13, 1918; s. Carl Hamilton and Maxie (Curtis) L.; m. Hildegard Bair, Dec. 7, 1946; children: Gregory Scott, Kimberly Kealani. Student, U. Tex., 1935-41, Advanced Mgmt. Program, Harvard, 1952; Sc.D., Clarkson Coll. Tech. With Am. Airlines, 1941-55, beginning as cargo research analyst, successively supr. spl. projects, mgr. econ. analysis br., dir. econ. planning div., 1941-54, asst. v.p. planning, 1954-55; exec. v.p. Hawaiian Airlines, 1955, pres., dir., chief exec. officer, 1955-64; sr. v.p., gen. mgr., dir. Eastern Air Lines, 1964-67, pres., chief operating officer, dir., 1967-69; gen. partner F. S. Smithers & Co., 1969—; chmn.; pres., chief exec. officer F. Smithers & Co., 1969-73. Chmn., chief exec. officer U.S. Ry. Assn., 1974-77; pres., dir., chief exec. officer Am. Bus Assn., 1977-82; chmn., chief exec. officer U.S. Africa Airways, 1990-94, bd. dirs., chmn. emeritus, cons.; chmn. bd. Airline Media Assocs., Inc.; organizer Consol. Ry. Corp., Conrail; organizer Nat. Ry. Passenger Corp., Amtrak; dir. Riegel Paper Corp., Rexham Corp., Bankers Security Life Ins. Soc., Bank of Commerce, Iroquois Brands Ltd., C. Brewer & Co., Bishop Trust Co., Internat. Bank; chmn. Mid Pacific Airlines, Honolulu; cons. airline moblzn., transp. div. Nat. Security Resources Bd., Korean War; cons. Def. Air Transp. Adminstrn., 1951-55, Dept. Transp., 1969. Bd. regents U. Hawaii; bd. govs. Pacific and Asian Affairs Council, Iolani Sch. Boys; bd. dirs. Hawaii Visitors Bur.; trustee, chmn. emeritus Clarkson Coll. Tech. Mem. Am. Mgmt. Assn. (dir., mem. exec. com.), Honolulu C. of C. (dir. 1958-59), Young Pres. Orgn., World Bus. Coun. (pres., dir. 1973-74), Conquistadores del Cielo (dir.), Burning Tree Club (Bethesda, Md.), Soc. of Sr. Aerospace Execs., Inc. (pres., dir. 1995-97).

LEWIS, AUDREY GERSH, financial marketing/public relations consultant; b. Phila., Dec. 1, 1933; d. Benjamin and Augusta (Fine) Gersh; divorced; children: Jamie Lewis Keith, Ruth-Ellen. Student, Temple U., 1951-53. Asst. mgr. accounts payable/receivable Turner Constrn. Co., Louisville, 1953-55; rep. sales, mktg., fin. depts. Benjamin Gersh Wholesaler Jeweler, Wyncote, Pa., 1955-69; registered rep. Seaboard Planning Corp. (formerly B.C. Morton Broker Del.), Greenwich, Conn. and Wyncote, 1969-72; placement counselor sales and mktg. dept. Greyhound Permanent Pers. subs. Greyhound Corp., Stamford, Conn., 1974-77; asst. v.p., mgr. investor rels.l, mktg. Am. Investors Corp., Greenwich, 1977-85; founder, pres. Audrey Gersh Lewis Cons. Ltd., 1985—. Chair Cancer Fund, Wyncote, United Fund Leadership Award, Wyncote, 1963-68; asst. treas. Republican Town Com., Greenwich, 1981-82; mem. Greenwich Town Alarm Appeals Bd., 1985-98. Mem. Assn. Corp. Growth (bd. dirs., v.p. mktg. and pub. rels. N.Y. chpt. 1989-92, mem. nat. ann. meeting planning com. 1992, 93, 94). Avocations: antiquing, walking, reading. Office: Audrey Gersh Lewis Cons Ltd Corp Exec Coach LLC PO Box 4644 Greenwich CT 06831-8644

LEWIS, BARRY KENT, cardiologist; b. Chgo., Aug. 2, 1949; s. Seymour and Esther (Rothfield) L.; m. Marsha Diane Berman, June 6, 1976; children: Jeremy Aaron, Ryan Allen. AB, Boston U., 1971; DO, Kirksville Coll. Osteo. Med., 1976. Diplomate Am. Bd. Internal Medicine, Sub-bd. Cardiology. Physician, asst. prof. Chgo. Coll. Osteo. Medicine, 1984-88; physician, cardiologist Cardiovascular Clin. Assocs., Farmington Hills, Mich., 1988—; asst. prof. Mich. State U. Coll. Osteo. Medicine, East Lansing, 1989—. Dir. cardiac catheterization lab. Botsford Gen. Hosp., Farmington Hills, 1989—. Capt. U.S. Army, 1977-80, Germany. Fellow Am. Coll. Cardiology, Am. Coll. Chest Physicians, Am. Coll. Osteo. Internists; mem. Am. Osteo. Assn., Am. Heart Assn., Am. Soc. Cardiovascular Interventionalists. Jewish. Avocations: music, photography. Home: 34662 Valley Forge Dr Farmington Hills MI 48331-3206 Office: Cardiovascular Clin Group Ste 300W 28080 Grand River Ave Farmington Hills MI 48336-5966

LEWIS, BASIL, investment company executive; b. London, May 11, 1922; came to U.S., 1977; s. Nathan Lewis and Ada Gran; m. Patricia Pearl Lewis, Sept. 12, 1951; children: David J., Jonathan A., Simon R. B of Commerce, London Sch. Econs., 1948. Mem. London Stock Exchange, 1959-77; fin. cons. Salomon Smith Barney, L.A., 1979-2000; v.p. investments Wachovia Securities, 2000—. Arbitrator Nat. Assn. Securities Dealers, L.A., 1996—. Capt. Brit. Army, 1942-46. Avocations: theatre, movies, opera, photography, reading. Office: Wachovia Securities 10877 Wilshire Blvd # 1500 Los Angeles CA 90024

LEWIS, BENJAMIN PERSHING, JR. pharmacist, public health service officer; b. Danville, Ky., June 2, 1942; s. Benjamin Pershing Lewis and Juanita Elizabeth Applewhite; m. Patricia Glover, 1968; children: Laura, Jason. BS in Pharmacy, Auburn U., 1966, MS in Pharmacy, 1972; PhD in Health Svcs. Mgmt., Century U., L.A., 1989. Registered pharmacist, Ky., Ala. Instr. Auburn (Ala.) U. Sch. Pharmacy, 1972-73, now affiliate asst. prof.; commd. lt. comdr. USPHS, 1976, advanced through grades to capt., 1985; pharmacy officer Bur. Drugs FDA, Rockville, Md., 1976-82, health scientist adminstr. orphan products devel., 1982-87, AIDS coord., 1987-89, spl. asst. to assoc. dir. Ctr. Biologics Evaluation-Rsch. Bethesda, 1989-92; dir. regulatory ops. divsn. of transfusion and emerging transmitted diseases FDA Ctr. Biologics Evaluation and Rsch., Rockville, 1993—2002; with Brand Inst., Inc., 2002—. Adj. prof. San Diego State U., 1998. Co-author: Veterinary Drug Index, 1982; editor: FDA Role in AIDS, 1988, The International Ramifications of Drug Development, 1988, Report of the Criticism Task Force on Career Development, 1989; co-editor: Poliovirus Attenuation: Molecular Mechanisms and Practical Aspects, 1993, Combined Vaccines and Simultaneous Administration, 1995; contbr. articles to profl. jours. Officer U.S. Army, 1972-76. Recipient letter of appreciation Sec. Md. Dept. Econ. and Employment Devel., 1991, Secs. award for disting. svc. Dept. Health and Human Svcs., 2001. Mem. COA of USPHS, Regulatory Affairs Profl. Soc. (Cert. Appreciation 1993), Am. Pharm. Assn., Am. Acad. Pharm. Rsch. and Sci., Sigma Xi. Methodist. Achievements include assignment by FDA to San Diego State U. to create one of the first Master of Science degrees in Regulatory Affairs in the U.S., 1998. Office: 1700 Rockville Pike Ste 400 Rockville MD 20852-1631 E-mail: blewis@brandinstitute.com.

LEWIS, BERNARD, Near Eastern studies educator; b. London, May 31, 1916; s. H. Lewis; m. Ruth Helene Oppenhejm, 1947 (div. 1974); 2 children. BA, PhD, U. London; postgrad., univs. of London and Paris; hon. doctorate, Hebrew U., Jerusalem, 1974, Tel Aviv U., 1979, SUNY, Binghamton, 1987, U. Pa., 1987, Hebrew Union Coll., 1987, Yeshiva U., 1991, Haifa U., 1991, Bar-Ilan U., 1992, Brandeis U., 1993, Ben-Gurion U., 1996, Ankara U., 1996. Asst. lectr. in Islamic history Sch. Oriental Studies, U. London, 1938, prof.

history Near and Middle East, Sch. Oriental and African Studies (formerly named Sch. Oriental Studies), 1949-74, hon. fellow, 1986; Cleveland E. Dodge prof. nr. ea. studies Princeton U., 1974-86, prof. emeritus, 1986—; A.D. White prof. at large Cornell U., 1984-90; dir. Annenberg Rsch. Inst., Phila., 1986-90; Ataturk prof. (hon.) Princeton (N.J.) U., 1992-93. Vis. prof. history UCLA, 1955-56, Columbia U., 1960, Ind. U., 1963; vis. prof. College de France, 1980, Ecole des Hautes Etudes, Paris, 1983-86; Class of 1932 lectr. Princeton U., 1964; vis. mem. Inst. for Advanced Study, Princeton, N.J., 1969, long-term mem., 1974-86; Gottesman lectr. Yeshiva U., 1974; Jefferson lectr. NEH, 1990; Tanner lectr. Oxford U., 1990; Weizmann lectr. in Humanities, 1991; Henry M. Jackson meml. lectr., 1992; Siemens Stiftung lectr., Munich, 1993; Merle-Curti lectr., Madison, Wis., 1993; lectr. N.Y. Pub. Libr., 1993. Author: The Origins of Ismailism, 1940, Turkey Today, 1940, British Contributions to Arabic Studies, 1941, Handbook of Diplomatic and Political Arabic, 1947, The Arabs in History, 1950, new edit., 1993, Notes and Documents from the Turkish Archives, 1952, The Emergence of Modern Turkey, 1961, rev. edit., 1968, (transl. from Ibn Gabirol) The Kingly Crown, 1961, Istanbul and the Civilization of the Ottoman Empire, 1963, The Middle East and the West, 1964, The Assassins, 1967, Race and Color in Islam, 1971, Islam in History, 1973, new edit., 1993, Islam from the Prophet Muhammad to the Capture of Constantinople, 2 vols., 1974, History Remembered, Recovered, Invented, 1975, Studies in Classical and Ottoman Islam, 7th-16th centuries, 1976, The Muslim Discovery of Europe, 1982, The Jews of Islam, 1984, Semites and Anti-Semites, 1986, rev. edit., 1997, The Political Language of Islam, 1988, Race and Slavery in Islam, 1990, Islam and the West, 1993, The Shaping of the Modern Middle East, 1994, Cultures in Conflict: Christians, Muslims and Jews in the Age of Discovery, 1995, The Middle East: A Brief History of the Last 2000 Years, 1996, The Future of the Middle East, 1997, The Multiple Identities of the Middle East, 1999, A Middle East Mosaic: Fragments of life, letters and history, 2000, Music of a Distant Drum, 2001, What Went Wrong? Western Impact and Middle Eastern Response, 2002; (with Amnon Cohen) Population and Revenue in the Towns of Palestine in the Sixteenth Century, 1978; author, editor: Land of Enchanters, 1948, The World of Islam: Faith, People, Culture, 1976; author, co-editor: Historians of the Middle East, 1962, Ency. of Islam, 1956-87; editor: (with others) The Cambridge History of Islam, vols. 1-11, 1971; co-editor: Muslims in Europe, 1992, Religionsgespräche im Mittelalter, 1992; also articles. Served with Royal Armoured Corps and Intelligence Corps, Brit. Army, 1940-41; with dept. Fgn. Office, 1941-45.Recipient Cert. of Merit for svcs. to Turkish culture, Turkish Govt., 1973, Harvey prize, 1978, Ataturk Peace prize, 1998; Univ. Coll. of London fellow, 1976. Fellow Brit. Acad., Royal Hist. Soc., Turkish Hist. Soc. (hon.), Sch. of Oriental and African Studies (hon.); mem. Am. Acad. Arts and Scis., Am. Philos. Soc., Am. Hist. Assn., Soc. Asiatique (hon.), Inst. d'Egypte (Cairo, assoc.), Inst. de France (corr.), Turkish Acad. Scis. (hon.). Office: Near East Studies Dept Princeton Univ Princeton NJ 08544-0001

LEWIS, BETTE LOUISE, school principal; b. Chandler, Ariz. m. Gladstone S. Lewis (dec. 1987); 1 child, Clinton H. BA, Marymount Coll., 1964; MA, U. Md., 1970. Cert. tchr., adminstr., supr., Md. Tchr. Palos Verdes (Calif.) Peninsula Unified Sch. Dist., 1963-65, Prince George's County Pub. Schs., Upper Marlboro, Md., 1965-69, vice-prin., 1969-72, prin., 1972—. Recipient Washington Post Dist. Ednl. Leadership Award, Prince George's County C. of C. Outstanding Adminstr. Award, Prince George's County Public Schools Outstanding Adminstr. Award, Sigma Sigma Sigma Alumna Achievement Award. Fellow Inst. Devel. Ednl. Activities (asst. dir. 1990); mem. ASCD, Am. Assn. Sch. Adminstrs., Nat. Assn. Secondary Sch. Adminstrs., Nat. Middle Sch. Assn., Md. Middle Sch. Assn., Md. Assn. Secondary Sch. Adminstrs., Rotary Internat., Sigma Sigma Sigma. Roman Catholic. Avocations: classical music, ballroom dancing, tennis, gardening, antiques. Office: Martin Luther King Jr Mid Sch 4545 Ammendale Rd Beltsville MD 20705-1113

LEWIS, BRIAN KREGLOW, computer consultant; b. Durban, Republic of South Africa, Sept. 2, 1932; s. Arthur Armington and Isabel (Kreglow) L.; m. Mary Helen Kidwell, July 14, 1953; children: Brian E., James A., Charles A., Carol J., Robert E., Sharon H. BS, Ohio State U., 1954; PhD, Tufts U., 1971. Biology tchr. Lincoln-Sudbury (Mass.) Regional High Sch., 1965-66; rsch. assoc. May Inst. for Med. Rsch., Cin., 1971-75; from asst. to assoc. prof. health sci. Grand Valley State U., Allendale, Mich., 1975-81; prin. Lewis Assocs., Sarasota, Fla., 1984—. Adj. asst. prof. physiology Cin. Coll. Medicine, 1972-75; assoc. prof. Ponce (P.R.) Sch. Medicine, 1981-84, prof., chmn. physiology, 1987-91; instr. Macintosh computer for beginners Sarasota County Tech. Inst., 1995-97. Contbr. revs. and articles to Computer Shopper, Proceedings Soc. Exptl. Biology Medicine, Am. Heart Jour., Atherosclerosis; developer business and ednl. software. Cubmaster, scoutmaster Boy Scouts Am., 1963-78; mem. ch. choir, St. Andrew Ch., Sarasota, 1984—, mem. fin. com., 1991-98, treas., 1999-2001; bd. dirs. Sarasota chpt. Soc. Preservation and Encouragement Barbershop Quartet Singing in Am., 1994, sec., 1995-99; active Village Voices, Greenhills, Ohio, 1972-75; active Meadows Chorus, 1996—; mem. Manatee chpt. SPEBSQSA, 2002—. Lt. Supply Corps USN, 1954-62. NIH fellow, 1965-71. Mem. Endocrine Soc., Soc. for Study Reproduction, Soc. for Study Fertility, Sarasota PC Users Group (spreadsheet SIG leader 1993-94, software reviewer 1992—, moderator TechForum 1996—), Sigma Xi. Office: 6423 Caracara St Sarasota FL 34241-9104 E-mail: brian_klewis@hotmail.com.

LEWIS, BROCK, investment company executive; b. New Bedford, Mass., July 16, 1930; s. Frank Edward and Mary (Brock) L.; m. Susan Wahl, Sept. 4, 1954 (div.); children: Juliana D., Christopher B., Josiah E., Victoria D. BA, Dartmouth Coll., 1952; LLB, Boston U., 1955; postgrad., NYU, 1959-61. Asst. v.p. Fidelity Union Trust Co., Newark, 1955-64; v.p., trust officer County Nat. Bank, Poughkeepsie, N.Y., 1964-67, Capital Nat. Bank, Houston, 1967-69; v.p. Lionel D. Edie & Co., 1969-72, Dominick Mgmt. Co., N.Y.C., 1972-75, Marine Midland Bank, N.Y.C., 1975-80; 1st v.p. Lehman Mgmt. Co., 1980-82; owner, pres. Brock Lewis Assocs. Ltd., Lawrenceville, N.J., 1982—; pres. SGI Internat., Inc., 1991—. Cons. State of N.J. Adminstrn. Office of Cts., Trenton, 1993—; dir. Inst. Social and Econ. Policy Middle East, Cambridge, Mass., 1993-99. Pres. Greater Trenton Symphony, 1993-2001, pres. emeritus, 2001—; dir. Steinway Soc., Princeton, 1990-2000; trustee emeritus Tabor Acad., Marion, Mass.; mem. Republican Presdl. Roundtable, 2000—. Mem. Nat. Assn. Bus. Economists (chmn. internat. Bus. Risk Mgmt., Danish Am. C. of C., European Am. C. of C., Princeton C. of C., Mercer County C. of C., Tabor Acad. Alumni Assn. (chmn. 1995-98, trustee 1995-98), Nassau Club, Pacific Club, Dartmouth Clubs of N.Y. and Princeton, Dartmouth Rowing Club, Union Boat Club Boston.

LEWIS, CALVIN FRED, architect, educator; b. Chgo., Mar. 27, 1946; s. Howard George and Fern Teresa (Voelsch) L.; m. L. Diane Johnson, Aug. 24, 1968; children: Nathan, Miller, Cooper, Wilson. BArch, Iowa State U., 1969. Architect Charles Herbert and Assocs., Des Moines, 1970-86; prin. Herbert Lewis Kruse Blunck Architecture, 1987—; prof., dept. arch chair Iowa State U., 2000—. Arch. nat. lectr.; AIA awards juror. More tha 50 projects published in profl. jours. Recipient Best in Design award Time mag.; named one of Top Young Architects in Country, Met. Home mag.; firm named Nat. AIA Firm of Yr., 2001. Fellow AIA (more than 70 Design awards 1972—, 3 Nat. Honor awards 1997, 2002, Internat Design award Bus. Week/Archtl. Record 1998, Internat. Design mag. awards 1998, 99, Nat. Design award AIA-AISC 1999). Avocations: sports, photography. Office: Herbert Lewis Kruse Blunk Architecture 202 Fleming Bldg Des Moines IA 50309-4081

LEWIS, CARL EDWIN, artist, photographer, designer; b. N.Y.C., June 1, 1951; s. Roman and Mabel Gertrude (Prescott) L.; m. Julia Jane Brown (div. 1974); m. Dorena Renise Rachall, Apr. 30, 1977. Student, U. Ariz., 1977-78; grad., Cathedral Choir Sch. of St. John the Divine. Designer Apple Unltd., Tucson, 1977-80; photographer The Grey Scale, Hartford, Conn., 1980-83; photographer/designer Zen D'Zins, Dallas, 1984-92; cmty. project program coord., dir., photographer/designer Crown Family Unity Programs ...And Lewis, Too?!, 1993—; internat. mktg. mgr. Ecotech Ag Inc., 1998. Mem. pub. art com. City of Dallas, 1991-98; dir. mktg. Global Environ. Group, 1996—; mem. Tex. Commn. on the Arts; artist-in-edn. dir. Skate Away From Violence; cons. Tex. Network of Youth Svcs.; pres., mem. U.S.-South African Fashion Inst., 1998; mem. U.S. Ghana Trade Mission, 1998; pres. The Universal Family, 2000, prin. AlchoSys/Sataurus Imaging Group, 1999. Project coord. Kente, the Sight and Sound, 1994; dir. Everybody Skate!, 1993; co-author Captured Light; exhibited in shows at Paul Mellon Art Ctr., Wallingford, Conn., 1984, 87, Mayor's Gallery, Stamford, Conn., 1990, U. Tex. at Dallas, 1991, Visions in Black Gallery, Bath House Cultural Ctr., 1993, Conduit Gallery, 1993, Amon Carter Mus., 1994, Houston Mus. Fine Arts, 1994, Irving Art Ctr., 1996others; represented in collections at U. Wis., Madison, Cathedral Choir Sch. of St. John the Divine, N.Y.C., San Antonio Mus. Art, Bklyn. Mus., Amon Carter Mus., Houston Mus. Fine Arts, Schomburg Ctr. Rsch. into Black Culture, Tex. Instruments, So. Meth. U. Served with USAF, 1971-76, Turkey. Recipient scholarships and awards; fellow Internat. Biog. Ctr., Cambridge, Eng. Mem. Royal Photography Soc. Avocations: collecting orchids, fencing, chess, inline skating, bodybuilding. Office: . . .and Lewis Too?! PO Box 820813 Dallas TX 75382-0813

LEWIS, CAROL E. academic administrator, management consultant; d. Otto A. and Edna M. Zunker(Stepmother); m. John S. Lewis, Aug. 28, 1938. BS, U. Fla., 1962, MS, 1966; PhD, Georgetown U., 1970; MBA, U. Alaska, 1978. Interim dean Sch. Agr. and Land Resources Mgmt. U. Alaska, Fairbanks, 2000—02, dean, dir. Sch. of Agr. and Land Resources Mgmt. and Agrl. and Forestry Expt. Sta., 2002—. From asst. to assoc. to prof. resources mgmt. U. Alaska, Fairbanks, 1973—, head dept. resources mgmt., 1989—98; rsch. physicist Dahlgren (Va.) Naval Weapons Lab., 1969—72; asst. prof. Clinch Valley Coll., U. of Va., Wise, Va., 1967—68. Mem.: Internat. 99s (pres. Midnight Sun chpt. 1993—97), Rotary Internat. (pres. College Rotary 1996—97), Phi Kappa Phi (pres. 1996—2002), Sigma Xi. Achievements include patents for ultrasonic imaging device /detection of tree disease and lumber/timber imperfections. Office: U Alaska 172 AHRB Box 757140 Fairbanks AK 99775-7140 Office Fax: 907-474-6567. E-mail: ffcel@uaf.edu.

LEWIS, CECIL DWAIN, minister; b. Dayton, Ohio, June 30, 1929; s. Clyde Dexter and Ina Candice (Harmon) L.; m. Jacqueline Ann Jones, July 29, 1951; children: Cynthia Lewis Parker, Constance Lewis Bunker. BA, Bob Jones U., 1951; MDiv, Grace Theol. Sem., Winona Lake, Ind., 1957; MA, Chapman Coll., 1972; postgrad., U.S.A. Chaplain Sch., 1973; PhD, Calif. Grad. Sch. Theology, Rosemead, 1991. Ordained to ministry Bapt. Ch., 1950. Asst. pastor Riverside Bapt. Ch., Decatur, Ill., 1951-54; pastor 1st Bible Ch., New Castle, Ind., 1961-64, Faith Baptist Ch., Flint, Mich., 1964-66; commd. 1st lt. U.S. Army, 1966, advanced through grades to lt. col., 1980, chaplain various places in U.S. and Vietnam, 1966-86, ret., 1986; pastor Harmony Bapt. Ch., Waynesville, Mo., 1988-89. Adj. prof. Drury Coll., 1984-90, John Brown U., 1992-93. Author: Training for Lay Leaders, 1981; tech. advisor, writer: (film) In Beginning, 1980; developer tng. programs for U.S. Army chaplaincy, 1978-82; contbr. articles to profl. jours. Chaplain Siloam Springs (Ark.) Police Dept. and Fire Dept.; bd. regents Liberty U., Linchburg, Va. Decorated Bronze Star (2), Air Medal, Meritorious Svc. medal, Valorous Unit award, Presdl. Unit Citation, Vietnamese Cross of Gallantry, Army Commendation award for heroism. Mem. VFW (life), Vietnam Vets. Am. (life), Am. Assn. Marriage and Family Therapists, Ret. Officers Assn. (life), Siloam Springs Country Club (bd. dirs.) Home: 706A Meghan St Siloam Springs AR 72761-5516 E-mail: cecill@ipa.net.

LEWIS, CHARLES EDWIN, epidemiologist, educator; b. Kansas City, Dec. 28, 1928; s. Claude Herbert and Maudie Friels (Holaday) Lewis; m. Mary Ann Gurera, Dec. 27, 1963; children: Kevin Neil, David Bradford, Matthew Clinton, Karen Carleen. Student, U. Kans., 1948—49; MD, Harvard, 1953; MS, U. Cin., 1957, ScD, 1959. Diplomate Am. Bd. Preventive Medicine (Occupl. Medicine). Intern, resident U. Kans. Hosp., 1953—54; trainee USPHS, 1956—58; fellow occupational health Eastman Kodak Co., 1958—59; asst. clin. prof. epidemiology Baylor U. Sch. Medicine, 1960—61; asso. prof. medicine U. Kans. Med. Sch., 1961—62, prof., chmn. dept. preventive medicine, 1962—69; coordinator Kan. Regional Med. Program, 1967—69; prof. social medicine Harvard Med. Sch., 1969—70; prof. pub. health, head div. health adminstrn. UCLA Med. Sch., 1970—72, prof. medicine, div. head, 1972—90; prof., 1972—89; prof. nursing Sch. Nursing UCLA Med. Sch., 1973—, head div. preventive and occupational medicine, 1991—93; dir. Health Svcs. Rsch. Ctr., 1991—93, UCLA Ctr. Health Promotion and Disease Prevention, 1991—; chair acad. senate UCLA, 1995—96. Cons. Getty Trust, Walt Disney Prodns.; mem. Nat. Bd. Med. Examiners, 1964—68, 1968—83, Jt. Commn. on Accreditation Health Care Orgns., 1989—95; mem. health svcs. rsch. study sect. USPHS, 1968—76; vis. scholar Annenberg Sch. Comm., U. So. Calif., 1980—81; mem. adv. bd. Hosp. Rsch. and Edn. Trust, 1972—75. Contbr. articles to profl. jours. Capt. USAF, 1954—56. Recipient Ginsberg prize medicine, U. Kans., 1954, Glasier award, Soc. Gen. Internal Medicine, 1988. Master: ACP (regent 1988—94, Rosenthal award 1980, Laureate award So. Calif. III 1994); fellow: APHA, Acad. Occupl. Medicine; mem.: Am. Assn. Physicians, Assn. Tchrs. Preventive Medicine (pres. coun. 1977—80), Internat. Epidemiology Soc. Home: 221 S Burlingame Ave Los Angeles CA 90049-3702 E-mail: lewis@ph.adm.ucla.edu.

LEWIS, CHARLES A. investment company executive; b. Orange, N.J., Oct. 23, 1942; s. F. Donald and Edna H. L.; m. Gretchen Smith, July 1967 (div.); m. Penny Bender Sebring, June 9, 1984. BA, Amherst Coll., 1964; MBA, U. Pa., 1966. Asst. to pres. Computer Tech., Inc., Skokie, Ill., 1969-70; 1st v.p. White, Weld, & Co., 1970-78; vice chmn. investment banking Merrill Lynch & Co., Chgo., 1978—. Life trustee Amherst Coll., Folger Shakespear Libr., 1989—, Chgo. Symphony Orch., 1989—; life dir. Juvenile Diabetes Rsch. Found. Greater Chgo.; vis. com. divsn. social scis. U. Chgo.; trustee Ravinia Festival, 1995—98; leadership coun. Chgo. Pub. Edn. Fund, 2000—; governing bd. North Kenwood/Oakland Charter Sch., 2000—; bd. dirs. Juvenile Diabetes Rsch. Found. Internat., 1994—95. Mem. Chgo.Club, Glen View Club, Econ. Club Chgo., Fisher Island Club. Office: Merrill Lynch & Co 5500 Sears Tower Chicago IL 60606 E-mail: calewis@exchange.ml.com.

LEWIS, CHARLES JEREMY (JERRY LEWIS), congressman; b. Spokane, Wash., Oct. 21, 1934; BA, UCLA, 1956. Former life ins. underwriter; field rep. for former U.S. Rep. Jerry Pettis; mem. Calif. State Assembly, 1968-78; vice chmn. rules com., chmn. subcom. on air quality; mem. U.S. Congress from 40th (formerly 35th) Calif. dist., 1979—; mem. appropriations com. Chmn. VA-HUD subcom., mem. defense subcom., select com. on intelligence, chmn. subcom. on human intelligence; co-chair Calif. Congl. Delegation. Republican. Presbyterian. Office: US Ho Reps 2112 Rayburn Ho Office Bldg Washington DC 20515*

LEWIS, CHARLES JOSEPH, journalist; b. Bozeman, Mont., July 10, 1940; s. Vern Edward James and Mary (Brooke) L.; m. Sarah Withers; children: Peter, Patrick, Barbara. BS in Humanities with Honors, Loyola U., Chgo., 1962; JD, Columbia U., 1965. Bar: Ill. 1965. Atty. McDermott, Will & Emery, Chgo., 1965-67; reporter City News Bur., 1967-68; reporter, editor Chgo. Sun-Times, 1968-73; with AP, 1974-89, reporter, editor, Washington, 1974-78, reporter, editor, L.A., 1978-80, personnel mgr., N.Y.C., 1981-83, bur. chief, Hartford, Conn., 1980-81, bur. chief, Washington, 1984-89; bur. chief Hearst Newspapers, Washington, 1989—. Bd. dirs. Nat. Press Found., Washington, 1985—, treas., 1987-88, vice chmn., 1988-90, chmn., 1990-92; dir. Reporters Com. for Freedom of the Press, 1993-98, SDX Found. Washington, 1996—; mem. adv. bd. Paul Miller Washington Reporting Fellowships, 1999—. Lance cpl. USMCR, 1963-67. Mem. Am. Soc. Newspaper Editors, Gridiron Club, Sigma Delta Chi (v.p. Washington chpt. 1988-89). Office: Hearst Newspapers 1701 Pennsylvania Ave NW Washington DC 20006-5889

LEWIS, CHARLES LEONARD, psychologist; b. Wellsville, Ohio, Jan. 6, 1926; s. Cleo L. and Charlotte (Hahn) L.; m. Charlotte J. Wynn, Sept. 8, 1948 (dec. Mar. 1987); children: Stephen C., Janet J., Judith A.; m. Jane E. McCormick, Oct. 1, 1988. BS in Edn. with honors, Ohio U., 1949; MA, U. Minn., 1953, PhD, 1955. Asst. dean of men Ohio U., 1948-50; assoc. dir. activities U. Minn., 1950-55; dean student affairs, assoc. prof. psychology U. N.D., 1955-62; exec. dean, assoc. prof. ednl. psychology U. Tenn., 1962-67; v.p. student affairs Pa. State U., 1967-72; exec. dir. Am. Personnel and Guidance Assn., Washington, 1972-74, exec. v.p., 1974-83, exec. v.p. emeritus, 1984—; pres. Charles L. Lewis & Assocs., Annandale, Va., 1983-85, Chuck Lewis et al, Lancaster, Pa., 1985—. Guest prof. U. Md., 1973; mem. Nat. Adv. Com. for Devel. Guidance Components-Career Edn., 1972-76. Founding editor Jour. Coll. Students Pers., 1958-64; mem. editl. bd. Pers. and Guidance Jour., 1954-57. Mem. Pres.'s Com. for Handicapped, 1972-80; bd. dirs. Ctr. Cmty. Hosps., Bellefonte, Pa. With U.S. Army, 1944-47. Recipient George Hill Disting. Alumni award Ohio U., 1981, Outstanding Alumnus Coll. Edn. Ohio U., 1988. Mem. APA, AAUP, Am. Assn. Higher Edn., Am. Coll. Pers. Assn. (pres. 1968-69), Nat. Assn. Student Pers. Adminstrs., Nat. Assn. Woman Deans and Counselors, Am. Pers. and Guidance Assn. (dir. 1967-70), Am. Assn. Univ. Adminstrs. (dir. 1973), Coun. Advancement of Stds. (bd. dirs.), Ohio U. Alumni Soc. and Friends Coll. Edn. (coun. 1985-92, bd. dirs. 1986-92), Willow Valley Computer Sig. (pres. 1999-2001), Psi Chi, Kappa Delta Pi, Beta Theta Pi, Chi Sigma Iota (founding dir. 1984-90). Episcopalian. E-mail: clewis5005@aol.com.

LEWIS, CHARLES RAYMOND, II, traffic engineer, consultant; b. Charleston, W.Va., May 29, 1947; s. Charles Raymond and Jane Ann (Veazey) L.; m. Constance Maria Gratop, Aug. 29, 1970; 1 child, Brian Anthony. BSCE, Ohio U., 1970; MEng in Civil Engring., Pa. State U., 1971. Registered profl. engr., W.Va., profl. surveyor, W.Va.; lic. master electrician, W.Va. Asst. planning and rsch. engr. W.Va. Dept. Hwys., Charleston, 1970-73; planning and rsch. engr. Dept. Transp. Traffic Engr. Divsn. W.Va. Divsn. Hwys., 1973—. Com. mem. Transp. Rsch. Bd., Washington, 1983—, com. chmn., 1984-90; project and synthesis panel mem. Nat. Coop. Hwy. Rsch. Program, Washington, 1991—. Asst. scoutmaster Boy Scouts Am., Charleston, 1991—; co-clerk Charleston Friends Meeting, 2001—. Fellow Automotive Safety Found.; recipient Silver Beaver award Boy Scouts Am., 1998, Lifetime Achievement award W.Va. Operation Lifesaver, 2001. Mem. Inst. Transp. Engrs., Am. Railway Engring. and Maintenance of Way Assn. Avocations: photography, geology, amateur astronomy. Office: Traffic Engring Divsn WVa Dept Transp 1900 Kanawha Blvd E Charleston WV 25305-0009

LEWIS, CHARLTON SCOTT, civil engineer; b. Hazlehurst, GA., Dec. 22, 1948; s. Earnest and Nancy Ann (Todd) L.; m. Paulette Gupton, Mar. 29, 1970; children: Stephanie Lynne, Lorinda Ruth, Anna Maria. BS in Civil Engring., Ga. Inst. Tech., 1971; MS in Engring., U. Calif., Berkeley, 1976. Registered profl. engr., Va. Civil engr. U.S. Forest Svc., Asheville, N.C., 1971-75, Berkeley, Calif., 1975-77, transp. planner Roanoke, Va., 1977-80, Cleveland, Tenn., 1980-87, s. zone engr., 1988—. Instr. Asheville-Buncombe Tech. Inst., Asheville, N.C., 1972, Road-Bridge Design Workshop, Chihuahua, Chihuahua, Mex., 1990. Composer: various songs, 1973—. Mem. ASCE, ASCAP. Mem. Church of God. Office: USDA Forest Svc 2800 Ocoee St N Cleveland TN 37312-5374

LEWIS, CHERIE SUE, lawyer, English language and journalism educator; b. Cleve., Feb. 6, 1951; d. Samuel D. and Evelyne P. L. BA, U. Mich., 1973; MS, Boston U., 1975; PhD, U. Minn., 1986; JD, Southwestern U., L.A., 1996. Cert. ESL tchr., Calif. Prof. Pa. State U., State College, 1988-89, Nat. Chengchi U., Taipei, Taiwan, 1989-91, Syracuse U., 1992-93, Nat. U., L.A., 1993—; atty.-advisor U.S. Social Security Adminstrn., 1998—. Cons. Pacific Rim Inst., L.A., 1992-95. Author: (book chpt.) Disability Rights, International, 1994, ednl. brochures, 1994; mng. editor Southwestern U. Jour. Law and Trade, 1995-96. Mem. AAUP, ABA. Avocations: music, skiing, internat. travel. Office: 6 Kenwood Ct Beachwood OH 44122-7501 E-mail: Cherie0206@hotmail.com.

LEWIS, CHERYL M. foundation executive; b. Tiffin, Ohio, Nov. 2, 1962; d. Jack R. and Madeline R. Staib; m. Murphy J. Lewis, May 5, 2000. AB in English, Heidelberg Coll., 1985, MEd, 1990. Cert. fundraising exec. English tchr. Clearcreek Schs., Springboro, Ohio, 1985-86; alumni dir. Heidelberg Coll., Tiffin, 1986-93; ann. fund dir. Youngstown (Ohio) State U., 1993-99; dir. devel. Shepherd's Found., Youngstown, 1999—. Vol. New Start Treatment Ctr., Warren, Ohio, 1995—. Mem. Assn. Fundraising Profls. (pres. Youngstown 2001—), Assn. Lutheran Devel. Execs., No. Ohio Planned Giving Coun. Office: Shepherd's Found 6000 Mahoning Ave Ste 410 Youngstown OH 44515 E-mail: clewis@shepherdofthevalley.com.

LEWIS, CLAUDIA JEAN, marketing professional; b. Washington, Sept. 3, 1947; d. Gerald O. and Shirley Ardith (Morris) Pearl; 1 child, Melissa P. Henriksen. BA in Speech Comm. summa cum laude, George Mason U., 1994, M Internat. Commerce and Policy summa cum laude, 1999. Community, client rels. mgr. Odin, Feldman & Pittleman, P.C., Fairfax, 1984—. Contbg. author: Military Lessons of the Gulf War, rev. edit., 1993, Theories of Communicative Interaction, 1994. Vol. Meridian Internat. Ctr., Washington, 1994—; mem. adv. com., "Care" award com. No. Va. Family Svcs., Falls Church, Va., 1994-99; mem. adv. com. Friends of The Women's Ctr., Vienna, Va., 1995-99; planning commr. City of Fairfax Planning Commn., 1995-97. Mem. Internat. Trade Assn. No. Va. (bd. dirs. 1997—, pres. 1998-2000), Nat. Assn. Law Firm Marketers (publicity chair 1991), Mid-Atlantic Legal Marketers Assn., Alpha Chi, Golden Key (Nat. Collegiate Comm. award winner, 1991, 92), Ctrl. Fairfax C. of C. (pres. 1990-91). Avocations: gardening, cooking, traveling, antiquing.

LEWIS, CLYDE A. lawyer; b. Hoquiam, Wash., June 20, 1913; s. J.D. Clyde and Loretta C. (Adelsperger) L.; m. Helen M. Judge, Sept. 22, 1936 (dec. Sept. 1985); m. Patricia Davis Judge, Oct. 1, 1988; children: Clyde A., John E. AB, U. Notre Dame, 1934; JD, Harvard U., 1939. Bar: N.Y. 1940, U.S. Supreme Ct. 1959. Mem. Lewis, Roger Kudrle & Meconi, P.C. and predecessor firms, Plattsburgh, NY. Comdr. in chief VFW, 1949-50, also served as sr. and jr. vice comdr. in chief, mem. nat. legis. com. Maj. USAAF, 1942-45. Decorated DFC with 2 oak leaf clusters, Air medal with 4 oak leaf clusters; recipient Croix de Guerre, France; invested Knight of Malta. Mem. ABA, N.Y. State Bar Assn., U.S. Strategic Inst., Def. Orientation Conf. Assn., Notre Dame Alumni Assn., Harvard Alumni Assn., Am. Legion. Clubs: Capitol Hill, K.C., Elks. Republican. Roman Catholic. Home: 12 New Hampshire St Plattsburgh NY 12903 Office: 53 Court St Plattsburgh NY 12901-2834

LEWIS, CORINNE HEMETER, psychotherapist, educator; b. N.Y.C., Nov. 28, 1925; d. Leslie Hall and Frances Pope Hemeter, m. Aug. 22, 1947 (div. 1984); children: Anne Marie, Richard Allyn, Timothy Hall; m. Ceylon S. Lewis Jr., Aug. 6, 1999. BSN, U. Pitts., 1947; MSW, U. Okla., 1978. Diplomate in clin. social work. Staff nurse St. Joseph's Hosp., Buckhannon, W.Va., 1947; head nurse Myer's Clinic, Phillipi, 1948; clin. instr., supr. Allegheny Valley Hosp., Tarentum, Pa., 1949; coord. psychiat. nursing edn. Hillcrest Med. Ctr., Tulsa, 1966-67; clin. staff mem. Tulsa Psychiat. Ctr., 1968-77; tchr. principles personality devel. Hillcrest Med. Ctr., 1966-75; supr., interns in psychotherapy Tulsa Psychiat. Ctr., 1971-77; pvt. practice psychotherapist Tulsa, 1978—. Dir. Drug Day Hosp., Tulsa Psychiat. Ctr., 1969, dir. nursing, 1970-71; adminstrv. cons. Family and Children's Svcs., Tulsa, 1978; renal dialysis unit cons. Hillcrest Med. Ctr., 1978; dir. Am. Cancer Soc. funded program Tulsa Psychiat. Ctr., 1977-79, cons. to dept. internal medicine, Tulsa Med. Coll., 1977-98. Jr. bd. mem. Women's Assn., Tulsa Boys Home, 1957-59; mem. Mental Health Assn. Tulsa, 1968-83, bd. dirs., 1982-83; vol. Jr. Assn., Tulsa Boys Home, 1958-59, Children's Med. Ctr., 1953-56; bd. dirs. Nursing Svc. Inc., Tulsa, 1982-83. Mem. Nat. Assn. Social Workers, Acad. Cert. Social Workers, Sigma Theta Tau. Democrat. Presbyterian. Avocations: classical music, reading. Home: 2300 Riverside Dr Apt 8F Tulsa OK 74114-2403

LEWIS, DALE KENTON, retired lawyer, mediator; b. Goodland, Kans., June 20, 1937; s. W. Homer and L. (Fern) L.; m. Constance L. Coover, Dec. 27, 1958; children— James W., Bari Lynn, Brad Kenton. BA, State U. Iowa, 1959; JD, Colo. U., 1962. Bar: Colo. 1962, Ind. 1968. Mem. firm Lewis & Ausenhus, Loveland, Colo., 1962-67; with Eli Lilly and Co., 1967-90; counsel Elanco Products Co., 1969-77; gen. counsel, sec. Elizabeth Arden, Inc., 1977-81, corp. asst. sec. and asst. gen. counsel, 1981-83, corp. asst. sec., dep. gen. counsel, 1983-86, sec., dep. gen. counsel, 1986-89; v.p., sec., gen. counsel DowElanco, Indpls., 1989-95; ret., 1995. Mem. Am. Corp. Counsel Assn., Order of Coif. Episcopalian.

LEWIS, DAN ALBERT, education educator; b. Chgo., Feb. 14, 1946; s. Milton and Diane (Sabath) L.; m. Stephanie Riger, Jan. 3, 1982; children: Matthew, Jake. BA cum laude, Stanford U., 1968; PhD, U. Calif., Santa Cruz, 1980. Rsch. assoc. Arthur Bolton Assocs., Sacramento, 1969-70; survey contr. Sci. Analysis Corp., San Francisco, 1971; dir. Stanford Workshops on Polit. and Social Issues Stanford (Calif.) U., 1971-74; projects adminstr. Ctr. Urban Affairs and Policy Rsch., Northwestern U., Evanston, Ill., 1975-80, asst. prof. edn., 1980-86, assoc. prof. edn., 1986-90, assoc. dir., chair grad. program human devel./social policy, 1987-90, prof. edn., 1990—. Vis. scholar Sch. Edn., Stanford U., 1990-91; mem. task force on restructuring mental health svcs. Chgo. Dept. Health, 1982; mem. human rights authority Ill. Guardianship and Advocacy Commn., 1980-82; adv. mem. com. on planning and inter-agy. coordination Commn. Mental Health and Devel. Disabilities, 1979; interim adv. com. on mental health City of Chgo., 1978; adv. mem. Gov.'s Commn. to Revise Mental Health Code Ill., 1975-77; presenter at profl. confs.; presenter workshops. Editor: Reactions to Crime, 1981; co-author: Fear of Crime: Incivility and the Production of a Social Problem, 1986, The Social Construction of Reform: Crime Prevention and Community Organizations, 1988, The Worlds of the Mentally Ill, 1991, The State Mental Patient in Urban Life, 1994, Race and Educational Reform, 1995; contbr. articles, book revs. to profl. publs. Bd. dirs. Designs for Change, Ill. Mental Health Assn.; rsch. adv. com. Chgo. Urban League, Chgo. Panel Pub. Sch. Finances, 1989-91; needs assessment tech. com. United Way Chgo., 1989-90; ednl. coun. Francis W. Parker Sch., Chgo., 1988-90; task force on restructuring mental health svcs. Chgo. Dept. Health, 1982; com. on mentally disabled Ill. State Bar Assn., 1983-89; rsch. policy com. Ill. Dept. Mental Health, 1978; bd. dirs. Mental Health Assn. Greater Chgo., 1977-84, v.p. pub. policy, 1979-83 Recipient Excellence in Tchg. award Northwestern U. Alumni Assn., 1998. Office: Northwestern Univ 2040 Sheridan Rd Evanston IL 60208-0855 E-mail: dlewis@northwestern.edu.

LEWIS, DANA KENNETH, human services/communications consultant, author; b. L.A., Aug. 24, 1945; s. Kenneth Robert and Ouida Jo (Norris) L.; m. Yoko Koshio, Sept. 12, 1969; 1 child, Michelle Cynthia. BA, Friends World Coll., Huntington, N.Y., 1976; MA, Goddard Coll., Plainfield, Vt., 1980. Cons. to pres. Emile, Inc., Osaka, Japan, 1976-77; residential houseparent Bethany Children's Home, Womelsdorf, Pa., 1977-78, cottage life supr., 1978-86, dir. home life, adminstr., 1986-94; co-founder, pres. Lewis Mktg., Inc. (formerly Pacific Rim Enterprises, Inc.), Fleetwood, 1989-98; founder The Metalog Group, 1993—. Instr. Pa. State U., 1981-83, Family Life Devel., Cornell U., 1982-85; presenter Treischman Conf., Boston, 1989; founder Yoko Trading, e-commerce, 1998. Author: Working with Children, 1981; author, speaker, audio cassettes Child Care and Communications, 1979—; mem. editorial bd. Jour. 1984; book reviewer, 1988; contbr. articles to profl. jours. Lectr. various local facilities, 1978—. Served as staff sgt., USAF. Mem. Child Care Assn. of Pa. (trainer, presenter 1979-87, keynote speaker regional confs. 1986, Dedicated Service award 1986). Avocations: computers, reading, poetry, writing, travelling. Home and Office: Metalog 22 Bick Rd Fleetwood PA 19522-9611 E-mail: danak01@fast.net.

LEWIS, DANIEL EDWARD, systems engineer, marketing engineer, computer company executive; b. Cleve., May 24, 1955; s. Arthur Edward and Vivian Jeanette (Davis) L.; m. Kimber Lea Thacher, Dec. 30, 1993. BSEE, Ohio State U., 1981; MBA, U. Akron, 1988. Registered profl. engr., Ohio. Sys. engr. Firestone Tire & Rubber, Akron, Ohio, 1981-83; software devel. mgr. Diebold Corp., Canton, 1983-85; computer product sales Arrow Electronics, Solon, 1985-86; sr. sys. analyst British Petroleum, Cleve., 1986-89; product mgr. Telxon Corp., Fairlawn, 1989-93; sr. mktg. mgr. Norand Corp., Cedar Rapids, Iowa, 1993-95, dir. mktg., 1995-97; v.p. sys. products Telxon Corp., The Woodlands, Tex., 1997-99; dir. strategy and bus. devel., comml. Internet svcs. divsn. Compaq Computers, Houston, 1999-2000; v.p., product mgr. ASP Application Svcs., Cable and Wireless Corp., 2000—. Contbr. articles to profl. jours. Mem. IEEE, Am. Mgmt. Assn., Assn. for Computing Machinery. Avocations: travel, skiing, sailing. Home: 39 Pebble Cove Dr The Woodlands TX 77381-3316 E-mail: delewis@compuserve.com.

LEWIS, DANIEL EDWIN, lawyer; b. Goshen, Ind., May 2, 1910; s. Daniel Arthur and Emma (Williams) L.; m. Annette Jean Fewell, July 28, 1934; children: Daniel E., Nancy Jean Haswell. A.B., Hanover (Ind.) Coll., 1932; M.S., Ind. U., 1939; J.D., Valparaiso U., 1949. Bar: Ind. 1949. Tchr. secondary schs., Ind., 1932-43; dir. indsl. relations Allis-Chalmers, LaPorte, Ind., 1943-55; ptnr. Newby, Lewis & Kaminski, LaPorte, after 1955, now of counsel. Treas., Health Care Fedn., 1982; pres. LaPorte Bd. Edn., 1952-55; vice chmn. Pottawatomie County Boy Scouts Am., 1963-69; pres. United Fund, 1957-65; chmn. LaPorte County ARC, 1948-49; pres. LaPorte YMCA, 1960-62; pres. LaPorte County Family Service, 1975-77; pres. LaPorte County Human Relations Bd., 1967-68. Recipient Alumni Achievement award Hanover Coll., 1965; inducted into the Football Hall of Fame, LaPorte. Fellow Ind. State Bar Found.; mem. ABA, Ind. State Bar Assn., LaPorte City and County Bar Assn., Soc. Profls. in Dispute Resolution, Kiwanis (Kiwanian of Yr. 1989), Elks (Elk of Yr. 1987), Masons. Presbyterian. Author: (fiction) At the Crossroads, 1980; So It Comes to Arbitration, 1982. Died Oct. 15, 1997. Office: 916 Lincolnway La Porte IN 46350-3412

LEWIS, DARRELL L. retail executive; b. Mason City, Iowa, Nov. 20, 1931; s. Milton Loren and Blanche Ione (Wilson) L.; m. Mary Jo Bahnsen, Oct. 22, 1950; children— John L., Lonnette Ann, Sherri Jo. MBA, Stanford U., 1970. With Osco Drug, Inc. subsidiary Jewel Cos., Inc., 1949-62; with Jewel Turn-Style, 1962; pres. Turn-Style Family Centers, Franklin Park, Ill., 1967-74, head Jewel Hypermarket, 1974; pres. Osco Drug, Inc., 1974-75, v.p. store and sales devel., 1976-77; pres. D.L. Lewis Drug Co. Inc., Bensenville, Ill., 1978—, chmn. bd., 1987—. Home: 12338 Sunset Dr Three Rivers MI 49093-9580 Office: DL Lewis Drug Co 12338 Sunset Dr Three Rivers MI 49093-9580

LEWIS, DAVE, professional hockey team coach; m. Brenda Lewis; children: Ryan, Meagan. Asst. and assoc. coach Detroit Red Wings, 1987—2002, head coach, 2002—. Achievements include 1997 and 1998 Stanley Cup Championships. Office: Detroit Red Wings Joe Louis Arena 600 Civic Center Detroit MI 48226*

LEWIS, DAVID CARLETON, medical educator, university center director; b. Hartford, Conn., May 19, 1935; s. Theodore and Lillian (Levin) L.; m. Eleanor Grace Levinson, Aug. 23, 1959; children: Deborah, Steven. AB magna cum laude, Brown U., 1957; MD, Harvard U., 1961. Intern Beth Israel Hosp., Boston, 1961-62, jr. resident, 1962-63, chief med. resident, 1966-67, dir. emergency unit and med. outpatient dept., 1969-71; sr. resident U. Hosps. Cleve., 1963-64, Parkland Meml. Hosp., Dallas, 1964-66; fellow U. Tex. Southwestern Med. Hosp., 1964-66; Sloan Found. fellow Harvard Med. Sch., Boston, 1971-72; med. dir. Washingtonian Ctr. for Addictions, 1972-77; dir. div. alcohol and substance abuse Roger Williams Gen. Hosp., Providence, 1976-82; dir. program in alcoholism and drug abuse Brown U., 1976-82, prof. medicine and community health, 1982—, Donald G. Millar prof. alcohol and addiction studies, 1987—, chmn. dept. community health, 1981-86, dir. Ctr. Alcohol and Addiction Studies, 1982-2000. Mem. nat. adv. coun. Nat. Alcohol Inst., Rockville, Md., 1981-85, cons. to dir., 1985-93; mem. sci. adv. bd. Children of Alcoholics Found., 1985-95; cons. WHO, 1986—, mem. WHO-cocaine global adv. com., 1992-95; chair Physician Consortium on Substance Abuse Edn., 1989—; mem. Carnegie Substance Abuse Adv. com., 1989-92; scholar-in-residence Nat. Inst. Med., 1991-92; mem. adv. panel to U.S. Pharmacopoeia, 1995—; mem. Drug Strategies Nat. Adv. Panel, 1994—, dir. WHO Collaborating Ctr. at Brown U., 1995-2000; mem. nat. adv. com. Robert Wood Johnson Found. Fighting Back program, 1996—. Author: The Drug Experience: Data for Decision Making, 1970; editor: Providing Care for Children of Alcoholics, 1986; editor Brown U. Digest of Addiction Theory and Application, 1986—; exec. editor Substance Abuse jour., 1984—; contbr. numerous articles to profl. jours. Med. dir. Beacon Hill Free Clinic, Boston, 1968—71; chmn. Mayor's Coun. on Drug Abuse, 1972—80; project dir. Physician Leadership on Nat. Drug Policy, 1997—. Grantee Nat. Alcohol and Drug Insts., 1986—, Robert Wood Johnson Found., 1996—, John D. and Catherine T. MacArthur Found., 1997—, Open Study Inst., 1997—; Edward John Noble fellow Harvard U. Med. Sch., 1957-91; receipient Assn. Med. Edn. and Rsch. in Substance Abuse award for Excellence in Medical Edn., 1986, Norman E Zinberg Meml. Lectr. award Harvard Med. Sch., 1996, AMA award, 1997, Excellence in Med. Edn. AMA-ERF, 1997. Fellow: ACP; mem.: Brown Med. Alumni Assn. (pres. 1974—76), Assn. Med. Edn. and Rsch. in Substance Abuse (pres. 1983—88, Excellence in Medicine award 1986), Inst. Medicine Study on Treatment Alcohol Problems, Am. Acad. on Physician and Patient (bd. dirs. 1998—2001), Am. Soc. Addiction Medicine (bd. dirs. 1995—), NAS, Sigma Xi, Phi Beta Kappa. Avocations: choral singing, sailing, photography. Office: Brown Univ Ctr Alcohol & Addiction Studies Box G Providence RI 02912 E-mail: David_Lewis@brown.edu.

LEWIS, DAVID EDWIN, chemistry educator; b. Tailem Bend, Australia, Nov. 21, 1951; s. Edwin and Shirley Cecile (Candy) L.; m. Deborah Anne Schurtz, May 7, 1978; children: Graeme Alexander, Veronica Anne. BSc, Adelaide U., 1972, BSc (Hons.), 1973, PhD, 1980. From asst. prof. to assoc. prof. Baylor U., Waco, Tex., 1981-88; from assoc. prof. to prof. S.D. State U., Brookings, 1989-97; prof. dept. chemistry U. Wis., Eau Claire, 1997—, chmn., 1997-99. Vis. asst. prof. U. Ill., Urbana, 1980-81; adv. bd. Custom Antibodies of Tex., Dallas, 1992—, adv. bd. MicroBioMed Corp., Dallas, 1992—, dir. chem. rsch., 1992-93, dir. rsch., 1993-97; adv. bd. Solus Biodefense, 1999—. Author: Organic Chemistry: A Modern Perspective, 1995; contbr. articles to profl. jours. Fellow Royal Australian Chem. Inst.; mem. Am. Chem. Soc., Sigma Xi. Achievements include discovery of antiviral compounds and uses of precursors to same for monitoring condition of combustion engines. Office: Dept Chemistry U Wis Eau Claire WI 54702 E-mail: lewisd@uwec.edu.

LEWIS, DAVID GENE, humanities educator; AA in Humanities, Santa Rosa Jr. Coll., 1993; BA in Humanities, U. Oreg., 1997, postgrad., 1997—99, MA, 2000. Grad. tchg. fellow Cross-Cultural Comm. Internat. Studies Program, 1997; intern Smithsonian Instn., 1998; rschr. S.W. Oreg. Rsch. Project II, Washington, 1998; grad. tchg. fellow dept. anthropology U. Oreg., 1999—. Cons. Horner Mus. Collection Oreg. State U., 2001; presenter in field. Editor (with Jason Younker and Mark Tveskov): Changing Landscapes, 2001; contbr. articles to profl. jours. Co-dir. Native Am. Student Union U. Oreg., 1995—96, mem. Associated Students Incidental Fee Com., 1996—97, bd. dirs. Multi-Cultural Ctr., 1996—97, mem. Longhouse Bldg. Com., 1995—98, organizer Longhouse Planning Group, 1999—2000, organizer Native Alumni Group, 1999—2000; vol. Celebrating Traditions Cultural Gathering, Eugene, 1996, 1998; exec. asst. Celebrating Traditions Cmty., 1996—97; vol. culture com. Grand Ronde (Oreg.) Tribe, 2000—. Fellow Smithsonian Instn. Rsch. for Am. Indians, 1998, grad. studies, Am. Indian Grad. Ctr., Albuquerque, 1999—2000; scholar Higher Edn., Confederated Tribes of Grand Ronde, 1997—. Mem.: Soc. Cultural Anthropology, Am. Ethnol. Assn., Nat. Assn. Student Anthropologists, Am. Anthropol. Assn. Office: Dept Anthropology U Oreg 3588 Sisters View Ave Eugene OR 97401

LEWIS, DAVID JOHN, lawyer; b. Zanesville, Ohio, Feb. 4, 1948; s. David Griff and Barbara Ann (Hoy) L.; m. Susan G. Smith; 1 child, Ann Elizabeth. BS in Fin., U. Ill., 1970, JD, 1973. Bar: Ill. 1973, D.C. 1974. Law clk. to Judge Philip W. Tone U.S. Dist. Ct. For North Dist. Ill., Chgo., 1973-74; assoc. Sidley Austin Brown & Wood, Washington, 1974-80, ptnr., 1980—. Comml. arbitrator Am. Arbitration Assn.; mem. Washington panel CPR Inst. Dispute Resolution. Mem. ABA. Office: Sidley Austin Brown & Wood 1501 K St NW Washington DC 20005 E-mail: dlewis@sidley.com.

LEWIS, DAVID L. lawyer; b. N.Y.C., Aug. 11, 1954; s. Albert B. and Sara Anne (Beresniakoff) L.; m. Carol Hayward, Dec. 21, 1983; children: Alexandra Hayward, Andrew Chase. BA, NYU, 1976; JD, Fordham U., 1979. Bar: N.Y. 1980, U.S. Dist. Ct. (ea. and so. dists.) N.Y. 1980, U.S. Ct. Appeals (2d cir.) 1981, U.S. Supreme Ct. 1983. Counsel to spk. pro tem N.Y. State Assembly, Albany, 1980-83; ptnr. Lewis & Fiore, N.Y.C., 1980—. Assoc. counsel to Senator Ray M. Goodman N.Y. State Senate, 2000, chief counsel, 2001. Columnist Decor mag., 1980-88. Mem. law com. Kings County Dem. Com., Bklyn., 1980—; pres. Bensonhurst Redevel. Corp., Bkyn., 1981-82. Mem. ATLA (author text on plea bargaining and settlement), NADCL (past bd. dirs.), N.Y. State Bar Assn., Assn. Bar City N.Y., N.Y. County Lawyers Assn., N.Y. State Assn. Criminal Def. Lawyers (bd. dirs., past pres.). Jewish. Office: Lewis & Fiore 225 Broadway Rm 3300 New York NY 10007-3050

LEWIS, DEBORAH ALICE, tax company executive, writer; b. Griffin, Ga., Mar. 26, 1947; d. Durward and Imogene Hinds L. AA, Miss. Gulf Coast Jr. Coll., Gulfport, 1973; student, William Carey Coll., 1973; BA in English cum laude, U. So. Miss., 1978. Vets. counselor Miss. Gulf Coast Jr. Coll., Gulfport, 1973-76; spl. agt. Dept of Def., 1976-84; instr., adj. faculty Phillips Coll., Gulfport, 1979-81; mgr. H&R Block Inc., Jacksonville, 1984—, tax edn. specialist Anniston, Ala., 1986—. Author: Duty, 1992, (poetry) Dan River Anthology, 1988; regional editor Feminist Lit., 1984. With USMC, 1965—68, with USMCR, 1968—75. Recipient Outstanding Young Women of Am. award, 1980. Mem. Nat. Tax Preparers Assn., Women Marines Assn., League for Animal Welfare (life mem.), Lambda Iota Tau. Avocation: historian. Office: H&R Block Inc 500 Pelham Rd Jacksonville AL 36265 Fax: 256-435-4189. E-mail: dlewis2233@aol.com.

LEWIS, DELANO EUGENE, ambassador, former broadcast executive; b. Arkansas City, Kans., Nov. 12, 1938; s. Raymond Ernest and Enna (Wordlow) L.; m. Gayle Carolyn Jones; children: Delano Jr., Brian, Geoffrey, Phillip. BA, U. Kansas, 1960; JD, Washburn U., 1963; LHD (hon.), Marymount U., 1988; D of Humane Letters, Bowie State U., 1992; D of Pub. Svc., George Washington U., 1991; DHL (hon.), Barry U., 1994, Kent State U., 1995, Lafayette Coll., 1996; LLD (hon.), Nova Southeastern U., 1997; DFA (hon.), So. Ill. U., 1997. Staff atty. U.S. Dept. of Justice, Washington, 1963-65, EEOC, Washington, 1965-66; assoc. dir., country dir. U.S. Peace Corps., Nigeria, Uganda, 1966-69; legis. asst. Sen. Edward Brooke Mass., Washington, 1969-71; adminstrv. asst. Congressman Walter Fauntroy, 1971-73; mgr. pub. affairs Chesapeake & Potomac Telephone Co., 1973-76, asst. v.p., 1976-83, v.p., 1983-88, pres., 1988-93; pres., CEO Nat. Public Radio, 1994-98; amb. to South Africa Dept. of State, Pretoria, South Africa, 1999-2001. Bd. dirs. Eastman Kodak, Africare, Colgate-Palmolive, Herman T's Smokehouse BBQ Rest. Pres. Greater Washington Bd. Trade, 1988; chmn. Mayor's Transition Com., 1978, D.C. Youth Employment Adv. Coun., 1992; co-chair D.C. Vocational Edn. and Career Opportunities Com., 1991, NPR Found.; emeritus bd. dirs. Washington Performing Arts Soc., 1990—; bd. dirs. Lincoln Theatre, Found. Schs., The Menninger Found., 1996. Named Washingtonian of Yr. Washingtonian mag., 1978, Man of Yr., Greater Washington bd. trustees, 1992; recipient Pres. medal Cath. U., Washington, 1978, Tree of Life award NCCJ, 1989, Social Responsibility award George Washington U. Sch. Bus., 1990, Spl. award Women of Washington, Disting. Alumni Citation U. Kans.; Disting. Leadership award Amnesty Internat., 1997, US Media Spotlight award, 1997. Mem. Kans. Bar Assn., D.C. Bar Assn., Georgetown Club. Democrat. Roman Catholic. Avocation: tennis. Address: PO Box 1389 Mesilla NM 88046 E-mail: delanolewis@zianet.com.

LEWIS, DENNIS CARROLL, writer, publisher, educator; b. Milw., Jan. 7, 1940; s. Carroll and Alyce Mae (Bryce) Lewis Paxton; m. Marie Benedicte Denizet, Nov. 1, 1973 (div. Dec. 1982); 1 child, Benoit. Student, U. Wis., 1957-61; BS, San Francisco State U., 1967. Computer programmer, analyst Levi Strauss, San Francisco, 1969-72; freelance book editor, 1972-73; book editor Miller Freeman Pub. Co., 1973-76; pub. rels. account exec. Paul Purdom & Co., 1977-81; ptnr. Hi-Tech. Publicity, 1981-84; pres. Hi-Tech. Pub. Rels., Inc. (acquired by Shandwick Plc, 1988), 1984-90. Owner Mountain Wind Pub., San Francisco, 1996—; Healing Tao instr. and Chi Nei Tsang practitioner, 1993—; instr. B.K. Frantzis Energy Arts, 1997—. Author: The Tao of Natural Breathing, 1997, Breathing as a Metaphor for Living, 1998; co-editor: Sacred Tradition and Present Need, 1975, On the Way to Self Knowledge, 1976; co-pub., editor Computer Publicity News, 1981-90; pub., editor Inner Alchemy jour., 1997-99; contbr. articles to newspapers and profl. jours. Mem. San Francisco Tennis Club. E-mail: info@authentic-breathing.com.

LEWIS, DONALD EMERSON, banker; b. Orange, N.J., Apr. 3, 1950; s. Donald Emerson Lewis and Marie (Gannon) Slaght; m. Suzanne Kimm, Oct. 12, 1974; children: Andrew Gannon, Meredith Marie, Carolyn Ann. AB, Villanova U., 1972; MBA, Boston Coll., 1974. V.p. Citibank N.A., N.Y.C., 1974-85, Boston Safe Deposit & Trust Co., N.Y.C., 1985-87; sr. v.p. United Jersey Banks, Princeton, N.J., 1987-91; v.p. Fleet Bank, N.A., Bridgewater, 1991-2000; prin. First Union Nat. Bank, Summit, 2000—. Mem.: Canoe Brook Country. Republican. Roman Catholic. Avocations: golf, platform tennis. Office: First Union Nat Bank 190 River Rd Summit NJ 07901-1412

LEWIS, DONALD JOHN, mathematics educator; b. Adrian, Minn., Jan. 25, 1926; s. William J. and Ellanora (Masgai) L.; m. Carolyn Dana Hauf, Dec. 28, 1953. BS, Coll. St. Thomas, 1946; PhD, U. Mich., 1950. Instr. Ohio State U., Columbus, 1950-52; asst. prof. U. Notre Dame (Ind.), 1953-57, assoc. prof., 1957-61, U. Mich., Ann Arbor, 1961-63, prof. maths., 1963-2000, prof. emeritus, 2000—, dept. chair, 1983-94; dir. Divsn. Math. Scis. Nat. Sci. Found., 1995-99. Mem. Inst. for Adv. Study, 1952-53, 90-91; vis. scientist U. Manchester (Eng.), 1959-61, Cambridge (Eng.), 1960-61; vis. fellow Trinity Coll., Cambridge, 1965, 69, Japanese Soc. for Promotion of Sci., Tokyo, 1974, Braesnose Coll., Oxford, Eng., 1975; visitor U. Heidelberg, Germany, 1980-81, 83; adv. bd. math. sci. NSF, 1983-86, math panel sci., 1993. Author: Introduction to Algebra, 1965, Calculus and Linear Algebra, 1970; editor: Proceedings of Symposia in Pure Math., 1971; contbr. 55 articles on number theory to profl. jours. Recipient Humboldt Preis award Alexander von Humboldt Soc., Germany, 1980, Disting. Svc. award Am. Math. Soc., 1995; fellow NSF, 1952-53, 59-61. Roman Catholic. Avocations: gardening. Home: 2250 Glendaloch Rd Ann Arbor MI 48104-2832 Office: U Mich Math Dept Ann Arbor MI 48109-1003 E-mail: djlewis@umich.edu.

LEWIS, DONNA CUNNINGHAM, banker, communications consultant; b. Salt Lake City, Aug. 23, 1945; d. Aloysius Cabre Cunningham and Margaret Louise (Jacobs) Brown; m. Gary K. Lewis, Dec. 10, 1976; children: Gary Alexander, Zoe Kit. Student, Ea. Mont. Coll., 1963-65, U. Mont., 1965, NYU, 1990. Mgr. telephone communications Bank of Calif., San Francisco, 1966-70; with Mfrs. Hanover Trust Co., N.Y.C., 1970—, asst. sec., mgr. video prodns., 1972-75, asst. v.p., dir. mgmt. communications, then v.p. and dir., 1975-88; v.p., mgr. internal comms., editor Topics Newspaper, 1988-96; employee communications, face to face comm. corp. campaigns J. P. Morgan Chase & CO. (formerly Chase Manhattan Corp.), N.Y.C., 1996—. Mem. Audio-Visual Mgmt. Assn. (chair membership com. 1986-89, assoc. Cert. of Accreditation 1988, Outstanding com. Chmn. 1988-89), Assn. Nat. Advertisers (chair audio visual communications com. 1980-85), Women in Communications, Inc., Jr. Achievement. Democrat. Home: 411 W End Ave New York NY 10024-5719 Office: JP Morgan Chase 270 Park Ave Fl 34 New York NY 10017-2014 E-mail: donna.m.lewis@jpmchase.com.

LEWIS, DOUGLAS, art historian; b. Centreville, Miss., Apr. 30, 1938; s. Charles Douglas and Beatrice Fenwick (Stewart) L. BA in History; BA in History of Art, Yale U., 1960, MA, 1963, PhD, 1967; BA in Fine Arts, Clare Coll., Cambridge (Eng.) U., 1962, MA, 1966. Asst. in instrn. Yale U., 1962-64; asst. prof. art Bryn Mawr Coll., 1967-68; vis. lectr. U. Calif., Berkeley, spring 1970, fall 1979; adj. prof. Johns Hopkins U., 1973-77; curator sculpture and decorative arts Nat. Gallery Art, Washington, 1968—. Professorial lectr. Georgetown U., 1980-93; adj. prof. U. Md., 1988-91, 93—; mem. art adv. coms. U. Va. Art Mus., Mt. Holyoke Coll. Art Mus., Lawrenceville Sch.; vice-chmn. nat. citizens stamp adv. com. U.S. Postal Svc.; adv. coun. Humanities West, San Francisco, 1991-98; adv. bd. Centro Palladiano, Vicenza, Italy. Author: The Late Baroque Churches of Venice, 1979, The Drawings of Andrea Palladio, 1981, rev. and enlarged edit., 2000, intro. to Renaissance Master Bronzes, 1986. Mem. Am. fellowship com. Belgian-Am. Ednl. Found. Recipient Copley medal Nat. Portrait Gallery, 1981; Chester Dale fellow; David E. Finley fellow Nat. Gallery Art, 1964-67; Rome Prize fellow Am. Acad. Rome, 1964-66, Bruce Curatorial fellow Nat. Gallery Art, 1997-98. Mem. Assn. for Art History (mem. adv. bd.), Coll. Art Assn. Am., Soc. Archtl. Historians, Nat. Trust Historic Preservation, Washington Collegium for the Humanities (adv. bd.), Manuscript Soc. Clubs: Yale (N.Y.C.); Falcons (Cambridge U.). Episcopalian. Office: Nat Gallery Art Washington DC 20565-0001 E-mail: d-lewis@nga.gov.

LEWIS, EDWARD B. biology educator; b. Wilkes-Barre, Pa., May 20, 1918; s. Edward B. and Laura (Histed) L.; m. Pamela Harrah, Sept. 26, 1946; children: Hugh, Glenn(dec.) , Keith. BA, U. Minn., 1939; PhD, Calif. Inst. Tech., 1942; Phil.D., U. Umea, Sweden, 1982; DSc, U. Minn., 1993. Instr. biology Calif. Inst. Tech., Pasadena, 1946—48, asst. prof., 1949—56, prof., 1956—66, Thomas Hunt Morgan prof., 1966—87, prof. emeritus, 1988—. Rockefeller Found. fellow Sch. Botany, Cambridge U., England, 1948—49; mem. Nat. Adv. Com. Radiation, 1958—61; vis. prof. U. Copenhagen, 1975—76, 1982; rschr. in developmental genetics, somatic effects of radiation. Editor: Genetics and Evolution, 1961. Capt. USAAF, 1942—46. Recipient Gairdner Found. Internat. award, 1987, Wolf Found. prize in medicine, 1989, Rosenstiel award, 1990, Nat. Medal of Sci., NSF, 1990, Albert Lasker Basic Med. Rsch. award, 1991, Louisa Gross Horowitz prize, Columbia U., 1992, Nobel Prize in Medicine, 1995. Fellow: AAAS; mem.: NAS, Am. Philos. Soc., Royal Soc. (fgn. mem.; London), Am. Acad. Arts and Scis., Genetics Soc. Am. (sec. 1962—64, pres. 1967—69, Thomas Hunt Morgan medal), Genetics Soc. Japan (hon.), Genetical Soc. Great Britain (hon.). Home: 805 Winthrop Rd San Marino CA 91108-1709 Office: Calif Inst Tech Divsn Biology 1201 E California Blvd Pasadena CA 91125-0001

LEWIS, EDWARD SHELDON, chemistry educator; b. Berkeley, Calif., May 7, 1920; s. Gilbert Newton and Mary (Sheldon) L.; m. Fofo Catsinas, Dec. 21, 1955; children— Richard Peter, Gregory Gilbert. BS, U. Calif., Berkeley, 1940; MA, PhD, Harvard U., 1947. NRC postdoctoral fellow UCLA, 1947-48; from asst. prof. to prof. chemistry Rice U., Houston, 1948-90, prof. emeritus, 1990—, chmn. dept. chemistry, 1963-67, 80-85. Vis. prof. U. Southampton, Eng., 1957, Phys. Chem. Lab., Oxford (Eng.) U., 1967-68, U. Kent, Canterbury, Eng., 1977, H.C. Ørsted Inst. , U. Copenhagen, 1980 Contbr. articles to profl. jours.; Editor: Investigation of Rates and Mechanisms of Reactions, 1974. Served with USNR, 1944-46. Guggenheim fellow, 1968. Fellow AAAS, Royal Irish Acad.; mem. Am. Chem. Soc. (S.W. regional award 1987), Royal Soc. of Chemistry, Phi Beta Kappa, Sigma Xi, Phi Lambda Upsilon. Home: 5651 Chevy Chase Dr Houston TX 77056-4004

LEWIS, EDWIN LEONARD, III, lawyer; b. Phila., Nov. 24, 1945; s. Edwin Leonard Jr. and Nancy (Hoffman) L.; m. Elisabeth C. Bacon, Oct. 6, 1984; children: Katharine Bacon, Caroline Huffington. BA, Lafayette Coll., 1967; JD, Temple U., 1970. bar: Pa. 1970, Ill. 1995. Assoc. MacElree, Platt & Harvey, West Chester, Pa., 1970-73; asst. gen. counsel Fidelity Mut. Life, Phila., 1973-76; sr. atty. Atlantic Richfield Co.; v.p. law Wells Fargo Alarm Svcs., King of Prussia, Pa., 1983-91; v.p., gen. counsel, sec. Borg Warner Protective Svcs., Parsippany, N.J., 1991-95, Borg Warner Security Corp., Chgo., 1995-97; pres. Atlantic Legal Found., N.Y.C., 1998-2000; v.p., gen. counsel Am. Sci. and Engring., Inc., Billerica, Mass., 2000—. Pub., editor Science in the Courtroom Review, 1998. Capt. M.I., USAR, 1970-76. Mem. Am. Corp. Counsel Assn., Phila. Bar Assn., Nat. Fedn. Ind. Bus. Legal Found. (legal adv. bd. 2000—). Avocations: marathon running, tennis, golf, sailing. Home: 59 Delafield Island Rd Darien CT 06820-6012 Office: Am Sci & Engring 829 Middlesex Turnpike Billerica MA 01821 E-mail: nlewis@as-e.com.

LEWIS, EDWIN REYNOLDS, biomedical engineering educator; b. Los Angeles, July 14, 1934; s. Edwin McMurtry and Sally Newman (Reynolds) L.; m. Elizabeth Louise McLean, June 11, 1960; children: Edwin McLean, Sarah Elizabeth. AB in Biol. Sci., Stanford U., 1956, MSEE, 1957, Engr., 1959, PhD in Elec. Engring., 1962. With research staff Librascope div. Gen. Precision Inc., Glendale, Calif., 1961-67; mem. faculty dept. elec. engring. and computer sci. U. Calif., Berkeley, 1967—, dir. bioengring. tng. program, 1969-77, prof. elec. engring. and computer sci., 1971-94, prof. grad. sch., 1994-99, prof. emeritus, 1999—, assoc. dean grad. div., 1977-82, assoc. dean interdisciplinary studies coll. engring., 1988-96. Chair joint program bioengring. U. Calif., Berkeley and San Francisco, 1988-91. Author: Network Models in Population Biology, 1977, (with others) Neural Modeling, 1977, The Vertebrate Inner Ear, 1985, Introduction to Bioengineering, 1996; contbr. articles to profl. jours. Grantee NSF, NASA, 1984, 87, Office Naval Rsch., 1990-93, NIH, 1975-2001; Neurosci. Rsch. Program fellow, 1966, 69; recipient Disting. Tchg. citation U. Calif., 1972, Berkeley citation, 1997; Jacob Javits Neurosci. investigator NIH, 1984-91. Fellow IEEE, Acoustical Soc. Am.; mem. AAAS, Assn. Rsch. in Otolaryngology, Soc. Neurosci., Toastmasters (area lt. gov. 1966-67), Sigma Xi. Office: U Calif Dept Elec Engring & Computer Scis Berkeley CA 94720-0001

LEWIS, EMANUEL RAYMOND, historian, psychologist, retired librarian; b. Oakland, Calif., Nov. 30, 1928; s. Jacob A. and Rose Lewis; m. Joan R. Wilson, Feb. 7, 1954; 1 son, Joseph J.; m. Eleanor M. Gamarsh, Aug. 24, 1967. BA, U. Calif., Berkeley, 1951, MA, 1953; PhD, U. Oreg., 1962. Asst. prof. psychology Oreg. Coll. Edn., 1961-62, Oreg. State U., 1962-67; project mgr. System Devel. Corp., Falls Church, Va., 1968-69; vis. postdoctoral research assoc. in Am. history Smithsonian Instn., Washington, 1969-70; chief historian, dir. research Contract Archeology, Alexandria, Va., 1971-73; librarian U.S. Ho. of Reps., Washington, 1973-95, libr. emeritus, 1995—. Author: Seacoast

Fortifications of the United States, 1970, 2d edit. 1979, 3d edit. 1993; editor: The Educational Information Center, 1969. Served with M.I. U.S. Army, 1954-56. NIMH research fellow, 1960

LEWIS, ERIC STEPHEN, elementary school educator; s. James Garnet and Pauline Lewis; m. Mary Lee Britts, July 31, 1993. AA, El Camino, Torrance, CA, 1972; BA, Calif. State U., Long Beach, 1975. Cert. tchr. Tchr. Nativity Sch., Torrance, 1981—96, Madrona Mid. Sch., Torrance, 1996—. Grantee Edn., Torrance Edn. Found., 2002. Mem.: SCVA, IAJE, Music Educators Nat. Conf. Avocation: sailing. Home: 2301 Danmar Ct Lomita CA 90717 Office: Madrona Mid Sch 21364 Madrona Ave Torrance CA 90503

LEWIS, EVELYN, management consultant; b. Goslar, Germany, Sept. 19, 1946; came to U.S., 1952, naturalized, 1957; d. Gerson Emanuel and Sala (Mendlowicz) L. BA, U. Ill., Chgo., 1968; MA, Ball State U., 1973, PhD, 1976. Rsch. analyst Office Comptr., State of Ill., Chgo., 1977-78; lectr. polit. sci. dept. Loyola U., 1977; asst. to commr. Dept. Human Svcs., 1978-81; group mgr. comm. Arthur Andersen & Co., 1981-84; dir. comm. and pub. rels. Heidrick and Struggles, Inc., 1984-88; assoc. ptnr. organization and human performance Accenture, 1989—. Mem. adj. faculty Sch. Bus. Adminstrn., Roosevelt U., 1988. Mem. Children of Holocaust, Chgo., 1982; bd. dirs. Internat. Children's Benefit Fund. Mem. B'nai B'rith. Jewish. Avocations: writing, poetry, bicycling, hiking. Office: Accenture 161 N Clark Chicago IL 60601

LEWIS, FELICE FLANERY, lawyer, educator; b. Plaquemine, La., Oct. 5, 1920; d. Lowell Baird and E. Elizabeth (Lee) Flanery; m. Francis Russell Lewis, Dec. 22, 1944. BA, U. Wash., 1947; PhD, NYU, 1974; JD, Georgetown U., 1981. Bar: N.Y. 1982. Dean Liberal Arts and Scis. L.I. Univ., Bklyn., 1974-78; assoc. Harry G. English, 1983-85, 91-01; adj. prof. polit. sci. L.I. Univ., 1983-2000. Author: Literature, Obscenity and Law, 1976; co-editor: Henry Miller, Years of Trial & Triumph, 1962-64, 1978. Home: 28 Whitney Cir Glen Cove NY 11542-1316

LEWIS, FLOYD WALLACE, former electric utility executive; b. Lincoln County, Miss., Sept. 23, 1925; s. Thomas Cassidy and Lizzie (Lofton) L.; m. Jimmie Etoile Slawson, Dec. 27, 1949; children: Floyd Wallace, Gail, Julie, Ann, Carol, Michael Paul. BBA, Tulane U., 1945, LL.B., 1949. Bar: La. 1949. With New Orleans Pub. Service Inc., 1949-62, v.p., chief fin. officer, 1960-62; v.p. Ark. Power & Light Co., Little Rock, 1962-63, sr. v.p., 1963-67; exec. v.p., dir. La. Power & Light Co., New Orleans, 1967-68, pres., 1968-70, chief exec. officer, 1968-71, chmn. bd., 1970-72; pres. Middle South Utilities, Inc., 1970-79, 80-85, chmn. bd., 1979-85, also dir., chief exec. officer, 1972-85. Pres., dir. Middle South Services, Inc., New Orleans, 1970-75, chmn., 1975-85, chief exec. officer, 1972-79; pres., dir. Middle South Energy, Inc., 1974-85; chmn. bd. System Fuels, Inc., 1972-85; dir. New Orleans br. Fed. Res. Bank, 1974-75, chmn., 1975; past dir. Fed. Res. Bank of Atlanta, Breeder Reactor Corp., New Orleans Pub. Service Inc., Ark. Power and Light Co., La. Power & Light Co., Miss. Power and Light Co., U.S. Chamber Commerce; mem. adv. com. Elec. Cos. Advt. Program, 1969-72, chmn., 1970-71; mem. electric utility adv. com. to Fed. Energy Adminstrn., 1975-76; chmn. Edison Electric Inst., 1976-77, mem. exec. com., 1974-78; mem. exec. com. Assn. Edison Illuminating Cos., 1973-80; dir. Electric Power Research Inst., 1977-82, chmn., 1979-81; dir. Am. Nuclear Energy Council, 1982-86; pres. Provident Housing Corp., 1999-2001. Mem. exec. bd. New Orleans area council Boy Scouts Am., 1967-80, v.p., 1970-74, pres., 1975-76, mem. regional exec. com., 1968-80; v.p. Com. for a Better La., 1975-76, sr. v.p., 1976-77, pres., 1977-78; bd. dirs. La. World Expn. Inc., 1976-89, chmn., 1980-81, 83-89, pres., 1981-83; chmn. Utility Nuclear Power Oversight Com., 1979-81; vice chmn. campaign United Fund, New Orleans, 1970, chmn., 1971; bd. dirs. New Orleans Symphony Soc., 1974-75, Atomic Indsl. Forum, 1982-86, vice chmn., 1985-86; bd. dirs. Pub. Affairs Research Council of La.; pres. New Orleans Bapt. Sem. Found., 1973-76, 91-92; trustee La. Coll., 1984-90; New Orleans Baptist Theol. Sem., 1954-62, 1968-78, v.p., 1970-78; bd. adminstrs. Tulane U., 1973-88, bd. visitors, 1968-71; bd. govs. Med. Center, 1969-73, vice chmn., 1969-71; chmn. alumni adv. council Grad. Sch. Bus., 1970-73; bd. dirs. U.S. Com. Energy Awareness, 1982-85, vice-chmn., 1983-84, chmn., 1985; v.p. Internat. House, 1970; trustee Com. Econ. Devel., 1972-87; mem. bd. Ochsner Med. Found., 1976-96, mem. exec. com., 1977-96; 1st chmn. Parents Council, Furman U.; mem. Parents Council, Wake Forest U., 1980-81; trustee La. Bapt. Found., 1995-2000, chmn. 1996; chmn. Kaken-Am. Found., 1999—. Served to ensign USNR, 1945-46. Recipient Silver Beaver, Silver Antelope Boy Scouts Am.; Oliver Townsend medal Atomic Indsl. Forum; Outstanding Alumni award Grad. Sch. Bus., 1970; Disting. Alumnus award Tulane U., 1983 Mem. Tulane Alumni Assn. (exec. com., treas. 1970), Order of Coif, Beta Gamma Sigma, Omicron Delta Kappa, Beta Theta Pi, Phi Delta Phi. Baptist (deacon).

LEWIS, FRANK LEROY, electrical engineering educator, researcher; b. Wurzburg, Germany, May 11, 1949; s. Frank Leroy and Ruth Evangeline (Shirley) L.; MBA in Elec. Enging. and Physics, Rice U., 1971, MEE, 1971; MS in Aero. Systems, U. West Fla., 1977; PhD in Elec. Engring., Ga. Tech., 1981. asst. prof. elec. engring. Ga. Inst. Tech., Atlanta, 1981-86, assoc. prof. 1986-90, prof., 1990; Moncrief-O'Donnell prof. electrical engring. U. Tex., Arlington, 1990—; cons. Lockheed-Ga., Marietta, 1983-87; cons./lectr. UN Umbrella Project, Warsaw, Poland, 1991. Author: Optimal Control, 1986, 2d edit. 1995; Optimal Estimation, 1986, Aircraft Simulation and Control, 1992, Applied Optimal Control and Estimation, 1992, Robot Control, 1992, Control of Robot Manipulators, 1993, Neural Network Control, 1999, High-Level Feedback Control Using Neurol Nets, 1999; editor Automatica, 1999; editl. bd. Internat. Jour. Intelligent Control and Systems, 1995—, others; contbr. over 120 articles to tech. jours. Lt. USN, 1971-77. NSF grantee, 1982, 86, 88, 90, 92, 94, 95, 98; Fulbright scholar, 1988; recipient Terman award Am. Soc. Engring. Edn., 1989, best faper award ARRI, 1992, 93, Excellence in Tchg. award Eta Kappa Nu, 1981. Fellow IEEE (Engr. of Yr. award Ft. Worth sect. 1995, other awards); mem. AAAS, NAE (com. on space sta. 1995—), Control Systems Soc. of IEEE (bd. govs. 1995, best paper award Dallas-Ft. Worth chpt. 1994), Sigma Xi (M. Ferst awards 1981, 84, Monie A. Ferst Best Paper award 1990). Current work: intelligent control, robotics, manufacturing, Subspecialty: Systems engineering, robotics, automation. Home: 704 Vail Dr Arlington TX 76012-2909

LEWIS, FRANK RUSSELL, JR. surgeon; b. Willards, Md., Feb. 23, 1941; m. Janet Christensen, 1996. AB in Physics, Princeton U., 1961; MD, U. Md., 1965; postgrad. in med. physics, U. Calif., Berkeley, 1970. Surg. dir. M/SICU San Francisco Gen. Hosp., 1973-80, dir. emergency dept., 1980-83, chief of staff, 1983-85, asst. chief of surgery, 1981-86, chief of surgery, 1986-92; prof. surgery Case Western Res. U., Cleve., 1994—; chmn. dept. surgery Henry Ford Hosp., Detroit, 1992—; exec. dir. American Board of Surgery, 2001—; mem. Cen. Surg. Soc., Western Surg. Soc., Am. Surg. Assn., Shock Soc. (pres.-coun. mem. 1978—), Am. Assn. for Surgery Trauma (pres. 1999-2002).; Fellow ACS (1st v.p. 1995-96, gov. 1988-93). Office: Henry Ford Hosp Dept Surg E 837 2799 W Grand Blvd Detroit MI 48202-2689 E-mail: flewis1@hfhs.org., frlewis@mediaone.net.*

LEWIS, FRED HARVEY, allergist, immunologist; b. N.Y.C., 1951; MD, N.Y. Med. Coll., 1976. Diplomate Am. Bd. Allergy and Immunology, Am. Bd. Internal Medicine. Intern Beth Israel Med. Ctr., N.Y.C., 1976-77, resident internal medicine, 1977-79; fellow allergy and immunology U. Mich. Med. Ctr., Ann Arbor, 1979-81; pvt. practice Olean, N.Y., 1983—; mem. staff Olean Gen. Hosp., 1983—; spl. cons. Children's Hosp., Buffalo, 1984—; clin. asst. prof. pedicatrics SUNY, 1984—. Fellow ACP, Am. Acad. Allergy, Asthma and Immunology, Am. Coll. Allergy, Asthma and Immunology. Office: 535 Main St Olean NY 14760-1513

LEWIS, FREDERICK D. science educator; b. Boston, Aug. 12, 1943; s. Richard Burnett and Emily Dunbar L.; m. Susan Rice, May 31, 1968; children: Gordon Rice, Katherine Jean. BA, Amherst Coll., 1965; PhD, U. Rochester, 1968. asst. prof. Northwestern U., Evanston, Ill., 1969-74, assoc. prof., 1974-79, prof., 1979—, assoc. dean, 1989-92. Assoc. editor: Jour. Physical Organic Chemistry, 1988-95. Recipient Tchr. Scholar award Dreyfus Found., 1973; fellow AP Sloan Found., 1975. Mem. AAAS, Am. Chem. Soc. (assoc. editor Jour. Am. Chem. Soc., 1995-99), InterAm. Photochem. Soc. (v.p. 1998-2000, pres. 2000-02). Avocations: music, travel, gardening, sailing. Office: Northwestern U 2145 Sheridan Rd Evanston IL 60208-0834

LEWIS, FREDERICK THOMAS, insurance company executive; b. Tacoma, Apr. 1, 1941; s. Arthur Thomas and June Louise (Levenhagen) L.; m. Sarah Carolyn Boyette, Apr. 18, 1971; adopted children: Johanna, Elizabeth, Sarah, Jonathan, Matthew. Student, Concordia Coll., Portland, Oreg., 1959-61, Dominican Coll., San Rafael, Calif., 1967-71. Registered health underwriter. Enroute coord. Trans World Airlines, N.Y.C., 1961-62, 64-66, customer svc. rep. Oakland, Calif., 1966-75; dist. rep. Aid Assn. for Luths., Twin Falls, Idaho, 1975-96, dist. mgr., 1984-88; pres. Luth. Care Ctr., Inc., Jerome, 2000—. Vocalist Oakland Symphony Chorus, 1972-75; soloist Magic Valley Chorale, Twin Falls, 1979-83. Cantor Immanuel Luth. Ch., Twin Falls, 1984-98; organizer Theos of Magic Valley, Filer, Idaho, 1984; dir. planned giving/major gifts Concordia U. Found., Portland, 1998—; chpt. leader So. Idaho Us Too!, 1998—. Mem.: Idaho Fraternal Congress (ins. counselor 1976, bd. dir. 1976—85, pres. 1981—82), Idaho State Assn. Life Underwriters (area v.p. 1988—89, sec. 1989—90, pres.-elect 1990—91, pres. 1991—92, state conv. exhibitor chmn. 1992—94, Bill Rankin Life Underwriter of Yr. award 1993), So. Idaho Health Underwriters (bd. dirs. 1986—88), So. Idaho Life Underwriters (pres. 1980—81, edn. chmn. 1984—86, nat. local com. mem. 1986—89), Nat. Assn.Life Underwriters (tng. coun. fellow 1984, Nat. Quality award, Nat. Sales Achievement award, Health Ins. Quality award 1978—96), Magic Valley Orchid Soc., Lions (local v.p. 1979—81, pres. 1982—83, organizer women's aux. 1983, sec. 1986—87, 1992—93, treas. 1993—94, sec.-treas. multiple dist. 39 1994—95, vice-dist. gov. 39W 1995—96, dist. gov. 39W 1996—97), Magic Valley Rose Soc. (bd. dir. 2000—01). Republican. Avocations: ceramics, numismatics, gardening, music. Home and Office: 1612 Targhee Dr Twin Falls ID 83301-3546 E-mail: flewis@cu-portland.edu.

LEWIS, GENE EVANS, retired medical equipment company executive; b. Terrell, Tex., May 17, 1928; s. John Evans and Helen Elizabeth (Patterson) L.; m. Sonya Dolishny, Jan. 21, 1950; children: Robert, Melissa. BSEE, Tex. A&M U., 1949. Sales, mktg. and engring. mgr. GE, Schenectady, Dallas, Pittsfield, Holyoke, Lynn, 1950-68, gen. mgr. various bus. Milw., 1970-77; group product mgr. Picker X-Ray, Cleve., 1968-70; pres. sci. instruments div. Am. Optical Corp., Southbridge, Mass., 1977-78, pres. internat. div., 1978-79, pres., 1979-84, Baker Instruments Corp., Allentown, Pa., 1985-88; bd. mem. Novecon Technologies, 1994-99. CEO Sterling Semicondr., Inc., 1996-2001. With Signal Corps U.S. Army, 1949. Mem. Calibogue Club, Sea Pines Country Club. Home: 25 Spartina Cres Hilton Head Island SC 29928-2925 E-mail: gelsl@aol.com.

LEWIS, GEORGE WITHROW, business executive; b. Berwyn, Ill., May 13, 1929; s. George Edward and Katherine (Withrow) L.; m. Ellen Freer Baker, Sept. 14, 1963 (div. Apr. 1987); children: George Baker, Martha Freer; m. Elizabeth Morgan Williams, Dec. 26, 1992. AB, Princeton, 1951; MBA, Harvard, 1955. With Ford Motor Co., 1955-62; cons. McKinsey & Co., N.Y.C., 1962-64; mng. dir. Rolls-Royce Motors Internat. Div., 1964-83. Vice-pres. fin. Eisenhower Exchange Fellowships, 1985-92. 1st lt., arty. AUS, 1952-53, Korea. Mem. Harvard Bus. Sch. Club of Phila. (past pres.). Episcopalian (vestryman). Home: 1004 N Adams St Wilmington DE 19801

LEWIS, GEORGIA EILEEN, counselor, school counselor; b. Peoria, Ill., Nov. 15, 1947; d. Frank George and Anna Louise Novotny; 1 child, Joshua Nathan. BA, No. Ill. U., 1970; MA in Counseling, Bradley U., 1998. Lic. clin. prof. counselor. Contact rep. Dept. Health and Human Svcs. Social Security Adminstrn., Peoria, 1980-94; domestic violence caseworker Ctr. for Prevention of Abuse, 1995-98; mental health clinician Luth. Social Svc., Galesburg, Ill., 1998-99; sch. counselor Pleasant Valley Sch. Dist. 62, Peoria, 1999—. Facilitator Pleasant Hill Sch., 2000; site facilitator Teen Dating Violence Grant, 2002; mem. sch. climate action team Pleasant Valley Sch., 2000—; spkr. in field. Vol, spkr. Ctr. for Prevention of Abuse, Peoria, 1994-98, co-facilitator Commonplace Ctr., 1997-98. Mem. ACA, Nat. Cert. Counselor, Ill. Counseling Assn., Toastmasters Internat. (competent award 1994), Phi Kappa Phi, Phi Lambda Theta, Chi Sigma Iota. Avocations: weight lifting, fitness activities. Home: PO Box 4411 Bartonville IL 61607 E-mail: NCC_LCPC@go.com.

LEWIS, GERALD JORGENSEN, judge; b. Perth Amboy, N.J., Sept. 9, 1933; s. Norman Francis and Blanche M. (Jorgensen) L.; m. Laura Susan McDonald, Dec. 15, 1973; children by previous marriage: Michael, Marc. AB magna cum laude, Tufts Coll., 1954; JD, Harvard U., 1957. Bar: D.C. 1957, N.J. 1961, Calif. 1962, U.S. Supreme Ct. 1968. Atty. Gen. Atomic, La Jolla, Calif., 1961-63; ptnr. Haskins, Lewis, Hugent & Newnham, San Diego, 1963-77; judge Mcpl. Ct., El Cajon, Calif., 1977-79, Superior Ct., San Diego, 1979-84; assoc.. justice Calif. Ct. of Appeal, 1984-87; dir. Fisher Scientific Group, Inc., 1987-98, Bolsa Chica Corp., 1991-93, Gen. Chem. Group, Inc., 1996—; of counsel Lathan & Watkins, 1987-97; dir. Invesco Mut. Funds, Denver. Adj. prof. evidence Western State U. Sch. Law, San Diego, 1977-85, exec. bd., 1977-89; dir. Invesco Mutual Funds, 2000—; faculty San Diego Inn of Ct., 1979— , Am. Inn of Ct., 1984— . Cons. editor: California Civil Jury Instructions, 1984. City atty. Del Mar, Calif., 1963-74, Coronado, Calif., 1972-77; counsel Comprehensive Planning Orgn., San Diego, 1972-73; trustee San Diego Mus. Art, 1986-89; bd. dirs. Air Pollution Control Dist., San Diego County, 1972-76. Served to lt. comdr. USNR, 1957-61. Named Trial Judge of Yr. San Diego Trial Lawyers Assn., 1984. Mem. Am. Judicature Soc., Soc. Inns of Ct. in Calif., Confrerie des Chevaliers du Tastevin, Order of St. Hubert (knight comdr.), Friendly Sons of St. Patrick (Irishman of Yr. 2000), The Irish 50 Aztec Big 50, Bohemian Club, La Jolla Country Club (dir. 1980-83), Prophets, The K Club (County Kildare), Pauma Valley Country Club. Republican. Episcopalian. Home: 6505 Caminito Blythefield La Jolla CA 92037-5806 Office: Latham & Watkins 701 B St Ste 2100 San Diego CA 92101-8197

LEWIS, GLADYS SHERMAN, nurse, educator; b. Wynnewood, Okla., Mar. 20, 1933; d. Andrew and Minnue Elva (Halsey) Sherman; m. Wilbur Curtis Lewis, Jan. 28, 1955; children: Karen, David, Leanne, Cristen. AB, Tex. Christian U., 1956; postgrad., Southwestern Bapt. Theol. Sem., 1959-60, Escuela de Idiomas, San Jose, Costa Rica, 1960-61; MA in Creative Writing, Ctrl. (Okla.) State U., 1985; PhD in English, Okla. State U., 1992. Mem. nursing staff various facilities, Okla., 1953-57; instr. nursing med. missionary Bapt. Mission and Hosp., Paraguay, 1961-70; vice chmn. edn. commn. Paraguay Bapt. Conv., 1962-65; sec. bd. trustees Bapt. Hosp., Paraguay, 1962-65, Paraguay, 1962-65; chmn. personnel com., handbook & policy book officer Bapt. Mission in Paraguay, 1967-70; trustee Southwestern Bapt. Theol. Sem., 1974-84, chmn. student affairs com., 1976-78, vice chmn. bd., 1978-80; ptnr. Las Amigas Tours, 1978-80, writer, conf. leader, campus lectr., 1959—; owner, publisher Greystone Press, LLC, 1998. Adj. prof. English Ctr. State U., Okla. (now U. Ctrl. Okla.),1990-91, faculty mem., asst. prof. English U., 1991-95, assoc. prof., 1995-2000, prof., 2000—; pub., owner Greystone Press; editor New Plains Rev., 2000--. Author: On Earth As It Is, 1983, Two Dreams and a Promise, 1984, Message, Messenger and Response, 1994, Loaves and Hyacinths, 1999; editor: The Jewish Roots of Christian Monotheism, 1999; also religious instructional texts in English and Spanish; editor Sooner Phusician's Heartbeat, 1979-82; contbr. articles to So. Bapt. and secular periodicals. Active Dem. com., Evang. Women's Caucus, 1979-80; leader Girl Scouts U.S.A., 1965-75; Okla. co-chmn. Nat. Religious Com. for Equal Rights Amendment, 1977-79; troup host Meier Internat. Study League, 1978-81. Mem. AAUW, Internat. and Am. Coll. Surgeons Women's Auxs., Okla. State, Okla. County Med Auxs., Am. Nurse Assn. Home: 2220 NE 131st St Edmond OK 73013-5728

LEWIS, GOLDY SARAH, real estate developer, corporation executive; b. West Selkirk, Man., Can., June 15, 1921; d. David and Rose (Dwor) Kimmel; m. Ralph Milton Lewis, June 12, 1941; children: Richard Alan, Robert Edward, Roger Gordon, Randall Wayne. BS, UCLA, 1943; postgrad., U. So. Calif., 1944-45. Pvt. practice acctg., L.A., 1945-57; law office mgr., 1953-55; dir., exec. v.p. Lewis Homes, Upland, Calif., 1955—, Lewis Construction Co. Inc., Upland, 1959—, Lewis Bldg. Co., Inc., Las Vegas, 1960—, Republic Sales Co., Inc., 1956—, Kimmel Enterprises, Inc., 1959—; mng. partner Lewis Homes of Calif., 1973—; mng. ptnr. Lewis Homes of Nev., 1972—, Western Properties, 1972—, Foothill Investment Co., 1971—, Republic Mgmt. Co., 1978—. Contbr. articles to mags., jours. Mem. Dean's Coun. UCLA Grad. Sch. Architecture and Urban Planning; mem. UCLA Found., Chancellor's Assocs.; endowed Ralph and Goldy Lewis Ctr. for Regional Policy at UCLA, 1989, Ralph and Goldy Lewis Hall of Planning and Devel. at U. S.C., 1989, others. Co-recipient Builder of Yr. award, Profl. Builder Mag., 1988, Housing Person of Yr. award, Nat. Housing Conf., 1990, Entrepreneur of Yr. award, Inland Empire, 1990; named Ralph and Goldy Lewis Sports Ctr. in their honor, City of Rancho Cucamonga, 1988, also several other parks and sports fields including Lewis Park in Claremont; named one of Women of Yr., Calif. 25th Senate Dist., 1989, (with husband Ralph M. Lewis) Disting. CEO, Calif. State U., San Bernadino, 1991, Mgmt. Leaders of the Yr., Univ. Calif., Riverside, 1993; recipient 1st award of distinction, Am. Builder mag., 1963, Homer Briggs Svc. to Youth award, West End YMCA, 1990, Spirit of Life award, City of Hope, 1993, Builder of Century award, Bldg. Industry Assn., Baldy View chpt., 1999. Mem. Nat. Assn. Home Builders, Bldg. Industry Assn. So. Calif. (Builder of Yr. award Baldy View chpt. 1988), Internat. Coun. Shopping Ctrs., Urban Land Inst. Office: Lewis Homes PO Box 670 Upland CA 91785-0670

LEWIS, GORDON GILMER, golf course architect; b. Shawnee, Okla., Sept. 7, 1950; s. Ted Eugene and Janet Garvin (Panner) L.; m. Karen Louise McKenzie, June 2, 1973 (div. Dec. 1981); children: Melanie Marie Lewis-Lehr, Katie McKenzie Lewis-Lehr; m. Susette Mamie London, June 11, 1988; children: London Marshall, Sarah June Victoria. B of Landscape Architecture, Kans. State U., 1974. Registered landscape architect, Ala., Kans., Fla. Golf course architect David Gill, St. Charles, Ill., 1974-75, Charles M. Graves Orgn., Atlanta, 1975-78, Gordon G. Lewis, Naples, Fla., 1978—. Prin. works include Meadowbrook Links, Rapid City, S.D. (Top 50 Pub. Courses in U.S.), The Hulman Links at Los Creek, Terre Haute, Ind. (Top 50 Pub. Courses in U.S.), Lagoon Park, Montgomery, Ala. (Top 75 Pub. Courses in U.S.), The Forest, Ft. Myers, Fla. (Top 50 Courses in Fla.), The Vines, Estero, Fla. (Golf Digest One of Top New Courses 1986), Worthington, Bonita Springs, Fla., Tsai-Hsing, Taipei, Taiwan, others. Republican. Presbyterian. Avocation: golf. Home: 5980 18th Ave NW Naples FL 34119-1216

LEWIS, GORDON RICHARD, lawyer; b. Rockford, Ill., June 12, 1949; s. H. Walter and Elizanne (Hanitz) L. BS in Environ. Sci., Mich. State U., 1971; JD, U. Mich., 1974. Assoc. atty. Warner Norcross & Judd LLP, Grand Rapids, Mich., 1974-79, ptnr., 1979—. Dir. Bay Plastics Machinery Corp., Bay City, Mich., 1997—; dir., sec. Scheer Bay Co., Bay City, 1998—. Dir. Little Manistee Watershed Conservation Coun., Irons, Mich., 1996—. Named to Best Lawyers in Am., Woodward-White, 1994—. Mem. Indian Club (dir., sec. 1986—), Kent Country Club. Avocations: fly fishing, golf, hunting. Office: Warner Norcross & Judd LLP 111 Lyon St NW Grand Rapids MI 49503-2406 E-mail: glewis@wnj.com.

LEWIS, GWENDOLYN L. sociologist, policy analyst; b. Sweetwater, Tenn., July 26, 1943; d. Robert Martin and Glenna Louise (Parker) L.; m. David Carey Montgomery, July 18, 1987. BA in Math., Reed Coll., 1965; MS in Sociology, San Jose State Coll., 1968; PhD in Sociology, Princeton U., 1975. Asst. prof. sociology U. Pitts., 1973-80; sr. rsch. assoc. Cornell U., Ithaca, N.Y., 1980; dir. premed. edn. project Associated Colls. of Midwest, Chgo., 1981-84; data svcs. officer Nat. Rsch. Coun., Washington, 1984-86; sr. policy analyst Coll. Bd., 1986-89; assoc. dir. sociology program NSF, 1989-91; sr. edn. specialist coop. state rsch. svc. USDA, 1991-95, dir. higher edn. programs, 1995-98. Cons. Am. Assn. State Colls. and Univs., Washington, 1991-92; mem. selection com. RJR Nabisco scholars Nat. Assn. State Univs. and Land-Grant Colls., Washington, 1987-89. Contbr. chpts. to Higher Education in American Society, 1987, The 1994 NEA Almanac, 1993, The 1995 NEA Almanac, 1994, The 1996 NEA Almanac, 1995, The 1997 NEA Almanac, 1996; co-author (publ.) Trends in Student Aid: 1980-89, 1989; contbr. articles to profl. jours. Pres. Reed Coll. Alumni Bd. Mgmt., Portland, Oreg., 1992-94, alumna trustee, 1994-98; mem. nat. adv. coun. Race and Ethnic Studies Inst. Tex. A&M U., College Station, 1991-92; mem. everyday sci. exhibit com. Mus. Sci. and Industry, Chgo., 1982-84; adult leader Hands On Sci. Program, 1998-99. Recipient Fulbright-Hayes Faculty Rsch. fellowship, 1976-77, grant NSF, 1986, Josiah Macy Jr. Found. Grant Renewal, 1982, N.Y. State Vocat. Edn. grant, 1980, Dissertation Rsch. grant NSF, 1973. Mem. AAAS, Am. Sociol. Assn. (chmn. status on women com. 1987-89, com. on coms. 1991-93), Assoc. Instl. Rsch., Am. Ednl. Rsch. Assn., Soc. Social Studies Sci. Home: 4512 Cortland Rd Chevy Chase MD 20815-3737

LEWIS, HAROLD ALLEN, childcare company executive; b. Bronx, Oct. 1, 1945; s. Barney and Bess S. (Feifer) L.; B.B.A., Hofstra U., 1970; M.B.A., N.Y.U., 1971; m. Helene A. Lipitz, May 25, 1968; children— Lyn C., Franci K. Asso. mgr. fin. planning and analysis Dun & Bradstreet Corp., N.Y.C., 1975-77, mgr. budgets/forecasts, 1977-78; mgr. strategic planning Reuben H. Donnelley Corp., N.Y.C., 1978-79; mgr. treasury ops. Dun & Bradstreet, N.Y.C., 1979-80; v.p. fin./planning Corinthian Broadcasting Corp., N.Y.C., 1980-85; v.p. fin. and adminstrn. Thomas Cook Travel, USA, 1985-86, sr. v.p., 1986, pres., 1986-89; chief oper. officer U.S. Travel Systems Inc., 1989-91; pres., chief exec. officer Childtime Learning Ctrs., 1991; mem. dean's exec. coun. Frank G. Zarb Sch. Bus., Hofstra U. With Army N.G., 1966-71. Mem. Hofstra U. Alumni Assn., NYU Alumni Assn. Home: 6659 Pleasant Lake Ct West Bloomfield MI 48322-4711

LEWIS, HELEN NATALIE, visual arts advisor; b. St. Louis, Oct. 2, 1946; d. Robert Alameda and Sylvia Krevin; m. Roy Lee Lewis (div.); m. Marvin Burton Meyer, Aug. 1, 1982. BA, Calif. State U., L.A., 1972, MA, 1974; cert. interior and environ. design, UCLA, 1991. Asst. curator Parsons Sch. Design, Otis Art Inst., L.A., 1974-79, asst. dir., curator, 1979-82, acting dir., 1982; dir. L.A. Louver Gallery, Venice, Calif., 1983; prin. Helen N. Lewis, Beverly Hills, 1982-88; ptnr. Lucoff/Lewis, 1988-91; prin. advisor in the visual arts Helen Alameda Lewis, 1991—. Ind. curator L.A. Mcpl. Gallery, L.A. Inst. Contemporary Art, 1977, Mt. St. Mary's Coll. Art Gallery, L.A., 1977. Jury mem. Angel City Links, L.A. City Sch. System, 1977, Bill of Rights Commemorative Com., L.A. Schs., 1977; bd. dirs. L.A. Mcpl. Art Gallery, 1988—; docent Venice Family Clinic Art Walk, 1990; founding mem. Mus. Contemporary Art, L.A. Nat. Endowment Arts Saab grantee L.A. Inst. Contemporary Arts, 1977; Fellows of Contemporary Art grantee, Otis Art Inst., 1982. Home and Office: 704 N Beverly Dr Beverly Hills CA 90210-3322 E-mail: hnlewis@pacbell.net.

LEWIS, HENRY DONALD, fundraising consultant; b. N.Y.C., Sept. 28, 1941; s. David and Ruth Lewis. BA, C.W. Post Coll., Greenvale, N.Y., 1966; MA, Adelphi U., Garden City, N.Y., 1972. Cert. fund raising exec. Prog. dir. Health Care Fin. Cons., Corona del Mar, Calif., 1977-79, Instl. Devel. Counsel, Bloomfield, N.J., 1979-81, v.p., 1981-82, sr. v.p., 1982-83; pres. Devel. Cons. Assocs., 1983—; sr. ptnr. Single Source Internat., 1985—. Cons. U.S. Merchant Marine Acad. Found., Kings Point, N.Y., 1985-98, Va. Mil. Inst., Lexington, 1980-90, N.J. Symphony Orch., Newark, 1988-90, Fla. Orch., Tampa, 1993; adj. faculty Kean U., Union, N.J., 1993-98; faculty Support Ctr. Washington, 1999—. Trustee Alumni Assn. of Bronx H.S. of Sci., 1986-91. With U.S. Army, 1961-64. Mem. Assn. Fundraising Profls. (bd. dirs. N.J. chpt. 1993-98, nat. curriculum com. 1999-2001, nat. diversity task force 2001—). Office: Devel Cons Assocs 1629 K St NW Ste 802 Washington DC 20006-1637

LEWIS, HENRY RAFALSKY, manufacturing company executive; b. Yonkers, N.Y., Nov. 19, 1925; s. Jasper R. and Freda (Rafalsky) L.; m. Barbara Connolly, June 15, 1957; children— Peter, Susan, Abigail. AB, Harvard U., 1949, MA, 1951, PhD, 1957. Group head Ops. Evaluation Group, Washington, 1955-57; staff electronic rsch. lab. RCA, Princeton, N.J., 1957-66, dir., 1966-70; v.p. R & D Itek Corp., Lexington, Mass., 1970-74; pres. Optel Corp., Princeton, N.J., 1974; sr. v.p. Dennison Mfg. Co., Waltham, Mass., 1974-85, vice-chmn., 1986-91, also bd. dirs.; CEO Celadon Scis. Inc., Boston, 1996-98. Bd. dirs. Dyax Corp., Cambridge, Celadon Sci.Boston, Pericor, Cambridge. Contbr. articles to profl. jours. Chmn. investment com. Powers (Mass.) Music Sch., 1978-90; mem. Harvard Grad. Soc. Coun., 1992-95. With U.S. Army, 1944-46. Mem. IEEE, Am. Phys. Soc., Harvard Club, Phi Beta Kappa, Sigma Xi. Clubs: Harvard. Home: 16A Louisburg Sq Boston MA 02108-1203 E-mail: hhrrlewis@aol.com.

LEWIS, HOMER DICK, retired nuclear engineer; b. Covington, Ky., Oct. 4, 1926; s. Homer Dewey and Viola Mabel Lewis; m. Marjorie Louise Hacker; children: Homer Daniel, Holly J., Laurel Marion Williams, Heather Eileen Wheat. BS Metallurgical Engring., U. Cin., 1952; MS Nuclear Engring., U. N.Mex., 1964, MS Materials Sci., 1971. Lic. N.Mex., 1957. Staff mem. Los Alamos Sci. Lab., N.Mex., 1952—57; lead engr. Boeing Airplane Co., Seattle,

1957—58; staff mem. Los Alamos Sci. Laboratory/Los Alamos Nat. Lab., 1958—86; lab. assoc./staff mem. Los Alamos Nat. Lab., 1986—94. Sect. leader - enriched uranium casting sect. Los Alamos Sci. Lab., 1953—57, prin. investigator/experimenter - measurement of high temperature phys., chem., properties of lmfbr fuels and fuel/clad interactions, 1975—79; sect. leader nonferrous and enriched uranium melting/casting tech. sect. Los Alamos Nat. Lab., 1981—86; lead engr. - manufacturing/welding rsch. Boeing Airplane Co., 1957—58. Contbr. articles to profl. jours. Instr./ assoc. dir. Los Alamos Ski Sch. at Pajarito Mtn., 1967—71. With USNR, 1944—49, capt. USAF, 1952—68. Mem.: Am. Soc. Metals (life), Los Alamos Ski Club (pres. 1962—63), NRA (life), Rocky Mountain Ski Instructors Ass./ Profl. Ski Instructors of Am., Emeritus mem., Sangre deCristo # 16 Knights Templar (comdr. 1970—71), Los Alamos York Rite, Col. Clay Lodge 159 Free and Accepted Masons (life), Phi Kappa Phi (life). Achievements include patents for powder metallurgy. Home: 3201 Wellington Pl Farmington NM 87402

LEWIS, HOWARD FRANKLIN, chiropractor; b. Havre de Grace, Md., July 27, 1944; s. Walter Lee and Ruby Jane (Moretz) L.; m. Margaret Colleen Bush, Apr. 8, 1963 (div. 1969); 1 child, Vaughn; m. Cynthia Marie Hoover, Apr. 4, 1970; children: Amy, David. D of Chiropractic, L.A. Coll. Chiropractic, 1971. Diplomate Am. Bd. Chiropractic Radiology; lic. chirpractor Calif., Md. Pvt. practice Lewis Chiropractic Ctr., Bel Air, Md., 1974-85, Fallston, 1985—. Fellow: Internat. Coll. Chiropractors; mem.: Found. Chiropractic Edn. and Rsch., Christian Chiropractors Assn., Sacro Occipital Rsch. Soc. (bd. dirs. 1992—95, cert.), Md. State Bd. Chiropractic Examiners (v.p. 1994—96, pres. 1996—99), Md. Chiropractic Assn. (chmn. bd. dirs. 1985—86, v.p. 1986, pres. 1987—89, 1999—2001, Leadership award 1989, Chiropractor of Yr. award 1990), Am. Chiropractic Coll. Radiology, Am. Chiropractic Assn. (mem. coun. on diagnostic imaging, coun. on nutrition). Republican. E-mai. Office: Lewis Chiropractic Ctr 1621 Bel Air Rd Fallston MD 21047-2745 E-mail: lewischiro@aol.com.

LEWIS, HUNTER, financial advisor, publisher; b. Dayton, Ohio, Oct. 13, 1947; s. Welbourne Walker and Emily (Spivey) L.; m. Elizabeth Sidamon-Eristoff, July 3, 1993. AB cum laude, Harvard U., 1969. Asst. to office of pres. Boston Co., 1970, v.p., 1972-73; pres. Boston Co. Fin. Strategies, Inc., 1971-72; co-founder Cambridge Assocs., Inc., Boston, 1973—. Author: The Real World War, 1982, A Question of Values, 1990; contbr. articles to N.Y. Times, Atlantic Monthly, Washington Post, others mags. and newspapers; author monographs on specialized fin. subjects. Former trustee, chmn. fin. com. Groton Sch.; former chmn. adv. bd. Dumbarton Oaks, affiliate of Harvard U.; former trustee Thomas Jefferson Found., Monticello; former mem. pension fin. com. World Bank; former dir. Worldwide Fund for Nature; former chmn. bd. dirs. Worldwatch Inst.; pres. emeritus, trustee Am. Sch. Classical Studies at Athens; bd. dirs., former treas. World Wildlife Fund; former trustee Pierpont Morgan Libr., N.Y.C.; chmn. bd. inst. Edn. Foster Children; former trustee Rockefelller Bros. Fund; chmn., dir. Nat. Environ. Trust. With USMC, 1969-70. Mem. Univ. Club (N.Y.C.), Knickerbocker Club (N.Y.C.), Met. Club (Washington). Office: 1110 N Glebe Rd Ste 1100 Arlington VA 22201-5763

LEWIS, JACK (CECIL PAUL LEWIS), publishing executive, editor; b. North English, Iowa, Nov. 13, 1924; s. Cecil Howell and Winifred (Warner) L.; m. Rueselle Gilbert, Mar. 1, 1996; children: Dana Claudia, Brandon Paul, Scott Jay, Suzanne Marie. BA, State U. Iowa, 1949. Publicist savs. bonds U.S. Treasury Dept., Des Moines, 1948-49; reporter Santa Ana (Calif.) Register, 1949-50; motion picture writer Monogram Pictures, 1950; reporter Daily Pilot, Costa Mesa, Calif., 1956-57; editor Challenge Pub., North Hollywood, 1957-60; pres. Gallant/Charger Publs. Inc, Capistrano Beach, 1960-98; editor, pub. Gun World, 1960-97. Author 12 novels, 30 other books, 11 TV shows, 8 motion pictures; editor 26 books; contbr. articles to mags. Served to lt. col. USMCR, 1942-46, 50-56, 58, 70. Decorated Bronze Star, Air medal (4), Meritorious Service medal, Navy Commendation medal. Mem. Writers Guild Am., U.S. Marine Corps Combat Corrs. Assn. (pres. 1970-71, 73-74, 80-81, chmn. bd. 1972-78), Sigma Nu, Sigma Delta Chi. Republican. Home: RR 2 Box 4783 Pahoa HI 96778-9779 E-mail: cleopatra54@earthlink.net.

LEWIS, JAMES EARL, financier; b. Chgo., Aug. 1, 1939; s. J. Earl and Elsie L. (Danneberg) L.; m. Patricia Ann Martin, Jan. 19, 1980. BA, DePauw U., 1961; MBA, U. Chgo., 1966. Analyst Harris Trust & Savs. Bank, Chgo., 1966-68; v.p. Paine, Webber, Jackson & Curtis, Boston, 1968-70; mgr. corp. loan component Gen. Electric Credit Corp., Stamford, Conn., 1971-77; v.p. Rauscher Pierce Refsnes Inc., Dallas, 1978-82; sr. v.p., mgr. corp. fin. dept. First Oklahoma Bancorp. Inc., Dallas and Oklahoma City, 1982-84; v.p., mgr. corp. fin. group PNC Mcht. Banking Co., Phila., 1984-87; v.p., dir. corp. fin. Ferris & Co., Inc., Washington, 1987-88; v.p. Washington Sq. Capital Markets Inc., Bala Cynwyd, Pa., 1988-90; pres., founder Mid. Atlantic Capital, Wayne, 1990-94; founder, pres. Phila. Factors, Inc., 1993—. Bd. dirs. Phila. Factors; founder, chmn., bd. dirs. PFI Capital Corp., 2002—. With U.S. Army, 1962—64. Mem.: Internat. Factoring Assn., Comml. Fin. Assn. (bd. dirs.), Greater Phila. Venture Group. Home: 852 Briarwood Rd Newtown Square PA 19073-2620 Office: 400 E Lancaster Ave Wayne PA 19087-4319

LEWIS, JAMES LEE, JR. actuary; b. Toungoo, Burma, June 11, 1930; s. James Lee and Lilly (Ryden) L.; m. Tamra Dell Johns, June 30, 1954; children: James Lee III, David Alexander, Stephen John, Susan Kim, Michael Ryden. BA, U. Mich., 1952, MA, 1956. Actuary Lincoln Nat. Life Ins. Co., Ft. Wayne, Ind., 1956-74; sr. v.p. Mutual Security Life Ins. Co., 1974-83; v.p., actuary Montlife Corp., Itaska, Ill., 1983-84; v.p., sr. actuary Covenant Life Ins. Co., Phila., 1984-94; actuary provident Mut. Life Ins. Co., 1994-96; ret., 1996. Pres. Associated Chs., Ft. Wayne., 1982; chmn. Project Commitment, Ft. Wayne, 1969. With U.S. Army, 1952-54. Fellow Soc. of Actuaries (com. chair 1988-91); mem. Am. Acad. of Actuaries (charter). Baptist. Avocations: racquetball, barbershop singing.

LEWIS, JAN PATRICIA, education educator; b. Seattle, Mar. 6, 1954; d. James Alfred and Jean Louise (Hamilton) L. BA in Edn., Oreg. State U., 1976; MA in Tchg., Lewis & Clark Coll., 1979; PhD in Curriculum and Instrn., U. Oreg., 1989. Cert. tchr. K-8 elem., 4-12 English, K-12 reading, Wash. Elem. tchr. Boring (Oreg.) Sch. Dist., 1976-86; grad. tchg. fellow U. Oreg., Eugene, 1986-89; asst. prof. Pacific Luth. U., Tacoma, 1989-95, assoc. prof., 1995—, dir. Ctr. for Tchg. and Learning, 1998—. Mem. adj. faculty Lewis and Clark Coll., Portland, Oreg., 1984-89; literacy cons., 1984—. Co-editor N.W. Reading Jour., 1993-2000; co-author: Building a Knowledge Base in Reading, 1997, Building a Knowledge Base in Reading: Teachers at Work, 1999. Mem. Internat. Reading Assn., Nat. Coun. Tchrs. of English, Wash. Orgn. Reading Devel. Office: Pacific Luth U Sch Edn Tacoma WA 98447-0001 E-mail: lewisjp@plu.edu.

LEWIS, JASON ALVERT, JR. communications executive; b. Clarksville, Tex., Aug. 17, 1941; s. Jason Allen and Mary (Dinwiddie) L. Student, Stockton Coll., 1959-60, San Jose Jr. Coll., 1962-63. Field engr. telephone tech. Pacific Bell, San Francisco, 1983-84; systems technician AT&T, 1984—. Patentee in field. With U.S. Army, 1964-66. Mem. Internat. Platform Assn., Cousteau Soc., Astron. Soc. Pacific, San Francisco Zool. Soc., Planetary Soc., U.S. Naval Inst. Democrat. Avocations: photography, astronomy. Home: 139 Pecks Ln South San Francisco CA 94080-1744

LEWIS, JEROME A. petroleum company executive, investment banker; b. 1927; married. BA in Engring., U. Okla. Geologist Shell Oil Co., 1950-51; pres. Lewmont Drilling Inc., 1951-65, Border Exploration Co., 1965-68; pres., chmn. bd., CEO Petro-Lewis Corp., 1968-87; pres. Princeps Ptnrs., Inc., 1987-97; dir. DenverAmerican Petrol., 1991-97. Bd. dirs. Denver Leadership Found., Trinity Forum, Downing St. Found. Mem. Ind. Petroleum Assn. Am., Oil Investment Inst. (founding gov.), World Pres.' Orgn., Am. Assn. Petroleum Geologists, Am. Petroleum Inst., Chief Execs. Orgn. Office: Downing Ptnrs Inc 50 S Steele St Ste 328 Denver CO 80209-2808

LEWIS, JERROLD See BOCK, JERRY

LEWIS, JERRY (JOSEPH LEVITCH), comedian; b. Newark, Mar. 16, 1926; s. Danny and Rae Levitch; m. Patti Palmer, 1944 (div.); children: Gary, Ron, Scott, Chris, Anthony, Joseph; m. Sandra Pitnick, 1983; 1 child, Danielle Sara. Edn., Irvington (N.J.) High Sch.; DHL (hon.), Mercy Coll., 1987. Prof. cinema U. So. Calif.; pres. JAS Prodns., Inc., P.J. Prodns., Inc. Began as entertainer with record routine at Catskill (N.Y.) hotel; formed comedy team with Dean Martin, 1946-56; performed as a single, 1956—; formed Jerry Lewis Prodns. Inc., prod., dir., writer, star, 1956; films include: My Friend Irma, 1949, My Friend Irma Goes West, 1950, At War with the Army, 1950, That's My Boy, 1950, Sailor Beware, 1951, The Stooge, 1952, Jumping Jacks, 1952, Scared Stiff, 1953, The Caddy, 1953, Money From Home, 1953, Three Ring Circus, 1954, Living it Up, 1954, You're Never Too Young, 1955, Artists and Models, 1955, Partners, 1956, Hollywood or Bust, 1956, The Delicate Delinquent, 1957, The Sad Sack, 1957, The Geisha Boy, 1958, Rockabye Baby, 1958, Don't Give Up the Ship, 1959, Li'l Abner, 1959, Visit to a Small Planet, 1960, The Bellboy, 1960, Cinderfella, 1960, The Ladies Man, 1961, It's Only Money, 1962, The Errand Boy, 1962, It's a Mad, Mad, Mad, Mad World, 1963, The Nutty Professor, 1963, Who's Minding The Store, 1963, The Patsy, 1964, The Disorderly Orderly, 1964, The Family Jewels, 1965, Boeing-Boeing, 1965, Three On A Couch, 1965, Way ... Way ... Out, 1966, The Big Mouth, 1967, Don't Raise the Bridge, Lower the Water, 1968, Hook, Line and Sinker, 1969, One More Time, 1969, Which Way To the Front?, 1970, Hardly Working, 1981, King of Comedy, 1983, Smorgasbord, 1983, Slapstick, 1984, To Catch A Cop, 1984, How Did You Get In?, 1985, Cookie, 1989, Arrowtooth Waltz, 1991, Mr. Saturday Night, 1992, Arizona Dream, 1993, Funny Bones, 1995; appeared on Broadway in Damn Yankees, 1995, on tour, 1995—; author: The Total Film-Maker, 1971, Jerry Lewis in Person, 1982; principal TV appearances include master of ceremonies ann. Labor Day Muscular Dystrophy Telethon, 1966—. Comdr. Order of Arts & Letters, France, 1984; nat. chmn. Muscular Dystrophy Assn. Recipient most promising male star in TV award Motion Picture Daily's 2nd Ann. TV poll, 1950, (as team), one of TV's 10 money making stars award Motion Picture Herald - Fame poll, 1951, 53-54, 57, best comedy team award Motion Picture Daily's 16th annual radio poll, 1951-53, Nobel Peace Prize nomination, 1978. Mem. Screen Producers Guild, Screen Dirs. Guild, Screen Writers Guild. Office: Jerry Lewis Films Inc 3160 W Sahara Ave # 16C Las Vegas NV 89102-6003 also: William Morris Agy Inc 151 S El Camino Dr Beverly Hills CA 90212-2704

LEWIS, JERRY M. psychiatrist, educator; b. Utica, N.Y., Aug. 18, 1924; s. Jerry M. and Margaret (Miller) L.; m. Patsy Ruth Price, Sept. 24, 1949; children: Jerry M., Cynthia Lewis-Reynolds, Nancy Minns, Tom. MD, Southwestern Med. Sch., Dallas, 1951. Diplomate Am. Bd. Psychiatry and Neurology. Staff psychiatrist Timberlawn Psychiat. Hosp., Dallas, 1957-63, chief women's svc., 1963-66, chief adolescent svcs., 1966-70, dir. profl. edn., 1970-79, psychiatrist-in-chief, 1979-88, dir. rsch., 1988-93. Dir. rsch. and tng. Timberlawn Psychiat. Rsch. Found., Dallas, 1967-88, sr. rsch. psychiatrist, 1988—; clin. prof. psychiatry, family practice and cmty. medicine Southwestern Med. Sch.; cons. in psychiatry Baylor U. Med. Ctr., Dallas. Author: No Single Thread, 1976, How's Your Family, 1978, To Be a Therapist, 1979, The Long Struggle, 1983, Swimming Upstream: Teaching Psychotherapy in a Biological Era, 1991, The Monkey-Rope, 1995, Marriage as a Search for Healing: Theory, Assessment & Therapy, 1997. Served with USN, 1943-45 Fellow Am. Coll. Psychiatrists (pres. 1985), Am. Psychiat. Assn., So. Psychiat. Assn. (pres. 1979); mem. Group for Advancement of Psychiatry (pres. 1987), Benjamin Rush Soc. (pres. 1994-95), AMA, Tex. Med. Assn. Office: PO Box 270789 Dallas TX 75227-0789

LEWIS, JESSICA HELEN (MRS. JACK D. MYERS), physician, educator; b. Harpswell, Maine, Oct. 26, 1917; d. Warren Harmon and Margaret (Reed) L.; m. Jack D. Myers, Aug. 31, 1946; children: Judith Duane (dec.), John Lewis, Jessica Read, Elizabeth Reed, Margaret Anne. AB, Goucher Coll., 1938; MD, Johns Hopkins U., 1942. USPHS Research fellow U. N.C., 1947-48, research assoc. dept. physiology, 1948-55; assoc. dept. medicine Duke Med. Sch., 1951-55; research assoc. dept. medicine U. Pitts., 1955-58, faculty, 1958-92, research assoc. prof., 1965-70, prof. medicine, 1970-92, prof. medicine emeritus, 1992—. Dir. research Central Blood Bank Pitts., 1969-74, v.p., 1974-85, med. dir. and sr. v.p., 1985-89, sci. dir., sr. v.p., 1985-92, sr. v.p., med. and sci. dir. emeritus, 1992—; dir. Hemophilia Center Western Pa., 1973-81 Author: Comparative Hemostasis in Vertebrates, also more than 250 sci. papers. Mem. Am. Physiol. Soc., Am. Soc. Clin. Investigation, Am. Fedn. Clin. Research, Soc. for Exptl. Biol. Medicine, Internat. Soc. Hematology, Am. Soc. Hematology, Sigma Xi. Achievements include rsch. on mechanism blood coagulation, fibrinolysis, hemorrhagic and thrombotic diseases and comparative vertebrate coagulation. Home: Dithridge House 220 N Dithridge St Apt 900 Pittsburgh PA 15213-1424 Office: Central Blood Bank Pitts 812 5th Ave Pittsburgh PA 15219-4701

LEWIS, JOHN BRUCE, lawyer; b. Poplar Bluff, Mo., Aug. 12, 1947; s. Evan Bruce and Hilda Kathryn (Kassebaum) L.; m. Diane F. Grossman, July 23, 1977; children: Samantha Brooking, Ashley Denning. BA, U. Mo., 1969, JD, 1972; LLM in Labor and Employment Law, Columbia U., 1978; diploma, Nat. Inst. Trial Advocacy, 1982. Bar: Mo. 1972, U.S. Ct. Appeals (8th cir.) 1973, U.S. Dist. Ct. (ea. dist.) Mo. 1974, U.S. Dist. Ct. (no. dist.) Ohio 1979, Ohio 1980, U.S. Ct. Appeals (6th cir.) 1982, U.S. Dist. Ct. (ea. dist.) Mich. 1983, U.S. Ct. Appeals (3d cir.) 1987, U.S. Supreme Ct. 1987, U.S. Dist. Ct. (no. dist.) Calif. 1987, U.S. Ct. Appeals (7th cir.) 1990. Assoc. Millar, Schaefer & Ebling, St. Louis, 1972-77, Squire, Sanders & Dempsey, Cleve., 1979-85; ptnr. Arter & Hadden, 1985-2001, Baker & Hostetler, Cleve., 2001—. Lectr. in field. Author: Employment Practices Self-Assessment Guide, 2d edit., 2000; contbr. articles to legal jours. Mem. Cleve. Council on World Affairs. Mem. ABA (sec. labor and employment law, com. EEO law, comm. law forum), Ohio State Bar Assn. (sec. labor and employment law), Greater Cleve. Bar Assn. (sec. labor law), St. Louis Met. Bar Assn., Am. Law Inst., Selden Soc., Ohio C. of C. (labor adv. com.), William K. Thomas Inn of Ct. (master bencher). Office: Baker & Hostetler 3200 Nat City Ctr 1900 E 9th St Cleveland OH 44114-3485 Business E-Mail: jlewis@bakerlaw.com.

LEWIS, JOHN FRANCIS, lawyer; b. Oberlin, Ohio, Oct. 25, 1932; s. Ben W. and Gertrude D. Lewis; m. Catharine Monroe, June 15, 1957; children: Ben M., Ian A., Catharine G., William H. BA, Amherst Coll., 1955; JD, U. Mich., 1958. Bar: Ohio 1958, U.S. Dist. Ct. (no dist.) Ohio 1959, U.S. Supreme Ct. 1973. Assoc. firm Squire, Sanders & Dempsey, Cleve., 1959—67; ptnr. Squire, Sanders & Dempsey LLP, 1967—, mng. ptnr. Cleve. office, 1985—2002. Co-author: Baldwin's Ohio School Law, 1980-91, Ohio Collective Bargaining Law, 1983. Trustee Ohio Found. Ind. Colls., Case Western Res. U., chmn., 1995-2001; trustee Playhouse Sq. Found., chmn., 1980-85; trustee, chmn. Ohio Aerospace Coun., 2001—; former mem. exec. com. Greater Cleve. Growth Assn.; trustee Musical Arts Assn., Univ. Circle, Inc., Ohio Foundn. Independent Coll.; hon. trustee Found. for Sch. Bus. Mgmt., Leadership Cleve., 1977-78; chmn. Cleanland Cleve., 1992-95. Recipient Malcolm Daisley Labor-Mgmt. Rels. award, 1991, Tree of Life award Jewish Nat. Fund, 1993, Nat. Conf. award, 1995, Franklin D. Roosevelt March of Dimes award, 1999. Mem. Cleve. Bar Assn., Ohio Bar Assn., ABA, Nat. Sch. Bd. Assn., Edn. Law Assn. (past pres.), Ohio Assn. Sch. Bus. Ofcls. (hon. life, Marion McGehey Edn. Law award 1998), Fifty Club of Cleve., Ohio Council Sch. Bd. Attys. (founding chair). Episcopalian. Home: 2 Bratenahl Pl Ste 7ef Bratenahl OH 44108-1183 Office: Squire Sanders & Dempsey 4900 Key Tower 127 Public Sq Ste 4900 Cleveland OH 44114-1304 E-mail: capeoceans@aol.com., Jlewis@ssd.com.

LEWIS, JOHN GIBBONEY, historian; b. Richmond, Va., June 26, 1930; s. Charles David and Louise Elizabeth (Gibboney) Lewis; m. Elizabeth Lyster Denby, Dec. 8, 1958 (div. Sept. 1986); 1 child Elisabeth Caillouet. Hist. archtl. cons., Winchester, Va., 1955—79. Contbr. Regional rep. Va. Hist. Landmarks Commn.; gov.'s appointee Chesapeake and Ohio Canal Nat. Hist. Park Citizens Adv. Commn.; chmn. citizen's com. Goose Creek Historic Dist. , 1977; chmn. Catoctin, Goose Creeks, 1974; mem. Loudoun County Hist. ., Leesburg, Va., 1955—80; mem. revolving fund Preservation of Hist. Winchester, 1980—; mem. Frederick County Hist. Soc., Winchester, 1980—, Music Theatre, Shennandoah U., Winchester, 1980—. With U.S. Army, 1952—54. Decorated Korean Svc. Medal with 3 bronze campaign stars, UN Svc. medal, Nat. Def. medal, Combat Infantry Badge; recipient award, U.S. Soil Conservation Svc., 1975, Resolution of Ho. of Dels. Com. on Conservation and Natural Resources, Commonwealth of Va., 1979, award, Winchester-Frederick County Hist. Soc., 1982, Ben Belchic award, Preservation of Hist. Winchester, Inc., 1986, The Elsie M. Rosenberger award, Preservation of Hist. Winchester and Winchester Frederick County C. of C., 1992, award, Thomas Balch Libr. Adv. Commn., 1995. Mem.: Va. Canals and Navigation Soc., Soc. Archtl. Historians, Assn. for Preservation Tech. Home: PO Box 85 Winchester VA 22604-0085

LEWIS, JOHN HARDY, JR. lawyer; b. East Orange, N.J., Oct. 31, 1936; s. John Hardy and Sarah (Ripley) L.; m. Mary Ann Spurgeon, June 25, 1960; children: Peter, David, Mark. AB magna cum laude, Princeton U., 1958; JD cum laude, Harvard U., 1961. Bar: Pa. 1962. Assoc. Morgan, Lewis & Bockius, Phila., 1965-69, ptnr., 1969-99, Montgomery McCracken Walker & Rhoads, LLP, Phila., 1999—. Trustee Blair Acad., Blairstown, N.J. Served to maj. USAF, 1962-65. Fellow Am. Coll. Trial Lawyers. Home: 1000 Green Valley Rd Bryn Mawr PA 19010-1912 Office: Montgomery McCracken Et Al 123 S Broad St Philadelphia PA 19109-1029

LEWIS, JOHN MILTON, cable television company executive; b. Slocomb, Ala., Mar. 29, 1931; s. Phil Truman and Vermell Beatrice (Avery) L.; m. Mary Lee Robledo, June 9, 1951; children: Janet Lee, Lee Michael. Grad. high sch., Slocomb, Ala. With Gulf Power Co., Panama City, Fla., 1949-56; self-employed Vehicle Svc. Co., 1956-58; dir. Burnup & Sims of Fla., Inc., W. Palm Beach, 1958-70; pres., bd. dirs. Wometco Cable Corp., Miami, Fla., 1970-94; pres., CEO SP1 Holding, Inc., Richardson, Tex., 1988-89; bd. dirs., CEO Spectradyne, Inc., 1988-89; pres. Key Capital Group, Inc., Miami, 1995—, St. Joe Comms., Inc., Port St. Joe, Fla., 1996—. Bd. dirs. Allied Waste Mgmt., Phoenix; pres. St. Joe Telephone Co., Inc., Port St. Joe, Fla.; cons. in field. Recipient Tower Club award So. TV Assn. Mem. Cable TV Pioneers, Masons. Republican. Office: Key Capital Group Inc PO Box 561009 9500 S Dadeland Blvd Ste 603 Miami FL 33156-2848

LEWIS, JOHN PRIOR, economist, educator; b. Albany, N.Y., Mar. 18, 1921; s. Leon Ray and Grace (Prior) L.; m. June Estelle Ryan, July 12, 1946; children— Betsy Prior, Sally Eastman, Amanda Barnum. Student, St. Andrews U., Scotland, 1939-40; AB, Union Coll., Schenectady, 1941; M.Pub. Adminstrn., Harvard, 1943, PhD in Polit. Economy and Govt, 1950; D.C.L., Union Coll., 1970. Instr., asst. prof. econs. and govt. Union Coll., Schenectady, 1946-50; mem. staff, asst. to chmn. Council Econ. Advisers, Exec. Office of Pres., Washington, 1950-53; cons. UN Korean Reconstrn. Agy., Pusan, Korea, 1953; assoc. prof. Ind. U., 1953-56, prof. bus. econs. and pub. policy, 1956-64, disting. service prof. bus. econs. and pub. policy, 1964, chmn. dept., 1961-63; mem. Council Econ. Advisers, Exec. Office of Pres., Washington, 1963-64; minister-dir. USAID mission to India, 1964-69; dean Woodrow Wilson Sch. Pub. Affairs, 1969-74; prof. econs. and internat. affairs Princeton (N.J.) U., 1969-91, prof. emeritus, 1991—; on leave as chmn. devel. assistance com. OECD, Paris, 1979-81, as DAC chmn. ann. OECD vols. on devel. cooperation, 1979-81; sr. advisor Overseas Devel. Coun., 1981—99. Sr. staff mem. in India Brookings Instn., Washington, 1959-60; mem. UN Com. on Devel. Planning, 1970-83, rapporteur, 1972-78 Author: Business Conditions Analysis, 1959, 2d edit., (with R.C. Turner), 1967, Quiet Crisis in India: Economic Development and American Policy, 1962, (with Ishan Kapur) The World Bank, Multilateral Aid, and the 1970's, 1973, (with V. Kallab) U.S. Foreign Policy and the Third World, 1983, Development Strategies Reconsidered, 1986, Strengthening the Poor, 1988, India's Political Economy, 1995, (with Devesh Kapur and Richard Webb) The World Bank: Its First Half Century, 1997. Served to lt. USNR, 1943-46, PTO. Home: 12 Valencia Ct Skillman NJ 08558-2354 Office: Princeton U Woodrow Wilson Sch Princeton NJ 08544-0001

LEWIS, JOHN R. congressman; b. Troy, Ala., Feb. 21, 1940; m. Lillian Miles, 1968; 1 child, John-Miles. BA, Am. Bapt. Theol. Sem., Nashville, 1961, Fisk U., 1963. Mem. City Coun., Atlanta, 1983—86, 100th-106th Congresses from 5th Ga. dist., Washington, 1987—, former chief dep. majority whip, mem. ways and means com.; community affairs dir. Nat. Consumer Coop. Bank, 1980—82. Civil rights leader; mem. Martin Luther King Ctr. for Social Change, African Am. Inst., Robert F. Kennedy Meml. Office: US Ho of Reps 343 Cannon 40 B Washington DC 20515-1005*

LEWIS, JOHN WILSON, political science educator; b. King County, Wash., Nov. 16, 1930; s. Albert Lloyd and Clara (Lewis) Seeman; m. Jacquelyn Clark, June 19, 1954; children: Cynthia, Stephen, Amy. Student, Deep Springs Coll., 1947-49; AB with highest honors, UCLA, 1953, MA, 1958, PhD, 1962; hon. degree, Morningside Coll., 1969, Lawrence U., 1986, Russian Acad. Sci., 1996. Asst. prof. govt. Cornell U., 1961-64, assoc. prof., 1964-68, Asst. prof. govt., 1961-64; prof. polit. sci. Stanford U., 1968-97, William Haas prof. Chinese politics, 1972-97, William Haas prof. emeritus, 1997—, co-dir. arms control and disarmament program, 1971-83, co-dir. NE Asia U.S. Forum on Internat. Policy, 1980-90, co-dir. Ctr. for Internat. Security and Arms Control, 1983-91, sr. fellow, 1991—; dir. Project on Peace and Cooperation in the Asian-Pacific Region, 1990—; chmn. Internat. Strategic Inst., 1983-89; chmn. joint com. on contemporary China Social Sci. Rsch. Coun.-Am. Coun. Learned Socs., 1976-79; mng. dir. Generation Ventures, 1994-99. Former vice chmn., bd. dirs. Nat. Com. on U.S.-China Rels.; cons. Senate Select Com. on Intelligence, 1977-81, Los Alamos Nat. Lab., 1987-92, Lawrence Livermore Nat. Lab., 1992-2002, Dept. of Def., 1994-96; mem. Def. Policy Bd., 1994-96; chmn. com. advanced study in China Com. Scholarly Comm. with People's Republic of China, 1979-82; mem. com. on internat. security and arms control Nat. acad. Scis., 1980-83; organizer first univ. discussion arms control and internat. security matters Chinese People's Inst. Fgn. Affairs, 1978, first academic exch. agreement Dem. People's Repb. of Korea, 1988; negotiator first univ. tng. and exch. agreement People's Rep. of China, 1978. Author: Leadership in Communist China, 1963, Major Doctrines of Communist China, 1964, Policy Networks and the Chinese Policy Process, 1986; co-author: The United States in Vietnam, 1967, Modernization by Design, 1969, China Builds the Bomb, 1988, Uncertain Partners: Stalin, Mao, and the Korean War, 1993, China's Strategic Seapower: The Politics of Force Modernization in the Nuclear Era, 1994; editor: The City in Communist China, 1971, Party Leadership and Revolutionary Power in China, 1970, Peasant Rebellion and Communist Revolution in Asia, 1974; contbr.: Congress and Arms Control, 1978, China's Quest for Independence, 1979, others; mem. editl. bd. Chinese Law and Govt.; mem. adv. bd. China Quarterly. Served with USN, 1954-57. Recipient Helios award, 2001. Home: 541 San Juan St Stanford CA 94305-8432 Office: Stanford U Encina Hall Stanford CA 94305-6105

LEWIS, JON RODERICK, political advisor; b. London, May 25, 1957; s. James Histed and Betty Prater L. Diploma, Internat. Sch. Geneva, 1975; AB in Internat. Rels., Polit. Sci., Am. U., 1979; postgrad., Brown U., 1979-86. Tchg. asst. Brown U., Providence, 1979-80; internat. editor Brown Jour. Internat. Assn., 1979-81; mem. adminstrn. staff Brown U., 1982-86; advisor on Brit.-Am. policy matters Washington, 1986—; pvt. sec. to Hon. James Histed Lewis, 1986-99. Election judge Montgomery County, Md., 1996-98. Democrat. Home: 8800 Clifford Ave Chevy Chase MD 20815-4745

LEWIS, JONATHAN JAMES, social worker, psychotherapist; b. Tulsa, Okla., Nov. 29, 1974; s. Jonathan Alan and Kendra Nelle (Kulow) Lewis; m. Tegan Shanti Bonga, May 16, 1998. BA, Wheaton Coll., 1997; MSW, Grand Valley State U., 2001. LCSW Mich. Assessor Kent County Cmty. Mental Health, Grand Rapids, Mich.; pvt. practice; case mgr. Touchstone Innware; psychiatric reports asst. Riverdell Ctr. for Behavioral Health, St. Johns. Cmty. crisis response team counselor. Mem.: NASW. Avocations: photography, poetry, non-fiction. Office: 15 Diamond St NE Grand Rapids MI 49504 E-mail: jjmsw@excite.com.

LEWIS, JONATHAN JOSEPH, surgical oncologist, molecular biologist, educator; b. Johannesburg, South Africa, May 23, 1958; s. Myer Philip and Maisie (Bagg) L.; m. Nanci Lynn Vicedomini, May 20, 1990. MB BCH, Witwatersrand U., Johannesburg, 1982; PhD, Yale U., 1990. Registrar in surgery Witwatersrand U. Sch. Medicine, 1982-87; postdoctoral assoc. Yale U. Sch. Medicine, New Haven, 1987-90, chief resident, surgery, 1990-92; fellow dept. surgery Meml. Sloan-Kettering Cancer Ctr., N.Y.C., 1992-94, attending surgeon, 1994—, asst. mem., 1994-99, assoc. mem., 1999—; chief med. officer Antigenics Inc., 2000—. Asst. prof. surgery Cornell Univ. Med. Coll., 1994-99, assoc. prof., 1999—; chief med. officer Antigenics Inc., N.Y.C., 2000—. Contbr. articles to profl. jours. Recipient Abelheim medal Med. Coun., 1982, Trubshaw medal Coll. of Surgeons, Johannesburg, 1984; Winston fellow Sloan-Kettering Inst., 1994-95. Fellow ACS, Royal Coll. Surgeons; mem. Am. Soc. Cell Biology, Am. Assn. Cancer Rsch., Am. Soc.

Clin. Oncology (Young Investigator award 1994), Assn. Acad. Surgeons, Soc. Surg. Oncology, N.Y. Acad. Scis. Jewish. Achievements include research in oncogenes, growth factors, signal transduction, immunotherapy, gene therapy. Office: Antigenics 630 5th Ave New York NY 10111 E-mail: jlewis@antigenics.com.

LEWIS, JORDAN DAVID, management consultant, author, international speaker, educator; b. Chgo., Aug. 9, 1937; s. Murray Robert and Ruth (Weinstein) L.; m. Lynn Lopata, Sept. 20, 1964; children: Matthew Michael, Katherine Anne. BSEngring. in Physics., BS Engring. in Math, U. Mich., 1960, MS Engring. in Instrumentation (fellow), MS Engring. in Nuclear Engring., U. Mich., 1963, PhD in Thermonuclear Physics, 1966. Instr. physics U. Mich. at Dearborn, 1962-64, research asst., 1964-66; with Battelle Devel. Corp., Columbus, Ohio, 1966-72, asst. mgr. devel. dept., 1968-70, mgr. gen. operations, 1970-72; dir. applied tech. programs Batelle Columbus Labs., Columbus, 1972; dir. presdl. tech. and econ. policy program Nat. Bur. Standards, Washington, 1973-77; exec. dir. A.T. Internat., 1977-79; mgmt. cons., 1979—; sr. lectr. Wharton Sch., U. Pa.; U.S. del. to OECD, Paris. Advisor strategic alliance to internat. corps.; fellow World Econ. Forum, Geneva, 1993, 94, 96, 98; chmn. Fed. Task Force on Energy Intensive Products, 1975, guest lectr. Wharton Kellowg, Columbia, Dartmouth Bus. Coll. Author: Partnerships for Profit: Structuring and Managing Strategic Alliances, 1990, The Connected Corporation: How Leading Firms Win Through Customer-Supplier Alliances, 1995, Trusted Partners: How Companies Build Mutual Trust and Win Together, 2000; editor: (with Lynn L. Lewis) Industrial Approaches to Urban Problems, 1972; guest columnist Wall St. Jour., N.Y. Times; contbr. articles to newspapers and profl. jours. Co-chmn. Columbus Outdoor Summer Concerts, 1968-70; chmn. bd. dirs. Columbus Inner-City Econ. Devel. Corp., 1969-71; pro-bono adv. Am. Cancer Soc., Internat. Ctr. Missing and Exhibited Children, bd. dirs. AEC fellow, 1964-66 Fellow AAAS (mem. council; chmn. indsl. sci. sect. 1975); mem. Am. Econs. Assn., Sigma Xi. Home: 3707 33rd Pl NW Washington DC 20008-3201

LEWIS, JOSEPH BRADY (JAY LEWIS), lawyer; b. Shreveport, La., Nov. 27, 1946; s. Joseph Peter and Gwendolyn (Pate) L. Student, U. So. Miss., 1964-67; BS summa cum laude, Troy State U., 1982; JD magna cum laude, Jones Sch. Law, Montgomery, Ala., 1991. Bar: Ala. 1992. News reporter Sta. WDAM-TV, Hattiesburg, Miss., 1968-69, Sta. KTVT-TV, Ft. Worth, 1969-70, Sta. WFAA-TV, Dallas, 1970-72; news anchor Sta. KTOK/Okla. News Network, Oklahoma City, 1972-74; editl. dir. Sta. WSFA-TV, Montgomery, Ala., 1974-77; pres. Ala. Info. Network, 1977-80, Amendment One, Inc., Montgomery, 1980-82; owner Lewis Comm., 1977-92; comm. dir. Augat Inc., 1983-92; ptnr. Prestwood, Lewis & Dickey, Montgomery, 1992—. Cons. Gen. TV Network, Montgomery, 1980-83; v.p., dir. Am. Community TV Assn., Montgomery, 1980-82. Contbr. articles to jours. and newspapers. Pres. Community Counseling and Guidance Ctr., Oklahoma City, 1973; trustee Ft. Toulouse Found., Montgomery. Named Communicator of Yr., Ala. Wildlife Fedn., 1977. Mem. ABA, Ala. Bar Assn., Ala. Criminal Def. Lawyers Assn., Ala. Trial Lawyers Assn., Montgomery County Trial Lawyers Assn., Montgomery County Bar Assn., Soc. Profl. Journalists (pres. chpt. 1974, 75, 78, Nat. Disting. Svc. award 1974, 78), Mensa, Citizens Against Fgn. Control of Am. (pres.), Alpha Epsilon Rho, Sigma Delta Kappa. Roman Catholic. Avocations: flying, sailing, tennis, golf, scuba diving. Office: 350 Adams Ave Montgomery AL 36104-2573

LEWIS, JOSEPHINE VICTORIA, retired marketing executive; b. Chgo., Dec. 3, 1936; d. Wincenty and Helena (Francyszczak) Gurbacki; m. Laurence Warren Lewis, Jan. 8, 1955; children: Laurence Michael, Michaleen Kay, Gregory Michael. AS in Mktg., Triton Coll., 1979; BA in Psychology, Benedictine U., 2001. Sec. Marsh & McLennan, Chgo., 1953-57; with factory prodn. Motorola, Franklin Park, Ill., 1969-70; with inventory control Reflector Hardware, Melrose Park, 1970-71; distbn./inventory supr. Jewel Imports (Osco Drug, Inc.), Oakbrook, 1971-83; Midwest regional mgr. Port of Seattle, 1983-96. Leader Dupage County coun. Girl Scouts U.S.A., 1968-71; den mother Thatcher county Boy Scouts Am., 1974-75; fundraiser United Way, Northlake, Ill., 1972-74; active Christian Family Movement, Marriage Encounter; vol. and mentor on transitional housing Cath. Charities, 1996—; vol. St. Margaret Mary Roman Cath. Ch., Naperville, 1992—, Morton Arboretum, 1999—. Mem. Women in Internat. Trade, Internat. Trade Assn. Greater Chgo., Customs Brokers and Fgn. Freight Forwarders Assn., Ocean Freight Agts. (sec. 1993, treas. 1994, v.p. 1995, pres. 1996, chmn. bd. 1997), Piggyback Assn. Chgo., Midwest Fgn. Commerce Club (bd. govs. 1996-97), Chgo. Transp. Club. Avocations: gardening, golf, stained glass, tap dancing.

LEWIS, JULIETTE, actress; b. San Fernando Valley, Calif., June 21, 1975; d. Geoffrey L. and Glenis Batley. TV appearances include Homefires (Showtime miniseries), I Married Dora, 1988, A Family For Joe, 1990; TV Movies include Too Young To Die, 1989; films include My Stepmother is an Alien, 1988, Meet the Hollowheads, 1989, National Lampoons Christmas Vacation, 1989, Cape Fear, 1991 (Academy Award nomination best supporting actress 1991), Crooked Hearts, 1991, Husbands and Wives, 1992, Kalifornia, 1993, That Night, 1993, What's Eating Gilbert Grape, 1993, Romeo is Bleeding, 1994, Natural Born Killers, 1994, Mixed Nuts, 1994, Strange Days, 1995, The Basketball Diaries, 1995, From Dusk Till Dawn, 1996, The Evening Star, 1996, Full Tilt Boogie, 1997, Somegirl, 1998, The 4th Floor, 1999, The Other Sister, 1999. Office: William Morris Agy care Norman Brokaw 151 S El Camino Dr Beverly Hills CA 90212-2775

LEWIS, KAREN MARIE, writer, editor; b. Syracuse, N.Y., Oct. 29, 1965; d. Stephan Joseph and Mary Josephine (Scully) L. Student, Simon's Rock of Bard Coll., 1982-83; BA in Linguistics cum laude, Barnard Coll., 1986; MA in Psychology, Brandeis U., 1989. Prodn. asst. Claremont Rsch. and Pub., N.Y.C., 1984-86; tchg. asst. Barnard Coll., 1984-86, Brandeis U., Waltham, Mass., 1988; freelance writer Great Barrington, 1989—; editl. asst. o.blek, 1992-93; ESL algebra tutor Lenox (Mass.) Meml. High, 1995; editor Construct, Inc., Great Barrington, 1994-97, tutor adult edn., 1996-98; intern The Artful Mind, 1997, office mgr., contbg. writer, editor, 1998; calendar prodr., 1999—2002; resident advisor Construct Inc., 1999—. Resident advisor Construct, Inc., 1999—. Contbr. articles to anthologies, newspapers and poetry jours. Roman Catholic. Home: 309 Main St Apt D Great Barrington MA 01230-1616

LEWIS, KENNETH D. bank executive; b. Meridian, Miss., Apr. 9, 1947; BA, Ga. State U., 1969. Pres. NCNB Nat. Bank Fla., 1986-88, NCNB Tex., Dallas, 1988-90, Gen. Bank NationsBank, Atlanta, 1991-93, NationsBank Corp., Charlotte, N.C., 1993-99; pres., COO Bank of Am. Corp., NC, 1999—2001, chmn., pres., CEO, 2001—. Bd. dirs. Health Mgmt. Assocs., Naples, Fla., Lowe's Companies Inc. Past chmn. bd. United Way of Cen. Carolinas Inc., Charlotte; dir. Homeownership Edn. and Counseling Inst.; chmn. bd. of trustees Nat. Urban League; chmn. Arts and Sci. Coun. campaign dr., Charlotte, 1998; bd. dirs. Presbyn. Hosp. Found., Charlotte. Office: Bank of Am Corp Ctr 100 N Tryon St Fl 58 Charlotte NC 28255-0001*

LEWIS, KIM, microbiologist; b. N.Y.C., Feb. 3, 1953; s. Tom John Lewis and Fainna Solasko; m. Tanya Genina, May 20, 1976; children: Alexandra, Maria. BS, Moscow U., 1976, PhD, 1980, D of Biology, 1984. Rschr. Moscow U., 1976-79, sr. rschr., 1979-84; rsch. assoc. U. Wis., Madison, 1987-88; asst. prof. MIT, Cambridge, Mass., 1988-94; assoc. prof. U. Md., Balt., 1994-97, Tufts U., Medford, Mass., 1997-2001; prof. biology Northeastern U., Boston, 2001—. Contbr. numerous papers to profl. jours. Rsch. grantee NSF, 1992, 94, 2001, ACS, 1992, NIH, 1996, 99, 2000, 2001, Dept. Energy, 1997. Mem.: Am. Chem. Soc., Soc. Indsl. Microbiology, Am. Soc. Microbiology. Avocations: reading, art, music. Office: Northeastern Univ Mugar 405 360 Huntington Ave Boston MA 02115 E-mail: k.lewis@neu.edu.

LEWIS, LINDA KATHRYN, librarian; b. Amarillo, Tex., Feb. 21, 1947; BA, U. Okla., 1968, MLS, 1969. Reference libr. U. N.Mex., Albuquerque, 1969-88, dir. collection devel., 1988—. Mem. exec. bd. Friends of U. N.Mex. Librs., Albuquerque, 1989—. Contbr. chpts. to books, articles to profl. jours. Mem. ALA, N.M. Libr. Assn., N.Am. Serials Interest Group. Office: U N Mex Gen Library Albuquerque NM 87131-0001

LEWIS, LLOYD ALEXANDER, priest, educator; b. Washington, Nov. 12, 1947; s. Lloyd Alexander and Alice Christine (Bell) L. AB, Trinity Coll., Hartford, Conn., 1969; MDiv, Va. Theol. Sem., 1972, DD, 1992; MA, Yale U., 1975, MPhil, 1981, PhD, 1985. Ordained deacon, Episcopal Ch., 1972, priest, 1972. Curate St. George's Parish, Bklyn., 1972-74; asst. minister St. Monica's Ch., Hartford, Conn., 1974-78, St. George's Parish, Washington, 1978-91; asst. prof. of NT Va. Theol. Sem., Alexandria, 1978-86, assoc. prof. of NT, 1986-91; dean Mercer Sch. of Theology, Garden City, N.Y., 1991—; hon. canon Cathedral of the Incarnation, 1991—. Adj. faculty Gen. Theol. Sem., 1995—. Trustee Va. Theol. Sem., 1995—. Recipient fellowship Rockefeller Doctoral Fund, 1974-76. Mem Soc. Biblical Lit., Soc. for Study of Black Religions. Democrat. Office: PO Box 16705 Alexandria VA 22302-0705

LEWIS, LOREN H. retired minister; b. Park County, Ind., Aug. 23, 1917; s. Fred I. and Bonnie Lewis; m. Peggy L. Lewis, Feb. 19, 1995; m. Moletia M. Belangee, May 30, 1941 (dec. June 6, 1993). BA, Earlham Coll., Richmond, Ill., 1955; MA, Garrett Coll., Evanston, Ill., 1959; student, Ecumenical Inst., Chgo., 1969—72; writing courses, U. Wis. Asst. foreman GM, Anderson, Ind., 1935—51; clergy United Meth.-North Ind. Conf., 1951—55, United Meth. Wis. Conf., 1955—86; mem. Com. on Social Concerns, 1965—70; tchr. theology and Bible courses Woodlawn UMC, Fla., 1987—2001; clergy rep. AAA, Rhinelander, Wis., 1966—68. Active chaplaincy program, Green Bay, Wis., 1980—84, Madison, Wis., 1974; active Radio Ministry, Rhinelander, 1965—70, Ripon, Wis., 1972. Contbr. Staff sgt. signal corps, 1942—45. Mem.: Kiwanis. Address: 545 Wildflower Ct Anderson IN 46013

LEWIS, LORRAINE, general counsel; b. Springfield, Mass., Feb. 25, 1956; d. Richard N. and Janet Claire (Howard) Pratte; m. Jacob M. Lewis, Sept. 28, 1985; 2 children. BA in History magna cum laude, Yale Coll., 1978; JD, Harvard Law Sch., 1981. Bar: D.C., Ill., 1982. Field atty. NLRB, Chgo., 1982-84; assoc. Feder & Edes, Washington, 1984-85; vol. atty. Washington Lawyer's Com. for Civil Rights, 1986; staff asst. Sen. John Glenn, 1986; asst. counsel then counsel and gen. counsel sen. com. on govtl. affairs, 1987-93; gen. counsel Office of Personnel Mgmt., 1993—. Office: Office of Personnel Mgmt 1900 E St NW Rm 7353 Washington DC 20415-0002*

LEWIS, LYNN C. English educator, writer; b. Nashville; d. Edward Clayton Jr. and Audrey Eubanks Lewis. MA in English, Tenn. State U., 1979; MBA, Columbia U., 1983; PhD in English, U. Mo., Columbia, 1999. Advt. salesperson Newspaper Printing Corp., Nashville, 1974-75; supr., staff specialist South Ctrl. Bell Tel. Co., Memphis and Birmingham, Ala., 1976-81; mktg./brand asst. Procter & Gamble Co., Cin., 1983-85; divsn. mgr., dir. job tng. Tenn. Valley Ctr., Memphis, 1985-88; instr. English U. Memphis, 1988-93; grad. rsch. asst. Ctr. for Studies in Oral Tradition U. Mo., Columbia, 1993-96; asst. prof. English Tenn. State U., Nashville, 1996—2002, assoc. prof. English, 2002—. Editor, manuscript proofreader U. Mo. Press, Columbia, 1995—; editl. asst. Ctr. for Studies in Oral Tradition, Columbia, 1994-96; advisor, mentor Lit. Guild of Tenn. State U., 1997—. Contbg. author: (preface) Not All Okies are White, 2000, (chpt.) Teaching Oral Traditions, 1998; contbr. poetry to jour. Mem. adv. bd. Beale St. Repertory Theater, Memphis, 1989-92. Recipient Leadership award Johnson & Johnson Cos., N.Y.C. and Milltown, N.J., 1981-83, Creative Writing award Memphis Arts Coun., 1988-90. Mem.: Coll. Lang Assn., Nat. Coun. Tchrs. English, Am. Soc. Authors, Composers and Pubs., Black Expressive Culture Studies Assn. (assoc.). Office: 3500 John A Merritt Blvd Nashville TN 37209-1500 E-mail: llewis@tnstate.edu.

LEWIS, MARIANNE H. psychiatric nurse practitioner; b. Frankfurt, Germany, Feb. 8, 1921; d. Emil B. and Jessie (Falk) Horkheimer; m. Harold S. Lewis, July 10, 1943; children: Harold S., Jr., Dale G. AAS in Nursing, Pace U., White Plains, N.Y., 1970; BS, 1976; MSN in Adult Psychiatric Nursing, Yale U., 1980. Registered profl. nurse, Conn., advance nurse practitioner, Fla., cert. ANA specialist in psychiatric-mental health nursing, 1983. Sr. staff nurse Psychiatry N.Y.U. Med. Ctr., 1971-73; dir. White Plains (N.Y.) Med. Ctr. Day Hosp., 1973-78; asst. clin. prof. Yale U. Sch. Nursing, 1981-91; clin. specialist Dept. Psychiatry VA Med. Ctr., West Haven, Conn., 1980-83; nurse counseling group Northwalk, 1983-88; clin. specialist Grand View Psychiatric Resource Ctr. Waterbury (Conn.) Hosp., 1988-90; psychiatric review specialist Aetna Life and Casualty Ins. Co., Middletown, Conn., 1991-92; advanced registered nurse practitioner Vis. Nurse Asn. of Southwest Fla., 1995-96. Apptd. ombudsman for long term care patients Gov., State of Fla., 1999-2001. Spkr. Pace U. Dedication of Lienhard Sch. Nursing Bldg., Pleasantville, N.Y., 1974; mem. recorder consort Ft. Myers, Fla., Sarasota Recorder chpt. Mem. ANA Coun. Clin. Specialists, Fla. Nurses Assn. Avocation: early music. Home: Kimball Farms Apt267 235 Walker St Lenox MA 01240

LEWIS, MARILEA WHATLEY, judge; b. Waco, Tex., Aug. 2, 1953; d. Thomas Howard and Della Frank (Shannon) Whatley; m. Danny Glen Lewis, Mar. 5, 1983; children: Thomas Hunter, Sheridan Frances. BA, Baylor U., 1975, JD, 1978. Bar: Tex. 1978; cert. Tex. State Bar Bd. of Legal Specialization. Assoc. Blassingame & Osburn, Dallas, 1978-80; asst. Atty. Gen. Tex., 1980; ptnr. Bradley & Schellhammer, 1980-83, Bradley & Lewis, Dallas, 1983-86; master, referee, magistrate 305th Dist. Ct., 1986-92; assoc. judge 330th Dist. Ct., 1992—. Bd. dirs., mem. Women's Guild United Cerebral Palsey, Dallas; mem. Jr. League, Dallas, 1990—; active La Fiesta de la Seis Banderas. Rsch. fellow Southwestern Legal Found. Fellow Tex. Bar Found.; mem. DAR, Tex. Acad. Family Law Specialists, Coll. of State Bar, State Bar Tex., Dallas Bar Assn. Republican. Episcopalian. Office: 330th Dist Court 600 Commerce St Dallas TX 75202-4616

LEWIS, MARION ELIZABETH, social worker; b. Los Alamos, Calif., Dec. 7, 1920; d. James Henry and Carolina Sophia (Niemann) Eddy; m. William Ernest Lewis, May 30, 1943 (dec. Oct. 1954); children: Doris Lenita, Paul William. Student, Jr. Coll., Santa Maria, Calif., 1939-40, Bus. Coll., Santa Barbara, Calif., 1940-41, Alan Hancock Coll., 1958-61; BA in Sociology cum laude, Westminster Coll., Salt Lake City, 1964. Office clk. Met. Life Ins. Co., Santa Barbara, 1942-43; sales clk. Sprouse Reitz Co., Laguna Beach, Calif., 1943-44; office clk. U.S. Army, Santa Maria AFB, 1944-45; sch. crossing guard Calif. Hwy. Patrol, Los Alamos, 1956-58; office clk. Holaday Children's Ctr., Salt Lake City, 1964; social worker Sonoma County Social Svc., Santa Rosa, Calif., 1964-78, ret., 1978. Sales rep. Avon Products, Los Alamos, 1957-61; sales clk. Gen. Store, Los Alamos, 1957-59; office clk. Sonoma County Pub. Health Dept., 1979-80. Deacon Presbyn. Ch., 1956—, moderator Presbyn. Women, First Presbyn. Ch., Santa Rosa, Calif., 1990-91, vice moderator, 1989-90, sem. rep., 1978-80, 92-94. Mem. AAUW, R.I. Geneal. Soc., Sonoma County Geneal. Soc., Calif. Automobile Assn., Sonoma County Assn. Ret. Employees, Sequoia Club, Westminster Coll. Alumni Assn., Alpha Chi. Democrat. Avocations: hiking, travel, gardening, crafts, genealogical research. Home: 61 Sequoia Cir Santa Rosa CA 95401-4992

LEWIS, MARK EARLDON, city manager; b. Boston, June 27, 1951; s Frederick Cole Lewis and Barbara (Forsyth) Corrigan; children: Anna Kristine, Benjamin Mark. BA, Washington State U., 1975; BS, We. State U., 1993, JD, 1995. Bar: Calif. 1996. Adminstrv. asst. City and Borough of Juneau, Alaska, 1975-77; city mgr. City of Valdez, 1978-82; commr. State of Alaska Dept. of Community and Regional Affairs, Juneau, 1982-83; dep. city mgr. City of South San Francisco, Calif., 1984-87, city mgr., 1987-88, City of Monterey Park, 1988-91, City of Colton, 1991-93, City of Union City, 1995-2001, City of Stockton, 2001—. Mem. State Bar Calif., Calif. City. Mgrs. Assn. (exec. com. 1996-98). Avocation: sailing. Home: 3901 Pine Lake Cir Stockton CA 95219 Office: 425 N El Dorado St Stockton CA 95202 E-mail: marklewis0627@aol.com.

LEWIS, MARK RICHARD, aerospace engineer, educator; b. Spokane, Feb. 4, 1962; s. Robert Mead and Patricia Ruby Jane (Gation) L. AA, Highline Coll., 1982; BS, U. Wash., 1986, MS, 1991. Performance engr. Boeing Aerospace, Seattle, 1987-88; assoc. U. Wash., 1991-92; adj. prof. Bellevue (Wash.) Coll., 1994-95; sr. propulsion engr. Boeing Comml. Airplane Group, 1996—. Adj. prof. Shoreline (Wash.) Coll., 1992, Highline (Wash.) Coll., 1993. Mem. AIAA, Seattle Profl. Engring. Employees Assn., Golden Key, Tau Beta Pi Assn., Phi Theta Kappa. Democrat. Avocations: weight lifting. Office: Propulsion Sys Divsn BCAG PO Box 3707 Seattle WA 98124-2207

LEWIS, MARSHALL EDWARD, psychiatrist, administrator, educator; b. Washington, Mar. 2, 1950; BA magna cum laude, Yale U., 1972; MD, Vanderbilt U., 1976. Diplomate Am. Bd. Psychiatry and Neurology, Am. Bd. Addiction Psychiatry. Clin. fellow in psychiatry Harvard U. Med. Sch., Boston, 1976-79; attending psychiatrist McLean Hosp., Belmont, 1979-83; med. dir. Las Encinas Hosp., Pasadena, Calif., 1983-85; CEO, med. dir. Psychiatric Inst. Pasadena, 1985-88; exec. med. dir. Rancho Park Hosp., El Cajon, Calif., 1991-92, St. Luke's Hosp., San Francisco, 1995-97; med. dir. Stanislaus County Dept. Mental Health, Modesto, 1997—; adminstr. Stanislaus Behavioral Health Ctr., 2002—. Lectr. in psychiatry Harvard U. Med. Sch., 1985-87; asst. clin. prof. U. So. Calif., L.A., 1984-89, U. Calif., San Diego, 1993—, Davis, 1998—. Mem. Drug Abuse Adv. Coun., Montgomery County, Md., 1990-91. Recipient Eight Ball award L.A. Press Club, 1984. Fellow Am. Psychiatric Assn.; mem. Calif. State Mental Health Assn. (bd. dirs. 1986-87), L.A. County Mental Health Assn. (bd. dirs. 1985-87), Ctrl. Calif. Psych. Soc. (pres.-elect 1999-2000, pres. 2000—), Calif. Psychiat. Assn. (mem. coun. 1999—). Office: Stanislaus County Dept Mental Health 1501 Claus Rd Modesto CA 95355-9711

LEWIS, MARTHA NELL, Christian educator, minister, expressive arts therapist; b. Atlanta, Mar. 4, 1944; d. Clifford Edward and Nell (Shropshire) Wilkie; m. Jeffrey Clark Lewis, Aug. 20, 1966 (div. Aug. 1986); children: John Martin, Janet Michelle Teal. BA, Tex. Tech. U., 1966; massage therapy, The Winters Sch., 1991; MA, Norwich U., 1994; MTS, Ch. Divinity Sch. Pacific, 2000. Cert. music practitioner, expressive therapist, massage therapist, therapeutic massage and bodywork, massage therapist instr., music instr. Geophys. analyst Shell Oil Co., Houston, 1966-68; photogravity specialist Photogravity, Inc., 1972-80; tchr. music Little Red Sch. House, 1974-75; sec., treas. Lewis Enterprises, Inc., 1976-83; regulatory supr. Transco Energy Co., 1983-92; expressive arts therapist Shalom Renewal Ctr., Splendora, 1995—, River Oaks Health Alliance, Houston, 1995-96; co-founder, past nat. exec. dir., pres., tchr. Music for Healing and Transition Program, 1994—. Massage therapist, expressive therapist, Houston, 1991—, Calif., 1996—; adj. prof. Holy Names Coll., Oakland, Calif., 1998-99; Sunday sch. coord. St. Stephen's Episc. Ch., Belvedere, Calif., 2000; min. Christian edn. St. Paul's Episc. Ch., Waco, Tex., 2000—. Advisor youth Corpus Christi Ch., Houston, 1970-80; vocalist, instrumentalist Sounds of Faith Folk Group, Houston, 1978—; harpist Houston Harpers Harp Ensemble, 1990-92; liturgical dancer Random Dance, Berkeley, Calif., 1997-2000; instr. exercise, body awareness Transco Energy Co. Fitness Ctr., Houston, 1990-92; vol. The Inst. for Rehab. and Rsch., Houston, 1989-90, Houston Hospice, 1992-96, Houston Healing Healthcare Project, 1993-96; vol. Healing Environ. Coun. St. Luke's Episc. Hosp., 1993-96; lay chaplain Cmty. of Hope, 1994—; founder The Winters Sch. Massage Therapy Care Team, Houston, 1991-96; vol. Ctr. for AIDS Svcs., Oakland, 1996-2000. Mem.: Nat. Assn. for Episcopal Edn. Dirs., Nat. Network Lay Profls., Christian Dance Fellowship USA, Nat. Sacred Dance Guild, Am. Massage Therapy Assn., Internat. Folk Harp Assn., Nat. Expressive Therapy Assn., Internat. Expressive Arts Therapy Assn., Sigma Kappa Alumnae Sorority (pres. Houston chpt. 1974—76, nat. collegiate province officer 1981—85, Houston Alumnae of Yr. 1981, Tex. Alumnae of Yr. 1980, Pearl Ct. award 1991), Houston Sigma Kappa Found. (bd. dirs.), Space City Ski Club (asst. trip coord. 1991—92). Roman Catholic. Episcopalian. Avocations: harp, piano, voice, dance, travel. Home: 1625 Wooded Acres #115 Waco TX 76710 E-mail: mlewis3444@aol.com., marthal@stpaulswaco.org.

LEWIS, MARTIN EDWARD, shipping company executive, foreign government concessionary; b. Chgo., Dec. 27, 1958; s. Martin Luther and Anna Adlene (Gaines) L. BA, Johns Hopkins U., 1981; postgrad., Rush Med. Coll., 1983-85. Chmn. bd., chief exec. officer Internat. Financier Inc., Chgo., 1987—; co. rep. Assn. S.E. Asia Nations Secretariat Gen., Jakarta, Indonesia, 1995—. Co. rep. OPEC, Vienna, 1988—, Supreme Coun. States of Cooperation Coun., Summit Confs. Countries of Cooperation Coun. for Arab States of Gulf, Secretariat Gen., Riyadh, Saudi Arabia, 1989—; corp. amb. plenipotentiary GM Overseas Ops., N.Y.C., 1977, Adam Opel, Russelsheim, Fed. Republic Germany, 1977. Mem. Asia Soc., Japan Soc. Republican. Avocations: golf, tennis, yachting, scuba diving. E-mail: info@ifiworld.com.

LEWIS, MARTIN R. paper company executive, consultant; b. Feb. 14, 1929; s. William and Ida (Goldman) L.; m. Renee Raines, Aug. 13, 1950 (div.); children: Jeffrey, Wendy, Lisa; m. Diane Carol Brandt, July 4, 1975. BA, NYU, 1949, LLB, 1951; LLM, U. Mich., 1952. CEO Williamhouse-Regency, Inc., N.Y.C., 1955-95; vice-chmn. DIMAC Corp., 1998-99; owner Martin Lewis Assocs., 1999—. Cons. in field. Bd. dirs. McBurney br. YMCA, N.Y.C. Mem. Envelope Mfg. Assn., Paper Club N.Y., N.Y. Jewish. E-mail: mrlewis@banet.net.

LEWIS, MARY ANN, nursing educator; b. Kansas City, Mo., Aug. 1, 1937; m. Charles Edwin Lewis, Dec. 27, 1963; children: Kevin, David, Matthew, Karen. BS in Nursing, U. Kans., 1962; MS in Nursing, Boston U., 1963; DrPH, UCLA, 1984. cert. adult nurse practitioner. Instr. pub. health nursing U. Kans., Kansas City, Mo., 1963-66; coordinator pub. health nursing Children's Mercy Hosp., 1966-68; research health specialist UCLA, 1971-73, project dir. Primex Family Nurse Practice, 1972-76, adj. asst. prof. nursing, 1976-80, adj. prof. nursing and medicine, 1980-86, asst. prof. nursing, 1986—, prof., 1989—; chair faculty UCLA Sch. Nursing, 1992-96, chair primary care sect., 1996—. Cons. internat. health Health Resources Adminstrn., Washington, 1978—; bd. dirs. Maxicare Rsch. and Edn. Found., L.A.; cons. Asthma and Allergy Found. Am., L.A., Washington; ad hoc reviewer NIH, Robert Wood Johnson Found. Author: Health Decision-Making, 1980; bd. dirs., editorial bd. The Nurse Practitioner, 1981—; contbr. articles to profl. jours. Com. mem. AIDS Project, Los Angeles, 1986-88. Fellow Am. Acad. Nursing; mem. AAUW, ANA, APHA, Assn. for History of Nursing, Chironians of UCLA Sch. Nursing (co-chmn. 1987—), Sigma Theta Tau. Office: UCLA Sch Nursing PO Box 956919 5-266 Factor Bldg Los Angeles CA 90095-6191 E-mail: mlewis@ucla.edu.

LEWIS, MARY JANE, film producer, director, scriptwriter, minister; b. Kansas City, Mo., July 22, 1950; d. J.W. Jr. and Hilda (Miller) L. BA, Stephens Coll., Columbia, Mo., 1971; MA, NYU, 1984, PhD, 1996. Cert. video prodr. Olelo Cmty. TV., Honolulu. Office mgr. Crazy Shirts, Inc., Honolulu, 1974-79; creator Exotic Exports, 1979-80; asst. buyer Bloomingdale's, N.Y.C., 1980-82; office mgr., media dir. Andiamo, Inc., 1982-85; freelance stylist Condé Nast, Inc., 1985-86; tchg. fellow NYU, 1988-90, adj. prof., 1990-92. Adj. faculty Fashion Inst. Tech., N.Y.C., 1983; lectr. U. Hawaii, creator adult edn. programs and credit classes, 1986—; lectr. NYU Sch. Continuing Edn., 1991-94; video stylist, asst. prodr. State of Hawaii Dept. Edn., Honolulu, 1994—; TV prodr. Office of the Mayor, City & County of Honolulu, 1998. Author: Careers in Fashion Manual, 1992; (TV/movie scripts) The Last Rose of Summer, 1992, The Mustard Seed, 1997 (Maui Writers Conf. Screenwriting Competition award 1998); prodr., dir., writer, narrator (video) Learning Through Community Service, 1998 (Communicator award 1998, Videographer award 1999); prodr. (live TV show) City Lights, Honolulu City Lights, 1998; prodr., dir., writer (documentary) Sarah Josepha Hale and The godey girls, 2002. Min. Global Aloha Weddings; mem. Friends of the Richards Free LIbr., Newport, NH. Mem. Women Make Movies, The Fashion Group Internat., Inc., NYU Alumni Assn., Nat. Trust for Historic Preservation, Kappa Alpha Theta Alumni (pres. pledge class 1968—). Avocations: psychic tarot readings, harpsicord, sailing, gardening, cats. Home: 91-513 B Hapalua St Ewa Beach HI 96706-2929 E-mail: mjlewisphd@verizon.net.

LEWIS, MARY THERESE, artist; b. Blue Island, Ill., June 21, 1951; d. Christian Henry and Marie Anne (Corcoran) Berns; m. Richard W. Lewis, Feb. 16, 1979. BA in Math. with highest honors, U. Ill., 1974; MS in Physics, U. Chgo., 1978; PhD in Phys. Oceanography, U. Del., 1996. Lead engr. rsch. & devel. robotics & artificial intelligence Boeing Mil. Airplane Co., Wichita, Kans., 1978-84; pvt. practice artificial intelligence engring., 1984-85; artist, writer, 1985—; artist, writer, owner NorthStar Studio Press, 1998—. Mm. Am. Geophys. Union. Home and Office: 2221 Inwood Rd Wilmington DE 19810-2807 E-mail: bernslewis@aol.com.

LEWIS, MELVIN, psychiatrist, pediatrician, psychoanalyst; b. London, May 18, 1926; came to U.S., 1956; s. Abraham George and Kitty (Merrick) L.; m. Dorothy S. Otnow, May 30, 1963; children: Gillian Io, Eric Anthony. M.B., BS, Guy's Hosp. Med. Sch., London, 1950; D.C.H., 1954; MA (hon.), Yale U., 1972. Diplomate Am. Bd. Psychiatry and Neurology, Am. Bd. Child Psychiatry; cert. in psychoanalysis, child and adolescent psychoanalysis. Intern Lambeth Hosp., 1950, Fulham Hosp., 1951 (both Eng); resident in pediatrics Yale U. Sch. Medicine, 1956-57, resident in psychiatry and child psychiatry, 1957-61; from instr. child psychiatry to sr. rsch. sci. Yale U. Child Study Ctr., New Haven, 1961—2002, sr. rsch. sci., 2002—. Author: Clinical Aspects of

Child and Adolescent Development, 1971, 3d edit. (with Fred Volkmar), 1991; editor: Jour. Am. Acad. Child & Adolescent Psychiatry, 1975-87, Child and Adolescent Psychiatry, A Comprehensive Textbook, 1991, 2d edit., 1996; cons. editor: Child and Adolescent Psychiatric Clinics of North America, 1991—. Served with M.C. Royal Army, 1951-53. Fellow: Royal Coll. Psychiatrists, Am. Psychiat. Assn., Am. Acad. Child and Adolescent Psychiatry; mem.: Am. Psychoanalytic Assn., Western New Eng. Psychoanalytic Inst. and Soc., Am. Pediat. Soc. Home: 10 St Ronan Ter New Haven CT 06520-7900 Office: Yale U Child Study Ctr 230 S Frontage Rd New Haven CT 06519-1124 E-mail: melvin.lewis@yale.edu.

LEWIS, MICHAEL RAY, encyclopedia editor; b. Hastings, Nebr., May 13, 1972; s. Thomas Ray and Joan Hilda Lewis. B Journalism, U. Nebr., Lincoln, 1994. News reporter Grand Island (Nebr.) Independent, 1995; pub. info. officer, editor Nebr. Blue Book, Nebr. Legislature, Lincoln, 1995-99; copy editor Britannica.com, Ency. Brit., 1999-2000, asst. editor, 2000; area studies/history editor World Book Ency., 2001—. Mem. Chicago coun. on fgn. relations Internat. Vis. Ctr. Mem. Chgo. Coun. Fgn. Rels., Inernat. Vis. Ctr. Chgo., Hemlock Soc. U.S.A., Summer Honors Program Alumni Assn. (founder, former pres.). Democrat. Home: 6825 N Sheridan Rd Apt 509 Chicago IL 60626-7856 Office: World Book Ste 2000 233 N Michigan Ave Chicago IL 60601 E-mail: mlewis10@msn.com.

LEWIS, MICHAEL SETH, health care executive; b. Bklyn., Dec. 11, 1953; s. Irving Abraham and Beatrice Rachel (Fishman) L.; m. Arlene Feigenbaum, June 27, 1976; children: Adam, Sara. BA, Bklyn. Coll., 1974; MS, Fordham U., 1975; MBA, Temple U., 1977. Grad. asst. Temple U., Phila., 1975-77; adminstrv. asst. Cherry Hill (N.J.) Med. Ctr., 1976-77; adminstr. Brachfeld Med. Assocs., Willingboro, N.J., 1977-94; v.p. Founders Health Care Inc., Phila., 1995-96; adminstrv. dir. dept. surgery Cooper Health Sys., Camden, N.J., 1997-99; exec. dir., CEO Ptnrs. in Primary Care, Berlin, 1999—. Pres. Congregation Beth Tikvah. Mem. Med. Group Mgmt. Assn., Beta Gamma Sigma. Home: 24 Abington Rd Mount Laurel NJ 08054-4720 Office: Ptnrs in Primary Care 114 Cross Keys Rd Ste 109 Berlin NJ 08009-9263 E-mail: mlewis@ppcdoc.com.

LEWIS, NANCY LOUINE LAMBERT, school counselor; b. Austin, Tex., Jan. 28, 1938; d. Claud Standard and Audrey Louine (Jackson) Lambert; m. Raymond Clyde Lewis, Dec. 27, 1958; children: Laura Beth, John Lambert. BA in English with highest honors, U. Tex., 1958, MEd in Guidance and Counseling, 1964. Lic. tchr. secondary English, counselor; lic. profl. counselor. Tchr. English Allan Jr. High Sch. Austin Ind. Sch. Dist., 1958-62, counselor Univ. Jr. High Sch., 1963-65; counselor Gary Job Corps Ctr., San Marcos, Tex., 1965-67; supr. student tchrs. English dept. curriculum and instrn. U. Tex., Austin, 1968-69, editor, writer, group leader Ctr. Pub. Sch. Ethnic Studies, 1969-76; counselor Allan Jr. High Sch. Austin Ind. Sch. Dist., 1976-80, counselor Martin Jr. High Sch., 1980-86, counselor Fulmore Mid. Sch., 1986-87, counselor Mendez Mid. Sch., 1987—. Instr. curr. studies U. Tex., Austin, 1968—. Contbr. articles to profl. jours. Vol. Dem. party, Austin, 1973—, First United Meth. Ch., Austin, 1955—; mem. Mayor's Task Force on Gangs, Crime and Drugs, City of Austin, 1990-91. Recipient Optimist Internat. Achievement in Edn. award, 1996. Mem. NEA, ACA, Am. Sch. Counselors Assn. (editl. bd. Sch. Counselor 1989-96), Tex. State Tchrs. Assn., Tex. Sch. Counselors Assn. (senator 1981-84, pres. 1985-86, chair counseling advocacy com. 1991-93, Mid. Sch. Counselor of Yr. 1993, Mid. Sch./Jr. H.S. v.p. 2000—), Tex. Counseling Assn. (senator 1981-84, publs. com. chair 1981-84, membership com. chair 1994-96), Tex. Mid. Sch. Assn., Capital of Tex. Counseling Assn. (pres. 1982-83), Edn. Austin (cons. com. 1990-93, Human Rels. award 1989-90), Pathways (bd. dirs.), Delta Kappa Gamma (pres. Lambda Iota chpt. 1990-92), Phi Beta Kappa. Avocations: travel, reading, playing bridge. Home: 1427 Salem Meadow Cir Austin TX 78745-2911 Office: Mendez Mid Sch 5106 Village Square Dr Austin TX 78744-4462 E-mail: nlewis1427@aol.com.

LEWIS, NATHAN SAUL, chemistry educator; b. L.A., Oct. 20, 1955; BS in Chemistry with highest honors, MS in Chemistry, Calif. Inst. Tech., 1977; PhD in Chemistry, MIT, 1981. Asst. prof. chemistry Stanford (Calif.) U., 1981-86, assoc. prof., 1986-88, Calif. Inst. Tech., 1988-90, prof., 1990—. Cons. Lawrence Livermore (Calif.) Nat. Lab., 1977-81, 84-88, Solar Energy Rsch. Assocs., Santa Clara, Calif., 1981-85, Am. Hosp. Supply, Irvine, Calif., 1983-85, Molecular Devices, Palo Alto, Calif., 1983-88; mem. U.S. Japan Joint Conf. Photochemistry and Photoconversion, 1983, Chem. Revs. Adv. Bd., 1989-92, long range planning com. Electrochem. Soc., 1991-94, Adv. Bd. Progress Inorganic Chemistry, 1992-94, vis. com. dept. applied sci. Brookhaven Nat. Lab., 1993—. Divisional editor Jour. Electrochemical Soc., 1984-90; mem. editorial adv. bd. Accounts Chem. Rsch., 1993—. Recipient Presdl. Young Investigator award, 1984-88, Fresenius award Phi Lambda Upsilon, 1990, Pure Chemistry award Am. Chem. Soc., 1991; Achievement Rewards Coll. Scientists Found. scholar Calif. Inst. Tech., 1975-77, Calif. State scholar, 1976-77, Carnation Co. Acad. Merit scholar, 1976-77, Camille and Henry Dreyfus Tchr. scholar, 1985-90; Fannie and John Hertz Found. fellow MIT, 1977-81, Alfred P. Sloan Rsch. fellow, 1985-87. Office: Calif Inst Tech Dept Chem 127 72 Pasadena CA 91125-0001 E-mail: nslewis@caltech.edu.

LEWIS, NELDA CONNER, social worker, therapist; b. Houston, Aug. 7, 1941; d. Hugh Lee adn Georga Norene (Patterson) Conner; m. Ronnie Eugene Lewis, June 25, 1964 (div. 1982); children: Ronda, Ronald, Renel. BA, Tex. So. U., 1962; MSW, Mich. State U., 1964; Doctorate, Tex. Women's U., 1989. Cert. social worker. Foster care social worker Negro Child Ctr., Houston, 1964-67; supr. Harris County Child Welfare Unit, 1967-69, DePelchin Children's Ctr., Houston, 1970-73, program dir., 1987—; team leader Mental Health/Mental Retardation Authority of Harris County, 1973-74; dept. chair Tex. So. U., 1974-87; program dir. De Pelchin Children's Ctr., 1987-95; dir. family devel. People In Partnership, 1995—. Presenter workship various profl. and community meetings. Program dir. health and human scvs. grant for teen parent program Tex. So. U.-United Way, 1984-86; mem. coun. adminstrn. YWCA., 1991. Honored, Harris County Ret. Tchrs. Assn.; named to Outstanding Young Women of Am., 1974. Mem. Acad. Cert. Social Workers, Assn. Black Social Workers (treas. 1991—), Nat. Assn. Social Workers (mem.-at-large 1991, membership chair 1991), Black Child Devel. Inst. Avocations: reading, listening to music. Home: 3208 Calumet St Houston TX 77004-7824 Office: People in Partnership 3000 Trulley St Houston TX 77004-1743

LEWIS, NINA, social worker; b. Cleve., July 21, 1953; d. William Paul and Gloria Louise (Pearch) L. BA in Sociology, Ohio State U., 1976, MSW, 1988. Lic. ind. social worker, Ohio. ACSW, rsch. asst. Disaster Rsch. Ctr. Ohio State U., Columbus, 1974-75; social worker Huckleberry House, 1976-78, North Cen. Community Mental Health Ctr., Columbus, 1979-80, CHOICES for Victims Domestic Violence, Columbus, 1980-90; social worker state HIV case, mgmt, cons. AIDS unit Ohio Dept. Health, 1990-93; dir. supportive housing dept. Lutheran Social Svcs. Central Ohio, 1992-97; HIV housing coord. Columbus Health Dept., 1997—. Adj. faculty Capital U., Ohio State U., Dominican Coll., Columbus State, Wright State. Coord. operation feed campaign Legal Aid Soc., Columbus, 1987. John H. Smith scholar, 1986-88, Anna Marie Mills scholar, 1986-88; recipient Walter and Marian English award, 1986-88, Social Worker of Yr. award Region V., 1996. Mem. NASW, Ohio State Coll. Social Work Alumni Assn. Office: Columbus Health Dept 240 Parsons Ave Columbus OH 43215-5331

LEWIS, ORME, JR. real estate investment company executive, land use adviser; b. Phoenix, Apr. 26, 1935; s. Orme and Barbara (Smith) L.; m. Elizabeth Bruening, Oct. 17, 1964; children: Joseph Orme, Elizabeth Blaise. BS, U. Ariz., 1958. Assoc. Coldwell Banker, Phoenix, 1959-64; v.p. Braggiotti Constrn., 1964-65; pvt. practice investment brokerage, 1966-69; dep. asst. sec. Dept. Interior, Washington, 1969-73; dir. devel. Ariz. Biltmore Estates, 1973-76; exec. World Resources Co., Phoenix and McLean, Va., 1978-91; mng. mem. Applewhite Laflin & Lewis, Phoenix, 1979-96; gen. ptnr. Equity Interests, 1982—; mng. dir. Select Investments, 1996—. Co-chmn. U.S. Adv. Com. on Mining and Mineral Rsch., Washington, 1982-94; mem. U.S. Emergency Minerals Adminstrn., 1987-01, Gov.'s Regulatory Rev. Coun., 1992-95, State Plant Site Transmission Line Com., Phoenix, 1974-85; co-chmn. Disease Control Rsch. Commn., 1995-2002; adv. bd. U.S. Minerals Mgmt. Svc., 2002—. Mem. Ariz. Senate, 1966-70; chmn. Phoenix Children's Hosp., 1981—; mem. Boyce Thompson Arboretum, 1999—; mem. governing bd. Polycystic Kidney Rsch. Found., Kansas City, Mo., 1983—, Ariz. Cmty. Found., 1986-91, Ariz. Parks and Conservation Coun., 1985-96, Ariz. State U. Found., Tempe, 1981—, Ariz. Hist. Found., 1984—; mem. governing bd. Desert Bot. Garden, 1987-89, Men's Art Coun., 1983-85. Recipient Dept. Interior Conservation Svc. award, 1996; inductee Wisdom Hall of Fame, 1997. Mem. Ariz. C. of C. (dir. 1990-96), Met. Club (Washington), Ariz. Valley Field Riding and Polo Club, Paradise Valley Country Club, Rotary. Republican. Home: 4325 E Palo Verde Dr Phoenix AZ 85018-1127 Office: Select Investments LLC 4350 E Camelback Rd Ste 260E Phoenix AZ 85018-8343 E-mail: adviser_az@msn.com.

LEWIS, PAUL LE ROY, pathology educator; b. Tamaqua, Pa., Aug. 30, 1925; s. Harry Earl and Rose Estella (Brobst) L.; m. Betty Jane Bixby, June 2, 1953; 1 child, Robert Harry. AB magna cum laude, Syracuse U., 1950; MD, SUNY, Syracuse, 1953. Diplomate Am. Bd. Pathology. Intern Temple U. Hosp., Phila., 1953-54; resident in pathology Hosp. of U. Pa., 1954-58, asst. instr., 1957-58; instr. pathology Thomas Jefferson U. Coll. Medicine, 1958-62, asst. prof., 1962-65, assoc. prof., 1965-75, prof., 1975-93, prof. emeritus, 1993—; pathologist Thomas Jefferson U. Hosp., 1958-91; attending pathologist Meth. Hosp., Phila., 1975-93, dir. clin. labs., chmn. dept. pathology, 1975-92, consulting pathologist, 1993—; pathologist pvt. practice, 1993—. Pres. Penndel Labs. Inc., Ardmore, Pa., 1974-85; cons. VA Hosp., Coatesville, Pa., 1976-85; mem. med. adv. com. ARC Blood Bank, Phila., 1978—. Contbg. author: Atlas of Gastrointestinal Cytology, 1983; contbr. articles to med. jours. 2d lt. USAAF, 1943-46. Fellow Am. Soc. Clin. Pathologists, Coll. Am. Pathologists; mem. AMA, Pa. Med. Soc., Philadelphia County Med. Soc., Internat. Acad. Pathology, Am. Soc. Cytology, Masons, Phi Beta Kappa, Alpha Omega Alpha, Nu Sigma Nu. Republican. Methodist. Avocations: photography, hiking. Home and Office: 521 Baird Rd Merion Station PA 19066-1301

LEWIS, PERRY JOSHUA, investment banker; b. San Antonio, Feb. 11, 1938; s. Perry Joshua and Zelime L. L.; m. Memrie Taylor Mosier, May 12, 1962 (div. 1994); children— Perry Joshua, IV, Memrie Fraser; m. Basha Szymanska, May 15, 1997. BA, Princeton U., 1959. Registered rep. Lee Higginson Corp., N.Y.C., 1960-63; comml. project mgr. Parsons & Whittemore, Inc., 1964-67; sr. v.p., mgr. corp. fin. div. Smith Barney, Harris Upham & Co. Inc., 1967-79; pres. MacKay-Lewis Inc., 1980-81; ptnr. Morgan Lewis Githens & Ahn, Conn., 1982—; sr. mng. dir. Heartland Indsl. Ptnrs., Greenwich, 2000—01; adv. dir. CRT Capital Group LLC, 2001—. Bd. dirs. Aon Corp., Chgo., Clear Channel Comm., Inc., San Antonio. Pres. bd. dirs. Performing Arts Ctr., Purchase, N.Y. With U.S. Army, 1959-60, 61-62. Mem.: Knickerbocker of N.Y., Doubles N.Y. Office: CRT Capital Group 262 Harbor Dr Stamford CT 06902 Fax: 203-438-8304 E-mail: pjlewis@sheffieldmb.com.

LEWIS, PHILIP, educational and technical consultant; b. Chgo., Oct. 23, 1913; s. Solomon and Fannie (Margolis) L.; m. Geraldine Gisela Lawenda, Sept. 1, 1947; 1 child, Linda Susan. BS, DePaul U., Chgo., 1937, MA, 1939; EdD, Columbia Tchrs. Coll., 1951. Chmn. dept. edn. Chgo. Tchrs. Coll.; also asst. prin., tchr. South Shore High Sch., Chgo., 1940-51; prin. Herman Felsenthal Elementary Sch., 1955-57; dir. Bur. Instructional Materials, Chgo. Pub. Schs., 1957-63, Bur. Research Devel. and Spl. Projects, 1963-67; pres. Instructional Dynamics Inc., Chgo., 1967-89, ret., 1989; ednl. and tech. cons., 1991—. Nat. cons. TV and instructional techniques, 1955— ; ednl. cons. to accrediting bur. Health Edn. Schs., 1971-89; chmn. adv. com. U.S. Office Edn., Title VII, 1964-67 Author: Educational Television Guidebook for Electronics Industries Association, 1961, also numerous articles.; mem. editorial bd. Nation's Schs. and Colls; multimedia tech. editor: Tech. Horizons in Edn; cons.: Jour. Ednl. Tech. and Communications; producer ednl., multimedia, tng. and mental health and human devel. materials. Served to lt. comdr. USNR, 1942-45. Mem. Soc. Programmed and Automated Learning (pres. 1960-65), NEA (v.p. dept. audiovisual instrn., chmn. commn. on tech. standards dept. audiovisual instrn. 1965-85), Nat. Assn. Ednl. Broadcasters, Am. Legion, Council for Ednl. Facilities Planners (editorial adv. bd. 1972-80) Ill. C. of C. (edn. com. 1970-77), Chgo. Assn. Commerce and Industry (chmn. edn. com. 1970-80), Nat. Audio-Visual Assn. (profl. devel. bd. 1969-76, chmn), Chgo. Press Club, Masons, Shriners, Rotary, Phi Delta Kappa. Home: 5212 Danbury Rd Bethesda MD 20814-2869

LEWIS, PHILIP M. computer science educator; b. N.Y.C., May 30, 1931; s. Morton Philip and Constance Arlene (Dreyfus) L.; m. Rhoda Yvonne Berman, Dec. 20, 1953; children: Michael Philip, Patricia Viola Lewis Susser. BEE, Rensselaer Poly. Inst., 1952; MS, MIT, 1954, PhD, 1956. Asst. prof. MIT, Cambridge, 1956-59; rsch. scientist GE R & D Ctr., Schenectady, NY, 1959-77, mgr. computer sci. br., 1977-87, cons., 1987—; leading prof., chmn. computer sci. dept. SUNY, Stony Brook, 1987—97, prof. computer sci. dept., 1996—. Adj. prof. Rensselaer Poly. Inst., Troy, N.Y., 1960-87. Co-author: Threshold Logic, 1967, Compiler Design Theory, 1976, Concurrency In Programming And Database Systems, 1993, Databases and Transaction Processing, 2002; co-editor: Software Engineering, 1980; contbr. articles to profl. jours.; patentee in field. V.p. Nat. Soc. for Autistic Children, Washington, 1977; pres. N.Y. State Soc. for Autistic Children, Albany, N.Y., 1980-82, Camary Corp. Residences for Autistic Adults, Albany, 1980-85; bd. visitors O.D. Heck Devel. Ctr., Schenectady, 1978-87. Fellow IEEE (chmn. tech. com. on founds. of computing 1971-73), Assn. for Computing Machines; mem. Soc. for Indsl. and Applied Math. (mng. editor Jour. on Computing 1972-74), Sigma Xi, Eta Kappa Nu, Tau Beta Pi. Home: 39 Annandale Rd Stony Brook NY 11790-2405 Office: SUNY Dept Computer Sci Computer Sci Bldg 1400 Stony Brook NY 11794-0001

LEWIS, RANDOLPH VANCE, molecular biologist, researcher; b. Powell, Wyo., Apr. 8, 1950; s. William (Jack) Fredrick and Evelyn Jean (Vonburg) L.; m. Lorrie Dale Emery, May 27, 1972; children: Brian, Daryl (dec.), Karren. BS in Chemistry, Calif. Inst. Tech., 1972; MS in Chemistry, U. Calif., San Diego, 1974; PhD in Chemistry, U. Calif., 1978. Postdoctoral fellow Roche Inst. Molecular Biology, Nutley, N.J., 1978-80; asst. prof. molecular biology U. Wyo., Laramie, 1980-84, assoc. prof., 1984-89, head dept., 1986-91, prof., 1989—; dir. NSF EPSCOR Program, 1990—. Cons. NIH, Bethesda, Md., 1985—91, Hoffman-LaRoche, Nutley, NJ, 1990—93, DuPont, Wilmington, Del., 1990—94, Protein Polymer Techs., San Diego, 1988—94, Nexia, 1999—; pres. Wyobigen, Laramie, Wyo., 1994—; bd. dirs. Wyo. Bus. Devel. Ctr. Author chpts. to books; contbr. articles to profl. jours. Mem. Jr. Livestock Sale Com., Laramie, 1991-98; pres. Albany County 4-H Coun., Laramie, 1994-98. Sloan Found. fellow, 1985; recipient Research Career Devel. award NIH, 1985, Jr. Faculty award Am. Cancer Soc., 1985, Burlington-North Faculty award U. Wyo., 1986. Mem. Am. Chem. Soc., Am. Soc. Biochemists and Molecular Biologists, N.Y. Acad. Scis., Protein Soc. Republican. Baptist. Achievements include discovery of opioid peptide precursor; sequencing of first spider silk protein genes; five product licenses; 4 patents. Avocations: fly fishing, bird hunting. Home: 1948 Howe Rd Laramie WY 82070-6889 Office: U Wyo PO Box 3944 Laramie WY 82071-3944

LEWIS, RAY, football player; b. May 15, 1975; children: Ray Anthony Lewis, Jr., Rayshad, Dymond Deseree. Degree in arts and scis. Profl. football player Balt. Ravens, 1996—. Vol. charitable orgns. Achievements include Became the 2nd player in NFL history to win both NFL Defensive MVP and Super Bowl MVP. Avocations: fishing, camping, swimming, basketball. Office: Balt Ravens Ravens Stadium 1101 Russell St Baltimore MD 21230 E-mail: inquiries@baltimoreravens.com.*

LEWIS, REBA JOLENE, secondary school educator, consultant; b. Duncan, Okla., July 18, 1949; d. Rube Ira and Loretha Corene Rose; m. Donald Lawrence Lewis, Aug. 29, 1969; children: Don, Joni, Thomas, Sunnie, Tyler. BS, Tex. A&M U., 1971; MEd, E. Ctrl. U., Ada, Okla., 1985. Cert. Nat. Bd. Tchg. Stds., secondary tchr. Okla., Tex. Tchr. English and speech Port Arthur (Tex.) Ind. Sch. Dist., 1972—75; tchr. Healdton (Okla.) HS, 1976—89, 1995—, Pampa (Tex.) HS, 1990—94; realtor Walker Realty, Healdton, 1995—98; instr. Murray State Coll., Ardmore, 1995—99. Cons. tchr. testing Okla. Dept. Edn., Oklahoma City, 1999. Del. to state conv. Tex. Rep. Com., Pampa, 1994. Mem.: NEA, Healdton Assn. Classroom Tchrs. (pres., treas., Tchr. of Yr. 1986), Okla. Edn. Assn. (del. 1975—89, Zone Tchr. of Yr. 1986). Republican. Baptist. Avocations: reading, writing, horses. Home: 320 Lamar Healdton OK 73438 Office: Healdton HS 432 W Texas Healdton OK 73438

LEWIS, RICHARD, SR. securities broker, consultant; b. Macon, Ga., Jan. 18, 1930; s. William Chapman and Florida (Zelius) L.; m. Iris Joy Clements, Sept. 10, 1949; children: Richard Jr., Linda Lee. Cert. pistol and rifle instr. State trooper Fla. Hwy. Patrol, various cities, 1951-72; pres. Gateway Shooters Supply, Inc., Jacksonville, Fla., 1972-82, Bobcat Enterprises Inc., 1983-84; broker Global Investments Securities Inc., Miami, 1985-86, Investacorp, Inc., Miami Lakes, Fla., 1986-89. Lobbyist Fla. Assn. of State Troopers, Tallahassee, 1988-89. With U.S. Army, 1952-54. Recipient cert. of appreciation, State of Fla., Tallahassee, 1972; Demolay Cross of Honor, Internat. Coun., Kansas City, Mo., 1973; cert. of commendation, State of Fla., 1972. Mem. NRA (life), Fla. Assn. State Troopers (legis. chmn. retirees 1987), High Meadow Landowners Assn. (pres. 2001—), V.F.W., Jacksonville Pistol Club (pres. 1968-72), Marion Dunn Masonic Lodge, Elks, Sons Am. Revolution, Sons Confederate Vets., Mil. Order Stars and Bars, Fraternal Order Police, Scottish Rite, Nobles Mystic Shrine (Ambassador-at-large). Republican. Methodist. Avocations: fishing, photography, competitive pistol shooting. Home: 461 High Meadow Trl Cleveland GA 30528-2324

LEWIS, RICHARD A. educational association administrator, writer; b. N.Y.C., May 15, 1935; s. Emanuel Paul Lewis and Frances Donner Weinberg; married; children: Amanda, Sascha, Sarah. BA, Bard Coll., 1958. Tchr. Art Ctr. of No. N.J., Englewood, 1961-64, Walden Sch., N.Y.C., 1963-64; instr. New Sch. for Social Rsch., 1964-73; drama and writing tchr. Manhattan-Country Sch., 1967-93; dir., founder Touchstone Ctr. for Children, 1969—. Adj. instr. Bank St. Coll. of Edn., N.Y.C., 1972-73; adj. prof. Rutgers U., New Brunswick, N.J., 1976-78, Western Wash. State U., Bellingham, 1980-82, Lesley Coll. Grad. Sch., Cambridge, Mass., 1981-84, Queens Coll., N.Y.C., 1988. Author: In the Space of The Sky, 2002, Each Sky Has its Words, 2000, Living By Wonder: Essays on the Imaginative Life of Childhood, 1998, German, 1999, Japanese, 2001, When Thought Is Young: Reflections on Teaching and the Poetry of the Child, 1992, All of You Was Singing: A Retelling of an Aztec Myth, 1994, In the Night Still Dark: A Retelling of the Hawaiian Creation Chant, 1988, The Park, 1968; editor: The Luminous Lanscape: Chinese Art and Poetry, 1981, I Breathe a New Song: Poems of the Eskimo, 1971, There are Two Lives: Poems by Children of Japan, 1970, The Way of Silence: Prose and Poetry of Basho, 1981, Still Waters of the Air: Three Modern Spanish Poets, The Poetry of Lorca, Machado and Jimenez, 1981, Muse of the Round Sky: Greek Lyric Poetry, 1969, Journeys: Prose by Children of the English-Speaking World, 1969, 2d edit., 1977, Of This World: A Poet's Life in Poetry-Poetry of Issa, 1969, In A Spring Garden, 1965; author, editor: (video) In the Spirit of Play, 1998, To Make A World, 1997; contbr. articles to profl. jours. Recipient Art Educator award N.Y. State Art Tchrs., 1997, Sch. and Cultural award Alliance for the Arts, 1988. Office: The Touchstone Ctr 141 E 88th St New York NY 10128

LEWIS, RICHARD ALLAN, financial planner, business consultant; b. Pitts., Feb. 25, 1952; s. Harry C. and Vera E. (Williams) L. BS in Econs., Allegheny Coll., 1974; MBA in Fin., U. Pitts., 1978. CFP. Trainee Mellon Bank, Pitts., 1974-75, various positions with, 1975-84, v.p. N.Am. ops., 1984-86; pres., COO WorkWell, 1987-89; sr. fin. planner The Acacia Group, 1989-97; ptnr. Lewis, McBeth & D'Ambrosio, LLP, 1997—. Mem. exec. com., bd. dirs. Arthritis Found., 1989—. Mem. Nat. Automated Clearing House Assn. (bd. dirs. 1981-86), Tri-State Automated Clearing House Assn. (pres. 1984-86, treas. 1980-83, v.p. 1984-85), Masons, Blue Lodge, Phi Beta Kappa, Delta Tau Delta (pres. house corp. 1976—). Republican. Methodist. Avocations: skiing, jogging, travel, gourmet cooking. Home: 106 Fairway Landings Dr Canonsburg PA 15317-9567 Office: 116 Federal St Pittsburgh PA 15212-5704

LEWIS, RICHARD HARLOW, urologist; b. San Diego, May 14, 1951; s. Charles William Jr. and Gene (Harlow) L.; m. Deanna Elma Boggs, March 14, 1950; children: Richard Harlow Jr., Sara-Grace Dean. BS, Guilford Coll., 1973; MD, Duke U., 1977. Intern Bethesda (Md.) Naval Hosp., 1977-78, residence, 1978-82; chief urology Orlando (Fla.) Naval Hosp., 1982-85; pvt. practice, Jacksonville, Fla., 1985—. Ptnr. McIver Urologic Clinic, Jacksonville, 1994-99. Mem. Christian Coalition, Duval County, Fla., 1987—; Rep. precinct rep., Duval County, 1987-90. Lt. comdr. USNR, 1973-85. Winner, Karl Storz Endoscope Photography Contest Karl Storz Corp., 1983. Fellow ACS, Am. Soc. Laser Medicine Surgery, Am. Bd. Laser Surgery, mem. Am. Urol. Assn., Am. Coll. Physician Execs., Med. Group Mgrs. Assn. (physician mem.), Rotary Internat. Avocations: tennis, computers, wine, travel. Home: 4900 Arapahoe Ave Jacksonville FL 32210-8336 Office: McIver Clinic 710 Lomax St Jacksonville FL 32204-4098

LEWIS, RICHARD LAURENCE, academic administrator, digital artist; b. Queens, N.Y., Oct. 9, 1955; s. Henry Louis and Joan Ann L.; m. Susan Roberta Ingalls, Aug. 2, 1981; 1 child Robert Andrew. BFA in Visual Arts, SUNY Coll., Purchase, 1977; MFA in Painting, U. Mich., Ann Arbor, 1983. Asst. prof. art Marist Coll., Poughkeepsie, N.Y., 1984-92, assoc. prof. art, 1992—, studio art coord., 1989-95, chair dept. art & art history, 1995-97, 2001—, dean acad. programs, asst. acad. v.p. N.Y., 1997-2000, chair faculty NY, 2002—. Mem. steering com. Joint Study with IBM Corp., 1992—. Author (with Susan I. Lewis): The Power of Art, 1995; author: (with James Luciana) Digital Media: An Introduction, 2002. Mem.: Coll. Art Assn., Am. Assn. Higher Edn. Office: Art and Art History Marist Coll 290 North Rd Poughkeepsie NY 12601-1326

LEWIS, RICHARD M. lawyer; b. Gallipolis, Ohio, Dec. 11, 1957; s. Denver E. and Mary Esther (Mobley) L.; m. Cheryl F. Hickman (div.); m. Diane K. Williams, Apr. 26, 1986. BA in Polit. Sci., Ohio State U., 1979; JD, Capital U., 1982. Bar: Ohio 1982, U.S. Dist. Ct. (so. dist.) Ohio 1984, U.S. Supreme Ct. 1986, U.S. Ct. Appeals (6th cir.) 1999; cert. civil trial advocacy Nat. Bd. Trial Advocacy. Pvt. practice law, 1982-83; assoc. Mary Bone Kunze, Jackson, Ohio, 1983-85; pvt. practice law, 1985-86; ptnr. Ochsenbein, Cole & Lewis, 1986-96, Cole & Lewis, Jackson, 1996-2000, The Law Firm of Richard M. Lewis, Jackson, 2001—. Lectr. in field; expert witness; appt. to Ohio Sup. Ct. Commn. Cert. of Attys. as Specialists, 2002-03. Mem. ABA, Assn. Trial Lawyers Am., Ohio State Bar Assn. (com. for Independent Judicracy and Unjust Criticism of Judges, 2001—), Jackson County Bar Assn. (past pres.), Ohio Acad. Trial Lawyers (bd. trustees 1993—, budget com. 1993-94, supreme ct. screening com. 1994, vice-chairperson family law com. 1994-95, chairperson-elect family law com. 1995—, chairperson family law com. 1995-96, exec. com., chair mem. com. 1996-97, co-chair regional CLE seminars 1997, exec. com. 1998-99, chair ADOPT task force 1998, editor Book of Complaints 2002). Home: 603 Reservoir Rd Jackson OH 45640-8714 Office: The Law Firm of Richard M Lewis 295 Pearl St Jackson OH 45640-1748

LEWIS, RICHARD PHELPS, physician, educator; b. Portland, Oreg., Oct. 26, 1936; s. Howard Phelps and Wava Irene (Brown) L.; m. Penny A. Brown, Oct. 12, 1982; children: Richard Phelps, Heather Brown. BA, Yale U., 1957; MD, U. Oreg., 1961. Intern Peter Bent Brigham Hosp., Boston, 1961-62, resident, 1962-63; Howard Irwin fellow in cardiology U. Oreg., Portland, 1963-65; sr. resident Stanford U., 1965-66, instr. dept. medicine, 1968-69; asst. chief cardiology Madigan Gen. Hosp., Tacoma, 1966-68; asst. prof. medicine div. cardiology Ohio State U., 1969-71, assoc. prof., 1971-75, prof., 1975-2000, dir. Divsn. Cardiology, 1972-86, dir., 1972-86, assoc. chmn. for hosp. and clin. affairs, 1980-86, prof. emeritus, 2000—. Mem. cardiovascular sect. Am. Bd. Internal Medicine, 1981-87, critical care medicine, 1988-92. Contbr. articles to profl. jours. Served with M.C. U.S. Army, 1966-68, col. res. Decorated Army Commendation medal Fellow ACP (gov. Ohio chpt. 1976-80, chmn. MKSAP cardiovascular sect. 1989-82), Am. Heart Assn. (coun. on clin. cardiology), Am. Coll. Cardiology (Ohio gov. 1988-91, chmn. bd. govs. 1990-91, trustee 1991-2000; editor self assessment program, 1991-96, 2000—, v.p. 1994-95, pres.-elect 1995-96, pres. 1996-97), Am. Clin. and Climatological Assn.; mem. Am. Fedn. Clin. Rsch., Ctrl. Soc. Clin. Rsch., Laennec Soc., Am. Heart Assn., Assn. U. Cardiologists, Alpha Omega Alpha. Republican. Episcopalian. Home: 5088 Stratford Ave Powell OH 43065-8771 Office: 473 W 12th Ave Columbus OH 43210-1240

LEWIS, RICHARD WARREN, advertising agency executive; b. N.Y.C., June 8, 1951; s. Stanley and Janet (Sweet) L.; m. Isabel Ellen Abrams, Mar. 19, 1977; children: Ariane, Amanda, Sam. BA, Hofstra U., 1973; MBA, NYU, 1978. Advt. exec., pres. GGK New York, 1978-84; mgmt. supr. Lois/GGK, N.Y.C., 1985-86; exec. v.p., mgmt. supr. TBWA Chiat/Day, 1987-95; sr. ptnr. worldwide account dir. Absolut TBWA, 1996—. Author: Absolut Book: The

Absolut Vodka Advertising Story, 1996 (N.Y. Times Bestseller List). Coach Dobbs Ferry (N.Y.) Baseball League, 1990-91, 2002. Recipient Clio award, 1989, Andy award Advt. Club N.Y., 1989, 91, Kelly award Mag. Pubs. Am., 1989; named one of '99 Advt. Age 100 Best Campaigns of the Century. Mem. Am. Advt. Fedn. (speaker). Office: TBWA CHIAT DAY 488 Madison Ave New York NY 10022-5702 E-mail: richard.lewis@tbwachiat.com.

LEWIS, RICHART DRAKE, columnist; b. Jeannette, Tenn., Jan. 8, 1958; s. James Eugene Lewis and Stella Jane Malott (Maiden Bryant), Darrell Eugene Malott (Stepfather); children: Shawnric Ryan, James Byron Dean, Glen Michael Leland. Grad. h.s., Tipton, Ind. Reporter, illustrator Devil's Doin' Newspaper, Tipton, Ind., 1974—78; contbr. writer Ft. Campbell (Ky.) Courier, 1979—80; columnist Inside Scoop, Indpls., 1995—97; writer, illustrator Darkangel Prodns., Decaturville, Tenn., 1997—. Reporter Internati. Coop. Tng., Tipton, 1977—78; contbr. writer Tipton Tribune, 1995—98. Author: Rock and Roll Dreams, 1992, Return to Me, 2000, Paint Me a Smile, 2001, The Summer of 72, 2002. Sgt. U.S. Army, 1978—81. Home and Office: 460 N West St Tipton IN 46072 Personal E-mail: rycster1313@yahoo.com.

LEWIS, RITA HOFFMAN, plastic products manufacturing company executive; b. Phila., Aug. 6, 1947; d. Roberg John and Helen Anna (Dugan) Hoffman; 1 child Stephanie Blake. Student, Jefferson Med. Coll. Sch. Nursing, 1965—67, Gloucester County Coll., 1993—. Gen. mgr. Sheets & Co., Inc. (now Flower World, Inc.), Woodbury, NJ, 1968—72; dir., exec. v.p., treas. Hoffman Precision Plastics, Inc., Blackwood, 1973—. Ptnr. Timber Assocs. Author: The Part of Me I Never REally Meant to Share, 1979, In Retrospect: Caught Between Running and Loving; editor (poetry): (singles mag.) SPOTLIGHTER; author: (columnist) Innovative Singles Mag., 1989—. Commr. N.J. Expressway Authority, 1990—, sec., 1990—91, treas., 1991—, chmn. pers., 1991—; apptd. mem. N.J. Senate Forum on Budget and Revenue Alternatives, 1991; guest spkr. various civic groups, 1974; mem. Coun. for Citizens of Glen Oaks, NJ, 1979—, Cloucester Twp. Econ. Devel. Com., 1981—, Cloucester Twp. Day Scholar Com., 1984—; mem. adv. coun. Gloucester Twp. Econ. Adv. Coun., 1985—; chairperson Gloucester Twp. Day Scholar Found., 1985—96; bd. dirs. Diane Hull Dance Co. Recipient Winning Eagle award, 1982, Mayor's award for Womens' Achievement, 1987, Outstanding Cmty. Svc. award Mayor, Coun. and Com., 1987, Don L. Stackhouse Achievement award, 1996. Mem.: NAFE, Soc. Plastic Engrs., Blackwood Businessmen's Assn., Sales Assn. Chem. Industry. Roman Catholic.

LEWIS, ROBERT, journalist, media executive; b. Montreal, Que., Can., Aug. 19, 1943; s. Leon R. and Margaret (Horan) L.; m. Sara Lewis, May 27, 1967; children: Christopher Robert, Timothy O'Neill. BA, Loyola Coll., 1964. Gen. reporter Montreal Star, 1964-65, Ottawa corr., 1965-66; chief Montreal bur. Time mag., 1967-68, Ottawa corr., 1968-70, Boston corr., 1970-72, chief Toronto bur., 1972-74; chief Ottawa bur. Maclean's Mag., 1975-82, mng. editor, 1982-93, editor-in-chief, 1993-2000; v.p. content devel. Rogers Media Inc., Toronto, 2000—. Office: Rogers Media Inc 777 Jarvis St 6th Toronto ON Canada M4Y 3B7 E-mail: rlewis@rci.rogers.com.

LEWIS, ROBERT KAY, JR. fundraising executive; b. Danville, Ky., Aug. 10, 1935; s. Robert K. and Mona (Hyden) L.; m. Wendy Gardiner, June 18, 1960; children: Mary Elizabeth, Mona Hyden, Robert K. III. BA, Ctr. Coll., Danville, 1957; MS, George Washington U., 1972. Advanced through ranks to lt. U.S. Navy, 1958-63; alumni/annual giving dir. Ctr. Coll., 1963-67; served to capt. U.S. Navy, 1967-81; alumni/pub. affairs dir. Ctr. Coll., 1981-83; pub. affairs dir. Va. Tech., Blacksburg, 1983-87; sr. v.p. Host Comm., Lexington, 1987-89; pres. Ky. C. of C., Frankfort, 1990, Global Advancement, Lexington, Ky., 1991—. Trustee Severn Sch., Severna Park, Md., 1979-83; bd. visitors McCallie Sch., Chattanooga, 1983-86; bd. dirs. Ky. Advocates for Higher Edn., Lexington, 1990—. Mem. Assn. Fund Raising Profls. (bd. dirs. Bluegrass chpt. 1991—), Henry Clay Found. (bd. dirs. Lexington, 1994—), Nat. Press Club, Coun. Advancement and Support of Edn. (bd. dirs. Ky. chpt. 1991-98). Assn. of Philanthropic Counsel (nat. bd. dirs. and exec. com. 2000—), Lexington Rotary Endowment (bd. dirs. 1995-2001). Presbyterian. Home: Forest Hill Farm 2667 Lexington Rd Danville KY 40422 Office: Global Advancement 333 W Vine St Ste 300 Lexington KY 40507-1626 E-mail: globaladvt@aol.com.

LEWIS, ROBERT DAVID GILMORE, retired editor; b. Chgo., Jan. 16, 1932; s. James Lee and Betty (Ryden) L.; m. Georgia Demopoulos, Aug. 4, 1956 (div. July 1988); children: Peter, Sarah, Mary, John, Elizabeth, Daniel, Susan; m. Jacqueline Mc Gregor, July 15, 1988; children: Jill, Katy, Sara. BA, Mich. State U., 1955. Reporter, city editor Galesburg (Ill.) Register-Mail, 1955-59; reporter, bus. editor Kalamazoo Gazette, 1960-64; state capitol corres. Booth Newspapers, Lansing, Mich., 1964-66, Washington corres. Washington, 1966-87, Newhouse Newspapers, Washington, 1987-91; sr. editor Am. Assn. Retired Persons Bull., 1991-99, ret., 1999; mng. dir. Lewis Properties, 2000—. Bd. visitors Les Aspin Ctr. for Govt., Marquette U., 1996—. Mem. Soc. Profl. Journalists (chmn. freedom info. com. 1978-83, sec.-treas., pres.-elect then pres., 1983-86, Wells Meml. Key award 1980), White House Corres. Assn., Nat. Press Club (chmn. bd. govs. 1975-77), Sigma Delta Chi Found. (bd. dirs. 1986-88), Cosmos Club, Supreme Ct. Hist. Soc., U.S. Capitol Hist. Soc. Avocations: antique furniture collecting, fishing. Home: 301 Constitution Ave NE Washington DC 20002-5921

LEWIS, ROBERT EDWIN , JR. pathology immunology educator, researcher; b. Meridian, Miss., Mar. 11, 1947; BA in Biology and Chemistry, U. Miss., 1969, MS in Microbiology, 1973, PhD in Pathology, 1976; specialty tng., Barnes Hosp., U. Miami Med. Ctr., U. Tenn. Ctr. for Health Scis., City of Memphis Hosps., St. Jude Children's Research Hosp. Instr. pathology, anesthesiology U. Miss. Med. Ctr., Jackson, 1976-77, asst. prof. pathology, 1977-84, asst. prof. anesthesiology, 1977-85, asst. dir. clin. immnuopathology lab., 1978-81, assoc. dir. tissue typing lab., 1980-84, dir. paternity testing lab., 1981—, assoc. dir. clin. immunopathology lab., 1981-84, asst. prof. nurse anesthesiology, 1981-85, assoc. prof. pathology, 1984-91, prof., 1991—, dir. clin. immunology, tissue typing lab., 1984—, mem. grad. council, 1981—, prof., 1991—. Co-author: Illustrated Dictionary of Immunology , 1995, 2d edit., 2003; editor (with J.M. Cruse): Concepts in Immunopathology, Vols. 1-8, 1985—91; co-author: Atlas of Immunology, 1999; editor: he Year in Immunology-1984-85, 1985, The Year in Immunology-1986-8, 1987, The Year in Immunology-1988, 1989, The Year in Immunology-1989-90, 1990, Progress in Experimental Tumor Research, Vol. 32, 1987, Contributions to Microbiology and Immunology, Vol. 8, 1986, Vol. 9, 1987, Vol. 10, 1989, Vol. 11, 1989, The Year in Immunopathology, 1987, Complement Profiles, Vol. 1, 1992; sr. editor: Pathology and Immunopathology Research, 1982—90, sr. editor: Immunologic Research, 1981, sr. editor: Transgenics, 1993—, sr. editor: Experimental and Molecular Pathology, 1999—, series editor: Concepts in Immunopathology, The Year in Immunology, Contributions to Microbiology and Immunology, —, vol. editor: Progress in Experimental Tumor Research, —, immunology editor: Dorland's Illustrated Medical Dictionary, 26th and 27th edits., —; ; contbr. Am. Cancer Soc. grantee, NIH grantee, Wilson Found. grantee, 1990-95. Fellow Royal Soc. Health; mem. AAAS, Am. Assn. Pathologists, Am. Assn. Immunologists, Clin. Immunology Soc., Can. Soc. Immunology, Reticuloendothelial Soc., Am. Soc. Microbiology, Am. Soc. Histocompatibility and Immunogenetics (chmn. publs. com. 2000—), Exptl. Biology and Medicine, N.Y. Acad. Scis., Miss. Acad. Scis., Sigma Xi. Office: U Miss Med Ctr Pathology Dept Dept Pathology 2500 N State St Jackson MS 39216-4500 E-mail: rlewis@pathology.umsmed.edu.

LEWIS, ROBERT ENZER, lexicographer, educator, editor; b. Windber, Pa., Aug. 12, 1934; s. Robert Enzer and Katharine Torrence (Blair) L.; m. Julie Fatt Cureton, May 14, 1977; children: Perrin Lewis Rubin, Torrence Evans Lewis; stepchildren: Sarah Cureton Kaufman, James S. Cureton. BA, Princeton U., 1959; MA, U. Pa., 1962, PhD, 1964. Tchr. English Mercersburg (Pa.) Acad., 1959-60; teaching fellow U. Pa., Phila., 1961-63; lectr. Ind. U., Bloomington, 1963-64, asst. prof., 1964-68, assoc. prof., 1968-75, prof. English, 1975-82, U. Mich., Ann Arbor, 1982—. Author: (with A. McIntosh) Descriptive Guide to the Manuscripts of the Prick of Conscience, 1982, (with others) Index of Printed Middle English Prose, 1985; editor: De Miseria Condicionis Humane (Lotario dei Segni), 1978; co-editor: Middle English Dictionary, 1982-83, editor-in-chief: vols. 8, 9, 10, 11, 12, 13, 1984-2001; gen. editor: Chaucer Libr., 1970—, chmn. editl. com., 1978-89, 97—. Bd. regents Mercersburg Acad., 1975-87. U.S. Army, 1954-56. Vis. rsch. fellow Inst. Advanced Studies in the Humanities, U. Edinburgh, 1973-74; Am. Coun. Learned Socs. fellow, 1979-80. Mem. Medieval Acad. Am. (mem. publs. com. 1987-92), Dictionary Soc. N.Am., New Chaucer Soc. Episcopalian. Office: U Mich Dept English 3187 Angell Hall Ann Arbor MI 48109-1003 E-mail: relewis@umich.edu.

LEWIS, ROBERT HENRY, lay worker; b. Chillicothe, Tex., Oct. 16, 1921; s. William Arnet and Minnie Easter (Stuckey) L.; m. Miriam Agnes Kothgassner, Mar. 10, 1946; children: Cindy Kaye Lewis Shaw, Pamela Jo Lewis Owens. BSin Elec. Engring., Tex. Tech U., 1952; postgrad., U. Ala., 1965-70. Registered elec. engr. Tex., Ala. Retired engr., 1981; treas., deacon Willowbrook Bapt. Ch., Huntsville, Ala., 1981-96; mem. Camden (Ala.) Bapt. Ch., 1997—. Deacon Camden Bapt. Ch., 1981. Mem. Rep. Presdl. Task Force. With U.S. Army, 1942-46. Mem. IEEE, Nat. Assn. Investors Corp., Nat. Assn. Investment Corp. (chmn. bd. Ala. chpt.). Home: 212 Broad St Camden AL 36726-1704

LEWIS, ROBERT JOHN CORNELIUS KOONS, university library director, consultant; b. Feb. 15, 1938; s. Frank Ashby and Dorothy Elaine (Koons) L.; m. Martha Marie Popejoy, Dec. 22, 1957 (div. 1964); 1 child, Stephen Ashley; m. Helena Barbara Vaughn Schumacker, Sept. 11, 1968 (div. 1976); children: Matthew, Randolph; m. Marguerita S. Kris, July 28, 1985 (dec. Feb. 2001). BA in History of Religion, George Washington U., 1961, MA in Secondary Edn., 1966; MSLS, Cath. U. Am., 1974. Intelligence analyst CIA, Washington, 1958-62; tech. libr. supr. Bell Aerospace, Tucson, 1968-70; info. officer Ambionics Inc., Washington, 1970-73; law libr. Patton, Boggs & Blow, 1973-75; rschr. George Washington U., 1976-78; libr. dir. Benjamin Franklin U., 1979—. Oriental art cons. Silverman Galleries, Alexandria, Va., 1978—; libr. dir. Cushman, Darby & Cushman, 1988-90, Nat. Geneal. Soc., 1990-93; libr. Met. Club, 1994—. Author, compiler: Brief History of the Rose Mount Branch of the Surles (Searles) Lewis Family of Virginia, 1976, collected poems: Quatrains based on the Love Poems of the 6th Dalai Lama and other poems, 1979, Lewis Patriarchs of Early Va. and Md., 1989, rev. edit., 1991, rev. 3d. edit., 1998, Welsh Family Coats of Arms, 1995. With U.S. Army, 1963-65. Awarded title of Gyalwa Karma Lozang Dondrup, by Kalu Rinpoche of Darjeeling, 1977; hon. grantee of arms Coll. of Arms, London, 1998. Mem. ALA (pres. com. 1982), Assn. Former Intelligence Officers, Spl. Librs. Assn., Nat. Geneal. Soc. (councilor 1990-93), Soc. Geneal. of London, Jamestowne Soc., The Augustan Soc., Mahikari of Am. Club, Subud Club, Theosophical Soc. Club, Sigma Phi Epsilon. Episcopalian. Home: 18612 Sage Way Germantown MD 20874-2041 Office: Met Club Libr 1700 H St NW Washington DC 20006-4601 E-mail: library@metroclub.com.

LEWIS, ROBERT LAWRENCE, lawyer, educator; b. N.Y.C., Sept. 25, 1919; s. Isador and Sadie (Holzinger) L.; m. Frieda Friedman, Nov. 24, 1940 (dec. 1961); children— Brian S., Paul E., David N.; m. Joanne Marcia Waxman, June 16, 1963; children— Pavia S., Eraclea S. AB, Hamilton Coll., 1940; LL.B., Case Western Res. U., 1948. With firm Ulmer & Berne, Cleve., 1948-64, ptnr., 1956-64; ret., 1964. Prof. law, dir. grad. div. Cleve.-Marshall Law Sch. (now Cleve. State U.), 1948-53; bd. dirs. Banner Industries, Inc., Cleve.; scholar-in-residence, prof. classics Cuayhoga C.C.; adj. prof. nonprofit governance Case Western Res. U., Cleve. Author: Five Angry Women, 1990, Agatharcus, 1993. Cons., evaluator North Central Assn. Colls. and Schs., Middle States Assn. Mem. Cleve. Area Arts Council, 1971-73; pres. Fairmount Center for Creative and Performing Arts, 1973-75; trustee, chmn. bd. Cuyahoga Community Coll.; trustee Cuyahoga Community Coll. Found., Playhouse Sq. Found., Cleve., Cleve. Commn. Higher Edn., Lake Erie Coll., Council for Interinstnl. Leadership, Pace Assn., New Orgn. for Visual Arts; bd. dirs. Assn. Governing Bds. Univs. and Colls.; bd. advisers Cleve. Ballet; trustee, v.p. New Cleve. Opera Co. Served to 1st lt., arty. and ordnance corps AUS, 1942-46, NATOUSA. Decorated Legion of Merit, Purple Heart Mem. Exec. Order Ohio Commodore, Phi Beta Kappa. Home: 2425 N Park Blvd Apt 4 Cleveland OH 44106-3154 Office: 900 Bond Ct Bldg Cleveland OH 44114 *There is neither a standard nor a uniform set of qualities which best fits one to be a member of society, and anyone who contends to the contrary, may be equated with the infamous and mythical Procrustes. I for one prefer the preservation of individuality. No one of us should be fitted to the bed of Procrustes. I prefer that we shall all survive; and each of us shall then be the richer for the survival of the other.*

LEWIS, ROBERT LEE, lawyer; b. Oxford, Miss., Feb. 26, 1944; s. Ernest Elmo and Johnice Georgia (Thirkield) L.; children: Yolanda Sherice, Robert Lee Jr., Dion Terrell, Viron Lamar, William Lovell. BA, Ind. U., 1970, JD, 1973; M in Pub. Service, West Ky. U., 1980. Bar: Ind. 1973, Ky. 1979, U.S. Ct. Claims, U.S. Ct. Internat. Trade, U.S. Tax. Ct., U.S. Ct. Mil. Appeals, U.S. Ct. Appeals (fed. cir.), U.S. Supreme Ct. Sole practice, Evansville, Ind., 1973-75, Gary, 1980—; atty., army officer U.S. Army, Ft. Knox, Ky., 1975-78; appellate referee Ind. Employment Security Div., Indpls., 1978-80. Mem. adv. com. Vincennes (Ind.) U., 1983—; bd. dirs. Opportunities Industrialization Ctr., Evansville, 1973-75. Served to sgt. JAGC, USMC, 1962-66, Vietnam, sgt. U.S. Army, 1975-78, lt. col. USAR. Named Ky. Col. Mem. ABA, Ind. Bar Assn., Ky. Bar Assn., Nat. Bar Assn., Ind. Bd. Realtors, Ind. U. Alumni Assn., Phi Alpha Delta. Methodist. Home and Office: 2148 W 11th Ave Gary IN 46404-2306

LEWIS, ROBERT TURNER, former psychologist; b. Taft, Calif., June 17, 1923; s. D. Arthur and Amy Belle (Turner) L.; m. Jane Badham, Mar. 23, 1946; children: Jane, William, Richard. BA, U. So. Calif., 1947, MA, 1950; PhD, U. Denver, 1952. Chief psychologist Hollywood Presbyn. Hosp., L.A., 1953-58; dir. psychol. svcs. Salvation Army, Pasadena, Calif., 1958-68; dir. Pasadena Psychol. Ctr., 1964-74; successively asst. prof., assoc. prof. and prof. Calif. State U., L.A., 1952-83, prof. emeritus, 1984—. Assoc. dir. Cortical Function Lab., L.A., 1972-84; clin. dir. Diagnostic Clinic, West Covina, Calif., 1983-85; dir. Job Stress Clinic, Santa Ana, Calif., 1985-95. Author: Taking Chances, 1979, A New Look at Growing Older, 1995, Money Hangups, 1995; co-author: Money Madness, 1978, Human Behavior, 1974, The Psychology of Abnormal Behavior, 1961. Lt (j.g.) USNR, 1943-46, PTO. Mem. APA, Calif. State Pscyhol. Assn. Republican.

LEWIS, ROGER KUTNOW, architect, educator, author; b. Houston, Jan. 9, 1941; s. Nathan D. and Betty K. Lewis; m. Eleanor Draper Roberts, June 24, 1967; 1 child, Kevin Michael. BArch, MIT, 1964, MArch, 1967. Registered architect, D.C., Va., Md. Vol. architect Peace Corps, Nabeul, Tunisia, 1964-66; designer Wilkes & Faulkner, Washington, 1967-68; ptnr. Chavarria/Lewis Assocs., 1968-71; prin. Roger K. Lewis AIA & Assocs., 1971-80; pres. Pecla Corp., 1971-81; ptnr. Chesapeake Design Group, Balt., 1980-81; prin. Roger K. Lewis FAIA, Architect & Planner, Washington, 1981—. Prof. U. Md. Sch. Arch., 1968—; mem. D.C. Com. on Design Arts, Washington, 1988-92; design advisor City of Alexandria, Va.; nat. peer profl. Gen. Svcs. Adminstrn. Pub. Bldg. Svc. Design Excellence Program. Author: Architect? A Candid Guide to the Profession, 1985, revised edit., 1998, Shaping the City, 1987; co-author Growth Management Handbook, 1989; author articles in jours.and periodicals, chpts. in books, encys.; columnist The Washington Post, 1984—. Trustee Capital Children's Mus. Recipient Fed. Design Achievement award Nat. Endowment for the Arts, Washington, 1988, numerous awards Am. Planning Assn., AAUW, 1985—. Fellow AIA (numerous design awards 1973—); mem. Faberge Arts Found. (bd. advs.), Cosmos Club. Home: 5034 1/2 Dana Pl NW Washington DC 20016-3441 Office: Univ Md Sch Of Architecture College Park MD 20742-0001 E-mail: rogershome@aol.com.

LEWIS, RON, congressman; b. Greenup County, Ky., Sept. 14, 1946; m. Kayi Gambill, 1966; children: Ronald Brent, Allison Faye. Student, Morehead State U.; BA in History and Polit. Sci., U. Ky., 1969; MA in Higher Edn., Morehead State U., 1981; student, USN Officer Candidate Sch. Ordained to ministry Bapt. Ch. With Ky. Hwy. Dept., Ea. State Hosp.; with sales various cos.; tchr. Watterson Coll., 1980-85; pastor White Mills Bapt. Ch.; owner small bus. Elizabethtown, Ky.; mem. 103d-106th Congresses from 2d Ky. Dist., 1994—, mem. ways & means com., subcoms., mem. govt. reform com. Past pres. Hardin and Larue County Jail Ministry. Named Guardian of Sr.' Rights, Tax Fairness Srs.; League Pvt. Property Rights, Coun. Citizens Against Govt. Waste, Nat. Fed. Ind. Bus. Mem. Severns Valley Ministerial Assn., Elizabethtown C. of C. Office: US Ho of Reps 2418 Rayburn Ho Office Bldg Washington DC 20515-1702*

LEWIS, RONALD WAYNE, lawyer; b. Buffalo, May 13, 1943; s. George Weber and Marianne (Parsons) L.; m. Lisa Scruggs; children: Joshua Byron, Kristopher Byron, Katherine Byron, Annalise N. AB, Dartmouth Coll., Hanover, N.H., 1965; MAT in French, Harvard U., 1969; JD, U. Miss., Oxford, 1978. Bar: Miss. 1978, U.S. Dist. Ct. (no. dist.) Miss. 1978, U.S. Ct. Appeals (5th cir.) 1979, U.S. Dist. Ct. (so. dist.) Miss. 1985, U.S. Supreme Ct. 1990, U.S. Claims Ct. 1991. Pvt. practice, Oxford, 1978-81; assoc. Hill, Lewis & Bell, 1981-83, Hill & Lewis, Oxford, 1983-86, Holcomb, Dunbar, Connell, Chaffin & Willard, Oxford, 1986-88; pvt. practice, 1988—. CJA criminal def. tng. coord. No. Jud. Dist., Miss., 1991—, CJA panel rep. to nat. confs., 1995—. Mem. Lafayette County Dem. Exec. Com., Oxford, 1985-96, chmn., 1987-91; bd. dirs. ACLU of Miss., 1989-90, Miss. Assn. for Children with Learning Disabilities, 1990-91; mem. instnl. rev. bd. U. Miss., 1999—. Mem. ABA, ATLA, Nat. Assn. Criminal Def. Lawyers, Miss. Trial Lawyers, Miss. Bar, Lafayette County Bar Assn., Am. Inn. of Ct. Ill. (bencher). Office: PO Box 207 607 S Lamar Blvd Oxford MS 38655-4428

LEWIS, ROY ROOSEVELT, physicist; b. Richmond, Va., Mar. 4, 1935; s. Jesse NMN and Elizabeth (Lewis) L.; m. Debra Blondell, Sept. 21, 1968 (div. Aug. 1974); 1 child, Roy Jr.; m. Linda Eleanor, Dec. 19, 1985. BS, Va. Union U., Richmond, 1958; MS, Howard U., 1962, UCLA, 1969, PhD, 1972. Asst. prof. UCLA, 1970-72; mem. tech. staff Hughes Rsch. Lab., Malibu, Calif., 1972-75, Aerospace Corp., El Segundo, 1977-81, TRW, Redondo Beach, 1981-82; dir. minority engring. Calif. State U., Long Beach, 1982-83, assoc. prof., 1982-86, Calif. State Polytech. U., Pomona, 1986-89; faculty fellow Jet Propulsion Lab. Calif. Inst. Tech., Pasadena, 1987-89, mem. tech. staff, 1989-93; pres. Roy Lewis & Assocs., a sci. cons. firm, Inglewood, Calif., 1993—. Author: LewLearns, Science Lessons For Children, 1977; contbr. articles to profl. jours. Mem. Am. Soc. Engring. Edn., Nat. Soc. Black Physicists, L.A. Coun. Black Engrs., IEEE, Inglewood Dem. Club, Sigma Xi, Alpha Phi Alpha, Sigma Phi Sigma. Episcopalian. Home: 1401 Overhill Dr Inglewood CA 90302-1346 E-mail: royphd@yahoo.com.

LEWIS, SAMUEL WINFIELD, retired government official, former ambassador; b. Houston, Oct. 1, 1930; s. Samuel Winfield and Sue Roselle (Hurley) L.; m. Sallie Kate Smoot, June 20, 1953; children: Pamela Gracelle, Richard Winfield. BA magna cum laude, Yale U., 1952; MA, Johns Hopkins U., 1954; PhD (hon.), Tel Aviv U., 1985, Hebrew U. Jerusalem, 1985, Weizman Inst. Sci., 1985; DHL (hon.), Hebrew Union Coll., 1986, Balt. Hebrew U., 1988; LLD (hon.), Salem-Teikyo U., 1991. Exec. asst. Am. Trucking Assn., Washington, 1953-54; fgn. svc. officer Dept. State, Washington, 1954-85; consular officer Naples, Italy, 1954-55; consul Florence, Italy, 1955-59; officer-in-charge Italian affairs Washington, 1959-61; spl. asst. to undersec. state, 1961; spl. asst. to spl. rep. of pres., 1961-63; dep. asst. dir. US AID Mission to Brazil, Rio de Janeiro, 1964-65; exec. officer embassy, 1965-67; dep. dir. Office Brazil Affairs, Washington, 1967-68; sr. staff mem. for Latin Am. Affairs Nat. Security Council, White House, 1968-69; spl. asst. for policy planning Bur. Inter-Am. Affairs, 1969; spl. asst. to dir. gen. Fgn. Svc., 1970-71; dep. chief mission and counselor embassy Kabul, Afghanistan, 1971-74; dep. dir. policy planning staff Dept. State, 1974-75, asst. sec. state for internat. orgn., 1975-77; U.S. ambassador to Israel, 1977-85; lectr., diplomat-in-residence Johns Hopkins Fgn. Policy Inst., Washington, 1985-86; pres. U.S. Inst. of Peace, 1987-93; dir. policy planning staff U.S. Dept. State, 1993-94, cons., 1994-95. Sr. internat. fellow The Dayan Ctr., Tel Aviv U., 1986-87; chmn. bd. overseers Harry S. Truman Rsch. Inst. for Advancement of Peace, Hebrew U., 1986-91; guest scholar The Brookings Inst., Washington, 1987; mem. bd. advisors Washington Inst. Near East Policy, 1986-93, 98—, counselor, 1995-98; adv. com. Search for Common Ground in the Mid. East, Washington, 1994—; vis. prof. Hamilton Coll., spring 1995, fall 1997, adj. prof. Sch. Fgn. Svc., Georgetown U., 1996; sr. advisor Israel Policy Forum, 1998—. Author: Making Peace Among Arabs and Israelis, 1991; contbg. author: The Middle East: Ten Years After Camp David, 1988, Soviet-American Competition in the Middle East, 1988, Israel: The Peres Era, 1987, The United States States and Israel: Evolution of an Unwritten Alliance, 1999; contbr. articles to profl. jours., also N.Y. Times, Washington Post. Bd. dirs. Inst. for Study Diplomacy, Georgetown U., 1994—; vice chmn. Ctr. Preventive Action, Coun. Fgn. Rels., 1994-97. Recipient William A. Jump award for outstanding service in pub. adminstrn., 1967, Meritorious Honor award Dept. State, 1967, Meritorious Honor award AID, 1967, Pres.' Mgmt. Improvement cert., 1971, Distinguished Honor award Dept. State, 1977, 85, Disting. Alumnus award Johns Hopkins U., 1980, Wilbur J. Carr award Dept. State, 1985; vis. fellow Princeton U., 1963-64. Mem. Am. Acad. Diplomacy (bd. dirs. 1995—, vice chmn. bd. dirs. 1995-99), Am. Fgn. Svc. Assn., U.S. Interreligious Com. for Peace in the Middle East, UN Assn., Coun. Fgn. Rels., Middle East Inst., Assn. Diplomatic Studies and Tng. (bd. dirs. 1995—), Inst. World Affairs (bd. dirs. 1996—), Cousteau Soc., Sierra Club, Phi Beta Kappa. Episcopalian. E-mail: sixtymeter@aol.com.

LEWIS, SANDRA COMBS, research psychologist, writer; b. Troup County, Ga., Oct. 8, 1939; d. Robert Milton and Imogene (Richardson) Combs; children: Virginia Susan Lewis , Charles James III. AB, Wesleyan Coll., 1961; MEd, Mercer U., 1972, Ga. State U., 1976; PhD, U. Ga., 1980. Personnel asst. Sears Roebuck & Co., Atlanta, 1961—62; rsch. asst. bd. regents U. Sys. Ga., 1962—63; asst. psychol. svcs. Bibb County Bd. Edn., Macon, 1972—73; instr. Macon Jr. Coll., 1973, 1982, Wesleyan Coll., 1973—75, 1981; psychometrist Middle Ga. Psychoednl. Ctr., 1975—76; instr. Mercer U., 1980—82. Presenter at profl. confs. Collaborator: (books) Christian Love and Problems of Living, 1992, God and Positive Christianity, 1998, Psychology for Life, 2000, A Revolutionary View of Education and Teaching for the Third Millennium, 2002. Pres. Macon Wesleyan Alumnae Club, 1973-74; bd. dirs. Family Counseling Ctr., Macon, 1975-76; ruling elder, clk. of session Northminster Presbyn. Ch., Macon, 1988-90, 94-96, vice moderator Presbyn. Women, 1989-90, 2002, moderator Presbyn. Women, 1990-91; v.p. Fore(In)Sight Found., 1991—. Mem.: APA, Mid. Ga. Psychol. Assn., Ga. Psychol. Assn. Avocations: gardening, photography. Home and Office: 4976 Oxford Rd Macon GA 31210-3059

LEWIS, SCOTT P. lawyer; b. Chgo., 1950; BA magna cum laude, Yale U., 1971; JD cum laude, Harvard U., 1974. Bar: Mass. 1974. Mem. Palmer & Dodge LLP, Boston, 1974—. Office: Palmer & Dodge LLP 111 Huntington Ave Boston MA 02199

LEWIS, SHARYN LEE, sculptor; b. Carmel, Calif., July 31, 1946; d. William Albert and Hazel Elisabeth Lewis; m. Robert John Western, Mar. 22, 1986. Asst. art tchr. Benin (Nigeria) Coll., 1974-76; comml. artist KTT Art Svc., Campbell, Calif., 1976-77; graphic artist, illustrator Intersil Corp., Santa Clara, 1977-80; sr. artist, graphic designer Pro-Log Corp., Monterey, 1980-83; freelance graphic designer, 1983-92; sculptor, 1992—. Sculptor: exhibitions include: Mystic Maritime Gallery, Mystic Seaport, Conn., 1995-96, 97-98, 99-2000, 2001-02, Big Horn Galleries, Carmel, Calif., 1995-96, Fifth Ann. Loveland (Colo.) Sculpture Invitational, 1996, Monterey Peninsula Art Found. Ann. Members Show, 1997, Monterey Mus. of Art, 1998, 99, 2000, 01, 02; also in many private collections in U.S. Mem. Internat. Sculpture Ctr., Washington, Nat. Sculpture Soc., N.Y.C., Nat. Mus. Women in Art, Washington, Met Mus. of Art, N.Y.C., Monterey Mus. of Art. E-mail: artnbrnz@mbay.net.

LEWIS, SHELDON NOAH, technology consultant; b. Chgo., July 1, 1934; s. Jacob Joseph and Evelyn (Mendelsohn) Iglowitz; m. Suzanne Joyce Goldberg, June 17, 1957; children: Sara Lynn, Matthew David, Rachel Ann. BA with honors, MS (Univ. fellow), Northwestern U., 1956; PhD (Eastman Kodak fellow), UCLA, 1959; postgrad. (NSF fellow), U. Basel, Switzerland, 1959-60; postgrad. cert. in research mgmt, Indsl. Research Inst., Harvard U., 1973. With Rohm & Haas Co., 1960-78, head lab., 1963-68, research supr., 1968-73, dir. splty. chem. research, 1973-74; gen. mgr. DCL Lab. AG subs., Zurich, Switzerland, 1974-75; dir. European Labs. Valbonne, France, 1975-76; corp. dir. research and devel. worldwide for polymers, resins and monomers Spring House, Pa., 1976-78; with The Clorox Co., Oakland, Calif., 1978-91, v.p. R&D, 1978, group v.p., 1978-84, exec. v.p., 1984-91, also bd. dirs.; pres. SNL Inc., Lafayette, 1991—. Mem. indsl. panel on sci. and tech. NSF. Referee: Jour. Organic Chemistry; patentee in field; contbr. articles to profl. publs. Mem. Calif. Inst. Adv. Bd., World Affairs Council, UCLA Chemistry Adv. Council, Bay Area Sci. Fair Adv. Bd., Mills Coll. Adv. Council for Sci. and Math. Recipient cert. in patent law Phila. Patent Law Assn., 1962, Roon award for coatings research Fedn. Socs. Coatings Tech., 1966, cert. of service Wayne State U. Polymer Conf. Series, 1967, cert. in mgmt. by objectives Am. Mgmt. Research, Inc., 1972 Mem. Soap and Detergent Assn. (bd. dirs.), Chem. Ind. Inst. of Toxicology (bd. dirs.), Indsl. Rsch. Inst., Am. Chem. Soc. (chmn. Phila. polymer sect. 1970-71), Soc. Chem. Industry London, Sigma Xi. Jewish. Office: SNL Inc 3711 Rose Ct Lafayette CA 94549-3030

LEWIS, SHERMAN RICHARD, JR. investment banker; b. Ottawa, Ill., Dec. 11, 1936; s. Sherman Richard and Julia Audrey (Rusteen) L.; m. Dorothy Marie Downie, Sept. 9, 1967; children: Thomas, Catherine, Elizabeth, Michael. AB, Northwestern U., 1958; MBA, U. Chgo., 1964. With investment dept. Am. Nat. Bank & Trust Co., Chgo., 1961-64; v.p. Halsey, Stuart & Co., N.Y.C., 1964-70, v.p. in charge corp. fin. dept., 1970-73; v.p. C.J. Lawrence & Sons, 1970; ptnr. Loeb, Rhoades & Co., 1973-76, ptnr. in charge corp. fin. dept., 1975-76, exec. v.p., bd. dirs., 1976-77, pres., co-chief exec. officer, 1977-78; vice chmn., co-chief exec. officer Loeb Rhoades, Hornblower & Co., 1978-79; pres. Shearson/Am. Express Inc., 1979-82, vice chmn., 1983-84, Shearson Lehman/Am. Express Inc., 1984-85, Shearson Lehman Bros. Inc., 1985-87, Shearson Lehman Hutton Inc., 1988-89; co-chief exec. officer, vice chmn., chmn. exec. com. Lehman Bros., 1990; vice chmn. Shearson Lehman Bros. Holdings, Inc., N.Y.C., 1990-93, Lehman Bros. Holdings, Inc., 1990—93, Lehman Bros. Inc., 1993—. Mem. Pres.'s Commn. on Housing, 1981-82, Pres.'s Coun. on Internat. Youth Exch., 1982-88; trustee Northwestern U., 1992—, regent, 1990-97; mem. bd. visitors Weinberg Coll. Arts and Scis., Northwestern U., 1981—, chmn., 1990-96; mem. coun. Grad. Sch. Bus., U. Chgo., 1991—; bd. dirs. The Korea Soc., U.S.-Greece Bus. Coun., N.Y. Eye and Ear Infirmary, U.S. Japan Bus. Coun. Commd. officer USMC, 1958-61. Mem. Coun. on Fgn. Rels., The Pilgrims, Bond Club, Univ. Club, Quogue Field Club, Shinnecock Yacht Club, Quantuck Beach Club. Office: Lehman Bros Inc 745 7th Ave New York NY 10019

LEWIS, SHIRLEY ANN REDD, college president; b. Winding Gulf, W.Va., June 11, 1937; d. Robert Fountain and Thelma Danese (Biggers) Redd; m. Ronal McGhee Lewis, Aug. 17, 1963; 1 child, Mendi Dessalines Shirley. BA, U. Calif., Berkeley, 1960, MSW, 1970; PhD, Stanford U., 1979; cert., U. London, U. Ghana, 1971. Tchr. Ravenswood City Schs., East Palo Alto, Calif., 1962-63, N.Y.C. Schs., 1964-65; counselor coordinator U. Calif., Berkeley, 1967-71; college instr. Los Altos (Calif.) Community Coll., 1970-72; researcher Stanford (Calif.) Sch. Edn., 1972-79; prof. Peabody Coll., Vanderbilt U., Nashville, 1980-81; prof., assoc. dean Meharry Med. Coll., 1982-85; asst. gen. sec. The Black Coll. Fund, 1986-94; pres. Paine Coll., Augusta, Ga., 1994—. Co-author: The Nairobi Method, 1972, The 1-2-3 Method, 1985. Bd. dirs. United Negro Coll. Fund, Ga. Bank & Trust, Morris Mus., United Way. Recipient Carnegie fellow, 1968-70; named Outstanding Contributor, Meharry Med. Coll. Pre Alumni Assn., 1986. Mem. Nat. Assn. of Ind. Colls. & Univs., Coun. Pres. (bd. dirs.), Alpha Kappa Al pha, The Links. Democrat. United Methodist. Avocations: reading, public speaking. Office: Paine Coll 1235 15th St Augusta GA 30901-3105

LEWIS, SHIRLEY JEANE, psychotherapist, educator; b. Phoenix, Aug. 23; d. Herman and Leavy (Hutchinson) Smith; m. Edgar Anthony Lewis (div.); children: Edgar Anthony (dec.), Roshaun, Lucy Ann Jonathan. AA, Phoenix C.C., 1957; BA, Ariz. State U., 1960; MS, San Diego State U., 1975, MA, 1986, Azusa Pacific U., 1982; PhD, U. So. Calif., 1983. Cert. tchr. Calif. Recreation leader Phoenix Parks and Recreation Dept., 1957-62; columnist Ariz. Tribune, Phoenix, 1958-59; tchr. phys. edn. San Diego Unified Schs., 1962—; adult educator San Diego C.C., 1973—; head counselor Gomper Secondary Sch./San Diego Unified Schs., 1998-2001. Instr. psychology, health, Black studies, 1977—, counselor, 1981—; cmty. counselor S.E. Counseling and Cons. Svcs. and Narcotics Prevention and Edn. Systems, Inc., San Diego, 1973-77; counselor educator, counselor edn. dept. San Diego State U., 1974-77; marriage, family, child counselor Counseling and Cons. Ctr., San Diego, 1977—; inservice educator San Diego Unified and San Diego County Sch. Dists., 1973-77; Fulbright Exch. counselor, London, 1994-96, asst. prin. Oceanside Unifed Sch. Dist., 1997-98; lectr. in field. Contbr. articles to profl. jours. Girl Scout phys. fitness cons., Phoenix, 1960-62; vol. cmty. tutor for high sch. students, San Diego, 1963; sponsor Tennis Club for Youth, San Diego, 1964-65; troop leader Girl Scouts U.S., Lemon Grove, Calif., 1972-74; vol. counselor USN Alcohol Rehab. Ctr., San Diego, 1978; mem. sch. coun.'s adv. bd. San Diego State U. Named Woman of Yr., Phoenix, 1957, One of Outstanding Women of San Diego, 1980; recipient Phys. Fitness Sch. award and Demonstration Sch. award Pres.'s Coun. on Phys. Fitness, Taft Jr. H.S., 1975, Excel award Corp. Excellence Edn., 1989; Delta Sigma Theta scholar, 1957-60; Alan Korrick scholar, 1956. Mem. NEA, Calif. Tchrs. Assn., San Diego Tchrs. Assn., Assn. Marriage and Family Counselors, Am. Personnel and Guidance Assn., Calif. Assn. Health, Phys. Edn. and Recreation (v.p. health), Am. Alliance of Health, Phys. Edn. and Recreation, Assn. Black Psychologists (corr. sec. 1993), Assn. African-Am. Educators, Delta Sigma Theta (Delta of Yr. 1987). Democrat. Baptist. Home: 1226 Armacost Rd San Diego CA 92114-3307 Office: Gompers Secondary Sch 1005 47th St San Diego CA 92102-3699 E-mail: slewis@mail.sandi.net. *Personal philosophy: High self-esteem, responsibility, self-discipline and striving to achieve personal goals are necessary for a healthful lifestyle regardless of one's personal, historical circumstances. The initial access to such characteristics, in reality, may only be in one's invention of fantasy.*

LEWIS, STANFORD, entrepreneur, educator; b. Hughes, Ark., Apr. 10, 1963; s. Oscar Lewis and Earlene Robinson; children: Wsir, Nika, Amen. Student, LeMoyne-Owen Coll., 1981, Oxford U., 1983; degree in Polit. Sci. & Philosophy, Fisk U., 1985; MST, Harvard U., 1991; M in Profl. Studies, Cornell U., 1994. Ordained minister. Student devel. specialist Seton Hall, East Orange, NJ, 1992; history & geography tchr. Chad Sci. Acad., Newark, 1993—95; vis. lectr. Rtugers U., Neward, 1993—96; prin., owner Stanford Lewis Enterprises, Maywood, Ill., 1996—. Vis. lectr. Lewis U., Romeoville, Ill., 1998—. Author: The Falsification & Fabrication of Ancient Egypt, 2002. Chmn. drug-free workplace Maywood C. of C., Maywood, 1996—2002; speech writer State Rep. 7 Dist., 2000—02; bd. trustee Maywood Libr., 2001—; bd. dir. Fred Hampton Scholarship, 1998. Fellow, Harvard U., 1985—87, Cornell U., 1989—90. Democrat. Avocation: travel. Home: 1416 South 21st Ave Maywood IL 60153 Office: Stanford Lewis Enterprise 1030 South 17th Ave Maywood IL 60153

LEWIS, STEPHEN RICHMOND, JR. economist, educator, academic administrator; b. Englewood, N.J., Feb. 11, 1939; s. Stephen Richmond Lewis and Esther (Magan) Lewish; m. Judith Frost, 1996; children from previous marriage: Virginia, Deborah, Mark. BA, Williams Coll., 1960, LLD, 1987; MA, Stanford U., 1962, PhD, 1963; LHD, Doshisha U., 1993. Instr. Stanford U., 1962—63; research advisor Pakistan Inst. Devel. Econs., Karachi, 1963—65; asst. prof. econs. Harvard U., 1965—66, Williams Coll., 1966—68, assoc. prof., 1968—73, prof., 1973—76, Herbert H. Lehman prof., 1976—87, provost of coll., 1968—71, 1973—77, spl. asst. to pres., 1979—80, dir. Williams-Botswana Project, 1982—88, chmn. dept. econs., 1984—86; vis. sr. research fellow Inst. Devel. Studies, Nairobi, Kenya, 1971—73; econ. cons. to Ministry of Finance and Devel. Planning, Govt. of Botswana, 1975—; vis. fellow Inst. Devel. Studies, Sussex, England, 1986—87; pres., prof. econs. Carleton Coll., Northfield, Minn., 1987—. Cons. econs. Ford Found., Edna McConnell Clark Found., World Bank, Orgn. Econ. Coop. and Devel., Govts. of Kenya, Philippines, Botswana; trustee Carnegie Endowment for Internat. Peace, 1988—. Author (with others): Relative Price Changes and Industrialization in Pakistan, 1969; author: Economic Policy and Industrial Growth in Pakistan, 1969, Pakistan: Industrialization and Trade Policy, 1970, Williams in the Eighties, 1980, Taxation for Development, 1983, South Africa: Has Time Run Out?, 1986, Policy Choice and Development Performance in Botswana, 1989, The Economics of Apartheid, 1989; mem. editl. bd.: Jour. Econ. Lit., 1985—87; contbr. chapters to books, articles to profl. jours. Exec. com. Indianhead coun. Boy Scouts Am., 1989—. Decorated Presdl. Order of Meritorious Svc. Botswana; recipient Disting. Eagle Scout award, 1993; fellow, Danforth Found., 1960—63, dissertation, Ford Found., 1962—63. Mem.: Am. Econ. Assn., Nat. Tax Assn., Coun. on Fgn. Rels., Phi Beta Kappa. Office: Carleton Coll Office Pres 1 N College St Ofc Pres Northfield MN 55057-4001

LEWIS, SYLVIA DAVIDSON, foundation executive; b. Akron, Ohio, Apr. 28, 1927; d. Harry I. and Helen E. (Stein) Davidson; m. Allen D. Lewis, Oct. 12, 1947; children: Pamela Lewis Kanfer, Randy, Daniel, Cynthia Lewis Lagdameo. Student, U. Mich., 1945-47, U. Akron, 1961-62. Editor Akron Jewish News, 1948-50; tchr. Revere Rd. Congregation, Akron, 1964-70; office mgr. Acme Lumber & Fence Co., 1970-85; nat. pres. NA'AMAT USA (Movement of Working Women & Vols.), N.Y.C., 1993-97. Pres. Planned Parenthood Summit Portage and Medina Counties, 1999-2001; founding mem. Govt. Affairs Com., Columbus, Ohio, 1981—, exec. com., 1988-89; v.p. Akron Jewish Cmty. Fedn., 1988-94, pres. women's divsn., 1987-90; elect mem. Akron Jewish Cmty. Bd., 1999—. Named Woman of Distinction, YWCA Summit County, 2001; named one of No. Ohio's Top Women Profls., No. Ohio Live mag., 1997; named to Ohio Women's Hall of Fame, 1995; recipient Golden Rule award, J.C. Penney, 1994, Vol. of Yr. award, Lippman Cmty. Day Sch., 1992, Commendation of Honor award, Ohio Gen. Assembly, 1993, Women of Achievement award, YWCA of Summit County, 1999. Democrat. Jewish. Avocations: reading, writing, travel, grandchildren. Home: 4389 Everett Rd Richfield OH 44286 E-mail: syllewis1@aol.com.

LEWIS, THOMAS PROCTOR, law educator; b. Ashland, Ky., Mar. 26, 1930; s. Blaine and Hallie Maud (Heal) L.; m. Nancy Ann Magruder, Sept. 27, 1949 (dec. 1984); children: Jean, Catherine, Jennifer, Blaine; m. Myrtle Blakley, Jan. 3, 1998. AB, U. Ky., 1959, LLB, 1954; SJD, Harvard U., 1964. Asst. prof. law U. Ky., 1957-59, assoc. prof., 1959-60, prof., 1961-65, acad. asst. to pres., 1964-65, dean Coll. of Law, 1976-82, prof., 1982-98, prof. emeritus, 1998—; prof. law U. Minn., 1965-72, Boston U., 1972-76. Of counsel Wyatt, Tarrant & Combs, 1982-86 ; vis. prof. U. Chgo., 1962, U. Wash., 1963-64; labor arbitrator, 1965—; spl. justice Ky. Supreme Ct., 1995, 97. Author: (with R. Levy, P. Martin) Social Welfare and the Individual, 1971; contbr. articles to law jours. Served with USNR, 1954-57. Mem. Ky., Mass. bar assns., Nat. Acad. Arbitrators, Am. Law Inst. Office: U Ky Law Coll Lexington KY 40506-0001

LEWIS, TONY LLOYD, pastor; b. Lake Charles, La., Sept. 4, 1951; s. Gloria Mae Lewis-Smith; m. Esther Ann Craven, Oct. 1, 1988; 1 child, Kimberly Josephine. Bachelors, Bishop Coll., 1979; Masters, Pitts. Theol. Sem., 1981; DD (hon.), Bethany Theol. Sem., 1987; D of Ministry, Triune Bible Coll. and Sem., 1990. Ordained to ministry, Bapt. Ch., 1980. Youth minister Prosperity Bapt. Ch., L.A., 1975-76; minister of evangelism Concord Bapt. Ch., Dallas, 1977-79; assoc. minister Ctrl. Bapt. Ch., Pitts., 1979-81; sr. pastor Morning Star Bapt. Ch., Portland, Oreg., 1982-91, Macedonia Bapt. Ch., Pomona, Calif., 1991—. Author: (tract) Whatever Happened to that Family Who Joined Our Church Last Month, 1993, From Bootcamp to the Battlefield, Read to Serve, 1996. Exec. bd. dirs. NAACP, Pomona, 1994; invitee White House Inauguration, 1988. Recipient Outstanding Leadership award Bapt. Ministers Fellowship of Portland, 1991, Cert. of Appreciation, Census Complete County Com., 1990. Mem. Nat. Bapt. Conv. Am. (bd. dirs. 1982—), San Gabriel Valley Bapt. Assn. of Pomona Calif. and Vicinity, Inc. (founder, exec. dir. 1991—). Avocations: chess, pool, computers. Office: 710 S Hamilton Blvd Pomona CA 91766-2823

LEWIS, VICTOR BRADLEY, philosopher, educator; b. Wayne, Mich., Feb. 20, 1965; s. Earl Clifford and Rachael Louise Hudson; m. Jody Vaccaro Lewis, July 10, 1999. BA, U. Md., 1987; MA, U. Notre Dame, 1989, PhD, 1997. Asst. prof. philosophy Cath. U. Am., Washington, 1997—. Cons. editor Communio: Internat. Catholic Rev., 1998—. Mem. Am. Philos. Assn., Am. Cath. Philos. Assn., Soc. Ancient Greek Philosophy, Soc. Greek Polit. Thought. Roman Catholic. Office: Cath U Am Sch Philosophy Washington DC 20064-0001 E-mail: lewisb@cua.edu.

LEWIS, W. WALKER, strategic and financial advisory company executive; b. Middletown, Ohio, Sept. 15, 1944; s. W. Walker Jr. and Emily S. (Spivy) L.; m. Ellen Anschuetz, Mar. 30, 1970; children: Walker, Alexandra (Sasha), Morgan. AB, Harvard U., 1967. Mgr. Boston Cons. Group, 1970-72; chmn. Strategic Planning Assocs., Washington, 1972-92; pres. Avon Products, N.Y.C., 1992-94; mng. dir. Kidder Peabody, 1994-96; sr. advisor Dillon Read & Co., 1997—; chmn. Devon Value Advisers, 1997—. Mem. Coun. on Fgn. Rels., Washington Inst. Fgn. Affairs. Office: Devon Value Advisers 399 Park Ave Fl 38 New York NY 10022-4616 E-mail: wlewis@devon-partners.com.

LEWIS, WALTER DAVID, historian, educator; b. Towanda, Pa., June 24, 1931; s. Gordon Cleon and Eleanor Esther (Tobias) L.; m. Carolyn Wyatt Brown, June 12, 1954 (div. 1980); children: Daniel Kent, Virginia Lorraine, Nancy Ellyn; m. Patricia L. Freeman, Apr. 26, 1986. BA cum laude, Pa. State U., 1952, MA, 1954; PhD, Cornell U., 1961. Instr. pub. speaking Hamilton Coll., Clinton, N.Y., 1954-57; fellowship coordinator Eleutherian Mills-Hagley Found., Wilmington, Del.; also lectr. history U. Del., 1959-65; assoc. prof. history SUNY, Buffalo, 1965-71, prof., 1971; Hudson prof. history and engring. Auburn (Ala.) U., 1971-95, disting. Univ. prof., 1994—. Dir. univ. project tech., human values and so. future, 1974-79; sr. fellow in Am. civilization Cornell U., 1958-59; vis. prof. history U. Tex.-Dallas, summer 1982, 83, 84; pres., dir. conf. on history of civil and comml. aviation (ICCA 92), Swiss Transport Mus., Lucerne, Switzerland, 1992; Charles A. Lindbergh prof. of aerospace history Nat. Air and Space Mus., 1993-94. Exec. co-prodr. (documentary film): About Us: A Deep South Portrait, 1977; author: From Newgate to Dannemora: The Rise of the Penitentiary in New York, 1965, Iron and Steel in America, 1976, Sloss Furnaces and The Rise of the Birmingham District: An Industrial Epic, 1994; co-author: Delta: The History of an Airline, 1979, Hopewell Furnace, 1983, The Airway to Everywhere: A History of All American Aviation, 1937-53, 1988; contbg. author: The Professions in America, 1965, Technology in Western Civilization, 1967, The Development of an American Culture, 1969, Notable American Women, 1971, Great Engineers and Pioneers in Technology, 1981, Technology in America, 2d edit., 1990, Science-Technology Relationships, 1993, Eli Whitney's Cotton Gin, 1793-1993, 1994, Bring History Alive, 1996; editor: Fighting the Flying Circus, 1997, Airline Executives and Federal Regulation: Case Studies in American Enterprise from the Airmail Era to the Dawn of the Jet Age, 2000, The Americanization of Edward Bok, 2000; co-editor: Economic Change in the Civil War Era, 1965, The Southern Mystique: Technology and Human Values in Changing Region, 1977; gen. editor Procs. of the Internat. Conf. on the History of Civil and Commercial Aviation, 1995; contbr. articles to profl. jours. Grantee NEH, 1973-79, 80—, Delta Airlines Found. 1973-79, Eleutherian Mills Hist. Libr., 1970-73, 80; postdoctoral fellow Nat. Humanities Inst., U. Chgo., 1978-79, Mellon fellow Va. Hist. Soc., 1988, 89, 92; recipient Leonardo da Vinci medal, (Soc. for the Hist. of Tech., 1993). Mem. Soc. History Tech., Ala. Hist. Assn., Lexington Group Transp. Historians, Phi Beta Kappa. Episcopalian. Home: 210 Lee Dr Auburn AL 36832-6722 Office: Auburn U Dept History 310 E Thach Ave Auburn AL 36830-5415

LEWIS, WAYNE H. investment company executive; b. N.Y.C., July 8, 1931; s. Harry Wayne and Eleanor (Diegoli) L.; m. Mary Jane Durnford, June 18, 1956; 1 child, Laura Alane. AB, Harvard U., 1953. Sales, instr. Exxon Corp., Boston, 1956-59; sales Conn. Gen. Life Ins. Co., Hartford, Conn., 1959-62; mgr. Mass. Gen. Life Ins. Co., Boston, 1962-67; v.p. sales Integon Corp., Winston-Salem, N.C., 1967-69; v.p. Lionel D. Edie & Co., N.Y.C., 1969-72; v.p. fin. planning 1st Pa. Bank, Phila., 1970-72; pres., owner Investor Svcs. Ltd., Villanova, Pa., 1972—. Chmn., bd. trustees Anthony Wayne Found., Paoli, 1991—; pres. Wayne Family Orgn., Paoli, 1988—; mem., oper. com. Wayne Mus., Paoli, 1984—. Mem. Union League Pa. (life), Merion Cricket Club, Desert Mountain Club, The Estancia Club, Chaine des Rotisseurs (officer exec. com. 1982—). Avocations: aerobics, off road driving & hiking, exploring nat. and state parks. Office: Investor Svcs Ltd PO Box 310 Villanova PA 19085-0310 Home: 1404 Mount Pleasant Rd Villanova PA 19085-2111

LEWIS, WAYNE WALTON, industrial engineer; b. Summerville, Ga., Mar. 5, 1951; s. Calvin Tipton and Annie Marie (Robbins) L.; m. Dianne Stone, Dec. 14, 1973 (div. June 1976); 1 child, Christopher Wayne; m. Marie Hardwick Mercer, July 8, 1991; 1 child, Jonathan Michael. AS in Bus. Adminstrn., Kennesaw State U., 1982, BBA in Bus. Adminstrn., 1987; AA in Psychology, Floyd Coll., 1986; A in Specialized Tech. in Indsl. Engring, Pa. State U., 1997. Jr. indsl. engr. Riegel Textile Corp., Trion, Ga., 1971-73; asst. indsl. engr. E.T. Barwick Industries, Barnwell, S.C., 1973-75; tech. svcs. supr. Pharr Yarns of Ga., Rome, 1975-95, Image Industries, Rome, 1995—. Mem. adv. bd. Berry Coll., Rome, Ga., 1991-93. Mem. campaign activities com. Ga. Ho. of Reps., Rome, 1978-98. Mem. Inst. Indsl. Engrs. (pres. 1973-98, Highest Growth award 1987), Grtr. Rome Engring. Assn. Republican. Methodist. Avocations: golf, tennis, lawn- and landscaping. Office: Image Industries 243 Huffaker Rd NW Rome GA 30165-1941 Home: 6 Etowah Dr SE Rome GA 30161-8466

LEWIS, WILBUR H. educational management consultant; b. Belmont, Ohio, Sept. 16, 1930; s. Charles W. and Lily B. (Dunfee) L.; m. Jean E. Lewis, Aug. 23, 1958; children— David, Deretta, Denise, Dawn, Darrin. Student, Miami U., Oxford, Ohio, 1948-51; BSBA, Ohio State U., 1953; M.Ed., Ohio U., 1961, PhD, 1964. Tchr. pub. schs., Scioto County, Ohio, 1957; tchr., adminstr. public schs. Belmont County, 1958-60; grad. asst. Ohio U., 1960-61; prin. high sch., adminstrv. asst. to supt. public schs. Athens, Ohio, 1961-64; asst. prof., adviser to Govt. of Nigeria, 1964-66; asst. supt. pub. schs. Athens, Ohio, 1966-67; prin. high sch. public schs. Wilmington, 1967-68; with Parma (Ohio) City Schs., 1968-77, asst. to supt., 1968-70, asst. supt., 1970-72, assoc. supt., 1972-75, supt., 1975-77, Tucson Unified Sch. Dist., 1977-79; cons. ednl. mgmt. Tucson, 1979—. Vice chmn. nat. adv. coun. Edn. Disadvantaged Children, 1972-80; supt. Ariz. State Schs. for Deaf and Blind, 1994-98. Planning divsn. United Way, Tucson, 1978-80; bd. dirs. Jr. Achievement, 1978-80. With U.S. Army, 1954-56. Recipient numerous civic awards for community service; Kettering Found. fellow, 1970 Mem. Am. Assn. Sch. Adminstrs., Buckeye Assn. Sch. Adminstrs., Masons, Shriners, Rotary Internat. (v.p. Tucson 1987—, past pres., dist. gov.'s rep. group study exch. dist. 9120 Nigeria, dist. 550 1990, chmn. group study exch. dist. 5490 1991-93), Phi Delta Kappa, Lambda Chi Alpha, Sigma Phi Epsilon. Achievements include rsch. in orgnl. devel., adminstrv. behavior patterns, tchr. job satisfaction, student achievement. Home: 7570 E Speedway Blvd Unit 609 Tucson AZ 85710-8823 E-mail: wlewis5@aol.com. *To achieve one must aspire. To aspire one must dream. But if dreams and aspirations are to become achievements one must persevere. The perseverance necessary to turn dreams and aspirations into achievements has always been made easier for me knowing that children and youth were the benefactors of my efforts.*

LEWIS, WILLIAM HENRY, JR. lawyer; b. Durham, N.C., Nov. 12, 1942; s. William Henry Sr. and Phyllis Lucille (Phillips) L.; m. Jo Ann Whitsett, Apr. 17, 1965 (div. Sept. 1982); 1 child, Kimberly N.; m. Peyton Cockrill Davis, Nov. 28, 1987. Student, N.C. State U., 1960-63; AB in Polit. Sci., U. N.C., 1965, JD with honors, 1969. Bar: Calif., D.C., U.S. Dist. Ct. (cen. dist.) Calif., U.S. Ct. Appeals (D.C. cir., 2nd and 5th cirs.), U.S. Supreme Ct. Assoc. Latham & Watkins, Los Angeles, 1969-74; exec. officer Calif. Air Resources Bd., Los Angeles and Sacramento, Calif., 1975-78; dir. Nat. Com. on Air Quality, Washington, 1978-81; counsel Wilmer, Cutler & Pickering, 1981-84; ptnr. Morgan, Lewis & Bockius LLP, 1984—, mgr. nat. environ. practice, 1999—2000. Spl. advisor on environ. policy State of Calif., L.A. and Sacramento, 1975; lectr. Law Sch. U. Va., 1993-97. Bd. dirs. For Love of Children, Inc., Washington, 1985-95, pres., 1987-91; bd. dirs. Advs. for Families, Washington, 1985-87, Hillandale Homeowners Assn., Washington, 1986-87, Thurgood Marshall Ctr. Trust, Washington, 1989-95; mem. EPA Clean Air Act Adv. Com., 1994—; chmn. bd. dirs., co-founder The Montpelier Found., 1998—. Mem. ABA. Home: 3900 Georgetown Ct NW Washington DC 20007-2127 also: 18454 Monteith Farm Rd Gordonsville VA 22942-7560 Office: Morgan Lewis and Bockius LLP 1111 Pennsylvania Ave NW Washington DC 20004

LEWIS, WILLIAM JOHN, aerospace engineer; b. Moncton, N.B., Can., Sept. 3, 1959; s. Ronald Lloyd and Marion Elizabeth (Dodge) L.; m. Shane Andrea Martin, July 16, 1983; children: Theodore William Dodge, Benjamin Peter Dodge. B in Engring., Royal Mil. Coll., Kingston, Ont., Can., 1981, M in Nuclear Engring., 1988; MBA, U. Man., Winnipeg, Can., 1985; B in Edn., Queen's U., Kingston, 1990, MEd, 1991; PhD in Nuclear Engring., Pacific Western U., 1992. Registered profl. engr., Ont. and Man. Commd. 2d lt. Can. Air Force, 1981; advance through grades to maj., 1994—; aerospace engring. officer Dept. Nat. Def., Winnipeg, 1982-85, Ottawa, Ont., 1985-86, maintenance analysis officer Trenton, 1991-94, aerospace engring. officer, 1994-97, Ottawa, 1997—2001; lectr. engring. Royal Mil. Coll., 1985-88, asst. prof., then assoc. prof., 1988-91, adj. prof., 1991—; aerospace engring. off. Dept. Nat. Def., Trenton, 2001—. Cons., pres. Software Aide, Kingston and Trenton, 1985—; mem. postgrad. adv. bd. Royal Mil. Coll., 1988-91. Contbg. author: Neutron Radiography, 3rd edit., 1990, 5th edit., 1997, Radiation Measurements and Applications, 1991. Scout leader Boy Scouts Am., 1994—. Grantee, Chief of Rsch. and Design, Ottawa, 1986—; recipient Can. 125 medal Govt. of Can., 1993, Can. Order of Mil. Merit, Govt. Can., 1999. Mem. AIChE, Am. Soc. for Engring. Edn., Can. Soc. Chem. Engring., Can. Soc. for Nondestructive Testing, Can. Neutron-Radiography Assn. (mem. conf. organizing com. 1990), Can. Nuclear Soc. (conf. organizing com. 1991), Masons, Shriners. Mem. United Ch. of Can. Achievements include design, installation and commission of world's first neutron radiography facility using small research reactor as neutron source; pioneer in investigation of advanced metal ceramics and composite aircraft flight controls using neutron radiography. Avocations: outdoor activities, visiting family cottage, recreational vehicles, hunting, fishing. Home: 49 Oak Ridge Dr RR #4 Brighton ON Canada K0K 1H0 Office: Royal Mil Coll Can Chem Eng PO Box 17000 Stn Forces Kingston ON Canada K7K 5L0 E-mail: bstblewis@sympatico.ca., lewis-w@rmc.ca.

LEWIS, WILLIAM HEADLEY, JR. manufacturing company executive; b. Washington, Sept. 29, 1934; s. William Headley and Lois Maude (Bradshaw) L.; m. Carol Elizabet Cheek, Apr. 22, 1967; children: Teresa Lynne, Bret Cameron, Charles William, Kevin Marcus. BS in Metall. Engring., Va. Poly. Inst., 1956; postgrad. Grad. Sch. Bus. Adminstrn., Emory U., 1978. Registered profl. engr., Calif. Various positions Lockheed Corp., Marietta, Ga., 1956-87, mgr. engring. tech. services, 1979-83, dir. engring. Getex divsn., 1983-86; mgr. Inspection Systems divsn. Lockheed Air Terminal, Inc., 1986-87; CEO Measurement Sys. Inc., Atlanta, 1987—. Chmn. Lockheed Corp. Task Force on NDE, 1980-86; mem. Com. to Study Role of Advanced Tech. in Improving Reliability and Maintainability of Future Weapon Systems, Office of Sec. of Def., 1984-85; co-founder Applied Tech. Svcs., Inc., 1967—; pres., CEO Applied Tech. Fin. Corp., Atlanta, 1983-86; mng. ptnr. Tech. Fin. Co., LLC; lectr. grad. studies and continuing edn. Union Coll., Schenectady, N.Y., 1977-82. Editor: Prevention of Structural Failures: The Role of Fracture Mechanics, Failure Analysis, and NDT, 1978; patentee detection apparatus for structural failure in aircraft. Served to 1st lt. USAF, 1957-60. Fellow: Am. Soc. for Nondestructive Testing (nat. dir. 1976—78, chmn. nat. tech. coun. 1977—78, chmn. aerospace com. 1972—74, nat. nominating com. 1982—85); mem.: NAS (mem. com. on compressive fracture 1981—83), AIAA, Am. Soc. for Metals, Brotherhood of the Knights of the Vine, Country Club Sapphire Valley, St . Ives Country Club. Home: 3127 St Ives C Club Pky Duluth GA 30097-2038 Office: 2152 Northwest Pkwy SE Ste B Marietta GA 30067-9306 E-mail: bill@measurements.com.

LEWIS, WILLIAM WALKER, management consultant; b. Roanoke, Va., Mar. 29, 1942; s. William Walker and Nancy Katherine (Phipps) L.; m. Jutta Maria Schwarzkopf, Dec. 27, 1966; children: Christopher William, Monica Gisela. BS in Physics with honors, Va. Poly. Inst. and State U., 1963; PhD in Theoretical Physics, Oxford U., 1966. Mem. staff Office of Asst. Sec. for Systems Analysis, Dept. Def., Washington, 1966-69; assoc. provost for resource planning, lectr. public and internat. affairs Princeton U., 1969-71; dir. office of analytical studies U. Calif., Berkeley, 1971-73; sr. ops. officer World Bank, 1973-77; prin. dep. asst. sec. for program analysis and evaluation Dept. Def., Washington, 1977-79; asst. sec. policy and evaluation Dept. Energy, 1979-81; pres. Dist. Heat and Power, Inc., 1981-82; ptnr. McKinsey & Co., Inc., 1982—; dir. McKinsey Global Inst., 1990—. Trustee, chmn. bd. dirs. Holy Cross Hosp.; trustee Ctr. for Econ. Rsch. and Grad. Edn. Charles U.; trustee George C. Marshall Found., Com. for Econ. Devel. Rhodes scholar, 1963-66 Office: 600 14th St NW Washington DC 20005-2008 E-mail: bill_lewis@mckinsey.com.

LEWIS-GRIFFITH, DOROTHY ELLEN, music educator, pianist; b. High Point, N.C., July 7, 1932; d. Fleet and Foda Lee (Blakeley) Lewis; m. David Griffith, Dec. 12, 1959 (div. 1967); children: Dorothy Lewis, David Fleet; m. Adrian Lafayette Shuford, Jr., July 28, 1985 (dec. Dec. 30, 2000). BS, Juilliard Sch., 1954, MS, 1955; D Mus. Arts, Johns Hopkins U., 1978. Grad. asst. Peabody Conservatory, Johns Hopkins U., Balt., 1971-72; assoc. prof. music

Valdosta State U., U. Ga. System, 1974-86; artist-in-residence Shuford Sch. Performing Arts, Catawba Coll., Salisbury, N.C., 1986—. Vis. prof. U. Wis., Superior, summer 1972, Steinway Artists Roster; artist-in-residence Catawba Coll., Salisbury, N.C., 1986-2000. N.Y. debut Town Hall, 1965, recitals at Abraham Goodman House, 1983, Weill Hall at Carnegie Hall, 1992; concerts in Germany, France, Brazil, Peoples Republic of China; soloist with Atlanta Symphony, Brevard Music Festival Orch., N.C. Symphony, Winston-Salem Symphony, Orchestre de la Cité Universitaire, Paris., Kunming, Yunnan (China) Symphony; recs. include Starer Sonata, Ginastera Sonata, 1965, A Christmas Celebration at the Piano, 1978, George Gershwin: A Piano Solo Album, 1994; contbr. to EPTA Music Jour. and New Grove Dictionary Am. Music and Musicians revised edit., New Grove Dictionary of Opera. Bd. dirs. Charlotte (N.C.) Symphony, 1963-65, Lowndes Art Commn., Valdosta, 1975-78, N.C. Symphony, Raleigh, 1988-90, N.C. Sch. Arts, 1994-98; mem. Jr. League Charlotte. Recipient diplôme Geneva Internat. Piano Competition, 1956, winner Brevard (N.C.) Music Festival Concerto Competition, 1965; Fulbright-Hays grantee, 1955, rsch. grantee Valdosta State Coll., 1983. Mem. Music Tchrs. Nat. Assn., Sigma Alpha Iota. Avocations: gardening, swimming.

LEWIS MILL, BARBARA JEAN, school psychologist, educator; b. Sacramento, Sept. 12, 1959; d. William Vasse and Mary Allene (Bridges) Lewis; m. Thomas Steven Mill, Oct. 17, 1981; 1 child, Thomas William. BA, U. Calif., Davis, 1981; MA, U. Calif., Santa Barbara, 1984. Pupil pers. svcs. credentials; cert. basic and sch. psychologist; cert. behavioral intervention case mgr. Pub. rels. asst. Coll. Agrl. and Environ. Scis., U. Calif., Davis, 1979-81; adminstrv. asst. libr. U. Calif., Santa Barbara, 1981-84; sch. psychologist intern Ventura (Calif.) County Supt. of Schs. Office, 1984-85, sch. psychologist, 1985-91, Rio Sch. Dist., Oxnard, Calif., 1985, Ojai (Calif.) Sch. Dist., 1991-92, Santa Paula (Calif.) Sch. Dist., 1991-2000, Ventura (Calif.) Unified Sch. Dist., 2000—. Coord. primary intervention program Santa Paula (Calif.) Sch. Dist., 1992-94; mem. planning com. Dropout Prevention/Outreach Program, Grace Thille Sch., Santa Paula, 1994; mem. local plan com. Ventura County Spl. Edn. Local Plan Area, 2000—. Mem. adv. bd. Pleasant Valley Rainbow Girls, Camarillo, Calif., 1986-89; bd. dirs. Strawberry Patch Presch., Oxnard, 1995-96; v.p. Rose Ave. Sch. PTA, 1997-98; co-pres. Hueneme Swimming Assn., 1998—; bd. dirs., asst. coach Channel Islands Aquatics, 1999—. Mem. ASCD, Nat. Assn. Sch. Psychologists (nat. cert. sch. psychologist), Internat. Reading Assn., Calif. Assn. Sch. Psychologists (Outstanding Sch. Psychologist region IV 1998; region VIII rep. 2000—, mem. mentoring com. 2001—, editl. bd. CASP Today 2002--), Ventura County Assn. Sch. Psychologists (exec. bd. 1987-91, 93-94, dir. pub. rels. 1991-93, 94-96, pres.-elect 1997-98, pres. 1998-99, past pres. 1999-2000, Outstanding Sch. Psychologist 1989, Meritorious Svc. award 1993), Hueneme Swimming Assn. (co-pres., bd. dirs. 1998—), Order Ea. Star, Rainbow for Girls (life, state officer Grand Scribe 1979). Avocations: parent education and outreach, conservation, creative arts, historical preservation, health and fitness.

LEWISON, EDWARD FREDERICK, surgeon; b. Chgo., Feb. 11, 1913; s. Maurice and Julia (Trockey) Lewison; m. Elizabeth Oppenheim, July 24, 1938 (dec. 1947); 1 child John Edward ; m. Betty Fleischmann, Mar. 21, 1948; children: Edward M., Robert S., Richard J. BS, U. Chgo., 1932; MD, Johns Hopkins U., 1936. Lic. MD Ill., Md., Fla., diplomate Am. Bd. Surgery. Chief, Breast Clin. Johns Hopkins Hosp., Balt., 1948-72; asst. prof. surgery Johns Hopkins U. Sch. Med., 1954-69, assoc. prof. surgery, 1969-80, assoc. prof. surgery, emeritus, 1980—. Vice-chmn. breast cancer com. WHO, Geneva, 1968—70; chmn. nat. conf. breast cancer Am. Cancer Soc., Washington, 1969, Swiss Cancer League, Lucerne, 1976; mem. H.S. Nat. Commn. Nat. Rsch. Coun., Washington, 1983—87; mem. adv. bd. Annie Casey Found., 1996—. Author: (book) Breast Cancer and Its Diagnosis and Treatment, 1955; editor: Breast Cancer, 1977, Conference on Spontaneous Regression of Cancer, 1974; co-author: Diagnosis and Treatment of Breast Cancer, 1981. Bd. dirs. United Way Md., Balt., 1986—94. Lt. col. M.C. U.S. Army, 1946. Named Disting. Citizen, Gov. State Md., 1980, Humanitarian of the Yr., Wyman Guild, 1990, oncology libr. in his honor, Johns Hopkins Hosp., 1980; recipient Cert. of Merit award, European Theater Ops., 1945. Fellow: ACS, AMA, Royal Soc. Medicine; mem.: Am. Bd. Surgery (diplomat 1946), Am. Cancer Soc. (life Vol. Leadership award 1984, Premier award 1995), N.Y. Acad. Scis. Achievements include invention of of rayable gauze for surgery. Home: 4100 N Charles St Baltimore MD 21218-1065

LEWITT, MILES MARTIN, computer engineering company executive; b. N.Y.C., July 14, 1952; s. George Herman and Barbara (Lin) L.; m. Susan Beth Orenstein, June 24, 1973; children: Melissa, Hannah. BS summa cum laude, CCNY Engring., 1973; MS, Ariz. State U., 1976. Software engr. Honeywell, Phoenix, 1973-78; architect iRMX line ops. systems, x86 line microprocessors Intel Corp., Santa Clara, Calif., 1978; engring. mgr. Intel, Hillsboro, Oreg., 1978-80, 1981-89, corp. strategic staff, 1981-82, engring. mgr. Israel, 1980-81; v.p. engring. Cadre Techs., Inc., Beaverton, Oreg., 1989-91; v.p. rsch. and devel. ADP, Portland, 1991—. Instr. Maricopa Tech. Coll., Phoenix, 1974-75. Contbr. articles to profl. jours. Bd. dirs. Portland Computer Tng. Inst., 1995—. Recipient Engring. Alumni award CCNY, 1973, Eliza Ford Prize CCNY, 1973, Advanced Engring. Program award, Honeywell, 1976, Product of Yr. award Electronic Products Mag., 1980. Mem. IEEE (sr.), IEEE Computer Soc. (voting mem.), Assn. Computing Machinery (voting mem.), Am. Electronics Assn. (exec. com. Oreg. Coun.). Democrat. Avocations: photography, internat. travel, beach walking.

LEWITT, SOL, artist; b. Hartford, Conn., 1928; BFA, Syracuse U., 1949. Instr. Mus. Modern Art Sch., 1964-67, Cooper Union, 1967, Sch. Visual Arts, N.Y.C., 1969-70, NYU, 1970. Contbr. articles on sculpture, drawing, conceptual art to jours., mags.; one-man shows include, Visual Arts Mus., N.Y.C., 1976, San Francisco Mus. Art, 1975, Wadsworth Atheneum, Hartford, Conn., 1981, Musee d'Art Contemporain, Bordeaux, France, 1983, retrospective travelling exhbn., Mus. Modern Art, N.Y.C., 1990-95, Mus. Contemporary Art, Montreal, Krannert Mus., Champaign, Ill., Mus. Contemporary Art, Chgo., La Jolla (Calif.) Mus., 1978-79, Stedelijk Mus., Amsterdam, 1984, Stedelijk Van Abbe Mus., Eindhoven, 1984, Musee d'Art Moderne de la ville de Paris, 1987, Tate Gallery, 1986, Walker Art Ctr., Mpls., 1988, Kunstlalle Bern, Switzerland, 1989, Touko Mus., 1990, Porticus, Frankfort, Fed. Republic Germany, 1990, Drawings 1958-92 Haags Gemeentemus., The Hague and tour, Structures 1962-93 Mus. Modern Art, Oxford and tour, 25 Years of Wall Drawings 1968-93 Addison Gallery, Phillips Acad., Andover, Mass., Prints 1970-95 Mus. Modern Art, N.Y.C., San Francisco Mus. of Art, 2000; group exhbns. include Sculpture Ann, Whitney Mus. Am. Art, N.Y.C., 1967, Minimal Art, The Hague, 1968, Documenta, Kassel, W. Ger., 1968, 72, 77, 82, Prospect, 1968, Dusseldorf, 1968, Stadtische Kuntshalle, Dusseldorf, 1969, La Jolla Mus. Contemp. Art, 1970, Tokyo Biennale, 1970, Guggenheim Internat., N.Y.C., 1971, Whitney Biennial, Whitney Mus. Am. Art, N.Y.C., 1979, Hayward Gallery, London, 1980, Internat. Sculpture exhbn., Basel, Switzerland, 1980, Westkunst, Cologne, Fed. Republic Germany, 1981, Musee Nat. d'Art Moderne, Paris, 1981, Art Inst. Chgo., 1982, Mus. Modern Art, N.Y.C., 1983, Mus. Contemporary Art, Los Angeles, 1986, Whitney Biennial, 1987, Skulptur Projekt, Münster, Fed. Republic Germany, 1987, Venice (Italy) Biennale, 1988, Zeitlos, Hamburg, Fed. Republic Germany; represented in permanent collections, Stedelijk Mus., Albright-Knox Art Gallery, Buffalo, Art Gallery Ont., Toronto, Los Angeles County Mus. Art, Los Angeles, Mus. Modern Art, N.Y.C., Tate Gallery, London, Centre Georges Pompidou, Paris, Whitney Mus. Am. Art, N.Y.C., Met. Mus. Art, N.Y.C., Art Inst. Chgo., Mus. Contemporary Art, Chgo.; work also in German, Swiss, Australian, Dutch, Belgian and Am. mus. Office: c/o Susanna Singer 50 Riverside Dr New York NY 10024-6555 E-mail: susanna50@aol.com.

LEWITT, WILFRED G. health products executive; BSc in Engring. and Bus., U. Toronto; MBA, U. Detroit. Formerly with W.R. Grace & Co., Cameroon; pres., CEO MDS Inc., 1970, CEO Canada, 1992—96, chmn. exec. mgmt. team Canada. Bd. dirs. MDS Inc.; bd. dirs. Hemosol, Inc., Internat. Group, Inc., Laidlaw Inc. Office: MDS Inc 100 International Blvd Toronto ON M9W 6J6 Canada Office Fax: 416-675-0688.*

LEWITTES, DON JORDAN, clinical psychologist; b. Bklyn., Jan. 21, 1950; s. Morton H. and Laura C. L.; m. Andrea D. Jordon, June 15, 1978; 1 child, Jason D. BA, NYU, 1971; PhD, SUNY, Albany, 1976. Diplomate Am. Bd. Med. Psychotherapists, Am. Bd. Forensic Examiners, Am. Bd. Forensic Medicine, Am. Bd. Psychol. Specialities. Instr. dept. psychiatry Albany Med. Coll., 1976-78; clin. affiliate, prof. of psychology St. John's U., 1983-85; sr. psychologist Schenectady Shared Svcs., Ellis Hosp., 1976-77; dir. adminstrv. and clin. inpatient svcs. South Richmond-South Beach Psychiat. Ctr., S.I., N.Y., 1977-81; chief psychologist South Nassau Cmty. Hosp., Oceanside, 1982-87; cons. Nassau Coalition on Child Abuse and Neglect, Hempstead, 1989-98. Psychol. cons. Gracie Sq. Hosp., N.Y.C., 1989-91; expert cons. N.Y.C. Office Legal Affairs/ACS, 1991—, Kings County and Bronx County Dist. Atty's. Office, 1994—; adjunct faculty Grad. Sch. Social Svc. Fordham U., 1995-96; intern dept. psychiatry Rutgers Med. Sch., Piscataway, N.J., 1974-75. Contbr. articles to profl. jours. Mem. Am. Psychol. Soc., Am. Profl. Soc. on the Abuse of Children. Home: 501 E 87th St New York NY 10128-7665 Office: 30 Hempstead Ave Rockville Centre NY 11570-4033

LEWITUS, MARLA BERMAN, lawyer; b. N.Y.C. d. Myron P. and Roslyn Berman. BS, Georgetown U., 1981; JD, NYU, 1985. Bar: N.Y. 1986. Corp. assoc. Parker Chapin Flattau & Klimpl, N.Y.C., 1985-91; sr. counsel Primerica Corp., 1991-93; asst. gen. counsel Travelers Group Inc. (formerly Primerica Corp.), 1993-98; assoc. gen. counsel Citigroup Inc. (formerly Travelers Group Inc.), 1998-99; sr. v.p., gen. counsel Travelers Life & Annuity, Hartford, Conn., 1999—. Mem. Phi Beta Kappa.

LEWITZ, AMY MAE, clinical nurse specialist, geriatrics psychiatry nurse; b. Chgo., Sept. 6, 1956; d. Thomas Louis and Florence (Gilberg) Rosenberg; m. Jack Arthur Lewitz; 1 child, Nathan David. BSN with honors, U. Ill., 1979, MS in Psychiat. Nursing, 1985. Cert. clin. specialist in adult psychiat. and mental health, ANCC. Staff nurse Northwestern Meml. Hosp., Chgo., 1979-84; clin. nurse specialist VA West Side Med. Ctr., 1985-97; nursing faculty U. Ill., North Park U., Oakton C.C., 1997—. Presenter in field. Active Nurses Network for a Nat. Health Program, Chgo., 1994—. Mem. ANA, Ill. Nurses Assn., Hadassah Nurses Coun., Sigma Theta Tau. Avocations: skiing, gardening, dancing, swimming. Home: 6942 N Kilpatrick Ave Lincolnwood IL 60712-2414 E-mail: jlewitz@earthlink.net.

LEWITZKY, BELLA, choreographer; b. Los Angeles, Jan. 13, 1916; d. Joseph and Nina (Ossman) L.; m. Newell Taylor Reynolds, June 22, 1940; 1 child, Nora Elizabeth. Student, San Bernardino Valley (Calif.) Jr. Coll., 1933-34; hon. doctorate, Calif. Inst. Arts, 1981; PhD (hon.), Occidental Coll., 1984, Otis Parsons Coll., 1989, Juilliard Sch., 1993; DFA, Santa Clara U., 1995; DFA (hon.), Calif. State U., Long Beach, 1997. Chmn. dance dept., chmn. adv. panel U. So. Calif., Idyllwild, 1956-74; founder Sch. Dance, Calif. Inst. Arts, 1969, dean, 1969-74; vice chmn. dance adv. panel Nat. Endowment Arts, 1974-77, mem. artists-in-schs. adv. panel, 1974-75; mem. Nat. Adv. Bd. Young Audiences, 1974—, Joint Commn. Dance and Theater Accreditation, 1979. Com. mem. Am. chpt. Internat. Dance Coun. of UNESCO, 1974—; trustee Calif. Assn. Dance Cos., 1976—, Idyllwild Sch. Music and Arts, 1986-95, Dance/USA, 1988-95, Calif. State Summer Sch. of Arts, 1988—; cons. the dance project WNET, 1987—. Co-founder, co-dir. Dance Dance Assocs., L.A., 1951-55; founder, 1966; artistic dir. Lewitzky Dance Co., L.A.; choreographer, 1948-97; founder, former artistic dir. The Dance Gallery, L.A.; contbr. articles in field; choreographed works include Trio for Saki, 1967, Orrenda, 1969, Kinaesonata, 1971, Pietas, 1971, Ceremony for Three, 1972, Game Plan, 1973, Five, 1974, Spaces Between, 1975, Jigsaw, 1975, Inscape, 1976, Pas de Bach, 1977, Suite Satie, 1980, Changes and Choices, 1981, Confines, 1982, Continuum, 1982, The Song of the Woman, 1983, Nos Duraturi, 1984, 8 Dancers/8 Lights, 1985, Facets, 1986, Impressions #1, 1987, Impressions #3, 1988, Agitime, 1989, Impressions #3, 1989, Episode #1, 1990, Glass Canyons, 1991, Episode #2, 1992, Episode #3, 1992, Episode #4, 1993, Meta 4, 1994, Four Women in Time, 1996. Mem. adv. com. Actors' Fund of Am., 1986—, Women's Bldg. Adv. Council, 1985-91, Calif. Arts Council, 1983-86, City of Los Angeles Task Force on the Arts, 1986—; mem. artistic adv. bd. Interlochen Ctr. for Arts, 1988—. Recipient Mayoral Proclamation, City of L.A., 1976, 1982, ann. award Dance mag., 1978, Dir.'s award Calif. Dance Educators Assn., 1978, Plaudit Award, Nat. Dance Assn., 1979, Labor's Award of Honor for Community Svc., L.A. County AFL-CIO, 1979, L.A. Area Dance Alliance and L.A. Junior C. of C. Honoree, 1980, City of L.A. Resolution, 1980, Distguished Artist Award, City of L.A. and Music Ctr., 1982, Silver Achievement award YWCA, 1982, California State Senate Resolution, 1982, 1984, Award of Recognition, Olympic Black Dance Festival, 1984, Distinguished Women's Award, Northwood Inst., 1984, California State U. Distinguished Artist, 1984, Vesta Award, Woman's Bldg, L.A., 1985, L.A. City Council Honors for Outstanding Contributions, 1985, Woman of the Year, Palm Springs Desert Museum, Women's Committee, 1986, Disting. Svc. award Western Alliance Arts Adminstrs., 1987, Woman of Achievement award, 1988, Am. Dance Guild Ann. award, 1989, So. Calif. Libr. for Social Studies & Rsch. award, 1990, Am. Soc. Journalists & Authors Open Book award, 1990, Internat. Soc. Performing Arts Adminstrs. Tiffany award, 1990, Burning Bush award U. of Judaism, 1991, 1st recipient Calif. Gov.'s award in arts for individual lifetime achievement, 1989; honoree L.A. Arts Coun., 1989, Heritage honoree, Nat. Dance Assn., 1991, Vaslav Nijinsky award, 1991, Hugh M. Hefner First Amendment award, 1991, Artistic Excellence award Ctr. Performing Arts U. Calif., 1992, Lester Horton Lifetime Achievement award Dance Resource Ctr. of L.A., 1992, Occidental Coll. Founders' award, 1992, Dance/USA honor, 1992, Visual Arts Freedom of Expression award Andy Warhol Found., 1993, Artist of Yr. award L.A. County High Sch. Arts, 1993, Freedom of Expression honor Andy Warhol Found. Visual Arts, 1993, Calif. Alliance Edn. award, 1994, Lester Horton Sustained Achievement award, 1995 Dance Resource Ctr. of L.A., Lester Horton award for Restaging and Revival, Dance Resource Ctr. of L.A., 1996, 97, Disting. Artists of 1996, High Sch. of Performing Arts, Houston Tex., Bill of Rights award, Am. Civil Liberties Union of So. Calif., Nat. Medal of Arts, 1996, Gypsy award Profl. Dancers Soc., 1997, We. Arts Alliance Emeritus Mem. award, 1999, Capezio ann. Dance award for Significant Conbns. to Dance in U.S., 1999, Lifetime Achievement award Calif. Arts Coun., 2001; grantee Mellon Found., 1975, 81, 86, Guggenheim Found., 1977-78, NEA, 1969-94; honoree Women's Internat. League Peace and Freedom, 1995; presented with Key to the City, Cin., 1997. Mem. Am. Arts Alliance (bd. dirs. 1977), Internat. Dance Alliance (adv. council 1984—), Dance/USA (bd. dirs. 1988), Phi Beta (hon.). Fax: 505-897-9259. *Dance is communicative of personal, emotive knowledge-- of sensory information common to all. The feel of the wind, the exhilaration of clear space, the headiness of an enormous height, the marvel of human power, one's personal worth-- can take shape and be illuminated in dance. How wonderful to work at something you love! How remarkable to be given the opportunity to utilize one's whole being, one's physical knowledge, intellectual capacity, imagination and creativity in a single persuit. How good to practice dance and know that it will not engage you in mass murders of warfare; it will not destroy our environment. It is capable of healing, celebrating, and sharing human resources. My philosophy is predicated on the belief that choreography is the taskmaster of us all. In each work, I attempt to discover again the truth of that statement.*

LEWKOWITZ, KAREN HELENE, orthodontist; b. Bklyn., Dec. 26, 1956; d. William A. and Janet B. (Kagan) L.; m. Robert Louis Shpuntoff, Dec. 18, 1983; children: Hilana Megan, Ariana Elizabeth. BA magna cum laude, CUNY, 1978; DDS, Columbia U., 1982; cert. in orthodontics, NYU, 1984. Researcher W. M. Krogman Ctr., Children's Hosp. Phila., Pa., 1976; ptnr. Bayside (N.Y.) Orthodontic Assocs., 1984—. Pres. med. awareness com. Queens Coll.-CUNY, 1977-78; attending orthodontist, lectr. Jamaica (N.Y.) Hosp., 1984—. Mem. Temple Torah, Little Neck, N.Y., 1988-94, Temple Israel, Great Neck, N.Y., 1994—, Hadassah, Great Neck, 1990—; v.p. of programming Orgn. Rehab. Thru Tng., Lake Success, N.Y., 1991. Mem. ADA, Acad. Gen. Dentistry, Am. Assn. Women Dentists, Am. Assn. Orthodontists, Queens County Dental Soc. (trustee 1985—, historian 1990, treas. 1991, sec. 1992, v.p. 1993, pres.-elect 1994, pres. 1995), Alpha Omega (pres. Columbia U. chpt. 1980-82, pres. Queens-Nassau chpt. 1984-87, Presdl. citation 1986, regent N.Y. met. area 1990, 91). Avocations: piano, tennis. Office: Bayside Orthodontics 59-01 Springfield Blvd Bayside NY 11364

LEWNES, PETER ANDREW, underwriting consultant; b. Queens, N.Y., Mar. 15, 1929; s. Andrew P. and Stamateke (Anagnostakos) L.; m. Barbara D. Pappas, Sept. 13, 1953; children: Andrew P., Christina G. Michalopoulos. MS in Fin. Svcs., Am. Coll., 1983. CLU, Am. Coll., Bryn Mawr, Pa., 1976; ChFC., 1983. Structural draftsman Voorhies, Walker, Foley & Smith, N.Y.C., 1950-55, Parco, Inc., N.Y.C., 1956-57; sr. structural draftsman Ford, Bacon & Davis, Inc., 1958-65; sales rep. Met. Life Ins. Co., Bkyln., 1965-93, sr. advanced underwriting cons. N.Y.C., 1993-98; fin. planner Metlife Securities, Inc., White Plains, 1986—. Moderator Life Underwriter Tng. Coun., Bklyn., 1976-79, White Plains, 1998—; lectr. SBA Workshop, N.Y.C., 1975-76; instr. distance course The Am. Coll., White Plains, 2002—. Trustee Three Hierarchs Greek Orthodox Ch., Bklyn., 1955-59; youth advisor Three Hierarchs Youth, Bklyn., 1955-65; mem. Holy Order of Three Hierarchs Ch., Bklyn., 1979—; vol. dean grad. studies N.Y. Ctr. for Fin. Studies, N.Y.C., 1995-2000. Mem. Nat. Assn. of Ins. and Fin. Advisors, Soc. of Fin. Svc. Profls., Fin. Planning Assn. Republican. Avocation: choral singing. Home: 58 Laurel Rd # 185 Lake Peekskill NY 10537-1544 E-mail: llewbob@aol.com.

LEWTER, HELEN CLARK, elementary education educator, retired; b. Millis, Mass., Jan. 14, 1936; d. Waldimar Kenville and Ida Mills (Currier) Clark; m. Alvin Council Lewter, June 18, 1966; children: Lois Ida, David Paul, Jonathan Clark. BA, U. Mass., 1958; MS, Old Dominion U., 1978. Tchr. Juniper Hill Sch., Framingham, Mass., 1960-63, Aragona Elem. Sch., Virginia Beach, Va., 1963-65, Park Elem., Chesapeake, 1965-67; edn. specialist Riverview Sch., Portsmouth, 1977-78; reading tchr. Truitt Jr. H.S., Chesapeake, 1979-83; reading resource tchr. Southeastern Elem., 1983-86; tchr. Deep Creek Elem. Sch., 1986-99, ret., 1999. Pers. task force, textbook adoption com. Chesapeake Pub. Schs., Va., 1984—85, employee handbook com., Va., 1986—87, K-6 writing curriculum com., Va., 1988—89. Active PTA, 1979—99; mem. mayor's adv. coun. City of Chesapeake, Va., 1988—89; tchr., workshop leader, dir., mem. various coms. Fairview Heights Bapt. Ch., Deep Creek Bapt. Ch., Va. So. Bapt. Retreats, 1968—; mem. summer missionary Va. So. Bapts., 1993. Mem.: NEA, Va. Reading Assn., Internat. Reading Assn., Chesapeake Reading Assn. (v.p., pres., honor and merit coun., chmn. various coms.), Chesapeake Edn. Assn., Va. Edn. Assn., Phi Kappa Phi, Kappa Delta Pi, Delta Kappa Gamma (legis. chmn.). Republican. Avocations: church related activities, reading. Home: 428 Plummer Dr Chesapeake VA 23323-3116

LEWTON, DIANE KAY, nurse practitioner; b. Ithaca, N.Y., Oct. 24, 1953; d. Wallace R. and Shirley L. (Withers) Nark; m. John Lewton; children: Stacey L., Brian S. AAS in Nursing, Broome Community Coll., 1978; BSN, Purdue U., 1988; MSN, Ball State U., 1995. RN, Ind., N.Y., Ohio; cert. family nurse practitioner; BLS, ACLS. Staff nurse, supr. Endicott (N.Y.) Nursing Home, 1979-81; charge RN rehab. and med.-surg. United Health Svcs. Wilson Hosp., Binghamton, N.Y., 1981-85; telemetry-rehab. nurse Parkview Hosp., Fort Wayne, Ind., 1985-88; med. svc. cons. Crawford & Co. Health & Rehab., 1988; dir. nursing Unicare Health System, 1989; nursing instr. Ivy Tech State Coll., Ft. Wayne, 1990-98; nurse practitioner in cardiology/internal medicine Med. Group Ft. Wayne, Ind., 1998—. Mem. Phi Theta Kappa, Sigma Theta Tau. Avocations: sewing, travel. Bus. Home: 9521 Fireside Ct Fort Wayne IN 46804-7778 Office: Med Group Ft Wayne 7836 W Jefferson Blvd Fort Wayne IN 46804-4138 E-mail: dlewton@mgfw.com.

LEWY, JOHN EDWIN, pediatric nephrologist; b. Chgo., Apr. 22, 1935; s. Stanley B. and Lucile (Mayer) L.; m. Rosalind Portnoy, June 9, 1963; children— Karen, Steven. BA, U. Mich., 1956; MD, Tulane U., 1960. Diplomate Am. Bd. Pediat. (oral examiner 1985-89, oral exam com. 1987-89, certifying exam. com. on clin. problems 1989-92, com. on rsch. and rev. 1992-98), Am. Bd. Pediatric Nephrology. Intern Michael Reese Hosp. Med. Center, Northwestern U., 1960-61, resident in pediatrics, 1961-62, Michael Reese Hosp. Med. Center, 1963-64, chief resident, 1964, pediatric nephrology fellow, 1965, dir. sect. pediatric nephrology, 1967-70; fellow dept. pediatrics Cornell U. Med. Coll., N.Y.C., 1966, research fellow physiology, 1966-67, asst. prof. pediatrics, 1970-71, assoc. prof., 1971-75, prof., 1975-78, dir. div. pediatric nephrology, 1970-78; Reily prof., chmn. dept. pediat. Tulane U. Sch. Medicine, New Orleans, 1978—; physician-in-chief Tulane Hosp. for Children, 1993—. Pediatrician La. Handicapped Children's Program; mem. exec. com., sci. adv. com. La. End Stage Renal Disease Coun.; mem. life options adv. bd. Rehab. Digest for Nephrologists, 1999—; mem. sci. adv. bd. Nat. Kidney Found., 1979—86, mem. health and sci. affairs com., 1989—95, mem. pub. policy com., 1990—96, chmn. pub. policy com., 1994—96, bd. dirs., 1994—96, mem. task force on early intervention and prevention, 1996—; mem. clin. sci. coun. Tulane U., chmn., 1980—90, 1995—, mem. exec. com. of clin. sci. coun., 1978—, mem. faculty senate, 1987—90; mem. task force on cmty. health care Tulane Sch. Pub. Health and Tropical Medicine, 1993—; bd. dirs. Kidney Found. La., 1984—, mem. med. adv. bd., 1981—, mem. sci. adv. bd., 1982—, rep., regional dir., 2000—, task force early intervention and prevention, 1996—. Contbr. over 200 articles and abstracts to profl. jours. Mem. profl. adv. com. Nat. Found. March of Dimes; sci. adv. com. U.S. Renal Data System, HHS, 1990—93; mem. com. on future of pediat. nephrology NIDDK, 1991—; spl. com. on ctrs. of excellence in kidney and urology diseases HHS Nat. Kidney and Urology Diseases Adv. Bd., 1994—96. Served with M.C. USAF, 1962—63. Named Intern of Year, Michael Reese Hosp. Med. Ctr., 1961; recipient award, La. Pediatric Soc., 1960, Ronald McDonald Children's Charities Gift of Love award, 1996, Disting. Svc. award, Nat. Kidney Found., 1996, Julio Figueroa Gift of Life award, Nat. Kidney Found. La., 1999, Disting. Svc. award, Tulane U. Med. Alumni Assn., 1999. Mem.: AAAS, APHA, Nat. Assn. Children's Hosps. (liason from comm. on Federal Gov. Affairs 2002), So. Soc. Pediatric Rsch., Greater New Orleans Pediatric Soc., Orleans Parish Med. Soc. (pub. health com. 1981—, media resource panel 1999—), Am. Soc. Artificial Internal Organs, Assn. Med. Sch. Pediatric Dept. Chairmen, La. State Med. Soc., Internat. Pediatric Nephrology Assn. (asst. sec. gen. 1977—78), Internat. Pediatric Chairs Assn., N.Y. Acad. Scis., Midwest Soc. Pediatric Research, Internat. Soc. Nephrology, Am. Soc. Nephrology, Am. Soc. Pediatric Nephrology (sec.-treas. 1974—80, pres. 1980—81, pub. policy com. 1991—94, 1996—2000, Founder's award 2000), Am. Pediatric Soc. (co-chair work group on pub. policy), Soc. Pediatric Rsch., Am. Acad. Pediat. (liaison from AMSPDC 1992—95, coun. fed. govt. affairs 1992—, task force on access 1999—, coun. on coms. 2002—, rsch./edn./orgn. action group 2002—, chmn. 2002, Henry L. Barnett award 1999), Am. Soc. Transplant Physics, Inst. Medicine (end stage renal disease com. 1989—91), Salt and Water Club, Alpha Omega Alpha (faculty advisor 1987—92). Home: 700 S Peters St New Orleans LA 70130-1663 Office: Tulane U Sch Medicine 1430 Tulane Ave New Orleans LA 70112-2699

LEWY, ROBERT MAX, physician; b. N.Y.C., Oct. 18, 1945; s. Martin and Ellen (Newmark) L.; m. Barbara, Oct. 4, 1987; children: Jennifer, Sarah. AB, U. Rochester, 1967; MD, U. Medicine and Dentistry N.J., Newark, 1971; MPH, Columbia U., 1977. Diplomate Nat. Bd. Med. Examiners, Am. Bd. Family Practice. Intern Dartmouth Affiliated Hosps., Hanover, N.H., 1971-72; resident Maine-Dartmouth Family Practice Program, Augusta, 1974-75; clin. scholar Columbia U., N.Y.C., 1975-77; dir. employee health svcs. Presbyn. Hosp., Columbia-Presbyn. Med. Ctr., 1977-88, dir. office physician affairs, 1988-91, sr. v.p. med. affairs, 1991-98; assoc. prof. medicine Columbia U., 1991—, sr. assoc. dean health scis., 1998—. Author: Preventive Primary Medicine, 1981, Employees at Risk, 1991; contbr. articles to profl. jours. With USPHS, 1972-74. Fellow Am. Occupational Med. Assn. (sec. chmn. 1984-88), Am. Coll. Preventive Medicine; mem. Am. Pub. Health Assn., N.Y. Occupational Med. Assn. (bd. dirs. 1985—). Home: 864 Bradley Pky Blauvelt NY 10913-1127 Office: Columbia U 630 W 168th St New York NY 10032-3795 E-mail: rl10@columbia.edu.

LEWYN, ANN SALFELD, English as a second language educator; b. N.Y.C., Dec. 1, 1935; d. Henry and Betty (Ahrens) Salfeld; m. Thomas Mark Lewyn, July 15, 1955; children: Alfred Thomas, Mark Henry. BA, Hunter Coll., 1967, MA, 1982. Mem. faculty UN Hospitality Extension Lang. Program, N.Y.C., 1974-86; adj. instr. ESL NYU, 1986-90, adj. asst. prof., 1990-95, adj. assoc. prof., 1995-2000; adj. prof., 2001—. Editor-in-chief (Newsletter) UN Hospitality Com., 1967-86. Mem. exec. bd. Small Press Ctr., N.Y.C., 1990-98; mem. adv. coun. Hospitality Com. for UN Dels. Inc., 1991-98; bd. dirs. Hunter Coll. Scholarship and Welfare Fund, N.Y.C., 1992—, sec., 1998-2000, 3d v.p., 2000-2001, 2d v.p., 2001—. Mem. Teachers of English as Second Lang. (author in Aug. 1990 newsletter), N.Y. State Tchrs. of English as Second Lang., Pi Sigma Alpha, Kappa Delta Pi. Avocations: travel, tennis, needlepoint. Home: 911 Park Ave New York NY 10021-0337 Office: NYU Am Lang Inst 48 Cooper Sq New York NY 10003-7154

LEWYN, THOMAS MARK, lawyer; b. N.Y.C., July 2, 1930; s. Oswald and Agnes (Maas) L.; m. Ann Salfeld, July 15, 1955; children— Alfred Thomas, Mark Henry. BA, Stanford, 1952, postgrad., 1952-54; LL.B., Columbia, 1955.

Bar: N.Y. 1957. Since practiced in, N.Y.C.; assoc. Simpson, Thacher & Bartlett, 1957-64, ptnr., 1965-75, sr. ptnr., 1976-90, of counsel, 1991—. Bd. dirs. Metro-Goldwyn-Mayer, Inc. Contbr. articles to profl. jours. Served to 1st lt., F.A. AUS, 1955-57. Mem. ABA, Assn. of Bar of City of N.Y., N.Y. State Bar Assn. Home: 911 Park Ave New York NY 10021-0337 Office: Simpson Thacher & Bartlett 425 Lexington Ave Fl 15 New York NY 10017-3954

LEY, RONALD, psychologist, educator; b. Buffalo, Oct. 19, 1929; s. August Andreas and Marie (Jerge) L.; m. Carmen De Brito, Jan. 16, 1965; 1 child, Jessica Elizabeth. BA, U. Buffalo, 1951; PhD, Syracuse U., 1963. Rsch. dir. Madison Area Project, Syracuse, 1962-63; asst. prof. psychology No. Ill. U., DeKalb, 1963-64, Grad. Faculty, New Sch. for Social Rsch., N.Y.C., 1964-66; prof. psychology and stats. SUNY, Albany, 1966-99, rsch. prof., 1999—. Cons. Nat. Inst. for Occupational Safety and Health; vis. prof. psychology U. P.R., 1969, cardiac dept., Charing Cross Hosp., London, 1988. Author: A Whisper of Espionage, 1990, Rumores de Espionaje: Wolfgang Köhler y los Monos en Tenerife, 1995; editor: Behavioral and Psychological Approaches to Breathing Disorders, 1994; mem. editl. bd.: Jour. Behavior Therapy and Exptl. Psychiatry, 1983—, mem. editl. bd.: Applied Psycholphysiology and Biofeedback, 1997—, guest editor: Biofeedback and Self-Regulation, 1994, guest editor: Behavior Modification, 2001; guest editor Behavior Modification (spl. issue in Respiratory Psychophysiology and the Modification of Breathing Behavior), 2002; contbr. Bd. dirs. Father's Assn. of the Albany Acad. for Girls, 1981-84. Rsch. fellow SUNY, 1967-68, 70, 74, 76, 78, 91, Rsch. grantee, 1967-72, 74-76, 78, 87-88, 91-92, 96-97, Nat. Inst. Occupl. Safety and Health grantee, 1982-83, 87-88, others. Fellow Am. Psychol. Soc., Behavior Therapy and Rsch. Soc.; mem. APA, Am. Statis. Assn., Assn. Advancement Behavior Therapy, Assn. Applied Psychophysiology and Biofeedback (chmn. sect. applied respiratory psychophysiology 1998-99), Author's Guild, Author's League Am., Ea. Psychol. Assn., Internat. Soc. Advancement Respiratory Psychophysiology (founder, pres. 1994-96), New Eng. Soc. Behavior Analysis and Therapy, Psychol. Assn. Northeastern N.Y. (sec. 1967-68, pres. 1983-84, Disting. Psychologist award 1996), N.Y. Acad. Scis., Soc. Psychophysiol. Rsch., Psychonomic Soc., Sigma Xi. Home: 22 Marion Ave Albany NY 12203-1823 Office: SUNY 1400 Washington Ave Albany NY 12222-1000

LEYBOLD-TAYLOR, KARLA JOLENE, college official; b. Lincoln, Nebr., Mar. 18, 1969; d. Norman Alfred and Marcella Ann (Stander) Leybold; m. Cameron Craig Taylor, May 28, 1994; 1 child, Amelia L. BA, Nebr. Wesleyan U., Lincoln, 1991; M in Theol. Studies cum laude, So. Meth. U., 1993. Assoc. registrar Thomas Nelson C.C., Hampton, Va., 1993-96; registrar Wells Coll., Aurora, N.Y., 1996—. Mem. Am. Assn. Collegiate Registrars and Admissions Officers, Mid. States Assn. Collegiate Registrars and Admissions Officers (new mems. orientation, mentoring and membership com. 1998—, chairperson 2000-2001, program com. 2001—, v.p. for profl. devel. and chair profl. activities com. 2002—), Va. Assn. Collegiate Registrars and Admissions Officers (hon., chmn. local arrangements 1995, mem. publs. com. 1995-96, Disting. Young Profl. award 1995), N.Y./N.J. Assn. Collegiate Registrars and Admissions Officers. Democrat. Roman Catholic. Avocations: travel, hiking, pets, reading, eucharistic ministry. Office: Wells Coll PO Box 500 Aurora NY 13026-0500 E-mail: kleybold@wells.edu.

LEYBOURN, CAROL, musician, educator; b. Toledo, Dec. 15, 1933; d. Charles Wilson and Esther Lenore (McCaughey) L.; m. Donald Herbert Kenney, Aug. 21, 1954 (div. 1981); children: James Herbert, Paul McLean, Laura Elizabeth, Matthew McLean; m. Jerry Frederick Janssen, May 26, 1984. MusB, U. Mich., 1955, MusM, 1957. Tchg. asst. U. Mich., Ann Arbor, 1955-57; concert pianist USIA, Kaiserslautern, Germany, 1957-61; dir., instr. Leybourn Studios, Ann Arbor, 1961-90; solo pianist, harpsichordist Kans., 1961-90; keyboardist, mgr. Sterling Chamber Players, 1975-90; keyboardist Ann Arbor Chamber Orch., 1980-90, Ann Arbor Symphony, 1980-90; pianist Leybourn Trio, Janssen Trio, 1986—; solo pianist, harpsichordist Libertyville, Ill., 1990-96; pianist Camerata Singers, Lake Forest, 1990-91; solo pianist, harpsichordist with cellist Laura Kenney , Indpls., 1996-98, Appleton, Wis., 1998—; pianist, harpsichordist Cappelli Chamber Music Soc., 1998—; pianist Lawrence U. Concert Choir, 2000; chamber music specialist Lawrence Univ. Arts Acad., WI, 1999—. Lectr., cons. various piano tchr. groups, 1975—; dir. Jr. Chamber Players, Ann Arbor, 1978-90, Junior Dixieland Jazz Players, Ann Arbor, 1984-90; dir. vocal music St. Gilbert's Elem. Sch. Grayslake, Ill., 1990-91; performer Nat. Conf. Women in Music, U. Mich., 1981, 83; adj. music instr. Ann Arbor Community Edn., 1984-90; instrumental music dir. Greenhills Sch., Ann Arbor, 1988-90; mem. piano faculty David Adler Cultural Ctr., Libertyville, Ill., 1990-96; adj. piano faculty Coll. of Lake County, 1993-96. Arranger : (Dixieland music books for 6th Graders) Combo!, 1987, musician concert appearances include (with cellist Laura Kenney). Bd. dirs. Ann Arbor Soc. Mus. Arts, 1962-90; dir. chamber music and jazz workshops David Adler Cultural Ctr., Libertyville, 1991-96; founder, chmn. bd. dirs. Lake County Youth Orch., 1994-96. Regents scholar U. Mich., 1951-55. Mem. Nat. Music Tchrs. Assn., Mich. Music Tchrs. Assn., Ind. Music Tchrs. Assn., Washtenaw Coun. for Arts, Women's City Club (Ann Arbor), Suzuki Assn. of the Ams., Mu Phi Epsilon (pres. Ann Arbor alumnae chpt. 1964-66), Pi Kappa Lambda. Republican. Presbyterian. Avocations: gardening, decorating, refinishing furniture, graphic arts. Fax: 920-954-9261.

LEYDA, JAMES PERKINS, retired pharmaceutical company executive; b. Youngstown, Ohio, Oct. 2, 1935; s. Walter Cletus and Dorothy Eleanor (Perkins) L.; m. Barbara Marie Dykstra, Sept. 9, 1967; children: Jason Walter, Jeffrey Albert, Justin Michael. BS in Pharmacy, Ohio No. U., 1957; MSc in Pharmacy, Ohio State U., 1959, PhD in Pharmacy, 1962. Registered pharmacist, Ohio. Devel. chemist Lederle Labs., Pearl River, NY, 1962—66; mgr. new product devel. Cynamid Internat., 1966—69; dir. new product devel. Merrell Internat., N.Y.C., 1969—81, Westport, Conn., 1969—81; dir. pharmacy rsch. Merrell Dow Pharm., Cin., 1981—84, dir. comml. devel., 1984—89; assoc. dir. product approval Marion Merrell Dow Inc. (name changed to Hoechst Marion Rousssel, Inc.), 1992—98; pres. Nova Cell Biotech., 1997—2000, Emerging Concepts, Inc., 1998—2002. Author: Pharmaceutical Chemistry, 1964; contbr. articles to profl. jours. Recipient Ohio No. U./Bristol Labs. Bristol award, 1957, Richardson Merrell Inc. Lunsford Richardson award, 1960, NIH Predoctoral Fellowship award, 1960. Mem. AAAS, Am. Pharm. Assn., Acad. Pharm. Scis., N.Y. Acad. Scis., Sigma Xi Avocations: tennis, golf. Home: 10597 Tanagerhills Dr Cincinnati OH 45249-3634 E-mail: jledya@cinci.rr.com.

LEYDEN, MICHAEL JOSEPH, II (LEI JIE MING), international business executive, educator, author; b. Feb. 26, 1950; m. Ivy Zhong Yu Xu, Nov. 1991. AA in Econs., Wenatchee Valley Coll., 1970; USVI, U. V.I., 1971; BA in Philosophy and Psychology, Ctrl. Wash. U., 1972; MA in Philosophy, Wash. State U., 1974; various mktg. diplomas, U. Hawaii, 1975-89; DBA, Newport U., Utah and Beijing, 1997. Corp. mgr., tng. dir. Colwell Bankers-Davenport Inc., Wenatchee, Wash., 1977-81; v.p. sales and mktg. John's Real Estate and Securities Corp., Bellevue, 1981-82; pres., founder Aero-Brokers Inc., Honolulu, 1983-86; gen. mgr. Tadashi & Sons Ltd., Truk Islands, Micronesia, 1987; CEO, adminstrv. and fin. mgr. Zorro's Pizza and Italian Restaurants, Honolulu, 1988; gen mgr. Coast Enterprises of Hawaii Inc., 1990; exec. v.p., gen. mgr. Eternity Internat. Trade Devel. Co., Ltd., China-U.S., 1992-93; prof. Sch. Internat. Bus. Nankai U., Tianjin, China, 1994; prof. dept. internat. politics Sch. Internat. Rels. Beijing U., 1995; prof. dept. econ. and mgmt. Qinghua (Tsinghua) U., Beijing, 1996; internat. bus. affairs dir. Michael Trading and Cons. Co. Ltd., Beijing City, 1997; prof. dept. econ. and mgmt. Shanghai U., People's Republic of China, 1998; dean, adminstrn. and devel. Coll. of Marshall Islands, Majuro, Micronesia, 1998; project dir., coord. not for profit orgn., Honolulu, 1999-2000. Spl. asst. to commr. edn. and rsch., statistician No. Marianas Islands Pub. Sch. Sys., 1991; Workforce Investment Act (WIA) program mgr. Samoan Svc. Providers Assn., Honolulu, 2001—. Author: (poems) Man Atop Banana Leaves, 1970, Intruders: Volcano Island Colours, 1975, Recruitment Strategies: A Model for Executive Decision-Making, 1980, Writing a Business Plan for the Five-Minute Reader, 1999, Guidelines for Entrepreneurs on How to Prepare an International Business Plan, 1992, "Magnus Opus" All the World Comes to Tientsen Via the Post, 2001, P.R. China (Tianjin) Postal and Cultural History 1887-1947, 2001, also articles. Chmn., mem. Shanghai Am. C. of C. Edn.-Pub. Com., 1997-99; mem. Tianjin and Beijing C. of C., 1995, 96. Mem. Pres.'s medal for leadership, 1970, Sophia Newspaper Editors award, 1973, Honolulu Mayor's award bus. honour, 1975, others. Mem. Am. Mgmt. Assn. (mem. pres. club 1980, 87, 92), N.Ctrl. Wash. Oriental Rug Soc. (editor Oriental Textile 1977-80), Royal Philatelic Soc. London, Am. Philatelic Soc., China Stamp Soc., N.C. Wash. Writers Guild, Executive Club of Honolulu (sec. 1987), Collectors Club (N.Y.), Lions, Rotary, Honolulu Downtown Club. Roman Catholic. Home: 3662-A Hilo Pl Honolulu HI 96816-3318 Office: Hawai Fgn Trade Co Inc PO Box 22124 Honolulu HI 96823-2124 Fax: 808-739-5057. E-mail: michaelleyden@yahoo.com.

LEYDON, DEBRA JEAN, food products executive; b. Bridgeport, Conn., Mar. 24, 1954; d. Thomas George and Joan Marie L. Materials specialist, receiving mgr. StorageTek Corp., Louisville, 1979-85; warehouse mgr. Mc-Data Corp., Broomfield, 1985-87; warehouse supr. Melco Industries, Westminster, 1987-92; master scheduler SPM/Denver, 1993-94; corp. warehouse mgr. Walker Component Group, Denver, 1994-95; materials mgr. DTM Products, Niwot, Colo., 1995-97; ops. mgr. Avalon Imaging, Boulder, 1997-99; pres., CEO Rocky Mountain Land & Sea Food Co., 1999—. Victim's adv. State of Colo., 2001—. Mem. Big Sisters, Denver, 1985-90. Mem. Am. Prodn. Inventory Control Soc. Home: 676 Monroe St Denver CO 80206-4451

LEYDORF, FREDERICK LEROY, lawyer; b. Toledo, June 13, 1930; s. Loftin Herman and Dorothy DeRoyal (Cramer) L.; m. Mary MacKenzie Malcolm, Mar. 28, 1953; children: Robert Malcolm, William Frederick, Katherine Ann, Thomas Richard, Deborah Mary Student, U. Toledo, 1948-49; BBA, U. Mich., 1953; JD, UCLA, 1958. Bar: Calif. 1959, U.S. Supreme Ct. 1970. Assoc. Hammack & Pugh, L.A., 1959-61; ptnr. Willis, Butler, Scheifly, Leydorf & Grant, 1961-81, Pepper, Hamilton & Scheetz, L.A., 1981-83, Hufstedler & Kaus, L.A., 1983-95. Lectr., cons. Calif. Continuing Edn. of Bar, 1965-92; mem. planning com. Probate and Trust Conf., U. So. Calif., 1984-92. Contbg. author: California Non-Profit Corporations, 1969; contbr. articles to profl. jours. Chmn. pub. adminstr.-pub. guardian adv. commn. Los Angeles County Bd. Suprs., 1972-73; v.p. J.W. and Ida M. Jameson Found., 1995—, bd. dirs., 1967—; bd. dirs. Western Ctr. on Law and Poverty, Inc., 1980-82, L.A. Heart Inst., 1988-90; mem. legal com. Music Ctr. Found., 1980-95; mem. lawyers adv. coun. Constl. Rights Found., 1982-85; mem. devel. adv. bd. U. Mich. Sch. Bus. Adminstrn., 1984-90; mem. adv. bd. UCLA-CEB Estate Planning Inst., 1979-92; Lt. USNR, 1953-55. Mem. Libbey H.S. Hall of Fame (Toledo), 1999. Mem. ABA, L.A. County Bar Assn. (bd. trustees 1973-75), State Bar Calif. (chmn. conf. dels. 1977, Alumnus of Yr. award, conf. of dels. 1983, mem. exec. com. estate planning, trust and probate law sect. 1979-80), L.A. County Bar Found. (pres. 1977-79, bd. dirs. 1975-87), Internat. Acad. Estate and Trust Law (v.p. N.Am. 1978-82), Life Ins. and Trust Coun. L.A. (pres. 1983-84), UCLA Law Alumni Assn. (pres. 1982), L.A. World Affairs Coun. (mem. internat. cir.), Chancery Club (pres. 1991-92), Jonathan Club, Laguna Hills Golf Club, Sunrise Country Club (Rancho Mirage, Calif.), Phi Delta Phi, Phi Delta Theta. Republican. Lutheran. Home: 75 Majorca Dr Rancho Mirage CA 92270-3826

LEYHANE, FRANCIS JOHN, III, lawyer; b. Chgo., Mar. 29, 1957; s. Francis J. and Mary Elizabeth (Crowley) L.; m. Diana M. Urizarri, May 8, 1982; children: Katherine, Francis J. IV, Joseph, Brigid Rose, James Matthew. BA, Loyola U., Chgo., 1977, JD, 1980. Bar: Ill. 1980, U.S. Dist. Ct. (no. dist.) Ill. 1980, U.S. Ct. Appeals (7th cir.) 1986. Assoc. Condon, Cook & Roche, Chgo., 1980-87; ptnr. Condon & Cook, 1988-98, Boyle & Leyhane, Ltd., Chgo., 1998—. Contbr. articles to profl. jours. Mem. Sch. bd. Immaculate Conception Parish, Chgo., 1993-96. Fellow Ill. Bar Found.; mem. Appellate Lawyers Assn. Ill., Ill. State Bar Assn. (mem. assembly 1987-90), Chgo. Bar Assn., Blue Key. Office: Boyle & Leyhane Ltd 11 E Adams Set 1600 Chicago IL 60603 E-mail: leyhane329@aol.com.

LEYVA, LUIS PABLO, JR. obstetrician/gynecologist; b. Cuba, Apr. 18, 1959; came to U.S., 1966; MD, U. UTESA, 1985. Diplomate Am. Bd. Ob-Gyn. Intern, then resident in ob-gyn. St. Agnes Hosp., Balt., 1987-89; resident in ob-gyn. Case West Rsch. U. Hosps., Cleve., 1989-90, W.Va. Sch. Medicine, 1990-92; attending South Miami (Fla.) Hosp., 1993—, Bapt. Hosp., Miami, Fla., 1995—, Columbia Kendall Regional Hosp., Miami, 1994—. Fellow ACOG. Office: Ste 103 9595 N Kendall Dr Miami FL 33176

LEZAK, SIDNEY IRVING, lawyer, mediator; b. Chgo., Nov. 8, 1924; s. Manny and Celia (Weiner) L.; m. Muriel Deutsch, June 26, 1949; children: Anne, David, Miriam. PhB, U. Chgo., 1946, JD, 1949. Bar: Oreg. 1949, U.S. Supreme Ct. 1962. Pvt. practice, Portland, Oreg., 1949-52; ptnr. Bailey, Lezak, Swink & Gates, 1951-61; U.S. atty. for Oreg., U.S. Dept. Justice, 1961-82; counsel Newcomb, Sabin, Schwartz & Landsverk, 1982—; mediator, 1982—. Mem. Oreg. Dispute Resolution Commn., Portland, 1989-91; mem. Dispute Resolution Adv. Coun. Oreg., Portland, 1987-89. 1st lt. USAAF, 1942-45, ETO. Decorated DFC, Air medal with three oak leaf clusters; recipient individual achievement award Willamette U. Dispute Resolution Ctr., 1990. Mem. ABA (cons. com. on dispute resolution 1989-92), Oreg. State Bar (chmn. dispute resolution com. 1986-88), Fed. Bar Assn. (pres. Oreg. 1963-64, chmn. alternative dispute resolution com. 1984-85). Democrat. Avocations: skiing, travel, hiking, France. Home: 1811 SW Boundary St Portland OR 97201-2172 Office: Newcomb Sabin Schwartz Landsverk 111 SW 5th Ave Ste 4040 Portland OR 97204-3643 E-mail: lezak@nsslaw.com.

L'GREEN, NEVILLE, music director; b. Melbourne, Australia, Sept. 20, 1960; s. Don and Joan L'Green. Student, NSW Conservatorium of Music, Sydney, NSW, Australia, 1985—86. Mus. dir. Christian City Ch., N.Y.C., 1999—. Author: (book) The Language of Music, 2000; dir.: (seminar) The Language of Music Workshop; , musician. Personal E-mail: nevlg@hotmail.com.

L'HEUREUX-DUBÉ, CLAIRE, judge; b. Quebec City, Can., Sept. 7, 1927; d. Paul H. and Marguerite (Dion) L'H.; m. Arthur Dubé (dec. 1978); children: Louise, Pierre (dec. 1994). BA magna cum laude, Coll. Notre-Dame de Bellevue, Que., 1946; LLL cum laude, U. Laval Law Faculty, Que., 1951; LLD (hon.), Dalhousie U., 1981, U. Montreal, 1983, Laval U., Que., 1984, Ottawa U., 1988, U. Que., 1989, U. Toronto, 1994, Queen's U., 1995, Gonzaga U., 1996. Bar: Que. 1952. Ptnr. Bard, L'Heureux & Philippon, 1969; sr. ptnr. L'Heureux, Philippon, Garneau, Tourigny, St. Arnaud & Assocs., 1952-73; Puisne judge Superior Ct. Que., 1973-79, Ct. Appeal of Que., 1979-87, Supreme Ct. Can., Ottawa, 1987—. Commr. Part II Inquiries Act Dept. Manpower and Immigration, Montreal, 1973-76; del. Gen. Coun. Bar of Que., 1968-70, com. on adminstrn. justice, 1968-73, others; pres. family law com. Family Ct. com. Que Civil Code Rev. Office, 1972-76; pres. Can. sect. Internat. Commn. Jurists, 1981-83, v.p., 1992—, pres. bd. dirs., 1998—. Editor: (with Rosalie S. Abella) Family Law - Dimensions of Justice, 1983; chmn. editorial bd. Can. Bar Rev., 1985-88; author articles, conf. proc., book chpt. Bd. dirs. YWCA, Que., 1969-73, Ctr. des Loisirs St. Sacrement, 1969-73, Ctr. Jeunesse de Tilly-Ctr. des Jeunes, 1971-77; v.p. Can. Consumers Coun., 1970-73; v.p. Vanier Inst. of the Family, 1972-73; lifetime gov. Found. Univ. Laval, 1980, bd. dirs., 1984-85; mem. Comité des grandes orientations de l'Univ. Laval, 1971-72; mem. nat. coun. Can. Human Rights Found., 1980-82, 82-84; mem. Can. del. to Peoples Republic China on Status of Women, 1981; mem. Nat. Coun. Can. Human Rights Found., 1980-84; v.p. Vanier Inst. of Family, 1972-73. Apptd. Queen's Counsel, 1969; recipient Medal of the Alumni, U. Laval, 1986, Médaille du Barreau de Que., 1987, Montreal Bar, 1994, Barrecece dee Quebec, 1995, Medal Internat. Yr. of the Famig, Que., 1994, Can. award, 1996 Can. Hadassah-WIZO, Prix de la Justice, Can. Inst. Adminstrn. Justice, 1997, Margaret Brent Women Lawyers Achievement award Am. Bar Assn. Commn. Women in the Profession, 1998. Mem. Can. Bar Assn. Can. Inst. Adminstrn. Justice, Internat. Soc. Family Law (hon. mem. 1988—, bd. dirs. 1977-88, v.p. 1981-88), Fedn. Internat. des Femmes Juristes, L'Assn. des Femmes Diplômées d'Univ., Assn. Québécoise pour l'Étude Comparative du Droit (pres. 1984-90), Am. Coll. Trial Lawyers (hon.), Am. Law Inst., Phi Delta Phi. Roman Catholic. Office: Supreme Ct Can Wellington St Ottawa ON Canada K1A 0J1

LHOTKA, SIDNEY BRUNO, tax accountant; b. Sevetin, Bohemia, Czechoslovakia, Apr. 4, 1926; came to U.S., 1956; s. Vaclav Vojtech and Helena (Valkova) L.; m. Jana M. Lhotka, Mar. 29, 1958. A in Acctg., U. Queensland, Australia, 1958, B in Comm., 1959. Acct., acctg. mgr. Bechtel Corp., San Francisco, 1956-61, product svcs. mgr., 1964-66, 68-83; asst. svcs. mgr. Transport Co. of Tex., Kwajalein, Mich., 1962-64; office mgr. systems and procedures RMK-BRJ Vietnam, Saigon, 1966-68; prin. Fin. and Tax Svcs., Concord, Calif., 1983—. Fellow Australian Soc. of Cert. Practicing Accts.; mem. Nat. Soc. of Pub. Accts., Nat. Assn. of Enrolled Agts., Internat. Assn. of Fin. Planning. Avocations: bicycle riding, swimming, walking. Home: 1314 Corte De Los Vecinos Walnut Creek CA 94598-2902 Office: Fin and Tax Svcs Concord CA 94520

LI, AN-PING, materials scientist, researcher; b. Dawu, Hubei, China; m. Liping Zhao, Dec. 25, 1990; 1 child, Yiwei Li. PhD, Peking U., Beijing, 1997. Engr. Electronic Industry China, Shijiazhuang, Hubei, China, 1991-94; rsch. scientist Max-Planck-Inst., Halle, Germany, 1997-99. Vis. scientist Mich. State U., East Lansing, 1999—. Contbr. articles to Jour. Advanced Materials. Guanghua fellow Peking U., 1996, Max-Planck-Inst. Soc. fellow, 1997. Mem. Materials Rsch. Soc. Office: Mich State U PA 16 East Lansing MI 48824 Fax: 517-432-5501. E-mail: apli@pa.msu.edu.

LI, BAO QIN, mathematician, researcher; b. Yangzhou, Jiangsu, China, June 4, 1962; s. Zheng Zhang Li and Mei Ying Qiao; m. Yi Zhi Yang. PhD, U. Md., 1993. Asst. prof. Hong Kong U. Sci. and Tech., 1995—97; assoc. prof. Fla. Internat. U., Miami, 1997—. Contbr. rsch. papers to profl. jours. Grantee, NSF, 2001—04, 1997—2000, Rsch. Grants Coun. Hong Kong, 1996—98, 1995—96. Personal E-mail: libaoqin@fiu.edu. Business E-Mail: libaoqin@fiu.edu.

LI, BENJAMIN DUNLOP, surgeon, researcher; b. Singapore, June 3, 1960; came to U.S., 1973; s. C.K. and Maisie Li; m. Mary K. Donovan, May 21, 1988; chidlren: Kathryn M., Jonathan M. BA, U. Hawaii, Manoa, 1982; MD, Yale U., 1986. Diplomate Am. Bd. Surgery. Intern Northwestern U., Chgo., 1986-87, resident in gen. surgery, 1987-89; fellow in surg. oncology Roswell Park Cancer Inst., Buffalo, 1989-91; asst. clin. instr. surgery McGaw Med. Ctr. Northwestern U., Chgo., 1991-92; clin. instr. Erie County Med. Ctr., Buffalo, 1992-95; clin. asst. instr. SUNY, 1992-95; attending surgeon Willis Knighton Hosps., Shreveport, La., 1996—, assoc. prof. surgery, 2000—; chief surg. oncology, asst. prof. La. State U. Health Scis. Ctr., 1996—; cons. surgeon Overton Brooks VA Med. Ctr., 1996—. Mem. clin. bd., coord. surg. multi-discipline tumor bd., chmn. cancer com. La. State U. Med. Ctr., 1996—. Author (book chpt.) Methods in Cell Biology, 1994, Surgical Oncology--An Altorithmic Approach; contbr. articles to Jour. Surg. Rsch., Jour. Surg. Oncology, Cancer, Head & Nedk, Internat. Jour. Cancer, European Jour. Cancer, Cancer, Jour. Oral Maxillofacial Surgery, Surg. Forum, Ann. Surg. Onogene, among others. Mem. ACS (cancer liaison physician 1996—), AMA, AAAS, Am. Soc. for Gastrointestinal Endocscopy, Am. Soc. Colon and Rectal Surgeons, Am. Soc. Clin. Oncology, Soc. Surg. Oncology, Am. Assn. Cancer Rsch., Am. Cancer Soc. (Clin. Oncology fellow 1994), Assn. for Acad. Surgery, N.Y. Acad. Scis., La. State Med. Soc., Roswell Park Surgery Soc., Shreveport Med. Soc., Shreveport Surg. Soc., S.W. Oncology Group, Southeastern Surg. Congress, Surg. Assn. La., Soc. Univ. Surgeons, So. Surg. Assn. Achievements include work with competitive PCR to quantify HER-2 amplification in FACS sorted breast cancer cells, overexpresion and breast cancer outcome. Office: La State U Health Scis Ctr 1501 Kings Hwy Shreveport LA 71103-4228 E-mail: bli@lsuhsc.edu.

LI, CHAOYING, biomedical researcher, researcher; b. Jingshan, Hubei, China, July 20, 1958; came to U.S., 1990; s. Yi Li and Yulan Liu; m. Chuli Yi, June 10, 1985; 1 child, Shu. MD, Tongji Med. U., Wuhan, Hubei, China, 1983, MS in Neurobiology, 1989. Asst. Tongji Med. U., Wuhan, 1983-89, lectr., 1989-90; vis. fellow NIH, Rockville, Md., 1990-94, intramural rsch. training award fellow, 1994-95, sr. staff fellow, 1995-98; prin. scientist AstraZeneca R&D, Boston, 1998-2000, AstraZeneca CNS Discovery, Wilmington, Del., 2000—. Author: Alcohol, Cell Membranes and Signal Transolution, 1993; contbr. articles to profl. jours. Mem. Soc. Neurosci. Achievements include first to demonstrate that alcohols affect the function of a neuronal membrane receptor by a direct interaction with the receptor protein, zinc potentiates excitatory action of ATP, copper enhances the function of P2X purinoceptors, protons potentiate ATP-gated ion channel responses to ATP and zinc, magnesium inhibits the function of P2X purinoceptors by decreasing the affinity of the receptor for ATP, inhibitory action of low micromolar concentrations of zinc on P2X purinoceptors, and differential modulation by copper and zinc of P2X receptor function, distinct ATP-activated currents in different types of neurons dissociated from adult rat DRG, ethanol-induced inhibition of a neuronal P2X receptor by an allosteric mechanism, ethanol inhibition of P2X receptors in mammalian central neurons, and novel mechanism of inhibition by PPADS of P2X receptors in neurons, histidine mutation of the rat P2X4 receptor alters agonist and antagonist sensitivities. Home: 10410 Flowerfield Way Potomac MD 20854 Office: Astra Zeneca CNS Discovery 1800 Concord Pike A-131 PO Box 15437 Wilmington DE 19850-5437 E-mail: chaoying.li@astrazeneca.com.

LI, CHENGZHI, research scientist; b. Xiamen, Fujia, China, Dec. 24, 1955; m. Xiaoying Xu, July 26, 1991. PhD, Texas A&M U., 1999. Postdoctoral staff dept. elec. and computer engring. Rice U., Houston, 1999—2001; rsch. scientist dept. computer sci. U. Va., Charlottesville, Va., 2001—. Mem.: IEEE. Achievements include research in predictable QoS for wired and wireless networks.

LI, CHIA-CHUAN, engineer, consultant; b. Taipei, Republic of China, Dec. 29, 1946; came to U.S., 1971; s. Wei-Tong and San (Huang) L.; m. Clemencia Vasquez, Nov. 26, 1983; children: Angie, Andrew. BS, Nat. Taiwan U., Taipei, 1969; MS, Rutgers U., 1974; PhD, U. Mich., 1977; MBA, Pepperdine U., 1986. Sr. engr. Gen. Atomic Co., San Diego, 1977-84; staff engr. Hughes Aircraft Co., El Segundo, Calif., 1984-85; project mgr. Electro Optical Ctr. Rockwell Internat. Corp., Anaheim, 1985—. Mem. Am. Soc. Metals, Sigma Xi. Democrat. Office: Rockwell Internat Corp 3370 E Miraloma Ave # 3107bd Anaheim CA 92806-1911

LI, CHING-CHUNG, electrical engineering and computer science educator; b. Changshu, Kiangsu, China, Mar. 30, 1932; came to U.S., 1954, naturalized, 1972; s. Lung-Han and Lien-Tseng (Hwa) L.; m. Hanna Wu, June 10, 1961; children: William Wei-Lin, Vincent Wei-Tsin. BSE.E., Nat. Taiwan U., 1954; MSE.E., Northwestern U., 1956, PhD, 1961. Jr. engr. analytical dept. Westinghouse Electric Corp., East Pittsburgh, Pa., 1957; inst. fellow Northwestern U., Evanston, Ill., 1957-59; asst. prof. elec. engring. U. Pitts., 1959-62, assoc. prof., 1962-67; vis. assoc. prof. elec. engring. U. Calif.-Berkeley, 1964; vis. prin. scientist Alza Corp., Palo Alto, Calif., 1970; faculty rsch. participant Pitts. Energy Tech. Ctr., Dept. Energy, Pitts., 1982, 83, 85, 88, 89; prof. elec. engring. U. Pitts., 1967—, prof. computer sci., 1977—; mem. Ctr. Multivariate Analysis, 1982-87, Ctr. for Parallel and Distributed Intelligent Systems, 1986—96; sabbatical leave Lab. for Info. and Decision Systems, MIT, 1988, Robotics Inst., Carnegie Mellon U., 1999. Mem. sci. adv. com. Horus Therapeutics, Inc., 1995-97. Guest editor: Jour. Cybernetics and Info. Sci., 1979, guest editor: Computerized Med. Imaging and Graphics, 1991, assoc. editor: Pattern Recognition, 1985—2001, mem. editl. bd.: Internat. Jour. Image and Graphics, 2000—; contbr. articles. Co-recipient cert. of merit Radiol. Soc. N.Am., 1979; rsch. grantee NSF, 1975-81, 85-87, Pa. Dept. Health, 1977-79, We. Pa. Advanced Tech. Ctr., 1983-84, 86-88, Health Rsch. and Svc. Found., 1985-86, Air Force Office Sci. Rsch., 1990-93, Pitts. Digital Greenhouse, Inc., 2000—). Fellow IEEE (tech. com., com. chmn. 1967—); mem. Biomed. Engring. Soc., AAAS, Pattern Recognition Soc., Sigma Xi, Eta Kappa Nu. Home: 2130 Garrick Dr Pittsburgh PA 15235-5033 Office: U Pitts Dept Elec Engring Pittsburgh PA 15261-0001

LI, CHU-TSING, art history educator; b. Canton, China, 1920; came to U.S., 1947; m. Yao-wen; children: Ulysses, Amy. BA, U. Nanking, 1943; MA in English Lit., U. Iowa, 1949, PhD in Art History, 1955. Instr. U. Iowa, 1954-55, 56-58, asst. prof., 1958-62, assoc. prof., 1962-65, prof., 1965-66; prof. art history U. Kans., Lawrence, 1966-78, dept. chmn., 1972-78, Judith Harris Murphy Disting. prof., 1978-90, prof. emeritus, 1990—, dir. NEH summer seminar on Chinese art history, 1975, 78, coordinator Mellon faculty seminar, 1979; acting asst. prof. Oberlin Coll., 1955-56; asst. prof. Ind. U., summer 1956; coordinator N.Y. state faculty seminar on Chinese Art History, SUNY, 1965; research curator Nelson Gallery of Art, Kansas City, 1966—. Vis. prof. fine arts Chinese U., Hong Kong, 1972-73, summer 1971, leader China visit group, 1973; vis. prof. Grad. Inst. Art History, Nat Taiwan U., 1990; vis. Andrew W. Mellon prof. U. Pitts., 1995; dir. NEH Summer Inst. Modern Chinese Art and Culture, 1991; participant Internat. Symposiums on Chinese Painting, Nat. Palace Mus., Taipei, 1970, Cleve. Mus. Art, 1981, Huangshan Sch. Painters, Hefei, Ahnui, Rep. China, 1984, on Words and Images in

Chinese Painting, Met. Mus. Art, N.Y.C., 1985, on the Elegant Brush: Chinese Painting under the Qianlong Emperor, Phoenix Art Mus., 1985, to celebrate 60th anniversary Nat. Palace Mus., Taipei, Taiwan, 1985, on History of Yuan Dynasty, Nanjing U., China, 1986, on art of Badashanren (Chu Ta), Nanchang, China, 1986; on Dunhuang Grottoes, China, 1987; on the Four Monk Painters, Shanghai Mus., 1987; on art of Chang Dai-chien, Nat. Mus. History, Taipei, 1988; Symposium on Contemporary Artistic Development, Nanjing, 1988; Symposium on Chinese Painting of Ming Dynasty Chinese U. Hong Kong, 1988; Symposium on Chinese Painting of the Ming and Qing Dynasties from the Forbidden City, Cleve. Mus. Art, 1989, Symposium on Hist. Studies, since 1911, Nat. Taiwan U., 1989, Symposium on 40th Anniversary of Founding of Liaoning Provincial Mus., Shenyang, China, 1989, Symposium on Painting of Wu Sch., Palace Mus., Beijing, 1990; Internat. Colloquium on Chinese Art History, Nat. Palace Mus. Taipei, 1991, Internat. Symposium on Art of Four Wangs, Shanghai, 1992, VIIeme Colloque Internat. de Sinologie, Chantilly, France, 1992, Symposium Painting at Close Qing Empire, Phoenix, 1992, Symposium on Ming & Qing Painting, Beijing, 1994, Symposium on Art of Zhao Meng-fu, Shanghai, 1995, Symposium on 20th Century Chinese Painting, Hong Kong Mus. Art, 1995, Symposium on Contemporary Chinese Painting, Biennale of Shanghai Art Mus., 1998; spl. cons. Chinese U., Hong Kong, 1971, Symposium on Painting and Calligraphy by Ming Loyalists, Early Ch'ing Period, 1975. Author: books and exhbn. catalogues including The Autumn Colors on the Ch'iao and Hua Mountains, A Painting by Chao Meng-fu, 1254-1322, 1965, Liu Kuo-sung: The Development of a Modern Chinese Artist, 1970, A Thousand Peaks and Myriad Ravines: Chinese Paintings in the Charles A Drenowatz Collection, 2 vols., 1974, Trends in Modern Chinese Painting, 1979; co-author: History of Modern Chinese Painting, Part 1: Late Qing, 1998, Part 2: Republican China, 2001; editor: Artists and Patrons: Some Social and Economic Aspects of Chinese Painting, 1990; co-editor: Chinese Scholar's Studio: Artistic Life in Late Ming, Asia Soc., 1987; contbr. , articles to books and catalogues. Ford Found. Fgn. Area Tng. fellow, 1959-60; grantee Am. Council Learned Socs. and Social Sci. Research Council, 1963-64, NEH, 1975, 78, 91, Com. for Scholarly Communication with People's Republic of China Nat. Acad. Scis., 1979, Am. Council Learned Socs., 1980, Asian Cultural Council, N.Y., 1981, Kans. U., summers 1966-80; U. Iowa research prof., 1963-64; Fulbright-Hayes faculty fellow, 1968-69 Mem. Coll. Art Assn. Am., Assn. for Asian Studies, Midwest Art History Soc., Internat. House of Japan, Min-chiu Soc. Hong Kong, Phi Tau Phi, Phi Beta Kappa (hon.), Phi Beta Delta. Home: 1108 Avalon Rd Lawrence KS 66044-2506 Office: Univ Kans Kress Found Dept Art History Lawrence KS 66045-0001 E-mail: ctsli@ku.edu., ctsli@juno.com.

LI, DAVID LEIWEI, English and Asian American studies educator; b. Shanghai, Nov. 23, 1959; came to U.S., 1985; s. Zhen Ting Li and Min Zhi Tao; 1 child, Art Ling. BA in English, Shanghai Fgn. Langs. Inst., 1982; MA in English/ESL, Indiana U. of Pa., 1986; PhD in English, U. Tex., 1991. Lectr. English dept. Shanghai Internat. Studies U., 1982-85; asst. prof. English U. So. Calif., L.A., 1991-97, assoc. prof. English, 1997-99; Collins disting. prof. humanities U. Oreg., Eugene, 1999—. Author: Imagining the Nation: Asian American Literature and Cultural Consent, 1998; editor: Globalization and the Humanities, 2001. Zumberg fellow U. So. Calif., 1994. Mem. MLA (chair Asian Am. discussion group, 1995, mem. exec. com. 1991-95). Office: U Oreg Dept English 1286 U Oreg Eugene OR 97403-1286

LI, DAVID WAN-CHENG, cell biologist; b. Heng Shan, Peoples Republic of China, Sept. 2, 1960; came to the U.S., 1986; s. Xi-Lin and Xin-Tao (Guo) L. BS, Hunan Normal U., 1982, MS, 1985; PhD, U. Wash., 1992. Adj. prof. biology Hunan Normal U., Chang Sha, People's Republic of China, 1995—; tchg. asst. U. Alta., Edmonton, Can., 1986; tchg. and rsch. asst. U. Wash., Seattle, 1986-92; rsch. scientist Columbia U., N.Y.C., 1992-95, asst. prof. ophthalmology, 1996-98; asst. prof. molecular biology UMDNJ-Sch. Medicine, Stratford, 1998—. Contbr. articles to profl. jours. Exec. pres. June 4th Found., Seattle, 1990-92, bd. dirs., 1989—. Mem. AAAS, Am. Soc. Cell Biology, Am. Soc. Biochemistry and Molecular Biology, Soc. Devel. Biology, Internat. Soc. Eye Rsch., N.Y. Acad. Sci., Assn. for Rsch. in Vision and Ophthalmology. Achievements include devel. of a set of biol. stds. for the hybrid yue carp and its parents; identification of pair of duplicated genes coding for two different isoelectric forms of insect pigment protein and cloning of these genes; discovery of a common cellular mechanism for stress induced non-congenital cataract formation in humans and animals. Office: U Medicine and Dentistry NJ Dept Molecular Biology 2 Med Ctr Dr Sci Ctr Rm 347 Stratford NJ 08084 E-mail: lidw@umdnj.edu.

LI, DORA HSI-CHUN, accountant; b. Hong Kong, Oct. 17, 1964; came to U.S., 1977; d. Chester C. and Mimi K. Li. BS, NYU, 1987. Bookkeeper Graphik Dimension Ltd., Flushing, N.Y., 1987-91; full charge bookkeeper Stereo Exch., Inc., N.Y.C., 1991-98; contr. Paging Source of Manhattan, 1998—. Avocations: travel, camping, fishing, playing tennis. Home: 68-61 Yellowstone Blvd Forest Hills NY 11375

LI, FUAN, marketing educator, researcher; b. Ning Yang, China, June 7, 1952; came to U.S., 1990; s. Tian You Li and Xiu Fang Ji; m. Bing Lan, Sept. 30, 1977; 1 child, Xiao Yi. BA in Philosophy, Shandong U., Jinan, China, 1982; MBA, Idaho State U., 1994; PhD in Marketing, Fla. Internat. U., 1999. Asst. prof. East China Normal U., Shanghai, 1985-90; vis. prof. St. Olaf Coll., Northfield, Minn., 1990-91; lectr. Fla. Internat. U., Miami, 1997-99; asst. prof. mktg. Mercyhurst Coll., Erie, Pa., 1999—2001; assoc. prof. mktg. William Paterson U., Wayne, NJ, 2002—. Author: Philosophical Logic and Philosophy of Logic, 1989; contbr. articles to profl. jours. Mem. Am. Mktg. Assn. (Doctoral Consortium fellow 1997), Acad. Mktg. Sci., Assn. Consumer Rsch., Soc. Consumer Psychology. Avocations: swimming, hiking, table tennis, tai chi. Home: 27 Harrier Ct Wayne NJ 07470 Office: William Paterson U 300 Pompton Rd Wayne NJ 07470-0001 E-mail: lif@wpunj.edu.

LI, FUHE, research scientist; b. Hubei, China; s. Wenshan Li and Rong Zhou; m. Kathleen H. Li; 1 child, Summer. BS, Nankai U., China, 1982; PhD, U. Vt., 1995. Chemist, project mgr. Semiconductor Rsch. Inst., Tianjin, China, 1982-88; postdoctoral U. Calif., Berkeley, 1995—97; mgr. thin film and chem. labs. Balazs Analytical Lab., Sunnyvale, Calif., 1997-98, tech. mgr., 1999—2001, Air Liquide Am. Corp., Fremont, 2001—. Vis. scientist McGill U., 1989-90. Contbr. articles to profl. jours. NSF grantee, 1996. Mem. Am. Chem. Soc. (semicondr. equipment and material internat. global chem. processing com.), San Francisco Internat. Volleyball Club. Home: 139 Lake Merced Hill 2C San Francisco CA 94132 Office: Air Liquide America Corp 46409 Landing Parkway Fremont CA 94538 Fax: 408-734-2276. E-mail: fli@balazs.com.

LI, GEORGE, cardiologist; b. Morristown, N.J., Jan. 29, 1958; s. Hsiao-Jun and Ven-Shun Li; m. Katherine Li; children: Sean, Shea, Brian. BS, Rensselaer Poly. Inst., 1980; MD, Baylor Coll. Medicine, 1984. Diplomate Am. Bd. Internal Medicine, specialty cardiovasc. diseases. Instr. medicine U. Tex. Med. Sch., Houston, 1990-92, asst. prof. medicine, 1992-94, clin. asst. prof. medicine, 1994—; with Internal Medicine Specialists, 1994—98, Houston Cardiovasc. Assocs., 1998—. Clin. instr. Baylor Coll. Medicine, Houston, 1994-98, clin. asst. prof. medicine, 1998—. Co-author: Molecular Biological Alterations in Heart Failure, Support and Replacement of the Failing Heart, 1995. Recipient Clin. Investigator Devel. award NIH, 1993, Henry Christen Meml. award Am. Fedn. Clin. Rsch., 1992. Fellow ACP, Am. Coll. Cardiology; mem. Am. Heart Assn. (rsch. fellow 1988), Alpha Omega Alpha. Office: Houston Cardiovasc Assocs 6560 Fannin St Ste 1654 Houston TX 77030-2734

LI, GUOHUA, epidemiologist, educator; b. Hubei, Mianyang, China, Jan. 11, 1963; arrived in U.S., 1989; s. Juxian Li and Fulan Xie; m. Xiaoying Ma, Dec. 15, 1987; children: Roland, Susan, Benjamin. MD, Beijing Med. U., 1984; MPH, Tongji Med. U., Wuhan, China, 1987; PhD, Johns Hopkins U., 1993. Lectr. Tongji Med. U., Wuhan, 1987-89; rsch. assoc. Johns Hopkins U. Sch. Hygiene and Pub. Health, Balt., 1992-95; asst. prof. Johns Hopkins U. Sch. Medicine, 1995-97, assoc. prof., 1997—2000, prof., 2001—. Mem. adj. faculty Johns Hopkins U. Sch. Hygiene and Pub. Health, 1995—. Co-author: Injury Fact Book, 2d edit., 1992; contbr. articles to profl. jours. Trustee Howard County Chinese Sch., Columbia, Md., 1998—. Recipient FIRST award Nat. Inst. on Alcohol Abuse and Alcoholism, 1995, Roche Epidemiology prize, 1999; grantee Nat. Inst. on Aging, NIH, 1997—, Nat. Inst. on Alcohol Abuse and Alcoholism, 1999—, Alcoholic Beverage Med. Rsch. Found., 1997-99, Ins. Inst. for Hwy. Safety, 1999—. Mem. Am. Pub. Health Assn., Aerospace Med. Assn., Soc. Acad. Emergency Medicine, Soc. Epidemiologic Rsch. Avocations: reading, writing, walking, team sports. Home: 4742 Leyden Way Ellicott City MD 21042-5989 Office: Johns Hopkins U 1830 E Monument St Baltimore MD 21204

LI, GUOSONG, mechanical engineering educator; b. Gaoyou, Jiangsu, China, May 9, 1965; s. Jiqing and Guixiang (Xu) L.; m. Ping Li, Feb. 27, 2002. BSc, Jiangsu Inst. Tech., Zhenjiang, China, 1985; MSc, Jiao Tong U., Shanghai, 1988, D Engring., 1991; PhD, Wright State U., 2000. Asst. prof. Jiao Tong U., Shanghai, 1991-92, assoc. prof. mech. engring., 1993-96, dep. dir. mfg. engring. divsn. dept. mech. engring., 1994-96; rsch. asst. Wright State U., 1996-2000; engring. analyst Hourglass Solutions Inc., Livonia, Mich., 2000—. Mem. youth commn. Prodn. Engring. Instn., 1992-96. Contbr. articles to profl. jours. Recipient Grade 2-prize for sci. and tech. progress The State Commn. of Edn. of People's Republic of China, Shanghai, 1993. Mem. AIAA, ASME, Soc. Mfg. Engrs., Chinese Mech. Engring. Soc. Avocations: classical music, Chinese chess, philosophy, fishing. Home: 7130 Foxthorne Dr Canton MI 48187 Office: Hourglass Solutions Inc Ste 424 17199 N Laurel Park Dr Livonia MI 48152 E-mail: guosong@gsli.net.

LI, HAIJUN, mathematician, educator, mathematician, consultant; b. Beijing, China, Feb. 12, 1958; arrived in U.S., 1987; s. Wenhua Li, Guixian Qiu; m. Sha Lisa Lu; children: Kevin. BS, Harbin Inst. Tech., China, 1982; PhD, U. Ariz., 1994. Lectr. Beijing Poly. U., 1982—87; asst. prof. Wash. State U., Pullman, 1994—2000, assoc. prof., 2000—. Cons. eCilitate Inc., Palo Alto, Calif., 2000—01. Recipient A Study of Synchronized Systems with Applications to Manufacturing, Communication and Reliability, NSF, USA, 1998—2002. Mem.: Inst. Ops. Rsch. and Mgmt. Sci., Inst. Math. Stats. Avocation: writing. Office: Wash State U Dept Math Pullman WA 99164 Office Fax: 509-335-1188. Personal E-mail: shaluli@msn.com. Business E-Mail: lih@math.wsu.edu.

LI, HANNA WU, music educator; b. Canton, China, Mar. 28, 1934; came to U.S., 1958, naturalized, 1972; d. Yat Chih and Wei Ying (Lo) Wu; m. Ching Chung Li, June 10, 1961; children: William Wei-Lin, Vincent Wei-Tsin. BA in Piano, Nat. Taiwan Normal U., 1956; MMus in Piano, Northwestern U., 1961. Instr. piano dept. music Nat. Taiwan Normal U., Taipei, 1956-58; instr. piano, prep. sch. dept. music Carnegie-Mellon U., Pitts., 1969-84, dir. piano, prep. sch., 1984—, instr. piano dept. music, 1974-78, artist lectr. in piano, 1979-88, assoc. prof. music, 1988—. Soloist, accompanist chamber music, Taipei, 1954—58; judge Young Musician Audition, Wheeling, W.Va., 1979, Wheeling, 95; adjudicator internat. piano competition Young Keyboard Artist Assn., Ann Arbor, Mich., 1985; judge Chiang Wen Yeh Internat. Young Artist Piano Competition, Washington, 1996; lectr. in U.S. and abroad; piano pedagogy workshop lectr., Shanghai, 93, Zhanjiang, China, 99, Grand Rapids, Mich., 99, Charleston, SC, 99, Charleston, 2001; adjudicator Chautauqua (N.Y.) Sch. Music, 1999; mem. com. on future of piano pedagogy World Piano Pedagogy Conf., 1996—. Recipient Presdl. Scholar's Disting. Tchr. award White House, 1997; students have won numerous awards and scholarships. Mem. Am. Music Scholarship Assn. (chmn. eastern region piano contest 1975—), Pitts. Concert Soc. (bd. dirs. 1984—), Pi Kappa Lambda. E-mail: hl2j+@andrew.cmu.edu. Home: 2130 Garrick Dr Pittsburgh PA 15235-5033 Office: Carnegie-Mellon U Sch Music Pittsburgh PA 15213

LI, HONGZHI, Falun Dafa founder, author; b. Jilin, China, May 13, 1951; came to U.S., 1996, permanent resident, 1998. m. Li Rui, 1981; 1 child, Li Meige. Qi-gong Master. Founder Falun Dafa, pres. Falun Dafa Inst., Beijing, 1992—; tchr. Falun Gong exercises, 1992-94. Lectr. over 450 on Falun Dafa, China, 1992-94, numerous lectures worldwide, 1995—. Author: China Falun Gong, 1993, Zhuan Falun (Best Selling book 1996, translated in over 20 langs.), 1994, Zhuan Falun II, 1995, Falun Dafa Exposition, 1996, Falun Buddha Law (Essentials for Further Advancement), 1997, Falun Buddha Law (Lecture in U.S.), 1997, Falun Dafa Explication, 1997, The Great Perfection Way of Falun Buddha Law, 1997, Falun Buddha Law (Lecture in Sydney), 1997, Falun Buddha Law (Lecture in European Falun Dafa Conference), 1999, Falun Buddha Law (Lecture in North America), 1999, Falun Buddha Law (Lecture in Changchun), 1999, Falun Buddha Law (Lecture in Singapore), 1999, Falun Buddha Law (Lecture in Switzerland), 1999, Hong Yin, 1999, Falun Buddha Law (Lecture in New Zealand), 2000, Falun Buddha Law (Lecture in Canada), 2000, Falun Buddha Law (Lecture in West America), 2000, Falun Budda Law (lecture in East America), 2000; videos include Falun Dafa 9 Day Lectures, Jinan, 1994, Falun Gong (5 sets) exercise instrn. tape, 1994; music cassette Falun Xuilian Dafa Exercise, 1994, others. Nominated Nobel Peace Prize, 2000, 2001; recipient Award for Advanced Boundary Sci. The Special Gold award, named Qi-gong Master most acclaimed by the masses, Oriental Health Expo., Beijing, 1993, Honor Cert. found. under Ministry of Pub. Security of China, 1993, Award Outstanding Svc., Ill., 1999, over 40 proclamations, resolutions, citations honor Master Li Hongzhi/Falun Dafa including Congl. Recognition of Achievement N.J., N.Y., Pa., Mass., Vt., others, 1999-2001, Internat. Religious Freedom award, Freedom House, U.S., 2001; Hon. Citizen and Goodwill amb., Houston, 1996, Hon. Citizen Atlanta, 1999, Hon. Georgia Citizen, Ga., 2000, Li Hongzhi Day/week proclaimed in over 20 cities, 1996-2001, Falun Dafa or Truth, Compassion, Forbearance day/week/month proclaimed in over 500 cities in U.S., Can., New Zealand, Australia, 1999-2001; honored Courage and Perserverance, N.Y.C., 2000. Avocation: cultivation. Mailing: 136-08 59th Ave Flushing NY 11355-5245

LI, HUA HARRY, computer scientist, electrical engineer; b. Tianjin, People's Republic of China, Nov. 22, 1956; came to U.S., 1982; s. Hua Sheng and Bao Ai Li; m. Maiying Lu, Nov. 4, 1982; children: Alen Lee, Kevin Lee. BS in Electronics Engring., Tianjin U., 1982; MSECE, U. Iowa, 1984, PhD in ECE, 1989. Lectr. Tianjin U., 1982; asst. prof. computer sci. Tex. Tech U., Lubbock, 1989-95, assoc. prof. computer sci., 1995-96; prin. engr. 53 Inc., Santa Clara, Calif., 1997; sr. computer architect Smedia Corp., San Jose. Computer cons., 1990—; inventor 1994 World Congress Neural Network Conf. Indsl. Neural Network Award; assoc. prof. computer engring. San Jose State U., 1997—. Author, editor: Vision Computing with VLSI Circuits, 1994, Fuzzy Logic and Intelligent Systems, 1995, Video Compression, 1996. Mem. IEEE. Avocations: camping, piano, fishing. Home: Redwood Shores 2200 Santa Ana St Palo Alto CA 94303-3137 Office: San Jose State Univ Computer Sci Dept Computer Engring Dept San Jose CA 95192-0001 Address: 37576 Summer Holly Cmn Fremont CA 94536-6569

LI, HUASHENG, scientist; b. Anyang, Henan, China, May 22, 1963; p. Fengren Li and Yuxiu Geng; m. Hua Shen, July 11, 1991; 1 child, Sijia. BS, Zhengzhou (China) Inst. Tech., 1982; MS, Taiyuan (China) U. Tech., 1985; PhD, Dalian (China) U. Tech., 1991. Asst. prof. Zhengzhou Inst. Tech., 1982-87, lectr., 1987-88, Beijing U. Chem. Tech., 1991-94, assoc. prof., 1994-95; vis. scientist Tokyo Inst. Tech., 1995-97; mgr. Ctrl. Computer Svcs. Co., Ltd., Tokyo, 1997-98, Aigis Sys., Inc., Bloomfield, N.J., 1998-99; sr. scientist Hi-Tec Sys., Inc., Egg Harbor Township, 1999—. Contbr. articles to profl. jours. Recipient Excellent Young Tchr. award Beijing Authority Culture and Edn., Huam Affair Bur., Beijing, Ednl. Labor Union Beijing, 1993, Beijing Exemplary Tchr. award Beijing Edn. Bur., 1994, Excellent Paper award soc. Computer Application and Chem. Engring., 1990. Mem.: Internat. Coun. Systems Engring., Chinese Younger's Assn. Chem. Engring. (standing com. 1994—96), Process Sys. Engring. China (com. 1997—99), Process Sys. Engring. Soc. Japan (com. 1997—99). Office: Hi-Tec Sys Inc 500 Scarborough Dr Ste 108 Egg Harbor Township NJ 08234 Home: 106 Ontario Ave Egg Harbor Township NJ 08234-4929 Fax: (609) 272-1888. E-mail: Huasli@hotmail.com.

LI, JIAN, chemical engineer, educator; b. Beijing, Sept. 3, 1957; came to U.S., 1997; s. Qinggui Li and Xinzhi Feng. B in Engring., Tianjin Inst. Light Industry, China, 1982; M in Engring., McGill U., 1986, PhD, 1989. Indsl. postdoctoral fellow Pulp and Paper Rsch. Inst. of Can., Pointe Claire, Que., 1989-90, rsch. scientist, 1990-97; assoc. prof. chem. engring. Inst. Paper Sci. and Tech., Atlanta, 1997-2000; prin. scientist Rayonier Rsch. Ctr., Jesup, Ga., 2000—. Invited spkr. Ekaman Day, Swedish Pulp and Paper Engr. Assn., 1997. Contbr. articles to profl. jours.; inventor in field. Rsch. grantee State of Ga., 1998. Mem. AIChE (ann. conf. program chair forest products divsn. 1999—), Tech. Assn. of Pulp and Paper Industry, Can. Pulp and Paper Assn. Office: 4474 Savannah Hwy Jesup GA 31545-5275 E-mail: jian.li@rayonier.com.

LI, JIN, environmental engineer, educator; b. Wuhan, Hubei, China, Sept. 24, 1972; arrived in U.S., 1977; d. Jianxin Li and Enqi Liu; married. PhD, U Cin., 2001. Rsch. fellow Hong Kong Polytech. U., HongKong, China, 1997; rsch. asst. U. Cin., 1997—2001; asst. prof. U. Wis., Milw., 2001—. Contbr., presenter U. Wis. Dept. Civil Engring., Milw., 2000—. Mem.: Am. Water Works Assn., Am. Soc. Microbiology, Am. Chem. Soc., Water Environ. Fedn., Internat. Water Assn., Assn. Environ. Engring and Sci. Profs., Sigma Xi. Office: Univ Wis Milw 3200 N Cramer St Milwaukee WI 53211 Office Fax: 414-229-6958. Business E-Mail: li@uwm.edu.

LI, JINPING, medical educator, researcher; b. Beijing, People's Republic of China, Oct. 11, 1963; s. Zhiyuan Li and Fatou Lou; m. Zhibin He, Aug. 16, 1989. B of Medicine, Hunan Med. Coll., People's Republic of China, 1985; MD, Peking Union Med. Coll., Beijing, 1990; PhD, Weizman Inst. of Sci., Israel, 1997. Attending physician China-Japa Friendship Hosp., Beijing, 1990-92; vis. scientist Hyogo (Japan) Med. Coll., 1993; postdoctoral fellow Stanford (Calif.) U., 1997-99, U. Tex., Dallas, 1999-2000, faculty mem., 2000—. Contbr. articles to profl. jours. Fellowship European Molecular Biology Orgn., 1996, Internat. Endocrinology Assn., 1996. Mem. AAAS. Office: Southwestern Med Ctr 5323 Harry Hines Blvd Dallas TX 75390-7208

LI, KAM WU, mechanical engineer, educator; b. China, Feb. 16, 1934; came to U.S., 1959; s. Yang Chung and Oy Lan Li; MS, Colo. State U., 1961; PhD, Okla. State U., 1965; m. Shui Mui Chan, Aug. 30, 1956; children: Christopher, Charles. Asst. prof. mech. engring. Tex. A&M U., Kingsville, 1965-67; assoc. prof. N.D. State U., Fargo, 1967-73, prof., 1973—, assoc. dean engring. and arch., 1989-91, chmn. dept. mech. engring., 1994-96; cons. Charles T. Main Inc., Boston, 1973-80, Center for Profl. Advancement, East Brunswick, N.J., 1982-84. Recipient cert. appreciation U.S. Navy, 1974; NSF fellow, 1966; Ford Found. fellow, 1972. Mem. ASME, N.Y. Acad Scis., Sigma Xi, Tau Beta Pi, Pi Tau Sigma, Kappa Mu Epsilon. Author: Power Plant System Design and Applied Thermodynamics. Contbr. numerous articles to profl. jours.; govt. engring. research, 1965—. Home: 2516 18th St S Moorhead MN 56560-4811 Office: ND State U University Ave Fargo ND 58105

LI, KEQIN, computer scientist, educator; b. Shanghai, China, May 26, 1963; s. Guoxing and Zongfen (Gu) L.; m. Ling Gao, May 21, 1987; children: Andrew, Charlotte, Christina. BS in Computer Sci., Tsinghua U., 1985; PhD in Computer Sci., U. Houston, 1990. Instr. U. Houston, 1987-88, rsch. asst., 1988-90; asst. prof. SUNY, New Paltz, 1990-96, assoc. prof., 1996-99, prof., 1999—. Assoc. editor-in-chief Internat. Assn. of Sci. and Tech. for Devel. jour., 1996-99; co-editor: Parallel Computing Using Optical Interconnections, 1998; co-editor conf. procs.; contbr. numerous articles to profl. jours. Recipient Best Paper award Internat. Conf. on Parallel and Distributed Processing Techniques and Applications, 1996, 49th Nat. Aerospace and Electronics Conf., 1997, Internat. Parallel and Distributed Processing Symposium, 2000. Mem. IEEE (sr.), IEEE Computer Soc., Assn. of Computing Machinery, Soc. for Indsl. and Applied Math., Internat. Assn. of Sci. and Tech. for Devel. Achievements include pioneered research on processor allocation and job scheduling in partitionable mesh connected systems which has inspired substantial subsequent research by numerous researchers and has created a very active and productive research area in parallel computing; co-inventor linear array with a reconfigurable pipelined bus system computing model which is now more and more popular in parallel computing using optical interconnections. Home: 21 Robin Rd Poughkeepsie NY 12601-5619 Office: SUNY 75 S Manheim Blvd New Paltz NY 12561-2499 E-mail: li@mcs.newpaltz.edu.

LI, LESLIE DENISE, novelist, journalist, playwright; b. N.Y.C., Nov. 21, 1945; d. Youlin and Genevieve (Louie) L.; 1 child, Anton Heinrich. BA, U. Mich., 1967; cinquieme degree, Alliance Francaise, Paris, 1969. Creator Taoist writing workshop, facilitator The Writers Voice of YMCA, N.Y.C., 1999-2000, N.Y. Open Ctr., N.Y.C., 1998-2001, Paris Writers Workshop, Paris, 2001; lectr. Asia Soc., Smithsonian Instn., Barnard Coll., Bowdoin Coll., Asian Studies Outreach, among others. Author: Bittersweet, 1992; co-author: Enter the Dragon, 2002; contbr. articles to profl. publs. including Travel & Leisure, Gourmet, Garden Design, Saveur, Modern Maturity, Writers Digest, N.Y. Times, The Internat. Herald Tribune, among others. Leo Maitland fellow, Millay Colony for the Arts, 1992; Freeman Found. grantee, 1998; recipient Tenn. Williams scholarship in fiction Sewanee Writer's Conf., 1999; resident Cottages at Hedgebrook, 1994. Mem.: Authors Guild. E-mail: leslieli@sover.net.

LI, LIN, physicist, biophysicist; b. Kaifeng, Henan, China, Dec. 3, 1969; came to U.S., 1992; s. Wu-Yi Li and Ding-Bi Zhao; m. Xin Li, Jan. 5, 1997. BS, Peking U., Beijing, 1991; MS, Northeastern U., Boston, 1994; PhD, U. Pa., 2000. Rsch. asst. Northeastern U., Boston, 1993—94, U. Pa., Phila., 1994—96, rsch. fellow, 1996—2000, postdoctoral rschr., 2000—01, rsch. assoc., 2001—. Mem. AAAS, Internat. Soc. Magnetic Resonance Medicine (Ednl. Student Stipend award), Internat. Yan Xin Qigong Sci. Assn., Am. Assn. Physicists Medicine. Office: MMRRCC B1 Stallar Chance La 422 Curie Blvd Philadelphia PA 19104 E-mail: lin@mail.mmrrcc.upenn.edu.

LI, MARY J. scientist, educator; b. Jinan, China; came to U.S., 1986; d. Jiawen and Changxian (Liu) Li; m. Liqin Len Wang; 1 child, Stefany C. Wang. BS, Ctrl.-South Inst. Tech., Changsha, China, 1982; MS, U. Md., 1989, PhD, 1992. Engr., instr. Xian (China) Mining Inst., 1982-86; tchg. asst. U. Md., College Park, 1986-92, rsch. scientist, 1992-98, assoc. dir., 1996-98, adj. prof., 1998-2001; prin. scientist Raytheon STX/NASA Goddard Space Flight Ctr., Greenbelt, Md., 1998-2001, chief scientist, 2000—. Panel reviewer NSF, Arlington, Va., 1995, 98. Contbr. chpt. to book, articles to profl. jours. Bd. dirs. Hope Chinese Sch., Md., 1996-98. Recipient Engring. Rsch. award NSF, 1995, Materials Rsch. award Army-DURIP, 1997, others. Mem. IEEE, Soc. Photo-Optical Instrumentation Engrs., Microscopy and Microanalysis Soc., Chinese-Am. Sci. and Tech. Assn. (bd. dirs. 1997—). Avocations: gardening, reading, water skiing, skiing. Office: Raytheon/NASA Goddard Space Flight Ctr Code 551 Bldg 22 Rm 390 Greenbelt MD 20771-0001

LI, MING, laser research scientist; b. Beijing, Sept. 4, 1968; m. Changqing Chen. PhD, U. Conn., 1999. Rsch. scientist Panasonic Boston Lab., Cambridge, Mass., 1999—. Indsl. affiliate MIT, Cambridge. Contbr. articles to sci. jours., including Japanese Jour. Applied Physics, Phys. Rev. Letters, Jour. Optical Soc. Am. B. Recipient outstanding rsch. award U.S. Immigration and Naturalization Svc., 2000. Mem. Optical Soc. Am., Materials Rsch. Soc., Am. Phys. Soc. Office: Panasonic Techs Inc 68 Rogers St Cambridge MA 02142 Fax: 617-577-1275. E-mail: phli@research.panasonic.com.

LI, NORMAN N. chemicals executive; b. Shanghai, China, Jan. 14, 1933; came to U.S.; naturalized, 1969. s. Lieh-wen and Amy H. Li; m. Jane C. Li, Aug. 17, 1963; children: Rebecca H., David H. BSChemE, Nat. Taiwan U., Taipei, 1955; MS, Wayne State U., 1957; PhD, Stevens Inst. Tech., 1963. Sr. scientist Exxon Rsch. and Engring. Co., Linden, NJ, 1963-81; dir. separation sci. and tech. UOP, Des Plaines, Ill., 1981-88; dir. engineered products and process tech. Allied-Signal Inc., 1988-92, dir. rsch. and tech., 1993-95; pres., CEO NL Chem. Technology, Inc., 1995—. Mem. NRC, 1985-89; lectr. AIChE, 1975-86. Editor 13 books on separation sci. and tech.; contbr. articles to jours. in field; patentee in field. Fellow: AIChE (dir. divsn. food, pharms. and bioengring. 1988—91, bd. dirs. 1992—94, Alpha Chi Sigma rsch. award 1988, Ernest Thiele award 1995, Chem. Engring. Practice award 2000, Lifetime Achievement award 2001); mem.: Acad. Sinica, Chinese Acad. Scis., N.Am. Membrane Soc. (pres. 1991—93, Perkin medalist 2000), Am. Chem. Soc. (Separation Sci. and Tech. award 1988), NAE. Home: 620 N Rolling Ln Arlington Heights IL 60004-5820 E-mail: nlchem@aol.com.

LI, PEARL NEI-CHIEN CHU, technology company executive; b. Jiangsu, China, June 17, 1946; came to U.S., 1968; d. Ping-Yung and Yao-Hwa (Li) Chu; m. Terry Teng-Fang Li, Sept. 20, 1969; children: Ina Ying, Ping Li. BA, Nat. Taiwan U., Taipei, 1968; MA, W.Va. U., 1971; cert. advanced study in info. studies, Drexel U., 1983. Cert. sr. libr., N.J. Instr. Nat. Tchr.'s Coll., Chang-Hua, Taiwan, 1977-78; reference libr. Camden County Libr., Voorhees,

N.J., 1981-82; libr. Kulzer and Dipadova, P.A., Haddonfield, 1982-87; libr. dir. Am. Law Inst., Phila., 1987-92; gen. mgr., info. specialist Unitek Internat. Corp. (Am.), Mt. Laurel, N.J., 1992-96; owner Universal Tech. Inc., 1997—. Tchr. South Jersey Chinese Sch., Cherry Hill, N.J., 1978-82. Editor: CLE Around the Country (annually), 1988-92; contbr. articles to profl. jours. Bus. mgr. Chinese Cmty. Ctr., Voorhees, 1981; mem. N.J. Dept. Commerce and Econ. Devel. for Small and Women and Minority Businesses, City of Phila. Minority/Women and Disadvantaged Bus. Enterprise, Md./D.C. Minority Supplier Devel. Coun., N.Y./N.J. Minority Purchasing Coun., N.Y./N.J. Port Authority Minority Bus. Enterprise. Home: 1132 Sea Gull Ln Cherry Hill NJ 08003-3113 Office: Universal Technology Inc 125 Gaither Dr Ste E Mount Laurel NJ 08054-1706 Fax: 856-235-0590. E-mail: ask@uti8.com.

LI, PETER WAI-KWONG, mathematics educator; b. Hong Kong, Apr. 18, 1952; came to U.S., 1971; s. Chun Tat and Lai Mui (Sum) L.; m. Glenna Marie Seaver, Oct. 30, 1982; children: Tiana, Natasha, Talia. BA, Calif. State U., 1974; MA, U. Calif., Berkeley, 1977, PhD, 1979. Rsch. mem. Inst. for Advanced Study, Princeton, N.J., 1979-80; asst. prof. Stanford (Calif.) U., 1980-83; assoc. prof. Purdue U., West Lafayette, Ind., 1983-85; prof. U. Utah, Salt Lake City, 1985-89, U. Ariz., Tucson, 1989-91, U. Calif., Irvine, 1991—, chair math. dept., 1993-96. Editor Rocky Mountain Jour. Math., 1989-91, Procs. of Am. Math. Soc., 1991—; Editor-in-Chief Comm. in Analysis and Geometry, 1992—. Grantee NSF, 1980—; fellowship Sloan, 1982-83, Guggenheim, 1989-90. Mem. Am. Math. Soc., Phi Beta Kappa. Avocations: swimming, skiing, cooking, wine-tasting. Office: U Calif Irvine Dept Math Irvine CA 92697-0001

LI, PINGAN, neurobiologist, educator; b. Yinchuan, Ningxia, China, Jan. 13, 1960; came to U.S., 1998; s. Baozhong Li and Fulian Zhang; m. Hellen Q. Li, June 31, 1987; 1 chlid, Eileena J. MD, Ningxia Med. Coll., Yingchuan, 1982; MS, Capital Med. U., Beijing, 1988; PhD, Lund (Sweden) U., 1996. Asst. prof. Ningxia Med. Coll., 1983-85, lectr., 1988-93; vis. scholar Lund U., 1993-94, assoc. rschr., 1996-97; assoc. prof. med. faculty U. Hawaii, 1998—. Prin. investigator Hawaiian Cmty. Found., 1999—. Scholar WHO, 1993-94, Lund U., 1995-96, Saskatoon (Can.) Rsch. Bd., 1996-97. Mem. Soc. for Neurosci. Avocations: chess, table tennis. Home: 98-897A Kaonohi St Aiea HI 96701 Office: Pacific Biomed Rsch Ctr LMP T312 1960 East West Rd Honolulu HI 96822

LI, QIN, television anchor, reporter, director, producer; came to U.S., 1999:; d. Jinkui and Hong Li. BA in Law, Chinese Youth Coll. Polit. Sc., Beijing, 1992; MS in Econs., Chinese Acad. Social Sci., Beijing, 1998; MS in Journalism, Columbia U., 2000. Cert. in pub. affairs. Reporter People's Daily, Beijing, 1992-94, editor, reporter Shanghai, 1994-99; TV anchor, news reporter Sino TV, Inc., N.Y.C., 2001—. Dep. editor-in-chief New Asia Culture Found. and Pub. House, Hong Kong, 1999—. Prodr.: (TV news documentary) Blue Sky Station: 8th Avenue—New York's 3d Chinatown, 2000 (Emmy award NATAS 2000); contbg. author: First-Hand Experience with China's Hope Project in One Hundred Counties, 1991; co-author: Japan: Another Miracle in the 21st Century?, 1993; contbr. feature stories to internat. publs. Mem. selection com. Internat. Fanzhian Scholarship, Hong Kong, 1998-2001 Recipient Best News award Chinese Nat. Journalists Assn. and Chinese Disability Assn., 1994, Best News award Chinese People's Polit. Consultative Conf., 1993; featured in Selected Works of Outstanding Chinese Editors and Reporters, 1996. Mem. Soc. Profl. Journalists. Home: Apt 2B 608 W 114th St New York NY 10025 Office Fax: 718-661-9138. E-mail: ql20@columbia.edu.

LI, QING'AN, scientist, researcher; b. Nei Mongul, China, Dec. 17, 1962; came to U.S., 1997; parents Hong and Xiu-yun Li; m. Jian Lu, June 13, 1987; 1 child, Yuan. BS, Nankai U., Tianjing, China, 1985; MS, Chinese Acad. Scis., Beijing, 1990; PhD, Chinese Acad. Scis. & Amsterdam U., Beijing and The Netherlands, 1993. Asst. prof. Nei Mongul U., Huhhot, 1985-87; asst. rsch. scientist Inst. Physics Chinese Acad. Scis., Beijing, 1993-96; postdoctoral fellow U. Tokyo, 1996-97; vis. scientist Argonne (Ill.) Nat. Lab., 1997—. Contbr. papers to profl. jours. Office: Argonne Nat Lab 9700 S Cass Ave Argonne IL 60439-4803 Fax: (630) 252-7777. E-mail: qli@anl.gov.

LI, QINGBO KIMBLE, chemist; s. Chenchuan Li and Yuying Zhou; m. Shuangyan Karen Li, July 14, 1988; children: Steven, Felix. PhD, Iowa State U., 1995. Rsch. assoc. Iowa State U., Ames, 1995—96; project leader SpectruMedix Corp, State College, Pa., 1995—98; head R&D SpectruMedix Corp., 1998—2001, v.p. genetics and customer applications, 2001—. Contbr. chapters to books, articles to profl. jours. Grantee Small Bus. Innovation Rsch. Phase I grant, U.S. Dept. Energy, 1997, Small Bus. Innovation Rsch. Phase II grant, 1998, Advanced Tech. Devel. grant, The Nat. Human Genome Rsch. Inst. , NIH, 2000. Mem.: AAAS, Am. Chem. Soc. Achievements include patents for multiplexed capillary electrophoresis system; automated system for multi-capillary electrophoresis having a two-dimensional array of capillary ends; automated parallel capillary electrophoretic system; electrically insulated capillary arrays for electrophoretic applications; detector having a transmission grating beam splitter for multi-wavelength sample analysis. Home: 2234 Autumnwood Dr State College PA 16801 Office: SpectruMedix Corp 2124 Old Gatesburg Rd State College PA 16803 Office Fax: 814-867-4513. Personal E-mail: qbli@aol.com. E-mail: qbli@spectrumedix.com.

LI, RAO, mathematician, computer scientist; b. Fushun, Liaoning, China, May 3, 1965; s. Jingyuan Li and Liangzhi Zhu; m. Yan Wu, Apr. 27, 1966; children: Dorothy. MA, U. of Pitts., 1994; MS in Computer Sci., PhD in Math., U. of Memphis, 1999. Asst. prof. Fushun Petroleum Inst., Fushun, China, 1988—91, lectr., 1991—92; asst. prof. Ga. Southwestern State U., Americus, Ga., 1999—2001, U. of S.C., Aiken, SC, 2001—. Contbr. articles to profl. jours. Mem.: ACM, Am. Math. Soc. Home: 3 Nancy Lane Apt 3A Aiken SC 29803 Office: University of South Carolina at Aiken 471 University Parkway Aiken SC 29801 Home Fax: 803-641-3726; Office Fax: 803-641-3726. Personal E-mail: raol@usca.edu. E-mail: raol@usca.edu.

LI, RICHARD T. retired library director, secondary school educator; b. Quidong, Hunan Province, China, Aug. 19, 1929; , naturalized, U.S., 1977; s. Town and Pan-Chin Li; m. Felisa T. Tan, Oct. 25, 1964; children: Ray, Joy. BA in English, Tamkang Coll. Arts and Sci., Taipei, Taiwan, 1965; MA in English, S.E. Mo. Coll., 1970; MLS, Kans. State Tchrs. Coll. Emporia, 1971; EdD, U. Kans., 1978. Tchg. cert. Kans. Engring. officer, army capt. Chinese Army, Taiwan, 1954—59; tchr. KW Tech Sch., Taaichung, Taiwan, 1959—61, Keelung 5th Mid. Sch., Keelung, Taiwan, 1965—67; tchr., libr. Eastern Heights H.S., Agra, Kans., 1973—74; head libr. media specialist Atchison (Kans.) H.S., 1974—78; asst. prof. Southwestern Okla. State U., Weatherford, 1978—80; Title III project officer Cameron U., Lawton, 1980—81; asst. dir. learning resources ctr. Tarrant County Jr. Coll., Fort Worth, 1982—97; ret., 1997. Author: Education and Career: An Immigrant's Journey in the Promised Land with Survival Tips, 1999, Where Can Find It? A Sources Handbook for New Immigrants, 2000, My God, It Missed Me! A Young Soldier's Accounts in the War Torn China 1940-50s, 2002. Capt. Army, 1954—59, Taiwan. Home: 4554 Rose Tree Ct Fort Worth TX 76137 Home Fax: 817-656-4138. Personal E-mail: w007745@airmail.net.

LI, SHIBO, medical genetics educator; b. Changchun, Jilin, People's Republic of China, Nov. 3, 1959; came to U.S., 1987; s. Yuliang and Zhongju (Gu) L.; m. Ying Zhao, May 18, 1985; 1 child, Lingshen. MD, Norman Bethune U. Med. Scis., Changchun, 1984. Resident, chief resident dept infectious disease First Teaching Hosp. of Norman Bethune U. Med. Scis., Changchun, 1984-87; postdoctoral fellow dept. lab. medicine and dept. genetics Yale U. Sch. Medicine, New Haven, 1987-93; clin. cytogenetic fellow, adj. asst. prof. U. South Ala. Coll. Medicine, Mobile, 1993-96, asst. prof., 1996—. Contbr. articles to profl. jours. Fellow Ministry of Pub. Health, People's Republic of China, 1987. Mem. AAAS, Assn. Chinese Geneticists in Am. (postdoctoral fellow ann. award 1990), Am. Human Genetics Soc. Home: 13504 Fox Creed Dr Oklahoma City OK 73131 Office: BSEB Rm 224 941 Stanton L Young Blvd Oklahoma City OK 73104-5019 E-mail: shibo-li@ouhsc.edu.

LI, SHU, electronics executive; b. Beijing, Dec. 12, 1958; s. Sitian Li and Xin Wang; m. Xiping Wu, May 26, 1995; children: Justin, Jason. PhD, Harvard U., 1987. Sr. v.p. Conexant Sys., Newport Beach, Calif., 2000—02; pres., CEO Jazz Semiconductor, 2002—, also bd. dirs. Office: Jazz Semiconductor 4321 Jamboree Rd Newport Beach CA 92660 Office Fax: 949-435-8756. Business E-Mail: shu.li@jazzsemi.com.

LI, SHUAN C. pathologist; b. Shanghai, China, Nov. 12, 1960; MD, 4th Mil. Med. U., China, 1985, MSc, 1987. Diplomate Am. Bd. Pathology, AP/CA, 1995. Intern 4th Mil. Med. U., 1884-85; fellow of pathology U. So. Calif., 1987-90; resident in pathology Ohio State U., Columbus, 1991-95, fellow CAP Found, 1995-96; fellow GI, liver pathology Johns Hopkins U. Med. Ctr., Balt., 1996-97. Staff pathologist Johns Hopkins Med. Ctr., Balt., 1997-98; asst. prof., attending pathologist U. Vt./Fletcher Allen Health Care, Burlington, 1998—. Mem. Coll. Am. Pathologists, Am. Soc. Clin. Pathologists. Office: U Vt/Fletcher Allen Health Care Dept Pathology Smith-2 Lab 111 Colchester Ave Burlington VT 05401-1473

LI, SHUHE, electrical engineer; b. Tianjin, China, Oct. 21, 1968; s. Zhenbao Li, Fanglan Zhou. PhD, Tianjin U., Tianjin, China, 1996. Postdoctoral rsch. assoc. Oreg. State U., Corvallis, 1998—2001; packaging engr. AXT Corp., Monterey Park, Calif., 2001—. Contbr. articles. Recipient 8th Five-Yr. Nat. Key Project award, China, 1997. Fellow: IEEE; mem.: Optical Soc. of Am. Office: American Xtal Tech 2019 Saturn St Monterey Park CA 91754 Office Fax: 323-278-0096. Business E-Mail: shuhel@axt.com.

LI, SHUI-CHI, research scientist; came to U.S., 1985; MS in Engring., Beijing U. Aero and Astro, 1980; PhD, Princeton U., 1990. Rsch. staff Beijing U. Aero and Astro, 1977-85; rsch. asst. Princeton (N.J.) U., 1985-88; from rsch. engr. to assoc. rsch. scientist U. Calif., La Jolla, 1988-97, assoc. rsch. scientist, 1997-2001, rsch. scientist, 2001—. Cons. BKM, In., San Diego, 1996—. Contbr. articles to profl. jours. Mem. AIAA, ASME, Internat. Gas Turbine Inst. (com. mem., best tech. paper award 1996, 98), Combustion Inst., Soc. Automotive Engrs. Home: 11139 Caminito Rodar San Diego CA 92126-6111 Office: Univ Calif San Diego 9500 Gilman Dr La Jolla CA 92093-5004 Fax: 619-534-5354. E-mail: scli@ucsd.edu.

LI, TIEN-SHUN, obstetrician, gynecologist, educator; b. Kaohsiung, Taiwan, Nov. 13, 1932; came to U.S., 1968; MD, Nat. Taiwan U., 1960. Diplomate Am. Bd. Ob-gyn. From intern to resident in ob-gyn. Nat. Taiwan U. Hosp., Taipei, 1961-64; resident in ob-gyn. St. Barnabas Med. Ctr., Livingston, N.J., 1971-73; attending staff Meadowlands Hosp. Med. Ctr., Secaucus, 1985—; clin. asst. prof. U. Medicine and Dentistry N.J., 1978—; pvt. practice Ft. Lee, N.J., 1978—. Fellow ACOG. Office: 2231 Lemoine Ave Fort Lee NJ 07024-6115

LI, TIEN-YIEN, mathematics educator; b. Hunan, China, June 28, 1945; came to the U.S., 1969; BS, Nat. Tsing Hua U., Taiwan, 1968; PhD, U. Md., 1974. Instr. U. Utah, Salt Lake City, 1974-76; asst. prof. Mich. State U., East Lansing, 1976-79, assoc. prof., 1979-83, prof., 1983-98, univ. disting. prof., 1998—. Contbr. articles to profl. jours. Guggenheim fellow, 1995. Home: 6439 E Island Lake Dr East Lansing MI 48823-9715 Office: Dept Math Mich State Univ East Lansing MI 48824 E-mail: li@math.msu.edu.

LI, TING-KAI, federal agency administrator, medical educator, researcher; BA in Chemistry and Biology, Northwestern U.; MD, Harvard U., 1959; DSc (hon.), Northeastern Ohio U. Dep. dir. biochemistry divsn. Walter Reed Army Inst. Rsch.; mem. faculty Ind. U. Sch. Medicine, Indpls., 1971—2002, disting. prof. medicine and biochemistry, assoc. dean rsch., 1986—2000; dir. Ind. Alcohol Rsch. Ctr.; dir. Nat. Inst. Alcohol and Alcoholism NIH, 2002—. Contbr. articles to profl. jours. Recipient Markle Scholar award in Academic Medicine, Disting. Rsch. award Rsch. Soc. on Alcoholism, James B. Isaacson award for Rsch. Excellence in Chem. Dependency, Jellinek award, W. George Pinnell award for Outstanding Svc., R. Brinkley Smithers Disting. Scientist award, Irwin Rsch. Scholar award, Mark Keller Hon. Lecture award Nat. Inst. on Alcohol Abuse and Alcoholism NIH. Fellow Soc. for Study of Addiction (hon.). Office: 6000 Executive Blvd Wilco Bldg Rm 400 Bethesda MD 20892-7003*

LI, TINGYE, electrical engineer; b. Nanjing, China, July 7, 1931; came to U.S., 1953, naturalized, 1963; s. Chao and Lily Wei-peng (Sie) L.; m. Edith Hsiu-hwei Wu, June 9, 1956; children: Deborah Chunroh, Kathryn Dairoh. BSEE, U. Witwatersrand, South Africa, 1953; MS, Northwestern U., Evanston, Ill., 1955, PhD, 1958; DEng (hon.), Nat. Chiao Tung U., Hsinchu, Taiwan, 1991. Mem. tech. staff AT&T Bell Labs., Holmdel, N.J., 1957-67; dept. head repeater techniques research dept. Bell Labs., 1967-76, lightwave media research dept., 1976-84, lightwave systems research dept., 1984-96; dept. head lightwave networks rsch. dept. AT&T Labs.-Rsch., Holmdel, N.J., 1996, divsn. mgr. Middletown, 1997-98, ret., 1998; ind. cons. Boulder, Colo., 1999—. Hon. prof. Tsinghua U., Shanghai Jiao Tong U., Beijing U. Posts and Telecomms., U. Electronic Sci. and Tech. of China, Qufu Normal U., No. Jiao Tong U., Tianjin U., Nankai U., Fudan U. Assoc. editor Optics Letters, 1977-78, topical editor, 1989-91; assoc. editor Jour. of Lightwave Tech., 1983-86; editor book series: Optical Fiber Telecommunications IV, Optical Fiber Communications, OSA Trends in Optics and Photonics Series; mem. editl. bd. Procs. IEEE, 1974-83, Microwave and Optical Tech. Letters, 1987-90, Internat. Jour. High Speed Electronics, 1990-95; contbr. articles on microwave antennas and propagation, lasers, coherent optics, optical comms., optical-fiber transmission, systems and networks to sci. jours., chpts. in books; patentee in field. Recipient Alumni Merit award Northwestern U., 1981, sci. and tech. medal AT&T, 1997. Fellow IEEE (W.R.G. Baker prize 1975, David Sarnoff award 1979), AAAS, Internat. Engring. Consortium, Photonics Soc. Chinese-Ams. (Achievement award 1998), Optical Soc. Am. (chmn. optical comms. tech. group 1979-80, bd. dirs. 1985-87, chmn. internat. activities com. 1988-90, chmn. photonics divsn. 1991-92, pres. 1995, John Tyndall award 1995, Frederic Ives medal 1997); mem. NAE, Chinese Inst. Engrs. U.S.A. (bd. dirs. 1974-78, Achievement award 1978), Academia Sinica (Taiwan), Chinese Acad. Engring., Chinese Am. Acad. and Profl. Assn. (bd. dirs. 1985-89, Achievement award 1983), Electromagnetics Acad., Sigma Xi, Eta Kappa Nu, Phi Tau Phi (pres. East Am. chpt. 1991-93). Clubs: F.F. Fraternity. E-mail: tinggeli@aol.com.

LI, TONGCHUAN, pharmacologist, researcher; b. Yongtai, Fujian, China, Oct. 11, 1955; s. Zongyu Li and Suying Lin; m. Xingxian Yan, July 29, 1955; children: Bing, Scion, Louisa, Mark. MD, Fujian Med U., Fujian, 1982; PhD, U. Minn., 1990. Instr. Fujian Med. U., Fuzhou, China, 1982—85; sr. scientist CytoMed, Cambridge, Mass., 1993—94; project mgr. Cubist Pharms., Inc., Lexington, 1995—. Guest prof. Fujian Med. U., Fuzhou, 2000. Recipient Bacaner Rsch. award, 1990. Mem.: AAAS, N.Y. Acad.Scis., Am. Soc. Pharmacology and Exptl. Therapeutics, Am. Assn. Fujian Med. U. Alumni (pres. 2002). Achievements include patents for epibatidine and derivatives thereof as cholinergic receptor agonists and antagonists. Home: 6 Salvi Dr Framingham MA 01701 Office: Cubist Pharms Inc 65 Hayden Ave Lexington MA 02421 Office Fax: 781-861-0566. Business E-Mail: tcli@cubist.com.

LI, TZE-CHUNG, lawyer, educator; b. Shanghai, China, Feb. 17, 1927; came to U.S., 1956; s. Ken-hsiang Li and Yun-hsien (Chang) Li; m. Dorothy In-lan Wang, Oct. 21, 1961; children— Lily, Rose LL.B., Soochow U., Shanghai, 1948; Diploma, Nat. Chengchi U., Nanking, 1949, China Research Inst. of Land Econs., Taipei, 1952; M.C.L., So. Meth. U., Dallas, 1956; LL.M., Harvard U., Cambridge, 1958; MS, Columbia U., N.Y.C., 1965; PhD, New Sch. for Social Research, N.Y.C., 1963. Judge Hwa-lien Dist. Ct., Hwa-lien, Taiwan, Republic of China, 1949-51; dist. atty. Ministry of Justice, Taipei, 1951-52; chief law sect. Ministry of Nat. Def., 1952-56; asst. prof. library sci. Ill. State U., Normal, 1965-66; asst. prof. polit. sci., library sci. Rosary Coll., River Forest, Ill., 1966-69, assoc. prof. library sci., 1969-70, 72-74, prof. library sci., 1974-82, dean, prof. Grad. Sch. Library and Info. Sci., 1982-88; prof. Dominican U., 1988-99, dean, prof. emeritus, 2000—; vis. assoc. prof. law Nat. Taiwan U., 1969; vis. assoc. prof. polit. sci. Soochow U., Taipei, 1969; dir. Nat. Central Library, 1970-72. Chmn. Grad. Inst. Library Sci., Nat. Central Library, Taipei, 1970-72; commr. Ministry of Examination, Examination Yuan, Taipei, 1971; chmn. com. on library standards, Ministry of Edn., Taipei, 1972; library cons. Soochow U., Nat. Chengchi U., Dr. Sun Yat-sen Meml. Library; mem. library adv. com. Ency. Britannica, 1982-95; hon. prof. library and info. sci. Jiangxi U., People's Republic of China, 1985—; vis. prof. law Suzhou U., Peking U., 1991, Nat. Taiwan U., 1991; hon. cons. univ. library, 1985—; hon. cons. Jiangxi Med. Coll., 1985—; adv. prof. East China Normal U., 1987—; cons. Nova U., 1987-88; mem. ad hoc adv. com. Chgo. Pub. Library Bldg. Planning, 1987-88; CEO LLD Group, 1972—; bd. chmn. Li Ednl. Found., 1977—. Author books including: Social Science Reference Sources, 1980, 2d edit., 1990, Mah Jong, 1982, 2d edit., 1991, An Introduction to Online Searching, 1985; also numerous articles in profl., scholarly jours.; editor Third World Librs., 1996—; founding editor Jour. Library and Info. Sci., 1975-80, mem. editl. bd. 1986-90; founding chmn., mem. editl. bd. Internat. Jour. of Revs., 1984-89; editor: World Libraries, 1996-99. Pres. Chinese Am. Ednl. Found., Chgo., 1968-70. Recipient Govt. Citation Republic of China, 1956, 1972, Philip D. Sang Excellence in Teaching award Rosary Coll., 1971, Disting. Service award Phi Tau Phi, Chgo., 1982, Service award HUD, Chgo. region, 1985, Disting. Service award Chinese Am. Librarians Assn., 1988. Mem. Chinese Am. Librarians Assn. (founding pres. 1976-80), Library Assn. China (Taipei), Phi Tau Phi (pres. 1985-87) Roman Catholic. Home: PO Box 444 Oak Park IL 60303-0444 Office: Dominican U 7900 Division St River Forest IL 60305-1066

LI, WEIYE, ophthalmologist, biochemist, educator; b. Zhejiang, China, Oct. 10, 1946; arrived in U.S., 1990; s. Zhao-ji and Qin (Yue) Li; m. Xnru Liu, Apr. 12, 1986; 1 child Yafeng. MD, Peking Second Med. Coll., China, 1970; postgrad., Acad. Med. Scis., China, 1978—80; PhD, U. Pa., 1984. Intern Chao Young Hosp., Peking, 1970—71, resident ophthalmology, 1971—78; rsch. fellow dept. ophthalmology and biochem. grad. sch. Sch. Medicine U. Pa., Phila., 1981—84, postdoctor, asst. prof. dept. ophthalmology Scheie Eye Inst. Sch. Medicine, 1984—85; asst. prof., attending physician ophthalmology Peking Union Med. Coll. Hosp., 1985—86, assoc. prof. ophthalmology, 1986—88, prof. ophthalmology, 1988—, chmn. dept. ophthalmology, 1989—99; prof. ophthalmology, dir. rsch. dept. ophthalmology, prof. pathology, mem. faculty interdepartmental program molecular biology and biotech. Hahnemann U., Phila., 1990—. Recipient Rsch. award, Internat. Juvenile Diabetes Found., 1984—86, 1st Class Sci. and Tech. Advances prize, Chinese Ministry Pub. Health, 1988; fellow postdoctoral fellow, Internat. Juvenile Diabetes Found., 1982—84; grantee, NIH, 1981—82, 1986—. Fight for Sight Inc., 1982—83, Am. Diabetes Assn., 1990—, Frank E. Snider Trust Fund, 1990—. Mem.: Assn. Chinese Ophthalmology Soc., Assn. Rsch. in Vision and Ophthalmology. Avocations: table tennis, bicycling, classical music. Office: Hahnemann U Dept Ophthalmology MS 209 219 N Broad St Philadelphia PA 19107 E-mail: weiye.li@drexel.edu.

LI, XIAO MING, engineering analyst; b. Wulumuzi, Sinjing, China, Nov. 6, 1960; came to U.S., 1984; s. Xue-Pu Li and Wei-Juan Chien; m. Josephine Wing Szeto, Feb. 10, 1988. BS in Mech. and Elec. Engring., Beijing Post and Telecom. Inst, 1982; MS in Mech. Engring., SUNY, Stonybrook, 1986, PhD in Mech. Engring., 1991. Elec. engr. Wulumuzi (China) Telephone and Telecomm. co., Sinjiang, 1982-84; rsch. asst. dept. orthopedics Health Sci. Ctr., Stony Brook, N.Y., 1985-86; rsch. asst. Lab. Exptl. Mechanics Rsch. SUNY, 1986-91; engring. analyst Navistar Internat. Transp. Corp. Tech. Ctr., Ft. Wayne, 1992-95; prin. engring. analyst automotive sales and engring. divsn. Citation Corp., Southfield, Mich., 1995-2000, program mgmt., tech. specialist sales and mktg. divsn. Novi, 2000—. Assoc. faculty dept. engring. Purdue U., Ft. Wayne, Ind., 1993. Contbr. articles to profl. jours. Mem. ASME, Soc. Mfg. Engrs., Materials and Info. Soc., Engring. Soc. for Advancing Mobility, Land, Sea, Air and Space. E-mail: xiaomingl@det.citioncorp.com.

LI, XIAOMING, pediatrics educator, psychologist; b. Shuyang, China, Nov. 30, 1956; s. Liangkai Tang and Yuzhen L.; m. Yu Yang, Jan. 1, 1983; children: Linda, Jonathan. PhD, U. Minn., Mpls., 1992. Asst. prof. U. Md. Sch. Medicine, Balt., 1992-98, assoc. prof., 1998-99; prof. W.Va. U., Morgantown, 1999—. Cons. UNICEF, Namibia, 1996-98; guest professorship Nanjing (China) U., 2000-03, Beijing Normal U., 2000-05; mem. US Substance Abuse and Mental Health Svc. Adminstrn. HIV/AIDS Standing Review Com., Bethesda, Md., 2000-02. Contbr. articles to profl. jours. Recipient Dissertation award Am. Psychol. Assn., 1991, Soc. Grad. Rsch. award, Minn. Edn. Alumni Soc., 1991, Eva O. Miller fellowship U. Minn., 1991-92; grantee U. Md. Sch. Medicine, 1993-94, World AIDS Found., 2000-02, Am. Acad. Pediatrics, 2001-02, NIMH, 2001-03. Mem. APS, NIMH, World AIDS Found., Am. Acad. Pediatrics. Office: W Va U PO Box 9214 Morgantown WV 26506-9214 Fax: 304-293-4341. E-mail: xli@hsc.wvu.edu.

LI, XIAO-RONG, electrical engineer, educator; b. Fuzhou, China, Sept. 21, 1959; m. Peizhu Li, Jan. 8, 1988; children: Helen W., Linda W. B of Engring., Zhejiang (China) U., 1982, M of Engring., 1984; MS, U. Conn., 1990, PhD, 1992. Rsch. assoc. U. Calgary (Can.), 1986-87; rsch. asst. U. Conn., Storrs, 1987-92; asst. prof. U. Hartford, West Hartford, Conn., 1992-94, U. New Orleans, 1994-99, assoc. prof., 1999—2002, prof., 2002—. Guest prof. Northwestern Poly. U., Xian, China, 1995—. Author: Estimation and Tracking, 1993, Multitarget Multisensor Tracking, 1995, Probability, Random Signals, and Statistics, 1999, Estimation with Applications to Tracking and Navigation, 2001; editor Comms. in Info. and Sys., 2000—. Recipient Rsch. Initiation award NSF, 1994, Faculty Early Career Achievement award U. New Orleans, 1996, Career award NSF, 1998. Mem. IEEE (sr., assoc. editor Transactions on Aerospace and Electronic Systems, 1995-96, editor 1996—, mem. program com. 35th Conf. on Decision and Control, Kobe, Japan 1996), Internat. Soc. Info. Fusion (steering chair internat. conf. on info. fusion 1998, 2000, gen. vice chair 1999, gen. chair 2002, bd. dirs. 1998—, v.p. for tech. activities 2000—), Chinese Profl. Assn. New Orleans (v.p. 1995-96). Achievements include work with novel methods for performance prediction and analysis of hybrid algorithms and target tracking algorithms; development of variable-structure multiple-model estimation techniques; estimation/track fusion; linear estimation, filtering, prediction, and smoothing. Avocations: swimming, poetry. Office: U New Orleans Electrical Engineering 2000 Lakeshore Dr New Orleans LA 70148-0001 E-mail: xli@uno.edu.

LI, YADONG, engineering educator; arrived in U.S., 1995; PhD, Tsinghua U., Beijing, 1992. Registered engring. intern. Rsch. asst. prof. U. Mo.-Columbia, 1995—2001; asst. prof. Jackson (Miss.) State U., 2002—. Mem.: ASCE, Assn. Environ. Engrs. and Sci. Profs. Office: Jackson State U 1400 J R Lynch St Jackson MS 39217-0168

LI, YAN, hematologist, oncologist; b. Beijing, July 15, 1966; came to U.S., 1990; MD, Beijing Med. U., 1990; PhD, Temple U., 1996. Resident in internal medicine Norwalk (Conn.) Hosp./Yale U. Sch. Medicine, 1996-99; hematology-oncology fellow U. Calif.-San Diego Sch. Medicine, 1999—. Contbr. articles to profl. jours. Grad. rsch. and study fellow Temple U., 1990-96. Mem. ACP, AMA, Am. Soc. Clin. Oncology, Am. Soc. Hematology. Avocations: tennis, opera, travel. E-mail: y4li@ucsd.edu.

LI, YAO-EN, chemical engineer; b. Shanghai, People's Republic of China, Oct. 24, 1958; m. Yi-Yin Ku, May 15, 1959; children: Kory, Katherine. MS, U. Ill., Chgo., 1986, PhD, 1988. Scientist Am. Air Liquide, Countryside, Ill., 1988-89, sr. scientist, 1989-2000; rsch. investigator Abbott Labs., Chgo., 2000—. Contbr. more than 20 articles to AIChE Jour., Jour. of Catalysis, Jour. Phys. Chemistry, Catalysis Letter, Vacuum; patentee in field. James scholar U. Ill., Chgo., 1984; grad. fellow U. Ill., Chgo., 1985-87; recipient Rsch. and Devel. award, 1997. Mem. AIChE, Am. Chem. Soc., Tau Beta Pi. Achievements include the invention & developing the first membrane - based perfluorcarbon compound recovery commercial process in the world, inventor of a hydrogen chloride purification process, invention of several metal surface passivation processes. E-mail: david_li@member.aiche.org.

LI, YUFENG, engineer; b. Ruicheng, Shanxi, China, Apr. 29, 1959; s. Liansheng and Dangdang (Liu) L.; m. Danzhu Lu, June 4, 1985; children: Linda, Steven. BS, Jiaotong U., 1982; MS, U. Wis., 1984, PhD, 1988. Postdoctoral rsch. scientist CMRR/U. Calif., San Diego, 1988-90; sr. adv. engr. Seagate Tech., Bloomington, Minn., 1990-95; sr. engring. mgr. Samsung Info. Systems Am., San Jose, Calif., 1995-98; prin. engr. Iomega Corp., Milpitas, 1998-99; sr. prin. engr. Read-Rite Corp., 1999—. Author chpt. to engring. handbook; contbr. articles to profl. jours. Recipient Math. Competition award Xi'an Jiaotong U., 1978. Mem. ASME (Best Paper award 1993). Achievements include major scientific/engineering contributions that include discovering the inherent shortcomings of optical profilometer in measuring non-homogeneous material and proposed the dual-wavelength solution; establishing the interface stiction theory with surface roughness and liquid film; theorized the I-beam strain gauge measurement system; conceiving the discrete laser-bump texture for tribiological application; demonstrated the accurate measurement of flash temperature with an MR head in nanoseconds; developing the standard for flying height calibration down to nanometers; developing the model for the efficient utilization of desiccant in packaging. Office: Read-Rite Corp 44100 Osgood Rd Fremont CA 94539-6401

LI, ZHANQING, meteorologist, educator; b. Luoyang, Henan, China, Sept. 17, 1963; s. Zhongtai Li, Bian Liang; m. Fengting Huang; children: Cary, Kelsey. BS, Nanjing Inst. of Meteorology, Nanjing, Jiangsu, China, 1982, MS, 1985; PhD, McGill U., 1991. Rsch. scientist Can. Ctr. for Remote Sensing, Ottawa, Canada, 1992—; prof. U. Md., College Park, 2001—. Team leader Can. Ctr. for Remote Sensing, Ottawa, Ontario, Canada, 1995—2000. Contbr. articles (4 National Awards received since 1998 (See the award section), 90s). Recipient Earth Sci. merit award, Natural Resource Can., 2000, Head of Pub. Svc. Aaard, Fed. Govt. of Can., 1998, Tech. in Govt. medal, Treasure Bd. Can., 1999, Agatha Bystram Info. award, Coun. Fed. Libr., 1999, Alouette award, Cana. Aero. and Space Inst., 2000, Earth Sci. merit award, Natural Resource Can., 1997. Mem.: Am. Meteorol. Soc., Am. Geophys. Union (atmosheric sci. com. 1992—). Office: ESSIC Univ Md 2207 CSS Bldg College Park MD 20742-2465 Office Fax: 301-405-8468. Business E-Mail: zli@atmos.umd.edu.

LI, ZHEN, medical researcher; b. Yanshan, China; d. Guoshun Li and Saifang Cheng; m. Juquan Song. MD, Sun Yat-Sen U. Med. Scis., Guangzhou, China, 1993, PhD in Immunology, 1998. Asst. prof. Sun Yat-Sen U. Med. Scis., Guangzhou, 1998-99; postdoctoral rsch. fellow U. Tex. Med. Br., Galveston, 1999—. Contbr. articles to profl. jours. Scholar Japanese 1st Medicine Industry, 1995; grantee Sun Yat-Sen U. Med. Scis., 1999. Mem. Am. Soc. Hematology, Am. Assn. Immunologists, Am. Soc. Microbiology, Am. Soc. Rickettsiology, Am. Soc. Tropical Medicine and Hygiene. E-mail: zhli@utmb.edu.

LI, ZHIJIE, ophthalmologist, immunologist; MS, Weifang Med. Coll., Weifang City, China, 1991; PhD, Jinan U., Guangzhou, China, 1994. Diplomate ophthalmology. Rsch. prof. Jinan U., Guangzhou, 1999—. Editl. bd. mem. Recent Advances in Ophthalmology, Xinxiang, Henan, 1999—. Editor: (book) Ocular Immunologic Diseases of the Eye, 2001, Current Ocular Therapy, 2000, Eye Banking, 1998, Corneal Disorders: Principles and Practi, 1994, Atlas of Ocular Anterior Diseases, 2001 (1st award of advancement of sci. and tech. State Coun. of China, 1998); author: Ocular Surface Diseases, 2001; contbr. papers to profl. jours. Named Excellent Young Tchr., HuoYingdong Edn. Found., Nat. Edn. Com. of China, 1995, 2000; recipient 2nd award of advancement of sci. and tech., Sci. and Tech. Com. of Henan Province, China, 2000, 3d award of advancement of sci. and tech., Sci. and Tech. Com. of Shandong Province, 1995.

LI, ZHILIN, mathematician, educator; b. Nanjing, Jiangsu, China, June 30, 1956; came to U.S., 1989; s. Wenfu Li and Guolan Cang; m. Xiaoyun Wang, Dec. 20, 1983; children: Miyuan Mike, Matthew S. BS in Math., Nanjing (China) Normal U., 1982, MS in Math., 1988; PhD in Applied Math., U. Wash., 1994. Instr. Nanjing Normal U., 1982-89; asst. prof. UCLA, 1994-96, Miss. State U., Starkville, 1996-97, N.C. State U., Raleigh, 1997—. Recipient Boeing Excellence award, 1991, Oak Ridge Jr. Faculty Enhancement award Oak Ridge Associated Univs., 1997. Mem. Soc. Indsl. and Applied Math., Am. Math. Soc. Office: NC State U Dept Math Box 8205 Raleigh NC 27695 E-mail: zhilin@math.ncsu.edu.

LIACOURAS, PETER JAMES, university president, lawyer; b. Phila., Apr. 9, 1931; s. James Peter and Stella (Lagakos) L.; m. Anne Locke Myers, Sept. 5, 1959; children: Lisa Ann, James Peter, Stephen Myers, Gregory Locke. Student, Coll. William and Mary, 1950-51; BS, Drexel U., 1953; JD, U. Pa., 1956; MA, Fletcher Sch. Law and Diplomacy, 1958; LLM, Harvard U., 1959; postgrad. (Sterling fellow), Yale U. Law Sch., 1964-65; LLD (hon.), Dropsie U., 1982; LHD (hon.), Drexel U., 1984. Bar: Pa. 1957. Atty. Defender Assn. Phila., 1956-57, 59; research assoc. Duke U. Law Sch. Rule of Law Research Center, 1959-63; asst. prof. law Temple U., 1963-65, asso. prof., 1965-67, prof., 1967—, dean Sch. Law, 1972-82, univ. pres., 1982—2000, chancellor, 2000—. Spl. dist. atty., Phila., 1969, 70; chmn. Select Commn. on Pa. Bar Exam. Procedures, 1970; co-chmn. sect. legal edn. World Peace Through Law Center, 1973-74; chmn. confidentiality com. Pa. Gov.'s Justice Commn., 1974-78; lectr. law schs., India, 1967, Rome, 1974, 75, Ghana, 1975; lectr. law schs. Hebrew U., Jerusalem, 1975, 76, 77, 78, 79, Tel Aviv, 1981, Greece, 1977, 78, 79, 81; cons. internat. law. Author: The International Court of Justice, 2 vols, 1962; contbr. numerous articles to law jours., 1957— . Recipient Human Rights award Nat. Conv. Women in Law, 1976, Ann. Human Relations award Am. Jewish Com., Phila., 1978, Disting. Am. award Am. Found. for Negro Affairs, 1987. Mem. Am. Bar Assn. (Post-Bakke Task Force 1978-80), Pa. Bar Assn., Phila. Bar Assn., Phila. Com. Fgn. Relations. Democrat. Greek Orthodox. Office: Temple University Chancellor's Office Barrack Hall Suite 300 Philadelphia PA 19122*

LIAKOS, JAMES CHRIST, business manager; b. Washington, Feb. 10, 1933; s. Christ and Xantippe (Franks) L.; m. Alexandra Avayanos, Jan. 1, 1956 (div. Jan. 1960); 1 child, Stephanie; m. Roberta Sue Katzman, May 31, 1963. B Comml. Scis., Benjamin Franklin U., 1956. Supr. acctg. dept. Bakery & Confectionery Union Industry Internat. Welfare and Pension Funds, Washington, 1955-66; adminstrv. asst. Am. Physiol. Soc., Bethesda, Md., 1966-76, asst. bus. mgr., bus. mgr., 1985—99. With U.S. Army, 1953-54, ETO. Mem. Nat. Soc. Pub. Acctg., Am. Soc. Assn. Execs. Greek Orthodox. Home: Apt 304 2121 S Ocean Blvd Pompano Beach FL 33062-8003

LIANG, EDISON PARKTAK, astrophysicist, educator, researcher; b. Canton, Republic of China, July 22, 1947; came to U.S., 1964; s. Chi-Sen and Siu-Fong (Law) L.; m. Lily K. Yuen, Aug. 7, 1971; children: Olivia, James, Justin. BA, U. Calif., Berkeley, 1967, PhD, 1971. Rsch. scientist U. Tex., Austin, 1971-73; assoc. instr. U. Utah, Salt Lake City, 1973-75; asst. prof. Mich. State U., East Lansing, Mich., 1975-76, Stanford (Calif.) U., 1976-79; physicist, group leader Lawrence Livermore Nat. Lab., Livermore, Calif., 1980-88, assoc. div. leader, 1988-91; prof. space physics and astronomy Rice U., Houston, 1991-2001, Andrew Hays buchanan prof. astrophysics, 2001—. Mem. NASA Rev. Panels, Washington, 1988—. Editor: (book) Gamma Ray Bursts, 1986. Named Sci. fellow and Anthony scholar U. Calif., Berkeley, 1967-69. Fellow Am. Physical Soc.; mem. Am. Astron. Soc., Internat. Astron. Union, Phi Beta Kappa, Sigma Xi. Office: Rice U Herman Brown Hall 6100 Main St MS108 Houston TX 77005-1892 E-mail: liang@spacsun.rice.edu.

LIANG, HONG, materials scientist; b. Beijing, China, Jan. 20, 1961; PhD, Stevens Inst. Tech., 1992. Sr. scientist Cabot Corp., Aurora, Ill., 1996—98; asst. prof. U. Alaska , Fairbanks, Alaska, 1998—2002. Mem.: ASME, Soc. Tribologists and Lubrication Engrs. (ann. meeting program com. 2002—), ASM International - HTS (Lectureship Award 1999). Business E-Mail: ffhl@uaf.edu.

LIANG, JEROME ZHENGRONG, radiology educator; b. Chongging, China, June 23, 1958; arrived in U.S., 1981; BS, Lanzhou U., China, 1982; PhD, CUNY, 1987. Rsch. instr. Albert Einstein Coll. Medicine, Bronx, NY, 1986—87; rsch. assoc. Duke U. Med. Ctr., Durham, NC, 1987—89, asst. med. rsch. prof., 1990—92; asst. prof. SUNY, Stony Brook, 1992—97, assoc. prof., 1997—2000, prof., 2000—, co-dir. biomed. engring., 1996—; founder Viatronix Inc. Mem. adv. bd. MDOL, Inc., 1999—; bd. dirs., v.p. R&D Viatronix, Inc., 2000—. Contbr. articles to profl. jours.; mem. editl. bd.: IEEE Transactions on Med. Imaging, 1999—. Recipient NIH awards, 1990—. AHA award, 1996—2001, N.Y. State Biotech. award, 1996—98, E-Z-EM award, 1997—98; grantee, Soc. Thoracic Radiology, 1994—95, ADAC Rsch. Lab., 1994—95. Achievements include development of Bayesian image processing, quantitative emission computed tomography, tissue segmentation from magnetic resonance images, virtual endoscopy, virtual realities in radiology. Avocations: swimming, fitness, tennis. Office: SUNY Stony Brook Dept Radiology 4th Fl Rm 120 Stony Brook NY 11794-8460

LIANG, JUNXIANG, aeronautics and astronautics engineer, educator; b. Hangzhou, Zhejiang, China, Aug. 17, 1932; s. Yigao and Yunruo (Yu) L.; m. Junxian Sun, Jan. 27, 1960; 1 child, Song Liang. Grad., Harbin Inst. Tech., 1960. Head control dept. Shenyang (Liaoning, China) Jet Engine R&D Inst., 1960-70, China Gas Turbine Establishment, Jiangyou, Sichuan, China, 1970-78, assoc. chief engr., 1978-83; vis. scientist MIT, Cambridge, Mass., 1984-86; prof. China Aerospace Inst. Systems Engring., Beijing, China, 1986—; grads. supr. Beijing U. Aero-Astronautics, 1986—; chief engr. Full Authority Digital Elec. Engine Control China Aerospace Industry Ministry, 1986-93. Mem. China Aerospace Sci. and Tech. Com., Beijing, 1983-94, Aero-engine R&D Adv. Bd., Beijing, 1991-95; bd. dirs. China Aviation Ency. Editl. Bd., Beijing, 1991-95; tech. support supr., mgmt. info. svc. dir. Am. PC, Inc., Union City, Calif., 1993—. Author: Nonlinear Control System Oscillation, 1964; contbr. articles to Jour. Aeronautics and Astronautics, Jour. Propulsion Tech., Internat. Aviation, Acta Aeronautica et Astronautica Sinica. Recipient Nat. Sci. and Tech. 2d award, China Nat. Sci. and Tech. Com., Beijing, 1965, Sic. and Tech. Progress award, China Aerospace Industry Ministry, 1991, Nat. Outstanding Sci. and Tech. Contbn. award, 1992. Mem. AIAA (sr.), Chinese Soc. of Aeronautical, Astronautical Engine Control (mem. commn. 1987—). Achievements include solution of oscillation problem on nonlinear control system; formulation of aircraft overall strategy, study and control of High Thrust/Weight Engine Rsch. Program.

LIANG, LANBO See LEONG, LAMPO

LIANG, PING, technology company executive, educator; b. Shaanxi, China; m. Linda Liang; children: Lusha, Biyonka. BS, Xi-an (China) Jiaotong U., 1982; MSEE, U. Pitts., 1983, PhD, 1987. 1997chair elect. engring. U. Calif., Riverside, 1995, assoc. prof.; founder, pres., CEO TransDimension Inc., Irvine, Calif., 1997—2002, chmn. bd., 2002—. Author: Neural Network Fundamentals, 1996; contbr. numerous articles to profl. jours. Rsch. grantee Def. Advanced Rsch. Project Agy., 1997, 98, AF Office of Scientific Rsch., 1999, Office of Naval Rsch., 1998, 99, NSF, 1995-96, Nat. Sci. and Engring. Rsch. Coun., 1988-92. Mem. IEEE (sr.). Avocations: business strategy, reading, music, fitness, travel. Office: TransDimension Inc 2 Venture Ste 500 Irvine CA 92618

LIANG, XU, civil engineer, educator; b. Chengdu, Sichuan, China, Jan. 21, 1963; d. Zengxiang Liang and Guifang Ju; m. Jing-Zhou Hou. MS in Civil Engring., U. of Wash., 1990, PhD, 1994. Post-doctoral rschr. Princeton U., Princeton, NJ, 1994—96; rsch. scientist joint ctr. for earth sys. tech. Goddard Space Flight Ctr., NASA U. of Md., Greenbelt, Md., 1996—98; asst. prof. U. of Calif., Berkeley, Calif., 1998—. Recipient Hellman award, U. of Calif. at Berkeley, 2000. Mem.: ASCE (Chi Epsilon award 1991), Internat. Assn. of Hydrologicalal Sci., Am. Meteorology Soc., Am. Geophys. Union. Office: University of Calif Berkeley CA 94720-1710

LIANG, YUE, engineer; b. Beijing, China, Aug. 2, 1959; came to U.S. s. Wenjie Liang; m. Ying Li Zhang, Aug. 30, 1990; 1 child, Xu. BS in Chem. Engring. and Process Control, Petroleum U., Beijing, 1984; MS in Chem. Engring., Kyoto U., Japan, 1990, PhD in Chem. Engring., 1993. Asst. prof. Petroleum U., Beijing, 1984-86; sr. engr. Furukawa Electric Ltd., Hiratsuka, Japan, 1993-97; rsch. engr. Mobil Tech. Co., Dallas, 1997-99; sr. engr. Fitel Techs., Phoenix, 1999—. Contbr. articles to profl. jours. Mem. ACS, AIChE. Office: 200 Westpark Dr Ste 190 Peachtree City GA 30269 Home: 117 Ardenlee Dr Peachtree City GA 30269-4204

LIAO, MARTHA, geneticist; b. Leeds, Eng., Feb. 9, 1948; came to U.S., 1967; d. Chung-Chou and Shirley Liao; m. Haojiang Tian, Mar. 18, 1991. BA, Bryn Mawr Coll., 1970; PhD, U. Pa., 1974. Inst. fellow Eleanor Roosevelt Inst., Denver, 1979-86; asst. prof. U. Colo. Health Scis. Ctr., 1982-88; sr. fellow Eleanor Roosevelt Inst., 1986-94; assoc. prof. dept. pediat. U. Colo. Med. Sch., 1988-95. Chmn. sci. adv. bd. Cancer League of Colo., Denver, 1989-91; reviewer VA Merit Rev. Bd., Washington, 1988-92; vis. assoc. prof. Albert Einstein Coll. Medicine, Bronx, N.Y., 1992-96; presenter in field. Contbr. articles to Porceedings NAS. Pres. Asian Performing Arts Colo., Denver, 1986—; chmn. rev. com. Denver Cultural Dist., 1989-91; bd. dirs. Asian Arts Assn., Denver Art Mus., 1989-91. Rsch. scholar to China NAS, 1981-82; Rsch. grantee NSF, 1984-86, Am. Cancer Soc., 1981-82, NIH, 1980-94. Mem. Am. Soc. Human Genetics, Am. Soc. for Cell Biology, AAAS, Soc. Chinese Bioscientist in Am. (rep. Denver 1988—), Assn. Chinese Geneticists in Am. (sec. 1989-91). Achievements include research in human chromosome 12 by molecular and cell genetics, human protein and its gene that helps AIDS virus multiply in humans. Home: 451 W Jamison Pl Littleton CO 80120-4264 Office: 150 Columbus Ave Apt 18D New York NY 10023-5969 Fax: 212-336-9487.

LIAO, MEI-JUNE, biopharmaceutical company executive; came to U.S., 1974; BS, Nat. Tsing-Hua U. Taiwan, 1973; MPh, Yale U., 1977, PhD, 1980. Tchg. asst. Nat. Taiwan U., 1973-74, Temple U., Phila., 1974-75, Yale U., New Haven, 1975-76, rsch. asst., 1976-79; postdoctoral assoc. MIT, Cambridge, 1980-83; sr. scientist Interferon Scis., Inc., New Brunswick, N.J., 1983-84; group leader Interferon Scis. Inc., 1984-85, dir. cell biology, 1985-87; dir. R&D Interferon Scis., Inc., 1987-94, v.p. R&D, 1995—. Contbr. articles to profl. jours.; inventor in field. Mem. Am. Soc. Biochemistry and Molecular Biology, Internat. Soc. Interferon and Cytokine Rsch., Internat. Cytokine Soc., Soc. Chinese Bioscientists in Am., N.Y. Acad. Sci. Office: Interferon Sci Inc 783 Jersey Ave New Brunswick NJ 08901-3660 E-mail: meijuneliao@yahoo.com.

LIAO, PAUL FOO-HUNG, electronics executive; b. Phila., Nov. 10, 1944; s. Tseng Wu and Tung Mei (Lin) L.; m. Karen Ann Pravetz, Aug. 31, 1968; children: Teresa S., Joanna S. BS, MIT, 1966; PhD, Columbia U., 1973. Rsch. assoc. Columbia U., N.Y.C., 1972-73; mem. tech. staff Bell Labs., Holmdel, N.J., 1973-80, dept. head., 1980-83; div. mgr. Bell Communications Rsch., Red Bank, 1984-89, asst. v.p., 1989-93, gen. mgr., 1993-95, v.p., 1995-96; v.p., chief tech. officer Matsushita Elec. Corp. Am., 1996—; pres. Panasonic Tech. Co., 1996—. Co-editor: Academic Press Quantum Electronics Book Series, 1980-96; contbr. over 75 articles to profl. jours.; holder over 12 patents in field. Bd. trustees Brookdale C.C. Fellow IEEE (Millennium medal 2000), Optical Soc. Am. (editor jour.), Am. Phys. Soc.; mem. Lasers and Electro Optic Soc. of IEEE (pres. 1987). Office: Panasonic Tech Inc 2 Research Way Princeton NJ 08540-6628

LIAO, SHUTSUNG, biochemist, oncologist; b. Tainan, Taiwan, Jan. 1, 1931; s. Chi-Chun Liao and Chin-Shen Lin; m. Shuching Liao, Mar. 19, 1960; children: Jane, Tzufen, Tzuming, May. BS in Agrl. Chemistry, Nat. Taiwan U., 1953, MS in Biochemistry, 1956; PhD in Biochemistry, U. Chgo., 1961. Rsch. assoc., 1960-63; asst. prof. U. Chgo., 1964-69; assoc. prof. dept. biochemistry and molecular biology Ben May Lab. Cancer Rsch., U. Chgo., 1969-71; prof. depts. biochemistry, molecular and cancer biology Ben May Inst. for Cancer Rsch., 1972—; dir. Tang Ctr. Herbal Medicine Rsch., 2000—. Cons. in field. Mem. editl. bd. Jour. Steroid Biochemistry and Molecular Biology, The Prostate, Receptors, Signal Transduction; assoc. editor Cancer Rsch., 1982-89; contbr. over 200 articles to profl jours. V.p. Chgo. Formosan Fed. Credit Union, 1977-79; trustee Taiwanese United Fund in U.S., 1981-85; mem. adv. com. Taiwan-U.S. Cultural Exch. Ctr., 1984-87. Recipient Sci-Tech. Achievement prize Taiwanese-Am. Found., 1983, Pfizer Lecture fellow award Clin. Rsch. Inst. Montreal, 1972, Gregory Pincus medal and award Worcester Found. for Exptl. Biology, 1992, Tzongming Tu award Formosan Med. Assn., 1993, C.H. Li Meml. Lecture award, 1994; NIH grantee, 1962—; Am. Cancer Soc. grantee, 1971-81. Fellow Am. Acad. Art and Scis.; mem. Am. Soc. Biochemistry and Molecular Biology, Am. Assn. Cancer Rsch., Endocrine Soc., N.Am.-Taiwanese Profs. Assn. (pres. 1980-81, exec. dir. 1981—), Nat. Acad. Taiwan. Achievements include discovery of androgen activation mechanism and androgen receptors; cloning and structural determination of androgen receptors and other novel nuclear receptors, and their genes, and receptor gene mutation in hereditary abnormalities and cancers; rsch. on regulation of hormone-dependent gene expression and cell growth, molecular bases of cancer cell growth and progression, chemoprevention, and therapeutic treatment of hormone-sensitive and insensitive cancers and diseases, molecular bases of cholestoral accumulation and control. Home: 5632 S Woodlawn Ave Chicago IL 60637-1623 Office: U Chgo Ben May Inst Cancer Rsch 5841 S Maryland Ave Chicago IL 60637-1463

LIAO, YEUN-JIAN (GENE), engineer, researcher; b. Taipei, Sept. 7, 1957; arrived in U.S., 1983; s. Der-Sheng Liao and Tsai-Lang Chen; m. Yao-Chu Judy Wang, Jan. 26, 1996; children: Allison C.Y., Alex H.Y. BS, Nat. Ctrl. U., Taiwan, 1981; MEng, U. Tex., 1984; grad., Columbia U., 1996; DEng, U. Mich., 1999. CAD/CAM sys. mgr. Carboloy Inc., Warren, Mich., 1985—91; mfg. process engr. Ford Motor Co., Dearborn, 1991—94; sr. project engr. Gen. Motors Corp., Pontiac, 1994—96, Warren, 1998—. Adj. prof. Lawrence Tech. U., Southfield, Mich., 2000, Wayne State U., Detroit, 2001—. Contbr. articles to profl. jours. Recipient Co-Primary Investigator award, NSF, 2002—, Postdoc. fellowship, Gen. Motors Corp., 1996—98. Mem.: ASME, Soc. Mfg. Engrs. (sr.). Achievements include patents for. Avocations: tennis, camping, biking. Office: Gen Motors Corp MC #480-305-200 6440 E 12 Mile Rd Warren MI 48090-9000 Office Fax: 586-986-8722. Business E-Mail: gene.l.liao@gm.com.

LIASHKOV, PETER, artist, educator; b. Rouen, France, Oct. 7, 1939; came to U.S., 1955; s. Maxim and Olga (Veger) L.; m. Ann Harvey; 1 child, Alexina. MFA, Otis Art Inst., L.A., 1968. Sr. instr. Art Ctr. Coll. of Design, Pasadena, Calif., 1975—. One-man shows include Spruce Street Forum, San Diego, 1996, Oculorum Gallery, L.A., Julie Rico Gallery, Santa Monica, Calif., 1999; exhibited in group shows at Kuhn Galerie, Aachen, West Germany, 1971, San Francisco Art Inst., 1977, 86, Baum-Silverman Gallery, L.A., 1980, 81, Koplin Gallery, L.A., 1984, Mcpl. Art Gallery, L.A., 1979, 86, 87, Bliss Gallery, Pasadena, 1989, Marble Palace, St. Petersburg, Russia, 1992, F. Riestra Gallery, Mexico City, 1993, Riverside (Calif.) Mus. of Art, 1996, San Diego Mus. Contemporary Art, 1997, others; represented in permanent collections Bklyn. Mus., Ill. Inst. Tech., Chgo., Pa. Acad. Fine Arts, Phila., AT&T, Chgo., N.Y. Pub. Libr., others. Office: Art Ctr Coll Design 1700 Lida St Pasadena CA 91103-1924

LIAU, GENE, medical educator; b. Hsing-Chu, Taiwan, Nov. 28, 1954; came to U.S., 1965; BS in Biology, U. N.C., 1977; DPhil, Vanderbilt U., 1982. Postdoctoral fellow Lab. Molecular Biology, Nat. Cancer Inst. NIH, Bethesda, Md., 1982-85; assoc. mem. dept. cell biology Revlon Biotech. Rsch. Ctr., Rockville, 1985-87; scientist I dept. molecular biology Am. Red Cross Jerome H. Holland Lab., 1987-90, scientist II, 1990-96, sr. scientist, 1996-98; assoc. prof. dept. anatomy George Washington U. Med. Ctr., Washington, 1995—; unit head metabolic and vascular disease group Genetic Therapy Inc., Gaitersburg, Md., 1998—; adj. prof. molecular biology Holland Lab., 1998—, sr. scientist, 1998—. Mem. AHA Vascular Wall Biology Rsch. Study Com., 1992-96, Pathology A Study Sect. NIH, 1994-98; invited spkr. in field. Contbr. articles to profl. jours. Arthritis Found. fellow, 1982-85; pub. health svc. grantee, 1988—; recipient Nat. Rsch. Svc. award NIH, 1977-81, Rsch. Career Devel. award, 1990-95. Mem. AAAS, Am. Soc. Cell Biology, Am. Heart Assn. Coun. Basic Sci. (Established Investigator 1990, Grant-in-Aid 1992-95, 95-98), Soc. Chinese Bioscientists, Sigma Xi. Office: Genetic Therapy Inc 9 W Watkins Mill Rd Gaithersburg MD 20878-4021

LIAUBA, DANUTE, music educator; b. Amsterdam, N.Y., Aug. 19, 1955; d. Vytautas and Adele Staskevicius; m. Rimas Liauba, Sept. 6, 1981. BS in Music Theory, Nazareth Coll., Rochester, N.Y., 1976; postgrad., Eastman Sch. Music, 1979-80; MusM in Musicology, Ind. U., 1982. Cert. tchr. music, N.Y. Lectr. Bucknell U., Lewisburg, Pa., 1981-83, U. Akron, Ohio, 1987—; pvt. practice instr. music Medina, 1987—. Vis. lectr. Vytuatas Magnus U., Kaunas, Lithuania, 1992. Co-author: Music of the Spheres, 1986, Curlionis: Painter and Composer, 1994. Mem. Music Tchrs. Nat. Assn., Ohio Music Tchrs. Assn. (pres. Akron chpt. 1995-97), Tuesday Musical Club (chair concert lecture 1999—). Avocations: skiing, scuba diving, travel. Home and Office: 3344 Forest Lake Dr Medina OH 44256-8733 E-mail: dliauba@hotmail.com.

LIAW, HANG MING, engineer; b. Taichung, Taiwan, Republic of China, Feb. 1, 1936; came to U.S., 1965; s. Der Wang and Young Tsing L.; m. Chau Yi, Mar. 3, 1939; children: Tsui Ying, Lucy, Sally. BS, Cheng Kung U., Tainan, Taiwan, 1959; MS, Pa. State U., 1967, PhD, 1970. Engr. Taiwan Sugar Corp., 1960-65; postdoctoral fellow U. S.C., Columbia, 1970-71; engr. Airtron. Litton Industry, Morrisplain, N.J., 1971-73, Semiconductor R & D Lab. Motorola, Phoenix, 1973-78, sect. mgr., 1978-90, dept. mgr., 1994—. Contbr. chpts. to books. Mem. IEEE, Electrochemical Soc. Home: 11540 N 104th St Scottsdale AZ 85260-6004 Office: Motorola Inc 5005 E Mcdowell Rd # 170 Phoenix AZ 85008-4229

LIBA, PETER MICHAEL, Canadian provincial government official; b. Winnipeg, Man., Can., May 10, 1940; s. Theodore and Rose Liba; m. Shirley Ann Collett, May 4, 1963; children: Jennifer Lacombe, Jeffrey, Christopher. DHL(hon.) , U. Manitoba, 2001. Reporter, news editor The Daily Graphic, The Neepawa Press, Portage la Prairie, Man., 1957-59; reporter The Winnipeg Tribune, 1959-67, city editor, 1967-68; ind. communications cons. Winnipeg, 1968-73; v.p. pub. affairs CanWest Broadcasting Ltd., 1974-75, exec. v.p., 1979-97; asst. gen. mgr. Sta. CKND-TV, 1975-79, mgr., 1980-87, gen. mgr., 1987-92; pres., CEO CKND TV Inc./SaskWest TV Inc., 1988-94; exec. v.p. CanWest Global Comm. Corp., 1993-97, exec. dir. corp. affairs, 1997-99; lt. gov. Province of Man., Can., 1999—. Bd. dirs. Global Comm. Ltd., Toronto, CanWest Broadcasting Ltd., Winnipeg, CanWest TV, Inc., Winnipeg, CanWest Prodns., Ltd., Winnipeg, CanWest Properties Ltd., Winnipeg, CanWest Maritime TV, Inc., Halifax, TV 3 Network, New Zealand, Network Ten (alternate), Australia; pres. Peli Ventures, Inc., 1975—. Trustee Transcona-Springfield Sch. divsn., Winnipeg, Canada, 1964—67; founding chmn. Variety Club Telethon, Canada; chmn. Winnipeg Conv. Ctr/; bd. dirs. Conv. Ctr. Corp. , Winnipeg, 1976—86, chmn. bd. dirs., 1981—84; bd. dirs. Atomic Energy of Can., Ltd., Ottawa, 1981—86, St. Boniface Gen. Hosp., Winnipeg, 1987—99. Decorated Order of Can., chancellor and 1st mem. Order of Manitoba; named Manitoban of Month, Mid Can. Commerce Mag., 1982, Knight of Justice, vice prior Order of St. John, 1999, citizen of yr., Manitoba Chinese Cmty., 2001; recipient Presidl. citation, Variety Clubs Internat., 1983, Internat. Media award, 1986, Commemorative medal, 125th Anniversary Can., 1992, Golden Dragon Citizen of Yr. award, 2001. Mem. Broadcasters Assn. Man. (pres. 1981-82), Western Assn. Broadcasters (pres. 1984-85, Broadcaster of Yr. award 1991, Broadcaster of Decade award 1994), Can. Assn. Broadcasters (chmn. bd. 1990-92, Spl. Gold Ribbon award 1999 named to Can. Broadcasters Hall of Fame, 1998), St. Charles Cluntry Club, Man. Club, Variety Club Man. (chief barker 1984-85). Office: Lieutenant Governor Ste 235 Legislative Bldg Winnipeg MB Canada R3C 0V8

LIBASSI, FRANK PETER, lawyer; b. N.Y.C., Apr. 20, 1930; s. Frank G. and Mary (Marino) L.; m. Mary Frances Steen, July 10, 1954; children: Thomas, Timothy, Jennifer. BA in Polit. Sci. cum laude, Colgate U., 1951; LLB, Yale U., 1954. Bar: N.Y. 1955, Conn. 1980. Enforcement atty. N.Y. State Housing and Rent Commn., 1954-56; regional dir. N.Y. State Commn. on Human Rights, Albany, 1956-62; dep. staff dir. U.S. Commn. on Civil Rights, 1962-66; spl. asst. to sec., dir. office for civil rights HEW, Washington, 1966-68; exec. v.p. The Urban Coalition, 1968-71; v.p. Am. City Corp., Columbia, Md., 1971-72; pres., CEO Greater Hartford Process Inc. (Greater Hartford Community Devel. Corp.), 1971-77; gen. counsel HEW, Washington, 1977-79; ptnr. Verner, Liipfert, Bernhard and McPherson, 1979-82; sr. v.p. Travelers Corp., Hartford, Conn., 1982-93; of counsel Verner, Liipfert, Bernhard & McPherson, Washington, 1993-95; dean Barney Sch. of Bus. and Pub. Adminstrn., U. Hartford, West Hartford, Conn., 1993-96; pres. Children's Fund of Conn., Hartford, 1996—2001, Child Health and Devel. Inst. of Conn., Hartford, 1997—2001. V.p. Ctr. for Global Bus. Studies, Paris, 1996-97; mem. Urban Land Inst., 1971-77; adv. bd. Bur. Nat. Affairs Housing and Cmty. Devel. Reporter, 1972-77; vis. lectr. Anderson Coll., Chatham Coll., Goddard Coll., Ohio Wesleyan U., 1974-76; adj. faculty Grad. Sch. Bus. and Pub. Adminstrn. U. Hartford, 1976-77; chmn. bd. dirs. Forstmann Corp., 1994-97. Author: The Negro in the Armed Forces, 1963, Family Housing and the Negro Serviceman, 1963, Equal Opportunity in Farm Programs, 1965, Revitalizing Central City Investment, 1977. Bd. dirs. legis. com. Am. Coun. Life Ins., 1987-90; bd. dirs., exec. com. Ins. Inst. Hwy. Safety, 1984-88; mem. pub. rels. policy com. Health Ins. Assn. Am., 1988-93; incorporator Inst. Living, 1973—, Hartford Hosp., 1973—, St. Francis Hosp., 1990—, Wheeler Clinic, 1996—; bd. dirs. Hartford Seminary, 2002—; adv. com. Dem. Nat. Com., 1974-77; chmn. Ct. Cmty. Care, Inc., 1980-86; com. on an aging soc. NAS, 1982-86; exec. com. Downtown Coun. Hartford, 1983-86, Greater Hartford Arts Coun., 1983-86; chmn. Gov.'s Commn. on Financing Long Term Care, 1986-87; nat. consumer adv. com. Am. Health Care Assn., 1985-86; com. on elderly people living alone The Commonwealth Fund, 1985-91; mem. Sec. Bowen's Task Force on Long-term Health Care Policies of Health Care Financing Adminstrn., 1986-87; bd. dirs. Alliance for Aging Rsch., 1986-91; mem. Nat. Retirees Vol. Ctr., 1988-90; mem. Pew Commn. on future of health profls., 1990-93; pub. affairs rsch. coun. conf. bd., 1990-93; mem. United Srs. Health Cooperative, 1990-91; health adv. coun. Johns Hopkins U., 1990-96, com. predicting future diseases Inst. Medicine, 1991-93; adv. bd. Nat. Acad. on Aging, 1992-95; U. Conn. Sch. Nursing, 1996—; trustee Conn. Pub. Expenditure Coun., 1991-95, bd. dirs., The Bushnel, 1998—; adv. com. on health care reform The Commonwealth Fund, 1993-98; bd. dirs. Duncaster

Cmty., 1993-97; Conn. Health Found., 1999—; bus. adv. bd. Conn. Commn. on Children, 1998—. Recipient Superior Performance award U.S. Commn. on Civil Rights, 1963, Meritorious Svc. award, 1965; Sec.'s spl. citation, 1967; Disting. Svc. award HEW, 1968, Friend of La Casa de Puerto Rico, Hartford, award, 1992; CT Assoc. Human Svcs., Exec Dirs. Awd., 1998; Woodrow Wilson sr. fellow, 1973-77. Mem. ABA, Fed. Bar Assn., N.Y. State Bar Assn., Conn. Bar Assn., Am. Assn. Retired Persons (nat. steering com. for new roles in soc. 1987-90), Greater Hartford C. of C. (bd. dirs. 1985-93, exec. com.). Clubs: Hartford. Home: 580 Mountain Rd Apt J Hartford CT 06117-1827 E-mail: libassi@attbi.com.

LIBAVA, JERRY RONALD, franchise consultant; b. Cleve., Oct. 6, 1936; s. Sanford and Dora (Friedlander) L.; m. Judith Rosalie Hollender, May 30, 1958; children: Joel, Jonathan, Janet. Hairdresser Bonwit Teller, Cleve., 1957-60; make-up artist, sales Revlon, Cleve. & N.Y.C., 1960-66; sales, sales mgr. Loreal-Lancome, Cleve., 1966-72; sales, regional mgr. Colonia, Inc., Stanford, Conn., 1981-83; dir. franchise devel. Physicians Weight Loss Ctrs., Akron, 1984-90; pres. Internat. Franchise Devel. LLC, Cleve., 1990—. Spkr. in field. With U.S. Army, 1957. Mem. Franchise Network (vice-chmn. 1993—). Jewish. Avocations: cycling, walking, golf.

LIBBER, SAMUEL MOGUL, pediatrician; b. Phila., Jan. 10, 1950; s. Leonard Mitchell and Gertrude (Mogul) L.; m. Sherie Lee Brook, July 9, 1978; children: Karen, David. BSc, U. Leeds, England, 1970; BA, Johns Hopkins U., 1972, MD, 1975. Diplomate Am. Bd. Pediatrics. Intern in pediat. Johns Hopkins Hosp., Balt., 1975-76, resident, 1976-78, fellow in pediatric endocrinology, 1981-83; ambulatory pediatrician Balt. City Hosps., 1978-81; pediatrician Annapolis (Md.) Pediatrics, 1983—; asst. prof. pediatrics Sch. Medicine Johns Hopkins U., Balt. Mem. Sch. Cmty. Action Network, Annapolis, 1994—. Fellow Am. Acad. Pediatrics; mem. Am. Diabetes Assn., Lawson Wilkins Pediatric Endocrine Soc., Juvenile Diabetes Found. Avocations: photography, music, painting, travel. Office: Annapolis Pediatrics 200 Forbes St Ste 200 Annapolis MD 21401-1599

LIBBEY, DARLENE HENSLEY, artist, educator; b. La Follettee, Tenn., Jan. 9, 1952; d. Charles Franklin and Geneva (Chitwood) Hensley; children: Michael Damon McLaughlin, Marina Auston. BFA in Painting, San Francisco Art Inst., 1989; MFA in Painting/Drawing, U. Tenn., 1994. Grad. asst. Alliance of Ind. Colls., N.Y.C., 1989; gallery asst. Holley Solomon Gallery, 1989; teaching assoc., instr. U. Tenn., Knoxville, 1991-94; lectr., instr. U. Tex.-Pan Am., 1994-97, South Tex. Cmty. Coll., 1995-96; instr. Pellissippi Tech. C.C., 1998—, U. Tenn., 1999—. Curator Belleza Salon, Knoxville, 1993-94; invitational rep. San Francisco Art Inst., N.Y. Studio Program, Alliance Ind. Colls., 1989; organizer Multi-Media Group Exhbn., San Francisco; lectr., instr. South Tex. C.C., McAllen; instr. Buck's Rock Camp, New Milford, Conn., summer, 1999. One-woman shows include U. Tex.-Pan Am., 1995, 96; exhibited in group shows at San Francisco Art Inst., 1985, 86, 87, 88, 89, Pacific Ctr., San Francisco, 1988, alliance of Ind. Colls., N.Y.C., 1989, San Francisco Mus. Modern Art, 1990, Bluxom Studios, San Francisco, 1991, Gallery 1010, Knoxville, 1991, 92, Ewing Gallery, U. Tenn., Knoxville, 1991, 92, 93, 94, SUNY, Syracuse, 1992, Printers Mark, Knoxville, 1993, Unitarian Ch., Knoxville, 1993, Tomato Head, Knoxville, 1994, Belleza Salon, Knoxville, 1994, U. Pan Am., 1995, 96; group show Museo Historico de Reynosa, Tamalipus, Mex., 1996. Vol. San Francisco Mus. Modern Art, 1990-91; founding mem. Grad. Student Union, U. Tenn., Knoxville, 1993; vol. instr. Knox County Schs., Knoxville, 1992-93; vis. artist Marin County Schs., San Anselmo, Calif., 1989. Tuition scholar San Francisco Art Inst., 1987; materials grantee U. Tenn., 1993, grantee Buck Found., 1987-89. Mem. Coll. Art Assn. Democrat. Unitarian Universalist. Avocations: cooking, reading. Home: 504 Longview Rd Knoxville TN 37919-3720

LIBBEY, JAMES K. education educator; b. Holden, Mass., May 16, 1942; s. Russell J. and Narcissa E. L.; m. Joyce M. Holmes, Dec. 28, 1963. BA, Miami U., Oxford, Ohio, 1964, BSEd, 1967; MA, Ea. Ky. U., 1971; PhD, U. Ky., 1976. Tchr. St. Michael Sch., Brookville, Ind., 1964-67; clk., typist U.S. Army, Bad Kreuznach, Germany, 1968-70; instr. U. Ky., Lexington, 1973-74; asst. prof. Ea. Ky. U., Richmond, 1974-79, assoc. dean, 1979-86; rschr. Flagler Coll., St. Augustine, Fla., 1986-93; assoc. prof. Embry-Riddle Aeronautical U., Daytona Beach, 1993—. Cons. So. W. Va. C.C., Logan, W.Va., 1975, University Press of Ky., Lexington, 1982, Miami U., Oxford, 1986. Author: (books) Alexander Gumberg and Soviet - American Relations, 1977, Dear Alben: Mr. Barkley of Kentucky, 1979, American - Russian Economic Relations, 1989, Russian - American Economic Relations, 1999. Co-chmn. Food Bank, Richmond, 1975-80; hope builder Habitat for Humanity, St. Augustine, Fla., 1992—; active Green Peace Action, 1986—. With U.S. Army, 1968-70, Germany. Grantee U. Ky., 1972, NEH, 1979, Kennan Inst. for Advanced Russian Studies, 1999. Mem. Am. Assn. Advancement of Slavic Studies, Soc. for Historians of Am. Fgn. Rels., Assn. for Gen. and Liberal Studies (exec. coun. mem. 1980-83, 94-97). Democrat. Roman Catholic. Avocations: walking, reading, travel, model building. Home: 258 Deltona Blvd Saint Augustine FL 32086-7355 Office: HU/SS Dept Embry-Riddle Aero Univ Daytona Beach FL 32114-3900 E-mail: libbeyj@cts.db.erau.edu.

LIBBIN, ANNE EDNA, lawyer; b. Phila., Aug. 25, 1950; d. Edwin M. and Marianne (Herz) L.; m. Christopher J. Cannon, July 20, 1985; children: Abigail Libbin Cannon, Rebecca Libbin Cannon. AB, Radcliffe Coll., 1971; JD, Harvard U., 1975. Bar: Calif. 1975, U.S. Dist. Ct. (cen. dist.) Calif. 1977, U.S. Dist. Ct. (no. dist.) Calif. 1979, U.S. Dist. Ct. (ea. dist.) Calif. 1985, U.S. Ct. Appeals. (2d cir.) 1977, U.S. Ct. Appeals (5th cir.) 1982, U.S. Ct. Appeals (7th cir.) 1976, U.S. Ct. Appeals (9th cir.) 1976, U.S. Ct. Appeals (D.C. cir.) 1978, U.S. Supreme Ct. 2001. Appellate atty. NLRB, Washington, 1975-78; assoc. Pillsbury Madison & Sutro LLP, San Francisco, 1978-83, ptnr., 1984-99; sr. counsel SBC Pacific Telesis Group, 1999—. Three Guineas fellow Harvard Law Sch., 1997; dir. Alumnae Resources, San Francisco, 1991-97. Mem. ABA (labor and employment sect.), State Bar Calif. (labor law sect.), Bar Assn. San Francisco (labor law sect.), Radcliffe Club (San Francisco). Office: SBC Pacific Telesis Group 140 New Montgomery St San Francisco CA 94105-3705

LIBBIN, JAMES DAVID, agricultural economics educator; b. Urbana, Ill., Oct. 24, 1950; s. David C. and Lois (Maddox) L.; m. Mary Bray, June 6, 1981; children: Zachary, Christina. BS in Agr., U. Ill., Urbana, 1972, MS in Agrl. Econs., 1975; PhD in Econs., Iowa State U., 1982. Rsch. asst. U. Ill., 1972-75; rsch. assoc. Iowa State U., Ames, 1975-79; prof. agrl. econs., extension farm mgmt. specialist N.Mex. State U., Las Cruces, 1979—. Adj. prof. Fla. Inst. Tech., White Sands Missile Range, N.Mex., 1985—. Author: Farm & Ranch Financial Records, 1987; contbr. over 300 articles and rsch. reports to profl. jours. Named State Farmer, N.Mex. Future Farmers Am., 1988. Mem. Am. Agrl. Econs. Assn., Western Agrl. Econs. Assn., Nat. Assn. Colls. and Tchrs. Agrl. (teaching award of merit 1989), Am. Soc. Farm Mgrs. and Rural Appraisers (sec.-treas. N.Mex. chpt. 1980—), Nat. Assn. Farm Bus. Analysis Specialists. Avocation: baseball. Home: 1108 Avenida De Quintas Las Cruces NM 88005-3501 Office: NMex State U PO Box 30003 Las Cruces NM 88003-8003

LIBBRECHT, GASPAR JOSEPH, civil engineer, educator; b. Roeselare, Belgium, Mar. 22, 1930; s. Pascal Leonard Libbrecht and Euphrasia Maria Vansteenkiste; m. Edna Deleu, July 15, 1961 (div. July 1993); children: Mieke, Katrien, Jan. Civil engr., U. Gent, 1955. Engr. Siemens, Brussels, 1957-58; prof. Katholieke Industriële Hogeschool, Oostende, Belgium, 1958-95; consulting engr. Roeselare, 1965—; prof. Katholieke Hogeschool Brugge Oostende, Brugge, Belgium, 1995-2000. Author: Computation of Machinery, 1961, Electrical Machinery, 1970, Control and Regulation, 1975, Servomechanism, 1975. Mem. Koninklijke Vlaamse Ingenieurs Vereniging, Koninklijke Vereniging Belgische Elektrotechnici, Order Architects Brussels. Avocation: recreational activities. Home: Mandeldreef 38 B 8800 Roeselare Belgium

LIBBY, GARY RUSSELL, museum director emeritus, writer; b. Boston, June 7, 1944; s. Charles W. and Sylvia P. Libby. BA, U. Fla., 1967, MA (NDEA fellow), 1968; MA, Tulane U., 1972. Instr. English Tulane U., 1968-71; asst. prof. Stetson U., Deland, Fla., 1972-77, vis. prof., 1977-86; dir. Mus. Arts and Scis., Daytona Beach, 1977—2001, dir. emeritus, 2002—. Reviewer Inst. Mus. Svcs.; panelist Mus. Assessment Program; reviewer Accreditation Commn. of Am. Assn. Mus. Author: (book) Two Centuries of Cuban Art, 1985, Cuba: A History in Art, 1997, Coast to Coast: The Contemporary Landscape in Florida, 1998, A Treasury of American Art, 2002; editor: (novels) Archipenko: Themes and Variations, 1989, Chihuly: Form From Fire, 1994 (Southeastern Mus. Conf. award, 1994), A Century of Jewelry and Gems, 1995, Celebrating Florida, 1995. Trustee Cuban Found.; mem. artists in edn. panel, visual arts panel, youth and children's mus. panel, sci. mus. panel A.D.A. statewide panel Fla. Arts. Coun.; panelist Challenge Grant Program, Cultural Instns. Program; mem. hist. mus. grants panel Fla. Divsn. History; mem. Halifax Area Advt. Authority, 1999—; mem. adv. bd. Daytona Beach Econ. Devel., 1999—; mem., chmn. adv. bd. Environ., Cultural, Hist., and Outdoors, 2001—; mem. Cultural Coun. Volusia County, 2002—. Mem.: Fla. Cultural and Ednl. Alliance (bd. dirs. 1995), Fla. Assn. Mus. (bd. dirs. 1992-98, 2000—, sec. 1995-96, 96-97, 97-98), Fla. Art Mus. Dirs. Assn. (govt. liaison 1990, pres. 1995-96, 96-97). Home and Office: 723 N Oleander Ave Daytona Beach FL 32118-3826

LIBBY, GENE ROGER, lawyer; b. Portland, Maine, Oct. 31, 1951; s. Leon and Doris (Jordan) L.; m. Mary J. Kerry, July 25, 1970 (dec. 1997); children: Jessica, Katie, Matthew, Lindsay. BS in Econs., U. So. Maine, 1974; JD, U. Maine, 1978. Bar: Maine 1978, U.S. Dist. Ct. Maine 1978. Ptnr. Cervizzi & Libby, Scarborough, Maine, 1978-79; asst. dist. atty. York County State of Maine, Alfred, 1979-80, dep. dist. atty. York County, 1980-81, dist. atty. York County, 1981-85; ptnr., gen. counsel, loss prevention officer Verrill & Dana, Kennebunk, Maine, 1986—. Bd. dirs. Sentencing Options, Portland, Maine. Bd. dirs. Maine Hwy. Traffic Safety Commn., 1982-83, Maine Cancer Found., 1999-, Mary's Walk Inc.; mem. Gov.'s Group on Child Abuse & Neglect, Maine, 1984; pres. Maine Prosecutor's Assn., 1984-85; chmn. York County Budget Com., 1993-97; councilor Saco City Coun., Ward 3. Mem. ABA, Maine Bar Assn., York County Bar Assn., Assn. Trial Lawyers Am., Nat. Assn. Criminal Def. Lawyers, Maine Trial Lawyers Assn. Democrat. Roman Catholic. Avocations: hockey, racquetball, jogging. Office: Verrill & Dana Lafayette Ctr PO Box 147 Kennebunk ME 04043-0147 E-mail: glibby@verrilldana.com.

LIBBY, JANE GAYTHORNE, archaeology writer, editor; b. Boston, June 27, 1934; d. Carl Estes and Esther May (Holton) L. BA in English, Bates Coll., 1956; student, Boston U., 1984. With Houghton Mifflin Co., Boston, 1956-60, assoc. editor, 1960-70, sr. editor, 1970-84; freelance editor various cos. including Charlesbridge Publ., Hackett Pub., 1985—; editor, crew mem. during field season Andover Found. Archeol. Rsch., Andover, 1986—, lab. dir. in China, 1993-96. Editor various materials including Excavation of Pintada Rockshelter, 1998, Late Pleistocene Human Friction Skin Prints from Pendejo Cave, N.Mex., 1996, 2d Ann. Report of the Sino-American Jiangxi Origin of Rice Project, 1997, Preliminary Investigations of the Archaic in the region of Las Cruces, New Mexico, 1993, Visit to a Coral Reef, 1992, A More Perfect Union, 1991, The Archaic Chihuahua Tradition, 1989, A History of the World, 1985, Planet Earth, 1976, The Mexican American, 1973, Astrology: The Divine Science, 1971, Reincarnation, 1968. Mem. Soc. for Am. Archaeology, Nat Wildlife Fedn. E-mail: condari@netway.com.

LIBBY, JOHN KELWAY, financial services company executive; b. Washington, June 13, 1926; s. John H. and Violet K. (Bamber) L.; m. Mary Seymour Kindel, Dec. 30, 1960; children: Carolyn K., Anne K., Virginia L. Osborne. BA, Haverford Coll., 1945; postgrad., Harvard U., 1946. With U.S. Dept. State, 1947-48, Capital Airlines Inc., 1949-51, S.G. Warburg & Co., London, 1954; assoc., v.p. Kuhn Loeb & Co., N.Y.C., 1955-66, gen. ptnr., 1966-77; mng. dir. Lehman Bros. Kuhn Loeb, Inc., N.Y.C., 1977-80, adv. dir., 1981-84; gen. ptnr. K.L. Assocs., 1985—; vice chmn. Caldwell Asset Mgmt., Inc., 2000—. Adviser Cen. Bank Venezuela, 1974-75; bd. dirs. various U.S. and fgn. corps. Lt. USN, 1944-46, PTO, 1951-53. Office: K L Assocs 450 Park Ave New York NY 10022-2605

LIBBY, RONALD THEODORE, political science educator, consultant, researcher; b. L.A., Nov. 20, 1941; s. Theodore Harold and Patricia Mildred (Griswold) L.; m. Kathleen Christina Jacobson, June 3, 1982; children: Kathleen Elizabeth Libby, Erin Kristin Jenne. BA, Wash. State U., 1965; MA, U. Wash., 1966, PhD, 1975. Lectr. U. Bostwana, Lesotho and Swaziland, 1973-75, U. Malawi, Zomba, 1975-76, U. Zambia, Lusaka, 1976-79; asst. prof. U. Notre Dame, South Bend, Ind., 1981-83; sr. lectr. U. W.I., Kingston, Jamaica, 1983-85; assoc. prof. Northwestern U., Evanston, Ill., 1985-86; sr. rsch. fellow Australian Nat. U., Darwin, 1986-87; sr. lectr. Victoria U., Wellington, New Zealand, 1987-89; prof. S.W. State U., Marshall, Minn., 1989-96; prof., chmn. dept. St. Joseph's U., Phila., 1996-2000; prof. polit. sci. U. North Fla., Jacksonville, 2000—. Treas. New Zealand Polit. Sci. Assn., Wellington, 1988-89. Author: Towards an Africanized U.S. Policy for Southern Africa, 1980, The Politics of Economic Power in Southern Africa, 1987, Hawke's Law, 1989 (Choice award 1991), Protecting Markets: U.S. Policy and the World Grain Trade, 1992, ECO-WARS: Political Campaigns and Social Movements, 1999; contbr. articles to profl. jours. With U.S. Army, 1962-64. Rsch. grantee Carnegie Endowment, 1971. Mem. Am. Polit. Sci. Assn., Internat. Studies Assn., Australian Polit. Sci. Assn. Roman Catholic. Avocations: tennis, handball, piano, singing. Office: U North Fla Dept Polit Sci 4567 St Bluff Rd S Jacksonville FL 32224 Home: 117 Turtle Bay Ln Ponte Vedra Beach FL 32082 E-mail: rlibby@unf.edu., rt12129@aol.com. *Through the many travails of life the one abiding principle that has guided me is intellectual honesty and integrity.*

LIBBY, RUSSELL CLARK, pediatrician; b. Washington, Feb. 26, 1952; s. William G. and Leona L.; m. Mary Elizabeth Schmidt, Mar. 23, 1996; children: Kristin, Katherine, Laura. BS in Zoology, George Washington U., 1974, MD, 1979. Diplomate Am. Bd. Pediats. Intern, then resident in pediats. Georgetown U. Hosp., Washington, 1979-82; pres., med. dir. Va. Pediat. Group Ltd., Fairfax, 1982—, Am. Pediat. Cons., Inc., Fairfax, 1992—; chmn., med. dir. Nat. Physician Care, 1993—. Mem. steering com. Partnership for Healthier Kids, Falls Church, Va.; clin. instr. U. Va., Med. Coll. Va., Georgetown U. Med. Sch., 1993—; chief gen. med. sect. Inova Fairfax Hosp. for Children. Contbr. ; editor: Va. Med. Quar., 1996—98, (newsletter) Managed Care Link, 1994—97; host, writer : TV series To Your Health. Named Best Pediatrician, Best for Families mag., 1993, 94, 97, 99, 2001, 2002. Fellow Am. Acad. Pediats. (sect. editor, author chpt. guidelines for pediat. home health care 2002); mem. AMA, Am. Acad. Home Care Physicians (cert. homecare med. dir., bd. dirs. 2002), Med. Soc. Va. (del.), Fairfax County Med. Soc. (exec. com., officer, contbr. to bull. 1995-98, pres.-elect 1999-2000, pres. 2001), No. Va. Med. Soc. (chmn. coun. 2001—), Pediat. Leadership Alliance. Avocations: stained glass art, writing. Office: Va Pediat Group Ltd 3020 Hamaker Ct Ste 200 Fairfax VA 22031-2220

LIBER, HILLARY SELESE JACOBS, foundation administrator; b. Balt., Apr. 25, 1953; d. Stanley J. Marmelstein; d. David Paul (stepfather) and Claire Beth (Kuff) Jacobs; m. Jeffrey Robert Liber, Aug. 5, 1972; children: Reuben Raphael, Seth Avram. BS in Edn., Kent State U., 1973; MS, SUNY, Buffalo, 1979. Intensive edn. instr. Cleveland Heights/University Heights Sch. Dist., Cleve., 1973-75; instr. for multi-handicapped Orleans Niagara BOCES, Lockport, N.Y., 1975-76; sales cons. Economy Co. Publishers, So. Calif., 1979-82; instr. gerontology sr. adult edn. Palomar Coll., San Marcos, Calif., 1979-86; instr. creative writing and current events sr. adult edn. Mira Costa Coll., Oceanside, 1979-88; regional dir. City of Hope, San Diego, 1989-91; vol. adult and teen educator Temple Solel, Encinitas, Calif., 1994—. Prin. Congregation Beth Am, Solana Beach, Calif., 1984-86; nat. field cons. supr. Hadassah, 1986-89. Contbg. author: Motivation, Career Striving and Aging, 1982, Touched by Adoption, 1999. Home: 4709 Vereda Luz del Sol San Diego CA 92130-8626 E-mail: hliber@aol.com.

LIBER, JOHN (JOHN DOUGLAS LIBER), lawyer; b. Salem, Ohio, Aug. 23, 1938; m. Nancy Bergren, Aug. 30, 1959; children: John R. II, Craig, Shannon. BS, Purdue U., 1960; JD, Ohio State U., 1963. Bar: Ohio 1963. Ptnr. Manchester, Bennett, Powers & Ullman, Youngstown, Ohio, 1963-72, Spangenberg, Shibley & Liber, Cleve., 1972—. Bd. dirs. Partnership for a Safer Cleve. Recipient Spangenberg award Cleve. Acad. Trial Attys., 1987. Fellow Am. Bar Found., Am. Bd. Trial Advocates, Am. Coll. Trial Lawyers, Internat. Soc. Barristers, Ohio Bar Found.; mem. Cleve. Acad. Trial Lawyers, Ohio Acad. Trial Lawyers (pres. 1985-86), Assn. Trial Lawyers Am. (bd. govs. 1987—), Shaker Heights (Ohio) Country Club, Wilderness Country Club (Naples, Fla.), Cleve. Bar Assn. (pres.), Ohio Met. Bar Assn. (pres.). Office: Spangenberg Shibley & Liber 1900 E 9th St Ste 2400 Cleveland OH 44114-3498

LIBERATI, MARIA THERESA, fashion production company executive; b. Phila., July 16, 1965; d. Edward Michael and Anna Maria Liberati. Student, Laval U., Que., Can., 1984; BS in Fgn. Lang. Edn., Temple U., 1986. Pres., bd. dirs. Sierra Ctr., Feasterville, Pa., 1988—; pres. M.T.L. Prodns., Phila., 1989—. Spokesperson Compassion for Animals, Phila., 1988—. Author: Fashion, Fun and Fitness, 1989, The Model's Guide, 1998; editor mab. Better Nutrition for Today's Living, 1990—. Named Miss Pa., 1985, Miss World, 1986; recipient Merit award Actors and Artists Assn., Rome. Mem. AFTRA, NAFE (adv. bd. 1988—). Avocations: reading, cooking. Office: MTL Prod PO Box 52457 Philadelphia PA 19115-7457 E-mail: marialib@hotmail.com.

LIBERMAN, GAIL JEANNE, editor; b. Neptune, N.J., Feb. 26, 1951; d. Si and Dorothy (Gold) L.; m. Alan Lavine, Dec. 20, 1991. BA, Rutgers U., 1972. Youth editor AP, N.Y.C., 1972-73; writer United Feature Syndicate, 1973; reporter, broadcast editor UPI, Phila. and Hartford, Conn., 1973-75; reporter Courier-Post, Camden, N.J., 1976-80, Bank Advt. News, North Palm Beach, Fla., 1981-82; editor Bank Rate Monitor, 1982-97. Author: Improving Your Credit and Reducing Your Debt, 1994 (endorsed Inst. CFPs), The Complete Idiot's Guide to Making Money With Mutual Funds, 1996, Love, Marriage and Money, 1998, Rags to Riches: Motivating Stories of How Ordinary People Achieved Extraordinary Wealth, 2000, Short and Simple Guide to Life Insurance, 2000, More Rags to Riches: All New Stories of How Ordinary People Achieved Extraordinary Wealth, 2002; columnist: Boston Herald, 1994—, America Online, 1996—, Investor Square, 1996—, Mutual Funds Interactive, 1996—, Quicken, 1998—, Palm Beach Daily News, 1998—, CNBC.com, 2000, Fasttrack mag., 2001—, Pitts. Post-Gazette, 2001; contbr. articles to profl. jours. Mem. Nat. Writers Union, Soc. Am. Bus. Editors and Writers.

LIBERMAN, ROBERT PAUL, psychiatry educator, researcher, writer; b. Newark, Aug. 16, 1937; s. Harry and Gertrude (Galowitz) L.; m. Janet Marilyn Brown, Feb. 16, 1973; children: Peter, Sarah, Danica, Nathaniel, Annalisa. AB summa cum laude, Dartmouth Coll., 1959, diploma in medicine with honors, 1960; MS in Pharmacology, U. Calif., San Francisco, 1961; MD, Johns Hopkins U., 1963. Diplomate Nat. Bd. Med. Examiners, Am. Bd. Psychiatry and Neurology. Intern Bronx (N.Y.) Mcpl. Hosp.-Einstein Coll. Medicine, 1963-64; resident psychiatry Mass. Mental Health Ctr., Boston, 1964-68; postdoctoral fellow in social psychiatry Harvard U., 1966-68, tchg. fellow in psychiatry, 1964-68; mem. faculty group psychotherapy tng. program Washington Sch. Psychiatry, 1968-70; asst. clin. prof. psychiatry UCLA, 1970-72, assoc. clin. prof., 1972-73, assoc. rsch. psychiatrist, 1973-76, rsch. prof. psychiatry, 1976-77, prof. psychiatry, 1977—. With nat. Ctr. Mental Health Svc., Tng. and Rsch., St. Elizabeths Hosp., also mem. NIMH Clin. and Rsch. Assocs. Tng. Program, Washington, 1968-70; dir. Camarillo-UCLA Clin. Rsch. Unit, 1970-97, dir. Clin. Rsch. Ctr. Schizophrenia and Psychiat. Rehab., 1977-2001; chief Rehab. Medicine Svc., West L.A. VA Med. Ctr., Brentwood divsn., 1980-92; cons. divsn. mental health and behavioral scis. edn. Sepulveda (Calif.) VA Hosp., 1975-80; practice medicine specializing in psychiatry, Reston, Va., 1968-70, Thousand Oaks, Calif., 1977—; staff psychiatrist Ventura County Mental Health Dept., 1970-75, Ventura County Gen. Hosp.; mem. med. staff UCLA Neuropsychiat. Inst. and Hosp., 1971—, Ventura Gen. Hosp., Camarillo State Hosp., 1970-97, West L.A. VA Med. Ctr.; dir. Rehab. Rsch. and Tng. Ctr. Mental Illness, 1980-85. Author: (with King, DeRisi and McCann) Personal Effectiveness: Guiding People to Assert Their Feelings and Improve Their Social Skills, 1975, A Guide to Behavioral Analysis and Therapy, 1972, (with Wheeler, DeVisser, Kuehnel and Kuehnel) Handbook of Marital Therapy: An Educational Approach to Treating Troubled Relationships, 1980, Psychiatric Rehabilitation of Chronic Mental Patients, 1987, (with DeRisi and Mueser) Social Skills Training for Psychiatric Patients, 1989, (with Kuehnel, Rose and Storzbach) Resource Book for Psychiatric Rehabilitation, 1990, Handbook of Psychiatric Rehabilitation, 1992, (with Yager) Stress in Psychiatric Disorders, 1993, (with Corrigan) Behavior Therapy in Psychiatric Hospitals, 1994, International Perspectives on Skills Training with the Mentally Disabled, 1998; mem. editl. bd. Jour. Applied Behavior Analysis, 1972-78, Jour. Marriage and Family Counseling, 1974-78, Jour. Behavior Therapy and Exptl. Psychiatry, 1975-2000, Behavior Therapy, 1979-84, Assessment and Intervention in Devel. Disabilities, 1980-85; assoc. editor Jour. Applied Behavior Analysis, 1976-78, Schizophrenia Bull., 1981-87, Internat. Rev. Psychiatry, 1988—, Psychiatry, 1993—; contbr. over 300 articles to profl. jours. and chpts. to books. Bd. dirs. Lake Sherwood Cmty. Assn., 1978—, pres., 1979-81, 90-92, v.p., 1992-95, sec., 1995-97; mem. Conejo Valley Citizens Adv. Bd., 1979-81. Served as surgeon USPHS, 1964-68. Recipient Noyes award for Rsch. in Schizophrenia, 1992, Kolb award in Schizophrenia, 1994, Human Rights award Psychosocial Rehab., Lilly Reintegration prize, Human Rights award WHO, 2000, Reintegration award Eli Lilly, 2000, Disting. Investigator award NARSAD, 2000-01; rsch. grantee NIMH, SSA, NIDA, VA, 1972—. Mem. Assn. Advancement Behavior Therapy (exec. com. 1970-72, dir. 1972-79), Am. Psychiat. Assn. (Hibbs and Van Ameringen awards, Inst. Psychiat. Svcs. Significant Achievement award), Assn. Clin. Psychosocial Rsch. (mem. coun. 1985-98, pres. 1995-97), Phi Beta Kappa. Home: 528 Lake Sherwood Dr Thousand Oaks CA 91361-5120 Office: 300 UCLA Med Plz Los Angeles CA 90095

LIBERT, DONALD JOSEPH, lawyer; b. Sioux Falls, S.D., Mar. 23, 1928; s. Bernard Joseph and Eleanor Monica (Sutton) L.; m. Jo Anne Murray, May 16, 1953; children: Cathleen, Thomas, Kevin, Richard, Stephanie. BS magna cum laude in Social Scis., Georgetown U., 1950, LL.B., 1956. Bar: Ohio. From assoc. to ptnr. Manchester, Bennett, Powers & Ullman, Youngstown, Ohio, 1956-65; various positions to v.p., gen. counsel and sec. Youngstown Sheet & Tube Co., 1965-78; assoc. group counsel LTV Corp., Youngstown and Pitts., 1979; v.p. and gen. counsel Anchor Hocking Corp., Lancaster, Ohio, 1979-87; pvt. practice, 1987—. Served to lt. (j.g.) USN, 1951-54. Mem. Ohio Bar Assn. (former chmn. sr. lawyers com.), Fairfield County Bar Assn. (mem. alt. dispute resolution com.), Lancaster Country Club, Rotary. Republican. Roman Catholic. Office: 127 W Wheeling St Lancaster OH 43130-3737

LIBERTINY, GEORGE ZOLTAN, automotive company research engineer; b. Szolnok, Hungary, June 14, 1934; came to U.S., 1963, naturalized, 1974; s. Arpad Pal and Ilona (Szendrei) L.; m. Anna Vizvardi, 1956; children: Thomas, Karen. B.Sc., U. Strathclyde, Glasgow, Scotland, 1959; PhD, U. Bristol, Eng, 1964. Engr. English Elec. Co., Ltd., Whetstone, Eng., 1959-60; asst. prof. mech. engring. U. Miami, Coral Gables, Fla., 1963-65, assoc. prof., 1965-68; assoc. prof. mech. and aerospace engring. Ill. Inst. Tech., Chgo., 1968-71; sr. research engr. Ford Motor Co., Dearborn, Mich., 1971-73, prin. research engring. assoc., 1973—. Adj. prof. mech. engring. U. Mich., Dearborn, 1982— ; cons. expert witness design, stress and materials related to product liability cases; ad hoc visitor Accreditation Bd. Engring. and Tech., 1977-83 Assoc. editor: Jour. Vibration, Acoustics, Stress and Reliability in Design, 1982-85; contbr. numerous articles to profl. jours.; patentee in field. Recipient Outstanding Engr. award Mich. Soc. Profl. Engrs., 1984. Ford Found. scholar, 1957-59, 60-63 Fellow ASME; mem. Soc. Automotive Engrs. (R.R. Teetor award 1967, Forest R. McFarland award 1983), Sigma Xi. Office: Ford Motor Co 330 Town Center Dr Ste 500 Dearborn MI 48126-2796 *There is nothing more important in life than freedom. No research engineer or scientist can be truly productive without being free. All my life I have fought to stay free. Both my success and the lack of greater success are due to my unwillingness to give up my freedom.*

LIBERTINY, SUSAN FRYC, mechanical engineer; b. Apr. 15, 1965; d. Richard and Beth Fryc; m. Thomas Libertiny. BS in mech. engring., Lawrence Tech. U., 1989; MS in mech. engring., Purdue U., 1995. Product design engr. Ford Motor Co., Dearborn, Mich., 1989-92, systems engr., 1992-95, mfg. process engr. Windsor, Ont., Can., 1995-96, engine strategy analyst Dearborn, 1996-98, team mgr., 1998-2001, site quality mgr. Windsor and Essex, Ont., Can., 2000—. Author, editor: (video) Engine Design 2000, 1995. Mem. vol. coun. Detroit Symphony Orch.; supporter Detroit Inst. Arts, Angela Hospice, Salvation Army, Am. Heart Assn. Nominated for Woman Engr. of Yr. Wards Automotive, 1994; winner 1st pl. award Eagle Talon Social Club Challenge, 1994; recipient award for Use of Magnesium in an Original Design Magnesium Coun. Am., 1989. Mem. ASME, Habitat for Humanity. Avocations: designing and manufacturing jewelry, charities. Office: Ford Motor Co Dearborn MI 48224 E-mail: libertinyt@asme.org.

LIBERTINY, THOMAS GABOR, mechanical engineer, administrator, stock broker; b. Miami, Fla., Mar. 26, 1966; s. George Z. and Anna (Vizvardi) L.; m. Susan Fryc. BSME, Lawrence Tech. U., 1990; MBA, Lawrence Technol. U., 1997. Applications engr. Octal, Inc., Southfield, Mich., 1987-88; mgr. Tensor Systems, Inc., Dearborn, 1988-92; engr. GSE Inc., Farmington, Mich., 1992-94; project mgr. Lucas Assembly and Test Sys., Livonia, 1994-96; mgr. engring., fin. AeroQuip-Vickers, Inc., Ann Arbor, 1996-98; pres. Ankur, Inc., Farmington Hills, 1998-99; fin. advisor Prudential Securities, Bloomfield Hills, 1999—2001; assoc. v.p. investments Raymond James & Assocs., Auburn Hills, 2001—. Lectr. in field. Patentee in field. Mem. Habitat ptnrs. coun. Habitat for Humanity, mem. fin. com., Detroit. Mem.: NSPE, ASME (leadership devel. intern coun. pub. affairs 1997—98, chmn. design edn. com. 1997—99, design engring. divsn. 1997—, futures com. 1999—2000, young engrs. coun. 1999—2000, sec. nat. nominating com. 1999—2002, chmn. SE Mich. sect. 2001—02, bd. on govt. rels. 2002—), Nat. Children's Advocacy Ctr., Soc. Exptl. Mechanics, Soc. Mfg. Engrs., Soc. Automotive Engrs. (full mem.), Mich. Soc. Profl. Engrs., Detroit Symphony Orch., Detroit Inst. Arts. Avocation: private pilot. E-mail: libertinyt@asme.org.

LIBERTO, JOSEPH SALVATORE, retired banker; b. Balt., Apr. 26, 1929; s. Cosimo and Anna (Serio) L.; m. Mary Jane Colandro, May 20, 1962; children— Joseph C., Grace Ann. Student, Balt. City Coll., 1945-47; certificate accounting, Balt. Coll. Commerce, 1949; grad., Nat. Assn. Bank Auditors and Comptrollers Sch. Banking, U. Wis., 1968. With Signet Bank, Md., Balt., from 1954; auditor Union Trust Co. Md., 1963-98, asst. v.p., security officer, 1979-98; ret. Served with AUS, 1951-53, Japan. Mem. Bank Adminstrn. Inst. (pres. Balt. 1968—), Inst. Internal Auditors. Home: 3219 Hiss Ave Parkville MD 21234-4724 Office: Signet Bank Baltimore St Baltimore MD 21202-1603

LIBERTY, ARTHUR ANDREW, judge; b. Oak Park, Ill., Nov. 7, 1954; s. Arthur and Patricia (Horton) L.; m. Jean Liberty, Nov. 22, 1980; children: Rebecca, Rachael. BS, Excelsior Coll., Albany, 1983; JD with honors, Ill. Inst. Tech., Chgo., 1987. Bar: Ill. 1987, U.S. Dist. Ct. (no. dist.) Calif. 1988, U.S. Dist. Ct. (no. dist.) Ill., 1992, U.S. Dist. Ct. (cen. dist.) Ill., 1995, U.S. Ct. Appeals (7th cir.) 1992, U.S. Ct. Appeals (9th cir.) 1989. Asst. dist. counsel U.S. Immigration and Naturalization Service, San Francisco, Chgo., 1987-88, 91-92; sector counsel U.S. Border Patrol, Livermore, Calif., 1988-91; ptnr. Azulay & Azulay, Chgo., 1992-95; pvt. practice Chgo. and Joliet, Ill., 1995-97; U.S. adminstrv. law judge Office of Hearings and Appeals, Detroit, 1997-98, chief U.S. adminstrv. law judge Evansville, Ind., 1998—. Spl. asst. U.S. atty. ea. dist. Calif., Fresno, 1988-91; instr. law and legal procedure Fed. Law Enforcement Tng. Ctr., Artesia, N.Mex., 1989-91; Assn. President, Hearing Office Chief Judges, 2001-; law & jud. procedure Office Hearings & Appeals Nat. Tng. Cadre, Falls Church, Va., 2001—. Contbr. articles to profl. books. Maj., pilot CAP, comdr. Evansville sr. squadron, 1999—. Mem. Brooks Am. Inns of Ct. (master). Avocations: flying, music, cooking. Office: HUD OALJ 409 3rd St SW Suite 320 Washington DC 20024

LIBERTY, JOHN JOSEPH, librarian; b. Sacramento, Dec. 14, 1927; s. John and Josephine (Zobac) L.; m. Irma Elizabeth Madsen, Aug. 25, 1951 (div. Oct. 1979); children: Kristine Elizabeth (dec. Aug. 1970), Marya Liberty. BA, Calif. State U., 1953; MA, U. Denver, 1963. Sr. law clk. Calif. State Libr., Sacramento, 1953-62, acquisitions libr., 1963-64, social sci. libr., 1964-92; faculty Calif. State U. Libr., 1963—; libr. emeritus, adj. faculty, dissent and social change collection Calif. State U. Libr., Sacramento, 1992—. Author: Currents on the Left, 1974, Facing Right, 1977, Journals of Dissent and Social Change, 7th edit., 1993. Mem. ACLU. Home: 5231 Carrington St Sacramento CA 95819-1609 Office: Calif State Univ Libr 2000 State University Dr E Sacramento CA 95819-6039

LIBIN, ALVIN G. business executive; LLD (hon.), U. Calgary. Co-owner Calgary Flames - NHL; chmn. Crownx Properties, Inc.; dir. Extendicare, Inc. (N.Am.). Chmn. Alta. Ingenuity Fund. Office: 255-5 Ave SW # 3200 Calgary AB Canada T2P 3G6

LIBIN, PAUL, theatre executive, producer; b. Chgo., Dec. 12, 1930; m. Florence Rowe, Sept. 25, 1956; children: Charles, Claire, Andrea. Student, U. Ill.; B.F.A., Columbia U., 1956. Producing dir., v.p. Jujamcyn Theaters, N.Y.C., 1990—. Producer (plays) including The Crucible, 1958, Six Characters in Search of an Author, 1963, Royal Hunt of the Sun, 1965, Circle in the Sq. Theatre, N.Y.C., 1965-90; co-producer (plays) Uncle Vanya, 1973, The Iceman Cometh, 1973, Death of a Salesman, 1975, The Lady from the Sea, 1976, The Night of the Iguana, 1976, The Club, 1976, Tartuffe, 1977, The Inspector General, Man and Superman, Spokesong, Loose Ends, 1978, Major Barbara, Past Tense, The Man Who Came to Dinner, 1979, The Bacchae, John Gabriel Borkman, The Father, Scenes and Revelations, 1980, Candida, MacBeth, Eminent Domain, 1981, Present Laughter, The Queen and the Rebels, The Misanthrope, 1982, The Caine Mutiny Court-Martial, Heartbreak House, Awake and Sing, 1983, Design for Living, 1984, Arms and the Man, Marriage of Figaro, 1985, You Never Can Tell, 1986, Coastal Disturbances, 1987, A Streetcar Named Desire, Juno and the Paycock, 1988, The Night of the Iguana, 1988, The Devil's Disciple, 1988, Ghetto, 1989, Sweeney Todd, 1989, Zoya's Apartment, 1990, The Miser, 1990; producing dir. plays I Hate Hamlet, 1991, Secret Garden, 1991, La Bete, 1991, Two Trains Running, 1992, Jelly's Last Jam, 1992, Tommy, 1993, Angels in America, 1993, My Fair Lady, 1993, Grease, 1994, Love! Valour! Compassion!, 1995, Smokey Joe's Cafe, 1995, My Thing of Love, 1995, Moon Over Buffalo, 1995, Patti LuPone on Broadway, 1995, Seven Guitars, 1996, A Funny Thing Happened on the Way to the Forum, 1996, Present Laughter, 1996, David Copperfield, Dreams and Nightmares, 1996, Annie, 1997, Young Man from Atlanta, 1997, The Sound of Music, 1998, Forever Tango, 1998, The Beauty Queen of Leenane, 1998, Death of a Salesman, 1999, The Civil War, 1999, The Weir, 1999, Swing, 1999, A Moon for The Misbegotten, 2000, Proof, 2000, King Hedley II, 2001, The Crucible, 2002. Served with U.S. Army, 1953-55. Recipient Obie award The Club, Village Voice, 1977, Tony award, 1976, 92, 93, 94, 95. Mem. 2d League Off Broadway Theatres and Producers (pres. emeritus), 1st League Am. Theatres and Producers (officer, exec. com., bd. govs.), Circle in the Square Theatre (owner, operator), Broadway Cares Equity Fights AIDS (pres.). Office: Jujamcyn Theaters St James Theatre 246 W 44th St New York NY 10036-3971

LIBKA, ROBERT JOHN, educational director, consultant; b. Pigeon, Mich., Sept. 19, 1951; s. Neil August and Joan Lois (Frank) L.; m. Bonnie Rae Borcher, June 16, 1973; children: Michelle, Kimberly, Jennifer. Cadet, U.S. Coast Guard Acad., 1969-71; BA in Edn., Concordia U., River Forest, Ill., 1975, MA in Edn., 1978. Cert. tchr. elem. & secondary schs., Ill., spl. guidance cert. Dir. residence hall Concordia U., River Forest, Ill., 1975-79, dir. student activities, 1975-87; dir. student ctr. dir. Koehneke Community Ctr., 1975-88; project coord. Khusrau translation Harvard U. and Smithsonian Instn., Boston, Washington, 1988-89; pres. Attitudinal Dynamics Internat., Inc., Maywood, Ill., 1970—; dir. guidance Walther Lutheran High Sch., 1989—; exec. dir. Luth. H.S. Assn. Kane and DuPage Counties, St. Charles, 1993-99; tchr. algebra Proviso West H.S., 2000—. Cons. Harvard U., Smithsonian Instn., Century Insur., Cook Cty. Sheriff's Officeand others, 1970—. Author: (Book) India: Price of Adventure, 1990; producer: Many videos of Internat. Religions and Cultures, 1988—; contbr. numerous articles to profl. and religious jours. Leader ARC, Chgo., 1975-85; mem. N. Maywood (Ill.) Community Orgn., 1975-85; pres. St. Paul Luth. Ch., 1987-88. Recipient Rsch. grant Smithsonian Instn., New Delhi, India, 1988. Mem. Am. Mgmt. Assn., Am. Personnel & Guidance Assn., Ill. Assn. Coll. Admissions Counselors, Luth. Edn. Assn. (life mem.), Gospel Music Assn., Nat. Assn. Campus Activities (bd. dirs. 1985-87). Avocations: travel, video production, distance running, photography. Home: 805 N 6th Ave Maywood IL 60153-1046 Office: Fox Valley Luth Acad 2400 E Main St Saint Charles IL 60174-2415

LIBKIND, JEAN SUE JOHNSON (JEAN SUE JOHNSON-LIBKIND), publishing executive; b. Racine, Wis., Apr. 4, 1944; d. John Bert and Loretta Laura (Richards) Johnson; m. D.M. Spradling, June 5, 1966 (div. Nov. 1971); 1 child, Eric David (dec.); m. Robert Lawrence Libkind, Oct. 13, 1991. Student, U. Oslo, Norway, 1965; BA in Journalism, U. Wis., 1966. Libr. asst. Racine (Wis.) Pub. Libr., 1962-64; mng. editor Daily Cardinal, Madison, 1965-66; project assoc. U. Wis.-Ctr. Sys., 1966-68; office mgr. Senrac Enterprises, 1968-71; prodn. jours. mgr. U. Wis. Press, 1971-72, asst. jours. mgr., 1972-77, asst. mktg. mgr., 1977-80; mktg. mgr. U. Ga. Press, Athens, 1980-84; sales, mktg. mgr. U. Penn Press, Phila., 1984-88; mktg. dir. Jewish Publ. Soc., 1988-91, dir. pub. ops., 1991-94; owner Johnson Libkind Pubs.' Agy., 1994-98; dir. Worldwide Books, Ithaca, NY, 1998—2001; owner Bookschlepper Rights Agy., 2001—. Speaker and cons. in field. Pres. Friends of Ea. State Penitentiary Park, 1996—98; treas. Commonland Cmty. Resident's Assn., 2000—01; program chair Unitarian Universalist Fellowship, Athens, 1982—84. Recipient Svc. award USMC, 1966, Svc. award After Sch. Day Care Assn., 1976; named Hon. Lt. Col., Ga. Militia, 1985. Mem. Women in Comms. (treas. 1990-91, sec. 1989-90, pres. 1970-71), Phila. Pub. Group (pres. 1990-92), Women in Scholarly Pub. (newsletter editor 1981-83, mentoring co-chair 1993-94, pres. 1998-99). Home: 837 N Woodstock St Philadelphia PA 19130-1408

LIBOFF, RICHARD LAWRENCE, physicist, educator; b. N.Y.C., Dec. 30, 1931; s. William and Sarah (Mell) L.; m. Myra Blatt, July 4, 1954; children: David, Lisa. AB, Bklyn. Coll., 1953; PhD, NYU, 1961. Asst. prof. physics NYU, 1961-63; prof. applied physics, applied math. and elec. engring. Cornell U., 1964—; prin. investigator Air Force Office Sci. Research, 1978-83, Army Research Office, 1984—. Cons. Batelle Columbus Lab. Author: Introduction to the Theory of Kinetic Equations, 1969, 79, Russian edit., 1974, Introductory Quantum Mechanics, 1980, 2d edit., 1991, Korean edit., 1992, 3d edit. 1998, Waveguides, Transmission Lines and Smith Charts, 1984, Kinetic Theory: Classical, Quantum and Relativistic Descriptions, 1990, 2d edit. 1998. Served with Chem. Corps U.S. Army, 1953-55. Recipient Founders Day cert. N.Y. U., 1961; Solvay fellow, 1972; Fulbright scholar, 1984 Fellow Am. Phys. Soc.; mem. Sigma Xi. Office: Cornell U Phillips Hall Ithaca NY 14853

LIBONATI, MICHAEL ERNEST, law educator, writer; b. Chgo., May 25, 1944; s. Roland V. and Jeannette K. Libonati; m. Yvonne M. Barber, Sept. 30, 1967; children: Michael, Emma. LLB, Yale U., 1967, LLM, 1969. Bar: D.C. 1968, Ill. 1975, Pa. 1976. Prof. law Temple U., Phila., 1972-90, Carnell prof., 1990—; cons. U.S. Adv. Commn. Intergovernmental Rels. Vis. prof. law U. Ala., Tuscaloosa, 1976, Cornell U., Ithaca, NY, 1977, Coll. William and Mary, Williamsburg, Va., 1987. Author (with Sands and Martinez): (book) Local Government Law, 4 vols., 1981—82; author: (with Hertzel and Williams) Legislative Law and Statutory Interpretation, 3d edit., 2001; author: Local Government Autonomy, 1993, Local Government Autonomy, Japanese edit., 1997, Local Government Autonomy, Spanish edit., 2000; author: (with Martinez) State and Local Government Law, 2000; asst. editor articles: Am. Jour. Legal History, 1971—82. Named Hon. Editor, Temple U. Law Quar., vol. 59, 1986; recipient Williams prize for Excellence in Tchg., 1985, 1990. Mem.: NAS (nat. rsch. bd., hwy. law project adv. commn.), Nat. Assn. Atty.'s Gen. (state constitution law project adv. bd.), Am. Law Inst. Office: Temple U Sch Law 1719 N Broad St Philadelphia PA 19122-6002

LIBRESCU, I. LIVIU, aeromautical and mechanical engineer, researcher; b. Ploiesti, Romania, Aug. 18, 1930; came to U.S., 1985; s. Isidor and Mina (Finkelstein) L.; m. Marilena Semian, Apr., 1966; children: Joseph, Lionel. B in Aero. Engring., Poly. Inst., Bucharest, Romania, 1952, MS, 1953; PhD, Acad. Scis. Romania, Bucharest, 1969; PhD (hon.), Poly. U., Bucharest, 2000. Prin. rsch. worker Inst. Fluid Mechanics Acas. Scis., Bucharest, 1953-69, Inst. Aerospace Constrns., Bucharest, 1970-75; prof. aero. mech. engring. Tel-Aviv U., 1979-86; prof. Va. Poly. Inst. and State U., Blacksburg, 1985—. Vis. prof. Terza U. degli Studi, Rome, 2000; academician Acad. Scis. Shipbuilding Ukraine, 2000; rschr. NASA Larc, Air Force Office of Sci. Rsch., NATO Rsch Office; lectr. in nat. and internat. confs.; organizer symposia and sessions with nat. and internat. confs.; reviewer for more than 40 jours. Author: Elasto-Statics and Kinetics of Anisotropic and Heterogeneous Shell-Type Structures, 1975; co-author: Random Vibrations and Reliability of Composite, 1992, Thermal Stresses IV, 1996, Series on Stability, Vibration and Control of Systems, vol. 4, 1997; contbr. over 250 articles to profl. jours.; adv. bd. editors Solid Mechs. Archives, 1975—; mem. editl. bd. Jour. Thermal Stresses, 1998, Internat. Jour. Non-Linear Mechs., 1997—, Jour. Thin-Walled Structures, 1999—; author of monographs; guest editor ASME. Recipient Traian Vuia prize Romanian Acad. Sci., 1972, Dean's award Excellence in Rsch., Va. Poly. Inst. and State U., 1999. Fellow Acad. Engring. Armenia; mem. Internat. Soc. Interaction Mechanics and Maths., N.Y. Acad. Sci., Commn. Astronautics Romanian Acad. Scis., Acad. Scis. of Shippbuilding Ukraine (academician 2000). Achievements include research that has resulted in seminal contributions brought within the disciplines: aeroelasticity, composite material structures, classical/non-classical shell, plate and beam theories, non-linear structural stability, unsteady magnetoaerodynamics, unsteady supersonic aerodynamics with chemical reactions, smart structures, vibration feedback control of aeronautical structures. Office: Va Poly Inst and State U MC 0219 Dept Engring Blacksburg VA 24061 E-mail: librescu@vt.edu.

LIBRETTO, JOHN CHARLES, television director; b. N.Y.C., Oct. 16, 1947; s. Charles and Esther (Boccuzzi) LiB.; m. Kristin Stromquist, Sept. 1, 1983; children: Katharine, Charles. BA in History, C. W. Post Coll., 1968. Mgr. NBC TV Network, N.Y.C., 1968-75, assoc. dir., 1975-85; dir. NBC Sports, 1985-87, NBC News, N.Y.C., 1987-98, 2000—, ABC-TV, N.Y.C., 1998-2000; sr. dir. NBC News, 2000—. Lectr. NATAS, N.Y.C., 1989. Dir.: (TV shows) World Championship Track and Field, 1983 (Monitor award 1984), Wimbledon Preview, 1983-86, Baseball Pre-Game, 1983-86, NFL Football, 1983-88, Donahue, 1985, Internat. Amateur Athletics Fedn. Track and Field, 1986, NBC Nightly News, 1987-88, XXIV Olympics, 1988, Decision '88, 1988, Today Show and Weekend Today, 1989-98, Rights and Lives, 1989, A Closer Look, 1991, Presidential Debates, 1992, Pope John Paul II in Central Park, 1995, The Faith Daniels Show, Ricki Lake Show, Tempestt, In Person With Maureen O'Boyle, Good Morning America, 1998-99, Dateline NBC, 2000—, convs. and elections, 2000. Sgt. USAF, 1969-71, Vietnam. Recipient Emmy award, 1984, 88, Emmy award nomination, 1979-80, 88, 96. Mem. NATAS, Dirs. Guild Am. Episcopalian. Avocations: music, travel, sports. Office: NBC 30 Rockefeller Plz New York NY 10112-0036 E-mail: john.libretto@nbc.com.

LIBRON, KEKE RENEE, secondary school educator; b. Bronx, N.Y. children: Dimin Renée, Jason Malik. BA, Herbert H. Lehman Coll., 2002. Receptionist Fox, Pheiffer, Frankel & Bachrach, Manhattan, NY, 1989; paraprofl. Dewitt Clinton H.S., Bronx, 1989—95, Health Opportunities H.S., Bronx, 1995—96, Evander Childs H.S., Bronx, 1996—. Author: Poetry.

LICATA, ARTHUR FRANK, lawyer; b. N.Y.C., June 16, 1947; BA in English, Le Moyne Coll., 1969; postgrad., SUNY, Binghampton, 1969-71; JD cum laude, Suffolk U., 1976. Bar: Mass. 1977, N.Y. 1985, U.S. Ct. Appeals (1st cir.) 1977, U.S. Dist. Ct. Mass. 1977, admitted Frank B. Murray, Jr. Inns of Ct. 1990-92. Assoc. Parker, Coulter, Daley & White, Boston, 1977-82; pvt. practice Arthur F. Licata P.C., 1982—. Prin. Ardlee Internat. Trading Co., Ea. and Ctrl. Europe and Russia, 1989-99; del. White House Conf. on Trade and Investment in Ctrl. Europe, Cleve., 1995; lectr. Mass. Continuing Legal Edn., Boston, 1982-90, mem. trial adv. com., 1984-88; mem. working group on drinking and drunk driving Harvard Sch. Pub. Health Ctr. for Health Comms., 1986; spkr. Conv. Nat. Fedn. Paralegal Assns., Boston, 1987; del. U.S.-People's Republic of China Joint Session on Trade, Investment and Econ. Law, Beijing, 1987; co-sponsor Estonian legal del. visit to Mass. and N.H. correctional instns., 1990; Boston host former Soviet legal del. visit, 1989; legal advisor Czech Anglo-Am. Bus. Inst., Prague, Czech Republic, 1989—, Russian Children's Fund, 1992-94, Estonia Acad. for Pub. Safety, 1992-94; adv. bd. Ford Found.'s Legal Resource Ctr., Czech Republic, 1994-96; participant U.S.-Russian Investment Symposium; spkr. Conf. on Proposed Tobacco Settlement and Tort Law, Harvard Law Sch., 1997; guest WGBH-Ch 2, TV, Greater Boston With Emily Rooney, 1999; chair seminar Mass. CLE, Boston, 2000. Panel mem. sta. WBZ TV, Boston; contbr. articles to profl. jours. U.S. Del. 6th People to People Juvenile Justice Program to USSR, Moscow, 1989; legal advisor Mass. chpt. MADD, Plymouth County, 1984-87; mem. State Adv. Com. Med. Malpractice, Boston, 1985; bd. dirs. Boston Ctr. for the Arts, 1990-94; mem. profl. adv. bd. Mass. Epilepsy Assn., 1986-93; counsel state coord. commn. MADD, Mass., 1984-86. Recipient Outstanding Citizen award Mothers Against Drunk Driving, 1986, Sacred Angelic Imperial Constanian Order of Saint George awarded by the Duke of Parma, Italy, 2000. Fellow Mass. Bar Found.; mem. ABA, ATLA, Mass. Bar Assn. (bd. dirs., young lawyers sect. 1979-80, 21st Century Club 1984), Mass. Acad. Trial Attys. (bd. dirs. 1991-99, exec. com. 1997-99), Nat. Bd. Trial Advocacy (bd. cert. civil trial advocate 1992— Avocation: travel. Office: Fed Res Plz 600 Atlantic Ave 27th Fl Boston MA 02210-2211 Fax: (617) 523-7743. E-mail: Licata@worldnet.att.net.

LICATA, PAUL JAMES, health products executive; b. Chgo., July 4, 1957; s. Alfonso and Carmela (Castrogiovanni) L.; m. Sandra Lynn Phinney, June 18, 1988; children: Julie Lynn, Andrea Carmela. BA in Econs., Bus. Adminstrn., Calif. State U., Fullerton, 1979, MBA, 1982. Gen. mgr. Calif. Nutritional Products, Huntington Beach, Calif., 1979—; project mgr. Schaads Hydro Ptnrs., 1985—, Fullerton Hydro Ptnrs., Ltd., Huntington Beach, 1986—; pres. World Organics Corp., Fountain Valley, Calif., 1989—, Nutrition Masters Inc., Huntington Beach, 1991—. CFO Nat. Inst. Nutrition Edn., Denver, 1986-88. Mem. Calvary Ch., Santa Ana, Calif., 1982—, class pres., 1982-84, 89-90, 95-96; v.p. Prince of Peace Sch. Parent Tchr. Fellowship, 1997-99, pres. 1999-01; leader Approved Workmen Are Not Ashamed, 1999. Mem. Nat. Nutritional Foods Assn. (chmn. 1982-84, bd. dirs. 1986-91, pres. 1989-90), Golden West Nutritional Foods Assn. (pres. 1986-87), Soc. for Advancement Mgmt. (pres. Orange County 1984-86, v.p. west region 1987-91, Mgmt. Honor Soc. award 1986). Republican. Avocations: travel, ch. related activities. Office: World Organics Corp 5242 Bolsa Ave Ste 3 Huntington Beach CA 92649-1054 E-mail: plicata@prodigy.net.

LICCIONE, ALEXANDER ANTHONY, artist; b. Rochester, N.Y., Jan. 28, 1948; s. James Anthony and Concetta Maria (Belluscio) L. BFA, Fla. Atlantic U., 1978. Internat. prof. fine arts Accademia di Belle Arti di Brera, Milan, 1968-72; art instr. Ctr. for the Arts, Vero Beach, Fla., 1996. Designer/painter/fabricator outdoor sports murals Indian River C.C., Ft. Pierce, Fla., 1976; painter/fabricator murals Hilton Hotel, N.Y.C., 1984, Citibank, N.Y.C., 1986, N.Y. Pub. Libr., 1988, La Campagna Restaurant, N.Y.C., 1993, Limoncello Restaurant, N.Y.C., 1996; painter MTV-Living Color Music Video, N.Y.C., 1990; works in permanent collection Casa Argentina en Jerusalem, Tierra Santa, Israel, 1993, Am. War Libr., Gardenia, Calif., 2002; author: (filmstrip) Metaphysical Art, 1976. Recipient awards for outstanding contbns. to Sesame St., Nat. Acad. TV Arts and Scis., 1992-93, One Life to Live, 1994-95; Daytime Emmy award As The World Turns, 2000-01. Fellow Fla. Philos. Assn. Roman Catholic. Avocation: photography. Home: 4 Heritage Ln Lagrangeville NY 12540

LICCIONE, MAUREEN T. lawyer; b. N.Y.C., Sept. 4, 1953; m. Kenneth F. Lindahl Jr., Nov. 27, 1981; children, Elizabeth Rogan Lindahl, Emily Nelson Lindahl. BA magna cum laude, Siena Coll., Loudonville, N.Y., 1975; JD, St. John's U., 1981. Bar: N.Y. 1982, U.S. Dist. Ct. (ea. and so. dists.) N.Y. 1982. Legis. aide N.Y. State Senate, 1972-78; student legal specialist City of N.Y., N.Y.C., 1978-81, asst. corp. counsel, 1981-85; ptnr. Twomey, Latham, Shea & Kelley, Riverhead, N.Y., 1985—. Mem. N.Y. State Bar Assn., Suffolk County Bar Assn. Office: Twomey Latham Shea & Kelley 33 W 2nd St # 398 Riverhead NY 11901-2701 also: 400 Townline Rd Hauppauge NY 11788-2838 also: 1 East Main St Ste 1 Bay Shore NY 11706 E-mail: mliccione@suffolklaw.com.

LICETTI, MARY ELIZABETH, business analysis director; b. N.Y.C., Nov. 2, 1954; d. Philip Carmelo and JoAnn (Milner) Licetti; m. George Guy Colagreco, Apr. 22, 1995; 1 child Anastasia Colagreco. BS in Acctg., Rutgers U., 1985; postgrad., Duke U., 1991, 92, Kenan Flagler Bus. Sch., Chapel Hill, N.C., 1995. Sr. acct. Johns-Manville, Manville, N.J., 1972-80; acctg. supr. Ortho Diagnostic Syss. (Johnson & Johnson), Raritan, 1981-87, bus. unit fin. mgr., 1988-90, project mgr., 1991-92, USA contr., 1992-95, dir. bus. analysis and fin. sys., 1995-98, dir. compliance, 1998-99; fin. dir. South Branch Watershed Assocs., Inc., Flemington, NJ, 2001—, South Br. Watershed Assn., 2001—. Chmn. supervisory com. Johns-Manville Employees Credit Union, Manville, 1977—80. Treas. Johns-Manville Employee Club; vol. audit com. United Way, Somerset, NJ, 1991—92; bd. dirs. Am. Liver Found., Commack, NY, 1995—99; vol. South Br. Watershed Assn., 2001—. Mem.: NAFE, Am. Mgmt. Assn., Inst. Mgmt. Accts. Avocations: bicycling, photography, art, musical composing. Home: 30 Madison Ave Flemington NJ 08822-3306 Office: South Branch Watershed Assocs 41 Lilac Dr Flemington NJ 08822 E-mail: maryli@att.net.

LICHENSTEIN, RICHARD, physician, health services administrator; b. Bklyn., Aug. 7, 1961; s. Bernard Eli and Rose Sarah Lichenstein; m. Maura Jacueline Rossman, May 7, 1998; children: Sarah, Michael. BS, CUNY, N.Y.C., 1981; MD, SUNY, Syracuse, 1984. Diplomate Am. Bd. Pediat., Am. Bd. Pediatric Emergency Medicine. Intern then resident in pediat. Columbia Presbyn. Med. Ctr., N.Y.C., 1984-87; fellow in gen. acad. and ambulatory pediat. Bronx Mcpl. Hosp. Ctr., 1987-88; asst., attending pediat. Bronx Mcpl. Hosp. Ctr., Jacobi Hosp., Bronx, N.Y., 1987-88; asst. prof. pediat. U. Md. Med. Ctr., Balt., 1988-94, dep. dir. pediat. emergency medicine, 1994—, dir. pediat. emergency dept., 1993—. Vice-chmn. region III Pediat. Emergency Med. Svc. Adv. Com., Balt., 1995-97, chmn., 1997—, assoc. pediat. med. dir., 1998—; Pediat. Analgesic Antipyretic Cons. Bd., McNeil Consumer Products, Princeton, N.J., 1999—. Editor internet jour. Soccer coach Soccer Assn. Columbia, Md., 1996-99. Recipient Innovations in Med. Edn. award Soc. Acad. Emergency Medicine, 1995. Fellow: Am. Acad. Pediatrics (sec.-treas. Md. chpt. 2000—, v.p. Md. chpt. 2002); mem.: Ambulatory Pediat. Assn. Avocations: tennis, travel. E-mail: rlichens@peds.umaryland.edu.

LICHLITER, WARREN EUGENE, surgeon, educator; b. Murphysboro, Ill., Jan. 24, 1952; s. Gene Estel and Dorothy Colleen (Williams) L.; m. Carol Jane Loftin, Nov. 3, 1979; children: Gary Edward, Christopher Warren, Adrienne Leigh, Abigail Meredith. BA, U. Tenn., 1974; MD, U. Tex., Galveston, 1978. Intern and resident in gen. surgery Baylor U. Med. Ctr., Dallas, 1979-83, resident in colon rectal surgery, 1983-84, mem. attending staff dept. colon rectal surgery, 1984—, assoc. dir. surg. edn., 1984—, program dir. dept. colon rectal residency, 2000—, chief dept. colon rectal surgery, 2000—; clin. asst. prof. surgery health sci. ctr. U. Tex., 1990—. Mem. adv. bd. Am. Cancer Soc., Dallas. Fellow ACS, Am. Soc. Colon Rectal Surgeons; mem. Tex. Surg. Soc., Dallas Soc. Surgeons, Alpha Omega Alpha. Avocations: running, cycling, sailing, kayaking, swimming. Office: 3409 Worth St Ste 500 Dallas TX 75246-2057

LICHO, ROBERT, physician, medical educator; b. N.Y.C., Dec. 13, 1958; s. Edward and Selene Licho; m. Margaret Licho, Sept. 5, 1993; children: Eric, William. BA, NYU, 1980; MD, Albany Med. Coll., 1985. Diplomate Am. Bd. Nuclear Medicine. Resident Albany (N.Y.) Med. Ctr., 1985-89, Stanford (Calif.) U., 1989-90; asst. prof. nuclear medicine U. Mass. Med. Sch., Worcester, 1990-99, asst. prof. radiology, 1999—2002, assoc. prof. radiology, 2002—. Contbr. articles to profl. jours. including Jour. Nuclear Medicine, IEEE Trans. Nuclear Sci., Cancer, Clin. Nuclear Medicine. Mem. Soc. Nuclear Medicine. Office: U Mass Meml Health Care 55 Lake Ave N Worcester MA 01655-0002 E-mail: lichor@ummhc.org.

LICHSTEIN, KENNETH LAWRENCE, psychologist, educator; b. Bklyn., July 20, 1947; s. Max and Sarah Lichstein; m. Betty J. Korr, Oct. 18, 1969; children: Benjamin, Jeremy, Jennifer. BBA, CCNY, 1968; PhD, U. Tenn., 1976. Lic. clin. psychologist. From asst. to full prof. psychology U. Memphis, 1976—. Adolescent psychiatry cons. St. Joseph Hosp., Memphis, 1980-91; insomnia cons. Sleep Disorder Ctr. Meth. Hosp., Memphis, 1990—. Author: Clinical Relaxation Strategies, 1988, Treatment of Late-Life Insomnia, 2000; contbr. over 70 articles to profl. jours., chpts. to 12 books. Grantee Nat. Inst. Aging, H.W. Durham Found., others. Mem. APA, Am. Acad. Sleep Medicine, Assn. Advancement of Behavior Therapy. Avocations: hiking, bird watching. Office: Dept Psychology U Memphis Memphis TN 38152-3230

LICHT, CHRISTOPH, medical professional; b. Karlsruhe, Baden, Germany, July 17, 1964; s. August and Anna-Elisabeth (Zimmermann) L.; m. Ulrike Hantel, Apr. 14, 1993; children: Johann-Christoph, Anna, Benedikt, Martin. Student, U. Essen, U. Heidelberg, U. Freiburg. Cert. pediatrician. Trainee in pediat. Children's Hosp., U. Cologne, 1992-99; rsch. fellow in nephrology U. Tex. S.W. Med. Ctr., Dallas, 1999—. Roman Catholic. Home: 10529 Sandpiper Ln Dallas TX 75230 Office: 5323 Harry Hines Blvd Dallas TX 75390-8856 E-mail: christoph.licht@utsouthwestern.edu.

LICHT, RICHARD A. lawyer; b. Providence, Mar. 25, 1948; s. Julius M. Licht and Irene (Lash) Olson; m. Roanne Sragow; children: Jordan David, Jeremy Michael, Jaclyn Rose, Jacob Adam. AB cum laude, Harvard U., 1968, JD cum laude, 1972; LLM in Taxation, Boston U., 1975. Law clk. to chief justice R.I. Supreme Ct., Providence, 1973-74; ptnr. Letts, Quinn & Licht, 1974-84; mem. R.I. Senate, 1975-84, chmn. judiciary com. and rules com., 1984; lt. gov. State of R.I., 1985-89; mng. ptnr. Tillinghast, Licht, Perkins, Smith & Cohen LLP, 1989—. Former chmn. R.I. Commn. on Racial, Religious and Ethnic Harrassment, Dr. Martin Luther King Jr. Holiday Commn., State Energy and Tech. Study Commn. rules com.; chmn. Coun. of State Govt., Intergovtl. Affairs Com., Nat. Focus Team, Bd. Gov. Higher Edn.; bd. regents Elem. and Secondary Edn.; mem. Pub. Telecom. Authority R.I., Univ. R.I. Found., Community Coll. R.I. Found. Bd. dirs., mem. corp. Roger Williams Hosp.; advisor Community Prep. Sch.; corporator Roger Williams Hosp.; trustee Save the Bay, Inc., Emma Pendleton Bradley Hosp.; bd. dirs. Temple Emanuel, Providence, Jewish Fedn. R.I., Samaritans; chmn. Small Bus. Adv. Council, Task Force on Teenage Suicide Prevention, CD Civil Preparedness Adv. Council, Urban League R.I., 1980-82, John Hope Settlement House, 1976-81; chair Am. Cancer Soc. Ball, 1989, Jewish Fedn. R.I. Passage to Freedom, 1989; chair R.I. chpt. Anti-Defamation League; mem. Women and Infants Corp., Dorcas Place, PARI, UNITAM, NCLG task force of Youth Suicide Prevention, Jewish Home for the Aged of R.I., bd. govs. for the handicapped; active YWCA of Greater R.I., Vols. in Action, Inc., Big Sister Assn. of R.I., Big Bros. R.I.; coordinator vols. gubernatorial campaigns Frank Licht, 1968, 70; active Jewish Community Ctr., Providence, 1975-83, East Side Sr. Citizens Ctr., 1975-76, R.I. Youth Guidance Ctr., Inc., 1987, Block Island Conservancy, Inc., Notre Dame Health Care Corp., 1987; Dem. candidate for U.S. Senate, 1988; chmn. ann. campaign Meeting Street Sch., 1990-91, mem. steering com. for capital fund drive, 1989-92; mem. corp. Womens and Infants Hosp.; Dem. candidate U.S. Senate, 2000. Named an Outstanding Young Man of R.I., R.I. Jaycees, 1979; recipient David Ben Gurion award State of Israel Bonds, 1977, Outstanding Pub. Service award Temple Torat Yisrael, 1985, Disting. Services to the Hispanic Community award Casa Puerto Rico, 1985, Hon. Pub. Service award Meeting St. Sch., 1986, Recognition award R.I. Day Care Dirs. Assn., 1986, award of Appreciation Child Care/Human Services, 1986, Govtl. Services award Ocean State Residences for the Retarded, 1987. Mem. R.I. Bar Assn., Hosp. Assn. R.I. (bd. dirs. 1997). Democrat. Office: Tillinghast Licht Perkins Smith & Cohen 10 Weybosset St Providence RI 02903-2818 Fax: 401-456-1210. E-mail: rlicht@tlslaw.com.

LICHTBLAU, JOHN H. economist; b. Vienna, Austria, June 26, 1921; came to U.S., 1939; s. Ernst and Alice (Fischer) Lichtblau-Lind; m. Charlotte M. Adelberg, Apr. 12, 1944; 1 child, Claudia L. Payne. B in Social Sci., CCNY, 1949; postgrad., NYU, 1950-53. Economist U.S. Dept. Labor, Washington, 1951-53, Conf. Bd., N.Y.C., 1953-54, Walter J. Levy Assocs., N.Y.C., 1955-56; research dir. Petroleum Ind. Research Found. Inc., 1956-61, exec. dir., 1961-72, chmn., 1972—, PIRA Energy Group, N.Y.C., 1977—. Hon. chmn. The Energy Forum NYU, 2001—. Contbr. articles to profl. jours., book chpts. Served with U.S. Army, 1944-47, ETO. Mem. Am. Petroleum Inst., Nat. Petroleum Council, Am. Econ. Assn., Internat. Assn. for Energy Economics (5th Ann. award for outstanding contbns. 1986), Council on Fgn. Relations. Office: Petroleum Industry Rsch Found 3 Park Ave New York NY 10016-5902

LICHTENBERG, BYRON K. futurist, manufacturing executive, space flight consultant, pilot; b. Stroudsburg, Pa., Feb. 19, 1948; s. Glenn John and Georgianna (Bierei) L.; children: Kristin, Kimberly; m. Tamara Miller, Mar. 14, 1997; children: Nathan, Jessanne. ScB, Brown U., 1969; MS, MIT, 1975, ScD, 1979. Rsch. scientist MIT, Cambridge, 1978-84; pres. Payload Systems, Inc., 1984-89, chief scientist, 1989-91; pres., chief exec. officer Omega Aerospace Inc., Virginia Beach, Va., 1991-96; pilot S.W. Airlines, 1994—. Contbg. author NASA Payload Specialist, 1979-92, Flew on Space Shuttle Mission #9, #45; contbr. articles to profl. jours. Trustee X-Prize Found., 1994—. Served to lt. col. USAF, Mass. Air N.G., 1969-93. Recipient NASA Space Flight award, 1983, 92, Spaceflight award VFW, 1983, Haley Spaceflight award AIAA, 1983. Mem. Assn. of Space Explorers (founder), Tau Beta Pi, Sigma Xi Avocations: golf, racquetball, windsurfing, skiing.

LICHTENBERG, ERIK RUSSELL, economics educator; b. Boston, Dec. 3, 1951; s. Philip and Elsa (Russell) Lichtenberg; m. Carol Ellen Mermey, July 7, 1979; children: Elinor, Jenny. BA in Linguistics, U. Chgo., 1973; PhD in Agrl. and Resource Econs., U. Calif., Berkeley, 1985. Vis. lectr., tchg. assoc. dept. agrl. and resource econs. U. Calif., Berkeley, 1982-86; dir. environ. econs. Western Consortium for the Health Professions, San Francisco, 1983-87; fellow Pew Health Policy Program Inst. for Health Policy Studies, U. Calif., 1987; asst. prof. dept. agrl. and resource econs. U. Md., College Park, 1988-92, assoc. prof. dept. agrl. and resource econs., 1992-98, prof. dept. agrl. and resource econs., 1998—. Topic leader for environ. econs. Am. Agrl. Econs. Selected Papers Com., 1991; mem. selected papers com. Assn. Environ. and Resource Economists, 1991-92; sr. economist for agr., natural resources and internat. grade Coun. Econ. Advisers, Exec. Office of the Pres., Washington, 1993-94; mem. Md. Power Plant Rsch. Program Acid Deposition Adv. Com., Md. Dept. Natural Resources, 1993-98; chair U.S. Econs. Panel, U.S.-Israel Binational Agrl. R&D Fund, 1994-95; mem. com. on assessing crop yield Nat. Rsch. Coun., 1996-97, mem. com. on genetically modified pest-protected plants, 1999-2000; presenter in field; cons. in field. Assoc. editor Am. Jour. Agrl. Economics, 1997—; mem. editl. bd. Agrl. and Resource Econs. Rev., 1994-95; contbr. articles to profl. jours. Fulbright scholar, Argentina, 1998; grantee U.S. Dept. Agr. Econ. Rsch. Svcs., U.S. Dept. Agr. Nat. Rsch. Initiative Competive Grants Program, Md. Agrl. Experiment Sta. Competitive Grants Program, N.E. Agrl. Pesticide Impact Assessment Program, Rockefeller Found., U.S. EPA, U.S. Dept. Agr., U.S. Geol. Survey, others. Mem. Am. Econ. Assn., Am. Agrl. Econs. Assn., Assn. Environ. and Resource Economists, Econometric Soc., Soc. for Risk Analysis, N.E. Agrl. and Resource Econs. Assn. Office: Univ Md 2200 Symons Hall College Park MD 20742-5535 E-mail: erikl@arec.umd.edu.

LICHTENBERG, LARRY RAY, chemist, consultant, researcher; b. Marceline, Mo., July 25, 1938; s. Kenneth Ray and Evelyn (Lauck) L.; m. Clarice Elaine Dameron, Dec. 23, 1961; children: Julia-Isabel Dameron. BS in Chemistry, Northeast Mo. State U., 1962. Chemist Bell & Howell, Chgo., 1962-62; jr. chem. engr. Magnavox Corp., Urbana, 1963-64; process engr. Gen. Electric Co., Bloomington, 1964-70; mfg. engr. Burr-Brown, Tucson, 1970-72; sr. staff scientist Motorola, Scottsdale, 1972—94, Phoenix, 1994—98, mem. corp. tech. coun., 1982—98; prin. scientist Process Optimization Specialists, Peoria, 1998—. Contbr. articles to profl. jours. Mem. Am. Chem. Soc., Internat. Soc. Hybrid Microelectronics (pres. Phoenix chpt. 1981-82). Republican. Baptist. Avocations: photography, sailing, amateur radio. Office: Process Optimization Specialists 9708 W Chino Dr Peoria AZ 85382-0944

LICHTENBERG, MARGARET KLEE, publishing company executive; b. N.Y.C., Nov. 19, 1941; d. Lawrence and Shirley Jane (Wicksman) Klee; m. James Lester Lichtenberg, Mar. 31, 1963 (div. 1982); m. William Shaw Jones, July 2, 2000; children: Gregory Lawrence, Amanda Zoe. BA, U. Mich., 1963; postgrad., Harvard U., 1963. Book rev. editor New Woman mag., 1972-73; assoc. editor children's books Parents Mag. Press, 1974; editor, rights dir. Books for Young People, Frederick Warne & Co., N.Y.C., 1975-78; sr. editor Simon & Schuster, 1979-80; dir. sales promotion Grosset & Dunlap, 1980-81; ednl. sales mgr. Bantam Books, 1982-84; dir. mktg. and sales Grove Press, 1984-86, dir. of sales, 1986-87; dir. sales Weidenfeld & Nicolson, N.Y.C., 1986-87; mktg. dir. Beacon Press, Boston, 1988-95; bus. and pub. coach, 1995—. Writer, freelance critic, 1961—. Contbr. articles, essays, stories, poetry, revs. to mags., newspapers and anthologies. Bd. dirs. Children's Book Council, 1978. Recipient 2 Avery Hopwood awards in drama and fiction, 1962, 2 in drama and poetry, 1963; coll. fiction contest award Mademoiselle mag., 1963; Woodrow Wilson fellow, 1963. Mem. Women's Nat. Book Assn. (past pres. N.Y. chpt.), Internat. Coach Fedn. (cert.), The Coaching Collective, Pubs. Mktg. Assn., N.Mex. Book Assn., SW Writers Workshop, PEN N.Mex Home and Office: 4 Cosmos Ct Santa Fe NM 87508-2285 E-mail: maggie@maggielichtenberg.com.

LICHTENSTEIN, CHASE WALTER, management consultant; b. Meriden, Conn., Sept. 22, 1936; s. Harry Charles and Josefa Rose (Weil) L.; m. Marie Agnes Sullivan, June 11, 1959; children: Helen, Paul, Jeremy, Caroline. B Chem. Engring., Cornell U., 1959. Registered profl. engr., N.J. Project mgr., plant engr. M&T Chems., div. Am. Can, Rahway, N.J., 1961-68; project mgr. E.R. Squibb, New Brunswick, 1968-72, prodn. mgr., 1972-74; plant mgr. Medi-Physics Inc., South Plainfield, 1974-75; mgr. corp. plant engring. and good mfg. practices Baxter Healthcare, Deerfield, Ill., 1975-78; dir. engring. Hyland div. Baxter Healthcare, Glendale, Calif., 1978-85; pres., owner Planning Masters, Newbury Park, 1985—. Contbr. articles to profl. jours. Chmn. Housing Authority, Edison, N.J., 1972-75. 1st lt. U.S. Army, 1959-61. Mem. Am. Soc. Tng. and Devel. (chpt. pres. 1989), Am. Inst Chem. Engrs., Nat. Soc. Profl. Engrs., Project Mgmt. Inst. Avocations: reading, camping, swimming. Home and Office: 3343 William Dr Newbury Park CA 91320-2931

LICHTENSTEIN, HARVEY, performing arts executive; b. Bklyn., Apr. 9, 1929; s. Samuel and Jennie (Meiner) L.; m. Phyllis Holbrook, Nov. 14, 1971; children: Saul, John. BA, Bklyn. Coll., 1951, LHD (hon.), 1986; postgrad., Bennington (Vt.) Coll., 1953; ArtsD (hon.), L.I. U., 1989; MusD (hon.), Mannes Coll. Music, 1989; LHD (hon.), Pratt Inst., 1993, Juilliard Sch., 1999, Bard Coll., 1999; DFA (hon.), Princeton U., 1999. Subscription and group sales mgr. N.Y.C. Ballet, also N.Y.C. Opera, 1965-67; pres., exec. producer Bklyn. Acad. Music, 1967-99; chmn. BAM Local Devel. Corp., N.Y.C., 1999—; Am. dir. Spoleto (Italy) Festival, 1971-73. Recipient Disting. Svc. to Arts award Am. Acad. Arts and Letters, 1999, Nat. Medal of Arts, 1999, Chevalier of Legion of Honor, France, 1998. Mem. Century Assn. (N.Y.C.).

LICHTENSTEIN, LAWRENCE MARK, allergy, immunology educator, physician; b. Washington, May 31, 1934; s. Samuel and Lillian (Colodny) L.; m. Carolyn Eggert, June 15, 1956; children: Elizabeth, Joshua, Rebekah. MD, U. Chgo., 1960; PhD, Johns Hopkins U., 1965. Diplomate: Am. Bd. Allergy and Immunology. Intern, Johns Hopkins Hosp., 1960-61, resident in medicine, 1965-66; asst. prof. medicine Johns Hopkins U. Sch. Medicine, 1966-70, assoc. prof., 1970-75, prof., 1975—, dir. Johns Hopkins Asthma and Allergy Ctr., 1989—. Mem. Nat. Adv. Allergy and Infectious Diseases Coun. Mem. editl. bd.: Clin. Immunology and Pathology, Immunology, Pulmonary, Allergy; editor 15 books; contbr. articles to profl. jours. Fellow ACP; mem. Am. Soc. Pharmacology and Exptl. Therapeutics, Am. Assn. Immunology (sec., treas.), Am. Fedn. Clin. Rsch., Am. Soc. Clin. Investigation, Am. Acad. Allergy and Immunology (past pres.), Am. Soc. Exptl. Pathology, Collegium Internat. Allergologicum (past pres.), Assn. Am. Physicians. Democrat. Jewish. Office: John Hopkins Asthma & Allergy Ctr 5501 Hopkins Bayview Cir Baltimore MD 21224-6821

LICHTENSTEIN, NATALIE G. lawyer; b. N.Y.C., Sept. 17, 1953; d. Abba G. and Cecile (Geffen) L.; m. Willard Ken Tom, June 10, 1979. AB summa cum laude, Radcliffe Coll., 1975; JD, Harvard U., 1978. Bar: D.C. 1978. Atty., advisor U.S. Dept. Treasury, Washington, 1978-80; prin. counsel World Bank, 1980-94, chief counsel East Asia and Pacific divsn. Legal Dept., 1994-99, adviser to v.p. legal, 1999-2001, chief counsel instnl. affairs, 2001—. Adj. prof. Chinese law Georgetown U., Washington, 1982-86. Contbr. articles on Chinese and Vietnamese law to profl. jours.

LICHTENSTEIN, ROBERT JAY, lawyer; b. Phila., Jan. 23, 1948; s. Irving M. and Marjorie J. (Weiss) L.; m. Sandra Paley, Aug. 14, 1971; children: David P., Kate. BS in Econs., U. Pa., 1969; JD, U. Pitts., 1973; LLM in Taxation, NYU, 1974. Bar: Pa. 1974, U.S. Tax Ct. 1978, U.S. Dist. Ct. (ea. dist.) Pa. 1979, U.S. Ct. Appeals (3rd cir.) 1982, U.S. Ct. Appeals (4th cir.) 1987. Ptnr. Saul, Ewing, Remick & Saul, 1978-88; assoc. Morgan, Lewis & Bockius, Phila., 1974-78, ptnr., 1988—; dir. Maritrans Inc. Instr. Main Line Paralegal Inst., Wayne, Pa., 1984-87, Paralegal Inst., Phila., 1987-90; adj. prof. law Villanova U. Sch. Law, 1991—, U. Pa. Sch. of Law, 1999—. Trustee Temple Brith Achim, King of Prussia, Pa., 1986-91. Mem. ABA, Pa. Bar Assn., Phila. Assn. Democrat. Avocations: skiing, tennis, reading. Office: Morgan Lewis Bockius LLP 1701 Market St Philadelphia PA 19103-2903 E-mail: rlichtenstein@morganlewis.com.

LICHTENSTEIN, SARAH CAROL, lawyer; b. East Orange, N.J., May 25, 1953; d. Carl and Hilda Ruth (Warshaw) L. BA, Wellesley Coll., 1975; JD, Columbia U., 1978. Bar: N.Y. 1979, U.S. Dist. Ct. (ea. and so. dists.) N.Y. 1979, U.S. Ct. Appeals (2d cir.) 1981. Assoc. Milbank, Tweed, Hadley & McCloy, N.Y.C., 1978-84, Dreyer and Traub, N.Y.C., 1984-87, ptnr., 1987-93, Shea & Gould, N.Y.C., 1993-94; arbitrator small claims ct. Civ. Ct. of the City of New York, 1988-93; ptnr. Morrison Cohen Singer & Weinstein LLP, N.Y.C., 1994-2000; counsel Lamb & Barnosky, LLP, Melville, N.Y., 2000—. Dir. Eleven Riverside Dr. Corp., 1986-89, 98-2000, pres., 1988-89; mem. panel of chpt. 7 trustees So. Dist. of N.Y., 1993-97; mem. mediation panel U.S. Dist. Ct. So. Dist. N.Y., Bankruptcy Ct. So. Dist. N.Y.; mem. faculty N.E. Deposition Program, Nat. Inst. Trial Advocacy. Contbr. articles to profl. jours. Trustee Stephen Wise Free Synagogue, 1987-90, officer, 1990-98. Wellesley scholar, 1975, Stone scholar Columbia U., 1977-78. Mem. ABA, Suffolk County Bar Assn. E-mail: scl@lambbamosky.com.

LICHTER, PAUL RICHARD, ophthalmology educator; b. Detroit, Mar. 7, 1939; s. Max D. and Buena (Epstein) L.; m. Carolyn Goode, 1960; children: Laurie, Susan. BA, U. Mich., 1960, MD, 1964, MS, 1968. Diplomate Am. Bd. Ophthalmology. Asst. to assoc. prof. ophthalmology U. Mich., Ann Arbor, 1971-78, prof., chmn. dept. ophthalmology and visual scis., 1978—. Chmn. Am. Bd. Ophthalmology, 1987. Editor-in-chief Ophthalmology jour., 1986-94. Served to lt. comdr. USN, 1969-71. Fellow: Am. Acad. Ophthalmology (bd. dirs. 1981—97, pres. 1996, sr. hon. award 1986, Lifetime Achievement award 2001); mem.: Acad. Ophthalmologica Internat., Internat. Coun. Ophthalmology, Assn. Univ. Profs. Ophthalmology (trustee 1986—93, pres. 1991—92), Mich. Ophthalmol. Soc. (pres. 1993—95), Washtenaw County Med. Soc., Mich. State Med. Soc., Pan Am. Assn.Ophthalmology (bd. dirs. 1988—, sec.-treas. English-speaking countries 1991—95, pres. 1999—2001), Am. Ophthalmol. Soc. (pres. 2000—01), AMA, Alpha Omega Alpha. Office: U Mich Med Sch Kellogg Eye Ctr 1000 Wall St Ann Arbor MI 48105-1912 E-mail: Plichter@umich.edu.

LICHTERMAN, MARTIN, history educator; b. N.Y.C., July 18, 1918; s. Joseph Aaron and Esther S. (Schacknowitz) L.; m. Charlotte Rottenberg, Oct. 7, 1945; children: Joshua David, Andrew Marc. BS, Harvard U., 1939, A.M., 1947; PhD, Columbia U., 1952. Instr. Rutgers U., Newark, 1948-51; instr., lectr. Princeton U., 1953-55; mem. research staff Princeton U. (Center for Research on World Polit. Instns.), 1951-53; asst. prof. M.I.T., 1955-60; dir. research to gov. Mass., 1959-60; exec. sec., dir. New Eng. Bd. Higher Edn., Winchester, Mass., 1961-66; dean Center Humanities and Social Scis. Union Coll., Schenectady, 1966-71; acting dean faculty Union Coll., 1971-72, dean faculty, 1972-76; prof. history Center Humanities and Social Scis. Union Coll., 1966-76, distinguished prof. history and higher edn., 1976-78; dean Empire State Coll., 1978-82, prof. history, 1982-83, prof. emeritus, 1983—; pres. Alternative Lifelong Learning, Berkeley, Calif., 1989-91. Cons. 20th Century Fund, N.Y.C., 1955-57, Friends World Coll., 1984-86; mem. Mass. Bd. Collegiate Authority, 1961-66; history docent Oakland Mus. of Calif., 1999—. Author: To the Yalu and Back, 1963; co-author: Political Community in the North Atlantic Area, 1957; contbr. articles to profl. jours. Vice chmn. bd. Mass. Com. Children and Youth, 1963-66, mem. exec. bd., 1961-66; adv. bd. Civil Liberties Mass., 1963-66; chmn. bd. New Eng. Council Advancement Sch. Adminstrn., 1961-63; vice chmn. Capital Dist. Civil Liberties Union, 1966-67; chmn. Freedom Forum, Inc., 1970-71, Schnectady Renewals, Inc., 1972-76; bd. dirs. Suffolk County chpt. N.Y. Civil Liberties Union, 1981-87; bd. dirs. Della Corte Internat., Inc., 1983-88; history docent Oakland Mus. of Calif., 1999—. Home: 2587 Hilgard Ave Berkeley CA 94709-1104 E-mail: clichty@dnai.com.

LICHTIG, LEO KENNETH, health economist; b. Bklyn., Oct. 20, 1953; s. Samuel and Alyne Norma (Strauss) L.; m. Susan Mary Walsh, May 15, 1977; children: Brielle Joy, Danica Jill. BS, MS, Rennselaer Poly. Inst., 1974, PhD, 1976. Asst. prof. SUNY, Albany, 1976-77; project specialist, econometrician N.J. State Dept. Health, Trenton, 1977-82; dir. utilization econs. and rsch. Empire Blue Cross/Blue Shield, Albany, 1982-90; v.p. rsch. and demonstration Health Care Rsch. Found., 1982-90; v.p. Network, Inc., Randolph, N.J., Latham, sr. v.p., chief info. officer Somerset, NJ, Latham, NY, 1994—2002; v.p. Aon Consulting, Inc., Somerset, 2002—. Pvt. practice cons., Latham, 1982-90; mem. nat. diagnosis related group steering com. health care fin. adminstrn. Yale U., Washington, 1979-81; mem. adj. faculty Russell Sage Grad. Sch. Health Adminstrn., Albany, 1986-94, Union Coll. Grad. Mgmt. Inst., Schenectady, N.Y., 1991-92; expert reviewer Health Care Financing Adminstrn., Washington, 1987, 89. Author: Hospital Information Systems for Case Mix Management, 1986; contbg. editor (newsletter) Nat. Report on Computers & Health, 1982-85; contbr. articles to profl. jours. Mem. tech. adv. com. Statewide Planning and Rsch. Coop. System, N.Y. State Dept. Health; mem. N.Y. State Universal Data Specifications Task Force, 1998—. Mem. Assn. for Health Svcs. Rsch., Am. Statis. Assn. (com. on privacy and confidentiality 1981-84, subcom. on quality and productivity measures 1988-90), Acad. for Health Svcs. Rsch. and Health Policy, Healthcare Fin. Mgmt. Assn., Internat. Arthurian Soc. (N.Am. br.). Avocation: Arthurian legends. Office: Aon Consulting Inc 270 Davidson Ave Somerset NJ 08873-4140 E-mail: lichtl@rpi.edu.

LICHTIN, LEON (JUDAH LEON LICHTIN), pharmacist; b. Phila., Mar. 5, 1924; s. Aaron and Rosa (Rosenberg) L.; m. Beverly I. Cohen, Aug. 6, 1950; children— Benjamin Lloyd, Alan Eli. BS in Pharmacy, Phila. Coll. Pharmacy and Sci., 1944, MS in Pharmacy, 1947; PhD in Pharmacy, Ohio State U., 1950. Asst. prof. pharmacy U. Cin., 1950-51, assoc. prof., 1951-64, prof., 1964-71, Andrew Jergens prof. pharmacy, 1971-91, Andrew Jergens prof. pharmacy emeritus, 1991—. Cons. in cosmetic sci. Contbr. articles to pharm. jours.; composer string music, vocal music, producer of CD JuChriLam in Celebration of Jerusalem 3000. Past pres. No. Hills Synagogue, Cin. Fellow AAAS, Soc. Cosmetic Chemists; mem. Rho Chi. Achievements include patents in field. Home: 801 Cloverview Ave Cincinnati OH 45231-6017 E-mail: Leon.Lichtin@uc.edu.

LICHTIN, NORMAN NAHUM, chemistry educator; b. Newark, Aug. 10, 1922; s. James Jechiel and Clara (Greenspan) L.; m. Phyllis Selma Wasserman, May 30, 1947; children— Harold Hirsh, Sara Marjorie Boyd, Daniel Albert. BS, Antioch Coll., 1944; MS, Purdue U., 1945; PhD, Harvard U., 1948. Faculty Boston U., 1947-93, prof. chemistry, 1961-93, prof. emeritus, 1993—, univ. prof., 1973-93, chmn. dept. chemistry, 1973-84, dir. divsn. engrng. and applied sci., 1983-87; chief scientist Synlize, Inc., 1987-90, Project Sunrise Inc., 1990-92, Photox Corp., Boston, 1993-97; chief sci. adviser, bd. dirs. NanoTek, Inc., Tucson, 1998—. Vis. chemist Brookhaven Nat. Lab., Upton, N.Y., 1957-58, research collaborator, 1958-70; guest scientist Weizmann Inst. Sci., Rehovoth, Israel, 1962-63; vis. prof. Inst. Phys. and Chem. Research, Wako, Japan, 1980, Hebrew U., Jerusalem, 1962-63, 70-71, 75-76, 80; Coochbehar lectr. Indian Assn. Cultivation of Sci., Calcutta, 1980 Assoc. editor Solar Energy, 1976-93; rsch. and publs. on mechanisms of chem. reactions including reaction of atomic nitrogen with organic compounds, influence of high energy radiation on organic compounds and photoredox reactions of dyes; photochem. conversion solar energy, ionization processes and ionic reactions in solutions in liquid sulfur dioxide, photo assisted solid-catalysis; catalytic and photocatalytic decomposition of organic and inorganic pollutants of air and water. Mem. alumni bd. Antioch Coll., 1996—2002. NSF sr. fellow, 1962-63. Fellow AAAS; mem. Am. Chem. Soc., Sigma Xi, Phi Beta Kappa (hon.) Home: 195 Morton St Newton MA 02459-1522 E-mail: norlichtin@aol.com.

LICHTMAN, ALLAN JAY, historian, educator, consultant; b. Bklyn., Apr. 4, 1947; s. Emanuel and Gertrude Louise (Cohen) L.; m. Katherine Martin Crane, June 6, 1970 (div.); 1 child, Kara Martin; m. Shelia Bradford, 1980 (div.); m. Karyn Lynn Strickler, June 8, 1991; 1 child, Samuel Allan. BA magna cum laude, Brandeis U., 1967; PhD, Harvard U., 1973. Dir. forensics Brandeis U., Waltham, Mass., 1968-71, Harvard U., Cambridge, 1971-72; asst. prof. history The Am. U., Washington, assoc. prof. history, 1977-78, prof. of history, 1978—, assoc. dean faculty and curricular devel. coll. arts & scis., 1985-87, chair dept. history, 1997—. Instr. Brandeis U., 1970; cons. Smithsonian Instn., 1974-79, John Anderson campaign for Pres., 1980, George Washington U., 1983, U.S. Dept. Justice, Washington, 1983—, V.P. Albert Gore, Jr., Washington, 1994-95; advisor Ted Kennedy for Pres. campaign, 1980; cons., commentator NBC spl. project on the history of the Am. Presidency; news cons. CBS; polit. commentator NBC News Nightside, Voice of Am., USIA, Am.'s Talking Cable Network; expert witness Com. for Civil Rights Under Law, 1983—, U.S. Dept. Justice, 1983—, pvt. attys., 1986—, various state, mcpl. and county jurisdictions, 1986—, ACLU, 1987—, So. Poverty Law Ctr., 1990, Legal Def. Fund, 1991, Puerto Rican Legal Def. and Edn. Fund, 1991—, NAACP, 1993-94, Reform Party, 1996, 2000, Reuters News Svc., 1996, 2000; columnist Montgomery Jour., Rockville, Md., 1990-98; columnist Montgomery Gazette, Gaithersburg, Md., 1998—; appeared on various radio and TV programs; spkr. at more than 50 confs. Author: Your Family History: How to Use Oral History, Personal Family Archives, and Public Documents to Discover Your Heritage, 1978, Prejudice and the Old Politics: The Presidential Election of 1928, 1979, The Keys to the White House, 1996; co-author (with Valerie French) Historians and the Living Past: The Theory and Practice of Historical Study, 1978, (with Laura Irwin Langbein) Ecological Inference, 1978; co-editor (with Joan Challinor) Kin and Communities: Families in America, 1979, (with Ken DeCell) The 13 Keys to the Presidency, 1990; series editor: Studies in Modern American History, 2000—; contbr. articles to profl. jours. and popular mags. Tchg. fellow Harvard U., 1969-73; rsch. grantee Am. U., 1978, 82; recipient Outstanding Young Men of Am. award U.S. C. of C. 1979-80, Top Spkr. award Nat. Conv. Internat. Platform Assn., 1983, 84, 87; Sherman Fairchild Distinguished Visiting scholar Calif. Inst. Tech., 1980-81; defeated twenty opponents on TIC TAC DOUGH, 1981. Mem. Am. Historian Assn., Orgn. Am. Historians, Social Sci. History Assn., Fed. City Club, Phi Alpha Phi, Phi Beta Kappa. Democrat. Jewish. Home: 9219 Villa Dr Bethesda MD 20817-3365 Office: The Am Univ Washington DC 20016

LICHTMAN, DAVID MICHAEL, military officer, health care administrator, orthopedist, educator; b. Bklyn., Jan. 14, 1942; s. Harry S. and Frances (Rubin) L.; m. Frances Lubin; children: James Matthew, Elisabeth Jill. Student, Tufts Coll., 1962; MD, SUNY, Bklyn., 1966. Diplomate: Am. Bd. Orthopaedic Surgery. Intern U. Minn. Hosp., 1966-67, Naval Aerospace Med. Inst., Pensacola, Fla., 1967; commd. lt. USN, 1967, advanced through grades to rear adm., 1988, flight surgeon Air Wing 3, 1968-69; mem. staff orthopaedic svc. Nat. Naval. Med. Ctr., Bethesda, Md., 1974-77, chmn. dept. orthopaedic surgery, head, hand surgery svc., 1984-87; dir. orthopaedic residency program Nat. Naval Med. Ctr., 1984-87; asst. chmn. dept. orthopaedic surgery Nat. Naval. Med. Ctr., 1975-77, chmn. dept. orthopaedic surgery, head hand surgery svc., dir. orthopaedic residency program, 1984-87; chmn. dept. orthopaedic surgery and rehab. Naval Hosp., Oakland, Calif., 1977-83, dir. orthopaedic residency program/dir. navy hand fellowship, 1977-83, head hand and microsurgery svc., 1977-83; mem. staff orthopaedic surgery, sr. hand/microsurgery cons., 1988-91; commanding officer, 1989-91; comdr. San Francisco Med. Command, Oakland, 1988-91; promoted to Rear Adm. (lower half), 1989; Rear Adm. (upper half), 1991; retired USN, 1994; John Dunn prof. orthopedic hand surgery Baylor Coll. Medicine, Houston, 1994-98; chmn. dir. ortho residency training John Peter Smith Hosp., Fort Worth, 1998—; clin. prof. Orthopedics Southwestern Coll. of Med., Dallas, 1998—. Cons. orthopaedic surgery asst. sec. def. for health affairs Dept. Def., Washington, 1988-94; specialty advisor naval surgeon gen. for orthopaedic surgery and hand surgery Bur. Medicine and Surgery Dept. Navy, Washington, 1983-86; prof. surgery and head divsn. orthopaedic surgery Uniformed Svcs. U. of Health Scis., Bethesda, 1984-94, ex-officio mem. bd. regents, 1991-94. Editor: The Wrist and Its Disorders, 1988, 2nd edit., 1997, Hand and Wrist Sect. Current Opinion in Orthopaedics.; contbr. articles to profl. jours. Mem. ACS (bd. govs. 1987-96), Am. Acad. Orthopaedic Surgeons, Am. Soc. for Surgery of the Hand (coun. 1999—, del. to AMA 2001—), Am. Orthopaedic Assn. (hon.), Mil. Surgeons U.S. (Philip Hench award 1982), Soc. Naval Flight Surgeons, Soc. Med. Consultants to the Armed Forces (coun. 1994—), Soc. Mil. Orthopaedic Surgeons (bd. dirs. 1987-90). Home: 4958 Overton Woods Ct Fort Worth TX 76109-2433 Office: John Peter Smith Hosp Dept Orthopedic Surgery 1500 S Main St Fort Worth TX 76104-4917 E-mail: dlicht@swbell.net.

LICHTMAN, JOAN, healthcare administrator, accountant, consultant; AB in Math. and Physics, Columbia U., 1965; MA in Edn., NYU, 1968; MS in Acctg., U. Hartford, 1981; postgrad., Georgetown U., 1992, Temple U., 1991-95, others. CPA, Conn., Pa.; cert. inhalation therapy tech. Acct., fin.

analyst Apter & Franklin, CPAs, Hartford, Conn., 1979-81, Siskin & Shapiro, CPAs, Hartford, 1977-78, Savs. and Loan League, East Hartford, 1975-77; asst. prof. acctg. Ctrl. Conn. State U., 1981-83. Therapist, instr., nursing aide, counselor Capital Dist. Psychiat. Ctr., Schenectady, N.Y., Albany Children's Home, VA Hosp., Newington, Conn., New Britain (Conn.) Gen. Hosp., various gen. and specialty hosps., Newark, N.Y.C., Hartford, Conn., Phila., 1957—; cons., rschr., educator Health Care Svcs. Sys./CREW, 1983—; presenter Am. Coll. Legal Medicine, Healthcare Fin. Mgmt. Assn., Am. Soc. Law and Medicine, Soc. for Health and Human Values, Ams. for Dem. Action, First/Second Presbyn. Ch., Mt. Holyoke Coll., Lawndale Meth. Ch., others; adj. faculty in math. Temple U., 1991, adj. faculty in health adminstrn., 1992-94; adj. faculty in physics, healthcare mgmt., epidemiology Peirce Coll., 2000. Contbr. articles to profl. publs. including PICPA, CPA Jour., Garden State Focus, Phila. Inquirer, Phila. Daily News, Bangor Daily News, Jour. Accountancy; editor The Phila. Examiner, 1998-2000; contbg. editor Nat. Online Discussion Leader, Managed Care, Healthcare Fin. Mgmt. Assn., 1995-97. Recipient S. June Schreibman award Women for Greater Phila., 1992, award United Way, 1992, Heroes Recognition award Phila. Daily News, 1992, Pub. Svc. award N.Y. Times, 1993. Mem. AICPA, Pa. Inst. CPAs, Healthcare Fin. Mgmt. Assn., Am. Coll. Legal Medicine, Am. Soc. Law, Medicine, and Ethics, Assn. Cert. Fraud Examiners. Office: Health Care Svcs Sys PO Box 927 Philadelphia PA 19105-0927

LICHTMAN, MARSHALL ALBERT, medical educator, physician, scientist; b. N.Y.C., June 23, 1934; s. Samuel and Vera Lichtman; m. Alice Jo Maisel, June 23, 1957; children: Susan, Joanne, Pamela. AB, Cornell U., 1955; MD, U. Buffalo, 1960. Diplomate Am. Bd. Internal Medicine. Resident in medicine Strong Meml. Hosp., 1960-63; surgeon USPHS, 1963-65; postdoctoral rsch. assoc. Sch. Pub. Health, U. N.C., 1963-65; chief resident, instr. medicine Strong Meml. Hosp., 1965-66; sr. instr. medicine, rsch. trainee in hematology U. Rochester Sch. Medicine, N.Y., 1966-67, asst. prof. medicine, 1968-70, spl. postdoctoral rsch. fellow hematology, 1968-70, assoc. prof. medicine, radiation biology and biophysics, 1971-74, prof. medicine, radiation biology and biophysics, 1974—, chief hematology unit dept. medicine, 1975-77, co-chief, 1977-89, sr. assoc. dean for acad. affairs and rsch., 1979-89, dean Sch. Medicine and Dentistry, 1990-95; exec. v.p. rsch. and med. affairs Leukemia Soc. Am., Inc., 1996—. Vis. prof. univs.; lectr. in field. Editor: Abnormalities of Granulocytes and Monocytes, 1975, Hematology for Practitioners, 1978, Hematology and Oncology, 1980, (with W.J. William, E. Beutler, A.J. Erslev) Hematology, 3d edit., 1983, 4th edit., 1990, (with E. Beutler, B. Coller, T.J. Kipps), 5th edit., 1995, 6th edit., 2001 (with E. Beutler, B. Coller, T.J. Kipps, U. Seligsohn), (with H.J. Meiselman and P.L. LaCelle) White Cell Mechanics: Basic Science and Clinical Aspects, 1984, Hematology: Landmark Papers of the Twentieth Century, 2000; contbr. articles to profl. jours.; mem. editl. bd. Blood Cells, 1978-84, Stem Cells, 1981-83, 93—, Blood, 1983-87, Internat. Jour. Cell Cloning, 1983-92, Exptl. Hematology, 1990-93, Blood Cells, Molecules and Diseases, 1995—, editor-in-chief, 2000—; mem. editl. bd. Am. Jour. Hematology, 2000—. Bd. govs. ARC, 1990-96. Recipient contracts U.S. Army Rsch., 1972-78, U.S. Dept. Energy, 1972-80; USPHS grantee, 1971-95. Master ACP; mem. NIH (hematology study sect. 1982-86), AAAS, Am. Fedn. Med. Rsch., Am. Soc. Hematology (pres. 1989), Internat. Soc. Hematology, N.Y. Acad. Scis., Am. Soc. Clin. Investigation, Assn. Am. Physicians, Am. Assn. for Cancer Rsch., Am. Physiol. Soc., Soc. Leuk Biology, Am. Soc. Cell Biology. Home: 64 Woodbury Pl Rochester NY 14618-3445 Office: U Rochester Sch Medicine & Dentistry Box 610 601 Elmwood Ave Rochester NY 14642-0001 E-mail: mal@urmc.rochester.edu.

LICHTOR, TERRY, neurosurgeon, neuro-oncologist; b. Kansas City, Mo., Nov. 5, 1953; s. Alexander and Lottie Lichtor; m. Malka Ann Mallin, Mar. 30, 1986; children: Alexandra, Sheridan, Herman, Leeber. BA in Chemistry, U. Chgo., 1975, PhD in Pathology, MD, U. Chgo., 1980. Diplomate Am. Bd. Neurol. Surgery, Nat. Bd. Med. Examiners. Intern in gen. surgery Mayo Grad. Sch. Medicine, Rochester, Minn., 1981-82; resident in neurol. surgery U. Chgo., 1982-87, rsch. fellow com. on neurobiology, 1987-89; rsch. assoc. dept. cell, molecular and structural biology Northwestern U., Chgo., 1989-90, rsch. asst. prof. dept. cell, molecular, structural biology, 1990-91; asst. prof. dept. surgery Harvard U., Boston, 1991-92; asst. prof. dept. neurol. surgery Rush U., Chgo., 1996-2000, assoc. prof. dept. neurol. surgery, 2000—; clin. assoc. prof. neurol. surgery Loyola U., 1996—. Attending neurosurgeon Cook County Hosp., Chgo., Edward Hines Hosp., Maywood, Ill., Ill. Masonic Med. Ctr., Chgo., Lake Forest (Ill.) Hosp., Rush Presby. St. Luke's Med. Ctr., Chgo.; online neurosurgery discussion group leader Physicians' Online, Tarrytown, N.Y., 1996—; neurosurgery reviewer Ctrl. Ill. Med. Rev. Orgn., Champaign, Ill., 1997—; lectr. Osler Inst., Terre Haute, Ind., 1997—; dept. editor neurosurgery Vets. Health Sys. Jour., 1998—. Recipient Resident award Am. Acad. Neurol. Surgery, 1985. Mem. AMA, ACS, Am. Assn. Neurol. Surgeons and Congress Neurol. Surgeons (joint sect. on tumors), Ill. Med. Soc., Chgo. Med. Soc., Rsch. Soc. Neurol. Surgeons, Chgo. Neurosurg. Soc., Soc. Neuro-Oncology, Maroon Key Soc., Phi Beta Kappa. Contbr. numerous articles, revs. to profl. jours. Avocations: tennis, photography. Office: Divsn Neurol Surgery 1835 W Harrison St # 3202 Chicago IL 60612-3701 E-mail: tlichtor@rush.edu.

LICHTSTEIN, DANIEL M. medical educator; b. N.Y.C., Dec. 12, 1949; s. Milton and Charlotte Louise Lichtstein; m. Shirley Ann Lichtstein, June 6, 1970; children: Jason, Michelle. Diplomate Am. Bd. Internal Medicine. Pvt. practice, West Palm Beach, Fla., 1978-96; assoc. prof. medicine U. Miami Sch. Medicine, 1996—. V.p. for med. affairs Intracoastal Health Sys., West Palm Beach, 1999—. Author: (book) Preparation for Medical Practice, 1998. Mentor Palm Beach County Schs., Palm Beach Gardens, 1994. Fellow ACP. Jewish. Avocations: golf, writing, traveling, community mentor. Office: Intracoastal Health Sys Ste 101 1401 Forum Way West Palm Bch FL 33401-2324

LICHTWARDT, HARRY EDWARD, physician, surgeon; b. Rio de Janeiro, Dec. 16, 1918; s. Henry Herman and Ruth (Moyer) L.; m. Genevieve Isabelle Merry, July 28, 1947; children: Ronald Arthur, Gregory Edward. AB, Oberlin Coll., 1940; MD, Washington, 1943. Diplomate Am. Bd. Urology. Intern Woman's Hosp., Detroit, 1943-44, surgery resident, 1946-47; resident surgery Dearborn VA Hosp., 1947-48; urology resident Wayne County Gen. Hosp., Eloise, Mich., 1948-51; practice medicine specializing in urology Royal Oak, 1951-83; chief urology William Beaumont Hosp., 1955-81; vice-chief urology, instr. Wayne County Gen. Hosp., 1958-65. Chmn. bd. mgmt. Birmingham (Mich.) YMCA, 1966-68. With M.C., AUS, PTO, 1944-46. Decorated Bronze Star. Fellow ACS; mem. AMA, Mich. Med. Soc., Oakland County Med. Soc., Am. Urol. Assn. (sec. North Cen. sect. 1971-74, pres. 1975, bd. dirs. 1980-97, historian 1988-97, Cert. Achievement award 1999), Orchard Lake Country Club. Home: 2160 Bordeaux Dr Orchard Lake MI 48323-3013

LICHTWARDT, ROBERT WILLIAM, mycologist; b. Rio de Janeiro, Nov. 27, 1924; s. Henry Herman and Ruth Moyer Lichtwardt; m. Elizabeth Thomas, Jan. 27, 1951; children: Ruth Elizabeth, Robert Thomas. AB, Oberlin Coll., 1949; MS, U. Ill., 1951, PhD, 1954. Postdoctoral fellow NSF, Panama, Brazil, 1954-55; postdoctoral rsch. assoc. Iowa State U., Ames, 1955-57; asst. prof. U. Kans., Lawrence, 1957-60, assoc. prof., 1960-65; sr. postdoctoral fellow NSF, Hawaii, Japan, 1963-64; prof. U. Kans., Lawrence, 1965-94, prof. emeritus, 1994—. Author: The Trichomycetes, Fungal Associates of Arthropods, 1986; contbr. 100 articles to profl. jours. Mem. Mycological Soc. Am. (life, pres. 1971-72, editor-in-chief 1965-70, William H. Weston award for tchg. excellence in mycology 1982, Disting. Mycologist award 1991), Brit. Mycological Soc. (hon.), Japan Mycological Soc. (hon.). Office: U Kans Dept Ecology Evol Biology Lawrence KS 66045-2106 E-mail: licht@ku.edu.

LICHTY, WARREN DEWEY, JR. lawyer; b. Colorado Springs, Dec. 17, 1930; s. Warren D. and Margaret (White) L.; m. Margaret Louise Grupy, Dec. 8, 1962. Student, Chadron State Coll., 1948-50; BS in Law, U. Nebr., 1952, JD, 1954. Bar: Nebr. 1954, U.S. Dist. Ct. Nebr. 1954, U.S. Ct. Appeals (8th cir.) 1973, U.S. Supreme Ct. 1979. Spl. agt. CIC, 1955-58; county judge Dawes County, Nebr., 1958-61; spl. asst. atty. gen. Nebr. Dept. Justice, Lincoln, 1961-69; mng. asst. atty. gen., chief counsel Nebr. Dept. Roads, 1969-97. Lectr. law Chadron State Coll., 1959-60; mem. com. on eminent domain and land use, transp. rsch. bd. NAS,-NRC, 1973-90. Served with U.S. Army, 1954-58. Named Grand Sovereign, United Grand Imperial Coun., Red Cross of Constantine, 2001. Mem. Nebr. Bar Assn., Lincoln Bar Assn., Am. Assn. State Hwy. and Transp. Ofcls. (subcom. on legal affairs 1969-97), Scottish Rite Rsch. Soc. (pres. 1990-95, bd. dirs. 1990—), Am. Legion, Internat. Supreme Coun. (hon., Order of DeMolay), Hiram Club (past pres.), Masons (33d degree, grand master Nebr. 1979, vice chmn. conf. Grand Masters N.Am. 1980, bd. dirs. Home Corp. Nebr. 1979-90, pres. George Washington nat. meml. assn.), Shriners, Royal Order Scotland, Scottish Rite (1st Grand Equerry, supreme coun. southern jurisdiction, U.S. and sovereign grand insp. gen. in Nebr. 1991—, bd. dirs. Found. Nebr. 1981-90, pres. bd. dirs. Found. Nebr. 1990—). Republican. Episcopalian. Home: PO Box 22559 Lincoln NE 68542-2559

LICK, DALE WESLEY, education educator; b. Marlette, Mich., Jan. 7, 1938; s. John R. and Florence M. (Baxter) L.; m. Marilyn Kay Foster, Sept. 15, 1956; children: Lynette (dec.), Kitty (dec.), Diana, Ronald. BS with honors, Mich. State U., 1958, MS in Math, 1959; PhD in Math, U. Calif., Riverside, 1965. Research asst. physics Mich. State U., East Lansing, 1958, teaching asst. math., 1959; instr., chmn. dept. math. Port Huron (Mich.) Jr. Coll., 1959-60; asst. to comptroller Mich. Bell Telephone Co., Detroit, 1961; instr. U. Redlands, 1961-63; teaching asst. math. U. Calif., Riverside, 1964-65; asst. prof. math. U. Tenn., Knoxville, 1965-67; postdoctoral fellow Brookhaven Nat. Lab., Upton, N.Y., 1967-68; assoc. prof. U. Tenn., 1968-69; assoc. prof., head dept. math. Drexel U., Phila., 1969-72; adj. assoc. prof. dept. pharmacology Med. Sch., Temple U., 1969-72; v.p. acad. affairs Russell Sage Coll., Troy, N.Y., 1972-74; prof. math. and computing scis. Old Dominion U., Norfolk, Va., 1974-78; also dean Old Dominion U. (Sch. Scis. and Health Professions); pres., prof. math. and computer sci. Ga. So. Coll., Statesboro, 1978-86; pres., prof. math. U. Maine, Orono, 1986-91, Fla. State U., Tallahassee, 1991-93, univ. prof. Learning Sys. Inst. and Dept. Edn. Leadership, 1993—. Cert. in tng. and cons., mng. orgnl. change. Author: Fundamentals of Algebra, 1970, (with C. Murphy) Whole-Faculty Study Groups: A Powerful Way to Change Schools and Enhance Learning, 1998, (with C. Mullen) New Directions in Mentoring: Creating a Culture of Synergy, 1999, (with C. Murphy) Whole-Faculty Study Groups: Creating Student-Based Professional Development, 2001; contbr. articles to profl. jours. Bd. dirs. Statesboro/Coll. Symphony, 1978-86, Statewide Health Coordinating Coun. Va., 1976-78, United Way of the Big Bend, 1992-98; chmn. higher edn. adv. bd. Cmty. of Christ, 1986—; mem. planning com. Bulloch Meml. Hosp., 1979-86; active Coastal Empire coun. Boy Scouts Am., 1982-86, Katalidin coun., 1986-91; bd. dirs. Health Care Ctrs. Am., Virginia Beach, Va., 1978, Ea. Va. Health Systems Agy., 1976-78; chmn., bd. dirs. Assembly Against Hunger and Malnutrition, 1977-78, pres., 1977-78; mem., high priest Cmty. of Christ. Mem. AAUP, AAAS, Am. Math. Soc., Math. Assn. Am., Am. Assn. Univ. Adminstrs., Am. Soc. Allied Health Professions, Am. Assn. State Colls. and Univs. (chmn. com. agr. resources and rural devel. 1981-86), Am. Assn. Higher Edn., Sigma Xi, Phi Kappa Phi, Pi Mu Epsilon (governing coun. 1972-77), Beta Gamma Sigma, Pi Sigma Epsilon. Office: Fla State U Learning Systems Inst C-4600 University Ctr Tallahassee FL 32306-2540 E-mail: dlick@lsi.fsu.edu., dlick@mailer.fsu.edu.

LICKE, WALLACE JOHN, lawyer; b. Bemidji, Minn., Jan. 23, 1945; s. George John and Lois (Sanford) L.; m. Martha Miriam Eddy, Dec. 19, 1969; children: Loriann, Paul. BA, U. Minn., 1967, MA, 1970, JD cum laude, 1973. Bar: Minn. 1973, U.S. Dist. Ct. Minn. 1973, U.S. Ct. Appeals (8th cir.) 1981, U.S. Supreme Ct. 1981. Instr. Itasca C.C., Grand Rapids, Minn., 1968—; assoc. Helgesen, Peterson, Engberg & Spector Attys. at Law (now Peterson, Engberg & Peterson), Mpls., 1972-75; sec., gen. counsel Blandin Paper Co. and UPM-Kymmene Inc., subs. UPM-Kymmene Corp., a Finnish Co., Helsinki, 1975—2002; pvt. practice, 2002—. Bd. dirs. Vol. Atty. Program Super Bd., Judy Garland Mus. and Children's Discovery Mus.; chmn. bus. retention and expansion strategies program U. Minn.; mem. panel of arbitrators Am. Arbitration Assn. Mem. bd. editors Minn. Law Rev. Area rep. Minn. awareness project Minn. Internat. Ctr./World Affairs Ctr.; Bd. dirs., pres. hon. bd. dirs. Itasca County Family YMCA, Itasca County Family YMCA, Grand Grand Rapids; bd. dirs., v.p., pres. Itasca County unit Am. Cancer Soc.; bd. dirs., pres. Myles Reif Performing Arts Ctr.; chmn., sec. post com. computer-small bus. explorer post Boy Scouts Am.; adult leader 4-H program Agrl. Extension Svc. U. Minn., St. Paul; mem. Bass Brook Twp. (Minn.) Econ. Devel. Com.; mem. promotion and prospecting com. Itasca Devel. Corp.; trustee Grand Rapids area community found; chmn. coop. solutions adv. bd. Grand Rapids, Minn.; trustee Libr. Found., Cmty. Libr. Found.; class rep. U. Minn. Law Sch.; bd. dirs. Judy Garland Mus. and Children's Discovery Mus., Grand Rapids, Minn. Recipient William Spurgeon III award Boy Scouts Am., 1988; NDEA Title IV fellow, 1967, Paul Harris fellow. Mem. ABA (com. mem.), Fed. Bar Assn., Minn. Bar Assn. (del., planning com.), Itasca County Bar Assn. (past sec., pres.), Minn. 15th Dist. Bar Assn. (com. mem.), Am. Corp. Counsel Assn. (charter), Am. Soc. Corp. Secs., Grand Rapids C. of C. (chmn. com., bd. dirs.), Rotary (bd. dirs., pres., sec. Grand Rapids, dist. rep.), Order of Ski U Mah, Phi Beta Kappa. E-mail: john_licke@yahoo.com.

LICKHALTER, MERLIN EUGENE, architect; b. St. Louis, May 4, 1934; s. Frank E. and Sophia (Geller) L.; m. Harriet Braen, June 9, 1957; children: Debra, Barbara. BArch, MIT, 1957. Registered arch., Mo., Ill., Calif., Fla., Mich., Wis., Nev., Tex., Ala., Okla., Va., Conn., La., Ga., B.C., Man. Ptnr. Drake Partnership, Architects, St. Louis, 1961-77; pres. JRB Architects, Inc., 1977-81; sr. v.p., mng. dir. Stone, Marraccini & Patterson, 1981-93; sr. v.p., dir. Cannon, 1993—. Owner, pres. mgmt. program Harvard U. Bus. Sch., 1992; cons. Dept. Def., Washington, 1977-78; lectr. Washington U. Sch. Medicine, 1989—. Prin. projects include The Mayo Clinic, Jacksonville, Fla., Washington U. Med. Ctr., St. Louis, U.S. Army Hosp., Frankfurt, Germany, Nat. AIDS Rsch. Ctr., NIH, Washington, Evanston (Ill.) Hosp., Loma Linda (Calif.) U. Med. Ctr., U. Mo. Health Scis. Ctr., Columbia, St. Louis U. Health Scis. Ctr., Children's Hosp. Rsch. Inst., New Orleans, U. Ala. Birmingham Sch. Medicine, U. Ala. Sch. Optometry. Trustee United Hebrew Cong., St. Louis, 1980-88, 93-98, 2000—; exec. com. bd. dirs. Arts & Edn. Coun. St. Louis, 1991—; pres. Acad. Architecture for Health Found. Capt. U.S. Army, 1957-59. Recipient Renovation Design award St. Louis Producers Coun., 1976, USAF Europe Design Award, 1990. Fellow: Am. Coll. Healthcare Architects; mem.: AIA (chmn. nat. acad. architect for health 1993), Acad. Arch. for Health Found. (pres. 2000—), Am. Assn. Health Planning, Am. Hosp. Assn., Hawthorne Found., St. Louis Regional Growth Assn., Frontenac Racquet Club, St. Louis Ambs., St. Louis Club, Masons. Jewish. Home: 160 N Brentwood Blvd Clayton MO 63105-3741 Office: Cannon Design One City Ctr Saint Louis MO 63101

LIDDELL, JANE HAWLEY HAWKES, civic worker; b. Newark, Dec. 8, 1907; d. Edward Zeh and Mary Everett (Hawley) Hawkes; AB, Smith Coll., 1931; postgrad. in art history, Harvard U., 1933-35; MA, Columbia U., 1940; Carnegie fellow Sorbonne, Paris, 1937; m. Donald M. Liddell, Jr., Mar. 30, 1940; children: Jane Boyer, D. Roger Brooke. Pres., Planned Parenthood Essex County (N.J.), 1947-50; trustee Prospect Hill Sch. Girls, Newark, 1946-50; mem. adv. bd., publicity and public relations chmn. N.J. State Mus., Trenton, 1952-60; sec., then v.p. women's br. N.J. Hist. Soc.; women's aux. prodn. chmn. Englewood (N.J.) Hosp., 1959-61; pres. Dwight Sch. Girls Parents Assn., 1955-57; v.p. Englewood Sch. Boys Parents Assn., 1958-60; mem. Altar Guild, women's aux. bd., rector's adv. council St. Paul's Episcopal Ch., Englewood, 1954-59; bd. dir. N.Y. State Soc. of Nat. Soc. Colonial Dames, 1961-67, rep. conf. Patriotic and Hist. Socs., 1964—; bd. dirs. Huguenot Soc. Am., 1979-86, regional v.p., 1979-82, historian, 1983-84, co-chmn. Tercentennial Book, 1983-85; bd. dirs. Soc. Daus. Holland Dames, 1965-82; nat. jr. v.p. Dames of Loyal Legion, USA; bd. dirs., mem. publs. com. Daus. Cin., 1966-72; bd. dirs. Ch. Women's League Patriotic Service, 1962—, pres., 1968-70, 72-74; bd. dirs., chmn. grants com. Youth Found., N.Y.C., 1974—; chmn. for Newark, Smith Coll. 75th Ann. Fund, 1948-50; pres. North N.J. Smith Club, 1956-58; pres. Smith Coll. Class 1931, 1946-51, 76-81, editor 50th anniversary book, 1980-81. Author: (with others) Huguenot Refugees in the Settling of Colonial America, 1982-85; contbr. The Dutch Contribution to the Development of Early Manhattan, 1969. Recipient various commendation awards. Republican. Mem. Colonial Dames Am. (N.Y.C. chpt.). Clubs: Colony, City Gardens, Church (N.Y.C.); Jr. League N.Y.; N.Y. Jr. League; Needle and Bobbin, Nat. Farm and Garden . Editor: Maine Echoes, 1961; research and editor asst., Wartime Writings of American Revolution Officers, 1972-75.

LIDDELL, W. KIRK, specialty contracting company executive; b. Lancaster, Pa., July 24, 1949; m. Pamela E. Trow; four children. AB in Econs. magna cum laude, Princeton U., 1971; MBA, JD, U. Chgo., 1976. Assoc. Covington & Burling, Washington, 1976-80; gen. counsel, v.p. AC and S Inc/Irex Corp., Lancaster, 1980-83; pres., CEO Irex Corp., 1984—. Bd. dirs. High Industries Inc., Splty. Products & Insulation Co., PCI Ins., Inc.; chmn. Lancaster City Partnership, 1986, Lancaster C. of C. and Industry, 1991; bd. dirs., pres. Econ. Devel. Co. Lancaster County, 1997—98; chmn. The Lancaster Alliance. Campaign chmn. United Way of Lancaster County, 1995. Lt. USAR, 1971—73. Leon Carol Marshall scholar U. Chgo. Grad. Sch. Bus., 1974-76; named Scholar-Athlete Nat. Football Found. Mem.: NAM (bd. dirs., asbestos steering com.), Nat. Insulation Assn. (chmn. long range planning 1998—), Pa. C. of C. and Industry (bd. dirs., mem. fin. com., mem. exec. com., chmn. policy com.). Office: Irex Corp 120 N Lime St Lancaster PA 17602-2923

LIDDLE, ALAN CURTIS, retired architect; b. Tacoma, Mar. 10, 1922; s. Abram Dix and Myrtle (Maytum) L. B.Arch., U. Wash., 1948; postgrad., Eidgenoissche Technische Hochschule, Zurich, Switzerland, 1950-51. Asst. prof. architecture U. Wash., 1954-55; prin. Liddle & Jones, Tacoma, 1957-67, Alan Liddle (architects), Tacoma, 1967-90, Liddle & Jacklin, Tacoma, 1990-98; ret., 1999. Architect oceanography bldgs, U. Wash., 1967, Tacoma Art Mus., 1971, Charles Wright Acad., Tacoma, 1962, Pacific Nat. Bank Wash., Auburn, 1965. Pres. bd. Allied Arts Tacoma, 1963-64, Civic Arts Commn. Tacoma-Pierce County, 1969; commr. Wash. Arts Commn., 1971; Bd. dirs. Tacoma Art Mus., Tacoma Zool. Soc., Tacoma Philharmonic, Inc. Served with AUS, 1943-46. Fellow A.I.A. (pres. S.W. Wash. chpt. 1967-68); mem. Wash. Hist. Soc., U. Wash. Alumni Assn. (all life) Home: 12735 Gravelly Lake Dr SW Lakewood WA 98499-1459 Office: 703 Pacific Ave Tacoma WA 98402-5207

LIDDLE, SIDNEY GEORGE, retired mechanical engineer, researcher; b. Salt Lake City, Feb. 27, 1933; s. Clare Maynard and Rozella (Gater) L.; m. Johanna Funkhouser, May 8, 1987 (dec. Aug. 1988). BSME, U. Utah, 1956; PhD in Mech. Engring., U. N.S.W., Sydney, Australia, 1970. Design engr. N.Am Aviation, Canoga Park, Calif., 1956-64; tchg. fellow U. N.S.W., Sydney, 1965-69; sr. engr. Rsch. Lab. GM, Warren, Mich., 1969-77, CalTech. Pasadena, Calif., 1977-85; project engr. Rand Co., Santa Monica, 1985-89; dir. Calif. Engring. Rsch. Inst., Pasadena, 1989-90; propulsion engr. GE Astro-Space, Princeton, N.J., 1990-92; ret., 1992. Contbr. numerous papers to profl. publs. Mem. ASME, AIAA, Soc. Automotive Engrs., Sigma Xi, Tau Beta Pi. Achievements include 5 patents. Avocations: gardening, travel, computers, book collecting. Home: PO Box 2928 Running Springs CA 92382 E-mail: sidliddle@earthlink.net.

LIDDY, EDWARD M. insurance company executive; b. 1945; married. Grad., Cath. U. Am., 1968; MBA, George Washington U., 1972. With Internat. Harvester Co., Ford Motor Co., Ryder Systems Inc., 1968-79; sr. v.p. G.D. Searle & Co., Skokie, Ill., 1979-85; with ADT Inc., N.Y.C., 1985-88, CFO, exec. v.p., dir., 1986-88; CFO Sears, 1988-94; pres., COO Allstate Ins Co., Northbrook, Ill., 1994-98, chmn., pres., CEO, 1999—. Bd. dirs. The Kroger Co., 3M, Ins. Information Inst. Chmn. elect, nat. gov. Boys & Girls Clubs Am.; bd. dirs. Northwestern Meml. Hosp., Jr. Achievement of Chgo. Mem.: Catalyst, Bus. Roundtable, Fin. Svcs. Forum. Office: Allstate Insurance Co 2775 Sanders Rd Northbrook IL 60062-6127*

LIDE, DAVID REYNOLDS, handbook and database editor; b. Gainesville, Ga., May 25, 1928; s. David Reynolds and Laura Kate (Simmons) L.; m. Mary Ruth Lomer, Nov. 5, 1955 (div. Dec. 1988); children: David Alston, Vanessa Grace, James Hugh, Quentin Robert; m. Bettijoyce Breen, 1988. BS, Carnegie Inst. Tech., 1949; PhD, Harvard U., 1952, AM, 1951. Physicist Nat. Bur. Standards, Washington, 1954-63, chief molecular spectroscopy sect., 1963-69, dir. standard reference data Gaithersburg, Md., 1969-88; editor-in-chief Handbook of Chemistry and Physics, CRC Press, 1988—. Pres. Com. on Data for Sci. and Tech., Paris, 1986-90. Author: Basic Laboratory and Industrial Chemicals, 1993, Handbook of Organic Solvents, 1995; (with G.W.A. Milne) Handbook of Data on Organic Compounds, 3rd edit., 1993, Names, Synonyms, and Structures of Organic Compounds, 1995; (with H.V. Kehiaian) Handbook of Thermophysical and Thermochemical Data, 1994; (with Milne) Handbook of Data on Common Organic Compounds, 1995, Properties of Organic Compounds and Properties of Organic Solvents Databases, 1996; (with G. L. Trigg and E. R. Cohen) AIP Physics Desk Reference, 2002, A Century of Excellence in Measurements, Standards and Technology, 2001, Handbook of Chemistry and Physics on CD-ROM, 2002; founding editor Jour. Phys. and Chem. Reference Data, 1972-92. Recipient Skolnik award for Chem. Info., Am. Chem. Soc., 1988, Patterson-Crane award, 1991, Presdl. Rank award in sr. exec. svc., 1986. Mem. Internat. Union Pure and Applied Chemistry (pres. phys. chemistry div. 1983-87). Achievements include use of microwave spectroscopy for studying hindered internal rotation, explanation of HCN laser, development of electronic databases of physical and chemical properties. Home and Office: 13901 Riding Loop Dr North Potomac MD 20878-3879

LIDICKER, WILLIAM ZANDER, JR. zoologist, educator; b. Evanston, Ill., Aug. 19, 1932; s. William Zander and Frida (Schroeter) L.; m. Naomi Ishino, Aug. 18, 1956 (div. Oct., 1982); children: Jeffrey Roger, Kenneth Paul; m. Louise N. DeLonzor, June 5, 1989. BS, Cornell U., 1953; MS, U. Ill., 1954, PhD, 1957. Instr. zoology, asst. curator mammals U. Calif., Berkeley, 1957-59, asst. prof., asst. curator, 1959-65, assoc. prof., assoc. curator, 1965-69; assoc. dir. Mus. Vertebrate Zoology, 1968-81, acting dir., 1974-75, prof. zoology, curator mammals, 1969-89, prof. integrative biology, curator of mammals, 1989-94, prof., curator emeritus, 1994—. Dancer Westwind Internat. Folk Ensemble, 1994-2000, Jubilee Am. Dance Theater, 1999—; contbr. articles to profl. jours. Bd. dirs. No. Calif. Com. for Environ. Info., 1971-77; bd. trustees BIOSIS, 1987-92, chmn., 1992; N.Am. rep. steering com., sect. Mammalogy IUBS, UNESCO, 1978-89; chmn. rodent specialist group Species Survival Commn., IUCN, 1980-89; mem. sci. adv. bd. Marine World Found. at Marine World Africa USA, 1987-98; pres. Dehnel-Petrusewicz Meml. Fund, 1985-97, sec.-treas., 1999. Fellow AAAS, Calif. Acad. Scis., Polish Acad. Scis. (fgn. mem.), Explorers Club; mem. Am. Soc. Mammalogists (dir. 1969—, 2d v.p. 1974-76, pres. 1976-78, C.H. Merriam award 1986, elected hon. mem. 1995), Am. Soc. Naturalists, Berkeley Folk Dancers Club (pres. 1969, tchr. 1984—, hon. mem. 2000). Office: U Calif Mus Vertebrate Zoology Berkeley CA 94720-0001 E-mail: lidicker@socrates.berkeley.edu.

LIDMAN, TOMAS ERIK, national librarian; b. Stockholm, June 30, 1948; s. Ivar and Gunhild (Andersson) L.; m. Kerstin Gårdbro, Aug. 19, 1972; children: Erica, Carl-Fredrik, Charlotte. PhD, U. Stockholm, 1979. Asst. libr. Royal Libr., Stockholm, 1971-79; sr. libr. Stockholm U. Libr., 1979-80; head dept. Delegation for Sci. Info., Stockholm, 1980-84; libr. Nordic Mus., 1984-85; dir. Nat. Libr. Psychology and Edn., 1985-92; libr. Stockholm U. Libr., 1992-95; nat. libr. Royal Libr., Stockholm, 1995—. Chmn. U. Borås, 1998—; bd. mem. Nordic Coun. Sci. Info., 2001--. Author: Party Politics in the House of Nobility in the 19th Century, 1979, Libraries in Sweden, 1990; co-author: Litteratursociologi, 1995; editor: Svenska Antikvariat, 1986. Mem. Swedish Assn. Bibliophiles (pres. 1992-97), Swedish Assn. Rsch. Librs. (pres. 1989-94), Scandinavian Fedn. Rsch. Librs. (pres. 1992-94), Nordic Coun. for Sci. Info. (v.p. 2002). Avocations: art, music, sports, travel. Office: Royal Libr PO Box 5039 S-10241 Stockholm Sweden

LIDOFSKY, STEVEN DAVID, medical educator; b. Bklyn., Jan. 19, 1954; s. Leon Julian and Eleanor Helen (Liebman) L.; m. Elisabeth Tang Barfod, May 3, 1982; children: Benjamin Barfod, Anna Barfod. BA, Columbia U., 1975, PhD, 1980, MD, 1982. Diplomate Am. Bd. Internal Medicine, Am. Bd. Gastroenterology. Intern U. Colo., Denver, 1982-83, resident, 1983-85, chief med. resident, 1985-86; fellow in gastroenterology U. Calif., San Francisco, 1986-90, asst. prof. medicine, 1990-97; assoc. prof. medicine and pharmacology, dir. hepatology U. Vt., Burlington, 1997—, dir. MD-PhD program, 2001—. Contbr. articles to profl. jours. Recipient Liver Scholar award Am. Liver Found., 1990-93, Rsch. award Am. Diabetes Assn., 1996. Mem. Am. Assn. for Study of Liver Diseases, Am. Gastroenterol. Assn. (Fiterman Found. Rsch. award 1994), Calif. Acad. Medicine, Western Soc. Clin. Investigation. Avocations: cartooning, cooking, running. Office: U Vt Rm 414 Burgess Burlington VT 05401 E-mail: steven.lidofsky@uvm.edu.

LIDONNICI, LESLIE, surgeon; b. Bklyn., Aug. 3, 1950; BA in Chemistry, Barnard Coll., 1972; MD, N.Y. Med. Coll., 1978. Diplomate Am. Bd. Surgery. Intern St. Vincent's Hosp., N.Y.C., 1978-79, resident in surgery, 1979, Downstate Med. Ctr., Bklyn., 1980-85, Flushing (N.Y.) Hosp. Med. Ctr., 1985-87; resident in thoracic and cardiovasc. surgery U. Alberta Hosp., Edmonton, Canada, 1989-91; fellow in surgery Astoria (N.Y.) Gen. Hosp., 1987-88; fellow in pediat. cardiac surgery Children's Hosp. N.J., Newark, 1988; asst. cardiothoracic surgeon Hackensack (N.J.) Med. Ctr., 1992-96, St. Francis Hosp., Roslyn, N.Y., 1996—. Mem. AMA, Assn. Women Surgeons, Women in Cardiothoracic Surgery, Am. Med. Women's Assn., Soc. Critical Care Medicine. Office: St Francis Hosp 100 Port Washington Blvd Roslyn NY 11576-1348

LIDSKY, ELLA, retired law librarian; b. Wilno, Poland; came to U.S., 1962; d. Leib and Sheina (Izygzon) Cwik; m. Alexander Lidsky, Feb. 20, 1963 (dec. Mar., 1996); 1 son, David Abraham. BA, Pedagogical Inst. Odessa, USSR; MS, Columbia U., 1966, MA, 1973. Cert. Russian and Hebrew lang. tchr. Tchr. high sch., Poland, 1948-51; elem. sch. Israel, 1961-62; asst. cataloger Tchrs. Coll. Columbia U., N.Y.C., 1966-68; cataloger Fairleigh Dickinson U., Teaneck, N.J., 1968-69, asst. dir. tech. services Madison, 1973-84; head cataloger Ramapo Coll., Mahwah, 1971-73; asst. libr. U.S. Ct. Internat. Trade Law Libr., N.Y.C., 1985-2000. Mem. Am. Assn. Law Libraries, Law Librarians of Greater N.Y., N.Y. Tech. Services Librarians, N.J. Law Librarians Assn. Democrat. Jewish. Avocations: music, travel. E-mail: Hella_@msn.com.

LIDSTONE, HERRICK KENLEY, JR. lawyer; b. New Rochelle, N.Y., Sept. 10, 1949; s. Herrick Kenley and Marcia Edith (Drake) L.; m. Mary Lynne O'Toole, Aug. 5, 1978; children: Herrick Kevin, James Patrick, John Francis. AB, Cornell U., 1971; JD, U. Colo., 1978. Bar: Colo. 1978, U.S. Dist. Ct. Colo. 1978. Assoc. Roath & Brega, P.C., Denver, 1978-85, Brenman, Epstein, Raskin & Friedlob, P.C., Denver, 1985-86; shareholder Brenman, Raskin & Friedlob, P.C., 1986-94; mem. Friedlob Sanderson Raskin Paulson & Tourtilott, LLC, 1995-98, Norton Lidstone, P.C., Greenwood Village, 1998—2002, Burns, Figa & Will, P.C., Englewood, 2002—. Adj. prof. U. Denver Coll. Law, 1985-2000; spkr. in field various orgns.; mem. state securities bd. Colo. Dept. Regulatory Agys., 1999—, v. chmn., 2001—, chair 2001-02. Author: Federal and State Securities Regulation for the General Practitioner in Colorado, 2000; editor U. Colo. Law Rev., 1977-78; co-author: Federal Income Taxation of Corporations, 6th edit.; contbg. author: Legal Opinion Letters Formbook, 1996, supplement, 1999; contbr. articles to profl. jours. Served with USN, 1971-75, with USNR, 1975-81. Mem. ABA (Am. Law Inst.), Colo. Bar Assn., Arapahoe County Bar Assn., Denver Assn. Oil and Gas Title Lawyers. Avocation: fluent Spanish language. Office: Burns Figa & Will PC Ste 1030 6400 S Fiddlers Green Cir Englewood CO 80111 E-mail: hklidstone@bfw-law.com.

LIDSTROM, NIKLAS, professional hockey player; b. Vasteras, Sweden, Apr. 28, 1970; With Detroit Red Wings, 1991—. Recipient Norris Trophy Award, 2000—01. Office: Detroit Red Wings Joe Louis Arena 600 Civic Center Detroit MI 48226*

LIDTKE, VERNON LEROY, history educator; b. Avon, S.D., May 4, 1930; s. Albert William and Aganeta (Boese) Lidtke; m. Doris Eileen Keefe, Apr. 21, 1951. BA, U. Oreg., 1952, MA, 1955; PhD, U. Calif., Berkeley, 1962. Tchr. high sch., Riddle, Oreg., 1953-55; instr. social sci. U. Calif., Berkeley, 1960-62; asst. prof. history Mich. State U., 1962-66, asso. prof., 1966-68; vis. asst. prof. U. Calif., Berkeley, 1963; asso. prof. Johns Hopkins U., 1968-73, prof., 1973—2001, chmn. dept. history, 1975-79, prof. emeritus, 2001—; pres. Friends of the German Historical Inst., Washington, 1991-94. Author: (book) The Outlawed Party: Social Democracy in Germany, 1878-1890, 1966, The Alternative Culture: Socialist Labor in Imperial Germany, 1985; mem ed bd: Jour Modern Hist, 1973—76, mem ed bd: Cent European Hist, 1982—89, mem ed bd: Int Labor and Working Class Hist, 1984—89; contbr. articles to profl jours. Fellow Fulbright Research, 1959—60, 1966—67, Nat Endowment Humanities, 1969—70, Davis Ctr Hist Studies, Princeton Univ, 1974—75, Wissenschaftskolleg zu Berlin, 1987—88, Max-Planck-Institut für Geschichte, Göttingen, 1996. Mem.: AAUP, Conf Group German Polit (officer 1975—83), Conf Group Cen European Hist (vpres 1985, pres 1986), Col Art Asn, Am Hist Asn (chair modern European sect 1992, Eugene Asher Distinguished Teaching Award 1999), Johns Hopkins Club. Home: 4806 Wilmslow Rd Baltimore MD 21210-2328 Office: Johns Hopkins U Dept History Baltimore MD 21218 Business E-Mail: Lidtke@jhu@edu.

LIDZ, BARBARA HOLLAND, geologist, researcher; b. N.Y.C., July 18, 1940; d. Edward Morton Jr. and Dorothy Provence (Mullins) Holland; m. Louis Lidz, May 27, 1960 (dec. Apr. 1967); children: Carolyn Elizabeth (dec.), Lauralee. BS, U. Miami, 1968. Rsch. aide Rosenstiel Sch. Marine and Atmospheric Sci. U. Miami, 1965-66, rsch. asst., 1966-70, rsch. assoc., 1970-74; geologic field asst. U.S. Geol. Survey, Miami, 1974-75, geologist, 1975-89, St. Petersburg, Fla., 1989—. Adj. faculty U. Miami, 1982—, U. South Fla., 1992—. Editor 15 books on carbonate sedimentology; contbr. more than 100 articles to profl. jours. Fellow Cushman Found. for Foraminiferal Rsch., 1992—; grantee Nat. Undersea Rsch. Ctr., 1991-92, Minerals Mgmt. Svc., U.S. Geol. Survey, 1992, U. Miami, 1991-94, Ctr. for Coastal Geology, 1991—. Mem. Miami Geol. Soc. (hon., pres. 1980-81), Geol. Soc. Am., Soc. for Sedimentary Geology (editor spl. publs. 1985-93). Achievements include production of the oldest carbonate depositional history for St. Croix and documented time of island emergence based on microscopic marine fossil evidence; described a new model for evolution of a windward margin (south Fla. reef tract) based on seismic geophysical evidence; discovered a new complex depositional component in 7 million year old sediments based on microscopic marine fossils leading to synthesis of regional eustatic tectonic and oceanographic processes spanning 65 million years in a world-class studied carbonate platform (Great Bahama Bank, Caribbean). Avocations: gardening, beachcombing, exploring reefs in the Bahamas and the Caribbean. Office: US Geol Survey 600 4th St S Saint Petersburg FL 33701-4802

LIE, YU-CHUN DONALD, electrical engineer; b. Taipei, Taiwan, Apr. 25, 1965; s. Kuo-Chin and Shu-Ling (Kung) Lie; m. Ching-Wen Wendy Yang, 1995; children: Paul Emmanuel, Titus Yuen. BSc, Nat. Taiwan U., Taipei, 1987; MSc, Calif. Inst. Tech., 1990, DPhil, 1995. Cert. engr.-in-tng., Calif. Comm., electronics, officer Taiwanese Army, 1987-89; head tchg. and rsch. asst. Calif. Inst. Tech., Pasadena, 1990-95; sr. process devel. engr. Rockwell Semiconductor Sys., Newport Beach, Calif., 1995-97, staff engr., 1997-99; mem. tech. staff Silicon Wave Inc., San Diego, 1999-2000; advisory RFIC designer Comm. Rsch. and Devel. Ctr. IBM Microelectronics, Encinitas, 2000—; vis. lectr. dept. elec. engring. U. Calif., San Diego, 2001—. Summer intern Motorola Inc., Phoenix, 1994, Jet Propulsion Lab., Pasadena, Calif., 1993. Contbr. over 30 articles to profl. jours., chpts. to books, internat. confs. Rotary Internat. scholar, Evanston, Ill., 1989-90; recipient Grad. Student award Internat. Union Material Rsch. Soc., 1994, various scholarships and contests. Mem.: IEEE (sr.). Achievements include patents on designing semiconductor circuits, devices and materials.

LIEB, DAVID BARRY, cardiologist; b. Chgo., Dec. 8, 1945; MD, U. Health Scis. - Chgo., Med. Sch., 1973. Diplomate Am. Bd. Internal Medicine, Am. Bd. Cardiovascular Diseases. Intern Michael Reese Hosp. Med. Ctr., Chgo., 1973-74, resident in internal medicine, 1974-76, fellow in cardiology, 1976-78, attending physician, 1978—; asst. clin. prof. medicine U. Ill. Coll. Medicine, 1991—. Mem. AMA, Am. Coll. Cardiology, Am. Coll. Physicians. Office: 111 N Wabash Ave Chicago IL 60602-1903

LIEB, ELLIOTT HERSHEL, physicist, mathematician, educator; b. Boston, July 31, 1932; s. Sinclair M. and Clara (Rosenstein) L.; m. Christiane Fellbaum; children: Alexander, Gregory. BSc, MIT, 1953; PhD, U. Birmingham, Eng., 1956; DSc (hon.), U. Copenhagen, 1979; Dr. (hon.), Ecole Poly. Fed. Lausanne, Switzerland, 1995. With IBM Corp., 1960-63; sr. lectr. Fourah Bay Coll., Sierra Leone, 1961; mem. faculty Yeshiva U., 1963-66, Northeastern U., 1966-68, MIT, Cambridge, 1968-75, prof. physics, 1963-68, prof. math., 1968-73, prof. math. and physics, 1973—, Princeton (N.J.) U., 1975—. Author: (with D.C. Mattis) Mathematical Physics in One Dimension, 1966, (with B. Simon and A. Wightman) Studies in Mathematical Physics, (with M. Loss) Analysis; also articles. Recipient Boris Pregel award chem. physics N.Y. Acad. Scis., 1970, Dannie Heineman prize for mathematical physics Am. Inst. Physics and Am. Phys. Soc., 1978, Prix Scientifique, Union des Assurances de Paris, 1985, Birkhoff prize Am. Math. Soc. and Soc. Indsl. Applied Math., 1988, Max-Planck medal German Phys. Soc., 1992, Boltzmann medal Internat. Union of Pure and Applied Physics, 1998, Onsager medal Norwegian U. Sci. and Tech., 1998, Rolf Schock prize in math. Swedish Acad. Scis., 2001, Levi L. Conant prize of Am. Math. Soc., 2002; Guggenheim Found. fellow, 1972, 78. Fellow AAAS, Am. Phys. Soc.; mem. NAS, Austrian Acad. Scis., Danish Royal Acad., Am. Acad. Arts and Scis., Internat. Assn. Math. Physics (pres. 1982-84, 97-99). Office: Princeton U Jadwin Hall-Physics Dept PO Box 708 Princeton NJ 08544-0001

LIEB, L. ROBERT, lawyer; b. Jersey City, July 15, 1941; s. Nathan Philip and Elizabeth (Blum) Lieb; m. Sherry Young, Sept. 11, 1971; children: Elizabeth Ann, Nathan Young. BA, U. Buffalo, 1962; LLB, NYU, 1965. Bar: N.J. 1967, N.Y. 1970, U.S. Dist. St. (so. and ea. dists.) N.Y. 1970. Law clk., appellate divsn. Superior Ct. N.J., 1965—66; sr. ptnr. Kimmelman, Lieb, Wolf & Samson, West Orange, NJ, 1972—77; chmn. Mountain Devel. Corp., West Paterson, 1978—, Bretton Woods Corp., NH, 1980—84. Chmn., bd. dirs. NorCrown Bank of Roseland, 1987. Officer The Children's Inst., Livingston, NJ; trustee Passaic County 200 Club, YMCA of the Oranges, Livingston Edn. Found.; co-chmn. Bryant Park Mgmt. Corp. Served 1st lt. JAGC USAF, 1966—72. Scholar Harry Rudin, NYU, 1963—65. Mem.: Essex County Bar Assn., Green Brook Country Club (North Caldwell, N.J.). Office: Mountain Devel Corp 3 Garret Mountain Plz Little Falls NJ 07424-3319

LIEBAU, FREDERIC JACK, JR. investment manager; b. Palo Alto, Calif., Sept. 30, 1963; s. Frederic Jack and Charlene (Conrad) L.; m. Carol Platt. BA, Stanford U., 1985. Press aide Office of V.P., Washington, 1982; intern L.A. Times, 1983; analyst Capital Rsch. Co., L.A., 1984-86; ptnr., portfolio mgr. Primecap Mgmt. Co., Pasadena, Calif., 1986—; owner Liebau Farms. Office: Primecap Mgmt Co 225 S Lake Ave Ste 400 Pasadena CA 91101-3093 E-mail: liebaufarm@aol.com.

LIEBELER, SUSAN WITTENBERG, lawyer; b. July 3, 1942; d. Sherman K. and Eleanor (Klivans) Levine; m. Wesley J. Liebeler, Oct. 21, 1971; 1 child, Jennifer. BA, U. Mich., 1963, postgrad., 1963-64; LLB, UCLA, 1966. Bar: Calif. 1967, Vt. 1972, D.C. 1988. Law clk. Calif. Ct. of Appeals, 1966-67; assoc. Gang, Tyre & Brown, 1967-68, Greenberg, Bernhard, Weiss & Karma, L.A., 1968-70; assoc. gen. counsel Rep. Corp., 1970-72; gen. counsel Verit Industries, 1972-73; prof. Loyola Law Sch., L.A., 1973—80; spl. counsel, chmn. John S. R. Shad, SEC, Washington, 1981-82; commr. U.S. Internat. Trade Commn., 1984-88, vice-chmn., 1984-86, chmn., 1986-88; ptnr. Irell & Manella, L.A., 1988-94; pres. Lexpert Rsch. Svcs., 1995—. Vis. prof. U. Tex., summer 1982; cons. Office of Policy Coordination, office of Pres.-elect, 1981-82; cons. U.S. Ry. Assn., 1975, U.S. EPA, 1974, U.S. Price Commn., 1972; mem. Adminstrv. Conf. U.S., 1986-88. Mem. editl. adv. bd. Regulation mag. CATO Inst.; sr. editor UCLA Law Rev., 1965-66; contbr. articles to profl. jours. Mem. adv. bd. U. Calif. Orientation in USA Law; bd. govs. Century City Hosp., 1992—2002, vice chair, 1997—99, chair, 1999—2001. Stein scholar UCLA, 1966. Mem. State Bar Calif. (treas., vice chair, chair exec. com. internat. law sect.), Practicing Law Inst. (Calif. adv. com.), Washington Legal Found. (acad. adv. bd.), Order of Coif. Jewish. E-mail: lexpert@lexpertresearch.com.

LIEBENDORFER, RICHARD ARTHUR, internist; b. Superior, Wis., Oct. 15, 1927; s. Joe and Nellie Marie (Starboard) L.; m. Priscilla Jean Hotle, Sept. 2, 1951 (dec. Oct. 1981); children: Kim Denise Brummett, Kurt R., Craig T.; m. Carole Lee Henderson, Nov. 18, 1982. BA, U. Iowa, 1949, MD, 1953. Diplomate Am. Bd. Internal Medicine. Intern U.S. Naval Hosp., Charleston, S.C., 1953-54; resident Univ. Hosps. U. Iowa, Iowa City, 1956-59; pvt. practice Tulsa; active staff St. John Med. Ctr., 1959—, pres. med. staff, 1989-90, bd. dirs., 1987-92. Med. dir. CompMed/Exel Care, Tulsa, 1994-96. Lt. USN, 1953-56. Fellow ACP; mem. Tulsa County Med. Soc. (pres. 1982), Okla. State Med. Assn. (trustee 1981-83). Avocations: tennis, golf, ranching, reading. Home: 3147 S Lewis Pl Tulsa OK 74105-2331 Office: Saint John Med Ctr 1919 S Wheeling Ave Ste 404 Tulsa OK 74104-5633 E-mail: rlieben@SJMC.org., rlieben@cox.net.

LIEBENOW, FRANKLIN EASTBURN, JR. English literature educator; b. Fredericksburg, Va., May 9, 1946; s. Franklin Eastburn and Katherine (Garrison) L.; m. Carolyn Lynch, July 3, 1971. BA, Randolph-Macon Coll., 1968; AM, U. Mich., 1969, PhD, 1984. Tchg. fellow, lectr. U. Mich., Ann Arbor, 1968-73, 74-75, 1978-79; lectr. Johannes Gutenberg U., Mainz, Germany, 1973-74; adj. instr. Rappahannock Coll., Warsaw, 1976-77; tech. writing cons. Naval Surface Weapons Ctr., Dahlgren, 1977; tech. writer UNISYS, 1984-86; tchr. Latin and German King George (Va.) H.S., 1987; asst. prof. Chgo. State U., 1987-92; assoc. prof., 1992-97; prof., 1997—; dept. asst. chair, 1994-96. Vis. lectr. in theater Mary Washington Coll. U. Va., Fredericksburg, Va., summer 1970, 71. Contbr. articles and reviews to profl. jours. Seminar fellow NEH, Emory U., 1993. Mem. MLA, Am. Soc. for Eighteenth-Century Studies, Midwestern Am. Soc. for Eighteenth-Century Studies, Eighteenth-Century Scottish Studies Soc., Sigma Upsilon, Eta Sigma Phi, Pi Delta Epsilon, Omicron Delta Kappa. Home: 1524 Carson Dr Homewood IL 60430 Office: Chgo State Univ 9501 S King Dr Chicago IL 60628-1501

LIEBENSON, GLORIA KRASNOW, interior design executive, freelance writer; b. Chgo., Apr. 6, 1922; d. Henry Randolph and Margaret (Rivkin) Krasnow; m. Herbert Liebenson, Mar. 11, 1944; children: Lauren Ward, Lynn Liebenson Green. Student, Internat. Inst. Interior Design, Washington, 1961; B Am. Studies, Dunbarton Coll., Washington, 1974. Numerous positions Journalism, Advt., editing, 1942-62; interior design exec. Creative Interiors, 1962—. Tchr. interior design YMCA, Washington, 1980-82. Mem. editorial staff Champlin Encyclopedia, 1945-47; journalist Shreveport Jour., 1944. Bd. dirs. Jewish Social Svc. Agy., Washington, 1983-85, Nat. Coun. Jewish Women. 1982-84; pres. Friends Nat. Museum African Art, 1983-85, D.C. Mental Health Assn., 1986-88. Democrat. Jewish. Avocations: theater, concerts, scrabble, reading, travel. Home: Ste 615 4200 Massachusetts Ave NW Washington DC 20016-4734 E-mail: glor15@juno.com.

LIEBENSON, HERBERT, economist, trade association executive; b. Chgo., July 26, 1920; s. Michael and Evelyn (Zimmerman) L.; m. Gloria Rachel Krasnow, Mar. 11, 1944; children: Lauren Ward, Lynn Green. BA, Roosevelt U., 1948; postgrad., U. Chgo., 1948, Am. U., 1949-52. Research assoc. United Mineworkers Pension and Welfare Fund, Washington, 1948-52; employee benefit/labor relations analyst C. of C. U.S., 1952-58; with Nat. Small Bus. Assn., 1958—, v.p., 1958-80, pres., 1980-86, sr. cons., 1986—; exec. dir. Small Bus. Legis. Council, 1980-86, chmn. tech. for new products and jobs, 1986—; mem. exec. com., chmn. com. on taxation SBA Nat. Adv. Council, 1982-86. Pres. del. White House Conf. on Small Bus., 1986; mem. Sec. Labor's mgmt. adv. com. on Landrum-Griffin Act, U.S. Employment Service Adv. Com.; mem. adv. com. on jobs Dept. Commerce Com. on Product Standards; alt. mem. Presdl. Pay Bd., 1973-74; mem. steering com. Nat. Com. to Preserve Family Bus., 1981; mem. nat. com. Am. Energy Week, 1981 Served with USAAF, 1942-46. Mem. Indsl. Relations Research Assn. (pres. chpt. 1961-62), Bus. Adv. Council Fed. Reports (bd. govs. 1970-85), Am. Soc. Assn. Execs. Clubs: Internat. Jewish. Home: Washington, DC. Died 2002.

LIEBER, ANNA, graphic designer; b. Germany, Aug. 13, 1947; came to U.S., 1949; d. Sol and Miriam (Scher) L. BA, Hunter Coll., 1969; postgrad., NYU, 1972-73; postgrad. in design, Sch. Visual Arts, 1981-83. Lic. tchr., N.Y. Asst. art dir. Archie Comics, N.Y.C., 1969-70; asst. prodn. mgr. Appleton-Century-Crofts Pub., 1970-71; tchr. art and English Beha Jr. High Sch., 1971-76; coord. After-Sch. Workshops Bd. Edn, 1971-76; prodn. dir. Nat. Rev. mag., 1976-86, art dir., 1986-87, prin. Lieber Design, 1983-89; ptnr. Lieber Brewster Design, Inc., 1989—. Designer Egglectric Light, 1983. Mem. Am. Inst. Graphic Arts, PRSA, NAWBO (bd. dirs.), Ad Club of N.Y. Avocations: skiing, horseback riding, painting.

LIEBER, CHARLES DONALD, publisher; b. Scheveningen, The Netherlands, Jan. 30, 1921; came to U.S., 1941, naturalized, 1944; s. Edmund Z. and Gabrielle (Lifczis) L.; m. Miriam Levin, July 17, 1960; children: John Nathan, James Edmund, George Theodore, Anne Gabrielle. Student, U. Brussels, 1938-40; BA, New Sch. for Social Research, 1948. With H. Bittner & Co. (Pubs.), N.Y.C., 1947-49; with Alfred A. Knopf, Inc., 1949-52, dir. coll. dept., 1960-64, Random House, N.Y.C., 1952-64; pub. Atherton Press, 1964-67; pres. Atherton Press, Inc., 1967-70; v.p. Aldine-Atherton, Inc., Chgo., 1971-72; pres. Lieber-Atherton, Inc., 1972—; gen. mgr. Hebrew Pub. Co., 1980-85, pres., 1985—, Lieber Publs., Inc., N.Y.C., 1981—. Author: (with A.D. Murphy) Great Events of World History, 1964; chmn. publ. com., mem. editl. bd. Reconstructionist mag., 1983-93. Chmn. West Side Jewish Cmty. Coun., Manhattan, 1978-82, mem.-at-large, 1974—; exec. bd. Jewish Reconstrn. Found., 1978-83, vice chmn., 1979-80, chmn., 1980-83, nat. bd. dirs., 1983-92; trustee St. Ann's Sch., 1983-89, Soc. for Advancement Judaism, 1974-90, treas., 1976-79, co-chmn., 1979-81; bd. dirs. Hebrew Arts Sch., 1974-82, Fedn. Reconstructionist Congregations, 1983-91; bd. dirs., treas. Close Encounters with Music, Inc., 1996—; founding mem. Lenox Hill Club, 1957; bd. dir. Millay Colony For the Arts, 2002-. Lt. AUS, 1942-46, CBI; v.p. bd. trustees Synagogue at Malden Bridge, 1999—. Recipient Mordecai M. Kaplan award Jewish Reconstructionist Found., 1988. Mem. Coll. Pubs. Group (chmn. 1965-66), Assn. Jewish Book Pubs. (pres. 1988-90). Office: Hebrew Publishing Co PO Box 222 Spencertown NY 12165-0222 E-mail: liebercd@aol.com.

LIEBER, CHARLES SAUL, physician, educator; b. Antwerp, Belgium, Feb. 13, 1931; came to U.S., 1958, naturalized, 1966; s. Isaac and Lea (Maj) L.; m. M. A. Leo; children: Colette, Daniel, Leah, Samuel, Sarah. Candidate in natural and med. sci., U. Brussels, 1951; MD, 1955. Intern, resident U. Hosp., Brugmann, Brussels, Belgium, 1954-56; research fellow med. found. Queen Elizabeth, 1956-58; research fellow Thorndike Meml. Lab., Harvard Med. Sch., 1958-60, instr., 1961; assoc. Harvard U., 1962; assoc. prof. medicine Cornell U., 1963-68; dir. liver disease and nutrition unit Bellevue Hosp., N.Y.C., 1963-68; chief sect. liver disease, nutrition and alcohol Tng. Program VA Hosp., Bronx, N.Y., 1968—; prof. medicine Mt. Sinai Sch. Medicine, 1969—, prof. pathology, 1976—, dir. Alcohol Research and Treatment Ctr., 1977—. Assoc. vis. physician Cornell Med. div. Bellevue, Meml., James Ewing hosps., 1964-69; Am. Coll. Gastroenterology disting. lectr., 1978, Henry Baker lectr., 1979 Recipient award of Belgian Govt. for rsch. on gastric secretion, 1956, Rsch. Career Devel. award NIH, USPHS, 1964-68, E.M. Jellinek Meml. award, 1976, A. Boudreau award Laval U., 1977, W.S. Middleton award highest honor for med. rsch. Dept. Vets. Affairs, 1977, Leahy Rsch. award highest honor for outstanding investigator, 1994, first Mark Keller award, NIAAA-NIH, 1996, AMA Scientific Achievement award, 1998. Fellow AAAS, Am. Soc. Nutritional Sci.; mem. ACP/Master, Assn. Am. Physicians, N.Y. Gastroent. Assn. (pres. 1974-75), Am. Soc. Biochemistry and Molecular Biology, Am. Soc. Addictive Medicine (pres. 1974-77, Sci. Achievement award 1989, Disting. Scientist award 1996), Assn. Clin. Biochemists (Kone award 1994), Am. Soc. Clin. Nutrition (McCollum award 1973, pres. 1975-76, Robert H. Herman Meml. award 1993), Am. Soc. Clin. Investigation, Am. Soc. Pharmacol. Exptl. Therapy, Am. Gastroent. Assn. (Disting. Achievement award 1973, Hugh R. Butt award for liver/nutrition 1992), Rsch. Soc. on Alcoholism (pres. 1977-79, Sci. Excellence award 1980, Disting. Svc. award 1992), Am. Coll. Nutrition (Outstanding Achievement award 1990), Am. Assn. Study Liver Diseases. Home: 6 Johnson Ave Englewood Cliffs NJ 07632-2107 Office: VA Med Ctr 130 W Kingsbridge Rd Bronx NY 10468-3904 E-mail: liebercs@aol.com.

LIEBER, DANIEL JOEL, oncologist; b. Amarillo, Tex., Oct. 27, 1952; BA, UCLA, 1972, MD, 1976. Intern and resident in medicine Harbor-UCLA Med. Ctr., 1976-79; pvt. practice Santa Monica, Calif., 1991—. Adj. asst. clin. prof. medicine UCLA. Mem.: ACP, Am. Soc. Clin. Oncology. Office: 2001 Santa Monica # 560W Santa Monica CA 90404

LIEBER, DAVID LEO, university president; b. Stryj, Poland, Feb. 20, 1925; came to U.S., 1927, naturalized, 1936; s. Max and Gussie (Jarmush) L.; m. Esther Kobre, June 10, 1945; children— Michael, Daniel, Deborah, Susan. BA, CCNY, 1944; B.Hebrew Lit., Jewish Theol. Sem. Am., 1944, M.Hebrew Lit., 1948, D.Hebrew Lit., 1951; MA, Columbia, 1947; postgrad., U. Wash., 1954-55, UCLA, 1961-63; LDH (hon.), Hebrew Union Coll., 1982—. Ordained rabbi, 1948. Rabbi, 1948, Sinai Temple, Los Angeles, 1950-54; dir. (B'nai B'rith Hillel), Seattle, Cambridge, 1954-56; dean students U. Judaism, Los Angeles, 1956-63, Samuel A. Fryer prof. Bible, pres., 1963-92, Skovron Disting. Svc. prof. Bibl. lit., 1990—, pres. emeritus, 1992—, L.A., 1992—; lectr. Hebrew UCLA, 1957-90; vice chancellor Jewish Theol. Sem., 1972-92. Mem. exec. coun. Rabbinical Assembly, 1966-69, v.p., 1994-96, pres., 1996-98; vice chmn. Am. Jewish Com., L.A., 1972-75; bd. dirs. Jewish Fedn. Coun., L.A., 1980-86, bd. govs., 1986—. Mem. editorial bd.: Conservative Judaism, 1968-70. Served as chaplain USAF, 1951-53. Recipient Torch of Learning award, Hebrew U., 1984, Simon Greenberg award, U. Judaism, 2002. Mem. Assn. Profs. Jewish Studies (dir. 1970-71), Phi Beta Kappa. Office: U Judaism 15600 Mulholland Dr Los Angeles CA 90077-1519 E-mail: dllieber@aol.com.

LIEBER, ROBERT JAMES, political science educator, writer; b. Chgo. m. Nancy Lieber; 2 children. BA in Polit. Sci. with high honors, U. Wis., 1963; postgrad. in Polit. Sci., U. Chgo., 1963-64; PhD in Govt., Harvard U., 1968. Asst. prof. Polit. Sci. U. Calif., Davis, 1968-72, assoc. prof., 1972-77, chmn. dept. Polit. Sci., 1975-76, 77-80, prof., 1977-81; postdoctoral rschr. St. Antony's Coll. Oxford (Eng.) U., 1969-70; prof. Georgetown U., Washington, 1982—, chmn. dept. govt., 1990-96, acting chmn. dept. psychology, 1997-99. Vis. prof. Oxford U., 1969, Fudan U., Shanghai, 1988; rsch. assoc. Ctr. Internat. Affairs, Harvard U., 1974-75; cons. U.S. Dept. State and Dept. Def., 1975—. Author: British Politics and European Unity, 1970, Theory and World Politics, 1972, Oil and the Middle East War: Europe in the Energy Crisis, 1976, The Oil Decade: Conflict and Cooperation in the West, 1983, No Common Power: Understanding International Relations, 1988, 4th edit., 2001; co-author: Contemporary Politics: Europe, 1976; editor, contbg. author: Eagle Adrift: American Foreign Policy at the End of the Century, 1997, Eagle Rules? Foreign Policy and American Privacy in the 21st Century, 2002; co-editor, contbg. author: Eagle Entangled: U.S. Foreign Policy in a Complex World, 1979, Eagle Defiant: U.S. Foreign Policy in the 1980s, 1983, Eagle Resurgent? The Reagan Era in American Foreign Policy, 1987, Eagle in a New World: American Grand Strategy in the Post-Cold War Era, 1992; editor: Will Europe Fight for Oil?, 1983; contbr. articles to Harper's, Politique étrangère, N.Y. Times, Washington Post, Christian Sci. Monitor, others, and profl. jours. Advanceman nat. campaign staff McCarthy for Pres., 1968; fgn. policy advising presdl. campaigns of Sen. Edward Kennedy, 1979-80, Walter Mondale. 1984, Bill Clinton, 1991-92; coord. Mid. East Issues presdl. campaign Michael Dukakis, 1988. Woodrow Wilson fellow, 1963, fellow NDEA, 1963-64, Harvard U., 1964-68, Social Sci. Rsch. Coun., 1969-70, Coun. Fgn. Rels., 1972-73, Guggenheim fellow, 1973-74, Rockefeller Found., 1978-79, Wilson Ctr. Smithsonian Inst., 1980-81, 99-00, Ford Found., 1981; vis. fellow Atlantic Inst. Internat. Affairs, Paris, 1978-79; guest scholar Brookings Inst., 1981. Mem. Coun. on Fgn. Rels., Internat. Inst. for Strategic Studies, Phi Beta Kappa. Office: Georgetown U Dept Of Government Washington DC 20057-1034 E-mail: lieberr@georgetown.edu.

LIEBERMAN, ANNE MARIE, retired financial executive; b. Jersey City, Aug. 28, 1946; d. Ralph Norman and Kathleen Celestine (Dooris) L.; m. Stephen Bruce Oshry, Sept. 21, 1986. BA, Sonoma State U., 1968; MLS, U. Calif., 1970, MBA, 1977. Cert. fin. planner; cert. fund specialist. V.p. Bank of Am., San Francisco, 1977-81, Lawrence A. Krause & Assocs., San Francisco, 1982-86; pres. Lieberman Assocs., San Rafael, Calif., 1986-98, ret., 1998. Author: Marketing Your Financial Planning Practice, 1986, Mastering Money, 1987; contbg. author: Financial Planning Can Make You Rich, 1987, The Expert's Guide to Managing a Successful Financial Planning Practice, 1988, About Your Future, 1988; columnist The Bus. Jour. Bd. dirs. Marin Gen. Found. Hosp., 1995; mem. pres.'s adv. bd. Sonoma State U., 2000. Selected by Worth mag. as one of 250 best fin. advisors in U.S., 1997, 98. Mem. Inst. Cert. Fin. Planners (Fin. Writer's award 1986), Nat. Endowment for Fin. Edn. (bd. dirs. 1996). Avocations: singing, ballroom dancing.

LIEBERMAN, ARCHIE, photographer, writer; b. Chgo., July 17, 1926; s. Sol and Rose (Schiff) L.; m. Esther Kraus, Jan. 11, 1948; children: Eric Joseph, Robert Charles Vories, Kurt Murrow Student, Inst. Design, Chgo., 1946-48; HHD (hon.), U. Dubuque, 1996. Contract photographer Time Mag., Chgo., 1950-51; staff photographer Black Star Pub. Co., N.Y.C., 1951-61. Adj. prof. Chgo. Theol. Sem., 1976-74; instr. Columbia Coll., Chgo., 1968-74; prof. art Knox Coll., Galesburg, Ill., U. Dubuque, Iowa. One man shows include Presbyn.-St. Luke's Hosp., Chgo., Chapel Hill Shopping Ctr., Akron, Ohio

Mchts. Assn., Flint, Mich., Arie Crown Theater, Chgo., Carson Pirie Scott & Co., Chgo., Prudential Bldg., Chgo., Agr. U.S.A., Soviet Union, U. Ill., Lake Forest Coll., Kodak Gallery, Grand Central Sta., N.Y.C., Rizzoli Gallery, Chgo., U. Dubuque (retrospective), 1987, Dubuque Mus. Art, Lands End Gallery, Dodgeville, Wis., 1991, Ford Ctr. Fine Art-Knox Coll., 1993, Elveahjem Mus., Madison, Wis., 1994, Freeport Art Mus., 1994, Lake Forest Coll., 1995; group shows include Jewish Mus., N.Y.C., Tower Gallery, Chgo., Garrett Bible Inst., Evanston, Met. Mus. Art, N.Y.C., Expo '67, Montreal, Art Inst. Chgo., 1986, Photography in Fine Arts, N.Y.C., San Diego Mus. Photographic Arts, 1986, Mitchell Mus., Mt. Vernon, Ill., 1987, 88, The Art Inst. of Chgo., 1986, 92, numerous others; author, photographer: The Israelis, 1965 (One of Best 50 Books award), Farm Boy (Friends of Lit. award), Neighbors, 1993; photographer books: Shalom, A Solitary Life, The Future of Religions, The Eternal Life, Holy Holy Land, The Story of Israel, Chicago In Color, Chicago, God Make Me Brave For Life, (with Ray Bradbury) The Mummies of Guanajuato, Chicago: A Celebration, 1990; photojournalist for mags. including: Look, Life, Saturday Evening Post, Collier's, Ladies Home Jour., Fortune, London Illustrated, Redbook, Farm Jour., Pageant, Parade, Bus. Week, Am. Weekly, Venture, U.S. News & World Report, Newsweek, Paris Match, Chgo. Mag.; indsl. photographer for corps. including Inland Steel, Acme Steel, Lands' End, Harvester, Gould Inc., McDonald's, Motorola, Grumman Corp., Internat. Minerals & Chem. Corp.; advt. photographs for: Allstate Ins., Phillip Morris, Schlitz, United Airlines, Jack Daniel, others Trustee Dubuque Mus. Art. Recipient Peter Lisagor award Headline Club of Sigma Delta Chi, 1980; Sinai Health Service award Mt. Sinai Hosp. Med. ctr., Chgo., 1985; various award U. Mo. Sch. Journalism Mem.: Galena Artists Guild, Dubuque Shooting Soc., Tavern Club, Chgo. Press Club, Arts Club of Chgo. Office: PO Box 61 Scales Mound IL 61075-0061 *People are not creative. There was only one creative act-The making of something out of a void-The creation itself. What people do is to discover that which has always been and position it in a new way. Therefore we must be discoverers to invent new things.*

LIEBERMAN, CAROL, healthcare marketing communications consultant; b. St. Louis, June 14, 1938; d. Norman Leonard and Ethel (Silver) Mistachkin; m. Malcolm P. Cooper, Aug. 25, 1962 (div. June 1977); children: Lawrence, Edward, Marcus; m. Edward Lieberman, Apr. 1992. BS, U. Wis., 1959; MA, N.Y. Inst. Tech., 1992; CTEFL, CTBE, Worldwide Tchr.'s Inst., 2000. Cert. tchr. english as foreign lang., tchr. of bus. english. Media buyer Lennen and Newell, Los Angeles, 1959-61; advt. mgr. Hartfield-Zodys, 1961-62, Haggarty's, L.A., 1962-63; sales rep. Abbott Labs., Bklyn., 1974-75; edn. dir. N.Y. and N.J. Regional Transp. Program, N.Y.C., 1975-78; account exec. Med. Edn. Dynamics, Woodbridge, N.J., 1978-79; dir. program devel. Kallir, Phillips & Ross Info. Media, N.Y.C., 1979-81; exec. v.p. sales and mktg. Audio Visual Med. Mktg., 1981-85; exec. v.p. Park Row Pubs./John Wiley & Sons Med. Div., 1985-88; pres., prin. Park Row Pubs., 1988-91; healthcare mktg. communications cons., Southampton, N.Y., 1991—; cons., prof. comms. and speech N.Y. Inst. Tech., 1991-95; exec. sec. Cardiopulmonary Bypass Consensus Panel, 1993—; asst. prof. profl. studies Southampton Coll., LI Univ., 2000—; asst. prof. U. Phoenix Online, 2001—. Cons. Am. Acad. Physician Assts., Washington, 1986-87, Am. Soc. Anesthesiologists, Chgo., 1986-88, Am. Acad. Family Physicians, 1987-91, Am. Psychiat. Assn., 1988, Am. Coll. Gen. Practitioners, 1988, N.Am. Soc. pacing and Electrophysiology, 1988-91, Internat. Immunocompromised Host Soc., 1996—; internet pub. Am. Assn. Thoracic Surgery, 1999—. Pub. CME Press. Mem. TESOL, IATEFL, Am. Women in Radio and TV, Soc. Tchrs. Family Medicine (cons.), Pharm. Advt. Council, Nat. Council Jewish Women, Hadassah. Avocations: tennis, writing fiction, classical piano. Home and Office: 41 Barkers Island Rd Southampton NY 11968-2702 E-mail: cmenetwork@mindspring.com.

LIEBERMAN, CHARLES, economist; b. Landsburg, Bavaria, Germany, July 25, 1948; s. Leo and Tola (Melcer) L.; m. Anne Rosenberg, Aug. 26, 1972; children: David, Michael, Jeremy. BS, MIT, 1970; AM in Econs., U. Pa., 1972, PhD in Econs., 1974. Asst. prof. U. Md., College Park, 1974-79; vis. assoc. prof. Northwestern U., Evanston, Ill., 1978-79; economist Fed. Res. Bank N.Y., N.Y.C., 1979-81; sr. economist Morgan Stanley, 1981-83; v.p., sr. economist Shearson Lehman Bros., 1983-86; mng. dir., dir. fin. market rsch. Chem. Securities Inc./Mfrs. Hanover Securities Corp., 1986-96; chief economist The Global Bank, Chase Manhattan Bank, 1996-97; mng. ptnr. Strategic Investors, N.Y.C., 1997—99; mng. mem. Lieberman Asset Mgmt. LLC, 1999—; CIO, chief economist Advisors Fin. Ctr., 2001—. Econs. commentator CNBC. Author: (newsletter) Market Commentary; contbr. articles to profl. jours. Sgt. U.S. Army Res., 1970-76. Stonier fellow, 1973, Fellow NSF, 1971. Mem. Forecasters Club N.Y. (treas. 1987-89, v.p. 1990-91, pres. 1991-92), Money Marketeers NYU (bd. govs., v.p., pres. 1992-93). Jewish. Avocations: tennis, skiing, classical music. Office: Advisors Fin Ctr 75 Montebello Rd Suffern NY 10901 *Work hard, play hard, and enjoy life.*

LIEBERMAN, DANIEL Z. psychiatrist; b. Buffalo, Feb. 20, 1964; BA, St John's Coll., Annapolis, Md., 1985; MD, NYU, 1996. Diplomate Am. Bd. Psychiatry and Neurology, 1997, diplomate addiction psychiatry Am. Bd. Psychiatry and Neurology, 1998. Clin. instr., chief resident NYU Sch. Med., 1995—96; dir. substance abuse treatment, asst. prof. George Washington U. Dept. Psychiatry, Washington, 1996—98, dir. outpatient psychiatry, asst. prof., 1998—. Contbr. articles. Mem.: Psychiatric Soc. Informatics, Am. Acad. Addiction Psychiatry, Group for the Advancement of Psychiatry, Am. Psychiatric Assn. Office: George Washington U 2150 Pennsylvania Ave NW 8 Fl Washington DC 20855

LIEBERMAN, EDWARD JAY, lawyer; b. Evansville, Ind., Apr. 8, 1946; s. Heiman George and Anna Sharp (Blacker) L.; m. Ellen Ackerman Wequsen, June 1, 1969; 1 child: Laura Amy. BSBA, Washington U., St. Louis, 1968, JD, 1971. Bar: Mo. 1971. Jr. ptnr. Bryan Cave, St. Louis, 1972-76; assoc. counsel 1st Nat. Bank in St. Louis, 1976-80; ptnr. Lowenhaupt, Chasnoff, Armstrong & Mellitz, St. Louis, 1980-84, Husch & Eppenberger, LLC, St. Louis, 1984—. Mem. ABA, Mo. Bar, Bar Assn. Met. St. Louis, Am. Coll. Mortgage Attys., Nat. Health Care Lawyers Assn. Office: Husch & Eppenberger, LLC 190 Carondelet Plz Ste 600 Saint Louis MO 63105 E-mail: ed.lieberman@husch.com.

LIEBERMAN, ELLIOTT, urologist; b. Paterson, N.J., May 14, 1951; s. Benjamin and Henrietta (Reback) L.; m. Lisa Lieberman; children: Brian Howard, Dana Elyse. BA in Biochemistry cum laude with distinction, Cornell U., 1972; MD, SUNY, Bklyn., 1976. Diplomate Am. Bd. Urology. Intern, resident in gen. surgery Mt. Sinai Hosp., N.Y.C., 1976-78; resident in urology SUNY-Downstate Med. Ctr., Bklyn., 1978-81; active attending staff North Shore U. Hosp., various cities, N.Y., co-chief divsn. urology Plainview, 1992—, chmn. med. bd., 2000—, assoc. chief dept. surgery, 2001—. Mem. adv. bd. Vis. Nurse Svc. N.Y.; mem. quality assurance com. White Oaks Nursing Home, Woodbury, N.Y. Mem. AMA, AUA, Med. Soc. State N.Y., Nassau County Med. Soc., N.Y. State Urol. Soc., Alpha Omega Alpha. Avocations: jogging, wine, music. Office: 875 Old Country Rd Ste 301 Plainview NY 11803-4934

LIEBERMAN, EUGENE, lawyer; b. Chgo., May 17, 1918; s. Harry and Eva (Goldman) L.; m. Pearl Naomi Feldman, Aug. 3, 1947; children: Mark, Robert, Steven. LLB, DePaul U., 1940, JD, 1941. Bar: Ill. 1941, U.S. Supreme Ct. 1963. Mem. firm Jacobs and Lieberman, 1954-60; sr. ptnr. Jacobs, Lieberman and Aling, 1960-74; spl. hearing officer U.S. Dept. Justice, 1967-78; hearing officer Ill. Pollution Control Bd., 1973—; pvt. practice Chgo. Contbr. articles to profl. jours. With U.S. Army, 1942-45. Recipient 1st in State award Moot Ct. Championship, 1940, gold award Philatelic Exhbn., Taipei, 1981, gold award World Philatelic Exhbn., Melbourne, 1984, Meritorious Svc. medal, bronze arrowhead award, others. Mem. Ill. State Bar Assn. (sr. counselor 1991), Chgo. Bar Assn., Appellate Lawyers Assn., Chgo. Philatelic Soc. (pres. 1964-68), Ill. Athletic Club. Home: 801 Leclaire Ave Wilmette IL 60091-2065

LIEBERMAN, FLORENCE, clinical social worker, educator; b. N.Y.C., Apr. 16, 1918; d. Simon and Fredericka (Joseph) Rosenblum; m. Lawrence Lieberman, Sept. 1, 1940; children: Joan, Paul. BA, Hunter Coll., 1938; MSS, Smith Coll., 1956; DSW, Columbia U., 1968. Diplomate Am. Bd. Examiners in Clin. Social Work. Social investigator Dept. Social Svcs., N.Y.C., 1939-46; researcher, cons. for various city govt offices, 1946-56; sr. social worker, student supr., group therapist Madleine Borg Child Guidance Clinic Jewish Family Svcs., 1956-66; prof. Hunter Coll. Sch. Social Work, 1966-86; vis. John Milner prof. U. So. Calif., 1988; psychotherapist Scarsdale, N.Y., 1968—. Author: Before Addiction, Clinical Social Work with Children; editor: Clinical Social Workers As Psychotherapists, Child & Adolescent Social Work Jour.; adv. editor Clin. Social Work Jour.; co-editor Aging in Good Health : A Quality Life Style for the Later Years, 1993; contbr. numerous articles to profl. jours. Recipient Van Ophuijsen Meml. award, Jewish Bd. of Guardians, 1964, Day-Garret award Smith Coll. Sch. of Social Work, 1986; named Disting. Practitioner in Social Work, 1983; elected Hall of Fame Hunter Coll. CUNY, 1994. Fellow Internat. Conf. for Advancement Pvt. Practice, Am. Orthopsychiat. Assn.(life); mem. Internat. Conf. for Advancement Pvt. Practice Clin. Social Work (pres. 2000—), NASW (charter), Am. Group Psychotherapy Assn., N.Y. State Soc. Clin. Social Work Psychotherapy (diplomate). Avocations: golf, gardening, theater. Office: 315 Wyndcliffe Rd Scarsdale NY 10583-4832 E-mail: Flieberman@msn.com.

LIEBERMAN, GAIL FORMAN, investment company executive; b. Phila., May 26, 1943; d. Joseph and Rita (Groder) Forman. BA in Physics and Math., Temple U., 1964, MBA in Fin., 1977. Dir. internat. fin. Standard Brands Inc., N.Y.C., 1977-79; staff v.p. fin. and capital planning RCA Corp., 1979-82; CFO, exec. v.p. Scali McCabe Sloves, Inc., 1982-93; v.p. fin., CFO, mng. dir. Moody's Investors Svc., N.Y.C., 1994-96; CFO TFPPG Thomson Corp., Boston, 1996-99; CEO Liquid Alternatives Inc., 2000; mng. ptnr. Rudder Capital LLC, 2001—. Bd. dirs. Allied Devices, Inc. Mem. Fin. Execs. Inst.

LIEBERMAN, GARY MITCHELL, mathematics educator; b. Chgo., May 30, 1952; s. Alvin and Tillie Bess (Lavin) L. BA, MS, Northwestern U., 1974; PhD, Stanford U., 1979. Instr. Iowa State U., Ames, 1979-80, asst. prof., 1980-84, assoc. prof., 1984-88, prof., 1988—. Contbr. articles to profl. jours. Bd. dirs. Octagon Orch., Ames, 1987. NSF rsch. grantee, 1984. Mem. Am. Math. Soc., Math. Assn. Am., Nat. Flute Assn. Office: Iowa State U Math Dept 400 Carver Hall Ames IA 50010

LIEBERMAN, HERBERT HENRY, writer; b. New Rochelle, N.Y., Sept. 22, 1933; s. Abraham Charles Lieberman and Sylvia Kissel; m. Judith Betsy Barksy, June 9, 1963; 1 child Zoe. BA, CCNY, 1955; MA, Columbia U., 1957. Editor MacMillan Pubs., N.Y.C., NY, 1960—65; mng. editor Reader's Digest, Chappaqua, 1967—96. Author: (plays) Matty & the Moron & Madonna, 1964, (novels) Crawlspace, 1971, City of the Dead, 1976. With U.S. Army, 1957—60. Recipient 1st prize, U. Chgo., 1962, Grand prix de Litérature, Policifar, 1978; fellow Guggenheim, 1964. Office: 136 E 57th St New York NY 10022

LIEBERMAN, JAMES S. physiatrist, neurologist; b. Mpls., Apr. 24, 1938; BS, U. Calif., 1960, MD, 1963. Instr., asst. prof. neurology SUNY, 1967-71; asst. prof. neurology Columbia U., 1971—72; from asst. prof. to prof. phys. medicine and rehab. and neurology U. Calif., Davis, 1972-91, chmn. rehab. medicine, 1982—91; prof., chmn. rehab. medicine Columbia U., N.Y.C., 1991—, sr. assoc. dean clin. svcs., asst. v.p. health sci., 1996—; prof. divsn. head rehab. medicine Cornell U., 2000—; physiatrist-in-chief N.Y. Presbyn. Hosp., 2000—. Mem. NAS Inst. Medicine, Am. Acad. Clin. Neurophysiology, Am. Acad. Neurology, Am. Acad. Phys. Medicine & Rehab. Office: Columbia U 630 W 168th St Unit 38 New York NY 10032-3795 E-mail: jsl12@columbia.edu.

LIEBERMAN, JOSEFA NINA, psychologist, educator, writer; b. Jaroslaw, Poland, May 16, 1921; came to U.S., 1946; d. David Samuel and Rosa Zerline (Leinwand) Margules; m. Meyer Frank Lieberman, Feb. 12, 1956. BS, Columbia U., 1957, MA, 1959, PhD in Ednl. Psychology, 1964. Lic. psychologist, N.Y. Lectr. Bklyn. Coll., 1964-65, asst. prof., 1965-71, assoc. prof., 1972-79, prof., 1979-83, prof. emerita, 1983—. Spkr. in field. Author: Playfulness: Its Relationship to Imagination and Creativity, 1977, Japanese translation, 1981, He Came to Cambridge, 1982, (chpt.) I Came Alone, 1990; contbr. articles to profl. jours. Mem., chair Hillel Found., Bklyn., 1964—83; founding mem. Solomon Schechter H.S.I, 1971; mem. Sr. Recreation, Woodstock, 1984—. Recipient fellowships and rsch. grants NIMH, 1958-78. Mem. APA, Phi Beta Kappa, Sigma Xi. Democrat. Avocations: languages, music, swimming, chess. Home: 648 Zena Rd Woodstock NY 12498 E-mail: Jnina@aol.com.

LIEBERMAN, JOSEPH ALOYSIUS, III, physician, educator; b. Oct. 15, 1938; s. Joseph Aloysius and Marie Catherine (McDermott) Lieberman; m. Judith Ann Dees, July 23, 1966; children: Lila, Lucy, Joseph Lieberman IV, Karl. BS, Georgetown U., 1960; MD, Jefferson Med. Coll., Phila., 1964; MA in Pub. Health, Rutgers U., 1989. Diplomate Am. Bd. Family Practice. Family physician Sr/Jr Partnership, Allentown, 1967—68; pvt. practice, 1968—71; sr. ptnr. West End Med. Group, 1971—77; faculty mem. Robert Wood Johnson Med. Sch., Piscataway, NJ, 1977—91; prof. family medicine Jefferson Med. Coll. Thomas Jefferson U., 1991—. Prof., chmn. dept. family medicine Robert Wood Johnson Med. Sch., Piscataway, 1982—91; chmn. dept. family and cmty. medicine Christiana Care Health Sys., 1991—2001. Contbr. Capt. USAF, 1965—67. Recipient Exceptional Merit award, U. Medicine and Dentistry of N.J., 1979—82; fellow Health Policy fellow, Inst. Medicine NAS, 1988—89. Republican. Roman Catholic. Office: Med Soc Delaware Ste 405 131 Continental Dr Newark DE 19713-1668 E-mail: jlieberman@jalmd.com.

LIEBERMAN, JOSEPH I. senator; b. Stamford, Conn., Feb. 24, 1942; s. Henry and Marcia (Manger) L.; m. Hadassah Freilich, Mar. 20, 1983; children: Matthew, Rebecca, Ethan, Hana. BA, Yale U., 1964, JD, 1967. Bar: Conn. 1967. Mem. Conn. Senate, 1971-81, senate majority leader, 1975-81; ptnr. Lieberman, Segaloff & Wolfson, New Haven, 1972-83; atty. gen. State of Conn., Hartford, 1983-89; U.S. senator from Conn., 1989—; chmn. govtl. affairs com. Mem. armed svcs. com., environment and pub. works com., small bus. com.; chmn. Dem. Leadership Coun., 1995-2000. Author: The Power Broker, 1966, The Scorpion and the Tarantula, 1970, The Legacy, 1981, Child Support in America, 1986, In Praise of Public Life, 2000. Candidate for v.p. U.S., 2000 Democrat. Jewish. Office: 706 Hart Senate Office Bldg Washington DC 20510-0001

LIEBERMAN, LAURENCE, poet, educator; b. Detroit, Feb. 16, 1935; s. Nathan and Anita (Cohen) L.; m. Bernice Clair Braun, June 17, 1956; children— Carla, Deborah, Isaac. BA, U. Mich., 1956, MA in English, 1958; postgrad., U. Calif.-Berkeley. Prof. English Coll. V.I., 1964-68; prof. English and creative writing U. Ill., Urbana, 1968—. U. Ill. Ctr. for Advanced Study Creative Writing fellow, Japan, 1971-72 Author: The Unblinding, 1968, The Achievement of James Dickey, 1969, The Osprey Suicides, 1973, Unassigned Frequencies: American Poetry in Review (1964-77), 1977, God's Measurements, 1980, Eros At the World Kite Pageant, 1983, The Mural of Wakeful Sleep, 1985, (poems) The Creole Mephistopheles, 1989, The Best American Poetry, 1991 (award), New and Selected Poems (1962-92), 1993, The St. Kitts. Monkey Feuds, 1995, Beyond the Muse of Memory: Essays on Contemporary Poets, 1995, Dark Songs: Slave House and Synagogue, 1996, Compass of the Dying, 1998, The Regatta in the Skies: Selected Long Poems, 1999, Flight From the Mother Stone, 2000; poetry editor poetry books program U. Ill. Press, 1970—; contbr. poetry to lit. jours., popular mags. Recipient award for Best Poems of 1968, Nat. Endowment for Arts, 1969, Jerome P. Shestack award Am. Poetry Rev., 1986; creative writing fellow U. Ill. Ctr. for Advanced Study, 2000—, Nat. Endowment Arts, 1986-87. Office: U Ill English Dept 608 S Wright St Urbana IL 61801-3630

LIEBERMAN, LESTER ZANE, engineering company executive; b. Newark, July 4, 1930; s. Herman P. and Cecile A. (Ashenfeld) L.; m. Judith Mazor, Aug. 11, 1957; children: Susan, Jane BS in Mech. Engring., Newark Coll. Engring., 1951, postgrad., 1953-58; DHL (hon.), Clarkson U., 1991. Registered profl. engr., N.J., Pa. Pres. Crest Engring. Inc., Newark, 1955-60; chmn., pres. Atmos Engring. Co. Inc., Kenilworth, N.J., 1960-78; pres., CEO, Clarkson Industries, Inc., N.Y.C., 1978-90; real estate investment and development Dowel Assoc., 1990—; partner, cons. Construction HUAC, 1990—. Bd. dirs. Lazard Fund, Cives Steel Corp. Trustee Clarkson U., Potsdam, N.Y.; chmn. Beth Israel Med. Ctr., Newark, 1970-96, N.J. Healthcare Found., 1996—. Named Alumnus of Yr., Newark Coll. Engring., 1980; recipient Friendship award Best Friends Newark, 1999, Humanitarian award St. Barnabas's Burn Found., 1999, Citizens award N.J. Acad. Medicine, 2000, Cmty. award Y Camps of N.J., 2000. Mem. ASHRAE (pres. 1964-65), Nat. Soc. Profl. Engrs., N.J. Soc. Profl. Engrs., Assn. Energy Engrs., Am. Acad. Environ. Engrs. (diplomate), Mason., Mountain Ridge Country Club (N.J.), Stockbridge Country Club (Mass.), Cornell Club (N.Y.), Morristown Club, Tau Beta Pi (Key award 1982). Lodges: Masons. Jewish. Avocations: skiing, sailing, tennis, golf. Home: Spring Valley Rd Morristown NJ 07960-7011 Office: 25 Lindsley Dr Morristown NJ 07960-4455 E-mail: leszl@aol.com.

LIEBERMAN, LOUIS (KARL LIEBERMAN), artist; b. Bklyn., May 7, 1944; s. Abraham and Jeannette (Feinberg) L. BFA, R.I. Sch. Design, 1969; cert., Bklyn. Mus. Art Sch., 1964; BA, Bklyn. Coll., 1966. Adj. lectr. Bklyn. Coll., 1971-78, Lehman Coll., Bronx, N.Y., 1972-75; vis. artist Ill. State U., Normal, 1978, Hamilton Coll., Clinton, N.Y., 1982. One-man shows include Vancouver Art Gallery, B.C., Can., 1969, James Yu Gallery, N.Y.C., 1973, 74, Nina Freudenheim Gallery, Buffalo, 1976, Root Art Ctr., Hamilton Coll., Clinton, N.Y., 1980, Harm Bouckaert Gallery, N.Y.C., 1981, John Davis Gallery, Akron, Ohio, 1983, 85, Columbus Mus. Art, Ohio, 1983, John Davis Gallery, N.Y.C., 1986; group shows include Aldrich Mus. Contemporary Art, Ridgefield, Conn., 1973, 74, Johnson Mus. Art, Ithaca, N.Y., 1981, Fine Arts Mus. L.I., Hempstead, N.Y., 1982, Cleve. Inst. Art, 1982, Met. Mus. Art, N.Y.C., 1983, Byer Mus. Art, Evanston, Ill., 1982, Visual Arts Ctr., Beer-Sheva, Israel, 1985, Kunsthauses, Zurich, Switzerland, McNay Art Mus., San Antonio, Phila. Mus. of Art, 1988, Erie (Pa.) Art Mus., 1988, Art Mus. of Santa Cruz, Calif., 1988, Hunter Mus., Chattanooga, 1989, others; represented in permanent collections including Kenan Ctr., Lockport, N.Y., Aldridge Mus. Contemporary Art, Ridgefield, Conn., Met. Mus. Art, N.Y.C., Phila. Mus. Art, Stamford (Conn.) Mus., Bklyn. Mus., Mus. Fine Arts, Budapest, Hungary, Istvan Kiraly Mus., Budapest, Ackland Art Mus., Chapel Hill, N.C.; art critic N.Y. Arts Jour., 1978-79. Recipient Sculpture award Creative Artist Pub. Service Found., 1971-72, Graphics award Creative Artist Pub. Svc. Found., 1980-81, Graphics award N.Y. Found. Arts, 1984-85; visual arts fellow Nat. Endowment for Arts, 1979-80; Pollack-Krasner Found. fellow, 1987; Adolf and Esther Gottlieb Found. grantee, 1989.

LIEBERMAN, MICHAEL JAY, ophthalmologist; b. N.Y.C., July 8, 1948; s. Murray H. and Bella (Adler) L.; m. Andrea Dina Kaplan, Aug. 3, 1969; children: Shira, Shelly, Devorah. BA, Yeshiva U., 1970; MD, N.Y. Med. Coll., Valhalla, 1974. Diplomate Am. Bd. Ophthalmology. Pvt. practice, Farmingdale, N.Y., 1978—. Staff physician Brunswick Hosp., Amityville, N.Y., 1978—, Mid Island Hosp. (now New Island Hosp.), Bethpage, N.Y., 1979—, North Shore Univ. Hosp., Plainview, N.Y., 1978—, North Shore U. Hosp., Syosset, N.Y., 1998—. Jewish. Office: 850 Fulton St Farmingdale NY 11735-3649

LIEBERMAN, MORRIS BARUCH, psychologist, educator, researcher; b. Warsaw, Poland, Nov. 8, 1925; came to U.S., 1959, naturalized, 1964; s. Aaron and Pearl D. (Orlinsky) L.; m. Bilha Reichberg, Jan. 26, 1948; children: Aaron, Shiloh I., Pearl T. Student, London U., 1943-44; diploma Indsl. Psych. and Bus. Adminstrn., I.C.S.U.S., 1961; RN, Geha Hosp., Pardes Katz, Israel, 1947; cert. pharmacology, Bklyn. Coll. Pharmacy, 1960; MS in Indsl./Sch. Psychology, L.I. U., 1965; PhD in Clin. Psychology, LIU, 1974. Diplomate Am. Acad. Behavioral Medicine, Am. Acad. Pain Mgmt., Am. Bd. Psychol. Examiners, Am. Coll. Forensic Examiners, Am. Coll. Advance Practice Psychologists; cert. Nat. Register Health Care Providers in Psychology; lic. psychologist, N.Y. Psychiat. nurse Kupat Holim, Israel, 1944-50, regional dir. Holon dist. Israel, 1952-59; pub. health educator N.Y. State Dept. Health, 1964; rschr. neuropsychol. labs. Einstein Coll. Medicine, N.Y., 1965-66; resident neurology and psychiatry dept. Kingsbrook Med. Ctr., Bklyn., 1966-68; sr. clin. psychologist, dir. neuro-psychiat. unit Bronx Psychiat. Ctr./Einstein Coll. Medicine, N.Y., 1968-72; dir. Heights Hill inpatient svcs., prin. psychologist South Beach Hosp. N.Y. State, SUNY, 1975-76; coord. psychiat. divsn. Workman Cir. Med. Dept., N.Y.C., 1976-85; prof. dept. psychology L.I. Univ. and Coll. Pharmacy, N.Y., 1976—. U.S. rep. Til Israel Inst. Orgnl. and Indsl. Psychology, N.Y., 1978-85; exec. dir. Psychol. Consulting Assocs., N.Y., 1978—; sr. staff mem. Nassau Pain and Stress Ctr., N.Y., 1985-87; tng., supervising and chief psychologist Am. Inst. Creative Living, S.I., N.Y., The Sklar and Gingerbread Learning Ctrs., S.I., 1986—. Author: (with others) Pscyhological Aspects in Physical Rehab. Regional dir. Am. Mental Health Affiliation with Israel, Israel Assn. Academicians and Students in Am., MDA Israeli Ambulance Emergency Svcs., Mapleton-Midwood Cmty. Mental Health Bd., N.Y. Maj. Israeli Def. Force, 1946-48, Israeli Def. Force Reserves, 1948-59. Decorated Haganah medal War of Independence medal, Sinai campaign medal, granted by IDF (Israel Defense Force); postgrad. fellowship analytic psychotherapist N.Y. Dept. Mental Hygiene/Advanced Inst. Psychoanalytic Psychotherapy, N.Y.C., 1969-72. Fellow Am. Assn. Marriage and Family Therapy, Am. Assn. Prescribing Psychologists, Am. Orthopsychiat. Assn.; mem. APA (Amer. Psychol. Assn.), AAAS (Amer. Assn. Advancement in Sci.), Am. Soc. Group Psychotherapy and Psychodrama, Am. Assn. Sex, Counselors and Therapists, Assn. Advancement Behavior Therapy, Am. Soc. Clin. Hypnosis, N.Y. Soc. Clin. Psychologists, Amer. Assn. Marriages and Family Therapy. Achievements include developer of psychological instrumentation, scales for assessment of cognitive and perceptual functioning. Home and Office: 114 Avenue N Brooklyn NY 11230-5507 also: 146 Hilltop Rd East Otto NY 14729

LIEBERMAN, PHILLIP LOUIS, allergist, educator; b. Memphis, Mar. 20, 1940; m. Barbara; children: Ryan, Lee, Jay. Student, London Sch. Econs., 1961; BA in Sociology, Tulane U., 1962; MD, U. Tenn., 1965. Intern City of Memphis Hosp. U. Tenn., 1965-66, asst. resident internal medicine, 1966-67, assoc. resident internal medicine, 1967-68, chief resident, 1968-69; fellow in allergy, immunology Northwestern U., Evanston, Ill., 1969-71; asst. prof., chief div. allergy, immunology U. Tenn., 1971-74, assoc. prof., chief div. allergy, immunology, 1974-79, prof., chief div. allergy, immunology, 1979—. Instr. internal medicine U. Tenn., 1968-69; mem. exec. bd. Joint Coun. of Allergy & Immunology, 1985-90, AAAI rep., 1990; AAAI rep. Mothers for Asthmatics, 1990. Co-editor: Asthma Edition: Abstract-a-Card System, 1991—; contbr. numerous articles, abstracts to profl. pubs.; author numerous presentations in field, book chpts., revs. Exec. bd. dirs. Asthma and Allergy Found. of Am., 1990—, mem. med. scientific coun., 1987, chmn., 1990—. Served to cpt. USAR, 1965-71. Mem. Am. Acad. Allergy (com. on alternative forms of therapy, 1980—), Am. Acad. Allergy and Immunology (exec. com. 1983-91, constitution and by-laws com. 1984-87, also chmn. 1985, undergraduate com. 1985, pres.-elect. 1987-88, pres. 1988-89, nominating com. 1987, also chmn. 1989, program com. 1987), Am. Coll. Allergists, Am. Assn. Allergists (sec. 1985), Am. Assn. Certified Allergists (2d v.p. 1986-87, pres. 1989-90), Am. Bd. Allergy and Immunology. Office: U Tenn 300 S Walnut Bend Rd Cordova TN 38018-7293 also: Allergy Assocs 920 Madison Ave Ste 909N Memphis TN 38103-3438

LIEBERMAN, ROBERT ARTHUR, physicist; b. Grand Rapids, Mich., May 22, 1950; s. Arthur A. and Margaret W. Lieberman; m. Jaye C. Lieberman, Feb. 14, 1988; children: Samson Robert, Leah Jaye. BS in Physics, Rensselaer Poly. Inst., 1971, MS in Physics, 1973; PhD in Physics, U. Mich., 1981. Mem. exec. com. local br. AFL-CIO, Ann Arbor, Mich., 1977; postdoctoral fellow biophysics rsch. divsn. U. Mich., 1981; mem. tech. staff AT&T Bell Labs., Murray Hill, N.J., 1981-91; dir. advanced fiber optics Phys. Optics Corp., Torrance, Calif., 1991-95, v.p. sensor systems, 1995-97, v.p. R&D, 1997-98; sr. v.p., chief tech. officer Intelligent Optical Systems, Inc., 1999—2001; chief tech. officer Optech Ventures LLC, 2001—. Assoc. editor: Jour. Measurement Sci. Tech., 1994-96, Optical Engring. jour. 1997—. Fellow SPIE (chmn. conf. on chem., biochem. and environ. sensors 1988-99, bd. dirs. 2001-2002); mem. IEEE (sr. mem.), AAAS, ASTM (vice-chmn. subcom. on fiberoptic chem. sensing), A m. Phys. Soc. Achievements include patents for fiber optic sensing, solid state physics and biophysics. Office: Intelligent Optical Systems Inc 2520 W 237th St Torrance CA 90505-5217

LIEBERMAN, ROBERT C(HARLES), political scientist; b. Boston, Sept. 26, 1964; s. Henry S. and Elizabeth (Caeser) Lieberman; m. Lauren M. Osborne, June 16, 1991; children: Benjamin, Martha, Aaron. BA, Yale U., 1986; MA, Harvard U., 1991, PhD, 1994. Asst. prof. polit. sci. and pub. affairs Columbia U., N.Y.C., 1994-2000, assoc. prof., 2000—. Author: Shifting the Color Line: Race and the American Welfare State, 1998. Recipient Leonard D. White award Am. Polit. Sci. Assn., 1995, Pres.'s Book award Social Sci.

History Assn., 1997, Thomas J. Wilson prize Harvard U. Press, 1997. Mem. Phi Beta Kappa. Jewish. Office: Columbia U Dept Polit Sci 420 W 118th St New York NY 10027-7213 E-mail: rcl15@columbia.edu.

LIEBERMAN, ROBERT J. federal audit agency administrator; m. Christine Lieberman; 1 child, Kimberly. BA magna cum laude, U. Notre Dame. Dir. internal audit followup Dept. Def., Arlington, Va., 1981-90, asst. inspector gen. for auditing Office of Inspector Gen., 1990-2000, dep. inspector gen., 2001—. Decorated Bronze Star, Presdl. Disting. Exec. and Meritorious Rank awards, Def. Meritorious Civilian Svc. awards, White House Y2K medal. Office: Dept Def 400 Army Navy Dr Arlington VA 22202-4704

LIEBERMAN, ROCHELLE PHYLLIS, relocation company executive; b. Bklyn., June 27, 1940; d. Solomon and Freda (Shapiro) Beller; m. Melvyn Lieberman, June 10, 1961; children: Eric Neil, Marc Evan. BA, Bklyn. Coll., 1961; M.Ed., Duke U., 1977. Tchr. Bklyn. pub. schs., 1961-64; instr. Carolina Friends, Durham, N.C., 1967-70; grad. intern Duke U., 1974-75, faculty adviser, 1975-76; sales assoc. Kelly Matherly, 1978-81; pres. Shelli, Inc., 1981—. Treas. Duke Forest Assn., Durham, 1980—85; mem. Nat. Rep. Congl. Com., Congl. Bus. Adv. Coun. Mem. LWV, Durham and Chapel Hill Bd. Realtors, Women's Council of Realtors (sec. 1980-81), Duke U. Eye Ctr. (adv. bd.), Kappa Delta Pi. Clubs: Duke Faculty, Duke Campus (Durham). Jewish. Avocations: piano, walking, knitting, writing, reading. Office: Shelli Inc 1110 Woodburn Rd Durham NC 27705-5738 E-mail: ShelliInc@aol.com.

LIEBERMAN, SEYMOUR, biochemist, educator; b. N.Y.C., Dec. 1, 1916; s. Samuel D. and Sadie (Levin) L.; m. Sandra Spar, June 5, 1944; 1 child, Paul B. BS, Bklyn. Coll., 1936; MS, U. Ill., 1937; PhD (Rockefeller scholar 1939-41), Stanford U., 1941; Traveling fellow, U. Basle, Switzerland, Eidgenoess. Tech. Hochschule, Zurich, Switzerland, 1946-47. Chemist Schering Corp., 1938-39; spl. rsch. assoc. Harvard U., 1941-45; assoc. Sloan-Kettering Inst., 1945-50; prof. biochemistry Columbia Coll. Physicians and Surgeons, 1950-87, prof. emeritus, 1987—, vice provost, 1988, assoc. dir. office sci. and tech., 1991-99; assoc. dean Columbus U. Inst. Health Scis. St. Luke's Roosevelt Hosp. Ctr., 1981-97, pres., 1981-97. Syntex lectr. Mexican Endocrine Soc., 1970; mem. Am. Cancer Soc. panel steroids, 1945-49, hormones, 1949-50, mem. com. pathogenesis of cancer, 1957-60; mem. endocrine study sect. NIH, 1959-63, chmn., 1963-65, mem. gen. clin. research centers, 1967-71; med. adv. com. Population Council, 1961-73; mem. endocrinology panel Cancer Chemotherapy Nat. Svc. Ctr., 1958-62; cons. WHO human reprodn. unit, 1972-74, Ford Found., 1974-77; hon. pres. Internat. Congress on Hormonal Steroids, 1982. Mem. editl. bd. Jour. Clin. Endocrinology and Metabolism, 1958-70, Jour. Biol. Chemistry, 1975-80; contbr. articles to profl. jours. Pfizer Traveling fellow McGill U., 1968; recipient Disting. Alumnus award Bklyn. Coll., 1971, Disting. Svc. award Columbia U., 1991. Fellow N.Y. Acad. Scis., NAS; mem. Am. Soc. Biol. Chemists, Am. Chem. Soc., Internat. Soc. Endocrinology (U.S. del. central com. 1964-76), Endocrine Soc. (Ciba award 1952, Koch award 1970, council 1970-73, pres. 1974-75, Roussel prize 1984, Dale medal 1986, Boehringer-Mannheim award lectr. 1992), Harvey Soc. Home: 515 E 72nd St New York NY 10021-4032 Office: 432 W 58th St New York NY 10019-1102 E-mail: sl22@columbia.edu.

LIEBERMAN-CLINE, NANCY, sports commentator, former professional basketball coach, former player; b. July 1, 1958; m. Tim Cline, 1988; 1 child, Timothy Joseph. Grad., Old Dominion U., 1981. Guard WBL's Dallas Diamonds, 1980-86, USBL's L.I. Knights, 1986-87, Washington Generals, 1987-88, Athletes in Action, 1996-97, WNBA - Phoenix Mercury, 1997-97; head coach, gen. mgr. WNBA - Detroit Shock, 1998—2000; now sports commentator. Women's basketball analyst NBA Broadcasting, ESPN, ABC, ESPN 2, Fox Sports NEtwork, NBC. Recipient Broderick Cup, 1979, 80, Wade Trophy (2), U.S. Olympic Silver medal, 1976; named All- Am., 1978-80, ODU Outstanding Female Athlete of Yr., 1977-80; mem. Women's Am. Basketball Championship team, 1985; Named to Basketball Hall of Fame, 1996.*

LIEBERMANN, LOWELL, composer, pianist, conductor; b. N.Y.C., Feb. 22, 1961; D in Musical Arts, Juilliard Sch.; studied with David Diamond, Vincent Persichetti, Jacob Lateiner, Laszlo Halasz. Composer-in-residence Dallas Symphony, 1999—. Composer (orchestra) War Songs for Bass Voice and Orch. Op. 7, 1981, Concertino for Cello and Chamber Orch. Op. 8, 1982, Symphony No. 1 Op. 9 (BMI award, 1st prize Juilliard Orch. Competition 1987), 1982, Three Poems of Stephen Crane Op. 11 for baritone, string orch., two horns, harp (Devora Nadworney award Nat. Fed. Music Clubs 1986) 1983, Concerto No. 1 for Piano and Orch. Op. 12, 1983, Sechs Gesaenge Nach Gedichten Von Nelly Sachs Op. 18 for soprano and orch., 1986, The Domain of Arnheim Op. 33, 1990, Concerto No. 2 for Piano and Orch. Op. 36, 1992, Flute Concerto Op. 39, 1992, Revelry for Orch. Op. 47, 1995, Concerto for Flute, Harp, and Orch. Op. 48, 1995; (opera) The Picture of Dorian Gray Op. 45, 1995, (chorus) Two Choral Elegies Op. 2 for SATB a capella (Fred Waring Choral award Nat. Fed. Music 1978), 1977, Missa Brevis Op. 15 for SATB chorus, tenor and baritone solos, organ (3d prize Ch. and Artist Composers Competition 1987), 1985; (piano solo) Piano Sonata Op. 1 (Outstanding Composition award Yamaha Music Found. 1982, 1st prize Nat. Composition Contest Music Tchrs. Nat. Assn. 1978), 1977, Piano Sonata No. 2 Sonata Notturna Op. 10, 1983, Variations on a Theme by Anton Bruckner Op. 19, 1987, Nocturne No. 1 Op. 20, 1987, Four Apparitions Op. 17, 1987, others; (chamber music) Sonata for Violoncello and Piano Op. 3, 1978, Two Pieces for Violin and Viola Op. 4, 1978, Sonata for Viola and Piano Op. 13 (1st Place Victor Herbert/ASCAP awards Nat. Fed. Music Clubs 1986, Brian Israel prize Soc. for New Music 1986), 1984, Sonata for Contrabass and Piano Op. 24, 1987, Fantasy on a Fugue by J.S. Bach Op. 27 for flute, oboe, clarinet, horn, bassoon, piano, 1989, Quintet for Piano and Strings Op. 34 for piano and string quartet, 1989, COncert for Trumpet and Orchestra Op. 64, 1999, Symphony No. 2 Op. 67, 1999; others; recordings: Piano Concerto on Hyperion with pianist Stephen Hough, James Galway plays Lowell Liebermann on BMG Classics; also organ music, voice and piano. Nominated for Grammy in 1997 for best classical contemporary composition for Piano Concerto No. 2. Mem. ASCAP, Corp. Yaddo (dir.). Democrat. Office: 820 W End Ave Apt 10B New York NY 10025-5384 E-mail: lowelll@lowellliebermann.com.

LIEBERSBACH, NORBERT JOHN, protective services official; b. Langdon, N.D., July 12, 1956; s. John Peter and Florence Gertrude Liebersbach; m. Susan Lynn Liebersbach, June, 19, 1982. AS, Monterey Peninsula Coll., 1977; BA, Golden Gate U., 1982; grad. FBI Nat. Acad., U. Va., 1993. Cert. C.C. tchr., Calif. Dep. sheriff Monterey County Sheriff's Dept., Salinas, Calif., 1977-80, correctional tng. officer, 1980-83, sgt., 1983-90, lt., 1990—. Sgt. U.S. Army, 1974-77. Recipient Cert. of Recognition, Calif. Bd. Corrections, 1983-91, Mgmt. Cert., peace Officers Stds. and Tng., 1993. Mem. Nat. Sheriff's Assn., Calif. State Sheriff's Assn., FBI Nat. Acad. Assocs., Am. Jail Assn. (cert. jail mgr.), Ctrl. Calif. Jail Mgrs. Assn. (pres. 1999), Monterey County Peace Officer Assn. (pres., bd. dirs. 1988-93), Am. Legion, Elis (Elk of Yr. 1997-98). Republican. Roman Catholic. Avocation: home repair. Home: 18570 Van Buren Ave Salinas CA 93906 E-mail: Liebersbachb@co.monterey.ca.us.

LIEBERSON, STANLEY, sociologist, educator; b. Montreal, Que., Can., Apr. 20, 1933; s. Jack and Ida (Cohen) L.; m. Patricia Ellen Beard, 1960; children— Rebecca, David, Miriam, Rachel. Student, Bklyn. Coll., 1950-52; MA, U. Chgo., 1958, PhD, 1960; MA (hon.), Harvard U., 1988; LHD (hon.), U. Ariz., 1993. Assoc. dir. Iowa Urban Cmty. Rsch. Ctr., U. Iowa, 1959-61, instr., asst. prof. sociology, 1959-61; asst. prof. sociology U. Wis., 1961-63, assoc. prof., 1963-66, prof., 1966-67; prof. sociology U. Wash., 1967-71, dir. Ctr. Studies Demography and Ecology, 1968-71; prof. sociology U. Chgo., 1971-74, assoc. dir. Population Rsch. Ctr., 1971-74; prof. sociology U. Ariz., Tucson, 1974-83, head dept., 1976-79; prof. sociology U. Calif., Berkeley, 1983-88, Harvard U., 1988-91, Abbott Lawrence Lowell prof. sociology, 1991—. Vis. prof. Stanford U., summer 1970; Claude Bissell disting. vis. prof. U. Toronto, 1979-80; Christensen fellow Oxford U., St. Catherine's Coll., 2001; mem. com. on sociolinguistics Social Sci. Rsch. Coun., 1964-70; mem. sociology panel NSF, 1978-81 Author: (with others) Metropolis and Region, 1960, Ethnic Patterns in American Cities, 1963; editor: Explorations in Sociolinguistics, 1967, (with Beverly Duncan) Metropolis and Region in Transition, 1970, Language and Ethnic Relations in Canada, 1970, A Piece of the Pie, 1980, Language Diversity and Language Contact, 1981, Making It Count, 1985, (with Mary C. Waters) From Many Strands, 1988, A Matter of Taste, 2000; assoc. editor: Social Problems, 1965-67, Sociol. Methods and Research, 1971-96; editorial cons. Sociol. Inquiry, 1965-67; adv. editor: Am. Jour. Sociology, 1969-74; editorial bd. Lang. in Society, 1972-74, Internat. Jour. Sociology of Lang, 1974-2000, Canadian Jour. Sociology, 1975-2000, Social Forces, 1980-83; adv. council Sociol. Abstracts, 1972-73, Language Problems and Language Planning, 1984-87; mem. editorial com. Ann. Rev. Sociology, 1992-96. Recipient Colver Rosenberger Ednl. prize, 1960; Guggenheim fellow, 1972-73, fellow Ctr. for Advanced Study in Behavioral Scis., 1995-96, Sackler Inst. for Advanced Study, Tel Aviv U., 1999. Fellow: NAS, Am. Acad. Arts and Scis.; mem.: Am. Name Soc., Sociol. Rsch. Assn. (exec. com. 1976—81, pres. 1981), Pacific Sociol. Assn. (v.p. 1984—85, pres. 1986—87), Internat. Population Union, Population Assn. Am. (dir. 1969—72), Am. Sociol. Found. (trustee 1992—96), Am. Sociol. Assn. (coun. mem. 1985—87, pres. 1990—91, Disting. Contbn. to Scholarship award 1982, co-winner book award culture sect. 2001). Office: Harvard U Dept Sociology William James Hall Cambridge MA 02138 E-mail: SL@WJH.harvard.edu.

LIEBES, RAQUEL, import/export company executive, educator; b. San Salvador, El Salvador, Aug. 28, 1938; came to the U.S., 1952, naturalized, 1964; d. Ernesto Martin and Alice (Philip) L.; m. Richard Paisley Kinkade, June 2, 1962 (div. 1977); children: Kathleen Paisley, Richard Paisley Jr., Scott Philip. BA, Sarah Lawrence Coll., 1960; MEd, Harvard U., 1961; MA, Yale U., 1963, postgrad., 1963-65; PhD, Oxford U., 1994. Tchg. fellow in Spanish Sarah Lawrence Coll., Bronxville, N.Y., 1958-60; econ. tchg. fellow Yale U., New Haven, 1964-65, instr. Spanish dept., 1964-66; exec. stockholder Import Export Co., San Salvador, 1968-89, also bd. dirs. Adj. prof. Am. U., Washington, 1989-91, dept. fgn. lang. and linguistics dept., fgn. studies Georgetown U., Washington, 1989-93; lectr. and conf. participation in Latin Am. art. Contbr. glossary of Spanish med. terms. Hon. consul Govt. of El Salvador, 1977-80; docent High Mus. of Art, Atlanta, 1972-77; vol. Grady Hosp., Atlanta, 1966-71; instr. Spanish for med. drs. Tucson Med. Ctr., 1966-71; chmn. Atlanta Coun. for Internat. Visitors, 1966-71; mem. Outreach Group on Latin Am., The White House, Washington, 1982-86; founding mem. John Kennedy Ctr. for Performing Arts, 1980—; mem. Folger/Shakespeare Libr., Smithsonian Inst., Agape, El Salvador; founding mem. Agape, El Salvador, 1981—, Concultura, El Salvador, 1999—, Libr. of Congress, Washington. Econ. fellow Yale U., 1964-65; Corcoran Mus. Art fellow, 1984-85; Smithsonian Mus. awardee, 1981-96. Mem.: AAUW, MLA, Rsch. Assn., Am. Biog. Inst., Jr. League of Washington, Concultura El Salvador, Yale Club, Harvard Club. Republican. Avocations: comparative literature, languages, international business, English literature, Shakespeare. Office: V I P Sal # 148 PO Box 52-5364 Miami FL 33152-5364 *Throughout my life, I have applied the tradition of ethics in each and every one of my activities and have expected. The self-same principle in each and everyone of those with whom I have surrounded myself. The persons I know, writers, artists, economists, musicians, and an array of scientists who are making leaps and bounds in our expanding economy. The art market also fascinates me. Collector of Latin and Columbian Art. So does music, especially of the baroque period.*

LIEBESKIND, DAVID, business management consultant, educator; b. Paterson, N.J., Nov. 30, 1931; s. Abraham Hyman and Jean (Elkin) L.; m. Judith Elinor Seibel, Feb. 9, 1957; children: Anne Michele, John Gary, Susan Amy. BS in Chemistry, Seton Hall U., 1954; MBA in Bus. Mgmt., Fairleigh Dickinson U., East Rutherford, N.J.; PhD in Bus. Adminstrn., N.Y.U., 1972. Tech. field rep. The Dow Chem. Co., Midland, Mich. and N.Y.C., 1956-61; asst. to pres. Chem. Insect Corp., Metuchen, N.J., 1962-63; various mktg. & sales positions Union Carbide Corp., N.Y.C., 1963-73, mgr. strategic planning, 1973-76, internat. area mgr. far east, 1976-80, ops. mgr. Danbury, Conn., 1980-82, dir. mktg., 1982-83, dir. health & safety Spl. Chems. Divsn., 1983-94; prin. Bus. Improvement Assocs., Stamford, 1994-96; pres. High Ridge Assocs., 1996—. Adj. prof. mgmt. N.Y.U., N.Y.C., 1994—; dir. Comml. Devel. Assn., Washington, 1977-79. Author: The Liebeskinds from My Perspective, 1994; contbr. articles to profl. jours. Bd. dirs. Stamford Jewish Cmty. Ctr., Jewish Cmth. Endowment Found. of Stamford. Capt. U.S. Army. Mem. Am. Chem. Soc., N.Y.U. Stern Sch. Alumni Assn. (past pres., dir.), Clifton Masonic Lodge. Avocations: jogging, hiking, sailing. Home: 233 Saddle Hill Rd Stamford CT 06903-2305

LIEBICH, MARCIA TRATHEN, community volunteer; b. Troy, N.Y., Mar. 10, 1942; d. Roland Henry and Ida Mae (Horsfall) Trathen; m. Donald Herbert Liebich, May 13, 1941; children: Kurt Roland, Mark Christian. BA, Elmira Coll., 1964. With Sunnyview Hosp. and Rehab. Ctr., Schenectady, 1982-96, dir. devel., 1992-94; CEO Sunnyview Hosp. Found., 1994-96. Co-founder Parent Anonymous Lay Therapy, Schenectady, 1974-80; trustee Elmira (N.Y.) Coll., 1978-94; bd. dirs. United Way, Schenectady, 1980-81, pres. 1985, bd. dirs. United Way, N.Y., 1991—, Sunnyview Rehab. Hosp., Schenectady, 1982, pres. 1988-91; social svcs. Women's Legis. Forum, Albany, 1984-91; bd. dirs. Leadership Schenectady, 1987-92, Schenectady C. of C., 1987-90, YMCA Capital Dist., 1991-94, WMHT Pub. Radio and TV, 1991-96; pres. Samaritan Counseling Ctr., Schenectady, 1988-91; bd. dirs., treas. Bridge Ctr. Drug Treatment, Schenectady, 1988-91; bd. dirs. Backstage Theater, 1999-2002; mem. Wood River Med. Ctr. Aux., 2002—. Recipient YWCA Community Vol. award, 1986, K.S. Rozendaal award Community Svc. Schenectady, 1987, Liberty Bell award Schenectady Bar Assn., 1990, Women of Vision Betty Bean award YWCA, 1990. Mem. AAUW (pres. 1978), PEO, Jr. League Schenectady (Vol. of Yr. award 1981), Summit Pub. Radio (treas. 1998-2002), Applause (sec. 1998-2002), Breckeridge Resort Chamber (amb. 1998-2002) , Phi Beta Kappa. Republican. Lutheran. Avocations: tennis, reading, knitting, skiing, watching hockey. Home: 196 Nez Perce Dr Hailey ID 83333-8573

LIEBLING, JEROME, photographer, educator; b. N.Y.C., Apr. 16, 1924; s. Maurice and Sarah (Goodman) L.; married, Nov. 11, 1949 (div. 1969); children: Madeline, Tina, Adam, Daniella, Rachel Jane. Student, Bklyn. Coll., 1942, 46, 48, New Sch. for Social Research, N.Y.C., 1948-49; LLD (hon.), Portland (Maine) Sch. Art, 1989. Prof. photography U. Minn., Mpls., 1949-69; prof. SUNY-New Paltz, 1957-58, Yale U., New Haven, 1976-77, Hampshire Coll., Amherst, Mass., 1970—. Author, photographer: Jerome Liebling Photographs (Best of Yr. 1982), Aperture, N.Y.C., 1988, The People Yes, The Photographs of Jerome Liebling, Aperture, 1995; editor: Photography-Current Perspective, 1977, Jerome Liebling: The Minnesota Photographs, 1997, The Dickinsons of Amherst, 2001. Served with U.S. Army, 1942-45, ETO, Africa. Fellow Mass. Arts Found., 1975; fellow Nat. Endowman Arts, 1979, Guggenheim, 1977, 81 Mem. Soc. Photog. Edn. Home: 39 Dana St Amherst MA 01002-2208 Office: Hampshire Coll West St Amherst MA 01002-2954

LIEBMAN, HOWARD MARK, lawyer; b. L.A., Dec. 20, 1952; s. Martin Irving and Frances (Weiner) L.; 1 child, Peter. AB, Colgate U., 1974, AM, 1975; JD, Harvard Law Sch., 1977. Cons. Office of Tax Analysis, U.S. Treasury Dept., Washington, 1975; assoc. Paul, Weiss, Rifkind, Wharton & Garrison, N.Y.C., 1976, Covington & Burling, Washington, 1977-79; ptnr. Oppenheimer, Wolff & Donnelly, Brussels, 1979-94, Morgan, Lewis & Bockius, Brussels, 1994-2000, Jones, Day, Reavis & Pogue, Brussels, 2000—. Co-author: Business Operations in the European Union (Bur. Nat. Affairs 1995); contbg. editor Tax Mgmt. Internat. Forum, 1980—, European Taxation, 1998—, Practical International Tax Planning, 1999—. Bd. dirs. Harvard Club of Belgium, Brussels, 1989-95, pres., 1993-95. Mem.: ABA, Am. C. of C. in Belgium (chair European Cmty. fiscal affairs subcom.). Office: Jones Day Reavis & Pogue 480 ave Louise 1050 Brussels Belgium

LIEBMAN, MONTE HARRIS, retired psychiatrist; b. Milw., July 20, 1930; s. William and Ida (Zaichek) L.; 1 child, Lori Kay Liebman Henrickson. BS, U. Wis., 1953, MD, 1957. Asst. clin. prof. Med. Coll. of Wis., Milw., 1961-90; pvt. practice, 1961-75; med. counselor Milw. and Hartland, Wis., 1975-85; child care provider Children's Day Child Care Ctr., Brown Deer, 1987-98; pres., counseling instr. Birthright of Waukesha, 1981—; pres., instr. People for Life, Milw., 1985—. Counseling instr. Pregnancy Aftermath Helpline, Milw., 1974-84; pianist Music of Love, Milw., 1986—. Author: Elements for Contemporary Counseling, 1977, (booklet) Introduction to Psychotherapy, 1977, What Is Love and How to Find It, 1977, Communications from the Private World of a Psychiatrist, 1977. Pres. Eyewitness for Life, Milw., 1993—; mem., cons. Parents as Tchrs. of Human Sexuality, Milw., 1978-95; Children's Day USA com., Lake Geneva, Wis., 1996-98; host, program mentor Lake Geneva Eastview Elem. Sch.; bd. dirs. Pregnancy Helpline of Walworth County, Inc., 2002. Capt. USAR, 1954-61. Fellow Am. Soc. of Psychoanalytic Physicians; mem. Live Poetry Soc. (co-founder), Wis. Fellowship of Poets, Univ. Faculty for Life (continuing mem.). Avocations: stamping, desktop publishing, composing original songs. Home: 1335 W Main St Apt 2 Lake Geneva WI 53147-1744 Office: 1335 W Main St Apt 2 Lake Geneva WI 53147-1744 E-mail: liebman@genevaonline.com.

LIEBMAN, NINA R. economic developer; b. Toledo, May 27, 1941; d. Jules Jay and Phyllis Gertrude (Kasle) Roskin; m. Theodore Liebman, Oct. 27, 1968; children: Sophie, Hanna, Tessa. Student, U. Marseilles, Aix-en-Provence, France, 1959-60, Skidmore Coll., 1960-61, NYU, 1961-63; cert. labor negotiator, Cornell U., 1993. Pub. info. officer Young Adult Inst., N.Y.C., 1978-81; U.S.A. dir. Rhone-Alps Econ. Devel. Assn., N.Y.C. and Lyon, France, 1981-85; internat. mktg. specialist N.Y. State Dept. Econ. Devel., N.Y.C., 1985-89, chief internat. programs, 1989-95; cons. Russian Fedn. Housing project The World Bank, 1995, cons. Russian Cmty. Social Infrastructure project, 1997. Exec. dir. Nat. Assn. Export Cos., 1997—99; assoc. dir. Architecture Rsch. Inst., 2000—; assoc. The Corcoran Group, 2002—. Co-author: Biz Speak: A Dictionary of Business Terms, Slang and Jargon, 1986. Vol., trained mediator Bklyn. Mediation Ctr.; mem. internat. adv. coun. Eisenhower Found.; mem. internat. adv. bd. Nat. Minority Bus. Coun., Bklyn. Philharmonic Chorus; bd. dirs. Murray Hill Neighborhood Assn.. Fellow Eisenhower Exch. Fellowship Program, 1993. Mem. UN Assn., Alliance Am. and Russian Women (bd. dirs.), U.S. Com. for UN, Devel. Fund for Women, Mcpl. Arts Soc. Democrat. Jewish. Avocation: choral singing. E-mail: nina.liebman@prodigy.net.

LIEBMAN, RONALD STANLEY, lawyer; b. Balt., Oct. 11, 1943; s. Harry Martin and Martha (Altgenug) L.; m. Simma Liebman, Jan. 8, 1972; children: Shana, Margot. BA, Western Md. Coll., Westminster, 1966; JD, U. Md., 1969. Bar: Md. 1969, U.S. Dist. Ct. Md. 1970, U.S. Ct. Appeals (4th cir.) 1972, D.C. 1977, U.S. Dist. Ct. D.C. 1982, U.S. Ct. Appeals (D.C. cir.) 1982, U.S. Ct. Appeals (5th cir.) 1985, U.S. Ct. Appeals (2nd cir.) 1988, U.S. Ct. Appeals (11th cir.) 1991, U.S. Ct. Appeals (9th cir.) 1992, U.S. Dist. Ct. (no. dist.) Calif. 1994, U.S. Supreme Ct. 1995, U.S. Ct. Appeals (7th cir.) 1996, U.S. Dist. Ct. (ea. dist.) Tex. 1999. Law clk. to chief judge U.S. Dist. Ct. Md., 1969-70; assoc. Melnicove, Kaufman & Weiner, Balt., 1970-72; asst. U.S. atty. Office of U.S. Atty., Dept. Justice, 1972-78; ptnr. Sachs, Greenebaum & Tayler, Washington, 1978-82, Patton Boggs, L.L.P., Washington, 1982—. Author: Grand Jury, 1983, Shark Tales, 2000; co-editor: Testimonial Privileges, 1983. Recipient spl. commendation award U.S. Dept. Justice, 1978. Mem. ABA, D.C. Bar Assn., Md. Bar Assn., Sergeants Inn Club (Balt.). Office: Patton Boggs LLP 2550 M St NW Ste 500 Washington DC 20037-1350

LIEBMAN, SHIRLEY ANNE, analytical research scientist; b. Boston, Sept. 4, 1934; d. John A. and Fay Glazier; m. Harmon L. Liebman, June 23, 1956; children: Robert C., David J. BS, Northeastern U., Boston, 1956; PhD, Temple U., Phila., 1969. Lab. technician MIT, 1953-55; jr. engr. Boeing Co., Seattle, 1956-58; rsch. chemist Monsanto Rsch. Corp., Everett, Mass., 1958-61; sr. rsch. scientist Armstrong World Ind., Lancaster, Pa., 1969-80; mgr. application and contract rsch. Chem. Data Systems, Oxford, 1980-83; sr. assoc. NRC-Ballistic Rsch. Lab., Aberdeen, Md., 1984-86; sr. scientist Geo-Ctrs., Inc., 1986-91; v.p., dir. contract rsch. and applications CCS Instrument Systems, West Grove, Pa., 1991-93. Sr. adv. bd. Environ. Rsch. Ctr., U. Nev., Las Vegas, 1990-95; cons. Computer Chem. Sys., Inc., Avondale, Pa., 1986-91, The CECON Group, Inc., Wilmington, Del., 1991—; founder and v.p. LL Sci. & Tech. Alliance, Inc., 1995-96; exec. Internat. Exec. Svc. Corps, 1995—. Co-editor: Pyrolysis and GC in Polymer Analysis, 1985; contbr. over 170 articles to profl. jours., chpts. to books. Citizens adv. coun. Lancaster Housing and Redevel. Authority, 1986—. Mem. AAAS, Am. Chem. Soc., Soc. for Applied Spectroscopy, Royal Soc. Chemistry (London). Republican. Unitarian Universalist. Achievements include patents in field; research in major disciplines of physical/analytical organic chemistry, chemical engineering and computers, polymer characterization, materials and environmental sciences, and the integrated intelligent instrument approach to analytical sciences. Home: 91 Pinnacle Rd W Holtwood PA 17532-9641

LIEBMAN, THEODORE, architect; b. Newark, May 7, 1939; s. Edward and Miriam (Applebaum) Liebman; m. Nina Roskin, Oct. 27, 1968; children: Sophie, Hanna, Tessa. B.Arch., Pratt Inst., 1962; M.Arch., Harvard U., 1963. Registered architect, Mass, NY, Colo, Ind, Fla, NJ, Pa. Project design officer Boston Redevel. Authority, mass., 1963-64; project dir. David A. Crane, Architect, Phila., 1966-69; chief architect N.Y. State Urban Devel. Corp., N.Y.C., 1969-75; prin. urban design and archtl. adviser Harvard Inst. Internat. Devel., Tehran, Iran, 1975-77; pres. HAUS Internat., Inc., N.Y.C., 1977-79, The Liebman Melting Partnership, Architects and Planners, N.Y.C., 1979—. Bd advisers Inst Urban Design, New York, NY, 1980—84; assoc prof urban design Pratt Inst, Brooklyn, NY, 1983—88; land develop mgr Russian Fed Housing Project-World Bank, 1995—96. Mem ed bd: Metropolis, 1981—88; contbr. articles to mags. Fellow, Am Acad, Rome, 1966, Wheelwright Travelling, Harvard Univ, 1971. Fellow: AIA (pres NY chpt 1983—84); mem.: Urban Land Inst (mem int coun). Office: The Liebman Melting Partnership 330 W 42nd St New York NY 10036-6902

LIEBMANN, GEORGE W(ILLIAM), lawyer; b. N.Y.C., June 20, 1939; s. William Liebmann and Margaret (Hirschman) Cook; m. Anne-Lise Grimstad, Apr. 29, 1967; children: Pamela, George, Franklin. AB, Dartmouth Coll., 1960; JD, U. Chgo., 1963. Bar: Md. 1964, Ill. 1964. With Chaucer Head Book Shop, Inc., N.Y.C., 1958-59; law clk. to chief judge Ct. Appeals Md., 1963-64; with Frank, Bernstein, Conaway and Goldman, Balt., 1964-79; asst. atty. gen. State of Md., 1967-69; exec. asst. to Gov. Md., Annapolis, 1979-80; prin. Liebmann and Shively, P.A., Balt., 1980—. Lectr. U. Md. Law Sch., 1977-78, Johns Hopkins U., 1991-92; mem. Gov.'s Commn. to Revise Annotated Code Md., 1974-83; alt. mem. State Planning Coun. on Radioactive Waste Mgmt., 1980-82; chmn. Gov.'s Task Force on Local Govt. Antitrust Liability, 1982-83, Gov.'s Commn. Health Care Providers' Profl. Liability Ins., 1983-84; gen. coun. Md. Econ. Devel. Corp., 1985—; vis. fellow U. Salford, Eng., 1996, Wolfson Coll., Cambridge, 1996, 98, 99; panelist U.S. Bankruptcy Trustee, 1980—. Author: Maryland District Court Law and Practice, 2 vols., 1976, Maryland Civil Practice Forms, 2 vols., 1984, The Little Platoons: Sub-Local Governments in Modern History, 1995, The Gallows in the Grove: Civil Society in American Law, 1997, Solving Problems Without Large Government, 1999, Six Lost Leaders: Prophets of Civil Society, 2001; mng. editor U. Chgo. Law Rev., 1962-63; contbg. author The American Enterprise, 1999—. Sec. Coalition Against the SST, Washington, 1969; trustee Hist. Annapolis Found., 1991-99; Rep. primary candidate U.S. Senate, 1998. Simon indsl. and profl. fellow U. Manchester, Eng., 1993-94. Mem. Am. Law Inst., Fed. Jud. Conf. 4th Cir., Libr. Co. Balt. Bar (bd. dirs. 1967—, pres. 1975-77), Engring. Soc. Md. (assoc.) Office: 8 W Hamilton St Baltimore MD 21201-5020

LIEBMANN, SEYMOUR W. construction consultant; b. N.Y.C., Nov. 1, 1928; s. Isidor W. and Etta (Waltzer) L.; m. Hinda Adam, Sept. 20, 1959; children: Peter Adam, David W. BSME, Clarkson U., 1948; grad., Indsl. Coll. Armed Forces, 1963, U.S. Army Command and Gen. Staff Coll., 1966, U.S. Army War Coll., 1971. Registered profl. engr., N.Y., Mass., Ga. Area engr. constrn. divsn. E.I. DuPont de Nemours & Co., Inc., 1952-54; constrn. planner Lummus Co., Inc., 1954-56; prin. mech. engr. Perini Corp., 1956-62; v.p. Boston Based Contractors, 1962-66, A.R. Abrams, Inc., Atlanta, 1967-74, pres., 1974-78, also bd. dirs. Founder Liebmann Assocs., Inc., Atlanta, 1979—; mem. nat. adv. bd. Am. Security Coun. Author: Military Engineer Field Notes, 1953, Prestressing Miter Gate Diagonals, 1960; contbr. articles to publs. Mem. USO Coun., Atlanta, 1968—, v.p., 1978, mem. exec. com., 1975-79; mem. Nat. UN Day Com., 1975; sr. army coord., judge Sci. Fair, Atlanta Pub. Schs., annually, 1979-88, 92—; asst. scoutmaster troop 298 Atlanta area coun. Boy Scouts Am., 1980-87, Explorer advisor, 1982-86, unit commr., 1985, dist. commr. North Atlanta Dist. Atlanta Area Coun., 1988-90, asst. coun. commr., 1990-95, mem. faculty Commrs. Coll., 1985-88, 92, mem. North Atlanta Dist. com., BSA, 1996—; mem. alumni adv. com. Clarkson Coll. Tech., 1981—, alumni bd. govs., 1983-94, Disting. Alumni Golden Knight award, 1983; mem. exec. com., zoning chmn. neighbor planning unit "A" City of Atlanta, 1982—, chmn., 1988, 95-2002, vice-chmn., 1989; pres. West Paces/Northside Neighborhood Assn., 1991—; apptd. civil engr. mem. to

City of Atlanta Water and Sewer Appeals Bd., 1992—; apptd. mem. to Mayor's Bond Oversight Com. City of Atlanta, 1995-96; chair City of Atlanta Nancy Creek Tech. Tunnel Adv. Com., 2002--; mem. blue ribbon panel Fulton County Juvenile Ct., 2001--; mem. Philmont Fall Adventure Trek, 2002; apptd. mem. Mayor's Svc. Commn., 2002—. Col. AUS Ret. Corps Engrs., 1948-52, Korea, Germany. Decorated Legion of Merit, Meritorious Svc. medal, USAR Achievement medal with oak leaf cluster; named to Old Guard of Gate City Guard, 1979; recipient cert. achievement, Dept. Army, 1978, Bronze DeFleury medal, U.S. Army Engr. Regiment, 1997, USO Recognition award, 1979, Order of Arrow award, Boy Scouts Am., 1983, 1987, Scouters Key, 1988, North Atlanta Dist. Merit award, 1989, Silver Beaver award, 1991, Disting. Commn. award, 1991, Engring. Profl. award, Am. Inst. Plant Engrs., 1987, Hands Across Atlanta award, 1997. Fellow: Soc. Am. Mil. Engrs. (life; program chmn. Atlanta post 1980—81, v.p. 1982, pres. 1983, chmn. readiness com. 1986—2000, bd. dirs. 1986—, program chmn. 1988, nat. meeting, asst. regional v.p. for readiness So. region 1991—, life dir. Atlanta Post 1994, James Lucas Chair Atlanta Post 1994, elected nat. dir. 1994—97, program chmn. S.Ea. regional site tng. conf. 1999, Nat. award of Merit 1982—83, Atlanta Post Leadership award 1988); mem.: NRA, NSPE, ASTM, Jt. Am. Counsel Engring. Cos. (chmn. 2002—), Am. Arbitration Assn. (panel arbitrators 1979—, constrn. adv. com. 1984—), Engrs. Club Boston, Met. Atlanta Engrs. (chmn. Engrs. Week 2000 and 2001 awards com.), Ga. Soc. Profl. Engrs. (mem. state licensing com. 2002—, bd. dirs. Buckhead chpt., state ethics com., Engr. of Yr. in Pvt. Practice 1990, Ga. Engr. Yr. 1991, Lifetime Achievement award for engring. excellence 2001), Am. Concrete Inst., Am. Cons. Engrs. Coun. (state and nat. pub. rels. coms., nat. ethics com., state legis. liaison com.), Army Engr. Assn. (life), U.S. Army Hist. Found., Atlanta Area Mil. Affairs Com., Vets. of the 1st U.S.Army Engr. Combat Bn., Atlanta Hist. Soc., Ga. Conservancy, Benyton Mackaye Trail Assn., Appalachian Trail Conf., Order of Engr., Mil. Order World Wars, Atlanta C. of C. (mil. affairs com. 1999), Downtown Atlanta Kiwanis, Cobb C. of C., Def. Preparedness Assn., Assn. U.S. Army (v.p. exec. com. local chpt. 1998—2000), Nat. Def. U. Found., Soc. 1st U.S. Inf., U.S. Army War Coll. Alumni Assn. (life), U.S. Army War Coll. Found. (life; Alumni Assn. Disting. Alumni Selection Com. 1997—), Res. Officers Assn. (life), Heros of 76, Civitan, Elks, Nat. Sojourners, Shriners, Masons (32d degree). Republican. Jewish. Home: 3260 Rilman Dr NW Atlanta GA 30327-2224 Office: Ste 700 210 Interstate North Pkwy SE Atlanta GA 30339-2111

LIEBOVICH, SAMUEL DAVID, retired steel executive; b. Rockford, Ill., Sept. 19, 1946; s. Albert A. and Dorothy (Pollard) L.; m. Erna Susan Horewitch, Oct. 1, 1966; children: Elaine Beth, Mitchell Phillip. BS magna cum laude, Bradley U., 1969; postgrad., U. Ill., 1969-70. Asst. dir. purchasing Liebovich Bros. Inc., Rockford, 1970-80, v.p. purchasing and inventory, 1980-82, pres. nat. sales, 1982-2000; ret., 2000. Allocations com. United Way, Rockford, 1987—88; bus. chmn. Statue of Liberty Com., 1986—87; pres. Wallenberg Com., 1988—89; adv. dir., chmn. corp. fundraising Mother House, 1997—99, adv. bd., 1997—2000; fin. sec., bd. dirs. Temple Beth El, Rockford, 1975—79, treas., 1993—94; v.p. Temple Bethel, 1995—98; chair United Jewish Appeal Greater Rockford Area, 1988—89; pres. Greater Rockford Jewish Fedn., 1989—92; fundraising com. Frenchman's Creek Jewish Fedn., Palm Beach, 2000—02, chmn., 2001—; bd. dirs. Rockford Symphony Orch., 1994—97, Palm Beach County Jewish Fedn., 2002—. Mem. ASTM, Nat. Assn. Aluminum Distbrs. (nat. com. 1979-85), Nat. Assn. Steel Distbrs. (bd. dirs. 1990-92, v.p. 1992-93, exec. v.p. 1994-95, pres. 1995-96, Pres. award 1993, 94, Steel Man of Yr. award 1996-97), Am. Soc. for Metal, Internat. Kiwanis (fellow award), Alpine Kiwanis (bd. dirs., sec., v.p., pres.-elect 1988-95, pres.), Ill.-Iowa Dist. 6 Kiwanis (lt. gov.-elect divsn. 12 1995-96, lt. gov. dist. 12 1996-97, George Hickson Triple Diamond award), Rockford B'nai B'rith (pres. 1973-76), Masons, Shriners, Frenchman's Creek Country Club, Alpine Kiwanis Club, Mau Nah Tee See Country Club. Republican. Jewish. Avocations: golf, racquetball, fishing, boating. Home: 900 N Lake Shore Dr Apt 809 Chicago IL 60611-1530 E-mail: sammie2116@aol.com.

LIEBOW, MARK, physician; b. Chgo., Sept. 16, 1953; s. Joseph and Razie Liebow; m. Tina Liebling, Oct. 20, 1985; children: David, Esther Hannah, Samuel Benjamin. BS with high honors, Mich. State U., 1974; MD, U. Ill., Chgo., 1978; MPH, Harvard U., 1986. Cert. Am. Bd. Internal Medicine. Resident internal medicine U. Wis. Hosps. and Clinics, Madison, 1978-81; staff physician North Care Med. Group, S.C., Evanston, Ill., 1981-85; assoc. dir. internal medicine residency prgm. St. Francis Hosp., 1986-93; dir. med. edn. and transitional year residency program St. Francis Hosp., 1989-93; cons. medicine Mayo Clinic, Rochester, Minn., 1994—; asst. med. dir. Mayo Mgmt. Svcs., Inc., 1996-2000; asst. prof. Mayo Med. Sch., 1995—. Mem. Pub. Programs Risk Adjustment Work Group, St. Paul, 1995—. Contbr. articles to profl. jours. Staff mem. Mikva for Congress Campaign, Skokie, Ill., 1974, 76. Fellow ACP; mem. AMA, Soc. Gen. Internal Medicine (chair health policy com. 1998-2001), Soc. for Med. Decision Making, Minn. Med. Assn., Zumbro Valley Med. Soc. Jewish. Avocation: bridge. Office: Mayo Clinic 200 1st St SW Rochester MN 55905-0002 E-mail: mliebow@aol.com.

LIEBOWITZ, LARRY ARNOLD, chemical engineer; b. Bklyn., June 19, 1943; s. Max and Estelle L. BChemE, CCNY, 1965; MChemE, NYU, 1968. Engring. group leader MEPCO divsn. NA Philips, Morristown, N.J., 1965-68; product mgr. Nytronics, Inc., Berkeley Heights, 1968-71; engring. mgr. KDI Pyrofilm Corp., Whippany, 1971-75; pres. LAL Technol. Corp., East Brunswick, 1975—. Founder, CEO Advanced Materials Tech. Corp. Mem. Soc. Plastics Engrs. (chmn. elec. and electronic divsn. 1970-71), Am. Chem. Soc., Am. Ceramics Soc. Achievements include development of monolithic multilayer ceramic capacitors, superior ceramic materials and chip structures and manufacturing techniques for electronic components and microcircuits which allow their use at microwave frequencies and broad band wireless comm. applications, log-slope method of predicting high-frequency performance of electronic devices, water based binders for electronic ceramics, replacing ones based on environment unfriendly volatile organic solvents; inventor split plate construction to promote flux cancellation for reduced inductance in multilayer capacitor chips, buried layer chip architecture for chips in microwave applicatons, design and method for manufacturing single layer ceramic capacitors with dielectric thickness less then .001 inch, SAFETURF (artificial turf engineered to reduce leg injuries); research in high temperature superconductor materials. Home and Office: PO Box 412 East Brunswick NJ 08816-0412 E-mail: laltec@aol.com.

LIEBOWITZ, NEIL ROBERT, psychiatrist; b. Bklyn., Feb. 5, 1956; s. Harold and Gertrude Liebowitz; m. Judith Linda Ross, Oct. 21, 1952; children: Sarah Michelle, Daniel Geoffery. BA, U. Va., 1978; MD, SUNY, Stony Brook, 1982. Cert. Am. Bd. Psychiatry and Neurology; cert. in clin. psychopharmacology Am. Soc. Clin. Psychopharmacology. Intern Greenwich Hosp. Assn., Greenwich, Conn., 1982-83; psychiatry fellow Yale Dept. Psychiatry, New Haven, 1982-86; chief resident psychiatry Yale New Haven Hosp., 1985-86; dir. consultation liaison psychiatry Newington VA Med. Ctr., Newington, Conn., 1986-87, chief mental hygiene clinic, 1986-88; asst. prof. psychiatry U. Conn., Farmington, 1986-92, asst. clin. prof. psychiatry, 1993—; dir. inpatient psychiatry Newington VA Med. Ctr., 1988-89; dir. ambulatory psychiatry John Dempsey Hosp., Farmington, 1989-91. Cons. psychiatrist Rocky Hill (Conn.) Vets. Home and Hosp., 1987-88; attending New Britain Gen. Hosp., 1992—; dir. Conn. Anxiety & Depression Treatment Ctr., Farmington, 1994—; founding mem., bd. dirs. PsychCare, Inc., 1996-98; bd. dirs. Psych Mgmt. Contbr. articles to profl. jours.; co-investigator clin. research Clin. Psychopharmocology, 1988—; mem. Integrated Neuroscis., Inc., 1999—. Mem. Am. Psychiat. Assn., Conn. Psychiat. Soc., Hartford Psychiat. Soc. (pres. 1997), Phi Beta Kappa. Office: Conn Anxiety & Depression Treatment Ctr Farmington CT 06032

LIEBSON, HERMAN, special education educator; b. Asbury Park, N.J., Feb. 10, 1951; s. Morris and Harriet L.; m. Eleanor Elizabeth Predmore, Aug. 30, 1988 (div. Aug. 1999); children: Avram David, Elijah Evan. B, SUNY, New Paltz, 1974, M, 1976. Cert. tchr., N.Y., English 7-12, spl. edn. Asst. mental hygiene therapy aide Dept. Mental Hygiene State of N.Y., Wassiac, 1974-77; insvc. tng. instr. Exception, Dawson Springs, Ky., 1977; tchr. spl. edn. Temple U., Phila., 1978; client treatment coord. Assn. Retarded Citizens, Rochester, N.Y., 1979-84; rehab. splst. Challenge Industries, Ithaca, 1984-90; resource room tchr. South Seneca Pub. Schs., Ovid, 1990-92; habilitation splst. I Dept. Developmental Disabilities, Rome, 1994-95; tchr. spl. edn. Dept. Corrections, Pine City, 1996—. Fellow to study spl. edn. N.Y. State Dept. Edn., 1975-76. Mem. Hist. Miniature Gaming Soc. (East). Avocations: role-playing games, military miniatures, historical boardgames, gardening. Home: PO Box 3091 Elmira NY 14905-0091

LIEBSON, MILT, sculptor, educator, author; b. N.Y.C., Dec. 12, 1923; s. Ely and Gertrude (Kern) L.; m. Lila Jacobs, Mar. 5, 1944; children: Richard, Ellen Liebson Porges, Donald. BS, St. John's U., 1948; MS, L.I. U., 1960. Tchr. Mercer Community Coll., West Windsor, N.J., 1987-99, Artworks, Princeton, 1989-96. One-man shows include Gallery 100, Princeton, N.J., George B. Markle Gallery, Hazelton, Pa., Bergen Mus., Paramus, N.J., Rutgers U., New Brunswick, N.J., Baron Art Ctr., Woodbridge, N.J., Monmouth Mus., Lincroft, N.J., AT&T Corp. Gallery, Hopewell, N.J., Ellarslie Mus., Trenton, N.J., Strand Gallery, Summit, N.J., Trenton City Mus., Mus. of Artists, Moscow, Delann Gallery, Plainsboro, N.J., Golden Door Gallery, New Hope, Pa., The Sculpture Showcase, New Hope, others; represented in various permanent collections; author: Direct Stone Sculpture, 1991, Direct Stone Sculpture II, 1992, Printmaking with Clay, 1996, Direct Wood Sculpture, 2001; video: Sculpting in Stone, 1995. With U.S. Army, 1942-44. Mem. Internat. Sculpture Ctr., Trenton Artists Workshop Assn., Allied Artists of Am. (assoc. mem.), Rho Chi. Avocations: tennis, golf, music. Home and Office: 69B Picea Plz Jamesburg NJ 08831-4143 E-mail: mil-lil@worldnet.att.net.

LIECHTI, HARRIS NELSON, writer, educator; b. Des Moines, Aug. 20, 1935; s. Frederick Simon and Dorothy Nelson Liechti; m. Marya Beth Adams, Oct. 31, 1970 (div. Sept. 21, 1989); children: Sean, Taya. BA, U. of Mich., Ann Arbor, MI, 1957, MA, 1958, Ph. D, 1968. Writer, prodr., dir. Armed Forces Radio & TV Svc., Hollywood, Calif., 1959—60; reports asst. US Office of Edn., Washington, 1962—63; tchg. fellow U. of Mich., Ann Arbor, Mich., 1964—66; asst. reports officer US office of Edn., Washington, 1966—68; speech educator U. of Wis., Oshkosh, Wis., 1968—90, communication educator, 1990—. Dir. Nat. Assn. of Ednl. Broadcasters, Washington, 1980—81; dir. of tv services U. of Wis., Oshkosh, Wis., 1969—74; faculty advisor Internat. Film Series, Oshkosh, Wis., 1981—86. Author: (lab manual) Basic TV Crew Positions, (book) Great Ideas in Film-Making; contbr. articles to profl. jour.; author: (plays) Adam and Eve and the Rest of Us, (book) Out of My Mind (Or Maybe Not). Mem. Peace Team, Ann Arbor, Mich., 1998—98. Sp4 U.S. Army, 1958—60, Hollywood, CA. Mem.: Dramatists Guild, Inc., World Future Soc. (panel chmn. 1987—87), Alpha Epsilon Rho, Phi Kappa Phi. D-Liberal. Unitarian Universalist. Avocations: writing, photography, acting, travel, reading. Home: 545 North State Street Apartment 5B Ann Arbor MI 48104 Personal E-mail: harrisliechti@comcast.net.

LIECHTY, DANIEL, social worker, educator; b. Beatrice, Nebr., May 2, 1954; s. Robert Lee and Miriam Janelle Liechty. PhD, U. Vienna, Austria, 1983; DMin, Grad. Theol. Found., Donaldson, Ind., 1994. Edn. specialist Inst. Pa. Hosp., Phila., 1990-93; psychol. counselor N.W. Ctr., 1993-95; psychosocial coord. Montgomery Hospital Hospice, Norristown, 1995-99; prof. social work Ill. State U., Normal, 1999—. Bd. dirs. Mid-Atlantic Acad. Religion, Phila. Author: Andreas Fischer and Anabaptism, 1988, Theology in Postliberal Perspective, 1990, Sabbatarianism in the Sixteenth Century, 1993, Early Anabaptist Spirituality, 1994, Transference and Transcendence, 1995, Death and Denial, 2003, Reflecting on Faith in a Post-Christian Society, 2003. Fellow Grad. Theol. Found.; mem. Mensa Ltd., Ernest Becker Found., Otto Rank Assn., Coun. Hospice Profls. Socialist. Avocation: folk music. Office: Ill State U 4650 Normal IL 61790-4650 E-mail: dliecht@ilstu.edu.

LIEDHOLM, CARL EDWARD, economics educator; b. Long Beach, Calif., July 22, 1940; s. George Edward and Marian (Folts) L.; m. Margaret Edith Osgood, Nov. 29, 1963; children: Kathleen Elizabeth, Erik Allen. BA, Pomona Coll., 1961; PhD, U. Mich., 1965. Adviser, acting dir. Econ. Devel. Inst., U. Nigeria, Enugu, 1965-67; asst. prof. econs. Mich. State U., East Lansing, 1967-69, chmn. econs. dept., 1969-74, prof. econs., 1972—, dir. off-farm employment project, 1977-83, dir. small enterprises approach to devel. project, 1982—. Cons. in field. NDEA fellow, 1961-65, Yale U. vis. fellow, 1974, Sussex (U.K.) U. vis. fellow, 1975; chmn. selection com. Internat. Doctoral Research Fellowship Program for Africa, Social Sci. Research Council, 1977-78 Author: (with Carl Eicher) Growth and Development of Nigerian Economy, 1970, The Indian Iron and Steel Industry: An Analysis of Comparative Advantage, 1972, Employment and Growth in Small-scale Industries: Empirical Evidence from Sierre Leone, 1985; assoc. editor: Rural Africana; co-editor: M.S.U. Internat. Development Papers; contbr. articles to profl. jours. Fellow African Studies Assn.; mem. Am. Econs. Assn., Nigeria, Royal econ. socs., U.S. Agy. for Internat. Devel. (rsch. adv. com.), Phi Beta Kappa. Clubs: Calif. Cello, Ann Arbor Track. Home: 830 Wildwood Dr East Lansing MI 48823-3049

LIEDKE, GUY ARTHUR, public administrator; b. Fond du Lac, Wis., May 1, 1954; s. Stanley Liedke and Carlaine Beer; m. Jean A. Pulvermacher, Feb. 9, 1974; children: Jennifer, Geoffery. AAS, C.C. of Air Force, 1988; BS in Sociology summa cum laude, St. Leo Coll., 1992; MPA, Troy State U., 1995. Enlisted USAF, 1972; advanced through grades to master sgt. USMC, 1987, ret., 1992; program specialist U.S. Dept. Vets. Affairs, Tampa, Fla., 1993—. Cons. VISN 8 Homeless Working Group, Fla. Mem. ASPA, Non-Commd. Officers Assn., Air Force Assn. Avocations: bicycling, woodworking, chip carving, reading, music. Office: Homeless Providers Grant and Per Diem Program 13000 B Downs Blvd Tampa FL 33612 Fax: (813) 979-3682. E-mail: Guy.Liedke@med.va.gov.

LIEF, HAROLD ISAIAH, psychiatrist; b. N.Y.C., Dec. 29, 1917; s. Jacob F. and Mollie (Filler) L.; m. Myrtis A. Brumfield, Mar. 3, 1961; Caleb B., Frederick V., Oliver F.; children from previous marriage: Polly Lief Goldberg, Jonathan F. BA, U. Mich., 1938; MD, NYU, 1942; cert. in psychoanalysis, Columbia Coll. Physicians and Surgeons, 1950; MA (hon.), U. Pa., 1971. Intern Queens Gen. Hosp., Jamaica, N.Y., 1942-43; resident in psychiatry L.I. Coll. Medicine, 1946-48; pvt. practice N.Y.C., 1948-51; asst. physician Presbyn. Hosp., 1949-51; asst. prof. Tulane U., New Orleans, 1951-54, assoc. prof., 1954-60, prof. psychiatry, 1960-67, U. Pa., Phila., 1967-82, prof. emeritus, 1982—, dir. div. family study, 1967-81; dir. Marriage Council of Phila., 1969-81, Ctr. for Study of Sex. Edn. in Medicine, 1968-82; mem. staff U. Pa. Hosp., 1967-81, Pa. Hosp., 1981—; clin. prof. psychiatry Jefferson Med. U., 1994—. Author: (with Daniel and William Thompson) The Eighth Generation, 1960; Editor: (with Victor and Nina Lief) Psychological Basis of Medical Practice, 1963, Medical Aspects of Human Sexuality, 1976, (with Arno Karlen) Sex Education in Medicine, 1976, Sexual Problems in Medical Practice, 1981, (with Zwi Hoch) Sexology: Sexual Biology, Behavior and Therapy, 1982, (with Zwi Hoch) International Research in Sexology, 1983, Human Sexuality With Respect to AIDS and HIV Infection, 1989; contbr. numerous articles to publs. Mem. La. State Commn. Civil Rights, 1958—67; Bd. dirs., chmn. Ctr. for Sexuality and Religion, 1988—2001; mem. adv. bd. False Memory Syndrome Found., 1992—. Maj. M.C. U.S. Army, 1943—46. Commonwealth Fund fellow, 1963-64; recipient Gold Medal award Mt. Airy Hosp., 1977, Lifetime Achievement award Phila. Psychiat. Soc., 1992, Gold Medal, World Assn. Sexology, 1999; named practitioner of yr. Phila. County Med. Soc., 1998. Fellow Phila. Coll. Physicians, Am. Psychiat. Assn. (50 yr. life), N.Y. Acad. Scis., AAAS, Am. Acad. Psychoanalysis (charter, past pres.), Am. Coll. Psychiatrists (founding), Am. Coll. Psychoanalysts (charter); mem. AMA, Am. Assn. Marriage and Family Therapists, Sex Info. and Edn. Coun. U.S. (past pres.), Group Advancement Psychiatry (life), Am. Soc. Adolescent Psychiatry, Am. Psychosomatic Soc., Assn. Psychoanalytic Medicine (life), Am. Psychoanalytic Assn., Internat. Psychoanalytic Assn., Internat. Acad. Sex Rsch., Soc. Sci. Study of Sex, Am. Soc. Sex Educators, Counselors and Therapists, Soc. Sex Therapists and Rschrs., World Assn. Sexology (past v.p.), Soc. Exploration of Psychotherapy Integration (adv. bd.), Pa. Med. Soc., Phila. Med. Soc., Columbia Club, Mich. Club of Greater Phila., Penn Club of N.Y., Sigma Xi, Al pha Omega Alpha, Phi Eta Sigma, Phi Kappa Phi. Home: 840 Montgomery Ave No 302 Bryn Mawr PA 19010-3344 Office: 987 Old Eagle School Rd Ste 719 Wayne PA 19087-1708 E-mail: halief@aol.com. *The conflict between individual gratification and the needs of society, between competition and cooperation, appears to me to be the most fundamental issue confronting mankind. My goal in life has been to steer a course that fosters service to others and to society without undue sacrifice of individual aspirations.*

LIEF, THOMAS PARRISH, sociologist, educator; b. N.Y.C., Oct. 4, 1931; s. Alfred and Zola Nina (Vogel) L. BA, U. N.Mex., 1955, MA, 1961; PhD, Tulane U., 1970. Bd. cert. substance abuse counselor, La.; case presentation evaluator. Counselor, archaeology asst. U. N.Mex., Albuquerque, 1959-60, 60-61; tchg. asst. dept. sociology Tulane U., New Orleans, 1961-64; instr. to asst. prof. dept. sociology Loyola U., 1964-69; assoc. prof. to prof. dept. sociology So. U., 1968-98; cons. on curriculum devel. Tuskegee Inst. Drug Abuse Human Svcs. Manpower Devel. Tng., 1973-78; adj. prof. sociology, assoc. grad. faculty mem. U. New Orleans, 1975-76; cons. various orgns., 1981-82; vis. prof. dept. sociology Tulane U., New Orleans, 1986; rev. com. mem. Alcohol, Drug Abuse & Mental Health Adminstrn. Office, 1987—. Bd. dirs. Nat. Assn. Alcoholism and Drug Abuse Counselors, 1990-91; pres. La. Assn. Substance Abuse Counselor and Trainers, 1990-91; adv. bd. Michael Halbrook Recovery Ctr. East Lake Hosp., 1990-92; mem. La. State Bd. Certification for Substance Abuse Counselors, 1988-92, Adv. Com. for Historically Black Colls. and Univs. Program for Substance Abuse Tng., 1987-89; tng. cons. Am. Indian Tng. Inst., Sacramento, Calif., 1985—; mem. La. Commn. on Alcohol and Drug Abuse, 1984-91, 97—; mem. L.A. Drug Control and Violent Crime Policy Bd., 1993—; contract cons. Ctr. for Substance Abuse Treatment, 1994-95; contract cons. Office Alcohol and Drug Abuse, Dept. Health and Hosps., 1998-99; founder, bd. dirs. Accreditation Coun.: Alcohol and Drug Counselor Program in Higher Edn.; mem. WWNO Pub. Radio adv. bd.; cons. in field. Contbr. numerous articles to profl. jours.; mem. editl. rev. com. Counselor, 1986—; co-author: Academic Linkages Resource Manual. Co-chair La. State-Wide Taskforce Counselor Manpower, 1984-90; pres., founder Nat. Assn. Substance Abuse Trainers and Educators, 1983—; bd. dirs. Nat. Commn. on Accreditation of Alcoholism and Drug Abuse Counselors, 1982-90, Certification Reciprocity Consortium/Alcohol and Other Drug Abuse, Inc., 1981-82; pres., founder La. Cert. Examining Bd. of La. Assn. Substance Abuse Counselor & Trainers, 1978-82; mem. Child Abuse Com. Dist. Atty.'s Office, 1976-80; co-dir. Insight House Adv. Bd., 1976-80. Mem. Am. Sociol. Assn., Am. Acad. Polit. and Social Scis., La. Assn. Substance Abuse Counselors and Trianers, La. Alcohol and Drug Abuse Assn., Nat. Assn. Alcoholism and Substance Abuse Counselors, Nat. Assn. Substance Abuse Trainers and Educators, Soc. for Applied Anthropology, Soc. for Study of Social Problems, So. Sociol. Soc., Substance Abuse Counselor Orgn., Nat. Commn. on Accreditation of Alcoholism and Drug Abuse Counselors Credentialing Bodies, Rotary.

LIEM, ANNIE, pediatrician; b. Kluang, Johore, Malaysia, May 26, 1941; d. Daniel and Ellen (Phuah) L. BA, Union Coll., 1966; MD, Loma Linda U., 1970. Diplomate Am. Bd. Pediatrics. Intern Glendale (Calif.) Adventist Hosp., 1970-71; resident in pediatrics Children's Hosp. of Los Angeles, 1971-73; pediatrician Children's Med. Group, Anaheim, Calif., 1973-75, Anaheim Pediatric Med. Group, 1975-79; practice medicine specializing in pediatrics Anaheim, 1979-96, Camas, Wash., 1996—. Fellow Am. Acad. Pediatrics; mem. Los Angeles Pediatric Soc., Orange County Pediatric Soc., Adventist Internat. Med. Soc., Chinese Adventist Physicians' Assn. Avocations: music, reading, gardening. Office: 411 NE 6th Ave Camas WA 98607-2037

LIEM, EDWIN T.H. lawyer; b. Jakarta, Indonesia, Mar. 16, 1963; M in Med. Sci., U. Amsterdam, The Netherlands, 1986, M in Netherlands Notarial Law, M in Netherlands Pvt. Law, U. Amsterdam, The Netherlands, 1989. Cert. Netherlands law practice, crown appt. civil law notary. Ptnr. Caron & Stevens/Baker & McKenzie, Amsterdam, 1989-96, Wouters Advt. & Notary/Andersen Legal, Amsterdam, 1998-2000. Contbr. articles to profl. jours. Mem. Royal Profl. Orgn. Civil Law Notaries. Office: Baker & McKenzie PO Box 2720 1000 CS Amsterdam Netherlands Fax: 31 20 5517554. E-mail: edwin.hiem@bahernet.com.

LIEM, KHIAN KIOE, medical entomologist; b. Semarang, Java, Indonesia, Jan. 11, 1942; came to U.S., 1969; s. Coen Ing T and Marie Soei-Nio (Goei) L.; m. Anita Tumewu, Apr. 3, 1980; children: Brian Dexter, Tiffany Marie, Jennifer Amanda, Ashley Elizabeth. BS, Bandung Inst. Tech., Bandung, Indonesia, 1964; MS, Bandung Inst. Tech., 1966, Eastern Ill. U., 1970; PhD, U. Ill., 1975. Registered profl. entomologist, vector ecologist. Grad. teaching asst. Bandung Inst. Tech., 1964-66, grad. instr., 1966-68; grad. rsch./teaching asst. Eastern Ill. U., 1969-70; grad. teaching asst. U. Ill., 1970-74; med. entomologist South Cook County Mosquito Abatement Dist., Harvey, Ill., 1974-76, mgr./dir. med. entomologist, 1977—. Cons. U.S. AID, Washington, 1979--. Recipient Community Svc. award Asian Am. Coalition, 1993. Mem. Am. Mosquito Control Assn. (chmn. resolution com. 1977-78, mem. editorial bd. 1980-83, mem. worldwide com. 1987—), Ill. Mosquito Control Assn. (pres. 1979-81), Entomol. Soc. Am. (com. on book revs.), Am. Tropical Medicine and Hygiene Assn., Am. Registry of Profl. Entomologists, Scientists Inst. Pub. Info., Soc. Vector Ecology, Sigma Xi, Phi Sigma. Roman Catholic. Avocations: soccer, tennis, martial arts, camping, classical music. Home: 8012 Binford Dr Orland Park IL 60462-2300 Office: Mosquito Abatement Dist 15440 Dixie Hwy Harvey IL 60426-2801 E-mail: sccmad@aol.com.

LIEN, BRUCE HAWKINS, minerals and oil company executive; b. Waubay, S.D., Apr. 7, 1927; s. Peter Calmer and LaRece Catherine (Holm) L.; m. Deanna Jean Browning, May 4, 1978. BS in Bus., Wyo. U., 1953; D in Bus. (hon.), S.D. Sch. Mines & Tech., 1996; hon. doctorate, SDSMT, 1996. Corp. exec. Pete Lien & Sons, Inc., Rapid City, S.D., 1944-60, bd. chmn., 1960—, Concorde Gaming Corp., 1990—, Browning Resources U.S., 1989—. Chmn. Cmty. Chest, Rapid City, S.D., 1956; pres. U. Wyo. Found., 1989-90; life bd. dirs. Salvation Army. 1st lt. U.S. Army, 1945-47, 50-52. Recipient Disting. Svc. award S.D. Sch. Mines, Rapid City, 1972, Disting. Svc. award Cosmopolitan Internat., Rapid City, 1983; named Disting. Alumnus, Wyo. U., Laramie, 1982, 1996. Mem. Internat. Lime Assn. (pres. 1973-75), Nat. Lime Assn. (pres. 1973-75, Merit award 1973, bd. dirs.), VFW, Am. Legion, Cosmopolitan Club, Masons, Elks. Republican. Lutheran. Home: PO Box 440 Rapid City SD 57709-0440 Office: Pete Lien & Sons Inc I 90 & Deadwood Ave PO Box 440 Rapid City SD 57709-0440

LIEN, PEI-TE, political scientist, educator; b. Hwa-lien, Taiwan, Mar. 24, 1957; came to U.S., 1979; d. Chien-kum Lien and Yu-cheng Chang; m. Wei Shyy, Jan. 3, 1981 (divorced); children: Albert, Alice. BA, Nat. Taiwan U., 1979; MA, U. Fla., 1991, PhD, 1995. Corr. World Jour., N.Y.C., 1989—91; assoc. prof. polit. sci. and ethnic studies U. Utah, Salt Lake City, 1995—. Co-chair Asian Pacific Am. Caucus, Washington, 1999—2001. Author: Political Participation of Asian Americans, 1997, Making of Asian America Through Political Participation, 2001. Bd. dirs. Utah Org. of Chinese Ams. NSF grantee, 1999-01, book award winner in Race, Ethnicity and Politics, Am. Polit. Sci. Assn. Fellow Social Sci. Rsch. Coun. (postdoctoral fellow 1999); mem. Am. Polit. Sci. Assn., Assn. Asian Am. Studies, Midwest Polit. Sci. Assn., So. Polit. Sci. Assn. Democrat. Avocations: gardening, hiking. Office: Dept Polit Sci U Utah 260 S Central Campus Dr 252 Salt Lake City UT 84112-9152 E-mail: plien@poli-sci.utah.edu.

LIENEMANN, DELMAR ARTHUR, SR. accountant, real estate developer; b. Papillion, Nebr., May 17, 1920; s. Arthur Herman and Dorothea M. (Marth) L.; m. Charlotte Peck, Jun 17, 1944 (dec. Mar. 1995); children: Delmar Arthur Jr., David (dec.), Diane, Douglas, Dorothy, Daniel, Denise. BS, U. Nebr., 1941. CPA, Nebr. Acct. Wickstrom Supply, Lincoln, Nebr., 1941, L.L. Coryell & Sons, Lincoln, 1942, Lester Buckley, CPA, Lincoln, 1943-45; pvt. practice, 1945—. Pres., v.p., sec., treas., bldg. chmn., charter mem. Christ Luth. Ch., Lincoln, 1949-70; co-commr. Lancaster County, Lincoln, 1954-58; pres. Lincoln Symphony Orch. Found., 1984—, Ethel S. Abbott Charitable Found. Mem. AICPA, N.E. Soc. CPA, Colo. Soc. CPA, Tex. Soc. CPA, Sertoma (sec.-treas. Lincoln chpt. 1952-68, Internat. Sertoman of Yr. 1962), Hillcrest Country Club, Nebr. Club, Nebr. Chancelors Club, Nebr. Touchdown Club, Nebr. Power Club, Nebr. Rebounders Club. Republican. Avocation: travel. Office: PO Box 81407 Lincoln NE 68501-1407

LIENHARD, JOHN HENRY, IV, mechanical engineer, educator; b. St. Paul, Aug. 17, 1930; s. John Henry and Catherine Edith Lienhard; m. Carol Ann Bratton, June 20, 1959; children: John Henry V, Andrew Joseph. AS, Multnomah Jr. Coll., 1949; BS, Oreg. State Coll., 1951; MSME, U. Wash., 1953; PhD in Mech. Engring., U. Calif., Berkeley, 1961; PhD (hon.), U. Houston, 2002, Sacred Heart U., 2002. Assoc. prof. mech. engring. Wash. State U., Pullman, 1961-67; prof. mech. engring. dept. U. Ky., Lexington, 1967-80; prof. mech. engring. U. Houston, 1980-89, M.D. Anderson prof.

mech. engring. and history, 1989—2000, prof. emeritus, 2000—. Clyde chair prof. U. Utah, Salt Lake City, 1981. Author (with C. L. Tien): (book) Statistical Thermodynamics, 1971, Statistical Thermodynamics, 2d edit., 1979; author: (with E. T. Layton) History of Heat Transfer, 1988; author: A Heat Transfer Textbook, 1991; author: (with J. H. Lienhard V) A Heat Transfer Textbook, 3d edit., 2001; author: (with others) James Turrell: Spirit and Light, 1997; author, host (radio) The Engines of Our Ingenuity; contbr. articles to profl. jours. Mem.: ASME (hon. Heat Transfer Meml. award, Charles Russ Richards award, Engr. Historian award 1998), Am. Soc. Engring. Edn. (Ralph Coates Roe Tchg. medal). Episcopalian. Home: 3719 Durhill St Houston TX 77025-4006 Office: U Houston Dept Mech Engring Houston TX 77204-0001 E-mail: jhl@uh.edu.

LIEPMANN, HANS WOLFGANG, physicist, educator; b. Berlin, Germany, July 3, 1914; arrived in U.S., 1939, naturalized, 1945; s. Wilhelm and Emma (Leser) Liepmann; m. Kate Kaschinsky, June 19, 1939 (div.); m. Dietlind Wegener Goldschmidt, 1954; 2 children. Student, U. Istanbul, 1933—35, U. Prague, 1935; PhD, U. Zurich, 1938; DEngring (hon.) , Tech. U. Aachen, 1985. Research fellow U. Zurich, 1938—39; mem. faculty Calif. Inst. Tech., Pasadena, 1939, prof. aeronautics, 1949—, dir. Grad. Aeronautical Labs., 1972—85, Charles Lee Powell prof. fluid mechanics and thermodynamics, 1976—83, Theodore von Kármán prof. aeronautics, 1983—85, Theodore von Kármán prof. aeronautics emeritus, 1985—. Mem. research and tech. adv. com. on basic rsch. NASA. Author (with A.E. Puckett): Aerodynamics of a Compressible Fluid, 1947; author: (with A. Roshko) Elements of Gasdynamics, 1957; contbr. articles to profl. jours. Recipient Physics prize, U. Zurich, 1939, Prandtl Ring, German Soc. Aeros. and Astronautics, 1968, Worcester Reed Warner medal, ASME, 1969, Michelson-Morley award, Case Inst. Tech., 1979, Nat. medal of Sci., U.S. Dept. Commerce, 1986, Guggenheim medal, Daniel Guggenheim Med. Bd. of Awards, 1986, Lord Found. award, 1990, Nat. medal of Tech., U.S. Dept. Commerce, 1993. Address: Calif Inst Tech 104-50 Dept Aeronautics 1200 E California Blvd Pasadena CA 91125-0001 also: 555 Haverrtorh Rd Flintridge CA 91011 E-mail: liepmann@cco.caltech.edu.

LIERMAN, EILEEN CLAIRE, health care administrator; b. Bklyn., Dec. 16, 1951; d. Stephen A. and Nancy (Cunningham) Myers; m. E. Paul Lierman, June 2, 1973. BA, Fordham U., 1973; MS, NYU, 1975; MBA, Fordham U., 1981; postgrad. Columbia U., 1984—. Supr. nuclear medicine Montefiore Hosp. Affiliation, Bronx, N.Y., 1978-85; dir. fin. St. Vincent-North Richmond, S.I., N.Y., 1985-86; adminstr. Beth Israel Med. ctr., N.Y.C., 1986—; mem. adv. bd. nuclear medicine Manhattan Coll., Bronx, 1981-85. Recipient Dir.'s award Montefiore Hosp. Affiliation, 1984. Mem. Health Care Fin. Mgmt., Nat. Assn. Female Execs., Soc. Nuclear Medicine. Roman Catholic. Avocations: antiques, hiking, tennis. Office: Beth Israel Med Ctr 10 Nathan D Perlman Pl New York NY 10003-3881

LIESEMER, RONALD NEWELL, plastics company executive; b. Toledo, Mar. 23, 1938; s. Newell Conrad and Vernice A. (Gensrick) L.; m. Karen Sue Lundgren, June 17, 1961; children: Jeffrey, Susan. BA, North Ctrl. Coll., Naperville, Ill., 1960; MS, Wayne State U., 1963, PhD, 1965. With DuPont Co., 1965-88, mktg. rsch. mgr. Del., 1977-79, sales mgr., Mylar, 1979-80, bus. mgr., Mylar Geneva, 1980-84, mgr. tech. svc. labs. Wilmington, 1984-88; v.p. tech. Am. Plastics Coun., Washington, 1988—2001. Contbr. chpt. to book, articles to profl. jours. Pres. Wessynton Homes Assn., Alexandria, Va., 1996. Mem. Am. Chem. Soc., Soc. Plastics Engrs. Office: Am Plastics Coun 1300 Wilson Blvd Ste 800 Arlington VA 22209-2321

LIESENFELD, VINCENT JOSEPH, lawyer; b. St. Paul, Feb. 16, 1947; s. Vincent Edward and Agnes Lillian L.; children: Patricia, Peter. BA summa cum laude, U. Minn., 1970; student, U. Reading, Eng., 1973-74; PhD, U. Wis., 1978; JD summa cum laude, Oklahoma City U., 1996. Bar: Colo., D.C., Minn., Okla., Tex., U.S. Supreme Ct., U.S. Tax Ct. Writer Minn. State Employment Svc., St. Paul, 1970, U. Wis. News and Publs., Madison, 1972; asst. prof. English U. Okla., Norman, 1977-83, assoc. prof., 1983-96; of counsel Salem Law Offices, 1996—. Vis. scholar UCLA, 1980; contbg. writer Am. Coll. Testing Program, Iowa City, 1982; rsch. cons. civil rights cases, Norman, 1982—. Author: The Licensing Act of 1737, 1984; editor: The Stage & the Licensing Act, 1981; contbr. articles and revs. to profl. jours. Vol. Spl. Olympics, Norman, 1990. Fulbright scholar, 1973-74; Woodrow Wilson fellow, 1969, W.A. Clark Libr. Mellon fellow, 1980, Rsch. fellow NEH, 1980-81; Rsch. grantee U. Okla., 1978, 79, 81, Coll. of State Bar of Tex., 2001, 02. Mem. ABA, Am. Intellectual Property Law Assn., William J. Holloway Jr Am. Inn of Ct., Phi Beta Kappa, Phi Delta Phi, Phi Kappa Phi. Avocations: amateur radio, running, computer programming. Office: Salem Law Offices 111 N Peters Ave Ste 100 Norman OK 73069-7235

LIETZ, JEREMY JON, educational administrator, writer; b. Milw., Oct. 4, 1933; s. John Norman and Dorothy B. (Drew) L.; m. Cora Fernandez, Feb. 24, 1983; children: Cheryl, Brian, Angela, Andrew, Christopher, Jennifer. BS, U. Wis., Milw., 1961; MS, U. Wis., Madison, 1971; EdD, Marquette U., 1980. Tchr. Milw. Pub. Schs., 1961-63, diagnostic counselor, 1968-71, sch. adminstr., 1971-95, hearing panel ombudsman, 1999—, acting student svcs. coord., 1999—; tchr. Madison (Wis.) Pub. Schs., 1964-65; rsch. assoc. U. Wis., Madison, 1965-67; instr. Marquette U., Milw., 1980-82, Milwaukee U. Sch., 2000—. Lectr. HEW Conf. on Reading, Greeley, Colo., 1973, NAESP Conf. on Reading, St. Louis, 1974, various state and nat. orgns.; co-founder, bd. dirs., cons. Ednl. Leadership Inst., Shorewood, Wis., 1980—; dir. Religious Edn. Program, Cath. Elem. East, Milw., 1985-86. Author: The Elementary School Principal's Role in Special Education, 1982; contbr. numerous articles, chpts., tests, revs. to profl. jours. V.p. PTA, 1961-62. With U.S. Army, 1954-56, ETO. Recipient Cert. of Achievement award NAESP, 1974. Mem. AAAS, Assn. Wis. Sch. Adminstrs. (mem. state planning com. 1977-79, lectr. 1982), Adminstrs. and Suprs. Coun. (mem. exec. bd. dist. 1977-79, mem. contract negotiations com. 1991-95), Filipino Am. Assn. Wis., U. Wis. Alumni Assn. (Madison), Milw. Mcpl. Chess Assn., U.S. Chess Fedn., Phi Delta Kappa. Home: 424 Susan Ln Thiensville WI 53092-1451 Office: Ednl Leadership Inst PO Box 11411 Milwaukee WI 53211-0411 E-mail: dcphil@prodigy.net.

LIETZAU, WILLIAM KENDALL, career officer, lawyer; b. Annapolis, Md., Nov. 9, 1960; s. Karl Ernest and Janice Mae L.; m. Diane Michelle, May 19, 1984; children: Rachel Anne, Zachary Thomas. BS, U.S. Naval Acad., 1983; JD, Yale U., 1989; LLM, U.S. Army JAG Sch., 1995. Bar: Conn. 1989, Ct. Mil. Appeals 1990, U.S. Supreme Ct. 1995. Rifle co. comdr. USMC, Kaneohe Bay, Hawaii, 1984-87, spl asst. U.S. atty. Jacksonville, N.C., 1989-91, lt. col., 1995; chief prosecutor Camp Lejeune, N.C., 1991-92; chief def. counsel Iwakuni, Japan, 1992-93; dep. sta. judge adv. Japan, 1993-95; head law armed conflict br. Navy JAG, Washington, 1996-97; dep. legal counsel to chmn. Joint Chiefs Staff, 1997-99; chief mil. judge Atlantic cir., 1999-2000; cmdg. officer 1st RTBn., San Diego, 2000—02; spl. asst. to Dept. Def. gen. counsel, 2002—. Adj. prof. Georgetown U., Washington, 1998-2000; spkr. in field. Contbr. articles to profl. jours. U.S. del. Ottawa Conv. Banning Landmines, Terrorist Bombing Conv., Nuc. Terrorism Conv., Rome Treaty Internat. Criminal Ct., Hague Cultural Property Protocol. Recipient Major Gen. Pugh award, 1995; named Career Mil. Lawyer of the Yr. Judge Adv. Assn., 1998. Avocations: running, biking, lifting. Office: Rm 4A923 1600 Defense Pentagon Washington DC Home: 1500 Arlington Blvd Arlington VA 22209-3501 E-mail: wklietzau@msn.com., lietzauw@osdgc.osd.mil.

LIETZEN, JOHN HERVY, human resources executive, health agency volunteer; b. Kansas City, Kans., July 17, 1947; s. Walter Edwin and Kathleen Mae (Griffith) L.; children: Gwendolyn Therese, Anne Gabrielle, Sarah Kathleen. BS, Mo. Valley Coll., 1974; MS, U. Mo., 1976; postgrad. U. Nebr., 1982-88. With Union Pacific R.R., 1971—, yard condr. Kans., 1971-77, pers. officer Omaha, 1977-78, pers. dir. Cheyenne, Wyo., 1978-79, sr. tng. officer dept. claims, 1979-83, mgr. staffing, 1983-84, mgr. affirmative action, 1984-86, human resources tng. and devel. cons. Omaha, 1986-89, 94—, Salt Lake City, 1989-94. Bd. dirs. Berkshire Village, Kansas City, 1976-77; mem. bd. ministries Valley View Meth. Ch., Overland Park, Kans., 1976-77; pastor and staff rels. com. Hanscom Pk. United Meth. Ch., 1980-81, lay leader, 1983; asst. leader Wyo. coun. Girl Scouts U.S.A., Cheyenne, 1978-79, asst. leader, Omaha, 1980-89, Salt Lake, 1989—, bd. dirs. Great Plains Girl Scout Coun., 1987-89; exec. bd. Nebr. affiliate Am. Diabetes Assn., 1981-89, pres. Midlands chpt., 1982-84, mem. planning and orgn. com., 1986-87, bd. dirs. Utah affiliate, 1990-94, co-founder Omaha Insulin Pump Club, 1986; loaned exec. United Way of Midlands, 1984. Sgt. U.S. Army, 1968-71, Germany. Mem. ASTD, Am. Soc. Pers. and Guidance Assn., Adult and Continuing Edn. Assn. Nebr. (mem. planning com. 1982-84), Nat. Soc. for Performance and Instrn. Republican. Office: 1416 Dodge St # Pf2 Omaha NE 68179-0001

LIEVERMAN, THEODORE MARK, lawyer; b. Hampton, Va., Dec. 1, 1949; AB, Vassar Coll., 1971; JD, Northeastern U., 1978. Bar: Mass. 1978, Pa. 1979, U.S. Dist. Ct. (ea. dist.) Pa. 1980, U.S. Dist. Ct. (so. dist.) N.Y. 1995, U.S. Ct. Appeals (3rd cir.) 1980, U.S. Dist. Ct. (mid. dist.) Pa. 1982, U.S. Ct. Appeals (11th cir.) 1982, U.S. Ct. Appeals (D.C. and fed. cirs.) 1984, U.S. Ct. Appeals (2nd cir.) 1995, U.S. Supreme Ct. 1986, N.J. 1988, U.S. Dist. Ct. N.J. 1988. Assoc. Kirschner, Walters & Willig, Phila., 1978-81; pvt. practice, 1982-88; assoc. Tomar, Simonoff, Adourian & O'Brien, Haddonfield, N.J., 1988-93; shareholder Tomar, Simonoff, Adourian, O'Brien, Kaplan, Jacoby & Graziano, Cherry Hill, 1994-2000; adj. prof. Rutgers-Camden Law Sch., 1991-94; lawyer Spector, Roseman & Kodroff, 2000—01, ptnr., 2002—. Of counsel Allan Kanner & Assocs., Phila., 1987-88; gen. counsel Phila. Area Project on Occupational Safety and Health, 1983-91, counsel to ct. apptd. election officer Internat. Bhd. of Teamsters, 1995-97; mem. AFL-CIO Lawyers Coordinating Com.; trustee N.J. Adv. Coun. on Safety and Health, 1994—. Mem. adv. bd. Lawyers Alliance for Nuclear Arms Control, Phila., 1984—88; vol. atty. ACLU, 1985—88. Mem. Phila. Bar Assn. E-mail: tlieverman@srk-law.com.

LIEVORE, RUSTON, pathologist, consultant; b. Colatina, Brazil, July 6, 1963; s. José Anselmo and Edith Pereira (Cardoso) L. Grad., U. Fed. do Espirito Santo, Vitória, Brazil, 1989. Med. diplomate; residence fo gen. physician diplomate, residence of clin. pathology diplomate, speciality of clin. pathology diplomate. Gen. physician Hucam-U. Fed. do Espirito Santo, Vitória, 1990-91; clin. pathologist Hosp. and Clinics-U. de São Paulo, Brazil, 1992-94; clin. pathologist, immunohematology chief Blood Bank of Hucam, Vitória, 1995—; clin. pathology, tech. dir. Pathology Lab., 1995—. Contbr. articles to profl. jours. Mem. AAAS, Am. Soc. for Microbiology, Am. Assn. for Clin. Chemistry. Roman Catholic. Avocations: reading, listening to classical music, painting, traveling, drawing. Home: Rua Miguel Jantorno 279 29043220 Vitória Brazil

LIEW, FAH POW, mechanical engineer; b. Kuala Lumpur, Selangor, Malaysia, Sept. 30, 1960; s. Yeam Shoon and Park Yuen (Yeong) L. BA in Computer Sci., SUNY, Buffalo, 1983; BS in Aerospace Engring., SUNY, 1983, MS in Mech. Engring., 1987. Tchg. asst. SUNY, Buffalo, 1983-85, rsch. asst., 1985-87; sr. mktg. rep. E.I. DuPont de Nemours & Co., Wilmington, 1988—. Mem. AIAA, ASME (assoc.), N.Y. Soc. Profl. Engrs., S.E. Asian Student Assn. (pres. 1980-81). E-mail: fah-pow-liew@usa.dupont.com.

LIEWENDAHL, BO KRISTIAN, clinical pathologist, nuclear physician; b. Helsinki, Aug. 21, 1941; s. Ernst August and Irina (Semenov) L.; 1 child, Kari Peter Nikolai. MD, U. Helsinki, 1966, PhD, 1968. Med. diplomate. Resident in clin. chemistry Helsinki U. Hosp., 1966-69, resident in medicine, 1969-72, cons. lab. dept., 1974-82; asst. prof., lectr. U. Helsinki, 1977-96, prof., 1996—; chief physician divsn. nuclear medicine Helsinki U. Hosp., 1983-99; NIH fellow U. Calif., San Francisco, 1972-73. Vis. scientist U. Wis., Madison, U. Va., Charlottesville, 1982; dir. nuclear medicine rsch. group Minerva Inst. Found., Helsinki, Finland, 1977—2002; sec. gen. Minerva Found., 1997—2002; sec. European Thyroid Assn. Congress, Helsinki, 1976; pres. European Nuclear Medicine Congress, Helsinki, 1984, Scandinavian Congress Nuclear Medicine, Helsinki, 1998; chmn. European Congress Clin. Chemistry, Tampere, Finland, 1995; del. nuclear medicine sect. European Union Med. Spltys., 1994—2002; del. European Bd. Nuclear Medicine, 1995—2002. Author, editor Scandinavian Jour. Clin. Lab. Investigation, 1986—96; mem. : editl. bd. European Jour. Nuclear Medicine, 1991—2002; contbr. articles to profl. jours. Recipient J.W. Runeberg Prize Finnish Med. Soc., 1969, Ann. Lecture Prize Finnish Med.Soc., 1973, T. Heiskanen Meml. Prize Finnish Radiol. Soc. and Finnish Nuclear Medicine Soc., 1985, Gold medal Minerva Found., Helsinki, 1989. Mem.: N.Y. Acad. Scis., Soc. Nuc. Medicine N.Y., World Fedn. Nuc. Medicine and Biology (del. 1988—, organizing com. 8th World Congress, Santiago, Chile 2002, mem. comgress sci. com. 1998—), European Thyroid Assn., European Assn. Nuc. Medicine (del. 1988—95, mem. organizing com. congress in Copenhagen 1996, Congress prize 1991), Finnish Soc. Nuc. Medicine (hon.; pres. 1996—98). Lutheran. Achievements include rsch. in thyroid function tests, particularly accurate assays for free thyroid hormone concentrations in blood, nuclear medicine procedures for diagnosis of oncological, hematological and neurological diseases. Office: Minerva Found Inst Biomedicum Helsinki Haartmansgatan 8 00290 Helsinki Finland

LIFCHITZ, MAX, composer, performer, music educator; b. Mexico City, Nov. 11, 1948; came to U.S. 1966; s. José Lifchitz and Betty Shumsky. MusB, The Juilliard Sch., 1970, MS, 1971; AM, Harvard U., 1973. Instr. Manhattan Sch. Music, 1976-77; asst. prof. music Columbia U., 1977-86; assoc. prof. music SUNY, Albany, 1986—, assoc. prof. Latin Am. studies, 1991—. Exec. dir. North/South Consonance, Inc., N.Y.C., 1980—; prodr. North/South Recs., 1992—. Composer, author: (piano) Affinities, 1979; (violin) Transformations #2, 1982; (orch.) Yellow Ribbons #17, 1983. Fellow Nat. Endowment Arts, Washington, 1975, ASCAP, 1979, Creative Artists Pub. Svc. Program, 1979, Guggenheim Found., 1982. Mem. Nat. Assn. Composers (treas. East Coast chpt. 1981—, pres. 1992—), Am. Soc. Composers (co-chmn. Region II 1986-96), Coll. Music Soc. (pres. N.E. chpt. 1996-2000). Office: SUNY Pac # 215 Albany NY 12222-0001 E-mail: ns.concerts@att.net.

LIFESO, ROBERT MURRAY, surgeon; b. Hamilton, Ont., Can., Apr. 19, 1945; s. Charles Murray and Josephine Rose (Dosman) L.; m. Susan Elizabeth Elliott, Dec. 20, 1968; children: Catherine Elizabeth, Erin Christine, David Charles. MD, U. Toronto, 1969. Diplomate Am. Bd. Orthopaedic Surgery. Rotating internship to chief resident Toronto Gen. Hosp., Hosp. for Sick Children, Toronto, 1969-70, 72-77; pvt. practice Kitimat, Northern B.C., Can., 1970-71, NSW, Australia, 1972; rsch. resident Toronto E. Gen. and Orthopaedic Hosp., 1972-73; asst. resident in neurosurgery Toronto-Wellesley Hosp., 1973, asst. resident in orthopaedics, 1974; chief resident orthopaedics Sunnybrook Med. Ctr., Toronto, 1977; chmn. dept. orthopaedic surgery King Faisal Specialist Hosp., Riyadh, Saudi Arabia, 1978-87; orthopaedic surgeon to King Fahad Bin Abdul Aziz, Saudi Arabia, 1981-87; chief orthopaedic surgery VAMC, Buffalo, 1987-91. Dir. Min-Rad, Inc., Buffalo; adj. prof. orthopaedic surgery, D'Youville Coll., Buffalo; clin. prof. SUNY, Buffalo; dir. Spinal Cord Injury Unit, Erie County Med. Ctr., Buffalo; cons. spine surgeon Roswell Park Cancer Inst., Buffalo; attending spine surgeon, Buffalo Gen. Hosp.; mem. faculty senate SUNY. Contbg. author books in field, including Principles and Practice of Genitourinary Oncology, 1996, Surgery of the Hand and Upper Extremity, 1996, Scanning of the Spine, 1983; contbr. numerous articles to profl. jours. Vol. spine surgeon Tribuvan U. Tchg. Hosp., Kathmandu, Nepal, 1986 others. Fellow Am. Coll. Surgeons, Royal Coll. Surgeons Can.; mem. Can. Med. Assn., Ont. Med. Assn., Acad. Medicine Toronto, Can. Orthopaedic Assn., Orthopaedic Overseas, Erie County Med. Soc., N.Y. Med. Soc., Am. Acad. Orthopaedic Surgeons, AMA, Medcin Sans Frontiers, Orthopaedic Trauma Assn. Home: 184 Halston Pkwy East Amherst NY 14051-1890 Office: Spine Ctr Erie County Med Ctr 462 Grider St Buffalo NY 14215-3021 Fax: 716-898-5713.

LIFFERS, WILLIAM ALBERT, retired chemical company executive; b. Union City, N.J., Jan. 12, 1929; s. William F. and Gertrude (Wildemann) L.; m. Mary Rafferty, Sept. 5, 1953; children— Steven, Linda, Wendy. BS in Bus. Adminstrn, Seton Hall U., 1953. With Am. Cyanamid Co., Wayne, N.J., 1953-93; v.p. Cyanamid Internat., 1972-74; pres. Cyanamid Internat. (Cyanamid Americas/Far East), 1974-76, corp. v.p., 1976-77, sr. v.p., dir., 1977-78, vice chmn., 1978-93; ret., 1993. Sr. advisor UN Devel. Programme, 1994; bd. dirs. Great Atlantic & Pacific Tea Co. Bd. dirs. Nat. Policy Assn., N.J. Inst. Tech. With Fin. Corps U.S. Army, 1951-53.

LIFLAND, WILLIAM THOMAS, lawyer; b. Jersey City, Nov. 15, 1928; s. Charles and Carolyn (Francks) L.; m. Nancy Moffat, May 29, 1954; children— Carol M., Charles C., J. Kerin, David T. BS, Yale U., 1949; JD, Harvard U., 1952. Bar: D.C. 1954, N.Y. 1955, N.J. 1965-2002; Senior Counsel, 2002-. Law clk. to Justice John M. Harlan U.S. Supreme Ct., 1954-55; assoc. Cahill Gordon & Reindel, N.Y.C., 1955-58, Paris, 1958-60, ptnr. N.Y.C., 1965—2002, sr. counsel, 2002—. Adj. prof. Fordham Law Sch., N.Y.C. Served as lt. USAF, 1952-54 Mem.: ABA, Assn. Bar City N.Y., D.C. Bar Assn., N.J. Bar Assn., N.Y. State Bar Assn., Nassau Club (Princeton, NJ), India House Club (N.Y.C.). Office: Cahill Gordon & Reindel 80 Pine St Fl 17 New York NY 10005-1790 E-mail: wlifland@cahill.com.

LIFSCHULTZ, PHILLIP, financial and tax consultant, accountant, lawyer; b. Oak Park, Ill., Mar. 5, 1927; s. Abraham Albert and Frances Rhoda (Siegel) L.; m. Edith Louise Leavitt, June 27, 1948; children: Gregory, Bonnie, Jodie. BS in Acctg., U. Ill., 1949; JD, John Marshall Law Sch., 1956. Bar: Ill. 1956; CPA. Tax mgr. Arthur Andersen & Co., Chgo., 1957-63; v.p. taxes Montgomery Ward & Co., 1963-78; fin. v.p., contr. Henry Crown & Co., 1978-81; prin. Phillip Lifschultz & Assocs., 1981—. Exec. dir. Dodi Orgn., 1987-90; v.p. Altra Travel, Northbrook, Ill., 1975—; v.p. Tax Execs. Inst., Chgo., 1977-78; pres. Great Lakes Shoe Co., Bannockburn, Ill., 1996—. Adv. coun. Coll. Commerce and Bus. Adminstrn., U. Ill., Urbana-Champaign, 1977-78; chmn. Civic Fedn. Chgo., 1980-82; chmn. adv. bd. to Auditor Gen. of Ill., 1965-73; project dir. Exec. Svc. Corps of Chgo., Chgo. Bd. Edn. and State of Ill. projects, 1980-87. With U.S. Army, 1945-46. Mem. Am. Arbitration Assn. (comml. panel 1983-94), Ill. Bar Assn., Chgo. Bar Assn., Am. Inst. CPAs, Ill. CPA Soc., Nat. Retail Merchants Assn. (chmn. tax. com. 1975-78), Am. Retail Fedn. (chmn. taxation com. 1971). Home and Office: 442 Kelburn Rd Apt 123 Deerfield IL 60015-4370 E-mail: papalif@aol.com.

LIFSHITZ, FIMA, pediatrician, endocrinologist; b. Mexico City, Apr. 24, 1938; s. Jose and Betty Lifshitz; m. Jere Ziffer, June 2, 1985; children: Eric, Karl. BS, Yavne Coll., Mexico City, 1955; MD, Nat. U., Mexico City, 1961. Diplomate Am. Bd. Pediatrics, Am. Bd. Pediatric Endocrinology. Prof. pediatrics Cornell U. Med. Ctr., N.Y.C., 1975-91; assoc. dir. pediatrics North Shore U. Hosp., Manhasset, N.Y., 1977-90, vice chmn. dept. pediatrics, 1990-91; prof. pediatrics SUNY Health Sci. Ctr., Bklyn., 1991—; chmn. dept. pediatrics Maimonides Med. Ctr., 1991-97; chief of staff Miami (Fla.) Children's Hosp., 1997—2000, chief nutrition scis., 2000—. Extraordinary prof. Serono chair for postdoctoral students U. Complutense, Madrid, 1998-99; dir. med. edn. St. George's Sch. Medicine, Grenada, W.I., 1999—; chmn. postgrad. course Miami Children's Hosp., 1997—; mem. adv. com. Internat. Soc. Pediat. Nutrition, 1992—. Named Man of Yr., Juvenile Diabetes Found., 1996. Fellow Am. Acad. Pediats., Am. Coll. Endocrinology, Lawson-Wilkins Pediat. Endocrine Soc.; mem. Soc. for Pediat. Rsch. (emeritus), Am. Coll. Physician Execs. Office: Miami Children's Hosp 3100 SW 62d Ave Miami FL 33155 E-mail: fima@drlifshitz.net.

LIFSON, KALMAN ALAN, retired management consultant, retail executive; b. Mpls., Oct. 15, 1926; s. Maurice Kalman and Gertrude (Shulkin) L.; m. Irene Londer, June 17, 1950 (dec. July 1968); m. Judith Abrams, Sept. 3, 1969; children: Valerie Leftwich, Kipp, Ione Spear, Stacey Dorfman, Grant Dorfman. BS in Naval Tech., U. Minn., 1946, MBA, 1949; PhD in Psychology, Purdue U., 1951. Commd. ensign USN, 1945, lt. (j.g), 1952; engring. officer Panama Canal Zone, 1945-46; supr. indsl. engring. Temco Aircraft, Dallas, 1951-52; mgmt. engring. officer USN, Washington, 1953-54, resigned; prin. Lifson, Wilson, Ferguson & Winick, Dallas, 1954-94, Pers. Decisions, Inc., Dallas, 1995-99; chmn. Harris'Dept. Stores, San Bernadino, Calif., 1980-94, Tex. Rsch. and Electronic Corp. and successors, Dallas, 1962-94, Electronic Mgmt. Info. Sys., 1970-94; chmn. emeritus B.R. Blackmarr & Assocs., Dallas, 1986-99; ret., 1999. Chmn. Fed. Home Loan Bank of 9th Dist., Little Rock, 1979-80; spkr. fields of psychology, retailing, banking, ops. rsch. Contbr. articles to profl. jours. Chmn. Congl. Commn. on Guaranteed Student Loans, Washington, 1975, Commn. on Orgn. of U.S. Dept. Labor, Washington, 1976; mem. Tex. Commn. on State Employee Productivity, Austin, Tex., 1985. Mem. Am. Psychol. Assn., World Pres. Orgn., Columbian Club (treas. 1950-54), Crescent Club, Sigma Xi. Jewish. E-mail: klifson906@aol.com. *"Winners" are those who can make the big play, who can turn the game around, who can conceive and institute dramatic changes. Those few of us who have been so endowed and developed must use our winnership to effect significant improvements to the well-being of those within our spheres of influence.*

LIFTIG, S. RICK, dentist, author; b. Conn., July 1953; s. Alvin Liftig. BA, U. Conn., Storrs, 1975; DMD, U. Conn., Farmington, 1979. Pvt. practice gen. dentistry, Waterbury, Conn., 1980-82, West Hartford, 1980—. Author: The Frugal Woodworker, 1985; editor/pub. Elmwood Gazette E-Mail Newsletter; contbr. articles to profl. jours. Com. chmn. cub. scout pack Boy Scouts Am., West Hartford, 1996-98; sec. West Hartford Vision, 1999—; chmn. Elmwood Day Celebration, 1999-2000. Fellow Acad. Gen. Dentistry; mem. ADA, Hartford Dental Soc., Conn. State Dental Assn., Rotary (West Hartford RYLA chmn.). E-mial. Office: 10 Princeton St West Hartford CT 06110-1893 E-mail: srick@snet.net.

LIFTIN, JOHN M. lawyer; Sr. v.p., gen. counsel Prudential Fin., Inc., Newark. Office: Prudential Financial Inc 751 Broad St Newark NJ 07102-3777

LIFTIN, JOHN MATTHEW, lawyer; b. Washington, June 25, 1943; children: Eric, Hilary. AB, U. Pa., 1964; LLB, Columbia U., 1967. Bar: N.Y. 1967, D.C. 1974, U.S. Dist. Ct. D.C. 1975, U.S. Ct. Appeals (D.C. cir.) 1975, U.S. Supreme Ct. 1980. Assoc. Sullivan & Cromwell, N.Y.C., 1967-71; spl. counsel to chmn. SEC, Washington, 1971-72, assoc. dir. market reg. div., 1972-74; ptnr. Rogers & Wells, 1974-85; pres. Quadrex Securities Corp., N.Y.C., 1985-87; sr. v.p., gen. counsel Kidder, Peabody Group Inc., 1987-96, Prudential Fin., Newark, 1998—. Mem. adv. bd. securities regulation and law reports Bur. Nat. Affairs, Inc., Washington, 1979—; mem. N.Y. Stock Exch. Legal Adv. Com., 2000—. Contbr. articles on securities law to profl. jours. Mem. ABA (former chmn. com. on fed. regulation of securities), Univ. Club. Office: Prudential Fin Inc Prudential Plz 751 Broad St Newark NJ 07102-3714

LIFTON, ROBERT KENNETH, diversified companies executive; b. N.Y.C., Jan. 9, 1928; s. Benjamin and Anna (Pike) L.; m. Loretta J. Silver, Sept. 5, 1954; children: Elizabeth Gail Lifton Hooper, Karen Grace Lifton Healy. BBA magna cum laude, CCNY, 1948; LLB, Yale U., 1951; doctorate (hon.), Bar Ilan U., Israel, 1993. Bar: N.Y. 1952. Assoc. Kaye, Scholer, Fierman, Hays & Handler, N.Y.C., 1955-56; asst. to pres. Glickman Corp., 1956-57; pres. Robert K. Lifton, Inc., 1957-61; chmn. bd. Terminal Tower Co., Inc., Cleve., 1959-63; pres. Transcontinental Investing Corp., N.Y.C., 1961-72, chmn. bd., 1969-72; ptnr. Venture Assocs., 1972-89; pres. Preferred Health Care Ltd., 1983-88; chmn. bd. dirs. Marcade Group, Inc., 1986-91, Medis El, 1993—, Cell Diagnostics, Inc., 1992-99; chmn. bd. dirs., CEO Medis Techs., Ltd., N.Y.C., 1999—. CEO, chmn. bd. dirs. Team Am., Inc., 1983-85; treas. Consol. Accessories Corp., 1980-88, Caron's Connection, Inc., 1985-89; bd. dirs. exec. investment com. Bank Leumi U.S.A., N.Y.C.; bd. dirs. Leumi Investment Svcs., Inc.; mem. faculty Columbia U. Law Sch., 1973-78, Yale U. Law Sch., 1972-75; guest lectr. Practicing Law Inst., Yale Law Sch., Pace Inst., NYU; founder Nat. Exec. Conf., Washington, Inc.; chmn. oversight com. for Masters Degree, NYU Real Estate Inst., 1987-88. Author: Practical Real Estate: Legal Tax and Business Strategies, 1978; contbr. articles to profl. jours. and handbooks (Graham and Dodd award for best article Fin. Analyst Jour. 1967). Mem. McGovern econ. adv. com., 1972-73; chmn. parents com. Barnard Coll., 1976-78; mem. com. of the collection Whitney Mus., 1976-79; trustee Yale U. Sch. Fund, 1974-77, NYU Real Estate Inst., 1983-89; chmn., bd. dirs. Fund for Religious Liberty, 1987-88; pres. Am. Jewish Congress, 1988-94; chmn. Internat. Bd. U.S. Mid. East Project com. fgn. rels., 1994—; pres. Israel Policy Forum, 1994—, chmn. bd., 1996-97, chmn. emeritus, 1997—; bd. dirs. Builders for Peace, 1993—, Abraham Fund, 1993—, Tel Aviv Mus., 1996—, Besa Inst., 1994—. HIAS, 1990-96; mem. exec. com. AIPAC, 1990—; vice-chmn. NJCRAC, 1994—; exec. com. AIPAC, 1993-96; trustee Am. Friends of Bar Ilan U., 1996—, mem. global bd. trustees, 1997—; bd. dirs. Pub. Health Rsch. Inst., 1996—, vice chmn., 1997-98, chmn., 1998—; co-chmn. Internat. Ctr. Pub. Health, 1999; trustee Bar Ilan Global, 1997—; bd. dirs. Georgia O'Keeffe Mus., 1999— . Lt. (j.g.) USN, 1952-55. Recipient Achievement award Sch. Bus. Alumni Soc. CCNY, 1984, James Madison award Fund for Religious Liberty, 1987, Stephen S. Wise award Am. Jewish Congress, 1993. Mem. Order of Coif, Beta Gamma Sigma. Home: 873 Park Ave New York NY 10028-0808 Office: 805 3rd Ave New York NY 10022-7513

LIGARE, KATHLEEN MEREDITH, strategy and marketing executive; b. Providence, Aug. 29, 1950; d. Kenneth MacAllister and Carol (Smith) Ligare. BA, Carleton Coll., 1972; MS, Yale U., 1976; MBA, Northwestern U., 1982. Sr. assoc. Booz, Allen & Hamilton, Chgo., 1978-82; mgr. mktg. and product devel. GE Capital Corp., Barrington, Ill., 1982-83, planning mgr., 1983-84, region mgr., 1984-85; sr. v.p. sales and mktg. Gen. Electric Capital Corp., 1992-93, sr. v.p. internat., 1993-96; prin. KML Enterprises, Inc., Chgo., 1985-92; dir. sales and mktg. GE Capital Europe, Brussels, Belgium, 1995-97; sr. v.p., mng. dir. GE Capital Asia Pacific, Hong Kong, Hong Kong, 1997-99; sr. v.p. mktg. long term care divsn. GE Fin. Assurance, San Rafael, Calif., 1999-2000, sr. v.p. mktg. and product mgmt. Richmond, Va., 2001—. Author: Illinois Women's Directory, 1977. Bd. dirs. Midwest Women's Ctr., Chgo., 1978-89; chair, bd. dirs. alumni ann. fund Carleton Coll., 1990-93, bd. dirs., 1987-94, mem. alumni bd., 1989, trustee, 1993—. Office: GE Fin Assurance 6620 W Broad St Richmond VA 23230

LIGENZA, ANDREA ANGELA, nurse; b. Lansford, Pa., Apr. 7, 1952; d. Stanley Walter and Mary Ligenza. Diploma in Nursing, Hosp. of U. Pa., 1973; BS in Nursing, U. Pa., 1976. CRNP; cert. nurse practitioner, Pa. Staff nurse Hosp. of U. Pa., Phila., 1973-79, nurse practitioner cardio-thoracic surgery sect., 1979-91; preceptor nursing students U. Pa., 1985-91; nurse practitioner Cardiothoracic Surg. Assocs. Pa. Hosp., 1988-89, Bryn Mawr (Pa.) Hosp., 1991-93, Primary Care, Drexel Hill, Pa., 1992—2001; orthop. nurse practitioner MCP Hosp, Phila., 2002—. Eucharistic min. Roman Cath. Ch. Mem. Puccini Inst., Sigma Theta Tau. Republican. Avocations: classical music, tennis, travel.

LIGEROS, M. SUE, transport refrigeration executive; b. Boulder, Colo., June 25, 1948; d. Michael George Ligeros and F. Evelyn (Summers) Leonard. Student Denver Woman's Coll. Mgr. Ohio Skate, Toledo, 1974-76; gen. mgr. M.G.L. Leasing Co., Denver, 1976-77, Thermo King Truck Sales of Denver, 1977-81, pres., gen. mgr., 1982— ; pres. Nissan Diesel Truck Sales of Denver, Inc., 1986—. Recipient Pres.'s award Thermo King Corp., 1982. Mem. Thermo King Dealer Adv. Council (sec.-treas. 1984-86). Republican. Greek Orthodox. Avocations: hiking; camping; outdoor sports. Office: Thermo King of Denver Inc 4990 Monaco St Commerce City CO 80022-4610

LIGETT, WALDO BUFORD, chemist; b. Middletown, Ohio, Nov. 2, 1916; s. Waldo Buford and Mabel Louise (Berkley) L.; m. Ann Elizabeth Hartwell, Aug. 29, 1940; children: Robert A., John D., Michael T., Steven D., Daniel L. BS, Antioch Coll., 1939; MS, Purdue U., 1941, PhD, 1944, D.Sc. (hon.), 1965; grad., Advanced Mgmt. Program, Harvard U., 1967. Chemist Eastman Kodak Co., Rochester, N.Y., 1935-38; research supr. Ethyl Corp., Detroit, 1944-51, asst. dir. chem., 1951-52, asso. dir. chem., 1952-62, dir. research and devel., 1962-63; v.p. Celanese Chem. Co., Corpus Christi, Tex., 1963-64, v.p. tech. and mfg., 1964-66; tech. dir. Celanese Corp., N.Y.C., 1966-67, v.p., 1967-72, Franklin Inst., Phila., 1973-81; pres. Franklin Inst. Research Labs., 1975-81. Dir. Franklin-Hahnemann Inst., 1974-81 Patentee in field. Fellow Am. Inst. Chemists; mem. Am. Chem. Soc., AAAS, Indsl. Research Inst., Research Soc. Am., N.Y. Assn. Research Dirs., Am. Nuclear Soc., Atomic Indsl. Forum. Home: 377 Carolina Meadows Villa Chapel Hill NC 27517-7521

LIGGETT, HIRAM SHAW, JR. retired diversified industry financial executive; b. St. Louis, Jan. 12, 1932; s. Hiram Shaw and Lucille (Gardner) L.; m. Margaret McGinness, Jan. 21, 1961; children: Lucille Gardner, Frances Shelby. BA, Colo. Coll., 1953; LLD (hon.), Maryville U., 1991. Cashier Brown Group, Inc., St. Louis, 1957-64, asst. treas., 1964-68, treas., 1968—, v.p., 1983-86 (ret.). Bd. dirs. Roosevelt Fed. Savs. and Loan, St. Louis Past trustee, vice chmn. bd. dirs. McKendree Coll., Lebanon, Ill., 1980-88; trustee, past chmn. bd. trustees Maryville U., St. Louis, 1982-91; past chmn. Provident Counseling, 1983; past v.p., bd. dirs. Jr. Achievement Miss. Valley, 1983; past dir. bi-state chpt. ARC, 1983; bd. dirs., pres. Cardinal Ritter Inst.; bd. dirs., chmn. devel. bd. Paraquad. Capt. USNR, 1953-79. Mem. Fin. Execs. Inst. (pres., dir. 1983—), St. Louis Coun. Navy League (bd. councilors 1982), Univ. Club (St. Louis, chmn. house com. 1975-78), Strathalbyn Farms Club (chmn. house com., pres. bd. dirs.), Alpha Kappa Psi, Tau Kappa Alpha. Republican. Presbyterian. E-mail: hligg498aol.com. Home: 64 Chesterfield Lakes Rd Chesterfield MO 63005-5400 Office: Liggett-Black & Co 8000 Bonhomme Ave #320 Saint Louis MO 63105

LIGGETT, LAWRENCE MELVIN, vacuum equipment manufacturing company executive; b. Denver, June 22, 1917; s. Thomas Harrison and Mary Deacon (Taylor) L.; m. Edith Irene Harris, June 20, 1943; children: Pamela Jane Liggett Schwartz, Betty Sue Liggett Brooks El Gammal. AB, Ctrl. Coll., Pella, Iowa, 1938; PhD in Chemistry, Iowa State Coll., 1943. Rsch. chemist NDRC, Iowa State Coll., 1941-43; plant mgr. Cardox Corp., Claremore, Okla., 1943-48; dir. inorganic rsch. Wyandotte Chems. Corp., 1948-55; dir. rsch., v.p. tech. dir. Airco Speer divsn. Airco, Inc., 1955-70, pres. Airco Electronics divsn., 1970-75; pres. Airco Temescal divsn. BOC Group, Berkeley, Calif., 1975-82; cons. bus. and tech., 1982—. Author; patentee in field. Mem. Am. Chem. Soc., Electronic Industries Assn. Republican. Home: 1856 Piedras Cir Alamo CA 94507-2820

LIGGETT, LUTHER LEROY, JR. lawyer; b. Marysville, Ohio, Mar. 1, 1956; s. Luther L. and Kathryn O. Liggett; m. Anne Liggett, June 25, 1983; children: Luther Alex, Katherine Ann. BA, George Washington U., 1978, JD, 1981. Bar: Ohio 1981. Atty. Liggett Law Offices, Marysville, 1981-83; asst. atty. gen. Ohio Atty. Gens. Office, Columbus, 1983-91; atty. Bricker & Eckler, 1991—. Mem. Futures Task Force, Hocking Coll., Nelsonville, Ohio. Democrat. Greek Orthodox. Avocations: politics, geology, stamps, coins, refinishing. Office: Bricker & Eckler 100 S Third St Columbus OH 43215-4291 Fax: 614-227-2390. E-mail: lliggett@bricker.com.

LIGGETT, MALCOLM HUGH, labor economist, educator; b. Balt., Sept. 3, 1929; s. Francis Marion and Neva Ruth (Crandall) L.; m. Suzanne LaPaugh, June 6, 1962. BA in Govt. with honors, U. Tex., 1957; PhD in Econs., Cornell U., 1967. Instr. Cornell U., Ithaca, N.Y., 1962-63; asst. prof. U. Calif., Santa Barbara, 1963-66, San Francisco State U., 1967-70; labor economist EEOC, Washington, 1970-73, U. Tex., Austin, 1973-75, Coun. on Wage and Price Stability, Washington, 1975-81; cons., 1981-83; assoc. prof. Pa. State. U. Harrisburg, Middletown, Pa., 1983-91; with Holland Point Enterprises, Vero Beach, Fla., 1994—. Faculty senate Pa. State U., 1986-88 Author: Employment Discrimination, 1978, Aluminum Prices, 1976; contrbr. articles to profl. jours. With USAF, 1950-53 Mem. Am. Arbitration Assn., Am. Econ. Assn., Assn. for Evolutionary Econs., Indsl. Rels. Rsch. Assn., Soc. Profls. in Dispute Resolution, Pi Sigma Alpha. Home: 1505 4th St Vero Beach FL 32962-2781 Office: Holland Point Enterprises 1505 4th St Vero Beach FL 32962-2781

LIGGETT, THOMAS JACKSON, retired seminary president; b. Nashville, May 27, 1919; s. Thomas Jackson and Lola Cleveland (Ballentine) L.; m. Virginia Corrine Moore, Aug. 12, 1941; children: Thomas Milton, Margaret Moore Liggett. AB, Transylvania U., 1940; MDiv, Lexington Theol. Sem., 1944, postgrad., 1950-52; LLD, Interam. U., 1965, Culver-Stockton Coll., 1959, Butler U., 1975; DHL, Transylvania U., 1969; DD, Eureka Coll., 1971, Phillips U., 1989. Ordained to ministry Christian Ch., 1940; pastor in Danville, Ky., 1943-45; missionary Argentina, 1946-57; prof. Union Theol. Sem., Buenos Aires, 1948-57; pres. Evang. Sem. of P.R., 1957-65; exec. sec. for Latin Am. Christian Ch., 1965-67, chmn. div. world mission, 1967-68; pres. United Christian Missionary Soc., 1968-74, Christian Theol. Sem., Indpls., 1974-86, ret., 1986. Del. World Council Chs. assembly in Uppsala, 1968, adviser assembly, Nairobi, Kenya, 1975; mem. governing bd. Nat. Council Chs., 1969-75, 85-87; moderator Disciples of Christ, 1985-87 Author: Where Tomorrow Struggles to be Born, 1970; Editor: Cuadernos Teologicos, 1954-55. Co-chmn. McGovern Task Force on Fgn. Policy in Latin Am., 1972, Democratic precinct committeeman, 1970-72. Mem. Disciples of Christ Hist. Soc. (life), Theta Phi. Home: 647 W Harrison Ave Claremont CA 91711-4537 E-mail: tjl22@juno.com.

LIGGETT, TWILA MARIE CHRISTENSEN, academic administrator, public television executive; b. Pipestone, Minn., Mar. 25, 1944; d. Donald L. Christensen and Irene E. (Zweigle) Christensen Flesher. BS, Union Coll., Lincoln, Nebr., 1966; MA, U. Nebr., 1971; PhD, 1977; DHL (hon.), Marymount Manhattan Coll., 2000. Dir. vocal and instrumental music Sprague (Nebr.)-Martell Pub. Sch., 1966-67; tchr. vocal music pub. schs., Syracuse, Nebr., 1967-69; tchr. Norris Pub. Sch., Firth, 1969-71; cons. fed. reading project pub. schs., Lincoln, 1971-72; curriculum coord. Westside Cmty. Schs., Omaha, 1972-74; dir. state program Right-to-Read Nebr. Dept. Edn., 1974-76; asst. dir. Nebr. Commn. on Status of Women, 1976-80; asst. dir. project admisntrn./devel. Great Plains Nat. Instructional TV Libr. U. Nebr., Lincoln, 1980-97; sr. v.p. for edn. Lancit Media Ent., Ltd. a Junior Net Co., N.Y., 1998-2001. Exec. prodr. Nebr. ETV Network/GPN a nat. PBS children's series Reading Rainbow, 1980—; cons. U.S. Dept. Edn., 1981; cons. Far West Regional Lab. Nebr. Edn. TV Network, San Francisco, 1978—79; panelist, presenter in field; Blue Ribbon panelist NATAS, 1991—2002; final judge Nat. Cable Ace Awards, 1991—92, 1997. Author: Reading Rainbow's Guide to Children's Books: The 101 Best Titles, 1994, rev. edit., 1996. Bd. dirs. Planned Parenthood, Lincoln, 1979-81. Recipient Grand award, N.Y., 1993, Gold medal, Internat. Film and TV Festival, 1996, 1999, World Gold medal, N.Y. Internat. Film and TV, 1995, Coun. on Internat. Nonthatrical Events Golden Eagle award, 1995, Image award, NAACP, 1994, 1996, 1999, 2002, 18 Nat. Emmy awards, 1985—2002. Mem. NATAS, Internat. Reading Assn. (panelist, presenter, Spl. award Contbns. Worldwide Literacy 1992), Am. Women in Film and TV, Phi Delta Kappa. Presbyterian. Home: 37 Crescent Pl Matawan NJ 07747 E-mail: Rrainbowl@aol.com.

LIGGIO, JEAN VINCENZA, adult education educator, artist; b. N.Y.C., Nov. 5, 1927; d. Vincenzo and Bernada (Terrusa) Verro; m. John Liggio, June 6, 1948; children: Jean Constance, Joan Bernadette. Student, N.Y. Inst. Photography, 1965, Elizabeth Seton Coll., 1984, Parsons Sch. of Design, 1985. Hairdresser Beauty Shoppe, N.Y.C., 1947-65; instr. watercolor N.Y. Dept. Pks., Recreation and Conservation, Yonkers, 1985-89, Bronxville (N.Y.) Adult Sch., 1989—. Substitute tchr. cosmetology Yonkers Bd. Edn., 1988-89; tchr. watercolor painting J.V.L. Watercolor Workshop of Fine Arts, Jakes Art Ctr., Mt. Vernon, N.Y. Paintings pub. by Donald Art Co., C.R. Gibson Greeting Card Co.; 12 watercolor paintings for Avon Calendar, Avon Cosmetics Co., 1994, 96; 12 florals for Avon-Can. Publ., 1996, 97; 12 floral paintings published by Enesco Corp., 1996; 2 floral greeting cards published by C.R. Gibson Co. Publ., 1996; floral greeting card printed by C.R. Gibson Co., 1997, boxed notecards by C.R. Gibson; floral watercolor painting on cover of C.R. Gibson Jour., 2000, floral watercolor painting on cover of C.R. Gibson Inspirational Jour.; pub. Friends Jour. Mag., Phila. Recipient 204 awards. Mem. Mt. Vernon Art Assn. (pres. membership com. 1983—, 203 awards), Scarsdale Art Assn. (publicity chmn. 1984-89), New Rochelle Art Assn., Hudson Valley Art Assn., Art Soc. Old Greenwich. Avocation: antiques. Home and Office: 166 Helena Ave Yonkers NY 10710-2524

LIGHT, ALFRED ROBERT, lawyer, political scientist, educator; b. Dec. 14, 1949; s. Alfred M. Jr. and Margaret Francis (Asbury) L; m. Mollie Sue Hall, May 28, 1977; children: Joseph Robert, Gregory Andrew. Student, Ga. Inst. Tech., 1967-69; BA with highest honors, Johns Hopkins U., 1971; PhD, U. N.C., 1976; JD cum laude, Harvard U., 1981. Bar: D.C. 1981, Va. 1982. Tax clk. IRS, 1967; lab technician Custom Farm Svcs. Soils Testing Lab, 1968; warehouse asst. State of Ga. Mines, Mining and Geology, 1970; clk.-typist systems mgmt. divsn., def. contract adminstrv. Def. Supply Agy., Atlanta, 1971; rsch. and teaching asst. dept. polit. sci. U. N.C., Chapel Hill, 1971-74; rsch. asst. Inst. Rsch. in Social Sci., 1975-77; program analyst Office of Sec. Def., 1974; asst. prf. polit. sci., rsch. scientist Ctr. Energy Rsch. Tex. Tech. U., Lubbock, 1977-78; rsch. asst. grad. sch. edn. Harvard U., 1978-79; assoc. Butler, Binion, Rice, Cook & Knapp, Houston, 1980, Bracewell & Patterson, Washington, 1980; Hunton & Williams, Richmond, Va., 1981-89; of counsel, 1989-93, 95-96; assoc. prof. St. Thomas U. Sch. Law, Miami, Fla., 1989-93, prof., 1993—. Interim dean, 1993-94; bd. advisors Toxics Law reporter, Bur. Nat. Affairs, Washington, 1987—. Contbr. articles to profl. jours. Charter mem. West Broward Cmty. Ch. Capt. USAR, 1971-85. Grantee NSF, Inst. Evaluation Rsch., U. Mass., Ctr. Energy Rsch., Tex. Tech. U., 1977-78; recipient Julius Turner award Am. Polit. Sci. Assn., 1977. Mem. ABA (vice-chmn.) tort and ins. practice sect. 1988-97, nat. res. and environ. sect. 1993-95, chmn. 1995-2000), Fed. Bar. Assn., Va. Bar Assn., Richmond Bar Assn., Phi Beta Kappa, Phi Eta Sigma. Democrat. Home: 1042 Woodfall Ct Fort Lauderdale FL 33326-2832 Office: St Thomas U Sch Law 16400 NW 32nd Ave Opa Locka FL 33054-6459 E-mail: alight@stu.edu.

LIGHT, ARTHUR HEATH, bishop; s. Alexander Heath and Mary Watkins (Nelson) L.; m. Sarah Ann Jones, June 12, 1954; children: William Alexander, Philip Nelson, John Page, Sarah Heath. BA, Hampden-Sydney Coll., 1951, DD, 1987; MDiv, Va. Theol. Sem., 1954, DD, 1970, St. Paul's Coll., 1979. Ordained priest Episcopal Ch., 1955. Rector West Mecklenburg Cure, Boydton, Va., 1954-58, Christ Ch., Elizabeth City, N.C., 1958-63, St. Marys Ch., Kinston, 1963-67, Christ and St. Luke's Ch., Norfolk, Va., 1967-79; bishop Diocese of Southwestern Va., Roanoke, 1979-96; pres. Province III Episcopal Ch., 1984-93. Mem. adv. coun. to presiding bishop, 1985-93; nominating com. 25th presiding bishop of the Episcopal Ch., 1994-97. Author: God, The Gift, The Giver, 1984. Bd. dirs. United Cmty. Fund, 1969-79, Norfolk Seamen's Friends Soc., 1969-79, Tidewater Assembly on Family Life, 1970-79, Friends of Juvenile Ct., 1975-79, Va. Inst. Pastoral Care, 1971-72; bd. dirs., exec. com. Va. Coun. Chs., 1979-97; bd. dirs. Roanoke Valley Coun. Cmty. Svcs., 1980-83, Virginians Organized for Informed Cmty. Effort, 1981-86; bd. dirs. Appalachian People's Svc. Orgn., 1981-91, pres., 1981-85, v.p., 1989-91; bio-med. ethics com. Ea. Va. Med. Sch., 1973-79, Lewis Gale Hosp., Salem, 1988—, Cmty. Hosp. Roanoke Valley, 1990-94; trustee Va. Episc. Sch., Lynchburg, 1979-96, Episc. H.S., Alexandria, 1979-96, Boys' Home, Covington, 1979-96, Stuart Hall Sch., Staunton, 1979-96, St. Paul's Coll., Lawrenceville, 1979-88; chmn. com. on continuing edn. Va. Theol. Sem., Alexandria, 1985-96, v.p. bd. trustees, 1987-96; bd. dirs., co-chmn. rural residency program Appalachian Ministries Ednl. Resource Ctr., Berea, Ky., 1985-87; mem. coord. cabinet Va. Coun. Churches, 1988-96, chmn. com. on church and soc., 1989-92; mem. Am. com. Kyosato Ednl. Experiment Project, 1990—, v.p., 1991-2001; mem. Gen. Conv. Standing Com. on World Mission, 1988-94, chmn., 1991-94; trustee Kanuga Conf. Ctr., 1991-95; bd. dirs. Conflict Resolution Ctr., 1996-98; cmty. rels. task force City of Roanoke, 1995—; bd. dirs. Habitat for Humanity, 1997-2000, Roanoke Valley Pastoral Counseling Ctr., 1998—, pres., 1999-2001; bd. mem. Nat. Com. for Cmty. and Justice, 2001—. Named One of Outstanding Men of Yr., Jaycees, 1961, 63; fellow St. George's Coll., Jerusalem, 1978, 89, fellow in biomed. ethics U. Va., 1989; recipient humanitarian award Nat. Conf. Cmty. & Justice, 2002. Democrat.

LIGHT, BETTY JENSEN PRITCHETT, former college dean; b. Omaha, Sept. 14, 1924; d. Lars Peter and Ruth (Norby) Jensen; m. Morgan S. Pritchett, June 27, 1944 (dec. 1982); children: Randall Wayne, Robin Kay Pritchett Church, Royce Marie Pritchett Bishop; m. Kenneth F. Light, Nov. 23, 1985 BS, Portland State U., 1965; MBA, U. Oreg., 1966; Ed.D., Oreg. State U., 1973. Buyer Rodgers Stores, Inc., Portland, Oreg., 1947-62; chmn. bus. div. Mt. Hood Community Coll., Gresham, 1966-70, dir. evening coll., 1970-71, assoc. dean instn., 1972-77, dean humanities and behavioral scis., 1977-79, dean devel. and spl. programs, 1979-83, dean communication arts, humanities and social scis., 1983-86. Mem. state com. for articulation between cmty. colls. and higher edn., 1976-78; mem. Gov.'s Coun. on Career and Vocat. Edn., 1977-86; former owner Effective Real Estate Mgmt., 1982—. Author: Values and Perceptions of Community College Professional Staff in Oregon, 1973; contbg. author: (case study) The Pritchett Study in Retailing, An Economic View, 1969. Mem. Gresham City Council, 1983-86. Mem.: Oreg. Vocat. Assn., Am. Vocat. Assn., Am. Assn. Higher Edn., Oreg. Bus. Edn. Assn., Danish Brotherhood, N.W. Danish Found., Danish Heritage Soc. Home: 1635 NE Country Club Ave Gresham OR 97030-4432

LIGHT, CHRISTOPHER UPJOHN, writer, computer musician, photographer; b. Kalamazoo, Jan. 4, 1937; s. Richard and Rachel Mary (Upjohn) L.; m. Lilykate Victoria wenner, June 22, 1963 (div. 1986); children: Victoria Mary, Christopher Upjohn Jr.; m. Margo Ruth Bosker, Jan. 2, 1994. AB, Carleton Coll., 1958; MS, Columbia U., 1962; MBA, We. Mich. U., 1967; PhD, Washington U., St. Louis, 1971. Editor, pub. Kalamazoo Mag., 1963-66; pres. Mich. Outdoor Pub. Co., Kalamazoo, 1965-68; product planner Upjohn Co., 1967-68; asst. prof. U. Utah, Salt Lake City, 1971-72; assoc. prof., chmn. fin. dept. Roosevelt U., Chgo., 1975-78; vis. prof. fin. No. Ill. U., 1978-79; freelance writer, computer musician, 1979—. Editor: Charles Dickens' Village Coquettes, 1992; mgr. spl. projects Sarasota Music Archive, 1992-96. Contbr. articles to profl. and microcomputer jours.; composer: Ten Polyrhytmic Etudes, 1991, Piano Sonata #1, 1992, (albums) Apple Compote, One-Man Band, 1985, Ultimate Music Box, Vol. I, 1988, Ulitmate Music Box, Vol. II, 1993; ;exhibitions include Aspects of Flowers, Ann Arbor, Mich., 1996, East Lansing, Mich., 1997, Kalamazoo, 1997, Aspects of Flowers II, Ann Arbor, 1997, Aspects of Flowers III, Fontana Festival, 1998, Portraits of Engines, Kalamazoo, 1998, Aspects of Flowers: Selections, Ann Arbor, 1999, Pathways, Kalamazoo, 1999, Aspects of Flowers IV, 2001, Landscapes, 2001. Trustee Harold and Grace Upjohn Found., 1965-85, 94—, pres., 1997—; trustee, bd. dirs. Kalamazoo Symphony Orch. Assn., 1990-99; trustee Sarasota Music Archive, 1990-95, Kalamazoo Coll., 1991-93; bd. dirs. Am. Symphony Orch. League, 1992-2000, sec., 1996-99; bd. dirs. Sarasota Concert Assn., 1998—. Recipient ann. press award Mich. Welfare League, 1967. Mem. ASCAP, NARAS (voting com.), Fin. Mgmt. Assn., Soc. Profl. Journalists, Univ. Club Chgo., Gull Lake Country Club, Columbia U. Club. N.Y. Office: 151 S Rose St Ste 820 Kalamazoo MI 49007-4715

LIGHT, JANE ELLEN, librarian; b. Crosby, N.D., May 4, 1948; d. Ralph W. and Ethel S. (Cady) Johnson; m. Donald Howard Light, June 19, 1979; children: Jessica, David. BA, Calif. State U., Sacramento, 1973; MLS, U. Calif., Berkeley, 1974. Project mgr. Peninsula Libr. Sys., San Mateo, Calif., 1974-78, sys. dir., 1979-83; program mgr. Coop. Libr. Authority, San Jose, Calif., 1978-79; asst. libr. dir. Redwood City (Calif.) Pub. Libr., 1983-84, libr. dir., 1984-97; city libr. San Jose Pub. Libr., 1997—. Libr. bldg. and mgmt. cons., Menlo Park, Calif., 1989—; del. On-line Computer Libr. Ctr. User's Coun., 1993-2000. Bd. dirs. Child Care Coordinating Coun., San Mateo, 1988-97, pres. 1992-93; bd. dirs. YMCA of Santa Clara Valley, 2001—. Mem. ALA, Calif. Libr. Assn., Pub. Libr. Assn. Office: San Jose Pub Libr Sys 180 W San Carlos St San Jose CA 95113-2005 E-mail: jane.light@ci.sj.ca.us.

LIGHT, JO KNIGHT, stockbroker; b. DeQueen, Ark., Mar. 15, 1936; d. Donald R. and Auda (Waltrip) Knight; m. Jerry T. Light, June 21, 1958 (dec. 1979); m. Victor E. Menefee Jr., Nov. 18, 1981; 1 child, Jerry T. Jr. BA cum laude, U. Ark., 1958. CFP. Travel cons. Comml. Nat. Bank, Little Rock, 1971-76; dist. mgr. Am. Express Co., N.Y.C., 1976-82; fin. advisor and retirement planning specialist Morgan Stanley, 1982—, registered investment advisor, 1996—, sr. v.p. investments, 1999—. Mem. Jr. League of Little Rock Sustainers; vol. Happiness Singers. Mem. Fin. Planning Assn., Internat. Assn. Fin. Planners (bd. dirs. 1992-98, pres. bd. 1995-96), U. Ark. Alumni Assn. (bd. dirs. 1974-77), Morgan Stanley Pres.'s Club, Morgan Stanley Dir.'s Club, Phi Beta Kappa, Kappa Kappa Gamma. Avocations: music, tennis, sailing, snow skiing. Office: Morgan Stanley 425 W Capitol Ave Ste 200 Little Rock AR 72201-3440 E-mail: jo.light@morganstanley.com.

LIGHT, JOHN RICHARD, sculptor; b. Kalamazoo, Oct. 11, 1940; s. Richard Light and Rachel Mary (Upjohn) L.; m. Frances Mary Hesser, June 21, 1969; 1 child, Aimee Upjohn. BA, Yale U., 1962. Asst. advt. mgr. Verson Allsteel Press Co., Chgo., 1967-68; pub. relations copywriter Barton Brands, 1970; investment cons., 1972-86; sculptor, 1986—. Editor: Impact Machining, 1968; exhbns. include Skokie (Ill.) Fine Arts Commn., 1991, Iron Feather Gallery, Sedona, Ariz., 1993, Auburn (Calif.) Art Ctr., 1994, Art Guild, Farmington, Conn., 1995, Art at Parkview Hills, Kalamazoo, 2000; represented in permanent collections Goulandris Mus. Cycladic Art, Athens, Greece, Harvard Med. Sch., Cambridge, Mass., Nat. Gallery Art, Washington, Nat. Mus. Ireland, Dublin, Pushkin Mus. Art, Moscow, U. Chgo., Yale U., New Haven. Bd. dirs. Juvenile Protective Assn., Chgo., 1975—, Kalamazoo Child Guidance Clinic, 1969—, Lakeside Boys and Girls Home, 1979—. Recipient Distinguished Service award Publicity Club Chgo., 1972. Mem. Internat. Sculpture Ctr., Nat. Sculpture Soc., Publicity Club (Chgo.) (dir. 1975-77, mgr. club publs. 1972-73, chmn. seminar com. 1976-77), Kiwanis (Kalamazoo and Chgo.). Roman Catholic. Home: 4020 Old Field Trl Kalamazoo MI 49008-3339 Office: Parks Trades Ctr Ste 313A 326 W Kalamazoo Ave Kalamazoo MI 49007

LIGHT, KENNETH FREEMAN, college administrator; b. Detroit, Jan. 22, 1922; s. Delbert Bertram and Hilma (Stolt) L.; m. Shirley Claire Bower, Jan. 7, 1944 (dec. 1984); children— Karen Christine, Kevin Harold, Brian Curtis; m. Betty Jensen Pritchett, Nov. 23, 1985 BS, U. Ill., 1949; MA, Mich. State U., 1952, PhD, 1967. Instr. mech. engring. dept. Mich. Tech. U., 1956-60, assoc. prof., coord. for tech. edn., 1960-65; vice chancellor for acad. affairs, v.p. for acad. affairs Lake Superior State Coll., Sault Ste. Marie, Mich., 1965-76, pres., 1982-86, Oreg. Inst. Tech., Klamath Falls, 1976-82. Pres. Upper Peninsula Health Edn. Corp., 1975-76; mem. Mich. Manpower Commn., 1973-74, Vocat. Edn. Adv. Council, 1973-76, Oreg. Career and Vocat. Adv. Council, 1977-82, Oreg. Manpower Commn., 1978-80; mem. Econ. Devel. Corp. Chippewa County, 1982-86. Served with USAF, 1942-45, to maj., USAFR. Mem. AAUP, Am. Soc. Engring. Edn., Am. Soc. Mil. Engrs., Air Force Assn., Phi Delta Kappa. Home: 6 Partridge Dr Kincheloe MI 49788-1303

LIGHT, MARION JESSEL, retired elementary education educator; b. San Antonio, Dec. 5, 1915; d. Marion Jackson and Kate Jessel (Cox) Parr; m. Marion Russell Light, Nov. 8, 1958 (dec. July 1983); children: Russell Jeffers, Paul Love. BA, So. Meth. U., 1936; MA, U. Tex., 1947. Cert. elem. and secondary sch. tchr., Tex. Elem. tchr. Dallas Ind. Sch. Dist., 1936-72. 1st v.p. The Cosmos Rev. Class, 1991-92, 97-98. Del. to 16th Senatorial Dist. Dem. Conv., 1988; moderator Presbyn. Women, 1st Ch., Dallas, 1989-90, co-moderator, 1994-95. Mem. AAUW (chmn. hobbies and crafts Dallas br. 1970s), Dallas Ret. Tchrs. Assn. (corr. sec. 1984-90), Dallas Women's Forum (rec. sec. Friday study 1987-89), Bay View Century Club (corr. sec. 1988-89, pres. 1993-95), Dallas Symphony Orch. League, Delta Kappa Gamma (pres. Delta Sigma chpt. 1956-58, Chpt. Achievement award 1979, Marion Parr Light Recruitment grantee named in her honor Delta Sigma chpt. 1958). Avocations: travel, photography, reading, gardening.

LIGHT, PAMELA DELAMAIDE, interior designer; b. Pittsburg, Kans., Sept. 16, 1950; d. Jack Riley and Pearl Darlene (Nelson) Delamaide; m. Kenneth Layne Light, July 25, 1970 (div. Apr. 1974); m. F. Dennie Pimental, Nov. 2, 1985. Student, Ohio U., 1968-70; BS in Environ. Design, Ball State U., 1973. Interior design apprentice Jon Wilding Studio, Anderson, 1970-71; interior designer Suniland Office Furniture, Houston, 1973-83; furniture rep. Reeves, Rice & Lights, 1983-84; interior designer H.O.K., San Francisco, 1986-87; sr. project designer, prin. Interior Archs., 1987-88; sr. designer, project mgr. Leason Pomeroy Assoc., Orange, 1988-90; sr. designer, v.p. Whisler-Patri, 1990-93; v.p. Reel Grobman, 1993-94; sr. v.p. HOK, 1995—. Cons. Front to Back, Houston, 1982-84. Mem.: Houston Humane Soc., Internat. Interior Designers Assn. (v.p. programs 1983, pres. South Tex. chpt. 1985, pres. No. Calif. chpt. 1987, nat. v.p. membership 1990), Archtl. Found. L.A. (exec. bd. 1995—), Citizens for Animal Protection. Republican. Methodist.

LIGHT, RICHARD JAY, statistician, education educator; b. N.Y.C., Sept. 10, 1942; s. Solomon Julius and Muriel (Szwarcman) L.; m. Patricia Kahn, June 27, 1965; children: Jennifer Susan, Sarah Elizabeth. BS, U. Pa., 1962, AM, 1964; PhD, Harvard U., 1969; LLD (hon.), U. Winnipeg, Can., 1991. Mem. faculty Harvard U., Cambridge, Mass., 1969—, prof. stats., 1975—. Dir. faculty studies John F. Kennedy Inst. Politics, 1971-76; mem. Bd. on Testing and Assessment, 2000—; mem. panel children's and family policy Nat. Acad. Scis., 1977—, chmn. panel on evaluation, 1982; panel program evaluation Social Sci. Research Council, 1977—; bd. dirs Huron Inst., Cambridge, Mass., 1971—; cons. World Bank, 1975—; dir. Harvard Assessment Seminar, Cambridge, 1986—; bd. testing and assessment Nat. Rsch. Coun. Co-author: Data for Decisions, 1982, Summing Up, 1984, By Design, 1990, Meta-analysis for Explanation, 1992; editor: Learning from Experience, 1982, Evaluation Studies Rev., 1983; author: Making the Most of College, 2001. Trustee Buckingham, Browne and Nichols Sch., Cambridge, 1977—, Wellesley Coll., 1998—; mem. policy adv. group Mass. Office of Children, 1977—; bd. dirs. Fund for Improvement Post-Secondary Edn., 1992-95. N.Y. State Advanced Coll. Teaching fellow, 1965; vis. fellow Ctr. Analysis Health Practices, Harvard U. Sch. Pub. Health, 1977-78; Sr. Research award Spencer Found., Chgo., 1978-84; research fellow Ford Found., N.Y.C., 1981; recipient Paul Lazarsfeld award for contbns. to sci., 1992. Fellow Am. Acad. Arts and Scis.; mem. Am. Assn. Higher Edn. Assn., Am. Ednl. Rsch. Assn., Am. Sociol. Assn., Am. Evaluation Assn. (pres. 1986), Coun. Applied Social Rsch.,

Evaluation Rsch. Soc. (Paul Lazarsfeld award 1991), Am. Assn. for Higher Edn. (nat. bd.), Fund for Improvement Postsecondary Edn. (nat. bd.). Home: 31 Dunbarton Rd Belmont MA 02478-2458 Office: John F Kennedy Sch Govt Harvard U Cambridge MA 02138

LIGHT, TERRY RICHARD, orthopedic hand surgeon; b. Chgo., June 22, 1947; BA, Yale U., 1969; MD, Chgo. Med. Sch., 1973. Asst. prof. Yale U., New Haven, 1977-80, Loyola U., Maywood, Ill., 1980-82, assoc. prof., 1982-88, prof., 1988-90, Dr. William M. Scholl prof., chmn. orthop. surgery and rehab, 1991—. Attending surgeon Hines (Ill.) VA Hosp., 1980—, Shriner's Hosp., Chgo., 1981—, Foster McGaw Hosp., Maywood, 1981—; hand cons. Chgo. White Sox, 1986—; bus. mgr. Jour. Hand Surgery, 1995-99. Editor Am. Acad. Orthop. Surgeons Hand Surgery Update, 1999, 2d edit. V.p. Frank Lloyd Wright Home and Studio Found., Oak Park, Ill., 1985-88, pres., 1988-90; chmn. bd. Fairfield Pub. Gallery, Sturgeon Bay, Wis., 1998-99; bd. dirs. Loyola U. Health Sys., 1999—. Fellow: ACS, Am. Acad. Orthop. Surgeons (chair Jour. Hand Surgery com.95 1995—99); mem.: Ill. Orthop. Soc. (v.p. 1995, pres.-elect. 1996, pres. 1997), Twenty-First Century Orthop. Assn. (pres. 1979—), Acad. Orthopaedic Soc. (second pres.-elect 1999—2000, first pres.-elect 2000—01, pres. 2001—02), Chgo. Soc. for Surgery of Hand (sec. 1985—87, pres.-elect 1987—88, pres. 1988), Am. Assn. Hand Surgery (bd. dirs. 1989—91), Am. Soc. for Surgery of Hand (treas.-elect 1998—99, treas. 1999—2002), Alpha Omega Alpha. Avocation: collecting American arts and crafts and pottery. Office: Loyola U Med Ctr 2160 S 1st Ave Maywood IL 60153-3304 E-mail: tlight@lumc.edu.

LIGHTBURN, FAYE MARIE, genealogist; b. Oakland, Calif., Aug. 9, 1928; d. Lloyd Michael and Alma Leone (Dennis) Brown; m. Jesse Leon Lightburn, Apr. 2, 1946; children: Sandra Jean Lightburn Stein (dec.), Steven Douglas, Marcia Faye Lightburn Blackwell, Janet Lightburn Powers. Student, Sacramento Jr. Coll., Mercy Hosp. Nursing, Sacramento. Food svc. mgr. Duval County Sch. Bd., Jacksonville Beach, Fla., 1964-86. Compiler and editor: Revolutionary Soldier Samuel Brown and some of His Family, 1993, supplement, 1994; compiler: The Palms Presbyterian Church History 1956-2000. Mem. DAR, Nat. Geneal. Soc., Mo. Geneal. Assn., Howard County Geneal Soc., St. Augustine Geneal. Soc., Federated Geneal. Soc., Va. Geneal. Soc., Assn. Profl. Genealogists, Boonslick Hist. Soc. Democrat. Presbyterian. Avocations: reading, traveling, gardening, researching.

LIGHTBURN, JEFFREY CALDWELL, corporate communications executive; b. Columbus, Ohio, June 17, 1947; s. Willis Caldwell and Nancy Ellen (Snyder) L.; m. Jeanne Kay McGraw, June 13, 1970; children: Nicole Ann, Benjamin Caldwell. BS, So. Ill. U., 1970. Editor base newspaper Fairchild AFB, USAF, Spokane, Wash., 1970-73; staff writer, reporter News Democrat, Belleville, Ill., 1973-76; editor, pub. rels. specialist Ralston Purina, St. Louis, 1976-78; sr. comm. specialist Frito-Lay, Inc., Dallas, 1978-81; mgr. comm. Curtis Mathes, 1981-83; dir. internat. comm. Pizza Hut, Wichita, Kans., 1983-90; sr. dir. comm. Taco Bell, Irvine, Calif., 1990-99, Tricon Global Restaurants, Irvine, 1999—. Mem. bd. edn. Sch. Dist. 118, Belleville, 1976-78. Recipient Excellence award Pub. Rels. Soc. Am., 1996, 97. Mem. Soc. Profl. Journalists - Sigma Delta Chi, Internat. Assn. Bus. Communicators (local chapter officer 1976—, Gold Quill awards 1976, 78, 84, 98). Republican. Methodist. Home: 6 Summitcrest Dove Canyon CA 92679-3410 Office: Taco Bell Corp 17901 Von Karman Ave Irvine CA 92614-6221 E-mail: jlightbu@tacobell.com.

LIGHTER, ERIC AARON, real estate and law enforcement software developer, consultant; b. Chico, Calif., Aug. 6, 1950; s. Bruce Clyde and Katherine Bernice (Stutsman) L.; m. Joan E. Prescott, Feb. 14, 1999. Grad., Realtors Inst., 1973; student, U. Hawaii. Salesman Fin. Security Life, Honolulu, 1970; founder, treas. 3d Eye Prodns., 1974-76; pres. Home Rent Hawaii, 1976, A Lighter Cons., Graphic and Media, Honolulu, 1977—; pres., CEO Lighter Properties Corp., Real Estate and Law Enforcement Software Developers, 1978—. Founder Quality Income Sys., Honolulu, 1983, Save Hawaii's Aloha Spirit Trustee's Assn., co-chair, 1992; CEO Credit Bur. Internat., Inc., 1984—; CEO, founder Constn. Coalition, Christian Tolerance Legal Reform Lobby, 1991—; pres. Wells Fargo Protective Alarm Svc. (White Collar Crime Investigation), 1992—; corp. owner, operator Waikiki Hotel; CEO Honolulu Inn and Volcano Inn, 1986, 96; investigative reporter The Am.'s Bull., Medford, 1992—; mem. Honolulu Realtor Pub. Rels. Com., 1983-84, Constnl. Rev. Forum, nat. dir.; CEO, Credit Bur. Internat., Inc., 1989—; innkeeper Volcano Inn, Hawaii, 1996—. Editor: Ke Alaka'i, 1984. Bd. dirs. Hawaii Alliance for Arts in Edn., 1984, Inst. Human Svcs., Honolulu, 1984; Hawaii Statue of Liberty Program mgr., 1986; pres. Royal Hawaiian Heritage, 1989—; investigator Western Iran-Contragate, 1987-98; founder Diamond Cross Ministries, 1985—; nat. media chmn. Gritz for U.S. Pres., 1992. Mem. Hawaii Assn. Realtors, Bldg. Industry Assn. Hawaii (Parade of Homes award of excellence 1983), Hawaii Jaycees (project initiator Silver Jubilee Project 1983, mgr. Outstanding Hawaii Jaycees program mgr., founding pres. Capital Dist. 182, King of King award 1982, 83), Nat. Assn. Bed and Breakfast, Swiss of Hawaii Club, Constn. Rangers Club (chief grand jury and investigations 1996—), Lions (Honolulu) (various offices including treas.). Avocation: playing Gospel guitar. Home: Honolulu Inn 1045 Spencer St Honolulu HI 96822-3749 E-mail: lightere001@hawaii.rr.com.

LIGHTER, JEREMIAH B. book designer, artist, illustrator, educator; b. Phila., Mar. 23, 1921; s. Julius and Sema (Tabachnick) L. BSS cum laude, CCNY, 1944. Asst. type dir. McCann-Erickson, N.Y.C., 1945-48; type dir. Kurt Volk, 1955-58, Young & Rubicam, N.Y.C., 1958-61; art dir. Harcourt Brace Jovanovich, 1961-81; pvt. practice, 1981—. Instr. Sch. Visual Arts, N.Y.C., 1971-74, Parsons Sch. Design, N.Y.C., 1974-94, Queens (N.Y.) Coll., 1979-81. Exhbns. include Phila. Print Club, HBJ Gallery, Wilburt's Gallery, L.A. County Fair, Parsons Gallery; group shows include Nexus Gallery, 2002, Stage Gallery, 2002; pvt. and pub. collections; illustrator books and mag. covers. Active Outdoors Club; pro bono Recording for Blind, Big Bros. Avocations: chess, bicycling, hiking, kite flying. Home: 2 Stuyvesant OvalApt 7G New York NY 10009-2111

LIGHTER, LAWRENCE, lawyer; b. Bklyn., Sept. 13, 1935; s. Abe and Frances (Laufer) L.; m. Gloria Rita Stiefel, June 28, 1959; children: Adam, Todd, Eric. BS in Acctg., Bklyn. Coll., 1956; JD, NYU, 1960. Bar: N.Y. 1962. Staff atty. S.E.S.A.C., N.Y.C., 1961-65; house counsel Mills Music Inc., 1965-68; N.Y. counsel Capitol Records, 1969-70; pvt. practice, 1970—. Guest lectr. St. John's U., Queens, N.Y., Five Towns Coll., Huntington, N.Y., NYU, N.Y.C., and others. Gen. legal editor: Encyclopedia of The Music Business, 1984. Office: 488 Madison Ave Fl 8 New York NY 10022-5702 Fax: 212 753 3630. E-mail: musicilawA1@aol.com.

LIGHTFOOT, DAVID WILLIAM, linguistics educator; b. Looe, Eng., Feb. 10, 1945; s. William Richard and Peggy May (Stevens) L.; m. Sarah Elizabeth Hairs, Feb. 7, 1946 (div. 1980); children: Kirsten, Heidi; m. Sari Ruth Hornstein, Nov. 24, 1955; children: Eric, Alexander. BA with honors, U. London, 1966; MA, U. Mich., 1968, PhD, 1971. Asst. prof. McGill U., Montreal, Que., Can., 1970-75, assoc. prof., 1975-78; prof. U. Utrecht, The Netherlands, 1978-83, U. Md., College Park, 1983-2001; dean grad. sch. Georgetown U., 2001—. Author: Natural Logic and Greek Moods, 1975, Principles of Diachronic Syntax, 1979, Explanation in Linguistics, 1981, The Language Lottery, 1982, How to Set Parameters, 1991, Verb Movement, 1994, The Development of Language, 1999, The Syntactic Effects of Morphological Change, 2002, The Language Organ, 2002 Mem. Linguistic Soc. Am., Linguistic Assn. Gt. Britain. Home: 7208 Heatherhill Rd Bethesda MD 20817-4657 Office: Grad Sch Georgetown U Washington DC 20057

LIGHTFOOT, EDWIN NIBLOCK, JR. retired chemical engineering educator; b. Milw., Sept. 25, 1925; married 1949, 5 children. BS, Cornell U., 1947, PhD in Chem. Engring., 1951. Asst prof., prof. biochem engr. U. Wis., Madison, 1953-80, prof. chem. engr., 1980-95, prof. emeritus, 1995—. Vis. prof. Tech. U. Norway, 1962, Stanford U., 1971, U. Canterbury, New Zealand, 1972. Author 14 books; contbr. articles to profl. jours. Recipient William H. Walker award Am. Inst. Chem. Engrs, 1975, Food, Pharm. and Bioeng award, 1979, Warren K. Lewis award, 1991. Mem. NAS, AAAS, Nat. Acad. Engr., Royal Norwegian Soc. Sci. & Letter, Am. Inst. Chem. Engr., Am. Chem. Soc. (E.V. Murphree award, 1994). Achievements include research on physical separation tech. mass transfer, biomedical engring. Office: U Wis 3639 Engineering Bldg 1415 Engineering Dr Madison WI 53706-1691 E-mail: lightfoot@engr.wisc.edu.

LIGHTFORD, MELVIN, minister; b. Brockton, Mass., Dec. 14, 1954; BS, U. Mass., 1978. Retired police officer City of Brockton, Mass.; evangelist Melvin Lightford Ministries, Inc., Brockton, Mass., 1999—. Vol. numerous church and civic orgns. Home: 78 Colonel Bell Dr Brockton MA 02301 Office: Melvin Lightford Minisitries Inc PO Box 1516 Brockton MA 02303

LIGHTMAN, ALAN PAIGE, physicist, writer, educator; b. Memphis, Nov. 28, 1948; s. Richard Louis and Jeanne (Garretson) L.; m. Jean Greenblatt, Nov. 28, 1976; children: Elyse, Kara. AB, Princeton U., 1970; PhD in Physics, Calif. Inst. Tech., 1974. Postdoctoral fellow Cornell U., Ithaca, N.Y., 1974-76; asst. prof. Harvard U., Cambridge, Mass., 1976-79; staff scientist Smithsonian Astrophys. Obs., 1979-88; prof. sci. and writing MIT, 1988-95; John E. Burchard prof., 1995—. Chair sci. panel NRC Astron. and Astrophys. Survey for 1990's. Author: Problem Book in Relativity and Gravitation, 1974, Radiative Processes in Astrophysics, 1976, Time Travel and Papa Joe's Pipe, 1984, A Modern Day Yankee in Connecticut Court, 1986, Origins: The Lives and Worlds of Modern Cosmologists, 1990 (Most Outstanding Sci. Book in Phys. Sci. award Assn. Am. Pubs.), Ancient Light, 1991, Great Ideas in Physics, 1992, Time for the Stars, 1992, Einstein's Dreams, 1993, Good Benito, 1995, Dance for Two, 1996. Recipient Gemant award Am. Inst. of Physics, 1996; Lit. Light of Boston Pub. Libr., 1995. Fellow AAAS, Am. Acad. Arts and Scis., Am. Phys. Soc.; mem. Am. Astron. Soc. (chmn. high energy astrophysics divsn. 1991). Office: MIT 77 Massachusetts Ave Cambridge MA 02139-4307

LIGHTMAN, HAROLD ALLEN, marketing executive; b. Gloucester, Mass., Oct. 23, 1925; s. Abraham and Gertrude (Chait) L.; m. Irma Shorell, Feb. 19, 1954; children: Timothy, Chip, Stacey. Student, Norwich U., 1943; student, Cambridge U., Eng., 1946; BBA, U. Miami, 1949; postgrad., Oxford (Eng.) U., 1996. Acct. exec. Grant Advt., Miami, Fla., 1948-50; advt. dir. Sears Roebuck & Co., Tampa, 1950-51; acct. exec. Robert Otto Internat., N.Y.C., 1952-53; acct. exec., field supr. Amos Parish & Co., 1954-56; acct. exec. Dowd, Redfield & Johnstone, 1957-59; chmn. bd. dirs. H. Allen Lightman Inc., 1959—. Bd. dirs. Irma Shorell Inc., N.Y.C.; pres., bd. dirs. Ind. Cosmetic Mfg. and Distbrs. U.S.A., v.p. nat. legis. affairs, 1974—; exec. v.p. Alfin Fragrances, Inc., 1985-87; pres. I.S. Labs. Inc., 1987-2000. Columnist: Seen & Heard, 1965-83; producer: Cable TV program Seen & Heard, 1978-87. Sgt. U.S. Army, 1943-46, ETO. Decorated Purple Heart, Bronze Star, European-African-Mid. Ea. Campaign medal with 3 battle stars, Combat Inf. Badge; recipient Pub. Rels. Gold Key award, 1987. Fellow Winston Churchill Meml. Libr., Harry S. Truman Meml. Libr.; mem. Nat. Fedn. Ind. Bus. (del. 1979), Internat. Platform Assn., Alpha Delta Sigma (founder, 1st pres. 1947-48), Miami Jr. C. of C. (publicity, pub. rels. dir. 1948-50), DAV, Am. Legion (vice comdr. 1948-49), Vets. of the Battle of the Bulge, The Jockey Club, Nat. Assn. Cosmetic Entrepreneurs (pres. 1997-98). Office: 75 E End Ave New York NY 10028-7909

LIGHTNER, SHARON GUTMAN, civic organization executive, poet; b. Worcester, Mass., May 22, 1949; d. Max (Marcus Heine) and Syma (Sternberg) Weissman; m. Paul Jerome Gutman, June 18, 1970 (dec. Sept., 1990); children: Rachel Z., Matthew A.; m. Charles Rand Lightner, June 26, 1993. BA, Bennington Coll., 1971; student, Hebrew Union Coll., N.Y.C., 1995—. Instr. Brit. fiction Beit Brl Tchrs. Coll., Tel Aviv, Israel, 1984-86; internat. coord. Remembering for the Future Internat. Conf., Berlin, 1991-93; v.p. Phila. Ctr. on the Holocaust, Genocide and Human Rights, 1991—, The Annual Scholars' Conf. on the Holocaust and the Chs., Phila., 1992—. Dir. Post Holocaust Generation in Diaglogue, N.Y.C., 1992—. Editor: Liturgies on the Holocaust: An Interfaith Anthology, 1995, A Modern Prophet: Letters to Franklin H. Littell, 1998; contbr. articles to profl. jours. including CCAR Jour.: A Reform Jewish Quar. Asst. U.S. dir. First Official Commemoration of Babi Yar, Kiev, Ukraine, 1992. Avocation: teaching meditation. Home: 518 Lawrence Ave Westfield NJ 07090-3118

LIGHTSEY, OWEN RICHARD, JR. psychologist; b. Biloxi, Miss., Dec. 9, 1956; s. Owen Richard and Nayna Ward (Warren) L.; m. Michaela Victoria Wells; 1 child, Richartd Michael. BA in Psychology, U. So. Miss., 1978, MS in Counseling Psychology, 1982; PhD in Counseling Psychology, U. Md., 1992. Lic. psychologist, Tenn. Counseling intern Singing River Mental Health Svcs., Pascagoula, Miss., 1982; employment counselor U. Miss., Hattiesburg, 1981-82; psychol. assoc. Hunt Correctional Ctr., Baton Rouge, 1982-87; coord. learning assessment promect Goucher Coll., Towson, Md., 1987-88; therapist, counselor M.K. Spodak, M.D. PA, 1988-89, Children of Separated and Divorced Parents Project, Columbia, Md., 1990; psychology assoc. Dundalk Counseling Ctr., Balt., 1990-91; predoctoral intern Counseling Ctr. U. Mo., Columbia, 1991-92; asst. prof. counseling psychology program U. Memphis, 1992—. Workshop facilitator Memphis City Police Officers and Sch. Counselors, 1993, Internat. Assn. Pers. in Employment Security Conf., 1995; site visitor/evaluator Collierville H.s., 1993; application reviewer Ryan White Funds, 1994-96; group leader Friends for Life, 1994; examiner State Psychology Licensure Exams, 1993, 94, 95; presenter in field. Contbr. articles to profl. publs. Mem. APA (divsn. 17 chair spl. task group 1994-96, mem. program com. 1992-95), ACA. Democrat. Avocations: writing, bicycling, hiking, travel. Home: 1337 Harbert Ave Memphis TN 38104-4504 Office: U Memphis Dept Counseling 100 Ball Edn Bldg Memphis TN 38152-0001

LIGHTSTONE, RONALD, lawyer; b. N.Y.C., Oct. 4, 1938; s. Charles and Pearl (Weisberg) L.; m. Nancy Lehrer, May 17, 1973; 1 child, Dana. AB, Columbia U., 1959; JD, NYU, 1962. Atty. CBS, N.Y.C., 1967-69; assoc. dir. bus. affairs CBS News, 1969-70; atty. NBC, 1970; assoc. gen. counsel Viacom Internat. Inc., 1970-75, v.p., gen. counsel, sec., 1976-80; v.p. bus. affairs Viacom Entertainment Group, Viacom Internat., Inc., 1980-82, v.p. corp. affairs, 1982-84, sr. v.p., 1984-87; exec. v.p. Spelling Entertainment Inc., L.A., 1988-91, CEO, 1991-93; chmn. Multimedia Labs. Inc., 1994-97; CEO, pres. New Star Media Inc., 1997-99, vice chmn., 1999-2000. Lt. USN, 1962-66. Mem. ABA (chmn. TV, cable and radio com.), Assn. of Bar of City of N.Y., Fed. Comm. Bar Assn.

LIGHTWOOD, CAROL WILSON, writer; b. Tacoma, Oct. 2, 1941; d. Harry Edward and Cora H. Wilson; m. Keith G. Lightwood (div. Dec. 1968); children: Miles Francis, Clive Harry. BA, Smith Coll., 1963. Writer various advt. agencies, 1968-82; v.p. Wakeman & DeForrest, Newport Beach, Calif., 1985-86; owner Lightwood Direct, Las Vegas, Nev., 1986—; pres. The Meeting Place, Inc., 2002. Author: Malibu, 1984; contbr. articles to profl. jours. Chair mus. coun. Long Beach Mus. Art, 1989; docent William O. Douglas Outdoor Classroom; bd. dirs. Friends of Channel 10. Mem. Sierra Club, Sisters in Crime. Episcopalian.

LIGHTY, FREDRICK W. lawyer; b. Danville, Pa., Mar. 18, 1967; s. Raymond G. and Geraldine A. (Brill) L. BA, Lycoming Coll., 1989; JD, Widener U., 1992. Bar: Pa. 1992, U.S. Dist. Ct. (mid. dist.) Pa. 1993, U.S. Ct. Appeals (3d cir.) 1993, U.S. Ct. Internat. Trade 1995. Private practice, Harrisburg, Pa., 1995—. Dir. Enviroquest, Inc., Harrisburg, 1995—. Office: PO Box 60312 Harrisburg PA 17106-0312 E-mail: Fredrick@lighty.net.

LIGI, BARBARA JEAN, architectural and interior designer; b. Binghamton, N.Y., June 13, 1959; d. Robert Richard and Helen Margaret (Wagner) Taylor; m. Alan Joseph Ligi, July 24, 1982; children: Curtis John, Ryan Robert, Janelle Anna. AA, Mt. Ida Coll., 1979; BFA, Syracuse U., 1982. Cert. Nat. Coun. for Interior Design Qualification. Designer Norman Davies, Architect, Binghamton, 1982—. Mem. adj. faculty design Broome C.C., Binghamton, 1987—. Active Nat. Trust for Hist. Preservation; mem. Preservation Assn. of Southern Tier. Mem. Am. Soc. Interior Designers (profl.), Gold Key. Democrat. Roman Catholic. Avocation: travel photography. Home: 2803 Robins St Endwell NY 13760-3314 Office: Norman J Davies Architect 783 Chenango St Ste 3 Binghamton NY 13901-1843

LIGOCKI, GORDON MICHAEL, artist, educator; b. Hammond, Ind., Sept. 7, 1943; s. Michael and Regina (Hlodnicki) L.; m. Rita K. Herdaliska, Jan. 25, 1968 (div. June 1980); 1 child, Ian Gabriel; m. Linda Lee Heinsen, Oct. 30, 1994. BFA, Ohio Wesleyan U., 1965; MA in Drawing, U. Iowa, 1967; MFA in Sculpture, U. Ill., 1968; postgrad., Gov.'s State U., 1987, 92. Writer Arts Ind., Indpls., 1987-91; writer, art critic Hammond (Ind.) Times, 1985-93; instr. life drawing Art Barn, Valparaiso, Ind., 1989—; assoc. prof. Purdue U., Hammond, 1992-97; gallery dir., adj. prof. Ind. U. N.W., Gary, 1992-2001; assoc. prof. Valparaiso U., 1990-2001; adj. prof. Ancilla Coll., 1998-2001. Panelist Ind. Arts Commn., Indpls., 1989; cons. on drawing Collegiate Press, Alta Loma, Calif., 1995; curator individual shows Midwest Mus. of Am. Art, Elkhart, Ind., 1991, No. Ind. Art Assn., Munster, Ind., Gary Comty. Mental Health, Hammond Pub. Libr. One-person shows include R.H. Love Gallery, Chgo., 1992, Herr Chambliss Gallery, Hot Springs, Ark., 1992; contbr. articles to newspapers and profl. publs. Named Friend of the Arts in Edn., Ind. Art Edn. Assn., 1991. Avocation: gardening. Home: 2142 N 125 E Winamac IN 46996-8520 Office: Tortuga Inn Bed & Breakfast 2142 N 125 E Winamac IN 46996-8520 E-mail: riparian@pwrte.com.

LIGON, PATTI-LOU E. real estate company executive, educator; b. Riverside, Calif., Feb. 28, 1953; d. Munford Ernest and Patsy Hazel L. BS, San Diego State U., 1983; BBA, Nat. U., San Diego, 1983, MA in Bus. Adminstrn., 1984. Cert. profl. counselor. Escrow asst., Cajon, Calif., 1978-79, Summit Escrow, San Diego, 1979-81; escrow officer Fidelity Nat. Title, 1982-84, Dawson Escrow, San Diego, 1984; owner, property mgr., investment adviser Ligon Enterprises, 1980—, cons., 1982—. Chmn. com., alumnae and assocs. San Diego State U., 1983-85; chmn. com. San Diego Zool. Soc., 1985; pres. Friends of Symphony, Riverside, Calif., 1978. Recipient commendation City and County of Honolulu, 1981. Mem. NAFE, Nat. Notary Assn., Calif. Escrow Assn., Am. Home Econs. Assn., Internat. Platform Assn., Calif. Bus. Edn. Assn., Jr. League of San Diego, Spinster Club (pres. 1981), Univ. Club (San Diego), Sigma Kappa (pres. 1974, v.p. sorority corp. 1976—). Republican. Methodist. Avocations: racquetball, clothing design, photography, travel. Home and Office: Ligon Enterprises PO Box 1642 La Mesa CA 91944-1642

LIGON-BORDEN, BETTY LEE, academic director; b. Greensboro, N.C., Apr. 13, 1945; d. John Ligon and Jo Anne Bertha Pittenger; m. John Robert Jones, Aug. 10, 1963 (div. Sept. 1990); children: Darrell, Douglas, Derrick, Julie Jones Gill; m. Gordon Trotter Borden, June 4, 1994; stepchildren: Justin, Matthew, Borden. BA (hons.) magna cum laude, Sam Houston State U., 1985; MA, Tex. A&M U., 1987; PhD, Rice U., 1993. Sr. adminstrv. asst. Baylor Coll. Medicine, Houston, 1991-92; sr. editor U. Tex. M.D. Anderson Cancer Ctr., 1992-95, U. Ark. for Med. Sci., Little Rock, 1995-96; acad. dir., adv. bd. dir. The Phoenix Acad., Houston, 1995—. Charter mem. N.W. Bible Fellowship, Spring, Tex., 1977; editl. cons. Word Rite Editl. Consulting, Houston, 1994—; mem. faculty Baylor Coll. Medicine, Houston, 1997—; adj. faculty U. St. Thomas, Houston, 1999-2001, U. Houston Downtown, 1989-99; owner Tapestries, ETC, Houston. Editor (monthly newsletter) Palmer Meml. Episcopal Ch., 1998—; mng. editor Seminars in Pediat. Infectious Diseases; guest editor Jour. Neuro-Oncology, 1994, 95; contbr. articles to profl. jours. Discussion leader Bible Study Fellowship, Conroe, Tex., 1978-83; tchg. leader Precept Upon Precept, Houston, 1999-2001; lic. lay chalice bearer/reader Episcopal Ch. Merit scholar Inst. in Brit. and Irish Studies, Dublin, Ireland, 1990. Mem. MLA, Soc. for Tech. Comm., Am. Med. Writers Assn., Rice Alumni Assn. Episcopalian. Avocations: home renovation, reading, needlepoint. Office: Baylor Coll Medicine One Baylor Plaza TCH A150 Houston TX 77030

LIGOTTI, EUGENE FERDINAND, retired dentist; b. N.Y.C., June 10, 1936; s. Eugene A. and Lee (D'Agata) L.; m. Corbina Theresa Loscalzo, Nov. 21, 1959; children: Gina Maria Ligotti Aliperti, Lisa Anne Ligotti Liberatoscioli. BA, Adelphi U., 1958; DDS, NYU, 1962. Pvt. practice, Huntington, N.Y., 1962-92; instr. operative dentistry NYU, N.Y.C., 1962-65. Author historic fiction, mystery novels, and screenplays; contbr. articles to profl. jours. and mags.; inventor ValueVac. Founder, pres. Upper Bay Civic Assn., Inc., Huntington, 1979—2001. Mem.: ADA, Suffolk County Dental Soc., N.Y. State Dental Soc., Huntington Hist. Soc. (trustee), German Shepherd Dog Club (pres. 1971—75), Chi Sigma, Xi Psi Phi (founder alumni chpt. 1981—82). Republican. Roman Catholic. Avocations: travel, writing. E-mail: eligotti@optonline.net.

LIGOURI, LORENE DELIA, obstetrician-gynecologist; b. Bklyn., 1954; d. Peter Ligouri and Sylvia Castro; m. Camillus Annesley Fernando, Aug. 20, 1977; children: Adrienne Lynn, Alex Christopher, Andrew William. BS in Med. Tech., NYU, 1976; MD, Mt. Sinai Sch. Medicine, N.Y.C., 1980; MBA, U. Fla., 1998. Diplomate Am. Bd. Ob-Gyn, Am. Bd. Managed Care Medicine. Resident in ob-gyn. Staten Island (N.Y.) Hosp., 1980-82, Beth Israel Med. Ctr., N.Y.C., 1982-85; staff Luth. Med. Ctr., Bklyn., N.Y. Meth. Hosp., N.Y.C., Beth Israel Med. Ctr. Office: Luth Med Ctr 150-55th St FHC Station 8 Brooklyn NY 11220

LIGTHART, JENNY ELISABETH, economist, researcher; b. Hoogkarspel, The Netherlands, Nov. 6, 1967; came to the U.S., 1997; PhD in Econs., U. Amsterdam, The Netherlands, 1995. Asst. prof. U. Amsterdam, 1995-97; economist IMF, Washington, 1997—. Author: Environment, Imperfect Markets and Public Finance, 1997. Office: Tilburg U Dept Econ PO Box 90153 5000 LE Tilburg Netherlands E-mail: jligthart@imf.org.

LIGUORI, PAUL ANTHONY, physician; b. Bronx, N.Y., Jan. 30, 1962; s. Frank and Lucy (DeAssis) L.; m. Kathleen Ann Liguori, Nov. 7, 1992. MD, SUNY, Buffalo, 1991. Intern Millard Fillmore Hosp./SUNY, Buffalo, 1991-92; resident U. Wash. Med. Ctr., Seattle, 1992-95; assoc. med. dir. Whittier Rehab. Hosp., Westborough, Mass., 1995—; cons. staff Hale Hosp., Haverhill, 1996—; assoc. staff Boston U. Sch. Medicine, 1996—; assoc. med. dir. Whittier Rehab. Hosp., Westboro, Mass., 1997-2000, med. dir. Haverhill, 2000—. Fellow Am. Acad. Phys. Medicine and Rehab.; mem. AMA, Assn. Acad. Physiatrists, Mass. Med. Soc. Office: Whittier Rehab Hosp 76 Summer St Haverhill MA 01830

LIH-BRODY, LISA, gastroenterologist; b. Aug. 3, 1963; MD, SUNY, Stony Brook, 1989. Asst. attending physician North Shore U. Hosp., Manhasset, N.Y., 1996-98; attending physician Pro Health Care Assocs., Lake Success. Office: 2800 Mascus Ave New Hyde Park NY 11042

LIHS, HARRIET, performing arts educator; b. Forest Hills, N.Y., Jan. 18, 1944; d. Howard L. and Belle (Friedman) Kane; m. Henry Viets Rivers, July 15, 1990; children: Nancy Suzanne Lewin, Daniel Jonathan Lewin. BS in Dance, U. Iowa, 1980, MS in Dance, 1983; MFA in Dance, Smith Coll., 1989. Instr. dance Wapello (Iowa) Dance Theatre, 1972-80; instr. Muscatine (Iowa) C.C., 1975-85; assoc. prof. Lamar U., Beaumont, Tex., 1984—. Vis. instr. Calif. State U., Fresno, 1994-95; yoga instr. India Cultural Ctr., Beaumont, 1997—. Author: Teaching Gymnastics, 1990, 3d edit., 2001, Jazz Dance, 1991, 2d edit., 1993, Appreciating Dance, A Guide to the World's Liveliest Art, 1998, 3d edit., 2002. Bd. dirs. Unitarian Ch., 2001—. Grantee S.E. Tex. Arts, 1998. Mem. NOW (pres. Golden Triangle chpt. 1993-94). Democrat. Avocations: painting, yoga. Home: 295 N Parkway Dr Beaumont TX 77705 E-mail: lihshr@hal.lamar.edu.

LIHS, MARILYN LOUISE, retired accountant; b. Burlington, Iowa, May 5, 1941; d. Omer C. and Geraldine E. (Berges) Wickerham; m. Craig E. Lihs, Mar. 26, 1961; children: Jeffrey A., Michael S. AA, S.E. Iowa C.C., Burlington, 1961; BBA, U. Iowa, 1986, MBA, 1991. Ch. organist Mil. Chapel, Bremerhaven, Germany, 1966-68; accts. payable clk. City of Burlington, 1968-71; accts. recieveable clk. Economy Advt., Iowa City, 1971-74; office mgr. Shay Electric, 1974-76; contr. Midwest Elect. Cont., 1976-82; from adminstrv. asst. to fin. analyst U. Iowa, 1982-86, adminstrv. acct., 1986-98, ret., 1998. Contbr. articles to Iowa Bus. Woman Mag. Pres. Bus. and Profl. Women Iowa Found., Des Moines, 1995—96; program facilitator Iowa City Cable TV, 1997; rep., com. chair U. Iowa Staff Coun., 1991—97; v.p. Village United Meth. Women, 2000—02, pres., 2002—. Mem. AAUW, Bus. and Profl. Women (Iowa pres. 1995-96, Iowa City pres. 1997-98, newsletter editor 1997-99, Woman of Yr. 1995-96, 98-99, Spa Area Women of Yr. 2001-2002), U. Iowa Alumni Assn. (life), Village Quilt Guild (pres. 2000-01). Democrat. Methodist. Avocations: travel, quilting, writing, genealogy. Home: 62 Promesa Dr Hot Springs Village AR 71909-7757 E-mail: MarilynLihs@netscape.net.

LIJOI, PETER BRUNO, lawyer; b. Suffern, N.Y., Sept. 2, 1953; s. Salvatore and Josephine (Gentile) L.; m. Christine Louise Confroy, Aug. 19, 1978; children: Jonathan Peter, Christopher Andrew. BA in History and Econs.,

Montclair State Coll., 1975; postgrad. in urban planning, Rutgers U., 1975-76; JD, Pace U., 1979; postgrad., Harvard U., 1992. Bar: N.J. 1981, N.Y. 1988. Rsch. intern N.J. Dept. Edn., Trenton, 1976; intern Office U.S. Atty., N.Y.C., 1977-78; energy coord. Rockland County, 1979-80; dep. dir., of counsel Pvt. Industry Coun., Pearl River, N.Y., 1980-91; pvt. practice law Summit, N.J., 1981—; dir., counsel County of Rockland Indsl. Devel. Agy., 1981-95; v.p., gen. counsel Rockland Econ. Devel. Corp., Pearl River, 1990-91. Cons. U.S. Dept. Energy, Washington, 1980; mem. program of instrn. for lawyers Law Sch., Harvard U., 1992; legal counsel and land acquisition mgr. K. Hovnanian Cos. North Jersey, Inc., 1993-95, K. Hovnanian Cos. Northeast, Inc., 1995-2001; v.p. land acquisition and legal counsel D.R. Horton Inc., N.J.; legis. counsel to Assemblyman Eric Munoz, N.J. State Legislature. Guest writer The Bond Buyer. Bd. dirs. Rockland County coun. Girl Scouts U.S., 1982-92; pres. Washington Elem. Sch. PTA, Summit, 1986-88; mem. Summit Planning Bd., desegregation grant adv. com. Summit Bd. Edn., 1992—; commr. tax bd. Union County, 1999—. Mem. ABA, N.J. Bar Assn., N.Y. Bar Assn., Union County Bar Assn., Assn. Trial Lawyers Am., Nat. Assn. Bond Lawyers. Roman Catholic. Avocations: running, coaching youth soccer. Home: 124 Canoe Brook Pkwy Summit NJ 07901-1436 Office: 20 Gibson Place Freehold NJ 07728 Home Fax: 908-273-6926; Office Fax: 732-577-1885.

LIKE, LANCE D. lawyer; b. Vincennes, Ind., Dec. 10, 1964; s. Cameron Keith and Sharon L. Like; m. Karen K. Yoshida, Apr. 25, 1992; children: Alexander, Noah. BS, U. Evansville, 1987; JD, Ind. U., 1990. Assoc. Lembke, Stewart & Coates, Englewood, Colo., 1990—93, Mallor Clendening Grodner & Bohrer LLP, Bloomington, Ind., 1993—2000, ptnr., 2000—. V.p. Hoosier Hills Estate Planning Coun., Bloomington, 1996—97, pres., 1997—98. V.p. Boys & Girls Club, Bloomington, 1995—97, bd. mem., 1994—2000, Bloomington Hosp. Found. Planned Gifts Com., 1999—2002. Mem.: ABA, Wealth-Counsel, LLC, Monroe County Ind. Bar Assn., Ind. State Bar Assn. Office: Mallor Clendening Grodner & Bohrer LLP 511 Woodscrest Dr PO Box 5787 Bloomington IN 47407

LIKE, RUSSEL C. economist, consultant, writer; b. Bklyn., June 14, 1967; m. Tatyana Like; 1 child Daniel. BA, BS, U. Pa., 1989; MS, U. N.C., 1992. Author Brunswick Galaxy Press, Highland Park, NJ, 1992—. Author: After the Blue, 1998. Office: Brunswick Galaxy Press PO Box 4213 Highland Park NJ 08904

LIKE, STEVEN, lawyer; b. Vincennes, Ind., Sept. 5, 1956; s. Cameron Keith and Sharon Lee (Smith) L.; m. Jane Elizabeth Lambert, June 2, 1979 (div.); children: Brandon, Christopher, Stephanie. BA in Econs., DePauw U., 1978; JD cum laude, Ind. U., 1981. Bar: Ind. 1981, Mich. 1984, U.S. Dist. Ct. (no. and so. dists.) Ind. 1981, U.S. Ct. Appeals (7th cir.) 1986. Assoc. Warrick, Weaver & Boyn, Elkhart, Ind., 1981-85, ptnr., 1986—95; exec. v.p., gen. counsel Patriot Homes, Inc., 1995—. Bd. dirs. Manufactured Housing Inst. Bd. dirs. United Way Elkhart County, 1982-88; bd. dirs. Assn. for Disabled of Elkhart County, 1984-91, pres., 1989; vice-chmn. MHI Govt. Rels. Com., 2001—; bd. govs. IMHA-RUIC, 1999—, pres., 2002—. Mem. ABA, Ind. Bar Assn., Mich. Bar Assn., Elkhart City Bar Assn. Republican. Methodist. Avocations: boating, fishing, golf, travel. Office: 307 S Main St Ste 200 Elkhart IN 46516-3102

LIKENS, GENE ELDEN, biology and ecology educator, administrator; b. Pierceton, Ind., Jan. 6, 1935; s. Colonel Benjamin and Josephine (Garner) L.; m. Phyllis Craig; children: Kathy, Gregory, Leslie. BS, Manchester (Ind.) Coll., 1957, DSc (hon.), 1979; MS, U. Wis., 1959, PhD, 1962; DSc (hon.), Rutgers U., 1985, Plymouth State Coll., U. N.H., 1989, Miami U., 1990; LHD (hon.), Union Coll., 1991; DSc (hon.), U. Bodenkultur, Vienna, Austria, 1993, Marist Coll., 1993; DSc, Wageningen Agrl. U., The Netherlands, 1998. Asst. zoology Manchester Coll., 1955-57; grad. teaching asst. U. Wis., 1957-59, vis. lectr., 1963; instr. zoology Dartmouth Coll., 1961, instr. biol. scis., 1963, asst. prof., then assoc. prof., 1963-69; mem. faculty Cornell U., 1969-83, prof. ecology, 1972-83, Charles A. Alexander prof. biol. scis., 1983, adj. prof., 1983—; v.p. N.Y. Bot. Garden, 1983-93; dir. Inst. Ecosystem Studies, Millbrook, NY, 1983—, pres., 1993—, G. Evelyn Hutchinson chair in ecology, 2000—; dir. Mary Flagler Cary Arboretum, 1983—; prof. biology Yale U., 1984—; prof. grad. field of ecology Rutgers U., 1985—. Vis. prof. Ctr. Advanced Rsch., also dept. environ scis. U. Va., Charlottesville, 1978-79; lectr. Williams Summer Inst. Coll. Tchrs., 1966, 67, Drew Summer Inst. Coll. Tchrs., 1968, Cornell U. Alumni Assn., 1978; Paul C. Lemon ecology lectr. SUNY, Albany, 1978; chmn. New Eng. div. task force conservation aquatic ecosystems U.S. Internat. Biol. Program, 1966-67; vis. assoc. ecologist Brookhaven Nat. Lab., 1968; C.P. Snow lectr. Ithaca Coll., 1979, 89; Robert S. Campbell lectr. U. Mo., 1980; A.E. Waller lectr. Ohio State U., 1990; Disting. Ecologist lectr. N.C. State U., 1980; Henry J. Oosting lectr. Duke U., 1985; Rilett vis. scholar Ill. State U., 1985; vis. scholar James Madison U., 1988; Class of 1960 vis. scholar, Williams Coll., Williamstown, Mass., 1988; Jack R. Hargis lectr. U. Minn., Duluth, 1988; Robert H. Woodworth lectr. in sci. Bennington (Vt.) Coll., 1988; mem. Nat. Commn. on Environment, 1991; Olin lectr. Environ. Fairfield U., 1990; lectr. Golden Series, Universität für Bodenkultur, 1991; William V. Kaesar Meml. scholar U. Wis., Madison, 1991; disting. scientist lecture series Bard Coll., 1991; Donnell Foster Hewett Lecture series Lehigh U., 1992; Miles C. Horton spl. lect. Va. Polytech. Inst., State U., 1993, Marine Biological Lab. Fri. evening lecture series Woods Hole, 1993; Granville Sewell disting. lectr. Columbia U., 1994; vis. disting. ecologist, Colo. State U., 1994; Raymond Lindeman Meml. lectr. U. Minn., 1996, Hans Jenny Meml. lectr. U. Calif., Berkeley, First N.M. Johnson lectr. Dartmouth Coll., 1996; Joseph Henry Sci. lectr., NY, 1997., Edward Bronfman Family Foundation Lecture, U. Vermont, 1998, Joan Milliken Stroud Meml. lectr. Stroud Water Rsch. Ctr., Avondale, Penn., 1998, Edwin Way Teale lectr. U. Conn., Storrs, 1998, Plenary lectr. ASLO Aquatic Scis., Santa Fe, 1999; plenary lectr. AIBS, 2000, U. Wis. Great Lakes Water Inst., 2000; cons. in field; mem. numerous govt. and sci. panels, 6th Huxley Lecturer, 2001, Institute of Biology, London; Walker Ames Professorship and lecturer, University of Washington, Seattle, 2001; participant numerous confs. Author 15 books; contbr. over 400 articles to sci. jours. Recipient Conservation award Am. Motors Corp., 1969, 75th Anniversary award U.S. Forest Svc., 1980, Disting. Achievement award Lab. Biomed. and Environ. Studies, UCLA, 1982, Regents medal of excellence SUNY, 1984, award N.Y. Acad. Scis., 1986, Internat. ECI prize for Limnetic Ecology, 1989, Disting. Svc. award N.Y. Bot. Garden, 1989, Disting. Svc. award Am. Inst. Biol. Scis., 1990, Lifetime Accomplishment award, 2000, Disting. Svc. award Hudson River Environ. Soc., 1997, The Garden Club Am. Spl. Citation, 1992, The Tyler World Environment prize U. So. Calif., 1993, Australia Prize, 1994; NATO sr. fellow, 1969, Guggenheim fellow, 1972-73; grantee NSF, EPA, Dept. Energy, USDA Forest Svc., NOAA, Disting. Svc. award Hudson River Environ. Soc., Inc., 1997, Vollenweider award and lecturship in Aquatic Sciences, Canada Ctr. for Inland Waters, Nat. Water Rsch. Inst., 1998, Storm King Award, Scenic Hudson Inc., 1998, Award of Excellence Nat. Coun. State Garden Clubs Inc., 1999. Fellow: AAAS; mem.: NAS (chmn . sect. 27 1986—89), Royal Danish Acad. Sci., Am. Inst. Biol. Scis. (pres. 2002—), Australian Acad. Scis. (Exch. fellow divsn. math. and natural scis. 2000), Australian Soc. Limnology, Internat. Water Resources Assn. (charter), Internat. Assn. Gt. Lakes Rsch., Freshwater Biol. Assn., Explorers Club, Am. Polar Soc., Royal Swedish Acad. Scis., Internat. Assn. Theoretical and Applied Limnology (v.p. 1998, pres. 2001, nat. rep., Naumann-Thienemann medal 1995), Am. Soc. Limnology and Oceanography (pres. 1976—77, v.p. 1975—76, 1st G.E. Hutchinson award for excellence in rsch. 1982), Ecol. Soc. Am. (chmn. study com. 1971—74, v.p. 1978—79, pres. 1981—82, Eminent Ecologist award 1995), Am. Acad. Arts and Scis., Brit. Ecol. Soc. (hon.), Am. Water Resources Assn. (hon.), Sigma Xi, Phi Sigma, Gamma Alpha. Methodist. Office: Inst Ecosys Studies Box AB Millbrook NY 12545 E-mail: likensg@ecostudies.org.

LIKENS, JAMES DEAN, economics educator; b. Bakersfield, Calif., Sept. 12, 1937; s. Ernest LeRoy and Monnie Jewel (Thomas) L.; m. Janet Sue Pelton, Dec. 18, 1965 (div.); m. Karel Carnohan, June 4, 1988 (div.); children: John David, Janet Elizabeth. BA in Econs., U. Calif., Berkeley, 1960, MBA, 1961; PhD in Econs., U. Minn., 1970. Analyst Del Monte Corp., San Francisco, 1963; economist 3M Co., Mpls., 1968-71; asst. prof. econs. Pomona Coll., 1969-75, assoc. prof. econs., 1975-83, prof. econs., 1983-85, Morris B. and Gladys S. Pendleton prof. econs., 1989—, dept. chair, 1998-2001. Vis. asst. prof. econs. U. Minn., 1970, 71, vis. assoc. prof., 1976-77; pres., dean Western CUNA Mgmt. Sch., Pomona Coll., 1975—; chmn. bd. 1st City Savs. Fed. Credit Union, 1978—; coord. So. Calif. Rsch. Coun., L.A., 1980-81, 84-85; mem. adv. coun. Western Corp. Fed. Credit Union, 1993—; cons. in field. Author: (with Joseph LaDou) Medicine and Money, 1976, Mexico and Southern California: Toward A New Partnership, 1981, Financing Quality Education in Southern California, 1985; contbr. articles to profl. jours. Served with USCG, 1961-67. Named Dir. of Yr., Calif. Credit UnionLeague, 1997, Credit Union Exec. Soc., 2001; recipient Leo H. Shapiro Lifetime Achievement award, Calif. Credit Union League, 2001; grantee rsch. grantee HUD-DOT, Haynes Found. Mem. ABA, Am. Econ. Assn., Western Econ. Assn. Home: 725 W 10th St Claremont CA 91711-3719 Office: Pomona Coll Dept Econs Claremont CA 91711 E-mail: jlikens@pomona.edu.

LIKINS, PETER WILLIAM, university administrator; b. Tracy, Calif., July 4, 1936; s. Ennis Blaine and Dorothy Louise (Medlin) L.; m. Patricia Ruth Kitsmiller, Dec. 18, 1955; children: Teresa, Lora, Paul, Linda, Krista, John. BCE, Stanford U., 1957, PhD in Engring. Mechanics, 1965; MCE, MIT, 1958; PhD (hon.), Lafayette Coll., 1983, Moravian Coll., 1984, Med. Coll. Pa., 1990, Lehigh U., 1991, Allentown St. Francis de Sales, 1993, Czech Tech U., 1993. Devel. engr. Jet Propulsion Lab., Pasadena, Calif., 1958-60; asst. prof. engring. UCLA, 1964-69, assoc. prof., 1969-72, prof., 1972-76, asst. dean, 1974-75, asso. dean, 1975-76; dean engring. and applied sci. Columbia U., N.Y.C., 1976-80, provost, 1980-82; pres. Lehigh U., Bethlehem, Pa., 1982-97, U. Ariz., Tucson, 1997—. Cons. in field. Author: Elements of Engineering Mechanics, 1973, Spacecraft Dynamics, 1982; Contbr. articles to profl. jours. Mem. U.S. Pres.'s Coun. Advisors Sci. and Tech., 1990-93. Ford Found. fellow, 1970-72; named to Nat. Wrestling Hall of Fame Fellow AIAA; mem. Nat. Acad. Engring., Phi Beta Kappa, Sigma Xi, Tau Beta Pi. Office: U Ariz PO Box 210066 Tucson AZ 85721-0066 E-mail: plikins@arizona.edu.*

LIKLEY, KATHERINE, retired retail executive, writer; b. Bakersfield, Calif., July 5, 1948; d. Newton Albert and Marion Louise (Clymer) L.; widowed; children: Ralph, James, Stuart; divorced; 1 child, Marion Louise. Student, Oxnard City Coll.; Yuba Coll., Butte Coll. V.p. Kties Thrift, Paradise, Calif.; pub. Writing Writers Mag.; pres. the Curiosity Shop, The Toy Attic, Paradise; trade coord. UTB-Oroville. Author of poems, short stories. With USNG, 1978—. Avocations: writing, grandchildren, pets. Office: 3925 Myers St Oroville CA 95966-6725 E-mail: alaskanme@yahoo.com.

LIKOSKY, WILLIAM HARRIS, neurologist, epidemiologist; b. Burlington, Vt., Feb. 23, 1940; s. Israel Nathan and Nettie Gertrude (Schobel) L.; m. Marilyn Jean Schron, June 27, 1965; children: David, Michael, Donald. BA, U. Vt., 1962, MD, 1966. Intern in medicine Yale U., New Haven, 1966-67, resident in medicine, 1967-68, resident in neurology, 1970-77; epidemiologist Communicable Disease Ctr., Atlanta, 1968-70; physician Kaiser Permanente, Santa Clara, Calif., 1978-90, dir. utilization Oakland, 1990-2000; chair dept. neurology Minor & James Med., Seattle, 2000—. Mem. Calif. Med. Rev. Inc., San Francisco, 1996—; dir. stroke care Swedish Med. Ctrs., Seattle. Mem. med. bd. MS Soc., Santa Clara, Calif., 1975-93. With Pub. Health Svc., 1978-70 Office: 515 Minor Ave Seattle WA 98104-2120 E-mail: BLikosky@pol.net.

LILES, CLIFTON ROY, software designer; b. San Antonio, Jan. 28, 1944; s. Roy Clifton and Lucy Mae Liles. BS in Physics, U. Houston, 1978. Software engr. Tex. Instruments, Richardson, Tex., 1978-90, Unisys, Houston, 1990-96; mem. computer sci. staff, software designer United Space Alliance, 1996—. With U.S. Army, 1967-71. Mem. IEEE, Assn. Computing Machinery, Am. Geophys. Union. Home: 2310 Longwood Dr Pearland TX 77581 Office: United Space Alliance 600 Gemini Ave Houston TX 77058 E-mail: c.r.liles@ieee.org., lilescr@acm.org.

LILEY, ELIZABETH ELLEN, journalist, educator; b. Lafayette, Ind., Nov. 14, 1964; d. Peter Edward and Elaine Elizabeth (Kull) Liley; m. Roman Goz, Aug. 31, 1997. BA, Purdue U., 1986. Reporter Jour. and Courier, Lafayette, 1986-89; reporter, acting bur. chief Gannett News Svc., Indpls., 1987-88; reporter, sr. writer, asst. metro editor Burlington (Vt.) Free Press, 1989-98; assoc. dir. pub. rels. Kelliher, Samets Volk Communicators, Burlington, Vt., 1998-99; dir. grants and spl. projects Burlington (Vt.) Sch. Dist., 1999—. Adj. prof. St. Michael's Coll., Colchester, Vt., 1993-98, Champlain Coll., Burlington, Vt., 1999-2001; ptnr., v.p. New Russia Imports Inc., St. Albans, Vt./St. Petersburg, Russia, 1994—. Pres. bd. dirs. Champlain Assn. for Retarded Citizens, Burlington, 1997—; vol. Hospice of Champlain Valley, Colchester, 1991—, bd. dirs., 1992-94; bd. dirs. Champlain Valley Jr. Svc., Burlington, 1991-92; pres. bd. dirs. Ledgewood South Condominium Assn., 1994—; mem. campaign cabinet United Way of Chittenden County, 2001—. Recipient Mavis Doyle award/Best Journalist in Vt., 1994, New Eng. Press Assn. award, Gannett Well Done awards, Vt. Press Assn. award, others. Lutheran. Home: 631 Maquam Shore Rd Swanton VT 05488-8449 Office: 150 Colchester Ave Burlington VT 05401-1422

LILEY, PETER EDWARD, mechanical engineering educator; b. Barnstaple, North Devon, Eng., Apr. 22, 1927; came to U.S., 1957; s. Stanley E. and Rosa (Ellery) L.; m. Elaine Elizabeth Kull, Aug. 16, 1963; children: Elizabeth Ellen, Rebecca Ann. BSc, U. London, 1951, PhD in Physics, DIC, U. London, 1957. With Brit. Oxygen Engring., London, 1955-57; asst. prof. mech. engring. Purdue U., West Lafayette, Ind., 1957-61, assoc. prof., 1961-72; assoc. sr. researcher Thermophys. Properties Research Ctr., Purdue U., 1961-72, prof. mech. engring., 1972-98; prof. emeritus, 1998—; sr. rschr. Ctr. for Info. and Numerical Data Analysis and Synthesis, Purdue U., West Lafayette, Ind., 1972-92. Cons. in field. Author: Sect. 2 Perry's Chemical Engineers Handbook, 7th edit., 1997, (with Hartnett et al.) Handbook of Heat Transfer Fundamentals, 2d edit., 1985, (with others) Marks Mechanical Engineers Handbook, 10th edit., 1996, Schaums 2000 Solved Problems in Mechanical Engineering Thermodynamics, 1988, Tables and Charts for Thermodynamics, 1995, Kutz Mechanical Engineers Handbook, 1998; co-author: Steam and Gas Tables with Computer Equations, 1985, Thermal Conductivity of Nonmetallic Liquids and Gases, 1970, Properties of Nonmetallic Fluid Elements, 1981, Properties of Inorganic and Organic Fluids, 1988; editor, mem. editl. bd. Internat. Jour. Thermophysics, 1980-86; contbr. chpts. to handbooks in field; contbr. articles to profl. jours.; reviewer profl. jours. Served with Royal Corps Signals, Brit. Army, 1945-48. Lutheran. Home: 3608 Mulberry Dr Lafayette IN 47905-3937 Office: Purdue U Dept Mech Engring Lafayette IN 47907 E-mail: eandpliley@insightbb.com.

LILIEN, ELLIOT STEPHEN, secondary education educator; b. Maplewood, N.J. s. Bernard Banner and Judith Batson (Mulally) L.; m. Louise Anne Hoehl, Jan. 29, 1965 (div. July 1968); m. Nancy Goddard Pierce, July 21, 1985. BA, U. Chgo., 1961; JD, Columbia U., 1964; MAT, Harvard U., 1965. Tchr. Concord (Mass.)-Carlisle H.S., 1965—, head coach fencing, 1965-85, head coach tennis, 1989—; curriculum coord. social studies K-12 Concord-Carlisle Schs., 1997. Head coach fencing Brown U., Providence, 1987-93; dir. Concord-Acad. Fencing Camp, 1975—. Author: German History 1815-1945, 1972, History of Greece and Rome, 1979, Competition Experiment, 1986. Commr. Northeast Fencing Conf., Boxboro, Mass., 1993—. Grantee Coun. for Basic Edn., 1983; elected to Concord-Carlisle Athetic Hall of Fame, 1996. Mem. Four Sch. Consortium (founder, pres. 1987), Concord-Carlisle Tchrs. (pres. 1972-94). Avocations: tennis, WWI poster collecting, swords, beer steins, autographs. Home: 62 Chester Rd Boxboro MA 01719-1808 Office: Concord-Carlisle H S 500 Walden St Concord MA 01742-3699

LILIEN, MARK IRA, executive; b. Kew Gardens, N.Y., Sept. 7, 1953; s. Robert Samuel and Annette Audrey (London) L. BS in Labor Relations, Cornell U., 1974; MBA in Entrepreneurial Mktg., U. Pa., 1976. Buyer, mdse. controller Korvettes Dept. Stores, N.Y.C., 1976-79; dir. mdse. adminstrn. Walden Books, Stamford, Conn., 1979-84; sr. assoc. Booz Allen & Hamilton, N.Y.C., 1985-86; v.p. Penguin USA, 1986-89, Barnes & Noble Bookstores, N.Y.C., 1989-92, Lechters, 1992-94, McGraw-Hill, N.Y.C., 1994-96; exec. v.p., COO Wilton Industries, 1997-2000; sr. v.p. ops. Lechters, 2000—01; COO, Kate's Paperie, 2002—. Usergroup chmn. JDA/ODBMS-WCC, 2000-01. Mem. editorial bd. Retail Systems Alert Newsletter, 1991-94. Schirer fellow Wharton Sch. Bus. U. Pa., 1975-76. Mem. Book Industry Systems Adv. Com. (vice chmn. 1983-84, chmn. 1988-89), Book Industry Study Group, Assn. Am. Pubs. (bus. mgrs. com., Pubnet com. 1986-89), Nat. Retail Fedn. (chmn. SpecNet com. 1990-92). Avocations: theatre, films. Home: 350 Bleecker St Apt 3E New York NY 10014-2631 E-mail: Marklilien@juno.com.

LILIENSTEIN, ROBERT WOLFGANG, anesthesiologist; b. Hamburg, Germany, Mar. 8, 1928; s. Theo Isidor and Hilde Johanna Lilienstein; m. Henrietta Mildred Robinson, Oct. 27, 1956; children: Joanne, Frieda, Peter, David. BA, NYU, 1951; MD, Finch U. Health Sci./Chgo. Med. Sch., 1955. Diplomate Am. Bd. Anesthesiology. Intern Los Angeles County Gen. Hosp., 1955-56; resident gen. practice San Luis Obisop Gen. Hosp., 1956-57; pvt. gen. practice, Half Moon Bay, Calif., 1957-60; resident in anesthesiology U. Calif. Med. Ctr., San Francisco, 1960-62; active med. staff St. Josephs Med. Ctr., Stockton, Calif., 1962-96; ret., 1996—; mem. staff emeritus Stockton Anesthesia Med. Group, Inc., 1996—. Mem. AMA, Calif. Med. Assn., Am. Soc. Anesthesiologists, Calif. Soc. Anesthesiologists, Internat. Anesthesia Rsch. Soc. Office: Stockton Anesthesia Med Group Inc PO Box 4057 2626 N California St Ste G Stockton CA 95204-5500 E-mail: rowli@softcom.net.

LILIENTHAL, ALFRED M(ORTON), author, historian, editor; b. N.Y.C., Dec. 25, 1913; s. Herbert and Lottye (Kohn) L. BA, Cornell U., Ithaca, N.Y., 1934; LLB, Columbia U., 1938, JD, 1969. Bar: N.Y. 1938. With Bennett, House & Couts, N.Y.C., 1939-41, State Dept., 1942-43, 45-48; cons. U.S. del. UN San Francisco Conf., 1945; adminstrv. practice, 1947-50; counsel Am.-Arab Assn. Commerce & Industry, 1960-65; editor, pub. Middle East Perspective (monthly newsletter), 1967-85. Lectr. on Middle East at numerous colls. and clubs throughout U.S. and fgn. countries, 1951-94, frequent guest TV and radio news commentator on Middle East devels., 1951-91; lectr. cultural symposium United Arab Emirates, Libya, Lebanon, Vienna, Baghdad, Prague; polit. columnist daily Al Qabas, Kuwait, 1976-77; accredited corr. to UN; chmn. Am. Coun. on the Middle East; cons. UN Internat. Conf. on Question Palestine, Geneva, 1983; participant Model Internat. Conf. on Middle East, Prague, 1988, 27 Middle East trips including West Bank and Gaza, 1953-94; guest of UN Sec.-Gen. at 50th Commemorative meeting, San Francisco, 1995. Author: Which Way to World Government, 1949, What Price Israel?, 1954, There Goes the Middle East, 1957, Studies in Twentieth Century Diplomacy, 1959, The Other Side of the Coin, 1965, Polish transl., 1966, The Zionist Connection, 1978, The Zionist Connection II, 1982, rev. Czechoslovakian edit., 1989, Japanese edit., 1991, This I Do Believe, 1994; contbr.: Zionism-The Dream and the Reality, 1974; monthly commentaries Washington Report on Middle East Affairs, 1988—; also numerous mag. articles and syndicated newspieces. Pres. Rep. First Voters League, 1940; Fusion Party candidate for N.Y.C. Coun., 1941; leader fight against Communist controlled Am. Youth Congress, 1941. With AUS, 1943-45. Papers housed in archives of Hoover Instn., Stanford, Calif. Mem. Nat. Rep. Club, Univ. Club, Capitol Hill Club, Nat. Press Club, Cornell Club Washington. Home and Office: 800 25th St NW Washington DC 20037-2207

LILIENTHAL, DAVID E. See ELY, DAVID

LILJEGREN, FRANK SIGFRID, artist, art association official; b. N.Y.C., Feb. 23, 1930; s. Josef Sigfrid and Ester (Davidsson) L.; m. Donna Kathryn Hallam, Oct. 12, 1957. Student, Art Students League, N.Y.C., 1950-55. Instr. painting, drawing, composition Westchester County Ctr., White Plains, N.Y., 1967-77, Art Students League, 1974-75, Wassenberg Art Ctr., Van Wert, Ohio, 1978-80, Wright State U. Br. Western Ohio Campus, Celina, 1981—. Corr. sec. Allied Artists Am., N.Y.C., 1967, exhbn. chmn., 1968— , pres., 1970-72, also bd. dirs. Exhibited at Suffolk Mus., Stonybrook, N.Y., Springfield (Mass.) Mus., Marion Kugler McNay Art Inst., San Antonio, Philbrook Mus., Tulsa, NAD, N.Y.C., New Britain (Conn.) Mus. Art, Ft. Wayne (Ind.) Mus. Art; represented in permanent collections Art Students League, Univ. Mus., S.E. Mo. State U., Cape Girardeau, Manhattan Savs. Bank, N.Y.C., Am. Ednl. Pubs. Inst., N.Y.C., New Britain Mus. Am. Art, Conn. With AUS, 1951. Recipient numerous awards for still life oil paintings. Mem. Fine Arts fedn. N.Y, Art Students League (life), Acad. Artists Assn., Coun. Am. Artists Socs., Artists Fellowship, Salmagundi. *The best advice I could give young artists is to first learn their craft to the fullest so that they can then be free to express themselves in what ever style and medium they then choose to work. Last but not least, they should have self-respect and great love for what they are doing.*

LILJESTRAND, JAMES STRATTON, physician administrator, internist; b. Wareham, Mass., May 8, 1941; s. Robert Stratton and Lyla Mae Liljestrand; div. 1978; children: Karin E., Norman N.; m. Alice Jane Romanker, Aug. 20, 1983; children: Amy A., Jennelle S. BS, Ohio State U., 1962; MD, Northwestern U., 1966; MPH, Harvard U., 1973. Diplomate Am. Bd. Preventive Medicine. Instr. Harvard Med. Sch., Boston, 1973-75; asst. dean Harvard Sch. Pub. Health, 1973-76; med. dir., sr. v.p. med. svcs. Healthsouth Braintree (Mass.) Rehab. Hosp., 1975-99; assoc. clin. coord. MassPro, Waltham, Mass., 1999—. Pres. Nat. Assn. Rehab. Facilities, Washington, 1991-93; chmn. bd. Rehab. Facilities Svcs., Inc., Washington, 1991-92; corp. med. liason Continental Med. Systems, Inc., Mechanicsburg, Pa., 1992-97. Contbr. articles to profl. jours. Pres. Alumni Assn. Harvard Sch. Pub. Health, 1980-83; assoc. clin. coord. Mass Pro; bd. dirs. Woods Hole Children's Sch. Sci.; clk. standing com. First Parish in Concord. With USPHS, 1967-69. Recipient Membership award Am. Acad. of Physical Medicine and Rehab., Chgo., 1991. Fellow Am. Heart Assn. (mem. stroke coun.), Am. Coll. Preventive Medicine, Am. Coll. Physician Execs. (cert.). Office: 235 Wyman St Waltham MA 02451-1231

LILLARD, JOHN FRANKLIN, III, lawyer; b. Cheverly, Md., Aug. 2, 1947; s. John Franklin Lillard Jr. and Madeline Virginia (Berg) Lillard; m. Kim Leslie Oliver, June 1, 1991 (div.); 1 child John Franklin Lillard IV. Bar: N.Y. 1972, D.C. 1974, Md. 1975. Assoc. Donovan, Leisure, Newton & Irvine, N.Y.C., 1971-74; ptnr. Lillard & Lillard, Washington, 1977—; trial atty. civil div. Dept. Justice, 1976-77. Instr. Dale Carnegie Course, 1988—97. Vice chair Village Coun. Friendship Heights, Chevy Chase, Md., 1975—77; chair Am. Solar Energy Assn.; founding mem. Nat. Adv. Coun. Ctr. for Study of the Presidency, 1970—99, Md. State Adv. Bd. on Spl. Tax Dists., 1976—77; alcoholic beverage adv. bd. Montgomery County, 1977—79; chair Eisenhower Centennial Meml. Com., 1990—97; candidate U.S. Congress 5th dist., Md., 1981. Recipient Eastman award, Am. Arbitration Assn., 1971. Mem.: Anne Arundel County Bar Assn., Prince George's County Bar Assn., Md. Bar Assn., Marlborough Hunt Club, Tred Avon Yacht Club (Oxford, Md.), Met. Club Washington. Republican. Episcopalian. Office: 8 Loudon Ln Annapolis MD 21401-1219

LILLARD, MARK HILL, III, computer consulting executive, former air force officer; b. Jacksonville, Fla., Sept. 1, 1943; s. Mark Hill Jr. and Cornelia Kingman (Callaway) L.; m. Marie-Jacques Le Guyader, June 3, 1972; children: Mark Hill IV, Michael Robert. BA, Bowling Green U., 1965; MS, St. Mary's U., San Antonio, 1976; MBA, Auburn U., 1977. Commd. 2d lt. USAF, 1965, advanced through grades to brig. gen., 1991; dir. spl. actions Combined Forces Command, Republic of Korea, 1980-83; comdr. 596 BMS, Barksdale AFB, La., 1983-85; dep. comdr. OPS, 2 BMS, 1985; chief force mgmt. Strategic Air Command Hdqrs, Offutt, Nebr., 1985-87; comdr. 64 ABG, Reese AFB, Tex., 1987, 64 FTW, Reese AFB, 1987-88; exec. to chief of staff SHAPE (NATO), Mons, Belgium, 1988-91; comdr. 57th Air Div., Minot AFB, N.D., 1991; ret., 1991; exec. v.p. Pilot Rsch. Assocs., Inc., Vienna, 1991—, also bd. dirs. Author: Simulation, 1976. Decorated Legion of Merit, Def. Superior Svc. medal, Def. Meritorious Svc. medal; Samil medal (Republic of Korea). Mem. Air Force Assn., Lions, Kiwanis, Phi Delta Theta. Republican. Avocations: tennis, golf. Home: 9516 Locust Hill Dr Great Falls VA 22066-2021 Office: Pilot Rsch Assocs Inc 1953 Gallows Rd Ste 350 Vienna VA 22182-4005

LILLEHEI, KEVIN OWEN, neurosurgeon, educator; b. Mpls., July 6, 1953; m. Anne Cheryl Hofmann; 1 child, Kira Anne. BS, Cornell U., 1975; MD, U. Mich., 1979—80, resident, 1980—85; asst. prof. surgery neurosurgery div. U. Colo. Health Scis. Ctr., Denver, 1985—2000, prof. neurosurgery, 2000—, chief sect. neuro-oncology, 1990—, vice chmn. dept. neurosurgery, 2001—; dir. neurosurg. intensive care unit Denver Gen. Hosp., 1986-87; chief neurosurgery Denver VA Hosp., 1987-90. Mem. AMA, Denver Med. Soc., Colo. Med. Soc., Colo. Neurosurg. Soc., Congress Neurol. Surgeons, Denver Acad. Surgery. Office: U Colo Health Scis Ctr 4200 E 9th Ave # 307C Denver CO 80220-3706

LILLEMOEN, HENRY DANIEL, retired writer; b. Pitts., Feb. 25, 1928; s. Daniel and Ella Maria (Kohring) L.; m. Betty Jane Veil, Aug. 19, 1950; children: Daniel, John, Richard, Randi, Erik. BA in Latin Am. Studies, U. Pitts., 1950. Supt. Harcliff Coal Co., East Brady, Pa., 1950-53; asst. mgr. Conn. Gen., Washington, 1953-58; sales mgr. Ward Mfg., 1958-68; nat. sales mgr. El Dorado Ind., Minneapolis, Kans., 1968-73; pvt. practice mfg. rep. Myrtle Beach, S.C., 1973-92; freelance writer Murrells Inlet, 1992—. Contbr. articles and short stories to popular mags. Lt. (j.g.) USNR. Mem. VFW, Am. Legion. Avocations: fishing, golf. Home: 763 Nelson Dr Murrells Inlet SC 29576-6305

LILLER, KAREN DESAFEY, public health educator; b. Pitts., Nov. 18, 1956; d. Thomas and Irene (Cenderelli) DeSafey; m. David Allen Liller, Aug. 30, 1980; children: Matthew Thomas Allen, Rebecca Irene Rose. BS, W.Va. U., 1978; MA, U. South Fla., 1982, EdS, 1986, PhD, 1988. Med. technologist Fla. Hosp., Altamonte Springs, 1978-81; lab. instr. Tampa (Fla.) Med. Coll., 1982-83; edn. dir. Sch. Med. Tech. Tampa Gen. Hosp., 1983-85; sci. advisor Mylan Pharms., Inc., Tampa, 1986-87; postdoctoral fellow Coll. Pub. Health, U. South Fla., 1988-90, asst. prof., 1990-96, assoc. prof., 1996—. Contbr. articles to profl. jours. Home: 16509 Cayman Dr Tampa FL 33624-1065 Office: U South Fla Coll Pub Health 13201 Bruce B Downs Blvd Tampa FL 33612-3805 E-mail: kliller@hsc.usf.edu.

LILLES, ANTHONY LYNN, church administrator, educator; b. Bethesda, Md., Nov. 13, 1964; s. John Cyprien Lilles and Elise Etna Mathias; m. Agnes Marie-Therese Kim Lilles, Sept. 21, 2002; children: John, Elisabeth, Marie. BA, Franciscan U., Stubenville, Ohio, 1987; STL, Pontifical Universtity of St. Thomas, Rome, Italy, 1992; STD, Pontifical U. of St. Thomas. Dir. of religious edn. Good Shephard Parish, Archdiocese of Denver, Denver, 1992—98; educator St. Thomas Sem., 1994—96; dir. of liturgy Archdiocese of Denver, Chancery, 1998—99; assoc. dir. of liturgy Arch Diocese of Denver, Chancerey, 1999—2001; theology faculty St. John Vianney Theol. Sem., 1998—99, chair of sacraments & liturgy depaartment, 1999—, prefect of studies, 2001—. Mem.: Fellowship of Cath. Scholars, Soc. of Cath. Liturgy. R-Consevative. Roman Catholic. Avocations: skiing, hiking, horseback riding, surfing. Home: 7743 West 62nd Way Arvada CO 80004 Office: St John Vianney Theological Seminary 1600 South Steele Street Denver CO 80210 Personal E-mail: lilles@archden.org.

LILLESAND, THOMAS MARTIN, remote sensing educator; b. Laurium, Mich., Oct. 1, 1946; m. Theresa Hofmeister, 1968; children: Mark, Kari, Michael. BS, U. Wis., 1969, MS, 1970, PhD in Civil Engring., 1973. Prof. remote sensing SUNY, Syracuse, 1973-78, U. Minn., 1978-82, U. Wis., Madison, 1982—. Cons., 1973—. Mem. ASCE (pres.), Am. Soc. Photogrammetry and Remote Sensing (Alan Gordon award 1979, 93, Talbert Abrams award 1984, Fennell award 1988), Soc. Am. Foresters, Am. Congress on Surveying and Mapping. Office: U Wis Environ Remote Sensing Ctr 1225 W Dayton St Rm 1239B Madison WI 53706-1612

LILLESTOL, JANE BRUSH, development consultant; b. Jamestown, N.D., July 20, 1936; d. Harper J. and Doris (Mikkelson) Brush; m. Harvey Lillestol, Sept. 29, 1956; children: Kim, Kevin, Erik. BS, U. Minn., 1969, MS, 1973, PhD, 1977; grad. Inst. Ednl. Mgmt., Harvard U., 1984. Dir. placement, asst. to dean U. Minn., St. Paul, 1975-77; assoc. dean, dir. student acad. affairs N.D. State U., Fargo, 1977-80; dean Coll. Human Devel. Syracuse (N.Y.) U., 1980-89, v.p. for alumni rels., 1989-95, project dir. IBM Computer Aided Design Lab., 1989—92; prin. Lillestol Assocs.; emeritus faculty Syracuse (N.Y.) U., 1995—. Charter mem. Mayor's Commn. on Women, 1986-90; NAFTA White House Conf. for Women Leaders, 1993. Bd. dirs. Univ. Hill Corp. Syracuse, 1983-93; mem. steering com. Consortium for Cultural Founds. of Medicine, 1980-89; trustee Manlius Pebble Hill Sch., 1990-94, Archbold Theatre, 1990-95, N.D. State U., 1992—. Recipient award U.S. Consumer Product Safety Commn., 1983, Woman of Yr. award AAUW, 1984, svc. award Syracuse U., 1992; named among 100 Outstanding Alumni Over Past 100 Yrs., U. Minn. Coll. Human Ecology, 2001; faculty practitioner, U. Phoenix Online, 2002. Office: 8046 E Via De Los Libros Scottsdale AZ 85258-3056 E-mail: lillestol@bigfoot.com.

LILLESTOL, MICHAEL JOHN, physician; b. Breckenridge, Minn., Nov. 8, 1947; s. Harvey S. and Mildred M. (Hager) L.; m. Mary L. Forsberg, Apr. 9, 1977; children: Kristopher, Kim, John, Karissa. BS in Pharmacy, N.D. State U., 1970; MD, U. Minn., 1974. Intern and resident Abbott/Northwestern Hosp.-Univ. Minn., Mpls., 1974-77; physician Physicians Clin. Profl. Assn., St. Paul, 1977-83, Internal Med. Assocs., Fargo, N.D., 1983-93, Dakota Heartland Health Sys., Fargo, 1994—2001, Internal Medicine Assocs., Fargo, 2002—. Staff sgt. UWAF, 1970-74. Fellow Am. Coll. Physicians; mem. AMA. Republican. Lutheran. Avocations: golf, tennis, Lionel trains. Office: 1707 Gold Dr South Fargo ND 58103

LILLEY, ALBERT FREDERICK, retired lawyer; b. Harrisburg, Pa., Dec. 21, 1932; s. Frederick Anthony and Jane Sander (Ingham) L.; m. Judith Carter Pennock, Sept. 1, 1956; children: Kirk Anthony, Kristin Sander, James Alexander. AB, Bowdoin Coll., 1954; LLB, U. Va., 1959. Assoc. Milbank, Tweed, Hadley & McCloy, N.Y.C., 1959-67, ptnr., 1967-96; ret., 1997. Trustee No. Highlands Regional H.S., Allendale, N.J., 1964-65; mem. Allendale Bd. Zoning Adjustment, 1965-66; bd. overseers Bowdoin Coll., 1976-88, overseer emeritus, 1988—; trustee Valley Hosp., Ridgewood, N.J., 1978-92, vice chmn. bd., 1985-89, chmn. bd., 1989-92; bd. dirs. Valley Care Corp., 1992-97, Valley Home and Cmty. Health Care, Inc., 1992-97; mem. alumni coun. U. Va. Law Sch., 1991-94, U.S. Can. Law Project Adv. Bd., 1990-95. 1st lt. U.S. Army, 1954-56. Mem. ABA, Am. Law Inst., U. Va. Law Sch. Alumni Assn. (class mgr. annual giving campaign), Chapel Hill Rotary Club (vocat. svc. dir. 1998-99, treas. 1999-2000, sec. 2000—). Home: 204 Laurel Hill Rd Chapel Hill NC 27514-4325 E-mail: alilll@nc.rr.com.

LILLEY, JOHN MARK, academic administrator, dean; b. Converse, La., Mar. 24, 1939; s. Ernest Franklin and Sibyl Arrena (Geoghagan) L.; children: Sibyl Elizabeth, Myles Durham; m. Geraldine Murphy; stepchildren: Benjamin Murphy, Jason Murphy. B in Music Edn., Baylor U., 1961, MusB, 1962, MusM, 1964; D of Musical Arts, U. So. Calif., 1971. Mem. faculty Claremont McKenna, Harvey Mudd, Pitzer and Scripps Colls., Claremont, Calif., 1966-76; asst. dean faculty Scripps Coll., 1973-76; asst. dean arts and scis. Kans. State U., Manhattan, 1976-80; provost, dean Pa. State U., Erie, 1980—2001; pres. U. Nev. Bd. dirs. Erie Conf., 1997—, Erie Plastics Corp., 1994—; mem. N.W. Pa. Indsl. Resource Ctr., 1987—. Condr. 1st performances Kubik, 1972, 76, Ives, 1974, (recording) Kubik, 1974. Bd. dirs., v.p. So. Calif. Choral Music Assn., L.A., 1971-76; mem. Archtl. Commn., Claremont, 1974-76; bd. dirs. Erie Philharm., 1980-86, Sta. WQLN Pub. Broadcasting of N.W. Pa., 1992—; bd. dirs. United Way of Erie County, 1981—, chair, 1998—; mem. Regents Commn. on Nursing Edn., Kansas City, Kans., 1978-79; pres. Pacific S.W. Intercollegiate Choral Assn., L.A., 1969-70. NEH grantee, 1978. Mem. Am. Assn. Higher Edn., Coll. Music Soc., Am. Choral Dirs. Assn., Am. Assn. State Colls. and Univs. (vice chair confs. and profl. devel. com. 1989, 97, chair 1990, bd. dirs. 1995—, govs. tuition account program adv. bd. 1996—), Erie Club, Kahkwa Club, Rotary (bd. dirs. Manhattan club 1979-80, Erie club 1981-88), Phi Mu Alpha Sinfonia, Omicron Delta Kappa. Republican. Presbyterian. Avocation: golf. Home: 3103 Marble Ridge Ct Reno NV 89511-5383 Office: U NV 1664 N Va St Reno NV 89557*

LILLEY, MILI DELLA, insurance company executive, entertainment management consultant; b. Valley Forge, Pa., Aug. 29; d. Leon Hanover and Della Beaver (Jones) L. MBA, Tex. Christian U., 1957, PhD, 1959. Various positions G & G Cons. Inc., Ft. Lauderdale, Fla., 1971-75; v.p. AMEX, Inc., Beverly Hills, Calif. and Acapulco, Mex., 1976-80; pres. The Hanover Group, Ft. Lauderdale, 1981—; personal and bus. mgr. entertainers including Ink Spots, 1984—, Lanny Poffo, Ft. Lauderdale, 1990—. Dist. agt. ITT Life Ins. Corp., also other leading cos. Named to All Stars Honor Roll Nat. Ins. Sales Mag., 1989. Mem. Fla. Assn. Theatrical Agents, Fla. Guild of Talent Agts., Mgrs., Producers and Orchestras. Office: The Hanover Group PO Box 70218 Fort Lauderdale FL 33307-0218

LILLEY, WILLIAM, III, information and communications business executive; b. Phila., Jan. 14, 1938; s. William, Jr. and Ida Weaver (Macklin) L.; m. Eve Auchincloss, Mar. 12, 1977; children— Buchanan Morgan, Brooke Carole, Whitman Elisa, Justin Weaver BA magna cum laude, U. Pa., 1959; MA, Yale U., 1961, PhD, 1965. Asst. prof. history Yale U., New Haven, 1962-69; prof. govt. U. Va., Charlottesville, 1977; co-founder, editor Nat. Jour., Washington, 1969-73; dep. asst. sec. HUD, 1973-75; dep., then dir. Council Wage and Price Stability, 1975-77; staff dir. Com. on Budget, Ho. of Reps., 1977-78; v.p. CBS, Inc., 1980-81, v.p. corporate affairs N.Y.C., 1981-84, sr. v.p. corporate affairs, 1985-86; pres. Am. Bus. Conf., 1986-88, Policy Communications Inc., Washington, 1988-2000; chmn., CEO InContext, Inc., 1992-2000, iMap Data Inc., Washington, 2000—. Bd. dirs. Econ. and Social Rsch. Inst., Stanford U. Social Sci. History Inst. Co-author: New Technologies Affecting Broadcasting, 1981, Economic and Social Impacts of Media Advertising, 1989, Impact of Advertising on the Competetive Structure of the Media, 1990, Impact of Media Advertising on International Competetiveness, 1991, Geographic Distribution of U.S. Businesses Which Advertise Heavily, 1991, Almanac of State Legislatures, 1994, State Atlas of Political and Cultural Diversity, 1996, State Legislative Elections: Voting Patterns and Demographics, 1997, Almanac of State Legislatures: Changing Patterns, 1990-97, 1998, The Economic Impact of the European Grands Prix, 1999; contbr. articles to profl. jours. Recipient U.S. Govt. Disting. Svc. award 1975, 76; Samuel F.B. Morse Rsch. fellowship, 1967-68; George Washington Eggleston prize; Most Disting. PhD Dissertation, humanities divsn., Yale U., 1965; Woodrow Wilson Fellowship, 1959-61. Mem. Yale Club, Merion Cricket, Cosmos, River Club, Chevy Chase, Met. Club. Clubs: Yale, Merion Cricket, Cosmos, River, Chevy Chase.

LILLGE, EUGENE FRANCIS, state official; b. Appleton, Wis., Nov. 17, 1950; s. Walter Henry Jr. and Rita Edna (Schreiter) L.; m. Laurel L. McCulloch, May 4, 1985 (div. Dec. 1994); children: Justin J., Crystal A., Benjamin D.; m. Debra L. Giuffre, Dec. 29, 1995 (div. July 2002); children: Tara L. Speck, Nicole S. Speck. BS in Edn., U. Wis., 1973. Cert. pub. mgr. From case worker to supr. Outagamie County Health and Human Svcs. Dept., Appleton, Wis., 1975-88; exec. coord. Outagamie County Office of County Exec., 1988-99; v.p. adminstrv. svcs. Badger State Lemonade LLC, 2000—; project dir. State of Wis. Dept. Workforce Devel., 2000—. Shareholder Green Bay Packers, Inc. Mem. bd. edn. Appleton Area Sch. Dist., 1975-81, 83-87; commr. City of Appleton Parks and Recreation Commn., 1978-79; chair Appleton Alcohol and Other Drug Abuse Prevention Com., 1980-81; mem. Wis. Cert. Pub. Mgmt. Program Policy Bd., 2001--. Mem. Nat. Assn. County Adminstrs., Nat. Assn. Counties (intergovernmental rels. steering com. 1996-99), Wis. Counties Assn. (county orgn. and adminstrn. steering com. 1990-99), Soc. of Wis. Cert. Pub. Mgrs. Roman Catholic. Avocations: golf, reading, crossword puzzles, computer games. Home: 3550 N Oneida St Appleton WI 54911-1038

LILLIBRIDGE, JOHN LEE, retired airline executive; b. Dover, Okla., Nov. 3, 1924; s. John Lee and Myra Ina (Munger) L.; m. Audrey Rae Hart, Aug. 22, 1948; 1 son, John Lee III. BS in Mech. Engring., Okla. A&M Coll., 1950; BS in Civil Engring., Tex. A&M Coll., 1956. Enlisted in U.S. Army, 1943, advanced through grades to col., 1970, ret., 1973—; officer Corps of Engrs., 1950-73; v.p. Eastern Airlines, Miami, Fla., 1973-86. Democrat.

LILLIE, HELEN, journalist, novelist; b. Glasgow, Scotland, Sept. 13, 1915; came to U.S., 1938; d. Thomas and Helen Barbara (Lillie) L.; m. Charles S. Marwick, Sept. 20, 1956. MA, U. Glasgow, 1938; postgrad., Yale U., 1938-40. Rsch. asst. info. divsn. Brit. Info. Svcs., N.Y.C., 1942-45, Brit. Security Coord., N.Y.C., 1945-46; asst. U.S. mgr., writer Media Reps., Inc., 1947-54; with advt. dept. Family Cir. Mag., 1955-56; Am. corr. The Glasgow Herald (now The Herald), 1956-94. Freelance feature writer, book reviewer Detroit Free Press, 1965-66. Author: The Listening Silence, 1970, Call Down the Sky, 1973, Home to Strathblane, 1993, Strathblane and Away, 1996, The Rocky Island, 1998, A New Kind of Life, 1999, History on My Doorstep, 2000; (columns) Inside USA, Helen Lillie's Washington Letter. V.p., acting pres. Cosmopolitan B PM Club of DC, 1972-73. Mem. Am. News Women's Club D.C., Soc. Women Geographers, Advt. Women of N.Y. (com. mem.). Presbyterian. Avocations: music, politic watching, travel, theater, reading. Home and Office: 3219 Volta Pl NW Washington DC 20007-2732

LILLIE, LLOYD, sculptor; b. Washington, May 20, 1932; s. Alfred Lloyd and Thelma (Folsom) Lillie; m. Barbara Ann Bailey, Dec. 4, 1954; children: Nina L., Warren T., Lisa M. Diploma with highest honors, Boston Mus. Sch.; student, Skowhegan Sch. Painting and Sculpture, Corcoran Sch. Art, Washington, Academia di Belle Arti, Florence, Italy. Mem. faculty Boston U., 1961—95, prof. art, 1974—95, prof. emeritus, 1995—. Camargo Found. fellow, Cassis, France, 1990; Boston Mus. Sch. traveling fellow, 59. One-man shows include St. Botolph Club, Boston, Falmouth (Mass.) Pub. Libr., Bumpus Gallery, Duxbury, Mass., Cambridge Art Assn., Mirsky Gallery, Boston, Mt. Ida Coll., Newton, Mass. , Milton (Mass.) Acad., exhibited in group shows at Corcoran Gallery Art, Washington, Nat. Sculpture Soc., N.Y.C., Art Inst. of Boston, Boston Pub. Libr., Palazzo Mediceo, Seravezza, Italy, NAD Invitational, 1998, Forest Hills Cemetery Invitational, Boston, 1998, Forest Lawn Cemetery Invitational, 1999, Nat. Sculpture Soc., 2000, others, Represented in permanent collections Boston Pub. Libr., Am. Embassy, Riyadh, Saudi Arabia, Coll. William and Mary, Va., U. Va., Charlottesville, Jefferson U., Phila. Recipient 1st prize in sculpture, NAD, 1994, Sydney Simon prize in sculpture, 1999, Gov.'s Design award, for Curley Park, Boston, 1st prize in sculpture, Boston Arts Festival, 1991, Bronze medal, Nat. Sculpture Soc., 1991. Mem.: NAD. Home: 19 Maple Ave Newton MA 02458

LILLIE, MARSHALL SHERWOOD, college safety and security director, educator; b. Corry, Pa., May 23, 1953; s. Lloyd G. and Jalean R. (Sherwood) L.; m. Anita M., Aug 16, 1975; children: Amanda M., Sarah N., Rebekah L., Reuben L. ASB, Erie Bus. Ctr., Pa., 1974; BA, Olivet Nazarene U., Kankakee, Ill., 1980; MS, Mercyhurst Coll., Erie, Pa., 1984. Cert. mcpl. police officer trainer, EMS technician. Dir., security Olivet Nazarene U., Kankakee, Ill., 1977-81; administr. asst. Mercyhurst Coll., Erie, Pa., 1981-86; dir., security Thiel Coll., Greenville, 1986—; owner Lillie Tng. Enterprises. Chmn. Western Pa. Security Dirs., 1989-90; instr. Thiel Coll., Greenville, Pa., 1990—, Mercyhurst Coll., Erie, 1992—; defensive tactics instr. Pressure Point Control Sys., 1995—; defensive driving instr. Nat. Safety Coun.; EMT, hazardous materials technician, ARC emergency response instr. Master Sunday Sch. Supr. Ch. of Nazarene, 1991; Mayor's Adv. com., Greenville, Pa., 1990. Mem. NRA, N.E. Coll. and Univ. Security Assn. (editor The Clipboard 1993-94, bd. dirs. 1992-96), Western Pa. Coll., Security Dirs. Assn., Am. Soc. Law Enforcement Trainers, Am. Soc. Indsl. Security (chmn. Lake Erie chpt. 1990-91). Republican. Mem. Ch. of Nazarene. Office: Thiel Coll 75 College Ave Greenville PA 16125-2186 E-mail: mlillie@thiel.edu.

LILLY, ARNYS CLIFTON, JR. physicist; b. Beckley, W.Va., June 3, 1934; s. Arnys Clifton and Ella Vay (McKeehan) L.; m. Agnes Madeline Micou, June 9, 1956; children: Gregory Alan, Diane Renee, James Clifton. BS in Petroleum Engring., Va. Poly. Inst., 1957, PhD in Physics, 1989; MS in Physics, Carnegie-Mellon U., 1963. Rsch. physicist Gulf Rsch. and Devel. Co., Pitts., 1957-65; prin. scientist Philip Morris Rsch. Ctr., Richmond, Va., 1965—, research fellow, 1984, dir. tech. assessment, 1988, v.p. tech. assessment, 1996. Mem. Am. Phys. Soc., Sigma Xi. Contbr. articles to physics jours.; patentee in field. Home: 9641 Waterfowl Flyway Chesterfield VA 23838-8905 Office: Philip Morris Rsch Ctr 4201 Commerce Rd Richmond VA 23234-2269

LILLY, CHARLES G. protective services official, consultant; b. Louisville, Aug. 24, 1956; s. Foster Dillard Lilly and Amber Helene Ament. MSc, Radford U., 1981. Pers. analyst Jefferson County Officer Pers. Mgmt., Louisville, 1982-85, City of St. Petersburg (Fla.), 1985-87; pers. examination analyst City of Louisville Civil Svc. Bd., 1987-98; dir. police human resources City of Louisville Divsn. Police, 1998—. Mem. Soc. Human Resource Mgmt., Louisville Soc. Human Resource Mgmt. Office: Louisville Divsn Police 633 W Jefferson St Louisville KY 40202 Fax: 502-574-7680. E-mail: glilly@lpdky.org.

LILLY, EDWARD GUERRANT, JR. retired utility company executive; b. Lexington, Ky., Oct. 29, 1925; s. Edward Guerrant and Elisabeth Read (Frazer) L.; m. Nancy Estes Cobb, Nov. 25, 1961; children: Penelope Read, Edward Guerrant III, Collier Cobb (dec.), Steven Clay. BS, Davidson Coll., 1948; MBA, U. Pa., 1949. Credit analyst Citizens and So. Nat. Bank, Charleston, S.C., 1949-50; asst. v.p. Wachovia Bank and Trust Co., Charlotte, 1952-55, v.p., 1956, v.p., loan adminstrv. officer Wilmington, N.C., 1956-60, sr. v.p., area exec. Kinston, 1961-62, Durham, 1963-70, sr. v.p., mgr. trust investment svcs. dept. Winston-Salem, 1970-71, also bd. dirs., 1971-88; sr. v.p., group exec. Carolina Power and Light Co., Raleigh, 1971-76, sr. v.p., chief fin. officer, 1976-81, exec. v.p., chief fin. officer, 1981-90, also bd. dirs. N.C. Bd. dirs. N.C. Enterprise Corp. Mem. U. N.C. bd. visitors, 1974-87; bd. dirs. Rsch. Triangle Found., Research Triangle Park; trustee Davidson Coll., 1976-88, Union Theol. Seminary. Served to lt., USNR, 1950-52, Mem. Edison Electric Inst. (chmn. fin. group 1979) Lodges: Rotary (Raleigh). Presbyterian.

LILLY, ELIZABETH GILES, mobile park executive; b. Bozeman, Mont., Aug. 5, 1916; d. Samuel John and Luella Elizabeth (Reed) Abegg; m. William Lilly, July 1, 1976; children: Samuel Colborn Giles, Elizabeth Giles. RN, Good Samaritan Hosp., Portland, Oreg., 1941; student, Walla Walla Coll., Lewis and Clark Coll. Bus., Portland. ARC nurse, tchr. area high schs., Portland; owner Welton Studio Interior Design; in pub. rels. Chas. Eckelman, Fairview Farms-Dairy Industry; owner, builder Mobile Park Plaza, Inc., Portland. Del. platform planning com. Rep. Party; mem. Sunnyside Seventh Day Adventist Ch., deaconess. Recipient Svc. award Multnomah County Commrs., 1984. Mem. Soroptimist Internat. (local bd. dirs., bd. dirs. Women in Transition), Rep. Women's Club (pres.), C. of C., World Affairs Coun., Toastmistress (pres.), Oreg. Lodging Assn. (pres. bd. dirs.), Rep. Inner Circle (life). Address: 19825 SE Stark St Portland OR 97233-6039

LILLY, EUGENE FRANCIS, retired publishing company executive; b. Huntingdon, Pa., May 24, 1932; s. Eugene Lawrence and Caroline Margaret (Geier) L.; m. Madeline Isabelle Dalton, Sept. 15, 1956; children: Kathleen Osborn (dec.), Marie Ragonese, Richard (dec.). BSBA, U. Rochester, 1954. CPA, N.Y. Staff acct. Price Waterhouse & Co., Rochester, N.Y., 1957-62, sr. acct., 1962-65; mgr. gen. acctg. & budgets Lawyers Co-op Pub. Co., 1965-72, contr., 1972-84, treas., contr., 1984-89, ret., 1989. Dir. Cath. Family Ctr., Rochester, 1976-96; treas., dir. Rotary Camp Haccamo, Rochester, 1976—; cons. Exec. Svc. Corps, Rochester, 1992—; mem., chmn. East Rochester Planning Bd. Lt. j.g. USN, 1954-57. Paul Harris fellow Rotary Internat. Mem. AICPA, N.Y. Soc. CPAs, Fin. Exec. Inst. Roman Catholic. Avocations: photography, golf, travel. Home: 254 W Hickory St East Rochester NY 14445-1814 E-mail: elilly1@juno.com.

LILLY, JOHN RICHARD, II, lawyer; b. Phila., July 20, 1962; s. John Richard Sr. and Elizabeth Anne (Brown) L.; children: John Richard III, Cameron Lewis. BA, Geoge Washington U., 1987; JD, U. Balt., 1991. Bar: Md. 1992, U.S. Dist. Ct. Md. 1995. Law clk. 7th Jud. Cir. Md., Upper Marlboro, 1991-92; asst. state's atty. State's Atty.'s Office Prince George's County Md., 1992-98; asst. atty. gen. Md. Atty. Gen.'s Office, Balt., 1998-2001; pvt. practice Glen Burnie, Md., 2001—. Adj. prof. U. Balt. Sch. Law, 1999-2000. Comments editor U. Balt. Jour. Environ. Law. Chmn. Oakland Mills Village Bd., Columbia, Md., 1990-92; pres. St. Stephen's Area Civic Assn., Crownsville, Md., 1994-95. Lt. USNR, 1988—. Mem. Anne Arundel Bar Assn. Avocations: tennis, sailing, reading, photography. Home: 133 Idlewild Rd Severna Park MD 21146 Office: 7439 Baltimore-Annapolis Blvd Glen Burnie MD 21061 E-mail: jrlillyesq@aol.com.

LILLY, JULIUS QUENTIN, engineering researcher; b. Lilly, W.Va., Aug. 6, 1933; s. James Willis and Elsie Mae (Pack) L.; m. Rose Joyce Hart, Dec. 28, 1953; children: Barry, Karen Regan, Kimberly Sawyer. BSME, W.Va. U. Inst. Tech., 1960; MSME, Va. Poly. Inst. and State U., 1962; postgrad., U. N.Mex., 1962-64; PhD in Mech. Engring., U. Ala., 1969. Engr.-in-tng., Ala. Staff asst. Los Alamos (N.Mex.) Lab., 1960; mem. staff Sandia Lab., Albuquerque, 1961-64; sr. engr. space divsn. Chrysler Corp., Huntsville, Ala., 1964-66; prin. engr. U.S. Army Missile Command, Redstone Arsenal, 1966-82; project engr. Army Ballistic Missile Def. Agy., Huntsville, 1982-84, Army Space and Missile Def. Command., Huntsville, 1984-99; pres., owner Julius Lilly Assoc., Madison, Ala., 1999—. Cons. Army Res. Office, Durham, N.C., 1976-88; R&D cons. Strategic Def. Initiative, Washington, 1984-90, Ballistic Missile Def. Orgn., Washington, 1990-99; advisor, cons. U.S. Army Sci. Bd., Washington, 1997-99. Contbr. articles to profl. jours. Cpl. U.S. Army, 1953-56. NSF grad. fellow, 1960. Mem. Am. Legion. Avocations: health, fitness, hiking, photography, camping. Home: 10466 Segers Rd Madison AL 35756 Office: Julius Lilly Assocs 10466 Segers Rd Madison AL 35756

LILLY, MARTIN STEPHEN, university dean; b. New Albany, Ind., Aug. 31, 1944; s. Raymond John and Amy Elizabeth (Peake) L.; m. Marilyn Ann MacDougall, Jan. 8, 1966; children— Matthew William, Mark Christopher, Rachel Marie, Martin Stephen, Jason Wood BA, Bellarmine Coll., Louisville, 1966; MA, Peabody Coll., Nashville, 1967, Ed.D., 1969. Instr. dept. spl. edn. Peabody Coll., 1967-69; asst. prof. edn. U. Oreg., 1969-71; research coordinator N.W. Regional Spl. Edn. Instructional Materials Center, 1969-71; research coordinator div. research Bur. Edn. for Handicapped U.S. Office Edn., 1971-72; assoc. prof. dept. spl. edn. U. Minn., Duluth, 1972-75; assoc. prof., chmn. dept. spl. edn. U. Ill., Urbana-Champaign, 1975-79, prof., chmn., 1979-81, assoc. dean grad. studies Coll. Edn., 1981-84; dean Coll. Edn. Wash. State U., Pullman, 1984-90, Calif. State U., San Marcos, 1990—. Cons. in field; U.S. Office Edn. fellow, 1966-69; pres. Tchr. Edn. Coun. State Colls. and Univs.; bd. dirs. San Diego County Childrens Initiative. Author: Children with Exceptional Needs: A Survey of Special Education, 1979, (with C.S. Blankenship) Mainstreaming Students With Learning and Behavior Problems, 1981; assoc. editor: Exceptional Children, 1969-79; cons. editor: Edn. Unltd, 1979-81; reviewer: Jour. Tchr. Edn, 1980— ; mem. editorial bd. Tchr. Edn. and Spl. Edn, 1980-83, co-editor, 1983-84; contbr. chpts. to books, articles to profl. jours. Mem. Coun. for Exceptional Children, Assn. Tchr. Educators, Am. Assn. Colls. Tchr. Edn., Phi Delta Kappa. Democrat. Roman Catholic. Office: Calif State U San Marcos CA 92096-0001

LILLY, MICHAEL ALEXANDER, lawyer, writer; b. Honolulu, May 21, 1946; s. Percy Anthony Jr. and Virginia (Craig) L.; children: Michael Jr., Cary J., Laura B., Claire F., Winston W. AA, Menlo Coll., Menlo Park, Calif., 1966; BA, U. Calif., Santa Cruz, 1968; JD with honors, U. of Pacific, 1974. Bar: Calif. 1974, U.S. Dist. Ct. (no., so. and ea. dists.) Calif. 1974, U.S. Ct. Appeals (9th cir.) 1974, Hawaii 1975, U.S. Dist. Ct. Hawaii 1975, U.S. Ct. Appeals (D.C. cir.) 1975, U.S. Supreme Ct. 1978, U.S. Ct. Appeals (7th cir.) 1979. Atty. Pacific Legal Found., Sacramento, 1974-75; dep. atty. gen. State of Hawaii, Honolulu, 1975-79, 1st dep. atty. gen., 1981-84, atty. gen., 1984-85; ptnr. Feeley & Lilly, San Jose, Calif., 1979-81, Ning, Lilly & Jones, Honolulu, 1985—. Author: If You Die Tomorrow-A Layman's Guide to Estate Planning. Dir. Diamond Head Theatre, U.S.S. Mo. Meml. Assn.; Lt. USN, 1968-71, Vietnam; capt. USNR. Named hon. Ky. col.; decorated Legion of Merit medal, 1997. Mem. Nat. Assn. Attys. Gen., Hawaii Law Enforcement Ofcls. Assn., Navy Res. Assn. (pres. 14th dist. 1986-89), Navy League (nat. dir., nat. dept. judge adv. to bd. Honolulu coun.), Outrigger Canoe Club. Home: 2769 Laniloa Rd Honolulu HI 96813-1041 Office: Ning Lilly & Jones 707 Richards St Ste 700 Honolulu HI 96813-4623 E-mail: michael@nljlaw.com. *Personal philosophy: Always do what you are afraid to do. Never give up. Forgive your enemies.*

LILLY, THOMAS GERALD, lawyer; b. Belzoni, Miss., Sept. 17, 1933; s. Sale Trice and Margaret Evelyn (Butt) L.; m. Constance Ray Holland, Dec. 29, 1962; children: Thomas Gerald Jr., William Holland, Carolyn Ray. BBA, Tulane U., 1955; LLB, U. Miss., 1960, JD, 1968. Bar: Miss. 1960. Assoc. firm Stovall & Price, Corinth, Miss., 1960-62; asst. U.S. atty. No. Dist. Miss., Oxford, 1962-66; assoc. firm Wise Carter Child & Caraway (and predecessor), Jackson, Miss., 1966-67, ptnr., 1967-94, Lilly & Wise, Jackson, 1994-2000, of counsel, 2001—. Served with USNR, 1955-88; rear adm. Res. ret. Decorated Legion of Merit, Navy Commendation medal. Mem. FBA (nat. coun. 1972—, rec. sec. 1975-76, gen. sec. 1976-77, 2d v.p. 1977-78, pres.-elect 1978-79, pres. 1979-80), Hinds County Bar Assn., Miss. State Bar, Miss. Bar Found., Democracy Devel. Inst. (bd. dirs. 1995—), Res. Officers Assn. (pres. Miss. dept. 1982-83), Naval Res. Assn., Ret. Officers Assn., Naval Order of U.S., Navy Supply Corps Assn., Navy League (pres. Ctrl. Miss. Coun. 1993), Mil. Order World Wars, Jackson Civil War Roundtable, Miss. Com. Employer Support Guard and Res., Lamar Order, Scabbard and Blade, Omicron Delta Kappa, Phi Delta Phi, Sigma Nu. Methodist. Office: Lilly & Wise 660 Katherine Dr Flowood MS 39208 E-mail: tomcomlilly@earthlink.net.

LILLY, WESLEY COOPER, marine engineer, ship surveyor; b. Phila., May 23, 1933; s. Richard Gladstone and Margaret Jane L.; m. Barbara Joan Newton, June 18, 1935 (div. Nov. 24, 1978); children: Pamela Lynn, Barbara Joan. BS in Engring., Pa. Mil. Coll., 1956-61. Apprentice machinist Phila. Naval Shipyard, 1951-53, prodn. shipbuilding, 1955-66, planning, design divsn., 1966-68; mem. shipbuilding testing specifications staff Naval Weapons Svc. Office, 1968-70; procurement prodn. Navy Dept. Navsea, Washington, 1970-86; pres., owner Marine Assocs., Amelia Island, Fla., 1972—; pres., founder Saturn Marine Engring., St. Augustine, 1986—. Programmer Basic, Fortran, and Cobol rev. bus. computech programs. Inventor, patentee in field. Served with U.S. Army, 1953-55. Mem.: Soc. Naval Archs. and Marine Engrs. (chmn. com. for small and medium shipyards/shipbldg.), Amelia Island PC Users Group, Antique Outboard Motor Club (dir.). Episcopalian. Avocations: accounting, computers, cruising, sailing. Home: 2757 1st Ave Fernandina Beach FL 32034-2345 Office: Marine Assocs Fernandina Beach FL 32034 E-mail: abcmarine2@hotmail.com., weslilly@netscape.net.

LILLY, WILLIAM ELDRIDGE, government official; b. Liberty, Tex., Aug. 25, 1921; s. Lawrence C. and Maude (McKinney) L.; m. Blanche Elizabeth Bromert, Jan. 18, 1944; children— Lizbeth Kristine, William Michael. AB, U. Calif. at Berkeley, 1950, grad. student, 1950-51. Program analyst Naval Ordnance Test Sta., China Lake, Calif., 1950-52; head estimates and analysis Naval Bur. Ordnance, Washington, 1952-54; dep. budget officer Nat. Bur. Standards, 1954-56; asst. dir. plans and programs Navy Polaris program, 1956-60; with NASA, 1960-82, asst. adminstr. for adminstrn., 1967-72, comptroller, 1972-82, ind. cons., 1982—. Pres. Arlington County (Va.) Youth Orgn., 1966-69. Served with USN, 1940-46. Recipient Exceptional Service medal NASA, 1966, 69, Disting. Service medal, 1973, 81; Career Service award Nat. Civil Service League, 1978; presdl. rank of Disting. Exec., 1980 Mem. Phi Beta Kappa, Pi Sigma Alpha. Home: PO Box 2028 Arlington VA 22202-0028 Office: P100 L'Enfant Plz N SW Washington DC 20024

LILLYMAN, WILLIAM JOHN, German language educator, academic administrator; b. Sydney, Australia, Apr. 17, 1937; came to U.S., 1963, naturalized, 1974; s. John and Christina Mary (Munro) L.; m. Ingeborg Wolz, Sept. 14, 1962; children: Gregory, Christina. AB, U. Sydney, 1959; PhD, Stanford U., 1964. Asst. prof. Stanford (Calif.) U., 1964-67; assoc. prof. U. Calif., Santa Cruz, 1967-72, prof. German Irvine, 1972—, dean humanities, 1973-81, vice chancellor acad. affairs, 1981-82, exec. vice chancellor, 1982-88, 98-00. Author: Otto Ludwig's Zwischen Himmel und Erde, 1967, Otto Ludwig: Romane und Romanstudien, 1977, Reality's Dark Dream The Narrative Fiction of Ludwig Tieck, 1979, Goethe's Narrative Fiction, 1983; co-editor; Probleme der Moderne, 1983, Horizonte Festschrift für H. Lehnert, 1990, Critical Architecture and Contemporary Culture, 1994. Mem. MLA, Am. Assn. Tchrs. German. Office: U Calif Exec Vice Chancellors Office 509 Administrn Bldg Irvine CA 92697-1000

LIM, ALEXANDER RUFASTA, neurologist, clinical investigator, educator, writer; b. Manila, Philippines, Feb. 20, 1942; s. Benito Pilar and Maria Lourdes (Cuyegkeng) Lim; m. Norma Sue Hanks, June 1, 1968; children: Jeffrey Allen, Kevin Alexander, Melissa Gail, Gregory Brian. AA, U. Santo Tomas, Manila, Philippines, 1959, MD, 1964. Intern Bon Secours Hosp., Balt., 1964-65; resident in internal medicine Scott and White Clinic Tex A&M U., Health Sci. Ctr. Coll. Medicine, Temple, Tex., 1965-67; resident in neurology Cleve. Clinic, 1967-69, chief resident in neurology, 1969-70, fellow clin. neurophysiology, 1970-71; clin. assoc. neurologist Cleve. Clinic Hosp., 1971-72; neurologist, co-founder, co-mng. ptnr. Neurol. Clinic, Corpus Christi, Tex., 1972—; pres., CEO Neurology, P.A., 1972-92. Chief neurology dept. Meml. Med. Ctr., Corpus Christi, Tex., 1975—90, Spohn Hosp., Corpus Christi, 1974—90, Reynolds Army Hosp., Ft. Sill, Okla., 1990—91; clin. assoc. prof. Sch. Medicine U. Tex. Health Sci. Ctr., San Antonio; cons., reviewer Tex. Medicine, 1995—. Active mentorship program for gifted and talented srs. South Tex. Area H.S. Lt. col. med. corps U.S. Army, 1990—91, Desert Shield/Desert Storm. Recipient Army Commendation medal, 1991, Nat. Def. medal, U.S. Army, 1991. Mem.: KC, AMA, Dana Alliance for Brain Initiatives, Tex. Neurol. Soc. (sec. 1986—88, pres. 1989—90), Tex. Med. Assn. (chmn. neurology 1985—86), Am. Acad. Pain Mgmt., So. Electroencephalographic Soc., Soc. Behavioral and Cognitive Neurology, Am. Acad. Immunotherapy, Am. Clin. Neurophysiology Soc., Am. Acad. Clin. Neurophysiology, Am. Epilepsy Soc. (editl. bd. mem. Neurocentral), Am. Acad. Neurology (spkrs. bur.), Acad. Am. Poets, Internat. Platform Assn. Republican. Roman Catholic. Avocations: tennis, philately, travel, skiing, bonsai. Home: 4821 Augusta Cir Corpus Christi TX 78413-2711 Office: The Neurological Clinic Christus Spohn Med Plaza 1415 3d St Ste 101 Corpus Christi TX 78404-2175 E-mail: anlim8@hotmail.com., alim@neurological_clinic.neurohub.net.

LIM, DANIEL VAN, microbiology educator; b. Houston, Apr. 15, 1948; s. Don H. and Lucy (Toy) L.; m. Carol Lee, Sept. 2, 1973. BA in Biology, Rice U., 1970; PhD in Microbiology, Tex. A&M U., 1973. Postdoctoral fellow Baylor Coll. Medicine, 1973-76; asst. prof. U. South Fla., Tampa, 1976-81, assoc. prof. microbiology, 1981-87, chmn. dept. biology, 1983-85, prof., 1987—. Pres. Micro Concepts Rsch. Corp; dir. Inst. Biomolecular Sci., 1988-93; cons. and expert witness in field. Author: Microbiology, 1989, 98, Introduction to Microbiology, 1995. Recipient Outstanding PhD Dissertation in U.S. award Phi Sigma, 1974, Outstanding Contbn. in Sci. and Tech. award Fla. Gov. Fellow Am. Acad. Microbiology; mem. Inter-Am. Soc. Chemotherapy (v.p. 1983-88), Am. Soc. Microbiology (pres. southeastern br. 1990-91, Carski award com. 1983-86, Margaret Green Outstanding Tchr. award). Achievements include inventor of bacteriological broth. Office: U South Fla Dept Biology SCA 110 4202 E Fowler Ave Tampa FL 33620-8000

LIM, DIANA MAGPAYO, internist; b. Manila, The Philippines, May 25, 1964; came to U.S., 1993; d. Thomas and Pacita King Magpayo; m. Kennedy Kaw, Mar. 18, 1992; children: Nicole Ann, Paul Nathan, Natalie Paige. BS in Med. Tech. cum laude, U. Santo Tomas, Manila, 1986, MD, 1990. Diplomate Am. Bd. Internal Medicine. Rotating intern U. Santo Tomas Hosp., Manila, 1990-91; intern, resident, mem. house staff Cath. Med. Ctr. Bklyn. and Queens, Inc., Jamaica, N.Y., 1993-96; mem. staff Christus Schumpert Bossier (formerly Bossier Med. Ctr.), Bossier City, La., 1996—, Willis Knighton Bossier Health Ctr., Bossier City, 1999—. Mem. AMA, ACP, La. State Med. Soc., Bossier Parish Med. Soc., Philippine Med. Assn., Manila Med. Assn. Office: Willis Knighton Bossier Internal Medicine Ste 420 2400 Hospital Dr Bossier City LA 71111-2391

LIM, ESTEBAN, JR. medical facility administrator, physician; b. Cebu City, The Philippines, July 19, 1958; came to U.S., 1983; s. Esteban T. and Natividad Lim; m. Daisy Y. Esparaz, Oct. 18, 1993; children: Nathaniel Stephen, Margaret Stacy. BA, Cebu Velez Coll., Cebu City, 1978; MD, Cebu Inst. Medicine, Cebu City, 1982. Diplomate Am. Bd. Psychiatry and Neurology. Intern and resident in psychiatry Bronx (N.Y.) Lebanon Hosp. Ctr., 1987-91, chief physician substance abuse unit, 1992-95; fellow cons./liaison psychiatry Montefiore Med. Ctr., Bronx, 1991-92; clin. dir. acute care Moccasin Bend Mental Health Inst., Chattanooga, 1995-97; med. dir. Lookout Mountain Cmty. Svcs., Lafayette, Ga., 1997—. Clin. inst. Albert Einstein Coll. Medicine, Bronx, 1992-93, asst. clin. prof., 1993-95; CEO, pres. ELC Trading Corp., Tuckahoe, N.Y., 1993—. Leo Davidoff Soc. award Albert Einstein Coll. Medicine, 1991. Mem. Am. Psychiat. Assn. (dist. treas. 1992-94), Acad. Psychosomatic Medicine, Am. Acad. Addiction Psychiatry. Roman Catholic. Avocations: computers, electronics, photography, travel. Office: Lookout Mountain Cmty Svc 501 Mize St PO Box 1027 La Fayette GA 30728-1027

LIM, HARRISON BING CHEUNG, social services administrator; b. China, Nov. 30, 1936; came to the U.S., 1970; s. Fook How and Oy Lin Lim; m. Margaret Ma, Nov. 24, 1965; children: Artina, Jackson, Rosana, Samson. M in Lit., Chinese U. Hong Kong, 1963, M in History, 1967. Coll. instr. Royden Coll., Hong Kong, 1963-70; dean Grammar Coll., 1963-70; coll. instr. Wilmington Coll., 1963-70; sr. counselor Pub. Health Dept./Mental Health Divsn., San Francisco, 1973-82; exec. dir., founder Charity Cultural Svcs. Ctr., 1983—, Crosscultural Cmty. Svcs. Ctr., San Jose, Calif., 1991—. Chinese-Am. del. chair 5th World Congress of Poets, 1981; bd. mem. Ctrl. Chinese H.S., San Francisco, 1985—, supt., 1987-91; supt. Asian Art Inst., San Francisco, 1991-92, Acad. Chinese Art, San Francisco, 1997—; bd. dirs. Nat. Am. Bank. Author: Bai Kuo Man, 1998; co-author: Silent River, 1961, Tong Tai Flower, 1961. Pres. Sino-Am. Cultural Assn., Calif., 1975—; founding bd. mem. Pres. Chiang Edn. Found., Calif., 1978—; presiding pres. Chinese Consol. Benevolent Assn., Calif., 1983; gen. sec. Dr. Sun Yat Sen's Free Prin. Assn., Calif., 1983-89; appointee Ex-Mayor Frank Jordan's Chinatown Econ. Task Force, San Francisco, 1992. Harrison B. Lim Day named in his honor by Sec. of State, San Francisco, 1990; named Unsung Hero/Asian Pacific Heritage, Sta. KQED-TV and San Francisco Examiner, 1995. Mem. Ning Yung Consol. Benevolent Assn., Lim Family Benevolent Assn. (pres. 1978-79). Avocations: writing, reading, teaching, traveling. Office: Charity Cultural Svcs Ctr 827 Stockton St San Francisco CA 94108-2120

LIM, HEETAEK, application developer; b. Mokpo, Jeonnam, Republic of Korea, July 12, 1964; s. Jongsul Lim and Youngdan Kim; m. Migyo Jeong; 1 child Mir. PhD, U. Calif., Berkeley, 2001. CAE engr. Samsung Engring. Co., Seoul, Republic of Korea, 1990—93; structural engr. Ssanyong Engring. and Constrn. Co., 1993—96; programmer Liftech Cons. Inc., Oakland, Calif., 1998—. Author: (paper) An explicit-implicit method for flexible-rigid multibody systems, 2001. Avocation: golf. Home: 1071 9th St Albany CA 94710 Office: U Calif Berkeley 760 Davis Hall Berkeley CA 94720-1710 Personal E-mail: limhitek@ce.berkeley.edu.

LIM, HENRY WAN-PENG, physician; b. Bandung, Indonesia, July 19, 1949; s. Budiman Ruslim and Nietje Tedjasuryani; m. Mamie Wong-Lim, July 20, 1975; children: Christopher T., Kevin T. BS in Biochemistry with honors, McGill U., 1971; MD cum laude, SUNY, Bklyn., 1975. Diplomate in dermatology, dermatol. immunology/diagnostic and lab. immunology Am. Bd. Dermatology; diplomate Nat. Bd. Med. Examiners. Intern Albert Einstein Coll. Medicine, Bronx, N.Y., 1975-76; resident dept. dermatology NYU Sch. Medicine, 1976-79, NIH fellow in dermatology, 1979, Dermatology Found. fellow, 1979-80, from instr. to assoc. prof. dermatology, 1979-93, prof. dermatology, 1993-97, asst. dean for vet. affairs, 1993-97; chmn. and Clarence S. Livingood chair dermatology Henry Ford Health Sys., Detroit, 1997—. Dir. acad. programs Henry Ford Med. Group; chief dermatology svc. N.Y. VA Med. Ctr., N.Y.C., 1985-94, chief staff, 1993-97, staff physician dermatology svc., 1994-97. Editor Photodermatology, Photoimmunology & Photomedicine, 2000—; mem. editl. bd. Jour. Am. Acad. Dermatology, 1993—; mem. editl. bd. Jour. Cut Med. Surg., 2000—. Recipient numerous awards; McGill U. scholar, 1968-70. Mem.: AMA, AAAS, Photomedicine Soc. (pres. 1992—99), Am. Assn. Immunologists, Am. Soc. for Photobiology (councilor 1998—2001, pres. 2002—), Am. Fedn. for Clin. Rsch., Assn. Profs. Dermatology (bd. dirs. 2000—), Am. Dermatology Assn. (chair membership com. 2002—), Dermatology Found., Soc. for Investigative Dermatology, Am. Acad. Dermatology (chair environ. com. 2000—, bd. dirs. 2002—), Alpha Omega Alpha. Avocations: travel. Office: Henry Ford Hosp Dept Dermatology 2799 W Grand Blvd Dept Detroit MI 48202-2689

LIM, JAE DOEG, systems engineer, researcher; b. Seoul, Korea (South), Oct. 3, 1962; arrived in U.S., 1985; s. Chang Lim, Jung Oh; m. Kon Lim, May 21, 1993; children: Jin, Amy. BS, U. Ala., 1990, MS, 1992, PhD, 1999. Rschr. Korea Telecom, Seoul, 1992—95; mgr. Dacom Corp., 1995—96; sr. sys. engr. Samsung Telecomm. Am., Richardson, Tex., 2000—. Cons. Dacom Corp., Tuscaloosa, Ala., 1996—96. Author: Radiation and scattering behavior of thin cylindrical antenna, 1992, Fixed Cell Assignment for Forward Link in Broadband Wireless Networks Supporting Internet Protocol Version 6 Mobility, 1999. Grantee, NSF, 1999, Tchg. Assistantship, U. of Ala., 1996—99, Rsch. Assistantship, 1990—92. Mem.: IEEE. Achievements include invention of method for increasing a data transmission rate in mobile wireles communication channels. Home: 2008 Londonderry Drive Allen TX 75013 Personal E-mail: jaedoeglim@hotmail.com.

LIM, JEFFREY JAMES, internist; b. Manila, The Philippines, Apr. 8, 1963; came to U.S., 1990; s. Henry Co and Emily (Weesit) L. BS in Biology, U. of the Philippines, 1984, MD, 1989. Diplomate Am. Bd. Internal Medicine. Intern SUNY, Bklyn., 1990-91, resident, 1991-93; clin. asst. instr. SUNY Health Scis. Ctr., 1990-93; attending physician Meml. Hosp. of Texas County, Guymon, Okla., 1994—, chief of staff, 2001—. Cons. physician Meml. Hosp. Tex. County Home Health, Guymon, 1994—, chmn. mortality & morbidity com., 1997—, chmn. ICU com., 1997—; clin. instr. U. Okla. Coll. Medicine, 2001—. Mem. ACP, AMA, Am. Soc. Internal Medicine, Soc. Critical Care Medicine, Am. Coll. Chest Physicians, Okla. Med. Assn., Okla. Soc. Internal Medicine. Roman Catholic. Avocations: swimming, basketball. Office: Internal Medicine Clinic 410 NE 12th S Guymon OK 73942

LIM, JOSEPH EDWARD, lawyer; b. Manila, Dec. 4, 1955; s. Protacio Jose Lim and Ellen Belle Galang; m. Blesilda Ladines; children: Joseph, Meilin. BS in Agribus., U. The Philippines, Laguna, 1978; MBA, U. The Philippines, Diliman, 1984; JD, U. Balt., 1992. Bar: Md. 1992. Agribus. specialist Tech. Resource Ctr., Makati, Philippines, 1978—80; divsn. mgr. Coop. Found. the Philippines, Quezon City, 1980—82; mktg. officer Nat. Home Mortgage Corp., Makati, 1982—86; with U.S. Army, Md., 1986—90; law clk. Md. State Atty.'s coord., Balt., 1990—91; claims examiner Injured Workers Ins., Towson, 1991—92; supervisory adminstrv. judge Office Employee Appeals, Washington, 1993—95, 1998—; pvt. practice Md., 1995—. Editor Agribus. Newsletter, 1977. Mem. Md. Trial Lawyers Assn., Nature Conservancy, World Wildlife Fund. Avocations: Chow dog breeding, photography, martial arts, writer. Home: 2018 Summit Ave Baltimore MD 21237-1334 Office: Office Employee Appeals 717 14th St NW Washington DC 20005-3200 E-mail: josephelim@hotmail.com.

LIM, LARRY KAY, university official; b. Santa Maria, Calif., July 4, 1948; s. Koonwah and Nancy (Yao) L.; m. Louise A. Simon, Aug. 15, 1988. BA, UCLA, 1970, teaching cert., 1971. Asst. engr. Force Ltd., L.A., 1969; tchg. asst. UCLA, 1970-71; tchr. L.A. Sch. Dist., 1971-82; dir. pre-coll. programs Sch. Engring., U. So. Calif., L.A., 1979—. Presenter minority math.-based intervention symposium U. D.C., Washington, 1988; presenter NEMEPA/WEPAN nat. conf., 1997. Newsletter editor, 1981-92. Bd. dirs. Developing Ednl. Studies for Hispanics, L.A., 1983-88. Named Dir. of Yr., Math., Engring., Sci. Achievement Ctr. Adv. Bd., 1986, 91, 92. Fellow Inst. Advancement Engring. (educator award); mem. Nat. Assn. Pre-Coll. Dirs., Nat. Assn. Minority Engring. Program Adminstr., Lotus/West Club (pres. 1981-92). Avocation: automobile racing. Office: U So Calif Sch Engring Ohe 104 Los Angeles CA 90089-0001

LIM, LEN GUI REMOLONA (MARK LIM), critical care and emergency nurse; b. Mauban, Quezon, Philippines, Mar. 2, 1951; came to U.S., 1978; s. Gui Kui Ama and Teofila (Remolona) L. Diploma, Quezon Meml. Hosp., 1974; BSN, Manila Cen. U., 1978. RN, Calif., N.Y., Ill.; cert. critical care nurse ACLS, mobile intensive care nurse. Staff nurse Mauban Emergency Hosp., Quezon, 1974-78; staff nurse med. surg. Dearborn (Mich.) Med. Ctr., 1978-80; rehab. charge nurse Fresno (Calif.) Community Hosp. and Med. Ctr., 1980-82; emergency dept. charge nurse Mary Thompson Hosp., Chgo., 1983-87; clin. nurse emergency dept. Cook County Hosp., 1988-90; staff med. nurse Rush Presbyn. St. Lukes Med. Ctr., 1990-91; staff emergency dept. Norwegian-Am. Hosp., 1990-95; staff Cook Co. Juvenile Detention Ctr., 1993—. Mem. ANA, Ill. Nurses Assn., Philippine Nurses Assn. Chgo., Mauban U.S.A. Home: 1926 W Harrison St Apt 504 Chicago IL 60612-3700

LIM, SALLYJANE, insurance and financial consultant, diversified financial services company executive; b. Manila; came to U.S., 1990; d. Teddy and Sonia (Yii) L.; children: Robin Michael, Rodney Jovin, Romelle Gavin Lim Velasco. AB-BSC magna cum laude, Coll. of Holy Spirit, Manila, The Philippines. CPA, The Philippines; Life Underwriters Tng. Coun. Fellow (LUTCF). Treas.-contr. Ky. Fried Chicken, Makati, Philippines, 1968-73; ins. rep. Insular Life Assurance Co., 1972-82; project analyst Pvt. Devel. Corp. of Philippines, 1972-78; account exec. Genbancor Devel. Corp., 1978-80; risk mgr. Filcapital Devel. Corp., 1978-82; pres. and gen. mgr., ins. broker Sally-Jane Multiline Insce. Consulting, Inc., Manila, 1978-90; real estate broker Sally-Jane Realty, Inc., 1980-90; ins. rep. and v.p. Macaulay Club Sun Life of Can., 1982-91; rep. Prudential Ins. Co. of Am.; registered rep. Pruco Securities Corp., L.A. Dist., South Pasadena, Calif., 1990-91, Asian Pacific Dist., 1991-98; ind. ins. broker John Hancock Life Ins. Co., UnumProvident Life & Disability, CNA Life, Conseco Life, Allianz Life, Lincoln Nat. Life, 1998—; registered rep. John Hancock Variable Life Ins. Co., 1998-2000; rep. New York Life Ins. Co., Pasadena, Calif.; registered rep. NYLIFE Securities, Inc., 2000—01; ins. broker Allianz Life, First Penn-Pacific Life, 2001—; registered rep. Signator Investors, Inc., 2001—. Flagbearer The Philippines Opening Ceremonies, Million Dollar Round Table 58th Ann. Meeting, San Francisco, 1985; guest fashion model A Company of Women Carnegie's Highlands Golf & Country Club, Idaho, 1999. Recipient Bronze statuette Most Outstanding Ins. Sales Exec. of the Philippines Consumers' Union of the Philippines, Manila, 1983, 88, Plasma 1 Million trophies Dept. Ins. the Philippines, 1988, 89, Young Achiever award Young Achiever Found., Quezon City, Philippines, 1988, Golden Scroll award Philippine Ednl. Youth Devel., Inc., Quezon City, 1988, Twelve Outstanding Profl. Svc. (T.O.P.S.) awards Nat. Achievement Rsch. Soc., Manila, 1988, Lahing Kayumanggi award Outstanding Lady Bus. Exec., Sons and Daughters Charity, Inc., the Philippines, 1988, Internat. Quality award (IQA) (Five Yrs. Qualification) Life Ins. Mktg. and Rsch. Assn., Hartford, 1989, Young Famous Celebrity Mother's trophy Golden Mother/Father Found., Quezon City, 1990, Recognition of Excellence cert., Merit award County of L.A., 8th Ann. Women of Achievement awards San Gabriel Valley YWCA, 1992, 1998 Grand Achievement award For Profl. Sector, People's Choice awards Ateneo U., the Philippines, cert. recognition, 1998, Parangal ng Bayan awardee, Nat. Consumers Coun., the Philippines, 1998, numerous others. Mem. Million Dollar Round Table (life), Nat. Assn. Ins. and Fin. Advisors, Calif. Assn. Ins. and Fin. Advisors, Arcadia C. of C., Asian Bus. Assn., Filipino-Am. C. of C., Greater Pasadena Assn. Ins. and Fin. Advisors, Chinese C. of C. (bd. dirs. L.A. 1992—). Avocations: Broadway musicals, ballet, fashion shows, concerts, ballroom dancing. Home and Office: 1006 Royal Oaks Dr Ste A Monrovia CA 91016-3737 E-mail: starSJ828@aol.com.

LIM, SHUN PING, cardiologist, educator; b. Singapore, Jan. 12, 1947; came to U.S., 1980; s. Tay Boh and Si Moi (Foo) L.; m. Sock Kian Ng, Dec. 9, 1972; children: Corinne Xian-Li, Damien Xian-Ming, Justin Xian-An. MB, BS with honors, Monash U., Melbourne, Australia, 1970, PhD, 1982. Diplomate Am. Bd. Internal Medicine, Am. Bd. Cardiovasc. Disease. Chief non-invasive cardiovasc. imaging U. Cin.-VA Med. Ctr., 1982-86; pvt. practice, Bismarck, N.D., 1986-89, Terre Haute, Ind., 1989-91, Marion, Ohio, 1991—; assoc. prof. cardiology Ohio State U., Columbus, 1994—. Chief cardiology U. N.D., Fargo VA Med. Ctr., N.D., 1991-93; pres. Inst. for Advanced Med. Tech., Marion, 1989—. Vol. physician Marion Free Med. Clinic, 1997—. Rsch. scholar Australian Nat. Health and Med. Rsch. Coun., 1978; rsch. grantee VA, Cin., 1985. Fellow ACP, Am. Coll. Cardiology, Am. Heart Assn. (rsch. grantee 1984), Royal Australasian Coll. Physicians, Acad. Medicine (Singapore), N.Y. Acad. Scis. (life); mem. Marion Acad. Medicine (pres.). Achievements include patent for in-vivo lactate sensor. Avocations: computers, travel, swimming. E-mail: 1011168002@webmd.com.

LIM, TEIK C. engineering educator, consultant; b. Seremban, Negeri Sembilan, Malaysia, Jan. 8, 1965; s. Kim Choon Lim and Kee Moi Tham; m. Yoon C. Voong, July 19, 1987; children: Alvin, Steven, Tiffany. BSME, Mich. Tech. U., Houghton, 1985; MSME, U. Mo., Rolla, 1986; PhD in Mech. Engring., Ohio State U., 1989. EIT EIT, Mich. Sr. project engr. SDRC, Milford, Ohio, 1990—96; rsch. scientist Ctr. for Automotive Rsch., Columbus, 1996—98; assoc. prof. U. Ala., Tuscaloosa, 1998—. Contbr. papers to numerous jours. and confs. Recipient Ferdinand P. Beer & E. Russell Johnston, Jr. Outstanding New Mechanics Educator award, ASEE, 2001, Southeastern Sect. New Faculty Rsch. 1st Pl. award, 2001; fellow presidential fellow, Ohio State U., 1989, faculty rsch. fellow, U. Mo.-Rolla, 1986. Mem.: AHS, ASA, ASME, INCE, SAE (assoc.; noise and vibration com. 1997—2002). Office: U Ala Box 870276 290 Hardaway Hall Tuscaloosa AL 35487

LIM, TOMAS Q., JR. physician; b. Vigan, Ilocos Sur, Philippines, Oct. 17, 1964; came to U.S., 1991; s. Tomas and Paula (Que) L. BS in Med. Tech., U. Santo Tomas, Manila, 1984, MD, 1988. Diplomate Am. Bd. Internal Medicine. Internal medicine intern St. Peter's Med. Ctr., New Brunswick, N.J., 1991-92; resident in internal medicine Luth. Med. Ctr., Bklyn., 1992-94; fellow in nephrology N.Y. Hosp./Cornell Med. Ctr., N.Y.C., 1994-96; primary care physician Salyersville (Ky.) Med. Ctr., 1996-2000, Albemarle Nephrology Assocs., Elizabeth City, N.C., 2000—. Mem. AMA, ACP. Roman Catholic. Avocations: travel, photography. Home: 1503 Emerald Lake Cir Apt 203 Elizabeth City NC 27909-3146 Office: Albemarle Nephrology Assocs 206 Hasting Ln Elizabeth City NC 27909 Fax: 252-335-4030.

LIMA, DONALD ROGER, retired computer programmer; b. San Luis Obispo, Calif., Jan. 9, 1935; s. Donald Joseph Lima and Vera Cora Moraga; m. Esther Hardin; 1 child, Gary. BA, Calif. State U., L.A., 1995. Programmer analyst City of L.A., 1975-95; ret., 1995. Author: (book) A Piece Is Missing, 1998; appearance in Theater Americana of Altadena, 1988-90. With U.S. Army, 1953-56. Democrat. Methodist. Avocation: pinochle. Home: # 210 124 Monterey Rd South Pasadena CA 91030-5033

LIMA, JACQUELINE DUTTON, artist, educator; b. Niagara Falls, N.Y., Oct. 28, 1949; d. Robert Emerson and Priscilla Ann (Tinker) Dutton; m. John Michael Lima; 1 child, Jessica Mae Lima McCarthy. BFA, Swain Sch. Design, New Bedford, Mass., 1978; MFA, CUNY, 1980. Tchr. drawing and painting, 1990-91; instr. Bklyn. Coll., CUNY, 1993-96, Fairleigh Dickinson U., Teaneck, N.J., 1994—. Tchr. N.Y. Acad. Art, N.Y.C., spring 1993, Western Carolina U., Cullowhee, N.C., summer 1997, Chosun U., Kwangju, Republic of Korea, spring 1999, William Paterson U., Wayne, NJ, 2000-; lectr. Hudson River Mus., Yonkers, N.Y., 1989, N.Y. Acad. Art, 1992, N.Y. Studio Sch., 1994, Sta. WFDU-TV, 1996, Woodstock TV, 1997, Chosun U., Kwangju, S. Korea, 1999, Wagner Coll., L.I. U., S.I., N.Y.C., 1999. One-woman shows Blue Mountain Gallery, N.Y.C., 1982, 84, 86, 88, 90, include Hobart and William Smith Colls., Geneva, N.Y., 1989, Suffolk C.C., L.I., 1993, 55 Mercer Street Gallery, N.Y.C., 1996, Schoolhouse GAlleries, Croton Falls, N.Y., 1997, Kentler Internat. Drawing Space, Bklyn., 1998, Fairleigh Dickinson U., 1998, Wagner Coll., 1999, Sussex County C.C., Newton, NJ, Farcountries.com; exhibited in group shows, including Kentler Internat. Drawing Space, 1991, 92, 96, 99, 2001, Blue Mountain Gallery, 1992, 99, 2001, Contemporary Realist Gallery, San Francisco, 1993, Rotunda Gallery, Bklyn., 1995, 98, Ceres Gallery, N.Y.C., 1997, 98, W.Va. Wesleyan U., Buckhannon, 1997, Franziska Pia Gallery, Bern, Switzerland, 1997, Western Carolina U., 1997, Eklektikos Gallery, Washington and Phoenix, 1998, Kleiner-James Gallery, Woodstock, N.Y., 1998, The Painting Ctr., N.Y.C., 1999, hereisnewyork.org, Reactions at Exit Art, Soho, NY, Atrium Gallery laguardia C.C.; permanent collections include Dickinson U. in Robeson Hall; work reviewed in various publs. Congregationalist. Home: RR 2 Box 2490 Canadensis PA 18325 E-mail: lima@fdu.edu.

LIMA, ROBERT, Hispanic studies and comparative literature educator; b. Havana, Cuba, Nov. 7, 1935; came to U.S., 1945; BA in English and Philosophy, Villanova U., 1957, MA in Theatre Arts and Drama, 1961; PhD in Romance Lits., NYU, 1968. Prof. Spanish and comparative lits. Pa. State U., University Park, 1965—2002, prof. emeritus, 2002—. Fellow Inst. for Arts and Humanistic Studies Pa. State U., 1986-2002, fellow emeritus, 2002-; vis. prof. comparative lit. Pontificia U. Cath., Peru; poet-in-residence U. Nat. Mayor de San Marcos, Peru, 1976-77; lectr. Romance langs. and lits. Hunter Coll. CUNY, 1962-65, USIA lectr., Peru, Cameroon, Equatorial Guinea. Author: The Theatre of Garcia Lorca, 1963, An Annotated Bibliography of Ramon del Valle-Inclan, 1972, (poetry) Fathoms, 1981, The Olde Ground, 1985, Mayaland, 1992, Dark Prisms Occultism in Hispanic Drama, 1995, Valle-Inclan. El Teatro de su Vida, 1995, Ramon lel Valle-Inclan: An Annotated Bibliography of Ramon del Valle-Inclan, 1999, (poetry) Sardinia/Sardegna, 2000; co-author: Dos Ensayos Sobre Teatro Español de los Veinte, 1984; editor, translator: Borges the Labyrinth Maker (A.M. Barrenechea), 1965, Valle-Inclan: Autobiography, Aesthetics, Aphorism, 1966; editor, contbr. Borges and the Esoteric, 1993, Cauda Pavonis issue on Leonora Carrington, 2000; translator: The Lamp of Marvels, Aesthetic Meditations (Ramon del Valle-Inclan), 1986, Savage Acts: Four Plays (Valle-Inclan), 1993; co-editor Readers Ency. Am. Lit., 1962, Homenaje A-- Tribute to Martha T. Halsey, 1995, Texts and Contexts: A Tribute to Beno Weiss, 2001; contbr. articles to profl. jours.; prodr., cons., TV and radio programs Centro de Estudios TV la U. Cath., Lima, Peru, 1976-77, Voice of Am., N.Y.C., 1961-62, Pendulum Prodns., 1960-61. Bd. dirs. Pa. Ctr. for Book. Recipient Founders Day award NYU, 1968, Play Translation prize Modern Internat. Drama, cert. of merit Writer's Digest Mag., 1982, Disting. Alumnus medal Villanova Univ., 1999; Rsch. grant Fund for Rsch. Pa. State U., Inst. for Arts and Humanistic Studies; Cintas Found. fellow in poetry Inst. Internat. Edn., 1971-72, fellow Commonwealth Speakers Program Pa. Humanities Coun., Sr. Fulbright fellow Coun. Internat. Exch. Scholars, 1976-77; others. Fellow Inst. for Arts and Humanistic Studies, Phi Kappa Phi (hon.), Phi Sigma Iota (hon.); mem. Internat. PEN, Poetry Soc. Am., Am. Assn. Tchrs. Spanish and Portuguese, Archaeol. Inst. Am., Am. Comparative Lit. Assn., Internat. Comparative Lit. Assn., Galician Studies Assn., Internat. Assn. Valleinclanistas, Am. Name

Soc., Am. Soc. Sephardic Studies, Poets and Writers, Hermetic Text Soc., Beast Fable Soc., Pa. Humanities Coun. (academician), N.Am. Acad. Spanish Lang., Fulbright Alumni Assn., Enxebre Orden da Vieira, Real Academia Española (corr.), Alpha Psi Omega. Home: 485 Orlando Ave State College PA 16803-3477 Office: Pa State U N-352 Burrowes Bldg University Park PA 06802 E-mail: rxl2@psu.edu.

LIMACHER, MARIAN CECILE, cardiologist; b. Joliet, Ill., May 4, 1952; d. Joseph John and Shirley A. (Smith) L.; m. Timothy C. Flynn, May 17, 1980; children: Mary Katherine Flynn, Brian Patrick Flynn. AB in Chemistry, St. Louis U., 1973, MD, 1977. Diplomate Am. Bd. Internal Medicine, Am. Bd. Cardiovascular Diseases. Resident in internal medicine Baylor Coll. Medicine, Houston, 1977-80, cardiology fellow, 1980-83, instr. medicine, 1983-84; dir. cardiology non-invasive labs. Ben Taub Hosp., 1983-84; asst. prof. medicine U. Fla., Gainesville, 1984-91, assoc. prof., 1991-97, prof., 1997—; dir. non-invasive labs. Gainesville VA Med. Ctr., 1984-99, chief cardiology, 1995-99. Dir. preventive cardiology program U. Fla., 1987—. Author (with others): Cardiac Transplantation: A Manual for Health Care Professionals, 1990, Geriatric Cardiology, 1992, The Role of Food in Sickness and in Health, 1993, Clinical Anesthesia Practice, 1994, Primary Care, 1994; mem. editl. bd.: Clin. Cardiology, 1990—, mem. editl. bd.: Preventive Cardiology, 1997—, assoc. editor: Jour. Watch Women's Health, 2001—, assoc. editor: Clin. Jour. Women's Health, 2001—; contbr. articles to profl. jours. Mem. bioethics commn. Diocese of St. Augustine, Jacksonville, Fla., 1990-94. Recipient Preventive Cardiology Acad. award NIH, 1987-92; grantee for Women's Health Initiative, NIH, 1994—. Fellow: ACP, Soc. Geriatric Cardiology (bd. dirs. 1997—, pres. 2002), Am. Coll. Cardiology (chair com. women cardiology 1998—2002, bd. trustees 1999—); mem.: Am. Heart Assn. (fellow coun. clin. cardiology, bd. dirs., pres. Alachua County divsn. 1986—89), Am. Soc. Preventive Cardiology (pres. 1998). Roman Catholic. Avocations: tennis, jogging, snow skiing, playing piano. Office: U Fla Coll Medicine PO Box 100277 Gainesville FL 32610-0277

LIMAN, ELLEN, painter, writer, arts advocate; b. N.Y.C. d. David and Gertrude (Edelman) Fogelson; m. Arthur Liman, Sept. 20, 1959 (dec.); children: Lewis, Emily, Doug. BA, Barnard Coll., 1957; student, N.Y. Sch. Interior Design, 1959. In pub. rels. Tex McCrary, Inc., 1957; interior designer Malanie Kahane Assocs., 1958-60; cons. on grants to the arts The Joe and Emily Lowe Found., 1975-92, pres./trustee, 1993-2000; pres. The Liman Found., 2000—; exec. asst. Adv. Commn. for Cultural Affairs, N.Y.C., 1981-82; dir. spl. projects, dir. City Gallery for N.Y.C. Dept. Cultural Affairs, 1980-84; chair N.Y.C. Adv. Commn. for Cultural Affairs, 1991-93. Author: The Money Savers Guide to Decorating, 1972, Decorating Your Country Place, 1973, Decorating Your Room, 1974, The Spacemaker Book, 1977, The Collecting Book, 1980, Babyspace, 1984, 2000, others; contbr. editor: Kid Smart Mag., 1995-96; contbr. articles to nat. mags. Founding trustee Internat. Ctr. of Photography, 1973—; trustee The Jewish Mus., 1974—, hon. trustee, 1993—; trustee The Ctr. for Arts Info., 1985-86, Mus. Am. Indian, 1998—, Westchester Coun. on Arts, 1994—; mem. N.Y.C. Commn. for Cultural Affairs, 1986-89; bd. dirs. Art Table, Inc., 1987-90, Trust for Cultural Resources, 1993-96, Am. Fedn. of Arts, 1994—; adv. bd. mem. Nat. Acad. Design, 1998—. Fax: 646-840-0211.

LI MANDRI, SALVATORE, computer programmer; b. Milan, Italy, July 20, 1952; s. Vincenzo and Angela Maria (Ardizzone) Li M.; m. Marie Varine Smith, May 16, 1981. BS in Engring. Tech. and Electronics, U. Ark., 1986. Draftsman Harvey Engring. Co., Hot Springs, Ark., 1975-77, jr. programmer, 1977-80, sr. programmer Little Rock, 1980-95; mgr. programming dept. USNR/HEMCO, Hot Springs, 1995—. Served to 2d lt. Italian Army, 1972-74. Avocations: tennis, guitar, electronics, chess. Home: 211 Pine Meadows Loop Hot Springs National Park AR 71901-8264 Office: UNSR/HEMCO 2505 E Grand Ave Hot Springs National Park AR 71901-9719

LIMANTOUR, PHILIPPE, computer science research executive, educator; b. Abidjan, Ivory Coast, Aug. 30, 1966; s. Jean-François and Anna (Morvan) L. Grad. computer sci. engr., Engr. Sch. in Computer Sci., Paris, 1990; higher studies degree in image art, Jussieu U., Paris, 1991; PhD, Orsay U., Paris, 1994; mgmt. degree, Conservatoire Nat. Arts Metier, Paris, 1998. Cert. in real time 3D computer graphics and multimedia engring. R & D engr. Videosystem, Paris, 1991-93; R & D project dir. Medialab, 1993-96; R & D rendering engr. Alias Wavefront/SGI, 1997-98; mng. dir., tech. dir. Sim Team, 1998-99; v.p. mktg. and devel. Cril Telecom, 1999-2000; mng. dir. Quantic Dream, 2000—. Instr. computer graphics Ecole Superieure d'Info. Elec. Automatique, 1990—; lectr. virtual reality and multimedia Ecole Superieure d'Info. Elec., Paris, 1994—; multimedia expert EEC, Brussels, 1997—. Mem. IEEE, Assn. for Computing Machinery, N.Y. Acad. Scis., AIR-ESIEA Assn. (founder, chmn. 1986-90). Avocations: rugby, sailing, scuba diving, travel. Office: Quantic Dream 56 Bd Davout F-75020 Paris France E-mail: plimantour@quanticdream.com.

LIMBACK, E(DNA) REBECCA, vocational education educator; b. Higginsville, Mo., Mar. 23, 1945; d. Henry Shobe and Martha Pauline Rebecca (Willard) Ernstmeyer; m. Duane Paul Limback, Nov. 9, 1963; children: Lisa Christine, Derek Duane. BE, Cen. Mo. State U., 1968, MEd, 1969, EdS, 1976; EdD, U. Mo., 1981. Cert. bus., English and vocat. tchr. Supervising tchr. Lab. Sch. Cen. Mo. State U., Warrensburg, 1969-76, asst. to grad. dean, 1977-79, asst. prof., asst. to bus. dean, 1981-83, assoc. prof. computer and office info. systems, 1984-95, 1986-95, prof. computer and office info. sys., 1996—. Mem. manual editing/revision staff State of Mo., Jefferson City, 1989-90; textbook reviewer Prentice-Hall, Englewood Cliffs, N.J., 1990-91. Author various curriculum guides; mem. editl. bd. Cen. Mo. State U. Rsch., 1982-92. Active Warrensburg Band Aides, 1989-93. Recipient Mo. Gov.'s Excellence in Tchg. award, 2001; grantee, RightSoft Corp., 1988. Mem. DAR, Nat. Bus. Edn. Assn. (conf. profl. opportunities com. 1989-99, info. processing editor Bus. Edn. Forum 1991), Assn. Career and Tech. Edn., North Cen. Bus. Edn. Assn. (Mo. rep., Collegiate Disting. Svc. award 1993), Mo. Bus. Edn. Assn. (all-chpt. pres. 1988-89, chair strategic planning com. 1999—, Postsecondary Tchr. of Yr. 1992), Assn. Bus. Comms., Mid-Mo. Artists, Phi Delta Kappa (all-chpt. pres. 1985), Delta Pi Epsilon (rsch. rep. 1989-92, nat. publs. com. 1993—). Lutheran. Avocations: archaeology, oil painting. Home: 1102 Tyler Ave Warrensburg MO 64093-2049 Office: Dockery 200-B/COIS Dept Cen Mo State U Warrensburg MO 64093 E-mail: limback@cmsu1.cmsu.edu.

LIMBAUGH, RONALD HADLEY, retired history educator, history center director; b. Emmett, Idaho, Jan. 22, 1938; s. John Hadley and Evelyn E. (Mortimore) L.; m. Marilyn Kay Rice, June 16, 1963; 1 child, Sally Ann. BA, Coll. Idaho, 1960; MA, U. Idaho, 1962, PhD, 1967. Hist. libr. Idaho State Hist. Soc., Boise, 1963-66; instr. Boise Coll., 1964-66; asst. prof. history U. of the Pacific, Stockton, Calif., 1966-71, archivist, curator, 1968-87, prof. history, 1977-2000, Rockwell Hunt chair of Calif. history, 1989-2000; dir. Holt-Atherton Ctr., U. of the Pacific, 1984-87. Exec. dir. Conf. of Calif. Hist. Socs., Stockton, 1973-76, 77-78, 82-86, 90-97; dir. John Muir Ctr. for Regional Studies, U. of Pacific, Stockton, 1989-2000; cons., evaluator NEH, 1983-86. Author: Rocky Mountain Carpetbaggers, 1982, John Muir's Stickeen and the Lessons of Nature, 1996; co-editor: (microform) John Muir Papers, 1986, (book) Guide to Muir Papers, 1986; contbr. articles to profl. jours. With U.S. Army, 1955-56. NDEA fellow, 1960; grantee Calif. Coun. Humanities, 1976, Nat. Hist. Publs. and Records Commn., 1980-82, NEH, 1983, Inst. European Studies, 1989, Hoover Libr. Assn., 1997. Mem. Western History Assn., Mining History Assn. Christian Humanist. Avocations: hiking, golf. Office: U Pacific 3601 Pacific Ave Stockton CA 95211-0197 E-mail: limbaugh@mcn.org.

LIMBAUGH, STEPHEN NATHANIEL, federal judge; b. Cape Girardeau, Mo., Nov. 17, 1927; s. Rush Hudson and Bea (Seabaugh) L.; m. DeVaughn Anne Mesplay, Dec. 27, 1950; children— Stephen Nathaniel Jr., James Pennington, Andrew Thomas. BA, S.E. Mo. State U., Cape Girardeau, 1950; JD, U. Mo., Columbia, 1951. Bar: Mo. 1951. Prosecuting atty. Cape Girardeau County, Mo., 1954-58; judge U.S. Dist. Ct. (ea. and we. dists.) Mo., St. Louis, 1983—. With USN, 1945-46. Recipient Citation of Merit for Outstanding Achievement and Meritorious Service in Law, U. Mo., 1982 Fellow Am. Coll. Probate Counsel, Am. Bar Found.; mem. ABA (ho. of dels. 1987-90), Mo. Bar Assn. (pres. 1982-83). Republican. Methodist. E-mail: stephen. Office: US Dist Ct Thomas F Eagleton Courthous 111 S Tenth St Ste 3.125 Saint Louis MO 63102 E-mail: limbaugh@moed.uscourts.gov.

LIMEHOUSE, HARRY BANCROFT, JR. real estate developer; b. Charleston, S.C., Dec. 3, 1938; m. Frankie Fennell, Jan. 18, 1961; children: Chip, Brien, Barry, Brad. BA in English, The Citadel, 1960, LLD (hon.), 1997; D in Hospitality (hon.), Johnson & Wales U., 1995; LLD (hon.), The Citadel, 1997; D in Bus. (hon.), Citadel, 1997. Lic. real estate broker, S.C. Mgmt. trainee Deering-Millikin, 1960-61; agt. Prudential Ins. Co., Charleston, 1962-67, mgr. W. Palm Beach, Fla., 1967-69; dir. campaign mgmt. divsn. Rep. Nat. Com., Washington, 1967-69; pres., founder Limehouse Properties, Charleston, 1970—. Bankruptcy trustee U.S. Trustee's Office, Columbia, S.C., 1988—. Mem. Pub. Rys. Commn. S.C., 1989-93, chmn., 1992-93; past pres. Carolina chpt. Real Estate Securities Inst.; charter pres. Charleston chpt. Comml. Income Properties Coun.; founding pres. Palmetto State Games; chmn. So. Govs. Conf., 1992; chmn. S.C. Dept. Transp. Commn., 1994-99. Named hotelier of Yr. S.C. Hospitality Assn., 1994; named to Order of the Palmetto, 1995; S.C. Transportation and Policy Counc., 1995, Man of the Year, 1996—; S.C. Wildlife Federation, Conservationist of the Year, 1996—; S.F. Taxpayers Assn., Man of the Year. Mem. Nat. Assn. Realtors, Aircraft Owners and Pilots Assn., Hibernian Soc., Downtown Athletic Club. Avocation: flying. Office: Limehouse Properties 8 Cumberland St Charleston SC 29401-2602

LIMPITLAW, JOHN DONALD, retired publishing executive, clergyman; b. N.Y.C., Jan. 4, 1935; s. Robert and Olga (Lang) L.; m. Susan Elizabeth Glover, May 21, 1960; children: Alison, Amy Elizabeth. BA, Trinity Coll., Hartford, Conn., 1956; MA in Religion, Yale U., 1992. With Marine Midland Bank Trust Co. N.Y., N.Y.C., 1956-61, Celanese Corp., N.Y.C., 1961-63; mgr. personnel Westvaco Corp., 1963-69; v.p. Warnaco Inc., Bridgeport, Conn., 1969-77, Macmillan Inc., N.Y.C., 1977-89; vicar Parish of Christ's Ch., Easton, Conn., 1992-97; bd. dirs. St. Mark's Day Care Ctr., Bridgeport, 1995—. Seminarian Yale Divinity Sch., New Haven, Conn., 1989-92; trustee Episcopal Investment Funds; bd. dirs. Inter-Ch. Residences, Inc., 3030 Park, Inc.; dir. Operation Hope; bd. dirs. Habitat, Easton, Conn., bd. ops., Fairfield, Conn., 1998—. Democrat. Episcopalian. Avocations: sailing, skiing. Home: PO Box 2004 140 Whidah Way Wellfleet MA 02667-7735 also: 6825 Grenadier Blvd Apt 1501 Naples FL 34108-7218 E-mail: jlimpitlaw@aol.com.

LIN, ALICE LEE LAN, physicist, researcher, educator; b. Shanghai, China, Oct. 28, 1937; came to U.S., 1960, naturalized, 1974; m. A. Marcus, Dec. 19, 1962 (div. Feb. 1972); 1 child, Peter A. AB in Physics, U. Calif., Berkeley, 1963; MA in Physics, George Washington U., 1974. Statis. asst. dept. math. U. Calif., Berkeley, 1961-63; rsch. asst. in radiation damage Cavendish Lab. Cambridge (Eng.) U., 1965-66; info. analysis specialist Nat. Acad. Scis., Washington, 1970-71; teaching fellow, rsch. asst. George Washington U., Catholic U. Am., 1971-75; physicist NASA/Goddard Space Flight Ctr., Greenbelt, Md., 1975-80, Army Materials Tech. Lab., Watertown, Mass., 1980—. Contbr. articles to profl. jours. Mencius Ednl. Found. grantee, 1959-60. Mem. AAAS, N.Y. Acad. Scis., Am. Phys. Soc., Am. Ceramics Soc., Am. Acoustical Soc., Am. Men and Women of Sci., Optical Soc. Am. Democrat. Avocations: rare stamp and coin collecting, art collectibles, home computers, opera, ballet. Home: 28 Hallett Hill Rd Weston MA 02493-1753

LIN, AMY YUH-MEI, industrial engineer, real estate investor; b. Chuang-Hua, Taiwan, Jan. 22, 1948; Came to U.S., 1973; d. Tu-To and Show-Lan (Wu) Tsai; m. Edward Yih-Ling Lin, Dec. 24, 1975; children: Shirley, Kenneth. BSBA, Cheng Kung U., Taiwan, 1971; MS in Indsl. Engring., W.Va. U., 1975. Supr. Yellow Springs (Ohio) Instrument Corp., 1977-78; indsl. engr. MSI Data Corp., Costa Mesa, Calif., 1978-79; sr. programmer, analyst MAI Basic Four Corp., Tustin, 1979-81; supr., sr. indsl. engr. LH Rsch., Inc., 1981-85; sr. indsl. engr. Rockwell Internat., Anaheim, Calif., 1985-90; pres., gen. mgr. Maylyne Creations, Irvine, 1990—, Fortune Investment & Mgmt., Irvine, 1989—. Sec. Cheng Kung U. Found., 1992, treas. 1994—; v.p., treas. Woodbridge High Sch. Chinese Parent Assn., Irvine, Calif., 1993—. Mem. Cheng Kung U. Alumni Assn. (treas. 1992, v.p. 1994—), Apt. Owners Assn. So. Calif., Internat. Inst. Indsl. Engring. Avocations: tennis, writing, reading, ping pong. Office: PO Box 18404 Irvine CA 92623-8404

LIN, BOR-LUH, mathematician, educator; b. Xiamen, Fujian, China, Mar. 4, 1935; s. Lam-Beng Lin and Yueh-Hwa Li; m. Hsin Lee Lin, Aug. 24, 1963; children: James, David, Michael. BS, Nat. Taiwan U., Taipei, Taiwan, 1956; MS, U. Notre Dame, Notre Dame, IN, 1960; PhD, Northwestern U., Evanston, IL, 1963. Prof. U. Iowa, Iowa City, 1963—94; chmn. Dept. Math., U. Iowa, 1994—2000; prof. U. Iowa, 2000—. Editor: (book) Banach Space Theory; co-author: Banach Spaces, Nonlinear and Convex Analysis. Recipient Hon. Prof., Harbin U. Sciences and Tech., Harbin, China. Mem.: Am. Math. Soc. Office: University Iowa Department of Mathematics Iowa City IA 52242 Office Fax: 319-335-0627. E-mail: bllin@math.uiowa.edu.

LIN, CHING-SHEN, pathologist; b. Ping-Tong, Taiwan, Republic of China, Sept. 11, 1934; s. Ten-Fu Lin and Chuang Chen; m. Lilly Lin, Nov. 25, 1962; children: John, Judith, Jane. MD, Nat. Taiwan U., 1960. Diplomate Am. Bd. Anatomic and Clin. Pathology. Clin. assoc. prof. pathology SUNY Downstate Med. Ctr., Bklyn., 1988-89; dir. autopsy pathology Mt. Sinai Med. Ctr., N.Y.C., 1989-99, assoc. prof. pathology, 1989-99. Bd. editors Am. Coll. Angiology, 1988—. V.p. Taiwan Ctr., N.Y.C., 1998-99. Ensign Chinese Navy, Taiwan, 1960-61. Fellow Am. Clin. Pathologists, Am. Coll. Angiology; mem. AMA, Nat. Taiwan U. Med. Coll. Alumni Assn. (pres. 1992-93), N.Y. Acad. Sci. Home: 26 Ebbtide Ln Dix Hills NY 11746 E-mail: cslin@mindspring.com.

LIN, CHUN, chemistry researcher; b. Fuzhou, Fujian, People's Republic of China, Dec. 3, 1969; arrived in U.S., 1993; BS, U. Sci. Tech. of China, Hefei, 1992; PhD, Fla. Inst. Tech., 1997. Rsch. assoc. dept. chemistry Tex. A&M U., College Station, 1997-2001; rsch. assoc. IBM T.J. Waston Rsch. Ctr., Yorktown Heights, N.Y., 2001—. Mem. AAAS, Am. Chem. Soc. (outstanding grad. student Orlando sect. 1995). Achievements include pioneering the study of metal-metal bonded supramolecular chemistry and its application in molecular electronics, 1997—, initiating the study of linear free energy relationship in dinuclear compounds, 1993-97. Office: IBM TJ Watson Rsch Ctr PO Box 218 Rte 134 Yorktown Heights NY 10598

LIN, FRANK CHIWEN, computer science educator; b. Shanghai, China, Aug. 28, 1936; came to U.S., 1953; s. Elmer C. and Virginia (Chang) Ling; m. Margareta Lundgren, Mar. 8, 1968 (div. Aug. 1979); children: Ulrika Lin, Sigrid Lin; m. Helen M. Baldado, Mar. 17, 1987. BECE, Yale U., 1957; postgrad., U. Goettingen, Germany, 1958; PhD in Theoretical Physics, Yale U., 1965; postgrad., Polytech. U. N.Y., 1980-82. Rsch. assoc. dept. theoretical physics Chalmers Tech. U., Goeteborg, Sweden, 1965-70; asst. to pres. Biomed. Scis. Inc., Fairfield, N.J., 1971-75; instr. physics, engring., and computer sci. L.B. Wallace State Jr. Coll., Andalusia, Ala., 1976-84; assoc. prof. computer sci. Western Conn. State U., Danbury, 1984-85; prof. computer sci. U. Md., Princess Anne, Md., 1986—. Vis. prof. physics Nat. Taiwan U., Taipei, 1970. Author: Elementary FORTRAN with Scientific and Business Applications, 1983, Structured BASIC for Mini- and Micro-Computers, 1985; (play) First Degree Murder, 1997; contbr. articles to profl. jours. Prin. investigator numerous grants, 1981-93. Mem. IEEE (treas./sec. local chpt. 1989-90, vice-chmn. local chpt. 1990-91), Assn. Computing Machinery, Yale Sci. and Engring. Assn., N.Y. Acad. Scis., Am. Assn. for Artificial Intelligence, Internat. Neural Network Soc., Am. Med. Informatics Assn., Tau Beta Pi. Avocation: classical music. Address: Inst Computacao Rue Passo da Patria 156 Bloc E 24210-240 Niteroi Rio de Janeiro Brazil

LIN, HENRY BAOHUA, consultant, writer; b. Fuchow, Fukien, China, Sept. 11, 1955; came to U.S., 1988; s. John Luchen and Mary Chih (Cheng) L. Master, Oreg. State U., 1990. Cons. feng shui design, natural health care methods, and face reading. Author: What Your Face Reveals, 1999 (Libr. award 2000), Chinese Health Care Secrets, 2000, The Art and Science of Feng Shui, 2000. E-mail: henry9us@yahoo.com.

LIN, HO-MU, engineering educator; b. Kaohsiung, Taiwan, July 12, 1938; s. Chao-Wu and Dean-Su L.; m. Su-Jung Wang, 1972; children: Eugene Ted, Jeffrey Eugene. BS, Nat. Taiwan U., 1962; Postgrad. Diploma, Tokyo Inst. Tech., 1966; PhD, Okla. State U., 1970. Sr. lectr., rsch. assoc. Okla. State U., 1970-73; rsch. fellow Rice U., 1974-75; tech. dir., sr. engr. Thermodynamics Rsch. Lab. Purdue U., 1975-87, sr. fellow, 1988-94; spl. chair Nat. Taiwan U., 1994, Nat. Taiwan Inst. Tech., 1994-97; prof., chmn. Nat. Taiwan U. Sci. and Tech., 1997—2001, v.p., 2001—. Sr. scientific adviser BIOS Indsl., Can., 1987—; cons. EXXON Rsch. and Engring. Co., 1984-85; sr. adviser Biotech. Svc. Internat., Can., 1984-87; spl. chair Nat. Sci. Coun., Taiwan, 1994-97. Editor (hon.) Jour. Chinese Inst. Chem. Engrs., Vol. 27 (No. 4), 1996, mem. editl. bd., 1997—;internat. monitor Jour. Chem. Engring. Japan, 1998—; contbr. 150 articles to tech. jours., 2 chpts. to books; patentee in field. Fellow UNESCO, 1965-66; recipient award Am. Petroleum Rsch. Funds, 1968, Rsch. Achievements award EXXON, Chevron, Amoco, 1983-87. Mem. Chinese Inst. Chem. Engrs. (dir. 1997—, editor (hon.) Chem. Engring. Vol. 45 1996), Am. Chem. Soc., AIChE, AAAS. Avocations: sports, gardening. Home: 3303 Hunter Rd West Lafayette IN 47906-5392 Office: Nat Taiwan U Sci & Tech 43 Keelung Rd Sec 4 Taipei 106 Taiwan

LIN, JAMES CHIH-I, biomedical and electrical engineer, educator; b. Dec. 29, 1942; m. Mei Fei, Mar. 21, 1970; children: Janet, Theodore, Erik. BS, U. Wash., 1966, MS, 1968, PhD, 1971. Engr. Crown Zellerbach Corp., Seattle, 1966-67; asst. prof. U. Wash., 1971-74; prof. Wayne State U., Detroit, 1974-80, U. Ill., Chgo., 1980—, head dept. bioengring., 1980-92, dir. robotics and automation lab., 1982-89, dir. spl. projects Coll. Engring., 1992-94, rsch. chair NSC, 1993-97, dir. Ctr. Wireless Tech. and Bioelectromagnetics, 1997—. Vis. prof., Beijing, Rome, Shan Dong, Taiwan Univs.; lectr. short courses, 1974—; cons. Battelle Meml. Inst., Columbus, Ohio, 1973-75, SRI Internat., palo Alto, Calif., 1978-79, Arthur D. Little Inc., Cambridge, Mass., 1980-83, Ga. Tech. Rsch. Inst., Atlanta, 1984-86, Walter Reed Army Inst. Rsch., 1973, 87, 88, Naval Aerospace Med. Rsch. Labs., Pensacola, 1982-83, U.R.S. Corp., San Francisco, 1985-87, CBS Inc., N.Y., 1988, U. Va., 1991-92, ACS Inc., Santa Clara Calif., 1989-90, Luxtron Corp., Mountainview, Calif., 1991-92, Commonwealth Edison, Chgo., 1991-95, Lucent Tech./Bell Labs., 1998-2000; program chmn. Frontiers of Engring. and Computing Conf., Chgo., 1985; chmn., convener URSI Jt. Symposium Electromagnetic Waves in Biol. Sys., Tel Aviv, 1987, Internat. Conf. on Sci. and Tech., 1989-91; chmn. Chinese-Am. Acad. and Profl. Conv., 1993; mem. Congrl. Health Care Adv. Coun., 13th dist., Ill., 1987-99; panelist NSF Presdl. Young Investigator award com., Washington, 1984, 89; mem. NIH diagnostic radiology, 1981-85, chmn. spl. study sect., 1986—; mem. U.S. Nat. Commn. for URSI, NAS, 1980-82, 90-99, chair Commn. K., 1990-99, Extremely Low Frequency Field monitoring com., 1995-97; mem. Pres. Com. Nat. Medal of Sci., 1992-93; mem. Nat. Coun. Radiation Protection and Measurement, 1992—, chmn. radio frequency sci. com., 1995—; chmn. Internat. Union of Radio Scis. Commn., Electromagnetics in Biology and Medicine, 1996-99; chmn. Internat. Sci. Meeting on Electromagnetics in Medicine, 1997; mem. citizen's adv. coun. Hinsdale Cen. H.S., 1988-93. Author: Microwave Auditory Effects and Applications, 1978, Biological Effects and Health Implications of Radiofrequency Radiation, 1987, Electromagnetic Interaction with Biological Systems, 1989, Mobile Comm. Safety, 1996; editor: Advances in Electromagnetic Fields in Living Systems, 1994—; columnist: ACM Mobile Computing and Comms. Rev., 1999—, columnist: IEEE Antennas and Propagation Mag., 1999—, columnist: IEEE Microwave Mag., 2000—, columnist: Radio Sci. Bull., 2001—, guest editor: EMB Mag., 1997—99, guest editor: Wireless Networks, 1996—97; contbr. articles to profl. jours. Recipient Nat. Rsch. Svcs. award 1982, Disting. Svc. award, Outstanding Leadership award Chinese Am. Acad. and Profl. Assn. MidAm., 1989. Fellow AAAS, AIMBE, IEEE (tech. policy coun. 1990-91, chmn. com. on man and radiation, 1990-91, assoc. and guest editor transactions on biomed. engring., guest editor transaction on microwave theory and techniques, disting. lectr. engring. in medicine and biology 1991—, Transaction Best Paper award 1975); mem. Biomed. Engring. Soc. (sr. mem.), Robotics Internat. (sr. mem.), Am. Soc. Engring. Edn., Bioelectromagnetics Soc. (charter, pres.-elect 1993-94, pres. 1994-95, chmn. ann. meeting 1994), Electromagnetics Acad., Marconi Found. (sci. com. 1996—), Golden Key, Sigma Xi, Phi Tau Phi (v.p.), Tau Beta Pi. Office: U Ill Coll Engring 1030 SEO MC/154 851 S Morgan St Chicago IL 60607-7042 E-mail: lin@uic.edu.

LIN, JAMES K. technology company executive, educator; b. Shanghai, China, Sept. 22, 1941; s. Hua Kun Lin and Sho Cheng Chiang; m. Ellen Lin; children: Vincent, Geoffrey, Charles. BS, Nat. Taiwan U., Taipei, 1965; MS, Pratt Inst., 1969; postgrad., U. Pa.; PhD, U. Southwestern La., 1977; DSc, U. Am., 1977. Sr. analyst, engr. mgr. RCA Global Comms., N.Y.C., 1975-77; mgr. timesharing ctr. CDC Taiwan, Taipei, 1977-81, sales mgr. country mktg., 1981-85; country mgr. CDC China/Hong Kong, Beijing, 1985-89; dep. gen. mgr. WANG Labs., Taipei, 1989-92; regional dir. EDS Asia, Hong Kong, 1992-94; gen. mgr. ABB China Ltd., 1994—. Prof. (part time) CUNY, 1973-74; spkr. in field. Mem. Chinese Academic and Profl. Assn. in Am. (pres. 1975-77), Chinese-Am. Assn. China (exec. dir. 1995-97), Am. C. of C. in China, Am. High Tech. Forum in China (treas. 1987-89), Comm. Network Assn. (exec. dir. 1992-94), Open Sys. Assn. Taiwan (mng. supr. 1989-91, Excellent Performances 1990). Avocations: swimming, basketball, music, travel. Home: 5257 Purdue Ave Culver City CA 90230-5349 Office: ABB China Ltd South Tower 14 East Third Ring Rd N 100026 Beijing China

LIN, JANET C. physician; b. Ann Arbor, Mich., Aug. 14, 1959; d. Shin R. and Agnes Li-Stu (Lee) L.; m. Sabino R. Torre, Sept. 24, 1988; children: Jennifer Lynn, Emily Anne. BA in Biology, Johns Hopkins U., 1981; MD, N.Y. Med. Coll., 1985. Diplomate Am. Bd. Internal Medicine. Clin. prof. Robert Wood Johnson Med. Sch., New Brunswick, N.J., 1992-2000, clin. instr., 1991-92, asst. clin. prof., 1992—2000, assoc. clin. prof. N.J., 2000—; epidemiologist Muhlenberg Regional Med. Ctr., Plainfield, NJ, 2001—, chief infectious diseases sect., 2001—. Contbr. articles to profl. jours. Scholar Johns Hopkins U., Balt., 1977-81. Fellow ACP, Infectious Diseases Soc. Am.; mem. N.J. Infectious Diseases Soc., Am. Soc. Microbiology, Alpha Omega Alpha, Omicron Delta Kappa. Avocations: travel, reading, theatre. Office: Muhlenberg Regional Med Ctr Park Ave and Randolph Rd Plainfield NJ 07061

LIN, JIIN-HUEY CHERN, engineering educator; b. Kaoshung, Taiwan, Republic of China, Feb. 19, 1949; d. Fen-Fu and Chung-Lin Lin Chen; m. Luh-Yuan Lin, July 5, 1973; children: Albert Isaac, Alice, Seraphina. BS in Physics, Chung Yuan Christian U., Taiwan, 1970; MS in Physics, N.E. La. U., 1974; PhD in Biomaterials, Northwestern U., 1983. Vis. specialist Nat. Yang-Ming U., Taipei, Tawian, 1984-85; asst. prof. Northwestern U., Chgo., 1985-89, vis. prof., 1996-97, Nat. Cheng-Kung U., Tainan, Taiwan, 1987-88, assoc. prof. Taiwan, 1989-95, prof. Taiwan, 1995—. Strategic com. Nat. Sci. Coun., Taipei, 1997-99. Jour. reviewer Dental Materials, Liverpool, U.K., 1995—, Jour. of Materials Chemistry and Physics, Liverpool, 1997—; contbr. numerous articles to profl. jours.; inventor in field. Recipient Excellent Rsch. award Nat. Sci. Coun. of Republic of China, 1990-2002, some 50 rsch. grants, 1990—; rsch. grantee Nat. Health Rsch. Inst., 1994—. Fellow The Acad. of Denal Materials; mem. Soc. of Biomaterials, Soc. of Dental Materials, Chinese Bioengring. Soc., Am. Ceramic Soc. Home: 911 Tower Rd Winnetka IL 60093-1935 Office: Nat Cheng-Kung U #1 University Rd Tainan 70101 Taiwan E-mail: chernlin@mail.ncku.edu.tw.

LIN, JOSEPH PEN-TZE, retired neuroradiologist; b. Foochow, China, Nov. 25, 1932; came to U.S., 1959, naturalized, 1974; s. Tai Shui and Chin Sien Lin; m. Lillian Y. Hsu, Dec. 23, 1959; children: James S., Carol W., Julia W. MD, Nat. Taiwan U., 1957. Diplomate Am. Bd. Radiology. Rotating intern Robert B. Green Meml. Hosp., San Antonio, 1959-60; resident in radiology Santa Rosa Med. Center, 1960-61, Bellevue Hosp. Center, N.Y.C., 1961-63; fellow in neuroradiology NYU Med. Ctr., 1963-65, instr. radiology, 1965-67, asst. prof., 1967-70, assoc. prof., 1970-74, prof., 1974-97; dir. neuroradiology sect. Univ. Hosp., N.Y.C., 1974-93; dir. neuroradiology Bellevue Hosp., 1993-97; ret., 1997. Cons. Manhattan VA Hosp., N.Y.C., 1974-97, Booth Meml. Hosp., N.Y.C., 1978-84, St. Vincent's Hosp., S.I., N.Y., 1978-85, New Rochelle (N.Y.) Hosp., 1978-85. Contbr. articles on neuroradiology to med. jours. Fellow Am. Coll. Radiology, Am. Heart Assn. (stroke coun.); mem. Am. Chinese Med. Soc. (pres. 1978), Am. Soc. Neuroradiology, Radiol. Soc. N.Am., Assn. Univ. Radiologists. Home: 15 Oxford Rd New Rochelle NY 10804-3712

LIN, JUCHUI RAY (JU-CHUI LIN), polymer scientist; b. Taoyuan, Taiwan, China, Apr. 25, 1947; came to U.S., 1974; s. Pai-Liang and Mai (Wang) L.; m. Jing-Fang Wang, Dec. 24, 1975; children: Amy Monica, Audrey Alice. BS in Chemistry, Nat. Taiwan Normal U., 1972; MS in Chemistry, Southwest Tex. State U., 1977; PhD in Macromolecular Sci., Case Western Res. U., 1985. Tchr. Taipei Gimmei Jr. High Sch., Taiwan, 1971-73; lab. instr. Nat. Ctrl. U., Chungli, Taiwan, 1973-74; chemist Sohio Rsch. Ctr., Warrensville Heights, Ohio, 1983, DPJ Rsch. Ctr., SCM Corp., Strongville, 1984-86; sr. scientist

Spectrum Control Rsch. Ctr., Erie, Pa., 1986-88; tech. mgr. Koch Membrane Systems, Inc., Wilmington, Mass., 1989-93; mgr. ion-exch. membrane technology Ionics, Inc., Watertown, 1993—. Author youth sci. books Youth Ency., 1970, also papers in field. Fellow Am. Inst. Chemists; mem. AIChE, Am. Chem. Soc., Soc. Plastics Engrs. Achievements include patents in field of conductive polymers, electrical active polymers, resins and coatings, elastomers, encapsulations for electronics, potting, ceramics, polymer blends, polymer surface modifications, membrane formulations, membrane processes; pioneer and inventor of cobalt chain transfer agents for living free radical polymerization, catalyzed grafting reaction of epoxide onto halogenated vinyl polymers, self-assembly surface coating technology, enzyme immobilization. Avocations: community service. Office: Ionics Inc 65 Grove St Watertown MA 02472-2882 E-mail: jlin@ionics.com.

LIN, JUNG-CHUNG, microbiologist, researcher; b. Ping Tung, Taiwan, Nov. 15, 1939; came to U.S., 1970; s. Wan-Ho and Kwei-Tzu (Chen) L.; m. Shou-Huei, July 19, 1967; children: Melissa, Richard. PhD, Temple U., 1974. Rsch. asst. unit 2 U.S. Naval Med. Rsch., Taipei, Taiwan, 1965-66; asst. prof. Nat. Def. Med. Coll., 1967-70; assoc. mem. Inst. of Zoology Academia Sinica, 1967-74; rsch. assoc. U. N.C., Chapel Hill, 1977-80, rsch. asst. prof., 1980-84, rsch. assoc. prof., 1984-90; chief molecular biology sect. Ctrs. for Disease Control, Atlanta, 1990—; chmn. dept. microbiology Tzu Chi U., Hualien, Taiwan, 1997—. Adj. prof. Emory U., Atlanta, 1992—. Author chpts. in books; contbr. over 90 articles to profl. jours. Grantee NCI, NIH, NIAID. Mem. AAAS, Am. Soc. for Microbiology, Am. Soc. for Virology, Am. Assn. for Cancer Rsch., Internat. Soc. for Antiviral Rsch., Internat. Assn. for Rsch. on Epstein-Barr Virus and Associated Diseases. Achievements include patent for design of antisense oligodeoxynucleotide to cure Epstein-Bar virus latent infection. Home: 3723 Toxaway Ct Atlanta GA 30341-4622 Office: Tzu Chi U No 701 Sect 3 Chung Yan Rd Hualien Taiwan E-mail: Jxl8@mail.tcu.edu.tw.

LIN, LAWRENCE SHUH LIANG, accountant; b. July 5, 1938; arrived in U.S., 67, naturalized, 79; s. Wan Chow and Inn Chi Lin; m. Grace Yu, July 31, 1966; children: Ray, Lester. LLB, Soochow U., 1963; MBA, Pepperdine U., 1970; JD, U. West L.A., 1998. Spl. project acctg. supr. Motown Records, Hollywood, Calif., 1975; chief acct. Elektra/Asylum/Nonesuch Records, Beverly Hills, 1976—77, United Artists Music Pub. Group, Hollywood, 1977—80; contbr.-adminstr. Pasadena (Calif.) Guidance Clinics (name now Pacific Clinics), 1980—86; v.p. Stew Kettle Corp., L.A., 1986—87, LKL Corp., L.A., 1987—89; internat. fin. cons. Pacific Capital Mgmt., Alhambra, 1990. Mem.: Nat. Assn. Security Dealers, Inst. Mgmt. Accts. Baptist. Office: Pacific Capital Mgmt 670 Monterey Pass Rd Monterey Park CA 91754-2419

LIN, LIANLIAN, management educator; b. Fushun, Liaoning, China, Aug. 22, 1956; d. Jiang Lin and Jianhua Sun; children: Nika Qiao. MA in Internat. Fin., Fudan U., Shanghai, China, 1985; LLM, U. Pa., Phila., 1988; PhD in Bus. Adminstrn., U. Tex., Austin, 1992. Faculty in mgmt. Calif. State Poly. U., Pomona, 1992—. Vis. prof. Peking U., Beijing, 2001. Contbr. articles. Mem.: Chinese Scholar Assn. So. Calif. (v.p. 1999—2002). Office: Calif State Poly U 3801 W Temple Ave MHR Pomona CA 91768

LIN, LIN, stock broker, insurance agent; b. Jan. 29; d. Boabing Lin and Qiuou Huang; m. Hua-Yun Xiao, Dec. 24, 1984 (div. Feb. 1994); children: Alexander Ronghui, Elizabeth Rong Fong. BA, Wuhan (China) Geol. U., 1983; BS, San Francisco State U., 1993. Clk. U.S. Post Office, San Francisco, 1986-99; broker WMA Securities, Daly City, Calif., 1997—. Mem. Chinese Engring. Soc. Office: WMA Securities 333 Gellert Blvd Ste 250 Daly City CA 94015-2614 E-mail: lin94010@yahoo.com.

LIN, LINDA I-LI, computer consultant, trainer; b. Brookings, S.D., July 22, 1966; d. Peck-Sun and Kwei-Chi (Ho) L.; m. Benjamin J. Miller, Aug. 13, 1995. BA, Harvard U., 1988; MBA, Kellogg Sch. Mgmt., 1993. Cons. Monitor Co., Cambridge, Mass., 1988-91; ind. graphic designer, 1991; product and program mgr. Microsoft Corp., Redmond, Wash., 1992; lead cons. Kellogg Computing Svcs., Evanston, Ill., 1992-93; cons. Boston Cons. Group, Boston, Chgo., 1993-95; ind. computer cons., trainer Chgo., Andover, Mass., Bedford, N.H., 1995—. Bd. dirs. Womens Bus. Ctr. Mem. ASTD, Beta Gamma Sigma. Avocations: figure skating, ethnic cooking, knitting.

LIN, MARIA C. H. lawyer; b. Kunming, Yunnan, China, Jan. 27, 1942; BSc, Coll. Mount St. Vincent, 1966; MSc, U. Kans., 1970; JD, Fordham U., 1978. Bar: N.Y. 1979, U.S. Dist. Ct. (so. and ea. dists.) N.Y. 1979, U.S. Ct. Appeals (Fed. cir.) 1982, U.S. Patent and Trademark Office, 1979, U.S Supreme Ct. 1985. Atty. Morgan & Finnegan, N.Y.C. Panelist World Intellectual Property. Mem. ABA, N.Y. State Bar Assn., World Intellectual Property Orgn. (domain name dispute panelist), N.Y. Intellectual Property Law Assn. (bd. dirs. 1979-88, internat. law and practice China com. 1979-85, fgn. patent law and practice 1986— chmn. 1990-91), Am. Intellectual Property Law Assn. (Chinese rels. com. 1983-87, internat. patent law and practice 1988—, chmn. 1995-96, co-chmn., China study group, 1997-2000), Internat. Intellectual Propery Soc. (chair 2000—). Office: Morgan & Finnegan LLP 345 Park Ave New York NY 10154-0053 E-mail: mclin@morganfinnegan.com.

LIN, MIN-CHUNG, obstetrician, gynecologist; b. Nan-Tou, Republic of China, Aug. 24, 1944; s. Chi-Hsien and Yue (Chen) L.; m. Miaw-Chyung, June 26, 1971; children: Susie, Judy, Nancy, Frances. MD, Tapei Med. Coll., Republic of China, 1970. Diplomate Am. Bd. Ob-Gyn. Chmn. ob-gyn dept. Cuba (N.Y.) Meml. Hosp., 1976-80, Ira Davenport Meml. Hosp., Bath, N.Y., 1980-95; med. staff ob-gyn. dept. Corning (N.Y.) Hosp., 1995—. Fellow: Am. Coll. Ob-Gyn. Republican. Presbyterian. Office: 123 Conhocton St Corning NY 14830

LIN, MING SHEK, allergist, immunologist; b. Taipei, Taiwan, Oct. 11, 1937; came to U.S., 1965; s. Joseph and Tong-Kai (Chan) Lynn; m. Mary Liao, Nov. 22, 1969; children: Jerry, Michael. MD, Nat. Taiwan U., 1964; PhD, U. Pitts., 1974. Diplomate Am. Acad. Allergy and Immunology, Am. Bd. Pediatrics. Asst. prof. U. Pitts. Grad. Sch. Pub. Health, 1976-80; asst. and assoc. prof. dept. pediatrics U. Pitts. Sch. Medicine, 1981—. Chief sect. of allergy and immunology Forbes Health System, Pitts., 1987—; pres. Pitts. Allergy Soc., 1995-97. Contbr. articles to Jour. Allery and Immunology, Internat. Congress of Immunology, Jour. Allergy, Jour. Pediatrics, Jour. Cellular Immunology, Immunology. Named Winklestan lectr., 1976. Fellow Am. Soc. for Microbiology; mem. AMA, Am. Acad. Allergy and Immunology. Home: 81 Locksley Dr Pittsburgh PA 15235-5117 Office: 4099 William Penn Hwy Ste 805 Monroeville PA 15146-2518

LIN, MING-CHANG, physical chemistry educator, researcher; b. Hsinpu, Hsinchu, Taiwan, Oct. 24, 1936; came to U.S., 1967, naturalized, 1975; s. Fushin and Tao May (Hsu) L.; m. Juh-Huey Chern, June 26, 1965; children: Karen, Linus H., Ellena J. BSc, Taiwan Normal U., Taipei, 1959; PhD, U. Ottawa, Ont., Can., 1966. Postdoctoral rsch. fellow U. Ottawa, 1965-67; postdoctoral rsch. assoc. Cornell U., Ithaca, N.Y., 1967-69; rsch. chemist Naval Rsch. Lab., Washington, 1970-74, supervisory rsch. chemist, head chem. kinetics sect., 1974-82, sr. scientist for chem. kinetics, 1982-88; Robert W. Woodruff prof. phys. chemistry Emory U., Atlanta, 1988—. Mem. adv. bd. Internat. Jour. Chem. Kinetics, 1990-93, Chemistry, World Sci. Pub. Co., Singapore, 1991—, Inst. Atomic and Molecular Sci., Taipei, 1991—; mem. young presdl. award com. NSF, Washington, 1990. Contbr. over 380 articles to profl. jours. 2d lt. Taiwan ROTC, 1960-62. Recipient Civilian Meritorious award USN, 1979, Humboldt award Humboldt Found., 1982, prize in sci. tech. Taiwanese-Am. Found., 1989, The Capt. Robert Dexter Conrad award U.S. Navy, 1998; Guggenheim fellow, 1982. Mem. Am. Chem. Soc. (Hillebrand prize 1975), Combustion Inst., Am. Vacuum Soc., Materials Rsch. Soc., N.Am. Taiwanese Profs. Assn., Sigma Xi (Pure Sci. award 1976 Naval Rsch. Lab. chpt.) Achievements include discovery of numerous chemical lasers, use of lasers to elucidate mechanisms of combustion, propulsion and gas-surface reactions; first use of lasers to ionize nonfluorescing radicals and to probe for radicals formed in heterogeneous catalytic reactions. Office: Emory Univ Dept Chemistry 1515 Pierce Dr NE Atlanta GA 30322-1003

LIN, PEN-MIN, electrical engineer, educator; b. Liaoning, China, Oct. 17, 1928; came to U.S., 1954; s. Tai-sui and Tse-san (Tang) Lin; m. Louise Shou Yuen Lee, Dec. 29, 1962; children: Marian, Margaret, Janice. BSE.E., Taiwan U., 1950; MSE.E., N.C. State U., 1956; PhD in Elec. Engring., Purdue U., 1960. Asst. prof. Purdue U., West Lafayette, Ind., 1961-66, assoc. prof., 1966-74, prof. elec. engring., 1974-94, prof. emeritus, 1994—. Author: (with L.O. Chua) Computer Aided Analysis of Electronic Circuits, 1975, Symbolic Network Analysis, 1991, (with R.A. DeCarlo) Linear Circuit Analysis, 1995, 2d edit., 2001. Fellow IEEE (life). Home: 3029 Covington St West Lafayette IN 47906-1107 Office: Purdue Univ Sch Of Elec Engring West Lafayette IN 47907

LIN, PING, mechanical engineer; b. Guangdong Province, China, Feb. 1, 1957; came to U.S., 1990; m. Qing Xiu Zhang, 1985; children: Jeffrey Y., Jessica Y. BS in Engring., Beijing Inst. Tech., 1982; MS in Mechanics, Northeastern U., Boston, 1992. Mfg. engr. Shanghai Machinery Co., 1982-84; mech. engr. People's Bank China, Beijing, 1984-86, engring. mgr., 1987-90; sr. project engr. Watts Regulator Co., North Andover, Mass., 1993-97; group leader MKS Instruments, Inc., Andover, 1997—2002; engring. mgr. Bio-Chem Valve Inc., Boonton, NJ, 2002—. Tchg. asst. Northeastern U., Boston, 1992-93. Recipient Nat. Engring. Excellence award Acad. Conf. Sci. Tech. China, 1986. Mem. ASME, Phi Kappa Phi. Achievements include 2 patents, 1 patent pending; research in fluid dynamics, thermal dynamics, mechanics and materials. Office: Bio-Chem Valve Inc Boonton NJ - E-mail: PLin@Bio-Chemvalve.com.

LIN, PI-TANG, physician; b. Chia-Yi, Taiwan, Feb. 15, 1946; MD, Taiwan U., 1972. Diplomate Am. Bd. Otolaryngology. Intern Hackensack (N.J.) Hosp., 1975-76; resident in surgery CMDNJ-Newark Med. Sch., 1976-77; resident in otolaryngology St. Luke's Hosp. Ctr., N.Y.C., 1977-80; fellow Columbia P&S, 1977-80; mem. staff Lenox Hill Hosp.; asst. prof. N.Y. Med. Coll., 1981-92. Mem. AMA, ACS, Am. Acad. Otolaryngology-Head and Neck Surgery. Office: 65 E 76th St Ste 1F New York NY 10021-1844 also: Ste 2C 13329 41st Rd Flushing NY 11355-3670

LIN, ROBERT KWANHWAN, language educator, consultant; b. Canton, Kwangtong, China, July 7, 1937; arrived in U.S., 1963; s. Chuan-fu Lin and Hui-Chin Cheng; m. Deborah Shieh, Feb. 22, 1964; children: Bryan Hsia-pin, Hsia-Lynn, Hsia-Min. BA, Nat. Taiwan U., Taipei, 1960; MA, U. Okla., 1965, U. Mich., 1971; PhD, U. San Francisco, 1983. Tchr. English Chung-li (Taiwan) H.S., 1961—62; instr. Woodbury U., L.A., 1965—66; instr., assoc. libr. Culver-Stockton Coll., Canton, Mo., 1966—70, assoc. prof. history, 1971—78; assoc. prof. English Nat. Taiwan U., Taipei, 1984—85; pub. Everyman's Bilingual Pub., 1985—87; cons. Lin's Bilingual Edn. Consulting, San Fracisco, 1987—. Fellow Yale U., New Haven, 1978; commentator World Jour., Millbrae, Calif., 2000—. Author: (book) English Composition, 1984, Parallels in English, 1985; contbr. articles to profl. jours. Adviser Ministry Econs., Taipei, 1984—85. Fellow, NEH, 1977, Fed. Bilingual, Dept. Edn., 1978—80. Avocations: carpentry, birdwatching, hiking, classical music, reading. Home and Office: 1959 44th Ave San Francisco CA 94116

LIN, STEPHEN HOUNG TZE, music educator; b. Louisville, May 20, 1953; s. Richard and Julia (Lam) L.; m. Sharon Elaine Brown, Aug. 20, 1977; 1 child, Stephen Wang Jr. B in Music Edn., Morehead State U., 1975; MEd, U. Louisville, 1980. Cert. tchr., Ky. Choral, gen. music tchr. Jefferson County Pub. Schs., 1975—; head music dept. Atherton High Sch., Louisville, 1976—. Chair All Jefferson County Sr. High Chorus, Louisville, 1979; guest conductor All-Dist. Jr. High Sch. Chorus, Cen. Ky. Music Educators Assn., Danville, 1986. Mem. So. Bapt. Theol. Sem. Oratorio Chorus, Louisville, 1975-76; deacon Broadway Bapt. Ch., Louisville, 1981-85; pres. bd. dirs. Louisville Youth Choir, 1982-83. Mem. NEA, Ky Educators Assn., Jefferson County Tchrs. Assn., Am. Choral Dirs. Assn. (co-chair nat. conv. 1987—), Ky. Music Educators Assn. (state choral chair 1985-87), Jefferson Dist. Music Educators Assn. (dist. choral chair 1981-85, pres.-elect 1988-89), Louisville Bach Soc. Republican. Home: 2607 Wareham Rd Louisville KY 40242-3216

LIN, STEVEN AN-YHI, economics educator, consultant; b. Taipei, Republic of China, Apr. 19, 1933; s. Ching-Ho Lin-Sheh and Wen (Chen) Lin; m. Yen-Yen Yeh, Jan. 27, 1961; 1 child: Anthony. BS, Nat. Taiwan U., Taipei, 1956; MS, Iowa State U., 1965, PhD, 1967. Asst. prof. U. Wis., River Falls, 1967-68, So. Ill. U., Edwardsville, 1968-71, assoc. prof., 1971-75, prof. econs., 1975—. Vis. prof. U. Chgo., 1975. Editor: Theory and Measurement of Economic Externality, 1975; editor Jour. Econs., 1974-76; contbr. numerous articles to profl. jours. Mem. Am. Econ. Assn., Mo. Valley Econ. Assn. (pres. 1978-79, sec. 1975-76). Home: 112 Sherwood Dr Glen Carbon IL 62034-1046 Office: So Ill Univ Dept Econs Edwardsville IL 62026-0001

LIN, THOMAS WEN-SHYOUNG, accounting educator, researcher, consultant; b. Taichung, Republic of China, June 3, 1944; came to U.S., 1970; s. Ju-chin and Shao-chin (Tseng) L.; m. Angela Kuei-fong Hou, May 19, 1969; children: William Margaret. BA in Bus. Adminstrn., Nat. Taiwan U., Taipei, 1966; MBA, Nat. Chengchi U., Taipei, 1970; MS in Acctg. and Info. Systems, UCLA, 1971; PhD in Acctg., Ohio State U., 1975. Cert. mgmt. acct., Calif. Internal auditor Formosa Plastics Group, Taipei, 1967-69, spl. asst. to the pres., 1969-70; asst. prof. U. So. Calif., L.A., 1975-80, assoc. prof., 1980-86, prof. acctg., 1986-90, acctg. cir. prof., 1990—, dir. doctoral studies acctg., 1982-86. Cons. Intex Plastics, Inc., Long Beach, Calif., 1979-81, Peat, Marwick, Mitchell, L.A., 1982, City of Chino, Calif., 1982; bd. dirs., audit com. chmn. FCB Taiwan Calif. Bank, 1997—. Author: Planning and Control for Data Processing, 1984, Use of Mathematical Models, 1986, Advanced Auditing, 1988, Using Accounting Information in Business Planning, Product Costing, and Auditing, 1991, Cost Management: A Strategic Emphasis, 1999; assoc. editor Internat. Jour. Bus., 1997—; mem. editl. bd. Taiwan Mgmt. Acctg., Quarterly Jour. Bus. and Econs., Am. Jour. Math. and Mgmt. Scis., Chinese Acctg. Rev., Hong Kong Jour. Bus. Mgmt., 1988—; contbr. articles to profl. jours. Bd. dirs. U. So. Calif. Acctg. Circle, L.A., 1986-88, 93-99, Taiwan Benevolent Assn. Am., Washington, 1986-89; pres. Taiwan Benevolent Assn. Calif., L.A., 1986-88, Chinese Am. Faculty Assn. So. Calif., 2000—. 2d lt. China Army, 1966-67. Recipient cert. appreciation L.A. City Mayor Tom Bradley, 1988, Congressman Martinez award for outstanding community svc., 1988; Faculty Rsch. scholar U. So. Calif. Bus. Sch., L.A., 1984-87. Mem. Am. Acctg. Assn. (bd. dirs. 1986-88), Chinese Acctg. Profs. N.Am. (founding pres. 1976-80), Inst. Cert. Mgmt. Accts. (cert. of disting. performance 1978), Inst. Mgmt. Accts. (coord. 1984—, Author's trophy 1978, 79, 81, 87), Inst. Mgmt. Scis. Republican. Baptist. Avocation: gardening. Home: PO Box 8023 Rowland Heights CA 91748-0023 Office: U So Calif Leventhal Sch Acctg Univ Park Acc 109 Los Angeles CA 90089-0001

LIN, TU, endocrinologist, educator, researcher, academic administrator; b. Fukien, China, Jan. 18, 1941; came to U.S., 1967; s. Tao Shing and Jan En (Chang) L.; m. Pai-Li, July 1, 1967; children: Vivian H., Alexander T., Margaret C. MD, Nat. Taiwan U., Taipei, 1966. Diplomate Am. Bd. Internal Medicine, Am. Bd. Endocrinology and Metabolism. Intern Episcopal Hosp.-Temple U., Phila., 1967-68; resident in medicine Berkshire Med. Ctr., Pittsfield, Mass., 1968-70; fellow in endocrinology Lahey Clinic, Boston, 1970-71, Roger Williams Gen. Hosp.-Brown U., Providence, 1971-73; rsch. fellow in med. sci. Brown U., 1971-73; chief, endocrine sect. WJB Dorn Vet. Hosp., Columbia, S.C., 1975—; asst. prof. U. S.C. Sch. Medicine, 1976-80, assoc. prof., 1980-84, prof. medicine, 1984—, prof., dir. divsn. endocrinology, diabetes and metabolism, 1992—. Merit review bd. endocrinology Dept. Vet. Affairs, 1990-94. Co-author: Disorders of Male Reproductive Function, 1996; mem. editl. bd. Biology of Reproduction, 1990-95, Jour. of Andrology, 1993-96; contbr. articles to profl. jours. Recipient Disting. Investigator award U. S.C. Sch. Medicine, 1981, 88, 95. Fellow ACP; mem. Endocrine Soc., Am. Soc. Andrology (chmn. ann. meeting, coun. 1993-96), Soc. for the Study of Reproduction, Am. Diabetic Assn., Am. Soc. Hypertension. Office: U SC Sch Medicine Med Library Bldg Ste 316 Columbia SC 29208-0001

LIN, TUNG YEN, civil engineer, educator; b. Foochow, China, Nov. 14, 1911; arrived in U.S., 1946, naturalized, 1951; s. Ting Chang and Feng Yi (Kuo) Lin; m. Margaret Kao, July 20, 1941; children: Paul, Verna. BSCE, Chiaotung U., Tangshan, Republic of China, 1931; MS, U. Calif., Berkeley, 1933; LLD, Chinese U. Hong Kong, 1972, Golden Gate U., San Francisco, 1982, Tongji U., Shanghai, 1987, Chiaotung U., Taiwan, 1987. Chief bridge engr., chief design engr. Chinese Govt. Rys., 1933—46; from asst. to assoc. prof. U. Calif., 1946—55, prof., 1955—76, chmn. div. structural engring., 1960—63, dir. structural lab., 1960—63; chmn. bd. T.Y. Lin Internat., 1953—87, hon. chmn. bd., 1987—92; pres. Inter-Continental Peace Bridge, Inc., 1968—. Chmn. World Conf. Prestressed Concrete, 1957, Western Conf. Prestressed Concrete Bldgs., 1960; chmn. bd. Lin Tung Yen, China, 1993—; cons. in field. Author: Design of Prestressed Concrete Structures, 1955, rev. edition, 1963; author: (with N.H. Burns) 3rd edit., 1981; author: (with B. Bresler, Jack Scalzi) Design of Steel Structures, 1968; author: (with S.D. Statesbury) Structural Concepts and Systems, 1981, 2d edit., 1988; contbr. articles to profl. jours. Named Alumnus of Yr., U. Calif. Alumni Assn., 1994; recipient Berkeley citation, 1976, Quarter Century award, NRC, 1977, Honor award, AIA, 1984, Pres.'s Nat. Med. of Sci., 1986, Merit award, Am. Cons. Engrs. Coun., 1987, John A. Roebling medal, Bridge Engring., 1990, Leadership award, Am. Segmental Bridge Inst., 1992, Outstanding Paper of Yr. award, Internat. Assn. Bridge and Structural Engring., 1993, Lifetime Achievement award, Asian Am. Archs. and Engring. Assn., 1993, Outstanding Achievement award of So. Calif., Prix Albert Caquot award, Assn. Française pour Constrn., 1995; fellow, U. Calif., Berkeley. Mem.: ASCE (hon. Wellington award, Howard medal, OPAL award), Chinese Acad. Sci., Prestressed Concrete Inst. (medal of honor), Internat. Fedn. Prestressing (Freyssinet medal), Academia Sinica, Chinese Acad. Sci., Nat. Acad. Engring., Am. Concrete Inst. (hon.), Chi Epsilon (hon.). Home: 8701 Don Carol Dr El Cerrito CA 94530-2734 Office: 315 Bay St San Francisco CA 94133-1923 *Fear incites fear; complex breeds complex. If one learns to control one's own fear and complex, and at the same time understands those of others, one will have gone a long way toward success and happiness.*

LIN, TUNG HUA, civil engineering educator; b. Chungkin, China, May 26, 1911; s. Yao-Ching and Yue (Kuo) L.; m. Susan Z. Chiang, Mar. 15, 1939; children: Rita P., Lin Wood, Robert P., James P. BS, Tangshan Coll., Chiaotung U., 1933; S.M., MIT, 1936; D.Sc., U. Mich., 1953. Prof. Tsing Hua U., China, 1937-39; chief engr. Chinese 2d Aircraft Co., Nancheun, Szechuan, 1939-44; prodn. mgr. Mfg. Factory, China, 1940-44; mem. tech. mission in charge of jet aircraft design, 1945-49; prof. aero. engring. U. Detroit, 1949-55; prof. engring. and applied scis. UCLA, 1955-78, prof. emeritus, 1978—. Cons.N.Am. Aviation, N.Am. Rockwell, L.A., 1964-74, Atomic Internat., Canoga Park, Calif., 1965-68, ARA Inc., Industry City, Calif., 1964-94. Author: Theory of Inelastic Structure, 1968; contbr. articles to profl. jours.; mem. editorial bd.: Jour. Composite Materials, 1966-75; patentee in field. Named Chinese Nat. fellow, Tsing-Hua U., 1933, prin. investigator, Office Naval Rsch., 1985—93, Air Force Office of Sci. Rsch., 1988—97; recipient medal for design of 1st Chinese twin-engine airplane, 1944, Disting. Svc. award Applied Mechanics Rev., ASME, 1966; grantee NSF, 54-78. Fellow ASME, Am. Acad. Mechanics; mem. ASCE (life, gen. chmn. engring. mechanics conf. 1965, Theodore von Karman award 1988); mem. NAE, Academia Sinica. Home: 906 Las Pulgas Rd Pacific Palisades CA 90272-2441 Office: UCLA Dept Civil Engring 405 Hilgard Ave Los Angeles CA 90095-9000 E-mail: thlin@seas.mcra.edu.

LIN, XI ERICK, physiologist, medical researcher; b. Chengdu, Sichuan, China, June 11, 1962; s. Yulao Lin and Xiyuan Xie; m. Ping Helen Chen; children: Anne, Alexander. PhD, U. Mich., 1993. Sect . chief Ho. Ear Inst., L.A., Calif., 1996—2002. Lab dir. Ho. Ear Inst., L.A., 1996—2002. Contbr. articles to jours. including Jour. Neurophysiology. Grantee grant, Am. Tinnitus Assn., 1998, rsch., NIH RO1, NIHR21, NIH RO3, DRF, ATA, 2001. Mem.: Soc. Neuroscience, Am. Physiology Soc., Am. Tinnitus Assn. Buddhist. Avocations: carpentry, travel, history readings. Office: Ho Ear Inst 2100 W Third Street Los Angeles CA 90057 Office Fax: 213-273-8088. Business E-Mail: xlin@hei.org.

LIN, YING-CHU See WU, SUSAN YING CHU LIN

LIN, YUEHE, research scientist; b. Longhai, Fujian, China, 1962; s. Bing Kang and Niu Lin; m. Hong Wu, 1995; 1 child Sophie. BS in Chemistry, Peking U., Beijing, 1984; PhD in Analytical Chemistry, Xiamen (China) U., 1991; PhD in Environ. Chemistry, U. Idaho, 1997. Postdoctoral fellow N.Mex. State U., Las Cruces, 1991—92; rsch. scientist U. Idaho, Moscow, 1992—94; sr. scientist Pacific N.W. Nat. Lab., Richland, Wash., 1997—. Mem.: Am. Chem. Soc. Achievements include patents in field. Avocations: tennis, volleyball, music. Home: 544 Fuller St Richland WA 99352 Office: Pacific NW Nat Lab Richland WA 99352

LIN, YUKWENG M. engineer, educator; b. Foochow, Fukien, China, Oct. 30, 1923; arrived in U.S., 1954, naturalized, 1964; s. Fa Been and Chi Ying (Cheng) Lin; m. Ying-yuh June Wang, Mar. 29, 1952; children: Jane, Della, Lucia, Winifred. BS, Amoy U., 1946; MS, Stanford U., 1955, PhD, 1957; D of Engring. (hon.), U. Waterloo, Can., 1994. Tchr. Amoy U., China, 1946-48, Imperial Coll. Engring., Ethiopia, 1957-58; engr. Vertol Aircraft Corp., Morton, Pa., 1956-57; rsch. engr. Boeing Co., Renton, Wash., 1958-60; asst. prof. U. Ill., Urbana, 1960-62, assoc. prof., 1962-65, prof. aero. and astron. engring., 1965-83; Charles E. Schmidt Eminent scholar chair Coll. Engring., dir. Ctr. for Applied Stochastics Rsch. Fla. Atlantic U., Boca Raton, 1984—. Vis. prof. mech. engring. MIT, 1967-68; sr. vis. fellow Inst. Sound and Vibration Research, U. Southampton, Eng., 1976; cons. Gen. Motors Corp., Boeing Co., Gen. Dynamics Corp., TRW Corp., Brookhaven Nat. Lab. Author: Probabilistic Theory of Structural Dynamics, 1967, Probabilistic Structural Dynamics: Advanced Theory and Applications, 1995; editor: Stochastic Structural Mechanics, 1987, Stochastic Approaches in Earthquake Engineering, 1987, Stochastic Structural Dynamics, 1990, Stochastic Dynamics and Reliability of Nonlinear Ocean Systems, 1994; contbr. articles to profl. jours. Recipient sr. postdoctoral fellowship, NSF, 1967—68, Alexander von Humboldt Sr. US Scientist award, 2000, J.P. Den Hartog award, ASME, 2001. Fellow: ASCE (Alfred M. Freudenthal medal 1984, Theodore von Karman medal 1998), Am. Acad. Mechs.; mem.: Am. Assn. Wind Engring., Earthquake Engring. Rsch. Inst., Internat. Assn. Structural Safety and Reliability, Russian Acad. Engring. (fgn. mem.), Nat. Acad. Engring., Sigma Xi. Home: 2684 NW 27th Ter Boca Raton FL 33434-6001 Office: Fla Atlantic U Coll Engring Boca Raton FL 33431 E-mail: linyk@fau.edu.

LIN, ZONGLI, electrical engineering educator; b. Fuqing, Fujian, China, Feb. 24, 1964; came to U.S., 1989; s. Changming Lin and Yuyan Chen; m. Jian K. Lin, June 22, 1992; children: Tony, Vivian. BS, Xiamen U., Fujian, 1983; M Engring., Chinese Acad. Space Tech., Beijing, 1989; PhD in Elec. Engring., Wash. State U., 1994. Engr. Chinese Acad. Space Tech., 1983-86; asst. prof. applied math. SUNY, Stony Brook, 1994-97; assoc. prof. elec. engring. U. Va., Charlottesville, 1997—. Author: Low Gain Feedback, 1998; co-author: Control Systems with Actuator Saturation: Analysis and Design, 2001; contbr. articles to sci. jours. Recipient young investigator award Office Naval Rsch., 1999. Mem.: IEEE (sr.; assoc. editor IEEE Transactions on Automatic Control). Office: U Va Dept Elec Engring Charlottesville VA 22903 E-mail: zl5y@virginia.edu.

LIN, ZONGZHU, mathematician, educator; PhD, U. Mass., 1989. From asst. to assoc. prof. Kans. State U., Manhattan, Kans., 1993—2002, prof., 2002—. Recipient Rsch. in Math. Sci. award, NSF, 1992—2002. Mem.: Am. Math. Soc. Office: Kansas State Univ Dept Math Cardwell 138 Manhattan KS 66506 Office Fax: 785-532-0546. E-mail: zlin@math.ksu.edu.

LINAKER, DAVID SCOTT, athletic trainer, educator; b. Lake Village, Ark., May 9, 1954; s. Charles Alan Linaker and Grace Marie Forte; m. Patricia Marie Kerth, Mar. 17, 1978; 1 child, Todd L. Webb. BS, U. Ariz., 1984, MS, 1985. Cert. athletic trainer. Athletic trainer, tchr. Peoria (Ariz.) Unified Sch. Dist., 1985-91, Amphitheatre Pub. Schs., Tucson, 1991—. Mem. Nat. Athletic Trainers Assn. (cert. 1985—, dist. dir., bd. dirs. 1998—), Rocky Mountain Athletic Trainers Assn. (cert. 1985—, dist. dir., pres. 1998—, dist. sec. 1992-98), Ariz. Athletic Trainers Assn. (cert. 1985—, pres. 1990-92, v.p. 1986-90), Ariz. Driver Safety Edn. Assn.

LINAWEAVER, WALTER ELLSWORTH, JR. physician; b. San Pedro, Calif., Oct. 16, 1928; s. Walter Ellsworth and Catherine Breathed (Bridges) L.; m. Lydia Anne Whitlock, Oct. 5, 1957; children: Catherine Ann, Nancy Alyn, Walter E. III. BA cum laude, Pomona Coll., 1952; MD, U. Rochester, 1956. Diplomate Am. Bd. Allergy and Immunology, Am. Bd. Pediatrics, Am. Bd. Pediatric Allergy. Intern pediatrics Med. Ctr. U. Rochester, N.Y., 1956-57, resident pediatrics Med. Ctr., 1958-59; asst. resident pediatrics Med. Ctr. UCLA, 1957-58; fellow allergy and immunology Med. Ctr. U. Colo., Denver, 1959-61, instr. pediatrics Sch. Medicine, 1961; pvt. practice Riverside (Calif.) Med. Clinic, 1962—. Asst. clin. prof. pediatrics Loma Linda U. Med. Sch., 1965—. Elder Presbyn. Ch. Staff sgt. U.S. Army, 1946-48. Inducted into Athletic Hall of Fame Pomona Coll., Claremont, Calif., 1979. Fellow: L.A.

Acad. Medicine, Southwestern Pediat. Soc. (emeritus, v.p. 1978), Am. Acad. Allergy, Asthma and Immunology, Am. Acad. Pediat.; mem.: AMA, Calif. Med. Assn., Riverside County Heart Assn. (pres. 1965—66), Riverside County Med.Soc. (councilor 1964—66). Republican. Avocations: gardening, American and British military history. Home: 1296 Tiger Tail Dr Riverside CA 92506-5475 Office: Riverside Med Clinic 3660 Arlington Ave Riverside CA 92506-3912

LINBURN, MICHAEL RICHARD, investment company executive; b. New York, Aug. 27, 1933; s. Richard Ernest and Mildred Adele (Jacobs) L.; m. Kathleen Burns Hoffman, July 12, 1997; children: Carol E. Linburn, Kimberly Moore Gonzalez, Alexandra Hoffman. BS in Indsl. Adminstrn., Yale U., 1954; MBA, Harvard Bus. Sch., 1959. V.p. Shearson Hammill and Co., New York, 1959-74, Oppenheimer Properties, New York, 1974-76, Balcor Am. Express, New York, 1978-83; sr. v.p. Angeles Securities, 1983-84; v.p. NHP Real Estate Securities, 1986-87; sr. v.p. Kimmins Securities, Inc., 1988-89; mng. dir. Morse Williams & Co., 1992—. Dir. Glosser Brothers, N.Y., 1969-75; bd. dirs. Real Estate Securities and Syndication Inst., 1970-75. Trustee Seawanhaka Corinthian Yacht Club. 1stLt., US Army, 1954-56. Republican. Episcopal. Avocations: chinese porcelains and bronzes, sailing, skiing, cooking, wines. Home: 418 E 50th St New York NY 10022-8002 Office: Morse Williams & Co Inc 230 Park Ave Rm 1635 New York NY 10169-1602 E-mail: mlinburn@yahoo.com.

LINCICOME, DAVID RICHARD, biomedical and animal scientist; b. Champaign, Ill., Jan. 17, 1914; s. David Rosebery and Olive Iola (Casper) L.; m. Dorothy Lucile Van Cleave, Sept. 1, 1941 (dec. Nov. 1952); children: David Van Cleave, Judith Ann; m. Margaret Stirewalt, Dec. 29, 1953. *David Lincicome's ancestor, Thomas Linthicum, arrived in the Port of Baltimore in 1658 from Great Britain (Wales) and became a wealthy landowner. The family migrated westward settling in what is now southwestern Pennsylvania. They later moved to Noble County, Ohio, where David's grandfather, Nathaniel Webster Lincicome, was born--the surname having been changed somewhere along the line to Lincicome from Linthicum. From Noble County, the family migrated to Brown County, Indiana, where David's father, David Rosebery Lincicome, was born. David has two children: David Van Cleave, who practices law and Judith Ann, who is a registered nurse specializing in paediatric intensive care and in handicapped children needing special care and education.* BS, MS with high honors, U. Ill., 1937; PhD in Tropical Medicine, Tulane U., 1941. Diplomate (emeritus) Am. Bd. Microbiology; diplomate Am. Coll. Animal Physiology; cert. animal scientist Am. Registry Profl. Animal Scientists. Asst. instr. U. Ill., 1937; asst. instr. tropical medicine Tulane U. Med. Sch., 1937-41; asst. prof. parasitology U. Ky., 1941-47, U. Wis. Med. Sch., 1947-49; sr. rsch. parasitologist Du Pont Co., 1949-53; from asst. prof. to full prof. biol. Scis. Howard U., 1953-70. Vis. sci. NIH, 1965-66; founder, registrar, Jacob Sheep Conservancy, 1988-96, bd. dirs., 1990-97, pres., 1996; vis. scholar Nat. Agrl. Libr., USDA, 1990-92; guest scientist USDA Exp. Sta., Beltsville, Md., 1978—, Naval Med. Rsch. Inst., 1954-62. Founder, editor Exptl. Parasitology, 1949-76; editor Transactions of the Ky. Acad. Sci., 1946-49, Transactions of the Am. Microscopical Soc., 1970-71, Internat. Rev. Tropical Medicine, 1953-63; founder Virology, 1950, Advances in Vet. Sci., 1952. Lt. col. Med. Svc. Corps, U.S. Army, World War II, PTO. Named Eminent Fellow, Wisdom Hall of Fame, 2001; recipient Anniversary award, Helminthological Soc., 1975, Sir Winston Churchill medal, Wisdom Soc. Advancement of Knowledge, Learning and Rsch. in Edn., 2001; grantee, NIH, 1958—68. Fellow: AAAS, Explorers Club (nat., N.Y.); mem.: Am. Soc. Tropical Medicine (emeritus), Va. State Dairy Goat Assn. (founder), Ut Prosim Soc. (Va. Poly. Inst. and State U.), Soc. Exptl. Biology & Medicine (sec. D.C. chpt. 1976, emeritus), Midwestern Conf. Parasitologists (1st sec. 1949, founder), Va. State Dairy Goat Assn. (pres. 1976, founder, Friend of VSDGA award 1999), Am. Livestock Breeds Conservancy (bd. dirs. 1994—97, 25th Anniversary award 2002), Nat. Tunis Sheep Registry (sec. 1991—92, bd. dirs. 1991—93), Jacob Sheep Soc. (Eng.), Jacob Sheep Breeders Assn., Natural Colored Wool Growers Assn. (bd. dirs. 1988—94), Nat. Pygmy Goat Assn. (bd. dirs. 1976—92, pres. 1979, founder), Am. Dairy Goat Assn. (bd. dirs. 1972—87, 1st sec. rsch. found. 1979, founder), Am. Goat Soc. (bd. dirs. 1990—96), Royal Soc. Tropical Medicine (emeritus), Am. Microscopical Soc. (emeritus), Am. Soc. Cell Biology, Am. Soc. Parasitologists, Am. Soc. Zoologists (emeritus), Soc. Invertebrate Zoology (emeritus), Am. Physiol. Soc. (emeritus), Helminthological Soc. (pres. 1958, emeritus), Greater Washington Area Soft-Coated Wheaten Terrier Club, Soft-Coated Wheaten Terrier Club Am. (mem. rescue com. 1993—99, mem. health com. 2000—), Univ. Ill. Pres. Coun., Univ. Ill. Found., Greater Washington D.C. Area Soft Coated Wheaten Terrier Club (pres. 1991—92, bd. dirs. 1999—2001, founder), Sigma Xi (pres. Howard chpt. 1962), Phi Beta Kappa. Achievements include breeding of two rare and endangered breeds of sheep, Jacob and Tunis, early breeder of West African Pygmy Goats and a rare dog, the Soft-coated Wheaten Terrier; founder and first sec. The Rsch. Found. of the Am. Dairy Goat Assn.; founder Midwestern Conf. of Parasitologists; founder four sci. jours. Exptl. Parasitology, Internat. Rev. Tropical Medicine, Virology, and Advances in Vet. Sci. Home: PO Box 13 4419 Cambria Ave Garrett Park MD 20896 E-mail: wheaten@bellatlantic.net., sheepman@frogmoor.org.com.

LINCK, CHARLES EDWARD, JR. English language educator; b. Lowemont, Kans., June 6, 1923; s. Charles Edward and Grace Elizabeth (Miller) L.; m. Alice Eugenie Meyer (div. Feb. 1964); 1 child, Charles Edward Lincoln; m. Ernestine Marie Porcher Sewell, Aug. 23, 1970. AB magna cum laude, St. Benedict's Coll., Atchison, Kans., 1951; MS, Kans. State Coll., 1953; PhD in English, U. Kans., 1962. Prof. English East Tex. State U., Commerce, 1958-91, prof. emeritus, 1991—. Owner, pub. Cow Hill Press; spkr. in field. Author, editor: Edgar Rye: North Central Texas Cartoonist and Journalist, 1972; co-editor: Bibliography of Evelyn Waugh, 1984; editor, pub. Evelyn Waugh in Letters by Terence Greeniage, 1994; editor, pub. Colleen, The Mountain Maid - A Story of War and Feud in Kentucky, 1994; editor: Bokay of Biscuits, 3 vols., 1997. With USN, 1943-46, PTO. Mem. MLA, Tex. Coll. English Assn. (pres. 1972), Am. Studies Assn., Tex. Folklore Soc. (pres. 1984). Democrat. Roman Catholic. Avocations: antique printing, native American Indian arts and crafts, photography. Home: Tex A&M U PO Box 3002 Commerce TX 75429-3002

LINCOLN, ALEXANDER, III, financier, lawyer, private investor; b. Boston, Dec. 1, 1943; s. Alexander Jr. and Elizabeth (Kitchel) L.; m. Isabel Fawcett Ross, Dec. 27, 1969. BA, Denver U., 1967; JD, Boston U., 1971. Bar: Colo. 1972, U.S. Ct. Appeals (10th cir.) 1972, U.S. Supreme Ct. 1979. Atty. Dist. Ct. Denver, 1973-78, Colo. Ct. Appeals, Denver, 1978-80; mng. ptnr. Alexander Lincoln & Co., 1980—. Mem. Colo. Bar Assn. (fin. com. 1975-76), Colo. Soc. Mayflower Descendants (life, bd. dirs. 1975—), Order of Founders and Patriots (life). Republican. Avocations: skiing, mountain climbing, horticulture. Home and Office: 121 S Dexter St Denver CO 80246-1052

LINCOLN, ANNA, company executive, foreign languages educator; b. Warsaw, Poland, Dec. 13, 1932; came to U.S., 1948; d. Wigdor Aron and Genia (Zalkind) Szpiro; m. Adrian Courtney Lincoln Jr., Sept. 22, 1951; children: Irene Anne, Sally Linda, Allen, Kirk. Student, U. Calif., Berkeley, 1949-50; BA in French and Russian with honors, NYU, 1965; student, Columbia Tchrs. Coll., 1966-67. Tchr. Waldwick (N.J.) H.S., 1966-69; chmn. Tuxedo Park (N.Y.) Red Cross, 1969-71; pres. Red Cross divsn. Vets. Hosp.; pres. China Pictures U.S.A. Inc., Princeton, N.J., 1994—; prof. fgn. rels. Fudan U., Shanghai, 1994—, prof. English and humanitarian studies, 1996—. Adv. bd. guidance dept. Waldwick (N.J.) H.S., 1966-69; hon. bd. dirs. Shanghai Fgn. Lang. Assn., 1994; hon. prof. Fudan U., Shanghai, 1994; leader seminars pm Chinat at top univs., 1996—. Author: Escape to China, 1940-48, 1985, Chinese transl., 1985, The Art of Peace, 1995, Anna Lincoln Views China, 2000; publ.: China Beyond the Year 2000 and the Nature of Love, 1997, Anna Lincoln Views China, 1999; co-dir. (TV docudrama) Escape to China 1941-48, 1998. Hon. U.S. Goodwill amb. for peace and friendship, China, 1984, 85, 86, 88; founder Princeton-Lincoln Found., Inc., 1985—. Named Woman of Yr. Am. Biog. Soc., 1993; recipient Peace Through the Arts prize Assn. Internat. Mujeres en las Artes, Madrid, 1993. Mem. AAUW, Women's Coll. Club (publicity chmn. 1991-96), Lit. Coll. Princeton, Present Day Club. Avocations: reading, swimming, bridge, seminars, ballroom dancing. Home and Office: China Pictures USA Inc 550 Rosedale Rd Princeton NJ 08540-2315

LINCOLN, BLANCHE LAMBERT, senator; b. Helena, Ark., Sept. 30, 1960; BA, Randolph-Macon Woman's Coll., 1982. Sr. assoc. The Pagonis & Donnelly Group, Inc., 1989-91; mem. U.S. Congress from 1st Ark. dist., 1992-96; U.S. senator from Ark., 1999—. Mem. agr. com., energy and natural resources com., spl. com. on aging; mem. Senate Social Security Task Force. Office: US Senate 355 Dirksen Senate Office Bldg Washington DC 20510-0001 also: 912 W Fourth St Little Rock AR 72201*

LINCOLN, EDMOND LYNCH, investment banker; b. Wilmington, Del., Aug. 3, 1949; s. Edmond Earl and Mary Margaret (Lynch) L.; B.A. magna cum laude, Harvard U., 1971, M.B.A., with distinction, 1974; m. Pamela Wick, Sept. 3, 1977; children: Lucy Arms, Emily Lord. Acting rare book librarian Henry Francis duPont Winterthur Mus. (Del.), 1971-72; with Kidder Peabody & Co., Inc., N.Y.C., 1974-94, asst. v.p., 1977-79, v.p. 1979-91, sr. v.p., 1991-94, mgr. govt. agy. fin., 1984-86, transp. group, 1986-94; mng. dir. PaineWebber Inc., N.Y.C., 1994—; pub. interest dir. Fed. Home Loan Bank of N.Y., 1987-89. Recipient Washburn History prize, Harvard U., 1971. Treas., Fed. Hall Meml. Assocs., 1981-87; mem. vis. com. Harvard Coll. Library, 1981-86, 88-94; exec. com. Friends of Harvard U. Track, 1972—, sec., 1976-87. Mem. Investment Assn. N.Y., Friends of Winterthur (trustee 1976-81, 87-93, sec. 1978-81, Winterthur Mus. acad. affairs com. 1992—), Assn. Internationale de Bibliophilie, Assn. of Fellows, The Pierpont Morgan Library, Club of Odd Volumes, Bond Club of N.Y., Grolier Club, Harvard Club (N.Y.C.), India House, Wilmington Club, Wilmington Country Club, Soc. of Naval Architects and Marine Engrs. (assoc.), Phi Beta Kappa. Republican. Roman Catholic. Home: 161 E 79th St New York NY 10021-0480 Office: PaineWebber Inc Apt 11C 1285 Avenue Of The Americas Fl Sconc New York NY 10019-6096

LINCOLN, MARGARET, library media specialist; b. N.Y.C., May 22, 1949; d. Irving Herman and Ann Ruth (Silver) Goldin; m. Gary Samuel Lincoln, June 5, 1971; children: Geoffrey, Benjamin, Ruth. AB in French, U. Mich., 1970, AMLS, 1973; Edn. Tech. Specialist, Mich. State U., 1996. Libr. media specialist Lakeview H.S., Battle Creek, Mich., 1973—. Computer skills and internet rsch. tchr. Battle Creek Area Pub. Schs., 1997—; chair, sec. REMC 12 Media Coun., Marshall, Mich., 1976%. Contbr. articles to profl. jours. Vol. libr., Sunday sch. tchr. Temple Beth El, Battle Creek, 1984—. Kellog Found. excellence in edn. grantee, 1994, 99; Am. Memory fellow Libr. of Congress, 2002; Mandel fellow U.S. Holocaust Meml. Mus., 2002. Mem.: Phi Beta Kappa, Beta Phi Mu. Home: 13166 11 Mile Rd Ceresco MI 49033-9769 Office: Lakeview HS 300 S 28th St Battle Creek MI 49015-2854

LINCOLN, SANDRA ELEANOR, chemistry educator; b. Holyoke, Mass., Mar. 11, 1939; d. Edwin Stanley and Evelyn Ida (Mackie) L. BA magna cum laude, Smith Coll., 1960; MSChem, Marquette U., 1970; PhD in Inorganic Chemistry, SUNY, Stony Brook, 1982. Tchr., prin. Oak Knoll Sch., Summit, N.J., 1964-74; tchr. Holy Child H.S., Waukegan, Ill., 1974-76; lectr. chemistry, dir. fin. aid Rosemont (Pa.) Coll., 1976-78; tchg. asst. SUNY, Stony Brook, 1978-82; prof. chemistry U. Portland, Oreg., 1982—, chmn. dept., 1999—. Contbr. articles to profl. jours. Cath. sister Soc. Holy Child Jesus, 1963—. Recipient Pres.'s award for Teaching, SUNY, Stony Brook, 1981; Burlington No. Outstanding scholar, 1987. Mem. Am. Chem. Soc., Phi Beta Kappa, Sigma Xi. Democrat. Home: 5937 N Denver Ave Portland OR 97217 Office: U Portland 5000 N Willamette Blvd Portland OR 97203-5743 E-mail: lincoln@up.edu.

LINCOLN, THOMAS L. pathologist, educator; b. Pitts., Jan. 4, 1929; s. John J. and Jean Gregg Lincoln; m. Nancy, Apr. 15, 1956 (dec. Feb. 1971); children: Elizabeth, John; m. Catherine de La Prée., May 30, 1972; 1 child, Iris. BS, Yale U., 1955, MD, 1960. Diplomate Nat. Bd. Med. Examiners, Am. Bd. Anat. Pathology. Intern in pathology Yale U., New Haven, 1960-61, resident, 1961-63; rsch. asst. prof. Inst. for Fluid Dynamics and Applied Math., U. Md., 1963-66; assoc. clin. prof., dept. pathology U. So. Calif. Cancer Ctr., L.A., 1975-77, assoc. prof., 1977-87, prof. rsch. pathology, 1987-96; prof. emeritus U. So. Calif.; sr. scientist Sunquest Info. Sys., Tucson, 1995-96, Rand Corp., Santa Monica, Calif., 1967—; prof. Coll. Health and Human Devel. Scis., U. Ill., Chgo., 1997—. Vis. prof. dept. clin. epidemiology and social medicine, St. Thomas's Hosp. Med. Sch., London, 1972; cons., rschr. in field. Contbr. articles to profl. jours. Mem. AMA, IEEE, Johns Hopkins Med. Soc., Leukemia Soc. Am. (patient advisor, L.A., 1970-82), Cosmos Club (Washington), Am. Soc. Clin. Pathology, Coll. of Am. Pathologists, Am. Assn. Med. Sys and Informatics, others. Episcopalian. Avocations: history, European politics, calendar algorithms. Home: 802 Franklin St Santa Monica CA 90403-2318 Office: Rand Corp 1700 Main St Santa Monica CA 90401-3297

LINCOLN, WALTER BUTLER, JR. marine engineer, educator; b. Phila., July 15, 1941; s. Walter Butler and Virginia Ruth (Callahan) L.; m. Sharon Platner, Oct. 13, 1979; children: Amelia Adams, Caleb Platner. BS in Math., U. N.C., 1963; Ocean Engr., MIT, 1975; MBA, Rensselaer Poly. Inst., 1982; MA, Naval War Coll., 1994. Registered profl. engr., N.H., Conn.; chartered engr., U.K. Ops. rsch. analyst applied physics lab. Johns Hopkins U., Silver Spring, Md., 1968-70; grad. asst. MIT, Cambridge, 1971-75; ocean engr. USCG R&D Ctr., Groton, Conn., 1976-78, chief marine systems divsn., 1983-97; program mgr. R&D, 1997—2002; prin. engr. Sanders Assocs., Nashua, N.H., 1978-83; lectr. U. Conn., Avery Point, 1986-95; prin. Lincoln Maritime, 2002—. Master, U.S. Mcht. Marine; comdg. officer res. unit U.S. Naval War Coll., 1999-2001. Contbr. articles to profl. jours. Capt. USNR, ret. Mem. SAR, Am. Soc. Naval Engrs., Am. Geophys. Union, Nat. Assn. Underwater Instrs. (instr. 1971—), Royal Inst. Naval Architects, Soc. Naval Architects & Marine Engrs. (chmn. New Eng. sect. 1996-97), Marine Tech. Soc. (exec. bd. New Eng. sect. 1980), Navy League, Naval War Coll. Found., Navy Sailing Assn. (ocean master), Pi Mu Epsilon. Achievements include discovery of rev. war ship Defense; rsch. in integrated systems modeling and engring. of deep ocean systems; devel. of algorithms for simulation of hydromechs. of ocean systems and ships; fuel cell power systems; engring. mgmt. of ship and marine environmental response and energy systems, rsch., devel., test and evaluation. Home and Office: 189 Avery Hill Rd Ledyard CT 06339 E-mail: waltnebula@aol.com.

LIND, ERIC HAWTHORN, sales executive; b. Montgomery, Ala., Aug. 30, 1956; s. Peter Malcom and Georgette (Davis) Lind; m. Deborah Ann Jermstad; 1 child Rachel. BS, Wash. State U., Pullman, 1978; JD, U.Puget Sound Sch. of Law, Tacoma, Washington, 1981; ThM, Andersonville Bapt.Sem., Carmilla, Ga., 1999. Gen. mgr./recreational vehicle sales Family Fun RV, Fife, Wash., 1994—99; sales Great Am. RV, 1999—2002. Bd. dirs. Spafford Children's Ctr., Bellevue, Wash., 1984—2001. Avocations: fly fishing, travel. Office: Great American RV 5800 Pacific Hwy. E. Tacoma WA 98424 Home Fax: 253-926-3079; Office Fax: 253-926-3079. Personal E-mail: rvconsultant@integrity.com.

LIND, JUDITH YANKIELUN, library director; b. Elizabeth, N.J., Nov. 2, 1953; d. Norbert Eugene and Emily Martha (Zienkowicz) Y.; m. Peter Eugene Lind, July 14, 1984; 1 child, Michael. BA, Kean Coll. N.J., 1975; MA, Rowan U., 1977, NYU, 1987. Lic. advanced media specialist, profl. libr., elem. tchr. Children's libr. Bloomfield (N.J.) Pub. Libr., 1977-79; head reference dept. Scotch Plains (N.J.) Pub. Libr., 1979-83, Berkeley Heights (N.J.) Pub. Libr., 1983-88; dir. Roseland (N.J.) Free Pub. Libr., 1988—. Cons. Magazines for Libraries, 6th, 7th, 8th. 9th and 10th edits.; contbr. articles and revs. to profl. jours. Mem. ALA, N.J. Libr. Assn. Office: Roseland Free Pub Libr 20 Roseland Ave Roseland NJ 07068-1235 E-mail: jlind@nplhub.org.

LIND, LANETTE MINA, piano teacher; b. Kokomo, Ind., Nov. 17, 1934; d. Percy Lelind Olaf and Pearl Marguerite (Schrepfer) Lind; married, Dec. 18, 1954 (div. 1971); children: Jennifer Teska, John Teska. Student Sch. of Music, Ind. U., 1952-55. Composer (symphony) The Toy Factory, 1984, Song of An American, 1986, Symphony No. 1 A Song of Thanksgiving, 1988, Primitive Dances, 1988, A Celebration of Spirituals, 1988, Symphony No. II The Ugly Duckling, 1993, Different Drummers, Same Songs, 1995, Toy Factory 2, (choral) Three Native American Prayers, Lullaby, We Are Brothers After All, When Tomorrow Comes, Song of the Earth Spirits, (mus. theater) The Emperor and The Nightingale, 1982, Carousel of Dreams, 1983, Beast, 1986, The Story of Dr. Charles Drrew, 1988, Frankenstein: The Monster Story, 1989, (concert) Moments, 1983, Three Shepherds, 1984, Please Go Away, 1989, Dances in Time, 1990, Dancing Toward the Light, 1993, Morpheus Sleeps, 1995, Alpha Beasts, 1995, Night Songs, Four Unknown Dances, The Manin Jackson Square. Mem. ASCAP, Am. Music Ctr., Am. Composer's Forum, Music Tchrs. Nat. Assn., Opera Am., Soc. Composers, Inc. Mem. Covenant Christian Ch.

LIND, LEVI ROBERT, classics educator, writer; b. Trenton, N.J., July 29, 1906; s. John Edward and Lydia (Nieminen) L.; m. Elena Marchant y Riquelme, Aug. 25, 1929; 1 dau., Rosa Elena (Mrs. D.C. Fuchs). BA, U. Ill., 1929, MA, 1932, PhD, 1936. Asst. prof., assoc. prof. classics Wabash Coll., Crawfordsville, Ind., 1929-40; successively asst. prof., assoc. prof., prof., Univ. Disting. prof. classics U. Kans., Lawrence, 1940—, chmn. dept., 1940-64. Vis. research prof. history medicine UCLA, summer 1959, U. Ill., summer 1937, 45; sec. Am. Com. on Medieval Latin Dictionary, UAI, 1937-41; U. Kans. rep. to adv. council Am. Acad. in Rome; pres. Central Labor Union, AFL, Lawrence, 1948-49 Author: Medieval Latin Studies: Their Nature and Possibilities, 1941, The Vita Sancti Malchi of Reginald of Canterbury: a critical edition, 1942, The Epitome of Andreas Vesalius, 1949, Lyric Poetry of the Italian Renaissance: an Anthology With Verse Translations, 1954, Ten Greek Plays in Contemporary Translations, 1957, Latin Poetry in Verse Translation, 1957, Ecclesiale by Alexander of Villa Dei, 1958, Berengario da Carpi, A Short Introduction to Anatomy, 1959, Vergil's Aeneid, 1963, Aldrovandi on Chickens: The Ornithology of Ulisse Aldrovandi (1600), 1963, Epitaph for Poets and Other Poems, 1966, Twentieth Century Italian Poetry: a Bilingual Anthology, 1974, Johann Wolfgang von Goethe, Roman Elegies and Venetian Epigrams, 1974, Studies in Pre-Vesalian Anatomy, 1975, Ovid, Tristia, 1975, André Chénier, Elegies and Camille, 1978, Gabriele Zerbi, Gerontocomia: On the Care of the Aged and Maximianus, Elegies on Old Age and Love, 1988, The Letters of Giovanni Garzoni: Bolognese Humanist and Physician (1419-1505), 1992, Berengario da Carpi, On Fracture of the Skull or Cranium, 1990, An Epitaph Years After, 1990; editor: Problemata Varia Anatomica, 1968. Fulbright research grantee Rome, Italy, 1954-55; NIH grantee in history of medicine, 1960-63; Am. Council Learned Socs. fellow, 1940 Mem. Am. Philol. Assn., Classical Assn. Middle West and South, Medieval Acad. Am., Soc. Ancient Medicine, Phi Beta Kappa (com. qualifications united chpts. 1955-61) Clubs: Discussion. Home: 4817 Baja Ct NE Albuquerque NM 87111-2711

LIND, MARSHALL L. academic administrator; b. Sept. 27, 1942; Ed.B., U. Wisc., Milwaukee; Ed.M, U. Mont, Missoula; PhD, Education, Northwestern U. Dean Sch. Extended and Grad. Studies U. Alaska, Juneau, until 1987, chancellor, 1987-99, Fairbanks, 1999—. Office: U Alaska Office Chancellor PO Box 757500 Fairbanks AK 99775-7500*

LIND, NIELS CHRISTIAN, civil engineering educator; b. Copenhagen, Mar. 10, 1930; s. Axel Holger and Karen (Larsen) L.; m. Veronica Claire Hummel, Nov. 29, 1957 (div. 1979); children: Julie Wilhelmina, Peter Christian, Adam Conrad; m. Virginia Patricia Cano Reynoso, Jan. 26, 1985 (div. 1996); 1 child, Andreas. MSc, Tech. U. Denmark, 1953; PhD, U. Ill., 1959. Design engr. Dominia Ltd., Copenhagen, 1953-54; engr. I Bell Telephone Co., Montreal, 1954-55; field engr. Drake-Merritt, Labrador, Nfld., 1955; asst. prof. U. Ill., Urbana, 1959-60; assoc. prof. civil engring. U. Waterloo, Ont., 1960-62, prof., 1962-91, disting. prof. emeritus, 1992, dir. Inst. Risk Research, 1982-88. Adj. prof. U. Victoria, B.C., 1993-95. Recipient Ostenfeld gold medal, 1978; recipient Cancam award Can. Congress Applied Mechanics, 1981, CERRA award Civil Engring. Reliability and Risk Assn., 1999. Fellow Royal Soc. Can., Am. Acad. Mechanics (pres. 1972-73). Home: 404-1033 Belmont Ave Victoria BC Canada V8S 3T4 E-mail: nlind@uvic.ca.

LIND, ROBERT CLARENCE, economist, educator; b. Seattle, June 23, 1937; s. Clarence Samuel and Harriet (Schreur) L.; m. Gretchen Gayle (div. 1967); m. Joan Squires-Lind, Feb. 21, 1968 (div. 1998); m. Elizabeth C. Wesman, Oct. 10, 1998; children: Jason Mark-Alexander, Vanessa Antonia-Alexandra. BA, Yale U., 1960; PhD, Stanford U., 1966. Asst. prof. econs. U. Wash., Seattle, 1966-67; asst. prof. engring., econs. systems Stanford (Calif.) U., 1967-70, assoc. prof., 1970-71, assoc. prof. grad. sch. bus., 1971-74; prof. econ. mgmt., pub. policy Cornell U., Ithaca, 1974—99, prof. emeritus, 1999—; sr. cons. Charles River Assocs., Hendersonville, NC, 2000—. Pres. The Washington Campus, Inc., 1979-85. Co-author: Discounting for Time and Risk in Energy Policy, 1982. Dir. Inst. for Pub. Policy Analysis, 1969-71. Recipient Leavey award Freedoms Found., 1983. Mem. Am. Law ans Econ. Assn., Acad. Mgmt., Am. Econ. Assn., Internat. Assn. Energy Econs., Yale Club N.Y., Cornell Club, Capital Hill Club. Home: PO Box 2708 Hendersonville NC 28793

LIND, THOMAS OTTO, barge transportation company executive; b. New Orleans, Apr. 24, 1937; s. Henry Carl Lind and Elinor (Rooney) Messersmith; m. Eugenia Niehaus, June 8, 1963; children: Elinor Ashley, Elizabeth Kelly. BSME, Tulane U., 1959, LLB, 1965. Cert. mech. engr., 1959. Assoc. Jones, Walker, Waechter, Poitevent, Carrere and Denegre, New Orleans, 1965-66; v.p., sec., counsel Ingram Corp., 1966-84; v.p. Gulf Fleet Marine Corp., 1984-85; v.p., regulatory counsel, sec. and asst. treas. New Orleans Pub. Svc., Inc. and La. Power and Light Co., 1985-92; regional counsel for La. Entergy Svcs., Inc., 1993-94; risk mgr. Canal Barge Co., Inc., New Orleans, 1994-97, sec., 1995—, gen. counsel, 1997—. Author: (Book) The Story of Herman des Norweger, 2002. Trustee Metairie Park Country Day Sch., 1991-95; mem. bd. govs. Trinity Sch., New Orleans, 1982-85; vestryman Trinity Ch., New Orleans, 1987-91; active Family of Cmty. and Utility Supporters, New Orleans, 1987-94. Lt. (j.g.) USN, 1959-62; comdr. USNR, 1962-79. Mem. Fed. Energy Bar Assn. (bd. dirs. New Orleans chpt. 1988-92, pres. 1992), La. Bar Assn. (bd. dirs. corp. law sect. 1973-75), La. Assn. Waterways Operators and Shipyards (bd. dirs. 1999—), New Orleans Bar Assn. (bd. dir. 1989-97, 2d v.p. 1989-90, sec. 1992-93, 1st v.p. 1993-94, pres.-elect 1994-95, pres. 1995-96, bd. dirs. New Orleans Pro Bono project 1994-96), La. Orgn. for Jud. Excellence (bd. dirs., sec. 1998-2000, v.p. 2000—), New Orleans Lawn Tennis Club (pres. 1986-88), Am. Bar Assn.(Ho. of Dels. 1996-97). Republican. Episcopalian. Avocations: tennis, numismatics. Home: 1126 Octavia St New Orleans LA 70115-3129 Office: Canal Barge Co Inc 835 Union St Ste 300 New Orleans LA 70112-1469 E-mail: tlind@canalbarge.com.

LINDA, GERALD, advertising and marketing executive; b. Boston, Nov. 25, 1946; s. Edward Linda and Anne Beatrice (Lipofsky) Coburn; m. Claudia Wollack, Sept. 24, 1978; children— Jonathan Daniel Rezny, Jessica Simone. BS in Bus. Adminstrn., Northeastern U., 1969, MBA, 1971; postgrad., U. Mich., 1971-75. Faculty U. Ky., Lexington, 1975-77; ptnr. Tatham-Laird & Kudner, Chgo., 1977-80; v.p. Marsteller, 1980-84; sr. v.p. HCM, 1984-86; pres. Gerald Linda & Assocs., 1986-89; prin. Kurtzman/Slavin/Linda, Inc., 1990-93, Kapuler Mkgt. Rsch., Chgo., 1993-94; pres. Gerald Linda & Assocs., Glenview, Ill., 1994—. Mem. editorial review bd. Jour. Current Issues and Rsch. in Advt., 1984—. E-mail: glamktg@aol.com.

LINDAHL, THOMAS JEFFERSON, retired university dean; b. Norwalk, Wis., July 4, 1937; s. Gust Adolf and Mabel Louise (Zietlow) L.; m. Lee Ann Snowberry, Dec. 22, 1962; children: Gary, Mark. BS, U. Wis., 1960; MEd, U. Ill., 1970; PhD, Iowa State U., 1977. Instr. Stockton (Ill.) Community High Sch., 1968-74, Highland Community Coll., Freeport, Ill., 1968-74; instr. Iowa State U., Ames, 1974-75; chmn. dept. Area I Vocat.-Tech. Sch., Calmar, Iowa, 1975-77; assoc. prof., chmn. agrl. bus. dept. U. Minn., Waseca, 1977-83, vice chancellor, 1983-90, acting chancellor, 1990-91; dean Coll. Agriculture U. Wis., Platteville, 1991-94, dean Coll. Bus. Industry, Life Sci. and Agr., 1994-98, sr. advancement officer, 1998-2000. Cons., evaluator North Ctrl. Assn. Commn. on Instns. Higher Edn., Chgo., 1985—; cons. Citizens Network for Fgn. Affairs, Ukraine, 1999-2001; cons. on coop. devel. and higher edn., 2000—; numerous presentations in field. Author: (with Bennie L. Byler) Professional Education In-Service Needs of Agriculture Instructors in Iowa Post Secondry Area Vocational Schools, 1977, (with Wayne Robinson and N.J. Guderon) Cooperative College of Kenya Feasibility Study for Expansion, 1980, (with Myron A. Eighmy) An Individualized Course in Getting Started, 1980, (with James L. Gibson) Associate Instructor Handbook, 1980; also articles and corr. courses. Lay speaker United Meth. Ch., 1980—; pres. Wis. Rural Leadership Program Bd., 1995-97. Recipient hon. state degree Wis. Future Farmers Am., 1993. Fellow Nat. Assn. Coll. Tchrs. Agr. (exec. com., v.p. 1991-92, pres. 1992-93, Disting. Educator award 1997); mem. NEA, Nat. Vocat. Agrl. Tchrs. Assn., Am. Vocat. Assn., Wis. Vocat. Assn., Minn. Vocat. Agrl. Tchrs. Assn. (25-yr. Tchg. award 1985), Iowa Vocat. Agrl. Tchrs. Assn.

(15-yr. Membership award), Wis. Assn. Inst. Agr., Am. Assn. Colls. and Schs. Agr. and Renewable Resources (v.p. 1995-96, pres. 1996-97), Phi Delta Kappa, Kappa Delta Pi, Phi Kappa Phi. Home: 295 Flower Ct Platteville WI 53818-1915 E-mail: lindahl@uwplatt.edu.

LINDARS, LAURENCE EDWARD, retired health care products executive; b. N.Y.C., Oct. 14, 1922; s. Arthur John and Florence Vera (Cunard) L.; m. Mary Gibson Grandy, Jan. 22, 1972; children— John L., William A., Nancy E. Student, Dartmouth Coll., 1943-44; BS, Columbia U., 1947. Sr. auditor Arthur Young & Co., N.Y.C., 1947-51; chief acct. Deering, Milliken & Co., 1951-53; treas., dir. Poloron Products, Inc., New Rochelle, N.Y., 1953-58; controller Atlas Gen., Inc., N.Y.C., 1958-59; controller, treas., dir. fin. planning Pepperidge Farm, Inc., Norwalk, Conn., 1959-67; with C.R. Bard, Inc., Murray Hill, N.J., 1967-88, dir., 1972-92, vice chmn., 1983-88. Mem. adv. bd. of Summit Trust Co., 1970-84 Trustee Overlook Hosp., 1973-79, Found., 1988-91, treas., 1989-90; trustee Epilepsy Found. N.J., 1985-90, pres., 1986-87, chmn., 1988-90. Lt. (j.g.) USNR, 1943-46. Mem. Fin. Execs. Inst., Canoe Brook Country Club, Harbour Ridge Yacht and Country Club, Delta Upsilon. Presbyterian. Home: 199 Woodland Ave Summit NJ 07901

LINDBERG, CHARLES DAVID, lawyer; b. Moline, Ill., Sept. 11, 1928; s. Victor Samuel and Alice Christine (Johnson) L.; m. Marian J. Wagner, June 14, 1953; children: Christine, Breta, John, Eric. AB, Augustana Coll., Rock Island, Ill., 1950; JD, Yale U., 1953; DHL, Augustana Coll., 2000. Bar: Ohio 1954. Assoc. Taft, Stettinius & Hollister, Cin., 1953-61, ptnr., 1961-85, mng. ptnr., 1985-98, of counsel, 1999—. Dir. Cin. Bengals Profl. Football Team; chmn. bd. dirs. Schonstedt Instrument Co., 1994—97. Editor Nat. Law Jour., 1979-90. Bd. dirs. Taft Broadcasting Co., Cin., 1973-87, Dayton Walther Corp., 1986-87, Gibson Greeting, Inc., 1991-2000; bd. dirs. Augustana Coll., 1978-87, 91-99, 2000—, sec., 1981-82, vice-chmn., 1982-83, chmn., 1983-86; pres. Cin. Bd. Edn., 1971, 74, Zion Luth. Ch., Cin., 1966-69; chmn. policy com. Hamilton County Rep. Com., 1981-90; mem. exec. com. Ohio Rep. Fin. Com., 1989-90; trustee Greater Cin. Ctr. Econ. Edn., 1976-91, pres., 1987-89, chmn., 1989-91; chmn. law firm divsn. Fine Arts Fund, 1985; trustee Pub. Libr. Cin. and Hamilton County, 1982—, pres., 1989, 96, 01. Mem. Cin. Bar Assn., Greater Cin. C. of C. (trustee 1985, exec. com., vice chmn. govt. and cmty. affairs com. 1989-91), Ohio Libr. Trustees Assn. (bd. dirs. 1986-87), Ohio C. of C. (bd. dirs. 1988-89), Queen City Club (sec. 1989-91), Commonwealth Club, Comml. Club (sec. 1994-96), Cin. Country Club, Optimists. Office: 1800 US Bank Tower 425 Walnut St Cincinnati OH 45202-3923 E-mail: lindberg@taftlaw.com.

LINDBERG, DONALD ALLAN BROR, library administrator, pathologist, educator; b. N.Y.C., Sept. 21, 1933; s. Harry B. and Frances Seeley (Little) L.; m. Mary Musick, June 8, 1957; children: Donald Allan Bror, Christopher Charles Seeley, Jonathan Edward Moyer. AB, Amherst Coll., 1954, ScD (hon.), 1979; MD, Columbia U., 1958; ScD (hon.), SUNY, 1987; LLD (hon.), U. Mo., Columbia, 1990. Diplomate Am. Bd. Pathology, Am. Bd. Med. Examiners (exec. bd. 1987-91). Rsch. asst. Amherst Coll., 1954-55; intern in pathology Columbia-Presbyn. Med. Ctr., 1958-59, asst. resident in pathology, 1959-60; asst. in pathology Coll. Physician and Surgeons Columbia U., N.Y.C., 1958-60; instr. pathology Sch. of Medicine U. Mo., 1962-63, asst. prof. Sch. of Medicine, 1963-66, assoc. prof. Sch. of Medicine, 1966-69, prof. Sch. of Medicine, 1969-84, dir. Diagnostic Microbiology Lab. Sch. of Medicine, 1960-63, dir. Med. Ctr. Computer Program Sch. of Medicine, 1962-70, staff, exec. dir. for health affairs Sch. of Medicine, 1968-70, prof., chmn. dept. info. sci. Sch. of Medicine, 1969-71; dir. Nat. Libr. of Medicine, Bethesda, Md., 1984—. Adj. prof. pathology U. Md. Sch. Medicine, 1988—, clin. prof. pathology U. Va., 1992—; dir. Nat. Coord. Office for High Performance Computing and Comms., exec. office of Pres., Office Sci. & Tech. Policy, 1992-95; mem. computer sci./engring. bd. Nat. Acad. Sci., 1971-74, chmn. Nat. Adv. Com. Artificial Intelligence in Medicine, Stanford U., 1975-84; U.S. rep. to Internat. Med. Info. Assn./Internat. Fedn. Info. Processing, 1975-84; bd. dirs. Am. Med. Info. Assn., 1992—, Health on the Net Found.; adv. coun. Inst. Medicine, 1992—. Author: The Computer and Medical Care, 1968; The Growth of Medical Information Systems in the United States, 1979; editor: (with W. Siler) Computers in Life Science Research, 1975; (with others) Computer Applications in Medical Care, 1982; editor Methods of Info. in Medicine, 1970-83, assoc. editor, 1983—; editor Jour. Med. Systems, 1976—, Med. Informatics Jour., 1976—; chief editor procs. 3d World Conf. on Med. Informatics, 1980; editorial bd. Jour. of AMA, 1991—; contbr. articles to jours. Recipient Silver Cord award Internat. Fedn. for Info. Processing, 1980, Walter C. Alvarez award Am. Med. Writers Assn. 1989, PHS Surgeon Gen.'s medallion, 1989, Nathan Davis award AMA, 1989, Presdl. Disting. Exec. Rank award, Sr. Exec. Svc., Outstanding Svc. medal Uniformed Svcs. U. Health Scis., 1992, Computers in Healthcare Pioneer award, 1993, recognition award High Performance Computing Industry, 1995, silver award U.S. Nat. Commn. on Librs. and Info. Scis., 1996, meritorious award Coun. Biol. Editors, 1996; Simpson fellow Amherst Coll., 1954-55; Markle scholar in acad. medicine, 1964-69; recipient pres.'s award Med. Libr. Assn., 1997, Morris F. Collen, M.D. award of excellence Am. Coll. Med. Informatics, 1997, Info. Frontier award N.Y. Acad. Medicine, 1999, Ranice W. Crosby Disting. Achievement award Johns Hopkins U. Sch. Medicine, 1998, Spl. Recognition award Coll. P&S Columbia U. Alumni, 2001. Fellow: AAAS; mem.: Am. Med. Informatics Assn. (pres. 1988—91), Gorgas Meml. Inst. Tropical and Preventive Medicine (bd. dirs. 1987—), Am. Assn. Med. Systems and Informatics (internat. com. 1982—89, bd. dirs. 1982, editor conf. procs. 1983, 1984), Salutis Initas (Am. v.p. 1981—91), Assn. for Computing Machines, Mo. Med. Assn., Coll. Am. Pathologists (commn. on computer policy and coordination 1981—84), Inst. Medicine of NAS, Cosmos (Washington) (award 2001), Sigma Xi. Democrat. Avocations: photography, riding. Home: 13601 Esworthy Rd Germantown MD 20874-3319 Office: Nat Libr of Medicine 8600 Rockville Pike Bethesda MD 20894-0002

LINDBERG, DUANE R. bishop, historian; b. Thief River Falls, Minn., Apr. 16, 1933; s. Edgar and Alice (Amundson) L.; m. E. Mardell Kvitne, June 6, 1954; children: Erik Duane, Karen Kristin Kelle, Karl Stephen, Martha Alice Stone, Kristian John. BS in Chemistry, U. N.D., 1954; MDiv in Theology, Luther Sem., St. Paul, 1961; MA in Am. Studies, U. Minn., 1969, PhD in Am. Studies, 1975. Rsch. chemist DuPont Co., 1954; tchg. asst. chemistry dept. U. Wis., Madison, 1956-57; chemist Minn. Farm Bur. Lab., St. Paul, 1957-59; pastor Epping and Wheelock (N.D.) Luth. Chs., 1961-68; rsch. historian Minn. State Hist. Soc., St. Paul, 1969-71; pastor Zion Luth. Ch., West Union, Iowa, 1971-78; sr. pastor Trinity Luth. Ch., Waterloo, 1978-87, Acension Luth. Ch., Waterloo, 1987—; nat. ch. body founder, presiding pastor Am. Assn. Luth. Chs., Mpls., 1987-99, presiding pastor emeritus, 1999—. Vis. prof. Upper Iowa U., Fayette, 1976-77; adj. prof. Am. Luth. Theol. Sem., St. Paul, 1996-2000. Author: Uniting Word, 1969, Men of the Cloth, 1980; contbr. articles to profl. jours. Bd. dirs. Palmer Meml. Hosp., West Union, Iowa, 1972-78, Allen Meml. Hosp., Waterloo, 1979—; founder, bd. mem. Buffalo Trails Mus., Epping, N.D., 1964-68; founder, bd. mem. Fayette County Hist. Soc., West Union, 1975-78; dean Decorah Conf. Am. Luth. Ch., 1976-78, exec. com. Iowa Dist., 1976-78; bd. dirs. Great Plains Inst. Theology, 1965-68; pres. Eastern Iowa Luth. H.S. Assn., 1997-. With U.S. Army, 1954-56. Recipient award of commendation Concordia Hist. Inst., St. Louis, 1980, Nehemiah award Abiding World Ministries, Mpls., 1990, award of excellence Allen Meml. Hosp., Waterloo, 1995. Mem. numerous profl. ministerial groups and ch. bds., Rotary, Sons of Norway. Address: Valley Lutheran High School 1024 W 8th St Waterloo IA 50702

LINDBERG, FRANCIS LAURENCE, JR. management consultant; b. Jacksonville, Fla., Mar. 13, 1948; s. Francis Laurence and Mildred Hortense (Parrish) L.; m. Anne Louise Stearns, Dec. 29, 1972 (div.); 1 child, Kristen Anne; m. Alexis Jean Parker, Nov. 12, 1983 (dec. May 1996). Student, Eckerd Coll., 1965-66; BA, Jacksonville U., 1969; MBA, U. North Fla., 1976. CPA, Ga. Actuarial asst. Gulf Life Ins. Co., Jacksonville, 1967-73; asst. actuary Am. Heritage Life, 1973-77; asst. sec.-treas., prin. acctg. officer Atlantic Am. Corp., Atlanta, 1977-84; assoc. v.p. fin. Security Benefit Group, Topeka, 1985-86; exec. v.p., chief fin. officer Am. Way Group of Cos., Southfield, Mich., 1986-87; prin. Lindberg Consulting Group, Inc. (formerly Lindberg Group), Atlanta, 1987-98, pres., 1998—. V.p. fin Carson-Brooks, Inc., Atlanta, 1991-93; treas., bd. advisors Good News Comm., Inc., 1986-94; dep. receiver USEC Ga., Atlanta, 1995—. Recipient Membership Achievement award, Inst. Mgmt. Accts., 1983, George E. Wilson award Inst. Mgmt. Accts., 1991. Mem. AICPA (MAS, PCPS divs.), Soc. Fin. Examiners, Ga. Soc. CPAs, Brotherhood St. Andrew. Republican. Episcopalian.

LINDBERG, RICHARD CARL, editor, author, historian; b. Chgo., June 14, 1953; s. Oscar Waldemar and Helen Marie (Stone) L.; m. Denise Kay, July 1, 1978. BA, Northeastern Ill. U., Chgo., 1974, MA, 1987. Mgr. Sears Roebuck, Chgo., 1971-84; scriptwriter Signature Group, Schaumburg, Ill., 1984-88; sr. editor Crime Books, Inc., Wilmette, 1989-92; editor-in-chief Ill. Police and Sheriffs News, Palatine, 1992-98; rschr., mktg. mgr. Search Internat., Schaumburg, 1998—. Team historian Chgo. White Sox Baseball Team, 1985—; speaker and lectr. on Chgo. history and baseball, Chgo. Author: Stuck on the Sox, 1978, Who's on Third?, 1983, The Chicago White Sox Encyclopedia, 1984, Chicago Ragtime: Another Look at Chicago 1880-1920, 1985, re-pub. as: Chicago by Gaslight: A History of Chicago's Netherworld 1880-1920, 1996, To Serve and to Collect: Chicago Politics and Police Corruption 1855-1960, 1991, Passport's Guide to Ethnic Chicago, 1992, Stealing First in a Two Team Town: The White Sox from Comiskey to Reinsdorf, 1994, Quotable Chicago, 1996, The White Sox Encyclopedia, 1997, The Armchair Companion to Chicago Sports, 1997, Return to the Scene of the Crime: A Guide to Infamous Places in Chicago, 1999, Review Again to the Scene of the Crime: A Guide to Even More Infamous Places in Chicago, 2001; contbg. writer Encyclopedia of Major League Team Histories, 1991, The Ballplayers, 1990, A Kid's Guide to Chicago, 1980, Encyclopedia of World Crime, 1990; contbr. articles to Chgo. History, USA Today mag., Screen Mag., The Reader, others. Recipient Disting. Alumni award Northeastern Ill. U. Found. Mem.: Ill. Acad. Criminology, Chgo. Press Vet. Assn., Chgo. Crime Commn., Soc. Midland Authors (pres. 1999—2001), Phi Alpha Theta (pres. chpt. 1988—91, Robert Zegger Meml. award 1987, Frederic Milton Thrasher award 2001). Republican. Methodist. Home: 5915 N Navarre Ave Chicago IL 60631-2628 E-mail: rclwriter@aol.com.

LINDBERG, TOD MARSHALL, editor, writer; b. Syracuse, N.Y., Feb. 25, 1960; s. Robert Sheridan and Dorothy Louise (Farris) L.; m. Christine Ann Tedeschi, Apr. 29, 1989; children: Abby Marshall, Molly Robins. BA, U. Chgo., 1982. Asst. editor Pub. Interest, N.Y.C., 1982-83, mng. editor, 1983-85; exec. editor Nat. Interest, Washington, 1985-86; sr. editor Insight, 1986, exec. editor news, 1987-90, dep. mng. editor, 1990-91; edtl. page editor The Washington Times, 1991-99; contbg. editor The Weekly Standard, 1995-96; media fellow The Hoover Instn., 1996-2000; editor Policy Rev., Washington, 1999—; rsch. fellow The Hoover Instn., Stanford U., 2001—. Editorial cons. Manhattan Inst., N.Y.C., 1983, Inst. for Ednl. Affairs, N.Y.C., 1983-85, Simon & Schuster, Pubs., N.Y.C., 1985; polit. columnist Washington Times, 1991—; mem. Coun. on Fgn. Rels., 2000—; bd. visitors Inst. on Polit. Journalism, Georgetown U., 1998—. Contbr. articles to profl. jours. Office: Ste 601 818 Connecticut Ave NW Washington DC 20006 also: Policy Review 818 Connecticut Ave NW Ste 601 20006 E-mail: lindberg@hoover.standford.edu.

LINDBLAD, RICHARD ARTHUR, retired health services administrator, drug abuse epidemiologist; b. Atlantic, Iowa, July 15, 1937; s. Clifford Robert and Emma Ruth (Dunham) L.; children: Julie, Richard, Mark. BS, San Jose State Coll., 1961; MS, U. Colo., 1965; M.P.H., Johns Hopkins U., 1971, Dr.P.H., 1974. Capt. USPHS, 1961, col., 1975, ret. capt., 1961-94; various assignments including adminstrn., epidemiology, research and prevention of substance abuse disorders Fed. Drug Abuse Treatment Hosp., Ft. Worth, Denver; dir. internat. programs Nat. Inst. on Drug Abuse, Rockville, Md.; cons. in drug abuse epidemiology WHO, UN; designed and supervised devel. of UN Internat. Drug Abuse Assessment System. Cons. on drug abuse rsch. and program devel. Designed and supervised devel. of the International Visiting Scientist and Technical Exchange program of the dept. of Health and Human Svcs.; Contbr. articles to profl. jours. Mem. Am. Public Health Assn., Md. Public Health Assn., Commd. Officers Assn. USPHS, Nat. Assn. Uniformed Services. Home: PO Box 179 Libertytown MD 21762-0179

LINDBLOM, LAURIE BETH, physician; b. Feb. 20, 1955; BFA, U. Wis., Milw., 1977; MD, U. Wis., Madison, 1989. Diplomate Am. Bd. Phys. Medicine and Rehab., Am. Bd. Spinal Cord Injury Medicine. Asst. prof. phys. medicine and rehab Ea. Va. Med. Sch., Norfolk, 1994—2001; chief spinal cord injury Hampton Vets. Hosp., 2001—. Mem. Va. Spinal Cord Injury Assn. (med. dir. 1999), Endependence Ctr. (bd. dirs. 1998-2002), Am. Acad. Phys. Medicine Rehab.

LINDE, HANS ARTHUR, state supreme court justice; b. Berlin, Germany, Apr. 15, 1924; came to U.S., 1939, naturalized, 1943; s. Bruno C. and Luise (Rosenhain) L.; m. Helen Tucker, Aug. 13, 1945; children: Lisa, David Tucker. BA, Reed Coll., 1947; JD, U. Calif., Berkeley, 1950. Bar: Oreg. 1951. Law clk. U.S. Supreme Ct. Justice William O. Douglas, 1950-51; atty. Office of Legal Adviser, Dept. State, 1951-53; pvt. practice Portland, Oreg., 1953-54; legis. asst. U.S. Sen. Richard L. Neuberger, 1955-58; from assoc. prof. to prof. U. Oreg. Law Sch., 1959-76; justice Oreg. Supreme Ct., Salem, 1977-90, sr. judge, 1990—. Fulbright lectr. Freiburg U., 1967-68, Hamburg U., 1975-76; cons. U.S. ACDA, Dept. Def., 1962-76; mem. Adminstrv. Conf. U.S., 1978-82, Oreg. Law Commn., 1997—; disting. scholar in residence Willamette U. Coll. Law, Salem, Oreg., 1994—. Author: (with George Bunn) Legislative and Administrative Processes, 1976. Mem. Oreg. Constl. Revision Commn., 1961-62, Oreg. Law Commn., 1997—, Oreg. Commn. on Pub. Broadcasting, 1990-93; bd. dirs. Oreg. Pub. Broadcasting, 1993-99. With U.S. Army, 1943-46. Fellow Am. Acad. Arts and Scis.; mem. Am. Law Inst. (council), Order of Coif, Phi Beta Kappa. Office: Willamette U Coll Law Salem OR 97301 E-mail: hlinde@willamette.edu.

LINDE, LUCILLE MAE (LUCILLE JACOBSON), motor-perceptual specialist; b. Greeley, Colo., May 5, 1919; d. John Alfred and Anna Julia (Anderson) Jacobson; m. Ernest Emil Linde, July 5, 1946 (dec. Jan. 27, 1959). BA, Colo. State Coll. of Edn., 1941, MA, 1947; EdD, U. No. Colo., 1974. Cert. tchr. Calif., Colo., Iowa, N.Y.; cert. ednl. psychologist; guidance counselor. Dean of women, dir. residence C.W. Post Coll. of L.I. Univ., 1965-66; asst. dean of students SUNY, Farmingdale, 1966-67; counselor, tchr. West High Sch., Davenport, Iowa, 1967-68; instr. grad. tchrs. and counselors, univ. counselor, researcher No. Ariz. U., Flagstaff, 1968-69; vocat. edn. and counseling coord. Fed. Exemplary Project, Council Bluffs, Iowa, 1970-71; sch. psychologist, counselor Oakdale Sch. Dist., Calif., 1971-73; sch. psychologist, intern Learning and Counseling Ctr., Stockton, 1972-74; pvt. practice rsch. in motor-perceptual tng. Greeley, 1975—. Rschr. ocumeter survey Lincoln Unified Sch. Dist., Stockton, 1980, 81, 82, Manteca (Calif.) H.S., 1981; spkr. Social Sci. Edn. Consortium, U. Colo., Boulder, 1993; mem. Monday Morning steering com. House Spkr. Newt Gingrich, 1997-98; mem. Attention Disorder Advocacy Group, 1997-2001; instr. seminars for ADD and ADHD, alleviating lag/dysfunctional in neural system noted, 1997-98, 1998-99, presenter seminars in field. Author: Psychological Services and Motor Perceptual Training, 1974, Guidebook for Psychological Services and Motor Perceptual Training (How One May Improve in Ten Easy Lessons!), 1992, Manual for the Lucille Linde Ocumeter: Ocular Pursuit Measuring Instrument, 1992, Motor-Perceptual Training and Visual Perceptual Research (How Students Improved in Seven Lessons!), 1992, Effects of Motor Perceptual Training on Academic Achievement and Ocular Pursuit Ability, 1992, Teaching University of Northern Colorado Laboratory Students and Greeley District 6 Students Motor-Perceptual Training Seminar, 2001; inventor ocumeter, instrument for measuring ocular tracking ability, 1989, target for use, 1991, cures for oculomotor dysfunction noted; patentee in field. Mem. Rep. Presdl. Task Force, 1989-96, trustee, 1991-92, charter mem., 1994—, life mem., 1994-95; mem. Rep. Nat. Com., 1990, 93-2002, Rep. Nat. Com. on Am. Agenda, 1993, Nat. Rep. Congl. Com., 1990, 92, 93, 95-2002, Nat. Fedn. Rep. Women, Greeley Rep. Women, 1996-2002; advisor Senator Bob Dole for Pres.; charter mem. Newt Gingrich's Speaker's Task Force, Senator Phil Gramm's Presdl. Steering Com.; at-large- del. Rep. Platform Planning Com.; team leader Nat. Rep. Rapid Response Network, Campaign America, 1996; active Heritage Found. (certificate as honored mem. leadership adv. bd., 1998-2000), Christian Bus. Men's Assn., Friends U. N.C. Librs., Citizens Against Govt. Waste, 1996-2001, Concerns of Police Survivors, 1996-98, Nat. Assn. of Police Orgn., elected to Libr. of Congress Nat. membership, 1997-2001; mem. WW II Vets. Com., 2000, 2001, Rep. Gov.'s Assn., 2001; mem. Rep. Gov.'s Policy Commn. Recipient Presdl. medal of merit and lapel insignia, 1990, Nat. Rep. Senatorial Com., 1991-2001, cert. of appreciation Nat. Rep. Congl. Com., 1992, 95, lapel pin Rep. Senatorial Inner Circle, 1990-96, Rep. Presdl. commemorative honor roll, 1993, Rep. Senatorial Freedom medal, 1994, Rep. Legion of Merit award, 1994, 96, Rep. Congl. Order of Freedom award, 1995, Senatorial Inner Cir. Lapel Pin, 1998, Lapel Pin award RNC, 1996, Leadership citation Rep. Senatorial Inner Cir./ Rep. Nat. Conv., 1996, Legion of Merit Rep. Presdl. exec. com., 1996, Honor cert. House Spkr. Newt Gingrich, 1996, Rep. Presdl. Legion of Merit medallion and matching lapel pin, 1994, Order of Merit, 1996, Conservative Leadership award Young Am.'s Found., 1999, Nat. Rep. Congl. Com. Rep. of the Yr. from Colo. award, 2000, Majority Leader's Commn. Cert., 2001, 2001 Conservative Patriot award The Pres., Ron Robinson and Bd. of Dirs. of The Young America's Found.; named to Rep. Na t. Hall of Honor, 1992. Mem. AAUP, NAFE, Nat. Assn. Sch. Psychologists and Psychometrists (spkr. conf. 1976), Rep. Senatorial Inner Cir. (name engraved on Ronald Wilson Reagan Eternal Flame of Freedom, 1995, on the Nat. Rep. Victory Monument, Washington, 1996, Rep. Sen. Inner Cir. (Conv. Medallion 1996, RNC Mems. Only pin 1996), 20th Century Rep. Leader, Rep. Sen. Inner Cir., 1998, The Smithsonian Assocs., Ronald Reagan Presdl. Libr. and Mus., Bush Presdl. Libr. and Mus., Nat. Trust for Hist. Preservation, Internat. Platform Assn., Friends of Newt Gingrich, 1998-99, Independence Inst., Assn. Children Learning Disabilities (spkr. internat. conv. 1976), Libr. of Congress Assn., 1999, CHADD (Chldrn. and Adults with Attention Deficit Disorder), Learning Disabilities Assn. of Colorado, Natl. Fragile X Found., Fraxa Rsch. Found., 1999, Pi Omega Pi, Pi Lambda Theta. Avocations: music, archtl. design. Home: 1954 18th Ave Greeley CO 80631-5208

LINDE, MAXINE HELEN, lawyer, business executive, private investor; b. Chgo., Sept. 2, 1939; d. Jack and Lottie (Kroll) Stern; B.A. summa cum laude, UCLA, 1961; J.D., Stanford U., 1967; m. Ronald K. Linde, June 12, 1960. Bar: Calif. 1968. Applied mathematician, reseach engr. Jet Propulsion Lab., Pasadena, Calif., 1961-64; law clk. U.S. Dist. Ct. No. Calif., 1967-68; mem. firm Long & Levit, San Francisco, 1968-69, Swerdlow, Glikbarg & Shimer, Beverly Hills, Calif., 1969-72; sec., gen. counsel Envirodyne Industries, Inc., Chgo., 1972-89; pres. The Ronald and Maxine Linde Found., 1989—; vice chmn. bd., gen. counsel Titan Fin. Group, LLC, Chgo., 1994-98. Mem. bd. visitors Stanford Law Sch., 1989-92, law and bus. adv. coun., 1991-94, dean's adv. coun. 1992-94. Mem. Order of Coif, Phi Beta Kappa, Pi Mu Epsilon, Alpha Lambda Delta.

LINDE, RONALD KEITH, corporate executive, private investor; b. L.A., Jan. 31, 1940; s. Morris and Sonia Doreen (Hayman) L.; m. Maxine Helen Stern, June 12, 1960. BS with honors, UCLA, 1961; MS (Inst. scholar), Calif. Inst. Tech., 1962, PhD (ARCS scholar, Rutherford scholar), 1964. Cons. Litton Industries, L.A., 1961-63, engr., 1961; materials scientist Poulter Labs., Stanford Rsch. Inst., Menlo Park, Calif., 1964; head solid state rsch. Stanford Rsch. Inst., 1965-67; chmn. shock wave physics dept., mgr. tech. svcs. Poulter Labs., 1967, dir. shock and high pressure physics div., 1967-68, chief exec. labs., 1968-69; dir. phys. scis. Stanford Rsch. Inst., 1968-69; chmn. bd., CEO Envirodyne Industries, Inc., Chgo., 1969-89; chmn. bd. The Ronald and Maxine Linde Found., 1989—. Co-chmn. bd. Titan Fin. Group, LLC, Chgo., 1994-98; law and bus. adv. coun. Stanford Law Sch., 1991-94, dean's adv. coun. 1992-94. Contbr. articles to various publs.; patentee in field. Mem. adv. bd. ARCS Found., Chgo., 1993-98; mem. Northwestern U. Assocs., 1978—; trustee Calif. Inst. Tech., 1989—, Harvey Mudd Coll., 1989-98, vice chmn., bd. trustees, 1993-98, vice chmn. emeritus, 1998—. Mem. Sigma Xi, Tau Beta Pi, Phi Eta Sigma. Office: Linde Found 180 E Pearson St Ste 5801 Chicago IL 60611-2182

LINDEBORG, RICHARD ANDREW, public affairs specialist; b. Lansing Mich., Dec. 24, 1946; s. Robert Gustav and Margaret Eloise (Isley) L.; m. Susan McCreight, Mar. 30, 1970. B.A., N.Mex. Highlands U., 1968; M.S., Syracuse U., 1973; student Dartmouth Coll., 1964-65. Acting chmn. dept. communication Baker U., Baldwin, Kans., asst. prof. journalism, 1974-76; adminstrv. technician USDA Forest Service, Sante Fe Nat. Forest, Pecos, N.Mex., 1976-78, sci. editor Rocky Mountain Forest and Range Expt. Sta., Fort Collins, Colo., 1979-82; chief sci. editor, head publs. U.S. Forest Products Lab., Madison, Wis., 1982-87; speech writer USDA Forest Service, Washington, 1987— ; instr. journalism Colo. State U., 1980, cons. speech research to pres., 1981-82. Bd. dirs. Larimer Choral Soc.; vice cmn. Community Devel. Block Grant program Ft. Collins, 1981; bd. dirs. Sante Fe County Red Cross, 1977-78, Capitol ACLU, 1982-83. Served with U.S. Army, 1968-71. Decorated Bronze Star, Army Commendation medal; recipient Forest Service Achievement award, 1978, 81, 83-86. Mem. Sigma Delta Chi. Democrat. Deacon, Presbyterian Ch. Contbr. articles to profl. jours. Office: US Dept Agrl 14th & Independence Ave SW Washington DC 20250-0001

LINDELL, EDWARD ALBERT, former college president, religious organization administrator; b. Denver, Nov. 30, 1928; s. Edward Gustaf and Estelle (Lundin) L.; m. Patricia Clare Eckert, Sept. 2, 1965; children: Edward Paul, Erik Adam. BA, U. Denver, 1950, MA, 1956, Ed.D., 1960, L.H.D. (hon.), 1975; Litt.D. (hon.), Tusculum Coll., 1979; D.H.L. (hon.), Roanoke Coll., 1981; Litt.D (hon.), Christ Coll., Irvine, 1992. Tchr. N. Denver High Sch., 1952-61; asst. dean Coll. Arts and Scis., U. Denver, 1961-65, dean, 1965-75; pres. Gustavus Adolphus Coll., St. Peter, Minn., 1975-80, Luth. Brotherhood Mut. Funds, Mpls., 1980—. V.p. Lutheran Brotherhood Found., 1980—, exec. dir. Exec. bd. Rocky Mountain Synod Lutheran Ch. Am., 1968—, Luth. Coun. U.S.A., v.p., 1975—; also pres. bd. coll. edn. and ch. vocations; trustee Midland Luth. Coll., Fremont, Nebr., Kans. Wesleyan U., Colo. Assn. Ind. Colls. and Univs., Luth. Med. Center, Wheatridge, Colo., Luth. Sch. Theology, Chgo., 1975—, St. John's U., Minn., 1978—; bd. dirs. Swedish Coun. Am., 1978—, pres., chmn.-elect, 2001, pres., 2002; adv. bd. Royal Swedish Acad. Scis., 1980; v.p. Am.-Swedish Inst., 1980; exec. v.p. external affairs Luth. Brotherhood, 1981—; pres. Nat. Fraternal Congress Am., 1988—; bd. dirs. Pacific Luth. Theol. Sem., 1978-80, Loretto Heights Coll., Colo., 1978-86, Gettysburg Theol. Sem., 1981-83, Wittenberg U., 1988, Bethany Coll., 1991—, Minn. Orch., 1983—, Am. Scandinavian Found., 1982—, Fairview Hosp., 1982—, U.S. Swedish Found. Internat. Sci. Rsch., 1981—, v.p. 1986—, Habitat for Humanity Internat., 1992—; pres. U.S. Wittenberg Found., 1996—. Named Outstanding Faculty Mem. Coll. Arts and Scis., U. Denver, 1964; decorated knight King of Sweden, 1976; recipient Suomi Disting. Svc. award, 1989. Mem. Good Samaritan Soc. (bd. dirs. 1997—, vice-chmn. 98-99, chmn.-elect 1999, chmn. 2000—), Swedish Pioneer Hist. Soc. (dir. 1979—), U. Denver Alumni Assn. (Career Alumni Achievement award 1994), Phi Beta Kappa. Office: Swedish Coun Am 2600 Park Ave S Minneapolis MN 55407 E-mail: edlindell@swedishcouncil.org.

LINDELOF, WILLIAM CHRISTIAN, JR. financial company executive; b. Wheeling, W.Va., June 21, 1946; s. William Christian and Ruth Elizabeth (Perkins) L.; m. Virginia Lee Partezana, May 5, 1973; children: Erik Christian, Alan Brent, Heather Catherine. AA, Ohio Valley Coll., Parkersburg, W.Va., 1967; BS, West Liberty State Coll., 1970. Cert. credit union exec. Salesman Univ. Guaranty Life Ins., Youngstown, Ohio, 1972-73; asst. mgr. Household Fin. Corp., 1974-76; loan officer 1st Wetzel Savs. and Loan (later 1st Wetzel Nat. Bank), New Martinsville, W.Va., 1976-79; mgr. Mobay Employees Fed. Credit Union, 1979-85; pres., chief exec. officer First Flight Fed. Credit Union, Havelock, N.C., 1985—. Chmn. exec. com. Gen. Sys. Users Group, New Martinsville, 1984-85; bd. dirs., sec. Marine Credit Union Network, 1988-91; bd. dirs. N.C. Credit Union Found., 1998—, vice chmn., 2000—. Mem. citizen's adv. coun. Adena Industries Workshop for Handicapped, New Martinsville, 1981-84; deacon, tchr. Bible class Morehead City (N.C.) Ch. of Christ; v.p. Carteret County chpt. Parents for Advancement Gifted Edn., 1987-91; bd/ dors/ Carteret County Econ. Devel. Coun., 1997-2001, sec.-treas., 1998-99. v.p., 2000-01. With U.S. Army, 1969-71. Recipient Medal of Merit, Ohio Valley Coll., 1989. Mem.: Nat. Credit Union Inst., Def. Credit Union Coun. (bd. dir. 1998—, sec. 1999—2001, treas. 2001—), Nat. Assn. Fed. Credit Unions (regulatory com. 1990—95, comm. com. 1996—97), NC Credit Union Network (bd. dir. East Carolina chpt. 1986—91, v.p. 1987—88, pres. 1988—90, edn. com. 1989—90, ann. meeting com. 1995—96, govtl. affairs com. 1997—98, bd. dir. 1998—), Credit Union Exec. Soc., Morehead City C. of C. (co-chmn.blueprint task force for Carteret C.C., mem. spkrs. bur., mil. liaison 1990—92), Havelock C. of C. (govtl. affairs com. 1990—95, bd.

dir. 1991—94, v.p. 1991—92, pres. 1992—93), Am. Legion (vice comdr. 1974—76), Delta Sigma Pi (life). Republican. Home: 3515 Meadow Dr Morehead City NC 28557-3013 Office: First Flight Fed Credit Union 1208 E Main St Havelock NC 28532-2405

LINDEMAN, JACK, retired literature educator, poet; b. Phila., Dec. 31, 1924; s. Samuel Lindeman and Elsie Teitelbaum. BS, West Chester State Coll. and U. Pa., 1949. Instr. English Lincoln U., Pa., 1961—62, Temple U., Phila., 1963—64, Kutztown (Pa.) State U., 1968—85, prof. emeritus, 1985—. Vis. writer in residence Russell Sage Coll., Troy, NY, 1966, U. Dayton, Ohio, 1968. Editor: (lit. mag.) Whetstone, 1955—61; poetry editor: Time Capsule, 1981—83; author: (Atlantis edit.) Twenty-One Poems, 1963, Appleseed Hollow, 2001; editor: The Conflict of Convictions, 1968, author poetry. Mem.: Friends of the Vatican Libr. Democrat. Humanist. Avocations: dogs and cats, reading, traveling, baseball, basketball. Home: 133 S Franklin St Fleetwood PA 19522-1810

LINDEMANN, ALBERT S. history educator; b. Santa Monica, Calif., May 19, 1938; s. Albert Enos and Clara Frances Shirk; m. Barbara S. Lindemann, Aug. 31, 1963; children: Timothy William, Erika Grace. BA, Pomona Coll., 1960; PhD, Harvard U., 1968. Prof. history U. Calif., Santa Barbara. Author: The Red Years, 1974, History of European Socialism, 1983, Jew Accused, 1991, Esau's Tears, 1997, Anti-Semitism Before the Holocaust, 2000. Home: 1470 Tunnell Rd Santa Barbara CA 93105 Office: U Calif Dept History Santa Barbara CA 93106 E-mail: lindeman@history.ucsb.edu.

LINDEMANN, CHARLES BENARD, cell biologist, researcher; b. S.I., Dec. 17, 1946; s. John Joseph and Mary Gaetana Lindemann; m. Linda S. Balden; 1 child Jessie Haglund 1 child Christopher ;1 child Laurel. PhD, SUNY, Albany, 1972. Avocations: juggling, harmonica. Office: Oakland U University Dr Rochester MI 48309 Office Fax: 248-370-4225. Business E-Mail: lindeman@oakland.edu.

LINDEMANN, JAN RUTH, social worker, governmental affairs consultant; b. Kankakee, Ill., Dec. 26, 1948; d. George A. and Ruth E. (Danker) Noffke; m. Paul F. Lindemann, May 22, 1971; children: Andrea, Jessica. BA, Valparaiso U., 1971; MSW, Ind. U., 1973. Cert. clin. social worker. Psychiat. social worker Larue Carter Hosp., Indpls., 1973-78; exec. dir. Ind. chpt. NASW, 1978-80; lobbyist, cons. Ind. Coalition Human Svcs., 1984—, Ind. Primary Health Care Assn., Indpls., 1993—. Adj. field instr. Sch. Social Work Ind. U., Indpls., 1973-95. Mem. pub. policy com. Mental Health Assn. Ind., Indpls., 1994—; mem. steering com. Kids Count, Indpls., 1994—; mem. Planned Parenthood, Indpls., 1987—; mem. adv. com. social svc. block grant State of Ind., 1987-90; del. White House Conf. Families, 1980; mem. adv. coun. Ind. U. Sch. Social Work. Named Social Worker of Yr. Ind. chpt. NASW, 1995. Mem. NOW, Govt. Affairs Soc. Ind. (bd. dirs. 1995—), Women's Polit. Caucus, Acad. Cert. Social Workers, Indpls. Press Club. Avocations: travel, reading, writing, golfing. Home and Office: 8132 Meadowbrook Dr Indianapolis IN 46240-2600

LINDEMER, LAWRENCE BOYD, lawyer, former utility executive, former state justice; b. Syracuse, N.Y., Aug. 21, 1921; s. George F. and Altamae (Reimers) L.; m. Jean Backus Lindemer; children— Lawrence Boyd, David G. Student, Taft Sch., 1939, Hamilton Coll., 1939-41; AB, U. Mich., 1943, LL.B., 1948. Bar: Mich. 1948. Asst. pros. atty., Ingham County, 1949-51; asst., commn. on orgn. Exec. Br. Govt., Hoover Comm., 1953-55; partner Foster, Lindemer, Swift & Collins (and predecessor firm), 1955-75; justice Mich. Supreme Ct., Lansing, 1975-76; sr. v.p., gen. counsel Consumers Power Co., 1977-86. Mem. Mich. Ho. of Reps., 1951-52; Republican state chmn., 1957-61; mem. Rep. Nat. Com., 1957-61; Rep. candidate atty. gen. Mich., 1966; bd. regents U. Mich., 1968-75; trustee Gerald R. Ford Found., 1985-98. Served with USAAF, 1943-45. Mem. ABA, State. Bar Mich. (commr. 1963-70), Mich. State Bd. Ethics, U. Mich. Alumni Assn. (pres. 1983-85), Am. Automobile Assn. (bd. dirs. 1987-96, chmn. 1993-95), Auto Club Mich. (b.d dirs. 1977-96, chmn. bd. 1985-87). Presbyterian (elder). Office: Foster Swift Collins & Smith PC 313 S Washington Sq Lansing MI 48933-2172 Home: 745 Lake Lotela Dr Avon Park FL 33825-9728

LINDEMULDER, LAURIE, piano educator, concert pianist; b. Detroit, Jan. 22, 1938; d. Ralph Leslie and Wilmine (Vanderveen) L.; m. Charles Thomas Harris, Jan. 15, 1966; children: Leslie Law Harris, Charles Jason Harris. MusB, U. Mich., 1959; MusM, U. Mich., 1961. Mem. faculty Kingswood Sch. Cranbrook, Bloomfield Hills, Mich., 1959-60, Detroit Inst. Musical Art, 1962-65, Detroit Cmty. Music Sch., 1962-65; self-employed, 1966-81; mem. faculty Wayne County C.C., Detroit, 1969-71; pianist Theater on Wheels, Houston, 1981-83; mgr., tchr. Loftis Music Studios, 1987-91; tchr. Houston Conservatory of Music, 1990-92; self-employed private studio, 1989—; tchg. artist Tex. Inst. Arts in Edn., 1996—. Founding mem. Music For a While Concert series, Grosse Pointe Woods, Mich., 1978-81; originator Arts Always, Houston, 1984-86; musician piano duet team with Alice Ellison, Detroit, 1963-94, with Norman Schack, Houston, 1994-2000. Vol. dir. camera person First Presbyn. Ch. Houston; founding sec. Cy-Fair Assn. for Edn. Academically Talented, 1984; chmn. cultural arts com. Post Elem. Sch., Cypress-Fairbanks Ind. Sch. Dist., Houston, 1984-86; bd. dirs. Bayou City Chamber Orch., 2001—. Travel grantee Cultural Arts Coun. Houston, 1999. Mem. Music Tchrs. Nat. Assn., Nat. Piano Tchrs. Guild, Tex. Music Tchrs. Assn., Houston Music Tchrs. Assn. (v.p., program chmn. 1994-97, pres.-elect 1997-98, pres. 1998-2000, immediate past pres. 2000—), Houston Music Tchrs. Assn. Edn. Found. (pres. 2000-02, bd. 2002-03), Bayou City Federated Music Club (founding pres. 1995-96), The Tuesday Musical Club (Houston). Home: 4507 Richmond Ave Houston TX 77027-6709

LINDEN, DAVID HUGH, engineering executive; b. South Amboy, N.J., Sept. 23, 1952; s. Douglas Edward and Mary Margaret (Beavis) L.; children: Christopher, Kimberly. BSME, Rutgers U., 1974. Project engr. Westinghouse Elec. Corp., Lester, Pa., 1974-76; steam turbine design engr. Ingersoll Rand Co., Phillipsburg, N.J., 1976-79; supr. expanded design engr., 1979-87; exec. v.p. Conmec, Inc., Bethlehem, Pa., 1987-98; pres. D.H. Linden & Assocs., Allentown, 1998—. Contbr. articles to profl. jours. Mem. ASME, ASTM, Am. Petroleum Inst., Nat. Assn. Corrosion Engrs. Home and Office: 720 Dorset Rd Allentown PA 18104-3386 E-mail: dhlinden@aol.com.

LINDEN, HAROLD ARTHUR, interior designer, consultant; b. N.Y.C., May 25, 1941; s. Moses Lindenman and Rose Barmack. BA in Art, CCNY, 1964, MA in Design, 1967. Merchandising mgr. Internat. Home, 1968-71; owner Mobili Internazionale, Ltd. Interior Design, 1964—. Design cons. Forecast Furniture, Inc., Winchester, Va., 1969-87; Charlton Co., Leominster, Mass., 1968-71; Archtl. CBT Corp., N.Y.C., 1971-86; designed (with others) Stonybrook, first mortarless masonry home in U.S., Matamoras, Penn. Designer Stonybrook House. Mem. Kappa Phi Omega (pledgemaster 1960, pres. 1961-64). Jewish. Avocations: painting, music, travel, theater, cooking. Office: PO Box 60 Matamoras PA 18336-0060

LINDEN, HENRY ROBERT, chemical engineering research executive; b. Vienna, Austria, Feb. 21, 1922; arrived in U.S., 1939, naturalized, 1945; s. Fred and Edith (Lermer) L.; m. Natalie Govedarica, 1967; children by previous marriage: Robert, Debra. BS, Ga. Inst. Tech., 1944; MChemE, Poly. U., 1947; PhD, Ill. Inst. Tech., 1952. Chem. engr. Socony Vacuum Labs., 1944-47; with Inst. of Gas Tech., 1947-78, various rsch. mgmt. positions, 1947-61, dir., 1961-69, exec. v.p., dir., 1969-74, pres., trustee, 1974-78; various acad. appointments Ill. Inst. Tech., Chgo, 1954-86, Frank W. Gunsaulus Disting. Prof. chem. engring., 1987-90, McGraw prof. energy and power engring. and mgmt., 1990—, interim pres., CEO, 1989-90, interim chmn., CEO Ill. Inst. Tech. Rsch. Inst., 1989-90; COO, GDC, Inc., Chgo., 1965-73; CEO Gas Devel. Corp. subs. Inst. Gas Tech., 1973-78, also bd. dirs.; pres., dir. Gas Rsch. Inst., 1976-87, exec. advisor, 1987-2000. Author tech. articles; holder U.S. and fgn. patents in fuel tech. Recipient award of merit oper. sect. Am. Gas Assn., 1956, Disting. Svc. award, 1974, Gas Industry Rsch. award, 1982, R&D award Nat. Energy Resources Orgn., 1986, Homer H. Lowry award for excellence in fossil energy rsch. U.S. Dept. Energy, 1991, award U.S. Energy Assn., 1993, Walton Clark medal Franklin Inst., 1972, Bunsen-Pettenkofer-Ehrentafel medal Deutscher Verein des Gas und Wasserfaches, 1978, Alumni medal Ill. Inst. Tech., 1995, Lifetime Achievement award The Energy Daily jour., 1996; named to Hall of Fame, Ill. Inst. Tech., 1982, Engring. Hall of Fame Ga. Tech., 1996. Fellow: AAAS, AIChE (Ernest W. Thiele award 2000); mem.: So. Gas Assn. (hon. life), Am. Chem. Soc. (chmn. divsn. fuel chemistry 1967, councilor 1969—77, H.H. Storch award), NAE. Office: Ill Inst Tech PH 135 10 W 33rd St Chicago IL 60616-3730

LINDEN, JAMES CARL, educator, consultant; b. Greeley, Colo., Sept. 12, 1942; s. Carl W. and Dorthy (Gray) L.; m. Susan Chapman, Dec. 26, 1968; children: Diana, Christina. BS in Chemistry, Colo. State U., 1964; PhD in Biochemistry, Iowa State U., 1969. Postdoctoral U. Muenchen, Fed. Republic of Germany, 1969-71, U. St. Louis, 1971-72; project leader G.W. Sugar Co., Loveland, Colo., 1972-76; chemist Adolf Coors Co., Golden, 1976-77; research scientist Colo. State U., Ft. Collins, 1977-85, prof. of microbiology and biochem. engring., 1996—. Vis. ETH (Biotech.), Zurich, 1980, Tech. U., Budapest, 1991, U. Regensburg, 1994. Contbr. articles to profl. jours. Recipient Alexander von Humboldt Stipendiate award, Bonn, Fed. Republic Germany, 1969-71, Rsch. Faculty award, Colo. State U., 1982, 85, 92. Mem. Am. Chem. Soc., Am. Soc. Plant Physiology, Soc. Indsl. Microbiology. Avocations: biking, gardening. Office: Colo State U 100 Glover Fort Collins CO 80523-1370

LINDEN, LYNETTE LOIS, bioelectrical engineer; b. Cheyenne, Wyo., Feb. 5, 1951; d. Byron Nels and Mary Ann (Savage) L. BA with honors, U. Calif., Santa Cruz, 1972; MS, MIT, 1974, PhD, 1988. Asst. engr. Burroughs Corp., Pasadena, Calif., 1969-70, engr., cons. La Jolla, 1971-73; teaching asst. U. Calif., Santa Cruz, 1974-76, MIT, Cambridge, Mass., 1973-75, tutor, 1976-79; engr. Lincoln Labs., Lexington, 1979-80; asst. prof. engring. Boston U., 1980—; ind. rsch. sci. Watertown, Mass., 1990—. Contbr. articles to profl. jours. Mem. AAAS, Am. Chem. Soc., N.Y. Acad. Scis., Soc. Women Engrs., Sigma Xi. Achievements include research in dimensionality constraints on color perception, application of group theory to computational models of neurons, visual perception, sensory systems, living systems, and biophysics of sensory systems. Office: PO Box 138 Watertown MA 02471-0138 E-mail: lynx@mit.edu.

LINDEN, PEPPY G. museum director; b. Louisville, Dec. 19, 1949; d. Bernard Sylvan and Helen Novitsky Goldstein; m. Russell Mathew Linden, May 9, 1971 (div. May 1979). BEd, U. Mich., 1971. Cert. elem. tchr. Program coord. Project Cmty., Ann Arbor, Mich., 1971-72; sr. rsch. asst. Inst. for Social Rsch., 1972-74; infant educator dept. pediats. U. Va., Charlottesville, 1975-76; pediat. admissions and adolescent coord. Kluge Children's Rehab. Ctr., U. Va. Med. Ctr., 1976-89; exec. dir. Va. Discovery Mus., 1990—. Mem. Cable TV Citizens' Adv. Com., Charlottesville, 1992-98; mem. Social Svcs. Adv. Bd., Charlottesville, 1996—. Judge Nat. History Day, Charlottesville, 1993-96; bd. dirs. Piedmont Coun. of Arts, Charlottesville, 1989-92, Charlotteville Regional Tourism Coun., 2001—; regional bd. dirs. Sorensen Inst. for Polit. Leadership, 2001—; sec., chair Charlottesville Electoral Bd., 1993-96; election ofcl. City of Charlottesville, 1991-93; pres., v.p. North Downtown Residents' Assn., Charlottesville, 1986-89; treas. Nat. Host Program, Charlottesville, 1993-94. Named Woman of Distinction, Va. Skyline coun., Girl Scouts U.S., 1993, Artist of Yr., Piedmont Coun. of Arts, 2001. Fellow Sorensen Inst. Polit. Leadership; mem. Leadership Charlottesville Alumni Assn. Jewish. Avocations: theater, water sports, politics, film, dance. Office: Va Discovery Mus 524 E Main St Charlottesville VA 22902-5336

LINDENBAUM, JEFFRY ALAN, osteopathic family physician, consultant; b. Phila., Nov. 26, 1948; s. Sidney Harvey and Elayne Judith (Steinberg) L.; m. Mimi Carole Jacobs, June 19, 1977; children: Scott, Andrew. BA in Biology with honors, Lehigh U., 1970; DO, Phila. Coll. Osteo. Medicine, 1975. Diplomate Am. Bd. Osteo. Examiners; cert. Am. Bd. Osteo. Family Physicians. Chief intern Del. Valley Hosp., Bristol, Pa., 1975-76; pvt. practice, 1976—, Bensalem, 1992—; pres. Jeffry A. Lindenbaum D.O., P.C. Staff Frankford Bucks Hosp., Langhorne, Pa., Lower Bucks Hosp., Bristol, Pa., Frankford Hosp., Phila; disability examiner Commonwealth Pa., 1979-97. Contbr. articles to profl. jours. Mem. B'nai Brith Men's Lower Moreland Lodge. Named Humanitarian Yr. Bucks County United Way, 1991. Fellow Am. Coll. Family Physicians (del.); mem. Am. Osteo. Assn. (del., trustee Poma dist. 14), Pa. Osteo. Med. Assn., Am. Coll. Osteo. Family Physicians (bd. dirs. Enclave of Fellows), Pa. Osteo. Family Physicians, Phila. Coll. Osteo. Medicine Alumni Assn. (life), Sigma Sigma Phi (v.p., bd. dirs.), Sigma Alpha Omicron. Avocations: golf, music, fine art, collectibles, travel. Office: Atrium of Bensalem Ste 108 Hulmeville and Byberry Rds Bensalem PA 19020 E-mail: jl-crackdoc@worldnet.att.net.

LINDENBAUM, SAMUEL HARVEY, lawyer; b. N.Y.C., Mar. 29, 1935; s. Abraham M. and Belle (Axelrad) L.; m. Linda Marion Lewis, June 16, 1957; children: Erica Dale Lindenbaum Tishman, Laurie Ellen. BA cum laude, Harvard U., 1956, JD cum laude, 1959; Fulbright fellow, Oslo U., Norway, 1959-60. Bar: N.Y. 1960. Assoc. Fried, Frank, Harris, Shriver & Jacobson, N.Y.C., 1960-62; mem. Lindenbaum & Young, Bklyn., 1962-74; sr. mem. Rosenman & Colin, N.Y.C., 1974-83, of counsel, 1983—2002; mem. Kramer Levin Naftalis & Frankel, 2002—. Mem. bd. overseers Albert Einstein Coll. Medicine; chmn. exec. com. Jewish Assn. for Svcs. for the Aged; mem. Counsel Assn. for Better NY; bd. govs., mem. exec. com., v.p. Real Estate Bd. NY; bd. dirs., chmn. exec. com. Am. Friends Israel Mus. Mem. Bklyn. Bar Assn., Harmonie Club, Harvard Club, Friars Club. Home: 998 5th Ave New York NY 10028-0102 Office: Kramer Levin Naftalis & Frankel 919 Third Ave New York NY 10022-2511

LINDENBERG, STEVEN PHILLIP, counselor, consultant; b. Lancaster, Pa., Dec. 6, 1945; s. Sidney David and Ruth Lillian (Levine) L.; m. Linda Kathleen Young, Aug. 26, 1967; children: Sara Michelle, Karen Rebecca, Elisabeth Claudine. BS, Millersville U., 1968; MEd, Shippensburg State U., 1974; PhD, U. Ga., 1977. Cert. sch. psychologist, Pa. Jr. high sci. tchr. Chambersburg (Pa.) Area Sch. Dist., 1972-74; grad. asst. dept. counseling edn. Univ. Ga., Athens, 1974-77; ptnr., clin. mental health counselor Hershey (Pa.) Psychiat. Assocs., 1977-93; founder Lindenberg Inst. for Therapy, 1993—. Sch. psychologist Ctrl. Dauphin (Pa.) Sch. Dist., 1998—; co-founder, 1st vice-chair Nat. Acad. Cert. Clin. Mental Health Counselors, Falls Church, Va., 1978-80; founder Lindenberg & David, Assocs., Hershey, 1990-99; mem. focus group task force Alternate Paths to Justice for 21st Century Pa. State Supreme Ct., 1996. Mem. editorial bd.: Jour. Mental Health Counseling, 1991-94, author: Group Psychotherapy with People Who Are Dying, 1983; contbr. articles to profl. jours. Founding bd. mem. Hospice of En. Pa., Enola, 1978-87, past pres., mem. bereavement com. 1978-93; mem. profl. devel. com. Am. Cancer Soc., Harrisburg, Pa., 1986-87; past pres., mem. bd. sch. dirs. No. Lebanon Sch. Dist., Fredericksburg, Pa., 1988-93; vol. victim/offender mediator Pa. Dept. Corrections, Office of Victim Advocate, 1998—. Decorated Am. Spirit of Honor medal Citizens Com. for Army, Navy and Air Force, Inc., Lackland AFB, Tex., 1968; recipient Jesse Heiges Disting. Alumnus award Shippensburg U., 1996. Mem. AACD (bd. dirs. 1979-80), Am. Mental Health Counselors Assn. (pres. 1979-80, profl. recognition awards 1981, 89, charter mem.), Pa. Mental Health Counselors Assn. (treas. 1993-95, pres. 1995-98), Pa. Alliance Counseling Profls. (pres.-elect 1995-96, pres. 1996-98) Pa. Counselor's Assn. (eminent practitioner 1988), Dauphin County Bar Assn. (task force mem. 1994-97), Phi Kappa Phi, Kappa Delta Pi. Avocations: writing, music composition and performance, gardening. Office: Lindenberg Inst Therapy 218 W Governor Rd Hershey PA 17033-1726 E-mail: drspl5@aol.com.

LINDENBERGER, HERBERT SAMUEL, writer, literature educator; b. L.A., Apr. 4, 1929; s. Hermann and Celia (Weinkrantz) L.; m. Claire Flaherty, June 14, 1961; children: Michael James, Elizabeth Celia. BA, Antioch Coll., Yellow Springs, Ohio, 1951; PhD, U. Wash., Seattle, 1955. From instr. to prof. English and comparative lit. U. Calif., Riverside, 1954-66; prof. German and English, chmn. program comparative lit. Washington U., St. Louis, 1966-69; Avalon prof. humanities Stanford (Calif.) U., 1969—2001, Avalon prof. emeritus, 2001—, chmn. program comparative lit., 1969-82; dir. Stanford Humanities Ctr., 1991-92. Author: On Wordsworth's Prelude, 1963, Georg Büchner, 1964, (play) Lear and Cordelia at Home, 1968, Georg Trakl, 1971, Historical Drama: The Relation of Literature and Reality, 1975, Saul's Fall: A Critical Fiction, 1979, Opera: The Extravagant Art, 1984, The History in Literature: On Value, Genre, Institutions, 1990, Opera in History: From Monteverdi to Cage, 1998, Dogstory: A Memoir in Hypertext, 1999; contbr. chpt. to book: Literature and the Other Arts, 2000; contbr. articles to profl. jours. Fulbright scholar Austria, 1952-53; Guggenheim fellow, 1968-69; Nat. Endowment Humanities fellow, 1975-76, 82-83; Stanford U. Humanities Ctr. Fellow, 1982-83 Mem. MLA (pres. 1997), Am. Comparative Lit. Assn. E-mail: lindenberger@stanford.edu.

LINDENFELD, JOANN, physician, educator; b. Benton Harbor, Mich., Feb. 11, 1948; d. Nelson Albert and Viola C. Lindenfield. MD, U. MIch., 1973. Diplomate in internal medicine, cardiology and critical care medicine Am. Bd. Internal Medicine. Asst. prof. medicine U. Colo., Denver, 1980-85, assoc. prof. medicine, 1985-90, prof. medicine, 1990—. Mem. cardiovenal adv. panel FDA, Washington, 1995—; cons. for pharm. firms. Author: Geriatric Internal Medicine, 1995, 99; contbr. articles to profl. jours. Recipient numerous awards U. Colo., Denver. Fellow Am. Coll. Cardiology, Am. Heart Assn. (clin. coun. rep.); mem. Internat. Soc. Heart and Lung Transplant, Am. Soc. Transplant Physicians. Avocations: hiking, poetry, gardening, writing. Office: U Colo Health Scis Ctr 4200 E 9th Ave B130 Denver CO 80262-0001 E-mail: JoAnn.Lindenfeld@uchsc.edu.

LINDENFELD, PETER, physics educator; b. Vienna, Austria, Mar. 10, 1925; came to U.S., 1948, naturalized, 1957; s. Bela and Elda (Lachs) L.; m. Lore Kadden, May 31,1953; children: Thomas, Naomi. Student, U. Man., Can., 1942-43; BASc., U.B.C., Can., 1946, MA Sc., 1948; PhD, Columbia U., 1954. Vis. lectr. Drew U., Madison, N.J., 1952-53; instr. Rutgers U., 1953-55, asst. prof. physics, 1955-61, asso. prof., 1961-66, prof., 1966-99, prof. emeritus, 1999—. Cons. summer inst. AID, Tirupati, India, 1965; regional counselor N.J. Am.. Inst. Physics, 1963-71; dir. NSF In-svc. Insts. High Sch. Tchrs., 1964-66; Rutgers Rsch. Coun. fellow and guest scientist Faculte de Scis., U. Paris-Sud, Orsay, France, 1970-71; vis. scholar Kyoto U., Japan, 1982. Contbr. articles to profl. jours. Recipient Warren I. Susman award for excellence in teaching, 1988, Robert A. Millikan Lecture award and medal Am. Assn. Physics Tchrs., 1989. Fellow Am. Phys. Soc.; mem. AAUP, Am. Assn. Physics Tchrs. (hon. mem. N.J. sect.). Home: 121 Harris Rd Princeton NJ 08540-3375 Office: Rutgers U Dept Physics and Astronomy Piscataway NJ 08854-8019

LINDENLAUB, JOHN CHARLES, electrical engineer, educator; b. Milw., Sept. 10, 1933; m. Deborah Hart, 1957; children: Brian, Mark, Anne, David. BS, MIT, 1955, MS, 1957; PhD in Elec. Engring., Purdue U., 1961. From asst. prof. to prof. Purdue U., West Lafayette, Ind., 1961-72, prof. elec. engring., 1972—99, dir. Ctr. Instrnl. Devel. Engring., 1977-81, prof. emeritus, 1999—. Mem. tech. staff Bell Telephone Labs., 1968-69; cons. Western Elec., N.Y. State Bd. Regents, Control Data Corp., J. Warren Rsch. in Higher Edn., Nat. Technol. U. Contbr. articles to profl. jours. Recipient Helen Plants award Frontiers in Edn. Conf., 1980, 87, 93; Danforth Found. assoc., 1966. Fellow IEEE (Edn. Soc. Achievement award 1984, Schmitz award FIE Conf.), Fellow Am. Soc. Engring. Edn. (Chester F. Carlson award 1988, Disting. Svc. citation 1993, E.R.M. Disting. Svc. award 1999). Office: Purdue Univ Elec Engring Bldg Lafayette IN 47907 E-mail: john.c.lindenlaub.1@purdue.edu.

LINDENMUTH, KEVIN J. film director, film producer, writer; b. Dearborn, Mich., July 10, 1965; s. John Philip Lindenmuth and Nancy Portugal; m. Audrey Anne Geyer. BA in Film and Video Studies, U. Mich., 1987. Prodn. mgr. B Video Inc., N.Y.C., 1989—98; owner Brimstone Prodns., 1992—2001, Brimstone Media Prodns., LLC, N.Y.C., 2001—. Author: (editor) Making Movies on Your Own, 1998, The Independent Film Experience, 2002; (dir., prodr., writer): Vampires & Other Stereotypes, 1992; Addicted to Murder, 1995; The Alien Agenda: Out of Darkness, 1996; The Alien Agenda: Under the Skin, 1997; Creaturealm: From the Dead, 1998; Addicted to Murder 2: Tainted Blood, 1998; (co-dir., prodr., writer): Twisted Tales, 1992; prodr.: Creaturealm: Demons Wake, 1998; co-prodr.: There & Back: Interviews with Near-Death Experiencers, 1998; (dir., prodr.): Walking Between the Raindrops, 1998; Addicted to Murder 3: Bloodlust, 1999; dir.: Rage of the Werewolf, 1999; (co-prodr., camera, co-editor): Caring for the Caregivers: Living with Cancer, 2000; (exec. prodr., co-dir.): The Alien Conspiracy: Evil Origin, 2001; The Alien Conspiracy: Time Enough, 2001; The Alien Conspiracy: Beyond the Lost World, 2001; Blood of the Werewolf; (exec. prodr., co-writer): Werewolf Tales; (co-prodr., co-dir.) (documentary) But You Look So Well... Mem.: Horror Writers Assn.

LINDENMUTH, RICHARD ALAN, electronics company executive; b. Phila., Dec. 28, 1944; s. Ralph Lester and Evelyn Josephine (Zimmerman) Dedel L.; m. Mary-Beth Anthony, Nov. 19, 1994; children: Michael, Carol Anne, Parker Stratton. BA in Internat. Affairs, U. Colo, 1970; MBA, Wharton Sch., U. Pa., 1971. Gen. mgr. North and West Africa Singer, Beirut, Lebanon, 1972-77; dir. internat. ops. Bendix Corp., Southfield, Mich., 1978-80; pres. Lexar Bus. Comms., Inc., Woodland Hills, Calif., 1980-82; v.p., gen. mgr. Imaging Sys. divsn. Burroughs Corp., Danbury, Conn., 1982-83; pres. Bus. and Consumer Comms. divsn. ITT, Raleigh, N.C., 1983-86; pres., CEO Robinson Nugent Inc., New Albany, Ind., 1986-90; pres. The Lindenmuth Group, 1990-91; pres., CEO Interpacific, 1991—; CEO Boulder INternat., 1993—, Quantegy, Inc., 1999—, Goproaudio.com, 2000—. With USN, 1962-66. Mem. Capital City Club (Raleigh). Republican. Presbyterian. Avocations: flying, sailing, scuba diving, travel, tennis. Office: PO Box 190 2230 Marvyn Pkwy Opelika AL 36803-0190

LINDER, BERTRAM NORMAN, foundation administrator, horse-breeder, actor; b. N.Y.C., Nov. 24, 1915; s. Albert Aaron and Bess (Newman) L.; m. Eleanor Jones (dec.); children: Robert Allan (dec.), Denise J.; m. Mary Ellen Smith. BA cum laude, Williams Coll., 1936; postgrad., Yale U., 1937-38, Columbia U., 1938-39. V.p. Linder Bros., Inc., Scranton, Pa., 1940-65, pres., treas., 1965-80, Albert A. & Bertram N. Linder Found., Inc., N.Y.C., 1965—; owner Hickory Hill Farm, Dalton, Pa., 1947—. Author: Songs to the Night, 1941. Pres. Jewish Fedn., Scranton, 1949-52; pres., co-founder Child Guidance & Psychiatry Ctr., Lackawanna County, Pa.; chmn. adv. bd. Salvation Army, Scranton, 1947-50; pres. United Way, Lackawanna County, 1960-63. 1st lt. inf. U.S. Army, 1943-46, ETO. (fought during D-Day Normany Invasion), 5 Campaign Stars, Presidential Citation. Decorated Bronze Star with V for Valor, Purple Heart, Belgian Fourragere; recipient Community Svc. award Scranton C. of C., 1949, Salvation Army, 1950, Citizenship award AFL-CIO, 1962, 65, Americanism award B'nai B'rith, 1965. Mem. AFTRA, SAG, Thoroughbred Owners and Breeders Assn., Thoroughbred of Am. Club (Lexington, Ky.), N.Y. Thoroughbred Breeders, Ky. Thoroughbred Assn., Penn Horse Breeders Assn., 4th U.S. Inf. Divsn. Assn., B'nai B'rith, Phi Beta Kappa. Republican. Jewish. Avocations: fishing, travel. Home: Hickory Hill Farm W Main St Dalton PA 18414-9522 Office: Linder Found Inc 305 E 40th St New York NY 10016-2189

LINDER, CARL H., III, diversified financial services company executive; BBA, U. Cinn., 1975. Co-pres. Am. Fin. Group, Inc., 1995—. Office: Am Fin Group Inc 1 E 4th St Cincinnati OH 45202-3717

LINDER, ELAINE B. social worker; b. Jamestown, N.Y., June 1, 1937; d. Clifford L. and Florence (Stanton) Bender; m. Lester W. Linder, Sept. 20, 1958 (dec.); children: Marshal Wayne, Marsden Wayne, Michele Elaine, Marla Noel. BMus., Houghton Coll., 1958; MSW, Syracuse U., 1986. Social worker Syracuse U., Geneva; music tchr. Phelps-Clifton Springs Cen. Sch. Dist., Clifton Springs; social worker-counselor Renaissance Group Home for Girls, Cmty. Counseling Ctr., Lyons, NY. Dir. music Coolspring Presbyn. Ch. Home: 158 Latonka Dr Mercer PA 16137-9360

LINDER, HARVEY RONALD, lawyer, arbitrator, mediator; b. Pitts., July 23, 1949; s. Charles Joseph and Rose (Ruben) Linder; m. Reva Rebecca Vertman, Aug. 14, 1971 (div.); children: Zalman F., Seth A.; m. Gail Lynne Silberman, May 26, 2002. BA, Duquesne U., 1971, JD, 1975. Bar: Pa. 1975, U.S. Dist. Ct. (we. dist.) Pa. 1975, U.S. Supreme Ct. 1979. Legal intern Dist. Atty.'s Office, Pitts., 1974-75; asst. mgr. arbitration U.S. Steel, 1975-80, mgr. labor rels., 1980-81, supt. employee rels. Clairton, Pa., 1981-83; corp. dir. employee rels. U.S. Steel Agri-Chemicals, Atlanta, 1984-86; corp. dir. law and human resources LaRoche Industries Inc., 1986-88, v.p., gen. counsel, 1988-96, Orion Mgmt. Svcs. Inc., 1996-97, SED Internat. Inc., 1997-99. Arbitrator, mediator, 1996—; pres. A.C.I.R.A., 1987-90. Contbr. poetry and photography to Duquesne Literary Mag., 1968-74. Exec. cons. Jr. Achievement, Pitts., 1978-83; head coach Atlanta Jewish Cmty. Ctr., Dunwoody, Ga., 1984—, bd. dirs., 1991—, v.p., 2001—; pres. B'nai Torah Synagogue, 1995-97, Hunter's Woods Homeowners' Assn., Dunwoody, 1986-87; commr.

Baseball & Soccer Leagues; bd. dirs. Atlanta Jewish Fedn., 1995-96, Atlanta YAD, 2000. Steel fellow Am. Iron and Steel Inst., 1977-85. Mem. ABA, Allegheny County Bar Assn., Indsl. Rels. Rsch. Assn., Duquesne U. Law Sch. Alumni Assn. (bd. dirs. 1980-84), B'nai B'rith (local v.p. 1975-80), Amer-Israel C. of C. (bd. dirs. 1993—). Democrat. Avocations: coaching, collecting books and sports memorabilia. Home and Office: 7025 Northgreen Dr Atlanta GA 30328-1453

LINDER, IRIS KAY, lawyer; b. Davenport, Iowa, May 3, 1952; d. Forrest Wesley and Josephine Jeanette (Barnett) Shaffer; 1 son, Eric Scott Socolofsky; m. Stephen J. Linder. BS, Mich. State U., 1976; JD, U. Mich., 1980. Bar: Mich. 1980, U.S. Dist. Ct. (we. and ea. dists.) Mich. 1980. Ptnr. Fraser, Trebilcock, Davis & Dunlap, P.C., Lansing., Mich., 1980—. Adj. faculty Cooley Law Sci., 1999—. Co-author: Michigan Usury Manual, 1982; contbr. chpt. to Litigation of the Commercial Case, 1992. Mem. planning bd. Ingham County Office for Young Children, 1986—87; mem. Mayor's Parking Adv. Com. , 1990—93; chair group com. Shared Vision Sys. and Rsch., 1994—96; bd. dirs. Capitol Area Girl Scouts USA, 1986—88, Capitol Area Polit. Action Com., 1990—96, chair, 1995; bd. dirs. Capitol Enterprise Forum, 1989—95, pres., 1993; bd. dirs. Capitol Area United Way1, 0994—2001, Infoguys, Inc., 1996—99, Congregation Kehillet Israel, Venture Ctr., Inc., 1996—2001, chair, 1999—2001. Recipient Book award U. Mich. Law Sch., 1980. Mem. ABA, Ingham County Bar Assn., State Bar Assn. Mich., Lansing Regional C. of C. (bus. women's coun. 1984-87, bd. dirs. 1987-92, dir. govt. affairs 1991-92, Tireless award 1992, Small Bus. Advocate of Yr. award 1993), Lansing Assn. Career Women (bd. dirs. 1985-87), Office Fin. and INs. Svcs. Securities Coun., Athena Found. (bd. dirs. 1986-87). Home: 2550 Dustin Rd Okemos MI 48864-2073 Office: Fraser Trebilcock Davis & Dunlap 1000 Michigan Nat Towers Lansing MI 48933 E-mail: ilinder@fraserlawfirm.com.

LINDER, JACQUES L. music educator, musician; b. Vincennes, Ind., Sept. 25, 1945; s. Walter Perry and Grace Lorene Linder. MusB in Edn., U. Evansville, 1967; MusM in Piano, U. Ill., 1969; pvt. piano instruction, Harriet Shirvan, 1973—78, Gabriel Chodos, 1983—88. Instr. piano Performing Art Sch. Worcester, Mass., 1972—75; pvt. piano tchr., 1974—90, St. Petersburg, Fla., 1991—. Instr. piano Clark U., Worcester, 1979—90, instr. primary theory, 1985—86; instr. piano U. South Fla., Tampa, 1990—2000, performance program coord., chairperson piano faculty cmty. music divsn., 1990—95, artistic dir., 1995—2000; founder, co-dir. The Commonwealth Competition for Young Pianists Clark U., Worcester. Musician: (soloist) Ill. Ctr. Orch., 1979, Ill. Ctrl. Orch., 1982, Worcester Consortium Orch., 1982, (solo recital) Belknap Mill Concert Series, 1984, 1986, Worcester Art Mus., 1985, 1986, 1987, Camargo Found., 1988, Colgate U., 1989, U. Md. Coll. Park Contemporary Music Festival, 1989, Fla. So. U., 1992, Eckerd Coll. Festival Performing Arts, 1996, U. South Fla., 1990—2000, (guest soloist) Conf. on Open Structure in 20th Century Music, 1986, (solo performance) Assn. U. Composers Conf., 1988, many others. Home: 816 25th Ave N Saint Petersburg FL 33704

LINDER, JAMES, pathologist, director; b. Omaha, Oct. 21, 1954; BS in Biochem. and Microbiology, Iowa State U. of Sci. & Tech., Ames, 1972—76; MD, U. of Nebr. Coll. of Medicine, Omaha, 1977—80. Cert. in Anatomic & Clinical Pathology 1980, Cytopathology Special Competence 1989. Asst. prof. Univ. of Nebr. Med. Ctr., Omaha, 1983—86, assoc. prof., 1986—89; prof. Univ. of Nebr. Coll. of Medicine, 1989—; vice chmn. Univ. of Nebr. Med. Ctr., 1992—96; assoc. dean Univ. of Nebr. Coll. of Medicine, 1995—98, interim dean, 1998—2000. V.p. Cytyc Healthcare Ventures, Boxborough, Mass., 2001—; chief med. officer Cytyc Corp., Boxborough, 1995—. Author: Atlas of Pathology, 1999, Bronchoalveolar Lavage, 1988; editor: Errors and Pitfalls in Diagnostic Cytology, 1997, Anderson's Pathology, 10th edit., 1996 (Excellence in Med. Publs., Am. Med. Writers Assn., 1996); contbr. over 100 peer reviewed articles. Bd. dirs. Omaha Children's Mus., Omaha, 2001—. Recipient Cert. of Recognition, US & Canadian Acads. of Pathology, 1990, 1994. Mem.: ACGME (accreditation appeals panel 1998), Am. Registry of Pathology (exec. bd. 1998), Am. Soc. Clin. Pathologists (patient safety initiative task force 2000, corp. devel. com. 2001, publs. adv. com. 2001, pres. 1998—99), US & Can. Acad. of Pathology (coun. mem. 2001—02). Avocations: Kempo, glass blowing, golf. Office: Univ of Nebr Med Ctr 983135 Nebr Med Ctr Omaha NE 68198-3135 Office Fax: 402-559-2990. Business E-Mail: jlinder@unmc.edu.

LINDER, JOHN E. congressman, dentist; b. Deer River, Minn., Sept. 9, 1942; s. Henry and Vera Elizabeth Davis L.; m. Lynne Leslee Peterson, 1963; children: Kristine Kerry, Matthew John. BS, U. Minn., 1964, DDS, 1967. Pvt. practice, Atlanta, 1969—82; mem. Ga. Ho. of Reps., 1975-80, 82-90; pres. Linder Fin. Corp., 1977-92; mem. U.S. Congress from 4th Ga. Dist., 1993-97, U.S. Congress from 11th Ga. Dist., 1997—. House rules com., subcom. on legis. process, steering com., former mem. Nat. Rep. Congl. Com. exec. com. U.S. Ho. of Reps., chmn. Founder I Care, 1970. Capt. USAF, 1967-69. Mem. ADA, Ga. Dental Assn., No. Dist. Dental Soc., Rotary. Republican. Presbyterian. Office: US Ho of Reps 1727 Longworth HOB Washington DC 20515-0001*

LINDERMAN, JEANNE HERRON, priest; b. Erie, Pa., Nov. 14, 1931; d. Robert Leslie and Ella Marie (Stearns) Herron; m. James Stephens Linderman; children: Mary Susan, John Randolph, Richard Webster, Craig Stephens, Mark Herron, Elizabeth Stewart. BS in Indsl. and Labor Rels., Cornell U., 1953; MDiv magna cum laude, Lancaster Theol. Sem., 1981; postgrad., clin. pastoral edn., Del. State Hosp., New Castle, 1981. Ordained priest, Episcopal Ch. Mem. pers. staff Hengerer Co., Buffalo, 1953-55; chaplain Cathedral Ch. St. John, Wilmington, Del., 1981-82; priest-in-charge Christ Episcopal Ch., Delaware City, 1982-87, vicar, 1987-91; assoc. rector St. Andrew's Episcopal Ch., Wilmington, Del., 1991-95, priest in charge, 1995-96; assoc. priest for pastoral care The Episc. Ch. of Sts. Andrew and Matthew, 1998—. Chair human sexuality task force, Diocese of Del., 1981-82, mem. clergy compensation com. and diocesan coun., 1982-86, pres. standing com., 1991—, com. on constitution and canons, 1989, designer and leader religious/spiritual retreats. Author, editor hist. study papers. Bd. dirs. St. Michael's Day Nursery, Wilmington, 1985-88; mem. secondary schs. com. Cornell U., bd. dirs., chmn. pers. com. Geriatric Svcs. of Del., 1989-96, sec. bd., 1993-96. Mem. Episcopal Women's Caucus, Del. Episcopal Clergy Assn., Nat. Assn. Episcopal Clergy, DAR (v.-regent Caesar Rodney chpt. 1996—), Mayflower Soc. (elder 2000—, surgeon 1983-95), Nat. Soc. Colonial Dames Am. Del., Dutch Colonial Soc. Del., Stoney Run Questers (pres.), Cornell Women's Club Del. (pres. 1966), Women of St. James the Less (pres. 1972-73), Women's Witnessing Cmty. at Lambeth, Patriotic Soc. in Del. (sec.-treas. conv. 1965-68), Chi Omega. Republican. Avocations: history, genealogy, travel. Home: 307 Springhouse Ln Hockessin DE 19707-9691 Office: The Episcopal Ch of Sts Andrew and Matthews Eighth And Shipley St Wilmington DE 19801 E-mail: linderjs@bellatlantic.net.

LINDERMAN, WILLIAM EARL, elementary school educator, writer; b. San Francisco, Mar. 22, 1955; s. Earl William and Marlene (Melamed) L.; m. Marilyn Monica Spitz, June 28, 1980; children: David William, Eva Alicia. BA in Elem. Edn., Ariz. State U., 1978, MA in Elem. Edn. Elem. sch. tchr., Ariz. Tchr. grade 3 Paradise Valley Sch. Dist., Phoenix, 1979—. Author: Calculator Fun, Hands on Math, One Minute Motivators; author or contbr. chpts. to 75 books; featured in ABC Radio Nat. News. Song leader at svcs. Towers Jail, Phoenix; lay minister singing scriptures ministry Phoenix 1st Assembly of God, food ministry Ch. on the St. Phoenix. Recipient Golden Bell award Ariz. Sch. Bd. Assn., Thanks to Tchrs. award Nat. Found. Improvement Edn./Nat. Alliance of Bus./Apple Computer; nominated as Author of the Month by McGraw-Hill Children's Pub. Co. Republican. Avocations: writing music, playing piano, guitar, helping children, writing books. Home: 18021 N 50th Pl Scottsdale AZ 85254-7567 Office: Copper Canyon Elem Sch 17650 E 54th St Scottsdale AZ 85254 E-mail: WLinderman@PVUSD.K12.az.us.

LINDES, DOROTHYANN MARLENE, physician; b. Pueblo, Colo., June 11, 1949; d. Nick J. and Dorothy M. (Zbacnik) Zakrasek; m. Conrad Lindes, Aug. 21, 1976 (div. 1992); children: Eli, Derek. BS in Biology, Creighton U., 1971; MD, U. Nebr., 1975. Diplomate Am. Bd. Family Practice. Resident in family practice Grant Hosp., Columbus, Ohio, 1975-78; physician North Fork Med. Clinic, Paonia, Colo., 1978-84; chief of staff Delta (Colo.) County Meml. Hosp., 1982, chief ob-gyn, pediat., 1983; physician S.W. Family Physicians, Inc., Cleve., 1984-2000; mem. staff S.W. Gen. Hosp., 1984-2000, chmn. pharmacy, therapeutics, infectious disease com., 1993-2000; physician East Oahu Med. Ctr., Honolulu, 2000—; mem. Queen's Med. Ctr. and Castle Med. Ctr., 2000—02, St. Francis Med. Ctr., Honolulu, 2002—. Vol. recycling hosp. supplies for third world countries Intervol. Preceptor med. students John A. Burns Sch. of Medicine, Honolulu, 2001. Mem. Am. Acad. Family Physicians, Intermed Internat. Inc. (bd. dirs. 2000—), Physicians Social Responsibility, Internat. Physicians Prevention Nuclear War, Cousteau Soc. Avocations: piano, ballroom dancing, interior decorating, aerobics. Office: East Oahu Med Ctr 850 W Hind Dr Ste 110 Honolulu HI 96821-1845

LINDESMITH, DIXIE LOU, retired geriatrics nurse; b. Butler, Ohio, Mar. 11, 1934; d. Gerald Edward and Aldine Marie (Barre) Beam; children: Daniel, Dennis, Denise; m. Ronald W. Lindesmith, Oct. 28, 2000. Lic. practical nurse, Timken-Mercy Hosp., Canton, Ohio, 1971; ADN, Walsh Coll., Canton, 1990. Cert. geriatric nurse, gerontol. nurse. Charge nurse Wyandot County Nursing Home, 1994-95; DON Hospitality House, Massillon, Ohio, 1995-97, with, 1997—2000; dir. nursing The Pines, Canton, 1998-2000; ret., 2000. Home: 2614 10th St NW Canton OH 44708-4274

LINDESMITH, LARRY ALAN, physician, administrator; b. Amarillo, Tex., July 27, 1938; s. Lyle J. and Imogene Agnes (Young) L.; m. Patricia Ann Brady, June 6, 1959 (div. Mar. 1973); children: Robert James, Lisa Ann; m. Diane Joyce Bakken, Nov. 22, 1973; children: Abigail Arleen, Nathan Lyle, David Alan. BA, U. Colo., 1959; MD, Bowman-Gray Sch. Medicine, Winston-Salem, N.C., 1963. Diplomate Am. Bd. Internal Medicine, Am. Bd. I.M.-Pulmonary Disease; cert. Am. Bd. Ind. Med. Examiners; cert. med. rev. officer Med. Rev. Officer Certification Coun.; Nat. Inst. Occupational Safety and Health B Reader; provider ACLS, advanced trauma life support. Medical intern U. Chgo. Hosps., Clinics, 1963-64; I.M. resident U. Colo. Med. Ctr., Denver, 1964-66; pulmonary disease fellowship U. Colo. Med. Ctr., Webb-Waring Lung Inst., 1966-67; asst. dir. infectious and pulmonary disease svc. Madigan Gen. Hosp., Tacoma, 1967-69; chief pulmonary disease Gundersen Clinic, Ltd., La Crosse, Wis., 1969-87, chief pulmonary and occupational medicine, 1979-89, chmn. dept. medicine, 1987-93; chief occupational health, preventive medicine, 1988-99; med. dir. of employee health and safety Gundersen Luth. Med. Ctr., 1997—2002, mem. emeritus staff, 2002—. Bd. govs. Gundersen Clinic, Ltd., 1987-93; adj. prof. phys. therapy U. Wis., La Crosse, 1977—; cons. VA Hosp., Tomah, Wis., 1977-93, Comty. Meml. Hosp., Winona, Minn., 1996-2002, Tomah Meml. Hosp., 1995-99; clin. asst. prof. internal medicine U. Wis., Madison, 1982-92, clin. assoc. prof., 1992—; med. dir. RESTOR U. Wis., La Crosse, 1986-95, Svcs. to Bus. and Industry Gundersen/Luth. Med. Ctr., La Crosse, 1987-94; mem. occupational medicine boardwriting com. Am. Bd. Preventive Medicine, 1992-97. Contbr. book chpts. and articles to profl. publs. Mem. Air Pollution Control Coun. State of Wis. Dept. Natural Resources, 1978-81; chmn. bd. dirs. Greater La Crosse Area C. of C., 1991; vice-chmn. bd. control Luther H.S., Onalaska, Wis., 1990-93, chmn. found. bd., 1999—. Maj. USAR, 1968-69. Boettcher Found. scholar, 1955-59; named Pagliara Tchr. of Yr. Gundersen Med. Found., 1984; recipient Dist. Svc. award Am. Lung Assn. Wis., 1988. Fellow Am. Coll. Chest Physicians, Am. Coll. Occupational and Environ. Medicine (assoc., chmn. pvt. practice coun., chmn. occupational lung disorders com., treas., med. ctr. occupl. health com. 1996-98, chmn. 1998-2000); mem. AMA, Am. Bd. Preventive Medicine (occupational medicine com. 1991-97), Am. Assn. Respiratory Therapy, Clin. Sleep Soc., Am. Thoracic Soc. (Wis. counselor 1978-81), Ctrl. States Occupational Medicine Assn. (bd. govs. 1984-95, pres. 1991), Am. Lung Assn. Wis. (pres. 1975-77), Wis. Thoracic Soc. (gen. conf. chmn. 1987), State Med. Soc. Wis. (chmn. environ. and occupational health com. 1989-91). Republican. Lutheran. Avocation: photography.

LINDGREN, A(LAN) BRUCE, church administrator; b. Grand Rapids, Mich., July 1, 1948; m. Carole Coonce; children: Stacey, Michael, David (dec.). BS in Sociology, Mich. State U., 1970; MDiv, St. Paul Sch. Theology, 1975. Ordained high priest. Campus minister Park Coll., 1975-77; dir. ministerial edn. Temple Sch., 1986-92; exec. min., World Ch. sec., exec. asst. to 1st presidency Cmty. of Christ, 1992—. Dir. devel. basic leadership curriculum Temple Sch., 1977-86. Editor: Leaders Handbook, 1985-92. Office: Cmty of Christ 1001 W Walnut Independence MO 64050

LINDGREN, CARL EDWIN, educational consultant, antiquarian, historian; b. Coeburn, Va., Nov. 20, 1949; s. Carl and Ruby (Corder) L.; m. Lynn Stewart, 1976 (div. 1979). A in Edn. with honors, N.W. Jr. Coll., 1970; BA in Edn., U. Miss., 1972, MEd, 1977, EdS, 1993; DEd, U. South Africa, 1999. FCP, Coll. of Preceptors, London, 1993. Coord. dept. edn. Delta Hills Edn. Assn., 1976-79; lectr. photography U. Miss., 1979-81; instr. health edn. Batesville Job Corps Ctr. U.S. Dept. Labor, 1980-82; pres., dir. Inst. for Ednl. and Hist. Rsch., London, England and Courtland, Miss., 1981—. Chair univ. faculty, chair Ctr. for Medieval Studies, Azaliah U., 2001--; mem. faculty Am. Mil. U. Contbr. over 200 articles to profl. jours. and mags.; author 10 books; mem. several adv., rev. and editl. bds. including London Inst. Sci. Tech., Ednl. Forum, Introductions, others; one-man shows and exhbns. U.S., Eng. and India. Capt., historian Brit. N.Am. Command Legion of Frontiersmen, 1999; lay assoc. the Priesthood, Handmaids of the Precious Blood, Cor Jesu Monastery; mem. Internet Franciscan Fraternity, Italy, Confraternity of the Most Holy Rosary (Dominican 15th Century); oblate novice Order of St. Benedict. Recipient Acad. Achievement award, 1970; EDPA fellow, 1973, Robert A. Taft fellow, 1977; Hon. Life Fellowship award (Jnana Ratna) World Jnana Sadhak Soc., Calcutta, 1978, Cert. of Excellence and Svc. Associateship award India Internat. Photog. Coun., New Delhi, 1991, Mahatma Gandhi Meml. award, 1994, Brotherhood of Blessed Gerard; decorated Order of St. Ignatius of Antioch (Vatican), Noble Compania de Ballesteros Hijosdalgo de San Felipe y Santiago. Fellow Royal Soc. Arts, Royal Asiatic Soc., Soc. Antiquaries of Scotland, Coll. Preceptors of Essex; mem. Royal Hist. Soc., Am. History of Edn. Soc., Humanitarian Soc., Commissione Internazionale Pre Lo Studio Degli Ordini Cavallereschi, Istituto Araldico Genealogico Italiano, Associazione Possessori di Certificazoni rilasciate dal Corpo dei Re d'Armi di Spagna, Cambridge U. Heraldic and Geneal. Soc., Am. Acad. Rsch. Historians of Medieval Spain, Soc. for Study of Crusades and the Latin East, Internat. Inst. Study of Chivalric Orders (vice chair), Am. Soc. for Chivalric Rsch. (pres.), Internat. Crusade for Holy Relics, DubhGhaill Usher (U.S.A.)-The Black Rod-Clann O Dubhghaill, Medieval Acad. Am., Asiatic Soc. Calcutta (affiliate), Phi Alpha Theta, Phi Delta Kappa, Kappa Delta Pi, Phi Theta Kappa, KC. Republican. Home: Avalon Woods 10431 Highway 51 Courtland MS 38620-9425 Office: 10431 Highway 51 Courtland MS 38620-9425 E-mail: lindgren@panola.com.

LINDGREN, CHARLOTTE HOLT, English language educator; b. Ipswich, Mass., Jan. 5, 1924; d. Hilmer Harold and Edith Grace (Whittier) L.; m. Donald James Winslow, Aug. 11, 1978. AB, Boston U., 1945, AM, 1947, PhD, 1961; MA (hon.), Emerson Coll., 1967. Tchr. Pinkerton Acad., Derry, N.H., 1945-46, Medfield (Mass.) H.S., 1947-49; adminstrv. asst. Boston Univ., 1949-60; prof. Emerson Coll., Boston, 1960-89, chmn. english dept., 1965-80, prof. emerita, 1989—. Co-leader Emerson Abroad Program, 1966-78; corporator Lasell Coll., Auburndale, Mass., 1997—. Co-author: William Barnes Dorset Engravings, 1986 (Mansell-Playdell award 1986), Gerald Warner Brace: Writer, Sailor, Teacher, 1998; editor: The Love Poems and Letters of William Barnes, 1986; contbr. articles to History Today, Dorset Yr. Book, T. Hardy Jour. Mem. Thomas Hardy Soc., William Barnes Soc., Herman Melville Soc., Women in Arts, Phi Beta Kappa. Avocations: photography, book reviewing. Home: 23 Maple St Auburndale MA 02466-2404 E-mail: lindwin24@aol.com.

LINDGREN, D(ERBIN) KENNETH, JR. retired lawyer; b. Mpls., Aug. 25, 1932; s. Derbin Kenneth and Margaret (Anderson) L.; m. Patricia Ann Ransier, Dec. 17, 1955; children— Christian Kenneth, Carol Ann, Charles Derbin BS, U. Minn., 1954, JD, 1958. Bar: Minn. 1958, U.S. Supreme Ct. 1968, U.S. Tax Ct. 1959, U.S. Ct. Appeals (D.C. cir.) 1981. Gen. practice law, Mpls., 1958-99; mem. Larkin, Hoffman, Daly & Lindgren, Ltd., 1960-95, of counsel, 1995; ret., 1995. Contbr. articles to profl. jours. Active Ind. Sch. Dist. 287 Bd. Edn. (Area Vocat. Tech. Coll.), 1979-83, Ind. Sch. Dist. 274 Bd. Edn., Hopkins, Minn., 1970-76, chmn., 1972-76; trustee Mpls. Soc. Fine Arts, 1982-88, Minn. Landscape Arboretum Found., 1989-99, pres., 1992-95; bd. overseers Mpls. Inst. Art, 1986-88, Mpls. Coll. Art and Design, 1980-86, vice-chmn., 1982-83, chmn., 1983-86, trustee, 1988-96; active Govs. Commn. on Reform Govt., 1983. Lt. USAF, 1955-57. Fellow Am. Coll. Trust and Estate Counsel; mem. ABA, Minn. Bar Assn., Hennepin County Bar Assn., Interlachen Country Club, Troon Golf and Country Club, Alpha Delta Phi, Phi Delta Phi. Presbyterian. Home: 11003 E Desert Vista Dr Scottsdale AZ 85255-8061 also: 4804 France Ave S # 2 Edina MN 55410-1756 E-mail: dklindgren@earthlink.net.

LINDGREN, JOHN RALPH, philosophy educator, writer; b. Oak Park, Ill., Oct. 8, 1933; s. J. Francis Lindgren and Leona G. Toussaint; m. Shirley A. Tryon, Dec. 27, 1958; children: Thomas, Michael, David, Timothy, Kathryn. BS, Northwestern U., 1959; MA in Philosophy, Marquette U., 1961, PhD in Philosophy, 1963. Instr. Coll. Holy Cross, Worcester, Mass., 1962-64, asst. prof. philosophy, 1964-65, Lehigh U., Bethlehem, Pa., 1965-69, assoc. prof. philosophy, 1969-79, prof. philosophy, 1979-95, William Wilson Selfridge prof. philosophy, 1985-88, Clara H. Stewardson prof. philosophy, 1989-95; prof. emeritus, 1995. Vis. scholar U. Pa. Sch. Law, Phila., 1977-78, Oxford (Eng.) U., 1986. Author: The Social Philosophy of Adam Smith, 1973, Sex Discrimination in Higher Education, 1984, The Law of Sex Discrimination, 1984, 88; editor: The Early Writings of Adam Smith, 1967, Horizon of Justice, 1995, Law and Ritual, 1997, Semiotics and the Human Sciences, 1998, The Law vs. the People, 2000. With U.S. Army, 1953-55. Mem. Internat. Assn. Philosophy of Law and Social Philosophy (exec. bd. 1981-83, 89-91), Nat. Soc. Philosophy and Pub. Affairs (exec. bd. 1987), Internat. Assn. Semiotics of Law. Democrat. Avocations: genealogy, gardening, photography. Office: Lehigh U Dept Philosophy 15 University Dr Bethlehem PA 18015-3057 E-mail: jrl3@lehigh.edu.

LINDGREN, RICHARD DAN, retired radiologist, healthcare administrator; b. Forest City, Iowa, June 17, 1931; s. Gilmore Rueben and Hazel Marie (Hill) L.; m. Ardeth Elaine Lindgren, Jan. 2, 1960; children: Laura, Eric, Mark, Amy. BA in Gen. Sci., U. Iowa, 1953, MD, 1956; BS in Mgmt., Upper Iowa U., 1988, BS in Acctg., 1992. Ret. radiologist. Capt. U.S. Army, 1960-62. Mem. Evangelical Covenant Ch. Home: 6006 Greentree Rd Madison WI 53711-3126

LINDGREN, TIMOTHY JOSEPH, supply company executive; b. N.Y.C., Dec. 7, 1937; s. Carl Herbert and Ruth Elizabeth (Pickering) L.; m. Barbara Fiorini, Feb. 7, 1957; children: Sharon, Mark, Susan. AA, Pierce Coll., Woodland Hills, Calif., 1959; BS in Prodn. Mgmt., Calif. State U., Northridge, 1961; MBA in Indsl. Relations, UCLA, 1962. Registered profl. engr., Calif. cert. tchr., Calif. Systems analyst, methods acct. Pacific Tel. & Tel., Van Nuys, Calif., 1964-65; dir. mfg. Olga Co., 1965-69; dir. prodn. Calif. Almond Orchards, Bakersfield, 1970-72, gen. mgr., 1972-73; pres. United Wholesale Lumber Co., Montebello, Calif., 1973-77; pres., chief exec. officer Fruit Growers Supply Co., Sherman Oaks, 1978—. Mem. Calif. C. of C. (chair com. on agrl. & natural resources). Office: Fruit Growers Supply Co 14130 Riverside Dr Sherman Oaks CA 91423-2313

LINDGREN, WILLIAM DALE, librarian; b. Peoria, Ill., Mar. 8, 1936; s. Hugh Gottfried and Olive Kathryn (Myer) L. BA, Bradley U., 1958, MA, 1959; MSLS, U. Ill., 1967. Tchr. Limestone High Sch., Bartonville, Ill., 1960-68; asst. dir. Learning Resources Ctr. Ill. Cen. Coll., East Peoria, 1968-73, dir., 1973—. Mem. transition bd. merger of four systems, 1993-94; bd. dirs. Alliance Libr. Sys.; mem. Ill. State Libr. Com. on Resolving the Unserved Problem, 1996—. Singer Ephphetha Schola Cantorum Gregoriana, 1996—. Chmn. East Peoria Oral History Com., 1983-84, Resource Sharing Alliance West Ctrl. Ill. Adv. Coun., 1985—; v.p. Ill. Valley Libr. System, pres. bd., 1988, 90—, treas., 1989, bd. dirs., 1990—; regional chair recruitment com. Am. Heart Assn., 1996—. Mem. ALA, Ill. Libr. Assn. (co-chair cracker barrels program ann. conf. 1989, 90, 91), Assn. Ednl. Media Tech., Assn. Ednl. Media and Tech. Ill., Coun. Libr. Tech., Creve Coeur Club (Peoria).

LINDH, PATRICIA SULLIVAN, banker, former government official; b. Toledo, Oct. 2, 1928; d. Lawrence Walsh and Lillian Winifred (Devlin) Sullivan; m. H. Robert Lindh, Jr., Nov. 12, 1955; children: Sheila, Deborah, Robert. BA, Trinity Coll., Washington, 1950, LL.D., 1975, Walsh Coll., Canton, Ohio, 1975, U. Jacksonville, 1975. Editor Singapore Am. Newspaper, 1957-62; spl. asst. to counsellor to Pres., 1974; spl. asst. to Pres., 1975-76; dep. asst. sec. state for ednl. and cultural affairs Dept. State, 1976-77; v.p., dir. corp. comms. Bank Am., L.A., 1978-84, corp. pub. rels. San Francisco, 1985-93. Trustee La. Arts and Sci. Center, 1970-73, Calif. Hosp. Med. Ctr., 1979-84; bd. dirs. Jr. League of Baton Rouge, 1969, Children's Bur. Los Angeles, 1979, 84, USO Northern Calif.; Rep. state vice chairwoman La., 1970-74; Rep. nat. committeewoman, La., 1974; mem. pub. affairs com. San Francisco World Affairs Coun., 1985; adv. bd. Jr. League Los Angeles, 1980-84; bd. visitors Southwestern U. Sch. Law. Roman Catholic. Home: 12380 Grandee Ct San Diego CA 92128-2120

LINDHEIM, RICHARD DAVID, television company executive, university official; b. N.Y.C., May 28, 1939; s. Gilbert R. and Pearl (Gruskin) L.; m. Elaine Lavis, Dec. 22, 1963; children: Susan Patricia, David Howard. BS, U. Redlands, 1961; postgrad, U. So. Calif., 1963. Adminstrv. asst. story dept. CBS, L.A., 1962-64; project dir. entertainment testing ASI Market Rsch., 1964-69; v.p. program research NBC, 1969-78, v.p. dramatic programs, 1978-79; producer Universal TV, 1979-81, v.p. current programs, 1981-85, sr. v.p. series programming, 1986-87, exec. v.p. creative affairs, 1987-91; exec. v.p. program strategy MCA TV Group, 1991-92; exec. v.p. Paramount TV Group, 1992-99; exec. dir. Inst. for Creative Techs., U. So. Calif., L.A., 1999—; with ICT, Marina Del Rey, Calif. Asst. prof. Calif. State U.; sr. lectr. U. So. Calif.; lectr. UCLA; reviewer NEH; bd. dirs. Am. Fgn. Svc. Intercultural Program-USA. Author: (with Richard Blum) Primetime: Network Television Programming, 1987, Inside Television Producing, 1991; contbr. articles to profl. jours. Mem. Acad. TV Arts and Scis., Producers Guild Am., Writers Guild Am. Democrat. Jewish. Avocations: model railroading, photography, music, traveling. Office: ICT 4676 Admiralty Way Ste 1001 Marina Del Rey CA 90292 *In this sophisticated society there are fewer and fewer opportunities for the individual. Technology has made most tasks too complex for one man. As a result the ability to work with other people and to provide leadership and management to groups of people has become vital. The key ingredients are communication, respect for others, and a feeling of belonging, while working in a relaxed, casual environment, where the leader is responsible and receptive.*

LINDHOLM, CLIFFORD FALSTROM, II, engineering executive, mayor; b. Passaic, N.J., Dec. 8, 1930; s. Albert William and Edith (Neandross) L.; m. Margery Nye (div.); children: Clifford, Elizabeth, John; m. Karen Cooper, Oct. 7, 1989. BS in Engrng., Princeton U., 1953; M in Engrng., Stevens Inst. Tech., 1957. Supr. prodn. GM, Linden, N.J., 1953-56; chmn. bd. Falstrom Co., Passaic, 1956—. Bd. dirs. N.J. Mfg. Ins. Co., Trenton, N.J. Reins. Co., Trenton, Albert Payson Terhune Found., N.J. Employers Assn. N.J. Mayor Twp. Montclair, N.J., 1988-92; pres. Montclair Bd. Edn., 1968-72. Mem. N.J. Bus. and Industry Assn. (bd. dirs. 1977—), Montclair Soc. Engrs. (pres. 1998-2000), Montclair Golf Club, Mantoloking Yacht Club. Republican. Mem. Ch. of Christ. Home: 10 Mountainside Park Ter Montclair NJ 07043-1209 Office: Falstrom Co 3 Falstrom Ct Passaic NJ 07055

LINDHOLM, DWIGHT HENRY, lawyer; b. Blackduck, Minn., May 27, 1930; s. Henry Nathanial and Viola Eudora (Gummert) L.; m. Loretta Catherine Brown, Aug. 29, 1958; children: Douglas Dwight, Dionne Louise, Jeanne Marie, Philip Clayton, Kathleen Anne. Student, Macalester Coll., 1948-49; BBA, U. Minn., 1951, LLB, 1954; postgrad., Mexico City Coll. (now U. of Ams.), 1956-57. Bar: Minn. 1954, Calif. 1958. Sole practice, Los Angeles, 1958-65, 72-81, 84—; ptnr. Lindholm & Johnson, 1965-69, Cotter, Lindholm & Johnson, Los Angeles, 1969-72; sole practice, 1972-81; of counsel Bolton, Dunn & Moore, 1981-84. Mem. Calif. Republican Central Com., 1962-63, Los Angeles Republican County Central Com., 1962-66; bd. dirs. Family Service Los Angeles, 1964-70, v.p., 1968-70; bd. dirs. Wilshire YMCA, 1976-77; trustee Westlake Girls Sch., 1978-81; hon. presenter Nat. Charity League Coronet Debutante Ball, 1984; bd. dirs. Calif. State U.-Northridge Trust Fund, 1989-93; bd. dirs. Queen of Angeles/Hollywood Presbyn. Med. Ctr., 1990-98; chmn., CEO Queen of Angels/Hollywood Presbyn. Found., 1997-2000; bd. dirs., corp. sec. QueensCare, 1998—. Served as capt. JAG Corps USAF, 1954-56. Recipient presdl. award Los Angeles Jr. C. of C., 1959 Mem. Calif. Bar Assn., L.A. County Bar Assn., Wilshire Bar Assn. (bd. govs. 1989-91), Internat. Genealogy Fellowship of Rotarians (founding pres. 1979-86), Calif. Club, Ocean Cruising Club Eng. (Newport Harbor port officer), Rotary (dir. 1975-78), Delta Sigma Pi, Delta Sigma Rho, Delta Theta Phi (state chancellor 1972-73). Presbyterian. Avocations: sailing, offshore cruising. Office: 3580 Wilshire Blvd Fl 17 Los Angeles CA 90010-2501 E-mail: dlindholm@earthlink.net.

LINDHOLM, FREDRIK ARTHUR, electrical engineering educator; b. Tacoma, Feb. 26, 1936; s. George Fred and Evelyn Blanche (Faul) L.; m. Susanne Shroad Howry, Aug. 22, 1959 (div. July 1966); m. Merle Elizabeth Flannery, Dec. 20, 1969. BS, Stanford U., 1958, MS, 1960; PhD, U. Ariz., 1963. Sr. engr. Motorola Corp., Phoenix, 1963-66; asst. prof. U. Ariz., Tucson, 1963-64, assoc. prof., 1964-66; prof. U. Fla., Gainesville, 1966—. Vis. prof. U. Leuven, Belgium, 1973-74; gen. chmn. Internat. Electron Devices Meeting Conf., Washington, 1974; program chmn. Internat. Photovoltaics Specialists Conf., Washington, 1978; cons. Jet Propulsion Lab., Pasadena, Calif., 1978-87, Los Alamos (N.Mex.) Nat. Lab., 1981-86. Author: Principles and Applications of Semiconductor Device Modeling, 1971; contbr. numerous articles to profl. jours.; patentee high-low emitter solar cell. Recipient Best Paper award Internat. Solid-State Cirs. Conf., 1963, 65, Outstanding Engring. Faculty award U. Fla., 1975, univ. tchr.-scholar, 1988. Fellow IEEE; mem. Am. Phys. Soc. Home: 4406 SW 17th Ter Gainesville FL 32608-3910 Office: U Fla Dept Elec-Computer Engring Gainesville FL 32611 E-mail: lindholm@ece.ufl.edu.

LINDHOLM, LORI ANN, naval officer; b. Gloversville, N.Y., Aug. 10, 1957; d. Frank and Beverly June (Daniels) Bolebruch; m. Ross Milton Lindholm, May 29, 1993. BA in Theatre Arts, SUNY, Oswego, 1979; MS in Systems Mgmt., U. So. Calif., 1988. Commd. ensign USN, 1980, advanced through grades to capt., 2002; pub. affairs officer Fleet Logistics Support Squadron-30, San Diego, 1980-82; student naval aviator Schs. Command, Pensacola, Fla., 1982-83; pilot under tng. Helicopter Anti-Submarine Warfare Squadron-10, San Diego, 1983-84; schedules officer, maintenance div. officer Fleet Composite Squadron-5, Philippines, 1984-86; asst. ops. officer Helicopter Combat Support Squadron-1, San Diego, 1986-88; flight deck officer USS Lexington, Pensacola, 1988-90; enlisted classification div. dir. Navy Occupational Devel. and Analysis Ctr., Washington, 1991-93; sr. analyst GPS Technologies, Inc., Arlington, Va., 1993-96; program mgr. Strategic Resources, Inc., Falls Church, 1996-99; dir. knowledge systems Lockheed Martin NE&SS-SS, 2002—. Instr. Presdl. Classrm., 1991-92. Contbr. articles to profl. jours. Ptnrs. in Edn. coord. USS Lexington/AA Dixon Sch., Pensacola, 1989-90; v.p. membership JET SET/Nat. Mus. Naval Aviation, Penacola., 1990; watch officer Navy Command Ctr., Naval Res., 1993-95, Office of Undersec. of Def./Policy, 1995-98; Chief Naval Ops. Exec. Panel, 1998—. Named regional finalist White House Fellowship, 1990. Mem. Women in Defense, Women Mil. Aviators, Tailhook Assn. (conv. com. 1987-91, Membership award 1989), Naval Helicopter Assn. (chpt. membership 1987-88), Oswego Alumni Assn., U. So. Calif. Inst. Safety and Systems Mgmt., Alumni Assn. Avocations: snow skiing, water skiing, golf, running. Home: 12 Chateau Cir Marlton NJ 08053-

LINDHOLM, RICHARD THEODORE, economics and finance educator; b. Eugene, Oreg., Oct. 5, 1960; s. Richard Wadsworth and Mary Marjorie (Trunko) L. m. Valaya Nivasananda, May 8, 1987. BA, U. Chgo., 1982, MA, 1983, PhD, 1993. Ptnr. Lindholm and Osanka, Eugene, 1986-89, Lindholm Rsch., Eugene, 1995—2001, owner, 1995—, The Lindholm Co., 1995—; ptnr. DBA Lindholm Rsch., Eugene, 2001—. Guest lectr. Nat. Inst. Devel. Adminstrn., Bangkok, Thailand, 1989; pres. Rubicon Inst., Eugene, 1988—; adj. asst. prof. U. Oreg., Eugene, 1988—. Campaign co-chmn. Lane C.C. Advocates, Eugene, 1988; coord., planner numerous state Rep. Campaigns, Oreg., 1988—; campaign mgr. Jack Roberts for Oreg. State Labor Commn., 1994; mem. staff Oreg. Senate Rep. Office, 1989-90; precinct committeeperson Oreg. Rep. Party, 1987-92, 94—; bd. dirs. Rubicon Soc., Eugene, 1987—, pres., 1993-98. Republican. Lutheran. Home: 3335 Bardell Ave Eugene OR 97401-8021

LINDHOLM, ULRIC SVANTE, engineering research institute executive, retired; b. Washington, Sept. 11, 1931; s. Svante Godfred and Hedwig (Krueger) L.; m. Laura Ann Carranza, July 6, 1962; children: Karl, Kirsten, Jon, Siri. BS, Mich. State U., 1953, MS, 1955, PhD, 1960. Rsch. instr. Mich. State U., East Lansing, 1959-60; sr. engr., mgr., dir., v.p. Southwest Rsch. Inst., San Antonio, 1960-94, ret., 1994. Lectr. St. Mary's U., San Antonio, 1961-62. Assoc. editor Soc. Exptl. Stress Analysis Exptl. Mechanics, 1979-82; contbr. numerous articles to profl. jours.; patentee in field. Chmn. bd. dirs. Healy-Murphy Ctr., San Antonio, 1970-81. With USN, 1955-57. Fellow ASME (assoc. editor Jour. Applied Mechanics 1981-83), AAAS; mem. Am. Soc. Metals. Democrat. Avocations: woodworking, antiques. Home: PO Box 367 Marlow NH 03456-0367

LINDHOLM, WILLIAM ROBERT, elementary school educator; b. Manitowoc, Wis., Oct. 7, 1955; m. Carol Ann Lindholm, Aug. 1, 1981; children: Carissa, Breanna. Degree in elem. edn., Lakeland Coll., 1979. 5th grade tchr. Melrose (Wis.) Elem. Sch., 1979—81; 6gh grade tchr. Lake Mills (Wis.) Mid. Sch., 1982—84, Howards Grove (Wis.) Elem. Sch., 1984—88; 6th and 7th grade tchr. Valders (Wis.) Mid. Sch., 1988—. Mem.: NEA, WEAL. Avocations: coaching, running, camping, boating. Home: 1683 Atlanta Cir Manitowoc WI 54220 Office: Valders Mid Sch 201 W Wilson Valders WI 54245

LINDLE, JANE CLARK, educator; b. Annapolis, Md., Jan. 28, 1954; d. Clifton Bob and Sue Helen Louise Clark; m. Garnett Adrian Lindle Jr., May 29, 1982; children: Rachel, Garnett III. BA, U. N.C., 1976; MS, U. Wis., 1982, PhD, 1983. Chair Student Consumer Action Union, Chapel Hill, N.C., 1974-75; tchr., lifeguard St. John's Episcopal Ch., Charleston, S.C., 1975-76; tchr. Luxemburg (Wis.)-Casco Schs., 1976-81; project asst. U. Wis., Madison, 1981-83; prin. St. Mary of Lake, Waunakee, Wis., 1983-84, Our Lady Queen of Peace, Madison, 1984-87; asst. prof. U. Pitts., 1987-91; prof. U. Ky., Lexington, 1991—. Tchr. N.C. Muscular Distrophy Camp, Raleigh, 1974; co-dir. UK/UL Joint Ctr. Study Edn. Policy, Lexington, 1996-2000. Mem. Am. Ednl. Rsch. Assn. (nominations com. chair 1998-2000), Politics Edn. Assn. (pres. 1994-96), U. Coun. Ednl. Adminstrn. (plenary rep. 1999-2001). Avocations: singing, travel, gardening. Office: U Ky 111 Dickey Hall Lexington KY 40506-0017 Fax: 859-257-1015. E-mail: jclind00@uky.edu.

LINDLEY, F(RANCIS) HAYNES, JR. foundation executive, lawyer; b. L.A., Oct. 15, 1945; s. Francis Haynes and Grace Nelson (McCanne) L.; m. Hollinger McCloud Lindley, Apr. 1, 1977; 1 child, Anne Hollinger Lindley. BA, Claremont (Calif.) Men's Coll., 1967; MFA, Claremont (Calif.) Grad. Sch., 1972; JD, Southwestern U., L.A., 1976. Bar: Calif. 1976, U.S. Supreme Ct. 1980. Deputy pub. defender Office of Pub. Defender, L.A., 1977-79; staff atty., Dept. Trial Counsel The State Bar of Calif., 1979-81; pvt. practice, 1981-90; pres. John Randolph Haynes and Dora Haynes Found., L.A., 1987-97, pres. emeritus, 1997—. Trustee John Randolph Haynes and Dora Haynes Found., L.A., 1978—. Mem. bd. dirs. TreePeople, L.A., 1985-87, So. Calif. Assn. Philanthropy, L.A., 1985-89; mem. bd. fellows Claremont (Calif.) U. Ctr. and Grad. Sch., 1987—; mem. bd. dirs. Marin Agrl. Land Trust, 1995—. Recipient Disting. Svc. award The Claremont (Calif.) Grad. Sch., 1994. Avocation: sailing, art history, banjo. Home: PO Box 1404 Ross CA 94957-1404 Office: John Randolph Haynes & Dora Haynes Found 888 W 6th St Ste 1150 Los Angeles CA 90017-2737

LINDLEY, JAMES DANIEL, lawyer; b. Paterson, N.J., May 24, 1948; s. Arthur Gugler and Dorothy Virgene (Roberts) L.; children: Maya Rachel, Joseph Samuel; m. Anita Martha Lemaire, June 30, 1996. BS in Acctg., U. N.C., 1973, PhD in Mktg., 1983; JD, Suffolk U., 1989. Bar: Mass. 1990, U.S. Dist. Ct. Mass. 1991, U.S. Bankruptcy Ct. 1991, U.S. Ct. Appeals (1st cir.) 1992, U.S. Supreme Ct. 1994. Sr. assoc. Antell & Assocs., Boston, 1990-96; pvt. practice law, 1996—. Asst. prof. Ohio U., Athens, 1978-84; assoc. prof. Suffolk U., Boston, 1984-89, Bentley Coll., Waltham, Mass., 1989-93. Fellow Nat. Employment Lawyers Assn., Univ. Club. Avocations: gardening, home repair, travel. Home: 120 Bynner St Jamaica Plain MA 02130-1043 Office: 8 Winter St 12th Flr Boston MA 02108-4705

LINDLEY, JEARL RAY, lawyer; b. Abilene, Tex., Mar. 12, 1934; s. Hardie Lindley and Hope Clement Mourant; m. Annabelle Sim Yee Lindley, May 22, 1954; children: Katheryn Ann, Michael Andrew, Carolyn Elizabeth. BS in Chemistry, N.Mex. State U., 1960; MD, U. Colo., 1964; MS, U. Ill., 1967; JD, South Tex. Coll. of Law, 1997. Asst. clin. prof. of surgery Rush Med. Coll. of Rush U., Chgo., 1969-71, U. Ill. Sch. of Medicine, Chgo., 1969-71; assoc. clin. prof. of surgery Tex. Tech. U. Sch. of Medicine, El Paso, 1976-80; atty., counselor Las Cruces, N.Mex., 1997—. Adj. prof. N.Mex. State U., Las Cruces, 1984-86. Author publs. in field (McNeil Meml. Rsch. award 1967). Bd. dirs. Meml. Gen. Hosp., Las Cruces, 1983, So. N.Mex. Regional Dialysis Ctr., Las Cruces, 1984-89; instr. ACLS, AHA, Las Cruces, 1980-86, ATLS, Am. Coll. Surgeons, Las Cruces, 1980-86; mem. emergency med. svcs. com. Dona Ana Emergency, Las Cruces, 1979, City County Hosp. Bd. Govs., Las Cruces, 1981-83; mem. internat. bd. dirs. N.Mex. State U. Alumni Assn., 1979-81; mem. bd. counselors Citizens Bank, Las Cruces, 1991-93. Named to Outstanding Young Men of Am., 1969, Marine of Yr., Marine Corps League, 1990, Guide to Am.'s Top Surgeons, 2002; commd. Ky. Col., State of Ky., 1989; proclamation of Jearl R. Lindley Day/Mayor of Truth or Consequences, N.Mex., 1990; recipient Disting. Citizen medal Dept. of N.Mex. Marine Corps League, others. Fellow Am. Coll. Surgeons, Internat. Coll. of Surgeons, Southwestern Surg. Congress; mem. Internat. Endovascular Soc., Soc. Clin. Vascular Surgery, AHA, Am. Legion, Marine Corps Assn., Marine Corps Heritage Found., Naval Inst., Marine Meml. Club, Air Force Assn., Marine Corps League (Commandant Dept. of N.Mex. 1990-91, Dept. Commandant's medal 1991, medal with bronze star 1988-90). Republican. Mem. Ch. of Christ. Avocations: shooting, photography, travel in an RV, reading, motorcycling. Home: 4566 Mockingbird St Las Cruces NM 88011-9616

LINDLEY, JUDITH MORLAND, cat registry administrator; b. Burbank, Calif., Mar. 25, 1948; d. Howard Paxson Conrow and Hazel Mary (Morland) Conrow-Caesar; m. William Ames (div. 1972); m. J. Lindley (div. 1983); widowed, 1990; children: Pamela Ames-Ortega, Jimmy J. Lindley, Joseph Bettoni, Patricia Bettoni. Grad in Animal Sci., Internat. Correspondence Sch., 1995. Pres., founder Calico Cat Registry, Morongo Valley, Calif., 1978—; pres., owner Animal Helpline, 1979—. Author: Calico Cat Registry Handbook, 1978, On Older Cats, 1996, Calicos and Kin, 1996; contbr. articles to mags. Avocations: animals, reading, writing. Home and Office: 48981 Oregon Trail PO Box 944 Morongo Valley CA 92256-0944

LINDLEY, NORMAN DALE, physician; b. Henrietta, Tex., July 18, 1937; s. Hardie Lindley and Hope (Clement) Mourant; m. Luise Ann Moser, May 29, 1964; children: Norman Dale Jr., Roger Paul. BS, N.Mex. Highlands U., 1960; MD, U. Colo., 1964. Diplomate Am. Bd. Ob-Gyn. Rotating intern Kans. City (Mo.) Gen. Hosp., 1964-65; resident in ob-gyn. St. Joseph Hosp., Denver, 1965-68; med. officer USAF, Cheyenne, Wyo., 1968-70; pvt. practice physician Alamogordo, N.M., 1970—. Dir. N.Mex. Found. for Med. Care, Albuquerque, 1985-88, N.Mex. Med. Rev. Assn., Albuquerque, 1985-88; physician liaison Am. Assn. Med. Assts., Chgo., 1987-93; physician advisor N.Mex. Soc. Med. Assts., 1984—. Bd. dirs. Otero County Boys and Girls Club, Alamogordo, 1977—, pres., 1979-81; bd. dirs. Otero County Assn. for Retarded Citizens, 1985-91, pres., 1989-90; bd. dirs. Otero County chpt. Am. Cancer Soc., 1970-72. Capt. USAF, 1968-70. Rsch. grantee NSF, 1959, 60. Fellow Am. Coll. Ob-Gyn.; mem. AMA, Am. Fertility Soc., Am. Inst. Ultrasound in Medicine, Am. Soc. Colposcopists and Cervical Pathologists, N.Mex. Med. Soc. (councilor 1985-88), Otero County Med. Soc. (pres. 1972-73, 83-84), Rotary (pres. White Sands chpt. 1981-82, bd. dirs. 1988-89, Svc. Above Self award 1979, Paul Harris fellow 1987). Avocations: watercolor painting, leatherworking, foreign languages. Home: 2323 Union Ave Alamogordo NM 88310-3849 Office: Thunderbird Ob-Gyn 1212 9th St Alamogordo NM 88310-5842

LINDLY, DOUGLAS DEAN, elementary school educator, administrator; b. San Diego, Aug. 22, 1941; s. George A. and Jessie V. L.; m. Brenda J., Oct. 22, 1971; children: Elizabeth, David. MA in Curriculum, Pepperdine U., 1967, student, 1975; credential edn., USC, 1971; student, U. Oreg., 1981-85, Oreg. State U., 1981-85; credential adminstrn., Calif. State U., Fullerton, 1991; cert. in spl. edn., Calif. State U., L.A., 1994. Cert. in profl. adminstrv. svcs., Calif., gen. teaching, Calif., standard designated adult edn., Calif., standard elem. teaching, Oreg., standard adminstrv., Oreg.; cert. lang. devel. specialist, Calif., Learning Handicapped and Resource Specialist credential. Supervising tchr. Imperial Schs., Pasadena, Calif., 1965-70; tchr. Charter Oak Unified Sch. Dist., Covina, 1970-78, Sweet Home (Oreg.) Unified Sch. Dist., 1978-81; prin. Lewis and Clark Sch. Dist., Astoria, Oreg., 1981-86, Barstow (Calif.) Unified Sch. Dist., 1986-88; spl. edn. dir. River Delta Unified Sch. Dist., Walnut Grove, Calif., 1988-89; resource specialist Los Angeles Unified Sch. Dist., 1990—. Tchr. motivational program Great Kids Club, 1982—. Author: A Handbook for Parents, 1967, Summer Education Handbook, 1970; contbr. numerous articles on ednl. programs to newspapers and mags., 1970-89. Vol. ARC, Pasadena/Covina, 1970-78; cubmaster Boy Scouts Am., Astoria and Barstow, 1982-88 (Outstanding Svc. award 1988); coach Little League, Astoria, 1985; leader youth group Ch. of God, 1975-81. Grantee Adventures in Success, 1976-78; scholar Future Tchrs. Am. and Eugene Tchrs. Assn., 1959; named San Gabriel Valley Outstanding Educator, San Gabriel Valley Endl. Consortium, 1977; recipient Outstanding Speaker award Toastmasters Internat., 1986, Outstanding Svc. award PTA, 1988. Mem. NEA, ASCD, Assn. Am. Educators, Calif. Assn. Gifted, Calif. Tchrs. Assn., Assn. Calif. Sch. Adminstrs. (assoc.), Kappa Delta Pi. Avocations: family, physical fitness, grandparenting, reading, travel. Home: 616 E Ghent St San Dimas CA 91773-1913

LINDNER, CARL HENRY, JR. sports team executive, insurance company executive; b. Dayton, Ohio, Apr. 22, 1919; s. Carl Henry and Clara (Serrer) L.; m. Edith Bailey, Dec. 31, 1953; children: Carl Henry III, Stephen Craig, Keith Edward. Co-founder United Dairy Farmers, 1940; pres. Am. Fin. Corp., Cin., 1959-84, chmn., 1959—, CEO, 1984—; owner, CEO Cincinnati Reds, 1999—. Bd. advs. Bus. Adminstrn. Coll., U. Cin. Republican. Baptist.

LINDNER, DANIEL GEORGE, program analyst; b. Bethlehem, Pa. s. George K. and Lorraine E. Lindner; m. Jenny Lindner; children: Eric, Alexander. BA in Govt., BA Econs., Lehigh U., 1977; MBA, George Washington U., 1984. Cert. profl. contracts mgr. Nat. Contract Mgmt. Assn. Sports announcer WLRN Radio, Bethlehem, 1973-74; sports dir., announcer WLTN-TV, 1973-77; contract negotiator Naval Regional Contracting Office, Phila., 1977-80; contract specialist Strategic Sys. Program Office, Washington, 1980-86; staff aide Office of Asst. Sec. of the Navy, Arlington, Va., 1986-90; contracting officer Dept. of the Navy, 1990-94; deployment mgr., program analyst Std. Procurement Sys. Program Office, Fairfax, Va., 1994-99, chmn. tech. working group and procurement working group, 1999—. Contbr. articles to profl. jours. Usher, mem. fin. com. Emmanuel Luth. Ch., Vienna, Va., 1989-98; counselor Fairfax (Va.) County Teen Living Program, 1993—; big bro. Big Bros. Am., Fairfax, 1995-96; coach Fairfax County Adult Volleyball League, 1994-95. Mem. Distributive Edn. Clubs Am. (judge regional and state competitions 1998—), Lehigh U. Alumni Assn. (recruiter 1989—, bd. mem. Washington chpt. 1993-97, dep. dir. campaign for preserving the vision 1994, dir. Lehigh Wrestling Club, 1995—). Avocations: travel, sports and history research, running, hiking. Office: PO Box 308 Clifton VA 20124-0308 E-mail: lindner_dan@hotmail.com.

LINDNER, JOSEPH, JR. physician, medical administrator; b. Cin., Apr. 5, 1929; s. Joseph and Mary (Apger) L.; m. Doris G. Beatty, July 29, 1961; children: Laura Lynn, Karen Leslie. AB, Dartmouth Coll., 1951; MD, U. Cin., 1955; MPH, Harvard U., 1977. Intern Cin. Gen. Hosp., 1955-56, resident in medicine, 1958-60, fellow in cardiology, 1960-61; mem. faculty dept. medicine U. Cin. Coll. Medicine, 1961-79, prof., 1975-79; sr. assoc. v.p. U. Cin., 1975-79, sr. assoc. dir., 1977-79; pres., chief exec. officer St. Barnabas Med. Ctr., Livingston, N.J., 1979-85, Trimark Corp., West Orange; ptnr. Cons. Assocs., Inc., 1991-92; pres. J. Lindner, Inc., Hilton Head, S.C., 1992—. Trustee Mt. St. Joseph Coll., 1972-76, The Asheville Sch., 1995-2002; bd. visitors, chmn. The Ashville Sch., 1995-2002; bd. dirs. MBL VCA-7. With USN, 1956-58. Fellow Am. Coll. Physician Execs.; mem. N.J. Med. Soc., Commonwealth Club, Baltusrol Golf Club, Country Club Hilton Head, Bear Creek Golf Club, Short Hills Club. Home and Office: 31 Old Fort Dr Hilton Head Island SC 29926-2601 E-mail: joelindner@aol.com.

LINDNER, LUTHER EDWARD, pathology educator; b. Toledo, Aug. 6, 1942; s. Arthur Edward and Lydia Clara (Holm) L.; m. Elizabeth Anne Rosenberry, May 24, 1969; children: Stephen James (dec.), Mary Irene, Martha Holm. BS, U. Toledo, 1964; MD, Case Western Res. U., 1967, PhD, 1972. Diplomate Am. Bd. Pathology. Intern, resident Inst. Pathology, U. Hosps. Cleve., 1967-72; asst. prof. U. Nev., Reno, 1975-82; assoc. prof. pathology Tex. A&M U., College Station, 1982—. Contbr. numerous articles to profl. jours. Maj. M.C., USAR, 1972-75. Fellow Coll. Am. Pathologists, Am. Soc. Clin. Pathologists; mem. U.S.-Can. Acad. Pathology. Home: 2507 Merrimac Ct College Station TX 77845-4109 Office: Tex A&M U Coll Medicine Dept Pathology And Lab Med College Station TX 77843-0001

LINDNER, RUDI PAUL, historian, educator; b. Stockton, Calif., July 17, 1943; s. Frank and Clare Lindner; m. Molly Morrow Mcglannan, Aug. 22, 1975; children: Clare, Beile. AB, Harvard U., 1965; MA, The U. of Wis., 1966; PhD, The U. of Calif., 1976. Jr. fellow Dumbarton Oaks, Washington, 1972—74; asst. prof. of history Tufts U., Medford, Mass., 1974—77; prof. of history The U. of Mich., Ann Arbor, Mich., 1977—. Vis. prof. history John Cabot U., Rome, 1993; vis. rsch. prof. Hebrew U. , Jerusalem, 2002. Author: (book) Nomads and Ottomans in Medieval Anatolia, 1983. Fellow Fulbright Hayes fellowship, 1992—93. Office: History DeptThe University of Michigan 435 S State St Ann Arbor MI 48109

LINDO, J. TREVOR, psychiatrist, consultant; b. Boston, Feb. 12, 1925; s. Edwin and Ruby Ianty (Peterson) L.; m. Thelma Elaine Thompson, Sept. 22, 1962. BA, NYU, 1946; cert. in pre-clin. studies, U. Freiburg, Switzerland, 1953; MD, U. Lausanne, Switzerland, 1957. Lic. psychiatrist, N.Y., Conn. Clin. instr. Columbia U., N.Y.C., 1965-75, asst. clin. prof., 1975-82, assoc. clin. prof., 1982-85; attending psychiatrist Bedford-Stuyvesant Cmty. Mental Health Clinic, Bklyn., 1976-86, med. dir., 1986—. Attending psychiatrist Harlem Hosp. Ctr., N.Y.C., 1964-75; vis. psychiatrist Interfaith Hosp., Bklyn., 1976-85; psychiat. cons. Bklyn. Bur. Cmty. Svc., 1980, Marcus Garvey Manor, Bklyn., 1982-86; candidate Nat. Bd. Forensic Examiners, 1995. Co-chairperson com. Dr. Thomas Matthew, N.Y.C., 1974. With U.S. Mcht. Marine, 1947-51. Fellow Am. Coll. Internal Physicians; mem. Nat. Med. Assn., Am. Psychiat. Assn., Provident Clin. Soc. (v.p. 1980-82, parliamentarian 1982—), Bklyn. Psychiat. Soc., Black Psychiatrists of Am. Avocations: travel, African art, sailing, swimming. Office: 1265 President St Brooklyn NY 11213-4237 also: Bedford Stuyvesant Cmty Mental Health Ctr 1406 Fulton St Brooklyn NY 11216-2606

LINDORFF, JOYCE ZANKEL, harpsichordist; b. Passaic, N.J., Jan. 19, 1950; d. Murray and Beryl (Cohen) Zankel; m. David Plimpton Lindorff, Jr., June 19, 1970; children: Ariel, Jed. BA, Sarah Lawrence Coll., Bronxville, N.Y., 1972; MusM, U. So. Calif., L.A., 1978, The Juilliard Sch., N.Y.C., 1980, DMA, 1982. Tchg. artist Lincoln Ctr. Inst., N.Y.C., 1981-87; music faculty Cornell U., Ithaca, N.Y., 1987-91; artistic dir. Music at Fishs Eddy (N.Y.), 1986—. Dir. Cornell Summer Harpsichord Workshop, Ithaca, 1988-92; vis. prof. Shanghai Conservatory of Music, China, 1991—; assoc. prof. Hong Kong Bapt. U., 1992-97; Fulbright prof. China-Xian Conservatory of Music, 1995; keyboard faculty Temple U., Phila., 1997; trustee Westfield Ctr. for Early Keyboard Studies, 1996—. CD recording Poglietti's Rossignolo; N.Y. solo debut Carnegie Recital Hall, 1980; numerous solo concerts and guest artist throughout the world. Nat. Endowment for Arts solo recitalist fellow, Washington, 1983; recipient Internat. Artist Sponsorship award Pro Musicis Found., N.Y.C., 1983—. Mem. Am. Musical Soc., Southeast Hist. Keyboard Soc., Royal Musical Assn., Pi Kappa Lambda, Mu Phi Epsilon, ACME.

LINDQUIST, DONALD AUGUST, lawyer; b. New Orleans, Sept. 28, 1924; s. Owen Henry and Anne (Grimes) L.; m. Fran C. Gorton, June 6, 1953; children: Christine Lindquist Smith, Catherine Lindquist Partridge, Donald C., Mary Fran Rosamond. BS, Mcht. Marine Acad., 1945; LLB, JD, Loyola U., New Orleans, 1951. Bar: U.S. Ct. Mil. Appeals, 1952, U.S. Supreme Ct. 1952, La. 1953, U.S. Dist. Ct. (ea. and mid. dists.) La. 1953, U.S. Ct. Appeals (5th cir.) 1953. Ptnr. Chaffe McCall Phillips Toler Sarpy, New Orleans, 1953—. Mem. judge Fed. Ct. Disciplinary Bd., 1983-88; former lectr. naval R & D, Tulane U. Adv. editor Tulane Maritime Law Jour. Bd. dirs. New Orleans Acad.; lectr. on prostate cancer at med. schs. and clins.; mem. permanent adv. bd. Tulane Admiralty Inst. Ensign USN, 1945-48, 51-52; comdr. USNR (ret.). Mem. ABA, La. Bar Assn., New Orleans Bar Assn. (past chmn. fed. ct. com.), Bar City N.Y., Maritime Law Assn. U.S (membership com.), Assn. Average Adjusters, Comité Maritime Internat., Mil. Order Fgn. Wars (bd. dirs.), Metairie Country Club, Bienville Club, Delta Theta Phi. Republican. Roman Catholic. Avocations: golf, hunting and fishing, sailing, travel, reading. Office: Chaffe McCall Et Al 2300 Energy Ctr 1100 Poydras St New Orleans LA 70163-1101 Fax: 504-585-7075.

LINDQUIST, EVAN, artist, educator; b. Salina, Kans., May 23, 1936; s. E.L. and Linnette Rosalie (Shogren) L.; m. Sharon Frances Huenergardt, June 8, 1958; children: Eric, Carl. BS, Emporia State U., 1958; MFA, U. Iowa, 1963. One-man shows include Mo. Arts Coun., 1973-75, Albrecht Art Mus., St. Joseph, Mo., 1975, 89, S.E. Mo. State U., 1977, Sandzen Gallery, Lindsborg, Kans., 1978, Galerie V. Kunstverlag Wolfbrum, Vienna, 1979, Poplar Bluff, Mo., 1987, Gallery V., Kansas CIty, Mo., 1988, Northwest Mo. State U., 1991, U. Iowa, Iowa City, 1995, WR Harper Coll., Palatine, Ill., 1996, Northwestern Coll., Orange City, Iowa, 1997, Art Ctr. of the Ozarks, Springdale, Ark., 1998, Fowler Ctr., Ark. State U., Jonesboro, 2001; group shows include Benjamin Galleries, Chgo., 1976, City of Venice, 1977, Boston Printmakers, 1971-87, Visual Arts Ctr. of Alaska, Anchorage, 1979, Western Carolina U., 1980, Pa. State U., 1980, Kans. State U., 1980, U. N.D., 1981, 92, Ariz. State U., 1981, 93, Barcelina, Cadaques, Girona, 1990, 93, 94, Tulsa, 1982, Jay Gallery, N.Y.C., 1983, Artists Books, German Dem. Rep., 1984, U. Tenn., Knoxville, 1985, Memphis State U., 1985, Ark. Arts Ctr., 1983, Miss. State U., 1986, Hunterdon Art Ctr., Clinton, N.J., 1986-87, 94, 95, Washington, 1988, Soc. Am. Graphic Artists/Printmakers, 1988-94, Boston, 1989-94, John Szoke Gallery, 1989, Woodstock, N.Y., 1990, 92, Silvermine Guild Galleries, New Canaan, Conn., 1992, 93, Woodstock Artists Assn., Littman Gallery, Portland State U., Galeria Brita Prinz, Madrid, Spain, 1992, U. Nebr., 1992,. Parkside Nat., Kenosha, Wis., 1993, 95, 2000, 2001, Minot, N.D., 1994, Fla. C.C., Jacksonville, 1995, Stonemetal Press, San Antonio, Tex., 1995, San Diego Art Inst., 1995, Schenectady (N.Y.) Mus., 1995, Fla. Printmakers, Jacksonville, 1996, Clemson U., S.C., 1996, U. Tex., Tyler, 1996, Old Print Shop, N.Y.C., 1997, Frederick Baker Gall., Chgo., 1997, Krasdale Gall., New york, 1998, Memphis Brooks Mus., 1998, Webster U., St. Louis, 1999, Bradley U., Peoria, Ill., 1999, 2001, Soc. of Am. Graphic Artists, New York, 1999, Hunterdon Art Ctr., Clinton, NJ, 1999, Irving Arts Ctr., Irving Tex., 1999, Payne Gall., Bethlehem, PA, 1999, U. Hawaii, Hilo, 2000; represented in permanent collections Albertina, Vienna, Art Inst. Chgo., Nelson-Atkins, Kansas City, Phoenix Art Mus., Ufizi Gall., Florence, Municipal Gall., Dublin, San Francisco Art Mus., Whitney Mus. Am. Art, N.Y.C., St. Louis Art Mus., Museo Reina Sofia, Madrid, others; staff artist Emporia State U., 1958-60; prof. Ark. State U., 1963—, pres. fell., 1981-82, 84-85; exhibition dir. Delta Nat. Small Prints Exhibition Ark. State U., 1996, 97. Mem. Soc. Am. Graphic Artists, Coll. Art Assn. Am., Mid-Am. Coll. Art Assn., Visual Artists and Galleries Assn. Office: PO Box 2782 State University AR 72467-2782 E-mail: elind@astate.edu.

LINDQUIST, LOUIS WILLIAM, artist, writer; b. Boise, Idaho, June 26, 1944; s. Louis William and Bessie (Newman) L.; divorced; children: Jessica Ann Alexandra, Jason Ryan Louis. BS in Anthropology, U. Oreg., 1968; postgrad., Portland State U., 1974-78. Researcher, co-writer with Asher Lee, Portland, Oreg., 1977-80; freelance artist, painter, sculptor, 1980-91, 98-99. Sgt. U.S. Army, 1968-71, Vietnam. Mem. AAAS, NRA Am., Am. Anthropol. Assn., N.Y. Acad. Scis., Acad. Am. Poets, Petersen's Sportsmen's Soc., N.Am. Hunting Club (life). Republican. Avocations: reading, beachcombing, listening to classical, jazz and native North American music. Home and Office: PO Box 991 Bandon OR 97411-0991

LINDQUIST, MICHAEL ADRIAN, career military officer; b. Cheyenne, Wyo., Nov. 12, 1946; s. Swen George and Beryl Esme (Edwards) L.; m. Frances Eleanor Arnold, Apr. 14, 1968; children: Michella, Michael, Patricia. BS in Econs., U. Tampa, 1975; MS in Logistics Mgmt., Fla. Inst. Technology, Melbourne, 1985; EdD in Orgnl. Leadership, U. Sarasota, 2002. Enlisted U.S. Army, 1966, advanced through ranks to col., staff officer 3d Support Command West Germany, 1980-83, exec. officer 8th Maintenance Group Hanau, West Germany, 1983-85, cmdr. 601st Ord BN Aberdeen Proving Ground, Md., 1986-88, dep. dir. tests Test & Evaluation Command, 1988-89, action officer The Joint Staff Pentagon, 1990-93, comdr. Tobyhanna (Pa.)

Army Depot, 1993-95, comdr. Combat Equipment Group Asia S.C., 1995-97; cons. Adrian Cons., 1998—; former exec. dir. Congl. Medal of Honor Soc. Mem. Assn. U.S. Army, VFW, Ret. Officers Assn., Ordnance Assn., Mil. Order of World Wars. Avocations: golf, coin collecting, stamp collecting. E-mail: colmal1@comcast.net.

LINDQUIST, RICHARD JAMES, portfolio manager; b. East Orange, N.J., June 22, 1960; s. Chester Edward and Rose Theresa (Grosso) L.; m. Clare Jacangelo, June 21, 1987; children: Matthew Cole, Kimberly Rose. BS, Boston Coll., 1982; MBA, U. Chgo., 1986. CFA; chartered investment counselor. Investment rsch. analyst N.Y. Life Ins. Co., N.Y.C., 1982-84; bond trader, v.p. T. Rowe Price Assocs., Inc., Balt., 1986-88; portfolio mgr., v.p. Prudential Ins. Co. Am., Newark, 1989; mng. dir., portfolio mgr. CS 1st Boston Investment Mgmt., N.Y.C., 1989-95, Credit Suisse Asset Mgmt., N.Y.C., 1995—. Mem. Assn. Investment Mgmt. & Rsch., Fin. Analysts Fedn., Inst. CFAs, Investment Coun. Assn. Am., N.Y. Soc. Security Analysts, N.Y. Athletic Club, Spray Beach Yacht Club, Boston Coll. Club, Sea Oaks Country Club. Avocations: golf, cycling, chess. Office: Credit Suisse Asset Mgmt 466 Lexington Ave 15th Fl New York NY 01001

LINDQVIST, GUNILLA, education educator; b. Uppsala, Sweden, Sept. 22, 1942; d. Lars and Margareta (Franzen) Kjellman; m. Jan Lindqvist; children: Jonas Alwall, Jesper Alwall, Klas Hermodsson, Sara Hermodsson, Alexander Lindqvist. PhD, U. Uppsala, 1995. Prefect U. Karlstad, Sweden, 1978-81, sr. lectr. Sweden, 1995—, rschr. dept. ednl. sci. Sweden, 1995—. Author: From Facts to Fantasy, 1989, Alone in the Big, Wide World, 1992, The Aesthetics of Play, 1995, The Possibilities of Play, 1996, Vygotsky and School, 1999, A Scenic Approach to History, 2000. Office: Dept Ednl Sci Univ Karlstad 65188 Karlstad Sweden E-mail: Gunilla.Lindqvist@kau.se.

LINDQVIST, GUNNAR JAN, management consultant, international trade consultant; b. Stockholm, July 12, 1950; s. Bengt Olof Sigfrid and Greta (Nyberg) L.; m. Mary Grady, June 23, 1984; children: Greta Louise, Mary Kerstin. Grad. with honors, Stockholm Sch. Econs., 1974. Lic. realtor, Ga. Asst. acctg. mgr. Granges Shipping, Stockholm, 1975-77; asst. budget mgr. Dynapac AB, 1978-79; asst. treas., contr. Peeples Industries, Savannah, Ga., 1980-83; owner, pres. Cash Mgmt., Inc., 1983—. Mem. The Carpenter's Order, Stockholm, 1978—. Served with Swedish Army. Mem. Scandinavian-Am. Found. of Ga. (bd. govs. 1988—), Savannah Area C. of C. (chmn. subcom. Small Bus. Coun. 1984-89), Swedish-Am. C. of C. Home and Office: 6800 Sandnettles Dr Savannah GA 31410-2317

LINDROS, ERIC BRYAN, professional hockey player; b. London, Can., Feb. 28, 1973; s. Carl and Bonnie L. Student, York U., Toronto. With Detroit Compuware, 1989—, Phila. Flyers, 1992—2000, NY Rangers, 2001—. Mem. Canadian Olympic Team, 1992, Cup All-Star team, 1989-90, OHL All-Star team 1990-91, NHL All-Star team, 1992-93; player NHL All-Star game, 1992-93. Recipient Plus/Minus award Canadian Hockey League, 1990-91, Red Tilson trophym 1990-91, Eddie Powers Meml. trophy, 1990-91; named Most Valuable Player World Jr. Hockey Championships, 1990, Most Valuable Player Ont. Jr. Hockey Assn., 1991, Player of the Year Canadian Hockey League, 1990-91, Hart Trophy, 1995, Lester B. Pearson Award, 1995, Nat. Hockey League. Office: Madison Square Garden 2 Penn Plaza New York NY 10121*

LINDROTH, JAMES TEODOR, music educator; b. South Weymouth, Mass., Nov. 21, 1968; s. Georg Teodor and June Carol Lindroth; m. Tracey Marie Falardeav, Dec. 19, 1993; children: Andrew James, Matthew Richard. B in Music Edn., U. Lowell, 1992; MA, U. Mass., Lowell, 1994. Cert. tchr. music K-12, cmty. coll. music. Music tchr. Beverly (Mass.) Pub. Schs., 1994—95, Miami (Ariz.) Pub. Schs., 1995—97, Brandon (Fla.) H.S., 1997—. Music dir. Tampa (Fla.) Bay Winds, 2000—. Mem.: Fla. Bandmasters Assn., Music Educators Nat. Conf. Mem. Lds Ch. Avocation: hockey. Office: Brandon High Sch 1101 Victoria St Brandon FL 33510 Business E-Mail: James.Lindroth@sdhc.k12.fl.us.

LINDROTH, LINDA (LINDA HAMMER), artist, curator, writer; b. Miami, Sept. 4, 1946; d. Mark Roger and Mae Lang Hammer; m. David George Lindroth, May 26, 1968 (div. Mar. 1985); m. Craig David Newick, June 6, 1987; 1 child, Zachary Eran Newick. BA in Art, Douglass Coll., 1968; studied with Gordon Matta-Clark, Rutgers U., 1975; studied with Garry Winogrand, N.Y., 1976; MFA in Art, Rutgers U., 1979; master class in non-fiction writing, Yale U., 1997. Adj. asst. prof. art Quinnipiac Coll., Hamden, Conn., 1998—. Exhibitions include Aetna Gallery, 1987, 1989, 1991, Franklin Furnace, N.Y.C., 1977, Conn. Commn. Arts, Hartford, 1985, 1996, Aldrich Mus. Contemporary Art, Ridgefield, Conn., 1987, 1987, Downey Mus. Art, Calif., 1989, Zimmerlo Art Mus. Rutgers U., 1989, Wesleyan U. Ctr. for Arts, 1990, Boston Pub. Libr., 1991, John Michael Kohler Art Ctr., Sheboygan, Wis., 1992, Joseloff Gallery U., Hartford, 1994, Artspace, New Haven, 1991, 1992, 1993, 1994, 1995, DeCordova Mus., Lincoln, Mass., 1995, Urban Glass, Bklyn., 1996, U. Conn. Atrium Gallery, 1999, Creative Arts Workship, 1999, New Haven Hist. Soc., 1999, Stedman Gallery, 1999, Rutgers U., 1999, others, Represented in permanent collections The Mus. Modern Art, N.Y.C., The Met. Mus. Art, The Mus. City of N.Y., Internat. Polaroid Collection/Artist Program, N.J. State Mus., Trenton, The Bibliotheque Nationale, Paris, Ctr. Creative Photography, Tucson, The Newark Mus., The Jane Voorhees Zimmerli Art Mus., New Brunswick, N.J., High Mus. Art, Atlanta, Yale U., Mus. d'art et d'histoire, Fribourg, Switzerland; co-author: Out of Bounds, 1994 (1st prize), Virtual Vintage, 2002. Dir. Artspace, Inc., New Haven; mem. Mayor's Task Force on Pub. Art, New Haven. Recipient Ann. Design Rev. award ID Mag., 1990, 91, 93, Honorable Mention, Nat. Peace Garden Design Competition, 1989, Pitts. Corning Archtl. Design Competition, 1988, Individual Artist fellow N.J. State Coun. on Arts, 1974-75, 83-84, Wilmer Shields Rich award Coun. Founds., 1995, Printing Industry Am. award, 1995; grantee Found. for Contemporary Performance Arts, Inc., 1989, 90, Fission Fusion NEA Inter-Arts, 1989, New Eng. Found. for Arts, 1992, Fairfield U., 1995, Ruth Chenven Found., N.Y.C., 1997, Ruth Chevnen Found., 1997; Conn. Commn. Arts fellow, 1995, New Eng. Found. Arts/NEA Regional Photography fellow, 1995-96; Emerging Voices lectr. Arch. League of N.Y., 1996; fellowship grantee in sculpture Conn. Commn. on the Arts, 2000. Studio: Lindroth & Newick 219 Livingston St New Haven CT 06511-2209

LINDSAY, DALE RICHARD, research administrator; b. Bunker Hill, Kans., Aug. 9, 1913; s. Charles Edwin and Iva (Missimer) L.; m. Sybil Anne McCoy, June 6, 1937; children: Martha Lou Lindsay Cover, Judith Anne Lindsay Clapp, Patricia Dale. AB, U. Kans., 1937, MA, 1938; PhD, Iowa State Coll., 1943. Entomologist Dept. Agr., summers 1937-39; teaching fellow, instr., research asso. Iowa State Coll., 1938-43; commd. officer USPHS, 1943—, scientist dir., 1955; assigned malaria control in war areas, 1943-45; entomologist charge operations Communicable Disease Center Activies, Pharr, Tex., 1945-48; chief Thomasville (Ga.) field sta., 1948-53; chief program evaluation sect., div. research grants NIH, 1953-55, asst. chief div., 1955-60, chief div., 1960-63; dep. to gen. dir. Mass. Gen. Hosp., Boston, 1963-65; spl. asst. to chancellor health scis. U. Calif. at Davis, 1965-67, asst. chancellor research and health scis., 1968-69; asso. commr. sci. FDA, 1969-71; asso. dir. med. and allied health edn. Duke U., 1971-75; asst. dir. for sci. coordination Nat. Center for Toxicol. Research, Jefferson, Ark., 1975-76; adj. prof. medicine U. Ark. Med. Sch., 1975-76; asso. dept. family and community medicine U. Ariz., 1977-82. Agrl. bd. Nat. Acad. Sci.-NRC, 1970-73; mem. exec. com., public trustee Nutrition Found., 1972-76, Environ. and Agrl. Found., 1974-79; chmn. sci. adv. bd. Nat. Center for Toxicol. Research, 1972-74. Fellow AAAS, Am. Public Health Assn.; mem. Entomol. Soc. Am. (gov. bd. 1958-62), Commd. Officer Assn. USPHS (treas. nat. exec. com. 1959-61) , Sigma Xi, Phi Kappa Phi, Gamma Sigma Delta.

LINDSAY, DIANNA MARIE, educational administrator; b. Boston, Dec. 7, 1948; d. Albert Joseph and June Hazelton Raggi; m. James William Lindsay III, Feb. 14, 1981. BA in Anthropology, Ea. Nazarene Coll., 1971; MEd in Curriculum and Instrn., Wright State U., 1973, MA in Social Studies Edn., 1974, MEd in Edn. Adminstrn., 1977; EdD in Urban History, Ball State U., 1976; MA in Counseling, U. Dayton, 2000. Supr. social edn. Ohio Dept. Edn., Columbus, 1976-77; asst. prin. Orange City Schs., Pepper Pike, Ohio, 1977-79; prin. North Olmsted (Ohio) Jr. High Sch., 1979-81; dir. secondary edn. North Olmsted City Schs., 1981-82; supt. Copley (Ohio)-Fairlawn City Schs., 1982-85; prin. North Olmsted High Sch., 1985-89, New Trier High Sch., Winnetka, Ill., 1989-96, Worthington Kilbourne H.S., Columbus, Ohio, 1996-2001; headmaster Columbus Jewish Day Sch., New Albany, 2001—. Bd. dirs. Harvard Prins. Ctr., Cambridge, Mass. Contbr. articles to profl. jours. Bd. dirs. Nat. PTA, Chgo., 1987-89 (Educator of Yr. 1989), Found. Human Potential, Chgo.,; bd. trustee Columbus Jewish Country Day Sch. Named Prin. of Yr. Ohio Art Tchrs., 1989, one of 100 Up and Coming Educators, Exec. Educator Mag., 1988, Milken Educator of the Yr. Ohio, 1999; recipient John Vaughn Achievements in Edn. North Cen. Assn., 1988; named Ohio Prin. of Yr, 2000. Mem. AAUW, Ill. Tchrs. Fgn. Lang., Rotary Internat., Phi Delta Kappa. Methodist. Avocations: stained glass, reading, travel, biking, harpist. Office: Columbus Jewish Day Sch 79 N High St New Albany OH 43054

LINDSAY, GEORGE CARROLL, former museum director; b. Cochranville, Pa., Sept. 28, 1928; s. J. George and M. Elizabeth (Copeland) L.; m. Mary-Edythe Shelley, June 27, 1953. BA, Franklin and Marshall Coll., 1950; student, Dickinson Sch. Law, 1950-53; MA (Wintherthur fellow early Am. culture 1953-55), U. Del., 1955. Asst. to dir. Henry Francis du Pont Wintherthur Mus., Del., 1955-56; asst. curator ethnology Smithsonian Instn., 1956-57, asso. curator cultural history, 1957-58, curator mus. service, 1958-66; dir. mus. services N.Y. State Mus., 1966-81, dir., 1981-83, dir. planning and program devel., 1983-86; exec. dir. Vanderbilt Mus., 1986-89. Lectr. early Am. decorative arts and architecture; cons. in field; v.p. Alexandria Assn., Va., 1961-62, pres., 1962-63, bd. dirs., 1963-66; bd. dirs. Greater Washington Ednl. TV Assn., 1964-66, mem. programming com., 1965-66; bd. dirs. No. Va. Fine Arts Assn., 1964-66, Mus. Audio-Visual Applications Group, 1962-70; mem. com. furnishing ofcl. reception room State Dept., 1960-75 Bd. dirs. Menands (N.Y.) Pub. Libr., 1970-86, Albany Symphony Orch., 1969-72, ARC, Albany, 1977-86; active Strasburg (Pa.) Borough Coun., 1992-96, pres., 1994-95; mem. planning commn. Strasburg Boro, 1995—; trustee Octoraro United Presbyn. Ch., 1993—, Strasburg Heritage Soc., 1997—. Mem. Am. Assn. Mus. (coun. 1969-72, v.p. 1970-71, chmn. profl. rels. com. 1974-80), N.Y. State Assn. Mus. (sec. 1968-77, pres. 1977-79, coun. 1985-89), N.E. Mus. Conf. (bd. govs. 1982-85, chmn. long range planning com. 1983-85), St. Andrew's Soc. (pres. Albany 1983-85), St. Andrew's Soc. Phila. Mem. Soc. Of Friends. Address: 255 Wallingford Rd Strasburg PA 17579-1448

LINDSAY, GEORGE PETER, lawyer; b. Bklyn., Feb. 22, 1948; s. Charles Joseph and Marie Antionette (Faraone) L.; m. Sharon Winnett, Sept. 8, 1973; children: William Charles, Kimberly Michelle. BA, Columbia U., 1969; JD, Harvard U., 1973. Bar: N.Y. 1974, Mass. 1985, U.S. Dist. Ct. (so. dist.) N.Y. 1974, U.S. Ct. Appeals (2d cir.) 1975. Assoc. White & Case, N.Y.C., 1973-82; ptnr. Miller, Wrubel & Dubroff, 1982-83, Sullivan & Worcester LLP, N.Y.C., 1983—. Mem. ABA, Assn. Bar City of N.Y., N.Y. State Bar Assn. Office: Sullivan & Worcester LLP 565 5th Ave New York NY 10017-2413 E-mail: gpl@sandw.com.

LINDSAY, JAMES WILEY, retired agricultural company executive; b. Des Moines, Sept. 13, 1934; s. Worthington U. Lindsay and Marsha E. (Wiley) Asher; m. Shirley L. Shutt, July 2, 1953 (div. May 1985, dec. 1990); children: Elizabeth Lindsay Foster, James W. II, Jennifer, Lindsay; m. Jean M. Baumann, Aug. 2, 1986; 1 child, Amanda Marie. Mgr. ops. Archer, Daniels, Midland, Fredonia, Kans., 1968-70, Lincoln, Nebr., 1970-72, mgr. export Decatur, Ill., 1972-74, v.p. western region Lincoln, 1974-76, v.p. ops. Cedar Rapids, Iowa, 1979-80, ops. mgr. Decatur, 1980-83; pres. Brazil ops. T.V.P., Inc., Campinas, Brazil, 1976-79; chief exec. officer AG Processing Inc., Omaha, 1983-2000; ret. Bd. dirs. ABC Ins., Des Moines; mem. adv. bd. U.S.Bank; pres., bd. dirs. Proagro and Protinal, Caracas, Venezuela. Mem. trade and environ. policy adv. com. U.S. Trade Rep.; bd. dirs. United Way, Elkhorn Sch. Found. Mem. Nat. Soybean Processors Assn. (chmn. 1987-91), Jaycees (pres. Fredonia chpt. 1963-64, bd. dirs. Des Moines chpt. 1960). Lodges: Masons. Republican. Roman Catholic.

LINDSAY, JUNE CAMPBELL MCKEE, communications executive; b. Detroit, Nov. 14, 1920; d. Maitland Everett and Josephine Belle (Campbell) McKee; m. Powell Lindsay, Nov. 25, 1967; 1 child, Kristi Costa-McKee. BA in Speech with honors (McGregor Fund Mich. grantee), U. Mich., 1943; cert. in electronics engring., Signal Corps Ground Signal Svc., 1943; postgrad. (Inst. Gen. Semantics grantee), U. Chgo., 1944-45; postgrad. (Armour grantee), NYU, 1945-46; postgrad., Columbia U., 1946-47, Wayne State U., 1960-64, U. Mich., 1964-70, 78—; MA, Specialist-in-Aging Cert., Inst. of Gerontology, 1982. Coord., activator McKee Prodns., Detroit, 1943-56, Being Unltd., Detroit, 1957—, InterBeing Inc., Detroit, 1979—, M.U.T.U-.A.L.A.I.D., 1981—. Info. dir. Suitcase Theatre Inc., Lansing and Ann Arbor; cons. Cornelian Corner Detroit Inc., 1957-63, Islamic Ctr. Found. Soc., Detroit, 1959-62, city Ann Arbor Human Rels. Commn., 1966-68, Urban Adult Edn. Inst., Detroit, 1968-69, Mich. Bell Tel. Co., Detroit, 1969, African Art Gallery Founders, Detroit Inst. Arts, 1964, WKAR-TV, Mich. State U., 1971—. Mem. Nat. Caucus, Ctr. for Black Aged; bd. dirs. Mus. Youth Internat., Saline, Mich., Ann Arbor Cmty. Devel. Corp.; chaplain's asst. U. Hosp., Ann Arbor, 1971-72; program dir. People-to-People, Ann Arbor, 1971-72; Suitcase Theatre tour coord. Brit. Empire's Leprosy Relief Assn., 1972—; assembly cons. Baha'i Faith, 1960—; mem. Comprehensive Health Planning Coun. S.E. Mich., Baha'i Internat. Health Agy., Inst. for Advancement of Health, Mission Helath, Catherne McAuley Health Ctr. Share and Care Support Group. Recipient Award for Excellence Mich. Ednl. Assn.,1971, Mich. Assn. Classroom Tchrs., 1972; exec. dir. Powell Lindsay Meml. Program in Theatre and Comm., Louhelen Baha'i Sch. and Residential Coll., U. Mich., Flint, Mott Cmty. Coll., 1988—. Mem. ACLU, Soc. for Individual Responsibility, Am. Women in Radio and TV, Broadcast Pioneers, Am. Fedn. Advt., Internat. Platform Assn., Gray Panthers, Planetary Citizens, Am. Assn. Adult and Continuing Edn., Am. Pub. Health Assn., Wellness Assocs., Mich. Assn. Holistic Helath, Internat. Health Found., Inst. Study Conscious Evolution, Am. Soc. on Aging, Mich. Health Coun., Nat. Coun. on Aging, U.S. Assn. Humanistic Psychology, Assn. Holistic Health, Internat. Soc. for Study of Subtle Energies and Energy Medicine, Nat. Inst. for Clin. Application of Behavioral Medicine, Assn. Baha'i Studies, Interfaith Coun. Peace and Justice, Mental Health Assn. in Mich., Mich. League Human Svcs., Mich. Soc. Gerontology, Comprehensive Health Planning Coun. Southeastern Mich., Subarea Adv. Coun., Washtenaw County Coun. on Aging, Nat. Coun. Sr. Citizens, Am. Assn. Ret. Persons, Nat. Assn. Pub. Health Policy, People's Med. Soc., Alliance for Democracy and Diversity, Giraffe Soc., Living Tao Found., World Future Soc., Nat. Trust for Historic Preservation, Orgn. Devel. Inst. (registered orgn. devel. profl.), UN Assn of U.S., Age-Groups United Relating On-site Respecting Autonomy (activator, troupe leader, prodr., developer of videotape vignettes and revues). Home: 2339 S Circle Dr Ann Arbor MI 48103-3442

LINDSAY, LESLIE, packaging engineer; b. Amsterdam, N.Y., Oct. 30, 1960; d. R. Gardner and Dorothy (Loucks) L. BA in Advt., Mich. State U., 1981, BS in Package Engring., 1982. Cert. profl. engr. in packaging. Constrn. inspector N.Y. State Dept. Transp., Albany, 1983; sr. package design engr. Wang Labs., Inc., Lowell, Mass., 1983-90; sr. packaging engr. Apple Computer, Inc., Cupertino, Calif., 1990-97; sr. pkg. engr. Bose Corp., Framingham, Mass., 1997—. Conf. speaker Internat. Safe Transit Assn., 1994; AmeriStar judge, 1999, 2000. Staff editor Packaging Horizons Mag. N.Y. State Regents scholar, 1977; recipient Silver Ameristar award for electronics packaging, 1993, 2000, ID mag. packaging award, 1993, Ameristar judges award for merit, 1995, Mem. Women in Packaging, Inst. Packaging Profls. (cert., mem. reduction, reuse, and recycling of protective packaging task group), Molded Pulp Environ. Pkg. Assn. (founding bd. mem., seminar spkr. 1997), Am. Contract Bridge League, Boston Women's Rugby Club (tour chmn. 1985), Wang Ultimate Frisbee (social chmn. 1986-89). Home: 193 Winter St Framingham MA 01702-2435

LINDSAY, NATHAN JAMES, space systems consultant, retired military officer; b. Monroe, Wis., May 24, 1936; s. Ralph Allen and Gertrude (Wartenweiler) L.; m. Shirley Rae Montgomery, Feb. 2, 1958; children: Lori E. Lindsay Smith, Anne, Nathan J. Jr., Susan E. Lindsay Brumett. BS in Mech. Engring., U.Wis., 1958, MS in Mech. Engring., 1965; MS in Systems Mgmt., U. So. Calif., L.A., 1976. Commd. 2d lt. USAF, 1958, advanced through grades to maj. gen., 1988; munitions officer USAF Weapons Ctr., Tripoli, Libya, 1959-61; weapons logistics officer USAF Europe, Wiesbaden, Germany, 1961-63; Titan III propulsion officer USAF Space Systems Divsn., L.A., 1965-69; aircraft guns devel. officer Air Force Armament Lab., Fla., 1969-70; grad. Armed Forces Staff Coll., Norfolk, Va., 1970; mgmt. auditor Air Force Systems Command, Andrews AFB, Md., 1971-73; grad. Def. Systems Mgmt. Coll., Ft. Belvoir, Va., 1973; space systems policy officer Air Force Office Special Projects, L.A., 1973-74, launch systems integration mgr., 1974-78; dir. policy and adminstrn. Air Force Office Space Systems, Pentagon, Washington, 1978-80; dir. space ops. support Air Force Space Divsn., L.A., 1980-82, program mgr. launch and control systems, 1982-84; comdr. Ea. Space and Missile Ctr., Patrick AFB, Fla., 1985-86; dep. comdr. for space launch and control systems Air Force Space Divsn., L.A., 1986-87; dir. NRO Program A, 1987-92; v.p. comml. programs Lockheed Martin Astrospace, 1993-97; v.p., gen. mgr. advanced launch sys. Lockheed Martin Astronautics, 1997-99. Mem. investigation task force NASA Challenger Accident, Kennedy Space Ctr., 1986; bd. dirs. RD-AMROSS Joint Venture, 1997-99, Comml. Launch Svcs. Co., 1997-99, Calif. Space and Tech. Alliance, 1999-2000. Co-chmn. Brevard County, Fla. Civilian-Mil. Affairs Coun., Cocoa Beach, 1984-86; elder Presbyn. Ch. Decorated Def. Disting. Svc. medal, NASA Disting. Svc. medal, Nat. Intelligence medal, Def. Superior Svc. medal, Legion of Merit with one oak leaf cluster, Meritorious Svc. medal with one oak leaf cluster, Joint Svc. Commendation medal, Air Force Commendation medal with one oak leaf cluster, Gen. Thomas White USAF Space trophy, 1992, AAS Mil. Astronautics award, 1993. Mem.: AIAA, Air Force Assn. (Bernard A. Shriever Space award 1989), Am. Legion, U. Wis. Alumni Assn. Avocations: hiking, travel, fishing, reading. Home: 1624 Tamarac Dr Golden CO 80401-8571 E-mail: n8shirley@aol.com.

LINDSAY, PATRICIA MAE, physician, medical administrator; b. Kilbourne, Ill., Aug. 26, 1942; d. William Louden and Virginia Mae (Sutton) L. BA, Drake U., 1964; MD, U. Ill., 1971. Assoc. med. dir. Ill. State U. Med. Ctr., Normal, 1978-81; chief of hypertension City of Faith, Tulsa, 1981-86; ptnr. Glass-Nelson Med. Clinic, 1986-88; med. dir. Med. Missions, 1983—; asst. prof. U. Okla. Med. Sch. Assoc. with med. dir. various med. hosps. and clinics, St. Petersburg, Russia, 1991—, also internat. clinics; video movie prodr., 1998—; Ky. cable TV prodr., 1995—. Vol. physician homeless and disabled patients and burn patients children, St. Petersburg, Russia, 1997; med. asst. Hurricaine Mitch's victims, 1998. NIH fellow, 1967-68; recipient Chem. Rubber Co. Physics Achievement award Drake U., 1961-62; Vsevolesk Hosp. wing named in her honor, St. Petersburg, Russia, 1994. Mem. AMA, ACP, Geriat. Med. Soc., Okla.Med. Soc., Tulsa Med. Soc., Beta Beta Beta. Office: Med Missions 2918 E 78th St Tulsa OK 74136-8732 also: Med Missions 19135 N 90th Ln Peoria AZ 85382-8565

LINDSAY, REGINALD CARL, judge; b. Birmingham, Ala., Mar. 19, 1945; s. Richard and Louise L.; m. Cheryl E. Hartgrove, Aug. 15, 1970. Cert., U. Valencia, 1966; AB in Polit. Sci. cum laude, Morehouse Coll., 1967; JD, Harvard U., 1970. Bar: Mass. 1971, U.S. Ct. Appeals (1st cir.) 1971. Assoc. Hill & Barlow, 1970-75, 78-79, ptnr., 1979-93; judge U.S. Dist. Ct. Mass., Boston, 1994—. Arbitrator, mem. comml. arbitration panel Am. Arbitration Assn., 1994—; commr. Mass. Dept. Pub. Utilities, Boston, 1975-77; pres. adv. bd. Mus. of Nat. Center of Afro-Am. Artists, 1975-81, v.p., 1981— ; trustee Thompson Islands Edn. Center, Boston, 1975-81; bd. dirs. United Way of Mass. Bay, 1981-84, Morgan Meml. Goodwill Industries, Boston, 1992—, Ptnrs. for Youth with Disabilities, Boston; mem. Nat. Consumer Law Ctr. (bd. dirs.), Mass. Commn. on Jud. Conduct, 1982-88; trustee Newton (Mass.) - Wellesley Hosp. Recipient Ruffin-Fenwick Trailblazer award Harvard Black Law Students Assn., 1994, Amanda V. Houston cmty. svc. award Boston Coll., 1998, Frederick E. Berry Expanding Ind. award Easter Seals, 1999, Heroes Among Us award Boston Celtics, 2001, Leadership award New Eng. Black Law Students Assn., 2001. Mem. ABA, Nat. Bar Found., Mass. Bar Assn., Boston Bar Assn. (coun. 1977—, citation jud. excellence 1999), Pi Sigma Alpha, Phi Beta Kappa. Office: 1 Courthouse Way Ste 5130 Boston MA 02210-3007

LINDSAY, ROGER ALEXANDER (BARON LINDSAY OF CRAIGHALL), investment executive; b. Dundee, Scotland, Feb. 18, 1941; s. Archibald Carswell Lindsay and Edith Paterson Bissett. Student, The Morgan Acad., Dundee, U. St. Andrews, Scotland. Asst. acct., office mgr. Andrew G. Kidd Ltd., Dundee, 1964-66; head office acct. Associated British Foods Ltd., London, 1966-71; sec., treas. Wittington Investments, Ltd., Toronto, 1971-95; exec. v.p. Wittington Investments Ltd., 1991-95; pres. Fort House Investments, 1989. Bd. dirs. United World Coll. Internat. Can., Inc., The W. Garfield Weston Found., Benedictine Heritage Ltd., Lydia Diamond Exploration Can. Ltd.; pres. St. John Coun. Ontario. Past moderator Presby. of East Toronto; aide-de camp Lt. Gov. of Ont.; vice chair bd. govs. Knox Coll. U. Toronto. Decorated comdr. Ven. Order Hosp. St. John. Fellow Chartered Inst. Mgmt., Inst. Dirs., Soc. Antiquaries Scotland; mem. Inst. Chartered Accts. Scotland, Royal Overseas League, The Nat. Club (Toronto), Coral Beach Club (Bermuda). Avocations: heraldry, antique silver, genealogy. Office: Fort House Investments 150 Heath St W Ste 1302 Toronto ON Canada M4V 2Y4 E-mail: fhilral@aol.com.

LINDSAY, WILLIAM KERR, surgeon; b. Vancouver, B.C., Can., Sept. 3, 1920; s. James Arthur and Lottie Mary (Early) L.; m. Frances Beatrice Ferris, Feb. 15, 1945; children— William Arthur, Barbara Susanne, Katherine Mary, Anne Louise. MD, U. Toronto, 1945, BS in Medicine, 1949, MS, 1959. Intern Toronto Gen. Hosp., 1945-46; resident Toronto Gen. Hosp. and Hosp. Sick Children, 1948-51, Montreal Gen. Hosp., 1951-52, Baylor U. Hosp., 1952-53; practice medicine, specializing in plastic surgery Toronto, 1953—; staff surgeon to head divsn. plastic surgery Hosp. for Sick Children, 1953-86, cons., 1965-86; project dir. Research Inst., 1954-85; faculty dept. surgery U. Toronto Faculty of Medicine, 1953-86, prof., 1968-86, chmn. interhospital com. for plastic surgery, 1965-86, prof. emeritus, 1986—. Chmn. med. dental staff com. Bloorview MacMillan Treatment Ctr. (formerly Hugh MacMillan Treatment Ctr. and Ont. Crippled Childrens Treatment Ctr.), 1958-63, cons., 1963—. Trustee McLaughlin Found., 1986—. With M.C., Royal Can. Army, 1943-46; surg. lt. Royal Can. Navy, 1946-47. Recipient Arbor award, 1994; Hon. head burn and plastic surgery dept. Gansu Provincial People's Hosp., Lanzhou City, China, 1994—. Fellow ACS, Royal Coll. Surgeons Can.; mem. Am. Assn. Plastic Surgeons (pres. 1970-71, Hon. award 1995), Can. Soc. Plastic Surgeons (pres. 1963), Easter Seal Soc. Ont. (chmn. med. adv. com. 1957-65, cons. 1952-95, mem. rsch. inst. 1979-95, Gold award 1995), Am. Soc. Plastic and Reconstructive Surgeons (Spl. Achievement award 1979), Am. Soc. Surgery of Hand, Am. Cleft Palate Assn., Brit. Soc. Surgery of Hand. Home and Office: 77 Clarendon Ave Apt 202 Toronto ON Canada M4V 1J2 E-mail: Wmlinds@aol.com.

LINDSEY, CASIMIR CHARLES, zoologist, educator; b. Toronto, Ont., Can., Mar. 22, 1923; s. Charles Bethune and Wanda Casimira (Gzowski) L.; m. Shelagh Pauline Lindsey, May 29, 1948. BA, U. Toronto, 1948; MA, U. B.C., Vancouver, 1950; PhD, Cambridge (Eng.) U., 1952. Div. biologist B.C. Game Dept., 1952-57; with Inst. Fisheries, also dept. zoology U. B.C., 1953-66; prof. zoology U. Man., Winnipeg, 1966-79; dir. Inst. Animal Resource Ecology, U. B.C., 1980-85; mem. Fisheries and Oceans Adv. Council, 1981-86; prof. emeritus U. B.C., 1988—. Bd. govs. Vancouver Pub. Aquarium, 1956—66, 1980—95; external assessor univs., Singapore and Nanyang, 1979—81; cons. in field. Author papers in field. Served with Can. Army, 1943-45. Recipient Publ. award Wildlife Soc., 1972; Saunderson award for excellence in teaching U. Man., 1977; Rh Inst. award, 1979; Nuffield Found. grantee, 1973; Killam sr. fellow, 1985-86. Fellow Royal Soc. Can.; mem. Can. Soc. Zoologists (pres. 1977-78), Can. Soc. Environ. Biologists (v.p. 1974-75), Am. Soc. Ichthyologists and Herpetologists (gov.), Fedn. Can. Artists. Office: U BC Dept of Zoology 6270 University Blvd Vancouver BC Canada V6T 1Z4

LINDSEY, DAVID ALLEN, retired geologist; m. Barbara Susan Gum, Aug. 13, 1966; children: Timothy, Joseph. PhD, Johns Hopkins U., Baltimore, MD, 1963—67. Scientist emeritus U.S. Geol. Survey, Lakewood, Colo., 1998—, geologist, 1967—97. Recipient Meritorious Svc., Dept. of Interior, 1988. Fellow: Geol. Soc. of Am. Achievements include research in Geology of Precambrian glacial deposits, syntectonic conglomerates, beryllium, copper, gold and uranium deposits.

LINDSEY, DAVID HOSFORD, lawyer; b. Kingsville, Tex., July 25, 1950; s. Ernest Truman and Helen Elizabeth (Hosford) L.; m. Marilyn Kay Williams, June 8, 1974; children: Seth Williams, Brooks Daniel. BS in Bus. Adminstrn.,

U. Mo., 1972; JD, Washburn U., 1975. Bar: Mo. 1975. With trust dept. Commerce Bank, Kansas City, Mo., 1974-75, asst. v.p., 1979-83, v.p., 1983-85, sr. v.p., 1985-94, chief credit officer, 1989—, exec. v.p., 2000—; mgr., sales dept. Pioneer Pallet, Inc., North Kansas City, 1976; asst. cashier Nat. Bank, 1977, asst. v.p., 1977-78, v.p., 1978-79. Vice chmn. planning and zoning com. City of Liberty, Mo., 1981-93; bd. dirs. Kansas City Met. YMCA. Mem. Mo. Bar Assn., Lawyers Assn. Kansas City, Kansas City Met. Bar Assn., Robert Morris Assn. (bd. dirs. Kansas City chpt.), Kansas City C. of C., Kansas City Alumni Assn. (bd. dirs.), Clayview Country Club, Phi Gamma Delta, Omicron Delta Kappa. Baptist. Home: 602 Camelot Dr Liberty MO 64068-1176 Office: Commerce Bank 1000 Walnut St Ste 730 Kansas City MO 64106-2123

LINDSEY, DAVID STEWART, entrepreneur; b. Youngstown, Ohio, Aug. 26, 1941; s. Haldean Stewart L. and Emma Jane Dixon Freeman; m. Mary Sue Stewart, Sept. 29, 1970 (div. Dec. 1975). BS, U. Oreg., 1964; MA, Bowling Green U., 1969; MBA, Ea. Wash. U., 1992, BA, 1996. Petroleum geologist Amerada Hess Corp., Tulsa, Okla., 1969-72; mine geologist Fed. Resources, Gas Hills, Wyo., 1972; petroleum geologist Cate Engring., Casper, 1973; geologist U.S. Bur. Mines, Spokane, Wash., 1974-76, phys. scientist, 1976-96; stock trader Lindsey Holdings, 1996—. Adj. prof. Ea. Wash. U., Cheney, 1997; tchr. Peace Corps, Borama, Somalia, 1964-66. Contbg. author U.S. Govt. Pubs. V.p. Park Terrace Condo Assn., Spokane, 1980-90; stephen min. 1st Presbyn. Ch., Spokane, 1994-96. Scholar Bowling Green U., Ohio, 1967; grantee NSF, 1968. Mem. Spokane Club, Spokane Mountaineers, Beta Gamma Sigma. Democrat. Home: 620 W 7th Ave #101 Spokane WA 99204 Office: Lindsey Holdings 620 W 7th Ave #101 Spokane WA 99204 E-mail: dslindsey@qwest.net.

LINDSEY, DOTTYE JEAN, marketing executive; b. Temple Hill, Ky., Nov. 4, 1929; d. Jesse D. and Ethel Ellen (Bailey) Nuckols; m. Willard W. Lindsey, June 14, 1952 (div.). BS, Western Ky. U., 1953, MA, 1959. Owner, Bonanza Restaurant, Charleston, W.Va., 1965; tchr. remedial reading Alice Waller Elem. Sch., Louisville, 1967-75, tchr., 1953-67, 1975-84, contact person for remedial reading, 1968—; regional mgr. A.L. Williams Fin. Mktg. Co., 1988—; profl. model Cosmo/Casablancas Modeling Agy., Louisville, 1984-89; with Primerica Fin. Svcs. (formerly A.L. Willams Fin. Svcs.), Louisville, 1988-98; model, 1984-89; regional mgr. Primerica Fin. Svcs., 1988-98. Treas. Met. Louisville Women's Polit. Caucus, 1980-88, Ky. Women's Polit. Caucus, 1988-91; bd. sponsor ROTC Western Ky. U., 1950; local precinct capt., 1987—; election officer, 1984—; treas. Ky. Women's Polit. Caucus, 1988-91; elected at-large mem. exec. com. Louisville/Jefferson County Dem., 1996—. Named Miss Ky., 1951. Mem. NEA, Ky. Edn. Assn., Jefferson County Tchrs. Assn., various polit. action coms., Internat. Reading Assn., Am. Childhood Edn. Assn. Baptist.

LINDSEY, ERIC W, social sciences educator; b. Blythville, Ark., Aug. 23, 1969; s. Thomas G. and Patricia E Lindsey. PhD, Auburn U., Alabama, 1997. Postdoctoral rsch. fellow U. N.C., Greensboro, 1997—99; asst. prof. of human devel. and family studies Tex. Tech U., Lubbock, Tex., 1999—. Contbr. articles to profl. jours., chpts. to books. Grantee Child Care Use among Mex.-Am. Families (Ongoing Study), Dept Human Health and Svcs., 2000-2003. Mem.: Soc. for Rsch. in Child Devel. Office: Texas Tech Univ P. O. Box 1162 Lubbock TX 79409 Office Fax: 806-742-0285. Business E-Mail: elindsey@hs.ttu.edu.

LINDSEY, GINA MARIE, airport executive; Gen. mgr. Seattle-Tacoma Internat. Airport, aviation dimension dir., 1997—, mng. dir. aviation divsn. Office: Seattle Tacoma Internat Airport PO Box 68727 Seattle WA 98168-0727*

LINDSEY, HUBERT ROLANE, judge; b. Jacksonville, Fla., July 15, 1933; s. Hubert Rush and Martha Mae (Johnson) L.; m. Elma Jean Bryan, Oct. 17, 1958; 1 child, Susan. BA, U. fla., 1957; JD, U. Fla., 1966. Bar: Fla. 1966; U.S. Dist. Ct. (so. dist.) Fla. 1968; U.S. Ct. Appeals (5th cir.) 1968; U.S. Supreme Ct. 1975. Tchr., English Duval County Sch. System, Jacksonville, 1958-61; asst. mgr. Fla. Nat. Bank, 1961-64; assoc. Farish & Farish, West Palm Beach, Fla., 1966-79; pvt. practice, 1979-86; cir. judge Fla. Judiciary, 1986—. Mem. Fla. Bar Assn., Palm Beach County Bar Assn., Fla. Trial Lawyers Assn., ABA. Avocations: gardening, travel, carpentry. Office: Palm Beach County Courthouse 300 N Dixie Hwy West Palm Beach FL 33401-4640

LINDSEY, JACQUELYN MARIA, editor; b. Buffalo, June 6, 1952; d. George Henry and Patricia Ann (Rott) Bilkey; m. Timothy Paul Murphy, Jan. 29, 1970 (div. May 1981); children: Paul Jeffrey, Jeremy Michael; m. Warren Lee Eckert, Dec. 5, 1987 (div. June 1992); m. Donald J. Lindsey, Nov. 5, 1994. Student, Ind. U., 1984. Adminstrv. asst. Western N.Y. Cath. Visitor, Buffalo, 1979-81; sec. religious edn. Our Sunday Visitor, Huntington, Ind., 1981-84, editl. asst. periodicals dept., 1985, staff editor periodicals and books, editor My Daily Visitor, 1985-91, coord. Diocesan edits., 1986-88, assoc. editor books, 1987-90, editor trade books, 1990-93, acquisitions editor trade books, 1991—, acquisitions editor religious edn., 1991-2001, editl. devel. mgr., 2001—. Co-founder, co-owner Specialty Tool & Engring., LLC, 1995—; bd. dirs. STE, Inc. Editor, compiler: Photo Directory of U.S. Catholic Hierarchy, 1987, 90, 93; editor Leaves Marianhill Missionaries, 1991—, Catholic Family Prayer Book, 2001, Catholic Pocket Prayer Book, 2002. Candidate for rep. Ind. Gen. Assembly 21st Dist., 1984; mem. LaFontaine Arts Coun., Huntington County, 1985-88; mem. Huntington County Dems., 1986-88. Mem. Cath. Press Assn. Office: Our Sunday Visitor Pub 200 Noll Plz Huntington IN 46750-4304

LINDSEY, JAMES KENDALL, civil engineer; b. Poteau, Okla., Jan. 15, 1924; s. Ray Vernett and Mattie Frances (Kendall) L.; m. Loah Joyce Crowley, July 14, 1946 (dec. 1996); children: Marcia Gay Morgan, Mark Ray, James Neill, John Kendall; m. Mary L. Chambers, Jan. 16, 1998. AS, Clemson U., 1944; BCE, Okla. State U., 1948; MS in Pub. Health, U. Mich., 1950. Registered profl. engr., Okla.; registered land surveyor, Okla. Mobile labs. engr. Okla. State Dept. Health, Oklahoma City, 1947-49, dist. engr., 1949-53; cons. engr. USA Ops. Mission, Addis Ababa, Ethiopia, 1954-55, various water and pollution control facilities, Okla., 1955—. Mem. environ. health com. Okla. Health Planning Coun., Oklahoma City, 1968-75. With U.S. Army, 1943-46. Named Okla. Water Pioneer Gov. of Okla., 1994. Mem. NSPE, Am. Waterworks Assn. (Okla. trustee 1958), Water Environ. Fedn., Okla. Water and Pollution Control Assn. (sec. 1948-53, pres. 1957), Lions (pres. Tahlequah club 1964-65), Tahlequah (Okla.) C. of C. Avocation: ranching. Home and Office: 1630 N Vinita Ave Tahlequah OK 74464-6222

LINDSEY, JANE WILLANN, minister; b. Spencer, Tenn., Oct. 13, 1936; d. William Ezra Keyt and Martha Jane Anderson; m. Jack Lee Lindsey; children: Michael, Deborah Boggs. Cert. pastor. Fl. mgr. Nationwide Jewelry Co., N.Y.C., 1965—69; office mgr. Davicon Jewelers,Inc., 1969—72. Bookkeeper Ctrl. Fla. Aluminum, Winter Haven, Fla., 1973—76; race rels. adv. Nationwide Jewelry Co., 1965—69. Author: Fantasy Come True, 1968 (Best of Poets award The Internat. Libr. of Poetry , 2002). Founder of mission for the needy Trinity Ho. Of Prayer, Winter Haven, Fla., 1979—85. Nominee Poet of the Yr., Internat. Soc. of Poets, 2002; recipient editor's choice award, 2002. Democrat. Pentecostal. Avocations: songwriting, painting, singing, poetry, gardening. Home: 519 Avenue K Northeast Winter Haven FL 33881-4154 Personal E-mail: jjandjlin@aol.com.

LINDSEY, JOANNE M. flight attendant, poet; b. Peoria, Ill., Aug. 27, 1936; d. George Edward and Elsie Rosetta (Mann) Lindsey; AA, El Camino Coll., Torrance, Calif., 1958. Exec. adminstrv. sec. Space Tech. Labs. (formerly Ramo-Woolridge), Hawthorne, Calif., 1958-64; flight attendant Am. Airlines, L.A., 1964—. Mem. acad. coun. Diplomatic Acad., London; vice consul Internat. Biographical Ctr. Contbr. poems to anthologies. Attended People to People Amb. Program's So. African Tour of Women Writers, 1998. Named to Internat. Libr. Poetry, 1996, 1997, 1998, 2001; recipient 7 Poetry Editor's Choice awards in anthologies. Mem.: Friends of Poets and Writers, L.A. World Affairs Coun., Internat. Soc. Poets, Audie Murphy Rsch. Found., Acad. Am. Poets. Avocations: gardening, writing, skiing, mountain biking, home refurbishing. Home: 846 American Oaks Ave Newbury Park CA 91320-5572

LINDSEY, JOHN HORACE, insurance agency executive; b. Waxahachie, Tex., July 28, 1922; s. Harry E. and Marie (Smith) L.; m. Sara Houstoun, Aug. 30, 1946; children: Edwin (dec.), David C. BA, Tex. A&M U., 1944. Propr. Lindsey Ins. Agy., Houston, 1953—; bd. of regents Texas A&M U System. Former v.p. Houston Mus. Fine Arts; former pres. Alley Theatre; bd. dirs. South Tex. Coll. Law, Tex. A&M Rsch. Found., College Station; pres. Tex. A&M U. Alumni, 1964; vice chmn. bd. visitors U.S. Mil. Acad.; bd. dirs. George Bush Presdl. Libr. Found. Recipient Disting. Alumni award Tex. A&M U. Home: 3640 Willowick Houston TX 77019-1114 Office: Ste 1100 2001 Kirby Dr Houston TX 77019-6081

LINDSEY, JONATHAN ASMEL, university official, librarian, educator; b. Bulloch County, Ga., June 9, 1937; s. Joel Wesley and Ethel Iora (Stickland) L.; m. Edythe Annette Loewer, Apr. 3, 1965; children— Julianna Elizabeth, Jonathan Edward AB, George Washington U., 1961; B.D., So. Bapt. Sem., Louisville, 1964; PhD, So. Bapt. Sem., 1968; MSL.S., U. Ala., 1975. Assoc. prof., librarian Judson Coll., Marion, Ala., 1967-77; assoc. dean, librarian Meredith Coll., Raleigh, N.C., 1977-83; librarian Baylor U., Waco, Tex., 1983-89, dir. found. devel., 1989-95, dir. donor info. and recognition, 1995-2001, asst. v.p. donor and info. svcs., 2001—. Author: (monographs) Free To Be, 1975, Change and Challenge, 1978, Professional Ethics and Librarians, 1985, Performance Evaluation: A Management Basic, 1986; editor: N.C. Libraries (H.W. Wilson award 1981), 1979-83, Publications in Librarianship, 1988-93; contbr. articles and book revs. to profl. publs. Mem. Waco Peace Alliance, PTA. Mem. ALA, Assn. Profl. Rschrs. in Advancement, Assn. FundRaising Profls., Coun. for Advancement and Support of Edn., Tex. Libr. Assn. Home: 8265 Mosswood Dr Waco TX 76712-2407 Office: Baylor U PO Box 97026 Waco TX 76798-7026 E-mail: jonathan_lindsey@baylor.edu.

LINDSEY, LAWRENCE BENJAMIN, economist; b. Peekskill, N.Y., July 18, 1954; s. Merritt Hunt and Helen Ruth (Hissam) Lindsey; m. Susan Ann McGrath, Aug. 28, 1982; 3 children. AB magna cum laude, Bowdoin Coll., Brunswick, Maine, 1976; MA, Harvard U., 1981, PhD, 1985; JD (hon.) , Bowdoin Coll., 1993. Economist Coun. Econ. Advisers, Washington, 1981—84; from asst. prof. to assoc. prof. Harvard U., Cambridge, Mass., 1984—90; faculty rsch. fellow Nat. Bur. Econ. Rsch., 1984—89; from assoc. dir. to spl. asst. to Pres., Office of Policy Devel., The White House, Washington, 1989—91; gov. Fed. Res. Bd., 1991—97; resident scholar Am. Enterprise Inst., 1997—2001; mng. dir. Econ. Strategies, Inc., 1997—2001; asst. to Pres. for econ. policy The White House, Washington, 2001—. Author: The Growth Experiment, 1990, Economic Puppetmasters: Lessons From the Halls of Power, 1999; contbr. articles to profl. jours. Recipient Walter Wriston award, Manhattan Inst., 1988, Disting. Pub. Svc. award, Boston Bar Assn., 1994. Office: The White House 1600 Pennsylvania Ave NW Washington DC 20502

LINDSEY, LINDA LEE, sociology educator; b. St. Louis, Aug. 16, 1947; d. Robert Houston and Ruth Margaret (Weimert) L. BA in Sociology and Edn., U. Mo., 1969; MA, Case Western Res. U., 1972, PhD in Sociology, 1974; MA in Counseling, St. Louis U., 1983. Cert. lifetime secondary social sci. tchr., Mo. Asst. prof. sociology John Carroll U., Cleve., 1973-78; mktg. rsch. supr. Southwestern Bell, St. Louis, 1978-79; assoc. prof. St. Louis Coll. Pharmacy, 1979-86; prof. social thought and analysis Washington U., St. Louis, 1981—; prof. sociology Maryville U., 1986—. Cons. Fact Finders Mktg. Rsch., 1982—; rep., co-chair Women's Program Coun. St. Louis, 1983—; rschr. Women in the Developing World, Washington U. and Maryville U., 1990—; spokesperson Tobacco-Free Mo., St. Louis, 1996—; presenter World Congress Sociology, 1978, UN Conf. on Women, Beijing, 1995; program evaluator Asian Studies devel. program East-West Ctr., 1999-2002; fellowship coord. Asian Studies Devel. Program, Pearl River Delta, Hong Kong, 2001. Author: Gender Roles: A Sociological Perspective, 1997; co-author: Sociology: Social Life and Social Issues, 2002; also articles. Trustee Children's Survival Fund, Carbondale, Ill., 1985-96; mem., chairperson advocacy com., bd. dirs. Luth. Family and Children's Svcs., St. Louis, 1992—; feedback supr. health focus group Med. Sch. St. Louis U., 1986—. Japanese culture fellow NEH, 1995; fellow Keizai Koho Ctr., Tokyo, 1990; NSF fellow Harvard U., 1989; Malone fellow Nat. Coun. U.S.-Arab Rels., Jordan, 1988; Fulbright fellow, India, 1981, Pakistan, 1986, India Inst., 1999; NEH summer Seminar awardee, Asian Studies Devel. Program summer Inst. award to Korea, 2000. Mem. Am. Sociol. Assn. (presenter 1995, 98), Global Health Coun., Japan Studies Assn., World Affairs Coun., Sociologists for Women in Soc., Midwest Sociol. Soc. (presenter 1979—), Mo. State Sociol. Soc. (pres. 1994-95, conf. presenter 1997-99). Democrat. Lutheran. Avocations: international travel, swimming, speaking, writing. Home: 29 Algonquin Wood Pl Saint Louis MO 63122-2013 Office: Maryville Univ 13550 Conway Rd Saint Louis MO 63141-7299 E-mail: lindsey@maryville.edu.

LINDSEY, LORI DAWN, lawyer; b. Dallas, Apr. 12, 1972; d. Marion Glenn and Judy Jo Lindsey. BA summa cum laude, U. Okla., 1994, JD with highest honors, 1997. Bar: Okla. 1997. Law clk., legal intern, atty. Norman, Edem, McNaughton & Wallace, Oklahoma City, 1995-98; assoc. Pray, Walker, Jackman, Williamson & Marlar, 1998-99; law clk. for U.S. Dist. judge Vicki Miles-LaGrange Western Dist. Okla., 1999—. Mem. ABA, ATLA, Okla. Trial Lawyers Assn. Avocations: tennis, puzzles. Office: US Dist Ct Western Dist of Okla 200 NW 4th St Ste 5011 Oklahoma City OK 73102-3031

LINDSEY, ROBERTA LEWISE, music researcher, historian; b. Munich, Apr. 23, 1958; d. Fred S. and Elsie E. (White) L. BMus, Butler U., 1980, MMus, 1987; PhD, Ohio State U., 1996. Pres., owner Profl. Typing Svcs., Indpls., 1980-84; mktg. specialist Merchants Mortgage Corp., 1985-87; exec. asst. Ind. Arts Commn., 1988-90; GTA Ohio State U., Columbus, 1990-94, music libr. asst., 1991-93, student coord. music in Ohio festival, 1993, vol. tutor coord., 1994-95, lectr. Marion, 1995; rsch. editor Ind. High Tech. Directory, 1995-97; lectr. Ind. U. Sch. Music, 1998, vis. asst. prof., 1999—2001, asst. prof. Indpls., 2001—. Rep. Susan Porter Meml. symposium Ohio State U., Columbus, 1995; mem. program com. AMS Midwest, 2001—02; vis. rsch. fellow Am. Music Rsch. Ctr., 1997; presenter in field; tchr. of record Digital Music Libr. Grant project Ind. U., 2000—; co-presenter Tech. Music Appreciation Symposium, 1999; spkr. in field. Book reviewer Ohioana Jour.; contbg. editor: Lenten Devotional, 2000, 2001; contbr. articles to profl. jours. Reader Ctrl. Ind. Radio Reading, Inc., Indpls., 1985-90; co-founder, mem. Grad. Music Students Assn., Ohio State U., Columbus; mem. multicultural diversity com. Coun. of Grad. Students, Columbus, 1992, mem. orgns. and elections com., 1992, co-chair orientation com., 1993; pre-concert lectr. Carmel Symphony Orch., 1998; mem. Inst. Rep. for the Arts, 1999—; adv. bd. Eiteljorg Mus., 1999—. Recipient Grad. Student Alumni Rsch. award, Ohio State U., 1993, Innovative Teaching Recognition award, Ind. U. Sch. Music, 2002; grantee Dena Epstein grantee, 2001, Ind. U. Purdue U. Indpls., 2001. Mem. Soc. Am. Music, Am. Musicol. Soc. (prof. com. 2001—, program com. midwest chpt. 2001-02), Coll. Music Soc. (Gt. Lakes chpt. conv. 2001, 02), Soc. Ethnomusicology, Am. Music Rsch. Ctr., Classic Ragtime Soc. Presbyterian.

LINDSEY, RUTH, retired physical education educator; b. Kingfisher, Okla., Oct. 26, 1926; d. Lewis Howard and Kenyon (King) L. BS, Okla. State U., 1948; MS, U. Wis., 1954; PEd, Ind. U., 1965. Registered kinesiotherapist, 1970. Instr. Okla. State U., Stillwater, 1948-50, Monticello Coll., Alton, Ill., 1951-54, DePauw U., Greencastle, Ind., 1954-56; prof. Okla. State U., Stillwater, 1956-75; vis. prof. U. Utah, Salt Lake City, 1975-76; prof. phys. edn. Calif. State U., Long Beach, 1976-88, prof. emeritus phys. edn., 1988—; freelance author, cons. Albuquerque; ret. Co-author: (originally titled Body Mechanics) Fitness for the Health of It, 6 edits., 1969-89, Concepts of Physical Fitness, 9 edits., 1997, Fitness for Life, 1st edit., 1979, 4th edit., 1997, Concepts of Physical Fitness and Wellness, 1st edit., 1994, 2d edit., 1997, The Ultimate Fitness Book, 1984, Survival Kit for Those Who Sit, 1989, A Menu of Concepts: Physical Fitness Concepts, Toward Active Lifestyles and Fitness and Wellness Concepts, Toward Healthy Lifestyles, 1996; contbg. author: Exercise and the Older Adult, 1998; editor, pub.: Why Don't You Salt the Beans, 1997, Kenyon's Songs, 1998; editor: Perspectives: Jour. of Western Soc. for Phys. Edn. Coll. Women, 1988-95; contbr. articles to profl. jours. Mem. Commn. on Aging, City of Westminster, 1998-2001 Amy Morris Homans scholar, 1964; recipient Disting. and Meritorious Svc. Honor award Okla. Assn. Health, Phys. Edn. and Recreation, 1970, Meritorious Performance award Calif. State U., 1987, Julian Vogel Meml. award Am. Kinesiotherapy Assn., 1988, Texty award Text and Acad. Authors Assn., 1997, William Holmes McGuffey award Tex. and Acad. Authors Assn., 1998. Fellow AAHPERD, Am. Kinesiotherapy Assn., Calif. Assn. Health, Phys. Edn., Recreation and Dance, Nat. Coun. Against Health Fraud, Western Soc. for Phys. Edn. of Coll. Women (Hon. Mem. award 1995), Phi Kappa Phi. Republican. Baptist. Avocations: golf, travel, writing.

LINDSEY, SANFORD CHAPDU, priest; b. Cin., Apr. 22, 1914; s. Clyde Lindsey and Caroline Amelia (Chapdu) L. AB, Kenyon Coll., 1948; MDiv, Episcopal Theol. Sch., Cambridge, Mass., 1950; MA, Gaulladet Sch., 1964. Ordained priest, 1951. Chaplain Phillips Acad., Andover, Mass., 1950; rector St. Andrew Parish, Washington County, Ohio, 1952-54, Trinity Parish, London, 1954-57; curate, tchr. St. Mark Acad., Cocoa, Fla., 1956-61; vicar, tchr. St. Peter Ch. and Sch., Plant City, 1961-64; dean's asst. and curator of mus. Washington Nat. Cathedral, 1964-71; rector St. Paul Parish, Logan, Ohio, 1971-73; curator Mary Johnston Mus., London, 1973-75; various to priest-in-charge St. Luke Parish, Cin., 1987—. Editor: (annual) Kenyon Coll. Reveille, 1947. Cpl. USAF, 1943-45. Avocations: painting drama scenic sets, woodcuts. Office: St Luke Parish 7350 Kirkwood Ln Cincinnati OH 45233-1030 Home: Apt 259 3550 Shaw Ave Cincinnati OH 45208-5414

LINDSEY, SETH MARK, lawyer, federal agency administrator; b. L.A., Oct. 18, 1947; s. Seth Rankin and Lela Belle L.; m. Susan Adelaide Badger, June 29, 1968; 1 child, Samantha. BA, U. So. Calif., L.A., 1968; JD, Yale U., 1971. Bar: Calif. 1972, U.S. Supreme Ct. 1984. Honors atty. Housing and Urban Devel., Washington, 1971-72, atty., 1972-76; asst. chief counsel Fed. Railroad Adminstrn., 1976-86, chief counsel, 1986—, acting adminstr., 1993, 2001. Spl. counsel for Conrail and Union Sta. Redevel. Fed. Railroad Adminstrn., 1984-86. Recipient Silver medal Dept. Transp., 1977, 83, Gold medal, 1984. Baptist. Office: Dept Transp Fed RR Adminstrn Adminstrn 1120 Vermont Ave NW Ms 10 Washington DC 20590-0001

LINDSEY, SHARON EUBANK, medical/surgical nurse, educator; b. Richmond, Va., Sept. 7, 1943; d. Hepburn Frederick and Virginia (Dunn) Eubank; m. Troy Newton Lindsey, July 20, 1963; children: Christine L. Schardt, Kimberly W. Cert., The Pan Am. Sch., Richmond, 1962—63; student, Va. Commonwealth U., Richmond, 1972—75; AS, John Tyler C.C., Chester, Va., 1975—78. RN Va. Clinic nurse J.B. Watkins Elem. Sch., Midlothian, Va., 1985—87; health svcs. nurse Psychiat. Inst. of Richmond, 1988; nutritional specialist NutriSystem, Richmond, 1989—91; nurse instr. Richmond Tech. Ctr., 1991—94; boutique fashion coord. Stein Mart, Richmond, 1994—2001. Mem. Richmond Assn. for Early Childhood Edn., 1980—83, Salisbury Women's Club, Midlothian, Va., 1985—2001, Am. Family Fitness, Midlothian, 1982—2001, Va. Mus. Fine Arts, Rep. Women's Club, Midlothian, Va., 1980—. Mem.: Aerobic and Fitness Assn. Am. (cert. fitness instr.), Salisbury Country Club, Phi Theta Kappa. Republican. Baptist. Avocations: dancing, gardening, aerobics, reading. Home: 2301 Castlebridge Rd Midlothian VA 23113-4012

LINDSEY, STEVEN W. astronaut, military officer; b. Arcadia, Calif., Aug. 24, 1960; s. Arden and Louise Lindsey; m. Diane Renee Trujillo; 3 children. BS in Engring. Scis., USAF Acad., Colo. Springs, Colo., 1982; MS in Aeronautical Engring., USAF Inst. Tech., Wright Field, Dayton, Ohio, 1990. Commd. 2d lt. USAF, Colo. Springs, 1982, advanced through grades to lt. col., student pilot Tex., 1982—83; pilot USAF 12th Reconnaissance Squadron , Bergstrom AFB, 1984—87; grad. student USAF Inst. Tech. , Wright AFB, Dayton, Ohio, 1987; test pilot student USAF Test Pilot Sch., Edwards AFB, Calif., 1989—90; test pilot USAF, Eglin AFB, Fla., 1990—93; grad. student USAF Air Command and Staff Coll. , Maxwell AFB, Ala., 1993—94; team leader integrated product USAF, Eglin AFB, 1994—95; astronaut NASA Johnson Space Flight Ctr., Houston, 1996—. Named Disting. Grad. Undergrad. Pilot Tng., USAF, 1983; recipient Leithen-Tittle award, USAF Test Pilot Sch. Class 89A, 1989, 3 Space Flight medals, NASA. Mem.: Soc. Exptl. Pilots, USAF Acad. Assn. Grads., Assn. Space Explorers. Achievements include 4500 flying hours using 50 different types of aircraft; 3 space flights, mission commander on 1, 896 hours in space. Avocations: camping, reading, racquetball, running, skiing. Office: Astronaut Office/CB Johnson Space Ctr Houston TX 77058

LINDSEY, SUSAN LYNDAKER, zoologist; b. Valley Forge, Pa., Aug. 23, 1956; d. Howard Paul and Lillian Irene (Whitman) Lyndaker; m. Kevin Arthur Lindsey, July 17, 1982; children: Ryan Howard, Shannon Marie. BS in Biology, St. Lawrence U., 1978; MA in Zoology, So. Ill. U., Carbondale, 1980; PhD in Zoology, Colo. State U., 1987. Rschr. St. Lawrence U., Kenya, East Africa, 1978; tchr. Beth Jacob H.S., Denver, 1986-87; rschr. mammal dept. Dallas Zoo, 1988-93; exec. dir. Wild Canid Survival and Rsch. Ctr., Eureka, Mo., 1993—. Adj. prof. Cedar Valley Coll., 1992-93, So. Ill. U., Carbondale, 1996—; mgmt. group mem. Red Wolf Species Survival Plan, Tacoma, Wash., 1994—, Mexican Gray Wolf Species Survival Plan, Albuquerque, 1993—, Maned Wolf Species Survival Plan, Washington, 1999—. Author: (with others) The Okapi: Mysterious Animal of Congo-Zaire, 1999; contbr. articles to profl. jours. Docent Denver Zool. Found., Denver Zoo, 1985-88. Mem. Acad. Sci. St. Louis, Am. Zoo and Aquarium Assn., Am. Behavior Soc., Am. Soc. of Mammalogists, Beta Beta Beta, Phi Beta Kappa, Psi Chi. Avocations: horseback riding, canoeing, gardening, photography, travel. Office: Wild Canid Survival Rsch Ctr Wash U PO Box 760 Eureka MO 63025-0760

LINDSKOG, DAVID RICHARD, lawyer; b. Aug. 4, 1936; s. Gustaf Elmer and Charlotte (Birely) L.; m. Elisabeth Lagg, Jan. 28, 1978; 1 child, Stefanie. BA, Yale U., 1958; LLB, U. Va., 1965. Bar: N.Y. 1966, conseil juridique France 1978, avocat 1992. Assoc. Curtis, Mallet-Prevost, Colt & Mosle, N.Y.C., 1965-72, ptnr., 1973-99; sr. v.p., gen. counsel Leach Holding Corp., Westport, Conn., 1999—. Lt. USNR, 1958-62. Mem. Internat. Bar Assn. Episcopalian. Home: 22 Shore Acre Dr Old Greenwich CT 06870-2130 Office: Leach Holding Corp 315 Post Road West Westport CT 06880

LINDSTROM, DONALD FREDRICK, JR. priest, consultant; b. Atlanta, July 18, 1943; s. Donald Fredrick Sr. and Elizabeth (Haynes) L.; m. Marcia Pace, Dec. 30, 1983; children: Christopher, Eric, Ashley, Ellison. ABJ, U. Ga., 1966; MDiv, Va. Theol. Sem., 1969; JD, Woodrow Wilson Coll. Law, 1977; postgrad., U. West Fla., 1984. Lic. marriage and family therapist, Fla., Ala. Broadcast journalist radio and TV, Atlanta and N.Y.C., 1961-68; priest Episcopal ch., 1969—; detective sgt. Atlanta Police Dept., 1970-75; rector St. Thomas Episcopal Church, Greenville, Ala., 1997—. Pvt. practice as marriage and family therapist, Pensacola, Fla., 1983-91; ecumenical officer Diocese of Ctrl. Gulf Coast, 1989-91, 2002—, Miss., 1992-97, mem. standing com., 2001—; bd. visitors Kanuga Conf. Ctr., 1993—; guest chaplain U.S. Ho. of Reps., 1994; mem. ecumenical staff gen. conv. Episcopal Ch., 1994. Writer, producer The Cry for Help, The Autumn Years; contbr. articles to profl. publs. Chaplain Atlanta Police Dept., 1975-78, Meridian Police Dept., 1995-97, Butler County (Ala.) Area Law Enforcement, 1998—; pres. N.W. Fla. chpt. Nat. Kidney Found., 1987-88; mem. Leadership Atlanta, 1975; bd. dirs. Leadership Pensacola; trustee Fla. Trust for Hist. Preservation. Mem. Am. Assn. for Marriage and Family Therapy (clin.), Mental Health Assn. (life, bd. dirs. Pensacola 1986-88), Internat. Conf. Police Chaplains, Rotary Internat., Navy League, Order of Holy Cross (assoc.), Chambellan Provincial, Bronze star of Excellence, Confrerie de la Chaine des Rotisseurs, Bailli Honoraire, Bailliage de Meridian, FOP, (officer), Alpha Tau Omega, Sigma Delta Chi, Di Gamma Kappa. Avocations: music, photography, traveling, fly fishing.

LINDSTROM, ERIC EVERETT, ophthalmologist; b. Helena, Mont., Nov. 28, 1936; s. Everett Harry and Nan Augusta (Johnson) L.; m. Nancy Jo Alexander, July 24, 1960; children: Laura Ann, Eric Everett. BS, Wheaton Coll., 1958; MD, U. Md., 1963; MPH, Harvard U., 1966. Diplomate Am. Bd. Preventive Medicine, Am. Bd. Ophthalmology. Intern Madigan Army Med. Ctr., Tacoma, 1963-64; resident in aerospace medicine Sch. Aerospace Medicine, Brooks AFB, Tex., 1966-68; resident in ophthalmology Brooke Army Med. Ctr., Ft. Sam Houston, 1972-75; surgeon 12th combat aviation group U.S. Army, Vietnam, 1968-69; chief profl. svcs. and aviation medicine Beach Army Hosp., Ft. Wolters, Tex., 1969-72; asst. chief ophthalmology clinic Madigan Army Med. Ctr., Tacoma, 1975-76; now with Lindstrom Eye Clinic; med. dir. Palo Pinto County (Tex.) Mental Health Clinic, 1970-72; ret. Cons. Tex. State Rehab. Com., 1971-72; chmn. bd. trustees South Cen. Regional Med. Ctr.; sr. aviation med. examiner, FAA; flight surgeon Miss. ANG. Deacon First Bapt. Ch., Laurel, 1978—; bd. dirs. Laurel Salvation Army, Good Shepherd Clin., Laurel. Decorated Bronze Star, Air medal with 2 oak leaf clusters, Meritorious Svc. medal. Fellow ACS, Am. Coll. Physician Execs., Am. Coll. Preventive Medicine, Aerospace Med. Assn. (assoc.), Am.

Acad. Ophthalmology; mem. AMA, FAA (sr. aviation med. examiner), Am. Acad. Cataract and Refractive Surgery, New Orleans Acad. Ophthalmology, Miss. Med. Assn. (trustee), Miss. Hosp. Assn. (bd. govs.), Miss. EENT Assn., South Miss. Med. Soc., So. Med. Assn., La.-Miss. EENT Assn., Flying Physicians Assn., Soc. Mil. Ophthalmologists, Soc. USAF Flight Surgeons, Alliance Air N.G. Flight Surgeons, Aircraft Owners and Pilots Assn., Kiwanis, Nu Sigma Nu. Home: 809 Cherry Ln Laurel MS 39440-1651 Office: Lindstrom Eye Clinic PO Box 407 Laurel MS 39441-0407 E-mail: drelindstrom@c-gate.net.

LINDSTROM, JANET ELENA, non-profit executive; b. Erie, Pa., Jan. 27, 1934; d. Charles and Emma Marie Ramandanes; m. Gary Edward Lindstrom, June 19, 1958 (wid. Jan. 1980); children: Maren, Jennifer. BS, Pa. State U., 1956; MA, Columbia U., 1960. Tchr. Erie Sch. Dist., 1956-58, New Canaan (Conn.) Schs., 1958-62, Foxglove Sch., New Canaan, 1982-83; exec. dir. New Canaan Hist. Soc., 1983—. Sec., DOVIA, 1992-94, v.p., 1994, dir. vol., Stamford, Conn., 1990-94; dir. vol., pres. 1989—; commr. Hist. Dist. Commn., New Canaan, 1989-95, sec. 1989-93, v.p. 1993-95; sec. Day Care Ctr. of New Canaan, 1992-96; pres. New Canaan H.S. Parent Facility, 1980-85, New Canaan Hist. Soc. bd. govs., 1983-85; co-chair NCHS Scholarship Found, New Canaan, 1982-84. Sec. Dirs. of Vols., Stamford, Conn., 1990-94, v.p. 1994-95, pres. 1996—. Bd. dirs. Lower Hudson Conf., 1996—, v.p., 1997-99. Mem. AAUW (pres. 1971-73, grantee 1973), Rep. Woman's Club, New Canaan Field Club, New Canaan C. of C. (bd. dirs. 1996-2000). Republican. Presbyterian. Office: The New Canaan Hist Soc 13 Oenoke Rdg New Canaan CT 06840-4195

LINDSTROM, JOYCE E. author; b. Rigby, Idaho, Jan. 8, 1931; d. Sheridan Stewart and Leah Emma (Ripplinger) Evans; m. Virgil Harold Lindstrom, Nov. 6, 1951; children: John Nils, Launa Joyce, Kurt Terry, Joni Marie, Todd Evan, Cecelia Ann, Janae Eleanor. Student, Idaho Falls Bus. Coll., summer 1949; AA, Ricks Coll., Rexburg, Idaho, 1989. Author: History of Lewisville, Idaho, 1982, Idaho's Vigilantes, 1984 (Writer of the Yr. award 1984), The Van Hoose, Van Hooser, Van Huss Family, 1993, Handcarts West, 1998 (Writer of the Yr. award 1999); contbr. numerous articles to various magr. Mem. Idaho Writers League (state v.p. 1990-91, pres. 1992-93, 2002-03, chpt. pres. 1994-95). Avocations: reading, travel. Home: 467 N 3200 E Lewisville ID 83431 E-mail: writejoy@srv.net.

LINDSTRÖM, LARS ERNST SIMON, education educator; b. Lund, Sweden, Sept. 8, 1943; s. Henning and Gunhild (Strindfors) L.; stepmother Ruth (Håkansson) L.; m. Barbara Kucha, July 13, 1996; children: Simon, Amanda. BA, Lund U., 1966, MA, 1970; PhD in Edn., Stockholm U., 1986. Lic. psychologist, Sweden. Lectr. Stockholm Sch. Social Work, Sweden, 1973-76; asst. prof. U. Coll. Arts, Crafts, and Design, Stockholm, 1976-90; rsch. assoc. Stockholm Inst. Edn./Stockholm U., 1990-94; prof. edn. Stockholm Inst. Edn., 1995—. Cons. The Municipality of Stockholm, 1975-80; vis. scholar Harvard U., Cambridge, Mass., 1991; chmn. Nordic Network Rschrs. in Visual Arts Edn., 1994-97; project coord. Comenius 3.1 program European Union, 1997-99; sci. prof. Linköping (Sweden) U., 1999; sci. adviser Nat. Swedish Bd. of Health and Welfare; mem. gov. bd. Stockholm Inst. Edn.; external evaluator Norwegian Min. Edn., 2001. Author: Managing Alcoholism, 1992; editor: Nordic Visual Arts Research, 1998, The Cultural Context, 2000; contbr. articles to profl. jours. Lutheran. Home: Urbergsvägen 20 S-16764 Bromma Sweden Office: Stockholm Inst Edn Box 34103 S-10026 Stockholm Sweden

LINDZEN, RICHARD SIEGMUND, meteorologist, educator; b. Webster, Mass., Feb. 8, 1940; s. Abe and Sara (Blachman) L.; m. Nadine Lucie Kalougine, Apr. 7, 1965; children: Eric, Nathaniel. AB, Harvard U., 1960, SM, 1961, PhD, 1964. Research assoc. U. Wash., Seattle, 1964-65; Research asso. U. Oslo, 1965-66; with Nat. Center Atmospheric Research, Boulder, Colo., 1966-68; mem. faculty U. Chgo., 1968-72; prof. meteorology Harvard U., 1972-83, dir. Center for Earth and Planetary Physics, 1980-83; Alfred P. Sloan prof. meteorology MIT, 1983—. Lady Davis vis. prof. Hebrew U., 1979; Sackler prof. Tel Aviv U., 1992; Vikram Sarabhai prof. Phys. Rsch. Lab., Ahmendabad, India, 1985; Lansdowne lectr. U. Victoria, 1993; Haurwitz lectr. Am. Meteorol. Soc., 1997; cons. NASA, Jet Propulsion Lab., others; corr. mem. com. on human rights NAS. Author: Dynamics in Atmospheric Physics; co-author: Atmospheric Tides; contbr. to profl. jours. Recipient Macelwane award Am. Geophys. Union, 1968 Fellow NAS, AAAS, Am. Geophys. Union, Am. Meteorol. Soc. (Meisinger award 1969, councillor 1972-75, Charney award 1985, Haurwitz lectr. 1997), Am. Acad. Arts and Scis., Norwegian Acad. Scis. and Letters; mem. Internat. Commn. Dynamic Meteorology, Institut Mondial des Scis. (founding mem.). Jewish. Office: MIT 54 1720 Cambridge MA 02139

LINDZEY, GARDNER, psychologist, educator; b. Wilmington, Del., Nov. 27, 1920; s. James and Marguerite (Shotwell) L.; m. Andrea Lewis, Nov. 28, 1944; children: Jeffrey, Leslie, Gardner, David, Jonathan. AB, Pa. State U., 1943, MS, 1945; PhD, Harvard U., 1949; LHD (hon.), U. Colo., 1990; DSc (hon.), Rutgers U., 1992. Research analyst OSRD, 1944-45; instr. psychology Pa. State U., 1945-46; teaching fellow Harvard U., Cambridge, Mass., 1946-47, research fellow, 1947-49, research assoc., asst. prof., 1949-53, lectr., chmn. psychol. clinic staff, 1953-56, prof., chmn. dept., 1972-73; prof. psychology Syracuse (N.Y.) U., 1956-57, U. Minn., 1957-64, U. Tex., 1964-72, chmn., 1964-68, v.p. acad. affairs, 1968-70, v.p. ad interim, 1971, v.p., dean Grad. Studies, prof. psychology, 1973-75; dir. Ctr. for Advanced Study in Behavioral Scis., Stanford (Calif.) U., 1975-89, dir. emeritus, 1989—. Mem. psychopharmacology study sect. NIMH, 1958-62, mem. program-project com., 1963-67, mem. adv. com. on extramural research, 1968-71; mem. com. faculty research fellowships Social Sci. Research Council, 1960-63, bd. dirs., 1962-76, mem. com. problems and policy, 1963-70, 72-76, chmn., 1965-70, mem. exec. com., 1970-75, chmn., 1971-75, mem. com. genetics and behavior, 1961-67, chmn., 1961-65; mem. com. biol. bases social behavior, 1967— ; mem. com. work and personality in middle years, 1972-77; mem. sociology and social psychology panel NSF, 1965-68, mem. spl. commn. social scis., 1968-69, mem. adv. com. research, 1974—, mem. Waterman award com., 1976-79; mem. exec. com., assembly behavioral and social sci. NAS-NRC, 1970—, mem. com. life sci. and pub. policy, 1968-74, mem. panel nat. needs for biomed. and behavioral research personnel, 1974—, mem. com. social sci. in NSF, 1975—, mem. Inst. Medicine, 1975—; mem. com. on drug abuse Office Sci. and Tech., 1962-63; mem. Presdl. Com. Nat. Medal Sci., 1966-69; bd. dirs. Found.'s Fund Research in Psychiatry, 1967-70; bd. dirs. Am. Psychol. Found., 1968-76, v.p., 1971-73, pres., 1974-76 Author: (with Hall) Theories of Personality, 1957, 70, 78; (with Allport and Vernon) Study of Values, 1951, 60; Projective Techniques and Cross-Cultural Research, 1961; (with J.C. Loehlin and J.N. Spuhler) Race Differences in Intelligence, 1975; (with C.S. Hall and R.F. Thompson) Psychology, 1975; also articles; editor: Handbook of Social Psychology, Vols. 1 and 2, 1954, Vols. 1-5, 1969, Assessment of Human Motives, 1958, Contemporary Psychology, 1967-73, History of Psychology in Autobiography, Vol. 6, 1974, vol. 7, 1980, vol. 8, 1989; assoc. editor Psychol. Abstracts, 1960-62, Ency. Social Scis., 1962-67; co-editor Century Psychology Series, 1960-74, Theories of Personality: Primary Sources and Research, 1965, History of Psychology in Autobiography, Vol. V, 1968, Behavioral Genetics: Methods and Research, 1969, Contributions to Behavior-Genetic Analysis, 1970 Fellow Ctr. Advanced Study Behavioral Scis., Stanford, 1955-56, 63-64, 71-72, Inst. Medicine, 1975— Fellow Am. Psychol. Assn. (bd. dirs. 1962-68, 70-74, mem. publs. bd., 1956-59, 70-73, chmn. 1958-59, mem. council of reps. 1959-67, 68-74, pres. divsn. social and personality psychology 1963-64, mem. policy and planning 1975, 78, pres. assn. 1966-67, mem. council of editors 1968-73, chmn. com. sci. award 1968-69, pres. divsn. gen. psychology 1970-71), Am. Acad. Arts and Scis., Am. Philos. Soc., Inst. Medicine, NAS, AAAS; mem. Am. Eugenics Soc. (bd. dirs. 1962-70), Soc. Social Biology (bd. dirs. 1972—, pres. 1978—), Am. Psychol. Assn. (dir. ins. trust 1973—), Univs. Research Assn. (bd. dirs. 1973-75) Home: 1100 Sharon Park Dr Apt 22 Menlo Park CA 94025-7004

LINE, WILLIAM GUNDERSON, lawyer; b. July 19, 1927; s. William Harrison and Lulu Mae (Gunderson) L.; children: Nancy Line Jacobs, Lindsey Line Natvig, Katherine Line Rasmussen, Julie Ann Line Bailey, Ashley E. Student, Nebr. State Tchrs. Coll., 1943-44; BSL, U. Nebr., 1948, JD, 1950. Bar: Nebr. 1950, U.S. Dist. Ct. Nebr. 1950, U.S. Supreme Ct. 1965. County atty. Dodge County, Nebr., 1955-59; ptnr. Kerrigan, Line & Martin, Fremont, 1962-95. Lectr. Nebr. State Patrol Tng. Camp, Ashland, 1959. Bd. dirs. Nebr. Civil Liberties Union, 1971-75. Mem. Nebr. Bar Assn., Dodge County Bar Assn. (pres. 1967), Phi Alpha Delta. Republican. Episcopalian. Office: PO Box 410 33 W 4th St Fremont NE 68026-0410

LINEBAUGH, DAVID EUGENE, fire marshal, educator; b. Colorado Springs, Colo., Aug. 26, 1955; s. Gary Eugene and Doris Irene (Llewellyn) Finch; m. Beverly Joan Good, Feb. 14, 1985; children: Christopher Aaron, Quinlan Scott. AAS, Pikes Peak C.C., Colorado Springs, 1992; BS, Colo. Christian U., 1994, MS, 1997. Dispatcher/patrolman Manitou Springs (Colo.) Police Dept., 1975-76, Colo. State Patrol, Colorado Springs, 1976-77; v.p. High Country Heat Pumps and Air Conditioning, 1978-84; combination inspector Regional Bldg. Dept., 1984-87; chief inspector Colorado Springs Fire Dept., 1987-90, dep. fire marshal, 1990-94, fire marshal, 1994—. Prof. fire sci. Pikes Peak C.C., 1994—; prof. mgmt. Colo. Christian U., 1998—. Contbr. articles to profl. jours. Mem. Regional Bldg. Commn., Pikes Peak Regional Bldg. Dept., Colorado Springs, 1983-84; mem. Pikes Peak leadership com. Citizens Goals, Colorado Springs, 1995-96; mem. cmty. action com. City of Colorado Springs, 1996; bd. dirs. Wagon Wheel Coun.-Girl Scouts Am., 1997. Recipient Achievement award Colorado Springs C. of C., 1993, Disting. Achievement award Colo. Christian U., 1994, Pikes Peak Leadership Grad. award Citizens Goals, 1995. Mem. Internat. Fire Code Inst. (chmn. edn. and cert. com. 1995—), Nat. Fire Protection Assn. (inspector qualification com. 1991—), Fire Marshals Assn. N.Am., Internat. Conf. Bldg. Ofcls., Fire Marshals Assn. Colo. (sec. 1993), Colo. Christian Univ. Alumni Assn. (bd. dirs. 1997). Republican. Methodist. Home: 2625 Whispering Ter Colorado Springs CO 80917-3600 Office: Colorado Springs Fire Dept Office Fire Marshal 31 S Weber St Colorado Springs CO 80903-1913

LINEBAUGH, KENT B. lawyer; b. Provo, Utah, Sept. 22, 1934; s. Glade Carleton and Thora Hawkins Linebaugh; m. Sherron Evelyn Bird, Jan. 12, 1962; children: Catherine, Mark B., Kent B. Jr., Elizabeth, Sarah. BS, U. Utah, 1958, JD, 1961. Bar: Utah 1961, U.S. Dist. Ct. Utah 1961, U.S. Ct. Appeals (10th cir.) 1969, U.S. Supreme Ct. 1995. Atty. Jones, Waldo, Holbrook & McDonough, Salt Lake City, 1965-70; gen. counsel Terracor, 1970-74; atty. Johnson & Linebaugh, 1974-76, Jardine, Johnson & Baldwin, Salt Lake City, 1976-78, Jardine, Linebaugh & Dunn, Salt Lake City, 1978-99, Jones, Waldo, Salt Lake City, 1999—. With USAF, 1962—65. Mem.: A. J. Anderson Inn of Ct. (past pres.). Mem. Lds Ch. Avocation: breeding and racing quarter horses. Home: 3000 Connor St Unit 3 Salt Lake City UT 84109-2463 Office: Jones Waldo 170 S Main St Ste 1500 Salt Lake City UT 84101-1644 E-mail: klinebaugh@joneswaldo.com.

LINEBERGER, WILLIAM CARL, chemistry educator; b. Hamlet, N.C., Dec. 5, 1939; s. Caleb Henry and Evelyn (Cooper) L.; m. Katharine Wyman Edwards, July 31, 1979. BS, Ga. Inst. Tech., 1961, MSEE, 1963, PhD, 1965. Rsch. physicist U.S. Army Ballistic Rsch. Labs., Aberdeen, Md., 1967-68; postdoctoral assoc. Joint Inst. for Lab. Astrophysics U. Colo., Boulder, 1968-70, from asst. prof. to prof. chemistry, 1970-83, E.U. Condon prof. chemistry, 1983—. Phi Beta Kappa nat. lectr., 1989. Capt. U.S. Army, 1965-67. Fellow AAAS, Joint Inst. for Lab. Physics, Am. Phys. Soc. (H.P. Broida prize 1981, Bomen Michelson prize 1987, Optical Sci. Am. Meggers prize 1988, Plyler prize 1992; mem. NAS, Am. Chem. Soc. (Irving Langmuir prize 1996), Am. Acad. Arts and Scis., Sigma Xi. Office: U Colo Joint Inst Lab Astrophysics Cb 440 Boulder CO 80309-0001

LINEBERRY, REBECCA J. municipal official, treasurer; b. Pulaski, Va., Feb. 12, 1963; d. Leroy Martin Sr. and Virginia (Whitt) Lineberry; div. Jan. 25, 2002. AAS in Acctg., New River C.C., Dublin, Va., 1983. Cert. govt. treas. U. Va.; master govt. treas. U. Va. Bookkeeper Bell Realty, Dublin, 1983; clk., sec. Town of Dublin, 1983-87, asst. treas., 1987-90, treas., 1990—. Mem. Va. Govt. Fin. Officers Assn., Treas.' Assn. Va., S.W. Va. Treas.' Assn. (vice chair 1997-99, chmn. 1999-2001), Assn. Govt. Accts. Avocations: archery, tennis, cross-stitch. Office: Town of Dublin PO Box 1066 Dublin VA 24084-1066 E-mail: rlineberry@dublintown.org.

LINEBERRY, SANDRA BEECH, accountant; b. Battle Creek, Mich., Nov. 22, 1946; d. Raymond August and Betty Jean (Bailey) Wank; m. James E. Beech, June 19, 1964 (div. June 1977); children: James Michael, Daniel Lee, Christina Rena; m. Terry Lineberry, Sept. 10, 1977 (div. June 1983). AA, Kellogg C.C., 1976; BA, Fla. Atlantic U., 1981. Bookkeeper Henry D. Bogaton, Lantana, Fla., 1978-81; acct. Darling & Rosasco CPA's, Palm Beach Garden, 1981-84, Rosasco & Lineberry CPA's, Royal Palm Beach, 1984-86, Peterson, Peterson & Rioux, Lake Worth, 1987—. Mem. AICPA, Fla. Inst. of CPA's. Republican. Methodist. Avocations: bowling, bike riding, jogging, softball, crocheting. Office: Peterson Peterson & Rioux CPAs 3003 S Congress Ave Ste 2C Lake Worth FL 33461-2169 Home: 200 NE 5th Ct Delray Beach FL 33444-3839

LINEHAN, ALLAN DOUGLAS, prosthodontist; b. L.A., Dec. 30, 1954; s. Charles K. and P. Alene (Rohrbaugh) L.; children: Chelsea L., Keegan H. BA, Lewis and Clark Coll., 1978; D in Dental Medicine, Oreg. Health Scis. U., 1983; MS in Prosthodontics, U. Tex., 1993. Diplomate Am. Bd. Prosthodontics. Gen. dental officer USAF Clinic Kadena, Okinawa, Japan, 1983-86, USAF Clinic Bitburg, Bitburg, Germany, 1986-90; prosthodontic resident Wilford Hall USAF Medical Ctr., San Antonio, 1990-93; chief of prosthodontics 10th Dental Squadron USAF Acad., Colorado Springs, Colo., 1993-97; dental lab. flight comdr. 81st Dental Squadron, Biloxi, Miss., 1997—2001. Vice chmn. prosthodontics for 2-yr. residence advanced edn. in clin. dentistry USAF, Keesler AFB, Miss., 1997—; flight comdr. Tri-Svc. Area Dental Lab., Peterson AFB, Colo., 2001—. Contbr. articles to profl. jours. Dir. for fundraising Explorer Elem. Sch., Colo. Springs, 1995-97. Recipient John J. Sharry Prosthodontic Rsch. competition award Am. Coll. Prosthodontics, 1993, Tylman Rsch. grant Am. Acad. Fixed Prosthodontics, 1992. Fellow Am. Coll. Prosthodontics; mem. Acad. Gen. Dentistry, Psi Omega (v.p. 1979-83). Avocations: automotive restoration, antique restoration, woodworking, metalworking, long distance running. Home: 3875 Weather Vane Dr Colorado Springs CO 80920 Office: 10th Dental Squadron OL-A/SGDA 1045 E Stewart Ave Bldg 2012 Colorado Springs CO 80914-9045

LINEHAN, WILLIAM MARSTON, urologic surgeon, cancer researcher; b. Tulsa, June 25, 1947; s. John Marston and Ella Marie (Bourg) L.; m. Tracey Ann Rouault, Sept. 29, 1979; children: Erin Louise, Emily Pauline. AB, Brown U., 1969; MD, U. Okla., Okla. City, 1973. Diplomate Am. Bd. Urology. Intern medicine U. Okla., 1973-74; intern and resident surgery Duke U., 1974-76, fellow cancer rsch., 1976-78, resident urologic surgery, 1978-82; chief urologic oncology br. Nat. Cancer Inst., Bethesda, Md., 1982—. Mem. urology interagy. coord. com. NIH, Bethesda, 1987—. Mem. editl. bd. Jour. Urology, 1990—; assoc. editor Jour. Nat. Cancer Inst., 1992—; contbr. articles to Nature Science, P.N.A.S., New Eng. Jour. Medicine, Jour. Nat. Cancer Inst. Recipient Gold Cystoscope award Am. Urological Assn., 1992. Fellow ACS; mem. Am. Urol. Assn., Soc. Univ. Surgeons, Am. Assn. Cancer Rsch., Am. Assn. Genitourinary Surgeons. Achievements include co-discovery of kidney cancer disease gene in sporadic renal cell carcinoma as well as in the familial renal cell carcinoma associated with von Hippel Lindau syndrome; co-discovery of hereditary papillary renal carcinoma gene; detailing of molecular genetic changes associated with initiation and progression of kidney cancer; evaluation of effect of interleukin-2 based immunotherapy in patients with advanced kidney cancer as well as effect of new anti-neoplastic agents for patients with advanced prostate carcinoma. Office: Nat Cancer Inst Surgery Br 9000 Rockville Pike Bethesda MD 20892-0001

LINES, SANDRA RAMSEY, forensic document examiner; b. Detroit, Dec. 8, 1940; d. Henry Alexander and Genevieve Agnes (Pilote) Habeeb; m. Richard Ramsey, Apr. 30, 1960 (div. 1965); children: Theresa L., Richard A., Renee A.; m. Ruskin R. Lines II, Sept. 9, 1998. AA, Scottdale (Ariz.) C.C., 1987; BA, U. Phoenix, 1989. Diplomate Am. Bd. Forensic Document Examiners; cert. pub. mgr. Sch. Pub. Affairs/Advanced Pub. Affairs Exec. Program Ariz. State U. Cert. peace officer, sgt. Cleve. Police Dept., 1973-82; investigator Ariz. Bd. Med. Examiners, Phoenix, 1983-84; cert. peace officer investigator Maricopa County Atty.'s Office, 1984-85; spl. agent cert. peace officer Office of Atty. Gen., 1985-96, forensic document examiner, 1991-96, Bur. Alcohol, Tobacco and Firearms, Walnut Creek, Calif., 1996-99; pvt. practice as forensic document examiner, Paradise Valley, Ariz., 1999—. Pub. lectr. Flandrau Sci. Ctr., U. Ariz., Tucson, 1990—92; lectr. astronomy camp Steward Obs., Tucson, 1991—92; project dir. Milky Way Galaxy exhibit gallery Adler Planetarium and Astronomy Mus.; presenter in field. Contbr. articles to profl. jours. Recipient Resolution for Achievements in Law Enforcement Cleve. City Coun., 1979, Committment and Support plaque Fraternal Order of Police, 1996. Fellow Am. Acad. Forensic Scis. (questioned document sect. 1996), Am. Soc. Questioned Document Examiners, S.W. Assn. Forensic Document Examiners; mem. ASTM (forensic scis. com.), Ariz. Women in Policing Assn. Republican. Mem. Maronite Cath. Ch. Achievements include being one of 14 women in 1973 to be the first women in uniform patrol and later the first woman in homicide unit of Cleve. Police Dept., establishment of forensic document lab. at Ariz. Atty. Gen.'s office; established and hosted study group meetings for Document Examiners No. Calif. Fax: 480-429-4677. E-mail: ramsylines@aol.com.

LINETT, DAVID, lawyer; b. Perth Amboy, N.J., Apr. 9, 1934; s. Jack K. and Anne L.; children: Jon, Peter, Maren. BA, Yale U., 1956; JD, Harvard U., 1959. Bar: D.C. 1959, N.J. 1960. Law sec. to assignment judge Superior Ct. NJ, 1959—60; assoc. Gross, Weissberger & Linett, New Brunswick, N.J., 1960-62, ptnr., 1962-77; prosecutor Somerset County, 1977-82; of counsel Lowenstein, Sandler, Brochin, Kohl et al and predecessor, Roseland and Somerville, 1982-85; ptnr. Gindin & Linett, Bridgewater, 1985—. Chmn. N.J. State Bar Com. on Programs for Law Enforcement Personnel, 1978-80; mem. com. on county dist. cts. N.J. Supreme Ct., 1980-82, mem. Post-Indictment Delay Task Force, 1980, dist. XIII ethics com., 1986-90, chair N.J. Supreme Ct. ethics fin. com., 1990-94, treas., 1992-94; gen. counsel United Heritage Bank, 1997-. Mem. N.J. Dem. State Com., 1973-77; bd. dirs. Somerset County Resource Ctr. for Women and Their Families, 1982-83; chmn. bd. trustees, Assn. for Advancement of Mentally Handicapped, 1987-89; commr. N.J. Election Law Enforcement Commn., 1987-2000, vice chair, 1996-2000; mem. Ct. House study com., Somerset County Bd. Freeholders, 1979-82; gen.chmn. Internat. Task Force on Edn. and Tng., 2001-02; gen. counsel United Heritage Bank, 1986—. Mem. ABA (corp., real property law sect.), Nat. Dist. Attys. Assn. (nat. treas., exec. com. 1981-82, Pres.'s award for outstanding svc. as chmn. fin. com. 1982), New Brunswick Bar Assn. (pres. 1974), N.J. Bar Assn. (land use sect., real property sect.), Somerset County Bar Assn., Somerset County C. of C. (bd. dirs. 1984-90, Outstanding Citizen of Yr. 1989), Rotary (pres. 1986-87, dist. gov. 1991-92). Office: PO Box 6135 1170 Rt 22 Bridgewater NJ 08807 E-mail: ginlin@aol.com.

LINFANTE, ITALO, physician, medical educator; b. Matera, Italy, Nov. 12, 1962; came to U.S., 1990; s. Felice Linfante and Carolina Atella. MD with honors, U. Rome, 1987. Diplomate Am. Bd. Psychiatry and Neurology. Vis. assoc. NIH, Bethesda, Md., 1990-94; resident George Washington U., Washington, 1994-95, Baylor Coll. Medicine, Houston, 1995-98; faculty Harvard Med. Sch., Boston, 1998—. Mem. Am. Heart Assn., Am. Acad. Neurology. Office: Harvard Med Sch BIDMC DA 779 330 Brookline Ave Boston MA 02215

LINFORD, RULON KESLER, physicist, engineer; b. Cambridge, Mass., Jan. 31, 1943; s. Leon Blood and Imogene (Kesler) L.; m. Cecile Tadje, Apr. 2, 1965; children: Rulon Scott, Laura Linford Williams, Hilary Linford Henderson, Philip Leon. BSEE, U. Utah, 1966; MS in ElecE, Mass. Inst. Tech., 1969, PhD in ElecE, 1973. Staff CTR-7 Los Alamos (N.Mex) Nat. Lab., 1973-75, asst. group leader CTR-7, 1975-77, group leader CTR-11, 1977-79, program mgr., group leader compact toroid CTR-11, 1979-80, program mgr., asst. div. leader compact toroid CTR divsn., 1980-81, assoc. CTR divsn. leader, 1981-86, program dir. magnetic fusion energy, 1986-89, program dir., div. leader CTR div. office, 1989-91, program dir. nuclear sys., 1991-93; staff LER, 1993-94; U. Calif. coord. sci. and tech., 1994-97; assoc. vice provost lab. programs Office of the Pres., U. Calif., Oakland, 1997—2001, assoc. vice provost, asst. v.p. lab. programs, 2002—. Contbr. articles to profl. jours. Recipient E. O. Lawrence award Dept. of Energy, Washington, 1991. Fellow Am. Physical Soc. (exec. com. 1982, 90-91, program com. 1982, 85, award selection com. 1983, 84, fellowship com. 1986); mem. Sigma Xi. Home: 1055 Aquarius Way Oakland CA 94611-1939 Office: U Calif Office Pres 1111 Franklin 11th Fl Oakland CA 94607-5200 E-mail: rulon.linford@ucop.edu.

LING, CHUNG-MEI, retired pharmaceutical company executive; b. Wen-Ling, Zhejiang, China, May 5, 1931; came to U.S., 1960; s. Hsin-Sao Ling and San-Mei Juan; m. Amy Hsieh; children: Dori, Ellen. BS, Nat. Taiwan U., 1958; MS, Ill. Inst. Tech., 1962, PhD, 1965. Head virology lab. Abbott Labs., North Chicago, Ill., 1968-81, rsch. fellow, 1978-84, mgr. rsch. and devel., 1981-84; founder, chmn. bd. dirs., chief sci. officer Gen. Biologicals Corp., Hsinchu, Taiwan, 1984-88, hon. chmn. bd. Taiwan, 1991—; prof. Nat. Tsing-Hua U., 1991-93. Asst. prof. Ill. Inst. Tech., Chgo., 1965-68; sci. specialist Nat. Inst. Preventative Medicine, Taipei, Taiwan, 1984-85; chief sci. cons. KangLing Biotech. Corp., Hsinchu, 1988—. Contbr. articles to profl. jours; patentee in field; inventor Hepatitis B diagnostics. Fellow Am. Acad. Microbiology; mem. Am. Soc. Biol. Chemists, Am. Clin. Chem., Sigma Xi. Avocations: sight-seeing, singing, interior design. Office: 571 Woodstork Ln Punta Gorda FL 33982

LING, DANIEL T. information technology executive; BSEE, MSEE, PhD in Elec. Engring., Stanford U. Various managerial pos., to sr. mgr.IBM Thomas J. Watson Rsch. Ctr.; sr. rschr., user interfaces and computer graphics; co-founder lab. Microsoft Rsch., Redmond, Wash., 1992—95, dir. lab., 1995—2000, corp. v.p., 2000—. Adv. com. U. Wash., Seattle, U. Calif., Berkeley. Mem.: Assn. Computing Machinery, Am. Phys. Soc., IEEE. Office: Microsoft One Microsoft Way Redmond WA 98052-6399*

LING, FREDERICK S. cardiology educator; b. N.Y.C., Dec. 14, 1960; AB, Columbia U., 1982; MD, NYU, 1986. Intern Beth Israel Hosp., Boston, 1986-87, resident in internal medicine, 1988-89; assoc. prof. cardiology U. Rochester (N.Y.) Sch. Medicine, 1993—. Cardiology fellow Yale U. Sch. Medicine, New Haven, Conn., 1989-93. Fellow Am. Coll. Cardiologists, Soc. Cardiac Angiography and Intervention; mem. AMA, Am. Heart Assn., Alpha Omega Alpha. Office: U Rochester Sch Medicine Dept Cardiology 601 Elmwood Ave # 679 Rochester NY 14642-0001

LING, HOE I. civil engineering educator; b. Sibu, Sarawak, Malaysia, Jan. 20, 1963; came to U.S., 1994; s. Kuek Khing and Teresa (Lau) L.; m. Li-Hwa Wang; children: Emi, Henry. BSc, Kyoto (Japan) U., 1988; MSc, U. Tokyo, 1990, PhD, 1993. Asst. prof. U. Del., Newark, 1994-98; asst. prof. civil engring. Columbia U., N.Y.C., 1998-99, assoc. prof. civil engring., 2000—. Recipient Presdl. career award NSF, 2001. Mem. ASCE, Japan Geotech. Soc. Office: Columbia U Dept Civil Engring 500 W 120th St New York NY 10027-6623 E-mail: ling@civil.columbia.edu.

LING, KATHRYN WROLSTAD, health association administrator; b. Watertown, Wis., Aug. 3, 1943; d. Jeffrey Harold and Constance Devina (Egre) Wrolstad; stepchildren: Renee Rainey, Roz Harper. BS in History and Polit. Sci., U. Wis., 1965; MDiv, Garrett-Evangelical Sem., 2001. Supr. recreation ARC, DaNang, Cam Ran Bay, VietNam, 1968; assoc. exec. dir. Am. Cancer Soc., Evanston, Ill., 1968-71, exec. dir., 1971-73, exec. dir. Montgomery County Unit Md., 1973-76, cons. income devel., 1976, dir., profl. edn. cancer incidence and end results, 1976-78, dir. income devel., 1978-82, exec. dir., 1982-84; assoc. exec. dir. Alzheimer's Disease and Related Disorders Assn., 1985-87, v.p. community svcs., 1988-91, sr. v.p. chpt. Family Svcs. and Edn. divsn., 1991-93. Cons. Nat. Aphasia Assn.; pres. The Leadership Edge, Chgo.; chmn. bd. dirs. Kaleidoscope. Past chair Kaleidoscope; bd. mem. ROTARY/One; founding bd. Ill. Vietnam Women's Project; pastor Union Ave. United Meth. Ch. Mem. Soc. Non-Profit Orgn. (chmn. bd. dirs., exec. v.p.). Home: 4356 S Union Ave Chicago IL 60609-3467

LING, NAM, educator; b. Singapore, Singapore, Dec. 9, 1956; s. Yu-Chich Ling and Siew-Chee Chen; m. Mei-Yan Lu, Dec. 3, 1994; children: Grace, Sophia. PhD, U. La., 1989. Product, process engr. Hewlett Packard, Singapore, 1981—83; asst. prof. Santa Clara (Calif.) U., 1989—94, assoc. prof., 1994—2001, prof., 2001—. Vis. cons. Nanyang Technol. U., Singapore, 1999—2001. Author: Specification and Verification of Systolic Arrays, 1999; contbr. articles over 75 articles to profl. jours., chapters to books. Interpreter Chinese Ch. in Christ, Mountain View, Calif., 1996—2000. Named IEEE Disting. Lectr., 2002—; recipient Rsch. Initiation award, NSF, 1990—93; grantee, Nortel Networks, 2000, New Japan Radio Corp., 1995—97,

1997—99, Medianix Semiconductor, Inc., 1997—98. Mem.: IEEE (sr.; assoc. editor 1990—, tech. com. chair 1990—), Am. Soc. for Engring. Edn., Assn. for Computing Machinery. Avocation: travel. Office: Santa Clara U 500 El Camino Real Santa Clara CA 95053

LING, ROBERT MALCOLM, banker, publishing executive; b. Akron, Ohio, July 6, 1931; s. Howard George and Catherine Zola (Smith) L.; m. Lois Claire Fisher Ling, Nov. 1, 1992; children: Shelly, Robert Jr., Amy, Beth, Patricia. BA in Journalism, Mich. State U., 1952. Asst. pres. Dike-O-Seal, Inc., Chgo., 1955-56; gen. mgr. Vollwerth Marquette (Mich.) Co., 1956-58, pres., 1958-75, Vandco Incorp., Marquette, 1975-85, Cable Americal Corp., Rancho Cordova, Calif., 1985-89, Romali Holdings, Inc., Rancho Cordova, 1989—. Chmn. Gold River Bank, Fair Oaks, Calif., 1990-92, Sacramento Safety Ctr., Inc., 1996—; publisher Grapevine-Independent newspaper, Rancho Cordova, Calif. Mayor City of Marquette, 1980-83, City of Rancho Cordova, Calif., 1986-87. Capt. U.S. Army, 1952-55. Republican. Home: 6032 Puerto Dr Rancho Murieta CA 95683-9313 Office: Romali Holdings Inc 3338 Mather Field Rd Rancho Cordova CA 95670-5966

LING, ROBERT WILLIAM, JR. biologist, educator; b. Oakland, Calif., Jan. 31, 1954; s. Robert William Ling and Jacqueline Laura (Roberts) Ling Mullen; children: Tami, Sheri, Robin, Cassandra, Amanda. AAS in Med. Tech., C.C. of Air Force, Maxwell AFB, Ala., 1981; BS in Biology, No. Mich. U., 1983, MA in Biology, 1985. Lectr. U. Md.-European divsn., 1987-92; mem. adv. bd. Clear Lake Edn. Ctr., Escanaba, Mich., 1992-97; dir. Clear Lake Edn. Ctr., 1992-97; mem. staff Cloud County C.C., 1997-99; biology prof. Kankakee C.C., 1999—. Mem. adv. bd. Northwoods Math.-Sci. Ctr., Escanaba, 1992-97, Delta Menominee Ground Water Edn. Ctr. Escanaba, 1994-97. Author: USAFE History of Desert Shield/Storm, 1991; (with others) Clec Master Plan Permit, 1993; contbr. articles to profl. jours. Capt. USAF, 1985-92. Mem. VFW, Soc. for the Study of Amphibians and Reptiles, Kiwanis, Sigma Xi. Democrat. Roman Catholic. Avocations: herpetoculture, hunting. Office: Kankakee CC PO Box 888 Kankakee IL 60901-0888 E-mail: bling@kcc.cc.il.us.

LING, STUART JAMES, music educator, composer; b. Youngstown, Ohio, Mar. 17, 1918; s. James Ira and Emma Catherine (Gill) Ling; m. Terry Wagner, Sept. 4, 1948; children: Kristine Holt, Karen Aczon, Katherine Olsen. MusB, Syracuse U., 1940, MusM, 1947, PhD in Music Edn., 1954. Supr. music Manlius (N.Y.) Bd. Edn., 1940—42; grad. asst. Syracuse (N.Y.) U., 1946—49; asst. prof. music, band dir. Coll. Wooster, Ohio, 1949—51, prof. music, band dir., 1952—84, prof. emeritus, 1984—. Cons. in field. Columnist Wooster Daily Record, 2000—; contbr. articles to profl. jours.; composer: numerous musical arrangements. Col. U.S. Army, 1942—46, Korea. Decorated Legion of Merit; recipient Disting. Achievement award, Edn. Press Assn. Am., 1997, Pres. award, Am. Fedn. Musicians, 2000; fellow Marvin Jones fellow, Lions Internat., 1999. Mem.: Music Educators Nat. Conf., Nat. Band Assn., Coll. Band Dirs. Nat. Assn., Ohio Music Edn. Assn. (adjudicator 1954—97, pres. 1980—82, Disting. Svc. award 1987), Sigma Nu, Phi Mu Alpha, Kappa Lambda, Phi Beta Mu. Episcopalian. Avocations: golf, stamp collecting, coin collecting, travel, reading. Home: 839 N Bever St Wooster OH 44691 E-mail: sling@wooster.edu.

LING, TA-YUNG, physicist; b. Shanghai, Feb. 2, 1943; married, 1969; 3 children. BS, Tunghai U., Taiwan, 1964; MS, U. Waterloo, Ont., Can., 1966; PhD in Physics, U. Wis., 1971. Rsch. asst. U. Wis., 1967-71; rsch. assoc. physics U. Pa., Phila., 1972-75, asst. prof., 1975-77; from asst. prof. to assoc. prof. Ohio State U., Columbus, 1977-83, prof. physics, 1983—. Recipient Outstanding Jr. Investigator award Dept. of Energy, 1977. Mem. Am. Phys. Soc. Achievements include research in experimental high energy physics; deep inelastic neutrino-nucleon scattering, neutrino masses and mixing, neutrino oscillations, deep inelastic electron-proton scattering, high energy proton-proton collisions. Office: Ohio State U High Energy Physics Lab Physics Dept/Smith Lab 174 W 18th Ave Columbus OH 43210-1106 E-mail: ling@mps.ohio-state.edu.

LINGAMPALLI, RAO GANGADHARA MOHAN, marketing professional; b. Ramachandrapuram, India, Apr. 2, 1966; came to U.S., 1989; s. Suryanarayana and Kamalavathi Lingampalli; m. Adilakshmi Ponguru, Dec. 23, 1994; children: Krishna, Kamal. B in Electronics and Comm. Engring., Jawaharlal Nehru Tech. U., 1987; MSEE, Stevens Inst. Tech., 1991. Telecomm. engr. Optical Comm. Labs., Hoboken, N.J., 1989-93; sr. engr. MCI Worldcom, Richardson, Tex., 1994-2000; sr. tech. mktg. mgr. Calient Networks, San Jose, Calif., 2000—. Presenter Internat. Symposium on Optics, Imaging, and Instrumentation Soc. Photo-Optical Engrs., San Diego, 1994. Mem. IEEE. Office: Calient Networks Dept 1054/107 5853 Rue Ferrari San Jose CA 95138 Home: 3320 Chemin De Riviere San Jose CA 95148-4309 E-mail: raolingampalli@calient.net., yao_lingampalli@hotmail.com.

LINGEL, NADA JO, optometry educator; b. Great Falls, Mont., May 15, 1957; d. Donald Stanley and Anna Marie (Lorang) L.; m. Dennis Lynn Smith, May 27, 1989. BS, Pacific U., 1979, D of Optometry, 1981, MS, 1988. Cert. of residency in hosp. based optometry. Pvt. practice, Hillsboro, Oreg., 1981-84; asst. prof. optometry Pacific U., Forest Grove, 1984-90, assoc. prof., 1990-96, prof., 1996—, asst. dean clin. affairs Coll. Optometry, 1993-96. Rsch. optometrist, clinic mgr. Cornea and Contact Lens Rsch. Unit, Sydney, NSW, Australia, 1987-88; consulting and attending dr. VA Med. Ctr., Portland, Oreg., 1994—. Author: (with others) Clinical Ocular Pharmacology, 1995, Clinical Optometric Pharmacology and Therapeutics, 1996; mem. editl. rev. bd. Jour. Optometric Edn., 1991—. Recipient 1st Annual Innovation in Edn. award Assn. Schs. and Colls. Optometry, 2000; named Best Instr., Phi Theta Upsilon, 1991. Fellow Am. Acad. Optometry; mem. Am. Optometric Assn. (mem. accreditation coun. optometric edn. 1995—, vice chair 2001-, Continuing Optometric Recognition award 1996, 97, 98, 99, 2000), Oreg. Optometric Assn. (mem. quality assessment appeal bd. 1994—), Beta Sigma Kappa. Avocations: watercolor painting, bicycling. Office: Pacific U Coll Optometry 2043 College Way Forest Grove OR 97116-1797 E-mail: lingelnj@pacificu.edu.

LINGELBACH, ALBERT LANE, lawyer; b. N.Y.C., July 19, 1940; s. Robert Lane and Sarah (Lewis) L.; m. Ann Norton, July 31, 1965; children: Albert Lane, Charity Ann. BS, U. Pa., 1962, LLB, 1965. Bar: N.Y. 1967, U.S. Tax. Ct. 1984. Assoc. Jackson & Nash, LLP, N.Y.C., 1965-72, ptnr., 1972—. Co-chmn. Port Washington (N.Y.) Cmty. Chest Fund Drive, 1972-73, bd. dirs. 1973-74, sec. 1974-75, v.p. 1975-76, exec. v.p. 1976-78, pres. 1978-80; elder Roslyn Presbyn. Ch. Mem. ABA (com. on significant new devels. in probate and trust law practice 1983-87), Assn. Bar of City of N.Y. (mem. com. on trusts estates and surrogates ct. 1980-83), N.Y. State Bar Assn., Am. Coll. Trust and Estate Counsel, Estate Planning Coun. N.Y.C. (dir. 1998-2001), Univ. Club (N.Y.C.), Southport (Maine) Yacht Club. Home: Ketch Lady Ann PO Box 472 Port Washington NY 11050-0104 Office: Jackson & Nash LLP 330 Madison Ave Fl 18 New York NY 10017-5095

LINGEMAN, RICHARD ROBERTS, editor, writer; b. Crawfordsville, Ind., Jan. 2, 1931; s. Byron Newton and Vera Frances (Spencer) L.; m. Anthea Judy Nicholson, Apr. 3, 1965; 1 child, Jenifer Kate. BA, Haverford Coll., 1953; postgrad., Yale U. Law Sch., 1956-58, Columbia U. Grad. Sch. Comparative Lit., 1958-60. Exec. editor Monocle mag., N.Y.C., 1960-69; assoc. editor, columnist N.Y. Times Book Review, 1969-78; exec. editor The Nation, N.Y.C., 1978-95, sr. editor, 1995—. Bd. dirs. Small Town Inst. Author: Drugs from A to Z, 1969, Don't You Know There's A War On?, 1971, Small Town America, 1980, Theodore Dreiser: At the Gates of the City 1871-1907, 1986, Theodore Dreiser: An American Journey, 1908-1945, 1990 (Chgo. Sun-Times Book of Yr.), Sinclair Lewis: Rebel from Main Street, 2002; mem. editl. bd. Dreiser Studies. With U.S. Army, 1953-56. NEH fellow. Mem. PEN, Authors Guild, Soc. Am. Historians, N.Y. Hist. Soc., Phi Beta Kappa. Office: Nation 33 Irving Pl New York NY 10003-2332

LINGENFELTER, SHERWOOD GALEN, university provost, anthropology educator; b. Hollidaysburg, Pa., Nov. 18, 1941; s. Galen Miller and Kathern Margaretta (Rogers) L.; m. Judith Elaine Beaumont, Aug. 10, 1962; children: Jennifer Elaine, Joel Sherwood. BA, Wheaton Coll., 1963; PhD, U. Pitts., 1971. Dir. acad. advising U. Pitts., 1964-66; instr. SUNY, Brockport, N.Y., 1966-67, asst. prof, 1969-74, assoc. prof., 1974-82, prof. anthropology, 1982-83; NIH predoctoral fellow U. Pitts., 1967-69; prof. Biola U., La Mirada, Calif., 1983-88, provost, sr. v.p., 1988-99; dean Sch. of World Mission Fuller Theol. Sem., Pasadena, 1999—2002, provost, 01—. Cons. in anthropology Summer Inst. Linguistics, Dallas, 1977-96, bd. dirs., 1999; tng. cons. Liebenzell Mission of Am., Schooleys Mountain, N.J., 1981-89; evaluating cons. Trust Terr. of the Pacific Islands, Saipan, Mariana Islands, 1969-74. Author: Yap: Political Leadership, 1975, The Deni of Western Brazil, 1980, Ministering Cross-Culturally, 1986, Transforming Culture, 1992, 2nd edit., 1998, Agents of Transformation, 1996; editor: Political Development in Micronesia, 1974, Social Organization of Sabah Societies, 1990. Bd. dirs. Christian Scholars Rev., 1989-95, Grace Brethren Internat. Missions, 1994—; mem. Sr. Accrediting Commn. Western Assn. Schs. and Colls., 2000—. Recipient Disting. Teaching award Biola U., 1987-88; grantee NSF, 1967-69, 79-81, SUNY Rsch. Found., 1970. Fellow Am. Anthrop. Assn., Soc. for Applied Anthropology, Am. Ethnol. Soc.; mem. Assn. Social Anthropology Oceania, Am. Conf. Acad. Deans. Democrat. Mem. Grace Brethern Ch. Office: Fuller Theol Sem Sch World Mission 135 N Oakland Ave Pasadena CA 91182-0001

LINGERFELT, ALAN THOMAS, civil engineer, real estate executive; b. Richmond, Va., Sept. 10, 1954; s. Luther Harold and Mildred Juanita (Corvin) L.; m. Gwendolynn Montes Ferguson, Aug. 9, 1975; children— Jonathan Ryan, Justin Michael, Daniel Kenton, Catherine Elizabeth. BSCE, Va. Poly. Inst., State U., 1976; postgrad. MBA program Va. Commonwealth U., 1980. Cert. profl. engr., Va. Founder, pres. Lingerfelt & Assoc., Inc., Richmond, 1977—, Lingerfelt Devel. Corp., 1978—, founder, pres. Lingerfelt Mgmt. Corp., 1980—. Mem. Children's Hosp. Building Fund Raising Campaign, Nat. Right to Work Com., Am. Security Council, Derbyshire Baptist Ch. Recipient Eagle Scout award Boy Scouts Am., 1972. Mem. Nat. Soc. Profl. Engrs., ASCE (pres. central Va. chpt. 1979, dir. Va. sect. 1982-83), Am. Cons. Engrs. Council, Constrn. Specifications Inst., Am. Water Works Assn., Water Pollution Control Fedn., Am. Pub. Works Assn., Richmond Joint Engrs. Council (found. chmn. 1979), Va. Soc. Profl. Engrs. (chmn. pvt. practice sect. central chpt. 1981-82), Inst. Real Estate Mgmt., Nat. Assn. Indsl. and Office Parks (pres. Va. chpt. 1982, outstanding service award 1982), Nat. Assn. Corp. Real Estate Execs., U.S. C. of C., Va. C. of C. (Entrepreneur of the Yr., 1987), Richmond Real Estate Group. Richmond Board Realtors, Urban Land Inst. W. Richmond Bus. Men's Assn., Jaycees (outstanding young man Am. award 1982). Assoc. Gen. Contractors Va., Inc. Clubs: Westwood Racquet, Downtown (Richmond), Va. Power Boat Assn., Skidmore Hunt, Engrs. (Richmond). Lodge: Rotary Internat. (Paul Harris fellow 1987). Home: 9812 Ridge Meadow Pl Richmond VA 23233-5576 Office: PO Box 12 S 3rd St Richmond VA 23219-3702

LINGERFELT, B. EUGENE, JR. minister; b. Highland Park, Mich., Dec. 18, 1955; s. Beecher Eugene and Nellie Beatrice (Sampson) L.; m. Suzanne Marie Martin, Aug. 7, 1976; children: Austin Stuart, Krystina Marie. BA, Cen. Bible Coll., Springfield, Mo., 1976; MDiv, Tex. Christian Univ., 1980; D of Ministry, Southwestern Bapt. Theol., Seminary, Ft. Worth, 1984. Ordained min. Cathedral of Praise Ch., 1984. Assoc. pastor Bethel Temple, Ft. Worth, 1978-82; missionary, guest lectr. East Africa Sch. of Theology, Nairobi, Kenya, 1982-83; marriage enrichment seminar speaker, 1983; founder and sr. pastor Cathedral of Praise, Arlington, Tex., 1984—. Founder Cathedral Christian Acad., 1988—; founder Overcoming Faith TV, 1994—. Author: The Spirit of Excellence, 1994, Compromise in the Modern Church, 1995, God's Very Own Child, 2000; co-author: Money: A Spiritual Force, 1985, You, Me & God, 1999; contbr. articles to religious jours. Named to Outstanding Young Men of Am., 1980. Republican. Office: Cathedral of Praise PO Box 121234 Arlington TX 76012-1234

LINGGOOD, RITA M. radiation oncologist; b. Eng., Jan. 18, 1942; came to U.S., 1975; d. Alfred James and Vera Olive (Evans) L.; m. Michael John Hudson, Apr. 30, 1977 (dec. 1999); children: Katherine, Julia. MB BS, U. London, 1965, MSc in Radiation Biology, 1973. Resident, fellow radiation oncology St. Bartholomew's Hosp., London, 1965-75, Mass. Gen. Hosp., Boston, 1975-93; attending physician radiation oncology Joint Ctr. for Radiation Therapy, Harvard U., 1993-99; with Binney Radiation Oncology Found. Harvard Med. Sch., 1999—2001; chief radiation oncology St. Annes Hosp., Fall River, Mass.; mem. Brigham and Women's Physician Orgn., 2002—. Mem. editl. bd. Jour. Neurooncology, Internat. Jour. Radiation Biology & Physics. Fellow Royal Coll. Radiology. Democrat. Episcopalian. Avocations: music, reading. Office: The Oncology Ctr 480 Hawthorn St North Dartmouth MA 02747-3713

LINGL, FRIEDRICH ALBERT, psychiatrist; b. Munich, Germany, Apr. 4, 1927; came to U.S., 1957, naturalized, 1962; s. Friedrich Hugo and Marie Luise (Lindner) L.; m. Leonore E. Trautner, Nov. 15, 1955; children— Herbert F., Angelika M. MD, Ludwig-Maxim U., Munich, 1952. Diplomate Am. Bd. Psychiatry and Neurology); cert. mental health adminstr. Intern Edward W. Sparrow Hosp., 1957-58; resident internal medicine City Hosp., Augsburg, Germany, 1953-54; resident psychiatry Columbus (Ohio) State Hosp., 1958-61; supt. Hawthornden State Hosp., Northfield, Ohio, 1963-66; dir. Cleve. Psychiat. Inst., 1966-72; pvt. practice, 1972-92; med. dir. Windsor Hosp., 1976-92, med. dir. emeritus, 1992—. Asst. clin. prof. Case Western Res. U., Cleve., 1970-97. Contbr. articles to med. jours. Fellow Am. Psychiat. Assn. (life); mem. AMA, Ohio Med. Assn., Ohio Psychiat. Assn., Am. Assn. Psychiat. Adminstrs., Cleve. Psychiat. Soc. Address: 40 Farwood Dr Chagrin Falls OH 44022-6848 E-mail: flingl@aol.com.

LINGL, JAMES PETER, lawyer; b. Appleton, Wis., Dec. 19, 1946; s. Peter Lawrence and Barbara (Verstegen) L.; children: Jason, Julie, Jameson. Student, Loyola U., Rome, 1967-68; BA, Rockhurst Coll., 1969; JD, U. Wis., 1975. Bar: Wis. 1975, U.S. Dist. Ct. (we. dist.) Wis. 1975, Calif. 1977, U.S. Dist. Ct. (cen. dist.) Calif. 1977. Ptnr. Bowman & Lingl, Depere, Wis., 1975-77, Taylor, Churchman & Lingl, Camarillo, Calif., 1977-83; prin. James P. Lingl & Assocs., 1983-98; of counsel Knopfler & Robertson, LLP, 1998-2001; prin. James P. Lingl & Assocs., 2001—. Author 13 pieces legis. State of Calif., 1987-90; chief editor Community Assn. Ref. Guide, 1990. Mem. Calif. Legis. Action Com., 1988-2000; advisor Calif. Assembly Housing Com., 1989; bd. dirs. Boys and Girls Club, Camarillo, 1977-89, pres. 1986, adv. bd., 1989—; bd. dirs. Camarillo Arts Council, 1984—, Make-a-Wish, Ventura, Calif., 1985-89; bd. dirs. Channel Islands chpt. Community Assns. Inst., 1987—, pres., 1989, chief editor ref. guide and newsletter, 1990. Recipient Am. Jurisprudence award Bancroft-Whitney, 1975. Mem. Ventura County Trial Lawyers Assn. (bd. dirs. 1983-84), Ventura County Bar Assn. (various offices 1981-86). Lodges: Rotary (bd. dirs. Camarillo 1982-83). Democrat. Roman Catholic. Avocations: sailing, golf. Office: 1200 Paseo Camarillo Ste 170 Camarillo CA 93010-6085

LINGLE, CRAIG STANLEY, glaciologist, educator; b. Carlsbad, N.Mex., Sept. 11, 1945; s. Stanley Orland and Margaret Pearl (Ewart) L.; m. Diana Lynn Duncan, Aug. 21, 1972; 1 son, Eric Glenn. BS, U. Wash., 1967; MS, U. Maine, 1978; PhD, U. Wis., 1983. Nat. rsch. coun. resident rsch. assoc. Coop. Inst. for Rsch. in Environ. Scis., U. Colo., Boulder, 1983-84, rsch. assoc., 1984-86; program mgr. polar glaciology divsn. polar programs NSF, Washington, 1986-87; cons. Jet Propulsion Lab., Pasadena, Calif., 1987-88; nat. rsch. coun. resident rsch. assoc. NASA Goddard Space Flight Ctr., Oceans and Ice Branch, Greenbelt, Md., 1988-90; rsch. assoc. prof. Geophys. Inst., U. Alaska, Fairbanks, 1990-2000, acting dir. Alaska synthetic aperture radar facility, 1997-98, rsch. prof. geophysics, 2000—. Contbr. articles to profl. jours. Recipient Antarctic Svc. medal of U.S., NSF, 1987, Rsch. Project of Month award Office of Health and Environ. Rsch., U.S. Dept. Energy, 1990, Group Achievement award NASA, 1992. Mem. AAAS, Internat. Glaciological Soc., Am. Geophys. Union, Sigma Xi. Avocations: downhill and cross-country skiing, canoeing, hiking. Office: U Alaska Geophys Inst PO Box 757320 Fairbanks AK 99775-7320

LINGLE, JOLYNN FLEISHMAN, writer, educator; b. Everett, Wash., June 20, 1938; d. Gustave A. and Sara M. Ruana; m. Ronald Martin Lingle, June 5, 1959; children: Kevin Todd, Gregory Scott. MS, Pepperdine U., Malibu CA, 1979; BA Home Economics, San Diego State U., San Diego CA, 1974. Cert. Childbirth Education U. of Calif., San Diego, 1978. Ibm machine operator US Airforce, Riverside, Calif., 1957—59; ibm keypunch / machine operator San Diego State U., San Diego, 1959—66, sr. clk., 1966—67; educator San Diego Unified Schools, 1975—77, San Diego CC, San Diego, 1991—99, San Diego Unified Schools, San Diego, 1977—99. Adminstrv. intern Twain Jr Sr H.S., San Diego, 1988—89; ged educator San Diego Unified Schools, San Diego, 1994—99; writing coord. Twain Jr Sr H.S., San Diego, 1995—97. Author: (feature article) Trailblazer, (directory) San Diego Unified Education Directory. Spkr. San Diego Cmty., San Diego, 1980—99. A2c US Airforce, 1957—1859, March AFB. Recipient Vol. of TheYear, San Diego Cmty. Svc. Assn., 1988-1989, Calif. State Tchr. of The Yr., CA Assn. of Family and Consumer Sciences, 1998, One of Top Ten Teachers In The Nation, Am. Assn. of Family and Consumer Sciences, 1998. Mem.: Am. Assn. of Family and Consumer Sciences, Creative Arts Com., Home and Cmty. Sect. of Colo. Assn. of Family and Consumer Sciences. Home: 9081A Yarrow Street Westminster CO 92103

LINGLE, KATHLEEN MCCALL, consultant, marketing executive, entrepreneur; b. Berea, Ohio, Aug. 24, 1944; d. Arthur Vivian McCall and Mary M. (Maxwell) Miller; m. John Hunter Lingle, Sept. 3, 1968 (div. 1991); 1 child, Michael Cameron; m. Sam F. Serrapede, Aug. 15, 1993. BA, Occidental Coll., 1966; MS, Ohio State U., 1977. Vol. Peace Corps, Chile and Venezuela, 1966, 69-72; project dir. Ohio State U. Hosp., Columbus, 1977-78; rsch. assoc. Ednl. Testing Service, Princeton, N.J., 1978-82; mgr. mktg. services Gulton Industries, 1982-84; rsch. dir. Rsch. 100, 1984-85; dir. mktg. planning and rsch. Applied Data Research, 1985-88; Western European sales mgr. Heuristics Software, Inc., Sacramento, 1988-89; pres., chief exec. officer Princeton Leadership Dynamics, 1989-90; rsch. dir. Families & Work Inst., N.Y.C., 1990-91, dir. tng., 1991-93; cons. Wyatt Co., N.Y.C., 1994-96; mgr. world class HR KPMG LLP, Princeton, N.J., 1996-97; sr. cons. Stromberg Cons., Purchase, N.Y., 1997-98; nat. work/life dir. KPMG LLP, Montvale, N.J., 1998—. Co-chair work-life leadership coun. Conf. Bd., 2001, chair, 2002. Vice pres. ops. Unitarian Ch. of New Brunswick (N.J.), 1983-84; mem. adv. com. Boston Coll. Ctr. Work Family Standards of Excellence. Mem. NAFE, Am. Mktg. Assn., Am. Mgmt. Assn., Bus. and Profl. Women (chmn. membership com., 1990-91), N.J. Assn. Women Bus. Owners, Princeton Network Profl. Women, Princeton Area C. of C. (membership com.), Am. Field Svc., Wharton Work/Life Roundtable, Boston Coll. Work/Life Roundtable, Conf. Bd. Work/Life Leadership Coun. (bd. dirs. 2002), Alliance Work/Life Profls. Democrat. Avocations: skiing, jogging, collecting modern art. Home: 1610 Rising Way Mountainside NJ 07092-1606

LINGLE, LINDA, political organization administrator, former mayor; b. St. Louis, 1953; Mayor County of Maui, Hawaii; chair. Democratic Party of Hawaii; mem. Maui County Coun., 1980—90; mayor Maui County , 1990—98; chmn. Hawaii Republican Party, 1999—2001; gubernatorial candidate for gov., 2002—. Recipient Evelyn McPhail award, 2000. Address: 1290 Ala Moana Blvd Honolulu HI 96825-0111 Office: County Maui 200 S High St Wailuku HI 96793-2135*

LINGLE, MARILYN FELKEL, freelance writer, columnist, author; b. Hillsboro, Ill., Aug. 16, 1932; d. Clarence Frederick and Anna Cecelia (Stank) Felkel; m. Ivan L. Lingle, Oct. 4, 1950 (dec. Aug. 2001); children: Ivan Dale, Aimee Lee Lingle Galligan, Clarence Craig. Sec. Ill. State Police, 1950; with welfare dept. Ill. Pub. Aid, Hillsboro, 1951-52; rschr. Small Homes Coun., Champaign, 1952-53; sec. Hillsboro Schs., 1954; office, payroll clk. Eagle Picher Zinc, Hillsboro, 1955-56; continuity dir. Sta. WSMI, Litchfield, Hillsboro, 1966-87. Adv. bd. Am. Savs. Bank/Citizens Savs. Bank, vice chmn., 1986-93. Contbr. poetry to profl. jours. Cmty. edn. bridge instr. Lincoln Land C.C.; fin. chmn. Hillsboro Hosp. Aux., 1972; lit. vol. Graham Correctional Ctr., Hillsboro, 1986-97; pres., bd. dirs. Montgomery Players and Encore Play Theatre, 1954-70. Recipient Vol. of Yr. award Graham Correction Ctr., 1995, award of Merit Ill. State Bd. Edn., 1994-95. Mem. Cousteau Soc., Internat. Wildlife Fedn., Nat. Wildlife Fedn., Phi Theta Kappa Internat., Hillsboro Country Club, Hillsboro Book Club. Democrat. Lutheran. Avocations: bridge, golf, gardening, travel, reading.

LINGLE, MURIEL ELLEN, retired elementary education educator; b. Sundown Twp., Minn., Sept. 15, 1927; d. Harold O. and Carrie H. (Ewald) Anderson; m. Dale A. Lingle, Aug. 21 (dec. June 1999); children: Barbara Jean, Tamara Jane. BS with distinction, Union Coll., Lincoln, Nebr., 1968; MA, U. Nebr., Lincoln, 1976. Cert. tchr., Nebr. Elem. tchr., Hallam, Nebr., 1959-62; tchr. Cen. Elem. and High Sch., Sprague-Martell, 1963-67, Helen Hyatt Elem. Sch., Lincoln, 1968-70; elem. tchr. Crete (Nebr.) Sch. System, 1970-91; ret., 1991. Recipient award for excellence in teaching Cooper Found., 1990-91, Internat. Woman of Yr. award, 1993-94. Avocations: reading, sewing, music, antique cars, collecting plates and die-cast precision automobile and truck models. Home (Winter): # 27 530 S Alma Sch Rd Mesa AZ 85210 Home (Summer): 4730 Hillside St Lincoln NE 68506

LINGLE, SARAH ELIZABETH, research scientist; b. Woodland, Calif., July 22, 1955; d. John Clayton and Dorothy Adelaide (Dubois) L.; m. Thomas Pratt Washington IV, May 20, 1989. BS, U. Calif., Davis, 1977; MS, U. Nebr., 1978; PhD, Washington State U., 1982. Lab. asst. U. Calif., Davis, 1975-77; rsch. asst. U. Nebr., Lincoln, 1977-78; rsch., teaching asst. Wash. State U., Pullman, 1979-82; rsch. assoc. Agrl. Rsch. Svc., USDA, Fargo, N.D., 1982-84, supr. plant physiologist Weslaco, Tex., 1984-97, acting rsch. leader, 1991-92, plant physiologist New Orleans, 1997—. Assoc. editor Crop Sci., 1991-97; contbr. articles to profl. jours., chpts. to 2 books. Mem. AAAS, Am. Soc. of Plant Physiologists, Am. Soc. Agronomy, Crop Sci. Soc. of Am., Sigma Xi. Episcopalian. Achievements include research in biochemistry and physiology of sugar deposition in sucrose-storing plant tissues. Office: USDA Agrl Rsch Svc 1100 Robert E Lee Blvd PO Box 19687 New Orleans LA 70179-0687

LINHARDT, ROBERT JOHN J, medicinal chemistry educator; b. Passaic, N.J., Oct. 18, 1953; s. Robert J. and Barbara A. (Kelley) L.; m. Kathryn F. Burns, May 31, 1975; children: Kelley, Barbara. BS in Chemistry, Marquette U., 1975; MA in Chemistry, Johns Hopkins U., 1977, PhD in Organic Chemistry, 1979; postgrad., Mass. Inst. Tech., 1979-82. Rsch. assoc. Mass. Inst. Tech., Cambridge, 1979-82; asst. prof. U. Iowa, Iowa City, 1982-86, assoc. prof., 1986-90, prof. medicinal and natural products chemistry, 1990—, prof. chem. and biochem. engring., 1996—, F. Wendell Miller Disting. prof., 1996, prof. chemistry, 1999—. Cons. in field.; interacad. exchange scientist to USSR NAS, 1988. Mem. editl. bd. Applied Biochemistry and Biotech., 1985—, Carbohydrate Rsch., 1990—, Jour. Carbohydrate Chemistry, 1995—, Jour. Biol. Chem., 1995-2000, Analytical Biochemistry, 1991-97, 2001—; contbr. numerous articles to profl. jours. Johnson and Johnson fellow MIT, 1981; NIH grantee, 1982—. Mem. AAAS, AACP (Volwiler award 1999), Am. Chem. Soc. (Horace S. Isbell award Carbohydrate Chemistry 1994), Soc. Glycobiology. Office: U Iowa Coll Pharmacy Phar # 303A Iowa City IA 52240 E-mail: robert-linhardt@uiowa.edu.

LINHARES, JUDITH YVONNE, artist, educator; b. Pasadena, Calif., Nov. 21, 1940; m. Philip E. Linhares June 15, 1961 (div. July, 1971); 1 child, Amanda Linhares Mason. Student, LA Otis Art Inst., 1960, San Francisco Art Inst., 1963; BFA, Calif. Coll. Arts & Crafts, 1964, MFA, 1970. Art tchr. San Francisco State Coll., 1969-71, San Jose City Coll., 1971-72, U. Calif., Davis, Berkeley, 1979, U. San Francisco, San Francisco Art Inst. other univs., Calif., N.Y., La., 1978—, Sch. of Visual Arts, N.Y.C., 1981—, NYU, 1990—. Lectr. at univs. and art insts. nationwide, 1974— One-woman shows include include Berkeley Gallery, San Francisco, 1972, one-woman shows include San Francisco Art Mus., 1976, Paule Anglim Gallery, San Francisco, 1978, 1980, 1982, 1984, 1988, 1989, 1994, Nancy Lurie Gallery, Chgo., 1981, 1989, 1990, Concord Gallery, N.Y.C., 1982, 1983, Ruth Siegel Gallery, 1985, Mo David Gallery, 1985, L.A. Louver Gallery, Venice, Calif., 1988, Julie Sylvester Edition, N.Y.C., 1989, The Gaibreath Gallery, Lexington, Ky., 1993, Greenville (S.C.) County Mus. of Art, 1994 (survey exhibition 1971-93), Sonoma (Calif.) State U., 1994, Edward Thorp Gallery, N.Y.C., 1997, 2001, exhibited in group shows at San Francisco Art Inst., 1973, Indpls. Mus. Art, 1984, Peninsula Mus., Monterey, Calif., 1987, Michael Walls Gallery, N.Y., 1987, Rosenberg Gallery, N.Y.C., 1992, pub. collections including, pub. collections. Recipient Adeline Kent award San Francisco Art Inst., 1976; grantee Nat Endowment for Arts, 1979, 87, 93-94, Gottlieb grantee, 1993; Guggenheim fellow, 1997, Anonymous Was a Woman grantee, 1999-2000. E-mail: judithlinhares@aol.com.

LINHART, EDDIE GENE, aerospace executive; b. Leachville, Ark., Mar. 8, 1941; s. Eddie Clifton and Della Inez (Towell) L.; m. Claudia Jean Benninger, May 25, 1962; children: William Gene, Bonnie Jean. BA, Calif. State U., Long Beach, 1975, MA, 1977; grad., Claremont Grad. Sch. Registered profl. engr. Calif. V.p. AVCO Aerostructures Divsn., Nashville, 1979-81, Northrop Corp., Hawthorne, Calif., 1981-85; pres. Western Gear Corp., CIty of Industry, 1985-88; pres., chief exec. officer Precision Aerotech, Inc., La Jolla, 1988-90, EGL Holdings, Inc., Laguna Hills, 1990—, Astech/MCI, Inc., Santa Ana, 1991-93; chmn. Advanced Metal Cos., Inc., Menlo Park, 1992—; chmn., CEO TFI Acquisition, Inc., 1995—. Dir. Calif. State U., L.A., 1983—. Bd. dirs. Boy Scouts Am., L.A., 1984—, dist. chmn., 1983-85. With USN, 1958-62. Recipient Disting. Engring. Achievement award San Fernando Valley Engrs. Coun., 1986; award for Achievement as chmn. Ind. Adv. Bd. Calif. State U., 1986, Frank E. Reeves Internat. Interprofl. award Ins. Mgmt. Engring., 1988. Fellow Soc. Mfg. Engrs. (dir. 1979—), Inst. Advancement of Engring.; mem. Am. Mgmt. Assn. (Silver Knight), Calif. Soc. Profl. Engrs., Soc. Automotive Engrs. (chmn. mfg. com. 1983-85, Achievement award 1985), Navy League. Republican. Lutheran. Avocations: golf, fishing, stamp collecting, coin collecting, restoring antique automobiles. Office: EGL Holdings Inc 8861 Kennelly Ln Anaheim CA 92804 E-mail: elinhart@trueform.com.

LINHART, JOSEPH WAYLAND, retired cardiologist, educational administrator; b. N.Y.C., Feb. 7, 1933; s. Joseph and Myrla Watson (Wayland) L.; m. Marilyn Adele Voight, Sept. 1, 1956; children: Joseph, Mary-Ellen, Richard, Jennifer, Donna-Lisa, Daria. BS, George Washington U., 1954, MD, 1958. Diplomate Am. Bd. Internal Medicine with subspecialty in cardiovascular diseases. Intern Washington Hosp. Ctr., 1958-59; resident George Washington U. Hosp., Washington, 1959-60, Duke U. Hosp., Durham, N.C., 1961, fellow, 1960, 62-63, Nat. Heart Inst./Johns Hopkins Hosp., Bethesda/Balt., Md., 1963-64; asst. prof. medicine U. Fla., Gainesville, 1964-67; clin. assoc. prof. U. Miami, Fla., 1967-68; assoc. prof. medicine U. Tex., San Antonio, 1968-71; prof., dir. cardiology Hahnemann Med. Coll., Phila., 1971-75; prof., chmn. dept. medicine Chgo. Med. Sch., 1975-79, Oral Roberts U., Tulsa, 1979-83; prof. medicine U. South Fla., Tampa, 1983-92; prof., regional chmn. medicine Tex. Tech. U., Odessa, 1992-93; prof. medicine La. State U., Shreveport, 1993-97; chief med. svc. VA Med. Ctr., 1993-97, acting chief of staff, 1996-97; ret., 1997. Cons. in cardiology and med./legal questions. Contbr. articles to profl. jours.; author 4 books. Mem. med. adv. com. YMCA, Niles, Ill., 1976-79; bd. govs. Phila. Heart Assn., 1972-75; mem. rsch. coun. Okla. Heart Assn., Tulsa, 1980-83. Fellow ACP, Am. Coll. Cardiology; mem. AAAS, Planetary Soc., Nat. Space Soc., Astron. Soc. of Pacific, Alpha Omega Alpha. Republican. Avocations: astronomy, history, model building, organ playing, music. Home: 625 Red Cedar Ct NE Saint Petersburg FL 33703-6203

LINHART, LETTY LEMON, editor; b. Pittsburg, Kans., Sept. 22, 1933; d. Robert Sheldon and Lois (Wise) Lemon; m. Robert Spayde Kennedy, June 8, 1955 (div. 1978); children: Carole Shea, Nancy Schrimpf, Nina Kennedy; m. Daniel Julian Linhart, June 9, 1986. BS, BA in English and Journalism, U.Kans., 1955; MS in Journalism, Boston U., 1975. Reporter Leavenworth (Kans.) Times, 1954; editor Human Resources Rsch. Office George Washington U., Washington, 1955-56; editor Behavior Rsch. Lab. Harvard Med. Sch., Boston, 1956-58; instr. Boston YMCA, 1960-64; freelance writer and columnist, 1975—; editor Somerville (Mass.) Times, 1975-77; pub. rels. dir. Lettermen of Lexington, Mass., 1978; instr. English Rollins Coll., Winter Park, Fla., 1978-79, Valencia Community Coll., Orlando, 1978-82, U. Cen. Fla., Orlando, 1979-82; tech. writer Kirschman Software, Altamonto Springs, Mass., 1980-81, Dynamic Control Software, Winter Park, Fla., 1981-82; editor Fla. Specifier, 1982-85, Mobile Home News, Maitland, Fla., 1985-86; instr. English, Seminole C.C., Sanford, 1986-94; Elderhostel instr. Canterbury Rsch. Ctr., 1994—; editor Oviedo (Fla.) Voice, 1994-95, 96, Tuscawilla Today Monthly Mag., 2000—01; columnist Oviedo Voice, Oviedo, Fla., 2001; reporter North County Times, Vista, Calif., 2001—. Resource person Am. on Line, 1996—. Author: Are These Extravagant Promises, 1989, Clues for the Clueless, 1996, Bits and Bytes of Recovery, 1998, Turn Your Eyes, 2002; contbr. articles to profl. jours. Pres. MIT Dames Boston, 1958-59, Boston Alumnae of Delta Delta Delta, 1959-62; dist. pres Delta Delta Delta, Tex., 1962-65; svc. provider, content provider, cmty. leader Am. On Line Addiction and Recovery Network, 1996—2000; cmty. leader media & journalism, AOL, 2000-. Named Outstanding Collegiate Delta Delta Delta, 1955. Mem. NAFE, Ctrl. Fla. Jazz Soc. (bd. dirs. 1983-93), Internat. Platform Soc., Soc. Women Execs., Altrusa Club (publicity com. 1980-83), Orlando Press Club (bd. dirs.), Mortar Bd., Phi Beta Kappa (Belmont, Mass. pres. 1965-78), Theta Sigma Phi, Sigma Delta Chi, Delta Sigma Rho. Avocations: swimming, singing, jazz. Home: 3408 Fairview Dr Vista CA 92084-1020 E-mail: oviedoletty@aol.com.

LINICK, ANDREW S. direct marketing expert; b. 1945; PhD in Indsl. Psychology, NYU, 1972. Chmn. bd. dirs. Linick Group Inc., Middle Island, N.Y. Office: Linick Group Inc The Linick Bldg PO Box 102 Middle Island NY 11953-0102 E-mail: LinickGrp@att.net.

LINK, E. G. (JAY LINK), corporate executive, family wealth counselor; b. Portsmouth, Va., Apr. 30, 1952; s. Edward and Hazel (Blalock) L.; m. Pamela Kay Kidwell, Jan. 19, 1955; children: Bethany, Anna, Kara, Lissa. BA, Cin. Bible Coll., 1974; MDiv, Cin. Christian Sem., 1979; BS, Am. Coll. Nutripathy, 1988; postgrad., Calif. Coast U., 1985-86. Ordained min. Chs. of Christ, 1974; cert. family wealth counselor. Min., Northern Ky., 1974-79; sales rep. Met. Life Ins., Joplin, Mo., 1979-81, sales mgr., 1981-82; founder, pres. E.G. Link Leasing Co., Inc., Franklin, Ind., 1982-87; founder, dir. Ind. Buying Club, 1986-99; co-founder, pres. Co-op Svcs., Inc., 1990-99; founder Shiloh Found., 1993—; founder, pres., owner Philanthro Dynamics, Inc., 1982-96, Family Wealth Counselors of Am., LLC, 1998—; founder, owner Thinking Beyond Technologies, LLC, 1998—2000. Nat. seminar spkr. on family wealth counseling; founder, pres. T.E.A.M. Products, Inc., 1993-2000; cons. to non-profit orgns.; founder Nat. Assn. Family Wealth Counselors; founder, pres. Profl. Mentoring Program, 1996-2000, Family Wealth Counselors Mgmt. Co., Inc., 1998-2000; founder, chmn. Family Wealth Counseling Cos., Inc., 1999-2000. Author: Family Wealth Counseling: Getting to the Heart of the Matter; editor Natural Alternatives, 1990-92, Thinking Beyond..., 1993-2000; contbr. articles to profl. jours. Founder, dir. Stewardship Ministries, Inc., Franklin, 1984-92. Mem. Nat. Assn. Family Wealth Counselors, Nat. Com. Planning Giving, Planned Giving Group Ind., Ind. Assn. Home Educators. Republican. Avocations: mission work, preaching, teaching Bible study, outdoor living. Home: 4363 E State Road 252 Franklin IN 46131-8164 Office: Family Wealth Counselors of Am 4363 E SR 252 Franklin IN 46131 E-mail: jlink@thinkingbeyond.net.

LINK, GEORGE HAMILTON, retired lawyer; b. Sacramento, Mar. 26, 1939; s. Hoyle and Corrie Elizabeth (Evans) L.; m. Betsy Leland; children— Thomas Hamilton, Christopher Leland. AB, U. Calif., Berkeley, 1961; LLB, Harvard U., 1964. Bar: Calif. 1965, U.S. Dist. Ct. (no., ea., ctrl. and so dists.) Calif. 1965, U.S. Ct. Appeals (9th cir.) 1965. Assoc. Brobeck, Phleger & Harrison, San Francisco, 1964-69, ptnr., 1970—2001, mng. ptnr. L.A., 1973-93, mng. ptnr. firmwide, 1993-96; ret., 2001. Chmn. Pacific Rim Adv. Coun., 1992-95. Bd. regents U. Calif., 1971-74; trustee Berkeley Found., Jr. Statesmen Am.; bd. govs. United Way, 1979-81; trustee, v.p. Calif. Hist. Soc., 1987—; bd. dirs. Ancient Egypt Rsch. Assocs. Fellow Am. Bar Found.; mem. ABA, Calif. Bar Assn., L.A. Bar Assn., U. Calif. Alumni Assn. (pres. 1972-75), Calif. Club, Bohemian Club, Jonathan Club. Republican. Methodist. Office: Brobeck Phleger & Harrison 550 S Hope St Los Angeles CA 90071-2627 E-mail: glink@brobeck.com., georgehlink@msw.com.

LINK, HENRY JOSEPH, environmental engineer; b. Hartford, Conn., 1946; s. Frank Joseph and Veronica Link. BSME, MIT, 1967; postgrad., Hartford Grad. Ctr., 1968. Registered profl. engr., Conn. Rsch. engr. United Techs. Corp., East Hartford, Conn., 1968-72, Met. Dist. Commn., Hartford, 1978; environ. engr. CE Maguire, Wethersfield, Conn., 1972-73; various positions, 1973-77; environ. engr. Conn. Health Dept., Hartford, 1978—. Dir., cons. Resource Recovery Sys., Essex, Conn., 1978—; bd. dirs., v.p. Performance Automotive, Glastonbury, Conn., 1970—. Bd. dirs. Hartford Ballet, 1982—. Mem. World Affairs Coun. (bd. dirs.), Wadsworth Atheneum, Hillstead Mus., New Britain Mus., MIT Club (bd. dirs. Hartford chpt. 1990—), Sigma Xi. Avocations: tennis, viewing performing or visual arts. Home: 45 Mountain St Hartford CT 06106-4240

LINK, PATRICK JAMES, electrical engineer; b. May 26, 1953; AAS, Milw. Sch. Engring., 1974, BS in Elec. Engring. Tech., 1976. Field svc. engr. Allis-Chalmers, Milw., 1976-80; devel. engr. Siemens, Roswell, Ga., 1980-86; sys. support engr. Allen-Bradley Co., Baton Rouge, 1986-92; regl. svc. mgr. ABB Indsl. Systems, Inc., 1992-96; drives cons. ABB Automation Inc., Duluth, Ga., 1996-99; pres. Adjustable Speed Drive Svcs., Inc., 1999—, 1999—. Home: 921 Sundew Dr Alpharetta GA 30005-4277 E-mail: plink@asdsinc.com.

LINK, ROBERT JAMES, lawyer, educator; b. Washington, May 25, 1950; s. Robert Wendell and Barbara Ann (Bullock) L.; m. Cheryl Ann Brillante, Apr. 22, 1978; children: Robert Edward, Holden James. BA, U. Miami, 1972, JD, 1975. Bar: Fla. 1975, U.S. Dist. Ct. (mid. dist.) Fla. 1980, U.S. Ct. Appeals (5th cir.) 1980, U.S. Ct. Appeals (11th cir.) 1981, U.S. Supreme Ct. 1984, U.S. Dist. Ct. (no. dist.) Fla. 1989. Asst. pub. defender City of Miami, Fla., 1975-78, City of Jacksonville, 1978-82; ptnr. Greenspan, Goodstein & Link, Jacksonville, 1982-84, Goodstein & Link, Jacksonville, 1984-85; pvt. practice, 1985-88; assoc. Howell, Liles & Milton, 1988-89; ptnr. Pajcic & Pajcic P.A., 1990—. Guest instr. U. Miami, 1976, U. Fla., 1979-88, Stetson U. Law Sch., 1984, Jacksonville U., 1987-88, U. North Fla., 1991. Atty. legal panel ACLU, Jacksonville, 1982-88. Mem. Fla. Bar Assn. (chmn. com. for representation of indigents criminal law sect. 1980, cert. criminal trial lawyer 1989), Jacksonville Bar Assn. (trial law sect.), Nat. Assn. Criminal Def. Lawyers (vice-chmn. post conviction com. 1990), Fla. Pub. Defender Assn. (death penalty steering com. 1980-82, instr. 1979—), Assn. Fla. Trial Lawyers (seminar spkr. 2000). Democrat. Methodist. Avocations: sailing, fishing, diving, softball. Home: 3535 Carlyon St Jacksonville FL 32207-5836 Office: 1900 Independent Dr Jacksonville FL 32202-5023

LINK, WILLIAM THEODORE, television writer, producer; b. Phila., Dec. 15, 1933; s. William Theodore and Elsie (Roerecke) L.; m. Margery Nelson, Sept. 5, 1980. BS, U. Pa., 1956. Bd. govs. The TV Acad., 1976 Writer, creator, producer (with ptnr. Richard Levinson) TV series Columbo, Mannix, McCloud, Murder, She Wrote, also others; writer, producer: made-for-TV movies The Storyteller; My Sweet Charlie, That Certain Summer, The Execution of Private Slovik, The Gun, Crisis at Central High, The U.S. vs. Salim Ajami, The Boys, The Bill Cosby Mysteries; Author: Fineman, 1973, Stay Tuned, 1981, The Playhouse, 1985, Off-Camera, 1986. Served with Signal Corps U.S. Army, 1956-58. Recipient Emmy awards Acad. TV Arts and Scis., 1970, 72, Golden Globe awards Hollywood Fgn. Press Assn., 1972 (2), Peabody award, Edgar Allan Poe award Mystery Writers Am., 1980, 81, 83, 84; Paddy Chayefsky Laurel award, 1986, Ellery Queen Lifetime Achievement award, 1989, Bouchercon Performance in the Arts award, 1989; inductee TV Hall of Fame, 1995. Mem. SAG, Writers Guild Am., Dramatists Guild, Mystery Writers Am. (pres. 2002, Marlow award 2001).

LINKE, SIMPSON, electrical engineering educator; b. Jellico, Tenn., Aug. 10, 1917; s. Meyer Lion and Bella Yetta L.; m. Esther Silverman, Sept. 15, 1946; children: Martha Ellen, Laura Miriam. BS in Elec. Engring., U. Tenn., 1941; M in Elec. Engring., Cornell U., 1949. Instr. elec. engring. Cornell U., Ithaca, N.Y., 1946-49, asst. prof. elec. engring., 1949-53, assoc. prof., 1953-63, prof., 1963-86, prof. emeritus, 1986—. Cons. N.Mex. Pub. Svc. Commn., Santa Fe, 1981; inactive mem. U.S. nat. com. of conf. internat. des Grands Réseaux Electriques a Haute Tension. Editor Connections, Cornell Elec. and Computing Engring. Newsletter, 1992—. Capt., U.S. Army, 1943-46. Recipient grants NSF, Office Naval Rsch., 1963-73; merit award Coun. Advancement and Support Edn., Ithaca, 1982. Fellow IEEE (life); mem. IEEE Power Engring. Soc., Sigma Xi, Eta Kappa Nu. Avocations: writing, music, theatre, opera, walking. Home: 383 The Parkway Ithaca NY 14850-2275 E-mail: SL78@cornell.edu.

LINKER, RAYMOND OTHO, JR. lawyer; b. Charlotte, N.C., Jan. 18, 1946; s. Raymond Otho Sr. and Frances (Baucom) L.; m. Nola Grady Jenning, June 24, 1969; 1 child, John Raymond. BS in Chem. Engring., N.C. State U., 1968; JD, Georgetown U., 1972. Bar: N.C. 1972, U.S. Dist. Ct. (we. dist.) N.C. 1972, U.S. Patent Trademark Office 1972. From assoc. to ptnr. Bell, Seltzer, Park & Gibson, Charlotte, 1972—; patent practice group leader Alston & Bird. Mem. N.C. Bar Assn., Am. Intellectual Property Assn., Carolinas Patent, Trademark and Copyright Law Assn. (past pres.). Presbyterian. Office: Alston & Bird LLP Bank of Am Plaza 101 S Tryon St Ste 4000 Charlotte NC 28280 E-mail: rlinker@alston.com.

LINK-JOBE, JANNICE LOUISE, education educator; b. Oregon City, Oreg., Apr. 8, 1947; d. Wilford Martin and Helen Louise (Hart) Link; m. Harvey Richard Jobe, May 31, 1973; 1 child, Tiffany Danielle-Louise. BS in Natural Scis., Oreg. Coll. Edn., Monmouth, Oreg., 1975, MS in Natural Scis. and Edn., 1977; EdD in Secondary Edn., Oreg. State U., Corvallis, 1996. Chemistry tchr. Ctrl. H.S., Independence, Oreg., 1977-89; asst. prin. Central High, 1989-91; prin. Talmadge Mid. Sch., Monmouth, 1991-96; prof. edn. Western Oreg. State U., 1996—, team leader proficiency based tchr. prep. program, 1997-98; prin. Sunrise Elem., Albany, Oreg., 1998—. Writer chemistry questions Am. Coll. Testing, Chgo., 1984-88; invited presenter 2d ann. U.S.-China Conf. on Edn., Beijing, 1998, Nat. Conf. Am. Assn. Colls. and Tchr. Edn., New Orleans, 1998, Nat. Stds. Based Tchg. and Learning Conf., Portland, Oreg., 1997; proficiency based evaluation sys. cons., 1998; lead rschr. China-U.S. Cmty. Edn. Project. Contbr. articles to Oreg. Sci. Jour., 1983-86. Bd. mem. Gang Task Force, Monmouth, 1991—; bd. dirs. YMCA, Salem, Oreg., 1995—. U.S. Presdl. finalist for sci. tchg. State of Oreg., 1985, 86., Tchr. of the yr., 1983-84. Fellow NAESP, ASCD, Confedn. Oreg. Sch. Adminstrs., Nat. Assn. Secondary Sch. Prins., Confederation of Sch. Adminstrn, Oregon Middle Level Assn., Phi Delta Kapa (v.p. Willamette Valley chpt., 1996—), Oreg. Counselors Assn. (hon., Adminstr. of Yr. State of Oreg., 1994, proficiency based evaluation sys. cons. 1998), Oreg. Sci. Tchrs. (pres. 1984-85). Avocations: sailing, hiking, reading, gardening, fishing, family activities. Home: 414 Stadium Dr S Monmouth OR 97361-1939 Office: Sunrise Elem Sch Albany OR 97321

LINKLATER, ISABELLE STANISLAWA YAROSH-GALAZKA (LEE LINKLATER), foundation administrator; b. Chgo., Sept. 15, 1939; d. Baron Stanislaw and Isabelle Lydia (Yarosh) Galazka. BE, Chgo. State U., 1959. Cert. tchr., Ill. Pub. rels. coord. Kelling Co., Chgo., 1955-57; tchr. Chg. Bd. Edn., 1957-89, coord. computer lab., 1989—; founder, pres., exec. dir. Assisi Animal Found. Edn. writer, coord. Elsa Internat. Wild Animal Appeal, Ill., 1985—; writer Lakeland Press, 1992. Bd. dirs. Townsquare Players, Woodstock (Ill.) Opera House, 1989-91. Recipient Outstanding Citizen award CBS Broadcasting, 1992. Mem. McHenry County Defenders (bd. dirs. 1989-91), East African Wildlife Soc. (U.S. rep.). Avocations: travel, music, theater. Office: Assisi Animal Found PO Box 143 Crystal Lake IL 60039-0143

LINKLATER, WILLIAM JOSEPH, lawyer; b. Chgo., June 3, 1942; s. William John and Jean (Connell) L.; m. Dorothea D. Ash, Apr. 4, 1986; children: Erin, Emily. BA, U. Notre Dame, 1964; JD, Loyola U., 1968. Bar: Ill. 1968, U.S. Dist. Ct. (no. dist.) Ill. 1968, U.S. Ct. Appeals (7th cir.) 1971, U.S. Supreme Ct. 1971, U.S. Ct. Appeals Washington, 1978, U.S. Ct. Appeals Washington 1978, Calif. 1981, U.S. Dist. Ct. (cen. dist.) Calif. 1981, U.S. Tax Ct. 1982, U.S. Dist. Ct. (no. dist.) Calif. 1983, U.S. Dist. Ct. (ea. dist.) Mich. 1989, U.S. Ct. Appeals (6th cir.) 1990, U.S. Dist. Ct. Hawaii, 1992. Atty. Fed. Defender Project, Chgo.; assoc. Baker & McKenzie, 1968-75, ptnr., 1975—. Contbr. articles to profl. jours. Mem.: Wong Sun Soc. San Francisco (internat. proctor), Chgo. Inn of Ct., Am. Bd. Criminal Lawyers, ACTL, Colo. Bar Assn., Calif. Bar Assn., Internat. inst., Chgo. Bar Assn. (pres. 2000—01, bd. mgrs. 1997—2002, past v.p. jud. candidates evaluation com., chmn. large law firm com.), 7th Cir. Bar Assn., Ill. Bar Assn., FBA, ABA (past co-chmn. com. on internat. criminal law criminal justice sect. , mem. criminal practice and procedure com. antitrust sect., others), Alpha Sigma Nu. Office: Baker & McKenzie 1 Prudential Plz Ste 3000 Chicago IL 60601

LINKLETTER, ARTHUR GORDON, radio and television broadcaster; b. Moose Jaw, Sask., Can., July 17, 1912; s. Fulton John and Mary (Metzler) L.; m. Lois Foerster, Nov. 25, 1935; children: Jack, Dawn, Robert (dec.), Sharon, Diane (dec.). AB, San Diego State Coll., 1934. Program dir. Sta. KGB, San Diego, 1934; program dir. Calif. Internat. Expn., 1935; radio dir. Tex. Centennial Expn., Dallas, 1936; San Francisco World's Fair, 1937-39; pres. Linkletter Prodns.; ptnr., co-owner John Guedel Radio Prodns. Chmn. bd. Linkletter Enterprises; owner Art Linkletter Oil Enterprises. Author: theme spectacle Cavalcade of Golden West, 1940; author and co-producer: theme spectacle Cavalcade of Am, 1941; writer, producer, star in West Coast radio shows, 1940-55; former star, writer: People Are Funny, NBC-TV and radio, Art Linkletter's House Party, CBS-TV and radio; Author: People Are Funny, 1953, Kids Say The Darndest Things, 1957, The Secret World of Kids, 1959, Confessions of a Happy Man, 1961, Kids Still Say The Darndest Things, 1961, A Child's Garden of Misinformation, 1965, I Wish I'd Said That, 1968, Linkletter Down Under, 1969, Oops, 1969, Drugs at My Door Step, 1973, Women Are My Favorite People, 1974, How to be a Super Salesman, 1974, Yes, You Can!, 1979, I Didn't Do It Alone, 1979, Public Speaking for Private People, 1980, Linkletter on Dynamic Selling, 1982, Old Age is not for Sissies, 1988; co-host (with Bill Cosby) series Kids Say the Darnedest Things, 1998—; lectr. convs. and univs. Nat. bd. dirs. Goodwill Industries; commr. gen. to U.S. Exhibit at Brisbane Expo 88, Australia, 1987; commr. gen. to rank of U.S. amb. to The 200th Anniversary Celebration, Australia, 1987—; bd. regents Pepperdine U.; pres. bd. advisors Ctr. on Aging, UCLA; chmn. bd. French Found. for Alzheimers Rsch. Recipient numerous awards. Address: 8484 Wilshire Blvd Ste 205 Beverly Hills CA 90211-3213

LINKONIS, SUZANNE NEWBOLD, probation officer, counselor; b. Phila., Aug. 24, 1945; d. William Bartram and Kathryn (Taylor) Newbold; m. Bertram Lawrence Linkonis, May 29, 1966; children: Robert William, Deborah Anne, Richard Anthony. AA in Psychology, Albany (Ga.) Jr. Coll., 1979; BA in Psychology, Albany (Ga.) State U., 1981; MS in Indsl. Psychology, Va. Commonwealth U., 1986. Office mgr., media buyer Long Advt. Agy., Richmond, Va., 1981-84; media mgr. Clarke & Assocs., 1984-85; human resources asst. Continental Ins., 1985; rsch. assoc. Signet Bank, N.A., 1986-87; program coord. Med. Coll. Va., 1988; personnel mgr. Bur. Microbiology, 1988-89; pers. specialist Va. State Dept. Corrections, 1989-90; human rights adv. Va. State Dept. Youth and Family Svcs., 1990-92, rehab. counselor, 1992-94, sr. rehab. counselor, 1994; pre-trial case mgr./counselor Henrico County Govt., 1994-97, cmty. corrections case mgr., counselor, 1997-2000, sr. county probation officer, counselor, 2001—. Future dir., cons. Mary Kay Cosmetics, Springfield, Va., 1975-77. Mem. APA. Republican. Roman Catholic. Avocations: professional journals in applied psychology, networking, walking, reading. Home: 401 Saybrook Dr Richmond VA 23236-3621 Office: 8600 Dixon Powers Dr Richmond VA 23228-2735 E-mail: blinkonis@cs.com.

LINKOUS, WILLIAM JOSEPH, JR. lawyer; b. Roanoke, Va., July 17, 1929; s. William Joseph and Mary Virginia (Lester) L.; m. Anita Marie Stedronsky, Oct. 15, 1960; children— William Joseph III, Brian Keith BA, Roanoke Coll., Salem, Va., 1951; MA in Econs., U. Va., 1954, JD, 1956. Bar: Va. 1956, Ga. 1957. Assoc. Powell, Goldstein, Frazer & Murphy, Atlanta, 1956-62, ptnr., 1962-79, 85—, mng. ptnr., 1979-85. Trustee Holy Innocents Episcopal Sch., Atlanta, 1974-80, Roanoke Coll., 1980-95, emeritus 1995—. Fellow Am. Coll. Trust and Estate Counsel, Am. Bar Found.; mem. State Bar Ga. (past chmn. fiduciary sect., co-chmn. Ga. trust law revision com. 1988-91, chmn. Ga. probate code revision com. 1991-97, chmn. Ga. guardianship code revision com.1997—), Va. State Bar, Am. Law Inst., Internat. Acad. Estate and Trust Law, Atlanta Estate Planning Coun. (pres. 1983-84). Avocation: tennis. Office: Powell Goldstein Frazer & Murphy 191 Peachtree St NE Ste 1600 Atlanta GA 30303-1700 Home: 6121 Ela Rd Whittier NC 28789-7610 E-mail: wlinkous@pgfm.com.

LINKOV, IGOR, conservationist, consultant; b. Berdichev, Ukraine, Mar. 26, 1967; s. Yuriy Linkov, Malvina Linkov; m. Elena Belinkaia, Feb. 12, 1990; children: Eugene. PhD, U. Pitts., 1995; MSc, Carnegie-Mellon U., 1995—95, Polytechnik Inst., St. Petersburg, Russia, 1990—90. Sr. risk assessor, mgr. Arthur D. Little, Inc., Cambridge, Mass., 2001—; sr. scientist Menzie-Cura & Assocs., Inc., Chelmsford, 1998—2001; rsch. assoc. Harvard U., Cambridge, 1997—98, postdoctoral fellow, 1996—97; rsch. assoc. U. Pitts., 1992—95; rsch. asst. Ioffe Phys.-Tech. Inst., St. Petersburg, Russia, 1988—92. Editor: Environmental Risk Assessment, 2001, Contaminated Forests, 1998, Air Pollution, 1997. Fellow Fellow, NAS, 1994, Sci. & Tech. Agy, Japan, 1998. Mem.: Internat. Union of Radioecology, Soc. Toxicology, Soc. Environ. Toxicology and Chemistry, Health Physics Soc., Soc. Risk Analysis (Conferences and Workshops Committee 2000—02). Office: Arthur D. Little, Inc. 20 Acorn Park Cambridge MA 02140 Office Fax: 617-498-7021. Business E-mail: linkov.igor@adlittle.com.

LINKS, ROBERT DAVID "BO", lawyer; b. San Francisco, Aug. 25, 1949; s. Milton Arnold and Roslyn (Morris) L.; 1 child, Alexis Jade. AB in Journalism, U. Calif., Berkeley, 1971; JD, UCLA, 1974. Bar: Calif. 1974, U.S. Dist. Ct. (no. dist.) Calif. 1974, U.S. Ct. Appeals (9th cir.) 1979, U.S. Supreme Ct. 1978. Assoc. Jacobs, Blanckenburg, May & Colvin, San Francisco, 1974-79; ptnr. Colvin Martin & Links, 1979-85; assoc. Harold S. Dobbs, 1985, Dobbs, Berger, Molinari, Casalnuovo, Vanelli & Nadel, 1985-86, ptnr., 1986-89, Dobbs, Berger, Molinari, Vanelli, Nadel & Links, 1989-94; spl. counsel Berger, Nadel & Vannelli. Student intern, Justice Mathew O. Tobriner, Calif. Supreme Ct., 1973. Editor: Toward Social Change, 1971, California Civil Practice Civil Rights Module, 1994—; author: Follow the Wind, 1995, Riverbank Tweed & Roadmap Jenkins, 2001. Bd. dirs. San Francisco-Bay area chpt. Am. Jewish Com., 1982—. Mem. Am. Arbitration Assn., Calif. Bar Assn., San Francisco Bar Assn., San Francisco Trial Lawyers Assn., Lake Merced Golf Club, Phi Beta Kappa. Democrat. Avocations: golf, photography, creative writing. Office: Berger Nadel & Vannelli 650 California St Fl 25 San Francisco CA 94108-2702 E-mail: bolinks@lmi.net.

LINMAN, JAMES WILLIAM, retired physician, educator; b. Monmouth, Ill., July 20, 1924; s. Chester E. and Ruth L. (Pearson) L.; m. Frances Firth, Aug. 31, 1946; children— John, Jean, James, Jeffrey. BS, U. Ill., 1945, MD, 1947. Intern, resident internal medicine Med. Sch., U. Mich., Ann Arbor, 1947-51, fellow in hematology, 1951-52, 54-56, asst. prof. internal medicine, 1955-56; chief hematology sect. VA Research Hosp. Chgo.; assoc. prof. medicine Med. Sch., Northwestern U., Evanston, Ill., 1956-65; prof. internal medicine Mayo Grad. Sch. Medicine, U. Minn., Mpls.; cons. hematology and head spl. hematology sect. Mayo Clinic-Found., Rochester, Minn., 1965-72; prof. medicine, dir. Osgood Leukemia Ctr., Health Sci. Ctr., U. Oreg., Portland, 1972-79, head hematology div., 1974-78; prof. medicine John A. Burns Sch. Medicine, U. Hawaii, Honolulu, 1979-92; emeritus prof., 1992—; chmn. admissions com. John A. Burns Sch. Medicine, U. Hawaii, Honolulu, 1983-92, asst. dean for admissions, 1988-92. Chmn. State of Hawaii Adv. Commn. on Drug Abuse and Controlled Substances, 1986-88; dir. med. edn. The Queen's Med. Ctr., Honolulu, 1987-88. Author: Principles of Hematology, 1966, Factors Controlling Erythropoiesis, 1960, The Leukemias, 1971, Hematology, 1975; Contbr. articles to profl. jours. Served with USAF, 1952-54. Recipient Tchr. of Year award Mayo Fellows Assn., 1970, Tchr. of Year award U. Hawaii, 1980, 81 Mem. Am. Soc. Clin. Investigation, Central Soc. Clin. Research, Am., Internat. socs. hematology, A.C.P., Western Assn. Physicians, Western Soc. Clin. Research, Pacific Interurban Clin. Club, Alpha Omega Alpha, Phi Kappa Phi. Clubs: Oahu Country. Home: 920 Ward Ave PH17HH Honolulu HI 96814-2100

LINN, CAROLE ANNE, dietitian; b. Portland, Oreg., Mar. 3, 1945; d. James Leslie and Alice Mae (Thorburn) L. Intern, U. Minn., 1967-68; BS, Oreg. State U., 1963-67. Nutrition cons. licensing and cert. sect. Oreg. State Bd. Health, Portland, 1968-70; chief clin. dietitian Rogue Valley Med. Ctr., Medford, Oreg., 1970—; clin. faculty, dietetic internship program Oreg. Health Scis. U., Portland, 2000—. Cons. Hillhaven Health Care Ctr., Medford, 1971-83; lectr. Local Speakers Bur., Medford. Mem. ASPEN, Am. Dietetic Assn., Am. Diabetic Assn., Oreg. Dietetic Assn. (sec. 1973-75, nominating com. 1974-75, Young Dietitian of Yr. 1976), So. Oreg. Dietetic Assn., Alpha Lambda Delta, Omicron Nu. Democrat. Mem. Christ Unity Ch. Avocations: sewing, needlecrafts, cooking, swimming, skiing. Office: Rogue Valley Med Ctr 2825 E Barnett Rd Medford OR 97504-8332

LINN, DIANA PATRICIA, elementary education educator; b. Perth, Australia, Dec. 31, 1943; came to U.S., 1948; d. Evan Andrew and Grace Henrietta (Springhall) Jarboe; m. Jim F. Erlandsen, July 9, 1966 (div. Mar. 1989); children: Rebecca, Tim, Jenny; m. Richard George Linn, Mar. 31, 1990; 1 stepchild, Cristal. AA, Olympic Coll., 1963; BA in Elem. Edn., Western Wash. U., 1965; MEd, U. Ariz., 1969. Cert. tchr., Wash. Tchr. Neomi B. Willmore Elem., Westminster, Calif., 1965-66; tchr. English and sci. Sunnyside Jr. H.S., Tucson, 1966-70; tchr. kindergarten All Seasons Sch., 1972-74; tchr. St.

Cyril's Sch., 1974-77; elem. tchr. Grace Christian Sch., 1977-80; kindergarten and elem. tchr. Ridgeview Christian Ctr., Spokane, Wash., 1983-85, Spokane Christian Schs., 1985-87; dir. Ridgeview Christian Learning Ctr., Spokane, 1987-88; tchr. kindergarten Arlington Elem. Sch., 1988-96, Grant Elem. Sch., Spokane, 1996—. Mem. curriculum study com. Sunnyside Sch. Dist., Tucson, 1967-68; chmn. accreditation and sch. bd. St. Cyril's Sch., Tucson, 1976-77; chair faculty involvement group, chair staff devel., chair wellness com. Arlington Elem., Spokane, 1992-93, sch. reporter, 1994-95; instr. reading readiness Family Learning Fair, Home Schooling Seminar, Spokane Falls C.C., Spokane, 1988; chair, coord. pre-sch. coop. Arlington Elem. with Spokane Falls C. C. of Spokane C.C., 1992-93; chair faculty involvement group, Arlington Elem., Spokane, 1995—, Grant Elem. Sch., 1996-97, also wellness chair, 1996-2001, site coun. faculty rep. 2001—, strategic plan equity com. Arlington Elem., Spokane, 1995-96. Coord. Christian edn. Valley Foursquare Ch., Spokane, 1982-87; coord. children's ch. Victory Faith Fellowship, Spokane, 1993—; Brownie troop leader Willmore Elem., Westminster, 1965-66; ednl. restructuring rep. for Arlington Elem., Spokane Sch. Dist. 81, 1992-93; mem. equity com., 1996-99, mem. early childhood com., 1996—, mem. strategic planning com., 1998—, wellness chmn., 1998-2000, mem. instrnl. team, 1999—; primary rep. Site Coun. Grant Elem., 2002. Scholar Naval Officer's Wives Club, 1961-62; recipient Eisenhower grant, 1990, 94, 96-97. Mem. ASCD, NEA, Wash. Edn. Assn., Spokane Edn. Assn. (Arlington Elem. rep. 1991-93), CPA Wives Club (sec., ball chair 1983-84), Alpha Delta Kappa (membership chair 1994-95, corr. sec. 1996-99). Republican. Avocations: collecting dolls, plates, swimming, quilt-making. Home: 1324 S Perry St Spokane WA 99202-3572 Office: Grant Elem Sch 1300 E 9th Ave Spokane WA 99202-2499 E-mail: dianaL.@sd81.k12.wa.us.

LINN, JAMES ELDON, II, insurance company executive; b. Kokomo, Ind., Sept. 6, 1943; s. James Eldon and Mary Jane (Smith) L.; m. Pamela Ann Moser, Sept. 6, 1968 (div. 1986); 1 child, Aaron Moser; m. Annalee Shriner, Nov. 20, 1986 (dec. Apr. 1998); stepchildren: Kris Firestone, Adam Firestone; m. Cynthia Webb, Nov. 29, 2001. BS in Bus. Adminstrn., Pacific Western U.; Assoc. Acctg., Lane Tech. Inst. CLU, Chartered Fin. Cons. Mgr. meat A & P, Indpls., 1961-63, Safeway, L.A., 1963-65; agy. mgr. Farm Bur. Ins., Lafayette, Ind., 1967-95; agt., owner Allstate Ins. Premier Svc. Agt., Brooksville, Fla., 1996—2001; ins. cons., 2001—. Instr. Life Underwriting Tng. Coun. Pres. West Cen. chpt. Kidney Found., Lafayette, 1981-83; bd. mem., sustaining membership chmn. Greater Lafayette YMCA, 1987-92; pres. Greater Lafayette YMCA Found., Inc., 1990-95. Sgt. U.S. Army, 1965-67. Mem. Am. Coll. Life Underwriters, Ind. Assn. Life Underwriters (pres. 1985-86, chmn. ethics com. 1991-95), Lafayette Soc. CLUs (pres. 1982-83), Nat. Assn. Life Underwriters (vice chmn. polit. involvement com. 1987-89), Internat. Soc. Financiers (cert. 1988), C. of C. (membership com. 1990-91), Farm Bur. Pres. Club (life), Frm Bur. Gov.'s Club (life), Hernando E. Rotary (sec. 1997—). Republican. Methodist. Avocation: jogging. Office: Linn Ins Svcs Unit 203 291 Scenic Gulf Dr Destin FL 32550-4943

LINN, RICHARD, federal judge; b. Bklyn., Apr. 13, 1944; BEE, Rensselaer Poly. Inst., 1965; JD, Georgetown U., 1969. Bar: Va., D.C. 1970, N.Y. 1994. Patent examiner U.S. Patent Office, 1965—68; patent agent U.S. Naval Research Lab., 1968—69; assoc. Brenner, O'Brien, Guay, Connors, 1970—71; patent advisor U.S. Naval Air Systems Command, 1971—72; assoc. Stepno & Neilan, 1972—73; partner Stepno, Schwabb & Linn, 1973—74, Imirie, Smiley & Linn, 1974—77, Marks & Murase, L.L.P., 1977—97, exec. comm., 1987—97; partner, pract. group leader intellectual prop. dept Foley & Lardner, 1997—99; judge U.S. Ct. Appeals (fed. cir.), Washington, 1999—.*

LINN, STUART MICHAEL, biochemist, educator; b. Chgo., Dec. 16, 1940; s. Maurice S. and Pauline L.; children: Matthew S., Allison D., Meagan S. BS with honors in Chemistry, Calif. Inst. Tech., 1962; PhD in Biochemistry, Stanford U., 1967. Asst. prof. biochemistry U. Calif., Berkeley, 1968-72, assoc. prof., 1972-75, prof., 1975-87, head div. biochemistry and molecular biology, 1987-90, 1995-2000. Mem. editl. bd.: Nucleic Acids Rsch., 1974—, Mem. editl. bd.: Jour. Biol. Chemistry, 1975—80, Mem. editl. bd.: Molecular and Cellular Biology, 1987—91; contbr. Helen Hay Whitney fellow, 1966-68; John Simon Guggenheim fellow, 1974-75; recipient USPHS Merit Grant award, 1988-97. Mem.: AAAS, Am. Soc. Microbiologists, Am. Soc. Biol. Chemists (coun.), Am. Acad. Arts and Scis. Office: U Calif Divsn Biochem & Molec Bio Barker Hall Berkeley CA 94720-3202 E-mail: slinn@socrates.berkeley.edu.

LINNA, TIMO JUHANI, immunologist, researcher, educator; b. Tavastkyro, Finland, Mar. 16, 1937; came to U.S., 1968, naturalized, 1981; foster s. Gustaf Lennart and Anne-Marie (Forsstrom) Ackell; m. Rhoda Margareta Popova, May 20, 1961; children: Alexander, Fredrik, Maria. MB, U. Uppsala, Sweden, 1959, MD, 1965, PhD, 1967. Intern, resident hosps., Sweden; pvt. practice medicine hosps. and clinic Sweden; asst. prof. histology U. Uppsala, 1967-71; asst. prof. microbiology and immunology Temple U., Phila., 1970-71, dir. lab. clin. immunology hosps., 1970-72, adviser clin. immunology, 1972-80, assoc. prof. microbiology, immunology, 1971-78, prof., 1978-80, research prof., 1980-90. Group leader immunology central research and devel. dept. E.I. duPont de Nemours & Co., Wilmington, Del., 1980-84, research supr., 1984-85, mgr. med. research products dept., 1986-87, assoc. med. dir., 1987-90; sr. dir. cellular immunology Applied Immune Scis., Inc., Menlo Park, Calif., 1990-91; sr. assoc. med. dir. inst. clin. immunology and infectious diseases, devel. rsch., Syntex (USA) Inc., Palo Alto, Calif., 1992-94, dir. med. rsch., 1994-95; dir. med. rsch. Roche Global Devel., Palo Alto, Calif., 1995-96; transplant med. liaison Roche Labs., Palo Alto, 1996—; immunology cons. UNDP/World Bank/WHO Spl. Program for Research and Tng. in Tropical Diseases, WHO, Geneva, 1978-79; mem. sci. adv. coun. Internat. Inst. Immunology Tng. and Research, Amsterdam, Netherlands, 1975-81. Author books; contbr. articles to profl. publs. USPHS Internat. postdoctoral research fellow, 1968-70; spl. research fellow U. Minn., 1970; Eleanor Roosevelt Am. Cancer Soc. fellow, 1976; grantee Swedish Med. Research Council, 1969-71; grantee NIH, 1972-80 Mem. Am. Assn. Cancer Research, Am. Assn. Immunologists (chmn. edn. com. 1975-80), Am. Assn. Pathologists, Am. Soc. Microbiology, Internat. Soc. Exptl. Hematology, Internat. Soc. Lymphology, N.Y. Acad. Scis., Reticuloendothelial Soc., Royal Lymphatic Soc. Uppsala, Scandinavian Soc. Immunology, Soc. Swedish Physicians, Swedish Med. Assn. Lutheran. Home: 260 Highland Ave San Carlos CA 94070-1911 Office: PO Box 10850 3401 Hillview Ave Palo Alto CA 94304-1320 E-mail: jlinna@prodigy.net.

LINNAN, JAMES DANIEL, lawyer; b. Olean, N.Y., Nov. 29, 1946; s. William Martine and Genevieve (Toohey) L.; married, June 5, 1971; 1 child, Brigid Mary. BS, Northeastern U., Boston, 1969; JD, Albany Law Sch., 1972. BAr: N.Y. 1973, U.S. Dist. Ct. (no. dist.) N.Y., 1973, U.S. Dist. Ct. Vt. 1976, U.S. Ct. Appeals (2d cir.), 1976, U.S. Supreme Ct. 1978, Fla. 1986. Spl. litigation counsel City of Albany, N.Y., 1976-85; assoc. Garry, Cahill & Edmunds, Albany, 1973-76; sole pratice, 1976-84; ptnr. Linnan, Shea & Flannery, 1987-89, Linnan Bacon & Meyer, 1989-92, Linnan & Fallon, 1992—. Founder, pres., v.p. Northeastern Family and Children's House, Inc., 1981; mem. Albany County Dem. County, 1976-93. Mem. Assn. Trial Lawyers Am., Am. Bd. Trial Advocates (nat. bd. dirs., past pres. Albany chpt.), N.Y. State Bar Assn., N.Y. Trial Lawyers, Capital Dist. Trial Lawyers. Democrat. Roman Catholic. Home: 61 Columbia St Albany NY 12210 Office: Linnan & Fallon LLP 61 Columbia St Albany NY 12210-2736 E-mail: jdlinnan@linnan-fallon.com.

LINNANE, JAMES FRANCIS, JR. internist, gastroenterologist; b. Boston, Apr. 12, 1962; s. James Francis and Joan Marie (Corcoran) L. BA, Holy Cross Coll., 1984; MD, Brown U., 1988. Diplomate Am. Bd. Internal Medicine with subspecialty in gastroenterology. Intern New Eng. Deaconess Hosp., Boston, 1988-89, resident, 1989-91; fellow Lahey Clinic Med. Ctr., Burlington, Mass., 1991-93; assoc. physician Forsythe Med. Specialists, Winston-Salem, N.C., 1993-95, Piedmont Health Care, 1995—. Mem.: AMA, ACP, Crohns and Colitis Found., Am. Coll. Gastroenterol. Endoscopy, Alpha Sigma Nu, Phi Beta KAppa. Home: 112 Big Oak Ln Statesville NC 28625-2702 Office: Piedmont Health Care Old Mocksville Rd Statesville NC 28625

LINNANSALO, VERA, engineer; b. Helsinki, Finland, Oct. 9, 1950; came to U.S., 1960, naturalized, 1969; d. Boris and Vera (Schkurat-Schkuropatsky) L. BS in Computer and Info. Sci., BME, Cleve. State U., 1974; MBA, U. Akron, 1983. Engring. assoc. B.F. Goodrich Co., Akron, Ohio, 1974-75, assoc. product engr., 1975-77, tire devel. engr., 1977-79, advanced tire devel. engr., 1979-84, quality devel. engr., 1984-85, sr. quality devel. engr., 1985-86; coord. GM-10 Uniroyal Goodrich Tire Co., 1986-88, sr. tire devel. scientist, 1988-89; mgr. design and product quality Pirelli Armstrong Tire Corp., New Haven, 1989-90; product design engr. truck ops. Ford Motor Co., Dearborn, 1990-93, vehicle quality and process specialist, corp. quality office, 1993-94, supr. econoline quality and reliability comml. truck, 1995-96, supr. ranger quality and reliablity light truck vehicle ctr., 1996-98, supr. explorer quality and reliability truck vehicle ctr., 1998-99, supr. tech. strategy, rsch. and advanced tech., 2000—02, performance cons. global core engring., 2002—. Mem. Am. Soc. Quality (sr., cert. quality engr.), Soc. Automotive Engrs., Mensa. Home: 9234 Mayflower Plymouth MI 48170 Office: WHQ The American Rd Dearborn MI 48124-3958 E-mail: vlinnans@ford.com.

LINNEHAN, RICHARD N. astronaut, veterinarian; b. Lowell, Mass., Sept. 19, 1957; BS in Animal Scis., U. New Hampshire, Durham, 1980; DVM, Ohio State U. Coll.Vet.Medicine, Columbus, 1985. Veterinarian Pvt. Practice, 1985—86; intern in Zoo animal medicine and comparative pathology Balt. Zoo and Johns Hopkins U. , 1987—89; commd. Capt. U.S. Army Vet. Corpso, 1989; chief clin. vet. USN Marine Mammal Program, San Diego, 1989—92; astronaut NASA Johnson Space Ctr. , Houston, 1992—. Faculty mem. N.C. State U. Coll. Vet. Medicine, Raleigh-Durham, NC, 1998—; bd. dir. Tulane/Xavier Astrobiology Ctr., New Orleans, 1998—. Recipient 3 NASA Space Flight medals, Alumni award, Ohio State U. Coll. Vet. Medicine, Disting. Alumni award, Ohio State U., 1997, 2002. Mem.: Assn. Space Explorers, Internat. Assn. Acquatic Animal Medicine, Am. Assn. Zoo Veterinarians, Am. Vet. Med. Assn. (president's award). Achievements include 3 space flights, 43 days in space including 3 space walks. Avocations: sports, natural history, oudoor activities. Office: Astronauts Office/CB Johnson Space Ctr Houston TX 77058

LINNELL, ROBERT HARTLEY, editor-in-chief; b. Kalkaska, Mich., Aug. 15, 1922; s. Earl Dean and Constance (Hartley) L.; m. Myrle Elizabeth Talbot, June 17, 1950; children: Charlene LeGro, Lloyd Robert, Randa Ruth, Dean Maxfield. BS, U. N.H., 1944, MS, 1948; PhD, U. Rochester, 1950. Asst. instr. U. N.H., 1942-44, instr., 1947; asst. prof. chemistry Am. U., Beirut, 1950-52, assoc. prof., chmn. chemistry dept., 1952-55; v.p. Tizon Chem. Corp., Flemington, N.J., 1955-58; assoc. prof. chemistry U. Vt., 1958-61; dir. Scott Research Labs., Plumsteadville, Pa., 1961-62; program dir. phys. chemistry NSF, 1962-65, planning assoc., 1965-67, program mgr. departmental sci. devel., 1967-69; dean Coll. Letters, Arts and Scis., U. So. Calif., Los Angeles, 1969-70; dir. Office Instl. Studies U. So. Calif., 1970-82, chmn. safety sci. dept., 1982-85, prof. emeritus, 1985—; pres. Harmony Inst., 1985-92. Cons. Reheis Corp., 1958-61, Coll. Chemistry Cons. Service, 1970-76, EPA, 1971-73, Lake Erie Environment Program, 1971-73 Author: Graduate Student Support and Manpower Resources in Graduate Science Education, 1968, Air Pollution, 1973, Hydrogen Bonding, 1971, Dollars and Scholars, 1982, Meeting The Needs of The Non-Smoking Traveler, 1986, Ignition Interlock Devices: An Assessment of Their Application to Reducing DUI, 1991; editor: my-oped.com, 1999—; contbr. articles to profl. jours. Mem. traffic adv. com. Auto Club So. Calif., 1985-93; treas. Norwich Congl. Ch., 1995-96, chair bus. com. 1996-98; coord. Concord Coalition, Upper Valley, N.H. and Vt., 1995—; mem. devel. bd. Upper Valley Tchr. Tng. Program, 1995-97; mem. scholarship com. Upper Valley Cmty. Found., 1996—; bd. overseers Dartmouth Hitchcock Med. Ctr., 1997—; bd. dirs. Upper Valley Habitat for Humanity, 1993-95. Recipient Outstanding Achievement award Coll. Tech., U. N.H., 1969 Mem. AAUP, Am. Chem. Soc. (program chmn. Washington 1968, divsn. chem. edn. 1971), Assn. Instl. Rsch., Am. Lung Assn. of Ctrl. Calif. (bd. dirs. 1986-92, pres. 1991-92), Rotary. Achievements include patents in chemistry field. Home: 82 Stagecoach Rd White River Junction VT 05001-9132

LINNEN, THOMAS FRANCIS, international strategic management consulting firm executive; b. Carbondale, Pa., Sept. 29, 1925; s. John Joseph and Marie Dolores (Fitzpatrick) L.; m. Mary Joanne, Dec. 28, 1951 ; children: Nancy, Paula, Michele, Thomas F. Jr., Mary J. Jr. BS, Georgetown U., 1949; postgrad., Am. U., Washington, 1951, U. Rochester, 1988. Writer Congl. News Reports, Washington, late 40's; congl. press asst., 1949; asst. for pub. relations office of pres. Georgetown U., 1950; officer psychol. and spl. ops. Aide Office Sec. Army USAF and U.S. Army, Ft. Bragg, N.C., 1951-55; mgr. Retail Credit Company, Atlanta, 1953-56, 59-72; various managerial assignments GM Equifax Inc., Chgo., 1972-80; regional mgr. ops. and sales Equifax Inc., Upstate, N.Y., 1980-89; pres. The NORAM Group Ltd., Buffalo, 1990-94, vice chmn., 1992, chmn., 1993, 94; pres. Am. Auto. Exports Inc., Russia, 1993, chmn., CEO Russia, 1994; chmn. AIG, Moscow, ABC, Moscow; pres. Thomas F. Linnen & Assocs., 1998—. Bd. dirs. Gaflin Comm. Group, Inc., Chgo.; on spl. assignment CIA, 1956-59; cons. to Russian govtl. units on market economy transition, 1952—; various positions with world affairs couns. and internat. insts. Pub. Russian internat. bus. newsletter "The Ural Region Focus"; contbr. articles to jours. and mags. Mem. adv. bd. Barat Coll., Buffalo Coun. on World Affairs, Internat. Inst. Buffalo, Chgo. Coun. Fgn. Rels., United Way Crusade of Mercy, Heart Fund Campaigns and other civic orgns.; chairmanship role in John F. Kennedy, Jimmy Carter and Jack Kemp campaigns for the Presidency. Maj. USAR ret. Mem. Res. Officers Assn. U.S. (former nat. officer), Mortgage Bankers Assn. Republican. Roman Catholic. Avocations: tennis, golf. Home and Office: 404 Clearwater Dr Ponte Vedra Beach FL 32082-4170 Office: 404 Clearwater Dr Ponte Vedra Beach FL 32082-4170 *Democracy, with all its warts and imperfections, remains the best form of government known to man. Yet, democracy, eroded by unbridled freedom and corrupt self-interests, lethally turns in upon itself. Freedom, devoid of individual responsibility and in mindless confrontation with man's God, will, over time, kill the democratic body politic itself.*

LINNEY, BEVERLY See HALLAM, BEVERLY

LINNEY, LAURA, actress; b. N.Y.C., Feb. 5, 1964; Motion picture and T.V. actress. Films include Lonrenzo's Oil, 1992, Searching for Bobby Fischer, 1993, Blind Spot, 1993, Dave, 1993, A Simple Twist of Fate, 1994, Congo, 1995, Primal Fear, 1996, The Truman Show, 1998, Lush, 1999, You Can Count on Me, 2000, The House of Mirth, 2000, Running Mates, 2000, Maze, 2000, The Laramie Project, 2002, The Mothman Prophecies, 2002 (T.V. films) Tales of the City, 1993, More Tales of the City, 1998, Love Letters, 1999, Wild Iris, 2001. Office: c/o CAA 9830 Wilshire Blvd Beverly Hills CA 90212-1804*

LINNEY, ROMULUS, author, educator; b. Phila., Sept. 21, 1930; s. Romulus Zachariah Linney and Maitland (Thompson) Clabaugh; m. Laura Callanan; children: Laura, Susan. BA, Oberlin Coll., 1953, LittD (hon.), 1994; MFA, Yale U., 1958; DLitt. (hon.), Applachian State U., 1995, Wake Forest U., 1998. Prof. Actors Studio MFA New Sch., N.Y.C. Lectr. U. N.C., Chapel Hill, Raleigh, U. Pa., Bklyn. Coll., Conn. Coll., Princeton U., Hunter Coll., Columbia U. Author: (novels) Heathen Valley, 1962, Slowly, By Thy Hand Unfurled, 1965, Jesus Tales 1980, (plays) The Sorrows of Frederick, 1968, Democracy and Esther, and the Love Suicide at Schofield Barracks, 1973, Holy Ghosts, and The Sorrows of Frederick, 1977, Old Man Joseph and His Family, 1978, The Captivity of Pixie Shedman, 1981, Tennessee, 1981 (Obie award), Childe Byron, 1981, The Death of King Philip, 1983, Laughing Stock, 1984, Sand Mountain, 1985, A Woman Without a Name, 1986, Pops, 1987, Juliet, Yancy and April Snow, 1989, Three Poets, 1989, Unchanging Love, 1990, '2', 1990, Ambrosio, 1991 (Obie award Sustained Excellence in Playwriting), Spain, 1993, True Crimes, 1995, Oscar Over Here, 1995, Mock Trial, 1996, Mountain Memory, 1996, A Christmas Carol (from Dickens), 1996, Gint (from Ibsen), 1998, A Lesson Before Dying (from novel by Ernest J. Gaines), 1998, The Unwritten Song (from a book by Willard R. Trask), 1999, Hisself, Goodbye, Oscar, 1999, others. Mem. Coll. of the Fellows of the Am. Theatre. With U.S. Army, 1954-56. Grantee NEA, Guggenheim Found., Rockefeller Found., others; recipient Lit. award AAAL, 1984, Award of Merit, 1999. Mem.: Fellowship of So. Writers, Ensemble Studio Theatre, Acad. Arts & Letters, Dramatists Guild (coun.), Am. Acad. Arts & Sci., Corp. of Yaddo (bd. dirs.). Address: 289 Dales Bridge Rd Germantown NY 12526-5222 E-mail: romuluslinney@msn.com.

LINOWES, DAVID FRANCIS, political economist, educator, corporate executive; b. N.J., Mar. 16, 1917; m. Dorothy Lee Wolf, Mar. 25, 1946; children: Joanne Linowes Alinsky, Richard Gary, Susan Linowes Allen (dec.), Jonathan Scott. Founder, ptnr. Leopold & Linowes (now BDO Siedman), Washington, 1946-62; cons. sr. ptnr. Leopold & Linowes, 1962-82; nat. founding ptnr. Laventhol & Horwath, 1965-76; chmn. bd, CEO Mickleberry Comm. Corp., 1970-73; chmn., CEO Perpetual Investment Co., Inc., 1950-88; dir. Horn & Hardart Co., 1971-77, Piper Aircraft, 1972-77, Saturday Rev./World Mag., Inc., 1972-77, Chris Craft Industries, Inc., 1958—, Work in Am. Inst., Inc.; prof. polit. economy, pub. policy, bus. adminstrn. U. Ill., Urbana, 1976—, Boeschensten prof. emeritus, 1987—. Cons. DATA Internat. Assistance Corps., 1962-68, U.S. Dept. State, UN, Sec. HEW, Dept. Interior; chmn. Fed. Privacy Protection Commn., Washington, 1975-77, U.S. Commn. Fair Market Value Policy for Fed. Coal Leasing, 1983-84, Pres.'s Commn. on Fiscal Accountability of Nation's Energy Resources, 1981-82; chmn. Pres.' Commn. on Privatization, 1987-88; mem. Council on Fgn. Relations; cons. panel GAO; adj. prof. mgmt. NYU, 1965-73; Disting. Arthur Young Prof. U. Ill., 1973-74; emeritus chmn. internat. adv. com. Tel Aviv U.; headed U.S. State Dept. Mission to Turkey, 1967, to India, 1970, to Pakistan, 1968, to Greece, 1971 ; U.S. rep. on privacy to Orgn. Econ. Devel. Intergovtl. Bur. for Informati cs, 1977-81, cons., N.Y.C., 1977-81; U.S. State Dept. mission to Chile, Argentina and Uruguay, July, 1988, Yugoslavia, May, 1991. Author: Managing Growth Through Acquistion, Strategies for Survival, Corporate Conscience; commn. report Personal Privacy in Information Society, Fiscal Accountablility of Nation's Energy Resources; editor: The Impact of the Communication and Computer Revolution on Society, Privacy in America, 1989, Creating Public Policy, 1998, Living Through 50 Years of Economic Progress with 10 Presidents-The Most Productive Generation in History 1946-1996, 2000; contbr. articles to profl. jours. Trustee Boy's Club Greater Washington, 1955-62, Am. Inst. Found., 1962-68; assoc. YM-YWHA's Greater N.Y., 1970-76; chmn. Charities Adv. Com. of D.C., 1958-62; emeritus bd. dirs. Religion in Am. Life, Inc.; former chmn. U.S. People for UN; chmn. citizens com. Combat Charity Rackets, 1953-58. 1st lt. Signal Corps, AUS, 1942-46. Recipient 1970 Human Relations award Am. Jewish Com., U.S. Pub. Service award, 1982, Alumni Achievement award U. Ill., 1989, CPA Distinguished Pub. Svc. award, Washington, 1989. Mem. AICPA (v.p. 1962-63), U. Ill. Found. (emeritus bd. dirs. 1), Coun. Fgn. Rels., Cosmos Club (Washington), Phi Kappa Phi (nat. bd. dirs.), Beta Gamma Sigma. Office: U Ill 308 Lincoln Hall Urbana IL 61801 also: 9 Wayside Ln Scarsdale NY 10583-2907 Home: # 524 120 SE 5th Ave Boca Raton FL 33432-5072

LINOWITZ, SOL MYRON, lawyer; b. Trenton, N.J., Dec. 7, 1913; s. Joseph and Rose (Oglenskye) L.; m. Evelyn Zimmerman, Sept. 3, 1939; children: Anne, June, Jan, Ronni. AB, Hamilton Coll., 1935; JD, Cornell U., 1938; LLD (hon.), Allegheny Coll., Amherst Coll., Bucknell U., Babson Inst., Brandeis U., Colgate U., Curry Coll., Dartmouth Coll., Elmira Coll., Georgetown U., Hamilton Coll., Hebrew Union Coll., Ithaca Coll., Marietta Coll., Johns Hopkins U., Oberlin Coll., St. John Fisher Coll., St. Lawrence U., Jewish Theol. Sem., Washington U., St. Louis, U. Miami, Muskingum Coll., Notre Dame U., U. Pacific, U. Pa., Rutgers U., Pratt Inst., Rider Coll., Roosevelt U., Chapman Coll., U. Mich., Govs. State U., U. Mo., Syracuse U.; LHD (hon.), Am. U., Loyola U., U. Rochester, Yeshiva U., U. Judaism, Wooster Coll.; PhD (hon.), U. Haifa. Bar: N.Y. 1938. Asst. gen. counsel OPA, Washington, 1942-44; ptnr. Sutherland, Linowitz & Williams, 1946-58, Harris, Beach, Keating, Wilcox & Linowitz, Rochester, N.Y., 1958-66; chmn. Nat. Urban Coalition, 1970-76; chmn. bd. dirs., chmn. exec. com., gen. counsel Xerox Corp., 1958-66; chmn. bd. dirs. Xerox Internat., 1966; sr. ptnr. Coudert Bros., 1969-84, sr. counsel, 1984-94; ambassador to OAS, 1966-69. Negotiator Panama Canal treaties, 1977-78; spl. Middle East negotiator for Pres. Carter, 1979-81; chmn. Am. Acad. of Diplomacy, 1984-89; co-chmn. Inter-Am. Dialogue, 1981-92; pres. Fed. City Coun., 1974-78; chmn. Pres. Commn. World Hunger, 1978-79; bd. dirs., co-founder Internat. Exec. Svc. Corps; chmn. State Dept. Adv. Com. on Internat. Orgns., 1963-66. Author: The Betrayed Profession, 1994, (memoir) The Making of a Public Man, 1985, This Troubled Urban World, 1974; contbr. articles to profl. jours. Trustee Hamilton Coll. (life), Cornell U. (emeritus), Johns Hopkins U. (emeritus), Am. Assembly; chmn. bd. overseers, bd. dirs. Jewish Theol. Sem., 1971-79. Lt. USNR, 1944-46. Recipient Presdl. Medal of Freedom, 1998. Fellow Am. Acad. Arts and Scis.; mem. Am. Assn. for UN (pres. N.Y. State), Rochester Assn. for UN (pres. 1952), Rochester C. of C. (pres. 1958), ABA, N.Y. Bar Assn., Rochester Bar Assn. (v.p. 1949-50), Am. Assn. UN (bd. dirs.), Council on Fgn. Relations, Order of Coif, Phi Beta Kappa, Phi Kappa Phi. Office: Acad for Ednl Devel 1875 Connecticut Ave NW Washington DC 20009-5728

LINSENMEYER, JOHN MICHAEL, lawyer; b. Columbus, Ohio, June 20, 1940; s. John Cyril and Ruth Theresa (Motz) L.; m. Barbara Panish, Aug. 12, 1961; children: Ann Elizabeth Linsenmeyer Nelson, Thomas More, Barbara Mary Linsenmeyer Malone. AB, Georgetown U., 1961, JD, 1964. Bar: Va. 1964, N.Y. 1965, U.S. Supreme Ct.1967, D.C. 1975. Assoc. Cravath, Swaine & Moore, N.Y.C., 1966-75; ptnr. Forsyth, Decker, Murray & Broderick, 1975-80, Morgan, Lewis & Bockius, N.Y.C., 1980—. Columnist Southern Conn. Newspapers, Greenwich, 1984—; contbr. articles to profl. jours. Police officer, sgt. Greenwich Police Dept. Special Div., 1966-87; cons. firearms Presdl. Commn. on the Causes and Prevention of Violence, 1968-69; bd. dirs. Fairfield County Fish and Game Agy., Newtown, Conn., 1973-77. Mem. N.Y. State Bar Assn., N.Y.C. Fed. Cts. Com., N.Y.C. Fed. Bar Coun., Univ. Club (N.Y.C.), Squadron A (N.Y.C.), Rocky Point Club (Old Greenwich, Conn.), Royal Can. Mil. Club (Toronto.), Republican. Roman Catholic. Avocations: hunting, shooting, horses, military history. Home: 9 Hendrie Ave Riverside CT 06878-1808 Office: Morgan Lewis & Bockius 43d Fl 101 Park Ave Fl 43D New York NY 10178-0002 E-mail: jlinsenmeyer@morganlewis.com.

LINSK, MICHAEL STEPHEN, real estate executive; b. L.A., Apr. 20, 1940; s. Abe P. and Helen Linsk; m. Wilma M. Stahl, Aug. 11, 1979; children by previous marriage: Cari E., Steven D. BSBA, U. So. Calif., 1965, MBA, 1969. CFO Larwin Group, Inc., Encino, Calif., 1970-75; v.p. fin., dir. Donald L. Bren Co., L.A., 1976-78; v.p., CFO, treas., dir. Wilshire Mortgage/Wilshire Diversified, Burbank, Calif., 1980-81; pres., dir. subs. Wilshire Mortgage Corp., 1981-84; pres., dir. Wilshire Realty Investments, 1981-84, Glenfed Investments Inc., subs. Glendale Fed. Savs., 1982-84; pres. Eastern Pacific Fin. Group, L.A., 1984-85; sr. v.p. Leisure Tech., Inc., 1985-87; CEO Investec Realty Group, Inc., Encino, 1987-88; sr. v.p. L.A. Land Co., 1988-91; mng. dir. real estate consulting Price Waterhouse Coopers, 1992—. Dir. Presdl. Savs. Bank, Jewel City Ins., Glendale, Verdugo Services, Inc., Glendale. Treas. Temple Judea, Tarzana, Calif., 1982-83, trustee, 1981-83; treas., bd. dirs. Am. Theater Arts; bd. dirs. North Hollywood Cultural Ctr., Inc., A Cmty. of Friends, Inc., 1998—. Mem. Bldg. Industry Assn. (dir. L.A. chpt. 1981-88), AICPA, Calif. Soc. CPAs, Urban Land Inst., Beta Gamma Sigma. Office: Price Waterhouse Coopers 400 S Hope St Ste 2300 Los Angeles CA 90071-2889 E-mail: michaellinsk@cswebmail.com., michael.linsk@us.pwcglobal.com.

LINSKY, MARTIN ALAN, public policy educator, consultant; b. Brookline, Mass., Aug. 28, 1940; s. Harold Max and Ruth Doran L.; m. Helen Roberts Strieder, Dec. 10, 1964 (div. Jan. 1979); children: Alison, Sam; m. Lynn H. Staley, July 7, 1979; 1 child, Max. BA, Williams Coll., Williamstown, Mass., 1961; JD, Harvard U., 1964. Asst. atty. gen. Commonwealth of Mass., Boston, 1967, chief sec. to the gov., 1992-95; mem. and asst. minority leader Mass. Ho. of Reps., 1967-72; editorial writer and reporter The Boston Globe, 1973-75; editor-in-chief The Real Paper, Cambridge, Mass., 1975-79; asst. dir. Inst. of Politics, John F. Kennedy Sch., 1981-85; instr. in law Boston Coll., Newton, Mass., 1973-85; lectr. in pub. policy John F. Kennedy Sch. of Govt. at Harvard, Cambridge, 1985-92, 95—; co-founder, prin. Cambridge Leadership Assocs., 2002—. Cons. seminars Ethics Ctr., Poynter Inst. for Media Studies, St. Petersburg, Fla., 1987-88, dir. ownership and leadership project, 1995-97; project dir. Revson Found., N.Y.C., 1982-85. Author: Impact: How the Press Affects Federal Policy Making, 1986, How the Press Affects Federal Policy Making: 6 Case Studies, 1986, (with Ed Grefe) The New Corporate Activism, 1995, (with Ronald Heifotz) Leadership on the Line: Staying Alive Through the Dangers of Leading, 2002; consulting editor: (books) Getting to Yes, 1981, Beyond the Hotline, 1985. Bd. dirs., selection com. Cavallo Found., Cambridge, 1988-96; bd. dirs. Ford Hall Forum, Boston, 1989-92; regular polit. commentator Monitor Network, Boston, 1992, WHDH-TV, CBS affiliate, Boston, 1990; bd. trustees Gaudino Meml. Fund, Williams Coll., 1992-

2002, chair, 1999-2002; chair selection com. William Bulger Excellence in Legislation Leadership award, 1999—. Recipient cash prize, second place essay competition, Woodrow Wilson Ctr. for Media Studies, Washington, 1990. Mem. Inst. for Alternative Journalism (bd. dirs. 1983-95, chair 1992-95), Poynter Inst. for Media Studies (bd. advisors 1981-97). Avocations: running marathons, Mexican food, collecting baseball cards. Home: 333 Central Park W Apt 26 New York NY 10025-7104 Office: John F Kennedy Sch Govt Harvard Univ Cambridge MA 02138 E-mail: marty@pipeline.com.

LINSON, ROBERT EDWARD, university administrator emeritus; b. Indpls., Dec. 10, 1922; s. William Albert and Anne Charlotte (Karstedt) L.; m. Nancy Sue Hughes, June 6, 1948; children: Cynthia, Lawrence, LuAnn. BS, Ball State U., Muncie, Ind., 1947; MS, Ball State U., 1948; EdD, U. Denver, 1957. Prin., acting supt. Jonesboro (Ind.) pub. schs., 1948-49; prin J.C. Knight Sch., Jonesboro, 1949-50, 51-52, Spiceland (Ind.) pub. schs., 1952-55; dir. alumni rels. Ball State Tchrs. Coll., Muncie, 1955-75; exec. dir. alumni and devel. Ball State U., 1975-80, v.p. univ. relations, 1980-87, v.p. univ. relations emeritus, 1987—. Cons. in field. Contbr. articles to profl. jours. Bd. dirs. Planned Parenthood of East Ctrl. Ind., 1988-91, United Way of Delaware County, Muncie, 1982-86, Muncie YMCA, 1980-84; mem. task force on govtl. rels. United Way of Ind., Indpls., 1985-91; founder Coun. Advancement and Support of Edn., 1974; bd. dirs. Ind. Basketball Hall of Fame. With USAF, 1943-46, 50-51. Named Outstanding U.S. Advancement Officer, Coun. for Advancement & Support of Edn., 1986; Alumni Disting. Svc. award, Ball State U., 1980, Ball State U. Athletic Hall of Fame, others. Mem. Am. Alumni Coun. (chmn. bd. dirs. 1972-73), Sagamore of the Wabash, Rotary. Democrat. Presbyterian. Avocations: travel, reading, intercollegiate athletics. Home: 909 N Meadow Ln Muncie IN 47304-3326

LINSTONE, HAROLD ADRIAN, management and systems science educator; b. Hamburg, Fed. Republic Germany, June 15, 1924; came to U.S., 1936; s. Frederic and Ellen (Seligmann) L.; m. Hedy Schubach, June 16, 1946; children: Fred A., Clark R. BS, CCNY, 1944; MA, Columbia U., 1947; PhD, U. So. Calif., 1954. Sr. scientist Hughes Aircraft Co., Culver City, Calif., 1949-61, The Rand Corp., Santa Monica, 1961-63; assoc. dir. planning Lockheed Corp., Burbank, 1963-71; prof. Portland (Oreg.) State U., 1970—. Pres. Systems Forecasting, Inc., Santa Monica, 1971-98; cons. 1973—. Author: Multiple Perspectives for Decision Making, 1984, Decision Making for Technology Executives, 1999; co-author: The Unbounded Mind, 1993, The Challenge of the 21st Century, 1994; co-editor The Delphi Method, 1975, Technological Substitution, 1976, Futures Research, 1977; editor-in-chief Technol. Forecasting Social Change, 1969—. NSF grantee, Washington, 1976, 79, 85. Mem. Inst. Mgmt. Scis., Ops. Rsch. Soc., Internat. Soc. Systems Scis. (pres. 1993-94). Avocation: photography. Office: Portland State U PO Box 751 Portland OR 97207-0751

LINSTROM, RICHARD CRISMAN, lawyer; b. Riverside, Calif., Dec. 19, 1956; s. Richard D. and Delores (Crisman) L.; m. Mie Mason, Aug. 13, 1988. Student, Columbia U., 1975, U. London, 1978; BS, U. San Francisco, 1979, JD, 1982. Bar: Nev., 1994, Hawaii, 1987, D.C., 1989. Sr. fin. analyst, mktg. mgr. Pacific Bell, San Francisco, 1983-87; dep. prosecuting atty. City and County of Honolulu, 1987-88; pvt. practice Honolulu and Las Vegas, 1989-95; chief dep. atty. gen. State of Nev., Las Vegas, 1995-2001; pvt. practice, 2001—. Mem. U.S.-Japan Vol. Assn. (bd. dirs., sec. 1990-95). Home: 10013 Summer Oak Ln #102 Las Vegas NV 89134-2625 Office: 723 S 3d St Las Vegas NV 89101-6702

LINSTROTH, TOD BRIAN, lawyer; b. Racine, Wis., Feb. 19, 1947; s. Eugene and Gloria L.; m. Jane Kathryn Zedler, June 23, 1972; children: Kathryn, Krista, Kassandre, Kyle. BBA in Acctg., U. Wis., 1970, JD, 1973. Bar: Wis. Assoc. Michael, Best & Friedrich, Madison, Wis., 1973-79, ptnr., mem. firm mgmt. com., 1980—. Chmn. Wis. Tech. Coun., Inc., 2001—. Bd. visitors Univ. Wis. Sch. Bus., 1991-94; mem. Wis. Gov.'s Sci. and Tech. Coun., Madison, 1993-95; pres. Madison Repertory Theatre. Mem. Greater Madison Area C. of C., Wis. Venture Fair (chair Steering Com. 1997—), Wis. Tech. Coun. (chair 2001—). Avocations: skiing, sailing, reading. Office: Michael Best & Friedrich 1 S Pinckney St Ste 700 Madison WI 53703-4236

LINTERIS, GREGORY T. astronaut; b. Demarest, N.J., Oct. 4, 1957; s. Lino Luigi and Helen Mary Linteris. BS in Chem. Engring., Princeton U., 1979; MS in Mech. Engring., Stanford U., 1984; PhD in Mech. and Aerospace Engring., Princeton U., 1990. Rsch. staff U. Calif., San Diego, 1990—92; rsch. staff, prin. investigator NASA microgravity combustion experiment NIST, 1992—; payload specialist, astronaut NASA STS-83, 1997, NASA STS-94, 1997. Contbr. articles to profl. jours. Fellow Guggenheim, 1985. Mem.: AIAA, Combustion Inst., Am. Phys. Soc., Sigma Xi. Avocations: running, skiing, board sailing, hiking, backpacking. Office: Astronaut Office/CB NASA Johnson Space Ctr Houston TX 77058*

LINTINGER, GREGORY JOHN, electrical engineer, educator; b. New Orleans, Oct. 8, 1946; s. Emile John Jr. and Lucy (Perez) L.; m. Barbara Gaudet, Mar. 14, 1965 (div. Sept. 1981); children: Gregory John Jr., Melissa Anne; m. Brenda Celeste Wambsgans, Dec. 12, 1981; 1 child, Emily Celeste. BS in Elec. Engring., U. New Orleans, 1985. Registered profl. engr., La., Tenn., Miss., Ark. Office mgr. Upper City Electric Co., New Orleans, 1967-72, elec. estimator, 1972-76, elec. designer, estimator, 1976-87, v.p. elec. design/estimating, 1987—; mgr., elec. and instrumental engring. dept. Wink Engring., 1994—. Instr. Associated Builders and Contractors, New Orleans, 1975-95. Pres. Young Men's Bus. Club of Greater New Orleans, 1975. Recipient Bush award Young Men's Bus. Club, New Orleans, 1973-75, Colomb award, 1975; named U. New Orleans Disting. Engring. Alumni, 1999. Mem. Illuminating Engrs. Soc. (sec. 1987-88), Inst. Electronic Engrs., Industry Application Soc. (exhibits chair 1997 annual meeting), Kiwanis (treas. 1986-87), A.B.C. (bd. dirs. New Orleans chpt. 1986-87). Republican. Roman Catholic. Avocations: piano, computers, music, philanthropy. Home: 639 Labarre Dr Metairie LA 70001-5442 Office: Wink Engineering Elect & Instrumental Engring Dept 4949 Bullard Ave Ste 100 New Orleans LA 70128-3147

LINTNER, DALE EDSEL, JR. accountant, construction company executive; b. Huntingdon Valley, Pa., Nov. 13, 1967; s. Dale E. Sr. and Norma R. (Curcillo) L.; m. Amelia L. Bozzi, Aug. 3, 1991; children: Dale E. III, Zachary J., Alexander J., Nicholas Q. BS Acctg., U. Del., 1991. Acct. Dale Construction Co., Glenside, Pa., 1989-93; controller Dale Corp., 1993-97, CFO, 1997—. Coach football Ancillae-Assumpta Acad., Wyncote, Pa., 1991—. Mem. Constrn. Fin. Mgrs. Assn., Bldg. Industry Assn. Phila. (treas. 1998—), Kappa Delta Rho (v.p. Alpha Beta chpt. 1989, pres. 1990). Roman Catholic. Avocations: coaching, golf. Office: Dale Corp 70 Limekiln Pike Glenside PA 19038-2924

LINTO, NANCY, medical unit director; b. Madison, Wis., Dec. 30, 1959; d. Roger H. and Ann L. (Coyle) Rebholz; m. Johnnie Linto Jr., June 27, 1987; children: William, Emily. BSN, Viterbo Coll., La Crosse, Wis., 1982; MS, Brenau U., 1999. Cert. in EKG monitoring, ACLS, med./surg. nursing, nurse practitioner. Staff nurse Sacred Heart Hosp., Eau Claire, Wis.; traveling nurse Boswell Meml. Hosp., Sun City, Ariz., McLeod Regional Med. Ctr., Florence, S.C., Lubbock (Tex.) Gen. Hosp., Morton F. Plant Hosp., Clearwater, Fla., Meml. Med. Ctr., Savannah, Ga.; Healthmaster Home Health, Augusta; asst. dir. med., C.A.R.E. coord., med. unit dir. Lanier Park Hosp., Gainesville. E-mail: njlinto@msn.com.

LINTON, HAROLD, architecture educator, writer; b. Pittsburgh, Pa., Oct. 1, 1947; s. Leonard and Ruth Linton; m. Nadyne M. Zolkower, Aug. 0, 1974; children: Joshua, Jonathan. BFA, Syracuse Univ., Syracuse, NY, 1969; MFA, Yale Univ., New Haven, CT, 1972. Asst. dean, coll. of architecture Lawrence Tech. Univ., Southfield, Mich., 1974—98; chmn., dept. of art Bradley Univ., Peoria, 1998—. Ceo ColorDesign 3D, Peoria, Ill., 1999—; design cons. Architecture & Indsl. Design, Peoria, Ill., 1999—. Author: (book) Color Forecasting, Portfolio Design, Color in Architecture. Fundraising team St. Francis Hosp., Peoria, Ill., 2000. Recipient Caterpillar Professorship, Bradley Univ., 2001, William Rainey Harper Award, 2001. Mem.: Nat. Assn. of Schools of Art & Design (evaluator 2000). Achievements include Author Of 14 Books On Color, Design, & Architecture. Avocations: traveling, traveling, art collecting. Office: Bradley Univ Dept of Art 1501 West Bradley Avenue Peoria IL 61625-0003 Office Fax: 309-677-3642. E-mail: linton@bradley.edu.

LINTON, JOY SMITH, primary school educator; b. Scranton, Pa., Dec. 9, 1952; d. Burnley J. and Josephine (Sbaraglia) Smith; m. William Howard Linton Jr., May 28, 1972; children: Kristy, David, Shelby. BSEd, West Chester State Coll., 1973. Minister St. Leo the Great Parish, Lancaster, Pa.; tchr. Apostles Community Preschool. Mem. bio-med. ethics com., mem. bio-med. edn. com. Ephrata Community Hosp; mem. subcom. med. and legal affairs Lancaster County Bar Assn. Mem. nat. bd. dirs., head family affairs commn. Nat. Coun. of Cath. Women, 1994-96 (pub. in Cath. Woman mag., submissions pub. in Bulletin Bd. publ.). Named St. Leo Woman of Yr., 1993; Hannah Kent Shopf Meml. scholar; Pa. Higher Edn. grantee. Mem. Nat. Assn. Edn. Young Children, Lancaster Assn. Edn. Young Children, Zeta Tau Alpha. Home: 808 Hillaire Rd Lancaster PA 17601-2221 E-mail: joy.linton@att.net.

LINTULA, MARGARET M. elementary and secondary school educator; b. Duluth, Minn., June 19, 1941; d. Yule Porter Eaton and Catherine Gurine Fleming Eaton Berg; m. John Elias Lintula, Aug. 17, 1963; 1 child, Maija Gurine Lintula Alexandrou. BS, U. Minn., 1963; MS, U. Wis., Superior, 1975. Lic. elem. tchr., K-12 reading specialist, Wis. Tchr. grade 4 Lakeside Elem. Sch., Duluth, 1963-66; tchr. grades 3-4 Boze Elem., Tacoma, 1967-71; tchr. English grades 7-8 Drummond (Wis.) Sch., 1971—2002, K-12 dist. reading specialist, 1976—2002; ret., 2002. Del. Dem. Nat. Conv., N.Y.C., 1992, state convs., 1988-97, vice-chmn. Dem. party, Bayfield County, 1986—. Named Secondary Tchr. of Yr., Wis. Congress Parents & Tchrs. Inc., 1989—90. Mem. NEA (bd. dirs. 1991-98, mem. women's issues com. 1998—), Wis. Edn. Assn. Coun. (bd. dirs. 1976-82, 88-98), Drummond Edn. Assn. (pres., chief negotiator 1980—), Wis. State Reading Assn., Internat. Reading Assn., Lions Club (Cable, Wis. chpt.). Democrat. Avocations: poetry, biking, painting, reading, travel. Home: PO Box 136 Drummond WI 54832-0136

LINTZ, BERNADETTE CELESTINE, French educator; b. Alsace, France; came to the U.S., 1977; Lic., U. Strasbourg, France, 1975; MA in English, U. Strasbourg, 1977; MA in French, Rice U., 1982, PhD in French, 1984. Tchg. fellow Rice U., Houston, 1979-81, instr., 1981-82; asst. prof. Colgate U., Hamilton, N.Y., 1983-89, assoc. prof., 1989—. Vis. assoc. prof. U. Mich., Dearborn, 2001—. Co-editor: Victor Hugo! Oeuvres et Critique (1981-83), 1992, The French Novel from Lafayette to Desvignes, 1995; contbr. articles to profl. jours. Grad. fellow Rice U., 1978-81; ACLS travel grantee, 1985; Sr. Picker Rsch. fellow Colgate U., 1990, Mellon grantee, 1999. Mem. MLA, Nineteenth Century French Studies Assn., Am. Assn. Tchrs. French, Assn. Internat. Zola Naturalism, Internat. Soc. Interdisciplinary Study, Groupe Inter-Univ. Victor Hugo. Avocations: travel, movies, photography. Office: Colgate U Dept Romance Langs & Lit 13 Oak Dr Hamilton NY 13346 E-mail: blintz@mail.colgate.edu.

LINTZ, ROBERT CARROLL, financial holding company executive; b. Cin., Oct. 2, 1933; s. Frank George and Carolyn Martha (Dickhaus) L.; m. Mary Agnes Mott, Feb. 1, 1964; children— Lesa, Robert, Laura, Michael. B.B.A., U. Cin., 1956. Staff accountant Alexander Grant, Cin., 1958-60; dist. mgr. Uniroyal, Memphis, 1960-65; v.p. Am. Fin. Corp., Cin., 1965— ; dir. Rapid-American Corp., McGregor Corp., Faberge Inc., all N.Y.C., H.R.T. Industries Inc., Los Angeles. Fisher Foods Inc., Cleve., Am. Agronomics, Tampa, Fla. Trustee, St. Francis-St. George Hosp., Cin., 1974-81. Served to capt. U.S. Army, 1956-58, 61-62. Republican. Roman Catholic. Home: 5524 Palisades Dr Cincinnati OH 45238-5620 Office: Am Fin Corp 1 E 4th St Cincinnati OH 45202-3717

LINVER, MICHAEL NORMAN, radiologist; b. Kansas City, Mo., Sept. 20, 1944; s. Joseph N. and Betty Jean (Levine) L.; m. Mina Jo Rosenbloom, July 30, 1967; children: Miriam, Elisheva, Daniel. BS, U. Mich., 1966; MD, U. Pitts., 1970. Diplomate Am. Bd. Nuclear Medicine, Am. Bd. Radiology. Staff radiologist St. Vincent's Hosp. and Med. Ctr., Toledo, 1976-78, Kino Cmty. Hosp., Tucson, 1978-80; ptnr. N.Mex. Radiologists P.C., Albuquerque, 1980-87; staff radiologist St. Joseph Northeast Heights Hosp., 1980—, St. Joseph Med. Ctr., Albuquerque, 1987—; ptnr. X-Ray Assocs. N.Mex. P.C., 1987—; assoc. clin. prof. radiology U. N.Mex., 1991—. Mem. nat. panel for quality determinants of mammography Agy. for Healthcare Policy and Rsch., Washington, 1992-94; mem. nat. mammography quality assurance adv. com. FDA, Washington, 1994-97; mem. N.Mex. Radiation Tech. Adv. Coun., Santa Fe, 1997-2000. Author: Emergency Radiology, 1986; co-author: Clinical Practice Guideline: Quality Determinants of Mammography, 1994. Bd. dirs. June Music Festival, Albuquerque, 1986-91, N.Mex. Symphony Orch., Albuquerque, 1992-99, Jewish Cmty. Ctr. of Greater Albuquerque, 1999—. Recipient Unsung Hero award Nat. Conf. of State Legislators, Nashville, 1990, People's Caring award People Living Through Cancer, 1996, Spirit of Hope award St. Joseph Healthcare Found., 1998. Fellow Soc. Breast Imaging; mem. Am. Cancer Soc. (chief lobbyist N.M. State Legis. 1990, state pres. 1992-93), Am. Coll. Radiology (breast task force, state pres. 1991-93, fellow 1994), Radiol. Soc. N.Am., Am. Roentoen Ray Soc., Am. Soc. Breast Disease. Avocations: arranging music, singing, performing, tennis, musical theater. Home: 6504 La Cuchilla NW Albuquerque NM 87107 Office: X-Ray Assocs NMex Ste 202 8020 Constitution Pl NE Albuquerque NM 87110 E-mail: mammomike@aol.com.

LINVILL, JOHN GRIMES, engineering educator; b. Kansas City, Mo., Aug. 8, 1919; s. Thomas G. and Emma (Crayne) L.; m. Marjorie Webber, Dec. 28, 1943; children: Gregory Thomas, Candace Sue. AB, William Jewell Coll., 1941; SB, Mass. Inst. Tech., 1943, SM, 1945, ScD, 1949; D of Applied Sci., U. Louvain, Belgium, 1966; DSc, William Jewell Coll., 1992. Asst. prof. elec. engring. Mass. Inst. Tech., 1949-51; tech. staff Bell Telephone Labs., 1951-55; assoc. prof. elec. engring. Stanford U., 1955-57, prof., dir. solid-state electronics lab., 1957-64, prof., chmn. dept. elec. engring., 1964-80, prof., dir. Center for Integrated Systems, 1980-90—, Canon USA prof. engring., 1988-89, prof. emeritus, 1989—; co-founder, dir. Tele Sensory Corp., 1971-2000; dir. Read-Rite Corp., 1992-2000. Author: Transistors and Active Circuits, 1961, Models of Transistors and Diodes, 1963; inventor Optacon reading aid for the blind. Recipient citation for achievement William Jewell Coll., 1963, John Scott award for devel. of Optacon, City of Phila., 1980, Medal of Achievement Am. Electronics Assn., 1983, Louis Braille Prize Deutscher Blindenverband, 1984. Fellow IEEE (Edn. medal 1976), AAAS; mem. Nat. Acad. of Engring., Am. Acad. of Arts and Scis. Home: 30 Holden Ct Portola Valley CA 94028-7913 Office: Stanford U Dept Elec Engring Stanford CA 94305

LINVILLE, MARY TODD, family nurse practitioner; b. Loogootee, Ind., Sept. 5, 1959; d. James Walter and Anna Margaret (Arvin) T.; m. Joe Linville, 1996; 1 child, B.J. BS in Social Work, St. Mary of the Woods Coll., 1982; AS in Nursing, Tenn. State U., 1989; MSN, Vanderbilt U., 1997. Cert. disaster nursing ARC; cert. family nurse practitioner ANCC; cert. trauma nursing Emergency Nurses Assn. Comty. organizer Rogers Park Tenants Com., Chgo., 1984-85; dir. Nashville Comys. Orgn. for Progress, Nashville, 1986-87, Tenn. Coun. Sr. Citizens, Nashville, 1987-89; staff nurse Nashville VA Med. Ctr., 1989-90; charge nurse Hartsville (Tenn.) Convalescent Ctr., 1990-94; quality assurance coord. ABC Home Health, Hartsville, 1992-93, adminstr. Lafayette, Tenn., 1994-95; charge nurse Trousdale Med. Ctr., Hartsville, 1995-97; family nurse practitioner, clinic mgr. Hartsville Family Health Ctr., 1997—2002, Trousdale Med. Ctr., 1998—, Fleming & Fleming & Assocs., 2002—. Presenter rural health conf. Meharry Med. Sch., Nashville, 1994; spkr. Tenn. rural Health Assn., 1995. Contbr., pub.: Love Passed On, 1991; contbr.: Photographic History of Martin County, 1993, Voices from the Hills, 1995; organizer, author: (disaster plan) Caring When it Counts, 1994. Bd. dirs., chair membership com. Mid. Cumberland Cmty. Health Agy., Nashville, 1992—, chair of bd., 2001—02; mem. Network, Washington, 1993—; organizer Trousdale County Cmty. Health Coun., Hartsville, 1992—; active Greenpeace, 1990—92; tchr. Confraternity of Christian Doctrine, Holy Family Cath. Ch., 1992, 1994, 1998, 1999, 2000, organizer Women's Club, 1999. Author winning entry The Evolving Woman Contest, 1998. Mem. ANA, Am. Acad. Nurse Practitioners, Tenn. Nurses Assn., Tenn. Assn. for Home Care, Tenn. Rural Health Assn., Trousdale County C. of C., Amnesty Internat., Health Profls. Network, Rural Tenn. Women's Support Group (organizer 1994), Sigma Delta Tau. Democrat. Avocations: Karate, music, writing. Home: 1640 Walnut Grove Rd Hartsville TN 37074-3630 Office: Fleming & Fleming & Assocs Ste 207 353 New Shackle Island Rd Hendersonville TN 37075 E-mail: mlinville40@hotmail.com.

LINVILLE, RAY PATE, educational administrator, analyst, editor, writer; b. Winston-Salem, N.C., Feb. 27, 1946; s. Clyde Burton and Nellie Pearl (Helm) L.; m. Mary Ann Slordal, July 30, 1970; children: Russell Pate, Rachel Ann. BA in Journalism, U. N.C., 1967; MS in Logistics Mgmt. with distinction, Air Force Inst. Tech., 1973. Commd. 2d lt. USAF, 1967, advanced through grades to col., 1989, materials mgr., 1973-76; mem. staff Tactical Air Command, Hampton, Va., 1976-79; plans officer UN Command, Seoul, Korea, 1980-81; staff analyst USAF, Washington, 1981-85; rsch. fellow Harvard U., Cambridge, Mass., 1985-86; chief combat support analysis Joint Chiefs of Staff, Washington, 1986-89; dir. logistics plans Strat. Air Command, Omaha, 1989-92; chief logistics plans and programs Air Combat Command, Hampton, 1992-93; ret. USAF, 1994; rsch. fellow Logistics Mgmt. Inst., McLean, Va., 1993-2000. Adj. prof. U. Va., Falls Church, 1986—88; grad. prof. Webster U., Washington, 1988—2000; adj. grad. prof. U. So. Calif., L.A., 1981; mgr. alumni edn. U. N.C. Gen. Alumni Assn., 2000—. Author: (monograph) Command and Control of Forces..., 1987; editor, asst. editor, mem. rev. bd. Logistics Spectrum, 1990-2000; contbr. articles to profl. jours. Dir., v.p., treas. Danbury Forest Com. Assn., Springfield, Va., 1982-84; youth group advisor, deacon Presbyn. Ch., Omaha and Fairfax, Va., 1986-99. Decorated Legion of Merit; recipient Outstanding Young Man of Am. award U.S. Jaycees, 1978. Mem. Internat. Soc. Logistics (sr., life, cert. profl. logistician, chpt. chmn. 1990-91, Bronze award 1991, Pres.'s award for Merit 1996, 97, 99), Air Force Assn. (life), U. N.C. Gen. Alumni Assn. (life), U.S. Chess Fedn. (life), Sigma Iota Epsilon. Avocations: writing, golf, piano, chess. Home: 845 St Andrews Dr Pinehurst NC 28374-9621 Office: U NC Gen Alumni Assn PO Box 660 Chapel Hill NC 27514-0660 E-mail: linville@carolina.net.

LINXWILER, LOUIS MAJOR, JR. retired finance company executive; b. Blackwell, Okla., Mar. 7, 1931; s. Louis Major and Flora Mae (Horton) L.; m. Susan Buchanan, July 27, 1963; children: Louis Major III, Robert William. BS, Okla. State U., 1953. Mgr. credit dept. Valley Nat. Bank, Tucson, 1957-60; sales rep. Vega Industries, Syracuse, N.Y., 1960-62; program dir. Am. Cancer Soc., Phoenix, 1962-67; v.p., mgr. credit dept. United Bank Ariz., 1967-76; dean edn. Am. Inst. Banking, 1976-80; cons., 1980-81, United Student Aid Funds Inc., 1981—88; also bd. dirs. Ariz. Student Loan Fin. Corp., founder, pres., CEO; founder, chmn., chief exec. officer Western Loan Mktg. Assn., Phoenix, 1984-90, also bd. dirs.; pres. Precision Design and Engring., Inc., Escondido, Calif., 1993—, Circulator Motor Co., Phoenix, 1996—; organizer, mng. ptnr. Energy Transition Products, L.L.C., 1998—. Editor: Money and Banking, 1978. Pres. City Commn. Sister Cities, Phoenix, 1986-87, Am. Inst. Banking, Phoenix, 1973-74, Phoenix YMCA Bd. Dirs., 1974-75; v.p. North Mountain Behavioral Inst., Phoenix, 1975-77. Served to 1st lt. U.S. Army, 1954-56. Mem. Shriners, Hiram Club, Rotary (bd. dirs. 1982-83, 93-94, 96-97), Beta Theta Pi. Republican. Presbyterian. Avocations: restoring automobiles, World War II history, travel. Home: 3624 N 27th Way Phoenix AZ 85016-7040 E-mail: loulinx@cox.net.

LINYARD, SAMUEL EDWARD GOLDSMITH, civil engineer; b. North Augusta, S.C., Jan. 7, 1937; s. David P. and Frieda (Goldsmith) L.; m. Margaret JoAnn Bell, Sept. 2, 1956 (dec. 1987); 1 child, Beth Louise; m. Sue Pardue, July 18, 1991; children: Susan Langley, David Rhett. Student, Augusta (Ga.) Coll., 1954-55, Clemson U., 1955-57. Registered profl. engr., S.C., Fla., N.C., N.H., Ky., W.Va. Engring. technician Patchen and Zimmerman, Augusta, 1957-58; engring. designer Michael Baker Jr., Columbus, Ohio, 1958-60, Rackoff Assocs., Columbus, 1960-61, Wilbur Smith Assocs., Inc., Columbia, S.C., 1961-69, assoc.-in-charge Orlando, Fla., 1969-72, Raleigh, N.C., 1972-85, sr. v.p. Columbia, 1985—. Mem. A. Pub. Works Assn., Cons. Engrs. S.C. (pres. 1987-89), S.C. Coun. Engring. Socs. (pres. 1989-91), S.C. Soc. Profl. Engrs. Episcopalian. Home: 230 King Charles Rd Columbia SC 29209-2257 Office: Wilbur Smith Assocs Inc 4500 Jackson Blvd Columbia SC 29209-1106

LINZ, ANTHONY JAMES, osteopathic physician, consultant, educator; b. Sandusky, Ohio, June 16, 1948; s. Anthony Joseph and Margaret Jane (Ballah) Linz; m. Kathleen Ann Kovach, Aug. 18, 1973; children: Anthony Scott, Sara Elizabeth. BS, Bowling Green State U., 1971; D.O., Des Moines U., 1974. Diplomate Nat. Bd. Osteo. Examiners; bd. cert., diplomate Am. Osteo. Bd. Internal Medicine, Internal Medicine, Med. Diseases of Chest and Critical Care Medicine. Intern South Pointe Hosp., Cleve., 1974-75; resident in internal medicine Brentwood Hosp., 1975-78; chief resident South Pointe Hosp., 1977-78; subsplty. fellow in pulmonary diseases Riverside Meth. Hosp., Columbus, Ohio, 1978-80; med. dir. pulmonary svcs. Sandusky (Ohio) Meml. Hosp., 1980-85; med. dir. cardio-pulmonary svcs. Firelands Community Hosp., Sandusky, 1985—. Cons. staff dept. medicine Good Samaritan Hosp., 1982—85, sect. internal medicine specializing pulmonary diseases; cons. pulmonary, critical care and internal medicine Firelands Cmty. Hosp., 1985—, active staff sect. internal medicine, chmn. dept. medicine, head div. pulmonary medicine, 1985—; cons. pulmonary, critical care, and internal medicine Providence Hosp., Sandusky, Mercy Hosp., Willard, Ohio; clin. prof. internal medicine Ohio U. Coll. Osteo. Medicine; clin. prof. medicine Univ. Health Scis. Coll. Osteo. Medicine, Kansas City, Mo.; clin. asst. prof. med. Med. Coll. of Ohio at Toledo; adj. prof. applied scis. Bowling Green State U., mem. respiratory tech. adv. bd. Firelands Campus, 1983—, med. dir. Respiratory Therapy program., 1984—; prof. osteopathic medicine U. Osteopathic Medicine and Health Scis., Des Moines; rep. Pub. Health Adminstrn., 2001—; exec. bd. pub. health student orgn. N.W. Ohio Consortium for Pub. Health. Author, contbr. articles and abstracts to profl. jours. Water safety instr. ARC, 1965—; med. dir., clin. rsch. investigator Camp Superkid Asthma Camp, 1984-97; bd. trustees Stein Hospice, 1986-90, chmn., 2000--; mem. adv. bd. Ams. with Disabilities Act, City of Sandusky, Ohio, chmn., 2001--; med. dir. in residence Camp Superkids Asthma Camp, 1984-97 Recipient Edward Ruff Comty. Svc. award Am. Lung. Assn., 1985, Master Clinician award Ohio U. Coll. Osteopathic Medicine, 1987, Golden Rule award J.C. Penney, 1990, Disting. Alumna/Alumnus award Firelands Coll., Bowling Green State U., 1995. Fellow: ACP-Am. Soc. Internal Medicine (Ohio chpt.), Am. Coll. Osteo. Internists, Am. Coll. Critical Care Medicine, Am. Coll. Chest Physicians; mem.: AAAS, Found. Critical Care (mem. Founder's Cir.), Ohio Pub. Health Assn., Am. Soc. Internal Medicine, So. Critical Care Medicine, Ohio Soc. Respiratory Care (med. adviser/dir. 1982—), Nat. Assn. Med. Dirs. Respiratory Care, Sandusky Yacht Club (corr.), Am. Lung Assn. (pres., 1st v.p., med. adv. bd. chmn., exec. bd. dirs., bd. dirs. Ohio's So. Shore sect. 1984—), Ohio Thoracic Soc., Am. Thoracic Soc., Am. Heart Assn., Ohio Osteo. Assn. (past pres., past v.p., past sec.-treas., acad. trustees 5th dist. acad.), Am. Osteo. Assn., European Thoracic Soc., Atlas Med. Fraternity, Pi Kappa Alpha, Beta Beta Beta, Alpha Epsilon Delta. Roman Catholic. Fax: (419) 621-0642. E-mail: doclinz@aol.com.

LINZ, GERHARD DAVID, psychologist, consultant; b. Waltershausen, Thuringia, Germany, Jan. 5, 1927; came to U.S., 1936; s. Leopold and Rita (Nussbaum) L.; m. Frances Ann Pierson; children: Christopher, Michael, Stephanie, Peter. B in Elec. Engring. with honors, Ga. Inst. Tech., 1948, MS, 1949; BDiv, Episcopal Theol. Sem. S.W., Austin, Tex., 1956; PhD, U. Tex., Austin, 1966. Diplomate Am. Bd. Profl. Psychology, Counseling Psychology. Rsch. engr. RCA Labs., Princeton, N.J., 1949-51; rsch. engr., Engring. Experiment Sta. Ga. Tech., Atlanta, 1951-53; rsch. engr., Def. Rsch. Lab. U. Tex., Austin, 1953-56; vicar All Saints Episcopal Ch., Warner Robins, Ga., 1956-59; assoc. rector Christ Ch. Episcopal, Macon, 1959; Episcopal chaplain U. Tex., Austin, 1960-66; asst. prof. Counseling Ctr. Mich. State U., East Lansing, 1966-70; from assoc. prof. to prof., assoc. dir. Counseling Ctr. Ga. State U., Atlanta, 1970-93, Alumni Disting. prof., 1984; pvt. practice Decatur, Ga., 1971—. Mem. dept. Christian Edn., Episcopal Diocese of Atlanta, 1957-59; bd. dirs. Inst. for Marital and Family Therapy, Atlanta. Author: Novice Notes-An Introduction to Cryptanalysis, 1990; contbr. articles to profl. jours. Chaplain Civitan Club, Warner Robins, Ga., 1958-59. With U.S. Army, 1945-46, ATO. Mem. Assn. Counseling Ctr. Tng. Agts. (v.p. 1979-85), Am. Psychol. Assn., Soc. for Clin. and Exptl. Hypnosis, Southeastern Psychol. Assn., Ga. Psychol. Assn., Ga. Coll. Pers. Assn. Episcopalian. Avocations: cryptography, bridge, photography, computers. E-mail: fs01gdl@panther.gsu.edu.

LINZ, WERNER MARK, international publishing executive; b. Cologne, Germany, Apr. 6, 1935; came to U.S., 1959, naturalized, 1976; s. George A. and Catherine B. (Wegener) L.; m. Helen Ruth Baumler, July 27, 1959; children: Julia, Alice. Student, U. Frankfurt, Germany, 1954-57, NYU, 1958. Successively treas., mktg. v.p., exec. v.p. Herder & Herder Pub. Co., N.Y.C.,

1958-71; pub., gen. mgr. Herder div. McGraw-Hill Book Co., 1971-73; pres., chief exec. officer Seabury Press, N.Y.C., 1973-80; founder, chmn., CEO Continuum Pub. Co. and Crossroad Pub. Co., 1980-92; chmn., CEO Continuum Pub. Group, 1992-2000; co-founder, v. chmn. Continuum Internat. Pub. Group, London and N.Y.C., 2000—; dir. Am. U. Press, Cairo, 1995—. Adj. prof. mktg. NYU, City U., Pace U. Charter mem. nat. adv. com. Ctr. for the Book Libr. of Congress; mem. Nat. Com. on Higher Edn. and Libr. Programs; bd. dirs. Peterson's, Princeton, N.J., Aperture Found., Jung Found., N.Y.C. Mem. Assn. Am. Pubs. (bd. dirs., chmn. edn. com.), Soc. Scholarly Pub. (charter) Clubs: University (N.Y.C.); Am. Yacht (Rye, N.Y.). Home: 230 Stuyvesant Ave Rye NY 10580-3115 Office: Continuum International Pub Group 370 Lexington Ave New York NY 10017-6503 also: Am U in Cairo 420 Fifth Ave New York NY 10017

LINZELL, DANIEL GATTNER, civil and structural engineer; b. Buffalo, Feb. 24, 1968; s. Charles Lewis and Carol Ann (Gattner) L.; m. Cindy Lynn Hammer, Aug. 3, 1991; 1 child, Kelsey Ann. BS in Civil Engring., Ohio State U., 1990; MS in Civil Engring., Ga. Inst. Tech., 1995. Registered profl. engr., Ga.; engr.-in-tng., Ohio. Drafter, lab. technician Resource Internat., Columbus, Ohio, 1989-90; engr. III Burgess and Niple, Ltd., 1990-94; rsch. asst. Ga. Inst. Tech., Atlanta, 1994—; assoc. engr. Constrn. Tech. Lab., Washington, 1998—. Mem. ASCE, NSPE, Tau Beta Pi, Chi Epsilon, Gamma Beta Phi. Avocations: fly fishing, basketball, reading.

LINZEY, JAMES FRANKLIN, minister, military officer, vocalist; b. San Diego, Sept. 26, 1958; s. Stanford Eugene and Verna May (Hall) L. BA in Religion, Vanguard U. So. Calif., 1979; MDiv, Fuller Theol. Sem., 1983; DD, Kingsway Theol. Sem., 2000. Ordained Assemblies of God Internat. Fellowship, 1977. Pastor of youth First Assembly of God, Huntington Park, Calif., 1979-80, assoc. pastor Sun Valley, 1982-83; telephone clk. World Vision Hdqrs., Pasadena, 1983; tchr. Santa Ana (Calif.) Unified Sch. Dist., 1983-85; commd. 1st lt. USAF, Norton AFB, Calif., 1985-89, advanced through grades to capt., 1989; Protestan chaplain USAFR, 1985—94, Vandenburg AFB, Calif., 1994-95; Protestant chaplain USAF, Laughlin AFB, Tex., 1995-98, 244th Quartermaster Bn., Ft. Lee, Va., 1998-2001, 249th Signal Bn. U.S. N.G., Dallas, 2001—. Tchr. L.A. Unified Sch. Dist., 1985-93, La Mirada-Norwalk Unified Sch. Dist., 1993-95; sr. pastor Cornerstone Cmty. Ch., Anaheim, Calif., 1986-88; chaplain Full Gospel Businessmen's Fellowship Internat., Knott's Berry Farm Chpt., Buena Park, Calif., 1992-94, v.p., 1992-94. Rec. artist (tape) Who Am I, 1993, (CD) You Were Always There, 1994, When the World Turns to God, 1995, Narrow Road, 2000; author: A Divine Appointment in Washington, D.C., 1999; contbr. articles to jours. Choir dir. First United Meth. Ch., La Palma, Calif., 1983-84; assoc. pastor Messenger Fellowship, Norwalk, Calif., 1985-86. Decorated Nat. Def. medal USAF, 1991, Achievement medal USAF, 1992, Commendation medal USAF, 1994. Mem. Nat. Assn. Evangelicals, Res. Officers Assn. (state chaplain 1991-94), Gospel Music Assn. Republican. Avocations: golfing, tennis, racquetball. Home: PO Box 5445 Gardena CA 90249

LINZEY, VERNA MAY, minister, writer; b. Coffeyville, Kans., May 17, 1919; d. Carey Franklin Hall Jr. and Alice May (Hart) Hall-Doyle; m. Stanford Eugene Linzey Jr., July 13, 1941; children: Stanford Eugene III, Virginia Darnelle Lemons(dec.) , Sharon Faye, George William, Vera Evelyn, Paul Edward, David Leon, James Franklin, Gena May English, Janice Ellen Drake. Student, Southwestern Assembly of God U., Waxahachie, Tex., 1938—39, Fuller Theol. Sem., Pasadena, Calif., 1945—. Lic. Minister Assembly of God. Asst. minister First Assembly of God, Baldwin Park , Calif., 1953—54; co-founder Holy Spirit Evangelism, Escondido, 1976—. Consultant Holy Spirit Evangelism, Escondido, Calif., 1976—; leader Pentecostal Movement Worldwide, 1976. Songwriter: O Blessed Jesus, 1971; contbr. articles to religious publs. Mem. nat. com. Dem. orgn., 1943—45; mem. nat. com. Republican Orgn., 1946—. Recipient Cert. of Recognition, Mayor of Escondido, Calif., 2001, Congressional Proclamation Rev. Dr. Verna May Linzey Day April 29th, 2001. Avocations: gardening, piano, photography, genealogy, singing. Home: 1641 Kenora Dr Escondido CA 92027 Office: Verna M Linzey 354 E Washington St Ste A Escondido CA 92025

LION, JOHN RENÉ, psychiatrist, educator; b. Fribourg, Switzerland, Sept. 16, 1938; came to U.S., 1941; s. Kurt S. and Elsa (Straus) L.; m. Jill A. Altschul, Dec. 29, 1963; children: DAvid M., Trina. AB, Harvard Coll., 1960; MD, Albany Med. Coll., 1965. Diplomate Am. Bd. Psychiatry and Neurology; lic. physician, Md. Intern George Washington U.-D.C. Gen. Hosp., Washington, 1965-66; resident Mass. Gen. Hosp., Boston, 1966-69; rsch. fellow in psychiatry Med. Sch. Harvard Coll., 1966-69, from asst. prof. to prof. psychiatry, 1971-77, prof., 1977-84; clin. prof. Sch. Medicine U. Md., Balt., 1984—; pvt. and forensic practice, 1972—. Dir. adult inpatient psychiat. svcs. U. Md. Hosp., 1978-84, dir., assoc. dir. hen cons. clin. rsch. program for violent behavior, 1972—; examiner Am. Bd. Psychiatry and Neurology, 1983, 89; participant conf. on assessment of dangerousness NAS/Nat. Inst. Medicine, 1981, mem. bd. health promotion and disease prevention, 1982; participant violence evaluation/mgmt. tng. program dept. health and mental hygiene State of Md., 1984-85; mem. adv. coun. on neurol. bases of abnormal behavior NIH, 1973-74; cons. Williams and Wilkins Pubs., Balt., 1974—, Westinghouse, 1990—, IBM, 1990—, Noxell Corp., 1990—, U.S. Postal Svc., 1990—, Bd. Physician Quality Assurance, 1985—, NIMH Violence and Traumatic Stress Rsch. Program, 1993; lectr. NIMH, Tokyo, 1992, Nat. Ctr. Neurology and Psychiatry, 1992, Keio U., Tokyo, 1992, others. Author: Evaluation and Management of the Violent Patient, 1972, The Art of Medicating Psychiatric Patients, 1978; editor: Personality Disorders, 1981, Assaults Within Psychiat. Facilities, 1981, Modern Hosp. Psychiatry, 1983; co-editor: APA Task Force Report on Clinician Safety, 1993; contbr. chpts. to over 35 books; mem. editorial bd. Violence and Victoms, 1989—, Jour. Family Violence, 1988—, Jour. Clin. Psychiatry, 1977-89; asst. editor Jour. Nervous and Mental Diseases, 1977-89; reviewer profl. publs.; prodr. audio/video presentations; contbr. numerous articles to sci. jours. Mem. Nat. Commn. on Causes and Preventions of Violence, Washington, 1969-71; bd. dirs. Nat. Coalition on TV Violence, 1982-83, Patuxent Instn., Jessup, Md., 1982-84; cons. civic orgns., including Cen. Md. Mental Health Systems Agy., Balt., 1976-77, Md. Dept. Health and Mental Hygiene, 1979—, Fellowship Halfway House, Balt., 1978-81, Md. Film Censor Bd., Balt., 1975-76, USPHS, Balt., 1973-78, others. Lt. comdr. USN, 1969-71. Fellow Am. Psychiat. Assn. (mem. various task forces 1971—), Group for the Advancement of Psychiatry; mem. Am. Acad. Psychiatry and Law, Internat. Soc. for Rsch. in Aggression, Md. Psychiat. Soc., Balt. City Med. Soc. (mem. coms. 1977, 80). Avocations: photography, woodworking, automobiles, house plants, writing. Office: 5100 Falls Rd # 328E Baltimore MD 21210-1914

LIONAKIS, GEORGE, architect; b. West Hiawatha, Utah, Sept. 5, 1924; s. Pete and Andriani (Protopapadakis) L.; student Carbon Jr. Coll., 1942-43, 46-47; BArch., U. Oreg., 1951; m. Iva Oree Braddock, Dec. 30, 1951; 1 dau., Deborah Jo. With Corps Engrs., Walla Walla, Wash., 1951-54; architect Liske, Lionakis, Beaumont & Engberg, Sacramento, 1954-86, Lionakis-Beaumont Design Group, 1986—. Mem. Sacramento County Bd. Appeals, 1967—, chmn., 1969, 75, 76; pres. Sacramento Builders Exchange, 1976. Served with USAAF, 1943-46. Mem. AIA (pres. Central Valley chpt., 1972—), Constrn. Specifications Inst. (pres. Sacramento chpt., 1962; nat. awards, 1962, 63, 65), Sacramento C. of C. (code com., 1970—). Club: North Ridge Country (pres. 1987). Lodge: Rotarian (pres. East Sacramento 1978-79). Prin. works include Stockton (Calif.) Telephone Bldg., 1968, Chico (Calif.) Main Telephone Bldg., 1970, Mather AFB Exchange Complex Sacramento, 1970, Base Chapel Mather AFB, Sacramento, 1970, Woodridge Elementary Sch., Sacramento, 1970, Pacific Telephone Co. Operating Center Modesto, Calif., 1968, Sacramento, 1969, Marysville, Calif., 1970, Red Bluff, Calif., 1971, Wells Fargo Banks, Sacramento, 1968, Corning, Calif., 1969, Anderson, 1970, Beale AFB Exchange Complex, Marysville, 1971, Cosumnes River Coll., Sacramento, 1971, base exchanges at Bergstrom AFB, Austin, Tex., Sheppard AFB, Wichita Falls, Tex., Chanute AFB, Rantoul, Ill., McChord AFB, Tacoma, Wash., health center Chico State U., Sacramento County Adminstrn. Center, Sacramento Bee Newspaper Plant. Home: 160 Breckenwood Way Sacramento CA 95864-6968 Office: Lionakis Beaumont Design Group 1919 19th St Sacramento CA 95814-6714

LIONE, SUSAN GARRETT, consultant; b. Boston, May 23, 1945; d. Charles Gerard and Josephine (Galgano) Garrett; m. Gerald Frederick Lione, Nov. 9, 1968; children: Mark Garrett, Christina Marie. BA in Econs., Immaculata Coll., 1966. Investment asst. Morgan Guaranty Trust, N.Y.C., 1966-69; portfolio mgr. Union Trust Co., Stamford, Conn., 1969-72; sales coord. Japan Air Lines, Hong Kong, 1977-84; mktg. coord. Hong Kong Tennis Patron Assn., 1982-84; ind. study on schs. Cen. Pk. Task Force, N.Y.C., 1990; sales assoc. Preferred Properties, New Canaan, Conn., 1991-96; cons. HTG Investment Advisors, Inc., 1997—. Pres. Am. Women's Assn., Hong Kong, 1977-78; sec. New Canaan CARES, 1989-90, v.p., 1990-91, pres., 1991-93, mem. adv. bd., 1998—. Bd. dirs. United Way New Canaan, 1994-2000, bd. sec., 1996-98, mem. allocations com., 1994—, allocations chmn., 1995-96, bd. chmn., 98-2000; bd. dirs. Vol. Ctr. Lower Fairfield County, 1996-99, sec., 1997-98, mem. adv. bd., 1999—; mem. lay adv. bd. St. Aloysius Ch., New Canaan, 1994, 95-98. Avocations: tennis. Office: HTG Investment Advisors 112 Main St New Canaan CT 06840-4730

LIONETTI, FRANK CARMINE, graphic design firm executive; b. Greenwich, Conn., Sept. 13, 1947; s. Alexander Joseph and Marcelline (Bria) L.; m. Leigh Maude Meeker, Sept. 7, 1969; children— Liza Meeker, Frank Alexander. A. in Fine Arts, Silvermine Coll. Art, 1969; B.F.A., Yale U., 1971, M.F.A., 1971. Graphic designer, projects coordinator Archtl. Graphics Assocs., New Canaan, Conn., 1971-73; pres. Frank C. Lionetti Design, Inc., Old Greenwich, Conn., 1973— . Designer U.S. postal stamp, 1974. Bd. dirs. Newington Children's Hosp., 1983—94. Mem. Conn. Art Dirs. Club (bd. dirs. 1984-89, pres. 1986-88), Am. Inst. Graphic Arts. Roman Catholic.

LIONNET, FRANCOISE, French and comparative literature educator; b. Mauritius, July 28, 1948; came to U.S., 1969; d. Joseph Louis L. and Madeleine Berenger; m. John A McCumber, May 8, 1972; children: Jonathan, Danielle. PhD in Comparative Lit., U. Mich., 1986. Prof. French & comparative lit. Northwestern U., Evanston, Ill., 1986-98; prof., chair French UCLA, L.A., 1998—. Vis. prof. Duke U., Durham, N.C., 1996. Author: Autobiographical Voices, 1989, Postcolonial Representations, 1995. Fellow Soc.Humanities, Cornell U., 1988-89, U. Calif. Humanities Rsch. Studies Inst., 1992, Rockefeller Found., 1991-92, Social Sci. Rsch. Coun., Mauritius, 1996, Fulbright fellow U.Mauritius, 1996-97. Mem. MLA (mem. exec. com. 1999—), Am. Philos. Soc., Am. Coun. Learned Socs., Am. Comparative Lit. Assn. Avocations: hiking, swimming, music. Office: UCLA 212 Royce Hl Los Angeles CA 90095-0001*

LIONS, JACQUES LOUIS, mathematician, educator; b. Grasse, France, May 2, 1928; s. Honore Antoine and Anne (Muller) L.; m. Andree Olivier, Aug. 21, 1950; 1 child, Pierre Louis. Degree in math., Ecole Normale Superieure, Paris, 1950; Dr es Sci., U. Paris, 1954; Dr (hon.), U. Liege, 1973, U. Madrid, 1976, U. Fudan, 1981, U. Goteborg, 1984, Heriot Watt U., Edinburgh, 1982, Poly. U. Madrid, 1988, St. Jacques de Compostella, 1994, U. Malaga, U. Santiago-Chile, 1997, Hebrew U., Jerusalem, 1997, Jian Tong U., Shanghai, 1998, Jian Jong U., Xian, 1998, BUAA, Beijing, 1998, U. Mex., 1998, U. Ctrl. Fla., 2000. Mem. faculty U. Nancy, France, 1954-62, U. Paris, 1962-73; prof. Coll. de France, Paris, 1973-98, hon. prof., from 1999. Prof. Ecole Poly., Paris, 1967-86; pres. Inst. Nat. de Rsch. en Informatique et en Automatique, 1980-84, Ctr. Nat. Etudes Spatiales, 1984-92; high sci. advisor DASSAULT industry, 1993—; pres. sci. bd. France Telecom, 1998—; sci. advisor ELF; chmn. sci. adv. com. Pechiney; bd. dirs. St. Gobain Pechiney Dassault Sys., Thomson Multi Media. Author: Les Inequations en Mecanique et en Physique, 1969, Some Methods in the Mathematical Analysis of Systems and of their Control, 1981, Controle des Systemes distribues Singuliers, 1983, others. Decorated comdr. Order Nat. de la Legion d'Honneur, G.O. Merite Nat. Awd., 1999, Order of the Rising Sun, Gold and Silver Star, 1998; recipient Japan prize, 1991, Harvey prize, 1991, Space award Aviation Week and Space Tech., W.T. and Idelia Reid prize SIAM, 1998, Lagrange prize, 1999, Hilbert Medal, 2000. Fellow Tata Inst. of Fundamental Rsch.; mem. Acad. des Scis. (pres. 1997-98), Pontificial Acad. Scis.; fgn. mem. Acad. Royale de Liege, Acad. Scis. Lombardie, Acad. Brasileira de Ciencias, Russian Acad. Scis., Ukraine Acad. Scis., Acad. Royale Belgium, Georgian Acad. Sci., Am. Acad. Arts and Scis., Internat. Acad. Astronautics, Acad. Sci. of Chile, Acad. Europae, Portugal Acad. Scis., Acad. Soc. Argentina, Royal Soc. London, Nat. Acad. Sci. U.S., Third World Acad. Sci., Royal Spanish Acad., Korean Acad. Sci. and Tech., Chinese Acad. Scis., Nat. Acad. Lincei, Acad. Tech. Paris. Home: Paris, France. Died June 17, 2001.

LIONTI, VINCENT JOSEPH, violist; b. Bethesda, Md., Apr. 9, 1959; s. C. Victor and Philomena A. (Paparo) L.; m. Kristin Allison Bostrup, Oct. 20, 1996; 1 child, Nicholas Vincent Lionti. MB, Juilliard Sch. Music, 1981, MusM, 1982. Violist Casals Festival Orch., P.R., 1980, N.Y. Philharm., N.Y.C., 1981-83, Detroit Symphony Orch., 1983-87, Ventura String Quartet, Detroit, 1983-87, Lyric Chamber Ensemble, Detroit, 1985-87; faculty Macomb Community Coll., 1983-87; violist Met. Opera Orch., N.Y.C., 1987—. Prin. viola Santa Fe Opera Orch., summer 1991; guest prin. viola Indpls. Symphony Orch., 1991, Am. Symphony Orch., 1994, N.J. Symphony Orch, 1994; condr. Westchester Jr. String Orch., 1993-97, Westchester Youth Symphony Orch., 1997&. Asst. dir. Fairlane Youth Chamber Music Guild, Detroit, 1986-87. Home: 2 Winthrop Dr Rye Brook NY 10573-1441 Office: Met Opera Orch Lincoln Ctr New York NY 10023

LIOTTA, PETER HEARNS, security affairs educator; b. Burlington, Vt., Sept. 16, 1956; BS, USAF Acad., 1978; MA, U. Okla., 1984, Cornell U., 1987, U.S. Naval War Coll., 1997; PhD, Salve Regina U., 1999. Attache U.S. Embassy, Athens, 1993-96; prof. nat. security affairs U.S. Naval War Coll., Newport, R.I., 1997—, Jerome E. Levy chair econ. geography and nat. security. Author ten books, including Dismembering the State: The Death of Yugoslavia and Why It Matters, 2001 (NEA Lit. fellow); contbr. numerous articles to profl. jours. Fulbright fellow Coun. for Internat. Exch. of Scholars, 1988-89. Office Fax: (401) 841-3893.

LIOTUS, SANDRA MARY, lighting designer, business owner, consultant; b. Pitts., Aug. 23, 1959; d. George A. Liotus and Marlene A. Rouse. BFA in Design, Carnegie Mellon U., 1984. Designer George Kovacs Lighting, Inc., N.Y.C., 1985-89; lighting designer with LeMar Terry N.Y.C. and Hoboken, N.J., 1993-95; lighting design cons. Sandra Liotus Lighting Design, N.Y.C. and Newport, R.I., 1995—. Spl. exhibits designer Redwood Libr. and Athenaeum, Newport, 1999—; lighting consulting design svcs. Preservation Soc. of Newport County, Newport, 1997—, Harvard U., Cambridge, Mass., 1995—, pvt. clients, 1995—, Robin Symes Ltd., London, 1999—, Mus. of the City of N.Y., 2000—, City of Boston Firemen-Vendome Meml., 2001—. Avocation: artist. Office: Sandra Liotus Lighting Design LLC 68 William St Newport RI 02840-3309 Fax: (401) 845-8949. E-mail: s.liotus@worldnet.att.net.

LIOU, KUO-NAN, atmospheric sciences educator, researcher; b. Taipei, Taiwan, Republic of China, Nov. 16, 1944; m. Agnes L.Y. Hung, Aug. 3, 1968; children: Julia C.C., Clifford T.C. BS, Taiwan U., 1965; MS, NYU, 1968, PhD, 1970. Rsch. assoc. Goddard Inst. for Space Studies, N.Y.C., 1970-72; asst. prof. atmospheric sci. U. Wash., Seattle, 1972-74; assoc. prof. U. Utah, Salt Lake City, 1975-80, prof., 1980-97, dir. grad. studies in meteorology, 1981-84, dir. Ctr. for Atmospheric and Remote Sounding Studies, 1987-97, chmn. dept. meteorology, 1996-97, rsch. prof. physics, 1992—; prof. UCLA, 1997—, dir. Inst. Radiation and Remote Sensing, 1997—, chair dept. atmospheric scis., 2000—. Adj. prof. geophysics U. Utah, Salt Lake City, 1992-97; vis. prof. UCLA, 1981, U. Ariz., Tucson, 1995; affiliated prof. Peking U., Beijing, Chinga, 1991—; vis. scholar Harvard U., 1985; cons. NASA Ames Rsch. Ctr., Moffett Field, Calif., 1984-94, Los Alamos (N.Mex.) Nat. Lab. 1984-88. Author: An Introduction to Atmospheric Radiation, 1980, Radiation and Cloud Processes in the Atmosphere, 1992; editor: Atmospheric Radiation Progress and Prospects, 1987; contbr. articles to profl. jours. Recipient Founders Day award NYU, 1971, Creativity award Atmospheric Scis. divsn. NSF, 1996; NRC fellow, 1970, Gardner fellow, 1978. Fellow AAAS, Optical Soc. Am., Am. Meterol. Soc. (chmn. atmospheric radiation com. 1982-84, Jule G. Charney award 1997), Am. Geophys. Union; mem. NAE. Home: 1488 Paseo De Oro Pacific Palisades CA 90272-1961 Office: UCLA Dept Atmospheric Scis 7127 Math Scis Bldg 405 Hilgard Ave Los Angeles CA 90095-9000

LIOZ, LAWRENCE STEPHEN, lawyer, accountant; b. N.Y.C., Sept. 24, 1945; s. William and Irma (Berksohn) L.; m. Carol Renee Skolnik, Nov. 20, 1971; children: Adam Russell, Randall Eric. BS, SUNY, Albany, 1967; JD, SUNY, Buffalo, 1970; LLM in Taxation, NYU, 1975. Bar: N.Y. 1970; CPA, N.Y. Mgr. Ernst & Whinney, N.Y.C., 1970-79; dir. tax affairs Azcon Corp., 1979-82; mgr. Deloitte Haskins & Sells, 1982-83, ptnr., 1983-84, Woodbury, N.Y., 1984-87, Margolin, Winer & Evens LLP, Garden City, 1987—. Speaker in field. Contbr. articles to profl. jours. Pres. Rolling Wood Civic Assn., Roslyn, N.Y., 1983—; trustee Flower Hill (N.Y.) Assn., 1985-87, Village of Flower Hill, 1987-92; treas. Roslyn Sch. Dist., 1986-99. Mem. ABA, AICPAs, N.Y. State Bar Assn., N.Y. State Soc. CPAs (chmn. fed. tax com. Nassau chpt. 1989-92, exec. bd. 1992—, pres. 2000-01). Jewish. Avocations: skiing, golf. Home: 84 Knollwood W Roslyn NY 11576-1319 Office: Margolin Winer & Evens LLP 400 Garden City Plz Fl 5 Garden City NY 11530-3317 E-mail: llioz@mwellp.com.

LIPAN, HOWARD KENNETH, information and technology consultant; b. N.Y.C., June 17, 1939; s. Irving and Rose Lipan; m. Nanci Lee Youngerman, May 28, 1971 (div. Feb. 1986); m. Marjorie Ann Morris, May 29, 1988. BS, Columbia U., 1966, postgrad., 1967-68. Computer programmer Met. Life, N.Y.C., 1968-69; sys. analyst Western Union, 1969-71; project leader, sys. architect E.F. Shelley & Co., 1971-75; dir. applications and sys. devel. NYU, 1975-76; pres. Digital Automation Enterprises, 1977-82; sr. cons., founding mem. The Yourdon Cons. Group, 1983-85; mng. cons. James Martin Assocs., Reston, Va., 1985; sr. cons., instr. McDonnell Douglas/Gane & Sarson IST, St. Louis, 1985-91; prin. cons., owner DAE, N.Y.C., 1991—. Cons. Inst. Mus. Svcs., Washington, 1979-80. Author course books and articles. Cadet CAP, Island Park, N.Y., 1950s; computer advisor Orpheus Chamber Orch., N.Y.C., 1994; mem. jr. com. N.Y.C. Ballet, 1995-98; mem. Ovation Soc. Carnegie Hall, N.Y.C., 1996—; founding mem. Nat. Campaign for Tolerance, 2001. Mem. AAAS, IEEE Computer Soc., Assn. for Computing Machinery, Am. Mgmt. Assn., Data Adminstrn. Mgmt. Assn., N.Y. Acad. Scis., Alumni Fedn. of Columbia U. Avocations: travel, photography, sailing, sculpture, tennis. Office: DAE LLC 300 E 71st St Ste 17E New York NY 10021-5242

LIPAN, PETRUTA E. semiotician, curator, artist; b. Braila, Romania, Oct. 18, 1957; d. Ene and Maria C. L. BFA, Washington Univ., 1991; MFA, PhD in Semiotic Studies, Ind. Univ., 1995. Instr. sculpture Ind. U., Bloomington, 1993-94, instr. 3-dimensional design, 1994-95; instr. sculpture Laumeyer Sculpture Mus., St. Louis, 1995-96; prof. art appreciation St. Louis U., 1996, assoc. curator S. Cuples House and McNamee Gallery, 1996—; mem. faculty Washington U., St. Louis, 1996-99; prof. art history St. Louis U., 1999-2000. Vis. artist Laumeier Sculpture Park, 1997, 1996, artist in residence, 1996; assisted in curating, organization and mktg. of shows including Edward Boccia: The Eye of the Painter, 1996, Ads With A Conscience, 1997, A Voice of Their Own, 1997, Mev Puelo: Witness to Life, 1997, Iridescence, 1998; curator Enduring Light: Fragility and Persistence, 1998, Passion for Color: Frederick Carder at Steuben Glass Works, 1999; presenter 5th Argentinian congress on Color, APHRA Behn Soc., Phila., 1999, Can. Semiotic Assn. Conf., Que., 1999, 7th Congress of IASS-AIS, Dresden, Germany, 1999, Math. Connections in Art, Music, and Sci., Winfield, Kans., 1999. Group exhibitions include Sioux City Art Ctr., 1997, Ind. Univ., 1996, Centre Interculturel Strathearn, 1996, The Editions Limited Gallery of Art, 1995, The Carver Cultural Ctr., 1995, Ind. Univ. Art Mus., 1995, Ind. Univ., 1993, 94, 95, San Diego Art Inst., 1993, Steinberg Gallery, 1991, Bixby Gallery, 1991, South Grand Gallery, 1986, numerous others. Mem. Nat. Sculpture Soc., Internat. Assn. for Semiotic Studies (presenter at confs.), Semiotic Soc. Am., Am. Assn. Mus., Assn. for Art History, Internat. Assn. for Visual Semiotics, Midwest Art History Soc. Home: 1129 Olivaire Ln Saint Louis MO 63132-3010 E-mail: lipanp@yahoo.com.

LIPCON, CHARLES ROY, lawyer; b. N.Y.C., Mar. 20, 1946; s. Harry H. and Rose Lipcon; m. Irmgard Adels, Dec. 1, 1974; children: Lauren, Claudia. BA, U. Miami, 1968, JD, 1971. Bar: Fla. 1971, U.S. Dist. Ct. (so. dist.) Fla. 1971, U.S. Ct. Appeals (5th cir.) 1972, U.S. Supreme Ct. 1976, U.S. Ct. Appeals (D.C. cir.) 1980, U.S. Dist. Ct. (so. dist.) Tex. 1982, U.S. Dist. Ct. (middle dist.) Fla. 2000, U.S. Ct. Appeals (11th cir.) 1994, U.S. Dist. Ct. Colo. 1999, U.S. Dist. Ct. (mid. dist.) Fla. 2000. Pvt. practice, Miami, Fla., 1971—. Lectr. U. Miami Sch. Law. Author: Help for the Auto Accident Victim, 1984, Seaman's Rights in the United States When Involved in An Accident, 1989; pub., editor The Cruise Line Law Reporter; contbr. articles to profl. jours. Named Commodore of High Seas, Internat. Seaman's Union. Mem. ABA, ATLA, Fla. Bar Assn., Fla. Trial Lawyers Assn., Dade County Bar Assn., Dade County Trial Lawyers, Fla. Admiralty Trial Lawyers Assn., Mensa. Office: 2 S Biscayne Blvd Ste 2480 Miami FL 33131-1803 E-mail: sealaw@aol.com.

LIPE, LINDA BON, lawyer; b. Clarksdale, Miss., Jan. 10, 1948; d. William Ray and Gwendolyn (Stickland) Lipe. BBA in Accountancy, U. Miss., 1970, JD, 1971. Bar: Miss. 1971, Ark. 1976, U.S. Dist. Ct. (no. dist.) Miss. 1971, U.S. Dist. Ct. (ea. dist.) Ark. 1976, U.S. Ct. Appeals (8th cir.) 1985. Sr. tax acct. Arthur Young & Co., San Jose, Calif., 1971-74, A.M. Pullen & Co., Knoxville, Tenn., 1975; legal counsel to gov. State of Ark., Little Rock, 1975-79; dept. pros. atty. 6th Jud. Dist. Ark., 1979-80; chief counsel Ark. Pub. Svcs. Commn., 1980-83; asst. U.S. atty. Ea. Dist. Ark., Dept. Justice, 1983—. Founding bd. dirs. Assn. Cert. Cruelty Investigators, Humane Soc. U.S.; bd. dirs., treas. Humane Soc. Pulaski County, 1997-2002. Mem. ABA, Miss. State Bar Assn., Ark. State Bar Assn. Episcopalian. Office: US Attys Office PO Box 1229 Little Rock AR 72203-1229

LIPEZ, KERMIT V. federal judge, former state supreme court justice; Former judge Maine Superior Ct.; assoc. justice Supreme Jud. Ct. of Maine, Portland, 1994—98; judge U.S. Ct. Appeals (1st cir.) Maine, 1998—. Office: 156 Federal St Portland ME 04101-4152

LIPFORD, ROCQUE EDWARD, lawyer, corporate executive; b. Monroe, Mich., Aug. 16, 1938; s. Frank G. and Mary A. (Mastromarco) L.; m. Marcia A. Griffin, Aug. 5, 1966; children: Lisa, Rocque Edward, Jennifer, Katherine. BS, U. Mich., 1960, MS, 1961, JD with distinction, 1964. Bar: Mich. 1964, Ohio 1964. Instr. mech. engring. U. Mich., 1961-63; atty. Miller, Canfield, Paddock & Stone, Detroit, 1965-66; asst. gen. counsel Monroe Auto Equipment Co., 1966-70, gen. counsel, 1970-72, v.p., gen. counsel, 1973-77, Tenneco Automotive, 1977-78; ptnr. firm Miller, Canfield, Paddock & Stone, Detroit, 1978—, mng. ptnr., 1988-91. Bd. dirs. La-Z-Boy Inc., Monroe Bank & Trust. Mem.: Knights of Malta, Legatus, Mich. Bar Assn., Mariner Sands Golf and Country Club, Monroe Golf and Country Club, North Cape Yacht Club, Otsego Ski Club, Pi Tau Sigma, Tau Beta Pi. Home: 1065 Hollywood Dr Monroe MI 48162-3045 Office: Miller Canfield Paddock & Stone 214 E Elm Ave Ste 100 Monroe MI 48162-2682 E-mail: lipford@mcps.com.

LIPHAM, WILLIAM PATRICK, principal, educator; b. Franklin, Ga., Oct. 15, 1950; s. William Taft and Claudie Evelyn (McCord) Lipham; m. Jane King, Aug. 11, 1973; children: Leslie Ann, William Brian. BA, West Ga. Coll., 1972, MEd, 1979, EdS, 1990. Cert. in secondary sci., adminstrn./supervision, Ga. Tchr. Heard County Bd. Edn., Franklin, Ga., asst. prin., prin. With U.S. Army Nat. Guard, 1972-78. Recipient Dave Edelson award, Boy Scouts Am., 1982, Dist. award of Merit, 1980. Mem. Ga. Assn. Educators, (v.p., pres., treas.), Ga. Assn. Edn. Leaders. Home: 2727 Ga 34 Hwy Franklin GA 30217 Office: Heard Elem Sch 150 Alford Dr Franklin GA 30217-6345

LIPIN, JOAN CAROL, healthcare executive, consultant; b. Denver, Aug. 25, 1947; d. Theodore and Kathe (Pardo) Lipin. BA, NYU, 1969; postgrad., MIT, 1973-74; MBA, Boston U., 1977; postgrad., N.Y. Law Sch., 2000—. Adminstrv. staff MIT, Boston, 1969, tech. asst., 1977; adminstr. Mass. Gen. Hosp., 1975-76, mgmt. cons., 1976; dept. head N.Y. Hosp., N.Y.C., 1977-80; exec. v.p. Gordon-Keeble, 1980-83; owner, pres. Thor Rsch., N.Y.C., 1983-86; sr. mgr. health svcs. ARC in Greater N.Y., 1986-88; cons. to pres. Nat. Inst. Life Threatening Illness and Loss, 1988-91; owner, pres. Thor Rsch., N.Y.C., 1989—; asst. to sr. atty. Wisehart & Koch, 1990—. Cons., mem. rev. bd. Ind. Testing Lab., N.Y.C., 1981-85, Forum Corp. Responsibility, 1981-82. Pub. poet; Libr. of Congress/Poetry Guild. Exec. mem., officer Lexington Dem. Club, 1994—; judicial del.-alt., 1995—; mem. county com. Dem. Party County of N.Y., 1994—; mem. Nat. Def. Counsel, Drs. Without Borders, Physicians for Social Responsibility; charter mem. So. Law Poverty Ctr., 2000; founding mem. Nat. Campaign for Tolerance, Earth Justice Legal Def. Fund.; mem. Women's Action Coun., 2001—; charter mem. women's action coun. Amnesty Internat.,

2001. Mem. ABA (student mem.), N.Y. State Bar Assn., N.Y. Acad. Sci., Am. Soc. Zoologists, Union Concerned Scientists, Amnesty Internat., Audubon Soc., World Wildlife Fund, Thanantology Found. (steering com., spl. asst. to pres. 1988-91), Amnesty Internat. (charter), Nat. Inst. Life (co-chairperson Threatening Illness and Loss symposium 1991), Pre-Hosp. Care Providers, Sierra Club. Home: 45 E 89th St Apt 14G New York NY 10128-1229 Office: Thor Rsch PO Box 1257 New York NY 10028-0009

LIPINSKI, ANN MARIE, newspaper editor; b. Trenton, Mich. Assoc. mng. editor for met. news. Chgo. Tribune, 1991—93, dep. mng. editor, 1994—95, mng. editor, 1995—2000, VP & exec. editor, 2000—01, Senior VP & exec. editor, 2001—. Recipient Pulitzer prize for series on politics and conflicts of interest Chgo. City Coun., 1988; grand prize, Robert F. Kennedy journ. award, 1993. Office: Chgo Tribune 435 N Michigan Ave Chicago IL 60611-4066*

LIPINSKI, BARBARA JANINA, psychologist, psychotherapist, educator, writer; b. Chgo., Feb. 29, 1956; d. Janek and Alicja (Brzozkiewicz) L. (dec.); m. Bernard Joseph Burns, Feb. 14, 1976 (div. 1985). B of Social Work, U. Ill., Chgo., 1978; MFCC, MA, U. Calif., Santa Barbara, 1982; PhD, U. So. Calif., 1992. Diplomate Am. Bd. Forensic Medicine; cert. tchr., Calif., psychology tchr., Calif.; cert. adminstr., non-pub. agent; lic. marriage, family and child therapist; bd. cert. forensic examiner; lic. psychologist. Police svc. officer Santa Barbara (Calif.) Police Dept., 1978-79; peace officer Airport Police, Santa Barbara, 1979-80; emergency comms. Univ. Police, 1980-82; facilitator, instr. Nat. Traffic Safety Inst., San Jose, Calif., 1981-87; assoc. dir. Community Health Task Force on Alcohol and Drug Abuse, Santa Barbara, 1982-86; instr. Santa Barbara C.C., 1987-88; patients' rights adv. Santa Barbara County Calif. Mental Health Adminstrn., 1986-89; pvt. practice psychotherapist Santa Barbara, 1985—; faculty mem., chair Pacifica Grad. Inst., Carpinteria, Calif., 1989-2000; police psychologist L.A. Police Dept., 2000; rsch. evaluator Miocrgrant, Ventura, 2002—. Intern clin. psychology L.A. County Sheriff's Dept., 1991-92, cons. Devereaux Found., Santa Barbara, 1993-95, Ctr. for Law Related Edn., Santa Barbara, 1986; cons., trainer Univ. Police Dept., Santa Barbara, 1982, 89. Author: In The Best Interest of the Patient: Ethical and Legal Issues in the Practice of Psychotherapy, 1999, Wisdom of the Oracle, 2000m, Feng Shui Wisdom, 2001, Heed the Call: Psychological Perspectives on Child Abuse, 2001, The Tao of Integrity: Legal, Ethical and Professional Issues in Psychology, 2002. Vol. crisis work Nat. Assn. Children of Alcoholics, L.A., 1987; crisis intervention worker Women in Crisis Can Act, Chgo., 1975-76; vol. counselor Santa Barbara Child Sexual Assault Treatment Ctr.-PACT, Santa Barbara, 1981-82. Recipient Grad. Teaching assistanship U. So. Calif., 1990-92. Mem. APA, Am. Profl. Soc. on Abuse of Children, Am. Coll. Forensic Examiners, Calif. Assn. Marriage and Family Therapists, Am. Psychotherapy Assn. (exec. adv. bd. 1997-99). Avocations: horticulture, aviculture, ecology. Office: Pacific Meridian 301 Los Cabos Ln Ventura CA 93001-1183 E-mail: pacificmeridian@aol.com.

LIPINSKI, JAMIE LYNNE, computer systems programmer, analyst; b. Balt., Aug. 13, 1962; d. Edward Eugene Jr. and Sylvia Lynne (Esslinger) L. BS, Towson State U., 1990. Bus. systems programmer, analyst Tex. Instruments, Hunt Valley, Md., 1984—. Mem. Digital Equipment Users Soc. Democrat. Roman Catholic. Avocations: music, sports, reading. Home: 5609 Sharon Dr Glen Arm MD 21057-9360 Office: Tex Instruments 10909 Mccormick Rd Cockeysville Hunt Valley MD 21031-1401

LIPINSKI, TARA KRISTEN, retired professional figure skater; b. Phila., June 10; Prof. figure skater Stars On Ice, 1998—. Competitive history includes placing 1st in Hershey's Kisses Challenge, 1997, 1st in World Championships, 1997, 1st in Champions Series Final, 1997, 1st Nat. Sr., 1997, 1st (team) U.S. Postal Svc. Challenge, 1996, 2d in Nations Cup, 1996, 3rd Trophy Lalique, 1996, 2nd place Skate Can., 1996, numerous others; recipient Mary Lou Retton award U.S. Olympic Festival, 1994; youngest-ever Olympic Festival gold medalist at age 12, 2nd place Nat. Champ., 1998, 1st place Skate, Rattle & Roll, 1998, 1st place Olympic Games, 1998, 1st place Champion Series Final, 1997,98. Avocations: reading, cooking, tennis.*

LIPINSKI, WILLIAM OLIVER, congressman; b. Chgo., Dec. 22, 1937; s. Oliver and Madeline (Collins) L.; m. Rose Marie Lapinski, Aug. 29, 1962; children: Laura, Daniel. Student, Loras Coll., Dubuque, Iowa, 1957-58. Various positions to area supr. Chgo. Parks, 1958-75; alderman Chgo. City Coun., 1975-83; mem. 98th-107th Congresses from 5th (now 3rd) Dist. Ill., 1983—, mem. transp. and infrastructure com. Dem. ward committeeman, Chgo., 1975—; del. Dem. Nat. Midterm Conv., 1974, Dem. Nat. Conv., 1976, 84, 88; pres. Greater Midway Econ. and Community Devel. Com.; mem. Chgo. Hist. Soc., Art Inst., Chgo., pres.'s coun. St. Xavier Coll.; mem. Congl. Competitive Caucus, Congl. Caucus for Women's Issues, Congl. Hispanic Caucus, Congl. Human Rights Caucus, Congl. Populist Caucus, Dem. Study Group, Export Task Force, Inst. for Ill., Maritime Caucus, N.E.-Midwest Congl. Coalition, Urban Caucus. Named Man of Yr. Chgo. Park Dist. 4, 1983; recipient Archer Heights Civic Assn. award 1979, 23d Ward Businessmen and Mchts. award Chgo., 1977, Garfield Ridge Hebrew Congregation award Chgo., 1975-77, Installing Officer award Vittum Park Civic Assn., 23d Ward Minuteman award, Friends of Vittum Park Polish award, Nathan Hale Grand award from S.W. Liberty Soc., S.W. Am. Edn. and Recreation program award, Sentry of Yr. award Stars & Stripes Soc., Ill. State Minuteman award 1991. Mem. Polish Nat. Alliance, Kiwanis (Disting. Svc. award, pres., Peace Through Strength Leadership award 1991). Democrat. Roman Catholic. Office: US Ho of Reps 2470 Rayburn House Office Bldg Washington DC 20515-0001 also: 5832 S Archer Ave Chicago IL 60638-1637*

LIPINSKY, CAROL, small business owner; b. Miami, Fla., Dec. 30, 1957; d. Murray and Helaine Lipinsky. Student, Guilford Coll., 1975-76; AA in Liberal Arts and Recreation, 1977; cert., Brown Coll. of Ct. Reporting, 1979. Owner, ct. reporter Lipinsky Reporting, Atlanta, 1982-86; sales rep. Atlantic Equipment Co., Miami, Fla., 1986-89; owner, tennis profl. The First Bounce, Inc., Atlanta and Poughkeepsie, N.Y., 1989—. Named Profl. of Yr. Ga. Profl. Tennis Assn. Avocations: photography, art.

LIPITZ, ELAINE KAPPEL, secondary education fine arts educator; b. N.Y.C., Oct. 5, 1924; d. Herman Kappel and Ceil (Friedson) Ferester; m. Elliott Alan Lipitz, Mar. 20, 1945; children: Linda Marsha Schreiber, Alice Lynn Lindholm. BFA, Pratt Coll., 1946; MA, Columbia U., 1955; MA in Adminstrn., St. Johns U., 1974. Fine Art tchr. Art & Design High Sch., N.Y.C., 1946-47, Jamaica High Sch., Queens, N.Y., 1949-70, fin art supr., 1970-75; coord. student affairs John Bowne High Sch., 1979-90, dir. community rels., 1990-93. Interior design cons., 1950-80; jewelry designer, 1950-62. One woman shows include Gallery of Manhasset, 1968, Booth Meml. Art Gallery, Queens, 1989; exhibited in group shows at Ctr. Kew Gardens Hills, 1966, Bklyn. Mus. Art, 1969, Park Ave. Christian Ch., 1969, N.Y. Regional Exhbn. Painting and Sculpture, 1969, Newsday Fed. Art Show, 1969 (1st Prize), 70 (2d Place award), Norfolk Mus., 1970, Gallery North, Setauket, N.Y., 1994, 95, Art Guild of Coconut Creek, 1995, 96, Schacknow Mus., 1997 (Spl. award), Coral Springs Artist Guild, 1997, Bailey Hall Gallery, 1998 (hon. mention), Schaknow Mus., 1998, Coral Springs Museum, 1999, 2000, 01, Serve Gallery (3d place spl. mention), 2000, 01. Recipient Mayor's Honor award for Cmty. Svc., 1989, 1st prize sculpture Govt. Ctr. Art Guild of Coconut Creek, Fla., 1994. Avocations: swimming, walking, traveling, concerts, theatre. Home: 3 Princess Tree Ct Port Jefferson NY 11777-1742

LIPKE, KATHRYN, artist, educator; b. Cooperstown, N.D., Dec. 16, 1939; d. Herluf O. Vigesaa and Ruth E. Vigessa; children: Tanya, Shannon. BS, N.D. State U., Fargo, 1962; MA, U. Calif., Berkeley, 1969. Prof. faculty fine arts Concordia U., Montreal, 1977—96, founder fibres, dept. sculpture, ceramic and fibres, 1977—96, assoc. dean rsch. faculty fine arts, 1992—96; docent prof. sculpture U. Lapland, Rovaniemi, Finland, 1997—. Vis. artist Goldsmiths Coll., U. London, Acad. Art and Design, Poland, U. Calif., Davis Emily Carr Coll. Art, Vancouver, Ont. Coll. Art and Harborfront, Toronto, Form Design Ctr., Malmo, Sweden; lectr. textiles Coll. of Marin, Kentfield, Calif., 1972, Ind. U., Bloomington, 1973; lectr. Hartford Arts Sch., U. Hartford, 1977; sculptor, with works in Calif., N.D., Vt., Corcoba Argentina, Kemijarvi and Levi Tunturi, Finland, Germany; numerous corp. commns.; solo and group art exhbns. in U.S., Can., Europe; prodr., dir. videos. Vol. art orgns., women's groups, environ. groups, 1969—. Recipient award. for outstanding documentary video prodn. Maya Women of Guatemala, 1993, 97, Saganash Fund for Acad. Innovation, Re-presenting Women, 1995-97; Nat. Endowment for Arts fellow, 1977-78. Mem.: RAVA (Assoc. Visual Arts), Textile Soc. Am., Assoc. Ind. Video and Filmmakers, USA. Home and Office: Dakota Prodns 6559 Vt Route 109 Belvidere Center VT 05442-9699

LIPKIN, BERNICE SACKS, computer science educator; b. Boston, Dec. 21, 1927; d. Milton and Esther Miriam (Berchuck) Sacks; m. Lewis Edward Lipkin; children: Joel Arthur, Libbe Lipkin Englander. BS in Biology, Chemistry, Northeastern U., 1949; MA in Psychology, Boston U., 1950; PhD in Experimental Psychology, Columbia U., 1961. Rsch. and devel. scientist Directorate Sci. and Tech., CIA, Washington, 1964-70; scientist dept. computer sci. U. Md., Greenbelt, 1971-72; health sci. adminstr. NIH, Bethesda, Md., 1972-88; cons. computerized text analysis, data exploration L+B and Co., 1989—. Author: String Processing and Text Manipulation in C, 1994; editor: Picture Processing and Psychopictorics, 1970, Latex for Linux, 1999; contbr. articles on computer-based text searches and data analysis to profl. publs. Cerebral Palsy Soc. fellow in neurophysiology, 1961-62; NIH trainee, 1955-58. Mem. AAAS, IEEE, APA, Optical Soc. Am., Assn. Computing Machinery, Sigma Xi. Jewish. Achievements include design of system for manipulation and analysis of text data files, documentation and instruction manuals; teaching children computer concepts and programming. Office: 9913 Belhaven Rd Bethesda MD 20817-1733 E-mail: bslipkin@erols.com.

LIPKIN, DAVID, chemist; b. Phila., Jan. 30, 1913; s. William and Ida (Zipin) L.; m. Silvia Stantic Alvarez, Nov. 10, 1973; children— Jeffrey Alan, Edward Walter. BS, U. Pa., 1934; PhD, U. Calif., Berkeley, 1939. Research chemist Atlantic Refining Co., Phila., 1934-36; research fellow U. Calif., Berkeley, 1939-42; research chemist Manhattan Project, 1942-43; research chemist, group leader Los Alamos Sci. Lab., 1943-46; mem. faculty Washington U., St. Louis, 1946—81, prof. chemistry, 1948-66, chmn. dept., 1964-70, William Greenleaf Eliot prof., 1966-81, emeritus, 1981—. Sr. vis. fellow Agrl. Research Council, Cambridge, Eng., 1960; vis. research scientist John Innes Inst., Norwich, Eng., 1971, 78; trustee Argonne Univs. Assn., 1969-71; cons. in field. Author; patentee in field. Guggenheim fellow, 1955-56 Mem. Am. Chem. Soc. (St. Louis award 1970), AAUP, Sigma Xi, Tau Beta Pi, Pi Mu Epsilon. Office: Washington Univ Chemistry Dept Saint Louis MO 63130

LIPKIN, EDWARD B. real estate developer; b. Phila., Aug. 15, 1945; s. Al and Sophie (Feldman) L.; children: Theodore, Jeremy; m. Jean Bauer; 1 stepchild, Andrew Bauer. BS in Fin., Temple U., 1967; DBA (hon.), Spring Garden Coll., 1984. Sr. tax assoc. Shearson Hayden Stone, Phila., 1975-76; pres. Nat. Property Analysts (name now EBL&S Inc.), 1976—. Founding mem. Wharton Real Estate Ctr. U. Pa. Pres. bd. dirs. Friends of Rittenhouse Sq., Phila., 1983—; mem. exec. com. Senator Bill Bradley, N.J., 1978—; bd. dirs. Woodlyne Sch., Stratford, Pa. With U.S. Army, 1967-73. Mem. Internat. Coun. Shopping Ctrs. (trustee 1986). Republican. Jewish. Office: EBL&S Inc 230 S Broad St Philadelphia PA 19102-4121 E-mail: eblipkin@cs.com.

LIPKIN, MARTIN, physician, scientist; b. N.Y.C., Apr. 30, 1926; s. Samuel S. and Celia (Greenfield) L.; m. Joan Schulein, Feb. 16, 1958; children: Richard Martin, Steven Monroe. AB, NYU, 1946, MD, 1950. Diplomate Nat. Bd. Med. Examiners. Mem. staff N.Y. Hosp., Meml. Hosp. for Cancer and Allied Diseases, 1972-96; prof. medicine Cornell U. Med. Coll., 1978—, prof. Grad. Sch. Med. Scis., 1978—; mem. and attending physician Meml. Sloan-Kettering Cancer Ctr., 1985-96; dir. clin. rsch. Strang Cancer Prevention Ctr., N.Y.C., 1996—. Vis. physician Rockefeller U. Hosp., 1981—; hon. lectr. Israel Med. Assn. and Gastroenterology Soc., 1982; nominator Nobel Prize for Physiology and Medicine, 1982; bd. dirs., officer The Med. Ednl. and Sci. Found. of N.Y.; bd. dirs. Internat. Soc. Cancer Chemoprevention; chmn. bd. Irving Weinstein Found. Mem. editorial bd. Cancer Rsch., Internat. Jour. Oncology, World Jour. Gastroenterology; editor: Gastrointestinal Tract Cancer, 1978, Inhibition of Tumor Induction and Development, 1981, Gastrointestinal Cancer: Endogenous Factors, 1981, Calcium, Vitamin D and Prevention of Colon Cancer, 1991, Cancer Chemoprevention, 1992; contbr. articles to profl. jours. Served as officer USN, 1953-55. Recipient NIH career devel. award, 1962-71; Albert F.R. Andresen ann. award and lectr. N.Y. State Med. Soc., 1971, medallion Nat. Cancer Ctr. Rsch. Inst., Tokyo, 1976, U. Padua, Italy, 1978. Fellow: ACP, Am. Coll. Gastroenterology; mem.: Am. Gastroenterol. Assn., Am. Assn. Cancer Rsch., Am. Physiol. Soc., Am. Soc. Clin. Investigation, Med. Soc. State of NY (chmn. sci. program com. 1990—91, chmn. edn. com. 1991—99). Office: 1230 York Ave New York NY 10021-6307 E-mail: lipkin@mail.rockefeller.edu.

LIPKIN, RANDIE TINA, novelist; b. Jan. 7, 1953; d. Isadore and Phyllis Glassman Lipkin. Author: Untitled (A Skier), 1994, Without, 1998.

LIPKIN, SEYMOUR, pianist, conductor, educator; b. Detroit, May 14, 1927; s. Ezra and Leah (Vidaver) L.; m. Catherine Lee Bing, Dec. 27, 1961 (div. 1983); 1 son, Jonathan Michael. MusB, Curtis Inst. Music, 1947; studied piano with, David Saperton, 1938-41, Rudolf Serkin, Mieczyslaw Horszowski, 1941-47; conducting with, Serge Koussevitzky, Berkshire Music Center, 1946, 48-49. Piano tchr. Juilliard Sch. Music, N.Y.C., 1986—. Faculty Manhattan Sch. Music, 1965-70, 72-86, NYU, 1980-86; piano faculty Curtis Inst. Music, 1969—, New Eng. Conservatory, 1984-86, faculty music dept. Marymount Coll., Tarrytown, N.Y., 1963-72, chmn. music dept., 1968-71. Condr. Bklyn. Coll. Orch., 1973-74; Ford Found. commn. to perform concerto by Harold Shapero, 1959; debut with Detroit Civic Orch., 1937; apprentice condr. to George Szell, Cleve. Orch., 1947-48; appearances as pianist other U.S. orchs. including Boston Symphony in Tanglewood; ann. tours including soloist, Buffalo and Nat. Symphony, soloist, asst. condr. N.Y. Philharm. tour, Europe and Russia, 1959; conducting debut Detroit Symphony, 1944; recitalist, 92d St YMHA, N.Y.C., 1981, 83, soloist N.Y. Philharm., N.Y.C., 1983, participant in chamber music, Spoleto Festivals, 1982, 83, co-condr. Curtis Inst. Orch., 1952-53, asst. condr. Goldovsky Opera Co. on tour, 1953, condr. N.Y.C. Opera Co., 1958, 1 of 3 asst. condrs. New York Philharm., 1959-60; mus. dir. Teaneck Symphony, N.J., 1961-70, L.I. Symphony, 1963-79, Scarboro Chamber Orch., N.Y., 1964-65, Joffrey Ballet, N.Y. City Center, 1966-68, 1972-79, prin. guest condr., 1968-72; artistic dir. Kneisel Hall Summer Chamber Music Sch. and Festival, 1987— (performed cycle of 32 Beethoven Sonatas 1988-90, Gardner Mus., Boston, 1996-99, Beethoven Soc., N.Y., 1997—, 10 Beethoven Violin Sonatas with Andrew Dawes 1995, Uto Ughi, Santa Cecilia, Rome, 1995, 5 cello sonatas with David Soyer 1989, Laurence Lesser, 1996, 5 piano concertos with Santa Fe Symphony 1993, complete sonatas of Schubert at Kneisel Hall, Gardner Mus., Boston, Kaye Playhouse, N.Y.C.); appearances as opera condr. Curtis Inst., Teatro Petruzzelli, Bari, Italy, 1986-87; participant in chamber music Norfolk Fest., 1984-85, Marlboro Fest., 1986; recorded Stravinsky Piano Cncerto and Concerto with N.Y. Philharm., Bernstein, Grieg, Saint-Saens, Strauss sonatas with Aaron Rosand (violin), Grieg, Dohnanyi, Weiner sonatas with Oscar Shumsky (violin), Franck Sonata, Chausson Concerto with Rosand, Beethoven Sonatas op. 106 and 109, Schubert Works and Weber Sonatas with Arnold Steinhardt (violin); artistic dir. internat. piano festival and William Kapell competition U. Md., 1988-92. Recipient 1st prize Rachmaninoff Piano Competition, 1948. Mem. Am. Guild Mus. Artists. Home: 420 West End Ave New York NY 10024-5708 Office: Perform Artist Internat 4417 Dunwick Ln Ste 300 Fort Worth TX 76109-2508

LIPMAN, DAVID, retired journalist, multimedia consultant; b. Springfield, Mo., Feb. 13, 1931; s. Benjamin and Rose (Mack) L.; m. Marilyn Lee Vittert, Dec. 10, 1961; children: Gay Ilene, Benjamin Alan. BJ, U. Mo., 1953, LHD (hon.), 1997. Sports editor Jefferson City (Mo.) Post-Tribune, 1953, Springfield Daily News, 1953-54; gen. assignment reporter Springfield Leader and Press, 1956-57; reporter, copy editor Kansas City (Mo.) Star, 1957-60; sports reporter St. Louis Post-Dispatch, 1960-66, asst. sports editor, 1966-68, news editor, 1968-71, asst. mng. editor, 1971-78, mng. editor, 1979-92; chmn. Pulitzer 2000 Pulitzer Pub. Co., St. Louis, 1992-96, multimedia cons., 1997-2000. Guest lectr. Am. Press Inst., Columbia U. Journalism Sch., 1967-70; chmn. bd. advisors U. Mo. Sch. Journalism, 1989-2001, chmn. bd. dirs. multi-cultural mgmt. program, 1995-97; bd. dirs. Columbia Missourian, 1989—, chmn. task force, 2001-2002. Author: Maybe I'll Pitch Forever, The Autobiography of LeRoy (Satchel) Paige, 1962, reissued, 1993, Mr. Baseball, The Story of Branch Rickey, 1966, Ken Boyer, 1967, Joe Namath, 1968; co-author: The Speed King, The Story of Bob Hayes, 1971, Bob Gibson Pitching Ace, 1975, Jim Hart Underrated Quarterback, 1977. Bd. dirs. Mid-Am. Press Inst., 1973-97, chmn., 1975-77; mem.-at-large nat. coun., bd. dirs. Am. Jewish Com. St. Louis, 1997—; bd. dirs. Rabbi Samuel Thurman Ednl. Found., 1997—; trustee United Hebrew Congregation, 1975-77; bd. dirs. Parkview Housing Corp.; chmn. com. 21st Century, U. Mo., 1993-94; vice chair Mo. Gov.'s Commn. on Info. Tech., 1994-95; chmn. ethics commn. City of Creve Coeur, 2001—, chair new tech. com., 1997-2001; mem. Creve Coeur Charter Commn., 2000-2001; cons. Mo. Press-Bar Commn., 1995—; mem. adv. bd. Jewish Light, 2001—. 1st lt. USAF, 1954-56. Recipient Univ. Mo. Faculty and Alumni award, 1988, Univ. Mo. Disting. Svc. in Journalism medal, 1989, St. Louis Jermiah award, 1991; named to Writers Hall of Fame of Am., Springfield, Mo., 2002. Mem. Am. Soc. Newspaper Editors, Newspaper Assn. Am. (mem. industry devel. com.-1993-96), Mo. Editors and Pubs. Assn. (pres. 1990-91), Mo. Soc. Newspaper Editors (bd. dirs. 1990-97, vice chmn. 1992-93, chmn. 1993), Mo. Press Assn. (1st v.p. 1994-95, pres. 1997, bd. dirs. 1998—), Mo. AP Mng. Editors Assn. (pres. 1990), U. Mo. Sch. Journalism Nat. Alumni Assn. (chmn. 1980-83), Press Club of St. Louis (chmn. 1987-94), Soc. Profl. Journalists (pres. St. Louis chpt. 1976-77), Kappa Tau Alpha, Omicron Delta Kappa. Jewish.

LIPMAN, FREDERICK D. lawyer, writer, educator; b. Phila., Nov. 16, 1935; s. Charles S. and Beatrice (Sanderow) L.; m. Gail Heller, July 25, 1965; children— L. Keith, Darren A. AB, Temple U.; LLB, Harvard Law Sch. Bar: Pa. 1960, N.Y. Practitioner, Phila., 1960-62; corp. counsel AEL Industries, Inc., Colmar, Pa., 1962-69; ptnr. Blank Rome Comisky & McCauley LLP, Phila., 1970—. Lectr. U. Pa. Law Sch., 1989-98, Temple U. Law Sch., 1989-94, Wharton Sch. of Bus., 1998—. Author: Going Public, 1994, How Much Is Your Business Worth, 1996, Venture Capital and Junk Bond Financing, 1998, Financing Your Business with Venture Capital, 1998, The Complete Going Public Handbook, 2000, Audit Committees, 2000, The Complete Guide to Employee Stock Options, 2001, The Complete Guide to Valuing and Selling Your Business, 2001. Bd. dirs. Phila. Ch. of Bezalel, 1989-91, Walnut St. Theatre, 1997-99, Phila. Geriatric Ctr., Penjerdel. Harvard Law Sch. scholar, 1957; Temple U. scholar, 1953. Mem. Phila. Bar Assn. (bd. govs. 1984-85), Greater Phila. C. of C. (bd. dirs., mem. exec. com. 1980-90, chmn. tech. council 1983-85), Harvard Law Sch. Assn. Greater Phila. (pres. 1988-89). Lodges: Masons. Democrat. Jewish. Avocation: tennis. Office: Blank Rome Comisky & McCauley LLP 1 Logan Sq Fl 3 Philadelphia PA 19103-6998 E-mail: lipman@blankrome.com.

LIPMAN, IRA ACKERMAN, security service company executive; b. Little Rock, Nov. 15, 1940; s. Mark and Belle (Ackerman) L.; m. Barbara Ellen Kelly Couch, July 5, 1970; children: Gustave K., Joshua S, M Benjamin. Student, Ohio Wesleyan U., 1958-60; LLD (hon.), John Marshall U., Atlanta, 1970; LLD (Hon.), Northeastern U., Boston, 1996. Salesman, exec. Mark Lipman Svcs. Inc., Memphis, 1960-63; v.p. Guardsmark, Inc., 1963-66, pres., 1966—, CEO, 1968—, chmn. bd., 1968—. Bd. dirs. Nat. Coun. on Crime and Delinquency, 1975—, chmn. fin. com., treas., 1978-79, vice chmn. bd. dirs., 1982-86, chmn. exec. com., 1986-93, chmn. bd. dirs., 1993-94, chmn. emeritus, 1993—, hon. chmn. 1997—; bd. dirs. Greater Memphis Coun. Crime and Delinquency, 1976-78, entrepreneurial fellow Memphis State U., 1976; mem. environ. security com., pvt. security adv. coun. Law Enforcement Assistance adminstrn., 1975-76; mem. conf. planning com. 2d Nat. Law Enforcement Explorer Conf., 1980. Author: How to Protect Yourself From Crime, 1975, 3d edit., 1989, 4th edit., 1997; contbr. numerous articles to profl. jours., mags. and newspapers. Bd. dirs. Memphis Jewish Cmty. Center, 1974, Memphis Shelby County unit Am. Cancer Soc., 1980-81, Memphis Orchestral Soc., 1980-81, Memphis Jewish Fedn., 1974-83; chmn. Shelby County com. U.S. Savs. Bonds, 1976; mem. president's coun. Memphis State U., 1975-79;, mem. visual arts coun., 1980-82; Memphis met. chmn. Nat. Alliance Businessmen, 1970-71; mem. task force Reform Jewish Outreach, Union Am. Hebrew Congregations, 1979-83; mem. young leadership cabinet United Jewish Appeal, 1973-78, mem. S.E. regional campaign cabinet, 1980; exec. bd. Chickasaw council Boy Scouts Am., 1978-81; bd. dirs., exec. com. Tenn. Ind. Coll. Fund, 1979; trustee Memphis Acad. Arts, 1977-81; mem. president's club Christian Bros. Coll., 1979-89; bd. dirs. Future Memphis, 1980-83, 83-86; nat. trustee NCCJ, 1980-92, exec. com., 1981-92, nat. Jewish co-chmn., 1985-88, nat. chmn., 1988-92, hon. chmn., past nat. chmn. Nat. Conf. Christians and Jews, 1992—; bd. dirs. Memphis chpt., 1980-85, life bd. dirs. Memphis chpt. 1985—; group II chmn. for 1982 campaign United Way Greater Memphis, 1981; v.p. exec. com. Internat. Coun. Christians and Jews, 1992-94; bd. govs. United Way of Am., 1992-99, bd. gov.'s liaison, 1991-92, chmn. ethics com., 1992-97, mem. exec. com., 1992-97, co-chmn. vol. involvement com., 1992—, mem. strategic planning com., 1994-96, diversity com., 1997-99; chmn. UWLC steering com. 1995-96; mem. Alexis de Tocqueville Soc. Nat. Leadership Coun., 1992-97, mem. emeritus, 1998—, mem. Second Century Initiative Vol. Involvement com., 1987-91; chair Task Force on Critical Markets, 1987-91, mem. exec. cabinet, 1990-91; trustee Memphis Brooks Mus. Art, 1980-83, Yeshiva U. of L.A., 1982-; trustee Simon Wiesenthal Ctr., 1982—, chmn. campaign com., 1983-92, mem. fin. and audit com., 1993—, exec. com., 1994—, co-chmn. budget and fin. com. Jerusalem Project, 1999-; bd. dirs. Nat. Alliance against Violence, 1983-85, Nat. Ctr. Learning Disabilities, 1989-94, United Way of Greater Memphis, 1984-85, gen. campaign chmn., 1985-86; founder, bd. overseers B'nai B'rith, 1980; bd. dirs. Tenn. Gov.'s Jobs for High Sch. Grads. Program, 1980-83; trustee Ohio Wesleyan U., 1988-97; vice chmn. spl. task force on endowment growth Ohio Wesleyan U., 1990-97; mem. bd. overseers Wharton Sch., U. Pa., 1991—, devel. com., 1995—, exec. adv. bd. Zicklin Ctr. Bus. Ethics Rsch., 1997—; assoc. trustee U. Pa., 1991—; mem. exec. com. Am. Israel Pub. Affairs Com., 1991-2001; bd. trustees Com. for Economic Devel., 1999—; adv. bd. dirs., Tenn. Titans, 1999-2000; mem. Hillel Internat. Bd. Govs., 2001—; bd. trustees, Fifth Ave. Synagogue, 2001—; Nat. Campaign Against Youth Violence (founding bd. mem.) 1999-2002; mem. Coun. on Fgn. Rels., 2002-; adv. bd. Ctr. for Values Based Leadership, Sacred Heart U., 2002-; mem. Soc. of Entrepreneurs, 2002-. Named one of Best Corp. Chief Exec. of Achievement, Gallagher Pres.'s Report, 1974; recipient Humanitarian of Yr. award, NCCJ, 1985, Outstanding Cmty. Sales award, Sales and Mktg. Execs. Memphis, 1987, Jr. Achievement Master Free Enterprise award, 1987, Alexis de Tocqueville Soc. award, 1995, Corp. Citizenship award, Com. for Econ. Devel., 2002. Mem. Internat. Assn. Chiefs Police, Am. Soc. Criminology, Internat. Soc. Criminology, Am. Soc. Indsl. Security (cert. protection profl.), 100 Club, B'nai B'rith, Econ. Club (bd. dirs. 1980-86, v.p. 1983-84, pres. 1984-85, chmn. exec. com. 1984-85). Republican. Office: Guardsmark Inc 10 Rockefeller Plz New York NY 10020-1903

LIPMAN, JOHN CRAWFORD, endovascular surgeon; b. Rochester, N.Y., Aug. 25, 1959; s. Earl Stanley and Jane Crawford Lipman; m. Jayne Pickering, June 4, 1988. BA in Gen. Sci., U. Rochester, 1980; MS in Physiology, Georgetown U., 1981, MD, 1985. Diplomate Am. Bd. Radiology, cert. added qualification vascular & interventional radiology. Clin. instr. Yale U. Sch. Medicine, New Haven, 1990—91; interventional radiologist Radiology Assocs. of Atlanta, 1991—. Author: Quick Reference to Radiology, 1995. Named one of Top Docs in Atlanta, Atlanta Mag., 2001. Fellow: Soc. Cardiovascular & Interventional Radiology. Office: Radiology Assocs of Atlanta Ste 505 1984 Peachtree Rd NW Atlanta GA 30309 Office Fax: 404-352-8176. Business E-Mail: jlipman@raadocs.com.

LIPMAN, LAURIE S. psychiatrist; b. Dec. 2, 1952; AB, U. Chgo., 1978; MD, Rush Med. Coll., 1986. Resident U. Chgo. Hosps., 1993; asst. prof. dept. psychiatry Northwestern U. Med. Sch., Chgo., 1993—; staff Mental Health Clin., Lakeside Veterans Admin., 1993—, med. co-dir., 1997—, dir., 2000—. Adv. edit., Jour. of the Amer. Soc. of Clin. Hypnosis. Contbr. articles to profl. jours. Office: Northwestern U Med Sch & Lakeside VA Dept Psychiatry 333 E Huron St # 116A Chicago IL 60611-3004

LIPMAN, MARVIN MATTHEW, medical educator; b. N.Y.C., Nov. 6, 1928; s. Louis B. and Bertha L.; m. Naomi L. Lipman, June 17, 1951; children: Barry D., Amy F., Mark A., Harry W. AB, Columbia Coll., 1949; MD, Columbia Coll. of Phys. & Surg., 1954. Intern, asst. resident Columbia-Presbyn. Med. Ctr., 1954-56; sr. resident Mass. Gen. Hosp., 1959-61; chief of medicine White Plains (N.Y.) Hosp. Ctr., 1985-90, chief of endocrinology, 1980-85, N.Y. Med. Coll., Valhalla, 1967-81, prof. clin. medicine, 1986—; chief med. advisor Consumers Union, Yonkers, NY, 1967—. Bd. trustees U.S. Pharmacopeia. Author: The Medicine Show, 1972, The Best of Health, 1998. Capt. U.S. Army, 1956-58. Fellow: Am. Coll. Endocrinology, ACP; mem.:

Am. Assn. Clin. Endocrinologists, Endocrine Soc., Am. Fedn. Med. Rsch., Am. Diabetes Assn., Alpha Omega Alpha. Avocations: theatre, opera, chamber music, squash. Office: Scarsdale Med Group 259 Heathcote Rd Scarsdale NY 10583

LIPMAN, MICHEL, writer, lawyer; b. San Francisco, June 11, 1913; s. Maurice and Frances Lipman. AA, San Jose State U., 1932; JD, Hastings Coll. of the Law, 1937. Bar: Calif. 1938, U.S. Dist. Ct. 1938. Corp. counsel Calif. Nurses Assn., San Francisco, 1969-71; pub. rels. dir. State Bar of Calif., 1971-76; v.p. Aeronautics, Inc., Burlingame, Calif., 1976-80; mng. ptnr. Univ. Concepts, San Francisco, 1991—. Writing cons. Bank of Am., San Francisco; condr. better writing seminars for various clients, San Francisco. Author: (instrn. manual) Safety Practices for Standard Oil Supervisors, (pharmacy publs.) Looking Better Through Plastic Surgery, Medical Law & Ethics, 1993, (with Angelo Capozzi) Change of Face, (with Herman Schwartz) Guidebook for the Hospital Patient; editor 12-set series annotated young people's books, 1971-72; writer, prodr.: (daily radio show) Point of Law, 1953—; creator Point of Law game; contbr. articles to profl. jours. Recipient 1st ann. award Bar Assn. San Francisco, 1954, George Washington Honor medal Freedom Found. of Valley Forge, 1953-54, 55, Silver Microphone award Advt. Group, 1999. Avocations: collecting rare books and stock certificates, opera. Office: University Concepts 719 Battery St San Francisco CA 94111-1501 Fax: (415) 956-2595.

LIPMAN, RICHARD PAUL, pediatrician; b. Cambridge, Mass., Aug. 1, 1935; s. Hyman Zelig and Betty (Likovsky) L.; m. Mary Alice Wilcox, Aug. 25, 1963; children: Gregory, Susan; m. Lora H. Higgins, July 6, 1996. AB magna cum laude, Harvard U., 1957; MD cum laude, Tufts U., 1961. Diplomate Am. Bd. Pediatrics. Intern Boston Floating Hosp., 1961-62, jr. resident, 1962-63, sr. resident, 1963-64, chief resident, 1964; rsch. fellow infectious disease Med. Sch. U. N.C., Chapel Hill, 1967-69; practice pediatrics Peabody and Salem, Mass., 1969—. Mem. staff North Shore Children's Hosp., Salem, Mass., assoc. chief of staff, 1974-76, pres., chief of staff, 1976-79, chief of medicine, 1979-83, trustee, 1980-84, corporator, 1985-86; mem. staff Tufts-New Eng. Med. Ctr., Boston, Boston Children's Hosp., North Shore Children's Hosp., Beverly Hosp., Melrose-Wakefield Hosp., Salem Hosp.; clin. instr. pediatrics Tufts U. Sch. Medicine, Boston, 1969-74, asst. clin. prof., 1974-78, assoc. clin. prof., 1978—; bd. dirs. Tufts Assoc. Health Maintenance Orgn., 1988-95, North Shore Health Systems, Inc., 1995-96. Contbr. articles to profl. jours. Capt. M.C., AUS, 1964-66. Fellow Am. Acad. Pediatrics; mem. AMA, Am. Soc. Microbiology, New Eng. Pediatric Soc., Mass. Med. Soc., Tufts Alumni Assn., Nat. Assn. Watch and Clock Collectors. Office: 1 Roosevelt Ave Peabody MA 01960-2200 also: 600 Loring Ave Salem MA 01970

LIPMAN-BLUMEN, JEAN, public policy and organizational behavior educator; b. Brookline, Mass., Apr. 28, 1933; AB, Wellesley Coll., 1954, AM, 1956; PhD, Harvard U., 1970; postdoctoral study, Carnegie-Mellon U., 1970-71, Stanford U., 1971-72. Asst. dir., Nat. Inst. Edn., dir women's rsch. program, 1973-78; spl. asst. Office of Asst. Sec. Edn.; fellow Ctr. for Advanced Study in Behavioral Scis., 1978-79; pres. LBS Internat., Ltd., Washington, 1979-84; prof. orgnl. behavior Claremont (Calif.) Grad. U., Thornton F. Bradshaw prof. pub. policy, 1983—. Vis. prof. sociology and orgnl. behavior U. Conn., 1979-80, U. Md., 1980-82; spkr. in field.; cons. Exec. Office of Pres., Dept. State, Dept. Labor, Dept. HHS, Dept. Agr., Dept. Edn., Bell Labs., Singapore Airlines, MarketIndex, Finland, also various fgn. govts.; tchr. exec. mgmt. and MBA programs. Author, editor: (with Jessie Bernard): Sex Roles and Social Policy, 1978; author: The Paradox of Success: The Impact of Priority Setting in Agricultural Research and Extension, 1984, Metaphor for Change: The USDA Competitive Grants Program, 1978-84, 1985, Gender Roles and Power, 1984, Women in Corporate Leadership: Reviewing a Decade's Research, 1996, The Connective Edge: Leading in an Interdependent World, 1996 (Pulitzer prize nomination), (with Harold J. Leavitt) Hot Groups: Seeding, Feeding, and Using Them to Ignite Your Organization, 1999, Connective Leadership: Managing in a Changing World, 2000. Recipient award for best bus. book Assn. Am. Pubs., 1999. Fellow AAAS. Office: Drucker Grad Sch Mgmt 1021 N Dartmouth Ave Claremont CA 91711 E-mail: jeanlipman@earthlink.net.

LIPNIC, VICTORIA A. federal agency administrator; Grad., Allegheny Coll., George Mason U. Spl. asst. to dir. bus. liaison, spl. asst. asst. sec. trade devel. Dept. Commerce, 1984—89; atty. pvt. practice; atty. employment and labor law dept. U.S. Postal Svc., 1994—2000; profl. staff mem., counsel U.S. Ho. Rels. Com. Edn. and the Workforce, 2000—02; asst. sec. employment stds. adminstrn. U.S. Dept. Labor, Washington, 2002—. Office: US Dept Labor FPB 200 Constitition Ave NW Washington DC 20210-0001*

LIPOMI, MICHAEL JOSEPH, health facility executive; b. Buffalo, Mar. 9, 1953; s. Dominic Joseph and Betty (Angelo) L.; m. Monica Lipomi; children: Jennifer, Barrett, Ryan, Eric. BA, U. Ottawa, 1976; MS in Health Adminstrn., U. Colo., 1994. Mktg. dir. Am. Med. Internat. El Cajon Valley Hosp., Calif., 1980-83; dir. corp. devel. Med. Surg. Ctrs. Am., 1983-85; CEO Stanislaus Surgery Ctr., Modesto, 1985—. Author: Complete Anatomy of Health Care Marketing, 1988; co-host med. TV talk show Health Talk Modesto. Bd. dirs. Am. Heart Assn., Modesto, 1988-89; pres. Modesto Community Hospice, 1987-88; active local govt.; sec.-treas. Modesto Industry and Edn. Council, 1989. Mem.: Am. Surg. Hosp. Assn. (bd. dirs. 2000—, legis. chmn. 2001), Modesto C. of C. (bd. dirs. 1989—92, 1997—), Federated Ambulatory Surgery Assn. (mem. govt. rels. com. 1988, bd. dirs. 1989—, chmn. govt. rels. com. 1990), No. Calif. Assn. Surgery Ctrs. (pres. 1986—88), Calif. Ambulatory Surgery Assn. (pres. 1988—89, mem. legis. com. 1994, mem. rsch. and edn. found. bd. 1994—), Rotary. Avocations: golf, tennis, skiing. Office: Stanislaus Surgery Ctr 1421 Oakdale Rd Modesto CA 95355-3359

LIPOVETSKY, STAN (STANISLAV LIPOVETSKY), statistician, mathematician; b. Moscow, Jan. 13, 1947; s. Simeon Eliezer Lipovetsky and Rebecca Abraham Sandalova; m. Natalia J. Smolianinkova, Oct. 24, 1994; children: Steven J.; m. Olga N. Tarasova, Dec. 19, 1970 (div. May 1, 1990); children: Lena, Daniel. MSc in Theoretical Physics, Moscow U., 1971, PhD in Math. Methods in Econs., 1989. Prof. faculty mgmt. Tel Aviv U., 1990—95; rsch. mgr. Custom Rsch. Inc., Mpls., 1998—. Mem. adv. bds.: internat. jours. on ops. rsch.; contbr. articles to profl. jours. Mem.: Internat. Soc. on Multiple Criteria Decision Making, Inst. Ops. Rsch. and Mgmt. Scis., Math. Assn. Am., Am. Statis. Assn. Office: Custom Research Inc 8401 Golden Valley Rd Minneapolis MN 55427 Office Fax: 763-542-0864. E-mail: lipovetsky@customresearch.com.

LIPPA, CAROL FRANCES, neurologist; b. Erie, Pa., Aug. 19, 1955; d. John Winn and Dorothy Marie (Zarembski) Ryan; m. Robert Leo Lippa, July 1982; children: Sara Marie, Alex Mitchell, Adam Lee. BA, McGill U., Montreal, Que., Can., 1978; MD, U. Mass., 1983. Diplomate Am. Bd. Psyhiatry and Neurology, Am. Bd. Neurorehab. Intern St. Vincent Hosp., Worcester, Mass., 1983-84; resident in neurology U. Mass. Med. Ctr., 1984-86, chief resident, 1986-87, resident in neuropathology, 1987-88, fellow neurobiology of aging, 1988-89, asst. prof. neurology, 1989-95, dir. brain donation program, 1993—, investigator clin. drug trials, 1992—; physician neurorehab. svc. Fairlawn Rehab. Hosp., 1992-96; prof. neurology Drexel U. Coll. Medicine, Phila., 1996—; chief neurology svc. Med. Coll. Pa.-Hahnemann U., 2000—, dir. Memory Disorders Ctr., 1996—. Contbr. more than 150 articles to profl. jours. Recipient 2d prize residents and fellows presentation, Boston Soc. Neurology and Psychiatry, 1985. Mem.: Am. Neurol. Assn., Am. Soc. Neurorehab., Soc. Neurosci., Am. Acad. Neurology. Home: 16 Radcliff Rd Bala Cynwyd PA 19004-2631 Office: Drexel U Coll Medicine Dept Neurology 3300 Henry Ave Philadelphia PA 19129-1191 E-mail: carol.lippa@drexel.edu.

LIPPA, LINDA SUSAN MOTTOW, ophthalmologist; b. Boston, Apr. 9, 1951; d. George and Edith Etelka Mottow; m. Erik Alexander Lippa, Mar. 6, 1980; 2 children. BA magna cum laude, Harvard U., 1973; MD, Columbia U., 1977. Diplomate Am. Bd. Ophthalmology. Intern St. Luke's Hosp. Med. Ctr., N.Y.C., 1977-78; resident in ophthalmology Albert Einstein-Montefiore Hosp., Bronx, N.Y., 1978-81; fellow ophthalmol. pathology Ill. Eye and Ear Infirmary, Chgo., 1981-82; attending ophthalmologist, ophthalmic pathologist Cook County Hosp., 1982-84, St. Paul (Minn.) Ramsey Med. Ctr., 1984-85; practice medicine specializing in ophthalmology Phila., 1985-93; clin. asst. prof. Thomas Jefferson Med. Coll., 1986-94; with Med. Eye Care Assocs. Med Eye Care Assocs., Norristown, Pa., 1989-93. Asst. surgeon Wills Eye Hosp., Phila., 1985-94; clin. instr., then clin. asst. prof. Loyola U.-Hines VA Hosp., Maywood, Ill., 1982-84; clin. asst. prof. U. Minn., Mpls., 1984-85; assoc. clin. prof. U. Calif., Irvine, dir. med. edn./ophthalmology, med. dir. ophthalmology faculty practice ; clin. investigator in ocular pharmacology Thomas Jefferson U., Phila., 1987. Contbr. to profl. publs. Fellow Soc. Heed Fellows; mem. Am. Acad. Ophthalmology. Avocations: music, gardening, reading, crafts. Office: U Calif Irvine Pavilion II 101 City Dr S 2d Fl Orange CA 92868-3201 E-mail: llippa@uci.edu.

LIPPARD, LUCY ROWLAND, writer, lecturer; b. N.Y.C., Apr. 14, 1937; d. Vernon William and Margaret Isham (Cross) L.; m. Robert Tracy Ryman, Aug. 19, 1961 (div. 1968); 1 child, Ethan Isham Ryman. BA, Smith Coll., 1958; MA in Art History, NYU, 1962; DFA (hon.), Moore Coll. Art, 1972, San Francisco Art Inst., 1984, Maine Coll. Art, 1994, Mass. Coll. Art, 1998. Freelance writer, lectr., curator, 1964—. Prof. Sch. Visual Arts, N.Y.C., Williams Coll., Queensland U., Brisbane, Australia, U. Colo., Boulder; mem. adv. bd. Franklin Furnace, N.Y.C., 1979—; bd. dirs. Printed Matter, N.Y.C., Ctr. for Study of Polit. Graphics, L.A., Time & Space Ltd., Hudson, N.Y., Sustainable Settings, Woody Creek, Colo.; co-founder W.E.B., Ad Hoc Women Artist's Com., Artists Meeting for Cultural Change, Heresies Collective and Jour., Artists Call Against U.S. Intervention in Ctrl. Am., Polit. Art Documentation/Distbn. Author: Overlay: Contemporary Art and the Art of Prehistory, 1983, Mixed Blessings: New Art in a Multicultural America, 1990, Pop Art, 1966, The Graphic work of Philip Evergood, 1966, Changing: Essays in Art Criticism, 1971, Tony Smith, 1972, Six Years: The Dematerialization of the Art Object, 1973, From the Center: Feminist Essays on Women's Art, 1976, Eva Hesse, 1976, (with Charles Simonds) Cracking (Brüchig Werden), 1979, Ad Reinhardt, 1981, Get the Message? A Decade of Art for Social Change, 1984, A Different War: Vietnam in Art, 1988, The Pink Glass Swan: Selected Feminist Essays on Art, 1995, The Lure of the Local: Senses of Place in a Multicentered Society, 1997, Florence Pierce: In Touch With Light, 1998, On the Beaten Track: Tourism, Art and Place, 1999, (with Alfred Barr and James Thrall Soby) The School of Paris, 1965, (novel) I See/You Mean, 1979; author, editor: Partial Recall: Photographs of Native North Americans, 1992; editor: Surrealists on Art, 1970, Dadas on Art, 1971; contbg. editor: Art in Am.; editor El Puente de Galisteo, 1997—; contbr. monthly columns Village Voice, 1981-85, In These Times, Z Mag., also numerous articles to mags., anthologies, and mus. catalogs, 1964—. Mem. Dem. Socialists Am., Atlatl, Nat. Writers Union; mem. planning and adv. com. Santa Fe County Open Land and Trails, 1999. Recipient Frederick Douglass award North Star Fund, 1994, Frank Jewett Mather award for criticism Coll. Art Assn., 1974, Claude Fuess award for pub. svc. Phillips Andover Acad., 1975, curating award Penny McCall Found., 1989, citation N.Y.C. mayor David Dinkins, 1990, Smith Coll. medal, 1992; Guggenheim fellow, 1968, ArtTable award, 1999; grantee Lannan Found., 2000. Avocations: hiking, rock art, local history. Home and Office: 14 Avenida Vieja Lamy NM 87540-9783

LIPPARD, STEPHEN JAMES, chemist, educator; b. Pittsburgh, Pa., Oct. 12, 1940; s. Alvin I. and Ruth (Green) L.; m. Judith Ann Drezner, Aug. 16, 1964; children: Andrew (dec.), Joshua, Alexander. BA, Haverford Coll., 1962; PhD, MIT, 1965; DSc (hon.), Tex. A&M U., 1995, Haverford Coll., 2000. Postdoctoral research fellow chemistry MIT, Cambridge, 1965-66, prof. chemistry, 1983-89, Arthur Amos Noyes prof. chemistry, 1989—, head chemistry dept., 1995—; asst. prof. chemistry Columbia U., N.Y.C., 1966-69, asso. prof., 1969-72, prof., 1972-82. Mem. study sect. metallobiochemistry NIH, 1973-77. Editor: Progress in Inorganic Chemistry, 1967-92; mem. editorial bd. Inorganic Chemistry, 1981-83, 89-91, assoc. editor, 1983-88; mem. editorial bd. Account Chem. Res., 1986-88, 99—; contbr. articles to profl. jours. Coach Demarest Borough Soccer Team, 1975-82, league adminstr., 1979-82. NSF fellow, 1962-66; Alfred P. Sloan fellow, 1968-70; Guggenheim fellow, 1972; recipient Tchr.-Scholar award Camille and Henry Dreyfus Found., 1971-76, Henry J. Albert award Internat. Precious Metals Inst., 1985, Alexander von Humboldt U.S. Sr. Scientist award, 1988, Am. Chem. Soc. award for Disting. Svc. in the Advancement of Inorganic Chemistry, 1994; sr. internat. fellow John E. Fogarty Internat. Center, 1979. Fellow AAAS; mem. NAS, Am. Acad. Arts and Sci., Nat. Inst. Medicine, Am. Chem. Soc. (chmn. bioinorganic subdiv. 1987-88, Inorganic Chemistry award 1987, Remson award 1987, Mallinckrodt Disting. Svc. award 1994, William H. Nichols medal 1995, Theodore W. Richards medal 2002, Basolo medal 2002, assoc. editor jour. 1989—, chmn. inorganic div., chmn. 1992), Am. Crystallographic Assn., Am. Soc. Biol. Chemists, Nat. Inst. Medicine, Max-Planck Soc. (hon. mem.), Royal Irish Acad., Italian Chem. Soc., Phi Beta Kappa. Home: Apt 602 975 Memorial Dr Cambridge MA 02138 Office: MIT Rm 18-498 77 Massachusetts Ave Cambridge MA 02139-4307

LIPPE, MELVIN KARL, lawyer; b. Chgo., Oct. 21, 1933; s. Melvin M. and Myrtle (Karlsberg) L.; children: Suzanne, Michael S., Deanna; m. Sandra M. Bauer, Jan. 5, 1974. BS, Northwestern U., 1955, JD, 1958; grad. cert., Grad. Sch. Banking, U. Wis., 1965; cert., Sr. Bank Officers Seminar, Harvard U., 1966. Bar: Ill. 1958; CPA, Ill. Assoc. D'Ancona, Pflaum, Wyatt & Riskind, Chgo., 1958-61; asst. to chmn. bd. Exchange Nat. Bank of Chgo., 1961-62, asst. v.p., 1962-64, v.p., 1964-66, sr. v.p., sec. to bd. dirs., 1966-69, exec. v.p., dir., 1969-74, vice chmn. bd., dir., 1974-76; dir. Am.-Israel Bank, Ltd., 1974-76; ptnr. Antonow & Fink, Chgo., 1977-88, Altheimer and Gray, Chgo., 1988—. Instr. Ill. Inst. Tech., 1960-63 Bd. dirs. Jewish Cmty. Ctrs. Chgo., 1972—, pres., 1980-82; bd. dirs. Chgo. chpt. Am. Jewish Com., 1974-78; life bd. dirs. Jewish Coun. for Youth Svcs., Chgo., pres., 1971; bd. dirs. Family Focus, 1992-98. With Ill. N.G., 1959. Mem. ABA, Chgo. Bar Assn., Phi Epsilon Pi, Beta Gamma Sigma. Jewish. Office: Altheimer & Gray 10 S Wacker Dr Ste 4000 Chicago IL 60606-7407 E-mail: lippem@altheimer.com.

LIPPER, KENNETH, investment banker, author, producer; b. N.Y.C., June 19, 1941; s. George and Sally (Hollander) L.; m. Evelyn Rebecca Gruss, June 12, 1966 (div. 2000); children: Joanna Helene, Daniella, Tamara, Julie BA, Columbia U., 1962; JD, Harvard U., 1965; LLM, NYU, 1966; postgrad., Faculté de Droit et Economique, Paris, 1967. Bar: N.Y. 1965. Assoc. Fried, Frank, Harris, Shriver & Jacobson, N.Y.C., 1967-68; dir. industry policy Office Fgn. Direct Investment, Washington, 1968-69; assoc., ptnr. Lehman Bros., N.Y.C., 1969-75; mng. dir., ptnr. Salomon Bros., 1976-82; dep. mayor City of N.Y., 1983-85; chmn. Lipper & Co., 1986—. Adj. prof. internat. affairs Sch. Internat. and Pub. Affairs, Columbia U., N.Y.C., 1976-83; mem. adv. bd. Fed. Res. Bank N.Y., 1994—, J.P. Morgan Chase Manhattan Bank, 1994—. Author: (novel) Wall Street, 1987 and chief tech. advisor movie, 1987; author, screenwriter, prodr. City Hall, 1996; prodr. film and play The Winter Guest, 1997; prodr. The Last Days, 1998 (Acad. award 1999); pub. Lipper Viking Penguin Biograph. Series, 1997—. Mem. adv. bd. John F. Kennedy Sch. Govt., Harvard U., 1994-99; exec. com. Harvard U. Resources, 1994—; bd. dirs. Case New Holland N.V., 1997—, Lincoln Ctr. Performing Arts, 1995-98, Sundance Inst., 1997—. John Simon Guggenheim Found., 2001—. Recipient medal of distinction City of N.Y., 1985; John Harvard fellow, 2001. Mem. Internat. Inst. Strategic Studies, Coun. Fgn. Rels., Econ. Club N.Y., Century Assn., Phi Beta Kappa Office: Lipper & Co 101 Park Ave Rm 6R New York NY 10178-0002*

LIPPER, STUART, b. Dec. 11, 1963; BS in Bus. Mktg., Ramapo Coll., 1986. Lic. series 3, 4, 7. Sales rep. Computerland, N.Y.C., 1986-90; sales mgr. 4G Data, 1990-94; stockbroker Triad Securities, 1994—. Office: c/o Triad Securities 111 Broadway New York NY 10006-1901

LIPPERT, CHRISTOPHER NELSON, dentist, consultant; b. N.Y.C., Apr. 17, 1952; s. Raymond Joseph and Shirley Ann (Nelson) L.; m. Valerie Jo Schlager, Nov. 4 1989. BS, U. Cin., 1975; DDS, Emory U., 1979. Dentist John W. Regenos DDS, Inc., Cin., 1979-87; pres., dentist Lippert & Wilkes DDS, Inc., 1987—. Cons. Teret's Syndrome Found., Cin., 1983—, Health Am., Cleve., 1985-90; lectr. Ohio State U., 1981-89. Bd. dirs. Creekwood Condominiums, Cin., 1985-86. Mem. ADA, Am. Acad. Fixed Prosthodontists, Ohio Dental Assn., Ohio Acad. Practice Adminstrn., Cin. Dental Soc. (peer rev. com. 1985—), Midwest Med. Found. (bd. dirs. 1984-88), Phi Eta Sigma, Sigma Alpha Epsilon, Psi Omega. Avocations: sailing, fishing, restoration of classic cars.

LIPPES, GERALD SANFORD, lawyer, business executive; b. Buffalo, Mar. 23, 1940; s. Thomas and Ruth (Landsman) Lippes; m. Sandra Franger; children: Tracy E, David S, Adam F. Student, U. Mich., 1958-61; JD, U. Buffalo, 1964. Bar: NY 1964. Sr. ptnr. Lippes, Silverstein, Mathias & Wexler, Buffalo, 1964—; sec., dir., gen. counsel Mark IV, Industries, Inc., Amherst, N.Y., 1969-2000. Chmn. Del. Photographic Products, Buffalo, 1970—88, Ingram Micro-D, Buffalo, 1982—86, Abels Bagels, Inc., Buffalo, 1972—75; bd. dirs. Gilbraltar Steel Corp., Buffalo Nat. Health Care Affiliates, Inc., The Wolf Group, Inc., Protective Industries, LLC. Bd dirs. Buffalo Fine Arts Acad., U. Buffalo Found., U. Buffalo Coun., N.Y. State Arts Coun.; chmn. bd dirs. Kaleida Health Sys., 2001—02. Named Entrepreneur of the Yr, 1993; recipient Distinguished Alumni Award, Univ Buffalo Law Sch, Citation Award, Nat Conf Christians and Jews, 1997; Jaeckle Award, SUNY, Bufflo. Mem.: Am Soc Corp Secys, Erie County Bar Asn, NY State Bar Asn. Office: Lippes Silverstein Mathias & Wexler 28 Church St Buffalo NY 14202-3908

LIPPIG, VIRGINIA ELLEN, tax accountant; b. Oak Park, Ill., Sept. 22, 1934; d. Walter C. and Irene Katherine Grottke; m. George Kenneth Lippig, Dec. 14, 1957; children: Larry, Ray, Sandra, Laura. Student Bus. and Fin., Valparaiso (Ind.) U., 1952-55, Northwestern U., Chgo., 1956-57. Acct. pvt. practice, Lombard, Ill. V.p. Police Pension Bd., Lombard, Ill., 1976-84, v.p. Davea Bd. of Accountancy, Addison, Ill., 1976-84, Good Samaritan Hosp. Adv. Bd., Downers Grove, Ill., 1980-84. Treas. Lombard Parade Com., 1970-84, Lombard Hist. Soc. 1980-84; mem. rep. Lombard Hist. Commn., 1976-80; chmn. bd. fin. St. John, 1976-92. Named Woman of Yr., Lombard (Ill.) Svc. League, 1978; recipient cert. appreciation, YWCA, 1976-95, Day Care Action Coun., Evanston, DeKalb, 1976-93, Davea Bd. of Accountancy. State of Ill., Downers Grove, Skokie, Wheaton, 1984. Mem. Nat. Soc. Pub. Accts. (Ill. chpt.), Ind. Accts. Assn. of Ill. (sec. 1978-80), Lombard C. of C. (pres. 1978). Republican. Lutheran. Avocations: swimming, fishing, singing. Office: Lombard Fin Svc Inc 108 S Main St Lombard IL 60148-2628

LIPPINCOTT, JAMES ANDREW, biochemistry and biological sciences educator; b. Cumberland County, Ill., Sept. 13, 1930; s. Marion Andrew and Esther Oral (Meeker) L.; m. Barbara Sue Barnes, June 2, 1956; children—Jeanne Marie, Thomas Russell, John James AB, Earlham Coll., 1954; A.M., Washington U., St. Louis, 1956, PhD, 1958. Lectr. botany Washington U., 1958-59; Jane Coffin Childs Meml. fellow Centre Nat. de la Recherche Scientifique, France, 1959-60; asst. prof. biol. scis. Northwestern U., Evanston, Ill., 1960-66, assoc. prof., 1966-73, prof., 1973-81, prof. biochemistry, molecular biology and cell biology, 1981-94, prof. emeritus Ill., 1994—, assoc. dean biol. scis., 1980-83. Vis. assoc. prof. U. Calif., Berkeley, 1970-71; vis. prof. Inst. Botany U. Heidelberg (Germany), 1974. Contbr. articles to profl. jours. Grantee NIH, NSF, Am. Cancer Soc., USDA Mem. Am. Soc. Biol. Chemists, Am. Soc. Plant Physiologists, Bot. Soc. Am., Am. Soc. Microbiology

LIPPINCOTT, JONATHAN RAMSAY, healthcare executive; b. Cin., Dec. 26, 1946; s. Morss d'Isay and Virginia Yvonne (Peugnet) L.; m. Nancy Todd Smith, Feb. 22, 1975; children: Jonathan J.E., Michael R.T. BA, Yale U., 1968; MLitt, Oxford U., 1972. Program research analyst human resources adminstrn. City of New York, 1973-76; exec. asst. to dir. med. ctr. U. Cin. Med. Ctr., 1977, asst. sr. v.p., 1977-84; fellow in HMO planning policy & mgmt. Harvard Community Health Plan, Brookline, Mass., 1985-86; assoc. sr. v.p. U. Cin. Med. Ctr., 1984-94; assoc. dir. U. Cin. Hosp., 1993-94; sr. v.p., chief strategic officer Health Alliance Greater Cin., 1994-97, exec. v.p., chief strategic officer, 1997—; exec. dir. bus. devel. Alliance Ptnrs., 1996-2000, bd. dirs., 2000—. Chmn., bd. Southwestern Ohio Sr. Svcs. Inc., Maple Knoll Village, 1993-96, trustee, 1988-97; bd. dirs., sec., treas. Univ. Health Maintenance Orgn., Inc., 1989-93; exec. bd. dirs. The Health Initiative, Cin.; co-dir. U. Cin. Inst. Health Policy and Health Svcs. Rsch., 1993-96, fellow, 2002—. Contbr. articles to cons. and acad. mags. Pres., bd. trustees Little Miami, Inc., Cin., 1984-85; steering com., chmn. health & human svcs. session Leadership Cin., 1983-84; vice chmn. Cin. Transp. Study Com., 1984-85. Mem. Am. Assn. Med. Colls. (midwest regional chmn. group on inst. planning 1991-93), Am. Coll. Health Care Execs., Cin. C. of C. (health care com.), Cin. Yale Club (exec. com.). Office: Health Alliance Greater Cin 3200 Burnet Ave Cincinnati OH 45229-3099

LIPPINCOTT, JOSEPH P. photojournalist, educator; b. Somerset, Pa., Mar. 12, 1940; s. Joseph Britton and Louise Frances (Picking) L.; widowed; children: Douglas B., David S.; m. Karen L. Krause, 1999. BA in Journalism, U. Iowa, 1968. Staff photographer The Miami (Fla.) Herald, 1964-67; pub. rels. dir. Lock Haven (Pa.) State Coll., 1967-68; mag. editor Caterpillar Tractor Co., Peoria, Ill., 1968-69; photo editor, photographer The Detroit Free Press, 1969-75; photo advisor The State News Mich. State U., East Lansing, 1975-84; instr. Lansing C.C., 1977-84; photo editor The Detroit News, 1984-87, The Patriot Ledger, Quincy, Mass., 1988-95; lectr. Boston U., 1990—. Author: An Introduction to Camera Maintenance, 1980, Care and Repair of Classic Cameras for Photographers and Collectors, 1999. Mem. Nat. Press Photographers Assn. (chmn. nat. portfolio critique 1994-96, Pictures of the Yr. awards). Avocation: unique photographic equipment. Home: PMB 291 95 Old Colony Ave Quincy MA 02170-2629

LIPPINCOTT, PHILIP EDWARD, retired paper products company executive; b. Camden, N.J., Nov. 28, 1935; s. J. Edward and Marjorie Nix (Spooner) L.; m. Naomi Catherine Prindle, Aug. 22, 1959; children: Grant, Kevin, Kerry. BA, Dartmouth Coll., 1957; MBA with distinction, Mich. State U., 1964. With Scott Paper Co., Phila., 1959-94, staff v.p. corp. planning, 1971, div. v.p., consumer products mktg., 1971-72, corp. v.p., mktg., 1972-75, sr. v.p., mktg., 1975-77, v.p., group exec. packaged products div., 1977—79, dir., 1978-94, pres., COO, 1980-94, chief exec. officer, 1982-94, chmn., 1983-94; ret., 1994. Chmn. bd. Campbell Soup Co., 1999-2001; bd. dirs. Campbell Soup Co., Exxon Mobil Corp.; trustee Penn Mut. Life Ins. Co. Chmn. bd. trustees Fox Chase Cancer Ctr., Phila.; mem. The Bus. Coun. Capt. U.S. Army, 1957-59. Mem. Pine Valley Country Club, Quail West Golf and Country Club, Park Meadows Country Club, Kappa Kappa Kappa, Pi Sigma Epsilon, Beta Gamma Sigma. Mem. Society Of Friends.

LIPPINCOTT, SARAH LEE, astronomer, graphologist; b. Phila., Oct. 26, 1920; d. George E. and Sarah (Evans) L.; m. Dave Garroway (dec.); m. Christian Zimmerman (dec.). Student, Swarthmore Coll., 1938-39, MA, 1950; BA, U. Pa., 1942; DSc (hon.), Villanova U., 1973. Research asst. Sproul Obs., Swarthmore (Pa.) Coll., 1941-50, research asso., 1951-72, dir., 1972-81, prof., 1977-81, prof. and dir. emeritus, 1981—, research astronomer, 1981—. Vis. assoc. in astronomy Calif. Inst. Tech., 1977. Author: (with Joseph M. Joseph) Point to the Stars, 1963, 3d edit., 1977, (with Laurence Lafore) Philadelphia, the Unexpected City, 1965; contbr. articles to profl. jours. Mem. Savoy Opera Co., Phila., 1947— ; bd. mgrs. Societe de Bienfaisance de Philadelphie, 1966-69. Recipient achievement award Kappa Kappa Gamma, 1966; Disting. Daus. of Pa. award, 1976; Fulbright fellow Paris, 1953-54; Jessie Kovalenko scholar, 1953-54. Mem. Am. Soc. Profl. Graphologists (treas. 1988-93), Rittenhouse Astron. Soc. (sec. 1946-48), Am. Astron. Soc. (lectr. 1961-84), Internat. Astron. Union (v.p. commn. 26, 1970-73, pres. 1973-75), Disting. Daus. Pa. (sec. 1988-99), Sigma Xi (pres. chpt. 1959-60). Home: 29 Kendal Dr Kennett Square PA 19348-2323 E-mail: zimlip@swarthmore.edu.

LIPPINCOTT, WALTER HEULINGS, JR. publishing executive; b. Phila., Jan. 16, 1939; s. Walter Heulings and Helen B. (Howe) L.; m. Caroline Seebohm, June 8, 1974 (div. June 1993); children: Sophie, Hugh. AB, Princeton U., 1960. With Morgan Guaranty Trust Co., N.Y.C., 1960-63; coll. traveler Harper & Row Pubs., 1963-65, editor, 1965-70, editor-in-chief, coll. dept., 1970-74; editorial dir. Cambridge Univ. Press, N.Y.C., 1974-81; assoc. dir. Cornell Univ. Press, 1982, dir., 1983-86, Princeton U. Press, N.J., 1986—. Mem.: Knickerbocker (N.Y.C.), Century (N.Y.C.). Home: 1 River Knoll Dr Titusville NJ 08560-1308 Office: Princeton U Press 41 William St Princeton NJ 08540-5237 E-mail: whl@pupress.princeton.edu.

LIPPITT, ELIZABETH CHARLOTTE, writer; b. San Francisco; d. Sidney Grant and Stella L. Student Mills Coll., U. Calif.-Berkeley. Writer, performer own satirical monologues, nat. and polit. affairs for 85 newspapers including Muncie Star, St. Louis Globe-Dem., Washington Times, Utah Ind., Jackson News, State Dept. Watch. Singer debut album Songs From the Heart; contbr. articles to 85 newspapers including N.Y. Post, L.A. Examiner, Orlando Sentinel, Phoenix Rep., The Blue Book; author: 40 Years of American History in Published Letters 1952-1992. Mem. Commn. for Free China, Conservative Caucus, Jefferson Ednl. Assn., Presdl. Adv. Commn. Recipient Congress of Freedom award, 1959, 71-73. Mem. Amvets, Nat. Trust for Hist. Preservation, Am. Security Coun., Internat. Platform Assn., Am. Conservative Union, Nat. Antivivisection Soc., High Frontier, For Our Children, Childhelp U.S.A., Free Afghanistan Com., Humane Soc. U.S., Young Ams. for Freedom, Coun. for Inter.-Am. Security, Internat. Med. Corps, Assn. Vets for Animal Rights, Met. Club, Olympic Club. Home: 2414 Pacific Ave San Francisco CA 94115-1238 *Personal philosophy: I believe in freedom of the individual.*

LIPPMAN, DOROTHY, nurse practitioner; b. Long Beach, Calif., Feb. 10, 1950; d. Emile Ferrer and Virginia Frances Lippman; children: Launa, Benjamin, Diana. ADN, Chaffey Coll., 1982; BSN, Calif. State U., Fullerton, 1995; MSN, UCLA, 1999. RN, Calif. Staff nurse St. Jude Med. Ctr., Fullerton, 1982—2002; nurse practitioner St. Jude Heritage Health, 1999—2002; outpatient wound care clin. St. Jude Med. Ctr., Calif., 1999-2000. Nursing dir. So. Calif. Am. Soc. Parenteral and Enteral Nutrition, 1995-99. Vol. We Care Program, Fullerton, 1999. Mem.: Americans Better Care of Dying, Am. Coll. Nurse Practioners, Calif. Coalition of Nurse Practioners, Nat. Conf. Gerontol. Nurse Practioners, Nat Gerontol. Nurse Assn., Nat. Acad. Nurse Prationers, Sigma Theta Tau.

LIPPMAN, JESSICA G. clinical psychologist, educator; b. Chgo., May 10, 1941; d. Solomon G. and Belle W. (Wineberg) Lippman; m. Harold M. Bornstein, June 18, 1961 (div. July 1976); 1 child, Amelia H. Barrett. BA in Social Work, NYU, 1963; MA in Learning Disabilities, Northeastern Ill. U., Chgo., 1973; PhD in Ednl. Psychology, Northwestern U., 1979. Registered clin. psychologist, Ill. Pvt. practice clin. psychology, Chgo., 1977-82; coord. clin. svcs., sr. staff Siegal Inst./Michael Reese Med. Ctr., 1979-86, chief psychologist, 1983-86; instr. clin. psychiatry and behavioral scis. Northwestern U. Med. Sch., 1991—. Orgnl. mgmt. cons., Chgo., 1996—. Contbr. articles to profl. jours.; presenter in field. Named One of Outstanding Therapists in U.S. Town & Country Mag., 1988. Mem. APA, Coun. for Nat. Register Health Svcs. Providers in Psychology. Office: 600 N McClurg Ct Chicago IL 60611-3044

LIPPMAN, LOUIS GROMBACHER, psychology educator; b. Whittier, Calif., Jan. 10, 1941; s. Robert Weiler and Ruth Major (Grombacher) L.; m. Marcia Zoe Luehrs, Dec. 21, 1965; children: Leah N., David R. BA, Stanford U., 1962; MA, Mich. State U., 1965, PhD, 1966. Teaching asst. Mich. State U., East Lansing, 1962-66; asst. prof. psychology Western Wash. U., Bellingham, 1966-69, assoc. prof., 1969-74, prof., 1974—. Vis. prof. San Diego State U., 1978. Author children's piano accompaniment book; editorial bd. mem. Jour. Irreproducible Results, The Annals of Improbable Research, 1984—; contbr. sci. and sci. humor articles to profl. jours. Mem. Am. Psychol. Soc., Psychonomic Soc., Rocky Mountain Psychol. Assn., Assn. Behavioral and Brain Scis. (assoc.), N.Am. Soc. for Psychology of Sport and Physical Activity, Northwestern Assn. Behavior Analysis, Nat. Assn. of Scholars, Sigma Xi, Psi Chi. Republican. Jewish. Avocations: walking, photography, piano. Office: Western Wash U Psychology Dept Bellingham WA 98225-9089

LIPPMAN, MURIEL MARIANNE, biomedical scientist; b. N.Y.C., Oct. 16, 1930; d. Louis George and Erna (Hirsch) L. BA, Syracuse U., 1951; MS, U. Pa., 1955; postgrad., Tufts U., 1965-66, Yale U., 1966-67; PhD, U. Chgo., 1970. Chmn. sci. dept. St. Agnes H.S., Rochester, N.Y., 1957-59, Nazareth Acad., Rochester, 1959-63; asst. prof. biology, rsch. dir. Nazareth Coll., 1963-65; scientist Retina Found., Boston, 1965-66; vis. scientist Karolinska Inst., Stockholm, 1967; assoc. prof. biology Seton Hall U., South Orange, N.J., 1970-71; sr. staff fellow Nat. Cancer Inst., Bethesda, Md., 1971-76; sr. scientist Food and Drug Adminstrn. Bur. Med. Devices, Silver Spring, 1976-77; sr. staff scientist Nat. Acad. Scis., Washington, 1977-78; dir. scientific planning and review Clement Assocs., 1978-79; pres. ERNACO, Inc., Silver Spring, 1979—, MMLI Biomed. Comm., Silver Spring, 1998—. Adj. prof. biology Am. U., Washington, 1981-83; vis. prof. Cook Coll., Rutgers State U., N.J., 1985-86; adj. prof. anatomy Frederick (Md.) C.C., 1991, No. Va. C.C., Sterling, 1992-96; vis. prof. biology U. Md., 1996, 97. Contbr. articles to profl. jours. Mem. Human Relations Commn. Montgomery County, Md., 1982-83. Recipient numerous grants and fellowships including Cancer Rsch. grantee Damon Runyon Found., 1964, Am. Cancer Soc. grantee, 1969-70, Biomedical rsch. grantee Evans Found., 1984-91, Nat. Heart, Lung and Blood Inst. NIH, 1986-87; U.S. Pub. Health fellow, 1965-66, KC Rsch. fellow, 1967, Danforth Teaching fellow U. Chgo., 1970; Teaching Excellence award Rochester Acad. Scis., 1963. Mem. Am. Med. Writers Assn., Drug Info. Assn., Sigma Xi. Office: ERNACO Inc PO Box 6522 Silver Spring MD 20916-6522

LIPPMAN, SHARON ROCHELLE, art historian, curator, art therapist, writer, artist, filmmaker; b. N.Y.C., Apr. 9, 1950; d. Emanuel and Sara (Goldberg) L. Student, Mills Coll., Columbia U., 1968; BFA, New Sch. Social Rsch., 1970, CCNY, 1972; MA in Cinema Studies, NYU, 1976, postgrad., 1987. Cert. secondary tchr., N.Y. Instr., dir., founder Sara Sch. of Creative Art, Sayville, N.Y., 1976-85; founder, exec. dir., tchr. Art Without Walls, Inc., Sayville and N.Y.C., 1985—; curator art exhbn. Heckscher State Park, East Islip, N.Y., 1985-87; exec. dir., curator Profl. Artist Network for Artists Internationally, 1991—; founder Art Without Walls, Inc., 1985—. Organizer Profl. Artist Network for Nat./Internat. Artists, 1994; curator Pub. Art in Pub. Spaces. Author: Patterns, 1968, College Poetry Press Anthology, 1970, America at the Millennium, 2000; exhibited in group shows at L.I. Children's Mus., Garden City, N.Y., 1995-97, Suffolk County Legislature, Hauppauge, N.Y., 1997, Bayport-Bluepoint Libr., 1997, East Islip Libr., 1997-98, U.S. Dept. Interior, Ft. Wadsworth, N.Y., 2001, Ellis Island Immigration Mus., N.Y., 2002, West Islip Libr., 2000, 2001, Battery Park, N.Y.C., 2002; pub. art mural History of L.I. Baymen, 1987, Immigration on the NYS Waterways, 2001; represented in permanent collection Devel. Disabilities Inst., Suffolk County Legis. Bldg., Polish Consulate, N.Y., West Islip Pub. Libr., East Islip Pub. Libr., Ctrl. Park Zoo, Coll. Art Assn. Bull. Conv. N.Y., Robert Moses State Park, N.Y., Smith Haven Mall Lake Grove, Garden City Mall, N.Y., Southside Hosp., Bayshore, N.Y. Vol. Good Samaritan Hosp., 1984, Southside Hosp., 1983, U. Stony Brook Hosp., 1985, Schneider Children's Hosp., New Hyde Park, N.Y., 1992, New Light-AIDS Patients, Smithtown, N.Y., 1993, Helen Keller Svcs. for the Blind, Hempstead, N.Y., 1993-94, St. Charles Hosp. and Rehab. Ctr., 1996, Nat. Health Bill Pub. Forum, Sayville Mid. Sch., 1996, Art Puzzles-Art Therapy Geriatrics Ward, Brookhaven (N.Y.) Meml. Hosp., 1990, Art Therapy Program Original Dept. Disabilities, Suffolk County, N.Y., 1988, Din-o-Soar Art Therapy Southside Hosp.-Pediatrics Ward, Bayshore, N.Y., 1999, Art Box-Art Therapy, Pediat. Ward Southside Hosp., Bayshore, 2000, It Takes Two Art Therapy, St. Charles Hosp., Port Jefferson, N.Y., 2000; mem. Whitney Mus., Guggenheim Mus., Mus. Modern Art, Met. Mus. Art, Jewish Mus., others; trustee Sayville Libr. Bd., 1996; bd. dirs. Friends of the Arts St. Joseph's Coll., N.Y., 1997; mem. Guggenheim Mus., Jewish Mus., Mus. of the City of N.Y., Art in Am., Art News, Am. Artist. Recipient Suffolk County New Inspiration award, 1990, Am. Artist Art Svc. award Am. Artists mag., 1993, Suffolk County Legis. proclamation, 1993, Newsday Leadership Vol. award Newsday newspaper, 1994, Nat. Women's Month award Town of Islip, 1996, Disting. Women's award Town of Islip, 1996, Nat. Poetry Press award, 1996. Mem. Orgn. Through Rehab. and Tng., Coll. Art Assn., Met. Mus. Art, Mus. Modern Art Univ. Film Assn., Sayville C. of C. Avocations: fine art, books, cinema, political science, inventions. Office: Art Without Walls Inc PO Box 341 Sayville NY 11782-0341 also: FDR Station PO Box 6344 New York NY 10150-6344 E-mail: artwithoutwalls@webtv.net.

LIPPMAN, WILLIAM JENNINGS, investment company executive; b. N.Y.C., Feb. 13, 1925; s. Henry J. and Fanny (Schapira) L.; m. Doris Kaplan, July 11, 1948; children— Howard Mark, Deborah Ellen. BBA cum laude, Coll. City N.Y., 1947; MBA, N.Y.U., 1957. Marketing mgr. Pavelle Color, Inc., N.Y.C., 1947-50; sales mgr. Terminal Home Sales Corp., 1950-55; div. mgr. King Merritt & Co., Inc., Englewood, N.J., 1955-60; pres., dir. Pilgrim Distbrs. Inc., Ft. Lee, 1960-86; pres. L.F. Rothschild Managed Trust L.F. Rothschild Fund Mgmt. Inc., N.Y.C., 1986-88, also dir.; pres. Franklin Managed Trust, New York, 1988—. Mem. faculty Fairleigh Dickinson U. Sch. Bus. Adminstrn., 1957-69; bd. govs. Investment Co. Inst. Contbg. author: Investment Dealer Digest. Mem. Nat. Assn. Securities Dealers (investment cos. com.) Home: 18 Daniel Dr Englewood NJ 07631-3736 Office: Franklin Managed Trust 1 Parker Plz Fort Lee NJ 07024-2937

LIPPMANN, MORTON, environmental health science researcher; b. Bklyn., Sept. 21, 1932; s. Samuel and Etta (Kleinfeld) L.; m. Janet Z. Gurian; children: Amy, Stanley, David. BChemE, Cooper Union, 1954; SM, Harvard U., 1955; PhD, NYU, 1967. Cert. indsl. hygienist. Indsl. hygiene engr. USPHS, Cin., 1955-57; indsl. hygienist U.S. AEC, N.Y.C., 1957-62; rsch. engr. Del Electronics Corp., Mt. Vernon, N.Y., 1962-64; rsch. scientist NYU, N.Y.C., 1964-67, asst. prof., 1967-70, assoc. prof., 1970-77, prof., 1977—. Mem. sci. adv. bd. EPA, Washington, 1982—, chmn. clean air sci. adv. com., 1983-87; mem. bd. sic. counselors NIOSH, Atlanta, 1988-93, chair, 1991-93. Lead author: Chemical Contamination in Human Environment, 1979; editor: Environmental Toxicants, 1992, 2000; contbr. over 260 sci. papers to profl. jours. Recipient David Sinclair award Am. Assn. Aerosol Rsch., 1990, Donald E. Cummings award Am. Indsl. Hygiene Assn., 1991, Herbert E. Stokinger award Am. Conf. Govtl. Indsl. Hygienists, 1993, Henry F. Smyth Jr. award Am. Acad. Indsl. Hygiene, 1996. Office: NYU Sch Medicine 57 Old Forge Rd Tuxedo Park NY 10987-5007 E-mail: lippmann@env.med.nyu.edu.

LIPPOLD, JUDITH ROSENTHAL, retired occupational therapist; b. Chgo., Feb. 27, 1931; d. Irving and Shulamite Hurwitz Rosenthal; m. Henry William Lippold, May 4, 1952; children: Luanne Joy, Laura Beth. BS in occupational therapy, U. Wisc., 1951. Occupational therapist Holladay Park Hosp., Portland, Oreg., 1952-53, Ruth Lodge Residential Tng. Ctr. for C.P. Children, Chgo., 1953-54, The Threshold, Champaign, Ill., 1968-72, Sacred Heart Hosp., Eau Claire, Wis., 1972-96, Next Step, Brotoloc Corp., Eau Claire, 1996-97; facilitator Renewing Life program Regional Cancer Ctr., Sacred Heart Hosp., 1997—. Leadership roles PTA and Girl Scout Am., Champaign, Ill., 1962-72; newsletter editor Chippewa Valley Ostomy Assn., 1992—. Avocations: reading, drawing, painting, writing. Home: 1304 Bradley Ave Eau Claire WI 54701-6523

LIPPOLD, RICHARD, sculptor; b. Milw., May 3, 1915; s. Adolph and Elsa (Schmidt) L.; m. Louise Greuel, Aug. 24, 1940; children— Lisa, Tiana, Ero. Student, U. Chgo., 1934-37; B.F.A., Art Inst. Chgo., 1937; D.F.A. (hon.), Ripon Coll., 1968. Tchr. Layton Sch. Art, Milw., 1940-41, U. Mich., 1941-44, Goddard Coll., 1945-47; head art sect. Trenton (N.J.) Jr. Coll., 1948-52; prof. Hunter Coll., N.Y.C., 1952-67. Works exhibited Inst. Arts, Detroit, 1946-47, St. Louis City Mus., 1946, Toronto (Ont.) Mus., 1947, Whitney Mus., N.Y.C., 1947, 49, 51-53, 76, Calif. Palace Legion of Honor, San Francisco, 1948, Fundacao de Arte Moderne, Sao Paulo, Brazil, 1948, Mus. Modern Art, N.Y.C., 1951-53, 63, Tate Gallery, London, 1953, Musée d'Art Moderne, Paris, 1955, Nat. Collection Fine Arts, Washington, 1976, Nat. Air and Space Mus., Washington, 1976, Biennale, Venice, 1988; one-man show Willard Gallery, N.Y.C., 1947-48, 50, 53, 62, 68, 73, Arts Club, Chgo., Layton Art Gallery, Milw., 1953, Haggerty Mus., Milw., 1990, 20th Century Sculpture, Nssau County Mus. of Art, NY, 1999, The Amer. Century, Whitney Mus. of Art, NY, 1999; represented in collections Addison Gallery Am. Art, Andover, Mass., Fogg Mus., Harvard U., Wadsworth Atheneum, Hartford, Mus. Modern Art, Whitney Mus., N.Y.C., Newark Mus., Met. Mus. Art, N.Y.C., Detroit Art Inst., Des Moines Art Inst., Brooks Gallery, Memphis, Mobile (Ala.) Art Mus., Musée de Vin, Pavillac, France, Munson-Williams-Proctor Inst., Utica, N.Y., Va. Mus. Fine Arts, Milw. Art Center, Yale U. Art Gallery, others, also pvt. collections, U.S. and Europe; commns. include Harvard U., 1950, Inland Steel Bldg, Chgo., 1958, Four Seasons Restaurant, Seagram Bldg., N.Y.C., 1959, Stage Set, Spoleto, Italy, 1959; Portsmouth (R.I.) Priory Ch, 1960, Pan Am Bldg., N.Y.C., 1961, Avery Fisher Hall, Lincoln Center, N.Y.C., 1961, Jesse Jones Hall, Houston, 1965, St. Mary's Cathedral, San Francisco, 1967, Christian Sci. Center, Boston, 1974, Hyatt Regency Atlanta, 1975, Fairlane Plaza, Dearborn, Mich., 1975; 115 foot stainless steel sculpture on mall in front, Air and Space Mus., Washington, 1976; King's Retiring Room, Riyadh, Saudi Arabia, 1977, Columbia (S.C.) Mall, 1977, Kish Island, Iran, 1978, Hyatt Regency, Milw., 1980, Shiga Sacred Garden, Kyoto, Japan, 1981; 250 foot sculpture Park Ave Atrium Bldg., N.Y.C., 1981, One Fin. Ctr., Boston, 1984, Deutsche Bank, Frankfurt, W. Ger., 1985, First Interstate Bank, Seattle, 1985, Sohio Hdqrs., Cleve., 1986, 200 foot high outdoor sculpture, Seoul, South Korea, 1986, Atrium Sculpture for Crystal City, Va., 1986, Marina Square, Singapore, 1986, Orange County Ctr. for Performing Arts, Costa Mesa, Calif., 1987, Atrium Sculpture and Tapestry, Alexandria, Va., 1988, Atrium Sculpture, San Diego, 1990, 95, Haggerty Mus. Retrospective, Marquette U., Milw., 1991, Montrone Residence, La Jolla, 1992, Conv. Ctr., Charlotte, N.C., 1995. Recipient 3d prize Internat. Sculpture Competition, Inst. Contemporary Arts, London, 1953, Creative Arts award Brandeis U., 1958, Silver medal Archtl. League N.Y., 1960, Honor award Mcpl. Art Soc. N.Y., 1963, Fine Arts medal AIA, 1970 Mem. Nat. Inst. Arts and Letters (v.p. 1966) Address: PO Box 248 Locust Valley NY 11560-0248

LIPPOLD, ROLAND WILL, surgeon; b. Staunton, Ill., May 1, 1916; s. Frank Carl and Ella (Immenroth) L.; m. Margaret Cookson, June 1, 1947; children: Mary Ellen Lippold Elvick, Catherine Anne Lippold Rolf, Carol Sue Lippold Webber. BS, U. Ill., 1940, MD, 1941. Diplomate Am. Bd. Surgery. Intern Grant Hosp., Chgo., 1941-42, resident in surgery, 1942-43, 47-48, St. Francis Hosp., Evanston, Ill., 1946-47; fellow in pathology Cook County Hosp., Chgo., 1947-48, resident in surgery, 1949-50; practice medicine specializing in surgery, 1950-53; also asst. in anatomy U. Ill., 1950-53; practice medicine specializing in surgery Sacramento, 1953-68; chief med. officer No. Reception Ctr.-Clinic, Calif. Youth Authority, 1954-68, chief med. services, 1968-79. Cons. in med. care in correctional instns.; cons. Calif. State Personnel Bd. Contbr. articles to med. publs. Chmn. Calif. Expn. Hall of Health, 1971-72. Comdr. M.C., USNR, 1943-73, PTO. Mem. Sacramento Surg. Soc., Sacramento County Med. Soc., Calif. Med. Assn., AMA, Sacramento Hist. Soc. (life). Republican. Lutheran. Home: 1811 Eastern Ave Sacramento CA 95864-1724

LIPPS, JERE HENRY, paleontology educator; b. L.A., Aug. 28, 1939; s. Henry John and Margaret (Rosaltha) L.; m. Karen Elizabeth Loeblich, June 25, 1964 (div. 1971); m. Susannah McClintock, Sept. 28, 1973; children: Jeremy Christian, Jamison William. BA, UCLA, 1962, PhD, 1966. Asst. prof. U. Calif., Davis, 1967-70, assoc. prof., 1970-75, prof., 1975-88, Berkeley, 1988—, prof. paleontology, 1988-89, prof. integrative biology, 1989—; dir. Mus. Paleontology, 1989-97. Dir. Inst. Ecology U. Calif., Davis, 1972-73, chmn. dept. geology, 1971-72, 79-84, chmn. dept. integrative biology, Berkeley, 1991-94. Contbr. articles to sci. publs. Fellow, dir. Cushman Found. Recipient U.S. Antarctic medal NSF, 1975; Lipps Island, Antarctica named in his honor, 1979. Fellow: CSICOP, AAAAS, Cushman Found. (pres. 1983—84), Geol. Soc. Am., Calif. Acad. Scis.; mem.: Coun. for Media Integrity, Paleontol. Soc. (pres. 1996—97). Avocation: scuba diving. Office: U Calif Mus Paleontology #4780 1101 Valley Life Sciences Bldg Berkeley CA 94720-4780 E-mail: jlipps@uclink4.berkeley.edu.

LIPPS, THOMAS W. lawyer; b. Oakland, Nebr., July 30, 1954; s. T. Wayne and Rita V. Lipps; m. Jayne Hansen, Nov. 23, 1984; children: Kirsten, Samuel. BS, U. Nebr., 1976, JD, 1979. Ptnr. Peterson & Lipps, Algona, Iowa, 1984—. Chmn., 5th Congl. Dist. Iowa Dem. Party, 2000—, mem. com., 1998. Mem. Iowa Trial Lawyers Assn. (bd. dirs. 1998-, Pub. Justice award 2000), Lions Club (pres. 1990-91). Lutheran. Avocations: bicycling, sailing. Office: Peterson & Lipps PO Box 575 Algona IA 50511 E-mail: tlipps@ncn.net.

LIPPY, KAREN DOROTHY FETHE, nurse psychotherapist; b. Balt., July 2, 1946; d. Vernon Harold and Dorothy Margaret (Wirth) Fethe; m. Robert Eugene Lippy, July 29, 1972; 1 child, Jarrod Blaire. BS in Nursing, U. Md., Balt, 1972, MS in Nursing, 1975. Cert. clin. specialist in adult psychiat./mental health nursing, master addictions counselor, critical incident stress mgmt., eye movement desensitization and reprocessing, diplomate Am. Coll. Profl. Mental Health Practitioners; cert. nursing adminstrn.-advanced, nurse psychotherapist. Clin. nurse specialist Springfield Hosp. Ctr., Sykesville, Md., 1975-79, asst. dir. nursing, 1979-86, dir. nursing, 1986-97; nurse psychotherapist Reentry Mental Health Svcs., Westminster, 1983—; mem. Carroll County Criticial Incident Stress Mgmt. Team, 1999—. Mem. task force on RN standards of practice Md. State Bd. Nursing; mem. patient rights, classification, RN job specification, and credentialing/privileging task forces Md. Mental Hygiene Adminstrn. Recipient Gov.'s Citation for Excellence, State of Md., Achievement in Nursing Adminstrn., Md. Dept. Mental Hygiene. Mem. ANA, Md. Nurses Assn. (dist. bd. dirs.), Internat. Critical Incident Stress Found., EMDR Internat. Assn., Sigma Theta Tau, Phi Kappa Phi. Home: 2519 Bird View Rd Westminster MD 21157-8309 Office: 40 S Church St Ste 105 Westminster MD 21157-5414

LIPS, SUSAN R. non-profit administrator; b. Atlanta, Sept. 23, 1949; d. Stanley and Gladys Renas; m. David Allan Lips, Sept. 20, 1970; children: Alan, Lisa, Gary, Renee. BA, Ga. State U., 1970. Asst. to dir. Ga. Heart Assn., Atlanta, 1970-71, Am. ORT, Atlanta, 1980-94, regional dir., 1995—. Pres. Epstein Sch. PTA, Atlanta, 1983-84, Shearith Israel Sisterhood, Atlanta, 1987-88; mem. Hadassah, v.p., 1981-82. Office: Am ORT 3781 Presidential Pkwy Atlanta GA 30340 E-mail: atlanta@aort.org.

LIPSCHULTZ, JEREMY HARRIS, communication educator; b. Chgo., Feb. 12, 1958; BA in Polit. Sci., U. Ill., 1980; MA in Reporting, Sangamon State U., 1981; PhD in Journalism, So. Ill. U., 1990. Adj. instr. U. Evansville, Ind., 1983; news dir., anchor-reporter Stas. WGBF-AM/WHKC-FM, Evansville, 1981-84; grad. asst., instr. So. Ill. U., Carbondale, 1985-88; prof. U. Nebr., Omaha, 1989—, chair grad. program com., 1995-2000, interim chair comm. dept., 2000. Author: Broadcast Indecency: F.C.C. Regulation and the First Amendment, 1997, Free Expression in the Age of the Internet: Social and Legal Boundaries, 2000, Crime and Local Television News: Dramatic, Breaking and Live From the Scene, 2002; editl. asst. Journalism Monographs, 1986-87; book reviewer: Communications and the Law, Journal of Radio Studies; editl. bd. Jour. of Broadcasting and Electronic Media, Jour. and Mass Comm. Edn., Jour. of Radio Studies, Comm. and the Law; contbr. articles to profl. jours. Mem. Assn. for Edn. in Journalism (chair law dvsn. rsch. 1991-92, profl. freedom and responsibility 1992-93, tchr. 1993-94), Nebr. Writers Guild. Office: U Nebr Coll Arts & Scis Arts and Sci Hall 107-C 6001 Dodge St Omaha NE 68182-0112 Fax: 402-554-3836. E-mail: jlipschultz@mail.unomaha.edu.

LIPSCHUTZ, MARIAN SHAW, secondary education educator, writer; b. Bklyn., Apr. 1, 1940; d. Melville Austin Shaw and Marguerite Frances (Van Dyke) Morgan; m. Ernst Lipschutz, Oct. 16, 1967 (dec. Sept. 1995); children: David Alexander, Sirene Rose Alexandra. BA, U. Mich., 1961; MA, Calif. State U., L.A., 1967; MFA, U. Calif., Irvine, 1977. Tchr. English, Westridge Sch., Pasadena, Calif., 1964—. Author: (novel) Land of Hunchbacks, 1988.

LIPSCHUTZ, MICHAEL ELAZAR, chemistry educator, consultant, researcher; b. Phila., May 24, 1937; s. Maurice and Anna (Kaplan) L.; m. Linda Jane Lowenthal, June 21, 1959; children: Joshua Henry, Mark David, Jonathan Mayer BS, Pa. State U., 1958; S.M., U. Chgo., 1960, PhD, 1962. Gastdocent U. Bern, Switzerland, 1964-65; from asst. prof. chemistry to assoc. head dept. Purdue U., West Lafayette, Ind., 1965—93, prof. chemistry, 1993—, assoc. head dept. of chemistry, 1993—2001; dir. chemistry ops. Purdue Rare Isotope Measurement Lab. (PRIME), 1990—2002. Vis. assoc. prof. Tel Aviv U., 1971-72; vis. prof. Max-Planck Inst. fuer Chemie, Mainz, Fed. Republic Germany, 1987; mem. panel space sci. experts Com. on Space Rsch., Space Agy. Forum of the Internat. Space Yr., Internat. Coun. Sci. Unions, 1990-92; cons. in field. Assoc. editor 11th Lunar and Planetary Sci. Conf., 3 vols., 1980; fin. editor Meteoritics and Planetary Sci., 1992-2000; contbr. numerous articles to profl. jours. Served to 1st lt. USAR, 1958-64 Recipient Cert. of Recognition, NASA, 1979, Cert. of Spl. Recognition, 1979, Group Achievement award, 1983, Cert. Appreciation, Nat. Commn. on Space, 1986; postdoctoral fellow NSF, 1964-65, NATO, 1964-65; Fulbright fellow, 1971-72 Fellow Meteoritical Soc. (treas. 1978-84, mem. joint com. on pubs. of Geochem. and Meteoritical Socs. 1985-93, fin. officer 1985-93, chmn. 1988-90); mem. AAAS, Am. Chem. Soc., Am. Geophys. Union, Planetary Soc., Internat. Astron. Union (U.S. rep. 1988—), Sigma Xi. Achievements include having minor planet named in honor of Lipschutz by Internat. Astronomical Union, 1987. Office: Purdue U Dept Chemistry West Lafayette IN 47907

LIPSCHUTZ-YEVICK, MIRIAM AMALIE, mathematician; b. Schevening, Holland, Netherlands, Aug. 28, 1924; came to U.S., 1940; d. Max and Pola (Majerczyck) L.; m. George Yevick, May 15, 1945; 1 child, David. BA, NYU, 1943; MS, MIT, 1945, PhD, 1947. Rsch. assoc. U. Md., College Park, 1951-52, Columbia U., N.Y.C., 1952-53; instr. CUNY, 1954-89; asst. prof. Adelphi Coll., Garden City, N.J., 1956-60; assoc. prof. Rutgers State U., Newark, 1964-87. Vis. fellow Princeton (N.J.) U., 1972-73, 82-83. Author: Mathematics for the Billions, ; contbr. articles to Am. Math. Soc., Am. Jour. Physics Mem. Am. Math. Soc. Inst. Math. Stats. Democrat. Jewish. Achievements include origination of field of holographic logic, special course on mathematics for life and society. Home: 22 Pelham St Princeton NJ 08540-5315

LIPSCOMB, ANNA ROSE FEENY, entrepreneur, arts organizer, fundraiser; b. Greensboro, N.C., Oct. 29, 1945; d. Nathan and Matilda (Carotenuto) L. Student langs, Alliance Francaise, Paris, 1967-68; BA in English and French summa cum laude, Queens Coll., 1977; diploma advanced Spanish, Forester Instituto Internat., San Jose, Costa Rica, 1990; postgrad., Inst. Allende San Miguel, Mex., 1991. Reservations agt. Am. Airlines, St. Louis, 1968-69, ticket agt., 1969-71; coll. rep. CBS, Holt Reinhart Winston, Providence, 1977-79; sr. aquisitions editor Dryden Press, Chgo., 1979-81; owner, mgr. Historic Taos (N.Mex.) In, 1981-89, Southwest Moccasin and Drum, Taos; pres., co-owner Southwest Products, Ltd., 1991—; owner, pres. All One Tribe, Inc., 1996—. Fundraiser Taos Arts Celebrations, 1989—; bd. dirs. N.Mex. Hotel and Motel Assn., 1986—; sem. leader Taos Women Together, 1989; founder All One Tribe Found., 1994, all One Tribe Drumming Festival, 1991—; mem. adv. bd. Drum Bus. Mag., 1996—; presenter workshop in field. Editor: Intermediate Accounting, 1980, Business Law, 1981; contbr. articles to profl. jours.; patentee in field. Bd. dirs., 1st v.p. Taos Arts Assn., 1982-85; founder, bd. dirs. Taos Spring Arts Celebration, 1983—; founder, dir. Meet-the-Artist Series, 1983—; bd. dirs., co-founder Spring Arts N.Mex., 1986; founder Yuletide in Taos, 1988, A Taste of Taos, 1988; bd. dirs. Music From Angel Fire, 1988—; founding mem. Assn. Hist. Hotels, Boulder, 1983—; organizer Internat. Symposium on Arts, 1985; bd. dirs. Arts in Taos, 1983, Taoschool, Inc., 1985-99, Roadrunner Recyclers, 1995—, TALKBACK, Taos, 1997-98; mem. adv. bd. Chamisa Mesa Ednl. Ctr., Taos, 1990—; organizer Drumming the Year 2000, 1996—. Recipient Outstanding English Student of Yr. award Queens Coll., 1977; named Single Outstanding Contbr. to the Arts in Taos, 1986. Mem. Millicent Rogers Mus. Assn., Taos Lodgers Assn. (mktd. task force 1989), Taos County C. of C. (1st v.p. 1988-89, bd. dirs. 1987-89, advt. com. 1986-89, chmn. nominating com. 1989), Taos Women Bus. Owners, Phi Beta Kappa. Home: Talpa Rte Taos NM 87571 Office: PO Drawer N Taos NM 87571

LIPSCOMB, JEFFREY JON, financial advisor; b. San Diego, May 8, 1946; s. Willis L. and Marjorie (Jones) L.; m. Jo Ann Elaine Nielsen, Oct. 1, 1983; 1 child, Amanda Nielsen. Student, Occidental Coll., 1964-68, Harvard U., 1971, New England Conservatory Music, 1972. Cert. fin. mgr. Chief cash flow analyst St. Johnsbury Co., Cambridge, Mass., 1970-81; pvt. investor San Diego, 1981-88; registered rep. New England Securities, Sacramento, 1988-97. Registered investment specialist Bankam. Investment Svcs., 1997-99; with Merrill Lynch Pvt. Client Group, 2000—. Columnist (fin. commentary) The Bus. Jour. Sacramento, 1990-91. Mem. East Sacramento (Calif.) Improvement Assn., 1988-97; pianist celebrity benefit concerts Stanford Children's Home, Sacramento, 1989. Mem. Inst. Cert. Fund Specialists, Internat. Assn. Fin. Planning (practitioner divsn. 1993—), New Eng. Leaders Assn., Sutter Lawn Tennis Club (pres. 1992-93), The Sutter Club, Investment Trust Boston Cornerstone Club. Republican. Presbyterian. Avocations: classical music, genealogy, tennis, chess. E-mail: jeff_lipscomb@ml.com., jefflipscomb@hotmail.com.

LIPSCOMB, OSCAR HUGH, archbishop; b. Mobile, Ala., Sept. 21, 1931; s. Oscar Hugh and Margaret (Saunders) L. STL, Gregorian U., Rome, 1957; PhD, Cath. U. Am., 1963. Ordained priest Roman Cath. Ch., 1956; consecrated bishop Roman Cath. Ch., 1980. Asst. pastor, Mobile, 1959-65; tchr. McGill Inst., 1959-60, 61-62; vice chancellor Diocese of Mobile-Birmingham, 1963-66, chancellor, 1966-80; pastor St. Patrick Parish, Mobile, 1966-71; lectr. history Spring Hill Coll., 1971-72; asst. pastor St. Matthew Parish, 1971-79, Cathedral Immaculate Conception, Mobile, 1979-80; adminstr. sede vacante Diocese of Mobile, 1980, now archbishop. Pres. Cath. Housing Mobile, Mobile Senate Priests, 1978-80; chmn. com. on doctrine Nat. Conf. Cath. Bishops, 1988-91. Author articles, papers in field. Chmn. bd. dirs.

Mobile Mus., 1966-88, Ala. Dept. Archives and History, 1979—, chmn., 1999—; chmn. bd. dirs. Cath. U. Am., Washington, 1983-98, Spring Hill Coll., Mobile, 1982—; chmn. NCCB Com. on Ecumenical and Interreligious Affairs, 1993-96, Cath. Common Ground Initiative, 1996—, chmn. com. on the liturgy, 1999—; mem. Mixed Internat. Commn. for Theol. Dialogue Between the Cath. Ch. and the Orthodox Ch., 1999-2002; chmn. bd. govs. N.Am. Coll., Rome, 1982-85; mem. Vox Clara commn. Congregation for Divine Worship, Rome, 2002--. Mem. Am. Cath. Hist. Assn., So. Hist. Assn., Ala. Hist. Assn. (pres. 1971-72, exec. com. 1981-88), Hist. Mobile Preservation Soc., Lions. Address: 36633 400 Government St PO Box 1966 Mobile AL 36633-1966

LIPSCOMB, STEPHEN LEON, mathematics educator, researcher; b. Junior, W.Va., Jan. 31, 1944; s. David Leon and Dema Ann (Alkire) L.; m. Patrecia Ann Skidmore, Sept. 15, 1962; children: Stephen Leon, Darrin Joel. BE, Fairmont State Coll., 1965; MMath, W.Va. U., 1967; PhD in Math., U. Va., 1973. High sch. tchr. and coach, Rehoboth Beach, Del., 1965-66; sr. mathematician Naval Surface Weapons Ctr., Dahlgren, Va., 1967-83; eminent scholar in math. Mary Washington Coll., Fredericksburg, 1983-84, chmn. dept. math. sci. and physics, 1984-86, chair dept. math., 1990-95. Adj. prof. math. Va. Poly. Int. and State U., 1976-92; sr. fellow Navy-Am. Soc. Engring. Edn., 1994, 95, 99-2001. Conbr. numerous articles to tech. jours. Mem. Am. Math. Soc. (author vol 46 in math. surveys and monograph series). Achievements include invention of Lipscomb's topological space, path notation in inverse semigroup theory, alternating semigroups; pioneering many mathematical concepts including first thurst integral programs for U.S. navy; chairing tiger team in the Tomahawk missile system prior to 1983 operational evaluation. Home: 8809 Robert E Lee Dr Spotsylvania VA 22553-3584 Office: Mary Washington Coll Dept Math Fredericksburg VA 22401 E-mail: slipscom@mwc.edu.

LIPSCOMB, THOMAS HEBER, III, information technology executive; b. Washington, Sept. 12, 1938; s. Thomas Heber and Louise Buchanan (Heiss) L.; m. Christine Young Jones, Aug. 22, 1981; children: Peter Scott, Adrienne Clare. BA, Coll. William and Mary, 1961; MA, Ind. U., 1965. Editor Bobbs-Merrill Co., 1965-67, Stein & Day Pubs., 1967-69; sr. editor Prentice-Hall, Inc., 1969-70; exec. editor, editor-in-chief Dodd, Mead & Co., 1970-73; pres. Mason & Lipscomb Pubs., 1973-74; ptnr. Hamilton Assocs., 1974-76; pres., CEO Times Books (N.Y. Times Book Co.), 1976-81; chmn. bd. New Capital Publs., Inc., 1981-85; pres. Delphi Assocs., N.Y.C., 1985-87; pres., CEO Cryptologics Internat., 1988-91, Infosafe Sys., Inc., N.Y.C., 1992-96, chmn., 1996-97, Ctr. for the Digital Future, 1997—. Chmn. bd. Atlantech Aquaculture Ltd., chmn., CEO Cardiact, Inc., 1999—. Contbr. articles to N.Y. Times, Wall St. Jour.nal, Washington Post, others; holder patents in digital tech. Mem. N.Y. Rep. County Com., 1971-80; mem. exec. bd. Am. Ctr. PEN, 1973-79; trustee Internat. Ctr. for Econ. Growth, Robert Coll., Istanbul, Turkey, 1973-81; mem. panel of advisors George Polk Award, 1977—, Mus. Digital Licensing Collection; chmn. N.Y. Vet.'s Leadership Program, 1985-88; dir. Giraffe Project, 1989—, NYU Ctr. Copyright in New Media. Served to lt. U.S. Army, 1961-64. Fellow Digital Copyright Forum; mem. Coun. on Fgn. Relations, Internat. Broadcast Inst., East-West Inst. Security Studies, Gibraltar-Am. Coun., St. Nicholas Soc., N.Y. Acad. Scis., Holland Lodge, Mid-Atlantic Club, Nat. Press Club. Office: 145 E 74th St Apt 4B New York NY 10021-3225 E-mail: tom@digitalfuture.org.

LIPSCOMB, THOMAS HEBER, JR. retired civil engineer; b. Lexington, Miss., Dec. 11, 1912; s. Thomas Heber and Lutie (Scott) L.; m. Louise Buchanan Heiss, June 6, 1935; children: Thomas III, Peg, Jane. BS, U.S. Mil. Acad., 1934; MS in Engring., Cornell U., 1938. Commd. 2d lt. U.S. Army, 1934, advanced through grades to maj. gen., 1962, ret., 1968; engr. U.S. Army Corps Engrs., various, 1938-62; exec. dir. Del. River Port Authority, Camden, N.J., 1968-70; gen. mgr. Southeast Mich. Transp. Authority, Detroit, 1970-74; pvt. practice Moorestown, NJ, 1974—94; ret., 1994. Cons. Met. Transp. Devel. Authority, San Diego, 1976-78. Fellow ASCE (S. Jersey br., N.J. sect. bd. dirs. 1984-86), Union League, Chi Epsilon. Achievements include constrn. of 3 dams on Columbian River and tributaries, 1951-54, serving as divsn. engr. N. Atlantic Divsn. U.S. Army Corps of Engrs., 1959-62, engr. U.S. Forces Far East, 1958-59, commdr. Ft. Leonard Wood, Mo., 1965-67. Home: 309 Bridgeboro Rd Apt 2345 Moorestown NJ 08057-1427

LIPSCOMB, WILLIAM NUNN, JR. physical chemistry educator; b. Cleve., Dec. 9, 1919; s. William Nunn and Edna Patterson (Porter) Lipscomb; m. Mary Adele Sargent, May 20, 1944; children: Dorothy Jean, James Sargent; m. Jean Craig Evans, 1983; 1 child Jenna. BS, U. Ky., 1941, DSc (hon.) , 1963; PhD, Calif. Inst. Tech., 1946; DSc (hon.) , U. Munich, 1976; DSc (hon.) , L.I. U., 1977; DSc (hon.) , Rutgers U., 1979, Gustavus Adolphus Coll., 1980; DSc (hon.) , Marietta Coll., 1981; DSc (hon.) , Miami U., 1983, U. Denver, 1985, Ohio State U., 1991; DSc (hon.) , Transylvania U., 1992. Phys. chemist Office of Sci. R&D, 1942—46; faculty U. Minn., Mpls., 1946—59, asst. prof., 1946—50, assoc. prof., 1950—54, acting chief phys. chemistry div., 1952—54, prof. and chief phys. chemistry div., 1954—59; prof. chemistry Harvard U., Cambridge, Mass., 1959—71, Abbott and James Lawrence prof., 1971—90, prof. emeritus, 1990—. Mem. U.S. Nat. Commn. for Crystallography, 1954—59, 1960—63, 1965—67; chmn. program com. 4th Internat. Congress of Crystallography, Montreal, 1957; mem. sci. adv. bd. Robert A. Welch Found.; mem. adv. bd. Mich. Molecular Biology Inst.; mem. adv. com. Inst. Amorphous Studies; mem. sci. adv. com. Nova Pharms., Daltex Med. Svc., Gensia Pharms., Binary Therapeutics. Author: The Boron Hydrides, 1963; author: (with G.R. Eaton) NMR Studies of Boron Hydrides and Related Compounds, 1969; assoc. editor: Jour. Chem. Physics, 1955—57; contbr. articles to profl. jours. Clarinetist, mem. Amateur Chamber Music Players. Named Robert Welch Found. lectr., 1966, 1971, Howard U. disting. lecture series, 1966, George Fisher Baker lectr., Cornell U., 1969, centenary lectr., Chem. Soc., London, 1972, lectr., Weizmann Inst., Rehovoth, Israel, 1974, Evans award lectr., Ohio State U., 1974, Gilbert Newton Lewis Meml. lectr., U. Calif., Berkeley, 1974, lectr., Mich. State U., 1975, U. Iowa, 1975, Ill. Inst. Tech., 1976; recipient Harrison Howe award in chemistry, 1958, Disting. Alumni Centennial award, U. Ky., 1965, Disting. Svc. in advancement inorganic chemistry, Am. Chem. Soc., 1968, George Ledlie prize, Harvard, 1971, Nobel prize in chemistry, 1976, Disting. Alumni award, Calif. Inst. Tech., 1977, First Outstanding Alumni award, U. Ky., 1999, Sr. U.S. Scientist award, Alexander von Humboldt-Stiftung, 1979, award lecture, Internat. Acad. Quantum Molecular Sci., 1980; fellow Guggenheim, Oxford U., Eng., 1954—55, Cambridge U., Eng., 1972—73, nSF sr. postdoctoral fellow, 1965—66, Overseas fellow, Churchill Coll., Cambridge, Eng., 1966, 1973. Fellow: Am. Phys. Soc., Am. Acad. Arts and Scis.; mem.: NAS, Academie Europeenne des Scis., des Arts et des Lettres, The Netherlands Acad. Arts and Scis. (fgn.), Math. Assn. Bioinorganic Scientists (hon.), Royal Soc. Chemistry (hon.), Am. Crystallographic Assn. (pres. 1955), Am. Chem. Soc. (chmn. Minn. sect. 1949—50, Peter Debye award phys. chemistry 1973), Phi Mu Epsilon, Sigma Pi Sigma, Phi Lambda Upsilon, Alpha Chi Sigma, Sigma Xi, Phi Beta Kappa. Office: Harvard U Dept Chemistry & Chem Biol 12 Oxford St Cambridge MA 02138-2902 E-mail: lipscomb@chemistry.harvard.edu.*

LIPSEY, JOSEPH, JR. water bottling company executive, retail and wholesale corporation executive; b. Selma, Ala., Sept. 12, 1934; s. Joseph and Anna (Bendersky) L.; m. Betty Fay Willian, June 5, 1960; children: Debora, Joseph III, Elizabeth, Tami. BA, La. State U., 1955, LLB, 1957; grad. Owner/Pres. Mgmt. Program, Harvard Grad. Sch. Bus., 1985. Bar: La. 1957, U.S. Dist. Ct. La. 1957, Korea 1959, Ryukyu Islands 1958. Ptnr. Howell & Lipsey, Baton Rouge, 1960-65; v.p. Lipsey's Wholesale, 1977—. Pres. So. Media Rsch. Co., Monroe, La., 1984-92; chmn. Composite Analysis Group, Inc., Alexandria, 1989—; CEO Lipsey Mountain Spring Water, Atlanta, 1990—, Nantahalla Spring Water Bottling Co., Highlands, N.C., 1994—; chmn., sec.-treas. EAS Pub. Co., Inc., 1994—; bd. dirs., ind. dir. Weingarten Golden Stae, Inc., Houston, 2001--; speaker OPM 10 Harvard U., 1985; lectr. La. State U. Law Sch., Baton Rouge, 1961-63, Furman Sch. Bus., Tulane U.; mem. chancellor's bd. Paul M. Hebert Law Ctr., La. State U., 2001--; chmn. Fashion Mchts. Conf., N.Y.C., 1977-81. Mem. exec. com. Com. for a Better La., Baton Rouge, 1971-86; pres. La. State U. Found., 1980-81. Capt. USAF, 1957-60. Inducted into La. State U. Law Sch. Hall Fame, 1987. Mem. La. State C. of C. (pres. 1973-75), Alexandria C. of C. (pres. 1971-72), Bus. Execs. for Nat. Security, Rotary. Democrat. Jewish. Business E-Mail: lipsey@lipseywater.com.

LIPSEY, RICHARD GEORGE, economist, educator; b. Victoria, B.C., Can., Aug. 28, 1928; s. Richard Andrew and Faith Thirell (Ledingham) L.; m. Diana Louise Smart, Mar. 17, 1960; children: Mark Alexander (stepson), Mathew Richard, Joanna Louise, Claudia Amanda. BA with honours, U. B.C., 1950, LLD (hon.) , 1999; MA, U. Toronto, 1953; PhD, London Sch. Econs., 1958; LLD (hon.) , McMaster U., 1984, Victoria U., 1985, Carleton U., 1986, Queens U., 1990; DSc (hon.) , Toronto U., 1992; DLitt (hon.) , Guelph U., 1993; LLD (hon.) , U. Western Ont., 1994; LL.D (hon.) , U. Essex, 1996; LL.D (hon.) (hon.) , U. B.C., 1999. Rsch. asst. B.C. Dept. Trade and Industry, 1950-53; from asst. lectr. to prof. econs. London Sch. Econs., 1955-63; prof. econs., chmn. dept., dean Sch. Social Studies, U. Essex, Eng., 1965-69; vis. prof. U. B.C., 1969-70, U. Colo., 1973-74; Irving Fisher vis. prof. Yale U., 1979-80; Sir Edward Peacock prof. econs. Queens U., Kingston, Ont., 1970-87; prof. Simon Fraser U., Vancouver, B.C., 1989-97, prof. emeritus, 1997—. Sr. rsch. advisor C.D. Howe Inst., 1983-89; dir. rsch. into growth in U.K. Nat. Econ. Devel. Coun. U.K., 1961-63; mem. coun. and planning com. Nat. Inst. Econ. and Social Rsch. U.K., 1962-69; mem. bd. Social Sci. Rsch. Coun. U.K., 1966-69. Author: An Introduction to Positive Economics, 9th edit, 1998, The Theory of Customs Unions: A General Equilibrium Analysis, 1971; co-author: An Introduction to a Mathematical Treatment of Economics, 3d edit, 1977, Economics, 12th edit., 1999, Mathematical Economics, 1976, An Introduction to the U.K. Economy, 1983, 4th edit., 1993, Common Ground for the Canadian Common Market, 1984, Canada's Trade Options in a Turbulent World, 1985, Global Imbalances, 1987, First Principles of Economics, 1988, 3d edit., 1996, Evaluating the Free Trade Deal, 1988, The NAFTA, What's In, What's Out, What Next, Business Economics, 1997, A Structuralist Assessment of Innovation Policies, 1998; editor: Rev. Econ. Studies, 1962-64. Decorated officer Order of Can.; Can. Inst. for Advanced Rsch. fellow, 1989—. Fellow Econometric Soc., Royal Soc. Can., Can. Inst. for Advanced Rsch., IC2 Soc. (Austin, Tex.); mem. Royal Econ. Soc. (council 1967-71), Econ. Study Soc. (chmn. 1965-69), Am. Econ. Assn., Can. Econ. Assn. (pres. 1980-81), Atlantic Econ. Soc. (chmn. 1986-87). Office: Simon Fraser U Harbour Centre 515 W Hastings St Vancouver BC Canada V6B 5K3 E-mail: rlipsey@sfu.ca.

LIPSEY, ROBERT EDWARD, economist, educator; b. N.Y.C., Aug. 14, 1926; s. Meyer Aaron and Anna (Weinstein) L.; m. Sally Irene Rothstein, Nov. 24, 1948; children: Marion (Mrs. William Greenlee), Carol (Mrs. William Hersh), Eleanor (Mrs. William Ho). BA, Columbia U., 1944, MA, 1946, PhD, 1961. Rsch. asst. Nat. Bur. Econ. Rsch., N.Y.C., 1945-53, rsch. assoc., 1953-60, sr. rsch. staff, 1960—, v.p. rsch., 1970-75, dir. internat. studies, 1975-78, dir. N.Y. Office, 1978—. Lectr. econs. Columbia U., 1961-64; prof. econs. Queens Coll. and Grad. Ctr., CUNY, 1967-95, prof. emeritus, 1995—; cons. Dept. Commerce, Fed. Res. Bd., UN, World Bank; mem. Pres. Adv. Bd. on Internat. Investment, 1977-78; bd. dirs. Rsch. Found. CUNY, 1994-95; exec. com. European Union Studies Ctr., CUNY, 1994—. Author: Price and Quantity Trends in the Foreign Trade of the U.S, 1963, (with Raymond W. Goldsmith) Studies in the National Balance Sheet of the U.S, 1963, (with Doris Preston) Source Book of Statistics Relating to Construction, 1966, (with Irving B. Kravis) Price Competitiveness in World Trade, 1971, (with Phillip Cagan) Financial Effects of Inflation, 1978, (with Irving B. Kravis) Saving and Economic Growth: Is the U.S. Really Falling Behind, 1987, (with Magnus Blomström and Lennart Ohlsson) Economic Relations Between the U.S. and Sweden, 1989, Measures of the Transnationalization of Economic Activity, United Nations, New York and Geneva, 2001; editor: (with Helen Stone Tice) The Measurement of Saving, Investment and Wealth, 1989, (with Robert E. Baldwin and J. David Richardson) Geography and Ownership as Bases for Economic Accounting, 1998, (with Alan Heston) International and Interarea Comparisons of Income, Output, and Prices, 1999, (with Jean-Louis Mucchielli) Multinational Firms and Impacts on Employment, Trade, and Technology, 2002; assoc. editor Rev. of Econs. and Stats., 1989-92; mem. editl. bd. Rev. of Income and Wealth, 1992—, Internat. Trade Jour., 1998—, Contemporary Econ. Policy, 2000—; contbr. articles to profl. jours. Fellow Am. Statis. Assn., N.Y. Acad. Scis.; mem. Acad. Internat. Bus., Nat. Assn. for Bus. Econs., Am. Econ. Assn., Internat. Assn. for Rsch. in Income and Wealth, Conf. on Rsch. in Income and Wealth, Econometric Soc., Internat. Trade and Fin. Assn. (pres. 1997), Western Econ. Assn. (bd. dirs. 1996-99), European Econ. Assn. Office: National Bureau Of Economic Research 365 5th Ave Fl 5 New York NY 10016-4309 E-mail: rlipsey@gc.cuny.edu.

LIPSHUTZ, LINDA KLEIN, social worker, employee assistance consultant; b. Mineola, N.Y., Sept. 9, 1952; d. Harold and Florence (Cohen) K.; children: Julie, David. BS, Cornell U., Ithaca, N.Y., 1974; MS in Social Work, Columbia U., N.Y.C., 1975. Lic. social worker, N.Y. Social worker Rockaway Youth Consultation Ctr., N.Y.C., 1975-77, Mt. Sinai Hosp., N.Y.C., 1977-78; sr. social worker Payne Whitney Clinic, 1978-81; social worker Fair Oaks Hosp., Summit, N.J., 1983-84; pvt. practice Plainview, N.Y., 1980—. Priorty systems, employee assistance cons., 1987—. Mem. NASW, ACSW, BCCSW. Office: 8243 Jericho Tpke Ste 220 Woodbury NY 11797-1805

LIPSHUTZ, ROBERT JEROME, lawyer, former government official; b. Atlanta, Dec. 27, 1921; s. Allen A. and Edith (Gavronski) L.; m. Barbara Sorelle Levin, Feb. 16, 1950 (dec.); children: Randall M., Judith Ann, Wendy Jean, Debbie Sue; m. Betty Beck Rosenberg, Feb. 10, 1973; stepchildren: Robert, Nancy Fay. JD, U. Ga., 1943. Bar: Ga. 1943, D.C. 1980. Practice in, Atlanta, 1947-77, 79—; ptnr. firm Lipshutz, Greenblatt & King, 1979—. Counsel to Pres. U.S., Washington, 1977-79 Past vice chmn. Ga. Bd. Human Resources; treas., legal counsel Jimmy Carter Presdl. campaign com., 1976; trustee The Carter Ctr.; adv. com. Jimmy Carter Libr. Lt. AUS, 1943-46. Mem. Am., Ga., Atlanta, D.C. bar assns., Atlanta Lawyers Club, Atlanta., B'nai B'rith (past pres., Disting. Svc. award). Jewish (past pres. The Temple). Office: Lipshutz Greenblatt & King Harris Tower 233 Peachtree St Ste 2300 Atlanta GA 30303-1504

LIPSIG, ETHAN, lawyer; b. N.Y.C., Dec. 11, 1948; s. Daniel Allen and Haddassah (Adler) L. BA, Pomona Coll., 1969; postgrad., Oxford U., 1969-70; JD, UCLA, 1974. Bar: U.S. Dist. Ct. (cen. dist.) Calif. 1974, U.S. Ct. Appeals (9th cir.) 1974, U.S Tax Ct. 1978. Author: Individual Retirement Arrangements, 1980, Downsizing, 1996. Mem. ABA (tax and labor rels. sect.), Calif. C. of C., Order of Coif, Soc. Fellows of Huntington Libr., Calif. Club, L.A. Men's Garden Club. Avocations: travel, horticulture, wine, music, art. Home: 280 California Ter Pasadena CA 91105-1515 Office: Paul Hastings Janofsky & Walker LLP 555 S Flower St Fl 23 Los Angeles CA 90071-2300

LIPSITT, LEWIS PAEFF, psychology educator; b. New Bedford, Mass., June 28, 1929; s. Joseph and Anna Naomi (Paeff) L.; m. Edna Brill Duchin, June 8, 1952; children: Mark, Ann. BA, U. Chgo., 1950; MS, U. Mass., 1952; PhD, U. Iowa, 1957. Instr. dept. psychology Brown U., Providence, 1957, asst. prof., 1958-61, assoc. prof., 1961-66, prof., 1966-96, dir. Child Study Ctr., 1967-92, Wriston lectr., 1993—, prof. emeritus psychology, med. sci. and human devel., 1996—, rsch. prof. psychology, 1996—. Mem. Gov.'s Adv. Commn. on Mental Retardation, 1963-66; cons. NIH; mem. edn. task force Model Cities Program, Providence, 1969-71; fellow Stanford Ctr. for Advanced Study in Behavioral Scis., 1979-80; vis. scientist NIMH, 1986-87; chair steering com. nat. child care project Nat. Inst. for Child Health and Human Devel., 1994-99, mem. adv. com., 1999-2001. Co-author: Child Development, 1979; founder, editor: Infant Behavior and Devel., 1978-82; founding co-editor: Advances in Child Development and Behavior, 1963-70, 78-82; co-editor: Research Readings in Child Psychology, 1963, Experimental Child Psychology, 1971, Advances in Infancy Research, 1981-99, Self-regulatory Behavior and Risk Taking, 1991, Progress in Infancy Research, 1991—; contbr. articles to profl. jours. Bd. dirs. Providence Child Guidance Clinic, 1960-63; trustee Butler Hosp., Providence, 1965-84; mem. bd. sci. counselors Nat. Ins. Child Health and Human Devel., 1984-88; nat. co-dir. Lee Salk Family Ctr., Kidspeace, Allentown, Pa., 1993—; participant White House Conf. on Child Care, 1998. Recipient Mentor award for lifetime achievement AAAS, 1995, Profl. Achievement citation U. Chgo., 1995; USPHS Spl. Rsch. fellow, 1966, Guggenheim fellow, 1972-73, USPHS fellow, 1973. Fellow AAAS (Lifetime Mentor award 1994), APA (exec. com. divsn. devel. psychology 1967-70, pres.-elect divsn. devel. psychology 1979-80, pres. divsn. devel. psychology 1980-81, bd. sci. affairs 1985-88, exec. dir. for sci. 1990-91, sci. officer 1991-92, Nicholas Hobbs award 1990, exec. com. divsn. gen. psychology 1997-2001, coun. of reps. 1997-2000, pres.-elect divsn. gen. psychology 1998-99, pres., 1999-2000, past pres. 2001, pres.-elect divsn. exptl. psychology 2001); mem. AAUP, Soc. Rsch. in Child Devel., Internat. Soc. Study of Behavioral Devel. (membership sec. 1981-83, exec. com. 1984-89), Am. Psychol. Soc. (founding mem., charter fellow, bd. dirs. 1989-90), Can. Inst. for Advanced Rsch. (chair adv. com. human devel. group 1995—), R.I. Psychol. Assn. (bd. dirs. 1995-98, Mental Health Svc. award 1998). E-mail: Lewis_Lipsitt@brown.edu.

LIPSITZ, LAWRENCE IRWIN, publishing executive; b. Paterson, N.J., July 24, 1937; s. Samuel and Rachel (Hammerman) L.; m. Janice Shapiro, July 3, 1966; children: David, Jill, Julie. BS, NYU, 1959, AM, 1960. Tchr. Saddle Brook (N.J.) High Sch., 1961-63; pub. rels. NYU, N.Y.C., 1963-69; pub. Ednl. Tech. mag., Tng. Rsch. Jour. and Ednl. Tech. Publs. Edn. Technology Publs., Englewood Cliffs, 1969—. Mem. adv. bd. ERIC Clearinghouse, Syracuse U. Editor: Technology and Education, 1972, Test Score Decline, 1978, Instructional TV, 1979, Telecommunications in Learning, 1991. Pres. Temple Emeth, Teaneck, N.J., 1984-87; chmn. alumni communications NYU, 1989—; com. mem. United Jewish Community, River Edge, N.J., 1986—. With USAF, 1960-61. Fellow Internat. Sys. Inst., Jewish Acad. Arts and Scis.; mem. NYU Alumni Fed. (com. chmn.). Jewish. Home: 1147 Trafalgar St Teaneck NJ 07666-1931 also: 154 Old Farms Rd Torrington CT 06790-2240 Office: Ednl Technology Publs 700 Palisade Ave Englewood Cliffs NJ 07632-0564 E-mail: edtecpubs@aol.com., LLipsitz@aol.com.

LIPSKY, BURTON G. lawyer; b. Syracuse, N.Y., May 29, 1937; s. Abraham and Pauline (Leichtner); m. Elaine B. Mannheimer, July 27, 1967; 1 child, Erika S., m. Carol S. Samberg, Feb. 4, 1973; 1 child, Andrew H. BBA, U. Mich., 1959; JD summa cum laude, Syracuse U., 1962. Bar: N.Y. 1962, U.S. Supreme Ct. 1967. Trial atty. U.S. Dept. Justice, Washington, 1962-67; assoc. Kaye, Scholer, Fierman, Hays & Handler, N.Y.C., 1967-72; ptnr. Delson & Gordon, 1972-87, Lipsky & Stout, N.Y.C., 1991-96; pvt. practice, 1996—. Mem. bd. visitors Syracuse U. Coll. of Law, 1989—; sec.-treas., dir. Robert Mapplethorpe Found., Inc., 1988—. Mem. ABA, N.Y. Bar Assn., Order of Coif, Justinian Soc., Am. Contract Bridge League (life master). Office: 100 Park Ave New York NY 10017-5586 E-mail: BurtLip@aol.com.

LIPSKY, IAN DAVID, business executive; b. Bklyn., May 26, 1957; s. Eugene Herman and Janet Dorothy (Heller) Lipsky; m. Cheryl Joy Weinberg; 1 child Ethan Maxwell. BS in Marine Engring., Maine Maritime Acad., 1979; MBA, U. San Francisco, 2000. Lic. eng contractor, Calif; US Coast Guard, Merchant Mariners Document steam & motor vessels. Third asst. engr. Interlake Steamship Co., Cleve., 1979-81; port engr. Exxon Internat. Co., Florham Park, N.J., 1981-84; prodn. supr. Alfred Conhagen Inc. Calif., Hercules, 1984-87, gen. mgr., 1987-89, v.p., 1989-2000; sr. mgr. facilities svcs. dept. Genentech, Inc., South San Francisco, Calif., 2001—. Mem.: Nat Soc Profl Engrs, Port Engrs San Francisco, Inst Marine Engrs (London), Marine Port Engrs NY, Soc Naval Architects & Marine Engrs. Democrat. Jewish. Avocations: golf, running, triathlons. Office: Genentech Inc 1 DNA Way South San Francisco CA 94080-4990 Home: 34 Madera Del Presidio Dr Corte Madera CA 94925-2068 E-mail: idlipsky@yahoo.com.

LIPSKY, JERRY, systems analyst; b. N.Y.C., June 11, 1951; s. Sidney and Harriet L.; m. Alice D. Jermyn, Jan. 7, 1989. AAS, Phila. C.C., 1972. Electronics tech. Talstar Computer Sys., Princeton, N.J., 1974-77, Atlanta Jour. and Constitution, 1977-78, sys. analyst, 1978-93, sys. mgr. online sys., 1993-97, datebase adminstr., 1997—. Avocations: photography, computer programming, reading. Office: The Atlanta Journal-Constitution 72 Marietta St NW Atlanta GA 30303-2899

LIPSKY, LINDA ETHEL, business executive; b. Bklyn., June 2, 1939; d. Irving Julius and Florence (Stern) Ellman; m. Warren Lipsky, June 12, 1960 (div. Sept. 1968); 1 child, Phillip Bruce; m. Jerome Friedman, Jan. 17, 1988. BA in Psychology, Hofstra U., 1960; MPS with hon. in Health Care Adminstrn., Long Island U., 1979. Child welfare social worker Nassau County Dept. Social Service, N.Y., 1960-64; adminstr. La Guardia Med. Group of Health Ins. Plan of Greater N.Y., Queens, 1969-72; cons. Neighborhood Svc. Ctr., Bronx, N.Y., 1973-78; dir. ODA Health Ctr., Bklyn., 1978-82; pres. Millin Assocs., Inc., Nassau, N.Y., 1982—. Mem. Health Care Fin. Mgmt. Assn., Nat. Assn. Community Health Ctrs., Nat. Assn. Female Execs., Cmty. Health Ctrs., Assoc. of N.Y., Hofstra U. Alumni Assn. (mem. senate 1984—, chairperson membership com. 1985—), Pi Alpha Alpha. Republican. Jewish. Avocations: cooking, writing, reading. E-mail: millin521@aol.com. Office: Millin Assocs Inc 521 Chestnut St Cedarhurst NY 11516-2244

LIPSKY, PAT, artist; b. N.Y.C., Sept. 21, 1941; d. Bernard G. and Bernice D. (Brown) Sutton; children: David Lipsky, Jonathan Lipsky. BFA, Cornell U., 1963; postgrad., Bklyn. Mus. Art Sch., 1960-61, Art Student's League, 1963; MA, Hunter Coll., 1968. Faculty Fairleigh Dickinson U., 1968-69, Hunter Coll., 1972, San Francisco Art Inst., 1974; assoc. prof. U. Hartford, 1983—2002. Guest lectr. Hirshhorn Mus., 1975, Va. Commonwealth U., Bennington Coll., 1977, U. Pitts., 1974, NYU, 1983, SACI, Florence, 1986, Springfield Mus., 1987-88, U. Miami, 1992, Pollock-Krasner House and Study Ctr., East Hampton, L.I., N.Y., 1995, Am. U., 1997, Muhlenberg Coll., 1999; guest lectr. Parsons Sch. Design, 1990, lectr., 1982-83, 90; instr. SUNY, Purchase, 1980-81; mem. adv. coun. Cornell U. Coll. Art and Architecture, 1988—. One-woman shows include Andre Emmerich Gallery, N.Y.C., 1970, 72, 74, 75, Deichter O'Reilly Gallery, 1976, Medici-Berenson Gallery, 1976, Everson Mus., 1970, Gloria Luria Gallery, Miami, 1988, Slater-Price Gallery, N.Y.C., 1986, Hartell Gallery Cornell U., 1989, Andre Zarre Gallery, 1991, Virginia Miller Gallery, Coral Gables, Fla., 1994, Bookstein Fine Arts, N.Y.C., 1997, The Kitchen, 1999, Elizabeth Harris Gallery, 1999, 2001, Piltzer Gallery, Barbizon, France, 2002; exhibited in group shows at Whitney Mus. Am. Art, 1971, Hirshhorn Mus. and Sculture Garden, 1975, Promenade Gallery, Hartford, 1984, U. Mass. Art Gallery, Amherst, 1987, Gloria Luria Gallery, 1988, 92, Andre Zarre Gallery, 1990, 95, Denise Renè Gallery, Paris, 1993, Gallery One, Toronto, Can., 1996, Snyder Fine Art, N.Y.C., 1996, Lori Bookstein/Fine Arts, 1997, Am. Acad. Arts & Letters, 2001; represented in permanent collections Herbert Johnson Mus., Itaca, N.Y., Witney Mus., Hirshhorn Mus., Walker Art Ctr., Hunter Coll., Fogg Art Mus., Harvard U., San Francisco Mus. Art, Bklyn. Mus., Blanton Mus. Art, U. Tex. at Austin, Wadsworth Atheneum, Hartford, Portland Mus. Art, Mus. Fine Arts, Houston; stage designer (play) Custody, Westbeth Theatre, N.Y.C., 1991. Recipient Childe Hassam Purchase prize AAAL, 2001; grantee N.Y. State Coun., 1972, N.Y. Found. Arts, 1992, Jerome Found., 1999, Adolph & Esther Gottlieb Found., 1999, Pollock-Krasner Found., 2000; sponsorship from Winsor and Newton Paint Co., 1992; fellow Va. Ctr. for Creative Arts, 1986, 93, Tyrone Guthurie Centre, Co., Moneghan, Ireland, 1996. Home: 410 W 24th St New York NY 10011-1303 Studio: 526 W 26th St Rm 1011 New York NY 10001-5541 E-mail: pslipsky@aol.com.

LIPSKY, STEPHEN EDWARD, engineering executive, electronics engineer; b. N.Y.C., Jan. 18, 1932; s. Arthur Arnold and Sophie (Malsbrook) Lipsky; m. Laura Roher, May 11, 1958 (div. 1978); children: Janice, Sharon, David; m. Hyla Schaffer, Apr. 7, 1979. B.E.E., NYU, 1953, M.E.E., 1962; PhD in Elec. Engring., Drexel U., 1993. Project engr. Fisher Radio Corp; div. mgr., staff scientist Loral Electronics, Yonkers, NY, 1958-63; corp. v.p. Polarad-Radiometrics, Lake Success, 1963-70; dir. advanced systems Gen. Inst. Corp., Hicksville, 1970-79; chief tech. officer, sr. v.p. Am. Electronic Labs., Lansdale, Pa., 1979-93; founder, chief tech. officer Bynetics Corp., Jenkintown, 1993—. Adj. univ. prof. Drexel U., Phila.; expert witness RF Comms. Author: (book) Microwave Passive Direction Finding, 1987; contbr. articles to profl. jours. Served to lt. U.S. Army, 1953—55. Decorated Bronze AFCEA medal. Fellow: IEE (assoc.), IEEE (life); mem.: Army Assn., Assn. Old Crows (bd. dirs. 1972—74, Sr. Gold Cert. merit 1990), Navy League, Am. Radio Relay League, Masons. Republican. Achievements include patents in field. Avocations: radio amateur, photography, stamp collecting, antique radios. E-mail: w2vvn@arrl.net.

LIPSMAN, RICHARD MARC, lawyer, educator; b. Bklyn., Aug. 17, 1946; s. Abraham W. and Ruth (Weinstein) L.; m. Geri A. Russo, 1979; children: Eric, Dara Briana. BBA, CCNY, 1968; JD, St. John's U., Jamaica, N.Y., 1972; LLM in Taxation, Boston U., 1976. Bar: N.Y. 1973, Mass. 1975, U.S. Dist. Ct. (ea. and so. dists.) N.Y. 1977, U.S. Supreme Ct. 1978, U.S. Tax Ct. 1979; CPA, N.Y., Mass. Tax atty. Arthur Young & Co., N.Y.C., 1972-74; assoc. Gilman, McLaughlin & Hanrahan, Boston, 1974-76, Lefrak, Fischer & Meyerson, N.Y.C., 1976-77; ptnr. Tarnow, Landsman & Lipsman, 1978; pvt. practice,

1979—. Adj. faculty Baruch Coll. CUNY, 1984-86, curriculum specialist Rsch. Found. CUNY, 1977-78; adj. faculty Pratt Inst., Bklyn., 1974, Queensboro Coll., Bayside, N.Y., 1978-80. Author, producer book/cassette program Learning Income Taxes, 1978—. Mem. ABA, AICPA, N.Y. State Bar Assn., Assn. of the Bar of the City of N.Y., N.Y. State Soc. CPA's. Jewish.

LIPSON, CHARLES BARRY, finance company executive; b. Bronx, N.Y., Apr. 9, 1946; s. Lawrence and Tesse (Ganz) L.; m. Lynn Beth Marcus, Oct. 22, 1972 (dec. Nov. 1998); 1 child, Marc Ira; m. Iris R. Morgan, May 27, 2001. BS in Bus. and Acctg., U. Conn., 1967; MBA in Fin., Iona Coll., 1970. With Colgate Palmolive, N.Y.C., 1969-73; dir. Helena Rubenstein (subs. of Colgate Palmolive), East Hills, N.Y., 1973-74, dir. internat. fin., 1974-76, contr. London, 1977-78; dir. plant assets Colgate Palmolive Co., N.Y.C., 1978-79, dir. fin., 1980-85; v.p., chief fin. officer Teledisc USA, 1986-88; pres., chief exec. officer HCS Brokerage Svcs., Inc., 1989-91; sr. v.p., chief ops. officer Home Capital Svcs., 1988-91. Sr. v.p., chief ops. officer Home Capital Svcs., N.Y.C., 1988-91; treas. Home Group Trust, N.Y.C., 1989-91; pres., founding ptnr. Rep. Asset Mgmt. Corp. (formerly M.D. Hirsch Investment Mgmt., Inc.), N.Y.C., 1991-95; pres. Freedom Capital Mgmt. Corp. M.D. Hirsch divsn., 1995-99; pres., CEO Fund Mgr. Trust, 1995-99; founding ptnr. The Lynnvest Group of Advest, Inc., 1999—. Editor: Conn. Daily Campus, 1966, sports editor, 1965. Mgr. Marlboro (N.J.) Twp. Little League, 1988-93; head coach Marlboro Recreation Basketball League, 1990-91; treas., bd. dirs. Temple Beth-El, North Bellmore, N.Y., 1982-83; dir., sec.-treas. Forsgate Cmty. Assn. Mem. Nat. Assn. Accts., Internat. Assn. Fin. Planners, Holland Orchards Country Club (pres. 1988-89), Forsgate Country Club. Avocations: coaching youth sports, golf, tennis, music. Office: Advest Inc The Lynnvest Group 1 Rockefeller Plz Fl 21 New York NY 10020-2105 E-mail: charles.lipson@advest.com.

LIPSON, CHARLES HENRY, political scientist, educator; b. Clarksdale, Miss., Feb. 1, 1948; s. Harry Mason Jr. and Dorothy (Kohn) L.; m. Susan Linda Bloom, July 13, 1980; children: Michael H., Jonathan S. BA, Yale Coll., 1970; MA, Harvard U., 1974, PhD, 1976. Rsch. assoc. Harvard Ctr. for Internat. Affairs, Cambridge, Mass., 1976-77; asst. prof. U. Chgo., 1977-84, assoc. prof., 1984—. Vis. scholar Harvard Ctr. for Internat. Affairs, 1979-80; founding dir. program on internat. politics, econs. and security U. Chgo., 1987—, chair com. on internat. rels., 1992-95; vis. fellow London Sch. Econs, 1988-89; mem. Chgo. Com., steering com. Midwest Consortium for Internat. Security Studies; ptnr. Capstone Entertainment. Author: Standing Guard: Protecting Foreign Capital in the 19th and 20th Centuries, 1985; editor: Theory and Structure in International Political Economy, 1999, Issues and Agents in International Political Economy, 1999, Rational International Institutions, 2001; mem. bd. editors Internat. Orgn., 1984-90, 96-2001, World Politics, 1998—; contbr. articles to profl. jours. Bd. dirs. Newberger Hillel Found. of U. Chgo., 1990—, mem. exec. com., 1993—, chmn. bd. dirs., 1994-99; bd. dirs. K.A.M. Isaiah Israel Congregation, Chgo., 1992—. Recipient Faculty Achievement award Burlington-No. Found., 1986; grantee German Marshall Fund U.S., 1983-84; fellow Rockefeller Found., 1979-81. Mem. Am. Polit. Sci. Assn. (sec. 1990-91), Am. Soc. for Internat. Law, Brit.-Am. Conf. for Successor Generation, Chgo. Com., Chgo. Coun. on Fgn. Rels., Internat. Inst. for Stratetic Studies, Internat. Studies Assn., Royal Inst. for Internat. Affairs. Jewish. Home: 5809 S Blackstone Ave Chicago IL 60637-1855 Office: U Chgo Dept Polit Sci 5828 S University Ave Dept Polit Chicago IL 60637-1515 E-mail: c-lipson@uchicago.edu.

LIPSON, JONATHAN MARK, psychologist; b. Providence, May 3, 1961; s. Sheldon Robert and Joan (Blum) L.; m. Yvonne Marie Lipson, Sept. 19, 1998. BA, Queen's U., Kingston, Ont., Can., 1984; MS, Okla. State U., 1988, PhD, 1993. Psychologist Saginaw (Mich.) Psychol. Svcs., 1993-95; postdoctoral fellow Genesys Regional Med. Ctr., Flint, Mich., 1995-97; dir. behavioral scis. Swedish Family Medicine Residency, Littleton, Colo., 1997—2002; ind. practice Lakewood and Conifer, 2002—. Cons. Physicians for Social Responsibility, Denver, 1997-98; citizen amb. del. People to People Internat., Eastern Europe, 1992. Contbr. chpt. to book, articles to profl. jours. Med. Explorer advisor Boy Scouts Am., Flint, 1996-97. Named Explorer Post of Yr., Tall Pine coun. Boy Scouts Am., 1997. Mem. APA, Colo. Psychol. Assn. Democrat. Jewish. Avocations: hiking, camping, skiing, bicycling. Office: 7596 W Jewell Ave Ste 200 Lakewood CO 80232 E-mail: jonlipsonphd@aol.com.

LIPSON, MELVIN ALAN, technology and business management consultant; b. Providence, June 1, 1936; s. Nathan and Esta (Blumenthal) L.; m. Jacqueline Ann Barclay, July 2, 1961; children: Donna, Robert, Michelle, Judith. BS, U. R.I., 1957; PhD, Syracuse U., 1963. Chemist ICI Organics, Providence, 1963, Philip A. Hunt Chem. Co., Lincoln, R.I., 1964-67, rsch. mgr., 1967-69; tech. dir. Dynachem div. Morton Thiokol Inc., Tustin, Calif., 1969-72, v.p., 1979-82, sr. v.p., 1972-82, 1982-85, exec. v.p., 1985-86, pres., 1986-89; v.p. tech. devel. Morton Internat. Inc., Chgo., 1989-92; pres. Lipson Assocs., Newport Beach, Calif., 1993—. Chmn. bd., CEO Aurelon, Inc., Huntington Beach, Calif., 1993-96, Pivotech., Inc., Newport Beach, Calif., 1996-98; CEO Meltex, Inc., Huntington Beach, Calif., 1998—. Home and Office: 1715 Plaza Del Sur Newport Beach CA 92661-1417

LIPSON, STEVEN MARK, clinical virologist, educator; b. Bklyn., May 25, 1945; s. Jonas and Ana (Soltz) L.; m. Heleen P. Bleiweiss, Apr. 25, 1971; children: Tracy J., Jennifer B. BS in Biology, L. I. U., 1967, MS in Microbiology and Marine Sci., 1972; PhD in Cell Biology and Microbiology, NYU, 1981. Cert. radioactive materials cert. N.Y. State Dept. Health, bd. cert. in virology Am. Soc. Clin. Pathologists. Rsch. assoc. hematology/oncology Bklyn. Hosp.-Caladonian Hosp., 1980-82; dir. virology and immunology N.Y. State Dept. Health, 1997; rsch. assoc. immunology lab. dept. neoplastic diseases Mt. Sinai Sch. Medicine, N.Y.C., 1982-84; chief virology lab., assoc. dir. divsn. microbiology Nassau County Med. Ctr., East Meadow, N.Y., 1984-90; dir. virology lab., rsch. asst. prof. microbiology/medicine North Shore U. Hosp.-NYU Sch. Medicine, Manhasset, 1990-00; acting dir. Flow Cytometry/Cellular Immunology Lab. North Shore U. Hosp.-NYC Sch. Medicine, 1995-97; chief Virology Lab., Columbia-Presbyn. Med. Ctr., N.Y.C., 2000; asst. prof. pathology Columbia U. Coll. Physicians and Surgeons, 2000; with Virology Cons., Inc., Bklyn., N.Y.C., NY, 2000—; rsch. biologist VA Med. Ctr., Northport, 2001—. Adj. prof., L.I. U., NY, 1987; cons. Enzo Biochem, N.Y.C., Becton, Dickenson and Co., Research Triangle Park, NC, Organon Teknika, Research Triangle Park, Roche Diagnostic Systems, Nutley, NJ, BioMerieux Vitek, Inc., Rockland, Mass., Bartels/Invitrogen, Issaquah, Wash., Pall Corp., Port Washington, NY; mem. profl. adv. panel Med. Lab. Advisor, 1994—; tchg. hosp. edn. specialist clin. microbiology lab. dept. pathology SUNY, Stony Brook, 2001—; rsch. scientist DVA, Northport, NY, 2001—; presenterover 75 abstracts at sci. meetings. Contbr.: Clinical Microbiology Procedures Manual (Virology), 1993, guest editl. bd. : Clin. Revs. in Microbiology, 1995, guest editl. bd. : Manual of Clin. Microbiology, 1995, guest editl. bd. : Jour. Infectious Disease, guest editl. bd. : Arch. Pathol. Lab. Med., guest editl. bd. : European Jour. Epidemiology, mem. editl. bd.: Med. Sci. Monitor, assoc. editor: Diagnostic Microbiol. Infectious Disease; contbr. articles to 67 profl. peer reviewed publs. Vol. lectr. Kiwanis Club, Long Island, 1985-90; vol. N.Y. Hall of Sci., Queens, 1996. Mem.: Long Island Infectious Disease Soc., N.Y. Infectious Diseases Soc., Am. Soc. for Microbiology (nat. and N.Y. City br.). Avocations: stamp collecting, swimming, riflery, travel, dining. Office: Virology Consultants Inc 2364 E 74th St Brooklyn NY 11234-6620 E-mail: montmor@aol.com.

LIPSTEIN, ROBERT A. lawyer; b. Wilmington, Del., Dec. 6, 1954; s. Eugene Joseph and Leona (Feld) L.; m. Cheryl A. Artibee-Wedlake, July 30, 1978; children: Rebecca Lynn, Matthew Wedlake. BA in Econs., Stanford U., 1975, JD, 1978. Bar: D.C. 1978, U.S. Dist. Ct. D.C., 1979, U.S. Ct. Appeals (D.C. cir.) 1980, U.S. Ct. Internat. Trade, 1984, U.S. Ct. Appeals (fed. cir.), U.S. Supreme Ct. 1990. Assoc. Morgan, Lewis & Bockius, Washington, 1978-84, Coudert Bros., Washington, 1984-86, ptnr., 1987-94; mng. ptnr. Lipstein, Jaffe & Lawson, L.L.P., 1994—. Mem. ABA (antitrust sect., law practice mgmt. sect.), D.C. Bar Assn., Phi Beta Kappa. Avocations: golf, wood working, Tae Kwon Do (3d degree black belt). Home: 511 Stonington Rd Silver Spring MD 20902-1545 Office: 190 M St NW Ste 700 Washington DC 20001-1219 E-mail: rlipstein@ljllaw.com.

LIPTON, AUDREY KING, lawyer, risk management consultant; b. N.Y.C., Jan. 30, 1942; BA, Columbia U., 1968; JD, NYU, 1972. Bar: N.Y. 1973. Atty. Sperry Corp., N.Y.C., 1972-76, GAF Corp., N.Y.C., 1976-78, customer svcs. pub. Keynote mag., dir. mktg. services, 1978-84; v.p. Telephonics Corp., Huntington, N.Y., 1984-89; pvt. practice N.Y.C., 1989—. Adj. faculty NYU; cons. UN, bd. dirs. N.Y. Law Sch., N.Y.C. Address: 20 Sutton Place South New York NY 10022

LIPTON, BRONNA JANE, marketing communications executive; b. Newark, May 10, 1951; d. Julius and Arlene (Davis) L.; m. Sheldon Robert Lipton, Sept. 23, 1984. BA in Spanish, Northwestern U., 1973. Tchr. Spanish Livingston (N.J.) H.S., 1973-78; profl. dancer Broadway theater, film, TV, N.Y.C., 1978-82; v.p., mgr. Hispanic mktg. svcs. Burson-Marsteller Pub. Rels., 1982-89; exec. v.p. Lipton Comms. Group, Inc., 1989-99, Latin Reports, 1996-99; v.p. Bienestar LCG Comms., Inc., 1999—. Mem. minority initiatives task force Am. Diabetes Assn., Alexandria, Va., 1987-90, mem. pub. rels. com., 1990-91, mem. visibility and image task force, 1991-92, bd. dirs. N.Y. Downstate affiliate, chmn. visibility and image com., 1992-93. Mem. rev. panel Hispanic Designers, Inc. Recipient Pinnacle award Am. Women in Radio and TV (N.Y. Chpt.), 1984, Value Added awards Burson-Marsteller, N.Y.C., 1982, 83, 84. Mem. Hispanic Pub. Rels. Assn. Avocations: ballet, jazz dance, tennis, fgn. travel, birding. Home: 1402 Chapel Hill Rd Mountainside NJ 07092-1405 E-mail: blipton@bienestar-lcg.com.

LIPTON, CHARLES, public relations executive; b. N.Y.C., May 11, 1928; s. Jack B. and Bertha (Lesser) L.; m. Audrey Williams, Nov. 11, 1951; children: Susan, Jack. AB, Harvard U., 1948. Market researcher Cecil & Presbury, Inc., N.Y.C., 1948-49; spl. events dir. 20th Century Fox Film Corp., 1949-52; account exec. Ruder & Finn, Inc., 1953-58, v.p., 1958-63, sr. v.p., 1963-69, vice-chmn., 1969-95; sr. counsel, 1995—; also bd. dirs. Guest lectr. Boston U., 1967-68. Mem. coun. Ctr. for Vocat. Arts, Norwalk, Conn., 1966—74; treas., mem. exec. com. Norwalk Symphony Soc., 1972—85; chmn. parents coun. Washington U., St. Louis, 1976—77, trustee, 1977—; chmn. Wycliffe Charities Found., 1998—; trustee Norwalk Jewish Ctr., 1966—70. Mem. Am. Soc. Colon and Rectal Surgeons (trustee), Internat. Pub. Rels. Assn., USIA (pub. rels., pvt. sector com. 1988-93), Nat. Emphysema Soc. (trustee), Nat. Investor Rels. Inst., Harvard Club, Harvard Varsity Club. Home: 4502 Hazleton Ln Lake Worth FL 33467-8633 Office: Ruder Finn Inc 301 E 57th St Fl 3 New York NY 10022-2900 E-mail: audles@aol.com.

LIPTON, CHARLES JULES, lawyer; b. N.Y.C., Oct. 26, 1931; m. Alice Garretson; children: Leah Jane, Emma Ely. AB, Syracuse (N.Y.) U., 1951; LLB, Yale U., 1954; LLM in Internat. Law, NYU, 1966. Bar: N.Y. 1955, U.S. Supreme Ct. 1958. Assoc. Hughes, Hubbard and Reed, N.Y.C., 1954-55; judge advocate, trial atty. U.S. Dept. of Air Force, Washington, 1955-57; assoc. Breed, Abbott and Morgan, N.Y.C., 1957-62; counsel Freeport Minerals Co., 1962-69; interregional legal advisor UN, 1969-74; sr. cons. UN Centre on Transnational Corps., 1976-90, chief legal adviser, 1991-92. Spl. counsel Am. Indian Coun. Energy Resource Tribes, Denver, 1978-84; bd. dirs. Havelock Asbestos Mines (Swaziland) Ltd., Sun Internat. of Lesotho Pty., Ltd., Dokolowayo Diamond Mines Ltd., Emaswati Coal Pty., Ltd.; cons. U.S. Commr. of Edn., 1965; legal advisor, cons. numerous govts. and internat. orgns.; comml. legal advisor to the Govt. of Lesotho, 1967-2001; legal advisor to Kings of Swaziland, 1969—; adj. prof. law NYU, 1975-88; vis. prof. law U. Swaziland, 1977-88, Nat. U. Lesotho, 1984-88; vis. lectr. in law U. Calif., Berkeley, 1974-82; vis. fellow U. NSW, Sydney, Australia, 1987; lectr. in field, participant in numerous workshops; Fulbright prof. law U. Tartu (Estonia), 1996. Contbr. articles to profl. jours. Capt. JAG, USAF, 1955-57. Mem. Am. Soc. Internat. Law, Am. Fgn. Law Assn., ABA (chmn. African law com. sect. on internat. and comparative law 1964-67), Assn. of Bar of City of N.Y., African Law Assn. in Am. (bd. dirs. 1969-72. Home: 1136 5th Ave New York NY 10128-0122

LIPTON, CLIFFORD CARWOOD, retired glass company executive; b. Huntington, W.Va., Jan. 30, 1920; s. Clifford Carwood and Zerelda (Adkins) L.; m. Alyce Jo Anne Eckley, Jan. 3, 1943 (dec. July 1975); children: Clifford Carwood III, Thomas Denton, Michael Forrester; m. Marie Hope Mahoney, May 26, 1976. B of Engring. Sci., Marshall U., 1948; postgrad. exec. mgmt. program, Pa. State U., 1959. Staff engr. Owens-Ill. Inc., Huntington, 1948-52, supr. engring. Streator, Ill., 1952-55, chief engr. divsn. Toledo, 1955-66; gen. mgr. Giralt Laporta SA, Madrid, 1966-71; dir. mfg. United Glass Ltd., London, 1971-74; mfg. and tech. dir. Owens-Ill. Internat., Geneva, 1974-82; dir. internat. devel. Owens-Ill. Inc., Toledo, 1982-83; ret., 1983. Cons. Owens-Ill., Inc., China, Greece and U.S., 1983-85, Internat. Exec. Svc. Corps., 1986-98. Mem. sch. bd. Am. Sch., Barcelona, Spain, 1966-67, Madrid, 1967-70; pres. Highland Trails Homeowners Assn., Southern Pines, N.C., 1987-93. 1st lt. Parachute Inf., U.S. Army, 1942-45. Mem. Benevolent and Protective Order Elks, 101st Airborne Divsn. Assn. Republican. Presbyterian. Avocations: travel, golf, reading, music, model engineering. Home: 104 Selkirk Trail Southern Pines NC 28387-7230 E-mail: clipton@pinehurst.net.

LIPTON, JEFFREY M. physician; b. N.Y.C., Apr. 27, 1947; s. Alfred and Thelma Lipton; m. Linda C. Rudolph, July 6, 1968; children: David, Joshua. BA, Queens Coll., CUNY, 1967; PhD, Syracuse U., 1972; MD, St. Louis U., 1975. Asst. in medicine Children's Hosp., Boston, 1979-84; asst. prof. pediats. Harvard Med. Sch., 1979—84; assoc. attending Columbia Presbyn. Med. Ctr., N.Y.C., 1984-87; assoc. prof. pediats. Columbia U. Coll. Phys. and Surg., 1984—87; chief pediatric hematology/oncology Mt. Sinai Med. Ctr., N.Y.C., 1987-99; prof. pediatrics Albert Einstein Coll. Medicine, 2001—; chief pediatric hematology/oncology and stem cell transplantation Schneider Children's Hosp., New Hyde Park, N.Y., 1999—. Advisor The Bone Marrow Found.-Resource and Ednl. Ctr., 1999—. Author more than 100 articles and book chpts. Mem. Am. Soc. Pediatric Hematology/Oncology (chair fin. com. 1999-2000), Soc. for Pediatric Rsch., Am. Soc. Hematology, Am. Soc. for Blood and Marrow Transplantation, N.Y. Soc. Study of Blood (pres. 1998), Pediatric Oncology Group (chair bone marrow transplant com. 1991—), Alpha Omega Alpha. Office: Schneider Children's Hosp 26901 76th Ave New Hyde Park NY 11040-1434 E-mail: jlipton@lij.edu.

LIPTON, JOAN ELAINE, advertising executive; b. N.Y.C., July 12, 1927; 1 child, David Dean. BA, Barnard Coll., 1948. With Young & Rubicam, Inc., N.Y.C., 1948-52, Robert W. Orr & Assocs., N.Y.C., 1952-57, Benton & Bowles, Inc., N.Y.C., 1957-64; assoc. dir. Benton & Bowles, Ltd., London, Eng., 1964-68; with McCann-Erickson, Inc. (advt. agy.), N.Y.C., 1968-85, v.p., 1970-79, sr. v.p., creative dir., 1979-85; pres. Martin & Lipton Advt. Inc., 1985—. Mem. Bus. Coun. for the UN Decade for Women, 1977-78; bd. vis. PhD program in bus. CUNY, 1986—. Recipient Honors award Ohio U. Sch. Journalism, 1976, Matrix award, 1979, YWCA award for women achievers, 1979, Clio Classic award; named Woman of Yr., Am. Advt. Fedn., 1974, Advt. Woman of Yr., 1984; named to Matrix Hall of Fame, 1998. Mem. Advt. Women N.Y. (1st v.p. 1975-76, v.p. Found. 1977-78), Women's Forum (bd. dirs. 1988-90), Women in Communications (pres. N.Y. chpt. 1974-76, named Nat. Headliner 1976). Office: 163 E 62nd St New York NY 10021-7613

LIPTON, JUDITH EVE, psychiatrist; b. Chgo., Mar. 7, 1951; d. Morris Abraham and Barbara (Steiner) L.; m. Peter Sisk, June, 1969 (div. Dec., 1974); m. David Philip Barash, Mar. 10, 1977; children: Jacob Sisk, Ilona Anne Barash, Nanelle Rose Barash. BA, Reed Coll., 1974; MD, U. N.C., 1974. Diplomate Am. Bd. Psychiatry & Neurology. Resident in psychiatry U. Wash., Seattle, 1975-78, clin. instr. dept. psychiatry and behavioral scis., 1979-80; consulting psychiatrist Family Counseling Ctr., Lynnwood, Wash., 1980-82; med. staff mem. Overlake Hosp., Bellevue, 1981-91; med. staff Evergreen Hosp., Kirkland, 1985-87; pvt. practice Meydenbauer Psychiat. Group, Bellevue, 1980-85, Redmond (Wash.) Med. Ctr., 1985-92, Woodinville, Wash., 1992-98; writer/rschr. Redmond, 1998—; cons. psychiatrist Comprehensive Breast Ctr., Providence campus Swedish Med. Ctr., Seattle, 1999—; clin. instr. dept. psychiatry U. Wash., 1999—. Co-author: (with D.P. Barash) Making Sense of Sex, 1997, The Myth of Monogamy: Fidelity and Infidelity in Animals and People, 2001, Gender Gap: The Biology of Male-Female Differences, 2002; contbr. articles to profl. jours. Leadership Redmond, Class of 1991. Recipient Merck award for Excellence in Med. Studies, 1972, Ralph Bunche award Wash. State Bar Assn., 1983, Woman of Distinction Matrix Table award Women in Comm. AAUW, 1987; scholar in residence Bellagio Study and Conf. Ctr., Rockefeller Found., Como, Italy, 1984; guest govt. USSR Forum on Nuclear Disarmament, Moscow, 1987. Fellow Am. Psychiat. Assn. (chmn. Com. on Nuclear Issues, 1987-89); mem. Wash. State Med. Soc., King County Med. Soc., Physicians for Social Responsibility (pres., founder Wash. Physicians for Social Responsibility 1979-83, rsch. and writing award 1983, Paul Beeson award 1986), nat. bd. dirs. 1980-86, spkr. fellowship 1983). Office: 2012 112th Ave NE Bellevue WA 98004 Fax: 425-882-2077. E-mail: drjudy@w-link.net.

LIPTON, LESTER, ophthalmologist, entrepreneur; b. N.Y.C., Mar. 14, 1936; s. George and Rita (von Steinbaum) L.; m. Harriet Arfa, June 25, 1960; children: Sherri, Brandi, Shawn BA, NYU, 1959; MD, Chgo. Med. Sch. 1964. Rsch. fellow Chgo. Med. Sch., 1959-60; intern Brookdale Hosp. Ctr., Bklyn., 1964-65; resident Harlem Eye and Ear Hosp., N.Y.C., 1965-68; assoc. attending Polyclinic French hosps., 1968-75; asst. attending physician, ophthalmologist, surg. instr. St. Clare's Hosp., 1975—; attending ophthalmologist Cabrini Med. Ctr., 1982—, St. Vincent's Hosp., N.Y.C., 1995—. Founder Lipton Eye Clinic, N.Y.C., 1981—; v.p. Van Arfa Realty, N.Y.C., 1984-88; pres. H&L Realty, Suffern, N.Y., 1981—; mem. bd. dirs. Salisbury (Conn.) Pub. Health Nursing Assn. Mem. U.S. Congl. Adv. Bd.; mem. bd. deacons Congregationalist Ch. With AUS, 1956-58. Named Internat. Amigo, OAS; recipient Presdl. Citation for outstanding community svc., 1991 Mem. N.Y. Med. Soc., Am. Assn. Individual Investors, Bronx High Sch. Sci. Alumni Assn., Sharon Country Club, United Shareholders Assn., Internat. Platform Assn., Wider Quaker Fellowship, Vanderbilt U. Cabinet Club. Republican. Home: Interlaken Estates Lakeville CT 06039 also: 1199 Park Ave New York NY 10128-1711 Office: Lipton Eye Clinic 51 E 90th St New York NY 10128-1205

LIPTON, LOIS JEAN, lawyer; b. Chgo., Jan. 14, 1946; d. Harold and Bernice (Reiter) Farber L.; m. Peter Carey, May 30, 1978; children: Rachel, Sara. BA, U. Mich., 1966; JD summa cum laude, DePaul Coll. Law, Chgo., 1974; postgrad., Sheffield (Eng.) U., 1966. Bar: Ky. 1974, U.S. Dist. Ct. (we. dist.) Ky. 1974, U.S. Ct. Appeals (6th cir.) 1974, Ill. 1975, U.S. Dist. Ct. (no. dist.) Ill. 1975, U.S. Ct. Appeals (7th cir.) 1976. Staff counsel Roger Baldwin Found. of ACLU, Inc., Chgo., 1975-79, dir. reproductive rights project, 1979-83; atty. McDermott, Will & Emergy, 1984-86, G.D. Searle, Skokie, Ill., 1988-90; sr. atty. AT&T, Chgo., 1990—. Del. White House Conf. on Families, Mpls., 1980. Recipient Durfee award, 1984. Mem. ACLU (v.p.), ABA, Chgo. Coun. Lawyers. Office: AT&T # R15 222 W Adams St Chicago IL 60606-5017 E-mail: llipton@att.com.

LIPTON, MARTIN, lawyer; b. N.J., June 22, 1931; s. Samuel D. and Fannie L.; m. Susan Lytle, Feb. 17, 1982; children: James, Margaret, Katherine, Samantha BS in Econs., U. Pa., 1952; LLB, NYU, 1955. Bar: N.Y. 1956. Ptnr. Wachtell Lipton Rosen & Katz, N.Y.C., 1965—. Mem. coun. Am. Law Inst. Chmn. bd. of trustees NYU; bd. trustees NYU Law Sch.; hon. chmn. Jerusalem Found.; chmn. bd. dirs. Prep for Prep; dir. Inst. Jud. Adminstrn. Mem.: Am. Acad. Arts and Scis. Office: Wachtell Lipton Rosen & Katz 51 W 52nd St Fl 29 New York NY 10019-6150

LIPTON, NINA ANNE, healthcare executive; b. N.Y.C., Oct. 6, 1959; d. Robert and Rita Kay (Wolfman) L. BA in Econs., Wellesley Coll., 1981; postgrad., London Sch. Econs., 1981-82. Rsch. asst. Nat. Econ. Rsch. Assocs., White Plains, N.Y., 1983-84; cons. A.T. Hudson and Co., Paramus, N.J., 1984; asst. economist Dean Witter Reynolds, N.Y.C., 1984-89; dir. market rsch. Platinum Guild Internat., 1989-94; v.p., exec. dir. Ctr. for Alternative Healthcare, Inc., Miami, Fla., 1995-98; exec. dir. Summit Med. Group, Conn., Ga., Ala., Mich., 1995—2001. Exec. dir., v.p. Aztec Mgmt. Co., 1995—. Writer This Week in Platinum weekly, 1989-94; contbr. articles to profl. jours. Recruiter, fundraiser, reunion com. chair Wellesley (Mass.) Coll. Alumnae Assn.,1982—, mem. spl. gifts com., 1991, co-chair 20th reunion 2000-2001, ann. giving rep. '81, 2001—; staff coord. Women for Bowles, Erskine Bowles for U.S. Senate, N.C., women's outreach dir., 2002—. Mem. Internat. Precious Metals Inst., Nat. Assn. Bus. Economists, Futures Industry Assn.

LIPTON, ROBERT STEPHEN, lawyer; b. Malone, N.Y., Apr. 19, 1942; BS in Aerospace Engring., U. Mich., 1964; postgrad., U. Wash., 1965-66; JD, Temple U., 1972. Bar: U.S. Patent and Trademark Office 1970, Pa. 1972, U.S. Dist. Ct. (ea. dist.) Pa. 1973, U.S. Ct. Appeals (fed. cir.) 1982. Wind tunnel test engr. The Boeing Co., Seattle, 1965-67, patent adminstr. Phila., 1967-70, patent agt., 1970-72, patent atty., 1972-75; pvt. practice law Media, Pa., 1975-84; ptnr. Lipton, Weinberger & Husick, 1984—. Mem. ABA, Pa. Bar Assn., Delaware County Bar Assn., Phila. Intellectual Property Law Assn., Am. Intellectual Property Law Assn., Am. Helicopter Soc. Office: Lipton Weinberger & Husick 201 N Jackson St Media PA 19063-2902

LIPTON, ROBERT STEVEN, lawyer; b. N.Y.C., May 12, 1946; s. Max and Mildred (Goodman) L.; m. Stephanie F. Kass, Aug. 8, 1971. BA, NYU, 1967, JD, 1971. Bar: N.Y. 1972, U.S. Ct. Appeals (2d cir.) 1972, U.S. Dist. Ct. (so. dist.) N.Y. 1973, U.S. Supreme Ct. 1975. Assoc. Curtis, Mallet-Prevost, Colt & Mosle, N.Y.C., 1971-80, ptnr., 1980-2001, of counsel, 2001—. Editor NYU Law Rev., 1969-71. Mem. ABA, Fed. Bar Council, N.Y. State Bar Assn., Assn. of Bar of City of N.Y., Phi Beta Kappa. Clubs: India House (N.Y.C.). Office: Curtis Mallet-Prevost Colt & Mosle 101 Park Ave Fl 34 New York NY 10178-0061 E-mail: rlipton@cm-p.com.

LIPTZIN, BENJAMIN, psychiatrist; b. N.Y.C., Sept. 17, 1945; s. David Murray and Mollie (Brody) L.; m. Sharon Leslie Rothstein, June 10, 1968; children: Shoshanna, Daniel, Deborah. BA, Yale U., 1966; MD, U. Rochester, N.Y., 1971. Diplomate Am. Bd. Psychiatry and Neurology. Resident in psychiatry U. Va. Hosp., Charlottesville, 1971-74; med. officer NIMH, Rockville, Md., 1974-78; dir. geriatric psychiatry McLean Hosp., Belmont, Mass., 1978-89, asst. gen. dir., 1989-90; chief dept. psychiatry Baystate Med. Ctr., Springfield, 1990—; prof., dep. chmn. dept. psychiatry Tufts U. Sch. Medicine, 1990—. Contbr. articles to profl. jours. With USPHS, 1972-78. Recipient Acad. award NIMH, 1983. Fellow Am. Psychiat. Assn. (trustee-at-large 1992-95); mem. AMA, Am. Coll. Psychiatrists. Democrat. Jewish. Office: Baystate Med Ctr Dept Psychiatry 759 Chestnut St Springfield MA 01199-1001 E-mail: benjamin.liptzin@bhs.org.

LIPUT, ANDREW LAWRENCE, lawyer, educator; b. Trenton, N.J., June 28, 1962; s. Andrew and Bernice Helen L.; m. Jacquelyn Anne Liput, Jan. 11, 1997; children: Mallory, Sloane. BA, Drew U., 1984; JD, Fordham U., 1987. Bar: N.J., 1987, N.Y., 1988, Conn., 1996. V.p., gen. cousel Parssine Group, Inc., NYC, 1988-91; sr. lawyer Hartman, Buhrman & Winnicki, Paramus, NJ, 1991-93; v.p., gen. counsel Marjam Supply Co., Inc., Bklyn., 1993-96; ptnr. Liput, Ricca, Donner LLP, Huntington, 1996—; adj. prof. Felician Coll., Lodi, NJ, 1994-97; assoc. prof. Suffolk C.C., Long Island, NY, 1998—, Briarcliff Coll., Bethpage, 2001—; prof. St. Joseph's Coll., 2001—. Trust officer, Neighborhood Cleaners Assn., N.Y.C., 1998—, Metropolitan Package Store Assn., Westchester, N.Y., 1997—. Author: Long Lost Tales of the Legendary Snarfdoodle, 2001; contbr. articles to profl. jours. Pres., dir. Bridge the Gap!, Long Island, 1999—, councilman, No. Plainfield, N.J., 1988-89. Mem. U.S. Rowing Assn., Aircraft Owners & Pilots Assn., N.Y. State Bar Assn., N.J. State Bar Assn., Conn. Bar Assn. Republican. Avocations: rowing, flying, reading, world travel. Office: Liput & Speregen PC 790 New York Ave Huntington NY 11743-4499

LIRANSO, TESFAYE F. statistician, researcher; b. Hosanna, Shoa, Ethiopia, Sept. 2, 1958; s. Tesfaye F. Liranso and Gesegesu D. Yemane, Fugago Liranso and Bubame Sewore; m. Gesegesu D. Yemane, Oct. 27, 1964; children: Yilak Tesfaye, Surafel Tesfaye; children: Nathan Tesfaye. PhD in Stats., Okla. State U., 1993. Sr. biostatistician Quintiles, Kans. City, Mo., 1999—2001, statis. sci., 2001—. Statis. and application cons. Multiple, Kans. City, 1995—97. Contbr. articles to profl. jours. Mem. PTA, Lee's Summit, Mo., 2001. Mem.: Am. Statstical Assn. Independent. Avocation: travelling by car. Office: Quintiles Inc 10245 Hickman Mills Drive Kansas City MO 64086

LIROFF, RICHARD ALAN, environmental association executive; b. Bklyn., June 21, 1948; BA in Politics cum laude, Brandeis U., 1969; Phd in Polit. Sci., Northwestern U., 1976. Project assoc. Environ. Law Inst., Washington, 1973-79; sr. assoc. The Conservation Found., 1979-89; dir. Ctrl. and Eastern Europe program World Wildlife Fund, 1989-95, policy dir. Wildlife and Contaminants program, 1997—. Author: A National Policy for the Environment, 1976, Protecting Open Space, 1981, Great Lakes, Great Legacy, 1990,

Reducing Reliance on Pesticides in the Great Lakes Basin, 1997. Co-founder, treas. Washington Area Bicyclist Assn., 1972; co-founder, sec. Webster House Tenant Assn., 1978. Mem. Brandeis U. Alumni Assn. (bd. dirs. 1972-87). Office: World Wildlife Fund 1250 24th St NW Fl 6 Washington DC 20037-1193

LIS, EDWARD FRANCIS, pediatrician, consultant; b. Chgo., Apr. 1, 1918; s. Stephen and Stephanie L.; m. Sonne Nadine Kowalsen, Apr. 3, 1944; children— Jeffrey Warren, James Bryan. Student, DePaul U., 1936-37; BS, MD, U. Ill. Pvt. practice, Park Forest, Ill., 1949-51; faculty U. Ill. Coll. Medicine, 1951-90, prof. pediatrics, also dir. div. services crippled children, 1959-90, prof. emeritus, 1990—. Dir. center handicapped children Univ. Hosp., U. Ill., 1955-90; cons. in field. Contbr. to profl. jours. Chmn. research adv. com. Children's Bur., HEW, 1964-67; mem. Ill. Commn. Children. Served to capt. AUS, 1944-46. Fellow Am. Acad. Pediatrics, Am. Pub. Health Assn.; mem. Sigma Xi. Home: 3003 Balmoral Cres Flossmoor IL 60422-1404 E-mail: edson639@aol.com.

LISA, JANICE P. auditor; b. Elizabeth, N.J., Apr. 15, 1957; d. Edward and Elizabeth Rose Bajgrowicz. BA in Acctg., Rutgers U., 1979; MPA in Pub. Adminstrn., Kean U., 1999. Corp. auditor Merrill Lynch, N.Y.C.; internal audit dir. County of Union, Elizabeth, NJ; asst. fin. mgr. Superior Ct./N.J. Union Vicinage. Mem. supervisory com., auditor Union County Credit Union. Rec. sec. Columbus Hosp. Aux. Found., Newark, 1997—. Mem.: ASPA, Inst. Internal Auditors, Pi Alpha Alpha. Roman Catholic. Avocations: speed walking, reading, touring museums, antiques. Home: 133 Liberty Ave Linden NJ 07036-3244 Office: State of NJ/Judiciary 2 Broad St Elizabeth NJ 07201

LISANBY, JAMES WALKER, retired naval officer; b. Princeton, Ky., Jan. 31, 1928; s. Alvin and Rebecca L.; m. Gladys Elnora Kemp, Nov. 18, 1951; children: Elizabeth Ann, Sarah Hollingsworth. BS in Elec. Engring, U.S. Naval Acad., 1950; Engrs. Degree in Naval Architecture, MIT, 1953-56; student, Program for Mgmt. Devel., Harvard U., 1967. Commd. ensign U.S. Navy, 1950, advanced through grades to rear adm., 1977; ship supt. Charleston Naval Shipyard, 1956-59; main propulsion asst. U.S.S. Antietam (CVS 36), 1959-61; asst. for ship materials, staff, comdr.-in-chief Atlantic Fleet, 1961-63; asst. for new constrn. cruisers and destroyers Naval Ship Systems Command, Dept. Navy, Washington, 1963-65, head procurement and prodn. br., fast deployment logistic ship project office, 1965-68, exec. asst. to comdr., 1969-70; dir. indsl. engring. office of asst. sec. of navy, installations and logistics, 1968-69; supr. shipbldg. Pascagoula, Miss., 1970-73; asst. for ship design, office chief naval ops., 1973-74; project mgr. LHA class amphibious assault ships, 1974-77; comdr. Naval Ship Engring. Center Navy Dept., Washington, 1977-79; dep. comdr. ship design and integration Naval Sea Systems Command, Dept. Navy, 1979-81, prin. dep. acquisition, 1981-83, ret., 1983; founder, pres. Naval Services Internat. Inc., Washington, 1983—, pres., chief exec. officer. Recipient Engr. of Yr. award Soc. Mfg. Engrs., 1979; decorated Legion of Merit Mem. Am. Soc. Naval Engrs. (nat. v.p. 1979-81), Soc. Naval Architects and Marine Engrs., Sigma Xi, Tau Beta Pi. Office: 1501 20th St S Arlington VA 22202

LISBOA-FARROW, ELIZABETH OLIVER, public and government relations consultant; b. N.Y.C., Nov. 25, 1947; d. Eleuterio and Esperanza Oliver; m. Jeffrey Lloyd Farrow, Dec. 31, 1980; 1 child, Hamilton Oliver Farrow; 1 stepchild, Maximillian Robbins Farrow. Student pvt. schs., N.Y.C. With Harold Rand & Co. and various other pub. rels. firms, N.Y.C., 1966-75; dir. pub. rels. N.Y. Playboy Club and Playboy Clubs Internat., 1975-79; pres., CEO Lisboa Assocs., Inc., N.Y.C., 1979—; founder, pres. Lisboa Prodns., Inc., Washington, 1994—. Counselor Am. Woman's Devel. Corp. Sec. Nat. Acad. Concert and Cabaret Arts; mem. nat. adv. coun. SBA, 1980-81, apptd., 1994—; exec. dir. Variety Club of Greater Washington Children's Charity, Inc., 1985-90; bd. dirs. Variety Myoelectric Limb Bank Found., 1990-91, Comcast, 2001, Hispanic Radio Network, 2001; trustee Hispanic Coll. Fund, 1995—, vice chair, 1996—; chair bd. trustees Southeastern U., 1997—; mem. adv. bd. Indsl. Bank, N.A., 1996; bd. dirs. Bell Multicultural H.S. Named Pub. Rels. Woman of Yr., Women in Pub. Rels., 1992, Empresaria del Milenio, Duodecimo Encuentro Empresarian, P.R., 2001, Hispanic Bus. Woman of Yr., Nat. Hispanic Bus. Coun., 1996, Hispanic of Yr. in Bus., La Nacion Newspaper, 1997, Entrepreneur of Yr., Hispanic Mag., 1999, Bus Woman of Yr., N.Y. State Hispanic Chambers Commerce; recipient Disting. award of Excellence, SBA, 1992, Women Bus. Enterprise award, U.S. Transp. Nat. Hwy. Transp. Safety Adminstrn., 1994, Civic Cmty. Achievement, Black Bus. and Profls. Network, 1999, Excellence in Entrepreneurship award, Dialogue on Diversity, Inc., 1995, Women of Distinction award, Nat. Conf. Coll. Women Student Leaders, 2000, Applause award, Women's Bus. Enterprise Nat. Coun., 2000, Imagen award, San Juan, P.R., 2001, Presdl. medal, Sistema U. Ana G. Mendez, U. Metropolitana, San Juan, 1999, Internat. Leadership award, Mex. Am. C. of C., 2001. Mem. U.S. Hispanic C. of C. (bd. dirs. 1998, Nat. Hispanic Businesswoman of Yr. 1996, vice chair 1999, chair 2000), D.C. C. of C. (pres. 2000), Small Bus. Adv. Coun., U.S. C. of C. (Blue Chip Enterprise award 1993), Advt. Coun., Am. Heart Assn., Hispanic Bus. and Profl. Women's Assn., Ibero-Am. C. of C. (bd. dirs. 1993, v.p. 1995, pres. 1997, pres. 1998, adv. chair 1999, Small Bus. award 1993, corp. of yr. award 2000), City Club Washington. Office: 1317 F St NW Washington DC 20004-1105

LISEK, NANCY ANN TARASEVICH, consulting company executive; b. Kingston, Pa., Sept. 28, 1941; d. Theodore and Mary M. (Muscavage) Tarasevich; m. Edward Martin Lisek, Nov. 10, 1962; children: Gregory Edward Paul, Damien Blair. Grad. Strayer's Bus. Sch., Balt., 1960, Barbizon, Towson, Md., 1983, Archdiocese Balt., 1976; student Essex Community Coll. Sec. Henry Rose, Balt., 1964-66, Lloyd's London, Balt., 1959-64; field mgr. Hamrah & Assocs., Glendale, Calif., 1984-85; pres., chief exec. officer, owner N.A.T.E.L. Enterprises, Balt., 1985—. Producer Renaissance Cities, Passport to Fun and Adventure; contbr. articles to profl. jours. Nat. legis. chmn. Md. P.T.A., Balt., 1978-80, sec., 1980-82, 1st v.p., 1982-84; mem. Washington legis. service com. Nat. P.T.A., 1979-85; mem. Md. Travel Council, 1986—; v.p. Balt. Tourism Assn., 1987; chmn. Md. Tourism Week, 1987; chmn. Md. P.T.A. Convention, Hunt Valley, 1983; co-ordinator Nat. P.T.A. Legis. Conf., Washington, 1984, 85; chmn. Md. Coalition to Save Pub. Edn., Balt., 1979; mem. White House Conf. on Families, Washington, 1980; mem. White House Conf. on Small Bus., 1985. Recipient Appreciation award St. Ursula's Cub Pack, Parkville, Md., 1976. Mem. Nat. Assn. Female Execs., Balt. Attractions Assn., Balt. Conv. Bur., Am. Entrepreneurs Assn. Roman Catholic. Avocations: travel; sewing; knitting. Home: 3511 Hiss Ave Baltimore MD 21234-4812 Office: NATEL Enterprises 3511 Hiss Ave Baltimore MD 21234-4812

LISENBY, DORRECE EDENFIELD, realtor; b. Sneads, Fla., Dec. 2, 1942; d. Neal McLendon and Linnie (McCroan) Edenfield; m. Wallace Lamar Lisenby, Nov. 18, 1961; children: Pamela Ann, Wallace Neal. BS in Tech. Bus. magna cum laude, Athens (Ala.) State Coll., 1991. Stenographer State of Fla., Tallahassee and Miami, Fla., 1960-62, Gulf Oil Corp., Coral Gables, 1962-64, Gulf Power Co., Pensacola, 1965-68; loan svc. asst. First Fed. Savs. and Loan Assn., Greenville, S.C., 1969-70; various real estate positions, 1978-85; adminstrv. asst. Charter Retreat Hosp., Decatur, Ala., 1986-91; broker/salesperson Ferrell Realty Plus, Inc., Tallahassee, 1995-2001; broker, owner Lisenby Realty, Inc., 2001—. Mem. Econ. Club Fla., Am. Legion (Citizenship award 1957), Tallahassee Symphony Soc., Avondale Forest Cmty. Club (pres. Taylors, S.C. chpt. 1969), Taylor's Garden Club (pres. Taylor's chpt. 1975-76), P.E.O. Sisterhood, Killearn Ladies Club (pres.). Republican. Baptist. Avocations: reading, music, bridge, gardening. Home: 2925 Shamrock St S Tallahassee FL 32309-3226 E-mail: dorrecel@msn.com.

LISETTI, CHRISTINE LAETITIA, computer scientist, educator; b. Nice, France; PhD, Fla. Internat. U., 1995. Postdoctoral rsch. fellow Stanford (Calif.) U., 1996—98; asst. prof. U. South Fla., Tampa, 1998—2001, U. Ctrl. Fla., Orlando, 2001—. Contbr. articles to profl. jours. Recipient Individual Rsch. Svc. award, NIH, 1998, Nils Nilsson award for integrating AI techs., 2000; grantee, Intel Corp., 1998, Interval Rsch. Corp., 1998—99, Office of Naval Rsch., 2000—. Mem.: Emotion Rsch. Soc., IEEE Soc. on Social Implications of Tech., IEEE Computer Soc., Assn. Computing Machinery, Am. Assn. Artificial Intelligence. Office: U Ctrl Fla University Blvd CSB Orlando FL 32816-2362 Business E-Mail: lisetti@cs.ucf.edu.

LISHAK, LISA ANNE, secondary education educator; b. Berlin, Nov. 27, 1960; (parents Am. citizens); d. Richard Edward Brogdon and Martha (Shuman) Gault; m. Robert Stephen Lishak, Apr. 22, 1989; 1 child, Trent Stephen. BS, Auburn U., 1989, postgrad., 2002—; MEd, Ala. State U., 1998. Cert in early adolescence/generalist category, Ala.; nat. bd. cert. tchr. Nat. Bd. for Profl. Tchg. Stds. Substitute tchr. Lee County, Auburn, Opelika Schs., Ala., 1989; tchr. math. Lanett (Ala.) Jr. High Sch., 1989-91, Opelika (Ala.) Mid. Sch., 1992-95; instr. math. So. Union C.C., Opelika, 1998-2000; tchr. algebra I and pre-algebra Russell County Middle Sch. formerly Jr. High Sch., Ala., 2000—. Usher Trinity Luth. Ch., Auburn, Ala., 1989—. Master sgt. USAF, 1978-84, mem. Res., 1978-2000, ret. Recipient plaque of appreciation Math-A-Thon, St. Jude's Children's Hosp., 1991; Ala. Power grantee, 1993-94, site-based mgmt. grantee Opelika Mid. Sch., 1994-95. Mem. NEA, Nat. Coun. Tchrs. Math., Chattahoochee Coun. Tchrs. Math., Ala. Edn. Assn., Columbia Regional Math. Collaborative, Phi Kappa Phi, Kappa Delta Pi, Pi Lambda Theta. Home: 789 Annabrook Dr Auburn AL 36830-7529 Office: Russell County Middle Sch PO Box 38 Seale AL 36875

LISHER, JAMES RICHARD, lawyer; b. Aug. 28, 1947; s. Leonard B. and Mary Jane (Rafferty) L.; m. Martha Gettelfinger, June 16, 1973; children: Jennifer, James Richard II. AB, Ind. U., 1969, JD, 1975. Bar: Ind. 1975, U.S. Dist. Ct. (so. dist.) Ind. 1975, U.S. Supreme Ct. 2000. Assoc. Rafferty & Wood, Shelbyville, Ind., 1976, Rafferty & Lisher, Shelbyville, 1976-77; dep. prosecutor Shelby County Prosecutor's Office, 1976-78; ptnr. Yeager, Lisher & Baldwin, 1977-96; pvt. practice, 1996—. Pros. atty. Shelby County, Shelbyville, 1983-95, pub. defender, 1995—, chief pub. defender, 2000—. Speaker, faculty advisor Ind. Pros. Sch., 1986. Editor: (manual) Traffic Case Defenses, 1982, First Law Office, 1998. Bd. dirs. Girls Club of Shelbyville, 1979-84, Bears of Blue River Festival, Shelbyville, 1982-2002; pres. Shelby County Internat. Rels. Coun., 1997-2002. Recipient Citation of Merit, Young Lawyers Assn. Mem. ATLA, Nat. Assn. Criminal Def. Lawyers, Ind. Pub. Defender Assn., Ind. State Bar Assn. (bd. dirs. young lawyer sect. 1979-83, bd. dirs. gen. practice sect. 1996-98, treas. 1997-98, vice-chmn. 1998-99, chmn. 2000-01), Shelby County Bar Assn. (sec.-treas. 1986, v.p. 1987, pres. 1988), Ind. Prosecuting Attys. Assn. (bd. dirs. 1985-95, sec.-treas. 1987, v.p. 1988, pres. 1990), Masons, Elks, Lions. Home: 106 Western Trce Shelbyville IN 46176-9765 Office: 407 S Harrison St Shelbyville IN 46176-2170

LISHKA, EDWARD JOSEPH, insurance underwriter; b. Chgo., Oct. 8, 1949; s. Edward John and Virginia Nelly (Powers) L.; m. Marie Ann Slawniak, June 7, 1975 (dec. Dec. 1993); 1 child, Ann. BS, Bradley U., 1971, MA, 1972. CPCU. Design engr. Forest Electric Co., Melrose Park, Ill., 1972-73; tech. writer Advance Schs. Inc., Des Plaines, 1973-74; design engr. Universal Oil Products, 1974-75; account engr. Oil Ins. Assn., Chgo., 1975-81; policy cons. CNA Ins. Co., 1981-85; underwriter Service Ins. Agy., Mount Prospect, 1985-86; sr. acct. underwriter Arkwright Mut. Inst. Co., Schaumburg Village, 1986-92; acct. analyst Mack & Parker, Chgo., 1992—2002; exec. risk mgmt. rep. Arthur J. Gallagher & Co., Itaska, 2002—. Mem. Schaumburg Village Ins. Com., 1983—. Mem. Soc. CPCUs (speaker 1987—, chmn. candidate devel. 1987-88, Profl. Devel. award 1986, 88, 89, 90, 92), Accredited Advisers in Ins. (assoc. in risk mgmt., assoc. in marine ins. mgmt.), Four Winds Ski Club (Itasca, Ill.). Republican. Roman Catholic. Avocations: skiing, golf, bicycling, fishing. Home: 100 Idlestone Ln Schaumburg IL 60194-4044 Office: Arthur J Gallagher & Co Two Pierce Pl Itasca IL 60143-2141 E-mail: EdLishka@aol.com., edward_lishka@ajg.com.

LISI, LORI A. (LORI FREDEKING), freelance/self-employed editor, writer; b. Fort Worth, July 28; d. Nelsie Ann Austin; m. James Lisi, Apr. 20, 2001. Student, U. Tex., Arlington, 1991—96. Freelance editor/writer, Garland, Tex., 1991—. Mem.: Nat. Writer's Union, Editl. Freelancers Assn. Home: PO Box 450475 Garland TX 75045 Personal E-mail: Lorifredeking@aol.com.

LISI, MARY M. federal judge; BA, U. R.I., 1972; JD, Temple U., 1977. Tchr. history Prout Meml. High Sch., Wakefield, R.I., 1975-76; law clk. U.S. Atty., Providence, 1976, Phila., 1976-77; asst. pub. defender R.I. Office Pub. Defender, 1977-81; asst. child advocate Office Child Advocate, 1981-82; also. pvt. practice atty. Providence, 1981-82; dir. office ct. appointed spl. advocate R.I. Family Ct., 1982-87; dep. disciplinary counsel office disciplinary counsel R.I. Supreme Ct., 1988-90, chief disciplinary counsel, 1990-94; U.S. Dist. judge Dist. Ct., Providence, Dist. R.I. (1st cir.), Providence, 1994—. Mem. Select Com. to Investigate Failure of R.I. Share and Deposit Indemnity Corp., 1991-92. Recipient Providence 350 award, 1986, Meritorious Svc. to Children of Am. award, 1987. Office: Fed Bldg and US Courthouse 1 Exchange Ter Ste 113 Providence RI 02903-1744

LISIECKI, DENISE THERESA, artist, educator; b. Cleve., Dec. 23, 1951; d. Leo Leonard and Anna Louise (Goldyn) L.; m. Kenneth Claude Freed, July 27, 1974; 1 child, Jacob Freed. BFA, Miami U. of Ohio, 1973; MA, SUNY, Oswego, 1974. Co-dir. Mich. Multiples Gallery, Richland, 1976-77; printmaking chair Kalamazoo Inst. Arts, 1983-84, 2-D dept. chair, 1984—, dir. Art Sch., 1997—. Adj. prof. Western Mich. U., Kalamazoo, 1977, Kalamzaoo Coll., 1997; vis. artist Mich. Coun. for the Arts, Alpena, 1977, Ferdale, Mich., 1979-80; juror watercolor competition Kans. Watercolor Soc., Wichita, 1996; cons. in field. Mem. coun. Edn. for the Arts Adv. Coun., Kalamazoo, 1997—. Arts Midwest fellow NAE, 1988; creative artist grantee Mich. Coun. of the Arts, 1981, 88; recipient Best of Show award Watermedia/Midland Arts, 1985. Avocations: gardening, yoga, reading. Home: 3210 East G Ave Kalamazoo MI 49004 Office: Kalamazoo Inst of Arts 314 S Park St Kalamazoo MI 49007 E-mail: denise_l@kiarts.org.

LISIO, DONALD JOHN, historian, educator; b. Oak Park, Ill., May 27, 1934; s. Anthony and Dorothy (LoCelso) Lisio; m. Susznne Marie Swanson, Apr. 22, 1958; children: Denise Anne, Stephen Anthony. BA, Knox Coll., 1956; MA, Ohio U., 1958; PhD, U. Wis., 1965. Mem. faculty overseas div. U. Md., 1958-60; from asst. prof. history to prof. emeritus Coe Coll., Cedar Rapids, Iowa, 1964—2002, prof. emeritus, 2002—. Author: (book) The President and Protest: Hoover, Conspiracy, and the Bonus Riot, 1974, Hoover, Blacks, and Lily-Whites: A Study of Southern Strategies, 1985; contbg. author: book The War Generation, 1975; contbr. articles to hist. jours. Mem. exec. com. Cedar Rapids Com. Hist. Preservation, 1975—77. With U.S. Army, 1958—60. Fellow William F. Vilas Rsch., U. Wis., 1963—64, NEH, 1969—70, Rsch., 1984—85, Am. Coun. Learned Socs., 1977—78; grantee, 1971—72, Rsch., U.S. Inst. Peace, 1990. Mem.: ACLU, AAUP, Am. Hist. Assn., Orgn. Am. Historians. Roman Catholic. Home: 4203 Twin Ridge Ct SE Cedar Rapids IA 52403-3950 Office: Coe Coll Cedar Rapids IA 52402

LISK, ALAN ROBERT, finance educator, consultant; b. Chgo., Dec. 1, 1942; s. Robert Duncan and Estelle Alice Lisk; m. Jean Marie Miller, June 12, 1965; 1 child Heather Rakosnik 1 child Travis. PhD, Temple U., 1998. Cert. Myers-Briggs Type Indicator 2001. Retail store divsn. mgr. Sears, Omaha, 1970—72, asst. purchasing agt. Chgo., 1972—74, asst. retail sales mgr., 1974—78, nat. retail sales mgr., 1978—79, asst. buyer Dubuque, Iowa, 1979—80, group mktg. asst. Chgo., 1980—81, nat. mktg. mgr., 1981—83, buyer, 1983—88, ops. mgr., 1988—89; chief operating officer Flying Colours USA, Inc., Geln Ellyn, 1989—91; exec. dir. degree completion program Eastern Coll., St. Davids, Pa., 1991—96; sr. assoc. trainer Temple U., Phila., 1994—98, grad. asst., 1996—98; dir. bus. rsch. ctr. Penn State U., Uniontown, 1998—2000, asst. prof. bus., 1998—2000; prin. ptnr. LJA Assocs., Dubuque, Iowa, 1996—; dir. U. Dubuque Inst. U. Dubuque, 2001—, assoc. prof. bus., 2000—. Cons. LJA Assocs., Dubuque, 1996—. Activist Presbyn. Ch. USA, Dubuque, 1985—. With U.S. Coast Guard, 1966—70. Mem.: ASTD, Orgnl. Devel. Inst. (co-chair annual internat. conf. 2001—), Assn. Psychological Type (cert. 2001—), Acad. Mgmt., Alpha Kappa Psi (advisor 1999—2000). Presbyterian. Avocations: reading, Web surfing, skiing, swimming. Office: U Dubuque 2000 University Ave Dubuque IA 52001 Office Fax: 563-589-3322.

LISK, EDWARD STANLEY, musician, educator, conductor; b. Oswego, N.Y., Feb. 1, 1934; s. Edward Andrew and Jennie (Segal) L.; m. Doris E. Thornber, Sept. 1, 1956; children: Janice, Carol, Jean. B Music Edn., Syracuse (N.Y.) U., 1956; postgrad., Ithaca (N.Y.) Sch. Music, 1965, Oswego State Coll., 1980. Cert. tchr., adminstr. Tchr. music Red Creek (N.Y.) Cen. Schs., 1958-70; band dir., K-12 music supr. Oswego (N.Y.) City Sch. Dist., 1970-91. Clarinetist Syracuse Symphony Orch., 1963-67; profl. musician Syracuse orchs., bands, 1960-90; clinician, lectr. Australian Nat. Band and Orch. Assn., Perth, Melbourne and Sydney, 1990, condr./clinician, 1995; clinician numerous convs., 1980—. Author: The Creative Director, 1987, Alternative Rehearsal Techniques Student Supplement, Books 1 and 2, 1993, A.R.T. Teaching Accessories, 1994, (video) A.R.T. and the V.C. University Wind Ensemble, 1994, Intangibles of Musical Performance, 1996; co-author: Teaching Music Through Performance in Band-Vol. 1,2&3.; contbr. articles to profl. jours. Sgt. U.S. Army, 1956-58. Named Tchr. of Yr., Oswego Classroom Tchrs. Assn., 1974, 83, Disting. Bandmaster Am., First Chair of Am., 1981, Area Educator of Yr., Phi Delta Kappa, 1983, Adminstr. of Yr., Oswego Bd. Edn./Adminstrn., 1989; recipient Sudler Order of Merit John Philip Sousa Found., 1997. Mem. Music Educators Nat. Conf., Nat. Band Assn. (1st v.p. 1988-90, pres. 1990-92, news editor 1992—, Citation of Excellence 1977), Am. Bandmasters Assn. (v.p. 1998-99, pres. 2000—), N.Y. State Band Dirs. Assn. (bd. dirs. 1981-96, named Outstanding Band Dir. 1995), N.Y. State Sch. Music Assn., World Assn. for Symphonic Bands and Ensembles, Phi Beta Mu. Roman Catholic. Avocations: computers, golf, travel. Home: 836 County Route 25 Oswego NY 13126-5716

LISKA, MARGARET NAYLOR, retired small business owner; b. Callaway, Nebr., July 27, 1922; d. James Corban and Ruth Frances (Snodgrass) Naylor; m. Arthur Joseph Liska, Apr. 5, 1946 (dec. 1995); children: Jo, A. James. BS, U. Denver, 1944. Auditor Conn. Gen. Life Ins., Hartford, 1944-45, mgr. Denver, 1945-46; co-owner Broadview (Ill.) Hardware, 1946-60, Ben Franklin Store, Batavia, Ill., 1962-93; pres. Liska Enterprises, Inc., 1962-93; owner Wedding Wisdom, 1982-93. Mem. AAUW (Rsch. and Project Endowment namee 1986), AARP, PEO (pres.), Am. Needlework Guild, Embroiders Guild of Am., St. Charles Country Club, Order of Eastern Star. Avocations: volunteerism, needlework, reading, cooking, golf. Home: 1500 S 14th St Unit 309 Saint Charles IL 60174-3772

LISKAMM, WILLIAM HUGO, architect, urban planner, educator; b. N.Y.C., Sept. 10, 1931; s. William J. and Johanne (Herz) L.; m. Karen Elizabeth Nunn, May 1979; children: Amanda Nunn, Mason Nunn; children by previous marriage— Erika, Thea, Fiona. B.Arch., Pratt Inst., 1954; Fulbright scholar, Technische Hochschule, Stuttgart, Germany, 1954-55; M.Arch., Harvard, 1956. Project architect maj. archtl. and urban planning programs, Calif. and N.Y., 1958-63; exec. v.p. Okamoto & Liskamm, Inc. (planners and architects), San Francisco, 1963-71; ind. archtl. and urban planning cons., 1971-74; pres. William H. Liskamm, AIA, AIP, Inc., 1974—; dir. planning Woodward-Clyde Consultants, San Francisco, 1978-79; dir. campus planning office U. Calif., Berkeley, 1984-90. Asst. prof. dept. architecture Coll. Environ. Design, U. Calif. at Berkeley, 1963-69, vice chmn., 1965-67, vis. sr. lectr. U. Coll., London, 1967-68; chmn. bd. Archtl. Found. No. Calif.; chmn. design rev. bd. San Francisco Bay Conservation and Devel. Commn., State of Calif., 1970-80; chmn. archtl. adv. com. Golden Gate Bridge Hwy. and Transp. Dist., 1980-81; prof., advisor more than 40 major planning and design competitions. Author: Appearance and Design Element, California Coastal Plan, 1974. Served to 1st lt. C.E. AUS, 1956-58. Recipient awards for profl. projects HUD; Am. Inst. Planners award for San Francisco Urban Design Plan, 1972; Wheelwright fellow Harvard, 1967-68; Nat. Endowment for Arts grantee. Mem. AIA (coll. of fellows).

LISLE, LAURIE, author; b. Providence, Sept. 11, 1942; d. Laurence Lisle and Adeline Cole Simonds; m. Robert I. Kipniss, Dec. 17, 1994. BA in English, Ohio Wesleyan U., 1965. Rschr. Newsweek mag., N.Y.C., 1970-78; assoc. prof. Southampton Coll. of L.I. U., 1981-82; ind. scholar So. Conn. Libr. Coun., Hamden, 1989—2002; spkr. N.Y. Coun. for the Humanities, N.Y.C., 2000—02. Author: Portrait of an Artist: A Biography of Georgia O'Keeffe, 1980, Louise Nevelson: A Passionate Life, 1990, Without Child: Challenging the Stigma of Childlessness, 1996. Active Dem. Town Com., Sharon, 1985—94. Mem. The Authors Guild, Am. Pen Ctr. Democrat. Unitarian Universalist. Home: PO Box 170 Ardsley On Hudson NY 10503 E-mail: llisle@ix.netcom.com.

LISLE, MARTHA OGLESBY, retired mathematics educator; b. Charlottesville, Va., June 29, 1934; d. Earnest Jackson and Lucy Elizabeth (Berger) Oglesby; m. Leslie M. Lisle, June 18, 1955 (div. June 1997); children: Lucie Austin, Karen B., John D. BA, Randolph-Macon Woman's Coll., 1955; MA, Fla. State U., 1957. Instr. various univ., 1957-69; tchr. Am. Sch., Khartoum, Sudan, 1971-72, Holton-Arms, Bethesda, Md., 1974-78, Rabat Am. Sch., Morocco, 1978-81, Stone Ridge Sch., Bethesda, 1981-82; instr. part-time Montgomery Coll., Takoma Pk., Md., 1982-83; assoc. prof. Prince George's Community Coll., Largo, 1983-97. Adj. prof. Md. Coll. Art and Design, 1997-99. Mem. DAR, Am. Math. Assn. Two Yr. Coll., Math. Assn. Am., Md. Math Assn. Two Yr. Coll., Assn. Women in Math., Pi Mu Epsilon. Democrat. Mem. Unitarian Ch. Avocations: sewing, working crafts, playing flute, singing in choir, quilting. Home: 11108 Woodson Ave Kensington MD 20895-1607 E-mail: mlisle@erols.com.

LISMAN, RICHARD D. ophthalmic plastic surgeon; b. N.Y.C., Apr. 24, 1950; s. Jack Victor and Sylvia Schwartz Lisman; m. Joan H. Hackett Lisman; children: Hilary, Cyrena, Daisy, Henry. BA, Hamilton Coll., 1972; MD, NYU, 1976. Chief preceptor fellowship program Am. Soc. Ophthalmic Plastic Surgery, N.Y.C., 1983—; clin. chief divsn. ophthalmic plastic surgery Manhattan Eye and Ear Hosp., 1983—, dir.; clin. prof. ophthalmology NYU Sch. Medicine, 1985—. Pres. Orbital Disease Edn. and Rsch. Found., N.Y.C., 1993—. Author/editor: (textbooks) Ophthalmic Plastic Surgery, 1986; editor: Ophthalmic Plastic Surgery, 1997; contbr. articles to profl. jours. Trustee St. Andrews Preservation Found.; asst. sec.-treas. St. Andrws Dune Ch., Southampton, N.Y. Fellow: Am. Soc. Ophthalmic Plastic Surgery, ACS; mem.: Manhattan Ophthal. Soc., County Med. Soc., Manhattan Ophthal.Soc., N.Y.Soc. Clin. Ophthalmology, N.Y. Orbit Soc., N.Y. State Ophthalmic Soc., N.Y. Ophthalmic Soc., N.Y. Acad. Medicine, Am. Acad. Ophthalmology, Lyford Cay, Southampton Club, Shinnecock Hills Golf Club, Bathing Corp. Southampton, Meadow Club Southampton. Office: 635 Park Ave New York NY 10021-6546 E-mail: RLisman@compuserve.com.

LISMAN, SUSAN R. anesthesiologist, educator; b. Newark, 1952; MD, Tufts U., 1978. Bd. cert. in anesthesiology, 1983. Surg. intern Dartmouth-Hitchcock, Hanover, N.H., 1978-79; resident in anesthesiology Tufts-New England Med. Ctr., Boston, 1979-81, fellow in neuroanesthesia and pediat. anesthesiology, 1981-82; staff New England Med Ctr, 1982-96; staff, dir. pediatric anesthesia Newton-Wellesley Hosp., Newton, Mass., 1996—; assoc. clin. prof. Tufts U. Sch. Medicine, Boston. Fellow Am. Acad. Pediat.; mem. Am. Soc. Anesthesiologists, Am. Soc. Rsch. in Anesthesia, Mass. Med. Soc., Mass. Soc. Anesthesiologists (sec. 1999—), Soc. Pediatric Anesthesia. Office: Newton-Wellesley Hosp Dept Anesthesiology 2014 Washington St Newton MA 02462-1699 E-mail: md.liss@nwh.org.

LISMON, GREGORY LAMONTE, SR. minister; b. Indpls., Aug. 22, 1961; s. James Scruggs and Sylvia Victoria Lismon-Bryant; m. Valencia O. Martin-Lismon, Apr. 24, 1995; children: Alexander Marcus Green, Gregory Lamont, Jr., Tiffany Christine, Jannelle A. Moniguette, Tyerelle Lamonte, Vincent Omar Lamonte. Traffic mgmt. diploma, USMC, 1984; grad. barber, Lovelle Barber Sch., 2000; B of Pastorial Theology, Beulah Bible Coll. and Sem., 2001. Min., Ind., 1978—; lifeguard Fall Creek YMCA, Indpls., 1988—90; aquatic mgr. Riverside Recreational Ctr., 1990—91; aquatic dir. Atkins Boys and Girls Club., 1992—93; barber Cuts by Gregory at the Hair Emporium, South Bend, 2000—01. CEO The Lords Kitchen, New Testament Ministries Worldwide, 1997; exec. bd. dirs. Southside Cmty. R Ross, Indpls., 1998—99; Chaplain King Park Area Neighborhood Orgn., 1995—96. Lt. cpl. USMC, 1980—84. Republican. Baptist. Avocations: aquatics, coaching, lifeguarding, administration, mentor. Home: 1034 Laurel Ct South Bend IN 46601

LISNER, CHARLES ALAN, internist; b. Cin., Aug. 16, 1967; s. Sheal David and Brenda (Glazer) Lisner; m. Diana Lynne Ellerman, Apr. 8, 1995; children: Samuel Ryan, Rachel Marie, Anna Elizabeth, Sarah Michelle. BA, U. Va., 1989, MD, 1993. Internal medicine physician Cons. in Internal Medicine, A Sentara Med. Group, Norfolk, Va., 1996—; assoc. med. dir. Exec. Evaluation Ctr.; intern U. Iowa Hosps. and Clinics, 1994, resident, 1996. Vol. physician Virginia Beach (Va.) Free Med. Clinic, 1996—. Mem. AMA, ACP, Norfolk Acad. Medicine. Office: Cons Internal Medicine 700 Wainwright Bldg 229 W Bute St Norfolk VA 23510

LISONI, GAIL MARIE LANDTBOM, lawyer; b. San Francisco, Mar. 11, 1949; d. William A. and Patricia Ann (Cruden) Landtbom; m. Joseph Louis Lisoni, Mar. 24, 1984. BA, Dominican Coll., Calif., 1971; JD, U. West L.A., 1978, cert. paralegal, 1974. Bar: Calif. 1979. Campaign treas. Calif. for Lisoni, Arcadia, 1979-81; assoc. Joseph Lisoni, Esq., L.A., 1981, Arnold S. Malter, Esq., L.A., 1982; ptnr. Lisoni & Lisoni, 1983—. Co-chair Dems. for James Rogan, 1996, 98; eucharistic minister St. Andrew's Ch., Huntington Meml. Hosp.; vol. Union Sta. Found. Homeless Shelter, Legal Aid Clinic. Mem. ABA, Assn. Trial Lawyers Am., Attys. Assn. L.A., Italian Am. Lawyers Assn., Sons of Italy, Centinela Valley Lodge. Roman Catholic.

LISS, HERBERT MYRON, communications executive, educator; b. Mpls., Mar. 23, 1931; s. Joseph Milton and Libby Diane (Kramer) L.; m. Barbara Lipson, Sept. 19, 1954; children: Lori-Ellen, Kenneth Allen, Michael David. BS in Econs., U. Pa., 1952. With mktg. mgmt. Procter & Gamble Co., Cin., 1954-63, Procter & Gamble Internat., various countries, 1963-74; gen. mgr. Procter & Gamble Comml. Co., San Juan, P.R., 1974-78; v.p., mgr. internat. ops. InterAm. Orange Crush Co. subs. Procter & Gamble Co., Cin., 1981-84; pres. River Cities (Ohio) Communications Inc, 1985—; pub. The Downtowner newspaper and others, Cin., 1985-96. Lectr. MBA and undergrad. bus. program Xavier U., Ohio, 1998—. Bd. dirs. Charter Com., Cin., 1958-63, Promotion and Mktg. Assn. U.S., 1978-81, Jr. Achievement, Cin., 1980-87, Inst. for Learning in Retirement, 1998—, Downtown Coun., Cin., 1985-94, treas., 1991-92; bd. dirs. Downtown Cin. Inc., 1995-98, mem. DCI retail mktg. com., 1995-98. Mem. Manila Yacht Club, Manila Polo, Club Escuela de Equitación De Somos Aquas (Madrid), Rotary Club. (Cin.). Home: 8564 Wyoming Club Dr Cincinnati OH 45215-4243

LISS, JEFFREY F. lawyer, educator; b. Balt., June 10, 1951; s. Solomon and Gertrude (Nadich) L.; m. Susan Michelson, July 30, 1972; children: Joanna M., Harrison S. BA, U. Mich., 1972, MA, JD, 1975. Bar: D.C. 1975, Md. 1981. Jud. law clk. U.S. Dist. Ct., Washington, 1975-77; from assoc. to ptnr. Wald, Harkrader & Ross, 1977-85; ptnr. Piper & Marbury (now Piper Rudnick), 1985—, COO, 1997—. Adj. prof. U. Mich. Law Sch., 1996, 2002, Georgetown Law Sch., 1985—, Am. U. Sch. Law, 1978-85. Co-author: Remedies in Business Torts Litigation, 1992. Bd. dirs. Washington Lawyers Com. for Civil Rights, Washington, 1992-98; pro bono counsel numerous orgns., Washington, 1977—; treas., Friends of Lt. Gov. Kathleen Kennedy Townsend, Md., 1996-. Fellow Am. Bar Found.; mem. Am. Law Inst., D.C. Cir. Hist. Soc. (bd. dirs.), Balt. Symphony Orchestra (exec. com., bd. dirs.). Democrat. Jewish. Avocations: baseball, reading, piano. Office: Piper Rudnick LLP 1200 19th St NW Fl 3 Washington DC 20036-2430 E-mail: Jeffrey.Liss@piperrudnick.com.

LISS, MATTHEW M. lawyer; b. Oak Park, Ill., 1966; BS in Acctg., BS in Fin., So. Ill. U., 1991, MS in Acctg., JD, So. Ill. U., 1994. Bar: Ill. 1994, Ga. 1998. Assoc. Phillip G. Neal and Assocs., Chgo., 1994-95; v.p. and gen. counsel Innovative Health Svcs., Inc., Tampa, Fla., 1995-98; with Swift, Currie, McGhee and Hiers, LLP, Atlanta, 1998—. Home: 4184 Nashoba Dr NE Roswell GA 30075-1667 Office: Swift Currie McGhee & Hiers LLP Ste 300 The Peachtree 1355 Peachtree St NE Atlanta GA 30309 Office Fax: 404-888-6199. E-mail: mml@scmhlaw.com.

LISS, NORMAN, lawyer; b. New York, May 7, 1932; m. Sandra Hirsch, Feb. 28, 1959. BS, NYU, 1952, LLB, 1955. Bar: N.Y. 1955, U.S. Dist. Ct. (so. dist.) N.Y. 1961, U.S. Dist. Ct (ea. dist.) N.Y. 1962. Assoc. Booth, Lipton & Lipton, New York, 1956-57, Seymour Detsky, New York, 1957-58; pvt. practice, 1958—. Cons. to Portugal Re-Cultural Events in U.S.; represented Norway in N.Y. proceedings to clear records of sailors arrested during 900th anniversary of Leif Ericson Voyage; jour. chair UJA Trial Lawyers USCG Acad. Law Day, 1987, 89, 94, 98. Contbr. articles to profl. jours. Chmn. Bronx County Bar div. United Jewish Appeal, Hist. Documents Exhbn., Operation Sail, 1986, USCG Acad. Law Day, 1987, 89; chmn. devel. Ellis Island Restoration Commn.; counsel N.Y. State Statue of Liberty Centennial Com., Mayor's Handicapped Citizens Adv. Bd., N.Y.C., Coun. on Arts; mem. Bronx County 350 Commn., N.Y.C. Commn. for Presdl. Conv.; rep., counsel N.Y.C. Com. on Bicentennial of U.S. Constitution; cons. Soc. Congl. Medal of Honor; commd. lt. col. N.Y. Guard Judge Advocate Gen. Unit; mem. exec. com. Am. Jewish Congress; trustee Am. Jewish Hist. Soc. Recipient Disting. Humanitarian award Inst. of Applied Human Dynamics, Meritorious Pub. Svc. award USCG, 1989; named Man of Yr. Am. Jewish Congress, Man of Yr. Kinneret Sch., 1985. Mem. ABA, N.Y. Bar Assn., Bronx County Bar Assn., Am. Arbitration Assn. (panel arbitrators), Assn. Trial Lawyers Am., Law Day Outreach Com., NYU Alumni Assn. (adv. coun.). Home: 2727 Palisade Ave Bronx NY 10463-1018 Office: 200 W 57th St New York NY 10019-3211

LISS, NORMAN RICHARD, insurance executive; b. Bronx, N.Y., May 29, 1947; s. Jacob Melvin and Terry Ruth (Stoppler) L.; student Athens (Ala.) Coll., 1965-67, U. Albuquerque, 1967; m. Orlinda P. Olivas, Apr. 11, 1970; children— Maria, Jacqueline Melissa. With First Nat. Life Ins. Co., Albuquerque, 1969-70; founder, pres. Ins. Planners of N.Mex., Albuquerque, 1970— . Active Heart Fund, United Way, Arthritis Found., Boy Scouts Am.; pres. N.Mex. Track Athletic Congress; bd. dirs. N.Mex. chpt. March of Dimes, N.Mex. Kidney Found. Served with USAF, 1967-69. Recipient various ins. sales awards, Dublin award for public service. Mem. Assn. Life Underwriters (local sec.-treas., bd. dirs., state chmn. pub. service, instr. and moderator Tng. Council), Million Dollar Round Table (life), Life Underwriter Tng. Coun. Fellow, Ct. of Table (charter mem.), Albuquerque Rotary Club Del Norte (charter, chmn. Ryla and Youth Exch. program, chmn. Rotary Ambassadorial Scholarship program, Rotarian of Yr. 1990-91, 91-92). Republican. Jewish. Home: 11433 Nassau Dr NE Albuquerque NM 87111-2741 Office: 3644 Thaxton Ave SE Albuquerque NM 87108-4385

LISSAUER, JACK JONATHAN, astronomy educator; b. San Francisco, Mar. 25, 1957; s. Alexander Lissauer and Ruth Spector. SB in Math., MIT, 1978; Phd in Applied Math., U. Calif., Berkeley, 1982. NAS-NRC resident rsch. assoc. NASA-Ames Rsch. Ctr., Moffett Field, Calif., 1983-85; asst. rsch. astronomer U. Calif., Berkeley, 1985, vis. rschr. dept. physics Inst. for Theoretical Physics Santa Barbara, 1985-87; asst. prof. astronomy program dept. earth and space scis. SUNY, Stony Brook, 1987-93, assoc. prof., 1993-96; space scientist NASA Ames Rsch. Ctr., 1996—. Rep. Univs. Space Rsch. Assn., SUNY, Stony Brook, 1987-96; vis. scholar dept. planetary scis. and lunar and planetary lab. U. Ariz., Tucson, 1990; guest prof. dept. physics U. Paris VII et Observatoire Paris, Meudon, France, 1990; mem. Lunar and Planetary Geoscis. Rev. Panel, 1989, 91, 99; vis. asst. rsch. physicist Inst. for Theoretical Physics, U. Calif., Santa Barbara, 1992, organizer Program on Plant Formation, 1992; rsch. assoc. Inst. d'Astrophysique, Paris, 1993; vis. scholar dept. astronomy U. Calif., Berkeley, 1994-95; adj. assoc. prof. SUNY, Stony Brook, 1996-2002; Yuval Ne'eman Disting. lectr. geophysics, atmosphere and space scis. Tel Aviv U., 2001, cons. prof. dept. geology and environ. sci. Stanford U., 2002. Planetary scis. editor New Astronomy Reviews; contbr. numerous articles on planet and star formation, extrasolar planets, spiral density wave theory, rotation of planets and comets to profl. jours. including Nature, Astron. Jour., Icarus, Sci., Astrophys. Jour. Letters, Astrophys. Jour., Jour. Geophys. Rsch., Astron. Astrophysics, Ann. Rev. Astron. Astrophysics, Revs. of Modern Physics. NASA Grad. student fellow, 1981-82, Alfred P. Sloan Found. fellow, 1987-91. Mem. Am. Astronomical Assn. (divsn. planetary scis., divsn. dynamical astronomy, Harold C. Urey prize divsn. planetary scis. 1992), Internat. Astronomical Union, Am. Geophys. Union. Achievements include research in planetary accretion, extrasolar planets, dynamics of planetary rings, cratering, binary and multiple star systems, circumstellar disks, resonances and chaos. Office: NASA Ames Rsch Ctr Space Sci Divsn 245-3 Moffett Field CA 94035

LISSKA, ANTHONY JOSEPH, humanities educator, philosopher; b. Columbus, Ohio, July 23, 1940; s. Joseph Anthony and Florence (Wolfel) L.; m. Marianne Hedstrom, Mar. 16, 1968; children: Megan Catherine, Elin Elizabeth. BA in Philosophy cum laude, Providence Coll., 1963; AM in Philosophy, St. Stephen's Coll., Dover, Mass., 1967; PhD in Philosophy, Ohio State U., 1971; Cert., Harvard U., Cambridge, 1979. Asst. prof. Denison U., Granville, Ohio, 1969-76, assoc. prof., 1976-81, dean of coll., 1978-83, prof. philosophy, 1981—, dir. honors program, 1987—2002, Charles and Nancy Brickman disting. svc. chair, 1998-2001. Vis. scholar U. Oxford, Eng., 1984; Aquinas lectr. Providence Coll., 2002; project reviewer NEH, Washington, 1979-90, evaluator; adv. bd. Midwest Faculty Seminar, Chgo., 1981-90; mem. scholarship com. Sherex Chem. Co., Dublin, Ohio, 1984-92; cons. Franklin Pierce Coll., Ringe, N.H., 1991, Hampden-Sydney (Va.) Coll., 1998; referee various philosophy jours. Author: Philosophy Matters, 1977, Aquinas's Theory of Natural Law, 1996, paperback edit. 1997; co-editor: The Historical Times, 1988-2002; contbr. numerous articles to profl. jours., chpts. to books. Bd. mgmt. Granville Hist. Soc., 1987-2002; precinct rep. Dem. Party, Granville, 1994—; convener Civil War Roundtable, Granville, 1989-95. Named Carnegie Prof. of Yr., Carnegie Found., 1994, Sears Found. Teaching award, 1990; NEH grantee, 1973, 77, 85. Mem. Am. Philos. Assn. (Teaching award 1994), Am. Cath. Philos. Assn., Nat. Collegiate Honors Coun., Soc. for Ancient Greek Philosophy, Soc. for Medieval and Renaissance Philosophy, Internat. Thomas Aquinas Soc. Democrat. Roman Catholic. Avocations: local history, photography. Home: 285 Burtridge Rd Granville OH 43023-1214 Office: Denison U Dept Philosophy Gilpatrick House Granville OH 43023 E-mail: lisska@denison.edu.

LIST, BOBYE GOODMAN, science foundation director; V.p. N.Y. C. of C. and Industry; exec. dir. summer jobs program N.Y.C. Partnership, 1989—; exec. dir. Literacy Vols., N.Y.C., 1994—; former dir. Bklyn. Children's Mus.; exec. dir The Emily Davie and Joseph S. Kornfeld Fdn., 2001—. Office: The Kornfeld Fdn. 41 Schermerhorn St, Suite 208 Brooklyn NY 11201*

LIST, ERICSON JOHN, environmental engineering science educator, engineering consultant; b. Whakatane, New Zealand, Mar. 27, 1939; came to U.S., 1962; s. Ericson Bayliss and Freda Helen (Sunkel) L.; m. Olive Amoore, Feb. 3, 1962; children: Brooke Meredith, Antonia Michael. B.E. with honors, U. Auckland, N.Z., 1961, B.Sc., M.E., U. Auckland, N.Z., 1962; PhD, Calif. Inst. Tech., 1965. Registered profl. engr., Calif., S.C. Sr. lectr. U. Auckland, 1966-69; asst. prof. Calif. Inst. Tech., Pasadena, 1969-72, assoc. prof., 1972-78, prof. environ. engring. sci., 1978-97, exec. officer, 1980-85, prof. emeritus, 1997; pres. Flow Sci. Inc., 1997—. Bd. dirs. Environ. Def. Scis., Pasadena; bd. chmn. Flow Sci. Inc., Pasadena, 1983— ; cons. So. Calif. Edison, Rosemead, Calif., 1973— , City and County of San Francisco, 1974— Author: (with Hugo B. Fischer et al), Mixing in Inland and Coastal Waters, 1979, (with W. Rodi) Turbulent Jets and Plumes, 1982, (with Roscoe Moss Co.) Handbook of Ground Water Development, 1990. Mem. Blue Ribbon Commn. City of Pasadena, 1976-78. Recipient Spl. Creativity award NSF, 1982 Fellow ASCE (editor Jour. Hydraulic Engring. 1984-89). Clubs: Athenaeum (Pasadena) (chmn. wine com. 1981-83). Republican. Office: Flow Sci Inc 723 E Green St Pasadena CA 91101-2111 E-mail: ejlist@flowscience.com.

LISTER, BRUCE ALCOTT, food scientist, consultant; b. Bklyn., Dec. 23, 1922; s. James Alan and Georgana Martha (Hunt) L.; m. Doris Ann Jonassen, May 20, 1990. BSChemE, Columbia U., 1943, MSChemE, 1947; cert. in Food Tech., MIT, 1952; PhD (hon.), Hofstra U., 1998. From lab. asst. to div. rsch. dir. General Foods Corp., Hoboken, N.J. and White Plains, N.Y., 1943-62; from mgr. tech. svcs. to v.p. corp. affairs Nestle Foods Corp., White Plains and Purchase, 1962-88; exec. dir., chmn. tech. com., bd. dirs. Tea Assn. U.S.A., N.Y.C., 1980-91; cons. food industry Baldwin, 1989—. Pres. Internat. Hydrolyzed Protein Coun., Washington, 1979-90; trustee cacao biogenetic rsch. project Pa. State U., State College, 1988-89; chmn. stds. regulations com. Nat. Coffee Assn., N.Y.C., 1968-88, tech. com. Chocolate Mfrs. Assn., McLean, Va., 1972-88; U.S. del., chmn. tea com., mem. coffee com. Internat. Stds. Orgn.; U.S. del., full commn., chocolate, soup, dietary foods, labeling coms. Codex Alimentarius; U.S. del., tea com. UN Commn. on Trade and Devel.; mem. govt. rels. com. Internat. Bottled Water Assn., 1987. Pres., v.p., bd. dirs., fin. chmn. Bethany Meth. Home, Bklyn., 1969—; treas., dir. Coun. Against Drug Abuse, Baldwin, 1969—; trustee, lay leader, fin. chmn. First Ch. Baldwin, United Meth., 1972—; mem. Nassau County Bd. Social Svcs., 1972-74; chmn. Nassau County Bd. Health, Mineola, N.Y., 1975-2000; pres., v.p., bd. dirs. R&D Assocs. U.S. Mil., 1966-76; vice chair, mem. adv. bd., chair scholarship com., cons. for new sci. bldg. Hofstra U., Hempstead, N.Y., 1982—, mem. engring. adv. bd. 1999—, mem. acad. affairs com., 2000—; pres. Rep. Club, Baldwin, 1967-68; mem. engring. sch. adv. bd. Columbia U., 1999—. Lt. (j.g.) USNR, 1944-46. Named Man of Yr., Baldwin Rep. Club, 1968, Nassau County (N.Y.) Sr. Citizen of Yr., 2000; recipient Hon. doctorate Nat. Assn. Food Equip. Mfrs., 1973, Cert. Appreciation for Patriotic Civilian Svc. U.S. Army, 1975. Fellow Am. Inst. Chemists; mem. AIChemE (profl.), Am. Chem. Soc. (emeritus), Inst. Food Technologists (emeritus, chmn. internat. div. 1985-88, mem. awards com. 1989, mem. codex com. 1996—, chair codex com. 1998—, liaison to Codex Alimentarius 1989-93), Phi Tau Sigma (nat. pres. 1989-90), Tau Beta Pi, Sigma Xi, Phi Lambda Upsilon. Achievements include patents in food formulations; working with NASA to supply menu items for all space missions from Mercury thru Shuttle. Home: 1976 Oakmere Dr Baldwin NY 11510-2739 Fax: (516) 223-0224..

LISTER, EARLE EDWARD, animal science consultant; b. Harvey, N.B., Can., Apr. 14, 1934; s. Earle Edward and Elizabeth Hazel (Coburn) L.; m. Teresa Ann Moore, June 4, 1983. BSc in Agriculture, McGill U., Montreal, Can., 1955, MSc in Animal Nutrition, 1957; PhD in Animal Nutrition, Cornell U., 1960. Feed nutritionist Ogilvie Flour Mills, Montreal, 1960—65; rsch. scientist rsch. br. Animal Rsch. Ctr. Agriculture Can., Ottawa, 1965—74, dep. dir. rsch. br. Animal Rsch. Ctr., 1974—78, program specialist ctrl. region rsch. br., 1978—80, dir. gen. Atlantic region rsch. br. Halifax, Canada, 1980—85, dir. gen. plant health and plant products and pesticides, food prodn. and inspection br. Ottawa, 1985—87, dir. rsch. br. Animal Rsch. Ctr., 1987—91; dir. Ctr. Food and Animal Rsch., 1991—92; cons., 1992—2001; chmn. Can. Found. for Conservation Farm Animal Genetic Resources, 1996—; hon. dir. Can. Farm Animal Genetic Resource Found. Presenter seminars in India, Hong Kong, Taiwan; mem. Can. del. to gen. FAO meetings. Co-chmn. United Way/Health Ptnrs. for Agriculture Can., Ottawa, 1991; former dir. N.S. Inst. Agrologists. McGill U. scholar, 1953-55; recipient Nat. Rsch. Coun. Post Grad. Spl. scholarship Cornell U., 1957-59. Fellow: Agrl. Inst. Can.; mem.: Ont. Inst. Agrologists, Can. Soc. Animal Sci. (former dir.). Achievements include research in the determination of nutrient requirements of beef cattle, determination of protein and energy levels and appropriate sources of nutrients for dairy calves; development of intensive feeding system for raising high quality beef from Holstein male calves. Home: 390 Hinton Ave Ottawa ON Canada K1Y 1B1

LISTER, HARRY JOSEPH, finance company executive, portfolio manager; b. Teaneck, N.J., Jan. 27, 1936; s. Harry and Arline Audrey (Pinera) L.; m. Erika Anna Maria Englisch, Sept. 3, 1960; children: Harry Joseph Jr., Karen P. Lister Lawson, Leslie M. Lister Fidler, Andrea A. Lister Lytle, Michael P. BS in Fin. and Econs., Lehigh U., 1958. Security analyst Calvin Bullock, Ltd., N.Y.C., 1959-61, assoc. dir. estate planning, 1961-65, dir. estate planning., 1965-72, asst. v.p., 1969-72; v.p. N.Y. Venture Fund, Inc., 1970-72; registered rep. Johnston, Lemon & Co., Inc., Washington, 1972—, dir., 1978-90, v.p., 1978-83, from corp. sec. to sr. v.p., 1978-90; v.p. Wash. Mgmt. Corp., 1972-81, corp. sec., 1978-81, exec. v.p., 1981-85, pres., CEO, 1985—, dir., 1978—; pres. JL Fin. Svcs., Inc., Washington, 1975-90; from v.p. to exec. v.p. Washington Mut. Investors Fund, Inc., 1972-85, corp. sec., 1978-81, pres., dir., 1985—; former pres., dir., vice chmn. bd. dirs. The Growth Fund of Washington, Inc. (now JP Morga Value Opportunities Fund), 1985—; registered prin., bd. dirs., pres. Washington Funds Distbrs., Inc., 1985-93. Former pres., trustee, vice chmn. bd. trustees The Tax Exempt Fund of Md., 1986—, The Tax Exempt Fund of Va., 1986—; vice chmn., bd. dirs. Washington Investment Advisers, Inc., 1991-2001; cons. Capital Group, Inc., L.A., 1972-2002; regent Coll. for Fin. Planning, Denver, 1979-84, mem. exec. com., 1980-84, chmn. bd. regents, 1981-83. Author: Your Guide to IRAs and 14 Other Retirement Plans, 1985. Bd. dirs. ctrl. Bergen chpt. ARC, Hackensack, N.J., 1968-72, chmn. exec. com., 1970-72; bd. dirs. Westwood (N.J.) Planning Bd., 1969-72, vice chmn., 1970-72; bd. dirs. Westwood Zoning Bd. Adjustment, 1970-72; bd. dirs. ICI Edn. Found., 1996—, chmn., 1997—. Mem.: Nat. Assn. Securities Dealers, Inc. (investment cos. com. 1984—87, bd. arbitrators 1987—98), Investment Co. Inst. (pension com., chmn. 1976—81, tax com., rsch. com., dirs. svc. com.), Mt. Vernon Ladies Assn. (mem. adv. com. 2001—), Lowes Island Club, Univ. Club, Met. Club. Home: Spinnaker Ct Reston VA 20191 Office: 1101 Vermont Ave NW Washington DC 20005-3521

LISTER, LINDA JOANNE, music educator, composer; b. Tarrytown, N.Y., June 30, 1969; d. Gordon Frank and Judith Smith Lister. AB in Voice, Vassar Coll., 1991; MMus in Voice, Eastman Sch. of Music, 1993; DMA in Voice, U. N.C., Greensboro, 1998. Instr. Sch. of Choral Studies, Saratoga Springs, NY, 1994, Hochstein Sch., Rochester, 1994—95; lectr. SUNY, Fredonia, 1993—95; dept. chair Music Acad. of N.C., Greensboro, 1997—; instr. Greensboro Coll., 1997—; asst. prof. Elon (N.C.) U., 2000—. Composer: (mini-operas) Tryst & Thereafter, 1989, How Clear She Shines, 2001, (musical) The Little Match Girl, 1984, (song cycles) Dependencies, 1995, Deep Dreams & Delicacies, 1996, The Landscape of Love, 2000; contbr. articles to profl. jours. Recipient Dissertation prize, Nat. Opera Assn., Washington, 1998, Jane Dillard award, Met. Opera Dist. Auditions, Charlotte, N.C., 2001. Mem.: Nat. Assn. Tchrs. of Singing, Phi Beta Kappa, Pi Kappa Lambda. Avocations: yoga, tennis, poetry.

LISTER, MARK WAYNE, clinical laboratory scientist; b. Panama City, Fla., June 30, 1954; s. Heamon Lee and Virginia (Hughes) L.; m. Elizabeth Ann Steger, Oct. 4, 1984; 1 child, Andrew Mark. Student, Monaco Med. Labs., Panama City, Fla., 1973-75; grad. with honors, Gulf Coast Coll., Panama City, Fla., 1979. Cert. med. technologist, Fla.; clin. lab. scientist, Nat. Cert. Agy.; specialist in hematology, immunohematology and cytogenetics. Lab. dir. Calhoun Gen. Hosp., Blountstown, Fla., 1979-82; evening shift supr. Hosp. Lab. Devel. Corp., Plantation, 1982-83; med. technologist Margate (Fla.) Gen. Hosp., 1983-84, Las Olas Hosp., Ft. Lauderdale, Fla., 1984; blood bank supr., coord. continuing edn. Fla. Med. Ctr., Lauderdale, 1984-89; evening shift supr. hosp. and reference lab. Westside Regional Med. Ctr., Plantation, 1989-2000, coord. continuing edn., 1989—, coord. ancillary blood glucose testing program, 1989—; mgr. transfusion svcs., hematology and flow cytometry Bethesda Meml. Hosp., Boynton Beach, Fla., 2000—. Mem. Broward County Tech. Adv. Com.; coord. continuing edn.; inspector Coll. Am. Pathologists; presenter Internat. Conf. on AIDS, Yokohama, Japan, 1994. Rschr. in human immunodeficiency virus; rsch. in immunology. Active Christ Ch. United Meth., Ft. Lauderdale, 1990—, Imperial Point Homeowners Assn., Ft. Lauderdale, 1991—; host parent Westminster Acad., Ft. Lauderdale, 1993. Mem. Am. Assn. Blood Banks, Fla. Assn. Blood Banks, Am. Med. Technologist, Fla. Soc. Med. Technologist. Avocations: woodworking, swimming, fishing, bicycling. Home: 2125 NE 56th Pl Fort Lauderdale FL 33308-2504 E-mail: markwlister@msn.com.

LISTER, THOMAS MOSIE, composer, lyricist, publishing company executive, minister; b. Empire, Ga., Sept. 8, 1921; s. Willis Waller and Orena Pearl (Holl) L.; m. Jewel Wylene Whitten, June 2, 1946; children— Brenda (Mrs. James Milton Vann), Barbara (Mrs. David Miller Williams). Attended, Rennsalaer Poly. Inst., 1944-45, Middle Ga. Coll., 1945-46, U. South Fla., 1968; studied privately at, Tampa U., 1958-63. Ordained to ministry Bapt. Ch., 1975. Founder, pres. Mosie Lister Publs., Atlanta, 1952-56, Tampa, 1956—. Choral dir. Composer, lyricist numerous gospel songs, 1940—; singer, Tampa, Fla., and Atlanta, 1941, 46-47; Compiler song. collections, hymnbooks, and others; arranger religious music for choral groups and ensembles; songs include I'm Feeling Fine, Where No One Stands Alone, His Hand in Mine; contbg. arranger profl. singing groups. Served with USNR, 1942-45. Named Bapt. Layman of Year for Tampa, 1971; inducted into Gospel Hall of Fame, 1976, Hall of Fame, So. Gospel Music Assn., 1997; recipient Humanist award Sesac, Inc., 1976; Mosie Lister Day named in his honor Tampa, 1974 Mem. Gospel Music Assn. (dir. 1970-71), Fla. Bapt. Ministers of Music Assn. (hon. life) Democrat. Address: 4304 65th St E Bradenton FL 34208-6622

LISTGARTEN, MAX ALBERT, periodontics educator; b. Paris, May 14, 1935; came to U.S., 1968; s. Samuel and Etla (Weber) L.; m. Eileen Anne Gregory, July 3, 1963; children: Karen, Sheralyn, Michael. DDS, U. Toronto, 1959; cert. in periodontics, Harvard U., 1963; MA (hon.), U. Pa., 1971; PhD (hon.), U. Athens, 1993. Research assoc. Harvard U., Boston, 1963-64; asst. prof. periodontics U. Toronto, Can., 1964-67, assoc. prof. Can., 1967-68, U. Pa., Phila., 1968-71, prof., 1971-2001, prof. emeritus, 2001—. Vis. prof. U. Gothenburg, Sweden, 1976—77, U. Berne, 1988—89, U. Calif., San Francisco, 2001—; cons. Nat. Inst. Dental Rsch., Bethesda, Md., 1979—88, FDA, Rockville, Md., 1992—, in field. Author textbooks and numerous articles on various aspects of periodontal anatomy, microbiology, histopathology, and diagnosis. Recipient Periodontology award William J. Gies Found., 1981; named Disting. Alumnus, Harvard U., 1986, U. Pa., 1994. Fellow AAAS, Am. Acad. Periodontology (Clin. Rsch. award 1987); mem. ADA, Am. Assn. for Dental Rsch. (pres. 1991-92), Internat. Assn. Dental Rsch. (award for basic rsch. in periodontology 1973). Jewish. Avocations: swimming, skiing, hiking, photography. E-mail: listgarten@netscape.net.

LISTON, ALBERT MORRIS, investor, administrator, educator; b. Aug. 6, 1940; s. Joseph Bostick and Hazel Marie (Smalley) L.; m. Angela Lynne Carbonatto, Jan. 1998. AB in Econs., U. Calif., Davis, 1963; MA in Govt., Calif. State U., Sacramento, 1970; postgrad., U. Calif., Santa Barbara, 1980—. Rsch. analyst polit. sci. dept. Ombudsman Activities Project, U. Calif., Santa Barbara, 1970-72; asst. prof. polit. sci. dept. CAlif. State U., Fullerton, 1973-79; investor, 1980—. Lt. Supply Corps, USNR, 1963-66. Mem. Kappa Sigma, Phi Kappa Phi. Democrat. Home: PO Box 8027 Missoula MT 59807-8027

LISTOPADZKI, DARIUSZ JAROSLAW, internist; b. Olsztyn, Poland, May 8, 1962; came to U.S., 1995; s. Romuald and Krystyna Listopadzki; m. Caren Listopadzki, Apr. 29, 1995; children: Thomas, Nina. Physician's diploma, Med. Acad. Bydgoszcz, Poland, 1986. Diplomate Am. Bd. Internal Medicine. Acad. tutor, rsch. worker dept. pathophysiology Med. Acad. Bydgoszcz, 1986-90, rotational intern, 1987-88, resident dept. and clinic cardiology and internal diseases, 1988-90; physician dept. ob-gyn. Edendale Hosp., Pietermaritzburg, South Africa, 1991-93, physician dept. medicine South Africa, 1993-95; resident internal medicine Hahnemann U. Hosp., Phila., 1995-98; internist Kimball (Nebr.) County Hosp., 1999—. Mem. AMA, ACP. Avocations: skiing, windsurfing, horseback riding. Office: Kimball County Hosp 505 S Burg St Kimball NE 69145-1313 E-mail: djlisto@megavision.com.

LITAN, ROBERT ELI, lawyer, economist; b. Wichita, Kans., May 16, 1950; s. David and Shirley Hermine (Krischer) Litan; m. Avivah D. Swirsky, Aug. 23, 1980. BS in Econs., U. Pa., 1972; MPhil in Econs., Yale U., 1976, JD, 1977, PhD in Econs., 1987. Bar: (D.C.) 1980. Rsch. asst. Brookings Instn., 1972-73; instr., then lectr. econs. Yale U., 1975-76; energy cons. NAS, 1975-77; regulation and energy specialist Pres.'s Coun. Econ. Advs., 1977-79; assoc. Arnold & Porter, Washington, 1979-82; assoc., then ptnr. and counsel Powell, Goldstein, Frazer & Murphy, 1982-90; sr. fellow Brookings Instn., 1984-92, dir. Ctr. for Econ. Progress, 1987-93; dep. asst. atty. gen. Dept. Justice, 1993-95; assoc. dir. Office of Mgmt. and Budget, 1995-96; v.p., dir. econ. studies Brookings Inst., Cabot family chair in econs. Cons. Inst. Liberty and Democracy, Lima, Peru, 1985—88; vis. lectr. Yale U. Law Sch., 1985—86; mem. Presdl. Congl. Commn. Causes of Savs. and Loan Crisis, 1991—92; cons. U.S. Dept. Treasury, 1996—97, 1999—2000. Author: Energy Modeling for an Uncertain Future, 1978, Reforming Federal Regulation, 1983, Saving Free Trade: A Pragmatic Approach, 1986, What Should Banks Do?, 1987, Liability: Perspectives and Policy, 1988, American Living Standards: Threats and Challenges, 1988, Blueprint for Restructuring America's Financial Institutions, 1989, Banking Industry in Turmoil, 1990, The Revolution in U.S. Finance, 1991, The Liability Maze, 1991, Down in the Dumps: Administration of the Unfair Trade Laws, 1991, The Future of American Banking, 1992, Growth With Equity, 1993, Assessing Bank Reform, 1993, Verdict, 1993, Financial Regulation in a Global Economy, 1994, Footing the Bill for Superfund Cleanups, 1995, American Finance for the 21st Century, 1997, Globaphobia: Confronting Fears of Open Trade, 1998, None of Your Business: World Data Flows and the European Privacy Directive, 1998, The GAAP Gap, 2000, Beyond the Dot.Coms, 2001, Hiking Together: The Israeli Experiment in Pluralism, 2002; contbr. articles to profl. jours. Recipient Class of 1964 award, U. Pa., W. Gordon award, 1972, Albert A. Berg award, 1971, 1972, Felix S. Cohen award, Yale U., 1976, Silver medal, Royal Soc. Arts, 1972; fellow Thouron, Eng., 1972. Mem.: ABA, Coun. on Fgn. Rels., Am. Econs. Assn. Democrat. Home: 3 Golden Crest Ct Rockville MD 20854-2982 Office: Brookings Instn 1775 Massachusetts Ave NW Washington DC 20036-2103 E-mail: rlitan@brook.edu.

LITANT, WILLIAM T. G. director; b. Bklyn., May 11, 1951; s. Irving and Raquel (Shafran) Litant; m. Michelle Order, June 8, 1980; children: Josiah, Micah. BFA, Emerson Coll., Boston, 1973. Cert. tchr secondary English Mass.

Media specialist Raytheon Co., Cambridge, Mass., 1973-76; dir. pub. rels. Mus. Transp., Boston, 1976-82; pub. affairs cons. Mass. Bay Transp. Authority, 1982-84, Mass. Hwy. Dept., Boston, 1984-86; dir. comms. and publs. Mass. Bar Assn., 1986-2001; comm. dir. aero.-astro. dept. MIT, Cambridge, 2001—. Editor: (book) Massachusetts Court Journalists Handbook, 1996, (newspaper) Lawyers Jour., (jour.) Mass Law Rev, Sect Revue. Mem.: New Eng Press Asn, Soc Prof Journalists, Nat Asn Bar Execs, Am Soc Asn Execs, BSA Club (pres 1978—). Avocations: flying, photography, motorcycling. Home: 276 Reed Farm Rd Boxboro MA 01719-1615 Office: MIT 77 Mass Ave 37-395 Cambridge MA 02139 E-mail: wlitant@mit.edu.

LITCH, C(HRISTOPHER) SCOTT, dental association administrator; b. Richmond, Va., July 31, 1961; s. Joseph and Christine Tisdale L.; m. Bonnie Kraus, Apr. 27, 1991; children: Arden Berenice, Emma Beatrice. BA, U. Md., 1983; MA, Duke U., 1986; JD, U. Md., 1988. Bar: Md. 1988, D.C. 1994, Ill. 2001. Legis. asst. Am. Assns. Dental Schs., Washington, 1988; legis. counsel Am. Asns. Dental Schs., 1989-96, gen. counsel, assoc. exec. dir., 1996-99; deputy exec. dir., gen. counsel Am. Acad. Pediat. Dentistry, Chgo., 1999—. Treas. Nat. Alliance Oral Health, Washington, 1996-99. Contbr. articles to profl. jours. Chair adult edn. com. Bethesda (Md.) Presbyn. Ch., 1992-96; vol. Big Bros. Nat. Capital Area, Silver Spring, Md., 1993-95. Recipient Pub. Svc. award Am. Assn. Pub. Health Dentistry, 2000. Mem.: Assn. Forum Chicagoland (govt. affairs com. 2001—), Am. Health Lawyers Assn., Am. Soc. Assn. Execs. (coun. legal sect. 2001—). Republican. Avocations: golf, running, reading, music. Office: Am Acad Pediatric Dentistry 211 E Chicago Ave Ste 700 Chicago IL 60611 E-mail: slitch@aapl.org.

LITCH, JOHN MICHAEL, lawyer; b. Detroit, Oct. 14, 1927; m. June E. Meyers, June 21, 1953; children: Brian M., Nancy A. Student, Detroit Coll. Law, 1951, LLB, 1957, JD, 1968. Mng. ptnr. Litch, Gordon & Assocs., Center Line, Mich., 1952—. Cpl. USAF, 1946-48. Mem. Fla. State Bar Assn., Mich. State Bar Assn., Macomb Probate Bar Assn., Macomb Fin. Planning and Probate Assn. Office: Litch Gordon & Assocs 26224 Van Dyke Ave Center Line MI 48015-1220

LITCHFIELD, BARBARA MAE SMITH, clergywoman; b. Providence, Apr. 14, 1935; d. Waldo Albert and Gertrude Wilbar (Palmer) Smith; m. Aug. 2, 1953 (div. Oct. 1971); children: William Sethares, Marilyn S. Nieuweboer; m. Chester Stanley Litchfield, May 11, 1980. BA cum laude, Boston U., 1968; ThM, Evangel Christian U., Monroe, La., 1992, ThD, 1993. Social worker Dept. Pub. Welfare, Watertown, Mass., 1969-86, supr. Waltham, 1986-90; assoc. min. Christian Renewal Ch., Salem, 1991-97, also bd. dirs.; co-pastor Shepherd's Staff Mins., Hollis, N.H., 1997—, also bd. dirs. Bd. dirs. Sar Shalom Ministries, Jerusalem, 1995—, Global Women of Faith Ministries, Wakefield, Mass., 1999—. Author: A Sheep's Eye View, 1990, All Is Not Well With Welfare, 1991, Bible Basics, 1995, Scriptural View of World Religions, 1996, Jesus in First Century Israel, 1996, From the Slime to the Sublime, 1997, The Battlefield, 1997, Israel My Love, 1998. Pentecostal. Avocations: raising goats and chickens, gardening, knitting. Home and Office: Shepherd's Staff Ministries PO Box 157 4 Baxter Rd Hollis NH 03049-5945

LITCHFIELD, JEAN ANNE, nurse; b. Gary, Ind., Oct. 6, 1942; d. Donald Kleine and Helen Louise (Sweet) Eller; m. Norman E. Stone, Dec. 27, 1965 (div. Aug. 1973); children: Diana, David, Julie; m. Frank Litchfield, Jan. 26, 1974. Lic. practical nurse, Ind. U. Vocat. Tech. Coll., 1973; AS in Biology, Richland C.C., 1991; BSN, Millikin U., 1993; MSN, Ind. State U., 1995. RN, Ind., Ill. Nurse asst. St. Anthony Hosp., Terre Haute, Ind., 1960-73, nurse, 1973-93; charge nurse psychiatric ward St. Mary's Hosp., Decatur, Ill., 1993-99; asst. prof. AD Nursing program Richland C.C., 1995—. Mem. student welfare com. Millikin U., Decatur, 1991-92. Recipient 1st place art award 1984, 85, 86, 2d place art award 1984, 85, 2d place County Fair, 1985, Gold Poet award World of Poetry, 1989, Silver Poet award, 1990, Outstanding Innovations in Tchg. and Learning award Richland C.C., 1997, 98, Excellence in Nursing Edn. award Decatur Area Task Force Nursing Edn., 2000; named Most Caring Nurse St. Mary's Hosp. 1990, Clara Compton scholar, St. Mary's Hosp., 1993, 94, scholar Am. Legion, 1992. Mem. Internat. Platform Assn., Barn Colony Artists (treas. 1986-88), Phi Theta Kappa, Beta Sigma Phi (treas. 1976-78), Alpha Tau Delta (treas. 1991-92, pres. 1992-93), Sigma Theta Tau Internat. Home: 1680 N 30th St Decatur IL 62526-5416

LITCHFIELD, JOHN EDWARD, chemist; b. Balt., Nov. 26, 1968; s. Clarence John and Patsy Ann Litchfield; m. Theresa Marie Wolfe, June 8, 1992 (dec. 1994); m. Jennifer Robin Lytle, July 21, 1997. BS, Frostburg (Md.) State U., 1991; PhD, U. S.C., 1996. Rsch. scientist Inst. for Diabetes Discovery, Branford, Conn., 1996—. Mem. AAAS, Am. Chem. Soc., Am. Soc. Mass Spectrometry. Office: Inst Diabetes Discovery 23 Business Park Dr Branford CT 06405 E-mail: jerl68@hotmail.com.

LITCHFIELD, ROBERT LATTA, JR. lawyer; b. Tucson, Apr. 6, 1949; s. Robert Latta Sr. and Mary Wyatt (Palmer) L.; m. Suzanne Kay Zerby, Dec. 29, 1971; children: Melissa Marie, Robert Latta III, Paul Andrew, James Ryan. BS, West Point Acad., 1971; MA, Miami U., 1977; JD, McGeorge Sch. Law, 1980. Bar: Oreg. 1980, U.S. Dist. Ct. Oreg. 1980, Calif. 1981, U.S. Dist. Ct. (ea. dist.) Calif. 1985. Assoc. Hershner, Hunter, Miller, Moulton & Andrews, Eugene, Oreg., 1980-83; pvt. practice, 1983-85; assoc. Felderstein, Rosenberg & McManns, Sacramento, 1985-86, Felderstein, Rosenberg, McManns, Diepenbrock, Wulff, et al., Sacramento, 1986-87; pvt. practice Grass Valley, Calif., 1987—. Adv. bd. Truckee River Bank, Grass Valley, 1992-94; radio talk show host KNCO Radio, Grass Valley, 1991-92. Author: The Man Who Had No Wings, 1977. Mem. adv. bd. Salvation Army, Grass Valley, 1991-94; team leader marriage encounter group Westminster Presbyn. Ch., Eugene, 1984—, deacon and elder, 1983-85; candidate Nev. County Superior Ct. Judge, 1996. Capt. USAF, 1971-77. Named Atty. of Yr., Consumer Bus. Rev., 1995. Mem. Nevada County Bar Assn., Tea Bag Tax Revolt (founder, chmn. 1990-94), Make a Difference, Inc. (bd. dirs. 1992-94), Angelian Soc. (founder, chmn. 1992—), Nevada County Gideons (pres. 1995). Republican. Avocations: scuba diving, writing, woodworking, Christian family enrichment. Office: 210 Magnolia Ave # 1 Auburn CA 95603-4823

LITEWKA, ALBERT BERNARD, communications and publishing company executive; b. N.Y.C., Feb. 5, 1942; s. Joel and Leah L. BA summa cum laude, UCLA, 1964; postgrad., U. Calif., Berkeley, 1964-65. Mgr. purchasing McGraw-Hill Book Co., N.Y.C., 1965-67; pres. Mktg. Innovations, Inc., 1967-69; v.p. Westinghouse Leisure Time Industries, 1972-75; exec. v.p. mktg. The Baker & Taylor Co. (W.R. Grace & Co.), 1975-77; pres. Pix of Am. (W. R. Grace & Co.), 1978; v.p. consumer services group W.R. Grace & Co., 1977-79; pres. Macmillan Gen. Books div., 1980-82; sr. v.p. Macmillan Pub. Co., Inc., 1980-82; pres. Warner Software, Inc., 1982-85; chmn., CEO Air Creative Group, Los Angeles and N.Y.C., 1986-98, Creative Domain, Inc., Los Angeles, Calif., 1991—. Author: Warsaw: A Novel of Resistance, 1989. Internat. Ladies Garment Workers Union Nat. scholar, 1959-64, U. Calif. Regents scholar, 1959-64; Woodrow Wilson Nat. Grad. fellow, 1964-65; recipient 1st prize Acad. Am. Poets, 1964 Mem. Am. Film Inst., Third Decade Coun., Authors Guild, Authors League Am., Acad. TV Arts & Scis. Office: Creative Domain Inc 9000 W Sunset Blvd Fl 9 Los Angeles CA 90069-5801

LITHERLAND, ALBERT EDWARD, physics educator; b. Wallasey, Eng., Mar. 12, 1928; emigrated to Can., 1953, naturalized, 1964; s. Albert and Ethel (Clement) L.; m. Anne Allen, May 12, 1956; children: Jane Elizabeth, Rosamund Mary. B.Sc., U. Liverpool, Eng., 1949, PhD, 1955; DSc (hon.), U. Toronto, 1998. Rutherford scholar Atomic Energy of Can., Chalk River, Ont., 1953-55, sci. officer, 1955-66; prof. physics U. Toronto, 1966-79, Univ. prof., 1979-93, Univ. prof. emeritus, 1993—. Contbr. articles to profl. jours. Recipient Rutherford medal Inst. Physics, London, 1974, Silver medal for accelerator-based dating techniques Jour. Applied Radiation and Isotopes, 1980; Guggenheim fellow, 1986-87. Fellow Royal Soc. Can. (Henry Marshall Tory medal 1993), Royal Soc. London, AAAS, Am. Phys. Soc.; mem. Can. Assn. Physicists (Gold medal for achievement in physics 1971) Home: Apt 801 120 Rosedale Valley Rd Toronto ON Canada M4W 1P8 Office: 60 St George St Toronto ON Canada M5S 1A7

LITHWICK, NORMAN HARVEY, economics educator; b. Ottawa, Ont., Can., Oct. 10, 1938; s. Arnold and Rose Lillian (Esar) L.; m. Yvonne Kate Baher, Mar. 12, 1964; children: Alexander, Dahlia, Hillel. BA with honors, U. Western Ont., 1960; AM, Harvard U., 1962, PhD, 1963. Asst. prof. econs. Carleton U., Ottawa, 1963-67, assoc. prof. econs., 1967-71, prof. econs., 1971—, chmn. econs., 1974-77, prof. pub. adminstrn., 1981—, supr. devel. adminstrn., 1985-90. Dir. Inst. Can. Studies Carleton U., 1972-73; vis. prof. econs. and geography Hebrew U., Jerusalem, 1977-78, 90-93; rsch. fellow Brookdale Instn., 1990—; vis. prof. Urban and Regional Econ. Devel. Beer Sheva, mng. dir. Negev Ctr. Regional Devel., asst. sec. Ministry Urban Affairs, Ottawa, 1970-71; advisor Prime Minister Can., Ottawa, 1984; cons. in field. Author: Economic Growth in Can., 1970, Urban Canada, 1970, Regional Policy in Can., 1978; contbr. articles to profl. jours. Mem. Jerusalem Com., 1981—; pres. Jewish Community Council, Ottawa, 1983-85; v.p. Nat. Budgeting Conf., Toronto, Ont., 1985—, Can. Jewish Congress, Montreal, Que., 1986-90; bd. dirs. Children's Hosp. Eastern Ont., Ottawa, 1982-85. Harvard U. grad. fellow, 1960-63, Lady Davis Trust fellow, 1977-78; Cen. Mortgage/Housing research grantee, 1966, Can. Council research grantee, 1968. Mem. Can. Econs. Assn., Can. Regional Sci. Assn., Can. Assn. Studies in. Devel. also: PO Box 845 85025 Metar Israel

LITKE, DONALD PAUL, business executive, retired military officer; b. Denver, Nov. 7, 1934; s. Walter Monroe and Alice Vivian (Fowler) L.; m. Myrna Kay McDonald, July 1, 1956; children— Bradley, Susan, Lisa BS in Econs., Colo. A&M U., 1956; MS in Internat. Affairs, George Washington U., 1966. Ops. and staff positions U.S. Air Force, 1956-79; vice comdr. Oklahoma City Air Logistics Ctr., 1979-81; dep. dir. logistics and security assistance U.S. European Command, Stuttgart, Germany, 1981-83; comdr. U.S. Logistics Group, Ankara, Turkey, 1983-85; dep. dir. Def. Logistics Agy., Alexandria, VA., 1985-86; pres. Bus. Devel. Internat., Alexandria and Niceville, Fla., 1986—. Contbr. articles to profl. jours. Mem. Air Force Assn. (Middle Mgr. of Yr. 1970, award of excellence 1977), Alpha Tau Omega Methodist. Avocations: automobile restoration; racquet sports. Home and Office: 2422 Edgewater Dr Niceville FL 32578-2305

LITMAN, BERNARD, electrical engineer, consultant; b. N.Y.C., Oct. 26, 1920; s. Nathan and Gussie (Friedman) L.; m. Ellen Ann Kaufman, Feb. 27, 1949; children— Barbara, Richard. BS in Elec. Engring, Columbia U., 1941, PhD, 1949; MS, U. Pitts., 1943. Design engr. energy equipment Westinghouse Electric Co., Pitts., 1941-47; with AMBAC Industries div. United Tech. Corp., Garden City, N.Y., 1949-83, tech. dir. guidance equipment Atlas intercontinental missile, 1962-63, chief engr. systems devel. and research, 1964-83; dir. advanced tech. Gull Electronics Systems Div., Parker Hannifin Corp., 1983-93; tech. cons., 1994-96; ret., 1996. Westinghouse lectr. U. Pitts., 1944; lectr. Adelphi U., Garden City. Co-author: Gyroscopics, 1961; patentee rotary amplifiers, axial motors, gravity pendulums, inductors, 2 axis accellerometers, ballistic missile safety devices, gyro attenuators, thrust retainers. William Petit Trobridge fellow, 1948 Asso. fellow Am. Inst. Aeros. and Astronautics (Achievement award L.I. sect. 1966); mem. IEEE (sr.), Am. Automatic Control Council, N.Y.-N.J. Trail Conf., Sigma Xi. Jewish. Home: 228 Wagon Wheel Ln Columbus NJ 08022-1119

LITMAN, BRIAN DAVID, communications executive; b. Kansas City, Mo., May 9, 1954; s. Marvin Wilbur and Louise Diane (Raskin) L. BJ, U. Mo., 1977. Promotion mgr. Atlanta br. CBS/Columbia Records, Atlanta, 1977-78; promotion mgr. CBS Records, Cleve., 1978-79; dir. mktg. Am. TV and Communications (subs. Time, Inc. Cable), Pitts., 1980-81; account mgr. Group W Satellite Communications, Stamford, Conn., 1981-82; dir. nat. accounts Hearst/ABC/NBC, N.Y.C., 1985-86, mng. dir. western divsn. L.A., 1986-90; pres. Entertainment and Comm. Holdings Orgn., West Hollywood, Calif., 1990-94; v.p. U.S. West/Interactive Video Enterprises, San Ramon, 1994-95; chmn. Entertainment & Comms. Holdings Orgn.; CEO Advanced Multimedia Products, 1997—. Chmn., CEO PlayMedia Sys. Inc., 1997—; chmn. Continuum Group, 1998—, PlayMedia Labs., 1998—, Subband Software, 2000—. Former dir. editorial bd. Emmy mag. Mem. L.A. World Affairs Coun., 1991—. Mem. Acad. TV Arts and Scis. (chmn. cable com. 1989-91), Hollywood Radio and TV Soc., L.A. Advt. Club, U.S.-Russia Trade and Econ. Coun. Office: 8170 S Eastern Ave Ste 4601 Las Vegas NV 89123-2579

LITMAN, HARRY PETER, lawyer, educator; b. Pitts., May 4, 1958; s. S. David and Roslyn M. (Margolis) L. BA, Harvard U., 1981; JD, U. Calif., Berkeley, 1986. Bar: Calif. 1987, U.S. Ct. Appeals (D.C. cir.) 1987, Pa. 1988, D.C. 1989, U.S. Ct. Appeals (9th cir.) 1990, U.S. Dist. Ct. (so. dist.) Tex. 1992, U.S. Supreme Ct. 1992, U.S. Dist. Ct. (ea. and we. dists.) Pa. 1993, U.S. Ct. Appeals (7th cir.) 1994, U.S. Dist. Ct. (ea. dist.) Va. 1997. Prodn. asst. feature films, N.Y.C., 1980-82; newsman, clk. baseball desk AP, 1982-83, sports reporter, 1983-86; law clk. to Hon. Abner J. Mikva U.S. Ct. Appeals (D.C. cir.), 1986-87; law clk. to Hon. Thurgood Marshall U.S. Supreme Ct., Washington, 1987-88, law clk. to Hon. Anthony M. Kennedy, 1989; asst. U.S. atty., dep. chief appellate sect. Dept. Justice, San Francisco, 1990-92, dep. assoc. atty. gen. Washington, 1992-93, dep. asst. atty. gen., 1993-98; U.S. atty. Western Dist. of Pa., 1998—2001. Adj. prof. Boalt Hall Sch. Law U. Calif., Berkeley, 1990-92, Georgetown U. Law Ctr., 1996-99, U. Pitts. Law Sch., 1999—. Editor-in-chief Calif. Law Rev., Vol. 73; author various articles. Presdl. scholar, 1976. Mem. Pa. Bar Assn., State Bar Calif., D.C. Bar, Order of Coif.

LITMAN, RAYMOND STEPHEN, financial services consultant; b. Kingston, Pa., Nov. 2, 1936; s. Stephen Vincent and Mary Helen (Wisnewski) Litman; m. Ann Mae Kosik, Nov. 24, 1960; children: Raymond Stephen II, A. Christine. BS in Commerce, Wilkes U., 1961. Credit mgr. ea. div. Sears Roebuck & Co., 1961—66; banking officer Phila. Nat. Bank, 1966—69; dir. Decision Dynamics Corp., Marlton, NJ, 1969—71; asst. v.p. Bankers Trust Co., N.Y.C., 1971—75; sr. banking officer Girard Bank, Phila., 1975—77; pres. World Wide Cons. Svcs., Plymouth Meeting, 1977—78; assoc. dir. bank card divsn. Am. Bankers Assn., 1978—80; mng. dir., sr. v.p. Chem. Bank, N.Y.C., 1981—92; pres., COO ECC Mgmt. Svcs. Inc., King of Prussia, Pa., 1992—93; pres., CEO Litman Assocs., Inc. Fin. Svcs. Cons. Mem. adv. coun. Credit Rsch Ctr. Purdue U. Served with USN, 1954—57, ETO. Mem.: VFW, Govt. Rels. Coun. and Banking Leadership, Am. Bankers Assn. (mem. bank card div. exec. com.), Internat. Assn. Credit Card Investigators (life; pres. Del. Valley chpt. 1976—77, dir. nat. chpt. 1976—77), Plymouth Meeting Hist. Soc., Montgomery County Police Chiefs Assn., Police Chiefs Assn. Southeast Pa., Frat. Order of Police, Am. Legion. Republican. Roman Catholic. Home: 2057 Sierra Rd Plymouth Meeting PA 19462-1826

LITMAN, RICHARD CURTIS, lawyer; b. Phila., May 2, 1957; s. Benjamin Norman and Bette Etta (Saunders) L.; m. Cheryl Lynn Goldstein, May 28, 1989; children: Amanda Rose, Jessica Brooke, Daniel Grant, Victoria Grace. BS, Union Coll., 1973; JD cum laude, U. Miami, 1979; LLM in Patent and Trade Regulation, George Washington U., 1980; M of Forensic Sci., Antioch Sch. Law, 1981. Bar: D.C. 1979, Fla. 1979, Pa. 1979, Va. 1980, Md. 1984, U. Ct. Appeals (fed. cir.), U.S. Patent and Trademark Office, U.S. Supreme Ct. Pvt. practice, Arlington, Va., 1983—. Instr. continuing legal edn.; organizer, dir. James Monroe Bank. Host Great Ideas Radio. com.; Contbr. articles to profl. jours. Fellow Food and Drug Law Inst., 1979-80; named Small Bus. of Yr. Arlington C. of C., 1995. Mem. ABA, Fed. Bar Assn., Am. Acad. Forensic Scis., Am. Intellectual Property Law Assn., Arlington County Bar Assn., Masons (32d degree Scottish Rite), Shriners. Office: Litman Law Offices Ltd Patent Law Bldg 3717 Columbia Pike Arlington VA 22204-4255 E-mail: litman@4patent.com.

LITMAN, ROBERT BARRY, physician, writer, television and radio commentator; b. Phila., Nov. 17, 1947; s. Benjamin Norman and Bette Etta (Saunders) L.; m. Niki Thomas, Apr. 21, 1985; children: Riva Belle, Nadya Beth, Caila Tess, Benjamin David. BS, Yale U., 1967, MD, 1970, MS, MPhil in Anatomy, 1972. Diplomate Am. Bd. Family Practice. Postdoct. rsch. fellow Am. Cancer Soc. Yale U., New Haven, 1970-73, USPHS fellow, 1974-75; resident in gen. surgery Bryn Mawr (Pa.) Hosp., 1973-74; pvt. practice in medicine and surgery Ogdensburg, N.Y., 1977-93, San Ramon, Calif., 1993—; mem. staff A. Barton Hepburn Hosp., 1977-93, John Muir Med. Ctr., 1993—, San Ramon Regional Med. Ctr., 1993—, also chmn. med. edn., chmn. dept. family practice, 1998-99. Commentator Family Medicine Stas. WWNY-TV and WTNY-Radio, TCI Cablevision, Contra Costa T.V.; moderator Ask the Dr.; clin. preceptor dept. family medicine State U. Health Sci. Ctr., Syracuse, 1978—. Author: Wynnefield and Limer, 1983, The Treblinka Virus, 1991, Allergy Shots, 1993; contbr. articles to numerous profl. jours. Pres. No. N.Y. chpt. AHA. Fellow Life Ins. Med. Rsch. Fund, U. Coll. Hosp., U. London, 1969-70; recipient We. Access Video Excellence award, 1998, 2001, Bay Area Cable Excellence award, 1999, Telly award, 1999, 2000, 01, 02. Fellow Am. Coll. Allergy, Asthma, and Immunology, Am. Acad. Family Physicians; mem. AMA (Physicians Recognition award 1970—), Calif. State Med. Assn., Alameda-Contra Costa County Med. Assn., Joint Coun. Allergy and Immunology, Nat. Assn. Physician Broadcasters (charter), Acad. Radio and TV Health Communicators, Book and Snake Soc., Gibbs Soc. Yale U. (founder), Sigma Xi, Nu Sigma Nu, Alpha Chi Sigma. Home and Office: PO Box 1857 San Ramon CA 94583-6857 E-mail: roblitmanmd@drlitman.com.

LITMAN, ROSLYN MARGOLIS, lawyer, educator; b. N.Y.C., Sept. 30, 1928; d. Harry and Dorothy (Perlow) Margolis; m. S. David Litman, Nov. 22, 1950; children: Jessica, Hannah, Harry. BA, U. Pitts., 1949, JD, 1952. Bar: Pa. 1952. Practiced in Pitts., 1952—; ptnr. firm Litman Law Firm, 1952—; adj. prof. U. Pitts. Law Sch., 1958—. Permanent del. Conf. U.S. Circuit Ct. Appeals for 3d Circuit; past chair dist. adv. group U.S. Dist. Ct. (we. dist.) Pa., 1991-94, mem. steering com. for dist. adv. group, 1991—; chmn. Pitts. Pub. Parking Authority, 1970-74; mem. curriculum com. Pa. Bar Inst., 1986—, bd. dirs., 1972-82. Bd. dirs. United Jewish Fedn., 1999—, cmty. rels. com., co-chair ch./state com.; bd. dirs. City Theatre, 1999—. Recipient Roscoe Pound Found. award for Excellence in Tchg. Trial Advocacy, 1996, Disting. Alumnus award U. Pitts. Sch. Law, 1996; named Fed. Lawyer of Yr., We. Pa. Chpt. FBA, 1999. Mem. ABA (del., litigation sect., anti-trust health care com.), ACLU (nat. bd. dirs., Marjorie H. Matson Civil Libertarian award Greater Pitts. chpt. 1999), Pa. Bar Assn. (bd. govs. 1976-79), Allegheny County Bar Assn. (bd. govs. 1972-74, pres. 1975, Woman of Yr. 2001), Allegheny County Acad. Trial Lawyers (charter), Order of Coif. Home: 5023 Frew St Pittsburgh PA 15213-3829 Office: One Oxford Centre 34th Fl Pittsburgh PA 15219

LITMAN, THEODOR JAMES, medical educator; b. Duluth, Minn., Aug. 7, 1932; s. Samuel N. and Leone Sylvia Litman; m. Brendalee Litman, Sept. 3, 1961; children: Greggory Robb, Scott Anthony. BA cum laude, U. Minn., 1954, MA, 1956, PhD, 1961. Asst. prof. program in hosp. adminstrn. U. Minn., Mpls., 1961-66, assoc. prof., 1967-70, prof. dept. healthcare mgmt., 1971-99, prof. emeritus dept. healthcare mgmt., 1999—. Cons. Nat. Ctr. Health Svcs. Rsch., Washington, 1976—. Book rev. editor Jour. Health and Human Behavior, 1963-66; author: Bibliography: The Sociology of Medicine and Healthcare-The First 50 Years, 1976; co-editor: Health Politics and Policy, 1987, 91, 97. With USAR, 1958-64. Fellow Am. Sociol. Assn., Am. Pub. Health Assn. Avocation: collegiate sports, little league baseball. Home: 3301 Gettysburg Ave S Minneapolis MN 55426-3723 Office: Dept Healthcare Mgmt 321 19th Ave S Minneapolis MN 55455-0438 E-mail: litmaa001@maroon.tc.umn.edu.

LITOFF, JUDY BARRETT, history educator; b. Atlanta, Dec. 23, 1944; d. John and Dorothy (Woodall) Barrett; children: Nadja Barrett, Alyssa Barrett. BA, Emory U., Atlanta, 1967; MA, Emory U., 1968; PhD, U. Maine, 1975. Asst. prof. history Bryant Coll., Smithfield, R.I., 1975-81, assoc. prof. history, 1981-87, prof. history, 1987—. Scholarly reader U. Ga. Press, Greenwood Press, U. Ill. Press, Prentice Hall, Univ. Press of Ky., Univ. Press of Colo.; project dir. U.S. Info. Agy. Grant, Minsk, Belarus, 1997—, higher edn. support program, Grant, Minsk, 1999. Author: American Midwives, 1978, American Midwife Debate, 1986; co-author: Miss You, 1990, Since You Went Away, 1991, Dear Boys, 1991, We're In This War, Too, 1994, European Immigrant Women, 1994, American Women in a World at War, 1997, Dear Poppa, 1997, What Kind of World Do We Want?, 2000; contbr. articles to profl. jours.; book reviewer many profl. jours. Bd. dirs. R.I. Hist. Soc., 1999—; bd. dirs., chair Goff Inst. for Ingenuity and Enterprise, 1998—; bd. dirs. R.I. Com. for Humanities, 1982-86; bd. overseers The Lincoln Sch., Providence, 1982-88, The Moses Brown Sch., Providence, 1984-93; leader Girl Scouts R.I., 1978-87. Recipient Disting. Faculty award Bryant Faculty Fedn., 1988, Bryant Alumni Assn., 1989, James Madison prize Soc. for History in Fed. Govt., 1994, Bryant Coll. Rsch. and Pub. award, 1997; Ford Career scholar Emory U., 1965-67. Mem. Orgn. Am. Historians, Am. Hist. Assn., So. Hist. Assn., R.I. Hist. Soc., Coordinating Com. on Women in the Hist. Profession, So. Assn. Women Historians, Phi Kappa Phi, Phi Alpha Theta. Avocations: skiing, hiking. Home: 248 Morris Ave Providence RI 02906-2424 Office: Bryant Coll 1150 Douglas Pike Smithfield RI 02917-1291 E-mail: jlitoff@bryant.edu.

LITOFF, RUTH ANNE, artist, educator; b. N.Y.C., Apr. 10, 1966; d. Ronald and Carole Litoff. Student, Sch. Visual Arts, 1985-87; BA in Philosophy and Bus., NYU, 1991. Fine arts photographer, N.Y.C., 1991—. Publ., editor-in-chief Fine Arts mag., 1983-84, On Seeing mag., 1986-89. Pub., editor-in-chief: Fine Arts mag., 1983—84, pub., editor-in-chief: On Seeing mag., 1986—89;exhibitions include Mus. Modern Art, N.Y.C., 2001, 2002. Winner Focal Pt. Gallery Internat. Juried Competition, 1994, Manhattan Arts Internat. 5th Ann. Arts Competition, 1996. Mem. Nat. Assn. Women Artists, Internat. Ctr. Photography (exec. com. 1997), Dalton Alumni Assn. (vis. artists com. 1994, arts com. 1995).

LITSCHGI, A. BYRNE, lawyer; b. Charleston, S.C., Dec. 31, 1920; s. Albert William and Mary Catherine (Byrne) L.; m. Mary Elaine Herring, Sept. 13, 1952. BBA, U. Fla., 1941; JD, Harvard U., 1948. Bar: Fla. 1948, D.C. 1950. Atty. Office Gen. Counsel, Treasury Dept., Washington, 1949-52; legis. asst. to U.S. senator, 1952; mem. firm Hedrick & Lane, Washington, 1953-60, Coles, Himes & Litschgi, Tampa, Fla., 1960-62, Shackleford, Farrior, Stallings & Evans, 1962-87, Dykema Gossett, Tampa, Fla., 1988-92; chmn. SL Industries, Inc., 1976-92; mem. firm Holland & Knight, Tampa, 1992—. Incorporator, dir. Communications Satellite Corp., 1962-64; mem. Fla. Jud. Council, 1965-68, U.S. Internal Revenue Commn. Adv. Group, 1967-68 Mem. Harvard Law Sch. Assn. (nat. council 1956-61), ABA (chmn. excise and miscellaneous tax com. tax sect. 1956-59), Fla. Bar, Bar Assn. D.C. Office: Holland & Knight PO Box 1288 Tampa FL 33601-1288

LITSCHGI, RICHARD JOHN, computer manufacturing company executive; b. St. Louis, July 1, 1937; s. William J. and Mary F. (Eynatten) L.; m. Christine Ewert, Aug. 21, 1968. BS, St. Louis U., 1959; MS, U. Okla., 1964. Cert. meteorology St. Louis U./USAF. Supr. Bellcomm, Inc., Washington, 1964-67; mgr. Computer Scis., Brussels, 1967-68, Intranet Computing Co., L.A., 1968-71, Xerox Corp., El Segundo, Calif., 1971-76; dir. Honeywell, Inc., L.A., 1976-80, v.p. Phoenix, 1980-85, Mpls., 1985-87, Honeywell Bull, Inc., 1987-88, Bull HN, Inc., Boston, 1988-89, Groupe Bull, Boston and Paris, 1990-93, Vanguard Automation, Inc., Tucson, 1993-94; ret., 1994. Bd. dirs. Arizonians for Cultural Devel., 1981-85; trustee Phoenix Art Mus., 1982-85. Capt. USAF, 1959-62. Home: 24 Tupelo Rd Falmouth MA 02540-1945

LITSKY, BERTHA YANIS, microbiologist, artist; b. Chester, Pa., Jan. 2, 1920; d. Edward Bernard and Hattie (Howell) Meade; m. Martin Yanis, June 27, 1942 (dec.); children: Libby Nesvold, Rosalind Yanishevsky; m. Warren Litsky, July 27, 1965 (dec. July 1994). BSc, Phila. Coll. Pharmacy, 1942; MPA, NYU, 1964; PhD, Walden U., 1974. Lic. med. technologist. Head dept. bacteriology Assoc. Labs., Phila., 1942-44; asst. supr. prodn. Nat. Drug Co., Swiftwater, Pa., 1944-45; rsch. bacteriologist U. Pa., Phila., 1945-50; cons. microbiologist, 1950-56; head dept. bacteriology S.I. Hosp., N.Y.C., 1956-65; rsch. assoc. U. Mass., Amherst, 1965—. Nurse cons. Bingham Assocs. Fund New Eng. Med. Ctr. Hosp., Boston, 1965-85 Author: An Administrative Program for Hospital Sanitation, 1966, Food Service Sanitation, 1973; contbr. chpts. to books; contbr. more than 115 articles to profl. jours. Troop mother Girl Scouts USA, S.I., 1953-60; judge Acad. Sci., N.Y.C., 1953-60; aided students in project for Sci. Fair, N.Y.C., 1953-62; mem. animal control com. Town of Amherst, 1978-80; sanitation cons. Town Hall, Amherst, 1994—; v.p. Friends of Amherst Stray Animals, 1980—; mem. fundraising com. MSPCA, Boston, 1995. Recipient scholarship NYU, 1964, Editl. award, Hosp. Mgmt., 1964, 65, 68, Annual Alumni award Phila. Coll. Pharmacy and Sci., 1979, Leonard A. Leipus award Am. Soc. for Hosp. Ctrl. Svc. Pers., 1982, 9th Annual Dr. John J. Perkins Meml. award Surgicot, Inc., 1983, Pub. Svc. award Assn. Surg. Technologists, 1983, 85, Appreciation award N.C. Assn. for Hosp. Ctrl. Svc. Pers., 1987, Pioneer in Infection Control award Smith Bros. Whitehaven, Ltd., 1992, among others. Mem. APHA, Am. Hosp. Assn., Am. Soc. Microbiology, Internat. Assn. for Hosp. Ctrl. Svc. Material Mgmt.

(Pres.'s award 1992), Amherst Club. Avocations: painting, working with homeless animals, playing the violin, teaching art history, international hospital work. Home: 21 Lowery Ln Mendham NJ 07945-3403 Office: U Mass Amherst MA 01003

LITT, MITCHELL, chemical engineer, educator, bioengineer; b. Bklyn., Oct. 11, 1932; s. Saul and Mollie (Steinbaum) L.; m. Zelda Sheila Levine, Sept. 6, 1955; children: Ellen Beth, Steven Eric. AB, Columbia U., 1953, BS in Engring, 1954, MS, 1956; D.Engring. Sci., Columbia, 1961. Research engr. Esso Research and Engring. Co., 1958-61; faculty U. Pa., 1961—, asso. prof. chem. engring., 1965-72, prof., 1972—, prof. bioengring., 1977—, chmn. dept. bioengring., 1981-90. Vis. prof. environ. medicine Duke, 1971-72; vis. prof. Weizmann Inst., Israel, 1979; v.p. research and devel. KDL Med. Techs. Inc., 1984-95; v.p. rsch. & devel. BioFlo Systems, Inc., 1995—. Co-editor: Rheology of Biological Systems, 1973; asso. editor: Biorheology; contbr. articles to profl. engrs. Mem. IEEE (engring. in medicine and biology soc.), Am. Inst. Chem. Engrs., Am. Soc. Engring. Edn., Am. Chem. Soc., Biomed. Engring. Soc., Internat. Soc. Biorheology, N.Am. Soc. Biorheology, Am. Inst. Med. Biol. Engring., Phi Beta Kappa, Sigma Xi, Tau Beta Pi, Phi Lambda Upsilon, Theta Tau. Achievements include spl. research biorheology transp. processes, chemically reacting systems, med. aspects engring. Home: 2420 Spruce St Philadelphia PA 19103-6423 Office: Univ Pa Dept Bio Engring Philadelphia PA 19104 E-mail: litt@seas.upenn.edu.

LITT, MORTON HERBERT, macromolecular science educator, researcher; b. N.Y.C., Apr. 10, 1926; s. Samuel Bernard and Minnie (Hertz) L.; m. Lola Natalie Abrahamson, July 7, 1957; children: Jonathan S., Jennifer A. BS, CCNY, 1947; MS, Bklyn. Poly. Inst., 1953, PhD, 1956. Turner and Newall fellow U. Manchester, Eng., 1956-57; sr. research fellow N.Y. State Coll. Forestry, Syracuse, N.Y., 1958-59; sr. scientist Allied Chem. Corp., Morristown, N.J., 1960-64, assoc. dir. research, 1965-67; assoc. prof. Case Western Res. U., Cleve., 1967-76, prof. macromolecular sci., 1976—. Cons. in industry and govt. Mem. adv. bd. Jour. Polymer Sci. and Polymer Chemistry; patentee in field. Fellow Am. Inst. Physics; mem. AAAS, Materials Rsch. Soc., Am. Chem. Soc., Chem. Soc. London, Electrochem. Soc. Home: 2575 Charney Rd Cleveland OH 44118-4402 Office: Case Western Res U Kent H Smith Bldg Cleveland OH 44106-7202 E-mail: MHL2@pop.cwru.edu.

LITTELL, MARCIA SACHS, Holocaust educator; b. Phila., July 12, 1937; d. Leon Harry Sobel and Selma Fisher Goldstein Lipson; m. Robert L. Sachs, Apr. 3, 1955 (div. June 1978); children: Jonathan R., Robert L. Jr., Jennifer Sachs-Dahnert; m. Franklin H. Littell, Mar. 23, 1980; children: Jennith Lawrence, Karen, Miriam, Stephen. BS in Edn., Temple U., 1971, MS in Edn., 1975, EdD, 1990. Internat. exec. dir. Anne Frank Inst., Phla., 1981-89; exec. dir. Ann. Scholars' Conf. on the Holocaust & the Chs., Merion, Pa., 1980—; prof., founding dir. MA program Holocaust & genocide studies The Richard Stockton Coll. N.J., 1997—. Adj. prof. Temple U., Phila., 1990-97; vis. prof. Phila. C.C., 1974-76; dir. Phila. Ctr. on the Holocaust, Genocide and Human Rights, 1989—; exec. com. Remembering for the Future, Oxford, Eng. and Berlin, 1986—; mem. edn. com. U.S. Holocaust Meml. Mus., Washington, 1987-89, chmn.'s adv. com., 1985. Mem. editl. bd. Holocaust & Genocide Studies, Oxford U. Press, 1987—, Bridges: An Interdisciplinary Journal of Theology, Philosophy, History and Science, 1995—; editor: Holocaust Education: A Resource for Teachers and Professional Leaders, 1985, Liturgies on the Holocaust: An Interfaith Anthology, 1986, rev. edit., 1996 (Merit of Distinction award), The Holocaust: Forty Years After, 1989, The Netherlands and Nazi Genocide, 1992, From Prejudice to Destruction: Western Civilization in the Shadow of Auschwitz, 1995, Remembrance and Recollection: Essays on the Centennial Year of Martin Neimoller and Reinhold Niebuhr, 1995, The Uses and Abuses of Knowledge: The Holocaust and the German Church Struggle, 1997, The Holocaust: Lessons For the Third Generation, 1997, Holocaust and Church Struggle: Religion, Power and the Politics of Resistance, 1996, Confronting the Holocaust: A Mandate for the 21st Century, part 1, 1997, part 2, 1998, A Modern Prophet, 1998, Hearing the Voices: Teaching the Holocaust to Future Generations, 1999. Exec. com. YM/YWHA Arts Coun., Phila., 1980—; adv. bd. Child Welfare, Montgomery County, 1975-80, Am. Friends the Ghetto Fighters House; bd. govs. Lower Merion Scholarship Fund, 1972-80. Named Woman of the Yr., Brith Sholom Women, Phila., 1993; recipient Eternal Flame award Anne Frank Inst., 1988; named to Hall of Fame Sch. Dist. of Phila., 1988. Fellow Nat. Assn. Holocaust Educators, Assn. of Holocaust Orgns. (founding sec. 1985-88), Nat. Coun. for the Social Studies. Democrat. Jewish. Avocations: walking, travel, reading. Office: PO Box 10 Merion Station PA 19066-0010 E-mail: Drlittell@aol.com.

LITTELL, RICHARD GREGORY, lawyer; b. Hartford, Conn., Feb. 7, 1931; s. Elliot Manning and Lilyan Ruth (Stiegel) L.; m. Barbara Anne Diggs, Mar. 31, 1962 (div. Dec. 1983); children: John Gregory, Susan Anne. BA, Cornell U., 1953; JD, Harvard U., 1956. Bar: D.C., Calif., N.Y. Asst. gen. counsel Civil Aeronautics Bd., Washington, 1967-69, assoc. gen. counsel, 1969-71, gen. counsel, 1973-74, Postal Rate Commn., Washington, 1971-73; ptnr. Dickstein, Shapiro & Morin, 1974-80, Bishop, Cook, Purcell & Reynolds, Washington, 1980-90; pvt. practice, 1990—. Author: Endangered and Threatened Species, 1992; contbr. numerous articles to profl. publs., gen. interest mags. and newspapers. Chmn. Air Pollution Adv. Com., Met. Washington Coun. of Govts., 1965-67. Mem. Cosmos Club, Nat. Press Club, Belle Haven Country Club. Avocations: flyfishing, tennis. Home: 613 S Fairfax St Alexandria VA 22314-3833 Office: 1220 19th St NW Ste 400 Washington DC 20036-2438 E-mail: rlittell@dgs.dgsys.com.

LITTEN, CHARLOTTE ELAINE, contractor, counselor, small business owner; b. Salyersville, Ky., Jan. 9, 1944; d. Henry Sterling and Lela May (Reed) Bailey; m. Arthur G. Litten, Sept. 23, 1962 (div. Jan. 1980); 1 child, Robert Mark Litten. Assoc. in Math. and Scis., Shawnee State U., 1986; BBA, Ohio U., 1987, MEd, 1990. Cert. counselor Nat. Bd. Cert. Counselors Inc.; cert. sec. Cert. Profl. Secs. With indsl. rel. Goodyear Atomic Corp., Piketon, Ohio, 1980-87; labor rels. specialist Martin Marietta Energy Sys., Inc., 1987-90, asst. to divsn. mgr., 1990-92, dept. mgr. cascade svcs., 1992-97; pres. Lockheed-Martin Inc., 1997—. Counselor, co-owner Hope Counseling Ctr., South Shore, Ky., 1991—. Bd. dirs. Pike County Joint Vocat. Sch. Adv. Bd., 1980—, Scioto County Vocat. Sch. Adv. Bd., Lucasville, 1980—, Atomic Employees Credit Union, Piketon, 1993—. Mem. Chi Sigma Iota, Phi Kappa Phi. Democrat. Avocation: counseling. Home: 2928 N Hill Rd Portsmouth OH 45662-2419 Office: Lockheed-Martin PO Box 628 Piketon OH 45661-0628

LITTERAL, DANIEL PACE, lawyer; b. Washington, Aug. 10, 1955; s. Kelley Litteral and Kathleen Margaret Olson; m. Katherine Hedwig Madson, Jan. 22, 1977 (div. Oct. 1998); 1 child, Jennifer Erin. BA, Wake Forest U., 1976; JD with honors, U. N.D., 1981. Bar: Md. 1981, Ariz. 2000, U.S. Dist. Ct. Md. 1982. Lawyer, prin. Litteral & Litteral Chartered, Silver Spring, Md., 1981-84, Rockville, 1984-88; pvt. practice law, 1988—2001; lawyer, assoc. gen. counsel U. Phoenix, 2002—. Adj. lectr. U. N.D., Grand Forks, 1980-81; lectr. Coll. Bd., Phila., 1997, Assn. Ind. Md. Schs., Potomac, 1998, lectr. ed. law assoc., 2001. Author (monthly column) Leisure Living, 1996-99, (profl. newsletter) Pvt. Ednl. Newsletter, 1998, 2001. Capt. U.S. Army/USAR, 1976-83. Mem. Md. State Bar Assn., Montgomery County Bar Assn, State Bar of Ariz. Avocation: private pilot. Office: U Phoenix 4615 E Elmwood Dr Phoenix AZ 85040

LITTIG, LAWRENCE WILLIAM, psychologist, educator; b. Madison, Wis., June 30, 1927; s. Lawrence Victor and Elsie Louise (Rosanske) L.; m. Iris Mark, June 15, 1957; children— Eve Alexandra, Amy Victoria, Sharon Elizabeth. BS, U. Wis., 1950, MS, 1955; PhD, U. Mich., 1959. Instr. dept. psychology U. Mich., Ann Arbor, 1958-59; asst. prof. psychology U. Buffalo, 1959-62; asst. program dir. instl. programs NSF, Washington, 1962-63; social psychologist W.E. Upjohn Inst. Employment Research, 1963-65; prof. social psychology Howard U., 1965-92, prof. emeritus social psychology, 1992—; prof. psychology Md. Inst. Coll. of Art, Balt., 1993—. Fulbright prof. U. Nottingham, 1961-62; vis. scholar U. London, 1971-72; cons. Brookings Instn., 1968-70, Dept. Labor, 1968-70; vis. prof. U. Wis., 1970 Cons. editor: Jour. Cross Cultural Psychology, 1969-74; contbr. articles to profl. jours. Port warden City of Annapolis, 1994—. U.S. Office Edn. grantee, 1965-70; NIMH research grantee, 1968-69; NSF research grantee, 1961-62; Nat. Inst. Child Health and Human Devel. grantee, 1971-73 Fellow AAAS, Am. Psychol. Assn., Am. Psychol. Soc., Soc. for Personality and Social Psychology; mem. Psychonomic Soc., Brit. Psychol. Soc., Sigma Xi. Clubs: Cosmos (Washington); Md. Capital Yacht, Eastport Yacht (Annapolis, Md.); Amateur Fencing (London). Home: 2 Wells Lndg Annapolis MD 21403-2316 Office: Howard U Dept Psychology Washington DC 20059-0001 E-mail: llittig@erols.com.

LITTLE, ALAN BRIAN, obstetrician, gynecologist, educator; b. Montreal, Que., Can., Mar. 11, 1925; emigrated to U.S., 1951, naturalized, 1959; s. Herbert Melville and Mary Lizette (Campbell) L.; m. Nancy Alison Campbell, Aug. 20, 1949 (div.); children: Michael C. (dec.), Susan MacF. and Deborah MacF. (twins), Catherine E., Jane A., Mary L.; m. Bitten Stripp, Mar. 31, 1983 BA, McGill U., 1948, MD, CM, 1950. Intern Montreal Gen. Hosp., 1950-51; resident Boston Lying-in and Free Hosp. for Women, 1951-55, asst. obstetrician, asso. obstetrician and gynecologist, 1955-65; teaching fellow, asst. prof. Harvard Med. Sch., 1952-65; prof. ob-gyn, then Arthur H. Bill prof. ob-gyn Case Western Res. U. Sch. Medicine, Cleve., 1965-82, chmn. dept. reproductive biology, 1972-82; prof. gynecology McGill U., Montreal, 1983—, chmn. dept. ob-gyn., 1983-94; clin. prof. ob-gyn. U. Medicine and Dentistry N.J., Newark, 1994—. Dir. dept. ob-gyn. Univ. Hosps., Cleve., to 1982, Royal Victoria Hosp., Montreal, 1983-94; mem. nat. adv. com. Nat. Inst. Child Health and Human Devel. Author: (with B. Tenney) Clinical Obstetrics, 1962; editor: (with others) Gynecology and Obstetrics-Health Care for Women, 1975, 2d edit., 1982; (with D. Tulchinsky) Maternal Fetal Endocrinology, 2d edit., 1994; contbr. articles to profl. jours. Served with RCAF, 1943-45. Fellow ACS, Royal Coll. Surgeons, Am. Coll. Obstetricians and Gynecologists; mem. AMA, Endocrine Soc., Am. Gynecol. and Obstet. Soc., Am., Central assns. ob-gyn., Assn. Profs. Ob-Gyn., Soc. Gynecol. Investigation, Soc. Ob-Gyn. Can. Office: UMDNJ MSB E506 185 S Orange Ave Newark NJ 07103-2757 E-mail: littleb1@umdnj.edu.

LITTLE, ANGELA CAPOBIANCO, nutritional science educator; b. San Francisco, Jan. 12, 1920; d. Alfredo Agosto and Elizabeth (Kruse) Capobianco; m. George Gordon Little, Nov. 8, 1947; 1 child, Judith Kristine. BA, U. Calif., Berkeley, 1940, MS, 1954, PhD, 1969. Specialist jr. to asst. to assoc. U. Calif., Berkeley, 1958-69, food scientist, 1969-85, assoc. prof. to prof, 1977-85, prof. emeritus, 1985—, acad. ombudsman, 1985-87, 89-91. Cons. in field; v.p., bd. dirs. Math/Sci. Network, Berkeley; vis. scholar U. Wash., Seattle, 1976-77, Kans. State U., Manhattan, 1972; mem. faculty Fromm Inst., U. San Francisco, 1992-96. Author: Color of Foods, 1962. Nutritional adv. bd. Project Open Hand, San Francisco, 1989-91, vol., 1988-91, UNICEF, San Francisco, 1986-89, Saint Francis Hosp., 1992—. Rsch. grantee Robert Woods Johnson Found., 1989-90, others 1960-85. Mem. AAUW, San Francisco Acad. Sci., San Francisco Mus. Soc., U. Calif. Berkeley Emeritii Assn. (pres. 1991-93), Am. Assn. for History of Medicine, Bay Area History of Medicine Club (pres. 1995-97), Sigma Xi. Avocations: music, books, travel, exercising, walking. Home: 85 Cleary Ct Apt 3 San Francisco CA 94109-6518 Office: U Calif Dept Nutritional Scis Berkeley CA 94720-0001 E-mail: aclittle@uclink.berkeley.edu.

LITTLE, BRENDA, ballerina; b. Montgomery, Ala. Student, Nat. Ballet Sch., Toronto, Ont., Can. Apprentice Nat. Ballet Can., Toronto, 1991—92, mem. corps de ballet, 1992—2001, second soloist, 2001—. Dancer (world premiere ballets) Pereault's The Comforts of Solitude, Dumais' the weight of absence, one hundred words for snow, Mrozewski's A Delicate Battle, Swan Lake, Serenade. Office: Walter Carsen Ctr for Nat Ballet Can 470 Queens Quay W Toronto ON Canada M5V 3Kr Office Fax: 416-345-8323.*

LITTLE, BRIAN KEITH, music educator; b. Bellflower, CA, Apr. 16, 1969; BS, U. So. Calif., L.A., 1991. Cert. tchr. 1993. Tchr. L.A. Sch. Dist., L.A., Calif., 1993—. Singer: (alternative rock band) Reciprocal of Ancient Ruins, 1999.

LITTLE, BRUCE WASHINGTON, professional society administrator; b. Feb. 22, 1936; m. Nancy J. Mains; children: Elizabeth, Thomas, David. BS, Kans. State U., 1963, DVM, 1965. Pvt. practice assoc., Normal, Ill., 1965-69; pvt. practice Americana Animal Hosp., Bloomington, 1969-85; asst. exec. v.p. AVMA, Schaumburg, 1986-96, exec. v.p., 1996—. Rabies control officer McLean County, Ill., 1968-72; instr. U. Ill. Extension Svc., 1974, adv. Mclean County Bd. of Health, 1980-85; pres., ops. mgr. Blooming Grove Farm, Inc., Bloomington, 1983-86; spkr. in field. Contbr. articles to profl. jours. Coach, Ill. 4-H Equine Judging Teams, 1974-76; bd. dirs. Mclean County Assn. Commerce Industry, 1983-85; v.p. Ill. State U. Athletic Booster Club, 1980-82, pres., 1982-84. With U.S. Army, 1955-57. Mem. AVMA, Ill. State Vet. Med. Assn., Chgo. Vet. Med. Assn., Rotary (Paul Harris Fellow), Alpha Zeta. Avocations: sports, golfing, reading, horse breeding. Office: Am Vet Med Assn 1931 N Meacham Rd Schaumburg IL 60173-4364

LITTLE, CARL MAURICE, performing arts administrator; b. Campbellton, N.B., Can., Mar. 17, 1924; s. George Everett and Ada (Boucher) L.; m. Frances R. Corner, Aug. 27, 1949; children: Christine, Jennifer, Geoffrey, Stephen; m. Barbara Wolfond, Dec. 8, 1978. BSc, Licentiate of Music, Dalhousie U., Halifax, N.S., Can., 1945, Diploma Engring., 1944; Assoc., Royal Coll. Music, London, 1952; Licentiate, Royal Acad. Music, London, 1952. Tchr. music public schs., Outremont, Que., Can., 1949-50; pvt. tchr. music Montreal, 1946-59, Toronto, Ont., 1959-70; producer music CBC Radio, Montreal, 1952-59, Toronto, 1959-65, nat. network supr. serious music, 1965-75; mgr. Nat. Arts Centre Orch., Ottawa, 1975-78; co-founder, pres. Little Gallery of the Arts, 1979-80; pres. Arts Connection, Victoria, B.C., 1980-98; exec. dir., festival adminstr. Courtenay Youth Music Centre (B.C.), 1983; organist Holy Trinity Anglican Ch., Saanichton, B.C., 1984-93. Pianist, 1945-52; juror for internat. music competitions including Scriabin Piano Competition, Oslo, Norway, Internat. String Quartet, Stockholm, Sweden, Let The Peoples Sing, Choir, London; jury chmn. Kathaumixw Internat. Choral Festival Powell River, B.C., Can. Mem. Can. Amateur Musicians Assn. (dir.; co-founder). Achievements include founding and administration of CBC competitions, CBC music projects and programs. Address: 109-134 5th Ave E Qualicum Beach BC Canada V9K 1Y7

LITTLE, CYNTHIA HAYES, guidance counselor; b. Burlington, Vt., Dec. 23, 1955; d. Norman Mailer and Priscilla (Green) Hayes; m. David Nelson Little, June 18, 1983; children: Eric, Matthew, Heather. BS in Elem. Edn., U. Vt., 1977, MS in Counseling, 1983. Cert. K-6 tchr., K-12 guidance counselor. Tchr. 3d grade Georgia (Vt.) Elem. Sch., 1977-84; K-4 guidance counselor Georgia Elem. and Mid. Sch., 1994—. Mem. PTA, ACA, NEA, Vt. Edn. Assn., Am. Sch. Counselors Assn., Vt. Counseling Assn. Baptist. Avocations: gardening, reading, skiing, swimming, walking. Home: 374 East Rd Milton VT 05468-3127

LITTLE, DANIEL EASTMAN, philosophy educator, university program director; b. Rock Island, Ill., Apr. 7, 1949; s. William Charles and Emma Lou (Eastman) L.; m. Ronnie Alice Friedland, Sept. 12, 1976 (div. May 1995); children: Joshua Friedland-Little, Rebecca Friedland-Little. BS in Math. with highest honors, AB in Philosophy with high honors, U. Ill., 1971; PhD in Philosophy, Harvard U., 1977. Asst. prof. U. Wis.-Parkside, Kenosha, 1976-79; vis. assoc. prof. Wellesley (Mass.) Coll., 1985-87; vis. scholar Ctr. Internat. Affairs Harvard U., 1989-91, assoc. Ctr. Internat. Affairs, 1991-95; asst. prof. Colgate U., Hamilton, N.Y., 1979-85, assoc. prof., 1985-92, prof., 1992-96, chmn. dept. philosophy and religion, 1992-93, assoc. dean faculty, 1993-96; v.p. academic affairs Bucknell U., Lewisburg, Pa., 1996-2000, prof. philosophy, 1996-2000; chancellor U. Mich., Dearborn, 2000—, prof. philosophy, 2000—. Teaching fellow Harvard U., 1973-76; participant internat. confs. Ctr. Asian and Pacific Studies, U. Oreg., 1992, Social Sci. Rsch. Coun./McArthur Found., U. Calif., San Diego, 1991, Budapest, Hungary, 1990, Morelos, Mex., 1989, Rockefeller Found., Bellagio, Italy, 1990, U. Manchester, Eng., 1986; mem. screening com. on internat. peace and security Social Sci. Rsch. Coun./MacArthur Found., 1991-94; manuscript reviewer Yale U. Press, Cambridge U. Press, Princeton U. Press, Oxford U. Press, Westview Press, Harvard U. Press, Can. Jour. Philosophy, Philosophy Social Scis., Synthese, Am. Polit. Sci. Rev.; grant proposal reviewer NSF, Social Sci. Rsch. Coun., Nat. Endowment for Humanities; tenure and promotion reviewer U. Tenn., Bowdoin Coll., Duke U., U. Wis.; faculty assoc. Inter-Univ. Consortium for Social and Polit. Rsch., 2000—. Author: The Scientific Marx, 1986, Understanding Peasant China: Case Studies in the Philosophy of Social Science, 1989, Varieties of Social Explanation: An Introduction to the Philosophy of Social Science, 1991 (Outstanding Book award Choice 1992), On the Reliability of Economic Models, 1995, Microfoundations Method and Causation: On the Philosophy of the Social Sciences, 1998; contbr. articles to profl. jours., books. Social Sci. Rsch. Postdoctoral fellow MacArthur Found., 1989-91, Rsch. grantee NSF, 1987, Woodrow Wilson Grad. fellow, 1971-72. Mem. Am. Philos. Assn., Assn. Asian Studies, Internat. Devel. Ethics Assn., Social Sci. History Assn., Soc. for the History of Tech., Phi Beta Kappa. Office: Chancellor U Mich Dearborn 4901 Evergreen Rd Dearborn MI 48128 E-mail: delittle@umich.edu.

LITTLE, DENNIS JAMES, small business owner; b. Indiana, Pa., Nov. 10, 1958; s. David Lowry and Elizabeth Ann (Fisher) L.; m. Cathy Rae Garrett, May 5, 1979; children: Dennis James II, Ginger Rae. Student, Penn State U., 1976, Ind. U. of Pa., 1981-82, Shippensburg U., 1989. Computer operator McCreary Tire & Rubber, Indiana, Pa., 1980-82, County of Indiana, Indiana, 1982; truck driver Mears Enterprises, Clymer, 1982-83; soil conservation technician USDA Soil Conservation Svcs., Indiana, 1983-87, Carlisle, Pa., 1987-90; pres. Little Enterprises Waste Hauling Inc., Newville, 1990—. Avocations: hunting, hiking.

LITTLE, FREDERICK ANTON, landscape architect, municipal administrator; b. Syracuse, N.Y., Jan. 18, 1945; s. Frederick Joseph and Anna Sofia (Peterson) L. Student in Agricultural Studies, SUNY at Cornell U., 1962-64; BS in Environ. Studies, SUNY at Syracuse U., 1972. Registered land arch., N.Y., Conn., cert. land arch., N.J. Landscape architect Hugh Stubbins Architects, Cambridge, Mass., 1972-74, Whitman and Howard Architects, Boston, 1974-76, HLW Architects, N.Y.C., 1976-78, Dept. Parks and Recreation City of N.Y., 1978—. Adj. lectr. Kingsbrough Coll., Bklyn., 1992; bd. trustees Tamarand Found., N.Y.C., 1993-95. Designer Hope Meml. Garden, 1993-94, George Rose Garden, 1995. Fundraiser, designer The Greening of Harlem, N.Y.C., 1990—95; vol. Gay Men's Health Crisis, 1990—95; fundraiser AIDS Monument Com., 2000—, Mr. Lure, 2000. Democrat. Buddhist. Avocations: genealogy, highland piping, antique collecting, motorcycling, gardening. Home: 486 9th Ave Apt 5 New York NY 10018-4105 Office: City of NY Dept Parks Olmsted Ctr Flushing Meadows Corona Pk Corona NY 11368

LITTLE, FREED SEBASTIAN, retired petroleum equipment manufacturing company executive; b. Ft. Smith, Ark., May 4, 1926; s. Jess Edward and Floy Kimbrough (Witt) L.; BA, U. Ark., 1950; m. Jana V. Jones, Dec. 9, 1951 (div.); 1 child, Mark McKenna. With Gilbarco Inc., Houston, 1964-90, cen. area mgr., Chgo., 1969-73, Western regional mgr., Houston, 1974-85, Western/Pacific regional mgr., 1986-90; founder, pres. Little and Assocs., Inc.; mgmt. cons., outsourcing placement specialist, 1990; bd. dirs. Wall St. Svcs., Inc. San Antonio, Waterhouse Fin. Mgmt. Group, Inc., San Antonio. Bd. dirs. Post Oak Family YMCA, Houston, Tex., 1990-95; patron Houston Mus. Fine Arts. Served with USAAF, 1945-46. Mem. Am. Petroleum Inst., Petroleum Equipment Inst., Am. Mgmt. Assn., Huguenot Soc., Sigma Alpha Epsilon, Houston City Club, Am. Legion. Presbyterian.

LITTLE, GAYLE ANNE, neonatal nurse practitioner; b. Coronado, Calif., Sept. 14, 1951; d. Edward William and Lorraine Catherine (Puetz) Campbell; m. James Lovell Little Jr., Aug. 7, 1971 (div. June 1984); children: Wendy Catherine, Christy Marie. Diploma, St. Luke's Hosp. Sch. Nursing, San Francisco, 1971; student, San Francisco City Coll.; ASN, Grossmont Coll., 1972; BSN, San Diego State U., 1985; MS in Neonatal Nurse Practitioner, U. Md., 1995. RN, Calif., Md., Oreg.; cert. BCLS instr., newborn resuscitation instr., newborn resuscitation regional trainer, pediatric advanced life support instr. Phys. therapy asst. St. Luke's Hosp., 1970-71; lic. vocat. nurse Coronado Hosp., 1971; grad. nurse med.-surg. units Sharp Meml. Hosp., San Diego, 1972, staff nurse newborn nursery, relief charge nurse GYN surgery, 1972-73, staff nurse per diem women's maternity-surg. unit, 1973-77, staff nurse cardio-vascular diversion unit, 1977-78, clin. nurse I spl. care nursery, 1978-83, clin. nurse IV level II nursery, 1986, clin. nurse III level II and level III NICU, 1983-93; dapa officer, edn. officer Naval Hosp. San Diego, 1988, staff nurse NICU, 1989, staff nurse pediatric unit, 1989-90, NICU/pediatric clin. cons., 1990-91; clinic charge nurse Navy Clinic Persian Gulf War, Bahrain, 1991; evening nurse supr. Naval Hosp. Camp Pendleton, Calif., 1992, asst. charge/charge nurse nursery, 1992-93, customer rels. program mgr., 1993-94; staff nurse per diem med., surg., spl. care and NICU Children's Hosp. San Diego, 1992-94; full ptnr. NICU U. Md. Med. System, Balt., 1994-95; CNIII, CRS Sharp Mary Birch Women's Ctr., 1995-97; neonatal nurse practitioner U.S. Naval Medicine Ctr., 1996-99; LCDR, NC, neonatal nurse practitioner Emanuel Children's Hosp., 1997—. Instr. phys. edn. U. San Diego, 1984; mem. edn. com. Sharp Meml. Hosp., 1986, mem. policy and procedure com., 1986, mem. std. care plan com., 1987; mem. stds. com. Naval Hosp. San Diego, 1989, mem. nurse corps ball com., 1990; change of command coord. USN, Bahrain, 1991; mem. stds. com. Naval Hosp. Camp Pendleton, 1993, mem. health care planning and access QMB com., 1994. Lt. USN, 1988-95, Persian Gulf War, 1991; with Naval Nurse Corps Res., 1994—, Lt. comdr. USN, 1995—. Decorated Navy Commendation medal. Mem. AWHONN (cert. neonatology), VFW, Nat. Assn. Neonatal Nurses, Assn. Mil. Surgeons U.S., Fleet Res. Assn. Democrat. Roman Catholic. Avocations: gardening, reading, walking, movies. Home: 530 C Ave Coronado CA 92118-1825

LITTLE, GEORGE DANIEL, clergyman; b. St. Louis, Dec. 18, 1929; s. Henry and Agathe Cox (Daniel) L.; m. Joan Phillips McCafferty, Aug. 22, 1953; children: Deborah Philips, Cynthia McCafferty (dec.), Alice Annette, Daniel Ross, Benjamin Henry. AB, Princeton U., 1951; MDiv, McCormick Theol. Sem., Chgo., 1954; LLD (hon.), Huron Coll., 1977. Ordained to ministry Presbyn. Ch., 1954; pastor East London Group Ministry, Presbyn. Ch. Eng., 1954-56, Friendship Presbyn. Ch., Pitts., 1956-62; assoc. dir. dept. urban ch., planning assoc. Bd. Nat. Missions, United Presbyterian Ch. U.S.A., N.Y.C., 1962-72; assoc. for budgeting Gen. Assembly Mission Council, 1973-76, exec. dir. council, 1976-84; pastor First Presbyn. Ch., Ithaca, N.Y., 1984-93; interim pres. McCormick Theol. Sem., Chgo., 1993-94; pastor-in-residence Village Presbyn. Ch., Prairie Village, Kans., 1995-96, Westminster Presbyn. Ch., Mpls., 1997-99; ret., 1999. Home: 13 Julia Cir Madison WI 53705-1033 E-mail: danglittle@aol.com.

LITTLE, GEORGE THOMAS, international relations educator, retired; b. Portland, Maine, July 28, 1918; s. George Tappan and Bertha Holbrook (Nelson) L.; m. Virginia Cole, May 24, 1942 (dec. Nov. 1984); children: George Thomas Jr., David Nelson, Katherine Joan; m. Elizabeth Born, May 4, 1989. AB, Bowdoin Coll., 1940; MA, Fletcher Sch. Law, 1941, Columbia U., 1943; PhD, Yale U., 1948. Asst. prof. Swarthmore (Pa.) Coll., 1947-48, U. Conn., Hartford, 1950; from asst. prof. to prof. U. Vt., Burlington, 1950-84, prof. emeritus, 1984—; prof. Taichung U., Taipei, Taiwan, Republic of China, 1955-57. Cons. N.Y. Edn. Dept., Albany, 1971-72; postdoctoral fellow Harvard U., Cambridge, Mass., 1972-74; chief of mission Quaker Relief, Vienna, 1948-50. Editor: International Relief Administration, 1943; editor Jour. Fgn. Studies Info. Svc., 1986, Jour. Vt. Coun. World Affairs, 1952-2000. Sec. Am. Civil Liberties Found. Vt., 1966. Recipient honor medal City of Vienna, 1949, hon. citizenship, Alaska, 1981; grantee Smith-Mundt Act, 1955, Ford Found., 1969, Nat. Def. Act, 1971. Mem. AAUP, Coun. Internat. Studies (sec.-treas. 1971-86), Am. Oriental Soc., Internat. Studies Assn. (pres. New Eng. 1982), Assn. for Asian Studies, Am. Polit. Sci. Assn., Am. Soc. Internat. Law, New Eng. Polit. Sci. Assn. (pres. 1983), Phi Beta Kappa. Avocations: sailing, stamps, travel. Home: 910 Wake Robin Dr Shelburne VT 05482-7583 Office: U Vt PO Box 849 Shelburne VT 05482-0849 E-mail: GLittle904@aol.com.

LITTLE, GRADY, professional athletics manager; Player-coach Yankee orgn., 1971—73; coach Ea. League, West Haven, Conn., 1974; minor league coach Balt., 1980, FSL, Miami; mgr. Appalachian League Oriole's Blufield rookieclub; mgr. minor league Atlanta, 1980—95, mgr., 1986, Richmond, 1993—95; coach bullpen Nat. League West Divsn. Championships , San Diego, 1996; bench coach Indians; bench coach, instr. Boston Red Sox , 1997—99, mgr., 2002—. Named Mgr. of Yr., Richmond, 1994; recipient Mgr. of Yr. awards, Baseball Am., Sporting News, 1992. Office: Boston Red Sox 4 Yowkey Way Boston MA 02215-3496*

LITTLE, JERRY JAMES, artist; b. Oakland, Calif. s. James Herman and Helen Janette (Bohannon) L.; m. Alma Jean Obusek, Aug. 29, 1970; children: Tyler, Todd. AA, Stockton (Calif.) Coll., 1950-51; student, Lane Cmty. Coll., Eugene, Oreg., 1963, U. Oreg., Eugene, 1964-65; studied with Millard Sheets,

Gerald, Brommer, Alan Haemer, others. Band leader Jerry Little and His Orch., Walnut Creek, Calif., 1948-51; mgmt. rep. AT&T Co., San Francisco, 1955-61; flight instr., comml. pilot Greens Flying Svc., Eugene, 1962-70; sales rep., graphic designer CPC Internat., Inc., 1963-88; owner Jerrys Fine Art, Walnut Creek, Calif., 1989—. Exhbn. co-chair arts Oreg. Watercolor Assn., Portland, 1982; art demonstrator, lectr., cons. Calif. Watercolor Assn., Orinda, 1995—; juror art show Ann. Napa Waercolor Art Show, Tiburon, Calif., 1996, Acad. Art Coll., 1998, Modesto Art League, 1998, Napa Ann. Art Show, 1998, Sacramento Art League Saint Helena Art Soc. '99; juror student awards Sacramento State Fair Alameda State Fair; exhbn. installer Exptl. Watercolor Soc., Alamo, Calif. 1995. Artist design ad formats, 1962-89, graphic design, 1962-89; artist: (art books) Collage Techniques, 1994, Best of Watercolor Places, 1996; featured in Internat. Artist Mag., The Artist Mag., others; exhibited in numerous pvt. collections. With USN, 1951-54. Recipient Best of Show award in visual art Western Oreg. Exposition, 1982, 1st awards in visual art Lane County Fair, Eugene, 1983, Valley Artists Assn., Pleasanton, Calif., 1993. Mem. Nat. Watercolor Soc. (signature mem.), Calif. Watercolor Assn. (signature mem., chmn. steering com. 1995, pres. 1998-99, outstanding achievement membership 1996), Am. Watercolor Assn. (assoc.), Alamo/Danville Watercolor Soc., Pleasanton Art Soc., Diablo Art Assn. (award 1993, 94, 95). Avocations: avid reader, snow skiing, water skiing, golf, travel. Home: 2549 Pine Knoll Dr Apt 4 Walnut Creek CA 94595-2023

LITTLE, JILL ANN, education educator; b. Syracuse, N.Y., Sept. 4, 1940; d. Wilfred Samuel and Frances Elgy (Webb) Lowe; m. Edward Serens Little, July 7, 1962; children: William Richard, Deanna Kristen, Kelly Anne. BS, Syracuse U., 1961; MEd, Temple U., 1966; PhD, Syracuse U., 1979. Elem. tchr. Jamesville Dewitt Schs., Dewitt, N.Y., 1961-62, Springfield Twp., Ambler, Pa., 1962-64; spl. tchr. Liverpool (N.Y.) Sch. Dist., 1964-66, B.O.C.E.S., East Syracuse, N.Y., 1966-67; adj. prof. LeMoyne Coll., Syracuse, 1979-88, asst. prof., 1988-91, adj. asst. prof., 1991—. Mem. N.Y. State Assn. Tchr. Educators (bd. dirs. 1984-86, 90—), Beta Kappa (rsch. com. 1989—). Republican. Roman Catholic. Home: 5760 Commons Park East Syracuse NY 13057-9400

LITTLE, JOHN BERTRAM, physician, radiobiology educator, researcher; b. Boston, Oct. 5, 1929; s. Bertram Kimball and Nina (Fletcher) L.; m. Francoise Cottereau, Aug. 4, 1960; children: John Bertram, Frederic Fletcher AB in Physics, Harvard U., 1951; MD, Boston U., 1955. Diplomate Am. Bd. Radiology. Intern in medicine Johns Hopkins Hosp., Balt., 1955-56; resident in radiology Mass. Gen. Hosp., Boston, 1958-61; fellow Harvard U., Cambridge, Mass., 1961-63; from instr. to assoc. prof. radiobiology Harvard Sch. Pub. Health, Boston, 1963-75, prof., 1975—, chmn. dept. physiology, 1980-83, James Stevens Simmons prof. radiobiology, 1987—, chmn. dept. cancer cell biology, 1997—, dir. Ctr. for Radiation Scis. and Environ. Health, 1998—; dir. Kresge Ctr. Environ. Health, 1982-98. Cons. radiology Mass. Gen. Hosp., Boston, 1965—, Brigham and Women's Hosp., Boston, 1968—; chmn. bd. sci. counsellors Nat. Inst. Environ. Health Sci., 1982—84; bd. sci. counsellors Nat. Toxicology Program, 1988—92; mem. sci. coun. Radiation Effects Rsch. Found., Hiroshima, Japan, 1992—98, chmn., Japan, 1996—98; bd. dirs. on radiation effects rsch. NAS, 1992—98, chmn., 1996—98; mem. Coun. Internat. Assn. for Radiation Rsch. Mem. editorial bd. numerous nat. and internat. jours.; contbr. chpts. to books and articles to profl. jours. Mem. coun. Nat. Coun. on Radiation Protection and Measurements, 1993—; trustee various hist. and cultural orgns. Capt. U.S. Army, 1956-58. Named one of Outstanding Investigator grantee, Nat. Cancer Inst., 1988—; recipient numerous rsch. and tng. grants, NIH, 1968—; grantee, Am. Cancer Soc., 1965—68. Mem. AAAS (coun. in med. scis. 1988-91), Radiation Rsch. Soc. N.Am. (pres.-elect 1985, pres. 1986-87), Am. Assn. Cancer Rsch., Am. Physiol. Soc., Health Physics Soc., Am. Soc. Photobiology, Internat. Assn. Radiation Rsch. (coun.). Avocations: music, architectural history. Office: Harvard U Dept Cancer Cell Biology 665 Huntington Ave Boston MA 02115-6021

LITTLE, JOHN DUTTON CONANT, management scientist, educator; b. Boston, Feb. 1, 1928; s. John Dutton and Margaret (Jones) L.; m. Elizabeth Davenport Alden, Sept. 12, 1953; children: John Norris, Sarah Alden, Thomas Dunham Conant, Ruel Davenport. SB in Physics, MIT, 1948, PhD, 1955; PhD (hon.), U. Liege, Belgium, 1992, Cath. U. of Mons, 1997; PhD (hon.) , U. London, 2002. Engr. Gen. Electric Co., Schenectady, 1949-50; asst. prof. ops. research Case-Western Res. U., 1957-60, assoc. prof., 1960-62; research asst. MIT, 1951-54, assoc. prof. mgmt., 1962-67, prof., 1967-78, George M. Bunker prof. mgmt., 1978-89, Inst. prof., 1989—, dir. Ops. Research Ctr., 1969-76, head mgmt. sci. group Sloan Sch. Mgmt., 1972-82, head behavioral and policy scis. area, 1982-88, chmn. undergrad. program, 1990—; pres. Mgmt. Decision Systems, Inc., 1967-80, chmn. bd. dirs., 1967-85; dir., advisor to bd. dirs. Info. Resources, Inc., 1985—. Cons. ops. rsch. indsl. govtl. orgns., 1958—; vis. prof. mktg. European Inst. Bus. Adminstrn., Fontainebleau, France, fall 1988; researcher math. programming, queuing theory, mktg., traffic control, decision support systems, e-commerce; bd. dirs. InSite Mktg. Technology, Inc., 1997-99. Assoc. editor: Mgmt. Sci, 1967-71; contbr. articles to profl. jours. Trustee Mktg. Sci. Inst., 1983-89. Served with AUS, 1955-56. Fellow AAAS (mem. coun. 2000—); mem. NAE, Ops. Rsch. Soc. Am. (coun. 1970-73, pres. 1979-80), Inst. Mgmt. Scis. (v.p. 1976-79, pres. 1984-85), Fellow Inst. for Ops. Rsch. and the Mgmt. Scis. (pres. 1995), Am. Mktg. Assn., Sigma Xi. Home: 37 Conant Rd Lincoln MA 01773-3912 Office: MIT Sloan Sch Mgmt Cambridge MA 02142-1347

LITTLE, JOHN WILLIAM, plastic surgeon, educator; b. Indpls., Mar. 12, 1944; s. John William Jr. and Naida (Jones) L.; m. Patricia Padgett Lea, May 26, 1969 (div. 1974); m. Teri Ann Tyson, Feb. 28, 1981 (div. 1982). AB, Dartmouth Coll., 1966, B in Med. Scis., 1967; MD, Harvard U., 1969. Diplomate Am. Bd. Med. Examiners, Am. Bd. Surgery, Am. Bd. Plastic Surgery. Intern Case Western Res. U., Cleve., 1969-70, resident in surgery, 1970-74, resident in plastic surgery, 1973-75; fellow in plastic surgery U. Miami, 1975-77; asst. prof. Georgetown U., Washington, 1977-82, assoc. prof., 1982-87, prof., 1987-92, clin. prof., 1992—, dir. div. plastic surgery, residency tng. program, plastic surgeon-in-chief univ. hosp., 1979-92; dir. Nat. Capital Tng. Program in Plastic Surgery affilitated hosps. Georgetown U. and Howard U., 1988-92; dir. Georgetown Plastic Surgery Fellowship in Breast and Aesthetic Surgery, 1990-92; pvt. practice Washington, 1992—. Prof. postgrad. edn. in plastic surgery Internat. Soc. Aesthetic Plastic Surgery, 1999—; chief plastic surgery Medlantic Ctr. for Ambulatory Surgery, Inc., 1993—, mem. med. adv. bd., 1993—; cons. Nat. Cancer Inst., NIH, Bethesda, Md., 1977-92, Washington VA Med. Ctr., 1981-92, Reach to Recovery program Nat. Capital chpt. Am. Cancer Soc., 1981—, RENU program in breast reconstrn., 1982; specialist site visitor plastic surgery residency rev. com. Accreditation Coun. for Grad. Med. Edn., 1982-95; vis. lect. various insts.; bd. govs. Nat. Endowment for Plastic Surgery, 1995—. Adv. editor Plastic and Reconstructive Surgery, 1997—, manuscript reviewer Plastic and Reconstructive Surgery, Annals of Plastic Surgery; assoc. editor Surgery of the Breast: Principles and Art, 1998; contbr. numerous articles to med. jours., numerous chpts. to books. Bd. dirs. Triann reconstructive surgery teams to Caribbean and S.Am., Georgetown Tissue Bank, 1986-88, Operation Luz del Sol; founder, pres., med. dir. Reconstructive Surgeons Vol. Program; bd. dirs. Washington Summer Opera Theater; trustee Washington Opera, 1993—, artistic com., 1994—; Domingo Circle, 1995—, Laureates' medal, 1999. Recipient Laureate medallion Domingo Cir., 1999, Mem. AMA, ACS (coord. plastic surgery audiovisual program Ann. Clin. Congress 1988-90, 92-93, bd. govs., Met. Washington chpt. councillor 1985-94, chmn. sci. program com. 1990-91, v.p. 1991-92, pres. 1992-93, bd. govs. 1998—), Nat. Capital Soc. Plastic Surgeons (sec. treas. 1982-83, pres. 1984-85), Am. Soc. Plastic Surgeons (audiovisual program dir. ann. meeting 1984-86, strategic planning com. 1987-96, fin. com. 1989-94, conv. policy com. 1993-96, ops. com. 1993-96, chmn. 1994-95, spokesperson network steering com. 1994-96, bd. dirs. 1994-96, exec. com. 1995-96, spokesperson 1998—, rep. to IPRAS 1999—), Am. Assn. Plastic Surgeons (co-chmn. various coms.), Plastic Surgery Ednl. Found. (bd. dirs. 1985-97, devel. com. 1991—, chmn. 1997-2000, chmn. various coms., rep. to Coun. Plastic Surg. Orgns. 1989-95, parliamentarian 1992-93, v.p. 1993-94, pres. adv. coun. 1993-96, commr. various commns., pres.-elect, 1995, pres. 1995-96, Maliniac fellow 1998—, Disting. Svc. award, 2000), Med. Soc. D.C. (chmn. plastic surgery sect. 1985), D.R. Millard Surg. Soc. and Ednl. Found. (pres. 1985-87), Am. Cleft Palate Assn., Am. Soc. Maxillofacial Surgeons, Washington Acad. Surgeons (coun. 1988-90), Am. Soc. Aesthetic Plastic Surgery (In Chun Sung award philanthropic svc. 2000), NE Soc. Plastic Surgeons (chmn. various coms., v.p. 1991-92, pres. 1992-93, historian 1994-99), Internat. Soc. Aesthetic Plastic Surgery (chmn. bylaws com. 1990-93, 95-97, parliamentarian 1990-93, mem. membership com. 1993-97, chmn. 1993-95, sec. gen. 1997-2000, rep. to IPRAS 1997-2000, prof. postgrad. edn. in aesthetic plastic surgery, others), Am. Alpine Workshop in Plastic Surgery (founder, pres. 1991-92, historian 1995—), Internat. Confedn. Plastic Reconstructive and Aesthetic Surgery (mem. exec. com. 1997-2000, coun. dels. 1999—), Nat. Endowment Plastic Surgeons (bd. govs. 1995—), Internat. Plastic, Reconstructive and Aesthetic Surgery Found. (bd. dirs. 1999—, ednl. program com. chmn. 1999—, vice chmn. devel. com. 1999—, publs. and videotape com.), European Assn. Plastic Surgeons (corr.), Turkish Soc. Plastic Surgeons (hon.), Argentine Soc. Plastic, Reconstructive and Aesthetic Surgeons (assoc.), Atlantic Soc. Plastic Surgeons (hon.), Soc. Am. and Italian Plastic Surgeons (founding mem. 1988—), Turkish Soc. Plastic Surgeons (hon. mem. 1996—), Argentina Soc. Esthetic Plastic Surgery and Repair (corr. mem. 1999—), European Assn. Plastic Surgeons (corr. mem 2000—), Atlantic Soc. Paltic Surgeons (hon. mem. 2000—), Mediterranean Soc. Plastic and Aesthetic Surgery (active mem. 2001—); fellow Am. Israeli Plastic Surgeons (charter mem. 1997—), Republican. Presbyterian. Home: 3030 K St NW Ph 212 Washington DC 20007-5107 Office: 1145 19th St NW Ste 802 Washington DC 20036-3700

LITTLE, LOREN EVERTON, musician, ophthalmologist; b. Sioux Falls, S.D., Oct. 28, 1941; s. Everton A. and Maxine V. (Alcorn) L.; m. Christy Gyles; 1 child, Nicole Moses; children from previous marriage: Laurie, Richard. BA, Macalester Coll., 1963; BS, U. S.D., 1965; MD, U. Wash., 1967. Prin. trumpeter Sioux Falls Mcpl. Band, 1956-65; trumpeter St. Paul Civic Orch., 1960-62; leader, owner Swinging Scots Band, St. Paul, 1960-63; trumpeter Edgewater Inn Show Room, Seattle, 1966-67, Jazztet-Arts Council, Sioux Falls, 1970-71, Lee Maxwell Shows, Washington, 1971-74; residency in ophthalmology Walter Reed Med. Ctr., 1974; co-leader, trumpeter El Paso (Tex.) All Stars, 1975; freelance trumpeter, soloist various casinos and hotels, Las Vegas, Nev., 1977—. Trumpeter (album) Journey by R. Romero Band, 1983, Sizenter, 1997; soloist for numerous entertainers including Tony Bennett, Burt Bacharach, Jack Jones, Sammy Davis Jr., Henry Mancini, Jerry Lewis Telethon, for video Star Salute to Live Music, 1989; with Stan Mark Band Nat. Pub. Radio Broadcast, 1994, 95; soloist on video Stan Mark Live at the 4 Queens Hotel, Las Vegas; pres. S&L Music, S&L Records; prodr. Carl Saunders Debut Album Out Of the Blue, 1996, Eclecticism, 2000. Trustee Nev. Sch. of the Arts, Las Vegas, 1983—; pres. S&L Music SNL Rec. Served to lt. col. U.S. Army, 1968-76, Vietnam. Decorated Silver Star, Purple Heart, Bronze Star, Air medal; fellow Internat. Eye Found., 1974; Dewitt Wallace scholar Readers Digest, 1963-65. Fellow ACS, Am. Acad. Ophthalmology; mem. Am. Fedn. Musicians, Nat. Bd. Med. Examiners. Presbyterian. Avocations: history, music, medicine, sports, skiing.

LITTLE, MARK MCKENNA, financial management executive; b. Hoisington, Kans., Mar. 30, 1957; s. Freed Sebastian Little and Jana Vaye (Jones) Hansen; m. Peggy Louise Kelly, June 24, 1988; 1 child, McKenna Louise. B of Gen. Studies, Tex. Christian U., 1980. Account exec. Liberty Mut. Ins. Co., San Antonio, 1981-83; cons. M. Little Fin. Enterprises, 1983-89; chmn., chief exec. officer Wall St. Svcs., Inc., 1989—. Pres., CEO Waterhouse Fin. Mgmt. Group, Inc., 1995—; mem. bd. advs. Clear Lake Nt. Bank, 1996-97. Bd. dirs. Mental Health Assn. in Greater San Antonio, United Way, 1988-92, pres., chmn., 1990, KLRN TV Cmty. Adv. Bd., San Antonio, 1990-94, pres., 1992-93; bd. dirs. N.E. Ind. Sch. Dist., chmn. bond com., 1998; bd. dirs. Kids Involvement Network, San Antonio, 1990—, chmn., 1990-93; bd. dirs. N.E. Ind. Sch. Dist.-Wide adv. bd., 1991-98, pres., 1991-92; del., bd. dirs. Jaycees Internat., Taipei, Taiwan, 1983; elected del. Tex. State Rep. Conv., 1992, White House Conf. Small Bus., 1995; trustee N.E. Ednl. Found.; vice chair allocations panel United Way, San Antonio, 1994; apptd. del. U.S. SEC-Govt. Forum on Small Bus. Capital Formation, 1995-2000; del., program co-chair Tex. Gov.'s Conf. on Small Bus., 1996; apptd. del. Congl. Small Bus. Summit, Washington, 1998; mem. World Affairs Coun., 1992-93. Recipient Edith Caldwell award Tex. Cmty. Edn. Assn., 1995, Jayne Nelson award, 1998, Citizen of Yr.-Cmty. Involvement award Nat. Cmty. Edn. Assn., 1999. Mem. San Antonio Area Coun. Pres., North San Antonio C. of C. (bd. dirs. 1991—, vice chmn. bd. 1991-92, 95, chmn. bd. 1997), San Antonio Jaycees (bd. dirs. 1982-83), North San Antonio Toastmasters (pres. 1990-91), Delta Tau Delta (Larry Abrahms award). Office: Wall St Svcs Inc 2313 Lockhill Selma Ste 216 San Antonio TX 78230

LITTLE, MILDRED MILLER, music educator, soloist; b. Bristol, Va., Aug. 27, 1939; d. DeWitt Pelton and Louise (Peavy) Miller; m. Richard M. Little, Oct. 7, 1972; 1 child, Patrick Miles. AA in Music magna cum laude, Brevard (N.C.) Jr. Coll., 1959; BM magna cum laude, Greensboro Coll., 1961; MA in Tchg., Winthrop Coll., 1972. Tchr., N.C. Elem. music tchr. Durham (N.C.) City Schs., 1962-64; pvt. music tchr. Charlotte, N.C., 1969-72; instr. freshman reading lab. Winthrop Coll., Rock Hill, 1970-72; pvt. reading splst., music tchr. Montgomery, Ala., 1974-76; reading splst. Lowdnes Acad., Lowdnes County, 1974-76; soloist Christian Sci. Ch., Montgomery, 1974-98; owner, tchr. Little Music Studio, Wetumpka, Ala., 1979—; music tchr. Edgewood Acad., Elmore, 1988-96. Author: Scales Without Tears, 1994; contbr. article to jour.; singer, soloist Montgomery (Ala.) Opera Guild, 1973-76. Mem. Am. Coll. Musicians (mem. faculty, chmn. local piano guild Montgomery, Ala. 1997—, Piano Guild Honor Roll 1990—), Nat. Fedn. Music Clubs, Ala. Fedn. Music Clubs (jr. counselor dist. IV 1981—, chair Ala. Jr. Festival 1988-92, chmn. Ala. Jr. Awards 1993—, Plaque dedicated in her honor 1995), Montgomery Music Study Club (dist. jr. counselor, Gold Cup chmn., counselor Intervals Jr. Music Club of Wetumpka). Republican. Methodist. Avocations: reading, crocheting, piano, theater, singing.

LITTLE, NANCY JANE, school director; b. Cleve., Sept. 26, 1946; d. Kenyon C. and Marion McClelland Cramer; m. Charles T. Little, Aug. 31, 1968; children: David Dalton, Peter Carskadon. BA, Case Western Res. U., 1968; MA in Art History, CUNY, 1977. Dir., libr. and archives Knoedler & Co. Art Gallery, N.Y.C., 1975-88; dir. authentication svc. Internation Found. for Art Rsch., 1993-96; exhbn. asst. Met. Mus. of Art, 1996-97; sch. dir. Nat. Acad. of Fine Arts, 1998—. Bd. dirs. Hudson River Mus. of Westchester, 1991-99, Sounview Prep Sch., Mt. Kisco, N.Y., 1999—; pres. Philipse Manor Hall Coalition, Yonkers, N.Y., 1991-94, Armour Villa Assn. Cmty. Group, Yonkers, N.Y., 1989-91. Recipient Cert., Key to City Yonkers Mayor, 1992, Citation of Spl. Merit for Cmty. Svc., Yonkers Hist. Soc., 1992. Avocations: skiing, biking, chorale singing, reading. Office: Nat Acad Design Sch 5 E 89th St New York NY 10128

LITTLE, R. DONALD, architect, administrator; b. Gastonia, N.C., Mar. 18, 1937; s. Coy Marshall and Stella May (Pruett) L.; m. Jacqueline Beatrice Mandel, June 10, 1967 (dec. Mar. 1995); Linda Lee Stoner; Sept. 7, 1999; children by previous marriage: Tina June Whitman, Diana Dawn Little, Laura Marie Van Meel; stepchildren: Keith, Don. BA, U. Md., 1972; BS in Architecture, Cath. U. Am., 1981, MArch, 1983. Ordained, chartered non-denominational minister, 1998. Blood bank and med. technologist Dr. Oscar B. Hunter Meml. Lab., Washington, 1961-66; biol. lab. technologist Naval Med. Rsch. Inst., Bethesda, Md., 1966-68; blood bank and med. technologist, supr. Ctrl. Lab. Doctor's Hosp., Washington, 1959-79; jr. architect VVKR Inc., University Park, Md., supr. architect; br. head design divsn. Naval Surface Weapons Ctr., Silver Spring, 1981-87; supr. architect, chief facility engring. br. Agrl. Rsch. Svc., USDA, 1987-96; area adminstrv. officer BARC Rsch. Svc., USDA, Beltsville, Md., 1996—. With USN, 1956-61. Mem. Am. Assn. Blood Banks, Am. Soc. Med. Technologists. Home: 13417 Rich Lynn Ct Highland MD 20777-9790 Office: BARC Rsch Svc/USDA Bldg 003 Rm 203 BARC-W 10300 Baltimore Ave Beltsville MD 20705-2325 E-mail: spirit77@bellatlantic.net.

LITTLE, RICHARD ALLEN, mathematics and computer science educator; b. Cochocton, Ohio, Jan. 12, 1939; s. Charles M. and Elsie Leanna (Smith) L.; children from previous marriage: Eric, J. Alice, Stephanie; m. Laura Ann Novosel, June 15, 1991. BS in Math. cum laude, Wittenberg U., 1960; MA in Edn., Johns Hopkins U., 1961; EdM in Math., Harvard U., 1965; PhD in Math. Edn., Kent State U., 1971. Tchr. Culver Acad., Ind., 1961-65; instr., curriculum cons. Harvard U., Cambridge, Mass. and Aiyetoro, Nigeria, 1965-67; from instr. to assoc. prof. Kent State U., Canton, Ohio, 1967-75; from assoc. prof. to prof. Baldwin-Wallace Coll., Berea, 1975—, dept. chair, 1978-83. Mathematician/educator Project Discovery Ohio Bd. Regents, 1992-96; vis. prof., math. Ohio State U., Columbus, 1987-88, 92-95; lectr. various colls. and univs.; pres. Cleve. Collaborative on Math. Edn., 1986-87, bd. dirs. 1985-2002; mem. policy bd. Ohio Resource Ctr. for Math. Sci. and Reading, 2000—, mem. exec. com. policy bd., 2001—, chair exec. com., 2002—. Contbr. articles to profl. jours. Bd. dirs. Canton Symphony Orch., 1973-75; Sunday sch. tchr. Bethany English Luth. Ch., Cleve., 1991—; bd. deacons Holy Cross Luth. Ch., Canton, 1968-74, chmn., 1971-74. Recipient Strosacker Excellence in Tchg. award and Student Senate Faculty Excellence award Baldwin-Wallace Coll., 1999. Mem. Nat. Coun. Tchrs. Math. (profl. devel. and status adv. com. 1987-90, program com. ann. meeting 1997), Ohio Coun. Tchrs. Math. (pres. 1974-76, v.p. 1970-73, sec. 1982-84, dir. state math. contest 1983-92, Christofferson-Fawcett award 1990), Ohio Math. Educators Leadership Coun. (pres. 1990-91, bd. dirs. 1988-92), Greater Canton Coun. Tchrs. Math. (pres. 1969-70), Math. Assn. Am. (pres. Ohio sect. 1983-84, editor 1977-83). Avocations: hiking, tennis, handball. Office: Baldwin-Wallace Coll Dept Math & Computer Sci 275 Eastland Rd Berea OH 44017-2005 E-mail: rlittle@bw.edu.

LITTLE, ROBERT ANDREWS, architect, designer, painter; b. Brookline, Mass., Sept. 9, 1915; s. Clarence Cook and Katherine Day (Andrews) L.; m. Ann Murphy Halle, Dec., 27, 1940; children: Sam Robertson, Revere (dec.). AB cum laude, Harvard U., 1937, M.Arch., 1939. Designer G.H. Perkins, Cambridge, Mass., 1939-41; architect U.S. Navy, Washington, 1941-43; ops. analyst Air Staff Intelligence, 1943-45; prin. Robert A. Little & Assos., Cleve., 1946-58, 67-69; partner Little & Dalton, 1958-67; dir. design Dalton-Dalton-Little-Newport, 1969-78; owner Robert A. Little, Design and Architecture, 1978—. Tchr., lectr. Harvard, U. Pa., Carnegie Inst. Tech., U. Mich., Smith Coll., U. Notre Dame, Kent State U. Exhibited art and graphics in Cleve., Phila., Boston., since 1970; works include Air Force Mus., Dayton, Ohio; one-person shows in Ohio, Maine, Mass. Trustee Cleve. Mus. Sci., 1952-56, Cleve. Inst. Music, 1956-58; mem. Cleve. Fine Arts Com. Served with U.S. Army, 1940. Fellow AIA (pres. Cleve. chpt. 1966-68, nat. and state design awards), Harvard Sch. of Design Alumni Assn. (past pres., internat. dir. of devel.) Home: 5 Pepper Ridge Rd Cleveland OH 44124-4904 Office: Robert A Little FAIA Design 5 Pepper Ridge Rd Cleveland OH 44124-4904 *As a child, I drew pictures all the time— and they were my current ideal— a face I thought pretty, a massive locomotive, a pine tree against the sea, or a castle in the sky. As an adult Designer and Artist, too, I have spent my whole life dreaming of beauty, and trying to create it— and, of course, never fully succeeding. But the great satisfaction has not been the results, but rather the breathless moments of the search itself, and the boundless horizons of the dream.*

LITTLE, ROBERT DAVID, library science educator; b. Milw., July 11, 1937; s. Kenneth Edwin and Grace Elizabeth (Terwileger) L. BA, U. Wis., Milw., 1959; MA, U. Wis., 1964, PhD, 1972. Tchr., sch. librarian Sevastapol Pub. Schs., Sturgeon Bay, Wis., 1959-62; sch. librarian Highland Park (Ill.) High Sch., 1962-63; supr. sch. libraries Sevastapol/Gilbraltor Pub. Sch., Sturgeon Bay, 1963-65; state sch. library supr. Wis. Dept. Pub. Instrn., Madison, 1965-69, program adminstr., 1969-70; asst. prof. libr. sci. U. Wis., Milw., 1970-71, acting dir. Sch. Libr. Sci., 1971; assoc. prof. libr. sci. Ind. State U., Terre Haute, 1971-77, prof., 1977-97, chmn. dept., 1971-93. Cons. Ind. Nat. Network Study, Terre Haute, 1978-79; cons., researcher Nat. Ctr. Edn. Stats., Washington, 1978-79; mem. Ind. State Libr. Adv. Coun., Indpls., 1981-91. Co-author: Public Library Users and Uses, 1988; editor: Cataloging, Processing, Administering AV Materials, 1972; contbr. articles to profl. jours. Pres. West Cen. Ind. chpt. Ind. Civil Liberties Union, 1988-92. Edn. Act fellow U. Wis., Madison, 1967, 68. Mem. ALA, Am. Assn. Sch. Librs., Assn. Ind. Media Educators (pres. 1981-82, Peggy Leach Pfeiffer Svc. award 1987). Methodist. Avocations: reading, travel. Home: 500 W 43rd St Apt 22H New York NY 10036-4335

LITTLE, ROBERT EUGENE, mechanical engineering educator, materials behavior researcher, consultant; b. Enfield, Ill., May 24, 1933; s. John Henry and Mary (Stephens) L.; m. Barbara Louina Farrell, Feb. 4, 1961; children: Susan Elizabeth, James Robert, Richard Roy, John William. BSME, U. Mich., 1959; MSME, Ohio State U., 1960; PhDME, U. Mich., 1963. Asst. prof. mech. engring. Okla. State U., Stillwater, 1963-65; assoc. prof. U. Mich., Dearborn, 1965-68, prof., 1968—. Author: Statistical Design of Fatigue Experiments, 1975, Probability and Statistics for Engineers, 1978 Mershon fellow Ohio State U., 1960 Mem. ASTM, Am. Statis. Assn. Home: 3230 Pine Lake Rd West Bloomfield MI 48324-1951 Office: U Mich 4901 Evergreen Rd Dearborn MI 48128-2406

LITTLE, THOMAS MAYER, public relations executive; b. Columbus, Ohio, Dec. 21, 1935; s. John William and Eulalia Josephine (Mayer) L.; m. Susan Mulford, Sept. 29, 1959; children: Carin Andrea, Debora Mayer, Sharon Mulford, Patricia Anne. BS in Journalism, Northwestern U., 1958; postgrad., Bradley U., 1958. Account supr. Philip Lesly Co., Chgo., 1962-77; v.p., account supr. Burson-Marsteller, N.Y.C., 1977; v.p. Foote Cone & Belding, Inc., 1977-78; pres. FCB Pub. Rels., 1978-81, Bus. Orgn., Inc. divsn. Carl Byoir & Assocs., N.Y.C., 1982, Tracy-Locke/BBDO Pub. Rels., Dallas, 1983-85; exec. v.p., gen. mgr. Manning, Selvage & Lee, N.Y.C., 1986; pres. T.J. Ross & Assocs., 1986-87; pres., gen. mgr. Golin/Harris Communication, N.Y., 1987-91; pub. rels. cons., 1992—. Bd. dirs. Damon Runyon-Walter Winchell Cancer Fund, N.Y.C. Lt. (j.g.) USN, 1959-62. Mem. Am. Mktg. Assn., Pub. Rels. Soc. Am. (S.C. and Ga. chpts.), Hilton Head Island C. of C., Publicity Club N.Y.C., Mt. Kisco (N.Y.) Country Club, Sea Pines Country Club (Hilton Head Island), Lotos Club (N.Y.C.), Sigma Alpha Epsilon. Roman Catholic. Home and Office: 2 Newhall Rd Hilton Head Island SC 29928-3112 E-mail: littlevthh@aol.com.

LITTLE, TRAVIS LANE, state senator, motel management executive; b. Corinth, Miss., Nov. 24, 1942; m. Doris Hall. Senator State of Miss., 1992—, pres., 2002—. Chmn. hwy. and transp. and mgmt. coms.; mem. county affairs, fin., ins., judiciary, pub. health and welfare, pub. property coms. Former Alcorn County supr. Recipient USAF Commendation Medal for Outstanding Svc., Govtl. Friend of Tourism award Miss. Tourism Assn., 1997. Mem. Internat. Franchise Assn. of Am., Franchise Adv. Coun., Corinth-Alcorn C. of C., Corinth Bd. of Realtors, Corinth Homebuilders Assn. Baptist. Office: State Capitol Bldg Rm. 303-NC Jackson MS 39215-1018*

LITTLE, W(ILLIAM) A(LFRED), foreign language educator, researcher; b. Boston, July 28, 1929; s. Wm. A. and Myrle A. (Holmes) L. BA, Tufts U., 1951; LTCL, Trinity Coll., London, 1952; MA, Harvard U., 1953, PhD, 1961. Asst. prof. Williams Coll., Williamstown, Mass., 1957-63; assoc. prof., chair Tufts U., Medford, 1963-66; chair U. Va., Charlottesville, 1966-72, prof., 1966-95, prof. German and music emeritus, 1995—. Vis. prof. musicology U. Rochester, N.Y., 1996. Author: G.A. Bürger, 1974; editor: Mendelssohn-Complete Organ Works, 5 vols., 1987-90; editor The German Quarterly, 1970-78; contbr. articles to profl. jours. Cpl. U.S. Army, 1953-55. Sesquicentennial fellow U. Va., 1972-73, 78-79, 88-89. Mem. MLA (chair comp. lit. 1970-72), Am. Assn. Tchrs. German (nat. exec. coun. 1968-78), Am. Guild Organists (registrar Mass. chpt. 1949-53, dean Charlottesville chpt. 1977-78, registrar, archivist Ctrl. Fla. chpt. 1995-99, nat. com. profl. edn. 1993—), Am. Mus. Soc., Orgn. Hist. Soc., Neue Bachgesellschaft (Leipzig). Home: 245 Terrell Rd West Charlottesville VA 22901 E-mail: wal@virginia.edu.

LITTLE, WILLIAM ARTHUR, physicist, educator; b. South Africa, Nov. 17, 1930; came to U.S., 1958, naturalized, 1964; s. William Henry and Margaret (Macleod) L.; m. Annie W. Smith, July 15, 1955; children— Lucy Claire, Linda Susan, Jonathan William. PhD, Rhodes U., S. Africa, 1953, Glasgow (Scotland) U., 1957. Faculty Stanford, 1958—, prof. physics, 1965-94; prof. emeritus, 1994—. Cons. to industry, 1960— ; co-founder, chmn. MMR Techs. Inc., 1980—, 3L&T, Inc., 1999—. Recipient Deans award for disting. teaching Stanford U., 1975-76, Walter J. Gores award for excellence in teaching, Stanford U., 1979, IR-100 award Indsl. Rsch. and Devel., 1981; NRC Can. postdoctoral fellow Vancouver, Can., 1956-58, Sloan Found. fellow, 1959-63, John Simon Guggenheim fellow, 1964-65, NSF sr. postdoctoral fellow, 1970-71 Fellow Am. Phys. Soc.; mem. Am. Chem. Soc. Achievements include spl. research low temperature physics, superconductivity, neural network theory cryogenics; holder 14 patents in area of cryogenics and med. instrumentation. Home: 15 Crescent Dr Palo Alto CA 94301-3106 Office: Stanford U Dept Physics Stanford CA 94305 E-mail: bill@mmr.com.

LITTLEFIELD, DANIEL CURTIS, historian, educator, researcher; b. Denison, Tex., Sept. 29, 1941; s. Elroy Littlefield and Ophelia Marie Williams; m. Valinda Whitted, June 23, 1990. AB, Sacramento State U., 1964; MA, Johns Hopkins U., 1973, PhD, 1977. Instr. York Coll. CUNY, N.Y.C., 1973-77; asst. prof. Va. Commonwealth U., Richmond, 1977-78; assoc. prof. La. State U., Baton Rouge, 1978-88; prof. U. Ill.-Urbana, Urbana-Champaign, 1988-99; Carolina prof. U. S.C., Columbia, 1999—. Coun. Omohandro Inst. Early Am. History and Culture, Williamsburg, Va., 1996-99. Author: Rice and Slaves, 1981, Revolutionary Citizens, 1997. Mem. Am. Hist. Assn., So. Hist. Assn. (mem. exec. coun. 1998-2000), South Caroliniana Soc., Orgn. Am. Historians. Office: U SC Dept History Columbia SC 29208

LITTLEFIELD, JOHN WALLEY, geneticist, cell biologist, pediatrician; b. Providence, Dec. 3, 1925; s. Ivory and Mary Russell (Walley) Littlefield; m. Elizabeth Lascelles Legge, Nov. 11, 1950; children: Peter P., John W., Elizabeth I. MD, Harvard U., 1947; MHS, Johns Hopkins U, 1992. Diplomate Am. Bd. Internal Medicine. Intern Mass. Gen. Hosp., Boston, 1947-48, resident in medicine, 1948-50, staff, 1956-74, chief genetics unit children's service, 1966-73; assoc. in medicine Harvard U. Med. Sch., 1956-62, asst. prof. medicine, 1962-66, asst. prof. pediatrics, 1966-69, prof. pediatrics, 1970-73; prof., chmn. dept. pediatrics Johns Hopkins U. Sch. Medicine, Balt., 1974-85; pediatrician-in-chief Johns Hopkins U. Hosp., 1974-85; prof., chmn. dept. physiology Johns Hopkins U. Sch. Medicine, Balt., 1985-92. Author: Variation, Senescence and Neoplasia in Cultured Somatic Cells, 1976. With USNR, 1952—54. Fellow Guggenheim, 1965—66, Josiah Macy Jr. Found., Oxford U., 1979. Mem.: NAS, Assn. Am. Physicians, Am. Pediatric Soc., Am. Soc. Human Genetics, Soc. Pediatric Rsch., Tissue Culture Assn., Am. Soc. Clin. Investigation, Am. Soc. Biol. Chemists, Am. Acad. Arts and Scis., Phi Beta Kappa, Delta Omega, Alpha Omega Alpha. Home: 304 Golf Course Rd Owings Mills MD 21117-4114 Office: Johns Hopkins U Sch Medicine Dept Physiology Baltimore MD 21205 E-mail: jlittlef@jhmi.edu.

LITTLEFIELD, PAUL DAMON, management consultant; b. Cambridge, Mass., June 8, 1920; s. W. Joseph and Sally Pastorius (Damon) L.; m. Emmy Farnsworth Neiley, June 19, 1943 (dec. Apr. 9, 1982); children: Diane Neiley Littlefield Ritsher, Elizabeth Damon Littlefield Lehman, Paul Damon Jr.; m. Lucy Jean Boyd, Dec. 30, 1983. AB, Harvard U., 1942, MBA with distinction (Baker scholar), 1948. Assoc., Freeport Minerals Co., N.Y.C., 1948-50, 52-62, treas., 1956-62; v.p. finance, treas. Arthur D. Little, Inc., Cambridge, 1962-73, sr. v.p., chief fin. officer, 1973-85, cons., 1985—; pres. Brynmere Assoc., Inc., 1991-92. Asst. to pres. Coty, Inc., 1951-52; bd. mem. Cambridge Trust Co., 1965-2000; mem. investment com. N.E. Health Sys., Inc. Hon. trustee, past chmn. Old Sturbridge Village. With destroyers and submarines to Lt. cmdr., 1942, USNR, 1945. Mem. Fin. Execs. Inst., Harvard Bus. Sch. Assn. Boston (past pres.), Treas.' Club of Boston, Cape Ann Hist. Assn. (bd. mgrs.). Home: 15 Norwood Heights Annisquam Gloucester MA 01930 Office: Acorn Pk Cambridge MA 02140

LITTLEFIELD, ROY EVERETT, III, association executive, legal educator; b. Nashua, N.H., Dec. 6, 1952; s. Roy Everett and Mary Ann (Prestipino) L.; m. Amy Root; children: Leah Marie, Roy Everett IV, Christy Louise. BA, Dickinson Coll., 1975; MA, Catholic U. Am., 1976, PhD, 1979. Aide U.S. Senator Thomas McIntyre, Democrat, N.H., 1975-78, Nordy Hoffman, U.S. Senate Sergeant-at-arms, 1979; dir. govt. rels. Nat. Tire Dealers and Retreaders Assn., Washington, 1979-84; exec. dir. Svc. Sta. and Automotive Repair Assn., 1984—; exec. v.p. Svc. Sta. Dealers of Am., 1994—. Cons. Internat. Tire and Rubber Assn., 1984, Tire Industry Assn.; mem. faculty Cath. U. Am., Washington, 1979—. Author: William Randolph Hearst: His Role in American Progressivism, 1980, The Economic Recovery Act, 1982, The Surface: Transportation Assistance Act, 1984; editor Nozzle mag.; contbr. numerous articles to legal jours. Mem. Nat. Dem. Club, 1978— Mem. Am. Soc. Legal History, Md. Hwy. User's Fedn. (pres.), Nat. Hwy. User's Fedn. (sec.), Nat. Capitol Area Transp. Fedn. (v.p.), N.H. Hist. Soc., Kansas City C. of C., Capitol Hill Club, Phi Alpha Theta. Roman Catholic. Home: 1707 Pepper Tree Ct Bowie MD 20721-3021 Office: 9420 Annapolis Rd Ste 307 Lanham Seabrook MD 20706-3061

LITTLEFORD, WILLIAM DONALDSON, retired publishing executive; b. Ft. Thomas, Ky., Aug. 4, 1914; s. Roger Seiter and Marjorie (Donaldson) L.; m. Mariana Weber, May 8, 1936 (dec. Feb. 1958); children: Anne, Michael; m. Marian Hastings Towne, Aug. 20, 1958; children: Joseph M. Towne, Marian Towne. Student, U. Cin.; grad. advanced mgmt. program, Harvard U., 1951. With Billboard Pub., Inc., Cin., 1934-85, gen. mgr., 1943-58, pres., 1958-76, chmn. bd., 1976-85, chmn. emeritus, 1985-99. Dir. Littleford Bros., Inc., 1948-2001, Advt. Coun., 1959-88; dir. Am. Bus. Press, 1954-65, chmn. bd., 1960-61; dir. Audit Bur. Circulations, 1959-67, Mag. Pubs. Assn., 1967-85, 2d Class Mail Publs., 1962-70, Pensord Press Ltd., Wales, U.K., 1969-86, United Color Press, Dayton, Ohio, 1970-87, Viegues Conservation and Hist. Trust, 1987-98. McAllister fellow Northwestern U., Chgo., 1987; named to the Pub. Hall of Fame, 1989; established William D. Littleford Found. for Corp. Cmty. Svc., 1998. Mem. Beta Theta Pi, Harvard Club (N.Y.C.). Episcopalian.

LITTLEJOHN, DAVID, writer; b. San Francisco, May 8, 1937; s. George Thomas and Josephine Mildred (Cullen) L.; m. Sheila Beatrice Hageman, June 10, 1963; children: Victoria Schoenke, Gregory David. BA, U. Calif., Berkeley, 1959; MA, Harvard U., 1961, PhD, 1963. Asst. prof. English, U. Calif., Berkeley, 1963-69, assoc. prof. journalism, 1969-76, prof., 1976-97, vice chmn. acad. senate, chmn. senate policy com., 1984-86, assoc. dean Grad. Sch. Journalism, 1974-78, 85-86, 87-89, prof. emeritus, 1997—. Arts critic Sta. KQED-TV, San Francisco, 1965-75, PBS nationwide, 1971-72; critic and corr. London Times, 1975-89, Architecture mag., 1984-89, Wall Street Jour., 1990—. Author: Architect: The Life and Work of Charles W. Moore, 1984, The Ultimate Art: Essays Around and About Opera, 1992, The Fate of the English Country House, 1997, The Real Las Vegas, 1999, also 9 other books, over 300 articles and 200 TV programs. Fulbright lectr., Montpellier, France, 1966-67; Am. Coun. Learned Socs. rsch. fellow, London, 1972-73; NEH grantee 1976-77. Mem. Arts Club (Berkeley, sec.). Democrat. Roman Catholic. Home and Office: 719 Coventry Rd Kensington CA 94707-1403

LITTLEJOHN, JOHN JOSEPH, petroleum engineer; b. Waco, Tex., Sept. 6, 1948; s. Lacy Welborn and Winfred Rachael (Young) L.; m. Susan Louise Ilse, 1972; children: Hillary, Elizabeth, Neal, Nathan. BS, Baylor U., 1971; MA, Harvard U., 1972, PhD, 1975. Explorationist Shell Oil Co, Houston, 1975-78; cons. various cos., 1978-81; pres. Rubicon Petroleum Inc., 1981-91, chmn., pres. Colorado Springs, Colo., 1978—. Vice-chmn. Advocates Internat., Annandale, Va., 1993—96; chmn. Internat. Tchg. Ministry, Dallas, 1994—. Mem. Am. Assn. Petroleum Geologists, Soc. Exploration Geophysics, Soc. Petroleum Engring. Baptist. Office: Rubicon Petroleum Inc 6 Pine Rd Colorado Springs CO 80906-4253

LITTLEJOHN, MARK HAYS, retired radiologist, artist; b. Detroit, Apr. 11, 1936; s. Maurice Mark and Elizabeth Dowell Littlejohn; children from previous marriage: M. Hays, Sara J.; m. Karla Ann McGinnis, Apr. 16, 1983; 1 stepchild, Bradford D. Schwartz. BS, Northwestern U., 1958, MD, 1961. Diplomate Am. Bd. Radiology, Am. Bd. Nuclear Medicine. Intern Luth. Hosp., Ft. Wayne, Ind., 1961-62; rsident VA Rsch. Hosp. and Northwestern U. Med. Sch., Chgo., 1962-65; staff radiologist Ireland Army Hosp., Ft. Knox, Ky., 1965-66, chief radiology, 1966-67; staff radiologist St. Mary Nazareth Hosp., Chgo., 1968-80, chief nuclear medicine, 1975-80; instr. in radiology Northwestern U. Med. Sch., 1968-71; dir. dept. radiology Cannon Meml. Hosp., Banner Elk, N.C., 1980-99, chief of staff, 1987-89; ret., 1999. Cons. 1st U.S. Army, 1966-67. Capt. U.S. Army, 1965-67. Mem. Am. Coll. Radiology, Am. Coll. Nuclear Physicians (charter), Am. Inst. Ultrasound Medicine, Radiology Soc. N.Am., Soc. Nuclear Medicine, Pi Kappa Epsilon. Home and Office: PO Box 188 Blowing Rock NC 28605-0188

LITTLEPAGE, GLENN E. social psychology educator; b. Dallas, Nov. 21, 1946; s. Gordon Ray and Mary Lucille Littlepage; 1 child from previous marriage, Nick; m. Anna Littlepage, June 1, 1986; 1 child, Morgan A. Jones. BS, U. N.Mex., 1969; MS, Kans. State U., 1971, PhD, 1974. Rsch. psychologist U.S. Army Retraining Brigade, Ft. Riley, Kans., 1971-73; prof. psychology dept. Mid. Tenn. State U., Murfreesboro, 1973—. Cons. editor Jour. Personality and Social Psychology, 2000-2001; assoc. editor Group Dynamics, 2001—. Contbr. articles to profl. jours. Mem. APA, Am. Psychol. Soc., Soc. Exptl. Social Psychology, Soc. Personality and Social Psychology, Soc. for Indsl. and Orgnl. Psychology. Avocations: bass fishing, woodworking, stained glass. Office: Mid Tenn State U Box 534 Murfreesboro TN 37132

LITTLER, GENE ALEC, professional golfer; b. San Diego, July 21, 1930; s. Stanley Fred and Dorothy (Paul) L.; m. Shirley Mae Warren, Jan. 5, 1951; children: Curt Michael, Suzanne. Student, San Diego State Coll. Mem. U.S. Ryder Cup Team, 61, 63, 65, 67, 69, 71, 75. Served with USN, 1951-54. Achievements include winning 29 PGA tour events including Nat. Jr. Championship, 1948, Nat. Amateur Championship, 1953, U.S. Open, 1961, Canadian Open, 1965, Tournament of Champions, 1955, 56, 57, World Series of Golf, 1966, Taheiyo Masters, Japan, 1974, 75, Australian Masters, 1980, 15 sr. tour titles and Coca Cola Grand Slam, Japan, 1983, 87.

LITTLETON, HARVEY KLINE, artist; b. Corning, N.Y., June 14, 1922; s. Jesse Talbot and Bessie (Cook) L.; m. Bess Toyo Tamura, Sept. 6, 1947; children— Carol Louise Littleton Shay, Thomas Harvey, Kathryn Tamra (dec.), Maurine Bess, John Christopher. Student, U. Mich., 1939-42, B in Design, 1947; MFA, Cranbrook Acad. Art, 1951; DFA (hon.) , Phila. U. of the Arts, 1982, RISD, 1996, U. Wis., 2000, Wis. Acad. Arts & Scis., 2001. Instr. ceramics Toledo Mus. Art, 1949-51; prof. art U. Wis., Madison, 1951-77, chmn. dept., 1964-67, 69-71, prof. emeritus, 1977—. Author: Glass Blowing - A Search for Form, 1971; one- and two-man exhbns. include Lee Nordness Galleries, N.Y.C., 1969-70, Maison de Culture, Liege, Belgium, 1974, J & L Lobmeyr, Vienna, 1974, Brooks Meml. Art Gallery, Memphis, 1975, Contemporary Art Glass Gallery, N.Y.C., 1977, 78, 79, Habatat Gallery, Detroit, 1980, 81, Heller Gallery, N.Y.C., 1980, 81, 82, 83, 84, 85, Glasmuseum Ebeltoft, Sweden, 1989, Royal Copenhagen Gallery, 1989, Finnish Glasmusem, Riihimaki, Finland, 1989, Kunsthaus am Mus., Cologne, Germany, 1990, Immenhausen, Germany, 1990, Glasmuseum, Frauenau, Germany, 1992, Yokohama (Japan) Mus. Art, 1995, retrospective exhbn. originated by High Mus. Art, Atlanta, 1984, traveling to the Renwick Gallery, Am. Craft Mus., Iowa State U., Milw. Art Mus. and Portland (Maine) Mus. Art, originated at Mint Mus. Craft & Design, Charlotte, N.C., 1999-2000, traveling to Ark. Art Ctr. Decorative Arts Mus., Little Rock, St. John's Mus. Art, Wilmington, N.C., Hunter Mus. Art, Chattanooga, Elvehjem Art Ctr., Madison, Wis.; represented in permanent collections, Victoria and Albert Mus., London, museums in, Germany, Holland, Switzerland, Belgium, Austria and, Czechoslovakia, also, Met. Mus. Art, N.Y.C., Mus. Modern Art, N.Y.C., Am. Craft Mus., N.Y.C., L.A. County Mus. Art., L.A., Corning Mus. of Glass, Toledo Mus. Art, Detroit Art Inst., Milw. Art Center, Smithsonian Instn., Washington, High Mus. Art, Atlanta, Chrysler Mus., Norfolk, Va., U. Mich., U. Ill., Ohio State U., Phila. Mus. Art, The White House, Washington, numerous other pub. and pvt. collections. Bd. dirs. Penland Sch., N.C., pres. bd. dirs., 1986-88; pres., chmn. Littleton Co., Inc., Spruce Pine, N.C., 1981—. With Signal Corps U.S. Army, 1942-45, ETO. Recipient diploma of honor Glass Mus. Frauenau, Germany, Fine Arts award Gov. N.C., 1987, Master of Medium award James Renwick Alliance, 1997, Disting. Alumnus award U. Mich. Sch. Art; named Living Treasure, State N.C.; Rsch. grantee U. Wis., 1954, 57, 62, 73, 75, Toledo Mus. Art, 1962, grantee Louis Comfort Tiffany Found. grantee, 1970-71, Corning Glass Works, 1974, Nat. Endowment for Arts, 1978-79. Fellow Am. Crafts Coun. (trustee 1957, 61-64, trustee emeritus, gold medal 1983), Corning Mus. Glass (Rakow award for excellence in art of glass); mem. Nat. Coun. for Edn. in Ceramic Arts (hon.), Glass Art Soc. (hon. life, lifetime achievement award 1993), Am. Ceramic Soc. (hon. life), Nat. Assn. Schs. Art and Designs (Disting. Svc. in Visual Arts citation 1996, Urbanglass award for Lifetime Achievement in Glass 1998). E-mail: glassman@m-y.net.

LITTLETON, ISAAC THOMAS, III, retired university library administrator, consultant; b. Hartsville, Tenn., Jan. 28, 1921; s. Isaac Thomas Jr. and Bessie (Lowe) L.; m. Dorothy Etta Young, Aug. 12, 1949; children— Sally Lowe Littleton Phillips, Thomas Young, Elizabeth Ann BA, U. N.C., 1943; MA, U. Tenn., Knoxville, 1950; MSLS, U. Ill., Champaign-Urbana, 1951, PhD, 1968. Circulation librarian, asst. librarian U. N.C., Chapel Hill, 1951-58; asst. dir. then dir. libraries N.C. State U., Raleigh, 1959-87, emeritus dir. libraries, 1987—. Mem. N.C. Libr. Networking Steering Com., Raleigh, 1982-85; bd. dirs. Southeastern Libr. Network, Atlanta, 1973-74, 83-86, chmn., 1985-86; chmn. Assn. Southeastern Rsch. Librs., 1969-71; mem. com. Gov.'s Conf. on Libr. and Info. Svcs., 1990. Author: The Literature of Agricultural Economics, 1969, State Systems of Higher Education and Libraries, 1977, D.H. Hill Library: An Informal History, 1993; editor: N.C. Union List of Scientific Serials, 1967. Bd. dirs., treas. Theater in Park, Raleigh, 1982-85, Friends of Wake County Pub. Librs.; sec. N.C. State U. Friends of Libr., Raleigh, 1964-87, bd. dirs., 1990-94, life mem. 1988; pres. Friends of N.C. Libr. for Blind and Physically Handicapped, 1989-93, bd. dirs. 1993—; v.p. Wake County UN Assn., 1994-95, sec., 1999-2000, pres., 2001—. Lt. (j.g.) USN, 1943-46, PTO. Council on Library Resources fellow, Washington, 1975-76 Mem. Southeastern Libr. Assn. (exec. bd. 1974-78), N.C. Libr. Assn. (exec. bd. 1969-71, hon. life), Torch Club (pres. Raleigh 1974-75), Raleigh Golden K Kiwanis Club (pres. 2001—). Mem. Community United Ch. of Christ. Avocations: theater; reading; concerts. Home: 4813 Brookhaven Dr Raleigh NC 27612-5706 E-mail: littletons@mindspring.com.

LITTLETON, JESSE TALBOT, III, radiology educator; b. Corning, N.Y., Apr. 27, 1917; s. Jesse Talbot and Bessie (Cook) L.; m. Martha Louise Morrow, Apr. 17, 1943 (dec. 1994); children: Christine, Joanne, James, Robert, Denise; m. Mary Lou Durizch, Mar. 25, 1995. Student, Emory and Henry Coll., 1934-35, Johns Hopkins U., 1935-39; MD, Syracuse U., 1943. Diplomate Am. Bd. Radiology. Intern Buffalo Gen. Hosp., 1943; resident in medicine, surgery and radiology Robert Packer Hosp., Sayre, Pa., 1946-51, assoc. radiologist, 1951-53, chmn. dept. radiology, 1953-76; prof. radiology U. South Ala., Mobile, 1976-87, prof. emeritus, 1987—. Cons. in field. Author 4 textbooks; contbr. chpts. to books and articles to profl. jkours., sci. exhibits to profl. confs. Served with M.C., U.S. Army, 1944-46, PTO. Fellow Am. Coll. Radiology; mem. AMA, Radiol. Soc. N.Am., Am. Roentgen Ray Soc., Ala. Acad. Radiology, Med. Assn. Ala., French Soc. Neuroradiology, Country Club of Mobile, Sigma Xi, Alpha Omega Alpha. Republican. Methodist. Achievements include research on conventional tomography, physical principles, equipment development and testing and clinical applications; transportation and radiology of acutely ill and traumatized patient; development of patient litter with removable top leading to placement of backboards in ambulances; development of dedicated trauma x-ray machine; angiography, development of first sheet film serialograph; development of equipment for sectional radiographic anatomy with Durizch. Home: 5504 Churchill Downs Ave Theodore AL 36582-9601 Office: U South Ala Med Ctr 2451 Fillingim St Mobile AL 36617-2238

LITTLETON, NAN ELIZABETH FELDKAMP, psychologist, educator; b. Covington, Ky., Oct. 23, 1942; d. William Albert and Norma Elizabeth (Smith) Feldkamp; m. O.W. Littleton, Oct. 4, 1969 (div. 1979). AAS, No. Ky. U., 1976, BS, 1978; MACE, Morehead State U., 1981; MA, U. Cin., 1986, PhD, 1995. Prof. No. Ky. U., Highland Heights, 1976—, dir. mental health and human svcs. program, 1989—. Officer, pres. Holly Hill Children's Home, Cold Spring, Ky., 1980-86; cons. Attituding Healing Ctr., Cin., 1990-94. Treas., editor So. Orgn. Human Svcs. Edn. Link, 1997—. Bd. dirs. Coun. for Stds. in Human Svc. Edn., Chgo., 1990-98—, Cancer Family Care, Cin., 1992-96. Mem. APA, Am. Psychol. Soc., Nat. Orgn. Human Svc. Edn., So. Orgn. Human Svc. Edn. (state rep. 1991—, treas., 1999—), Nat. Assn. Women in Edn., Nat. Women's Studies Assn., Assn. Humanistic Psychologists. Home: 333 W 17th St Covington KY 41014-1007

LITTLETON, TAYLOR DOWE, humanities educator, educator; b. Birmingham, Ala., Mar. 14, 1930; s. M. Taylor and Florence (Longcrier) L.; m. Lucy Williams, Aug. 7, 1954; children: Dowe, George, Franklin, Mary Wood. BS, Fla. State U., 1951, MA, 1952, PhD, 1960. Tchg. fellow Fla. State U., Tallahassee, 1954-57; from instr. to prof. dept. English Auburn U., Ala., 1957—, dean undergrad. studies, 1968-71, v.p. for acad. affairs, 1972-83, W. Kelly Mosley prof. sci. and humanities, 1983—. Author: Advancing American Art: Painting, Politics, and Cultural Confrontation at Mid-century, 1989, Athletics and Academe: An Anatomy of Abuses and a Prescription for Reform, 1991, The Color of Silver: William Spratling, His Life and Art, 2000; author, editor: To Prove A Villain: The Case of King Richard III, 1964, The Idea of Tragedy, 1965; editor: multi-vol. series The Franklin Lectures in Sci. and Humanities: Approaching the Benign Environment, 1970; The Shape of Likelihood, 1974, A Time To Hear and Answer, 1977, The Rights of Memory, 1985; assoc. editor So. Humanities Rev., 1967-70. With U.S. Army, 1952-54. Mem. So. Atlantic MLA, Phi Kappa Phi, Omicron Delta Kappa Democrat. Episcopalian. Home: 415 Norman Cir Auburn AL 36830-6307 Office: Auburn U Dept English & Humanities Haley 9030 Auburn AL 36830

LITTLEWOOD, DOUGLAS BURDEN, business brokerage executive; b. Buffalo, Sept. 24, 1922; s. Frank and G. Joan (Burden) L.; m. Jevene Hope Baker, July 2, 1949; children— Douglas Baker, Dean Houston, Laurie Littlewood Vogelsang BS in Mech. Engring, Rensselaer Poly. Inst., 1945; MBA, Harvard, 1947. Sales engr. Otis Elevator Co., 1948-49; asst. to sec. Nat Gypsum Co., Buffalo, 1949-52, sec., 1952-67; investment banker Hornblower & Weeks, 1967-68; pres. Littlewood Assocs., Inc., 1968-95, chmn. bd., 1995—. Past pres. Greater Niagara Frontier coun. Boy Scouts Am.; active Buffalo YMCA, United Fund; bd. dirs. Presbyn. Homes of Western N.Y.; bd. dirs., chmn. emeritus Salvation Army; v.p. N.E. region Boy Scouts Am. Served to lt. (j.g.) USNR, 1943-46. Recipient Silver Beaver, 1965; recipient Silver Antelope, 1978, Disting. Eagle, 1979 Mem. Country Club of Sebring, Buffalo Jr. C. of C. (past dir., chmn. bd.), Am. Soc. Corp. Secs., Buffalo Canoe Club (past commodore), Buffalo Country Club. Home: 1925 SE Lakeview Dr Sebring FL 33870-4938 Office: 22 Dawnbrook Ln Buffalo NY 14221-4930 *If you truly believe you are happy and successful then, and only then, you truly are.*

LITTLEWOOD, THOMAS BENJAMIN, retired journalism educator; b. Flint, Mich., Nov. 30, 1928; s. Thomas Nelson and Louise Engela (Grebenkemper) L.; m. Barbara E. Badger, June 9, 1951; children: Linda S. Johnson, Lisa L. Ratchford, Thomas S., Leah J. Hamrick. Student, DePauw U., 1948-51; BS, Northwestern U., 1952, MS, 1953. Reporter Chgo. Sun-Times, 1953-76, chief Springfield State Capital Bur., 1955-64, corr. Washington Bur., 1965-76; prof. journalism U. Ill., Urbana-Champaign, 1977-96; prof. emeritus, 1996—; head dept. U. Ill., Urbana-Champaign, 1977-87. Author: Bipartisan Coalition in Illinois, 1959, Horner of Illinois, 1969, The Politics of Population Control, 1977, Coals of Fire, 1988, Arch, 1990, Calling Elections, 1999. John F. Kennedy Inst. Politics Harvard U. fellow, 1975. Mem. Soc. Profl. Journalists (SDX Nat. award 1988), Ill. State Hist. Soc., N.Am. Soc. Sports History, Kappa Tau Alpha. E-mail: tbbblittlewood@prodigy.net.

LITTMAN, BURT A. obstetrician-gynecologist; b. N.Y.C., Dec. 11, 1952; MD, Georgetown U., 1977. Diplomate in ob-gyn. and reproductive endocrinology Am. Bd. Ob-Gyn. Intern R.I. Hosp., Providence, 1977-78; resident in ob-gyn. Women & Infants Hosp., 1978-81; fellow in reproductive endocrinoogy NIH, Bethesda, 1981-83; pvt. practice Rockville, Md. Mem. staff Shady Grove Advent Hosp., Rockville, Holy Cross Hosp., Silver Spring, Md., George Washington U. Hosp, Washington; clin. prof., George Washington U. Sch. Medicine, Washington, 1983—. Mem. ACOG, Am. Soc. Reproductive Medicine, Endocrine Soc., Soc. Reproductive Endocrine, Soc. Reproductive Surgeons. Office: 9711 Med Ctr Dr Ste #214 Rockville MD 20850-3323

LITTMAN, DAVID BERNARD, lawyer; b. Plainfield, N.J., Oct. 16, 1949; s. Alexander and Muriel Roslyn (Block) L.; m. Deborah Joy Fields, Nov. 9, 1980; 1 child, Alexandra Ellen Pauline. AB, Lafayette Coll., 1970; JD, Rutgers U., 1973. Bar: N.J. 1974, U.S. Dist. Ct. N.J. 1974, U.S. Supreme Ct. 1983; cert. criminal trial atty. Assoc. Winetsky & Winetsky, Linden, N.J., 1973-76; pvt. practice, 1976—. Mcpl. pub. defender Scotch Plains Twp., N.J., 1999. Mem. ABA, N.J. Bar Assn., Union County Bar Assn., Linden Bar Assn. (pres. 1977-80), N.J. Trial Lawyers, Masons (sec. Highland Park lodge 1979-86, treas. 1987—, gen. counselor M.W. grand lodge 1991—). Democrat. Jewish. Home: 1557 Ashbrook Dr Scotch Plains NJ 07076-2854 Office: 129 N Wood Ave Linden NJ 07036-4227

LITTMAN, EARL, advertising and public relations executive; b. Jan. 29, 1927; s. David and Cele Littman; m. Natalie Carol Jacobson, Dec. 21, 1948; children: Erica Humphrey, Bonnie Likover, Michael L. Littman. BS, NYU, 1948. With George N. Khan, N.Y.C., 1948-50, Jones & Brown, Pitts., 1950-52; chmn., CEO Goodwin, Dannenbaum, Littman & Wingfield Inc., Houston, 1952-92; pres. The Advertizing Firm, Inc., 1992, Two Nerds and a Suit, Inc., 1994. Bd. dirs. Ctr. for Am. History, U. Tex., mem. Chancellor's Coun.; chmn. Anti-Defamation League, Tex., 1984; bd. dirs. Am. Heart Assn., Houston, Glassell Sch, Houston chpt. World Pres. Orgn., Ctr. for Am. History, U. Tex.; active End Hunger Network, Houston, 1984; active NCCJ; founder, exec. dir. Drugs Kill Prevention/Edn. Program, 1997; exec. dir. Drugs Kill. With USN, 1944-45. Recipient Silver medal Am. Advt. Fedn., 1989, Outstanding Vol. award Savvy, 1990, Anti-Defamation League Popkin award, 1990, End Hunger Network award, 1992; Am. Heart Assn. honoree, 1988, John McMahon award Am. Heart Assn., 1996; Heritage award Am. Women in Radio and TV, 1992, Cmty. Champion award Tex. Commn. Alcohol and Drug Abuse, 2000; named Mktg. Man of Yr., Am. Mktg. Assn., 1999. Mem. Affiliated Advt. Agys. Internat. (pres. 1979-80), Am. Advt. Agy. Assn. (gov. Houston chpt. 1990, Paul Dudley White award 1991), Houston Advt. Fedn. (Living Legend award 1993), Winedale Hist. Assn. (former pres.), Marathon Assn. E-mail: papaearl@hotmail.com.

LITTMAN, HOWARD, chemical engineer, educator; b. Bklyn., Apr. 22, 1927; s. Morris and Gertrude (Goldberg) L.; m. Arline F. Caruso, July 3, 1955; children— Susan Joy, Vicki Kim, Paul William. BChemE, Cornell U., 1951; PhD, Yale U., 1956. Asst., then assoc. prof. Syracuse U., 1955-65; on leave to Brookhaven Nat. Lab., summer 1957, Argonne Nat. Lab., 1957-59; faculty Rensselaer Poly. Inst., Troy, N.Y., 1965—, prof. chem. engring., 1967—, chmn. faculty council, 1975-76. Vis. prof. Imperial Coll., London, 1971—72, Chonn'am Nat. U., Kwangju, Republic of Korea, 1988; Fulbright lectr. U. Belgrade, Yugoslavia, 1972. Patentee in field; contbr. articles to profl. jours. A founder Onondaga Hill Free Library, 1961, trustee, 1961-65, pres., 1965; a founder Onondaga Library System, 1962, trustee, 1962-65, v.p., 1965; trustee Capital Dist. Library Council, 1969-75, pres., 1970, 73. Served with USN, 1945-46. IREX grantee U. Belgrade, summer 1973; recipient Disting. Faculty award Rensselaer Poly. Inst., 1988. Mem. Am. Inst. Chem. Engrs., Am. Chem. Soc., Sigma Xi. Home: 7 Tulip Tree Ln Schenectady NY 12309-1837 Office: Rensselaer Poly Inst Troy NY 12180-3590

LITTMAN, MARLYN KEMPER, information scientist, educator; b. Mar. 26, 1943; d. Louis and Louise (Jacobs) Janofsky; m. Bennett I. Kemper, Aug. 1, 1965 (dec. June 1987); children: Alex Randall, Gari Hament, Jason Myles; m. Lewis Littman, Apr. 22, 1990. BA, Finch Coll., 1964; MA in Anthropology, Temple U., 1970; MA in Info. Sci., U. South Fla., 1983; PhD in Info. Sci., Nova Southeastern U., 1986. Dir. Hist. Broward County Preservation Bd., Hollywood, Fla., 1979—87; automated systems libr. Broward County Main Libr., Ft. Lauderdale, 1984—86; assoc. prof. info. sci. Nova U., 1987—94, dir. info. sci. doctoral program, 1987—94; prof. info. sci. Nova Southeastern U., 1995—. Weekly columnist Ft. Lauderdale News, 1975—79; contbg. editor Hyper NEXUS-Jour. Hypermedia and Multimedia Studies, 1996—; assoc. editor Jour. On-Line Learning, 1997—. Author: A Comprehensive Documented History of the City of Pompano Beach, 1982, A Comprehensive History of Dania, 1983, A Comprehensive History of Hallandale, 1984, A Comprehensive History of Deerfield Beach, 1985, A Comprehensive History of Plantation, 1986, A Comprehensive History of Davie, 1987, Networking: Choosing a LAN Path to Interconnection, 1987, Building Broadband Networks, 2002; author: (with others) Mosaics of Meaning, New Ways of Learning, 1996; contbr. articles to Microcomputer Environment: Management Issues, also to pro, chapters to books. Pub. info. officer Broward County Hist. Commn., 1975—79; vice chmn. Broward County Adv. Bd., 1987—92; bd. dirs. Ctrl. Agy. Jewish Edn., 1992—94. Recipient Judge L. Clayton Nance award, 1977, Broward County Hist. Commn. award, 1979. Mem.: IEEE, ALA, Assn. Computing Machinery, Internat. Soc. for Tech. in Edn., Phi Kappa Phi, Beta Phi Mu. Home: 2845 NE 35th St Fort Lauderdale FL 33306-2007 Office: Nova U Sch Computer and Info Sci 3100 SW 9th Ave Fort Lauderdale FL 33315-3025 E-mail: marilyn@nova.edu.

LITTMAN, RICHARD ANTON, psychologist, educator; b. N.Y.C., May 8, 1919; s. Joseph and Sarah (Feinberg) L.; m. Isabelle Cohen, Mar. 17, 1941; children— David, Barbara, Daniel, Rebecca. AB, George Washington U., 1943; postgrad., Ind. U., 1943- 44; PhD, Ohio State U., 1948. Faculty U.

Oreg., 1948—, prof. psychology, 1959—, chmn. dept., 1963-68, vice provost acad. planning and resources, 1971-73. Vis. scientist Nat. Inst. Mental Health, 1958-59 Contbr. articles to profl. jours. Sr. postdoctoral fellow NSF, U. Paris, 1966-67; sr. fellow Nat. Endowment for Humanities, U. London, 1973-74; Ford Found. fellow, 1952-53; recipient U. Oreg. Charles H. Johnson Meml. award, 1980. Mem. APA, Western Psychol. Assn., Am. Psychol. Soc., Soc. Research and Child Devel., Psychonomics Soc., Animal Behavior Soc., Soc. Psychol. Study of Social Issues, Internat. Soc. Developmental Psychobiology, History of Sci. Soc., Am. Philos. Assn., AAUP, Sigma Xi. Home: 3625 Glen Oak Dr Eugene OR 97405-4736 Office: U Oreg Dept Psychology Eugene OR 97403 E-mail: rlittman@darkwing.uoregon.edu.

LITTON, ANDREW, musical director; b. N.Y.C., May 16, 1959; BS, MBA, Juilliard Sch. Music. Music dir. Dallas Symphony, 1994—. Office: Morton H Meyerson Symphonic Ctr 2301 Flora St Ste 300 Dallas TX 75201-2404*

LITTON, DAPHNE NAPIER RUDHMAN, special education educator; b. Schenectady, July 28, 1952; d. James Napier and Mary (Stathas) Rudhman; m. John Shelby Litton, Oct. 5, 1984; children: Christian Napier, Erin Elizabeth. BS in Elem. Edn., Ind. U., South Bend, 1974, MS in Elem. Edn., cert. learning disabled, Ind. U., South Bend, 1978; cert. emotionally disturbed, Ind. U.-Purdue U., Indpls., 1982. Tchr. remedial reading, dir. motor skills, tchr. summer sch. Olive Twp. Elem. Sch., New Carlisle, Ind., 1976; tchr. learning disabled, gifted, remedial reading Ox Bow Elem. Sch., Elkhart, 1976-85, dir. motor skills, 1976-85; tchr. learning disabled Stafford (Va.) Community Schs., 1985-87; tchr. emotionally disturbed Elvin Hill Elem. Sch., Columbiana, Ala., 1987-88; dir., adminstr. Riverchase Presbyn. Presch./Mother's Day Out, Birmingham, 1989-90; tchr. learning disabled Yorkshire Elem. Sch., Manassas, Va., 1993-95, Piney Grove Elem. Sch., Kernersville, N.C., 1995—. Mem. Ind. State Com. for Svc. Personnel Devel., Elkhart, 1979-85; asst. girl's volleyball coach Ox Bow Elem. Sch., Elkhart, 1985-87; asst. dir. Sports Medicine 10K Run Vols., South Bend, 1986. Contbr. Active Am. Cancer Soc., South Bend, 1975, Girl Scouts. Recipient Editor's Choice award, Nat. Libr. of Poetry, 1997. Mem. Coun. Exceptional Children. Republican. Presbyterian. Avocations: musical instruments, choir, travel, swimming, genealogy. Home: 1820 Glenridge Dr Kernersville NC 27284-8666

LITTON, RANDALL GALE, lawyer; b. Idaho Falls, Idaho, July 13, 1939; s. Ralph John and Inez Evelyn (Petersen) L.; m. Sandra Byrne, Aug. 19, 1961 (div. 1993); children: Sean B., Stephanie L., Emily R.; m. Jo Ann Foerster, July 22, 2000. BSEE, U. Idaho, 1961; LLB, George Washington U., 1965. Bar: Mich. 1965, U.S. Dist. Ct. (ea. dist.) Mich. 1966, U.S. Dist. Ct. (we. dist.) Mich. 1967, U.S. Ct. Appeals (6th cir.) 1971, U.S. Ct. Appeals (8th cir.) 1979, U.S. Ct. Appeals (Fed. cir.) 1984, U.S. Ct. Appeals (7th cir.) 1993, U.S. Supreme Ct. 1993. Examiner U.S. Patent Office, Washington, 1962-64; ptnr. Price, Heneveld, Cooper, DeWitt & Litton, Grand Rapids, Mich., 1965—. Mem. ABA, Mich. Bar Assn. Presbyterian. Avocations: hunting, fishing, skiing. Office: Price Heneveld Cooper DeWitt & Litton 695 Kenmoor Ave SE Grand Rapids MI 49546-2375 E-mail: rlitton@priceheneveld.com.

LITTRELL, CARL PAUL, civil engineer; b. St. Louis, Aug. 14, 1946; s. Carl Ess and Mary Ann (Heaven) L.; m. Jane Marie Schmitz, July 12, 1969; children: John Carl, David Scott, Joseph Robert. BSCE, U. Notre Dame, 1968, MSCE, 1973. Registered profl. engr., Ind., Mich. Pres. Shilts, Graves and Assocs., South Bend, Ind., 1970-91; dir. engring. City of South Bend, 1991-98, city engr., 1998—. Fellow ASCE; mem. Nat. Soc. Profl. Engrs., Am. Pub. Works Assn. Democrat. Roman Catholic. Avocation: baseball umpire. Office: City of South Bend 1316 County-City Bldg South Bend IN 46601 E-mail: sbblue53@aol.com., clittrell@ci.south-bend.in.us.

LITTRELL, DAVID A. music educator, conductor; b. Columbia, Mo., Aug. 1, 1949; s. J. Harvey and Louise Miller Littrell; m. Laurel Ann Wilkens, Sept. 2, 1994; children: Nathan, Matthew. MusB, Kans. State U., 1971; MusM, U. Tex., 1972, D of Mus. Arts, 1979. Asst. prof. U. Wis., Kenosha, 1973—75; sect. cellist Denver Symphony Orch., 1975—77; assoc. prof. U. Evansville, Ind., 1979—87; Univ. Disting. prof. Kans. State U., Manhattan, 1987—. Founder, music dir., condr. Gold Youth Orch., Manhattan, 1989—. Editor: ASTA String Syllabus, 1997, Teaching Music through Performance in Orchestra, 2001; cellist (CD) Pastorale, 1998. Mem.: Music Educators Nat. Conf., Suzuki Assn. Am., Am. String Tchrs. Assn. (nat. pres. 2002—). Republican. Evangelical Free. Avocations: Bible study, gardening. Home: 400 Oakdale Manhattan KS 66502-3736 Office: Kans State Univ 109 McCain Auditorium Manhattan KS 66506-4702

LITTRELL, DENNIS ALLEN, writer; s. Marvin and Beulah (Heavener) Littrell; children: Deja Herbers. BA, UCLA, L.A., 1969. Cert. Tchr. Calif., 1989. Newspaper reporter Asbury Pk. (N.J.) Press, 1969—71; tchr. Mira Costa H.S., Manhattan Beach, Calif., 1989—95. Gaming cons. SuperWinners, Inc, Las Vegas, Nev., 1974—78; yoga instr. Dennis Littrell Sch. of Am. Yoga, Torrance, Calif., 1978—84. Author: (novels) A Perfectly Natural Act, 1974, (book) Beating the Verbal SAT, 1992, (short stories) The Nancine Blues, 2000, Garbage Sam and the Bill Passer, 2000. Basketball coach Redondo Beach Recreation Dept., Redondo Beach, Calif., 1973—75. Specialist four/pro-1 US Army, 1960—63, France. Mem.: LA Futurists. Yoga. Avocations: stock trading, chess, writing. Personal E-mail: dalittrell@yahoo.com.

LITTRUP, PETER JOHN, radiologist, cancer researcher; b. Flint, Mich., Nov. 12, 1959; co-investigator, Am. Cancer Soc.-Nat. Prostate Cancer Detection Project, State of Mich. Cancer Consortium, Mich. Dept. Cmty. Health, Lansing, 2000—. s. Gunnar and Gerda Marie Littrup; m. Martha Appledorn, Nov. 23, 1985; children: Gerrit Lee, Gunnar Vagn. BS with honors, U. Mich., 1980, MD, 1985. Rsch. fellow Radiol. Soc. N.Am., Chgo., 1990-92; dir. rsch., dept. radiology Wayne State U./St. Joseph Mercy, Ann Arbor, Mich., 1991-93; dir. radiol. rsch. Wayne State U., Detroit, 1994; dir. med. technology devel. Karmanos Cancer Inst., 1999—; prof. radiology WayneState U., 2001—. Contbr. over 60 articles and revs. to profl. jours., 5 chpts. to books; presenter over 50 abstracts at nat. meetings. Recipient Citizen of Week award, Detroit Airport and WWJ Radio, 1996, Jr. Faculty award, Nat. Cancer Soc., 1992. Mem. Soc. Uroradiology (Best Scientific Paper award 1998), Soc. Radiologists in Ultrasound, Am. Coll. Radiology, Am. Inst. Ultrasound in Medicine, Radiol. Soc. N.Am. Avocations: Masters swim team, golf, guitar, basketball, kids' sports. Office: Harper Hosp Dept Radiology 3990 John R Rd Detroit MI 48201 E-mail: plittrup@med.wayne.edu.

LITVAK, EUGENE, medical educator; b. Kiev, Ukraine, May 26, 1949; s. Izrail and Anna Litvak; m. Ella Tsenter; children: Mark. PhD, Moscow Inst. Physics and Tech. Prof. health care and ops. mgmt. Boston U. Sch. Mgmt., 2000—. Dir. Program for Mgmt. of Variability in Health Care Delivery Boston U., 2001—; adj. lectr. Sch. Pub. Health Harvard U., Boston, 1990—; Dozor vis. prof. Ben Gurion U., Israel, 2001; prin. investigator, emergency room diversion study Mass. Dept. Pub. Health, 2001—02. Contbr. more than 50 articles to profl. jours., chpts. to books. Mem. Mass. Emergency Rm. Diversion Task Force, Boston, 2001. Recipient sr. investigator, cost-effective strategies for blood screening award, USAID, 1999—; grantee, NIH, 1995—2000, Mass. Gen. Hosp., 1995—. Mem.: Soc. Med. Decision Making, Inst. Ops. Rsch. and Mgmt. Sci. Avocations: teaching, reading, travel. Office: Boston U Sch Mgmt 595 Commonwealth Ave Boston MA 02215 Business E-Mail: litvak@bu.edu.

LITVAK, ISAIAH A. finance educator, consultant; b. Shanghai, China, Oct. 1, 1936; arrived in U.S., 1999; s. Matthew Max Litvak and Basia Daitch; m. Marilyn Kenigsberg Litvak, Sept. 21, 1958; 1 child Matthew Kenneth. B in Commerce, McGill U., Montreal, Can., 1957; MS, Columbia U., 1959, PhD, 1964. Prof. McMaster U., Hamilton, Canada, 1961—70, Carleton U., Ottawa, Canada, 1970—78; prof., Pierre Lassonde chair in internat. bus. York U., Toronto, Canada, 1978—99; Eugene and Christine M. Lynn eminent scholar, chair internat. bus. Fla. Atlantic U., Boca Raton, 1999—. Cons. Galeos Ltd., Toronto, 1978—99. Author: Marginalization of Corporate Canada, 2001; contbr. articles to profl. jours. Mem.: Acad. Internat. Bus., Acad. Mgmt. Office: Fla Atlantic Univ 777 Glades Rd Boca Raton FL 33431

LITVAK, RONALD, psychiatrist; b. Cleve., Aug. 11, 1938; s. Albert and Ruth (Jaffe) L.; m. Betty Ann Resnick, Aug. 14, 1960; children: Alan, Diane, Amy. BA, Case Western Res. U., 1960; MD, Ohio State U., 1964, MS, 1968. Diplomate Am. Bd. Psychiatry and Neurology, Am. Bd. Forensic Psychiatry; lic. Ohio. Intern in internal medicine Ohio State U. Hosp., Columbus, 1964-65, resident in psychiatry, 1965-68; chief resident in psychiatry Profl. Staff Ohio State U. Hosp., 1967-68; practice medicine specializing in psychiatry Ohio, 1964—. Dir. outpatient svcs. Harding Hosp., Worthington, Ohio, 1979-83, pres. med. staff, 1980; cons. Ohio Dept. Mental Health and Mental Retardation, 1970-78, Chillicothe VA Hosp., 1970-71, Columbus Police Dept., Worthington Police Dept., Ohio State Hwy Patrol, Indsl. Commn. of Ohio, Ohio Atty. Gen., State Med. Bd. of Ohio, Supreme Ct. of Ohio, Bd. of Commrs. and Grievances and Discipline of the Bar, Columbus City Atty., U.S. Dept. Labor, U.S. Dept. State. Contbr. articles to profl. jours. Served to maj. Med. Service Corps, U.S. Army, 1968-70. Recipient Cert. of Achievement Comdr. U.S. Walson Army Hosp., Ft. Dix, N.J., 1970, Letters of Commendation, Officers in Tng. Brigade, Ft. Dix, N.J. Fellow Am. Psychiat. Assn.; mem. AMA, Ohio State Med. Assn., Ohio Psychiat. Assn., Psychiat. Soc. Cen. Ohio, Acad. Medicine of Columbus and Franklin County, Am. Acad. Psychiatry and the Law. Home: 1195 Circle On The Grn Columbus OH 43235-1208 Office: 1170 Old Henderson Rd Ste 201 Columbus OH 43220-3623

LITVIN, INESSA ELIZABETH, piano educator; b. Gorky, Russia, Sept. 13, 1939; came to U.S., 1980; d. Aron J. and Elizabeth I. (Shapiro) Frenkel; m. Edward J. Litvin, Aug. 22, 1975. MA in Piano Performing magna cum laude, Conservatory, Leningrad, Russia, 1965. Prof. music Ctrl. Music Sch., Leningrad, 1965-79; pvt. instr. piano Encinitas, Calif., 1980—. Recipient prize Shostakovich Piano Competition, Leningrad, 1964, recognition for exceptional artistic achievements of students Nat. Found. Advancement in Art, Miami, Fla., 1999. Mem. Calif. Assn. Profl. Music Tchrs., Music Tchrs. Assn. Calif. Home: 1632 Jerrilynn Pl Encinitas CA 92024-4757 E-mail: ielitvin@adelphia.net.

LITVINOV, DMITRI, advisory development engineer; b. Donetsk, Ukraine, July 5, 1970; s. Alexander Litvinov and Natalia Litvinova; m. Julia Novikov; 1 child Alexandra. BS in Gen. and Applied Physics, Moscow Inst.Physics and Tech., Dolgoprudny, Moscow Dist., Russia, 1992; MS in Physics, U. Miami, Coral Gables, Fla., 1994; MS in Elec. Engring., U.Michigan, Ann Arbor, 1997, PhD, 1999. Rsch. asst. Inst. Solid State Physics, Chernogolovka, 1990—92, U. Miami, Coral Gables, Fla., 1992—94, U. Mich., Ann Arbor, 1994—97, Horace H. Rackham fellow, 1998; vis. scientist Carnegie Mellon U., Pitts., 1999—2000; rschr. Seagate Rsch., 1998—. Peer reviewer Am. Inst. Physics, Argonne, 1997—; peer reviewer Elsevier Publs., Amsterdam, Netherlands, 1998—, Publs. IEEE Magnetics Society, Pitts., 1999—; co-chair North American Perpendicular Magnetic Recording Conference, Coral Gables, 2001—02; adj. prof. U. Miami, Coral Gables, Fla., 2001—; co-chair Joint N.Am. Perpendicular Magnetic Rec. Conf. and Japanese Perpendicular Magnetic Rec. Conf., Monterey, Calif., 2002—. Author: (Research) Cubic Boron Nitride, 1999 (Horace H. Rackham Fellowship, 1998); contbr. articles to profl. jours. Mem.: IEEE (publs. chair Transactions on Magnetics 2001—), Am. Phys. Soc., Materials Rsch. Soc. Achievements include 76 provisional patents filed in data storage field, 1999—; 26 utility patent applications filed Magnetic Recording Tech., 1997—; research in general contributions to materials and device engineering. Office: Seagate Technology 1251 Waterfront Pl Pittsburgh PA 15222 Home Fax: 419-791-3337. Personal E-mail: dmitri.litvinov@ieee.org.

LITWACK, GERALD, biochemistry researcher, educator, administrator; b. Boston, Jan. 11, 1929; s. David and Edith Jean (Berkman) Lytell; m. Patricia Lynn Gorog, Feb., 1956 (div. 1973); 1 child, Claudia; m. Ellen Judith Schatz, Aug. 31, 1973; children: Geoffrey Sandor, Katherine Victoria. BA, Hobart Coll., 1949; MS, U. Wis., 1950, PhD, 1953. Postdoctoral fellow Biochem. Labs. U. Paris, 1953-54; asst. prof. Rutgers U., New Brunswick, N.J., 1954-60; trainee Oak Ridge Inst. Nuc. Studies, 1955; assoc. prof. U. Pa., Phila., 1960-64; Carnell prof., dep. dir. Fels Inst., Sch. of Medicine Temple U., 1964-91; prof., chair dept. pharmacology Thomas Jefferson U., 1991-96, also dep. dir. Kimmel Cancer Inst., 1991-97; assoc. dir. for basic sci. Kimmel Cancer Ctr., 1992-97, chmn. dept. biochemistry and molecular pharmacology, 1996—, dir. Ctr. Apoptosis Rsch., assoc. dean sci. affairs, 1996-2001, vice dean for rsch., 2001—. Chmn. adv. com. am. Cancer Soc., N.Y.C., 1977-80; mem. adv. panel NSF, Washington, 1980-84; mem. ad hoc panels NIH, Bethesda, 1985, 89, reviewer, 1977, 84, 91, cons. Nat. Inst. Environ. Health Scis., 1982; mem. ad hoc panels Israel Cancer Rsch. fund Sci. Rev. Panel, 1992-93, U.S. Army Breast Cancer Study Sect., 1994; mem. U.S. Army Neurotoxicology and Neurodegeneration Study Sect., 1997, others; councilor Soc. for Exptl. Biology and Medicine, N.Y.C., 1984-88; cons. Franklin Inst., 1976, Georgetown U., 1980; reviewer Haverford Coll., 1976, NIH programs, 1984, 91; mem. adv. bd. Diabetes Rsch. Ctr. U. Pa., 1996—; mem. joint steering com. for pub. policy Rockville, Md., 1997—; evaluator Roswell Park Meml. Inst., 1978; mem. sci. adv. bd. Norris Cotton Cancer Ctr. Dartmouth Med. Sch., 1984—; Jefferson rep. U. Catania, Sicily, 1994—, U Naples, Italy, 2001--; mem. subcom. B study sect. NIH, NIDDK, 1998; mem. subcom. on rsch. Sharpe-Strumia Found., 1998—; external reviewer NICHD, NIH, 1999; vis. prof. U. Calif., Berkeley, 1956, U. Calif., San Francisco, 1972; hon. prof. biochemistry Rutgers U., 1957-60; vis. scientist Courthauld Inst. Biochemistry, U. London, 1971; mem. study sect. SPORE breast and prostate cancer rsch., NIH and NCI, 2000-01. Author/co-author: Experimental Biochemistry, 1960, Hormones, 1987, 2d edit., 1997; editor: Biochemical Actions of Hormones, Vol. XIV, 1970-87, Receptor Purification, 1990; founder, editor-in-chief Receptor, 1990-96, re-named Receptors and Signal Transduction, 1996-98; editor-in-chief Vitamins and Hormones, 1992—; co-editor Actions of Hormones on Molecular Processes, 1964; assoc. editor Encyclopedia of Hormones, 2001—; mem. editl. bd. Chemtracts, Cancer Comm., Cancer Rsch., Endocrinology, Anticancer Rsch., Oncology Rsch., 1992, Oncology Reports, 1993—, Critical Revs.,d Eukaryotic Gene Expression,94—, Apoptosis, 1995—. Bd. dirs. Sharpe-Strumia Found. Bryn Mawr Hosp., 1997—. Recipient Rsch. Career Devel. award NIAMD, NIH, 1963-69, Pub. Svc. award Chapel of Four Chaplains, 1977, Faculty Rsch. award Temple U., 1987. Mem. Endocrine Soc. (program com. 1991-93, sci. and edn. com. 1992-93, ann. meeting steering com. 1990-93, com. on sci. and ednl. programs 1992-93), Am. Soc. Biochemistry and Molecular Biology, Am. Soc. Pharmacology and Exptl. Therapeutics, Am. Assn. Cancer Rsch. (chair task force on endocrinology 1995, mem. endocrinology and signal transduction subcom., program com., 1995-96), Am. Chem. Soc., Assn. of Am. Med. Colls. (mem. GREAT group 1997—, congl. liaison 1998—, mem. GRAND group 2000--), Assn. for Med. Sch. Pharmacology, Assn. of Med. and Grad. Dept. of Biochemistry. Achievements include discovery and identification of the glucocorticoid receptor; co-discovery of ligandin (glutathione S-Transferase family) mechanism of glucocorticoid receptor activation, studies in apoptosis, immunophilin signal transduction, basic studies in asthma. Home: 380 Montgomery Ave Wynnewood PA 19096-1815 Office: Thomas Jefferson U 10th and Locust St Philadelphia PA 19107-3197 E-mail: gerry.litwack@mail.tju.edu.

LITWACK, LEON FRANK, historian, educator; b. Santa Barbara, Calif., Dec. 2, 1929; s. Julius and Minnie (Nitkin) L.; m. Rhoda Lee Goldberg, July 5, 1952; children: John Michael, Ann Katherine. BA, U. Calif., Berkeley, 1951, MA, 1952, PhD, 1958. Asst. prof., then assoc. prof. history U. Wis., Madison, 1958-65; mem. faculty U. Calif., Berkeley, 1965—, prof. history, 1971—, Alexander F. and May T. Morrison prof. history, 1987—; dir. NDEA Inst. Am. History, summer 1965. Vis. prof. U. S.C., 1975, Colo. Coll., Sept. 1974, 79, La. State U., 1985; Fulbright prof. Am. history U. Sydney, Australia, 1991, Moscow (USSR) State U., 1980; vis. lectr. Peking U., (China), 1982; Walter Lynwood Fleming lectr. La. State U., 1983; Wentworth scholar-in-residence U. Fla., Spring 1983; mem. Nat. Afro-Am. History and Culture Commn., 1981-83; mem. screening com. Fulbright Sr. Scholar Awards, 1983-86; bd. acad. advisors The American Experience Sta. WGBH-TV, 1986—, Africans in America, WGBH-TV, 1990-98; Ford Found. prof. So. studies U. Miss., 1989; mem. exec. com. of dels. Am. Coun. of Learned Socs., 1993-96. Author: North of Slavery: The Negro in the Free States, 1790-1860, 1961, Been in the Storm So Long: The Aftermath of Slavery, 1979, Trouble in Mind: Black Southerners in the Age of Jim Crow, 1998; (film) To Look for America, 1971; co-author: The United States, 1981, rev. edit., 1991, Without Sanctuary: Lynching Photography in America, 2000; editor: American Labor Movement, 1962; co-editor: Reconstruction, 1969, Black Leaders in the Nineteenth Century, 1988, Harvard Guide to African American History, 2001. Mem. Bradley Commn. on History in Schs., 1987-90, Schomburg Commn. for the Preservation of Black Culture; trustee Nat. Coun. for History Edn., 1990-96, mem. steering com. 1994 NAEP History Consensus Project; chair U. Calif. Acad. Senate Libr. Com. 1995-97. Served with AUS, 1953-55. Recipient Excellence in Teaching award U. Calif., Berkeley, 1967, 95, Disting. Tchg. award, 1971, 95 Mem. Orgn. Am. Historians (chmn. nominations bd. 1975-76, exec. bd. 1983-85, pres. 1986-87), Am. Hist. Assn. (chmn. program com. 1980-81), So. Hist. Assn., Soc. Am. Historians, Am. Acad. Arts and Scis., Am. Antiquarian Soc., U. Calif. Alumni Assn., Assn. for the Study African Am. Life and History, PEN Am. Ctr. Office: U Calif Dept History 3229 Dwinelle Hall Berkeley CA 94720-2550

LITWEILER, JOHN BERKEY, writer, editor; b. South Bend, Ind., Feb. 21, 1940; s. John Ernest and Pauline Lucile (Yoder) L. BA, North Cen. Coll., Naperville, Ill., 1962. Indexer-researcher Urban Rsch. Corp., Chgo., 1970-74; editor Maher Publs., 1974-75, 79-81; instr. Am. Sch., 1975-79; writer, editor Ency. Brittanica, 1992-99; free-lance writer, editor, jazz critic Chgo., 1981—. Vis. instr. Sch. of Art Inst., Chgo., 1982. Author: The Freedom Principle, 1984, Ornette Coleman: A Harmolodic Life, 1993; contbr. numerous articles to Reader, Chgo. Tribune, N.Y. Times Book Rev., Kulchur, Down Beat, Jazz Times, other publs. Bd. dirs. Jazz Inst. of Chgo., 1977-88; com. mem. DeMichael Jazz Archives, 1977-88, Chgo. Jazz Festival, 1984-88, 98—. Jazz Criticism Inst. Music Critics Assn. fellow, 1974, NEH fellow, 1981. Home: 5633 S Kenwood Ave Chicago IL 60637-1687 E-mail: jlitweil@megsinet.net.

LITWICKI, ELLEN M. history educator; BA, No. Ariz. U., 1976; MBA, Ariz. State U., 1980; PhD, U. Va., 1992. Asst. prof. U. Utah, Salt Lake City, 1990-92, SUNY, Fredonia, 1992-99, assoc. prof., 1999—. Author: America's Public Holidays, 1865-1920, 2000; contbr. Mem. Am. Studies Assn., Orgn. Am. Historians. Office: SUNY Coll at Fredonia Dept History Fredonia NY 14063

LITWIN, BURTON HOWARD, lawyer; b. Chgo., July 26, 1944; s. Manuel and Rose (Boehm) L.; m. Nancy Iris Stein, Aug. 25, 1968; children: Robin Meredith Litwin Levine, Keith Harris, Jill Stacy. BBA with honors, Roosevelt U., 1966; JD cum laude, Northwestern U., 1970. Bar: Ill. 1970, U.S. Dist. Ct. (no. dist.) Ill. 1970, U.S. Tax Ct. 1971, U.S. Ct. Fed. Claims 1983; CPA, Ill. Of counsel Neal, Gerber & Eisenberg, Chgo., 2002—. Author chpts. of books; contbr. articles to profl. jours. Recipient Gold Watch award Fin. Execs. Inst., Chgo., 1965. Mem. ABA (chmn. nonfiler task force for No. Ill. 1992-94), Chgo. bar Assn. (chmn. adminstrv. practice subcom., fed. taxation subcom. 1982-83) Avocations: roses, painting, photography. Office: Neal Gerber & Eisenberg Two N LaSalle St Ste 2200 Chicago IL 60602-3801 E-mail: burtl@attbi.com., blitwin@ngelaw.com.

LITWIN, SHARON, orchestra executive; Asst. dir. devel. New Orleans Mus. Art, 1988-99; exec. dir. La. Philharm. Orch., New Orleans, 1999—. Staff writer Times-Picayune, New Orleans. Office: La Philharm Orch 305 Baronne St Ste 600 New Orleans LA 70112-1619*

LITWINOWICZ, ANTHONY, information specialist, researcher; b. Jelenia Gora, Poland, July 29, 1952; came to U.S., 1978; s. Anthony and Anna (Zdrojewski) L.; m. Catherine Veronica Gajdos, June 30, 1979; children: Catherine, Anthony, John Paul, Peter. MA in History and Philosophy, Lodz U., Poland, 1976; MS in Info. Studies, Drexel U., 1984, postgrad., 1985-90. Cert. in info. mgmt. Sr. info. specialist Laventhol & Horwath CPAs, Phila., 1984-89; instr. info. sci. Delaware Valley Coll., Doylestown, Pa., 1989-91; dir. Info. Ctr. Samsung Electronics, Ridgefield Park, N.J., 1992—. Author: Nazi Occupation of Poland, 1978; contbr. articles to profl. jours. Mem. Am. Soc. for Info. Sci. Republican. Roman Catholic. Avocations: collecting antiques, reading, martial arts. Home: 108 W Pumping Station Rd Quakertown PA 18951-4214 Office: Samsung Electronics Am 105 Challenger Rd Ridgefield Park NJ 07660-2113

LITZENBOERGER, WOLFGANG, software engineering executive, industrial consultant; b. Hannover, Germany, June 10, 1935; s. Ernst Joachim and Martha Emma (Althoff) L.; m. Ingeborg Meinhold, May 26, 1940; children: Dominique, Wolf-René, Nathalie. Ed., U. Bari (Italy), 1959-60, U. Sorbonne, Paris, 1961, U. Barcelona, Spain, 1962, U. Bologna, Italy, 1963, Pacific Western U., L.A., 1982-83. Gen. mgr. Pisani and Rickertsen, Istanbul, 1956-59; pres., ptnr. INHA Internat. AG, Mauren, Switzerland, 1963-73; mng. dir., owner IDC Indsl. Devel. Cons. GmbH, Duesseldorf, Fed. Republic Germany, 1972-92. Owner, mng. dir. PDC Planning and Devel. Cons. GmbH, Duesseldorf, 1981-85; mng. dir., shareholder Indsl. Informatics GmbH, Freiburg, Fed. Republic Germany, 1985-92. Contbr. articles to profl. jours. Fellow Inst. of Dirs. (London); mem. Institut fuer Interdisziplinäre Denkschulung und Publikationen (v.p. 1984—). Avocations: golf, horseback riding, language and philosophy studies. Office: Taomed Lda Caixa 19 Tunes Gare P-8365 Armacão de Pêra Algarve Portugal Fax: 282 338 131. E-mail: F.Serpa@netc.pt.

LIU, AGATHA H. researcher; b. Taipei, Taiwan, Jan. 10, 1973; d. Leh-Fu Liu and Chia-Jung Chen. BS, Columbia U., 1995; M of Engring., Cornell U., 1996; PhD, U. Wash., 2002. Tchg. asst. Columbia U., N.Y.C., 1993—94; rsch. asst. Purdue U., West Lafayette, Ind., 1994; programmer Columbia U., N.Y.C., 1995; tchg. asst. Cornell U., Ithaca, NY, 1995—96; tech. staff Oracle Corp., Redwood Shores, Calif., 1996—97; rsch. asst. U. Wash., Seattle, 1997—2000; co-op IBM T. J. Watson Rsch., Yorktown Heights, NY, 2000—02. Jour. referee IBM T. J. Watson Rsch., Yorktown Heights, NY, 2000—02; tech. coord. European Genetics Found., Bologna, Italy, 2000. Fellow Distbd. Mentoring Project fellow, Computing Rsch. Assn., 1994; grantee grad. rsch. fellow, NSF, 1997—2000. Mem.: Tau Beta Pi.

LIU, ALAN FONG-CHING, mechanical engineer; b. Canton, China, Mar. 25, 1933; came to U.S., 1958; s. Gee Call and Shuk Hing (Chen) L.; m. Iris P. Chan, Sept. 2, 1962; children: Kent, Willy, Henry. BSME, U. Chiba, Japan, 1958; MSME, U. Bridgeport, 1965. Sr. structures engr. Lockheed Calif. Co., Burbank, Calif., 1968-73; sr. tech. specialist/project mgr. Rockwell Internat. Space divsn., Downey, 1973-76; sr. tech. specialist Northrop Corp. Aircraft divsn., Hawthorne, 1976-88; sr. engring. specialist/projectmgr. Rockwell Internat./N.Am. Aircraft, El Segundo, 1988-95; pvt. practice West Hills, 1995—. Author: Structural Life Assessment Methods, 1998; developer structural life analysis methodologies in support of various aircraft projects; contbr. articles to Jour. of Aircraft, AIAA Jour., Res Mechanica, Jour. Engring. Materials and Tech., Engring. Fracture Mechanics, ASM Handbook Vol. 19, Fatigue and Fracture, 1996; presenter in field. Fellow AIAA (assoc.); mem. ASTM, Am. Soc. Metals Internat. Achievements include research on fatigue and fracture of metallics and composites, on durability and damage tolerance of airframe structures. E-mail: future2000@yahoo.com.

LIU, ALFRED JITFU, otolaryngologist; b. Tokyo, Sept. 22, 1952; BA, U. San Diego, 1975; MD, Baylor U., 1979. Diplomate Am. Bd. Otolaryngology. Intern in surgery U. Hawaii J.A. Burns Sch. Medicine, Honolulu, 1979-80, resident in surgery, U. Wash., Seattle, 1981-86; clin. prof., chief ENT divsn. U. Hawaii, 1986—. Mem. staff Queens Med. Ctr., Honolulu; clin. prof. dept. surgery U. Hawaii J.A. Burns Sch. Medicine. Fellow ACS; mem. AMA, ACS, Am. Acad. Otolaryngology-Head and Neck Surgery, Hawaii Soc. Otolaryngology-Head and Neck Surgery. Office: 1329 Lusitana St Ste 407 Honolulu HI 96813-2412

LIU, ANPING, electrical engineering researcher; b. Anlu, Hubei, China, Apr. 15, 1966; s. Zhiming Liu and Wanhua Xiong; m. Shan Ying, July 20, 1991; 1 child, Jiesi. PhD, U. Electro-Comm., Tokyo, 1997. Sr. rsch. engr. PC Photonics, Waterford, Conn., 1999-2000; sr. rsch. scientist Corning (N.Y.) Inc., 1999—. Mem. IEEE (sr.). com. Home: 363 County Rd 64 Apt 5D Elmira NY 14903 Office: Corning Inc SP-AR-02-04 Corning NY 14831 E-mail: liua@corning.com., ap@fedu.uec.ac.jp.

LIU, BAODONG, political scientist, consultant; b. Huaiyin, Jiangsu, China, Dec. 16, 1965; s. Guohan Liu and Ding Fang; m. Lu Yao Liu, July 7, 1989; children: Rebecca, Daniel. B of Laws, East China Inst. Polits./Law, 1987; MA in Polit. Sci., Okla. State U., 1995; PhD in Polit. Sci., U. New Orleans, 1999. Bar: China. Atty. AnDe Law Firm, Nanjing, Jiangsu, China, 1993; asst. prof. polit. sci. Stephens Coll., Columbia, Mo., 1999—2002, U. Wis., Oshkosh, 2002—. Polit. commentator St. KFRU Radio Sta., Columbia, 2000; statist. advisor of grad. program Stephens Coll., Columbia, 1999-2002, strategic planning and budgeting com., chair Harry Truman scholarship com. 2000-02, . Mem. editl. bd. Turbulent Voyage: Readings in African Am. Studies, 2000—

Recipient Ted Robinson award Southwestern Polit. Sci. Assn., 1999. Mem. Am. Polit. Sci. Assn. (Asian Pacific Am. caucus 2000—, travel grant 1999, Byran Jackson award 1999), Japan Study Group, Pi Sigma Alpha. Office: Univ Wis Dept Polit Sci Oshkosh WI 54901 E-mail: bblpo@yahoo.com.

LIU, BEDE, electrical engineering educator; b. Shanghai, China, Sept. 25, 1934; came to U.S., 1954, naturalized, 1960; s. Henry and Shan (Yao) L.; m. Maria Agatha Sang, Jan. 31, 1959; 1 dau., Beatrice Agatha. BS in Elec. Engring., Nat. Taiwan U., 1954; M.E.E., Poly. Inst. Bklyn., 1956, D.E.E., 1960. Equipment engr. Western Electric Co., N.Y.C., 1954-56; intermediate engr. A.B. DuMont Lab., Clifton, N.J., summer 1956; mem. tech. staff Bell Telephone Labs., Murray Hill, 1959-62, summers 1957, 58, 66; mem. faculty Princeton U., 1962—, prof. elec. engring., 1969—; dept. chmn., 1994-97. Vis. prof. Nat. Taiwan U., 1970-71, U. Calif., Berkeley, 1971, Shanghai Jiao Tong U., 1979; hon. prof. Chinese U. Electronics Sci. and Tech., 1997. Co-author: Digital Signal Processing, 1976; editor: Digital Filters and the Fast Fourier Transform, 1975; patentee in field. Recipient Tech. Achievement award IEEE Signal Processing Soc., 1985, Edn. award IEEE Cir. and Systems Soc, 1988, Mac Van Valkenburg award 1997, IEEE Signal Processing Soc. award, 2000, Golden Jubilee medal, 2000, Millennium medal, 2000; named Hon. Prof. Inst. Acoustics, Inst. Electronics, Academia Sinica, 1988. Fellow IEEE (bd. dirs., 1984-85, Centennial medal 1984, Best Paper award IEEE Trans Video Technology, 1994, 96); mem. IEEE Circuits and Systems Soc. (v.p. 1979, pres. 1982, Edn. award 1988), Nat. Acad. Engring. Home: 248 Hartley Ave Princeton NJ 08540-5656 Office: Princeton Univ Dept Elec Engring Princeton NJ 08540 E-mail: liu@ee.princeton.edu.

LIU, BEN-CHIEH, economist; b. Chungking, China, Nov. 17, 1938; came to U.S., 1965, naturalized, 1973; s. Pei-juang and Chung-su L.; m. Jill Jyh-huey, Oct. 2, 1965; children— Tina Won-ting, Roger Won-jung, Milton Won-ming. BA, Nat. Taiwan U., 1961; MA, Meml. U. Nfld., 1965, Washington U., St. Louis, 1968, PhD, 1971. Economist Chinese Air Force and Central Customs, Taiwan, 1961-63; resource economist Canadian Land Inventory and Forest Services, Nfld., 1963-65; research project dir. St. Louis Regional Indsl. Devel. Corp., 1968-72; prin. econs. Midwest Research Inst., Kansas City, Mo., 1972-80; mgr. Energy and Environ. Systems Div., Argonne (Ill.) Nat. Lab., 1980-81. Prof. econs., assoc. dir. rsch. Oklahoma City U., 1981-82; prof. mgmt., mktg. and info. systems Chgo. State U., 1982—; pres. Liu & Assocs., Inc., 1982—; vis. prof. econs. U. Mo., 1970-78, Nat. Taiwan U., 1991-92; Fulbright prof., dir. Internat. Enterprises Inst., Nat. Dong-Hwa U., Taiwan, 1997-98; dean Coll. Bus., Chung-Yuan Christian U., Taiwan, 2000-01; cons. UN, NSF; mem. Gov. Thompson's Adv. Com. on Agrl. Export, 1985-87, Congressman Fawell's Adv. Com. on Sci. and Tech., 1985-98; commr. Nat. Commn. on Librs. and Info. Svcs., 1991-94. Author: Interindustrial Structure Analysis: An Input-Output Study for St. Louis Region, 1968, The Quality of Life in the United States, 1970, Rating, Index and Statistics, 1973, Quality of Life Indicators in U.S. Metropolitan Areas, 1975, Physical and Economic Damage Functions for Air Pollutants by Receptors, 1976, Earthquake Risk and Damage Functions, An Integrated Model, 1981, Income, Energy and Quality of Life: An Information Systems Approach to Decisions, 1988; mem. editorial bd.: Internat. Jour. Math. Social Sci, Am. Jour. Econs. and Sociology, Hong Kong Jour. Bus. Mgmt., Internat. Jour. of Bus.; Internat. Jour. Mgmt.; contbr. articles to profl. jours. Recipient rsch. study award Am. Indsl. Devel. Coun., 1969—, Fulbright Scholar awards, 1992, 96, Faculty Meritorious awards Chgo. State U., 1983, 86, 89, 90, Disting. Prof. Advancement Increase awards, 1990, 96, Outstanding Rsch. award Nat. Sci. Coun., 1997-98; U.S. Econ. Devel. Adminstrn. fellow, 1967-68; Korean Govt. scholar, 1963-65; Fulbright scholar Mgmt. Devel. Inst., Delhi U., 1992. Fellow Am. Statis. Assn. (com. mem.); mem. Am. Econ. Assn. (com. mem.), Econometric Soc., Royal Econ. Soc., Internat. Statis. Instn., Assn. for Social Econs. (com. mem.), Tax Inst. Am., Chinese Acad. and Profl. Assn. (pres. 1984-85), Chinese Econ. Assn. in N.Am. (pres. 1988-90), Chinese Am. Profs. Assn. (pres. 1996—). Home: 5360 Pennywood Dr Lisle IL 60532-2032 Office: Chgo State U Chicago IL 60628 E-mail: benclin678@hotmail.com. *The joy of living may temporarily rest on present or past glory, but it is the immersion in planning for the future— the living ahead of one's time— which ensures permanently the flourishing of the joy of life. In a commonwealth society, happiness does not come from doing what we like to do, but from liking what we have to do for the less-well-to-do-ones.*

LIU, BENJAMIN YOUNG-HWAI, engineering educator; b. Shanghai, China, Aug. 15, 1934; s. Wilson Wan-su and Dorothy Pao-ning (Cheng) L.; m. Helen Hai-ling Cheng, June 14, 1958; 1 son, Lawrence A.S. Student, Nat. Taiwan U., 1951-54; BS in Mech. Engring., U. Nebr., 1956; PhD, U. Minn., 1960; doctorate (hon.), U. Kupio, Finland, 1991. Asso. engr. Honeywell Co., Mpls., 1956; research asst., instr. U. Minn., 1956-60, asst. prof., 1960-67, asso. prof., 1967-69, prof., 1969-93, regent's prof., 1993—, dir. Particle Tech. Lab., 1973-95; dir. Ctr. for Filtration Rsch., 1995—. Vis. prof. U. Paris, 1968-69; patentee in field. Contbg. author: Aerosol Science, 1966; editor: Fine Particles, 1976, Application of Solar Energy for Heating and Cooling Buildings, 1977, Aerosols in the Mining and Industrial Work Environment, 1983, Aerosols: Science, Technology and Industrial Application of Airborne Particles, 1984; editor-in-chief: Aerosol Sci. and Tech., 1983-93; contbr. articles to Ency. Chem. Tech., Ency. Applied Physics. Guggenheim fellow, 1968-69; recipient Sr. U.S. Scientist award Alexander von Humboldt Found., 1982-83. Mem. ASME, ASHRAE, Inst. Environ. Scis. (v.p. 1993-95), Air and Waste Mgmt. Assn., Am. Assn. for Aerosol Rsch. (pres. 1986-88), Chinese Am. Assn. Minn. (pres. 1971-72), NAE (Fuchs' prize 1994), Am. Filtration and Separation Soc. Home: 1 N Deep Lake Rd North Oaks MN 55127-6504 Office: U Minn Particle Tech Lab 111 Church St SE Minneapolis MN 55455-0150

LIU, BRIAN CHEONG-SENG, urology and oncology educator, researcher; b. Hong Kong, Jan. 15, 1959; came to U.S., 1968; s. Keh Ming and Yin Man (Au) L. BS in Microbiology summa cum laude, UCLA, 1980, PhD in Molecular Biology, 1984. Postdoctoral fellow in tumor immunology and tumor biology Sch. Medicine UCLA, 1984-88; instr. dept. urology Mt. Sinai Sch. Medicine, N.Y.C., 1988-89, asst. prof. dept. urology, dir. urologic rsch., 1989-98; dir. molecular urology rsch. labs. Brigham & Women's Hosp., Harvard Med. Sch., Boston, 1999—. Sr. rsch. fellow Jonsson Comprehensive Cancer Ctr., 1985-88; vis. investigator dept. pathology Henry Ford Hosp., Detroit, 1987-88. Mem. editl. bd. Jour. Urology, 1996—; contbr. articles to profl. jours. Recipient Edwin Beer award N.Y. Acad. Med., 1991-93, New Investigator award Am. Found. Urologic Diseases, 1994—, Cancer of the Prostate Rsch. award Capcure Found., 1995, Merck Young Investigator award in Urology, 1996; Nat. Cancer Inst. grantee, 1991—. Mem. ABA, Am. Urologic Assn., Soc. Basic Urologic Rsch. (treas.), Sigma Xi. Office: Brigham & Women's Hosp Divsn Urology 45 Francis St Boston MA 02115-6105 E-mail: DrLiu@aol.com.

LIU, CHAO-MIN, biochemist, biotechnologist, researcher; b. Min-hsiung, Taiwan, Aug. 9, 1936; came to U.S., 1963; s. Shin-ruh and She-O (Yu) L.; m. Sharon Shih, Aug. 10, 1969; children: Franklin, Daniel. BS, Nat. Taiwan U., 1958, MS in Phytopathology, 1960; MS in Biochemistry, U. Wis., 1967, PhD in Biochemistry, 1969. Rsch. asst. Nat. Taiwan U., Taipei, 1961-62; instr. biochemistry Taipei Med. Coll., 1962-63; rsch. asst. U. Wis., Madison, 1963-69; rsch. assoc. Waksman Inst., New Brunswick, N.J., 1970-72; sr. scientist Hoffmann-La Roche Inc., Nutley, 1972-79, rsch. fellow, 1979-85, rsch. investigator, 1985-91, rsch. leader, 1991-2001, sr. rsch. leader, 2001—. Contbr. over 40 articles to profl. jours. including Jour. Antibiotics, Jour. Biol. Chemistry, Anti-microbial Agts. and Chemotherapy, Jour. Am. Chem. Soc.; mem. editl. bd. Jour. Antibiotics, 1992—. Life mem. Art Students League N.Y. Fellow Am. Acad. Microbiology; mem. Am. Chem. Soc., Soc. Indsl. Microbiology, European Soc. Animal Cell Tech., Am. Soc. Microbiology, Art Students League N.Y. (life). Achievements include 21 U.S. patents on new antibiotics and processes for their production; discovery of ionomycin as a Ca^{++} ionophore; discovery of antibiotic X-14868A as an anti-coccidial agt. trade name Cygro. Avocation: oil painting. Home: 36 Rockledge Pl Cedar Grove NJ 07009-1627 Office: Hoffmann-La Roche Inc 340 Kingsland St Nutley NJ 07110-1199 E-mail: chao-min.liu@roche.com.

LIU, CHARLES, astrophysicist; With Steward Obs., Tucson, 1997; cons. astrophysicist Ralph Appelbaum Assoc., N.Y.C., 1997—99; astrophysicist Am. Mus. Natural History; rsch. scientist dept. physics and astronomy Barnard Coll. Office: Am Mus Natural History Dept Astrophysics Central Park West at 79th St New York NY 10024*

LIU, CHIEN, sociologist, educator; b. Beijing, China, Jan. 20, 1959; came to U.S., 1985; s. Hongmei and Xingzeng (Tan) L.; m. Xiaoyan Zhang, May 14, 1996; 1 child, Alexander Hanqing. BA, Beijing Second Fgn. Lang. Inst, 1982; MA, Baylor U., Waco, Tex., 1987; PhD, Fla. State U., 1993. Vis. asst. prof. U. Memphis, 1993-95; prof. dept. sociology/anthropology Wagner Coll., N.Y.C., 1995—. Contbr. articles to profl. jours. NSF grantee, 2000. Mem. Am. Sociol. Assn. (Advancement of the Discipline award 1997). Avocations: reading, classical music, ping pong. Office: Wagner College Dept Sociology One Campus Rd Staten Island NY 10301 E-mail: chienliu@wagner.edu.

LIU, CHIU, transportation engineer, educator; b. Bo Luo, Canton, China, Oct. 25, 1964; came to U.S., 1984; parents Cho-hung Liu and Yan Jiang; m. Yan-hong Cheng, Aug. 7, 1996. BS, Calif. State U., 1986; PhD in Physics, U. Tex., 1993, MSCE, 1994, PhD in Civil Engring., 1997. Tchg. asst. U. Tex., Austin, 1987-93, 95; rsch. eng. asst. Ctr. Transportation Rsch., Tex., 1995-97, rsch. engr. assoc., 1997; mem. staff Dept. Civil Engring., El Paso, 1998; transportation engring. dir. Tex. Ctrs. Border Econ. Devel., 1998—. Adv. panel Tex. Dept. Transportation, Austin, 1998—; com. mem. Nat. Rsch. Coun., Washington, 1998—. Contbr. articles to profl. jours. including Jour. Transportation Engring., Transportation Rsch. Record, others. Adv. panel Metropolitan Planning Org., El Paso, 1998; coord. NAFTA Inst., El Paso, 1998. Fellow Advanced Inst. Transportation Engring., U. Tex., Austin, 1995-97. Mem. Nat. Soc. Profl. Engrs., Am. Soc. Civil Engrs., Am. Physical Soc., Sigma Xi. Achievements include development of sound theoretical frameworks for understanding the dynamic response of layered structures, eg. road structure to response tovehicle-road interaction, sound theoretical framework for predicting the evolution of surface profile of a layered road structure by linking together the vehicle dynamic characteristics, road surface characteristics and dynamic material properties of the road structures, a sound theoretical framework for rehabilitating road surfaces; rsch. in the control of vehicle flow, the geometric and physical design of roads, the theory of traffic flow, the transportation planning, and the evolution of pavement distress due to vehicle loading. Office: Tex Ctrs for Border Economic Devel Univ Tex El Paso TX 79968-0001

LIU, DAVID SHIAO-KUNG, physical scientist; b. Chung King, China, Aug. 27, 1940; s. Chen and Betty Shih Liu; m. Emily Tsai; children: John, Jeffrey, Joanne, Joanne. BSc, Nat. Cheng Kung U., Taiwan, 1962; MS, U. Calif., Berkeley, 1965; PhD, NYU, 1972. Registered profl. engr., N.Y., civil engr., Calif. Sr. scientist RAND Corp., Santa Monica, Calif., 1971—91; pres. Gen. Sys., Malibu, 1990—. Sr. advisor Sci. Adv. Bd., Office Prime Min., Taipei, Taiwan, 1987—2000; sr. cons. RAND Corp., Santa Monica, 1995—2000; prof. oceanographic engring. Nat. Cheng-Kung U., Tainan, Taiwan, 1980—87; adj. assoc. prof. U. So. Calif., L.A., 1977—85; sr. cons. Ministry of Econ. Affairs, Taipei, Taiwan, 1989—2000; sr. advisor Cen. Weather Bur., Taipei, Taiwan, 1986—2000; sr. cons. Coun. Econ. Devel., Taiwan, 1994—97, Naval Hydrographic Bur., Taiwan, 1981—96. 2d lt. mil. police, 1962—63, Taiwan. Achievements include development of 3-dimensional numerical model, water quality of N.Y. Harbor. Home: 3706 Oceanhill Way Malibu CA 90265-5640

LIU, DONALD C. mechanical engineer; b. Ithaca, N.Y., June 6, 1936; s. Chung Lo and Dorothy (Sze) L.; m. Elizabeth L. Hsu, Feb. 16, 1961; children: Thomas, Robert, Richard, William. BSME, Tsing Hua U., Beijing, 1958; MSME, Rsch. Inst. Machine Bldg. Industry, Fuzhou, China, 1962. Registered profl. engr., Conn. Tech. advisor Design Inst. Machine Bldg. Industry, Fujian, China, 1958-61; rsch. engr. Rsch. Inst. Machine Bldg. Industry, 1961-70; tech. suprervisory controller Sanming (Fujian) Gear Factory, 1970-74; supervisory controller Beijing Tech. Exch. Ctr., 1976-80; chief engr., tech. dir. Beijing Camera Factory, 1975-80; mech. specialist Lummus Co., Bloomfield, N.J., 1980-82; sr. project engr., project mgr. Moore Spl. Tool Co., Bridgeport, Conn., 1982-90; sr. project engr. Productor Machine Co., 1990-91; mgr. mech. engring. Thermatool Corp., East Haven, 1992-98; mgr. engring. Van Staal Corp., Stratford, 1998—2002. Contbr. articles to profl. jours. Mem. Soc. Mech. Engrs. (sr.). Home and Office: 39 Robinwood Rd Trumbull CT 06611-4923 E-mail: donaldliu@msn.com., dcliun@netscape.net.

LIU, ERNEST K. H. international banking executive, international financial consultant; b. Hong Kong, Oct. 4, 1950; came to U.S., 1979; s. Sun-Ip and Mei-Choi (Man) L.; m. Lily Chan, Dec. 5, 1979; children— Aimee On-On, Alvin Lok-Tin B.Social Sci., Hong Kong U., 1974; MBA in Fin., NYU, 1986. Lending officer Bank of Am. NT and SA, Hong Kong, 1974-76; market officer Hong Kong Trade Devel. Council, 1976-79, mgr. N.Y.C., 1979-82; asst. v.p. mktg. Honkong and Shanghi Banking Corp, 1982-83; sr. account exec. Citibank, N.A., 1984-88; asst. v.p. Merrill Lynch Internat. Pvt. Client Svcs., 1988-91; dir. Asia-Pacific Internat. Trade Promotion Ltd., 1991—. E-mail: ernestkliu@aol.com.

LIU, FENGHAI, engineer; b. Baotuo, China, Aug. 11, 1967; s. Erren Liu and Yuhua Zhou; m. Xiulan Chang, Aug. 12, 1992; 1 child, Tong. B in Electronic Engring., Tsinghua U., Beijing, 1990, M in Electronic Engring., 1992. Prof. asst. Tsinghua U., Beijing, 1992-94, lectr., 1994-97, assoc. prof., 1997—. Guest researcher Tech. U. Denmark, Lyngby, 1997-98. Contbr. articles to profl. jours.; inventor temperature controller. Mem. IEEE, Assn. Chinese Students and Scholars in Denmark. Avocations: sports, music, stamp collecting. Office: Mintera Corporation 1 Lowell Research Center 847 Rogers St Lowell MA 01852 Fax: 978-937-9790. E-mail: fenghai.liu@mintera.com.

LIU, GANGHUA, biologist, physician; b. Anshan, Liaoning, China, May 12, 1962; d. Jiouqiao Liu and Linan Peng; children: Xinqi (Mike) Ren. PhD IN BIOLOGY, Univ.Of Texas At San Antonio, San Antonio, Tx Usa, 1997—2001; MEDICINE DEGREE (MD), China Medical University, China, 1979—84. Postdoctoral fellow UNIV. OF TX HEALTH SCIENCE CENTER AT SAN ANTONIO, San Antonio, 2001—02; doctoral researcher UNIV. OF TX AT SAN ANTONIO, 1997—2001. Research assistant UNIV. OF TX AT SAN ANTONIO, San Antonio, 1995—97; doctor and scientist INSTITUTE OF BIOLOGY AND CHILDREN'S HOSPITAL, Nanchang, Jiangxi, China, 1984—96. Author: (doctoral dissertation) CARDIOVASCULAR AND BEHAVIORAL EFFECT OF SEROTONIO 1 A RECEPTORS IN THE DORSAL DENTATE GYRUS OF THE HIPPOCAMPUS IN RATS, 2001. Mem.: INTERNATINAL BEHAVR NEUROSCIENCE. Home: 4060 Medical Dr. #804 San Antonio TX 78229 Office: Univ. Of Texts Health Science Center 7703 Floyd Curl San Antonio TX 78229 Personal E-mail: gliu_98@yahoo.com. Business E-Mail: liug0@uthscsa.edu.

LIU, HANLI, biomedical engineer, educator; b. Beijing, China, Mar. 6, 1960; d. Li-ya Wang and Zhongcheng Liu; m. Anqi Wu, July 6, 1957; children: Eric Wu, Rodney Wu. PhD in Physics, Wake Forest U., Winston-Salem, N.C., 1994. Rsch. assoc. U. City Sci. Ctr., Phila., 1992—96; post-doctoral fellow U. of Pa, 1994—96; asst. prof. of biomed. engring. U. of Tex. , Arlington, 1996—2001, assoc. prof. of biomedical engring., 2001—. Adj. faculty mem. joint program in biomed. engring. U. Tex. Southwestern Med. Ctr., Dallas, 1996—2002. Recipient Outstanding Young Scientist award, Houston Soc. for Engring. in Medicine and Biology, 1998, Outstanding Young Faculty Award, Coll. of Engring. , U. of Tex., Arlington, 1999. Mem.: IEEE, Optical Soc. of Am. Home: 706 Gunnison Ct Arlington TX 76006 Office: Univ Texas at Arlington P.O. Box 19138 Arlington TX 76019 Office Fax: 817-272-2251. Business E-Mail: hanli@uta.edu.

LIU, HAN-SHOU, space scientist, researcher; b. Hunan, China, Mar. 9, 1930; came to U.S., 1960, naturalized, 1972; s. Yu-Tin and Chun-Chen (Yeng) L.; m. Sun-Ling Yang Liu, May 2, 1957; children: Michael Fu-Yen, Peter Fu-Tze. PhD, Cornell U., 1963. Rsch. asst. Cornell U., 1962-63; rsch. assoc. Nat. Acad. Sci., Washignton, 1963-65; scientist NASA Goddard Space Flight Ctr., Greenbelt, Md., 1965—. Contbr. articles to profl. jours. Pres., Mei-Hwa Chinese Sch., 1980-81. Fellow AAAS; mem. AIA, Am. Astron. Soc., Am. Geophys. Union, Planetary Soc. Office: NASA Goddard Space Flight Ctr Code # 921 Greenbelt MD 20771-0001 E-mail: hanshou@core2.gsfc.nasa.gov.

LIU, HENRY, engineering educator, researcher, consultant; b. Peking, China, June 3, 1936; came to U.S., 1961; s. Yen-Huai and Remei (Bardina) L.; m. Susie Dou-Mei Chou, Dec. 16, 1964; children: Jerry B., Jason C., Jeffrey H. BS, Nat. Taiwan U., Taipei, 1959; MS, Colo. State U., 1963, PhD, 1966. Registered profl. engr., Mo. Asst. prof. U. Mo., Columbia, 1965-69, assoc. prof., 1969-76, prof. engring., 1976—, Natural Gas Pipeline Co. prof. engring., 1983-90; James C. Dowell prof. engring., 1990—. Dir. Capsule Pipeline Rsch. Ctr., 1991—; vis. expert Nat. Taiwan U., Taipei, 1980; vis. prof. U. Melbourne, Australia, 1980; cons. wind energy Taiwan Power Co., Taipei, 1982—. Contbr. articles to profl. jours.; patentee in coal-log and capsule pipelines; inventor coal log pipeline. Recipient Disting. Lecture award Internat. Symposium on Freight Pipelines, 1982 Mem. ASCE (chmn. aerodynamics com. 1976-80, chmn. exec. com. aerospace divsn. 1988-89, chmn. pipeline rsch. com. 1991-94, Aerospace Sci. & Tech. award 1983, Bechtel Pipeline Engring. award 1992), Am. Soc. Engring. Edn. (mem. exec. com. mechanics divsn. 1982-85), Internat. Freight Pipeline Soc. (pres. 1989-94), U.S. Wind Engring. Rsch. Coun. (bd. dirs. 1985-89). Unitarian Universalist. Home: 3212 Woodbine Dr Columbia MO 65203-0976 Office: Univ Mo Dept Civil Engring Columbia MO 65211-0001

LIU, HSIEN-TUNG, dean; b. Canton, China, Feb. 17, 1935; s. Chiu-Nan Liu and Shiu-Fan Wu; m. Li-Ping Hsieh, June 5, 1964; children: Benjamin, Lisa. BA, Nat. Taiwan U., 1958; MA, Calif. State U., Chico, 1962; PhD, Claremont Grad. U., 1967. Asst. prof. Calif. State U., Chico, 1965-67, Point Park Coll., Pitts., 1967—78, v.p., dean, 1987-91, prof., 1978—91; dean Bloomsburg (Pa.) U., 1991—. Reviewer IREX, U.S. Info. Agy., Washington, 1983. Author: Border Disputes Between Imperial China and Tsarist Russia, 1968; editor Bull. Internat. Soc. Ednl. Cultural Scientific Interchanges, 1974-78. Mem. adv. bd. mil. vet. edn. Pa. Dept. Edn., Harrisburg, 1987-91, charter sch. commn., 1997—; mem. charter sch. adv. bd. Am. Acad. Liberal Edn., Washington, 2000—. Recipient stipend NEH, 1975; Douglas MacArthur scholar Calif. State U., 1961-62, Inst. for Ednl. Mgmt. scholar Harvard U., 1995; Claremont Grad. U. fellow, 1962-64. Mem. Am. Polit. Sci. Assn., Am. Assn. Univ. Adminstrs., Coun. Colls. Arts Scis. Office: Bloomsburg U Pa 400 E 2nd St Bloomsburg PA 17815

LIU, JIE, chemist; PhD, Harvard U., 1996. Asst. prof. Duke U., Durham, NC, 1999—. Office: Duke U Dept Chemistry Durham NC 27708 Office Fax: 919-660-1605. Business E-Mail: j.liu@duke.edu.

LIU, JING-QIU, education educator; b. Beijing, China, Sept. 15, 1951; came to U.S., 1987; m. Luzheng Shen, June 26, 1979; 1 child, Yu Lisa. MS, Iowa State U., 1989, PhD, 1992. Sr. tchr. Baoding H.S., China, 1977-87; rsch. asst. Iowa State U., Ames, 1987-92, rsch. assoc. Rsch. Inst. for Studies in Edn., 1993, temp. instr. Sch. Edn., 1993-94; asst. prof. edn. Troy (Ala.) State U., 1994-98, Eastern Wash. U., 1998—, assoc. prof. edn., 2001—. Contbr. articles to profl. jours. Recipient Women Tchr. Awards for excellence in instrn. Baoding Dist., China, 1979, 86; Ctr. for Internat. Edn., Coll. of Edn., Iowa State U. Grad. Asst. award, 1992; Internat. Peace scholar, 1988-89. Mem. Nat. Assn. Multicultural Edn., Am. Edn. Assn., Phi Kappa Phi, Phi Delta Kappa. E-mail: Jane.Liu@mail.ewu.edu.

LIU, JINGZHI, biophysicist, neuroscientist; b. Qingdao, China, Feb. 6, 1970; s. Yanchuan Liu and Shuxiang Bing; m. Aihua Cong, May 2, 1997; children: Kelvin, Katherine. PhD, Case Western Res. U., 2000. Rsch. engr. Cleve. Clinic Found., 1998-2000, project staff, 2000—. Adj. prof. Case Western Res. U., Cleve., 2000—, Cleve. State U., 2001—. Contbr. articles to profl. jours. Kang Youwei scholarship The Kang Youwei Found., 1987, Zhang Zongzhi scholarship U. Sci. and Tech. of China, 1992. Mem. AAAS, Am. Phys. Soc., The Biomed. Engring. Soc., The Biophys. Soc., Internat. Soc. for Magnetic Resonance in Medicine, Internat. Brain Rsch. Orgn., Soc. for Neurosci., Am. Physiol. Soc. Avocations: fishing, reading. Office: Cleve Clinic Found BME-ND20 9500 Euclid Ave Cincinnati OH 44195 E-mail: liuj@bme.ri.ccf.org.

LIU, KATHERINE CHANG, artist, art educator; b. Kiang-si, China; came to U.S., 1963; d. Ming-fan and Ying (Yuan) Chang; m. Yet-zen Liu; children: Alan S., Laura Y. MS, U. Calif., Berkeley, 1965. Instr. U. Va. Ext., Longwood Coll.; mem. tchg. staff Intensive Studies Seminar, Santa Fe, 1995, 96, 97, 98, 99, 2000, 2002; invited mem. L.A. Artcore Reviewing and Curatorial Bd., 1993; invited juror, lectr. over 75 exhbns. and orgns., Kans., S.C. Watercolor Socs., 1998, Alaska, Ga., Tex. and Okla. Watercolor Soc. Anns., 1997, Adirondacks Nat. Show, N.Y., 1999, Ann. Exhibit Watercolor Ohio, 1999, Watercolor Soc. Oreg., 1999, The Collage Soc. Am., 1999; juror, lectr. Ala. Watercolor Soc. Ann., 1996, Midwest Watercolor Soc. Nat. Exhibit, 1996, Watercolor West Nat. Open, 1996, Charlotte County Open Nat., Fla., 2000; sole juror The Taos (N.Mex.) Exhbn. Am. Watercolor, 2000, Va. Watercolor Soc. Ann., Richmond, 2001, Rocky Mountain Nat. Competition, 2001, also others; chmn. jury selection Nat. Watercolor Soc. 80th Annual Competition Exhbn., 2000; sole juror Rocky Mountain Nat. Watermedia Competition, Colo., 2001, ann. show Va. Watercolor Soc., 2001, Collage/Assemblage/USA I, Ventura (Calif.) Coll. 2001, Collage/Assemblage/USA II, 2002. One-woman shows include Harrison Mus., Utah State U., Riverside (Calif.) Art Mus., Ventura (Calif.) Coll., Fla. A&M U., Gail Harvey Gallery, Santa Monica, 1998, J.J. Brookings Gallery, San Francisco, 1998, Louis Newman Galleries, L.A., L.A. Artcore, Lung-Men Gallery, Taipei, Republic of China, Lew Allen Contemporary, Santa Fe Drawing Exhibit, Golden West Collage Gallery, 1999, Rosaline Koener Gallery, Westhampton, N.Y., 2000, AMA Gallery, Turku, Finland, 2001, Gail Harvey Gallery, Santa Monica, Calif., 2001, Rosaline Koener Gallery, LI, N.Y., 2002, Galerie Egelund, Copenhagen, 2002; invitational shows include: Crossing Cultures, Lewallen Contemporary, 1998, State of the Arts International Biennial, Parkland Coll. Ill., 1989, 91, 97, Treasures for the Community: The Chrysler Mus. Collects, 1989-96, 97, Watercolor U.S.A. Hon. Soc. Invitational, 1989, 91, 93, 95, 97, Hunter Mus. Art, Tenn., 1993, Bakersfield Art Mus., 1994, Sandra Walters Gallery, Hong Kong, 1994, Horwitch-Newman Gallery, Scottsdale, Ariz., 1995, Hong Kong U. Sci. and Tech. Libr. Art Gallery, 1996, J.J. Brookings Gallery, San Francisco, 1996, 97, 98, John N Joe Gallery, L.A., 1996, Bill Armstrong Gallery, Springfield, Mo., 1996, Chrysler Mus. Fine Art, Norfolk, Va., 1997, U. B.C. Art Gallery, 1992, U. Sydney Art Mus., 1992, Ruhr-West Art Mus., Wise, 1992, Macau Art Mus., 1992, Rosenfeld Gallery, Phila., 1994, Mandarin Oriental Fine Arts, Hong Kong, 1994, Hampton U. Mus., 2000, Fukuoka Asian Art Mus., 2001, Lew Allen Contemporary Gallery, N.Mex., 2001, Asian Am. Artists, Calif. State Channel Islands, Calif., 2002, What About Beauty, Invitational Foothills Art Ctr., Golden, Colo., 2002; contbr. works to 24 books and 46 periodicals. Co-curator Taiwan-USA-Australia Watermedia Survey Exhbn., Nat. Taiwan Art Inst., 1994; sole juror San Diego Watermedia Internat., 1993, Triton Mus. Open Competition, 1994, Northern Nat. Art Competition, 1994, Watercolor West Nat., 1993, Tenn., Utah, Hawaii, N.C. Watercolor Socs., North Am. Open, Midwest Southwest and over 30 state-wide competitions in watermedia or all-media; co-juror Rocky Mountain Nat., San Diego Internat. and West Fedn. Exhibits. Recipient Rex Brandt award San Diego Watercolor Internat., 1985, Purchase Selection award Watercolor USA and Springfield (Mo.) Art Mus., 1981, Gold medal, 1986, Mary Lou Fitzgerald meml. award Allied Arts Am. Nat. Arts Club, N.Y.C., 1987, Achievement award of Artists Painting in Acrylic Am. Artists Mag., 1993; NEA grantee, 1979-80. Mem. Nat. Watercolor Soc. (life, chmn. jury 1985, pres. 1983, Top award 1984, cash awards 1979, 87; chmn. jury selection 80th ann. open competition exhibit 2000), Watercolor U.S.A. Honor Soc., Nat. Soc. Painters in Casein and Acrylic (2nd award 1985), Rocky Mountain Nat. Watermedia Soc. (juror 1984, awards 1978, 80, 86). E-mail: KchangLiu@aol.com.

LIU, KE JIAN, medical educator; b. Xian, Shaanxi, China, Sept. 19, 1961; s. Huanqi and Kun (Liao) L.; m. Jiao Ding, Oct. 20, 1989; children: Sarah, Evan. BSc, Beijing U., 1982; PhD, U. Leeds, 1988. Rsch. assoc. U. Norte Dame, South Bend, Ind., 1988-89; rsch. spl. U. Ill., Urbana, 1990-93; asst. prof. Dartmouth Coll., Hanover, N.H., 1993—. Contbr. articles to profl. jours. Mem. Am. Chemical Soc., Am. Assoc. Adv. Sci., Internat. EPR Soc. Office: Dartmouth Med Sch 7785 Vail Hanover NH 03755 E-mail: jliu@unm.edu.

LIU, KEVIN H. research scientist, computer scientist; b. Beijing, Jan. 23, 1970; B Engring., Beijing U. Sci. and Tech., 1991; grad. diploma in computer sci., Royal Melbourne Inst. Tech., Australia, 1992; M Bus. Sys., Monash U., Melbourne, 1993; PhD in Computer Sci., Victoria U. Tech., Melbourne, Australia, 1997. Rsch. asst. Victoria U. Tech., 1994-96, lectr., 1996-97; mem.

rsch. faculty Rutgers U., New Brunswick, N.J., 1997-98; rsch. scientist Telcordia Techs., Red Bank, 1998—. Mem. tech. program com. IEEE Internat. Conf. on Computer Comm. and Networks, 2000-01. Contbr. articles to profl. jours., including IIEEE Transactions on Comms., IEEE Jouur. Lightwave Tech., IEEE Jour. on Selected Areas in Comm., IEEE Network Mag., others; author: IP over WDM, 2001. Mem. IEEE, Assn. for Computing Machinery. Office: Telcordia Techs 850 NW Island Terr A8 Beaverton OR 97006 Office Fax: 503-439-9108. Business E-Mail: kliu@iee.org.

LIU, LIN SHU, biomaterials scientist; b. Shangtou, China, Nov. 15, 1948; came to U.S., 1990; s. Shu Zheng Liu and Zheng Ying Wang; 1 child, Xing Liu. BS, South China Normal U., Gang Zhou, China, 1976, MS, 1982; PhD, Kyoto (Japan) U., 1990. Asst. prof. South China Normal U., 1982-85; postdoctoral assoc. dept. chem. engring. MIT, Cambridge, 1990-92; rsch. scientist Telios Pharm., Inc., San Diego, 1992-94; principal scientist Advanced Polymer Sys., Inc., Redwood City, 1994-96; sr. scientist Orquest, Inc., Mountain View, 1996-99, prin. scientist, 1999—2001, BiolMed Inc, San Luis Obispo, 2001—02; rsch. chemist USDA, ARRS, ERRC, Phila., 2002—. Vis. scientist Kyoto U., 1985-87. Contbr. chpts. to books and articles to sci. jours. Recipient Sci. Progress award Guandong, China, 1987; Imanishi scholar Kyoto U., 1988-90; grantee Commn. of European Communities, 1990. Mem. Am. Chem. Soc., Controlled Release Soc., Soc. for Biomaterials. Achievements include patents for biomaterials of implantable and injectable matrices for growth factor, cytokine, protein delivery, and for bone/cartilage repair, wound healing, design and synthesis. Home: Apt 18-0 7600 Stenton Ave Philadelphia PA 19118 Office: USDA ARS Ea Region Rsch Ctr 600 E Mermaid Ln Glenside PA 19038 E-mail: isliu@arserrc.gov.

LIU, LINDA, endocrinologist; b. Geneva, May 11, 1954; d. Tsing-Chang and Eileen (Lee) Liu; m. Cheng-Yunn Willia Wuu, Dec. 5, 1986; children: Stanley Yen, Roland Yen. BA, Wellesley Coll., 1976; MD, Brown U., 1980. Intern, resdient Hahnemann U. Hosp. Ctr., Phila.; intern, resident Hahnemann U. Hosp., 1980-82; resident Meml. Hosp., Worcester, Mass., 1982-83; rsch. fellow NIH, Bethesda, Md., 1986-88, andrology cons., 1988-90, 93—; pvt. practice, Rockville. Fellow ACP; mem. Am. Diabetes Assn., Endocrine Soc., Montgomery County Med. Soc., Phi Beta Kappa. Office: Endocrine/Diabetes Assocs 6001 Montrose Rd Ste 211 Rockville MD 20852-4872 E-mail: lliu511@msn.com.

LIU, LUMEI, chemistry researcher; b. Cheng-du, China, Apr. 20, 1939; came to U.S., 1985; d. Feng-Wu Liu and Zon-sheiw Lue; m. Dezhao Wang, Aug. 1, 1961; children: Yu Wang, Xin Wang. Bachelor, Beijing Normal U., 1959, PhD, 1988. Asst. prof. Beijing Normal U., 1959-82; TV lectr. Dept. Chinese Edn., Beijing, 1979-83; assoc. prof. Beijing Normal U., 1988-89; postdoctoral dept. chemistry U. Houston, 1989-92; rschr. U. Houston Superconductor Ctr., 1992—96; rsch. assoc. U. Houston Materials Ctr., 1996—2001; scientist, rsch. faculty U. Houston, 2001—. Vis. scholar U. Houston, 1985-87. Author: Inorganic Chemistry, 1990; contbr. articles to profl. jours. Named one of Women at Their Best, Glamour Mag., Dec. 1999. Mem. Chinese Assn. Profl. Sci. and Tech. Office: Univ Houston Dept Chemistry Calhoun 4800 Houston TX 77204-0001 E-mail: lliu@mail.uh.edu.

LIU, MARGARET C. music educator; b. Canton, China, Aug. 10, 1947; came to the U.S., 1972; d. Man-Hymn Wong and Shau-Chung Ng; m. John Pui-Chee, July 28, 1973; children: Amos Tao-Peng, Deborah Tao-En. BA, Hong Kong Bapt. U., 1970; M in Ch. Music, Southwestern Bapt. Theol. Sem., 1975. Freelance vocal and keyboard performer, various cities, 1972—; pvt. music tchr., 1975; music dir. 1st Chinese Bapt. Ch., Atlanta, 1976-80, 85-89, Chinese Bapt. Ch., College Park, Md., 1980-83; pres., CEO Cambridge Acad. Music and Arts, Atlanta, 1999—. Bd. mem. Alliance Theatre Edn. Adv. Coun., Atlanta, 1996-99; pres. North Dekalb Music Tchrs. Assn., Atlanta, 1997-99; Ga. local rep. Associated Bd. of the Royal Schs. Music, London, 1997—. Deacon Hanley Rd. Bapt. Ch., St. Louis, 1984. Mem. Music Tchrs. Nat. Assn., Music Educators Nat. Conf., Nat. Guild Piano Tchrs., Kindermusik Educators Assn.

LIU, MARGARET M. fabric company executive; b. China, July 24, 1946; d. I-Yung and K-Ming (Huan) L.; m. Shau-Chung Hu, Feb. 14, 1984; 1 child. Z.G. BA, Christian Coll., Taipei, Taiwan, 1974; MBA, Lincoln U., 1983; BBA, Nat. Acad. Mgmt., Taipei, 1980. Dir., pres. Am. Hubei Assoc., N.Y.C.; dir. Nat. Acad. Mgmt., Taipei; dir., pres. China Natural Fabric Corp., Bklyn. Hostess TV and radio program Computer and You, China TV Co., Cen. Radio Sta., 1970-73. Mem. Nat. Rep. Congl. Com. Recipient award Fend Chia U., Taipei, Taiwan Internat. Conf. on Computerized Bus. Simulations, 1976, Taiwan Merchants Assn. N.Y., Inc. Home: 1025 45th St Apt 1D Brooklyn NY 11219-1904 Address: PO Box 190716 Brooklyn NY 11219-0716

LIU, MAW-SHUNG, physiologist, dentist; b. Taiwan, Republic of China, Feb. 2, 1940; came to U.S., 1968; s. Chao-Tung and Chian (Hwang) L.; m. Min-Chau Chang, Sept. 15, 1966; 1 child, Chien-Ye. DDS, Kaohsiung Med. U., Taiwan, 1964; PhD, U. Ottawa, Can., 1976. Cert. by Coun. Nat. Bd. Dental Examiners. Intern in pathology U. Ky., Lexington, 1968-69; instr. physiology La. State U. Med. Ctr., New Orleans, 1974-76, asst. prof., 1976-78; assoc. prof. Sch. of Medicine, Wake Forest U., Winston-Salem, N.C., 1978-82; prof. St. Louis U. Sch. Medicine, 1982—. Vis. prof. Beijing Med. U., 1984-, Zhejiang Med. U., 1986, Kaohsiung Med. U., 1989-, Chang Gung Med. Coll., 1989-; mem. surgery, anesthesiology and trauma study sect. NIH, 1988—92. Mem. editl. bd. Circulatory Shock, 1982-93, Shock, 1993—; contbr. over 90 articles and 90 papers to profl. jours. Named hon. prof. Nanjing Med. Univ., 1984, Hunan Med. Univ., 1988; grantee Nat. Heart Lung and Blood Inst., Inst. Gen. Med. Sci., 1977—. Mem. Internat. Soc. Heart Rsch., Am. Physiol. Soc., The Shock Soc. Achievements include first to significant contribution to the understanding of molecular pathogenesis of myocardial and hepatic dysfunction during shock, sepsis and trauma. Office: St Louis U Sch Medicine Dept Pharm and Physiol Sci 1402 S Grand Blvd Saint Louis MO 63104-1004 E-mail: Lium@slu.edu.

LIU, MEILIN, electrochemical educator; m. Xueying Zhang; children: Elbert, Allen. PhD, U. Calif., Berkeley. CPA. Prof. Ga. Inst. Tech., Atlanta, 1992—2002. Recipient National Young Investigator Award, NSF, 1993-98. Mem.: Electrochemical Soc. (Executive Member of High Temperature Materials Division 1996—2002). Office: Ga Inst Tech 771 Ferst Dr Atlanta GA 30332-0245 Office Fax: 404-894-9140.

LIU, MICHAEL MINORU FAWN, federal agency administrator; b. Honolulu, Sept. 7, 1953; s. George Y. H. and Marian (Doi) L.; m. Susan Orlando, May 1, 1988; 1 child, Nicholas. BA, Stanford U., 1974; JD, U. Hawaii, 1977. Bar: Hawaii 1977, U.S. Ct. Appeals (9th cir.). Chief minority atty. State Ho. of Reps., Hawaii, 1978-80, state rep., 1980-82; mktg. chief, counsel Knight Devel. Corp., 1981-83; state rep. State Ho. of Rep., 1984-90; owner Advantage Land Co., 1989-91; dep. under sec. small community and rural devel. USDA, Washington, 1991-92, dep. asst. sec. natural resource and environ., 1992-93; acting adminstr. Rural Electrification Adminstn., 1991-92; v.p. community reinvestment act & govt. affairs Bank of Am., Honolulu, 1993—; state senator State of Hawaii, 1994—; asst. secy. public indian housing U.S. Dept. H.U.D., Washington, 2001—. Republican. Office: US Dept HUD Public & Indian Housing 451 7th St SW Washington DC 20410-9000*

LIU, PAMELA PEI-LING, landscape architect, graphics designer; b. Taipei, Taiwan, Jan. 31, 1951; came to U.S., 1968; d. Hoh-Tu and Julia C.Y. (Sheng) L. BS, Marywood Coll., 1972; MLA , U. Va., 2002. Calligrapher Geyer Studio, N.Y.C., 1972-74; artist James Bell Graphic Design, 1974-75; freelance artist, designer, art dir., 1975-81; ptnr. Triptic Graphics Inc., 1981-91; pres. LIU Comms. & Design, Inc., 1991—2001. Mem. AABGA, US/ICOMOS, NOW, Am. Soc. Landscape Archs., Women in Arts (charter), Nat. Trust for Hist. Preservation, New Eng. Garden History Soc., Sierra Club. Avocations: Chinese and French languages, travel, gardening, photography.

LIU, PETER ANDREW, psychologist; b. London, Mar. 11, 1955; arrived in Hong Kong, 1957; s. Tse-Ming Benjamin and Anne-Marie (Marent) L.; m. Gillian Ann Choa, Mar. 1, 1990 (div. Nov. 1996); children: Alexandra Marie, George Benjamin. BSc with honors, U. Toronto, Ont., Can., 1975, PhD, 1981; MA, U. Guelph, Toronto, 1976. Registered profl. psychologist. Cons., psychologist Toronto Bd. Edn., 1981-88; prin. cons. Hay Mgmt. Cons., Hong Kong, 1988-89; assoc. exec. dir. Inst. Mgmt. U. Hong Kong, 1990-97; mng. dir., bus. cons. Forum Asia Ltd., Hong Kong, 1997-99; gen. mgr. The Psychol. Corp., Toronto, 2000—. Vis. lectr. Ludwig Maximillian U., Munich, 1983-85; Can. Coun. fellow Children's Hosp., Ottawa, Ont., 1977-79; intern Polyclin., U. Zürich, 1982. Contbr. articles to profl. publs. Mem. Ont. Club (Toronto, non-resident). Roman Catholic. Avocations: tennis, Chinese antiques, modern art, jazz. Home: 1002-20 Avoca Ave Tornto ON Canada M4T 288 Office: Harcourt Canada Ltd 55 Horner Ave Toronto ON Canada M82 4X6 E-mail: peter_lie@harcourt.com.

LIU, RALPH YIEH-MIN, investment management and banking executive; b. Taiwan, Republic of China, Aug. 24, 1958; came to U.S., 1983; m. Laura Liu. BSE, Nat. Taiwan U., l981; M ChemE, Rice U., l984; postgrad., U. Mich., l985; MBA, MSE, U. Pa., Wharton Bus. Sch., l987; postgrad., NYU, 1989. Assoc. 1st Boston Corp., N.Y.C., 1986; investment rep. Morgan Stanley & Co., 1987-89; pres. RYL Corp., 1989—; currency options dealer Global Securities and Fgn. Exch., Chem. Banking Corp., 1989-90; pres., chief exec. officer RYL Corp., 1990—; treas. AT&T Capital Corp., Morristown, N.J., 1990-91; derivative products mgr., head trader Equitable Capital Mgmt. Corp., N.Y.C., 1991-92; v.p. trading, sales and risk mgmt. Union Bank of Switzerland, Singapore, 1992-93; mng. dir. Chase Manhattan Asia Ltd., Hong Kong, 1993-95, Advanced Risk Mgmt. Solutions Pte Ltd., Singapore, 1995—; chmn., CEO Advanced e-Fin. Techs., Inc., 2000—. Co. chair, Singapore Dinner Cmte., Intl. Assn. of Fin. Engrs. Author software Portfolio Analysis, 1996, VaR and VaR Derivatives, 1997, Pricing Issues of VaR Deribatives, 1998. Mem. coun. Fresh Air Fund, N.Y.C., 1988—, Fedn. Protestant Welfare Agys., N.Y.C., 1988—, Morris-Jumel Mansion, Inc., N.Y.C., 1992—. Rice U. fellow, 1983, Rackham grad. fellow U. Mich., l984, IBM Mgmt. Info. fellow U. Pa., 1986. Mem. IEEE, Am. Inst. Chem. Engrs., Ops. Rsch. Soc. Am., Am. Mgmt. Soc., Asian Fin. Soc., Princeton Club, Wharton Bus. Sch. Club N.Y., Am. Stock Exch. Club, Internat. Assn. Fin. Engrs. (co-chmn. Singapore dinner com.). Avocations: travel, reading, golf, tennis, squash. E-mail: ralph.liu.wg87@wharton.upenn.edu., ryliu@yahoo.com.

LIU, RHONDA LOUISE, librarian; b. Honolulu; d. David Yuk Fong Liu and Shirley May Chong Liu. BA, U. Hawaii at Manoa, Honolulu, 1974, M of Libr. Info. Studies, 1991; grad., FBI Citizens Acad., 1998. Remote regions/homework ctrs. outreach libr. Alu Like Native Hawaiian Libr. Project, 1992; libr. II Hawaii State Libr., 1992; fgn. expert libr. studies in English program Beijing Fgn. Studies U., 1992—93; info. specialist Savs. & Cmty. Bankers of Am., Washington, 1993—94; staff specialist III Md. State Dept. Edn., Md. State Libr. for Blind and Physically Handicapped, Balt., 1995—99; asst. project mgr. Serial Record Holdings Conversion Project/LSSI Libr. of Congress, Washington, 2000; reference libr. George Washington U. at Mt. Vernon Coll., 2000—01; sr. technician, serial record divsn. Libr. of Congress, 2001—02, serials control specialist, serial record divsn., 2002—. Libr. asst. Legis. Reference Bur. Libr., 1989-90; asst. rschr. Legis. Info. Sys. Office, 1984-85; ESL tutor Keimei Gakuen, Tokyo, 1979; exhibit facilitator Smithsonian Instn., 1999. Active Friends of the Md. State Libr. for Blind and Physically Handicapped, 1994-99, Md. State Dept. Edn. Employees' Adv. Coun., 1998-99; sec. Coalition Opposed to Violence and Extremism, State of Md., 1997-99; v.p., sec. U. Hawaii Sch. Libr. and Info. Studies, 1990-91. Alu Like Native Hawaiian Libr. fellow, 1990-91; Kamehameha Schs./Bishop Estate scholar, 1991. Mem. U. Hawaii Alumni Assn., U. Hawaii Sch. Lib. and Info. Studies Alumni Assn., Kamehameha Schs. Alumni Assn. (East Coast region), Lung Kong Kung Shaw Soc., Libr. Congress Profl. Assn. Avocations: gourmet cooking, multi-cultural activities, overseas travel, hula. E-mail: rliu@loc.gov.

LIU, ROGER KIM SING, accountant; b. Honolulu, July 25, 1934; s. Roger O.K. and Alice (Mar) L.; m. Sandra Jean Ching, Aug. 9, 1958; children: Rouen, RoJeanne, RoAnne, Ian, Royd. BA, U. Hawaii, 1956; postgrad., Golden Gate U., 1957. CPA, Hawaii. Acct., sr. tax auditor Peat, Marwick, Mitchell, Honolulu, 1958-62; pvt. practice acctg., 1963—. Account exec. E.A. Buck Co., Inc.; dir., officer Broadcast Svcs., Inc., Honolulu, Ellaric Corp., Honolulu, Chadel; lectr. U. Hawaii, Honolulu C.C. Bd. dirs. Cath. Youth Orgn., Honolulu, 1983, Palolo Chinese Home, 1997, Friends of Royal Hawaiian Band, Hawaii Found. for Chinese Culture and Arts; treas. Jeremy Harris Mayor of Honolulu Campaign Com., 1997-98; treas. PTA, Honolulu, 1981; treas. Hawaii Chinese History Ctr., 1983, now pres., chmn. 1994 Conf. from Memories to Aspirations: The Chinese Am. Experience; pres. U. Hawaii Art Assn., 1984, Waialae Iki Ridge Cmty. Assn.; founder Chinese Cmty. Action Coalition; pres. Tai Koong Chinese Sch., 2000. Mem. AICPA, Hawaii Soc. CPA's (chmn. edn. com., lectr., taxation cons., chmn. legis com.), Nat. Fedn. Ind. Bus., Am. Assn. Ind. Investors (life), Acad. Arts, Honolulu Contemporary Mus., U. Hawaii Alumni Asn. (life), U.S. C. of C., Honolulu Opera, Honolulu Symphony, Honolulu Jaycees (bd. dirs. 1966-68), Newman Club (bd. dirs. 1954-56), Peng Hui (pres. 1954-56, conf. chmn. 1994). Home: 1531 Ipukula St Honolulu HI 96821-1419 Office: 1221 Kapiolani Blvd Penthouse Blackfield Bldg Honolulu HI 96814

LIU, RUTH WANG, educator, researcher; b. China, Feb. 25, 1945; d. James D. and Anna H. Wang; m. C.Y. Liu, Feb. 21, 1975; children: Brian, Lora. BS, Union Coll., 1966; MS, U. Calif., San Francisco, 1967; EdD, U. Tenn., 1997. Asst. prof. Sch. of Nursing Loma Linda U., Calif., 1968-72; clin. nurse specialist Cmty. Mental Health, San Francisco, 1972-75; adminstr. Chattanooga Women's Laser Ctr., 1976-95; coord. East Tenn. Consortium for Higher Edn. U. Tenn., 1998—, postdoctoral rsch. assoc., 1998-2000; dir. Institutional Rsch. and Planning, So. Adventist U., Collegedale, Tenn., 2000—. Adj. prof. So. Adventist U., Collegedale, Tenn., 1996-2000, cons. 1975; lectr., rschr., cons., 1990—; cons. Taiwan Adventist Hosp., Taipei, Taiwan, 1974, Atlantic Union Coll., South Lancaster, Mass., 1970; adv. bd. Kiddie Kampus, Collegedale, 1994—; bd. dirs. Cmty. Trust & Banking, Ooltewah, Tenn. Contbr. articles to profl. jours. Exec. com. Ga. Cumberland Conf. of Seventh-day Adventists, Calhoun, Ga., 1997—; adv. bd. Seventh-day Adventist Ch., Collegedale, 1999—; bd. dirs. Good Samaritan Sanitarium and Hosp., Knoxville, Ill., 1970—; trustee, bd. dirs. Chinese Internat. Missions, Dunlap, Tenn., 2001—. Mem. Am. Assn. for Higher Edn., Assn. for Instnl. Rschrs., Soc. Coll. and Univ. Planners, Sigma Theta Tau, Phi Kappa Phi. Seventh-day Adventist. Avocations: music, swimming, hiking.

LIU, SHENGSHENG, chemistry research scientist; b. Anqin, Anhui, China, Dec. 22, 1966; s. Fangan Liu and Xiaoxia Zhu; m. Yunqiu Jia, July 12, 1994; children: Brenda Xihe, Stephen Yimeng. BS in Chemistry, Anhui Normal U., Wahu, China, 1991; MS in Polymer Sci., Chinese Acad. of Scis., Changchun, China, 1994, PhD, 1997. Postdoctoral research assoc. Penn. State U., 1997—. Research scientist Penn. State U., 1997—. Author: Ethylene/a-olefin copolymerization with supported Cp2ZrCl2 catalysts, Chinese Jour. of Applied Chemistry, 1995, Soluble Metallocene catalysts for olefin polymerization, Orgaometallic Chemistry and Catalysis, 1997, Polymerization of ethylene by zinconocene / B(C6F5)3 catalysts with aluminum compounds, Jour. of Applied Polymer Science, 1997, Polymer-supported titanium catalysts for ethylene polymerization, Chinese Polymeric Materials Science and Engineering, 1998, Preparation of polymer-supported metallocene catalysts for alefin polymerization, Journal of Applied Polymer Science, 1999, Synthesis of novel graft-like copolymer of syndiotactic polystyrnen with polybutadiene, Macromolecular Rapid Communications, 1999, Real-time crystallization and melting study of ethylene-based copolymer by SAXS, WAXD and DSC techniques, ACS Symposium Series, 2000, Novel aluminum-based, transition metal-free, catalytic system for homo and copolymerization alkens, Journal of the American Chemical Society, 2000, Synthesis of syndiotactic-polystyrene-graft-polymethyl methacrylate, syndiotactic-polystyrene-graft-polymethyl acrylate and syndiotactic-polystyrene-grafy-atactic polystyene with defined structure, 2000, Grafting of Syndiotactic polystyrene by branched oligomeric polythylene using Ni compound / AlCl3 catalyst, Journal of Polymer Science, 2001, Synthesis of novel linear polyethlene-based graft copolymer, Macromolecules, 2001. Recipient first prize for distinguished students, Anhui Normal U., 1988, 1990, second prize for disting. students, 1989, Chinese Acad. of Scis., 1997. Mem. Sigma Xi, Am. Chem. Soc. Patents in Preparation of high molecular weight, highly liner polymers of ethlene and a-olefins in the presence of a transition metal-free catalyst system, 1998, Process for polymerization of allylic compounds, 2000, Novel polymer-supported metallocene catalysts for ethlene polymerization, 2000.Avocations: music, fishing, travel, basketball, cooking. Office: Dept of Chemistry Pennsylvania State U. 152 Davey Lab State College PA 16802 Home: Apt 101 425 Waupelani Dr State College PA 16801-4554 Fax: (814) 863-8403. E-mail: sxl50@psu.edu.

LIU, SHENGZHONG (FRANK LIU), chemist, researcher; b. China, 1963; came to U.S., 1989; BSc, Shaanxi Tchrs. U., China, 1983; MSc, Lanzhou U., China, 1986, PhD, Northwestern U., 1992. Tchg., rsch. fellow Lanzhou (China) U., 1986-89; material chemist Argonne (Ill.) Nat. Lab., 1992-94; sr. scientist QQC, Inc., Dearborn, Mich., 1994-97; scientist SI Diamond Tech. Inc., 1997-98; sr. scientist Solarex Corp., Toano, Va., 1998—. Contbr. articles to Sci., Nature. Mem. ASM Internat., Materials Sci. Soc., Am. Chem. Soc., Minerals, Metals, Materials Soc. Achievements include patents for synthesis of diamond and related materials, methods of joining metal components, preparation of nanoscale materials. E-mail: liuf@bpsolar.com.

LIU, SHIYAO, statistician; s. ChunZhi Liu and ShuQin Li; m. Yan Yin, Aug. 30, 1968; children: Tommy, Raymond, Frank. BA, N.E. Univ. Tech., Shenyang, China, 1985; MS, Beijing Normal U., 1987, U. Nebr., 1995. Asst. prof. N.E. U. Tech., Shenyang, China; statis. MDS/Harris, Lincoln, Nebr., 1995—97; statis./programmer ASG, Cary, NC, 1997—98; rsch. scientist Mylan Pharm., Inc., Morgantown, W.Va., 1998—2000; sr. rsch. scientist II Mylan Pharm. Inc., Morgantown, WV, 1998—. Home: 667 Bellaire Dr Morgantown WV 26505 Office: Mylan Pharmaceuticals Inc 3711 Collins Ferry Road Morgantown WV 26505 Office Fax: 304-285-6446. Personal E-mail: shiyao_liu@hotmail.com. E-mail: sliu@mylanlabs.com.

LIU, SI-KWANG, veterinary pathologist; b. Kwangsi, China; came to U.S., 1959; s. Yeeshao and Shinmei (Yeh) L.; m. Sing-ping Chueh, Dec. 20, 1961; children: Davis, Ernest, Diana, Phillip. DVM, Chinese Vet. Coll., Anshun Kweichow, 1950; PhD, U. Calif., Davis, 1964. Chief veterinarian Taitung Agrl. Rsch. Sta., Taiwan, 1951-56; instr., chief Nat. Taiwan U. Vet. Hosp., Taipei, 1956-59; rsch. asst. U. Calif. Sch. Vet. Med., Davis, 1959-64; pathologist, sci. fellow N.Y. Zool. Soc., Bronx, 1964-88, 88—; pathologist, chief, sr. staff mem. Animal Med. Ctr., N.Y.C., 1964-97; fellow in pathology VA Gen. Hosp., Bronx, 1965-68; sr. pathologist, chmn. dept. pathology Animal Med. Ctr., N.Y.C., 1997-98; from asst. assoc. prof. to prof. N.Y. Med. Coll., 1966-90; sr. pathologist, assoc. dir. Caspary Rsch. Inst., 1998—. Cons. Pig Rsch. Inst., Taiwan, 1984—; vis. expert Nat. Sci. Coun., Taipei, 1976, 83, 88, 91; vis. prof. Nat. Taiwan U., Taipei, 1976, 88, 91, Nat. Chung Hsing U., Taichung, Taiwan, 1983; adj. prof. medicine Cornell U. Med. Coll., N.Y.C., 1998—; condr. some 300 lectrs., acad. presentations, and discussions in biomed. and sci. confs., U.S. and abroad. Author: An Atlas of Cardiovascular Pathology, 1989; contbr. more than 250 articles to Jour. Vet. Med. Assn., Am. Jour. Pathology, others. Elder Presbyn. Ch. of Newtown, Elmhurst, N.Y., 1970-80. Recipient rsch. award Ralston Purina Co., 1982, Feline Disease award Cornation, 1984, Rsch. Excellence award Beecham, 1986, comparative pathology award Chinese Pathology Soc., 1989, Outstanding Svc. award N.Y.C. Vet. Assn., 1991, Outstanding Svc. award N.Y. State Vet. Medicine Soc., 1991, Rsch. award Japanese Vet. Cardiol. Soc., 1992, Rsch. and Svc. award Chinese Vet. Med. Assn., 1992, award Chinese Vet. Med. Assn., 1993, 95, Postgrad. Edn. award Chinese Vet. Med. Assn., 1995, Rsch. Excellence in Cardiovasc. Diseases award Pig Rsch. Inst., Taiwan, 1995, Disting. Svc. award Animal Med. Ctr., 1999. Mem. Internat. Acad. Pathology, Internat. Skeletal Soc., Internat. Cardiovascular Pathology Soc., N.Y. Acad. Scis., Am. Vet. Med. Assn., Vet. Med. Assn. N.Y.C. (hon.), N.Y. State Vet. Medicine Soc. Office: Animal Med Ctr 510 E 62nd St New York NY 10021-8314

LIU, WEIHONG, art critic; b. China, Dec. 31, 1956; naturalized, 1997; MA, Wachong Tchr. U., Wuhan, China, 1981, PhD, 1983; MA, Bridgeport U., 1995. Rschr. Iron-Road Tech. Acad., 1983-84; assoc. prof. dept. art history TV U., 1984-86, Sarega Edn. Coll., 1986-90; dir. The Weih Fine Arts Appraisal, Inc., 1991—; chmn. dept. contemporary art Soho Fine Arts Inst., 1998—. Art cons. Nat. Edn. Inst., N.Y.C., 1996—, Internat. Art League, N.Y.C., 1998—, China Acad. Arts and Famous Figures, 1996—, Windsor (Conn.) Gallery, 1998—; hon. dean Acad. Oriental Arts, 1999—; sr. hon. advisor Sin-shenzou Art Gallery, Singapore, 1997—; hon. lifetime curator Xubozong Mus. Art, China, 1997—. Author: (texts) Contemporary Art, 1986, Abstract Art, 1988, (plays) The Song of Teachers, 1975 (award of excellent play), Unfathomable Enigma, 1993, The Day of Wedding, 1996; editor-in-chief: Comtemporary Art Am., 1999; art exhibited in group shows at Ringwood (N.Y.) Arts Assn., 1997 (3d pl.), Suburban Art League, Woodbury N.Y., 1997, 98 (award of merit 1997, 98), Queens (N.Y.) Artists Alliance, 1998 (Best in Show), AQA Gallery, Queens, 1998 (People's Choice award), Manhattan Art Internat., N.Y.C., 1998 (Artist Showcase award), Singapore Internat. Art competition, 1998 (award of excellence), Famous Figures Works Exhbn. of Arts Circles, China, 1998 (Silver medal). Named One of 100 Outstanding Artists in China, 1998; recipient Omega award Ringwood Manor Assn. Arts, 1998, 1st prize award Nat. Art League, N.Y., 2000. Mem. Singapore Arts Inst. (sr. hon. academician), Assn. Art Historians, Playwrights Assn., Coll. Art Assn., Appraisers Assn. Am. (cert.), Allied Artists Am. Home: 94-46 85th Rd Apt 2H Woodhaven NY 11421 Fax: 718-846-6540.

LIU, WILLIAM SHIO, psychotherapist, holistic physician, minister; b. Formosa, Taiwan, Dec. 15, 1968; came to U.S. 1975; s. Frank Ju-Feng and Fanny Zy Liu; m. Terri Lynne Wagoner, Nov. 10, 1995; 1 child, Maile Midori. BA in Psychology, BA in Anthropology, U. Tex., 1991; grad. Inst. Bible Studies, Internat. Sch. Theology, 1992; (hon.) PhD in Religion, PhD in Clin. Psychology, U. Tex., Austin, 1994. Cert. hypnotherapist Am. Bd. Hypnotherapy, transpersonal hypnotherapist Nat. Assn. Transpersonal Hypnotherapists; lic. master G-Jo accupressure G-Jo Natural Health Inst.; ordained reverend title and ministerial lic. Universal Life Ch./World Christianship Ministries, 1996-98; 4th deg. black belt Mano de Guerra Internat. Wing Chun Martial Arts Assn. Campus counselor, adj. faculty staff U. Nebr., Kearney, 1992-94; acupressure physician William S. Liu Enterprises, Kearney, Lahaina, Orlando, Hawaii, Fla., 1992—. pres., surfing psychotherapist Lahaina, Maui, 1994-95; d. Tchr. Found. for Inner Peace, Unity Ch. Maui, Wailuku, Hawaii, 1992—; exercise physiologist, personal fitness trainer Powerhouse Gym, Bally Total Fitness, World Gym, Orlando, Fla., 1995-97; cons. Michael and Assocs., Orland; mental health specialist Jammers Coffeehouse, Orlando. Author: (tng. book) Why Is Gilligan Skinny and the Skipper Fat?: A Simple and Light Hearted Guide to Health and Fitness, 1996, (children's lit.) Shio's Surfing School, 1997, (self-help book) Dr. Shio's Stories for the Soul, 1997; creator: (psychotherapy method) Jungian Playground, 1997. Fellow Am. Assn. of Psychotherapists; mem. APA, Am. Holistic Health Assn. (practitioner mem.), Inst. Noetic Scis. (VIP press pass 1999 internat. conf.). Presbyterian. Avocations: surfing, reading, swimming. Office: 469 S Deerwood Ave Orlando FL 32825-8010 E-mail: williamsliu@usaf.org.

LIU, WING KAM, mechanical and civil engineering educator; b. Hong Kong, May 15, 1952; came to U.S., 1973, naturalized, 1990; s. Yin Lam and Siu Lin (Chan) L.; m. Betty Hsia, Dec. 12, 1986; children: Melissa Margaret, Michael Kevin. BSc with highest honors, U. Ill., Chgo., 1976; MSc, Calif. Inst. Tech., 1977, PhD, 1981. Registered profl. engr., Ill. Asst. prof. mech. and civil engring. Northwestern U., Evanston, Ill., 1980-83, assoc. prof., 1983-88, prof., 1988—. Prin. cons. reactor analysis and safety div. Argonne (Ill.) Nat. Lab., 1981—. Co-author: Nonlinear Finite Elements for Continua and Structures, 2000; co-editor: Innovative Methods for Nonlinear Problems, 1984, Impact-Effects of Fasts Transient Loadings, 1988; musician: Computational Mechanics of Probabilistic and Reliability Analysis, 1989. Recipient Thomas J. Jaeger prize Internat. Assn. for Structural Mechanics in Reactor Tech., 1989, Ralph R. Teetor award Soc. Automotive Engrs., 1983; named among 93 most highly cited rschrs. in engring. Inst. for Sci. Info., 2001; grantee USF, Army Rsch. Office, NASA, AFSOR, ONR, GE, Ford Motor, Chrysler. Fellow ASCE, ASME (exec. mem. applied mechanics divsn. 2001, Melville medal 1979, Pi Tau Sigma gold medal 1985, Gustus L. Larson Meml. award 1995), U.S. Assn. Computational Mechanics (pres. 2000—, Computational Structural Mechs. award 2001), Am. Acad. Mechanics. Office: Northwestern U Dept Mech Engring 2145 Sheridan Rd Evanston IL 60208-0834 E-mail: w-liu@northwestern.edu.

LIU, XIANG, optical physicist, optical engineer; b. Chengdu, Shichuan, China, Mar. 5, 1970; came to U.S., 1994; s. Zhongren and Shuirong (Lei) L.; m. Hongou Deng, Aug. 8, 1994; 1 child, Daniel J. BS, Beijing Normal U., 1989; MS, Chinese Acad. of Scis., 1994, Cornell U., 1998, PhD, 2000. Engr.

Inst. of Physics, Chinese Acad. of Scis., Beijing, 1989-94; rschr. U. Del., Newark, 1994-96, Cornell U., Ithaca, N.Y., 1996-2000; mem. tech. staff Lucent Techs., Holmdel, N.J., 2000—. Presenter in field. Contbr. numerous articles to profl. jours. Recipient First Class award Advances of Sci. and Tech., 1994, 98. Mem. Optical Soc. of Am., Am. Physics Soc. Achievements include 11 patents on optical communications formats and devices, novel laser design, and optical solutions in fibers and quadratic nonlinear media. Office: 101 Crawfords Corner Rd Holmdel NJ 07733-1900

LIU, XIAO, ophthalmologist, neurobiologist; b. Shanghai, China, Feb. 11, 1967; s. Benren Liu and Ke Hu; m. Mei Li. MD, Shanghai Med. U., China, 1990; PhD, Kyoto U., Japan, 1999. Ophthalmologist Huadong Hosp., Shanghai, China, 1990-94, Nagata Eye Hosp., Ikoma Gen. Hosp., Japan, 1995-98; predoctoral rsch. fellow Northwestern U. Med. Sch., Chgo., 1998-99; postdoctoral rsch. fellow Doheny Eye Inst., U. So. Calif. Keck Sch. Medicine, L.A., 1999-01; rsch. fellow dept. ophthalmology U. Calif., San Francisco, 2001—. Recipient Eye Rsch. award Meml. Eye Rsch. Fund, Tokyo, 1994, Travel award Japan Med. Assn., 1995, Toyobo Bio-tech. Travel award, Tokyo, 1997, Eye Rsch. award, China-Japan Med. Assn., 1998. Mem. AAAS, N.Y. Acad. Scis., Assn. Rsch. in Vision and Ophthalmology, Assn. Online Ophthalmologists, Fedn. of Am. Socs. for Exptl. Biology, Am. Assn. Anatomists. Achievements include research in cataract, glaucoma and retina surgery; cell adhesion study; transgenic mice study; nerve regeneration and growth cone study. Office: UCSF Beckman Vision Ctr Dept ophthalmology 10 Kirkham St San Francisco CA 94143 Fax: 415-476-6289. E-mail: xiaoliu98@hotmail.com.

LIU, XIAOQING FRANK, computer scientist, educator; b. Xiangtan, Hunan, China, June 24, 1962; came to U.S., 1991; s. Mingzhang and Shengnan L.; m. Xiaoxia Linda Liu, May 17, 1988; 1 child, Jesse. BS, Changsha (China) Inst. Tech., 1982; MS, Southeast U., Nanjing, China, 1985; PhD, Tex. A&M U., 1995. Lectr. dept. computer sci. Southeast U., Nanjing, 1985-90; asst. prof. dept. computer sci. U. Mo., Rolla, 1995—, dir. software engrng. lab., 1996—. Gen chmn. Nat. Conf. Young Computer Profls., Nanjing, 1989; program com. N.Am. Fuzzy Info. Processing Symposium, Berkeley, Calif., 1996, 98, 99, Internat. Conf. Software Engrng. Knowledge Engrng., San Francisco, 1998, 99, 2000. Contbr. articles to Internat. Jour. Concurrent Engrng., Rsch. Application, IEEE Potential, Internat. Jour. Sys. Software, others. Mem. IEEE, Assn. Computing Machinery. Queen's U. Grad. fellow, 1991; grantee U. Mo.,1996-97, NSF, 1996—. Achievements include research in imprecise software requirement specification and analysis methodology, intelligent house of quality, high-order object model, case-based process planning for agile manufacturing.

LIU, XIAOYUE, mechanical engineer; b. Shanghai, China, Feb. 19, 1963; s. Jianyou Liu and Qin Xie; m. Yi Zhang, June 6, 1964; children: Siyao, Stanley. BS, Beijing U. Aeronautics and Astronautics, 1984; MS, Third Rsch. Acad. Aerospace Ministry, 1987; PhD, Rensselaer Poly. Inst., 1998. Mech. engr. Beijing Precision Machinery Co., 1987—94; sr. engr. Adapco, Melville, NY, 1998—99; sr. CFD engr. Valeo Climate Control Co., Auburn Hills, Mich., 1999—2001; sr. mech. engr. GE Corp. R&D Ctr., Niskayuna, NY, 2001—. Contbr. articles to profl. jours. Mem.: AAAS, ASME.

LIU, XU-DONG, mathematics educator; b. Shanghai, China, Mar. 7, 1962; s. Kai-Ben Liu and Xiu-Feng Yang; m. Xiaohui Lu, Aug. 8, 1987; 1 child, Evan. MA, UCLA, 1990, PhD in Applied Math., 1993. Vis. mem. Courant Inst. of Math. Scis., NYU, 1993-96; assoc. prof. U. Calif., Santa Barbara, 1996—. Contbr. articles to profl. jours. including Jour. of Computational Physics. Grantee NSF, 1998—. Home: 961 W Campus Ln Goleta CA 93117 Office: U Calif Dept Math Santa Barbara CA 93106 E-mail: xliu@math.ucsb.edu.

LIU, YANGANG, atmospheric scientist; b. Yantai, Shandong, China, Nov. 26, 1962; s. Shuheng Liu and Cunlan Sun; m. Lan Xie, Apr. 1990; 1 child, Miao Linda. PhD, U. Nev., Reno, 1998. Rsch. scientist Chinese Acad. Meteorol. Scis., Beijing, 1983-86; rsch. asst. Nanjing (Jiang Su, China) Inst. Meteorology, 1986-89; asst. rsch. prof. Chinese Acad. Meteorol. Scis., Beijing, 1989-93; rsch. asst. Desert Rsch. Inst., Reno, 1993-98; rsch. assoc. Brookhaven Nat. Lab., Upton, NY, 1998—, asst. scientist, 2001—. Contbr. articles to sci. jours. Mem. AAAS, Am. Geophys. Union, Am. Meteorol. Soc., Soc. for Indsl. and Applied Math. Office: Brookhaven Nat Lab Bldg 815E 75 Rutherford Dr Upton NY 11973-5000 Office Fax: 631-344-2887. E-mail: lyg@bnl.gov.

LIU, YIJUN, engineering educator, researcher; b. Xi'an, Shaanxi, China, Oct. 26, 1959; BS, Northwestern Poly. U., Xi'an, Shaanxi, China, 1982, MS, 1984; PhD, U. Ill., 1991. Lectr. dept. aerospace engrng. Northwestern Poly. U., Xi'an, China, 1984—87; postdoctoral rsch. assoc. Ctr. for Nondestructive Evaluation, Iowa State U., Ames, 1992—94; CAE analyst Advanced Vehicle Tech., Ford Motor Co., Dearborn, Mich., 1995—96; asst. prof. Mech. Engrng. Dept., U. Cin., 1996—2000, assoc. prof., 2000—. Contbr. articles. Grantee, NSF, 1998. Mem.: ASME, Internat. Assn. for Boundary Element Methods, U.S. Assn. for Computational Mechanics, Internat. Assn. for Computational Mechanics, Sigma Xi. Avocations: photography, travel, swimming. Office: Univ of Cincinnati Dept Mech Engrng PO Box 210072 Cincinnati OH 45221-0072

LIU, YONG-YU, molecular biologist; b. Weinan, Shannxi, China, Jan. 2, 1957; came to U.S., 1997; s. Zhen-Rong and Miao-Yuan (Shi) L.; m. Min-Hong Dai, June 15, 1985; 1 child, Xiao-Tian. MD, Suzhou Med. Coll., China, 1984; PhD, Shanghai U. of TCM, 1989. Postdoctoral fellow U. Rome, 1993-96, U. Man., Winnipeg, 1996-97, John Wayne Cancer Inst., Santa Monica, Calif., 1997-99, jr. mem., 1999-2000, asst. mem., 2000—. Asst. prof. Suzhou Med. Coll., 1989-93. Contbr. articles to profl. jours.; inventor in field. Mem. AAAS, The Endocrine Soc. (assoc.), Am. Assn. for Cancer Rsch., Am. Soc. for Biochemistry and Molecular Biology. Office: John Wayne Cancer Inst 2200 Santa Monica Blvd Santa Monica CA 90404-2302

LIU, YOUNG KING, biomedical engineering educator; b. Nanjing, China, May 3, 1934; came to U.S., 1952; s. Yih Ling and Man Fun (Teng) L.; m. Nina Pauline Liu, Sept. 4, 1964 (div. July 1986); children— Erik, Tania; m. Anita Beeth, Aug. 14, 1994 (div. Aug. 2000). BSME, Bradley U., 1955; MSME, U. Wis.-Madison, 1959; PhD, Wayne State U., 1963. Cert. acupuncturist, Calif. Asst. prof. Milw. Sch. of Engrng., 1956—59; instr. Wayne State U., Detroit, 1960—63; lectr. then asst. prof. U. Mich., Ann Arbor, 1963—69; assoc. prof. then prof. Tulane U., New Orleans, 1969—78; prof. biomed. engrng., dir. dept. U. Iowa, Iowa City, 1978—93; pres. U. No. Calif., Petaluma, 1993—; interim pres., CEO Calif. Coll. Podiatric Medicine, 2000—01. COO 3DMetrics, Inc. Contbr. articles to profl. jours., chpts. to books NIH spl. research fellow, 1968-69; recipient Research Career Devel. award NIH, 1971-76 Mem. Internat. Soc. Lumbar Spine (exec. com., ctrl. U.S. rep. 1983-88), Orthopedic Research Soc., Am. Soc. Engrng. Edn., Sigma Xi Democrat. E-mail: admits@uncm.edu., ykingliu@yahoo.com.

LIU, YUAN HSIUNG, drafting and design educator; b. Tainan, Taiwan, Feb. 24, 1938; came to U.S., 1970; s. Chun Chang and Kong (Wong) L.; m. Ho Pe Tung, July 27, 1973; children: Joan Anshen, Joseph Pinyang. BEd, Nat. Taiwan Normal U., Taipei, 1961; MEd, Nat. Chengchi U., Taipei, 1967, U. Alta., Edmonton, 1970; PhD, Iowa State U., 1975. Cert. tchr. Tchr. indsl. arts and math. Nan Ning Jr. H.S., Tainan, Taiwan, 1961-64; tech. math. instr. Chung-Cheng Inst. Tech., Taipei, 1967-68; drafter Sundstrand Hydro-Transmission Corp., Ames, Iowa, 1973-75; assoc. prof. Fairmont (W.Va.) State Coll., 1975-80; per course instr. Sinclair C.C., Dayton, Ohio, 1985; assoc. prof. Miami U., Hamilton, 1980-85, Southwest Mo. State U., Springfield, 1985—. Cons. Monarch Indsl. Precision Co., Springfield, 1986, Gen. Electric Co., Springfield, 1988, Fasco Industries, Inc., Ozark, Mo., 1989, 95, Springfield Remfg. Corp., 1990, 92, Ctrl. States Indsl., Intercont Products, Inc., L&W Industries, Inc., ZERCO Mfg. Co., 1994-95, Paul Mueller Co., 1996. 2d lt. R.O.C. Army, 1962-63. Recipient Excellent Teaching in Drafting award Charvoz-Carsen Corp., Fairfield, N.J., 1978. Mem. Am. Design Drafting Assn. Avocations: walking, TV. Office: SW Mo State U Dept Indsl Mgmt 901 S National Ave Springfield MO 65804-0094 E-mail: yhl045f@smsu.edu.

LIU, ZENGHE, research scientist; b. Wuan, Hebei Province, China, May 9, 1965; s. Xijin Liu and Ronde Bai; m. Yankun Gong; 1 child Amy. PhD, Calif. Inst. Tech., 2001. Research chemist Central Iron and Steel Research Institute, Beijing , China, 1988—94; Research Assistant Baylor University, Waco, TX, 1994—97; Senior Scientist TheraSense, Inc., Alameda, CA, 2002—02. Contbr. Electrochem. Soc. Interface, Pennington, 2000—; Reviewer Analytical Chemistry, Columbus, 2002—. Contbr. papers to profl. jours. Fellow Dow Chem. fellow, Calif. Inst. Tech., 2000—01; scholar Li Ming scholar, 1998—99. Mem.: Electrochem. Soc. (dept. energy summer rsch. fellow 2000, nat. meeting travel grantee 1999, 2001), Am. Chem. Soc. Home: #216 544 Central Ave Alameda CA 94501 Office: TheraSense Inc 1360 S Loop Rd Alameda CA 94502 Home Fax: 510-239-2799. Business E-Mail: zach.liu@therasense.com.

LIU, ZHONG-PING (PETER LIU), natural medicine specialist, actor; b. Beijing, June 5, 1958; came to U.S., 1986; s. De-Rang Liu and Yin-Mei Zhang. BS in Plant Protection, Hunan Agrl. U., Changsha, Hunan, China, 1981; AAS in Data Processing Tech., Del. Tech., Wilmington, 1990; BS in Computer Info. Systems, Goldey-Beacom Coll., Wilmington, 1991; MS in Oriental Medicine, Samra U., L.A., 1996; cert. in ESL, Nanjing Normal U. Cert. in advanced English as a second lang., Del. Tech.; cert. in ornamental hort. Longwood Gardens, Inc.; tng. in Chinese opera, drama, singing, dance, film acting and Qigong. Gardener Gaotian Econ. Plant Garden, Shaodong, Hunan, China, 1975-78; asst. rschr. Hunan Inst. Plant Protection, Changsha, China, 1982-84; curator Jiangsu Inst. Botany/Nanjing Bot. Garden Mem. Sun Yat-Sen, Nanjing, Jiangsu, China, 1984-86; horticulturist Longwood Gardens, Inc., Kennett Square, Pa., 1986-87; computer lab. asst. Goldey-Beacom Coll., Wilmington, Del., 1990-91, sr. asst./computer cons., 1991-94; observer, intern Samra U., L.A., 1995-96. Prin. actor in film, TV, theatre, voice-over and commls.; contbr. rsch. articles to profl. jours. Mem. SAG, AFTRA, Calif. Chinese Medicine Assn., Internat. Assn. Traditional Chinese Qigong. Avocations: Chinese opera, pop and classical music, stamp collecting, basketball, cycling. Home: PO Box 3273 Alhambra CA 91803-0273

LIU, ZI-KUI, materials science and engineering educator; b. Xiang Dong Tungsten Mine, Cha-Ling, China, Jan. 21, 1963; came to the U.S., 1996; s. Kecai Liu and You Ling Song; m. Weiming Huang; children: Erik, David. BS, Ctrl. South U. Tech., Changsha, China, 1982; MS, U. Sci. and Tech., Beijing, 1985; PhD, Royal Inst. Tech., Stockholm, 1992, docent, 1996. Tchg. staff U. Sci. and Tech., Beijing, 1985-87; rschr. Royal Inst. Tech., Stockholm, 1992-96; rsch. assoc. U. Wis., Madison, 1996-98; sr. rsch. scientist Questek Innovations LLC, Evanston, Ill., 1998; asst. prof. Pa. State U., University Park, 1999—. Editor-in-chief: CALPHAD; contbr. articles to profl. jours. Bd. mem. Chinese Lang. Sch., Madison, 1996-98. Recipient 3rd pize China Nat. Key Projects, Ministry Metallurgy, China, 1988; China State Coun. expert lecturing scholar, 1998, Career award NSF, 1999. Mem. The Mineral, Metals and Materials Soc. (TMS Young Leader 1998), Am. Soc. Metals, Materials Rsch. Soc., Sigma Xi. Avocation: tennis, skiing, squash, golf. Office: Pa State Univ 209 Steidle Bldg University Park PA 16802-5006 E-mail: zikui@psu.edu.

LIU, ZIMING, science educator; b. Shantou, Guangdong Province, China, June 3, 1965; m. Shuping Chen. PhD, U. Calif., Berkeley, 1996; MS, Zhongshan U., Guangzhou, China, 1990. Rsch. scientist Ricoh Sillicon Valley, Inc., Menlo Park, Calif., 1996—98; vis. asst. prof. U. Wash., Seattle, 1998—2000; asst. prof. San Jose State U., Calif., 2000—. Contbr. Recipient Mary E. Wood award, Mary E. Wood Found., 1995. Office: San Jose State U One Washington Square San Jose CA 95152

LIUZZI, ROBERT C. chemical company executive; b. Boston, 1944; married. AB, Coll. of Holy Cross, 1965; LLB, U. Va., 1968. V.p., gen. counsel U.S. Fin., Inc., 1969-74; with CF Industries, Inc., Long Grove, Ill., 1975—, exec. v.p., CFO, 1977-80, exec. v.p., operating officer, 1980-84, pres., CEO, 1985—. Chmn. ad hoc com. Domestic Nitrogen Prodrs., Washington; chmn. bd. dirs. Can. Fertilizers Ltd.; bd. dirs. The Fertilizer Inst., Nat. Coun. Farmer Coops., Fla. Phosphate Coun., Tallahassee; mem. Nat. Forum Nonpoint Source Pollution sponsored by Nat. Geographic Soc. and Conservation Fund of Washington. Mem. coun. Internat. Exec. Svc. Corps, Stamford, Conn.; mem. bus. adv. coun. Law Sch. U. Va., Charlottesville. Mem. Ill. Bus. Roundtable, Northwestern U. Assocs., Coun. of 100, Tampa Fla., Internat. Fertilizer Industry Assn. (mem. coun.). Office: CF Industries Inc One Salem Lake Dr Long Grove IL 60047-8402

LIUZZO, JOSEPH ANTHONY, food science educator; b. Tampa, Fla., Dec. 16, 1926; s. Joseph and Annie (Minardi) L.; m. Elaine Grammer, Nov. 30, 1951; children: Paul Arthur, Patricia Joyce, Jolaine Marie. BS, U. Fla., 1950, MS, 1955; postgrad., U. So. Calif., 1952-53; PhD, Mich. State U., 1958. Microbiologist Stokely-Van Camp Co., Tampa, 1950; head divsn. microbiology Nutrilite Products, Inc., Buena Park, Calif., 1951-54; asst. prof. biochemistry La. State U., Baton Rouge, 1958-62, assoc. prof. food sci., 1962-69, prof., 1969-97, prof. emeritus, 1997—, faculty chmn. athletics, 1979-83, prof. emeritus, 1997—. Chmn. Am. Legion Baseball Program, 1976-82, 97—. Contbr. articles to profl. jours. With U.S. Army, 1945-46. Recipient Outstanding Alumnus award Food Sci. and Human Nutrition, Mich. State U., 1994. Fellow AAAS, Am. Inst. Chemists, Inst. of Food Technologists; mem. Am. Inst. Nutrition, Am. chem. Soc., Kiwanis (pres. 1988-89, div. lt. gov. 1990-91), Sigma Xi, Phi Tau Sigma, Gamma Sigma Delta, Phi Sigma, Omicron Delta Kappa. Republican. Mem. Ch. of Christ. Office: La State U Dept Food Science Baton Rouge LA 70803-0001 E-mail: jliuzzo@agcenter.lsu.edu.

LIVA, EDWARD LOUIS, eye surgeon; b. Lyndhurst, N.J., Aug. 30, 1925; s. Paul Francis and Lucy Agnes (Andreozzi) L.; m. Dorothea Lucille Carter, Aug. 29, 1946; children: Edward Jr., Bradford, Douglas, Jeffrey, Elaine. SB, Harvard U., 1946, MD, 1950. Diplomate Am. Bd. Ophthalmology. Intern Med. Coll. Va., Richmond, 1950-51; fellow in eye pathology Mass. Eye and Ear, Boston, 1951; resident Brooklyn Eye and Ear, N.Y., 1952-53; chief ophthalmic examiner Workman's Compensation Bd., N.Y.C., 1957-63; sr. ophthalmic surgeon Hackensack (N.J.) Med. Ctr., 1957—, Valley Hosp., Ridgewood, N.J., 1963-99; sr. ophthalmic surgeon, resident instr. oculoplastics Manhatten Eye, Ear and Throat, N.Y.C., 1957-96, emeritus, 1996—. Pres. Bergen Surg. Ctr., Paramus, N.J., 1991—, Eye Inst. of Paramus, 1987—. Author: Advances in Ophthalmic Plastic, 1983. Active Rep. Club, Ridgewood, 1960—. Capt. USAF, 1955-57. Fellow AMA, Am. Acad. Ophthalmology, Internat. Coll. of Surgeons, Am. Soc. of Ophtalmic Plastic and Reconstructive Surgery (chartered). Republican. Roman Catholic. Achievements include development of new lid flaps oculoplastics, prototype of lid canal laceration repair, major modification of ptosis surgical procedures widely used, disproved Trichromatic theory of color vision in 1952. Office: Liva Eye Ctr One West Ridgewood Ave Paramus NJ 07652 Home: # Lph 2600 S Ocean Blvd Boca Raton FL 33432-8385

LIVADARY, PAUL JOHN, lawyer; b. L.A., Oct. 6, 1937; s. John Paul and Helen (Loomis) Livadary; m. Marcia Forstmann Day, Apr. 6, 2002; children: Sarah Elizabeth, Catherine Carter, Emily Elene, John Matthew. BA in Econs., Stanford U., 1959; LLB, U. Calif., Berkeley, 1964. Bar: Calif. 1965, U.S. Dist. Ct. Calif. 1965. Assoc. O'Melveny & Myers, L.A., 1965-75; ptnr. Parker, Milliken, Clark, O'Hara & Samuelian, 1975-93; pvt. practice, 1993—. Bd. dirs. Children's Hosp. of L.A., 1982-93, Greater L.A. Zoo Assn., 1989-01; founder, bd. trustees Pasadena Waldorf Sch., Altadena, Calif., 1978-92; bd. trustees Republican Assocs., L.A., 1970-92. 1st lt. U.S. Army, 1959-61. Mem. Valley Hunt Club. Office: 2029 Century Park E Ste 437 Los Angeles CA 90067-2905 E-mail: plivadary@aol.com.

LIVELY, CAROL A. retired professional society administrator; b. Chgo., Sept. 2, 1935; d. William Mann and Lillian (Juske) Haycock; m. E. Raymond Platig; children: Richard B., Laura Jean. L.P.N., Los Angeles Sch. Nursing, 1953; student, Columbia U., 1954, Boston U., 1956-57. Program dir. United Fund, Pittsfield, Mass., 1966-71; exec. dir. Western Mass. Health Council, 1971-74; asst. exec. dir. Genesse Health Council, Rochester, N.Y., 1974-76; dir. devel. Shimer Coll., Mt. Carroll, Ill., 1976-77; assoc. dir. Am. Hosp. Assn., Chgo., 1977-80; dir. health div., v.p. Smith Bucklin Assn., Washington, 1980—96, ret., 1996. Mem. Achievement Rewards Coll. Scientists, Washington, 1980-96, Meridan House, 2000—, Black Tie Club, Inc., 1993—; cons. Dept. Health Rep. Haiti, Washington, 1976— Contbg. author: Politics of Health Planning, 1962; contbr. articles to profl. jours. Bd. dirs. Jacobs Pillow Dance Theatre, Pittsfield, 1968, Albany Regional Med. Program, N.Y., 1971-74. Symphony Soc.; v.p. Symphony Guild; mem. Jr. League, 1965—; mem. Commn. Drug Abuse Council, Boston, 1971-74; mem. women's bd. Washington Ballet, 1998-2001; trustee Shimer Coll.; mem. Fla. Internat. Music Festival Guild, Mus. Arts and Scis., Daytona Beach. Recipient Woman of Yr. award Bus. and Profl. Women, 1971 Fellow Am. Coll. Nuclear Physicians; mem. New Eng. Pub. Health Assn., Mass. Council on Aging, Am. Soc. Hosp. Planning, Am. Pub. Health Assn., Nat. Rehb. Hosp. Bd. Assn. Home: 1 Old Trl Ormond Beach FL 32174-4312

LIVELY, JOHN POUND, magazine editor, publisher; b. Chattanooga, May 3, 1945; s. John Jefferson and Janet Florence (Pound) Lively Ledford; m. Cheryl Lynn Weinberg, Oct. 20, 1967; children— Tiffany Wynne, Joshua; m. Ruth Rohde Haskell, Sept. 14, 1991. BA in English, Centre Coll. Ky., 1967; MA, N. Tex. State U., 1971, postgrad., 1971-75. Tchr. English Selwyn Sch., Denton, Tex., 1975-77; cabinetmaker, designer Dallas, 1977-79; asst. editor Fine Woodworking Mag., Newtown, Conn., 1979-80, assoc. editor, 1980-81; editor Fine Homebuilding Mag., 1981—; editorial dir. Taunton Press Inc., 1987-88; assoc. pub. for Fine Woodworking and Fine HomeBuilding mags., 1988-89; pub. Fine Woodworking, Fine Homebuilding, Newtown, Conn., 1989—, corp. chief of staff, 1991, corp. editorial dir., 1992—, editor-in-chief, v.p., 1993, pres., CEO, 2000—. Contbr. articles to profl. jours. Mem. Am. Soc. Mag. Editors, Mag. Pubs. Assn., Cooper Hewitt Mus. Avocations: cabinetmaking, carpentry, furniture design. E-mail: jlively@taunton.com.

LIVELY, PIERCE, federal judge; b. Louisville, Aug. 17, 1921; s. Henry Thad and Ruby Durrett (Keating) L.; m. Amelia Harrington, May 25, 1946; children: Susan, Katherine, Thad. AB, Centre Coll., Ky., 1943; LL.B., U. Va., 1948. Bar: Ky. 1948. Individual practice law, Danville, Ky., 1949—57; mem. firm Lively and Rodes, 1957—72; judge U.S. Ct. Appeals (6th cir.), Cin., 1972—, chief judge, 1983—88, sr. judge, 1988—97, ret., 1997. Mem. Ky. Commn. on Economy and Efficiency in Govt., 1963—65, Ky. Jud. Advisory Com., 1972. Trustee Centre Coll. With USNR, 1943—46. Mem.: ABA, Am. Judicature Soc., Raven Soc., Order of Coif, Omicron Delta Kappa, Phi Beta Kappa. Presbyterian.

LIVENGOOD, CHARLOTTE LOUISE, employee development specialist; b. L.A., June 18, 1944; d. James Zollie and Zela (Cogburn) L. BS in Secondary Edn., Tex. A & I U., 1968; MEd in Pers. Guidance and Counseling, North Tex. U., 1971. Cert. secondary teaching, Tex.; cert. counselor, Tex. Counselor Gus Grissom H.S., Huntsville, Ala., 1971-72; tchr. West Springfield H.S., Springfield, Va., 1972-73; edn. specialist U.S. Dept. Def., El Paso, Tex., 1975-78; instr. El Paso (Tex.) C.C., 1977-78; employee devel. specialist U.S. Office Pers. Mgmt., Dallas, 1978-79; pers. mgmt. specialist Dept. Vets. Affairs, Houston, 1979-87; labor rels. specialist Dept. Vets. Affairs, VA Med. Ctr., 1987-89; pers. staffing specialist Dept. Vets. Affairs, 1989-90; employee devel. specialist, acad. tng. officer HUD, Ft. Worth, 1990-95; assoc. prof. Ariz. State U., 1995—; Bur. of Engraving and Printing Ctr. Excellence tng. officer Dept. Treasury, Ft. Worth, 1995—. EEO investigator Dept. Vet. Affairs, 1984-87, fed. women's program mgr., 1984-85; mem. standing panel for pers. specialists/fed. suprs./mgrs. Merit Systems Protection Bd., 1996—; mem. design team Dept. Treasury, 2001; speaker in field. Editor: Pipline, 1980—87; co-author: Plate Printer Apprenticeship Standards, 2002. Chaperon, forensics coach Jr. High Sch. Speech Dept., 1968-69; tchr. S. Grand Prairie H.S., 1969-71; mem. Dallas/Ft. Worth Quality Control Coun., Tex. War on Drugs Com., 1990—; hon. mem. Dallas/Ft. Worth Fed. Exec. Bd., 1993-94. Recipient Future Secs. of Am. scholarship, 1962. Mem. ASTD, AAUW, Am. Pers. and Guidance Assn., Assn. for Quality Participation, Internat. Transactional Analysis Assn., Tex. State Tchrs. Assn., Tex. Classroom Tchrs. Assn., Fed. Bus. Assn., VA Employee Assn., Intergovernmental Tng. Assn., Intergovernmental Tng. Coun. (chairperson 1993-94), Federal Women's Program Mgr., Merit Sys. Protection Bd. Standing Panel for Personnel Specialists, Federal Supv., Mgrs. Mem. Church of Christ. Avocations: reading, travel, bridge, fishing, theater. Office: US Dept Treasury Bur Engraving & Printing Western Currency Facility 9000 Blue Mound Rd Fort Worth TX 76131-3304

LIVERMORE, DOUGLAS CARL, educator, consultant; b. Oto, Iowa, Mar. 27, 1947; s. Carl Orlando and Irene Ellen Livermore; m. Vicki Lee Livermore, Feb. 9, 1974; children: Stephanie, K.C. AAS, Western Iowa Tech., 1967; BS, Wayne State Coll., 1973, MSE, 1976; EdD, U. No. Colo., 1986. Electronics technician Barber Coleman Co., Rockford, Ill., 1967-69; mktg. mgr. Burroughs Corp., Sioux City, Iowa, 1973-75; asst. prof. mktg. Wayne (Nebr.) State Coll., 1975-80; prof., divsn. chair Morningside Coll., Sioux City, 1980—. Ptnr. HLLA, LLP, Sioux City, 1997-2000. Chair troop com. Boy Scouts of Am., Sioux City, 1995—. Named Faculty Person of Yr., Omicron Delta Kappa, 1984. Mem. Midwest Mktg. Assn. Roman Catholic. Home: 4167 Sherwood Ter Sioux City IA 51106 Office: Morningside Coll 1501 Morningside Ave Sioux City IA 51106 E-mail: livermor@morningside.edu.

LIVERS, CATHERINE MCGHEE, writer; b. Indianapolis, IN, June 11, 1953; d. Martha McGhee, Phillip McGhee; m. Fred L. McGhee; children: Shereka, Marcus, Victoria. Associate Bachelor of Arts, Rehoboth Christian College, Indianapolis, IN, 1998. College Instructor/Hebrew & Greek Language Rehoboth Christian College, Indianapolis, IN, 1995—99; College Instructor/Greek Language Simmons Bible College, 1998—99. Director Shahar Institute, Indianapolis, IN, 1997—2002; CEO Shahar Publishing, Indianapolis, IN, 1999—2002. Author: (Book) Biblical History of Black Mankind, 1999 (1999 Merit Award-Writers Digest, 2000 Book of the Year Award-UBUS Communications Systems, 2001 Meet the Artist XIII Award-Indpls Marion Co Pub Library). Mem.: Indiana African-American Genealogy Group (Member), African American Authors Helping Authors (Promotions 2001—02). Office: Shahar Publishing 8605 Allisonville Rd. #283 Indianapolis IN 46250 Business E-Mail: shaharpublishing@hotmail.com.

LIVERS, THOMAS HENRY, fundraiser for nonprofit organizations; b. Louisville, Sept. 15, 1946; s. Henry Edgar and Katherine (Ellison) L.; m. Karen Culter, June 13, 1970 (div. June 1988); children: Zehra Livers Hudson, Floyd Forrest; m. Beverly Morgan Dennis, June, 1996; children: Eric, Jarrett Dennis. BA, U. Louisville, 1970; postgrad., Butler U., Indpls., U. Conn., Bridgeport. Cert. fund raising exec. Elephant zookeeper Louisville Zoo, 1968-70; curator Indpls. Zoo, 1970-72; zoo dir. Breadsley Park Zoo, Bridgeport, 1972-75; exec. dir. East Bay Zool. Soc., Oakland, Calif., 1975-77; zoo supt. Lafayette Zool. Park, Norfolk, Va., 1977-82; exec. dir. Nature Ctr. of Charlestown, Devault, Pa., 1982-85, Cmty. Health Task Force, Phila., 1985-86; regional dir. Nat. Soc. to Prevent Blindness, Harrisburg, Pa., 1986-89; exec. dir. Nat. Kidney Found., Ind., 1990-92; mortgage broker, loan officer Louisville, 1992-94; dir. devel. Holy Rosary Acad., 1994-96, Presbyn. Cmty. Ctr., Louisville, 1996-98, Cedar Lake Found., LaGrange, Ky., 1998-2000, Bridgehaven, Inc., Louisville, 2000-01; assoc. dir. Cmty. Found. of South Ala., Mobile, 2001—. Cons. Conn. Gen. Assembly, Hartford, Conn., 1973-75; bd. dirs. Ind. Organ Donors Adv. Bd., Indpls., 1990-92. Writer newspaper column Phoenixville News, 1983-85; contbr. articles to mags. Bd. dirs. earth day Louisville Zoo, Louisville Audubon Soc., Louisville Nature Ctr., Kentuckiana Children's Ctr., Gulf Coast chpt. Assn. Fundraising Profls., Fair Housing Ctr.; chair bd. cert. AFP Greater Metro Louisville. Mem. Assn Fund Raising Profls. (cert.), Focus Louisville, U. Club Louisville, Exch. Club U.S. (hon. life). Avocations: oil painting, gardening, reading, writing, travel. Office: Cmty Found South Ala PO Box 990 Mobile AL 36601 E-mail: tlivers12@cs.com., tlivers@communityendowment.com.

LIVERSAGE, RICHARD ALBERT, cell biologist, educator; b. Fitchburg, Mass., July 8, 1925; s. Rodney Marcellus and Hazel Mildred (Huntting) L.; m. June Patricia Krebs, June 19, 1954; children: John Walter, Robert Richard, James Keith, Ross Andrew. BA, Marlboro Coll., 1951; A.M., Amherst Coll., 1953, Princeton U., 1957, PhD, 1958. Fellow Bowdoin Coll., Brunswick, Maine, 1953-54; instr. Amherst Coll., 1954-55, Princeton, 1958-60; mem. faculty U. Toronto, 1960—, prof. zoology, 1969—, grad. sec. dept., 1975-77, asso. chmn. grad. affairs dept., 1978-84, acting chmn., 1980-81. Investigator Huntsman Marine Lab., St. Andrews, N.B., Can., 1968-71; vis. prof. Strangeways Rsch. Lab., Cambridge, Eng., 1972. Contbr. numerous articles on role of nerves and endocrine secretions and the genetic basis of vertebrate appendage regeneration to sci. jours. Served as flight engr. USAAF, 1943-45. Recipient 5 decorations. Mem. Royal Can. Inst., Sigma Xi (exec. com., v.p., pres. U. Toronto chpt.). Home: 48 Ferndell Cir Unionville ON Canada L3R 3Y8 Office: U Toronto Ramsay Wright Zool Lab Toronto ON Canada M5S 3G5 E-mail: liversag@zoo.utoronto.ca.

LIVESAY, THOMAS ANDREW, museum administrator, lecturer; b. Dallas, Feb. 1, 1945; s. Melvin Ewing Clay and Madge Almeda (Hall) L.; m. Jennifer Clark, June 15, 1985 (div.); 1 child, Russell; m. Amanda Haralson, Nov. 12, 1994; children: Heather Marie, Seth Stover. BFA, U. Tex., Austin, 1968, MFA, 1972; postgrad., Harvard U. Inst. Arts Adminstrn., 1978. Curator Elisabet Ney Mus., Austin, 1971-73; dir. Longview (Tex.) Mus. and Arts Center, 1973-75; curator Amarillo (Tex.) Art Center, 1975-77, dir., 1977-80; asst. dir. for adminstrn. Dallas Mus. Fine Arts, 1980-85; dir. Mus. of N.Mex., Santa Fe, 1985-2000, Whatcom Mus. History and Art, Bellingham, Wash., 2000—. Mem. touring panel Tex. Commn. Arts; mem. panel Nat. Endowment Arts, Inst. Mus. Svcs.; adj. prof. U. Okla., Coll. Liberal Studies, 1992—, U. N.Mex., 1992—; chmn. N.Mex. State Records and Archives Commn., 1986—. Author: Young Texas Artists Series, 1978, Made in Texas, 1979; editor: video tape American Images, 1979, Ruth Abrams, Paintings, 1940-85, NYU Press. Served with U.S. Army, 1969-71. Mem. Am. Assn. Mus. (coun. 1986-89, commn. on ethics 1992—, accreditation commn. 1994—, chmn. acreditation commn. 1997—), Tex. Assn. Mus. (v.p. 1981, pres. 1983), Rotary. Presbyterian. Office: Whatcom Mus History & Art 121 Prospect St Bellingham WA 98225 E-mail: tlivesay@cob.org.

LIVESAY, VALORIE ANN, security program analyst; b. Greeley, Colo., Sept. 9, 1959; d. John Albert and Mary Magdalene Yurchak. BA in Edn., U. No. Colo., 1981; M in Computer Info. Sys., U. Denver, 1991; AAS in Fashion Mktg., Colo. Inst. Art, 1996. Drafter Computer Graphics, Denver, 1981, Advanced Cable Sys., Inc., Denver, 1981-82, Am. TV Comm. Corp., Englewood, Colo., 1982-83; janitor Rockwell Internat., Golden, 1983-84, analytical lab tech., 1984-86, metall. operator, 1986-88; nuclear material coord. EG&G Rocky Flats Inc., 1988-92, lead security analyst, 1992-95; adminstr., coord. Colo. Inst. Art, Denver, 1996-97. Active Channel 6, Denver, 1985, World Wildlife Fund, Westminster, Colo., 1987, Denver Dumb Friends League, 1987, The Nature Conservancy, Boulder, Colo., 1989. Mem. NAFE, Am. Soc. Insdl. Security. Avocations: scuba diving, mountain biking, skiing, reading, boating. Home: 7445 Sarasota Ln Santa Fe NM 87505 Office: U Calif Los Alamos Nat Lab Los Alamos NM 87545

LIVICK, STEPHEN, fine art photographer; b. Leeds, Yorkshire, Eng., Feb. 11, 1945; arrived in Can., 1947; Student, Sir George Williams U., Montreal, Can., 1963-66. Self employed artist, 1970—. One man shows include Centaur Gallery, Montreal, 1972, London Art Gallery, Ont., 1973, George Eastman House, Rochester, N.Y., 1975, David Mirvish Gallery, Toronto, 1976, 77, Photography Gallery, Bowmanville, Ont., 1976, 77, Balt. Mus. Art, 1978, Lunn Graphics, Washington D.C., 1978, Gallery Graphics, Ottawa, 1978, Jane Corkin Gallery, Toronto, 1979, 80, 81, U. Western Ont., London, 1981, 93, George Dalsheimer Gallery, Balt., 1982, MacDonald Stewart Art Ctr., Guelph, 1983, 94, New Brunswick Craft Sch., Fredericton, 1986, Winnipeg Photographers Group, 1987, Galerie Sequence, Quebec, 1988, U .Sherbrooke, 1990, Can. Mus. Contemporary Photography, Ottawa, 1992, MacKenzie Art Gallery, Regina, 1994, Meml. U. Art Gallery, St. John's, 1994, Beaverbrook Art Gallery, Fredicton, 1995, Art Gallery Windsor, 1995, Columbia U., N.Y., 1996, Tokyo Art Gallery, Ginza, Japan, 1998; travelling exhibitions include George Eastman House, 1978-81, London Regional Art Gallery, 1976-77, Nat. Film Bd., 1976-84, Art Gallery Ont., 1980, 81, Can. Mus. Contemporary Photography, 1986, 87; exhibited in group shows at Nat. Art Gallery, Ottawa, 1975, London Pub. Art Gallery, 1976, Nat. Film Bd., Ottawa, Can., 1977, Mendal Art Gallery, Saskatoon, Can., 1977, Neikrug Galleries, N.Y.C., 1978, Banff-London Exchange, Alberta, Can., 1978, Smithsonian Instn., Washington, 1981, Carpenter Ctr. Visual Arts, Cambridge, Mass., 1981, U. Calgary, 1982, Saidy Bronfman Mus., Montreal, 1984, Photographers Gallery, London, Eng., 1984, Presentation House, Vancouver, B.C., 1985, Photo Union Gallery, Hamilton, Ont., 1986, Film In The City, St. Paul, 1989, Corcoran Gallery Art, Washington, 1989, London (Can.) Regional Art Mus., 1990, Can. Mus. Contemporary Photography, Ottowa, 1992, others; represented in permanent collections Nat. Art Gallery Can., Can Mus. Contemporary Photography, Art Gallery Ont., Can. Art Bank, Nat. Archives Can., Mus. Modern Art, N.Y., George Eastman House, Rochester, N.Y., Carnegie Mus. Art, Pitts., Mus. Fine Arts, Houston, Fogg Art Mus., Cambridge, Mass., Balt. Mus. Art, George Washington U., Washington, Norton Gallery Art, West Palm Beach, Fla., Syracuse (N.Y.) U., Middlebury (Vt.) Coll., Hickory (N.C.) Mus. Art, U. Iowa Mus., U. No. Iowa, Art Gallery Hamilton, Can., High Mus. Art, Atlanta, Ga., London Regional Art Gallery, Corcoran Gallery Art, Washington, Queens U., Kingston, Can., Winnipeg (Can.) Art Gallery, Sarnia (Ont.) Art Gallery, U. Western Ont., London, Macdonald Stewart Art Ctr., Guelph, Ont., numerous pvt., corp. collections. B level grantee Can. Coun., Ottawa; sr. grantee Ont. Arts Coun., Toronto. Home and Office: 22A Maitland St Studio London ON N6B 3L2 Canada N6B 3L2 E-mail: slivick@livick.com.

LIVINGOOD, WILSON S. law enforcement official; b. Phila., Oct. 1, 1936; s. Clarence S. and Louise S. L.; m. Mari Louise Vatter, Feb. 21, 1998; stepchildren: Sarah, Elizabeth, Anne. BS in Police Adminstrn., Mich. State U., 1961. Spl. agt. U.S. Secret Svc., Dallas, 1961-69, spl. agt. in charge, 1969-86, deputy asst. dir., 1986-89, exec. asst. to dir., 1989-95; sgt. at arms U.S. Ho. of Reps., Washikngton, 1995—. Bd. dirs. Fed. Law Enforcement Tng. Ctr., Glynco, Ga. With USN, 1954-57. Mem. Nat. Sheriffs Assn., Internat. Assn. Chiefs of Police (exec. com. 1993-2001), Belle Haven Country Club (past bd. dirs.). Epsicopalian. Avocations: tennis, running, skiing, sailing, golf. Office: US Ho of Reps H-124 The Capitol Washington DC 20515-0001

LIVINGSTON, ALAN WENDELL, communications executive; b. McDonald, Pa. s. Maurice H. and Rose L. (Wachtel) L.; m. Nancy Olson, Sept. 1, 1962; children: Peter, Laura, Christopher. BS, U. Pa., 1940. Exec. v.p. Capitol Records, Inc., Hollywood, Calif., 1946-55, pres., chmn., 1960-68; v.p. programming NBC, Burbank, 1955-60; pres. Mediarts, Inc., Los Angeles, 1968-76; exec. v.p., pres. entertainment group 20th Century Fox Film Corp., Beverly Hills, Calif., 1976-80; pres. Pacific Rim Entertainment, Los Angeles, 1980-95; novelist, cons. Access Fund and Atlanta Investment Fund, Inc., Beverley Hills, 1995—. Creator various children's books, records and Bozo the Clown, 1946—; author: Ronnie Finklehof, Superstar, 1988; writer, producer (animated film) Sparky's Magic Piano, 1988. Bd. dirs. Ctr. Theater Group, Los Angeles. Served to 2d lt. inf. U.S. Army, 1943-46. Mem. ASCAP, Nat. Acad. Rec. Arts and Scis., Acad. TV Arts and Scis., Acad. Motion Picture Arts and Scis.

LIVINGSTON, ALFRED JAMES, archaeologist, consultant; b. Gallup, N.Mex., Mar. 14, 1967; s. Wilbur James Livingston and Marie Jean Yazzie. AA, York (Nebr.) Coll., 1988; BA, No. Ariz. U., 1995. Archaeol. aide Bur. Indian Affairs, Ft. Defiance, Ariz., 1988—89; archaeologist tech. II Navajo Nation Hist. Preservation, Window Rock, 1990; archaeologist Office of Contract Archaeology, Albuquerque, 1991; archaeologist II Navajo Nation Archaeology Dept., Flagstaff, Ariz., 1991—97; archaeologist Navajo Housing Authority, Window Rock, 1997—. Archaeologist Dept. of State of Baden Wurttem, Karlsruhe, Germany, 1995; vol. archaeologist Dept. So. Archaeology, Aix en Provence, France, 1995. Mem.: Soc. Am. Archaeology, Am. Anthropol. Assn. Avocations: travel, painting, walking, hiking, exploring. Mailing: PO Box 1579 Fort Defiance AZ 86504 Fax: 928-729-6602. E-mail: alivingston@hooghan.org.

LIVINGSTON, ANN CHAMBLISS, lawyer; b. Mpls., July 25, 1952; d. Johnston Redmond and Patricia A. Livingston. BA, Trinity U., San Antonio, 1974; JD, St. Mary's U., San Antonio, 1979. Bar: Tex. 1979, U.S. Ct. Appeals (5th cir.) 1981, U.S. Patent and Trademark Office, 1986, Ct. Appeals (fed. cir.) 1988. Briefing atty. Supreme Ct. of Tex., Austin, 1979-80; assoc. Groce, Locke & Hebdon, San Antonio, 1980-85; ptnr. Gunn, Lee & Jackson, 1985-89; assoc. Baker, Mills & Glast, 1989-90, Baker & Botts, San Antonio, 1990—. Exec. editor St. Mary's U. Law Jour., 1978-79. Mem. Tex. Bar Assn., Phi Delta Phi. Home: 1201 Loop 165 Dripping Springs TX 78620-4725 Office: Baker & Botts 98 San Jacinto Blvd Ste 1600 Austin TX 78701-4078

LIVINGSTON, BOB (ROBERT LINLITHGOW LIVINGSTON JR.), lawyer, former congressman; b. Colorado Springs, Colo., Apr. 30, 1943; s. Robert L. and Dorothy (Godwin) Livingston; m. Bonnie Robichaux, Sept. 13, 1965; children: Robert Linlithgow III, Richard Godwin, David Barkley, SuShan Alida. BA in Econs., Tulane U., 1967, JD, 1968; postgrad., Loyola Inst. Politics, 1973. Bar: La. 1968. Ptnr. Livingston & Powers, New Orleans, 1976—77; asst. U.S. atty., dep. chief criminals divsn. U.S. Attys. Office, 1970—73; chief spl. prosecutor, chief armed robbery divsn. Orleans Parish Dist. Atty.'s Office, 1974—75; chief prosecutor organized crime unit La. Atty. Gen.'s Office, 1975—76; mem. 95th-106th Congresses from 1st La. Dist., 1977—99; chair appropriations com., 1996—98; founder The Livingston Group, Washington, 1999—. Bd. dirs. Holcim, Inc., 2000—. Mem. nat. adv. bd. Young Ams. for Freedom; bd. suprs. Smithsonian Inst., 1995—98; bd. dirs. Internat. Rep. Inst. Ctr. for Democracy, 1996—. Named Outstanding Asst. U.S. Atty., 1973. Mem.: ABA, New Orleans Bar Assn., La. Bar Assn., Fed. Bar Assn., Am. Legion, Navy League. Roman Catholic. Office: The Livingston Group 499 S Capitol St SW Ste 600 Washington DC 20003

LIVINGSTON, CRAIG, history educator; b. Provo, Utah, Dec. 30, 1959; BA, Brigham Young U., 1985, MA, 1991; PhD, Temple U., 2002. Rschr. Smith Inst. Brigham Young U., Provo, Utah, 1990-92; history tchr. Valley Forge Mil. Acad., Wayne, Pa., 1993-95; prof. history Montgomery Coll., Conroe, Tex., 1995—. Contbr. articles to profl. jours. Capt. U.S. Army, 1986-89. Mem.: Soc. Historians Am. Fgn. Rels., Mormon History Assn. Avocations: military miniatures, bagpipes. Office: Montgomery Coll 3200 College Park Dr Conroe TX 77384-4500 E-mail: craigl@nhmccd.edu.

LIVINGSTON, DAVID MORSE, biomedical scientist, physician, internist; b. Cambridge, Mass., Mar. 29, 1941; s. Arthur Joshua and Phyllis Freda (Kanters) Livingston; m. Jacqueline Gutman, June 23, 1963 (div. 1983); m. Emily Rabb, Jan. 25, 1986; children: Catherine Ellen, Julie. AB cum laude, Harvard U., 1961; MD magna cum laude, Tufts U., 1965. Diplomate Am. Bd. Med. Examiners, Am. Bd. Internal Medicine. Intern, resident Peter Bent Brigham Hosp., Boston, 1965—67; rsch. assoc., sr. staff fellow, sr. investigator NCI-NIH, Bethesda, Md., 1967—69, 1971—73; rsch. fellow in biol. chemistry Harvard Med. Sch., Boston, 1969—71, asst. prof. medicine, 1973—76, assoc. prof. medicine, 1976—82, prof. medicine, 1982—92, Emil Frei prof. medicine, 1992—; v.p. Dana-Farber Cancer Inst., Boston, 1989—91, dir., physician-in-chief, 1991—95; Emil Frei prof. medicine and genetics Harvard Med. Sch., 1998—, chmn. exec. com. rsch., 1995—2000. Dep. dir., mem. exec. com. Dana-Farber Harvard Cancer Ctr., 1999—. Mem. editl. bd. Virology , 1989—97, MOI & Cell Biology , 1998—2000; editor: BBA Revs. on Cancer, 1988—2001; contbr. articles to profl. jours. Comdr. USPHS, 1967—73; mem. sci. adv. com. Damon Runyan-Walter Winchell Cancer Fund, N.Y.C., 1988—92, chmn. sci. adv. com., 1989—92; vice chmn. sci. adv. com. Pezcoller Found., Trento, Italy, 1994—; mem. sci. adv. bd. Inst. Cancer Rsch., Fox Chase, Pa., 1991—96, Lineburger Comprehensive Cancer Ctr., U. N.C., Chapel Hill, 1993—95, MIT Cancer Ctr., 1994—; mem. ext. adv. com. Fred Hutchinson Cancer Rsch. Ctr., 1992—96, Ctr. Cancer Rsch. MIT, 1994—; chmn. bd. sci. advisers NIC/NIH, 1995—99; Cancer Rsch. Fund, 1992—; pres. bd. Cancer Rsch. Fund, 1997—, mem. exec. com., 1994—. Recipient Claire & Richard Morse award for Rsch., Dana-Farber Cancer Inst., 1991, Baxter award, AAMC, 1997, Brinker award, Susan Komen Found., 1997, Lila Gruber award, 2001. Mem.: NAS, Inst. Medicine of NAS, Am. Soc. Virology, Am. Soc. Biol. Chemistry and Molecular Biology, Assn. Am. Physicians, Am. Soc. for Clin. Investigation, Harvard Club (N.Y.C., Boston), St. Botolph Club, Met. Club Washington, Alpha Omega Alpha. Achievements include discovery of important aspects of the neoplastic transforming process and of the mechanisms governing control of the mammalian cell cycle. Office: Dana-Farber Cancer Inst 44 Binney St Boston MA 02115-6084

LIVINGSTON, DOUGLAS MARK, lawyer; b. Lawton, Okla., Nov. 2, 1945; s. Oscar Calloway and Irene (Norton) L.; m. Vicki Sue Ratts, Dec. 21, 1969; children: Lisa Marie, Stephen Mark, Anna Lee, Micah James. BS, Okla. Christian Coll., 1967; MPH, U. Okla., 1969, JD, 1980; MEd, Wayne State U., 1981; Grad., USAF War Coll., 1994, U.S. Army War Coll., 1998. Bar: Okla. 1980, U.S. Dist. Ct. (we. dist.) Okla. 1987, U.S. Army Ct. Mil. Rev. 1989, U.S. Ct. Appeals for Armed Forces 1995, U.S. Ct. Appeals (fed. cir.) 1995, U.S. Supreme Ct. 2000. Intern Cleveland County Dist. Atty., Norman, Okla., 1979-80; gen. counsel, dir. Delphi Devel., Ltd., 1980-81, Pepco Devel., Inc., Norman, 1981-85; gen. counsel Pepco, Inc., 1981-85; owner, ptnr. Payne, Livingston & Harold, P.C., Oklahoma City, 1985-86, Livingston Law Office, Norman, 1986-92, 93-94; staff atty. U.S. Dept. of Army, Ft. Sill, Okla., 1992-93, labor atty., 1994-2000; atty.-advisor Dept. Air Force, Tinker AFB, 2000—. Ptnr. Concord Investments, Ltd., Norman, 1982-88; team dir. 33d judge adv. gen. detachment, Oklahoma City, 1988-91, 29th judge adv. gen. detachment, Tulsa, 1991-93; staff judge adv. 4003d U.S. Army Garrison, Ft. Chaffee, Ark., 1993-95, 122nd USAR Command, North Little Rock, Ark., 1995; comdr. 1st Legal Support Orgn., San Antonio, 1995-98; staff judge adv. 90th Regional Support Command, North Little Rock, Ark., 1998-2001. Editor coll. newspaper Talon, 1966; note editor Am. Indian Law Rev., 1979-80. Bd. dirs. Big Bros./Big Sisters, Norman, 1983-85, Rock Creek Youth Camp, Norman, 1985-94; Rep. precinct chmn., Oklahoma City, 1971. Capt. U.S. Army, 1973-77; col. USAR. Named one of Outstanding Young Men of Am., 1973. Mem. Okla. Bar Assn., Fed. Bar Assn., Cleveland County Bar Assn., Res. Officers Assn., Assn. U.S. Army., Sr. Army Res. Comdr.'s Assn., U.S. Army JAG Sch. Alumni Assn., U.S. Army War Coll. Alumni Assn. Mem. Ch. of Christ. Avocations: family activities, reading, running. Home: 911 S Lahoma Ave Norman OK 73069-4509 Office: Office of Staff Judge Adv 7460 Arnold St Sewing Tinker AFB OK 73145-9002 E-mail: douglas.livingston@tinker.af.mil.

LIVINGSTON, GIDEON ELEAZAR (GUY LIVINGSTON), food and nutrition scientist, consultant; b. Rotterdam, The Netherlands, Feb. 1, 1927; came to U.S., 1940, naturalized, 1945; s. Morris S. and Rachel (Grunfeld) L.; m. Cilla Mahr, Sept. 18, 1948 (div. Apr. 1987); children: David J., Gary M., Nina J. Livingston Phillis; m. Joan Bendel Adams, July 13, 1991. BA, NYU, 1948; MS, U. Mass., 1951, PhD, 1952. Cert. nutrition specialist, 1995, N.Y. State cert. dietician and nutritionist, 1996. Asst. prof. U. Mass., Amherst, 1951-53, assoc. prof., 1953-59; pres. Food Sci Assocs., Dobbs Ferry, N.Y., 1956—. Pres. Eli Gilde, Ltd., Dobbs Ferry, 1995—; adj. prof. Columbia U., N.Y.C., 1966-72, Pratt Inst., Bklyn., 1972-78, NYU, N.Y.C., 1978-89; chmn. food and nutrition coun. Am. Health Found., N.Y.C., 1970-91, chmn. Inst. Food Technologists's commemoration of 250th Anniversary Nicolas Appert, 1999; bd. dirs. DeLuca Pasta Co., 1987-96, Sierra Sunset, Inc., 1988—, Mitchell Lane Kitchens, Inc., 1991-93. Author: Happiness Is...a Celebration of Life and Love, 1996; co-author: Food Service Systems: Analysis, Design and Implementation, 1979; editor: Nutritional Status Assessment of the Individual, 1989; editor-in-chief Pioneers in Food Sci., 1993—; co-editor: Role of Product Development in Implementing Dietary Guidelines, 1982, Environmental Aspects of Cancer, 1984. With U.S. Army, 1945-47, ETO. Recipient Rsch. award U. Mass. chpt. Sigma Xi, 1957. Fellow AAAS, Am. Coll. Nutrition, Inst. Food Technologists (pres. N.Y. sect. 1969-70, Carl R. Fellers award 1993, Foodservice Disting. Achievement award 1996); mem. Am. Chem. Soc., Rsch. Devel. Assocs. for Mil. Food and Packaging Sys. (hon.), N.Y. Acad. Scis. Avocation: writing fiction and biographies.

LIVINGSTON, JAMES DUANE, physicist, educator; b. Bklyn., June 23, 1930; s. James Duane and Florence (Boullee) L.; m. Nancy Lee Clark, June 27, 1953 (div. 1976); children: Joan, Susan, Barbara; m. Sharon Hood Penney, Mar. 30, 1985. B in Engring. Physics, Cornell U., 1952; PhD in Applied Physics, Harvard U., 1956. Physicist R & D GE, Schenectady, N.Y., 1956-89; sr. lectr. dept. material sci. and engring. MIT, Cambridge, 1989—. Author: Driving Force: The Natural Magic of Magnets, 1996, Electronic Properties of Engineering Materials, 1999; author, co-author over 100 publications in field. Coolidge Fellow Gen. Electric Corp. R & D, 1987; recipient Disting. Career award Hudson-Mohawk chpt. AIME, 1986. Fellow Am. Soc. Metals, Am. Phys. Soc.; mem. Nat. Acad. Engring., IEEE, AAAS, Materials Rsch. Soc., The Minerals, Metals and Materials Soc. Democrat. Unitarian Universalist. Achievements include 7 patents; advanced research in superconducting, ferromagnetic, and mechanical properties of materials. Home: 90 Albee Dr Braintree MA 02184-8252 Office: MIT 13 4066 Cambridge MA 02139 E-mail: jdliv@mit.edu.

LIVINGSTON, JEFFERY C. history educator; b. Dayton, Ohio, Aug. 20, 1957; s. Charles Hugh and Nancy Carol Livingston; m. Julie Ann Archer, June 6, 1987; children: Jade, Levi. BA, Miami U., Oxford, Ohio, 1980; MA, U. Toledo, Ohio, 1985, PhD, 1989. Prof. history Calif. State U., Chico, 1989—, campus master tchr., 1999—. Prin. investigator North State History-Social Sci. Project, Chico, 1995—; cons. U.S. Dept. Edn. Jacob Javits Fellowship, Washington, 1993-95, Calif. Commn. on Tchr. Credentialing, 1994-95. Contbr. numerous articles to profl. jours. Vol., mem. program coun. KZFR Cmty. Radio, Chico, 1997—; mem. Chico Peace and Justice Ctr., 1997—. Mem. Orgn. Am. Historians, Soc. for Historians of Am. Fgn. Rels., ACLU, Amnesty Internat., Phi Alpha Theta, Phi Kappa Phi, Phi Eta Sigma. Avocations: sports, music, travel. Home: 721 Brookwood Way Chico CA 95926-1732 Office: Calif State U History Dept Chico CA 95929-0001 E-mail: jlivingston@csuchico.edu.

LIVINGSTON, JOHN H. retired other: engineering, retired military officer; b. Mo., Sept. 8, 1912; s. Alfred W. Livingston and Ida Catherine Fink; m. Sarah Hester Eilyeen Broyles, Apr. 3, 1943 (dec. Apr. 30, 1998); children: John H. Jr., Joseph W., Mary E. Attended, Air Force Sch. Tech.; MSChemE, La. State U., 1948; BS in civil engring. , Mo. Sch. of Mines, 1939. Engr. State of Mo., 1949, State of La., 1956—70. Mem. Phelps County Heritage Soc., Rolla, Mo.; donator South Bossier Vol. Fire Dept.; donator 3,000 books Centenary Coll., Shreveport, La. Lt. U.S. Army, 1939—49, maj. U.S. Army, 1942, capt. U.S. Army, 1942, 1st lt. U.S. Army, 1941, served USAR, 1940, 2nd lt. U.S. Army, 1939—40. Recipient purple heart, U.S. Army, bronze star, commendation ribbon. Mem.: Alumni Adv. Bd. Found., Soc. Am. Mil. Engrs. (pres.), Veterans of Foreign Wars, Heroes of '76, La. Engring. Soc., Retired Officers Assn. (life), Mil. Order of Purple Heart (life), Atkins Lodge. Home: PO Box 178 Elm Grove LA 71051-0178

LIVINGSTON, JOHNSTON REDMOND, manufacturing executive; b. Foochow, China, Dec. 18, 1923; s. Henry Walter V and Alice (Moorehead) Livingston; m. Caroline Johnson, Aug. 17, 1946 (dec.); children: Henry, Ann, Jane, David; m. Patricia Karolchuck, Sept. 4, 1965. BS in Engring. with honors, Yale U., 1947; MBA with distinction, Harvard U., 1949. With Mpls.-Honeywell Regulator Co., 1949-55; with Whirlpool Corp., 1956-66, v.p., until 1966, Redman Industries, Dallas, 1966-67; dir. Constrn. Tech., Inc., 1967—, pres., chmn. bd. dirs. Denver, 1974-89; chmn. bd. dirs. Enmark Corp., 1979-90. Pres. Marcor Housing Sys., Inc., Denver, 1971-74. Past mem. industry adv. com. Nat. Housing Ctr.; bd. dirs., past pres. Nat. Home Improvement Coun.; pres., chmn. bd. dirs. Denver Symphony Assn., 1977-81; bd. dirs., past chmn. bd. dirs. Rocky Mountain Regional Inst. Internat. Edn.; trustee, pres. Bonfils-Stanton Found., Denver, 1979—; hon. trustee Inst. Internat. Edn., N.Y. Baker scholar, Harvard U., 1949. Mem. Rocky Mountain World Trade Assn. (bd. dirs., past chmn. bd. dirs.), Denver Country Club, Yale Club N.Y., Sigma Xi, Tau Beta Pi. Home: 2800 S University Blvd No 27 Denver CO 80210 Office: 5070 Oakland St Denver CO 80239-2724

LIVINGSTON, JOYCE TORBIC, civilian military employee; b. Lumberton, N.C., Sept. 12, 1953; d. Myles and Rena Mae Torbic; m. Edwin Charles Livingston; children: Kristi. BS in Bus., Troy State U., 1985. Audit clk. IRS, Columbus, Ga., 1976—81; mgmt. analyst Civil Svc., Ft. Benning, 1981—. Author: (novels) Borrowed Memories, 2000, The Edge of Good-bye, 2001. Vol. Animal Human Soc., Columbus, 2000—02. Methodist. Avocations: physical fitness, reading, gardening. Home: 308 Turkey Tr Fortson GA 31808 Office: Western Hemisphere Inst 7011 Morrison Ave Ridgway Hall Fort Benning GA 31905-2611 Business E-Mail: livingstonj@benning.army.mil.

LIVINGSTON, KATHRYN E. writer; b. Schenectady, N.Y., Jan. 11, 1953; d. Abram Fryer Livingston, Virginia Kathryn Swart; m. Mitchell Kriegler, June 5, 1977; 3 children. BA, Kirkland Coll., Clinton, N.Y., 1975; MA, Hunter Coll., N.Y.C., 1979. Freelance writer, 1983—. Author: Special Effects Photography, 1985, Patrick Demarchelier: Fashion Photographer, 1984, Secrets of Studio Still Life Photography, 1984, Photographing Your Baby, 1984; co-author: Parenting Partners (St. Martins), 1999, The Secret Life of the Dyslexic Child, 2002; contbr. Mailing: 143 Highview Pl Bogota NJ 07603

LIVINGSTON, LEE FRANKLIN, real estate and finance consultant; b. Boston, Feb. 20, 1942; s. William and Frances (Turner) L.; m. Elaine Wiesenfeld, June 9, 1968; children: Eli, Jed. Student, Sch. Visual Arts, 1959-62, Georgetown U., 1964. Mem. staff pub. rels. and promotion dept. Newsweek, N.Y.C., 1965-70; mng. dir., sec., treas. Anasarca Corp., North Brunswick, 1971—. Pres. Imperial Cons., Inc.; ptnr. Bess & Co., Phila. Stock Exch.; cons. on charitable fund raising to various charities, 1971—. Active charities for retarded citizens and women and children victims of abuse, also Spl. Olympics; trustee, pres. Anshe Emeth Meml. Temple; treas. Jewish Social Svcs.; bd. dirs. Women Aware. With C.E., U.S. Army, 1962-64. Recipient Am. Svc. award Girl Scouts U.S., Bronze Svc. award Spl. Olympics, Svc. award Spl. Edn., 1989, 91, N.J. Person of Yr. award, 1992. Mem. Greenacres Country Club, Phila. Stock Exch. Club. Democrat. Home: 12 Derby Ln # 4 North Brunswick NJ 08902-4729 also: 3300 S Ocean Blvd Palm Beach FL 33480-5637 Office: 850 Us Highway 1 New Brunswick NJ 08902-3312

LIVINGSTON, MARGARET GRESHAM, civic leader; b. Birmingham, Ala., Aug. 16, 1924; d. Owen Garside and Katherine Milton (Morrow) Gresham; m. James Archibald Livingston, Jr., July 16, 1947; children: Mary Margaret, James Archibald, Katherine Wiley, Elizabeth Gresham. Grad., The Baldwin Sch., Phila., 1942; AB, Vassar Coll., 1945; MA, U. Ala., 1946. Acting dir. Birmingham Mus. Art, 1978-79, 81, chmn. bd. dirs., 1978-86, mem. exec. bd., 1978—. Bd. dirs. Birmingham Civic Ctr. Authority, 1988-95; bd. dirs. Altamont Sch., Birmingham, 1963—, chmn. bd., 1986. Named Woman of Yr., Birmingham 1986; named to Ala. Tennis Hall of Fame, 1994. Mem. Am. Assn. Mus., Jr. League, Ala. Tennis Assn. Episcopalian.

LIVINGSTON, MARGERY ELSIE, missionary, clinical psychologist; b. Petoskey, Mich., Oct. 29, 1940; d. David Eugene and Beryle Mae (Herrington) L. BS with honors, Taylor U., Upland, Ind., 1962; MA with high honors, Wheaton (Ill.) Coll., 1983; student, U. Paris Sorbonne, 1970. Lic. psychologist, Pa., limited lic. psychologist, Mich. Tchr. Waterford (Mich.) Sch. Sys., 1962-64; ednl. missionary, county dir. BCM Internat., Union County, N.J., 1965-69; ednl. missionary BCM Internat. and AIM Internat., Albertville and Paris, France, 1969-70, ednl. missionary, technician Watsa, Democratic Republic of Congo, 1970-81; counselor, therapist BCM Internat./AIM Internat. Amani Counseling Ctr., Nairobi, Kenya, 1983-84; organizer, dir. counseling dept., counselor, cons. BCM Internat., Upper Darby, Pa., 1985-97, organizer, dir. mem. care ministries, 1998-2000, mem. care ministries, cons., 2000—. Guest lectr. Bunia (Dem. Rep. Congo) Theol. Sem., 1984, Adi (Dem. Rep. Congo) Bible Inst., 1978, Aru (Dem. Rep. Congo) Bible Inst., 1978, Todro (Dem. Rep. Congo) Bible Inst., 1980; organizer/facilitator Missions and Mental Health-East, Mt. Bethel, Pa., 1995-97; guest lectr. Communauté Evangelique Ctr. de l'Afrique Chs., Dem. Republic of Congo, 1991; spkr. in field. Editor: Commit They Way, 1994; author: (Bible study series) Living in Community, 1980, translator (illustrator) Bible lessons from English to Lingala for use in Congo; contbr. articles to profl. jours. Spkr., adj. staff Rockford (Mich.) Bapt. Ch., 1965—, Haven Reformed Ch., Kalamazoo, 1978—2002, Clinton Hill Bapt. Ch., Union, NJ, 1965—, Silvercrest Bapt. Ch., Waterford, Mich., 1966—, First Congl. Ch., Rockford, 1985—, North Plainfield (N.J.) Bapt. Ch., 1988—; facilitator Bible Club work Democratic Republic of Congo, 1985—; fundraiser, facilitator printing and distbn. Christian lit. Democratic Republic of Congo, 2001—. Billy Graham Evangelistic Assn. scholar, 1981-83. Mem.: APA (assoc.), Midwest Mem. Care Network (charter), Christian Therapists Bible Study, Assn. N.Am. Missions, Am. Assn. of Christian Counselors (charter, spkr. regional conf. 1999). Baptist. Avocations: writing poetry, clarinet, walking, aerobic weight-lifting, swimming. Office: 309 Colonial Dr Box 249 Akron PA 17501-0249 also: BCMI Western Mich 710 Baldwin St Jenison MI 49428-9706 E-mail: worship@rockfordbaptist.com.

LIVINGSTON, MYRAN JAY, author, film writer, director and producer; b. N.Y.C., Mar. 19, 1934; s. Myran Jabez and Anne Josephine (White) L.; m. Elizabeth Rasmussen, July 28, 1956 (div. May 1971); 1 child, Lisa Browning; m. Bernice Helen Beck, Nov. 8, 1971; children: Simon Jabez, Sarah Gustine. Student, Kenyon Coll., 1952-56, U.C.L.A., 1957-58. Writer/dir. CBS TV Network, L.A., 1956-64, McCann-Erickson, San Francisco, 1965-71, Eastman Kodak, Rochester, N.Y., 1980-83; owner, operator Promethean Prodns., L.A., 1983-96. Guest lectr. Coll. of Marin, San Francisco, 1972-73, Loyola Marymount U., L.A., 1979, Rochester Inst. of Tech., 1982. Author: (novels) The Prodigy, 1979, The Synapse Function, 1985, Tchr. in comml. prodn. San Francisco Women in Advertising, 1976, The Del Monte Corp., San Francisco, 1970, Van Nuys (Calif.) H.S., 1980, Mira Catalina Sch., Palos Verdes, Calif., 1986. Recipient 7 Golden Eagle awards Coun. on Internat. Theatrical Events, 1982-84, 1st place Gold Camera award U.S. Indsl. Film Festival, 1984, CLIO for "Most Beautiful Spot" award Bullocks, 1978, 4 Telly Silver and Bronze awards 14th and 17th Ann. Competition, 1993,96. Mem. Writer's Guild of Am., The Author's Guild. Episcopalian. Avocations: classical piano, songwriting. Home and Office: Promethean Prodns 170 Honey Run Rd Chico CA 95928-8847 E-mail: promeprod@aol.com.

LIVINGSTON, PAMELA A. corporate image and marketing management consultant; b. Richmond Hill, N.Y., Nov. 21, 1930; d. Paul Yount and Anna Margaret (Altland) L. BA, Adelphi U., 1951; postgrad., NYU, 1952, Columbia U., 1959, Am. Acad. Dramatic Art, 1954, IBM Sys. and Mktg. Schs., 1967-70, Brandon Sch. Electronic Data, 1973, Pa. State U., 1993. Pers. and pub. rels. depts. Am. Can Co., N.Y.C., 1951-60; exec. sec. to pres. York (Pa.) divsn. Borg-Warner Corp., 1962-65; freelance writer, 1965-67; mktg. ofcl. IBM Corp., 1967-70; rsch. analyst, dir. new EDP bus. Ins. Co. N.Am., 1971-74; asst. to v.p. corp. affairs IU Internat., Phila., 1974-75; comm. and mktg. mgmt. cons. specializing in corp. identity, 1975—. Corp. image cons., 1984—; freelance writer, spkr. on identity, 1994—. Contbr. articles to tech jours. Recipient various journalism awards, award in mktg. and sales IBM, 1969-70, award for innovative product application, 1969. Mem. AAUW, Sales/Mktg. Execs. Internat., Art Alliance, Pub. Rels. Soc. Am., Econs. Club of York C. of C., Phila. Club Advt. Women, Phila. Acad. Fine Arts, World Affairs Coun., English-Speaking Union, Kappa Kappa Gamma. Home and Office: 108 S Rockburn St York PA 17402-3467

LIVINGSTON, RICHARD ALAN, retired secondary education educator; b. Johnstown, Pa., Nov. 3, 1935; s. James Dean and Mary Eva (Harshberger) L. BA, Juniata Coll., 1957; MDiv, Bethany Theol. Sem., Richmond, Ind., 1962; MusM, Northwestern U., 1964, PhD, 1977. Cert. secondary tchr., Ill. Tchr. English, Wendell Phillips H.S., Chgo., 1962-63, Reavis H.S., Burbank, Ill., 1964-68, Niles East H.S., Skokie, 1968-80, Niles North H.S., Skokie, 1980-93; ret., 1993. Mem. chorus Ch. of Ascension (Episcopal), Chgo., 1962-72, Chgo. Symphony Chorus, 1972— Pianist Highland Avenue Ch. of Brethren, Elgin, Ill., 1991—. Mem. Am. Guild Mus. Artists (Chgo. Symphony Chorus union del. 1977-80, nat. bd. govs. 1978—, chmn. exec. com. midwest area 1995-96), Niles Twp. H.S. Retirees Assn. (sec. 1994—). Avocations: attending opera, concerts, plays, hiking, reading, travel. Home: 1633 Winnetka Rd Glenview IL 60025-1823

LIVINGSTON, ROBERT A. brewing company executive; b. Dallas, Aug. 9, 1950; s. Stanley R. and Alberta L. Livingston. AA, Moorpark Coll., 1976; BA in Polit. Sci., U. Calif., Santa Barbara, 1980. Educator and tng. rep. U.S. VA, L.A., 1974-77; mgr. Beer and Wine Store, Santa Barbara, 1977-80; sales mgr. TAB Distributing Co., 1980-82; regional brewery rep. Coors Brewing Co., Golden, Colo., 1982-87, govtl. affairs mgr., 1987—. Spkr. in field. Mem. vets. adv. coun. U. Calif., Santa Barbara, 1978-79. Sgt. USMC, 1970-74, Viet Nam. Mem. VFW (award 1977), Tenn. Assn. Bus. (pub. affairs com. 1997—), Am. Legion, Pub. Affairs Coun., Rotary. Methodist. Avocations: coins, motorcycling, classical music events, foreign travel. Office: Coors Brewing Co PO Box 40685 Nashville TN 37204-0685

LIVINGSTON, ROBERT BOYD, oncologist, educator; b. Tulsa, June 3, 1941; s. Lee Shepherd and Helen Virginia Livingston; m. Shirley Leona Malarchuk, Apr. 6, 1974; children: Anne, Nicolas, Darcie. BA, U. Okla., 1963, MD, 1967. Diplomate Am. Bd. Internal Medicine, Am. Bd. Med. Oncology. Sr. asst. surgeon USPHS, Bethesda, Md., 1968-70; asst. prof. U. Tex. Health Scis., Houston, 1973-76, assoc. prof. San Antonio, 1976-79; chief hematology/oncology Cleve. Clinic, 1979-82; prof. U. Wash., Seattle, 1982—. Mem. editl. bd. Jour. Clin. Oncology, 1993—. Contbr. over 130 articles to profl. jours. Recipient Jeffrey A. Gottlieb Meml. award M.D. Anderson Hosp., 1998. Mem. Am. Soc. Clin. Oncology, Am. Assn. Cancer Rsch. Democrat. Avocations: jogging, cross-country skiing, tennis. Office: U Wash Med Ctr PO Box 356043 Seattle WA 98195-6043

LIVINGSTON, ROBERT GERALD, historian, journalist; b. N.Y.C., Nov. 17, 1927; s. Robert Teviot and Geraldine (Gray) L.; m. Jeanne Andrée Nettel, May 12, 1955; children: Catherine Schuyler Livingston Fernandez, Robert Eric. AB, AM, Harvard U., 1953, PhD, 1959. Fgn. svc. officer U.S. Dept. State, Washington, 1956-74; v.p. German Marshall Fund U.S., 1974-77, pres., 1977-81; writer, 1981-83; acting dir. Am. Inst. for Contemporary German Studies, Johns Hopkins U., 1983-87, dir. Am. Inst. for Contemporary German Studies, 1987-94, chief devel. officer, 1995-96; sr. vis. fellow German Hist. Inst., 1997—. Commentator "Die Woche," Hamburg, 1998—. Co-author, editor: The Federal Republic in the 1980s, 1983, West German Political Parties, 1986; contbr. over 300 articles to polit. jours. and newspapers. Sgt. U.S. Army, 1946-49. Mem. German Studies Assn. U.S., Harvard Grad. Sch. Alumni Assn. Coun., Coun. on Fgn. Rels., N.Y. Soc. Cons. of Cincinnati, Cosmos Club, Chevy Chase Club, Barnstable Yacht Club (Mass.), Phi Beta Kappa. Democrat. Episcopalian. Avocations: hiking, swimming, tennis. Office: German Historical Inst 1607 New Hampshire Ave NW Washington DC 20009-2562 E-mail: jliving844@aol.com.

LIVINGSTON, WILEY FREEMAN, JR. software engineer; b. Macon, Ga., Dec. 20, 1962; s. Wiley Freeman and Mary Virginia L.; m. Sandra Lynn Tackett, Apr. 22, 1988; children, Brian, Myra. BSEE, Auburn U., 1987. Registered profl. engr., Ga. Project mgr. USAF, Robins AFB, Ga., 1987—. Active PTO, Family Support Alliance for Mentally Ill. Mem. IEEE, Mid. Ga. Hemerocallis Soc. (1st v.p. 1998-2001). Roman Catholic. Avocations: gardening, computers. Home: 314 Cliff Howard Dr Warner Robins GA 31088-7944 Office: WR-ALC/LYSBB Richard Ray Blvd Robins AFB GA 31098 Fax: 775-402-1474. E-mail: wileylivingstone@cs.com.

LIVINGSTON, WILLIAM SAMUEL, university administrator, political scientist; b. Ironton, Ohio, July 1, 1920; s. Samuel G. and Bata (Elkins) L.; m. Lana Sanor, July 10, 1943; children: Stephen Sanor, David Duncan. BA, MA, Ohio State U., 1943; PhD, Yale U., 1950. Asst. prof. U. Tex., Austin, 1949-54, asso. prof., 1954-61, prof. govt., 1961—, chmn. dept. govt., 1965-69, Jo Anne Christian centennial prof. Brit. studies, 1982-95, asst. dean Grad. Sch., 1954-58, chmn. Grad. Assembly, 1965-68, chmn. faculty senate, 1973-79, chmn. comparative studies program, 1978-79; vice chancellor acad. programs U. Tex. System, 1969-71; v.p., dean grad. studies U Tex. Austin, 1979-95; acting pres. U. Tex. Austin, 1992-93; sr. v.p., 1995—. Vis. prof. Yale U., 1955-56, Duke U., 1960-61; sec.-treas. Assn. Grad. Schs., 1982-85; bd. dirs. Council Grad. Schs. in U.S., 1983-86. Author: Federalism and Constitutional Change, 1956; contbg. author: World Pressures on American Foreign Policy, 1962, Teaching Political Science, 1965, Federalism: Infinite Variety in Theory and Practice, 1968, Britain at the Polls 1979, 1981; editor: The Presidency and Congress: A Shifting Balance of Power, 1979; co-editor: Australia, New Zealand and the Pacific Islands Since the First World War, 1979; editor, contbr. author: Federalism in the Commonwealth, 1963, A Prospect of Liberal Democracy, 1979, The Legacy of the Constitution: An Assessment for the Third Century, 1987; book rev. editor: Jour. Politics, 1965-68, editor-in-chief, 1968-72; mem. editl. bd. Publius: Jour. of Federalism, 1971-95; mem. bd. editors: P.S, 1976-82, chmn., 1978-82. Served to 1st lt. FA AUS, 1943-45. Decorated Bronze Star, Purple Heart.; Recipient Teaching Excellence award, 1959; Ford Found. fellow, 1952-53; Guggenheim fellow, 1959-60; USIS lectr. in U.K. and India, 1977 Mem. Am. Polit. Sci. Assn. (exec. coun. and adminstrv. com. 1972-74, chmn. nominating com. 1973-74, 78-79), So. Polit. Sci. Assn. (exec. coun. 1964-67, pres. 1974-75), Southwestern Polit. Sci. Assn. (pres. 1973-74), Hansard Soc. (London), Philos. Soc. Tex., Austin Soc. for Pub. Adminstrn. (pres. 1973-74), Southwestern Social Sci. Assn. (pres. 1977-78), Phi Beta Kappa, Omicron Delta Kappa, Phi Gamma Delta, Pi Sigma Alpha (nat. coun. 1976-84, nat. pres. 1980-82). Home: 3203 Greenlee Dr Austin TX 78703-1621 Office: U Tex Office Sr VP Austin TX 78712

LIVINGSTONE, CAROL, academic administrator; b. Ridgewood, N.J., Oct. 11, 1953; d. Edward and Jane Margaret Livingstone; m. Daniel Richard Grayson, Aug. 29, 1976; children: Paul, David. BS, MIT, 1975; PhD, Columbia U., 1981, MBA, 1983. Cons. Sibson & Co., Princeton, NJ, 1981—82; acting dir. MBA program U. Ill., Urbana, 1983—84, dir. divsn. mgmt. info., 1984—, assoc. provost, 2000—. Bd. dirs. McKinley Found., Champaign, Ill., 2001—. Recipient J. Frederick Miller Vol. Svc. award, U. YMCA, Champaign, 1989. Mem.: Ill. Assn. Instnl. Rsch. (pres. 2001). Presbyterian. Home: 2409 S Vine St Urbana IL 61801

LIVINGSTONE, HARRISON EDWARD, writer, publisher; b. Urbana, Ill., May 23, 1937; s. Harry E. and Elsie (Harrison) L. BA, Harvard U., 1970; JD, U. Balt., 1963. Pres., owner The Conservatory Press, Balt., 1976—. Author: David Johnson Passed Through Here, 1971, The Wild Rose, 1985, HARVARD, John, 1987, High Treason, 1989 (N.Y. Times Bestseller), rev. edit., 1998, High Treason 2, 1992 (N.Y. Times Bestseller), Killing the Truth, 1993, Killing Kennedy, 1995, Baltimore, 1998, The Zapruder Film: Deceipt and Deception, 1999, Stunning New Evidence from the U.S. Govt. in the JFK Case, 2000, also numerous poems. Recipient Cert. of Honor, Balt. City Police, 1964; inductee Nat. Police Hall of Fame, 1964. Avocations: model railroading. Office: care The Conservatory Press PO Box FB Pacific Grove CA 93950

LIVINGSTONE, JOHN LESLIE, accountant, management consultant, business executive, educator; b. Johannesburg, South Africa, Aug. 29, 1932; m. Trudy Dorothy Zweig, Aug. 7, 1977; children: Roger Miles, Adrienne Jill, Graham Ross, Robert Edward. B of Commerce, U. Witwatersrand, South Africa, 1956; MBA, Stanford U., 1963, PhD, 1966. CPA, N.Y., Tex.; cert. in bus. valuation. Budget dir. Edgars Stores Ltd., South Africa, 1958-61; asso. prof. Ohio State U., Columbus, 1966-69, Arthur Young Disting. prof., 1970-73; Fuller E. Callaway prof. Ga. Inst. Tech., Atlanta, 1973-78, mem. exec. bd., 1976-78; ptnr. Coopers & Lybrand, N.Y.C., 1978-81; prin., v.p. Mgmt. Analysis Center, Inc., Cambridge, Mass., 1975-90; prof., chmn. div. acctg. and law Babson Coll., 1985-89, adj. prof., 1990-99. Cons. FPC, SEC, HEW, also maj. corps. Author 10 books including Accounting for Changing Prices: Replacement Cost and General Price Level Adjustments, 1976, Management Planning and Control, 1987, The Portable MBA: Finance and Accounting, 1992, 3d edit., 2002; assoc. editor: Decision Scis., 1973-78; mem. editl. bd. The Acctg. Rev., 1969-72, 76-78, Acctg., Orgns. and Socs., 1975-78, Jour. Acctg. and Pub. Policy, 1983-95; contbr. numerous articles to profl. jours. Mem. AICPA, Fla. Inst. CPAs, N.Y. Soc. CPAs, Inst. Bus. Appraisers, Nat. Assn. for Forensic Econs., Nat. Assn. Bus. Economists, Am. Arbitration Assn. (arbitrator comml. panel), Tex. Soc. CPAs, Pres. Country Club (West Palm Beach). Office: 2300 Palm Beach Lakes Blvd Ste 306 West Palm Beach FL 33409-3303 E-mail: les561@hotmail.com.

LIVINGSTONE, SUSAN MORRISEY, federal agency administrator; b. Carthage, Mo., Jan. 13, 1946; d. Richard John II and Catherine Newell (Carmean) Morrisey; m. Neil C. Livingstone III, Aug. 30, 1968. AB, Coll. William and Mary, 1968; MA, U. Mont., 1973; postgrad., Tufts U., 1973, Fletcher Sch. Law and Diplomacy, 1973—. Rschr. Senator Mark O. Hatfield, Washington, 1969-70; chief legis. and press asst. Congressman Richard H. Ichord, 1973-75, adminstrv. asst., 1975-81; cons. Congressman Wendell Bailey, 1981; exec. asst. VA, 1981-85, assoc. dep. adminstr. logistics and mgmt., 1985-86, sr. procurement exec., 1985-89, assoc. dep. adminstr. logistics, 1985—89; asst. sec. Army U.S. Dept. of Def., 1989-93; v.p. health and safety svcs. ARC, 1993-97; cons., 1997-2001; under sec. of Navy U.S. Dept. Navy, Washington, 2001—. Mem interagy. com. on women's bus. enterprise The White House, 1985-89; mem. Pres.'s Coun. on Mgmt. Improvement, 1985-86; cons. Def. Sci. Bd., 1998, 2000; mem. adv. bd. Martin Inst. U. Idaho, 2000-01. Vice chair White House Commn. on Nat. Moment of Remembrance, 2002—. Mem. Exec. Women in Govt., Procurement Round Table (bd. dirs. 1994-2001), Assn. U.S. Army (bd. dirs. 1994-96, mem. coun. trustees 1996-2001, CEO, dep. chmn. 2000-01), Women in Internat. Security (mem. adv. bd. 1994-97), Navy League. Episcopalian. Office: Under Sec Navy Rm 4E732 1000 Navy Pentagon Washington DC 20350-1000*

LIVINGSTONE, TRUDY DOROTHY ZWEIG, dancer, educator; b. N.Y.C., June 9, 1946; d. Joseph and Anna (Feinberg) Zweig; m. John Leslie Livingstone, Aug. 7, 1977; 1 child, Robert Edward. Student, Charles Lowe Studios, N.Y.C., 1950-52, Nina Tinova Studio, 1953-56, Ballet Russe de Monte Carlo, 1956-57, Bklyn. Coll., 1964-66; BA in Psychology cum laude, Boston U., 1968, MEd, 1969; postgrad., Serena Studios, Carnegie Hall Ballet Arts, N.Y.C., 1973-74. Tchr. Millis (Mass.) Pub. Schs., 1969-72, Hebrew Acad. Atlanta, 1974-76; profl. dancer various orgns. including Rivermont Country Club, Jewish Community Ctr., Callanwolde Performing Arts Ctr., Atlanta, 1974-84; founder, owner, instr. dance Sasha Studios, 1974-77; owner Trudy Zweig Livingstone Studios, Wellesley, Needham, Mass., 1987-88, Palm Beach, Fla., 1989—. Judge dance competition Atlanta Council Run-Offs, 1976. Vol. League Sch., Bklyn., 1965, Kennedy Meml. Hosp., Brighton, Mass., 1969, Nat. Affiliation for Literacy Advances, Santa Monica, Calif., 1982. Mem. Am. Alliance for Health, Phys. Edn., Recreation and Dance, Poets of the Palm Beaches, L.A. Athletic Club, Wellesley Coll. Club, Governor's Club (West Palm Beach). Avocation: writing poetry.

LIVINGSTON-MACIRELAN, JOAN PERSILLA, artist; b. Wenatchee, Wash., Oct. 9, 1940; d. Herbert Edgar and Maxine Lucina (Irelan) Macy; m. David Warner Livingston, June 15, 1958 (div. Apr. 1981); children: Dolly Jo, Jennifer Lynn. Student in oil painting, Old Town Gallery, Auburn, Calif., 1966; student, Ft. Mason Art Ctr., San Francisco, 1989. Cert. cosmetologist, Calif., Wash. Salon owner TJ's Hair Factory/Hair Today, Auburn, 1969-79; photographer's stylist Ed Young Photography, San Francisco, 1985-86; studio painter Studio Nine, Sausalito, 1986-90, 94-96; designer sculptor Poupee Millet, San Rafael, 1990-91; studio painter Studio Nine, 1991-94; wilderness artist Studio Nine Cabin Studio, Stehekin, Wash., 1996-98, Seattle, 1998-99; studio painter, art tchr. Studio Nine, Cashmere, 1999, studio painter, graphic designer, 2000—01. Exhibited in one-woman and group exhbns. in, San Francisco, Sausalito, also Palm Beach, Fla., Sanibel Island, Fla., Santa Fe, Wenatchee, Wash., over 30 pvt. collections. Recipient awards for art Placer County Fair, 1957-60, The Artists Mag., 1988, 91, 95, Gallery 76, Wenatchee, 2001. Mem. Nat. Mus. Women in the Arts, Artist's Trust (Seattle). Avocations: writing children's stories, writing poetry, flamenco dance, hiking. E-mail: josstudio9@msn.com.

LIVOLSI, FRANK WILLIAM, JR. lawyer; b. Stamford, Conn., June 6, 1938; s. Frank Sr. and Rose M. Livolsi. BA, Pa. Mil. Coll., 1962; JD, Fordham U., 1965. Bar: Ct. 1968. Ptnr. Plotkin & Livolsi, Stamford, 1970—. Served to capt. U.S. Army, 1965-67, Vietnam. Home: 155 Thornwood Rd Stamford CT 06903-2616 Office: Plotkin & Livolsi 1035 Washington Blvd Stamford CT 06901-2294

LIVSEY, ROBERT CALLISTER, lawyer; b. Salt Lake City, Aug. 7, 1936; s. Robert Frances and Rosezella Ann (Callister) L.; m. Renate Karla Guertler, Sept. 10, 1962; children: Scott, Rachel, Daniel, Benjamin. BS, U. Utah, 1962, JD, 1965; LLM, NYU, 1967. Bar: Utah 1965, Calif. 1967. Prof. Haile Selassie U., Addis Abbaba, Ethiopia, 1965-66; spl. asst. to chief counsel IRS, Washington, 1977-79; assoc., then ptnr. Brobeck, Phleger & Harrison, San Francisco, 1967—. Adj. prof. U. San Francisco Law Sch., 1970-77; mem. adv. com. IRS Dist. Dirs., 1986-89; mem. western region liason com IRS (chmn. 1989). Research editor U. Utah Law Rev., 1964-65; editor Tax Law Rev., 1966-67; contbr. articles to profl. jours. Bd. dirs. Gilead Group, 1986-88, East Bay Habitat for Humanity, 1987-88, Morning Song, 1992-94. Mem. ABA (chmn. subcom. real estate syndications 1981-84), State Bar Calif. (chmn. taxation sect. 1984-85), San Francisco Bar Assn. (chmn. taxation sect. 1982), Am. Coll. Tax Counsel, Am. Law Inst., Tax Litigation Club (pres. 1986-87), Order of Coif, Beta Gamma Sigma. Democrat. Mem. Evangelical Covenant Ch. Club: Commonwealth (San Francisco). Home: 128 La Salle Ave Piedmont CA 94610-1233 Office: Brobeck Phleger & Harrison 1 Market Plz Fl 31 San Francisco CA 94105-1100 E-mail: rlivsey@brobeck.com.

LIZANICH-ARO, SUZANNE, health care consultant; b. Newark, Sept. 17, 1953; d. Frank and Natalie Ann Lizanich; m. Karl Stephen Aro, July 1, 1978; children: Stephen Christopher, Caroline Mei. AAS in Nursing, County Coll. Morris, 1973; BA in English, Fairleigh Dickinson U., 1975; MA in Am. Studies, Seton Hall U., 1976; MPH in Health Svcs. Adminstrn., Johns Hopkins U., 1982. RN, Md., D.C., N.J. Relief charge nurse, staff nurse Dover (N.J.) Gen. Hosp., 1973-76; student health nurse Student Health Ctr. Fairleigh Dickinson U., Madison, N.J., 1973-75; chief occupational health nurse Nat. Health Svcs., Inc., Washington, 1976-77; community health nurse Vis. Nurse Assn., 1977-78; program asst., ambulatory care mgr. Nat. Capital Med. Found., Inc., 1978-81; program mgr., project mgr., rev. specialist United Mineworkers Health & Retirement Funds, 1982-85; dir. utilization rev. Am. PsychMgmt. Inc., 1985-86; health systems cons. SLA Cons., Inc., Silver Spring, Md., 1986-96; sys. design cons. SLA Consulting, 1997—. Program devel. cons. Green Spring Health Svcs., Columbia, Md., 1989—94; program cons. CMG Health Inc., Owings Mills, Md., 1994—95; sys. design cons. Blue Cross/Blue Shield of Del., 1996, Medecision Inc., Berwyn, Pa., 1987—2000. Bd. dirs. St. Luke's House, Bethesda, Md., 1997—. Office: SLA Cons 1008 Balmoral Dr Silver Spring MD 20903-1303 E-mail: lizaro@toad.net.

LIZARDOS, EVANS JOHN, mechanical engineer; b. N.Y.C., Mar. 25, 1936; s. John George and Pearl (Arapoudis) L.; m. Helen Samaras, May 15, 1960; children: John E., Paul E., Lynn Lizardos Bloecker. B in Mech. Engring., Poly. U., Bklyn., 1960. Lic. profl. engr., N.Y. Draftsman Clinton Bogert Assocs., N.Y.C., 1953-56; designer Guy B. Panero, 1956-60; assoc. Piccirillo & Brown, 1960-65; pres., CEO Lizardos Engring. Assocs., Albertson, N.Y., 1965—. Contbr. chpts. to books and articles to profl. jours. Treas. L.I. Heart Coun., 1992-94, chmn. bd., 1992-98; contbr. Guide Dog Assn. for Blind. Fellow ASHRAE (bd. govs. 1974-75, rec. sec. 1975-76, v.p. 1977-78, pres. 1978-79, chmn. handbook); mem. Cons. Engrs. Coun. N.Y. State (pres. 1986-87), Assn. Energy Engrs. (charter), Am. Solar Energy Soc., ASME, Am. Soc. Plumbing Engrs. (charter, chpt. sec. 1975-77), Constrn. Specification Inst. (profl.), Internat. Dist. Energy Assn., Inst. Noise Control Engring., Instrument Soc. Am. (sr.), Internat. Solar Energy Soc., Nat. Fire Protection Assn., NSPE, Refrigeration Engrs. and Techs. Assn. (mem.-at-large). Greek Orthodox. Avocations: model railroading, running. Office: 200 Old Country Rd Mineola NY 11501-4235

LIZT, SARA ENID VANEFSKY, lawyer, educator; b. USSR, Mar. 10, 1913; came to U.S., 1921; d. Max and Yocheved (Koval) Vanefsky; widowed. LLB, CUNY, Bklyn., 1941, LLM, 1962. Bar: N.Y. 1946, U.S. Dist. Ct. (so. and ea. dists.) N.Y. 1946. Pvt. practice Bklyn., 1946—. Prof. CUNY, Bklyn., 1966-80. Address: 2060 E 19th St Brooklyn NY 11229-3943

LJUBICIC DROZDOWSKI, MILADIN PETER, consulting engineer; b. Zajecar, Yugoslavia, Sept. 28, 1921; came to U.S., 1959; s. Peter Miladin and Martha Jovan (Viktorovic) Ljubicic; m. Dusica Cile Pavic, Sept. 9, 1948. Diploma in engring., U. Belgrade, Yugoslavia, 1951, 52; ancien éleve, Ecole Nationale Superieure de l'Armement, Paris, 1956; MSME, UCLA, 1964, PhD in Mec. Engring., 1971. Design and test engr. Fed. Mogul Bower, El Monte, Calif., 1959-62; chief advanced armament analytical support Hughes Helicopters, Culver City, 1962-78; engring. supr. Bechtel Power Corp., Norwalk, 1978-80; engring. adviser Bechtel Espana, Madrid, 1980-87; v.p. Koach Engring., Sun Valley, Calif., 1987; engring. cons. Mission Viejo, 1987—. Asst. to chmn. continuum mechanics, Belgrade, 1955-56; guest lectr. Sch. Engring. and Applied Sci., UCLA, 1971; prof., Loyola Marymount U., L.A., 1978-80. Contbr. to profl. publs. Mem. Am. Soc. Mech. Engrs., Am. Def. Preparedness Assn., Spanish Nuclear Soc. Avocations: European history, art history, archeology, photography, sculpting. Home and Office: 26426 Lope De Vega Dr Mission Viejo CA 92691-3316

LLAMAS, LUIS, pathologist; b. Mexico City, Apr. 28, 1948; came to U.S., 1975; s. Leopoldo and Rosalia (Cervantes) L.; m. Helia Nunez-Medina, Apr. 26, 1974; children: Elisa, Luis Leopoldo. BS, U. Mex., Mexico City, 1966; intern, IMSS, 1972; MD, U. Mex., Mexico City, 1973. Diplomate Am. Bd. Pathology. Resident in pathology Creighton U. Affiliated Hosps., Omaha, 1975-76, U. Tex. M.D. Anderson Cancer Ctr., Houston, 1976-79, U. Tex. Med. Sch., Houston, 1982-84, asst. prof. clin. pathology, 1984-86; pathologist Doctors' Hosp., Laredo, Tex., 1986-88; dir. labs. Mercy Regional Med. Ctr., Lardeo, 1988—. Home: 8310 Albany Ave Lubbock TX 79424-3426 Office: Covenant-Meth Hosp Pathology Dept 3709 19th St # 165 Lubbock TX 79410-1204

LLANOS, LUIS SOCORRO, retired public administrator, mediator, arbitrator, public affairs consultant; b. St. Croix, V.I., June 30, 1940; s. Felix and Eulogia (Encarnacion) L.; m. Joycelyn Louise Bough, Oct. 23, 1964; children: Elaine Eulogia Schuster, Luis Socorro, Eric Andre Farid. Cert. adminstrv. law, U. Nev., Reno, 1984; cert. occupl. safety and health mgmt., U. So. Calif., 1984; BS, Western States U., 1986, MBA, 1993; cert. labor rels. studies, Cornell U., 1988; cert. stratgic leadership, Duke U., 1991; cert. mediation theory and practice, Ctr. for Dispute Resolution, 1993; cert. arbitration, VI-PERB, 1994; cert. mediation, U. Mo., 1994. Cert. hazard control mgr. Compliance officer Divsn. Occupl. Safety and Health V.I. Dept. Labor, 1973-74, chief compliance officer, 1974-76, supervisory compliance officer, 1976-77, asst. dir., 1977-80, asst. commr.-OSH, 1980-87, asst. commr. labor, 1987-89, commr. of labor, 1989-94. Served on V.I. Bd. of Tax Rev., 1979-89, V.I. Pub. Employees' Rels. Bd., 1983-89, Vocat. Edn. Adv. Coun., 1984-89, V.I. Territorial Emergency Mgmt. Coun., 1989-94, Gov.'s Overall Econ. Devel. Com., 1990-94, V.I. Water and Power Authority, 1991-94. Elected mem. Holy Cross Parish Coun., St. Croix, 1982; mem. Holy Cross choir, 1958; sec. V.I. Wage Bd., 1991-94, V.I.-PERB, 1989-94; chmn. Labor Task Force, Turnbull-James '98 Transition Team, 1998. Served with U.S. Army, 1962-64. Recipient recognition certs. U.S. Dept. Labor-OSHA, V.I. Labor-Mgmt. Com., U.S. Bur. Labor Statistics, Hispanos Unidos, Fed. Mediation and Conciliation Svc., others. Fellow Acad. Polit. Sci., 1994-98; mem. KC, (charter St. Croix, treas. 1974-75). Democrat. Roman Catholic. Avocations: photography, classical guitar, choir, woodwork. Office: PO Box 850 Kingshill VI 00851-0850

LLARULL, MARCELO, mathematician, educator, researcher; s. Marcelo A and Mira Llarull. PhD, SUNY, Stony Brook, 1982—88, MA, 1982—87; Licenciado, Universidad Nacional de Córdoba, Cordoba, Argentina, 1976—81. Prof. of math. William Pateson U., Wayne, NJ, 1990—; hans rademacher instr. U. of Pa, Philadelphia, Pa., 1988—90; asst. Universidad Nacional de Cordoba, Argentina, 1981—82. Mem.: Math. Assn. of Am., Am. Math. Soc. Achievements include research in Scalar curvature estimates.

LLAURADO, JOSEP G. nuclear medicine physician, scientist; b. Barcelona, Spain, Feb. 6, 1927; s. José and Rosa (Llaurado) Garcia; m. Deirdre Mooney, Nov. 9, 1966; children: Raymund, Wilfred, Mireya; m Catherine D. Entwistle, June 28, 1958 (dec.); children: Thadd, Oleg, Montserrat. BS, BA, Balmes Inst., Barcelona, 1944; MD, Barcelona U., 1950, PhD in Pharmacology, 1960; MSc in Biomed. Engring., Drexel U., 1963. Diplomate Am. Bd. Nuclear Medicine. Resident Royal Postgrad. Sch. Medicine, Hammersmith Hosp., London, 1952-54; fellow M.D. Anderson Hosp. and Tumor Inst., Houston, 1957-58, U. Utah Med. Coll., Salt Lake City, 1958-59; asst. prof. U. Otago, Dunedin, New Zealand, 1954-57; sr. endocrinologist Prizer Med. Rsch. Lab., Groton, Conn., 1959-60; assoc. prof. U. Pa., Phila., 1963-67; prof. Med. Coll. Wis., Milw., 1970-82, Marquette U., Milw., 1967-82; clin. dir. nuc. medicine svc. VA Med. Ctr., 1977—82; chief nuc. medicine svc. VA Hosp., Loma Linda, Calif., 1983—; prof. dept. radiation scis. Loma Linda U. Sch. Medicine, 1983—. U.S. rep. symposium on dynamic studies with radioisotopes in clin. medicine and rsch. IAEA, Rotterdam, The Netherlands, 1970, Knoxville, Tenn., 1974. Hon. editor Internat. Jour. Biomed. Computing; dep. editor Environ Mgmt. and Health; contbr. numerous articles to profl. jours. Merit badge counselor Boy Scouts Am., 1972—; pres. Hales Corners (Wis.) Hist. Soc., 1981-83. Recipient commendation cert. Boy Scouts Am., 1980, Joan d'AlÓs prize Cardiovasc. Ctr. St. Jordi, Barcelona, 1999, XII Batista-Roca prize Inst. Exterior Projection of Catalan Culture, 2000. Fellow Am. Coll. Nutrition; mem. IEEE (life), Royal Acad. Medicine of Catalonia/Barcelona, Soc. Nuc. Medicine (computer and acad. couns.), IEEE in Medicine and Biology Soc. (nat. adminstrv. com. 1986-89), Biomed. Engring. Soc. (charter), Am. Physiol. Soc., Am. Soc. Pharmacology and Exptl. Therapeutics, Soc. Math. Biology (founding), Endocrine Soc., Am. Soc. Nuc. Cardiology, Soc. Catalana Biologia, Casal dels Catalans Calif. (pres. 1989-91)_, Calif. Med. Assn. (sci. adv. panel on nuc. medicine 1983—). Office: VA Hosp Nuclear Med Svc Rm 115 11201 Benton St Loma Linda CA 92357-0001

LLERA, TAMUELA L. television producer; b. Richmond, Va., Dec. 16, 1963; d. Thomas Franklin and Sarah Ann Virginia (Hendricks) Anderson; m. Juan Carlos Llera, Jan. 26, 2001; 1 child Sarah Isabel. Student, Mary Baldwin Coll., 1982; BS in Biology, Radford U., 1986. Art dir. On-Site Media, Boston, 1986—92; editor, prodr. Hot Source Media, Washington, 1992—93; freelance editor, prodr., 1993—95; supervising prodr. Discovery Channel, Miami, Fla., 1995—. Mem. AIDS Action Com., 1986—92, Children's Def. Fund, 1992—2000, Hands On Miami, 2000—02; vol. Big Sisters, 1986—92. Avocations: roller blading, tennis, fishing, scuba diving, drawing. Office: Discovery Channel 6505 Bwelagoon Dr Miami FL 33126 E-mail: tamllera@discovery.com.

LLEWELLYN, JOHN SCHOFIELD, JR. former food company executive; b. Amsterdam, N.Y., Jan. 10, 1935; s. John S. and Dorothea (Breedon) L.; m. Mary Martha Pallotta, June 9, 1962; children: Mary M., John S. III, Robert J., James P., Timothy J. AB, Holy Cross Coll., 1956; MBA, Harvard U., 1961. With mktg. Gen. Foods Corp., White Plains, N.Y., 1961-69, Sunshine Biscuit div. Am. Brands, N.Y.C., 1973-77; exec. v.p. Morton Frozen Foods div. ITT Continental Baking Co., Charlottesville, Va., 1977-79; gen. mgr. Continental Kitchens ITT Continental Baking Co., Rye, 1980-81; sr. v.p. Ocean Spray Cranberries Inc., Plymouth, Mass., 1982-86, exec. v.p., chief operating officer, 1986-87, pres., chief exec. officer, 1988-97; ret., 1997. Bd. dirs. Dean Foods Co. Trustee St. Sebastian's Country Day Sch., Needham, Mass., 1991—; bd. dirs. Mass. Environ. Trust, 1991—; mem. bd. advisors Boardroom Consultants. Capt. USMC, 1957-63. Mem. Nat. Food Processors Assn. Roman Catholic. Home: Steamboat Ln Hingham MA 02043 E-mail: jsllewe@attbi.com.

LLEWELLYN, LEONARD FRANK, real estate broker, investment company executive; b. Harlowton, Mont., Oct. 31, 1933; s. Ralph Emory and Frances Louise (Ewing) L.; m. Patricia Lockrom, Aug. 16, 1951 (div. 1955); m. Corrie J. Spruit, Apr. 21, 1974 (div. 1995); m. Anna N. McKinney, 1997. BSEE, Eastern Mont. Coll. Edn., 1955. Enlisted USMC, 1957, advanced through grades to capt., 1960, ret., 1967; owner Capitol Fla. Assn., Inc., Alexandria, Va., 1966-74; pres., owner Fla. Properties, Inc., Balt., 1968-74; chmn. Marco Beach Realty, Inc., Marco Island, Fla., 1975-82, 82—, Cons., Inc. of S.W. Fla., Marco Island, 1982—; mng. dir., founding ptnr. Capital Mgmt. Co., 1999—. Served as presdl. pilot for presidents Kennedy and Johnson, 1963-66; bd. dirs. Founders Nat. Bank and Trust Co.; mem. adv. bd. Founding Ptnrs. Capital Mgmt. Co., co-mng. dir., 1999—. Author: (manual) Aero-Gunnery Tactics, 1958. Bd. dirs. Collier County Conservancy, 1978-83; trustee Naples (Fla.) Cmty. Hosp., 1980-83, Cmty. Found. Collier County, 1990-94; sheriff's commr., Collier County, Fla., 1990—. Named Top Gun, USN, USMC, 1958, Citizen of Yr. Marco Island N.Y. Times and Marco Island Eagle, 1982. Mem. Marco Island Bd. Realtors (pres. 1982), Marco Island C. of C. (pres. 1981-82, pres. emeritus 1984), Naples Forum (pres. 1985-86), Nat. Aviation Club, Nat. Assn. Sales Masters, Rotary Club. Republican. Home: PO Box 825 852 Bald Eagle Dr Marco Island FL 34145-2543 Office: Newgate Ctr Ste 119 5100 N Tamiami Trail Naples FL 34103 E-mail: lenllew@aol.com.

LLEWELLYN, LINDA GARRISON, foundation executive; b. Lockport, N.Y., July 25, 1953; d. Robert Groves and Mary Jean Garrison; m. John Frederick Llewellyn, Apr. 15, 1989; 1 step-daughter, Sharon J. BS, Regents Coll., Albany, 1995; D (hon.), Pepperdine U., 1997. V.p. Headline Brokers, Secaucus, N.J., 1976-85; mgr. Forest Lawn Meml. Pks., Glendale, Calif., 1985-89; v.p. Forest Lawn Found., 1994-98, pres., 1998—. Dir., officer Goodwill Industries So. Calif., L.A., 1994-2001; dir., mem. exec. com. ARC, L.A., 1994-2000; dir. Children's Bur. So. Calif., L.A., 1998—. Mem. So. Calif. Assn. Philanthropy (bd. dirs. 2000—). Office: Forest Lawn Found 1712 S Glendale Ave Glendale CA 91205-3320

LLEWELLYN, RALPH ALVIN, physics educator; b. Detroit, June 27, 1933; s. Ralph A. and Mary (Green) L.; m. Laura Diane Alsop, June 12, 1955; children: Mark Jeffrey, Rita Annette, Lisa Suzanne, Eric Matthew. BS in Chem. Engrng. with high honors, Rose-Hulman Inst. Tech., 1955; PhD in Physics, Purdue U., 1962. Mem. faculty Rose-Hulman Inst. Tech., Terre Haute, Ind., 1961-70, assoc. prof. physics, 1964-68, prof., 1968-70, chmn. dept. physics, 1969-70; prof., chmn. dept. Ind. State U., 1970-72, 74-80; dean Coll. of Arts and Scis. U. Ctrl. Fla., Orlando, 1980-84, prof., 1980—. Exec. sec. Energy Bd., staff officer environmental Studies Bd. NAS/NRC, Washington, 1972-74; vis. prof. Rensselaer Poly. Inst., Troy, N.Y., 1964; cons. Commn. on Coll. Physics, 1987-89, NSF, 1965-66; mem. Ind. Lt. Gov.'s Sci. Adv. Coun., 1974-80; adv. bd. Ind. Gov.'s Energy Extension Svc., Fla. Solar Energy Ctr., policy coun. Fla. Inst. Govt., Fla. Radon Adv. Coun., 1988—; mem. environ. adv. com. Fla. Inst. Phosphate Rsch.; mem. grievance com. Fla. Bar, nat. adv. coun. Nat. Commn. on Higher Edn. Issues, 1982. Author: (with others) Physics 3E, 1991, Elementary Modern Physics, 1992, Modern Physics 3E, 1999; assoc. editor: Phys. Rev. Letters; contbr. articles to profl. jours.; producer instructional films and TV. Trustee Merom (Ind.) Inst. Recipient Tchg. Incentive award Fla. State Univ. Sys., 1994, 97; NSF Coop. fellow, 1959-60, Am. Coun. Edn. Acad. Adminstrn. Internship Program fellow. Fellow Ind. Acad. Sci. (chmn. physics divsn. 1969-70, Spkr. of Yr. award 1975, pres.-elect 1980); mem. AAAS, AAUP, Am. Phys. Soc., Am. Assn. Physics Tchrs. (pres. Ind.), N.Y. Acad. Scis., Fla. Acad. Scis. (endowment com.), Internat. Oceanographic Found., Ind. Acad. Sci., Sigma Xi, Tau Beta Pi. Home: 1463 Palomino Way Oviedo FL 32765-9304 Office: U Cen Fla Dept Physics Orlando FL 32816-0001 E-mail: ral@physics.ucf.edu.

LLINÁS, RODOLFO RIASCOS, medical educator, researcher; b. Bogota, Colombia, Dec. 16, 1934; came to U.S., 1959, naturalized, 1973; s. Jorge Enrique (Llinas) and Bertha (Riascos) L.; m. Gillian Kimber, Dec. 24, 1965; children: Rafael Hugo, Alexander Jorge. BS, Gimnasio Moderno, Bogota, 1952; MD, U. Javeriana, Bogota, 1959; PhD, Australian Nat. U., 1965; MD (hon.), U. Salamanca, Spain, 1985; PhD (hon.), U. Barcelona, Spain, 193, U. Nacional Bogota, Colombia, 194; D, Univ. Complutense, Madrid, 1997. Research fellow Mass. Gen. Hosp.-Harvard U., 1960-61; NIH research fellow in physiology U. Minn., Mpls., 1961-63, assoc. prof., 1965-66; assoc. mem. AMA Inst. Biomed. Research, Chgo., 1966-68, mem., 1970, head neurobiology unit, 1967-70; assoc. prof. neurology and psychiatry Northwestern U., 1967-71; guest prof. physiology Wayne State U., 1967-74; professorial lectr. pharmacology U. Ill.-Chgo., 1967-68, clin. prof., 1968-72; prof. physiology, head neurobiology div. U. Iowa, 1970-76; prof., chmn. physiology and biophysics NYU, N.Y.C., 1976—, Thomas and Suzanne Murphy prof. neurosci., 1985—. Mem. neurol. sci. research tng. com. Nat. Inst. Neurol. Diseases and Stroke, NIH, 1971-73; mem. neurology A study sect. div. research grants NIH, 1974-78; assoc. neurosci. research program MIT, 1974-83; mem. U.S. Nat. Com. for IBRO, 1978-81; acting chmn. U.S. Nat. Com. For IBRO, 1982, chmn., 1983-89, exec. com., 1985—; mem. sci. adv. bd. Max-Planck Inst. for Psychiatry, Munich, 1979-83; professorial lectr. Coll. de France, Paris, 1979, Nat. Poly. Inst., Mexico City, 1981; IBRO internat. lectr., S.Am., 1982; McDowall lectr. King's Coll., London, 1984 Author: (with Hubbard and Quastel) Electrophysiological Analysis of Synaptic Transmission, 1969; editor: Neurobiology of Cerebellar Evolution and Development, 1969, (with W. Precht) Frog Neurobiology: A Handbook, 1976; chief editor: Neurosci., 1974— ; mem. editorial bd.: Jour. Neurobiology, 1980— ; mem.: Pfluegers Archives, 1981— , Jour. Theoretical Neurobiology, 1981— . Recipient John C. Krantz award U. Md., 1976, Einstein Gold medal UNESCO, 1991, Signoret award in cognition, Fondation Ipsen La Salpâtrière, Paris, 1994. Mem. NAS, Soc. For Neurosci. (council 1974-78), Am. Physiol. Soc. (Bowditch Lectr. 1973), Am. Soc. Cell Biology, Biophys. Soc., Harvey Soc., Internat. Brain Research Orgn., N.Y. Acad. Scis., Am. Acad. Arts & Scis., Am. Philosophical Soc., Real Academia Nacional de Medicina, Nat. Deafness and Other Communication Disorders, Nat. Inst. of Health (adv. coun.), Alpha Omega Alpha (hon.) Office: NYC Sch Med 550 1st Ave New York NY 10016-6402

LLITERAS, DANIEL SERAFIN, writer; b. Bronx, N.Y., July 13, 1949; s. Frank Serafin and America Lliteras; m. Susan Kathleen Touchstone. BA, Fla. State U., Tallahassee, 1973; MFA, Fla. State U., 1976. Corpsman and Diver U.S. Navy and Marine Corps, 1967—70; theatrical dir. Numerous Legitimate Theaters, N.Y.C., Fla., Washington, 1976—79; mem. Merchant Marines, 1979—80; Lt. (diving and salvage) U.S. Navy, 1981—85; fire fighter Norfolk (Va.) Fire Dept., 1986—2000. Author: (poetry/photography) In a Warrior's Romance, 1991, (novels) In the Heart of Things, 1992, Into the Ashes, 1993, Half Hidden by Twilight, 1994, The Thieves of Golgotha, 1998, Judas the Gentile, 1999, 613 West Jefferson, 2001; author: (also poetry, haiku, short stories). Mem.: Internat. Assn. Fire Fighters. Home: PO Box 5216 Virginia Beach VA 23471

LLORENS, MERNA GEE, elementary education educator, music educator; b. Ofahoma, Miss., Oct. 4, 1939; d. Junior McKinley and Birdie Rose Smith; m. Ramon James Llorens Sr., Oct. 1, 1960; children: Regina Llorens Dominguez, Ramon James Llorens Jr. BS, Western Mich. U., 1971. Sec. Follet Pub. Co., Chgo., 1960-62, Mohawk Tablet Co., Chicago Heights, 1963-65; elem. tchr. St. Basil Cath. Sch., South Haven, Mich., 1965-79, South Haven Pub. Schs., 1979—. Chair Jubilee 100th Ann. St. Basil, faith and vision campaign com. Mem.: South Haven Edn. Assn. (chair courtesy com. 1985—2000), Black History Leadership Soc. (charter, treas., publicity/program chair, Spl. Tribute Role Model of Yr. award 2001), St. Basil Altar Rosary Women's Svc. Guild (treas. 2002—, Woman of Yr. 1990), Lions Club (3d v.p.), Delta Sigma Theta Sorority, Inc. (pres. 1999—2001, Benton Harbor/St. Joseph Alumnae chpt.). Democrat. Roman Catholic. Avocations: crafts, camping, gardening, Minnie Pearl impersonator. Home: 67556 County Rd 338 South Haven MI 49090-8372 E-mail: mergee@aol.com.

LLORENTE, ALEX JERONIMO, educator, lawyer; b. Havana, Cuba, Aug. 20, 1959; came to US 1965; s. Carlos O. L. and Aida Rodriguez; m. Evelyne N. Havan, July 2, 1988; children: Ariel, Adrian. BA, U. South Fla., 1978, MA in Econs., 1980; MBA in Acctg., U. Houston, 1983; JD, Western State U., 1994. Bar: Calif. 1995. CPA Tex., 1984. Tax auditor IRS, Tampa, Fla., 1979-81; assoc. prof. Brazosport Coll., Lake Jackson, Tex., 1982-84; prof. Saddlebrook Coll., Mission Viejo, Calif., 1984—; pvt. practice Laguna Hills, 1995—. Office: 24031 El Toro Rd Ste 210 Laguna Hills CA 92653-3152 E-mail: alex@llorente.com.

LLOYD, ALEX, lawyer; b. Atlantic, Iowa, Aug. 13, 1942; s. Norman and Ruth (R.) L.; m. Jacqueline Roe, Aug. 24, 1963; children: Erin, Andrea, John, Peter. BA in Econs., Colby Coll., 1964; LLB, Law Sch., Yale U., 1967. Bar: Conn., U.S. Dist. Ct. Conn., U.S. Ct. Appeals (2d cir.), U.S. Tax Ct., U.S. Supreme Ct. Assoc. Shipman & Goodwin, 1967-72, ptnr., 1972—, chmn. mgmt. com., 1985-96. Bd. dirs. Hartford Hosp., Conn. Health Sys., Inc., Conn. Bar Found. Recipient Dist. Svc. award, Conn. Legal Svcs. Fellow Am. Bar Found., Conn. Bar Found.; mem. ABA, Am. Soc. of Hosp. Attys., Conn. Bar Assn. (Charles J. Parker award). Avocations: golf, boating, fishing, raquet sports, piano. Office: Shipman & Goodwin 1 American Row Hartford CT 06103-2833 E-mail: alloyd@goodwin.com.

LLOYD, BOARDMAN, investment executive; b. Concord, N.H., Jan. 8, 1942; s. Francis Vernon and Elisabeth (Boardman) L.; m. Barbara Horwich, Mar. 20, 1966 (div. 1999); children: Pamela, Amy, Emily. BA, Yale U., 1964; JD, U. Chgo., 1967. Bar: N.Y. 1968, Mass. 1971. Assoc. Casey, Lane & Mittendorf, N.Y.C., 1967-69, Choate, Hall & Stewart, Boston, 1969-76, ptnr., 1976-90; pres. Harris & Lloyd Inc., Cambridge, Mass., 1991—. Chmn. Cambridge United Way, 1975-82, Yale U. Parents Com., 1986-90, com. mem., 1986-90, chmn., 1989-90; bd. dirs. Greater Boston Legal Svcs., 1986—; trustee First Night, Boston, 1987-90, Shady Hill Sch., Cambridge, 1980-84; trustee Coydog Found., 1996—. Mem. N.Y. Bar Assn., Boston Bar Assn. Office: Harris & Lloyd Inc 80 Trowbridge St Cambridge MA 02138-3102

LLOYD, CECIL RHODES, pediatric dentist; b. Corpus Christi, Tex., Aug. 18, 1930; s. Cecil Rhodes Hilbun and Cidney W. (Linxwiler) Lloyd; m. Donna Mae Thomas, Dec. 31, 1955 (div. 1973); children: James Michael, Leigh Ann, Lisa Kendall; m. Glenda Sue Williams, Dec. 31, 1979; children: Lauren Cecily, Sutton Rhodes. Student, La. State U., 1949, La. Tech. Inst., 1950, Centenary Coll., 1952-54; DDS, Loyola U., New Orleans, 1958. Pvt. practice pediatric dentistry, Shreveport, La., 1958—. Cons. in pediatric dentistry Barksdale AFB, La., 1970—; mem. staff and surg. com. Christus Schumpert Hosp., Shreveport. Chmn. Cen. YMCA, Shreveport, 1974, met. bd., 1969, Ind. Bowl Football Classic, Shreveport, 1984, 85, Fellowship Christian Athletes, 1986; bd. dirs. Riverside Hosp., Bossier, La., 1982-84; pres.-elect Sports Found., 1989, pres., 1990; founder Sports Mus. of Champions, Shreveport-Bossier; interim mem. Shreveport City Coun., 1990. With USMC, 1950-52. Named Southwestern Handball Hall of Fame, 1996. NW La. Dental Assn., La. Dental Assn., ADA, Am. Acad. Pediatric Dentistry, La. Bd. Dentistry (pres., 1969-70, 77-78, 83-84), Ark.-La.-Tex. Dental Congress (chmn. 1979-80). Republican. Baptist. Avocation: theatre. Office: 927 Shreveport Barksdale Hwy Shreveport LA 71105-2205

LLOYD, CHARLES ALLEN, lawyer; b. Hickory, N.C., Mar. 27, 1944; s. Charles Edward and Maude (Shuford) L.; m. Cheryl Ann Taylor, Aug. 20, 1966; children: Susan Taylor, Rebecca Ann. BA, Davidson Coll., 1966; JD, U. N.C., 1969. Bar: N.C. 1969, U.S. Dist. Ct. (ea., mid. and we. dists.) N.C. 1970, U.S. Ct. Appeals (4th cir.) 1972, U.S. Supreme Ct. 1974; bd. cert. specialist in criminal law. Law clk. to presiding chief judge U.S. Dist. Ct. for Eastern Dist. N.C., Clinton, 1969-70; asst. atty. gen. Office of N.C. Atty. Gen., Raleigh, 1970-74; ptnr. Smith, Patterson, Follin, Curtis, James & Harkavy, Greensboro, N.C., 1974-87, Carrington & Lloyd, Greensboro, 1987-88; pvt. practice, 1988—. Lectr. continuing legal edn. seminars, 1982—. Mem. ABA, N.C. Bar Assn. (chmn. criminal justice sect. 1986-88), Nat. Criminal Def. Lawyers Assn., Greensboro Criminal Def. Lawyers Assn. (pres. 1981, 88, 94). Avocation: running. Home: 5300 Sequoia Ct Greensboro NC 27455-2184 Office: 301 S Greene St Ste 100 Greensboro NC 27401-2660

LLOYD, CHRISTOPHER, actor; b. Stamford, Conn., Oct. 22, 1938; m. Jane Walker Wood. Actor, Neighborhood Playhouse, N.Y.C.; actor: summer stock and off-Broadway, including title role in Kaspar, 1973 (Obie award, Drama Desk award); Broadway appearances include White and Maddox, Macbeth, N.Y. Shakespeare Festival; films include Butch and Sundance, 1969, Three Warriors, One Flew Over the Cuckoo's Nest, 1975, Goin South, 1978, The Onion Field, 1979, The Black Marble, 1980, The Legend of the Lone Ranger, 1981, Mr. Mom, 1983, To Be or Not to Be, 1983, Star Trek III, 1984, Adventures of Buckaroo Banzai, 1984, Joy of Sex, 1984, Back to the Future, 1985, Clue, 1985, Who Framed Roger Rabbit, 1988, Walk Like a Man, 1987, Eight Men Out, 1988, Track 29, 1988, Why Me, The Dream Team, 1989, Back to the Future, Part II, 1989, Back to the Future, Part III, 1990, The Addams Family, 1991, Suburban Commando, 1991, Dennis the Menace, 1993, Twenty Bucks, 1993, Addams Family Values, 1993, Angels in the Outfield, 1994, The Pagemaster, 1994, Camp Nowhere, 1994, The Radioland Murders, 1994, Things To Do in Denver When You're Dead, 1995, Changing Habits, 1996, Cadillac Ranch, 1996, Quicksilver, 1997, Highway, 1997, Real Blonde, 1997, Amastasia, 1997, My Favorite Martian, 1999, Man on the Moon, 1999, Baby Geniuses, 1999, Wit, 2001, Interstate 60, 2002; TV films include Lacy and the Mississippi Queen, 1978, The Word, 1978, Stunt Seven, 1979, Money on the Side, 1982, September Gun, 1983, Avonlea, 1991 (Emmy award, Best Actor in a Drama Series, 1992), Dead Ahead: Exxon Valdez, 1992, T-Bone N Weasel, 1992, Rent-A-Kid, 1995, The Ransom of Red Chief, 1996, The Right to Remain Silent, 1996, Alice in Wonderland, 1999; appeared as regular in TV series Barney Miller, 1975, Taxi, 1978-83 (Best Supporting Actor Emmy award 1982, 83), Cheers, 1982, Amazing Stories, 1985, Road to Avonlea, 1990, Back to the Future, 1991-92, Deadly Games, 1995, Spin City, 1996, The Tick, 2002. Office: The Gersh Agency c/o Bob Gersh 252 N Canon Dr Beverly Hills CA 90210-5302

LLOYD, DAVID DILSWORTH TALBOTT, emeritus educator; b. Montclair, N.J., May 9, 1930; s. Dilsworth Talbott and Marion F. Wescoe; s. Richard G. Lloyd (stepfather); m. Martha Cornelia Walker, Nov. 15, 1955 (div. Apr. 1974); 1 stepchild, David Brantley; m. Maureen Catherine Doudy, Mar. 23, 1979; children: Cassandra, Susan, Cynthia, Douglas and Paul (twins), Robert. BA, Monclair State Tchrs., 1952; MA in Speech/Theater, Mich. U., 1957. Cert. tchr. Asst. prof. Olivet (Mich.) Coll., 1957-59; from asst. prof. to assoc. prof. Glassboro (N.J.) State Tchrs. Coll. (name now Rowan U.), 1959-2000, chmn. speech, theater, dance, 1986-93; chmn. journalism/creative writing dept. Rowan U., Glassboro, 1997-2000, adj. prof. N.J., 2000—, Gloucester County Coll., Sewell, 2000—. Active Poet in the Classroom, N.J. Sch. Arts/N.J. Coun on Arts. Author, illustrator: The Circle, 1974, Snowman, 1979, 2 edit., 1999, Norton's The Haiku Anthology, 1999. With USN, 1952-55. Mem. Omega Club. Avocations: painting, drawing, haiku, poems, plays. Home and Office: 17 4th Ave Pitman NJ 08071-1419

LLOYD, DAVID NIGEL, performer, lyricist; b. Mombasa, Kenya Protectorate, Mar. 16, 1954; came to U.S., 1962; s. Gerald Lloyd and Madeline Jean (Cooke) Steinberg; m. Elizabeth Shannon Meehan, July 31, 1976 (div. 1979); m. Gita Freimann, June 21, 1982; 1 child, Ursula Jane. Student, Seneca Coll., Willowdale, Ont., Can., 1971-73. Social worker Met. Toronto Assn. for Mentally Retarded, 1975; sales clk. Montgomery Ward, Canoga Park, Calif., 1976-79; prodn. asst. Spungbuggy Works, Hollywood, 1979-81; composer/performer, 1980-83; shift mgr. Bodhi Tree Books, 1983-89; West Coast tour mgr. Robin Williamson Prodns., Hollywood, also Cardiff, Wales, 1991-93, 99; song poet/performer California Hot Springs, 1990—. Film composer Low End Prodns., L.A., 1983, 95; film composer, poet, Spike Stewart Films, L.A., 1991-95. Author: (chap book/poetry) Death in Los Fumos, 1994, How to Write a Traditional Song (chap book), 2000; composer/performer: (music recordings) Dark Ages, 1984, An Age of Fable, 1987, Death in Los Fumos, 1994, How Like Ghosts Are We, 1998. Vol. folk music tchr. Hot Springs Elem. Sch., California Hot Springs, 1991-96; folk music fundraising concert dir. Hot Springs Parent Group, 1994-95; artist-in-residence Kern County Calif. schs. sponsored by the Arts Coun. of Kern, 1998—; mem. Kern County Supr. Sch. writing team to prepare guidelines for Kern County Arist in Residence program, 1999-2000. Mem. N.Am. Folk and Dance Alliance. Avocation: Sequoia trees. Home: Rte 4 Box 695 California Hot Springs CA 93207 E-mail: davidnigellloyd@yahoo.com.

LLOYD, DAVID THOMAS, writer, English educator; b. Utica, N.Y., Feb. 25, 1954; s. Richard Glynne and Mair Elvira (Thomas) L.; m. Kim Gayle Waale. Student, U. Wales, 1973-74; BA in English cum laude, St. Lawrence U., 1975; MA in English and Am. Lit., U. Vt., 1978; MA in Creative Writing, PhD in English Lit., Brown U., 1985. Grad. instr. U. Vt., 1976-78, adj. instr., 1978-79, 80, 81; grad. instr. Brown U., 1982-84, adj. prof., summer 1984, 85; dir. S.I. Newhouse Writing Ctr. Le Moyne Coll., Syracuse, N.Y., 1985-91, asst. prof., 1985-91, assoc. prof., 1991-95, prof., 1995—, chair dept. English, 1992-96, dir. creative writing program, 1997—. Editor, author: (poetry anthology) The Urgency of Identity, 1994, (interview anthology) Writing on the Edge, 1997; author: (poetry chapbook) The Everyday Apocalypse, 2002; contbr. articles to profl. jours.; author of poems and short stories. Recipient stipends Welsh Nat. Gymanfa Ganu Assn., 1986, 87, Travel to Collections award NEH, 1992; named scholar of yr. Le Moyne Coll., 1995; fellow Watson Found., 1975; Fulbright disting. scholar U. Wales, Bangor, 2001. Mem. MLA, Am. Conf. for Irish Studies, N.Am. Assn. for the Study of Welsh Culture and History (exec. bd. mem. 1995—). Office: Dept English Le Moyne Coll Syracuse NY 13214

LLOYD, DOUGLAS SEWARD, physician, public health administrator; b. Bklyn., Oct. 16, 1939; s. Heber Hughes and Virginia Seward (Chamberlin) L. AB in Chemistry, Duke U., 1961, MD, 1971; postgrad., Old Dominion U., 1965-67; MPH in Health Planning, U. N.C., 1971. Diplomate Am. Bd. Preventive Medicine. Intern Duke U., Durham, N.C., 1971-72, clin. scholar, 1972, resident in family practice, 1972-73; commr. health Conn. Dept. Health Services, 1973-87; assoc. med. dir. Nat. Med. Rsch. Corp., Hartford, Conn., 1987-89; pres. Doug Lloyd Assocs., Farmington, 1989-92; dir. Ctr. Pub. Health Practice Health Resources and Svcs. Adminstrn., Rockville, Md., 1992-98; with Assn. Schs. Pub. Health, Washington, 1999—. Lectr. Yale U., Conn., 1973-87; chmn. bd. Pub. Health Found., 1984-87. Contbr. articles to profl. jours. Capt. USNR, ret. Recipient Lange Publ. award, 1971, McCormick award for excellence in pub. health, 1987, Ervin award for creative vision, The Pub. Health Found., 2001. Fellow Am. Coll. Preventive Medicine; mem. AMA, Am. Pub. Health Assn., Assn. State and Territorial Health Ofcls. (past pres.). Home: 10804 Bird Song Path Columbia MD 21044-3693 Office: Ctr for Pub Health Parklawn 8-103 5600 Fishers Ln Rockville MD 20857 Office Fax: 301-443-1164. E-mail: dLloyd@hrsa.gov.

LLOYD, ERIC, actor; b. Glendale, CA, May 19, 1986; T.V. and movie actor. Appeared in films Heart and Souls, 1993, Greedy, 1994, The Santa Clause, 1994, Dunston Checks In, 1996, Deconstructing Harry, 1997, Batman & Robin, 1997, Luminous Motion, 1998, The Santa Clause 2, 2002; T.V. series include Laurie Hill, 1992, Jesse, 1998; T.V. movies include A Family Torn Apart, 1993, Seasons of the Heart, 1994, A Christmas Memory, 1997, others; also voice characterizations and T.V. guest appearances.*

LLOYD, EUGENE WALTER, retired construction company executive; b. Bklyn., Apr. 9, 1943; s. Walter Vincent and Mary Regina L.; m. Julia Ann Bain Menzies, May 6, 1967; children: Deborah Ann, Doreen Marie. AA in Constrn., N.Y. Tech. Coll., 1960-63. With Stephen H. Falk & Assocs., Great Neck, N.Y., 1962-65, Builder's Estimating Service, N.Y.C., 1965-67; estimator Humphreys & Harding, Inc., 1967-68; chief estimator, corp. sec. Conforti & Eisele, Inc., 1968-76; exec. v.p. Torcon, Inc., Westfield, N.J., 1976-93; v.p., dir. The Henderson Corp., Raritan, 1994-98; contract mgr. Huber, Hunt & Nichols, Inc., Indpls., 1998; ret., 1998. Served with U.S. Army, 1963-69. Republican. Roman Catholic. Home: 6910 E Bobwhite Way Scottsdale AZ 85262-8526

LLOYD, FRANCIS LEON, JR. lawyer; b. Winchester, Va., Dec. 1, 1955; s. Francis Leon Sr. and Jeannette Marie (Dove) L.; m. Myra Denise DuBose, Sept. 18, 1982. BA in English and French, U. Richmond, 1978; JD, U. Va., 1981. Bar: Va. 1981, Tenn. 1982, U.S. Dist. Ct. (ea. dist.) Tenn. 1982, U.S. Ct. Appeals (6th cir.) 1984. Assoc. Herndon, Coleman, Brading & McKee, Johnson City, Tenn., 1981-86, ptnr., 1987-88; of counsel The Taylor Group, Ltd., 1983; law clk. to judge U.S. Dist. Ct. (ea. dist.) Tenn., Knoxville, 1988-98; assoc. London & Amburn, PC, 1998-99, mem., 1999—. Bd. dirs. Assn. Retarded Citizens Washington County, Inc., Johnson City, 1982-88. Avocations: literature, music, hiking. Home: 8804 Regent Ln Knoxville TN 37923-1640 Office: London & Amburn PC 1716 W Clinch Ave Knoxville TN 37916-2408 E-mail: fllmail@latlaw.com.

LLOYD, HUGH ADAMS, lawyer; b. Pine Apple, Ala., Oct. 5, 1918; s. James Adams and Kate (Compton) L.; m. Lydia Douglas, Sept. 18, 1942; children: Kathryn Lloyd Allen, Sally Douglas (Mrs. Charles Proctor), Elizabeth Anne (Mrs. Thomas Goodman), Hugh Adams Jr. Student, Oglethorpe U., 1936-37; AB, U. Ala., 1941, LL.B., 1942. Bar: Ala. 1942, U.S. Supreme Ct 1958. Adjudicator VA, Montgomery, Ala., 1946-47; partner firm Lloyd, Dinning, Boggs & Dinning, Demopolis, 1947—. Chmn. bd. dirs., chief exec. officer Robertson Banking Co., Demopolis, ret., 1995. Active Boy Scouts Am.; chmn. Demopolis Indsl. Devel. Com., 1970; mem. Regional Com. Juvenile Delinquency, 1970; chmn. Marengo County Devel. Bd., 1972-73; mem. Demopolis City Coun., 1974; chmn. Indsl. Devel. Bd. Marengo County, 1980; pres. Marengo County Port Authority, 1987—, Demopolis City Schs. Found., 1995—; trustee Judson Coll., Marion, Ala., 1981, vice-chmn. bd., 1989, chmn., 1991; bd. dirs. Judson Coll.-Marion Inst. Joint Found. With AUS, 1943-45. Decorated Bronze Star; recipient Silver Beaver award Boy Scouts Am., 1972, Paul Harris Fellow award Rotary Found., 1998, award for cmty. svc. West Ala. Mental Health Bd., 1998, Demopolis Citizen of Yr. award, 1998. Mem. ABA, Am. Judicature Soc., Ala. Bar Assn., 17th Jud. Circuit Bar Assn. (pres.), Marengo County Hist. Soc. (v.p. 1980), Demopolis C. of C. (pres., Citizen of Yr. award 1998, Lifetime Cmty. Svc. award 2002), Ala. Law Inst. (coun.), Bus. Coun. Ala. (dir. 1995), Ala. Safety Coun. (former dir.), Demopolis Country Club (pres. 1967-68), Kiwanis (dist. gov. 1967, chmn. internat. com. Key clubs 1969, internat. com. on boys and girls work 1972, dist. chmn. laws and regulations com. Ala. dist. 1979). Baptist (past chmn. ch. bd. deacons, by-laws com. Ala. State Bapt. Conv. 1997). Home: 1408 Colony Dr Demopolis AL 36732-3443 Office: PO Drawer 740 501 N Walnut Ave Demopolis AL 36732-2037

LLOYD, JACQUELINE, English language educator; b. N.Y.C., Aug. 21, 1950; d. R.G. and Hortense (Collins) L. BA, Fisk U., 1972; MEd, U. North Fla., 1989. Instr. English, dir. Writing Ctr. Edward Waters Coll., Jacksonville, Fla., 1983, 90—. Mem. Nat. Coun. Tchrs. English. Democrat. Presbyterian. Avocation: movies. Home: 5006 Andrew Robinson Dr Jacksonville FL 32209-1002

LLOYD, JAMES D. federal agency administrator; BSME with honors, Union Coll.; M Indsl. Engring., Tex. A&M U. Safety engr. U.S. Army Aviation Sys. Command, St. Louis; prin. safety engr., chief program evaluation U.S. Army Materiel Command, Alexandria, Va., dir. field safety activity, 1979—87; with NASA Hdqrs., Washington, 1987—, dir. product assurance, dir. safety and risk mgmt. divsn. Office of Safety and Mission Assurance, 1993—. Office: NASA Hdqrs Mail Code Q 300 E St SW Washington DC 20546

LLOYD, JEAN, early childhood educator, television producer; b. Montgomery, Ala., Mar. 3, 1935; d. James Jack and Dorothy Gladys (Brown) L.; 1 child, Jamie Angelica. BA, Queens Coll., 1957; MA, NYU, 1960, PhD, 1976. Tchr. jr. h.s. N.Y.C. Bd. of Edn., 1961, dir. head start ctr., 1966, 67 summer, tchr. early childhood, 1961-69, tchr. kindergarten, 1984—; instr., asst. prof. U. Coll. Rutgers U., Newark, 1969-83. Cons. Bd. Examiners, N.Y.C., 1982, Dept. of Pers., N.Y.C., 1985; rsch. cons. Seymour Laskow CPA, 1983; chmn. bd. dirs. Your Family Inc., N.Y.C., 1989—; prodr. New Ventures cable TV show (Manhattan), 1987—. Author: Sociology and Social Life, 1979; contbr. over 10 articles to profl. jours. Recipient Ed Press award Ednl. Press Assn., 1968; Project Synergy fellow Tchrs. Coll., Columbia, 1991-93. Mem. ASCD, United

Fedn. of Tchrs., Delta Kappa Gamma. Democrat. Methodist. Avocations: writing poetry and feature articles, singing in church choir. Home: 180 W End Ave New York NY 10023-4902 Office: PS 207 41 W 117th St New York NY 10026-1901

LLOYD, JOHN, composer, educator; b. Wilkinsburg, Pa., July 22, 1938; s. John Samuel and Dorothy Lloyd. MA Music, Duquesne U., Pittsburgh, Pennsylvania, 1969; LGSM, Guild Hall Sch. of Music and Drama, London, England, 1965; BA Music Edn., Otterbain Coll., Westerville, Ohio, 1960. Organist First Presbyn. Ch., London, 1995—; music educator Churchill Area Schools, Pittsburgh, Pa., 1961—93; vocalist Chautauqua Opera, Chautauqua, NY, 1956—67. Recipient Composition Award, Nat. Sch. Orch. Assn., 1994. Presbyterian. Home: 231-B North Madison Road London OH 43140-2014 Office: First Presbyterian Church 211 Garfield Avenue London OH 43140

LLOYD, JOHN RAYMOND, mechanical engineering educator; b. Mpls., Aug. 1, 1942; s. Raymond Joseph and Wilma Mable (Epple) L.; m. Mary Jane Whiteside, Dec. 20, 1963; children: Jay William, Stephanie Christine. BS in Engring., U. Minn., 1964, MSME, 1966, PhDME, 1971; D in Tech. Sci. (hon.), Russian Acad. Scis., 2000. Devel. engr. Procter & Gamble Co., Cin., 1966-67; prof. mech. engring. U. Notre Dame, South Bend, Ind., 1970-83; disting. prof. Mich. State U., East Lansing, 1983—, chmn. dept. mech. engring., 1983-91, dir. Inst. Global Engring. Edn., 1997—2001. Cons. LeRoy Troyer & Assocs., Mishawaka, Ind., 1980—90, Azdel Inc., Shelby, NC, 1987—90; advisor NSF, Washington, 1987—90; Nat. Bur. Stds. assessment panel NRC, Washington, 1987—93; sci. coun. Internat. Ctr. Heat and Mass Transfer, Yugoslavia, 1986—; chmn. Midwest Energy Consortium, 1993—2000; adv. editor McGraw Hill, Inc., 1990—. Adv. editor Internat. Jour. Heat and Fluid Flow, 1985—, Jour. Engring. Physics and Thermodynamics, 1993—; contbr. over 100 articles to profl. jours., chpts. to books. Recipient Outstanding Faculty award U. Notre Dame, 1975, 82, Ralph R. Teetor Edn. award Soc. Automotive Engrs., 1986. Fellow: ASME (nat. bd. comm. 1983—90, rsch. and tech. devel. bd. 1985—99, editor Jour. Heat Transfer 1989—95, coun. on edn., critical techs. com. 1991—93, sr. v.p. engring. 1999—2002, v.p. rsch. 1995—98, Outstanding Paper award 1977, Melville medal 1978, Heat Transfer Meml. award 1995, Dedicated Svc. award 1999). Office: Mich State U Dept Mech Engring 2242 Engring Bldg East Lansing MI 48824 E-mail: lloyd@egr.msu.edu.

LLOYD, JOHN LEWIS, music educator, gospel music historian, soloist; b. Phila., Jan. 7, 1960; s. John Lewis and Frances Virginia (Boardley) L. Student, Settlement Music Sch., Phila., 1979-82, 97—, Combs Coll. Music, 1983-86, Temple U. Dir. Wayland Temple Bapt. Ch. Male Chorus, Phila., 1980-92, Reunion Choir of Phila., Phila., 1988—, F.C. Singers, 1988—; head tchr. Rainbow Cmty. Headstart, 1989-99. Voice major Dorothy Pearson Studio Music; nat. supr. Nat. Soloist Bur.; lectr. in field. Prodr. (CD) Gospel Music of the Masters, vol. I & II, 2000; pub. hymns and spirituals in gospel form; contbr. articles to profl. jours. Organizer, pres. Greater Phila. Choral Chpt.; dir. Reunion Choir Phila., 1988—; bd. trustees Ctr. for Econ. & Law Charter Sch. Recipient City Coun. Citation, Senate Pa. U.S. Ho. of Reps., Phila. Mem. Nat. Conv. Gospel Choirs and Choruses (organizer Greater Phila. chpt., bd. dirs.). Baptist. Avocations: collecting old gospel sheet music and records. E-mail: themusicman2@aol.com.

LLOYD, MICHAEL JEFFREY, recording producer; b. N.Y.C., Nov. 3, 1948; s. John and Suzanne (Lloyd) Sutton; m. Patricia Ann Varble, Sept. 6, 1980; children: Michael, Christopher, Jeni, Deborah. Student, U. So. Calif. V.p. artists and repertoire MGM Records, Inc., 1969-73; ind. record producer, 1973—; pres. Heaven Prodns., 1975—, Michael Lloyd Prodns., 1979—, Taines-Lloyd Film Prodns., 1984-85; music dir. TV series Happy Days; music dir. Kidsongs, Living Proof, NBC-TV movie, Kidsongs Videos; prodr. Love Lines, NBC-TV movie Swimsuit; pres., co-founder Studio M, Beverly Hills, Calif., 2000—. Guest lectr. UCLA, Pepperdine U.; judge Am. Song Festival. Composer: (music for feature films) Tough Enough, If You Could See What I Hear, Dirty Dancing, All Dogs Go to Heaven, (music and lyrics) Rudolph the Red Nose Reindeer - The Movie, 1998, Coyote Ugly, Driven, Angel Eyes, music for 8 Movies of the Week, 12 TV Spls., 28 TV series and 58 motion pictures. Recipient 51 Gold Album awards, 26 Platinum Album awards, 26 Gold Single awards, 2 Platinum Single awards, 3 Grammy awards, 43 Chart Album awards, 100 Chart Single awards, 10 Broadcast Music Inc. awards, Am. Music award, Dove award, 2 Nat. Assn. Record Mrcts. Mem.: AFTRA, NARAS, SAG, ASCAP (12 awards), Am. Fedn. Musicians.

LLOYD, MICHAEL L. nursing administrator, educator; b. Miami, Ariz., Jan. 17, 1954; s. James Warren and Willa Mae (Jackson) Lloyd; m. Glynnis Morrill; 1 child, Amanda. Diploma, Mesa (Ariz.) Community Coll., 1974; BSN, Ariz. State U., 1976. RN, Colo., Ariz. Instr. nursing Gateway Community Coll., Phoenix, 1984-90; dir. nurses PRN, 1990-93; staff nurse post anesthesia care unit Montrose (Colo.) Meml. Hosp., 1993-96, dir. surg. svcs., 1996—. Contbr. articles to profl. jours. Mem. Assn. Post Anesthesia Nurses, Assn. Operating Rm. Nurses, Ariz. Assn. Health Care Agys., Ariz. Nurse Network, Ariz. Nurses Assn., Colo. Nurses Assn. E-mail: mike&glynnis@montrose.net or mikel@mmh.hbocvan.com.

LLOYD, RAY DIX, health physicist; b. Mar. 10, 1930; s. Ray Ernest and Dixie (Penrose) L.; m. Louise Mortensen, July 10, 1954; children: Thomas R., Janna L. Brady, Alan T., Christopher R., Heather L. Smith. BS, U. Utah, 1954, MS, 1956, PhD, 1974; postgrad., U. Southwestern La., 1959, La. State U., 1960. Diplomate Am. Bd. Health Physics. From rsch. asst. radiobiology divsn. to rshc. prof. U. Utah, 1961—84, rsch. prof. dept. pharmacology, radiobiology divsn., 1984-92; part-time rsch. prof. U. Utah Sch. Medicine, 1992—. Adj. asst. prof. dept. mech. engring. U. Utah, 1975-90; adj. prof. engring. U. Utah, 1997—, rsch. prof. radiology, 1998—; cons. in field; mem. Nat. Coun. Radiation Protection and Measurements, 1980-92, consociate mem., 1992—; mem. radiol. health adv. com. Utah State Divsn. Health. Assoc. editor: (jour.) Health Physics, 1990-92; (book) Delayed Effects of Bone Seeking Radionuclides; reviewer: Radiation Rsch., Health Physics, Radiat. Protection, Internat. Jour. Radiation Biology, others; contbr. articles to profl. jours., chpts. to books; patentee radiation detector. Master sgt. U.S. Army, 1951—52, Korea. Fellow Health Physics Soc.; mem. Am. Acad. Health Physics, Radiation Rsch. Soc., Health Physics Soc. (Great Salt Lake chpt.), Utah br. Am. Assn. for Lab. Animal Sci., Internat. Radiation Protection Assn., Sigma Xi, Phi Kappa Phi, Gamma Theta Upsilon. Office: U Utah Radiobiology 729 Arapeen Dr 2334 CAMT Salt Lake City UT 84108-1218

LLOYD, ROBERT ALBERT, retired foundation administrator; b. Pitts., Apr. 21, 1930; s. Robert Morgan and Martha Elizabeth (Sauter) L. Student, Carnegie Mellon U. Adminstrv. supr. Pitts. Inf. Sch., USAR, 1951-71, ret., 1971; asst. mgr. meml. dept. Sears Roebuck & Co., Pitts., 1960-71, mem. staff, 1971-91, ret. Chmn. Boro of Dormont (Pa.) Rep. Com., 1974-76, committeeman 7th Dist., Allegheny County, 1970-76; bd. dirs., past v.p. Concerned Citizens of Dormont Boro Inc.; sch. dir. Commonwealth of Pa.; bd. dirs. Keystone Oaks Sch. Dist., treas., 1997-98, trustee Golden Winds Found.; active Cath. Hist. Soc., Holy Family Soc., Opus Dei, St. Pius X Roman Cath. Ch.; bd. dirs. Keystone Oaks Sch. Dist., 2000—. With USAR, 1951-90. Decorated Legion of Honor, Order of DeMolay, Commendation medal, U.S. Army; recipient Good Citizenship medal SAR, 1943, Citizen of Yr. award Sears, 1996-97. Mem.: St. Vincent de Paul Soc. (treas. 2000—), Cath. Soc. History (bd. dirs.), Order of St. Lawrence (grand knight comdr.), Cath. Knights Am. (area rep.), Genesis, Sons of Union Vets. of Civil War, Am. Legion, K.T. (life sponsor Eye Found.), KC (4th deg., Color Corps, Bd. dirs. Pitts. coun., Knight of Month 1995, Knight Family of Month 1996, Dep. Grand Knight 2001), Sons of Italy (trustee Grand Loddge of Pa.), Rotary. Home: 3089 Pinehurst Ave Pittsburgh PA 15216-2434

LLOYD, ROBERT BALDWIN, political science educator; b. Toms River, N.J., Oct. 11, 1961; s. Robert Baldwin Sr. and Elspeth Yvonne Lloyd; m. Ann Denise Lloyd, Dec. 18, 1982; children: Ellyn, Owen, David. BA, U. Ariz., 1983; MRP, Cornell U., 1985; PhD, Johns Hopkins U., 1998. Asst. area dir. African area SIL Internat., Nairobi, Kenya, 1988-90, dir. Mozambique program Maputo, 1990-93, govt. affairs specialist Washington, 1993-97; coord. internat. studies Pepperdine U., Malibu, Calif., 1998-2000, dir. Ctr. for Internat. Studies and Langs., 2000—. Contbr. articles to profl. jours. Mem. Internat. Studies Assn., Am. Polit. Sci. Assn. Republican. Presbyterian. Office: Pepperdine U 24255 PCH Malibu CA 90263 E-mail: robert.lloyd@pepperdine.edu.

LLOYD, R.W. psychiatrist; AB, Princeton U., 1968; PhD, U. S.C., 1975; MD, U. Ariz., 1986. Diplomate Am. Bd. Psychiatry and Neurology. Resident and intern U. Ariz. Affiliated Hosps., Tucson, 1986-90; clin. asst. prof. psychiatry, Coll. Medicine U. Ariz., 1991—95; chief in patient psychiatry Tucson VA Med. Ctr., 1990—94, chief substance abuse treatment unit, 1992—94.

LLOYD, SALLY-HEATH FAHNESTOCK, artist; b. Glen Cove, N.Y., Aug. 22, 1942; d. J. Sheridan Fahnestock and Margaret Fahnestock Lewis; m. Douglas Wray Lloyd, Jr., March 9, 1964; children: Wendy, Douglas. AA, St. Mary's Coll. of Md., 1962; BFA, Ariz. State U., 1989. Studio artist, Scottsdale, Ariz., 1989—. Mem. Soc. No. Am. Goldsmiths, Am. Craft Coun., Ariz. Designer Craftsmen (juried mem., state bd. pres. 1997-99), Ariz. Masterworks Chorale, Ariz. State U. Nelson Art Mus., Phoenix Art Mus. Avocations: hiking, choral singing, travel. Home: 23645 N 83rd Pl Scottsdale AZ 85255-3508 E-mail: sally-heath@lloydtardis.com.

LLOYD, THOMAS BLAIR, research scientist, consultant; b. Reedsville, W.Va., Aug. 29, 1921; s. Hazen C. and A. Dolvena (Buchanan) L.; m. Barbara Sprinthall, Oct. 8, 1944; children: Thomas B., Judith E., Althea. BS, Washington and Jefferson Coll., 1942; MS, Western Res. U., 1946, PhD, 1948. Asst. prof. Muhlenberg Coll., Allentown, Pa., 1948-54; supr. rsch. N.J. Zinc Co., Palmerton, 1954-83; rsch. scientist Lehigh U., Bethlehem, 1983—. Cons. to numerous corps. and law firms. Contbr. chpts. to books, articles to profl. jours. Mem. Northampton County Dem. Com., 1989—; chmn. Sch. Bd., Palmerton, 1960-66. Served with USN, 1944-46, PTO. Mem. Am. Chem. Soc. (chmn. Lehigh Valley sect. 1955), Engrs. Club Lehigh Valley (pres. 1960), Sigma Xi. Episcopalian. Achievements include many proprietary advances in TiOz pigment manufacture and adhesion science. Home: 127 Bridle Path Rd Bethlehem PA 18017-3870

LLOYD-JONES, DADIVA BOCOBO, nursing assistant, writer; b. Tarlac, Philippines, Nov. 7, 1931; arrived in U.S., 1989; d. Alfredo Santiago Perez and Inez Dupitas Bocobo; m. Bernardo Villanueva Aperocho, Aug. 27, 1951 (div.); children: Butch Aperocho(dec.) , Darius, Norman, Noel, Rey(dec.) ; m. Leon Thomas Lloyd-Jones, Mar. 12, 1992. BS in Edn., U. of the East, Manila, Philippines, 1955; MA, Ateneo de Manila, 1964; EdD, U. Pangasinan, Dagupan, Philippines, 1977. Cert. nursing asst., Wash. H.S. English tchr. Gerona Inst., Tarlac, 1956—64; prof. Feati U., Manila, 1964—71, U. Pangasinan, 1971—81; speech and drama tchr. Ramon Magsaysay, Manila, 1981—89; home health aide Olympic Peninsula Home Health, Wash., 1991—94, nursing asst., 1995—97, Dynamic Corp., L.A., 1995—. Co-author: Speech and Drama, 1988; author: (poems) Of Tears and Flowers, 1999, Heart and Soul, 2000. Recipient Editor's Choice awards (4), Internat. Libr. Poetry, 1998—2000, Editor's Choice awards (6), Nat. Libr. of Poetry, 1998—99. Mem.: Internat. Soc. Poets. Avocations: writing poems and essays, piano, singing. Home: 357 N Edunburgh Ave Los Angeles CA 90048

LLOYD-STILL, JOHN DASHWOOD, pediatrician, educator; b. London, Dec. 21, 1936; came to U.S., 1968; a. Robert Merrick and Vera Sybil L-S.; m. Dorothy Malm, May 24, 1959; children: Robert, Sarah. MB BS, U. London, 1960; MRCP, Royal Coll. Physicians, 1964. Diplomate Am. Bd. Pediatrics. Sr. resident Children's Hosp. and Med. Ctr., Boston, 1968-69; sr. registrar St. Mary's Hosp. U., London, 1968-70; fellow in nutrition Harvard Med. Sch., 1970-72; asst. prof. pediatrics Pa. State U., Hershey, 1972-74; assoc. prof. Northwestern U., Chgo., 1974-85, prof., 1985-96, Rush Med. Coll., Chgo., 1994—; dir. Cystic Fibrosis Ctr. Rush-Presbyn.-St. Luke's Med. Ctr., 1996—. Fellow Nat. Cystic Fibrosis Found., Atlanta, 1970-72. Editor: (book) Malnutrition and Intellectual Development, 1974, Textbook of Cystic Fibrosis, 1983. Recipient Larkin prize in medicine U. London, 1960, Brenneman award Chgo. Pediatric Soc., Fulbright fellowship, 1968-69. Mem. Royal Coll. Physicians, Am. Acad. Pediatrics, N.Am. Soc. Pediatrics, Gastroenterology & Nutrition, Am. Gastroent. Assn., Am. Assn Study Liver Disease. Avocations: golf, fishing, travel. Home: 806 Clinton Pl Evanston IL 60201-1764 Office: Rush Presbyn St Lukes Med Ctr 1725 W Harrison St Chicago IL 60612-3828 E-mail: jdlloydstill@yahoo.com.

LLUBIÉN, JOSEPH HERMAN, psychotherapist, counselor; b. San Juan, PR, July 14, 1943; s. Herman LLubién-Torres and Guilliermina Diaz Asad-LLubién; children: Sanjay Alexander, Jiang Carlos, Jose Lorenzo, Jill Ann Jo Garcia; m. Patricia Deveda, 1995; 1 child, Michael D'Angelo; 1 adopted child, Darius Johann LLubién Ricks. BA in Psychology and English, Fordham U., 1973; MA in Lit. and Creative Writing, CUNY, 1981; PhD, Sch. for Social Rsch., 1984; PhD in Psychology and Human Svcs., Walden U. Inst. for Advanced Studies, Mpls., 1995. Adj. prof. English and poetry Coll. Human Scis., Fordham U. Alumni Fedn., N.Y.C., 1969-70; nat. adminstr., dir. counseling Employment Tng. Adminstrn. U.S. Labor Dept., Washington, 1970-82, nat. dir. counseling/tng. Comty. Employment Tng. Adminstrn., 1971-82; adj. prof. English and poetry Coll. Human Svcs., 1979-80; adjunct prof. English and Composition Malcolm King Coll., N.Y.C., 1984; substance abuse treatment counselor, psychotherapist Alcohol Drug Addiction Svcs. Adminstrn. D.C. Gen. Hosp., Washington, 1989-90; psychotherapist, crisis counselor, bilingual guidance counselor, clin. mental health specialist JMC Assocs., Inc., 1990-91; bilingual guidance counselor D.C. Pub. Schs. Bancroft Elem. Sch., 1991-93; clin. mental health specialist, bilingual Dept. Human Svcs., Commn. on Mental Health, 1993; psychol. treatment counselor II Nat. Capital Systems, Inc. Methadone Therapy Treatment Ctr., 1993-95; behav. therapist, activity coord. P.S.I. Assocs., Inc., 1995—; clin. counselor Vesta Found., Inc., 1995—; social worker Bancroft Elem. D.C. Pub. Schs., 1995-98; edn. counselor Jefferson Jr. H.S. Washington Pub. Schs., 1998—; case investigator McKenney, DeApolis, Gordon & Lightfoot. Curriculum co-writer Substance Abuse Prevention Curriculum for Pre-kindergarten and Primary Edn.; assisted in devel. of bilingual activity workbook for elem. schs. with U.S. Dept. Justice and Nat. Crime Prevention Coun., 1992; mem. youth coun. U.S. State Dept. Fgn. Desk, 1972-81. Author: (poetry) From the Belly of the Shark, 1978, For Neruda La Luz Que Llega, 1979, Black Yellow Red Indian Songs, 1999, Black Streams, 1999. Vol. counselor Apache reservation in southern Tex., 1986-87, Northern Cheyenne reservation, Lamedeer, Mont.; vol. trainer for guidance counselors Howard U. in substance abuse prevention, 1988-92. With USAF, 1961-67, Vietnam, USAR, 1982-90. Doctoral fellow Walden U. Inst. Advanced Studies, 1991. Mem. NAACP, ACA, Princeton U. Club, N.Y., Assn. of Sch. Counselors, La Raza Unida, U.S. Karate Assn., Am. Karate Assn., U.S. Tai Chi Assn., Japan-USA Akeido Fedn., Internat. Kung Fu Assn., All Japan Am. Akeido Fedn., Tai Chi Chinese Fedn., Tae Quan Do Am. Karate Fedn., Kung Fu Am. Fedn. Home: Apt C401 4660 Martin Luther King Jr Ave C401 Washington DC 20032-4991

LNENICKA, WADE SHERIDAN, purchasing official, councilman; b. Kansas City, Mo., Nov. 1, 1951; s. William Joseph and Georgia Marie (Ericksen) L.; m. Robin Ann Brown, June 22, 1985. BS in Mgmt., Ga. Tech., 1973; MBA, U. Mich., 1978; grad. with honors, U.S. Army Command and Gen. Staff Coll., 1983; grad., Nat. Def. U., 1991. Cert. purchasing mgr. Nat. Assn. Purchasing Mgmt., Inc. Bus. mgr. Wink Davis Equipment Co., Inc., Atlanta, 1978-79; order control supr. Printpack Inc., 1980-82, purchasing supr., 1982-87, purchasing mgr., 1987-2000; mem. Smyrna (Ga.) City Coun., 1988—; v.p. purchasing CPG-Pepsi Bottlers, Inc., Atlanta, 2000—. Mem. civic adv. com. Emory-Adventist Hosp. Home Health, 1997—; mem. Emory-Adventist Hosp. Sr. Oasis, 1998—2000; mem. adv. bd. Small Cities newsletter, 1998—; bd. dirs. Ridge Assisted Living, Inc. at Ridgeview Inst., 1998—. 1st lt. U.S. Army, 1973—76, maj. USAR, 1976—95. Mem. Am. Legion, Vets. Meml. Assn. of Smyrna, Ga., Inc., U.S. Intercollegiate Lacrosse Assn., U.S. Lacrosse, Cobb Mcpl. Assn. (sec. 1992, treas. 1993, v.p. 1994, pres. 1995). Avocations: bridge, lacrosse, military history, politics. Home: 3950 Glenhurst Dr SE Smyrna GA 30080-5896 Office: CPG-Pepsi Bottlers Inc 2849 Paces Rd Ste 240 Atlanta GA 30339 E-mail: wlnenicka@yahoo.com., wslnenicka@cpgpepsi.com.

LO, ARTHUR WU-NIEN, electrical engineering educator; b. Shanghai, China, May 21, 1916; came to U.S., 1945, naturalized, 1957; s. Liang-Kan and Shou-Pan (Heng) L.; m. Elizabeth H. Shen, Aug. 24, 1950; children: Katherine E., James A. BS, Yenching U., 1938; MA, Oberlin Coll., 1946; PhD, U. Ill., 1949. Mem. tech. staff RCA Research Labs., 1951-60; mgr. advanced devel., data systems div. IBM Corp., 1960-62, mgr. exploratory devel., components div., 1962-64; prof. elec. engring. Princeton U., 1964-86, prof. emeritus, 1986—. Cons. in field, 1964—, spl. research digital electronics and computer systems. Author: Transistor Electronics, 1955, Introduction to Digital Electronics, 1967; also papers in field; patentee in field. Fellow IEEE; mem. Sigma Xi, Eta Kappa Nu, Pi Mu Epsilon. Home: 102 Maclean Cir Princeton NJ 08540-5623 E-mail: eandalo@aol.com.

LO, CLARENCE Y. H. sociology educator, writer; b. Phila., Oct. 15, 1948; s. Chien-Pen and Lucy Chu Lo; m. Laurie Ann Castro, Feb. 15, 1980 (div. Nov. 1992); children: Nigel C., Julian C.; m. Darlaine Claire Gardetto, June 19, 1999. AB, Harvard U., 1970; MA, U. Calif., Berkeley, 1973, PhD, 1978. Lectr. U. Calif., San Diego, La Jolla, 1978-79; asst. prof. UCLA, 1979-87; assoc. prof. U. Mo., Columbia, 1987—. Cons. BBC TV, London, 1996; cons. Ednl. Testing Svcs., Princeton N.J., 1994—. Author: Small Property Vs. Big Government, 1990; author, editor: Social Policy and the Conservative Agenda, 1998; contbr. articles to profl. jours. Radio appearances interviews and commentaries KWMU, KBIA, KPFK, KCEO, St. Louis, Columbia, L.A., 1980—; chair Peace Studies faculty, U. Mo., 1993-95; active electoral campaign initiative, Mo., 1994. Grantee Calif. Coun. for the Humanities in Pub. Policy, San Diego Calif., 1979-80. Mem. Am. Sociol. Assn. (various offices and adv. bds., minority fellowship program), Harvard Club. Avocations: astronomy, surfing. Office: U Mo Sociology Dept Columbia MO 65211-6100 E-mail: LoC@missouri.edu.

LO, FU-CHEN, economist, educator, ambassador; b. Chia-yi, Taiwan, May 8, 1935; s. Chian-Tien and Tan-Baih Lo; m. Vickie Chin-fun Mao, June 15, 1962; children: Theadore Tse-shin, David Tse-yen. BA, Nat. Taiwan U., 1958; MA, Waseda U., Tokyo, 1963; PhD, U. Pa., 1968. Chief comparative studies UN Ctr. Regional Devel., Nagoya, Japan, 1973-80; sr. rsch. fellow East-West Ctr., Honolulu, 1981-82; affiliated faculty U. Hawaii, 1981-84; rsch. coord. Asia and Pacific Devel. Ctr., Kuala Lumpur, Malaysia, 1985-89; prin. acad. officer UN U., Tokyo, 1990-95, dep. dir./prof. Inst. Advanced Studies, 1995-2000, prof. emeritus Inst. Advanced Studies, 2000—; dir. Modern Culture Found., 2000—; Taiwan ambassador to Japan. Vis. prof. U. Pa., Phila., 1982-84; founder, organizer Future of Asian-Pacific Economy Conf., 1985-89; bd. dirs. Taiwan Soc., 1991-94; founder, pub. Taiwan Tribune, N.Y., 1981-87. Author: Growth Pole Strategy and Regional Development Policy, 1978, Asian and Pacific Economy Toward the Year 2000, 1987, Global Adjustment and the Future of Asia-Pacific Economy, 1989, Emerging World Cities in Pacific Asia, 1995. Founding mem., ctr. com. mem. World United Formosans for Independence, N.Y., Taipei, 1970—; bd. dirs. Amnesty Internat., Tokyo, 1975-77; founding mem., bd. dirs. Formosan Assn. for Pub. Affairs, 1982. Grantee Toyota Found., 1977-78, Internat. Devel. Ctr. Japan, 1993-94, Environment Agy. of Japan, 1995-96. Mem. Am. Econ. Assn., Japan Soc. for Internat. Devel. (founding mem.), Internat. Geog. Union (founding mem., mem. working group on urbanization in developing countries). Office: Taipei Econ and Cultural Rep Office 5-20-2 Shirokanedai Minato-ku Tokyo 108-0071 Japan

LO, HOI-KWONG, research scientist; b. Hong Kong, Mar. 21, 1967; arrived in U.S., 1999; s. Lee-Gun and Chung-Chun Lo. BA in Math., Trinity Coll., Cambridge, U.K., 1989; MS in Physics, Caltech, 1991, PhD in Physics, 1994. Mem. Inst. for Advanced Study, Princeton, N.J., 1994-96; rsch. cons. Hewlett-Packard Labs., Bristol, U.K., 1996-97, sr. mem. tech. staff, 1997-99; chief scientist, sr. v.p. R&D MagiQ Techs., Inc., N.Y.C., 1999—. Co-editor, co-author: Introduction to Quantum Computation and Information, 1998. Prince Philip scholar Friends of Cambridge U., Hong Kong, 1986. Mem. Am. Phys. Soc. Achievements include co-inventor and patentee quantum cryptographic system with reduced data loss. Office: MagiQ Techs Inc 275 7th Ave Fl 26 New York NY 10001-6708 E-mail: hoi_kwong@magiqtech.com.

LO, JIEN-CHUNG, electrical engineer; b. Taichung, Taiwan, Dec. 27, 1960; s. Chang-Kuei Lo and Yu-Shuang Lo-Kuo; m. Shu-Ying Shung; children: Wenchau Albert, Wenyen Agatha. PhD, U. La., 1989. Field svc. engr. Digital Equipment Corp. Taiwan, Taipei, 1983—85; asst. prof. U. R.I., Kingston, 1989—94, assoc. prof., 1994—99, prof., 1999—. Dir. Lab. Electronic Testing, Kingston, 1999—; patentee in field. Editor: IEEE Transactions on Computers, 2001; author: An Introduction to the Fundamentals of Fault-Tolerant Computing, 1994; contbr. articles. Recipient, Champlin Found., 1999, State of R.I. and Cherry Semiconductor Inc., 1999—2000; fellow, NSF and Global Collaboration Program, Japan, 1996; grantee, Office of Naval Rsch., 1994—96, NSF, 1999—2001. Mem.: IEEE (gen. chair North Atlantic workshop 1999, gen. chair symposium defect and fault tolerance in VLSI sys. 2001). Office: Dept Electrical & Computer Engring 4 E Alumni Ave Kingston RI 02881 Office Fax: 401-782-6422. Business E-Mail: jcl@ele.uri.edu.

LO, PATRICK PUNCHUK, physician; b. Hong Kong, Nov. 26, 1952; came to U.S., 1972; s. Yuen and City-Yu (Cheung) L.; m. Daisy Yawluan Sim, Dec. 19, 1982; 1 child, Jeffrey. BS in Pharmacy, U. Okla., 1977; DO, Okla. State U., 1982. Diplomate Am. Bd. Osteo. Gen. Practice; registered pharmacist, Okla. Intern Hillcrest Health Ctr., Oklahoma City, 1982-83; physician Corn Med. Clinic, 1983—. Mem. Am. Osteo. Assn., Okla. Osteo. Assn., Am. Coll. Gen. Practice, Lions. Office: Corn Med Clinic 1506 S Agnew Ave Oklahoma City OK 73108-2432

LO, SHUI-YIN, physicist; b. Canton, Oct. 20, 1941; came to the U.S., 1959; s. Long tin and Ty-Fong (Chow) L.; m. Angela Kwok-Kie Lau, Dec. 18, 1969; children: Alpha Wei-min, Fiona Ai-ming, Hao-min. BS, U. Ill., 1962; PhD, U. Chgo., 1966. Rsch. assoc. Rutherford High Energy Lab., Chilton, United Kingdom, 1966-69, Glasgow (United Kingdom) U., 1969-72; sr. lectr. U. Melbourne, Australia, 1972-89; pres. Inst. for Boson Studies, Pasadena, Calif., 1986-92; CEO Infrared Health Co., 2000—. Dir. Sinotronic Co., Hong Kong; exec. v.p., dir. rsch. Am. Environ. Tech. Group, Monrovia, Calif., 1993-2000; vis. faculty Calif. Inst. Tech., 1994-98. Author: Scientific Studies of Chinese Character, 1986; author, editor: Geometrical Picture of Hadron Scattering, 1986; ed. Physical, Chemical and Biological Properties of Stable Water Clusters, 1998, contbr. over 100 articles to profl. jours. Prin. Chinese Sch. of Chinese Fellowship Victoria, Australia, 1977-84. Fellow Australian Inst. Physics; mem. Am. Phys. Soc. Achievements include patents for Chinese computer and BASER, water-based catalyst; and creator of IE technology; research in quantum theory of meridians in acupuncture.

LO, YEE ON, composer; b. Chong Qing, Si Chuan, China, Sept. 29, 1945; came to U.S., 1966; p. Kei-Pak and Bih-Tang Lo. AB, U. Calif., Berkeley, 1972, MS, 1979; PhD, Stanford U., 1987. Composer Wings II: Portrait, Dream I - Shattered, When That Call Shudders 'cross..., Duo Concertant - Le Conte du Troubadour, The Interrupted Serenade, Three Postludes, Dreams-Sequence, River Through Time, Night Space. Recipient Program Music prize Bourges Concours Internat., Bourges, France, 1997 . Mem. ASCAP (awards 1997, 98, 99), Audio Engring. Soc. Home and Office: PO Box 62 Palo Alto CA 94302-0062 Fax: 650-329-9655. E-mail: acoustic@olagrande.net.

LOACH, PAUL ALLEN, biochemist, consultant, biophysicist, educator; b. Findlay, Ohio, July 18, 1934; s. Leland Oris and Dorothy Elizabeth (Davis) L.; m. Patricia A. Johnson, Dec. 27, 1957; children: Mark, Eric, Jennifer; m. Pamela Sue Parkes, Apr. 19, 1986; children: Matthew, Sarah, Andrew. BS, U. Akron, 1957; PhD (NIH fellow), Yale, 1961. Research assoc. Nat. Acad. Scis.-NRC; postdoctoral fellow U. Calif. at Berkeley, 1961-63; asst. prof. chemistry Northwestern U., 1963-68, assoc. prof., 1968-73, prof., 1973-74, prof. biochemistry and molecular biology, and chemistry, 1974—. Mem. BBCA study sect. NIH, 1978-82. Assoc. editor: Photochemistry and Photobiology, 1973-80, Biophysics of Structure and Mechanism, 1973-82; Contbr. articles, revs. to profl. jours. Recipient C.P. award U. Akron, 1957, Research Career Devel. award USPHS, 1971-76 Mem. Am. Soc. Biol. Chemists, AAAS, Biophys. Soc., Am. Soc. Photobiology (pres. 1985-86). E-mail: p_loach@northwestern.edu.

LOADER, JAY GORDON, retired utility company executive; b. Plainfield, N.J., Aug. 3, 1923; s. Carl and Madalyn (Wright) L.; m. Joan Merrell, Aug. 19, 1965; children: Michael Jay, Sandra Lee, Gigi Ann. BS, U. Ala., 1951. C.P.A., Ga. Auditor Arthur Andersen & Co., Atlanta, 1951-55; with Fla. Power Corp., St. Petersburg, Fla., 1955-82, asst. sec., asst. treas., 1960-67, sec.-treas., 1967-82, v.p., 1980-89; v.p., sec. Fla. Progress Corp., St. Petersburg, 1983-89;

ret., 1989. Served with AUS, 1943-44. Mem. AICPA, Am. Soc. Corp. Secs., Fin. Analysts Soc. Ctrl. Fla., U. Ala. Alumni Assn., St. Petersburg Yacht Club, Phi Eta Sigma, Beta Gamma Sigma, Beta Alpha Psi. Home: 13325 108th Ave Largo FL 33774-4649

LOAR, PEGGY ANN, foundation administrator, museum administrator; b. Cin., May 14, 1948; d. Jerome Vincent and Elizabeth (Ranz) Wahl. BA in History of Art, U. Cin., 1970, MA in History of Art, 1971. Summer intern Met. Mus. Art, N.Y.C., 1968; curator edn. Indpls. Mus. Art, 1971-76, asst. to the dir., 1974-75, asst. dir., 1975-77; asst. dir. programs and policy Inst. Mus. Svcs., 1977-80; dir. Smithsonian Inst. Traveling Exhbn. Svc., Washington, 1980-87, Wolfsonian Found., Miami, Fla., 1987-96; exec. dir. COPIA: The Amer. Ctr. Wine, Food and Arts, Napa, Calif., 1997—. Lectr. art history U. Cin., 1970-71; lectr. art appreciation and criticism Ind. U., Purdue U., 1975-77; guest lectr. in field. Project dir.: The Art of Cameroon Exhibition Catalog, 1984, Treasures from the Smithsonian Inst. Exhibition Catalog, 1984, Paris Style 1900: Art Noveau Bing, 1986, Hollywood: Legend & Reality Exhibition Catalog, 1988. Travel grantee Japan Found., 1984; Swedish Inst. grantee; Aspen Inst. Humanistic Studies fellow, 1986-87, recipient Smithsonian Gold Medal for Disting. Service, 1987. Mem. Am. Assn. Museums (mus. ethics com. 1980), Internat. Coun. Museums (pres. U.S. nat. com., 1996-2002, US dir.), Com. Internat. Musees d'Art Moderne. Avocations: biking, hiking, dogs, food, wine. Office: COPIA Am Ctr Wine Food & Arts 500 1st St Napa CA 94559

LOARIE, THOMAS MERRITT, healthcare executive; b. Deerfield, Ill., June 12, 1946; s. Willard John and Lucile Veronica (Finnegan) L.; m. Stephanie Lane Fitts, Aug. 11, 1968 (div. Nov. 1987); children: Thomas M., Kristin Leigh Soule. BSME, U. Notre Dame, 1968; Student, U. Minn., 1969-70, U. Chgo., 1970-71, Columbia U., 1978. Registered profl. engr., Calif. Prodn. engr. Honeywell, Inc., Evanston, Ill., 1968-70; various positions Am. Hosp. Supply Co., 1970-83, pres. Heyer-Schulte divsn., 1979-83; pres. COO Novacor Med. Corp., Oakland, Calif., 1984-85, also bd. dirs.; pres. ABA Bio Mgmt., Danville, 1985-87; chmn., CEO Keravision, Inc., Fremont, 1987-2001; founder, chmn., med. device CEO Roundtable, 1993—; founder, chmn., CEO Learnings, Danville, Calif., 2001—; co-founder, chmn. CardioProfile, Inc., 2002—. Asst. prof. surgery Creighton U. Med. Sch., Omaha, 1986-94; guest lectr. Anderson Sch. Mgmt., U. Calif., L.A., 2001—; sprk. in field. Contbr. articles on med. tech. and pub. policy to Wall St. Jour., others. Bd. dirs. Marymount Sch. Bd., 1981-84; bd. dirs. United Way Santa Barbara, 1981-84, assoc. chairperson, 1982-83, treas., 1983. Named One of 50 Rising Stars: Exec. Leaders for the 80's Industry Week mag., 1983. Mem. Assn. for Rsch. in Vision and Ophthalmology, Contact Lens Assn. Ophthalmology, Health Industry Mfrs. Assn. (spl. rep. bd. dirs. 1993-96, bd. dirs. 1997—, exec. com. 1997—, treas. 1998-00, chmn.-elect 2000—), Am. Entrepreneurs for Econ. Growth, Med. Tech. Leadership Forum, Calif. Healthcare Inst. (bd. dirs. 1998—, exec. com. 2000—). Roman Catholic. Achievements include leading development of Intacs corneal ring segments for treatment of nearsightedness (named One of Top 10 Medical Advances by Health Magazine/CNN 1999). Avocations: snow skiing, backpacking, oil painting, the arts.

LOATMAN, ROBERT BRUCE, computer scientist, researcher; b. Washington, Aug. 23, 1945; s. Paul John and Miriam Joyce (Barna) L.; m. Carol Ann Chalmers, June 6, 1969 (div. 1991); children: Thomas, Cynthia, Ryan, Michael; m. Konthip Prabhailakshana, Sept. 7, 1996. BA, Fordham U., 1967, PhD, 1976. Programmer Gen. Electric Co., Schenectady, N.Y., 1968-69; math. instr. Georgetown U., Washington, 1973-76; mem. tech. staff Mitre Corp., McLean, Va., 1978; tech. dir. Killalea Assocs., Inc., Alexandrai, 1976-80; computer scientist PRC Inc., Rsch. and Devel. div., Mclean, 1980-84; dir., artificial intelligence PRC Inc., Tech. div., 1984-92, chief scientist, 1990-2000; advanced tech. architect SpaceWorks Inc., Rockville, Md., 2000-01; sr. tech. staff Explore Reasoning Sys., Catharpin, Va., 2000; sr. prin. cons. Keane Fed. Systems, McLean, 2001—. Judge Fairfax (Va.) County Sci. Fair, 1988—; mentor Rsch. Sci. Inst., McLean, 1984-91, Soc. for Indsl. and Applied Math., 1996-97. Contbr. numerous articles to profl. jours. Vol. advisor Fin. Edn. Ctr., Fairfax, 1990-91. Named one of Top 10 High-Tech Talents Wash. Tech. newspaper, 1989; recipient Parallax prize Emhart Corp., 1988, Advanced Technology Achievement award Litton Industries, Inc., 1996. Mem. AAAS, Am. Math. Soc., Am. Assn. Artificial Intelligence, Assn. for Computational Linguistics. Roman Catholic. Achievements include patent for natural language understanding system. Home: 10991 Clover Hunt Ct Reston VA 20194-1431 Office: Keane Fed Systems 1410 Spring Hill Rd Mc Lean VA 22102 E-mail: rbloatman@comcast.net., bruce_loatman@ers.com.

LOBACH, KATHERINE S. pediatrician, educator; b. Akron, June 2, 1927; d. Titus Breinig and Katherine M. (Slawik) L.; m. Richard Joseph Kaufman, Oct. 10, 1953; children: James Lobach, Susan Elizabeth, John Roger. AB, Smith Coll., 1948; MD, Columbia U., 1952. Diplomate Am. Bd. Pediats. Instr. pediats. Southwestern U. Sch. Medicine, Dallas, 1955-57; instr., asst. prof. pediats. Albert Einstein Coll. Medicine, Bronx, 1957-69, 69-75, assoc. prof. pediats., then prof., 1975-87, dir. Comprehensive Family Care Ctr., 1970-87, clin. prof. pediats., 1988—; asst. commnr. for child health City of N.Y. Dept. Health, 1987-94; dir. Child Health Clinics N.Y.C. Health and Hosps. Corp., 1994-98. Mem. health prof. adv. bd. March of Dimes of Greater NY, 1980—2001; mem. health svcs. adv. com. The Children's Aid Soc., NYC, 1992—; chmn. adv. com. Infant, Child Health Assessment Program, NYC, 1992—; mem. advocacy coun. Citizen's Com. for Children of NYC, 1998—. Contbr. articles to sci. and profl. jours., chpts. to books. Co-chmn. City Wide Coalition for Immunization Initiatives, NYC, 1992—2001; mem. Mayoral Commn. on future of Child Health in NYC, 1987—89; bd. dir. Bronx Com. Health Network, 1998—. Statewide Youth Advocacy, 2000. Recipient Sloan Pub. Svc. award Fund for City of N.Y., 1993, Haven Emerson award Pub. Health Assn. of N.Y.C., 1993. Fellow Am. Acad. Pediats. (pres. N.Y.C. chpt. 1985-88, chair nat. nominating com. 1997), N.Y. Acad. Medicine (chmn. pediats. sect. 1994-96); mem. Ambulatory Pediat. Assn. (pres. 1973-74), Am. Pediat. Soc., Phi Beta Kappa, Sigma Xi. Avocations: reading, travel, tennis, gardening, music. Home: 238 Kensington Oval New Rochelle NY 10805-2917

LOBANOV-ROSTOVSKY, OLEG, management consultant; b. San Francisco, July 12, 1934; s. Andrei and Grace S. (Pope) L-R.; m. Susan Waters, Sept. 8, 1979; 1 child, Alexandra; children by previous marriage: Christopher, Nicholas. BA, U. Mich., 1956. Cmty. concert rep. Columbia Artists Mgmt. Inc., 1958-59; mgr. Columbus (Ohio) Symphony Orch., 1959-62, Hartford (Conn.) Symphony Orch., 1962-65, Balt. Symphony, 1965-69; program officer div. humanities and arts Ford Found., 1969-75; exec. dir. Denver Symphony Orch., 1975-76; mng. dir. Nat. Symphony Orch., Washington, 1977-80; cons. Fed. Coun. on Arts, 1980-81; exec. dir. Del. Ctr. for Performing Arts, 1981-82; from exec. v.p., mng. dir. to pres. Detroit Symphony Orch., 1982-89; ind. cons., 1989-90; mng. ptnr. Middle Am. divsn. Jerold, Panas, Young & Ptnrs. Inc., Chgo., 1990-91; pres. Calif. Ctr. for the Arts, Escondio, Calif., 1991-96; sr. ptnr. Jerold Panas, Linzy & Ptnrs., Inc., Chgo., 1996—.

LOBAO, LINDA MARY, sociologist, educator; b. Beverly, Mass., Aug. 9, 1952; d. George and Helen (Baschuk) L.; 1 child, Erick. BA in Sociology, Boston U., 1974; MA in Sociology, U. South Fla., 1981; PhD in Sociology, N.C. State U., 1986. Asst. prof. Ohio State U., Columbus, 1986-90, assoc. prof. , rural sociology, sociology and geography, 1990-97, prof., 1997—. Author: Locality and Inequality: Farm and Industry Structure and Socio-Economic Conditions, 1990; co-author: Beyond the Amber Waves of Grain: An Examination of Social and Economic Restructuring in the Heartland, 1995; contbr. articles to profl. publs. Grantee NSF, 1988, USDA, 1993, 2000, 2001. Mem. Am. Sociol. Assn., Rural Sociology Soc. (mem. coun. 1985—, v.p. 1997-98, pres. 2002-2003).

LOBAY, IVAN, mechanical engineering educator; b. Koltuny, Ukraine, Oct. 4, 1911; came to U.S., 1961, naturalized, 1968; s. Stephan and Clementina (Maret) Lobay; m. Halyna Makarenko, Apr. 25, 1943; children: Maria Ivanna, Halyna Blahoslava. Mech. Engr., Inst. Tech., Brno, Czechoslovakia, 1940, Cen. U. Venezuela, Caracas, 1956. Registered profl. engr., Conn. Engr., designer Erste Bruenner Maschinenfabriksgesellschaft, Brno, 1940-41; asst. prof. dept. mech. engring. Inst. Tech., Lviv, Ukraine, 1942-43, sci. asst. dept. mech. engring. Brno, 1943-45; engr. san. and civil engring. Ministry San. Affairs, Caracas, Venezuela, 1948-59; prof. dept. civil engring. U. Santa Maria, 1957-60; prof., chmn. divsn. tech. machines & prodn Cen. U. Venezuela Mech. Engring. Sch., 1956-62; prof. dept. mech. engring. U. New Haven, West Haven, 1963-77, 83-84, prof. emeritus, 1984—; prof. gas sect. Inst. Algerien du Petrole, Boumerdes, Algeria, 1977-82. Cons. Ministry of Edn., Ukraine, Kyiv, 1993. Author: Lecciones de Elementos de Maquinas, No. 3, 1960, No. 2, 1961, Estudio Sobre Descarga de Aguas de Lluvia, 1962, Free Lateral Discharge from an Open Triangular Channel, 1993, Education of Engineering Squads in USA, 1996, Workload of University Professors in USA, 1996, Faculty in Higher Education in USA, 1997, Governance in Higher Education in USA, 1999, Memoirs, 1999. With U.S. Army, 1945-47. Decorated Hramota and Cross of Merit Bukovynian Battalion, 1995; recipient Hramota award Govt. in Exile of Ukrainian Nat. Republic, 1992. Mem. AAUP, AAAS, ASME, NSPE, Conn. Soc. Profl. Engrs., N.Y. Acad. Scis., Ukrainian AAUP, Ukrainian Engrs. Soc. Am., Coll. Engrs. Venezuela, Assn. Profs. U. Ctrl. Venezuela, Acad. Engring. Scis. Ukraine. Home: 873 Orange Center Rd Orange CT 06477-1712

LOBB, CYNTHIA JEAN HOCKING, lawyer; b. San Francisco, June 12, 1962; d. Thomas Messinger and Diane (Knight) Hocking; m. Jerry Mark Lobb, Dec. 1, 1990; children: Sean Thomas, Kevin Joseph, Braden McMillan. BA in Polit. Sci., UCLA, 1984; JD, Golden Gate U. Law Sch., U. San Diego Law Sch., 1993. Bar: Ca., 1993. Asst. Congressman W. Dannemeyer, Washington, 1987-88; legal sec. Fulbright & Jaworski, 1988; law clerk MCI Internat. Divsn., Rye Brook, NY, 1990, Kern County Counsel, Bakersfield, Calif., 1991; lawyer Lobb & Cliff, Riverside, 1997-98, Law Office of Cynthia Hocking, Menifee, 1995—. Spanish tchr. Good Shepard Lutheran Sch., Menifee, Calif., 1996-99. Mem. Riverside Repub. Women's Federated, Temecula Repub. Women's Federated, Lake Menifee Women's Club, 1998—2002; Assoc. mem. Calif. Repub. Party, 1980—; pub. rels. dir. St. Martha's Ch., 1998—2002, Bible sharing leader, 1994—97; bd. dirs. Mothers and Others, 1999—2002. Mem. Alpha Delta Chi (named Most Outstanding mem. 1984, Outstanding Young Women of Am., 1985). Republican. Roman Catholic. Avocations: fitness training, jazzercize, scrapbooking, Spanish and French, travel. Home: 23782 Dijon Ct Menifee CA 92584 Office: Lobb & Cliff 1650 Spruce St Ste 500 Riverside CA 92507-2436

LOBB, WILLIAM ATKINSON, financial services executive; b. Arlington, Pa., Apr. 21, 1951; s. Anthony William and Annamarie (Hilpert) L.; m. Maureen Veronique O'Hagan, July 7, 1977; children: William Atkinson III, Anthony Hagan. BS, Georgetown U., 1977. Account exec. Johnston Lemon, Washington, 1977-78; sr. account exec. Merrill Lynch, Alexandria, Va., 1979-83; asst. v.p. E.F. Hutton, Washington, 1983-85; mng. dir., ptnr.-in-charge CIBC Oppenheimer, Inc., Atlanta, 1985—. Bd. trustees Madison Morgan Cultural Ctr.; bd. dirs. Atlanta Charity Clays, Atlanta Opera. Mem. Nat. Securities Traders Assn., Ga. Securities Assn., Univ. Club, Army-Navy Club, Burge Plantation Hunt Club, Piedmont Driving Club. Avocation: squash. Office: CIBC Oppenheimer Inc 1200 Monach Plz 3414 Peachtree Rd NE Atlanta GA 30326-1153 E-mail: will.lobb@us.cibc.com.

LOBDELL, DAVID HILL, pathologist; b. Erie, Pa., July 9, 1930; s. Webster Alexander Lobdell, Christine (Kern) Lobdell. AB, Kenyon Coll., 1952; MD, U. Mich., 1956. Diplomate Am. Bd. Pathology 1961. Resident Pathology Bellevue-NYU Med. Ctr., 1956—60; pathologist St. Vincent's Med. Ctr., Bridgeport, Conn., 1960—63, chair Dept. Lab. Medicine, 1963—95, sr. pathologist, 1996—. Asst. clin. prof. Pathology NYU Sch. Medicine, 1961—69; assoc. clin. prof. Allied Health U. Conn., Storrs, 1984—95. Contbr. Sec., bd. dirs. St. Vincent's Med. Found., Bridgeport. Fellow: Am. Soc. Clin. Pathology, Coll. Am. Pathologists (del. House of Dels. 1991—97); mem.: Conn. Soc. Pathologists (pres. 1982—87), Alpha Omega Alpha, Phi Beta Kappa. Avocation: philately. Office: St Vincent Med Ctr 2800 Main St Bridgeport CA 06606

LOBDELL, FRANK, artist; b. Kansas City, Mo., 1921; m. Ann Morency, 1952; children: Frank Saxton, Judson Earle; m. Jinx Rowam, 1996. Studied, St. Paul Sch. Art, 1938-39, Calif. Sch. Fine Arts, 1947-50, Academie de la Grande Chaumiere, Paris, France, 1950-51. Tchr. Calif. Sch. Fine Arts, 1957-65; prof. art, Stanford, 1965—. One man shows, Lucien Labaudt Gallery, 1949, Martha Jackson Gallery, 1958, 60, 63, 72, 74, de Young Meml. Mus., San Francisco, 1959, Ferus Gallery, 1962, Pasadena Art Mus., 1961, San Francisco Mus. Art, 1969, Benador Gallerie, Geneva, Switzerland, 1964, Gallerie Anderson-Mayer, Paris, 1965, Smith-Anderson Gallery, San Francisco, 1982, Oscarsson Hood Gallery, N.Y.C., 1983, 84, 85, John Berggruen Gallery, San Francisco, 1987, Campbell-Thiebaud Gallery, San Francisco, 1988, 90, 92, 95, Printworks Gallery, Chgo., 1988-96, Stanford Mus. Art, 1988, Hackett Freedman Gallery, 2002, retrospective show, Pasadena Art Mus. and Stanford Mus., 1966, San Francisco Mus. Modern Art, 1983, Stanford Mus., 1993, Saint Mary's Coll., 1998, Western Mich. U. Art Gallery; exhibited group Shows, Salon du Mai, Paris, 1950, III Sao Paulo Biennial, 1955, Whitney Mus. Am. Art, 1962-63, 72, Guggenheim Mus., N.Y.C., 1964, Van Abbemuseum, Eindhoven, Holland, 1970, Corcoran Gallery Art, Washington, 1971, U. Ill., 1974, 15 Calif. Modernists, Fresno Art Mus., 1995; represented in permanent collections, San Francisco Mus. Art, Oakland Mus. Art, L.A. County Mus., Nat. Gallery Washington, others. Served with AUS, 1942-46. Recipient Nealie Sullivan award San Francisco Art Inst., 1960, award of merit AAAL, 1988. Home: 2769 Octavia St Apt 3 San Francisco CA 94123-4311

LOBEL, MARTIN, lawyer; b. Cambridge, Mass., June 19, 1941; s. I. Alan and Dorothy W. l.; m. Geralyn Krupp, Mar. 15, 1981; children: Devra Sarah, Rachel Melissa, Hannah Krupp. AB, Boston U., 1962; JD, 1965; LLM, Harvard U., 1966. Bar: Mass. 1965, D.C. 1968, U.S. Supreme Ct. 1968. Ptnr. Lobel & Lobel, Boston, 1965-66; asst. prof. law U. Okla., Norman, 1967; congl. fellow Washington, 1968; legis. asst. to Senator William Proxmire, 1968-72; ptnr. Lobel, Novins & Lamont, Washington, 1972—. Lectr. Law Sch. Am. U., Washington, 1972—; resellers referee, U.S. Dist. Ct., Wichita; chmn. Tax Analysts, 1972—. Contbr. articles to legal jours. Chmn. tax notes/tax analysis. Mem. ABA, Mass. Bar Assn., D.C. Bar Assn. (ch,m. consumer affairs com. 1976-77, chmn. steering com. on antitrust and consumer affairs sect.), Order of Coif, Harvard Club (Washington), Boston U. Club (Washington). Home: 4525 31st St NW Washington DC 20008-2130 Office: Lobel Novins & Lamont 1275 K St NW Ste 770 Washington DC 20005-4048 E-mail: lobel@lnllaw.com.

LOBEL-ANGEL, MEREDITH ANNE, lawyer; b. San Francisco, Nov. 7, 1956; d. Charles I. and Julia V. Lobel; m. Frank P. Angel; 1 child, Fiona. BA, Stanford U., 1978, MA in Latin Am. Studies, 1979, MA in French, 1982, JD, 1983; postgrad., U. Paris, 1977-78. Bar: Calif. 1983, N.Y. 1984, D.C. 1985. With firm Chadbourne, Parke, Whiteside & Wolff, 1983-85, Kadison, Pfaelzer, Woodard, Quinn & Rossi, L.A., 1985-86, Tenenbaum & Ardi, L.A., 1986-87; with Viacom Prodns. Inc., Universal City, Calif., 1988-90; sole practioner Malibu and Hillsborough, 1990-96; dir. legal affairs Inscape, L.A., 1996-97; gen. counsel Graphix Zone Inc., 1997, Allstate Comms., Inc., Chatsworth, Calif., 98, Dream Works, L.L.C., 1998-99; dir. bus. devel. Riffage.com, 1999-2000. Hon. consulate of Luxembourg, 1993—; arbitrator Los Angeles County Superior and Mcpl. Cts., 1994-96; judge pro tem small claims divsn. Malibu Mcpl. Ct., 1993-94; land trust dir. People for Parks, 1995-97. Mem. bd. visitors Stanford Law Sch., 1996-97. Contbr. chpts. to books, articles to profl. jours. Home: 2961 Valmere Dr Malibu CA 90265-2971

LO BELLO, JOSEPH DAVID, bank executive; b. Northampton, Mass., Feb. 5, 1940; s. Joseph Vincenzo and Marie (Mandella) Lo B.; m. Karen Suzanne Martin, June 21, 1969; children: Mark, Kara, Kimberly. BS, Babson Coll., 1961; MBA, U. Mass., 1963; postgrad., Harvard Bus. Sch., 1987. Loan officer Third Nat. Bank Hampden County, Springfield, Mass., 1963-65, v.p., 1965-75, sr. v.p., 1975-81; exec. v.p. Bank of New Eng. West, N.A., 1981-90; regional pres. Bank of New Eng. N.A., 1990-92; pres., chief exec. officer Peoples Savs. Bank, Holyoke, Mass., 1992—. Dir. Mass. Indsl. Fin. Agy., Boston, 1987, Conn. Online Computer, 1994, Credit Data Svcs., Inc., 1993; treas., trustee Basketball Hall of Fame, Springfield, 1985; trustee Springfield Coll., 1984; chmn. Baystate Health System, Springfield, 1983. Mem. Rotary Club. Avocations: golf, hiking, theatre, travel. Home: 152 Meadowbrook Rd Longmeadow MA 01106-1341

LOBENHERZ, WILLIAM ERNEST, container company/association executive, lawyer; b. Muskegon, Mich., June 22, 1949; s. Ernest Pomeroy and Emajean (Krautheim) L.; m. Carla Rae Krieger; children: Jessica Anne, Rebecca Jean, Christopher William, Andrew William. BBA, U. Mich., 1971; JD cum laude, Wayne State U., 1974. Bar: Mich. 1974. Legal counsel Mich. Legis. Services Bur., Lansing, Mich., 1974-77; legal legis. cons. Mich. Assn. of Sch. Bds., 1977, asst. exec. dir. for legal legis. affairs, 1977-79; asst. v.p. state and congl. relations Wayne State U., Detroit, 1979-81, assoc. v.p. state relations, 1981-82, v.p. govtl. affairs, 1982-87; assoc. Dykema Gossett, Lansing, Mich., 1987-89; pres., CEO, Mich. Soft Drink Assn., 1989—, MSDA Svc. Corp., Lansing, 1997—. Guest lectr. in govtl. affairs, Wayne State U., U. Mich., U. Detroit; referee Mich. Tax Tribunal, 1993-97. Contbr. chpt. Mich. Handbook for School Business Officials, 1979, 2nd edit., 1980; also articles to profl. jours. and mags. Mem. govtl. affairs com. New Detroit Inc., 1984-87, chmn. state subcom. of govtl. affairs com., 1986-87; chmn. ind. schs. campaign Greater Metro Detroit United Fund Torch Dr., 1979, chmn. Colls. and Univs. campaign, 1980; bd. dirs. Mich. Epilepsy Ctr., 1991-97, Coun. for Mich. Pub. Univs., 1991—, Tourism Industry Coalition of Mich., vice-chair, 1998—; mem. Mich. Recycling Partnership, 1997—. Recipient Book award Lawyer's Coop. Pub. Co., 1973, Outstanding Svc. award Mich. Assn. for Marriage and Family Therapy, 1992, 95, Silver scholar key Wayne State U. Law Sch., 1974; named among Top 10 Single Interest Lobbyists, Inside Mich. Politics, 2001. Mem. Mich. Bar Assn., NAACP, Coun. for Advancement and Support of Edn. (Mindpower citation 1982), Mich. Delta Found. (bd. dirs. 1977-97, sec. 1981-84, v.p. 1987-88), Greater Metro Detroit C. of C. (contact interviewer bus. attraction and expansion coun. 1984-86), City Club. Home: 900 Long Blvd # 365 Lansing MI 48911 Office: Mich Soft Drink Assn 634 Michigan National Tower Lansing MI 48933-1707 E-mail: msda@voyager.net.

LOBER, LIONEL M. screenwriter, producer; b. Alexandria, Egypt, Nov. 13, 1933; s. Louis and Eva (Horowitz) L.; m. Mati Elpern, June 20, 1961 (dec. Nov. 1983); children: Sharon Nadine, Alma Nora. BA in Theater, English, Brandeis U., 1955. Assoc. prodn. mgr., asst. to Otto Preminger Exodus, 1960; exec. asst. to exec. v.p. United Artists Corp., N.Y.C., 1961-63; v.p. European prodn. Metro-Goldwyn-Mayer, 1963-65; exec. in charge of prodn. D.E.A.R. Studios, Rome, 1965-70; v.p. Prodigal Prodns., Paris, 1970-75; writer, producer Warner Bros. TV, United Artists Corp., Cannon Films, N.Y.C., Los Angeles, London, 1975-78. Lectr. on film writing and prodn. Calif. State U., Northridge. Screenwriter: A Candle for the Dead, 1969, Black Madonna, 1972, Who Stole Irving, 1975, The Second Coming, 1979, He and She, 1983, Slit Throat, 1987, The Corsican Brothers, 1987, Final Scream, 1988, Danger Girl, 1989, Cop Out, 1990, Checkmate, 1991, Double Impact, 1992, Turnabout, 1994, An Ideal Husband, 1995, (play) Shadow of Guilt, 1996, Lost Soul, 1998, With A Bang!, 1999. Capt. USMC, 1956-60. Mem. Writers Guild Am. West, Brit. Acad. Film and TV Arts (L.A.). Democrat.

LOBIG, JANIE HOWELL, special education educator; b. Peoria, Ill., June 10, 1945; d. Thomas Edwin and Elizabeth Jane (Higdon) Howell; m. James Frederick Lobig, Aug. 16, 1970 (dec. Dec. 2001); 1 child Jill Christina. BS in Elem. Edn., So. Ill. U., 1969; MA in Spl. Edn. Severely Handicapped, San Jose State U., 1989. Cert. elem. tchr., Calif., Mo., Ill., handicapped edn., Calif., Mo.; ordained to ministry Presbyn. Ch. as deacon, 1984. Tchr. trainable mentally retarded children Spl. Luth. Sch., St. Louis, 1967-68; tchr. trainable mentally retarded and severly handicapped children Spl. Sch. Dist. St. Louis, 1969-80, head tchr., 1980-83; tchr. severly handicapped children San Jose (calif.) Unifed Sch. Dist., 1983-86; tchr. autistic students Santa Clara County Office Edn., San Jose, 1986—; tchr. Suzanne Dancers, 1991-92. Vol. Am. Cancer Soc., San Jose, 1986—89, 1992, Am. Heart Assn., 1985—, Multiple Sclerosis Soc., 1990—, Wildlife Ctr. Silicon Valley, 1998—; moderator bd. deacons Evergreen Presbyn. Ch., 1986—89. Mem. Council for Exceptional Children, Assn. for Severly Handicapped, Nat. Edn. Assn., Calif. Tchrs. Assn. Avocations: golf, motor home travel, bridge, needlework. Home: 3131 Creekmore Way San Jose CA 95148-2805 Office: James Franklin Smith Elem Sch 2220 Woodbury San Jose CA 95121 E-mail: JanieAngel@aol.com.

LOBIONDO, FRANK A. congressman; children: Adina, Amy. BA in Bus. Adminstrn., St. Joseph's U., 1968. Ops. mgr. LoBiondo Bros. Motor Express, Inc., Rosenhayn, N.J., 1968-94; mem. Cumberland County Bd. Chosen Freeholders, 1985-88; mem. First Legis. Dist. N.J. Gen. Assembly, 1988-94; mem. house transp. & infrastructure com., small bus. com. U.S. House Reps., 1995—. Pres. Cumberland County Guidance Ctr., 1982—84; founder Cumberland County Environ. Health Task Force, 1987; chmn. Cumberland County chpt. Am. Heart Assn., 1989—90; hon. chmn. ann. fund raising drive Cumberland County Hospice, 1992; bd. dirs. YMCA, trustee, 1981—84, 1990—94. Office: US House Reps 225 Cannon Ho Office Bldg Washington DC 20515-0001

LOBL, HERBERT MAX, lawyer; b. Vienna, Austria, Jan. 10, 1932; s. Walter Leo and Minnie (Neumann) L.; m. Dorothy Fullerton Hubbard, Sept. 12, 1960; children: Peter Walter, Michelle Alexandra. AB magna cum laude, Harvard U., 1953, LLB cum laude, 1959, Avocat honoraire, 1993. Bar: N.Y. 1960, U.S. Tax Ct. 1963, French Conseil Juridique 1973; French avocat. mem. Paris bar, 1992, avocat hon., 1993. Assoc. Davis, Polk & Wardwell, N.Y.C., 1959-90, N.Y.C. and Paris, 1963-69, ptnr., 1969-92, sr. counsel, 1993—; assoc. counsel to Gov. Nelson Rockefeller Albany, N.Y., 1960-62. Lectr. law Columbia U., N.Y.C., 1993-95; supervisory bd. mem. CII-HB International, Amsterdam, The Netherlands, 1977-82. Gov. Am. Hosp. Paris, 1981-83, 88-93; bd. trustees Am. Libr., Paris, 1969-81, Nantucket (Mass.) Cottage Hosp., 1996-99, dir. Nantucket Arts Coun., 2000—. Served to 1st lt. USAF, 1954-56. Fulbright scholar U. Bonn, Germany, 1954. Mem. Am. C. of C. (bd. dirs. France 1988-90), Univ. Club, Harvard Club. Address: PO Box 2488 Nantucket MA 02584-2488 also: PO Box 118 Rye NY 10580-0118 also: Davis Polk & Wardwell 450 Lexington Ave New York NY 10017-3911

LOBO, REBECCA, professional basketball player; b. Hartford, Conn., Oct. 6, 1973; BA in Polit. Sci., U. Conn. Basketball player USA Women's Nat. Team, N.Y. Liberty, 1997—2001, Houston Comets, 2001—. Mem. 1992 U.S. Olympic Festival East Team, 1992 Jr. World Championship Qualifying Team, 1993 USA Jr. World Championship Team, launched the Ruth Ann & Rebecca Lobo Scholarship in Allied Health at U. of Conn., 2001. Co-author: The Home Team, 1996. Recipient Wade trophy and named Nat. Player of Yr., Naismith, U.S. Basketball Writers Assn., 1995, 1994 and 1995 Kodak All-Am. First Team, Big East Conf. Player of Yr., Big East Tournament Most Outstanding Player, 1994 and 1995 Big East Conf. Women's Basketball Scholar Athlete of Yr. Office: Houston Comets Two Greenway Plaza Ste 400 Houston TX 77046*

LOBO, ROGERIO A. obstetrician and gynecologist; b. Hong Kong, 1949; MD, Georgetown U., 1974. Diplomate Am. Bd. Ob-Gyn. Intern U. Chgo. Hosps., 1974-75, resident in obstetrics, 1975-78; fellow in reproductive endocrinology L.A. County-U. So. Calif. Med. Ctr., 1980; physician Presbyn. Hosp., NYC, 1995—; dir. Sloane Hosp. for Women Columbia-Presbyn. Med. Ctr., 1995—2002; Willard C. Rappleye prof. ob-gyn. Columbia Coll. Physicians and Surgeons. Editor Jour. Soc. for Gynecol. Investigation, 1993—. Mem. ACOG, Am. Soc. Reproductive Medicine, Endocrinology Soc., Soc. Gynecol. Investigation (past pres.). Office: Columbia Presbyn Med Ctr 622 W 168th St Rm 16-28 New York NY 10032-3720

LOBOSCO, ANNA FRANCES, state program development specialist; b. Binghamton, N.Y., Nov. 13, 1952; d. James H. and Marie A. (Wilcox) Mee; m. Charles M. Lobosco, Apr. 27, 1974; children: Charles Jr., Amanda, Nicholas, Dennis. BA in History, Marist Coll., Poughkeepsie, N.Y., 1974; MS in Edn./Spl. Edn., Coll. St. Rose, Albany, 1978; PhD in Curriculum and Instrn., SUNY, Albany, 1989. Cert. tchr. elem., secondary and spl. edn., N.Y. Diagnostic remedial tchr. Orange County Assn. for Help of Retarded Children, Middletown/Newburgh, N.Y., 1973-78; instr., supr. student tchrs. Mt. St. Mary Coll., Newburgh, 1980-82; rsch. asst., assoc. dir. evaluation consortium SUNY, Albany, 1985-89; devel. disability program planner/prevention specialist N.Y. State Developmental Disabilities Planning Coun., 1989-2001, dep. exec. dir., 2001—. Cons. N.Y. State Edn. Dept. Edn., 1987-89, N.Y. State Unified Tchrs., 1988-89, N.Y. State Coun. on Children's Families, 1986-88, N.Y. State Assn. Counties, 1987-88; instr. Coll. St. Rose, Albany, 1989-90; adj. faculty dept. ednl. theory and practice U. Albany/SUNY, 1997-2000. Contbr. articles to profl. jours; exec. producer viedeos Mary's Choice: The Effects of Prenatal Exposure to Alcohol and Other Drugs, 1992, Its Up to You, 1995. Mem. sch. bd. Saratoga Ctrl. Cath. H.S., 1996—, v.p., 1998—2000, pres.,

2000—02. Named Advocate of the Yr., N.Y. Libr. Assn., 1993. Mem. Coun. Exceptional Children, Am. Evaluation Assn., Am. Ednl. Rsch. Assn., Am. Assn. Mental Retardation, Kappa Delta Pi. Avocations: needlework, sports, reading. Bus. Office: NYS Devel Disabilities Planning Coun 155 Washington Ave Fl 2 Albany NY 12210-2329 E-mail: alobosco@ddpc.state.ny.us.

LOBOSKY, JEFFREY, physician, neurosurgeon; b. Hammond, Ind., Aug. 31, 1951; s. Julian Arthur and Patricia Marian Lobosky; m. Diana Lee Lobosky, June 24, 1972; children: Hollie Marie, Kimberly Brooke, Grayson Michael. BS, U. Notre Dame, 1973; MD, U. Calif., Irvine, 1977. Diplomate Nat. Bd. Med. Examiners, Am. Bd. Neurol. Surgery. Resident in pathology U. Calif. Irvine Med. Ctr., Orange, 1978, resident in surgery, 1978-79, resident in neurosurgery, 1978-80, U. Iowa Hosps., Iowa City, 1980-84; pvt. practice neurosurgery Chico, Calif., 1984—. Mem. staff N.T. Enloe Meml. Hosp., Chico, 1984—, Chico Cmty. Hosp., 1994—98, Oroville (Calif.) Med. Ctr., 1984—, Feather River Hosp., Paradise, Calif., 1984—, St. Elizabeth Hosp., Red Bluff, 1988—; adj. prof. Sch. Nursing Calif. State U., Chico, 1988—; assoc. clin. prof. dept. neurol. surgery U. Calif., San Francisco, 1991—; vis. prof. and guest lectr. Contbr. articles to profl. jours. Recipient numerous awards. Fellow ACS; mem. AMA, Calif. Med. Assn., Calif. Assn. Neurol. Surgeons, San Francisco Neurol. Soc., Congress Neurol. Surgeons, Am. Assn. Neurol. Surgery, Butte-Glenn Med Soc. Roman Catholic. Avocations: golf, skiing, tennis, cycling, reading. Office: Ste 370 251 Cohasset Rd Chico CA 95926-2239 E-mail: jlobosky@aol.com.

LOBRON, BARBARA L. speech educator, writer, editor, photographer; b. Phila., Mar. 19, 1944; d. Martin Aaron and Elizabeth (Gots) L. Student, Pa. State U., 1962-63; BA cum laude, Temple U., Phila., 1966; student art therapy, Erika Steinberger, N.Y.C., 1994—; MS, Coll. Mt. St. Vincent, 2001. Reporter, writer Camden (N.J.) Courier-Post, 1966-68; editl. asst. Med. Insight mag., N.Y.C., 1970-71; mng. editor Camera 35 mag., 1971-75; also assoc. editor photog. anns. U.S. Camera/Camera 35, 1972, 73; freelance editor as Word Woman N.Y.C., 1975-77, 79-99; acct. exec. Bozell & Jacobs, 1977-79; copy editor Camera Arts mag., 1981-83; editl. coord. Ctr. mag. Nat. Ctr. Health Edn., 1985; editl. coord. Popular Photography mag., 1986-95; assoc. editor Sony Style, 1995; tchr. speech improvement N.Y.C. Bd. Edn., 1995—. Contbg. editor: Photograph; participant 3M Editor's Conf. (1st woman), 1972; photography group exhbns. include Internat. Women's Art Festival, N.Y.C., 1975, Rockefeller Ctr., N.Y.C., 1976, Photograph Gallery, N.Y.C., 1981; acrylic painting exhbns. Tchrs. Coll., N.Y.C., 1994, Warwick Hotel, N.Y.C., 1995; represented in collection Libr. Calif Inst. Arts, Valencia; copy editor: The Complete Guide to Cibachrome Printing, 1980, The Popular Photography Question and Answer Book, 1979, The Photography Catalog, 1976, Strand: Sixty Years of Photography, 1976, You and Your Lens, 1975; contbr. articles to comml. publs., chpts. to books. Tchr. Sch. Vol. Program, N.Y.C. Recipient 1st pl. honors Dist. 1, Internat. Assn. Bus. Communicators, 1977. Mem. Soka Gakkai Internat. Buddhist. Avocations: dancing, reading, photography, origami, walking. Home: 85 Hicks St Apt 7 Brooklyn NY 11201-6825 E-mail: freedom@con2.com.

LOCALIO, MARCIA JUDITH, medical/surgical nurse; b. Phila., June 14, 1947; d. Herman Julius and Mildred Barbara (Brown) Bandarsky; m. Anthony Bernard Localio, Feb. 25, 1967; children: Jennifer Hope, David Anthony. Diploma in nursing, Bucks County Vocat. Tech. Sch., 1984; ADN, Bucks County C.C., 1989; student, Ctr. for Nursing Excellence; BSN, Thomas Edison State Coll., 1999; grad., Janus Computer Tng. Microsoft Office, 2000. RN, N.J., Pa.; cert. EMT, instr. CPR, first aid; cert. phlebotomist Am. Soc. Clin. Pathology. Instr. CPR and EMT State of N.J., Princeton; nurse instr. IV therapy and venipuncture State of N.J., North Princeton Devel. Ctr. Habilitation plan coord. State of N.J.; complaint investigator N.J. Dept. Health, Office of Managed Care; pub. health rep. Tuberculosis Program, N.J. Dept. Health. Notary pub. State of N.J. Recipient Sustained Achievement award N.J. Dept. Human Svcs., 1991-92, Recognition award North Princeton Devel. Ctr., 1986, 95, 15 Yr. Career Svc. award State of N.J.; State of N.J. nursing scholar. Mem. Am. Soc. Clin. Pathologists (assoc.), N.J. Nursing Assn., Intravenous Nurses Soc.

LOCASCIO, PETER CAESAR, humanities educator; b. Passaic, N.J., June 28, 1956; s. Caesar Ralph Locascio, Dorothy Locascio. BA in Art History, Montclair State Coll., 1978; MA in Art History, NYU, 1982. Cert.: (paralegal studies program cert.) 1986; Cert. tchr. ESL 1997. Instr. Southwestern C.C., Chula Vista, Calif., 2000; adj. prof. Art History and Humanities Huron Internat. U., San Diego, 1998; instr. EF Internat. Lang. Sch., 1996—97; instr./lectr. Adult Continuing Edn. Program Wayne Adult Sch., Wayne, NJ, 1983—91; curator visual resources Calcia Fine Arts Libr. Montclair State U., Upper Montclair, 1986; adj. prof. History Art and Architecture Kean College, Union, 1983—84. Spl. guest lectr. History Art San Diego Mus. Man, Balboa Park, San Diego, 1997; special guest lectr. Art History Sch. Continuing Edn. NYU, 1985; guest lectr. Art History Summit Art Ctr., Summit, NJ, 1983. Author: Vocabulary Vantage: A Course Book for Students of English as a Second Language (ESL) and a Review for Native Speakers of English, 1998, The Scepter and the Double Crown: A History of Ancient Egypt and its Art, 1996, Enjoying Piano, 1996. Mem.: Coll. Art Assn. (not applicable N/A—A). Avocation: Avocations: singing, swimming, cooking, travel. Home Fax: 619-276-7271.

LOCATELLI, PAUL LEO, academic administrator; b. Santa Cruz, Calif., Sept. 16, 1938; s. Vincent Dino and Marie Josephine (Piccone) L. BS in Acctg., Santa Clara U., 1961; MDiv, Jesuit Sch. Theology, 1974; DBA, U. So. Calif., 1971. CPA, Calif.; ordained priest Roman Cath. Ch., 1974. Acct. Lautze & Lautze, San Jose, Calif., 1960-61, 73-74; prof. acctg. Santa Clara (Calif.) U., 1974-86, assoc. dean Bus. Sch., acad. v.p., 1978-86, pres., 1988—. Campus compact Assn. Jesuit Colls. and Univs., JV:SV Network, NCCJ, Am. Leadership Forum Silicon Valley; bd. trustees Jesuit Sch. Theology, Berkeley; exec. com. Ind. Colls. and Univs. of Calif., Parents Helping Parents; past rector Jesuit Cmty. at Loyola Marymount U. Co-author: (assessment) The New Curriculum: A Guide to Professional Accounting, 1995. Past trustee U. San Francisco, Seattle U., St. Louis U., Loyola Marymount U., Regis U.; past mem. Sr. Commn. Western Assn. Schs. and Colls., Acctg. Edn. Change Commn.; adv. coun. John Gardner Ctr. for Youth and Their Cmtys.; mem. acad. adv. bd. Panetta Inst. Mem. AICPA, Calif. Soc. CPAs (Disting. Prof. of the Yr. award 1994), Am. Acctg. Assn., Assn. Governing Bds. (pres.' coun.), Commonwealth Club Silicon Valley. Democrat. Office: Santa Clara U 500 El Camino Real Santa Clara CA 95053-0015

LOCH, JOHN ROBERT, university administrator; b. Aug. 25, 1940; s. Robert Addison and Mary Virginia (Beck) L. Student, Waynesburg Coll., 1958; AB, Grove City Coll., 1962; postgrad., Pitts. Theol. Sem., 1962; MEd, U. Pitts., 1966, PhD, 1972, Harvard U., 1984. Cert. program planner. Asst. to dean of men, program planner U. Pitts., 1963-64, dir. student union, 1964-70, dir. student affairs rsch., 1970-71, dir. suburban ednl. svcs. Sch. Gen. Studies, 1971-75; dir. continuing edn. and pub. svc. Youngstown (Ohio) State U., 1975-82, dir. univ. outreach, 1990—. Chief adminstrv. officer Metro Coll., 1996-98; assoc. mem. grad. faculty, 1980-95; rsch. assoc. Pres.'s Commn. on Campus Unrest, 1970; chmn. program com. Park Vista Retirement Cmty., 1994-95, vice chair bd. dirs., 1995-96, mktg. com., 1999—; trustee Ohio Presbyn. Retirement Cmtys., 1993-99, program com., 1993-99. Trustee Mahoning Shenango Area Health Edn. Network, 1976-91, Career Devel. Ctr. for Women, 1978-80; trustee Youngstown Area Arts Coun., 1980-85, pres., 1981-83; bd. dirs. Protestant Family Svcs., 1981-83; active Older Adults Task Force, Mahoning County, 1992-96; trustee Mahoning County RSVP, 1983-89, chmn. evaluation com., 1983-84, chmn. pers. com., 1984-85, chmn. bd. trustees, 1986-87; coord. fund raising Nat. Unity Campaign, Mahoning County, 1980; state chmn. Young Rep. Coll. Coun. Pa., 1960. Mem. AAUW, Assn. Continuing Higher Edn. (chair-elect region VI 1997-98, chair 1998-99), Adult Edn. Assn. USA, Nat. U. Continuing Edn. Assn., Ohio Coun. Higher Continuing Edn. (pres. 1979-80), Ohio Continuing Higher Edn. Assn. (hon. life mem., co-chmn. constn. com. 1982, v.p. state univs. 1984-85, pres.-elect 1985-86, pres. 1986-87, historian 1988-96, chmn. awards and honors com. 1989-92, editor Voluntary Continuing Edn. Requirements 1993-95, Spl. Svc. award 1989), Ohio-Pa. Higher Edn. Network (chmn. 1989-90), Learning Resources Network (Univ. Coun. Gt. Lakes rep. 1996—), Youngstown Traffic Club (hon. life mem.), Youngstown Club, Kiwanis (dir. 1981-82), Youngstown Dist., Purchasing Mgrs. Assn., Omicron Delta Kappa, Kappa Kappa Psi, Phi Kappa Phi (pres. 1980-81, pres. 1994-95, 96-97, Disting. Mem. award 2000), Alpha Phi Omega, Alpha Sigma Lambda, Phi Delta Kappa. Presbyterian. Home: 242 Upland Ave Youngstown OH 44504-1849 Office: Met Coll Southwoods Commons 100 De Bartolo Pl Youngstown OH 44512 E-mail: jrloch@ysu.edu.

LOCHANKO, ELIZABETH ALEXANDRA, communications executive; b. Toronto, Ontario, Can., Apr. 30, 1957; came to U.S., 1960; d. Adam and Alexandra Lochanko. BA, Rutgers U., 1979; M of Music, Johns Hopkins U., 1982. Office mgr. Simos C. Dimas Esquire, N.Y.C., 1982-84; pub. rels. mgr. 'K' Lines/Cloud Tours, 1984-86; sr. acct. exec. Peter Martin Assocs., 1986-88; sr. v.p. corp. communications Sony Pictures Entertainment, L.A., 1988-96; cons., 1996-99; chief comm. State Controller Calif., 1999—. Mem. NAFE, Women in Comms., Johns Hopkins Alumni Assn., Douglass Rutgers Alumni Assn., Phi Beta Kappa. Avocations: music, hiking, reading, biking, travel.

LOCHBIHLER, FREDERICK VINCENT, lawyer; b. Chgo., Jan. 30, 1951; s. Frederick Louis and Marion Helen (Rutkauskas) L.; m. Darlene Gotfryde Wantuch, Nov. 8, 1952; 1 child, Frederick Karlman. AB in Govt. summa cum laude, U. Notre Dame, 1973; JD with honors, U. Chgo., 1976. Bar: Ill. 1976, U.S. Dist. Ct. (no. dist.) Ill. 1977, U.S. Ct. Appeals (7th cir.) 1980, U.S. Ct. Appeals (8th cir.) 1981, U.S. Supreme Ct. 1982, U.S. Dist. Ct. (ctrl. dist.) Ill. 1983, U.S. Dist. Ct. Ariz. 1991, U.S. Ct. Appeals (fed. cir.) 2001. Assoc. Chapman and Cutler, Chgo., 1976-84, ptnr., 1984—. Mem. Phi Beta Kappa, Order of Coif. Avocations: military history, literature, travel. Home: 605 Waukegan Rd #1F Glenview IL 60025 Office: Chapman and Cutler 111 W Monroe St Ste 1700 Chicago IL 60603-4006

LOCHHEAD, ROBERT BRUCE, lawyer; b. St. Louis, June 20, 1952; s. Angus Tulloch and Matilda Evangeline (Thurman) L.; m. KLynn Walker, June 21, 1974; children: Robert, Richard, Cynthia, Melinda, Rebekah, Elizabeth. BA, Brigham Young U., 1975; JD, Columbia U., 1978. Bar: D.C. 1979, Utah 1980, U.S. Dist. Ct. Utah 1980, U.S. Ct. Appeals (10th cir.) 1980, U.S. Supreme Ct. 1986. Law clk. to judge U.S. Ct. Appeals (10th cir.), Salt Lake City, 1978-79; assoc. Hogan & Hartson, Washington, 1979-80, Larsen, Kimball, Parr & Crockett, Salt Lake City, 1980-82; shareholder Parr, Waddoups Brown, Gee & Loveless, 1982—. Judge pro tem Small Claims Ct., Salt Lake City, 1985-88; mem. panel of arbitrators U.S. Bankruptcy Ct., Dist. Utah, 1995—. Harlan Fiske Stone scholar, 1976-78. Mem. ABA, Am. Bankruptcy Inst. Mem. Lds Ch. Home: 492 N Flint St Kaysville UT 84037-9777 Office: Parr Waddoups Brown Gee & Loveless 185 S State St Ste 1300 Salt Lake City UT 84111-1537

LOCHMILLER, KURTIS L. real estate entrepreneur; b. Sacramento, Dec. 30, 1952; s. Rodney Glen and Mary Margaret (Frauen) L.; m. Mariye Susan Mizuki, Nov. 9, 1951; children: Margaux Sian, Chase Jordan. BA in Econs. and Fin., U. Denver, 1975. Dist. sales mgr. Hertz Truck Div., Denver, 1975-76; drilling foreman Shell Oil, Alaska, Mont., Colo., 1976-79; pres., owner Kurtex Mortgage & Devel. Co., Denver, 1979—. Kurtex Properties Inc., Denver, 1980-86; pres., chief exec. officer Kurtex Inc., 1981—. Bankers Pacific Mortgage, Denver, 1980—. Bankers Fin. Escrow Corp., Denver, 1984—, Northwest Title & Escrow, Denver, 1984—. Pres., chief exec. officer Steamboat Title, Steamboat Springs, Colo., 1985—, First Escrow, Denver, 1986—, Fidelity-Commonwealth-Continental Escrow, Denver, 1984—; pres. Colonnade Ltd., Denver, 1981-88; pres., bd. dirs. Breckridge (Colo.) Brewery. V.p., founder Colfax on the Hill, Denver, 1984; mediator, arbitrator Arbitrator/Mediation Assn., Denver, 1986; mem. Police Athletic League, Denver, 1988. Recipient Pres. Spl. Achievement/Founder award Colfax on the Hill, Denver, 1984, Spl. Mayor's award, City & County of Denver, 1985. Mem. Nat. Assn.of Real Estate Appraisers, Internat. Brotherhood of Teamsters, Colo. Mortgage Bankers Assn., Mortgage Banking Assn., Denver C. of C., Phi Beta Kappa, Omicron Delta Epsilon. Clubs: U.S. Karate Assn. (Phoenix) (3d degree Black Belt), Ferrari (Portland). Lodges: Internat. Supreme Council Order of Demolay. Avocations: collecting cars, karate, fishing, art collecting. Home: 1 Carriage Ln Littleton CO 80121-2010 Office: Bankers Fin Escrow Corp 9655 E 25th Ave Ste 101 Aurora CO 80010-1056

LOCHNER, PHILIP RAYMOND, retired communications executive, consultant; b. New Rochelle, N.Y., Mar. 3, 1943; s. Philip Raymond and Maryl (Browning) L.; m. Sally Soth, July 23, 1973; children: Lauren Soth, John Philip. BA, Yale U., 1964, LLB, 1967; PhD, Stanford U., 1971. Bar: N.Y., D.C. Assoc. dean, asst. prof. law SUNY, 1971-73; assoc. Cravath Swaine & Moore, N.Y.C., 1973-78; various legal staff positions, including gen. counsel Time Inc., 1978-90; commr. U.S. Securities and Exch. Commn., Washington, 1990-91; sr. v.p., chief adminstrv. officer Time Warner, Inc., N.Y.C., 1991-98; ret., 1998; dir., cons. Greenwich, Conn., 1998—. Bd. dirs. Apria Healthcare Group, Inc., Costa Mesa, Calif., Clarcor, Inc., Rockford, Ill., Gtech Holdings Inc., West Greenwich, R.I., Bklyn. Bancorp, N.Y.C.; bd. advs. Republic N.Y. Corp., N.Y.C., 1997—, Am. Stock Exch., N.Y.C., 2002--; past mem. bd. advs. Investment Mgmt. Advs., Inc.; adj. faculty Law Sch. Columbia U. Contbr. articles to profl. jours., newspapers. Bd. dirs. Canterbury Sch., Investor Responsibility Rsch. Coun. Fulbright fellow U. London, 1968. Mem. Nat. Assn. Securities Dealers (bd. advisors), Phi Beta Kappa. Avocations: kayaking, sailing, hiking. Office: 699 Lake Ave Greenwich CT 06830-3333

LOCHOTZKI, PAULINE A. (PAULA LOCHOTZKI), psychologist, educator; b. Sandusky, Ohio, July 28, 1949; d. Norbert C. Lochotzki and Anna Belle Spieldenner. BA in Edn., Mary Manse, 1974; MA in Psychology, Marywood, 1988. Cert. practioner neuro-linguistic programming Columbus, Ohio. Contbr. chapters to books. Named Poet of Yr., Orange County, Calif., 1995. Home: 426 Williams St Fremont OH 43420

LOCHRIDGE, LLOYD PAMPELL , JR. lawyer; b. Austin, Tex., Feb. 3, 1918; s. Lloyd Pampell and Franklyn (Blocker) L.; m. Frances Potter, Jan. 23, 1943; children: Anne, Georgia, Lloyd P. III, Patton G., Hope N., Frances P. AB, Princeton U., 1938; LLB, Harvard U., 1941. Bar: D.C. 1942, Tex. 1945, U.S. Ct. Appeals (5th cir.), U.S. Supreme Ct. Assoc. Law Office Vernon Hill, Mission, Tex., 1945-46; ptnr. Hill & Lochridge, 1946-49, Hill, Lochridge & King, Mission, 1949-59, McGinnis, Lochridge & Kilgore, Austin, 1959—. Mem. adv. bd. Salvation Army, Austin, 1962—; mem. vestry Ch. Good Shepherd, Austin, 1968-73; trustee Austin Lyric Opera, 1986—. Comdr. USNR, 1941-46, ETO. Mem. ABA (bd. govs. 1989-92), State Bar Tex. (pres. 1974-75), Travis County Bar Assn. (pres. 1970-71), Hidalgo County Bar Assn. (pres. 1954-55). Episcopalian. Avocations: tennis, squash, sailing. Office: McGinnis Lochridge & Kilgore Capitol Ctr 919 Congress Ave Ste 1300 Austin TX 78701-2499 E-mail: llochridge@mcginnislaw.com.

LOCHRIDGE, STANLEY KEITH, cardiovascular and thoracic surgeon; b. Tupelo, Miss., Jan. 24, 1947; s. Oscar Wendell and Willie Lou (Stidham) L.; m. Tracy Lynn Lochridge; children: Kirby, Kristin, Erin, Kalin. BS, U. Ala., Tuscaloosa, 1968; MD, U. Ala., Birmingham, 1972. Diplomate Am. Bd. Surgery, Am. Bd. Thoracic Surgery. Intern and resident Carraway Meth. Med. Ctr., Birmingham, Ala., 1972-76; cardiac fellow U. Iowa Hosps., Iowa City, 1976-78; cardiac surgeon CardioThoracic Surgeons, P.C., Birmingham, 1978-89, Norwood Clinic, P.C., Birmingham, 1989—. Major, U.S. Army N.G., 1972-79, Birmingham. Fellow ACS, Am. Coll. Cardiology, Am. Coll. Chest Physicians; mem. Internat. Cardiovasc. Soc., Soc. Thoracic Surgeons, So. Soc. Thoracic Surgeons, Alpha Omega Alpha. Republican. Methodist. Avocations: hiking, boating, skiing. Office: Norwood Clinic PC 1528 Carraway Blvd Birmingham AL 35234-1991 E-mail: skl00742@aol.com.

LOCIGNO, PAUL ROBERT, public affairs executive; b. Cleve., Sept. 17, 1948; s. Paul Robert and Anna Mae (Zingale) L.; m. Ki Cho Rim; children: Paul III, Tammy, Robert. AA, Cuyahoga C.C., Parma, Ohio, 1974; BA, Case Western Res. U., 1976; postgrad., Cleve. State U., 1977-78. Part-time faculty Cuyahoga Community Coll., 1979-83; vice-chmn. Presdl. Inaugural Labor Com., Washington, 1980-81; vice-chmn. labor com. Presdl. Inaugural Com., 1984-85; legis. agt. Internat. Brotherhood of Teamsters, 1977-90, dir. govt. internat. affairs, 1983-89, dir. Asian/Pacific br. Taipei, Taiwan, 1985-88; spl. rep. of chmn. Hill & Knowlton Pub. Affairs Worldwide, Washington, 1989-91; pres., founding ptnr. Rollins Internat. Ltd., Alexandria, Va., 1997—; CEO Ganeden Biotech Inc., San Diego. Bd. dirs. Nanjing Ya Dong Corp. Mem. Pres.'s Export Coun., 1988-89; mem. Asia adv. com. Bicentennial of U.S. Constitution, 1990; bd. govs. Am. League for Exports and Security Assistance, 1989; mem. Nat. Commn. for Employment Policy, Washington, 1981-86; bd. dirs. Children's Right Coun., Washington, 1997—. With USMC, 1968-70, Vietnam. Republican. Roman Catholic. Avocations: archery, golf, fishing. Home: 15100 Hawksbill Ct Woodbridge VA 22193-5831 Office: Ganeden Biotech Inc 1228 Euclid Ave Ste 900 Cleveland OH 44115-1845

LOCK, ALBERT LARRY, JR. financial services company executive; b. St. Louis, Nov. 20, 1947; s. Albert Larry and Bernadine Helen (Syron) L.; m. Barbara Ann Harding, Feb. 13, 1971; children: Brian C., Sean M. Student, U. Mo., St. Louis, 1966-68; AA, Northwest Mo. State U., 1975; MS in Fin. Svcs., The Am. Coll., 1998. CLU, 1979, ChFC, 1983. Ins. agt. Western and So. Life, St. Louis, 1970-74; field underwriter Home Life of N.Y., 1975—84; owner, fin. advisor Universal Fin. Group Inc., 1984—. Cons. fin. planning workshop St. Louis C.C., 1983-90; mem. broker/dealer Pres.'s Coun. Mutual Svc. Corp., 1992--; bd. dirs., legis. chmn. St. Louis Assn. Ins. and Fin. Advisors, mem. Top-of-the-Table Million Dollar Round Table. Pres. St. Paul Sch. Bd., 1990-91; bd. dirs. Bishop DuBourg H.S., 1997—, Marianist Retreat Ctr., St. Louis, 1997--. Sgt. U.S. Army, 1968-70, Vietnam. Decorated Bronze star, Air medals. Mem. St. Louis Soc. Fin. Svcs. Profls. (pres. 1988-89. chair fin. counseling sects.), Nat. Assn. Securities Dealers (registered prin.), Million Dollar Round Table. Roman Catholic. Avocation: racquetball. Office: Universal Fin Group Inc 7751 Carondelet Ave Saint Louis MO 63105-3316

LOCK, GERALD SEYMOUR HUNTER, retired mechanical engineering educator; b. London, June 30, 1935; arrived in Can., 1962, naturalized, 1973; s. George and Mary (Hunter) L.; m. Edna Burness, Sept. 19, 1959; children: Graeme, Gareth, Grenville. B.Sc. with honors, U. Durham, Eng., 1959, PhD, 1962. Asst. prof. mech. engring. U. Alta. (Can.), Edmonton, 1962-64, assoc. prof., 1964-70, prof., 1970-93, dean interdisciplinary studies, 1976-81; cons. mech. engr., Edmonton, 1993—. Chmn. Internat. Arctic Sci. Commn. Regional Bd., 1993-96. Vice chmn. Alta. Manpower Adv. Coun., 1979-84, chmn., 1984-89; chmn. Salvation Army Red Shield Appeal, 1980-82; bd. govs. Alta. Coll., chmn., 1982-85; founding pres. Alta. Poetry Festival Soc., 1981. Recipient Queen Elizabeth II Silver Jubilee medal, 1977 Fellow Engring. Inst. Can, Can. Soc. Mech. Engring. (pres. 1977-78), ASME; mem. Sci. Coun. Can., Can. Polar Commn. Mem. Progressive Conservative Party. Anglican. Home: 11711 83rd Ave Edmonton AB Canada T6G 0V2 Office: U Alta Edmonton AB Canada T6G 2G3

LOCK, RICHARD WILLIAM, packaging company executive; b. N.Y.C., Oct. 5, 1931; s. Albert and Catherine Dorothy (Magnus) L.; m. Elizabeth Louise Kenney, Nov. 2, 1957; children— Albert William, Dorothy Louise Lock Kuhl, John David. BS, Rutgers U., 1953; MBA, N.Y. U., 1958. Acct. Gen. Electric Co., 1953-54, Union Carbide Co., N.Y.C., 1956-58; div. controller St. Regis Paper Co., Houston, 1959-62, Owens-Illinois, Inc., Toledo, 1962-64, supr. programmer office methods and data processing, 1964-65, asst. mgr. data processing procedures, 1965-67, mgr. systems analysis and devel., 1967-68, mgr. corp. systems analysis and devel., 1968-70, dir. corp. systems and data processing, 1970-72, gen. mgr. electro/optical display, 1972-75, treas., 1975-80, v.p., dir. corp. planning, 1980-84, v.p., asst. chief fin. officer, treas., 1984-88; mng. dir. Magnus Assocs., 1989—. Mem. adv. bd. Toledo Salvation Army, 1973—, chmn., 1974-77; pres. Toledo Area Govtl. Research Assn., 1978-79; bd. dirs. Riverside Hosp. Found., Toledo, 1982—. Served with USAF, 1954-56. Mem. Fin. Execs. Inst., Am. Soc. Corp. Secs., Phi Beta Kappa. Clubs: Toledo. Republican. Lutheran. Home: 5831 Monroe St Apt 406 Sylvania OH 43560-2256

LOCK, RICK E. private investigator; b. Spokane, Wash., Jan. 15, 1954; s. Stuart George and Dorothy I. Lochead; m. Virgil Elizabeth Flores, Sept. 25, 2000; 1 child Christine Elizabeth ; m. Jennifer Lea Elliott, Apr. 19, 1976 (div. Jan. 1986). AA, Mira Costa C.C., Oceanside, Calif., 1978; BA in Journalism, San Diego State U., 1980, MA, 1982. Cert. physical therapist Calif. Hockey player Kansas City (Mo.) Blues, 1971; with VA Regional Office, San Diego, 1978—82; physical therapist Physical Therapist Assoc., 1983—85; with dept. corrections CCI, Tehachapi, 1985—89; pvt. practice Poway, 1989—. Active Com. to Present RFK with the Medal of Freedom, L.A., 1989—; campaign mgr. Dem. Convention, Oceanside, 1976; campaign worker Rep. Convention, San Diego, 1992, campaign worker, monitor, 1996. Sgt. USMC, 1973—77, Vietnam. Decorated Bronze Star, Purple Heart. Mem.: NRA. Republican. Roman Catholic. Avocations: theater , one-act plays. Home: 13609 Frame Rd Poway CA 92064 Office Fax: 858-748-9577.

LOCK, ROBERT JOSEPH, accountant; b. Jefferson City, Mo., June 20, 1955; s. Elmer Joseph and Clara Barbara (Luebbert) L.; m. Cheryl Lynne Garoutte, Apr. 20, 1985 (div. Jan. 1988); m. Susan C. Springhower, Nov. 16, 1991. BSBA in Acctg., U. Mo., 1977. CPA, Mo. Sr. Mo. State Auditor's Office, Jefferson City, 1977-82; ptnr. McBride, Lock & Assocs., Kansas City, Mo., 1982—. Past. pres. Picture Hills Homeowners Assn., 1994-96; treas. Northwood Hills Homes Assn., 2001. Mem. Am. Inst. CPA's, Mo. Soc. CPA's, Assn Govtl. Accts. Lodges: KC. Roman Catholic. Avocations: golf, tennis, photography. Home: 5735 N Polk Dr Kansas City MO 64151-2697 Office: McBride Lock & Assocs 1221 Baltimore Ave Ste 406 Kansas City MO 64105-1952

LOCKAMY, ARCHIE, III, operations management educator; b. El Paso, Tex., July 24, 1957; s. Archie Jr. and Corrine Ann Lockamy; m. Vicki G. Glover, Dec. 19, 1981. B of Chem. Engring., Ga. Inst. Tech., 1979; MBA, Atlanta U., 1983; PhD, U. Ga., 1990. Cert. in prodn. and inventory mgmt.; cert. fellow in prodn. and inventory mgmt.; acad. Jonah. Corp. mgmt. intern TRW, Inc., Cleve., 1983-85; prodn. supt. TRW Motor Divsn., Dothan, Ala., 1985-87; asst. prof. ops. mgmt. U. Mich., Ann Arbor, 1990-92; interim asst. v.p. for acad. affairs Fla. A&M U., Tallahassee, 1996-97, prof. ops. mgmt., 1992-2000, Samford U., Birmingham, Ala., 2000—. Mem. bd. examiners Malcolm Baldridge Nat. Quality Award, 1997—; acad. quality improvement project design cons. North Cen. Assn. Colls. and Schs., 1999-2000. Co-author: (book) Reengineering Performance Measurement, 1994; contbr. articles to profl. jours.; mem. editl. rev. bd. Benchmarking: An Internat. Jour., 1995—, Jour. Ops. Mgmt., 1994—; referee Mfg. Rev., 1991, Internat. Jour. Prodn. Rsch., 1992—, Jour. Sys. Improvement, 1994—, Ann. Advances in Bus. Cases, 2000—, Prodn. and Inventory Mgmt. Jour., 2000—; contbr. APICS Dictionary, 1992-97. Bd. dirs. Innovation Investment Program, Tallahassee, 1996, APICS E&R Found., 1998-2000, sec., 1999, v.p., 2000. Recipient Cert. of Appreciation for Outstanding Svc. to the Nation, U.S. Dept. Commerce, 1997, 98, 99, 2000. Mem. APICS, AIChE, Decision Scis. Inst., Prodn. and Ops. Mgmt. Soc., Performance Measurement Assn., Beta Gamma Sigma (pres. Sanford U. chpt. 2001). Avocations: chess, racquetball, music. Office: Samford U 800 Lakeshore Dr Birmingham AL 35229 Office Fax: 205-726-2464. E-mail: aalockam@sanford.edu.

LOCKART, BARBETTA, fabric designer, textile and fine artist, jeweler, art educator; b. Sacramento, Feb. 28, 1947; d. Bernard Elwood and Naomi Joyce (Wilson) L.; m. Michael Stanley Ray, Dec. 29, 1982 (div.). AA in English, Southwestern Coll., Chula Vista, Calif., 1974; BA, San Diego State U., 1975; MA in Edn. Adminstrn., N.Mex. State U., Las Cruces, 1979; MA in Counseling and Guidance, N.Mex. State U., 1981. Sec., interim coord., tchr. Indian edn. project Palm Springs (Calif.) Unified Sch. Dist., 1976-79; outreach coord. Tecumseh House/Boston Indian Coun., 1980-81, asst. dir., 1981; acad. counselor, coord. native Am. Affairs Ea. N.Mex. U., Portales, 1981-82; ind. rschr. in field of counseling Albuquerque, 1982-89, Sacramento, 1987-97; owner Dearwater Designs, Albuquerque, 1985-88, Sacramento, 1988-90, Barbetta's Beads & Art, Sacramento, 1990-97, ITSA, 1997—. Instr. in fabric design. Author: Resolving Discipline Problems for Indian Students: A Preventative Approach, 1981, Auctions and Auction Going: Make Them Pay Off for You; contbr. articles to profl. jours. Rockefeller Found. fellow, 1978-79, Nat. Inst. Edn. fellow, 1979-80. E-mail: bb@itsastudio.com.

LOCKE, CARL EDWIN, JR. academic administrator, engineering educator; b. Palo Pinto County, Tex., Jan. 11, 1936; s. Carl Edwin Sr. and Caroline Jane (Brown) L.; m. Sammie Rhae Batchelor, Aug. 25, 1956; children: Stephen Curtis, Carlene Rhae. BSChemE, U. Tex., 1958, MSChemE, 1960, PhD-ChemE, 1972. Rsch. engr. Continental Oil Co., Ponca City, Okla., 1959-65; prodn. engr. R.L. Stone Co., Austin, Tex., 1965-66; prodn. rsch. engr. Tracor Inc., 1966-71; vis. assoc. prof. U. Tex., 1971-73; from asst. prof. to prof., dir. chem. engring. U. Okla., Norman, 1973-86; dean engring. U. Kans., Lawrence, 1986—. Co-author: Anodic Protection, 1981; contbr. articles to profl. jours. Disting. Engring. grad. U. Tex., 1993, Kansas Engr. of Yr. Kansas Engring. Soc., 1996. Fellow Am. Inst. Chem. Engrs.; mem. ASTM, Nat. Assn.

Corrosion Engrs. (regional chair 1988-89, Eben Junkin award South Cen. region 1990), Am. Soc. Engring. Edn. (vice-chair engring. deans coun. 1999-2001, chair 2001—), Lawrence C. of C., Rotary (pres. 2001—). Democrat. Presbyterian. Office: U Kans Sch Engring Rm 4010 1530 W 15th St Lawrence KS 66045-7526 E-mail: lok@ku.edu.

LOCKE, EDWIN ALLEN, III, psychologist, educator, retired; b. N.Y.C., May 15, 1938; s. Edwin Allen and Dorothy (Clark) L.; m. Anne Hassard, June 13, 1968. BA, Harvard U., 1960; MA, Cornell U., 1962, PhD, 1964. Assoc. research scientist Am. Inst. Research, 1964-66, research scientist, 1966-70; asst. prof. psychology U. Md., College Park, 1967-69, assoc. prof., 1969-70, assoc. prof. bus., mgmt. and psychology, 1970-73, dean's prof. of leadership & motivation, 1973-96; chmn. faculty mgt. and orgn. Coll. Bus. and Mgmt. U. Md., College Park, 1984-96, prof. emeritus, 2001. Author: A Guide to Effective Study, 1975; co-author: Goal Setting: A Motivational Technique That works, 1984, A Theory of Goal Setting and Task Performance, 1990, The Essence of Leadership, 1991, The Prime Movers: Traits of the Great Wealth Creators, 2000; editor: Generalizing from Laboratory to Field Settings, 1986, Handbook of Principles of Organizational Behavior, 2000; contbr. articles to profl. jours. Office Naval Research grantee, 1964, 79; NIMH grantee, 1967; Army Rsch. Inst. grantee, 1993. Fellow APA, Acad. Mgmt., Am. Psychol. Soc., Soc. Indsl. and Orgnl. Psychology (Disting Scientific Contbn. award 1993). E-mail: elocke@rhsmith.umd.edu. *The most important literary/philosophical influence in my life has been Ayn Rand. Her philosophy of Objectivism demonstrates that man's highest moral purpose is the achievement of his own happiness and that reason is his only means to achieve it. Her novels, which portray man as an heroic being, are an inspiration to every man to achieve the best within him.*

LOCKE, ELIZABETH HUGHES, foundation executive; b. Norfolk, Va., June 30, 1939; d. George Morris and Sallie Epps (Moss) Hughes; m. John Rae Locke, Jr., Sept. 13, 1958 (div. 1981); children: John Rae III, Sallie Curtis. BA magna cum laude, Duke U., 1964, PhD, 1972; MA, U. N.C., 1966. Instr. English U. N.C., Chapel Hill, 1970-72; dir. univ. pubs. Duke U., Durham, N.C., 1973-79; corp. contbns. officer Bethlehem (Pa.) Steel Corp., 1979-82; dir. edn. divsn. & comm. Duke Endowment, Charlotte, N.C., 1982-96, exec. dir., 1996-97, pres., 1997—. Vis. prof. English Duke U., 1972-73. Editor: Duke Encounters, 1977, prospectus for Change: American Private Higher Education, 1985, (mag) Issues, 1985-96. Pres. Angier B. Duke Meml., Inc., 1997—, The Duke Endowment, 1997—, Nanaline H. Duke Fund, 1997—, Doris Duke Trust, 1998, Jr. League, Durham, 1976, Hist. Preservation Soc., Durham, 1977, Charlotte Area Donors Forum; past pres. Comm. Philanthropy, Washington, Sch. of Arts, Charlotte; mem. legis. com. Coun. on Founds., 1997-, Washington, 1995; trustee Southeastern Coun. of Founds., 1997—, Wing Haven Found.; commr. So. Assn. Colls. & Schs., 1998—; bd. visitors Davidson Coll., Charlotte Country Day Sch., Duke U., Johnson C. Smith U.; trustee Winghaven Found. Recipient Leadership award Charlotte C. of C., 1984; Danforth fellow, 1972. Mem. Nat. Task Force, English Speaking Union, The Most Venerable Order of St. John of Jerusalem (officer sister), Charlotte City Club (bd. govs.), Phi Beta Kappa. Democrat. Epsicopalian. Office: 100 N Tryon St Ste 3500 Charlotte NC 28202-4001 E-mail: elocke@tde.org.

LOCKE, GARY, governor; b. Jan. 21, 1950; s. James and Julie Locke; m. Mona Lee, Oct. 15, 1994; children: Emily Nicole, Dylan James. BA in Polit. Sci., Yale U., 1972; JD, Boston U., 1975. Dep. prosecuting atty. State of Wash., King County; mem. Wash. State Ho. of Reps., 1983—94; gov. State of Washington, 1996—. Cmty. rels. mgr. U.S. West; chief exec. King County, 1994—97. Named First in effectiveness among Puget Sound area lawmakers Seattle Times, 1990. Office: PO Box 40002 Olympia WA 98504-0002

LOCKE, HAROLD OGDEN, chemist; b. Camden, N.J., Sept. 14, 1931; s. Harold Glenwood and Grace Reynolds (Ogden) L.; m. Elizabeth Janet Bellmer, Aug. 22, 1959; children: Bruce Charles, David Edward. BA, Wesleyan U., Middletown, Conn., 1953, MA, 1955; PhD, Rutgers U., 1962. Chemist Armstrong Cork Co., Lancaster, Pa., 1961-65; analytical chemist GAF Corp., Wayne, N.J., 1965—. Patentee on insoluble vinyl lactam clarifiers. With U.S. Army, 1958. Mem. ASTM (vice chmn. com. D12.12, 1976—), Am. Chem. Soc. Republican. Episcopalian. Avocation: folk dancing. Home: 816 Pine St Easton PA 18042-4219 Office: GAF Corp 1361 Alps Rd Wayne NJ 07470-3687

LOCKE, JOHN HOWARD, retired lawyer; b. Berryville, Va., Sept. 4, 1920; s. James Howard and Mary Elizabeth (Hart) L.; m. Frances Rebecca Cook, Feb. 23, 1946; children: Anne Locke Evans, Nancy Locke Curlee, Rebecca Locke Leonard. BS, U. Richmond, 1941; LLB, U. Va., 1948. Bar: Va. 1948. Ptnr. Gentry, Locke, Rakes & Moore, Roanoke, Va., ret., 1985. Apptd. Hearing Officer Supreme Ct. Va., 1987; founder, pres. Big Bros., Roanoke, 1960. With USN, 1942-46. Fellow Am. Coll. Trial Lawyers, Internat. Soc. Barristers (pres. 1970); mem. ABA, Va. State Bar, Va. Bar Assn., Roanoke City Bar Assn. (pres. 1970-71), Internat. Assn. Ins. Counsel, 4th Cir. Jud. Conf., Omicron Delta Kappa, Raven Soc., Shenandoah Club (Roanoke, Va.). Presbyterian.

LOCKE, MICHAEL, zoology educator; b. Nottingham, Eng., Feb. 14, 1929; came to U.S., 1961; s. R.H. and K.N. (Waite) L.; m. J. V. Collins; children by previous marriage, Vanessa , John, Timothy, Marius. BA, Cambridge U., 1952, MA, 1955, PhD, 1956, Sc.D., 1976. State scholar, found. scholar St. John's Coll., 1949-56; lectr. zoology Univ. Coll. W.I., 1956-61; guest investigator Rockefeller Inst., N.Y.C., 1960; assoc. prof. biology Case Western Res. U., Cleve., 1961-67, prof. biology, 1967-71; prof., chmn. dept. zoology U. Western Ont., London, Can., 1971-85, prof. zoology, 1985-94; prof. emeritus, 1994—. Raman prof. U. Madras, India, 1969; vis. dir. rsch. Internat. Ctr. Insect Physiology and Ecology, Nairobi, Kenya, 1977-81; chmn. Gordon Conf. on Lysosomes, 1970. Editor Monographs on Ultrastructure, 1970—; mem. editorial bd. Tissue and Cell, 1968—, Jour. Insect Physiology, 1978—, Insect Sci. and Its Applications, 1979-89; former editor: Growth Soc. Symposia; editor, contbr. vols. 11 A, B, C, Insecta-Microscopic Anatomy of Invertebrate, 1998; contbr. over 200 articles to profl. jours. Served with RAF Named Disting. Lectr. in Life Sci., Cornell U., 1988; recipient Disting. Internat. award in insect morphology and embryology gold medal, 1988, Wigglesworth medal and lectr., Internat. Entomol. Congress, Brazil, 2000, Helmuth Prize, U.W.O., 2001, Cert. of Distinction, Internat. Entomol. Congress, Brazil; fellow, Killam fellow, 1988—90. Fellow Royal Soc. Can., AAAS, Am. Soc. Entomol. (hon.), Royal Soc. Entomol. of London (hon.); mem. Am. Soc. Cell Biology. Avocations: lapidary, gemologist, bone, ivory, horn antiquities. Office: Dept Zoology U Western Ont London ON Canada N6A 5B7 Fax: 519-433-4166. E-mail: mlocke@.uwo.ca.

LOCKE, NORTON, hotel management and construction company executive; b. Mpls., May 22, 1927; s. Ben and Harriet (Markus) L.; m. Peggy Jane Smith, Nov. 6, 1959; children: Alexandria, Jonina, Elizabeth, Victoria. BS, U. Wis., 1951; MBA, Mich. State U., 1957, cert. food and beverage exec., 1984, cert. hotel adminstr., 1986, cert. food service profl., 1988. Corp. dir. food and beverage Kahler Corp., Rochester, Minn., 1970; gen. mgr., chief exec. officer Carolando Corp., Orlando, Fla., 1971-74; also dir.; gen. mgr. Radisson Muehlebach Hotel, Kansas City, Radisson Cadillac Hotel, Detroit, 1974-79; v.p., gen. mgr. White Co. Hospitality Div., Merrillville, Ind., 1979-80; dist. dir. I.D.M. Mgmt. Co., Chgo., 1980-83; v.p., gen. mgr. Skirvin Plaza Hotel, Oklahoma City, 1983-87; v.p., dir. ops. SBI Mgmt. Co., 1987-91; v.p., gen. mgr. Anaheim (Calif.) Plz. Hotel, 1991-93; corp. dir. Midwest Hospitality Mgmt., Anaheim, Calif., 1993-99. Faculty Vallencia Coll., 1971-74; adj. prof. Oklahoma City C.C., 1983-89, Century Coll., San Diego, 1996-98, ITT Tech. Coll., San Diego, 1997-99 Author: Hard Times Cook Book, World Without Milk Cookbook, Land of Milk and Honey, Heritage, A Taste of Tradition. Bd. dirs. U. Minn. Tech. Coll., 1970-75, Am. Hotel and Motel Assn. Sch., 1975-79, Detroit Conv. and Visitors Bur. Served with inf. AUS, 1944-46. Mem. Internat. Food Service Execs. Assn. (dir. 1971-74), Am. Hotel and Motel Assn. (cert.), Am. Chefs Assn., Mich. and Ind. Hotel Assn., Nat. Restaurant Assn., Hotel Sales Mgrs. Assn., Am. Fisheries Inst. (dir. 1970-71), Okla. State Hotel Assn. (Innkeeper of Yr. 1985, Bd. Mem. of Yr. 1986) Clubs: Masons (Scottish Rite 32 degree), Shriners, Rotary, SKAL Internat, Toastmasters Internat. Republican.

LOCKE, THOMAS BERNARD, federal agency administrator; b. Bridgeport, Conn., Nov. 3, 1948; s. Bernard Ray and Marion Jewel (Johnson) Locke; m. Alice Frances McCabe, Apr. 17, 1971 (div. 1983); children: Thomas John, James Tennant; m. Gina Rae Robinson, May 21, 1983 (div. 1993); 1 child Erin Brittany ; m. Tina Suzanne Gentry, Aug. 28, 1993 (div. 1999); m. Tabitha Jill Odom, Dec. 2, 1999. AB, Catholic U. Am., 1970. With FBI, 1970—; supr. exch. program Drug Enforcement Adminstrn., Washington, 1985-87; asst. spl. agt. in charge FBI, Knoxville, 1987-95; insp. FBI Hdqrs., 1995-97; spl. agt. in charge FBI, Memphis, 1997—99; dep. asst. dir. FBI Hdqs., 1999—. Author spl. report Black Tar Heroin in the U.S., 1986. Exec. com. Ea. Dist. Narcotics Unit, Tenn., 1988-95. Recipient Achievement award N.Y.C. Police Dept., 1980; Secret Service plaque U.S. Secret Service, 1984. Mem. Am. Soc. Indsl. Security, FBI Agts. Assn., Hon. Legion of Police Dept. N.Y.C. (Valor award 1986). Republican. Methodist. Office: FBI Headquarters 935 Pennsylvania Ave NW Washington DC 20535

LOCKE, WILLIAM, retired endocrinologist; b. Morden, Man., Can., Mar. 16, 1916; s. Corbet and Ruby Louise (Brown) L.; m. Katherine Elizabeth Acer Russell, Sept. 29, 1945 (dec.). MD, U. Man., Winnipeg, 1938; MS in Medicine, U. Minn., 1947. Diplomate Am. Bd. Internal Medicine. Intern Winnipeg (Man., Can.) Gen. Hosp., 1937-38; fellow in medicine Mayo Found., Rochester, Minn., 1938-40, 46-48; rsch. fellow Harvard U., Boston, 1948-50; staff Ochsner Clinic, New Orleans, 1950-2000, sr. cons., 1987-2000; clin. prof. medicine Tulane U., 1968-86, prof. emeritus, 1986-2000, ret., 2000. Sec. Alton Ochsner Med. Found., New Orleans, 1950—; pres. med. staff Ochsner Found. Hosp., New Orleans, 1954-55, trustee, 1978—; cons. in endocrinology Ochsner Found. Hosp., New Orleans, 1998—. Author, editor: Hypothalmus and Pituitary in Health and Disease, 1972; contbr. chpts. to books and articles to profl. jours. Lt. comdr. RCNVR, 1940-46. NIH grant, 1958-62. Fellow ACP; mem. Am. Diabetes Assn., Endocrine Soc., Sigma Xi. Republican. Episcopalian. Home: 150 Broadway St Apt 1104 New Orleans LA 70118-7612 Office: Ochsner Clinic 1514 Jefferson Hwy New Orleans LA 70121-2483 E-mail: wmlocke@bellsouth.net.

LOCKE, WILLIAM HENRY, lawyer; b. Eagle Pass, Tex., Nov. 14, 1947; s. William Henry and Genevieve (Moss) L.; children: William Henry III, Elizabeth Madeleine. AA with honors, Del Mar Coll., 1967; BA, U. Tex., 1969, JD with honors, 1972. Bar: Tex. 1972; cert. in real estate law. Exec. dir. The Kleberg Law Firm, Corpus Christi, Tex., 1972-99, Graves, Dougherty, Hearon & Moody, Austin, 2000—. Co-dir. advanced real estate law course State Bar of Tex., 1986-87. Author: Seizure of Lender's Collateral Under Drug Enforcement Laws, 1990, Contractual Indemnity in Texas, 1991, Civil Forfeiture Actions, 1993, Shifting of Risk: Contractual Provisions for Indemnity, Additional Insureds, Wavier of Subrogation and Exculpation, 1995, Texas Foreclosure Manual, 1995, Risk Management: Through Contractual Provisions for Indemnity, Additional Insureds Waiver of Subrogation, Releases and Exculpation, 1997, 2002, Sales Contracts: A Framework for Risk Allocation, 1998, Due Diligence in the Acquisition of Income Producing Properties, 2000; contbg. author: Texas Construction Law, 1988. Chmn. Corpus Christi Planning Commn., 1984-85, Corpus Christi Airport Zoning Commn., 1985; bd. dirs., sec. Leadership Corpus Christi, 1984-85; pres. Palmer Drug Abuse Program, Corpus Christi, 1985-87, pres., 2002; treas. St. James Episcopal Elem. Sch., 1987-91. Fellow Tex. Bar Found. (life), Tex. Coll. Real Estate Law (dir. 1990-2001), Coll. Law of State Bar Tex.; mem. ABA, Corpus Christi Bar Assn. (pres. 1987-88), Rotary (bd. dirs. Corpus Christi 1987-88, sec. 1989, Disting. Svc. Above Self award 1985, Corpus Christi merit award 1987), Beta Theta Pi. Democrat. Episcopalian. Fax: 512-478-1976. E-mail: blocke@gdhm.com.

LOCKE LLOYD, JENNIFER C. elementary school educator, consultant; b. Chgo., Apr. 22, 1951; d. Aldridge and Dorothy Locke; m. Carlton (Tony) Carpenter, Sept. 21, 1976 (div. July 1978); children: Rachel C., Carleton Carpenter II; m. John Lloyd, July 1995; 1 child, Rachel. BA, Chgo. State U., 1974; MEd, Nat. Louis U., 2000. Art tchr. Chgo. Bd. Edn., 1975-98, primary sch. tchr., 1989—; pres. Arts n' Us Fine Gifts, Chgo., 1998—. Artists cons. Locke Lloyd Prodns., Chgo., 1995—; planner spl. events. Artist, face painter, body artist, sculptor; creator masks for plays; presenter folktales and drama sems. Mem. South Shore Art Coalition, 1995-2001, Coalition for Improvement of Edn. in south Shore, 2001. Tchr. Incentive grantee Oppenheimer Fund, 1985-87; equipment grantee Chgo. Bd. Edn. Cultural Arts Dept., 1997-99; grantee Chgo. Found. for Edn., 1989. E-mail: lockelloyd@aol.com.

LOCKE MONDA, ROBIN, graphic designer, artist; b. Lowell, Mass., Apr. 17, 1950; d. Newton and Jean Woodman (Emery) Locke; m. Robert Monda, July 15, 1972. Student, Cooper Union, 1968-69; BA in Art summa cum laude, Bklyn. Coll., 1989. Owner Robin Locke Monda: Graphic: Arts, N.Y.C., 1994—; adj. instr. desktop publishing and graphic design CUNY, Coll. Staten Island, 1997—, instr. adult edn. dept., 1998—; adj. instr. Sch. Visual Arts, N.Y.C., 1999; instr. adult edn. dept. Parsons Sch. Design, 1999—. Vis. instr. Pratt Manhattan, 1999—. One person show at 55 Mercer Gallery, N.Y.C., 1990; exhibited in group shows at Herron Test Site, N.Y.C., 1992, Thread Waxing Space, N.Y.C., 1994, Katonah (N.Y.) Mus. Art, 1994, Newhouse Gallery Contemporary Art, Snug Harbor Cultural Ctr., Staten Island, N.Y., 1997, N.Y. State Mus., Albany, 1998; illustrator jour. Menninger Perspective, 1993, Pierogi 2000 Flat Files, 2002--; editor, art dir. for book: Bloody Wymmin Comix, I, 1994, II, 1995, III, 1998; author: A to Z: An Adult Alphabet, 1990; artist for book: Crash: Nostalgia for the Absence of Cyberspace, 1994. Bd. dirs., mem. visual arts adv. bd. Snug Harbor Cultural Ctr., S.I., N.Y., 1995—. Grantee Artist Space, 1990. Mem. Women's Caucus for Art, Coun. on Arts and Humanities for S.I., The Art Dirs. Club, N.Y. Mac Users Group, Alpha Sigma Lambda. Democrat. Home and Office: Robin Locke Monda: Grafik/Arts 36 Hamilton Ave Staten Island NY 10301-1816

LOCKER, DAN LEWIS, career officer; b. San Antonio, June 23, 1946; BS in Biology, S.W. Tex. State Coll., 1967; MD, U. Tex., 1973. Diplomate Am. Bd. Surgery. Commd. 2d lt. USAF, 1970, advanced through grades to brig. gen., 1997; resident in family practice USAF Med. Ctr., Scott AFB, 1973-75, resident in gen. surgery Keesler AFB, Miss., 1975-79; chief surg. svcs. 366th Tactical Fighter Wing, Mountain Home AFB, Idaho, 1979-83; chief gen. surgery, dir. USAF Regional Med. Ctr., Wiesbaden, West Germany, 1983-86; dep. comdr. for hosp. svcs. 48th Tactical Fighter Wing, Royal AF Lakenheath, Eng., 1986-89; comdr. 96th Strategic Hosp., Dyess AFB, Tex., 1989-91, 82nd Med. Group, Sheppard AFB, 1991-94; dir. med. svc. office mgmt. AF Mil. Pers. Ctr., Randolph AFB, 1994-95; command surgeon Hdqrs. USAF in Europe, Ramstein Air Base, Germany, 1995-97; comdr. 81st Med. Group, Keesler AFB, Miss., 1997—. Cons. to surgeon gen. for gen. surgery, 1986. Contbr. articles to profl. jours. Decorated Legion of Merit; recipient Award for Gen. Surgery Surgeon Gen., 1979. Fellow ACS; mem. Soc. of Air Force Clin. Surgeons. Office: 81 MDG/CC 301 Fisher St Ste 101 Keesler AFB MS 39534-2508

LOCKER, GERSHON YEHUDA, oncologist, educator; b. N.Y.C., Aug. 8, 1948; s. Joseph and Edith (Kurtzman) L.; m. Louise Ann Chapman, Nov. 9, 1980; children: Rachel Z., Joshua D. BA summa cum laude, Columbia U., 1969; MD, Harvard U., 1973. Cert. in internal medicine, Am. Bd. Internal Medicine; cert. in med. oncology. Resident in internal medicine U. Chgo., 1973-75; fellow in med. oncology Nat. Cancer Inst., Bethesda, Md., 1975-78; chief med. oncology St. Joseph Hosp., Chgo., 1978-81; dir. oncology edn. Evanston (Ill.) Hosp., 1982—97; chief divsn. hematology/oncology Evanston Northwestern Healthcare, 1998—; assoc. prof. medicine Northwestern U., Evanston, 1993—2002, prof. medicine, 2002—; Kellogg Scanlon chair in oncology Evanston Northwestern Healthcare, 2000—. Study sect. mem. NIH Spl. Study Sects. Small Bus. Initiatives, Bethesda, 1994-98; mem. NIH Clin. Oncology Study Sect., 2000—; chief med. advisor Y-Me Breast Cancer Support Orgn., Chgo., 1995-97; co-dir. Kellogg Cancer Care Ctrs. Contbr. articles to profl. jours. Bd. trustees Y-Me Nat. Breast Cancer Orgn., Chgo., 1987-92, 95-97; adv. bd. Cancer Wellness Ctr., Northbrook, Ill., 1989—; oncology adv. com. Blue Cross Blue Shield Ill., Chgo., 1994-96. Lt. comdr. USPHS, 1975-78. Named Outstanding Tchr., Evanston Hosp., 1983; recipient Alumni Svc. award Columbia Coll. Alumni Bd., 1988, Scv. award Y-Me Breast Cancer Orgn.; rsch. grantee Ill. Cancer Ctr., 1987-88, Nat. Cancer Inst., 2000—. Fellow Am. Coll. Physicians, Inst. Medicine Chgo.; mem. Am. Soc. Clin. Oncology (mem. breast and colon cancer marker guidelines com. 1994-96), Am. Assn. Cancer Rsch., Ea. Coop. Oncology Group, Ill. Med. Oncology Soc. (bd. dirs. 1990-99). Office: Kellogg Cancer Ctr Rm 3134 Evanston Hosp 2650 Ridge Evanston IL 60201 E-mail: gylocker@northwestern.edu.

LOCKER, J. GARY, university official, civil engineering educator; b. Kenora, Ont., Can., Nov. 19, 1937; s. Lorne John and Gladys Sarah (Kirk) L.; m. Elaine June Letawsky, May 25, 1963; children: Laura Lee, Tiffany Dawn. BSCE, U. Man., Winnipeg, Can., 1961; MS, U. Alta., Edmonton, Can., 1963, PhD, 1969. Registered profl engr., Ont. Lectr. dept. civil engring., Royal Mil. Coll., Kingston, Ont., 1963-66, asst. prof., 1968-71; assoc. prof. faculty engring. U. Regina, Sask., Can., 1971-73; chmn. dept. civil engring. Lakehead U., Thunder Bay, Ont., 1973-76, dir. Sch. Engring., 1976-94, dean Faculty Engring., 1994-97; exec. dir. Native Access Program for Engring. Mem., past. chmn. Coun. Ont. Deans Engring., Nat. Coun. Deans Engring and Applied Sci.; mem.-at-large Can. Engring. Accreditation Bd. Can. Coun. Profl. Engrs. Fellow Engring. Inst. Can.; mem. Can. Geotech. Inst., Profl. Engrs. Ont. (order of honor), Internat. Soc. Soil Mechanics and Found. Engring., Thunder Bay Fly Fishing Club. Geotech. engring. rsch. in organic soils and clay shales. Avocations: fly fishing and tying, gardening, trailer travel. Office: Lakehead U Faculty Engring Nape Lakehead U Oliver Rd Thunder Bay ON Canada P7B 5E1

LOCKETT, JAMES, history educator; Degree in polit. sci., Morehouse Coll.; MS in Libr. Svc., PhD, Atlanta U.; MA, Case Western Res. U.; postgrad., U. for Svcs., NYU, U. Ala., 1991, U. Fla., U. Dar es Salaam, Tanzania, 1993. Prof. history, Afro-Am. history, polit. sci., geography Stillman Coll., 1990—. Lectr. Stillman Coll. Elderhostel, 1993; mem. faculty Univ. Coll. Belize, 1994; cons., presenter in field. Contbr. numerous articles to profl. publs. Mem. econ. devel. adv. coun. Ala. Conf. Black Mayors, Inc.; chmn. bd. dirs. Ala. Afro-Am./Black Hall of Fame; mem. adv. bd. Ala. Hist. Commn.; assoc. commr. Ala. Elections Commn.; mem. west Ala. oral history project West Ala. Planning and Devel. Coun.; bd. dirs. Murphy African Am. Mus. Found.; campus coord. Exxon/Kettering Pub. Leadership; mem. adv. com. Gov.'s Salute to Great Black Alabamans; coord. so. regional edn. bd./fund for improvement of postsecondary edn. Stillman Coll.; mem. Pres.'s Colloquium Series Com.; mem. project to preserve history of black Tuscaloosa in Ala. Recipient cert. of recognition IRS, 1991. Fellow Royal Geog. Soc.; mem. Assn. for Study of Afro-Am. Life and History (pres. West Ala. chpt.), Phi Alpha Theta (chairperson faculty orgn. 1997, rep. Rhodes Scholarship Trust). Avocations: golf, football, basketball, baseball, track. Home: 2745 Elm St Lot 11 Tuscaloosa AL 35401-6457

LOCKETT, LANDON JOHNSON, former linguistic educator, researcher; b. Ft. Benning, Ga., May 22, 1929; s. Landon Johnson and Roberta Blye (Davies) J.; m. Carol Yvonne Ramsay, Aug. 11, 1990. BA, U. Tex., 1954, LLB, 1957, PhD, 1968; M of Comparative Law, So. Meth. U., 1959. Bar: Tex. Atty. Raymond M. Hill and Assocs., Houston, 1957-61; NDEA fellow U. Tex., Austin, 1962-65, instr. Portuguese, 1965-69, asst. prof. Portuguese lang. & linguistics, 1969-75; assoc. prof. linguistics Univ. Fed. Rio Grande North, Natal, Brazil, 1982-83. Vis. prof. linguistics Pontificia Univ. Cath. Rio Grande South, Porto Alegre, Brazil, 1970, Univ. Autonoma Guadalajara, Mex., 1976-77, Univ. Fed. Rio Grande North, 1978-82; conservation rschr., advocate. Author: O Uso do Infinitivo num Corpus de Portugues Coloquial Brasileiro, 1969; contbr. articles to profl. jours. Cadet U.S. Cadet Corps, 1948-50. Recipient Nancy benedict Meml. award Native Plant Soc. Tex., 1994. Mem. Tex. Acad. Sci., Tex. State Hist. Assn. Achievements include discovery of wild population of Sabal mexicana palm trees 200 miles north of what was believed to be northern limit of range; led successful effort to protect unique population of apparent Sabal mexicana X, minor hybrid palms. Home: 3210 Stevenson Ave Austin TX 78703-2242

LOCKETT, TYLER CHARLES, state supreme court justice; b. Corpus Christi, Tex., Dec. 7, 1932; s. Tyler Coleman and Evelyn (Lemond) L.; m. Sue W. Lockett, Nov. 3, 1961; children: Charles, Patrick. AB, Washburn U., 1955, JD, 1962. Bar: Kans. 1962. Pvt. practice law, Wichita, 1962—; judge Ct. Common Pleas, 1971-77, Kans. Dist. Ct. 18th Dist., 1977-83; justice Supreme Court Kans., Topeka, 1983—. Methodist. Office: Kans Supreme Ct 374 Kansas Judicial Ctr Topeka KS 66612-1502*

LOCKETTE, DAPHNEY D. elementary education educator; b. N.Y.C., Sept. 30, 1973; BA, Va. State U., 1995; M in Elem. Edn., Fairleigh Dickinson U., 2001; postgrad. studies in instructional tech., Farleigh Dickinson U., Teaneck, N.J., 2001—. Technology coord. Americorps/Project First, N.Y.C., 1995—97; substitute tchr. Bergen County Bd. of Edn., Englewood, NJ, 1997; adminstrv. asst. Silver Palate, Cresskill, 1997; kindergarten tchr. My Friend's Day Sch., Teaneck, 1997—99; tchr. asst. First Grade Englewood on the Palisades Charter Sch., Englewood, 1999—. Tutor computer tech. and lang. arts Esteem Acad., Englewood. Author: Secrets from the Depths of My Soul, 2000. Treas., Praise Ministries, 2000—. Mem. Alpha Kappa Alpha.

LOCKEY, RICHARD FUNK, allergist, educator; b. Lancaster, Pa., Jan. 15, 1940; s. Stephen Daniel and Anna (Funk) L.; m. Carol Lee Madill, July 3, 1982; children: Brian Christopher, Keith Edward BS, Haverford Coll., 1961; MD, Temple U., 1965; MS, U. Mich., 1972. Diplomate Am. Bd. Internal Medicine, Am. Bd. Allergy and Immunology. Intern Temple U. Med. Sch., Phila., 1965-66; asst. resident internal medicine Univ. Hosp. U. Mich., Ann Arbor, 1966-67, resident, 1966-68, fellow in allergy and immunology, 1969-70; asst. prof. medicine U. South Fl. Coll. Medicine, Tampa, 1973-77, assoc. prof. medicine, 1977-83, asst. dir. div. allergy and immunology, 1979-82, dir. allergy and immunology, 1982—, prof. medicine, 1983—, prof. pediats., 1983—, prof. pub. health, 1987—; asst. chief sect. allergy and immunology VA Hosp., 1973-82, chief sect. allergy and immunology, 1983—, Joy McCann Culverhouse endowed prof. allergy and immunology, 1997. Mem. allergenic adv. com. FDA, 1985-89. Editor: Allergy and Clinical Immunology, 1980; co-editor: (with S.C. Bukantz) Fundamentals of Immunology and Allergy, 1987, (with S.C. Bukantz) Principles of Immunology and Allergy, 1987, JAMA Primer on Allergic and Immunologic Diseases, 1987, (with S. C. Bukantz) Allergen Immunotherapy, 1991, (with M. Levine) Monograph on Insect Allergy, 1995, (with S. Bukantz) Allergens and Allergen Immunotherapy, 1999, (with D. Ledford) Immunotherapy: A Practical Review and Guide, 2000, (with S. Kemp) Diagnostic Testing of Allergic Disease, 2000; mem. edit. bd. Jour. on Allergy and Immunology, 1999-04; contbr. more than 300 articles to profl. jours. and chpts. to books; author monographs. Served to maj. USAF, 1971-73 Named Outstanding Med. Specialist, Town and Country Mag., 1989, Claude P. Brown Meml. lectr. Assn. Clin. Scientists, ADA, 1981, Disting. Visitor Ann. Meeting of Coll. of Medicine, Republic of Costa Rica, 1979, spl. mem. Internat. Sci. Bd. Pharmacia Allergy Rsch. Found., 1992—; recipient Alumni Achievement award Temple U. Sch. of Medicine Alumni Assn., 1990, Outstanding Leadership in Chpt. Devel. and Patient Support, Nat. Asthma and Allergy Found. of Am. award, 1992, Cert. of Appreciation, Fla. Med. Assn., 1992, medalist Fla. Acad. Scis., 2000, Disting. Svc. award Univ. S. Fla., 2001. Fellow ACP, AAAS, AMA, Am. Coll. Chest Physicians, Am. Acad. Allergy and Immunology (chmn. com. on insects 1978-81, chmn. undergrad. and grad. edn. com. 1982-88, com. on occupational lung disease 1982—, chmn. com. on standardization of allergenic extracts 1983-86, exec. com. mem. at large 1986-88, historian 1988-89, sec. 1989-90, treas. 1990-91, pres.-elect 1991-92, pres. 1992-93, Am. Bd. Allergy and Immunology (bd. dirs. 1993-98), World Allergy Assn. (bd. dirs. 1997—), Internat. Assn. Allergology (clin. immunology bd. dirs.), Soc. Allergy and Immunology of Cordoba, Argentina (hon.), John M. Sheldon U. of Mich. Allergy Soc. (councilor 1977-80, pres. 1980-82), Fla. Allergy and Immunology Soc. (sec.-treas. 1979-80, pres. 1981-82), Southeastern Allergy Assn., Hillsborough County Med. Assn., Joint Coun. Allergy and Immunology, Clin. Immunology Soc., Fla. Thoracic Soc., Univ. Club, Aliva Country Club. Avocation: antique cut glass and tools. Home: 3909 Northampton Way Tampa FL 33624-4443 Office: U So Fla VA Hosp #502 13801 Bruce B Downs Blvd Tampa FL 33613-3946

LOCKHART, AILEENE SIMPSON, retired dance, kinesiology, physical education educator and editor; b. Atlanta, Mar. 18, 1911; d. Thomas Ellis and Aileene Reeves (Simpson) Lockhart. BS, Tex. Woman's U., 1932; MS, U. Wis., 1937, PhD, 1942; DSc (hon.), U. Nebr., 1967. Mem. faculty Mary Hardin Baylor Coll., Belton, Tex., 1937-42, U. Wis., 1941-42; asst. prof., then assoc. prof. phys. edn. and pharmacology U. Nebr., 1942-49; assoc. prof., then prof. U. So. Calif., 1949-73; dean, prof. Coll. Health, Phys. Edn., Recreation and Dance Tex. Woman's U., 1973-78, Cornaro prof., 1973-78, prof. dance and phys. edn., chmn. dept. dance, 1978-83, adj. prof., 1983-88, Rachel Bryant Meml. lectr., 1997. Clare Small lectr. U. Colo., 1975; Ethel Martus Lawther lectr. U. N.C., 1978; Army Morris Homans lectr., Milw., 76; Donna Mae Miller Humanities scholar/lectr. U. Ariz., Tucson, 1989; vis. prof./lectr. Iowa State U., univs., Wash., Oreg., Wiss., Mass., N.C., Colo., N.H., Calif., State U., Long Beach, Springfield Coll., Mass., Smith Coll., Wellesely Coll., U. Maine-Presque Isle, Dunfermline Coll., Edinburgh, Scotland, U. Brazil, Brasilia; cons. editor William C. Brown Pub. Co., Dubuque, Iowa, 1954—95. Author or co-author: 12 books; contbr. articles to profl. jours.; cons. editor or editor: over 300 books. Recipient Alumnae award, Tex. Woman's U., 1971, Disting. Alumnae award, U. Wis.-Madison, 1981, Cornaro award, 1980, Honor award, Ministry Edn., Taiwan, 1981, Heritage award, Nat. Dance Assn., 1985, honra ao Merito, Ministerio de Educator and Cultura Brazilla, Brazil, 1977; fellow Amy Morris Homans, 1961—62; scholar Minnie Stevens Piper Found., State of Tex., 1983, Nat. Dance Assn., 1986—87, Tex. Assn. Health, Phys. Edn., Recreation and Dance, 1986. Fellow: Am. Acad. Phys. Edn. (pres. 1980—81, Hetherington award 1992), Am. Alliance Health, Phys. Edn., Recreation and Dance (Honor award 1963, Luther Halsey Gulick medal 1980), Am. Coll. Sports Medicine; mem.: Nat. Assn. Phys. Edn. in Higher Edn., So. Assn. Phys. Edn. Coll. Women, Nat. Dance Assn., Nat. Assn. Girls and Women in Sports (Honor award 1991, Rachel Bryant Meml. lectr. 1997), Phi Kappa Phi. Presbyterian. *That my students, many now well respected scholars, others eager neophytes in the journey of learning, exemplify some of the goals, ideals and visions, the high standards and high expectancies we have shared together is to me the most meaningful and fulfilling aspect in my life as an educator.*

LOCKHART, GEMMA, producer, writer; b. Rapid City, S.D., Dec. 5, 1956; d. Jim and Teena L.; children: Mica, Nakca, Aaron. BA in English, Creative Writing, Dartmouth Coll., 1979. TV news reporter Duhamel Broadcasting Enterprises, Rapid City, S.D., 1974-80; TV producer Rural Ethnic Inst., 1981-83; instr. Oglala Lakota Coll., Kyle, S.D., 1983-86; horse rider Black Hills; TV producer S.D. Pub. TV, Vermillion, 1989-90; ind. producer, 1990—; CEO Wambli Win Prodns., 1994—, Anpao Studio, Rapid City, 1995—. Auditor Lakota Elders, Dakota Land, 1975—; freelance columnist various publs. including USA Today. Presdl. scholar, 1975, 85. Mem. NAFE, Dartmouth Coll. Alumni Coun., Nature Conservancy (bd. dirs. 1995-96). Republican. Avocation: walking. Home: Box 8044 Rapid City SD 57709-8044 also: Dark Canyon Rapid City SD 57702

LOCKHART, GREGORY GORDON, prosecutor; b. Dayton, Ohio, Sept. 2, 1946; s. Lloyd Douglas and Evelyn (Gordon) L.; m. Paula Louise Jewett, May 20, 1978; children: David H., Sarah L. BS, Wright State U., 1973; JD, Ohio State U., 1976. Bar: Ohio 1976, U.S. Dist. Ct. (so. dist.) Ohio 1977, U.S. Ct. Appeals (6th cir.) 1988, U.S. Supreme Ct. 1993. Legal advisor Xenia and Fairborn (Ohio) Police Dept., 1977-78; asst. pros. atty. Greene County Prosecutor, Xenia, 1978-87; ptnr. DeWine & Schenck, 1978-82, Schenck, Schmidt & Lockhart , Xenia, 1982-85, Ried & Lockhart, Beavercreek, Ohio, 1985-87; asst. U.S. atty. So. Dist. of Ohio, Columbus, 1987-2001, U.S. atty. Dayton, 2001—. Adj. prof. Coll. Law U. Dayton, 1990—, Wright State U., Dayton, 1979—. Co-author: Federal Grand Jury Practice, 1996. Pres. Greene County Young reps., Xenia, 1977-79. With USAF, 1966-70; Vietnam. Mem. Fed. Bar Assn. (chpt. pres. 1994-95), Dayton Bar Assn., Kiwanis (pres. 1983-84, lt. gov. 1986-87), Jaycees (pres. 1976-79), Am. Inns of Ct. (master of bench emeritus). Methodist. Avocations: golf, tennis, hiking, camping. Office: US Attorney Federal Bldg 200 W 2d St Rm 602 Dayton OH 45402 E-mail: gregory.lockhart@usdoj.gov.

LOCKHART, JAMES BICKNELL, III, federal agency administrator; b. White Plains, N.Y., May 13, 1946; s. James Bicknell Jr. and Mary Ann (Riegel) L.; m. Carolyn Strahan Zoephel, June 17, 1972; children: James Bicknell IV, Grace Strahan. BA, Yale U., 1968; MBA, Harvard U., 1974. Asst. treas. Gulf Oil (E.H.), London, 1979-80; fin. dir. Gulf Oil Belgium, Brussels, 1980-81; sr. mgr. Gulf Oil Corp., Pitts., 1981-82, asst. treas., 1982-83; v.p., treas. Alexander and Alexander Services, N.Y.C., 1983-89; exec. dir. Pension Benefit Guaranty Corp., Washington, 1989-93; mng. dir., head pvt. fin. group Smith Barney, Inc., N.Y.C., 1993-95; sr. v.p. fin. Nat. Reins. Corp., 1996; mng. dir., CFO NetRisk, Greenwich, Conn., 1997—2001; dep. commr., COO, Social Security Adminstrn., Washington, 2002—. Contbr. articles to profl. jours. Treas. Reps. Abroad, London, 1978-80. Served to lt. (j.g.) USNR, 1969-72. Fellow Assn. Corp. Treas. (Eng.); mem. Assn. Pvt. Pension and Welfare Plans (bd. dirs. 1993-95). Office: Social Security Admin Off of Comnr Altmeyer Bldg 6401 Security Blvd Baltimore MD 21235-6401 Office Fax: 410-966-1463.

LOCKHART, JOHN HARDY, JR. civil engineer; b. Stephensville, Tex., Mar. 8, 1937; s. John Hardy and Isla Beth (Cathey) L.; m. Virginia Bess Greenslit, June 24, 1961; children: John Hardy III, Elizabeth Lockhart Huxford, Erin Irene, Drew Henderson. Student, Tarleton State Coll., 1955-57; BS in Petroleum Engring., Tex. Tech. U., 1960; MS, Ga. Inst. Tech., 1972. Registered profl. engr., Tex. Hydrologist U.S. Army C.E., Ft. Worth, 1960-65, hydraulic engr. Jacksonville, Fla., 1965-67, civil engr. Atlanta, 1967-79, Washington, 1979—. Liaison to U.S. Army Corps of Engrs. Coastal Engring. Rsch. Bd., Vicksburg, Miss., 1968—, liaison to com. on tidal hydraulics, Vicksburg, 1979-80. Mem. ASCE, Nat. Soc. Profl. Engrs., Am. Shore and Beach Preservation Assn., Coastal Soc. Home: 36 Little Creek Ln Fredericksburg VA 22405-3621 Office: U S Army Corps Engrs 20 Massachusetts Ave NW Washington DC 20314-0001

LOCKHART, JOHN MALLERY, management consultant; b. Mellen, Wis., May 17, 1911; s. Carl Wright and Gladys (Gale) L.; m. Judith Anne Wood, Feb. 26, 1938 (dec. June 1991); children: Wood Alexander, Gale, Thomas; m. Frances Whittaker, Jan. 7, 1993. BS, Northwestern U., 1931; JD, IIT, 1938. CPA, Ill. Teaching fellow Northwestern U., 1931; asst. v.p. Welsh, Davis & Co. (investment bankers), Chgo., 1935-41; treas. Transcontinental & Western Air, Inc., Kansas City, Mo., 1941-47; exec. v.p., CEO TACA Airways, S.A., 1944-45; v.p., dir. The Kroger Co., 1947-71, exec. v.p., 1961-71; pres. Kroger Family Ctr. Stores, 1969-71, Lockhart Co. (mgmt. cons.), 1971—; v.p. corp. fin. Gradison & Co., 1973-86. Chmn. bd. dirs., CEO Ohio Real Estate Investment Co., Ohio Real Estate Equity Corp., 1974-76; bd. dirs. Employers Mut. Cos., Des Moines, Witt Co.; chmn. bd. dirs. Autotronics Systems, Inc., 1976-78; bd. dirs. Vectra Internat., Inc., Hamilton Mut. Ins. Co. Chmn. Hamilton County Hosp. Commn., 1965-84; mem. adv. bd. Greater Cin. Airport, 1961-86. Mem. Comml. Club, Cin. Country Club, Conquistadores del Cielo Club. Home and Office: 2770 Walsh Rd Cincinnati OH 45208-3425

LOCKHART, KEITH ALAN, conductor, musician, teacher; b. Poughkeepsie, N.Y., Nov. 7, 1959; s. Newton Frederick and Marilyn Jean (Woodyard) L. BA summa cum laude in German, MusB summa cum laude Piano Performance, Furman U., 1981; MFA in Orch. Conducting, Carnegie-Mellon U., 1983; D (hon.), Boston Conservatory, 1996, Northeastern U., 1998, Furman U., 2000. Mem. condrs. faculty Carnegie-Mellon U., 1983-89; music dir. Pitts. Civic Orch., 1987-90; asst. condr. Akron Symphony Orch., 1988-90, Cin. Symphony Orch., Cin. Pops Orch., 1990-92, assoc. condr., 1992-95; music dir. Cin. Chamber Orch., 1992-99, Boston Pops Orch., Boston Symphony Orch. Youth Concerts, 1995—, Utah Symphony Orch., 1998—. Guest condr. Chgo. Symphony Orch., Cleve. Orch., L.A. Philharmonic, L.A. Chamber Orch., Toronto Symphony, Mont. Symphony Orch., Indpls. Symphony, N.Y. Philharm., Phila. Orch., Houston Symphony, Milw. Symphony, Dallas Symphony, Orch. Sinfonica de Tucuman (Argentina), New Japan Philharm.; mem. adv. bd. Music Educators Nat. Conf.; pres. nat. adv. bd. Brevard Music Ctr., 1996—. Co-editor, arranger performance edition opera John Gay: The Beggar's Opera, 1985; recordings: Telarc, Christmas Songs with Mel Torme, 1992, works by Galbraith, Alonso-Crespo, 1995, New Energy from the Americas with Cin. Chamber Orch., 1996, Runnin Wild: The Boston Pops Play Glenn Miller, 1996, American Visions, 1997, The Celtic Album, 1998, Holiday Pops, 1998, Splash, 1999, The Latin Album, 2000, My Favorite Things: A Richard Rodgers Celebration, 2002. Mem. Conductor's Guild Am., Symphny Orch. League, Am. Fedn. Musicians. Avocations: reading, cooking, skiing, raquetball, outdoor sports. Office: The Boston Pops Orchestra 301 Massachusetts Ave Symphony Hall Boston MA 02115 E-mail: klockhart@bso.org.

LOCKHART, MACK L. city official; b. Greenville, S.C., 1946; BS in Bus. Orgn. and Mgmt., Bluefield Coll. Sr. appraiser City of Richmond, Va., 1989-93, city assessor, 1993—. Mem. Nat. Forum for Black Pub. Officials, Internat. Assn. Assesssing Officers, Nat. Negro Golf Assn. Office: Office of City Assessor 900 E Broad St Rm 802 Richmond VA 23219-1907

LOCKHART, MADGE CLEMENTS, educational organization executive; b. Soddy, Tenn., May 22, 1920; d. James Arlie and Ollie (Sparks) Clements; m. Andre J. Lockhart, Apr. 24, 1942 (div. 1973); children: Jacqueline, Andrew, Janice, Jill. Student, East Tenn. U., 1938-39; BS, U. Tenn., Chattanooga and Knoxville, 1955, MEd, 1962. Elem. tchr. Tenn. and Ga., 1947-60, Brainerd H.S., Chattanooga, 1960-64, Cleveland (Tenn.) City Schs., 1966-88; owner, operator Lockhart's Learning Ctr., Inc., Cleveland and Chattanooga, 1975—; co-founder, pres. Hermes, Inc., 1973-79; co-founder Dawn Ctr., Hamilton County, Tenn., 1974; apptd. mem. Tenn. Gov.'s Acad. for Writers. Author poetry, short stories and fiction; contbr. articles to profl. jours. and newspapers. Pres. Cleveland Assn. Retarded Citizens, 1970, state v.p., 1976; pres. Cherokee Easter Seal Soc., 1973-76, Cleveland Creative Arts Guild, 1980; bd. dirs. Tenn. Easter Seal Soc., 1974-77, 80-83; chair Bradley County Internat. Yr. of Child; mem. panel for grants Coun. Govts. S.E. Tenn. Devel. Dist., 1990-92; mem. Internat. Biog. Centre Adv. Coun., Cambridge, Eng., 1991-92; mem. mayor's com. Mus. for Bradley County, Tenn., 1992—. Recipient Service to Mankind award Sertoma, 1978, Gov.'s award for service to handicapped, 1979; mental health home named in her honor, Tenn., 1987. Mem. NEA (life), Tenn. Edn. Assn., Am. Assn. Rehab. Therapy, S.E. Tenn. Arts Coun., Cleveland Edn. Assn. (Service to Humanity award 1987). Mem. Ch. of Christ. Clubs: Byliners, Fantastiks. Home: 3007 Oakland Dr NW Cleveland TN 37312-5281

LOCKHART, PAUL S. astronaut, military officer; b. Amarillo, Tex., Apr. 28, 1956; s. Leo (Stepfather) and Joy Wiley; m. Mary Theresa Germaine. BA in Math., Tex. Tech. U., 1978; MS in Aerosace Engring., U. Tex., Austin , 1981. Commd 2d lt. USAF, 1981, student pilot, 1981—83; pilot USAF 49th Fighter Interceptor Squadron, 1983—86; operations pilot F-4 USAF in Germany, 1986—87; instr. pilot for F-4 and F-16 crews surface to air missile suppression USAF, Germany, 1987—90, test pilot trainee Calif., 1991—92; from test wing pilot to ops. officer USAF 39th Flight Test Squadron, Eglin AFB, Fla., 1992—96; astronaut NASA Johnson Space Ctr., Houston, 1996—. Fellow Exchange fellow U. Innsbruck and U. Vienna Summer Schs., Rotary Club, 1978—79. Achievements include 4000 flight hours using 30 different aircraft. Avocations: camping, hunting, outdoor sports. Office: Astronaut Office/CB Johnson Space Ctr Houston TX 77058

LOCKHEAD, GREGORY ROGER, psychology educator; b. Boston, Aug. 8, 1931; s. John Roger and Ester Mae (Bixby) L.; m. Jeanne Marie Hutchinson, June 9, 1957; children: Diane, Elaine, John. BS, Tufts U., 1958; PhD, Johns Hopkins, 1965. Psychologist rsch. staff IBM Research, Yorktown Heights, N.Y., 1958-61; rsch. assoc., instr. Johns Hopkins U., Balt., 1961-65; asst. prof. psychology Duke U., Durham, N.C., 1965-68, assoc. prof., 1968-71, prof., 1971-2001, chmn. dept. exptl. psychology, 1991-97, prof. dept. psychol. and brain scis., 2001—. Scholar Stanford U.; rsch. assoc. U. Calif., Berkeley, 1971-72; fellow Wolfson Coll., Oxford (Eng.) U., 1980-81; scholar Fla. Atlantic U., 1981; cons. in human engring. Cons. editor: Perception and Psychophysics, 1972-92; contbr. articles to profl. jours., co-author, editor chpts. in books. With USN, 1951-55. NSF grantee, 1966-69, 79-84, USPHS grantee, 1963-69, 70-79, Air Force Office Sci. Rsch., 1983-91. Fellow APA, Am. Psychol. Soc., Soc. Exptl. Psychologists; mem. Psychonomic Soc., Internat. Soc. Psychophysics, Sigma Xi, Phi Beta Kappa (hon.). Home: 2900 Montgomery St Durham NC 27705-5638 Office: Duke U Dept Exptl Psychology Durham NC 27708

LOCKHEED, MARLAINE ELIZABETH, sociologist, World Bank official; b. Los Angeles, Sept. 20, 1942; d. John Allan and Patricia (Maser) L.; children: E. Graham Katz, Khalida K. BA, Reed Coll., 1964; PhD, Stanford U., 1972. Sr. research scientist Edn. Testing Service, Princeton, N.J., 1972-85; sociologist World Bank, Washington, 1985-97, mgr., 1997—. Editor, author: Contribution of Social Science to Education Policy and Practice, 1986, Improving Primary Education in Developing Countries, 1990, Effective Schools in Developing Countries, 1993, Primary Education in India, 1997; editor, author: jour. articles and book chpts.

LOCKINGTON, DAVID, conductor; b. Eng. arrived in U.S., 1978; m. Dylana Jenson; 3 children. BA, U. Cambridge, Eng.; MA in cello performance, Yale U. Prin. cellist Nat. Youth Orch. Great Britain; cellist New Haven Symphony Orch.; asst. prin. cellist Denver Symphony Orch., asst. conductor; music dir. Cheyenne Symphony Orch., Denver Young Artist's Orch., Boulder Bach. Festival; founder, conductor Acad. Wilderness Chamber Orch.; asst. conductor Opera Colo., Balt. Symphony Orch., 1992, assoc. conductor, 1993-95; music dir. N.Mex. Symphony Orch., 1995—2000, Ohio Chamber Orch., Long Island Philharmonic, 1996—97, 1999—2000, Grand Rapids Symphony, Grand Rapids, Mich., 1999. Guest conductor St. Louis Symphony, Colo. Symphony, Grand Rapids (Mich.) Symphony, Pacific Symphony, Wichita (Kans.) Symphony, Honolulu Symphony, Harrisburg (Pa.) Symphony, Fla. Orch., Dayton (Ohio) Philharmonic, La. Philharmonic, World Youth Symphony, Interlochen Arts Acad. Office: Grand Rapids Symphony Ste 1 169 Louis Campau Promenade NW 1 Grand Rapids MI 49503-2629*

LOCKLAIR, GARY HAMPTON, computer science educator; b. Sacramento, May 1, 1956; s. Oliver Hampton and Frances Eleanor (Snyder) L.; m. Karen Ann Kellar, Aug. 13, 1977; children: Joshua, Sabrina, David, Daniel, Valerie. BA in Chemistry, Calif. State U., Sacramento, 1979, BS in Computer Sci., 1980; MS, U. Idaho, 1986; PhD in Computer Sci., Nova Southeastern U., 2002. Programmer, analyst Calif. Dept. Transp., Sacramento, 1977-79; mem. tech. staff Hewlett-Packard Co., Cupertino, Calif., 1980-81, software quality engr. Corvallis, Oreg., 1981-83, software program mgr. Boise, Idaho, 1983-86; asst. prof. Concordia U. Wis., Mequon, 1986—, chair computer sci. dept., 1986—, dir. computer ctr., 1986-93. Computing cons., Milw., 1986—. Author: All of the Above, 1992; contbr. articles to profl. jours. Dist. computer cons. Philomath (Oreg.) Sch. Dist., 1981-83. Recipient HP Customer Svc. award Hewlett-Packard and Exxon Corp., 1985. Mem. IEEE, Assn. for computing Machinery. Lutheran. Avocation: photography. Office: Concordia U Wis 12800 N Lake Shore Dr Mequon WI 53097-2418 E-mail: locklair@luther.cuw.edu.

LOCKLEAR, JR. WILLIAM FRANK, composer, small business owner; b. Trion, Ga., Sept. 7, 1947; s. William Frank and Lillian Ruth Locklear; m. Dora Suzanne Dreckhrah, Dec. 29, 2000; children: Joseph William Locklear; m. Lynda Jo Gray, Aug. 16, 1969 (dec. Sept. 0, 1999). BS Music Ed., Jacksonville State Univ., Jacksonville, AL, 1973. Band dir. Name of H.S.?, City?, Ga., 1969—98; bus. owner Bill Locklear Custom Music, Summerville, 1998. Composer and arranger of more than 1000 compositions since 1970. Recipient Award of Merit, Coll. Band Directors Nat. Assn., 1993. Mem.: Ga. Music Educators Assn., Music Educators Nat. Conf., Jaycees, Rincon, GA. Achievements include composed music for 1996 olympics, for the Atlanta Braves, and for the City of Atlanta. Home: 4171 Hair Lake Road Summerville GA 30747-6439 Office: Bill Locklear Custom Music 4171 Hair Lake Road Summerville GA 30747-6439 E-mail: mail@marchingbandmusic.com.

LOCKLEDGE, JACK E. retired principal; b. West Pittston, Pa., Oct. 6, 1928; s. Louis Frank Lockledge and Edna Mae Curnow; m. Mary Anne Potter, Aug. 10, 1957 (div. June 1984); children: David Evans, Jeffrey Carleton, Scott Potter. BA in Psychology, U. Ariz., 1954; BA in Fgn. Trade, Am. Inst. Fgn. Trade, 1955; MS in Edn., Hofstra U., 1960; student, Lehigh U., 1962-63; EdD, Nova U., 1982. Fgn. trade salesperson E.I. Dupont de Nemours, Wilmington, Del., 1955-56; tchr. Porterville (Calif.) Union H.S., 1956-57, Newbridge Rd. Sch., East Meadow, N.Y., 1958-61, Linden Sch., Doylestown, Pa., 1961-62, Hancock Elem. Sch., Norristown, 1962-63; prin. Ichabod Crane Ctrl. Schs., Kinderhook, N.Y., 1963-65, Highland (N.Y.) Ctrl. Sch., 1965-67, Canton (Pa.) Area Sch. Dist., 1967-86; headmaster St. Andrew's Elem. and Middle Sch., Annapolis, Md., 1986-91; ret., 1992. Founder Open Space Sch., 1968. With USN, 1946-49. NDEA Inst. Fgn. Langs. scholar Pa. State U., U. Knas., 1962, 63. Mem. Md. Child Care Assn. (legis. com.), Masons, Rotary (past pres.), Venice Opera Guild (grant officer), Lambda chpt. Phi Delta Epsilon (past pres.), Gamma Epsilon, Kappa Alpha (past pres.). Republican. Episcopalian. Avocations: hiking, swimming, opera, furniture refurbishing, painting and sculpting. Home: 225 Laurel Hollow Dr Nokomis FL 34275-4014 E-mail: jack@lockledge.com.

LOCKLEY, MARTIN G. geologist, educator; b. St. Helier, Jersey, United Kingdom, 1950; s. Ronald Mathias Lockley and Eileen Mary Gaudin Stocker; life ptnr. Mary Lynne Rossick; children: Peter, Katherine; children: , Gavdin, Katherine, , Thresa, Magguerite, Thresa. BCS Geocogy, Queens U., Belfast Northern IRELAND, 1970—74; Phd. Geocogy, Birmingham U., England, 1974—77. Post doctoral Glasgow, Scotland, England, 1977—80; rsch. U., England; prof. of geocogy U. of Colo., Denver, 1980. Founder mem. & bd. mem. Friends Of Dinosaur Ridge (501C), Morrison, Colo., 1889. Author: (book) Tracking Dinosaurs , Dinosaur Tracks , The Enternal Trail. Recipient Paeonrological Rsch., NSF, Western USA, 1987 TO 1997, Paleoncological Rsch., Nat. Geog. Sci., 1995. Home: 31110 Robinson Hill Road Golden CO 80403 Home Fax: 303-556-6197.

LOCKLIN, KENNETH ROBERT, international venture capitalist, merchant banker; b. N.Y.C., May 29, 1949; s. Wilbert Edwin and Olga Maria (Osterwald) L.; m. Helen D. Weiland, Sept. 10, 1983; children: Kayla Weiland, Connor Weiland. BA in Psychology and History, Yale U., 1972. Mgmt. trainee Hartford (Conn.) Nat. Bank, 1972-73, fin. analyst, 1973-74, sr. fin. analyst, 1974; v.p. project devel. Equator Bank Ltd., Hartford, 1974-81, v.p. corp. fin., 1982-83; exec. dir. Equator Adv. Svcs. Ltd., 1983-85; chief adminstr. officer Equator Holdings, Nassau, Bahamas, 1986; founder, mgr. Africa Growth Fund, L.P., Washington, 1987-91; pres. Advantage Fin. Svcs., Inc., Storrs, Conn., 1990-97; ptnr. EIF Group, Washington, 1997—; founder, mgr. Renewable Energy and Energy Efficiency Fund, 2000—. Sr. advisor, dir. environ. investment and fin. A.T. Internat., Washington, 1991-97; bd. dirs. Washington, Sch. for Field Studies, Boston, NESEA, Greenfield, Mass. Mem. Internat. Wilderness Leadership Found., Nature Conservancy, N.E. Sustainable Energy Assn., Club of 1000. Office: EIF Group Ste 200 2000 L St NW Washington DC 20036

LOCKLIN, WILBERT EDWIN, management consultant; b. Washington, Apr. 2, 1920; s. Wilbert Edwin and Margaret Mae (Franklin) L.; m. Olga Maria Osterwald, June 28, 1947; children: Kenneth, Patricia, Randall. BS, Johns Hopkins U., 1942; LLD, George Williams Coll., 1966; DHum, Springfield Coll., 1994. Vice-pres. Nat. Bur. Pvt. Schs., N.Y.C., 1947-49; account exec. Reuel Estill & Co., 1949-51; asst. dir. admissions Johns Hopkins, 1945-47, asst. to pres., 1955-65; v.p. Johns Hopkins Fund, 1960-65; pres. Springfield (Mass.) Coll., 1965-85, Locklin Mgmt. Services, 1985—. Chmn. bd. dirs., mem. exec. com., salary com., charitable funds com.; chmn. trust com. Bay Bank Valley Trust Co., 1966-91; mem. exec. com. Assn. Ind. Colls. and Univs. in Mass., 1971-83; founding mem. Cooperating Colls. of Greater Springfield.; pres. Cooperating Colls. of Greater Springfield, 1982-83; mem. exec. com., bd. dirs. Business Friends of Arts. Bd. dirs. Springfield Symphony Orch., 1973-83; campaign dir. Elms Coll., 1992-94; sr. advisor Mass. Soc. for Prevention of Cruelty to Animals, 1995-99, Loomis Communities, 1998—. Served with USAAF, 1942-45. Decorated DFC, Air medal. Home: # 7242 2400 S Ocean Dr Apt 7242 Fort Pierce FL 34949-8082 E-mail: welocklin@worldnet.att.net.

LOCKMAN, STUART M. lawyer; b. Jersey City, July 18, 1949; s. Albert Korey and Edna Sally (Easton) L.; m. Deena Laurel Young, Dec. 27, 1970; children: Jeffrey, Susan, Karen. BA, U. Mich., 1971, JD, 1974. Bar: Mich. 1974, Fla. 1991; bd. cert. health law specialist, Fla. Ptnr. Honigman Miller Schwartz and Cohn, Detroit, 1974—. Office: Honigman Miller Schwartz & Cohn 2290 1st National Bldg Detroit MI 48226 E-mail: sml@honigman.com.

LOCKNER, VERA JOANNE, farmer, rancher, legislator; b. St. Lawrence, S.D., May 19, 1937; d. Leonard and Zona R. (Ford) Verdugt; m. Frank O. Lockner, Aug. 7, 1955; children: Dean M., Clifford A. Grad., St. Lawrence (S.D.) High Sch., 1955. Bank teller/bookkeeper First Nat. Bank, Miller, S.D., 1963-66, Bank of Wessington, 1968-74; farmer/rancher Wessington, 1955-2000. Sunday sch. tchr. Trinity Luth. Ch., Miller, 1968-72; treas. PTO, Wessington, 1969-70; treas., vice chmn., chmn., state com. woman Hand County Dems., Miller, 1978—; mem. S.D. Dem. Exec. Bd., 1997-2000. Named one of Outstanding Young Women of Am., Women's Study Club, Wessington, 1970. Mem. Order of Ea. Star (warder, marshall, chaplain 1970—). Avocations: oil painting, crafts, gardening, photography. Home and Office: 301 3rd St NW Saint Lawrence SD 57373-2324

LOCKRIDGE, ALICE ANN, exercise physiologist; b. Gread Bend, Kans., Mar. 27, 1951; d. Richard Lee and Madeleine McMillan; m. Patrick Henry Lockridge, Jan. 1, 1988. AS, Pratt (Kans.) Community Coll., 1971; BS, U. Kans., 1973; MS in Phys. Edn., U. Wash., 1977. Cert. fitness instr. , phys. fitness specialist/trainer; accredited exam preparation trainer Am. Coun. on Exercise. Tchr. Kansas City (Kans.) Pub. Schs., 1973-74, Highline Pub. Sch. Dist., Seattle, 1974-76; fitness instr. Seattle Fire Dept., 1977-79; insvc. trainer various sch. dists., 1984—; prog. instr./health fitness technologist Renton (Wash.) Vocat. Tech. Inst., 1985-87; fitness instr. Apprenticeship and Non-Traditional Employment for Women, Renton, 1981-87; exercise physiologist Seattle City Light and Snohomish, 1988—; owner PRO-FIT, Renton, 1983—, Exercise Express, Renton, Wash., 1995—. Fitness cons. police dept., Seattle, 1991; testing cons. police, fire, electric and water depts., various cities, 1991; tchr. tng. lectr., various sch. dists., 1984—. Author: (book/study cards) PRO-FACTS, 1986, (edn. chart) Training Heart Rate Chart, 1983, (slide show series) Do It Right...Teach It Safe, 1985, (consumer edn. series) Never Exercise with a Jerk, 1990. Recipient Presdl. Sports awards, Presdl. Coun. on Phys. Fitness, 1978-86, Outstanding Support award Apprenticeship and Non-Traditional Employement for Women, 1988, Top-Ten Movers and Shapers award Seattle Times. Mem. IDEA, AAHPERD, Assn. for Fitness Profls. (com. mem.), Am. Coun. on Exercise (cert. com. 1986, cert. trainer of fitness instrs., accredited exam prep. trainer, 1989—), Wash. Alliance of Health, Physical Edn., Recreation and Dance, Nat. Speakers Assn. (Pacific N.W. chpt. bd. dirs. 1992-93), Nat. Dance Assn. (advocacy com.). Avocations: coaching rugby, weight lifting, walking, gardening. Office: PRO-FIT's Exercise Express 12012-156th Ave SE Renton WA 98059-6317 E-mail: alice@exercisexpress.com.

LOCKSHIN, MICHAEL DAN, rheumatologist; b. Columbus, Ohio, Dec. 9, 1937; s. Samuel Dan and Florence (Levin) L.; m. Jane Toby Roberts, Sept. 2, 1965; 1 child, Amanda. AB, Harvard U., 1959, MD, 1963. Diplomate Am. Bd. Internal Medicine. From asst. prof. to prof. Cornell U. Med. Coll., N.Y.C., 1970-89; attending physician Hosp. for Spl. Surgery and N.Y. Hosp., 1970-89; dir. extramural program Nat. Inst. Arthritis & Musculoskeletal Skin Diseases/NIH, Bethesda, Md., 1989-97, acting dir., 1994-95; dir. Barbara Volcker Ctr. Hosp. for Spl. Surgery, N.Y.C., 1997—. Prof. Cornell U. Med. Coll., N.Y.C., 1997—. Contbr. over 150 articles to jours., chpts. to books. Mem. Am. Rheumatism Assn. (2d v.p. 1984-85), La Sociedad Chilena de Reumatologica (hon.), Alpha Omega Alpha. Office: 535 E 70th St New York NY 10021-4872 E-mail: volckerctr@hss.edu.

LOCKSPEISER, NANCY FLANDERS, artist, designer; b. Boston, Oct. 9, 1941; d. Louis Hequembourg Flanders Jr. and Florence Lucille Reiter; m. Lester Lockspeiser, Oct. 3, 1969; children: Tai Mara, Brett Louis. BA, Cornell U., 1963; postgrad., U. Colo., 1972-73. Copywriter Cabot, Cabot & Forbes, Boston, 1963-69; copywriter, acting art dir. N.Y. State Urban Devel. Corp., N.Y.C., 1969-72; pub. rels., promotion Hugh Stubbins & Assocs., Cambridge, Mass., 1973-75; art dir., designer Children's Diabetes Found., Denver, 1976-92; prin. Lockspeiser Graphic Design, 1976—. Commd. print Dr. Henry Kissinger, 1979, Rocky Mountain Hebrew Acad., 1979, Ctrl. City Opera Ho. Assn., 1981, Nat. Multiple Schlerosis, 1989. Guest lectr. Denver Audubon Soc., 1977; mem. Denver Art Mus. Alliance Contemporary Art, 1978—, Guild Children's Diabetes Found., Denver, 1979—, Nat. Mus. Women Arts, 1981—; artist Denver Sister Cities Internat., 1998—, Arthritis Found., Nat. Multiple Schlerosis. Recipient Halo award Denver Advt. Fedn., 1997. Mem. Acad. Am. Poets. Home and Office: 770 Lafayette St Denver CO 80218-3503

LOCKTON, DAVID BALLARD, business executive; b. Indpls., Mar. 28, 1937; s. Richard Curtis and Violet (Ballard) L.; m. Mary Shullenberger, Aug. 1961 (div. Dec. 1969); children: Jennifer Anne Barker, Mary Wendell; m. Kathy Austin, Apr. 3, 1971; 1 child, Richard A. BA, Yale U., 1959; JD, U. Va.,

1962; postgrad., Stanford U., 1972. Ptnr. Lockton and Scopelitis, Inc., Indpls., 1965-70; founder, pres., chief exec. officer Ontario (Calif.) Motor Speedway, 1968-71; chief exec. off., publisher, owner Calif. Bus. Mag., L.A., 1972-75; pres., chief exec. officer Lola Grand Prix, Ltd., 1976-79; founder, chief exec. officer Data Broadcasting, Inc., San Mateo, Calif., 1980-85; chmn., founder, CEO Interactive Network, Inc., 1986-99; pres. Lockton Ventures, 1996—; bus. adv. coun. U. Va. Law Sch., 1997—. Co-founder, bd. dirs. A.Z.L. Resources, Inc., 1964-75; creator, developer Internat. Race of Champions (IROC) TV Racing Series, 1972—, co-founder, chmn. Repair Shop Systems, Inc., 1986; nationwide lectr. on entrepreneurship and info. tech. Patentee in interactive TV and wireless data. Dir. U.S. Auto Club, 1967-70. Recipient Meritorious Svc. award Soc. Automotive Engrs., 1970. Mem. Jonathan Club (L.A.), Crooked Stick Golf Club (co-founder) (Indpls.), Carmel Valley Ranch, Penrod Soc. (co-founder, Indpls.). Republican. Episcopalian. Avocations: jazz piano, golf. Office: Lockton Ventures Suite 389 225 Cross Roads Blvd Carmel CA 93923-8649

LOCKWOOD, FRANK JAMES, manufacturing company executive; b. San Bernadino, Calif., Oct. 30, 1931; s. John Ellis and Sarah Grace (Roberts) L.; children from previous marraige: Fay, Frank, Hedy, Jonnie, George, Katherine, Bill, Dena; m. 2d. Crystal Marie Miller, 1986. Student, Southeast City Coll., Chgo., 1955, Ill. Inst. Tech., 1963-64, Bogan Jr. Coll., Chgo., 1966. Foreman Hupp Aviation, Chgo., 1951-60; dept. head UARCO, Inc., 1960-68; pres. XACT Machine & Engring., 1968—. Chmn. bd., pres., bd. dirs. Lockwood Engring., Inc., Chgo.; Ill. Nat. Corp., Chgo., and cons. engr., Chgo. Patentee printing equipment, beverage cans, gasoline pump dispenser "Super Pin", bus. forms equipment. Participant Forest Land Mgmt. Program; mem. Ill. Ambassadors; commr. Econ. Devel. Commn., Mt. Vernon, Ill., 1985; mem. bd. County of Jefferson, Ill., 1992—; mem. exec. com., legis. com. Ill. County Bds. Coun. Named Chgo. Ridge Father of the Yr., 1964. Mem. Ill. Divers' Assn. (pres. 1961-62). Lodges: Masons (32 degree), Shriners (past master 2). Home: RR 1 Texico IL 62889-9801 Office: 7011 W Archer Ave Chicago IL 60638-2201

LOCKWOOD, GARY LEE, lawyer; b. Woodstock, Ill., Dec. 3, 1946; s. Howard and Luella Mae (Behrens) L.; m. Cheryl Lynn Wittrock, Jan. 5, 1967; children: Jennifer, Lee, Cynthia. BA magna cum laude, Iowa Wesleyan Coll., 1969; student, Albert Ludwig U., Freiburg in Breisgau, Fed. Republic Germany, 1968-69; JD, Northwestern U., 1976. Bar: Ill. 1976, U.S. Dist. Ct. (no. dist.) Ill. 1976, U.S. Ct. Appeals (7th cir.) 2000. Assoc. Lord, Bissell & Brook, Chgo., 1976-85, ptnr., 1985—. Bd. dirs. McHenry Sch. Dist. 15, Ill., 1974-85, pres., 1979-80. Served to sgt. U.S. Army, 1970-72. Mem. ABA (bus. and ins. com. 1985—). Methodist. Avocations: sports. Home: 333 N Canal St Chicago IL 60606 Office: Lord Bissel & Brook 115 S La Salle St Fl 3600 Chicago IL 60603-3902 E-mail: glockwoo@lordbissell.com.

LOCKWOOD, HELSHI, advertising executive; b. East Orange, N.J., May 18, 1941; d. Warren Sewell and Ann Frances (Gleason) L.; m. Bertram A. Tunnell Jr., Dec. 13, 1969 (div. Oct. 1976); children: Bertram A. III, Tory Lockwood; stepchildren: John, Mark, Tracy, Wendy, Jan, Kate; m. William B. Hewson Jr., May 30, 1981; 1 child, Charles W.; stepchildren: William B. III, Andrew L., Elizabeth S. BA, Pa. State U., 1963. Promotion asst. Vogue Mag., London, 1963-64; advt. sales rep. Brides Mag., 1964-65; west coast mgr. Status Mag., L.A., 1965-67, asst. advt. mgr. N.Y.C., 1968-69; advt. sales rep. Eye Mag., 1967-68; N.Y. mgr. Phil. and Boston Mags., 1969-76; v.p. Metro Mag., 1976-78; exec. v.p., ptnr. Catalyst Communications, 1978-80; account mgr. Dun's Rev., 1980-82; ea. advt. dir. Dun's Bus. Month, 1982-84, advt. dir., 1984-85; dir. nat. accounts Chgo. Mag., 1986; ea. advt. mgr. Mediatex Nat. Sales, 1987-88, v.p., nat. sales dir., 1989-94, v.p., mng. dir., 1994-98; pres. Emmis Pub. Nat. Sales (acquired by Emmis Comm.), 1998—. Deacon Brick Ch., N.Y.C., 1983. Mem. Advt. Women N.Y. Republican. Presbyterian. Home: 8 Hanson Rd Darien CT 06820-2502 Office: Emmis Publ Nat Sales 60 E 42d St Ste 1103 New York NY 10165

LOCKWOOD, JOANNE SMITH, mathematician educator; b. Quebec City, Can., Nov. 9, 1946; d. Donald William MacKay and Sylvia Eleanor (Howard) Smith; m. Bryce M. Lockwood Jr., Aug. 10, 1968; children: Daren MacKay, Keith McLellan. BA in English, St. Lawrence U., 1968; MBA, Plymouth State Coll., 1980, BA in Math., 1985. Editor Houghton Mifflin Co., Boston, 1969-86; tchr. New Hampton (N.H.) Sch., 1974-76, 80-81; lectr. Plymouth (N.H.) State Coll., 1988—. Author: (textbooks) Beginning Algebra with Applications, 1989, 92, 96, Intermediate Algebra with Applications, 1989, 92, 96, Business Mathematics, 1988, 94, Introductory Algebra with Basic Mathematics, 1989, 96, Algebra with Trigonometry for College Students, 1991, A Review of Geometry, 1993, Prealgebra, 1994, Algebra for College Students: A Functions Approach, 1994. Mem. Am. Math. Assn. of Two Yr. Colls., Text and Acad. Authors Assn. Home: RR 1 Box 180 New Hampton NH 03256-9717

LOCKWOOD, JOHN LEBARON, plant pathologist, educator; b. Ann Arbor, Mich., May 28, 1924; s. George LeBaron and Mary Bonita (Leininger) L.; m. Jean Elizabeth Springborg, Mar. 21, 1959; children: James L., Laura A. Student, Western Mich. Coll., 1941-43; BA, Mich. State Coll., 1948, MS, 1950; PhD, U. Wis., 1953. Asst. prof. Ohio Agrl. Expt. Sta., Wooster, 1953-55, Mich. State U., East Lansing, 1955-61, assoc. prof., 1961-67, prof., 1967-90, prof. emeritus, 1990—. Served with U.S. Army, 1943-46 NSF research fellow, 1970-71. Fellow Am. Phytopathol. Soc. (pres. 1984-85).

LOCKWOOD, MARY KATHERINE KAFOGLIS, zoology educator, physiology consultant; b. Columbus, Ohio, June 28, 1955; d. Milton Z. Kafoglis and Madelyn McClintock Lockhart; m. James Wayne Lockwood, Sept. 5, 1981; children: Andrew, Meredith. BS in Biology, Davidson Coll., 1977; MS in Physiology, Pa. State U., 1981; PhD in Biol. Nutrition, UCLA, 1989. Technician Pa. State U., University Park, 1977-80; rsch. specialist U. Fla., Gainesville, 1980-81; rsch. assoc. Emory U., Atlanta, 1981-84; tech. assoc. UCLA, 1984-88, instr., 1985-87, Rivier Coll., Nashua, N.H., 1990-94, U. N.H., Durham, 1994—. Cons. McGraw-Hill, Dubuque, Iowa, 1997—, MKK Lockwood, Pathophysiologist, Amherst, N.H., 1998—. Contbr. articles to profl. jours. EMT-intermediate Amherst Rescue Squad, 1988—; leader Girl Scouts-Swiftwater Coun., N.H., 1996-2001; active Libr. Friends Bd., Amherst Town Libr., 1996-2001; co-chair PTA, Amherst, 2000-01. Proctor-Gamble Rsch. grantee Am. Inst. Nutrition, 1987, Gladys Emerson Rsch. grantee UCLA, 1988. Mem. World Assn. Girl Scouts Girl Guides, Amherst Rescue Assn., Sigma Xi. Avocation: needlework. Home: 11 Roberge Dr Amherst NH 03031 Office: Dept Zoology Univ NH Durham NH 03824 E-mail: mkkl@cisunix.unh.edu.

LOCKWOOD, RHONDA J. mental health services professional; b. Jacksonville, N.C., Apr. 4, 1960; d. George Barton and Sally Lynn (Hassell) L. BA, Newberry Coll., 1982; MS in Edn., Youngstown State U., 1988. nat. cert. counselor. Corrections/tng. officer Geauga County Sheriff's Dept., Chardon, Ohio, 1982-87; forensic counselor Human Svcs. Ctrs., Inc., New Castle, Pa., 1987-89; dir. children & family svcs. Marion Citrus Mental Health Ctrs., Inc., Ocala, Fla., 1989-96; clin. social worker Fla. Dept. Juvenile Justice, Alachua Halfway House, 1996-97; coord. TANF/Interface Youth Program Corner Drug Store, Inc., Gainesville, Fla., 1997—. Co-founder Sexual Abuse Intervention Network, Ocala, 1990-96, chair, 1990-92, Family Svcs. Planning Team, 1992-94; cons. Health & Human Svcs. Bd. Dist. 13, 1993-96; mem. Eckerd Youth Comprehensive Treatment Program adv. bd., 1997-99; adj. fculty Webster U., Ocala campus, 1999—. Pol. vol. state campaigns Dem. Party, Warren, Ohio, 1978-85; mem. Sexual Abuse Prevention Edn. Network, New Castle, 1987-88; cons. to gov.'s task force Sex Offenders and Their Victims; cons. Mad Dads Orgn., Ocala, 1993; mem. Juvenile Justice Coun., Ocala, 1993-94; mem. Hamilton, Lafayette, Suwannee and Columbia Counties Juvenile Justice Couns., 1997—; children's svc. rep. Fla. Coun. for Cmty. Mental Health, 1995-96; instr. counselor edn. program, Webster U., Ocala, Fla., 1998—. Recipient Outstanding Teen Vol. award Am. Red Cross, 1977. Fellow N. Eastern Ohio Police Benevolent Assn.; mem. Nat. Mus. for Women in the Arts, Nat. Bd. Cert. Counselors, NGLTF, Ind. Prodr. Womens Music, Human Rights Campaign Fund, Chi Sigma Iota, Phi Kappa Phi. Democrat. Avocations: softball, volleyball, golf, fishing. Home: 201 E Main St Archer FL 32618-5517

LOCKWOOD, ROBERT W. management consultant; b. Boise, Idaho, June 11, 1924; s. Walter Thomas and Elizabeth C. (Chamberlain) L.; m. Lois M. Minely, Feb. 19, 1945; children— Linda Kay Lockwood Johnson, Craig H. BS, U. Calif., Berkeley, 1949, MBA, 1950; LL.D. (hon.), Northrop U., 1971. Civilian chief mgmt. Los Angeles procurement dist. U.S. Army, 1955-56; cons. Booz Allen and Hamilton, Los Angeles, 1956-58; v.p. United Calif. Bank, 1958-75; v.p. acad. affairs Northrop U., 1975-76; asst. to pres. Bradston Hurricane, 1979-80; pres. Diversified Baby Products Internat., West Covina, Calif., 1980—. Grad. prof. mgmt. Northrop U., Nat. U., San Diego. Served to 1st lt. USAR, 1942-45. Fellow Am. Inst. Indsl. Engrs. (pres. 1971-72) Clubs: Masons.

LOCKWOOD, THEODORE DAVIDGE, former academic administrator; b. Hanover, N.H., Dec. 5, 1924; s. Harold John and Elizabeth (Van Campen) L.; m. Elizabeth Anne White, Apr. 13, 1944 (dec. Feb. 1980); children: Tamara Jane Lockwood Quinn, Richard Davidge, Mavis Ferens Borak, Serena Katherine; m. Lucille LaRose Abbot, Sept. 7, 1980. BA, Trinity Coll., 1948, Litt.D. (hon.), 1981; MA, Princeton, 1950, PhD, 1952; L.H.D., Concord Coll., 1968; LL.D., Union Coll., 1968, U. Hartford, 1969; L.H.D., Wesleyan U., Middletown, Conn., 1970. Instr. great issues Dartmouth, 1952-53; asst. prof. history Juniata Coll., Huntingdon, Pa., 1953-55, Mass. Inst. Tech., 1955-60; dean faculty Concord Coll., Athens, W.Va., 1960-64; provost, dean faculty Union Coll., Schenectady, 1964-68; pres. Trinity Coll., Hartford, Conn., 1968-81, Armand Hammer United World Coll. of Am. West, Montezuma, N.Mex., 1981-93. Chmn. Greater Hartford Consortium for Higher Edn., 1972-81 Author: Mountaineers, 1945, Studies in European Socialism, 1960, Our Mutual Concern: The Role of the Independent College, 1968, Dreams and Promises: The Story of the Armand Hammer United World College, 1997. Bd. dirs. Vols. Internat. Tech. Assistance, 1965-85, chmn., 1966-71; Bd. fellows Trinity Coll., 1962-64, trustee, 1964-81; corporator Hartford Hosp., 1978-81, Hartford Pub. Libr., 1969-81; bd. dirs. Inst. for Living, 1969-81, Edn. Commn. of States, 1969-71, Am. Coun. on Edn., 1977-81; trustee Northwood Sch., Lake Placid, N.Y., 1969-78; dir. adv. coun. Audubon Soc. Expdn. Inst., 1978-90; bd. dirs. Harry Frank Guggenheim Found., 1979—, Nepal adv. com. World Wildlife Fund, 1985-95; dir. Ars Publica, 1989-95. With U.S. Army, 1943-45. Belgian-Am. Fellow, 1959 Mem. Assn. Am. Colls. (dir. 1973-78, chmn. 1976-77, mem. project on undergrad. edn. 1981-85), Greater Hartford C. of C. (dir. 1977-81), Phi Beta Kappa, Pi Gamma Mu. Unitarian Universalist. E-mail: luted@together.net.

LOCKYER, BILL, state attorney general; b. Oakland, Calif., May 8, 1941; 1 child Lisa. BA in Polit. Sci., U. Calif., Berkeley; cert. in sec. tchg., Calif. State U., Hayward; JD, U. of the Pacific. Past tchr., San Leandro, Calif.; Mem. Calif. State Assembly, 1973; state senator State of Calif., 1982; pres. pro tem, chmn. senate rules com., chmn. senate jud. com. Calif. State Senate, 1994—98; atty. gen. State of Calif., 1999—. Active San Leandro Sch. Bd., 1968—73. Past chair Alameda County Dem. Ctrl. Com. Named Legislator of Yr., Planning and Conservation League, 1996, Calif. Jour., 1997. Office: Office Atty Gen Dept Justice PO Box 944255 Sacramento CA 94244-2550*

LOCKYER, CHARLES WARREN, JR. corporate executive; b. Phila., Apr. 6, 1944; s. Charles Warren and Mary Alice (Underwood) L.; m. Karen A. Damiani, Jan. 22, 1966; children: Charles Warren III, Larissa A., Daphne M. BA, Fordham U., 1966; MA, Princeton U., 1968, PhD, 1971; JD, Georgetown U., 1995. V.p. Fidelity Bank, Phila., 1970-79; v.p., chief fin. officer Pubco Corp., Glenn Dale, Md., 1980-82; exec. v.p. Perpetual Savs. Bank, F.S.B., Alexandria, Va., 1982-90; pres. Alleco Inc., Cheverly, Md., 1991—95; assoc. Fred, Frank, Harris, Schriver & Jacobson, Washington, 1996—. Dir. Gulfstream Land & Devel. Corp., Plantation, Fla., 1980-86. Trustee Jeanes Hosp., Phila., 1973-87; dir. Foulkeways at Gwynedd, Pa., 1975-80; mem. adv. com. classics Princeton U., 1978-83. Woodrow Wilson fellow, 1966. Mem. Phi Beta Kappa. Home: 4409 Glenridge St Kensington MD 20895-4255 Office: Fried Frank Harris Schriver & Jacobson 1001 Pennsylvania Ave NW Washington DC 20004-2505 E-mail: lockych@ffhsj.com.

LOCSIN, ENRIQUE LOPEZ, company executive; b. Manila, Jan. 28, 1946; s. Teodoro M. and Rosario (Lopez) L.; m. Susan Romualdez. Student, Letran Coll., Manila, La Salle Coll., Bacolod City and Manila, Asian Inst. Mgmt., Makati City, The Philippines, Alexander Hamilton Inst. Pres., gen. mgr. Philippines Free Press, The Philippines, 1986—, LR Publs., Inc., The Philippines, 1988—; pres. El Crown Merchant, Inc., The Philippines, 1997—, Today Newspaper, The Philippines, 1999. Agt. Nat. Bur. Investigation, Manila. Mem. Makati Sports Club, Alabang Country Club, Manila Club. Avocations: golfing, football, bowling. Office: Unit D-2 2d FL DPSI Bus Ctr 210 Nicanor Garcia St Bel-Air Makati Philippines E-mail: freepress@epic.net.

LODDE, GORDON MAYNARD, health physics consultant; b. Lafayette, Ind., Aug. 19, 1933; s. Herman Morris and Eva Grace (Robinson) Lodde; m. Nancy Jean Caldwell, Aug. 21, 1955; children: Gordon A., Bruce C., Melissa J. BS, Purdue Univ., 1958; MS, Univ. Rochester, 1964. Health physist U.S. Army, 1959-79; health physics cons. Porter Cons., Ardmore, Pa., 1979-84; cons. engr. GPU Nuclear, Middletown, 1984-94; health physics cons. Mt. Joy, 1994—. Contbr. Scoutmaster Boy Scouts Am., White Sands, N.Mex., 1967—70, Edgewood, Md., 1975—79, post adv., 1976—80. With Med. Svc. Corp U.S. Army, 1959—79. Decorated Commendation medal with two oak leaf clusters, , Legion of Merit; recipient Merit award, Boy Scouts Am., 1976, Silver Beaver award, 1978. Mem.: N.Y. Acad. Scis., Am. Assn. Physicists in Medicine, Am. Indsl. Hygiene Assn., Am. Conf. of Gov. Hygienists, Am. Nuc. Soc., Health Physics Soc. Home and Office: 742 Ferndale Rd Mount Joy PA 17552-9384

LODDER, ROBERT ANDREW, chemistry and pharmaceutics educator; b. Cin., May 31, 1959; BS, Xavier U., Cin., 1981, MS, 1983; PhD, Ind. U., 1988. Teaching asst. Xavier U., 1981-83, Ind. U., Bloomington, 1983-85, rsch. asst., 1985-87; asst. prof. chemistry and pharmaceutics U. Ky., Lexington, 1988-94, assoc. prof., 1994—. Contbr. articles to profl. jours.; patentee in field. Recipient 100 award R & D mag., 1988, Tomas Hirschfeld award Pitts. Conf., 1988; 1st prize IBM Supercomputing Competition, 1990, NSF New Young Investigator award 1992, Paper award ASAE, 1993, Buchi NIR award, 2001; Technicon near-infrared analysis rsch. fellow, 1987. Mem. AAAS, ASTM, Coun. for Near-Infrared Spectroscopy (del.-at-large to nat. bd. dirs.), Am. Chem. Soc., Am. Assn. Pharm. Scientists, Am. Pharm. Assn., Ky. Acad. Sci. Office: U Ky Coll Pharmacy Rose St Lexington KY 40536-0001

LODER, JOHN MARK, lawyer; b. Minot, N.D., Sept. 22, 1958; s. LeRoy Albert and Ann Louise (Hennes) L.; m. Elizabeth Janet Wentz, June 1, 1985; children: Thomas A., Stephen A.C. AB, Harvard U., 1980, JD, 1983. Bar: Mass., 1985. Law clk. Judge Myron H. Bright U.S. Ct. Appeals (8th Cir.), Fargo, N.D., 1983-84; assoc. Ropes & Gray, Boston, 1984-92, ptnr., 1992—. Avocations: mountain biking, music. Home: 36 Marsh St Dedham MA 02026-4306 Office: Ropes & Gray 1 International Pl Boston MA 02110-2624 E-mail: jloder@ropesgray.com.

LODER, RANDALL THOMAS, orthopedic surgeon; b. Lincoln, Nebr., Aug. 12, 1954; s. Ervin Lee and Dorothy Johanna Loder; m. Christine Ann Loder, Aug. 10, 1985; children: Andrew, Wendy, David. BA, U. Colo., 1976; MD, Washington U., 1980. Diplomate Am. Bd. Orthopedic Surgery. Asst. prof. Med. Coll. Ohio, Toledo, 1986-87, Wayne State U., Detroit, 1987-90; asst. prof., then assoc. prof. U. Mich., Ann Arbor, 1990-99; chief of staff Shriners Hosp., Mpls., 1999—. Mem. question task force Am. Bd. Orthpedic Surgery, mem. written exam. com., 1996—. Mem. editl. bd. Jour. Pediat. Orthopedics, 1996—; contbr. articles to sci. and profl. jours. Fellow Am. Acad. Pediats. (exec. com. 1996—); mem. Pediat. and Orthopedic Soc. N.Am. (rsch. dir. 1993-96, Best Paper award 1999), Am. Acad. Orthopedic Surgeons (editor 1996-99), Southview C.C., Alpha Omega Alpha. Avocations: hiking, photography, stamp collecting. Office: Shriners Hosp for Children 2025 East River Pkwy Minneapolis MN 55414

LODER, VICTORIA KOSIOREK, information broker; b. Batavia, N.Y., May 27, 1945; d. Leon Stanley and Jennie Joann (Amatrano) Kosiorek; m. Ronald Raymond Loder, Nov. 6, 1965. BS in Bus. Mgmt., Roberts-Wesleyan Coll., Rochester, N.Y., 1989; MLS, SUNY, Buffalo, 1992; postgrad. in Religious Study, Liberty U., 1993—; postgrad., Faith Bible Bapt. Coll., 1999—2001. Tech. info. specialist Eastman Kodak Co., Rochester, 1985-92; reference libr. Xerox Corp., Webster, N.Y., 1993-95, mgr. XPS strategy and integration libr. Fairport, 1995-97, mgr. PSG Strategy and Bus. Info. Resource Ctr., 1997-99. V.p., treas. Victron Design Svc. USA, Kent, N.Y., 1988—; pres., owner Alpha Omega Info Source, Kent, N.Y., 1993—. Avocations: clothing design/construction, horticulture/landscape design, floral design.

LODEWICK, PHILIP HUGHES, equipment leasing company executive; b. Bklyn., Dec. 31, 1944; s. Robert John and Louise Mary (Bockhold) L.; m. Christine Helen Lobeck, July 5, 1969; children: Alyssa Erin, Kendra Blythe. BS, U. Conn., 1966, MBA, 1967. With sales dept. IBM Corp., N.Y.C., 1969-71; officer Boothe Fin. Corp., San Francisco, 1971-80; pres. The Tradewell Corp., equipment leasing co., Ridgefield, Conn., 1980—. Gen. ptnr. Sierra Assoc. IV, San Francisco, 1981-88; CFO Wicklo's Maple Hill Farm, Ridgefield, 1983—; bd. dirs. Ancora Coffee Roasters Inc., U. Conn. Found., Project Graphics, Inc.; bd. overseers U. Conn. Bus. Sch.; chmn. bd. trustees U. Conn. Found. Trustee U. Conn. Found.; bd. dirs. St. Andrew's Luth. Ch., Ridgefield, 1979—; mem. Conn. Refugee Resettlement Commn., 1985-88; bd. dirs., treas. Family Y in Ridgefield, 1985-89; founder, dir. Discovery Ctr., 1986—; founder, pres. A Better Chance in Ridgefield, 1987—; founding dir. Internat. Forgiveness Inst., Madison, Wis. With AUS, 1967-69, Korea. Mem. Computer Lessors and Dealers Assn., Golden Bridge Hounds, L.I. Golden Retreiver Club (pres. 1979-80), Golf Club on the Internet (bd. dirs.). Republican. Lutheran. Avocations: golf, tennis, basketball, travel, reading. Home and Office: Tradewell Corp 201 Spring Valley Rd Ridgefield CT 06877-1229

LODGE, ARTHUR SCOTT, mechanical engineering educator; b. Waterloo, Lancashire, Eng., Nov. 20, 1922; s. Wilfred Claude and Jean Dea (Scott) L.; m. Helen Catherine Bannatyne, July 18, 1945; children: Keith Bannatyne, Alison Mary Shambrook, Timothy Patrick. BA, U. Oxford, 1945, MA, D.Phil., U. Oxford, 1948. Jr. sci. officer Admiralty, Eng., 1942-45; theoretical physicist NRC, Montreal, Que., Can., 1945-46, Brit. Rayon Research Assn., Manchester, Eng., 1948-60; sr. lectr. Math Inst. Sci. and Tech., U. Manchester, 1961-68; prof. dept. engring. mechanics U. Wis., Madison, 1968-91, Hougen vis. prof., 1991, prof. emeritus, 1991—; v.p. Bannatek Co., Inc., 1981—2001. Author: Elastic Liquids, 1964 (citation classics award 1981), Body Tensor Fields..., 1974, An Introduction to Elastomer Molecular Network Theory, 1999; contbr. articles to profl. jours.; patentee stressmeter. Recipient Byron Bird award U. Wis.-Madison, 1980; grantee U.S. govt. agys. Fellow Inst. Physics London; mem. NAE, Soc. Rheology (Bingham medal 1971), Brit. Soc. Rheology (Gold medal 1983). Republican. Episcopalian. Avocation: piano playing. E-mail: aslodge@facstaff.wisc.edu.

LODGE, EDWARD JAMES, federal judge; b. 1933; BS cum laude, Coll. Idaho, 1957; JD, U. Idaho, 1961. With Smith & Miller, 1962-63; probate judge Canyon County, Idaho, 1963-65; judge Idaho State Dist. Ct., 1965-88; U.S. bankruptcy judge State of Idaho, 1988—89; dist. judge, chief judge U.S. Dist. Ct. Idaho, 1989—. Mem. Ninth Cir. Jud. Coun., 1997-98; chair Chief Dist. Judges for Ninth Cir., 1998-99. Recipient Kramer award for excellence in jud. adminstrn., award of legal merit U. Idaho Law Sch., 2000; named three time All-Am., disting. alumnus Coll. Idaho, Boise State U., Professionalism award Idaho State Bar, 1997; named to Hall of Fame Boise State U., Coll. Idaho. Mem. Idaho Trial Lawyer Assn., Idaho State Bar Assn. (Professionalism award 1997), U.S. Fed. Judges Assn., Boise State Athletic Assn., Elks Club. Office: US Dist Ct MSC 040 550 W Fort St Fl 6 Boise ID 83724-0101

LODGE, GEORGE C(ABOT), business administration educator; b. Boston, July 7, 1927; s. Henry Cabot Jr. and Emily (Sears) L.; m. Nancy Kunhardt, Apr. 23, 1949 (dec. Feb. 1997); children: Nancy Lodge Burmeister, Emily Lodge Pingeon, Dorothy Lodge Peabody, Henry, George Jr., David; m. Susan Alexander Powers, Aug. 2, 1997. AB cum laude, Harvard U., 1950; hon. doctorate, INCAE, 1994. Polit. reporter, columnist Boston Herald, 1950-54; dir. info. U.S. Dept. Labor, Washington, 1954-58, asst. sec. labor for internat. affairs, 1958-61, U.S. del. to ILO, chmn. governing body, 1960-61; lectr. Grad. Sch. Bus. Adminstr., Harvard U., Boston, 1961-68, assoc. prof., 1968-72, prof. bus. adminstrn., 1972-91, Jaime and Josefina Chua Tiampo prof. bus. adminstrn., 1991-98, prof. emeritus, 98—. Author: Spearheads of Democracy: Labor in the Developing Countries, 1962, Engines of Change: United States Interests and Revolution in Latin America, 1970, The New American Ideology, 1975 (Ann. Book award Am. Acad. Mgmt. 1995), The American Disease, 1984, Perestroika for America, 1990, Comparative Business-Government Relations, 1990, Managing Globalization in the Age of Interdependence, 1995; co-author: Ideology and National Competitiveness, 1987; editor: U.S. Competitiveness in the World Economy, 1984. Rep. candidate U.S. Senate, Mass., 1962; vice-chmn. Inter-Am. Found., 1970-77. With USN, 1945-46. Named one of 10 Outstanding Youn Men in U.S., U.S. Jr. C. of C., 1961; recipient Arthur S. Fleming award, 1961, McKinsey award Harvard Bus. Rev., 1970, 74, Disting. Svc. award Harvard Bus. Sch., 2001; Lee Kuan Yew fellow Gov. of Singapore, 1991. Mem. Coun. Fgn. Rels., Carnegie Endowment for Internat. Peace (emeritus trustee), Robert F. Kennedy Meml. (trustee). Office: Harvard U Bus Sch Soldiers Fld Boston MA 02163-1317 E-mail: glodge@hbs.edu.

LODGE, HENRY SEARS, physician; b. Oct. 20, 1958; BA, U. Pa., 1981; MD, Columbia U., 1985. Diplomate Am. Bd. Internal Medicine. Intern Columbia U. Presbyterian Med. Ctr., N.Y.C., residency; attending physician N.Y. Presbyterian Hosp., 1988—; asst. clin. prof. Coll. Physicians and Surgeons Columbia U., N.Y.C., 1989—; pvt. practice specializing internal medicine and prevention. Chmn., CEO N.Y. Physicians LLP; past pres. Presbyn. Hosp. Alumni Assn., N.Y. Clin. Soc., Soc. Practitioners of Columbia Presbyn. Med. Ctr. Mem. Am. Coll. Physicians. Office: 635 Madison Ave New York NY 10022-1009

LODHA, ANURAG, chemical engineer; b. Calcutta, Mar. 23, 1975; came to U.S., 1998; s. Vimal Chand and Saroj Lodha. BSChemE with honors, Regional Engring. Coll., Jaipur, India, 1996; MSChemE, Clemson U., 2000. Intern Karnataka Soaps and Detergents Ltd., Bangalore, India, 1994, Tata Chems. Ltd., Jamnagar, India, 1995; rsch. fellow Indian Inst. Tech., Bombay, 1996-98; officer Essar Investments Ltd., 1998; grad. rsch. asst. dept. chem. engring. Clemson (S.C.) U., 1998-2000; adv. mfg. engr. Seagate Tech., Bloomington, Minn., 2000—. Contbr. articles to profl. jours. Vol. Indian Inst. Tech., 1996-97. Recipient Best Paper award U. Roorkee, 1996. Mem. IEEE. Avocations: cricket, tennis, reading, philosophy. Office: Seagate Tech 1 Disc Dr Bloomington MN 55435 E-mail: anurag.lodha@seagate.com.

LODI, EDWARD, writer, publisher; b. Wareham, Mass., June 24, 1943; s. Edward John and Mary Louise L.; m. Yolanda Lodi, Sept. 15, 1996. B, Boston U., 1965, M, 1968. Instr. Shaw U., Raleigh, N.C., 1967-70, Mass. Maritime Acad., Buzzards Bay, 1972-74. Spkr. in field. Author: Deep Meadow Bog, 1999, Shapes That Haunt New England, 2000, Cranberry Chronicles, 2000, Murder on the Bogs, 2001, Haunters of the Dusk, 2001, Cranberry Gothic, 2002. Avocations: wildlife conservation, gardening. Home: 41 Walnut St Middleborough MA 02346 Office: Rock Village Pub 41 Walnut St Middleborough MA 02346

LODICO, CHERYL MADELINE, secondary education educator; b. Bklyn., Aug. 24, 1944; d. Philip and Helen (Kutner) Miller; m. Nicholas Joseph Micucci, Feb. 13, 1969 (dec. Aug. 1987); m. Emanuel Joseph Lodico, Jan. 15, 1989; stepchildren: Diana Lynn, William Maurice. BA, Cortland State Coll., 1966; MS in Edn. in English, Queens Coll., 1971. Permanent cert. to teach English grades 7-12. English tchr. grade 9 Jerusalem Ave. Jr. H.S. North Bellmore, L.I., N.Y., 1966; English tchr. grades 7, 8, 9, also grade 6 gifted Lawrence Middle Sch., 1966-96; ret., 1996; tchr. ECC Acad., Bayside, N.Y., 1997-98; writer, 1998—. Sponsor, editor Creative Writing Club. Contbr. articles to profl. jours.; author of poetry. Mem. Nat. Coun. Tchrs. English. E-mail: lc2345567. Home: 14712 15th Dr Whitestone NY 11357-2509

LODISH, LEONARD MELVIN, marketing educator, entrepreneur; b. Cleve., Aug. 1, 1943; s. Nathan H. and Sylvia (Friedman) L.; m. Susan Joyce Fischer, July 11, 1965; children: Max, Jacob, Chaim. AB magna cum laude, Kenyon Coll., 1965, LLD (hon.), 1999; PhD, MIT, 1968. Asst. prof. mktg. U. Pa., Phila., 1968-71, assoc. prof., 1971-75, prof. mktg., 1975-87, chmn. mktg. dept., 1991-92., 1984-88, Samuel R. Harrell prof., 1988—, vice dean Wharton West, 2001—; founding dir. Evergreen Health Group, Inc., 1984-91; founder, chmn. The Wharton Global Cons. Practicum, 1995—. Bd. dirs. Info. Resources, Inc., Chgo., Franklin Electronic Pub. Inc., Mt. Holly, N.J., J&J Snack Foods, Inc., Pennsauken, N.J.; co-founder, prin. Mgmt. Decisions Sys., Inc.,

Waltham, Mass., 1967-85; co-founder, dir. Shadow Broadcast Svcs., Bala Cynwyd, Pa., 1991-98. Author: The Advertising and Promotion Challenge: Vaguely Right or Precisely Wrong?, 1986, Entrepreneurial Marketing: Lessons from Wharton's Pioneering MBA Course, 2001; mem. editl. bd. Mgmt. Sci., Jour. Mktg. Sci., Jour. Advt. Rsch., Jour. Personal Selling and Sales Mgmt.; contbr. articles to profl. jours. Pres. Temple Beth Hillel/Beth El, Wynnewood, Pa., 1983-85, bd. dirs. 1975-98, 99, trustee, 1995—. Recipient Odell award for best impact article, 2000. Mem. Inst. Mgmt. Scis. (Franz Edelman award 1987), Ops. Research Soc. Am., Am. Mktg. Assn. (winner 1st Paul E. Green award 1996), Phi Beta Kappa. Jewish. Home: 301 Kent Rd Wynnewood PA 19096-1814 Office: U Pa Wharton Sch Dept Mktg Philadelphia PA 19104

LODOWSKI, CHARLES ALAN, business association executive; b. Dallas, May 10, 1945; s. Charles Harry and Genevieve (Gowaty) L.; m. Patricia Anne Snead, May 27, 1967; children: Charles, Tracy, Amy. BBA in Fin., U. Tex., 1968. Pres. East Tex. Citizens Credit Union, Palestine, Tex., 1978-86; dist. rep. Nat. Fedn. Ind. Bus., Nashville, 1987-88, regional tng. mgr., 1991-93, div. mgr., 1989-90, 94-96, dir. sales ops., 1996—. Republican. Avocations: woodworking, gardening. Office: Nat Fedn Ind Bus 53 Century Blvd Nashville TN 37214-3693 Home: 6132 Brentwood Chase Dr Brentwood TN 37027-4443 E-mail: lodowski@comcast.net., charles.lodowski@NFIB.org.

LODWICK, GWILYM SAVAGE, radiologist, educator; b. Mystic, Iowa, Aug. 30, 1917; s. Gwylim S. and Lucy A. (Fuller) Lodwick; m. Maria Antonia De Brito Barata; children from previous marriage: Gwilym Savage III, Philip Galligan, Malcolm Kerr, Terry Ann. Student, Drake U., 1934—35; BS, State U. Iowa, 1942, MD, 1943. Resident pathology State U. Iowa, 1947—48, resident radiology, 1948—50; fellow, sr. fellow radiologic and orthopedic pathology Armed Forces Inst. Pathology, 1951; asst., then assoc. prof. State U. Iowa Med. Sch., 1951—56; prof. radiology, chmn. dept. U. Mo. at Columbia Med. Sch., 1956—78, rsch. prof. radiology, 1978—83, interim chmn. dept. radiology, 1980—81, chmn. dept. radiology, 1981—83, prof. bioengring., 1969—83, acting dean, 1959, assoc. dean, 1959—64; assoc. radiologist Mass. Gen. Hosp., 1983—88, radiologist, 1988—91, hon. radiologist, 1991—; vis. prof. dept. radiology Harvard Med. Sch., 1983—93. Cons. in field; vis. prof. Keio U. Sch. Medicine, Tokyo, 1974; chmn. sci. program com. Internat. Conf. on Med. Info., Amsterdam, 1983; trustee Am. Registry Radiologic Technologists, 1961—69, pres., 1964—65, 1968—69; mem. radiology tng. com. Nat. Inst. Gen. Med. Scis., NIH, 1966—70; com. radiology Nat. Acad. Scis.-NRC, 1970—75; chmn. com. computers Am. Coll. Radiology, 1965, Internat. Commn. Radiol. Edn. and Info., 1969—73; cons. to health care tech. divsn. Nat. Ctr. for Health Svcs., Rsch. and Devel., 1971—76; dir. Mid-Am. Bond Tumor Diagnostic Ctr. and Registry, 1971—83; adv. com. mem. NIH Biomed. Image Processing Grant Jet Propulsion Lab., 1969—73; nat. chmn. MUMPS Users Group, 1973—75; mem. radiation study sect. divsn. rsch. grants NIH, 1976—79, mem. study sect. on diagnostic radiology and nuc. medicine divsn. rsch. grants, 1979—82, chmn. , 1980—82; mem. bd. sci. counselors Nat. Libr. of Medicine, 1985, chmn., 1987—89; dir. radiology Spaulding Rehab. Hosp., 1986—92. Adv. editl. bd.: Radiology, 1965—86, cons. to editor: , 1986—91, adv. editl. bd.: Current/Clin. Practice, 1972—88, mem. editl. bd.: Jour. Med. Systems, 1976—, mem. editl. bd.: Radiol. Sci. Update divsn. Biomedia, Inc., 1975—83, mem. editl. bd.: Critical Revs. in Linguistic Imaging, 1990, mem. cons. editl. bd.: Skeletal Radiology, 1977—92, mem. cons. editl. bd.: Contemporary Diagnostic Radiology, 1978—80, assoc. editor: Jour. Med. Imaging, 1988—. Served to maj. U.S. Army, 1943—46, ETO. Decorated Sakari Mustakallio medal Finland; named Most Disting. Alumnus in Radiology, State U. Iowa Centennial, 1970; recipient Sigma Xi Rsch. award, U. Mo., Columbia, 1972, Gold medal, XIII Internat. Conf. Radiology, Madrid, 1973, Founder's Gold medal, Internat. Skeletal Soc., 1990, Disting. Alumni Achievement award, U. Iowa, 2002. Fellow: AMA (radiology rev. bd. coun. med. edn., coun. rep. on residency rev. com. for radiology 1969—74), Am. Coll. Radiology (co-chmn. ACR-NEMA standardization com. 1983—90, NEMA Med. Tech. Leadership award 1995); mem.: Phila. Roentgen Ray Soc., Ind. Roentgen Soc., Tex. Radiol. Soc., Salutis Unitas, Mo. Radiol. Soc. (1st pres. 1961—62), Finnish Radio Soc. (hon.), Portuguese Soc. Radiology and Nuc. Medicine (hon.), Assn. Univ. Radiologists, Radiol. Soc. N.Am. (3d v.p. 1974—75, chmn. ad hoc com. representing assoc. scis. 1979—87, chmn. assoc. scis. com. 1981—87), Nat. Acad. Practice in Medicine, Am. Coll. Med. Informatics (founding), NAS Inst. Medicine, Cosmos, Harvard of Boston Club, Rotary, Alpha Omega Alpha. Home: 3900 Galt Ocean Dr Apt 307 Fort Lauderdale FL 33308-6622 E-mail: lodwickmd@aol.com.

LODWICK, JUDITH LYNNE, nursing educator; b. New Orleans, Feb. 20, 1954; d. Frank Tillman Jr. and Grace Evelyn (Hilty) L. BSN, La. State U., 1976. RN, La.; cert. CPR, ACLS instr., advanced trauma life support coord., med.-surg. nurse, cert. emergency nurse. Head nurse hematology-oncology endocrinology Ochsner Found. Hosp., New Orleans, 1978-82, unit instr., head nurse Ochsner emergency dept., 1983-88, staff nurse emergency dept., 1989-91; staff nurse, relief charge nurse, preceptor E. Jefferson Gen. Hosp., Metairie; clin. instr. post ICU East Jefferson Gen. Hosp., 1991-96, supr. post ICU, 1996-98. Coord. orientation workshops and preceptorships, affilate faculty Charity Delgado Sch. of Nursing, 1996-97, educator N.A. advancement PCT program; chairperson universal chart order post ICU flowsheet East Jefferson Gen. Hosp. Mem. Nat. Oncology Soc., Emergency Nursing Assn. (sec. emergency dept. quality assurance program com.), Critical Care Nurses Assn. (chmn. post ICU quality assurance com, competency based edn. com.), Nursing Edn. Com., Policy and Procedure Com., ICU flowsheet com. (chmn.). Home: 2056 Lafitte St La Place LA 70068-2029

LODWICK, MICHAEL WAYNE, lawyer; b. New Orleans, Sept. 21, 1946; s. Frank Tillman Jr. and Grace Evelyn (Hilty) L.; children: Sarah Peirce, Jane Durborow, Elizabeth Hilty; m. Mary League, June 15, 1991. BA, La. State U., 1968; MA, Tulane U., 1972, PhD, 1976; JD, Loyola U., New Orleans, 1981. Bar: La., U.S. Dist. Ct. (ea. dist.) La. 1981, U.S. Ct. Appeals (5th cir.) 1981, U.S. Ct. Appeals (D.C. cir.) 1982, U.S. Ct. Appeals (11th cir.) 1986, U.S. Ct. Appeals (9th cir.) 1990, U.S. Ct. Appeals (2d cir.) 1996, U.S. Ct. Appeals (4th cir.) 1996, U.S. Supreme Ct., 1987, Calif. 1990, U.S. Dist. Ct. (ctrl., no. and so. dists.) Calif. 1990. Instr. to asst. prof. Tulane U., New Orleans, 1976-78; assoc. Barham & Churchill, 1981-83, O'Neil, Eichin & Miller, New Orleans, 1983-87, ptnr., 1987-89, Fisher & Porter, 1989-97, Porter, Groff & Lodwick, 1997—. Editor, co-founder and pub. Plantation Soc. in Americas jour., 1979-83, 86—; editor-in-chief Loyola Law Rev., 1980-81; contbr. articles to profl. jours. Mem. New Orleans Symphony Chorus, 1985-89, Pacific Chorale, 1989—. Tulane U. fellow, 1970-72; recipient Loyola U. Law Rev. Honor award, 1981, Loyola Law Alumni award, 1981. Mem. ABA, La. State Bar Assn., State Bar Calif., Fed. Bar Assn., Assn. Transp. Law, Logistics and Policy, Maritime Law Assn. U.S. Home: 20241 Seashell Cir Huntington Beach CA 92646-4436 Office: Porter Groff & Lodwick 110 Pine Ave Fl 11 Long Beach CA 90802-4430

LÖE, HARALD, retired dentist, educator, researcher; b. Steinkjer, Norway, July 19, 1926; s. Haakon and Anna (Bruem) Löe; m. Inga Johansen, July 3, 1948; children: Haakon, Marianne. DDS, U. Oslo, 1952; D in Odontology, 1961; hon. degree, U. Gothenburg, 1973, Royal Dental Coll., Aarhus, 1980, U. Athens, 1980, Cath. U., Leuven, 1980, U. Lund, 1983, Georgetown U., 1983, U. Bergen, 1985, U. Md., 1986, Med. U. N.J., 1987, Royal Dental Coll., Copenhagen, 1988, U. Toronto, 1989, U. Detroit, 1990, S.C. Med. U., 1990, U. Helsinki, Finland, 1992, Pacific U., 1993, U. Milan, Italy, 1994. Instr. Sch. Dentistry, Oslo U., 1952-55; rsch. assoc. Norwegian Inst. Dental Rsch., 1956-62; Fulbright rsch. fellow, rsch. assoc. dept. oral pathology U. Ill., Chgo., 1957-58; Univ. rsch. fellow Oslo U., 1959-62, asso. prof. dept. periodontology, 1960-61; prof. dentistry, chmn. dept. periodontology Royal Dental Coll., Aarhus, Denmark, 1962-72, assoc. dean, dean-elect, 1971-72; prof., dir. Dental Rsch. Inst., U. Mich., Ann Arbor, 1972-74; dir. Nat. Inst. Dental Rsch. Nat. Inst. Dental Rsch., Bethesda, Md., 1983-96; dean, prof. periodontology U. Conn. Health Ctr. Sch. Dental Medicine, Farmington, 1974-82, univ. prof., 1994-97; vis. prof. U. Bern, Switzerland, 1997—. Vis. prof. periodontics Hebrew U., Jerusalem, 1966—67; hon. prof. Med. Scis. U. Beijing, 1987; cons. WHO, NIH. Contbr. With Norwegian Army, 1944—48. Decorated Knight of Danebrog Queen of Denmark, Comdr. of Royal Norwegian Order of Merit King of Norway; recipient 75th Anniversary award, Norwegian Dental Assn., 1958, prize, Aalborg Dental Soc., 1965, William J. Gies Periodontology award, 1978, Alfred C. Fones medal, U.S. Surgeon Gen.'s medal and Exemplary award, 1988, Internat. award, Swedish Dental Assn., 1989, Harvard medal, 1992, Scandinavian Pub. Health award, 1994. Mem.: ADA (Gold medal 1994, Callahan medal 1995, Spenadel medal 1995), AAAS, Mass. Dental Soc. (Internat. award), Am. Soc. Preventive Dentistry (Internat. award), Scandinavian Assn. Dental Rsch., Danish Dental Assn., Am. Assn. Dental Rsch. (hon.), Am. Acad. Periodontology, Am. Coll. Dentists, Inst. Medicine NAS, Internat. Assn. Dental Rsch. (pres. 1980, Basic Rsch. in Periodontology award 1969), Internat. Coll. Dentists.

LOEB, ARTHUR L. design science educator; b. Amsterdam, The Netherlands, July 13, 1923; s. L. Herbert and Nelly (Isaac) L.; m. Charlotte I. Aarts, Sept. 22, 1956. BSCh, U. Pa., 1943; AM in Physics, Harvard U., 1945, PhD in Chem. Physics, 1949. Rsch. assoc. in chemistry MIT, 1950-54, staff, digital computer lab., 1952-58; vis. staff U. Utrecht, Netherlands, 1954; lectr. to assoc. prof. elec. engring. MIT, 1956-63; staff scientist Kennecott Cooper Corp., Lexington, Mass., 1963-73; hon. assoc., lectr. visual and environ. studies Harvard U., Cambridge, 1970—, sr. lectr., 1975—; curator of teaching collection Carpenter Ctr. of Visual Arts, Harvard U., 1973-93; master of Dudley House Harvard U., 1982-88, hon. assoc. Dudley House, 1988—, mem. faculty Grad. Sch. Edn., 1995—. Editor: The Design Sci. Collection, Birkhauser, Boston, Basel, Switzerland, Berlin; author: Color and Symmetry, 1973, Space Structures, 1976, Concepts and Images, 1992, others; contbr. articles to profl. jours. Trustee exec. com. Radcliffe Coll., 1988-92; bd. dirs., mem. corp. Boston Early Music Festival, 1989—; adv. bd. Fuller Inst., 1986, Cambridge Ctr. for Behavioral Studies; resident Rockefeller Found., 1990; chmn. adv. coun. Internat. Soc. for Interdisciplinary Study of Symmetry; bd. dirs. Soc. for Aesthetics in Math.; overseer Boston Baroque. Recipient Golden Door award, Internat. Inst. Boston, 1987. Fellow Am. Inst. Chemistry (life), Royal Soc. Arts (life); mem. Acad. Memt., Harvard Mus. Assn., The Shop Club, St. Botolph Club. Unitarian Universalist. Avocations: music, history. Home: 29 Shepard St Cambridge MA 02138-1504 Office: Harvard U Carpenter Ctr Visual A Cambridge MA 02138

LOEB, BEN FOHL, JR. lawyer, educator; b. Nashville, May 15, 1932; s. Ben Fohl and Frances (Paysinger) L.; m. Anne Nelson, Sept. 23, 1961 (div. 1982); children: Charles Nelson, William Nelson. BA, Vanderbilt U., 1955, JD, 1960. Bar: Tenn. 1960, U.S. Supreme Ct. 1966, N.C. 1975. Assoc. Crownover, Branstetter & Folk, Nashville, 1960-64; asst. dir. Inst. Govt. U. N.C., Chapel Hill, 1964—, prof. pub. law and govt. Sch. Govt., 1972—. Counsel to N.C. legis. coms. on motor vehicle law and transp., Raleigh, 1973-83; cons. on alcohol beverage control, 1985-89; cons. on wildlife, natural and scenic areas, 1989-93; mem. U. N.C. Faculty Coun., 1994-97. Author: Traffic Law and Highway Safety, 1970, Alcohol Beverage Control Law, 1971, Motor Vehicle Law, 1975, Legal Aspects of Dental Practice, 1977, Eminent Domain Procedure, 1984, Punishments for Crimes and Motor Vehicle Offenses, 1999; assoc. editor Vanderbilt Law Rev., 1959-60. 1st lt. U.S. Army, 1955-57. Mem. ABA, Tenn. Bar Assn., Phi Beta Kappa, Phi Delta Phi, Pi Kappa Alpha (chpt. pres. 1954-55), Carolina Club (Chapel Hill). Democrat. Baptist. Home: 17 Bluff Trail Chapel Hill NC 27516-1603 Office: U NC Sch of Govt Cb 3330 Knapp Bldg Chapel Hill NC 27599-3330 E-mail: loeb@iogmail.iog.unc.edu.

LOEB, JEFFREY T. English language educator; b. Junction City, Kans., Oct. 13, 1947; s. Dan Benoit and Bonnie Heck Loeb; m. Jane More, Oct. 5, 1942; 1 child, Andi Catherine. BA, U. Kans., 1972, MA, 1978, PhD, 1995. Asst. city mgr. Junction City Cable TV, 1978-79, regional mgr., 1979-83; owner, mgr. Studio Prints Photography, Junction City, 1983-90; instr. U. Kans., Lawrence, 1990-95; chair English Pembroke Hill Sch., Kansas City, Mo., 1995—. Faculty advisor Voice, Pembroke Hill Sch., Kansas City, 1996-2001 Editor, afterword author: (book) Memphis Nam Sweden, 1997 (reissue), Black Prisoner of War, 2000 (reissue); contbr. articles to profl. jours. Pres., v.p., mem. Junction City Bd. Edn., 1981-89. Cpl. USMC, 1967-69, Vietnam. Mem. MLA, Popular Culture Assn., Journalism Educators of Greater Kansas City. Home: 8849 Lamar Shawnee Mission KS 66207 Office: Pembroke Hill Sch 5121 State Line Rd Kansas City MO 66214 E-mail: jeffloeb@wonderlink.net.

LOEB, JOHN LANGELOTH, JR. investment counselor; b. N.Y.C., May 2, 1930; s. John Langeloth and Frances (Lehman) L.; children: Nicholas, Alexandra. Grad., Hotchkiss Sch., 1948; AB cum laude, Harvard, 1952, MBA, 1954; LL.D. (hon.), Georgetown U. With Loeb, Rhoades & Co., N.Y.C., from 1956, gen. ptnr., mem. mgmt. com., 1964-73, mng. ptnr., pres., 1971-73, ltd. ptnr., 1973-84; chmn. bd. Holly Sugar Co., Colo., 1969-71; amb. to Denmark Copenhagen, 1981-83; chmn. John L. Loeb, Jr. Assocs., N.Y.C., 1984—. U.S. del. to 38th session Gen. Assembly of UN; spl. advisor environ. matters to Gov. Nelson A. Rockefeller, 1967-73; chmn. Gov. N.Y. Coun. Environ. Advisors, 1970-75; pres. Winston Churchill Found., 1981—; trustee Ednl. Testing Svc., Princeton, N.J., 1986-93; bd. dirs. Am.-Scandinavian Found. Bd. trustee Monefiore Hosp. and Med. Ctr. , Mus. City, NY, 1962—94; bd. trustees John and Frances L. Loeb Found., 1957—98; mem. Harvard Vis. Com. Loeb Drama Ctr., 1988—94, N.Y. State Coun. on the Arts, 1996—; pres. John L. Loeb Jr. Found., 1963—; bd. dirs. Am.-Scandinavian Found., 2002—. Lt. USAF, 1954—56. Lord of the Manor of Brinsley; Decorated Grand Cross of the Order of Dannebrog (Denmark); recipient Lee Max Friedman award Am. Jewish Hist. Soc., Disting. Patriot award SAR; Hon. Comdr. of the Most Excellent Order of the Brit. Empire. Mem. Downtown Assn. (N.Y.C.), Harvard Club, Century Country Club, Sleepy Hollow Club (Westchester, N.Y.), Buck's Club, Brooks's Club, Hurlingham Club (London), Royal Danish Yacht Club (Copenhagen), Royal Swedish Yacht Club (Stockholm), Lyford Cay Club (Nassau, Bahamas). Home: Ridgeleigh 194 Anderson Hill Rd Purchase NY 10577-2101 Office: John L Loeb Jr Assocs Inc 50 Broad St Rm 1137 New York NY 10004-2307 E-mail: johnloeb@aol.com.

LOEB, LARRY MORRIS, communications company executive; b. Morgan City, La., Oct. 13, 1940; s. Richard Levy and Pauline Endler (Forgotston) L.; m. Maria-Luisa Elvira Achino, Apr. 5, 1968; children: Maddalena, Leonora. BA, Tulane U., 1962; postgrad., Columbia U., 1962-63, JD, 1966. Bar: N.Y. 1967. Staff atty. ABC Inc., N.Y.C., 1966-68, gen. atty., 1968-80; v.p., dir. bus. affairs ABC Video Enterprises Inc., 1980-86; v.p. legal and bus. affairs Video Enterprises and Pub. Capital Cities/ABC Inc., 1986-93; v.p. cable and internat. devel., legal ABC Inc., 1993-97; legal counsel The Hearst Corp., 1998—. Mgmt. com. A & E Networks, N.Y.C., 1981-96, Lifetime, 1983-85; adv. coun. TMM (RTL2), 1996-97; mng. dir. Hearst Enterprises, B.V.; bd. dirs. Tevecap S.A., Brazil. Bd. dirs. Theater for a New Audience, N.Y.C., 1981—. Woodrow Wilson fellow, 1962-63. Mem. N.Am. Nat. Broadcasters Assn. (pres. 1996-97), European Broadcasting Union (legal com. 1973-97). Democrat. Jewish. Avocations: piano, theatre, reading, travel, languages. Home: 164 W 94th St New York NY 10025-7015 Office: The Hearst Corp 959 8th Ave New York NY 10019-3795 E-mail: lmloeb@hearst.com.

LOEB, MARCIA JOAN, research psychologist; b. N.Y.C., Mar. 26, 1933; d. Nathan and Anne Mermelstein; m. George Irwin Loeb, Aug. 30, 1953; children: Alex, Daniel. BA, Bklyn. Coll., 1953; MS, Cornell U., 1957; PhD, U. Md., 1970. Rsch. asst. dept. zoology Cornell U., Ithaca, N.Y., 1956-57, rsch. asst. Sch. Nutrition, 1957-59; rsch. asst. NIH, Bethesda, Md., 1961-62; grad. asst. dept. zoology U. Md., College Park, 1964-68, rsch. asst. Natural Resources Inst., 1968-70; NRC-Naval Rsch. Lab. postdoctoral rsch. assoc. Naval Rsch. Lab., Washington, 1970-72; rsch. assoc. Nat. English Rsch. Coun. unit Marine Sci. Labs. Univ. Coll. North Wales, 1973-74; rsch. physiologist Chem. and Biophys. Control Lab. USDA, Beltsville, Md., 1978-80, rsch. physiologist Insect Reprodn. Lab., 1980-91, rsch. physiologist Insect Neurobiology and Hormone Lab., 1991-96, rsch. physiologist Insect Biocontrol Lab., 1996—. Vis. asst. prof. invertebrate zoology The Am. U., Washington, 1977-78, Western Md. Coll., Westminster, Md., 1976-77; adj. prof. invertebrate zoology, anatomy and physiology The Am. U., Washington, 1975-76; instr. biology, human anatomy and physiology No. Va. C.C., Annandale, 1972-73; adj. assoc. prof. Howard U., 1993-97, 99—; organizng com. Internat. Conf. on Insect Neurochemistry and Neurophysiology, College Park, Md., 1983, organizing com., publicity chmn., sect. chmn., 1986, organizing com., local arrangements chmn, sect. chmn., 1989; co-organizer 13th Ann. of IX Internat. Conf. on Invertebrate Cell Culture, San Francisco, 1996; participant and spkr. internat. sci. confs. Vol. editor: Internat. Conf. on Insect Neurochemistry and Physiology, 1993; co-editor: Invertebrate Cell Culture: Looking Toward the Twenty First Century...Proceedings of the IX International Conference on Invertebrate Cell Culture, 1997; contbr. numerous articles to profl. jours. Internat. Soc. for Invertebrate Reprodn. (sect. chmn. internat. meetings 1983, 86), Am. Soc. Zoologists (divsns. comparative endocrinology, devel. and invertebrate zoology), Soc. for In Vitro Biology (nat. Capitol area br., symposium organizer 2000), Sigma Xi. Office: USDA Insect Biocontrol Lab Bldg 011A Rm 211 BARC West Beltsville MD 20705 E-mail: loebm@ba.ars.usda.gov.

LOEB, MARSHALL ROBERT, journalist; b. Chgo., May 30, 1929; s. Monroe Harrison and Henrietta (Benjamin) L.; m. Elizabeth Peggy Loewe, Aug. 14, 1954; children: Michael, Margaret. BJ, U. Mo., 1950; postgrad., U. Goettingen, Germany, 1950-51. Reporter Garfield News and Austinite, Chgo., 1944-45; reporter, columnist Garfieldian and Austin News, 1946-47, 49-51; reporter Columbia Missourian, 1948-50; staff corr. UP, Frankfurt, Germany, 1952-54; reporter St. Louis Globe-Democrat, 1955-56; contbg. editor Time mag., 1956-61, assoc. editor, 1961-65, sr. editor, 1965-80, econs. editor and columnist, 1978-80; mng. editor Money Mag., 1980-84; editor Time Inc. Mag. Devel., 1984-86; mng. editor Fortune, 1986-94, editor-at-large, 1994-95, columnist, 1996; editor Columbia Journalism Rev., 1997-99; columnist, adv. bd. mem. CBS Marketwatch.com, 1999—. Daily commentator CBS Radio Network; assoc. fellow Yale U., Berkeley Coll., 1977—; bd. dirs. priceline.com. Author (with William Safire): Plunging Into Politics, 1962; author: Marshall Loeb's Money Guide, 1983, ann. edits., 1985—94, Money Minutes, 1986, Lifetime Financial Strategies, 1996, 52 Weeks to Financial Fitness, 2001; editor (with Andrew Leckey): Best Business Stories of the Year , 2001. Bd. dirs. Nat. Neurofibromatosis Found., Recording for the Blind and Dyslexic; overseer NYU Stern Sch. Bus.; bd. advisors Knight-Bagehot Fellowship. Recipient Gerald M. Loeb award UCLA Sch. Mgmt., 1974, Lifetime Achievement award, 1996, Journalism medal U. Mo., 1988, TJFR Bus. Journalism Luminaries award 1990, 2000, Disting. Achievement award Soc. Am. Bus. Editors and Writers, 1998. Mem. Econ. Club of N.Y., Coun. Fgn. Rels., Am. Soc. Mag. Editors (pres. 1988-90), Overseas Press Club Am. Jewish. Home: 31 Montrose Rd Scarsdale NY 10583-1129 Office: CBS MarketWatch dot com 1697 Broadway New York NY 10019-2925 Business E-Mail: mloeb@marketwatch.com.

LOEB, PETER KENNETH, money manager; b. N.Y.C., Apr. 8, 1936; s. Carl M. and Lucille H. (Schamberg) L.; m. Jeanette Winter, Nov. 1, 1980; 1 child, Alexander Winter; children by previous marriage: Peter Kenneth Jr., Karen Elizabeth, James Matthew. BA, Yale U., 1958; MBA, Columbia U., 1961. Security analyst Loeb, Rhoades & Co., N.Y.C., 1961-66, syndicate dept. ptnr., 1966-71, with trading/instl. sales sect., 1971-79; mng. dir. Shearson Corp., 1979-83; mng. dir., portfolio mgr. PaineWebber Inc., 1983-92; ptnr. Shufro, Rose & Co., 1992-97; pres. Delta Capital Mgmt., 1997-01; mng. dir. Neuberger Berman, 2001—. Mem. com. on securities Am. Stock Exch., 1978-80; mem. del. to Beijing symposium N.Y. Stock Exch., 1986. Coach, games ofcl. Manhattan Spl. Olympics, 1980—; bd. dirs., co-chmn. devel. com. N.Y. Spl. Olympics, 1985-89; chmn. devel. com. Spl. Olympics Internat., 1986-97, bd. dirs.; mem. com. on univ. investments Columbia U., 1977-85, trustee, 1979-85, vice-chmn. alumni adv. bd., 1986-92; fund chmn. Columbia U. Bus. Sch., 1964-66, mem. alumni counseling bd., 1970—, pres. Columbia Bus. Sch. Assocs., 1971-73, mem. bd. overseers, 1976—; bd. dirs. City Ctr. Theatre Found., City Harvest, Food Chain, 1996-99; trustee Allen Stevenson Sch., 1969-97, trustee emeritus, 1997—; trustee Langeloth Found., 1972—; bd. dirs., 1998; trustee N.Y. Infirmary-Beekman Downtown Hosp., 1978-85; mem. adv. bd. Atoms Track Club Bedford-Stuyvesant, 1970—; cert. track ofcl. USA Track and Field, 1985—; mem. marshals com. Westchester Golf Classic, 1970—, exec. com. 2001—, tournament vice chmn. 2001—; contbg. mem. Mus. Modern Art, Met. Mus. Art; mem. Statue of Liberty/Ellis Island Found., Friends of Kennedy Ctr., Friends of the Philharm., Friends of Carnegie Hall; mem. Wall St. com. N.Y. Urban Coalition, 1969-71; mem. exec. bd. new leadership divsn. Fedn. Jewish Philanthropies, 1963-64; vice-chmn. Pacesetter com. Greater N.Y. coun. Boy Scouts Am., 1966-67. Recipient Alumni medal for conspicuous service Columbia U., 1975, Alumni medal for disting. service Columbia U. Bus. Sch., 1976, Disting. Svc. award Atoms Track Club, 1995, Founder's award Westchester Golf Classic, 1997. Mem. SAR, Securities Traders Assn. N.Y., Investment Assn. N.Y. (exec. bd. 1969), Securities Industry Assn. (governing council 1977-79, minority capital com. 1980-85, trustee Econ. Edn. Found. 1986—, vice chmn. 1992—), Nat. Assn. Security Dealers (chmn. dist. 12 com. 1981, gov. 1982-85, chmn. corp. fin. com. 1983-86, vice-chmn. fin. 1984, mem. arbitration com. 1986-89, NASDAQ qualifications com. 1989—), N.Y.C. Baseball Fedn. (pres. 1968-91, chmn. 1992-99, award for disting. service 1976), Club 101, Doubles Club, Bond Club, Century Country Club, Beta Gamma Sigma, Alpha Kappa Psi, Phi Gamma Delta. Office: Neuberger Berman 605 3rd Ave New York NY 10158-3698

LOEB, RONALD MARVIN, lawyer; b. Denver, Sept. 24, 1932; s. Ellis and Lillian (Mosko) L.; m. Shirley Ross; children: Joshua Ross, Gabriel Ross, Daniel Seth, Jennifer Miriam, Rachel Sarah.. AB with highest honors, UCLA, 1954; LLB cum laude, Harvard U., 1959. Bar: Calif. 1960. Assoc. Irell & Manella, L.L.P, L.A., 1959-64, ptnr., 1964-97, of counsel, 1997-99; acting CEO Mattel, 2000; sr. v.p., gen. counsel Williams Sonoma, Inc., 1999—. Instr. Stanford Law Sch. Director's Coll., 2001-02, bd. dirs. Mattel, Inc., Ehama Inst.; course presenter The Esalen Inst., 1994; instr. corp. governance and social responsibility KVK Raju Internat. Leadership Acad., Hyderabad, India; task force on social cohesion sponsored by Danish Min. Pub. Affairs. Co-editor: Duties and Responsibilities of Outside Directors, 1978. Trustee Crossroads Sch. Arts and Scis., Santa Monica, Calif., 1987-99; past chmn. Pacific Crest Outward Bound Sch.; past founding trustee, dir. World Bus. Acad. Mem. ABA, State Bar Assn. Calif., Office: Williams Sonoma Inc 3250 Van Ness Ave San Francisco CA 94109 E-mail: rloeb@wsgc.com.

LOEBACH, MICHAEL CLAUD, otolaryngologist; b. South Bend, Ind., Jan. 2, 1946; s. Edward Raymond Loebach and Mary Jean (Brooker) Follett; m. Kathryn Jean Negles, Nov. 11, 1972; James Christopher, Christina Marie, Edward Michael. BA, St. Mary's Coll., Winona, Minn., 1968; MD, Northwestern U., 1972, MBA, 1988. Diplomate Am. Bd. Otolarynology. Intern Rush-Presby. St. Luke's Hosp., Chgo., 1972-73; resident in otolaryngology U. Ill. Eye and Ear Infirmary, 1975-78; staff physician Dreyer Med. Clinic, Aurora, Ill., 1978—, vice-chmn. bd. dirs. Bd. dirs. Dreyer Clinic S.C.; chief of staff Provena Mercy Ctr. Svcs., 1997-2000. Chmn. cubscout pack com. Boy Scouts Am., Aurora, 1982-85. Served to lt. USN, 1973-75. Mem. Am. Acad. Otolaryngology, Am. Coll. Physician Execs., Alpha Omega Alpha. Republican. Roman Catholic. Avocations: downhill skiing, travel, gardening. Email: (business). Office: Dreyer Med Clinic 1221 N Highland Ave Aurora IL 60506-1404 E-mail: Michael.Loebach@dreyermed.com.

LOEBER, THOMAS STANTON, retired biologist; b. San Francisco, Sept. 2, 1922; s. Charles Stanton Loeber, Lydia Annette Brown; m. Rachelle Colver Mathews; m. Eunice Ann Young (div. June 1944); children: Lucy Ann Lowry, Mary Ellen Huckstep, Thomas Stanton Loeber Jr. BA in Zoology, Pomona Coll., 1948; MS in Entomology, U. Mass., 1950; MA in Internat. Rels., UCLA, 1963. Cert. Vector Control Specialist Calif. Dept. Health, 1955, Fundamentals of Procedure Writing Gen. Physics Corp., 1985. Dir. Nat. Malaria Eradication Svc. Hashemite Kingdom of Jordan, 1957—60; rsch. analyst State Libr., Salem, Oreg., 1963—67; instr. Mt. Angel Coll., 1966—73; program exec. Oreg. Dept. Transp., Portland, 1978—81; tech. writer Nuc. Generating Sta. So. Calif. Edison, San Onofre, Calif., 1983—86; biol. cons. Pacific SW Biol. Svcs., National City, 1986—87. Malariologist internat. divsn. USPHS, 1956—60; instr. SW Oreg. C.C., 1967—73, Nat. U., San Diego, 1984; U.S. rep. Regional Conf. WHO, Baghdad, 1957, Addis Ababa, 59; cons. Gov.'s Commn. for Handicapped, Salem, Oreg., 1968, Manpower Study Prudential Properties, Agoura, Calif., 1974. Author: Foreign Aid Our Tragic Experiment, 1961, Three Case Studies in Public Library Development, 1966, A Brief History of Time Since 1960, 1999; co-author: A Computer-Based Approach to Planning in Underdeveloped Areas, 1965. Dir. UCLA Internat. Student Ctr., 1962—63. Cpl., journalist USAF, 1944—45, lt. jg. USPHS, 1956—60. Grantee, Ford Found., 1962. Mem.: Sigma Xi, Pi Gamma Mu, Pi Sigma Alpha. Achievements include development of first computerized library catalog Oregon State Library. Avocation: Avocations: Audubon Christmas count, docent Santa Margarita River conservation area, fly fishing, history, writing. Home: 310 Via Spolador Fallbrook CA 92028

LOEBLICH, HELEN NINA TAPPAN, paleontologist, educator; b. Norman, Okla., Oct. 12, 1917; d. Frank Girard and Mary (Jenks) Tappan; m. Alfred Richard Loeblich, Jr., June 18, 1939; children: Alfred Richard III, Karen Elizabeth Loeblich, Judith Anne Loeblich Covey, Daryl Louise Loeblich Valenzuela. BS, U. Okla., 1937, MS, 1939; PhD, U. Chgo., 1942. Instr. geology Tulane U., New Orleans, 1942-43; geologist U.S. Geol. Survey, Washington, 1943-45, 47-59; mem. faculty UCLA, 1958—, prof. geology, 1966-84, prof. emeritus, 1985—, vice chmn. dept. geology, 1973-75. Research assoc. Smithsonian Instn., 1954-57; assoc. editor Cushman Found. Foraminiferal Research, 1950-51, incorporator, hon. dir., 1950—. Author: (with A.R. Loeblich Jr.) Treatise on Invertebrate Paleontology, part C, Protista 2, Foraminiferida, 2 vols., 1964, Foraminiferal Genera and Their Classification, 2 vols., 1987, Foraminifera of the Sahul Shelf and Timor Sea, 1994; author: The Paleobiology of Plant Protists, 1980; mem. editl. bd. Palaeoecology, 1972-82, Paleobiology, 1975-81; contbr. articles to profl. jours., govt. publs. and encys. Recipient Joseph A. Cushman award Cushman Found., 1982; named Woman of Yr. in Sci. Palm Springs Desert Mus., 1987; Guggenheim fellow, 1953-54. Fellow Geol. Soc. Am. (sr., councilor 1979-81); mem. Paleontol. Soc. (pres. 1984-85, patron 1987, medal 1982), Soc. Sedimentary Geology (councilor 1975-77, hon. mem. 1978, Raymond C. Moore medal 1984), UCLA Med. Ctr. Aux. (Woman of Yr. medal), AAUP, Internat. Paleontological Assn., Paleontol. Rsch. Inst., Am. Microscopical Soc., Am. Inst. Biol. Scis., Phi Beta Kappa, Sigma Xi. Home: 1556 W Crone Ave Anaheim CA 92802-1303

LOEBNER, HUGH GENE, manufacturing company executive; b. N.Y.C., Mar. 26, 1942; s. William Loebner and Virginia Whitehead; m. Elaine Sideri, June 8, 1968 (div. Dec. 1974). BA, Johns Hopkins U., 1963; MA, NYU, 1964; PhD, U. Mass., 1972. Asst. dir. computing U. Md. Baltimore County, Catonsville, 1975-80; pres., CEO Crown Industries, Inc., East Orange, N.J., 1981—. Sponsor Loebner prize for artificial intelligence, 1990. Author: Manifesto of Sexual Freedom, 1996. Treas. Marijuana Reform Party N.Y., N.Y.C., 1999-2001. Home: 220 W 98th St New York NY 10025 Office: Crown Industries inc 155 N Park St East Orange NJ 07017 Fax: 973-672-7536. E-mail: hugh@loebner.net., hugh@gocrown.com.

LOEFFLER, FRANK JOSEPH, physicist, educator; b. Ballston Spa, N.Y., Sept. 5, 1928; s. Frank Joseph and Florence (Farrell) L.; m. Eleanor Jane Chisholm, Sept. 8, 1951; children: Peter, James, Margaret, Anne Marie. BS in Engring. Physics, Cornell U., 1951, PhD in Physics, 1957. Research asso. Princeton U., 1957-58; mem. faculty Purdue U., Lafayette, Ind., 1958-97, prof. physics, 1962-97; prof. emeritus, 1997—; vis. prof. Hamburg U., Germany, 1963-64, Heidelberg U., Germany, CERN, Switzerland, 1971, Stanford U. Linear Accelerator Ctr., 1980-83. Trustee, mem. exec. com., chmn. high energy com. Argonne Univs. Assn., 1972-76, 78-79, mem. com. on fusion programs, 1979-80; vis. prof. U. Hawaii, 1985-86. Contbr. to profl. publs. Recipient Antarctic Svc. medal NSF/USN, 1990, Ruth and Joel Spira award for outstanding tchg., 1992. Fellow Am. Phys. Soc., Sigma Xi, Tau Beta Pi. Achievements include developing and manufacturing undergraduate physics laboratory experiments and lecture demonstration apparatus. Exptl. research in astrophysics, high energy gamma ray astronomy, high energy particle interactions and on-line data acquisition-processing systems. Established gamma ray astronomy lab. at South Pole, Antarctica, 1989, 91, 92. Home: 341 Hokulani St Makawao HI 96768-8612 Office: Purdue U Dept Physics Lafayette IN 47907

LOEFFLER, JAMES JOSEPH, lawyer; b. Evanston, Ill., Mar. 7, 1931; s. Charles Adolph and Margaret Bowe L.; m. Margo M. Loeffler, May 26, 1962; children— Charlotte Bowe, James J. BS, Loyola U.; JD, Northwestern U. Bar: Ill. 1956, Tex. 1956. Assoc. Fulbright & Jaworski, Houston, 1956-69, ptnr., 1969-86, sr. ptnr., 1986, Chamberlain, Hrdlicka, White, Johnson & Williams, Houston, 1986-90; pvt. practice law, 1990-2000. Mem. Ill. Bar Assn., Tex. Bar Assn., Houston Country Club.

LOEFFLER, RICHARD HARLAN, retail and technology company executive; b. Kansas City, Mo., Sept. 15, 1936; s. Sidney A. and Lily (Cowell) L.; m. Sheila Kay Gilligan, July 7, 1984; children: Kimberly Anne, Melissa Anne; stepchildren: Patrick K. Gilligan, Todd M. Gilligan. Student, U. Mo.; MBA, Pepperdine U., 1975. Ptnr. Foristall & Co., L.A., 1960-65; pres. Beverly Hills Film Corp., Calif., 1962-65; v.p. Buttes Gas and Oil Corp., Oakland, 1965-66; exec. v.p. TRE Corp., Beverly Hills, 1966-72; chmn., pres. Simplex Industries, Adrian, Mich., 1972-76; pres., chief oper. officer TRE Corp., L.A., 1976-86; chmn., CEO, MemTech Corp., Beverly Hills, 1987-91; chmn. Am. Builders Hardware Corp., Calif., 1991-93; chmn., CEO RHL Mgmt. Group, Inc., 1992-99; pres., COO, bd. dirs. Standard Brands Paint Co., Torrance, 1992-93; chmn., CEO, pres. Hawaiian Grocery Stores, Ltd., Honolulu, 1996-99; mng. dir. Camden Ptnrs., N.Y.C., 1999—. Bd. dirs. Future Flow Sys. Inc., Newbury Park, Calif. Mem. bus. coun. Nat. Democratic Com., Washington, 1983—; trustee Internat. Assn. for Shipboard Edn. Office: Dolphin Enterprises 4201 Long Beach Blvd Ste 206 Long Beach CA 90807-2020

LOEFFLER, WILLIAM ROBERT, quality productivity delivery specialist, engineering educator; b. Cleve., Aug. 31, 1949; s. Harry T. and Frances R. (Pearson) L.; children: Kelly Lynn, Robert Jason. BA, Wittenberg U., 1971; MA, SUNY, Stony Brook, 1972; EdS, U. Toledo, 1979; PhD, U. Mich., 1984. Dir. alt. learning ctr. Lucas County Schs., Toledo, 1977-79; dir. chem. and metall. svcs. Toledo Testing Lab., 1979-82; pres. Chem. Resources, Lambertville, Mich., 1982-83; v.p. Benchmark Techs., Toledo, 1983-86; pres. Loeffler Group, Inc., 1986—. Pres. Tech. Soc. Toledo, 1985-86; conf. chmn. Am. Soc. Quality Control, Deming Conf., Toledo, 1984; mem. Nat. Task Force ALARA Atomic Indsl. Forum, Washington; congl. sci. counselor PACCOS, Ohio; Ford Motor Co. prof., endowed chair Statis. Quality Studies Ea. Mich. U., 1986; examiner, trainer Malcolm Baldridge Nat. Quality Award, 1988-90. Editor: Jour. Toledo Tech. Topics, 1982-92; asst. editor: Jour. English Quar., 1976-77; contbr. articles to profl. jours. Vice-chmn. Pvt. Industry Coun., Monroe County, Mich., 1983, 84; chmn. Bus.-Industry-Edn. Day Toledo & Detroit C. of C., 1984-85; trustee Bedford Pub. Schs., Mich., 1982-85; chmn. Robotics Internat., 1985; bd. dirs., trustee Wittenberg U., 1991-95, Franciscan Health Sys., 1991-94, Riverside Health Group, 1993-98, North Coast Health Sys., 1994-98, Corp. for Effective Govt., 1995-96. Recipient Harvard Book award, 1967, Internat. Man of Yr. award for total quality mgmt. Cambridge Ctr., Eng., 1992; fellow SUNY, Stony Brook, 1975-76, Cambridge U., 1976-77. Fellow Am. Psychol. Soc.; mem. Am. Chem. Soc. (chmn. Toledo chpt. 1984), Am. Soc. Non-Destructive Testing, U. Mich. Club, Rotary, Phi Delta Kappa, Phi Kappa Phi. Methodist. Address: PO Box 857 Perrysburg OH 43552-0857 Office: PO Box 857 Perrysburg OH 43552-0857

LOEH, CORINNE RACHOW, artist, art collector; b. Livingston, Ill., Apr. 6, 1918; d. Tipmer Charles and Mae Leona (Batemon) Rachow; m. Hugo William Loeh (dec.); children: Sandra Mae Blaeser, Danna Clare Koschkee (dec.). Grad., Blackburn Coll., 1937; BS in Edn., Greenville Coll., 1950; MS in Art Edn., So. Ill. U., 1958. Tchr. pub. schs., Ill., 1937-52; art supr. Unit Dist. #1, Carlyle, 1952-55; tchr. art high sch., supr. K-9 Unit Dist. #2, Greenville, 1955-65, title one author, dir., 1965-69; prof. art Greenville Coll., 1956-65; art dir. Unit Dist. #46, Elgin, Ill., 1969-77; freelance artist Oro Valley, Ariz., 1982—; founder CLO Arts Inc., Andover, Mass., 2002. Founder CLO Arts, Inc., 2002; art collector CLO Art Gallery, Oro Valley, 1982—; cons. in field. Author: Prescription for Titans, 1971; editor: Ill. Art Edn. Assn. News, 1972, 77; one-woman shows include Judson Coll., Elgin, 1979, Western Gallery, Tucson, Ariz., 1985, 87, Blaeser Estate, Andover, Mass., Retrospective Art Show, Andover, 2000; represented in permanent collections at Archives of Nat. Mus. Women in Arts, Washington. Mem.: Tucson Art Mus., Fiber Arts Internat., Surface Designers, Nat. Mus. Women in Arts (charter mem.). Republican.

LOEHDEN, OTTO LOUIS, retired surgeon; b. Orenco, Oreg., June 14, 1933; MD, U. Oreg., 1958. Diplomate Am. Bd. Surgery. Intern USPHS Hosp., Norfolk, Va., 1958-59, resident New Orleans, 1959-61, resident in gen. surgery San Francisco, 1961-63; mem. staff Forest Grove Cmty. Hosp., Hillsboro, Oreg., Tuality Cmty. Hosp., Hillsboro; ret., 2000. Mem. ACS, Oreg. Med. Assn., Portland Surg. Soc., Washington County Med. Soc. E-mail: oloehden@aol.com.

LOEHLIN, JOHN CLINTON, psychologist, educator; b. Ferozepore, India, Jan. 13, 1926; s. Clinton Herbert and Eunice (Cleland) L.; m. Marjorie Leafdale, Jan. 2, 1962; children— Jennifer Ann, James Norris. AB, Harvard U., 1947; PhD, U. Calif., Berkeley, 1957. With rsch. dept. McCann-Erickson, Inc., Cleve., 1947-49; instr. to asst. prof. psychology U. Nebr., Lincoln, 1957-64; mem. faculty U. Tex., Austin, 1964—, prof. psychology and computer scis., 1969-92, prof. emeritus, 1992—. Author: Computer Models of Personality, 1968, Latent Variable Models, 1987, Genes and Environment in Personality Development, 1992; co-author: Race Differences in Intelligence, 1975, Heredity, Environment and Personality, 1976, Introduction to Theories of Personality, 1985. With USNR, 1945-47, 51-53. Fellow Ctr. Advanced Study Behavioral Scis., 1971-72. Fellow Am. Psychol. Soc.; mem. Behavior Genetics Assn., Soc. Multivariate Exptl. Psychology. Home: 304 Almarion Dr Austin TX 78746-5644 Office: U Tex Dept Psychology Austin TX 78712 E-mail: loehlin@psy.utexas.edu.

LOEHR, STEPHANIE SCHMAHL, school social worker; b. Watertown, N.Y., Dec. 14, 1941; d. John Schmahl and Helene (Mosely) Kay. AB in Elem. Edn., Ripon Coll., 1964; MSW, U. Wis., Milw., 1969, MA in Urban Affairs, 1973; cert. in marriage and family studies, Chgo. Family Inst., 1983. Diplomate Am. Bd. Examiners in Clin. Social Work; cert. ind. clin. social worker, Wis. Clinician Philstan Psychiat. Clinic, Milw., 1977-86; psychotherapist Psychiat. Consultation Assocs., 1986-89, Charter Behavioral Health Svcs., 1990—2000; sch. social worker Milw. Pub. Schs., 1989—; case work supr. Milwaukee County Dept. Social Svcs., Milw., 1974-77. Field instr. Sch. Social Welfare, U. Wis., Milw.; presenter workshops; pvt. practice psychotherapy. Mem. Nat. Assn. Social Workers (past state and local chpt. officer), Acad. Cert. Social Workers. Democrat. Unitarian-Universalist. Avocations: piano, singing, photography. Office: Milw Pub Schs Victory 2222 W Henry Ave Milwaukee WI 53221-4920

LOEHWING, RUDI CHARLES, JR. publicist, radio broadcasting executive, journalist; b. Newark, July 26, 1957; s. Rudy Charles Sr. and Joan Marie (Bell) L.; m. Claire Popham, Sept. 4, 1987; children: Aspasia Joyce, Tesia Victoria, Rudi Douglas, Anna Marie, Samantha Diane, Ian Ryan. Student, Biscayne U., 1975, Seton Hall U., 1977, Hubbard U., 1980. Announcer radio sta. WHBI FM, N.Y.C., 1970-72; producer Am. Culture Entertainment, Belleville, N.J., 1973-74, exec. producer Hollywood, Calif., 1988-94; CEO Broadcaster's Network Internat., La Crescenta, 1989—, U.K., 1989—. Bd. dirs. First Break, Hollywood, also U.K., 1988—. Author: Growing Pains, 1970; dir. exec. producer TV documentaries and comml. advertisements, 1983; patentee in field. Devel. dir. Tricentennial Found., Washington, 1989-90; bd. dirs. Civic Light Opera of South Bay Cities, 1998—, Tax Edn. Assn., Just Say No to Drugs, L.A., 1989, Hands Across the Atlantic, Internat. Country Top 10, The Rock of Russia, Job Search, Hollywood, U.K. and Russia. Named Youngest Comml. Radio Producer and Announcer for State of N.Y., Broadcaster's Network Internat., 1972 Mem. Nat. Press Club, Broadcasters Network Assn. (bd. dirs. 1977—), Profl. Bus. Comms. Assn. (founder 1989), BNI News Bur. (chmn. 1991—), Civic Light Opera of South Bay Cities (bd. dirs. 1996—). Avocations: flying, music, writing, photography, martial arts (recipient awards). Office: BNI Comms 2750 Pineridge Plz Tujunga CA 91042

LOEN, LINDA MICHEL, social worker, artist; b. New Haven, June 16, 1948; d. Benjamin and Roslyn Zelda (Pessin) Montlick; m. John A. Michel, May 4, 1975 (div. 1986); 1 child, Jason Michel; m. John Anthony Loen Jr., June 20, 1986; 1 child, Sandra Lynn Daignault. MS in Rehab. Counseling with honors, So. Conn. State U., New Haven, 1982, MSW with honors, 1994. Lic. clin. social worker; cert. in HIV case mgmt. Social worker Dept. Mental Retardation, 1975-80; social svc. case mgr. Conn. Cmty. Care, New Haven, 1990-97; behavioral health case mgr. Blue Cross/Blue Shield Managed Care HMO, Hamden, Conn., 1997-99; dir. of social svc. Gladeview Healthcare Ctr., 1999—. Mem. APA, NASW, NAMI. Roman Catholic. Avocations: art, canoeing, swimming, photography, oil painting. Home: 810 N Madison Rd Guilford CT 06437-1711 Office: Gladeview Nursing Home 70 Audubon St Old Saybrook CT 06475

LOENGARD, JOHN BORG, photographer, editor; b. N.Y.C., Sept. 5, 1934; s. Richard Otto and Margery (Borg) L.; m. Eleanor Sturgis, Aug. 25, 1963 (div. 1987); children: Charles, Jennifer, Anna BA, Harvard Coll., 1956. Staff photographer Life mag., N.Y.C., 1961-72, picture editor, 1973-87; freelance photographer, 1987—; columnist Popular Photography mag., N.Y.C., 1987, Am. Photographer, N.Y.C., 1988—. Author: Pictures Under Discussion, 1987, Life Classic Photographs: A Personal Interpretation by John Loengard, 1988, Life Faces: Commentary by John Loengard, 1991, Celebrating the Negative, 1994, Georgia O'Keeffe at Ghost Ranch, 1995, Life Photographers: What They Saw, 1998; essays in Life mag., The Shakers, 1967, Georgia O'Keeffe, 1968, Vanishing Cowboys, 1970, Photographers Over 80, 1982, Henry Moore, 1983, Interstate 80, 1989. Recipient Ansel Adams award Am. Soc. Mag. Photographers, 1987, Lifetime Achievement award Photographic Adminstrs., Inc., 1996. Home: 20 W 86th St New York NY 10024-3604 E-mail: loenpics@aol.com.

LOENGARD, RICHARD OTTO, JR. lawyer; b. N.Y.C, Jan. 28, 1932; s. Richard Otto and Margery (Borg) L.; m. Janet Sara Senderowitz, Apr. 11, 1964; children: Maranda C., Philippa S.M. AB, Harvard U., 1953, LLB, 1956. Bar: N.Y. 1956, U.S. Dist. Ct. (so. dist.) N.Y. 1958. Assoc. Fried, Frank, Harris, Shriver & Jacobson, predecessor firms, N.Y.C., 1956-64, ptnr., 1967-97; of counsel Fried, Frank, Harris, Shriver & Jacobson, 1997—; dep. tax legis. counsel, spl. asst. internat. tax affairs U.S. Dept. Treasury, Washington, 1964-67. Mem. Commerce Clearing House, Riverwoods, Ill. Editl. bd. Tax Transaction Libr., 1982-94; contbr. articles to profl. publs. Fellow Am. Coll. Tax Counsel; mem. ABA, N.Y. State Bar Assn. (exec. com. tax sect. 1984—, sec. 1994-95, vice chair 1995-97, chair 1997-98), Assn. Bar City N.Y. Office: Fried Frank Harris Shriver & Jacobson 1 New York Plz New York NY 10004-1980 E-mail: loengri@ffhsj.com.

LOERKE, WILLIAM CARL, art history educator; b. Toledo, Aug. 13, 1920; s. William Carl and Anna Louisa (Stallbaum) L.; m. Helen Trautmann, 1944; children— Anna Hurd, Timothy, Eric, Alison, Lisa Huff, Ellen, Martha. BA, Oberlin Coll., 1942; M.F.A., Princeton U., 1948, PhD, 1957. Acad. positions history of art Brown U., 1949-59; assoc. prof. Bryn Mawr Coll., 1959-64; prof. art history U. Pitts., 1964-71, chmn. fine arts dept., 1964-69; prof. Byzantine art Harvard U., Dumbarton Oaks Research Library, 1971-88, prof. emeritus, 1988—; dir. studies Ctr. Byzantine Studies, 1971-77; vis. prof. Cath. U. Am., 1978-88. Vis. prof. U. Md., 1988-92; mem. adv. bd. Ctr. for Advanced Study in Visual Arts, Nat. Gallery Art, Washington, 1979-82, 89-92, 97-2000. Co-author: The Place of Book Illumination in Byzantine Art, Princeton, 1975, Monasticism and the Arts, 1984, Codex Rossanensis, Commentarium, Rome, 1987, Architecture: Fundamental Issues, N.Y., 1990; contbr. Byzantine East, Latin West: Art Historical Studies in Honor of Kurt Weitzman, 1995; contbr. articles to profl. jours.; contbr. Dictionary of Byzantium, 1991. Served with USNR, 1943-46. Jr. fellow Princeton U., 1946-48, Dumbarton Oaks Harvard U., 1948-49, Danforth Tchr. fellow, 1956-57; Fulbright Rsch. scholar Am. Acad. Rome, 1952-53; recipient A.K. Porter prize Coll. Art Assn., 1961. Mem. Coll. Art Assn., Medieval Acad. Am., Soc. Fellows, Am. Acad. at Rome, Internat. Ctr. Med. Art. Home: 227 Gralan Rd Catonsville MD 21228-4835 E-mail: bloerke@aol.com.

LOESBERG, JONATHAN, humanities educator; b. N.Y.C., June 30, 1950; s. Burton and Gertrude Loesberg; m. Gail Grella, Aug. 9, 1975. AB, Brown U., 1972; MA, Cornell U., 1975, PhD, 1977. Acting asst. prof. Cornell U., Ithaca, N.Y., 1978-79; vis. asst. prof. Brandeis U., Boston, 1979-80; asst. prof. Holy Cross U., Worcester, 1980-82; from asst. to assoc. prof. Am. U., Washington, 1982-1991, prof., 1991—, chair dept. lit., 1995—2002. Fellow Rutgers Ctr. for Critical Analysis of Contemporary Culture, 2002—. Author: Fiction of Consciousness, 1986, Aestheticism and Deconstruction, 1991 (Award 1995, ACLS award 1995-96). Mem. N.E. Victorian Studies Assn. (pres.). Office: American U 4400 Massachusetts Ave Washington DC 20016 E-mail: jloesbe@american.edu.

LOESCH, KATHARINE TAYLOR (MRS. JOHN GEORGE LOESCH), communication and theatre educator; b. Berkeley, Calif., Apr. 13, 1922; d. Paul Schuster and Katharine (Whiteside) Taylor; m. John George Loesch, Aug. 28, 1948; 1 child, William Ross. Student, Swarthmore Coll., 1939-41, U. Wash., 1942; BS, Columbia U., 1944, MA, 1949; grad., Neighborhood Playhouse Sch., 1946; postgrad., Ind. U., 1953; PhD, Northwestern U., 1961. Instr. speech Wellesley (Mass.) Coll., 1949-52, Loyola U., Chgo., 1956; asst. prof. English and speech Roosevelt U., 1957, 62-65; assoc. prof. comm. and theatre U. Ill., 1968-87, assoc. prof. emeritus, 1987—. Contbr. articles to profl. jours.; author numerous poems; performer of poetry. Active ERA, Ill., 1975-76. Am. Philos. Soc. grant, 1970. Mem. MLA, Am. Soc. for Aesthetics, Linguistic Soc. Am., Chgo. Linguistic Soc. (co-chmn. 1954-56), Nat. Comm. Assn. (chair interpretation divsn. 1979-80, Golden Ann. award 1969), Celtic Studies Assn. N.Am., Pi Beta Phi. Episcopalian. Home: 2129 N Sedgwick St Chicago IL 60614-4619 Office: U Ill Dept Performing Arts M/C 255 1040 W Harrison St Chicago IL 60607-7130 E-mail: dpa@uic.edu.

LOESCH, MABEL LORRAINE, social worker; b. Annandale, Minn., July 1, 1925; d. Rudolph and Hedwig (Zeidler) Treichler; m. Harold Carl Loesch, Oct. 19, 1945; children: Stephen, Gretchen, Jonathan, Frederick. BS, La. State U., 1972, MSW, 1974. Cert. Acad. Cert. Social Worker, bd. cert. diplomate. Tchr. Am. schs., Tegucigalpa, Honduras, 1960-61, Guayaquil, Ecuador, 1962-66, La Ceiba, Honduras, 1966-67; supr. clin. svc. Blundon Home, Baton Rouge, 1974-81; social worker, cons. Dhaka, Bangladesh, 1981-85; social worker Manna Food Bank, Pensacola, Fla., 1986—. Adj. instr. social work dept. Southern U., Baton Rouge, 1976-81. Author: Generations in Germany and America, 1995, 300 Years in the Family, 1998, Family Farms, 2001, Exiled to America, 2001; editor: Making Do, 1989, Making Do II, 1994. Mem. adv. com. Luth. Ministries of Fla., 1993-97. Mem. NASW, Mensa (local sec. 1986-90, chair scholarships com. 1992—), InterTel, Phi Kappa Phi. Democrat. Lutheran. Avocation: genealogy. Home: 2140 E Scott St Pensacola FL 32503-4957

LOESCHER, RICHARD ALVIN, gastroenterologist; b. Brockton, Mass., Feb. 6, 1940; s. Vernon Alvin and Anna Marie (Good) L.; m. Linda Rockwell Clifford Loescher, June 5, 1965 (div. Jan. 1982); children: Steven Clifford Loescher, Laura May Loescher. BA, De Pauw U., 1961; MD cum laude, Harvard U., 1965. Diplomate Am. Bd. Internal Medicine, 1972, Am. Bd. Gastroenterology, 1973. Chief Med. Svc. U.S. Pub. Health Svc. Hosp., Lawton, Okla., 1967-69; chief Med. Staff, 1968-69; svc. unit dir., 1969; attending physician Seattle, 1970-71, U. Hosp., 1970-71; active staff Sacred Heart Med. Ctr., Eugene, Oreg., 1973—, Eugene (Oreg.) Hosp., 1972-88; courtesy staff McKenzie-Williamette Hosp., Springfield, Oreg., 1982—. Recipient Rector scholarship DePauw U., 1957-61, Maimonides award Harvard Med. Sch., 1965. Mem. AMA, ACP-Am. Soc. Internal Medicine, Lane County Med. Soc., Oreg. Med. Assn., Am. Soc. for Gastrointestinal Endoscopy, Am. Acad. Med. Acupuncture, Alpha Omega Alpha, Phi Beta Kappa. Democrat. Unitarian Universalist. Avocations: physical fitness, personal growth, magic, outdoor activities. Home: 2345 Patterson St Apt 34 Eugene OR 97405-2974 Office: 1162 Willamette St Eugene OR 97401-3568

LOESCH-FRIES, LORETTA SUE, virology educator; b. Ventura, Calif., Sept. 5, 1947; d. Frank James and Helyn Mildred (Stenson) L.; m. Robert Edward Fries, Feb. 14, 1976; children: Michael, Matthew. BS, Wash. State U., 1969; PhD, U. Wis., 1974. Sr. scientist Agrigenetics, Madison, Wis., 1981-88; asst. adj. prof. U. Wis., 1987-91; asst. prof. virology Purdue U., West Lafayette, Ind., 1991—. Panel mem. for grant rev. panels USDA, 1985, 86, Dept. of Energy, 1988. Asst. editor Molecular Plant Microbe Interactions, 1988-95, Virology, 1993-95, Jour. Virology, 1996—; contbr. articles to profl. jours. Mem. Am. Phytopathological Soc., Am. Soc. Virology, Internat. Soc. Plant Molecular Biology. Achievements include patents for trangenic virus-resistant plants. Office: Purdue U Dept Botany/Plant Pathology Agriculture Rsch Bldg West Lafayette IN 47907-1057

LOESENER, OTTO ROBERT, aerospace engineer; b. Guatemala, Sept. 29, 1960; s. Eduard and Margoth (Diaz) L.; m. Eloi Viana, Jan. 17, 1992. MSc, U. Hamburg, Germany, 1987; PhD, U. Stuttgart, Germany, 1993. R&D engr. U. Stuttgart, 1987-92, cons., 1993; project mgr. Physikalisch-Technische Bundesanstalt, Braunschweig, Germany, 1994-98; prof. indsl. engring. U. Del Valle, Guatemala City, Guatemala, 1995-98; quality auditor Digart, Switzerland, 1998—, DGQ, Germany, 1998—, EOQ, Europe, 1998—; mng. dir. Integral Quality Cons., S.A., Guatemala City, 1999—; indsl. devel. mgr. UN Indsl. Devel. Orgn., Vienna, Austria, 2000—. Cons. UN/Guatemalan Govt., San José, Costa Rica, 1990. Author: Pyrometrische Temperaturmessungen, 1993; contbr. articles to profl. jours. Treas. Artentinian Club Germany, Stuttgart, 1993. Grantee U. Del Valle, 1978-81, U. Hamburg, 1981-87. Mem. AIAA (sr.), Am. Astronaut. Soc. (founding mem.), German Phys. Soc., German Engring. Soc. Roman Catholic. Achievements include patent for linearpyrometer for investigations of thermal protection systems of spacecraft; arrangement for pyrometric temperature measurements on re-entry vehicles;far-infrared pyrometer for radiation temperature measurements on aerospace materials in an arc-heated wind tunnel. Office: UNIDO VIC Rm D2139 PO Box 300 A-1400 Vienna Austria

LOESER, HANS FERDINAND, lawyer; b. Kassel, Germany, Sept. 28, 1920; s. Max and Cecilia H. (Erlanger) L.; m. Herta Lewent, Dec. 14, 1944; children— Helen, Harris M., H. Thomas. Student CCNY, 1940-42, U. Pa., 1942-43; LL.B. magna cum laude, Harvard U., 1950. Bar: Mass. 1950, U.S. Supreme Ct. 1968. Asso. firm Foley, Hoag & Eliot, Boston, 1950-55, ptnr., 1956— ; hon. consul-gen. Republic of Senegal; mem. Mass. Bd. Bar Overseers; trustee Vineyard Open Land Found., Martha's Vineyard, Mass.; mem. exec. com. and nat. bd. Lawyers' Com. for Civil Rights Under Law, steering com. and past chmn. Lawyer's Com. for Civil Rights Under Law of Boston Bar Assn.; incorporator Univ. Hosp., Boston, Mt. Auburn Hosp., Cambridge, Mass. Served to capt. U.S. Army, 1942-46. Decorated Bronze Star, Purple Heart; hon. fellow U. Pa. Law Sch., 1978-79, commencement speaker, 1978. Fellow Am. Bar Found., Mass. Bar Found.; mem. ABA, Mass. Bar Assn., Boston Bar Assn. Clubs: Union, Harvard, Cambridge. Office: Foley Hoag & Eliot 1 Post Office Sq Ste 1700 Boston MA 02109-2175

LOESER, JOHN DAVID, neurosurgeon, educator; b. Newark, Dec. 14, 1935; s. Lewis Henry and Rhoda Sophie (Levy) L.; m. Susan Winifred Becker, June 11, 1961 (div. 1974); children: Sally Ann, Thomas Eric, Derek William; m. Karen Winslow, Dec. 29, 1977; 1 child, David Winslow. BA, Harvard U., 1957; MD, NYU, 1961. Diplomate Am. Bd. Neurol. Surgery; cert. Nat. Bd. Med. Examiners.; lic. neurosurgeon, Wash. Intern dept. surgery U. Calif., San Francisco, 1961-62; resident neurol. surgery U. Wash., Seattle, 1962-67; asst. prof. neurosurgery U. Calif., Irvine, 1967-68; asst. prof. neurol. surgery U. Wash., Seattle, 1969-75, assoc. prof., 1975-80, prof., 1980—, dir. Multidisciplinary Pain Clinic, 1983-97; chief div. of neurosurgery Children's Hosp. & Med. Ctr., 1987-93. Fulbright sr. scholar, Australia, 1989-90. Contbr. articles to profl. jours.; editor profl. books Served as maj. U.S. Army, 1968-70. Fellow AAAS; mem. Internat. Assn. Study of Pain (sec. 1984-90, pres. 1993-96), Am. Pain Soc. (treas. 1980-85, pres. 1986-87), Am. Assn. Neurol. Surgeons, North Pacific Soc. Neurology and Psychiatry, Wash. Assn. Neurosurgery, Western Neurosurg. Soc., Am. Acad. Pain Medicine, King County Med. Soc., Neuromodulation Soc., Conf. Neurol. Surgeons, Phi Beta Kappa, Alpha Omega Alpha. Avocations: skiing, woodcarving. Office: U Wash Dept Neurol Surgery PO Box 356470 Seattle WA 98195-6470

LOETE, STEVEN DONALD, pilot; b. Tacoma, Aug. 21, 1959; s. Donald Kenneth and Ida Lorraine (Buck) L.; m. Jodi Christine Barnett, 1998; children: Samantha, Tiffani, Joshua. BA, Pacific Luth. U., 1984. Pilot contracting office USAF, Williams AFB, Ariz., 1985; flight instr. Clover Park Tech. Coll., Tacoma, 1986, 99; charter pilot Stellar Exec., Chandler, Ariz., 1986-87; pilot, airline capt. Maui Airlines, Guam, 1987; airline capt., checkairman Westair Airlines, Fresno, Calif., 1987-98; airline pilot Air Wis., 1998—; owner Northwestern Properties; corp. pilot Exec. Jet Mgmt., Cin., 1999—. Contbr. Save the Children, 1988-90; mem. Angel Flight, U. Puget Sound, 1981-83; bd. dirs. aviation adv. com. Clover Park Tech. Coll., 1991—. 1st lt. USAF, 1983-93. Mem. Airline Pilots Assn. (chmn. organizing com. 1989, chmn. coun. 1989-91). Republican. Methodist. Avocations: racquetball, fishing. Home and Office: Box 760 Spanaway WA 98387 E-mail: northwesternproperties@attbi.com.

LOETHER, HERMAN JOHN, sociologist, educator; b. Pitts., Feb. 27, 1930; s. Herman Carl Loether and Evelyn M. Hester; m. Carolyn Louise Jackson, June 15, 1957; 1 child, Christopher Paul Loether. BA in Sociology, Calif. State U., L.A., 1951; MA in Sociology, U. Wash., 1953, PhD in Sociology, 1955. From asst. prof. to prof. sociology Calif. State U., L.A.,

1957-67; prof. sociology Calif. State U. Dominguez Hills, Carson, 1967-97, prof. emeritus, 1997—. Cons. Calif. Commn. on Crime Control and Violence Prevention, 1981-82, SWRL Ednl. Rsch. and Devel., Los Alamitos, Calif., 1984-85, Dominguez Hills accreditation task force Calif. State U., Carson, 1999. Author: Problems of Aging, 1967, 75, Social Impacts of Infectious Diseases, 2000; co-author: Descriptive and Inferential Statistics, 1976, 80, 88, 93, Social Research, 1999, 2002. With USN, 1955-57. Mem. AAUP, Am. Sociol. Assn., Am. Statis. Assn., Alpha Kappa Delta Internat. Sociology Honor Soc. (internat. pres. 1974-76). Avocations: genealogy, travel. Home: 6564 Monero Dr Palos Verdes Estates CA 90275-3264

LOEVINGER, LEE, lawyer, science writer; b. St. Paul, Apr. 24, 1913; s. Gustavus and Millie (Strouse) L.; m. Ruth Howe, Mar. 4, 1950; children: Barbara L., Eric H., Peter H. BA summa cum laude, U. Minn., 1933, JD, 1936. Bar: Minn. 1936, Mo. 1937, D.C. 1966, U.S. Supreme Ct., 1941. Assoc. Watson, Ess, Groner, Barnett & Whittaker, Kansas City, Mo., 1936-37; atty., regional atty. NLRB, 1937-41; with antitrust div. Dept. Justice, 1941-46; ptnr. Larson, Loevinger, Lindquist & Fraser, Mpls., 1946-60; assoc. justice Minn. Supreme Ct., 1960-61; asst. U.S. atty. gen. charge antitrust div. Dept. Justice, 1961-63; commr. FCC, 1963-68; ptnr. Hogan & Hartson, Washington, 1968-85, of counsel, 1986—; v.p., dir. Craig-Hallum Corp., Mpls., 1968-73. Dir. Petrolite Corp., St. Louis, 1978-83; U.S. rep. com. on restrictive bus. practices Orgn. for Econ. Coop. and Devel., 1961-64; spl. asst. to U.S. atty. gen., 1963-64; spl. counsel com. small bus. U.S. Senate, 1951-52; lectr. U. Minn., 1953-60; vis. prof. jurisprudence U. Minn. (Law Sch.), 1961; professorial lectr. Am. U., 1968-70; chmn. Minn. Atomic Devel. Problems Com., 1957-59; mem. Adminstrv. Conf. U.S., 1972-74; del. White House Conf. on Inflation, 1974; U.S. del. UNESCO Conf. on Mass Media, 1975, Internat. Telecomms. Conf. on Radio Frequencies, 1964, 66. Author: The Law of Free Enterprise, 1949, An Introduction to Legal Logic, 1952, Defending Antitrust Lawsuits, 1977, Science As Evidence, 1995; author first article to use term: jurimetrics, 1949; contbr. articles to profl. and sci. jours.; editor, contbr.: Basic Data on Atomic Devel. Problems in Minnesota, 1958; adv. bd. Antitrust Bull., Jurimetrics Jour. Served to lt. comdr. USNR, 1942-45. Recipient Outstanding Achievement award U. Minn., 1968; Freedoms Found. award, 1977, 84. Fellow Am. Acad. Appellate Lawyers; mem. ABA (del. of sci. and tech. sect. to Ho. of Dels. 1974-80, del. to joint conf. with AAAS 1974-76, co-chair 1990-93, liaison 1984-90, 93-98, chmn. sci. and tech. sect. 1982-83, coun. 1986-89, standing com. on nat. conf. groups 1984-90), AAAS, Minn. Bar Assn., Hennepin County Bar Assn., N.Y. Acad. Sci., D.C. Bar Assn., FCC Bar Assn., Broadcast Pioneers, U.S. C. of C. (antitrust coun. 1980-94), Am. Arbitration Assn. (comml. panel), Atlantic Legal Found. (adv. coun.), Cosmos Club (pres. 1990), City Club (Washington), Phi Beta Kappa, Sigma Xi, Delta Sigma Rho, Sigma Delta Chi, Phi Delta Gamma, Tau Kappa Alpha, Alpha Epsilon Rho. Home: 5600 Wisconsin Ave Apt 17D Chevy Chase MD 20815-4414 Office: Hogan & Hartson 555 13th St NW Ste 800E Washington DC 20004-1109 Fax: 202-637-5910. E-mail: loevil@hhlaw.com. *With age I come increasingly to believe that life is, and should be, a learning experience. This involves a peculiar paradox: Ignorance increases faster than knowledge, as each new fact or principle opens new frontiers for intellectual exploration. Thus, with greater learning comes intellectual humility and skepticism. So, after reaching 75 I am less certain of anything than at 25 I was of everything.*

LOEW, BRENDA, publisher; b. Boston, Apr. 1, 1951; d. Kenneth F. and Florence (Rosoff) Loew; m. Ira R. Tatelbaum, Aug. 1970 (div. May 1983); children: Laura Rani, Max Loew. BA, Boston U., 1971, postgrad., 1980-83; MA, Brown U., 1973; Hon. Cultural Doctorate Internat. Comm., World U., 1992; cert. paralegal profl. program, Northeastern U., 2000; grad., Newton Civilian Police Acad., 2000, Bojack Acad., 2001. Cert. manicurist Mass., English, speech tchr. Mass. Library asst. John D. Rockefeller Library, Providence, 1973; speech therapist Dartmouth (Mass.) Pub. Schs., 1974-79; pub., editor Eidos mag., Boston, 1984—; pres., treas., bd. dirs. Brush Hill Press, Inc., 1984-88; founder and pub. Tatelbaum Assn. Pub. Rels. & Fund Raising, 1987; recruiter Newbury Coll., Brookline, Mass., 1998; circulation sales Cmty. Newspapers, Needham, 1998-99; team leader Smarter Kids.Com, 1999; customer care Toysmart.com, Waltham, 1999; prodr. Newton (Mass.) TALK, 2000—. Active fundraising and pub. rels. Bill Baird AIDS Awareness Fund., 1987, Boston U. Ad Hoc Com. for Reproductive Freedom, 1987; chair Bill Baird Pro-Choice Def. League, Boston, 1989—99; participant numerous radio, TV, news broadcasts; cons. Bojack Acad., West Roxbury, Mass., 2000—; owner 4 Paws Dog Walking Svc. ; instr. Boston Learning Soc., Needham, Mass., Cambridge (Mass.) Ctr. for Adult Edn. Author: Eden Poems, 1982, Life Evolves From Living, 1983; short stories; editor: Boston Collection of Women's Poetry, 1983; editor (mag.) Eidos; contbr. articles to profl. jours., mags.; contbg. writer Community Advocate, Marlborough, Mass. Nat. Coalition Against Censorship; instr. Boston Learning Soc. , Needham, Mass., Cambridge Ctr. Adult Edn.; vol. instr. citizenship program ARC, Boston; media coord. Emerson Coll. Polit. Awareness Orgn.-Safer Sex March, 1987; cand. Newton Sch. Com., 1999, Newton Bd. Aldermen, 2001; dir. Nat. AIDS Telethon, Boston, 1987, Newton Taxpayers Assn., 2001. Recipient Lifestyle award, 1993, Golden Phallus award, 1996, Patriotic Citizen award VFW; named Saint, Universal Life Ch., Inc., 1997; named to Playboy Online Hall of Fame. Fellow: World Lit. Acad.; mem.: Am. Holistic Health Assn., Notary Pub., Internat. Massage Assn., Coop. Am. Bus. Network, Nat. Kidney Found. (life), Ind. Press. Assn., Mass. Fully Informed Jury Assn. (contact 1997—2001), Internat. Platform Assn., Pet Sitters Internat., Nat. Writers Union, Hadassah (life). Democrat. Avocations: politics, law, writing, canoeing, golf. E-mail: eidos@eidos.org.

LOEW, FRANKLIN MARTIN, college president, biologist, consultant; b. Syracuse, N.Y., Sept. 8, 1939; s. David Franklin and Sarah (Adelaide) Loew; children: Timothy, Andrew. BS, Cornell U., 1961, DVM, 1965; PhD, U. Sask., 1971; DHL, Becker Coll., Worcester, Mass., 1998. Cert. Lic. veterinarian. Rsch. asst. Tulane U., New Orleans, 1966—67; prof. U. Sask., Saskatoon, 1967—77; dir. comparative medicine Johns Hopkins U., Balt., 1977—82; dean Sch. Vet. Medicine, Tufts U., Boston, 1982—95, Henry and Lois Foster prof. comparative medicine, 1985—95; v.p. Tufts U. Devel. Corp. Inc., 1991—95; dean Coll. Vet. Medicine Cornell U., Ithaca, 1995—97; pres., CEO Med. Foods, Inc., Cambridge, Mass., 1997—98; pres. Becker Coll., Worcester, 1998—. Cons. Can. Coun. Animal Care, Ottawa, 1969—84; mem. life scis. com. Nat. Acad. Sci., Washington, 1981—88; N.B. Lectr. Am. Soc. Microbiology; mem. nat. adv. bd. Ctr. on Bioethics Lit., Kennedy Inst. Georgetown U., 1986—; Scholfield lectr. U. Guelph, Canada; Smith lectr. U. Saskatachwen; Schalm lectr. U. Calif.; univ. lectr. Tex. A&M U.; bd. dirs. Mass. Health Resources Inst.; sci. and tech. avd. com. State of Mass., 1988—92; mem. Sec.'s Avd. Com. nat. Rsch. Initiative USDA , 1992—95; trustee Marine Biol. Lab., 1990—94, New Eng. Aquarium, 1991—98, Guys Drug Rsch. Unit., England; mem. panel animal health Nat. Rsch. Coun., 1992—; mem. Tuskegee Bioethics Adv. Com., 1998—; vis. scientist MIT, 1998—; chmn. Med. Foods, Inc., Cambridge, 1998—. Author: (novels) Vet in the Saddle, 1978; editor Laboratory Animal Medicine, 1984; contbr. Chmn. bd. trustees Boston Zool. Soc., 1984—88; trustee Worcester Acad., 1984—90, 1999—; Humane Soc. U.S., 1999—; mem. adv. coun. Nat. Ctr. Rsch. Resources, NIH, Blue Ribbon USDA, 1987—91; bd. dirs. Mass. SPCA, 1996—; mem. bus. bd. Pharmacia & Upjohn, 1996—98. Decorated Queen Elizabeth II Jubilee medal Gov.-Gen. Can.; named Vet. of Yr., Mass. SPCA, 1989; recipient Charles River prize, Am. Vet. Med. Assn., 1988, Disting. Svc. award, Mass. Vet. Med. Assn., 1992; grantee Med. Rsch. Coun. Can. fellow, 1969—71. Mem.: Am. Antiquarian Soc., Am. Socs. for Exptl. Biology, Assn. Am. Vet. Colls. (pres. 1985—86), Am. Inst. Nutrition, AAAS, NAS/Inst. Medicine. Office: Becker Coll 61 Sever St Worcester MA 01609-2165 E-mail: floew@beckercollege.edu.

LOEWEN, ERWIN G. precision engineer, educator, consultant; b. Frankfurt, Germany, Apr. 12, 1921; came to U.S., 1937; s. Franz L. and Gladys M. (Marx) L.; m. Joanna M. Wills, Sept. 5, 1952 (div. 1996); children: Oliver F., Heidi R.; m. Anita Rosenfeld, Mar. 1999; children: Stefynie, Valerie. BMechE, NYU, 1941; MS, MIT, 1949, MMechE, 1950, ScD, 1952. Tech. dir. Taft-Pierce Mfg. Co., Woonsocket, R.I., 1952-60; dir. gratings and metrology Bausch & Lomb, Rochester, N.Y., 1960-85; v.p. R&D Milton Roy Co., 1985-87; prof. optics U. Rochester, 1988-97. Author: Diffraction, Gratings and Applications, 1997; contbr. articles on metal cutting, precision engring., and diffraction grating to profl. jours., chpt. to book. Staff sgt. U.S. Army, 1944-46, PTO. Recipient Civic Sci. and Tech. award Rochester C. of C., 1991. Fellow ASME (v.p. standardization), Optical Soc. Am. (David Richardson medal, 1984, Robert M. Burley prize 1993, Fraunhofer medal 1993, Rochester Engr. of Yr. 1992), Soc. Mfg. Engrs.; mem. Am. Soc. Precision Engrs. (hon.), Soc. Photoinstrumentation Engrs., Internat. Instn. Prodn. Engring. Rsch., Sigma Xi. Avocations: photography, skiing, swimming. Home: 8 Menlo Pl Rochester NY 14620-2718 E-mail: eloewen@aol.com.

LOEWENBERG, GERHARD, political science educator; b. Berlin, Germany, Oct. 2, 1928; came to U.S., 1936, naturalized, 1943; s. Walter and Anne Marie (Cassirer) L.; m. Ina Perlstein, Aug. 22, 1950; children: Deborah, Michael. AB, Cornell U., 1949, A.M., 1950, PhD, 1955. Mem. faculty Mount Holyoke Coll., 1953-69, chmn. dept. polit. sci., 1963-69, acting academic dean, 1968-69; prof. polit. sci. U. Iowa, Iowa City, 1970—, chmn. dept., 1982-84, dean Coll. Liberal Arts, 1984-92, dir. Comparative Legis. Research Center, 1971-82, 92—; vice chair East-West Parliamentary Practice Project, 1990-2000. Vis. assoc. prof. Columbia, UCLA, 1966, U. Mass. summer session at Bologna, Italy, 1967, Cornell U., 1968; mem. council Inter-Univ. Consortium for Polit. Research, 1971-74, chmn., 1973-74 Author: Parliament in the German Political System, 1967, Parlamentarismus im politischen System der Bundesrepublik Deutschland, 1969, Modern Parliaments: Change or Decline, 1971; co-author: Comparing Legislatures, 1979; co-editor: Handbook of Legislative Research, 1985, Legis. Studies Quar., Legislatures: Comparative Perspectives on Representative Assemblies, 2002; contbr. articles to profl. jours. Trustee Mt. Holyoke Coll., 1971-84, chmn., 1979-84. Fulbright fellow, 1957-58; Rockefeller fellow, 1961-62; Social Sci. Research Council faculty research fellow, 1964-65; Guggenheim fellow, 1969-70 Mem. Am. Polit. Sci. Assn. (coun. 1971-73, v.p. 1990-91, Frank J. Goodnow award 2001), Midwest Polit. Sci. Assn., Phi Beta Kappa, Phi Kappa Phi, Pi Sigma Alpha. Office: U Iowa 336 Schaeffer Hall Iowa City IA 52242-1409

LOEWENSTEIN, LENORE CECILE, retired school librarian; b. Far Rockaway, N.Y., July 11, 1932; d. Bernard and Anna (Goldberg) Pearlman; m. Walter Bernard Loewenstein, June 21, 1959; children: Mark, Marcia. BEd, SUNY, Potsdam, 1954; MLS, San Jose State U., 1984. Tchr. East Meadow (N.Y.) Sch. Dist., 1954-57, Plainview (N.Y.)-Old Bethpage Sch. Dist., 1957-59, Downers Grove (Ill.) Sch. Dist., 1960-61; substitute libr. Palo Alto, Menlo Park and Mountain View Sch. Dists., Calif., 1974-78; elem. sch. libr. Palo Alto Sch. Dist., 1978-83, mid. sch. libr., 1984-85; elem. sch. libr. Burlingame (Calif.) Sch. Dist., 1985-90, 2d and 3d grade tchr., 1990-92. Vol. cons. East Palo Alto Sch. Dist., 1985; mem. sch. site coun. Burlingame Sch. Dist., 1986-88. Author curriculum materials for elem. grades. Recipient J. Russell Kent award San Mateo County Bd. Suprs., Redwood City, Calif., 1989. Mem. AAUW. Avocations: writing children's stories, swimming, hiking. Home: 515 Jefferson Dr Palo Alto CA 94303-2834

LOEWENSTEIN, WALTER BERNARD, nuclear power technologist; b. Gensungen, Hesse, Germany, Dec. 23, 1926; came to U.S., 1938; s. Louis and Johanna ((Katz) L.; m. Lenore C. Pearlman, June 21, 1959; children: Mark Victor, Marcia Beth. BS, U. Puget Sound, 1949; postgrad., U. Wash., 1949-50; PhD, Ohio State U., 1954. Registered profl. engr., Calif. Rsch. asst., fellow Ohio State U., Columbus, 1951-54; rsch. asst. Los Alamos Nat. Lab., 1952-54; sr. physicist, divsn. dir. Argonne (Ill.) Nat. Lab., 1954-73; dept. dir., dep. divsn. dir. Electric Power Rsch. Inst., Palo Alto, Calif., 1973-89, profl. cons., 1989—, mem. large aerosol containment experiment project bd., 1983-87. Mem. Marviken project bd. Studsvik Rsch. Ctr., Stockholm, 1978-85; mem. LOFT project bd. Nuclear Energy Agy., Paris, 1982-89; mem. tech. adv. com. nuclear safety Ontario Hydro Corp., 1990-98; mem. nuclear engring. dept. adv. com. Brookhaven Nat. Lab., 1992-96; mem. advanced tech. divsn. adv. com. Los Alamos Nat. Lab., 1994-99; mem. nuclear engring. dept. adv. com. U. Calif., Berkeley, 1994—. With USNR, 1945-46. Recipient Alumnus Cum Laude award U. Puget Sound, 1976. Fellow Am. Phys. Soc., Am. Nuclear Soc. (v.p., pres. 1988-90); mem. Am. Assn. Engring. Socs. (sec., treas. 1990), Nat. Acad. Engring. Jewish. Avocations: history, golf. Home and Office: 515 Jefferson Dr Palo Alto CA 94303 E-mail: wblo3@aol.com.

LOEWENSTEIN, WERNER RANDOLPH, physiologist, biophysicist, educator; b. Spangenberg, Germany, Feb. 14, 1926; came to U.S., 1957; naturalized, 1965. s. Siegfried and Adele (Muller) von Loewenstein; m. Birgit Rose, Oct. 7, 1971; children: Claudia, Patricia, Harriett, Stewart. BS, U. Chile, 1945, PhD, 1950. Instr. physiology U. Chile, Santiago, 1951-53, assoc. prof., 1955-57; fellow in residence Wilmer Inst., Johns Hopkins U., Balt., 1953-54; rsch. zoologist UCLA, 1954-55; asst. prof. physiology Columbia U. Coll. Physicians and Surgeons, N.Y.C., 1957-59, assoc. prof., 1959-66, prof., 1966-71, dir. cell physics lab., 1963-71; prof. physiology and biophysics, chmn. dept. U. Miami (Fla.) Sch. Medicine, 1971-95, prof., chmn. emeritus, 1995—; dir. lab. cell comm. Marine Biol. Lab., Woods Hole, 1995—. Block lectr. U. Chgo., 1960; lectr. Royal Swedish Acad. Sci., 1966; Max Planck lectr., 1967, Claude Bernard lectr., Coll. de France, 1970; Fulbright disting. prof., 1970, USSR Acad. Sci. lectr., Leningrad, 1975; Humboldt lectr., 1988, Humbolt lectr., Munich, 1988, Lauger lectr., Konstanz, 1991, Hillarp lectr., Munich, 1993; mem. Pres. Ford's Biomed. Rsch. Adv. Panel, 1975-77, USAF Sci. Adv. Panel, 1982-86 Author: The Touchstone of Life, 1999, Penguin Books, 2000; editor Biochimica et Biophysica Acta, 1967-74; editor in chief Jour. Membrane Biology, 1969—; editor Handbook of Sensory Physiology, 51 vols., 1971-77; contbr. numerous articles on membrane biophysics, physiology of intercellular communication, neurophysiolog and cancer rsch. to profl. jours. Kellogg internat. fellow in physiology, 1953-55; Commonwealth Fund internat. fellow, 1967; NSF, NIH Rsch. grantee. Mem. N.Y. Acad. Scis.; mem. Am. Physiol. Soc., Biophys. Soc., Soc. Gen. Physiologists, The Harvey Society, Soc. Neuroscience, Marine Biol. Lab. Woods Hole (corp. mem.), Quisset Yacht Club. Office: Marine Biol Lab Lab Cell Comm 7 M B L St Woods Hole MA 02543-1015

LOEWENTHAL, NESSA PARKER, intercultural communications consultant; b. Chgo., Oct. 13, 1930; d. Abner and Frances (Ness) Parker; m. Martin Moshe Loewenthal, July 7, 1951 (dec. Aug. 1973); children: Dann Marcus, Ronn Carl, Deena Miriam; m. Gerson B. Selk, Apr. 17, 1982 (dec. June 1987). BA in Edn. and Psychology, Stanford U., 1952. Faculty Stanford Inst. for Intercultural Communication, Palo Alto, Calif., 1973-87; dir. Trans Cultural Svcs., San Francisco, 1981-86, Portland, Oreg., 1986—. Dir. dependent svcs. and internat. edn. Bechtel Group, San Francisco, 1973-81, internat. edn. cons., 1981-84; mem. adv. com. dept. internat. studies Lesley Coll., Cambridge, Mass., 1986—; mem. Oreg. Ethics Commns., 1990—; mem. Bay Area Ethics Consortium, Berkeley, 1985-90; chmn. ethics com. Sietar Internat., Washington, 1987—, mem. governing bd., 1992-95; mem. faculty Summer Inst. for Internat. Comms., Portland, Oreg., 1987-97; core faculty Oreg. Gov.'s Sch. Svc. Leadership, Salem, 1995-97. Author: Professional Integration, 1987, Update: Federal Republic of Germany, 1990, Update: Great Britain, 1987; author, editor book series Your International Assignment, 1973-81; contbr. articles to profl. jours. Mem. equal opportunity and social justice task force Nat. Jewish Coun. on Pub. Affairs; bd. dirs. Kids on the Block, Portland, Portland Jewish Acad., 1996—, Portland Ashkalon Sister City Assn., Portland Jewish Fedn., 1999—, Coalition to Eliminate Bias and Hate Crimes in Oreg., 1999—; bd. dirs., co-chair ethics com. Soc. Humanistic Judaism, 1996-99; task force on Racism and Violence, Portland, Oreg.; mem. Lafayette (Calif.) Traffic Commn., 1974-80; bd. dirs. Ctr. for Ethics and Social Policy, 1988-91; mem. exec. bd. and planning com. Temple Isaiah, Lafayette, 1978-82; bd. dirs. Calif. Symphony, Orinda, 1988-90; mem. exec. com. overseas schs. adv. com. U.S. Dept. State, 1976-82; bd. dirs. Jewish Fedn. Oregon; mem. cmty. rels. com. Portland Jewish Fedn.; mem. Nat. Jewish Cmty. Rels.; mem. Task Force on Racism, Ethnicity and Pub. Policy, 1998—. Named Sr. Interculturalist, Sietar Internat., 1986. Mem. ASTD (exec. bd. internat. profl. performance area 1993-97, 99), Soc. for Intercultural Edn. Tng. and Rsch. (chmn. 1986-87, nomination com. 1984-86, co-chmn. 1989-90, chmn. ethics com. 1989-98, governing bd. 1992-95), World Affairs Coun. Democrat. Avocations: photography, swimming. Office: 2399 NW Hosmer Lake Dr Bend OR 97701-5475 E-mail: nessa@transport.com.

LOEWINGER, KENNETH JEFFERY, lawyer; b. Washington, Sept. 22, 1945; s. Myron Arthur and Lenore Loewinger; m. Margaret Irene Krol, May 5, 1978. BA, Georgetown U., 1967, JD, 1971. Bar: U.S. Dist. Ct. D.C. 1971, U.S. Ct. Mil. Appeals 1972, U.S. Ct. Appeals (D.C. cir.) 1972, U.S. Supreme Ct. 1979. Law clk. to judge D.C. Superior Ct., Washington, 1971-72; law clk. to presiding judge D.C. Ct. Appeals, 1972-74; sr. ptnr. Loewinger, Brand & Kappstatter, 1975-95, Loewinger & Brand, PLLC, Washington, 1995—. Pres. N.Am. Title and Escrow Co., Inc., 1976—; mem. D.C. Superior Ct., 1976—; mem. adv. com. U.S. Bankruptcy Ct., 1985-86. Author: Loewinger on Landlord and Tenant, 1986. Commr. Housing Prodn. Com., D.C., 1986-87. Mem. ABA, D.C. Bar Assn., Supreme Ct. Hist. Soc. Office: Loewinger & Brand 471 H St NW Washington DC 20001-2617

LOEWY, KATHY, social worker, therapist; b. Logan, Utah, Mar. 27, 1948; d. Roy and Donna Cook; m. James Loewy, May 22, 1969; children: Krystal, Steve. BS in Psychology, U. Utah, 1986, MSW, 1988. Lic. and cert. clin. social worker. Adminstrv. asst. U. Utah, Salt Lake City, 1984-88; social work intern Youth Svcs. Ctr., 1987; P.A.T. clinician Olympus View Hosp., 1988-89; social work intern LDS Social Svcs., Sandy, Utah, 1988; contract social worker LDS Social Svcs. Sandy, 1988-93; svcs. dir., social worker Nat. Multiple Sclerosis Soc., Salt Lake City, 1991—, dir. program svcs., 1991-92; social worker Health South Rehab. Hosp., 1995-99. Vol. U. Utah Sch. on Alcohol & Drug Abuse, Salt Lake City, 1985-87; vol. speaker local sch. dist., 1988—; women's conf. speaker LDS Ch., American Fork, Utah, 1988; edn. support group leader various chs., Salt Lake City, 1987-88; mem. continuing edn. com. Grad. Sch. Social Work, U. Utah, 1994—. Mem. NASW, Assn. Mormon Counselors and Psychotherapists, Golden Key, Phi Kappa Phi, Psi Chi, Phi Eta Sigma. Democrat. Mem. Lds Ch. Avocations: piano, travelling, oil painting, cooking. Office: Twin Peaks Elem Sch 5325 South 1045 East Salt Lake City UT 84117

LOFFREDI, DEBORAH LYNN, music educator, actress; b. Clearfield, Pa., Feb. 7, 1974; d. Helen Ruth Loffredi. BFA in Music Theater, Point Pk. Coll., 1999. Performer Walt Disney World, Orlando, Fla., 1994—95; dir., founder Musically Yours, Clearfield, Pa., 1990—. Dir. CAST Children's Theatre, Clearfield, 1992—; pvt. acting, dance & voice tchr., Clearfield, 1990—. Lutheran. Avocations: animal activism, performing.

LOFGREN, ANNE ELIZABETH, musician, educator; b. Rochester, Minn., May 11, 1948; d. Karl Adolph and Jean Frances Lofgren; m. Sawa Popoff, Aug. 30, 1983 (div. June 1989). BA in Music summa cum laude, BS in Music Edn. with high distinction, U. Minn., 1971; MS of Music in Clarinet, Mich. State U., 1974; MA in TESOL, Columbia U., 1992; diploma in oboe, Mozarteum, Salzburg, Austria, 1978, Konservatorium der Stadt Wien, Vienna, 1981. Tchr. clarinet and recorder Salzburger Musikschulwerk, Salzburg, Austria, 1974-78; tchg. asst. English Austrian Ministry of Edn. and Arts, 1976-77; tchr. oboe Musikschulen der Stadt Wien, Vienna, 1980-85; oboist Vereinigte Buhnen Wien, 1984-90; adj. lectr. ESL Kingsborough Cmty. Coll., Bklyn., 1991-93; tchr. ESL Jewish Cmty. House of Bensonhurst, 1992-93, Sprachinstitut der Industrie, Vienna, 1993-96; oboist Orquesta Filarmonica de Queretaro, Mex., 1996-2000; tchr. English Oxford Sch. English, Mestre, Italy, 2000; oboist Orquesta Sinfonica, Monterrey, Mex., 2001—. Mem. Phi Beta Kappa, Pi Kappa Lambda. Avocations: literature, foreign languages, Flamenco dancing, sewing. Home: 211 2nd St NW Apt 1916 Rochester MN 55901-3101 E-mail: oboe@mailcity.com.

LOFGREN, CHARLES AUGUSTIN, legal and constitutional historian, history educator; b. Missoula, Mont., Sept. 8, 1939; s. Cornelius Willard and Helen Mary (Augustin) L.; m. Jennifer Jenkins Wood, Aug. 6, 1986. AB with great distinction, Stanford U., 1961; AM, 1962, PhD, 1966. Instr. history San Jose State Coll., 1965-66; asst. prof. Claremont McKenna Coll., 1966-71; assoc. prof., 1971-76; prof., 1976—; Roy P. Crocker prof. Am. history and politics, 1976—. Author: Government form Reflection and Choice, 1986, The Plessy Case, 1988, Claremont Pioneers, 1996; contbr. articles to profl. jours. Served with USAR, 1957-63. Mem. Am. Soc. Legal History, Orgn. Am. Historians, Am. Hist. Assn. Republican. Roman Catholic. Office: Claremont McKenna Coll Dept History 850 Columbia Ave Claremont CA 91711-6420

LOFGREN, DONNA LEE, geneticist; b. Bay Shore, N.Y., Apr. 13, 1957; d. Carl Oscar and Esther Louise (Kustes) L. BS, Cornell U., 1979; MS, Va. Polytech. Inst. and State U., 1981, PhD, 1984. Postdoctoral rsch. assoc. Dept. Animal Scis. Purdue U., West Lafayette, Ind., 1985-90, prof. assoc. in animal breeding, 1990—. Mem. Am. Soc. Animal Sci., Am. Dairy Sci. Assn., Sigma Xi (rsch. award 1985). Office: Dept Animal Sci Purdue U 1151 Lilly Hall West Lafayette IN 47907-1151 E-mail: dlofgren@purdue.edu.

LOFGREN, KARL ADOLPH, surgeon, educator; b. Killeberg, Sweden, Apr. 1, 1915; s. Hokan Albin and Teckla Elizabeth (Carlsson) L.; m. Jean Frances Taylor, Sept. 12, 1942; children: Karl Edward, Anne Elizabeth. Student, Northwestern U., 1934-37; MD, Harvard U., 1941; MS in Surgery, U. Minn., 1947. Diplomate Am. Bd. Surgery. Intern U. Minn. Hosps., Mpls., 1941-42; Mayo Found. fellow in surgery, 1942-44, 46-48; asst. surgeon Royal Acad. Hosp., Uppsala, Sweden, 1949; asst. to surg. staff Mayo Clinic, Rochester, Minn., 1949-50, cons. sect. peripheral vein surgery, 1950-81; instr. in surgery Mayo Grad. Sch. Medicine, 1951-60, asst. prof. surgery, 1960-74; comdg. officer USNR Med. Co. Mayo Clinic, 1963-67, head sect. peripheral vein surgery, dept. surgery, 1966-79, sr. cons., 1980-81. Assoc. prof. surgery Mayo Med. Sch., 1974-79, prof., 1979-81, emeritus prof., 1982— ; cons. surg. staff Rochester Meth. Hosp., St. Mary's Hosp. Contbr. chpts. to textbooks, articles to profl. jours. Mem. adv. bd. Salvation Army, Rochester, 1959-81, 82— , pres., 1962-63. Served to capt. M.C. USNR, 1944-46. Decorated Bronze Star Fellow ACS; mem. Soc. Vascular Surgery, Midwestern Vascular Surgery Soc., Internat. Cardiovascular Soc., Minn. Surg. Soc., Swedish Surg. Soc. (hon.), Swiss Soc. Phlebology (co-worker), So. Minn. Med. Assn. (pres. 1972-73), Scandinavian Soc. Phlebology (hon.), Am. Venous Forum, Rotary Club, Sigma Xi. Baptist. Office: Mayo Clin Rochester MN 55905-0001 Home: 211 2nd St NW Apt 1916 Rochester MN 55901

LOFGREN, ZOE, congresswoman; b. San Mateo, Calif., Dec. 21, 1947; d. Milton R. and Mary Violet Lofgren; m. John Marshall Collins, Oct. 22, 1978; children: Sheila Zoe Lofgren Collins, John Charles Lofgren Collins. BA in Polit. Sci., Stanford U., 1970; JD cum laude, U. Santa Clara, 1975. Bar: Calif. 1975, D.C. Adminstrv. asst. to Congressman Don Edwards, San Jose, Calif., 1970-79; ptnr. Webber and Lofgren, 1979-81; mem. Santa Clara County Bd. Suprs., 1981-94, U.S. Congress from 16th Calif. dist., 1995—. Mem. com. on stds. of ofcl. conduct, jud. com., sci. com.; part-time prof. law U. Santa Clara, 1978-80. Exec. dir. Cmty. Housing Developers, Inc., 1979-80; trustee San Jose C.C. Dist., 1979-81; bd. dirs. Cmty. Legal Svcs., 1978-81, San Jose Housing Svc. Ctr., 1978-79; mem. steering com. sr. citizens housing referendum, 1978; del. Calif. State Bar Conv., 1979-82, Dem. Nat. Conv., 1976; active Assn. Immigration and Nationality Lawyers, 1976-82, Calif. State Dem. Ctrl. Com., 1975-78, Santa Clara County Dem. Ctrl. Com., 1974-78, Notre Dame H.S. Blue Ribbon Com., 1981-84, Victim-Witness Adv. Bd., 1981-94. Recipient Bancroft-Whitney award for Excellence in Criminal Procedure, 1973. Mem. Santa Clara County Bar Assn. (trustee 1979—), Santa Clara County Women Lawyers Com. (exec. bd. 1979-80), Santa Clara Law Sch. Alumni Assn. (v.p. 1977, pres. 1978), Nat. Women's Polit. Caucus, Assn. of Bay Area Govts. (exec. bd. 1981-86). Office: US Ho Reps 227 Cannon Ho Office Bldg Washington DC 20515-0516 also: 635 N 1st St Ste B San Jose CA 95112-5110*

LOFLAND, GARY KENNETH, cardiac surgeon; b. Milford, Del., Mar. 5, 1951; s. Joseph Sudler and Doris Louise (Peters) L.; m. Janice Marie Show, Feb. 3, 1979; children: Kiernan Sudler, Glennis Kathleen. BA cum laude, Boston U., 1969, MD cum laude, 1975. Diplomate Am. Bd. Surgery, Am. Bd. Thoracic Surgery; lic. physician, Va., N.Y., Mont., N.C. Intern, jr. asst. resident in surgery Duke U. Med. Ctr., Durham, N.C., 1975-81, rsch. fellow dept. surgery, 1979-81, sr. asst. resident in surgery, 1981-84, chief resident in surgery, 1984-85, teaching scholar in cardiac surgery, 1985-86; sr. registrar in cardiothoracic surgery Hosp. for Sick Children, London, 1986-87; dir. cardiovascular surgery Children's Hosp. of Buffalo, 1987-88; asst. prof. surgery SUNY, Buffalo, 1987-88; assoc. prof. surgery/pediatrics, Med. Coll. Va., Richmond, 1988-94, dir. pediatric cardiac surgery/med. dir. cardiac surgery ICU, 1988-94; clin. prof. surgery Georgetown U., Washington, 1994-97; dir. Columbia/HCA Ctr. Congenital Heart Disease, Richmond, 1994-97; dir. cardiovascular surgery Children's Mercy Hosp., Kansas City, Mo., 1997—; prof. surgery U. Mo. Kansas City Sch. Medicine, 1997—, Joseph Boon Gregg chair sect. cardiac surgery. Editor (in chief): Progress in Pediat. Cardiology, 2002—; mem. editl. rev. bd.: , —, mem. editl. rev. bd.: Year Book of Thoracic Surgery, —; contbr. articles. Pres. Am. Heart Assn., Richmond; mem. bd. trustees Transplant Found. Lt. comdr. USPHS, 1977-79. Recipient Univ. Hosp. Trustees award, Boston, 1975; HEW/USPHS commendation medal, 1979. Mem. AMA, Am. Heart Assn., Assn. for Acad. Surgery, Internat. Soc. for Heart Transplantation, Med. Soc. Va., Richmond Acad. Medicine, Richmond Surg. Soc., So. Thoracic Surg. Assn., Soc. for Thoracic Surgeons, Congenital Heart Surgeons Soc., , Alpha Omega Alpha. Home: PO Box 126 Crozier VA 23039-0126 Office: Children's Mercy Hosp Divsn Cardiovascular Surgery 2406 Gillham Rd Kansas City MO 64108

LÖFSTEDT, BENGT TORKEL MAGNUS, classics educator; b. Lund, Sweden, Nov. 14, 1931; arrived in U.S., 1967; s. Ernst Martin Hugo and Sigrid (Johanson) L.; m. Maija-Leena Kekomäki, Oct. 15, 1961; children: Ragnar, Torsten, Ritva, Ingvar. MA, U. Uppsala, Sweden, 1954, Fil. Lic. (PhD), 1957, Fil. doktor, 1961. Asst. prof. Latin U. Uppsala, 1962-67; asso. prof. Mediaeval Latin U. Calif. at Los Angeles, 1967-68, prof., 1968—. Contbr. Swedish newspapers Fria Ord, Vägen Framät. Author: Studien Über die Sprache der langobardischen Gesetze, 1961, Der hibernolateinische Grammatiker Malsachanus, 1965, Zenonis Veronensis Tractatus, 1971, Ars Laureshamensis, 1977, Sedulius Scottus: In Donati artem minorem, in Priscianum, in Eutychem, 1977, Sedulius Scottus: in Donati artem maiorem, 1977; author: (with G.J. Gebauer) Bonifatius: Ars Grammatica, 1980; author: Ars Ambrosiana, 1982, Beauts Liebanensis: Adversus Elipandum, 1984; author: (with L. Holtz and A. Kibre) Smaragdus: Liber in Partibus Donati, 1986; author: (with Leena Löfstedt) Maturin Cordier: De Corrupti Sermonis Emendatione, 1989; author: Sedulius Scottus: Kommntar zum Evangelium nach Matthäus 1, 1-11,1, 1989, Sedulius Scottus: Kommentar zum Evangelium nach Matthäus, 11,2 bis Schluss, 1991; author: (with B. Bischoff) Anonymus ad Cuimnanum, 1992; author: Vier Juvenal-Kommentare aus dem 12. Jh., 1995; author: (with Scott Talkovic) Diego Valadés: Catholicae Assertiones, 1998; author: Ausgewählte Aufsätze, 2000, Hrabanus Maurus: Expositio in Matthaeum, 2000; contbr. articles. Served to lt. Swedish Army, 1959-60. Alexander von Humboldt-Stiftung fellow Munich, 1961-62; Humanities Inst., U. Calif. grantee, 1968, 71; Am. Philos. Soc. grantee, 1971, 74; Am. Council Learned Socs. grantee, 1972, 75 Lutheran. Office: UCLA Dept Classics 405 Hilgard Ave Los Angeles CA 90095-1417

LÖFSTEDT, LEENA (MAIJA LEENA LÖFSTEDT), Romance philology educator; b. Helsinki, Finland, July 17, 1937; came to U.S., 1967; d. Paavo and Maire Anelma (Sormunen) Kekomäki; m. Bengt Torkel Magnus Löfstedt, Oct. 15, 1961; children: Ragnar, Torsten, Ritva, Ingvar. MA, Helsinki U., 1960, PhD, 1966. Assoc. prof. Romance philology U. Helsinki, 1976-78, periodical tchg. of Romance philology, 1980—; prof. Romance philology U. Jyväskylä, Finland, 1978-81; rsch. assoc. Ctr. for Medieval and Renaissance Studies, UCLA, 1989—. Mem. Adv. Coun. RomancePhilology, Berkeley, Calif., 1996—; mem. Com. Sci., RLiR, Nancy, France, 1998—; adv. coun. Neuphilologische Mitteilungen, Helsinki, 2001—. Author: Les expressions du commandement et de la défense en latin, 1966, Textual criticism: editions of Old French translations of Vegetius by Jean de Meun, 1979, Jean de Vignay, 1982, the anonymous of 1380, 1989, and the editio princeps of an Old French translation of Gratian's Decretum, 1992, 93, 96, 97, 2001, (with Bengt Löfstedt) Maturin Cordier, De Corrupti sermonis emendatione, 1989; contbr. numerous articles to profl. jours. Mem. Société Néophilologique, Medieval Acad. Am., Academia Scientiarum Fennica, N.Y. Acad. Scis. Lutheran. Avocations: family activities, hiking, gardening. E-mail: lofstedt@humnet.ucla.edu.

LOFSTROM, MARK D. lawyer, educator, communications executive; b. Mpls., May 11, 1953; s. Dennis E. and Dorothy Dee (Schreiber) L. BA in Art History, Carleton Coll., 1979; MBA, Columbia U., 1989; JD, U. Hawaii, 1992. Bar: Hawaii 1992, Minn. 1995. Pub. rels. asst. Honolulu Acad. Arts, 1979, pub. rels. rep., 1980-84, pub. rels. officer, 1984-87; law clk. Kiefer Oshima Chun Fong and Chung, Honolulu, 1990-91; assoc. Cades Schutte Fleming & Wright, 1991-95; pvt. practice Law Offices of Mark D. Lofstrom, Mpls., 1995-97; rep. sales mgr. Guthrie Theater and Minn. Orch., Minn., 1997-99; class counsel Milberg Weiss et al., 1999-2000; atty. Patterson, Thuente et al., Mpls., 2000-01. Instr. internat. bus. law/bus. law for accts. U. Hawaii Coll. Bus., 1995-96; instr. art law U. Hawaii summer session, 1995-96; organizer artists and writers exhbn., 1981; coord. rep. program Carleton Coll. Alumni Assn., Hawaii, 1984-87; co-editor and mktg. assoc. Pacific Telecomms. Coun., 1988-92, intern East-West Ctr., 1992. Editor mag. on preservation; exec. editor U. Hawaii Law Rev., 1991-92; co-editor: (newsletter) Pacific Comm. Coun. Procs., 1990-92; bd. editors Hawaii Bar Jour., 1992-97; contbr. articles on current exhbns., intellectual property, art, and internat. law. Sec., bd. dirs. Arts Coun. Hawaii, 1985-86, chmn. ways and means com., 1986-87, pres. bd. dirs.; bd. dirs. Hawaii Alliance for Arts Edn., 1994-95, chmn.-elect, 1995-97; mem. St. Mathias Twp. Comprehensive Devel. Plan Com., 1997-99; dir. Minn. Stonewall DFL, 2000—; v.p. Rainbow Health Initiative, 2001—. Recipient NCR Stakeholders award, 1988, legal rsch. and writing award Hawaii State Bar Assn. Young Lawyers Div., 1991. Mem. ABA, Hawaii State Bar Assn. (sec. internat. law sect. 1994, chair internat. law sect. 1995-96), Minn. Bar Assn. Office: PO Box 3605 Minneapolis MN 55403-0605

LOFTIN, RICHARD BOWEN, physics and computer science educator, researcher; b. Hearne, Tex., June 29, 1949; s. Richard and Dorothy Mae (Weems) L.; m. Karin Christiane John Cibula, Nov. 23, 1972; children: Elisabeth Christiane, Benjamin Bowen. BS, Tex. A&M U., 1970; MA, Rice U., 1973, PhD, 1975. Asst. physics prof. Tex. A&M U., Galveston, 1975-76; asst. prof. U. Houston-Downtown, 1976-80; assoc. prof. U. Houston, 1980-88; prof. physics U. Houston-Downtown, 1988-94; prof. computer sci. U. Houston, 1994—; faculty assoc. software tech. br. NASA Johnson Space Ctr., 1986—. Cons. McDonnell Douglas Space Systems Co., 1990-92, LinCom, 1992-93. Contbr. articles to Innovative Applications of Artificial Intelligence, Machine Mediated Learning, ASCE Monograph, Internat. Advances in Nondestructive Testing, Jour. of Applied Physics and numerous others. Mem. bd. Ministerial Edn. Wis. Luth. Synod, 1990—, dist. coord. parish edn. south cen. dist., 1991—. Recipient Space Act award NASA, 1992, Pub. Svc. medal NASA, 1993. Mem. AIAA (vice chmn. com. on stds. for space automation and robotics 1990-93, tech. com. on artificial intelligence 1992—), Am. Assn. Artificial Intelligence, Am. Assn. Physics Tchrs., Am. Phys. Soc., Assn. for Computing Machinery. Achievements include co-design of architecture for intelligent computer-aided training systems; patent in computer software. Office: U Houston One Main St Houston TX 77002

LOFTIS, JOHN, JR. (JOHN CLYDE LOFTIS JR.), English language educator; b. Atlanta, May 16, 1919; s. John Clyde and Marbeth (Brown) L.; m. Anne Nevins, June 29, 1946; children: Mary, Laura, Lucy. BA, Emory U., 1940; MA, Princeton U., 1942, PhD, 1948. Instr. English Princeton, 1946-48; instr., then asst. prof. English UCLA, 1948-52; faculty Stanford U., 1952-81, prof. English, 1958-81, Bailey prof. English, 1977-81, Bailey prof. emeritus, 1981—, chmn. dept., 1973-76. Author: Steele at Drury Lane, 1952, Comedy and Society from Congreve to Fielding, 1959, La Independencia de la Literatura Norteamericana, 1961, The Politics of Drama in Augustan England, 1963, The Spanish Plays of Neoclassical England, 1973, (with others) The Revels History of Drama in English, Vol. V, 1976, Sheridan and the Drama of Georgian England, 1977, Renaissance Drama in England and Spain: Topical Allusion and History Plays, 1987; editor: (Steele) The Theatre, 1962, Restoration Drama: Modern Essays in Criticism, 1966, (with V.A. Dearing) The Works of John Dryden, Vol. IX, 1966, (Sheridan) The School for Scandal, 1966, (Nathaniel Lee) Lucius Junius Brutus, 1967, (Addison) Essays in Criticism and Literary Theory, 1975, The Memoirs of Anne, Lady Halkett and Ann, Lady Fanshawe, 1979, (with D.S. Rodes and V.A. Dearing) The Works of John Dryden, Vol. XI, 1978, (with P.H. Hardacre) Colonel Bampfield's Apology, 1993; co-editor Augustan Reprint Society, 1949-1952, English Literature, 1660-1800: A Current Bibliography, 1951-56; gen. editor: Regents Restoration Drama Series, 35 vols, 1962-81; mem. editorial bd.: Studies in English Literature, 1966-76, Huntington Library Quar., 1968-76, Wesleyan Edit. Works Henry Fielding, 1970-83 , Augustan Reprint Soc., 1985-90. Served with USNR, 1942-46, PTO. Fellow Fund Advancement Edn., 1955-56; Fulbright lectr. Am. studies Peru, 1959-60; Guggenheim fellow, 1966-67; fellow Folger Shakespeare Library, 1967; NEH fellow, 1978-79 Mem. MLA, Phi Beta Kappa, Kappa Alpha. Home: 7 Arastradero Rd Portola Valley CA 94028-8012 Office: Stanford Univ Dept English Stanford CA 94305

LOFTIS, REBECCA HOPE, psychologist; b. Ferndale, Mich., Aug. 19, 1958; d. Harold Lewis and Virginia (Warren) L.; m. Leonard H. Chyet, Oct. 8, 1988. BA, Salem (Mass.) State Coll., 1985; MA, U. Hartford, Conn., 1987; PsyD, Mass. Sch. Profl. Psychology, 1997. lic. mental health counselor, marriage and family therapist, psychologist. Psychotherapist Lynn (Mass.) Youth Resource Bur., 1988-92; practicum Atlantic Care Mental Health Ctr., Lynn, 1992-93, Lynn Youth Resource Bur., 1993-94; intern Tewksbury Hosp., 1994-96; clin. dir. Westboro Secure Treatment Program, 1997-98, Health and Edn. Svcs., Salem, Mass., 1998—; dir. psychol. svcs. Norfolk County Sheriff's Office and Correctional Ctr., Dedham, 1999—. Avocations: karate, equestrienne, bonsai collecting, cooking. Office: Norfolk County Sheriff's Office 200 West St Dedham MA 02026-5528

LOFTON, KENNETH, professional baseball player; b. East Chicago, Ind., May 31, 1967; Student, U. Ariz. Baseball player Houston Astros, 1988-91, Cleveland Indians, 1991-96, Atlanta Braves, 1996-97, Cleve. Indians, 1997—2001, Chicago White Sox, 2002, San Francisco Giants, 2002—. Ranked 1st in Am. League for stolen bases, 1992; recipient Am. League Gold Glove award, 1993-96; named to All-Star Team, 1994-96. Office: San Francisco Giants Pacific Bell Park 24 Willie Mays Plaza San Francisco CA 94107*

LOFTON, KEVIN EUGENE, medical facility administrator; b. Beaumont, Tex., Sept. 29, 1954; BS, Boston U., 1976; M Health Care Adminstrn., Ga. State U., 1979. Adminstrv. resident Meml. Med. Ctr., Corpus Christi, Tex., 1978-79; adminstr. emergency svcs. Univ. Hosp., Jacksonville, Fla., 1979-80, adminstr. material mgmt., 1980-81, asst. exec. dir. ambulatory care, 1981-82, asst. v.p. ambulatory svcs., 1982-83, v.p. profl. svcs., 1983-86; exec. v.p. Univ. Med. Ctr., 1986-90; exec. dir. Howard Univ. Hosp., Washington, 1990-93, U. Ala. Hosp., Birmingham, 1993-98; group pres. Cath. Health Initiative, Louisville, 1998-99, COO Denver, 1999—. Contbr. articles to profl. publs. Fellow Am. Coll. Health Care Execs. (R.S. Hudgens award 1993); mem. Am. Hosp. Assn. (bd. dirs.), Nat. Assn. Health Svcs. Execs. (past pres., bd. dirs.). Office: 199 Broadway Ste Denver CO 80202

LOFTON, THOMAS MILTON, lawyer; b. Indpls., May 12, 1929; s. Milton Alexander and Jane (Routzong) L.; m. Betty Louise Blades, June 20, 1954; children: Stephanie Louise, Melissa Jane. BS, Ind. U., 1951, JD, 1954, LLD (hon.), 2000, Wabash Coll., 2001. Bar: Ind. 1954, U.S. Ct. Appeals (7th cir.) 1959, U.S. Supreme Ct. 1958. Law clk. to justice U.S. Supreme Ct., Washington, 1954-55; ptnr. Baker & Daniels, Indpls., 1958-91. Dir. Ind. U. Found., Bloomington, 1978-91, Clowes Fund, 1980-2001; chmn. bd. Lilly Endowment, Indpls., 1991—; mem. bd. visitors Ind. U. Law, Bloomington, 1976—. Editor-in-chief Ind. Law Jour., 1953. Trustee Earlham Coll., 1988—91; dir. Allen Whitehill Clowes Charitable Found., 1990—. 1st lt. U.S. Army, 1955—58. Recipient Peck award Wabash Coll., 1982, Disting. Alumni Svc. award Ind. U., 1997. Mem.: Ind. Acad., Masons, Order of Coif, Sigma Nu, Beta Gamma Sigma. Republican. Presbyterian. Home: 9060 Pickwick Dr Indianapolis IN 46260-1714 Office: Lilly Endowment 2800 N Meridian St Indianapolis IN 46208-4713

LOFTUS, ELIZABETH F. psychology educator; b. L.A. d. Sidney and Rebecca Fishman; m. Geoffrey Loftus, June 30, 1968 (div. Jan. 1991). BA, UCLA; MA, PhD, Stanford U.; DSc (hon.), Miami U.; D (hon.), Leiden U.; LLD (hon.), John Jay Coll. Criminal Justice; DSc (hon.), U. Portsmouth, Eng. Prof. U. Wash., Seattle, 1973—2002; Disting. Univ. prof. U. Calif., Irvine, 2002—. Author: Eyewitness Testimony, 1979, 2d. edit., 1996, Witness for the Defense, 1991, Myth of Repressed Memory, 1994.

LOFTUS, JAMES MICHAEL, entertainer; b. Phila., May 21, 1961; s. James Bernard and Leonida (Michaud) L. Student, Allentown Coll. of St. Francis De Sales, 1979-81. News, weather reporter Sta. WAEB/WXKW, Allentown, Pa., 1981; disc jockey Sta. WZZO-FM, Bethlehem, 1981-82; keyboardist, singer Vagabond, Lehigh Valley, 1982-83; featured actor, singer Shepherd Hills Dinner Theater, Wescosville, 1984-87; actor, comedian Sturdy Beggars Comedy Show Twin County Cable/Manhattan Cable, Allentown, N.Y.C., 1986—; pianist, singer various Lehigh Valley restaurants and hotels, 1986—. Pianist/vocalist State Theatre, Easton, Pa., 1992, Ga. World Conf. Ctr., Atlanta, 1995, Las Vegas Convention Ctr., 1996, Plaza Hotel, N.Y.C., 1996, Waldorf-Astoria, N.Y.C., 1996; opening act Regis Philbin, State Theatre, Easton, Pa., 1992; pianist tribute functions for Rosetta LeNoire, Douglas Fairbanks Jr., 1996, Milton Berle, 1996; pianist Theatre Hall of Fame induction dinner for Julie Andrews, 1997. Featured actor local prodns. including Jesus Christ Superstar, 1984, The Best Little Whorehouse in Texas, 1985, Evita, 1985, Bedroom Farce, 1986, Brighton Beach Memoirs, 1987; film: Your's Truly, Harry C. Trexler, 1986, Eddie, 1996; pianist, vocalist Sam's Restaurant, N.Y.C., 2001—; appeared on TV: New York News, CBS, 1995; composer (music and lyrics) Ghosts on Broadway, John Houseman Theatre, N.Y.C., 1995; composer (CD) The Fame Game, 2000. Composer, performer title song for Dream Come True orgn., Allentown, 1987. Mem. Cath. Actors Guild (pianist 1991). Roman Catholic. Avocations: drawing, designing. Home: 3738 Geryville Pike Green Lane PA 18054-2118

LOFTUS, KAY DOUGLAS COLGAN, social worker; b. Bad Axe, Mich., July 27, 1941; d. James Fletcher and Myrtle Irene (Krueger) Colgan; m. Stephen Deane Loftus, Jan. 2, 1965; children: Amy Loftus Tuitel, Anna. BA, Alma Coll., 1963; MA, Bowling Green State U., 1966; MSW, Western Mich. U., 1983. Cert. social worker; Healthy Families Am. cert. trainer; lic. marriage and family therapist. Clin. social worker Barry County Cmty. Mental Health Svcs., 1983-95; program mgr. Healthy Families Barry County, Hastings, Mich., 1995-98; cons. Children;s Charter of the Cts. of Mich., Lansing, 1999—. Bd. dirs. Barry County Child Abuse Coun., Hastings, 1977. Office: Childrens Charter of Cts Mich 324 N Pine St # 1 Lansing MI 48933-1024 E-mail: loftuskay@atti.com., kaydc@iserv.net.

LOFTUS, STEPHEN EDWARD, elementary art educator, sculptor; b. Stoughton, Wis., Sept. 17, 1949; s. Edward Henry and Gladys Lillian (Lange) L. BS, U. Wis., Platteville; M in Art Edn., U. Wis., 1995. Cert. tchr., Wis. Art tchr. Wausau (Wis.) Pub. Schs., 1981—. Sculpture judge State Visual Arts Classic Competition, Madison; presenter in field. Contbr. Jour. on Japan's Edn. in Art, 1991; sculptor; songwriter. Vol. tchr. Ctr. for the Visual Arts; sculpture judge State Visual Arts Classic Competition MATC, Madison; citizen amb. Japan art educators, People to People Program, Wausau, summer 1991; soapbox derby judge, art advisor Boy Scouts Am.; vol. Meals on Wheels; councilor, choir mem. United Meth. Ch.; representer WAEA Cranbrook Estate western region state's ann. meeting art edn. issues, Mich. Recipient Award of Excellence for mixed media painting, State Wis. Art. Edn. Assn. Conf., 2000, Award of Excellence for sculpture, Ctr. Visual Arts Wausau, Resolution of Commendation, Pres. Philip R. Albert, MD, Wausau Pub. Schs. Sch. Bd., 2000, 2d Resolution Commendation bringing recognition to Wausau Pub. Schs., Christine A. Bremer Pres. Bd. Edn., Wausau, Wis. . Mem. Nat. Art Edn. Assn. (v.p. North Ctrl. region bd. 1993-95, pres.-elect del. at dels. assembly nat. spring conf. 2002), NEA, State Edn. Assn., Wis. Art Edn. Assn. (Art Educator of Yr. 2000), Wis. Alliance Arts Edn. (Disting. Svc. award within the arts edn. profession 2000). Home: 1243 Sunset Dr Wausau WI 54401-4256 Office: 2701 Robin Ln Wausau WI 54401

LOFTUS, THOMAS DANIEL, lawyer; b. Nov. 8, 1930; s. Glendon Francis and Martha Helen (Wall) L. BA, U. Wash., 1952, JD, 1957. Bar: Wash. 1958, U.S. Ct. Appeals (9th cir.) 1958, U.S. Dist. Ct. Wash. 1958, U.S. Ct. Mil. Appeals 1964, U.S. Supreme Ct. 1964. Trial atty. Northwestern Mut. Ins. Co., Seattle, 1958-62; sr. trial atty. Unigard Security Ins. Co., 1962-68, asst. gen. counsel, 1969-83, govt. rels. counsel, 1983-89; of counsel Groshong, LeHet & Thornton, 1990-98; mem. Wash. Commn. on Jud. Conduct (formerly Jud. Qualifications), 1982-88, vice-chmn., 1987-88; judge pro tem Seattle Mcpl. Ct., 1973-81; mem. nat. panel of mediators Arbitration Forums, Inc., 1990—. Sec., treas. Seattle Opera Assn., 1980-91; pres., bd. dirs. Vis. Nurse Svcs., 1979-88; pres., v.p. Salvation Army Adult Rehab. Ctr., 1979-86; nat. committeeman Wash. Young Rep. Fedn., 1961-63, vice-chmn, 1963-65; pres. Young Reps. King County, 1962-63; bd. dirs. Seattle Seafair, Inc., 1975; bd. dirs., gen. counsel Wash. Ins. Coun., 1984-86, sec., 1986-88, v.p., 1988-90, Am. Mediation Panel of Mediators, 1990-96; bd. dirs. Arson Alarm Found., 1987-90; bd. visitors Law Sch. U. Wash., 1993—. 1st lt. U.S. Army, 1952-54, col. Res., 1954-85. Fellow Am. Bar Found.; mem. Am. Arbitration Assn. (nat. panel arbitrators 1965—, nat. panel mediators 2000—), Am. Arbitration Forums, Inc. (nat. panel arbitrators 1992), Nat. Assn. Security Dealers (bd. arbitrators 1997—), Am. Mediation Panel, Wash. Bar Assn. (gov. 1981-84), Seattle King County Bar Assn. (sec., trustee 1977-82), ABA (ho. of dels. 1984-90), Internat. Assn. Ins. Counsel, U.S. People to People (del. Moscow internat. law-econ. conf. 1990), Def. Rsch. Inst., Wash. Def. Trial Lawyers Assn., Wash. State Trial Lawyers Assn., Am. Judicature Soc., Res. Officers Assn., Judge Advocate Gen.'s Assn., Assn. Wash. Gens., U. Wash. Alumni Assn., Coll. Club Seattle, Wash. Athletic Club, Masons, Shriners, English Spkg. Union, Ranier Club, Pi Sigma Alpha, Delta Sigma Rho, Phi Delta Phi, Theta Delta Chi. Republican. Presbyterian. Home: 3515 Magnolia Blvd W Seattle WA 98199-1841 Office: Coll Club Bldg 505 Madison St Ste 300 Seattle WA 98104-1123

LOGA, SANDA, physicist, educator; b. Bucharest, Romania, June 13, 1932; came to U.S., 1968; d. Stelian and Georgeta (Popescu) L.; m. Karl Heinz Werther, Mar. 1968 (div. 1970); m. Radu Zaciu, 1996. MS in Physics, U. Bucharest, 1955; PhD in Biophysics, U. Pitts., 1978. Asst. prof. faculty medicine and pharmacy, Bucharest, 1963-67; rsch. asst. Presbyn./St. Luke's Hosp., Chgo., 1968-69; assoc. rsch. scientist Miles Labs., Elkhart, Ind., 1969-70; rsch. asst. U. Pitts., 1971-78; rsch. assoc. Carnegie-Mellon U., Pitts., 1978-80; health physicist VA Med. Ctr., Westside, Chgo., 1980; med. physicist, VA Med. Ctr. N. Chgo, 1980-97. Assoc. prof. Chgo. Med. Sch., N. Chgo., 1985-98. Mem. Am. Assn. Physicists in Medicine, Health Physics Soc. Office: Chgo Med Sch U Health Scis 3333 Green Bay Rd North Chicago IL 60064-3037

LOGAN, BERNARD J. obstetrician; b. Boston, May 8, 1941; MD, Tufts U., 1966. Diplomate Am. Bd. Ob-Gyn. Intern Phila. Gen. Hosp., 1966-67; resident Boston City Hosp., 1967-70; staff Malden (Mass.) Hosp., 1973—99, chmn. ob-gyn., 1986-98; staff Lawrence Meml. Hosp., Melrose Wakefield Hosp.; clin. instr. Tufts U. Sch. Medicine, Boston. Clin. instr. Tufts U. Sch. Medicine., 1990—. Fellow Am. Coll. Ob-Gyn., Am. Coll. Gynecol. Laparascopy, Am. Fertility Soc., Mass. Med. Soc. Office: 101 Main St Ste 217 Medford MA 02155-4530

LOGAN, BETTY MULHERIN, human services specialist; b. Augusta, Ga., July 14, 1926; d. James B. and Mayclare (Rice) Mulherin; m. Vance Earle Logan, Jr. June 30, 1951; children: James V., Charles E., Mayclare Scherer, Anne Marie Harvey, Vance E III, E. Carson Johnson. Student, Fontbonne Coll. Tchr. St. Mary's and Aquinas Schs., Augusta, Ga., 1960-76; ret. vol., 1998. Organist St. Mary's Ch., Augusta, 1960-76; treas. parish coun. PCCW, Augusta, 1956-57, chmn. various coms., 1957-70; pres. deanery Coun. Cath. Women, Augusta and Savannah, 1970-72, 76-78; founder, dir. Cmty. Clothing Ctr., Augusta, 1967-76; founder Right to Life, 1969—; founder, treas., bd. dirs., trustee Birthright, Augusta, 1971—; chair Am. Cancer Soc. of Augusta, 1960-66; rep. Savannah Diocese Ga. Legis. Forum, 1978-82; pres. Augusta coun. Cath. Savannah Diocesan Coun. Coun. Cath. Women, 1976-78. Mem. Nat. Hist. Soc., Sacred Heart Cultural Ctr. (aux.). Roman Catholic. Avocations: swimming, learning computers, writing memoirs. Home: 2624 Raymond Ave Augusta GA 30904-5379 Office: Birthright Augusta Inc St Joseph Hosp 2260 Wrightsboro Rd Augusta GA 30904-4764

LOGAN, CHARLES WILBUR, urologist; b. Nashville, Sept. 12, 1934; s. J. Wilbur and Lillie Mae (Polk) L.; m. Joyce Whitley Martin, Apr. 18, 1964; children: Russell, Christopher, Karen. BA in English Lit., So. Meth. U., 1956; MD, Vanderbilt U., 1960. Diplomate Am. Bd. Urology. Intern surgery Cornell Med. Ctr., N.Y.C., 1961-62; resident gen. surgery Baylor Med. Ctr., Houston, 1963, resident urology surgery, 1963-65; assoc. prof. urology U. Ark., Little Rock, 1967—; staff Bapt. Med. Ctr., 1967—, St. Vincent Infirmary, Little Rock, 1967—, chief surgery, 1980-84; vice chief urology Doctors Hosp., 1993-94, chief urology, 1995—. Bd. dirs. Vis. Nurses Assn., 1989—; past bd. dirs. Our House, Little Rock, St. James United Meth. Ch. Capt. U.S. Army, 1965-67. Recipient Founders medal Vanderbilt Med. Sch. Mem. AMA (alt. del. 1994), ACS (Ark. chpt., past pres., past sec., gov. 1990-96), Am. Assn. Clin. Urologists (bd. dirs. 1993-96, sec. 1997—), Am. Urol. Assn. (South Ctrl. sect. health policy coun. rep.), Ark. Med. Soc. (chmn. coun., pres.-elect, pres. 1997-98), Ark. Urol. Assn. (past pres., past sec., South Ctrl. sect. rep.), Ark. Lithotripsy Inst. (pres.), Pulaski County Med. Soc. (past pres., councilor), Endourol. Soc., Pediat. Urol. Soc., Ark. Travelers Baseball Club (bd. dirs., v.p.), Ark. Gov.'s Task Force on Healthcare, Blue Cross-Blue Shield Med. Svcs. Rev. Com. and Carrier Adv. Com., Am. Coll. Surgeons (sec. bd. govs.), Rotary, Phi Beta Kappa, Alpha Omega Alpha. Avocations: hunting, gardening, golf, running. Office: Urology Assocs PA 500 S University Ave Little Rock AR 72205-5302

LOGAN, DAN, investor, writer; b. Chgo., Dec. 10, 1946; s. David S. and Reva (Frumkin) L.; m. Gloria Jean Blasz, July 8, 1973; children: Elizabeth, Andrew. BA, Knox Coll., 1969. Sr. speechwriter, asst. Ill. Gov. Daniel Walker, Springfield, Ill., 1975-76; spl. asst. U.S. Sen. Joseph Biden, Jr., Washington, 1977; speechwriter, cons. U.S. Rep. Max Baucus Senate campaign, 1978; speechwriter Charles Ferris, chmn. FCC, 1980; exec. dir. Free Men, Inc., 1980-87; co-founder Nat. Congress for Fathers and Children, 1981. Ptnr. Mercury Investments, Chgo., 1988—. *Dan Logan conceived and wrote Walker's 1976 campaign slogan, which was featured in David Garth's commercials. He also wrote the well-known Ferris speech promoting robust broadcast programming in wake of "seven dirty words" Supreme Court decision. Save Jazz 90 hired Media Access Project to successfully prevent precedent of commercial stations purchasing a noncommercial one. His op-ed pieces on men's issues have appeared in many of the nation's largest newspapers. Fine art photographs have been exhibited at galleries. He has freelanced speeches for U.S. Senators Edmund Muskie and Gary Hart. He was also involved in presidential campaigns for Vice President Hubert H. Humphrey in 1968 and U.S. Senator George McGovern in 1972.* Contbr. articles to newspapers. Founder Save Jazz 90, 1997; bd. dirs. Reva and David Logan Found., 1998—. Mem. Nat. Writers Union. Unitarian Universalist.

LOGAN, DAVID BRUCE, health care administrator, nurse; b. Grand Rapids, Mich., Jan. 30, 1942; s. Wesley Goldsmith and Ernestine (Sovereen) L.; m. Joann Fern Jordan, Nov. 5, 1961; children: Jennifer, Julie, Jeanine, David II, Douglas, Dean. MusB, U. Mich., 1964; B Zoology with honors, Mich. State U., 1970; MBA, U. Ill., 1978. Tchr. sci. Flint (Mich.) Pub. Schs., 1970-71; health care adminstr. USAF, Mpls., 1971-75; asst. chief, med. adminstrn. svc. trainee VA, 1975-76, asst. chief med. adminstrn. svc. Danville, Ill., 1976-78; asst. med. dist. coord. VA Med. Dist. 15, Indpls., 1978-80; med. dist. coord. VA Med. Dist. 8, Durham, N.C., 1980-87; nat. disaster med. system mgr. VA, Salisbury, 1987-99, ret. Dir. choir Kirk of Kildaire Presbyn. Ch., 1981-85; asst. scoutmaster, scoutmaster Boy Scouts Am., 1978-94. Capt. USAF, 1964-68, lt. col. Res. ret. Fellow Am. Coll. Healthcare Execs., Soc. Air Force Res. Med. Officers, Air Force Assn., Res. Officers Assn. (bd. dirs. Minn. 1973-74, jr. v.p. for air 1974-75).

LOGAN, DAVID SAMUEL, investment banker; b. Chgo., Jan. 10, 1918; children: Daniel Joel, Richard Elliot, Jonathan Charles. BA, U. Chgo., 1939, JD, 1941; D of Pub. Svc. (hon.), St. Xavier U., 1998. Bar: Ill., 1941, U.S. Supreme Ct., 1950. Lawyer Bd. of Econ. Warfare, Washington, 1942-46; mng. ptnr. Associated Hotels, Chgo., 1947-55, Mercury Investments, Chgo., 1955—. Mem. Chgo. adv. com. Cultural Facilities Fund; exec. com. Nat. Archives Coun., Chgo., 1975-80, Ill. State Art Coun., Chgo., 1977—; mem. photography and libr. coms. Art Inst. Chgo., U. Chgo.; donor: Reva and David Logan grants in support of new writing on photography, Reva and David Logan Ctr. for Clin. Rsch. U. Chgo., Reva and David Logan Gallery Legion of Honor, San Francisco. Recipient civil govt. award U. Chgo., svc. recognition Ill. Alliance for Arts Edn., 1993, Pub. Svc. citation U. Chgo. Alumni Assn., 1994, Gov.'s Spl. Recognition award Ill. Arts Coun., 1995. Mem.: Chgo. Bar Assn., Ill. State Bar Assn., Grolier Club (N.Y.C.), Arts Club. Jewish. Home: 209 E Lake Shore Dr Chicago IL 60611-1307 Office: Mercury Investments 919 N Michigan Ave Ste 3301 Chicago IL 60611-1688

LOGAN, DON, publishing executive; BA, Auburn U.; MA, Clemson U. Pres. Oxmoor House, 1978—84; exec. v.p. Southern Progress Corp., 1984—85, chmn. CEO, 1985—92; pres., COO Time Inc., N.Y.C., 1992—94, pres., CEO, 1994—97, chmn, 1997—2002; chmn. media & comm. grp. AOL Time Warner Inc., 2002—. Office: AOL Time Warner Inc 75 Rockefeller Plz New York NY 10019-6990

LOGAN, DOUGLAS ORR, magazine editor; b. New Haven, Dec. 17, 1955; s. John Arthur and Ann Orr L.; m. Elizabeth Joslin Dunham, Aug. 25, 1984 (div. Aug. 1991); m. Melissa Harmon Logan, Sept. 21, 1994; children:

Nicholas Henley, Jane Orr. BA, Trinity Coll., 1978. Assoc. editor Dodd, Mead & Co., N.Y.C., 1979-85; mng. editor Sailing World Mag., Norwalk, Conn., 1985-89, cons. editor, feature writer, 1989-95, exec. editor, 1998-99; webmaster Cruising World, Sailing World, Newport, R.I., 1995-99; editor-in chief Practical Sailor mag., Clinton, Conn., 2001—. Editor 42 books; contbr. articles to profl. publs. Sports amb. People-to-People Sports com. Mem. Thimble Islands Sailing Club.

LOGAN, EARL STEVEN, sales professional, artist; b. South Bend, Ind., Oct. 20, 1956; s. Earl and Barbara Jean L. BS in Bus., Ind. U., 1985. Real estate agt. Cressy and Everett Better Homes and Gardens, Mishawaka, Ind., 1985-89; quality control supr. Qualex, South Bend, 1990; retail assoc. Montgomery Ward, 1991; retail specialist L.S. Ayres, Mishawaka, 1992—. Exhibited in group shows at Colfax Cultural Ctr., South Bend, Ind., 1995, Mus. Sci. and Industry, Chgo., 1995, 96, Elkhart Regional Juried Art Competition, 1995, 96, 99, 17th Ann., 1995 (Makielski Merit award), 18th Ann., 1996 (Best Drawing), 21st Ann., 1999 (Best Painting, Louise J. Anes Meml. Purchase award 1999), Midwest Mus. Am. Art, Elkhart. Avocations: reading, astronomy, basketball, meditation.

LOGAN, FRANCIS DUMMER, lawyer; b. Evanston, Ill., May 23, 1931; s. Simon Rae and Frances (Dummer) L.; m. Claude Riviere, Apr. 13, 1957; children: Carolyn Gisele, Francis Dummer. BA, U. Chgo., 1950; BA Juris, Oxford U., 1954; LL.B., Harvard U., 1955. Bar: N.Y. 1956, Calif. 1989. Assoc. Milbank, Tweed, Hadley & McCloy, N.Y.C., 1955-64, ptnr. N.Y.C. and L.A., 1965-96, chmn., 1992-96. Mem. vis. com. U. of Chgo. Coll.; bd. dirs. Pasadena Symphony Orchestra. Mem. Calif. State Bar, Coun. on Fgn. Rels., Am. Law Inst., Pacific Coun. on Internat. Policy, N.Y. State Bar. Home: 1726 Linda Vista Ave Pasadena CA 91103-1132

LOGAN, FRIEDA MAE, painter, educator; b. Springfield, Mo., Apr. 30, 1929; d. Carl and Anna Julia Elizabeth (Hollingshead) Oberlander; m. Glenn Woodrow Logan, Dec. 9, 1951; children: Glenn Kerry, Leslie Logan Stapinski. BA, Kansas City Art Inst., 1951, postgrad., 1980, Penn Valley Coll., 1982-84. Stylist Ricemor Coats & Suits, Kansas City, Mo., 1951-52; stylist, designer Brand & Puritz Inc., 1952; designer Dan-Deb Mfrs., 1953-58; freelance illustrator for various retail cos., 1958-75, 79-84; staff artist Ray Advt., 1976-77, Macy's, Kansas City, 1977-79; ind. painter Springfield, 1984—. Mem. Pub. Sch. Com. to Evaluate Curriculum for Visual Arts, Springfield, 1993; exhibits dir. Image Point Gallery, 1996-97; tchr. watercolor classes Springfield Art Mus., 1996-99; tchr. pvt. studio classes, 1996-99. Exhibited works in numerous nat. and regional exhibits; contbr. articles to art mags. Mem. Springfield Visual Arts Alliance (membership dir. 1995-96, exhibits dir. 1996-98). Avocations: needlework, photography. Office: Frieda Logan's Studio 706 E Westchester Ct Springfield MO 65810-2822

LOGAN, HENRY VINCENT, retired transportation executive; b. Phila., Nov. 7, 1942; s. Edward Roger and Alberta L.; m. Mary Genzano, Sept. 28, 1963; children: Michele Leah, Maureen Laura, Monica Lynn. BS in Commerce, DePaul U., 1975; M in Mgmt., Northwestern U., 1984. Successively supr. corp. acctg., asst. mgr. gen. acctg., mgr. gen. acctg., dir. corp. acctg. and taxes TTX Co., Chgo., 1962-70, contr., 1970-78, dir. fin. planning, 1978-83, mng. dir., fin. adminstr., 1983-85, CFO, v.p., 1985-88, sr. v.p. fleet mgmt., 1988—. Bd. dirs. Calpro, Co., Mira Loma, Calif., RailGon Co., Chgo. Treas. TTX Co. Polit. Action Com., Chgo., 1980; vol Sch. Dist. 87 Task Force, Glen Ellyn, Ill., 1986. Hon. fellow U. Denver Intermodal Transp. Inst., 1999. Mem. Nat. Freight Transp. Assn., Intermodal Assn. N.Am. (chmn. legis. com. 1992-94), Rlwy. Supply Assn. (bd. dirs., treas., sec., v.p., chmn. fin. com., pres. 2001), Union League Club (mem. reception com. 1987-92, fin. com. 1993-95), Medinah (Ill.) Country Club, Willoughby Golf Club, Fla. Republican. Roman Catholic. Avocations: golf, music, reading, bicycling. Home: 4522 SE Waterford Dr Stuart FL 34997

LOGAN, HOWARD G. science and technology educator; b. Rock Springs, Wyo., Sept. 26, 1948; s. Kenneth D. and Margaret M. Logan; m. Susan F. Logan, Feb. 14, 1976; 1 child, Grant. BS in Biology, U. Wyo., 1972. Cert. in biology; cert. tchr. endorsement, Wyo.; cert. firefighter, Wyo., cert. officer, Wyo., cert. arson investigator, Wyo., cert fire officer II, Wyo., cert. fire instr., Wyo. Sci. and tech. educator Sweetwater County Sch. Dist. #2, Green River, Wyo., 1972—. Presenter Internet Trona Symposium, 1994; owner, CEO Logan/Ruhaak Corp., Green River, 1988-2000; com. mem. Found. Com., City of Green River, 1980—. Capt., firefighter, chief officer Green River Vol. Fire Dept., 1974-99; Y2K compliance coord. City of Green River, 1999-2000; dir. Y2K compliance Tech. Help Desk Educator, Green River, 1984-99; exec. bd. dirs. Associated Parents of U. of Wyo., Laramie, 1999—. Mem. Green River Edn. Assn. (pres., v.p., treas. 1975-78). Avocations: technology, family, travel. Home: 580 Lombard Green River WY 82935 Office: Green River HS 1615 Hitching Post Dr Green River WY 82935 E-mail: loganho@sw2.k12.wy.us.

LOGAN, J. MURRAY, investment manager; b. Balt., Mar. 15, 1935; s. Lloyd and Helen Mildred (Gilbert) L.; m. Mary Page Cole, June 19, 1987 (dec. Sept. 1993); 1 child by previous marriage, Maria Charlotte. BA, Johns Hopkins U., 1959. Securities analyst Merrill Lynch Pierce Fenner & Smith, N.Y.C., 1959-62; ptnr. Wood Struthers & Winthrop, 1962-70; v.p. EFC Mgmt. Corp., L.A., 1970-73, Faulkner, Dawkins & Sullivan, Inc., N.Y.C., 1973-75; chmn. investment policy com. Rockefeller & Co., Inc., 1975-97; mng. ptnr. L-R Global Ptnrs. Bd. dirs. World Trust Fund, Luxembourg, Berkshire Opera Co., Camphill Found., Camphill Village, U.S.A., pres.; trustee U.K. Fund, N.Y.C. Trustee Johns Hopkins U., Balt., 1984-91. With USCG, 1954-56. Mem.: Town Tennis Club, The Leash, Racquet and Tennis Club. Office: 320 Park Ave Fl 28 New York NY 10022

LOGAN, J. PATRICK, lawyer; b. Buffalo, Oct. 4, 1950; BA, Coll. Holy Cross, 1972; JD, Temple U., 1976. Bar: Pa. 1977, Ala. 1977. With Burr & Forman, Birmingham, Ala. Mem. ABA, Ala. State Bar (chmn. labor and employment law sect. 1989-90), Birmingham Bar Assn. Office: Burr & Forman 3100 S Trust Twr 420 20th St N Ste 3000 Birmingham AL 35203-3284

LOGAN, JAMES KENNETH, lawyer, former federal judge; b. Quenemo, Kans., Aug. 21, 1929; s. John Lysle and Esther Maurine (Price) Logan; m. Beverly Jo Jennings, June 8, 1952; children: Daniel Jennings, Amy Logan Sliva, Sarah Logan Sherard, Samuel Price. AB, U. Kans., 1952; LLB magna cum laude, Harvard U., 1955. Bar: Kans. 1955, Calif. 1956. Law clk. U.S. Cir. Judge Huxman, 1955—56; with firm Gibson, Dunn & Crutcher, LA, 1956—57; asst. prof. law U. Kans., 1957—61, prof., dean Law Sch., 1961—68; ptnr. Payne and Jones, Olathe, 1968—77; judge U.S. Ct. Appeals (10th cir.), 1977—98; pvt. practice Logan Law Firm LLC, Olathe, 1998—2001, Foulston Siefkin LLP, Overland Park, 2002—. Ezra Ripley Thayer tchg. fellow Harvard Law Sch., 1961—62; vis. prof. U. Tex., 1964, Stanford U., 1969, U. Mich., 1976; sr. lectr. Duke U., 1987, 91, 93; commr. U.S. Dist. Ct., 1964—67; mem. U.S. Jud. Conf. Adv. Com. Fed. Rules of Appellate Procedure, 1990—97, chair, 1993—97. Author (with W.B. Leach): Future Interests and Estate Planning, 1961; author: Kansas Estate Administration, 5th edit., 1986; author: (with A.R. Martin) Kansas Corporate Law and Practice, 2d edit., 1979; author: The Federal Courts of the Tenth Circuit: A History, 1992, also articles. Candidate for U.S. Senate, 1968. Served with U.S. Army, 1947—48. Recipient Disting. Svc. citation, U. Kans., 1986, Francis Rawle award, ABA-ALI, 1990; scholar Rhodes Scholarship, 1952. Mem.: ABA, Kans. Bar Assn., Order of Coif, Phi Delta Phi, Alpha Kappa Psi, Pi Sigma Alpha, Omicron Delta Kappa, Beta Gamma Sigma, Phi Beta Kappa. Democrat. Presbyterian. E-mail: jlogan@foulston.com.

LOGAN, JAMES SCOTT, SR. federal agency administrator; b. Stanford, Ky., June 18, 1948; s. James M.H. and Lillian Elizabeth (Givens) L.; m. Rose Marie Helm, Aug. 31, 1968; children: James Matthew, Tasha Marie. AA, Columbia (Mo.) Coll., 1990, BS/BA cum laude, 1992; postgrad., U. Colo., 1992—. Unit adminstr. USAR, Lakewood, Colo., 1972-82; continuity of govt. planner Fed. Emergency Mgmt. Agy. Region VIII, 1983-90, tech. hazards program specialist, 1991-92, sr. tech. hazards program specialist, 1992-95, team leader state and local programs Colo., 1995—; emergency analyst Office of Regional Dir., Denver, 1995—, dir. preparedness tng. and exercises divsn., 1998—2000, dir. readiness, response and recovery divsn., 2001—. Chmn. bd. dirs. Rocky Mountain Human Svcs. Coalition, 1995-99, bd. dirs. 1998—, pres., 1998-99. Mem. NAACP, Denver, 1992; mem. NCOA NCO Assn., Denver, 1979—; mem. citizen's adv. com. polit. sci. dept. U. Colo., Denver; chmn. bd. dirs. Rocky Mt. Human Svcs. Coalition, 1995—, pres., 1998-99; bd. dirs. City Club Denver, 2000. With U.S. Army, 1968-71, Vietnam, USAR, 1972. Decorated Legion of Merit. Mem. VFW, Am. Legion, Denver City Club, Pi Sigma Alpha. Democrat. Baptist. Avocations: reading, computers, political science. Home: 16952 E Bates Ave Aurora CO 80013-2243 Office: FEMA Region VIII PO Box 25267 Bldg 710A Denver CO 80225-0267 E-mail: scott.logan@fema.gov.

LOGAN, JOHN A., III, hospital administrator; b. Dec. 16, 1937; BS, Western Ky. U., 1958; MD, Vanderbilt U., 1961. Intern Toledo (Ohio) Hosp., 1961-62; pvt. practice Henderson, Ky., 1962-86; chief of staff Meth. Hosp., 1967-86, med. dir., 1986—. Author: Innovation, 1992. Pres. YMCA, Henderson. Named Citizen of Yr., Henderson C. of C., 1993. Mem. Rotary (pres.). Address: 1305 N Elm St # 48 Henderson KY 42420-2783 E-mail: jalogan@methodisthospital.net.

LOGAN, JOHN ARTHUR, JR. retired foundation executive; b. Chgo., Dec. 8, 1923; s. John Arthur and Dorothea (Halstead) L.; m. Ann Orr deForest, Aug. 30, 1960. Grad., Taft Sch., Watertown, Conn., 1942; BA, Yale, 1949, MA, 1951, PhD, 1954; LL.D., Western Md. Coll.; L.H.D., Hollins Coll. Faculty Yale, 1949-61, asst. prof. history, 1958-61; pres. Hollins Coll., 1961-75, Ind. Coll. Funds Am., N.Y.C., 1975-86. Vis. lectr. Salzburg Seminar in Am. Studies, 1961. Author: No Transfer: An American Security Principle, 1961. Served to capt. AUS, 1942-46. Fellow Saybrook Coll., Yale, 1950— Mem. Phi Beta Kappa. Clubs: Elizabethan (New Haven); Century Assn. (N.Y.C.), Yale (N.Y.C.). Home: 88 Notch Hill Rd Apt 353 North Branford CT 06471-1853

LOGAN, JOHN FRANCIS, electronics company executive, management consultant; b. Norristown, Pa., Apr. 10, 1938; s. Francis Michael and Elizabeth V. L. BS in Bus. Adminstrn., Drexel U., 1961. CPA, N.Y. Auditor Hurdman and Cranston CPA's (merger KPMG Peat Warwick), N.Y.C., 1961-69; v.p. fin., chief fin. officer, treas. Aero Flow Dynamics, Inc., 1969-84; v.p. fin. and adminstrn., chief fin. officer, treas. Codenoll Tech. Corp., Yonkers, N.Y., 1985-90; v.p. fin., chief fin. officer, treas. VTX Electronics Corp., Farmingdale, 1991-92; mgmt. cons. Comtex Info. Systems, Inc./KLMB Group Inc., N.Y.C., 1992-95; v.p. fin., CFO, treas. M-Power Corp., Stamford, Conn., 1995-2000; mgmt. cons. Resources Connection, N.Y.C., 2000—. With U.S. Army, 1962-64. Mem. AICPAs, N.Y. State Soc. CPA's, Pa. Soc.

LOGAN, JOYCE POLLEY, education educator; b. Providence, Sept. 18, 1935; d. Vernon and Hattie Alice Polley; m. Jewell Wyatt Logan (dec.), June 4, 1956; 1 child, James Edward. BS, Murray State U., 1956, MA, 1960; EdD, Vanderbilt U., 1988. Cert. bus. tchr., vocat. adminstrn. Student sec. Murray (Ky.) State U., 1954-56; bus. tchr. Hopkins County Schs., Madisonville, Ky., 1956-68; regional coord. Vocational Region 2 Ky. Dept. Edn., 1968-83; prin. Health Occupations Sch., 1983-88; voc., tech. adminstr. Ky. Dept. Edn., Frankfort, 1988-90; asst. prof. dept. adminstrn. and supervision Coll. Edn. U. Ky., Lexington, 1991—99; state dir. Ky. Com. for Secondary and Middle Schs. So. Assn. Colls. and Schs., 1995-98; assoc. prof. dept. adminstrn. and supervision Coll. Edn. U. Ky., Lexington, 2000—. Evaluator Distance Edn. Training Coun., Washington, 1981—; field coord. military evaluations, Am. Coun. on Edn., Washington, 1984—. Author: (with A.C. Krizan) Basics of Writing, 1993, 2000. Mem. alumni bd. Murray (Ky.) State U. Coll. Bus., 1988—; fundraiser Ky. Spl. Olympics, Madisonville, 1983, YMCA, Madisonville, 1984; mem. edn. com. Greater Leadership Program Madisonville, Ky. C. of C., 1987-88. Recipient Exceptional Svc. award Coll. Edn., U. Ky., 1999; named FFA Hon. State Farmer, Ky. FFA., 1979, Woman of the Year, Lion's Club, Madisonville, Ky., 1987, Outstanding Tchr. Educator, 1992, Exceptional Achievement award for svc. U. Ky., 1999. Mem. Nat. Bus. Edn. Assn., Am. Vocat. Assn., Ky. Vocat. Assn., Southern Assn. of Colls. and Schs. (trustee 1973, 1976-78, chmn. Commn on Occupational Ednl. Insts. 1973), Ky. Assn. for Sch. Adminstrs., Assn. for Supervision and Curriculum Devel., Phi Delta Kappa, Omicron Delta Kappa (hon.). Avocations: jogging, tennis, reading, piano playing. Home: 2956 Tabor Oaks Ln Lexington KY 40502-2898 Office: U Ky 111 Dickey Hall Coll of Edn Lexington KY 40506

LOGAN, KATHLEEN V. personnel consultant; b. Detroit, Apr. 5, 1942; d. Yeatman Lee and Joan Marshall Vestal; m. Carl Flack Logan, July 24, 1971; 1 child, Kelly Flack. BA in Elem. Edn., U. Mich., 1964; MS in Mgmt., U.S. Naval Postgrad. Sch., 1971; MA in Marriage and Family Therapy, U.S. Internat. U., San Diego, 1981. Tchr. elem. schs., Fremont, Calif., 1964-65, Ann Arbor, Mich., 1965-67; officer USN, San Diego, Monterey, Calif., 1967-74, Norfolk, Va., 1967-74, cons., trainer, 1981—; cons. Ketron, Inc., Washington, 1981-83; counselor USN Family Advocacy, Yokosuka, Japan, 1983-84; instr. St. Leo Coll., Norfolk, Va., 1986-88; coord. employee assistance program Bapt. Hosp., Pensacola, Fla., 1990-96; cons., 1997—. Contbr. articles to profl. jours. Mem. Mayor's Task Force on Violence, Pensacola, 1994; sec. Girl Scout Coun. of N.W. Fla., Pensacola, 1994—; chmn. Pensacola Ctr. for Creative Cmty. Solutions, 1995—. Lt. USN, 1967-74. Avocations: reading, biking, canoeing, piano, cooking. Home and Office: 129 Chanteclaire Cir Gulf Breeze FL 32561-4061

LOGAN, LEE ROBERT, orthodontist; b. L.A., June 24, 1932; s. Melvin Duncan and Margaret (Seltzer) L.; m. Maxine Nadler, June 20, 1975; children: Chad, Casey. BS, UCLA, 1952; DDS, Northwestern U., 1956, MS, 1961. Diplomate Am. Bd. Orthodontics. Gen .practice dentistry, Reseda, Calif., 1958-59; practice orthodontics Northridge, 1961—; pres. Lee R. Logan DDS Profl. Corp. Mem. med. staff Northridge Hosp.; owner Maxine's Prodn. Co.; owner Maxine's Talent Agy.; guest lectr. UCLA, U. So. Calif. Contbr. articles to profl. jours. Achievements include patent and licensing agreement with 3M for a device to attach braces, 2001. Served to lt. USNR, 1956-58. Named 1st Pl. winner, Autistic Jogathon, 1981—2001, (with wife) Couple of Yr., Autistic Children Assn., 1986; recipient Nat. Philanthropy award, 1987. Mem. ADA, San Fernando Valley Dental Assn. (pres. 1998), Am. Assn. Orthodontists, Pacific Coast Soc. Orthodontists (dir., pres. so. sect. 1974-75, chmn. membership 1981-83), Foudn. Orthodontic Rsch. (charter mem.), Calif. Soc. Orthodontists (chmn. peer rev. 1982-93), G.V. Black Soc. (charter) Angle Soc. Orthodontists (pres. 1981-82, bd. dirs. 1982-2001, nat. pres. 1985-87), U. S.C. Century Club Fraternity, Xi Psi Phi, Chi Phi. Home: 4830 Encino Ave Encino CA 91316-3813 Office: 18250 Roscoe Blvd Northridge CA 91325-4226 E-mail: orthologan@aol.com.

LOGAN, LYNDA DIANNE, elementary education educator; b. Detroit, June 22, 1952; d. Horatio Bernard and Ruby (Newsom) Graham; m. Keith L. Logan, Aug. 16, 1980 (div); 1 child, Lauren Nicole. BS, Ea. Mich. U., 1974, MA, 1980. Cert. tng. program quality rev., Calif.; cert. tchr., Calif., Miss., Mich.; cert. Lang. Devel. Specialist (CLAD), 1996; lic. guidance counselor basic related edn., Miss.; cert. counselor pupil pers. svc. credential, Mich., Calif. Substitute tchr. Detroit Pub. Schs., 1974-76; mid. sch. tchr. Inkster (Mich.) Pub. Schs., 1976-80; CETA vocat. counselor Golden Triangle Vocat.-Tech. Ctr., Mayhew, Miss., 1980-82, basic related educator, 1980-82; elem. tchr. Inglewood (Calif.) Unified Sch. Dist., 1982-93, reading resource specialist, 1993-96; tchr. Crozier Magnet Mid. Sch., Inglewood, Calif., 1996—. Advisor Assn. Student Body, 2000-2001; tchr.-mentor The Gear-Up Program, 2000--; mem. forecast adv. bd. COED Mag., N.Y.C., 1979-80; advisor/founder Newspaper Club Fellrath Mid. Sch., Inkster, 1979-80; mem. interviewing com. Golden Triangle Vocat.-Tech. Ctr., Mayhew, 1980-82, evaluation and follow-up com., 1980-82; pronouncer spelling bee Inglewood Unified Sch. Dist., 1991, 94; organizer student study team meetings Worthington Sch., Inglewood, 1993-96, coord. reading program, 1993-96; mem. interviewing com., 1987-95; co-chair yearbook com., 1993-94, prin. adv. bd., 1987-92, ct.-liaison and child welfare attendance rep. L.A. County Edn., 1995-96, sch. leadership team mem., 1991—, supt. adv. coun., 1995-96, reading is fundamental coord., 1993-96, mem. team earthquake preparedness com., 1994-96, coord. after-sch. tutoring program, 1998-99, curriculum coun. rep. 1998-99, mentor tchr.-gear up program, 2000--, grant proposal writer, 2000-01, mem. sch. site coun.; adult edn. tchr. CBET Program, 2001--; supervising tchr. Calif. State U., Dominguez, 1987, 94, 2002--, Nat. U., 1987, 94, UCLA, 2001-02. Youth co-chairperson March of Dimes, Detroit, 1976-80; com. mem. Nat. Coun. Negro Women, L.A. chpt., 1982-84; com. mem. Cmty. Action Program, Eternal Promise Bapt. Ch., L.A., 1991, pres. choir, 1991, v.p. hospitality com., 1987-88; co-chmn. women's com., 1990; mem. parent adv. com. Knox Presbyn. Ch. Nursery Sch., L.A., 1988-89; mentor, tchr. UCLA. Mem. ASCD, AAUW, NAFE, Black Women's Forum, Ladies Aux. Knights of St. Peter Claver, Ea. Mich. U. Alumni Assn., Phi Gamma Nu. Avocations: bike riding, community organizational activities, travel, movies, theater. Office: Crozier Magnet Middle School 151 N Grevillea Ave Inglewood CA 90301-1705 E-mail: pontiaclyn@aol.com.

LOGAN, MARIANNE MCNEIL, poet; b. Sturgis, S.D., Sept. 12, 1929; d. John Frederick and Elleene (Allison) McFarland; m. Grant Smith McNeil, Mar. 3, 1950 (dec. Apr. 19910); m. Claude Herman Logan, Mar. 23, 1994. Organizer cowboy poets for Old West Days celebration, Amarillo, Tex., 1986, monthly Cowboy Poetry Breakfasts, Amarillo, 1991, monthly cowboy poetry prorams Barnes and Noble bookstores, Amarillo; presenter cowboy poetry over S.W., performing at Nat. Cowboy Poet Hall of Fame, Spearfish, S.D., Nat. Cowboy Hall of Fame, Oklahoma City, Nat. Cowgirl Hall of Fame, Hereford, Tex., Trinity Writers' Conf., Ft. Worth, Inspirational Writers Alice! Conf., Amarillo, Poetry Soc. Tex. Ann. Summer Conf., McKinney. Author: (poetry) Celebration for Sonneteers, 1986, Girls Write Cowboy Too, 1990, Designed by Heritage, 1998. Recipient Tex. winner for arts Col. Sanders Super Achiever Nat. Contest, 1996. Mem. Poetry Soc. Tex. (councilor-at-large), S.W. Cowboy Poets Assn. (organizer, coord. 1991—), Hi-Plains Soc. (pres. 1998—), Writers Assn. Golden Spread Moderator 1999), Amerillo Sr. Citizens Writers's Group (organizer, coord.), Panhandle Profl. Writers (lifetime award 1998). Republican. Presbyterian. Avocations: reading, playing pool, dancing, travel. Home: 27 S Roosevelt Amarillo TX 79103

LOGAN, MARIE-ROSE VAN STYNVOORT, literature educator, editor; b. Brussels, Belgium, May 26, 1944; d. Jean Stevo and Marie-Rose (Mabille) Van Stynvoort; m. John Frederick Logan, Sept. 7, 1968 (div. 1997); 1 child, Franklin. Licence, U. Brussels, 1966; MA, Yale U., 1970; MPhil, 1972, PhD, 1974. Instr. Yale U., New Haven, 1972-74; asst. prof. Columbia U., N.Y.C., 1974-83; assoc. prof. Rice U., Houston, 1983-93, Goucher Coll., Balt., 1993-96; assoc. prof. dept. English Temple U., Phila., 1996—. Gen. editor Annals of Scholarship Quar. in Humanities and Social Scis., 1994—; assoc. editor Columbia Dictionary in European Lit., N.Y., 1978-81; lectr. in field. Editor: Contending Kingdoms, 1992, Gerard Genette Figures of Literary Discourse, 1981; author: Michel de Ghelderode, 1996; contbr. over 100 articles to profl. jours. and over 200 lectures at major instutions in the U.S. and abroad. Pres. Annals of Scholarship, Inc., 1995—. Recipient Chevalier de l'Ordre des Palmes Academiques Govt. of France, 1980; Nat. Endowment of Humanities fellow, 1981-88, Harvard U. fellow, 1975-76, Inst. for Advanced Study in Humanities fellow U. Edinburgh, 1989. Mem. Soc. Fellows in Humanities Columbia U., Elizabethan Club Yale U. Home: 4041 Ridge Ave # 4-416 Philadelphia PA 19129-1550 Office: Temple U Coll Arts and Scis Dept English Philadelphia PA 19129 E-mail: mlogan@nimbus.temple.edu.

LOGAN, MARY CALKIN, development and public relations consultant; b. Washington, Jan. 23, 1941; d. Loren Malcolm and Edith Garrison Calkin; m. Richard Lewis Logan, Jan. 6, 1962; children: Ashley Logan Drews, Austin Lewis. BA, U. Tex., 1963. Tchr. Tex. State Sch. for the Deaf, Austin, 1963-64; exec. sec. Dewar, Robertson & Pancoast, 1964-69; devel. dir. St. Joseph High Sch., Victoria, Tex., 1989-94; vol. dir. comty. rels. Hospice of S. Tex., 1994-96. Author, producer video; author script. Vice-chair Govs. Commn. for Women, State of Tex., 1989-90, Victoria County (Tex.) Rep. Orgn., 1988-94; chmn. Tex. Women's Hall of Fame, 1988; v.p. Palmer Drug Abuse Program, 1990-91, Womens Crisis Ctr., Victoria, 1987-89; sec. Boys Club, Victoria, 1981-83; mem. steering com. Nat. Pub. Radio, Victoria, 1992-94, 1997-2001, Victoria Performing Arts Ctr. Capital Campaign, 1999-2000; bd. dirs. Victoria Coll., 1996, Bronte Club of Victoria, 1998—, sec., 2000, 1st v.p., 2001, pres., 2002--; bd. dirs. Victoria Symphony Soc., 1999—, Victoria Women's Clubhouse, 1999--; master gardener, 2002. Mem. Jr. League Victoria (pres. 1985-86, Oustanding Sustainer Recognition award 1996, Sustainer chmn. 1999—), Ct. Six Flags (sec. 1989-90, treas. 1993-94, chmn. 1999, corr. sec. 2001), Victoria Preservation, Inc. (sec., founding mem., pres. 1994-96), Victoria Country Club (pres. 1989-90), Settlement Club Austin. Episcopalian. Avocations: needlepoint, gardening, walking, baseball card collecting, reading. Home and Office: 303 Turtle Rock Dr Victoria TX 77904-1137 E-mail: marich@cox-internet.com.

LOGAN, MATHEW KUYKENDALL, journalist; b. Norman, Okla., Aug. 19, 1933; s. Leonard Marion and Floy-Elise (Duke) L.; m. Linda Dianne Elderkin, Dec. 31, 1964. BA in Journalism, U. Okla., 1955. Reporter UPI, 1957—58; city editor Daily Oklahoman, 1958—69; asst. mng. editor Houston Post, 1969—76, mng. editor, 1976—83, Sta. KHOU-TV, 1984—87; asst. dean for community affairs Med. Sch. U. Tex., 1987—92; v.p. pub. affairs and mktg. Hermann Hosp., 1992—97; v.p. corp. comm. Meml. Hermann Healthcare Sys., 1997—2002; vis. prof. journalism Sam Houston State U., Huntsville, 2002—. Served with AUS, 1957. Mem. UPI Editors Tex. (pres. 1977), Tex. AP Mng. Editors Assn. (pres. 1983), Sigma Chi. Methodist. Home: 24 Sunlit Forest Dr The Woodlands TX 77381-2986 Fax: 281-367-2686. E-mail: kuyklogan@flex.net.

LOGAN, MICHAEL J. veterinary medical officer; b. Springfield, Mo., Jan. 19, 1951; s. John Ronald and Joan (Andrus) L.; m. Paula Ann Gamble, Aug. 14, 1971 (div. Dec. 1992); children: Wesley Brian, Stephanie Gayle, Rebecca Dawn; m. Wilma Jean Boyd, May 28, 1993. Student, S.W. Mo. State U., 1969-71; DVM, U. Mo., 1976; MPH, Tex. A&M U., 2002; postgrad., City U., Renton, Wash., 1997-98, Tulane U., 2000—. Intern Auburn Univ., Auburn, Ala., 1976-77; assoc. clinican Niceville Animal Clinic, Niceville, Fla., 1977-79; owner, practitioner Crane Animal Health Ctr., Crane, Mo., 1979-90; vet. medical officer U.S. Dept. Agr. FSIS, Decatur, Ark., 1990-91; supr. vet. medical officer Food Safety Inspection Svc., Batesville, 1991-92; SVMO inspector in charge USDA, FSIS, Conagra, 1992—. Recipient Cert. of Commendation USDA, 1991, 92, 93, 94, 95, 96, 97, cert. merit, 1998 (2), 99, 2000, 2001. Mem. AVMA, Am. Assn. Food Hygiene Vets., Ark. Vet. Med. Assn., Nat. Assn. Fed. Vet., Mo. Vet. Med. Assn., Am. Assn. Bovine Practitioners, Nat. Assn. Bus. Owners, Alpha Zeta, Phi Zeta, Gamma Sigma Delta. Avocations: gardening, piano, guitar. Home: 10 Lakeview Dr Newport AR 72112-5047 Office: USDA FSIS 10 D035 P383 PO Box 2127 Batesville AR 72503-2127 E-mail: mwlogan@swbell.net.

LOGAN, NANCY ALLEN, library media specialist; b. Rochester, N.Y., Mar. 27, 1933; d. Warren William and Dorothea Amelia (Pund) Allen; m. Joseph Skinner Logan, Dec. 29, 1952; children: Joseph Skinner Logan Jr., Susan, Annette Logan Miller, Jennifer Logan Haber. Student, Middlebury Coll., 1951-52; BA, Cornell U., 1955; MLS, SUNY, Albany, 1967; cert. legal asst., Marist Coll., 1983. Cert. libr. media specialist, social studies tchr. N.Y. Libr. media specialist Hyde Park (N.Y.) Sch. Dist., 1971-93. Editor: Dear Friends, 1989; editor: (newsletter) Sch. Libr. Media Specialists, 1984—85, Jamestown Hist. Soc., 1997—2001. Arts chmn. Jr. League, Poughkeepsie, NY, 1967—69; dir. Jr. Arts Ctr., 1967—69, edn. chmn., 1970—71; sec. bd. dirs. Poughkeepsie Tennis Club, 1973—79; indexer periodicals Dutchess County Hist. Soc., Poughkeepsie, 1979—93; county rep. Sch. Libr. Media Specialists, 1982, exhibits chmn. ann. meeting, 1983, 1984; indexer Jamestown (R.I.) Press, 1993—; bd. dirs. Friends of Jamestown Philomenian Libr., 1994—97, trustee, 1999—; mem. Jamestown Planning Commn., 1999; stewardship chair Conanicut Island Land Trust, 2002—. Mem.: Beavertail Lighthouse Assn. (bd. dirs. 1994—97). Avocation: reading, sailing, swimming, travel, bicycling. Home: 149 Seaside Dr Jamestown RI 02835-3117 E-mail: jslogan@compuserve.com.

LOGAN, P. BRADLEY, music educator, church musician; b. Decatur, Ill., Jan. 28, 1954; s. Charles Harold III and E. Jo-Ann (Kashefska) L.; m. Dawn Marie Henning, Dec. 27, 1974; 1 child, Erin Marie. BS in Music Edn., N.D. State U., Fargo, 1976; MA in Choral Music, Calif. State U., Long Beach, 1978; DMA in Choral Lit. and Conducting, U. Ill., 1986. Cert tchr., Ala., N.D. Grad. tchg. asst. Calif. State U., Long Beach, 1977-78, instr. choral/vocal music, 1978-79; grad. tchg. asst. U. Ill., Urbana, 1980-82; dir. choral activities, asst. prof. La. Coll., Pineville, 1982-86; dir. choral activities, assoc. prof. U. Montevallo, Ala., 1987-93; dir. music First United Meth. Ch., Alabaster, 1988-95; dir. choral music Pelham (Ala.) H.S., 1995-98; dir. choral activities, assoc. prof. Bemidji (Minn.) State U., 1998—. Executor Dr. Edwin R. Fissinger's Mus. Estate, 1990—; founder, artistic dir. Ctrl. Ala. Women's Chorus and Chamber Choir, Pelham, 1993—95; founder, dir. Logan Chamber Singers, L.A., 1977—79; co-editor Meadowlark Music Pubs.; condr. 3d

Internat. Festival of Choirs, Siena, Italy, 2001, Carnegie Hall, N.Y.C., 2002. Author: The Choral Music of Edwin R. Fissinger, 1986; contbr. articles to profl. jours. Dir. music ministry Mt. Chapel United Meth. Ch., Birmingham, Ala., 1997; interim dir. music ministries Pineville Park Bapt. Ch., Pineville, 1987; dir. music ministries First United Meth. Ch., Urbana, 1981-82; dir. choral music Our Redeemer Luth. Ch., Garden Grove, Calif., 1977-79. Recipient Founders awrd Internat. Peanut Festival, 1995. Mem. Am. Choral Dirs. Assn. (life; coll./univ. chmn. 1983-84, 87-93, La. pres. 1985-87, Ala. pres. 1991-93, Minn. bd. dirs. 2000—), Music Educators Nat. Conf., Coll. Music Soc., Nat. Asns. Tchrs. of Singing, N.D. State U. Student Alumni Assn. (founder, pres.). Avocations: golf, yardwork, softball. Home: 4629 Cherry Ln NE Bemidji MN 56601-5293 E-mail: plogan@bemidjistate.edu.

LOGAN, PAULA M. entertainment company executive, accountant; b. Bklyn., Nov. 23, 1971; d. Charles L. Price and Vyris Logan; 1 child, Tyrone T. BS in Acctg. and Econs., L.I. U., 1999. Account exec. Blanksteen Cos., N.Y.C., 1990-93, property and casualty ins. broker, 1993; account exec. Rude Boy Internat. Sounds, Bklyn., 1989—, Vy's Bake Shop, Bklyn., 1989—, Lady P's Party Cons. Co., Bklyn., 1989-93, v.p., 1993—. Vol. income tax assistance program, IRS, Bklyn., 1997—; youth counselor St. Mary's Ch. of Christ, 1993—. Mem. AICPAs, Lions. Democrat. Pentecostal. Avocations: collecting teddy bears and porcelain dolls, stamps and coins, reading, dancing. Office: Lady P's Party Cons 166 St Marks Ave Brooklyn NY 11238 E-mail: PLoganGrant@netscape.net., Lady_P_01@hotmail.com.

LOGAN, RALPH ANDRE, physicist; b. Cornwall, Ont., Sept. 22, 1926; s. Joseph A. and Lucy T. (Carter) L.; m. Aug. 26, 1950; children: Howard, Mary, Marguerite, Anthony, Enid, Alisa, Ruth, John, Thomas. BSc, McGill U., Montreal, 1947, MSc, 1948; PhD, Columbia U., N.Y.C., 1952. Tech. staff mem. AT&T Bell Labs Research Div., Murray Hill, N.J., 1952-94. Author: numerous tech. pubs.; patentee in field. Fellow IEEE, Am. Physics Soc.; mem. NAE, Optical Soc. Home: 7 Cindy Dr Manahawkin NJ 08050-4230

LOGAN, RICHARD, radiologist; b. Carrollton, Ill., May 7, 1932; MD, U. Ill., Chgo., 1958. Cert. Am. Bd. Radiology. Intern St. Louis City Hosp., 1958-59, resident in internal medicine, 1959-60; pvt. practice Polo, Ill., 1960-65; resident in radiology U. Wis. Hosps., Madison, 1965-68; staff Meriter Hosp., 1968-99; clin. prof. U. Wis. Med. Sch. Mem. Am. Coll. Radiology, Radiol. Soc. N.Am., Wis. Radiol. Soc. Office: 14016 La Mesita Rd NE Albuquerque NM 87112-6512

LOGAN, RODMAN EMMASON, retired jurist; b. West Saint John, N.B., Can., Sept. 7, 1922; s. Gilbert Earle and Emma Zela (Irwin) L.; m. Evelyn Pearl DeWitt, June 19, 1948 (dec.); children: John Bruce DeWitt, Ian David Alexander, Mary Jane Irwin Hill, Bruce Rodman Hans. BA, U. N.B., 1949, BCL, 1951, DCL (hon.), 1988; DCL, St. Thomas U., Fredericton, N.B., 1974. Bar: N.B. 1951, created Queen's Counsel 1972. Partner firm Logan, Bell and Church, Saint John, N.B., 1951-70; elected to Legis. Assembly, 1963, 67, 70, 74, 78; minister of labor and provincial sec. Province of N.B., 1970-77; atty.-gen. and minister of justice, 1977-82; justice Ct. of Queen's Bench, 1982-96. Served with Can. Armed Forces, 1942-45, U.K., N.W. Europe and Ctrl. Mediterranean Forces; hon. col. Royal N.B. Regt. Mem. Royal Commonwealth Soc., St. Andrew's Soc., Royal United Svcs. Inst. Clubs: Royal Can. Legion, Carleton and York Regtl. Anglican. Home: 273 Nerepis Rd Westfield NB Canada E5K 2Z9

LOGAN, SAMUEL PRICE, lawyer; b. Lawrence, Kans., Dec. 26, 1964; s. James Kenneth and Beverly Jo L. BA magna cum laude, Duke U., 1987; JD, U. Kans., 1990. Bar: Mo. 1990, U.S. Dist. Ct. (we. dist.) Mo. 1990, Kans. 1991, U.S. Dist. Ct. Kans. 1991, U.S. Ct. Appeals (10th cir.) 1994. Assoc. Spencer Fane Britt & Browne, Kansas City, Mo., 1990-95, Stinson, Mag & Fizzell, P.C., Kansas City, 1995-96; pvt. prac. Logan Law Firm, LLC, 1998—. Mem. Johnson Co. Bd. Realtors. Mem. Kans. Bar Assn., Kansas City Met. Bar Assn., Johnson County Bar Assn. (v.p. 2001—), Order of Coif. Democrat. Presbyterian. Avocations: golf, reading, music. Home: 5604 Cherry St Kansas City MO 64110-2722 Office: 153 W 151st St Ste 110 Olathe KS 66061-5300 E-mail: loganlawfirm@worldnet.att.net.

LOGAN, SANDRA JEAN, economics and business educator; b. Dayton, Ohio, Jan. 3, 1940; d. Max B. and Edna E. (Sanderson) Parrish; m. John E. Logan, Apr. 25, 1964. BA, Drew U., 1962; MBA, Columbia U., N.Y.C., 1964; PhD, U. S.C., 1976. Piano tchr., Whippany, N.J., 1957-64; lab. analyst Bear Creek Mining Co., Morristown, summer 1957, 58; rsch. asst. Drew U., Madison, summer 1962; staff asst. N.J. Bell Telephone Co., Newark, summer 1963, 64-67; instr. bus. U. Toledo, 1967-69; asst. prof. econs. and bus. S.C. State Univ., Orangeburg, 1970-76; prof. econs. and bus. Newberry (S.C.) Coll., 1976—, acting v.p. acad. affairs, 1993-95. Cons. econs., Ohio and S.C., 1967—, N.J. Bell Telephone Co., Newark, 1968; lectr. bus. Ea. Mich. U., Ypsilanti, spring 1969. Active Coldstream Home Owners Assn., Columbia, S.C., 1972-80; officer St. Andrews Woman's Club, Columbia, 1969-76. Rsch. grantee U. S.C. and S.C. State U., 1974-75. Mem. Am. Econs. Assn., So. Econs. Assn. Republican. Presbyterian. Home: 112 Smiths Market Ct Columbia SC 29212-1923 Office: Newberry Coll College St Newberry SC 29108

LOGAN, THADDEUS SUMNER, III, architect; b. Arlington, Va., June 7, 1955; s. Thaddeus Sumner Jr. and Mary Gertrude (Boehling) L.; m. Patricia Ruth Eisemann, Oct. 6, 1984; children: Thaddeus Sumner IV, Devitt August Henry. BS in Arch., U. Va., 1977; MS in Urban Planning, Columbia U., 1982. Lic. arch., N.Y. Project mgr., planner N.Y. City Dept. Ports and Terminals, 1981-84, dir. port and aviation devel., 1984-86; project mgr. Coopers & Lybrand, N.Y.C., 1986-93; dir. property mgmt. The Bank of N.Y., 1994—. Co-author: Hatton Grange Mill, 1976. Mem. parish coun. Holy Innocents Parish, Pleasantville, N.Y., 1992-93; mem. phase I, II citizens com. Pleasantville Sch. Bd., 1998. William Kinne fellow Columbia U., 1981; recipient Outstanding Student award Am. Planning Assn., 1981. Mem. Real Estate Bd. N.Y. (mem. institutional owners com. 1995-97). Roman Catholic. Office: The Bank of NY 100 Church St New York NY 10286-0001 Home: 75 Park Pl New York NY 10286

LOGAN, THOMAS WILSON STEARLY, SR. priest; b. Phila., Mar. 19, 1912; s. John Richard and Mary (Richardson) L.; m. Hermoine Hill, Sept. 3, 1938; 1 son, Thomas Wilson Stearly. AB, Lincoln U., 1935, LLH (hon.), 1985; cert., Gen. Theol. Sem., 1938; STM, Phila. Divinity Sch., 1941; DD, Va. Sem., 1988; LLH (hon.), St. Augustine Coll., 1984; D of Sacred Theology, Episcopal Sem., Cambridge, Mass., 1994. Ordained priest Episcopal Ch., 1938. Vicar St. Philip Ch., N.Y.C., 1938-40, St. Michael's and All Angels Chs., Phila., 1940-45; rector Calvary Ch., 1945-84, rector emeritus, 1984—. Pres. worker's conf. Episcopal Ch., 1951-61; canon St. Mary's Cathedral, Phila.; dean Schykill (Pa.) Deanery; former pres. Hampton (Va.) Mins. Conf., 1960-61; mem. diocesan coun.; police chaplain; chaplain Phila. Gen. Hosp.; S.T.D. Gen. Theol. Sem., N.Y.C., 1998. Bd. dirs. YMCA, Black Mus., Phila.; trustee Haverford State Hosp.; pres. Downington (Pa.) Sch.; life mem. Lincoln (Pa.) U. Mem. NAACP (life), Alpha Phi Alpha (life), Masons (33 degree, past grand master Pa.), Shriner (imperial chaplain). Home: 46 Lincoln Ave Yeadon PA 19050-2822

LOGANBILL, G. BRUCE, pathologist; b. Newton, Kans., Sept. 06; s. Oscar and Warrene L. BA, Bethel Coll., Kans., 1956; MA, U. Kans., 1958; PhD, Mich. State U., 1961; postdoctoral fellow, Inst. Logopedics, 1965-66. Mem. faculty Kalamazoo Coll., 1961-63; mem. faculty Fresno (Calif.) State U., 1966-68, Calif. State U., Long Beach, 1968—, prof., 1975—; voice cons., aesthetic performance cons. Nat. Coll. Psychiatry, Paris. Lectr. on voice modification/pathologies and interpretive comm., Argentina, Denmark, France, Hong Kong, Estonia, Switzerland, Japan, Can., India, Scotland, Czechoslovakia, USSR, Singapore, Germany, Netherlands, People's Republic of China; U.S. rep. 2d Internat. Congress de Melodie-Therapie du Language en accord Nat. Coll. Psychiatry, Paris, 1990; cons. aesthetic comms., Ferrand Exhbn. Embassy of France, Washington. Author: The Bases of Voice, Articulation and Pronunciation, 1974, 6th edit., 1997, also in Japanese, 1980; contbr. more than 30 articles to profl. jours. Mem. Speech Comm. Assn., Am. Speech and Hearing Assn., Western States Comm. Assn., Internat. Assn. Logopedics and Phoniatrics, Internat. Phonetics Assn., Internat. Assn. Art Therapy (v.p. 1996—), Assn. Calif. State U. Profs. (univ. chpt. pres. 1985), Assoc. Internat. Melodic Therapy and Language (v.p. 1997-2000), Big Ten Club of L.A., others. Republican. Episcopalian. Office: Calif State U 1250 N Bellflower Blvd Long Beach CA 90840-0006

LOGANI, KULBHUSHAN LAL, civil and structural engineer; b. Mardan, Panjab, India, Oct. 20, 1943; came to U.S., 1969; s. Sulakhan Mal and Shankri Devi L.; m. Suresh Logani, Jan. 24, 1965; children: Sanjay, Monica, Ronica. BSCE, Panjab U., 1961; ME in Structural Engring., Iowa State U., 1970, PhD, 1973. Registered profl. engr., lic. structural engr. Design engr. Bhakra & Beas Design Orgn., New Delhi, 1961-65; engring. cons. Ministry of Agr., Ghana, West Africa, 1965-69; rsch. asst. Iowa State U., Ames, 1969-73; consulting engr. Harza Engring. Co., Chgo., 1973-86; v.p., dir. Facilities Cons. Ltd., 1986-93; pres. KL Cons. Ltd., Glenview, Ill., 1991—. Cons. dam design and constrn. Dept. Hydraulic Resources, San Juan, Argentina, 1979-83; cons. devel. of instrumentation under artesian conditions Reza Shah Kabir Dam, Iran, 1978-79. Author publs. in field including Proceedings of VII Pan Am. Conf. on Soil Mechanics and Found. Engr.-Can., 1983, Transaction of the 14th Internat. Congress on Large Dams - Brazil, Proceedings of the Internat. Conf. on Recent Advances in Geotechnical Earthquake Engring., U. Mo., Rolla, 1981, various others confs. in field; contbg. author ency. article, 1988; contbr. articles to profl. jours. Founding mem. Assn. of Indian in Am., Chgo. Rsch. grantee Def. Nuclear Agy., Washington, 1970-73. Fellow ASCE; mem. ASTM (com. on soil and rock 1984—), Internat. Soc. Soil Mechanics and Found. Engring., Instn. of Engrs. India. Achievements include math. model for rock creep and progressive failure, math. formulation to model rock failure in plane-strain, devel. of equipment and technique to install instruments under high pore water pressure condition and deep water. Home and Office: 1144 Bette Ln Glenview IL 60025-2429

LOGANI, MAHENDRA KUMAR, biomedical physics educator; b. Sialkot, Punjab, India, May 15, 1941; came to U.S. 1968; s. Khem Chand and Kartar Devi L.; m. Shashi Prabha, May 16, 1968; children: Anupma L. Kulkarni, Deependra K. BS, Aligarh (India) U., 1957, MS, 1961, PhD, 1967. Lectr. in chemistry Dharam Samaj Coll., Aligarh, 1961-64; postdoct. fellow Smith Coll., Northampton, Pa., 1968-69; rsch. assoc. Temple U., Phila., 1969-72, asst. prof. dermatology, 1972-77, assoc. prof. dermatology, 1977—, prof. biomed. physics, 1994—. Vis. scientist Oak Ridge (Tenn.) Nat. Lab, 1981-82, Nagoya (Japan) U., 1980, U. Padova (Italy), 1980; co-investigator Nat. Inst. Environ. Health; prin. investigator NIH, 2000—. Contbr. articles to profl. jours., chpt. to book. Pres. India Cultural and Religious Ctr., Phila., 1985—; v.p. Coun. Indian Orgns., Phila., 1996-98, vice-chmn., 1998-00. Postdoct. fellow Sloan Found., 1968-69. Mem. ACS, Am. Oil Chemists' Soc., AAAS, Bioelectromagnetic Soc., Sigma Xi. Avocations: gardening, jogging, music. Home: 3261 Farragut Ct Bensalem PA 19020-1822 Office: Temple U Sch Medicine 3440 N Broad St Philadelphia PA 19140-5104 E-mail: mklogani@hotmail.com.

LOGAN-SUTTON, FLORETTA R. educator; b. Elizabeth City, N.C., Mar. 13, 1930; d. Ivy Hillard and Rosa Lillian (Stewart) Roach; m. Chester C. Sutton, Sept. 19, 1949 (dec. 1988); children: Gwen Omari, Chester Jr., Karen Bailey, Fred, Renee, Verona Dunn; m. Ben L. Logan; stepchildren: Tyrone, Karen Graham, Kathy, Darryl, Victor, Christopher. BA, Elizabeth City State U., 1955; MA, Glassboro (N.J.) State Coll., 1962. Tchr. grades 1-5 Bd. Edn., Atlantic City, tchr. basic skill improvement program. Contbr. rsch. to profl. jours. Mem. NEA, NAACP, Internat. Assn. Ministers' Wives and Ministers' Widows, Inc., N.J. Ret. Edn. Assn. Atlantic County, N.J. Edn. Assn., Atlantic City Edn. Assn., Phi Delta Kappa, Alpha Bettes. Home: 1910 Marmora Ave Atlantic City NJ 08401-2014

LOGE, PETER MARTIN, organization administrator; b. L.A., Mar. 5, 1965; BS in Speech, Emerson Coll., 1987; MS in Speech, Syracuse (N.Y.) U., 1989; MA in Polit. Sci., Ariz. State U., 1992. Instr./dir. forensics Clemson (S.C.) U., 1989-91; dir. constituent svc. Congressman Sam Coppersmith, Tempe, Ariz., 1993-95; sr. assoc. Progressive Comm., 1994; reporter The Bus. Jour., Phoenix, 1995; dep. to chief of staff/sys. adminstr. Senator Edward Kennedy, Washington, 1995-96; regional field dir./dir. tech. The Concord Coalition, 1996-97; campaign mgr./press sec. Sherman for Congress, Woodland Hills, Calif., 1998; chief of staff/comm. dir. Congressman Brad Sherman, Washington, 1997-99; dir. The Justice Project, 1999—. Commentator NPR, BBC. Vice chmn. Maricopa County Dems., Phoenix, 1992-94; mem. alumni bd. Emerson Coll. Alumni Assn., 2000—. Democrat. Avocation: soccer. Office: The Justice Project 50 F St NW Ste 1070 Washington DC 20001-1532

LOGENDRAN, RASARATNAM, industrial engineer, educator; b. Kopay, Jaffna, Sri Lanka, Aug. 2, 1953; came to U.S., 1981; s. Vythilingam and Nageswari Rasaratnam; m. Jayanthi Logendran, Dec. 30, 1985; children: Verni, Vathani. BSc with honors, U. Sri Lanka, Katubedda, 1975; M in Engring., Asian Inst. Tech., Bangkok, 1980; PhD, Okla. State U., 1984. Mech. engr. Sri Lanka Sugar Corp., Hingurana, 1976; rsch. officer Ceylon Inst. Sci. and Indsl. Rsch., Colombo, Sri Lanka, 1976-78; rsch. assoc. Asian Inst. Tech., Bangkok, 1980-81; asst. prof. So. Ill. U., Edwardsville, 1984-89; assoc. prof. Oreg. State U., Corvallis, 1989—. Faculty rsch. assoc. McClellan AFB, Sacramento, 1995. Co-editor: Group Scheduling and Cellular Manufacturing - Methodologies and Applications, 1998; contbr. articles to profl. jours. Grantee NSF, 1991-93, 94-95, 2001—; Faculty fellow Boeing Co., 1996, Faculty Rsch. fellow NASA, 1997; Fulbright scholar U. Sains Malaysia, 2000. Mem. Inst. Indsl. Engrs. (sr.), Inst. Ops. Rsch. and Mgmt. Sci., Soc. Mfg. Engrs., Am. Soc. Engring. Edn., Alpha Pi Mu (faculty advisor 1994—). Avocations: gardening, travel, music, running. Home: 1204 NE Conroy Pl Corvallis OR 97330 Office: Oreg State U Dept Indsl Mfg Engring 118 Covell Hall Corvallis OR 97331-2407 Fax: 541-737-5241. E-mail: logendrr@engr.orst.edu.

LO GERFO, FRANK WILLIAM, surgeon; b. Middletown, N.Y., Sept. 15, 1940; MD, U. Rochester, 1966. Diplomate Am. Bd. Surgery. Intern Boston U. Hosp., 1966-67, resident in surgery, 1967-71; chmn. dept. surgery Beth Israel Deaconess Med. Ctr., Boston, 1987—. Prof. surgery Boston U., 1973-87, Harvard U. Med. Sch., 1991—. Maj. USMC, 1971-73. Fellow Am. Coll. Surgeons; mem. Am. Surg. Assn., Internat. Soc. Cardiovascular Surgery, Soc. Univ. Surgeons, Soc. Vascular Surgeons, Am. Bd. Surgery (dir.). Office: Beth Israel Deaconess MC 110 Francis St Ste 3A Boston MA 02215-5501

LOGGIE, JENNIFER MARY HILDRETH, medical educator, physician; b. Lusaka, Zambia, Feb. 4, 1936; arrived in U.S., 1964, naturalized, 1972; d. John and Jenny (Beattie). M.B., B.Ch., U. Witwatersrand, Johannesburg, South Africa, 1959. Intern Harare Hosp., Salisbury, Rhodesia, 1960-61; gen. practice medicine Lusaka, 1961-62; sr. pediatric house officer Derby Children's Hosp., also St. John's Hosp., Chelmsford, Eng., 1962-64; resident in pediatrics Children's Hosp., Louisville, 1964, Cin., 1964-65; fellow clin. pharmacology Cin. Coll. Medicine, 1965-67; mem. faculty U. Cin. Med. Sch., 1967—, prof. pediatrics, 1975-98, assoc. prof. pharmacology, 1972-77, prof. emeritus pediatrics, 1998—. Contbr. articles to med. publs.; editor Pediatric and Adolescent Hypertension, 1991. Grantee Am. Heart Assn., 1970-72, 89-90 Mem. Am. Pediatric Soc. (Founder's award 1996), Midwest Soc. Pediatric Rsch. Episcopalian. Home: 1133 Herschel Ave Cincinnati OH 45208-3112

LOGGIODICE, SUSAN REBECCA, small business owner; b. Chadron, Nebr., Mar. 8, 1969; d. Charles Alan and Crystal Eve (Licthe) Staetz; m. Walter Edward Bancroft, June 18, 1988 (div. Oct. 1991); 1 child, Crystal Marie; m. Omar Raphael Loggiodice Adrian, Apr. 15, 1993. BA, LaSalle U., 1991, MA, 1992; MS in Computer Tech., Cleve. Inst. Electronics, 1993; JD, LaSalle U., 1996. Field rschr. Networking Agy., Inc., Richboro, Pa., 1988-90; sys. designer CMG Internat., Inc., Boonton, N.J., 1991-93; graphic designer Chadron Record, Inc., 1992-93; Internet site adminstr., owner TOPS BBS, Smyrna, Ga., 1993—. Team leader Software Devel. Group, Santa Ana, Calif., 1992—; advisor Team/OS2, Smyrna, 1994—. Author: Undocumented OS Calls, 1991, Society's Ghost: Manic Depression, 1993. Advocate Pendulum, 1992—. Mem. NAFE, Internat. Shareware Group. Avocations: painting, computers, boating, travel.

LOGIE, JAMES WALLACE, surgeon, retired; b. Grand Rapids, Mich., Jan. 31, 1911; m. Jean N. MD, U. Mich., 1935. Diplomate Am. Bd. Surgery. Intern U. Mich. Hosp., Ann Arbor, 1935-36, resident gen. surgery, 1936-38, 40-42, resident pathology, 1939-40; pvt. practice Grand Rapids, Mich., 1942-82; ret., 1982. Chief of staff Blodgett Meml. Hosp., Grand Rapids, 1959-60. Fellow ACS (pres. Mich. chpt. 1965-66); mem. AMA, Ctrl. Surgery Assn., Mich. State Med. Soc. Home: 3604 E Fulton St Apt 249E Grand Rapids MI 49546-1398 E-mail: DOB41@aol.com.

LOGIE, JOHN HOULT, mayor, lawyer; b. Ann Arbor, Mich., Aug. 11, 1939; s. James Wallace and Elizabeth (Hoult) L.; m. Susan G. Duerr, Aug. 15, 1964; children: John Hoult Jr., Susannah, Margaret Elizabeth. Student, Williams Coll., 1957-59; BA, U. Mich., 1961, JD, 1968; MS, George Washington U., 1966. Bar: Mich. 1969, U.S. Dist. Ct. (we. and ea. dists.) Mich. 1969, U.S. Ct. Appeals (6th cir.) 1987. Assoc. Warner, Norcross & Judd, Grand Rapids, Mich., 1969-74, ptnr., 1974—2001, of counsel, 2002—; mayor City of Grand Rapids, 1992—. Chmn. civil justice adv. group U.S. Dist. Ct. (we. dist.) Mich. 1995-99; program coord. condemnation law sect. Inst. CLE; guest lectr. Grand Rapids C.C., Grand Valley State U., Western Mich. U., Mich. State U.; bd. vis. Sch. Bus. and Pub. Mgmt. George Washington U, 1995—; instr. U.S. Naval Acad., 1964-66. Trustee Grand Valley State U. Found., 1998—; chmn. Clarke Hist. Libr./Ctrl. Mich. U., 2000—; pres. Grand Rapids PTA Coun., 1971-73, Heritage Hill Assn., 1976, pres., trustee, 1971-84; chmn. Grand Rapids Urban Homesteading Commn., 1975-80, Grand Rapids Hist. Commn., 1985-90, Grand Rapids/Kent County Sesquicentennial Com., 1986-88; mem. Headlee Blue Ribbon Commn., 1993-94, Mich. Workforce Invesment Bd., 2002; v.p., bd. dirs. Goodwill Industries, Grand Rapids, 1973-79, Am. Cancer Soc., Grand Rapids, 1970-81; pres., trustee Hist. Soc. Mich., 1984-90. Lt. USN, 1961-66. Recipient Lifetime Achievement award Mich. Hist. Preservation Network, 2000. Mem. ABA (forum com. on healthlaw 1980—), Am. Health Lawyers Assn., Mich. Bar Assn. (chmn. condemnation com. real property sect. 1985-88), Grand Rapids Bar Assn. (dir. young lawyers sect. 1970), Mich. Soc. Hosp. Attys. (pres. 1976-77), Univ. Club (dir. 1979-82, pres. 1980-82), Peninsular Club, Williams Club (N.Y.C.). Avocations: motor cruising, hunting, fishing. Home: 601 Cherry St SE Grand Rapids MI 49503-4726 Office: Warner Norcross and Judd 111 Lyon St NW Ste 900 Grand Rapids MI 49503-2487 also: Office of Mayor 300 Monroe Ave NW Grand Rapids MI 49503-2206 E-mail: logiejh@wnj.com.

LOGIUDICE, ELAINE A. nursing administrator; b. Sellersville, Pa. d. William and Miriam (Yoder) Anders; m. Guy LoGiudice. BS, Columbia U.; MSN, Cath. U. Am., 1982. Cert. nurse adminstr., advanced. Dept. chairperson/instr. Washington Hosp. Ctr. Sch. Nursing, Washington, 1974-82; MCH dir. Prince George's Gen. Hosp., Cheverly, Md., 1982-85; dir. maternal-child health/psychology D.C. Gen. Hosp., Washington, 1986-96, project dir. RWJ grant, 1994-96; coord. NSG standards & practice Bon Secours St. Joseph Hosp., Port Charlotte, Fla., 1996-97; NSG dir. CMS State of Fla., Ft. Myers, 1997—. Mem. ANA. E-mail: elaine_logiudice@doh.state.fl.us.

LOGOTHETIS, NICKOLAS, management consultant, researcher, educator; b. Kavala, Macedonia, Greece, Aug. 19, 1952; s. John and Helen (Papadopoulou) L.; m. Elena Nicolaidou, Dec. 29, 1985; children: John, Antigoni. Diploma in Math., Patras Coll., Greece, 1975; MSc in Stats., U. Sheffield, Eng., 1977; PhD, U. Nottingham, Eng. Chartered statistician, England. Rsch. advisor London Sch. Econs., 1980-84; head of stats. GE Co., London, 1985-88; sr. cons. Brit. Telecom, 1989-91; mng. dir. TQM Hellas, Athens, Greece, 1991—. Sr. vis. rsch. fellow City U., London, 1987-90; councillor, supr. MBA program Brit. Consul, Athens, 1994—. Author: (books) Probability Distributions, 1985, Quality Through Design, 1989, Managing for Total Quality, 1992; also contbr. articles to profl. jours.; mem. editl. com. Applied Stats., 1987-90, Internat. Jour. TQM, Eng., 1988-90. V.p. Overseas Students Bur., U. Nottingham, 1978-79, pres. 1979-80. With Greek Army, 1988. Named EFQM representative Fedn. of Greek Industries, Athens, 1992, Unconditional Consultant, Cyprus Inst. Tech., 1993. Mem. Greek Orthodox Ch. Avocations: music, tennis, basketball, chess, reading. Office: TQM Hellas Mavili 3 11141 Athens Attiki Greece E-mail: tqmstv@hol.gr.

LOGRONO, ROBERTO, cytopathologist; b. New Britain, Conn., Apr. 21, 1956; s. Miguel Angel Logrono-Batlle and Blanca Yolanda Di Vanna; m. Nancy Altagracia Marti, Oct. 28, 1983; children: Natalie B., Paula Y. MD, U. Autonoma Santo Domingo, Dominican Republic, 1982. Diplomat Am. Bd. Pathology, Am. Bd. Cytopathology. Resident in anatomic clin. pathology St. Barnabas Med. Ctr., Livingston, NJ, 1986—91, chief resident, 1990—91; assoc. pathologist Katherine Shaw Bethea Hosp., Dixon, Ill., 1991-92, Cmty. Gen. Hosp. Med. Ctr., Sterling, 1991-92; chief anatomic pathology and cytology Clinica Corazones Unidos, Santo Domingo, 1992-94; asst. instr. cytopathologist U. Wis., Madison, 1995-97; dir. cytopathology U. Tex. Med. Br., Galveston, 1997—, asst. prof. pathology Ill., 1997-2000, assoc. prof. pathology, 2000—. Asst. prof. pathology U. Nat. Pedro Henriquez Urena, Santo Domingo, 1992-93, U. Iberoamericana, Santo Domingo, 1993-94. Contbr. articles to profl. jours. Fellow: Am. Soc. Clin. Pathologists, Coll. Am. Pathologists (del. resident's forum 1990—91); mem.: Tex. Soc. Cytology, Am. Soc. Cytopathology (ednl. devel. com. 1997—2001), Internat. Acad. Cytology. Office: U Tex Med Br 301 U Blvd Galveston TX 77555-0548 Fax: (409)772-8437. E-mail: rologron@utmb.edu.

LOGSDON, CINDY ANN, small business owner; b. Webb City, Mo., Oct. 22, 1960; d. Donald Joseph Dicharry and Rae Marie (Bourgeois) Tuttle; m. Wayne Joseph Logsdon, Dec. 18, 1982; children: Brandy Marie, Ashley Renee, Laura Lynne (dec.). Student, Mo. So. State Coll., 1978-79. Office mgr. Anchala N. Reddy, M.D., Joplin, Mo., 1980-82, Vodur C. Reddy, M.D., Joplin, 1984-85, Joel Dean, D.O., Joplin, 1985-88; co-owner, treas. Tint 'N More, Inc., 1991—; co-owner/operator Profl. Svcs. Plus, 1988—, PM Resource, Joplin, 1999—. Bus. cons. Bernard F. Bettasso, M.D., Joplin, 1988-91. Mem. Profl. Assn. of Resume Writers, Joplin C. of C., Nat. Assn. of Resume Writers. Roman Catholic. Avocations: gourmet cooking, volleyball, racquetball. Office: Professional Services Plus 2230 S Main St Ste B Joplin MO 64804-2048

LOGSDON, JOHN MORTIMER, III, aerospace analyst, educator; b. Cin., Oct. 17, 1937; s. John M. Jr. and Marcella C. (Ludwig) L.; m. Roslyn Leibson, Jan. 20, 1962; children: David, Michael. BS in Physics, Xavier U., 1960; PhD in Polit. Sci., NYU, 1970. Asst. prof. Cath. U. Am., Washington, 1966-70; from asst. prof. to prof. George Washington U., 1970—, dir. grad. program in sci., tech. and pub. policy, 1972-88, dir. Space Policy Inst., 1987—, dir. Ctr. for Internat. Sci. and Tech. Policy, 1989-2001. Mem. V.P.'s Space Policy Adv. Bd., 1992; bd. dirs. The Planetary Soc., Pasadena, Calif.; cons. various pub., pvt. and internat. orgns. Author: Decision to Go to the Moon, 1970; contbr. articles to profl. and popular jours. Recipient NASA Disting. Svc. medal, 2001; Woodrow Wilson Ctr. fellow, 1974, 2000. Fellow AAAS, AIAA; mem. Internat. Acad. Astronautics. Home: 7460 Westlake Ter Bethesda MD 20817-6502 Office: Space Policy Inst George Washington U Washington DC 20052-0001 E-mail: logsdon@gwu.edu.

LOGSDON, MARGE A. English educator; b. Pitts., Apr. 24, 1946; d. Harry Reynolds and Dorothy (Barrett) Logsdon. B in English Edn., Slippery Rock U., 1969; M in Liberal Arts, Duquesne U., 1983; PhD, U. Pitts., 2000. Adv. coun. Internat. Poetry Forum, Pitts., 1998-2000. Avocations: writing, golf, travel. Home: 549 Indus St Pittsburgh PA 15207-1234 Office: Oakland Cath HS 144 N Craig St Pittsburgh PA 15213-2701

LOGSDON, ROSLYN, artist, educator; b. Bklyn., Aug. 13, 1940; d. Aaron and Evelyn Leibson; m. John M. Logsdon, Jan. 20, 1962; children: David, Michael. BA, Bklyn. Coll., 1961, postgrad., 1961-64. One-woman shows include Herkimer (N.Y.) C.C., 1993, Fed. Courthouse Gallery, Greenbelt, Md., 1997, Greenbelt Libr., 1996, Columbia (Md.) Art Gallery, 1994, Glenview Mansion Gallery , Rockville, Md., 1999, Montpelier Cultural Art Ctr., Laurel, Md., 2001, exhibited in group shows at Mid. Am. Art Coun., 1995—98, Anderson Gallery , Pontiac, Mich., 1996, Lexington (Ky.) Art League, 1997, U.S. Embassy , Turkey, Wenham (Mass.) Mus., 1998, Rochester (Minn.) Art Ctr., 1998, Spruill Art Ctr., Atlanta, 1999; author: People and Places: Imagery in Fiber, 1998; contbr. articles to profl. jours. Grantee Md. State Arts Coun., 1997-98, Prince George's Art Coun., 1989, 91, 92, 93, 94, 96, 97. Avocations: travel, reading, cooking. Office: Montpelier Cultural Arts Ctr 12826 Laurel Bowie Rd Laurel MD 20708-9700 E-mail: roz.logsdon@verison.net.

LOGUE, ALEXANDRA WOODS, higher education administrator, psychologist; b. Phila., Aug. 21, 1952; d. James Gibson and Camille (Woods) Logue; m. Ian Scott Shrank, June 23, 1974; 1 child, Samuel Logue Shrank. AB, Harvard U., 1974, PhD, 1978. Asst. prof. dept. psychology SUNY, Stony Brook, 1978-84, assoc. prof., 1984-89, prof., 1989-95, assoc. dean divsn.

social and behavioral scis., 1989-91, chair dept. psychology, 1992-95; dean Weissman Sch. Arts and Scis. Baruch Coll.-CUNY, N.Y.C., 1995—, prof. dept. psychology, 1995—. Doctoral faculty in psychology CUNY, 1995—. Author: The Psychology of Eating and Drinking: An Introduction, 1991, Self-control: Waiting Until Tomorrow for What You Want Today, 1995; cons. editor Jour. Exptl. Psychology: Animal Behavior Processes, 1987—, mem. editl. bd. Jour. Exptl. Analysis of Behavior, 1988-91, 93-96, 99—, Jour. Applied Behavior Analysis, 1994-96; contbg. editor Nutrition Revs., 1986-92. NSF grad. fellow, 1975-78; Rsch. grantee NSF, 1985-88, NIMH, 1981-82. Fellow APA (chair divsn. 3 fellows com. 1996-97, divsn. 25 exec. com. 1989-92, awards com. 1989-95, Hake award 1996, chair divsn. 6 fellows com. 2000-01), AAAS, Am. Psychol. Soc.; mem. Golden Key, Sigma Xi, Phi Eta Sigma. Office: Baruch Coll Weissman Sch Arts & Scis 17 Lexington Ave # A1621 New York NY 10010-5518 E-mail: alexandra_logue@baruch.cuny.edu.

LOGUE, DENNIS EMHARDT, financial economics educator, consultant; b. Bklyn., Mar. 28, 1944; s. Joseph Paul and Helen Rose (Emhardt) L.; m. Marcella Julia Watson, June 11, 1966; children: Dennis E. Jr., Patrick G. AB, Fordham U., 1964; MBA, Rutgers U., 1966; PhD, Cornell U., 1971. Asst. prof. Ind. U., Bloomington, 1971-73; sr. economist U.S. Treasury, Washington, 1973-74; prof. bus. Tuck Sch., Dartmouth Coll., Hanover, 1974—2001; chair Michael F. Price Coll. Bus. Univ. Okla. Founding bd. dirs. Ledyard Nat. Bank; bd. dirs. Sallie Mae (GSE), Waddell and Reed Fincancial Inc. Author: Legislative Influence on Corporate Pension Plans, 1979, The Investment Performance of Corporate Pension Plans, 1988, editor: Handbook of Modern Finance, 1998; co-editor Fin. Mgmt., 1978-81. Former trustee Crossroads Acad., Josiah Bartlett Ctr. for Pub. Policy Rsch. Served to 1st lt. U.S. Army, 1966-68. Mem. Am. Econ. Assn., Am. Fin. Assn. (bd. dirs. 1981-84), Fin. Mgmt. Assn. (bd. dirs., pres. 1995—), Knights of Malta, Order Holy Sepulchre, Beta Gamma Sigma. Republican. Roman Catholic. Office: Price Coll of Bus Adams Hall Univ of Okla Norman OK 73019 Home: 1000 Riviera Dr Norman OK 73072-7623

LOGUE, JAMES NICHOLAS, epidemiologist; b. Duryea, Pa., June 18, 1946; s. James and Lucille (Polen) L.; m. Mary Frances Carey, Nov. 25, 1972; children: Melissa, Jimmy, Jeffrey. BS, Kings Coll., 1968; MPH, U. Mich., 1971; DrPH, Columbia U., 1978. Statistician Warner Lambert Co, Morris Plains, N.J., 1969-70, 71-73; sr. med. biostatistician Ciba-Geigy Co., Summit, 1973-78; epidemiologist GEOMET Technologies, Inc., Rockville, Md., 1978-80; supervisory epidemiologist US FDA, 1980-82; dir. divsn. environ. health assessment Pa. Dept. Health, Harrisburg, 1982—. Office: Pa Dept Health PO Box 90 Harrisburg PA 17108-0090

LOGUE, JEAN EVELYN, music educator, educator; b. Chgo., Mar. 14, 1918; d. John Philip and Annaline Hazel Jeffrey; m. Osby Russell Logue, Mar. 12, 1938; children: Eleanor Jean Buckner, Jeffrey, Don, Anne. Student, Cornell Coll., 1935-38; BS in History, Ea. Ill. U., 1968, MA in Music, 1977. Pvt. practice piano tchr., Springfield, Ill., 1977-96, Chesterfield, Mo., 2001—. Dir. ch. camps, bell choir and childrens choir; historian Farmington Genealog. Assn. Mem. Am. Guild Organists, Decatur Music Tchrs. Assn. (past v.p., sec.). Democrat. Methodist. Avocations: organ, quilting. Home: 1466 Westmeade Dr Chesterfield MO 63017-4643 E-mail: jelogue@hotmail.com.

LOGUE, JOHN J(OSEPH), psychologist; b. Phila., Nov. 16, 1929; s. Edwin J. and Ellen V. (Mallon) L.; m. Evelyn Bortnick, Apr. 24, 1954; 1 child, Eileen Logue Handel. BS, Temple U., 1954, MEd, 1958, EdD, 1966. Lic. psychologist Pa., Md., N.J., Del. Ptnr., sr. cons. RHR Internat., Phila., 1966-88; pvt. practice Jenkintown, Pa., 1988—. With U.S. Army, 1954-56. Mem. APA (indsl., orgn., cons., counseling, edn. divsns.), The Three Seasons Yacht Club. Home: 1942 Greymont St Philadelphia PA 19116-3926

LOGUE, JOSEPH CARL, electronics engineer, consultant; b. Phila., Dec. 20, 1920; s. Percival J. and Mathilda (Moser) L.; m. Jeanne Martha Neubecker, Mar. 31, 1943; children: Raymond, Marilyn, Paul. BEE, Cornell U., 1944, MEE, 1949. Instr. Cornell U., Ithaca, N.Y., 1944-49, asst. prof., 1949-51; engr. IBM, Poughkeepsie, 1951-86, dir. rsch. divsn. Yorktown Heights, 1986; CEO Lorex Industries Inc., Poughkeepsie, 1986—. 30 patents in field; contbr. papers to profl. publs. IBM fellow. Fellow IEEE, AAAS; mem. NAE, Rsch. Soc. Am. Avocations: scuba diving, photography. Home: 52 Boardman Rd Poughkeepsie NY 12603-4228 E-mail: jclogue@msn.com.

LOGUE, JUDITH FELTON, psychoanalyst, educator, professional coach; b. Phila., Aug. 21, 1942; d. Martin and Laura (Goldman) Kirshenbaum; m. Stephen Felton, Feb. 8, 1966 (div. Aug. 1989); 1 child, Jane Jennifer; m. A. Douglas Logue, Feb. 14, 1990. AB in Govt., Wheaton (Mass.) Coll., 1963; MSW, Rutgers U., 1966, PhD, 1983; grad., N.Y. Ctr. Psychoanalytic Tng., 1978. Diplomate Am. Bd. Psychotherapy, Am. Bd. Forensic Medicine, Am. Bd. Examiners Clin. Social Worker, Am. Bd. Forensic Examiners, Am. Bd. Psychol. Specialties. Clin. social worker VA, Newark, 1967; psychotherapist Santa Barbara (Calif.) Mental Health Svcs., 1967-69; supr. Santa Barbara Counselling Ctr., 1967-69; pvt. practice psychoanalysis, 1969—. Psychoanalyst, therapist Fifth Ave. Ctr. for Psychotherapy, N.Y.C., 1969-72; instr. Marymount Manhattan Coll., 1971; psychotherapy supr. clin. faculty, dept. psychiatry Rutgers Med. Sch., New Brunswick, N.J., 1972-75, tchg. asst. Grad. Sch. Social Work, 1974-76; vis. lectr. Bryn Mawr Coll. Sch. Social Work and Social Rsch., 1980; mem. faculty N.Y. Ctr. for Psychoanalytic Tng., 1980—, N.J. Inst. Psychoanalysis and Psychotherapy, 1982—; adv. bd. Am. Bd. Forensic Social Workers, 1999; chair adv. bd. Am. Bd. Forensic Social Workers, 2000; pres. Goldilox Co., Inc., ShAIRing, Inc. Mem. editl. bd. jour Current Issues in Psychoanalytic Practice, 1983—; contbr. articles to profl. jours. Bd. dirs. N.Y. Ctr. for Psychoanalytic Tng., Inst. for Psychoanalysis and Psychotherapy N.J. Faculty, 1982—. Recipient Disting. Faculty award Atlantic County Psychoanalytic Soc., 1987; NIMH fellow, 1965. Fellow N.J. Soc. for Clin. Social Work; mem. AAUP, NASW, APA (div. 39, sect. 1), Am. Coll. Forensic Examiners (Outstanding Svc. award 2000), Conf. Psychoanalytic Psychotherapists, Nat. Assn. for Advancement of Psychoanalysis, Groves Conf. on Family, Acad. Cert. Social Workers, Soc. for Psychoanalytic Tng. (bd. dirs. 1983—, dir. social sci. program 1983-86), Am. Acad. Experts Traumatic Stress (cert.), Internat. Coach Fedn. Home and Office: 159 Valley Rd Princeton NJ 08540-3442 E-mail: DrJudith@judithlogue.com.

LOGUINOV, DMITRI, computer scientist, educator; b. Moscow, Russia, Mar. 12, 1974; s. Seguei Loguinov and Irina Loguinova. BS, Moscow State U., Moscow, 1995; PhD, CUNY, New York, 2002. Rsch. asst. Philips Rsch. USA, Briarcliff Manor, NY, 1998—2001. Contbr. scientific papers to confs. articles to profl. jours. Mem.: IEEE, Assn. Computing Machinery.

LOH, ARTHUR TSUNG YUAN, finance company executive; b. Shanghai, People's Republic of China, Dec. 2, 1923; came to U.S., 1948; s. Chengor and Kwei N. (Wang) L.; m. Monica K.L. Chen, Apr. 16, 1955; children: Stephanie T.L., Pamela T.K. BA, St. John's U., Shanghai, 1945; MS, U. Ill., 1949, PhD, 1952. V.p., co-owner R.W. Pressprich & Co., N.Y.C., 1952-69; exec. v.p. fin. GAC Corp., Allentown, Pa., 1970-71; v.p., co-owner N.Y. Securities Co., N.Y.C., 1972-74; sr. v.p., chief fin. officer Govt. Employees Ins. Co., Criterion Ins. Co., Washington, 1974-80; chief fin. officer Rotary Internat., Evanston, Ill., 1981-88; founder, chmn. Loh Assocs., Greenwich, Conn., 1988—. Chmn. bd. GAC Securities Co., Ft. Lauderdale, Fla., 1973-74. Chmn. devel. com. Travelers Aid Soc., N.Y.C.; active Rep. Nat. Com., Washington, Heritage Found.; dir. Mid. Patent Rural Cemetery. Mem. Assn. for Investment Mgmt. and Rsch., Internat. Soc. Security Analysts, Am. Econ. Assn., Fin. Execs. Inst., Inst. Chartered Fin. Analysts (chartered), N.Y. Soc. Security Analysts, Wall Street Club, Bankers Club Am., Windmill Club, Greenwich Polo Club, Rotary, Downtown Assn. (N.Y.C.), City Midday Club (N.Y.C.). Methodist. Avocations: tennis, swimming, skiing, travel. Home: 9 North Ln Armonk NY 10504-2238 also: East of Rte 7 Danby VT 05739 Office: Loh Assocs 2001 W Main St Stamford CT 06902-4501

LOH, GERHARD, librarian; b. Leipzig, Saxony, Germany, Jan. 24, 1937; s. Artur and Gertrud (Kuhn) L.; m. Elke Martina Teichmann, Feb. 20, 1964; children: Andre, Gerald, Hjalmar. Libr., Fachschule, Leipzig, Germany, 1956; Diploma Okonom, Univ. Leipzig, 1970, PhD, 1983, U. Berlin, 1990. Libr. U. Leipzig, 1956-70, scientific asst., 1970-75, leader of dept. catalogues, 1975-87, vice-dir., 1987-90, leader dept. econs., law, sports, 1990—. Author: Volkerschlacht bei Leipzig, 1963, Internationale Bibliographie der Antiquariats-Auktions- und Kunstkataloge, 1960-96, Bibliographie der Antiquariats-Auktions-und Kunstkataloge, 1975-2001; co-editor: Zeitschriftenbestandsverzeichnis der Universitatsbibliothek Leipzig, 1977-89, Verzeichnis der Kataloge von Buchauktionen und Privatbibliotheken aus dem deutschsprachigen Raum, 1995-99, Die europaeischen Privatbibliotheken und Buchauktionen, 1997-2000, others. Office: Universitatsbibliothek Beethovenstrasse 6 Saxony Leipzig D-04107 Germany

LOHF, KENNETH A. librarian, writer; b. Milw., Jan. 14, 1925; s. Herman A. and Louise (Krause) Lohf. AB, Northwestern U., 1949; AM, Columbia U., 1950, MS in Library Sci., 1952. Asst. librarian spl. collections Columbia U., N.Y.C., 1957-67, librarian rare books and manuscripts, 1967-92. Author: Thirty Poems, 1966, Conrad at Mid-Century: Editions and Studies, 1957, The Achievements of Marianne Moore: A Bibliography, 1958, Yvor Winters: A Bibliography, 1959, Frank Morris: A Bibliography, 1959, Sherwood Anderson: A Bibliography, 1960, An Index to the Little review, 1914-1929, 1961, The Collection of Books, Manuscripts and Autograph Letters in the Library of Jean and Donald Stralem, 1962, Indices to Little Magazines, 1953—64, The Literary Manuscripts of Hart Crane, 1967, The Jack Harris Samuels Library, 1974, The Centenary of John Masefield's Birth, 1978; author: (poems) Seasons, 1981, Arrivals, 1987, Fictions, 1990, Passages, 1991, Places, 1992, Endings/Beginnings, 1994; editor: Hart Crane, Seven Lyrics, 1966, Collections and Treasures of the Rare Book and Manuscript Library of Columbia University, 1985, Poets in a War, 1995, Hours, 1996, Moon and Sun, 1997, Columbia Library Columns, 1981—92, A Hymn of Simon Peter, 1998, Red Unto White, 1999, The Book of Twelve, 2000; contbr. ; author: (novels) East West, 2002. Sec.-treas. Friends of Columbia U. Librs., 1973—92; mem. coun. Am. Mus. Britain; mem. vestry St. Thomas Ch. of Fifth Ave. 1st lt. USAF, 1943—46. Mem.: Coun. Fellows Pierpont Morgan Libr., Order of St. John of Jerusalem, Grolier Club (coun., sec. 1987—90, pres. 1990—94), Century Club, Knickerbocker Club. Episcopalian. Home: 560 Riverside Dr Apt 21B New York NY 10027-3236

LOHMAN, GORDON RUSSELL, retired manufacturing executive; b. 1934; BS, MIT, 1955. Rsch. metallurgist, project engr. Amsted Industries, Inc., Chgo., 1958-61; project engr. Amsted Rsch. Labs., 1961-67; dir. rsch. Amstead Industries, Inc., 1967-68, pres. rsch., 1968-76, pres. MacWhyte divsn., 1976-78, v.p., 1978-87, exec. v.p., then pres., 1987-88, pres., COO, 1988-90, pres., CEO, 1990-1999; ret., 1999. Trustee Ill. Inst. Tech.; bd. dirs. Fortune Brands Inc., Ameren. Lt. USAF, 1955-58.

LOHMAN, LORETTA CECELIA, social scientist, consultant; b. Joliet, Ill., Sept. 25, 1944; d. John Thomas and Marjorie Mary (Brennan) L. BA in Polit. Sci., U. Denver, 1966, PhD in Am. History, 1996; MA in Social Sci., U. No. Colo., 1975. Lectr. Ariz. State U., Tempe, 1966-67; survey researcher Merrill-Werthlin Co., 1967-68; edn. asst. Am. Humane Assn., Denver, 1969-70; econ. cons. Lohman & Assocs., Littleton, Colo., 1971-75; rsch. assoc. Denver Rsch. Inst., 1976-86; owner, rsch. scientist Lohman & Assocs., Littleton, 1986-99; affiliate Colo. Water Resources Rsch. Inst., Ft. Collins, Colo., 1989-91; Colo. Nonpoint source info./edn. coord. coop. ext. Colo. State U., 1999—. Tech. adv. com. Denver Potable Wastewater Demo Plant, 1986—90; cons. Constrn. Engrng. Rsch. Lab., 1984—; peer reviewer NSF, 1985—86, Univs. Coun. Water Resources, 1989; WERC consortium reviewer N.Mex. Univs.-U.S. Dept. Energy, 1989—, Co-Alliance Environ. Edn. Adv. Bd., 2000—; course cons. Regis Coll., Denver, 1992—. Contbr. articles to profl. jours. Vol. Metro Water Conservation Projects, Denver, 1986-90; vol. handicapped fitness So. Suburban Parks and Recreation. Recipient Huffsmith award Denver Rsch. Inst., 1983; Nat. Ctr. for Edn. in Politics grantee, 1964-65. Mem. ASCE (social and environ. objectives com.), Orgn. Am. Historians, Pub. Hist. Assn., Sigma Xi, Pi Gamma Mu, Phi Alpha Theta. Avocations: vegetable and xeriscape gardening, traveling, miniature boxes. Home and Office: 3375 W Aqueduct Ave Littleton CO 80123-2903 E-mail: llohman@juno.com. *Personal philosophy: Recognition of biological, social, and cultural interdependence leads to a cooperative spirit emphasizing sharing and openmindedness. This allows one to be true to oneself.*

LOHMANN, GEORGE YOUNG, JR. neurosurgeon, hospital executive, international business executive, artist; b. Scranton, Pa., Aug. 9, 1947; s. George Young Lohmann and Elizabeth (Nichols) Frantzen; m. Joette Calabrese, May 15, 1973 (div. 1981); m. Rosemary Ei-Ling Ma, Sept. 24, 1988 (div. 1998); 1 child, Norelle Christa Victoria. AB in Chemistry with honors, Hobart Coll., 1968; MD, SUNY, Buffalo, 1972. Diplomate Am. Bd. Neurol. Surgeons, Am. Acad. Pain Specialists, Am. Bd. Forensic Medicine, Am. Acad. Disability Analysts. Resident gen. surgery Wesley Meml. Hosp., Chgo., 1972-73; asst. med. dir. West Side Orgn., 1973-74; emergency physician St. James Hosp., Chicago Heights, Ill., 1973-74; from jr. resident to chief resident neurosurgery Georgetown U. Hosp., Washington, 1975-79; chief resident neurosurgery Washington Vets. Hosp., 1978; pvt. practice Baton Rouge, 1979-81, 81-84; dir. dept. neurosurgery Brookdale Hosp. Med. Ctr., Bklyn., 1984-93; pres. Bklyn. Neurosurg. Svcs., Inc., 1985—; pvt. practice Midland, Tex., 1994-96; founding pres. Dragongate Adoption Cons., Inc. Mem. Med. Dir. Com., Risk Mgmt. Com., Exec. Quality Assurance Com., 1987-93; mem. Med. Bd. Com., 1985-93, Exec. Bd. Com., 1984-93, Pain Mgmt. Com., 1988-91; regional dir. Tex. Physicians Resource Coun., 1996-97. Contbr. articles to profl. jours.; actor: (in amatur theatre). Mem. adv. bd. Ctr. Latin Affairs, Baton Rouge, 1982-84; mem. Senatorial Inner Cir., 1988, mem. presdl. roundtable, 1991; mem. Presdl. Roundtable, 1992; trustee Christian Victory Ctr., Hempstead, N.Y., 1986-88; vol. Appalachian Project, 1970. Named to Compton-Connolly Guide to Best Physicians in the N.Y. Met. Area; selected by peers as one of Best Doctors in America Ctrl. Region, 1996-97. Fellow ACS, Am. Coll. Pain Mgmt., Am. Coll. Forensic Examiners, Am. Coll. Disability Analysts; mem. AMA, Am. Assn. Neurol. Surgeons (sect. intensive care), Christian Med. and Dental Soc., Am. Assn. Neurologic Surgeons, N.Y. State Neurosurg. Soc., N.Y. Soc. Neurosurgery, Congress Neurologic Surgeons (spine sect., sect. on trauma, sect. on intensive care), Tex. State Med. Soc., So. Med. Soc. Presdl. Roundtable (presdl. transition team 1980-81), West Tex. Cigar Soc., Physicians Resource Coun. (Tex. regional dir.), Argentier Honoraire Confrerie de la Chaine des Rotisseurs, Bailli Foundateur de Midland-Confrerie de la Chaine des Rotisseurs, Midland Confrerie de la Chaine des Rotisseurs (Bailli Honoraire), Chaine des Rotisseurs (commdr.), Consul de L'Ordre Mondial des Gourmets Degustateurs, Brilliat-Savarin Soc., Shanhai Tiffin Club, Donyin Sister City Assn., Midland Arts Assn., Midland C. of C., Midland-Odessa Symphony and Choral Soc., Midland Arts Assn. Avocations: skiing, painting, poetry, music, cooking.

LOHMANN, KEITH HENRY, police department official, consultant; b. Dec. 26, 1955; s. Henry August and June Dorothy (Friberg) L.; m. Margaret Lynch, Mar. 31, 1984; 1 child, Katarina. AS in Law Enforcement, Guilford Coll., 1977, BS in Adminstrn. of Justice, 1981; M in Pub. Affairs, U. N.C., 1987. Ops. mgr. H. Lohmann and Son, Brookhaven, 1973-75, 81-82; ops. supr. Powers Detective and Patrol, Greensboro, N.C., 1975-81; pub. safety officer Chapel Hill (N.C.) Police Dept., 1982-84, police planner, 1984-87; coord. law enforcement dist. N.H. U.S. Dept. Justice, Concord, 1987-89; spl. asst. U.S. Atty., Washington, 1989-92; prof. criminal justice N.H. Tech. Inst., 1992-93; lt. N.H. Police Stds. & Tng. Coun., Concord, 1993-95, maj., 1996—. Security cons. Hotel Europa, Inc., Chapel Hill, 1982-83. Mem. Nat. Coun. Law Enforcement Edn. and Tng., Internat. Assn. Dirs. of Law Enforcement Stds. and Tng., N.H. Assn. Chiefs of Police. Lutheran. Avocations: golf, tennis, snow skiing. Office: NH Police Stds & Tng Coun 17 Fan Rd Concord NH 03301-7424

LOHMULLER, MARTIN NICHOLAS, bishop; b. Phila., Aug. 21, 1919; s. Martin Nicholas and Mary Frances (Doser) L. BA, St. Charles Borromeo Sem., Phila., 1942; D.Canon Law, Catholic U. Am., 1947. Ordained priest Roman Catholic Ch., 1944; officialis Diocese Harrisburg, Pa., 1948-63; vicar for religious Diocese of Harrisburg, 1958-70; pastor Our Lady of Good Counsel parish, Marysville, Pa., 1954-64, St. Catherine Laboure Parish, Harrisburg, 1964-68; consecrated Bishop of Ramsbury, 1970; vicar gen. Archdiocese Phila., 1970-94; aux. bishop of Phila., 1970-94; pastor Old St. Mary's Parish, Phila., 1976-89, Holy Trinity Parish, Phila., 1976-89. E-mail: bishiplo@aoc.1p01.web.

LOHN, ROGER LOWELL, management consultant; b. Wessington Springs, S.D., Feb. 6, 1934; s. Kenneth Fairbairn and Irma Gladys Lohn; m. Eleanor Terlinden, Nov. 7, 1958; children: Cinty Lou, Mark David, Matthew Eric. Student, Phoenix Jr. Coll., 1958-60, Ariz. State U., 1960-63. Quality assurance technician Sperry Phoenix, 1958-60; engr. Motorola Mil., 1961-65; reliability product mgr. Siemens, Scottsdale, Ariz., 1965-67; dir. quality assurance Motorola Mobile Comm. Products, Fort Worth, 1967-83; dir. quality and productivity Codex-Phoenix Ops., 1983-86; mgr. reliability and quality assurance Motorola, Inc., Schaumburg, Ill., 1986—, mem. semiconductor group, 1987-91, cons., 1991—. Editor: The Quality System, 1981, revised, 1990.contbr. articles to profl. jours. Lst lt. USAF, 1952-57. Mem. Am. Soc. Quality Control (various com. positions). Home: 145 N Centennial Way Mesa AZ 85201-6750

LOHNES, WALTER F. W. German language and literature educator; b. Frankfurt, Germany, Feb. 8, 1925; came to U.S., 1948, naturalized, 1954; s. Hans and Dina (Koch) L.; m. Claire Shane, 1950; children: Kristen, Peter, Claudia. Student, U. Frankfurt, 1945-48, Ohio Wesleyan U., 1948-49, U. Mo., 1949-50; PhD, Harvard U., 1961. Asst., Inst. German Folklore, U. Frankfurt, 1947-48; instr. German U. Mo., 1949-50; head dept. German, Phillips Acad., Andover, Mass., 1951-61; asst. prof. Stanford (Calif.) U., 1961-65, assoc. prof., 1965-68, prof., 1969-95, prof. emeritus, 1995—, dir. NDEA Inst. Advanced Study, 1961-68, chmn. dept. German studies, 1973-79, dir. Inst. Basic German, 1975-95, prin. investigator NEH grant, 1978-80. Vis. prof. Woehler-Gymnasium, Frankfurt, 1956-57, Middlebury Coll., 1959, U. N.Mex., 1980, 81, 86, U. Vienna, 1990, Coll. de France, Paris, 1992; mem., chmn. various coms. of examiners Ednl. Testing Svc. and Coll. Bd.; chmn. German Grad. Record Exam. Author: (with V. Nollendorfs) German Studies in the United States, 1976, (with F. W. Strothmann) German: A Structural Approach, 1968, 4th rev. edit., 1988; (with E.A. Hopkins) Contrastive Grammar of English and German, 1982, (with Martha Woodmansee) Erkennen und Deuten, 1983, (with J.A. Pfeffer) Grunddeutsch, Texte zur gesprochenen deutschen Gegenwartssprache, 3 vols., 1984, (with D. Benseler and V. Nollendorfs) Teaching German in America: Prolegomena to a History, 1988; contbr. numerous articles to profl. jours.; editor: Unterrichtspraxis, 1971-74 Bd. dirs. Calif. Youth Symphony, 1977-78, Oakland (Calif.) Symphony Youth Orch., 1978-80, Peninsula Dem. Coalition, 1998—. Decorated Fed. Order of Merit (Germany); Medal of Honor in Gold (Austria); German Govt. grantee, 1975, 76, 78. Mem. MLA, Am. Assn. Tchrs. German (v.p. 1961-62, 70-71, Outstanding Educator award 1994; hon. 1995), Am. Assn. Applied Linguistics, Am. Coun. on Teaching Fgn. Langs., German Studies Assn., Internat. Vereinigung Germanische Sprach und Literaturwissenschaft. Home: 733 Covington Rd Los Altos CA 94024-4903 Office: Stanford U Dept German Studies Stanford CA 94305-2030

LOHR, Mrs. BENJAMIN FRANKLIN See DAVIS, RUTH MARGARET

LOHR, HAROLD RUSSELL, retired bishop; b. Gary, S.D., Aug. 31, 1922; s. Lester ALbert and Nora Helena (Fossum) L.; m. Theola Marie Kottke, June 21, 1947 (div. Dec. 1973); children: Philip Kyle, David Scott, Michael John; m. Edith Mary Morgan, Dec. 31, 1973. BS summa cum laude, S.D. State U., 1947; PhD, U. Calif.-Berkeley, 1950; MDiv summa cum laude, Augustana Theol. Sem., Rock Island, Ill., 1958. Ordained to ministry Augustana Luth. Ch., 1958; installed as bishop, 1980. Research chemist Argonne Nat. Lab., Lemont, Ill., 1950-54; pastor Luth. Ch. of Ascension, Northfield, 1958-70; assoc. exec. Bd. Coll. Edn., N.Y.C., 1970-73; dir. research Div. Profl. Leadership, Phila., 1973-77, assoc. exec., 1977-80; synodical bishop Luth. Ch. in Am., Fargo, N.D., 1980-87, Evang. Luth. Ch. in Am., Moorhead, Minn., 1988-91, ret., 1991. Mem. exec. council Luth. Ch. in Am., N.Y.C., 1982-87; mem. commn. of peace and war, 1983-85. Contbg. author: Growth in Ministry, 1980; also articles to sci. jours. Bd. dirs. Gustavus Adolphus Coll., 1980-87, Luther Northwestern Sem., St. Paul, 1980-87, Concordia Coll., Moorhead, Minn., 1988-91; mem. ch. coun. Evang. Luth. Ch. in Am., Chgo., 1990-91, disciplinary hearing officer, 1992-97, interim dir. synodical rels., 1993-94; mem. bd. govs. Chgo. Ctr. Religion and Sci., 1987-99, Zygon Ctr. Religion and Sci., Chgo., 1999—; mem. Summit on Environ., Joint Appeal in Religion and Sci., Washington, 1992; mem. adv. bd. Ctr. for Faith and Sci. Exch., Concord, Mass., 1995-99, mem. exec. bd., 1999-2001. Recipient Suomi award Suomi Coll., 1983. Mem. Phi Kappa Phi. Democrat. Home: 47 Brook Ln Berlin MA 01503-1671 E-mail: hrlohrs@aol.com.

LOHR, JACOB ANDREW, physician, pediatrician, educator; b. Lexington, N.C., Aug. 15, 1940; s. Dermot and Blanche (Grimes) L.; m. Elizabeth Waite, June 19, 1967 (div. 1978); m. Lura Galloway, Nov. 27, 1993; children: Jason Merrill, Lara Jane Parker, Jonathan Waite, Elizabeth Brice. AB, U. N.C., 1962, MD, 1967. Diplomate Am. Bd. Pediats. Chief resident dept. pediats. U. Va., Charlottesville, 1969-70, prof., 1984-90, divsn. chief, assoc. chair, 1976-90; prof. dept. pediats. U. N.C., Chapel Hill, 1990—, divsn. chief, assoc. chair, 1990-98, vice chair dept. pediats., 1998-2000; pediatrician-in-chief N.C. Children's Hosp., 1999-2000, sr. cliinician, 2000—; exec. dir. Gov.'s Inst. Alcohol and Substance Abuse, 1998—. Cons. to task force on urinary tract infections Am. Acad. Pediats., 1992-99, WHO Com. on Hospitalized Children at Risk, Geneva, 1999-2000. Editor: Pediatric Outpatient Proceedings, 1992, Guidelines for Nurse Practitioners, 1994, 5th edit., 1999, Essence of Pediatrics, 2000; med. editor Am. Bd. pediats., 1996—; contbr. articles to profl. jours. Bd. dirs. Head Start, Charlottesville, 1973-76, Ronald McDonald House, 1980-82, Orange County Ptnrship. for young Children, Chapel Hill, 1994-96; trustee Bowman Fund, U. Va., 1972—. Lt. comdr. USN, 1970-72. Fellow Am. Acad. Pediats.; mem. Am. Soc. for Microbiology, Ambulatory Pediat. Assn., Pediat. Infectious Disease Soc., Infectious Disease Soc. Lutheran. Avocations: golf, boating. Office: U NC Dept Pediats 639 Burnett Wommack Chapel Hill NC 27599-0001 E-mail: JLohr@med.unc.edu.

LOHR, WALTER GEORGE, JR. lawyer; b. Balt., Mar. 3, 1944; s. Walter George and Janet Louise (Cartee) L.; children: Lila Meredith, Walter George III, Frederick Boyce. AB, Princeton U., 1966; LLB, Yale U., 1969. Bar: Md. 1969. Law clk.to Hon. Harrison L. Winter U.S. Cir. Ct., Richmond, Va., 1969-70; assoc. Piper & Marbury, Balt., 1970-74, ptnr., 1977-88, Hogan & Hartson, Washington, 1992—; asst. atty. gen. State of Md., Balt., 1974-76; prin. Walter G. Lohr Jr., 1988-92. Bd. dirs. Danaher Corp., Washington, Cmty. of Sci., Inc., Balt., iSky, Inc., Laurel, Md., chmn.; mem. adv. bd. Prudential Venture Ptnrs., N.Y.C., 1985-93. Trustee Balt. Mus. Art, 1986-1998, 2000-. Office: Hogan & Hartson 111 S Calvert St Ste 1600 Baltimore MD 21202-6191 E-mail: wglohr@hhlaw.com.

LOHRER, RICHARD BAKER, investment consultant; b. Boston, Nov. 30, 1932; s. Leo and Elizabeth Louise (Kaiser) L.; m. Ruth Willa Gutekunst, Feb. 15, 1958; children: Richard Baker, William L., Elizabeth L. Hall, Andrew M. AB, Harvard U., 1954; MBA, NYU, 1961. Asst. sec. comml. lending Irving Trust Co. (now Bank of N.Y.), N.Y.C., 1957-64; asst. to v.p. fin. and treas. Nat. Dairy Products Corp. (now Kraft Foods Divsn. of Philip Morris, Inc.), 1964-71; asst. treas. Martin Marietta Corp. (now Lockheed Martin Corp.), 1971-74; with Northrop Corp. (now Northrop Grumman Corp.), L.A., 1974-90, treas., 1977-87, v.p. trust investments, 1987-90; prin., pres. R.B. Lohrer Assocs., Inc., Palos Verdes Estates, Calif., 1990—. Bd. dirs. Cmty. Helpline, Inc., 1988-98, pres., 1992-97; bd. dirs. Presbyn. Ch. (U.S.A.) Investment and Loan Program, Inc., 1995—, vice chmn., 1995-2000, chmn. 2001—; bd. dirs., chmn. endowment fund trustees Palos Verdes Art Ctr., 1996—. Mem. L.A. Treas. Club (pres. 1981), Boston Latin Sch. West Coast Alumni Assn. (bd. dirs., pres. 1982-84), Fin. Exec. Internat., Harvard Club of So. Calif., Palos Verdes Golf Club, Masons. Republican. Presbyterian.

LOHRLI, ANNE, retired English language educator, writer; b. Bake Oven, Oreg., Feb. 9, 1906; d. Gottfried and Anna (Hüsser) L. BA, Occidental Coll., L.A., 1927, MA, 1928, Columbia U., 1932; PhD, U. So. Calif., 1937. Tchr. L.A. city schs., 1937-45; prof. English N.Mex. Highlands U., Las Vegas, 1945-65. Vis. prof. U. Trieste, 1954. Compiler: Household Words, List of Contributors, etc., 1973; contbr. some 40 articles in Dickensian, Princeton U. Libr. Chronicle, Victorian Studies, Pacific Historian, others, 1963-94. Mem. Phi Beta Kappa, Phi Kappa Phi. Home: 901 Marlene St Apt 3 Ukiah CA 95482-5987

LOHSE, AUSTIN WEBB, banker; b. N.Y.C., Jan. 22, 1926; s. Henry Vincent and Gertrude (Schroeder) L.; m. Virginia Meyer Butler, May 14, 1949; children: Constance Butler, John Daniel. BA, Dartmouth Coll., 1947. Credit analyst Irving Trust Co., N.Y.C., 1947-52; with Am. Express Internat. Banking Corp., 1952-73, asst. v.p., 1958-61, v.p., 1961-68, sr. v.p., 1968-73; v.p. Charterhouse Group Internat. Inc., N.Y.C., 1973-78, R.T. Madden & Co. Inc., N.Y.C., 1978-81; pres. A.W. Lohse & Co. Inc., 1981-96. Former dir. Am. Express Bank G.M.B.H., Frankfurt, Germany, Am. Express Bank S.P.A., Rome, Am. Express Securities S.A., Paris, LB/Amex Ltd., London, Eng. Mem. Casque and Gauntlet Soc., Beta Theta Pi. Clubs: Short Hills (N.J.); Knickerbocker (N.Y.C.). Republican. Episcopalian. Home: 105 Old Short Hills Rd Short Hills NJ 07078-2128

LOHSE, SUSAN FAYE, county official, educator; b. Fergus Falls, Minn., Dec. 23, 1952; d. Philip Irving and Harriet Elinor Arlene (Hanson) Berg; m. Robert Wayne Lohse, July 7, 1973; children: Trevor Robert, Trisha Sue, Thomas Roger, Tana Ruth. BS, Bemidji State U., 1973; cert. sr. accredited assessor, U. Minn., 1993. Tchr. Kensington Pub. Schs., 1973-75; sub. tchr. Elbow Lake (Minn.)-Wendell Pub. Schs., 1975-80, tchr., 1982-83, Ashby Pub. Schs., 1981, Elbow Lake Cmty. Edn., 1976—82, Elbow Lake Cmty. Edn., 1996—; assessor's clk. Grant County Assessor's Office, 1983, dep. assessor, office mgr., 1985—94, county assessor, 1994—. Instr. U. Minn. Ext. Svcs., Elbow Lake, 1993—99, Elbow Lake, 2000. Mem.: West Ctrl. and Minn. Assessment Pers. (pres. 1990—92), Minn. Assn. Assessing Officers (sec. region 7 1999, treas. 2000, pres. 2001). Lutheran. Avocations: sewing, crocheting, volleyball, camping. Office: Grant County Assessor 10 2d St NE Elbow Lake MN 56531

LOHUIS, ARDYTH JUNE, musician, educator; b. Melrose Park, Ill., June 29, 1939; d. Delmont John and Charlotte Carolyn Solack. B of Sacred Music, Ill. Wesleyan U., 1960; MM, Northwestern U., 1962; D of Mus. Arts, U. Cin., 1970. Organist Barrington (Ill.) Presbyn. Ch., 1960-62, 1st Presbyn. Ch., Haddonfield, N.J., 1962-66; dir. music, organist Mt. Washington Meth. Ch., Cin., 1967-69; prof. music Va. Commonwealth U., Richmond, Va., 1969—; dir. music, organist Bethlehem Luth. Ch., 1988-89. Touring artist Va. Commn. for Arts, Richmond, 1990-92; mem. Whikehart Chorale, Bloomington, 1960-68. Musician: (recs.) Murray/Lohuis Duo Performs Works for Violin and Organ, Vol. I, 1991, "Rondo" The Murray/Lohuis Duo Performs Works for Violin and Organ, Vol. 2, 1993, "Breached Borders" The Murray/Lohuis Duo Performs Works for Violin and Organ, Vol. 3, 1996, "Airs and Romances" The Murray/Lohuis Duo Performs Works for Violin and Organ, Vol. 4, 2000, Chamber Works of Allen Blank ("Dualisms" and "Elegie"), 2000. Pres. Neighborhood Sch. of Arts, Richmond, 1997-99, exec. bd., 1993-2000; v.p. Southeastern Hist. Keyboard Soc., 1996-97, 2000-2002, pres. 2002-; mem. Organ Hist. Soc. Mem. Am. Guild Organists (Va. state chmn, 1983-89, dean South Jersey chpt. 1963-66, dean Richmond chpt. 1978-80), Coll. Music Soc., Pi Kappa Lambda (pres. Va. Commonwealth U. chpt. 1976-78), Delta Omicron (life mem., Star of Delta Omicron 1981), Sigma Epsilon Sigma. Home: 9409 Redington Dr Richmond VA 23235-4043 Office: Va Commonwealth U Music Dept 922 Park Ave Box 842004 Richmond VA 23284-2004 Office Fax: 804-827-0230. E-mail: ajlohuis@vcu.edu.

LOIELLO, JOHN PETER, diplomat; b. Oceanside, N.Y., Aug. 16, 1943; s. Rosario Paul and Mary Agnes (Butler) L.; m. Elaine Margaret Robinson, June 14, 1944. BA in History, Fordham U., 1965; MA in History, SUNY, Buffalo, 1973; PhD in African History, U. London, 1980. Tchr. history The Gow Sch., South Wales, N.Y., 1967-71; instr. U. Md. (U.K.), London, 1976-78; exec. dir. Dem. Party Com. Abroad, Washington and London, 1978-80; sr. cons. Assn. Am. Chambers of Commerce in Latin Am., Washington, 1980; spl. asst. to chmn. NEH, 1978-82; assoc. dir. Democracy Prog., 1982-83; founding exec. dir. Nat. Dem. Inst. for Internat. Affairs, 1983-85; pres. Gowran Internat., 1985-93, 2000—; assoc. dir. ednl. and cultural affairs U.S. Info. Agy., 1994-98, sr. advisor to dir., 1999-2000. Pres. Alcide de Gaspari Found. (USA), Washington, 1987-89. Contbr. articles to profl. jours. Commr. Commn. on Platform Accountability, Dem. Nat. Com., Washington, 1981-85, chmn. fgn. policy subcom., 1980, platform com., 1980; sec. Tax Equity for Ams. Abroad, London, 1977-79; sec. Dems. Abroad, London, 1976-79. Recipient Commdr. of Order of Lion Senegal, 1999; African Studies scholar, U. London, 1974-78, grantee, 1975. Mem. Nat. Italian Am. Found., Royal African Soc. Democrat. Roman Catholic. Avocations: travel, racquetball, swimming.

LOIGNON, GERALD ARTHUR, JR. nuclear engineer; b. N.Y.C., June 25, 1950; s. Gerald Arthur Loignon Sr. and Nancy MacLean (Walker) Bucknell; m. Margaret Mary Hamburger, Aug. 7, 1971; children: Brian MacLean, Matthew Thomas, Teresa Marie. BS in Nuc. Engring., N.C. State U., 1976. Registerd profl. engr., S.C.; lic. sr. reactor operator Nuc. Regulatory Commn. Health physics technician nuc. fuel divsn. Westinghouse, Columbia, S.C., 1970-72; office equipment technician Cavin's Inc., Raleigh, N.C., 1973-76; quality assurance engr. Met. Edison Co., Reading, Pa., 1976-79; shift tech. advisor Met. Edison Co., Gen. Pub. Utility, Harrisburg, 1979-81, S.C. Electric and Gas Co., Jenkinsville, 1981-83, assoc. mgr. performance and results, 1983-88, shift engr., 1988-91, test unit supr., 1992-95, coord. nuc. ops. project, 1995-96, sr. PRA engr., 1996-2001, quality assurance supr., 2001—. Mem. choir, dir. religious edn. St. Marks Parish, Newberry, S.C., 1991—. Mem. Am. Nuc. Soc. (chair S.C. chpt. 1985-86, profl. engring. exam. com. 1987—, Nuclear Installation Safety Divsn. program com. 1997—, cert. of appreciation 1985, cert. of governence 1986), Profl. Reactor Operator Soc. Roman Catholic. Home: 3137 Jalapa Rd Kinards SC 29355-9380 Office: SC Electric and Gas Co VC Summer Nuc Sta PO Box 88 Jenkinsville SC 29065-0088 E-mail: gloignon@scana.com.

LOIN, E. LINNEA, retired social work administrator; b. Middletown, Conn., Nov. 20, 1942; d. Alfred William Skinner and Ada Patricia Moore; m. Peter Michael Loin, Sept. 16, 1972. BA, U. Conn., 1965. Social worker State of Conn., Middletown and Hartford, 1964-69, case supr. Hartford, 1969-74, program supr. Hartford, Manchester and Rockville, Hartford, 1984-90, Willimantic, 1990-97; ret., 1997. State liaison Nat. Ctr. for Child Abuse and Neglect, Washington, 1985-90. Editor: Connecticut's Children, 1985, Common Ground, 1987-89. Avocations: swimming, walking, reading, travel, water sports. Home: 29 Cowles Rd Willington CT 06279-1705

LOK, SILMOND RAY, pharmaceutical executive; b. Columbus, Ohio, Dec. 14, 1948; s. Fee and Oilene (Yee) L.; 1 child, Drake Carlyle. BS in Pharmacy, Ohio State U., 1973; MBA, Capital U., 1982. Registered pharmacist. Pharmacist, Federated Stores, Columbus, Ohio, 1975-82; pharm. salesman Ives Labs., Columbus, 1982, Squibb, Columbus, 1982-85; dir. pharmacy services Wendt-Bristol Co., 1985-89; dir. pharmacy dept. St. Anthony Med. Ctr., 1989-92; dir. pharmacy Fraizer Health Ctr., Orient Correctional Inst., 1992-93; dir. pharmacy Corrections Med. Ctr., 1993—. Mem. Grove City Civic Assn. 1st lt. USAF, 1973-75. Mem. Cen. Ohio Acad. Pharmacy, Sigma Phi Epsilon, Kappa Psi (grand regent grad. chpt. 1973-75). Avocation: Kenpo karate (black belt, 1st degree). Home: 6378 Seneca Way Grove City OH 43123-9220

LOKEN, BARBARA, marketing educator, social psychologist; b. Owatonna, Minn., Aug. 22, 1951; d. Gordon Keith and June Rosaline (Iverson) Anderson; 1 child, Elizabeth Loken Diebel. BA in Psychology magna cum laude, U. Minn., 1973; MA, NYU, 1976; PhD in Social Psychology, U. Ill., 1981. Rsch. and statis. asst. Nat. Soc. Prevention Blindness, N.Y.C., 1974-76; rsch. asst. dept. psychology U. Ill., 1976, 78-80, instr., 1977-78; NIMH trainee in measurement, 1979-80; asst. prof. dept. mktg. U. Minn., 1980-86, assoc. prof., 1986-92, prof., 1992—. Co-dir. edn. evaluation Minn. heart health project Sch. Pub. Health, 1982-88, adj. assoc. prof. dept. psychology, 1987-92, adj. prof., 1992—; vis. assoc. prof. mktg. UCLA, 1988. Assoc. editor: Jour. Consumer Rsch., 1996-99; contbr. articles to profl. jours. Rsch. grantee Sch. Mgmt., U. Minn., 1981-84, 86, 88-99. Mem. Am. Psychol. Assn., Am. Mktg. Assn., Assn. Consumer Rsch., Assn. for Consumer Rsch. 2000 (treas.).

LOKEN, JAMES BURTON, federal judge; b. Madison, Wis., May 21, 1940; s. Burton Dwight and Anita (Nelson) Loken; m. Caroline Brevard Hester, July 30, 1966; children: Kathryn Brevard, Kristina Ayres. BS, U. Wis., 1962; LLB magna cum laude, Harvard U., 1965. Law clk. to chief judge J. Edward Lumbard U.S. Ct. Appeals (2d Cir.), N.Y.C., 1965—66; law clk. to assoc. justice Byron White U.S. Supreme Ct., Washington, 1966—67; assoc. atty. Faegre & Benson, Mpls., 1967—70, ptnr., 1973—90; gen. counsel Pres.'s Com. on Consumer Interests, Office of Pres. of U.S., Washington, 1970; staff asst. Office of Pres. of U.S., 1970—72; judge U.S. Ct. Appeals (8th cir.), St. Paul, 1990—. Editor: Harvard Law Rev., 1964—65. Mem.: Minn. State Bar Assn., Phi Kappa Phi, Phi Beta Kappa. Avocations: golf, running. Office: US Courthouse 300 S 4th St Ste 11W Minneapolis MN 55415-0848 also: US Ct Appeals 8th Cir 111S 10th St Rm 24.32 St Louis MO 63102*

LOKEY, FRANK MARION, JR. broadcast executive, consultant; b. Ft. Worth, Oct. 15, 1924; s. Frank Marion Sr. and Corinne (Whaley) L. Student, Smith-Hughes Evening Coll., 1955-59. Announcer, newscaster, disc jockey, morning personality Stas. WAPI, WBRC and WSGN, Birmingham, Ala., 1941-52; pres. Sta. WRDW-TV, Augusta, Ga., 1952-55; asst. gen. mgr., mgr. sales, news anchor Sta. WLW-A TV (now WXIA-TV), Atlanta, 1955-66; co-owner, gen. mgr. Sta. WAIA, 1960-62; S.E. news corr., talk show host CBS News N.Y., N.Y.C., 1960-66; asst. to owner, gen. mgr. Sta. WBIE-AM-FM, Atlanta, 1962-64; asst. to pres., gen. mgr. Stas. KXAB-TV, KXJB-TV, KXMB-TV, Aberdeen, Fargo, Bismarck, S.D., N.D., 1966-67; exec. v.p., gen. mgr. St. WEMT-TV, Bangor, Maine, 1967-70; pres., gen. mgr. Stas. KMOM-TV, KWAB-TV, Odessa-Midland, Big Spring, Tex., 1970-75; exec. v.p., gen. mgr. Sta. KMUV-TV (now named KRBK-TV), Sacramento, 1975-77; CEO Lokey Enterprises, Inc., Sacramento, L.A., El Centro, 1977—, also chmn. bd. dirs. Cons., troubleshooter 18 TV stas. nationwide, 1977—; cons., actor 6 movie prodn. cos., Hollywood, Calif., 1980—; cons., outside dir. Anderson Cons., Manhattan, L.I., N.Y., 1981—; network talk show host/news corr. for 7 news orgns. worldwide, 1984—; bd. dirs. Broadcast Audience Behavior Rsch., Manhattan, 1986—, mem. inner circle, 1986—; mem. bd. advisors Men of Achievement, Cambridge, Eng.; owner/franchiser The Party Place; motivational spkr. Creator, originator approach to real estate mktg.; prodr. swing/ballroom dance parties, LA., Palm Spring, Calif., Las Vegas, Nev., London, Paris, Dublin, Ireland, Sydney Australia. Hon. mem. Imperial County Bd. Suprs., El Centro, 1986—, El Centro City Coun., 1987—. Mem. Am. Legion. Baptist. Avocations: producer big bands parties, movie acting, ancient history, tracing family tree. Home and Office: 2709 US Highway 111 Imperial CA 92251-9772

LOKEY, LINDA H. music educator; b. Buffalo, Sept. 1954; m. Charles G. Lokey; children: Peter, Dawn. A.Fine Arts, St. Petersburg (Fla.) Jr.Coll., 1985; BMus in Piano Performance/Piano Pedagogy, U. South Fla., 1990. Nat. cert. tchr. music. Music tchr. Palm Harbor (Fla.) Montessori Sch., 1986-88; ch. pianist First Bapt. Ch., Dunedin, Fla., 1988-91; coll. staff accompanist Reinhardt Coll., Waleska, Ga., 1993-95; tchr. pvt. and group piano, 1972—. Music com. Cherokee County (Ga.) Arts Coun., 1994-95; adjudicator for music Music Tchrs. Assn. festivals, Federated Music Clubs; active Cherokee Cmty. Chorale, 1992—, chorale grant com. chair, 2002-. U. South Fla. Talent Grant award, 1985-86. Mem. Music Tchrs. Nat. Assn., Ga. Music Tchrs. Assn., Cherokee Music Tchrs. Assn. (pres. 1993-95, fundraising com. 1993-99, 3rd v.p. publicity 1995—, pres.-elect 2001), Ga. Music Tchrs. Assn. (exec. bd. 2000-02), Cobb Music tchrs. Assn., Am. Coll. Musicians, Cherokee County Arts Coun. (bd. dirs. 2002-, program com. chair 2002-), Blue Ridge Mountain Arts Assn., Golden Key. Avocations: travel, hiking, sailing, charity work. Home and Office: 866 Valley Dr Canton GA 30114

LOKKEN, STEVEN LEE, chiropractor, nutritionist, internist; b. Thief River Falls, Minn., Apr. 1, 1950; s. Leroy Albert and Delores May (Johnson) L.; m. Kathryn Ann Ehret, Feb. 5, 1977; children: John, Ryan, Shane, Stephanie. D Of Chiropractic, Palmer Coll. Chiropractic, Davenport, Iowa, 1972. Diplomate Am. Bd. Chiropractic Internists, Am. Bd. Clin. Nutrition; cert. clin. nutritionist; bd. cert. naturopathic physician. , Calif., 1973-92; pvt. practice Colorado Springs, Colo., 1993—. Fellow Am. Acad. Chiropractic Physicians; mem. Am. Chiropractors Assn. (mem. coun. internal diagnosis and family practice), Am. Diabetes Assn., Am. Assn. Clin. Nutritionists, Internat. Assn. Clin. Nutritionists, Am. Acad. Anti-Aging Medicine, Am. Naturopathic Med. Assn. Avocations: ultramarathon running, mountain biking, fly fishing, four-wheeling. Office: 815 E Platte Ave Colorado Springs CO 80903-3546

LOKMER, STEPHANIE ANN, international business development consultant; b. Wheeling, W.Va., Nov. 14, 1957; d. Joseph Steven and Mary Ann (Mozney) L. BA in Comm., Bethany Coll., 1980; cert., U. Tübingen, Germany, 1980, Sprach Inst., Tübingen, 1980. V.p. Wheeling Coffee and Spice, W.Va., 1981—; pres. Lokmer & Assocs., Inc., McLean, 1986-2000; v.p. strategic devel. Telia Internat. Carrier, Inc., 2000—. Mem. com. regulatory and internat. affairs Comptel; mem. com. Comptel Regulatory and Internat. Couns. Bd. dors. Am. Found. of Ivory Coast. Mem. Pub. Rels. Soc. Am., World Affairs Coun., Regulatory and Internat. Affairs Com., Counselors Acad., Comptel (regulatory an dinternat. affairs com.), Zeta Tau Alpha. Republican. Roman Catholic. Avocations: tennis, reading, flying, politics.

LOLAS, ANTHONY JOSEPH, SR. health and environmental business executive; b. Detroit, Mar. 27, 1942; s. Charles and Doris (Rutkowski) L.; m. Marilyn Ruth Hickey, June 7, 1967 (div. Jan. 1989); children: Anthony J. Jr., Nicole E.; m. Patricia Smith Dod, Dec. 9, 1995. BS in Engring. Mgmt., USAF Acad., 1967; MBA in Bus. Ops. Analysis, UCLA, 1968; EdS in Adminstrn. and Supervision, Troy State U., 1980; PhD in Adminstrn. and Leadership, U. S.C., 1994. CEO Bus. Svcs., Charleston, S.C., 1980-91; chief bus. mgmt. S.C. Dept. Health and Environ. Control, Columbia, 1992—. Cons. various cos., Charleston, 1973-89; adj. prof. computer resource mgmt. Webster U., 1993—. Author: (books) Education Objectives, 1980, Crisis in Confidence, 1994. Cons., advisor Future Bus. Leaders, Charleston, 1994-96. Lt. col. USAF, 1967-90. Decorated D.F.C., Meritorious Svc. medal, 4 Air medals. Mem. S.C. Govt. Assn. Purchasing Ofcls., S.C. Fleet Mgmt. Assn., Profl. Risk Mgmt. Assn., Judo Assn. Am. (life), Mensa, S.C. C. of C. (issues com.). Home: 4700 Carter Hill Dr Columbia SC 29206-4604 Office: DHEC Bus Mgmt 2600 Bull St Columbia SC 29201-1797

LOLLAR, THOMAS WILLIAM, ceramics department head; b. Detroit, Mar. 19, 1951; s. Harold Robert and Marjorie Bernice (Rowe) L. BFA, W. Mich. U., Kalamazoo, 1973, MA, 1979. Ceramics faculty Kalamazoo Art Inst., Kalamazoo, 1973-79, Parsons Sch. of Design, N.Y.C., 1979-82; dir. Shippee Gallery, 1984-87; ceramics faculty Crafts Students League, 1982-89; head Tchrs. Coll. Columbia U., N.Y., 1989—. Art cons., Upjohn Co., Kalamazoo. Mich., Revlon, Inc., N.Y.C.; juror, N.Y. State Art Competition, Albany, N.Y. Prin. works include Homage to Albany clay mural, 1988, Manhattan mural, 1990, Washington mural, 1990. Mem. Artist Equity of N.Y. Home: 50 W 106th St New York NY 10025-3819

LOLLEY, WILLIAM RANDALL, minister; b. Troy, Ala., June 2, 1931; s. Roscoe Lee and Mary Sara (Nunnelee) L.; m. Clara Lou Jacobs, Aug. 28, 1952; children: Charlotte, Pam. AB, Samford U., 1952, DD (hon.), 1980; BD, Southeastern Sem., 1957, ThM, 1958; ThD, Southwestern Sem., 1962; DD (hon.), Wake Forest U., 1971, U. Richmond, 1984; LLD (hon.), Campbell U., 1986; LittD (hon.), Mercer U., 1988. Ordained to ministry So. Bapt. Conv., 1951. Pastor First Bapt. Ch., Winston-Salem, N.C., 1962-74; pres. Southeastern Bapt. Theol. Sem., Wake Forest, 1974-88; pastor First Bapt. Ch., Raleigh, 1988-90, Greensboro, 1990-96, ret., 1996. Author: Crises in Morality, 1963, Bold Preaching of Christ, 1979, Servant Songs, 1994. Mem. Coop. Bapt. Fellowship, Rotary. Democrat. Home: 11508 Old Creedmoor Rd Raleigh NC 27613-6910

LOLLI, ANDREW RALPH, industrial engineer, former army officer; b. Seatonville, Ill., Oct. 15, 1907; s. Joseph Fredrick and Adolfa (Fiocchi) L. Student Armed Forces Staff Coll., 1950, Nat. War Coll., 1957, N.Y. Inst. Fin., 1971; BS, Dickinson Coll., 1952; postgrad. Fordham U., 1952. Enlisted in U.S. Army, 1940, advanced through grades to maj. gen., 1960; chief plans and priorities Allied Forces So. Europe, 1952-56; comdr. Air Def. units, N.Y. and San Francisco, 1957-60; comdr. XX U.S.A. Corps, 1961-62, XV, 1962-63, comdr. Western NORD Region, Hamilton AFB, Calif., 1963-66; ret., 1966; exec. asst. Hughes Aircraft Co., Fullerton, Calif., 1967; dir. gen. services State of Calif., Sacramento, 1967-70; v.p. Sigmatics, Newport Beach, Calif., 1970-73, Intercoast Investments Co., Sacramento, 1975-76; pres. Andrew R. Lolli Assocs. Inc., San Francisco, 1973—, Lolman Inc., San Francisco, 1976—; commr. Small Bus. Adv. Commn., San Francisco, 1989-93; pres. bd. trustees Commonwealth Equity Trust, 1974-80; vice chmn. Calif. Pub. Works bd., 1967-69; mem. adv. panel Nat. Acad. Scis. and Engring. in Research, Washington, 1968-70; mem. fed., state and local govt. adv. panel Fed. Gen. Services, Washington, 1968-69. Bd. dirs. Columbia Boys Park Club, San Francisco, Lab. for Survival, San Francisco; mem. Presido of San Francisco Restoration Adv. Bd., 1994. Decorated D.S.M., Legion of Merit with oak leaf cluster, Bronze Star with oak leaf cluster; named Man of Year, Italian Sons of Am., 1964. Mem. Nat. Assn. Uniformed Services, Assn. U.S. Army, Ret. Officers Assn. Roman Catholic. Developed short notice inspection system for army air def. missiles, 1960. Home: 1050 N Point St San Francisco CA 94109-8302 Office: 286 Jefferson St San Francisco CA 94133-1126

LOLLI, DON R(AY), lawyer; b. Macon, Mo., Aug. 9, 1949; s. Tony and Erma Naomi (Gerlich) L.; m. Deborah Jo Mrosek, May 29, 1976; children: Christina Terese, Joanna Elyse, Anthony Justin. BA in Econs., U. Mo., 1971, JD, 1974. Bar: Mo. 1974, U.S. Dist. Ct. (we. dist.) Mo. 1974, U.S. Dist. Ct. (ea. dist) Mo. 1996, U.S. Dist. Ct. Kans. 1998, U.S. Ct. Appeals (8th cir.) 1976, U.S. Ct. Appeals (10th cir.) 1979, U.S. Ct. Appeals (3rd cir.) 1992, U.S. Supreme Ct. 1979, U.S. Tax Ct. 1981. Assoc. Beckett & Steinkamp, Kansas City, Mo., 1974-79; mem. Beckett, Lolli and Bartunek, 1980-96, Swanson, Midgley, LLC, Kansas City, 1997—. Lectr. CLE seminar U. Mo. Sch. Law, Kansas City, 1984, 89. Vol. coach Visitation Sch.; co-chair St. Teresa's Acad. Fundraising. Mem. ABA, Mo. Bar Assn., Kansas City Bar Assn., Lawyers Assn. Kansas City, U. Mo. Alumni Assn., Rotary, Beta Theta Pi (asst. gen. sec. 1997—, Tiedman Inn 1973-74, Merit cert. 1974), Phi Delta Phi (pres.). Roman Catholic. Home: 645 W 62nd St Kansas City MO 64113-1501 Office: Swanson Midgley LLC Crown Ctr 2420 Pershing Rd Ste 400 Kansas City MO 64108-2505 E-mail: dlolli@swansonmidgley.com.

LOLLMAN, MATTHEW TOBIAS, music educator; b. Kansas City, Mo., Mar. 17, 1971; s. Kenneth Michael and Karel Ann Lollman. BA in Edn., Northeastern St. U., 1995. Cert. Tchr. Okla., 1995. Band dir. Valliant Pub. Sch., Valliant, Okla., 1995—99, Vinita Pub. Sch., Vinita, 1999—. Band dir. after sch. program Vinita Pub. Sch., 2001—, dir. four yr. plan com., 2001. Musician, composer: (albums) Pyramid, 1994. Named Tchr. of Yr., Valliant Pub. Schs., 1997. Mem.: NEA, Okla. Edn. Assn., Okla. Music Educators Assn., Music Educators Nat. Conf., Northeastern Band Dir. Assn. (sec. 2000—02). Conservative. Methodist. Avocations: camping, music, sports. Home: 914 W North Avenue Vinita OK 74301 Office: Vinita Public Schools 226 N Miller Vinita OK 74301 Personal E-mail: bandman@junct.com.

LOMAN, MARY LAVERNE, retired mathematics educator; b. Stratford, Okla., June 10, 1928; d. Thomas D. and Mary Ellen (Goodwin) Glass; m. Coy E. Loman, Dec. 23, 1944; 1 child, Sandra Leigh Loman Easton. BS, U. Okla., 1956, MA, 1957, PhD, 1961. Grad. asst., then instr. U. Okla., Norman, 1956-61; asst. prof. math. U. Ctrl. Okla., Edmond, 1961-62, assoc. prof., 1962-66, prof., 1966-93, prof. emeritus, 1993—. NSF fellow, 1965-67. Mem. Math. Assn. Am., Nat. Coun. Tchrs. Math., Okla. Coun. Tchrs. Math. (v.p. 1972-76), Higher Edn Alumni Coun. Okla., VFW Aux., Delta Kappa Gamma. Home: 2201 Tall Oaks Trl Edmond OK 73003-2325 *Strive to do each task to the best of your ability. Then don't look back, saying "If only I had ...", but look forward to the next, knowing you gave your very best effort.*

LOMANO, LANCE ALAN, chemist, educator; b. Columbus, Ohio, Aug. 29, 1970; s. Michael Earl Lomano, Patricia Kay Lomano; children: Anthony Rauft-Lomano. BS, Bowling Green State U., 1992. Cert. tchr. Fla., 1994. Tchr. Pinellas County Schs., St. Petersburg, Fla., 1994—. Avocations: sports, movies. Office: Northeast High Sch 5500 16th St N Saint Petersburg FL Personal E-mail: lancebrick11@yahoo.com.

LOMAS, CHARLES GARDNER, engineering educator, retired; b. Ft. Peck, Mont., Dec. 5, 1934; s. George Edward and Evelyn Gardner (Carr) L.; m. Arletta Pelekaluhi Akamine, Apr. 27, 1957; 1 child, Kathleen Pelekaluhi Lomas. BS in Edn., U. Md., 1957, BSME, 1964, MS in Mech. Engring., 1975. Instr. U. Md., College Park, 1971-77; engr. Dantec Electronics, Ramsey, N.J., 1977-80; instr. Lafayette Coll., Easton, Pa., 1980-82; freelance writer Greenbelt, Md., 1982-85; asst. prof. Rochester (N.Y.) Inst. Tech., 1985-86; assoc. prof. Northampton Community Coll., Bethlehem, Pa., 1986-88, Calif. Poly. State U., San Luis Obispo, 1988-92, Oreg. Inst. Tech., Klamath Falls, 1992-97. Author: Fundamentals of Hot Wire Anemometry, 1985. Achievements include patents for fluidic pressure regulator, sonic detector. Home: 3881 Rio Vista Way Klamath Falls OR 97603

LOMAS, ERIC JAMES, investment banker; b. N.Y.C., Mar. 12, 1947; s. James and Florence (Marletti) L.; m. Florence Jean Mauchant, Jan. 18, 1992. BS cum laude, L.I. U., 1970; MBA, NYU, 1972. Cert. CFA. Analyst Troster, Singer & Co., N.Y.C., 1972-76; cons. Deloitte Haskins & Sells, 1976-85; mng. dir. Gruntal & Co., 1985-89; pres. Hill Thompson Group, Ltd., 1989-98. Chmn. Rexel, Inc., Coral Gables; dir. Goodland Foods, Inc. Mem. adv. bd. Long Island U., grad. sch. bus. NYU. With USNR, Vietnam. Mem. N.Y. Athletic Club. Avocations: skiing, sailing, biking, photography. Office: Hill Thompson Group Ltd 437 Madison Ave New York NY 10022-7001

LOMAS, LYLE WAYNE, agricultural research administrator, educator; b. Monett, Mo., June 8, 1953; s. John Junior and Helen Irene Lomas; m. Connie Gail Frey, Sept. 4, 1976; children: Amy Lynn, Eric Wayne. BS, U. Mo., 1975, MS, 1976; PhD, Mich. State U., 1979. Asst. prof., animal scientist S.E. Agrl. Rsch. Ctr., Kans. State U., Parsons, 1979-85, assoc. prof., 1985-92, prof., 1992—, head, 1985—. Contbr. articles to refereed sci. jours. Mem. Am. Soc. Animal Sci., Am. Registry Profl. Animal Scientists, Am. Forage and Grassland Coun., Rsch. Ctr. Adminstrs. Soc. (bd. dirs. 1993—, sec. 1999-2000, 2d v.p. 2000-01, v.p. 2001-02, pres. 2002-03), Rotary (bd. dirs. Parsons 1992—96 v.p. 1994-95, pres. 1995-96), Phi Kappa Phi, Gamma Sigma Delta. Presbyterian. Achievements include research in ruminant nutrition, forage utilization by grazing stocker cattle. Home: 24052 Douglas Rd Dennis KS 67341-9014 Office: Kans State U SE Agrl Rsch Ctr PO Box 316 Parsons KS 67357-0316 E-mail: llomas@oznet.ksu.edu.

LOMAX, KENNETH MITCHELL, agricultural engineering educator; b. Wilmington, Del., Nov. 4, 1947; s. Ernest S. and Martha W. (Mitchell) L.; m. Nancy R. Beltz, Oct. 16, 1971. BS in Chem. Engring., Lafayette Coll., Easton, Pa., 1969; MS in Entomology, U Del., Newark, 1971; PhD in Agrl. Engring., U. Md., College Park, 1976. Registered profl. engr., Del. Asst. prof. Horn Point Environ. Labs. U. Md., Cambridge, 1976-80; asst. prof. agrl. engring. U. Del., Newark, 1980-85, assoc. prof. agrl. engring., 1985—, dept. chairperson, 1998—. Pres. faculty senate U. Del., 1992-93. Contbr. articles to profl. jours. Recipient Excellence In Teaching award U. Del. and Lindbach Found., 1988; named Faculty Mem. of Yr., Panhellenic Coun., 1993. Mem. ASHRAE, Am. Soc. Agrl. Engrs., Am. Mushroom Inst. (dir. 1987-90). Avocation: outdoor activities. Office: U Del Bioresources Engring Dept Newark DE 19717 E-mail: kml@udel.edu.

LOMAX, MICHAEL LUCIUS, college president; Former instr. Morehouse/Spelman Colls., Emory U., Ga. Inst. Tech., U. Ga.; pres. Dillard U., New Orleans, 1997—. Former pres. Nat. Faculty, Atlanta. Bd. govs. United Way of Am., Greater New Orleans Edn. Found.; founding chmn. Nat. Black Arts Festival; trustee Studio Mus. in Harlem; mem. presdl. adv. d. Historically Black Colls and Univs.; mem. Nat. Mus. African Am. History and Cultural Plan Action Presdl. Commn. Office: Dillard Univ 2601 Gentilly Blvd New Orleans LA 70122-3043

LOMBARD, JOHN CUTLER, retired lawyer; b. Berkeley, Calif., Oct. 9, 1918; s. Norman and Ellen (McKeighan) L.; m. Dorothy Brandt, July 9, 1946; children: Lawrence, John, David, Laurie. BA, Principia U., 1946; JD, Northwestern U., 1949. Assoc. Jones, Birdseye & Grey, Seattle, 1950-60; ptnr. Hamley & Lombard, 1960-70, Day, Taylor, Lombard & Kiefer, Seattle, 1970-85; pvt. practice, 1985—. Mem. com. Jud. Counsel, 1980-84. Trustee King County Mcpl. League, 1980-84. With USAF, 1941-45. Decorated D.F.C., 5 Air medals, presdl. citation. Mem. Seattle King County Bar Assn. (chmn. probate com. 1975-76, chmn. lawyer referral com. 1989-90), Rainier Club. Avocations: golf, skiing, bridge, playing piano. Home: 2315 NE 65th St # 402 Seattle WA 98115

LOMBARD, JOHN JAMES, JR. lawyer, writer; b. Phila., Dec. 27, 1934; s. John James and Mary R. (O'Donnell) L.; m. Barbara Mallon, May 9, 1964; children: John James, William M., James G., Laura K., Barbara E. BA cum laude, LaSalle Coll., 1956; JD, U. Pa., 1959. Bar: Pa. 1960. Ptnr. Obermayer, Rebmann, Maxwell & Hippel, Phila., 1959-84; mgr. personal law sect. Morgan Lewis & Bockius LLP, 1985-90, vice-chair personal law sect., 1990-92, chair, 1992-99; spl. counsel McCarter & English LLP, 2000—. Sec., dir. Airline Hydraulics Corp., Phila., 1969—; adv. com. on decedents estates laws Joint State Govt. Commn., 1992—, mem. subcom. on powers of atty., 1993—; co-chair So. Jersey Ethics Alliance, 1993-97. Co-author: Durable

Powers of Attorney and Health Care Directives, 1984, 3d edit. 1994; contbr. articles to profl. jours. Bd. dirs. Redevel. Authority Montgomery County, Pa., 1980-87, Gwynedd-Mercy Coll., Gwynedd Valley, Pa., 1980-89, LaSalle Coll. H.S., Wyndmoor, Pa., 1991-97. Recipient Treat award Nat. Coll. Probate Judges, 1992. Mem. ABA (chmn. com. simplification security transfers 1972-76, chmn. mem. com. 1972-82, mem. coun. real property, probate and trust law sect. 1979-85, sec. 1985-87, divsn. dir. probate div. 1987-89, chair elect 1989-90, chair 1990-91, co-chair Nat. Conf. Lawyers & Corp. Fiduciaries), Pa. Bar Assn. (ho. of dels. 1979-81), Phila. Bar Assn. (chmn. probate sect. 1972), Am. Coll. Trust and Estate Counsel (editor Probate Notes 1983, bd. regents 1986-91, mem. exec. com. 1988-91, elder law com. 1993—), internat. Acad. Estate and Trust Law (exec. com. 1984-88, 90-94), Am. Bar Found., Internat. Fish and Game Assn., Union League Club (Phila.), Ocean City Club (N.J.), Marlin and Tuna Club, Ocean City Yacht Club. Office: McCarter & English LLP Mellon Bank Ctr Ste 700 1735 Market St Philadelphia PA 19103

LOMBARD, KAREN VIRGINIA, economist; b. Oak Lawn, Ill., Apr. 10, 1965; d. George Eugene and Elizabeth Anne Lombard; m. Alexander Galanos Taber; children: Geordie Lombard Taber. BA in Econs., St. Mary's Coll., Notre Dame, Ind., 1987; MA in Econs., PhD in Econs., U. Chgo., 1993. Asst. prof. econs. U. Miami, Coral Gables, Fla., 1993—97; v.p. Econ. Analysis LLC, L.A., 1998—. Contbr. Fellow Bradley Found. fellow, U. Chgo., 1992—93; scholar Chgo. Bus. Fellow scholar, 1986. Mem.: Western Econs. Assn., Am. Econs. Assn.

LOMBARD, RICHARD SPENCER, lawyer; b. Panama Canal Zone, Jan. 28, 1928; s. Eugene C. and Alice R. (Quinn) L.; m. Arlene Olson, Dec. 27, 1952; children: Anne, James. AB, Harvard U., 1949, JD, 1952. Bar: N.Y. 1953, Tex. 1971. Assoc. Haight, Gardner, Poor & Havens, N.Y.C., 1952-55; mem. law dept. Creole Petroleum Corp., Caracas, Venezuela, 1955-65, mgr. Venezuela, 1963-65; gen. counsel Esso Chem. Co., N.Y.C., 1966-69; assoc. gen. counsel Humble Oil & Refining Co., Houston, 1969-71; asst. gen. counsel Exxon Corp., N.Y.C., 1971-72, assoc. gen. counsel, 1972-73, gen. counsel, 1973-93, v.p., 1980-93; counsel Baker & Botts, Dallas, 1993-96. Trustee Parker Sch. Fgn. and Comparative Law, Columbia U., 1977—, chmn. bd. trustees, 85—. Author: American-Venezuelan Private International Law, 1965. Served with USAAF, 1946-47. Fellow Am. Bar Found.; mem. Am. Law Inst., Am. Arbitration Assn. (bd. dirs., chmn. bd. 1983-86), Assn. Bar City of N.Y., State Bar of Tex., Univ. Club (N.Y.C.).

LOMBARDI, CORNELIUS ENNIS, JR. lawyer; b. Portland, Oreg., Feb. 12, 1926; s. Cornelius Ennis and Adele (Volk) L.; m. Ann Vivian Foster, Nov. 24, 1954; children— Cornelius Ennis, Gregg Foster, Matthew Volk. BA, Yale, 1949; JD, U. Mich., 1952. Bar: Mo. Since practiced in, Kansas City, Mo.; mem. firm Blackwell, Sanders, Matheny, Weary & Lombardi, 1957-92, of counsel. Former pres. Kansas City Mus. Assn., Estate Planning Coun. of Kansas City; trustee Pembroke Country Day Sch.; chmn. soc. of fellows Nelson Gallery Found.; bd. dirs., Mo. Parks Assn. Mem.: Kansas City Country Club, Order of Coif, Phi Alpha Delta. Home: 5049 Wornall Rd Kansas City MO 64112-2423 Office: 2 Pershing Sq 2300 Main St Ste 1100 Kansas City MO 64108-2416

LOMBARDI, DAVID ENNIS, JR. lawyer, lecturer, mediator; b. Mar. 5, 1940; s. David E. and Ruth Harriet (Harrison) L.; m. Susanna C. Woodbury, June 20, 1970; children: Sara Ennis, Eric David. BA, U. Calif., Berkeley, 1962; postgrad., U. Florence, Italy, 1964; JD, Yale U., 1966. Bar: Calif. 1966. John woodman Ayer fellow at law U. Calif., Berkeley, 1963; assoc. Brobeck, Phleger & Harrison, San Francisco, 1967-73; adj. prof. bus. law U. Md., NATO Hdqrs., Belgium and Italy, 1974-75; sr. atty. Crown Zellerbach Corp., San Francisco, 1975-76; sr. ptnr. Lombardi & Lombardi, 1976-83, Steinhart & Falconer, San Francisco, 1983-92; spl. counsel Bianchi, Engel, Keegin & Talkington, San Rafael, Calif., 1992. Chief cir. mediator U.S. Ct. Appeals (9th cir.), San Francisco, 1992—; lectr. on negotiation, mediation U. Calif. Sch. Law, Davis, U. San Francisco Sch. Law, U. Santa Clara Sch. Law, Stanford Law Sch., U. Wash. Sch. Law, U. Cairo Faculty of Law, Sch. Law Nat. U. India, Coll. Law U. Calcutta, others; mem. chancellor's com. for univ. affairs U. Calif. 1962-63; cons. on law reform and mediation for Ministry of Justice, Egypt, India, Israel, Hawaii, others; mem. alumni adv. com. U. Calif., 1968-69. Trustee Head Royce Sch., 1983-86, San Domenico Sch., 1986-90, Kentfield Schs. Found., 1985-90. Mem. ABA, Calif. Bar Assn. (prin. referee Calif. State Bar Ct. 1977-86), San Francisco Bar Assn., Am. Soc. Internat. Law, Yale U. Law Sch. Alumni Assn. (pres. No. Calif. 1989—), Olympic Club, Fgn. Svc. Assn. No. Calif. Home: 1650 Lake St San Francisco CA 94121-1343 Office: US Ct Appeals PO Box 193939 San Francisco CA 94119-3939 E-mail: david_lombard@ca9.uscourts.gov.

LOMBARDI, DAVID RICHARD, lawyer; b. Bremerton, Wash., Mar. 27, 1949; s. Richard Caesar and Virginia Elizabeth (Smallridge) L.; m. Judith Ann Rummell, June 1, 1974; children: Rebecca, Katherine. BA, Stanford U., 1971; JD, U. Santa Clara, 1976. Bar: Idaho 1976, U.S. Dist. Ct. Idaho 1976, U.S. Ct. Appeals (9th cir.) 1985; cert. civil trial specialist. Ptnr. Langroise, Sullivan & Smylie, Boise, Idaho, 1976-84; of counsel Holland & Hart, Langroise & Sullivan, 1984-85; ptnr. Imhoff & Lynch, 1985-90, Givens Pursley, LLP, Boise, 1990—. Mem. Am. Health Lawyers Assn., Def. Rsch. Inst., Am. Inns of Ct. Roman Catholic. Avocations: fly fishing, skiing, performing and visual arts. Office: Givens Pursley LLP Ste 200 277 N 6th St Boise ID 83702-7720

LOMBARDI, DENNIS M. lawyer; b. L.A., May 15, 1951; s. Peter Joseph and Jean (Nelson) L.; m. Suan Choo Lim, Jan. 9, 1993; children: Alexis Jeanne, Erin Kalani. BA, U. Hawaii, 1974; JD summa cum laude, U. Santa Clara, 1977. Bar: Calif. 1977, U.S. Dist. Ct. Hawaii, 1981. Assoc. Frandzel & Share, Beverly Hills, Calif., 1977-79; pvt. practice Capistrano Beach, 1979-81; ptnr. Case, Bigelow & Lombardi, Honolulu, 1982—. Office: Case Bigelow & Lombardi 737 Bishop St Fl 26 Honolulu HI 96813-3201

LOMBARDI, DON DOMINICK, art critic, artist; b. Bronx, N.Y., Dec. 16, 1954; s. Richard William and Mariana Frances (LaCroce) Lombardi; m. Diane Carmela Amenta, Aug. 24, 1980; 1 child Lora Amenta. AS, Westchester C.C., Valhalla, N.Y., 1975; BS, SUNY, 1995. Adj. prof. Westchester C. C., Valhalla, N.Y., 1988—; curator exhibn. Castle Gallery, Coll. New Rochelle (N.Y.), 1996, 97, 98, Choate House Pace U. Gallery, Pleasantville, N.Y., 1997. Art critic Art New Eng., Brighton, Mass., 1997-99, New Art Examiner, Chgo., 1997, The N.Y. Times, 1999—, Sculpture Mag., Washington, 1999—, Juxtapiz Mag., 2002-; exhibns. include Art Cologne, Germany, 1989, 90, 91, 92, Portico Fine Art, N.Y.C., 1990, Katonah Mus., 1995, 98, Art/Ex Gallery Stamford Mus., 1997, 2000, Stamford Mus., 1997. Recipient Dorothy Mayhall Meml. award Stamford (Conn.) Mus., 1997, Spl. Opportunity Stipend N.Y. Found. Arts, 1998. Mem. Internat. Assn. Art Critics. Home: 186 Prospect Ave Valhalla NY 10595

LOMBARDI, EUGENE PATSY, retired orchestra conductor, violinist, educator; b. North Braddock, Pa., July 7, 1923; s. Nunzio C. and Mary (Roberto) L.; m. Jacqueline Sue Davis, Mar. 1955; children: Robert, Genanne. BA, Westminster Coll., 1948; MA, Columbia U., 1948; Edn. Specialist, George Peabody Coll., 1972; MusD, Westminster Coll., 1981. Band dir. Lincoln H.S., Midland, Pa., 1948-49; orch. dir. Male H.S., Louisville, 1949-50, Phoenix Union H.S., 1950-57; orch. dir., prof. Ariz. State U., Tempe, 1957-89; ret., 1989. Condr. Phoenix Symphonette, 1954-61, 70-73, Phoenix Symphony Youth Orch., 1956-66, Phoenix Pops Orch., 1971-83, Fine Arts String Orch., Phoenix, 1995-97 With USAAF, 1943-46. Decorated Bronze Star; recipient Alumni Achievement award Westminster Coll., 1976, gold medal Nat. Soc. Arts and Letters, 1973, Disting. Tchr. award Ariz. State U. Alumni, 1974, Phoenix appreciation award, 1983 Mem. Music Educators Nat. Conf., Am. String Tchrs. Assn. (pres. Ariz. unit 1965-67), Am. Fedn. Musicians, Ariz. Music Educators Assn. (pres. higher edn. sect. 1973-75, Excellence in Teaching Music award 1989), Ind. Order Foresters, Phi Delta Kappa, Phi Mu Alpha, Alpha Sigma Phi. Republican. Methodist. Home: 920 E Manhatton Dr Tempe AZ 85282-5520

LOMBARDI, FREDERICK MCKEAN, lawyer; b. Akron, Ohio, Apr. 1, 1937; s. Leonard Anthony and Dorothy (McKean) L.; m. Margaret J. Gessler, Mar. 31, 1962; children: Marcus M., David G., John A., Joseph F. BA, U. Akron, 1960; LLB, Case Western Res., 1962. Bar: Ohio 1962, U.S. Dist. Ct. (no. and so. dists.) Ohio 1964, U.S. Ct. Appeals (6th cir.) 1966. Prin., shareholder Buckingham, Doolittle & Burroughs, Akron, 1962—, chmn. comml. law and litigation dept., 1989-99. Bd. editors Western Res. Law Rev., 1961-62. Trustee, mem. exec. com., v.p. Ohio Ballet, 1985-93; trustee Walsh Jesuit H.S., 1987-90; life trustee Akron Golf Charities, NEC World Series of Golf; bd. mem. Summa Health Sys. Found., Downtown Akron Partnership, St. Hilary Parish Found. Mem. Ohio Bar Assn. (coun. of dels. 1995-97), Akron Bar Assn. (trustee 1991-94, 97-2000, v.p., pres.-elect 1997-98, pres. 1998-99), Case Western Res. U. Law Alumni Assn. (bd. govs. 1995-98), Case Western Res. Soc. Benchers, Fairlawn Swim and Tennis Club (past pres.), Portage Country Club, Pi Sigma Alpha. Democrat. Roman Catholic. Office: Buckingham Doolittle & Burroughs 50 S Main St Akron OH 44308-1828 E-mail: flombardi@bdblaw.com.

LOMBARDI, GIANCARLO, Italian language educator; b. Rome, Mar. 6, 1965; s. Fernando Lombardi and Maria Luisa Basili. PhD, Cornell U., 1996. Asst. prof. Italian, Smith Coll., Northampton, Mass., 1996-99, CUNY, Staten Island, 1999—. Author: Roomes With a View: Feminist Diary Fiction, 2002; contbr. articles to profl. jours. Mem. MLA. Office: Coll Staten Island CUNY 2800 Victory Blvd Staten Island NY 10314 E-mail: lombardi@postbox.csi.cuny.edu.

LOMBARDI, JOHN V. university administrator, historian; b. Los Angeles, Aug. 19, 1942; s. John and Janice P. Lombardi; m. Cathryn Lee; children: John Lee, Mary Ann. BA, Pomona Coll., 1963; MA, Columbia U., 1964, PhD, 1968. Prof. contratado Escuela de Historia, Universidad Central de Venezuela, Caracas, 1967; lectr. history Ind. U. S.E., Jeffersonville, 1967-68, asst. prof., 1968-69; vis. asst. prof. Ind. U., Bloomington, 1968-69, asst. prof. history, 1969-71, assoc. prof., 1971-77, prof., 1977-87, dir. Latin Am. studies program, 1971-74, dean Internat. Programs, 1978-85, dean Coll. Arts and Scis., 1985-87; prof. history Johns Hopkins U., 1987-89, provost, vp. for acad. affairs, 1987-89; pres. U. Fla., Gainesville, 1989-99, prof. history, dir. The Ctr., 1999—; chancellor Univ. of Mass., 2002—. Author: (with others) Venezuelan History: A Comprehensive Working Bibliography, 1977, People and Places in Colonial Venezuela, 1976, Venezuela: Search for Order, Dream of Progress, 1982; Mem. editorial bd.: (with others) UCLA Statis. Abstracts Latin Am, 1977— ; contbr. (with others) articles to profl. jours. Fulbright-Hayes research fellow, 1965-66 Mem. Am. Hist. Assn., Latin Am. Studies Assn., Pan Am. Inst. Geography and History, Academia Nacional de la Historia (corr. mem .) Office: University of Mass at Amherst Chancellor's Office Amherst MA 01003 E-mail: lombardi@ufl.edu.*

LOMBARDI, KENT BAILEY, insurance company administrator; b. Keene, N.H., Nov. 24, 1955; s. Louis Richard Lombardi and Jean (Thurston) Tacy; m. June M. Havas, Aug. 12, 1978; children: Marina, Anthony. BS in Mktg. & Mgmt., Siena Coll., 1977. CPCU. Claims adjuster Crawford & Co., Poughkeepsie, N.Y., 1977-78, adjuster-in-charge Middletown, 1978-82, 83-85; adjuster Ft. Orange Claims, Clifton Park, 1982-83; claims examiner Frontier Ins. Co., Monticello, 1985-87, asst. claims mgr. property & casualty, 1987-92, asst. claims mgr. med./dental malpractice Monticello & Rock Hill, 1992-94, v.p., claims mgr. med./dental malpractice Rock Hill, 1993-96, v.p. med./dental malpractice, 1996—. Mem. Mid Hudson Claims Assn. Avocations: skiing, golf, music. Office: Frontier Ins Co Lake Louise Marie Rd Rock Hill NY 12775

LOMBARDI, VALENTINO DENNIS, lawyer; b. Providence, Feb. 5, 1943; s. Joseph and Angelina (DiDonato) L.; m. Linda Ann Dardeen, Sept. 5, 1966; children: Valerie Lynn, Nicole Maria, Joseph Thomas. AB, Providence Coll., 1966; JD, Suffolk U., 1971. Bar: R.I. 1971, U.S. Dist. Ct. R.I. 1971. Sole practice, North Providence, 1971—. Legal counsel dept. labor and tng. State of R.I., 1978—, dept. social and rehabilitative services, 1972-73, dept. corrections, 1973-76, chief legal counsel, 1976-78; assoc. judge mcpl. ct. Town of North Providence, R.I., 1986—. Chmn. businessman's athletic club YMCA, Providence, 1976-80; bd. dirs. and sec. Iannotiti Scholarship Fund. Mem. Providence Coll. Alumni Assn. (class agt. 1981—), Sons of Italy (treas. 1995—, 1st v.p. 1997, pres. 2001—). Democrat. Roman Catholic. Avocations: golf, running, sports spectating. Home: 11 Stephanie Dr Providence RI 02904-2913 Office: 959 Mineral Spring Ave North Providence RI 02904-4934 E-mail: VnL66@aol.com.

LOMBARDO, DAVID ALBERT, actor, writer, speaker, aviation educator; b. Chgo., Jan. 31, 1947; s. Ignace Palmeri and Diane Marion (Balducci) L. BS, U. Ill., 1974, MEd, 1977. Tchr. York Community High Sch., Elmhurst, Ill., 1974-75; instr. Coll. Edn., U. Ill., Urbana, 1975-77, asst. dir. career devel. and placement, 1977-79; with Accelerated Ground Schs., 1978-81, dir. Nat. Flying Inst. refresher clinics; dir. program devel. Airmanship, Inc., Rockford, Ill., 1981-82; gen. aviation cons. Lombardo & Assocs., 1981—; asst. prof. profl. aviation La. Tech. U., Ruston, 1982-85; dir. tng. Frasca Internat., Urbana, Ill., 1985-88; asst. prof., aerotech. program leader Bowling Green (Ohio) State U., 1988-91; assoc. dean aviation Lewis U., Romeoville, Ill., 1991-93. Chief instr. Greater St. Louis Flight Instrs. Assn., 1980-81; accident prevention counselor FAA, 1980—. Author: Aircraft Systems: Understanding Your Airplane, 1988, Advanced Aircraft Systems, 1993, Aircraft Systems, 1998; assoc. editor Images, 1988-90; editor Simulation Newsletter, 1985-91, contbg. editor Pvt. Pilot Mag., 1984-87, Aviation Maintenance Mag., 1995-2000, Rotor and Wing Mag., 1999-2000; staff editor, Aviation Internat. News, 1999—; contbr. articles to profl. jours. Bd. dirs. Ruston Community Theater, 1983-85; founder, bd. dirs. Hill Country Arts Coun., 1983-85; dep. sheriff Will County Sheriff's Aux., 1994—. With AUS, 1966-69, Vietnam. Decorated Vietnamese Gallantry Cross; recipient Ark. Traveler award Gov. of Ark., 1978, Plaque of Appreciation, Greater St. Louis Flight Instrs. Assn., 1981, Excellence award La. Tech. U., 1984, Instr. Yr. award Aerotech Program Bowling Green State U., 1989, numerous others. Mem. Univ. Aviation Assn. (chmn. FAA/Univ. Aviation Assn. flt. tng. device task force 1990-93, chmn. simulation com. 1987-93, mem. publs. com. 1985-88, nat. treas. 1992-93), Aviation/Space Writers Assn. (Midwest region Journalism award of Excellence 1989), Assn. Aviation Psychologists, Human Factors Soc., Soc. Automotive Engrs., Alpha Eta Rho (advisor 1983-85, 88-91), Chi Gamma Iota, Phi Delta Kappa, Epsilon Pi Tau. Republican. Roman Catholic. Home and Office: 1113 S Raven Rd Shorewood IL 60431-9165

LOMBARDO, DAVID DOMENIC, human resources executive; b. West Reading, Pa., Nov. 20, 1939; s. Anthony D. and Mary A. (Piscitello) L.; m. Maryann V. Widnick, Jul. 12, 1969; children: Michelle Ann, David Anthony. BA in Polit. Sci., Albright Coll., 1961; MA in Internat. Rels., N.Y. Univ., 1964, PhD in Human Resources, 1978. Accredited Sr. Profl. in Human Resources by HR Cert. Inst., 2000. Pers./ind. rels. specialist U.S. Atomic Energy Commn., N.Y., 1967-71; chief employee/labor rels. U.S. Social Security Adminstrn., Flushing, N.Y., 1971-73, chief pers., 1973-77; chief. recruit & placement Libr. of Congress, Washington, 1977-90, chief human resources ops., 1990-95; adj. prof. mgmt., human resources Univ. Md., College Park, 1987—; dir. human resources Anne Arundel Co. Publ. Schs., Annapolis, Md., 1995—. Mem. rsch. com. Soc. for Human Resource Mgmt., Alexandria, Va., 1993—. Pres. Crofton Civic Assn., Crofton, Md., 1984-88, Rules Com., chmn., 1990-92. With U.S. Army, 1963-65. Mem. Acad. of Mgmt., Am. Assn. of Sch. Pers. Admin., Ind. Rels. Rsch. Assn., Md. Assn. of Sch. Pers. Admin. (pres. 1998-99), Md. Negotiation Svc., Soc. For Human Resource Mgmt., Annapolis Soc. Human Resource Mgmt. (founder, 1st pres. 1999-2000). Office: Anne Arundel Co Pub Schs 2644 Riva Rd Annapolis MD 21401-7305

LOMBARDO, FREDRIC ALAN, pharmacist, educator; b. New Castle, Pa., May 11, 1948; s. Valentine Frank and Clara Eleanor (Cugini) Lombardo; m. Loretta D. Patts, May 22, 1971; children: Alan John, Lauren Beth, Leslie Anne. BS in Pharmacy, Duquesne U., 1971, PharmD, 1974; MS, Fla. Inst. Tech., 1979. Lic. pharmacist Pa., Va., D.C., Tex., cert. Am. Coll. Clin. Pharmacists. Resident in hosp. pharmacy Mercy Hosp., Pitts., 1973; commd. 2nd lt. U.S. Army, 1974, advanced through grades to lt. col., 1993; chief clin. pharmacy support svc. Brooke Army Med. Ctr., Ft. Sam Houston, Tex., 1980-85; chief outpatient pharmacy svc. Walter Reed Army Med. Ctr., Washington, 1985-86, chief cancer treatment sect., chief hematol.-oncol. pharmacy, 1986-92; resigned active duty entered U.S. Army reserve, 1993; sr. clin. pharmacy supr. Nat. Heart, Lung and Blood Inst., NIH, Bethesda, Md., 1992-95; asst. prof. clin. and adminstrv. pharmacy sci. Howard U., Washington, 1995—, asst. prof. psychiatry Coll. Medicine, assoc. prof. cmty. medicine and family practice; asst. prof. U. Md. Asst. prof. pharmacology Cath. U., Washington, 1995—, H. Lee Med. Sch., USUHS, Bethesda, Md., 1995—; asst. prof. pharmacology Cancer Ctr., Ctr. Sickle Cell Disease Howard U. , 1995—, asst. dir. Cancer Ctr., 1997; prof. Found. Advancement Edn. Sci., Grad. Sch. NIH, 1996—; mem. Mid-Atlantic Oncology Adv. Group, Washington, 1997; mem. coun. experts com. Oncologic Diseases USP. Co-host Ask the Pharmacy Doctor program Sta. WRC-980, Washington, 1997—, guest various TV and radio programs. Active Urban Health U., Urban Family Inst., Washington, 1996—97. Lt. col. USAR, 1993—. Grantee Rsch., Ortho-McNeil Pharm., Washington, 1996—97. Fellow: Am. Soc. Cons. Pharmacists; mem.: Nat. Pharm. Assn., Am. Soc. Health Professions, Am. Pharm. Assn. (bd. cert. in pharmacotherapy nutrition support, oncology, psychopharmacology, and geriatrics), KC, Am. Legion. Democrat. Roman Catholic. Avocations: military history, mathematics. Home: 13503 Apple Barrel Ct Herndon VA 20171-4006 Office: Howard Univ Coll Pharmacy and Pharm Sci 2300 4th St NE Washington DC 20002-1220

LOMBARDO, JOHN WYNNE, eye surgeon; b. N.Y.C., Dec. 26, 1948; s. Josef Vincent and Beatrice Silvy Lombardo; m. Alix Sandra Dragnich, Mar. 21, 1981; children: Marisa Silvy. BA, Columbia U., 1969, MD, 1973. Diplomate Am. Bd. Ophthalmology, Am. Bd. Psychiatry and Neurology. Intern in internal medicine Mt. Sinai Hosp., N.Y.C., 1973-74; resident, chief resident in psychiatry Columbia-Presbyn. Med. Ctr., 1974-77, instr. dept. psychiatry, 1977-79; resident, chief resident ophthalmology Manhattan Eye, Ear & Throat Hosp., N.Y.C., 1979-82; pvt. practice Bklyn., 1982—. Trustee Park Ave. Meth. Ch., N.Y.C., 1988-94, 98—; trustee Marymount Sch., N.Y.C., 1997—. Laughlin fellow Am. Coll. Psychiatrists, 1976. Fellow ACS, Am. Acad. Ophthalmology; mem. Med. Soc. State of N.Y., N.Y. State Ophthalmologic Soc., The Univ. Club, Alpha Omega Alpha. Avocations: karate, opera, sporting clay shooting, golf. Home: 1172 Park Ave New York NY 10128-1213 Office: Lombardo Ophthalmology of Bay Ridge PC 7801 4th Ave Brooklyn NY 11209-3701 E-mail: jwlombardo@earthlink.net.

LOMBARDO, JOSEPH SAMUEL, acoustical engineer; b. Chgo., Aug. 16, 1946; s. Joseph and Frances Lombardo; m. Maureen Frick, May 25, 1974; children: Christopher, Jennifer. BS in Elec. Engring., U. Ill., 1969; MS in Elec. Engring., Johns Hopkins U., 1974. Registered profl. engr., Ill. Instrumentation specialist Johns Hopkins U./Applied Physics Lab., Laurel, Md., 1970-78, sect. supr. acoustics group, 1978-84, program mgr. Navy undersea rsch., 1984—, program mgr. for info. tech. devel., 1996—. Com. mem. Adv. Group to Asst. Sec. of Navy, Washington, 1990. Contbr. articles to profl. jours. Bd. govs. Cape St. Claire (Md.) Improvement Assn., 1985. Mem. IEEE, Nat. Security Indsl. Assn. (com. 1992-95), Cape St. Claire Yacht Club (commodore 1984-86), Eta Kappa Nu, Tau Beta Pi, Sigma Tau. Achievements include patents for vibration sensor, large aperture element location sys., towing configuration hardware for geophys. exploration sys.; avocation: sailing. Office: Johns Hopkins U Applied Physics Lab Johns Hopkins Rd Laurel MD 20723

LOMBARDO, MICHAEL JOHN, lawyer, educator; b. Willimantic, Conn., Mar. 25, 1927; s. Frank Paul and Mary Margaret (Longo) Lombardo; children: Nancy C., Claire M. BS, U. Conn., 1951, MS, 1961, JD, 1973. Bar: Conn. 1974, U.S. Dist. Ct. Conn. 1975, U.S. Supreme Ct. 1979, U.S. Ct. Appeals (2d cir.) 1980. Div. controller Jones & Laughlin Steel Corp., Willimantic, 1956-67; adminstrv. officer health ctr. U. Conn., Hartford, 1968-69; dir. adminstrv. svcs. South Central Community Coll., New Haven, 1969-70; asst. dir. adminstrn. Norwich (Conn.) Hosp., 1970-77; asst. atty. gen. State of Conn., Hartford, 1977-92; pvt. practice, Willimantic, 1992—. Adj. asst. prof. U. Hartford, 1961-70; adj. prof. bus. Old Dominion U., 1973-81; adj. lectr. in law and bus. Ea. Conn. State U., 1973-2000, disting. adj. faculty, 1990. Vol. Windham Ctr. (Conn.) Fire Dept. Sgt. U.S. Army, 1945-46, 1st lt. USAFR, 1951-53, col. USAFR, 1953-87, col. USAF ret., 1987. Decorated Air Force Meritorious Svc. medal, 1980; named Disting. Mil. Grad., U. Conn., 1950. Mem. AAUP, VFW, ATLA, Internat. Platform Assn., Retired Officers Assn., Conn. Bar Assn., Windham County Bar Assn., Assn. Trial Lawyers Am., Mensa Internat., Am. Legion, Lions (bd. dirs. Willimantic chpt. 1960-64). Home: 35 Oakwood Dr Windham CT 06280-1520 E-mail: ecsuprof@aol.com.

LOMBARDO, PETER CHARLES, dermatologist; b. Rochester, N.Y., Dec. 4, 1935; s. Charles J. and Constance R. (Inguaggiato) L. BA, U. Rochester, 1955; MD, Union U., 1959. Diplomate Am. Bd. Dermatology. Intern Mary Imogene Bassett Hosp., Cooperstown, N.Y., 1959-60; resident in dermatology Columbia Presbyn. Med. Ctr., N.Y.C., 1962-65; resident in internal medicine St. Luke's Hosp. Ctr., 1965-66; pvt. practice, 1966-97; with Sutton Pl. Dermatology, 1997—. Faculty dept. dermatology Coll. Physicians and Surgeons Columbia U., N.Y.C., 1966-97, assoc. clin. prof. dermatology, 1997—; case rev. Med. Liability Mutual Ins. Co., N.Y.C., 1985—, Office of Profl. Med. Conduct Dept. Health N.Y. State, N.Y.C., 1995—. Author: (with others) Clinical Geriatrics, 1979, Dermatology and Person Threatening Diseases, 1996; manuscript rev. Jour. Am. Acad. Dermatology, 1986; contbr. articles to profl. jours. Del. Govs. Conf. on Librs., Albany, N.Y., 1978. Mem. Internat. Soc. Tropical Dermatology, Am. Acad. Dermatology (adv. coun. 1992—, mem. ethics com. 1995—, mem. exec. com. rep. N.Y. 1997—), Med. Soc. County N.Y. (grievance com. peer rev. 1992—, chair grievance com. 1997—), N.Y. State Soc. Dermatology (bd. dirs. 1992—), Individual Practice Assn. Met. N.Y. (credentials com. 1995—), N.Y. State Soc. Dermatology (bd. dirs. 1992—), N.Y. Acad. Medicine (Fred Wise Meml. award 1965), N.Y. Dermatol. Soc. (bd. dirs. 1992—, pres. 1993)Manhattan Met. Dermatol. Soc., Riverside Practitioners Soc., N.Y. Athletic Club, Met. Opera Club. Avocations: opera, travel. Office: Sutton Pl Dermatology 445 E 58th St New York NY 10022-2302 E-mail: drlombardo@suttonplacedermatology.com.

LOMBARDO, PHILIP JOSEPH, broadcasting company executive; b. Chgo., June 13, 1935; s. Joseph Pete and Josephine (Franco) L.; m. Marilyn Ann Tellefsen, June 22, 1963; children: Dean, Jeffrey. Student, U. Ill., 1953-55; BA in Speech, Journalism and Radio/TV, postgrad. speech, U. Mo., 1958; grad. advanced mgmt. program, Harvard U., 1976. Account exec. Sta. WWCA, Ind., 1959-60; producer-dir. Sta. WBBM-TV, Chgo., 1960-65; program mgr., acting gen. mgr. Sta. WLWT, Cin., 1965-67; v.p., gen. mgr. Sta. WGHP-TV, N.C., 1968-73; pres., chief exec. officer Corinthian Broadcasting Corp., N.Y.C., 1973-82; chmn., pres., chief exec. officer Champlain Communications Corp., 1982-84; mng. gen. ptnr. Citadel Communications Co. Ltd., 1982—; chmn., pres., chief exec. officer Citadel Communications, Co. Ltd., C.C.C. Communications Corp., Lombardo Communications II, Inc., P.J.L. Investments, Inc., 1984—; mng. gen. ptnr., nat. sales rep. U.S. and Can. TV stas. Can. Communications Co., Toronto, 1985—; mng. gen. ptnr. Coronet Communications Co., N.Y.C., 1985—, Capital Comm. Co., Inc., 1994—, Citadel Comm., LLC, 1995—. Bd. dirs. The Gabelli Group, The Lynch Corp., N.Y.C. Mem. adv. bd. Salvation Army; com. budget, bd. dirs. United Fund; mem. com. High Point (N.C.) United Schs.; 1st vice chmn. Central Carolina chpt. Nat. Multiple Sclerosis Soc., 1968-73; bd. dirs. High Point Arts Council, 1968-73. Served with AUS, 1959, 62. Recipient Disting. Svc. award Freedom Found., Am. Legion, High Point (N.C.) Youth Coun. Mem. Dirs. Guild Am., Internat. Radio and TV Soc. (bd. govs.). Clubs: Winged Foot Golf, Marco Polo, Board Room, Bronxville Field, Chgo. Press. Lodges: Rotary, Kiwanis. Home: 24 Masterton Rd Bronxville NY 10708-4804 Office: Citadel Comm Co 99 Pondfield Rd Bronxville NY 10708-3902 E-mail: citnyltd@aol.com.

LOMBARDO TROSTORFF, DANIELLE MARIA, lawyer, educator; b. Buffalo, Dec. 31, 1951; d. Daniel M. and D. Anne (Bezer) Lombardo; m. Alexander Peter Trostorff, June 30, 1984; children: Alexander Peter Jr., Lauren. BS, Cornell U., 1972; MSW, Washington U., St. Louis, 1976, JD, 1977. Bar: N.Y. 1978, D.C. 1978, U.S. Dist. Ct D.C. 1979, U.S. Ct. Appeals (D.C. cir.) 1980, La. 1981, U.S. Dist. Ct. (ea. dist.) La. 1981, U.S. Ct. Appeals (5th and 11th cirs.) 1981, U.S. Dist. Ct. (mid. and we. dists.) La. 1983. Legal asst. Michael LoPinto, Atty., Ithaca, N.Y., 1973; intern Pub. Defender's Office State of Ill., Belleville, 1974; legal asst. hon. judge Betty Friedlander, Ithaca, summer 1975; with personal trust new bus. dept. Irving Trust Co., N.Y.C., 1977-78; staff atty., acting mng. atty. family law unit Neighborhood Legal Svcs., Washington, 1978-80; trial atty. Office of Corp. Counsel spl. litigation sect. Commonwealth of D.C., 1980-81; ptnr. Donna D. Fraiche, 1981-84; chairperson health law sect. Broadhurst, Brook, Mangham & Hardy, New Orleans, 1984-87; ptnr. Brook, Morial, Cassibry, Fraiche & Pizza, 1987-91; shareholder Locke Purnell Rain Harrell, 1991-99; ptnr. Locke Liddell & Sapp, LLP, 1999—; ptnr., chairperson Healthcare Practice Group. Adj. prof. health care law Tulane U. Sch. Pub. Health and Tropical Medicine, New Orleans, 1989-93. Contbr. articles to profl. jours. Mem. adv. bd. Agenda for Children, New Orleans, 1990—; co-pres. Child Abuse Coun. of Greater New Orleans, 1989-90; past pres. Greater New Orleans Women's Healthcare Exec. Network. Mem. Am. Coll. Healthcare Execs. (regent's adv. coun. La.), La. Soc. Hosp. Attys. of La. Hosp. Assn. (pres. 1983-85), Cornell U. Alumni Assn. (chair-person admissions network 1989—). Office: Locke Liddell & Sapp LLP 601 Poydras St Ste 2400 New Orleans LA 70130-6036 E-mail: dtrostorff@lockeliddell.com.

LOMET, DAVID BRUCE, computer scientist; b. Neptune, N.J., Aug. 2, 1939; s. Pierre and Helen (Foster) L.; m. Charlotte Jean Vandermark, Aug. 15, 1964; children: Bruce, Kevin. BS in Physics, Lafayette Coll., Easton, Pa., 1961; MS in Math., George Washington U., Washington, 1966; PhD in Computer Sci., U. Pa., Phila., 1969. Vis. researcher U. Newcastle (U.K.)-upon-Tyne, 1975-76; mem. rsch. staff IBM Corp., Yorktown Heights, N.Y., 1969-85; prof. computer sci. Wang Inst. Grad. Studies, Tyngsboro, Mass., 1985-87; sr. info. cons. Digital Equipment Corp., Nashua, N.H., 1987-89, sr. cons. engr. and mem. rsch. staff Cambridge, Mass., 1989-94; sr. rschr., mgr. database rsch. group Microsoft Corp., Redmond, Wash., 1995—. Grant reviewer VLDB, SIGMOD; chmn. program com. FODO93; vice-chmn. program com. ICDE, 1995, co-chmn. program com., 2000, conf. co-chmn., 01. Editor ACM Transactions on Database Systems, Data Engring. Bull., VLDB Jour., Parallel and Distributed Database Sys. Jour., ACM SIGMOD Digital Revs; contbr. over 60 articles to profl. publs. Mem., v.p. Bd. Edn., Yorktown Heights, N.Y., 1980-85. Recipient 2 Best Paper awards SIGMOD Conf.; IBM resident grad. fellow, 1966. Mem. IEEE (sr. mem., Outstanding Contbn. award, Golden Core Mem. Meritorious Svc. award), AAAS, Assn. Computer Machinery (editor Transactions on Database Sys.), Phi Beta Kappa. Democrat. Achievements include 21 patents; research in database systems, programming languages, computer architecture and distributed systems. Office: Microsoft Rsch One Microsoft Way Redmond WA 98052

LOMHOFF, PETER GEORGE, lawyer; b. N.Y.C., Jan. 21, 1945; BA, Reed Coll., 1966; MA, U. Chgo., 1970; postgrad., Harvard U., 1970-71; JD, U. Calif. at Berkeley, 1974. Bar: Calif. 1974, U.S. Dist. Ct. (no. dist.) Calif. 1974, U.S. Ct. Appeals (9th cir.) 1974. Law clk. Judge William T. Sweigert, U.S. Dist. Ct. (no. dist.) Calif., San Francisco, 1975-77; assoc. Law Office John Diaz Coker, Pittsburg, Calif., 1974-75; instr. Lincoln U. Sch. Law, San Francisco, 1977-80; atty. pvt. practice, Oakland, Calif., 1977—. Speaker in field. Contbr. to profl. handbooks. Democrat. Office: 1 Kaiser Plz Ste 1725 Oakland CA 94612-3681

LOMICKA, WILLIAM HENRY, investor; b. Irwin, Pa., Mar. 9, 1937; s. William and Carabel L.; m. Carol L. Williams, Feb. 14, 1979; 1 son, Edward W. BA, Coll. Wooster, Ohio, 1959; MBA, U. Pa., 1962. Sr. securities analyst Guardian Life Ins. Co., N.Y.C., 1962-65; treasury svcs. mgr. L.B. Foster Co., Pitts., 1966-68, Welch Foods Co., Westfield, N.Y., 1969-70; asst. treas. Ashland Oil, Inc., Ky., 1970-75; sr. v.p. fin. Humana Inc., Louisville, 1975-85; pres., fin. cons. Old South Life Ins. Co., 1985-87; sec. econ. devel. Commonwealth of Ky., 1987-88; acting pres. Citizens Security Life Ins. Co., Louisville, 1988-89; pres. Mayfair Capital, Inc., 1988-99; chmn. Coulter Ridge Capital, Tucson, 1999—. Bd. dirs. Pomeroy Computer Resources, Inc., Counsel Corp. Served with USAR, 1962-63. Home and Office: 7406 N Secret Canyon Dr Tucson AZ 85718-1435

LOMINAC, HARRY GENE, retired theater educator, designer; b. Asheville, N.C., Nov. 30, 1930; s. Harry and Pauline (Woodbury) L.; m. Mary Billie Ashe, Jan. 30, 1959; children: Tory Leigh, Tanya Leah. MA in Drama, U. N.C., 1962. Chair dept. Judson Coll., Marion, Ala., 1962-64; instr., tech. dir. Ky. State U., Frankfort, 1964-68; asst. prof., tech. dir. Baker U., Baldwin City, Kans., 1968-70; supr. prodn. and tng. N.C. Svcs. for Blind, Raleigh, 1972-85; food svc. designer Hickory Farms, 1985-88, Food Lion, Raleigh, 1988-95. Vis. instr. U. N.C., Chapel Hill, summer 1962. Author: The Carolina Dramatic Assn.: Its History 1922-1962, 1962; contbr. poetry to books, jours.; actor Unto These Hills, Cherokee, N.C., 1963, The Daniel Boone Story, Harrodsburg, Ky., 1964. Staff sgt. USAF, 1953-57. Avocations: landscaping, gardening. Home: PO Box 234 Tuckasegee NC 28783-0234

LOMKE, EVANDER, publishing executive; b. Mt. Vernon, N.Y., Sept. 6, 1953; s. Lester and Leah Polizzotti L.; m. Fotini Stavros, Nov. 29, 1980; 1 child, Elizabeth Leah. BA, City Coll. of N.Y., 1975; MA, U. Toronto, Ont., 1976. Assoc. editor Frederick Ungar Publishing, N.Y.C., 1982-86; assoc. mng. editor Crossroad/Ungar/Continuum, 1986-87; mng. editor Continuum Pub. Group, 1987-95, v.p., mng. editor, 1995-99, Continuum Internat. Pub. Group, N.Y.C., 1999—2002, v.p., sr. editor, 2002—. Bd. dirs., chmn. editl. com. Am. Mental Health Found. William Bradley Otis fellow CCNY, 1975. Mem. Phi Beta Kappa. Home: 3215 Arlington Ave Apt 6H Bronx NY 10463-3334 E-mail: evander@continuum-books.com.

LOMMEL, JAMES M. information technology manager; b. Evanston, Ill., Feb. 7, 1932; s. Edward J. and Florence Marie Lommel; m. Mary Ann Ryan; children: Joan Mintz, Patricia Bruttomesso. BS, Ill. Inst. Tech., 1953, MS, 1954; PhD, Harvard U., 1958. R & D staff GE Global Rsch., Schenectady, NY, 1957—93, mgr. tech. info., 1993—. Gen. chmn. adv. com. Magnetism and Magnetic Materials Com., N.Y.C., 1974; mem. pub. policy com. Am. Inst. Physics, N.Y.C., 1982—87. Contbr. articles to profl. jours. Bd. chmn., bd. mem., facilities com. chair Schenectady Arts Ctr. and Theatre, 1977—; pres. Schenectady Civic Players, 1962—64; exec. sec. N.Y. State Cmty. Theatre Assn., 1965—75; trustee Engring. Info., Inc., N.Y.C.; spl. librs.adv. com. OCLC, Dublin, 1995—98; treas. Schenectady Symphony Orch. Assn., 1998—; pres. pastoral coun. St. Helen's Ch., 1997—2000, trustee, 2002—. Mem.: IEEE (pres. Magnetics Soc. 1981—82), Am. Inst. Mining, Metallurgy and Petroleum Engrs.-Metall. Soc. (life). Office: GE Global Rsch PO Box 8 Schenectady NY 12301 Personal E-mail: lommel@earthlink.net. Business E-Mail: lommel@research.crd.ge.com.

LOMON, EARLE LEONARD, physicist, educator, consultant; b. Montreal, Nov. 15, 1930; came to U.S., 1951, naturalized, 1965; s. Harry and Etta (Rappaport) L.; m. Ruth Margaret Jones, Aug. 4, 1951; children: Martha Glynis, Christopher Dylan, Deirdre Naomi. B.Sc., McGill U., Montreal, 1951; PhD, MIT, 1954. NRC Can. overseas research fellow Inst. Theoretical Physics, Copenhagen, 1954-55; fellow Weizmann Inst., Rehovoth, Israel, 1955-56; research assoc. lab. nuclear studies Cornell U., Ithaca, N.Y., 1956-57; assoc. prof. theoretical physics McGill U., Montreal, 1957-60; assoc. prof. physics MIT, Cambridge, 1960-70, prof., 1970-99, prof. emeritus, 1999—. Vis. staff mem. Los Alamos Nat. Lab., 1968—; project dir. Unified Scis. and Math. for Elem. Schs., Cambridge, 1970-77; adj. prof. U. Louvain-la-Neuve, Belgium, 1980; vis. prof. U. Paris, 1979-80, 86-87, UCLA, 1983, U. Wash., 1985, Nanjing U., 2002; vis. rschr. Kernforschungsanlage Jülich, 1986-92, U. Geneva, 1993, CERN, Geneva, 1994, IPN, Orsay, 1994; Lady Davis vis. prof. Hebrew U., Jerusalem, 1993-94; vis. rschr. U. Tübingen, 1997; vis. fgn. scientist KEK (Tanashi br.), Tokyo, 1999-2000, fgn. faculty mem., Nanjing Univ., Nanjing, 2002. Contbr. articles to profl. jours. Guggenheim Meml. Found. fellow CERN, Geneva, 1965-66; Dupont fellow, 1952-53; Ossabaw Island Project fellow (Ga.), 1978; Sci. Research Council fellow U. London, 1980 Fellow Am. Phys. Soc.; mem. Can. Assn. Physicists Office: MIT 6-302 77 Mass Ave Cambridge MA 02139-4307 E-mail: lomon@mitlns.mit.edu.

LOMONACO, SALVATORE JOHN, protective service official; b. N.Y.C., Nov. 23, 1947; s. Lawrence J. and Nettie Lomonaco; m. Josephine T. Poidomani, Mar. 28, 1971 (div. Mar. 1996); children: Michael, Caryn, Steven. BS in Criminal Justice with honors, Rollins Coll., 1976, MS in Bus. Mgmt. with honors, 1984. Hostage team comdr. Orlando (Fla.) Police Dept., 1978—, patrol ops. comdr., 1983-87, property crimes investigative comdr., 1987-91, dep. divsn. comdr. airport ops., 1991-94, drug enforcement comdr., 1994-97, spl. ops. comdr., capt., 1997—. Assoc. prof. Seminole C.C., Sanford, Fla., 1990-94; advanced curriculum instr. Valencia C.C., Orlando, 1996—. Lectr. in field. Pres., v.p., bd. dirs. Spouse Abuse Inc., 1978-94; bd. dirs. Crisis Nursery Inc., 1990-92, Childrens Home Soc., 1992-94; commr. gender bias commn. State of Fla. Supreme Ct., 1988-96; steering com. gov.'s domestic violence task force State of Fla., 1993—; stakeholder Ctrl. Fla. Healthy Cmty. Initiatives, Orlando, 1995—. With USNR, 1966-68. Mem. Police Benevolent Assn. (bd. dirs. 1994—). Republican. Avocations: boating, fishing. Office: Orlando Police Dept PO Box 913 Orlando FL 32802-0913

LOMONOSOFF, JAMES MARC, marketing executive; b. Van Nuys, Calif., Apr. 29, 1951; s. Boris Marc and Eileen Fairfax (Thomson) L.; m. Elisabeth Maas, June 12, 1982; children: Marc Frederik, James Forrest. BA in Econs., Colgate U., 1973; MBA in Gen. Mgmt., U. Va., 1975. With Saatchi and Saatchi Advt., N.Y.C., 1975-93, v.p., account supr., 1975-85, sr. v.p., mgmt. supr., 1986-87, exec. v.p., mgmt. dir., 1987-93, pres. Collateral Plus divsn., 1987-90; CEO, pres. Saatchi & Saatchi Specialized Comm., 1991-92; account dir. VDB/Compton B.V., Amsterdam, The Netherlands, 1980-83; acct. dir. Saatchi and Saatchi Compton S.A., Madrid, 1983-84; regional acct. dir. Saatchi and Saatchi Compton Worldwide, London, 1984-86; mng. dir., CEO BSB/Saatchi and Saatchi, Prague, 1992-93; v.p. internat. mktg. Walt Disney Attractions Inc., Lake Buena Vista, Fla., 1994-98, v.p. internat. mktg. and sales L.Am. Coral Gables, 1999; sr. v.p. mktg. Celebrity Cruises Inc., Miami, 1999—2001. Mem. Beta Theta Pi. Republican. Home: 4211 Monserrate St Coral Gables FL 33146-1207 Office: Celebrity Cruises Inc 1050 Caribbean Way Miami FL 33132-2028 E-mail: jameslomonosoff@netscape.net.

LONABAUGH, ELLSWORTH EUGENE, retired lawyer; b. San Diego, Feb. 24, 1923; s. Alger Wellman and Marion G. (Bailey) L.; m. Carol W. Marr, Dec. 29, 1949 (div. June 1965); children: Marr, Ellsworth, Carol; m. Jean LaValle Miterenga, Dec. 29, 1967; 1 child, Jason. JD, U. Colo., 1950. Bar: Wyo. 1950, Tex. 1951, U.S. Dist. Ct. (so. dist.) Tex. 1951, U.S. Dist. Ct. (fed. dist.) Wyo. 1953, U.S. Ct. Appeals (10th cir.) 1963, U.S. Supreme Ct. 1971. Assoc. Williams & Thornton, Galveston, Tex., 1951-53; ptnr. Lonabaugh & Lonabaugh, Sheridan, Wyo., 1953-71; sr. ptnr. various law firms, 1971-79, Lonabaugh & Riggs, Sheridan, 1980-98, of counsel, 1998-2001. Mem. uniform state laws commn. State of Wyo., 1963-77; city atty. City of Sheridan, 1957; mem. Wyo. Ho. of Reps., Cheyenne, 1955-56, 67-71. Commr. Wyo. Bar, 1972-74; sr. warden St. Peter's Episcopal Ch., 1962-63; chmn. county ctrl. com. Rep. Party, 1966-70. Staff sgt. U.S. Army, 1942-45, ETO. Decorated Bronze Star; recipient Spl. 76 award Sheridan County Commrs., 1976. Mem. Am. Bar Found. (life), Sheridan County Bar Assn. (pres. 1960-61), Sheridan County C. of C. (pres. 1974-75, named Man of Yr., 1975), Am. Legion, DAV, Sheridan Country Club (sec. 1955-59, Phi Delta Phi, Rotary (pres. local chpt. 1972-73), Elks, Shriners, Sigma Chi (pres. 1946-47). Episcopalian. Avocations: golf, sports. Home (Winter): 56 Durango Circle Rancho Mirage CA 92270 Office: PO Dr 5059 Sheridan WY 82801

LONCAR, MIROSLAV, music educator; b. Karlovac, Croatia, May 29, 1964; s. Anka Loncar, Miroslav Loncar; m. Natasa Klasinc; children: Maya, Nina. MusD, U.So.Miss., 1996. Prof. music William Carey Coll., Hattiesburg, Miss., 1994—. Musician: (albums) Con Spirito, 1995, Images, 1998; author: Pieces for Guitar, 1999. Mem.: Coll. Music Soc., Music Tchr. Nat. Assn. (Tchrs. Enrichment grant). Office: William Carey College 498 Tuscan Avenue Hattiesburg MS 39401

LOND, HARLEY WELDON, editor, publisher; b. Chgo., Feb. 5, 1946; s. Henry Sidney and Dorothy (Shaps) L.; m. Marilyn Moss, Aug. 20, 1981; 1 child Elizabeth. BA in Journalism, Calif. State U., L.A., 1972. Adminstrv. dir. Century City Ednl. Arts Project, L.A., 1972-76, hon. dir., 1982—; founder, editor Intermedia mag., 1974-80; prodn. mgr. FilmRow Publs., 1981; assoc. editor Box Office mag., Hollywood, Calif., 1981-84, editor, assoc. pub., 1984-94; dir. publs. Entertainment Data, Inc., 1994-95; pres. CyberPod Prodns., 1995—; asst. news editor The Hollywood Reporter, 1995-2000, news editor, 2000—. Syndicated columnist Continental Features, Washington, Tel-Aire Publs., Dallas, 1986—; hon dir. Monterey (Calif.) Film Festival, 1987; mem. media adv. bd. Cinetex Internat. Film Festival, 1988; cons. Take 3 Info. Svc.; web architect-master, OnVideo website, 1995—. Editor: Entertainment Media Electronic Info. Svc.; contbg. editor: (video) Family Style Mag.; contbr. articles to profl. publs. Calif. Arts Council grantee, 1975, Nat. Endowment for Arts grantee, 1976-77. Mem. MLA, Soc. Profl. Journalists, Assn. for Edn. in Journalism and Mass Communication, Speech Communication Assn., Soc. for Cinema Studies. Home and Office: PO Box 17377 Beverly Hills CA 90209-3377

LONDON, ANDREW BARRY, film editor; b. Bronx, N.Y., Jan. 1, 1949; s. Max Edward and Nellie (Steiner) L. BA in Cinema magna cum laude, U. So. Calif., 1970. Represented by Mont. Artists, Santa Monica, Calif. Prin. works include: (features) Big Eden, 2000, The Meteor Man, 1993, F/X 2, 1991, Rambo III, 1988, Planes, Trains and Automobiles, 1987, Link, 1986, Cloak & Dagger, 1984, Psycho II, 1983, The True Story of Eskimo Nell, 1975, (TV shows) The Soul Collector, 1999, A Memory in My Heart, 1999, Murder at 75 Birch, 1999, Before He Wakes, 1997, Perfect Crime, 1997, Divided By Hate, 1997, The Crying Child, 1996, Evil Has a Face, 1996, Don't Talk to Strangers, 1994, Day of Reckoning, 1993, Mortal Sins, 1992, Running Delilah, 1992, True Tales, 1992, Sweet Poison, 1991, Tales from the Crypt, 1989-90, Beauty and the Beast Pilot, 1987, The Christmas Star, 1986; sound editor: Wolfen (MPSE Golden Reel award 1982), Hammett, Roadgames, Psycho II, I'm Dancing As Fast As I Can, Perfect, Protocol, Coal Miner's Daughter, The Long Riders, others. Mem. Acad. Motion Picture Arts and Scis., Motion Picture Sound Editors (Golden Reel award 1982), Phi Beta Kappa. Office: 3085 St George St #3 Los Angeles CA 90027-2532

LONDON, CHARLOTTE ISABELLA, secondary education educator, reading specialist; b. Guyana, S.Am., June 11, 1946; came to U.S., 1966, naturalized, 1980; d. Samuel Alphonso and Diana Dallett (Daniels) Edwards; m. David Timothy London, May 26, 1968 (div. May 1983); children: David Tshombe, Douglas Tshaka. BS, Fort Hays State U., 1971; MS, Pa. State U., 1974, PhD, 1977. Elem. sch. tchr., Guyana, 1962-66; secondary sch. tchr., 1971-72; instr. lang. arts Pa. State U., University Park, 1973-74; reading specialist/ednl. cons. N.Y.C. C.C., 1975; dir. Skills Acquisition and Devel. Ctr. Stockton (N.J.) State Coll., 1975-77; reading specialist Pleasantville (N.J.) Pub. Schs., 1977—, supr. English dept., supr. gifted and talented program, 1999—. Ind. specialist United Nations Devel. Programme, Guyana, 1988—; v.p. Atlantic County PTA, 1980-82; del. N.J. Gov.'s Conf. Future Edn. N.J., 1981; founder, pres. Guyana Assn. Reading and Lang. Devel., 1987. Sec. Atlantic County Minority Polit. Women's Caucus. Mem. Internat. Reading Assn., Nat. Coun. Tchrs. English, ASCD, AAUW, Pi Lambda Theta, Phi Delta Kappa (sec.). Mem. African Meth. Episcopal Ch. Home: 6319 Crocus St Mays Landing NJ 08330-1107 Office: Pleasantville Pub Schs W Decatur Ave Pleasantville NJ 08232

LONDON, DAVID L. lawyer; b. N.Y.C., Mar. 3, 1967; s. Jack and Charlotte (Lord) L.; m. Penelope London, June 18, 1994. BA magna cum laude, Yale U., 1989, JD, 1993. Bar: N.Y. 1994, U.S. Dist. Ct. (so. and ea. dists.) N.Y. 1995, Colo. 1997, U.S. Dist. Ct. Colo. 1997, U.S. Tax Ct. 1998. Jud. clk. to Hon. John C. Lifland U.S. Dist. Ct. for N.J., Newark, 1993-94; assoc. Simpson Thacher & Bartlett, N.Y.C., 1994-97, Hogan & Hartson LLP, Denver, 1997—. Mem. Colo. lawyers com. Housing Task Force, Denver, 1997—; mem. Denver Downtown Partnership Housing Task Force, 2000—. Office: Hogan & Hartson LLP 1200 17th St Ste 1500 Denver CO 80202-5840 E-mail: dllondon@hhlaw.com.

LONDON, HERBERT IRA, humanities educator, institute executive; b. N.Y.C., Mar. 6, 1939; s. Jack and Esta (Epstein) L.; m. Joy Weinman, Oct. 13, 1942 (div. 1974); children: Staci, Nancy; m. Vicki Pops, Nov. 18, 1950; 1 child, Jaclyn. BA, Columbia U., 1960, MA, 1961; PhD, N.Y. U., 1966; DL, U. Aix.-Marseille, Aix-en-Province, France, 1982, Grove City Coll., 1993. Teaching fellow N.Y. U., N.Y.C., 1963-64, instr., 1964-65, asst. prof., 1967-68, univ. ombudsman, 1968-69, assoc. prof., 1969-73, prof., 1973—, dean Gallatin div., 1972-92, John M. Olin U. Prof. Humanities, 1992—; instr. New Sch. for Social Research, 1964-65; research scholar Australian Nat. U., Canberra, Australia, 1966-67; pres. Hudson Inst., 1997—. Bd. overseers Ctr. for Naval Analysis, Washington, 1983-93; trustee Hudson Inst., Indpls., 1979—, research fellow 1974—; sr. fellow Nat. Strategy Info. Ctr. Created TV programs: Myths That Rule America, The American Character; contbr. numerous articles to profl. jours. Bd. dirs., former chmn. Nat. Assn. Scholars, N.Y.C., 1986; bd. advisors Coalition for Strategic Def. Initiative, Washington, 1986; candidate for mayor of N.Y.C., 1989; conservative candidate for gov., N.Y., 1990, 94; candidate for comptroller of N.Y. State, 1994. Named Danforth Assoc., Danford Found., 1971; recipient Anderson award, NYU, 1965, Fulbright award, U.S. Govt., 1966—67, Def. Sci. award, Def. Sci. Jour., 1985, Martin Luther King award, Congress of Racial Equality, 1995, Peter Shaw Meml. award, Exemplary Writing Nat. Assn. Scholars, 1996, Jacques Maritain Humanitarian award, Am. Maritain Assn., 1996, Ellis Island Medal of Honor, 2000, Am. Jewish Congress award, 2001, Libery and Media award, 2002. Mem. Freedom House, Am. Hist. Assn., Edn. Excellence Network, Heritage Found (assoc. scholar 1983—), Ethics and Pub. Policy Ctr. (assoc. scholar 1985—), Nat. Strategy Info. Ctr., Coun. Fgn. Rels. Republican. Jewish. Avocations: writing, tennis. Home: 2 Washington Square Vlg New York NY 10012-1732 Office: NYU 113 University Pl New York NY 10003-4527

LONDON, IRA D. lawyer; b. N.Y.C., July 9, 1931; s. Murray M. and Janet (Weiss) Lichtenstein; m. Phyllis I. Kagel, May 30, 1956; children: Roberta Silverstein, Elyssa Weitzer, Suzanne Corbin. BA in English, NYU, 1956; JD, Bklyn. Law Sch., 1960. Bar: N.Y. 1960. Asst. dist. atty. Kings County Dist. Attys. Office, Bklyn., 1962-67; pvt. practice, N.Y.C., 1967—. Instr., lectr. Harvard Law Sch., Cardozo Law Sch., Yeshiva U., N.Y.C., 1983—, Hofstra U., Hempstead, N.Y., 1984—, Nat. Criminal Def. Coll., Macon, Ga., 1986—; lectr. various nat. and state bar assns. Author: Intra Family Homicide: The Battered Family, 1987. Cpl. U.S. Army, 1953-55. Fellow Am. Bd. Criminal Lawyers (pres. 1990); mem. ABA (def. function com. 1988—), N.Y. State Bar Assn. (exec. com. 1990—), Kings County Criminal Bar Assn. (bd. dirs. 1986-89), Nat. Assn. Criminal Def. Lawyers (bd. dirs. 1986-91), N.Y. State Assn. Criminal Def. Lawyers (v.p. 1986-94, pres. 1995-96), L.I. Mens Tennis League (pres. 1987-89), Lawrence Tennis Club (pres. 1971). Office: 475 Park Ave S New York NY 10016-6901 E-mail: iradlondon@aol.com.

LONDON, IRVING MYER, physician, educator, retired physician; b. Malden, Mass., July 24, 1918; s. Jacob A. and Rose (Goldstein) London; m. Huguette Piedzicki, Feb. 27, 1955; children: Robert L.J., David T. B in Jewish Edn., Hebrew Coll., 1938; AB summa cum laude, Harvard U., 1939, MD, 1943; DSc (hon.) , U. Chgo., 1966. Sheldon Traveling fellow Harvard U., 1939—41, Delamar research fellow med. sch., 1940—41; intern Presbyn. Hosp., N.Y.C., 1943, asst. resident, 1946—47, asst. physician, 1946—52, assoc. attending physician, 1954—55; Rockefeller fellow in medicine Coll. Physicians and Surgeons, Columbia U., 1946—47; instr. Columbia U., 1947—49; asso. in medicine Coll. Phys. and Surg., Columbia U., 1949—51; asst. prof. Coll. Phys. and Surg., Columbia, 1951—54, assoc. prof., 1954—55; prof., chmn. dept. medicine Albert Einstein Coll. Medicine, N.Y.C., 1955—70, vis. prof. medicine, 1970—; prof. biology MIT, 1969—89, prof. emeritus, 1989—; vis. prof. medicine Harvard Med. Sch., 1969—72, prof. medicine, 1972—89, prof. emeritus, 1989—; dir. div. health scis. and tech. Harvard and MIT, 1969—85, prof. medicine, 1972—, Grover M. Hermann prof. health scis. and tech., 1977—89, prof. emeritus, 1989—; dir. Whitaker Coll. Health Scis., Tech. and Mgmt., MIT, 1978—83; dir. med. service Bronx Mcpl. Hosp. Center, 1955—70. Delta Epsilon lectr. U. Colo., 1962, Harvey lectr., 61; Jacobaeus lectr., Stockholm, 64; vis. scientist Pasteur Inst., Paris, 1962—63; Commonwealth Fund fellow, 1962—63; Alpha Omega Alpha lectr. Yale, Boston U., Columbia, SUNY Downstate Med. Ctr., U. Chgo.; Harry L. Alexander vis. prof. Washington U., St. Louis, 1968; Alpha Omega Alpha vis. prof. Johns Hopkins U., 1970; Eugene A. Stead Jr. vis. lectr. Duke Med. Ctr., 1970; cons. to Surgeon Gen. AUS, 1957—60; chmn. metabolism study sect. USPHS, 1961—63; Med. fellowship bd. NAS, NRC, 1955—64; mem. bd. sci. cons. Sloan Kettering Inst., 1960—72; bd. sci. counselors Nat. Heart Inst., 1964—68; exec. com. Health Rsch. Coun., City N.Y., 1958—63; mem. sci. adv. coun. Pub. Health Rsch. Inst., N.Y.C., 1958—63; mem. adv. com. to dir. NIH, 1966—70, nat. cancer adv. bd., 1972—76; physician Brigham and Women's Hosp., 1972—83, sr. physician, 1983—; chmn. rsch. group Nat. Commn. on Arthritis, 1975—76; chmn. adv. com. Divsn. Health Scis., Inst. Medicine, 1979—82; mem. Bd. Sci. Counselors, NIADDK, 1979—83; bd. dirs., cons. Johnson and Johnson, 1982—89; founder Genetix Pharms., 1996. Assoc. editor: Jour. Clin. Investigation, 1952—57, mem. editl. bd.: Am. Jour. Medicine, 1965—79. Bd. trustees Hebrew Coll., 2000—; bd. dirs. Philippe Found. Capt. U.S. Army, 1944—46. Recipient Bloomfield medal and lectr., Lady Davis Inst., 1986. Mem.: NAS (med. bd. medicine 1967—70, founding mem. Inst. Medicine 1970), AAAS (Theobald Smith award in med. scis. 1953), Assn. Am. Physicians, Internat. Soc. Hematology, Am. Soc. Hematology, Am. Soc. Clin. Investigation (pres. 1963—64), Am. Soc. Biol. Chemists, Alpha Omega Alpha, Phi Beta Kappa. Office: Harvard U-MIT Div Health Scis and Tech 77 Massachusetts Ave Cambridge MA 02139-4301 E-mail: imlondon@mit.edu.

LONDON, JOHN RUTHERFORD, III, aerospace program administrator; b. Rock Hill, S.C., June 8, 1953; s. John Rutherford Jr. and Harriette Chandler (Iler) L.; m. Joyce Louellen Low, Aug. 19, 1978; children: Elizabeth Jordan, Sarah Louellen Inga, Joshua David, Hannah Gloria Rimma, Mary Annadell Valentina, Samuel Stephen Victor. BS in Engring. Tech., Clemson U., 1975; MS in Engring. Mgmt., Fla. Inst. Tech., 1983. Commd. USAF, 1975, advanced through grades to lt. col., 1992, congl. liaison, 1993-95, dep. missile def. architect, 1995-96, program mgr. space based laser, 1996-97, ret., 1997; mgr. X-34 Program NASA, Marshall Space Flight Ctr., Ala., 1997, mgr. Future-X Pathfinder Program, 1998—2000, mgr. test and evaluation dept. Ala., 2000—. Author: LEO on the Cheap, 1994; contbr. articles to profl. jours. Fellow AIAA (assoc., sect. chmn.), Brit. Interplanetary Soc.; mem. Phi Delta Theta. Episcopalian. Avocation: collecting military antiques. Home: PO Box 1095 Madison AL 35758-5095 Office: NASA Space Transp Directorate Huntsville AL 35812

LONDON, MICHAEL JEFFREY, public relations executive; b. Waterbury, Conn., Apr. 20, 1952; s. Sherman David and Arlene Dolores (Freedman) L.; m. Allison Brook Spitzer, June 27, 1976; 1 child, Jordan Maxwell. BA, U. Conn., 1974; MS, Rensselaer Poly. Inst., 1987. Pub. rels. assoc. Combined Ins. Co. Am., Chgo., 1974; reporter The Hartford (Conn.) Courant, 1975-78, asst. bus. editor, 1978-80, bur. chief, 1980-82; news rep. Northeast Utilities, Hartford, 1982-83, sr. news rep., 1983-85; dir. corp. rels. Lone Star Industries, Inc., Stamford, Conn., 1985-90; prin. Michael J. London and Assocs., Trumbull, 1990—. Instr. U. Conn., Storrs, 1981-82; comms. chair Share Our Strength, New Haven, 1997. Recipient Bronze Quill award Internat. Assn. Bus. Communicators, 1993. Mem. Nat. Investor Rels. Inst., Pub. Rels. Soc. Am., Soc. Profl. Journalists, Newcomen Soc. N.Am., Internat. Assn. Bus. Communicators. Jewish. Avocation: photography. Office: Michael J London & Assocs 4 Daniels Farm Rd Ste 330 Trumbull CT 06611-2233

LONDON, RAY WILLIAM, consultant, mediator, arbitrator, researcher; b. Burley, Idaho, May 29, 1943; s. Loo Richard and Maycelle Jerry (Moore) L. AS, Weber State Coll., 1965; BS, 1967; MSW, U. So. Calif., 1973; PhD, 1976, Exec. MBA, 1989; postgrad. cert. dispute resolution, Pepperdine Law Sch., 1993; LLM, Strathcylde Sch. Law, 2000. Diplomate: Am. Bd. Psychol. Hypnosis (dir. 1984-97, pres. 1989-97, forensic and ethics divsn.), Am. Acad. Behavioral Med., Internatl. Acad. Med. and Psychol. (dir. 1981-90, pres. 1981-85), Am. Bd. Profl. Neuropsychology, Am. Bd. Adminstrv. Psychol., Am. Bd. Examiners Clinic Social Work, Am. Bd. Profl. Psychol., NASW Clin. Social Work Bd., Am. Bd. Psychol. Specialties, Am. Bd. Forensic Med., Am. Acad. Pain Mgmt., Am. Acad. Experts in Traumatic Stress, Am. Bd. Forensic Examiners, Cyberlex. Global Info. Tech. Law Forum; cert. Soc. Med. Analysts; cert. mgmt. cons., profl. cons. to mgmt.; registered internat. cons. Registry of Arbitrators. Congrl. asst. U.S. Ho. of Reps., 1964-65; rsch. assoc. Bus. Advs., Inc., Ogden, UT, 1965-67; dir. counseling and cons. svcs. Meaning Found., Riverside, Calif., 1966-69; mental health and mental retardation liasion San Bernardino Cty. Social Svcs., San Bernardino, CA, 1968-72; clin. trainee VA Outpatient Clin., Los Angeles, 1971-72, Childrens Hosp. of L.A., 1972-73; clin. fellow, 1973-74; clin. trainee Reiss David Child Study Ctr., Los Angeles, 1973-74, L.A. Cty. - U. So. Calif. Med. Ctr., 1973; group facilitator conflict resolution Benjamin Rush Ctr., Orange, CA, 1973-75; psychologist Orange Police Dept., Calif., 1974-80; COO London Assocs. Internat., 1974-80; clin. and consulting psychology postdoctoral intern Orange Cty. Mental Health, Orange, CA, 1976-77; postdoctoral fellow U. Calif. - Irvine-Calif. Coll. Med., 1978; cons. to pub. schs., agys., hosps., bus. Natl. and Internatl., 1973—; cons. qualitative-quantitative rsch., dispute resolution and assessment Santa Ana, Calif., 1974—; pres. bd. govs. Human Factor Programs, 1976-86; CEO Human Studies Ctr., 1987—; pres., CEO London Consult Orgn. Behavioral-Crisis-Devel. Info. and Knowledge, Conflict Resolution, Change and Rsch. Cons., 1980—. Rsch. affil. Ctr. for Crisis Mgmt., U. So. Calif. Grad. Sch., Bus. Adminstrn., 1988-90; presenter nat. and internat. lectures, seminars and workshops; mem. faculty UCLA, U. So. Calif., Calif. State U., U. Calif., Irvine, Calif. Coll. Med., Internat. Cong. of Psychosomatic Med., Internat. Coll., U. Strathclyde Sch. of Law; Arbitration Trained World Intellectual Property Orgn.; rsch. assoc. Nat. Commn. for Protection of Human Subjects of Biomed. and Behavioral Rsch., 1976; rschr. E-commerce, info. tech., info. security, intellectual property, defective software law, liability in info. age, Internet telecomm. law U. Strathclyde Sch. Law, 1998-2000; mem. EEOC Mediator panel. Author: Encyclopedia of Telecommunications Regulation and Policy; editor: Internat. Bull. Med. and Psychol., 1980—90, A.B.C.D. Report, 1988—, Behavioral Med., Australian Jour., 1980, Internat. Bull. Conflict Resolution, 1993—; editor-in-chief LondonConsult.com, —; adv. editor: Internat. Jour. Clin. and Exptl. Hypnosis, 1981—92, mng. editor: , 1991—97, assoc. editor: , 1992—97; cons. editor Internat. Jour. Psychosomatics, 1984—90, Experimentalle und Klinische, 1987—, pub. London Behavioral Med. Assessment, 1982, A Behavioral-Crisis-Devel. newsletter, ABCD newsnote; prodr.: (TV series) Being Human, 1980; contbtg. author: World Book Ency. and books; contbr. articles to profl. jours. Recipient Congl. recognition U.S. Ho. of Reps., 1978, Morton Prince Awd., 1993; named scholar laureate Erickson Advanced Inst., 1980. Fellow: Soc. Clin. and Exptl. (bd. dirs. 1985—87, treas. 1987—89), Am. Coll. Forensic Psychol., Soc. Clin. Social Work (dir. 1979—80), Royal Soc. Health, Inst. for Soc. Scientists Rsch. Coun., Inst. for Social Influence Studies; mem.: ABA (assoc., ethics and tech. coms.), Am. Arbitration Assn., Internat. Dispute Resolution Ctr., London Ct. of Internat. Arbitration, Profl. Mediation Assn., Calif. Dispute Resolution Coun., So. Calif. Mediation Assn., Soc. Profls. in Dispute Resolution, Qualitative Rsch. Cons. Assn., Soc. for Computers in Psychology, Assn. Internet Rschrs., Toastmasters, Lamda Iota Tau, Pi Rho Phi, Tau Kappa Alpha, Delta Sigma Rho, Phi Delta Kappa. Office: London Consult 17955 Sky Park Cir Ste E Irvine CA 92614-6373 E-mail: rwl@londonconsult.com.

LONDON, STEVE NORMAN, obstetrician-gynecologist, educator; b. Ardmore, Okla., Apr. 22, 1952; MD, U. Okla., 1977. Bd. cert. in ob-gyn.; subspecialty in reproductive endocrinology. Asst. prof., dir. divsn. reproductive endocrinology U. Ark. Health Sci. Ctr., Little Rock, 1986-90; assoc. prof., dir. divsn. reproductive endocrinology U. Ky., Lexington, 1990-94; prof., chmn. dept. ob-gyn. La. State U. Health Sci. Ctr., Shreveport, 1994—, program dir. ob-gyn. residency, 1998—. Examiner Am. Bd. Ob-Gyn., Dallas, 1994—. Author: (book) Menopause Clinical Concepts, 3d edit., 1999. Bd. trustees Noel Meth. Ch., Shreveport, 1997—; scoutmaster Boy Scouts Am., Shreveport, 1994—. Fellow ACOG; mem. Soc. for Reproductive Endocrinology, Am. Soc. Reproductive Endocrinology. Avocations: gardening, camping. Office: La State U Dept Ob-Gyn 1501 Kings Hwy Shreveport LA 71103-4228 E-mail: slondo@lsuhsc.edu.

LONDRÉ, FELICIA MAE HARDISON, theater educator; b. Ft. Lewis, Wash., Apr. 1, 1941; d. Felix M. and Priscilla Mae (Graham) Hardison; m. Venne-Richard Londré, Dec. 16, 1967; children: Tristan Graham, Georgianna Rose. BA with high honors, U. Mont., 1962; MA, U. Wash., 1964; PhD, U. Wis., 1969. Asst. prof. U. Wis. at Rock County, Janesville, 1969-75; asst. prof., head theatre program U. Tex. at Dallas, Richardson, 1975-78; assoc. prof. U. Mo., Kansas City, 1978-82, prof. theatre, 1982-87, curators' prof., 1987—; women's chair in humanistic studies Marquette U., 1995. Dramaturg Mo. Repertory Theatre, Kansas City, 1978-2001, Nebr. Shakespeare Festival, 1990—; guest dramaturg Gt. Lakes Theater Festival, 1988; mem. archives task force Folly Theatre, 1982-83; artistic advisor New Directions Theatre Co., 1983-90; hon. lectr. Mid.-Am. State Univs. Assn., 1986-87; mem. U.S.-U.S.S.R. Joint Commn. on Theatre Historiography, 1989; mem.adv. bd. Contemporary World Writers, 1991—; lectr. univs. Budapest, Pecs, Debrecen, Hungary, 1992; vis. prof. Hosei U., Tokyo, 1993. Author: Tennessee Williams, 1979, Tom Stoppard, 1981, Federico Garcia Lorca, 1984, (play) Miss Millay Was Right, 1982 (John Gassner Meml. Playwriting award 1982), The History of World Theater: From the English Restoration to the Present, 1991 (Choice Outstanding Acad. Book award 1991), Chow Chow Pizza, 1995 (Kansas City Gorilla Theatre First Prize, winner Stages '95 Competition, Dallas), (book) Love's Labour's Lost: Critical Essays, 1997; (opera libretto) Duse and D'Annunzio, 1987; (with Daniel J. Watermeier) The History of North American Theater: The United States, Canada, and Mexico from Pre-Columbian Times to the Present, 1998; co-editor: Shakespeare Companies and Festivals: An International Guide, 1995; book rev. editor: Theatre Jour., 1984-86; assoc. editor: Shakespeare Around the Globe: A Guide to Notable Postwar Revivals; mem. editl. bd. Theatre History Studies, 1981-87, 89—, Studies in Am. Drama, 1945 to the present, 1984-93, 19th Century Theatre Jour., 1984-95, Bookmark Press, Tennessee Williams Rev., 1985-87, Dramatic Theory and Criticism, 1986—, On-Stage Studies, The Elizabethan Rev., 1992-99, Theatre Symposium, 1994—, The Oxfordian, 1998—, Estreno Contemporary Spanish Plays, 1998—, So. Ill. U. Press Theater in the Americas series, 2000—; contbr. articles and book and theatre revs. to profl. publs. Hon. co-founder, bd. dirs. Heart of Am. Shakespeare Festival, 1991—, v.p., 2000—; bd. dirs. Edgar Snow Meml. Fund, 1993—; active UMKC Grad. Coun., 2001—, acad. stds. com. Coll. Arts and Scis., 2001—. Fulbright grantee U. Caen, Normandy, France, 1962-63, NEH grantee, 1971, 80, faculty rsch. grantee U. Mo., 1985, 86, 90, 91, tchr. seminar grantee Mo. Humanities Coun., 1993, 96, Disting. Alumni award U. Mont., 1998; grad. fellow U. Wis., 1966-67, Trustees fellow U. Kansas City, 1987-88; inductee Coll. Fellows Am. Theatre, bd. mem., 2000—, sec., 2001—. Mem. MLA, Am. Soc. Theatre Rsch. (mem. exec. com. 1984-90, program chair 1995), Shakespeare Theatre Assn. Am. (sec. 1991-93), Internat. Fedn. for Theatre Rsch. (del. gen. assembly 1985), Am. Theatre Assn. (commn. on theatre rsch. 1981-87, chmn. 1984-86), Theatre Libr. Assn., Dramatists Guild, Literary Mgrs. and Dramaturgs Am., Shakespeare Oxford So., Mid.-Am. Theatre Conf. (chair grad. rsch. paper competition 1985), Am. Theatre and Drama Soc. (v.p. 1995-97, pres. 1997-99), Nat. League of Am. PEN Women (bd. mem. Kansas City-Westport br.), Assn. for Theatre in Higher Edn. (v.p. for awards 2001—, Outstanding Tchr. award 2001), Internat. Al Jolson Soc., Lewis and Clark Heritage Found. Roman Catholic. Avocations: travel, theatre, continental cuisine. Home: 528 E 56th St Kansas City MO 64110-2769 Office: Mo Repertory Theatre Dept Theatre 5100 Rockhill Rd Kansas City MO 64110-2481 Fax: (816) 235-6532. E-mail: LondreF@umkc.edu.

LONDRIGAN, PAUL JAMES, business educator; b. Flint, Mich., Sept. 23, 1942; s. James A. and Evelyn L. (Ptaszenski) L.; children: Heather Lynn, Francie Leah; m. Desiree Dawn Wellsted, Aug. 13, 1977; children: Jason James, Erika Dawn, Sean Patrick. Student, Flint Jr. Coll., 1960-62; BBA, Western Mich. U., 1965, M of Bus. Edn., 1969. Sr. clk. Fisher Body Flint Plant #1, 1965-70; tchr. driver's edn. Grand Blanc (Mich.) High Sch., 1971-76; tchr., coach Algonac (Mich.) High Sch., 1970-71, Southwestern High Sch., Flint, 1971-74; instr. Montcalm Community Coll., Sidney, Mich., 1988-89; prof., advisor, coord. mktg. mgmt. program Mott Community Coll., Flint, 1974—. Coach Am. Youth Soccer Orgn., Grand Blanc; basketball coach Holy Family Cath. Sch., Grand Blanc, 1990-91, 97-98; head boys soccer coach Flint No. H.S., 1997. Recipient Talented Tenth Support award Beta Psi Club, 1983, 84, 89; Named Tchr. of Yr. Sch. of Bus., 1987-88, 90-91. Mem. Am. Mktg. Assn. Home: 5224 Copley Square Rd Grand Blanc MI 48439-8642 Office: Mott Community Coll 1401 E Court St Flint MI 48503-6208

LONE, RITA JOAN, retired linen service manager; b. New Castle, Ind., Jan. 29, 1938; d. Alva Dale and Edna Jane (Walker) L. BS in Edn., Ind. Wesleyn U., 1961. Registered exec. housekeeper, laundry and linen dir. Tchr. Avilla (Ind.) High Sch., 1961-63, Peru (Ind.) Jr. High and High Sch., 1963-66, R.J. Basket Jr. High Sch., Jonesboro, Ind., 1966-67; asst. chemist Marion (Ind.) Gen. Hosp., 1967-71, supr. 2nd shift, 1971-79, med. technologist, 1979-81, instr. ednl. svcs., 1981-88, mgr. environ. and linen svcs., 1988-94. Instr. Ind. Wesleyan U., Marion, 1976-78. Vol. Am. Cancer Soc., Marion, 1981-87; instr. Arthritis Found., Marion, 1985-88; active, instr. CPR, Am. Heart Assn. Mem. Nat. Assn. Instnl. Linen Mgmt. (chair ednl. affairs com. 1995—), Ind. Assn. Instnl. Linen Mgmt. (treas.), Nat. Exec. Housekeepers Assn. (chpt. pres., 2d vice gov. Cen. dist., gov. 1995—). Avocations: reading, hiking, canoeing, traveling, spectator sports. Home: 11959 Lancewood Dr Roscommon MI 48653-9006

LONECK, BARRY MARTIN, social work researcher, educator; b. Erie, Pa., Dec. 5, 1954; s. Francis and Mary Gertrude (Gent) L.; m. Andrea Bernice Fabrizi, Aug. 6, 1977; children: Heather, Gabrielle, Kimberly, Stephanie. BA, Case Western Res. U., 1976, MS in Social Adminstrn., 1978, PhD in Social Welfare, 1985. Alcoholism counselor, researcher The Lakeland Inst., Lorain, Ohio, 1981-89; asst. prof. Sch. of Social Welfare, SUNY, Albany, 1989-97, assoc. prof., 1997—. Co-author: (monograph) Research and Development of An Alcohol Abuse Prevention Program at Case Western Res. U., 1980; editl. adv. bd. Jour. of Social Work Practice in the Addictions; contbr. numerous articles to profl. jours. Faculty mem. Ctr. for Study of Issues in Publ. Mental Health, Albany; bd. dirs. Pahl, Inc., Troy, N.Y., Pahl Facilities, Inc., Troy. Rsch. fellow Nat. Assn. State Mental Health Program Dirs. Rsch. Inst., 1991-93. Mem. NASW, Acad. Cert. Social Workers (cert.), Soc. for Social Work and Rsch., United Univ. Professions. Roman Catholic. Avocation: amateur radio. Home: 15 Cedar Ln Gansevoort NY 12831-1055 Office: SUNY Sch Social Welfare 135 Western Ave Albany NY 12203-1011 Business E-Mail: loneck@csc.albany.edu.

LONEGAN, THOMAS LEE, retired restaurant corporation executive; b. Kansas City, Mo., July 4, 1932; s. Thomas F. and Edna L. (Payton) L.; m. Donna F. Ednie, Apr. 11, 1958; children: Timothy L., John M. BSME, Gen. Motors Inst., 1955; MS in Mgmt., USN Post Grad Sch., 1963; grad., Indsl. Coll. Armed Forces, Washington, 1970; postgrad., Calif. State U., Long Beach, 1979-83; grad., Coll. for Fin. Planning, Denver, 1984. Registered profl. engr., Mass.; CFP. Commd. ensign USN, 1956, advanced through grades to comdr., 1978; dir. pub. works, officer in charge of constrn. Naval Weapons Sta., Seal Beach, Calif., 1974-78; ret., 1978; dir. cen. staff McAthco Enterprises, Inc., Camarillo, Calif., 1985, exec. v.p., CFO, 1986-90, pres., CEO, 1991-93, exec. v.p., CFO, 1994-95; ret. Bd. dirs. McAthco Enterprises; exec. v.p. engring. Orange County Engring. Coun., 1977-78. Author: Analysis and Attenuation of Air Borne Noise in Industrial Plants, 1955, Formalized Training of Maintenance Personnel, 1963. Vol. various couns. Boy Scouts Am., 1968-76. Decorated Bronze Star with combat device, Meritorious Svc. medal, Jt. Svcs. Commendation medal, Navy Achievement medal; decorated Order of Chamoro (Guam); named Sr. Engr./Arch. Yr. Naval Facilities Engr. Command, 1972; recipient Silver medal Boy Scouts Am., 1974. Fellow Soc. Am. Mil. Engrs., Ret. Officers Assn., GM Inst. Robots Honor Soc.; mem. Beta Gamma Sigma. Avocations: reading, theater, music, foreign travel. E-mail: tomlonegan@socal.rr.com.

LONERGAN, KEVIN, lawyer; b. Racine, Wis., Oct. 2, 1954; s. Ralph and M. Janet L.; m. Elizabeth Ison, Oct. 10, 1981; children: Lindsey, Kristen, Emily, Marc. BS, USAF Acad., 1976; JD, U. Wis., 1979. Bar: Wis. 1979, U.S. Dist. Ct. (we. dist.), Wis. 1979; cert. Nat. Bd. Trial Advocates. Commd. 2nd lt. USAF, 1976, med. retirement, 1977; asst. dist. atty. Eau Claire County, Eau Claire, Wis., 1979-81; assoc. Thompson, Parke & Heim, Ltd., LaCrosse, 1981-82; ptnr., v.p. Herrling, Clark, Hartzheim & Siddall, Ltd., Appleton, 1982—. Apptd. ct. commr. Outagamie County, 1994—; host (TV program) You and the Law, 1988—; regular guest WHBY "Open Line" Radio show, 1995—. Bd. dirs. Eau Claire Kinship Program, 1981; bd dirs., v.p., pres. Casa Clare Half-Way House, Appleton, 1984-87; mem. United Way Cabinet, 1988, 90. Mem. ATLA, Wis. Acad. Trial Lawyers (bd. dirs. 1991—, treas. 1996, sec. 1997, v.p. 1998, pres.-elect 1999, pres. 2000, past pres. 2001), Outagamie County Bar Assn. (sec. 1992-93, v.p. 1993-94, pres. 1994-95). Roman Catholic. Avocations: family, physical fitness. Home: 44 N Crestway Ct Appleton WI 54913-9510 Office: Herrling Clark Hartzheim & Siddall 800 N Lynndale Dr Appleton WI 54914-3017 E-mail: LKonergan@HerrlingClark.com.

LONERGAN, THOMAS FRANCIS, III, criminal justice consultant; b. Bklyn., July 28, 1941; s. Thomas Francis and Katherine Josephine (Roth) L.; m. Irene L. Kaucher, Dec. 14, 1963; 1 son, Thomas F. BA, Calif. State U., Long Beach, 1966, MA, 1973; MPA, Pepperdine U., L.A., 1976; postgrad., U. So. Calif., L.A., 1973-76. Dep. sheriff Los Angeles County Sheriff's Dept., 1963-70; U.S. Govt. program analyst, 1968—; fgn. service officer USIA, Lima, Peru, 1970-71; dep. sheriff to lt. Los Angeles Sheriff's Office, 1971-76, aide lt. to div. chief, 1976-80; dir. Criminal Justice Cons., Downey, Calif., 1977—. Cons. Public Adminstrv. Service, Chgo., 1972-75, Nat. Sheriff's Assn., 1978, 79; cons. Nat. Inst. Corrections, Washington, 1977-89, coordinator jail ctr., 1981-82 ; tchr. N. Calif. Regional Criminal Justice Acad., 1977-79; lectr. Nat. Corrections Acad., 1980-83; spl. master Chancery Ct. Davidson County, Tenn., 1980-82, U.S. Dist. Ct. (no. dist.) Ohio, 1984-85, Santa Clara Superior Ct. (Calif.), 1983-89, Calif. Supreme Ct., 1984-87; U.S. Dist. Ct. Ga., Atlanta, 1986-87, U.S. Dist. Ct. (no. dist.) Calif., 1982-93—, U.S. Dist. Ct. (no. dist.) Idaho, 1986, U.S. Dist. Ct. Oreg. 1986, U.S. Dist. Ct. Portland 1987, U.S. Dist. (no. dist.) Calif. 1984-89, 95-97. Author: California-Past, Present & Future, 1968; Training-A Corrections Perspective, 1979; AIMS-Correctional Officer; Liability-A Correctional Perspective; Liability Law for Probation Administrators; Liability Reporter; Probation Liability Reporter; Study Guides by Aims Media. Mem. Nat. Sheriff's Assn. Roman Catholic.

LONERGAN, WALLACE GUNN, economics educator, management consultant; b. Potlatch, Idaho, Mar. 18, 1928; s. Willis Gerald and Lois (Gunn) L.; m. Joan Laurie Penoyer, June 1, 1952; children: Steven Mark, Kevin James. BA, Coll. Idaho, 1950; MBA, U. Chgo., 1955, PhD, 1960. Asst. dir., asst. prof. bus. Indsl. Relations Ctr. U. Chgo., 1960-70, assoc. dir., assoc. prof., 1970-74, dir., prof., 1974-84; vis. prof. Rikkyo U., Tokyo, 1985; vis. fellow Merton Coll. Oxford (Eng.) U., 1986; chair, prof. bus., econs. divsn. Albertson Coll. Idaho, Caldwell, 1987—. V.p. Human Resources Research Cons., Chgo., 1980-87. Author: Leadership and Morale, 1960, Group Leadership, 1974, Performance Appriasal, 1978, Leadership and Management, 1979. Chmn. Episcopal Commn. on Higher Edn., Chgo., 1970-80, mgmt. com. United Way Chgo., 1982-85. 1st lt. U.S. Army, 1950-53, Korea. Named Disting. Alumni Coll. Idaho, 1962; vis. scholar Internat. Anglican Exchange, N.Y.C., 1976, Tokyo, 1986. Mem. Internat. House Japan, Internat. Indsl. Relations Research Assn., Acad. Mgmt., Rotary. Avocations: power walking, hiking. Home: 812 E Linden St Caldwell ID 83605-5335 Office: Albertson Coll Idaho Bus Econs Divsn 2112 Cleveland Blvd Caldwell ID 83605-4432

LONEY, GLENN MEREDITH, drama educator; b. Sacramento, Dec. 24, 1928; s. David Merton and Marion Gladys (Busher) L. BA, U. Calif., Berkeley, 1950; MA, U. Wis., 1951; PhD, Stanford U., 1953. Teaching asst. U. Calif., Berkeley, 1949-50, Stanford U., Calif., 1952-53; instr. San Francisco State U., 1955-56, U. Nev., Las Vegas, 1956; prof. U. Md., Europe, N. Africa, Middle East, 1956-59; instr. Hofstra U., Hempstead, N.Y., 1959-61, Adelphi U., Garden City, 1959-61; prof. speech and theater Bklyn. Coll. and City U. Grad. Ctr., 1961-71, prof. theater, 1971—. Author: Briefing and Conference Techniques, 1959, Peter Brook Midsummer Night's Dream, 1974, The Shakespeare Complex, 1974, Young Vic Scapino, 1980, The House of Mirth-The Play of the Novel, 1981, Twentieth Century Theatre, 1983, California Gold Rush Drama, Musical Theatre in America, 1984, Unsung Genius, 1984, Creating Careers in Music Theatre, 1988, Staging Shakespeare, 1990, Peter Brook: Oxford to Orghast, 1997; editor: The Modernist; chief correspondent N.Y. Theatre wire and N.Y. Mus. Wire, Curator's Choice on Internet, 1996—, founding editor, project dir., Modern Theatre Online, NYU. Served with AUS, 1953-55. Fellow Am. Scandinavian Found.; mem. AAUP, Am. Theatre Critics Assn., Outer Critics Circle (sec.), Am. Music Critics Assn., Am. Soc. Theatre Research, Internat. Fedn. Theatre Research, Theatre Library Assn., Theatre Hist. Soc., Internat. Assn. Theatre Critics, Phi Beta Kappa, Alpha Mu Gamma, Phi Eta Sigma, Phi Delta Phi. Democrat. Office: 3 E 71st St New York NY 10021-4154

LONG, ALFRED B. former oil company executive, consultant; b. Aug. 4, 1909; s. Jessie A. and Ada (Beckwith) L.; m. Sylvia V. Thomas, Oct. 29, 1932; 1 child, Kathleen Sylvia (Mrs. E.A. Pearson, II). Student, S. Park Jr. Coll., 1928-29, Lamar U., 1947-56, U. Tex., 1941; grad., Citizens Police Acad. With Sun Oil Co., Beaumont, Tex., 1931-69, driller geophys. dept., surveyor engring. dept., engr. operating dept., engr. prodn. lab., 1931-59, regional supr., 1960-69, cons., 1969—. Inventor oil well devices. Sr.'s bd. dirs. Bapt. Hosp., Beaumont; chaplain sr.'s vols. bd. dirs. S.E. Tex. Rehab. Hosp., Beaumont, Srs.-Lawmen Coun.; chaplain; Jefferson County Program Planning Com., 1964; tech. adv. group Oil Well Drilling Inst., Lamar U., Beaumont. Recipient Nat. Jefferson award for Outstanding Pub. Svc. Am. Inst. for Pub. Svc., 1992, Cmty. Svc. award Quarter Century Wireless Assn., 1994, Sensational Srs. of the U.S. honor CBS TV, 1994, Hometown Heroes Sta. CH6TV, 1995, Nat. CBS Cable The Best of US, 1997, Eye on the People, 1997 Ageless Hero Cmty. Involvement Year 2000 award Blue Cross-Blue Shield; Olympic Torch bearer, 1996, Police 100 Club (life mem. 1998), Pub. Svc. award Beaumont Police Dept., 2000. Mem. IEEE, Soc. Petroleum Engrs., Am. Petroleum Inst., Am. Assn. Petroleum Geologists, Houston Geol. Soc., Gulf Coast Engring. and Sci. Soc. (treas. 1962-65), U.S. Power Squadron, Soc. Wireless Pioneers, Citizen Police Acad. (life), Sheriff's Assn. Tex.

LONG, ANDRE EDWIN, law educator, lawyer; b. San Francisco, Dec. 28, 1957; s. Edwin John and Anna (Suss) L.; m. Michele Jean Dubinsky, Oct. 4, 1986; children: Christian Andre, Katrina Marie. BA, U. Pacific, 1979; MBA, Golden Gate U., 1981; JD, Southwestern U., 1982. Bar: Hawaii 1984, D.C. 1990, Wash. 2001, U.S. Ct. Appeals (9th cir.) 1984. Legal counsel Pure Water, Ltd., Manama, Bahrain, 1982-84; pvt. practice Honolulu, 1984-85; sr. contracts negotiator Litton Data Systems Corp., Van Nuys, Calif., 1985-87; contracts mgr. Eaton, Am. Nucleonics Corp., Westlake Village, 1987-92; owner, broker A. Long Realty, Ridgecrest, 1989—; asst. prof. contract law Air Force Inst. Tech., Dayton, 1992-99; assoc. counsel Navy Office of Gen. Counsel, China Lake, 1999—. Lectr. Tech. Tng. Corp., 1991-92; instr. Oxnard Coll., 1990-92, George Washington U. Law Sch./ESI Govt. Contract Law Program; asst. adj. prof. Embry-Riddle U. Author: U.S. Immigration and Visa Laws Made Simple, 1985, 2d edit., 1991, Government Contract Law, 1995, 96, 98, 99, Negotiating Government Contracts, 1996; editor The Clause, 1995-2000, Contract Mgmt. Jour., 1998-2000, Jour. Pub. Procurement.. Fellow Nat. Contract Mgmt. Assn. (pres. China Lake chpt. 2001-02); mem. Hawaii Bar Assn., D.C. Bar Assn., Aircraft Owners and Pilots Assn., Bd. Contracts Appeals Bar Assn. (chmn. publs. com. 1995-2000, bd. govs. 1997-2000), Canyon Ranch Assn. (chmn. 2000—). Avocations: scuba diving, snow skiing, sailing, flying. Office: NAWCWD Code 111000D 1 Adminstration Cir Ridgecrest CA 93555 E-mail: longae@navair.navy.mil.

LONG, ANN MARIE, health facility administrator; b. Hartford, Conn., Oct. 9, 1945; d. John and Bridie (Griffin) O'Connell; m. Michael T. Long, Sept. 9, 1967; children: Michael, Maura, Deirdre. Diploma, St. Francis Hosp., Hartford, 1966; BSN magna cum laude, U. Hartford, 1978; M. in Health Care Mgmt., The Hartford Grad. Ctr., 1987. RN, Conn.; cert. in advanced continuity of care; cert. in nursing adminstrn.; cert. in case mgmt. Critical care staff nurse St. Francis Hosp. and Med. Ctr., Hartford, 1966-67, continuing care coord., 1978-83, nursing supr., 1983-90, dir. continuing care, 1990—, Mt. Sinai Hosp., Hartford, 1992—; nursing instr. St. Francis Sch. Nursing, 1967-68; dir. of continuing care St. Francis Hosp. and Med. Ctr., Mt. Sinai Hosp., 1992-95; dir. divsn. continuum of care mgmt. St. Francis Hosp. and Med. Ctr., 1995. Profl. adv. com. Vis. Nurses Assn. Farmington Valley. Justice of the Peace, Simsbury, Conn. Mem. Conn. Nurses Assn., Conn. Hosp. Assn. (continuing care coords. conf.), Conn. Assn. Continuity Care, Case Mgmt. Soc. Am., Case Mgmt. Soc. New Eng., Am. Orgn. Nurse Execs., Sigma Theta Tau, Alpha Chi. Home: 9 Metacom Dr Simsbury CT 06070-1851 E-mail: along@stfranciscare.org.

LONG, ANTHONY ARTHUR, classics educator; b. Manchester, Eng., Aug. 17, 1937; came to U.S. 1983; s. Tom Arthur and Phyllis Joan (LeGrice) L.; m. Janice Calloway, Dec. 30, 1960 (div. 1969); 1 child, Stephen Arthur; m. Mary Kay Flavell, May 25, 1970 (div. 1990); 1 child, Rebecca Jane; m. Monique Marie-Jeanne Elias, Mar. 22, 1997. BA, U. Coll. London, 1960; PhD, U. London, 1964. Lectr. classics U. Otago, Dunedin, N.Z., 1961-64; lectr. classics U. Nottingham, Eng., 1964-66; lectr. Greek and Latin U. Coll. London, 1966-71; reader in Greek and Latin U. London, 1971-73; Gladstone prof. Greek U. Liverpool, Eng., 1973-83; prof. classics U. Calif., Berkeley, 1982—; pub. orator U. Liverpool, Eng., 1981-83; Irving Stone prof. lit. U. Calif., Berkeley, 1991—, chmn. dept. classics, 1986-90. Mem. Inst. Advanced Study, Princeton, N.J., 1970, 79; vis. prof. U. Munich, 1973, Ecole Normale Supérieure, Paris, 1993, 2001; Cardinal Mercier prof. philosophy U. Louvain, Belgium, 1991; mem. Mellon Fellowships Selection Com., 1984-90; mem. selection com. Stanford U. Humanities Coun., 1985-86; Corbett lectr. U. Cambridge, 1998-99; Faculty Rsch. lectr. U. Calif., Berkeley, 1999-2000. Author: Language and Thought in Sophocles, 1968 (Cromer Greek prize 1968), Problems in Stoicism, 1971, 96, Hellenistic Philosophy, 1974, 2d edit., 1986, (with Fortenbaugh and Huby) Theophrastus of Eresus, 1985, (with Sedley) The Hellenistic Philosophers, 1987, (with Dillon) The Question of Eclecticism, 1988, 96, (with Bastianini) Hierocles, 1992, (with others) Images and Ideologies, 1993, Stoic Studies, 1996, 2d edit., 2001, Cambridge Companion to Early Greek Philosophy, 1999, Epictetus, 2002; editor: Classical Quar., 1975-81, Classical Antiquity, 1987-90; gen. editor: (with Barnes) Clarendon Later Ancient Philosophers, 1987—. Served to lt. Royal Arty., Eng., 1955-57 Named hon. citizen City of Rhodes, Greece; sr. fellow humanities coun. Princeton U., 1978, Bye fellow Robinson Coll., Cambridge, 1982, Guggenheim fellow, 1986-87, sr. fellow Ctr. for Hellenic Studies, 1988-93, fellow NEH, 1990-91, Wissenschaftskolleg fellow, Berlin, 1991-92, William Evans fellow U. Otago, New Zealand, 1995. Fellow Am. Acad. Arts and Scis., Brit. Acad. (corr.); mem. Classical Assn., Aristotelian Soc., Am. Philol. Assn., Phi Beta Kappa (hon.). Avocations: music, walking, travel, bridge. Home: 32 Sunset Dr Kensington CA 94707-1139 Office: U Calif Dept Classics Berkeley CA 94720-0001 E-mail: aalong@uclink4.berkeley.edu.

LONG, BERT LOUIS, JR. artist; b. Houston, Sept. 27, 1940; s. Bertran Louis and Constance (Morris) L.; m. Connie Dianne Kelly, Aug. 15, 1964; children: Deborah Denise Foster, John Alan, Bertran Louis III. Class A tchg. credential adult edn., UCLA, 1972. Tchr. adult edn. L.A. (Calif.) Unified Sch. Dist., 1972-75; owner, exec. chef Berts Gourmet Restaurant, Klamath Falls, Oreg., 1975-76; sous chef Hilton Hotels, Las Vegas, Nev., 1976; exec. sous chef Ritz Carlton Hotels, Chgo., 1976-77, Hyatt Regency Hotel, Houston, 1977-78; exec. chef Holiday Inn, 1978-79. Chmn. Artists in Action, 1979-83; visual arts panelist allocations com. Cultural Arts Coun., visual arts subpanelist selection com., 1988; adv. panel appointee Task Force Midtown Arts Ctr.; exec. com. mem. Houston Arts Alliance; panelist visual arts Tex. Commn. on the Arts, 1990; presenter in field. One-man shows include Butler Gallery, Houston, 1988, Art Mus. S.E. Tex., Beaumont, 1987-88, Dallas (Tex.) Mus. Art, 1988, Tex. A&M Meml. Student Ctr., College Station, 1989, Barry Whistler Gallery, Dallas, 1989, Allan Stone Gallery, N.Y.C., 1990, Lew Allen Gallery, Santa Fe, 1991, Contemporary Arts Mus., Houston, 1991, Lyons Matrix Gallery, Austin, 1992, The Fabric Workshop Mus., Phila., 1993, complejo Cultural San Francisco, Spain, 1996, San Francisco/Ctr. de Expericiones San Jorge de Caceres, others; exhibited in group shows at Dallas (Tex.) Mus. Art, 1990, Calif. Afro-Am. Mus., L.A., 1990, Duke U. Mus. Art, Durham, N.C., 1990, Studio Mus. in Harlem, N.Y.C., 1990, Palm Springs (Fla.) Desert Mus., 1990, Alternative Mus., N.Y.C., 1991, Contemporary Arts Mus., Houston, 1991, Barry Whistler Gallery, Dallas, 1991, Sala 1, Rome, 1991, Am. Acad. in Rome, Italy, 1991, Lewallen Gallery, Santa Fe, 1991, Dishman Art Gallery, Beaumont, 1991, The Painted Bride Gallery, Phila., 1993, Lyons Matrix Gallery, Dallas, 1993, Mus. Fine Arts, Houston, 1993, The Galveston (Tex.) Arts Ctr., 1993, Amazing Space, Cleveland, Tex., 1994, First Interstate Bank, 1994, Irving Arts Ctr., Tex., 1996, others; represented in permanent collections including Huntington Art Gallery, U. Tex., Mus. Fine Arts, Houston, Dallas (Tex.) Mus. Art, Bell Telephone, Met. Mus. Art, Dinos of Calif., Spikes Pers., Erenwert Produce, Pfeffer Interests, Fleming Prodns., Craig Washington Law Firm, Highland Distributing, Mus. Comtemporary Art, Chgo. Libr., Ajuntamiento Berzocana, Fabric Workshop Mus., Mus. S.E. Tex., Inst. Mario Roso de Luna, Spain; pub. Houston ArtScene, 1979-88; performances include Fire/Falla Installations Canermero, Cáceres, Spain, 1994-96; contbr. articles to profl. jours. With USMC, 1959-64. Recipient proclamation State of Tex., Tex. Senate, 1990; named Outstanding Texan, State of Tex. Ho. of Reps., 1991. Fellow Soc. Fellows Am. Acad. in Room; mem. Tex. Fine Art Assn. (internat. bd. dirs. 1992—). Avocations: traveling, reading, gardening, photography, writing. Office: Lyons Matrix Gallery 5715 Sam Houston Cir Austin TX 78731-3336

LONG, BEVERLY GLENN, retired lawyer; b. Omaha, Mar. 1, 1923; d. Max Edgar and Allise Katherine Dorothea (Nielsen) Glenn; m. Jacob Emery Long, May 6, 1950 AB in Econs., U. Chgo., 1944; LLB, Columbia U., 1947. Bar: N.Y. 1948, R.I. 1951, U.S. Dist. Ct. (so. dist.) N.Y. 1949, U.S. Tax Ct. 1949, U.S. Dist. Ct. R.I. 1951, U.S. Ct. Appeals (2d cir.) 1949, U.S. Ct. Appeals (1st cir.) 1958, U.S. Ct. Claims 1960, U.S. Supreme Ct. 1960. Assoc. Edwards & Angell LLP, Providence, 1950-59, ptnr., 1959-86, of counsel, 1986—. Adv. com. child welfare svcs. R.I. Dept. Social Welfare, 1959-66; pers. com. Big Bros. R.I., 1964-67; mem. Gov.'s Com. on Status of Women, 1965; chmn. R.I. Children's Code Commn., 1967-74; fundraiser Columbia U. Sch. Law,

1947-88, R.I. area for U. Chgo., 1951—; bd. dirs. Child Welfare League of Am., Inc., 1975-80, Children's Friend and Svc., Inc., 1966-75, 77-79, Providence chpt. ARC, 1967-72; bd. dirs. St. Mary's Home for Children, 1966-80, v.p., 1978-80; bd. dirs. R.I. Conf. Social Work, 1961-66, Coun. Cmty. Svcs., Inc., 1957-64; task force evaluation of criminal justice program LEAA, 1974-78; active United Way Southeastern New Eng., Inc., 1951-81, ad hoc adv. com., exec. budget com., 1971-78, bd. dirs., 1973-74, ABA sr. lawyers divsn. coun., 1986-91, sec., 1991-95. Recipient citation for pub. service U. Chgo., 1959 Fellow Am. Bar Found., R.I. Bar Found.; mem. ABA (Outstanding State Membership Chmn. award 1984), R.I. Bar Assn. (ho. dels., exec. com., pres., Merit award 1990), New Eng. Bar Assn. (bd. dirs. 1982-85), Fed. Bar Assn., Am. Law Inst., Am. Judicature Soc. (bd. dirs. 1988-90), U.S. Supreme Ct. Hist. Soc., U. Club R.I. Republican. Home: 200 Elmgrove Ave Providence RI 02906-4233

LONG, CARL FERDINAND, engineering educator; b. N.Y.C., Aug. 6, 1928; s. Carl and Marie Victoria (Wellnitz) L.; m. Joanna Margarida Tavares, July 23, 1955; children: Carl Ferdinand, Barbara Anne. S.B., MIT, 1950, S.M., 1952; D.Eng., Yale U., 1964; A.M. (hon.), Dartmouth Coll., 1971. Registered profl. engr., N.H. Instr. Thayer Sch. Engring., Dartmouth Coll., Hanover, N.H., 1954-57, asst. prof., 1957-64, assoc. prof., 1964-70, prof., 1970-94, assoc. dean, 1970, dean, 1972-84, dean emeritus, 1984—; prof. emeritus, 1994—; dir. Cook Design Ctr. Thayer Sch. Engring., Dartmouth Coll., 1984-94. Engr. Western Electric Co., Alaska, 1956-57; v.p. ops., dir. Controlled Enivronment, 1975-81; pres., dir. Q-S Oxygern Processes, Inc., 1979-84; N.H. Water Supply and Pollution Control Com., U.S. Army Small Arms Systems Agy.; mem. New Eng. Constrn. Edn. Adv. Coun., 1971-74; mem. adv. com. U.S. Patenta and Trademark Office, 1975-79; mem. ad hoc vis. com. Engrs. Coun. for Profl. Devel., 1973-81; pres., dir. Roan of Thayer, Inc., 1986-93; bd. dirs. Micro Tool Co., Inc., Micro Weighing Systems, Inc., 1986-91, Roan Ventures, Inc., 1987-91; pres., dir. Hanover Water Works Co., 1989-97. Mem. Hanover Town Planning Bd., 1963-75, chmn., 1966-74; trustee Mt. Washington Obs., 1975-92; bd. dirs. Eastman Community Assn., 1977-80; mem. corp. Mary Hitchcock Meml. Hosp., 1974—. NSF Sci. Faculty fellow, 1961-62; recipient Robert Fletcher award Thayer Sch. of Engring., 1985, Fellow Members awd., Am. Soc. for Engineering Education, 1992. Fellow AAAS, ASCE, Am. Soc. Engring. Edn. (chmn. New Eng. sect. 1977-78, chmn. council of sects. Zone 1, dir. 1981-83); mem. Sigma Xi, Chi Epsilon, Tau Beta Pi. Republican. Baptist. Home: 25 Reservoir Rd Hanover NH 03755-1311

LONG, CECIL LENEIR, engineer; b. Philadelphia, Miss., Dec. 8, 1938; s. John Cecil and Sudie Elizabeth (Fulton) L.; m. Wanda Jo Lyle, May 30, 1963; children: John Andrew, Dana Elizabeth. BA in Chemistry, Miss. So. Coll., 1961; postgrad. U. So. Miss., 1971-72; MSEE, Southeast Inst. Tech., 1983. Quality control mgr. Johnson & Johnson Co., Chgo., 1963-65; supr., prodn. supt. May Alumnium Inc., El Campo, Tex., 1965-68; chemist Dow Chem. Co., Russellville, Ark., 1969-70; prodn. supr. Armstrong Rubber Co., Natchez, Miss., 1970-73; quality assurance mgr. Coyne Cylinder Co., Huntsville, Ala., 1973-79; systems analyst Delta Rsch. Inc., Huntsville, 1979-87; sr. engr. CAS, Inc., Huntsville, 1987-91; sr. systems analyst, Johnson Controls, 1992-94; quality assurance cons. Fairbanks Scales, Meridian, Miss., 1994-95; sr. engr. EG&G Spl. Projects, Las Vegas, 1995—. Patentee in field. Served to 1st. lt. U.S. Army, 1961-63. Recipient Disting. Svc. award U. So. Miss., 1983, Alumni Continuous Svc. award, 1989. Mem. NRA, Am. Soc. for Quality Control, Am. Def. Preparedness Assn., Jaycees (past officer El Campo), U. So. Miss. Alumni Assn. (Huntsville chpt. pres. 1982-83, 87-88), Assn. Old Crows, Masons, Kappa Alpha. Republican. Baptist. Home: 200 Foxgate Ave # 25-g Hattiesburg MS 39402-1851

LONG, CEDRIC WILLIAM, health research executive; b. Mpls., Mar. 4, 1937; s. Tracy Steven and Clarice Cecilia (Robertson) L. BA, UCLA, 1960, MA, 1962; PhD, Princeton U., 1966. Postdoctoral fellow U. Calif., Berkeley, 1966-68; instr. NYU Med. Sch., N.Y.C., 1968-70; lab. chief Flow Labs., Rockville, Md., 1970-76, Litton Industries, Frederick, 1976-80; preclin. chief NIH, Nat. Cancer Inst., DCT, Bethesda, 1980-86; gen. mgr. Nat. Cancer Inst.-Frederick Cancer R&D Ctr., 1986-97; spl. asst. to dir. Nat. Cancer Inst. - Divsn. Extramural Activities, 1997-2000, asst. dir., 2000—. Home: 2 Basildon Cir Rockville MD 20850-2724

LONG, CHARLES FARRELL, insurance company executive; b. Charlottesville, Va., Nov. 19, 1933; s. Cicel Early and Ruth Elizabeth (Shifflett) L.; m. Ann Tilley, May 28, 1960; children: C. Farrell, Linda. CLU; chartered fin. analyst. Founder, pres. Casualty Underwriters, Inc., Charlottesville, 1959-72, Group Underwriters, Inc., Charlottesville, 1959—. Trustee P.A.I. Ins. Trust. Mem. Assay Commn. of U.S., 1975; bd. dirs. Am. Heart Assn.; mem. U. Va. Student Aid Found. With USN, 1954-58. Mem. Am. Soc. CLUs, Ctrl. Va. CLUs Assn. (dir.), Va. Press Assn., Inland Press Assn. Chgo., Million Dollar Round Table. Creator Queen's medal for Queen Elizabeth, 1976. Home: 1400 W Leigh Dr Charlottesville VA 22901-7719 Office: Madison Park Charlottesville VA 22903

LONG, CHARLES FRANKLIN, retired corporate communications executive; b. Norman, Okla., Jan. 19, 1938; s. James Franklin and Mary Katherine (Nemecek) L.; m. Joan Hampton, Sept. 16, 1961; children: Charles Franklin, David Hampton, Stephen Andrew. BA, U. Okla., 1961. Sports writer San Angelo (Tex.) Standard-Times, 1961-62; news reporter Norman Transcript, 1962-63; assoc. editor Sooner mag., U. Okla., 1963-66; news editor Quill mag., Chgo., 1967-71, editor, 1971-80; sr. editor Cahners Pub. Co., Des Plaines, Ill., 1981-83; mgr. internal communications Beatrice Cos., Inc., Chgo., 1983-86, dir. communications, 1986-88; dir. corp. communications Tellabs, Inc., Lisle, Ill., 1989-99. Author: With Optimism for the Morrow, 1965. Bd. dirs. Wheaton (Ill.) Youth Outreach, 1988-94, Western DuPage Spl. Recreation Assn. Found., 1994-98; chmn. exec. com. Wheaton Grand Theatre, 1999-00. Named to Okla. Journalism Hall of Fame, 1979. Mem. Internat. Assn. Bus. Communicators (Spectra Excellence award Chgo.), Soc. Profl. Journalists-Sigma Delta Chi, Beta Theta Pi. United Methodist. Home: 1106 N Washington St Wheaton IL 60187-3860 E-mail: charlielong@prodigy.net. *My parents, through gentle persuasion and by their own example, taught their sons to be curious and conscientious. I suppose it was those principles which eventually led me into a career in journalism and to come to realize that the supreme test of any good journalism is the measure of its public service— to serve the truth; to subscribe to ethical standards; to enlighten the public as to the nature and meaning of journalistic pursuits, especially in how those efforts support the American people's stake in their First Amendment to the Constitution.*

LONG, CHARLES THOMAS, lawyer, history educator; b. Denver, Dec. 19, 1942; s. Charles Joseph and Jessie Elizabeth (Squire) L.; m. Susan Rae Kircheis, Aug. 9, 1967; children: Brian Christopher, Lara Elizabeth, Kevin Charles. BA, Dartmouth Coll., 1965; JD cum laude, Harvard U., 1970. Bar: Calif. 1971, U.S. Dist. Ct. (cen. dist.) Calif. 1971, U.S. Ct. Appeals (9th cir.) 1975, D.C. 1980, U.S. Dist. Ct. D.C. 1981, U.S. Ct. Claims 1995. Assoc. Gibson, Dunn & Crutcher, Los Angeles, 1970-77, ptnr., 1977-79, Washington, 1979-83; dep. gen. counsel Fed. Home Loan Bank Bd., 1984-85; ptnr. Jones, Day, Reavis & Pogue, 1985-98; grad. tchg. asst. hist. dept. George Washington U., 1998—. Bar: Calif. 1971, U.S. Dist. Ct. (ctrl. dist.) Calif. 1971, U.S. Ct. Appeals (9th cir.) 1975, D.C. 1980, U.S. Dist. Ct. 1981, U.S. Ct. Fed. Claims 1995. Contbr. articles to profl. jours. Mem. Chesapeake Bay Maritime Mus., Friends of the Nat. Maritime Mus., Greenwich, Eng.; pres. Leigh Mill Meadows Assn., Great Falls, Va., 1980. Served to lt. USNR, 1965-67. Mem. ABA, Calif. Bar Assn., D.C. Bar Assn., Coun. for Excellence in Govt., Women in Housing and Fin., Dartmouth Lawyers Assn., Herrington Harbour Sailing Assn. (sec.-treas. 1996), Soc. for Mil. History, N.Am. Conf. on Brit. Studies, Navy Records Soc. (London), U.S. Naval Inst., Chesapeake Bay Maritime Mus., Friends of the Nat. Maritime Mus. (Greenwich, Eng.), Westwood Country Club (Vienna, Va.), Am. Hist. Assn. Republican. Methodist. Avocations: sailing, photography, computers, naval history.

LONG, CHRISTOPHER, toxicologist; b. Woodside, N.Y., June 13, 1949; s. Walter Anthony and Jeanne (Bishop) L.; m. Maureen Ann Otremba, Jan. 2, 1978; children: Elizabeth Marie, Matthew Christopher. BA in Chemistry, Marist, 1971; MS in Biomedicine, L.I. U., 1974; MS in Pharm./Toxicology, St. John's U., 1979, PhD in Toxicology, 1981. Diplomate Am. Bd. Forensic Toxicology. Toxicologist, supr. Nat. Health Labs., East Meadow, N.Y., 1972-73, N.Y. Med. Labs., Great Neck, 1973-74; adj. faculty St. John's U., Jamaica, 1983-85; toxicologist Nassau County Med. Examiner, East Meadow, 1974-85; adj. faculty So. Ill. U. Med. Sch., Springfield, 1986-88; chief toxicologist Ill. State Police, 1985-88; dir. toxicology, asst. prof. St. Louis U. Med. Sch., 1988—. Expert toxicologist, cons. FDA, 1990-94; chief toxicologist St. Louis County, 1991—. Contbr. articles to profl. jours. Leader Cub Scouts, 1991. Recipient Ednl. Rsch. award Soc. for Toxicology, 1981. Fellow Am. Acad. Forensic Scis.; mem. Soc. Forensic Toxicology, Internat. Soc. Forensic Toxicology, N.Y. Acad. Scis. Roman Catholic. Office: Saint Louis U Med Sch 1402 S Grand Blvd Saint Louis MO 63104-1004

LONG, CLARENCE DICKINSON, III, lawyer; b. Princeton, N.J., Feb. 7, 1943; s. Clarence Dickinson and Susanna Eckings (Larter) L.; children: Clarence IV, Andrew, Amanda, Victoria, Stephen. BA, Johns Hopkins U., 1965; JD, U. Md., 1971; postgrad., Judge Adv. Gen.'s Sch., 1979-80. Bar: Ct. Appeals Md. 1972, U.S. Dist. Ct. D.C. 1972, U.S. Ct. Mil. Appeals 1975, U.S. Supreme Ct. 1976, N.C. 1978, U.S. Ct. Claims 1982, U.S. Ct. Appeals (fed. cir.) 1990. Asst. state's atty., Balt., 1973-74; trial atty., trial team chief Office Chief Trial Atty. Contract Appeals Divsn., U.S. Army, Washington, 1980-84; chief atty. Def. Supply Svc., 1984-87; trial team chief contract appeals divsn. U.S. Army, 1987-92; sr. atty. Sec. Air Force, Office of Gen. Counsel, 1992—. Contbr. articles on Am. Civil War to various periodicals. Lt. col. U.S. Army. Decorated Silver Star, Soldier's medal, Bronze Star, Purple Heart (2), Meritorious Svc. medal (2), Army Commendation medal (2), Cross of Gallantry with gold star, Combat Infantryman's badge, Legion of Merit. Mem. D.C. Bar Assn., N.C. Bar Assn., BCA Bar Assn. (bd. govs.), Federalist Soc., Grant Monument Assn. (trustee). Federalist Soc. Home: 5328 Danbury Forest Springfield VA 22151-1702 E-mail: longc@pentagon.af.mil., long2502@aol.com.

LONG, CLARENCE WILLIAM, accountant; b. Hartford City, Ind., Apr. 17, 1917; s. Adam and Alice (Weschke) L.; m. Mildred Bernhardt, Aug. 8, 1940; children: William Randall, David John, Bruce Allen. BS, Ind. U., 1939. With Ernst & Young, Indpls., 1939-78, ptnr., 1953-78, ret., 1978. Mem. econ. exec. com. Gov. Ind., 1968-73. Mem. nat. budget and consultation com. United Way of Am., 1966-70; bd. dirs. United Fund Greater Indpls., 1966—, treas., 1968—; bd. dirs. Jr. Achievement, Ind., 1966-67; mem. exec. com. Nat. Jr. Achievement, 1966-67; mem. fin. com. Indpls. Hosp. Devel. Assn., 1966-67; trustee Ind. U., 1975-84; trustee Art Assn. Indpls., pres., 1977-86; mem. adv. com. to dir. NIH, 1986-92. Mem. Am. Inst. C.P.A.'s (council 1959-62), Ind. Assn. C.P.A.'s, Nat. Assn. Accountants, Ind. C. of C. (dir.), Delta Chi, Beta Alpha Psi, Alpha Kappa Psi. Clubs: Woodstock (Indpls.) (dir. 1958-60), Columbia (Indpls.) (dir. 1971-77, pres. 1976), Royal Poinciana Golf Club (Naples, Fla.). Republican. Lutheran. Home: 607 Somerset Dr W Indianapolis IN 46260-2924 Office: 1 Indiana Sq Indianapolis IN 46204-2004

LONG, DANIEL A. ophthalmologist; b. Donaldsonville, La., Nov. 19, 1950; s. Joseph Calvin and Mary Alice Montero L.; m. Monica, July 12, 1974; children: Danielle, Lisa. BA in Psychology, Tulane U., 1972; MD, La. State U., 1976. Diplomate Am. Bd. Ophthalmology. Chief ophthalmology So. La. Med. Ctr., Houma, 1980-82; pvt. practice ophthalmology New Orleans, 1982-84, Gretna, La., 1984—. Chief surgery Meadowcrest Hosp., Gretna, 1991-93, vice chief med. staff, 1993-95, chief med. staff, 1995-97; adv. bd. Allergan Pharms., Irvine, Calif., 1987. Fellow Am. Acad. Ophthalmology (achievement award, 2002); mem. Internat. Soc. Refractive Surgery, New Orleans Acad. Ophthalmology (chair program com. 1991, 95, 97, 2000; editor ann. meeting transactions; sec. 2000-02), La. Ophthalmology Assn. (pres. 1999—, councelor, 2002—). Avocations: golf, skiing, hiking, scuba diving, cycling. Office: 120 Meadowcrest St Ste 330 Gretna LA 70056-5249

LONG, DAVID G. engineering educator; BS, Brigham Young U., 1982, MS, 1983; PhD, U. So. Calif., 1989. Project engr. Jet Propulsion Lab. Calif. Tech. U., Pasadena, 1983-90; prof elec. and computer engring. dept. Brigham Young U., Provo, 1990—. Dir. Ctr. for Remote Sensing, Brigham Young U., Provo, 1999—. Recipient Achievement awards NASA, 1997. Mem. IEEE (sr.). Mem. Lds Ch. Office: Brigham Young U 459 Clyde Bldg Provo UT 84602 E-mail: long@ee.byu.edu.

LONG, DAVID MICHAEL, JR. biomedical researcher, cardiothoracic surgeon; b. Shamokin, Pa., Feb. 26, 1929; s. David Michael and Elva (Christ) L.; m. Donna Rae Long, Feb. 26, 1954; children: Kurt, Raymond, Carl, Grace, Carolyn, Ruth. BS magna cum laude, Muhlenberg Coll., Allentown, Pa., 1951; MS, Hahnemann U., Phila., 1954, MD, 1956; PhD, U. Minn., 1965. Lic. physician, Ariz., Calif., Colo., Ill., Md., Minn., Pa., Tex.; diplomate Nat. Bd. Med. Examiners, Am. Bd. Surgery, Am. Bd. Thoracic Surgery; cert. trauma provider, advanced life support; advanced cardiac life support. Intern Hahnemann U. Hosp., Phila., 1956-57; resident in surgery U. Minn., Mpls., 1957-65, fellow in surgery, 1957-61, 63-65, fellow in physiology, 1959-61; pres., chmn. bd. Long Labs., San Diego, 1984-85; chmn., dir. rsch. Fluoromed Pharm., Inc., 1985-89; chmn., dir. sci. Alliance Pharm. Corp., La Jolla, 1989-91; pres., chmn. Abel Labs., Inc., Spring Valley, 1991—, Biofield Corp., Spring Valley, 2000—. Mem. faculty Hahnemann U., 1953-54, U. Calif., San Diego, 1973-92, U. Minn., 1959-61, 63-64, Naval Med. Sch., 1962, Chgo. Med. Sch., 1965-67, Cook County Grad. Sch. Medicine, 1965-73, U. Ill., 1967-73; cons. Chgo. State Tuberculosis Sanitarium, 1967-72; asst. dir. dept. surg. rsch. Hektoen Inst. for Med. Rsch. of Cook County Hosp., 1965-68, dir., 1968-73, assoc. attending staff, 1965-73; attending staff West Side VA Hosp., 1966-73, U. Ill. Hosp., 1967-73, Villa View Hosp., 1973-85, AMI Valley Med. Ctr., 1973-85, Grossman Dist. Hosp., 1973-85, Alvarado Cmty. Hosp., 1973-85, Sharp Meml. Hosp., 1973-84; head divsn. cardiovasc. and thoracic surgery U. Ill., 1967-73; cons. continuing med. edn. com. Grossmont Dist. Hosp., 1985—; mem. continuing med. edn. com. Sharp Healthcare Sys., 1994—; cons. Docent Corp., 1975-76; com. mem. consensus devel. com. Thrombolytic Therapy in Thrombosis, NIH/FDA, 1980; trustee N.Y. Acad. Art, N.Y.C., 1997—; bd. govs., chmn. Hahnemann U. Hosp./Tenet Healthcare, Phila., 1999—. Contbr. numerous articles and abstracts to profl. jours., chpts. to books; editl. bd. Current Surgery, 1967-89; co-editor Hematrix, 1982-85. Bd. dirs. Rsch. Assocs. of Point Loma Nazarene coll., San Diego, chmn., 1984-85; bd. trustees Muhlenberg Coll., Allentown, Pa., 1992—, chmn., 1994—; bd. dirs. Grossmont Hosp. Found., Grossmont Hosp., La Mesa, Calif., 1992—; co-chmn. Calif. divsn. of campaign of Muhlenberg Coll., 1992-93; chmn. Campaign of Grossmont Hosp. Found. for David and Donna Long Cancer Treatment Ctr. and Cardiac Diagnosis Ctr., 1992-94; co-chmn. Campaign for Health Ctr., Point Loma Nazarene Coll., San Diego, 1992-94. Rsch. fellow Heart Assn. Southeastern Pa., 1953-54, Student Senate of Hahnemann U., 1955; trainee Nat. Cancer Inst., 1957-58, Nat. Heart Inst., 1958-60, 63-64; spl. rsch. fellow Nat. Heart Inst., 1960-61; established investigator Minn. Heart Assn, 1964-65; Muhlenberg Coll. scholar, 1947-51, Hahnemann U. scholar, 1952-55, Luth. Brotherhood Leadership scholar, 1951 Fellow ACS, Am. Coll. Chest Physicians (sec. cardiovascular surgery com. 1976-78), Am. Coll. Cardiology; mem. AAAS, AMA, Am. Assn. Thoracic Surgery, Am. Assn. Anatomists, Internat. Cardiovascular Surgery Soc., Internat. Soc. for Artificial Cells and Immobilization Biotechnology, Am. Heart Assn., Am. Physiol. Soc., Am. Thoracic Soc., Assn. for Advancement of Med. Instrumentation, Cajal Soc. Neuroanatomy, Calif. Med. Assn., Internat. Soc. Surgery, Internat. Soc. Hemorheology (founding mem.), N.Y. Acad. Sci., San Diego County Med. Soc., Soc. Thoracic Surgeons, Soc. Univ. Surgeons, Warren H. Cole Soc., Western Thoracic Surg. Soc. Lutheran. Achievements include 17 U.S. patents and 11 fgn. patents. Avocations: hiking, gardening, philanthropic programs, books on Winston Churchill. Office: Abel Laboratories Inc 2737 Via Orange Way Ste 108 Spring Valley CA 91978-1750

LONG, DAVID RUSSELL, academic program director; b. Worcester, Mass., Feb. 12, 1942; s. Wendell Russell and Eleanor May (Ohlund) L.; children: Daphne Ruth Evdokia, Payson David Cheslov. BA, Emerson Coll., 1965; MS in Ednl. Communication, U. Albany, 1970, MS in Ednl. Adminstrn., 1977. TV producer-dir. U. Albany, N.Y., 1968-69, dir. audio-visual svc., 1969—. Pres., cons. Media Assocs., Scotia, N.Y., 1982—; asst. to dir. White Funeral Home, Scotia, 1982—. Creator slide programs for fire chiefs, police, children's mus.; author: (videotape) Children's Participation Play (selected for inclusion in Libr. of Congress). Fin. sec., mem. pub. rels com. Scotia Fire Dept., 1975-85, commr., 1985-88; bd. dir. Scotia-Glenville Children's Mus., 1980-84, Schenectady Acess Cable Coun., 1980-84. With U.S. Army, 1966-67, Vietnam. Recipient Chancellor's award for excellence in profl. svc. U. Albany, 1982. Mem. Capital Dist. Media Assn., Hudson-Mohawk Vol. Fireman's Assn., Glenville Fire Fighters Assn. (pub. rels. com. 1978-86). Republican. Methodist. Avocations: walking, swimming, reading, travel, exercise. Home: 144 Van Aernem Rd Ballston Spa NY 12020-3800 Office: U Albany 1400 Washington Ave Albany NY 12222 E-mail: drl14@albany.edu.

LONG, DONALD GREGORY, financial services consultant; b. Lima, Ohio, Mar. 19, 1937; s. Chester Vernon and Margaret Francis (Packard) L.; m. Linda Ann Bosking, Aug. 1, 1964: Karen Elizabeth, Joanne Deborah. BS, U. Ill., Urbana, 1959; MBA, Stanford U., 1964. Systems engr. IBM Corp., N.Y.C., 1964-68, product mgr. Princeton, N.J., 1969-75, elec. funds transfer project mgr., 1975-78, industry cons., 1979-89, Charlotte, N.C., 1989-91; chmn. CCM, Inc., 1990—; ind. fin. svcs. cons., 1992—; chmn. McLong, Inc., 1992—. IBM liaison pres.'s nat. commn. elec. funds transfers, Washington, 1975-77; faculty mem. Stonier Grad. Sch. Banking, Rutgers U., N.J., 1979-83, Grad. Sch. Banking, U. Wis., 1978-85, Grad. Sch. Retail Bank Mgmt., U. Va., 1980-85, Sch. Elec. Funds Transfer, Northwestern U., 1985-90, Payment Systems Inst., U. Colo., 1986-90; bd. dirs. Montgomery Nat. Bank, Rocky Hill, N.J., 1981-89; trustee New Money Inst., Washington, 1987. Contbr. articles to fin. mags. Pres. Rep. orgn., Belle Mead, N.J., 1976-77; chmn. Montgomery Township N.J. planning bd., Belle Mead, 1981-88; trustee Foundation for Hosp. Art, Atlanta, 1986—; del. S.C. Rep. Conv., 1996. Served to capt. with USAF, 1960-62. Mem. Elec. Funds Transfer Hall of Fame, Princeton Area C. of C., Elec. Funds Transfer Assn. (bd. dirs. 1982—), Nat. Assn. Watch and Clock Collectors, Antique Auto Club, Masons, Shriners, Lions, River Hills Country Club (bd. dirs. 1992—, v.p. 1993—, pres. 1994), Lake Wylie C. of C. (bd. dirs. 1994—). Republican. Methodist.

LONG, DONLIN MARTIN, surgeon, educator; b. Rolla, Mo., Apr. 14, 1934; s. Donlin M. and Davene E. (Johnson) L.; m. Harriett Page, June 13, 1959; children: Kimberley Page, Elisabeth Merchant, David Bradford. Student, Jefferson City Jr. Coll., 1951-52; MD, U. Mo., 1959; PhD in Neuroanatomy, U. Minn., 1964. Diplomate Am. Bd. Neurol. Surgery. Intern U. Minn. Hosps., Mpls., 1959-60; resident in neurol. surgery U. Minn. Health Sci. Ctr., 1960-64, Peter Bent Brigham and Children's Hosp. Med. Center, Boston, 1965; practice medicine specializing in neurosurgery Balt., 1973—; asst. prof. dept. neurosurgery U. Minn. Hosps., 1967-70, neurosurgeon, 1967-73, assoc. prof., 1970-73; neurosurgeon-in-chief dept. neurosurgery Johns Hopkins Hosp., 1973-2000; prof. and chmn. dept. neurosurgery Johns Hopkins U., 1973—, mem. prin. staff Applied Physics Lab., 1976—. Cons. neurosurgery Mpls. VA Hosp., 1967-73, John F. Kennedy Inst., 1977, Balt. City Hosp., 1973— Contbr. numerous articles on neuropathology and surgery to profl. jours.; contbr. to book chpts. in field. Served with USPHS, 1965-67. Mem. Soc. Neurosci., Am. Assn. Neuropathologists, Soc. Neurol. Surgeons, AAAS, AMA, Balt. Neurol. Soc., Internat. Assn. Study of Pain, Internat. Soc. Pediatric Neurosurgery, William T. Peyton Soc., Congress Neurol. Surgeons, Johns Hopkins Med. and Surg. Assn., Electron Microscopy Soc. Am., Md. Neurosurg. Soc., Am. Acad. Neurosurgery, Am. Assn. Neurol. Surgery, Neurol. Soc. Am., Cajal Club, Sigma Xi, Omicron Delta Kappa, Alpha Omega Alpha, Phi Eta Sigma, Pi Mu Epsilon, Mystical 7. Home: 9 Blythewood Rd Baltimore MD 21210-2401 Office: Johns Hopkins Hosp Dept Neurosurgery 600 N Wolfe St Carnegie 466 Baltimore MD 21287-7709 Fax: 410-955-6407. E-mail: dmlong@jhmi.edu.

LONG, DONNA ELAINE, fundraising executive; b. Monroe, Mich., July 12, 1946; d. Joseph Edward and Ada Jane (Osgood) L. BS, Ctrl. Mich. U., 1968. Asst. dir. fund dept. Nat. Urban League, N.Y.C., 1969-85; dir. devel. and pub. affairs N.Y. Urban League, 1985-87; dir. devel. Nat. Minority Supplier Devel. Coun., 1988—. Bd. dirs. Howard Meml. Fund, N.Y.C., 1989—; mem. adv. bd. Ralph Ellison Meml. Project, 1998—. Democrat. Lutheran. Office: Nat Minority Supplier Devel Coun 1040 Avenue Of The Americas New York NY 10018-3703

LONG, EDWARD ARLO, business consultant, retired manufacturing company executive; b. Detroit, May 5, 1927; s. Arlo Russell and Florence Viola (Magown) L.; m. Lorraine Ruth Nordin, May 21, 1947; children: Karin Louise Long Schelke, Marian Elizabeth Long Benton. BS, Wayne State U., 1956, MBA, 1964. Mfg. mgr. Ex-Cell-O Corp., Detroit, 1950-68; v.p. mktg. Colonial Broach & Machine, Warren, Mich., 1968-70; group v.p. Blue Bird Body Co., Fort Valley, Ga., 1970-75; pres. tool equipment div. Chgo. Pneumatic Tool, Franklin, Pa., 1975-77; group v.p. Joy Mfg. Co., Pine Bluff, Ark., 1977-87; v.p., gen. mgr. Wheeling Machine Products Co./Cooper Industries, 1987-94; ret., 1994. Dir. Security Nat. Bank, Wheeling, W.Va. Bd. dirs. Franklin Hosp., 1976-76, Oglebay Inst., Wheeling, 1981-83, Ohio Valley Hosp. Trust, Wheeling, 1982-83, Ark. Ind. Colls., 1984, Jefferson County Indsl. Found., 1985, Pine Bluff Fifty for the Future, 1985, Pine Bluff Symphony Orch., 1987, Leadership Pine Bluff, 1990; apptd. zoning commr., Pine Bluff, 1995. Served with USCG, 1945-46. Scholar Nat. Office Mgmt. Assn., 1952, Beta Gamma, Detroit, 1953 Mem. AIME, Am. Petroleum Inst., Duquesne (Pitts.) Club, Rotary, Alpha Kappa Psi, Psi Chi, Sigma Iota Epsilon. Democrat. Roman Catholic. Home and Office: 7409 S Laurel St Pine Bluff AR 71603-8121 Fax: 870-534-2773. E-mail: longtrapper2@aol.com.

LONG, EDWIN TUTT, surgeon; b. St. Louis, July 23, 1925; s. Forrest Edwin and Hazel (Tutt) L.; m. Mary M. Hull, Apr. 16, 1955; children: Jennifer Ann, Laura Ann, Peter Edwin. AB, Columbia U., 1944, MD, 1947. Diplomate Am. Bd. Surgery, Am. Bd. Thoracic Surgery. Rotating intern Meth. Hosp., Bklyn., 1947-478; surg. intern U. Chgo. Clinics, 1948-49, resident in gen. surgery, 1952-55, resident in thoracic surgery, 1955-57; asst. prof. surgery U. Chgo., 1957-59; thoracic and cardiovasc. surgeon, chief surgery dept. Watson Clinic, Lakeland, Fla., 1960-69; assoc. prof. surgery U. Pa., Phila., 1970-73; thoracic and cardiovasc. surgeon Allegheny Cardiovasc. Surg. Assocs., Pitts., 1973-88; exec. v.p. Mailings Clearing House and Roxbury Press, Inc., 1988-90, pres., 1990-96, chmn. bd. dirs., 1991—. Dir. Watson Clinic Rsch. Found., 1965-69; with Physicians Nat. Health Program, 1999—; bd. dirs. Roxbury Press, Inc., Cardiac Telecom, Inc., Pitts.; Disting. lectr., curriculum advisor healthcare leadership program Herzberg Sch. Mgmt., Rockhurst U., 2001—. Patentee gas sterilizer, 1969. Mem. bd. regents Rockhurst U., 2000—. Capt. USAF, 1950-52. Pressure Vectorography rsch. grantee Alfred P. Sloan Found., 1963; Nelson-Atkins Mus. fellow, 1997—. Mem. ACS, Am. Coll. Cardiology, Internat. Soc. for Cardiovasc. Surgery, Nat. Assn. Pacing and Electrophysiology (charter), Allegheny Vascular Soc. (pres. 1987), Ea. Vascular Soc. (founding mem.), Soc. Thoracic Surgery (founding mem.), Midwest Bioethics Ctr., Kansas City Concensus, Woodside Club, Rotary, Sigma Xi, Beta Theta Pi. Home: 4550 Warwick Blvd # 1204 Kansas City MO 64111-7725 Office: 4550 Warwick Blvd # 1209 Kansas City MO 64111 also: Roxbury Press Inc 601 E Marshall St Sweet Springs MO 65351-0295 E-mail: elongmd@kc.rr.com.

LONG, ELAINE (LOTUS LONG), writer, editor; b. Sterling, Colo., Jan. 12, 1935; d. Guy William and Evelyn Irene (Simpson) Mullenax; m. Thomas John O'Rourke, Aug. 17, 1963 (dec. Feb. 1965); 1 child, Mary Kendall; m. Arthur Warren Long, Oct. 4, 1969. BA, U. Colo., 1955. Tchr. Portland (Oreg.) Pub. Schs., 1955-57, Denver Pub. Schs., 1957-58, U.S. Civil Svc., Upper Heyford, Eng., 1958-59; copywriter KBOL Radio, Boulder, Colo., 1959-61; ranch hand Guy Mullenax, Gillette, Wyo., 1961-62; copy and feature writer, traffic mgr. KKAR Radio, Pomona, Calif., 1962-63; freelance writer Denver, 1966—. Editor Boulder, Buena Vista, Colo., 1974—. Author: Jenny's Mountain, 1987, Bittersweet Country, 1991; cons. editor: Separate Lives: The Story of Mary Rippon, 1999; contbr. ; cons. editor: A Texas Tragedy: Orphaned by Bootleggers, 2001, cons. editor: Dancing with Principle: Hanya Holm in Colorado, 1941-1983, 2001; ; author: (short stories) The Violinists Story, 2002. Mem. Western Writers Am. (Spur awards chmn. 1993, Svc. award 1994, 95, bd. dirs. 1994-95), Aircraft Owners and Pilots Assn., Women Writing the West, Author's Guild N.Y., Colo. Authors' League (bd. dirs. 1987-88). Avocations: flying, songwriting, singing, hiking, reading.

LONG, EUGENE THOMAS, III, philosophy educator, administrator; b. Richmond, Va., Mar. 16, 1935; s. Eugene Thomas and Emily Joyce (Barker) L.; m. Carolyn Macleod, June 25, 1960; children: Scott, Kathryn. BA, Randolph-Macon Coll., 1957; BD, Duke U., 1960; PhD, U. Glasgow, Scotland, 1964. Asst. prof. philosophy Randolph-Macon Coll., 1964-67, assoc. prof., 1967-70, U. S.C., Columbia, 1970-73, prof., 1973—2002, prof. emeritus, 2002—, chmn. dept., 1972-87. Author: Jaspers and Bultmann, 1968, Existence, Being and God, 1985, Twentieth Century Western Philosophy of Religion, 1900-2000, 2000; contbr., editor: God, Secularization & History,

1974, Experience, Reason and God, 1980, Prospects for Natural Theology, 1992; editor: Handbook of Contemporary Philosophy of Religion, 1995—; editor-in-chief Internat. Jour. for Philosophy of Religion, 1990—; assoc. editor Internat. Jour. Philosophy of Religion, 1975-90, So. Jour. Philosophy, 1978-83; contbr., co-editor: God and Temporality, 1984, Being and Truth, 1986; mem. adv. editl. bd. The Works of William James, 1974-88, The Correspondence of William James, 1988—; contbg. editor: God, Reason and Religions, 1995; ; editor, contbr. Issues in Contemporary Philosophy of Religion, 2001; contbr. articles to profl. jours. Mem. S.C. Com. for Humanities, 1980-85; mem. adv. bd. The Franklin J. Matchette Found., 1992—. Recipient Rsch. award NEH, 1968, Duke U./U. N.C. Coop. Program in Humanities, 1968-69. Mem. Soc. Philosophy in Religion (pres. 1980-81), Metaphys. Soc. Am. (sec. treas. 1977-81, exec. coun. 1991-94, v.p./pres.-elect 1996-97, pres. 1997-98), So. Soc. Philosophy and Psychology (exec. coun. 1976-79), Am. Philos. Assn. (sec. treas. eastern divsn. 1985-94). Office: U SC Dept Philosophy Columbia SC 29208-0001

LONG, FRANCIS MARK, retired electrical engineer, educator; b. Iowa City, Nov. 10, 1929; s. Frank B. and Hilda B. (Rohret) L.; m. Mary Ann Coyne, June 8, 1964 (dec. Apr. 1994); children: Ann Brett, Mary Bronwyn, Thomas Martin Carver, Caitlin Frances. BS, U. Iowa, 1953, MS, 1956; PhD, Iowa State U., 1961; NIH fellow, Stanford U. and Lawrence Livermore Lab, 1972-73. With Collins Radio Co., Cedar Rapids, Iowa, summers 1952, 55, Douglas Aircraft Co., Santa Monica, Calif., summer 1953, USNAMTC, Point Mugu, summer 1956, Good All Electric Co., Ogallala, Nebr., summer 1957, Lawrence Radiation Lab., Livermore, Calif., summer 1967, Globe Union Co., Milw., summer 1975, Naval Rsch Lab., Washington, 1988, 89, 91; instr. U. Wyo., Laramie, 1956-58, prof. elec. engring., 1960-95, prof. emeritus, 1995—, head elec. engring. dept., 1977-87; instr. Iowa State U., 1958-60. Dir. Wyo. Biotelemetry, Inc., Rocky Mountain Bioengring. Symposium; pres. Alliance for Engring. in Medicine and Biology, 1983, 84, mem. exec. com., 1979-89; conf. chmn., procs. editor 1st, 2d, 3d and 5th Internat. Conf. on Wildlife Biotelemetry; adj. prof. Univ. Denver, 1996—, Colo. Tech. Univ., 1997—, U. Colo., Denver, 1999—. Author: (with E.M. Lonsdale) Introductory Electrical Concepts, 1967, rev. edit., 1977; co-author: (with R.G. Jacquot) Introduction to Engineering Systems, 1988. Trustee St. Paul's Newman Center Parish, 1969-72; mem. City of Laramie Planning Commn., 1970-72. Served with C.E. U.S. Army, 1953-55. Decorated citation Republic of Korea Army C.E.; recipient G.D. Humphrey Outstanding Faculty award U. Wyo., 1973, Western Electric Fund award for engring. teaching, 1978 Mem. IEEE (life, edn. activities com. chmn. Denver sect. 1997), Am. Soc. Engring. Edn. (v.p., dir., 1st Outstanding Biomed. Engring. Educator award biomed. engring. divsn. 1981, chmn. Elec. Engring. divsn. 1986-87), Internat. Soc. for Hybrid Microelectronics (v.p. Rocky Mountain chpt. 1996-97, pres. 1998), Sigma Xi. Republican. Home: 1888 S Jackson St Apt 701 Denver CO 80210-3918 E-mail: flong30989@aol.com.

LONG, FRANK WESLEY, JR. chemist; b. Springfield, Ill., Aug. 26, 1925; s. Frank Wesley and Elizabeth Margaret (Franke) L.; m. Thelma Elizabeth Keil Long, Nov. 17, 1951; children: Stephen Wesley, William Douglas, Valerie Elizabeth Long Feiss. BS, U. Ill., 1946; PhD in Organic Chemistry, State U. Iowa, 1950. Grad. asst. State U. Iowa, Iowa City, 1946-50; lab. chemist 3M Co., Mpls., summer 1948, Ethyl Corp., Ferndale, Mich., summer 1949, GAF Corp., Easton, Pa., 1950-52; project mgr. textile dyeing and finishing U.S. Army Quartermaster, Phila., 1952-53; sec. mgr. sales devel. Hooker Electrochem. Co., Niagara Falls, N.Y., 1953-64; dir. product devel. Princeton (N.J.) Chem. Rsch. Inc., 1964-67; product dir. ARCO Chem. Co. (subsidiary of Atlantic Richfield Co.), Phila., 1967-83; owner Riverside Assocs., Princeton, 1983—; dir. bus. devel. Princeton Advanced Tech., 1991—. Expert witness in field. Contbr. chpts. to books: Chemicals in Plastics, 1967, U.S. Petrochemical Industry, 1974, Fundamentals of the U.S. Petroleum Industry, 1980. Pres. elem. sch. PTA, Niagara Falls, 1963. Mem. Comml. Devel. Assn. (bd. dirs. 1976-78, Golden C award 1991), Am. Chem. Soc. (bd. dirs. chem. mktg. divsn. 1974-76), Am. Assn. Textile Chemists and Colorists, Chem. Cons. Network, Princeton Ind. Cons., Chemist's Club. Achievements include development of flame retardant chemicals and plastics, heat resistant plastics, petrochemicals. Avocations: hunting, fishing, coins, Indian artifacts. Home and Office: Riverside Assocs 292 Riverside Dr Princeton NJ 08540-5432 Fax: (609) 924-8227. E-mail: fwlong@att.net.

LONG, GARY, civil engineer, educator; b. Berwyn, Ill., Jan. 9, 1943; s. Don A. and Reta (Staff) L.; m. Jane Shaffer, Sept. 22, 1973. BSC.E., Bradley U., 1967; MS, Tex. A&M U., 1968, PhD, 1973; postgrad., Law Sch., U. Notre Dame, 1976-77. Registered profl. engr., Ill., Fla. cert. in data processing. Engr. trainee, jr. engr. De Leuw, Cather & Co. (Cons. Engrs.), Chgo., 1961-65; engring. research asso. Tex. Transp. Inst., College Station, 1966-71; prin. engr.-planner Wilbur Smith and Assos. (Cons. Engrs. and Planners), Houston, 1971-75; prof. civil engring. U. Notre Dame, Ind., 1975-77, U. Fla., Gainesville, 1977—; asst. dean U. Fla. (Grad. Sch.), 1981-83. Cons. to research agys. and law firms. Contbr. articles to profl. jours. Fellow Inst. Transp. Engrs. (Past Pres.'s award 1972, Tech. Council award 1977); mem. Transp. Research Bd., Transp. Research Forum, Ops. Research Soc. Am., Sigma Xi. Home: 101 NW 28th St Gainesville FL 32607-2510 Office: U Florida Dept Civil Engring Gainesville FL 32611

LONG, GARY JOHN, chemistry educator; b. Binghamton, N.Y., Dec. 3, 1941; s. Clifford James and Margaret (Goodnow) L.; m. Fernande Grandjean, Nov. 20, 1992; 1 child, Jeffrey Robert. BS, Carnegie-Mellon U., 1964; PhD, Syracuse U., 1968. Asst. prof. chemistry U. Mo. Rolla, 1968-74, assoc. prof. chemistry, 1974-83, prof. chemistry, 1983—. Contbr. over 260 articles to profl. jours. Recipient Internat. Francqui chair professorship, Belgium, 2002—; fellow Fulbright fellow, Liege, Belgium, 1993. Office: Dept Chemistry U Mo Rolla Rolla MO 65409-0010 E-mail: glong@umr.edu.

LONG, GREGORY ALAN, lawyer; b. San Francisco, Aug. 28, 1948; s. William F. and Ellen L. (Webber) L.; m. Jane H. Barrett, Sept. 30, 1983; children: Matthew, Brian, Michael, Gregory. BA magna cum laude, Claremont Men's Coll., Calif., 1970; JD cum laude, Harvard U., 1973. Bar: Calif. 1973, U.S. Dist. Ct. (ctrl. dist.) Calif. 1973, U.S. Ct. Appeals (9th cir.) 1976, U.S. Supreme Ct. 1977, U.S. Ct. Appeals (fed. cir.) 1984. Assoc. Overton, Lyman & Prince, L.A., 1973-78, ptnr., 1978-87, Sheppard, Mullin, Richter & Hampton, L.A., 1987—. Arbitrator L.A. Superior Ct. Fellow Am. Bar Found.; mem. ABA (young lawyers divsn. exec. coun. 1974-88, chmn. 1984-85, ho. of dels. 1983-89, exec. coun. litigation sect. 1981-83), Calif. Bar Assn. (del. 1976-82, 87-88), L.A. County Bar Assn. (exec. com. 1979-82, trustee 1979-82, barristers sect. exc. coun. 1976-82, pres. 1981-82, exec. coun. trial lawyers sect. 1984-88, chair amicus briefs com. 1989-92). Office: Sheppard Mullin Richter & Hampton 333 S Hope St Los Angeles CA 90071-1406 E-mail: glong@smrh.com.

LONG, H. OWEN, retired economics educator, fiction writer; b. Decatur, Tenn., Mar. 6, 1921; s. Thomas Frank and Mattie Lena (Powers) L.; m. Mary Virginia Patrick, Dec. 20, 1951; children: Belinda Jane Long Stevens, John Owen Long. BA, Maryville (Tenn.) Coll., 1943; MS, U. Tenn., 1947; PhD, Vanderbilt U., 1952. Asst. prof. econs. Carson-Newman Coll., Jefferson City, Tenn., 1947-48; assoc. prof. Maryville Coll., 1948-50; prof., dean, registrar, co-founder Ky. Wesleyan Coll., Owensboro, 1951-60; prof., registrar, dean admissions, scholarship officer Evansville (Ind.) U., 1960-62; prof., head dept. bus. and econs. Pensacola (Fla.) Jr. Coll., 1962-86; ret., 1986; writer fiction, history and econs., 1986—. Author: Long-Told Tales, 1990, The Long Path to the Western Waters, 1991, Tales of the Gulf Coast, 1992, Tales of Pleasant Grove, 1992, Tales with a Smile, 1992, A Medley of Tales, 1992, Tales de Guerre, 1993, Get Three Out..Unto a Land (History of Kentucky Wesleyan College), 1994, Tales of Father Gander, 1994, Outline of the Principles of the Science of Economics: Macro-Economics and Micro-Economics 2 vols., 1994, More Tales of the Gulf Coast, 1994, Tales of the River Country, 1995, Tales of the 50 States and the D.C., 1996, Tales of the Uncivil War Era, 6 vols., 1998, Up From the Dawning: A Story of Atlantis, 1998, The Fury of the Tempest, 1999, On the Rocky Road to Rome: Worle War II Novel, 2000, Animal Tales, 2000, Tales D'Amour, 2000, Myths and Legends, 2000, Oma's Favorite Tales, 2000, Opa's Favorite Tales, 2000, Selected Tales, 2000, The Beautiful Red Sunset, 2000, Winds of Change, 2000, Richmond Rampage, 2001, Counter-Stroke, 2001, Whites Seeing Red, 2002, Two Can't See Red, 2002, The Big Third Goes All the Way, 2002, Southern Tales, 2002, Tales for Carter and Patrick, 2002, Tales for Sarah and Meredith, 2002, Tales for Brandon and Ryan, 2002, Book of Games and Amusements, 2002, Beholding the Golden Mist 4 vols., 2002. Named Hon. Order Ky. Cols., 1958. Mem. Am. Econ. Assn. (life), Alpha Beta Gamma (life). Home: The Long White House 1712 N Whaley Ave Pensacola FL 32503-5733

LONG, HARRY (ON-YUEN ENG), chemist, science and technology executive, consultant; b. Passaic, N.J., June 22, 1932; s. Eng Yick and Yue York (Ng) L.; m. Linda Lai-King Yu, Sept. 18, 1960; 1 child, Steven Eng Park-Ning BS, N.J. Inst. Tech., Newark, 1959. Asst. devel. engr., belts and splty. products Uniroyal, Inc., Passaic, 1959-62, devel. engr. hose and expansion joints, 1962-67, sr. process engr., 1967-71; chief devel. engr. Raybestos-Manhattan, Inc., 1971-72; chief chemist Goodall Rubber Co., Trenton, N.J., 1972-76, tech. mgr., 1976-90; v.p. tech. Pelmor Labs., Inc., Newtown, Pa., 1990—. Editor, author: Basic Compounding and Processing of Rubber, 1985. Mem. AAAS, ASTM, Am. Chem. Soc. (area dir. Rubber div. 1990-92, Spl. Svc. award Rubber div. 1985), Phila. Rubber Group (chmn. 1980). Achievements include development of the rubber technology course used by the subdivisions of the rubber division of American Chemical Society throughout the U.S., Canada, Mexico and Colombia; organization of national symposium on rubber compounding. Office: Pelmor Labs Inc 401 Lafayette St Newtown PA 18940-2167

LONG, HELEN HALTER, writer, educator; b. St. Louis, Nov. 19, 1906; d. Charles C. and Ida (May) Halter; m. Forrest E. Long, June 22, 1944. AB, Washington U., St. Louis, 1927, AM, 1928; PhD, NYU, 1937. Grad. fellow Washington U., 1927-28; tchr. social studies Venice, Ill., 1928-30; asst. prof. social sci. N.Y. State Coll. for Tchrs., Albany, 1930-38; tchr. Mamaroneck, NY, 1938-42; prin. elem. and jr. high schs., 1942-54; asst. supt. schs., 1954-61; dir. Inst. Instructional Improvement, N.Y.C., 1962-88; pres. Books of World, Sweet Springs, Mo., 1962-86; bd. dirs. Roxbury Press, 1987—96, emeritus, 1997—. Teaching fellow, instr. Sch. Edn. NYU, 1936-43; assoc. editor Clearing House, 1935-55. Author: Society in Action, 1936, National Safety Council Lesson Units, 1944-52, (with Forrest E. Long) Social Studies Skills, 8th edit, 1976 (with Forrest E. Long). Mem. Phi Beta Kappa, Pi Gamma Mu, Kappa Delta Pi, Alpha Xi Delta (Diamond Jubilee Outstanding Women award 1968) Home: The Gatesworth One McKnight Pl Apt 155 Saint Louis MO 63124 Office: Roxbury Press Inc 601 E Marshall Sweet Springs MO 65351-0295

LONG, HOWARD CHARLES, physics educator emeritus; b. Seizholtzville, Pa., Dec. 12, 1918; s. Howard William and Isabella Geneva (Reese) L.; m. Frances Monroe Hoke, Apr. 16, 1945; children— Howard Charles, David William, Carol Joyce. BA, Northwestern U., 1941, postgrad., 1941-42; PhD, Ohio State U., 1948. Asst. prof. physics Washington and Jefferson Coll., 1948-51; head Electromagnetism Influence Fields sec., U.S. Naval Ordnance Lab., 1951-52; assoc. prof., dept. chmn. physics Am. U., 1952-53; prof. physics, chmn. dept. Gettysburg Coll., 1953-59; prof. physics Dickinson Coll., 1959-81, chmn. dept., 1963-75, Joseph Priestley Chair of Natural Philosophy, 1973, prof. emeritus, 1981—. Cons. physicist Naval Ordnance Lab., White Oak, Md., 1952-73, McCoy Electronics Co., Mt. Holly Springs, Pa., 1958-59 Contbr. articles to ednl. jours. Active Boy Scouts Am. Served with USNR, 1944-45. Mem. Am. Assn. Physics Tchrs. (sec.-treas. Central Pa. sect. 1958-59, v.p. 1959-60, pres. 1960-61), A.A.U.P. (sec.-treas. Dickinson chpt. 1963-64, v.p. 1964-65, pres. 1965-66), A.A.A.S., Am. Phys. Soc., Cumberland Conservancy. Methodist (chmn. adminstrn. bd. 1961-62, chmn. ofcl. bd. 1957-59, mem. conf. bd. edn. 1971-73). Home: 240 Belvedere St Carlisle PA 17013-3501 Office: Dickinson Coll Carlisle PA 17013

LONG, JAMES JAY, lawyer; b. Pitts., Jan. 23, 1959; s. James E. and Barbara E. (Holsberg) L.; m. Tamara Rae Beer, Sept. 7, 1985. AB, U. Chgo., 1981; JD magna cum laude, U. Minn., 1984. Bar: Ill. 1984, U.S. Dist. Ct. (no. dist.) Ill. 1984, Minn. 1988, U.S. Dist. Ct. Minn. 1989. Atty. Winston & Strawn, Chgo., 1984-87; assoc. Briggs & Morgan, St. Paul, 1987-91, shareholder, 1991—. Contbr. articles to profl. jours. Mem. St. Paul Jaycees (v.p. 1989-90, pres. 1993-94), Order of Coif. Democrat. Avocations: travel, sports, horse racing. Office: Briggs & Morgan 2400 IDS Center 80 S 8th St Ste 2400 Minneapolis MN 55402-2157

LONG, JEANINE HUNDLEY, state legislator; b. Provo, Utah, Sept. 21, 1928; d. Ralph Conrad and Hazel Laurine (Snow) Hundley; m. McKay W. Christensen, Oct. 28, 1949 (div. 1967); children: Cathy Schuyler, Julie Schulleri, Kelly M. Christensen, C. Brett Christensen, Harold A. Christensen; m. Kenneth D. Long, Sept. 6, 1968. AA, Shoreline C.C., Seattle, 1975; BA in Psychology, U. Wash., 1977. Mem. Wash. Ho. of Reps., 1983-87, 93-94, mem. Inst. Pub. Policy; mem. Wash. Senate, Dist. 44, Olympia, 1995—. Ranking mem. Human Svcs. and Corr. com., Wash. Senate. Mayor protem, mem. city coun. City of Brier, Wash., 1977-80. Republican. Office: PO Box 40482 Olympia WA 98504-0482 E-mail: long_je@leg.wa.gov.

LONG, JIM, race car driver; Mechanic D.K, Ulrich, NC, 1984—85; crew chief Hendrick Motor Sports, Charlotte, 1986—. Office: Hendricks Motorsports 4400 Papa Joe Hendrick Blvd Charlotte NC 28262

LONG, JOAN HAZEL, accountant; b. Colchester, Vt., Sept. 26, 1952; d. Ray Lawrence Sr. and Bernice Ethel (Reynolds) Wells; m. Joseph Andre Long (dec. Jan. 1996); 1 stepchild, Tracy Kendrew Long Stevens. A in Acctg., C.C. Vt., St. Albans, 1990. Cert. motorcycle rider tng. instr. Vt. Dept. Motor Vehicles, cert. motorcycle lic. examiner. Receptionist, sec. Vis. Nurse Assn., Burlington, Vt., 1971-72; accts. receivable bookkeeper Surg. Assocs., Inc., 1972-73; sec., bookkeeper Munson Earth Moving, South Burlington, Vt., 1973-74; upholsterer, owner Essex Upholstery Shop, Winooski, 1974—; corp. sec., acct. Engelberth Constrn., Inc., 1975-82; acct. Joan Long Acctg. Svcs., 1983—; scheduling coord. Vt. Rider Edn. Program, 1996-98; mgr., owner Wells Properties, 1997; site mgr. Vt. Rider Edn. Program, 1999—. Contbr. poem to East of Sunrise (Editor's Choice award Nat. Libr. Poetry), 1995. Activist, pres. Vt. Motorcyclist Rights Orgn., Essex Junction, 1975-78; govtl. affairs dir. Freedom of the Rd.-Vt., Inc., 1991-93; elected mem. com. Vt. Motorcycle Safety Adv. Com., 1993, 94; tax vol. AARP, 1990—. Avocations: motorcycling, fly fishing, horseback riding, golf, reading.

LONG, JODI L. office manager; b. Wilmington, N.C., Sept. 23, 1964; d. Jimmy Ray and Betty Elaine (Teague) L. BA in speech comm., U. N.C. Wilmington, 1986. Cert. Am. Bd. Opticians. Gen. mgr. LensCrafters, Hyattsville, Md., 1991-96; office mgr. Hour Eyes, Reston, Va., 1997—. Mem. Am. Paint Horse Assn. Avocation: horseback riding. Office: Hour Eyes 11130 S Lakes Dr Ste L Reston VA 20191-4395

LONG, JOHN A. plant consultant; b. Lewistown, Mont., Sept. 1, 1927; s. Philip and Nellie Long (Deceased); m. Jean Long, July 4, 1950; children: Timothy, Mark, Deborah, Christine Ungar. BS, Univ. Idaho, Moscow, ID, 1952; MS, Wash. State Univ., Fullman, WA, 1954; PhD, Tex. A&M Univ., College Station, TX, 1961. Asst. in agronomy N.Mex State Univ., Las Cruces, N.Mex., 1954—56, Tex. A&M Univ., College Station, 1956—61; dir. A.M. Scott & Sons Co., Marysville, 1961—91; ptnr. Long Bater Consultants, 1991—. Pres. Nat. Coun. of Comml. Plant Breeders, Washington, 1979—80; chmn. The Fertilizer Inst., Turf & Garden Cmte., Washington, 1987—88. Author: (book) Cytology of St. Augustine Grass; contbr. articles to profl. jours. Pres. Friends of Marysville Pub. Libr., Marysville, Ohio, 2001—02; pres. pta Marysville Pub. Schools, 1970. T-5 U.S. Army, 1941—48, US; Korea. Recipient Excellence in Rsch. Award, O.M. Scott Co. Mem.: Ohio Acad. of Sci. D-Liberal. Protestant. Achievements include development of developed & patented first St. Augustine grasses and wrote the first plant patent on a seed propagated Kentucky Bluegrass. Avocation: gardening. Home: 17 Scott Circle Marysville OH 43040-1048 Home Fax: 937-642-2664. Personal E-mail: jlong@midohio.net.

LONG, JOHN BROADDUS, JR. economist, educator; b. Bklyn., Feb. 28, 1944; s. John Broaddus and Katherine Lumpkin (Wicker) L.; m. Carol Elaine Stephens, Aug. 6, 1966; children— Jennifer Tipton, Owen Rosser, John McCauley BA, Rice U., 1966; PhD, Carnegie-Mellon U., 1971. Asst. prof. U. Rochester, N.Y., 1969-74, assoc. prof., 1974-84, prof., 1984—. Editor Jour. Fin. Econs., 1982-96, adv. editor, 1996-98; contbr. articles to profl. jours. Office: U Rochester William E Simon Grad Sch Bus Adminstrn Wilson Blvd Rochester NY 14627 E-mail: long@simon.rochester.edu.

LONG, JOHN D. retired insurance educator; b. Earlington, Ky., July 21, 1920; s. John Boyd and Effie (Yates) L.; m. Hazel Elinor Schnyder; children: Douglas P., Martha S. Caughey, Elinor J. Badanes. BS, U. Ky., 1942; MBA, Harvard U., 1947; D. Bus. Adminstrn., Indiana U., 1954. CLU, CPCU. Instr. De Pauw U., Greencastle, Ind., 1947, Indiana U., Bloomington, 1947—, asst. prof., 1954-56, assoc. prof., 1956-59, prof., 1959-90, acting dean sch. bus., 1983-84, Arthur M. Weimer prof. bus., 1985-90, Arthur M. Weimer prof. bus. emeritus, 1990; ret., 1990. Bd. dirs. Meridian Ins. Cos., Indpls., 1975-92; property-liability ins. cons. and expert witness. Author: Ethics, Morality, and Insurance, 1971, The Bible in English, 1998, What Think Ye of Christ? (Book for Intellectual Skeptics), 1998, Living Christ's Gospel, 2002; co-editor: Property and Liability Insurance Handbook, 1965; editor: Issues in Insurance, 1978; author numerous ins. related monographs; contbr. articles to profl. jours. Served to capt. U.S. Army, 1943-46, 51-52 Mem. Soc. CPCUs, Am. Risk and Ins. Assn. (pres. 1966-67, Elizur Wright award 1975), Am. Inst. Propery and Liability Underwriters (trustee 1978-89). Republican. E-mail: long@indiana.edu.

LONG, JOHN MICHAEL, neuroradiologist; b. Washington, Dec. 24, 1941; s. Bernard James and Catherine Ryan (Crego) L.; m. Nancy Gail Shepard, May 13, 1967; children: John M., Thomas Eric, Michaela L., Brian A., Bianca E. BS in Biology, Coll. Holy Cross, 1963; MD cum laude, Georgetown U., 1967. Med. and pediatrics intern Cleve. Clinic, 1967-68; resident in diagnostic radiology Yale U., New Haven, 1968-71, fellow in neuroradiology, 1970-71, instr. radiology, 1970-71; chief of neuroradiology Tripler Army Med. Ctr., Honolulu, 1971-74; assoc. prof. radiology, asst. prof. neurosurgery U. Ky., Lexington, 1974-75; neuroradiologist Eastern Maine Med. Ctr., Bangor, 1975—, chief radiology svc., 1977—; dir. Spectrum Med. Group, Maine, 1996-2001; chief radiology Acadia Hosp., 1997—. Contbr. articles to profl. jours. Maj. U.S. Army, 1971-74. Decorated Army Commendation medal. Fellow Am. Coll. Radiology; mem. Am. Soc. Neuroradiology (sr.), Radiol. Soc. N.Am., Maine Radiology Soc. (pres. 1980-81), Bangor Rotary, Alpha Omega Alpha. Roman Catholic. Avocations: skiing, golf, choral music. Home: 101 Trillium Trl Bangor ME 04401-2150 Office: Eastern Maine Med Ctr 489 State St Bangor ME 04401-6616

LONG, JUDITH ANN, nurse anesthetist; b. Warrensburg, Mo., Sept. 30, 1944; d. Ernest Edwin and Pansy Orene (Maxwell) L. A of Nursing, Coll. of Med. Arts, 1970; degree in nurse anesthesia, Ohio State U., 1974; BA in Health Adminstrn., Ottawa (Kans.) U., 1984; postgrad., 2000—. Staff nurse Kettering (Ohio) Med. Ctr., 1970-72; staff nurse anesthetist St. Lukes Hosp., Duluth, Minn., 1974-76, dir. anesthesia dept., 1979-85; staff nurse anesthetist St. Mary's Duluth Clinic, 1986—. Mem. adv. dept. design St. Mary's Med. Ctr. Duluth, 1994-96. Author: (novel) Last Mass of Knight Templars, 1998. Adoptive sponsor Christian Found. for Children, Colombia, 1996—, Nairobi, Kenya, 1997—. Mem. Am. Assn. Nurse Anesthetists, Minn. Assn. Nurses, Lake Superior Writers, Benedictine Oblate. Republican. Roman Catholic. Avocations: gardening, sailing, biking, tennis, sporting clays. Office: St Mary's Duluth Clinic 407 E 3d St Duluth MN 55805 E-mail: jlong79049@aol.com.

LONG, KENNETH D. marketing research administrator; b. Cleve., Mar. 13, 1952; s. Donald C. and Gertrude J. L.; m. Marian H. Long, Nov. 17, 1979; children: Steven, Kristen. BA in psychology, Ohio State Univ., 1974; MBA, Cleve. State Univ., 1984. Interviewer Princeton Survey Rsch. Ctr., Princeton, N.J., 1975; rsch. analyst Penton Media, Inc., Cleve., 1975-78, mgr. of mktg., econ. analysis, 1978-88, dir. info. svcs., 1988-93, dir. rsch. svcs., 1993-99; dir. rsch. ops. The Pat Henry Group, 2000-01; industry analyst The Freedonia Group, 2001—. Speaker at confs. Editor: Industry Inquiry Trends, 1998; contbr. articles to profl. jours. Avocations: musician, running. E-mail: k d. Office: The Freedonia Group 767 Beta Dr Cleveland OH 44143-2326 E-mail: long@hotmail.com.

LONG, KERRY BLAIR, lawyer; b. N.Y.C., Jan. 19, 1950; s. Frederick R. and Hazel A. (MacGregor) L.; m. Barbara E. McGann. AB, Colgate U., 1972; postgrad. Tulane U., 1977-78; JD magna cum laude, Cornell U., 1980. Bar: D.C., N.Y., U.S. Dist. Ct. (so. and ea. dists.) N.Y. Assoc. White & Case, N.Y.C., 1980-85, Perkins Coie LLP, Washington, 1985-88; ptnr., 1989-2000; ptnr. Fulbright and Jaworski LLP, Washington, 2001—. Lt. USN, 1972-77. Republican. Baptist. Office: Fulbright & Jaworski LLP 801 Pennsylvania Ave NW Washington DC 20004-2615

LONG, LELAND TIMOTHY, geophysicist educator, seismologist; b. Auburn, N.Y., Sept. 6, 1940; s. Walter K. and Carmalita Rose Long; m. Sarah Alice Blackard, Mar. 1970; children: Sarah Alice, Katherine Rose, Amy Virginia. BS in Geology, U. Rochester, 1962; MS in Geophysics, N.Mex. Inst. Mining and Tech., 1964; PhD in Geophysics, Oreg. State U., 1968. Registered profl. geologist, Ga. From asst. to assoc. prof. Sch. Earth and Atmosphere Scis. Ga. Inst. Tech., Atlanta, 1968-81, prof., 1981. Cons. in seismology, near-surface seismic imaging, seismic road vibrations and gravity data analysis. Contbr. articles to profl. jours. Office: Ga Inst Tech Earth And Atmospheric Scis Atlanta GA 30332-0340 E-mail: tim.long@eas.gatech.edu.

LONG, LINDA ANN, lawyer; b. Durham, N.C., Feb. 8, 1952; d. Grover Cleveland and Ellen (Parnell) L. BA, U. Del., 1974; JD, Widener U., 1979. Bar: D.C. 1989. Lobbyist Legis. Svcs., Inc., Dover, Del., 1977-79; campaign staff Connally for Pres., Arlington, Va., 1979-80; exec. dir. Reagan-Bush Com. Del., Wilmington, 1980; asst. for legis. affairs Gov. Pierre S. duPont IV, Dover, 1981; regional rep. pub. affairs Gulf Oil Corp., Phila., 1981-83, dir. GULF-PAC, area dir. pub. affairs Pitts., 1983-85; pres. Long Cons. Inc., 1985-89; dir. press & pub. liaison with NASA for Christa McAuliffe Challenger 51-L Mission, 1985-86; atty. Montgomery, McCracken, Walker & Rhoads, Washington, 1989-94, Blank, Rome, Comisky & McCauley, Washington, 1994-96; pvt. practice Wilmington, 1996—. State & fed. legislation regulatory affairs, & non profit adv. to state senate campaigns, Del., 1998; adv. to Del. gubanatorial candidate, 1998—; counsel Pa. House Legis. Redistricting, 1991; gen. counsel Women Execs. in State Govt., 1990-95; counsel Nat. Policy Forum, 1993-96; lectr. Internat. Rep. Inst., election law for Macedonia Parliamentary Party Mem., 1992; del. Internat. Observer Mission-Romania Parliamentary & Presdl. Elections, 1992; mem. comml. space transp. adv. com. U.S. Dept. Transp., 1988-90; bd. dirs., exec. com. Air and Space Heritage Coun., 1987—; loaned exec. pub. affairs dept. NASA, 1984-85; sr. adv. to convention mgr. 1992 Rep. Convention. Mem. Rep. Bus. Coun. Del., 1982-83; cons., asst. to chmn. Rep. Nat. Com., 1986-89, dep. polit. counsel, 1987-89, dep. to gen. counsel, 1992-96, life mem.; me. women's adv. bd. Internat. Rep. Inst.; mem. Gov.'s Commn. Status of Women Spkrs. Bur., 1981-83; mem. Wright Meml. Dinner Com., 1985; dir. contract negotiations-ops. 1989 Am. Bicentennial Presdl. Inaugural Com.; mem. Del. Lawyers for George W. Bush for Pres. Mem. Women in Govt. Rels., Am. Petroleum Inst. (com. pub. rels. 1981-84), Rep. Nat. Lawyers Assn. (bd. dirs. 1993—), U.S. Dept. Transp. Comml. Space Transp. (adv. com. 1988-90), Charter 100, Capitol Hill Club. Office: 32 Harlech Dr Greenville DE 19807 E-mail: lalong1@aol.com.

LONG, LINDA SUE, special education educator; b. Marshall, Mo., Oct. 14, 1947; d. Thomas Arnet and Helen Louise (Ray) Meads; m. Robert Earl Long, Aug. 7, 1999; 1 child from previous marriage Lisa Susanne Meads Casey. Student, Mo. Valley Coll., Marshall, Mo., 1966-67; AA, Longview C.C., Lee's Summit, Mo., 1987; BS in Edn. cum laude, Cen. Mo. State U., Warrensburg, 1990; MS in Edn., 1996. Technician AT&T, Lee's Summit, Mo., 1969-87; tchr. spl. edn. Lee's Summit Sch. Dist., 1990, Midway Sch. Dist., Cleveland, Mo., 1990—. Dist. coord. HIV/AIDS edn. Midway Sch. Dist.; guest speaker on the impact of HIV/AIDs on families. Recipient Crystal Apple award for excellence in teaching, 1995. Mem. Coun. Exceptional Children, Learning Disabilities Assn., Kappa Delta Pi, Phi Kappa Phi. Home: 5613 NW Hutson Rd Kansas City MO 64151-2831 Office: Midway Sch Dist Cleveland MO 64734

LONG, MADELEINE J. mathematics and science educator; b. N.Y.C. d. Harry L. and Irma (Silverman) L. BA, Queens Coll., 1960; M.Ed., Harvard U., 1963; Ed.D., Columbia U., 1967. Tchr. Westbury (N.Y.) Sch. System, 1960-61; teaching fellow Harvard U., 1962-63; prof. edn. L.I. U., asst. to dean, 1967-69, chmn. dept., 1969-76, dir. div. edn., dir. grad. programs at Westchester br. campus, 1977-83, dir. Inst. Advancement Math. and Sci., 1983-91; program officer (on leave from L.I. U.) NSF, Washington, 1991-96; v.p. The Implementation Group, 1996-99; program dir. math., sci., tech. and extended day programs AAAS, 1999—. Vis. scientist, spl. asst. comprehensive design planning NSF, 1992-93, sr. program officer Urban Systemic Initiative, 1993-96, reader, 1973, 77, 79, 85, 88, 90, career access panelist and chair, 1988; dir. summer tng. programs N.Y.C. Bd. Edn., 1978, 79, 81; reader Fund for Improvement Postsecondary Edn., 1984, 85, 87, N.J. Bd. Higher Edn., Minority Instns. Sci. Improvement Program; cons. to various univs. and sch. sys.; lectr. in field; apptd. coun. on excellence and equity in math. and sci. edn. N.Y. State, 1986-91; v.p. The Implementation Group, 1996-99; mem. adv. bd. L.A. Collaborative Tchr. Edn., 1997—, Tchrs. Am. Math. & Sci. Programs, 1996—. Mem. editorial bd. Jour. Coll. Sci. Teaching, 1986-89; contbr. articles to profl. jours. Mem. edn. subcom. Mayor's Commn. on Sci. and Tech., 1989-91. Columbia U. fellow, 1963-64, grantee NSF, 1972, 78, 79, 80, 81, 84-87, 87-91, 91-94, Career Edn., 1975, Fund for Improvement Postsecondary Edn., 1983-87, Title II Edn. for Econ. Security Act N.Y. State. Fellow Philosophy of Edn. Soc.; mem. AAAS (chair sect. Q, Sci. Edn., chmn. edn. section, program dir. 1999—), Assn. Supervision and Curriculum Devel., N.Y. Acad. Sci., Nat. Sci. Tchrs. Assn., Nat. Coun. Tchrs. Math., Am. Ednl. Rsch. Assn., Kappa Delta Pi. Office: NSF 4201 Wilson Blvd Arlington VA 22230-0001

LONG, MARK CHISTOPHER, English educator; b. LaJolla, Calif., Nov. 30, 1959; s. Wendell Oliver and Mary Ellen (Ricketts) L.; m. Rebecca Elizabeth Todd, Sept. 10, 1994; children: Nathaniel Carroll Todd Long, Ellinore Ruth Todd Long. BA, Ithaca (N.Y.) Coll., 1990; MA, U. Wash., 1992, PhD, 1996. Profl. ski instr., back-country guide Profl. Ski Instrs. of Am., Calif., 1980-86; tchg. asst. U. Wash., Seattle, 1991-96, asst. dir. writing ctr., 1992-93, asst. dir. expository writing program, 1993-95, acting instr. dept. English, 1996-98; asst. prof. English and Am. studies Keene (N.H.) State Coll., 1998—. Acting instr. U. Wash., 1996-98. Author: U.S. Marine Corps Ski Instruction Manual, 1994; contbr. articles to profl. jours. Mem. MLA, Nat. Coun. Tchrs. English, Assn. for Study of Lit. and the Environment, Phi Alpha Theta, Phi Kappa Phi. Democrat. Unitarian Universalist. Avocations: Nordic skiing, climbing, sea kayaking, wilderness travel. Home: 113 Village Rd Surry NH 03431-8312 Office: Keene State Coll Dept English Keene NH 03435-1402 E-mail: mlong@keene.edu.

LONG, MARTIN E. lawyer; b. Parsons, Kans., Dec. 29, 1955; s. Richard Harvey Long and Francie Ann (Westhoff) Moccioni; m. Joann Rose Ficker, Sept. 17, 1988. BBA in Polit. Sci., Western State Coll., Gunnison, Colo., 1976; JD, U. Denver, 1980. Bar: Colo. 1983, U.S. Dist. Ct. Colo. 1983. Landman Fairway Energy Corp., Denver, 1981-83; pvt. practice, 1984—. Mem. Kiwanis, Denver, 1987-89. Republican. Presbyterian. Avocations: skiing, tennis, hunting, biking. Office: 303 E 17th Ave Ste 800 Denver CO 80203-1299

LONG, MAXINE MASTER, lawyer; b. Pensacola, Fla., Oct. 20, 1943; d. Maxwell L. and Claudine E. (Smith) M.; m. Anthony Byrd Long, Aug. 27, 1966; children: Deborah E., David M. AB, Bryn Mawr Coll., 1965; MS, Georgetown U., 1971; JD, U. Miami, 1979. Bar: Fla. 1979, U.S. Ct. Appeals (5th cir.) 1980, U.S. Dist. Ct. (so. dist.) Fla. 1980, U.S. Ct. Appeals (11th cir.) 1981, U.S. Dist. Ct. (mid. and no. dists.) Fla. 1987. Law clk. to U.S. dist. judge U.S. Dist. Ct. (so. dist.) Fla., Miami, 1979-80; assoc. Shutts & Bowen, 1980-90, of counsel, 1990-92, ptnr., 1992—. Mem. Fla. Bar Assn. (cert. bus. litigator, mem. bus. litigation cert. com. 1995-99, vice chair, 1996-97, past chair bus. litigation com., sec./treas. bus. law sect.) Dade County Bar Assn. (mem. fed. cts. com., recipient pro bono award/Vol. Lawyers for the Arts 1989). Office: Shutts & Bowen 201 S Biscayne Blvd Ste 1500 Miami FL 33131-4308 E-mail: mlong@shutts-law.com.

LONG, MEREDITH J. art dealer; b. Joplin, Mo., Sept. 14, 1928; s. Emery Meredith and Martha M. (Attebury) L.; m. Cornelia Cullen, June 23, 1967; children: Meredith, Jenny, Gretchen, Martha Katherine. BA, U. Tex., 1950, postgrad. Law Sch., 1950-51, 53-54. Exec. Curtis Mathes Corp., Houston, 1953-57; owner Meredith Long & Co., 1957—, Meredith Long Contemporary, N.Y.C., 1977-80; prin. Davis & Long, 1974-80, Watson-de Nagy and Co., Houston, 1974-80. Dir. Bank S.W., 1975-84, S.W. Bancshares, 1984; bd. dirs. MCorp, Quintana Petroleum Corp., 1984-94, dir. 1983—. Editor: Americans at Home and Abroad Catalogue, 1971, Tradition and Innovation-American Paintings 1860-1870 Catalogue, 1974, Americans at Work and Play, 1845-1944 Catalogue, 1980. Chmn. mcpl. arts, City of Houston, 1976-78; bd. dirs., exec. com., trustee Mus. Fine Arts, 1977-79; bd. dirs., mem. exec. com. Houston, Alley Theatre, Houston, 1975—, chmn., 1989-93; trustee Houston Ballet Found., 1974-76, exec. com., 1976-77, adv. com., 1979-80; mem. exec. com. Contemporary Arts Mus., 1975-77; mem. pres.'s adv. bd. John F. Kennedy Center of Performing Arts, until 1980; v.p. devel. Houston Symphony Soc., dir., 1986, adv. bd., 1987—, past bd. dirs., pres.'s counc. Houston Grand Opera; mem. adv. council U. Tex. Coll. Fine Arts, Austin, 1979—; chmn. emeritus, 1993; trustee Houston chpt. Multiple Sclerosis Soc., 1981, Archives of Am. Art, 1989-95, Cultural Arts Coun. City of Houston, 1991—; chmn. Tex. Heart Inst., 1991—. Mem. Am. Assn. Museums, Am. Fedn. Arts, Visual Artists and Galleries Assn. (dir. 1977-78), Art Dealers Assn. Houston (past pres.), Ducks Unlimited Inc. (nat. trustee 1969-80, sponsor of yr. 1979), River Oaks Country Club, Bayou Club, Coronado (bd. dirs.), Ramada-Tejas, The Houstonian, Doubles Club (N.Y.C.), Knickerbocker Club (N.Y.C.). Home: 3722 Knollwood St Houston TX 77019-1110 Office: 2323 San Felipe St Houston TX 77019-3494

LONG, MICHAEL ALAN, musician, writer; b. Chgo., Oct. 14, 1945; s. Irving Robert and Libby (Zasser) L.; m. Isola Charlayne Jones, Aug. 3, 1989 (div. Oct. 1995). BA in English, Ariz. State U., 1967; MusM, Phila. Inst. Music, Kharkov Ukraine, 1993; Mus D, Philharm. State Inst. Music, Kharkov, Ukraine, 1997. Artist in residence Ariz. State U., Tempe, 1968-73; investment banker Bancom Fin. Corp., Phoenix, 1972-83. Edn. dir. U.S. Office Econ. Opportunity, Phoenix, 1969-72; pres. Solaris Classics, Phoenix, 1997—; internat. mgr. Russian Fed. Orch., Moscow, 1995-00; artist adv. U.S. Coun. of the Arts, Phoenix, 1970-75; cons. Ministry of Culture of Republic of Ukraine; vis. prof. Philharm. Inst., Kharkov, 1997-00; internat. mgr. State Symphony of Russian Republic; cons. concerts in field, worldwide. Classical recordings include Hovhaness Symphony for Guitar, Music of the Royal Courts, Hovhaness Mystery of the Holy Martyrs, Tristeza de Amor, Partitas of J.S. Bach; writer, prodr., performer Mr. Cobb's Corner, 1978, PBS TV series In Concert, CBS series Perimeter; dramatist: Il Valentino, 1996, Don Carlos, 1997. Recipient Best Documentary Sound Track, U.S. Coun. of the Arts, 1969, Internat. Gold medal Swedish Arabian Horse Assn., Stockholm, 1982, Gold Medal Premio Roma, 5 Grammy award nominations. Jewish. Avocations: weightlifting, collecting books and art, ancient numismatics, breediing horses. Office: 3550 N Central Ave Ste 701 Phoenix AZ 85012-2109

LONG, MICHAEL CHRISTIAN, forester; b. Lock Haven, Pa., July 29, 1946; s. David C. and Marie (Dickey) Mapes; m. Linnetta Ann Ryan Long, Mar. 24, 1969; 1 child, Douglas Michael. Student, Utah State U., 1964-65; AAS in Forestry, Paul Smiths Coll., 1971; BS in Resource Mgmt., Syracuse U., 1972. Cert. pub. mgr., Fla. Clay County forester Fla. Divsn. Forestry, Ft. Myers, 1972-74, Ft. Myers dist. forester, 1974-79, chief fire control bur., 1979-96, asst. divsn. dir., 1996—. Incident command team Nat. Wildfire Coord. Group, 1981-85; chmn. Nat. Fire Weather Adv. Group, 1986-94. Co-author: National Wildfire Coordinating Group, 1985. Vol. firefighter Jefferson County Emergency Svcs., Monticello, Fla., 1998—. With U.S. Army, 1966-69. Decorated with 3 Purple Hearts, 2 Bronze Stars, 2 Army Commendation medals; recipient Achievement award Nat. Assn. State Foresters, 1994, Silver Smokey Bear award U.S. Forest Svc./Nat. Advt. Coun., 1996, Sustained Superior Achievement award Fla. Dept. Agr. and Consumer Svcs., 1998; recipient lifetime achievement award Nat. Assn. State Forests, 2000; named Monticello, Fla.'s Firefighter of Yr., 2000. Mem. Fla. Fire Chiefs Assn. (Fire Chief of Yr. award 1995), Fla. State Firemens Assn., Forestry Conservation Comm. Assn. (past pres.), Nat. Fire Protection Assn. (bd. dirs. Wildland Fire sect.). Avocations: running, hunting, fishing, backpacking. Office: Fla Divsn Forestry 3125 Conner Blvd Tallahassee FL 32399-6576 E-mail: longm@doacs.state.fl.us.

LONG, MICHAEL ELDON, government and history educator; b. Charleston, W.Va., Aug. 15, 1950; s. Roy Eldon and Alice Mae (Leonard) Long; m. Marilyn Sue Branscome, May 25, 1970 (div. Sept. 1997); children: Lisa Michelle, Michael Brent. BA, U. Charleston, 1973; postgrad., George Washington U., 1974-75, U. Hawaii-Manoa, 1983; MS, Cen. Mich. U., 1985; postgrad., Marshall U., 1999, U. S. Fla., 2002. Enlisted U.S. Army, 1977, commd. officer, 1978-97; maj. (ret.) USAR , 1997; instr. history and polit. sci. Pasco-Hernando C.C., 2001—. Adj. prof. govt. and history Southside Va. C.C., 1992—93, St. Petersburg Jr. Coll., Fla., 1999—2001, U. Charleston, W.Va., 1999, Pasco-Hernando C.C., Fla., 2000—01, Fla. Met. U., Tampa, 2000—01; cons. Discussant Southwestern Polit. Sci. Assn., 2001. *Michael Long has thirty years of dedicated public service (1973-2003) as a college educator, local government official, and a commissioned Army officer. As Instructor of History and Political Science at Pasco-Hernando Community College (2001-present), his most recent accomplishments include the establishment of an honors-level course for undergraduate students in American History. While serving in Virginia local government (1989-1996) Mr. Long received the Marsha Mashaw Memorial Award for outstanding service as an Assistant City Manager. Maj. Michael E. Long, USAR (Ret.) held a variety of command and staffing assignments in the Army and U.S. Army Reserve and has received numerous military awards and decorations.* Manuscript/book reviewer: Jour. Politics, manuscript/book reviewer: White Ho. Studies, manuscript/book reviewer: Fla. Hist. Qur., manuscript/book reviewer: W.Va. History, manuscript/book reviewer: Richmond Times-Dispatch, manuscript/book reviewer: Mil. Rev. Dir. Ft. Scammon Hist. Assn., South Charleston, W.Va., 1964—65; seasonal ranger-historian Nat. Pk. Svc., Petersburg Nat. Battlefield, Va., 1972; curator divsn.hist. preservation Fairfax County Pk. Authority, Annandale, 1973—75; participant Woodlawn Conf. Hist. Site Adminstrn., Mt. Vernon, 1974; curator collection and exhibits Hist. Bethlehem, Inc., Pa., 1975—76; exec. dir. Parkersburg (W.Va.) Arts Ctr., 1976—77; bd. dirs. Meherrin River Arts Coun., Emporia, Va., 1990—91, South Charleston Mus. Found., 1998—99. Mem.: So. Polit. Sci. Assn. (panel chair 2001), Am. Polit. Sci. Assn., Acad. Polit. Sci., Am. Hist. Assn., Assn. U.S. Army Club (Suncoast chpt.), Am. Legion. Republican. Roman Catholic. Avocation: historic preservation. Home: 5143 50th Ave West Bradenton FL 34210 Office Fax: 727-816-3321. Business E-Mail: longm@phcc.edu.

LONG, MICHAEL HOWARD, urban planner, landscape architect; b. Rochester, N.Y., July 20, 1956; s. Howard M. and Barbara K. (Leonard) L.; m. Diane M. Olshefski, Mar. 11, 1979; children: Kristan M., Jessica A., Brendan M., Gregory M. AAS in Architecture, Dutchess Community Coll., 1976; BS in Environ. Design, SUNY, Syracuse, 1979, B Landscape Architecture, 1980; MA in Pub. Adminstrn., Syracuse U., 1992; M Landscape Arch., SUNY, Syracuse, 1992. Registered landscape architect, N.Y. Constrn. foreman Landscape Concepts, Millbrook, N.Y., 1976-80; site designer, estimator F.W. Cunningham, Inc., Auburn, 1980; landscape architect Environ. Design and Research, Skaneateles, 1981-84; sr. planner Cayuga County Planning Bd., Auburn, 1980-92; Capital Improvement Program mgr. City of Auburn, Office of Planning and Econ. Devel., 1992—; cons. Brennan Lorenzini Architects, Auburn, 1984-88; sec.-treas. New Directions Therapeutics, Inc., 1989—; mng. ptnr. E.A. Huntington House Partnership, 1990—. Prin., cons. Liberatore, Long Preservation Planners, Auburn, 1987; co-dir. Willard Meml. Chapel Project, 1988-92; spkr. historic preservation program Cornell U., 1992—. Basketball coach Cath. Youth Orgn., 1980-84, 95-2000; chmn. Cmty. Preservation Com., Inc., Cayuga County, N.Y., 1984-88, City of Auburn Hist. Resources Adv. Bd., 1987-92; trustee Cayuga Mus. History and Art, 1985-92; bd. dirs. Auburn Bicentennial Com., 1991-94; coord. White House Millenium Coun. tour to the Harriet Tubman House, 1998; total quality mgmt. facilitator City of Auburn, 1994-98; spkr. leadership Cayuga/C. of C., 1990—; spkr. N.Y. Conf. of Mayors, 1995; parish rep., 2000; treas. Cath. Youth Orgn. Bd., 2000. Grantee Fulbright scholarship, Greece, 1979; recipient award Preservation League N.Y. State, 1990. Mem. Am. Soc. Landscape Architects (juror nat. student awards design competition 1986, 88, 90), Am. Planning Assn. (spkr. upstate N.Y. chpt. 1996, nat. conf., 1998, treas. ctrl. N.Y. chpt. 1999-2000, treas. upstate N.Y. chpt. 2000—), Nat. Trust for Hist. Preservation. Avocations: house restoration, coaching, golf. Office: City of Auburn Office Planning and Econ Devel 24 South St Meml City Hall Auburn NY 13021

LONG, MICHAEL JOHN, public health sciences educator, researcher; b. Oxford, Eng., Jan. 30, 1932; s. George Henry and Annie Maud (Carpenter) L.; m. Elizabeth Caroline Johnston (div. Mar. 1984); children: Adrian, Sean, Ashley; m. Mary Ann Lescoe, May 26, 1984. BLS, U. Okla., 1971, MA in Econs., 1973; PhD, U. Mich., 1978. Asst. prof., dir. grad. program dept. cmty. medicine Wayne State U., Detroit, 1977-82; assoc. prof., dir. health adminstrn. program Ea. Mich. U., Ypsilanti, 1982-86; prof., assoc. chmn. dept. health adminstrn. Med. U. S.C., Charleston, 1986-88; prof., chmn. dept. health policy and adminstrn. Pa. State U., State Coll., 1988-91; prof., dir. grad. program dept. health adminstrn.-cmty. med. U. Edmonton, Alta., Can., 1991-94; prof., chmn., MPH dir. dept. health svcs. orgn. and policy Wichita (Kans.) State U., 1994-96, prof. dept. pub. health scis., 1996—. Faculty cons. W.K. Kellogg sponsored Health Adminstrn. Baccalaureate Curriculum, Washington, 1986-87; cons. Ont. Coun. on Grad. Studies, Can., 1991-94; inaugural lectr. Calgary (Alta.) WHO Ctr. Series in Mental Health, 1993. Author: The Medical Care System: A Conceptual Model, 1994, Health and Healthcare in the United States, 1998; also articles. Dissertation grantee Nat. Ctr. for Health Svcs. Rsch., 1977. Avocations: running, reading, household remodeling. Home: 1223 N Rutland Wichita KS 67206 Office: Wichita State U Dept Pub Health Scis 1845 Fairmount St Wichita KS 67260-0001 Fax: 316-978-3025. E-mail: long@chp.twsu.edu.

LONG, NICHOLAS TROTT, lawyer; b. Bethlehem, Pa., Jan. 24, 1947; s. John Cuthbert and Mary Catherine (Parsons) L.; m. Abigail Brooks, Oct. 11, 1981; 1 child, Gabriel Parsons Brooks Long. BA, Cornell U., 1968; JD, Columbia U., 1972. Bar: Pa., R.I. Asst. dist. atty., Phila., 1972-73; pvt. practice, 1973-77, 92—; asst. pub. defender State of R.I., Providence, 1977-79; gen. counsel U. R.I., Kingston, 1979-86; chief asst. A.G. civil divsn. State of R.I., 1987-90, spl. prosecutor and counsel to the atty. gen., 1987-91, counsel to commn. of higher edn., 1992-2000; gen. counsel R.I. Coll., Providence, 2000—. Ednl. cons. Co-author: The Legal Deskbook for Administrators of Independent Colleges and Universities, 1993, rev., 1999, Managing Liability and Overseas Programs, 1999; author: Strategic Legal Planning: The College and University Legal Audit, 1998. Bd. dirs. Internat. Inst. R.I., Providence, 1990—, 1st v.p., 1997-99; pres. Sakonnet Preservation Assn., Little Compton, R.I., 1994-98, bd. dirs., 1985—. Mem. Nat. Assn. Coll. and Univ. Attys. Avocations: sailing, theatre. Office: 101 Dyer St Ste 400 Providence RI 02903 E-mail: nicholas@ntlong.com.

LONG, PAMELA OLIVIA, historian; b. Quakertown, Pa., Mar. 17, 1943; d. Winslow Nielson and Barbara Jane (Henry) L.; m. Robert A. Korn, July 18, 1979; 1 child, Allison Rachel. BA with honors, U. Md., 1965, MA in History, 1969, PhD in Renaissance/Reformation History, 1979; MSW, Cath. U., 1971. Asst. prof. Barnard Coll., N.Y.C., 1981-82; copyright examiner Libr. of Congress, Washington, 1983-86; tutor St. John's Coll., Annapolis, Md., 1991-92; freelance writer, 1993; vis. asst. prof. Johns Hopkins U., 1995-98. Adj. asst. prof. NYU, 1982, Marymount Manhattan Coll., 1982, Trinity Coll., Washington, 1983, U. Md., College Park, 1987, 93; conf. coord. Sci. and Tech. in Medieval Soc., Medieval and Renaissance Studies Program, Barnard Coll., 1983; bd. dirs. AVISTA, Inc. (Assn. Villard de Honnecourt for the Interdisciplinary Study of Medieval Tech., Sci. and Art, 1987-92; presenter in field. Author: Openness, Secrecy, Authorship: Technical Arts and the Culture of Knowledge from Antiquity to the Renaissance, 2001; editor Sci. and Tech. in Medieval Soc., Annals of the N.Y. Acad. Scis., 1985; editor-in-chief AVISTA FORUM, 1987-88, reviews editor, 1992—; editl. adv. bd. Tech. and Culture, 1992—; contbr. articles to profl. jours. Recipient Fulbright-Hays award for Italy, 1979-80, Abbott Payson Usher prize Soc. for the History of Tech., 1993, Morris D. Forkosch prize for best book in intellectual history, 2001; grantee NSF, 1986, 91-92, 98-2000; travel grantee NRC, 1989; Jr. fellow Folger Inst. Renaissance and Eighteenth Century Studies, 1974, 75, 78; Grad. fellow U. Md., 1976-79; Jr. Post-Doctoral fellow Soc. for the Humanities, Cornell U., 1980-81; Dibner Libr. fellow Nat. Mus. Am. History, Washington, 1993; NEH long-term fellow Folger Shakespeare Libr., 1994-95, Sr. fellow Dibner Inst. History Sci. and Tech. MIT, Cambridge, Mass., 2000-01. Home: #137 3100 Connecticut Ave NW Apt 137 Washington DC 20008-5100

LONG, PETER AVARD CHIPMAN, retired rear admiral United States Navy; b. Montreal, Quebec, Can., Feb. 19, 1944; m. Janet Elaine Hall; children: Melinda, David. BS, U.S. Naval Acad., 1967; MS in Pers. Mgmt., Naval Postgrad. Sch., Monterey, Calif., 1972; PhD in Learning Tech., Nova Southeastern U., Ft. Lauderdale, 1991. Commd. ensign U.S. Navy, 1967, advanced through grades to rear admiral, 1994; main propulsion asst., damage control asst. USS Dennis J. Buckley, 1967-69; engr. officer USS Hepburn, 1972-75; cmmdg. officer USS Moctobi, Pearl Harbor, Hawaii, 1975-76; exec. officer USS Albert David, 1980-81; commanding officer USS David R. Ray, 1985-87, USS Reeves, 1991-93, Cruiser-Destroyer Group 5, Kitty Hawk Battle Group, 1996-98, commdr., 1993—, rear admiral, 1994—. Addtl. shore duties include: exec. officer Navy Recruiting Dist., San Diego, Placement Office and Detailer at Naval Mil. Pers. Command, Washington, CNO Chair Industrial Coll. of the Armed Forces, commanding office Naval Sta., Mayport, Fla.; commdg. officer Naval Sta., Pearl Harbor, Hawaii, cmmdr. Logistics Group We. Pacific, Singapore, dep. chief of staff for shore installation mgmt., U.S. Pacific fleet; provost Naval War Coll., 1998-2000; pres. Valley Forge Mil. Acad. and Coll., 2000—. Decorated Navy DSM, Legion of Merit with 4 gold stars, Navy Commendation medal with gold star; recipient Navy Achievement medal. Office: Valley Forge Mil Acad 1001 Eagle Rd Wayne PA 19087-3613 E-mail: plong@VFMAC.com.

LONG, PHILIP LEE, information systems executive; b. Cleve., Jan. 24, 1943; s. Philip Joseph and Anne Catherine (Woodward) L.; BEE, Ohio State U., 1968, MSc, 1970; m. LeAnn Boyack Edvalson, Apr. 22, 1982; children: Sarah J., Caitlin T.; children by previous marriage: Philip Imants, Michael Oskar; Assoc. dir. Ohio Coll. Libr. Ctr., 1969-73; asso. for computer systems devel. SUNY, Albany, 1974-75; pres. Philip Long Assos., Inc., Salt Lake City, 1975-81; v.p. Novell Data Systems, 1981-82; v.p. Telerate Systems, Inc., 1983-93; pres. Philip Long Assocs., Ltd., South Orange, N.J., 1993—; instr. computer sci. Ohio State Univ., libr. sci. SUNY, Catholic U. Am.; cons. to UNESCO, Bibliotheque National de France, Lib. Congress, Nat. Comm. Library and Info. Sci. Grantee, Nat. Rsch. Coun., Nat. Acad. Sci., 1971. Mem. Am. Soc. Info. Sci., IEEE, ALA, Assn. Computing Machinery, Am. Nat. Stds. Inst. Contbr. articles to profl. jours. Office: 397 Thornden St South Orange NJ 07079-1423

LONG, RALPH STEWART, clinical psychologist; b. Pitts., Feb. 23, 1926; s. Ralph S. and Virginia (Hawk) L.; m. Vera Lazorchak, June 16, 1951; children: Karen Virginia, Brian Reed, Lauri Michelle. BS, Lock Haven U., 1950; MEd, Pa. State U., 1951; PhD, Washington U., St. Louis, 1965. Lic. psychologist, Tex. Commd. 2d lt. USAF, 1951, advanced through grades to lt. col., 1968, psychologist various hosps. U.S. and Europe, 1951-71; ret., 1971; dir. psychol. svcs. Community Ctr. Mental Health, Mental Retardation, Wichita Falls, Tex., 1971-72; psychol. cons. Family Counseling Ctr., 1972-74; dir. psychol. svcs. Nueces County Mental Health-Mental Retardation Community Ctr, 1974-77; dir. Corpus Christi Counseling Ctr./Physicians-Surgeons Hosp., Tex., 1977-79, Psychol. Cons., Corpus Christi, 1979-82; exec. dir. Personal Dynamics Inst., 1982—, dir., 1988—. Instr. dept. psychology McKendree Coll., Lebanon, Ill., 1962-63; instr. So. Ill. U., 1962-64; adj. prof. human rels. Webster U., Webster Groves, Mo., 1976-79, 88-93; adj. prof. psychology Del Mar Coll., Corpus Christi, 1977-83, adj. prof. bus. adminstrn., 1991-93; cons. Tex. Dept. Corrections, 1988-90; bd. dirs. Ctr. Creative Living, 1986—; cons., trainer Crisis Svcs., 1980—; profl. adv. bd. North Tex. Regional Coun. Alcoholism, 1971-74, Mental Health Assn. Coastal Bend, 1974-83, Wichita Mental Health Assn., 1965-67, 70-74; adj. prof. Embry-Riddle U., Corpus Christi, 1991-93; clin. dir. Shoreline Chem. Dependency Treatment Ctr., 1989-92; consulting psychologist Nueces County Juvenile Justice Ctr., Corpus Christi, 1992—, Warm Springs Rehab. Ctr., Corpus Christi, 1992—. MCC Managed Behavioral Care, Inc., Eden Prairie, Minn., 1992—, Champus Provider, 1972—; bd. dirs. Consumer Credit Counseling Svc. South Tex., 1983-92, emeritus, 1993—. Contbr. to profl. jours.; presenter in field. Active Tex. chpt. ARC; founding mem. Nat. Campaign for Tolerance; charter sponsor Air Force Meml. Found., Statue of Liberty-Ellis Island Found.; mem. Nat. Com. to Preserve Social Security and Medicine. With USNR, 1944—51. Named Am. Man Sci., 1962. Fellow Soc. Air Force Clin. Psychologists; mem. APA, DAV, VFW, Am. Inst. Hypnosis, U.S. Holocaust Meml. Mus. (charter), Libr. of Congress Assocs. (charter), Tex. Assn. Mental Health (exec. com. 1980-83), Air Force Assn., Nat. Register Health Svc. Providers in Psychology, Smithsonian, Sierra Club, Am. Assn. Ret. Persons, Ret. Officers Assn., Am. Mil. Soc., Am. Legion, U.S. Naval Inst., Common Cause, Nat. Air and Space Soc. (founding mem.), WWII Meml. Soc. (charter mem.), Earth Justice Legal Def. Fund, Nat. Arbor Day Found., United Srs. Assn., Theosophical Soc. Am., Nat. Wildlife Fedn., Nat. Mus. Am. Indian (charter), F.D. Roosevelt Meml. (founding), Am. Air Mus. in Britain (charter), Nat. Trust for Hist. Preservation, Masons, Shriners, Sigma Xi. Avocations: painting, writing, travel, camping, fishing. Office: Personal Dynamics Inst 1819 S Brownlee Blvd Corpus Christi TX 78404-2901

LONG, REGINALD ALAN, lawyer, educator; b. Pitts., Jan. 9, 1960; s. William Bryant and Betty (Holmes) L.; m. Lisa D. Love, Apr. 26, 1987; children: Reginald Alan Jr., Bryant A. BS, California (Pa.) State Coll., 1981; MBA, Fordham U., 1990; JD, N.Y. Law Sch., 1996. Bar: N.Y. 1997, N.J. 1998, U.S. Dist. Ct. (no. dist.) N.J. 1998. Sys. analyst Pa. Dept. Transp., Harrisburg, 1981-84; bus. analyst Pa. Blue Shield, Camp Hill, 1984-87; assoc. dir. TIAA-CREF, N.Y.C., 1987-98; ptnr. Love and Long, L.L.P., Newark, 1997—. Adj. prof. real estate Rutgers U. Grad. Sch. Bus., Newark, 1998—. Mentor Youth Emergency Ctr., Newark, 1987; counselor, vol. Youth Crisis Ctr., Newark, 1987; mem. Bro. to Bro. Mentor Program, East Orange, N.J., 1998. Mem. ABA, N.Y. Bar Assn., Omega Psi Phi (Man of Yr. award 1993). Avocations: winemaking, basketball, golf. Home: 338 Warwick Ave South Orange NJ 07079-2445 Office: Love & Long LLP 108 Washington St Newark NJ 07102-3024

LONG, RICHARD PAUL, civil engineering educator, geotechnical engineering consultant; b. Allentown, Pa., Nov. 29, 1934; s. Peter Anthony and Matilda (Stier) L.; m. Mary Elizabeth Doyle, Aug. 29, 1964; children: Marybeth, Christopher. BCE, U. Cin., 1957; MCE, Rensselaer Poly. Inst., 1963, PhD, 1966. Registered profl. engr., Conn. NSF postdoctoral fellow Rensselaer Poly. Inst., Troy, N.Y., 1966-67; from asst. to assoc. prof. civil engring. U. Conn., Storrs, 1967-77, prof., 1978-97, head dept., 1977-90, prof. emeritus, 1997—. Com. mem. Transp. Research Bd., Washington, 1971—. Contbr. articles to profl. jours.; co-inventor, patentee prefabricated subsurface drain, stress laminated timber bridges. Pres. Mansfield Middle Sch. Assn., Storrs, 1977-79; commr. Mansfield Housing Authority, Storrs, 1987—, chmn., 1988-93. 1st lt. U.S. Army, 1958-61. Recipient T.A. Bedford prize Rensselaer Poly. Inst., 1966, AT&T Found. award for Teaching Excellence, 1988, Recognition award Conn. Soc. Profl. Engrs., 1989. Fellow ASCE; mem. Conn. Soc. Civil Engrs. (sec. 1986-88, pres.-elect 1988-89, pres. 1989-90), Am. Soc. Engring. Edn. Roman Catholic. Avocations: jogging, travel. Home: 31 Westgate Ln Storrs Mansfield CT 06268-1506 E-mail: long@uconnvm.uconn.edu., rpmelong@earthlink.net.

LONG, ROBERT HOWARD, JR. lawyer; b. Granville, N.Y., Sept. 13, 1938; s. Robert Howard and Sarah Rebecca (McCauley) L.; div.; children: Nicole Aimeé, Sarah Rebecca. BA, Shippensburg U., 1965; JD, Dickinson Sch. Law, Carlisle, Pa., 1968. Bar: Pa., Fla., U.S. Supreme Ct. Ptnr. Rhoads & Sinon LLP, Harrisburg, Pa., 1968—. Course planner and panalist fundamentals of mcpl. fin. Pa. Bar Inst.; lectr. mcpl. fin. and investments Special Coun. to Pa. State Treas. Del. Rep. Nat. Conv., 1976, 80, 84, 88, 90; panelist Pa. Newsmakers, Harrisburg, 1999; bd. dirs., com. chair Shippensburg Univ. Found., 1990—; legis. task force on sch. district and local govt. investments. Mem. ABA (taxation sect.), Nat. Assn. Bond Lawyers, Pa. Bar Assn., Fla. Bar Assn., Masons, Scottish Rite, York Rite, Shriners. Republican. Avocations: current affairs, financial markets, economics, big game hunting. Home: 665 Saint Johns Dr Camp Hill PA 17011-1339 Office: Rhoads & Sinon 1 S Market Sq Fl 12 Harrisburg PA 17101-2132 E-mail: rlong@rhoads-sinon.com.

LONG, ROBERT EMMET, author; b. Oswego, N.Y., June 7, 1934; s. Robert Emmet and Verda (Lindsley) L. BA, Columbia Coll., 1956; MA, Syracuse U., 1964; PhD, Columbia U., 1968. Instr. SUNY, Cortland, 1962-64; asst. prof. Queens Coll., CUNY, N.Y.C., 1968-71; writer, 1971—. Author: The Great Succession: Henry James and the Legacy of Hawthorne, 1979, The Achieving of the Great Gatsby, 1979, Henry James: The Early Years, 1983, John O'Hara, 1983, Nathanael West, 1985, Barbara Pym, 1986, James Thurber, 1988, James Fenimore Cooper, 1990, The Films of Merchant Ivory, 1991, Ingmar Bergman: Film and Stage, 1994, The Films of Merchant Ivory: Newly Updated Edition, 1997, Broadway, the Golden Years: Jerome Robbins and the Great Choreographer-Directors, 2001; editor numerous books, including John Huston: Interviews, 2001, George Cukor: Interviews, 2001; contbr. articles to profl. jours. and popular mags. Democrat. Episcopalian. Avocations: films, theater, ballet, jazz, travel. Address: 254 S 3rd St Fulton NY 13069-2356

LONG, ROBERT EUGENE, banker; b. Yankton, S.D., Dec. 5, 1931; s. George Joseph and Malinda Ann (Hanson) L.; m. Patricia Louise Glass, June 19, 1959; children: Malinda Ann, Robert Eugene, Jennifer Lynn, Michael Joseph. BS in Acctg., U. S.D., 1956; MBA, U. Mich., 1965; grad., Madison Grad. Sch. Banking, 1973, Nat. Comml. Lending Grad. Sch., U. Okla., 1977. Cert. comml. lender. Financial analyst Chrysler Corp., 1958-59; supr. finance Ford Motor Co., 1966-67; with First Wis. Bankshares Corp., Milw., 1967—, v.p. fin., 1973—; exec. v.p. 1st Wis. Fond du Lac, 1978—; dir. 1st Wis. Nat. Bank of Southgate, Waukesha and Fond du Lac; exec. v.p., dir. West Allis State Bank, 1979-81, pres., dir., 1981—, chief exec. officer, 1983—; sr. v.p. adminstrn. Park Banks, 1987—; chmn., pres., CEO Robert E. Long & Assoc., L.L.C., 2002—. Speaker/chmn. banking seminars Am. Mgmt. Assn., 1970—. Pres. local br. Aid Assn. Luth., 1970—, corp. bd. dirs., 1982—, vice chmn. bd., 1989—; pres. Mt. Carmel Luth. Ch., Milw., 1972; team capt. Re-elect Nixon campaign, 1972; bd. dirs. Luth. Social Svcs. of Wis. and Upper Mich., 1978—, chmn. bd., 1983—; bd. dirs. Luther Manor, 1981, Luther Manor Found., 1984, pres. bd. dirs. United Luth. Program for Aging, 1986—; bd. dirs. Wis. Inst. Family Medicine, 1985, pres., 1992—, elected corp. adv. coun., 1996; vice chmn. adv. coun. West Allis Meml. Hosp., 1993—; bd. dirs. Luth. Sem. Theology at Chgo., 1997. With USAF, 1951-52. Recipient Good Citizenship award Am. Legion, 1948 Mem. Wis. Assn. Family Practice (bd. dirs. 1992—), Wauwatosa C. of C. (bd. dirs. 1992—), Alpha Tau Omega. Clubs: Western Racquet (Elm Grove, Wis.) (dir. 1976—); Bluemound Golf and Country; Elmbrook Swim (pres. 1977-78). Lodges: Masons, Shriners, Jesters, Scottish Rite. Lutheran. Home and Office: N21w24052 Dorchester Dr Unit 6D Pewaukee WI 53072-4692 E-mail: PattyLou4@aol.com.

LONG, ROBERT GLENDON, pediatrician; b. Hartford, Conn., Mar. 7, 1937; s. Glendon Rodney and Alice (Owen) L.; m. Judith Rogers, June 18, 1966; children: Elizabeth Ann Long Turner, David, Daniel, Rebecca Long Helsby. BA, U. Conn., 1959; MD, Albany Med. Coll., 1964. Diplomate Am. Bd. Pediats. Resident in pediats. U.S. Army Tripler Gen. Hosp., Honolulu, 1967; chief pediats. U.S. Army Kue Gen. Hosp., Okinawa, Japan, 1968-70; dir. Hoa Khanh Children's Hosp., Danang, Vietnam, 1970-75; med. dir., pediatrician Logefeil Meml. Hosp., Taitung, Taiwan, 1977-98; pediatrician Quang Nam Gen. Hosp., Tamky, Vietnam, 1998-2000, Logefeil Meml. Hosp., Taitung, 2000—. Mem. missionary TEAM, Wheaton, Ill., 1977—. Lt. col. U.S. Army, 1963-70. Recipient award for svc. to Vietnamese, Vietnamese Govt., 1972, award for svc. in remote area Taiwan, 1990, Fgn. Friend medal Ministry of Interior of Taiwan, 2002, 1st class medal Coun. Indigenous Affairs, Taiwan, 2002. Fellow Am. Acad. Pediats.; mem. AMA, Christian Med. and Dental Soc. Avocations: photography, writing. Home: 15 Woodpine Ct Columbia SC 29212- Office: Logefeil Meml Hosp 350 Kaifeng St Taitung 950 Taiwan

LONG, ROBERT MERRILL, retail drug company executive; b. Oakland, Calif., May 19, 1938; s. Joseph Milton and Vera Mai (Skaggs) L.; m. Eliane Quilloux, Dec. 13, 1969. Student, Brown U., 1956-58; BA, Claremont Men's Coll., 1960. With Longs Drug Stores Inc., Walnut Creek, Calif., 1960—, dist. mgr., 1970-72, exec. v.p., 1972-75, pres., 1975-77, pres., chief exec. officer, 1977-91; chmn., chief exec. officer Longs Drug Stores, 1991-2000, chmn., 2000—. Mem. Nat. Assn. Chain Drug Stores (dir.) Office: Longs Drug Stores Corp PO Box 5222 141 N Civic Dr Walnut Creek CA 94596-3858

LONG, ROBERT RADCLIFFE, fluid mechanics educator; b. Glen Ridge, N.J., Oct. 24, 1919; s. Clarence D. and Gertrude (Cooper) L.; m. Cristina Nersing, 1962; children: John Radcliffe, Robert W. AB in Econs, Princeton, 1941; MS in Meteorology, U. Chgo., 1949, PhD, 1950. Meteorologist U.S. Weather Bur., Paris, France, 1946-47; asst. prof. Johns Hopkins U., Balt., 1951-56, assoc. prof., 1956-59, prof. fluid mechanics, 1959-88, prof. emeritus, 1988—, dir. hydrodynamics lab., 1951-88. Assoc. dept. aero. and mech. engring. Ariz. State U. Author: Mechanics of Solids and Fluids, 1960, Engineering Science Mechanics, 1964; also articles in field. Home: 3989 Myrtle St Sarasota FL 34235-5157 E-mail: rrlong4@comcast.net.

LONG, ROGER LEONARD, artist; b. Jackson, Tenn., Oct. 26, 1978; s. Roger Long, Linda Marie Long; m. Athena Adele Wilson, May 22, 1999. Owner, artist Portrait Phenomena, Ridgeland, Miss., 1998—; art, dance instr. Smarty Pants Ednl. Svcs., Jackson, 2000; art, dance instr./asst. mgr. Basic Skills Learning Ctr., Madison, 2001. Owner, choreographer Go Long Prodns., Ridgeland, Miss., 2001—; instr., choreographer Choreorobics, Jackson, Miss., 2001—; dir., cons. Artual Minds, Jackson, 2001—. (Scholastic award, 1994), (Clarion Ledge Elvis Drawing Contest award, 1993); choreographer performer Tribute to a Young Man, 2001. Min. Christian Congregation Jehovah's Witness, Jackson, 1995—. Avocation: Avocations: dancing, drawing, writing, music. Office: Portrait Phenomena 526 Evergreen St Ridgeland MS 39157 Home: 526 Evergreen St Ridgeland MS 39157

LONG, RONALD ALEX, real estate and financial consultant, lawyer, educator; b. Scranton, Pa., Dec. 9, 1948; s. Anthony James and Dorothy Agnas (Posgay) L.; m. Geraldine Sinneway, July 17, 1976; 1 child, Elizabeth Dorothy. BA, Bethany Coll., Lindsburg, Kans., 1971; MAT, Trenton (N.J.) State Coll., 1973; BS, Spring Garden Coll., 1980; MBA, St. Joseph's U., Phila., 1985; JD, Widener U., 1996; cert. new home sales profl., Grad. Realtor Inst., 1990. Bar: Pa. 1997, U.S. Supreme Ct.; cert. real estate instr. Substitute tchr. Hackettstown and Roxbury (N.J.) Sch. Bds., 1971-72; prof., chmn. bus. adminstrn. dept. Spring Garden Coll., Phila., 1973-92; sales assoc. Red Carpet Real Estate, Doylestown, Pa., 1980—; cons. real estate, 1980—; atty., 1997—. Cons. mgmt. Budd Wheel Corp., Phila., 1978-82; pres., prin. Aladdin Fin. Svcs., Inc.; prin. Loan Finders, Inc.; dir. Met. Real Estate Sch., Doylestown, 1991-95;cons. The Princeton Group Telecom. Specialist, 1993-96; adj. prof. Pa. State U., Thomas Edison Coll., Dept. Treasury; mktg. specialist IRS, 1997-98. Co-author: Explorations in Macroeconomics, 1988, Explorations in Microeconomics, 1989; contbr. articles to area newspapers. Site dir. ARC Blood Mobile, 1975-91; bd. dirs Buckingham (Pa.) PTA, 1984-88. Recipient Legion Honor award Chapel of the 4 Chaplains, Phila., 1984, Profl. Devel. award, Mgrs. award IRS, 1997. Mem. Nat. Assn. Realtors, Bar Supreme Ct. U.S., Pa. Assn. Realtors, Bucks County Assn. Realtors, U.S. Power Squadrons, U.S. Coast Guard Aux., Profl. Assn. Diving Instrs. (cert.), Moe Levine Trial Advocacy Honor Soc. (cert. achievement land transactions, ocean and coastal law, alcohol), Alcohol, Vehicle and the Law, Bus. Club (treas. 1969-71, pres. 1970-71), Alpha Chi, Pi Sigma Chi, Eta Beta Phi, Delta Theta Phi. Republican. Avocations: scuba diving, karate, surface and underwater photography, running. Home: 2698 Cranberry Rd Doylestown PA 18901-1770

LONG, RUSSELL CHARLES, academic administrator; b. Alpine, Tex., Oct. 9, 1942; s. Roy Joel and Lovis Lorene (Graham) L.; m. Elaine Gresham, May 8, 1964 (div. Jan. 1986); 1 child, Mark Roy; m. Natrelle Hedrick, Mar. 28, 1986. BS, Sul Ross State U., Alpine, 1965; MA, N.Mex. State U., 1967; PhD, Tex. A&M U., 1977. Assoc. prof. Schreiner Coll., Kerrville, Tex., 1967-69; instr. Tarleton State U., Stephenville, 1969-72, asst. prof., 1972-77, assoc. prof., 1977-85, prof., 1985-92, asst. v.p. acad. adminstrn., 1987-90, chair dept. English and Lang., 1990-92; provost and v.p. acad. adminstrn. West Tex. A&M U., Canyon, 1992-94, interim pres., 1994-95, pres., 1995—. Office: West Texas A&M Univ Wt Sta 2501 4th Ave Canyon TX 79016-0001 E-mail: rlong@mail.wtamu.edu.

LONG, SARAH ANN, librarian; b. Atlanta, May 20, 1943; d. Jones Lloyd and Lelia Maria (Mitchell) Sanders; m. James Allen Long, 1961 (div. 1985); children: Andrew C., James Allen IV; m. Donald J. Sager, May 23, 1987. BA, Oglethorpe U., 1966; M in Librarianship, Emory U., 1967. Asst. libr. Coll. of St. Matthias, Bristol, Eng., 1970-74; cons. State Libr. Ohio, Columbus, 1975-77; coord. Pub. Libr. of Columbus and Franklin County, 1977-79; dir. Fairfield County Dist. Libr., Lancaster, Ohio, 1979-82, Dauphin County Libr. Sys., Harrisburg, Pa., 1982-85, Multnomah County Libr., Portland, Oreg., 1985-89; sys. dir. North Suburban Libr. Sys., Wheeling, Ill., 1989—. Chmn. Portland State U. Libr. Adv. Coun., 1987-89. Contbr. articles to profl. jours. Bd. dirs. Dauphin County Hist. Soc., Harrisburg, 1983-85, ARC, Harrisbiry, 1984-85; pres. Lancaster-Fairfield County YWCA, Lancaster, 1981-82; vice chmn. govt. and ednl. divsn. Lancaster-Fairfield County United, Lancaster, 1981-82; sec. Fairfield County Arts Coun., 1981-82; adv. bd. Portland State U., 1987-89; mentor Ohio Libr. Leadership Inst., 1993, 95. Recipient Dir.'s award Ohio Program in Humanities, columbus, 1982; Sarah Long Day established in her honor Fairfield County, Lancaster, Bd. Commrs., 1982. Mem. ALA (pres. 1999-2000, elected coun. 1993-97, chair Spectrum fund faising com. 2001—), Pub. Libr. Assn. (pres. 1989-90, chair legis. com. 1991-95, chair 1998, nat. conf. com. 1995-98), Ill. Libr. Assn. (pub. policy com. 1991-97, Librarian of Yr. award 1999), Ill. Libr. Sys. Dirs. Orgn. (pres. 2000—), North Suburban Libr. Found. (bd. dirs. 1995—). Office: N Suburban Libr Systems 200 W Dundee Rd Wheeling IL 60090-4750

LONG, SARAH ELIZABETH BRACKNEY, physician; b. Sidney, Ohio, Dec. 5, 1926; d. Robert LeRoy and Caroline Josephine (Shue) Brackney; m. John Frederick Long, June 15, 1948; children: George Lynas, Helen Lucille Corcoran, Harold Roy, Clara Alice Lawrence, Nancy Carol Sieber. BA, Ohio State U., 1948, MD, 1952. Intern Grant Hosp., Columbus, Ohio, 1952-53; resident internal medicine Mt. Carmel Med. Ctr., 1966-69, chief resident internal medicine, 1968-69; med. cons. Ohio Bur. Disability Determination, 1970—. Physician student health Ohio State U., Columbus, 1970-73; sch. physician Bexley (Ohio) City Schs., 1973-83; physician advisor to peer rev. Mt. Carmel East Hosp., Columbus, 1979-86, med. dir. employee health, 1981-96; physician cons. Fed. Black Lung program U.S. Dept. Labor, Columbus, 1979-98. Mem. AMA, Gerontol. Soc. Am., Ohio Hist. Soc., Ohio State Med. Assn., Franklin County Acad. Medicine, Alpha Epsilon Delta, Phi Beta Kappa. Home: 2765 Bexley Park Rd Columbus OH 43209-2231

LONG, SARAH SUNDBORG, pediatrician, educator; b. Portland, Oreg., Oct. 31, 1944; MD, Jefferson Med. Coll., 1970. Diplomate Am. Bd. Pediat. Intern St. Christopher Hosp. for Children, Phila., 1970-71, resident, 1971-73, fellow pediat. and infectious diseases, 1973-75, staff, 1975—2002; prof. pediat. Drexel U. Coll. Medicine, 2002—. Chief editor: Principles and Practice of Pediatric Infectious Diseases, 1997; assoc. editor Jour. Pediatrics, 1997—; contbr. over 100 articles to med. jours. Mem. Am. Acad. Pediat., Soc. for Pediat. Rsch., Am. Pediat. Soc., Pediatric Diseases Soc. (pres. 1999-2001). Office: St Christopher Child Hosp Sect Infectious Diseases Erie Ave at Front St Philadelphia PA 19134

LONG, STEPHEN CARREL MIKE, lawyer; b. Roswell, N.Mex., Sept. 22, 1951; s. R.E. (Mike) and Evelyn Marie (Row) Long; m. Barbara I. Lowe, July 19, 1980; children: Jennifer Lynn, Joel Raymond Matthew. BBA with honors, N.Mex. State U., 1973; JD, U. N.Mex., 1977. Bar: N.Mex. 1977, U.S. Dist. Ct. N.Mex. 1977, U.S. Tax Ct. 1977, U.S. Ct. Appeals (10th cir.) 1977, U.S. Supreme Ct. 1982, U.S. Ct. Mil. Appeals 1982. Pvt. practice, Albuquerque, 1977-82, 85-87; assoc. Wheeler, Nye, McElwee & Martone, 1982-84; v.p. Wheeler, McElwee, Sprague & Long, P.C., 1984-85; pres. Long Law Firm, P.A., 1987-90; dir. Long & Thomas, P.A., 1990-91; pvt. practice Placitas, N.Mex., 1992-94; assoc. Ron Koch, P.A., Albuquerque, 1994-2001, Bill Gordon & Assocs., Albuquerque, 2001—. Staff judge adv. N.Mex. Dept. Mil. Affairs, 1980—92; adj. prof. Wayland Bapt. U., 1999—2000. Author: Consumer Bankruptcy Law in New Mexico, 3d edit., 1991; editor Nat. Resources Jour., 1976-77; staff N.Mex. Law Rev., 1975-76; contbr. articles to profl. jours. Trial coach N.Mex. Law Related Edn. Project, 1983-88, 99-2000; bd. dirs., Christian Legal Aid & Referral Svcs., Inc., Albuquerque, 1982-88; chmn., bd. dirs., Hosanna, Inc., Albuquerque, 1986-94. Served to col., N.Mex. Dept. Mil. Affairs. Mem.: N.Mex. Criminal Def. Lawyers Assn., N.Mex. State Bar Assn. (bd. dirs. bankruptcy sect. 1990—94, chmn.-elect 1993), Nat. Assn. Criminal Def. Lawyers, Sigma Pi, Delta Theta Phi. Republican. Baptist. Avocations: cowboy, team roper. Office: 2501 Yale SE Ste 204 Albuquerque NM 87106 E-mail: stevelong@qwest.net.

LONG, STEPHEN PAUL, anesthesiologist, pain medicine; b. Harrisonburg, Va., Oct. 16, 1959; s. Paul Richard and Dolores (Whitten) L.; m. Georganne Wells, July 25, 1987; 3 children. BS with hons., Randolph Macon Coll., 1982; MD, Va. Commonwealth U., 1986. Intern then resident in surgery Med. Coll. Va. Hosp., Richmond, 1986-88, resident in anesthesiology, 1988-91, fellow in pain medicine, 1990-91, dir. acute pain svc., 1991-97; pvt. practice pain medicine, 1998—. Bd. dirs. FOCUS; gov.'s commn. study pain Commonwealth Va., 1993-97; adminstrv. assoc. office of pres., co-dir. pain mgmt. ctr. Va. Commonwealth U., Richmond, 1997-98; commr., City of Richmond Human Rels. Commn., 1993-96; gov's commn. Mandated Healthcare Benefits, 1998—. Bd. dirs. Randolph-Macon Coll., 1993—97, Athletes for Jesus, 1994—97, Children's Mus. Richmond, 1996—2000, Fellowship Christian Athletes, 1999—2001, Va. Commonwealth U. Health Sys., 2000—. Grantee Syntex Labs. 1994, Roche Labs, 1997. Mem.: Va. Soc. Anesthesiologists (bd. dirs., pres.-elect), So. Pain Soc., Med. Soc. Va. (chmn. pain com.), Am. Soc. Anesthesiology, Am. Soc. Regional Anesthesia, Internat. Assn. Study Pain, Am. Acad. Pain Medicine, Am. Pain Soc., Phi Beta Kappa. Episcopalian. Avocations: skiing, tennis, golfing. Office: Commonwealth Pain Specialists Ste 170 5700 Old Richmond Ave Richmond VA 23226-1828 Fax: 804-288-7245.

LONG, THAD GLADDEN, lawyer; b. Dothan, Ala., Mar. 9, 1938; s. Lindon Alexander and Della Gladys (Pilcher) L.; m. Carolyn Frances Wilson, Aug. 13, 1966; children: Louisa Frances, Wilson Alexander. AB, Columbia U., 1960; JD, U. Va., 1963. Bar: Ala. 1963, U.S. Dist. Ct. (no. dist., so. dist., mid. dist.) Ala., U.S. Ct. Appeals (11th cir., 5th cir.), U.S. Supreme Ct. Assoc. atty. Bradley, Arant, Rose & White, Birmingham, Ala., 1963-70, ptnr., 1970—. Adj. prof. U. Ala., Tuscaloosa, 1988—2002, Samford U., Birmingham, 1999—, Cumberland Law Sch., 1999—2002. Co-author: Unfair Competition Under Alabama Law, 1990, Protecting Intellectual Property, 1990; mem. editl. bd. The Trademark Reporter; contbr. articles to profl. jours. Chmn. Columbia U. Secondary Schs. Com. Ala. Area, 1975—, Greater Birmingham Arts Alliance, 1977-79; trustee, pres. Birmingham Music Club, 2000—; trustee Oscar Wells Trust for Mus. Art, Birmingham, 1983—, Canterbury Meth. Found., 1993—, sec., 1993—; chmn. Entrepreneurship Inst. Birmingham, 1989; vice chmn., trustee Sons Revolution Found., Ala., 1994-2002; pres. Birmingham-Jefferson Hist. Soc., 1995-97; trustee Birmingham Music Club Endowment, 1995—; mem. Birmingham Com. Fgn. Rels. Mem. U.S. Patent Bar, Internat. Trademark Assn., Am. Law Inst., Ala. Law Inst., Birmingham Legal Aid Soc., Ala. Bar Assn. (chmn., founder bus. torts and antitrust sect.), Biotechnology Assn. of Ala., Inc. (sec. 1998-2001), U. Va. Law Alumni (chmn. Birmingham chpt. 1984-89), S.R. (pres. 1994-95), Gen. Soc. S.R. (gen. solicitor 1994-2000), Am. Arbitration Assn., Order of the Coif, Omicron Delta Kappa. Republican. Methodist. Avocations: travel, writing, table tennis. Home: 2880 Balmoral Rd Birmingham AL 35223-1236 Office: One Federal Place Birmingham AL 35203 E-mail: thadlong@aol.com.

LONG, THOMAS LESLIE, lawyer; b. Mansfield, Ohio, May 30, 1951; s. Ralph Waldo and Rose Ann (Cloud) L.; m. Peggy L. Bryant, Apr. 24, 1982. AB in Govt., U. Notre Dame, 1973; JD, Ohio State U., 1976. Bar: Ohio 1976, U.S. Dist. Ct. (so. dist.) Ohio 1976, U.S. Dist. Ct. (no. dist.) Ohio 1977, U.S. Ct. Appeals (6th cir.) 1978. Assoc. Alexander, Ebinger, Fisher, McAlister & Lawrence, Columbus, Ohio, 1976-82, ptnr., 1982-85, Baker & Hostetler, Columbus, 1985—. Mem. ABA, Ohio Bar Assn., Columbus Bar Assn., Fed. Bar Assn., Assn. Trial Lawyer Am. Clubs: Capitol (Columbus). Democrat. Roman Catholic. Home: 2565 Leeds Rd Columbus OH 43221-3613 Office: Baker & Hostetler 65 E State St Ste 2100 Columbus OH 43215-4260

LONG, TIMOTHY SCOTT, chemist, consultant; b. Racine, Wis., Dec. 20, 1937; s. Leslie Alexander and Esther (Sand) L.; m. Karen M. Koniarski, July 13, 1985; children by previous marriage: Corinne, Christine. BS in Chemistry, Winona State U., 1975. Staff chemist IBM, Rochester, Minn., 1962-77, adv. chemist Harrison, N.Y., 1977-80, IBM Instruments, Inc., Danbury, Conn., 1980-81, mgr. Midwest Instrument Ctr. Chgo., 1981-85; mgr. corp. environ. engring. IBM, Stamford, Conn., 1985-89, industry cons. White Plains, N.Y., 1989-92; environ. cons. Geraghty & Miller, Inc., Rochelle Park, N.J., 1992-94, Indpls., 1994-97. Mem. World Environ. Ctr., N.Y.C., 1985-89; adv. bd. Coop. Ctr. Rsch. in Hazardous and Toxic Substances, Newark, 1985-89. Author: Testing for Prediction of Material Performance, 1972, Methods for Emissions Spectrochemical Analysis, 1977, 2d edit., 1982; contbr. articles to Applied Spectroscopy, Plating, Polymer Engring. and Sci. Mem. ASTM (com. emission spectroscopy), Soc. Applied Spectroscopy (chmn. Minn. sect. 1976-77), Soc. Plastics Engrs. (bd. reviewers 1975-76). Achievements include demonstration of world's first application using ion chromatography in the analysis of indsl. waste water. Home: 2 Calle Final Placitas NM 87043-9214

LONG, VIRGINIA, state supreme court justice; m. Jonathan D. Weiner; 3 children. Grad., Dunbarton Coll. of Holy Cross; JD, Rutgers U., 1966. Dep. atty. gen. State of N.J.; assoc. Pitney, Hardin, Kipp and Szuch; dir. N.J. Divsn. Consumer Affairs, 1975; commr. N.J. Dept. Banking, 1977-78; judge N.J. Superior Ct., 1978-84, Appellate Divsn. N.J. Superior Ct., 1984-95, presiding judge, 1995-99; assoc. justice Supreme Ct. N.J., 1999—. Office: Supreme Ct NJ PO Box 023 Trenton NJ 08625-0970*

LONG, WILLIAM ALLAN, retired forest products company executive; b. Columbus, Ohio, Aug. 25, 1928; s. Allan C. and Dorothy (Crates) L.; m. Ann Cors, Aug. 27, 1954; children: Leslie, David, Steven, Jeffrey. BA, Ohio Wesleyan U., 1951. Vice pres. Diamond Internat., N.Y.C., 1951-70; exec. v.p. Overhead Door Corp., Dallas, 1970-75; v.p. St. Regis Paper Co., N.Y.C., 1975-79; group v.p. Inland Container Corp., Indpls., 1979-93; ret., 1993. Sgt. U.S. Army, 1946-47. Republican. Presbyterian. Home: 8073 Clymer Ln Indianapolis IN 46250

LONG, WILLIAM JOSEPH, software engineer; b. Kokomo, Ind., Feb. 1, 1956; s. George Alexander and Rebecca Bethina (Burgan) L. BA, Harvard U., 1979; cert. in project mgmt., U. Calif., Berkeley, 1994. Cons. Bechtel Corp., San Francisco, 1982-85; assoc. prof. Dalian (Liaoning, China) Inst. Tech., 1985-86; software engr. Bechtel Corp., San Francisco, 1986-92; EDI project mgr. Pacific Gas & Electric Co., 1992-94; software engr. Am. Pres. Lines, Oakland, Calif., 1994-95. Mem. adv. bd. Synetics, Inc., San Francisco, 1987—; owner William J. Long and Assocs., Oakland, Calif., 1990—. Vol. English tutor, Oakland, Calif., 1983—. Rsch. grantee Smithsonian Astrophys. Obs., Cambridge, Mass., 1976. Mem. IEEE, Assn. Computing Machinery, Am. Assn. Artificial Intelligence, Math. Assn. Am. Avocations: languages, photography, playing hammer dulcimer, jogging. Home and Office: William J Long and Assocs 2225 7th Ave #33 Oakland CA 94606-1969

LONG, WILLIAM MCMURRAY, physiology educator; b. Greenville, S.C., Nov. 9, 1948; s. William McMurray and Cecile Mae (Ariail) L.; m. Kathleen Webb, Mar. 18, 1971 (dec. Oct. 1990); m. Marianne Castrén, July 22, 1992. BA, Tulane U., 1970, BS, 1974; PhD, La. State U., 1980. Rsch. assoc. Med. Ctr. La. State U., New Orleans, 1974-75; pathology extern Charity Hosp. of La., 1975-80; Nat. Rsch. Svc. Award fellow Pa. State Med. Ctr., Hershey, 1980-82; rsch. assoc. Mt. Sinai Med. Ctr., Miami Beach, Fla., 1983-89; rsch. physiologist VA Med. Ctr., Miami, 1982-89; asst. prof. medicine U. Miami, 1982-89; asst. prof. physiology U. N.D., Grand Forks, 1989-94; CFO OBI Lab. Co., 1994-2000, dir., 2000—. Cons. VA Med. Ctr., Miami, 1991; ad hoc reviewer Am. Jour. Physiology, Bethesda, Md., 1990-91, Va. Ctrl. Office, 1987-90; dir. Minority Access to Rsch. Careers, U. N.D., Ah'jo'gun to the Baccalaureate. Author: Non-Steriodal Agents in Sepsis Syndrom, 1989, (with others) Airways: Asthma, Bronchietasis and Emphysema, 1992; contbr. articles to profl. jours. Chmn. Nat. Letter-In Com., New Orleans, 1968, Cliff Solar Fund, New Orleans, 1973; cood. Spring Jazz Festival, New Orleans, 1970. Recipient Rsch. award Bush Found., 1990, Nat. Rsch. Svc. award NIH, 1980-82; grantee NIH, 1986-89, Fla. Lung Assn., 1984-85, VA, 1986-90, Am. Heart Assn. Dakota affiliate, 1991-93, Nat. Inst. Gen. Med. Scis., 1992—. Mem. Am. Physiol. Soc., Am. Thoracic Soc., N.Y. Acad. Scis., Da Vinci Soc. (sec. 1987-88). Achievements include research in modification of cardiac proteolysis with amino acid methyl esters, in inefficacy of steroids in treatment of septic shock syndrome, in differentiation of histamine effects on bronchial flow and bronchomotor tone, on protein profiles in differentiating mechanisms of pulmonary edema, in role of bronchial blood flow in allergic airway disease and pharmacologic modification of that response; establishment of research and science education program for minorities and statewide tribal colleges; differential accumulation in brain of radon daighters in Alzheimer's Disease and Parkinson Disease. Home: 1339 Clara Brown Rd Prosperity SC 29127 Office: OBI Labs 1339A Clara Brown Rd PO Box 718 Prosperity SC 29127-0718

LONG, WILLIS FRANKLIN, electrical engineering educator, researcher; b. Lima, Ohio, Jan. 30, 1934; s. Jesse Raymond and Cerelda Elizabeth (Stepleton) L.; m. Ginger Carol Miller; children: Andrew Mark, Kristin Kay, David Franklin. BS in Engring. Physics, U. Toledo, 1957, MSEE, 1962; PhD, U. Wis., 1970. Registered profl. engr., Wis. Project engr. Doehler Jarvis div. Nat. Lead Co., Toledo, 1957, 59-60; instr. U. Toledo, 1962-66; mem. tech. staff Hughes Rsch. Labs., Malibu, Calif., 1969-73; asst., then assoc. prof. depts. extension engring. and elec. engring. U. Wis., Madison, 1973-80, prof., chair dept. extension engring., 1980-83, prof. depts. engring., profl devel. and elec. and computer engring., 1985—, prof. emeritus, 2001—; dir. ASEA Power System Ctr., New Berlin, Wis., 1983-85. Prin. Long Assocs., Madison, 1973—; cons. Dept. Energy, Washington, 1978—, ABB Power Systems, Raleigh, N.C., 1985—. Editor EMTP Rev., 1987-91; contbr. articles to profl. jours.; patentee power switching. Mem. adv. com. energy conservation Wis. Dept. Labor, Industry and Human Rels., 1976-77; mem. rural energy mgmt. coun. Wis. Dept. Agrl., Trade and Comsumer Protection, 1999-2001; chmn. Wis. chpt. Sierra Club, 1977; pres. bd. dirs. Madison Urban Ministry, 1993-95. 2d lt. Signal Corps., U.S. Army, 1958. Recipient Disting. Engring. Alumnus award U. Toledo, 1983, award of excellence U. Wis.-Extension, 1987; Sci. Faculty fellow NSF, 1966. Fellow IEEE (life, Meritorious Achievement in Continuing Edn. award 1991); mem. Internat. Coun.. on Large Electric Systems (expert advisor 1979—). Mem. United Ch. of Christ. Avocation: canoeing. Home: 125 N Hamilton St #906 Madison WI 53703 Office: U Wis 432 N Lake St Rm 737 Madison WI 53706-1415

LONGABERGER, TAMI, home decor accessories company executive; BBA in Mktg., Ohio State U., 1984. Joined Longaberger Co., Newark, 1984, pres., 1994, CEO. Trustee Ohio State U.; bd. dirs. John Glenn Inst. for Pub. Svc. and Pub. Policy. Named to Ohio Women's Hall of Fame; recipient Women Mean Business award. Mem. Direct Selling Assn. (chmn. bd. dirs.), Ohio Fed. Bus. and Profl. Women.

LONGAKER, RICHARD PANCOAST, political science educator emeritus; b. Phila., July 1, 1924; s. Edwin P. and Emily (Downs) L.; m. Mollie M. Katz, Jan. 25, 1964; children— Richard Pancoast II, Stephen Edwin, Sarah Ellen, Rachel Elise. BA in Polit. Sci, Swarthmore Coll., 1949; MA in Am. History, U. Wis., 1950; PhD in Govt, Cornell U., 1953. Teaching asst. Cornell U., 1950-53, vis. asso. prof., 1960-61; asst. prof. Kenyon Coll., 1953-54, asso. prof., 1955-60; asst. prof. U. Calif., Riverside, 1954-55, faculty Los Angeles, 1961-76, chmn. dept. polit. sci., 1963-67, prof., 1965-76, dean acad. affairs grad. div., 1970-71; prof. Johns Hopkins U., Balt., 1976-87, provost and v.p. for acad. affairs, 1976-87, prof. emeritus, cons. western states office Santa Monica, Calif., 1987—; prof. in residence UCLA, 2001—. Author: The Presidency and Individual Liberties, 1961; co-author: The Supreme Court and the Commander in Chief, 1976, also articles, revs. Served with AUS, 1943-45. Mem. Am. Polit. Sci. Assn. Office: 16550 Chalet Ter Pacific Palisades CA 90272-2344 E-mail: longaker@ucla.edu.

LONGAN, GEORGE BAKER, III, real estate company executive; b. Kansas City, Mo., Apr. 20, 1934; s. Benjamin Hyde and Georgette Longan O'Brien; divorced; 1 child, Nancy Ann Longan LaPoff. BSBA, U. Ariz., 1956; postgrad., U. Kans., 1956-57. Cert. real estate broker. Sr. v.p., gen. mgr. Paul Hamilton Co., Kansas City, 1963-84; pres. Eugene D. Brown Co., 1984-93; v.p. J.C. Nichols Real Estate, 1993-94. Bd. dirs. Genesis Relocation Network, N.J. Served to staff sgt. USAF, 1958-62. Mem. Nat. Real Estate Assn. (bd. dirs. 1991-94, 99, 2000), Mo. Real Estate Assn. (bd. dirs. 1987-90), Ariz. Real Estate Assn. (bd. dirs. 1999, 2000), Real Estate Bd. Kansas City (bd. dirs. 1987-90), Met. Kansas City Real Estate Bd. (pres. 1992), Beta Sigma Psi, Sigma Chi. Episcopal. Avocations: antique collecting, swimming. Office: Long Realty Co 5683 N Swan Rd Tucson AZ 85718-4565

LONGARDNER, CRAIG THEODOR, manufacturing executive; b. Ft. Wayne, Ind., June 2, 1955; s. Joseph Bernell and Dolores Waneta (Kiel) L.; m. Marsha Elaine Lessig, July 9, 1983; children: Joseph Simon, Jacob Kiel. BA, Ind. U., 1977; MBA, Butler U., 1985. Cert. purchasing mgr. Divisional buyer Eaton Corp., Cleve., 1977-80; purchasing mgr. Hurco Cos., Inc., Indpls., 1980-85; materials mgr. Ransburg Corp., 1985-88; purchasing mgr. Nucor Steel Corp., Crawfordsville, Ind., 1988-94; mgr. materials & transp. Steel Dynamics, Inc., Butler, 1994—. Instr. bus. statistics Kellogg Community Coll., Battle Creek, Mich., 1977. Mem. John Wayne Found. (life); fundraiser Nat. Leukemia Soc. Jr. Achievement. Mem. AISE, Nat. Assn. Purchasing Mgrs., Ind. U. Alumni Assn. (life), Midwest Assn. Rail Shippers. Republican.

Presbyterian. Avocations: basketball, hunting, racquetball, camping, short stories. Home: 3016 Wilderness Rd Fort Wayne IN 46845-1652 Office: 4500 County Road 59 Butler IN 46721-9747

LONGDEN, CLAIRE SUZANNE, retired financial planner, investment advisor; b. Sheffield, Yorkshire, Eng., June 2, 1938; came to U.S., 1964; d. John Stewart and Daisy (Heath) L. Diploma in pvt. sec., Coll. Commerce & Tech., Sheffield, 1956; cert. in Fin. Planning, Coll. Fin. Planning, 1979. Sec., Sheffield, 1956-62; G-4 asst. UN/WHO, Geneva, Switzerland, 1962-64; pvt. sec. Arthur Wiesenberger, N.Y.C., 1966-70; v.p. Alex Brown & Sons, 1970-75; 1st v.p. Butcher & Singer, 1975-89; pres. Claire Longden Assocs., Rhinebeck, N.Y., 1989-98. Adj. prof. fin. planning NYU, 1981-82. Conf. speaker 1980-86; contbr. articles to profl. jours. Bd. dirs. No. Dutchess Hosp., Rhinebeck, 1989-98, pres., 1995-96; bd. dirs. Cross River Healthcare, 1997-98, No. Dutchess Hosp. Found., 1997-99. Named one of Top Planners Nationwide, Money mag., 1987. Mem. Inst. CFPs (nat. bd. dirs. 1984-86, founder, N.Y.C. chpt. 1982-86, N.E. regional dir. 1985-86, bd. of ethics 1993-95, Cert. Fin. Planner of Yr. 1984), Womens Bond Club N.Y. (pres. 1982-84), Inst. Am. Fin. Planners (bd. dirs. 1983-85), Registry Fin. Planning Practitioners, Rotary (pres. Rhinebeck chpt. 1993-94). Avocations: gardening, swimming, walking, riding, skiing.

LONGENECKER, MARK HERSHEY, JR. lawyer; b. Akron, Ohio, Feb. 16, 1951; s. Mark Hershey and Katrina (Hetzner) L.; m. Ruth Rounding, June 17, 1978 (div.); children: Emily Irene, Mark Hershey III. BA, Denison U., 1973; JD, Harvard U., 1976. Bar: Ill. 1976, Ohio 1979. Atty. Lord, Bissell & Brook, Chgo., 1976-79; ptnr. Frost Brown Todd LLC (and predecessor firms), Cin., 1979—, chmn. bus.-corp. dept., 1996—2002. Dir. ST Media Group Internat. Bd. govs. Ohio Fair Plan Underwriting Assn., Columbus, 1989-92; dir. Salvation Army, Cin., 2000—. Mem. Cin. Country Club, Queen City Club, Gyro Club, Harvard Club (Cin. pres. 1993-94). Office: Frost Brown Todd LLC 2500 PNC Ct 201 E 5th St Ste 2500 Cincinnati OH 45202-4182 E-mail: mlongenecker@fbtlaw.com.

LONGER, WILLIAM JOHN, lawyer; b. Vinton, Iowa, Oct. 20, 1951; s. Hal Owen and Patricia Diane (Milroy) L.; m. Deborah Ann Dagenais, Aug. 7, 1976; 1 child, Kathryn Johanna. BA, Valparaiso U., 1974, JD, 1977. Bar: U.S. Dist. Ct. (no. dist.) Ind. 1978. Assoc. John D. Breclaw & Assocs., Griffith, Ind., 1977-79; sole practice Hobart, 1979—; judge Hobart (Ind.) City Ct., 1992—. Dep. pros. atty., Lake County, Ind., 1982-91; asst. city atty., Hobart, Ind., 1986-87; instr. bus. law Calumet Coll., Hammond, Ind., 1978-79; atty. Sch. City Hobart, 1988—. V.P. Hobart Family YMCA, 1985-86, pres. 1987-88. Mem. ABA, Ind. Bar Assn., Lake County Bar Assn., Hobart Bar Assn. (pres. 1985, sec. 1983-84), Hobart C. of C. (pres. 1986). Methodist. Home: 514 N Lake Shore Dr Hobart IN 46342-5016 Office: 651 E 3rd St Hobart IN 46342-4419 E-mail: wilonger@netnitco.net.

LONGFELLOW, CHARLES ALFRED, information officer; b. Dover, Del., Oct. 13, 1967; s. Charles Alfred Sr. and Theresa T. (Ricci) L. BA in Math. Scis., U. Del., 1990; MS in Libr. and Info. Sci., Drexel U., 1993; MBA, Del. State U., 1998. Bibliographic instrn. libr. Del. State U. Libr., Dover, 1993-94, asst. coord. tech. svcs., 1995-98; sr. application support splst. computer ctr. Del. Tech. and C.C., 1998-99; data mgr., assessment analyst Del. Dept. Edn., 1999-2000; chief info. officer Christina Sch. Dist., Newark, 2000—. Faculty senator Del. State U., 1995-98. Editor: Directory of Delaware Libraries, 1997. Treas. exec. bd. Westfield Maintenance Corp., 1997-98. Mem. ALA, Del. Libr. Assn. (coll. and rsch. librs. divsn. treas. 1994-97, sec. exec. bd. 1997-99). Office: Christina Sch Dist Technology Office 925 Bear Corbitt Rd Bear DE 19701-1324 E-mail: longfellowc@christiana.k12.de.us.

LONGFIELD, WILLIAM HERMAN, health care company executive; b. Chgo., Aug. 8, 1938; s. William A. and Elizabeth (Beringer) L.; m. Nancy Shofstall, June 10, 1961; children: William, Scott. BS, Drake U., 1960; grad. bus. mgmt. program, Northwestern U., 1972. Pres. Convertors divsn. Am. Hosp. Supply, Evanston, Ill., 1961-82; exec. v.p., dir. Lifemark, Inc., Houston, 1982-83; pres., CEO Cambridge Group, Inc., Dallas, 1983-89; chmn., CEO C.R. Bard, Inc., Murray Hill, N.J., 1989—, also bd. dirs. Bd. dirs. Atlantic Health Sys., Manor Care, Inc., Toledo, West Pharm. Svcs., Pa., Horizon Health Corp., Dallas; bd. dirs. Internat. Non-Wovens Assn., N.Y.C., 1975-82; chmn. AdvaMed; bd. dirs. Cytyc. Chmn., bd. dirs. Deerfield (Ill.) Youth Orgn., 1975-80. Recipient Pres.' award Nat. Nurse Cons. Assn., 1980. Mem. Baltrusol Golf Club, Echo Lake Country Club, Metedeconk Country Club. Republican. Presbyterian. Avocations: golf, tennis. Office: C R Bard Inc 730 Central Ave New Providence NJ 07974-1199

LONGHOFER, GORDAN ALLEN, art educator, performance artist; b. Wichita, Kans., May 14, 1960; s. Donald Eugene and Erma Maxine Longhofer; m. Karen Lynn Byrd, Aug. 16, 1983; children: Blake, Dean, Luke, Abby. MusB, MusB in Edn., Okla. Bapt. U., 1983; MusM, U. Okla., 1984. Educator's cert. Fla., Okla., Kans. Vocal music instr. Carnegie (Okla.) Pub. Schs., Carnegie, Okla., 1984—87, Barber County N. USD #254, Medicine Lodge, Kans., 1987—88, Palm Beach County Sch. Dist., West Palm Beach, Fla., 1988—91, 1999—2001; instr. voice Palm Beach Atlantic Coll., 1991—97; lead instr. Palm Beach Opera, 1998—2001, edn. and outreach coord., 2001—. Condr., messiah Barber County Choral Soc., Medicine Lodge, 1988; musica dir. Santaluces Cmty. H.S., Lantana, 1990. Singer: (Operas) Tosca, 1990, 1998, Madama Butterfly, 1991, 1997, La traviata, 1992, 1996, Aïda, 1992, Rigoletto, 1993, 1997, 2001, Il barbiere di Siviglia, 1994, 2001, 2000, Il trovatore, 1993, La Bohème, 1993, Carmen, 1994, Salome, 1995, Eugene Onegin, 1996, The Merry Widow, 1996, 2001, Turandot, 1996, Così fan tutte, 1995, 1997, La bohème, 1998, 2000, Manon, 1999, Un ballo in maschera, 2000, Der Fliegende Holländer, 2000, Norma, 2001, Luisa Miller, 2001; singer: (bass soloist) (oratorio) Mozart Requiem, 1985, 1991, Messa di Gloria, 1993, Petite Messe Solennelle, 1994, Messiah, 1990, 1995, 1997, Creation, 1987, 1991, 1995, 1996, 1997, Mass in C Major by Beethoven, 1990, 2000; actor: (musical) "M" Madeline and Merlin's Magic at Midnight, 2001. Deacon Westside Bapt. Ch., Boynton Beach, Fla., 1994—97; mem. cultural edn. com. Palm Beach County Cultural Coun., West Palm Beach, 2001—02; mental health month planning com. Mental Health Assn. of Palm Beach County, West Palm Beach, 2002—02. Named Nat. Finalist Stewart Awards Operatic Voice Competition, Okla. Symphony Orch., 1986, Semi-Finalist, Luciano Pavarotti Internat. Voice Competition, 1995; recipient Encouragement award, Tulsa Dist. Met. Opera Nat. Coun., 1985, Most Promising Singer award, 1986; scholar Benton-Schmidt Vocal, U. Okla., 1983-1984. Mem.: NEA, Fla. Edn. Assn., Fla. Vocal Assn., Fla. Music Educators Assn., Music Educators Nat. Conf. Avocations: golf, reading, fishing. Office: Palm Beach Opera 415 S Olive Ave West Palm Beach FL 33401

LONGHOFER, RONALD STEPHEN, lawyer; b. Junction City, Kans., June 30, 1946; s. Oscar William and Anna Mathilda (Krause) L.; m. Elizabeth Norma McKenna; children: Adam, Nathan, Stefanie. BMus, U. Mich., 1968, JD, 1975. Bar: Mich. 1975, U.S. Dist. Ct. (ea. dist.) Mich., U.S. Ct. Appeals (6th cir.), U.S. Supreme Ct.; cert. chartered fin. analyst. Law clk. to judge U.S. Dist. Ct. (ea. dist.) Mich., Detroit, 1975-76; ptnr. Honigman, Miller, Schwartz & Cohn, 1976—, chmn. litigation dept., 1993-96. Co-author: Courtroom Handbook on Michigan Evidence, 2002, Michigan Court Rules Practice, 1998, Mich. Court Rules Practice-Evidence, 2002, Courtroom Handbook on Michigan Civil Procedure, 2002; editor Mich. Law Rev., 1974-75. Served with U.S. Army, 1968-72. Mem. ABA, Detroit Bar Assn., Fed. Bar Assn., U. Mich. Pres.' Club, Order of Coif, Phi Beta Kappa, Phi Kappa Phi, Pi Kappa Lambda. Home: 974 Penniman Ave Plymouth MI 48170 Office: Honigman Miller Schwartz & Cohn 2290 1st National Bldg Detroit MI 48226 E-mail: rsl@honigman.com.

LONGHURST, ROBERT RUSSELL, retired secondary school educator; b. Montgomery, Ala., Feb. 28, 1921; s. Lawrence Alston and Margaret Earlene (King) L.; m. Anne McMahon, Nov. 26, 1952 (div. 1982). Student, Vanderbilt U., 1942; BA in Econs., Peabody Coll., 1949, MA, 1950. Cert. tchr., Tenn. Various positions Stinson Aviation & Consol.-Vultee Aircraft Corp., 1940-43; tech. rep. Lockheed Overseas Corp., British Isles, 1943-44; tchr. Nashville Bd. Edn., 1950-77, coordinator vocat. edn., 1977-87; ret., 1987. Nat. defense course in aeronautics, Vanderbilt U., 1942. Served as petty officer USNR, 1944-46, PTO. Mem. NEA, Tenn. Edn. Assn., Met. Nashville Edn. Assn., Am. Vocat. Assn., Am. Legion, Pi Gamma Mu. Mem. Ch. of Christ. Avocations: woodworking, music, financial planning, investing. Home: 2421 Eastland Ave Nashville TN 37206-1101

LONGIN, THOMAS CHARLES, education association administrator; b. Lewistown, Mont., Nov. 17, 1939; s. Charles Otto and Anne Dorothy (Vavrovsky) L.; m. Nancy Tillinghast; children: Kevin C., Teresa L., Karl T., Anne M. BA in History, Carroll Coll., 1962; MA in History, Creighton U., 1965; PhD in Am. History, U. Nebr., 1970. Instr. Carroll Coll., Helena, Mont., 1965-67; asst. prof. Va. Poly. Inst. and State U., Blacksburg, 1970-73; asst. prof., then assoc. prof. Ithaca (N.Y.) Coll., 1973-82, dean humanities and scis., 1976-82, provost, 1985-96; v.p. acad. affairs Seattle U., 1982-85; v.p. programs and rsch. Assn. of Governing Bds., Washington, 1997—. Office: Assn of Governing Bds 1 Dupont Cir NW Ste 400 Washington DC 20036-1136 E-mail: tlongin@agb.org.

LONGINI, PETER RICHARD, communications executive; b. Pitts., June 4, 1944; s. Richard Leon and Muriel Jeanette (Davis) L.; m. Margery Joyce Lubet, June 12, 1983; children: Kate, Andrea, Sarah. BA, Coll. Wooster, 1966; MS in Comm. Rsch., U. Pitts., 1968, PhD of Comm. Rsch., 1970. Asst. prof. U. Pitts., 1970-75; prof. Bklyn. Coll., 1975-79; sr. writer PPG Industries (formerly Pitts. Plate Glass), 1980-92; pres. Peter Longini Comm., Wexford, Pa., 1992—. Columnist The News Record, 1992-97; corr. The Pitts. Post Gazette, 1994-99 Avocations: performing arts, transportation. E-mail: plongini@nauticom.net.

LONGINO, THERESA CHILDERS, nurse; b. Jacksonville, Fla., Feb. 17, 1959; d. Harold David and Eleanor Theresa (McHarg) Childers; m. Matthew Ray Longino, July 11, 1987. Student, Stetson U., 1977-78; ADN, Fla. C.C., Jacksonville, 1981; student, U. North Fla., 1985-86; BSN, U. Phoenix, 2000. RN, Fla. RN Meth. Hosp., Jacksonville, 1981, Meml. Med. Ctr., Jacksonville, 1981-86, Good Samaritan Home Health, Jacksonville, 1986, Kimberly Nurses, Jacksonville, 1986, St. Vincents Med. Ctr., Jacksonville, 1986—. Catechist Prince of Peace Cath. Ch., Jacksonville, 1990-91, 97-98, lectr., reader, 1991—, youth min., 1996. Mem. Jacksonville Jaguars Booster Club, Sigma Theta Tau (Omicron Delta chpt.). Republican. Roman Catholic. Home: 4135 Hudnall Rd Jacksonville FL 32207-5766 E-mail: tclongino@webtv.net.

LONG-KELLY, JENNIFER, therapist; b. Maryville, Mo., Nov. 20, 1973; d. John Francis and Janice Fay Long; divorced; 1 child, Amanda Blair. BS in Psychology, Family Life, and Resource Mgmt. cum laude, N.W. Mo. State U., 1996, MS in Counseling, 1999. Lic. profl. counselor, Mo. Case mgr. Tarkio (Mo.) Acad., 1995-98; instr. N.W. State U., Maryville, 1996-99; social svcs. worker II State Mo. Divsn. Family Svcs., 1998-2000; resource specialist Cath. Charities, St. Joseph, Mo., 1999—; children's therapist Family Guidance Ctr., Maryville, 1999—; instr. Ind. Living program, choices program through Mo., 2001—. Mem. United Meth. Ch., Mound City, Mo. Mem. ACA, APA, Alpha Sigma Alpha. Republican. Avocations: exercising, travel, photo albums. Home: 19307 Burke Rd Rock Port MO 64482 Office: Family Guidance Ctr Summit Dr Maryville MO 64468

LONGLEY, CHRISTOPHER QUENTIN MORI, financial service executive; b. Mpls., May 23, 1961; s. Robert William and Frances Margaret (Heil) L.; m. Nancy Mori, Dec. 13, 1985; children: Christopher Hideo, Mariko Ann Frances, Charles Stratton. BA, St. Thomas U., 1987; JD, William Mitchell Coll. of Law, 1992. Bar: Minn. Staff asst. Senator Rudy Boschwitz, St. Paul, 1980-81; fundraiser Congressman Arlen Erdahl, Osseo, Minn., 1982; legis. asst. Senator Rudy Boschwitz, Washington (D.C.), 1982-83; fin. dir. People for Boschwitz, Mpls., 1984-89; cons. Longley & Assoc., St. Paul, 1986-96; chief devel. officer St. Thomas Acad., 1989-92; assoc. Hessian, McKasy & Soderberg, P.A., Mpls., 1992-94; pes. Quantum Comms. Group, Inc., Eden Prairie, Minn., 1994-96; pres., CEO Quantum Wireless Solutions, Inc., Bloomington, 1996-97; v.p., COO Internet Fin. Svcs., LLC, Mpls. Bd. dirs. QAI Corp., St. Paul, Newtel Europe, LLC, QWSI, Inc. Bd. dirs. Welcome Neighbor Time Savers, Inc., DoTheGood.com; co-founder Rep. Victory Club PAC, Cambodian Children's Edn. Fund. Named Outstanding Young American, OYM, Inc., N.Y., 1986. Mem. U.S. Supreme Ct. Bar Assn., Minn. State Bar, Ramsey County Bar. Home: 726 Summit Ave Saint Paul MN 55105-3440 Office: Internet Fin Svcs Ste 900 120 S 6th St Minneapolis MN 55402-1812

LONGLEY, MARJORIE WATTERS, newspaper executive; b. Lockport, N.Y., Nov. 2, 1925; d. J. Randolph and Florence Lucille (Craine) Watters; m. Ralph R. Longley, Oct. 1, 1949 (dec.). BA in English with highest honors cum laude, St. Lawrence U., 1947. Sports editor, feature writer Lockport Union Sun and Jour., 1945; with N.Y. Times, N.Y.C., 1948-88, asst. to v.p. consumer mktg., 1975-78, circulation sales mgr., 1978-79, sales dir., 1979-81, dir. pub. affairs, 1981-88; pres. Gramercy Internat., Inc. (mktg. and pub. rels.), 1988—; assoc. pub. The Earth Times, 1996—. Dir. pub. affairs and pub. info., N.Y.C. Off-Track Betting Corp., 1990-94; mem. Nat. Newspapers' Readership Coun., 1979-82; mem. adv. coun. API, 1980-85. Author: America's Taste, 1960. Trustee St. Lawrence U., 1969-75, 77—; chmn. bd. dirs. Am. Forum for Global Edn., 1977-98, chmn. emerita, 1999—; pres. N.Y. City Adult Edn. Coun., 1974-77, Grmercy Pk. Lot Owners Assn., Inc., 1995—; mem. N.Y. State Adv. Coun. for Vocat. Edn, 1976-81, postsecondary edn., 1978-81, Mayor's Coun. Environment of N.Y.C., 1983-96; bd. dirs. Nat. Charities Info. Bur., 1983-96, Literacy Ptnrs., Inc., 1996—; chmn. 42d St. Edn., Theatre, Culture, 1984-88, chmn. emeritus, 1988—. Mem. Nat. Inst. Social Scis., Am. Mgmt. Assn. (nat. mktg. coun. 1972-89, bd. dirs. 1986-88), Nat. Arts Club, Overseas Press Club, Phi Beta Kappa. Democrat. Baptist. Office: Gramercy Internat Inc 34 Gramercy Park E New York NY 10003-1731

LONGMAN, ANNE STRICKLAND, special education educator, consultant; b. Metuchen, N.J., Sept. 17, 1924; d. Charles Hodges and Grace Anna (Moss) Eldridge; m. Henry Richard Strickland, June 22, 1946 (dec. 1960); m. Donald Rufus Longman, Jan. 20, 1979 (dec. 1987); children: James C., Robert H. BA in Bus. Adminstrn., Mich. State U., 1945; teaching credentials, U. Calif., Berkeley, 1959; postgrad., Stanford U., 1959-60; MA in Learning Hand, Santa Clara U., 1974. Lic. educator. Exptl. test engr. Pratt & Whitney Aircraft, East Hartford, Conn., 1945-47; indsl. engr. Marchant Calculators, Emeryville, Calif., 1957-58; with pub. rels. Homesmith, Palo Alto, 1959-62; cons. Right to Read Program, 1978-79; monitor, reviewer State of Calif., Sacramento, 1976-79; tchr. diagnosis edn. Cabrillo Coll., Aptos, Calif., 1970-79; lectr. edn. U. Calif., Santa Cruz, 1970-79; cons. Santa Cruz Bd. Edn., 1970-79; reading rschr. Gorilla Found., Woodside, Calif., 1982—. Bd. mem. Western Inst. Alcoholic Studies, L.A., 1972-73; chmn. Evaluation Com., Tri-County, Calif., 1974; speaker Internat. Congress Learning Disabilities, Seattle, 1974; ednl. cons. rsch. on allergies, 1993—. Author: Word Patterns in English, 1974-92, Cramming 3D Kids, 1975—, 50 books for migrant students, 1970-79; contbr. articles on stress and alcoholism and TV crime prevention for police, 1960-79. Founder Literacy Ctr., Santa Cruz, 1968-092; leader Girl Scouts U.S.A., San Francisco, 1947-50; vol. Thursday's Child, Santa Cruz, 1976-79, Golden Gate Kindergarten, San Francisco, 1947-57; vol. Yosemite Nat. Pk. Recipient Fellowships Pratt & Whitney Aircraft, 1944, Stanford U., 1959. Mem. Internat. Reading Assn. (pres. Santa Cruz 1975), Santa Clara Valley Watercolor Soc., Los Altos Art Club (v.p. 1992), Eichler Swim and Tennis Club. Republican. Episcopalian. Avocations: watercolor painting, travel, drama. Home and Office: 651 Sinex Ave #J211 Pacific Grove CA 93950

LONGMIRE, WILLIAM POLK, JR. physician, surgeon; b. Sapulpa, Okla., Sept. 14, 1913; s. William Polk and Grace May (Weeks) L.; m. Jane Jarvis Cornelius, Oct. 28, 1939; children— William Polk III (dec.), Gill, Sarah Jane. AB, U. Okla., 1934; MD, Johns Hopkins, 1938; MD hon. degrees, U. Athens, Greece, 1972, Northwestern U., 1976, U. Lund, Sweden, 1976; MD (h.c.), U. Heidelberg, Germany, 1974. Diplomate Am. Bd. Surgery (chmn. 1961-62). Intern surgery Johns Hopkins Hosp., Balt., 1938-39, resident surgery, 1944, surgeon in charge plastic out-patient clinic, 1946-48, surgeon, 1947-48; Harvey Cushing fellow exptl. surgery Johns Hopkins, 1939-40, Halsted fellow surg. pathology, 1940, successively instr., asst. prof. assoc. prof. surgery, 1943-48; prof. surgery UCLA, 1948-81, prof. emeritus, 1981—, chmn. dept., 1948-76. Cons. surgery Wadsworth VA Hosp., Los Angeles County Harbor Hosp., 1945-76, VA disting. physician, 1982-87; guest prof. spl. surgery Free U. Berlin, Fed. Republic Germany, 1952-54; vis. prof. surgery Mayo Grad. Sch. Medicine, 1968, Royal Coll. Physicians and Surgeons of Can., 1968; chmn. surgery study sect. NIH, USPHS, 1961-64; mem. Conf. Com. on Grad. Edn. in Surgery, 1959-66, chmn., 1964-66; mem. spl. med. adv. group to med. dir. VA, 1963-68, vice chmn., 1967-68; chmn. surgery tng. com. NIH, 1969-70; mem. pres.' cancer panel Nat. Cancer Inst., 1982-91; Wade vis. prof. Royal Coll. Surgeons Edinburgh, 1972; nat. civilian cons. surgery Air Surgeon USAF; surg. cons. Surgeon Gen. U.S. Army, 1961-88; commr. Joint Commn. on Accreditation of Hosps., 1975-80. Editor: Advances in Surgery, 1975-76; editorial bd.: Annals of Surgery, 1965— . Served as maj. USAF, 1952-54; spl. cons. Air Surgeon Gen.'s Office. Recipient hon. certificate for advancement cardiovascular surgery Free U. of Berlin, 1954, certificate for high profl. achievement USAF, 1954, Gold medal UCLA, 1980, prize Societe Internationale De Chirurgie, 1987, Disting. Med. Alumni award Johns Hopkins Univ. Sch. Medicine, 1999; inducted into Okla. Hall of Fame, 1980. Fellow ACS (chmn. forum com. fundamental surg. problems 1961-62, regent 1962-71, chmn. bd. regents 1969-71, pres. 1971-73, Sheen award N.J. chpt. 1987); hon. fellow Assn. Surgeons Great Britain and Ireland, Royal Coll. Surgeons Ireland, Royal Coll. Surgeons Edinburgh, Royal Coll. Surgeons Eng., Italian Surg. Soc., Association Française de Chirurgie, Japan Surg. Soc.; mem. AMA (mem. council on med. edn. 1964-69), Soc. Scholars of Johns Hopkins U., Soc. Clin. Surgeons, Am. Surg. Assn. (pres. 1967-68), Pacific Coast Surg. Assn., Western Surg. Assn., So. Surg. Assn., Soc. U. Surgeons, Internat. Soc. Surgery, Internat. Fedn. Surg. Colls. (pres. 1984-87), Internat. Surgical Group, (pres. 1993), Am. Assn. Thoracic Surgery, Pan-Pacific Surg. Assn., Los Angeles Surg. Soc. (pres. 1956), Bay Dist. Surg. Soc., Soc. Surgery Alimentary Tract (pres. 1975-76), Calif. Med. Assn. (sec. surg. sect. 1950-51, chmn. sci. bd. 1966-67, Golden Apple award 1990), James IV Assn. Surgeons (pres. 1981), Soc. Surg. Chairmen (pres. 1970-72), Sociédad Argentina di Cirugia Digestiva (hon.), So. Surg. Assn. (hon.), Italian Surg. Soc. (hon.), Phi Beta Kappa, Alpha Omega Alpha; corr. mem. Deutsche Gesellschaft fur Chirugie. Home: 10102 Empyrean Way Bldg 8 Los Angeles CA 90067-3825 Office: U Calif Med Ctr Los Angeles CA 90024

LONGNECKER, DAVID EUGENE, anesthesiologist, educator; b. Kendallville, Ind., 1939; MD, Ind. U., 1964, MA in Anesthesiology, 1968. Diplomate Am. Bd. Anesthesiology. Intern Blodgett Meml. Hosp., Grand Rapids, Mich., 1964—65; resident in anesthesiology U. Ind., 1965—69; asst. prof. dept. anesthesiology U. Mo., 1970—73; assoc. prof. dept. anesthesiology U. Va., Charlottesville, 1974—78, prof., 1978—88; Robert D. Dripps prof., chmn. dept. anesthesia U. Pa., Phila., 1999—, sr. v.p., chief med. officer, 2002—. With USPHS, 1968—70. Mem.: Inst. Medicine, Am. Soc. Anesthesiologists. Office: U Pa Health Sys Dept Anesthesia 3400 Spruce St Philadelphia PA 19104-4283 E-mail: delongnecker@uphs.upenn.edu.

LONGO, DANIEL ROBERT, health services researcher, medical educator; b. Jersey City, Feb. 20, 1952; s. Frank and Rose (Liguori) L.; m. Karen Ann Ludy, Sept. 4, 1976; children: Gregory Seton, Alexis Seton. BS cum laude, Villanova U., 1974; M of Hosp. Adminstrn., George Washington U., 1976; ScD in Health Policy Mgmt., Johns Hopkins U., 1982. Cons. Am. Hosp. Assn. , Chgo., 1980-82; dir., multi-hosp. systems project Joint Commn. on Accreditation of Healthcare Orgns., 1982-85; dir. rsch. Joint Commn.on Accreditation of Healthcare Orgns., 1984-86; asst. exec. dir. quality mgmt. Ancilla Systems Inc., Chgo. Affiliated Healthcare Group, 1986-87; v.p. quality assurance Hosp. Assn. N.Y. State, Albany, 1987-89; pres. Hosp. Rsch. Ednl. Trust, Chgo., 1989-92; assoc. prof. family and cmty. medicine Sch. Medicine U. Mo., Columbia, 1992-99, prof. family and cmty. medicine, 1999—. Bd. dirs. Inst. on Quality of Care and Patterns of Practice, Hosp. Rsch. Ednl. Trust, Chgo., 1991-92, Assn. Health Svcs. Rsch., Washington, 1990-93; adv. com., Quality Improvement Task Force, Chgo., 1988-93; liaison com., Inst. Medicine, Washington, 1990-92; adj. faculty Columbia U.; vis. scholar Northwestern U., Evanston, Ill., 1984-92; sr. faculty assoc. Johns Hopkins U., Balt., 1990-92; adj. assoc. prof. St. Louis U., 1993—; quality of care advisor Mo. Dept. Health, 1993—. Author: Integrated Quality Assessment, 1989, Inventory of External Data, 1990; editor: Quantitative Methods in Quality Management, 1990; contbr. articles to profl. jours. Lt. USNR, 1975-79. Rsch. fellow Sisters Mercy Health Corp., 1983-87. Mem. Am. Pub. Health Assn. (program chmn. 1987), Assn. Health Svcs. Rsch. (bd. dirs. 1990-93), Soc. Tchrs. Family Medicine (Best Rsch. Paper Yr. award 1997). Home: 2291 W Ridley Wood Columbia MO 65203 Office: U Mo Sch Medicine 306 Med Sci Bldg Columbia MO 65212-0001

LONGO, LAWRENCE DANIEL, physiologist, obstetrician-gynecologist; b. Los Angeles, Oct. 11, 1926; s. Frank Albert and Florine Azelia (Hall) L.; m. Betty Jeanne Mundall, Sept. 9, 1948; children: April Celeste, Lawrence Anthony, Elisabeth Lynn, Camilla Giselle. BA, Pacific Union Coll., 1949; MD, Coll. Med. Evangelists, Loma Linda, Calif., 1954. Diplomate Am. Bd. Ob-Gyn. Intern L.A. County Gen. Hosp., 1954-55, resident in internal medicine, 1955-58; asst. prof. ob-gyn UCLA, 1962-64; assoc. prof. physiology and ob-gyn U. Pa., 1964-68; prof. physiology and ob-gyn Loma Linda U., 1968—; dir. ctr. for perinatal biology Loma Linda U. Sch. Medicine, 1974—. Perinatal biology com. Nat. Inst. Child Health, NIH, 1973-77; co-chmn. reprodn. scientist devel. program NIH; NATO prof. Consiglio Nat. delle Rsch., Italian Govt. Editor: Respiratory Gas Exchange and Blood Flow in the Placenta, 1972, Fetal and Newborn Cardiovascular Physiology, 1978, Charles White and A Treatise on the Management of Pregnant and Lying-in Women, 1987; co-editor: Landmarks in Perinatology, 1975-76, Classics in Obstetrics Gynecology, 1993; editor classic pages in ob-gyn. Am. Jour. Ob-Gyn.; contbr. articles to profl. jours. Served with AUS, 1945-47. Founder Frank A. and Florine A. Longo lectureship in faith, knowledge, and human values Pacific Union Coll., 1993. Fellow Royal Coll. Ob-Gyns., Am. Coll. Ob-Gyns.; mem. Am. Assn. History Medicine (coun.), Am. Osler Soc. (bd. govs., sec.-treas., pres.), Am. Physiol. Soc., Assn. Profs. Ob-Gyn., Perinatal Rsch. Soc., Soc. Gynecologic Investigation (past pres.), Neurosci. Soc., Royal Soc. Medicine. Adventist. Office: Loma Linda U Sch Medicine Ctr Perinatal Biology Loma Linda CA 92350-0001

LONGO, PAUL ALBERT, retired industrial engineer, consultant; b. N.Y.C., May 30, 1916; s. Anthony and Theresa (DeFranco) L.; m. Frances Abruscatto, Sept. 24, 1939; children: Robert, Virginia Lorey, Dennis, James, Dina Miller. Student, NYU, 1942-43, Columbia U., 1953-54, Indsl. Coll. Armed Forces, 1954-55; diploma, U.S. Army Logistics Mgmt. Ctr., 1958, U.S. Army Chem. Corps Sch., 1965. Registered profl. engr., cert. mfg. engr. Field project engr. Dept. Def., N.Y.C., 1940-65; supervisory indsl. engr. Aberdeen Proving Grounds, Edgewood, Md., 1966-70, programs mgr., 1970-71, chief indsl. ops., 1971-75, disposal engr., 1975-77. Chmn. indsl. planning coun. Dept. Def. Munitions Bd., 1954-58; chmn. Armed Svcs. Indsl. Readiness Coun., 1954-56; bd. dirs., v.p. Sci. Experiments Corp., N.Y.C., 1956-58; chief field engr. Jones Engrng., Towson, Md., 1978-79; engrng. cons. ICI Ams., Inc., Wilmington, Del., 1979-81; tech. instr. Harford C.C., Bel Air, Md., 1968; mil. instr. Army Chem. Sch., Ft. McClellan, Ala., 1968; tech. advisor Dept. Def., 1965-70. Author books, 1986-90; co-author: Fundamentals of Tool Design, 1983-84; contbr. articles to profl. jours.; editor: Jigs and Fixture Design, 1983; developer integrated Cad-Cam system for transition of design of army chem. ordnance to manufacturing, 1966-70; patentee in field. Dir.-at-large Beach Pkwy. Civic Assn., Cape Coral, Fla., 1991-97. Lt. col. ret. U.S. Army Res., 1949-69. Recipient Dept. Def. Meritorious Civilian Svc. award Army Chem. Corps, 1945, Meritorious Svc. medal U.S. Army, 1969, 1st pl. trophy award Ralph H. Landes Indsl. Mgmt. Soc., Chgo., 1970, 2d pl., 1973, multiple merit awards Soc. Mfg. Engrs., Dearborn, Mich., 1960-79. Mem. Ret. Officers Assn. (life), Engrng. Soc. Cape Coral, Md. Res. Officers Assn. (pres. Edgewood chpt. 1965), Internat. Soc. Mfg. Engrs. Tech. (sem. chmn. 1969). Republican. Roman Catholic. Avocations: golf, boating, swimming, tennis, fishing. Home and Office: 1907 SE 40th Ter Cape Coral FL 33904-8007

LONGO, RONALD ANTHONY, lawyer; b. Schenectady, N.Y., Nov. 17, 1952; s. Vito Frank and Frances (Scardamaglia) L.; m. Susan Fraioli, Nov. 15, 1980; children: Kristen, John Michael. BS, Cornell U., 1974; JD, Pace U., 1980. Bar: N.Y. 1981, U.S. Dist. Ct. (so. dist.) N.Y. 1984, U.S. Supreme Ct. 1984. Asst. dir. labor rels. Onondaga County, Syracuse, N.Y., 1974-75; dir. employee rels. Ardsley (N.Y.) Sch. Dist., 1975-80; assoc. Plunkett & Jaffe, White Plains, N.Y., 1980-86, ptnr., 1986-93, Keane & Beane, P.C., White Plains, 1993—. Dep. town atty. Town of Clarkstown, New City, N.Y., 1985—; adj. assoc. prof. Iona Coll., New Rochelle, N.Y., 1982-90; adj. prof. L.I. U., Brookville, N.Y., 1986-88; instr. labor rels. studies program Cornell U., 1991-92. Author: (with others) Public Sector Labor and Employment Law,

1988, 98. Mem. ABA, N.Y. State Bar Assn., N.Y. State Pub. Employer Labor Rels. Assn. (sec., treas. 1979-81, pres. 1982-83, Disting. Svc. award 1983). Office: Keane & Beane PC 1 N Broadway Ste 700 White Plains NY 10601-2319

LONGO, SALVADOR EUGENE, biomedical engineer; b. New Orleans, Dec. 7, 1940; s. Joseph C. and Ruth (Cenas) L.; m. Pamela Marie Martina, Aug. 18, 1962; children: Sherri Anne, Debbie Marie, Michele Theresa, Salvador Eugene Jr. BSEE, La. State U., 1963, MSEE, 1966; PhD in Physics, Tulane U., 1971. Registered profl. engr., La., Tex., Ga., Miss., Wyo. Rsch. engr. Boeing Aerospace Co., New Orleans, 1966-70; dir. Campbell MC Cool Laser Lab., 1966-70; instr. dept. surgery Tulane Med. Sch., 1966-70; med. physicist Ochsner Hosp., Metairie, La., 1970-71; pres. Applied Rsch. Corp., New Orleans, 1971—; pres., cons. Dr. Salvador E. Longo & Assocs., Inc., 1971—; pres. Managed Biomed. Svcs., Inc., 1996—. Contbr. articles to profl. jours. Chief of comm. Jefferson Parish Civil Def., Metairie, 1963-66. NSF Rsch.. fellow, 1966-67, NIH Cancer Rsch. fellow, 1967-70. Mem. Am. Assn. Physicists in Medicine, Am. Coll. Clin. Engring. (charter), Am. Coll. Med. Physicists, Nat. Fire Protection Assn. (com. mem.), Am. Radio Relay League, Sigma Pi Sigma. Republican. Roman Catholic. Avocations: amateur radio, model trains, stamps, hunting, fishing.

LONGOBARDI, PAMELA SCOTT DODGEN, artist, educator; b. Montclair, N.J., Oct. 1, 1958; d. Jerome Clyde and Patricia Joy (Gammons) Dodgen; m. Harry Gennaro Longobardi, Apr. 18, 1981 (div. Mar. 1984). BFA, U. Ga., 1981; MFA, Mont. State U., 1985. Freelance sci. illustrator, dept. zoology U. Ga., Athens, 1980-81; sci. illustrator Mus. of the Rockies, Bozeman, Mont., 1982-84; cartographer Red Bluff Archeol. Survey, Mont. Com. for Humanities, 1984-85; instr. Mont. State U., 1985; conservator prints Permanent Collection, Mont. State U., Bozeman, 1986; printer Teaberry Press, San Francisco, 1986; collaborative printer Exptl. Workshop, 1986; artist in residence Ucross Found., Clearmont, Wyo., 1986; assoc. prof. art U. Tenn., Knoxville, 1987-97, Ga. State U., Atlanta, 1997—, assoc. dean fine arts, 2001—. Vis. artist, lectr. Acad. Fine Arts, Helsinki, 1993; vis. artist Fine Arts Inst., Lahti, Finland, 1993; vis. critic Acad. Fine Arts, Bratislava, Slovakia, 1993; vis. lectr. Temple U. Program in Rome, 1993. Exhibited in solo shows Kathryn Sermas Gallery, N.Y.C., 1991, 92, Lowe Gallery, Santa Monica, Calif., 1992, Lowe Gallery, Atlanta, 1991, 93, 94, 98, 2000, Instituto de Estudios Norteamericanos, Barcelona, 1991, others; solo multimedia installation at MUUry Gallery of New Media, Helsinki, 1993, Czech Cultural Ctr., Bratislava, 1993; represented in permanent collection 1st Tenn. Bank/ MBL Life Assurance Corp., Memphis, Fulton County Med. Examiners Facility. Recipient Artist Prematis award Taller Galeria Fort, Barcelona, 1989, others; U. Tenn. rsch. grantee abroad, 1990, 91, 92, 94, SAF/NEA Visual Artist fellow, 1994, Tenn. State Arts Commn. Visual Artist fellow, 1996, Rsch. grant Ga. State U., 1998, 99. Mem. Coll. Art Assn., So. Graphics Coun. Home: 1090 Standard Dr NE Atlanta GA 30319-3320 Office: Ga State U Sch Art & Design PO Box 4107 Atlanta GA 30302-4107

LONGOBARDO, ANNA KAZANJIAN, engineering executive; b. N.Y.C. d. Aram Michael and Zarouhy (Yazejian) Kazanjian; m. Guy S. Longobardo, July 12, 1952; children: Guy A., Alicia. Student, Barnard Coll., 1947; BSME, Columbia U., 1949, MSME, 1952. Sr. systems engr. Am. Bosch Arma Corp., Garden City, N.Y., 1950-65; rsch. sect. head Sperry Rand Corp., Gt. Neck, 1965-68, rsch. sect. head systems mgmt., 1968-73; mgr. engring. personnel utilization Sperry Corp., 1973-77, mgr. systems mgmt. program planning, 1977-81, mgr. planning systems mgmt. group, 1981-82, dir. tech. svc. sys. devel., 1982-89, dir. field engring., 1989-93; dir. strategic initiatives Unysis Corp., 1993-95; bd. dirs. Engring. Found. Gateway Engring. Edn. Coalition, 1998—, also bd. dirs.; vice chmn. Engring. Conf. Found. Bd., 2001—. Chmn. exec. compensation com. Woodward-Clyde Group, Denver, 1989-97. Contbr. articles to profl. publs. Trustee Columbia U., N.Y.C., 1990-96, trustee emerita, 1996—; mem. Columbia Engring. Coun., 1987—, chmn., 1987-91; mem. Bronxville (N.Y.) Planning Bd.; chmn. Bronxville Design Rev. Com., 1993—; pres. Soc. Columbia Grads., 1998-2000. Recipient hon. citation Wilson Coll. Centennial, 1970, Alumni medal for conspicuous svc. Columbia U., 1980, Egleston medal for disting. engring. achievement Columbia U., 1997; named One of 100 N.Y. Women of Influence, New York Woman mag., 1986. Fellow Soc. Women Engrs. (founder, pioneer); mem. AIAA (sr.), ASME (sr.), Columbia U. Engring. Alumni Assn. (pres. 1977-81), Columbia U. Alumni Fedn. (pres. 1981-85), Bronxville Field Club.

LONGONE, DANIEL THOMAS, chemistry educator emeritus; b. Worcester, Mass., Sept. 16, 1932; s. Daniel Edward and Anne (Novick) L.; m. Janice B. Bluestein, June 13, 1954. BS, Worcester Poly. Inst., 1954; PhD, Cornell U., 1958. Research fellow chemistry U. Ill., Urbana, 1958-59; mem. faculty dept. chemistry U. Mich., Ann Arbor, 1959—, assoc. prof., 1966-71, prof., 1971-87, emeritus prof., 1988—. Cons. Gen. Motors Research Co., 1965-77 Am. Chem. Soc.-Petroleum Research Fund internat. fellow, 1967-68; Fulbright scholar, 1970-71 Mem. Am. Chem. Soc., Sigma Xi, Tau Beta Pi, Phi Lambda Upsilon. Home: 1207 W Madison St Ann Arbor MI 48103-4729 Office: U Mich 3533 Chemistry Ann Arbor MI 48109 E-mail: dtlongwfl@netscape.com.

LONGSTREET, RENEE SCHONFELD, television writer, producer; b. Los Angeles, July 19, 1940; d. Morrey and Faye (Zeiler) Schonfeld; m. Jack Silas, Nov. 19, 1961 (div. Dec. 1973); children: Julie Lynne, Carolyn Jo, Sean Michael; m. Harry Stephen Longstreet, Jan. 9, 1977. BA in English, UCLA, 1961. Staff writer Julie Farr M.D. Paramount Pictures, Hollywood, Calif., 1977-78; exec. story cons. Cliffhangers Universal TV, Universal City, 1978-79, producer, writer various shows, 1982-83, 20th Century Fox, Inc., Los Angeles, 1983; supervising producer NBC Prodns., 1984-85, Warner Bros. TV, Los Angeles, 1985; exec. producer, writer Fame, Rags to Riches MGM-TV, Culver City, Calif., 1986-88; with series devel. Evergreen Dream, Inc., Los Angeles, 1988—. Author: (screenplay) Gathering Part II, 1979, The Promise of Love, 1981, The Sky's No Limit, 1984; exec. producer, writer CBS TV show Night Walk, 1989, With A Vengeance, 1992, Test of Love, 2000; writer The Jennifer Graham Story, Gunsmoke: One Man's Justice, 1994, Alien Nation: Body and Soul, 1995, To Face Her Past, 1996, Alien Nation, The Udara Legacy, 1997, Chance of a Lifetime, 1997, Marriage of Convenience, 1998, A Memory in My Heart, 1999, Forget Me Never, 1999; prodr. Sex, Love and Cold Hard Cash, 1992; writer, prodr. A Vow to Kill, 1995, The Perfect Daughter, 1996. Mem.: Acad. TV Arts and Scis, Writers Guild of Am.

LONGSTREET, STEPHEN (CHAUNCEY LONGSTREET), author, painter; b. N.Y.C., Apr. 18, 1907; m. Ethel Joan Godoff, Apr. 22, 1932; children: Joan, Harry. Student, Rutgers Coll., Harvard U.; grad., N.Y. Sch. Fine and Applied Art, 1929; student in Rome, Paris. Ind. artist, writer, 1930—. Staff lectr. Los Angeles Art Assn., 1954, UCLA, 1955, 58-59, lectr. Los Angeles County Mus., 1958-59; staff mem. arts and humanities dept. UCLA, 1965—; prof. art, dir. dept. Viewpoints Inst. of Gen. Semantics, Los Angeles, 1965; prof. modern writing U. So. Calif., Los Angeles, 1975-80. Began as painter; contbr. to French, Am. and English mags.; also cartoonist; radio writer for NBC, CBS, and other networks, writer shows for Rudy Vallee, Deems Taylor, John Barrymore, Bob Hope, Ellery Queen; writer popular series detective stories for Lippincott and Morrow under pen name Paul Haggrad, 1936; film critic Saturday Rev., 1941; mem. editorial staff Time mag., 1942, Screenwriters mag., 1947-48; critic L.A. Daily News, Book Pages, 1948; assoc. producer Civil War series The Blue and Gray, NBC, 1959—; author: All or Nothing, 1983, Delilah's Fortune, 1984, Our Father's House, 1985; painting exhibited: L.A., 1946, 48, N.Y., 1946, London, 1947; one-man shows include Padlia Galleries, L.A., 1970, Memphis Mus., 1979, Erie Mus., 1981, Coll. of Libr. of Congress, 1980, Jazz Age Revisited, 1983, Smithsonian Nat. Portrait Gallery, 1983, Sr. Eye Gallery, Long Beach, Calif., 1990, Columbus (Ohio) Mus. Art, 1992, tour of Japan, 1994; retrospective show Longstreet the Mature Years, L.A., 1983, Jazz-The Chgo. Scene, Regenstein Libr. U. Chgo., 1989, Columbus (Ohio) Mus. Fine Arts; author: The Pedlocks, 1951, The Beach House, 1952, The World Revisited, 1953, A Century of Studebaker on Wheels, 1953, The Lion at Morning, 1954, The Boy in the Model-T, 1956, Real Jazz, 1956, The Promoters, 1957, The Bill Pearson Story, 1957, (in French), Complete Dictionary of Jazz, 1957, Man of Montmartre, 1958, The Burning Man, 1958, The Politician, 1959, The Crime, 1959, Geisha, 1960, Gettysburg, 1960, A Treasury of the World's Great Prints, 1961, Eagles Where I Walk, 1961, The Flesh Peddler, 1962, A Few Painted Feathers, 1963, War In Golden Weather, 1965, Pedlock & Sons, 1965, The Wilder Shore: San Francisco '49 to '06, 1968, A Salute to American Cooking, (with Ethel Longstreet), 1968, War Cries on Horseback, An Indian History, 1970, The Canvas Falcons, 1970, Chicago: 1860-1920; a history, 1973, The General, 1974, (with Ethel Longstreet) World Cookbook, 1973, Win or Lose, 1977, The Queen Bees, 1979, Storm Watch, 1979, Pembroke Colors, 1981, From Storyville to Harlem - 50 years of the Jazz Scene, 1987, Magic Trumpets--The Young Peoples Story of Jazz, 1989, (poems) Jazz Solos, 1990, My Three Nobel Prizes; Life with Faulkner, Hemingway and Sinclair Lewis, 1994, Up River-The Jazz of Kansas City and Chicago, 1997; editor, illustrator: The Memoirs of W.W. Windstaff Lower Than Angels, 1993; writer screen plays including Uncle Harry, 1943, Rider on a Dead Horse, The Imposter, First Travelling Saleslady, Stallion Road, 1946, The Jolson Story, 1947, Helen Morgan Story, 1956, plays including High Button Shoes, 1947, Gauguin, 1948, All Star Cast, Los Angeles, A History, 1977, (TV series) Playhouse 90, TV writer for Readers Digest Theatre, 1955; contbr. dialogue for films Greatest Show on Earth, Duel In the Sun. Pres. Los Angeles Art Assn., 1973-90. Recipient Stafford medal London, 1946, Bowman prize, 1948, Photo-Play mag. Gold medal for The Jolson Story, 1948, Billboard-Donaldson Gold medal for High Button Shoes, 1948. Mem. Motion Picture Acad. Arts and Letters, Writers Guild Am. (bd. dirs. 1948), Phi Sigma (charter mem.). Clubs: Sketch, Daguerreotype Society, Winadu Players. *I seem to have stumbled into the most dangerous world history since the fall of Rome. This time little of civilization may survive. The vulgarization of the culture by TV and lack of an American greatness in the White House can bring Orwell's world into being. But mankind will most likely remain in some form in his polluted planet, recalling what was the past. Man will always remain an undomesticated animal; rather kill than think.*

LONGSTREET, WILMA S. curriculum and instruction educator; b. N.Y.C., July 3, 1935; d. Hyman Steinberg and Estelle Rosa; widowed; stepchildren: Patricia, Robert, Richard Engle. BA, Hunter Coll., 1956; MS, Ind. U., 1968, PhD, 1970. Cert. tchr., N.Y.C. Asst. prof. U. Ill., Champaign/Urbana, 1970-72; from assoc. prof. to prof. edn. U. Mich., Flint and Ann Arbor, 1972-78; dean, prof. edn. DePaul U., Chgo., 1978-82; dean edn. U. New Orleans, 1982-85, prof. curriculum and instrn., 1982—. Mem. Coll. and Univ. Faculty Assembly, 1970—, pres., 1999; cons. to sch. sys., Gary, Ind., Flint, Mich., New Orleans, State of Ind. Author: Aspects of Ethnicity, 1978, The Leaders and the Led, 1979; co-author: A Design for Social Education, 1972, (with Shirley H. Engle) Curriculum for a New Millennium, 1993; contbr. over sixty articles to profl. jours. Mem. Profs. of Curriculum (factotum, chair nominating com. 2001), Phi Delta Kappa. Democrat. Unitarian-Universalist. Home: 49 Gull St New Orleans LA 70148 Office: U New Orleans Coll Edn New Orleans LA 70148 E-mail: wlongstr@uno.edu.

LONGSTRETH, BEVIS, lawyer; b. N.Y.C., Jan. 29, 1934; s. Alfred Bevis and Mary Agnes (Shiras) L.; m. Clara Seymour St. John, Aug. 10, 1963; children: Katherine Shiras, Thomas Day, Benjamin Hoyt. BS cum laude, Princeton U., 1956; LL.M., Harvard U., 1961. Bar: N.Y. 1962. Assoc. Debevoise & Plimpton, N.Y.C., 1962-70, ptnr., 1970-81; commr. SEC, Washington, 1981-84; ptnr. Debevoise & Plimpton, 1984-97, of counsel, 1997—2000. Lectr. Columbia U. Law Sch., N.Y.C., 1975-81, adj. prof., 1994-99; cons. Ford Found., 1971-72; cons. to Comptroller Gen. of U.S.; mem. pension fin. com. World Bank, 1987-95; bd. govs. Am. Stock Exch., 1992-98; bd. dirs. AMVESCAP, plc, Coll. Ret. Equities Fund. Author books numerous articles on investment, securities and law. Trustee Nathan Cummings Found., 1991-97, 1999—, trustee; New Sch. U., 1987—; chmn. fin. com. Rockefeller Family Fund, 1986—. Lt. USMC, 1956-58. Mem. Am. Law Inst., Assn. of Bar of City of N.Y., Coun. Fgn. Rels. Democrat. Home: 322 Central Park W New York NY 10025-7629 Office: Debevoise & Plimpton 919 3rd Ave New York NY 10022-6225 E-mail: blongstreth@mindspring.com., blongstreth@debevoise.com.

LONGSWORTH, ELLEN LOUISE, art historian, consultant; b. Auburn, Ind., Aug. 21, 1949; d. Robert Smith and Alice Louise (Whitten) L.; m. Frederic Sanderson Stott, Sept. 1, 1973 (div. 1981); m. Joseph Nicholas Teta, June 15, 1991. BA, Mt. Holyoke Coll., 1971; MA, U. Chgo., 1976; PhD, Boston U., 1987. Trainer, designer Polaris Enterprises Corp., Quincy, Mass., 1981-82, asst. v.p., 1982-84, cons., 1989-93; from asst. prof. to assoc. prof. Merrimack Coll., N. Andover, 1985-95, prof., 1995—, chmn. dept., 1993-2000. Adj. instr. art and art history Bradford Coll., Haverhill, Mass., 1975-80; vis. lectr. art history Lowell (Mass.) U., 1981-82, Boston U., 1982-86, 88, 91, Babson Coll., Wellesley, Mass., 1984-85. Active Merrimack Valley Coun. on the Arts and Humanities, Haverhill, 1975-78, Friends of Kimball Tavern, Bradford Coll., Haverhill, 1975-80, Haverhill Arts Commn., 1996-2002; bd. dirs. Winnekenni Found., Haverhill, 1990— Grantee Faculty Devel., Merrimack Coll., 1989-90, 92-93, 95, 97, 2002, Kress Summer Travel, Boston U., 1980, 86, recipient in-house Ciejek fellowship for humanistic rsch., 1998; Boston U. fellow, 1980-82, 85; recipient internship Isabella Stewart Gardner Mus., Boston, 1979-80. Mem. AAUW, Coll. Art Assn., South-Ctrl. Renaissance Conf. (exec. com. 1998-2002), Italian Art Soc., Renaissance Soc. Am. Republican. Methodist. Avocations: reading, playing the piano, painting and drawing, weight training, swimming. Home: 649 Main St Haverhill MA 01830-2647 Office: Merrimack Coll North Andover MA 01845 E-mail: ellen.longsworth@merrimack.edu.

LONGUET, GREGORY ARTHUR, automation engineer, consultant; b. Pensacola, Fla., Nov. 1, 1945; s. Harry Charles and Gretchen (Gregory) L.; m. Elaine Gail Shuler, July 11, 1970; children: Ondreja N., Courtney E. BS, Ga. State U., 1974; MS in Mech. Engring., Ga. Inst. Technology, 1975. Cert. mfg. specialist. Toolmaker GM, Doraville, Ga., 1970-74; mfg. engr. Gen. Dynamics Corp., Ft. Worth, 1974-79; automation engr., cons. IBM, Lexington, Ky., 1979-91, design team cons., rep., 1985-91, mfg. consulting engr. Ala., Miss. trading area Montgomery, Ala., 1991-94; sr. mfg. info. sys. cons., mgr. Tech. Consulting, Inc., Louisville, 1994—. Dir. ops. sys. Gen. Cable Corp., Highland Heights, Ky. Elder Presbyn. Ch., Lexington, 1980—; mem. Habitat for Humanity, Girl Scouts U.S., South Ctrl. Ala. Capt. U.S. Army, 1966-70, Vietnam. Mem. Am. Prodn. and Inventory Control Soc., Soc. Mfg. Engrs., Nat. Mgrs. Assn., Masons, Beta Phi Gamma. Avocations: sports cars, aircraft, astronomy. Office: Tech Consulting Inc 1800 Meidiogen Tower Louisville KY 40202

LONGWELL, HARRY, oil company executive; b. Bunkie, La., July 20, 1941; BS in Petroleum Engring., La. State U., 1963. Engr. drilling Exxon Mobil Corp., New Orleans, mgr. ops. Corpus Christi, 1974, L.A., 1974, divsn. mgr., 1977, mgr. ops. dept. prodn., v.p. Houston, 1980-85, v.p. exploration and prodn. in Europe London, England, 1986, exec. asst. N.Y.C., 1986, v.p. exploration and prodn. Florham Park, N.J., 1987, exec. v.p., 1990; pres. Exxon Co., U.S.A., 1992; sr. v.p., dir. Exxon Mobil Corp., Irving, Tex., 1995—2001, exec. v.p., dir., 2001—. Mem. exec. com. bd. dirs. Nat. Action Coun. for Minorities in Engring.; bd. dirs. U. Dallas; mem. bd. visitors, mem. exec. com. U. Tex. M.D. Anderson Cancer Ctr.; mem. adv. bd. Dallas Area Habitat for Humanity. Office: Exxon Mobil Corp 5959 Las Colinas Blvd Irving TX 75039-4202 E-mail: hjlongwell@exxonmobil.com.

LONGWELL, JOHN PLOEGER, chemical engineering educator; b. Denver, Apr. 27, 1918; s. John Stalker and Martha Dorothea (Ploeger) L.; m. Marion Reed Valleau, Dec. 11, 1945; children: Martha Reed, Elizabeth Ann, John Dorney. BSME, U. Calif., Berkeley, 1940; ScD in Chem. Engring, MIT, 1943. With Exxon Rsch. & Engring. Co., Linden, N.J., 1943-77; dir. Exxon Rsch. & Engring. Co. Central Basic Rsch. Lab., 1960-69, sr. sci. adv., 1969-77; prof. chem. engring. MIT, Cambridge, 1977-89. Contbr. articles to profl. jours. Recipient Sir Alfred Egerton medal for contbns. to combustion Nat. Acad. Engring., 1976 Mem. Am. Chem. Soc., Combustion Inst. (past pres.), Am. Inst. Chem. Engrs. (award 1979), Sigma Xi, Tau Beta Pi. Republican. Achievements include patents in field. Home: PO Box 1876 Kingston WA 98346-1876

LONGWELL, ROBERT LEROY, writer; b. Denver, Mar. 24, 1926; s. Harry Vernon and Ahlene Stella (Feikert) Longwell; m. Irene LaJean Randall, Nov. 30, 1946; children: Wanda Lorraine, Larry Vernon(dec.) , Lavonna Faye. BA, U. Nebr., Kearney, 1950; MA, U. No. Colo., 1961; PhD, U. Colo., 1971. Cert. tchr. secondary sch. Instr., dept. chair various h.s., Nebr., 1950—62; faculty U. No. Colo., Greeley, 1963—, prof. English and Speech, 1979—86, prof. emeritus comm., 1986—, prof. emeritus edn., 1989—, mem. tchr. edn. faculty, 1981—89. Cons. Monfort of Colo. Corp., Greeley, 1968—72; corres. Omaha World-Herald, 1955—62. Contbr. Precinct com. chair Rep. Party, Greeley, 1975—92; reading tutor Right to Read Programs, 1991—; mem. Greeley City Mus., 1996—2001. With USN, 1944—46. Mem.: Emeritus Faculty Assn. U. No. Colo. (pres. 1991—92), Colo. Speech Assn. (exec. coun. 1963—65), Friends of the U. No. Colo. Librs., Kiwanis (past pres.). Republican. Methodist. Avocations: photography, camping, travel, singing, woodworking. Home: 1226 25th St Greeley CO 80631

LONGWORTH, RICHARD COLE, journalist; b. Des Moines, Mar. 13, 1935; s. Wallace Harlan and Helen (Cole) L.; m. Barbara Bem, July 19, 1958; children: Peter, Susan. BJ, Northwestern U., 1957; postgrad., Harvard U., 1968-69. Reporter UPI, Chgo., 1958-60, parliamentary corr. London, 1960-65, corr. Moscow, 1965-68, Vienna, 1969-72, diplomatic corr. Brussels, 1972-76; econ. and internat. affairs reporter Chgo. Tribune, 1976-86, bus. editor, econ. columnist, 1987-88, chief European corr., 1988-91, sr. writer, 1991—2002, sr. corr., 2002—; internat. affairs commentator Sta. WBEZ-FM, Chgo., 1984—. Adj. prof. Northwestern U., 1998—, guest scholar, 2001. Author: Global Squeeze: The Coming Crisis for First-World Nations, 1998, Global Chicago, 2000. With U.S. Army, 1957-58. Nieman fellow, 1968-69; recipient award for econ. reporting U. Mo., 1978, 80, John Hancock, 1978, 79, 82, Gerald Loeb award for econ. reporting, 1979, Media award for econ. understanding Dartmouth Coll., 1979, award Inter-Am. Press Assn., 1979, Peter Lisagor award Sigma Delta Chi, 1979, Sidney Hillman award, 1985, Lowell Thomas award for travel writing, 1985, Beck award for fgn. corr., 1986, Domestic Reporting award, 1987, Overseas Press Club award, 1994, 97, Alumni Merit award Northwestern U., 2000. Mem. Coun. Fgn. Rels. N.Y., Chgo. Com. of Council Fgn. Rels., Assn. Am. Corrs. in London, Internat. Music Found. (dir.), Ednl. Found. for Nuclear Sci. (dir.). Office: Chicago Tribune 435 N Michigan Ave Chicago IL 60611-4066 E-mail: rlongworth@tribune.com.

LONIGAN, PAUL RAYMOND, language professional, educator; b. N.Y.C., May 27, 1935; s. William Raymond Maloy and Irene Rita (Hickman) Lonigan; m. Cynthia Ann Hartley, June 5, 1965; children: Jennifer, Cynthia. BA magna cum laude, Queens Coll., 1960; PhD, Johns Hopkins U., 1967. Instr. Russell Sage Coll., Troy, N.Y., 1963-65; assoc. prof. SUNY, Oswego, 1963-65, Queens Coll., CUNY Grad. Ctr., N.Y.C., 1967-83, prof., 1983—, dep. exec. officer PhD program in French, 1969-72, coord. French program, 1982-85, 91-96. Author: Gormont et Isembart, 1976, Chrétien's Yvain, 1978, The Early Irish Church, 1989, The Druids, 1996; editor: Respuetas del Corazón by Maria Carreño. Sponsor Le Cercle Français. With U.S. Marine Corps, 1954-62. Decorated Chevalier Dans L'Ordre Des Palmes Académiques (France). Mem. Phi Beta Kappa, Delta Phi Alpha. Avocations: numismatics, philately, writing poetry, hunting, fishing. Office: Queens Coll King 207 65-30 Kissena Blvd Flushing NY 11367

LONNGREN, KARL ERIK, electrical and computer engineering educator; b. Milw., Aug. 8, 1938; s. Bruno Leonard and Edith Irene (Osterlund) L.; m. Vicki Anne Mason, Feb. 16, 1963; children: Sondra Lyn, Jon Erik. BS in Elec. Engring., U. Wis., 1960, MS, 1962, PhD, 1964. Postdoctoral appointment Royal Inst. Tech., Stockholm, 1964-65; asst. prof. elec. engring. U. Iowa, Iowa City, 1965-67, assoc. prof., 1967-72, prof., 1972—. Vis. scientist Inst. Plasma Physics, Nagoya, Japan, 1972, Math Rsch. Ctr., Madison, 1976, Los Alamos (N.Mex.) Sci. Labs., 1979, 80, Inst. Space and Astron. Sci., Tokyo, 1981, Danish Atomic Energy, Riso, 1982, others. Author: Introduction to Physical Electronics, 1988, Electromagnetics with MATLAB, 1997; co-author: Introduction to Wave Phenomena, 1985; co-editor: Solitons in Action, 1978. Recipient Disting. Svc. citation U. Wis. Madison, 1992. Fellow Am. Phys. Soc., IEEE Presbyterian. Home: 21 Prospect Pl Iowa City IA 52246-1932 Office: U Iowa Dept Elec & Computer Engring Iowa City IA 52242 E-mail: lonngren@eng.uiowa.edu.

LONNQUIST, GEORGE ERIC, lawyer; b. Lincoln, Nebr., Mar. 29, 1946; s. John Hall and Elizabeth Claire (Hanson) L.; m. Wendi Ann McDonough; children: Alethea, Courtenay, Barrett. BS, U. Tenn., 1968; JD, U. Nebr., 1971; LLM, NYU, 1974. Bar: Calif. 1983, Oreg. 1972, Nebr. 1971. Law clerk Oreg. Supreme Ct., Salem, 1971-72; dep. legis. counsel Oreg. Legislature, 1972-73; ptnr. Meysing & Lonnquist, Portland, 1974-78; v.p., assoc. gen. counsel Amfac, Inc., Portland and San Francisco, 1978-84; sr. v.p., gen. counsel Homestead Fin. Corp., Millbrae, Calif., 1984-91, Homestead Savs., Millbrae, 1984-93; pvt. practice, San Francisco, 1993—. Democrat. Roman Catholic. Avocation: woodcarving. Home: 1945 Beach Park Blvd Foster City CA 94404-1326 Office: 4000 E 3rd Ave Foster City CA 94404-4805 E-mail: lonn@legacypartners.com.

LOO, BEVERLY JANE, publishing company executive; b. L.A. d. Richard Y. and Bessie E. Sue Loo. BA, U. Calif., Berkeley. Dir. subs. rights Prentice-Hall, Inc., N.Y.C., 1957-59; fiction editor McCall's mag., 1959-62; exec. editor and dir. subs. rights, gen. books div. McGraw-Hill Book Co., N.Y.C., 1962-82; pres. Beverly Jane Loo Assocs., Inc., 1982-85; sr. editor, dir. subs. rights World Almanac Pharos Books, 1985-88; dir. mktg. and subs. rights Paragon House, 1988-91; dir. mktg. and sales Thomasson-Grant, Charlottesville, Va., 1991-93; dir. pub. and comm. inst. U. Va. Sch. Continuing Edn. & Profl. Studies, 1993—. Mem.: Arts (London); Overseas Press (N.Y.C.); Va. Writers; U. Va. Faculty. Home: Lewis & Clark Sq # 701 250 W Main St Charlottesville VA 22902-5079 Office: Zehmer Hall 104 Midmont Ln Charlottesville VA 22903-2449

LOO, MARCUS HSIEU-HONG, urologist, physician, educator; b. N.Y.C., Aug. 12, 1955; s. David Wei and Patricia (Pai) L.; m. Donna C. Wingshee, Oct. 3, 1987; children: Christopher, Courtney. BSEE with distinction, Cornell U., 1977, MD, 1981. Diplomate Am. Bd. Urology. Asst. attending urologist N.Y. Hosp.-Cornell Med. Ctr., N.Y.C., 1988—; clin. asst. prof. urology Cornell U. Med. Coll., 1994-2000, clin. assoc. prof. urology, 2000—. Admissions com. Cornell U. Med. Coll.; mem. operating bd. Columbia Cornell Care, LLC.; cons. Chinatown Health Cilnic; clin. dir. Asian Am. Cancer Awareness Rsch. and Tng. grant. Author: The Prostate Cancer Source Book, 1998. Mem. oper. bd. Columbia Cornell Care L.L.C. Fellow ACS; mem. AMA, IEEE, Am. Assn. Clin. Urologists, Am. Urol. Assn., Soc. Internat. Urology, Cornell U. Med. Coll. Alumni Assn. (bd. dirs.), Chinese Am. Med. Soc. (pres., bd. dirs. 1990-97), Fedn. Chinese Am. and Chinese Can. Med. Socs. (bd. dirs., v.p.), Tau Beta Pi, Eta Kappa Nu, Phi Tau Phi. Office: 53 E 70th St New York NY 10021-4941

LOO, MARITTA LOUISE, nurse, national guard officer; b. Denver, Feb. 6, 1945; d. William Del Rio and Audrey Elaine (Fromholz) Dugan; m. Albert W.S. Loo, June 26, 1971 (div. Apr. 1976). Diploma, St. Mary's, Kansas City, Mo., 1966; BS in Health Svcs. Adminstrn., Calif. U., Navato, 1986; student, Army War Coll., 1986-87; MBA, Am. U., 2000, PhD Bus. Ethics, 2001. RN, Tex. From staff to head nurse Kansas City Gen. Hosp., Mo., 1966-69; shift charge, emergency nurse St. Mary's Hosp., Kansas City, 1969-71; rsch. nurse office of Dr. J. Willoughby, 1970-71; dir. critical care Dallas-Ft. Worth Med. Ctr., Grand Prairie, Tex., 1974-86; rev. supr. Tex. Med. Found., 1988-92; dir. home health and rehab. Dallas-Ft. Worth Med. Ctr., Grand Prairie, 1993-2000; COO Cert. Care Givers, LLC , 2001—; dir. crisis care Vitas, Dallas, 2002—. Freelance leadership trainer and mgmt. cons., 1985—93, 2000—; owner, pres. Masavic Properties, Inc., Ft. Worth, 1979—; co-chmn. Tex. Adj. Gen.'s adv. coun., Austin, 1985—86; spl. advisor Am. Security Coun., Washington, 1985, nat. advisor, 1985—87; rep. Partnership for Peace Program, Prague, 1995; mem. congl. bd. for candidate selection Annapolis Acad., 1995; comdr. med. squadron Tex. Air Nat. Guard, 1995—2000, state med. officer hdqs., 1994—95, 2000—01; mem. Cong. Bd. for Candidate Selection for Sr. Mil. Acads., 1995—; motivational spkr.; chief ops. officer Cert. Care Givers, LLC, 2001; bd. dirs. Tarrant Coun., 2001—, fin. dir., 2002; pres. 136 Silver Eagles Assn., 2000—. Contbr. articles to mags. Resource coord. ARC, Carlisle, Pa., 1986—87; mem. humanitarian mission Joint-Forces BRAVO to Honduras, 1997; state med. officer Tex. ANG Hdqs., 1994—95, 2000—01; bd. dirs. Tarrant Coun., 2001—, v.p. bd. dirs., 2002; mem. Cath. Adults, Irving, Tex. Capt. USAF, 1971—74, col. Air Nat. Guard, 1975—2001, 1989, Desert Shield, 1989—90, Desert Storm. Recipient Honored Vol. award ARC, 1982, Profl. Devel. award Tex. Adj. Gen.'s Adv. Coun., 1986, Rare Joint Forces award, 1995; named one of Notable Women of Tex., 1985. Mem.: AACN (bd. advisors 1983, office Ft. Worth chpt. 1984—86), DAV (bronze leader comdrs.

club), ANA, Air Force Assn., N.G. Assn. (del. 1984—2001), Silver Eagle Assn. (pres. 2000—), Am. Legion. Republican. Roman Catholic. Avocations: theater, music. Home: 2433 Parkwood Dr Grand Prairie TX 75050-1727 E-mail: masavic@juno.com.

LOO, THOMAS S. lawyer; b. 1943; BS, JD, U. So. Calif. Bar: Calif. 1969. Ptnr. Greenberg Traurig, Santa Monica, Calif., 2001—. Office: 2450 Colorado Ave Ste 400E Santa Monica CA 90404

LOOCKERMAN, WILLIAM DELMER, educational administrator, retired; b. Phila., Feb. 24, 1939; s. William Delmer and Kathleen (Cullen) L.; m. Alice Clara Winnemore, June 9, 1962; 1 child, Alice B. BS in Health and Phys. Edn., West Chester (Pa.) State U., 1962, MS in Health and Phys. Edn., 1967; EdD in Phys. Edn., Temple U., 1970; cert. sch. dist. adminstr., Niagara U., 1974. Tchr. Upper Darby (Pa.) Schs., 1965-68; teaching assoc. Temple U., Phila., 1968-70; asst. prof. SUNY, Buffalo, 1970-73; dir. health, phys. edn. and recreation Orchard Park (N.Y.) Cen. Schs., 1973-81; registered sch. bus. adminstr. Springville (N.Y.) Griffith Inst. Cen. Sch. Dist., 1981-2001, ret., 2001, adminstr. emeritus, 2001—. Adj. asst. prof. Niagara U., Niagara Falls, NY, 1975—77; adj. prof. Canisius Coll., Buffalo, 1979—81; statewide rep. Group 491 Ins. Safety Program, Albany, NY, 1983—2001, trustee, NY, 1991—2001, mem. exec. com., NY, 1991—2001, chair, NY, 1996—2001; spkr. local, state, nat. and internat. meetings. Contbr. articles to profl. jours. Capt. USNR ret. Recipient spl. honor award N.Y. State Coaches Assn., 1980, honor award N.Y. State Assn. Health, Phys. Edn. and Recreation, 1979, conf. dedication, 1980. Mem. Internat. Assn. Sch. Bus. Ofcls. (mem. choir 1989—, song leader Opening Gen. Session 1997, appreciation award 1990, 94), N.Y. State Sch. Bus. Ofcls. (chpt. exec. com. 1983-85), AMVETS, Naval Order U.S. (chpt. comdr. 1987-96, 2000-2001, companion to gen. coun. 1997-99, Naval Res. Assn. (chpt. pres., nat. budget/fin. com. 1995—, nat. v.p. 1997-99, 2001--, treas. 1999-2001, mem. nat. adv. com . 1987—, Nat. award of Merit 2001), Am. Legion; mem. WNY Armed Forces Week com. 1980—), Springville Cmty. Choir 1997. Republican. Episcopalian. Avocation: woodworking. Home: 7643 Lewis Rd Holland NY 14080-9625

LOOGES, PETER JOHN, systems engineer, architect; b. East Orange, N.J., Mar. 4, 1963; s. Edwin John and Ida Claire (Jacobus) L.; m. Heather Marta Evans, Apr. 6, 1989 (dec.); 1 child, Adrian; m. Suzanne Marie Luehks; 1 child, Zachary Michael. BS in Computer Sci., Rensselaer Poly. Inst., 1985; MS in Computer Sci., Old Dominion U., 1991, PhD in Computer Sci., 1992. Commd. ensign USN, 1985, advanced through grades to lt., resigned, 1992; researcher, adj. prof. Old Dominion U., Norfolk, Va., 1992-93, adj. computer sci. prof., 1993-99; global telecomm. chief architect, corp. v.p. Sci. Applications Internat. Corp., Hampton, Va., 1993—. Contbr. articles to profl. jours. Mem. IEEE, Assn. for Computing Machinery, Software Engring. Inst. Avocations: scuba, sky diving, raquetball. Office: Sci Applications Internat Corp 10260 Campus Point Dr San Diego CA 92121-1522 E-mail: loogesp@saic.com.

LOOK, PAUWILO, creative media developer, architecture marketer; b. Honolulu, Dec. 22, 1964; m. Stanley James Wilson, Aug. 22, 1987 (div. Sept. 1992); 1 child, Raelyn; Carlson Chun Ping Look, May 22, 1995; children: BrayDn, Sarah Champayn, LonDyn Sydney. Degree in Comms., Honolulu C.C./U. Hawaii; grad. with honors, Columbia Sch. Broadcasting. Sales asst., spl. events prodr. KHON-TV 2, Honolulu, 1992-94; news dir. KCCN AM and FM/KINE Radio, 1994-95; live events prodr., promotions coord. Oceanic Cable, a Time Warner affiliate, Mililani, 1995-98; telethon host Muscular Dystrophy Assn. Hawaii, Honolulu, 1998—; mktg. specialsit Coca-Cola Bottling Co. of Hawaii, 2000—. Prodr., writer, voiceover Taste Hawaii with Hari, 1999; prodr., writer, host ann. TV spls. Road to Fame Talent Search, 1995—, Kiddieoke Kids Talent Search, 1995—; prodr., writer, narrator ann. TV spl. Christmas Mele, 1995—. Bd. dirs. Coalition for a Drug-Free Hawaii, Honolulu, Crimestoppers, Honolulu. Named Internat. Queen of Queens, Ms. Profl. Woman Internat., 1998, Ms. Asia Profl. Woman Internat., 1999, Ms. Hawaii Am. Achievement, 1998, 99, Ms. US Internat. Beauty, 2000-01, 01-02, Mrs. Asia Pacific Universal Achievement, 2001, Ms. Hawaii, 2001; recipient award Mother-Dau. Hawaii World of Pageants, 1998, Mrs. Am. Achievement Nat. Career award, 2000. Mem. NAFE, Assn. Broadcasters, Hawaii Music Awards. Avocation: pageants. Office: PO Box 970306 Waipahu HI 96797-0306 E-mail: hawaii_1@theglobe.com.

LOOMAN, JAMES R. lawyer; b. Vallejo, Calif., June 5, 1952; s. Alfred R. and Jane M. (Halter) L.; m. Donna G. Craven, Dec. 18, 1976; children: Alison Marie, Mark Andrew, Zachary Michael. BA, Valparaiso U., 1974; JD, U. Chgo., 1978. Bar: Ill, 1978, U.S. Dist. Ct. (no dist.) Ill. 1978, U.S. Claims Ct. 1979. Ptnr. Sidley Austin Brown & Wood, Chgo., 1986—. Fellow Am. Coll. Comml. Fin. Lawyers; mem. ABA, Chgo. Bar Assn., Chgo. Athletic Assn., Skokie Country Club, Mid-Day Club. Lutheran. Office: Sidley Austin Brown & Wood Bank One Plz Chicago IL 60603-2003 E-mail: jlooman@sidley.com.

LOOMIE, EDWARD RAPHAEL, lawyer; b. N.Y.C., Aug. 18, 1918; s. Leo Stephen Loomie and Loretta F. Murphy; widowed; children: Christine, Paul. AB, Columbia U., 1940, JD, 1942. Pvt. practice. Pres. Internat. Copyrights Inc., Resources Plus Inc. Mem. 7th Regiment Vets. Assn. (v.p.).

LOOMIS, CHRISTOPHER KNAPP, metallurgical engineer; b. San Francisco, May 6, 1947; s. Richard and Evaline Elsie (Crandal) L.; m. Merril Ellen Purdy, Dec. 8, 1968; 1 child, Nicole Lee; m. Sandra Lee Marsh, Feb. 14, 1993. Profl. Engring. degree, Colo. Sch. Mines, 1969. Process engr. Alcan Aluminum Corp., Riverside, Calif., 1969-73, prodn. supt., 1973-76, process engr. Oswego, N.Y., 1976-78, maintenance engr., 1978-80; metall. engr. Hazelett Strip-Casting Corp., Colchester, Vt., 1980-81; chief engr. ARCO Metals Co., Chgo., 1981-84; maintenance supt. Cerro Metal Products, Paramount, Calif., 1984-85, mgr. engring. and maintenance, 1985-86; supt. tech. svcs. Golden Aluminum Co., Ft. Lupton, Colo., 1987-88, process devel. engr. Lakewood, 1988-91, corp. environ. and process engr., 1991; engr. IV Coors Brewing Co., Golden, 1991-93, materials engr. V, 1993-96, supr. maintenance svcs., 1999—; gen. ptnr. Loomis Engring. and Design, 1996-99. Mem. Am. Soc. for Metals, Metall. Soc., Colo. Sch. Mines Alumni Assn., Am. Soc. for Quality Control, Fedn. Fly Fishers (life), Trout Unltd. (life). Episcopalian. Avocations: fishing, camping, mechanics, home repair. Office: Coors Brewing Co PO Box 4030 Golden CO 80401-0030 E-mail: loomiseng@att.net., chris.loomis@coors.com.

LOOMIS, EARL ALFRED, JR. psychiatrist; b. Mpls., May 21, 1921; s. Earl Alfred and Amy Louise (Shore) L.; m. Victoria Malkerson, June 2, 1994 (div.); children: Rebecca Marie Keith, Kathleen V. Loomis, Jennifer Lee; m. Lucile Meyer, July 1, 1962 (dec. 1967); 1 child, Amy W. Loomis-Rossman; m. Anita Muriel Peabody, Mar. 22, 1969. MD, U. Minn., 1945. Diplomate Am. Bd. Psychiatry and Neurology, Am. Bd. Adult and Child Psychiatry; cert. Am. Soc. Addiction Medicine. Intern in internal medicine, pediatrics Univ. Hosp., Boston, 1945-46; resident Western Psychiat. Hosp., Pitts., 1946-48, Hosp. U. Pa., Phila., 1948-50; assoc. prof. child psychiatry U. Pitts. Sch. Medicine, 1952-56; prof. psychiatry and religion Union Theol. Sem., N.Y.C., 1956-63; chief div. child psychiatry St. Luke's Hosp., 1956-62; rsch. fellow U. Geneva (Switzerland) Inst. Jean-Jacques Rousseau, 1962-63; med. dir. Blueberry Treatment Ctr./Severly Emotionally Ill Children, Bklyn., 1963-81; prof. psychiatry Med. Coll. Ga., Augusta, 1980-90; pvt. practice, cons. Vet. Hosp., Charter Hosp. of Augusta, 1985-95; cons. U.S. VA Hosp., Augusta, 1985-95. Cons. Gracewood Sch. and Hosp., Augusta, 1983-89, Eisenhower Army Med. Ctr., Augusta, 1983-2000. Author: The Self in Pilgrimage, 1960; contbr. articles to profl. jours. Lt. (j.g.) USNR, 1950-52. Rsch. grant NIMH, 1956-63, travel grant, 1962-63, U.S. Info. Svcs., 1963. Fellow Am. Psychiat. Assn. (chair psychiatry and religion 1955-60); Group for the Advancement of Psychiatry (chair psychiatry and religion 1959-62), Am. Psychoanalytic Assn., Psychoanalytic Study Group of S.C. (founder, pres. 1981-88). Achievements include development of techniques for studying ego functions in psychotic, retarded and normal children via play pattern observations. Home and Office: PO Box 697 125 Cove Cir Greenport NY 11944

LOOMIS, EDWARD WARREN, writer, educator; b. Newport News, Va., Aug. 8, 1924; s. Arthur Kirkwood and Ethel (Morgan) L.; m. Ruth Fetzer, July 6, 1924 (dec. Feb. 1975); children: Jessica, Andrea, Abby; m. Mary I. O'Connor, Jan. 1, 1976. AB in English, Case Western Res. U., 1947; MA in English, PhD in English, Stanford U., 1959. Instr. English U. Ariz., Tucson, 1955-59; acting chancellor Deep Springs Coll., Calif., 1962-64; prof. U. Calif., Santa Barbara, 1959-87. Author: End of a War, 1958, The Charcoal Horse, 1959, Men of Principle, 1963, Clean and Sober, 2000, Romeo and Juliet in L.A., 2000, Heroic Spain, 2000; also stories. With U.S. Army, 1943-45, ETO. Home: 6591 Camino Venturoso Goleta CA 93117-5525 E-mail: ED910@cox.net.

LOOMIS, HOWARD KREY, banker; b. Omaha, Apr. 9, 1927; s. Arthur L. and Genevieve (Krey) L.; m. Florence Porter, Apr. 24, 1954; children: Arthur L. II, Frederick S., Howard Krey, John Porter. AB, Cornell U., 1949, MBA, 1950. Mgmt. trainee Hallmark Cards Inc., kansas City, Mo., 1953-56; sec., contr., dir. Mine Svc. Co. Inc., Ft. Smith, Ark., 1956-59; contr., dir. Electra Mfg. Co., Independence, Kans., 1959-63; v.p., dir. The Peoples Bank, Pratt, 1963-65, pres., 1966-2001, chmn., dir., 1998—. Pres., dir. Gt. Plains Leasing Inc., Pratt, 1966-80, Ctrl. States Inc., Pratt, 1970-76; pres. Krey Co. Ltd., Pratt, 1978-99, chmn., dir. 1999—; fin. chmn. Econ. Lifelines, Topeka; bd. dirs. All Ins. Inc., Pratt, Kans. Wildscape Found. Past pres. Pratt County United Fund; past chmn. Cannonball Trail chpt. ARC; bd. dirs., past comdg. gen. Kans. Cavalry; past pres. Kanza coun. Boy Scouts Am. With U.S. Army, 1950-52. Mem. Kans. C. of C. and Industry (past transp. chmn., dir., v.p.), Pratt Area C. of C. (past pres., bd. dirs.), Kans. Bankers Assn. (past bd. dirs.), Fin. Execs. Inst., Park Hills Country Club (past pres.), Elks, Rotary, Sigma Delta Chi, Chi Psi. Republican. Presbyterian. Home: 502 Welton St Pratt KS 67124-0928 Office: The Peoples Bank 222 S Main St Pratt KS 67124-1102

LOOMIS, JAMES COOK, educator, navigator; b. Long Beach, Calif., Sept. 22, 1935; s. Joseph Gray and Elizabeth Cook L.; children: Gannon, Megan Leslie Loomis Powers. BS, U. Calif., 1958, MA, 1961; postgrad., U. Mich., 1962. Dept. head math. Culver City (Calif.) H.S., 1962-70; dir. Cetacean Rels. Soc., Maui, Hawaii, 1976-98, Planetary Healing Pageants, Maui, 1976-98. Fellshp., Mental Health Rsch. Inst., Genetic Algorithms, under John Holland and dir. J.G. Miller, Living Systems; spkr., U Hawaii Matsunaga Peace Inst., 1st Global Peace Rsch. Conf., 1994, SHE PEACE: A World Peace Beadgame; Creating Future Friendly ECO-GEO-CEO's; mem., Proj. Jonah Grant, 1976, Deep Breathold diving Dolphin Entertainer; creator, Y2Kaper FOANA-TUNUP-HAS Flags of All Nations and The United Nations Underwater Parade Honoring All Species for the Global Millenuium Television network 2001, 24 hr. Broadcast. Author: Saving The Cosmos ('il Tuesday), 1995, Strange Fluke, 1990 (1st prize Maui Writers Conf. 1994). Address: PO Box 958 Paia HI 96779-0958

LOOMIS, JANICE KASZCZUK, artist; b. New Britain, Conn., June 26, 1952; d. William and Pauline Teresa (Archacki) Kaszczuk; m. Richard Wager Loomis, Oct. 1, 1977 (div. 2000); children: Richard Ward, Brian William. BA cum laude, U. Hartford, 1987. Vis. artist West Hartford Sch. Sys., 1990, 94, Glastonbury Sch. Sys., 1989; chair instrn. and scholarship com. West Hartford Art League, 1996—. Group exhbns. include Internat. Sculpture Ctr., Washington, 1987, Joseloff Gallery, Hartford, 1987, Gallery on the Green, Canton, 1990, Farmington (Conn.) Village Libr. Gallery, 1990, First Ch. Gallery, Springfield, Mass., 1991, Cast Iron Gallery Show, N.Y.C., 1993, Budapest, Hungary, 1994, Am. Medallic Sculpture Show, 1994-95, Am. Numismatic Assn. Medallic Show, 1994, U. Conn. Invitational Sculpture Show and Sale, 1994, Newark Mus. Medallic Show, 1995, Canon House Rotunda, Washington, 1996, Saltbox Gallery, West Hartford, 1996. Recipient award for sculpture Acad. Artists Assn., 1994, Honor award for sculpture Acad. Artists Nat. Juried Exhbn., 1996, Gilroy Roberts scholarship Am. Numismatic Assn., 1994, 96. Mem. Nat. Sculpture Soc. (assoc.), Conn. Women Artists (bd. dirs. 1997-99), Soc. Conn. Sculptors (founding pres. 1992-93, sec. 1994-95), Am. Medallic Sculpture Assn. (bd. dirs. 1994-97, sec. 1996-97), Canton Artist's Guild. Avocations: people, dogs. E-mail: jkloomis@ix.netcom.com.

LOOMIS, NORMA IRENE, marriage and family therapist; b. Dunlap, Ind., May 6, 1941; d. Edwin Clifford and Lucille DeVere (Hall) Dick; m. Edwin Dale Loomis; children: William Dale, James Vernon. BS in Edn., Western Mich. U., 1973, MA in Edn., 1976; PhD in Christian Counseling, Rocky Mountin Inc., 1990. Cert. marriage and family therapist. Tchr. Cassopolis (Mich.) Schs., 1973—; counseling Christian Counseling Svcs., Goshen, Ind., 1985—. Presenter Elkhart (Ind.) Pub. Schs., 1992—95, Middlebury (Ind.) Pub. Schs., 1992—94, Elkhart Ct., 1995—97; pres. Champion Reality Inc., Elkhart, 1983—; founder, pres. Soaring As Women of Value, 2001. Contbr. articles to profl. publs.; author tchg. materials Hot Shots Prodns. Mem. Cmty. Corrections Adv. Bd., Elkhart County, 1994—; pres. Juniper Beach Assn., Mears, Mich., 1985-96, Women in Action, Elkhart, 1985-94. Mem. ACA, Am. Mental Health Counselors Assn., Ind. Counselors Assn. for Alcohol and Drug Abuse, Am. Assn. Christian Counselors, Christian Assn. Psychol. Studies. Republican. Mem. Bretheran Ch. Avocations: swimming, boating, bowling, crafts. Home: 22650 Lake Shore Dr Elkhart IN 46514-9570 Office: Christian Counseling Svcs 333 E Madison St Goshen IN 46526-3429 E-mail: ml641@juno.com.

LOOMIS, NORMAN RICHARD, physician; b. Forest Hills, N.Y., Feb. 18, 1927; s. Leon Charles and Mabel Clare (Copley) L.; m. Laura Russell; children: Jane, Lynne, Richard. AB, Oberlin Coll., 1948; MD, State U. Coll. Medicine, Syracuse, N.Y., 1952. Diplomate Am. Bd. Family Practice. Pvt. practice, Ontario, N.Y., 1954-97; chief dept. family practice Rochester (N.Y.) Gen. Hosp., 1965-97; clin. assoc. prof. dept. family practice U. Rochester. Bd. dirs. Med. Liability Mutual Ins. Co.; cons. Monroe Plan for Med. Care, Rochester, 1994-97; med. adv. com. on Medicaid N.Y. State Dept. Health, Albany, 1997—; chmn. medicaid com. Med. Soc. of State of N.Y., 1996—. Founder, cons. Ontario (N.Y.) Vol. Ambulance. Named Citizen of Yr. Ontario, 1973. Mem. N.Y. State Acad. Family Practice (pres. 1976-77), Am. Acad. Family Practice (alt. del. 1983-93, chmn. drugs and devices com. 1992), Masons, Ontario C. of C., Ontario-Walworth Rotary. Republican. Presbyterian. Avocations: sailing, tennis, photography. Home and Office: 7736 Tamarack Ln Ontario NY 14519-9713

LOOMIS, ROBBIE, race car driver; Crew chief Petty Enterprises. Rondleman, NC, 1991—99, Hendrick Motorsports, Charlotte, 2000—. Office: Hendrick Motorsports 4400 Papa Joe Hendrick Blvd Charlotte NC 28262

LOOMIS, ROBERT ARTHUR, retired sales executive; b. Oelwein, Iowa, June 27, 1936; s. Irving McArthur and Elsie Pauline (Brickman) L.; m. Karen Lee McKiney, Dec. 27, 1958; children: Duane Robert, Debra Lee, David Craig, Douglas Irving. Grad. high sch., Arlington, Iowa, 1954. With Rath Packing Co., Waterloo, Iowa, 1954-62; salesman Firestone Tire & Rubber Co., 1961-64, plant mgr. Aberdeen, S.D., 1964-66, Wichita, Kans., 1966-70; asst. br. mgr. Myers Tire Supply, Kansas City, Mo., 1970-71; sales devel. mgr. Bandag, Inc., 1971-98; ret., 1998. Cubmaster Boy Scouts Am., Excelsior Springs, Mo., 1971-74; asst. scoutmaster 1974-78. With U.S. Army, 1955-57. Mem. Elks. Republican. Lutheran. Avocations: grandchildren, gardening, travel. Home and Office: PO Box 1111 Penitas TX 78576-1111

LOOMIS, ROBERT DUANE, publishing company executive, author; b. Conneaut, Ohio, Aug. 24, 1926; s. Kline C. and Louise C. (Chapman) L.; m. Gloria Colliani, Apr. 12, 1956 (div.); 1 dau., Diana Rachel; m. Hilary Paterson Mills, Sept. 18, 1983; 1 child, Robert Miles. BA, Duke U., 1950. Assoc. editor Rinehart & Co., N.Y.C., 1956-58; v.p., exec. editor Random House, Inc., 1958—. Author: Story of the U.S. Air Force, 1959, Great American Fighter Pilots, 1961, All About Aviation, 1964. Served with USAF, 1945. Recipient Roger Klein award for creative editing, 1977 Home: 68 W 11th St New York NY 10011-8673 Office: Random House Inc 299 Park Ave New York NY 10171

LOOMIS, SALORA DALE, psychiatrist; b. Peru, Ind., Oct. 21, 1930; s. S. Dale Sr. and Rhea Pearl (Davis) L.; m. Carol Marie Davis, Jan 3, 1959; children: Stephen Dale, Patricia Marie. AB in Zoology, Ind. U., 1953, MS in Human Anatomy, 1955, MD, 1958. Diplomate Am. Bd. Psychiatry and Neurology. Intern Cook County Hosp., Chgo., 1958-59; resident in psychiatry Logansport (Ind.) State Hosp., 1959-60, Ill. State Psychiat. Inst., Chgo., 1960-62; staff psychiatrist Katharine Wright Psychiat. Clinic, 1962-65, dir., 1965-92. Cons. Ill. Youth Commn. 1962-64; instr. psychiatry Northwestern U. Med. Sch., Chgo., 1962-64, assoc. 1964-67; asst. dir. Northwestern U. Psychiat. Clinics, Chgo., 1963-65; attending psychiatrist St. Joseph Hosp., Chgo., 1964—; lectr. psychiatry and neurology Loyola U. Med. Sch. Chgo., 1964-65, assoc. 1965, asst. prof. 1965-73, lect. 1980-89, clin. assoc. prof., 1989-2002, clin. prof., 2002—; psychiat. cons. Ill. Dept. Pub. Health, 1967—; sr. attending psychiatrist, chmn. dept. psychiatry Ill. Masonic Med. Ctr., Chgo. 1970-92, chmn. emeritus, 1992—; assoc. prof. psychiatry U. Ill. Coll. Medicine, Chgo., 1973—. Fellow Am. Coll. Psychiatrists, Am. Psychiat. Assn. (life), Acad. Psychosomatic Medicine; mem. AMA, Ill. State Med. Soc. (chmn. council on mental health and addiction 1974-75, chmn. joint peer rev. com. 1975-76), Ill. Psychiat. Soc. (chmn. ethics com. 1974-75, chmn. peer rev. com. 1976-78), Chgo. Med. Socs. Fax: 630-845-9145.

LOONEY, CLAUDIA ARLENE, health facility administrator; b. Fullerton, Calif., June 13, 1946; d. Donald F. and Mildred B. Schneider; m. James K. Looney, Oct. 8, 1967; 1 child, Christopher K. BA, Calif. State U., 1969. Dir. youth YWCA No. Orange County, Fullerton, Calif., 1967-70; dir. dist. Camp Fire Girls, San Francisco, 1971-73, asst. exec. dir. L.A., 1973-77; asst. dir. cmty. resources Childrens Hosp., 1977-80; dir. cmty. devel. Orthopaedic Hosp., 1980-82; sr. v.p. Saddleback Meml. Found./Saddleback Meml. Med. Ctr., Laguna Hills, Calif., 1982-92; v.p. planning and advancement Calif. Inst. Arts, Santa Clarita, 1992-96; pres. Northwestern Meml. Found., Chgo., 1996-99; sr. v.p. Childrens Hosp., L.A., 1999—. Instr. U. Calif., Irvine, Univ. Irvine; mem. steering com. U. Irvine. Steering com. United Way, L.A., 1984-86. Fellow Assn. Healthcare Philanthropy (nat. chair-elect, chmn. program Nat. Edn. Conf. 1986, regional dir. 1985-89, 98, fin. com. 1988—, pres., com. chn. 1987—, Give To Life com. chmn. 1987-91, mid-west regional conf. chmn. 1998, Orange County Fund Raiser of Yr. 1992, L.A. County fund raiser of yr. 1996); mem. Nat. Soc. Fund Raising Execs. Found. (cert., vice chmn. 1985-90, chair 1993—, mem. Chgo. conf. com. 1997, 98), So. Calif. Assn. Hosp. Devel. (past pres., bd. dirs.), Profl. Ptnrs. (chmn. 1986, instr. 1988—), Philanthropic Ednl. Orgn. (past pres.). Avocations: swimming, sailing, photography. Office: Children's Hosp LA 4650 Sunset Blvd Ste 29 Los Angeles CA 90027

LOONEY, GERALD LEE, medical educator, administrator; b. Bradshaw, W.Va., Nov. 22, 1937; s. Noah Webster and Anna Belle (Burris) L.; m. Linda Louise Pluebell, Oct. 19, 1962 (div. Apr. 1975); children: Deborah Lynn, Catherine Ann, Karen Marie, Kelli Rachelle. AB, Johns Hopkins U., 1959, MD, 1963; MPH, Harvard U., 1968. Diplomate Am. Bd. Preventive Medicine, Am. Bd. Pediatrics. Resident pediatrics Tufts-New Eng. Med. Ctr., Boston, 1965-67; physician-in-chief Kennedy Meml. Hosp., 1969-71; asst. prof. family and cmty. medicine U. Ariz. Coll. Medicine, Tucson, 1971-72; asst. prof. emergency medicine U. So. Calif. Sch. Medicine, L.A., 1972-77; assoc. clin. prof. medicine U. Calif., Irvine, 1991—; emergency dept. dir. Glendale (Calif.) Adventist Med. Ctr., 1978-84, Orthopaedic Hosp., L.A., 1985-88; urgent care dir. Bay Shore Med. Group, Torrance, Calif., 1988-93; med. dir. Surecare and LAX Clinics Centinela Hosp., Inglewood, 1993-95; dir. med. svc. Boeing Co. Mil. Aircraft, Long Beach, 1996—. Bd. dirs. Beach Cities Health Dist., Redondo Beach, Calif., 1992-93. Avocation: history. Home: 8801 Bayside Circle Las Vegas NV 89117

LOONEY, ROBERT DUDLEY, lawyer; b. Tishomingo, Okla., Mar. 25, 1919; s. M.A. and Helen (Dudley) L.; m. Caroline Ambrister, Dec. 19, 1941; children: Caroline H. Hill, Robert D., John A. BA, Okla. U., 1941, LLB, 1943. Bar: Okla. 1942, U.S. dist. ct. Okla., 19, U.S. ct. apls. (10th Cir.) Okla., 1946. Sr. ptnr. Looney Nichols et al, Oklahoma City, 1942—; prof. law Oklahoma City U. Sch. Law, 1971-73; lectr. U. Okla. Sch. Law. Mem. exec. bd. Wesleyan Youth Inc., 1958-97. Served with USCGR, 1942-45. Fellow Am. Coll. Trial Lawyers, Internat. Coll. Trial Lawyers, Internat. Acad. Trial Lawyers; mem. Oklahoma County Bar Assn. (dir.), ABA, Okla. Bar Assn., Oklahoma City Rotary (pres. 1961-62, dist. gov. internat. 1964-65), Masons. Presbyterian. Home: 2617 NW 58th St Oklahoma City OK 73112-7103 Office: 528 NW 12th St Oklahoma City OK 73103-2407

LOONEY, WILLIAM FRANCIS, JR. lawyer; b. Boston, Sept. 20, 1931; s. William Francis Sr. and Ursula Mary (Ryan) L.; m. Constance Mary O'Callaghan, Dec. 28, 1957; children: Willam F. III, Thomas M., Karen D., Martha A. AB, JD, Harvard U. Bar: Mass. 1958, D.C. 1972, U.S. Supreme Ct. 1972, U.S. Dist. Ct. (ea. dist.) Mich. 1986. Law clk. to presiding justice Mass. Supreme Jud. Ct., 1958-59; assoc. Goodwin, Procter & Hoar, Boston, 1959-62; chief civil divsn. U.S. Attys. Office, 1964-65; ptnr. Looney & Grossman, Boston, 1965-94, sr. counsel, 1995—. Asst. U.S. atty. Dist. Mass., 1962-65; spl. hearing officer U.S. Dept. Justice, 1965-68; mem. Mass. Bd. Bar Overseers, 1985-91, vice-chmn., 1990-91; corp. mem. Greater Boston Legal Svcs., Inc., 1994—. Mem. Zoning Bd. of Appeals, Dedham, Mass., 1971-74; bd. dirs. Boston Latin Sch. Found., 1981-85, pres. 1981-84, chmn. bd. dirs., 1984-86; trustee Social Law Libr., 1994-97; chmn. ADR adv. com. U.S. Dist. Ct., 1998—. Fellow Am. Coll. Trial Lawyers (state com. 1996-2001); mem. Mass. Bar Assn. (co-chmn. standing com. lawyers responsibility for pub. svc. 1987-88, chmn. fed. ct. adv. com. Alternative Dispute Resolution 1998—), Boston Bar Assn. (pres. 1984-85, coun. mem. 1985-90, chmn. sr. lawyers sect. 1992-94, Maguire award for professionalism 1995), Nat. Assn. Bar Pres.'s, Boston Latin Sch. Assn. (pres. 1980-82, life trustee 1982—, Man of Yr. 1985), USCG Found. (bd. dirs. 1987-2000, dir. emeritus 2000—), Norfolk Golf Club, Harvard Club, Harvard U. Alumni Assn. (bd. dirs. 2001—). Democrat. Roman Catholic. Home: 43 Coronation Dr Dedham MA 02026-6230 Office: 101 Arch St Fl 9 Boston MA 02110-1112 E-mail: wlooney@lgllp.com., h.wlooney@socialaw.com.

LOOP, FLOYD D. health, medical executive; b. Lafayette, Ind., Dec. 17, 1936; s. Floyd Addison and Marie D. L.; m. Bernadine P. Healy, Aug. 17, 1985; children: Alison, Frederick, Kendall, Bartlett, Marie. BS, Purdue U., 1958; MD, George Washington U., 1962. Diplomate: Am. Bd. Surgery, Am. Bd. Thoracic Surgery. Intern, resident in gen. surgery George Washington U., 1962-64, chief resident, 1967-68; fellow in cardiac surgery Cleve. Clinic Found., 1967-70, staff surgeon thoracic and cardiovascular surgery, 1971-75, chmn. dept. thoracic and cardiovascular surgery, 1975-89, chmn. bd. govs., CEO, 1990—; bd. dirs. Tenet Healthcare, Santa Barbara, 1999—. Trustee Healthcare Leadership Coun. Mem. Editorial bd. Jour. Thoracic and Cardiovascular Surgery, 1979-85, Am. Jour. Cardiology, 1978-83, Am. Heart Jour, 1980— , Clin. Cardiology, 1979— , Jour. Cardiac Surgery, 1986— , Jour. Cardiothoracic Anesthesia, 1986— , Cleve. Clinic Jour. Medicine, Perfusion. With M.C. USAF, 1964-66. Decorated Brazilian Order of Merit Fellow ACS (adv. council for cardiothoracic surgery 1986—), Am. Coll. Cardiology (Theodore and Susan B. Cummings Humanitarian award 1975); mem. Am. Assn. Thoracic Surgery (treas. 1984—, mem. council 1984—), Am. Surg. Assn., Soc. Thoracic Surgeons, Am. Coll. Chest Physicians (bd. regents 1986—), Thoracic Surgery Dirs. Assn., Am. Heart Assn. (exec. com. of council on cardiovascular surgery 1985—, Paul Dudley White citation for internat. service 1980), Am. Soc. Artificial Internal Organs Soc. Vascular Surgery. Office: Cleve Clinic Found 1 Clinic Ctr 9500 Euclid Ave Cleveland OH 44195-0001*

LOORY, STUART HUGH, journalist; b. Wilson, Pa., May 22, 1932; s. Harry and Eva (Holland) L.; m. Marjorie Helene Dretel, June 19, 1955 (div. July 1995); children: Joshua Alan, Adam Edward, Miriam Beth; m. Nina Nikolaevna Kudriavtseva, Aug. 17, 1995. BA, Cornell U., 1954; MS with honors, Columbia U., 1958; postgrad., U. Vienna, Austria, 1958. Reporter Newark News, 1955-58, N.Y. Herald Tribune, 1959-61, sci. writer, 1961-63, Washington corr., 1963-64, fgn. corr., 1964-66; sci. editor Metromedia Radio Stas., 1962-64, Moscow corr., 1964-66; sci. writer N.Y. Times, 1966; White House corr. Los Angeles Times, 1967-71; fellow Woodrow Wilson Internat. Center for Scholars, Washington, 1971-72; exec. editor WNBC-TV News, 1973; Kiplinger prof. pub. affairs reporting Ohio State U., Columbus, 1973-75; assoc. editor Chgo. Sun-Times, 1975-76, mng. editor, 1976-80; v.p., mng. editor Washington bur. Cable News Network, 1980-82, Moscow bur. chief, 1983-86, sr. correspondent, 1986, exec. producer, 1987-90; exec. dir. internat. rels. Turner Broadcasting System, Inc., Atlanta, 1988—; editor-in-chief CNN World Report, 1990-91; v.p. CNN, 1990-95; exec. v.p. Turner Internat. Broadcasting, Russia, 1993-97; v.p., supervising prodr. Turner Original Prodns., 1995. Lee Hills chair of free press studies U. Mo., Columbia, 1997—; lectr. in field. Author: (with David Kraslow) The Secret Search for Peace in Vietnam, 1968, Defeated: Inside America's Military Machine, 1973, (with Ann Imse) Seven Days That Shook the World: The Collapse of Soviet Communism, 1991; Editor IPI Report (Internat. Press Inst.), 1998—, IPI Global Journalist, 1999—; contbr. articles mags. and encys. Recipient citation Overseas Press Club, 1966; Raymond Clapper award Congl. Press Gallery, 1968; George Polk award L.I.U., 1968; Du Mont award U. Calif. at, Los

Angeles, 1968; Distinguished Alumni award Columbia, 1969; 50th Anniversary medal Columbia Sch. Journalism, 1963; Edwin Hood award for diplomatic corr. Nat. Press Club, 1987; Pulitzer traveling scholar, 1958. Jewish. Office: U Mo Sch Journalism 132A Neff Annex Columbia MO 65211-1200 E-mail: loorys@missouri.edu.

LOOS, JOHN THOMPSON, business owner; b. West Palm Beach, Fla. s. John T. and Margaret (Browning) L.; children: Amy, John, Melissa. BSBA, U. Fla., 1970. Co-founder, v.p., bd. dirs. Am. Mktg. and Mgmt., Inc., Ft. Lauderdale, Fla., 1970-78; pvt. practice real estate investor, 1978—. Bd. dirs. DiMar Industries, Davie, Fla.; pres. 1st Lauderdale Investments-Di-Mar Properties. Active Ft. Lauderdale Riverwalk Com., 1987-91, Jud. Nominating Commn., Broward County, Fla., 1988-92; bd. dirs. Broward County YMCA, 1982—, past pres.; bd. dirs., vice-chmn., chmn. North Broward Hosp. Dist., 1989-93; bd. dirs., vice-chmn. Downtown Devel. Authority, Ft. Lauderdale, 1990, 93, 96, chmn., 1990-94, active, 1988-2000, 2001—; chmn. Cmty. Svcs. Bd., Ft. Lauderdale, 1986-90; bd. dirs. North Lauderdale-Progreso Devel. Dist., 1990-91, Broward County Planning Coun., 1993-95, Broward County Charter Rev. Com., 1994-96, Broward County Partnership for the Homeless, 1997-98; bd. dirs. Downtown Coun. Named Downtowner of Yr., Ft. Lauderdale, 1997, Person of Yr., Ft. Lauderdale Riverwalk, 2002. Mem. Ft. Lauderdale C. of C. (bd. govs. 2001). Republican. Home: PO Box 399 Fort Lauderdale FL 33302-0399

LOOS, RANDOLPH MEADE, financial planner; b. Warren, Ohio, May 22, 1954; s. Donald Ambert and Kathleen Jean (Woods) L.; m. Jolene Lora Turkoc, Aug. 3, 1985. BSBA, U. Fla., 1977. CFP. Rsch. cons. Fla. State U., Tallahassee, 1977-78; exec. sec. Chi Phi Fraternity, Atlanta, 1978-79, nat. dir., 1979-80; systems rep. Burroughs Corp., Chgo., 1980-81, sr. systems rep., 1981-82; account exec. Prudential-Bache Securities, Charlotte, N.C., 1982-84; investment broker A. G. Edwards & Sons, Clearwater, Fla., 1984—, sr. investment broker, 1991-92, v.p. investments, 1992-2000, sr. v.p. investments, 2001—, trust specialist, 1995—. Musical dir. Toast of Tampa Show Chorus, 1986-97, internat. champions 1994. Mem. Inst. CFP. Republican. Avocations: golf, barbershop harmony, wine collecting. Office: A G Edwards & Sons Inc 28100 Us Highway 19 N Ste 500 Clearwater FL 33761-2686

LOOSBROCK, CAROL MARIE, information management professional; b. Dubuque, Iowa, Aug. 21, 1936; d. Julius Carl and Elizabeth Cecilia (Kurz) L. BA, Clarke Coll., 1958; postgrad., Art Inst. Chgo., 1959-63; MS, Am. U., 1979. With Dept. Def., Washington, 1968—, specialist, 1979—. Mem. AAAS, Assn. Computing Machinery (Washington D.C. symposium steering coms. 1980-81, exec. coun. 1981-84); N.Y. Acad. Scis. (life), Am. Mgmt. Assn., Am. Security Coun. Found. (U.S. congl. adv. bd. 1984—, coalition for peace through strength leadership award, coalition for Desert Storm, coalition for internat. security), Am. Mus. Natural History. Republican. Home: 4514 Connecticut Ave NW Washington DC 20008-4327 Office: The Pentagon Washington DC 20310-0001

LOOSE, JOHN W. sales company executive; BA, Earlham Coll.; diploma, Harvard Bus. Sch. Various sales, mktg. mgmt. positions Corning Inc., 1964-85, v.p., gen. mgr. Asia Pacific, 1985-88, v.p. internat., 1988-90, exec. v.p., Info. Display Group, 1990-93, pres., CEO, 1993-96, co-COO, sector pres., 1996—. Office: Corning Inc 1 Riverfront Plz Corning NY 14831-0002*

LOOSE, MARY ELLEN, musician; b. Santa Monica, Calif., May 23, 1954; d. Robert John and Beverly Elvina (Baker) Reese; m. Timothy Neil Loose, Feb. 9, 1980; children: Leslie Alane, Laura Christine, Steven Timothy, Samuel Thomas. Student, Brigham Young U., 1972, Coll. of the Canyons, 1973, Valley Coll., 1975. Music copyist Embryo Music Co., Studio City, Calif., 1978; profl. accompanist so. Calif., 1978—; ptnr. Reese-Loose Music Co., North Hollywood, Calif., 1982—; composer, arranger so. Calif., 1982—; composer, arranger, profl. accompanist Mesa, Ariz., 1987—. Pianist Bob Hope USO Club, Hollywood, Calif., 1979, Embryo Music Co., Studio City, Calif., 1975-76; mus. arranger Grand Land Singers, Cerritos, Calif., 1974-79, Maryann Mendenhall Women's Chorale, Granada Hills, Calif., 1981—. Composer vocal duets, piano solos; mus. arranger (record) Sweet Hour of Prayer, 1984; performer recording of own compositions Peaceful Morning, 1989. Mem. ASCAP, Tempe-Mesa Music Tchrs. Assn., Associated Latter-day Media Artists, Ariz. Mormon Songwriters Assn. Republican. Mem. Lds Ch. Avocations: sewing, aerobics, weight-lifting, embroidery, teaching children. Home: 1026 E Garnet Ave Mesa AZ 85204-5811

LOOSE, STEPHANIE JOY, accountant; b. Jamestown, N.D., July 7, 1957; d. Lawrence Walter and Ardelle Delores (Ziesch) L.; 1 child, Peter Loose-Montano. AA in Gen. Edn., Hartnell Coll., 1982; BS in Acctg., Golden Gate U., 1995. CPA, Calif. Sec. to Hayashi & Wayland, CPAs, Salinas, Calif., 1977-79; from sec. to CPA Ingraham & Loose, CPA's, 1979-93, ptnr., 1993—. Vol. cmty. mem. Salinas Union H.S., 1996. Vol. Dorothy's Kitchen, Steinbeck Festival, Calif. Internat. Airshow; mem. Leadership Salinas—, Planned Parenthood; treas. Save our Svcs.-Save Our Salinas; bd. dirs. Oldtown Salinas Assn. Mem. LWV Salinas Valley (voter svc. com. 1992-95, 98-99, 2001, v.p. 1994-95, in-charge of election for Clinica Del Salad Del Valle De Salinas 1995, pres. 2002), ACLU Monterey County (bd. dirs. 1992-95). Avocations: gardening, reading, dancing, dining. Office: Ingraham & Loose CPAs 412 S Main St Salinas CA 93901

LOOSEN, PETER THOMAS, medical educator; b. Freiburg, Germany, Mar. 19, 1944; s. Otto and Maria L.; children; Max. Alex. MD, U. Munich, Germany, 1970. Assoc. prof. psychiatry U. N.C., Chapel Hill, 1979-83; prof. psychiatry Duke U., Durham, N.C., 1983-86; prof. psychiatry & medicine Vanderbilt U., Nashville, 1986—. Sr. fellow John F. Kennedy Ctr. Rsch. Human Devel., Peabody Coll., Nashville, 1996—. Fellow Collegium Internat. Neuro-Psychopharm.; mem. AAAS, Am. Psychiat. Assn., Soc. Biol. Psychiatry, N.Y. Acad. Scis., Am. Coll. Neuropsychopharmacology, Am. Coll. Psychiatrists, Endocrine Soc., Internat. Soc. Psychoneuroendocrinology, Endocrine Soc., Am. Psychosomatic Soc., Soc. Neuroscis, Deutsche Gesellschaft Psychiatrie und Nervenheilkunde. Home: 156 Valley Forge Dr Nashville TN 37205 Office: VA Med Ctr (116A) 1310 24th Ave S Nashville TN 37212-2367 Fax: 615-385-1455. E-mail: ptloosen@aol.com.

LOOSER, DEVONEY KAY, English language educator; b. St. Paul, Apr. 11, 1967; d. LeRoy Joseph and Sharon LeAnn (Sarslow) L.; m. George Lewis Justice, 1996. BA, Augsburg Coll., 1989; PhD, SUNY, Stony Brook, 1993. Instr. English SUNY, Stony Brook, 1989-93; asst. prof. English Ind. State U., Terre Haute, 1993-98, acting dir. women's studies, 1997-98; asst. prof. women's studies U. Wis., Whitewater, 1998-2000; vis. asst. prof. English Ariz. State U., 2000-2001; asst. prof. English La. State U., 2001—02, U. Mo., Columbia, 2002—. Author: British Women Writers and the Writing of History, 1670-1820, 2000 (Choice Outstanding Acad. Title award 2001); editor: Jane Austen and Discourses of Feminism, 1995; co-editor: (with E. Ann Kaplan) Generations: Academic Feminists in Dialogue, 1997; contbr. articles to profl. jours. NEH fellow, 1994. Mem. MLA, Am. Soc. Eighteenth Century Studies, Jane Austen Soc. N.Am. (bd. dirs. 2000—), Nat. Women's Studies Assn., N.Am. Soc. Study of Romanticism. Office: U Mo Columbia Dept English Columbia MO 65211 E-mail: looserd@missouri.edu.

LOOSER, DONALD WILLIAM, academic administrator; b. Lufkin, Tex., June 14, 1939; s. William E. and Mildred H. (Wageneck) L.; m. Elsa Jean Albritton, Aug. 20, 1966; 1 child, William Gregory. B in Music Edn., B in Music Edn., MusB, Baylor U., 1962; MusM, Northwestern U., 1963; PhD, Fla. State U., 1972. Instr. Miss. Coll., Clinton, 1963-64; asst. prof. Houston Bapt. U., 1964-68, asst. to pres., 1968-72, dean gen. edn., 1972-77, v.p. adminstrv. affairs, 1977-83, v.p. acad. affairs, 1983—. Pres. Conf. Deans Faculties and Acad. V.P.s, 1985-86; participant Harvard U. Inst. Edn. Mgmt., 1985; mem. adv. bd. Tex. Edn. Agy., Austin; mem. innovation in undergrad. edn. panel So. Regional Edn. Bd., Atlanta; pres. Nat. Conf. Acad. Deans, 1990-91. Mem. editorial adv. bd. Audio-Visual Inst. Mag.; contbr. articles to profl. jours.; rec. artist A Jubilant Song, 1983. Mem. adv. bd. Houston Symphony Orch., Houston Grand Opera, S.W. Consortium on Internat. Study, Dallas; staff Tallowood Bapt. Ch., 1965-88; pianist Second Bapt. Ch., Houston, 1988-98. Mem. Am. Assn. Higher Edn., Houston Philos. Soc., Rotary, Phi Delta Kappa, Omicron Delta Kappa, Pi Kappa Lambda, Kappa Delta Pi. E-mail: dlooser@hbu.edu.

LOOTS, JAMES MASON, lawyer; b. Iowa City, May 24, 1958; s. Robert James and Mary (Ladd) L.; m. Ann Marie Stockmeyer; children: Mason S., Karl R. BSJ, Northwestern U., Evanston, Ill., 1980; JD cum laude, Mich. Law Sch., 1984. Bar: D.C. 1984, U.S. Dist. Ct. D.C. 1985, U.S. Dist. Ct. Md., 1992, U.S. Ct. Appeals (D.C. cir.) 1985, U.S. Tax Ct. 1990, U.S. Ct. Fed. Claims 1998, U.S. Ct. Appeals (4th cir.) 2000. Assoc. Skadden, Arps, Slate, Meagher & Flom, Washington, 1984-89, Jones, Day, Reavis & Pogue, Washington, 1989-92; ptnr. Barrymore & Loots, 1992-95, Perry, Simmons & Loots, Washington, 1995-99, Goldstein & Loots, Washington, 1999—2002, Ford & Harrison LLP, Washington, 2002—. Treas. Worldly Goods, Inc., Washington, 1988-94; adj. prof. Am. U. Wash. Coll. Law, 1990-96. Editorial Bd. Mich. Law Rev., 1982-84. Vol. VISTA, Baton Rouge, 1980-81; v.p. Bedford Springs (Pa.) Festival, 1987-89; adv. bd. Washington Legal Counsel for the Elderly, 1988-97; mem. D.C. Small Bus. Adv. Bd., 1990-99; chmn. D.C. Commn. Human Rights, 1991-2001; bd. dirs. Capitol Hill Assn. Merchants & Profls., 1994-97. Mem. D.C. Bar Assn. (Pro Bono Lawyer of Year, 1988), Washington Coun. Lawyers. Office: Ford & Harrison LLP 1300 19th St NW # 700 Washington DC 20036 Mailing: PO Box 76852 Washington DC 20013 E-mail: jloots@fordharrison.com.

LOPACH, JAMES JOSEPH, political science educator; b. Great Falls, Mont., June 23, 1942; s. John Ernest and Alma Marie (Schapman) L.; divorced, Dec. 10, 1991; children: Christine, Paul. AB in Philosophy, Carroll Coll., 1964; MA in Am. Studies, U. Notre Dame, 1967, MAT in English Edn., 1968, PhD in Govt., 1973. Mgr. Pacific Telephone, Palo Alto, Calif., 1968-69; adminstr. City of South Bend, Ind., 1971-73; prof. U. Mont., Missoula, 1973—, chmn. dept. polit. sci., 1977-87, assoc. dean Coll. Arts and Scis., 1987-88, acting dir. Mansfield Ctr., 1984-85, spl. asst. to the univ. pres., 1988-92, assoc. provost, 1992-95, spl. asst. to provost, 1995-96. Cons. local govts., state agys., tribal govts., law firms, 1973—; expert witness. Author, editor: We the People of Montana, 1983, Tribal Government Today, 1990, 98, Planning Small Town America, 1990; contbr. articles to profl. jours. Roman Catholic. Office: U Mont Dept Polit Sci Missoula MT 59812-0001 Business E-Mail: lopach@selway.umt.edu.

LOPACKI, EDWARD JOSEPH, JR. lawyer; b. Bklyn., June 4, 1947; s. Edward Joseph and Lillian Jane (Wallace) L.; m. Crystal May Miller, June 21, 1969; children: Edward Joseph III, Elizabeth Jane. BA in sociology, Villanova U., 1971; JD, Vt. Law Sch., 1980. Bar: Fla. 1981, U.S. Dist. Ct. (mid. dist.) Fla. 1983, U.S. Ct. Appeals (11th cir.) 1986. Mgmt. trainee Bankers Trust Co., N.Y.C., 1968-72; counselor N.J. State Employment Svcs., Red Bank, 1972-77; pvt. practice Bradenton, Fla., 1981—. Adj. prof. of law Nova U., Ft. Lauderdale, Fla., 1981, Manatee C.C., Bradenton, Fla., 1994-96; cons. Suncoast Ctr. for Ind. Living, 1999-2001. Mem. Fla. Ind. Living Coun., 1996-2000, dist. VI adv. coun. Fla. Dept. Health and Rehabilitative Svcs., 1988-92, Manatee County Health Care Adv. Bd., 1993—, Manatee County Coun. on Access for the Disabled, 1994—, Suncoast Ctr. for Ind. Living, 1995-99; pres. Cen. Soccer Assn., 1981-82; mem. De Soto Boys Club, 1982-87, sec., 1986-87; chmn. edn. com. Manatee Area c. of C., 1983; mem. Manatee Area Youth Soccer Assn., 1981-82, Manatee Coun. on Aging, 1986-87, Boys' Club Manatee County, 1986-87; bd. dirs. Manatee County G.T. Bray Little League East, 1988-89. Mem. Nat. Orgn. Social Security Claimants Reps., Manatee County Bar Assn. (bd. dirs. 1988-89), KC (advocate 1984-85, 88-91), Lions (pres. Manatee River 1985-86, treas. 1987-88, 90-91, sec. 1988-89, Lion of Yr. award 1988, 94). Democrat. Roman Catholic. Avocations: reading, advocacy for civil rights of people with disabilities. Home: 6612 27th Avenue Dr W Bradenton FL 34209-7405 Office: 5515 21st Ave W Ste C Bradenton FL 34207-3901 E-mail: LopackiLaw@aol.com.

LOPACZYNSKI, WLODZIMIERZ, endocrinologist; b. Olsztyn, Poland, Mar. 14, 1955; came to U.S. 1988; s. Stanislaw and Daniela (Czarnecka) L.; m. Joanna Renata Olesinska, July 31, 1982; children: Justyn, Martyna, Adrienne. MD, Med. Sch. Bialystok, Poland, 1980; PhD, 1985. Resident Univ. Hosp., Bialystok, Poland, 1980-81; asst. dept. chemistry Med. Sch. Bialystok, 1980-83, sr. asst., 1983-84, sr. asst. endocrinology dept., 1984-88, asst. prof. endocrinology, 1988—; scientist endocrine sect. Metabolism Br., NCI-NIH, Bethesda, Md., 1988—; scientist U. N.C. Chapel Hill. Author textbook in Polish: Introduction to Clinical Immunopathology, 1984; contbr. articles to profl. jours. Internat. Soc. Endocrinology travel grantee, Kyoto, 1988. Mem. Am. Endocrinology Soc., Polish Biochem. Soc., Polish Endocrinology Soc. Roman Catholic. Achievements include development in characterization of eucaryotic ribosomes, in modification of ELISA test for diagnosis of autoimmunologic diseases; research in experiments using cyclic nucleotide independent kinase and peptide hormones, new methodological aspects for determination of interactions and phosphorylation of IGFI receptor. Home: 8024 Inverness Ridge Rd Potomac MD 20854-4011 Office: Dept Nutrition U NC Chapel Hill Cb Hl # 7400 Chapel Hill NC 27599-0001

LOPATA, MARTIN BARRY, business executive; b. Bronx, N.Y., Apr. 6, 1939; s. Julius A. and Rose (Silverman) L.; m. Sarah G. Lopata, July 4, 1965 (div. 1978; children: Warren A., Lawrence M.; m. Lynette Wyrick, May 6, 1989 (div. 1991). Grad., H.S. Art and Design, N.Y.C.; student, N.Y.C. C.C., Bklyn. Ordained minister Ch. of Divine Sci., 1983; cert. realty investment assoc. Sales mgr. H. Natoway Co., L.A., 1961-62; contract mgr. A.S. Aloe Co., 1962-64; merchandise mgr. S.E. Rykoff Co., 1964-70; v.p. Kirby Sales, 1970-71; pres. MBL Industries Inc., Santa Ana, Calif., 1971-87, Unicorn Seminars Inc., Huntington Beach, 1987-88, Unicorn Investments Internat., Huntington Beach, 1988-91; chair Yes Ednl. Sys., Reno, 1995-97; v.p. gen. mgr. Dayva Internat. Inc., Huntington Beach, Calif., 1999—; v.p. Dayva Internat. Inc., 2000—; bus. cons. Maintex Inc., Industry, Calif., 1999-2000; v.p. Dayva Internat. Inc., 2000-01; v.p., realtor Orange Coast Properties, 2001—. Chmn. Soviet Am. Internat. Co., 1988-92; joint venture Sovaminco Soviet Am. Internat. Co. #104, Moscow; pres. Coastal-West Industries, 1991-92. Patron Am. Mus. Nat. History, N.Y.C., 1984-91; bus. chmn. Ctr. for Soviet-Am. Dialogue, Washington, 1987-91; chmn. Com. on Bus.-A New Way of Thinking in a New Age, Moscow, 1987; bd. dirs. Three Mountain Found., Lone Pine, Calif., 1987-88, Inside Edge, Irvine, Calif., 1987-94, found. pres., 1993-94; vice chmn. United Ch. Religious Science, Los Angeles, 1986-87, pres. Huntington Beach Ch. Religious Sci., 1985; min. Cmty. Ch. by the Bay, 1983—; chmn. Blissful Wisdom Found., 1996—. Avocation: boating. Home: 3103-A Mace Ave Costa Mesa CA 92626-2529

LOPATA, VASILI IVANOVICH, artist; b. Nova Basan, Ukraine, Apr. 28, 1941; s. Ivan Mykolayovich and Hanna Antonivna Lopata; m. Regina V. Lopata, Sept. 23, 1969; 1 child, Olga V. Lopata. MA, Acad. of Arts, Kyiv, Ukraine, 1970; PhD, USSR Acad. of Arts, Moscow, 1972. Cons. Radyansky Pismennik, Kyiv, 1967, Radyanska Shcola, Kyiv, 1968-89, Dnipro, Kyiv, 1970-88, Veselka, Kyiv, 1970-93, Tavria, Simpheropol, Ukraine, 1972, Melbourne, Australia, 1974, Molodaya Gvardiya, Moscow, 1976, Voronezh, Russia, 1980; author design of Ukrainian currency Govt. of Ukraine, 1991-92. Illustrator, designer Pobratimy, 1972 (2d prize 1972), Poltava, 1980 (2d prize 1980), Ballady, 1982 (2d prize 1982), Topolya, 1984 (1st prize 1984), Slovo o Polku Igorevim, 1986, 1989 (1st prize 1986), History of Ukraine, 1993 (1st prize 1993), The Lord is the Strength of His People, 1996; over 600 woodcuts, linocuts and etchings; artist portrait John Paul II, 1993 (Privet Gift from his holyness 1993); painter numerous oils, pastels, watercolors; author: Somewhere Within My Heart, Hope and Disappointment; contbr. articles to profl. jours.; work collected in numerous museums. With Soviet Army, 1961-64. Named honored citizen, City Hall of Winnipeg, Can., 1990, City Hall of Brundon, Can., 1990, honored artist of Ukraine, 1979, Order of Honor, Govt. of Ukraine, 1988, nat. artist, 2001; recipient First Pl. Book-Plate Competition, London, 1989, Shevchenko prize laureate, Govt. of Ukraine, 1992, First prize, Prominvestbank, 1998. Mem. Union of Artists of Ukraine. Avocations: collector old and new prints and books. Home: 1800 22nd Ave Apt 103 San Francisco CA 94122-4449 E-mail: vilopata@yahoo.com.

LOPATIN, ALAN G. lawyer; b. New Haven, May 25, 1956; s. Paul and Ruth (Rosen) L.; m. Debra Jo Engler, May 17, 1981; children: Jonah Adam, Asa Louis. BA, Yale U., 1978; JD, Am. U., 1981. Bar: D.C. 1981, U.S. Supreme Ct. 1985. Law clk. FMC, Washington, 1980-81; counsel com. on post office and civil svc. U.S. Ho. of Reps., 1981-82, counsel com. on budget, 1982-86, dep. chief counsel, 1986-87, counsel temp. joint com. on deficit reduction, 1986, dep. gen. counsel com. on post office and civil svc., 1987-90, gen. counsel com. on edn. and labor, 1991-94; pres. Ledge Counsel, Inc., 1995—; exec. dir. Nat. and Cmty. Svc. Coalition, 1995-99; ptnr. Valente Lopatin & Schulze, Washington, 1998—. Mem. presdl. task force Cable Reform, Washington, 1993. Mem. ABA, D.C. Bar Assn., Nat. Assn. Thrift Savs. Plan Participants (pres. 1999—), Nat. Dem. Club, Yale Club (Washington). Democratic. Jewish. Home: 4958 Butterworth Pl NW Washington DC 20016-4354 Office: Valente Lopatin & Schulze 600 14th St NW Fl 5 Washington DC 20005 E-mail: ledgecnsl@aol.com.

LOPATIN, SERGEY DMITRIEVICH, microelectronic scientist, electrochemist; b. Belarus, USSR, July 11, 1964; came to U.S., 1996; s. Dmitri and Mariya Lopatin; m. Marina Polyanskaya, Dec. 21, 1997; children: Valentin, Dima, Kim. MS, Radioengring. Inst., Minsk, USSR, 1988; PhD, U. Comp. Sci./Radioelectronics, Minsk, Belarus, 1994. Engr. Integral Semiconductor Inc., Minsk, Belarus, 1988-92; scientist Acad. Scis., 1992-94; sr. scientist U. Computer Sci. and Radioelectronics, 1994-96; vis. scientist Cornell U., Ithaca, N.Y., 1996-97; mem. tech. staff, sr. engr. Advanced Micro Devices, Sunnyvale, Calif., 1997—. Instr., lectr Berkeley U., Burlingame, Calif., 1998; lectr. in field; mentor of SRC projects. Contbr. numerous articles to profl. jours. Grantee SEMATECH, 1996-97, DARPA, 1997; recipient Best Paper award IITC and Stanford U., 2000. Mem. IEE, Am. Chem. Soc., Materials Rsch. Soc., Electrochem. Soc. Achievements include patents in field. Avocations: travel, fine arts, family activities, sports. Home: 1000 Kiely Blvd Apt 66 Santa Clara CA 95051-4842 Office: Advanced Micro Devices 1 Amd Pl # Ms160 Sunnyvale CA 94085-3905 E-mail: sergy.lopatin@amd.com.

LOPATKA, SUSANA BEAIRD, women's health nurse, consultant; b. White Plains, N.Y., May 1, 1937; d. Paul J. and Dorothy V.L. (Jewell) Grueninger; m. John Rudolph Lopatka, Sept. 6, 1975. AB in Polit. Sci., Duke U., 1959; BSN, Columbia U., 1962; MA in Parent/Child Nursing, NYU, 1975. RN, Ill. Staff nurse Columbia-Presbyn. Med. Ctr., N.Y.C., 1962; pub. health nurse Dept. of Health, City of N.Y., 1962-66; pub. health nurse high-risk maternal and infant care project N.Y. Med. Coll., 1966-67; nursing coord. Brownsville East N.Y. Ctr. Maternal and Infant Care Project City of N.Y., 1967-69; asst. supr. ambulatory care Mt. Sinai Med. Ctr., 1969-70, sr. supr. ambulatory care, 1970-72, asst. DON ambulatory care, 1972-75; clin. specialist in maternity Chgo. Lying-In Hosp., U. Chgo. Med. Ctr., 1976-80, DON, 1980-86; maternal/child health nurse cons. Ill. Dept. Human Svcs., 1986—. Mem. perinatal nursing adv. coun. Greater Ill. chpt. March of Dimes, Chgo., 1979—. Founding pres., bd. dirs. Am. Scandinavian Assn. Ill., Chgo., 1983-95; active Chgo. Coun. Fgn. Rels., 1976—, Chgo. Hist. Soc., 1994—. Recipient Nurses Recognition award Greater Ill. chpt. March of Dimes, 1993; fellow Ill. Pub. Health Leadership Inst., 1998-99. Mem. ANA, APHA, Ill. Nurses Assn., Chgo. Nurses Assn. (dist. 1), Ill. Pub. HealtAssn. (chmn. maternal-child health sect. 1992-94, asst. chmn. 1990-92), Ill. Assn. Maternal-Child Health (pres. 1992-94, bd. dirs. 1989-96), Sigma Theta Tau, Pi Sigma Alpha. Avocations: hiking, bicycling, classical music. Office: Ill Dept Human Svc 1112 S Wabash 3d Fl Chicago IL 60605-1218

LOPCHINSKY, RICHARD ALAN, surgeon, educator; b. N.Y.C., Mar. 21, 1950; MD, Albert Einstein Coll. Medicine, 1975. Diplomate Am. Bd. Surgery. Resident in gen. surgery Maimonides Med. Ctr., Bklyn., 1975-79; fellow in head and neck surgery Sloan-Kettering Meml. Ctr., N.Y.C., 1979-80; staff Mt. Sinai Med. Ctr.; chief divsn. head and neck surgery Flushing (N.Y.) Hosp. Med. Ctr., 1990-98; staff Lenox Hill Hosp., N.Y.C. Clin. asst. prof. Mt. Sinai Sch. Medicine. Fellow: ACS; mem.: Am. Thyroid Assn., N.Y. Met. Breast Cancer Group, Soc. Head and Neck Surgery, N.Y. Head and Neck Soc. (treas. 2000—02), Am. Soc. Breast Disease, Am. Soc. Head and Neck Surgery (publ. com. 1997—98, mem.com. 1995—97). Office: 5 E 94th St New York NY 10128-1913 E-mail: richard.lopchimsky@mssm.edu.

LOPER, CARL RICHARD, JR. metallurgical engineer, educator; b. Wauwatosa, Wis., July 3, 1932; s. Carl Richard S. and Valberg (Sundby) Loper; m. Jane Louise Loehning, June 30, 1956; children: Cynthia Louise Loper Koch, Anne Elizabeth. BS in Metall. Engring., U. Wis., 1955, MS in Metall. Engring., 1958, PhD in Metall. Engring., 1961; postgrad., U. Mich., 1960. Metall. engr. Pelton Steel Casting Co., Milw., 1955-56; instr., rsch. assoc. U. Wis., Madison, 1956-61, asst. prof., 1961-64, assoc. prof., 1964-68, prof. metall. engring., 1968-88, prof. materials sci. and engring., 1988-2001, ret. prof. materials sci. and engring., 2001, assoc. chmn. dept. metall. and mineral engring., 1979-82; pres. CRL Corp., 1979—, CRL Corp., Ltd., 1985—. Rsch. metallurgist Allis Chalmers, Milw., 1961; adj. prof. materials U. Wis., Milw., 2002—; cons., lectr. in field. Author: (book) Principles of Metal Casting, 1965; contbr. articles to profl. jours. Chmn. 25 Anniversary Ductile Iron Symposium, Montreal, Canada, 1973; pres. Ygdrasil Lit. Soc., 1989—90. Recipient Adams Meml. award, Am. Welding Soc., 1963, Howard F. Taylor award, 1967, Svc. citation, 1969, 1972, others, Silver medal award, Sci. Merit Portuguese Foundry Assn., 1978, medal, Chinese Foundrymen's Assn., 1989; fellow Foundry Ednl. Found., 1953—55, Wheelbrator Corp., 1960, Ford Found., 1960. Fellow: AIM, Am. Soc. Metals (chmn. 1969—70); mem.: Tau Beta Pi, Foundry Ednl. Found., Korean Inst. Metals and Materials (hon.), Am. Welding Soc., Am. Foundrymen's Soc. (bd. dirs. 1967-70, 76-79, Foundry Ednl. Found. dirs. award 1994, Best Paper award 1966, 67, 85, John A. Penton gold medal 1972, Hoyt Meml. lectr. 1992, Aluminum Divsn. award sci. merit 1995), Blackhawk Country Club, Torske Klubben (bd. dirs., co-founder 1978—, Foundry Hall of Honor 2001), Gamma Alpha, Alpha Sigma Mu, Sigma Xi. Lutheran. Achievements include significant contributions to understanding the solidifcation and metallurgy of ferrous and non-ferrous alloys; recognized authority of solidification and cast iron metallurgy, and on education in metallurgy and materials science. Office: U Wis Cast Metals Lab 1509 University Ave Madison WI 53706-1538 E-mail: loper@engr.wisc.edu.

LOPER, D. ROGER, retired oil company executive; b. Mpls., Dec. 14, 1920; s. Donald Rust and Agnes (Yerxa) L.; m. Sylvia Lee Brainard, Aug. 16, 1946 (dec. Apr. 1973); children: Ann Kathleen, Michael Brainard, Joyce Elizabeth, Nancy Jean Loper Woods; m. Genevieve Jean Kusles, May 4, 1974. BSMetE, Carnegie Tech. Inst., 1947. Registered chem. engr., Calif. Div. supr. Standard Oil of Calif., San Francisco, 1958-64, asst. chief engr., 1964-74; gen. mgr. Chevron Petroleum, London, 1974-80; pres. Chevron Shale Oil Co., Denver, 1980-82; v.p. Chevron Overseas Petroleum, San Francisco, 1982-85; cons. Loper Assocs., Carmel, Calif., 1985—. Inventor hydrocracking reactor, remote inspection device. Pres. Our Saviour Luth. Ch., Lafayette, Calif., 1971-72; foreman Monterey County Civil Grand Jury, 1997. Maj. U.S. Army, 1942-46. Republican. Home and Office: 2804 Pradera Rd Carmel CA 93923-9717

LOPER, DAVID ERIC, geophysics educator, mathematics educator; b. Oswego, N.Y., Feb. 14, 1940; married, 1966; 4 children. BS, Carnegie Inst. Tech., 1961; MS, Case Inst. Tech., 1964, PhD in Mech. Engring., 1965. Sr. scientist Douglas Aircraft Corp., 1965-68; from asst. prof. to assoc. prof. Fla. State U., Tallahassee, 1968-77, prof. math., 1977-97, prof. geology and math., 1997—; dir. Geophysical Fluid Dynamics Inst., 1994—. Nat. Ctr. Atmospheric Rsch. fellow, 1967-68, sr. vis. fellow U. Newcastle-upon-Tyne, Eng., 1974-75, Cambridge U., Eng., 1990; H.C. Webster fellow U. Queensland, Australia, 1983. Fellow Am. Geophys. Union; mem. Sigma Xi. Achievements include research on boundary layers in rotating, stably stratified, electrically conducting fluids; evolution of the earth's core including stratification, heat transfer, solidification and particle precipitation; karst hydrology. Office: Fla State U Geophys Fluid Dynamics Inst 18 Keen Bldg Tallahassee FL 32306 E-mail: loper@gfdi.fsu.edu.

LOPER, LINDA SUE, special collections librarian; b. Wakefield, R.I., Jan. 28, 1945; d. Delmas Field and Dora Belle (Hanna) Sneed; children: Matthew Lee Mathany, Amanda Virginia Mathany Van DerHeyden, Morgan Lynnclare Loper. BA, Peabody Coll., Nashville, 1966, MLS, 1979; EdD in Ednl. Adminstrn., Vanderbilt U., Nashville, 1988. Tchr. Parkway Sch., Chesterfield, Mo., 1966-68, Charlotte Mecklenburg Schs., Charlotte, N.C., 1968-71; dir. city libr. Jackson George Regional Libr. System, Pascagoula, Miss., 1979-82; media ctr. specialist Pascagoula Mcpl. Sch. Dist., 1982-83, Moore County Sch. System, Lynchburg, Tenn., 1983-91; ref. libr. Motlow State C.C., Tullahoma, 1983-85; dir. learning resource ctr. Columbia (Tenn.) State C.C., 1991-99; CEO Grant Seekers, Inc., 1996-99; CEO Loper Literary Agy., 1999—2001; accounts svcs. mgr. E.B. Stephens Co. (EBSCO), 1999-2001; spl. collections divsn. mgr. Nashville Pub. Libr., 2001—. Presenter TLA Ann. Conv., Knoxville, 1998, Am. Assn. Women in C.C.s Regional Conf., 1997, LEAP State Dept. Edn. Conf. for Libr., Chattanooga; career ladder participant

Tenn. Edn. Dept. Level II; TIM trainer Dept. Edn., Nashville; exec. dir. Tenn. Bd. of Regents Media Consortium, 1993-96; chair profl. staff orgn. Columbia State C.C., 1998-99; presenter, judge 6th Ann. Cumberland Writers Conf., Cookeville, Tenn. Author: Bibliography for Tennessee Commission on Status of Women, 1979; contbr. article to profl jour. Pres. Moore County Friends of Libr., Lynchburg, Tenn., 1991; bd. dirs. Moore County Hist. and Geneal. Soc., Lynchburg, 1991; mem. Tenn. Bicentennial Com., Giles County, 1996; co-dir. So. Tapestry, a Bicentennial oral history project; sec., mem. exec. bd. Hope House Domestic Violence Shelter, 1993-96, mem. adv. bd., 1996—; mem. steering com. Bus., Industry, Edn. Partnership, 1994-99. Recipient Gov.'s Acad. award State Dept. of Edn., U. Tenn., 1988, Inst. for Writing Tenn. History, U. Tenn., 1990, Gov.'s Conf. on Info. Sci., Nashville, 1990. Mem. ASCD, ALA, S.E. Libr. Assn., Tenn. Libr. Assn. (co-chair strategic planning com. 1996-99), TENNSHARE (chair collection devel. com. 1996-99), Moore County Edn. Assn. (treas., chair tchrs. study coun., chair polit. action commn. 1989-91), Giles County Edn. Found. UDC, DAR (historian), Tenn. Acad. Libr. Collaborative (exec. coun. 1996-99), Phi Delta Kappa, Beta Phi Mu, Delta Kappa Gamma. Democrat. Episcopalian. Avocations: French hand sewing, crosstitch, sewing, reading, gardening. Office: Nashville Pub Libr Spl Collections Divsn 615 Church St Nashville TN 37219 E-mail: sue.loper@metro.nashville.org.

LOPER, WARREN EDWARD, computer scientist; b. Aug. 2, 1929; s. Leon Edward and Belva Fannin) L.; m. Ruth M. Wetzler, June 17, 1967; 1 child, Mary Katherine. BS in Physics, U. Tex. at Austin, 1953; BA in Math (hon.), 1953. Commd. ensign U.S. Navy, 1953; advanced through grades to lt., 1957; physicist U.S. Naval Ordnance Test Sta., China Lake, Calif., 1956-61; operational programmer U.S. Navy Electronics Lab., San Diego, 1962-64; project leader, sys. programming br., digital computer staff U.S. Fleet Missle Sys. Analysis & Eval. Group, Corona, 1964-65; sr. sys. analyst digital computer staff U.S. Naval Ordnance Lab., 1965-69; head sys. programming br. Naval Weapons Ctr. Corona Labs, 1969; computer specialist compiler and ops. sys. devel. Naval Electronics Lab. Ctr., San Diego, 1969-76; project leader langs., op. sys. and graphics Naval Ocean Sys. Ctr., 1977-90; employee emeritus, 1990-93; retired, 1993. Navy rep. on tech. subgroup Dept. Def. High Order Lang. Working Group, 1975-80. Recipient Disting. Svc. award Dept. Def., 1983. Democrat. Roman Catholic. Home: 6542 Alcala Knolls Dr San Diego CA 92111-6947

LOPES, DAVEY, former professional baseball manager; b. Providence, May 3, 1946; 1 child, Vanessa Lin. Grad., Washburn U., Topeka, 1969. Profl. baseball player Dodgers, Athletics, Cubs, Astros, 1972-87; dugout and first base coach Tex. Rangers, 1988-91; mgr. Ariz. Fall League; first base coach Balt. Orioles, 1992-94, San Diego Padres, 1995-99; mgr., head coach Milw. Brewers Baseball Club, 1999—2002. Office: Milw Brewers County Stadium PO Box 3099 Milwaukee WI 53201-3099*

LOPES, MARIA FERNANDINA, commissioner; b. Ganda, Angola, Portugal, Dec. 12, 1934; came to U.S., 1963; d. Rodrigo do Carmo and Maria Jose Fernandes (Mendes) Marques; m. Fernandes Esteves Lopes, Aug. 11, 1962; children: Lisa Maria Lopes Moss, Mark Esteves Lopes. Student, Lisbon (Portugal) Comml. Inst., 1953, Massasoit Community Coll., Brockton, Mass., 1988. With archives dept. Portuguese Govt., Lisbon, 1958-62; congl. aide Congresswoman Margaret M. Heckler, Fall River, Taunton, Mass., 1972-74; mem. Taunton (Mass.) Sch. Com., 1976-93; commr., chairperson Bristol County, Mass., 1991—. Founder Day of Portugal, 1974. Avocations: traveling, politics, antiques, music. Home: 28 Worcester St Taunton MA 02780-2041 Office: Office County Commissioners Superior Courthouse PO Box 208 Taunton MA 02780-0208

LOPES, MYRA AMELIA, writer; b. Nantucket, Mass., July 9, 1931; d. Leo Joseph and Mary Ellen (Moriarty) Powers; m. Curtis Linwood Lopes, June 25, 1955; children: Dennis, Sherry, Kathy, Curtis, Bekcy. BS, Bridgewater, 1954; diploma, Inst. Children's Lit., 1982, N.Y. Inst. Journalism, 1984. Cert. elem. educator Mass. Tchr. Fairhaven (Mass.) Sch. Sys., 1954-58; prin. Sheri Ka Kindergarten, 1960-76. Author: (novels) Look Around You, 1990, Looking Back, 1991, Seeing It All, 1992, But Then There Was More, 1993, (book) Captain Joshua Slocum: A Centennial Tribute, 1994, Captain Slocum's Life Before and After the Spray, 1997, The Rogers Legacy, 1997, The Castle on the Hill, 1998, My Town, 1999, (documentary) Joshua Slocum: New World Columbus, 2001, Around the Kitchen Table, 2002, A Piece of the Rogers Mansion: The Mitchell House, 2002. Bd. dirs. Fairhaven Improvement Assn., 1986—98, chair membership, 1986—96, pres., 1990—93; bd. dirs. YWCA, New Bedford, 1982—88, chair cmty. rels., 1982—83, nominating chair, 1983—84, chair pers. bd., 1984—88; trustee Millicent Libr., 1993—; bd. govs. Am. Biog. Instn., 1997—; bd. dirs. Fairhaven H.S. Hall of Fame, 1999—. Named Woman of the Yr., New Bedford Std.-Times and cmty., 1999; named to Hall of Fame, Fairhaven H.S., 1997. Mem.: Joshua Slocum Soc. Internat. (historian 1997—2000, bd. dirs. 2001—02), Rotary (bd. dirs. 1998—99, v.p. 2000—, pres.-elect 2001, pres. Fairhaven chpt. 2002—, Paul Harris fellow 2000). Democrat. Roman Catholic. Avocations: gardening, reading, walking, crafts, music. Home: 71 Fort St Fairhaven MA 02719-2811 Personal E-mail: clopes7081@aol.com.

LOPEZ, ANGEL R. PAGAN, dean, dentist; DDS Dental-Endodontics, U. P.R. Sch. Dentistry, 1988. Pvt. practice as a dentist; dean. U. P.R., 1999—. Office: PO Box 365067 San Juan PR 00936 Address: 1280 Main St Worcester MA 01603-6619*

LOPEZ, ANGELO CAYAS, freelance illustrator; b. Norfolk, Va., Mar. 29, 1967; s. Felizardo Pardo and Teresita (Cayas) L. BS in Graphic Design, San Jose State U., 1992. Cashier Marriott's Great Am., Santa Clara, Calif., 1985; page tech. svc. dept. Sunnyvale (Calif.) Pub. Libr., 1985-90, tech. svc. clk., 1993—; intern Palo Alto (Calif.) Fast Stats, 1990-91; framer Aaron Bros., Sunnyvale, 1991-92; cashier Linden Tree Children's Bookstore, Los Altos, Calif., 1992-94. Executed murals Beryessa br. San Jose Pub. Libr., 1995, Grace Cmty. Covenant Ch., Los Altos, Calif., 1998, Shields Elem. Sch., San Jose, 2000. Contbr. illustrations to books including Two Moms A Zark and Me, 1993, Night Travelers, 1994, Cherubic Children's New Classic Storybook, Vol. 2, 1998; contbr. illustrations, cartoons to mags. Vol. Arts Project, Santa Clara, 1990; tutor San Jose (Calif.) Chinese Alliance Ch., 1993-95; active Santa Clara U. Mission Ch., 1992-95; mem. local Svc. Employees Internat. Union of Sunnyvale Pub. Libr., 1995—. Democrat. Avocations: reading, painting, basketball, watching old movies. Home: 231 N 15th St San Jose CA 95112-1839

LOPEZ, BARRY HOLSTUN, writer; b. Port Chester, N.Y., Jan. 6, 1945; s. Adrian Bernard and Mary Frances (Holstun) L.; m. Sandra Jean Landers, June 10, 1967 (div. Jan. 16, 1999). BA cum laude, U. Notre Dame, 1966, MA in Teaching, 1968; postgrad., U. Oreg., 1968-69; LHD (hon.), Whittier Coll., 1988, U. Portland, 1994, Tex. Tech. U., 2000; LHD in Environ. Studies (hon.) , Utah State U., 2002. Free-lance writer, 1970—. Assoc. Media Studies Ctr. at Columbia Univ., N.Y.C., 1985—; mem. U.S. Cultural Delegation to China, 1988; residency fellow Lannan Found., 1999, MacDowell Colony, 2001. Author: Desert Notes, 1976, Giving Birth to Thunder, 1978, Of Wolves and Men, 1978 (John Burroughs Soc. medal 1979, Christophers of N.Y. medal 1979, Pacific Northwest Booksellers award in nonfiction 1979), River Notes, 1979, Winter Count, 1981 (Disting. Recognition award Friends Am. Writers in Chgo. 1982), Arctic Dreams, 1986 (Nat. Book award in nonfiction Nat. Book Found. 1986, Christopher medal 1987, Pacific Northwest Booksellers award 1987, Frances Fuller Victor award in nonfiction Oreg. Inst. Literary Arts 1987), Crossing Open Ground, 1988, Crow and Weasel, 1990 (Parents Choice Found. award), The Rediscovery of North America, 1991, Field Notes, 1994 (Pacific Northwest Booksellers award in fiction 1995, Critics' Choice award 1996), Lessons From the Wolverine, 1997, About This Life, 1998, Apologia, 1998, Light Action in the Caribbean, 2000; also numerous articles, essays and short stories; contbg. editor Harper's mag., 1981-82, 84—, N.Am. Rev., 1977—, Ga. Rev., 2000—; works translated into Japanese, Swedish, German, Dutch, Italian, French, Norwegian, Chinese, Finnish, Spanish, Arabic. Recipient award in Lit., Am. Acad. Arts and Letters, 1986, Antarctic Svc. medal U.S. Congress, 1989, Gov.'s award for Arts, 1990, Lannan Found. award, 1990, Internat. Environ. award Prescott Coll., 1992, John Hay award, The Orion Soc., 2002, St. Francis of Assisi award DePaul U., 2002; HEA Title V fellow, 1967, John Simon Guggenheim Found. fellow, 1987; grantee NSF, 1987, 88, 91, 92, 99. Fellow Explorers Club; mem. PEN Am. Ctr., Authors Guild, Poets and Writers, Nature Conservancy (hon. life).

LOPEZ, CONSTANCE R. nursing administrator; b. N.Y.C., Apr. 2, 1953; d. Saverio and Mary (Catania) L.; m. Stephen Sanborn, Apr. 22, 1997; children: Lindsay Lopez-Rodkin. BSN summa cum laude, Herbert H. Lehman Coll., 1975; MS, Rutgers U., 1987. Assoc. dir. nursing svcs. Daus. of Jacob, Bronx, N.Y.; dir. nursing svcs. Kingsbridge Heights Manor; asst. v.p. nursing svcs. Benedictine Hosp., Kingston, N.Y., v.p. mental health svcs.; v.p. critical care svcs., dir. nursing, sr. v.p. nursing svc The Kingston Hosp. Mem. ANA, N.Y. State Nurses Assn.

LOPEZ, DAVID, lawyer; b. N.Y.C., May 9, 1942; s. Damaso and Carmen (Gonzalez) L.; m. Nancy Mary Cea, Aug. 29, 1964; children: David, Jonathan. AB, Cornell U., 1963; JD, Columbia U., 1966. Bar: N.Y. 1966. Assoc. firm Leon, Weill & Mahoney, N.Y.C., 1966-67, Bressler & Meislen, N.Y.C., 1967-70; individual practice law, 1970—. Chmn. bd. A.T.I. Adv. Svcs., Inc., 1979—; dir. Nancy Lopez, Inc., Southampton, N.Y. Mem. ABA, N.Y. State Bar Assn., Suffolk County Bar Assn. Office: 171 Edge of Woods Rd PO Box 323 Southampton NY 11969-0323 E-mail: davidlopezesq.com@aol.com.

LOPEZ, DAVID TIBURCIO, lawyer, educator, arbitrator, mediator; b. Laredo, Tex., July 17, 1939; s. Tiburcio and Dora (Davila) L.; m. Romelia G. Guerra, Nov. 20, 1965; 1 child, Vianei López Robinson. *Wife Romelia G. López came with her family from Mexico speaking Spanish, enrolled in U.S. schools, and graduated valedictorian of her class. She has been office manager for López law firm in Houston for more than 20 years. Daughter Vianei López Robinson is an accomplished lawyer and a popular actress and dancer in civic theater productions in Abilene, Texas. Vianei and her husband, N. Keith Robinson, Jr., M.D., a very well-regarded internist in private practice, collect art and fine wines. Father, Tiburcio López, was born in 1902 in Mexico and lives in Laredo, Texas.* Student, Laredo Jr. Coll., 1956-58; BJ, U. Tex., 1962; JD summa cum laude, South Tex. Coll. Law, 1971. Bar: Tex. 1971, U.S. Dist. Ct. (so. dist.) Tex. 1972, U.S. Ct. Appeals (5th cir.) 1973, U.S. Dist. Ct. (we. dist.) Tex. 1975, U.S. Ct. Claims 1975, U.S. Ct. Appeals (fed. cir.) 1975, U.S. Supreme Ct. 1976, U.S. Dist. Ct. (ea. dist.) Tex. 1978, U.S. Dist. Ct. N.Mex. 2000, U.S. Ct. Appeals (11th cir.) 1981, U.S. Ct. Appeals (9th cir.) 1984; cert. internat. com. arbitrator Internat. Ctr. for Arbitration; mediator tng. Atty.-Mediator Inst. Reporter Laredo Times, 1958-59; cons. Mexican Nat. Coll. Mag., Mexico City, 1961-62; reporter Corpus Christi (Tex.) Caller-Times, 1962-64; state capitol corr. Long News Svc., Austin, Tex., 1964-65; publs. dir. Interam. Regional Orgn. of Workers, Mexico City, 1965-67; nat. field rep. AFL-CIO, Washington, 1967-71, publs. dir. Tex. chpt. Austin, 1971-72; pvt. practice Houston, 1971—. Adj. prof. U. Houston, 1972-74, Thurgood Marshall Sch. Law, Houston, 1975-76; mem. adv. com. nat. Hispanic ednl. rsch. project One Million and Counting Tomas Rivera Ctr., 1989-91; mem. adv. bd. Inst. Transnat. Arbitration; charter mem. Resolution Forum Inc.; mem. adv. bd. South Tex. Ctr. Profl. Responsibility; mem. nat. panel of neutrals JAMS/ENDISPUTE, 1996-2000. *Before graduating first in his law school class in 1971, David T. López was a prize-winning journalist in Texas and public relations executive in Mexico. His litigation experience includes civil rights, employment, international venture and intellectual property cases. Trained as a mediator and international commercial arbitrator, he was appointed in 1996 as a panelist by J*A*M*S/Endispute. He has worked in Latin America, travelled extensively in Europe, Asia and the Middle East, and written and lectured at professional seminars in English and Spanish on international labor issues, dispute resolution, and cross-cultural negotiation and communication.* Bd. dirs. Pacifica Found., N.Y.C., 1970-72, Houston Community Coll., 1972-75; mem. bd. edn. Houston Ind. Sch. Dist., 1972-75. With U.S. Army. Mem. ABA (co-chair, diversity in litig. com.), FBA, Tex. Bar Assn. (com. on pattern jury changes), Houston Bar Assn. (com. on alternative dispute resolution), Internat. Bar Assn., Interam. Bar Assn., Bar of U.S. Fed. Cir., Mex.-Am. Bar Assn., Inter-Pacific Bar Assn., Tex.-Mex. Bar Assn. (chair labor com.), Hispanic Bar Assn., World Assn. Lawyers (chair internat. lab. sect.), Am. Judicature Soc., Indsl. Rels. Rsch. Assn., Sigma Delta Chi, Phi Alpha Delta. Democrat. Roman Catholic. Home: 28 Farnham Ct Houston TX 77024 Office: 3900 Montrose Blvd Houston TX 77006-4959 E-mail: dtlopez@lopezlawfirm.com.

LOPEZ, FLOYD WILLIAM, lawyer; b. Albuquerque, Sept. 7, 1952; s. J. Joseph and Eleanor (Marron) L.; m. Susan Templeton, Dec. 27, 1980; children: Kathleen, Melinda, Michael, Carolyn, Owen. BA in English and Spanish, Amherst Coll., 1974; JD, U. N.Mex., 1982. Bar: N.Mex. 1982, U.S. Dist. Ct. N.Mex. 1983, U.S. Ct. Appeals (10th cir.) 1983. Senate intern N.Mex. Legis., Santa Fe, 1979; messenger Modrall, Sperling, Roehl, Harris & Sisk, Albuquerque, 1979; pvt. practice in constn., 1979; legal extern Marron & McKinnon, 1979-81; law clk. to judge Edwin L. Mechem U.S. Dist. Ct., 1982-84; counsel Gov.'s Organized Crime Prevention Commn., 1984-86; asst. county atty. County of Bernalillo, 1991-95; pvt. practice, 1985—. Mem. ethics com. Bernalillo County; analyst N.Mex. Senate, 1993. Mem. Albuquerque Bar Assn. (bd. dirs. 1990-93), Legal Aid Soc. (bd. dirs. 1990-94, Pro Bono award 1986-89). Democrat. Roman Catholic. Avocations: skiing, golf. Office: Lopez & Simms LLP 618 Manzano St NE Albuquerque NM 87110

LOPEZ, FRANCISCO, IV, health care administrator; b. San Jose, Costa Rica, Costa Rica, Aug. 31, 1956; s. Francisco III and Myriam (Bolanos) L.; m. Marie Jeanne de Lassus; children: Matthew Chase, Kathryn Louise, Elizabeth Myriam Jane, James Austin. BS, La. State U., 1976; MHA, Tulane U., 1980. Adminstrv. asst. Mercy Hosp. of New Orleans, 1980-81, asst. v.p., 1981-82, v.p., 1982-85, exec. v.p., 1985-86, chief operating officer, 1986—; exec. v.p. Mercy Health Sys., 1995—; pres. St. Mary's/Mercy Hosp., 1995—; CEO St. Mary's Regional Med. Ctr., 2000—. Bd. cons. St. John's Place, New Orleans, 1986—. Bd. dirs. Enid Beautiful; trustee Enid Telecomms. Authority; v.p. Calhoun/Palmer Neighborhood Assn., New Orleans, 1984-85; bd. dirs. Holy Name of Jesus Sch., New Orleans, 1985, United Cerebral Palsy, New Orleans, 1986, Mount St. Mary H.S., Okla. Cath. Health Care Assn., bd. dirs. YMCA, Rotary Club; trustee Vance Devel. Authority, Phillips U., YMCA. Recipient Associated U. Programs in Health Adminstrn. scholarship, 1979, Nat. Hispanic scholarship, 1980. Fellow Am. Coll. Health Care Execs. (Foster G. McGaw scholarship 1979); mem. Am. Hosp. Assn., Enid C. of C. (trustee), So. Yacht Club (New Orleans), Oakwood Country Club. Clubs: So. Yacht (New Orleans). Avocations: tennis, travel, swimming. Home: 2029 Oak Leaf Cir Enid OK 73703-2330 Office: St Mary's Reg Med Ctr PO Box 232 Enid OK 73702-0232

LOPEZ, GUILLERMO, obstetrician-gynecologist, educator; b. Bogota, Colombia, Oct. 3, 1919; came to U.S., 1944; s. Pedro P. and Sofia (Escobar) L.; m. Jeannie Pareja, July 16, 1955; children: Monica, Diana, Roberto, John G. MD, U. Nacional, Bogota, 1943; MS in Ob-Gyn, St. Louis U., 1947; asst. etranger, U. Paris, 1954. BE Am. Bd. Ob-Gyn. Intern Hosp. San Juan de Dios, U. Nacional, Bogota, 1942-43; resident in ob-gyn St. Louis U. Group Hosps., 1944-47; head gynecol. svc. San Juan de Dios Hosp., U. Nacional, Bogota, 1949-53, prof. of ob-gyn, 1951, assoc. dean clin. scis., 1965-66; head dept. gynecol. Inst. Nacional Cancer, 1950-68; rsch. assoc. UCLA Harbor Gen. Hosp., 1967-68; head population div. Colombian Assn. Med. Schs., Bogota, 1969-73; head dept. gynecology, obstetrics and reproduction Centro Medico de los Andes, Fundacion Santa Fe, 1981-88; rsch. prof. dept. community and family health Coll. Pub. Health, U. South Fla., Tampa, 1989—. Seminar cons., tchr. mother and child care Peruvian Assn. Acad. Med. programs, Paracas, Peru, 1970; pres. Corp. Cen. Regional Population, Bogota, 1973-89; cons. Pan-Am. Health Orgn. (WHO), UN Fund for Population Activities (UNFPA), 1989—; bd. dirs. Bogota Health Div., 1981-82; presenter in field. Editor: Reproduction, 1979, editor Reproductive Health in Americas, 1992; contbr. articles to profl. jours., including Am. Jour. Ob-Gyn., Med. Cir., Panamerican Health Orgn., Editorial Fotolito Garcia e Hijos, others. Bd. dirs. Floridians for a Sustainable Population. Fellow ACS, Am. Coll. Ob-Gyn.; mem. N.Y. Acad. Scis., Am. Fertility Soc., Nat. Acad. Medicine Colombia, Fla. Ob-Gyn. Soc., Am. Pub. Health Assn. Office: U South Fla Coll Pub Health 13201 Bruce B Downs Blvd Tampa FL 33612-3805 Home: 5918 Bayview Cir S Gulfport FL 33707-3930

LOPEZ, HUGO FERREIRA, materials engineering, educator; b. Luis Potosi, Mex., Dec. 10, 1952; came to U.S., 1980; s. Francisco and Maria (Ferreira) L.; m. Emilia Dearbeloa, Mar. 22, 1981; children: Jessica Emilia, David Joseba. BA in Indsl. Engring., Saltillo (Mex.) Tech., 1975; MS in Metallurgy Engring., Ohio State U., 1982, PhD in Metallurgy Engring., 1983. Rsch. prof. Saltillo Tech.; asst. prof. U. Wis., Milw., assoc. prof.; prof.; chair materials dept. U. Wis., Milw. Contbr. articles to profl. jours. Mem. U.S. bd. NACE-Latin Am., Cancun, Mex., 1997-98. Mem. Nat. Assn. Corrosion Engrs. (bd. dirs. Latin Am.). Office: Univ Wis Milw 3200 N Cramer St Milwaukee WI 53211-3029 E-mail: hlopez@uwm.edu.

LOPEZ, JEAN ENGEBRETSEN, neuroscience nurse, researcher; b. Alliance, Nebr., June 23, 1950; d. John Peter and Helen LaRue (Vyzourek) Engebretsen; m. Samuel Lopez, Dec. 22, 1979. BSN, U. Nebr., 1973; cert. in neuro nursing, Montreal Neurol. Inst., Que., Can., 1978; MSN, Ariz. State U., 1987. RN, Ariz.; cert. clin. rsch. coord. Cert. neuroscience RN U.S. Peace Corps, Kuala Lumpur, Malaysia, 1973-74; staff nurse, charge nurse neuro ICU Barrow Neurolog. Inst. of St. Joseph's Hosp. and Med. Ctr., Phoenix, 1974-89, neuro-oncology and head injury rsch. nurse clinician, 1989-99; clin. rsch. nurse coord. Sun Health Rsch. Inst. Ctr. for Clin. Rsch., Sun City, Ariz., 1999—. Mem. Am. Assn. Neuro Nurses (past. sec. Ariz. chpt., chpt. coun. rep. for S.W.). Office: Sun Health Rsch Inst Ctr for Clin Rsch 10515 W Santa Fe Dr Sun City AZ 85351-3020 E-mail: jean.lopez@sunhealth.org.

LOPEZ, JENNIFER, actress, dancer, singer; b. Bronx, N.Y., July 24, 1970; m. Cris Judd, 2001 (div. 2002). Appeared in films Money Train, 1995, Jack, 1996, Blood and Wine, 1996, Anaconda, 1997, Selena, 1997, My Family, 1995, U-Turn, 1997, Antz (voice), 1998, Out of Sight, 1998, Thieves, 1999, Pluto Nash, 1999, The Cell, 2000, The Wedding Planner, 2001, Angel Eyes, 2001; released Latin music albums: On the 6, 1999, J.Lo, 2001, J to Tha L-O!: The Remixes, 2002. Recipient ALMA award 1998, Lasting Image award 1998, Lone Star Film and TV award 1998; nominated for Blockbuster Entertainment award, 1998, Golden Globe, 1998, Independent Spirit award 1996, MTV Movie award 1999, ShoWest Female Star of the Yr., 2002. Office: Internat Creative Mgmt 8942 Wilshire Blvd Beverly Hills CA 90211-1934*

LÓPEZ, JESUS M. writer; b. Orocovis, Puerto Rico, July 29, 1935; s. Jesus Maria López, Rosa Jiménez de la Torre; m. Minerva Correa, May 29, 1962; children: Maria, Martin, Floragnes. BA, Cath. U. Puerto Rico, 1960. Coord. sales Crown Zellerbach Paper Co., San Juan, PR, 1961—65, Internat. Paper Co., San Juan, 1965—71; owner Santa Rita Bakery, Veca Alta, PR, 1971—82; mgr. Microsat Co., Washington, 1982—85; writer, rschr. Waterbury, 1986—. Biographer Antonio Paoli Edicionea Linican, Waterbury, 1997—. Republican. Roman Catholic. Avocations: reading, collecting records, collecting stamps, collecting coins. Home: 14 Pine St Waterbury CT 06710

LOPEZ, JOSEPH JACK, oil company executive, consultant; b. N.Y.C., July 26, 1932; s. Florentino Estrada and Leah (Bodner) L.; m. June Elliott, June 20, 1953; children: Karen Marie Lopez Romino, Debra Jo Lopez, Laura Jean Lopez Berrell. Student, CCNY, 1955-59. Project estimator Chem. Constrn.-Engrs., N.Y.C., 1960-64, Dorr Oliver-Engrs., Stamford, Conn., 1964-66; chief estimator R.M. Parsons-Engrs., Frankfurt, Germany, 1966-74; mgr. project svcs. A.G. McKee-Engrs., Berkley Heights, N.J., 1974-76; mgr. tech. svcs. Rsch. Cottrell Corp., Sommerville, 1976-78; cons. Booz Allen & Hamilton, Abu Dhabi, United Arab Emirates, 1978-84; v.p. XL Tech. Corp., N.Y.C., 1984-87; cons. Qatar Gen. Pete Corp., Doha, 1987-90; pres. J. Lopez Cons., Babylon, N.Y., 1990—. Estimator Combustion Engring. Co., N.Y.C., 1955-60; cons. Mobil Oil, Paulsboro, N.J., 1990-93, Houston, 1996-97; cons. Ultramar Oil, Wilmington, Calif., 1994-95, Mobil Oil, Beamount, 1997-99. With USAF, 1950-54. Mem. Am. Assn. Cost Engrs., Project Mgmt. Inst. Republican. Roman Catholic. Home and Office: 15 Hinton Ave Babylon NY 11702-1407

LOPEZ, KATHRYN JEAN, editor, reporter; b. N.Y.C., Mar. 22, 1976; d. Joseph Patrick and Bernadette Carroll Lopez. BA, Cath. U. Am., 1997. With Heritage Found., Washington; assoc. editor Nat. Rev., N.Y.C., 1997—; exec. editor Nat. Rev. Online, 2001—. Dir. campus media network Cardinal Newman Soc. for Preservation of Cath. Higher Edn., 2001—. Appearances (TV) CNN, FOX, MSNBC, NPR, oxygen; contbr. articles to profl. jours. Roman Catholic. Office: National Review 215 Lexington Ave New York NY 10016 E-mail: klopez@nationalreview.com.

LOPEZ, LINDA CAROL, social sciences educator; b. N.Y.C., Dec. 26, 1949; d. Ralph B. and Miriam (Tayor) L. BA, U. Wis., Madison, 1972; MA, Ohio State U., 1974, PhD, 1976. Vis. asst. prof. U. Wis., Eau Claire, 1976-77; instr., asst. prof. SUNY, Oneonta, 1977-83; assoc. prof. Rockford (Ill.) Coll., 1983—89; prof. dept. social scis. Western N.Mex. U., Silver City, 1989—, dir. field experience, 1989-91. Contbr. articles to profl. jours., including Psychol. Reports, Internat. Jour. Addiction, Hispanic Jour. Behavioral Scis., Jour. Genetic Psychology, Jour. Employment Counseling, Perceptual and Motor Skills, Reading Improvement, Counseling and Values, Social Studies Jour. Recipient best paper award New Eng. Rsch. Orgn., 1979; postdoctoral faculty fellow Northeastern U., Boston, 1980-81. Mem. Midwestern Ednl. Rsch. Assn., Phi Delta Kappa. Avocations: walking, reading. Home: PO Box 1479 Bayard NM 88023

LOPEZ, MANUEL M. mayor; Mayor, Oxnard, Calif. Address: 300 W 3rd St Oxnard CA 93030-5790*

LOPEZ, NANCY, professional golfer; b. Torrance, Calif., Jan. 6, 1957; d. Domingo and Marina (Griego) Lopez; m. Ray Knight, Oct. 25, 1982; children: Ashley Marie Knight, Erinn Shea Knight, Torri Heather Knight. Student, U. Tulsa, 1976-78. Author: (book) The Education of a Woman Golfer, 1979. Named first victory winner, Bent Tree Classic, Sarasota, Fla., 1978, AP Athlete, 1978, Rolex Rookie of the Yr., 1978, Rolex Player of the Yr., 1978, 1979, 1985, winner, Sunstar Classic, 1979, Sahara Nat. ProAm, 1979, Women's Internat., 1979, Coca-Cola Classic, 1979, Women's Kemper Open, 1980, Sara Coventry, 1980, Rail Charity Classic, 1980, Ariz. Copper Classic, 1981, Colgate Dinah Shore, 1981, J&B Scotch Pro-Am, 1982, 1983, Mazda Japan Classic, 1982, Elizabeth Arden Classic, 1983, Uniden LPGA Invitational, 1984, Chevrolet World Championship Women's Golf, 1984, Chrysler-Plymouth Charity Classic, 1985, LPGA Championship, 1985, Mazda Hall of Fame Championship, 1985, Henredon Classic, 1985, Portland PING Championship, 1985, Sarasota Classic, 1987, Cellular One-PING Golf Championship, 1987, Mazda Classic, 1988, Ai Star/Centinela Hosp. Classic, 1988, Chrysler-Plymouth Classic, 1988, Mazda LPGA Championship, 1989, Atlantic City Classic, 1989, Nippon Travel-MBS Classic, 1989, MBS LPGA Classic, 1990, Sara Lee Classic, 1991, Rail Charity Golf Classic, 1992, PING-Cellular One LPGA Golf Championship, 1992, Youngstown-Warren LPGA Classic, 1993, Chick-fil-A Charity Championship, 1997, others; named to LPGA Hall of Fame, 1987, PGA World Golf Hall of Fame, 1989; recipient Vare Trophy, 1978. Mem.: LPGA (Player and Rookie of the Yr. 1978). Republican. Achievements include winning 48 LPGA Tour events, 3 maj. championships. Office: care Internat Mgmt Group 1360 E 9th St Ste 100 Cleveland OH 44114-1715

LOPEZ, NILO C. writer; b. Key West, Fla., Sept. 21, 1919; s. Juan Nepomuceno Lopez, Herminia Alonzo; m. Onelia Fernandez Lopez, Oct. 29, 1943. Author: (book) Memories of Old Key West, 1997, Thirties and Later Years, 1998, The Key West Hemingway Loved, 2000. Democrat. Roman Catholic. Avocations: reading, sports. Home: 2310 Seidenberg Ave Key West FL 33040

LOPEZ, PEDRO FELIPE, social worker, educator, playwright, writer; b. Havana, Cuba, Aug. 23, 1938; s. Pedro Lopez and Josefa Margarita Bravo. D Pedagogy, Santa Clara U., versity, Cuba., 1959. Cert. Tchr. of Spl. Edn. , Enseñanza Diferenciada, Cuba 1962. Med. social worker N.Y.C. HHC, 1968—2001. Trainer child abuse and maltreatment recognition Lincoln Med. and Mental Health Ctr., N.Y.C., 1991—2001. Home: 452 Fort Washington Avenue Apt. # 40 New York NY 10033-4618

LOPEZ, PETER EDWARD, artist; b. Las Vegas, N.Mex., May 14, 1940; s. Pedro (Pete) Ernest and Maria Emma (Chavez) L.; children: Kathryn Gouveia, Yvette Navarro. BA in Art Edn., U. N.Mex., 1976. Employment rep. N.Mex. Dept. Labor, Santa Fe. Instr. Rancho Valmora (N.Mex.) Sch., 1996; spkr. in field. Exhibited in group shows Tri-Cultural Arts Exhibit, Espanola, N.Mex., 1987, Gallinas River Gallery, Las Vegas, 1990, Montez Gallery, Santa Fe,

1993-95, Arrott Art Gallery, N.Mex. Highlands U., Las Vegas, 1994-95, Fiesta Artistica Hispanic Art Market, Albuquerque, 1997, Spanish Colonial Traditional Arts Market, Santa Fe, 1990—. Bd. dirs. Las Vegas Arts Coun., 1998; Retablo wood relief demonstrator El Rancho de las Golondrinas, N.Mex., 1997. Recipient Invitation award Imagenes de la Fe Exhibit, Espanola, 1994, 1st pl. Retablo art Tri-Cultural Arts, 1987, 1st place award N.Mex. State Fair, Retablos, 1998. Mem. Spanish Colonial Arts Soc. (Spanish Market Poster award 1993). Avocations: encouraging art for young people, hiking, camping, gardening, reading. Home: PO Box 183 Montezuma NM 87731-0183

LOPEZ, RALPH AURELIO, civil engineer, educator; b. Havana, Cuba, Oct. 26, 1944; came to U.S., 1961; s. Rafael and Caridad (Martinez) L.; m. Lois Ann Colonel Rudloff, 1966 (div. 1975); 1 child, Paul Christopher; m. Angela Batista do Nascimento, Jan. 3, 1994. BS in Civil Engring., U. Fla., 1966. Diplomate Am. Acad. Environ. Engrs., Am. Bd. Forensic Engring. and Tech.; registered civil engr., Calif.; registered profl. engr., Fla., Ga., S.C. Asst. engr. L.A. County Flood Control Dist., L.A., 1967-70; assoc. engr. North Marin Water Dist., Novato, Calif., 1970-73; project mgr. Sverdrup Corp., Gainesville, Fla., 1973-76; cons. wastewater treatment Miami, 1976-79; assoc. dir. engring. Mayes, Suddeth & Etheredge, Inc., Orlando, 1979-84; v.p., dir. engring. Donald McIntosh Assocs., Inc., Winter Park, 1984-88; cons. water resources and environ. engring. Miami, 1988-93; cons. water resources, prof. Physics State of Minas Gerais, Brazil, 1993-96; dir. spl. projects Thomas & Hutton Engring. Co., Savannah, Ga., 1996—. Lectr. in field. Office: Thomas & Hutton Engring Co 50 Park Of Commerce Way Savannah GA 31405-1358

LOPEZ, RUBEN, information scientist; b. Apr. 7, 1943; Degree in Elec. and Phys. Scis., U. Havana, 1962; Degree in Math. and Computer Scis., St. Thomas U., Miami, Fla., 1982; MBA, U. Miami, 1986. Cumputer jr. engr. RCA, Palm Beach, Fla., 1967-70; design engr. Control Data, Mpls., 1970-71; sys. analysts mgr. Sperry Univac, Miami, 1973-83; asst. v.p. U. Miami, 1983-99; v.p. CBS Sportsline, Ft. Lauderdale, Fla., 1999; v.p., CIO Intermedia Comms., Tampa, 2000—. Office: Intermedia Communications 1 Intermedia Way Tampa FL 33647-1752 E-mail: Rplopez@intermedia.com.

LOPEZ-ALGERIA, MICHAEL E. astronaut; b. Madrid, May 30, 1958; s. Eladio and Louise Lopez-Alegria; m. Daria Robinson; 1 child. BS in Systems Engring., U.S. Naval Acad., 1980; MS in Aeronautical Engring., U.S. Naval Postgrad. Sch., 1988; grad. Sr. Execs. in Nat. and Internat. Security Program, Harvard U. Commd. ensign USN, 1980, advanced through grades to capt.; flight instr. Pensacola, Fla., 1981—83; pilot, mission comdr.; engring. test pilot, program mgr. Naval Air Test Ctr., Patuxent River, Md.; astronaut NASA, Houston, 1992—, with Astronaut Office, crew rep. Kennedy Space Ctr., dir. ops. Yuri Gagarin Cosmonaut Tng. Ctr., Star City, Russia, head ISS Crew Ops. br. of Astronaut Office. Mem.: Assn. Naval Aviation and Assn. of Space Explorers, Soc. Exptl. Test Pilots. Achievements include logged over 4,500 flight hours in over 30 different types of aircraft; logged over 27 days in space; flight engr. STS-73 Columbia (1995); crew STS-92 Discovery (2000). Avocations: sports, travel, cooking, national and international political, economic and security affairs. Office: Astronaut Office/CB NASA Johnson Space Ctr Houston TX 77058*

LOPEZ CALIX, JOSE ROBERTO, economist; b. San Salvador, El Salvador, Oct. 25, 1956; came to U.S., 1994; s. Roberto Lopez and Melba Calix; m. Deborah Talavera; children: Daniela, Pablo, Sebastian. MA in Econs. with distinction, Cath. U. Louvain, Belgium, 1981; PhD in Econs. with distinction, 1996; MA in Internat. Fin. and Econs., U. Pitts., 1989. Cons. U.S. Congress, Pitts., 1989; gen. dir. Ministry of Planning, San Salvador, 1990-92; project chief economist Interam. Devel. Bank, San Jose, Costa Rica, 1992-94; economist The World Bank, Washington, 1994-96, resident rep. Guatemala, 1996-99, sr. economist, 1999—. Coord. reconstrn. plan Ministry Planning, San Salvador, 1991; coord. monetary/macro integration Ctrl. Am. Program Interam. Devel. Bank, San Jose, 1992; advisor peace negotiations World Bank, Guatemala, 1996—, advisor fiscal issues, Washington, 1999—. Author: Guatemala: Medium-Term Investment Review (best practice), 1997, Guatemala: Post-Conflict Reform, 1999; contbr. chpt.: Protocol of Monetary/Macro Integration of Central America, 1994. Fin. sponsor PRONADE Primary Edn. Program, Guatemala, 1999. Disting. fellow new generation of young economists Ctrl. Am. Assn., San Jose, 1992; named Best Bachelor of El Salvador, Jesuit Externado San Jose, San Salvador, 1974, Best World Bank Project for Guatemala Fin. Mgmt., 1999, Ctrl. Bank Guatemala award paper on monetary/fiscal, 2001. Mem. Econometric Soc., Internat. Econs. Assn., Latin Am. Studies Assn. Roman Catholic. Avocations: chess, tennis. Home: 11414 Empire Ln Rockville MD 20852 Office: World Bank 1818 H St NW Washington DC 20433 E-mail: jlopezcalix@worldbank.org.

LOPEZ-COBOS, JESUS, conductor; b. Toro, Spain, Feb. 25, 1940; m. Brigitte Elm, Aug. 13, 1998; 3 children. PhD in philosophy and music, U. Madrid, 1964; diploma composition, Madrid Conservatory, 1966; diploma conducting, Viennna (Austria) Acad., 1969. Gen. music dir. Deutsche Oper Berlin, 1981-90; prin. guest condr. London Philharm., 1981-86; prin. condr., artistic dir. Spanish Nat. Orch., 1984-89; music dir. Cin. Orch., 1986—2001, Orchestre de Chambre de Lausanne, Switzerland, 1990—2000, condr. Switzerland. Also condr. concerts Edinburgh Festival, London Symphony, Royal Philharm., N.Y. Philharm., L.A. Philharm., Chgo. Symphony, Cleve. Orch., Phila. Orch., Berlin Philharm., Berlin Radio Orch., Amsterdam Concertgebouw, Vienna Philharm., Swiss Romande, Muncih Philarharm., Hamburg NDR, Oslo Philharm., Zurich Tonhalle, Israel Philharm., opera prodns. at Royal Opera House, Covent Garden, London, La Scala, Milan, Italy, Met. Opera, N.Y.C., Paris Opera, others; recs. include Lucia di Lammermoor New Philham. Orch., Otello, recital and operatic disc with José Carrera and London Symphony Orch., Liszt's Dante Symphony with Swiss Romande, Falla's Three-Cornered Hat, R-K Capricio Espagnole, Chiabrier's Espana with L.A. Philharm., others. Decorated iffucer Arts and Letters (France); recipient 1st prize Besancon Internat. Condr.'s Competition, 1969, Prince of Astrurias award Spanish Govt., 1981, 1st Class Disting. Svc. medal Fed. Republic of Germany, 1989, medalla Bellas Artes (Spain), 2001. Address: 8 Chemin Bellerive 1007 Lausanne Switzerland Office: ICM Artists Ltd 40 W 57 St New York NY 10019

LOPEZ CRUZ, HUMBERTO J. foreign language educator; b. Oct. 15, 1959; PhD in Spanish, Fla. State U., 1995. Adj. lectr. Fla. Internat. U., Miami, 1994-96; asst. prof. U. Ctrl. Fla., Orlando, 1996—. Office: U Ctrl Fla Dept Fgn Langs Orlando FL 32816-0001 E-mail: hlopez@pegasus.cc.ucf.edu.

LOPEZ-DAVILA, LIANA ESTHER, radiologist; b. San Juan, P.R., July 1, 1963; d. Eliud Lopez-Velez and Yvonne Davila-Chacon; m. Agustin Antonio Rodriguez-Gonzalez, May 1, 1993; children: Agustin Andres, Claudia Sofia, Alvaro Agustin. BA, Smith Coll., 1985; MD, U. P.R., San Juan, 1990. Diplomate Am. Bd. Radiology, Nat. Bd. Med. Examiners. Intern in surgery Boston Med. Ctr., 1990-91; radiology resident Beth Israel Med. Ctr., N.Y.C., 1991-94, chief resident in radiology, 1994-95; body imaging fellow Tufts-New Eng. Med. Ctr., Boston, 1995-96; staff radiologist Somascan, Hato Rey, P.R., 1996—. Mem. AMA, Radiol. Soc. N.Am., Roentgen Ray Soc., Colegio de Medicos-Cirujanos de P.R. Home: 1924 Calle Sauco San Juan PR 00927-6718

LOPEZ DEL CASTILLO, ALFREDO, anesthesiologist; b. Manila, 1940; came to U.S., 1971; MD, Coll. Med. U. Philippines, 1964. Diplomate Am. Bd. Anesthesiology, cert. in anesthesiology and pain mgmt. Intern Philippine Gen. Hosp., 1963-64, resident surgeon, 1964-69; resident anesthesiologist Mt. Sinai Hosp., N.Y.C., 1979-81; mem. staff Victory Meml. Hosp., Bklyn. Mem.: Am. Soc. Orthop. Medicine, Richmond County Med. Soc., Med. Soc. State of N.Y., N.Y. State Soc. Anesthesiologists, Am. Soc. Anesthesiologists. Office: 126 Wieland Ave Staten Island NY 10309-2214

LOPEZ-LYLES, LUZ MARIA, visual artist; b. Comayagüela, Honduras, May 29, 1944; d. Andrés Felipe and Reina Magarita (Flores) López; children: Maria del Carmen Brisolara, William André Jr. BA magna cum laude, Southeastern La. U., 1995. Grants rev. panelist La. Divsn. of Arts, Baton Rouge, 1997; represented by Fraser Gallery, Washington, Baton Rouge Gallery, LeMieux Gallery, New Orleans, Pascal Robinson Galleries One-person exhbns. at Ven Norman Studio, Covington, 1995-96, Nicholls State U., Thibodeaux, La., 1997, Thomas V. Robinson Galleries, Houston, 1997, Le Mieux Galleries, 1998, Southeastern La. U., 1999; exhibited in groups at Imperial Calcasieu Mus., Lake Charles, La., Contemporary Arts Ctr., New Orleans, 1998, Caffery Stained Glass Gallery, 1995, Gallery Latreuo, Jacksonville, Fla., 1995, Baton Rouge Gallery, 1995, 96-97, Slidell (La.) Cultural Ctr., 1996, 97, Delgado C.C., 1996, George E. Ohr Arts & Cultural Ctr., Biloxi, Miss., 1996, Argosy Atrium, Baton Rouge, 1996, Fraser Gallery, Washington, 1997, Mus. L.Am. Art, Calif., 1998, Alexandria Mus. Art, 1998, La. Div. Art, 2001 (Liquitex Purchase, Artist of Yr. 2001); work displayed in Trophies of Honor project Griffith U., Queensland, Australia/Miss. State U. Recipient Excellence in Art award Liquitex, 1995; artist fellow La. Divsn. of Arts, 1996-97. Mem. St. Tammany Parish Art Assn., La. Profl. Artists Network, Baton Rouge Gallery, Hammond Regional Arts Ctr., La.

LOPEZ LYSNE, ROBIN, cultural organization administrator; b. Rockford, Ill., Nov. 3, 1953; d. Robert Edward and Martha Virginia (Lysne) Heerens; m. Carter Blocksma, Nov. 1, 1976 (div. Jan. 18, 1985); m. Ernesto Lopez-Molina, July 26, 1998; children: Chris, Matt, Mari Luna del Sol Lopez-Lysne(dec.). BFA cum laude, U. Wis., Milw., 1975; MA in Spirituality and Psychology, Holy Names Coll., 1988. Art tchr. Battle Creek (Mich.) Art Ctr., 1979—85, Detroit (Mich.) Art Horse Lectrs., 1979—85, Ella Sharp Mus., Jackson, 1979—85, curator of exhibits and edn., 1980—85; self-employed energy medicine practitioner Boulder Creek, Calif., 1985—; cmty. organizer Mountain Cmty. Resources, Ben Lomond, 1999—. Mem. Somatics Group, Marin County, Calif., 1989—95; presenter, lectr. in field. Author: (non-fiction and poetry) Dancing Up the Moon, 1995, Living a Sacred Life, 1997, 1999. Exec. bd. Together for Youth-United Way, Santa Cruz, Calif., 1999—. Grantee, Friends of Creation, Oakland, 1988, Flow Fund, N.Y., Calif., 1992, Rockford (Ill.) Arts Coun., 1996, 1997, Santa Cruz Mountain Art Ctr., Ben Lomond, 2000. Mem.: Valley Unity Action Group (dir. 1999—).

LOPEZ-NAKAZONO, BENITO, chemical and industrial engineer; b. Nuevo Laredo, Tam., Mex., Oct. 26, 1946; came to U.S., 1968; s. Benito and Ayko (Nakazono) Lopez-Ramos; m. Anastacia Espinoza, June 22, 1981; children: Benito Keizo, Tanzy Keiko, Aiko Michelle. BSc in Chem. Engring. & Indsl. Engring., ITESM, Monterrey, Mexico, 1968; MS in Chem. Engring., U. Houston, 1971. Prof. chem. engring. ITESM, Monterrey, 1971-72; vessel analytical design engr./process engr. M.W. Kellogg, Houston, 1973-79, 81; product mgr. Ind. Del Alcali, Monterrey, 1980-81; sr. process engr. Haldor Topsoe, Inc., Houston, 1982-2000; project mgr. Monarch Separators, Inc., 2001—. Bd. trustees San Marcus UMC, Baytown, Tex.; pres. adminstrv. coun. United Meth. Ch., Houston, 1990-92, lay leader, 96, trustee, 2001. ITESM fellow, 1963, U. Houston fellow, 1968. Mem. Tex. Soc. Profl. Engrs., Sigma Xi. Achievements include development and design of hydrogen, ammonia, methanol, formaldehyde and SNOx/WSA plants, pre-commissioning, commissioning and start-up supervision of ammonia plants in Mexico, U.S., Canada., Russia, Somalia, India and Bangladesh; design of oil/water separators; project management and installation of reactors and catalysts loading; operation and startup supervision and energy optimization. Home and Office: 1805 Lanier Dr League City TX 77573-4720 E-mail: benl@monarchseparators.com.

LOPICCOLO, JOSEPH, psychologist, educator, author; b. L.A., Sept. 13, 1943; s. Joseph E. and Adeline C. (Russo) Lo P.; m. Leslie Joan Matlen, June 20, 1964 (div. 1978); 1 child, Joseph Townsend; m. Cathryn Gail Pridal, Dec. 20, 1980; 1 child, Michael James. BA with highest honors, UCLA, 1965; MS, Yale U., 1968, PhD, 1969. Lic. psychologist, Mo. Asst. prof. U. Oreg., Eugene, 1969-73; assoc. prof. U. Houston, 1973-74; prof. SUNY, Stony Brook, 1974-84, Tex. A&M U., College Station, 1984-87; prof. psychology U. Mo., Columbia, 1987—, chmn. dept., 1987-90. Vis. scholar Cambridge (Eng.) U., 1991. Author: Becoming Orgasmic, 1976, 2d edit., 1988, also book chpts.; editor: Handbook of Sex Therapy, 1978; contbr. numerous articles to profl. jours. Woodrow Wilson Found. fellow; NIH rsch. grantee, 1973-84 Fellow Am. Psychol. Assn.; mem. Internat. Acad. Sex Rsch., Soc. for Sci. Study of Sex (pres. 1983-84, Alfred Kinsey Meml. Rsch. award), Soc. for Sex Therapy and Rsch. (Masters and Johnson Rsch. award 1997), Phi Beta Kappa, Sigma Xi. Office: U Mo Dept Psychology 210 Mcalester Hall Columbia MO 65211-2500 E-mail: LoPiccoloJ@missouri.edu.

LOPKER, ANITA MAE, psychiatrist, researcher; b. San Diego, May 25, 1955; d. Louis Donald and Betty Jean (Sayman-Campbell) L. BA magna cum laude, U. Calif., San Diego, 1978; MD, U. Rochester, 1982. Diplomate Nat. Bd. Med. Examiners, Am. Bd. Forensic Examiners, Am. Bd. Forensic Medicine. Intern in internal medicine Yale U. Sch. Medicine-Greenwich Hosp., 1982-83; resident in psychiatry Yale U. Sch. of Medicine, 1983-86; postdoctoral fellow Yale U. Sch. Medicine, New Haven, 1982-86, clin. instr., 1986-88; pvt. practice specializing eating disorders and Lyme disease Westport, Conn., 1987—. Cons. psychiatrist Yale-New Haven Hosp Lyme Disease Study Clinic, 1987-94, Yale U. Lyme Disease Rsch. Project, 1986—, Alcoholism and Drug Dependency Coun., Inc., 1989-90; internat. lectr. on Lyme psychiat. syndrome; nat. lectr. on eating disorders, substance abuse. Contbr. articles to profl. jours. Founding mem. Nat. Mus. for Women in the Arts, Washington, 1986; patron Menninger Found., 1990-94, Met. Opera, 1993-95; bd. dirs. The Fairfield Orch., 1993-96. Recipient Benjamin Rush prize in psychiatry U. Rochester Sch. Medicine, 1982, citation for Scholastic Achievement Am. Med. Women's Assn., 1982. Mem. AAAS, Am. Psychiat. Assn., Conn. Psychiat. Soc., World Fedn. Mental Health (life), N.Y. Acad. Scis., Menninger Found., Alpha Omega Alpha, Phi Beta Kappa. Achievements include discovery of preventable neuropsychiatric disorders associated with Lyme disease and tachyphylaxis as key to rapid reversal of tardive dyskinesia by verapamil, a calcium channel blocker. Avocations: classical dressage, modern dance, classical guitar. Home: 101 Regents Park Westport CT 06880-5532 Office: 18 Burr Rd Westport CT 06880-4219 E-mail: alopker@snet.net.

LOPPNOW, MILO ALVIN, clergyman, former church official; b. St. Charles, Minn., Jan. 13, 1914; s. William and Doretta (Penz) L.; m. Gertrude Stoltz, Feb. 6, 1942; children— Donald, Bruce, David. BA, Moravian Coll., 1937; M.Div., Moravian Theol. Sem., 1940, D.D., 1970. Ordained to ministry Moravian Ch. in Am., 1940; pastor congregations nr. Wisconsin Rapids, Wis., 1940-41, Waconia, Minn., 1941-53, Lakeview Ch., Madison, Wis., 1953-64; dist. pres. Western Dist. Moravian Ch., 1965-78; elected bishop, 1970. Chmn. Youth Commn., Madison, 1957-63; Trustee Moravian Coll., 1954-78, Moravian Theol. Sem., Bethlehem, Pa.; former chaplain, dir. devel. Marquardt Meml. Manor, Watertown, Wis. E-mail: malopp@GDI.com.

LOPREATO, JOSEPH, sociologist, writer; b. Stefanaconi, Italy, July 13, 1928; arrived in U.S., 1951; s. Frank and Marianna (Pavone) L.; m. Carolyn H. Prestopino, July 18, 1954; (div. 1971); children: Gregory F., Marisa S. Schmidt; m. Sally A. Cook, Aug. 24, 1972 (div. 1978). BA in Sociology, U. Conn., 1956; MA in Sociology, Yale U., 1957, PhD in Sociology, 1960. Asst. prof. sociology U. Mass., Amherst, 1960-62; vis. lectr. U. Rome, 1962-64; assoc. prof. U. Conn., Storrs, 1964-66; prof. sociology U. Tex., Austin, 1968-98, chmn. dept. sociology, 1969-72. Vis. prof. U. Catania, Italy, 1974, U. Calabria, Italy, 1980; steering com. Council European Studies, Columbia U., 1977-80; chmn. sociology com. Council for Internat. Exchange Scholars, 1977-79; mem. Internat. Com. Mezzogiorno, 1986-88; Calabria Internat. Com., 1988-90. Author: Italian Made Simple, 1959, Vilfredo Pareto, 1965, Peasants No More, 1967, Italian Americans, 1970, Class, Conflict and Mobility, 1972, Social Stratification, 1974, The Sociology of Vilfredo Pareto, 1975, La Stratificazione Sociale negli Stati Uniti, 1945-1975, 1977, Human Nature and Biocultural Evolution, 1984, Evoluzione e Natura Umana, 1990, Mai Più Contadini, 1990, Crisis in Sociology: The Need for Darwin, 1999; contbr. articles to profl. jours. Mem. Nat. Italian-Am. Com. for U.S.A. Bicentennial; mem. exec. com. Congress Italian Politics, 1977-80. Served to cpl. U.S. Army, 1952-54. Fulbright faculty research fellow, 1962-64, 73-74; Social Sci. Research Council faculty research fellow, 1963-64; NSF faculty research fellow, 1965-68; U. Tex. Austin research fellow, 1973-74, spring 1985, spring 1993; Guido Dorso award for U.S.A., Italy, 1992. Mem.: AAAS (behavioral sci. rsch. prize com. 1992—94), Internat. Soc. Human Ethology, So. Sociol. Soc. (assoc. editor Am. Sociol. Rev. 1970—72, Social Forces 1987—90, Jour. Polit. and Mil. Sociology 1980—90), Evolution and Behavior Soc., European Sociobiol. Soc., Internat. Sociol. Assn. Catholic-Episcopalian. Home and Office: 1801 Lavaca St Apt 10A Austin TX 78701-1307

LOPREST, FRANK JAMES, JR. lawyer; b. N.J., Oct. 6, 1960; s. Frank James and Jane Ann (Stables) L.; m. Theresa Beth Moser, May 10, 1997. AB, Cornell U., 1982; postgrad., NYU, 1984; JD, U. Notre Dame, 1989. Bar: Calif. 1989, N.Y. 1991. Law clk. to Hon. David G. Larimer U.S. Dist. Ct. (we. dist.) N.Y., Rochester, 1989-90; assoc. Paul, Hastings, Janofsky & Walker, L.A., 1990-92; special asst. U.S. atty. U.S. Dist. Ct. (so. dist.) N.Y., N.Y.C., 1992—. First Lt. U.S. Army, 1984-85. Roman Catholic. Office: Office US Atty State Dept 100 Church St New York NY 10007-2601

LOPRETE, JAMES HUGH, lawyer; b. Detroit, Sept. 17, 1929; s. James Victor and Effie Hannah (Brown) LoP.; m. Marion Ann Garrison, Sept. 11, 1952; children: James Scott, Kimberly Anne, Kent Garrison, Robert Drew. AB, U. Mich., 1951, JD with Distinction, 1953. Bar: Mich. 1954. Practiced law, Detroit, 1954—; atty. Chrysler Corp., 1953; assoc. firm Monaghan, LoPrete, McDonald, Yakima & Grenke, P.C. and predecessor firms, from 1954, mem. firm, 1966—, pres., 1979—. Bd. dirs. Drake's Batter Mix Co.; instr. legal writing Wayne State U., Detroit, 1955-57 Trustee U. Mich. Club of Detroit Scholarship Fund, 1967, pres., 1982—; trustee Samuel Westerman Found., 1971—, pres., 1984; trustee John R. & M. Margrite Davis Found.; pres. Louis & Nellie Sieg Found., 2000—, Frank G. and Gertrude Dunlap Found., 2001—. Fellow Am. Coll. Trust and Estate Counsel, Internat. Acad. Estate and Trust Law; mem. ABA, Oakland County bar assns., State Bar Mich., Detroit Athletic Club (dir. 1983-88, sec. 1986-88), Orchard Lake Country Club, U. Mich. of Greater Detroit (pres. 1966). Home: 2829 Warner Dr Orchard Lake MI 48324-2449 Office: Monaghan LoPrete McDonald et al 40700 Woodward Ave Ste A Bloomfield Hills MI 48304-5110 E-mail: monaghan@bignet.net.

LOPUCKI, LYNN MICHAEL, law educator; b. Detroit, Dec. 22, 1944; s. Anthony and Irene (Olszynski) LoP. AB, U. Mich., 1965, JD, 1967; LLM, Harvard U., 1970. Bar: Fla., Calif. Ptnr. Schwartz, Schwartz, LoPucki & Deering, Gainesville, Fla., 1972-74, LoPucki & LoPucki, Gainesville, 1974-80; assoc. prof. law U. Mo., Kansas City, 1980-84, U. Wis., Madison, 1984-88, prof. law, 1988-93; William R. Orthwein prof. of law Washington U., St. Louis, 1993-96; A. Robert Noll prof. of law Cornell Law Sch., 1996-99; prof. law UCLA Law Sch., 1999—. Scholar-in-residence Heller, Ehrman, White & McAuliffe, San Francisco, 1992, 93; cons. People's Republic of China, Beijing, 1993-95. Co-author: Commercial Transactions: A Systems Approach, Strategies for Creditors in Bankruptcy, 1985, 2d edit., 1991; co-author: Secured Credit, 1995; editor: Directory of Bankruptcy Attorneys, 1986-90; contbr. articles to profl. publs.; mem. editl. adv. bd. Jour. of Banker Law and Practice; law advisor bd. contbg. editors Norton Bankruptcy. Grantee NSF, 1986, Nat. Conf. Bankruptcy Judges, 1992, 93. Mem. ABA, Am. Law Inst. (adviser transnat. insolvency project 1994), Am. Bankruptcy Inst., Law and Soc. Assn. Office: Cornell Law Sch Myron Taylor Hall Ithaca NY 14853

LORANGE, JOANNE, foundation administrator, former college administrator; b. Southbridge, Mass., Jan. 2, 1946; d. Albert Lucien and Lorraine Marguerite (Briere) Lorange; B.A., St. Elizabeth Coll., 1968; M.A., Columbia U., 1971, M.A. in Higher and Adult Edn., 1972; m. Ronald Davis Herron, May 18, 1974; 1 dau., Jocelyn Lorange-Herron. Dir. residential programming, adminstrv. asst. for housing Tchrs. Coll., Columbia U., 1969-72; dir. fin. aid Richmond Coll., CUNY, S.I., 1972-76; asso. dean students Barnard Coll., Columbia U., 1975-77; dir. admissions/external relations Antioch/New Eng. Grad. Sch., Keene, N.H., 1978-86; ptnr. Marketplace Gourmet, Keene, 1985-89; dir. devel. Wykeham Rise Sch., Washington, Conn., 1988-89; exec. dir. Women's Crisis Ctr., Norwalk, Conn., 1989—; instr. New Eng. Coll., Henniker, N.H., 1977-78, Sch. for Lifelong Learning, N.H., 1982-84; cons. Upward Bound, Keene State Coll., N.H., 1982—. Jour. reviewer Nat. Assn. Student Pers. Adminstrs. Region I. Advisor Women's Center, Richmond Coll., S.I., 1972-75; judge N.H. Jr. Miss Contest, 1980; fund-raising trainer United Way; bd. dirs. Grand Monadnock Arts Council, Keene Summer Theatre, Family Planning Services Southwestern N.H.; asst. Campaign chmn. Monadnock United Way. Mem. N.H. C. of C., N.H. Women in Higher Edn. (pres.), Nat. Assn. Women Deans, Counselors and Adminstrs., Nat. Assn. Student Personnel Adminstrs., Coun. for Advancement and Support Edn. (Gold award 1985), Kiwanis. Home: 11 Old Woods Rd Brookfield CT 06804-3630 Office: Women's Crisis Ctr 5 Eversley Ave Norwalk CT 06851-5821

LORANT, JOHN HERMAN, retired economist, health policy analyst; b. Duesseldorf, Germany, Mar. 25, 1932; came to U.S., 1941; s. Hugo and Lilly Lorant; m. Susan Haas, June 30, 1968; children: Mandy, Jenny. BS, U. Wis., 1953; MBA, Harvard U., 1957; PhD, Columbia U., 1966. Dir. human resources AMA, Chgo., 1977-79, sr. health policy assoc., 1989-97; prof. bus. Lake Forest (Ill.) Coll., 1980-83; dir. human resources Chgo. Osteo. Med. Ctr., 1983-85; prin. Chrysalis Group, Highland Park, Ill., 1985-87; cons. Blue Cross and Blue Shield Assn., Chgo., 1987-89; sr. health policy analyst AMA, 1989—97. Author: The Role of Capital-Improving Innovations in American Manufacturing During the 1920's, 1975; contbr. articles to profl. jours. 1st lt. U.S. Army, 1954-55. Woytinsky scholar, 1962-63. Home: 1185 Linwood Ave Prescott AZ 86305-2868

LORBER, BARBARA HEYMAN, communications executive; b. N.Y.C. d. David Benjamin and Gertrude (Meyer) Heyman; divorced. AB in Polit. Sci., Skidmore Coll., 1966; MA, Columbia U., 1973, postgrad., 1973-76. Asst. dir. young citizens divsn. Dem. Party, 1966-68; exec. asst. to dean Albert Einstein Coll. Medicine, Bronx, N.Y., 1968-72; exec. asst. to v.p. devel. Vanderbilt U., Nashville, 1976-77; spl. projects dir. Am. Acad. in Rome, N.Y.C., 1977-78; pub. affairs dir. Met. Opera, 1978-84; sr. v.p. Hill and Knowlton, 1985-88; pres. Lorber Group, Ltd., 1989-95; v.p. comms. and planning N.Y.C. Partnership and C. of C., 1996-98; sr. v.p. planning and devel. N.Y.C. & Co./Major Events, 1998—. Guest lectr. Arts and Bus. Coun., N.Y.C., Internat. Soc. Performing Arts Adminstrs., N.Y.C., NYU Sch. Continuing Edn., Nat. Media Conf., Nat. Soc. Fund Raising Execs., N.Y.C.; exec. prodr., prodr., writer N.Y. Internat. Festival Arts, N.Y.C., 1988. Contbr. chpts. to book; contbr. articles to profl. jours. Office: NYC & Company/Major Events 810 7th Ave 3d Fl New York NY 10019-5818

LORBER, DANIEL LOUIS, endocrinologist, educator; b. N.Y.C., Sept. 21, 1946; s. Jerome Zachary Lorber and Ruth (Frank) Cook. AB, Columbia U., 1968; MD, Albert Einstein, 1972. Diplomate Am. Bd. Internal Medicine, Endocrinology and Metabolism. Intern medicine Bronx (N.Y.) Municipal Ctr., 1972-73; resident medicine Albert Enstein, Bronx, 1973-75; fellow in endocrinology Vanderbilt U., Nashville, 1975-77; from asst. prof. to asst. dean NYU Sch. Medicine, N.Y.C., 1977-84; from asst. clin. prof. to assoc. clin. prof. Albert Einstein Coll. Medicine, Bronx, 1984-94; clin. assoc. prof. Cornell U. Med. Coll., 1994—; dir. endocrinology N.Y. Hosp. Med. Ctr. of Queens, N.Y., 1994—. Med. dir. Diabetes Control Found., Flushing, N.Y., 1985—. Editor in chief Practical Diabetology Magazine, 1987—. Fellow ACP; mem. Am. Diabetes Assn. (bd. dirs. N.Y. State affiliate 1982-94), Endocrine Soc. Democrat. Jewish. Avocations: skiing, tennis, sailing. Address: Lorber Tibaldi MD PC 59-45 161st St Flushing NY 11365-1414 E-mail: dll55@columbia.edu., ltrendo@aol.com.

LORBER, MORTIMER, retired physiology educator; b. N.Y.C., Aug. 30, 1926; s. Albert and Frieda (Levin) L.; m. Eileen Segal, May 20, 1956; children: Kenneth, Stephanie. BS, NYU, 1945; DMD cum laude, Harvard U., 1950, MD cum laude, 1952. Diplomate Nat. Bd. Med. Examiners. Rotating intern A.M. Billings Hosp., 1952-53; resident in hematology Mt. Sinai Hosp., N.Y.C., 1953-54, asst. resident in medicine, 1957; asst. resident medicine Georgetown U. Hosp., Washington, 1958; instr., asst. prof. dept. physiology and biophysics Georgetown U., 1959-68, assoc. prof., 1968-97; ret., 1997. Lectr. physiology U.S. Naval Dental Sch., Bethesda, Md., 1962-70, Walter Reed Army Inst. Dental Rsch., Washington, 1963-70; guest scientist Naval Med. Rsch. Inst., Bethesda, 1978-83. Contbr.: The Merck Manual, 14th-17th edits., 1982, 87, 92, 99; contbr. articles to profl. jours. Lt. USNR, 1954-56. Recipient Lederle Med. Faculty award Lederle Co., Pearl River, N.Y., 1960-63, USPHS Rsch. Career Devel. award Nat. Inst. Dental Rsch., Bethesda, 1963-70; grantee Am. Cancer Soc., USPHS. Mem. Am. Physiol. Soc., Am. Soc. Hematology, Assn. Rsch. in Vision and Ophthalmology, Internat. Assn. Dental Rsch. Jewish. Achievements include discovery that the ground substance is masked but not lost in calcification, removal of spleen is followed by a reticulocytosis that is permanent in dogs, dogs have many more young reticulocytes in their blood than man, stretching of skin increases mitoses in the rat showing physical factors can modulate DNA and cell division, adult Gaucher cells contain iron secondary to erythrophagocytosis, the spleen protects against insecticide-induced hematoxicity, biological armature provides internal stability to exocrine glands, rat lacrimal glands are stretched by their attachments and contain somatostatin, mastication reflexly increases gastroduodenal motility. Home: 5823 Osceola Rd Bethesda MD 20816-2032 E-mail: melorber@aol.com.

LORCH, ERNEST HENRY, lawyer; b. Frankfurt, Germany, Oct. 11, 1932; came to U.S., 1940; s. Alexander and Kate (Freundt) L. AB, Middlebury Coll., 1954; JD, U. Va., 1957; LLD (hon.), Fairfield U., 1987. Bar: N.Y. 1958. Assoc. Olwine, Connelly, Chase, O'Donnell & Weyher, N.Y.C., 1957-65, ptnr., 1965-84; pres., chief oper. officer Dyson-Kissner-Moran Corp., 1984-90, pres., chief exec. officer, 1990-91; chmn., chief exec. officer, 1991-92; ret., 1992; of counsel Whitman, Breed, Abbott & Morgan, N.Y.C., 1992—. Chmn. bd. dirs. Varlen Corp., Chgo.; bd. dirs. Tyler Corp., Dorsey Trailers, Inc. Dir. various inner city athletic assns., N.Y.C., 1959—; The DYSM Found., N.Y.C., 1985-92; trustee, officer, dir. The Riverside Ch., N.Y.C., 1961—; treas., dir. Wheelchair Charities Inc., Religion in American Life, 1993-96. Mem. ABA, N.Y. State Bar Assn. Office: Whitman Breed Abbott & Morgan 200 Park Ave New York NY 10166-0005

LORCH, KENNETH F. lawyer; b. Indpls., July 24, 1951; BSBA, Washington U., 1973; JD, John Marshall Sch. Law, 1976. Bar: Ill. 1976, U.S. Dist. Ct. (no. dist.) Ill. 1977; CPA, Ill. Ptnr. Wildman, Harrold, Allen & Dixon, Chgo. Mem. planned giving adv. coun. Chgo. Symphony Orch.; pres. Chgo. bd. Am. Technion Soc.; mem. planned giving steering com. City of Hope; bd. dirs. Chgo. Coun. on Planned Giving, Coun. for Jewish Elderly; mem. profl. adv. com. Chgo. Cmty. Trust. Mem. Chgo. Bar Assn. (exec. com., Cook County Probate Ct. rules and forms com., mem. legis. com., mem. probate practice com. 1991, mem. trust law com., chmn. estate planning com., mem. young lawyers sect. 1983-85), Chgo. Estate Planning Coun., Jewish Fedn. Chgo. (past chair profl. adv. com.). Office: Wildman Harrold Allen & Dixon 225 W Wacker Dr Ste 3000 Chicago IL 60606-1224

LORCH, MARISTELLA DE PANIZZA, medieval and Renaissance scholar, writer; b. Bolzano, Italy, Dec. 8, 1919; came to U.S., 1947, naturalized, 1951; d. Gino and Giuseppina (Cristoforetti) de Panizza Inama von Brunnenwald; m. Claude Bové, Feb. 10, 1944 (div. 1955); 1 child, Claudia; m. Edgar R. Lorch, Mar. 25, 1956; children: Lavinia Edgarda, Donatella Livia. *Daughters: Claudia Valeani, resident of Paris since 1969, professor of English Studies Lycee Mistral (Fresne), and Institute Universitaire Formation des Maitres. Children: Celia, Charles. Lavinia E. Lorch, PhD of Greek Literature, Columbia University, Preceptor Humanities CU and Chamberlain Fellow, assistant professor classics, Vassar College; director, Scuola New York, 1986-92, director, English Section Lycee francais de New York, 1992-99. Donatella Lorch, BA, Barnard College, MA, MIA, Columbia University, Chinese History, Oriental Studies, correspondent, New York Times, 1989-97 (Bureau Chief, East Africa), NBC foreign correspondent, London, 1997-99, correspondent, Newsweek, 1999—.* Ed., Liceo Classico, Merano, 1929-37; Dott. in Lettere e Filosofia, U. Rome, 1942; DHL (hon.), Lehman Coll., CUNY, 1993. Prof. Latin and Greek Liceo Virgilio, Rome, 1941-44; assoc. prof. Italian and German Coll. St. Elizabeth, Convent Station, N.J., 1947-51; faculty Barnard Coll. and Columbia U., 1951-90; prof. Barnard Coll., 1967—, chmn. dept., 1951-90, co-founder, chmn. medieval and renaissance program, 1972-90. Founder, dir. Ctr. for Internat. Scholarly Exch., Barnard Coll., 1980-90; dir. Casa Italiana, Columbia U., 1969-76, chmn. exec. com. Italian studies, 1980-90, founding dir. Italian Acad. Advanced Studies in Am., 1991-96, dir. emerita and dir. external rels., 1996—. Author: Critical edit. L. Valla, De vero falsoque bono, Bari, 1970, (critical edit.) Michaelida (with W. Ludwig), 1976, On Pleasure (with A. K. Hieatt), 1981, A Defense of Life: L. Valla's Theory of Pleasure, 1985, Folly and Insanity in Renaissance Literature, 1986, (with E. Grassi) All' America, 1990, Italy at the Millennium, 2001; editor: Il Teatro Italiano del Renascimento, 1981, Humanism in Rome, 1983, La Scuola, New York, 1987; mem. editorial bd. Italian jour. Romanic Review; also articles on Renaissance lit., philosophy and theater. Chmn. Am. Ariosto Centennial Celebration, 1974; chmn. bd. trustees La Scuola N.Y., 1986-92; trustee Lyceé Française de N.Y., 1986—; mem. adv. bd. Marconi Found., 1998. Decorated Cavaliere della Repubblica Italiana, 1973, Commendatore della Repubblica Italiana, 1988, Grande Ufficiale della Republica Italiana, 1996; recipient AMITA award for Woman of Yr. in Italian Lit., 1973, Columbus '92 Countdown prize of excellence in humanities, 1990, Elen Cornaro award Sons of Italy Woman of Yr., 1990, Father Ford award, 1994, hon. mem. Legendary Women, 1997. Mem. Medieval Acad. Am., Renaissance Soc. Am., Am. Assn. Tchrs. Italian, Am. Assn. Italian Studies (hon. pres. 1990-91), Internat. Assn. for Study of Italian Lit. (Am. rep., assoc. pres. 8th Congress 1973), Acad. Polit. Sci. (life), Pirandello Soc. (pres. 1972-78), Arcadia Acad. (Asteria Aretusa 1976). Home: 445 Riverside Dr New York NY 10027-6801 Office: Columbia Univ Italian Acad Adv Study Casa Italiana New York NY 10027

LORD, BARBARA JOANNI, lawyer; b. Bay Shore, N.Y., Aug. 7, 1939; d. Theodore and Doris Aileen (Smith) Joanni; m. Robert Wilder Lord, June 24, 1967. BA, U. Miami, 1961; JD, NYU, 1966. Bar: N.Y. 1967, Fla. 1978, U.S. Supreme Ct. 1991. Asst. editor Am. Best Co., N.Y.C., 1961-64; contract analyst Guardian Life Ins. Co., 1964-66; legal trainee N.Y. State Liquor Auth., 1966-67, atty., 1967-70, sr. atty., 1970-80, assoc. atty., 1980—. Mem. ABA, N.Y. State Bar Assn., Fla. Bar Assn., Order Ea. Star. Office: N Y State Liquor Authority 11 Park Pl New York NY 10007-2801

LORD, EVELYN MARLIN, mayor; b. Melrose, Mass., Dec. 8, 1926; d. John Joseph and Mary Janette (Nourse) Marlin; m. Samuel Smith Lord Jr., Feb. 28, 1948; children: Steven Arthur, Jonathan Peter, Nathaniel Edward, Victoria Marlin, William Kenneth. BA, Boston U., 1948; MA, U. Del., 1956; JD, U. Louisville, 1969. Bar: Ky. 1969, U.S. Supreme Ct. 1973. Exec. dir. Block Blight Inc., Wilmington, Del., 1956—60; mem. Del. Senate, Dover, 1960—62; administrv. asst. county judge Jefferson County, Louisville, 1968—71; corr. No. Ireland News Jour. Co., Wilmington, 1972—74; legal adminstr. Orgain, Bell & Tucker, Beaumont, Tex., 1978—83; v.p. Tex. Commerce Bank, 1983—84; councilman City of Beaumont, 1980—82, mayor pro tem, 1982—84, mayor, 1990—94, 2002—. Tourism chmn. U.S. Conf. Mayors, 1994, adv. bd., chmn. arts, culture and recreation, 1992—94; sr. counselor Ky. Bar, 2002—. Bd. dirs. Symphony Soc. S.E. Tex., 1990-98, 2002-, Found. S.E. Tex., 1990—, Evelyn M. Lord Teen Ct., 1993—, Lincoln Inst., 1994-2001, Beaumont Pub. Schs. Found., 1999, Ptnrs. for Children, Child Protective Svcs.; trustee United Way, Beaumont, 1990—, pres., 1994, 97; mem. adv. bd. Boy Scouts Am., Three Rivers, 1978-84, 89-94, mem. exec. bd., 2000—; mem. adv. bd. Lamar U. Found., 1997-99, trustee, 1999—; pres. Girl Scouts Am., Kentuckiana Coun., 1966-70, Tex. Energy Mus., 1995-2001; active Sister City Commn.; chmn. Fed. Emergency Mgmt. Agy., 1997-98; bd. dirs., trustee Leadership Edn. Found., 1995-2001, Lincoln Found., 1994-2001; chmn. Spindletop 2001 Com. Named Disting. Law Alumni, U. Louisville, Citizen of Yr., Sales and Mktg. Assn., 1990, Beaumont Man of the Yr., 1993, Womann with Heart, Am. Heart Assn., 2000, Free Ent. Person of the Yr., Assn. Bldg. Contrs., 2000, Newsmaker of the Yr., Press Club Jefferson County, 2001, Hurricane Evelyn, ARC, 2001; recipient Silver Beaver award, Boy Scouts Am., Beaumont, 1979, Disting. Alumni award, Boston U., 1983, Disting. Leadership award, Nat. Assn. Leadership Orgns., Indpls., 1991, Labor-Mgmt. Pub. Sector award, 1991, Disting. Grad. award, Leadership Beaumont, 1993, Rotary Svc. Above Self award, 1994, Excellency award, Tex. State Hist. Commn., 2001. Mem. LWV (Del. state pres. 1960-62, bd. dirs. Tex. 1978-80), Bus. and Profl. Women Assns. (Woman of Yr. 1983), 100 Club (pres. 1995-97), Girl Scouts Am. (life), Rotary (hon.), Sigma Kappa (life), Phi Kappa Phi, Delta Kappa Gamma (hon.), Sigma Iota Epsilon (hon.). Avocations: writing, reading, African violets, genealogy. Home: 1240 Nottingham Ln Beaumont TX 77706-4316 *Basically - I believe in "blooming where you're planted". Life with my husband has taken me all over the world but we've always managed to be "at home" wherever we've been able to give a bit of ourselves.*

LORD, GEORGE DEFOREST, English educator; b. N.Y.C., Dec. 2, 1919; s. George deForest and Hazen (Symington) L.; m. Ruth Ellen du Pont, Mar. 22, 1947 (div. 1978); children: Pauline, George deForest Jr., Edith (dec.), Henry; m. Louise Robins Hendrix, 1978 (div. 1992); m. Marcia Adkisson Babbidge, 1993. BA, Yale U., 1942, PhD, 1951. Instr. English Yale U., New Haven, 1947-66, prof., 1966—. Master Trumbull Coll., 1963-66, dir. directed studies, 1968-70, assoc. chmn. English dept., 1983-86; dir. Fiduciary Trust, N.Y., 1969-91; cons. PBS TV program Transformations of Myth Through Time, 1982-90; lectr. in field. Author: Homeric Renaissance: the "Odyssey" of George Chapman, 1956, Poems on Affairs of State, 1963, Andrew Marvell, Complete Poetry, 1968, rev. edit., 1985, Andrew Marvell: A Collection of Critical Essays, 1968, Anthology of Poems on Affairs of State, 1975, Heroic Mockery: Variations on Epic Themes from Homer to Joyce, 1977, Trials of the Self: Heroic Ordeals in the Epic Tradition, 1983, Classical Presences in Seventeenth-Century English Poetry, 1987 (Outstanding acad. book 1987 Choice mag.); gen. editor Poems on Affairs of State: Augustan Satirical Verse: 1660-1714, 7 vols., 1963-75; contbr. articles, revs. to acad. jours. Trustee Winterthur Mus., 1952-80, Mary Holmes Coll., West Point, Miss., 1971-80, Fair Haven Housing, 1972-78; trustee, advisor Outward Bound USA, 1977-92; vestryman Calvary Episcopal Ch., Stonington, Conn., 1986-89. Morse fellow 1954-55, NEH sr. fellow, 1982. Mem. MLA, English Inst., Renaissance Soc. Am., Am. Acad. in Rome, The Century Assn. Home: 3 Diving St Stonington CT 06378-1405 Office: Yale U Dept English New Haven CT 06520 E-mail: glord63452@aol.com.

LORD, HAROLD WILBUR, electrical engineer, electronics consultant; b. Eureka, Calif., Aug. 20, 1905; s. Charles Wilbur and Rossina Camilla (Hansen) L.; m. Doris Shirley Huff, July 25, 1928; children: Joann Shirley (Mrs. Carl Cook Disbrow), Alan Wilbur, Nancy Louise (Mrs. Leslie Crandall), Harold Wayne. BS, Calif. Inst. Tech., 1926. With GE, Schenectady, N.Y., 1926-66, electronics engr., 1960-66; pvt. cons. engr. Mill Valley, Calif., 1966-90. Contbr. articles to profl. jours.; patentee in field. Fellow IEEE (life, tech. v.p. 1962, Centennial medal 1984, IEEE Magnetics Soc. Achievement award 1984, 3d Millenium medal 2000). Home: 1565 Golf Course Dr Rohnert Park CA 94928-5638

LORD, JACQUELINE WARD, accountant, photographer, artist; b. Andalusia, Ala., May 16, 1936; d. Marron J. and Minnie V. (Owen) Ward; m. Curtis Gaynor, Nov. 23, 1968. Student U. Ala., 1966, Auburn U., 1977, Huntingdon Coll., 1980, Troy State U., 1980; BA in Bus. Adminstrn., Dallas Bapt. U., 1985. News photographer corr. Andalusia (Ala.) Star-News, 1954-59, Sta. WSFA-TV, Montgomery, Ala., 1954-60; acct., bus. mgr. Reihardt Motors, Inc., Montgomery, 1962-69; office mgr., acct. Cen. Ala. Supply, Montgomery, 1969-71; acct. Chambers Constrn. Co., Montgomery, 1972-75; pres. Foxy Lady Apparel, Inc., Montgomery, 1973-76; acct. Rushton, Stakely, Johnston & Garrett, attys., Montgomery, 1975-81; acctg. supr. Arthur Andersen & Co., Dallas, 1981-82; staff acct. Burgess Co., C.P.A.s, Dallas, 1983; owner Lord & Assocs. Acctg. Svc., Dallas, 1983—; tax acct. John Hasse, C.P.A., Dallas, 1984-86; Dallas Bapt. Assn., 1986—. Vol. election law commr. Sec. of State of Ala. Don Siegelman, Montgomery, 1979-80; mem. Montgomery Art Guild, 1964-65, Ala. Art League, 1964-65, Montgomery Little Theatre, 1963-65, Montgomery Choral Soc., 1965. Recipient Outstanding Achievement Bus. Mgmt. award Am. Motors, 1968. Mem. Am. Soc. Women Accts. (pres. Montgomery chpt. 1976-77, area day chmn. 1978, del. ann. meeting 1975-78), Soroptimists Internat. (pres. elect Montgomery chpt. 1975-76), Nat. Assn. Ch. Bus. Adminstrn. Home: 5209 Meadowside Dr Garland TX 75043-2731

LORD, JAMES GREGORY, organizational and philanthropic counsel to consultants; b. Cleve., Aug. 23, 1947; s. James Nelson and Esther L.; children: Michael Richard, Rebecca Esther. Student U. Md., Far East Campus, 1966-68, Cleve. State U., 1968-72; m. Wendy Franklin, July 10, 1977. TV news prodr. Far East Network, Tokyo, 1965-68; wire editor News-Herald, Willoughby, Ohio, 1968-69; pub. rels. assoc. United Way, Cleve., 1969-70; free-lance pub. rels. person, Cleve., 1970-72; dir. pub. rels. Ketchum, Inc., Pitts., 1972-77; cons. devel. philanthropic instns., Cleve., 1977—; cons. White House Endowment Fund, Washington, 1983-94, Vatican Info. Svc., Vatican City, 1993, Nat. 4-H, Chevy Chase Md., 1994-95, United Religions, San Francisco, 1996; assoc. Cambridge (Eng.) Partnership for Orgnl. Transformation, Cambridge U., 1995—; chief devel. officer Cleve. Mus. Art, 1984-85; vis. fellow St. Mary's Coll., 1993; chair Mgmt. of Change Think Tank, 1993; disting. fellow Mt. Vernon Inst., 1995; developer The Philanthropic Quest Methodology, 1995-97; del. United Religions Charter Writing Summit, 1996; frequent keynote spkr. including United Way of Can., Ottawa, 1995; sponsor Crossing Boundaries: Building Creative Partnerships Conf., 1996; presenter Embarking on the Quest seminar, Cambridge (Eng.) U., 1995-97; founder Philanthropic Quest Internat., 1995. With USN, 1964-68, Japan. Author: Philanthropy and Marketing, 7th edit., 1981, The Raising of Money, 1983 (nat. and internat. bestseller), Communicating with Donors, 1984, Building Your Case, 1984, The Campaign Manuals, 1985, The Development Consultant, 1985, Guide for the Professional, 2d edit., 1986, Philanthropic Quest series of 9 books, 1996, The Practice of the Quest series of 5 books, 1998, Translating the Quest to Volunteers Monograph, 1996, The Age of Possibility, 2002, presenter, Embarking on the Quest Seminar, Cambridge Univ., Eng., 1995-2002; editor: Results! Time Management System, 1986, Market Smart, 1988, The Campaign Letter, Non-Profit Mgmt. Report; contbr. numerous articles on philanthropy, mktg. and quality of life in Am. cities to various publs.; developed one-man photography exhbns., 15 worldwide sites, 1968-72; founder Appreciative Inquiry Consulting, 2001. Home: 28050 S Woodland Rd Cleveland OH 44124-5638

LORD, JERE JOHNS, retired physics educator; b. Portland, Oreg., Jan. 3, 1922; s. Percy Samuel and Hazel Marie (Worstel) L.; m. Miriam E. Hart, Dec. 30, 1947; children— David, Roger, Douglas. Physicist U. Calif. Radiation Lab., Berkeley, 1942-46; research asso. U. Chgo., 1950-52; asst. prof. physics U. Wash., Seattle, 1952-57, assoc. prof., 1957-62, prof., 1962-92, prof. emeritus, 1992—. Fellow AAAS, Am. Phys. Soc.; mem. Am. Assn. Physics Tchrs. Home: 720 Seneca St Apt 1004 Seattle WA 98101-2766 Office: U Wash Dept Physics Box 351560 Seattle WA 98195-1560

LORD, KATHLEEN VIRGINIA ANDERSON, fundraising executive, educator; b. Lakewood, Ohio, Feb. 11, 1934; d. Wallace Matthew and Ernestine (McNutt) Anderson; m. Donald Charles Lord, Feb. 9, 1954 (div. June 1978); children: Maurita Beth, Sean Christopher. Student, Oberlin Coll., 1951-52; BS in Theater and Music with honors, Tex. Woman's U., 1972, MA in English and Drama, 1974; postgrad., Ohio U., 1977-80. Advt. supr. Cleve. Plain Dealer, 1954-61; devel. dir. Denton (Tex.) Christian Pre-Sch., 1970-72; asst. prof. Unity (Maine) Coll., 1972-80; dir. alumni rels. and ann. fund Ashland (Ohio) U., 1980-85; dir. devel. Pa. Stage Co., Allentown, 1985-86; dir. devel. and pub. rels. Singing City Choir, Phila., 1986-88; pvt. practice cons. for philanthropy and pub. rels., 1988-92; dir. major gifts/planned giving Luther Care, Lititz, 1992-98; adj. prof. Lebanon Valley Coll., Annville, 1998—2000. Contralto Dallas Civic Opera Co., 1966-72. Author: (drama) Once There Was A Camelot, 1973. Pres. Pa./Md. chpt. ALDE, 1995-98; bd. dirs., pres. Opera Outreach, Harrisburg, Pa., 1997—; v.p. Central Pa. Luth. Credit Union, 1996-2001. Coun. Advancement and Support of Edn. scholar, 1981. Mem. Nat. Soc. Fund Raising Execs. (cert., Franklin Form com., chair diversity com., membership com. presenter 1986—), Ohio Conf. Women in Minorities in Higher Edn. (exec. com. 1983-84, adv. com.), Ind. Coll. Adminstrs. Assn. of Ohio (bd. dirs., exec. com. 1982-83), Coun. Advancement and Support Edn. (presenter, moderator 1982-83). Lutheran. Avocation: singing.

LORD, M. G. writer; b. La Jolla, Calif., Nov. 18; d. Charles Carroll and Mary (Pfister) L.; m. Glenn Horowitz, May 19, 1985 BA, Yale U. Reporter N.Y. Bur., Wall Street Jour., N.Y.C.; editl. artist Chgo. Tribune; editl. cartoonist, columnist Newsday, N.Y.C., 1979-94. Cartoons syndicated L.A. Times Syndicate, 1984-89; column syndicated Copley News Svc., 1989-94; resident humanities fellow U. Mich., 1986-87. Author: Mean Sheets, 1982, Prig Tales, 1990, Forever Barbie: The Unauthorized Biography of a Real Doll, 1994; columnist Preservation, 1996—. Resident humanities fellow U. Mich., 1986-87. Office: care Eric Simonoff Janklow & Nesbit Assoc 445 Park Ave New York NY 10022-2606

LORD, MARVIN, apparel company executive; b. N.Y.C., Sept. 22, 1937; s. Harry and Irene (Taub) L.; m. Joan Simon, Aug. 5, 1961; children— Elisa Anne, Michael Harris BS, Long Island U., Bklyn., 1959. Mdse. mgr. Oxford Industries, Inc., N.Y.C., 1964-66, gen. mdse. mgr., 1966-70, v.p., gen. mgr., 1970-73; pres. Holbrook Co., Inc. Div Oxford Industries, Inc., 1970-85; pres., chief exec. officer Crystal Brands, Inc.-Youthwear Group, 1985—; pres. Cluett Shirtmakers, 1988—, M.L. Enterprises, Roslyn Heights, N.Y., 1990—; pres., chief oper. officer Sanyo Fashion House, N.Y.C., 1991—; pres., CEO MAternity Resources Inc., 1994—; exec. v.p. E.A. Hughes & Co., 1996—. Chmn. Fathers Day Coun., N.Y.C., 1984—; bd. dirs. Nat. Conf. Cmty. and Justice, 1997, Fashion Inst. of Tech., 1997. Recipient Disting. Alumni award L.I. U., 1987. Mem. Mens Fashion Assn., Young Menswear Assn. Jewish. Avocation: tennis. Home: 53 Parkway Dr Roslyn Heights NY 11577-2705 Office: E A Hughes & Co 146 E 37th St New York NY 10016-3108 Business E-Mail: mlord@eahughes.com.

LORD, MIA W. world peace and disarmament activist; b. N.Y.C., Dec. 2, 1911; m. Robert P. Lord (dec. Nov. 1977); children: Marcia Louise, Alison Jane. BA in Liberal Arts cum laude, Bklyn. Coll., 1935; postgrad., San Francisco State U., 1984—99. Hon. sec. Commonwealth of World Citizens, London; membership sec. Brit. Assn. for World Govt.; sec. Ams. in Brit. for U.S. Withdrawal from S.E. Asia, Eng.; organizer Vietnam Vigil to End the War, London; pres. Let's Abolish War chpt. World Federalist Assn., San Francisco State U. Appointed hon. sec. Commonwealth of World Citizens, London; officially invited to Vietnam, 1973; organizer Vietnam Vigil to End the War, London. Author: The Practical Way to End Wars and Other World Crises: the case for World Federal Government: listed in World Peace through World Law, 1984, and in Strengthening the United Nations, 1987, War: The Biggest Con Game in the World, 1980. Hon. sec., nat. exec. mem. Assn. of World Federalists-U.K.; founder, bd. dirs. Crusade to Abolish War and Armaments by World Law. Nominated for the Nobel Peace Prize, 1975, 92, 93; recipient four Merit awards Pres. San Francisco State U. Mem. Secretariat of World Citizens USA (life), Assn. of World Federalists USA, Brit. Assn. for World Govt. (membership sec.), Crusade to Abolish War and Armaments by World Law (founder, dir.), World Govt. Orgn. Coord. Com., World Fed. Authority Com., Campaign for UN Reform, Citizens Global Action, World Constitution and Parliament Assn., World Pub. Forum, Internat. Registry of World Citizens. Home: 174 Majestic Ave San Francisco CA 94112-3022

LORD, RICHARD DENNIS, photographer; b. Cleve., June 22, 1951; s. James Nelson and Esther (Pollock) L.; m. Patricia L. Michelsen, July 14, 1974 (div. Apr. 1987); children: Tanya, Michele, Arthur; m. Michelle Nante, Nov. 23, 2001. BA, Boston U., 1973, MA, 1975; postgrad., U. Copenhagen, 1974-75. Pres. The Mgmt. Group, N.Y.C., 1987-91; pvt. practice photographer, 1991—. Lectr. NYU, N.Y.C., 1989, Seton Hall U., West Orange, N.J., 1989-90, Pace U., White Plains, N.Y., 1990-91; cons. in field, 1986-90. Author: The Management Reports, 1987, The Non Profit Problem Solver, 1989; photo exhibits at UN Gen. Assembly, Parsons Gallery, N.Y.C., Boston Ctr. for the Arts, Otis Art Inst., L.A. Trustee City and County Sch., N.Y.C., 1986-88; mem. Hells Kitchen Neighborhood Assn., N.Y.C. Recipient Photography awards Religious Communicators Coun., UMAC. Mem. Advt. Photographers of Am., Am. Soc. Media Photographers, United Meth. Assn. Comm., Phi Beta Kappa. Office: 408 W 34th St Apt 2E New York NY 10001-2340 E-mail: rlord@rlordphoto.com.

LORD, ROBERT WILDER, retired editor and writer; b. Keene, N.H., May 14, 1917; s. Edward Brown Lord and Alice Maria Buffum; m. Helen Burgess, Aug. 31, 1940 (div. 1965); children: Rowena Lord Soteros, Robert W. Jr., Richard E.B.; m. Barbara Lillian Joanni, June 24, 1967. AB with honors, Middlebury Coll., 1939; MA, NYU, 1964. Chartered Life Underwriter, Am. Coll., Bryn Mawr, Pa., 1944. Writer Prudential Ins. Co. of Am., Newark, 1939-44; editor Flitcraft, Inc., Oak Park, Ill., 1944-48; editor, v.p. Flitcraft A.M. Best Co., N.Y.C., 1948-65; editor, v.p. Communication Channels, 1966-74; freelance writer, 1974-96; ret., 1996. Cons. to ins. orgns.; dir. ins.-connected corps. and ins. co. Author: Running Conventions, Conferences, and Meetings, 1981; former editor 25 books, mags. and newsletters; contbr. numerous articles to ins. publs., newspapers, and mags. Active in neighborhood improvement orgns., N.Y.C. Recipient Vol. of Yr. award, Conf. of Patriotic and Hist. Socs. N.Y., 2001, Conf. of Patriotic and Hist. Socs., N.Y.C., 2001. Mem. Soc. Fin. Svc. Profls., Alden Kindred Am., Buffum Family Assn., Wilder Assn., Soc. Mayflower Descs., Soc. Colonial Wars, Sons of the Revolution (bd. mgrs.), Soc. War of 1812, Sons of Union Vets. of the Civil War, Sons of Confederate Vets., Navy League of U.S., Masons. Avocations: military history, languages, coins, books, military relics, travel. Home: 61 Jane St Apt 12P New York NY 10014-5138

LORD, TIMOTHY CHARLES, philosophy educator; b. Elizabethtown, Ky., Nov. 5, 1960; s. David George and Maizie Joyce (Holmes) L.; m. Nancy Cecile DeJoy, Dec. 23, 1995 (div. Dec. 2000). BA, Cedarville Col., 1985; MA, Iowa State U., 1987, Purdue U., 1991, PhD, 1995. Prof. of Philosophy Heartland C.C., Bloomington, Ill., 1993—. Chair Philosophy/Religion Dept. Heartland C.C., Bloomington, Ill., 1993-99. Contbr. articles to profl. jours.; manuscript reviewer profl. jours. Mem. Am. Philosophical Assn. (mem. philosophy in 2-yr. colls. com. 2000-03), Soc. for Phenomenology and Existential Philosophy, Am. Soc. for Aesthetics, Internat. Assn. for Philosophy and Literature, Am. Assn. for Philosophy Tchrs., R.G. Collingwood Soc., Phi Kappa Phi. Office: Heartland CC 1500 W Raab Rd Normal IL 61761 E-mail: tim.lord@hcc.cc.il.us.

LORDI, KATHERINE MARY, lawyer; b. Jersey City, Mar. 24, 1949; d. Peter G. and Hilde E. (Illy) L. AB, Trinity Coll., Washington, 1971; JD, Fordham U., 1975. Bar: N.J. 1975, U.S. Supreme Ct. 1983, U.S. Dist. Ct. N.J. 1975, U.S. Ct. Appeals (3rd cir.) 1989. Clk. Friedman & D'Allessandro, East Orange, N.J., 1974-75; assoc., 1975-76; pvt. practice Bloomfield, N.J., 1976—. Adj. instr. Coll. St. Elizabeth, Convent Station, N.J., 1978-86, adj. prof., 1986—; legal adviser Mcpl. Ct. Clks. Assn., 1977-84. Notes editor: Fordham Urban Law Jour., 1974-75. Trustee Cath. Family and Cmty. Svcs, 1980—, v.p., 1986—; mem. adv. bd. Acad. St. Elizabeth, Convent Station, N.J., 1980-84; mem. Essex County Adv. Bd. Status on Women, 1983-92, chmn., 1985-88, co-chair, 1990-92; trustee New Sch. for Arts, 1988-89, Family Svc. League, Inc., 1986-2000, pres. 1991-94. Fellow: Royal Soc. Encouragement of Arts, Manufactures and Commerce; mem.: ATLA, ABA, Bloomfield C. of C. (trustee 1986—94, v.p. legis. 1990—94), Essex County Bar Assn., NJ Bar Assn., Bloomfield Lawyers Club (pres. 1983—84). Roman Catholic. Office: 54 Fremont St Bloomfield NJ 07003-3428 E-mail: k.lordi@worldnet.att.net.

LORDI, WILLIAM MICHAEL, psychiatrist, child psychiatrist; b. N.Y.C., Apr. 5, 1923; s. Michael Angelo and Lillian Elizabeth Lordi; m. Elizabeth Ann Lordi, June 20, 1948 (div. Sept. 1972); m. Beverly Cooke, Sept. 24, 1972; children: Jeanine, Randall, Deidre. BS, Colgate U., 1945; MD, L.I. Coll. Medicine, 1949. Intern USN Hosp., N.Y.C., 1949-52; resident in psychiatry and child psychiatry USPH Hosp., Lexington, Ky., 1950-54, U. Ohio Med. Sch., Cin., 1950-54, Louisville Child Guidance Clinic, 1952—; resident child psychiatry Columbus Child Med Ctr., 1955-57; med. dir. Meml. Guild Clinic, Richmond, Va., 1957-66, Meml. Found. Home, Richmond, 1957—; CEO, med. dir. Commonwealth Psychiat. Hosp., 1971-81. Dir. group psychotherapy group, 1971-81. Contbr. articles to profl. publs. Cons. Chesterfield Pub. Schs., 1957-90, Ea., Ctrl. and Western State Hosp., 1957-90. Surgeon USPHS, 1950-54. Life fellow Am. Psychiatric Assn.; mem. Am. Psychiat. Assn. Avocations: painting, music. Home and Office: 7100 Covebrook Ln Mechanicsville VA 23116-4833

LORD MARSHALL OF KNIGHTSBRIDGE, See LORD MARSHALL, COLIN

LORE, MARTIN MAXWELL, lawyer; b. Milw., June 13, 1914; s. Michael and Jean (Dinerstein) L.; m. Doris Silver, Mar. 19, 1944; children: Amy L. Kovner, Dr. Cathy Jo. BA, U. Wis., 1934, LLB, 1936; LLM, Harvard, 1937; BCS, Strayer Coll. Accountancy, 1939. Bar: Wis. 1936, N.Y. 1946, D.C. 1947, Fla. 1977, U.S. Supreme Ct. 1939; CPA, D.C. Assoc. Rubin, Zabel & Ruppa, Milw., 1936-37; with Office Undersec. Treasury, 1937-38; spl. atty. office chief counsel, bur. IRS, 1938-40; trial counsel IRS (New Eng. div. tech. staff), 1940-42, IRS (N.Y. div.), 1945-47; tax counsel S.J. Foosaner, Newark, 1947-48; pvt. law practice N.Y.C., 1948-72; mem. firm Zissu Lore Halper & Robson, 1972-76, counsel, 1976-80; ptnr. Lore & Levy, N.Y.C., 1981—. Pres. bd. Fed. Tax Forum, Inc.; lectr. Tax Workshop, 1953-55, law sch. St. John's U., 1954, Fairleigh Dickinson U., 1955-56; specialist fed. tax matters, lectr. taxation NYU, 1946-50, 65, Practising Law Inst., 1947-48, Tax Inst., 1948, Pa. State Coll., 1949-50, U. W.Va., U. San Francisco, 1951, SUNY, Stony Brook, 1978-79; tax cons. Med. Econs.; pres. Estate Planning Coun. N.Y.C., 1968-69;

part-time employee Melnik & Karan, Milw., 1933-36. Author: The Administration of The Federal Income Tax Through the United States Board of Tax Appeals, 1937, How to Win a Tax Case, 1955, Thin Capitalization, 1958; co-editor: Jour. of Taxation; chmn. bd. editors: How To Work with the Internal Revenue Code of 1954; contbr. articles to legal and accounting jours. Lt. comdr. Office Gen. Counsel, USNR, 1942-44. Mem. ABA (com. income taxation estates and trusts), N.Y. State Bar Assn., Assn. Bar City of N.Y. (taxation com., com. on trusts, estates and surrogate's cts.), FBA (chmn. com. fed. taxation), AICPA (sec. fed. tax lawyers com.), D.C. Accts., County Lawyers Assn. (taxation com.), Seawane Club (bd. govs.), Lawyers Club (N.Y.C.), Harvard Club (N.Y.C.), Barristers (Washington). Home: 46 Broome Ave Atlantic Beach NY 11509-1214 Office: Lore & Levy 711 3rd Ave Fl 15 New York NY 10017-4014

LOREDO, LINDA S. marketing executive; b. Newark, Mar. 30, 1959; d. Charles Frances and Mary Josephine Loredo. With Dolls by Consolidated Enterprise, Roselle Park, N.J. Office: Dolls by Consolidated 440 E Westfield Ave Roselle Park NJ 07204-2432

LORELLI, MICHAEL KEVIN, consumer products and services executive; b. N.Y.C., Apr. 17, 1951; s. Domenic and Effie (Stankevich) L.; m. Nancy Buck; children: Karen, Elizabeth. BE, NYU, 1972, MBA in Mktg., 1973. Dir. mktg. Clairol Co., N.Y.C., 1973-81, v.p., gen. mgr. divsn. Almay cosmetics, 1983-84; v.p., gen. mgr. internat. div. Playtex, Stamford, Conn., 1981-84; v.p. mktg. Apple Computer, Cupertino, Calif., 1984-85; exec. v.p. Pepsi-Cola Co., Somers, N.Y., 1985-88; pres. Pepsi-Cola East, 1989-92, Pizza Hut Internat., 1993-95; pres. America's divsn. Tambrands, Inc., White Plains, N.Y., 1995-96; ptnr. Bryant Ptnrs. L.L.C., 1997-99; v.p., chief devel. officer Air Express Internat., Darien, Conn., 1999-2001; pres., CEO Strategic Optical Holdings, Inc., Yonkers, NY, 2001—; CEO Lens Express Inc., Deerfield Beach, Fla., 2001—. Mem. Inst. for Cancer Prevention. Author: (children's book) Traveling Again, Dad? Bd. dirs. Trident Internat., Inc., Closure Inc., Keep Am. Beautiful, Rosenbluth Travel; trustee Sarah Lawrence Coll., Madison Sq. Boys and Girls Club. Republican. Roman Catholic. Avocations: flying, golf, running.

LOREN, DONALD PATRICK, naval officer; b. N.Y.C., Mar. 17, 1952; s. Nicholas A. and Helen T. (Carrado) L.; m. Maureen M. Lynch, Jan. 12, 1991. BS in Ops. Analysis, U.S. Naval Acad., 1974; MS in Edn., Old Dominion U., 1983; postgrad., Harvard U., 1993-94, MIT, 1994-95. Commd. ens. USN, 1974, advanced through grades to rear adm., combat sys. officer, Destroyer Squadron Thirty-One, 1978; ops. officer USS Peterson, 1979-80; ops. and readiness officer Destroyer Squadron Two Staff, 1981-82; asst. chief of staff for comms. Cruiser Destroyer Group Eight Staff, 1983-85; exec. officer USS John Hancock, 1985-86; flag sec. to comdr. in chief U.S. Naval Forces, Europe, 1986-88; NATO policy officer Strategic Plans and Policy Directory, Joint Staff, 1989-91; comdg. officer USS Elrod FFG-55, 1991-93; doctrine devel. officer Naval Doctrine Command, 1993; fed. exec. fellow Ctr. for Internat. Affairs Harvard U., Cambridge, Mass., 1993-94; profl. staff mem. Ind. Commn. on Roles and Missions of Armed Forces, 1993-94; comdr. Destroyer Squadron Twenty-eight, Norfolk, Va., 1995-97; dep. dir. strategy and policy divsn. Office the the Chief of Naval Ops., 1997-98; exec. asst. to comdr. in chief U.S. Naval Forces Europe, 1998—2001; and comdr. in chief Allied Forces So. Europe, 1998—2001; exec. asst., prin. advisor to operational comdr. NATO Combat Forces, 1999—2001; dep. dir. surface ships Office of the Chief of Naval Ops., 2001—. Fellow MIT, Seminar XXI, fgn. politics, internat. rels. and the nat. interest, 1994-95. Author: Shape Up! A Shipboard Program for Physical Fitness, 1981; contbr. articles to profl. publs. Mem. Phi Kappa Phi, Sigma Iota Epsilon. Avocations: jogging, weight training, classical music, ballet, opera. Office: Dir Surface Ships Office of the Chief of Naval Ops N76E, 2000 Navy Pentagon Washington DC 20350-2000

LOREN, SOPHIA, actress; b. Rome, Sept. 20, 1934; d. Riccardo Scicolone and Romilda Villani; m. Carlo Ponti, Apr. 12, 1967; children: Carlo Ponti, Edoardo. Student, Scuole Magistrali Superiori. Films include E Arrivato l'Accordatore, 1951, Africa sotto i Mari, La Favorita, La Tratta Delle Bianche, 1952, Aida, Tempi Nostri, Ci Troviamo in Gellera, La Domenica Della Buona Genti, Il Paese dei Campanelli, Un Giorno in Pretura, Due Notti con Cleopatra, Pelegrini d'Amore, Attila, Carosello Napoletano, 1953, Miseria e Nobilta, Gold of Naples, Woman of the River, Too Bad She's Bad (Best Actress award Buenos Aires Festival), 1954, Lucky To Be A Woman, Sign of Venus, The Millers Wife, Scandal in Sorrento, 1955, Pride and Passion, Boy on a Dolphin, Legend of The Lost, 1957, Desire Under the Elms, Houseboat, The Key (Best Actress award Japan), 1958, That Kind of Woman, Black Orchid, 1959 (Best Actress Venice Festival, David Di Donatello award Italy, Victoire Popularity award France), Heller in Pink Tights (Best Actress Rapallo Festival Italy), It Started in Naples, A Breath of Scandal, The Millionaires, 1960, Two Women, (11 Best Actress awards including Oscar, Hollywood, Di Donatello award, Cannes Film Festival, N.Y. Critics, Golden Globe, Brit. Film Acad., others from Ireland, Japan, Belgium, Spain, France, W. Ger., also other awards), El Cid, Madame, Bocaccio 70, 1961, The Condemned of Altona, Five Miles to Midnight, 1962, Yesterday, Today and Tomorrow, (Best Actress Di Donatello award, Golden Globe award), 1963, The Fall of the Roman Empire, Marriage Italian Style, 1964 (Best Actress Di Donatello award, Golden Globe award, Alexander Korda award Brit. Film Inst., others), Operation Crossbow, Lady L, Judith, 1965, Arabesque, A Countess From Hong Kong, 1966, Happily Ever After, Ghosts, Italian Style (Best Fgn. Actress Diploma USSR), 1967, More Than A Miracle, (Ramo d'Oro award Italy, other awards), 1968, Sunflower (Best Actress Di Donatello award), 1969, The Priest's Wife, 1970, Lady Liberty, White Sister, 1971, Man of La Mancha, 1972, The Voyage (Di Donatello award), 1973, Brief Encounter, The Verdict, 1974, The Cassandra Crossing, A Special Day, 1977, Firepower, 1978, Brass Target, 1979, Blood Feud, 1981, Grumpier Old Men, 1995, Messages, 1996, Soleil, 1997, Destinazione Verna, 1999; TV film appearances include Sophia Loren: Her Own Story, 1980, Angela, 1982, Aurora, 1985, Mother Courage, 1986, The Fortunate Pilgrim (Best Actress of Yr. for TV mini-series), 1987, La Ciociara, 1989, Ready to Wear (Prêt-à-Porter), 1994. Recipient numerous awards including Nastro d'Argento, Italy, 14 Bambi and Bravo Popularity awards, Fed. Republic Germany, 3 Prix Uilenspiegol Fiamingo award, Belgium, Popularity awards Am. Legion, Tex. Cinema Exhibitors, 4 Snosiki Popularity awards, Finland, 2 Best Actress awards Bengal Film Journalists Assn., India, Box-Office Favourite Medal, Italy, Helene Curtis award, U.S.A., Simpatia Popularity award, Italy, Rudolph Valentino Screen Svcs. award, Italy, Best Actress award Moscow Film Festival, Hon. Acad. award, 1990; named Most Popular Actress in Italy. Address: c/o La Concordia Ranch 1151 Hidden Valley Ranch Rd Thousand Oaks CA 91361

LORENCE, JAMES J. historian, educator; b. Racine, Wis., Nov. 18, 1937; s. Leonard F. Lorence and Ruth E. Parmenter; m. Donna May Nyiri, Aug. 20, 1960; children: Christine, Juliet. BS, U. Wis., Milw., 1960, MS, 1964; PhD U. Wis., Madison, 1970. Prof. history U. Wis.-Marathon County, Wausau, 1966—2001; Eminent Scholar of History Gainesville (Ga.) Coll., 2001—. Project dir. History Tchg. Alliance, Wausau, 1986—2001; founder, project dir. Marathon County History Tchg. Alliance; chmn. dept. history U. Wis. Colls.; chmn. senate U. Wis. Colls. Author: Suppression of Salt of the Earth, 1999, Organizing the Unemployed, 1996, G.J. Boileau and the Progressive Farmer-Labor Alliance, 1994. Recipient Gov.'s award, Wis. Humanities Coun., 2000, Kenneth Kingery award, Coun. Wis. Writers, 2000, Carnegie/Case Wis. Professor of Year award, 1994. Mem.: Soc. Historians of Am. Fgn. Rels., Orgn. Am. Historians (nom. bd. 2001—), Am. Hist. Assn. (tchr. divsn. 1993—95). Democrat. Unitarian Universalist. Home: 4709 Plantation Dr Flowery Branch GA 30542 Office: Gainesville Coll PO Box 1358 Gainesville GA 30503

LORENSEN, FREDERICK HAMILTON, educational administrator, consultant; b. Bridgeport, Conn., Nov. 12, 1943; s. Frederick Irving and Virginia Francis (Hamilton) L.; m. Ruth Ann Hogan, July 8, 1967; children: Lisa, Erik, Kevin. BA, Fairfield (Conn.) U., 1965, MEd, 1966; PhD, U. Conn., 1979. Tchr. social studies Masuk H.S., Monroe, Conn., 1966-67; admissions counselor Fairfield U., 1967-69, assoc. dir. admissions, 1969-79; dir. admissions Duquesne U., Pitts., 1979-91, dir. freshman devel. and spl. student svcs., 1991—. Cons. scholarships Ednl. Teseting Svc., Princeton, N.J., 1986—, Alcoa, Pitts., 1991-99; ednl. cons. Northwood Realty, Pitts., 1986-96; presenter numerous workshops. Mem. acad. excellence com. North Allegheny H.S., Wexford, Pa., 1986; Cub Scout pack leader Boy Scouts Am., Wexford, 1980-82. Recipient Loyola award Fairfield (Conn.) U., 1965, Svc. award Nat. Assn. Coll. Admissions Counselors, 1985, Presdl. Staff Excellence award, Duquesne U., 2000; Glee Club scholar Fairfield U., 1964-65, Dissertation fellow U. Conn., 1978. Mem. Nat. Orientation Dirs. Assn., Middle States Assn. Registrars and Officers of Admissions (pres. 1990-91, named hon. mem. 1999), Assn. on Higher Edn. and Disability. Roman Catholic. Avocations: reading, swimming. Office: Duquesne U 309 Duquesne Un Pittsburgh PA 15282-0001 E-mail: lorensen@duq.edu.

LORENTE, RODERICK DANA, optometrist; b. Lynn, Mass., Mar. 9, 1949; s. Roderick Mariano and Cassie V. (Petrykowski) L.; m. Carol Ann London, Jan. 1, 1972 (div. 1987); m. Mary Carlstrom, June 13, 1993. BA, Northeastern U., 1971; OD, New Eng. Coll., 1975. Optometrist G. Burtt Holmes & Assoc., Worcester, Mass., 1975-83, Peabody Med. Assocs. (was Med. East Community Health Plan), Peabody, 1986-98, D'Ambrosio Eye Care, 1998; pvt. practice Belmont, Mass., 1979-84; mgr. clin. programs Soft Contact Lens div. Am. Optical (named changed to Ciba Vision Care), Framingham, 1984-86, Atlanta, 1984-86. Asst. prof. New Eng. Coll. Optometry, Boston, 1983—; dir. opt. residency program D'Ambrosio Eyecare, Inc., 1998—. Contbr. articles to profl. jours. Mem. Am. Optometric Assn., New Eng. Coun. Optometrists, Mass. Soc. Optometrists (contact lens com. 1980-84), Belmont Lions, Beta Nu. Home: 39 Whitney Rd Harvard MA 01451-1405 Office: DAmbrosio Eye Care 100 Hospital Rd Ste 2 Leominster MA 01453-2253

LORENTZEN, JAMES CLIFFORD, radiologist; b. Ardmore, Okla., Apr. 15, 1957; s. Clifford Leslie and Doris Lorraine (Thompson) L.; m. Tracey J. Smith, Apr. 4, 1992; children: Abigail, Andrew. BA, Baylor U., 1979; MD, Baylor Coll. Med., 1983. Diplomate Am. Bd. Internal Medicine, Am. Bd. Radiology. Intern Baylor Coll. of Medicine, 1983-84, resident, 1984-86; staff physician Okla. City Clinic, 1986-92; resident Health Sci. Ctr. U. Okla., 1992-96; pvt. practice radiology, 1997—. Clin. asst. in medicine Med. Sch. U. Okla., 1987-92. U. Okla. fellow, 1996-97. Mem. AMA, Am. Coll. Radiology, Radiol. Soc. N.Am., Phi Beta Kappa, Alpha Omega Alpha, Pi Kappa Alpha. Republican. Baptist. Avocations: music, literature, flying. E-mail. Home: 105 Brugg Ct New Bern NC 28562 Office: Coastal Radiology 720 Newman Rd New Bern NC 28562 E-mail: LorentzenJ@aol.com.

LORENTZEN, ROBERT ROY, JR. producer; b. Omaha, Feb. 21, 1942; s. Robert Roy Sr. and Frances (Johnson) L.; m. Marianne Louise Bury, Sept. 23, 1973; children: Brian, Kristin. Student, Iowa State U., 1960-63, Calif. State U., Los Angeles, 1965-66. Nat. mgr. vote collection CBS-TV news, N.Y.C., 1968, assignment desk/reporter, 1968-69, asst. bur. chief/S.E. Asia producer Saigon, Vietnam, 1969-71, asst. fgn. editor N.Y.C., 1971-72, bur. chief Chgo., 1972-75; exec. producer Sta. WTTW-TV, 1975-77; asst. prof. journalism Northwestern U., Evanston, Ill., 1977-79; pres., exec. producer Video Techniques, Bradenton, Fla., 1979—. Cons. Medill Sch. Journalism News Service, Northwestern U., Washington, 1985—. Dir., author, producer (documentary) You Can Make It (Emmy award 1984). Planning commr. Manatee County, Fla. Mem. Dirs. Guild Am., Radio/TV News Dirs. Assn., Fla. Motion Picture and TV Assn., Manatee C. of C., Delta Tau Delta. Republican. Methodist. Avocation: water sports. Office: Video Techniques Inc 3306 26th St W Bradenton FL 34205-3608

LORENZ, DENISE EILEEN, physician assistant; b. Dickinson, N.D., Sept. 3, 1962; d. Norris Lee Chase and Erlis Beverly (Paulson) Swenson; m. James Allen Lorenz, May 30, 1986 (div. Nov. 2001); children: Stacey, Dustin Faris, Brittany, James W. Cert. Physician Asst., U. N.D., 1994; ADN, Dickinson State U., 1985. Physician asst. St. Alexius-Garrison (N.D.) Clinic, 1994-95, St. Alexius-Hazen (N.D.) Clinic, 1995—. Fellow Am. Acad. Physician Assts, N.D. Acad. Physician Assts. (bd. dirs., membership chair 1993-96, v.p. 1996-97, pres.-elect 1998-99, pres. 1999—). Lutheran. Avocation: crosstitch, reading, crafts, sports. . Home: 414 4th Ave NE Hazen ND 58545 Office: Hazen Clinic 301 4th Ave NE Hazen ND 58545-4434

LORENZ, HANS ERNEST, photographer; b. Karlsbad, Czechoslovakia, Sept. 11, 1940; came to U.S., 1950; naturalized, 1954. s. Hugo and Maria (Gareis) L.; m. Pamela Marie Carswell, May 27, 1978; 1 child, April Nicole. BA, Okla. Bapt. U., 1962. Tchr. pub. schs., Prince George County, Va., 1964-65; sr. curatorial photographer Colonial Williamsburg (Va.) Found., 1965—. Writer, lectr. 19th Century photographic history. Contbr. photographs to numerous books on 18th Century antiques. Mem. Am. Photographic Soc., Nat. Stereoscopic Assn., Am. Numismatic Assn. Baptist. Home: 116 Walnut Hills Dr Williamsburg VA 23185-3433 Office: Colonial Williamsburg Fnd Dept Collections-Photog 309 1st St Williamsburg VA 23185-4306 E-mail: hlorenz@cwf.org.

LORENZ, HILARY S. artist; b. Muskegon, Mich., Oct. 20, 1964; d. James D. and Beverly J. (Reschutz) L. BS, Western Mich. U., 1987; MA, U. Iowa, 1992, MFA, 1993. Instr. Bob Blackburn Printmaking Workshop, N.Y.C., 1993-96; asst. prof. Alfred (N.Y.) U., 1996-97, Md. Inst., Balt., 1997—2000, L.I. U., Bklyn., 2001—. One-woman shows include Carnegie Arts Ctr., Kans., 1997, Seton Hall U., NJ, 1997, Barret House Gallery, N.Y., 1997, Kansas City (Mo.) Artist Coalition, 1997, McHenry County Coll., Ill., 1998, 1708 Gallery, Va., 1998, Nat. Acad. for the Arts, Taipei, Taiwan, 1998. A.I.R. Gallery, N.Y.C., 1998, Lower East Side Printshop, N.Y.C., 1999, Ctr. for Book Arts, N.Y.C., 2001, Locus Media, N.Y.C., Aramona Gallery, NY, 2002, Sara Nightingale Gallery, NY, 2002; group shows include Bronx Printmakers, 1995-97, Haggin Mus. Art, Calif., 1994, Allentown Mus. Art, Pa., 1994, Galerie Bodek, Germany, 1994, The Painted Bride Gallery, Pa., 1995, Hostos Coll., NY, 1996, Abrazo Interno Gallery, NY, 1996, Wright State Coll., Ohio, 1997, Art and Sci. Mariboe Gallery, Seton Hall U., N.J., 1997, 8th Internat. Bicentennial Print and Drawing, Taipei Fine Art Mus., Taiwan, 1997, Side St. Project, Santa Monica, Calif., 1998, U. Conn., Storrs, 1998, Goya Girl Press, Balt., 1998, Kanagawa Art Found., Japan, 1998, Cinema Rex, Belgrade, Yugoslavia, 1998, Evergreen House, Balt., 1999, Duncan and Miller Gallery, Washington, 1999, Md. Art Pl., Md. Park Sch., Balt., 2000, Sharjah Art Mus., 2000, Gallery ad Miskok, Hungary, 2000, Scandinavian-Am. Mus., Pa., 2000, Great Hall of Sci., NY, Silicon Gallery, Pa., 2001, City Without Walls, NJ, 2002, Bronx River ARt Ctr. Recipient artist fellowship NEA Mid-Atlantic, Balt., 1996, Helen Stiles scholarship Manhattan Graphics Ctr., N.Y.C., 1995, Book Grant, U. Iowa Cultural Ctr., Iowa City, 1992, Spl. Editions. residency Lower East Side Printshop, N.Y.C., 1997; Frans Misereel fellow, Belgium, Fulbright sr. fellow, 2001; Taiwan Faculty Rsch. grantee, L.I. U., NY. Mem. Coll. Art Assn. Home: PO Box 20483 New York NY 10009-8972 Studio: 155 Suffolk St Fl 2D New York NY 10002-1622

LORENZ, HUGO ALBERT, retired insurance executive, consultant; b. Elmhurst, Ill., July 5, 1926; s. Hugo E. and Linda T. (Trampel) L. BS, Northwestern U., 1949; LL.B., Harvard U., 1952. Bar: Ill. 1954. Mem. patent staff Bell Telephone Labs., Murray Hill, N.J., 1952-53; atty. First Nat. Bank Chgo., 1954-58; gen. counsel N.Am. Life Ins. Co. of Chgo., 1958-73; dir., v.p., gen. counsel, sec. Globe Life Ins. Co., Chgo., 1973-95; v.p. Union Fidelity Life Ins. Co., 1993-96; sec. Gt. Equity Life Ins. Co., 1977-80, Pat Ryan & Assos. Inc., Va. Surety Co., Chgo., 1977-96. Bd. dirs. Sr. Ctrs. Met. Chgo., 1977-93, pres., 1983-85; trustee Hull House Assn., 1983-88. With USNR, 1944-46. Mem. Assn. Life Ins. Counsel, Connoisseurs Internat (bd. dirs. 1972—, pres. 1980-95), Internat. Wine and Food Soc. Chgo. (gov. and oenologist 1980—). Unitarian Universalist. Home: 950 N Clark St # A Chicago IL 60610-8701

LORENZ, JOHN DOUGLAS, college official; b. Talmage, Nebr., July 2, 1942; s. Orville George and Twila Lucille (Larson) L.; m. Alice Louise Hentzen, Aug. 26, 1967; 1 child, Christian Douglas. BS, U. Nebr., 1965, MS, 1967, PhD, 1973. Systems analyst U. Nebr., Lincoln, 1967-73; asst. prof. Kettering U., Flint, Mich., 1973-74, assoc. prof., 1974-78, prof., 1978—, dept. head, 1984-87, asst. dean, 1986-88, provost, dean faculty, 1988-92, Richard L. Terrell prof. acad. leadership, 1990—, v.p. for acad. affairs, provost, 1992—. Cons. GM, Detroit, 1973-82, various orgns. Contbr. articles to profl. jours. Judge Internat. Sci. and Engring. Fair, various locations, 1989—. Mem. NSPE, Soc. Mfg. Engrs. (sr.), So. Automotive Engrs., Accreditation Bd. for Engring. and Tech., Am. Soc. Engring. Edn., Antique Auto Racing Assn., Model Engine Collectors Assn., Antique Model Race Car Club. Home: 8165 Shady Brook Ln Flushing MI 48433-3007 Office: Kettering U 1700 W 3rd Ave Flint MI 48504-4898 E-mail: jlorenz@kettering.edu.

LORENZ, JOHN GEORGE, librarian, consultant; b. N.Y.C., Sept. 28, 1915; s. John W. and Theresa T. (Virtel) L.; m. Josephine R. Trumbull, Oct. 1, 1944; children: Laurence T., Janice R. BS (Library fellow), CCNY, 1939; BS in L.S, Columbia U., 1940; MS in Pub. Adminstrn., Mich. State U., 1952. With Queens Borough (N.Y.) Library, then Schenectady Pub. Library, 1940-44; chief reference div. Grand Rapids Pub. Library, 1944-46; asst. librarian Mich. State Library, 1946-56; with U.S. Office Edn., 1957-65, dir. div. library services and ednl. facilities, 1964-65; dep. librarian of congress Library of Congress, Washington, 1965-76; exec. dir. Assn. Research Libraries, 1976-80; library cons., 1980—; interim dir. libraries Cath. U. Am., 1982-83; liaison mem. com. sci. and tech. info. exec. office, 1966-73; interim dir. CAPCON, 1985; spl. asst. to librarian Georgetown U. Library, 1985-87; interim dir. Washington Research Library Consortium, 1987-88; coord. libr. stats. program Nat. Commn. on Librs. and Inf. Sci., 1988-97. Exec. com. Nat. Book Com., 1968-74 Author numerous articles in field; contbr. to books. Presdl. appointee Nat. Hist. Publs. and Records Commn., 1979-83. Recipient Superior Svc. award HEW. Mem. ALA (coun. 1960-64, 69-73, chmn. panel UNESCO 1965-70, exec. bd. 1970-75, Lippincott award 1993), D.C. Libr. Assn., Internat. Fedn. Libr. Assn. (mem. program devel. group 1974-78), Am. Nat. Stds. Inst. (treas. libr. stds. com. 1980-88), Cosmos Club. Home: 100 Norman Dr Apt 311 Cranberry Township PA 16066-4229

LORENZ, KATHERINE MARY, banker; b. Barrington, Ill., May 1, 1946; d. David George and Mary (Hogan) L. BA cum laude, Trinity Coll., 1968; MBA, Northwestern U., 1971; grad., Grad. Sch. for Bank Adminstrn., 1977. Ops. analyst Continental Bank, Chgo., 1968-69, supr. ops. analysis, 1969-71, asst. mgr. customer profitability analysis, 1971-73, acctg. officer, mgr. customer profitability analysis, 1973-77, 2d v.p., 1976, asst. gen. mgr. contr.'s dept., 1977-80, v.p., 1980, contr. ops. and mgmt. svcs. dept., 1981-84, v.p., sector contr. retail banking, corp. staff and ops. depts., 1984-88, v.p., sr. sector contr. pvt. banking, centralized ops. and corp. staff, 1988-90, v.p., sr. sector contr. bus. analysis group/mgmt. acctg., 1990-94, mgr. contrs. dept. adminstrn. and tng., 1990-94; v.p., chief of staff to chief adminstrv. officer Bank Am. Ill., 1994-96, sr. v.p., mgr. adminstrv. svcs., 1996-97, mng. dir., mgr. adminstrv. svcs., 1998-99; sr. v.p., Chgo. adminstrn. exec. Bank Am., 1999—. Mem. Execs. Club Chgo., Trinity Coll. Alumnae Assn. (bd. dirs.). Office: Bank of Am 231 S La Salle St Rm 1320 Chicago IL 60604-1407

LORENZ, LEE SHARP, cartoonist; b. Hackensack, N.J., Oct. 17, 1932; s. Alfred Lloyd and Martha (Castagnetta) L.; m. Jill Allison Runcie, Sept., 1986; children: Christopher, Matthew, Martha, Ava. Student, Carnegie Inst. Tech., 1950-51; BFA, Pratt Inst., 1954. Staff cartoonist New Yorker mag., 1958—, art editor, 1973—; profl. cornetist, 1955—; cons., 1997—. Cartoonist: Here it Comes, 1968; author, illustrator: Scornful Simkin, 1980; collection Npw Look What You've Done, 1977; illustrator: Real Men Don't Eat Quiche, 1982, A Bridge Bestiary, 1986, Collection the Golden Age of Trash, 1987; author, illustrator: A Weekend in the Country, 1985; author: The Art of the New Yorker, 1995. Trustee Swann Coll. of Cartoon and Caricature, 1978—; dir. Mus. for African Art. Mem. Century Club. Home: PO Box 117 Easton CT 06612-0117

LORENZ, NANCY, artist; BFA in Painting and Printmaking, U. Mich., 1985; MFA in Painting, Tyler Sch. Art, Phila. and Rome, 1988. Instr. R.I. Sch. Design, 1996; lectr. in field. One-person shows include Temple U., Rome, 1988, Willoughby Sharp Gallery, N.Y., 1990, Genovese Gallery, Boston, 1990, 91, 94, others; exhibited in group shows at Helander Gallery, N.Y., 1989, 90, 91, 92, 93, Helander Gallery, Palm Beach, 1989, 90, 91, N.Y. Pub. Lib., 1994, Austin Ackles Studio, N.Y., 1995, PDX, Portland, Oreg., 1996, 98, 2000, Galerie Verneil des Saints-Péres, Paris, Galerie Xippas, Paris; numerous others; represented in permanent collections Senayan Hotel, Jakarta, Yokahama Hotel, Japan, Soho Grand Hotel, N.Y., MIA Ins., Pan Am. Bldg., San Francisco, Muscat Hilton, Oman, David Barton Gym, N.Y. Pub. Lib., Champion Paper, Ohio, Shinwa Med. Inc., Nagoya, Japan, Aero Studios, N.Y., The Boston Co., numerous others. Guggenheim fellow, 1998. Office: c/o PDX Gallery 604 NW 12th Ave Portland OR 97209-3002 E-mail: pdxgallery@aol.com.

LORENZ, RALPH D. research scientist, writer; s. Detlef E. Lorenz and Margaret B. Muir; m. Elizabeth P. Turtle, 1996. B in Engring., U. Southampton, Eng., 1990; PhD, U. Kent, Canterbury, Eng., 1994. Young grad. European Space Agy., Noordwijk, Netherlands, 1990—91; sr. rsch. assoc. Lunar and Planetary Lab. U. Ariz., Tucson, 1994—. Fellow: Royal Astron. Soc.; mem.: Brit. Interplanetary Soc., Am. Geophys. Union, Royal Aero. Soc. Office: U Ariz 1629 E University Blvd Tucson AZ 85721-0092

LORENZ, RONALD THEODORE, manufacturing executive; b. Chgo., Apr. 9, 1936; s. Raymond W. and Olga (Hagel) L.; m. Elizabeth L. Lehning, Nov. 26, 1960 (div. 1970); children: Dane B., Drenna D.; m. Phyllis J. Scordato, May 5, 1972 (div. May 1989); children: Amy J., Adam R. Cert. stationary engr. Asst. engr. Conrad Hilton Hotel, Chgo., 1953-55, engr., 1957-59, Kemper Ins. Co., Chgo., 1959-67; pres. Capitol Music Ctrs., Elgin, Ill., 1967-81, Rapco Internat., Jackson, Mo., 1982-91, Allied Industries, Cape Girardeau, 1992—. Served with U.S. Army, 1955-57. Mem. Jackson C. of C. (officer 1987-88), Nat. Assn. Music Mchts. (officer trade show com. 1987-90). Republican. Avocations: music, walking, boating, swimming. Home and Office: PO Box 689 Ocean Springs MS 39566-0689 E-mail: RonLorenz@prodigy.net.

LORENZEN, DONALD ROBERT, lawyer; b. Chgo., Aug. 29, 1964; BS in Computer Sci., Loyola U., Chgo., 1986; JD, U. Mich., 1991. Bar: Ill. 1991, Minn. 1993, Colo. 1993. Sr. cons. Andersen Cons., Chgo., 1986-88; assoc. Sidley & Austin, 1991-93, Holleb & Coff, Chgo., 1993-98, ptnr., 1999, Sachnoff & Weaver, Ltd., Chgo., 2000—. Mem. ABA, Ill. Bar Assn., Chgo. Bar Assn. Office: Sachnoff & Weaver Ltd 30 S Wacker Dr 29th Fl Chicago IL 60606 E-mail: dlorenzen@sachnoff.com.

LORENZEN, ROBERT FREDERICK, ophthalmologist; b. Toledo, Mar. 20, 1924; s. Martin Robert and Pearl Adeline (Bush) L.; m. Lucy Logdson, Feb. 14, 1970; children: Roberta Jo, Richard Martin, Elizabeth Anne. BS, MD, Duke U., 1948; MS, Tulane U., 1953. Intern Presbyn. Hosp., Chgo., 1948-49; resident Duke U. Med. Ctr., 1949-51, Tulane Grad. Sch., 1951-53; practice medicine specializing in ophthalmology Phoenix, 1953—. Bd. dirs. St. Vincent de Paul Eye Clinic; mem. staff St. Joseph's Hosp., St. Luke's Hosp., Good Samaritan Hosp., Surg. Eye Ctr. of Ariz. Pres. Ophthalmic Scis. Found., 1970-73; chmn. bd. trustees Rockefeller and Abbe Prentice Eye Inst. of St. Luke's Hosp., 1975— Editor in chief Ariz. Medicine, 1963-66, 69-70. Recipient Gold Headed Cane award, 1974; named to Honorable Order of Ky. Colls. Fellow ACS, Internat. Coll. Surgeons, Am. Acad. Ophthalmology and Otolaryngology, Pan Am. Assn. Ophthalmology; mem. Am. Assn. Ophthalmology (sec. of ho. of dels. 1972-73, trustee 1973-76), Ariz. Ophthal. Soc. (pres. 1966-67), Ariz. Med. Assn. (bd. dirs. 1963-66, 69-70), Royal Soc. Medicine, Rotary (pres. Phoenix 1984-850). Republican. Office: 3333 E Camino Sin Nombre Paradise Valley AZ 85253

LORENZI, VIRGINIA, nursing administrator, pediatrics nurse, educator; b. Port Chester, N.Y., Jan. 31, 1958; d. William and Virginia (Bishop) K.; married. BSN, Columbia U., 1980, MA, 1986, MEd, 1990. Cert. in staff devel. and continuing edn., in child and adolescent nursing, ANA, diabetic educator ADA. Staff nurse Greenwich (Conn.) Hosp. Assn., head nurse pediatrics, staff educator. Recipient Excellence in Oncology Nursing award, Fairfield County Am. Cancer Soc., 1986, Helen Meehan Nurse Day award, 2000. Mem. Sigma Theta Tau (past 2d v.p. Alpha Zeta chpt.), Kappa Delta Pi.

LORENZO, MICHAEL, engineer, government official, real estate broker; b. Newton, N.J., 1920; m. Anastasia Hackett; 5 children. BS in Chemistry and Physics, Pa. State U., 1947; MEA, George Washington U., 1956, postgrad., 1975-78, USDA Grad. Sch. Registered profl. engr., D.C., Md.; cert. Internat. Property Specialist (CIPS), FIPC. Field instrumentation engr. Fischer and Porter Co., Harboro, Pa., 1947-52; aerospace engr. Dept. Def., 1952-65; with Westinghouse Electric Corp., Friendship, Md., 1965-81; mgr. Air Resources Westinghouse Mgmt. Services, Inc., 1966-70, dir. environ. quality control, 1970-73; founder, pres. Tech. Protection Engring. Co., 1982—; dep. under-sec. def. Washington, 1981-82; founder, prin. broker First Lady Realty Corp., 1986—. Author: (with others) Chemical Equipment Costs, 1950; assoc. editor: Missile and Rockets, 1958-61; contbr. articles to profl. jours.; patentee stall surge sonic sensor. Rear Admiral AC USN, World War II, Korea. Decorated D.S.M., D.F.C. (2), Air medals (7) Mem. Profl. Tennis Registry. Office: First Lady Realty Corp 3126 Shadeland Dr Falls Church VA 22044-1726 *Healthy mind requires healthy body and vice versa. Per Winston Churchill "A Democracy is one of the worst forms of Government invented, except for all the others." It's my time in life to give back. You don't get a second chance to make a good first impression.*

LORI, WILLIAM E. bishop; b. Louisville, May 6, 1951; BA, St. Pius X Sem., Covington, Ky., 1973; MA, Mount St. Mary's Sem., Emmitsburg, Md., 1977; STD, Cath. U. Washington, 1982. Ordained priest Roman Cath. Ch., 1977. Sec. to James Cardinal Hickey, 1983-94; chancellor/vicar gen., moderator of Curia, 1994-95; titular bishop Diocese of Bulla, 1995-2001; aux. bishop, vicar gen./moderator of Curia, Archdiocese of Washington, 1995-2001; bishop of Bridgeport, Conn., 2001—. Chmn. Archdiocesan Commn. for Ecumenical and Interreligious, 1982—86; theol. advisor to Archbishop, 1982—94; mem. com. in edn. USCC, 1996, mem. com. on human values, 96; trustee Cath. U. Am., 1997—, chair acad. affairs com., 1998—; mem. USCCB Comm. on Doctrine, 2001; mem. USCCB Com. on Pro Life Activities; chmn. bd. trustees Sacred Heart U., Fairfield, Conn., 2001—; bd. dirs. St. Luke Inst., Silver Spring, Md., Blessed Pope John XXIII Sem., Boston. Office: 238 Jewett Ave Bridgeport CT 06606

LORIA, MARTIN A. lawyer; b. N.Y.C., Apr. 11, 1951; s. Daniel Bernard and Estelle Miriam (Barasch) L.; m. Carol Berkowitz, June 3, 1973; children: Alyson, Marissa. BA, SUNY, Albany, 1972; JD, Suffolk U., 1975. Bar: Mass. 1975, U.S. Dist. Ct. Mass. 1976, U.S. Supreme Ct. 1979. Atty. New Eng. states counsel Lawyers Title Ins. Corp., Boston, 1979-82; ptnr. Adelson, Golden & Loria, P.C., 1983-2000, Cherwin Theise Adelson & Loria LLP, Boston, 2001—. Contbg. author Massachusetts Continuing Legal Education Crooker's Notes. Mem. ABA, Mass. Bar Assn., Boston Bar Assn., Mass. Conveyancers Assn. (pres. 1991, bd. dirs. 1988-2000), Abstract Club (bd. dirs., pres.). Office: Cherwin Theise Adelson & Loria One Internat Place Boston MA 02110 E-mail: mloria@ctallaw.com.

LORIE, JAMES HIRSCH, business administration educator; b. Kansas City, Feb. 23, 1922; s. Alvin J. and Adele (Hirsch) L.; m. Sally Rosen, June 16, 1948 (div. 1953); 1 child Susan; m. Nancy A. Wexler, June 19, 1958 (dec. 1966); stepchildren: Katherine Wexler, Jeffrey Wexler; m. Vanna Metzenberg Lautman, Aug. 27, 1967; stepchildren: Erika Lautman, Victoria Lautman, Karl Lautman. AB, Cornell U., 1942, A.M., 1945; PhD, U. Chgo., 1947. Research asst. Cornell U., Ithaca, N.Y., 1944-45; mem. staff seminar Am. civilization Salzburg, Austria, 1947; mem. faculty U. Chgo. Grad. Sch. Bus., 1947-92, prof. bus. adminstrn., asso. dean, 1956-61; dir. Center Research in Security Prices, 1960-75. Cons. divsn. rsch. and statistics bd. govs. Fed. Res. Sys., 1950-52; cons. U.S. Treas. Dept., 1973-74; bd. dirs. Thornburg Mortgage Co., Inc., Chgo.; mem. Nat. Market Adv. Bd., 1975-77. Author: (with Harry V. Roberts) Basic Methods of Marketing Research, 1951, (with Richard A. Brealey) Modern Developments in Investment Management, 1972, (with Mary T. Hamilton) The Stock Market: Theories and Evidence, 1973; Contbr. articles to profl. jours. Served with USCGR, 1942-44. Mem. Am. Econ. Assn., Mont Pelerin Soc., Nat. Assn. Securities Dealers (dir. 1972-75), Phi Beta Kappa. Clubs: Arts (Chgo.); Quadrangle (U. Chgo.). Home: 2314 N Lincoln Park W Chicago IL 60614-3455

LORI-GENE, artist, educator; b. Hackensack, N.J., Mar. 2, 1956; d. Arthur Andrew Jr. and Dolores Gertrude (Savage) Miller; m. Kenneth R. Fenster, Mar. 21, 1997. BA of Visual Arts, Ga. State U., 1979, MFA in Sculpture, 1991; postgrad., Tex. Tech. U., 1985. Instr. DeKalb Coll., Clarkston, Ga., 1987-99; asst. prof. Ga. Perimeter Coll. (formerly DeKalb Coll.), 1999—. Creator numerous sculptures and paintings, 1979--. Recipient grant Bur. Cultural Affairs, Atlanta, 1989, Ga. Coun. for the Arts, 1986-87, 94-95, De Kalb Coun. for the Arts, 1984, Fulton County Arts Coun., 1991, Banff Ctr. for the Arts, 1993; fellow The Hambidge Found., 1989; Fulbright-Hays grantee, 1998. Mem. Nat. Coun. for Edn. in Ceramic Arts, Fulbright Assn. Avocations: music, culinary arts, dancing, outdoors. Home: 2388 Oxbow Cir Stone Mountain GA 30087-1217

LORIMER, CLARK D. small business owner; b. Williamsport, Pa., Feb. 27, 1947; s. Clark and D. Jean Lorimer; children: Craig A., Duane C. Owner AGS Electrical, Williamsport, Muncy, Pa., 1968—. With USNR, 1965-68. Mem. NRA (life). Avocations: fishing, boating, hunting.

LORIMER, SIR DESMOND, retired chartered accountant; b. Belfast, Ireland, Oct. 20, 1925; s. Thomas Berry and Sarah (Robinson) L.; m. Patricia Doris Samways, Mar. 12, 1957; 2 daus. DSc, U. Ulster, 1987, Queens U., Belfast, 1993. Sr. ptnr. Harmood Banner Smylie & Co., Belfast, 1960-74; chmn. No. Ireland Electricity, 1991-94, Lamont Holdings, Belfast, 1973-96, No. Bank Ltd., Belfast, 1986-97, Old Bushmills Distillery Co. Ltd., Belfast, 1986-98; dir. Irish Distillers Group PLC, Dublin, Ireland, 1986-98. Pres. Inst. Chartered Accts., Ireland, 1968—69. Avocations: golf, gardening. Home: 6A Circular Rd W Cultra Hollywood BT18 0AT Northern Ireland Office: Purdys Lane Newtownbreda Belfast BT8 7AR Northern Ireland

LORINCE, L(OIS) MARGARET, music educator; b. Amarillo, Tex., Feb. 3, 1926; d. William Fred and Lois Kathleen (Hartzog) Scott; m. Frank Edell Lorince, Jr., Aug. 19, 1950; children: Frank Russell, Nancy Lorince Hill. BM, Oklahoma City U., 1948; MM, Eastman Sch. Music, Rochester, N.Y., 1950. Double bassist Oklahoma City Symphony, 1944-47; instr. piano, theory Oklahoma City U., 1948-49; pvt. piano tchr. Morgantown, W. Va., 1953-60; gen. music instr. pub. schs., Rochester, N.Y., 1960-62; chmn. music preparatory dept., mem. music faculty W.Va. U., Morgantown, 1963-86, prof. music, piano and piano pedagogy, 1979-86, asst. chair divsn. music, 1983-86, prof. emeritus, 1986; pvt. piano tchr. Isle of Palms, S.C., 1986—. Adjudicator, mem. panel D.W. Baldwin Fellowships, 1989-97; bd. dirs. Charleston Symphony Orch. League, 1992—. Contbr. articles to profl. jours.; mem. editl. bd. Am. Music Tchr., 1995-97. Trustee, pres. Music Tchrs. Nat. Assn. Found., 1989-95; co-chair Conf. on Women and Creativity, Morgantown, W. Va., 1983-84. Mem. Music Tchrs. Nat. Assn. (pres. ea. divsn. 1974-78, nat. pres. 1991-93, profl. cert. in piano, chair nat. pedagogy com. 1995—), W. Va. Music Tchrs. Assn. (founding, pres. 1965-69), Charleston Music Study Club (v.p. 1995-97), Pi Kappa Lambda. Avocations: gardening, travel. Home: 105 Sparrow Dr Isle Of Palms SC 29451-2504

LORING, ARTHUR, lawyer, financial services company executive; b. N.Y.C., Oct. 13, 1947; s. Murray and Mildred (Rogers) L.; m. Vicki Hootstein, June 4, 1978 BS in Commerce, Washington and Lee U., 1969; JD cum laude, Boston U., 1972. Bar: Mass. 1972. Atty. Fidelity Mgmt. & Research Co., Boston, 1972-98, sr. legal counsel, 1980-82, v.p., gen. counsel, 1984-93; sr. v.p., gen. counsel, 1993-98; v.p.-legal FMR Corp., Boston, 1982-98; sec. Fidelity Group of Funds, 1982-98; dir. Fidelity Capital Publs. Inc., 1991-98; v.p. Fidelity Distbr. Corp., Boston, 1984-98; sr. v.p., gen. counsel Fidelity Investments Instnl. Svcs., Inc., 1994-98; mng. dir. Cypress Holding co., 1998-2000; mng. dir., mem. exec. com. Spyglass Investments LLC, Boston, 2000—. Bd. govs. Investment Co. Inst., 1988-90; chmn. ICI SEC Rules Com., 1990-95; adv. bd. Fund Directions, 1993-98; bd. dirs. New River Investor Com., chmn. audit com., 1998—; dir. Global Alliance Value Investors, Ltd., 1999-2000; dir. Cypress Tree Sr. Floating Rate Fund, N. Am. Sr. Floating Rate Fund, 1998-2000; dir. Advantage Bank, chmn. investment com., 2000—. Case editor Boston U. Law Rev., 1971-72. Mem. adv. bd. Sch. of Commerce, Washington and Lee U., 1996—; bd. dirs. Jewish Fedn. of Palm Beach, 2001—, chmn. found. com., 2001—; bd. dirs. Morse Geriatric Ctr., 2001—, pres. found., 2001—, v.p., 2002—; bd. dirs. Kramer Sr. Svc. Agy., 2000—. Mem.: ABA (securities regulation com.), Boston Bar Assn., Palm Beach Country Club (bd. dirs. 2002—), Pine Brook Country Club (bd. dirs. 1996—, v.p. 2000—), Cavendish Club (bd. dirs. 1981—84), Boston Chess Club (pres. Brookline, Mass. 1981—83). Republican. Jewish. Avocations: golf, bridge, exercise. Home: 209 Via Tortuga Palm Beach FL 33480-3638 Office: Spyglass Investments LLc 4 S Market Bldg Boston MA 02109

LORING, GLORIA JEAN, singer, actress; b. N.Y.C., Dec. 10, 1946; d. Gerald Louis and Dorothy Ann (Tobin) Goff; m. Alan Willis Thicke, Aug. 22, 1970 (div. 1986); children: Brennan Todd, Robin Alan; m. Christopher Beaumont, June 18, 1988 (div. 1993); m. René Lagler, Dec. 20, 1994. Grad. high sch. Owner Glitz Records, L.A., 1984—; pres. Only Silk Prodns., 1985-90; owner Silk Purse Prodns., 1992—. Began profl. singing, Miami Beach, 1965; appeared in numerous TV shows; featured singer: Bob Hope's Ann. Armed Forces Christmas Tour, 1970; featured several record albums; featured actress: Days of Our Lives, 1980-86; composer: TV themes Facts of Life, 1979, Diff'rent Strokes, 1978; author: Days of Our Lives Celebrity Cookbook, 1981, Vol. II, 1983, Living the Days of Our Lives, 1984, Kids, Food and Diabetes, 1986, Parenting a Diabetic Child, 1991, The Kids Food and Diabetes Family Cookbook, 1991, Parenting a Child with Diabetes, 1999. Celebrity chmn. Juvenile Diabetes Rsch. Found. Recipient Humanitarian of Yr. award Juvenile Diabetes Rsch. Found., 1982, 88, Lifetime Commitment award Juvenile Diabetes Rsch. Found., 1999, Woman of Achievement award Miss Am. Orgn., 1999. E-mail: gloria@glorialoring.com. *Life is a constant amazement!.*

LORING, HONEY, small business owner; b. Phila. BA in Psychology, U. Md., 1970; MEd, Wash. U., St. Louis, 1971. Lic. psychologist-master Vt.; directress cert. Assn. Montessori Internat. Counselor Gardenville Diagnostic Ctr., St. Louis, 1971-72; tchr. Early Learning Pre-Sch., 1972-74; music dir., cabin counselor Follow Through Day Camp, Brattleboro, Vt., 1972-74; tchr. Montessori Sch., Dublin, 1974-75; ednl. cons. children's books Left Bank Books, St. Louis, 1975-76; program dir. day camp Brattleboro Child Devel., 1975-79; behavioral therapist Behavioral Medicine Unit, Dartmouth Med. Sch., 1979-84; pvt. therapist Brattleboro, Vt., 1984-85; founder, pres. Gone to the Dogs, Inc., Putney, 1984—. Dog groomer, 1979-92; founder, dir. Camp Come to the Dogs., 1990—; mfr. dog collars, 1984—; founder Tails Up Inn, 1995-98; took wolves around U.S. to do ednl. environ. programs with the Clem and Jethro Lectr. Svc., 1974-76. Author: (with Jeremy Birch) You're On. . .Teaching Communication Skills, 1984, The Big Good Wolf; contbr. articles to profl. jours. Leader 4-H Dog Club; helper Riding for the Physically Handicapped, St. Louis, 1974. Home and Office: PO Box 600 Putney VT 05346-0600

LORING, JOHN ROBBINS, artist, writer; b. Chgo., Nov. 23, 1939; s. Edward D'Arcy and China Robbins (Logeman) L. BA, Yale U., 1960; postgrad., Ecole Beaux Arts, Paris, 1960-63; D in Arts (hon.), Pratt Inst., 1996. Disting. vis. prof. U. Calif., Davis, 1977; bur. chief Archtl. Digest mag., N.Y.C., 1977-78; design dir. Tiffany and Co., N.Y.C., 1979—; mem. acquisitions com. dept. prints and illustrated books Mus. Modern Art, N.Y.C., 1990-99. Contbg. editor: Arts mag., 1973-79, Archtl. Digest mag., 2000—; books include: The New Tiffany Tablesettings, 1981, Tiffany Taste, 1986, Tiffany's 150 Years, 1987, The Tiffany Wedding, 1988, Tiffany Parties, 1989, The Tiffany Gourmet, 1992, A Tiffany Christmas, 1996, Tiffany's 20th Century, 1997, Tiffany Jewels, 1999, Paulding Farnham, Tiffany's Lost Genius, 2000, Magnificent Tiffany Silver, 2001, Louis Comfort Tiffany at Tiffany & Co., 2002; one-man exhbns. include Balt. Mus. Art, 1972, Hundred Acres Gallery, N.Y., 1972, Pace Edits., 1973, 77, Long Beach Mus. Art, 1975, A.D.I. Gallery, San Francisco, 1976; group exhbns. include Phila. Mus. Art, 1971, N.Y. Cultural Ctr., 1972, Biennale graphic Art, Ljubljana, Yugoslavia, 1973, 77, Intergrafia 74, Krakow, Poland, 1974, Bklyn. Mus. Nat. Print Exhbn., 1974, Art Inst. Chgo., 1975, R.I. Sch. Design, 1976; represented in permanent collections Mus. Modern Art, N.Y.C., Whitney Mus. Am. Art, Chgo. Art Inst., Boston Mus. Fine Arts, R.I. Sch. Design, Balt. Mus. Art, Yale U. Art Gallery; commd. by U.S. Customhouse, N.Y.C., Prudential Ins. Co. Am. Eastern Home Office, Woodbridge, N.J., City of Scranton, Pa., Western Savs., Phila., Tivoli Garden, Copenhagen. Recipient Edith Wharton award Design & Art Soc., 1988, Distinction in Design award Fashion Group Internat., 1996. Office: Tiffany & Co 600 Madison Ave New York NY 10022-2580 also: Harry N Abrams 100 5th Ave Fl 6 New York NY 10011-6903 *I look on whatever talents I may have as natural resources to be given freely wherever needed. A lot has been given out; a lot has come in.*

LORING, RICHARD WILLIAM, psychotherapist; b. Bronx, N.Y., May 26, 1928; s. William Maurice and Jeannette Edith (Bass) Loring; m. Janet Teetor, Aug. 22, 1953; children: Steven, David, Lynne. BA, DePauw U., 1952; MA, Ind. U., 1954; PhD, Columbia Pacific U., 1982. Psychiat. social worker Richmond (Ind.) State Hosp., 1954—56; asst. dir. Tippecanoe County Mental Health Center, Lafayette, 1956—62; exec. dir. Venango County Mental Health Center, Oil City, Pa., 1962—71; adminstr. Mental Health/Mental Retardation Authorities, 1970—71; dir. Venango Human Svcs. Ctr., Franklin, 1971—75; clin. program dir., dir. consultation and edn. Erie County Mental Health Dept.; pvt. practice psychotherapy Oil City, 1976—2001. Mem. staff dept. psychiatry Oil City Hosp.; sr. psychotherapist Vets. Adminstrn. Vietnam Vets. Outreach Program, 1986—; part-time prof. sociology DePauw U., 1956—62; part-time prof. psychology Pa. State U., 1968—69; field prof. U. Pitts., 1969—74; part-time prof. sociology Clarion State Coll, 1972—73; part-time prof. mental health counseling Gannon Coll., 1975; clin. advisor Physician Asst. Preceptorship, 1986—95; spl. cons. Corps Chaplains U.S. Army, 1971—75; mem. profl. adv. com. Crippled Children and Adults Com., 1971—75, Clarion State Coll. Sch. Nursing, 1981—94. Editor: Selected Papers of Psychiatric Outpatient Centers, 1967, Psychiatric Outpatient Centers and Low Income Populations, 1968. Del., mem. task force White House Conf. on Aging, 1971; del. Nat. Conf. on Mental Health, 1975; chmn. N.W. Pa. Family Planning Coun., 1974; bd. dirs. Pa. Mental Health Assn., 1969—77, mem. exec. com., 1973—77; bd. dirs. Franklin Light Opera Co., 1970—74; chmn. project rev. com. Venango Regional Comprehensive Health Planning, 1973—75; chmn. Gt. Lakes Forum on Primary Prevention in Mental Health, 1976; mem. N.W. region steering com. Pub. Com. for Humanities in Pa., 1971—74. Served with AUS, World War II. Named Boss of Yr., Ft. Venango chpt. Nat. Secs. Assn., 1972. Fellow: Am. Assn. Social Psychiatry; mem.: APHA, ACA, Am. Coll. Clinic Adminstrs., Am. Assn. Mental Health Counseling, Psychiat. Outpatient Centers Am. (exec. sec. 1966—74). Home: 406 W 7th St Oil City PA 16301-3040 Office: Venango Int Med Assocs U Pitts Med Ctr 1 Memorial Dr Oil City PA 16301-1341

LORING, STEPHEN HATHAWAY, b. Boston, July 9, 1946; s. Oliver Leland and Elizabeth Brewster L.; m. Hilary Rodd, Aug. 8, 1970; children: Benjamin, Sarah. BA, Amherst (Mass.) Coll., 1968; BMS, Darmouth Med. Sch., 1970; MD, Harvard Med. Sch., 1973. Intern in internal medicine U. Hosp., Boston, 1973-74; rsch. fellow in physiology Harvard Sch. of Pub. Health, 1974-77, rsch. assoc. in physiology, 1977-80, asst. prof. physiology, 1980-85, assoc. prof. physiology, 1985-91, 93—; assoc. prof. anesthesia Harvard Med. Sch., 1991—; scientific dir. respiratory therapy Beth Israel Deaconess Med. Ctr., Boston, 1991—. Mem. Am. Thoracic Soc. Office: Beth Israel Deaconess Med Ctr Dana 717 330 Brookline Ave Boston MA 02215

LORING, THOMAS JOSEPH, forest ecologist; b. Haileybury, Ont., Can., May 27, 1921; s. Ernest Moore and Margaret Evangeline (Bacheller) L.; m. Beth Rogers McLaughlin, Oct. 29, 1966; children: John Francis, Christopher Thomas. BSc in Forestry, Mich. Tech. U., 1946; M Forestry, N.Y. State Coll. Forestry, 1951. Forester McCormick Estates, Champion, Mich., 1947; cons. Porteous and Co., Seattle, 1948-49; forester Penokee Veneer Co., Mellon, Wis., 1951-53; cons. E.M. Loring Consulting, Noranda, Que., Can., 1954-55; forester USDA Forest Svc., Albuquerque, 1956-81; cons. Tom Loring, Cons., Victoria, B.C., Can., 1986—. Mem. Parks and Recreation Commn., Victoria, 1988-92, mem. environment adv. com., 1993-97. Editor: Directory of the Timber Industry in Arizona and New Mexico,1 972; co-editor: Ecology, Uses and Management of Pinyon-Juniper Woodlands, 1977. Pres. Shawnigan Lake Residents and Rate Payers Assn., B.C., 1985-86. Mem. Soc. Am. Foresters (sect. chair 1960-62), Ecol. Soc. Am., Forest Products Soc. (regional rep. 1980-81), Can. Inst. Forestry, Soc. Ecol. Restoration. Home: 59 Moss St Victoria BC Canada V8V 4M1

LORIO, PENNY, playwright, composer; b. Kalamazoo, Feb. 23, 1958; d. Jerry Gene Lorio and Patricia Ann Kelly. Student, Western Mich. U., 1980—85, Kalamazoo Valley C.C., 1988—90. Resident playwright, composer Actors and Playwrights Initiative Theatre, Kalamazoo, 1993—98; assoc. prodr. Pussycat Theatre Co., Balt., 2000—. Author: (plays) Behind a Masquerade of Rhymes, 1996, .and the Scent of Tiger Lilies, 1997 (Finalist Midwest Theatre Network New Play Competition, 1998), P.L.P.D.; a little insurance never hurts, 1997, EXPENSES, 1990, (plays) Four Scenes: A Hungarian Trilogy, 2000 (3rd Pl. Best Prodn. Balt. Playwrights Festival, 2000); composer (with ll bennett, book by bryan zocher) Ebenezer!, 1995; author Assorted Short Works. Mem.: Internat. Ctr. for Women Playwrights, Dramatists Guild, The Mobtown Players (assoc.). Avocations: antique restoration, tennis, golf. Personal E-mail: applejax2@earthlink.net.

LORNITZO, FRANK, retired chemist; b. N.Y.C., Dec. 18, 1926; s. Frank Karl Lornitzo and Michela Krupicka; m. Elspeth M. Colwell, Aug. 18, 1958 (div. Mar. 1983); children: Steven Frank, Morris Frederick, Hannah Jan; m. M. Sherry, 1994. Student, Antioch Coll., Yellow Springs, Ohio, 1944-46; BS in Chemistry, U. R.I., 1955; MS in Chemistry, U. Wis., 1956, MS in Philosophy, 1958. Tchg. asst. dept. chemistry U. Wis., Madison, 1956-57, project asst./assoc., 1957-70; scientist project assoc. VA Hosp. TB Lab. and Enzyme Inst./U. Wis., 1958-70, sr. rsch. specialist dept. physiol. chemistry, 1970-86; sr. rsch. specialist fellow U. Wis., Milw., 1987-94; ret., 1994. Writer instrumentation manuals U. Wis., Milw., 1991-93, programming tutorial Molecular Modeling, Milw., 1992-94, data retrieval computation Molecular Models, 1993-94; contbt. to book Methods in Enzymology, 1981; contbr. articles to profl. jours.; patentee in field. Contbr. to book: Methods in Enzymology, 1981; contbr. articles to profl. jours.; patentee in field. Recipient citation U.S. Surgeon Gen., 1964. Fellow Am. Inst. Chemists; mem. AAAS, Am. Chem. Soc., N.Y. Acad. Scis. Avocations: writing, walking, music, plays, reading. E-mail: blessdkrumheit@yahoo.com.

LORO, ANTONIO, artist; b. Nove, Italy, May 6, 1934; came to U.S., 1949; s. Giuseppe and Evelina (Menegotto) L.; m. Gretchen; children: Brooks, Clark. PhD in Humanities, Occidental U. St. Louis, 1978; PhD in Art Sci., Greenwich U., 1991. Founder, dir. St. Mark Acad. Art Conservation Sci., Houston, Caribbean Fine Arts Sch., P.R., First Mus. Art Aguadilla; vis. prof. emeritus U. Ariz. Art restorer. Executed murals Hall Ford Motor Co., Gral Pacheco, Argentina, Adminstrn. Bldg. U. P.R., Arecibo Regional Libr. Coll. U. P.R., Borinquen Internat. Airport, Coliseum Aguadilla, Hall BMW, Houston, Assumption Cath. Ch., Houston; exhibited in group shows at Met. Mus. Fine Art, N.Y.C. Recipient Silver, Gold medals Nat. Salon Arts, Grand Prize of Honor, Argentina, Internat. Grand Mcpl. prize, Italy, Cross and Title Cavalier, Pres. Italian Republic, City Hall Recognition, City of Nove, Italy, 1998. Mem. Appraisers Assn. Am., Am. Chem. Soc., Am. Inst. Conservation Historic Artistic Works, Internat. Inst. Conservation Restoration, Scottish Soc. Conservation Restoration, Internat. Assn. Conservation Books Ppaer Archival Material, Australian Inst. Conservation Cultural Material, Internat. Soc. Fine Arts Appraisers (sr.). Address: 1612 W Alabama St Houston TX 77006-4102

LORRANCE, ARLEEN, foundation administrator; b. N.Y., Feb. 26, 1939; d. Irving and Rose (Karpincus) Udoff; m. Richard, Apr. 13, 1964. AA, Bklyn. Coll., 1960, BA, 1963, MFA, 1971. Profl. actor TV Stage Film, N.Y., 1956-71; tchr. speech, drama Jefferson High, 1965-71, acting chairperson, speech, drama, 1970-71; exec. dir. The Love Project, San Diego, 1972-91; artistic dir. The Theatre of Life, 1981—; exec. dir. Teleos Inst., 1992—; consciousness cons. Author (with Diane K. Pike): Channeling Love Energy; author: Why Me? How to Heal What's Hurting You, The Love Project, The Love Principles, The Two: A Spiritual Thriller. Mem. Actors' Equity Assn., Am. Fed. Radio, TV Artists, SAG. Home and Office: 7119 E Shea Blvd Ste 109 PMB418 Scottsdale AZ 85254

LORSUNG, THOMAS NICHOLAS, news service editor; b. Milw., June 9, 1938; s. Nicholas A. and Margaret (Senger) L.; m. Mary Jelen, Aug. 27, 1960; children: Kristin Lorsung Shulder, Anne Lorsung Quinn, Erin Lorsung Krauss. BJ, Marquette U., 1960. Reporter Journal-Times, Racine, Wis., 1961-63; reporter, photographer, news editor Cath. Rev., Balt., 1963-69; photo, copy editor The Sentinel, Milw., 1969-72; photo editor Nat. Cath. News Svc., Washington, 1972-75, news editor, 1975-76, mng. editor, 1976-89; dir., editor-in-chief Cath. News Svc. (formerly Nat. Cath. News Svc.), 1989—. Chmn. bd. dirs. Carroll Pub., Washington, 1993-95; cons. Pontifical Coun. for Social Comms., 1995—. Recipient By-Line award Marquette U., 1997. Mem. Cath. Press Assn. (bd. dirs. 1991—, sec. 1998-2000, v.p. 2000—, St. Francis de Sales award 1995), Internat. Cath. Union of the Press, Fed. Cath. News Agencies (v.p. 1992). Avocations: photography, biking, choral singing. Home: 5367 Iron Pen Pl Columbia MD 21044-1812 Office: Catholic News Svc 3211 4th St NE Washington DC 20017-1106 E-mail: tlorsung@catholicnews.com.

LORTI, DANIEL CAESAR, engineer; b. Dec. 13, 1936; s. Dante Antonio, Marie Therese (Butrago) L.; m. Jane Susann Perkins, Aug. 15, 1959 (div. Feb. 1979); children: Daniel C., Dean J., Susan D., David S.; m. Gloria Jean Hooper, May 3, 1980. BSEE summa cum laude, Ariz. State U., 1966, MS in Engrng., 1967; postgrad., U. Calif., Irvine, 1968-69. Registered profl. engr., Ariz. Mem. radar systems analysis staff Ford Aeronutronic, Newport Beach, Calif., 1966-68; mem. tech. staff Gen. Rsch. Corp., Santa Barbara, 1968-71, Spectra Rsch. Systems, Newport Beach, 1971-74, 75-76; pres. Data Tec, Irvine, 1974-81; v.p. Corp. Benefit Cons., Tustin, Calif., 1974-75; sr. scientist Xonics, Inc., L.A., 1976-78, v.p. Van Nuys, Calif., 1979-80; v.p., prin. XonTech, Inc., 1980-85; chief radar engr., dir. adv. systems bus. devel. Northrop Electronics Sys. Divsn., Hawthorne, Calif., 1985-94; gen. mgr., v.p. Mekel Engring, Inc., Brea, 1995—99; pres. Tecom Industries, Inc., Chatsworth, 2000—01. Contbr. articles to profl. jours.; patentee precision ignition adjustment device. With USAF, 1955-59. Mem. IEEE, Phi Kappa Phi, Tau Beta Pi, Eta Kappa Nu. Home: 425 Vista Parada Newport Beach CA 92660-3528

LORTIE, JOHN WILLIAM, solar research company executive; b. Chgo., July 11, 1920; s. William Arthur and Alice Marie (McNamee) L.; m. Mary Elaine Sullivan, Sept. 21, 1946; children: Colleen, Kevin, Timothy. Student, Ill. Inst. Tech., 1940-42, U. Ala., 1976. Radar technician Western Electric Co., Westchester, Ill., 1946-50; pres. William A. Lortie & Sons, 1950-65, Monark Instant Homes, Ocean Springs, Miss., 1965-75; dir. rsch. Energy Rsch. Corp., Mobile, Ala., 1974-88; pres. Essential Solar Products, 1980—. Pres. Energy Internat. Innovations, Mobile, Ala., 1981—; solar cons.; bd. dirs. Internat. Solar Acad., 1988—; head dept. solar tech. Carver State Tech. Coll., 1976-81; internat. rep. Barclay Group Fin. With U.S. Army, 1942-46. Mem. Ala. Acad. Scis., Ala. Solar Energy Assn. (state chmn.), Ala. Solar Industries Assn. (bd. dirs., pres.), Internat. Solar Energy Soc., Nat. Assn. Solar Contractors. Republican. Roman Catholic. Achievements include research subspecialties in combustion processes, fuels and sources, solar pond power generation, solar aeration fish ponds, solar desalination, super conductivity/solar cells, patent research, laser guidance systems, design of flexible amorphous silicon photovoltaic cloth, magnetic energy recovery from earth core, ultra high power projection through the atmosphere. Fax: (251) 340-0492. E-mail: jhnjckl1@aol.com.

LORTON, LEWIS, researcher, computer executive, dentist; b. N.Y.C., Nov. 3, 1939; s. Frederick S. and Rosell (Engel) L.; divorced; children: Elizabeth, Mark, Michael S.; m. Jacqueline Carol Andor, Aug. 3, 1982; children: Michael E., Erin. BA, Brandeis U., 1960; DDS, U. Pa., 1964; MSD, Ind. U., 1978. Pvt. practice, West Medway, Mass., 1964-66; commd. lt. U.S. Army, 1966, advanced through grades to col., 1983, researcher, tchr., 1976—. Cons. Armed Forces Inst. Pathology, Washington, 1986-97; chief info. mgr. Henry M. Jackson Found., 1989-91; v.p. Klemm Analysis Group, Inc., 1991-92; pres. Lorton Assoc., 1992-94; exec. dir. Health Care Open Systems & Trials, Inc., 1994-98, mng. ptnr. Intersect Assocs., LLC, 1998—; adminstr. FPSH, 1998; chmn., founder HIPAADocs Corp. Contbr. numerous articles to profl. jours. Recipient Carl Schlack award Assn. Mil. Surgeons U.S., 1988. Fellow Am. Forensic Soc.; mem. Am. Med. Informatics Assn., Health Info. Mgmt. ys. Soc. Avocations: bicycling, computers, fly fishing, squash. Office: 6852 Oak Hall Ln Columbia MD 21045-3609

LORTON, ROBERT E., JR. publishing executive; BA, U. Tulsa, 1964. Publ. Tulsa World World Publ. Co., ceo, also chmn. bd. dirs. Bd. dirs. F&M Bank and Trust Co. Trustee U. Tulsa; bd. dirs. Philbrook Art Ctr., Boy Scouts Coun., Salvation Army, Sutton Avian Rsch. Ctr.; past chmn. Tulsa Port of Catoosa Authority, Philbrook Mus. Art, , Tulsa Area United Way, chmn. drive, 1984. Mem. Tulsa C. of C. (past chmn.). Office: PO Box 1770 Tulsa OK 74102-1770*

LOS, CORNELIS ALBERTUS, financial economist, portfolio manager, educator; b. Purmerend, The Netherlands, Dec. 14, 1951; s. Klaas and Adriaantje (Nieuwland) Los; m. Diane Nichols, June 10, 1979 (div. 1984); 1 child Francesca R. E. ; m. Elizabeth M. Ten Houten, June 18, 1986 (div. 1991); 1 child Marguerita E. A. ; m. Rose Lee Haubenstock, May 5, 1994. Candidatus cum laude (BA Hon), U. Groningen, 1974, Doctorandus (MPhil), 1976; rsch. student London Sch. Econs., Sch., Slavonic & E. European Studies, 1975-76; diploma, Inst. Social Studies, The Hague, 1977; MPhil, Columbia U., 1980, PhD, 1984. Tchg. asst. Columbia U., N.Y.C., 1978-80, preceptor, 1979, instr., 1980-81; economist Fed. Res. Bank of N.Y., 1981-85, sr. economist, 1985-87, Nomura Rsch. Inst. (America) Inc., 1987-90; chief U.S. economist NMB Postbank Group/ING Bank/ING Capital, N.Y.C., 1991-93; assoc. prof. banking and fin. Nanyang Tech. U., Singapore, 1995-99; assoc. prof. fin. U. Adelaide, Australia, 2000; vis. assoc. prof. fin. Deakin U., 2001; assoc. prof. Kent State U., 2000—. Adj. lectr. Hunter Coll., N.Y.C., 1980, CCNY, 1980—81; adj. prof. Baruch Coll., N.Y.C., 1985—86; rsch. assoc. Ctr. Math. Sys. Theory U. Fla., Gainesville, 1986—92; pres. EMEPS Assocs. Inc., 1986—; lectr. numerous profl. confs., U.S. and fgn. countries; cons. World-bank, 1994—, Inter-Am. Devel. Bank, 1994—, Asian Devel. Bank, 1996—. Author: (book) Computational Finance-A Scientific Perspective, 2001; contbr. articles to profl. jours., chapters to books. Mem. acad. bd. Nanyang Tech. U., 1997—99; bd. dirs. The Netherland-Am. Found., INc., 1991—95. Recipient Lady Van Renswoude of The Hague Found. awards, 1974—75, MAOC Countess Van Bylandt Found. award, 1976, Scholten Cordès Found. awards, 1976—77; scholar Fulbright-Hays, 1977. Fellow: Am. Coll. Forensic Examiners (life); mem.: AIMR, IEEE (sr.), Singapore Soc. Fin. Analysts, Nat. Econ. Club, N.Y. Acad. Sci., Am. Math. Soc., Am. Fin. Assn., Am. Econ. Assn., Am. Statis. Assn., Internat. Assn. Math. and Computer Modeling, Internat. Assn. Fin. Engrs., Econometric Soc., Math. Assn. Am., Australasian Inst. Banking and Fin. (sr. assoc. 1999—2000), London Goodenough Trust, World Coun. Alumni Internat. Ho. (N.Y.C.), Grad. Faculties Alumni Columbia U., Nanyang Bus. Sch. Alumni Assn., Columbia U. Club (Singapore) (found. treas.). Avocations: history of the Silk Road and the American Revolution, travel, hiking, jogging, rowing. Office: Kent State U Coll Bus Adminstrn & Gradh Sch Mgmt Dept Fin Rm 416 Kent OH 44242-0001 Fax: +1-330-672-9006. E-mail: clos@bsa3.kent.edu.

LOS, MARINUS, retired agrochemical researcher; b. Ridderkerk, The Netherlands, Sept. 18, 1933; arrived in U.S., 1960; s. Cornelis and Neeltje (Zoutewelle) Los; m. Lorraine Betty Lowe, May 11, 1957; children: Simon, Sija, Michael, Martin(dec.). BS, Edinburgh U., Scotland, 1955, PhD, 1957. Sr. rsch. chemist Am. Cyanamid Co., Princeton, NJ, 1960—71, group leader, 1971—84, sr. group leader, 1984—86, mgr. crop protection chems., 1986—88, assoc. dir. crop scis. N.J., 1988-92, rsch. dir. crop scis. NJ, 1992—96; ret., 1996. Recipient Disting. Inventor of 1990 award, Intellectual Property Owners, Inc., Washington, 1990, Thomas Alva Edison Patent award, R&D Coun. of N.J., 1991, Nat. Medal of Tech., NSF, 1993, Achievement award, Indsl. Rsch. Inst. Inc., 1994. Mem.: AAAS, Plant Growth Regulator Soc., Am. Chem. Soc. (Perkin medal 1994, Creative Invention award 1995, Heroes of Chemistry 1999, Internat. award for rsch. in agrochemicals 2002). Achievements include patents in field. E-mail: LosMar@aol.com.

LOSANOFF, JULIAN EMILOV, surgeon, educator; b. Sofia, Bulgaria, June 26, 1961; s. Emil Krumov and Margarita Hristova (Stambolieva) L.; m. Krassimira Sabeva Ivanoff, Nov. 12, 1987; 1 child, Christian Julianov. MD, Med. U., Sofia, 1987; Diploma, Higher Inst. Econs., 1996. Diplomate Bulgarian Bd. Gen. Surgery. Gen. med. practice, Drenovets, Bulgaria, 1987-91; clin. fellow Tokushukai Med. Corp., Japan, 1997; resident in gen. surgery Mil. Med. Acad., Sofia, 1991-99, surgeon, asst. prof., 1991-2000; rsch. assoc. dept. surgery U. Mo., Columbia, 2000—01, rsch. instr., 2001—. Contbr. articles to profl. jours. With Bulgarian Army, 1979-81. Mem. N.Y. Acad. Scis., Internat. Soc. Surgery, Nat. Geog. Soc., Sofia Surg. Soc. (sec.), Bulgarian Med. Assn., Bulgarian Mil. Med. Soc. (sec.), European Soc. Emergency Medicine. Greek Orthodox. Avocation: painting. Home: 1326 Ashland Rd Apt I Columbia MO 65201 E-mail: jelosanoff@yahoo.com.

LOSASSO, THOMAS JAMES, anesthesiologist; b. Chgo., Mar. 26, 1959; s. Guido Reno and Mary Ann (Barretto) L.; m. Jane Carol Wollenberg, Sept. 12, 1986. BSEE, Marquette U., 1981; MD, Loyola U., 1985. Diplomate Nat. Bd. Med. Examiners, Am. Bd. Anesthesiology. Intern then resident in anesthesiology Mayo Clinic, Rochester, Minn., 1985-89, asst. prof. anesthesiology, 1989-95; cons. Anesthesia Assocs., Duluth, 1995—. Vis. prof. dept. anesthesiology St. Lukes Hosp., 1992, U. Colo. Health Scis. Ctr., 1993, U. Pa., 1994; lectr. in field. Contbr. articles to profl. jours. Grantee Anaquest, 1989, ICI Pharmaceuticals, 1991; recipient 2d pl. award Midwest Anesthesia Conf., 1992. Mem. Am. Soc. Anesthesiologists (subcom. on clin. neurosci. 1994-95), Minn. Soc. Anesthesiologists (exec. com. 1997-2002), Minn. Med. Assn. Office: Valley Anesthesiology Cons PA Ste 20 14700 28th Ave North Plymouth MN 55447

LOSCALZO, ANTHONY JOSEPH, lawyer; b. Bklyn., May 13, 1946; s. Frank Anthony and Frances (Puliatti) L.; m. Kathryn Mary Pica, Aug. 4, 1973. BBA, St. John's U., 1967, JD, 1969. Bar: N.Y. 1969, Fla. 1971, U.S. Dist. Ct. (so. and ea. dists.) N.Y. 1973, U.S. Ct. Appeals (2d cir.) 1975, U.S. Supreme Ct. 1975. Ptnr. Loscalzo & Loscalzo, P.C., N.Y.C., 1981—. Mem. ABA, Assn. Trial Lawyers Am., Fla. Bar Assn., N.Y. State Trial Lawyers Assn., N.Y. State Bar Assn. Office: Loscalzo & Loscalzo PC Ste 408 14 E 4th St Apt 408 New York NY 10012-1141 E-mail: aloscalzo@loscalzolaw.com.

LOSCALZO, JOSEPH, cardiologist, biochemist; b. Camden, N.J., Oct. 26, 1951; s. Joseph and Dolores Rita (Ventura) L.; m. Anita Beth Sendrow, Mar. 10, 1974; children: Julia, Alexander. AB summa cum laude, U. Pa., 1972, MD and PhD, 1978. Diplomate Am. Bd Internal Medicine; cert. in cardiovascular disease. Postdoctoral fellow U. Pa., Phila., 1978; resident in internal medicine Brigham and Women's Hosp., Boston, 1978-81, clin. fellow cardiology, 1981-83, chief med. resident, 1983-84, instr. medicine, 1983-85; clin. fellow medicine Harvard Med. Sch., 1978-81, asst. prof. medicine, 1985-88, assoc. prof., 1989-93; chief cardiol. sect. Brockton West Roxbury VA Med. Ctr., 1989-93; disting. prof. medicine, prof. biochemistry Boston U., 1994—, dir. Whitaker Cardiovasc. Inst., Sch. Medicine, 1994—, vice chmn. dept. medicine, chief cardiovasc. medicine, 1994-96, Wade prof., chmn. dept. medicine. Chair rsch. rev. com. Am. Heart Assn., 1988—; rsch. rev. coms. Nat. Heart, Lung and Blood Inst., Bethesda, Md., 1990—; dir. NIH Specialized Ctr. Rsch. in Ischemic Heart Disease, 1995—; chair cardiovasc. disease bd. Am. Bd. Internal Medicine, 1999—; mem. bd. sci. counselors Nat. Heart, Lung and Blood Inst., Bethesda, 2000—, chair, 2001—. Author, or editor 14 books on vascular biology and medicine, thrombosis and hemostasis; assoc. editor New Eng. Jour. Medicine; contbr. mem. editl. bd. Circulation, Circulation Rsch., Jour. Am. Coll. Cardiology, Jour. Thrombosis and Thrombolysis, Vascular Medicine, Am. Jour. Cardiology; contbr. over 350 articles to profl. jours. Recipient med. scientist tng. award NIH, 1972-77, rsch. career devel. award, 1989-94, clin. scientist award Am. Heart Assn., 1983-88. Fellow ACP, Am. Coll. Cardiology; mem. Am. Fedn. Clin. Rsch., Am. Soc. Clin. Investigation, Assn. Am. Physicians, Assn. Univ. Cardiologists, Am. Soc. Biol. Chemistry, Phi Beta Kappa, Alpha Omega Alpha. Achievements include 20 patents related to nitric oxide congeners. Office: Boston U Sch Medicine Whitaker Cardiovasc Inst 700 Albany St Boston MA 02118-2518

LOSCHEN, EARL LEE, psychiatrist, educator; b. Minden, Nebr., Jan. 10, 1944; s. Herman George and Agnes Anna (Garrelts) L.; m. Marilyn Jean Reinhardt, June 15, 1974; children: Rebecca, Elizabeth. BS, Midland Luth. Coll., 1966; MD, U. Nebr., Omaha, 1970; MS in Edn., So. Ill. U., 1988. Diplomate Am. Bd. Psychiatry and Neurology. Asst. prof. U. Nebr., Omaha, 1973-74, So. Ill. U., Springfield, 1974-80, assoc. prof., 1980-95; prof., 1995—; asst. chmn. dept. psychiatry So. Ill. U., Springfield, 1980-92, chmn. dept. psychiatry, 1992—. Cons. Ill. Dept. Pub. Health, Springfield, 1976-88, Ill. Dept. Rehab. Services, Springfield, 1977-88, Aid to Retarded Citizens, Springfield, 1981—, Macoupin County Mental Health, Carlinville, Ill., 1974-95; mem. psychiat. panel Health Care Financing Adminstrn., 1986—. Contbr. chpts. to books. Mem. com. rights of minors Ill. Commn. Children, 1974-77, com. youth and law, 1977-79; del. 1980 Ill. White House Conf. on Children, 1980, Ill. Conf. Children's Priorities of 1980's, 1981. Fellow Am. Psychiat. Assn.; mem. AMA, NADD (bd. dirs. 2000-01), Nat. Assn. Rural Mental Health (bd. dirs. 1985-91, pres. 1988-89), Ill. State Med. Soc. (coun. mental health and addiction 1985-88, com. on drugs and therapeutics 1995—), Ill. Psychiat. Soc. (downstate counselor 1996-2001, pres.-elect 2001-02, pres. 2002—), Am. Assn. Mental Retardation. Avocations: photography, gardening. Office: So Ill U Sch Medicine PO Box 19642 Springfield IL 62794-9642 E-mail: eloschen@siumed.edu.

LOSCHIAVO, LINDA BOSCO, library director; b. Rockville Ctr., N.Y., Aug. 31, 1950; d. Joseph and Jennie (DelRegno) Bosco; m. Joseph A. LoSchiavo, Sept. 7, 1974. BA, Fordham U., 1972, MA, 1990; MLS, Pratt Inst., 1974. Picture cataloguer Frick Art Reference Libr., N.Y.C., 1972-75; sr. cataloguer Fordham U. Libr., Bronx, N.Y., 1975-87, head of retrospective conversion, 1987-90, systems libr., 1990-91, dir. libr. at Lincoln Ctr., 1991—. Libr. cons. Mus. Am. Folk Art Libr., N.Y.C., 1985-90; indexer Arco Books, N.Y.C., 1974. Editor: Macbeth, 1990, Julius Ceasar, 1990, Romeo and Juliet, 1990. Mng. producer Vineyard Opera, N.Y.C., 1981-88. Mem. ALA, N.Y. Tech. Svcs. Librs., Beta Phi Mu, Alpha Sigma Nu. Home: 317 Collins Ave Mount Vernon NY 10552-1601 Office: Fordham Univ Library 113 W 60th St New York NY 10023-7404

LOSEE, FERRIL ANDREW, retired electrical engineer; b. Lehi, Utah, June 5, 1928; s. Andrew Fredrick Losee and Ardella Elizabeth Anderson; m. Dona Jean Hansen, Dec. 15, 1953; children: Chris, Anne, Bonnie, Joan, Don, Thomas, Nannette, Jonathan, Melinda. BSEE, U. Utah, 1953; MSEE, U. So. Calif., 1957. Elec. engr. Hughes Aircraft Co., Culver City, Calif., 1953—59; engr. Aeronutronic, Newport Beach, 1959—65; prof. elec. engring. Brigham Young U., Provo, Utah, 1965—83; elec. engr. SRS Tech., Newport Beach, Calif., 1983—88, EG&G Spl. Projects, Las Vegas, 1988—93; ret., 1993. Cons. Aerospace Corp., San Bernardino, Calif., 1965—69, various industries, 1965—93. Author: RF Systems, Components and Circuits Handbook, 1997, Anderson Family History, 1999, Losee Family History, 2000. Bishop LDS Ch., Newport Beach, 1963—65. Achievements include 5 patents. Avocation: genealogy. Home: 3145 Bannock Dr Provo UT 84604-4259

LOSEE, JOHN FREDERICK, JR. manufacturing executive; b. Milw., Apr. 27, 1951; s. John Frederick and Helen (Joslyn) L.; m. Jane Agnes Trawicki, Aug. 25, 1973; children: Nicole Marie, John Michael. BSME, Marquette U., 1973, MS in Indsl. Engring., 1982. Registered profl. engr., Wis.; cert. numerical control mgr., Wis. Mfg. engr. OMC-Evinrude div. Outboard Marine Corp., Milw., 1975-78, mfg. engr. supr., 1978-80, mgr. tool engring., 1980-85, mgr. process and tool engring., 1985-86, dir. mfg. engring., 1986-88; v.p. ops. Rytec Corp., Jackson, Wis., 1988-90; v.p. adminstrn. Custom Products Corp., 1990-91; part-owner Nat. Mfg. Co. Inc., Milw., 1991-96; owner JFL Mfg., Inc., Sussex, Wis., 1996—. Mem. Numerical Control Soc., Soc. Mfg. Engrs., Computer and Automated Systems Assn. Republican. Roman Catholic. Home: W264 N6565 Hillview Dr Sussex WI 53089-3452 E-mail: jflmfg27@aol.com.

LOSEE, MICHAEL PATRICK, music director; b. Milton, Fla., July 26, 1955; s. Patrick J. and Anne Melvin Losee. AA, Pensacola Jr. Coll., 1978; BA, U. W. Fla., 2000. Lic. cosmetologist Dept. Rehab. Svcs., State of Fla., 1984. Dir. music East Side Bapt. Ch., Milton, Fla., 1984—88; deptl. acct. U. W. Fla., Pensacola, 1996—98, opera scenes accompanist, 1997—98; dir. music St. Sylvester Cath. Ch., Gulf Breeze, 2000—01, St. Rose of Lima Cath. Ch., Milton, 2001—. Accompanist Pensacola Little Theatre, 1994; dir. music Emerald Coast Chorale, Pensacola, 1999—2001; music dir. Chamber Ensemble St. Sylvester Cath. Ch., Pensacola. Mem. Santa Rosa County Rep. Party, Milton. Named All-Am. Scholar, All-Am. Collegiate Soc., 1998—; scholar Gittenstein scholar, U. W. Fla., 1997, Maude Kelly scholar, 1998. Mem.: Fla. Music Tchrs. Assn., Music Tchrs. Nat. Assn., Coll. Music Soc., Golden Key, Delta Omicron. Roman Catholic. Home: 6136 Arnie's Way Milton FL 32570 Office: St Rose of Lima Cath Ch 6451 Park Ave Milton FL 32570 Home Fax: 850-626-4150. Personal E-mail: farrosee@juno.com. Business E-mail: loseem@ptdiocese.org.

LOSEN, STUART MELVIN, clinical psychologist; b. N.Y.C., Apr. 12, 1930; s. Michael and Jean (Pistchal) L.; m. Joyce Elissa Garskof, Dec. 25, 1952; children: Laurie, Daniel. BA, CCNY, 1952, MA, 1953; PhD, U. Buffalo, 1959. Lic. psychologist, Conn. Psychologist trainee Buffalo VA Hosp., 1955-59; mental health cons. North Haven (Conn.) Pub. Schs., 1960-65; spl. svcs. coord. New Canaan (Conn.) Pub. Schs., 1965-83; pvt. practice Westport, Conn., 1983—. Part-time lectr. Yale U., New Haven, 1960-65; part-time assoc. prof., lectr. So. Conn. State U., New Haven, 1962-89; part-time pvt. practice, Westport, 1968-83; lectr. Fairfield (Conn.) U., 1986—. Co-author: Parent Conferences in Schools, 1978, Special Education Team, 1985; columnist Westport News, 1989-93; author chpt. to book; contbr. articles to profl. jours. Mem. adv. bd. Ret. Sr. Vol. Program, Norwalk, Conn., 1990—, Conn. Assn. Children with Learning Disabilities, Norwalk, 1990—; mem. town com. Dem. Party, Westport, 1993—; cons. Westport Pub. Schs., 1990—, Wilton (Conn.) Pub. Schs., 1990—. Recipient Outstanding Svc. citation New Eng. Assn. for Children with Disabilities; named to Hall of Fame Svc. to Children, Conn. Assn. Children with Disabilities. Fellow APA, Conn. Psychol. Assn. (past pres. 1970-71); mem. Conn. Assn. Sch. Psychologists (chmn. ethics com. 1975-85, Disting. Svc. to Children award 1983), Conn. State Bd. Examiners (apptd. gov. 1978-83), Conn. Assn. Pupil Pers. Adminstrn. (past pres. 1978-79). Democrat. Avocations: percussionist, singing, dancing, tennis, beach. Home: 6 Wild Oak Ln Westport CT 06880-1813 Office: 260 Riverside Ave Westport CT 06880-4804

LOSER, JOSEPH CARLTON, JR. dean, retired judge; b. Nashville, June 16, 1932; s. Joseph Carlton and Pearl Dean (Gupton) L.; m. Mildred Louise Nichols, May 25, 1972; 1 child, Joseph Carlton III. Student, U. Tenn., 1950-51, Vanderbilt U., 1952-55; LLB, Nashville YMCA Night Law Sch., 1959. Bar: Tenn. 1959. Pvt. practice, 1959-66; judge Gen. Sessions Ct., Davidson County, Tenn., 1966-69, Cir. Ct. 20th Jud. Dist. Tenn., 1969-86; dean Nashville Sch. Law, 1986—. Mem. ABA, Tenn. Bar Assn., Nashville Bar Assn., Am. Legion, Masons, Shriners, Sigma Delta Kappa, Kappa Sigma. E-mail: jcloser@prodigy.net.

LOSH, SAMUEL JOHNSTON, engineering administrator; b. Hershey, Pa., Nov. 11, 1932; s. Charles Seibert and Esther Dora (Johnston) L.; m. Llewellyn Mathews Hall, Sept. 26, 1964 (div. Oct., 1994); children: Elizabeth Mathews, Stephen Johnston; m. Lorna Gail Gordon, Mar. 20, 2001. BSME, MIT, 1954; postgrad., Syracuse U., Utica, 1956-57, UCLA, 1968-74, U. So. Calif., 1975-81. Cert. profl. mgr. Inst. Cert. Profl. Mgrs. Engr. RCA, Camden, N.J., 1954-55; instr. Syracuse U., Utica, 1956; mem. tech. staff TRW, L.A., 1957-59; systems engr. Hoffman Electronics, L.A, 1959-62; spacecraft systems engr. Lockheed Calif. Co., Burbank, 1962-64; sr. systems specialist Xerox Spl. Info. Systems, Pasadena, Calif., 1964-87; sr. systems engr. Datametrics Corp., Chatsworth, 1987-89; pres. Milner Street, Inc., Pasadena, 1980—. Sec. Regina Properties, Inc., Pasadena, 1981-92. Chmn. L.A. chpt. MIT Ednl. Coun., 1978-2001; facilitator Math. Standards Program, L.A. Unified Sch. Dist., 1994. Recipient George Morgan award MIT Ednl.Coun., 1987; named Silver Knight of Mgmt., Nat. Mgmt. Assn., 1980. Mem. IEEE, AIAA, MIT Alumni Assn. (bd. dirs. 1981-83). Republican. Unitarian Universalist. Avocations: skiing, travel, apt. mgmt. Home and Office: PO Box 50368 Pasadena CA 91115-0368 E-mail: samlosh@alum.mit.edu.

LOSH, SUSAN CAROL, education educator, researcher; b. Detroit, May 30, 1946; d. Rubin Losh and Naomi Lois Hendelman; m. Neil Bernard Betten, Aug. 18, 1984; children: Reuben Losh-Betten. BA Psychology, U. Mich., 1971, MA Sociology, PhD Sociology, U. Mich., 1973. Asst. prof. sociology Fla. State U., Tallahassee, 1973—78, assoc. prof. sociology, 1978—2000, assoc. professor ednl. rsch., 2000—. Cons. United Faculty of Fla., Tallahassee, 1984—. Contbr. over 2 dozen articles to profl. jours., over 80 contbns. to various confs. (awards for tchg. and tech. innovation in tchg.). Cons. AAUW, Tallahassee, 2001—, City of Tallahassee, 1975—81; sec. Tallahassee Area Shetland Sheepdog Assn., Tallahassee, 1995—; exec. com. mem. Southern Sociological Soc., Atlanta, 1980—82. Avocation: Shetland Sheepdogs, Housing Renovation. Office: Dept Ednl Rsch Fla State U Tallahassee FL 32306-4453 Office Fax: 850-644-8776.

LOSI, MAXIM JOHN, medical communications executive; b. Jersey City, Dec. 27, 1939; s. Maxim Fortune and Carrie (Rivoli) Losi; m. Mary Ann De Grandis, May 30, 1968; children: Christopher, Benjamin. AB, Princeton U., 1960; postgrad., N.Y. Med. Coll., 1960-61, Albert Einstein Coll. Medicine, 1961-62; PhD in English, NYU, 1972. Lectr. English, C.W. Post Coll., L.I. U., Greenvale, N.Y., 1965-67; instr. English, Centenary Coll. for Women, Hackettstown, N.J., 1967-71, chmn. dept., 1970-71; med. abstractor, indexer Coun. for Tobacco Rsch., N.Y.C., 1972-73; freelance med. writer, 1973-74; sr. clin. info. scientist Squibb Inst. Med. Rsch., Princeton, N.J., 1974-77, project team leader, 1975-77; chief med. writer ICI Ams., Wilmington, Del., 1977-79; dir. biomed. comm. Revlon Health Care Group, Tuckahoe, N.Y., 1979-86; exec. dir. documentation mgmt. and regulatory submissions Covance Clin. and Peri-Approval Svcs. Inc., Princeton, 1987-97; v.p. regulatory affairs Scirex Corp., Blue Bell, Pa., 1997-98; pres. Max Losi Assocs. Pharm. Regulatory Cons. & Comm., Trenton, NJ, 1998—. FDA cons. Microbiol. Assocs., Bethesda, Md., 1973; mgmt. cons. Robert S. First Assocs., N.Y.C., 1974; vis. lectr. med. writing techniques St. George U. Med. Sch., Grenada, W.I., 1977; adj. asst. prof. English, Rider U., Lawrenceville, N.J., 1999—. Mem.: Drug Info. Assn., Am. Med. Writers Assn. (pres. N.Y. chpt. 1984—85, nat. pres. 1987—88). Roman Catholic.

LOSO, CHRISTI BALL, television producer; b. Wharton, Tex., July 18, 1963; d. Wilbur Allen and LaWanda (Gersbach) Ball; m. Derik Evan Loso, May 18, 1996. BA in English, BJ, U. Tex., 1985. Reporter, assoc. prodr. KTVV-TV, Austin, 1985-86; prodr. TV news KCPM-TV, Chico, Calif., 1987-88, KSBW-TV, Salinas, 1988-89; prodr. 1st in the morning TV news KIRO-TV, Seattle, 1989-92; video svcs. editor Miller Ptnrs., Inc., 1993; pub. affairs prodr. KCPQ-13, 1993-98; dir. mktg., comms., Wash. chpt. March of Dimes, 1998—. Writer, prodr.: (pub. affairs TV program) N.W. Focus, 1993-98. Mem. Seattle Art Mus., 1994-98; vol. Wash. Literacy, Seattle, 1992. Recipient Broadcast Media award for pub. svc. programming, Internat. Reading Assn., 1998. Mem. NATAS (bd. govs. Seattle chpt. 1995-96, officer 1996-98, Emmy nominee 1994, Emmy award 1998), Pub. Rels. Soc. Am. Office: March of Dimes 1904 3rd Ave Ste 230 Seattle WA 98101-1181 E-mail: closo@modimes.org.

LOSS, JOHN C. architect, retired educator; b. Muskegon, Mich., Mar. 6, 1931; s. Alton A. and Dorothy Ann (DeMars) Forward; m. LaMyrna Lois Draggoo, June 7, 1958. B.Arch., U. Mich., 1954, M.Arch., 1960. Registered architect, Md., Mich. Architect Eero Saarinen & Assocs., Bloomfield Hills, Mich., 1956-57; owner John Loss & Assocs, Detroit, 1960-75; prof., acting dean Sch. Architecture, U. Detroit, 1960-75; prof., head dept. architecture N.C. State U., Raleigh, 1975-79; assoc. dean. Sch. Architecture U. Md., College Park, 1981-83, prof. architecture, 1979-93, prof. emeritus architecture, 1993—; dir. Architecture and Engring. Performance Info. Ctr., 1982-93; pvt. practice, Annapolis, College Park, 1979-93, Whitehall, Mich., 1993—. Mem. com. NRC-NAS, 1982-93; mem. bldg. diagnostics com. Adv. Bd. on Build Environ., 1983-93; mem. com. on earthquake engring. NRC, 1983-93; leader survey team for tornado damage in Pa. and Ohio, 1985. Author: Building Design for Natural Hazards in Eastern United States, 1981, Identification of Performance Failures in Large Structures and Buildings, 1987, Analysis of Performance Failures in Civil Structures and Large Buildings, 1990, Performance Failures in Buildings and Civil Works, 1991; works include med. clinic, N.C.; Aldersgate Multi Family Housing, Oscoda, Mich. Advisor Interfaith Housing Inc., Detroit, 1966-74; advisor Detroit Mayor's Office, 1967-69, Interim Housing Com. Mich. State Housing Devel. Authority, Lansing, 1969-71, Takoma Park Citizens for Schs., Md., 1981-82; advisor, cons. Hist. Preservation Commn., Prince George's County, Md.; planning commn. Blue Lake Twp., Mich., 1994—; art and environ. commn. Grand Rapids Diocese of Cath. Ch., 1996-2002; vol. tchr. St. James Sch., Montague, Mich., 2001-. With U.S. Army, 1954-56. NSF grantee, 1978-84, 86-90; named one of Men of Yr., Engring. News Record, 1984. Fellow AIA; mem. K.C. (charter Grand Knight 2001-). Democrat. Roman Catholic. *To participate, as an architect, in the continuing saga of the creation of the built environment and, as a teacher, in the continuing rebirth of our intellectual and spiritual lives remains a very special honor. I feel a sincere debt of gratitude to my mother who read to me when I was a very small child and who launched me on a life of reading and service. Happiness is a spiritual thing - not a physical thing! Success (our happiness) begins with what we aspire to be - not what we have or want.*

LOSS, MARGARET RUTH, lawyer; b. Phila., June 17, 1946; d. Louis and Bernice Rose (Segaloff) L.; 1 child, Elizabeth Loss Johnson. BA, Radcliffe Coll., 1967; LLB, Yale U., 1970. Bar: Conn. 1970, N.Y. 1973. Assoc. Sullivan & Cromwell, N.Y.C., 1971-77; with Equitable Life Assurance Soc. U.S., 1977-88, asst. gen. counsel, 1979-85, v.p. and counsel, 1985-88; counsel LeBoeuf, Lamb, Greene & MacRae, 1988-98. Mem. com. Yale Law Sch. Fund. Mem. ABA, Am. Law Inst., Conn. Bar Assn., Assn. of Bar of City N.Y. Home and Office: 201 E 80th St # 12A New York NY 10021-0516 E-mail: margaretloss@compuserve.com.

LOSSE, CATHERINE ANN, pediatric nurse, critical care nurse, educator, clinical nurse specialist, family nurse practitioner; b. Mount Holly, N.J., Mar. 12, 1959; d. David C. and Bernice (Lewis) Losse. Diploma, Helene Fuld Sch. Nursing, 1980; BSN magna cum laude, Thomas Jefferson U., 1986; MSN, U. Pa., 1989; Family Nurse Practitioner Cert., Widener U., 1997. RN N.J., Pa. Staff nurse adult med.-surg. Meml. Hosp. Burlington County, Mount Holly, N.J., 1980-81; staff nurse pediatric home care Newborn Nurses, Moorestown, 1986-87; clin. nurse II surg. intensive care Deborah Heart & Lung Ctr., Browns Mills, 1986-87, clin. nurse III pediatric cardiology, 1981-86, 87-97; ednl. nurse specialist critical care The Children's Hosp., Phila., 1992-94; instr. nursing of families, maternal-child health, pediat., geriatrics Burlington County Coll., 1994-96; staff nurse pediatric home care Bayada Nurses, Burlington, N.J., 1995; family nurse practitioner Alliance Family Medicine Ctr. Fam. Med. Res. Prog., Mt. Holly, 1997-99; nurse practitioner long term care The Masonic Home of N.J., Burlington, 1999—. Clin. instr. pediat. Thomas Jefferson U., 1990; clin. instr. adult med. surg. Burlington County coll., 1991. Rep. Congress on Policy and Practice: Gerontol. Health rep., 2001—. Mem.: AACN, ANA, Congress on Policy and Practice (rep. gerontologic health 2001—), Am. Geriatrics Soc., Am. Heart Assn., N.J. State Nurses Assn. (cabinet on continuing edn. rev. team III 1992—96, advanced practice forum 1994—), Sigma Theta Tau. Home: 253 Spout Spring Ave Mount Holly NJ 08060-2041 Fax: 609-386-0414.

LOSSE, JOHN WILLIAM, JR. mining company executive; b. St. Louis, Mar. 16, 1916; s. John William and Claire (Schmedtje) L.; m. Marjorie West Penney, Mar. 7, 1942; children: John William IV, Georgia Shane, Barbara Stevens, Mary Coulter, Penney Gregersen, Jane Momberger. BS, Washington U., St. Louis, 1937; MBA, Harvard U., 1939. Sec.-treas. J.W. Losse Tailoring Co., St. Louis, 1939-41, 45-55; treas., contr., asst. sec. Uranium Reduction Co., Salt Lake City, 1955—61; v.p. fin. Atlas Minerals div. Atlas Corp., 1962-64; asst. v.p., asst. treas. Am. Zinc Co., St. Louis, 1965-66, v.p. fin., treas., 1966-70; v.p. fin. Conrad, Inc., St. Louis, 1970-71; v.p., sec., dir. Fed. Resources Corp., Salt Lake City, 1971-82, pres., CEO, dir., 1982-84, 85-86, CFO, dir., 1986-88, v.p., treas., 1988—2001, also bd. dirs., 1988-89; sec.-treas. Madawaska Mines Ltd., Bancroft, Canada, 1976—82, pres., bd. dirs., 1983—2001; pres. Camp Bird Colo., Inc., Ouray, 1983-92. Pres. Utah Natural Resources Council, 1964; tax com. and fin. adv. com. Am. Mining Congress, 1965-84; bd. dirs. Episcopal Mgmt. Corp., Salt Lake City, 1988-99. Bd. dirs. St. Mark's Hosp., Salt Lake City, 1987-88, Arthritis Found., Salt Lake City, 1988-97; vice chmn., bd. dirs. St. Mark's Charities, Salt Lake City, 1987-92; mem. investment com. Corp. of the Bishop, Salt Lake City, 1989-96; mem. investment adv. com. Perpetual Trust of St. Peter and St. Paul, 1995-96. Lt. comdr. USNR, 1941-45. Mem. Utah Mining Assn. (bd. dirs., legis. and tax coms. 1971-91), Alta Club of Salt Lake City, Phi Delta Theta. Republican. Episcopalian.

LOSSER, MARIE-REINE MARTHE, anesthesiologist, researcher; b. Selestat, Alsace, France, June 12, 1964; d. François Hubert and Anne-Marie Losser. MD, U. Paris XIII, 1993, PhD, 1998. Cert. in anesthesiology and intensive care, Paris, 1993. Anesthesiologist Hosp. Lariboisiere, Paris, 1995—; residentpub. assistance Paris Hosp. Mem. French Soc. Anesthesia Reanimation, European Soc. Intensive Care Medicine, French Coll. Anesthesia Reanimation. Avocations: opera, jazz, natural history. Office: Montreal Gen Hosp Dept Anesthesia 687 Pine Ave Montreal QC Canada HSA 1A4 E-mail: lossermr4621@aol.com., losser@hotmail.com.

LOTAS, JUDITH PATTON, advertising executive; b. Iowa City, Apr. 23, 1942; d. John Henry and Jane (Vandike) Patton; children: Amanda Bell, Alexandra Vandike. BA, Fla. State U., 1964. Copywriter Liller, Neal, Battle and Lindsey Advt., Atlanta, 1964-67, Grey Advt., N.Y.C., 1967-72; creative group head SSC&B Advt., 1972-74, assoc. creative dir., 1974-79, v.p., 1975-79, sr. v.p., 1979-82, exec. creative dir., 1982-86; founding ptnr. Lotas Minard Patton McIver, Inc., 1986—. Active scholarship fund raising; bd. dirs. Samuel Waxman Cancer Rsch., Found., N.Y.C., 1981-88; fundraiser Nat.

Coalition for the Homeless, N.Y.C., 1986—. Recipient Clio award, Venice Film Festival award, Graphics award Am. Inst. Graphic Artists, 1970, Effie award, Grad. of Distinction award Fla. State U., 1993; named Woman of Achievement, YWCA, One of Advt.'s 100 Best Women Ad Age, 1989. Mem. Advt. Women N.Y. (1st v.p. 1984-87, bd. dirs. 1981-87, Advt. Woman of Yr. 1993), The Ad Coun. (mem. creative rev. bd. 1994—, bd. dirs. 1995—), Partnership Drug-Free Am. (mem. creative rev. bd.), Women's Venture Fund (bd. dirs. 1995—), Kappa Alpha Theta. Democrat. Home: 45 E 89th St New York NY 10128-1251 E-mail: jlotas@lmpnyc.com.

LOTEMPIO, JULIA MATILD, accountant; b. Budapest, Hungary, Oct. 14, 1934; came to U.S., 1958, naturalized 1962; d. Istvan and Irma (Sandor) Fejos; m. Anthony Joseph LoTempio, Mar. 11, 1958. AAS in Lab. Tech. summa cum laude, Niagara County C.C., Sanborn, N.Y., 1967; BS in Tech. and Vocat. Edn. summa cum laude, SUNY, Buffalo, 1970; MEd in Guidance and Counseling, Niagara U., 1973, BBA in Acctg. summa cum laude, 1983, MBA in Mgmt., 1998. Sr. analyst, rschr. Gt. Lakes Carbon Co., Niagara Falls, N.Y., 1967-71; tchr. sci. Niagara Falls Schs., 1973-75; tchr. sci. and English Starpoint Sch. System, Lockport, N.Y., 1975-77; club adminstr., acct. Twinlo Racquetball, Inc., Niagara Falls, 1979-81; bus. cons. Twinlo Beverage, Inc., 1981-85; staff acct. J.D. Elliott & Co. PC, CPAs, Buffalo, 1986-87; acct. Lewiston, 1988—2001; instr. applied chemistry Niagara County C.C., Sanborn, 1979, instr. acctg. principles, 1989—2001. Bd. dirs. Niagara Frontier Meth. Home Inc., Niagara Frontier Nursing Home Inc., The Blocher Homes Inc., Buffalo. Mem. faculty continuing edn., speaker, chairperson fin. and community rels. coms. United Meth. Ch., Dickersonville, N.Y., 1985-90; guest speaker, counselor, tchr. Beechwood Svc. Guild, Buffalo, 1987-91; bd. dirs. Niagara Frontier Meth. Home, Inc., Getzville, N.Y., 1988-2001; bd. dirs., mem. fin., investment, pension, ins., and community rels. coms. Niagara Frontier Nursing Home Co., Inc., Getzville, 1988-2001, Blocher Homes, Inc., Williamsville, N.Y., 1988-2001; asst. sec., bd. dirs., mem. exec., quality and assurance coms., chmn. community rels. com. Beechwood/Blocher Community, Buffalo, 1990-2001; mem. Coop. Parish Coun., Sanborn, N.Y., 1991-94; mem. adminstrv. bd., chmn. outreach com. Pekin (N.Y.) United Meth. Ch., 1992-2000; sec. to bd. dirs. Beechwood/Blocher Found., Amherst, N.Y., 1992-93, asst. treas., 1993-94, treas., 1994, vice chmn., 1994-2001. Mem. NAFE, Nat. Soc. Pub. Accts., Nat. Assn. Accts., Nat. Fedn. Bus. and Profl. Women's Club, Internat. Platform Assn., Niagara U. Alumni Assn., SUNY Coll. Buffalo Alumni Assn., Niagara County C.C. Alumni Assn. Avocations: public speaking, walking, travel, reading, computers. Home and Office: 1026 Ridge Rd Lewiston NY 14092-9704 E-mail: ajlotempio@juno.com.

LOTH, STANISLAW JERZY, director of photography, researcher; b. Pabianice, Lodz, Poland, Jan. 21, 1929; came to U.S., 1981; s. Emilian and Zofia (Kindler) L.; m. Lidia Cichocka, 1969; 1 child, Anna. Student, Panstwowa Wyzsza Szkola Teatralna I Filmowa, Lodz, 1950-54. Dir. photography, Poland, U.S., 1958—. Researcher three-dimensional systems N.Y., 1981, Arriflex Corp. N.Y., 1983, Panorama film system N.Y., 1985; cons. Jaws III (three-dimensional film), 1983, Acueity, Larkspur, Calif., 2000. Dir. photography: (feature films) The Certificate Origin (1st prize Cannes Film Festival, 1964), The Nightingale Boys (1st prize Venice Film Festival, 1971), Pearl of the Crown, 1973, Days and Nights (Acad. award nominee, 1977), The Wall, Polish-Am. Prodns., 1980; scriptwriter (short films) The Purple Symphony, The Trace Symphony, The Cloud Symphony, Crumbs of Life; author: (novel) This Body, 1994, (novel and script) Lili, 1994, The Blue World, Brochia, 1998, The Castle, 1999; 8 patents camera equipment, 1986-93, 3 patents film camera equipment, 1994-96, 2 patents film camera equipment, 1997-99, 3 patents depth of field/Dofi, 1998-99. Avocation: gliding. Home: 4421 Hunter Run Dr Clemmons NC 27012 Office: Acueity 700 Larkspur Landing Cir Larkspur CA 94939-1715

LOTHERY, SHAWNE LAMARR, writer, multimedia designer; b. Toledo, Dec. 12, 1969; s. Michael James Sr. and Delores Louise L.; 1 child James Coleman. Cert. of Completion, U. Toledo, 1989. Achievements include invention of Lothery's Electronic Dictionary. Home: 1026 1/2 Belmont St Toledo OH 43607-4264

LOTKE, PAUL A. orthopedic surgeon; b. Sept. 9, 1937; m. Dorothy Sue Lotke; 3 children. MD, U. Pa., 1963. Intern Univ. Hosp., Madison, Wis., 1963-64; resident Hosp. for Spl. Surgery, N.Y.c., 1964-71; prof. orthopedic surgery U. Pa. Hosp., Phila., 1971—. Editor: (book) Master Techniques of Knee Surgery, 1995; contbr. numerous articles to med. jours., chpts. to med. texts. Lt. USN, 1964-66. Mem. Knee Soc. (pres. 1985), Phila. Orthopedic Soc. (pres. 1985), Phila. Rheumatism Soc. (pres. 1986), Hosp. Spl. Surgery Soc. (pres. 1994). Office: Hosp Univ Pa 3400 Spruce St Philadelphia PA 19104-4206 E-mail: paul.lotke@uphs.upenn.edu.

LOTOCKY, WALTER LUBOMYR, music educator; b. Manhattan, N.Y., Jan. 29, 1959; s. Michael Lotocki and Rose Wasylyna Motruk; m. Anna Mary Maksymowich, Nov. 14, 1987; children: Kathryn, Tatiana, Daria, Taisa, Sonya, Wolodymyr. BS in Music, Mercy Coll., 1981; BS in Music, Westchester Conservatory Music, White Plains, N.Y., 1981. Rt. sales assoc. Haagen-Dazs, Miami, Fla., 1992—99; account exec. Lynk Sys., Inc., Ft. Lauderdale, 1999—2000; tchr. music Pompano Beach H.S., 2001—. Ukrainian Catholic. Avocations: scuba diving, swimming, fishing, boating. Home: 9015 SW 51 Pl Cooper City FL 33328 Office: Pompano Beach HS 1400 NE 6th St Pompano Beach FL 33060 Personal E-mail: wlotocky@yahoo.com.

LOTSPEICH, ELLIN SUE, elementary education educator; b. Spring Valley, Ill., July 2, 1952; d. Donald Robert and Mary Rita (Smith) Mason; m. Thomas Grant Weaver, Jan. 26, 1974 (dec. July 1989); children: Jennifer, Michelle, Patrick; m. Michael Charles Lotspeich, Apr. 9, 1994; children: Michael Charles II, Charles David. BS, Western Ill. U., 1974, M Ednl. Adminstrn., 1995. Unit art specialist Winola Unit Dist., Viola, Ill., 1974-84, Al Wood Unit Dist., Woodhull, 1984—; discipline based art cons. Getty Ctr. for Edn. in Arts, 1989—; prin. Apollo Elem. Sch., Carbon Cliff, Ill., 1998-2001; ednl. specialist Western Ill. U., 2001—; prin. Irving Elem. Sch., Kewanee, Ill. Exec. bd. Commn. on Edn. Diocese of Peoria, Ill., 1993—, exec. chmn. Religious Edn. Com., 1994—. Mem. Nat. Art Edn. Assn., Ill. Art Edn. Assn. (exec. bd. 1980—, state youth art chmn. 1990-93), Ill. Rembrandt State Assn. (editor newsletter 1987-90, bd. dirs.), Ill. Alliance for Arts, Henry Stark H.S. Art Tchrs. (pres. 1984-96). Home: 621 E Prospect St Kewanee IL 61443-3021 Office: Irving Elem 609 W Central Blvd Kewanee IL 61443

LOTSTEIN, JAMES IRVING, lawyer; b. Steubenville, Ohio, Jan. 27, 1944; s. Jack and Dorothy (Nach) L.; m. Paulette L. Gutcheon, June 25, 1972; children: Melissa A., Amanda J. BSBA, Northwestern U., 1965; JD, U. Conn., 1968. Bar: Conn. 1969, U.S. Ct. Appeals (2d cir.) 1971, U.S. Supreme Ct. 1972. From assoc. to ptnr. Hoppin, Carey & Powell, Hartford, Conn., 1969-86; ptnr. Cummings & Lockwood, 1986—96, ptnr.-in-charge, 1988-95, chmn. dept. Mergers and Acquisitions Practice Group, 2001—. Author: An Introduction to the Connecticut Business Corporation Act, 1994, Ten Things You Can Do Now to Prepare for the New Connecticut Business Corporation Act, Connecticut Business Corporation Act Sourcebook, New Indemnification Provisions of the Conneticut Business Corporation Act, 1997, Why Choose Connecticut? Advantages of the Connecticut Business Corportion Act Over the Delaware General Corporation Law, 2000, Update on Connecticut Corporation Law, Corporate Governance of Connecticut Nonprofit Corporations, 2002. Trustee Conn. Pub. Broadcasting, Inc., Conn. Pub. Broadcasting, Inc.; mem. Sec. of State's bus. adv. com. State of Conn.; active Am. Coll. Investment Counsel; mem. Econ. Devel. Agy., Canton, Conn., 2001— 1st lt. JAGC, USAR, 1968-74. Mem. ABA (chmn. dirs. and officers task force, mem. corp. laws com. 1992), Conn. Bar Assn. (chmn. mcpl. law and govtl. svc. com. 1981-82, chmn. bus. law sect. 1990-92, co-chmn. Conn. bus. corp. act task force 1993-98). Office: Cummings & Lockwood LLC City Pl I Hartford CT 06103

LOTT, ALFRED DAVIS, assistant city manager; b. Detroit, Mar. 7, 1954; s. George Edward Jr. and Muriel Davis L.; children: Alfred Davis II, Ingrid Nicole; m. Carolyn Gibson Lott, May 15, 1999. BS in Polit. Sci., Tuskegee U., 1976; MPA, U. Ctrl. Tex., 1994. Commd. 2nd lt. U.S. Army, 1976, advanced through grades to lt. col., 1998; comdr. Aviation Tng. Co., Fort Rucker, Ala., 1985-86; ops. officer Aviation Bn. Fort Hold, Killeen, Tex., 1991-92; divsn. chief aviation divsn. U.S. Army III Corps, 1993; chief pub. affairs WWII com. Dept. Def. Pentagon, Washington, 1993-95; chief pub. affairs U.S. Army, L.A., 1995-97; pub. affairs plans officer Dept. Def. Pentagon, Washington, 1997-98; asst. city mgr. City of College Park, Md., 1998—. Active Neighborhood Watch, College Park, 1998—. Mem. Am. Legion, Internat. Assn. Bus. Communicators, Ret. Officers Assn., ICMA. Democrat. Methodist. Avocation: chess. Office: City of College Park 4500 Knox Rd College Park MD 20740-3390

LOTT, BRENDA LOUISE, insurance company executive; b. Clinton, Ind., July 29, 1955; d. John and Thelma Louise (Anderson) Pastore; m. Robert Ralph Rundle, June 16, 1974 (div. July 1985); children: Danielle Marie Rundle, John Robert Rundle; m. Mark Lee Lott, July 4, 1985. BA in Polit. Sci., Colo. Women's Coll., Denver, 1976; student, Ins. Inst. of Am. Claim adjuster Allstate Ins. Co., Englewood, Colo., 1973-83; field claim adjuster Transamerica Ins. Co., 1983-86; claim examiner Colonial Ins. Co., Denver, 1986-87, examiner/supr., 1987-89, regional claim mgr., 1990-92; dir. financial and insurance svcs. Innovative Svcs. Am., Golden, Colo., 1992—. Staff speaker Western Ins. Info. Svc., Denver, 1983-85; participant, invited faculty mem. 5-day lecture series Colonial Univ., Anaheim, Calif., 1990. Sponsor Plan Internat. foster parents program, 1989—. Mem. NAFE, LWV, NAACP (mem.-at-large), Ins. Women of Denver, Internat. Customer Svc. Assn., Colo. Claims Assn. (bd. dirs. 1986-88), Claim Mgrs. Coun., Denver Claims Assn., PGA Tours Ptnrs. Avocations: raquetball, co-ed flag football, basketball, tennis, golf. Office: Innovative Svcs of Am 13922 Denver West Pkwy Ste 200 Golden CO 80401-3142

LOTT, DOLORES MAXINE, retired school system administrator; b. Rockdale, Tex., July 17, 1930; d. Isaac Hanibal and Ada (Green) Woods; m. Frank White II, Feb. 12, 1951 (div. Sept. 1955); children: Andrea Lynn, Frank III; m. Rufus Lott, July 25, 1956 (dec.); children: Rufus Jr., Vernon Keith, David. BA, Prairie View (Tex.) A&M U., 1951; EdM, Our Lady of the Lake U., San Antonio, 1963; EdD, Nova U., 1986. From procurement clk. to asst. supr. Kelly AFB, San Antonio, 1951-57; libr., counselor J.W. Riley Elem. Jr. H.S., 1957-65; counselor J.W. Riley Mid. Sch., 1965-71, Jefferson H.S., San Antonio, 1971-73; personnel dir. San Antonio Ind. Sch. Dist., 1973-83, dir. program coordination, 1983-89; ret. Lectr. Our Lady of the Lake U., summers 1971, 72. Precinct chmn. San Antonio Dem. Party, 1988—; commr. City of San Antonio Civil Svc., 1993-96; mayor pro-tem San Antonio City Coun., 1996, mem. coun., 1996-97; pres. Saturday Morning Breakfast Club, 1986—; mem. Coalition of 100 Black Women. Recipient Cmty. Svc. award Prarie View A&M Alumni Assn., 1982; fellow Our Lady of the Lake U., 1963, 65. Mem. Tex. State Tchrs. Assn., Tex. Ret. Educators Deferred Dividend Assn., San Antonio Area Tchrs. Assn. Baptist. Avocations: reading, motivational speaking, teaching church school, playing bridge, dancing. Home: 202 Morningview Dr San Antonio TX 78220-3121 E-mail: dmlott1@aol.com.

LOTT, IRA TOTZ, pediatric neurologist; b. Cin., Apr. 15, 1941; s. Maxwell and Jeneda (Totz) L.; m. Ruth J. Weiss, June 21, 1964; children: Lisa, David I. BA cum laude, Brandeis U., 1963; MD cum laude, Ohio State U., 1967. Intern Mass. Gen. Hosp., Boston, 1967, resident in pediatrics, 1967-69, resident in child neurology, 1971-74; clin. assoc. NIH, Bethesda, Md., 1969-71; from clin. rsch. fellow to asst. prof. Harvard Med. Sch., Boston, 1971-82; clin. dir. Eunice Kennedy Shriver Ctr. for Mental Retardation, Waltham, 1974-82; assoc. prof. U. Calif., Irvine, 1983-91, prof., 1992—, chmn. dept. pediat., 1990-2000, dir. clin. neurosci. devel., 2000—. Chmn. dept. pediatrics U. Calif., Irvine, 1990-2000 , dir. pediatric neurology, 1983—, clin. neuroscience devel., 2000—; pres. Prof. Child Neurology, Mpls., 1992—. Editor: Down Syndrome-Medical Advances, 1991; contbr. articles to profl. jours. Sec., treas. Child Neurology Soc., Mpls., 1987-90. Lt. comdr. USPHS, 1969-71. NIH grantee, 1974—; recipient Career Devel. award Kennedy Found., 1976. Fellow Am. Acad. Neurology; mem. Am. Pediatric Soc., Am. Neurol. Assn., Nat. Down Syndrome Soc. (sci. acad. bd. 1985—), Western Soc. for Pediatric Rsch. (councillor 1989-91). Achievements include research in relationship of Down Syndrome to Alzheimer's disease, neurometabolic disease, extracorporeal membrane oxygenation in infants. Office: U Calif Irvine Med Ctr Dept Pediatrics 101 The City Dr S # 2 Orange CA 92868-3201

LOTT, PETER F. chemist; BS, St. Lawrence U., 1949, MS, 1950; PhD, U. Conn., 1956. Assoc. prof. U. Mo., Rolla, 1956—61; chemist Pure Carbon Co., St. Mary's, Pa., 1961—63; assoc. prof. St. John's Univ., Jamaica, L.I., NY, 1963—65; prof. U. Mo., Kansas City, 1965—95; owner Specialized Scientific Svcs., LLC, Mo., 1995—. Contbr. articles. Sgt. U.S. Army, 1945—46. Mem.: Am. Indsl. Hygiene Assn., Am. Chem. Soc. Home: 5414 Holmes St Kansas City MO 64110 Office: Specialized Scientific Svcs LLC 5000 Oak St Twin Oaks N Lobby Box 151 Kansas City MO 64112

LOTT, ROGER RICHARD STANLEY, priest; b. St. Paul, Mar. 18, 1922; s. Edward Richman and Violet Marguerite Susan Lott. AB, Spring Hill Coll., 1947; LLB, Vanderbilt U., 1949, MA in English, 1957, MLS, 1958. Ordained priest Roman Catholic Ch., 1954. Prof. St. Bernard Coll., Cullman, Ala., dir. of libr.; spiritual cons. St. Bernard Abbey, cons. chem. dependency. Bd. dirs. St. Bernard Prep Sch., Cullman. Sgt. U.S. Army, 1942-45. Avocations: travel, reading. Home: St Bernard Abbey 1600 St Bernard Dr SE Cullman AL 35055-3057 E-mail: rogerlott@yahoo.com.

LOTT, TRENT, senator; b. Grenada, Miss., Oct. 9, 1941; s. Chester P. and Iona (Watson) L.; m. Patricia E. Thompson, Dec. 27, 1964; children— Chester T., Jr., Tyler Elizabeth. B.P.A., U. Miss., 1963, JD, 1967. Bar: Miss. 1967. Assoc. Bryan & Gordon, Pascagoula, Miss., 1967; adminstrv. asst. to Congressman William M. Colmer, 1968-72; mem. 93d-100th Congresses from 5th Miss. dist., 1973-89; Rep. whip 97th-100th Congresses from 5th Miss. dist., mem. Ho. Rules com.; U.S. senator from Miss., 1989—; Sen. armed svcs. com., budget com., energy, natural resource; 102d Congress, sec. Senate Rep. Conf., 103d Congress; majority whip 104th Congress; majority leader 104th-105th Congress. Field rep. for U. Miss., 1963-65; acting alumni sec. Ole Miss Alumni Assn., 1966-67; named as observer from House to Geneva Arms Control talks; chmn. Commerce, Sci. & Transp.; mem. Senate Republican Policy Com., Commerce, Fin. Com., 1996, Rules Com., 1996. Recipient Golden Bulldog award, Guardian of Small Bus. award. Mem. ABA, Jackson County Bar Assn., Sigma Nu, Phi Alpha Delta. Lodges: Mason. Republican. Baptist. Office: 487 Russell Senate Office Bldg Washington DC 20510-0001 also: 911 Jackson Ave, Ste.127 Oxford MS 38655*

LOTT, WAYNE THOMAS, systems engineer; b. Pitts., Mar. 20, 1959; s. Wayne Thomas Lott Sr. and Patricia Julia (Malanowski) Lott Martin; m. Diane Mary Phillips, Sept. 11, 1982; children: Sarah Marie, Justin Thomas. AS in Computer Sci., C.C. Allegheny County, Pitts., 1984; BSBA in Info. Sys., Robert Morris U., 1986; MS in Mgmt. Info. Sys., Am. U., 1997. Intern, programmer Thrift Drug Co., Pitts., 1986; contract programmer Comsource Tech. Svcs., 1986-87; programmer Tippins Inc., 1987; initial designer tng. AT&T, Herndon, Va., 1988, tech. tester, 1988-89, sys. analyst Va., 1989-92; sys. engr. AT&T Bell Labs., 1992-94, AT&T, Herndon, 1995-97, tech. mgr. ordering software devel., 1998-2000; dist. mgr. ordering software devel. IBM Global Svcs., 2000—, IT cons., delivery mgr., 2001—. Mem. IEEE, Upsilon Pi Epsilon. Roman Catholic. Home: 12779 Misty Creek Ln Fairfax VA 22033-1728 E-mail: Lott_Wayne@hotmail.com.

LOTTA, TOM (ANTHONY TOM LOTTA), artist; b. Rochester, N.Y., Mar. 28, 1924; s. Joseph and Julia (Roncone) L.; m. Rosemary Alionello, June 18, 1949; children: Tom, Karen. AS, Rochester Inst. Tech., 1950. Freelance artist, Rochester, 1951—. Committeeman Rep. Cen. Com., Greece, N.Y., 1970—. Sgt. U.S. Army, 1943-45. Named to, Boxing Hall of Fame, Can., 1977, Rochester Boxing Hall of Fame; recipient numerous awards for paintings, 58 awards in the arts. Mem. Am. Watercolor Soc., Soc. Illustrators, Rochester Art Club (pres. 1976-77). Roman Catholic. Studio: 1337 Beach Ave Rochester NY 14612-1846

LOTTEN, LARRY LYNN, architect; b. Carmel, Calif. s. Arthur Alfred and Alta May (Winslow) L.; m. Carmelita Mandawe, Mar. 25, 1995; children: Keith Allen, Brent Andrew. BArch, Calif. Poly. State U., San Luis Obispo, 1972. Lic. architect, Calif. Archtl. draftsman Duerr/Architect, Gilroy, Calif., 1972-86; field coord. PJHM Architects, San Jose, 1986-92, project architect, 1992-98, studio dir., 1998-00, AEDIS Architecture and Planning, San Jose, 2000—. 1st lt. U.S. Army, 1964-69. Mem. AIA. Democrat. Roman Catholic. Avocations: piano, basketball, dancing. Home: 851 Promenade Ct San Jose CA 95138-1306 Office: AEDIS Architecture Planning 1494 Hamilton Ave Ste 100 San Jose CA 95125-4537 E-mail: llotten@aedisgroup.com.

LOTTES, PATRICIA JOETTE HICKS, foundation administrator, retired nurse; b. Balt., Aug. 18, 1955; d. James Thomas and Linda Belle (Cadd) Hicks; m. Jeffrey Grant Gross, Aug. 18, 1979 (div. 1981); m. William Melamet Lottes, Sept. 10, 1983 (div. 1997). Diploma in practical nursing, Union Meml. Hosp., 1978. Staff nurse Union Meml. Hosp., Balt., 1978-79, critical care nurse, 1979-81; vis. critical care nurse, 1981-84; head nurse Pharmakinetics, Inc., 1984-85; dir. Arachnoiditis Info. and Support Network, Inc., Ballwin, Mo., 1991—2001, dir. nat. support groups, 1992—. Nat. support group leader Arachnoid, 1993-2002. Sec., treas. O'Fallon (Mo.) Elks Ladies Aux., 1989-91, treas., 1991-92, incorporator, 1991, bd. dirs., 1991-94; co-chairperson 303d Field Hosp., U.S. Army Family Support Group, St. Louis, 1990-94. Mem. Nat. Disaster Med. Systems (assoc.), Elks Benevolent Trust, Elks Nat. Home Perpetual Trust. Republican. Baptist. Avocation: quilting. Home: 606 Barbara Dr O'Fallon MO 63366-1306

LOTUACO, LUISA GO, pathologist; b. Gapan, The Phillipines, Jan. 29, 1938; d. Galicano Yuzon and Alicia (Go) L.; m. George Garrett Shepherd; 1 child, Lara. MD cum laude, U. Santo Tomas, Manila, 1960. Diplomate Am. Bd. Pathology. Adj. resident North Gen. Hosp., Manila, 1960-62; intern Mercy Hosp., Pitts., 1962-63, resident in pathology, 1963-65, Ball Meml. Hosp., Muncie, Ind., 1965-66, Henry Ford Hosp., Detroit, 1966-67; pathologist Manila Sanitarium and Hosp., 1969-72; mem. faculty dept. pathology U. Kans., Kansas City, 1972, 74-93; pathologist St. Catherine Hosp., East Chicago, Ind., 1973-74; pathologist, dir. clin. labs. VA Med. Ctr., Kansas City, Mo., 1974-94; chief pathology and lab. medicine John Pershing VA Med. Ctr., Poplar Bluff, 1994-96, chief staff, 1995—. Fellow: Am. Assn. Clin. Pathologists, Coll. Am. Pathologists; mem.: Sr. Execs. Assn., Philippine Med. Soc., Philippine Med. Soc. Kansas City (pres. 1981—83), Am. Med. Women's Assn., Am. Assn. Blood Banks, U.S. and Can. Acad. Pathologists, Am. Coll. Healthcare Execs, Rotary (pres. Poplar Bluff 1998—99, Paul Harris fellow 1996). Avocations: stamps, ceramics, antiques, opera, classical music. E-mal. Home: 14111 Christy Ln Poplar Bluff MO 63901-9751 Office: John Pershing VA Med Ctr 1500 N Westwood Blvd Poplar Bluff MO 63901-3318 E-mail: lglggs@socket.net., luisa.lotuaco@med.va.gov.

LOTVEN, HOWARD LEE, lawyer; b. Springfield, Mo., Apr. 8, 1959; s. Isadore and Gytel (Tuchmeier) L.; m. Charlotte Lotven. BA, Drake U., 1981; JD, U. Mo., Kansas City, 1984. Bar: Mo. 1984, U.S. Dist. Ct. (we. dist.) Mo. 1984. Pvt. practice, Kansas City, 1984—; asst. prosecutor City of Kansas City, 1985. Prosecutor City of Harrisonville (Mo.), 1989-91, atty., 1989-91; prosecutor City of Napoleon, Mo., 2001—. Mem. Hyde Park Crime Patrol, 1985—91, Hyde Park Assn. Zoning and Planning Commn., 1993—97; vol. Heartland United Way, 1995; trustee Pilgrim Chapel, 2001—, Heart of Am. Stand Down, 2001; judge Mo. Sta H.S. Moot Ct. Competition, 1992. Mem. ABA, Mo. Bar Assn. (young lawyers coun. 1986-88, lectr. 1987-90, criminal law com. 1989—, gen. practice law com. 1990—, co-chair criminal law com. 1991-92, exec. coun. gen. practice law com. 1993-99, Law Day spkr. 1986, 96, lectr. 1987-90, 92, 97), Kansas City Bar Assn. (chmn. mcpl. cts. com. 2002, Vol. Atty. Project, 1992—, Vol. Atty. Project award winner 1994, continuing edn. spkr. 2000—), House Rabbit Soc., Delta Theta Phi, Omicron Delta Kappa, others. Democrat. Jewish. Avocation: sports. Office: 1125 Grand Blvd Ste 915 Kansas City MO 64106

LOTWIN, STANFORD GERALD, lawyer; b. N.Y.C., June 23, 1930; s. Herman and Rita (Saltzman) L.; m. Judy Scott, Oct. 15, 1994; children: Lori Hope, David. BS, Bklyn. Coll., 1951, LLB, 1954, LLM, 1957. Bar: N.Y. 1954, U.S. Supreme Ct. 1961, Pa. 1986. Ptnr. Blank Rome Tenzer, Greenblatt LLP, N.Y.C., 1987—; of counsel Frankfurt, Garbus, Klein & Selz, 1983-87. Served with U.S. Army, 1954-56. Fellow Am. Acad. Matrimonial Lawyers (bd. of mgrs. 1984—); mem. N.Y. State Bar Assn. (family law sect.), N.Y. County Trial Lawyers (lectr. 1980—), Internat. Acad. Matrimonial Attys. Office: 405 Lexington Ave New York NY 10174-0002

LOTZ, GEORGE MICHAEL, retired computer graphics executive, graphic designer, photographer; b. Balt., Aug. 28, 1928; s. Michael Henry and Mina Catherine Lotz; m. Anna Mae Carlson, July 21, 1951; 1 child, Georgeanna. Student, Md. Inst. Art, 1956-58, Johns Hopkins U., 1957-58, Catonsville C.C., 1975, Essex C.C., 1976-78. Mech. draftsman, designer Sinclair Scott Canning House Machinery Co., Balt., 1948-50; illustrator, designer Comm. divsn. Bendix Corp., Towson, Md., 1950-69, supr. graphic arts, photography, 1969-73, supr. computer graphics and drafting, 1972-81, mgr. tech., publs., engring. libr., transformer design, multilith dept., spl. svcs. lab., engring. print dept. graphic arts & photography depts., 1981-83; mgr. elec. pub. & tech. svcs. depts. Allied Signal Co. (formerly Bendix Corp.), 1983-93; ret., 1993; owner George M. Lotz Designer/Photographer, 1993—. Art dir., pres. Glen Arm Graphic, 1963-74; advisor Md. State Dept. Art Edn., 1973-78, U. Md. Coll. Human Ecology, 1981—, Essex C.C. Computer Graphics, 1981—, C.C. Balt. Graphics, 1978—, Goucher Coll., 1991—; mem. panel Nat. Endowment Arts, 1977-78; conf. chmn. Indsl. Graphics Internat., U. Md., 1974, adv. Coll. of Human Ecology & Art Design, 1981—; advisor graphic arts C.C. Balt., 1978—, Essex C.C., 1981—; tchr. tech. writing Goucher Coll.; guest spkr. various locals colls., 1973, 77, profl. groups, 1967-78. Contbr. articles on graphic art and edn. to profl. jours. Judge Jr. Miss. Pagent, Reisterstown, Md., 1971, 72. With USNR, 1947-48. Recipient 38 nat. awards for art direction, graphics design including 1st pl. newsletter design Nat. Assn. Indsl. Artists, 1970, 1st pl. award Assoc. Printing Industries Am., 1976, award of excellence Printing Industries Md., 1978, 79, 1st pl. in photography 1982 World's Fair Design Competition. Mem. Indsl. Graphics Internat. (pres. 1975-77, exec. dir. 1980—, award of merit 13th ann. design competition for promotional photography Vancouver, B.C., Can., 1986), Coun. Comm. Soc. (dir. 1984-85), Advt. Assn. Balt. (dir. 1971-78), Soc. Tech. Comm. (1st place award 1977), Bendix Emblem Club, Bendix Mgmt. Club (pres. 1982-83), Balt. Camera Club. E-mail: G. Home and Office: 11212 Old Carriage Rd Glen Arm MD 21057-9415 E-mail: g-lotz@msn.com.

LOTZ, JOAN THERESA, public relations company executive; b. N.Y.C., Feb. 22, 1948; d. Andrew J. and Joan (McCartney) L. BA, Lehman Coll., 1970. Libr. asst. Met. Mus. Art, N.Y.C., l969-74; office mgr. York Cable Corp., Inc., 1974-77, Mobile Communications, Inc., N.Y.C., 1977-78; lease mgr. Major Muffler Ctrs., Inc., 1978-81; v.p., asst. to chmn. Rowland Worldwide, 1981-93; pres. JL Enterprises, 1993—. N.Y. State Regent's scholar, 1965-69. Mem. Nat. Scholastic Soc. Democrat. Roman Catholic. Avocation: ballet.

LOTZE, EVIE DANIEL, psychodramatist; b. Roswell, N.Mex., Mar. 6, 1943; d. Wadsworth Richard and Lee Ora (Norrell) Daniel; m. Christian Dieter Lotze, June 9, 1963; children: Conrad, Monica. BA cum laude, La. State U., 1964; MA, Goddard Coll., 1975; PhD, Union Inst., Cin., 1990. Dir. Casa Alegre, Hogares, Albuquerque, 1979-80; pvt. practice Riyadh, Saudi Arabia, 1980-83, Silver Spring, Md., 1983-85; dir. Gulf States Psychodrama Tng., Houston, 1986-88; founder, dir. Innerstages Psychodrama Tng., Houston and Washington, 1988-99; program devel. cons. in tng. Children's Nat. Med. Ctr., Washington, 1994-96; pvt. practice Paris, 1996-97; mem. sr. profl. staff Pretrial Svcs. Resource Ctr., Washington, 1998-2001; mem. Work Culture Transformation Bd., USAF, 2001; cons. Work Transformation Group, 2001—. Supr. Houston Area psychodramatists, 1988—98; tng. cons. Assn. Applied Psychologists, Moscow, 1992—97; cons. in field. Author: (tng. manual) Clinical Psychodrama Training Manual, 3 vols., 1990, Pretrial Services Reference Book, 1999. Bd. dirs. Interact Theater, Houston, 1992. Recipient Fulbright sr. scholars award for Russia. Democrat. Lutheran. Avocations: cross-country skiing, biking, hiking, camping, reading. Home: 2250 Leetown Pike Kearneysville WV 25430 E-mail: evielotze@hotmail.com.

LOTZENHISER, GEORGE WILLIAM, music educator, university administrator, composer; b. Spokane, Wash., May 16, 1923; m. Kathryn Tuttle, 1944; children : William (dec.), Jon. BA cum laude, Ea. Wash. U., 1946, BEd in Social Sci., 1947; MusM, U. Mich., 1948; EdD, U. Oreg., 1956. Prof. music U. Ariz., Tucson, 1948-60; prof. Ea. Wash. U., Cheney, 1960-83, dir. H.S. creative arts summer series, 1960-83; dean Ea. Wash. U. Sch. Fine Arts, 1960-83, dean emeritus, 1983—. Cons. and lectr. in field; tchg. fellow U. Mich., 1947-48, U. Oreg., 1955-56. Author: A Study of Faculty Loads in Member Schools of the National Association of Schools of Music, 1963, A

Study of the Selection Process of Administrators of the Fine Arts in Colleges and Universities in the U.S., 1970, Music 200: A Programmed Music Theory Text; numerous solo and ensemble compositions; contbr. articles to profl. jours.; profl. condr./trombonist symphony, opera, musical theatre, ballet, circus, etc. Mem. Wash. State Music Adv. Com., 1967-83, exec. com. Alliance for Arts Edn., 1972-83; mem. Spokane Riverfront Festival of the Arts, 1976-78, Allied Arts of Wash. State, 1977-83. Served to rear adm. USNR, 1942-82. Decorated Legion of Merit; named Disting. Eagle Scout, Boy Scouts Am. Mem. ASCAP, Nat. Assn. Schs. Music (accreditation com. chmn. 1960—), Nat. Music Educators Research Council, N.W. Assn. Accreditation Com., Western Assn. Schs. and Colls. Com. Congregationalist. Home: PO Box 1528 Coupeville WA 98239-1528 E-mail: glotz@whidbey.net.

LOTZER, GERALD BALTHAZAR, lawyer; b. Moorehead, Minn., May 28, 1951; s. Clem B. and Erna (Jeschke) L.; m. Nancy Louise Martin, June 1, 1974; children: Jonathan, Benjamin. BA, U. North Tex., 1973; JD, Baylor U., 1988. Bar: Tex. 1988, U.S. Dist. Ct. (no. dist.) Tex. 1988. Supr. br. Liberty Mut., Dallas, 1974-80; supr. home office Trinity Universal, 1980-82; supr. region Comml. Union Ins. Co., 1982-86; dir. Fanning, Harper & Martinson, 1994—. Mem. ABA, Tex. Bar. Office: Fanning Harper & Martinson PC 2 Energy Sq 4849 Greenville Ave Ste 1300 Dallas TX 75206- E-mail: glotzer@fhnlaw.com.

LOU, JIANFENG, research scientist; b. Zhejiang, China, 1968; came to U.S., 1993. m. Wei Li; 1 child, Michelle B. BSChemE, Zhejiang U., Hangzhou, China, 1989, MS in Polymer Materials, 1991; MS in Chem. Engring. Practice, MIT, 1996, PhD in Chem. Engring., 1998. Rsch. asst. State Key Lab. of Polymer Reaction Engring., Hangzhou, 1991-93; scientist Elf Atochem N.Am., King of Prussia, Pa., 1998—. Contbr. articles to profl. jours., chpt. to book. Mem. AIChE, Am. Chem. Soc., Sigma Xi. Achievements include study on the application of microwave technology for chemical processing application; advances in the understanding of how microwaves interact with chemical mixtures to generate heat. Avocations: sports, swimming, hiking, travel. Office: Elf Atochem NAm 900 1st Ave King Of Prussia PA 19406-1308

LOU, ZHENG (DAVID), technical specialist; b. Changshu, Jiangsu, Peoples Republic China; came to U.S., 1982; s. Gui-Xin and Pei-Ling Lou; m. Min Yu, 1984; children: Katherine, Paul, Craig. BE, Zhejiang U., Hangzhou, China, 1982; PhD, U. Mich., 1990. Asst. rsch. scientist Transp. Rsch. Inst. U. Mich., Ann Arbor, 1990-93; tech. specialist Ford Motor Co., Ypsilanti, Mich., 1993-2000, Visteon Corp., Plymouth , 2000—. Contbr. articles to Jour. Rheology, Jour. Biomechanics, others. Grantee NASA, 1992-94, U.S. Army, 1992-94. Mem. ASME, SAE, N.Y. Acad. Scis., Tau Beta Pi, Sigma Xi. Achievements include first to research in nonlinear dynamic interaction between an electrorheological fluid and a viscometer of electrorheological valves and dampers; for heat transfer model in hyperthermia as a tumor therapy, engine valve control, pressure regulators, powertrain thermal systems; patents in field. Home: 11200 Fellows Creek Dr Plymouth MI 48170-6382 Office: Visteon Corp Cube C236 45000 Helm St Plymouth MI 48170 E-mail: zlou@visteon.com.

LOUARD, AGNES A. social work educator; b. Savannah, Ga., Mar. 10, 1922; d. Jospeh B. and Agnes (Hollinger) Anthony; m. V. Benjamin Louard (dec. Aug. 1986); children: Rita Jean, Diane C. Louard-Michel, Kenneth A. BA, U. Pa., 1944; MA, Fisk U., 1945; MSW, Columbia U., 1948; postgrad., NYU Sch. Edn., 1970-72. Asst. to dir. South Broad St. U.S.O., Phila., 1945-46; supr. children and teen activity Manhattanville Neighborhood Ctr., N.Y.C., 1948-50, supr. children's div., 1950-52; dir. recreation and edn. Union Settlement Assn., 1952-57; dir. East Harlem Project, 1958-59; sr. caseworker Speedwell Svcs. for Children, Inc., 1959-61, Leake and Watts Children's Home, Yonkers, N.Y., 1962-63; dir. recreation A. Holly Patterson Home for Aged and Infirmed, Uniondale, 1963-65; field instr. Sch. Social Work Columbia U., N.Y.C., 1965-67, asst. prof. Sch. Social Work, 1967-71, assoc. prof. sch. social work, 1971-92; adj. prof. Sch. Social Work Columbia U., 1992—. Couns. Harlem Youth Bd., N.Y.C., Headstart Program, N.Y.C., 1966-68, James Weldon Johnson Ctr., N.Y.C., 1967-69, CCNY Psychol. Ctr., 1969-70, Volt-Headstart Op., Schenectady, N.Y., 1970, Atlantic City, 1972, Harlem Hosp., 1971-73, Spence Chapin Foster Care and Adoption Svcs. Agy., N.Y.C., 1973—; trainer summer Headstart Progs., NYU, 1967-68; mem. staff E.P.D.A. Guidance Inst., Queens Coll., 1969. Trustee Union Chapel, Oak Bluffs, Martha's Vineyard, Mass., 1975—, Union Chapel, Oak Bluffs, 1975—, sec., 1995—; mem. adv. bd. YWCA, New Harlem, N.Y., 1985-88; bd. dirs., past pres. Harriet Tubman Cmty. Ctr., Hempstead, N.Y., 1964-86; bd. dirs. Pleasant Ave. Day Care Ctr., 1987—, Peninsula Counselling Ctr., Woodmere, N.Y., 1972—, pres., 1985-88, Schomburg Corp., 1989—, trustee, 1994-96, 97—; v.p. Allen Neighborhood Care Team, 1995-97. Mem. NAACP, NASW, ACLU, Common Cause, Women's City Club. Democrat. Avocations: reading, travel, jazz music. Home: 560 Riverside Dr Apt 6L New York NY 10027-3240 Office: Columbia U Sch Social Work 622 W 113th St New York NY 10025-7982

LOUARD, RITA JEAN, endocrinologist, educator; b. N.Y.C., June 15, 1954; d. Vernon Benjamin and Agnes Anthony L. AB, Bryn Mawr Coll., 1976; MD, Columbia U., 1981. Diplomate Am. Bd. Internal Medicine and Endocrinology. Intern, then resident Boston City Hosp., 1981-84; clin. instr. Peninsula Hosp., Far Rockaway, N.Y., 1984-85; attending physician Harlem Hosp., N.Y.C., 1985-86; instr. clin. medicine Columbia U. Coll. Physicians and Surgeons, 1985-86; fellow in endocrinology Yale U., New Haven, 1986-89, assoc. rsch. scientist, 1989-94; med. dir. eastern blind rehab. svc. West Haven (Conn.) VA Med. Ctr., 1992-94; dir. Comprehensive Diabetes Care Ctr., assoc. prof. Med. Coll. Ga., Augusta, 1994-2000; attending physician Atlanta Med. Ctr., 2000—, sect. chief endocrinology, co-dir. diabetes metabolic ctr., 2000—. Chair diabetes adv. coun., Atlanta Med. Ctr., 2001—, Ga. diabetes adv. council, 2001—; instr. Nat. Diabetes Ednl. Initiative, 1997-99; dir. diabetes metabolic ctr., 2001—. Mem. editl. bd. Diabetes Lifeline, 1997—, Ethnicity and Disease, 1997—. Hannah E. Longshure Meml. Med. scholar Bryn Mawr Coll., Pa., 1977. Fellow Am. Coll. Endocrinology; mem. ACP, Internat. Soc. Study Hypertension in Blacks, Am. Diabetes Assn. (bd. dirs. South Coastal region 1999, pres. 2002-03, nat. com. 2000--), Am. Women's Med. Assn., Endocrine Soc., Am. Assn. Clin. Endocrinologists, Alpha Omega Alpha. Democrat. Episcopalian. Avocation: quilting. Home: 760 Palatine Ave Atlanta GA 30316 E-mail: rita.louard@etenethealth.com.

LOUARGAND, MARC ANDREW, real estate executive, financial consultant; b. San Francisco, July 3, 1945; s. Andrew Louargand and Edna Antoinette McNeil (dec.); m. Elizabeth A. Warner, June 18, 1966 (div. Oct. 1978); m. J. R. McDaniel, Feb. 14, 1986. BA, U. Calif., Santa Barbara, 1967; MBA, UCLA, 1974, PhD, 1982. Asst. prof. Calif. State Polytech. U., Pomona, 1975-77; assoc. prof. Calif. State U., Northridge, 1977-83, U. Mass., Boston, 1983-88; sr. lectr. Ctr. for Real Estate Devel. MIT, Cambridge, 1986-93; 2d v.p., sr. officer Mass. Mut. Life Ins. Co., Springfield, Mass., 1993-94; mng. dir., co-founder Cornerstone Real Estate Advisors, 1993—. Chmn. Mile Square Farm Inc., Vt. Only of Mile Square Farm; cons. in field. Author: CRE2000: Managing the Fifth Strategic Resource, Study Guide to Financial Management, 1986, (with others) Principles and Techniques of Appraisal Review, 1980, Handbook of Real Estate Portfolio Management; co-editor Jour. Real Estate, Portfolio Mgmt.; assoc. editor Jour. Real Estate Lit., Jour. Corp. Real Estate (UL), Briefings in Real Estate Fin., (UK); contbr. articles to profl. jours. Bd. dirs. Beverly Glen Assn., Bel Air, Calif., 1973-77, Citronia Homeowners Assn., Northridge, Calif., 1978-83; chmn. Carlisle (Mass.) Bd. Assessors, 1985-93. Fellow, Homer Hoyt Inst. Fellow Am. Real Estate Soc. (dir.); mem. Nat. Coun. Real Estate Investment Fiduciaries (chair portfolio strategy com.). Republican. Avocations: tree farming, skiing, building restoration. Home: 32 Longmeadow St Longmeadow MA 01106-1015

LOUBE, SAMUEL DENNIS, physician; b. Rumania, Aug. 26, 1921; came to U.S., 1922, naturalized, 1927; s. Harry and Rebecca (Pollack) L.; m. Emily Wallace, Apr. 14, 1976; children— Julian M., Jonathan B., Susan C., Karen E., Patricia A., Pamela B., Brian R. AB, George Washington U., 1941, MD cum laude, 1943. Diplomate: Am. Bd. Internal Medicine. Intern, then resident in medicine Gallinger Municipal Hosp., Washington, 1943-46; physician US-PHS, 1946-48; postdoctoral fellow NIH, 1948-50; research fellow in endocrinology Michael Reese Hosp., Chgo., 1948-49; research fellow in metabolism and endocrinology May Inst. Jewish Hosp., Cin., 1949-50; mem. faculty George Washington U. Med. Sch., 1950-89, clin. prof. medicine, 1975-89, prof. emeritus, 1989. Practice medicine specializing in endocrinology and metabolic diseases, Washington, 1950-88, mem. Washington Internal Medicine Group, 1965-88; former chmn. dept. medicine, chief sect. endocrinology Sibley Meml. Hosp. Contbr. articles to med. jours. Fellow ACP; mem. AMA, Am. Diabetes Assn., Endocrine Soc., Am. Soc. Internal Medicine, Diabetes Assn. D.C. (past pres.), Jacobi Med. Soc. (past pres.). Jewish.

LOUCK, JAMES DONALD, physicist, researcher; b. Grand Rapids, Mich., Dec. 13, 1928; m. Margaret Carolyn Marsh, 1960; children: Samuel, Thomas, Joseph. BS, Ala. Poly. Inst., Auburn, 1950; MS, Ohio State U., 1952, PhD, 1958. Staff mem. Los Alamos (N.Mex.) Sci. Lab., 1958-60, 63-83, lab. fellow, 1983-90; assoc. rsch. prof. Auburn (Ala.) U., 1960-63, lab. assoc., ret. fellow, 1991—; adj. prof. Nankai U., Tianjin, China, 1996—, hon. dir. ctr. combinatorics China, 1998—; pres. Nicholas C. Metropolis Math. Found., 1998—. Co-author: (book) Quantum Theory of Angular Momentum, 1981, The Racah-Wigner Algebra in Quantum Theory, 1981, Symbolic Dynamics of Trapezoidal Maps, 1986; assoc. editor: Annals of Combinatorics, 1996—, mem. adv. bd.: Jour. Molecular Spectroscopy, 1975—85, mem. editl. bd.: Jour. Math. Physics, 1989—91; contbr. articles to profl. jours. Lt. (j.g.) USN, 1952—55. Mem.: AAAS, Am. Phys. Soc. Achievements include discover and development of numerous mathematical advances in physical applications of symmetry methods and their combinatorial interpretations. Avocation: gardening. Home: 54 Wildflower Way Santa Fe NM 87506-2116

LOUCKS, DANIEL PETER, environmental systems engineer; b. Chambersburg, Pa., June 4, 1932; s. Emerson Hunsberger and Eleanor Wright (Johnson) L.; m. Marjorie Ann Grant, June 24, 1967; children: Jennifer Lee, Susan Louise. BS, Pa. State U., 1954; MS, Yale U., 1955; PhD, Cornell U., 1965. Asst. prof. environ. engring. Cornell U., Ithaca, N.Y., 1965-70, assoc. prof., 1970-74, prof., 1974—, chmn. dept., 1974-80; assoc. dean research and grad. studies Cornell U. (Coll. Engring.), 1980-81. Rsch. fellow Harvard U., Cambridge, Mass., 1968; economist IBRD, Washington, 1972-73; vis. prof. MIT, Cambridge, 1977-78; rsch. scholar Internat. Inst. for Applied Sys. Analysis, 1981-82; vis. disting. prof. U. Colo., 1992, U. Adelaide, 1992, Tech. U. Aachen, Germany, 1993, U. Tech., Delft, The Netherlands, 1995; cons. NATO, UN, WHO, FAO, UNESCO, IRBD on water resources and regional devel. projects in Asia, Western and Eastern Europe, Africa and L.Am., 1970—, EPA on water quality planning USSR, 1975-77; vis. prof. Internat. Inst. Hydraulic and Environ. Engring., Delft, 1976-80, 86—; environ. adv. bd. U.S. Army Corps Engrs., 1994-98, chmn. 1996-98; dir. NATO Advanced Rsch. Workshops, 1990, 95. Contbr. articles to jours. and books on math. models. for mng. water resources systems and environ. quality. Bd. dirs. Wilderness Corp., Plymouth, Vt., 1968-96, treas., 1987-96; pres. Cmty. Improvement Assn., Ithaca, 1976-77, 99-2000. Capt., aviator USNR, 1956-81. Recipient U.S. Sr. Rsch. award Alexander von Humboldt Found., 1992, Joy Wyatt Challenge (EDUCOM) award, 1991, Disting. Lecture award Nat. Rsch. Coun. Taiwan, 1990, 99, Warren A. Hall medal Univs. Coun. Water Resources, 2000; Fulbright-Hayes fellow Yugoslavia, 1975. Fellow and honorary mem. ASCE (Walter Huber rsch. award 1970, Julian Hinds award 1986); mem. AAAS, NAE, Am. Geophys. Union, Inst. Mgmt. Scis., Internat. Water Resources Assn., Am. Water Resources Assn., Internat. Assn. Hydraulic Rsch., Internat. Assn. Hydrologic Scis., Sigma Xi. Home: 116 Crest Ln Ithaca NY 14850-2704 Office: Cornell U Hollister Hall Ithaca NY 14853 E-mail: DPL3@cornell.edu.

LOUCKS, RALPH BRUCE, JR. investment company executive; b. St. Louis, Dec. 10, 1924; s. Ralph Bruce and Dola (Blake) L.; m. Lois Holloway, June 4, 1949 (dec. Sept. 1983); children: Elizabeth, Mary Jane; m. Mary Sutliffe Stahl, June 2, 1984. BA, Lake Forest Coll., 1949; postgrad. U. Chgo., 1950-52. Investment fund mgr. No. Trust Co., Chgo., 1950-53, Brown Bros. Harriman & Co., Chgo., 1953-55; investment counsel, pres. Tilden, Loucks & Grannis, Chgo., 1955-80; sr. v.p. Bacon, Whipple & Co., 1981-88; mng. dir. Tilden, Loucks & Woodnorth, 1988—. Served with 11th Armored Divsn., AUS, 1943-45. Decorated Bronze Star medal, Purple Heart. Mem. Investment Counsel Assn. Am., Huguenot Soc. Ill. (pres. 1960-61), Nat. Assn. Security Dealers (registered prin.), Soc. Colonial Wars. Office: 150 S Wacker Dr Chicago IL 60606-4103

LOUCKS, TERRY LEE, writer, retired biosystems executive; b. Loveland, Colo., Feb. 10, 1936; BS in Petroleum Engring., U. Tulsa, 1960, MS in Petroleum Engring., 1961; PhD in Physics, Pa. State U., 1963. Prof. physics Iowa State U., 1963-68; dir. Rockwell Sci. Ctr., 1969-78; pres., CEO, Compuchem, Raleigh, N.C., 1980-82, ETCC, Inc., Raritan, N.J., 1982-83; dir. Vitesse (Calif.) Electronics, 1987-88; v.p. tech. Norton Co., Worcester, Mass., 1983-88; cons. Rothschild Ventures, N.Y.C., 1988; pres., CEO, chmn. PerSeptive Biosystems, Cambridge, Mass., 1988-90, ret., 1991. Cons. Rothschild Ventures, N.Y.C., 1988. Author: Burning Words, 1998. Recipient Disting. Alumni award U. Tulsa, 1990, Alumni Fellow award Pa. State U., 1992. Home: 13611 Mc Queens Ct Jacksonville FL 32225-4912 E-mail: zloucks@aol.com.

LOUCKS, VERNON R., JR. retired medical technologies executive; b. Evanston, Ill., Oct. 24, 1934; s. Vernon Reece and Sue (Burton) L.; m. Linda Kay Olson, May 12, 1972; 6 children. BA in History, Yale U., 1957; MBA, Harvard U., 1963. Sr. mgmt. cons. George Fry & Assos., Chgo., 1963-65; with Baxter Travenol Labs., Inc. (now Baxter Internat. Inc.), Deerfield, 1966—99, exec. v.p., 1976, also bd. dirs., chmn., 1980, CEO, 1990—99. Bd. dirs. Dun & Bradstreet Corp., Emerson Electric Co., Quaker Oats Co., Anheuser-Busch Cos.; bd. advisors Nestlē U.S.A. Trustee Rush-Presbyn.-St. Luke's Med. Ctr.; assoc. Northwestern U. 1st lt. USMC, 1957-60. Recipient Citizen Fellowship award Chgo. Inst. Medicine, 1982, Nat. Health Care award B'nai B'rith Youth Svcs., 1986, William McCormick Blair award Yale U., 1989, Yale medal, 1997, Semper Fidelis award USMC, 1989, Disting. Humanitarian award St. Barnabas Found., 1992, Alexis de Tocqueville award for community svc. United Way Lake County, 1993, Industrialist of Yr. award Am. Israel C. of C., 1996; named 1983's Outstanding Exec. Officer in the healthcare industry Fin. World; elected to Chgo.'s Bus. Hall of Fame, Jr. Achievement, 1987. Mem.: Bus. Coun., Bus. Roundtable (conf. bd., mem. policy com.), Health Industry Mfrs. Assn. (chmn. 1983), Chgo. Club.

LOUDEN, ROBERT BURTON, philosopher, educator; b. Lafayette, Ind., Apr. 8, 1953; s. Robert Kurz and Anne (Zimmerman) L.; m. Lucinda Baker, June 15, 1980 (div. Sept. 1982); m. Tama Silverstein, May 19, 1985; children: Elizabeth Mary, Sarah Rebecca. BA, U. Calif., Santa Cruz, 1975; MA, U. Chgo., 1976, PhD, 1981. Vis. asst. prof. philosophy Iowa State U., Ames, 1980-82; asst. prof. philosophy U. Southern Maine, Portland, 1982-86; assoc. prof. philosophy U. South Maine, 1988-96, prof. philosophy, 1996—. Series editor Ethical Theory SUNY Press, 1988-94; vis. prof. philosophy Göttingen (Germany) U., 1992, Emory U., Atlanta, 1995. Author: Morality and Moral Theory, 1992, Kant's Impure Ethics, 2000; editor: The Greeks and Us, 1996, Am. Kant Soc. Publ. Series, 2001-, Friedrich Schleiermacher Lectures on Philosophical Ethics, 2002; contbr. articles to profl. jours. Am. Coun. Learned Socs. fellow, 1989-90; Humboldt Found. rsch. fellow, 1991-92, 96-97; NEH fellow, 1996. Mem. Am. Philos. Assn. (rsch. fellow 2002-03), No. New Eng. Philos. Assn. (pres. 1986-87), Maine Philios. Inst. (pres. 1985-86). Avocations: violin music, cycling. Home: 96 Clinton St Portland ME 04103 Office: U So Maine 96 Falmouth St Portland ME 04103-4864 E-mail: louden@maine.edu.

LOUDEN, WILLARD CHARLES, artist, environmental consultant; b. Trinidad, Colo., Jan. 16, 1925; s. Roy D. and Zita P. (Bradley) L.; m. Virginia M. Hudson, Juen 1964 (div. 1969); 1 child, Tamara; m. Mary Ann Thiel, Jan. 1, 1973. AA, Trinidad (Colo.) State Coll., 1947; BA, U. Mo., 1949; postgrad., Colo. State U., 1973. Rancher, Branson, Colo., 1946-86; tchr. Branson High Sch., 1952-57; wildlife cinematographer Branson, 1955-62; vol. Peace Corps, Iran, 1962-64; geology, anthropology, mus. tech. instr. Trinidad State Coll., 1973-76; bldg. renovator Trinidad, 1977-95; environ. cons. Branson, 1977—; mus. dir., curator A.R. Mitchell Mus. & Gallery, Trinidad, 1980-98. Bd. dirs. Louden-Henritze Archeol. Mus., 1990—. One man shows include Columbian Hotel, Trinidad, Colo., 1960, Colo. Bank and Trust, Delta, Colo., La Rennaisance, Pueblo, Colo., 1993; three person show A.R. Mitchell Mus. and Gallery, Trinidad, 1985; exhibited in group shows at Folsom Art Group, Folsom, N.Mex., Trinidad, 1960-67, Trinidad Roundup Shows, 1975-87, Nat. Art Shows, LaJunta, Colo., 1979-90, Wildlife Art Exhbn., Denver, 1983, Artists of the West Show, Colorado Springs, 1988, Santa Fe Trail Days Show, Trinidad, 1989-90; included in permanent collections: Trinidad Nat. Bank, Otero Jr. Coll., LaJunta, Nuzum Nurseries, Boulder, Bob Doak Oil Explorations, Albuquerque. Pres. So. Colo. Heritage Conservancy, Pueblo, 1987—, S.E. Colo. Area Health Edn. Ctr., 1990—, Friends of Purgatory, 1993—; adv. com. Pinon Canyon Manuever Area Land Utilization Tech. Adv. Com., 1984—; chmn. bd. Mid-Town Investment Corp., Trinidad, 1975-87. With U.S. Army, 1943-46. Recipient Outstanding Svc. award, Colo. Nature Conservancy, 1986, Internat. Peace Prize, Beyond War, 1987, Stephen Hart award, Colo. State Hist. Soc., 1988, Outstanding Svc. award, A.R. Mitchell Mus. and Gallery, 1990, Chenoweth award for outstanding cmty. svc., 1996. Mem. Colo. Archaeol. Soc. (chpt. pres.), Trinidad Art League (pres. 1975-77), Trinidad Hist. Soc. (hon. life mem.). Avocations: photography, backpacking, archaeology, Western history, organic gardening. Home: 83500 County Rd 10 Branson CO 81027-9501 Office: AR Mitchell Mus & Gallery PO Box 95 Trinidad CO 81082-0095

LOUDENSLAGER, LARRY NEAL, safety and environmental coordinator; b. Thomas, Okla., Aug. 19, 1949; s. Samuel Grover and Twila Mae (Valentine) L.; m. diana Caroll Reber, June 27, 1969; children: Kimberly, Larry Neal, Lori. BA, Southwestern Okla. State U., 1972; M Ed, 1976. Cert. tchr., Okla.; registered environ. mgr. Nat. Registry Environ. Mgrs. Instr. art and indsl. arts instr. Okeene Pub. Schs., Okla., 1972-78; sys. operator Delhi Gas Pipeline, Canton, 1978-80; safety technician, 1980-82; dist. safety environ. coord. Ozark Gas Pipeline, Fort Smith, 1982-90, TXO Prodn., 1984-90; regional safety coord. Sonat Exploration Co., 1990-99; prin. safety and health rep. El Paso Prodn., 1999—. Pres. Ark. One-Call System, Little Rock, 1994-95. Feature artist We. Plains Libr. sys., 1971p designer tng. aids trailer; inventor emergency security latch; designer counterweight relief valve vent cap. Asst. scoutmaster Gt. Salt Plains coun. Boy Scouts Am., Okeene, 1976-77; mem. sch. bd. Okeene Pub. schs., 1981-82. Recipient cert. Nat. Safety Coun. Mem. Am. Soc. Safety Engrs. (cert.), Okla. Air Nat. Guard (hon.), Masons.

LOUDERBACK, KEVIN WAYNE, business owner; b. Mt. Vernon, Ill., Mar. 10, 1971; s. Richard Lynn and Wilberta Maxine (Anderson) L. Draftsman, civil engr. Finley Engring. Co., Inc., Lamar, Mo., 1988-91; civil engr. GTE North, Sun Prairie, Wis., 1991-92; with Empiregas Corp., Lebanon, Mo., 1992-93; EMT-A Breech Paramedics Ambulance Svc., 1993-94; EMT Lake of the Ozarks Ambulance Svc., 1994—; owner, chmn., pres. Ozark Jerky Co., Inc., Conway, 1992—; v.p., CFO J&K Enterprises, Inc., 1997—; owner, ptnr. Ecclectic Collections, ltd., Lebanon, 1997—. Vol. EMT-P Conway Rescue Group, 1993-95, EMT-P Dallas County Rescue, 1995—. Vol. fireman Barton County Alert Squad, Lamar, 1989-92; mem. Barton County Disaster Team, 1989-92, Barton County Haz-Mat Squad, 1988-92, Mo. Emergency Preparedness Assn., 1989-92; dir. Dallas County First Responders, 1995—. Baptist. Avocations: flying private planes, golf, photography, travel. Office: 2011 S Jefferson Ave Lebanon MO 65536-4285 Home: 603 Gibbs Ave Mount Vernon MO 65712-1618

LOUDERBACK, PETER DARRAGH, accountant, consultant; b. July 16, 1931; s. Darragh and Constance (Clemens) L.; m. Roberta Wildow, Jan. 7, 1978; children by previous marriage: John, Jim, Susan, Tom. BA, U. Vt., 1955. With Bell Telephone of Pa., Phila., 1955-61, supr. revenue acctg., 1959-61; cons. Peat, Marwick, Mitchell & Co., Newark, 1962-71, ptnr. in charge comml. bank cons. practice, 1979-81, dir. fin. instns. cons. practice, 1981-85; prin., owner earnings performance group, 1985-90; dir. fin. svcs. cons. AGS Info. Svcs., 1990-91; owner Cons. Cooperative, Inc., 1991—. CEO Spatial Decision Mgmt. Windermere, Fla., 1994-97; dir., cons. svcs. Medici Tech., Inc., Lebanon, N.H., 1997-98; ind. bank cons., 1999—. Served to capt. U.S. Army, 1961. Republican. Episcopalian. Home: 2 Bayberry Ln Nantucket MA 02554-2800 E-mail: plouder@attbi.com.

LOUDERBACK, TOM, auditor; b. Washington, Apr. 23, 1953; s. Warren Clinton and Jacqueline Emelia Louderback; m. Carolyn Joan Louderback, May 10, 1975; 1 child, Sarah Christine. AB, U. Louisville, 1975, MS, 1992. CPA, Ky. Audit supr. Welenken, Himmelfarb & Co., Louisville, 1984-87; contr. Mus. History and Sci., 1987-89; quality reviewer Welenken, Himmelfarb & Co., 1989-91; audit supr. Cotton & Allen, P.S.C., 1991-92; sys. support analyst Humana, Inc., 1992-2000; tax auditor Revenue Commn., 2000—. Editl. contbr. to Courier Jour., other newspapers and mags., 1980—. Sec.-treas. Common Cause Ky., 1984—; constrn. vol. Habitat for Humanity, 1998—; treas. Ohio Valley Unitarian Universalist Dist., Indpls., 1993-97, HELP Ministries Ctrl. Louisville, 1994-98. Lt. comdr. USNR, 1975-83. Mem. Am. Amateur Press, Ky. Soc. CPAs. Democrat. Unitarian Universalist. Avocations: writing letters, volunteering.

LOUDERBACK, TRUMAN EUGENE, environmental project manager; b. Sterling, Colo., Jan. 17, 1946; s. George DeWayne and Lillian Louise (Harrach) L.; m. Dena Marie Chambers, June 1, 1985; children: Nicole Marie, Kyle Eugene, Matthew Joseph. BS, Colo. State U., 1968; postgrad., U. Colo., 1974-75. Registered environ. mgr., Nat. Registry of Environ. Profls. Project investigator and biologist, research inst. Colo. Sch. Mines, Golden, 1972-78; adminstr. quality assurance Cleveland-Cliffs Iron Co., Casper, Wyo., 1979, dir. environ. affairs, 1980-83, Rifle, Colo., 1984-88, Cliffs Engring., Inc., Rifle, 1984-88; pvt. practice cons. Lakewood, 1978-79, 96-97, Rifle, 1988-89; sr. project mgr., quality assurance mgr. Roy F. Weston, Inc., Lakewood, Colo., 1989-96; sr. project mgr., assoc. Burns & McDonnell, Kansas City, Mo., 1997-98; sr. project mgr., sr. assoc. 3D/Internat., Houston, 1998-2000; environ. divsn. mgr. Aviles Engring. Corp., 2000—. Chmn. environ. com. Pacific Shale Project, Rifle, 1983-87, also mgr. environ. impact statement, 1983-84. Contbr. articles to profl. jours. Industry rep. Colo. Joint Rev. Process Team, Colo. Dept. Nat. Resources, 1983; organizer Denver Environ. Forum, 1995; developer, dir. environtl. project mgmt. tng. programs. Mem. Willowbridge Homeowners Assn. (mem. archtl. control com.). Lodges: Rotary (bd. dirs. Rifle chpt. 1984), Masons. Republican. Methodist. Avocations: travel, fishing, photography. Home: 9302 Stone Porch Ln Houston TX 77064-7492 Office: Aviles Engring Corp 5790 Windfern Houston TX 77041 E-mail: louderback5@msn.com.

LOUDERMILK, MARY RUTH, local government volunteer; b. Washington, Sept. 27, 1944; d. Richard Raymond and Bessie Delores (Collins) Higgins; m. Wilmer Eugene Loudermilk, Sept. 26, 1964; children: Delores, Richard. Operator Bell Phone, Lawrenceville, Ill., 1963-64; coun. person ward 2 Cedar Lake (Ind.) Town Coun., 1984-91, 95-99, pres., 1996. Vol. Boy Scouts Am., Cedar Lake, 1977—; team chmn., life mem. Girl Scouts, 1973-83; mem. Cedar Lake Plan Commn., Ambulance Commn., Derlick Bldg. Commn., 1984-91; vice chmn. Cedar Lake Dem. Orgn., mem. De. Precinct Com.; past mem. Band Boosters, Hanover, Cedar Lake PTA, Cedar Lake Little League, Cedar Lake Girls Softball; past honor queen of Job's Daughters, past Gardine treas. of Jobs, coun. person. Named Woman of Yr. in Govt., Women Jaycees, Cedar Lake, 1984-85. Mem. Cedar Lake Profl. Bus. Women, Order Ea. Star, Job's Daugs. (past honor queen). Democrat. Methodist. Home: PO Box 238 Cedar Lake IN 46303-0238 E-mail: maryruth238@yahoo.com.

LOUDIERE, DANIEL, administrator; b. Colombiers, France, Oct. 3, 1943; s. Louis and Delaunay L.; m. Ebba Petersen, Apr. 12, 1967; children: Alain, Carola, Cornelia, Aeneas, Cordula, Artus, Akilles, Attico. Engring. degree, Ecole Nat. Gref, 1968, Ecole Polytech, 1965. Engr. CTGREF, Paris, 1969-77; head divsn. CEMAGREF, Antony, France, 1977-83, dir. France, 1984-86; dir. rsch. Ecole Nat. Génie l'Eau et l'Environement, Strasbourg, France, 1991-92, gen. mgr. France, 1993—. Cons. in field. Mem. Soc. Hydrotecnic, Commn. on Large Dams (sec. 1978-84). Office: ENGEES 1 Quai Koch 67000 Strasbourg France

LOUDON, CRAIG MICHAEL, video specialist; b. Chgo., June 23, 1950; s. Howard Edgar and Laverne Anne (McKeeta) L. BS in Broadcast Prodn., So. Ill. U., 1976. Lic. radiotelephone operator, FCC. Announcer, engr. Sta. WGSB, St. Charles, Ill., 1976-77, Sta. WVVX-AM-FM, Highland Park, 1977; video tape operator, editor, cameraman ABC-TV, Chgo., 1977-84; video tape operator, editor Sta. KABC-TV, Hollywood, Calif., 1984, The Video Tape Co., North Hollywood, 1985-86, Bluth Video Systems, Burbank, 1986-87; video tape operator NBC-TV, 1987-89, Paramount Pictures, Hollywood, 1989—. Avocations: volleyball, coin collecting. Home: PMB 194 9135-A Reseda Blvd Northridge CA 91324 E-mail: winwoodie@aol.com.

LOUDON, DOROTHY, actress; b. Boston, Sept. 17, 1933; d. James E. and Dorothy Helen (Shaw) L.; m. Norman Paris, Dec. 18, 1971 (dec.) Student, Syracuse U., 1950-51, Emerson Coll., summers 1950, 51, Alviene Sch. Dramatic Art, 1952, 53, The Am. Acad. Dramatic Art. Appeared in nat. repertory cos. of The Effect of Gamma Rays on Man in the Moon Marigolds, 1970, Plaza Suite, 1971, Luv, 1965, Anything Goes, 1967; appeared in Broadway prodns. Nowhere to Go But Up, 1962 (Theatre World award), Sweet Potato, 1968, Fig Leaves Are Falling, 1969 (Tony nominee), Three Men on a Horse, 1969 (Drama Desk award), The Women, 1973, Annie (Tony award, Drama Desk award, Outer Critics Circle award), 1976 (Dance Educators Am. award), Ballroom, 1979 (Tony nominee), Sweeney Todd, 1980, West Side Waltz, 1981 (Sarah Siddons award), Noises Off, 1983 (Tony nomination), Jerry's Girls, 1985 (Tony nomination), Driving Miss Daisy, 1988, Annie 2, 1990, Comedy Tonight, 1994, Love Letters, 1995, Showboat, 1996, N.Y. Encore series, 1997; appeared in film Garbo Talks, 1984, Midnight in the Garden of Good and Evil, 1997; numerous appearances on TV variety and talk shows; latest TV appearances In Performance at the White House, A Salute to Stephen Sondheim at Carnegie Hall, 1992; star TV show Dorothy, 1979; appeared in supper clubs The Blue Angel, Le Ruban Bleu, Persian Room; rec.: (CDs) Saloon, Broadway Baby. Mem. SAG, AFTRA, Actors Equity. Office: care Lionel Larner Agy 119 W 57th St New York NY 10019-2303 *I have no "thoughts on my life" that do not include my late husband, Norman Paris. He loved the theatre, as do I, and was my reason for being and my constant inspiration to persevere. That perserverance brought me the coveted Tony award for Miss Hannigan in "Annie." My husband lived to share that glorious moment with me. The award is small consolation, indeed-but the letters of love and encouragement from people all over the country is wondrous. It is a tribute to my husband as well as to me. I will devote my life to the justification of the faith he had in me-and to the faith of all those everywhere who love the theatre.*

LOUDON, JOHN VINCENT, publishing executive; b. Toronto, Ont., Can., Oct. 16, 1945; arrived in U.S., 1946; s. John Alexander Loudon, Doris Rose (Doherty) Loudon; m. Sharon Lebell, Mar. 10, 1985; children: Kyle D. Loudon Lebell, Michal S. Loudon Lebell, Danya S. Loudon Lebell, Noah Jacob Lebell Loudon. BA summa cum laude, Fortham U., 1968; MA cum laude, U. Toronto, 1970; PhD, Claremont Grad. U., 1972; diploma, Radcliffe Publ. Course, 1974. Vis. prof. U. San Francisco, 1972—73, Loyola Marymount U., L.A., 1973—74; editor Parabola Mag., N.Y.C., 1975—77, Harper & Row, N.Y.C., 1977—79; mgr. editl. Harper San Francisco, 1979—87, exec. editor, 1987—. Co-author: Maps to Ecstasy, 1990; contbr. . Mem.: Soc. Bibl. Lit., Am. Acad. Religion. Office: Harper Collins San Francisco 353 Sacramento St #500 San Francisco CA 94111

LOUGEE, DAVID LOUIS, lawyer; b. Worcester, Mass., Mar. 20, 1940; s. Laurence H. and Erma Virginia (MacAllister) L.; m. Mary Anne Strebb, July 15, 1979; children: Adam, Sara, Barbara, Laurence. AB, Bates Coll., 1962; LLB, Duke U., 1965. Bar: Mass. 1965. Ptnr. Mirick O'Connell, DeMallie & Lougee, Worcester, 1965—, mng. ptnr., 1985—2001. Bd. dirs. Commonwealth Bio Ventures, Inc., Meridian Med. Techs., Inc., Radius Capital Ptnrs., LLC, Unitas Corp., G&C Corp. Named Woodward White, The Best Lawyers in Am. Home: 78 Ridge Rd Hardwick MA 01037 Office: 100 Front St Worcester MA 01608-1425

LOUGEE, WENDY PRADT, library director; b. Rhinelander, Wis., Aug. 9, 1950; d. Alan Emmons Pradt and Marie Elizabeth Wendland; m. Michael Durand Lougee, Aug. 25, 1973; 1 child, Mariel. BA, Lawrence U., 1972; MS, U. Wis., 1973; MA, U. Minn., 1977. Head grad. libr. U. Mich. Libr., Ann Arbor, Mich., 1984—93, assoc. dir., 1993—2002; libr., McKnight presdl. prof. U. Minn., Mpls., 2002—. Contbr. articles to profl. jours. JSTOR Project grantee Mellon Found., 1996. Mem. ALA (life), Am. Soc. Info. Sci. Office: U Minn 499 O Meredith Wilson Libr 309 19th Ave S Minneapolis MN 55455

LOUGHARY, THOMAS MICHAEL, dentist; b. Beardstown, Ill., June 13, 1959; s. Thomas Giels and Beverly Ann (Marshall) L.; m. Vicki Lynne Shaneman, May 25, 1986 (div.); children: Thomas Michael II, Victoria Paige. Student, Knox Coll., 1977-80; DMD, So. Ill. U., Alton, 1984. Dentist Pla. Dental Ctr., Jacksonville, Ill., 1984-90, Dental Assocs. of Jacksonville, 1991—; gen. practice dentistry Beardstown Dental Assocs., 1985-98; staff dentist Passavant Hosp., Jacksonville, Ill.; mng. ptnr. BTS Outdoors Inc., Bear Creek Farms; ptnr. Stokes Bay Corp., a Canadian Fishing Lodge Enterprise. Cons. Cass County Cancer Assn., Virginia, Ill., 1986—, Beardstown Board Edn., 1980—. Soloist Jacksonville Symphony Soc., 1984, 87; dir. Beardstown Community Theater, 1990-91, Jacksonville Theater Guild, 1990; chmn. Cass County Cancer Soc., 1989—. Recipient monetary cert. Phi Gamma Delta Ednl. Found., 1980. Mem. ADA, Chgo. Dental Soc., G.V. Black Dental Soc., Jacksonville C. of C., Kiwanis, Elks, Internat. Assn. of Orthodontics and Edn. (chmn. St. Louis advanced orthodontic study club), Internat. Assn. of Orthodontics (bd. dirs.). Republican. Lutheran. Avocations: sports, hunting, fishing, raising Irish Setters. Home: 2180 Clark Rd Arenzville IL 62611-3043 Office: Dental Assocs Jacksonville 1515 W Walnut St Ste 10 Jacksonville IL 62650-1158

LOUGHEAD, JEFFREY LEE, physician; b. Mystic, Conn., May 11, 1957; s. Lawrence L. and Alice M. L.; m. Melinda K., Apr. 29, 1995; children: Brittany, Molly, Connor. BA, Miami U., 1979; MD, U. Cin., 1983; postgrad. in bus. adminstrn., Wright State U., 1997-98. Intern Children's Hosp. Med. Ctr., Cin., 1983-84, resident, 1984-86, chief resident, 1986-87; fellow in neonatal-perinatal medicine U. Cin., 1987-90; med. dir. spl. care unit Good Samaritan Hosp., Dayton, 1991-95; dir. quality assurance Children's MEd. Ctr., 1991-97, physician advisor nursing rsch. com., 1993-97; clin. dir. Children's Med. Ctr., 1995-97; dir. neonatal intensive care unit Ctrl. Dupage Hosp.; dir. strategic ops. Midwest Neoped Assocs. Ltd., 1998—. Author: (chpts.) Principles of Perinatal and Neonatal Metabolism, 1991, 2d edit., 1998, Current Pediatric Therapy, 1996; nutrition editor: Neonatal Network, 2000—. Fellow Am. Coll. Nutrition (Young Investigator award 1988), Am. Acad. Pediatrics (diplomate pediatrics, neonatal perinatal medicine); mem. PHi Beta Kappa, Alpha Omega Alpha, Beta Gamma Sigma. Avocation: amateur and profl. auto racing driver. Office: 900 Jorie Blvd Ste 186 Oak Brook IL 60523-3808

LOUGHEED, ARTHUR LAWRENCE, investment advisor, tax and pension consultant; b. Fresno, Calif., Aug. 11, 1944; s. Evan Archabald and Irene Elizabeth (Westby) L.; m. Margaret Ickes, Feb. 19, 1965 (div. Dec. 1983); children: Christopher, Jennifer Lougheed Branaugh, Evan; m. Nancy Lee Sanderson, May 11, 1985. Postgrad., U. So. Calif., 1964-65; MS in Fin. Svcs., Am. Coll., Bryn Mawr, Pa., 1980, MS in Mgmt., 1985. Registered investment advisor; enrolled agt.; CFP, ChFC, CLU, CPCU. Regional v.p. life and mut. fund ops. Farmers Ins. Group New World Life Ins. Co., L.A., 1965-74; mgr. pension and profit sharing plans Aetna Life & Casualty Aetna Fin. Group, Hartford, Conn., 1974-76; nat. dir. mktg. and sales tng. CNA Cos., Chgo., 1976-81; COO Lawrence-Lee, A Calif. Corp., Palm Springs, Calif., 1981—. Assoc. editor: CAL Underwriter Mag., 1975-76; contbr. tech. articles to profl. mags. and jours. Mem. faculty curriculum adv. com. Ext. Sch. Bus. & Mgmt., U. Calif., San Diego, 1986-94; mem. faculty internat. ins. exec. edn. U. Calif., Irvine, 1984; coll. and h.s. sports ofcl. CIF-Calif. Mich H.S. & Coll. Athletic Assn., 1962-74. Recipient Coll. News Photographer 1st pl. AP, 1963. Mem. Internat. Assn. for Fin. Planning (bd., v.p. edn. 1990-92), Am. Soc. CLU and ChFC (various offices), Am. Soc. Pension Actuaries (assoc. profl., fin. com. 1996—), Nat. Assn. Life Underwriters, Internat. Bd. CFS, Nat. Soc. Enrolled Agts., Calif. Assn. Ind. Accounts (pres. 1994), San Diego Assn. Life Underwriters (bd. dirs. 1982-84), Verdugo Hills Assn. Life Underwriters (bd. dirs. 1975-77), San Diego Lodge Masons (master), Al Bahr Temple Shriners (noble). Avocations: golf, photography, literature. Home and Office: 466 S Via Las Palmas Palm Springs CA 92262-4250

LOUGHEED, PETER, lawyer, former Canadian premier; b. Calgary, Alta., Can., July 26, 1928; s. Edgar Donald and Edna (Bauld) L.; m. Jeanne Estelle Rogers, June 21, 1952; children— Stephen, Andrea, Pamela, Joseph. BA, U. Alta., 1950, LL.B., 1952; MBA, Harvard U., 1954. Bar: Alta 1955. With firm Fenerty, Fenerty, McGillivray & Robertson, Calgary, 1955-56; sec. Mannix Co., Ltd., 1956-58, gen. counsel, 1958-62, v.p., 1959-62, dir., 1960-62; individual practice law, from 1962; formerly mem. Alta. Legislature for Calgary West; formerly leader Progressive Conservative Party of Alta., 1965-85; premier of Alta., 1971-85; ptnr. Bennett Jones, Calgary, 1986-99, counsel, 1999—. Office: Bennett Jones LLP 855 2nd St SW 4500 Bankers Hall Calgary AB Canada T2P 4K7

LOUGHLIN, KEVIN RAYMOND, urological surgeon, researcher; b. N.Y.C., Aug. 10, 1949; s. Raymond Gerard and Josephine (McGrath) L. AB, Princeton U., 1971; MD, N.Y. Med. Coll., 1975; MBA Boston U., 2000. Diplomate Nat. Bd. Med. Examiners, Am. Bd. Urology. Surgery instr. Harvard Med. Sch. Brigham & Women's Hosp., Boston, 1983-86, asst. prof. surgery Harvard Med. Sch., 1986-90, dir. urologic rsch., 1987—, assoc. prof. surgery Harvard Med. Sch., 1991—99; prof. surgery Harvard Med. Sch., 1999—. Staff urologist Dana Farber Cancer Inst., Boston, 1991—; dir. urologic rsch. Brigham and Women's Hosp., Boston, 1987—. Author, editor, co-editor 6 books, contbr. over 150 articles to profl. jours. Fellow Am. Cancer Soc., 1982-83, Nat. Kidney Found., 1980-81. Fellow ACS; mem. AAAS, Am. Soc. Andrology, Am. Soc. Clin. Oncology, Am. Urologic Assn., Boston Surg. Soc., Soc. for Basic Urologic Rsch. Achievements include patent in laparoscopic surg. instruments, and design of other surg. instruments. Home: 61 Pinckney St Boston MA 02114-4801 Office: Brigham & Womens Hosp 75 Francis St Boston MA 02115-6106

LOUGHMAN, BARBARA ELLEN, immunologist researcher; b. Frankfurt, Ind., Oct. 26, 1940; d. Jimmie Jewel and Ruth Eileen (Hoyer) Evers; m. Terry B. Loughman, June 28, 1962 (dec.); children: Lance Evers Loughman, Chad Elliott Loughman. BS, U. Ill., 1962; PhD, Notre Dame U., 1972. Rsch. scientist Ames Rsch. Labs., Elkhart, Ind., 1962-72; staff fellow NIH, Balt., 1972-74; from rsch. assoc. to rsch. mgr. The Upjohn Co., Kalamazoo, 1974-84; dir. immunology rsch. Monsanto Co., St. Louis, 1984-85; sr. dir. immunology diseases rsch. G.D. Searle/Monsanto Co., 1986-88; dir. project mgmt. Rorer Ctrl. Rsch., Horsham, Pa., 1988-91; dir. internat. drug regulating affairs Marion Merrell Dow, Kansas City, Mo., 1991-95; v.p. devel. svcs. Internat. Med. Tech. Cons., Inc., Lenexa, Kans., 1995-97, Pharm. Rsch. Assoc., Inc., Lenexa, Kans./Ohio, 1997-98; assoc. rsch. prof. medicine Loma Linda (Calif.) U., 1998—; v.p., drug devel. and medical affairs, COO Encore Pharmaceuticals, Inc., Loma Linda, Calif., 1998—. Contbr. over 20 articles to profl. jours. Mem. AAAS, Am. Acad. Asthma Allergy and Immunology, Am. Assn. Immunology. Avocations: singing, golf. Home and Office: 7153 Champions Ln West Chester OH 45069-4635 E-mail: bloughman@earthlink.net.

LOUGHRAN, JAMES NEWMAN, philosophy educator, college administrator; b. Bklyn., Mar. 22, 1940; s. John Farley and Ethel Margaret (Newman) L. AB, Fordham U., 1964, MA, 1965, PhD in Philosophy, 1975; PhD (hon.), Loyola Coll., Balt., 1985. Joined S.J., 1958; ordained priest Roman Catholic Ch., 1970. Instr. philosophy St. Peter's Coll., Jersey City, 1965-67; asst. dean Fordham U., Bronx, N.Y., 1970-73, tchr. philosophy, 1974-79, 82-84, dean, 1979-82; pres. Loyola Marymount U., L.A., 1984-91; acting pres. Bklyn. Coll., 1992; Miller Prof. Philosophy John Carroll U., Cleve., 1992-93; interim pres. Mount St. Mary's Coll., Emmitsburg, Md., 1993-94; interim acad. v.p., Fordham U., Bronx, N.Y., 1994-95; pres. St. Peter's Coll., 1995—. Contbr. numerous articles and revs. to popular and scholarly jours. Mem. (ex-officio) N.J. Commn. for Higher Edn.; trustee St. Peter's Coll., Jersey City, 1972—78, 1994—, Xavier U., Cin., 1981—84, Canisius Coll., Buffalo, 1994—2001, Fordham U., 2000—; chair N.J. Presidents' Coun. Mem. Am. Philos. Assn. Avocation: tennis. Email: Loughran. E-mail: loughran_j@spc.edu.

LOUGHREY, F. JOSEPH, manufacturing executive; b. Holyoke, Mass., Oct. 27, 1949; s. F. Joseph and Helen T. (Barrett) Loughrey; m. Deborah Jane Welsh, July 23, 1988; 1 stepchild Blair Edward Welsh. BA in Econs., African Studies, U. Notre Dame, 1971. Pres. AIESEC-U.S. Inc., N.Y.C., 1971-73; mgr. corp. employment Cummins Engine Co., Columbus, Ind., 1974-75, mgr. internat. personnel, 1975-79, dir. personnel (mktg.), 1979-81, dir. personnel (mktg. and subs.), 1981-83, dir. internal mgmt., 1983-84; mng. dir. Holset Engring. Co. Ltd., Huddersfield, Eng., 1984-86; v.p. employee rels. Cummins Engine Co., Columbus, Ind., 1986-87, from. v.p. So. Ind. ops. to v.p. heavy duty engines, 1988-90, group v.p. worldwide ops., 1990-95, exec. v.p., group pres. indsl. and chief tech. officer, 1996-99, pres., 1999—. Sr. mem. nat. adv. bd. Tauber Mfg. Inst. U. Mich.; mem. adv. coun. coll. arts and letters U. Notre Dame; pres. bd. dir. Developmental Svcs., Inc.; bd. dir. Tower Automotive, Inc., Sauer-Danfoss, Inc., Cummins Found. Trustee Columbus Child Care Ctr. Fellow: Brit. Inst. Mgmt.; mem.: AIESEC Internat. (sr.), Jr. Achievement (bd. dir.). Democrat. Roman Catholic. Office: Cummins Engine Co PO Box 3005 Columbus IN 47202-3005 E-mail: Joe.Loughrey@Cummins.com.

LOUGHRIDGE, JOHN HALSTED, JR. lawyer; b. Chestnut Hill, Pa., Oct. 30, 1945; s. John Halsted Sr. and Martha Margaret (Boyd) L.; m. Amy Claire Booe, Aug. 3, 1980 (div. Apr. 1995); 1 child, Emily Halsted. AB, Davidson Coll., 1967; JD, Wake Forest U., 1970. Bar: N.C. 1970, U.S. Dist. Ct. 1970, U.S. Ct. Mil. Appeals 1986, U.S. Supreme Ct. 2002. Divsn. head, v.p., counsel Wachovia Mortgage Co., Winston-Salem, N.C., 1971-79; sr. v.p., counsel Wachovia Bank, 1980—. Continuing legal edn. program planner N.C. Bar Found., 2000—01. Mem. cabinet, chair profl. divsn. United Way Forsyth County, 1994. Col. JAGC, USAR, 1970-2000. Mem.: UCC (Article 5 drafting com. N.C. Gen. Statutes Commn. 1999), ABA (corp. banking and bus. law sect. 1970—, internat. law and practice sect. 1999—), N.C. Bar Found. (continuing edn. program planner 2000—01), Mortgage Bankers Assn. Am. (legal issues com. 1982—92, fin. affiliates com. 1988—92), Am. Corp. Counsel Assn. (bd. dirs. N.C. chpt. 1988—98, 2001—, v.p.), Forsyth County Bar Assn., N.C. Coll. Advocacy, N.C. State Bar, N.C. Bar Assn. (real property sect. 1971—, bus. law sect. 1971—, internat. law sect. 1984—, fin. instns. com. 1985—, corp. counsel sect. 1989—, real property curriculum com. 1990—93, governing coun. 1992—98, treas. 1999—2000, bus. law curriculum com. 1999—2001, sec. 2000—01, vice chair 2001—02), Res. Officers Assn. (chpt. pres. 1996—97, sec. 1997—), Davidson Coll. Alumni Assn. (bd. dirs. 2001—), Rotary, Forsyth Country Club, Twin City Club (sec. 1990—97, gov. 1994—, pres. 1997—2001), Union League Phila., Phi Delta Theta, Phi Delta Phi. Republican. Presbyterian. Avocations: golf, tennis. Home: 615 Arbor Rd Winston Salem NC 27104 Office: Wachovia Bank 301 S College St Charlotte NC 28288-0630 E-mail: john.loughridge@wachovia.com.

LOUGHRIN, JAY RICHARDSON, mass communications educator, consultant; b. Mankato, Minn., Oct. 21, 1943; s. J. Richardson and Jane Aileen (Smith) L.; m. Helen Marie Struyk, Aug. 8, 1964 (div. Sept. 1985); children: Jennifer, Amy; m. Yolanda Christina Ramos, July 17, 1986; children: Tawny, Heather. BA in Drama, Calif. State U., Los Angeles, 1968; postgrad., San Diego State U., 1968-69, UCLA, 1970-71, U. Redlands, Calif., 1983-84, Fla. State U., 1990; MA, Whittier (Calif.) Coll., 1992. Prodn. asst. Andrews-Yagemann Prodns., Hollywood, Calif., 1961-63; with merchandising, sales Sta. KTTV-TV, 1963-64; assoc. producer Born Losers Am. Internat. Pictures, 1964; assoc. producer V.P.I. Prodns., 1964, Ralph Andrews Prodns., North Hollywood, Calif., 1965; producer Stein Erikson Ski Films, 1965, F.K. Rocket Films, North Hollywood, 1966-68; dir. promotion and publicity Sta. KCST-TV, San Diego, 1968-69; prof. mass communication Rio Hondo Coll., Whittier, 1969—; sales mgr. Warren Miller Films, Hermosa Beach, Calif., 1984-85, cons., 1985-86; exec. producer Echo Prodns., Hollywood, 1985-87. Cons. Radio Concepts, Los Angeles, 1978-80, Tom Cole Prodns., Los Angeles, 1985-87, Chuck Richards Whitewater, Lake Isabella, Calif., 1984-86; media relations cons. Police Officers Standards and Training, Sacramento, 1986—; venue mgr. Los Angeles Olympic Organizing Com., Long Beach, Calif., 1984. Winter sports writer Kern Valley Sun; contbr. articles to Review Publs., Orange Coast mag., Jet Am. mag., Ted Randall Report. Pres. Rue Le Charlene Homeowners Assn., Palos Verdes, Calif., 1984, Hilltop Homeowners Assn., Walnut, Calif., 1989-90; v.p. West Walnut Homeowners Assn., 1988-89. Recipient Pub. Service Programming award Advt. Council, N.Y.C., 1982; named Adviser of Yr., U. So. Calif.'s 50th Annual Journalism Awards, Los Angeles, 1985. Mem. Acad. TV Arts and Scis., Rio Hondo Coll. Faculty Assn. (pres. 1978), So. Calif. Broadcasters Assn. (Pub. Service award 1978), N.Am. Snowsport Journalists Assn. Republican. Avocations: sailing, skiing, whitewater rafting, motorcycling, bicycling. Office: Rio Hondo Coll 3600 Workman Mill Rd Whittier CA 90601-1616 E-mail: jloughrin@rh.cc.ca.us.

LOUI, ALEXANDER C.P. electrical engineer, researcher; b. San Fernando, Trinidad and Tobago, Feb. 20, 1961; came to U.S., 1990; s. John Sue-Tang and Mary Loui; m. Jessie S. Chong, May 25, 1991; children: Rachel, Madeline, Alicia. BSc in Elec. Engring., U. Toronto, 1983, MSc in Elec. Engring., 1986, PhD in Elec. Engring., 1990. Rsch. asst. Atomic Energy of Can. Ltd., Chalk River, Ont., 1982; teaching asst. dept. elec. engring. U. Toronto, 1983-89, rsch. assoc. signal processing lab., 1985-90; mem. tech. staff applied rsch. Bellcore, Red Bank, N.J., 1990-94; rsch. scientist Applied Rsch., Bellcore, 1995-96; rsch. assoc. Networked Imaging Tech. Ctr. Eastman Kodak Co., Rochester, N.Y., 1996-98, tech. leader, rsch. assoc. Imaging Sci. Tech. Lab., 1998—, group leader Multimedia Comm., Imaging Sci. & Tech. Lab., 1998—; adj. prof. dept. elec. and computer engring. U. Toronto, Can., 1999—. Mem. tech. com. IEEE Internat. Conf. on Image Processing, 1994-96, 2001; assoc. chair tech. program com. IEEE Internat. Symposium on Circuits and Sys., 1999; invited tutorial spkr. Internat. Symposium on Multimedia Info. Processing, Taipei, Taiwan, 1999; spkr. in field. Contbr. articles to profl. jours.; assoc. editor Jour. Electronic Imaging, 1998—, IEEE Transactions on Multimedia, 2000—. Founding mem., past pres. Jarvis Multicultural Soc., Toronto, 1988-90. Wallbery Undergrad scholar, 1981-82, NSERC postgrad. scholar, 1983-87. Mem. IEEE (sr. mem. 1997, chair spl. session internat. conf. on image processing 2000, mem. tech. program com. Internat. Conf. on Multimedia and Expo 2000-02, mem. tech. program com., area chair Internat. Conf. on Multimedia and Expo 2001, Tokyo, mem. tech. program com. Pacific Rim Conf. on Multimedia Beijing 2001), Soc. Imaging Sci. Tech., Internat. Soc. for Optical Engring. Baptist. Avocations: table tennis, skating, reading, hi-fi systems, travel. Office: Eastman Kodak Co Mail Code 01816 1700 Dewey Ave Rochester NY 14650-1816 E-mail: alexander.loui@kodak.com.

LOUIE, DAVID MARK, lawyer; b. Oakland, Calif., Oct. 8, 1951; s. Paul and Emma (Woo) L.; m. Johanna C. Chuan, Sept. 6, 1986; children: Ryan David, Jenna Rachel. AB cum laude, Occidental Coll., 1973; JD, U. Calif., Berkeley, 1977. Bar: Calif. 1977, U.S. Dist. Ct. (no. Dist.) Calif. 1977, U.S. Ct. Appeals (9th cir.) 1977, Hawaii 1978, U.S. Dist. Ct. Hawaii 1978. Ptnr. Case & Lynch, Honolulu, 1977-88; sr. ptnr. Roeca, Louie & Hiraoka, 1988—. Faculty mem. Profl. Edn. Systems, Inc. (PESI) Seminars: Hawaii Ins. & Tort Update, 1995, 1996, Depositions (Strategies, Tactics & Mechanics), 1990, Nat. Bus. Inst. (NBI) Seminars: Arbitrating and Trying the Automobile Injury Case in Hawaii, 1993, Ins. Litigation in Hawaii, 1992, Pacific Law Inst. (PLI) Seminars: Premises Liability, 1995, Hawaii State Bar Assn. Depositions, 1997, Mediation Techniques, 2001, miscellaneous seminars: Hawaiian Bitumuls & Paving Co., Job Site Accidents, 1994, Hawaiian Dredging Construction Co., Job Site Accidents, 1993; mem. Def. Rsch. Inst., 1990—. Contbg. author: Going Back, 1972, Hawaii Tort Liability Issues in Work Site Accident Cases, 1989, Trying the Automobile Accident Case, 1991, Hawaii Tort Law Update, 1992, 94. Bd. dirs. Jr. Achievement Hawaii, Honolulu, Aloha Towers Devel. Corpo., 1998—, chmn., 1999—; Sec., v.p., dir. Ohana Ins. Co. Hawaii, Inc., 1994-95. Mem. ABA (sects. on tort and ins. practice litigation 1978—, minority couns. demonstration program 1994), Hawaii State Bar Assn. (bd. dirs. 1994-98, v.p. 2000, pres. 2001), Calif. State Bar Assn., Hawaii Def. Lawyers Assn. (bd. dirs. 1990—, sec.-treas. 1994-99), Nat. Asian Pacific ABA (Hawaii chpt. pres. 1992-95, bd. dirs. 1996—), Mensa, Pacific Club (chmn.). Home: 4122 Pakolu Pl Honolulu HI 96816-3930 Office: Roeca Louie & Hiraoka 841 Bishop St Ste 900 Honolulu HI 96813-3917

LOUIE, STEVEN, multimedia courseware developer, nurse; b. L.A., Jan. 3, 1951; s. Quan Ying and Ngit Seem (Der) L.; m Judith Anne LeFevre, Aug. 16, 1984; children: David Christopher, Linda Danielle, Cameron Quan. Diploma in nursing, U. Ariz., 1977, student, 1984—. RN, Ariz. Mktg. dir. Bus. Computers, Tucson, 1982-84; program coord. Cerebral Palsy Found., 1984-85; systems analyst U. Ariz. Coll. Medicine, 1987-91; pres. synap TRIX, 1992—. Dir. Tucson Learning Ctr., 1984-86; interim dir. Children's Mus., Tucson, 1986-87; cons. Burroughs Computer/Cemcorp, Detroit, 1985. Contbr. articles to profl. jours. Bd. dirs. Disability Resources of Tucson, 1988-89, UN Assn., Tucson, 1984-85. Lt. USNR, 1969—. Mem. Apple Programmers and Developers Assn., Naval Res. Officers Assn. Democrat. Avocations: running, art.

LOUIE, STEVEN J. allergist, immunologist; b. N.Y.C., Feb. 3, 1952; s. Henry and Corinne Louie. BA, SUNY, Potsdam, 1973; MD, SUNY, Bklyn., 1978. Diplomate Am. Bd. Allergy & Immunology, Am. Bd. Internal Medicine. Intern Nassau County Med. Ctr., East Meadow, N.Y., 1978-79, resident in internal medicine, 1979-81; fellow in allergy & immunology U. South Fla., Tampa, 1981-83; pvt. practice Atlantis, Fla. Mem. staff JFK Hosp., Atlantis, West Palm Beach, Fla., Palm Beach Gardens (Fla.) Med. Ctr., Good Samaritan Hosp., clin. prof. U. South Fla. Coll. Medicine, 1983-84. Fellow Am. Acad. Allergy & Immunology, Am. Coll. Allergy Asthma & Immunology, Allergy & Immunology Soc.; mem. Fla. Med. Assn., Palm Beach County Med. Soc., Fla. Allergy Asthma and Immunology Soc. Office: 5507 S Congress Ave Ste 140 Atlantis FL 33462-1139

LOUIS, BARBARA R. psychologist, educator, consultant; b. Fond du Lac, Wis., Sept. 30, 1950; d. H. J. and Mary Anne (Reichard) Mueller; m. Stanley D. Louis, Jan. 20, 1974 (div. May. 1988); children: Joshua, Justin. BFA, U. Wis., Milw., 1973; MS, Rutgers U., 1988, PhD, 1992. Diplomate Am. Bd. Psychol. Spltys.; lic. psychologist. Comml. artist, 1972-75; freelance artist, 1975-83; tchg. asst. Rutgers U., New Brunswick, N.J., 1985-90, instr. dept. psychology, 1987-89; predoctoral fellow Robert Wood Johnson Med. Sch. U. Medicine and Dentistry N.J., 1986-90, instr. pediat., 1990-92, asst. prof., 1992-2001, assoc. prof., 2001—. Admissions cons. Hunter Coll. Campus Schs., N.Y.C., 1994—; program dir. Gifted Child Clinic, New Brunswick, 1995—. Mem. editl. bd. Roeper Rev.; contbr. articles to profl. jours. Grad. scholar Rutgers U., 1990. Mem. APA, Nat. Assn. Gifted Children, Internat. Soc. Infant Studies, Soc. Rsch. Child Devel., N.J. Assn. Gifted Children (trustee 1994-2000). Office: U Medicine and Dentistry NJ Robert Wood Johnson Med Sch 97 Paterson St New Brunswick NJ 08901-2160 Fax: 732-235-6189. E-mail: louisba@umdnj.edu.

LOUIS, GLENN, music educator; b. Brooklyn, May 3, 1951; B, Juilliard Sch., 1973. Lic. tchr. N.Y. Clk. IRS, Holtsville, NY, 1976; music tchr., 1973—. Mem.: Am. Fedn. Musician. Avocations: golf, tennis. Home: 2928 Ruddell Rd #123 Lacey WA 98503-7829

LOUIS, KENNETH MALIQ, neurosurgeon, educator; b. Detroit, May 14, 1953; s. John Maliq and Della (Galip) L.; m. Catherine Jordan, July 3, 1976; children: Jennifer Jordan, Michael Kenneth, Daniel Alexander. Grad., U. Mich., 1973; MD, Wayne State U., 1977. Diplomate Am. Bd. Neurol. Surgery. Intern, fellow in gen. surgery John Hopkins Hosp., Balt., 1977-78; postdoctoral fellow in neuroendocrinology Columbia-Presbyn. Med. Ctr., 1978-79; asst. resident in neurol. surgery Columbia U., N.Y.C., 1978-82, chief resident in neurol. surgery, 1982-83; neurosurgeon Neurol. Surgery Assocs., Tampa, Fla., 1983—; clin. asst. prof. neurosurgery sect. U. S. Fla., 1983-96, clin. assoc. prof. neurosurgery sect., 1996—99, clin. asst. prof. dept. radiology, 1991-96, clin. assoc. prof. dept. radiology, 1996—2001, clin. asst. dept. anesthesiology, 1993-96, clin. assoc. dept. aneshtesiology, 1996—2001. Attending neurosurgery Tampa Gen. Hosp., St. Joseph's Hosp., Tampa; cons. Women's Hosp., Tampa, Shriner's Hosp., Tampa, Meml. Hosp., Tampa. Contbr. articles to profl. jours. Grantee NIH. Fellow: ACS; mem.: AOA, AMA, Hillsborough County Med. Soc., Fla. Assn. Pediatric Tumors, Fla. Neurosurg. Soc., Fla. Med. Assn., Fla. Spine Soc., Soc. Neurosurg. Soc., N.Am. Spine Soc., Internat. Soc. Craniomaxillofacial Soc., Congress of Neurol. Surgeons, Am. Assn. Neurol. Surgeons, Phi Beta Kappa. Avocations: fishing, magic, running, ballroom dancing, martial arts. Office: Neurol Surgery Assocs 3000 E Fletcher Ave Ste 340 Tampa FL 33613-4645

LOUIS, LESTER See BROWN, LES

LOUIS, PAUL ADOLPH, lawyer; b. Key West, Fla., Oct. 22, 1922; s. Louis and Rose Leah (Weinstein) L.; m. Nancy Ann Edgeworth Lapof, Dec. 28, 1971; children: Louis Benson, IV, Connor Cristina and Marshall Dore (twins). BA, Va. Mil. Inst., Lexington, 1947; LL.B., U. Miami, Fla., 1950, JD, 1967. Bar: Fla. 1950, U.S. Dist. Ct. (so. dist.) Fla. Asst. state atty., 1955-57; atty. Beverage Dept. Fla., 1957-60; spl. asst. atty. gen. State of Fla., 1970-71; partner firm Sinclair, Louis, Heath, Nussbaum & Zavertnik (P.A.), Miami, 1960—; mem. Fed. Jud. Nominating Commn., 1977-80; mem. peer rev. com. U.S. Dist. Ct. for So. Dist. Fla., 1983-85. Author: Defamation, How Far Can You Go, Trial and Tort Trends, 1969; contbr.: chpts. to Fla. Family Law, 1967, 72. Founder mem. Palm Springs Gen. Hosp. Scholarship Com., 1968; mem. Dade County Health Facilities Authority, 1979-82; trustee Fla. Supreme Ct.

Hist. Soc., 1994—. Served to 1st lt. USAAF, 1943-45, ETO, maj. USAF Res., 1962. Decorated Air medal with five oak leaf clusters, Bronze Star (7), Purple Heart. Mem. ABA, Fla. Bar (bd. cert. civil trial lawyer and marital and family law, bd. govs. 1970-74), Dade County Bar Assn. (dir. 1954-55, 66-69), Am. Judicature Soc., Va. Mil. Inst. Alumni Assn. Clubs: Miami, Bath. Democrat. Jewish. Home: 4411 Palm Ln Miami FL 33137-3346 Office: 1125 A I duPont Bldg 169 E Flagler St Miami FL 33131-1210

LOUIS, WILLIAM JOSEPH (JOHN GARVIE MONKS), theater educator, actor, director, artist, poet; b. Castorland, N.Y., Mar. 5, 1928; s. Loren A. and Laura Ruth Louis. Cert., Sch. St. Philip Neri, Boston, 1951; BA in English, Boston Coll., 1957, MA in Comparative Dramatic Lit., 1959; PhD in Speech and Theatre and Humanities, Stanford U., 1969; postdoctoral, U. Nice, France, 1967-68, 69, Lee Strasberg Acting Inst., Hollywood, Calif., summer 1976; BA in Studio Art, Avila Coll., 1990. Novice Trappist Monastery, Spencer, Mass., 1951. Instr. LeMoyne Coll., Syracuse, N.Y., 1958-60; asst. prof. theatre U. B.C., Vancouver, Can., 1968-70; coord. drama Western N.Mex. U., Silver City, 1971-73; chmn. performing and visual arts dept. Avila Coll., Kansas City, Mo., 1973-87, prof. humanities, 1987-91; ret., 1991. Actor; originator dept. comm. Avila Coll., 1976, artist-in-residence, 1991—. Mem. screening com. Mo. Arts Coun., 1975. With U.S. Army, 1947-48. Named Hon. Citizen of Silver City, 1971. Mem. Actors Equity, Nat. Jesuit Honor Soc., Kansas City Artists Coalition, Kansas City Clay Guild, Friends of Art, Order of Cross and Crown (Boston Coll.), VFW, Alpha Sigma Nu. Democrat. Roman Catholic. Avocations: painting, sculpting, poetry, aerobics. Home: 109 Glen Arbor Rd Kansas City MO 64114-5163 Office: Art Divsn Avila Coll 11901 Wornall Rd Kansas City MO 64145-1007 E-mail: wjlouis@juno.com.

LOUIS, WILLIAM ROGER, historian, educator; b. Detroit, May 8, 1936; s. Henry Edward and Bena May (Flood) L.; m. Dagmar Cecilia Friedrich; children: Antony Andrew, Catherine Ann BA, U. Okla., 1959; MA, Harvard U., 1960; PhD, Oxford U., 1962, DLitt, 1979; DLitt (hon.), Westminster Coll., 1998. Asst. prof., then assoc. prof. history Yale U., 1962-70; prof. history U. Tex., Austin, 1970-85, dir. Brit. Studies, 1975—, Kerr chair English history and culture, 1985—, disting. teaching prof., 1998—. Supernumerary fellow St. Antony's Coll., U. Oxford, Eng., 1986-96, hon. fellow, 1996—; fellow Brit. Acad., 1993—; Chichele lectr. All Souls Coll., U. Oxford, Eng., 1990; Disting. lectr. London Sch. Econs., 1992; Cust lectr. Nottingham (Eng.) U., 1995; Brit. Acad. Elie Kedorie Meml. lectr., 1996; Churchill Meml. lectr., 1998; history faculty lectr. U. Oxford, Eng., 2001; disting. vis. prof. Am. U. in Cairo, 2001; dir. summer seminars NEH, 1985, 88, 90, 91, 96, 00. Author: Ruanda-Urundi, 1963, Germany's Lost Colonies, 1967, (with Jean Stengers) The Congo Reform Movement, 1968, British Strategy in the Far East, 1919-1939, 1971, Imperialism at Bay, 1977 (History Book Club), British Empire in the Middle East, 1984 (George Louis Beer prize Am. Hist. Assn. and Tex. Inst. Letters award), In The Name of the God Go! Leo Amery and the British Empire in the Age of Churchill, 1992; editor British Documents on the End of the Empire, 1988—; editor-in-chief Oxford History of the British Empire, 1992—; editor: (with P. Gifford) Britain and Germany in Africa, 1967, France and Britain in Africa, 1971, The Origins of the Second World War: A.J.P. Taylor and His Critics, 1972, National Security and International Trusteeship in the Pacific, 1972, Imperialism: The Robinson and Gallagher Controversy, 1976, (with William S. Livingston) Australia, New Zealand and the Pacific Islands Since the First World War, 1979, (with P. Gifford) The Transfer of Power in Africa, 1982, (with R. Stookey) End of the Palestine Mandate, 1986, (with H. Bull) The Special Relationship: Anglo-American Relations Since 1245, 1986, (with P. Gifford) Decolonization and African Independence, 1988, (with James Bill) Musaddiq, Iranian Nationalism and Oil, 1988, (with Roger Owen) Suez 1956: The Crisis and Its Consequences, 1989, (with Robert A. Fernea) The Iraqi Revolution of 1958, 1991, (with Robert Blake) Churchill, 1993, Adventures with Britannia, 1995, More Adventures with Britannia, 1998, (with Michael Howard) The Oxford History of the Twentieth Century, 1998, (with Judith Brown) The Oxford History of the British Empire: The Twentieth Century, 1999, (with Ronald Hyam) The Conservative Government and the End of Empire, 1957-64, 2000, Festschrift: The Statecraft of British Imperialism: Essays in Honor of William Roger Louis, 1999. Woodrow Wilson fellow Harvard U., 1959-60, Marshall scholar Oxford U., 1960-62, NEH fellow, Am. Inst. Indian Studies fellow, Guggenheim fellow, vis. fellow All Souls Coll., U. Oxford, overseas fellow Churchill Coll., U. Cambridge, Eng., fellow Woodrow Wilson Internat. Ctr.; guest scholar Brookings Instn.; disting. visitor hist. dept. Peking U., Beijing; named hon. Comdr. of Brit. Empire Queen of Eng., 1999. Fellow Royal Hist. Soc.; mem. Am. Hist. Assn. (life), Coun. on Fgn. Rels. (N.Y.C.), Tex. Inst. Letters, Reform Club (London), Century (N.Y.C.), Met. Club (Washington), Am. Hist. Assn. (pres. 2001). Democrat. Office: U Texas Dept History Austin TX 78712

LOUIS-COTTON D'ENGLESQUEVILLE, FRANCOIS PIERRE, automobile company executive; b. Neuilly Seine, France, Sept. 4, 1929; came to U.S., 1955; s. Georges Auguste and Paule Marie Cotton (d'Englesqueville) L.; m. Martine Combaluzier, Apr. 30, 1965 (div.); 1 child, Veronique; m. Mary Elizabeth Thames, June 14, 1986; children: George, Timothy, Jennifer, Mary Beth. BEE, Ecole Brequet, Paris, 1952. Engr. Demarais Freres, Paris, 1954-55, Cadillac Motor Cars div. GM, Detroit, 1955-58; nat. svc. mgr. Peugeot, S.A., N.Y.C., 1958-60; engr. Michelin Tire Group, Woodside, N.Y., 1960-61, Port Authority N.Y. and N.J., N.Y.C., 1962-68; dir. Renault USA, Inc., Washington, 1968-94; cons. Garden City, N.Y., 1994—. Mem.: The European Inst. (Washington, D.C.), Assn. Internat. Automobile Mfrs. (bd. dirs. 1974—94), Soc. Automotive Engrs., Conseiller du Commerce Exterieur de la France, Cercle Militaire (Paris), Army and Navy Club (Washington). Avocations: photography, travel, cooking. Fax: 631-653-8932. E-mail: Francois@optonline.net.

LOUKAITOU-SIDERIS, ANASTASIA, urban planner, educator, urban planner, consultant; b. Athens, Greece, May 12, 1958; arrived in U.S., 1983; d. Elias Loukaitis and Electra Loukaitou; m. Athanasios Sideris, Aug. 27, 1983; children: Constantine Sideris, Elias Sideris. BA in Arch., Nat. Tech. U., Athens, 1983; MA in Arch., M in Planning, U. So. Calif., L.A., 1985, PhD in Urban Planning, 1988. Registered arch., Greece. Lectr. urban planning program UCLA, 1989—91, asst. prof. dept. urban planning, 1991—97, assoc. prof. dept. urban planning, 1997—2001, prof., vice chair dept. urban planning, 2001—02, chair dept. urban planning, 2002—. Project mgr. L.A. Neighborhood Initiative, L.A., 1997—2000; cons. Greek Ministry Nat. Edn., Greece, 1997, Greece, 99, Greece, 2002, Transp. Edn. Rsch. Bd., Washington, 2001—. Author: Urban Design Downtown, 1998; guest editor: spl. issue Jour. Archl. and Planning Rsch., 2002. Recipient Excellence in Academia award, Young Pres. Orgn.-So. Calif. chpt., 1999, Project award, Am. Inst. Cert. Planners, Washington, 1999, Acad. Merit award, Am. Planning Assn. Calif. chpt., Sacramento, 1999. Mem.: Tech. Chamber Greece, Greek Assn. Registered Archs., Assn. Greek Urban and Regional Planners, Assn. Collegiate Schs. of Planning. Avocations: travel, photography, acoustic guitar. Home: 326 S Berkeley Ave Pasadena CA 91107 Office: UCLA Dept Urban Planning 405 Hilgard Ave Los Angeles CA 90095

LOUNDMON-CLAY, JUANITA L. educator, academic administrator; b. Charleston, W.Va., Aug. 11; d. Albert D. and Mattie L. (Collins) L.; m. Earl Clay Jr. (dec.); children: Pamela Clay-Mitchell, Kimberly Clay-Clay, Dana Clay-Braddock. BA, W.Va. State Coll.; MSW, W.Va. U.; MA, Ind. U.; PhD, Fla. State U., 1978. Psychologist Navistar Corp., Indpls., 1978-80; pvt. practice psychology, 1980-84; clin. psychologist Lakeview Mental Health Ctr., Pensacola, Fla., 1984-85; pvt. practice A Better Way Christian Counseling Ministry, Tallahassee, 1985-88; prof. Regent U., Virginia Beach, Va., 1988-89; assoc. prof. Am. U. of Les Cayes, Haiti, 1989-91; mental health cons. to Christian Orgns., Ft. Wayne, Ind.; pres., CEO A Better Way Counseling and Cons. Agy.; v.p. student affairs, assoc. prof. Bluefield State Coll. Cons. Washington Project, 1989—, Haiti Mins. Conf., Port-Au-Prince, 1989; founder, dir. first group treatment home for adolescent girls in State of Ind.; founder A Better Way Counseling and Diagnostic Agy. Author: New Career Development Strategies For The Black Working Poor, 1977; prodr. Black-on-Black Pub. Svc. TV Program. Precinct chmn. Rep. Exec. Com., Tallahassee, 1987-88; bd. mem. City Coun. EEO Commn., Tallahassee, 1987-89, Bluefield Cmty. Ctr., 2000-01; former pres. Ind. Conf. Social Welfare, Indpls.; bd. dirs. Cmty. Action of N.E. Ind., Ft. Wayne Ballet, Old Fort br. YMCA; life mem. NAACP, mem. cmty. access network TV, Martin Luther King Breakfast Club Inc.; candidate Ind. Legislature, 1996; vol. docent Lincoln Mus.; spkr., motivator Christian Women's Groups. Fla. U. Systems grantee, 1976; named one of Outstanding Young Women Am., 1978; recipient Cmty. Svc. award City of Pensacola, 1974, YMCA, C. of C., Ft. Wayne, Ind., 1970, Ebony in Excellence award, 1997. Mem. Am. Assn. Counseling and Devel., Va. Assn. Counseling and Devel., Ind. Psychology Assn. (life), Kiwanis Internat. Office: 219 Rock St Bluefield WV 24701 E-mail: JCandJesus@Juno1.com.

LOUNSBURY, HELEN MARIE, education educator, consultant; b. N.J., Mar. 14, 1939; d. Joseph Anthony Sr. and Helen Teresa Golden; m. Patrick Lounsbury Sr., Jan. 30, 1960; children: Patrick Jr., Elaine Teresa, Amy Jo. BS with distinction, SUNY, 1960; MA in Lit., Vt. Coll., 1993. Tchr. Mohanasen Ctrl. Sch., Rotterdam, N.Y., 1960-62, Berne-Knox-Westerlo Ctrl. Sch., Berne, 1962-96; clin. edn. regional supr. SUNY, Oneonta, 1996—; instr. Coll. St. Rose, Albany, N.Y., 1996-98; themes advisor Albany Sch. Humanities, 1997—2001; scorer Nat. Testing Svc., 2001—. Presenter in field; cons. U.S. Dept. Edn.; bd. dirs. Albany County Reading Assn., v.p., 1996-99; pres. bd. edn. Berne-Knox-Westerlo Ctrl. Sch. Dist.; reviewer N.Y. State Dept. Edn., 1997—, CTB McGraw-Hill, 1999--, WESTAT, 1998--. Co-author: DeBeers, A Factory Family, 1985, Chances Are: Investigations in Probability, 1995. Bd. dirs. Hilltown Cmty. Rsch. Ctr., Berne, 1982-94, Albany County (N.Y.) Rural Housing Alliance, 1984-99, Albany City Reading Coun.; coord. Arts Connection Learning Partnership, Albany, 1992-95. Named N.Y. Tchr. of Excellence, 1993; NEH Masterworks Study grantee, 1995, N.Y. Found. of the Arts grantee, 1993, 94, Pioneering Partner Found. grantee, 1996, 98. Mem. ASCD, PTA (hon. life, Disting. Svc. award 1996)), N.Y. State Reading Assn., N.Y. State Math. Assn., Internat. Reading Assn., Assn. Math. Tchrs. N.Y. State, N.Y. State English Tchrs., Hodge Podge Soc., Civil War Roundtable, Kiwanis, Kappa Delta Pi. Avocations: travel, reading, genealogy. Office: Lounsbury Cons East Berne NY 12059

LOUNSBURY, JAMES RICHARD, retired broadcaster, pilot, writer; b. Ames, Iowa, Feb. 24, 1923; s. George Lloyd and Nell Amelia (Parsons) L.; m. Reba Janet Smith, Sept. 10, 1949 (div. 1963); children: Steven Richard, Kelly Katrina. BME, Drake U., 1945. Sports and news announcer Stas. KSO and KRNT Radio, Des Moines, 1943-46; announcer, disc jockey Sta. WHAS Radio, Louisville, 1946-48, Sta. WIND Radio, Chgo., 1949-53; announcer, disc jockey, TV host Sta. WGN-WGN TV, 1954-57; TV dance party host Sta. WBKB (WLS-TV), 1957-63; staff announcer, disc jockey, newscaster ABC Radio-TV, N.Y.C., 1964-70; anchorman, reporter UPI News Radio Network, 1971-79; news dir., anchorman Sta. KTHI-TV, Fargo, N.D., 1980-82; anchorman, reporter UPI News Radio Network, Washington, 1983-91. Author: Hey, Look, I'm on TV, 2000. Named Host of Chgo.'s Best Audience Participation TV Show, TV Guide, 1955. Mem. Ariz. Pilots Assn. (bd. dirs. 2000—). Methodist. Avocations: flying, swimming, jogging, reading. Home: 5300 W Flying Circle St Tucson AZ 85713-4336

LOUNSBURY, JOHN FREDERICK, geographer, educator; b. Perham, Minn., Oct. 26, 1918; s. Charles Edwin and Maude (Knight) L.; m. Dorothea Frances Eggers, Oct. 3, 1943; children— John Frederick, Craig Lawrence, James Gordon. BS, U. Ill., 1942, MS, 1946; PhD, Northwestern U., 1951. Asst. dir. rural land classification program Insular Govt., P.R., 1949-52; cons., research analyst Dayton Met. Studies, Inc., Ohio, 1957-60; chmn. dept. earth scis., prof. geography Antioch Coll., 1951-61; prof. geography, head dept. geography and geology Eastern Mich. U., 1961-69; chmn. dept. geography Ariz. State U., 1969-77; dir. Ctr. for Environ. Studies, 1977-80; prof. emeritus Ariz. State U., 1987—. Project dir. Geography in Liberal Edn. Project, Assn. Am. Geographers, NSF, 1963-65, project dir. commn. on coll. geography, 1965-74; dir. environment based edn. project US. Office Edn., 1974-75; dir. spatial analysis of land use project NSF, 1975-85 Author articles, workbooks, textbooks. Mem. Yellow Springs Planning Commn., Ohio, dir. research, 1957-60; mem. Ypsilanti Planning Commn., 1961-66; research com. Washtenaw County Planning Commn., 1961-69; mem. cons. Ypsilanti Indsl. Devel. Corp., 1961-63. Served with AUS, 1942-46, ETO. Named Man of Yr., Yellow Springs C. of C., 1956-57 Fellow Ariz.-Nev. Acad. Sci.; mem. Assn. Am. Geographers (chmn. East Lakes div. 1959-61, mem. nat. exec. council 1961-64, chmn. liberal edn. com. 1961-65), Nat. Council Geog. Edn. (chmn. earth sci. com. 1961-68, regional coord. 1961-63, mem. exec. bd. 1968-71, 77-83, v.p. 1977-78, pres. 1979-80, Disting. Svc. award 1988, Disting. Mentor award 1990), Mich. Acad. Sci. Arts and Letters (chmn. pub. relations com. 1964-69, past chmn. geography sect.), Ohio Acad. Sci. (past exec. v.p.), Mich. Acad. Sci., Ariz. Acad. Sci., Am. Geog. Soc., AAAS, Sigma Xi, Delta Kappa Epsilon, Gamma Theta Upsilon. Home: 2426-2 Quarterback Ct Ypsilanti MI 48197 Office: Ariz State U Dept Geography Tempe AZ 85281

LOUNSBURY, STEVEN RICHARD, lawyer; b. Evanston, Ill., July 26, 1950; s. James Richard and Reba Jeanette (Smith) L.; m. Dianne Louise Daley, Apr. 16, 1983; children: Jimson, Cody, Richard. BA, U. Calif., Santa Barbara, 1973; JD, U. West L.A., 1977. Bar: Calif. 1979, Oreg. 1997, U.S. Dist. Ct. (cen. dist.) Calif. 1979, U.S. Dist. Ct. Oreg. 1999. Pvt. practice, L.A., 1979-83; contract atty. FAA, 1981; trial atty. Hertz Corp., 1983-86; mng. counsel 20th Century Ins. Co., Woodland Hills, Calif., 1986-94; mng. atty. Lounsbury and Assocs., Brea, 1986-94; sr. trial atty. Bollington, Lounsbury and Chase, 1994-99; asst. Coos County counsel, Coquille, Oreg., 1999—2002; co. counsel Coos County, 2002—. Arbitrator Orange County Superior Ct., Santa Ana, Calif., 1992-99. Dir. internat. rels. Rotary Internat., Venice-Marina Club, Calif., 1980-81; dir. L.A. Jr. C. of C., 1981-82, chmn. westside com. 1980-81. Mem. ABA, Calif. Bar Assn., Oreg. Bar Assn., Calif. House Counsel (bd. dirs., chmn. membership 1993-94). Avocations: music (flute, choral), travel. Office: Coos County Office Legal Counsel 250 N Baxter St Coquille OR 97423-1852 E-mail: slounsbury@co.coos.or.us.

LOURENCO, RUY VALENTIM, physician, educator; b. Lisbon, Portugal, Mar. 25, 1929; came to U.S., 1959, naturalized, 1966; s. Raul Valentim and Maria Amalia (Gomes-Rosa) L.; children: Peter Edward, Margaret Philippa. MD, U. Lisbon, 1951. Intern Lisbon City Hosps., 1951-53, resident internal medicine, 1953-55; instr. U. Lisbon, 1955-59; fellow dept. medicine Columbia U.-Presbyn. Med. Ctr., N.Y.C., 1959-63; asst. prof. medicine N.J. Med. Sch., 1963-66, assoc. prof., 1966-67; practice medicine specializing in pulmonary medicine, 1967—; assoc. prof. medicine and physiology U. Ill. Coll. Medicine, Chgo., 1967-69, prof., 1969-89, Foley prof. medicine, 1978-89, chmn. dept. medicine, 1977-89, exec. head dept. medicine, 1983-89; dir. respiratory rsch. lab. Hektoen Inst., 1967-71; dir. pulmonary medicine Cook County Hosp., 1969-70; attending physician U. Ill. Med. Ctr., 1967-89, dir. pulmonary sect. and labs, 1970-77, physician-in-chief, 1977-89, pres. med. staff, 1980-81; prof. medicine and physiology, dean N.J. Med. Sch. U. Medicine and Dentistry N.J., Newark, 1989—2000, dean emeritus, 2001—. Cons. task force on rsch. in respiratory diseases NIH, 1972, mem. pathology study sect., 1972-76; mem. rev. bd. Spl. Ctrs. of Rsch. program, 1974; cons. career devel. program VA, 1972-90; mem. nat. com. Rev. Sci. Basis of Respiratory Therapy, 1973-74; chmn. exec. com. U. Hosp., Newark, 1989-2000; mem. bd. govs. Hackensack U. Hosp., 1993-2001; mem. fin. com. USMLE, 2000; mem. Nat. Bd. Med. Examiners, 1994—. Mem. editl. bd. Jour. Lab. and Clin. Medicine, 1973-77, 84-91, Am. Rev. Respiratory Diseases, 1985-91; contbr. numerous articles on pulmonary diseases, respiratory physiology and biochemistry to med. jours. Fellow AAAS, ACP, Am. Coll. Chest Physicians (pres. Ill. chpt. 1974-75, vice chmn. com. on environ. health 1981-82, gov. 1988-90, 93-95); mem. Assn. Am. Med. Colls. (coun. of deans 1989—, exec. com. project 3000 by 2000), Am. Fedn. Clin. Rsch., Am. Heart Assn., Am. Physiol. Soc., Am. Soc. Clin. Investigation, Am. Thoracic Soc. (chmn. sci. assembly 1974-75, bd. dirs. 1987-90, chmn. com. on internat. rels. 1989-91), Assn. Am. Physicians, Chgo. Soc. Internal Medicine (pres. 1988-89), Am. Lung Assn. (com. smoking and health 1981-84), Internat. Acad. Chest Physicians and Surgeons (chmn. nominating com. 1984-90), Chgo. Lung Assn. (bd. dirs. and mem. exec. com. 1974-82), Soc. Exptl. Biology and Medicine, Hispanic Serving Health Professions Schs. (pres. 1998-2001), Sigma Xi, Alpha Omega Alpha, Phi Kappa Phi. Office: NJ Med Sch 185 S Orange Ave Rm C671 Newark NJ 07103-2757

LOURIE, ALAN DAVID, federal judge; b. Boston, Jan. 13, 1935; AB, Harvard U., 1956; MS, U. Wis., 1958; PhD, U. Pa., 1965; JD, Temple U., 1970. Bar: Pa. 1970. Chemist Monsanto Co., St. Louis, 1957-59; lit. scientist, chemist, patent agt. Wyeth Labs., Radnor, Pa., 1959-64; counsel Smith Kline Beecham Corp., Phila., 1964-90; successively as patent agt., atty., dir. corp. patents, asst. gen. counsel, v.p. corp. patents Smith Kline Beecham Corp.; cir. judge U.S. Ct. Appeals (fed. cir.), Washington, 1990—. Mem. Judicial Conf. Com. on Financial Disclosure, 1990-98; mem. U.S. del. to Diplomatic Conf. on Revision of Paris Conv. for Protection of Indsl. Property, 1982, 84; vice chmn. industry functional adv. com. to U.S. Trade Rep. and Dept. Commerce, 1987-90; chmn. U.S. group of U.S.-Japan Bus. Coun. Task Force on Patents. Bd. visitors Law Sch., Temple U. Mem. ABA, Phila. Patent Law Assn. (pres. 1984-85), Am. Intellectual Property Law Assn. (bd. dirs. 1982-85), Assn. Corp. Patent Counsel (treas. 1987-89), Pharm. Mfrs. Assn. (chmn. patent com. 1981-86), Am. Chem. Soc., Cosmos Club, Harvard Club Washington. Office: US Ct Appeals Fed Cir 717 Madison Pl NW Washington DC 20439-0002

LOUTZENHISER, CAROLYN ANN, retired elementary education educator; b. Rochester, Minn., Sept. 18, 1942; d. Frank Arnold and Mae Nellie (Walters) Mahnke; m. John William Loutzenhiser, July 1, 1967; 1 child, Amy. BS, Wis. State U., 1966. Lic. tchr., Minn. First grade tchr. St. Paul Pub. Schs., 1966-67; first grade tchr. Dist. 535 Rochester Pub. Schs., Rochester, Minn., 1967-73; reading tchr. Rochester Pub. Schs., 1974-2000, ret., 2001. Presenter Chpt. I tchr. aides, Rochester, 1974-76; speaker, presenter Chpt. I workshop for parents, Rochester, 1974-88, So. Minn. Edn. Coop. Svc. Unit, Rochester, 1984, 91, 92; WSS trainer Rochester Pub. Schs., 2000-02. Legis. chmn. PTA, Churchill Sch., Rochester, 1982-84; mem. PTA, Rochester; guardian coun. mem. Jobs Daughters Bethel 13, Rochester, 1971, 86-88. Mem. NEA, AAUW (study group chmn. 1973-74), Minn. Edn. Assn., Rochester Edn. Assn., Order Eastern Star (worth matron Rochester chpt. 1975-76), White Shrine of Jerusalem (worthy high priestess Rochester chpt. 1981-82), Alpha Delta Kappa (pres. Delta chpt. 1990-92). Republican. Congregationalist. Avocations: golf, writing, reading, traveling, Am. hist. Home: 5154 Edgewater Dr Savage MN 55378-5615

LOUX, GORDON DALE, company executive; b. Souderton, Pa., June 21, 1938; s. Curtis L. and Ruth (Derstine) L.; m. Elizabeth Ann Nordland, June 18, 1960; children: Mark, Alan, Jonathan. Diploma, Moody Bible Inst., Chgo., 1960; BA, Gordon Coll., Wenham, Mass., 1962; BD, No. Bapt. Sem., Oak Brook, Ill., 1965, MDiv, 1971; MS, Nat. Coll. Edn., Evanston,Ill., 1984; LHD (hon.), Sioux Falls Coll., 1985. Ordained to ministry, Bapt. Ch., 1965. Assoc. pastor Forest Park (Ill.) Bapt. Ch., 1962-65; alumni field dir. Moody Bible Inst., Chgo., 1965-66, dir. pub. rels., 1972-76; dir. devel. Phila. Coll. Bible, 1966-69; pres. Stewardship Svcs., Wheaton, Ill., 1969-72; exec. v.p. Prison Fellowship Ministries, Washington, 1976-84, pres., CEO, 1984-88, Prison Fellowship Internat., Washington, 1979-87; pres. Internat. Students, Inc., Colorado Springs, Colo., 1988-93, Gordon D. Loux & Co., LLC, Colorado Springs, 1994—, Trinity Cmty. Found., 1996—. Author: Uncommon Courage, 1987, You Can Be a Point of Light, 1991; contbg. author: Money for Ministries, 1989, Dictionary of Christianity in America, 1989. Bd. dirs. Evang. Coun. for Fin. Accountability, Washington, 1979-92, vice chmn., 1981-84, 86-87, chmn., 1987-89; vice chmn. Billy Graham Greater Washington Crusade, 1985-85; bd. dirs. Evang. Fellowship of Mission Agys., 1991-94, Ctr. for Christian Jewish Dialogue, Colorado Springs, 1996—, Hope and Home, Colorado Springs, 1998—, C2ure, Mechanicsburg, Pa., 1999—, Global Leaders Initiative. Named Alumnus of Yr., Gordon Coll., 1986. Mem. Broadmoor Golf Club (Colo. Springs). Republican. Home: 740 Bear Paw Ln N Colorado Springs CO 80906-3215 Office: PO Box 38898 Colorado Springs CO 80937-8898

LOUX, JONATHAN DALE, business development consultant; b. Oak Park, Ill., Mar. 23, 1966; s. Gordon Dale and Elizabeth (Nordland) L.; m. Jan Mary Peters, July 22, 1989; children: Kara Leigh, Kurtis Dale, Kenton Stanley, Kourtney Grayce. BS, Eastern Coll., St. Davids, Pa., 1988. CPA, Ill. Acctg. supr. Capin, Crouse, LLP, Wheaton, Ill., 1989-93; supr. internal audit Select Beverages, Ind., Darien, 1993-94; pres. Gordon D. Loux Co., LLC, Colorado Springs, Colo., 1994—, Loux Group, LLC, Colorado Springs, 1996—; v.p. Cure Internat., Lemoyne, Pa., 2002—. Trustee Eastern Coll., St. Davids, Pa., 2000—. Republican. Presbyterian. Home and Office: 1003 4th St New Cumberland PA 17070

LOUX, RICHARD CHARLES, retired research executive, accountant; b. Ottawa, Kans., Apr. 2, 1929; s. John Peter and Zelma Orpha (Sutherland) L.; m. (div. 1984); children: Chrysa, Marilyn, Joan, Judy, Richard, Mary, Paula. BS in Acctg., Wichita State U., 1951. CPA, Kans. Acct. Witherspoon and Co. CPAs, Wichita, Kans., 1952-55; ptnr. Loux, Gose and Co. CPAs, 1955-75; commr. Kans. State Corp. Commn., Topeka, 1975-85; dir. Kans. Electric Utilities Rsch. Program, 1985-93. Pres. Wichita Estate Planning Coun., 1966, Kans. Advocacy and Protective Svcs. for Developmentally Disabled, Inc., Manhatter, 1978-88; bd. dirs. Nat. Regulatory Rsch. Inst., Columbus, Ohio, 1980-85, Cerebral Palsy Rsch. Found. Kans., Wichita, 1974-97; exec. com. Nat. Assn. Regulatory Commrs., Washington, 1980-85. Mem. AICPAs, Wichita CPAs (pres. 1965). Home: PO Box 1 Wichita KS 67201-5001 Fax: 316-315-0512. E-mail: rloux@msn.com.

LOVAAS, JOHN L. foreign aid executive, community activist; b. Washington, Mar. 27, 1943; s. Lloyd C. and Mary Alyce Lovaas; m. Frances C. Andersen, July 31, 1965; children: Deron, Terrence, Jennifer. BS, U. Md., 1967. Chief program officer U.S. AID, Tegucigalpa, Honduras, 1974-79, dep. dir. Niamey, Niger, 1981-83, Panama, Panama, 1983-86, asst. dir. Office Caribbean Affairs Washington, 1986-88, dir. ops. task force humanitarian assitance Ctrl. Am., 1988-89, dep. dir. Office Ctrl. Am. Affairs, 1989-90, dep. mission dir. San Salvador, El Salvador, 1990-94; v.p. Cambridge Consulting Corp., McLean, Va., 1996-98; spl. asst. to pub. Connection Newspapers, 1998—. Cons. World Bank, Tegucigalpa, 1996. V.p. Reston Assn., 1996—99; pres. Alliance Better Cmty., Reston, 1997, Reston Citizens Assn., 1999—2000; master marketer Reston Homegrown Farmers Market, 1997—; chmn. Reston 2000 Transp. Com., 1998—; mem. steering com. ARC Fairfax County, Herndon, Va., 2001—; vol. Rucker Homeless Shelter, 2001—, FISH, 2001—; vice chair Fairfax County Dem. Com., Falls Church, Va., 1995—96; mem. ctrl. com. Va. Dem. Party, 1998—; co-chair Hunter Mill Dist. Dem. Com., Reston, 1997—98. Mem. Sierra Club. Avocations: travel, gardening, theatre, reading. Home: 11437 Washington Plaza W Reston VA 20190 Office: Connection Newspapers 7913 Westpark Dr Mc Lean VA 22102 E-mail: jlovaas@aol.com.

LOVANO, SALVATORE CHARLES, II, music educator; b. Lakewood, Ohio, Apr. 2, 1961; s. Salvatore Charles Lovano and Joy Lee Theobald; m. Joyce Ann Riley; children: Jessica, Christopher, Feran. B in Music Edn., Ohio U., 1983. Music tchr. Frontier Local Schs., New Matamoras, Ohio, 1983—84; instrumental music tchr. West Liberty-Salem (Ohio) Local Schs., 1984—85, Youngstown (Ohio) City Schs., 1985—88, Maysville Local Sch. Dist., South Zanesville, 1988—96, Edison Local Sch. Dist., Richmond, 1996—. Dir. Canfield (Ohio) Cmty. Band, Ohio, 1985—88, Y-City Barbershop Chorus, Zanesville, Ohio, 1993—96; assoc. dir. Toronto (Ohio) Cmty. Band, Ohio, 1996—. Mem.: NEA, Ohio Edn. Assn., Ohio Music Edn. Assn., Music Educators Nat. Conf. Avocations: music, woodworking, computers. Home: 447 Mellwood Dr Toronto OH 43964 Office: Edison High Sch 9890 SR 152 Richmond OH 43944 Home Fax: 740-544-5594; Office Fax: 740-765-4961. E-mail: scl2@clover.net.

LOVBORG, UFFE, diagnostic research company executive; b. Kolding, Denmark, June 2, 1954; came to the U.S., 1999; s. Carl and Ingelise (Christiansen) L. Degree in Zoology, Aarhus (Denmark) U., 1976; Degree in Biochemistry, Copenhagen U., 1978, PhD in Immunology, 1981. R&D scientist NUNC, Roskilde, Denmark, 1981-85, Novo Nordisk, Bagsvaerd, Denmark, 1985-93; core scientist Novo Nordisk Symbion, Copenhagen, 1993-95; rsch. fellow Sydney (Australia) U., 1995-99; mgr. Borg-Biomed. & Diagnostic Consulting, Sydney, Australia, 1998-99; sr. exptl. scientist CSIRO, 1999; project mgr. Dako Corp., Carpinteria, Calif., 1999—. External tchr. Copenhagen U., 1987-95; referee Australian Asthma Fund, 1998-99. Author: Monoclonal Antibodies, 1982, Guide to Solid Phase Immunoassay, 1984; contbr. articles to profl. jours. Achievements include patents for rendering proteins non-allergenic through changing their molecular structure. Avocations: walking, nature, travels. Office: Dako Corp 6392 Via Real Carpinteria CA 93013-2921 E-mail: ulovborg@hotmail.com., uffe.lovborg@dakousa.com.

LOVE, BEN HOWARD, retired organization executive; b. Trenton, Tenn., Sept. 26, 1930; s. Ben Drane and (Whitehead) Virginia; m. Ann Claire Hugo, Mar. 4, 1933; children: Ben H. Jr., Phillip H.(dec.) , Leigh Anne, Mark E. BS,

Lambuth Coll., 1955, HHD (hon.), 1986; Dr. Philanthropy (hon.), Pepperdine U., 1987; LHD (hon.), Montclair State U., 1991. With Boy Scouts Am., 1955—, dist. exec. Tenn., 1955-60, scout exec. Delta area council, Clarksdale, Miss., 1960-64, dir. Nat. council, North Brunswick, N.J., 1964-68, scout exec. Longhorn council, Ft. Worth, 1968-71, scout exec. Sam Houston council, Houston, 1971-73, dir. Northeast region, Dayton, N.J., 1973-85, chief scout exec. Nat. council, Irving, Tex., 1985-93. Bd. dirs. Am. Gen. Series Portfolio Co., U.S. Life Income Fund. Served with U.S. Army, 1951-52. Recipient Gold medal SAR, Bronze Wolf award World Scout Orgn. Mem. La Cima Club (bd. dirs. Irving chpt. 1985-99), Diamond Oaks Country Club. Republican. Presbyterian. Avocations: tennis, golf, swimming, reading, spectator sports. Office: 4407 Eaton Cir Colleyville TX 76034-4653

LOVE, BRENDA ZEJDL, administrative assistant; b. Temple, Tex., Dec. 13, 1950; d. Johnnie James Billings and Robbie Erlene (Frazier) Welch; m. Lee James Harwell (div.); 1 child, Clinton Dee; m. Frank Lincoln Leary III, Feb. 14, 1982 (div. 1987); m. Mark K. Zejdl, Oct. 16, 1996. Student, Austin C.C., 1978-80, Foothill Coll., 1984-93; BA, Trinity Coll. and U., 1990; PhD, Hamilton U., 1992—; postgrad., Inst. Advanced Study, San Francisco, 1993—. Emergency med. tech.; lic. pilot. Emergency med. tech. Breckenridge Hosp., Austin, Tex., 1979, Santa Clara Valley (Calif.) Med. Ctr., 1980; outside sales rep. Bus. Equipment Co., San Francisco, 1981-82; counselor Nat. Sexually Transmitted Disease Hotline, Palo Alto, 1984-86, Nat. AIDS Hotline, Palo Alto, 1986-87, San Francisco Sex Information Switchboard, San Francisco, 1987-88; adminstrv. asst. ALZA Corp., Palo Alto, 1983—2001; adminstrn. Alexza MDC, Calif., 2002—. Lectr., researcher Inst. for Advanced Study of Human Sexuality; bus. mgr. Frank Leary Racing, 1981-83; adminstrv. asst. to chief adminstrv. law judge Tex. Comptroller Pub. Accounts, 1978-80. Author: Encyclopedia of Unusual Sex Practices, 1992; co-producer: (video) 500 Unusual Sex Practices, 1992; contbr. articles to profl. jours. Mem. Author's Guild, Inst. for Advanced Study of Human Sexuality, Am. Assn. Sex Educators, Counselors and Therapists, Soc. for Sic. Study of Sex, Calif. Writers Club, Mystery Writers Am. Libertarian. Jewish. Avocations: flying, sky diving, skating, photography. Office: Alexza MDC 1001 E Meadow Cir Palo Alto CA 94303 E-mail: lovezejdl@hotmail.com.

LOVE, DANIEL JOSEPH, consulting engineer; b. Fall River, Mass., Sept. 27, 1926; s. Henry Aloysius and Mary Ellen (Harrington) L.; m. Henrietta Maurisse Popper, June 10, 1950 (dec. Mar. 1986); children: Amy, Timothy (dec.), Terence, Kevin; m. Adeline Aponte Esquivel, Feb. 11, 1989; stepchildren: Eric, Brian, Jason. BSEE, Ill. Inst. Tech., 1951, MSEE, 1956; MBA, Calif. State U., Long Beach, 1973. registered profl. engr., Calif., Ariz., Ill., La.; cert. fire protection, Calif. Test engr. Internat. Harvester Co., Chgo., 1951-52; designer Pioneer Svc. & Engring. Co., 1952-53; project engr., ops. mgr. Panellit Co., Skokie, Ill., 1953-60; mktg. mgr. Control Data Co., Mpls., 1961-62; mktg. mgr., asst. to pres. Emerson Electric Co., Pasadena, Calif., 1963-65; pres., gen. mgr. McKee Automation Co., North Hollywood, 1965-68; engring. specialist Bechtel Co., Vernon and Norwalk, 1968-80, chief elec. engr. Madrid, 1980-83, engring. specialist Norwalk, Calif., 1983-87; cons. engr. Hacienda Heights, 1987—. Contbr. articles to jours. in field. Pres. Wilson High Sch. Band Boosters, Hacienda Heights, 1971-73. With USN, 1944-46. Named Outstanding Engr., Inst. for Advancement Engring., 1986; recipient 3d place prize paper award Industry Application Soc., 1995. Fellow IEEE (disting. lectr., chmn. Met. L.A. sect. 1973-74, chmn. L.A. coun. 1977-78, chmn. protection com. 1990-91, Richard Harold Kaufmann award 1994, Ralph H. Lee prize paper award 1995); mem. NSPE, Nat. Acad. Forensic Engrs., Instrument Soc. Am. (sr.), Soc. Fire Protection Engrs. Republican. Roman Catholic. Avocations: duplicate bridge, travel, walking, writing. Home: 16300 Soriano Dr Hacienda Heights CA 91745 E-mail: dan.love@ieee.org.

LOVE, DARRYL LEWIS, quality engineer; b. Meridian, Miss., June 29, 1966; s. D.L. and Lettye Mae (Bruton) Love; m. Najma Baniche Hogan, Dec. 23, 1995 (div. July 2001). BS in Mech. Engring. Tech., U. So. Miss., Hattiesburg, 1988. Cert. quality auditor. Quality control engr. Irvin Automotive, Greenwood, Miss., 1989-90; quality supr. Amoco, Andalusia, Ala., 1990-91; process engr. Wellman Inc., Fayetteville, N.C., 1991-98; sr. quality process engr. Moen Inc., New Bern, NC, 1999—. Lead auditor cert. BSI/Wellman, Fayetteville, 1993—. Mem. ASME, Am. Soc. Quality, Toastmasters Internat., Phi Beta Sigma (v.p. 1997—), Phi Beta Sigma (pres. 1999—). Democrat. African Methodist Episcopal Zion. Avocations: hunting, fishing, golf, physical fitness, martial arts. Home: PO Box 14188 New Bern NC 28561-4188 Office: Moen Inc 101 Industrial Dr New Bern NC 28562-9607

LOVE, HAROLD GIBSON, agricultural economics educator; b. Taylorsville, Ky., Apr. 30, 1928; s. Samuel Marion and Bertie Gibson Love; m. Louise Nadine Schwers, July 31, 1949; children: Michael Douglas, Harold Alan. BS in Agr., U. Ky., 1949, MS, 1963; PhD, U. Mo., 1969. Vocation agr. tchr. Spencer County Bd. Edn., Taylorsville, Ky., 1949-52; proof dir. U.S. Army Ordnance, Madison, Ind., 1952-54; asst. county agrl. agt. Coop. Ext. U. Ky., Harrodsburg, 1954-57, ext. agrl. mktg. agt. dept. agrl. econs. Louisville, 1957-66, ext. prof. agrl. econs. Lexington, 1969-86; chief of party Western U. agrl. edn. project U. Ky./USAID, Palembang, Indonesia, 1986-90; agribus. cons. Lexington, 1991—. Vis. prof. U. São Paulo, Piracicaba, 1992; agribus./mktg. cons. ACDI/VOCA, Republic of Armenia, 1994-99, also U.S. and 25 fgn. countries, 1966—; designer mktg. sys. for fruit and vegetables in India NDDB/Govt. India, New Delhi, 1984. Author, project leader: (book, instrnl. materials) Managing Farm Supply Cooperatives, 1975; author: (book/plan) Rural Marketing Strategy for Armenia, 1999. Recipient Outstanding Ky. Ext. Specialist award Ky. Ext. Specialists Assn., 1975. Mem. Internat. Assn. Agrl. Econs., Am. Agrl. Econs. Assn. (Profl. Excellence award in Comm. 1977), So. Agrl. Econs. Assn. (Lifetime Achievement award 1999), Assn. Coop. Educators (dir.-at-large 1977-82, Disting. Svc. award 1981), Epsilon Sigma Phi. Southern Baptist. Avocations: running/road racing, writing, traveling. Home: 991 Cooper Dr Lexington KY 40502-2508 Office: U Ky Dept Agrl Econs Lexington KY 40546-0001 E-mail: haroldlove@earthlink.net.

LOVE, JAMES SANFORD, III, communications executive; b. Jackson, Miss., Aug. 4, 1944; s. James Sanford Jr. and Jo Ellis (Buie) L.; m. Barbara Ann Harris, June 11, 1966 (div. Oct. 1981); children: James S. IV, Caroline E., Gillian M. BBA in Bus. and Govt., U. Miss., 1966; MBA, U. Va., 1968. Acct. exec. J. Walter Thompson, N.Y.C., 1968-70; rsch. analyst, asst. v.p. Dean Witter Co., 1970-73; chmn., CEO Love Broadcasting Co., Biloxi, Miss., 1972-91, Lakewood Meml. Pk., Jackson, 1972-91; rsch. analyst Baker Weeks & Co., N.Y.C., 1973-75; rsch. analyst, v.p. Paine Webber & Co., 1975-77; chmn., CEO Love Comm. Co., Jackson, 1991—. Cosn. Norberg Capital, N.Y.C., 1979-97; co-founder Millsaps Buie House Bed and Breakfast Inn, 1987—; owner White House Hotel, Biloxi, Miss., 1989—. Exec. prodr.: Miss. News Tonight, 1991-92. Trustee Millsaps Coll., Jackson, 1989—, Land Trust for the Miss. Coastal Plain, Miss. chpt. Nature Conservancy, 1990—, chmn. bd. trustees, 1996—97; chmn. leadership bd. Boys and Girls Club of Miss. Gulf Coast, 1994—96; mem. adv. bd. Salvation Army, 1997—. Named to All-Am. Rsch. Team, Instl. Investor Mag., 1974-75; recipient George Foster Peabody award U. Ga., 1989, regional Emmy award, 1990, 50th Anniversary Hero award The Nature Conservancy Miss. Chpt. Mem. Boston Club (New Orleans), Windance Country Club (Gulfport, Miss.), Univ. Club (Jackson), Biloxi Yacht Club. Episcopalian. Avocations: gardening, photography, salt water fishing, history. Home: 12137 Hickman Rd Biloxi MS 39532-9429 Office: Love Comm Co 240 Eisenhower Dr Bldg C Biloxi MS 39531-3601

LOVE, JOSEPH L. history educator, former cultural studies center administrator; b. Austin, Tex., Feb. 28, 1938; s. Joseph L. Sr. and Virginia (Ellis) L.; m. Laurie Reynolds, Dec. 23, 1978; children: Catherine R., David A.; children from previous marriage: James A., Stephen N. AB in Econs. with honors, Harvard U., 1960; MA in History, Stanford U., 1963; PhD in History with distinction, Columbia U., 1967. From instr. to prof. U. Ill., Urbana-Champaign, 1966—, dir. ctr. Latin Am. and Caribbean studies, 1993-99. Rsch. assoc. St. Antony's Coll. Oxford U.; vis. prof. Pontifical Cath. U., Rio de Janeiro, 1987; presenter in field. Author: Rio Grande do Sul and Brazilian Regionalism, 1882-1930, 1971, Sao Paulo in the Brazilian Federation, 1889-1937, 1980, Crafting the Third World: Theorizing Underdevelopment in Rumania and Brazil, 1996; editor: (with Robert S. Byars) Quantitative Social Science Research on Latin America, 1973, (with Nils Jacobsen) Guiding the Invisible Hand: Economic Liberalism and the State in Latin American History, 1988, (with Werner Baer) Liberalization and its Consequences: A Comparative Perspective on Latin America and Eastern Europe, 2000; bd. editors Latin Am. Rsch. Rev., 1974-78, Hispanic Am. Hist. Rev., 1984-89, The Americas, 1995-99; contbr. articles to profl. jours. Fulbright-Hays Rsch. grantee; fellow Social Sci. Rsch. Coun., IREX, Guggenheim; vis. fellow U. São Paulo, Inst. Ortega y Gasset, Madrid; sr. rsch. fellow NEH, others; sr. univ. scholar U. Ill., 1993-96. Mem. Am. Hist. Assn., Conf. Latin Am. History (chair Brazilian studies com. 1973, mem. gen. com. 1983, Conf. prize 1971), Latin Am. Studies Assn. Unitarian Universalist. Office: U Ill Dept History 309 Gregory Hall 810 S Wright St Urbana IL 61801-3644 E-mail: j-love2@uiuc.edu.

LOVE, JUSTIN WILLIS, music educator, educator; b. South Bend, Ind., Nov. 11, 1974; s. Robert E. and Tara S. Love; m. Elizabeth (Bee) N Townley, June 16, 2001. MusB Edn. with distinction, U. of Kans., 1998. Cert. K-12 music tchr. Kans. Dir. of instrumental music Ulysses (Kans.) Unified Sch. Dist., 1998—2000; dir. of bands De Soto (Kans.) H.S., 2000—. Low brass instr. Hume Music, Lawrence, Kans., 1995—98; sectional condr. Midwestern Music Camp, Lawrence, 1997—, resident dir., 2000—00, recreation dir., 1996—99; trombonist Heart of Am. Wind Symphony, 2001, Shawnee Concert Band, 2002—. Bldg. rep. De Soto Teacher's Assn. - NEA, 2001—02. Mem.: Kans. Bandmaster's Assn., Kans. Music Educator's Assn., Kappa Kappa Psi. Avocations: travel, reading. Office: De Soto HS 35000 W 91st St De Soto KS 66018 E-mail: jlove@usd232.org.

LOVE, KEITH SINCLAIR, communications executive; b. Apr. 26, 1947; s. James and Ruth L. BA, NYU, 1980. Editor N.Y. Times, N.Y.C., 1973-79; editor, polit. writer L.A. Times, 1979-90; asst. to v.p. ops. McClatchy Newspapers, Inc., 1990-92; pub. Ellensburg (Wash.) Daily Record, 1992-98; comm. dir. Gov. State of Washington, Olympia, 1998-99; v.p. comm. Stimson-Lane Vineyards & Estates, Woodinville, Wash., 1999—. Office: Stimson Lane Vineyards State Wash PO Box 1976 Woodinville WA 98072-1976

LOVE, KENNETH EDWARD, real estate, investment and business consultant; b. Bamberg, S.C., Dec. 8, 1941; s. Murray Eugene and Mozelle (Bodiford) L.; widowed; children: Kenneth E. II, Karen C., Kimberly Ann. Student, So. Meth. U., 1960, Columbia Coll., 1961; BS in History, U. S.C., 1963. Magistrate State of S.C., Columbia, 1970-73; real estate broker Crown KEL, Inc., 1973-87; exec. v.p. McDaniels So. Chems., 1984—; pres. Crown KEL, Inc. Pub. Co., 1986—, Comput-MED, Inc., 1987—. Owner Antiques Inc., Columbia, 1978—. Trustee Allen U., Columbia, 1973; mem. exec. com. S.C. Dem. Party, Columbia, 1962-74, chmn. 1971—; mem. U.S. Fgn. Affairs Panel, 1986—; chmn. So. East Dem. Regional Dist., 1994; mem. White Ho. Com. Policies; exec. dir. S.C. Citizens and Merchants' Assn., 1992—; chmn., CEO Carolina Hist. Found. Soc., Inc., 1996—. Served to sgt. U.S. Army, 1957-59. Named Outstanding Young Man Columbia City, 1972, Outstanding Dem. Nat. Dem. Party, 1992. Mem. S.C. Citizens and Merchants Assn. (pres. 1994—, exec. dir. 1995—), Greater Columbia Assn., Carolina Hist. Found. Soc. Inc. (chmn. bd. 1996—). Avocations: woodworking, medical research reading, politics. Office: Ken Love and Assoc 609 Columbia Ave Lexington SC 29072-2619

LOVE, MARSHA LYNN, interior decorator; b. West Palm beach, Fla., Nov. 14, 1944; d. James Luther and Blanche Louise (Morrison) L. BA, Fla. State U., 1966; MA, U. N.C., 1970. Lic. secondary sch. tchr., Fla. Tchr. Forest Hill H.S., West Palm Beach, 1967-68; counselor, dean women Fla. Atlantic U., Boca Raton, 1971, asst. to dean student affairs, 1971-74, asst. dean students, 1974-81; interior decorator Tulane Kidd Interiors, 1981—. Adj. instr. Palm Beach C.C., Boca Raton, 1981—. Author: The Vitamin Parade, 1990; contbr. articles to profl. jours. Pres. Delray Beach (Fla.) Hist. Soc., 1986, Jr. League of Boca Raton, 1984; founding chmn. Cason Cottage Mus., Delray Beach, 1988; exhibits chmn. Singing Pines Mus., Boca Raton, 1980. Mem. Order of the Crown of Charlemagne, Soc. Colonial Govs., Washington Family Descendants, Daus. of the Cincinnati, Colonial Dames of Am. (chpt. pres. 1997-00), Mortar Bd., Garnet Key, Phi Theta Kappa, Kappa Kappa Gamma (field rep. 1966-67). Republican. Methodist. Avocations: needlepoint, art, antiques, travel, genealogy. Home: 2000 S Ocean Blvd Apt 402 Delray Beach FL 33483-6411

LOVE, MARY ANN E. state legislator; b. West Pittston, Pa., Feb. 21, 1940; married; 2 children. Grad., Wilkes-Barre (Pa.) Bus. Sch., 1959. State legis. dist.32 Md. Ho. Reps., Annapolis, 1993—, mem. econ. matters com. Chmn. Anne Arundel County Delegation, 1999—. Bd. dirs. Providence Ctr., Hospice of the Chesapeake. Recipient County Achievement award Nat. Assn. Counties, 1986-89, Anne Arundel Trade Coun. Legis. of Yr. award, 1997. Mem. No. Anne Arundel County C. of C. (Pres.'s award 1996). Office: Md Ho of Reps 214 Lowe House Office Bldg Annapolis MD 21401

LOVE, MICHAEL JOSEPH, lawyer; b. Chicopee, Mass., Mar. 1, 1958; BA, U. Mass., 1984; student, Vanderbilt U., 1991-92; JD, U. Denver, 1992. Bar: Tenn., U.S. Dist. Ct. (mid. dist.) Tenn. 1992. Ptnr. Zellar, Cartwright & Love, PLLC, Clarksville, Tenn., 1994-96, Cartwright & Love, PLLC, Clarksville, 1996—. Gen. editor U. Denver Law Rev. Mem. legal com. NORML. With U.S. Army, 1975-78. Mem. Nat. Assn. Criminal Def. Lawyers (life), Tenn. Bar Assn. (exec. com. criminal def. sect.), Tenn. Assn. Criminal Def. Lawyers (NORML legal com.). Democrat. Office: Cartwright & Love PLLC 215 S 2nd St Clarksville TN 37040-3629 E-mail: MichaelJLove@msn.com.

LOVE, MILDRED ALLISON, retired secondary school educator, historian, writer, volunteer; b. Moultrie, Ga., Mar. 12, 1915; d. Ulysees Simpson Sr. and Susie Marie (Dukes) Allison; m. George Alsobrook Love, Aug. 24, 1956 (dec. 1978). BSEd, U. Tampa (Fla.), 1941; MS in Home Econs., Fla. State U., 1953; MA in History, U. Miami, Coral Gables, Fla., 1969. Cert. tchr., Fla. Vocat. home econs. tchr. Hamilton County Pub. Schs., Jasper, Fla., 1941-43, Pinellas County Pub. Schs., Tarpon Springs, 1946-51, Dade County Pub. Schs., Miami, 1951-61, history tchr., 1961-73; supr. food svcs. Ft. Jackson (S.C.), 1944-46. Chmn. subcoun. for crime prevention Brickell Area, City of Miami, 1983-87; mem. Crisis Response Team, Miami Police Dept., 1983—; vol. VA Hosp., Miami, 1987—; historian, vol. vets affairs VFW Aux., Miami, 1988-89; precinct worker presdl. election, 1976, 80; sponsor history honor soc. Miami Edison Sr. H.S., 1961-73; mem. Mus. of Sci., St. Stephen's Episc. Ch., Coconut Grove, Fla.; mem. Dade Heritage Trust; charter mem. Libr. Congress Assocs.; mem. Arthritis Found., Consumer Union. Mem. AAUW, VFW (aux. post 471 Miami, Fla.), Am. Assn. Ret. Persons, Hist. Assn. S. Fla., U. Miami Alumni Assn., Fla. Ret. Educators Assn., Nat. Wildlife Fedn., Am. Legion (aux. post 29 Miami, Fla.), Nat. Trust Hist. Preservation, Coll. of Arts and Scis. Assn. U. Miami, Fla. Vocat. Home Econs. Tchrs. (pres. 1947), Fla. Vocat. Home Econs. Assn. (pres. 1948-49), Dade Heritage Trust, Woman's Club of Miami Beach, Sierra Club, Phi Alpha Theta. Democrat. Episcopalian. Avocation: foreign languages. Home: 2411 S Miami Ave Miami FL 33129-1527

LOVE, NANCY LORENE, communication and political strategist, educator; b. Dallas, Oct. 4, 1947; d. H. Mack and Helen (Hardin) L. BS, So. Meth. U., 1970; MS, North Tex. U., 1975. Speechwriter, strategist Love & Assocs., Atlanta, 1975-95; exec. dir. Crisis Aid, 1977-82; instr. comm. and polit. strategy DeKalb Tech. Inst., 1995-2000, Ga. Perimeter Coll., 2000—; assoc. exec. dir. Ga. Tech. YMCA, 2000—01. Advisor Am. Parliamentary Assn. Contbr. articles to profl. publs. Arbitrator BBB, Atlanta, 1982—; Ga. coord. Sister Cities, Inc., Washington; pres. N.E. Ga. chpt., exch. dir. Friendship Force; account exec. United Way, Atlanta; chmn. bd. SSS Ga., Atlanta. Mem. AAUW, Rotary (youth exch. officer North DeKalb coun., Rotarian of Yr. award 1996), Am. Parliamentary Assn., Phi Theta Kappa (advisor 1995-99, leadership instr.). Methodist. Avocations: gourmet cusine, travel, international politics. E-mail: nancy.love@ymca.gatech.edu.

LOVE, RICHARD EMERSON, equipment manufacturing company executive; b. N.Y.C., Dec. 15, 1926; s. Emerson C. and Ruth A. (Mealley) L.; m. Margaret A. Lloyd, June 24, 1950; children— Mary-Ann, Nancy, Jane, Thomas. Grad., N.Y. State Maritime Coll., 1946; AAS, Hofstra Coll., 1955. Group v.p. Crane Co., N.Y.C., 1967-72, U.S. Filter Co., N.Y.C., 1972-75; group pres. Peabody Internat. Corp., Stamford, Conn., 1975-77, exec. v.p., 1978-85; group v.p. Pullman Co. (merged with Peabody Internat. Corp.), 1985-87; v.p. ops. Hosokawa Micron Internat. Inc., N.Y.C., 1987-93; dir., cons. Hosokawa Micron Internat., 1993-95; ret., 1995. Pres. Internat. Area Mgmt., Hilton Head, S.C., 1995—. Served with USN, 1948-49. Mem. ASME, Instruments Soc. Am. Office: Internat Area Mgmt 16 Old Fort Dr Hilton Head Island SC 29926-2698

LOVE, ROBERT LYMAN, educational consulting company executive; b. Oswego, N.Y., July 28, 1925; s. Robert Barnum and Marion Alberta (Peavy) L.; m. Janet May Fuller, June 26, 1948; children: Robert H., Andrew L., Charles D., Cynthia S. Student, U. Rochester, 1943-44; AB, Syracuse U., 1945, postgrad., 1946-48, MEd, 1949; postgrad., Cornell U., 1963-64. Sci. tchr. Middlesex Valley Central Sch., Rushville, N.Y., 1949-53; mem. faculty Agrl. and Tech. Coll., SUNY-Alfred, 1953-81; prof., dean Agrl. and Tech. Coll., SUNY (Sch. Allied Health Techs.), until 1981, dean emeritus, 1981—; pres. Edn. Cons. Services, Alfred Station, N.Y., 1981—. Former mem. bd. dirs. Nat. Tech. Inst. Deaf Med. Records program; program evaluation steering com. AMA; allied health reviewer HEW; mem. health sub-com. 39th Congl. Dist. Author: He and She, An Introduction to Human Sexuality and Birth Control, 1970; editor: Upward Mobility for Lab Personnel, 1970. Fin. sec., mem. adminstrv. bd. Alfred United Meth. Ch., bd. dirs. preschool and day care ctr., 1992—, pres., 1998—; mem. Roving Vols. in Christ's Svc., 1982-91, bd. dirs. 1984-86, 89-91, chmn. bd. dirs., 1989-90; mem. Selected Vols. in Christ's Svc., 1987-88; litercy vol.; pres., bd. dirs. Genesee Valley Habitat for Humanity, Inc., 1993-95; treas. 1995-98; Allegany County Office for Aging Handyman's Svc. Fellow Sci. Tchrs. Assn. N.Y. State, Am. Soc. Allied Health Professions; mem. Gideons Internat. (past pres. Hornell Camp), Literacy Vols. Am. (bd. dirs. Allegany County chpt. 1990-93), Masons, Order Eastern Star. Republican. Office: Loves Angels Stained Glass and Edn Cons Svc 5366 Jericho Hill Rd Alfred Station NY 14803-9736 *Having had the opportunity to work with young people has kept me young and knowing the Lord has saved me.*

LOVE, SANDRA RAE, information specialist; b. San Francisco, Feb. 20, 1947; d. Benjamin Raymond and Charlotte C. Martin; m. Michael D. Love, Feb. 14, 1971. BA in English, Calif. State U., Hayward, 1968; MS in L.S., U. So. Calif., 1969. Tech. info. specialist Lawrence Livermore (Calif.) Nat. Lab., 1969—. Mem. Beta Sigma Phi. Democrat. Episcopalian. Office: Lawrence Livermore Nat Lab PO Box 808 Livermore CA 94551-0808

LOVE, SHARON IRENE, elementary education educator; b. Pontiac, Mich., July 27, 1950; d. James and Ethlyn (Cole) M.; married; 1 child, Sheralyn Reneé. BS, Western Mich. U., 1964; postgrad., Oakland U., Rochester, Mich. Cert. elem. educator, early childhood educator, Mich. Tchr. kindergarten Pontiac Bd. Edn., 1964-69, 76-83, 87—, tchr. 1st grade, 1965-66, tchr. 4th grade, 1983-84, tchr. 2d grade, 1984-87. Tchr. trainer triple I.E. classroom instruction Emerson Elem. Sch., Pontiac, 1988-89; trainer Math Their Way, Pontiac Sch. Sys., 1989, leadership, 1990; trainer Mich. Health Model Oakland Schs., Waterfort, 1987; co-chair com. for developing and writing new Fine Arts curriculum for Pontiac Sch. Dist., 1993-94; chmn. coordinating coun. Webster Elem. Sch., 1994-95; head tchr. kindergarten pilot Bethune Elem. Sch., 1995-96. Co-author: kindergarten sci. curriculum for Pontiac Sch. Dist., 2000—02. Chair coord. coun. Walt Whitman Elem. Schs., Pontiac, 1987-91; mem. PTA, 1970-90; chair coord. coun. Webster Elem. Sch., 1993-94, Bethune Elem. Sch., 1999-2000, mem. sch. improvement com., 1999-2000, mem. tech. com., 1999-2000. Creative Art grantee Pontiac PTA, 1965; recipient cert. Appreciation Pontiac Blue Ribbon Com., 1991, cert. for outstanding educator Mich. Gov. Engler, 1991, Mark Twain Elem. cert. for excellence, 2001, AIDS Awareness cert. City of Pontiac, 2001, others. Mem. NAACP, Mich. Edn. Assn., Pontiac Edn. Assn. (del. 1965-66). Avocations: art, writing poetry, sewing. Office: Pontiac Bd Edn 350 Wide Track Dr E Pontiac MI 48342-2243

LOVE, SUSAN DENISE, accountant, consultant, small business owner; b. Portland, Oreg., Aug. 5, 1954; d. Charles Richard and Betty Lou (Reynolds) Beck; m. Daniel G. Oliveros, Dec. 21, 1979 (div. Nov. 1983); m. Michael Dean Love, Aug. 24, 1984 (div. Mar. 1989); m. Michael Eugene Watson, July 28, 1990 (div. Dec. 1994); m. David Phillip Dulaney, Aug. 22, 1998. BA in Graphic Design, Portland State U., 1976. Office mgr. Rogers Machinery Co., Portland, 1972-77; exec. sec. Creighton Shirtmakers, N.Y.C., 1977-80; dir. adminstrn. Henry Grethel div. Manhattan Industries, 1980-81; exec. asst. S.B. Tanger and Assocs., 1981-83; exec. asst., bookkeeper M Fin. Corp., Portland, 1983-84; acct. cons., owner Office Assistance, 1984—; owner WE LOVE KIDS Clothing Store, 1985—; owner, pres. Oreg. Music and Entertainment, 1989—99; v.p. Coral Sales Co., 2002—. Sec./treas. Designers' Roundtable, Portland, 1985-88; co-owner, The Tuxedo Club, 1992-95. Mem. Oreg. State Pub. Interest Rsch. Group, Portland, 1985-90, Oreg. Fair Share,Salem, 1987, mem. adv. bd. career and life options program Clackamas Community Coll., 1989-91. Mem. Women Entrepreneurs Oreg. (bd. dirs. 1988-98, pres. 1992-95, Mem. of Yr. award 1991, 95), Brentwood-Darlington Neighborhood Assn. (treas. 1993-2000), Parkside Homeowners Assn. (treas. 2002—), North Clackamas County C. of C., Nat. Fedn. Ind. Bus., Outer S.E. Coalition. Democrat. Avocations: bicycling, aerobics, sewing, hiking, music, graphic design. Office: Office Assistance PO Box 1784 Clackamas OR 97015-1784

LOVE, TERRY, federal agency specialist; b. Clinton, Okla., July 1, 1953; d. Lavera Reyes; m. Lavern Birdshead, Oct. 17, 1973 (div. May 1975); 1 child, Roman L. Birdshead; m. Wilbur R. Love, July 1, 1981. AA, Haskell Ind. Jr. Coll., Lawrence, Kans., 1975; BA, S.W. Okla. State U., 1980, MEd, 1997. Indian child welfare caseworker Cheyenne, Arapaho Tribes Okla., Concho, 1983-87, indian child welfare coord., caseworker, 1987-90; child protection specialist Bur. Indian Affairs, Anadarko, Okla., 1991-94, social svc. rep., 1994-96, 98-99, ct. clk. Pawnee, 1996-98, realty asst. El Reno, 2000; child welfare specialist Crow Creek Sioux Agy./Bur. Indian Affairs, Ft. Thompson, S.D., 2001—. With Substance Abuse Treatment Ctr., Concho, Okla., 1992-94; youth guidance counselor Iowa Tribe Okla., Perkins, 1996-98. Democrat. Baptist. Avocations: Native American activities, walking, swimming, skating, movies. Home: PO Box 569 Fort Thompson SD 57339

LOVE, WILLIAM EDWARD, lawyer; b. Eugene, Oreg., Mar. 13, 1926; s. William Stewart and Ola A. (Kingsbury) L.; m. Sylvia Kathryn Jaureguy, Aug. 6, 1955; children: Kathryn Love Petersen, Jeffrey, Douglas, Gregory. BS, U. Notre Dame, 1946; MA in Journalism, U. Oreg., 1950, JD, 1952. Bar: Oreg. 1952. Newspaper reporter Eugene Register Guard, 1943-44, 47-52; asst. prof. law, asst. dean Sch. Law U. Wash., Seattle, 1952-56; ptnr. Cake, Jaureguy, Hardy, Buttler & McEwen, Portland, Oreg., 1956-69; pres., chmn., CEO Equitable Savs. & Loan, 1969-82; sr. ptnr. Schwabe, Williamson & Wyatt, 1983—. Chmn. Oreg. Savs. League, 1976; dir. Portland Gen. Electric, 1976-83, Fed. Home Loan Bank of Seattle, 1976-79, 85-96, adv. council Fed. Nat. Mortgage Assn., Washington, 1978-80; exec. dir. Oreg. Facilities Authority, 1990—. Author: (with Jaureguy) Oregon Probate Law and Practice, 2 vols., 1958; contbr. articles to profl. jours. Commr., past chmn. Oreg. Racing Commn., 1963-79; pres. Nat. Assn. State Racing Commrs., 1977-78; commr. Port of Portland, 1979-86, pres. 1983; referee Pac-10 football, 1960-81, Rose Bowl, 1981; active United Way, Boy Scouts Am., Portland Rose Festival, polit. campaigns; mem. adv. coun. Jockey's Guild, Inc., 1990-01. Served to lt. (j.g.) USN, 1944-47. Mem. Oreg. Bar Assn., Multnomah County Bar Assn., Multnomah Athletic Club, Golf Club (Portland). Republican. Home: 10225 SW Melnore St Portland OR 97225-4356 Office: Schwabe Williamson & Wyatt 1211 SW 5th Ave Ste 1800 Portland OR 97204-3713

LOVECCHIO, JOSEPH A. music educator, conductor; b. Berwick, Pa., May 2, 1952; s. Angelo Michael and Marguerite Delrose Lovecchio; m. Alice Mae Bright; children: Joseph Jr., Maria, Michael. BS, Pa. State U., 1974; MA, Coll. N.J., 1979. Permanent tchg. cert., Pa. Instrumental music dir. Centennial Sch. Dist., Warminster, Pa., 1975—. Music dir., condr. Warminster Symphony Orch., 1995—. Mem. NEA, Internat. Jazz Educators Assn., Music Educators Nat. Conf., Nat. Band Assn. (Pa. state chair 1998), Pa. Music Educators Assn. (dist. II advocacy chair), Pa. Edn. Assn. E-mail: LoveJo@CentennialSD.org., Jallov@aol.com.

LOVEJOY, GEORGE MONTGOMERY, JR. real estate company executive; b. Newton, Mass., Apr. 15, 1930; s. George Montgomery and Margaret (King) L.; m. Ellen West Childs, June 30, 1956; children: George Montgomery III, Edward R., Philip W., Henry W. BA, Harvard U., 1951. V.p. Minot, DeBlois & Maddison, Boston, 1955-72; exec. v.p. Meredith & Grew, Inc., 1972-78, pres., 1978-88, chmn., 1988-95, Fifty Assocs., Boston, 1988-94, pres., 1994—2001. Trustee various Scudder Kemper Inc. mut. funds, 1975-2000. Mem. Weston (Mass.) Planning Bd., 1961-68, chmn., 1965-67; mem. Bd. Selectmen, 1968-71, chmn., 1970-71; bd. dirs. Boston Mcpl. Rsch. Bur., 1966—, chmn., 1982-84; mem. com. Fund for Preservation Wildlife and Natural Areas, 1985-94, chmn., 1992-94; trustee New Eng. Aquarium, 1969—, pres. 1992-94, chmn. 1994; trustee Radcliffe Coll., 1987-95; mem. Corp. Northeastern U., 1983-2002; bd. dirs. Pioneer Inst. for Pub. Policy Rsch. Mem. Counselors of Real Estate (past pres., bd. dirs.), Greater Boston Bldg. Owners and Mgrs. Assn. (past pres.), Inst. Real Estate Mgmt. (past pres. New Eng. chpt.), Greater Boston Real Estate Bd. (past pres.), Mass. Assn. Realtors, Nat. Assn. Realtors, Nature Conservancy (mem. Mass. adv. bd., chmn. 1994-97), Harvard Club Boston (past pres.). Avocations: outdoor activities, land conservation. Home: 54 Beacon St Boston MA 02108-3531 Office: Fifty Assoc 50 Congress St Boston MA 02109-4002

LOVEJOY, JEAN HASTINGS, social services counselor; b. Battle Creek, Mich., July 1, 1913; d. William Walter and Elizabeth (Fairbank) H.; m. Allen Perry, March 27, 1912; children: Isabel L. Best, Linda L. Ewald, Elizabeth L. Fulton, Margaret L. Baldwin, Helen L. Battad. BA, Mt. Holyoke Coll., So. Hadley, Mass., 1935. Traveling sec. Student Volun. Movement, N.Y.C., 1935; bookkeeper Hartford Consumers Co-operative, Conn., 1944; tchr. Pre-School, Congl. Ch., W Hartford, 1944-45; instr. St. John's U., Shanghai, China; tchr. Edn., 1st Congl. Ch., Berkeley, Calif., 1958-59; instr. Tunghai U., Taiwan, 1960-63; sec. Pres. Tunghai U., Taichung, Taiwan, 1960-63. Pres. Ecumenical Assn. for Housing, San Rafael, 1971, 78-80; founding mem. Hospice of Havasu, 1982, pres. bd. dirs., 1985-87, vol. trainer, 1987-92; bereavement vol. Cmty. Hospice, Tucson, 1993-96; vol. friendly visitor N.W. Interfaith Ctr., Tucson, 1995—;vol. libr. La Rosa Health Ctr., Tucson, 1998—. Recipient OACC Sr. Achievement award, 1991; named Vol. of Yr., Marin County, Calif., 1970, 79; street named Lovejoy Way in her honor Novato (Calif.) City Coun., 1980. Mem. LWV (program v.p. Pierce County chpt. 1967, pres. cen. Marin County chpt. 1973-75, legis. analyst land use 1979-80, Calif. chpt.). Mem. United Ch. of Christ (Stephen min.) Home: Apt 8208 7500 N Calle Sin Envidia Tucson AZ 85718-7363

LOVEJOY, KIM BRIAN, English educator; b. Burlington, Vt., Aug. 8, 1952; s. Norman Robert Sr. and Rita Blanche (Frenette) L.; m. Mary Elizabeth Sugg, Aug. 1, 1980; children: Rebecca Elizabeth, Joseph Franklin. BA, St. Michael's Coll., 1974; MA, Purdue U., 1977; PhD, U. Mo., Columbia, 1987. Grad. tchr. Purdue U., West Lafayette, Ind., 1974-77; instr. William Woods U., Fulton, Mo., 1977-81; grad. tchr. U. Mo., Columbia, 1981-87; asst. prof. Ind. U., Indpls., 1987-93, assoc. prof., 1993—, assoc. chair English dept., 1996-98, acting chair, 1997-98. Adv. bd. Readerly-Writerly Tests, Eastern N.Mex. State U., 1995—. Author: Writing: Process, Product, & Power, 1993; mng. editor Jour. of Tchg. Writing, 1987—; contbr. articles to profl. jours. Fellow U. Mo., 1985. Mem. MLA, Nat. Coun. Tchrs. English (lang. policy com. 1994—), Conf. Coll. Composition and Comm. (exec com., rsch. network forum), Ind. Tchrs. Writing. Democrat. Roman Catholic. Avocations: golf, racquetball, biking. Office: Ind U Purdue U Indpls Dept English CA 501M 425 University Blvd Indianapolis IN 46202-5148 Home: 810 Copperfield Ln Danville IN 46122-2515 Fax: 317-278-1287. E-mail: klovejoy@iupui.edu.

LOVELACE, DOROTHY LOUISE, volunteer; b. Birmingham, Ala., Dec. 24, 1921; d. Walter Louis and Dorothea Christina (Sayers) Howard; m. Larry Clark Lovelac, Dec. 23, 1941 (dec. 2002); children: Larry C. (dec.), Susan Lovelace Weaver, Claude Thomas II. Student, Birmingham So. Coll., 1938-40. Extra (HBO movies) From the Earth to the Moon, 1997. Girl scout leader, den mother Keesler AFB, Biloxi, Miss., 1950—52; mem. Orlando Civic Theatre Guild, publicity chmn., 1973—80; pres. Top of the Hill Drama Club, 1989—93, Roadside Theatre Co. of Orlando, 1988—89; vol. ARC, Keesler AFB, Miss., South Ruislip AFB, London, Scott AFB, Ill., Patrick AFB, Fla., 1953—71, Orlando Tng. Ctr. Chapel, 1971—98, vol. libr., 1980—82; vol. tchr. Head Start, Patrick AFB, Fla., 1971—72; Sunday sch. tchr., choir; mem. Protestant Women of the Chapel, Orlando Naval Tng. Ctr., 1972—97, pres., 1992—96, v.p., 1987—91, hospitality chmn., 1980—87; guitar instr. Winter Park Presbyn. Ch., 1992. Recipient 2d pl. award Smucker's Strawberry Festival Recipe Contest, 1998. Mem. Fla. Assn. for Family and Cmty. Edn. (treas. 1984-92, v.p. 1992-97, Best of Show 1990, First Pl. of Collection of Christmas Songs, 1991, Best of Show for Quilt, 1992, First Pl. for Song, 1992, Best of Show for Indian Beading, 1993, Best of Show children's Poetry book, 1994, Best of Show Dried Flower Art, 1995). Avocations: writing, music, needle work, drama, gardening. Home: 2518 Sweetwater Trail Maitland FL 32751-5017

LOVELACE, ELDRIDGE HIRST, retired landscape architect, city planner; b. Kansas City, Kans., Mar. 16, 1913; s. Charles Wilson and Eva (Hirst) L.; m. Marjorie Van Evera, May 15, 1937; children: Jean (Mrs. William C. Stinchcombe), Richard. B.F.A. in Landscape Architecture, U. Ill., 1935. Registered profl. engr., Mo. With Harland Bartholomew & Assocs., Inc., St. Louis, 1935— 81, mem. firm, 1943-79, chmn. bd., 1979— 81; cons., 1981—; prepared comprehensive city plans numerous cities including Toledo, Baton Rouge, Oklahoma City, Vancouver, Waco, Lincoln, Washington; master plans for naval facilities Hawaiian Islands and P.I.; also plans parks, subdivs., housing projects. Vice pres. Internat. Fedn. Landscape Architects, 1975-77, sec. gen., 1980— 81 Author: Harland Bartholomew: His Contributions to American Urban Planning. Mem. bd. commrs. Tower Grove Park, 1971—, pres. 1986-94. Fellow Am. Soc. Landscape Architects (past pres.), ASCE; mem. Am. Inst. Cert. Planners. Clubs: Mo. Athletic (St. Louis). Home: 8600 Delmar Blvd Saint Louis MO 63124-1973 E-mail: marjorielovelace@aol.com.

LOVELACE, GEORGE DAVID, JR. quality engineer; b. Pampa, Tex., Aug. 9, 1952; AS, Clarendon (Tex.) Coll., 1972; BS, Oklahoma City U., 1985, MBA, 1992. Cert. quality engr. Engring. aide Dayton Tire subs. Bridgestone/Firestone, Inc., Oklahoma City, 1973; sr. engring. aide Bridgestone/Firestone, Inc., 1973-75, tech. asst., 1975-83, sr. tech. asst., 1983-85, statis. engr., 1985-87, sr. statis. engr., 1987-90, Dayton Tire, Oklahoma City, 1991-92, sect. mgr. quality assurance, 1992-99, area bus. mgr. curing/final inspection, 1999—2001, sect. mgr., 2001, sr. environ. coord., 2002—. Mem. bd. of elders Grace Chapel, Mustang, Okla., 1977—; tchr. Grace Chapel Sunday Sch., 1977—, chmn., 1987—. Mem. Am. Soc. for Quality (sr., Okla. sect., program chmn. 1984-85, vice chmn. 1985-86, chmn. 1986-87). Republican. Avocations: leathercraft, numismatics, personal computer. Home: 1320 Grand View Way Mustang OK 73064-7233 Office: Dayton Tire Div Bridgestone Firestone N Am Tire LLC 2500 S Council Rd # 24011 Oklahoma City OK 73128-9501

LOVELACE, JULIANNE, former library director; b. Jackson, Miss., July 30, 1941; d. Benjamin Travis and Julia Elizabeth (Knight) Robinson; m. William Frank Lovelance, July 6, 1963 (div. Mar. 17, 1972); 1 child, Julie Lynn. BA in History, So. Meth. U., 1963; MLS, U. North Tex., 1970. Clk. Dallas Pub. Libr., 1963-64, children's libr. asst., 1964-66, children's libr., 1966-69; libr. Richardson (Tex.) Pub. Libr., 1971-72, supr. pub. svcs., 1972-87, dir., 1987-2001; pres. 4womenShopping, Inc., 2000—. Active Richardson Adult Literacy Ctr., Altrusa Internat., Inc. Richardson, Leadership Richardson Alumni Assn., Friends of the Richardson Pub. Libr., Citizens Police Acad. Alunmni Assn., Baylor/Richardson Med. Ctr. Found. Bd.; women's adv. coun. Baylor/Richardson Med. Ctr.; exec. com. Wildflower Arts & Music Festival; steering com. opening gala events Eisemann Ctr. for the Performing Arts. Named one of 21 for the 21st Century, Collin County Bus., 2000. Avocations: horseback riding, blackjack. E-mail: jl3430@swbell.net.

LOVELACE, LINDA DIANE, court administrator; b. Hamilton, Ohio, Oct. 3, 1948; d. Joseph Weber and Martha M. (Morris) White; children: Brent David, Kerri Leigh. BA in Polit. Sci., BA in French, Otterbein Coll., 1970. Cert. data processing Internat. Data Processing. Receptionist Boyd Chiropractic Clinic, Hamilton, Ohio, 1966-70; admitting clk. Univ. Hosp., Columbus, 1970-72; sec., youth dir. Park Ave Unite Meth. Ch., Hamilton, 1973-80; admitting clk. Ft. Hamilton Hughes Hosp., 1980; clk. Area II Ct., 1981-82, Area I, II and III Cts., Hamilton, 1983-86; ct. adminstr. Butler County Domestic Rels. Ct., 1987-93; ct. adminstr. gen. div. Butler County Common Pleas Ct., 1992—. Lectr. Butler County Alcoholism Coun., Hamilton, 1983-86. Pres. Butler County Women's Rep. Club, Hamilton, 1988-90; mem. Rep. Party Exec. Com., Hamilton, 1985—; pres. S.W. Ohio Ct. Clks. Assn., 1983; bd. dirs., trustee Ohio Assn. Mcpl. Cts., 1981-86; chair Butler County Computer Task Force, 1991—; mem. security task force Butler County Ct. Common Pleas, 1992—; mem. Butler County Coalition on Domestic Violence, 1991—. Named for Community Svc., Alcoholism Coun. Butler County, 1986. Mem. ABA (assoc.), Nat. Ctr. for State Cts. (assoc.), Soc. Human Resource Mgmt., Search Task Force, Am. Judicature Soc., Nat. Assn. Ct. Mgmt. (pres. 1990-91), Nat. Fedn. Republican Women. Methodist. Avocations: tennis, reading, traveling, biking. Office: Butler County Domestic Rels Ct 101 High St Fl 2D Hamilton OH 45011-2727

LOVELACE, ROSE MARIE SNIEGON, federal space agency administrator; b. Sweet Hall, Va., Feb. 19, 1937; d. Adolph and Annie (Mickel) Sniegon; m. William Wayne Lovelace, Aug. 11, 1962. Degree in bus., Longwood Coll., 1957. Adminstrv. aide Dept. of Navy, Washington, 1957-60; adminstrv. asst. Joint Blood Coun.-Pvt., 1960-63; exec. staff NASA, 1963-73, program analyst-specialist, 1973-80, chief adminstrv. ops. and Congl. affairs br., 1980-92; ret., 1992. Cons. NASA, 1992—. Editor, author: (pamphlet) Space Operations, 1989, (video) Space Communications, 1991. Pres. Jr. Achievement Co., 1953-55, Kettering Recreation Coun., Largo, Md., 1974-76; league coord. U.S. Tennis Assn., Anne Arundel County, Md., 1989-91, team capt., 1984-99, 2001; active various civic orgns. including LWV, ch., community and county functions, 1957—. Recipient Jr. Achievement Exec. award and Nat. Speakers award, 1954, Gold medal Parks and Planning, Prince Georges County, Md., 1976, Exceptional Svc. award NASA, 1983, Exceptional Svc. medal NASA, 1992. Mem.: Annapolis Opera, Inc., Anne Arundel County Tennis Assn., Am. Heart Assn. (Heart Ball com. fundraiser 2000), Sportfit Racquet and Fitness Club, Severn Town Club (pres. 1996—98, chair Holly Ball fundraiser 1998—99). Republican. Methodist. Avocations: tennis, gardening, flower arranging, organizing social and tennis events, designing and painting wearable art.

LOVELAND, ANNE CAROL, history educator; b. Jamaica, N.Y., Dec. 23, 1938; d. John Wayne and Edith Ellen Loveland; m. John Kenneth Edmiston, Aug. 11, 1973 (div. Feb. 1988); m. Otis Bullard Wheeler, Mar. 23, 1991. BA, U. Rochester (N.Y.), 1960; MA, Cornell U., 1963, PhD, 1968. From instr. to prof. history dept. La. State U., Baton Rouge, 1964-93, T. Harry Williams prof. Am. history, 1993-2000, chair history dept., 1993-96, T. Harry Williams prof. emerita, 2000—. Author: Emblem of Liberty, 1971, Southern Evangelicals and the Social Order, 1980 (Mackemie award), Lillian Smith, 1986 (Rose award), American Evangelicals and the U.S. Military, 1996; co-author: Lafayette, 1989 (Moe award); contbr. articles, essays to profl. publs. Fellow Woodrow Wilson Found., 1960-61, Gertrude Gilmore fellow Cornell U., 1963-64, Younger Humanist fellow NEH, 1973-74; La. State U. fellow, 1989; grantee La. State U. Coun. on Rsch., 1968, 71, 75, 77, 81, So. Regional Edn. Bd., 1985, U.S. Army Mil. History Inst., 1986, Inst. for Study of Am. Evangelicals, 1989. Mem. Phi Beta Kappa. Address: 657 Highland Oaks Dr Baton Rouge LA 70810-5348

LOVELAND, DONALD WILLIAM, retired computer science educator; b. Rochester, N.Y., Dec. 26, 1934; s. Roger Platt and Dorothy (Dobbin) L.; m. Amy Straw, May 21, 1966; children: Robert Philip, Douglas Roger. AB, Oberlin Coll., 1956; SM, MIT, 1958; PhD, NYU, 1964. Mathematician, programmer IBM, Yorktown Heights, N.Y., 1958-59; asst. prof. math. NYU, 1964-67; asst. prof., then assoc. prof. math. and computer sci. Carnegie-Mellon U., Pitts., 1967-73; prof., chmn. dept. computer sci. Duke U., Durham, NC, 1973—78, 1991—92, 1998—99, prof. computer sci., 1973—2001. Disting. faculty visitor IBM Rsch. Ctr., Yorktown Heights, 1979-80; program chmn., editor procs. 6th Conf. on Automated Deduction, 1982, trustee corp. controls, 1994-97. Author: Automated Theorem Proving: A Logical Basis, 1978; co-editor: (with W.W. Bledsoe) Automated Theorem Proving: After 25 Years, 1984; mng. editor book series Artificial Intelligence, 1983-92; editl. bd. Artificial Intelligence, 1983-93, Jour. Automated Reasoning, 1983-2001. Recipient Herbrand award for disting. contbns. to automated reasoning, 2001; grantee NSF, 1970-73, 75-77, 88-92, 92-96, Air Force Office Sci. Rsch., 1981-86, Army Rsch. Office, 1984-91. Fellow Assn. for Computing Machinery, Am. Assn. Artificial Intelligence; mem. Assn. for Symbolic Logic, AAAS. Home: 182 Montrose Dr Durham NC 27707-3929

LOVELAND, EUGENE FRANKLIN, petroleum executive; b. Anderson, Ind., Sept. 11, 1920; s. Irving Eugene and Clare (McFarlane) L.; m. Joan King, Aug. 4, 1944; children: Jeffrey, David C. and Peter F. (twins), Mark, Laurie E. BA, Wesleyan U., Middletown, Conn. With Shell Oil Co., 1946-80, v.p. central mktg. region, 1968-71, v.p. oil products, 1972-80; pres. Transworld Oil USA, Inc. (formerly T.W. Oil Inc.), 1981—; chmn., chief exec. officer T.W. Oil Inc., 1983-89, ret., 1989. Bd. dirs. Transworld Oil Ltd., Bermuda. Bd. dirs. Lyric Theatre, Houston, Am. Dance Cos.; chmn. Houston Ballet Found., Combined Arts Corp., Campaign, Houston, Greater Houston Skating Coun., vice chmn. Better Bus. Bur., Houston; hon. counsul gen. Republic of Malta in Tex.; dir. Cultural Arts Coun. Houston, 1989-93; chmn. Greater Houston Ice Skating Coun., 1989—; mem. exec. com. Houston Internat. Festival, 1992; chmn. devel. commn. Fay Sch., 1992. With USNR, 1943-45. Decorated D.F.C., Air medal (2); recipient Disting. Alumnus award Wesleyan U., 1993. Mem. Mil. and Hospitaller Order St. Lazarus Jerusalem. Office: Transworld Oil USA Inc 910 Travis St Ste 800 Houston TX 77002-5806

LOVELESS, A. SCOTT, lawyer, consultant; b. Ely, Nev., Oct. 13, 1951; s. George K. Loveless and Esther (Hopkins) Stoddard; m. Cheri Anderson, Nov. 22, 1974. BA in German, Brigham Young U., 1975, JD, 1978, PhD in Family Studies, 2000. Bar: D.C. 1979, U.S. (D.C. dist.) Dist. Ct. 1979. Atty. Wigman & Cohen, Arlington, Va., 1979, Sughrue, Rothwell, Mion, Zinn & Macpeak, Washington, 1979-80; pvt. practice McLean, Va., 1980-81; atty., advisor Office of the Solicitor, Dept. of the Interior, Washington, 1981-90, Office of the Solicitor, Salt Lake City Field Office, 1991—2000; exec. dir. World Family Policy Ctr. J. Reuben Clark Law Sch., Brigham Young U. Office: Brigham Young U 519 JRCB Provo UT 84602

LOVELESS, EDWARD EUGENE, education educator, musician; b. Lafayette, Ind., July 29, 1919; s. Benjamin Moses and Belva Lucille (Bowles) L.; m. Jean Evelyn Skinner, May 18, 1941; children: Linda Louise Loveless Reeder, Kathleen Beal Loveless Bodine, Stephen Edward, Melissa Jane Loveless Campbell, Benjamin Warwick. BS, Purdue U., 1940, MS, 1941; Ed.D., Stanford U., 1960. Tchr., prin., supt. public schs., Ind., 1941-57; asst. Stanford U., 1957-60; prin. public schs. Palo Alto, Calif., 1961-65; asst. prof. sch. adminstrn. San Francisco State Coll. and assoc. prof. San Jose State Coll., 1960-65; assoc. prof. U. Nev., Reno, 1965-72, prof., 1972-85, prof. emeritus, 1986—. Vis. prof. Purdue U., summers 1965, 68, 75; prof. exec. devel. program USAF, Crete, spring 1973. Author: (with Frank Krajewski) The Teacher and School Law: Cases and Materials in the Legal Foundations of Education, 1974, (with J. Clark Davis) The Administrator and Educational Facilities, 1982; contbr. over 70 articles to profl. jours.; editor: Who's Who in Northern Nevada Education, 1976; spkr. on sch. vandalism; clarinetist, saxaphonist, vocalist Jean and Ed (musical duo), 1984—; musical tours Ms World Discoverer, Singapore, The South Seas, New Guinea, Western Samoa, Tonga, Fiji, Tahiti, others, 1984-85; performance South Pacific Coll., Stanford U. Alumni Assn., 1985; royal command performance King Tauf-ahau Tupou IV, Tonga, 1985; commd. performance Trident submarine USS Nev., 1986; concert U.S. Embassy, Geneva, 1987; recs. include Songs of the 30's and 40's, The Gershwin Bros., The Best of Irving Berlin, Jerome Kern Favorites, Hoagy & Benny Revisited, An Evening with Cole Porter, We Like Rodgers & Hart, The Genius of Duke Ellington, Easy Listening, Songs of Jule Styne, A Tribute to Jimmy Van Heussen, A Geriatric Jam with Jean, Ed and Nancy Wilson, 1998, Rodgers and Hammerstein Music, 1989, cassette tape series for Wickenburg (Ariz.) Hist. Mus., 1989, Golden Anniversary performance Purdue U., 1990, 74th Birthdays Cassette, 1993, Nat King Cole Songs, 1996. Performer, concert artist for retirement homes and hosps., Palo Alto, Calif., 1990—. Recipient Commendations for providing benefit concerts and performances Sierra Health Care Ctr., 1985, Salvation Army Family Emergency, 1986, VA Hosp., 1988, Daus. of Norway, 1988, Westwood Retirement Home, 1989, State of Nev. Employees Assn., 1989; recipient Certs. of Appreciation Riverside Hosp., 1986, Carson Convalescent Ctr., 1987, Reno Lions Club, 1987, Thank-U-Gram Physicians Hosp., 1988, Manor at Lakeside, 1988, award Washoe County Sr. Citizens Ctr., 1989, Sharon Heights Convalescent Hosp., Palo Alto, Calif., 1993. Mem. NEA, Nev. Edn. Assn., Internat. Soc. Gen. Semantics, Nat. Soc. Profs., Navy League, Kappa Sigma, Phi Delta Kappa (cert. for disting. service 1974, placque of appreciation Gamma Psi chpt. 1976) Democrat. Presbyterian (elder). Home: 2170 Princeton St Palo Alto CA 94306-1325 *Providing musical entertainment for retired and/or hospitalized people has a therapeutic effect that medicine cannot provide. Wynton Marsalis says that "music washes away the dust of everyday life from your feet".*

LOVELESS, GEORGE GROUP, retired lawyer; b. Baldwinsville, N.Y., Sept. 16, 1940; s. Frank Donald and Mayme (Lont) L.; m. Shirley Morrison, Nov. 27, 1965; children: Michael, Peter. BS, Cornell U., 1962, MBA, 1963; JD, U. Md., 1968. Bar: Pa. 1969, U.S. Dist. Ct. (ea. dist.) Pa., U.S. Ct. Appeals (3d cir.). Ptnr. Morgan, Lewis & Bockius LLP, Phila., 1968-2000; ret., 2000. With USAFR, 1963-68. Republican. Presbyterian. Home: 11 Rose Valley Rd Media PA 19063-4217 Office: Morgan Lewis & Bockius LLP 1701 Market St Philadelphia PA 19103-2921 E-mail: GGL1@cornell.edu.

LOVELESS, KATHY LYNNE, client services executive; b. Corsicana, Tex., Mar. 7, 1961; d. Vernon Ray and Barbara Alice (Brown) L. BA, Baylor U., 1983. Adminstrv. asst. InterFirst Bank, Dallas, 1983-85, Chaparral Steel Co., Midlothian, 1985-89, audio/visual coord., 1989-93; freelance computer instr. Duncanville, 1993-94; tng. specialist U. Tex. Southwestern Med. Ctr., Dallas, 1994-95, supr. client svcs. ctr., 1995-97, database coord., 1997-98; tester, trainer The Sabre Group, Ft. Worth, 1998-2000, product mgr., 2000—. Bd. dirs. Richardson Theatre Ctr., 1999—; pres., v.p. Midlothian Cmty. Theatre, 1990-93, mem., 1987-94; v.p. Lovers Ln. United Meth. Ch. Choir, Dallas, 1994, 95, Adminstrv. Bd., 1995-96, 1999—, chmn. broadcast com., 2001; chmn. worship and mem. care com. Elmwood United Meth. Ch., 1990, 91; bd. dirs. Trinity River Mission, Dallas, 1994, 95, 96. Mem. NAFE, AAUW, Soc. for Theatrical Artists Guidance and Enhancement, Women in Tech., Inc. Avocations: sports, films, music, books, theatre. E-mial. Home: 9947 Knoll Krest Dr Dallas TX 75238 E-mail: ilvmovies@aol.com.

LOVELESS, PEGGY ANN, social work administrator; b. Decatur, Ill., June 9, 1952; d. William Walter and Rose Marie (Sheppard) L. Student, Ill. State U., 1970-72; BA, U. Ill., 1974, MSW, 1976. Cert. lic. clin. social worker; cert. in health care ethics; diplomate Am. Bd. Examiners in Clin. Social Work. Social worker Met.-Police Social Svcs., Urbana, Ill., 1976-80; clin. supr. Ctr. Children's Svcs., Danville, 1980-84; med. social worker Sarah Bush Lincoln Health Ctr., Mattoon, 1984-86, Portland (Oreg.) Adventist Med. Ctr., 1986-88; dept. supr., social worker Oreg. Health Scis. U., Portland, 1988-92, interim dir. social work, 1992-93, asst. dir. social work Ctr. Ethics, 1993-96, mem. ethics consulting svc., 1991-96; behavioral health case mgr. PacifiCare Behavioral Health, 1996-98; case mgr. Pacific Gateway Hosp., Portland, Oreg., 1998-99; clin. supr. Multnomah County, Behavioral Health Divsn. Managed Care Program, 1999—. Vol. Goose Hollow Family Homeless Shelter, Portland, 1993-94, vol. supr., 1994-95, bd. dirs., 1996-97. Mem. Soc. Social Work Adminstrs. Health Care (com. nominations 1995-96, chair, pres. meeting planning com. 1994, com. mem. devel. 1997), Oreg. Soc. Social Work Adminstrs. Health Care (pres. elect 1993, pres. 1994, chair/conf. com. 1995). Avocations: reading, walking, skiing, travel. Office: Multnomah County Behavioral Health Divsn Managed Care Program 421 SW Sixth Ave 166/5 Portland OR 97204

LOVELESS, RALPH PEYTON, lawyer; b. Birmingham, Ala., Apr. 8, 1936; s. Ralph Peyton Sr. and Arbrette Inez (Loveless) Anderson; m. Mary Katherine Rushing, Dec. 30, 1957; children: Laura Katherine, Linda Arbrette. BS, U. Ala., 1957, LLB, 1959. Bar: Ala. 1959, U.S. Dist. Ct. (so. dist.) Ala. 1959, U.S. Dist. Ct. D.C. 1969, U.S. Ct. Appeals (5th cir.) 1966, U.S. Supreme Ct. 1969, U.S. Ct. Appeals (11th cir.) 1981. Assoc. Caffey, Gallalee & Caffey, Mobile, Ala., 1959-63; ptnr. Caffey, Gallalee, Edington & Loveless, 1963-67; atty. Fed. Trade Commn., Washington, 1967-69; asst. dist. atty. Mobile County, Ala., 1969-71; assoc. Marr & Friedlander, Mobile, 1971-72; ptnr. Marr, Friedlander & Loveless, 1972-74; pvt. practice, 1974-79; ptnr. Loveless & Banks, 1979-91, Loveless, Banks & Lyons, Mobile, 1991-96, Loveless & Lyons, Mobile, 1996—. Mcpl. judge Citronelle, Ala., 1990-91, Bayou La Batre, Ala., 1990-94; bd. dirs. Ala. Law Sch. Found., Tuscaloosa. Co-author: FTC Staff Report on Automobile Warranties, 1969. Bd. dirs. Mobile Track and Field Assn., 1960-67; pres. Am. Field Svc., Mobile, 1965-67; mem. County Dem. Exec. Com., Mobile, 1962-67. Mem. ABA, Ala. Bar Assn., Ala. Trial Lawyers Assn. (exec. com. 1983-87), Ala. Law Inst. (partnership law adv. com.), U. Ala. Nat. Alumni Assn. (pres., exec. com. 1985-90), Civitan Club, U.S. Power Squadron. Methodist. Avocations: boating, travel, reading. Home: 4100 Woodhill Cir Mobile AL 36608-2431 Office: Loveless and Lyons 56 Saint Joseph St Ste 711 Mobile AL 36602-3407

LOVELL, CARL ERWIN, JR. lawyer; b. Riverside, Calif., Apr. 12, 1945; s. Carl Erwin and Hazel (Brown) L.; m. Danna I. Wale; children: Carl Erwin III, Timothy C., Tishia R., Ashley P., Garrett T. BA, Vanderbilt U., 1966, JD, 1969. Bar: Nev. 1969, D.C. 1971, U.S. Supreme Ct. 1973. Jr. editor Land and Water Law Rev., 1973-89; instr. bus. law U. Nev., Las Vegas, Clark County C.C.; city atty. City of N. Las Vegas, 1970-73; elected city atty. City of Las Vegas, 1973-77; v.p., sec.-treas., legal counsel Circus Circus Hotels, Inc., Las Vegas, 1977-83; sr. ptnr. Lovell, Bilbray & Potter, 1984-89; pvt. practice, 1989—; v.p., dir. Air Nev. Airlines, Inc. Chmn. Nat. Inst. Mcpl. Law Officers Consumer Protection Adv. Com., 1973-77, Nev. Crime Commn. Bd., 1974-77; U.S. rep. to China-U.S. Internat. Trade and Law Talks, Beijing, 1987; arbitrator, AAA, 1989—. Bd. dirs., v.p. BBB, 1983-91; chmn. NCCJ; pres. Clark County Young Dems., 1971-72; bd. dirs. Nat. Kidney Found.; pres., trustee Nev. Donor Network, Inc., 1992-96. With USAF, 1966-68. Mem. ABA, ATLA, Nev. State Bar, Nev. Trial Lawyers Assn., Elks (justice Las Vegas chpt. 1985-88). Office: 2801 S Valley View Blvd Ste 1B Las Vegas NV 89102-0116 E-mail: dcarl@wealthprotectionconcepts.com., lovellachieve4u@earthlink.net.

LOVELL, EDWARD GEORGE, mechanical engineering educator; b. Windsor, Ont., Can., May 25, 1939; s. George Andrew and Julia Anne (Kopacz) L.; m. Roxann Engelstad; children: Elise, Ethan BS, Wayne State U., 1960, MS, 1961; PhD, U. Mich., 1967. Registered profl. engr., Wis. Project engr. Bur. Naval Weapons, Washington, 1959, Boeing Co., Seattle, 1962; test engr. Ford Motor Co., Troy, Mich., 1960; instr. U. Mich., Ann Arbor, 1963-67; design engr. United Tech., Hartford, Conn., 1970; prof. engring. U. Wis., Madison, 1968—, chmn. dept. engring. mechanics and astronautics, 1992-95. Cons. structural engring. to govt. labs., indsl. orgns., mgj. textbook pubs., 1968—. Contbr. numerous articles to profl. jours. Postdoctoral research fellow Nat. Acad. Sci., 1967; NATO Sci. fellow, 1973; NSF fellow, 1961 Mem. Wis. Fusion Tech. Inst., Wis. Ctr. for Applied Microelectronics, Sigma Xi, Tau Beta Pi, Phi Kappa Phi Office: U Wis Dept Mech Engring 1513 University Ave Madison WI 53706-1539

LOVELL, EMILY KALLED, freelance/self-employed journalist; b. Grand Rapids, Mich., Feb. 25, 1920; d. Abdo Rham and Louise (Claussen) Kalled; m. Robert Edmund Lovell, July 4, 1947. Student, Grand Rapids Jr. Coll., 1937-39; BA, Mich. State U., 1944; MA, U. Ariz., 1971. Copywriter, asst. traffic mgr. Sta. WOOD, Grand Rapids, 1944-46; traffic mgr. KOPO, Tucson, 1946-47; reporter, city editor Alamogordo (N.Mex.) News, 1948-51; Alamogordo corr., feature writer Internat. News Svc., Denver, 1950-54, El Paso Herald-Post, 1954-65; Alamogordo news dir., feature writer Tularosa (N.Mex.) Basin Times, 1957-59; co-founder, editor, pub. Otero County Star, Alamogordo, 1961-65; newscaster KALG, 1964-65; freelance feature writer Denver Post, N.Mex. Mag., 1949-69; corr. Electronic News, N.Y.C., 1959-63, 65-69; Sierra Vista (Ariz.) corr. Ariz. Republic, 1966; freelance editor N.Mex. Pioneer Interviews, 1967-69; asst. dir. English skills program Ariz. State U., 1976; free-lance editor, writer, 1977—. Part-time tchr., lectr. U. Pacific, 1981-86; part-time interpreter Calif., 1983-91, Interpreters Unlimited, Oakland, 1985-91; sec., dir. Star Pub. Co., Inc., 1961-64, pres., 1964-65, 3d v.p., publicity chmn. Otero County Cmty. Concert Assn., 1950-65; mem. Alamogordo Zoning Commn., 1955-57; mem. founding com. Alamogordo Ctrl. Youth Activities Com., 1957; vice chmn. Otero County chpt. Nat. Found. Infantile Paralysis, 1958-61; charter mem. N.Mex. Citizens Coun. for Traffic Safety, 1959-61; pres. Sierra Vista Hosp. Aux., 1966; pub. rels. chmn. Ft. Huachuca chpt. ARC, 1966; mem. nat. bd. Hospitalized Vets. Writing Project, 1972-99; vol. instr. autobiography & creative writing, 1991—. Author: A Personalized History of Otero County, New Mexico, 1963, Weekend Away, 1964, Lebanese Cooking, Streamlined, 1972, A Reference Handbook for Arabic Grammar, 1974, 77; contbg. author: The Muslim Community in North America, 1983.

Recipient 1st Pl. awards N.Mex. Press Assn., 1961, 62, Pub. Interest award Nat. Safety Coun., 1962, 1st Pl. award Nat. Fedn. Press Women, 1960, 62; named Woman of Yr. Alamogordo, 1960, Editor of Week Pubs. Aux., 1962, adm. N.Mex. Navy, 1962, col. A.D.C. Staff Gov. N.Mex., 1963, Woman of Yr., Ariz. Press Women, 1973. Mem. N.Mex. Press Women (past sec.), Ariz. Press Women (past pres.), N.Mex. Fedn. Womens Clubs (past dist. pub. rels. chmn., hon. life Alamogordo), N.Mex. Hist. Soc. (life), N.Mex. Fedn. Bus. and Profl. Womens Clubs (past pres., hon. life Alamogordo), Pan Am. Round Table Alamogordo, Theta Sigma Phi (past nat. 3d v.p.), Phi Kappa Phi. Democrat. Moslem. Home: 3400 Wagner Heights Rd Apt 226 Stockton CA 95209-4855 *Personal philosophy: You have to live with yourself...an idle grouch is bad company.*

LOVELL, FRANCIS JOSEPH, investment company executive; b. Mar. 21, 1949; s. Frank J. and Patricia Anna (Donnellan) L. BBA, Nichols Coll., 1971. With Brown Bros. Harriman & Co., Boston, 1971—2002, v.p., 1990—. Mem. New Eng. Hist. Gen. Soc., Union Club of Boston. Republican. Home: 25 Pomfret St West Roxbury MA 02132-1809 also: 48 Hidden Village Rd West Falmouth MA 02574 Office: 40 Water St Boston MA 02109-3604

LOVELL, FREDERICK WARREN, pathologist, medical legal consultant; b. Astoria, Oreg., June 13, 1922; s. Sherman Watson and Ruby Jane (Dunn) L.; m. Mary Margaret Jones, Aug. 21, 1950 (div. July 1980); children: Margaret Spah, Sherman, Robert, Mary Jo Blazina, Santina Brynsvold; m. June Anne Hendrickson, June 13, 1981. BS, U. Oreg., 1949; MS, Northwestern U., 1952, MD, 1953. Diplomate Am. Bd. Pathology. Pilot U.S. Army Air Corps, Pacific theatre, 1943-45; advanced through grades to col. USAFR, 1969; intern Presbyn. Hosp., Chgo., 1953-54; fellow in pathology UCLA Med. Ctr., 1954-55; resident in pathology Swedish Hosp., Seattle, 1955-57; med. officer USAF, Washington, 1957-60, ret., 1970; chief pathologist Northwest Hosp., Seattle, 1960-79; clin. prof. U. Wash., 1961-80; chief med. examiner Ventura County, Ventura, Calif., 1981-93; med. legal cons., 1993—. Cons. FAA, Washington, 1960-72, NASA, 1959-60. Contbr. numerous med. and aviation safety articles to jours. Decorated Air medal with clusters. Recipient Profl. Svc. citation FAA, 1972. Fellow Am. Acad. Forensic Sci.; mem. Nat. Assn. Med. Examiners, Rotary, Phi Beta Kappa, Delta Upsilon. Episcopalian. Avocation: sailing. Home and Office: 5401 Topa Topa Dr Ventura CA 93003-1148 E-mail: fwlmd@aol.com.

LOVELL, HOWELL, JR. non profit organization executive; b. San Jose, Calif., Oct. 12, 1938; s. Howell and Rebecca (Oser) L.; m. Donna Lovell, Apr. 21, 1965 (div. Apr. 1994); children: Howell III, Eric, Kathleen. BA, Stanford U., 1960, JD, 1963. Pvt. practice lawyer, San Francisco, 1965-92; exec. dir. Pets in Need, Redwood City, Calif., 1992-93, Recording for The Blind & Dyslexic, Palo Alto, 1995—. Sec. Palo Alto Family YMCA, 1990-91, 93-94, 97-98, vice chair, 1998—, bd. dirs. 1993—. Mem. Nat. Soc. Fund Raising Execs. (bd. dirs., v.p. programs 1998—), Palo Alto C. of C., Ferne Ave. Home Owners Assn. (pres. 1996—), Internat. Domino Assn. (bd. dirs., treas. 1994-98), San Francisco Down Town Garden Club (pres. 1994), Kiwanis (bd. dirs., pres.-elect Palo Alto chpt.), YWCA fin. comm., 1998—. Avocations: genealogy, photography, sports. Home: 124 Ferne Ave Palo Alto CA 94306-4644 Office: Recording for The Blind & Dyslexic 488 W Charleston Rd Palo Alto CA 94306-4103

LOVELL, JOAN ELLEN, mental health professional; b. Alton, Ill., Oct. 24, 1955; d. Lee Roy and Arlou (Brown) Waller; 1 child, Frank. AS, RN, Monticello Coll., Godfrey, Ill., 1974; BA in Social Work, Calif. State U., Northridge, 1977; MA in Psychology, Calif. Grad. Inst., Westwood, 1988, PhD in Psychology, 1996. RN, Calif.; registered psychologist Calif. Nurse, asst. head nurse St. Francis Med. Ctr., 1977-80; crisis resolution unit nurse Dept. Mental Health L.A. County, L.A., 1983-85, homeless coord., 1985-87, patient rights advocate, 1987-92, children and youth svc. coord., 1993—; mental health cons. Fed. Project 90044, 1992-93; owner Medi Fact Rsch., Huntington Beach, Calif., 1992-97. Cons. Philippine-Am. Orgn., Long Beach, Calif., 1985-87. Ct. advocate for victims of rape L.A. Commn. Against Assaults on Women, L.A., 1977, rape hotline counselor, 1976-77. Mem. APA (affiliate), Calif. Psychol. Assn.

LOVELL, MALCOLM READ, JR. public policy institute executive, educator, former government official, former trade association executive; b. Greenwich, Conn., Jan. 1, 1921; s. Malcolm Read and Emily (Monihan) L.; m. Celia Coghlan, 1978; children by previous marriage: Lucie, Sara. Annette, Caroline. Student, Brown U., 1939-42; I.A., Harvard U., 1943; MBA, Harvard, 1946. With Ford Motor Co., Dearborn, Mich., 1946-58; mgr. employee services Am. Motors Corp., Detroit, 1958-61; chmn. State Labor Mediation Bd., 1963; dir. Mich. Office Econ. Opportunity, 1964, Mich. Employment Security Commn., Detroit, 1965-69; exec. asso. Manpower, Urban Coalition, 1969; dep. asst. sec. of labor and manpower adminstr., 1969-70; asst. sec. of labor for manpower, 1970-73; pres. Rubber Mfrs. Assn., 1973-81; asst. dir. Office Policy Coordination and Econ. Affairs, Office Pres.-Elect, 1980; undersec. Dept. Labor, Washington, 1981-83; vis. scholar Brookings Instn., 1983-85; disting. vis. prof. govt. and dir. Labor Mgmt. Inst., George Washington U., 1985-92, 99—; pres. Nat. Policy Assn., 1992-99; sr. fellow Hudson Inst., 1985-88; exec. Exec. Coaching Network, 1999—; exec. in residence George Washington U. Sch. Bus. and Pub. Mgmt., 1999—. Mem. Nat. Adv. Coun. on Vocat. Edn., 1975-79, Nat. Commn. for Manpower Policy, 1977-79; chmn. sec. labor Task Force on Econ. Adjustment and Worker Dislocation, 1985-86; mediator Collective Bargaining Forum, 1983-2000. V.p. Birmingham (Mich.) Sch. Bd., 1956-60; bd. dirs. Nat. Alliance Bus., 1984—; bd. dirs. Travelers Aid of Washington, 1983-86, pres., 1985-86. Lt. USNR, 1943-46. Sr. fellow Hudson Inst., 1985-88. Mem. Clean Plate (Washington), Cosmos Club (Washington), Alpha Delta Phi. Mem. Soc. Of Friends. Office: 2033 K St NW Ste 230 Washington DC 20006-1033

LOVELL, MARY ANN, secondary education educator; b. Magnolia, Ark., May 30, 1943; d. Dezzy and Priscilla (Glover) Biddle; m. Clearence Edward Lovell, June 4, 1966 (div. 1975); children— Clearesia Ann, Delia Marie, Dezzy Aquib. BA, U. Ark., 1965; MS, Ouachita Bapt. U., 1972; MS in Criminal Justice, Grambling State U., 1997. Tchr. high sch., Stutgart, Magnolia, Arkadelphia and Eudora, Ark., 1964-75, Milw., 1981— ; tchr. Ethan Allen Sch., Dept. Health and Human Svcs. State of Wis., 1986; job svc. specialist CETA, Wis. Dept. Industry, 1975-76; spl. project, coord. Milwaukee County Civil Svc. Commn., 1976-78. Mem. Internat. Reading Assn., Wis. State Reading Assn., Wis. Edn. Assn. (coun. 1989-90), Milw. Tchrs. Edn. Assn., Milw. Inner City Arts Coun., Inc., Milw. Area Reading Coun., Educators' Politically Involved Coun., Am. Mgmt. Assn., State of Wis. Edn. Profls. (Local 3271), Nat. Assn. Blacks in Criminal Justice, Alpha Phi Sigma. Democrat. Pentecostal. Club: Playboy (Chgo.).

LOVELL, TERRY JEFFRY, business educator; b. Sacramento, Mar. 26, 1953; s. Charles C. and Maxine (Carter) L.; m. Shannon Lynn Pribble, Mar. 17, 1992; children: Jared Cameron, Terry Jessica. BA in Sociology, U. Mont., 1975; MBA, Ariz. State U., 1985; PhD in Bus., Greenwich U., 1993. Tchr./rsch. asst. Ariz. State U., Tempe, 1983-88; asst. prof. bus. U. Alaska, Anchorage, 1988-90; prof. bus. Yavapai Coll., Prescott, Ariz., 1990—. Presenter, rschr. in field. Contbr. articles, rsch. papers in field. Home constrn. vol. Habitat for Humanity, Prescott, 1995—; pres. faculty senate Yavapai Coll., 1995. Mem. APA, Acad. Mgmt., Am. Sociol. Assn. Avocation: woodworking. E-mail: bc. Office: Yavapai Coll 1100 E Sheldon St Prescott AZ 86301-3220 Fax: (520) 776-2160. E-mail: terry@yavapai.cc.az.us.

LOVELL, THEODORE, electrical engineer, consultant; b. Paterson, N.J., May 10, 1928; s. George Whiting and Ethel Carol (Berner) L.; m. Wilma Syperda, May 8, 1948 (div. Oct. 1961); m. Joyce Smelik, July 15, 1962; children: Laurie, Dorothy Jane, Valerie, Cynthia, Karen, Barbara. BEE, Newark Coll. Engring., 1948; postgrad., Canadian Inst. Tech., 1950. Exec. dir. Lovell Electric Co., Franklin Lakes, N.J., 1955-82; ptnr., exec. dir. Lovell Design Services, Swedesboro, 1982—. Author engring. computer software, 1982. Bd. dirs., treas. Contact "Help" of Salem County, 1991-93; pres. Bloomingdale Bd. Edn., N.J., 1970-82; mem. Mcpl. Planning Bd., Bloomingdale, 1980-82, Swedesboro/Woolwich Bd. Edn., 1987-94, v.p., 1990-92, pres. 1993-94; mayoral candidate Borough of Bloomingdale, 1982; v.p. Woolwich Twp. Rep. Club, 1996—; chmn. Woolwich Twp. Bus. Adv. Com., 1997—; mem. Gloucester County Econ. Devel. Coun., 1998—. Recipient Outstanding Service award Lake Iosco Co., Bloomingdale, 1985, 20 Yr. Svc. award N.J. Sch. Bd. Assn., 1994. Fellow Radio Club Am.; mem. Soc. Engring. Technicians, Dickinson Theater Organ Soc. Presbyterian. Avocations: Lincoln history, theatre organ music. Home: 16 Liberty Ct Swedesboro NJ 08085-3010 Office: Lovell Design Svcs PO Box 366 Swedesboro NJ 08085-0366 *It has become apparent to me, slowly perhaps that as I progress through life, the things that bring lasting joy and satisfaction are not personal achievements, but those things that help others.*

LOVELL, WALTER BENJAMIN, secondary education educator, radio broadcaster; b. Cottonwood, Ariz., Jan. 7, 1947; s. Walter William Lovell and Mary Katherine (MacDonald) Bruce; m. Patsy Nichols, July 16, 1965 (div. Nov. 1986); children: Katherine Vi, Walter Kenneth, Karen Jennifer, Kristin Diane; m. Karen Lynn Bird, Mar. 3, 1990. AA, Ea. Ariz. Coll., 1966; B of Music Edn., No. Ariz. U., 1969, MusM, 1975; PhD in Music Edn., Hamilton U., 2002. Dir. of bands Kingman (Ariz.) High Sch., 1968-70; asst. dir. bands Phoenix Union High Sch., 1970-71; dir. bands Carl Hayden High Sch., Phoenix, 1971-73, Mohave High Sch., Bullhead City, Ariz., 1973-78, Elko (Nev.) High Sch., 1978—. Condr. numerous winning, competitive performances with Elko H.S. Band, including Grand Champions Holiday Bowl Parade, Field and Jazz competition, 1994, pre-game performance and field show, Nat. Freedom Bowl, Anaheim, Calif., 1988, 90, Disneyland Parade, Anaheim, 1990, pre-game and half-time performances Weber State U., Ogden, Utah, 1990-97, U. Utah, 1995, Concert Band Festival, Boise (Idaho) State U., 1990-97, U. Nev.-Las Vegas Band Competition, 1988, Fiesta Bowl Parade, Phoenix, 1985, Tournament of Roses Parade, Pasadena, 1983, 95, 99, Presdl. Inaugural Parade, Washington, 1981, No. Nev. Youth Band Tour of Great Britain, 1982, Macy's Thanksgiving Day Parade, 1979, 2000, Performances in Washington, 1981, 2000, Hollywood Christmas Parade, 2002; assoc. dir. All-Ariz. Bi-Centennial Band, 1976. Composer: (concert band compositions) Suite For Band, 1975, Tranquility, 1988, (jazz band compositions) Maybe Tuesday, 1974, Sunday Afternoon, 1987. Recipient Gubernatorial Proclamation for Elko H.S. Band, 1981, 83, 86, 88, 90, 92, 94, 96, 98, Proclaimed The Pride of Nev., 1995, 96, 2000, Proclaimed Nev.'s Mus. Amb., 1998, 2000; Gubernatorial Proclamation No. Nev. Youth Band, 1982, Nat. Sch. Band Achievement awards, 1981, 82; recipient Disting. Svc. award U. Nev.-Reno Bands, 1986, Citation of Excellence Nat. Band Assn., Nev. State Bd. Edn., 1983, Disting. Bandmaster of Am. award, 1981, Nev. State Marching Band Champion award, 1983-86, 92-94, 97, 99, 2001, Holiday Bowl Jazz Festival Grand Champion award, 1992, Nev. Music Educator of Yr., 1999; inducted Nev. Broadcasters Hall of Fame, 2001. Mem. Nat. Band Assn. (citation of Excellence 1987), Am. Sch. Band Dirs. Assn., Nev. Music Educators Assn., Music Educators Nat. Conf., Ariz. Band and Orchestra Dir.'s Assn., Internat. Assn. Jazz Educators, Nat. Assn. Jazz Educators, Ariz. Music Educators Assn. Office: Elko High Sch 987 College Ave Elko NV 89801-3419 E-mail: bandguy@elko-nv.com.

LOVELL, WALTER CARL, engineer, inventor; b. Springfield, Vt., May 7, 1934; s. John Vincent and Sophia Victoria (Klementowicz) L.; m. Patricia Ann Lawrence, May 6, 1951; children: Donna, Linda, Carol, Patricia, Diane, Walter Jr. B of Engring., Hillyer Coll., Hartford, Conn., 1959. Project engr. Hartford Machine Screw Co., Windsor, Conn., 1954-59; design engr. DeBell and Richardson Labs., Enfield, 1960-62; cons. engr. Longmeadow, Mass., 1962—; freelance inventor Wilbraham, 1965—. Numerous patents include Egg-Stir mixer, crown closure sealing gasket, circular unleakable bottle cap, sonic wave ram jet engine, solid state heating tapes, card key lock; composer over 50 country-and-Western songs. Achievements include patents for sonic wave ram jet engine, solid state heat and resistor tape, card key lock, security lock system, heat producing paints and ceramics; innovations include discovery of monothermal electric effect and micro-inductive film that replaces ballast in fluorescent lights.

LOVELL, WHITFIELD, artist; b. N.Y.C., 1959; BFA, Cooper Union Sch. Art, 1981. One-person shows include Interchurch Ctr., N.Y., 1982, Galeria Morivivi, N.Y., 1984, John Jay Coll., N.Y., 1985, Harlem Sch. Arts, N.Y., 1987, Jersey City (N.J.) Mus., 1988, Lehman Coll. Art Gallery, N.Y., 1993, South Ea. Ctr. Contemporary Art, Winston Salem, N.C., 1997, DC Moore Gallery, N.Y., 1997, 2000, 2002, The Andy Warhol Mus., Pitts., 1998, U. N.Tex. Art Gallery, Denton, 1999, Studio Mus., Harlem, N.Y., 2000, Neuberger Mus. Art, N.Y., 2000, Montclair Art Mus., N.J., 2001, Tubman African Am. Mus., Ga., 2001, Jones Ctr. Contemporary Art, Tex., 2000, Knoxville Mus., Tenn., 2001, Boston U. Art Gallery, Mass., 2001, Hand Workshop, Richmond, Va., 2001, Evansville Mus., Ind., 2002, U. Wyo. Art Mus., Laramie, 2002, Columbus (Ga.) Mus., 2002; exhibited in group shows at AIR Gallery, N.Y., 1981, 82, ABC No Rio, N.Y., 1982, Cayman Gallery, N.Y., 1983, Kenkeleba Gallery, N.Y.C., 1984, 85, Howard U. Gallery of Art, Washington, 1985, Bronx River Art Gallery, N.Y.C., 1985, Longwood Arts Gallery, N.Y.C., 1986, Met. Life Gallery, N.Y., 1987, Aljira Gallery, Newark, 1988, Cinque Gallery, N.Y., 1989, Snug Harbor Cultural Ctr., N.Y., 1990, Pepsico Gallery, N.Y., 1991, Boston Mus. Fine Arts, 1991, Allen Meml. Art Mus., Miami, Fla., 1992, Intar Gallery, N.Y., 1993, Agustin Barrios Gallery, Asuncion, Paraguay, 450 Broadway Gallery, N.Y., 1994, Puffin Found., N.Y.C., 1994, Exit Art, N.Y.C., 1995, Ark. Arts Ctr., Little Rock, 1995, DC Moore Gallery, N.Y., 1995, 96, 98, Round 3 Inst. Project Row Houses, Houston, 1996, Atrium Gallery, Morristown, N.J., 1997, David Klein Gallery, Birmingham, Mich., 1997, Sexta Bienal, Havana, Cuba, 1997, Craven Gallery, West Tisbury, Mass., 1998, Bronx Mus. Arts, N.Y., 1999, 2000, Nat. Mus. Am. Art, Washington, 1999, Seattle Art Mus., Washington, 2000, Yale U. Art Gallery, Conn., 2000, Megura Mus., Tokyo, 2001; represented in pub. collections The Ark. Arts Ctr. Found., Little Rock, The Lib. of Congress, Washington, Met. Mus. Art, N.Y.C., New Sch. Social Rsch., N.Y.C., Seattle Art Mus., Washington, Yale U., Art Gallery, Conn., Neuberger Mus. Art, N.Y.C., Nat. Mus. Am .Art, Washington, Hunter Mus. Art, Tenn., Ark. Arts Ctr., The Promise of Learnings Collection, N.Y.C. Grantee Joan Mitchell Found., 1996; Jerome Found. fellow to Robert Blackburn Printmaking Workshop, 1982; Robert Blackburn Printmaking Workshop fellow, 1985; Regional fellow Mid-Atlantic Nat. Endowment Arts, 1992; fellow N.Y. Found. Arts, 1997; Eastman scholar Skowhegan Sch. Painting and Sculpture, 1985; N.Y. State Coun. Arts grantee, 1986, 87; Penny McCall Found. grantee, 1990; Artists Homeless Shelter Collaborative grantee, 1991; N.Y. Found. Arts grantee, 1991; artist in residence Mousem D'Asilah, Morocco, 1988, Art Awareness, Lexington, N.Y., 1991, Warhol Mus., Pitts., 1998, U. No. Tex., 1999, Hand Workshop Art Ctr., Richmond, Va., 2000, Ctr. for Documentary Studies Duke U., Durham, N.C., 2001. Office: care DC Moore Gallery 724 5th Ave New York NY 10019-4106 Fax: 212-247-2119.

LOVELY, CYNTHIA JANE, reading educator; b. Santa Monica, Calif., Apr. 18, 1945; d. Kent K. and Dora Virginia Patton; m. John M. Lovely, Aug. 12, 1967; children: John Kent, James Paul. BA, Colo. Women's Coll., 1966; MA in Elem. Edn., No. Ariz. U., 1994. Tchr. 1st grade Aurora (Colo.) Pub. Schs., 1967, Huntington Park (Calif.) Day Sch., 1967-70; substitute tchr. Hawthorne Christian Sch., Huntington Beach, Calif., 1978-79; instr. income tax H&R Block, Flagstaff, Ariz., 1981-92; instr. adult edn. No. Ariz. Inst. Tech., 1991; substitute Flagstaff Pub. Schs., 1989-97, reading tchr., 1992-96; owner individual tax prepartion and bookkeeping co., 1993—; 1st grade tchg. asst. St. Mary's Parochial Sch., Flagstaff, Ariz., 1997-98; 1st grade tchr. Carden of the Peaks, 1998-99, 5th & 6th grade tchr., 2000—; mid. sch. math and history tchr. SonRise Christian Sch., 1999-2000. Instr. tax Yavapai Coll., Flagstaff, 1984. Mem. Ariz. Reading Assn., Internat. Reading Assn. Baptist. Home: 1130 Shullenbarger Dr Flagstaff AZ 86001-8959

LOVELY, ERNA SUSAN, retired primary school educator; b. N.Y.C., Jan. 1, 1930; d. George Fritz and Susan M. Muller; m. Thomas Dixon Lovely, June 16, 1956; children: Thomas John, Richard Robert. BA, U. Mich., 1951; MA, Adelphi U., 1965. Cert. elem. and secondary tchr. Primary sch. tchr. Westbury (N.Y.) Pub. Schs., 1955-58, Garden City (N.Y.) Pub. Schs., 1969-87; ret., 1987. Vice-chair bd. trustees SUNY Nassau C.C., Garden City, 1986—. Pres. Garden City PTA, 1969-71; chair pers. com. Nassau C.C., 1988—; mem. Mayoral Selection com., 1986-88; chair Adelphi U. Anniversary, 1981-82, Sons Am. Revolution Ball com., 1993—. Enterprise fellow Adelphi U., 1984. Mem. AAUW (bd. dirs. Garden City chpt.), U. Mich. Alumni Assn., Garden City C. of C., Marco Island Yacht Club. Republican. Roman Catholic. Avocations: reading, writing, travel. Home: 1780 Addison Ct Marco Island FL 34145-5912 Home (Summer): PO Box 1005 Sag Harbor NY 11963-0029

LOVELY, THOMAS DIXON, banker; b. N.Y.C., Apr. 2, 1930; s. Thomas John and Margaret Mary (Browne) L.; AB, Adelphi U., 1954, MA, 1956, MBA, 1958; m. Erna Susan Fritz, June 16, 1956; children: Thomas John Hall, Richard Robert. Treas., Pepsi Cola Bottling Co., Garden City, N.Y., 1957-60; assoc. prof. mgmt. and communications CUNY, 1958-77; dist. adminstr. Lido Beach (N.Y.) Pub. Schs., 1971-80; chmn. bd., pres. Fidelity Fed. Savs. and Loan Assn., Floral Park, N.Y., 1980-82, chmn. bd., pres. Fidelity N.Y., 1982—; bd. trustees, 1991-95, fin. and investment com., 91-95, SUNY; v.p., dir., N.Y. Enterprise Co. Trustee, SUNY, 1992, chmn. bd. SUNY Old Westbury Coll. Found., 1989—, vice chmn. bd.rustees Adelphi U., 1967-91, chmn. bd. govs. Univ. Sch. Banking and Money Mgmt., 1975—; trustee Nassau County (N.Y.) Med. Center, 1982—; exec. v.p., treas. Nassau County coun. Boy Scouts Am., 1986—, pres., 1989-92; regional chmn. campaign U.S. Treasury Savs. Bonds Sales, Long Island, 1987—; pres., trustee Meadowbrook Med. Edn. Found., Inc., 1987—. Mem. SAR, L.I. Insured Savs. Group (v.p.). Clubs: Pinehurst Country (N.C.), Marco Island, Fla. Yacht Club, Cherry Valley Country (Garden City). Home: PO Box 1005 Sag Harbor NY 11963-0029 Office: Fidelity NY Fed Savs Bank 1000 Franklin Ave Garden City NY 11530-2910 E-mail: dixonern@aol.com.

LOVELY, THOMAS JOHN, neurosurgeon, educator; b. N.Y.C., June 29, 1957; s. Thomas Dixon and Erna Susan (Fritz) L.; m. Alice Mannion, May 7, 1983; children: Stephen Thomas, Kevin William, Laura Elizabeth, Colleen Ann. BS, U. Mass., 1979; MD, U. Pa., 1983. Diplomate Am. Bd. Neurol. Surgery. Surg. intern North Shore U. Hosp.-Cornell Med. Ctr., Manhassett, N.Y., 1983-84; neurosurg. resident Temple U. Hosp., Phila., 1984-88, neurosurg. chief resident, 1988-89; asst. prof. neurosurgery Albany (N.Y.) Med. Coll., 1989-94; asst. prof. neurol. surgery Sch. Medicine U. Pitts., 1994-98; attending surgeon U. Pitts. Med. Ctr., 1994-98; clin. assoc. prof. surgery Albany Med. Coll., 1999. Mem. biomed. instnl. rev. bd., mem. faculty credentials com. Sch. Medicine U. Pitts., 1995-98. Contbr. articles to profl. publs., chpts. to books, also abstracts and presentations in field. Mem. cmty. adv. bd. WQED-Pitts. pub. TV, 1995-98; baseball coach Brad-Mar-Pine Athletic Assn., Wexford, Pa., 1995-98. Fellow ACS; mem. Am. Assn. Neurol. Surgery, Congress Neurol. Surgeons, Soc. for Rsch., Sigma Xi, Phi Beta Kappa, Phi Kappa Phi. Office: Albany-Troy Neurosurgical Associates 319 S Manning Blvd Ste 110 Albany NY 12208-1748 E-mail: lovely@atnsa.com.

LOVEN, ANDREW WITHERSPOON, environmental engineering company executive; b. Crossnore, N.C., Jan. 31, 1935; s. Andrew Witherspoon Loven and Annie Laura (Crowell) Stewart; m. Elizabeth Joann DeGroot, June 20, 1959 (dec.); children: Laura Elizabeth, James Edward. BS, Maryville Coll., 1957; PhD, U. N.C., 1962. Registered profl. engr., Colo., Ga., La., Md., N.C., S.C., D.C., Ohio, Fla., Mich., Va. Rsch. assoc. U. N.C., Chapel Hill, 1962-63; sr. rsch. chemist Westvaco Corp., Charleston, S.C., 1963-66, mgr. carbon devel., 1966-71, mgr. wastewater cons. svc., 1967-71; mgr. engring. concepts Engring.-Sci. Inc., McLean, Va., 1971-74, v.p., regional mgr. Atlanta, 1974-80, group v.p., 1980-86; pres., CEO Engring. Sci. Inc., Pasadena, Calif., 1986-95, also chmn. bd. dirs.; exec. v.p. Parsons Engring. Sci. Inc., 1995; pres., CEO Millennium Sci. & Engring., Inc., McLean, Va., 1995—. Contbr. articles to profl. jours. NSF grantee, 1958-59; recipient Maryville Coll. Alumni Citation award, 1992. Mem. AIChE, NSPE, Am. Acad. Environ. Engrs. (diplomate, membership com. 1985—), Water Environment Fedn., Am. Water Works Assn., Am. Pub. Works Assn., Constrn. Industry Pres. Forum, Country Club Roswell, Sigma Xi, Alpha Gamma Sigma. Avocations: golf, hiking. Home: 1512 Barksdale Ct Kennesaw GA 30152 Office: Millennium Sci & Engring Inc 6145 Barfield Rd Ste 110 Atlanta GA 30328

LOVENTHAL, MILTON, writer, playwright, lyricist; b. Atlantic City; s. Harry and Clara (Feldman) L.; m. Jennifer McDowell, July 2, 1973. BA, U. Calif., Berkeley, 1950, MLS, 1958; MA in Sociology, San Jose State U., 1969. Researcher Hoover Instn., Stanford, Calif., 1952-53, spl. asst. to Slavic Curator, 1955-57; librarian San Diego Pub. Library, 1957-59; librarian, bibliographer San Jose (Calif.) State U., 1959-92. Tchr. writing workshops, poetry readings, 1969-73; co-producer lit. and culture radio show Sta. KALX, Berkeley, 1971-72; editor, pub. Merlin Press, San Jose, 1973—. Author: Books on the USSR, 1951-57, 57, Black Politics, 1971 (featured at Smithsonian Inst. Special Event, 1992), A Bibliography of Material Relating to the Chicano, 1971, Autobiographies of Women, 1946-70, 72, Blacks in America, 1972, The Survivors, 1972, Contemporary Women Poets an Anthology, 1977, Ronnie Goose Rhymes for Grown-Ups, 1984; co-author: (Off-Off-Broadway plays) The Estrogen Party to End War, 1986, Mack the Knife, Your Friendly Dentist, 1986, Betsy & Phyllis, 1986, The Oatmeal Party Comes to Order, 1986, (plays) Betsy Meets the Wacky Iraqi, 1991, Bella and Phyllis, 1994; co-writer (mus. comedy) Russia's Secret Plot to Take Back Alaska, 1988; lyricist Intern Girl, 1998, Smithsonian, 2002. Recipient Bill Casey Award in Letters, 1980; grantee San Jose State U., 1962-63, 84. Mem. Assn. Calif. State Profs., Calif. Alumni Assn., Calif. Theatre Coun., Am. Assn. for Advancement of Slavic Studies, Soc. for Sci. Study of Religion. Office: PO Box 5602 San Jose CA 95150-5602

LOVERIDGE-SANBONMATSU, JOAN MEREDITH, communication studies and women's studies educator; b. Hartford, Conn., July 5, 1938; d. Gilbert Thomas and Rosabel Frances (Nowry) Loveridge; m. Akira Sanbonmatsu, Aug. 29, 1964; children: James Michael, Kevin Yosh. BA, U. Vt., 1960; MA, Ohio U., 1963; PhD, Pa. State U., 1971. Writer, programming radio/tv WRUV, WCAX, Burlington, Vt., 1956-60, WOUB, Athens, Ohio, 1962-63, AFKN, Korea, 1960-61; unit head ARC, Japan, Korea, 1960-61; asst. prof. SUNY, Brockport, 1963-77, prof. comm. studies and women's studies Oswego, 1977-98, prof. emerita, 1999—, instr. intensive English summer program, 1993—, co-coord. women's studies program, 1978-80, 82, instr. internat. studies infusion program, 1985-91. Vis. prof. Rochester (N.Y.) Inst. Tech., 1971; assoc. adj. prof. Monroe C.C., Rochester, 1972-76; instr. Pa. State, State College, 1966-67; cons. for oral history project ARC Overseas Assn., 1994—; cons. Cazenovia Coll., N.Y., 1988-89; pres. bd. dirs. Woman's Career Ctr. Inc., Rochester, 1975-76; invited Japan Lecture Tour, 1997. Co-author: Feminism and Woman's Life, 1995; contbg. author: Public Speakers in the US, 1925-1993, Vol. 2, 1994; contbr. poetry to publs., 1986—; poetry editor/editl. bd.: Lake Effect, 1985-92; contbr. articles to profl. jours. including Howard Jour. Comms., Comm. Edn., Phoebe and Feminist Jour. Religious edn. team tchr. May Meml. Unitarian Soc., Syracuse, 1979-81; mem. adv. parent com., Oswego H.S., 1986-87. Recipient Unsung Heroine award Ctrl. N.Y. NOW, Syracuse, 1987, presdl. citation for social change ARC Overseas Assn., 1998; rsch. grantee Pa. State U., 1970, SUNY, Oswego, 1978, 91, 92, 94, 95, 96, N.Y. State United Univ. Professions Profl. Devel. and Quality of Working Life grantee, 1985, 87, 93, 94, 98; fellow U. Ill., Chgo., 1983. Mem. N.Y. Asian Studies Assn., Nat. Comm. Assn. (women's caucus job placement dir., exec. bd. 1977-78), Ea. Comm. Assn., N.Y. Speech Comm. Assn., Soc. for Intercultural Edn., Tng. and Rsch., Nat. Women's Studies Assn., Speech Comm. P.R. Assn., N.Y. State Women's Studies Assn., ARC Overseas Assn. (v.p. 1999-2001). Avocation: poet. Home: 23 McCracken Dr Oswego NY 13126-6011

LOVERN, TERRANCE LEE, production manager; b. Spokane, Oct. 8, 1945; s. Theodore and Tressa Clar (Adams) L. Grad. high sch., N.Y.C. Prin. understudy Ice Capades, 1963-64; prin. skater, dancer Casa Carioca Ice Revue, Garmisch, Germany, 1964-66; prin. skater Holiday on Ice, U.S. & South Am., 1966; prin. skater, dancer Conrad Hilton Hotel Ice Revue, Chgo., 1966-68; dancer Tropicana Hotel, Las Vegas, 1968-72, Lido de Paris, Las Vegas, 1972-74; dancer, singer Bobbie Gentry Show, 1974-76; prin. skater, dancer Flamingo Hilton, 1976-81; dancer, singer Lido deParis Show, Stardust Hotel, 1976-81; instr. ice skating Ice Land Ice Arena, 1983-88; skater, dancer Flamingo Hilton, 1986-89; co. mgr. Stardust Hotel, 1989-91, prodn. mgr., 1991-2000; prodn. stage mgr. Wayne Newton Show, Stardust Resort & Casino, 2000—. Artistic dir. Civil Ballet, Las Vegas, 1988-95. Bd. dirs. Golden Rainbow Las Vegas, 1997. Recipient Can. Figure Skating Gold medal, Vancouver, B.C., 1963. Home: 6113 Edgewood Cir Las Vegas NV 89107-2596 Office: Stardust Resort & Casino 3000 Las Vegas Blvd S Las Vegas NV 89109-1932

LOVETRI, JEANNETTE LOUISE, voice educator; b. Southampton, N.Y., Apr. 2, 1949; d. James John and Aline Rita (Zimmer) L. Student, Manhattan Sch. Music, 1967-68, Julliard Sch., 1971-72, pvt. dance, piano & vocals, Greenwich, Conn., 1970-75, pvt. dance, piano & vocals, N.Y.C., 1975—. Tchr.

voice music dept. Upsals Coll., East Orange, N.J., 1976-81; founder, dir. The Voice Workship, 1983—. Guest lectr. Boston Conservatory of Music, 1987—, Faculty Internat. Symposium Care of Profl. Voice, N.Y., 1987—, 1st Internat. Congress Arts Medicine, N.Y.C., 1992, British Voice Assn., Actors Ctr., London, 1993, 1st Internat. Music Theatre Tng., Austraila, 1994, 96, Wagner Coll., N.Y., 1994, Loyola Coll. Balt., 1994, Towson State Coll., Balt., 1996, N.A.T.S. Va. Chpt., 1996; lectr., workshop leader, various U.S. cities, Amsterdam, Copenhagen, Stockholm, London, Sydney, Berlin, Hamberg; sci. rschr. on vocal acoustics Royal Swedish Tech. Inst., 1990; guest vocal coach for Meredith Monk at Houston Grand Opera, 1992; cons. Mount Sinai Hosp., Grabscheid Voice Ctr., N.Y.C., 1997—; faculty drama dept. voice NYU, N.Y.C., 1997—, Sch. Edn. NYU, 1999, Brigham Young U., 2000, Shenandoah Conservatory, 2000; dir. vocal studies Bklyn. Youth Chorus, 1992—; spkr. in field. Contbr. articles to profl. jours. Van Lawrence fellow The Voice Found., Phila., 1999. Mem. Am. Acad. Tchrs. Singing, N.Y. Singing Tchrs. Assn. (bd. dirs., pres., former chmn. Music Theatre Com. Am. Symposium), Nat Assn. Tchrs. Singing (spkr., panelist winter workshop 2001). Achievements include having students on Broadway, TV, film and in concert halls. E-mail: voiceworkshop@erols.com.

LOVETT, CLARA MARIA, university administrator, historian; b. Trieste, Italy, Aug. 4, 1939; came to U.S., 1962; m. Benjamin F. Brown. BA equivalent, U. Trieste, 1962; MA, U. Tex., Austin, 1967; PhD, U. Tex., 1970. Prof. history Baruch Coll. CUNY, N.Y.C., 1971-82, asst. provost, 1980-82; chief European divsn. Libr. of Congress, Washington, 1982-84; provost, v.p. acad. affairs George Mason U., Fairfax, Va., 1988-93; on leave, dir. Forum on Faculty Roles and Rewards Am. Assn. for Higher Edn., 1993-94; pres. No. Ariz. U., Flagstaff, 1994-2001, pres. emerita, 2001—; sr. fellow, dir. Ctr. for Competency Based Edn. Inst. for State Studies, 2002—. Vis. lectr. Fgn. Svc. Inst., Washington, 1979-85. Author: Democratic Movement in Italy 1830-1876, 1982 (H.R. Marraro prize, Soc. Italian Hist. Studies); Giuseppe Ferrari and the Italian Revolution, 1979 (Phi Alpha Theta book award); Carlo Cattaneo and the Politics of Risorgimento, 1972 (Soc. for Italian Hist. Studies Dissertation award), (bibliography) Contemporary Italy, 1985; co-editor: Women, War, and Revolution, 1980, (essays) State of Western European Studies, 1984; contbr. sects. to publs., U.S., Italy. Organizer Dem. clubs Bklyn., 1972-76; mem. exec. com. Palisades Citizens Assn., Washington, 1985-87; vestry mem. St. David's Episc. Ch., Washington, 1986-89; bd. dirs. Blue Cross Blue Shield Ariz., 1995—; trustee Western Govs. U., 1996—; mem. Ariz. State Bd. Edn., 1999-2001. Fellow Guggenheim Found., 1978-79, Woodrow Wilson Internat. Ctr. for Scholars, 1979 (adv. bd. West European program), Am. Coun. Learned Socs., 1976, Bunting Inst. of Radcliffe Coll., 1975-76, others; named Educator of Yr. Va. Fedn. of Bus. and Profl. Women, 1992. Mem. Am. Assn. Higher Edn. (cons. 1979—), Soc. for Italian Hist. Studies, Assn. Am. Coll. and Univs. (bd. dirs. 1990-93). Avocations: choral singing, swimming. Office: 2715 N 3d St Phoenix AZ 85003 E-mail: clara.lovett@nau.edu.

LOVETT, DANIEL JAY, SR. broadcast executive; b. Rapid City, S.D., Dec. 26, 1940; s. Mildred J. Colontonio; m. Olivia L. Von Buvinghausen; children: Daniel Lovett, Jr., Kelly Kay Kreminski, Zachary William. Disc jockey KPID Radio, Payette, Idaho, 1957—59; announcer KWOS Radio, Jefferson City , Mo., 1959—63; news anchor KRCG-TV, Jefferson City, 1960—63; news reporter/anchor KILT Radio, Houston, 1963—66; news/sports reporter KTRH Radio, 1966—67; sports dir./anchor KTRK-TV (ABC), 1967—73; radio play-by-play voice Houston Oilers, 1970—73; sports anchor WABC-TV, N.Y.C., NY, 1973—76; play-by-play ABC NCAA Regional Football, DC, 1976; sports dir./anchor WJLA-TV, Washington, 1976—80; radio play-by-play voice WASHINGTON REDSKINS, 1977—80; sports commentator ABC RADIO NETWORK, N.Y.C., NY, 1980—88; sports anchor ABC World News Weekend, 1980—85; sports commentator WFAN Radio, 1987—88; sports dir./anchor KGO-TV (ABC), San Francisco, 1988—96; dir. video comm. ICED, Cypress, Tex., 2000—. Sec. Houston Acad. Radio/Tv/Music Artists, Houston, treas. Contbr. articles to mags.; prodr.: (films) "Lone Star 500" Nascar, 1972; actor: (plays) "The Boy Friend", 1962. Recipient Tex. Sportscaster of Yr. award, Associated Press, 1970, 1971, 1972. Office: ICED 12715 Telge Rd. Cypress TX 77429-2289 Personal E-mail: Dannolove@aol.com.

LOVETT, FRANCIS WILLIAM, JR. adult education educator; b. Northampton, Massachusetts, July 9, 1922; s. Francis William Lovett and Elizabeth Claire Costello; m. Shirley Virginia Green, June 19, 1948; children: Francis William Lovett III, Jane L. Schenderlein, Susan L. Dahl. BS with distinction, Wesleyan U., Middletown, Conn., 1948; MS, Northwestern U., 1953. Cert. tchr. N.Y., Ohio. Prin. Latin Sch. of Chgo., 1948—57; headmaster Hillsdale Sch., Cin., 1957—66; counselor Culver Mil. Acad., Ind., 1966—69; headmaster Moravian Acad., Bethlehem, Pa., 1971—74; dir. Duluth Cathedral Sch., Minn., 1975—77; curriculum dir. Univ. Sch., Milw., 1979—86; lectr SUNY , Plattsburgh, 1987—94; ret., 2000. Lectr. Ohio U., Chillicothe, 1996—2000. Author (literary drama): Intempestuous Storm, 1948 (award of Distinction, 1948); author: (historical novel) Six Colors for a Champion, 2002; contbr. Pfc 10th Mt. Divsn. U.S. Army, 1942—45, Italy. Decorated Bronze Star with 2 Oak Leaf Clusters. Mem.: Am. Conf. for Irish Studies, 10th Mt. Divsn. Nat. Assn., Int. Fed. Mt. Soldiers. Avocation: Avocations: writing, lecturing, travel in Ireland, travel in Greece. Home: 304 Robin Rd Waverly OH 45690-1521

LOVETT, JOHN ROBERT, retired chemical company executive; b. Norristown, Pa., June 17, 1931; s. James and Margaret (Creighton) L.; m. Sandra Miller, May 26, 1956; children: Judy, Jackie, John Robert Jr. BS, Ursinus Coll., 1953; MS, U. Del., 1955, PhD, 1957. Rsch. chemist Exxon Rsch., Linden, N.J., 1957-64; lab. dir. Exxon Rsch./Exxon Chem., 1964-70; v.p. Paramins Exxon Chem., Houston, 1970-74, tech. mgr. Linden, 1974-76; v.p. rsch. Air Products and Chems., Inc., Allentown, Pa., 1976-81; pres. Europe Air Products and Chems., Inc., Hersham, Eng., 1981-88; group v.p. chems. Air Products and Chems., Inc., Allentown, 1988-92, exec. v.p. gases & equipment, 1992-93, exec. v.p. strategic planning and tech., 1993-96. Mem. AICE, Chem. Mfrs. Assn. (bd. dirs. 1990-95), Am. Chem. Soc., Soc. Chem. Industry. Home: 2830 W Liberty St Allentown PA 18104-4748

LOVETT, LAURENCE DOW, retired real estate and steamship executive; b. Jacksonville, Fla., Apr. 13, 1930; s. William Radford and Agnes Nisbet (Dow) L. BA, Harvard U., 1951, LL.B., 1954. Vice pres. Eric Boulton, Inc., N.Y.C., 1958-60; vice pres. Eastern Steamship Lines, Miami, Fla., 1960-65, Suwanee Steamship Co., N.Y.C., Jacksonville, 1965-78; pres. Burgoyne Properties, 1978-85; v.p. Piggly Wiggly Corp., 1965-82. Chmn. bd. dirs. Met. Opera Guild, 1979-86; chmn. Save Venice Inc., 1987-98, Venetian Heritage, Inc., 1998—; chmn. bd. dirs. Chamber Music Soc. of Lincoln Ctr., 1989-93. Served with AUS, 1955-57. Mem.: Knickerbocker, The Brook. Address: Palazzo Sernagiotto Canareggio 5723 Venice Italy also: 11 Ave Princess Grace Monte Carlo 98000 Monaco

LOVETT, MILLER CURRIER, management educator, clergyman; b. Lynn, Mass., Mar. 18, 1923; s. Charles William and Phoebe Frances (Miller) L.; m. Dorothy Johnsen, Feb. 14, 1946 (div.); children: Anne E., Celeste M., Peter W., Rebecca J.; m. Virginia Lavelli, May 26, 1979. BSBA, Boston U., 1944, STB, 1946, PhD, 1964; postgrad., MIT, Boston U., 1970-72. Pastor Wesley United Meth. Ch., Medford, Mass., 1946-52; sr. pastor United Meth. Ch., Ellensburg, Wash., 1952-62, Congl. Ch., Laconia, N.H., 1965-70; assoc. prof. bus. adminstrn. Belknap Coll., Center Harbor, 1970-73; prof. bus. adminstrn. Bunker Hill Community Coll., Charlestown, Mass., 1973-77; assoc. prof. mgmt. Boston State Coll., 1977-82, U. Mass., Boston, 1982—2002; ret., 2002. Founder and exec. dir. Social Ventures Trust, Lexington, Mass., 1985—; mem. cmty. econ. devel. projects, Peru, USA, 1985-97, Boston, 1990—, N.H., 1995—. Contbr. articles to profl. jours. Lt. col. CAP USAF, 1955—. Recipient Disting. Svc. award Ellensburg Jr. C. of C., 1956. Mem. Mass. Tchrs. Assn., Assn. Enterprise Opportunity, Masons. Avocations: stamp and coin collecting. Home: PO Box 1669 25 Spindle Point Rd Meredith NH 03253-6748 Office: U Mass Coll Pub & Community Svc Boston MA 02125-3393

LOVETT, RADFORD DOW, marine terminal real estate and investment company executive; b. Jacksonville, Fla., Sept. 6, 1933; s. William Radford And Agnes (Dow) L.; m. Katharine R. Howe, June 25, 1955 (dec. Jan. 1991); children: Katharine, William Radford, Philip, Lauren; m. Susan Wylie Rogers, June 16, 1995; children: Nick, Peter, Teddy Rogers. With Merrill Lynch, Pierce, Fenner & Smith Inc., N.Y.C., 1958-78; mng. dir. Capital Markets Group, 1975-78; pres. Piggly Wiggly Corp., Jacksonville, Fla., 1978-82; chmn. bd. Commodores Pt. Terminal Corp., 1978—. Chmn. Southcoast Capital Mgmt. Corp., Jacksonville, 1995—; bd. dirs. Wachovia Corp., Fla. Rock Industries Inc., Patriot Transp., Inc., Winn-Dixie Stores, Inc. Trustee Drew U., 1976-79, St. Vincent's Found., Jacksonville Zool. Soc. Lt. F.A. U.S. Army, 1955-57. Mem. Coastal Conservation Assn. Fla. (bd. dirs.). Episcopalian. Office: Ste 1600 One Independent Dr Jacksonville FL 32202-5009

LOVETT, WENDELL HARPER, architect, educator; b. Seattle, Apr. 2, 1922; s. Wallace Herman and Pearl (Harper) L.; m. Eileen Whitson, Sept. 3, 1947; children: Corrie, Clare. Student, Pasadena Jr. Coll., 1943-44; BArch, U. Wash., 1947; MArch, MIT, 1948. Architect, designer Naramore, Bain, Brady & Johanson, Seattle, 1948; architect, assoc. Bassetti & Morse, 1948-51; pvt. practice architect, 1951—; instr. architecture U. Wash., 1948-51, asst. prof., 1951-60, assoc. prof., 1960-65, prof., 1965-83, prof. emeritus, 1983—. Lectr. Technische Hochschule, Stuttgart, 1959-60 Prin. works include nuclear reactor bldg. U. Wash., 1960, Villa Simonyi, Medina, Wash., 1989; patentee in field. Pres. Citizen's Planning Coun., Seattle, 1968-71; bd. dirs. Seattle Baroque Orch., 1998—. With AUS, 1943-46. Recipient 2d prize Progressive Architecture U.S. Jr. C. of C., 1949; Internat. design award Decima Triennale di Milano, 1954; Arch. Record Homes awards, 1969, 72, 74; Interiors award, 1973; Sunset-AIA awards, 1959, 62, 69, 71; Fulbright grantee, 1959; AIA fellow, 1978 Mem. AIA (sec. Wash. chpt. 1953-54, bd. dirs. Found. Seattle chpt. 1991-92, Seattle chpt. medal 1993, pres. sr. coun. 1991-92), Plestcheeff Inst. (bd. dirs. 1992). Home and Office: 420 34th Ave Seattle WA 98122-6408

LOVETT, WILLIAM ANTHONY, law and economics educator; b. Milw., Sept. 2, 1934; AB, Wabash Coll., 1956; JD, NYU, 1959; PhD in Econs., Mich. State U., 1969. Bar: N.Y. 1960. Atty. U.S. Dept. Justice, Washington, 1962; economist FTC, 1963-69; prof. Tulane U., New Orleans, 1969—, dir. internat. law, trade and fin. program, 1985—. Joseph Merrick Jones prof. law and econs., 1991—. Author: Inflation and Politics, 1982, Banking and Financial Institutions Law, 1984, 88, 92, 97, World Trade Rivalry, 1987, U.S. Shipping Policies and the World Market, 1996, U.S. Trade Policy, 1998. Root-Tilden scholar, 1956-59. Mem. ABA, Am. Econs. Assn., Am. Soc. Internat. Law, Phi Beta Kappa. Office: Tulane Law Sch New Orleans LA 70118

LOVEWELL, MARJORIE KLINGENSMITH, secondary school educator; b. Mpls., Aug. 19, 1938; d. Medford Shirley and Margaret Isabel (Jepson) Klingensmith; m. Hubart S. Lovewell Jr., Aug. 6, 1960 (div. Dec. 1981). BS, U. Minn., 1960; MEd, U. Ga., 1974. Cert. secondary edn. tchr., Minn., Ga. Tchr. Ind. Sch. Dist. #281, Robbinsdale, Minn., 1961-69, Dekalb County Bd. Edn., Decatur, Ga., 1969—. Curriculum writer State Dept. Edn., Atlanta, 1989-90. Bd. dirs. Ga. chpt. Myasthenis Gravis Found., 1999—. Mem.: Brain Injury Assn. Ga. (bd. dirs. 2000—), Ga. Assn. Familu and Comsumer Sci. (dist. M treas. 1996—), Am. Assn. Family and Consumer Scis. (cert.), Atlanta Alliance Theater Guild (corr. sec. 2001—02), Delta Kappa Gamma, Delta Zeta Found. (sec. 1989—93, treas. 1993—95, v.p. 1995—97, pres. 1997—2001, spl. advisor 2001—), Delta Zeta Sorority (alumnae pres. Atlanta chpt. 1974, 1983). Episcopalian. Home: 96 The Prado NE Atlanta GA 30309-3370

LOVICK, NORMAN, accountant; b. Wilson, N.C., July 10, 1942; s. Henry J. and Ella (Lovick) Webb; children: Norman Lovick Jr., Michael D. BS, Durham (N.C.) Coll., 1963; AA, N.C. Cen. Coll., Durham, 1961; MS, Am. U., 1964; Adv. Deg., USDA Grad. Sch., Washington, 1971. Acctg. analyst U.S. Dept. Treasury, Washington, 1967-76; fin. analyst Midland Nat. Corp., Wheaton, Md., 1976-78; cpa, cert. fin. planner Lovick's Fin. Assocs., Hyattsville, 1978-88, chief exec. officer, pres., 1985—. Gen. agt. Bankers United, Cedar Rapids, Iowa, 1977-79; notary pub. With U.S. Army, 1965-67. Mem. Nat. Assn. Accts., D.C. Life Underwriters Assn., Nat. Assn. Life Underwriters, Nat. Soc. Pub. Accts., Am. Inst. Profl. Bookkeepers, D.C. Soc. Ind. Accts., Am. Mgmt. Assn., Masons (32 deg., chaplain). Democrat. Pentecostal Ch. Avocations: fishing, boating, reading, dancing. Office: Lovick's Fin Assoc Inc 3601 Hamilton St Ste 201 Hyattsville MD 20782-3946

LOVIN, KEITH HAROLD, university administrator, philosophy educator; b. Clayton, N.Mex., Apr. 1, 1943; s. Buddie and Wanda (Smith) L.; m. Marsha Kay Gunn, June 11, 1966; children: Camille Jenay, Lauren Kay BA, Baylor U., 1965; postgrad., Yale U., 1965-66; PhD, Rice U., 1971. Prof. philosophy Southwest Tex. State U., San Marcos, 1970-77, chmn. dept. philosophy, 1977-78, dean liberal arts, 1978-81; provost, v.p. acad. affairs Millersville U., Pa., 1981-86; provost, v.p. acad. and student affairs U. So. Colo., Pueblo, 1986-92; pres. Maryville U. St. Louis, 1992—. Contbr. articles on philosophy of law, philosophy of religion to profl. publs.; mem. adv. bd. Southwest Studies in Philosophy, 1981-90. Bd. dirs. St. Louis Symphony Orch., 1995-2001, United Way of Greater St. Louis, 1992-99, Boys Hope, Jr. Achievement Mississippi Valley, Inc., 1992-2001, St. Luke's Hosp., Nat. Coun. Alcohol and Drug Abuse Adv. Bd., St. Louis Intercollegiate Athletic Conf., Higher Edn. Coun.; bd. dirs., pres. Ind. Colls. and Univs. of Mo. Mem. Chesterfield C. of C., Univ. Club, Media Club, Gov. Bus. Edn. Roundtable. Avocation: fly fishing. Home: 13664 Conway Rd Saint Louis MO 63141-7234 Office: Maryville U 13550 Conway Rd Saint Louis MO 63141-7299 E-mail: klovin@maryville.edu.

LOVING, DEBORAH JUNE PIERRE, lawyer, real estate broker; b. Omaha, Jan. 21, 1953; d. Thomas Eukis and June (Dawson) L.; children: La Shaun, Ronald, Mignion. BA, Mills Coll., 1977; JD, U. Iowa, 1979. Bar: Hawaii 1987, U.S. Dist. Ct. (no. dist.) Calif. 1987, U.S. Dist. Ct. Hawaii 1987, U.S. Ct. Mil. Appeals 1987; lic. real estate broker, Calif.; tchg. credential Calif. C.C. Pvt. practice, Oakland, Calif., 1987—. Real estate developer, Cancun, Mex. and U.S., 1991—; officer, bd. dirs. Cmty. Based Developers, Oakland, 1992—; mem. adv. bd. Bayview Med. Group, Vallejo, Calif., 1995—. Mem. Oxford Club. Avocations: sailing, travel, tennis, art. Office: 3911 Harrison St Oakland CA 94611-4536 E-mail: pierre@jps.net.

LOVING, SUSAN BRIMER, lawyer, former state official; m. Dan Loving; children: Lindsay, Andrew, Kendall. BA with distinction, U. Okla., 1972, JD, 1979. Asst. atty. gen. Office of Atty. Gen., 1983-87, 1st asst. atty. gen., 1987-91; atty. gen. State of Okla., Oklahoma City, 1991-94; ptnr. Lester, Loving & Davies, Edmond, Okla., 1995—. Master Ruth Bader Ginsburg Inn of Ct., 1995-97. Vice-chmn. Pardon and Parole Bd., 1995; mem. Gov.'s Commn. on Tobacco and Youth, 1995—97; mem. med. steering com. Partnership for Drug Free Okla., Inst. for Child Advocacy, 1996—97; bd. dirs. Bd. for Freedom of Info., Okla. Inc., 1995—2001, Legal Aid of West Okla., 1995—2001, Legal Aid Svcs. of Okla., 2002—. Recipient Nat. Red Ribbon Leadership award Nat. Fedn. Parents, Headliner award, By-liner award Okla. City and Tulsa Women in Comm., First Friend of Freedom award, Freedom of Info., Okla., Dir. award Okla. Dist. Attys. Assn. Mem.: Oklahoma County Bar Assn. (bd. dirs. 2001—), Okla. Bar Assn. (mem. ho. dels. 1996—, grievance com. 1999—, task force on professionalism and civility 1999—, past chmn. adminstrv. law sect., chmn. adminstrn. of justice com., chmn. profl. responsibility comm., Spotlight award 1997), Phi Beta Kappa. Office: Lester Loving & Davies PLLC 1505 Renaissance Blvd Edmond OK 73013-3018 E-mail: sloving@lldlaw.com.

LOVING, WILLIAM RUSH, JR. writer, consultant; b. Norfolk, Va., Sept. 14, 1934; s. William Rush and Margaret Elizabeth (Billups) L.; m. Jane Parker, July 1963 (div. Dec. 1987); children: Katharine G., Margaret Borden, Leslie R.; m. Marsha Thaler, June 30, 1989 (div. June 1994); m. Jane Dillard Gregory, Nov. 18, 2000. BA, U. Richmond, 1956. Lt. U.S. Army, 1957-59; reporter Richmond (Va.) Times-Dispatch, 1959-62, bus. editor, 1965-69; reporter The Virginian-Pilot, Norfolk, 1962-63; info. coord. Va. Mus. Fine Arts, Richmond, 1963-65; assoc. editor Fortune mag., N.Y.C., 1969-79; asst. dir. U.S. Office Mgmt. and Budget, Washington, 1979-80; pres. Loving Assocs. Ltd., 1980—; mem. firm Sitrick & Co., 1999—. Editor: How To Protect What's Yours, 1983; contbr. articles to various mags. Bd. dirs. Alfred I. duPont Fund. Mem. Nat. Press Club, Bucks County C. of C., Va. Hist. Soc., Newcomen Soc., Cosmos Club, Springfield Golf and Country Club. Avocations: photography, painting. Home: 6425 Murray Hill Rd Baltimore MD 21212 E-mail: rushloving@mindspring.com.

LOVINGER, SOPHIE LEHNER, child psychologist; b. N.Y.C., Jan. 15, 1932; d. Nathaniel Harris and Anne (Rosen) Lehner; m. Robert Jay Lovinger, June 18, 1957; children: David Fredrick, Mark Andrew. BA, Bklyn. Coll., 1954; MS, City Coll., N.Y.C., 1959; PhD, NYU, 1967. Diplomate Am. Bd. Profl. Pschology. Sr. clin. psychologist Bklyn. State Hosp., 1960-61; grad. fellow NYU, N.Y.C., 1964—67; psychotherapy trainee Jamaica (N.Y.) Ctr., 1964-67; asst. prof. Hofstra U., Hempstead, N.Y., 1967-70; prof. Cen. Mich. U., Mt. Pleasant, 1970-98; psychotherapist, psychoanalyst Mich., 1964-98, Charleston, S.C., 1999—. Author: Learning Disabilities and Games, 1978, Language-Learning Disabilities, 1991, Child Treatment from Intake Interview to Termination, 1998; contbr. articles to profl. jours. Fellow: Am. Acad. Clin. Psychology; mem.: APA, Nat. Register Health Svc. Providers. Office: 4 Carriage Ln Ste 300B Charleston SC 29407-6065 E-mail: sllov@earthlink.net.

LOVINGER, WARREN CONRAD, emeritus university president; b. Big Sandy, Mont., July 29, 1915; s. Wilbur George and Ruth Katherine (Hokanson) L.; m. Dorothy Blackburn, Aug. 14, 1937; children— Patricia Mae, Jeanie, Warren Conrad BA, U. Mont., 1942, MA, 1944; EdD, Columbia U., 1947. Tchr., prin. Pub. Schs. Mont., 1937-43; instr. history U. Mont., Missoula, 1943-44; pres. No. State U., Aberdeen, S.D., 1951-56, Central Mo. State U., Warrensburg, 1956-79, pres. emeritus, 1979—. Exec. sec. Am. Assn. Colls. for Tchr. Edn., 1947-51, nat. pres., 1963-64; nat. pres. Am. Assn. State Colls. and Univs., 1974-75; mem. del. to study effects of Marshall Plan on Western Europe, 1950; leader study of tchr. edn. in Fed. Republic of Germany, 1964; leader del. People's Republic of China, 1975; mem. comparative study tour of Republic of China, 1976 Author: General Education in Teachers Colleges, 1948; contbr. articles to profl. jours. Served as lt. USNR, 1944-46, ETO Recipient Silver Beaver award Boys Scouts Am., 1970; Outstanding Civilian Service award Dept. Army, 1979 Mem. Mo. Tchrs. Assn., Am. Assn. Sch. Adminstrs., Mo. Assn. Sch. Adminstrs., Columbia U. Alumni Assn., Stover C. of C. , Am. Legion, Gideons Internat., Phi Kappa Phi, Phi Delta Kappa, Kappa Delta Pi, Lodges: Masons, Shriners, Rotary, Lions. Baptist. Avocations: travelling; writing; fishing; farming.

LOVINGOOD, REBECCA BRITTEN, elementary school educator; b. Bethlehem, Pa., June 5, 1939; d. Clyde Robert and Helen Cauffiel (Britten) L. BS, Syracuse U., 1961; MA, Guildhall Sch. of Music, London, 1962; cert., Jagiellonian U., Krakow, Poland, 1985. Cert. tchr., N.Y., Pa., N.J. Del.; LPN, Pa. Newspaper reporter The Christian Sci. Monitor, Boston, 1963-65; music tchr. Devereux Found., Devon, Pa., 1965-66; elem. sch. tchr. The Episcopal Acad., Merion, 1966-90; tchr. Diocese of Wilmington Schs., 1991-92; tchr. 2d grade King of Peace Italian Sch. Archdiocese of Phila., Phila., 1992—. Edn. tchr. U. Ala., Tuscaloosa, 1988; dir. children's theater, Saratoga Performing Arts, Saratoga Springs, N.Y., 1969; dir. music events, Aldeburgh Music Festival, Suffolk, Eng., 1970. Author numerous children's plays. Vol. The Musical Fund Soc., Phila., The Coll. of Physicians. Recipient Legion of Honor, Chapel of Four Chaplains, Phila., 1981; travel grant, Kosciuszko Found., N.Y.C., 1985. Mem. Am. Assn. for the History of Medicine. Democrat. Roman Catholic. Avocations: masters swimming, piano and cello concerts, miniature dachshunds, Johnstown Symphony. Home: 165 Dartmouth Ave Johnstown PA 15905-2306 Office: Fourth Grade Tchr West End Catholic Sch 317 Power St Johnstown PA 15906-2730

LOVINS, L. HUNTER, public policy institute executive; b. Middlebury, Vt., Feb. 26, 1950; d. Paul Millard and Farley (Hunter) Sheldon; m. Amory Bloch Lovins, Sept. 6, 1979; 1 child, Nanuq. BA in Sociology, BA in Polit. Sci., Pitzer Coll., 1972; JD, Loyola U., L.A., 1975; LHD, U. Maine, 1982. Bar: Calif. 1975. Asst. dir. Calif. Conservation Project, L.A., 1973-79; co-CEO, co-founder Rocky Mountain Inst., Snowmass, Colo., 1982—. Vis. prof. U. Colo., Boulder, 1982; Henry R. Luce vis. prof. Dartmouth Coll., Hanover, N.H., 1982; pres. Nighthawk Horse Co., 1993. Co-author: Brittle Power, 1982, Energy Unbound, 1986, Least-Cost Energy Solving the CO2 Problem, 2d edit., 1989, Natural Capitalism, 1999. Bd. dirs. Point Found., Basalt and Rural Fire Protection Dist., Nighthawk Horse Co., Rocky Mountain Inst., Windstar Land Conservancy; vol. EMT and firefighter. Recipient Mitchell prize Woodlands Inst., 1982, Right Livelihood Found. award, 1983, Best of the New Generation award Esquire Mag., 1984, Nissan prize, 1995, Lindbergh award, 1999, Bd. Govs.' award Loyola Law Sch., 2000, LOHAS award for svc. to bus., 2001, Shingo Prize for Excellence in Mfg. Rsch., 2001. Mem. Calif. Bar Assn., Am. Quarter Horse Assn., Am. Polocrosse Assn. Avocations: rodeo, fire rescue, polocrosse. Office: Rocky Mountain Inst 1739 Snowmass Creek Rd Snowmass CO 81654-9199

LOVISCKY, DOUGLAS CHARLES, financial planner; b. Sharon, Pa., Aug. 14, 1968; s. Charles E. and Barbara K. Loviscky; m. Kelly Winkelman, July 17, 1993; 2 children: Kendall Jordan, Andrew Douglas. BS in Fin., Pa. State U., 1990; JD, U. Pitts., 1996. Bar: Pa. 1996; CPA, Pa. CPA Price Waterhouse, Pitts., 1991-93; tax atty. Williams Coulson, 1996-2000; fin. planner Fleck & Assocs., Ltd., State College, 2000—. Bus. editor Jour. Law and Commerce, 1995-96. Mem. ABA, Pa. Bar Assn. Bus. Office: Fleck & Assocs Ltd 409 S Pugh St State College PA 16801-5308 E-mail: loviscky@efleck.com.

LOVISI, GARY, writer; b. New Hyde Park, N.Y., Apr. 28, 1952; s. Aldo Mario and Vivian Maria (DeGaetano) L.; m. Pat Mastronardi, Nov. 22, 1975 (div. Jan. 1981); m. Lucille Cali, Nov. 7, 1999. AAS in Bus. Adminstrn., Kingsborough C.C., 1984. Founder Gryphon Books; founder, sponsor N.Y. Collectible Book Expo. Author: Science Fiction Detective Tales, 1986, Sherlock Holmes: The Great Detective in Paperback, 1990, Dashiell Hammet and Raymond Chandler, 1994, Hellbent on Homicide, 1995, Extreme Measures, 1996, Sarasha, 1997, Blood in Brooklyn, 1999, The Sexy Digests, 2001; editor, pub. Paperback Parade, Hardboiled Mag.; contbr. articles to profl. jours.

LOVITZ, JON, actor, comedian; b. Tarzana, Calif., July 21, 1957; Attended, U. Calif.-Irvine; studied acting, Film Actors Workshop. Began performing in comedy improvisation with the Groundlings, L.A.; TV work includes (series) Foley Square, 1985, Saturday Night Live, NBC, 1985-90, The Critic, 1994—, (voice); feature films include The Last Resort, 1986, Ratboy, 1986, Jumpin' Jack Flash, 1986, Three Amigos, 1986, Big, 1988, My Stepmother is an Alien, 1988, Brave Little Toaster, 1989 (voice), Mr. Destiny, 1990, An American Tail: Fievel Goes West, 1991 (voice), A League of Their Own, 1992, Mom and Dad Save the World, 1990, Coneheads, 1993, National Lampoon's Loaded Weapon I, 1993, City Slickers II: The Legend of Curley's Gold, 1994, North, 1994, Trapped in Paradise, 1994, High School High, 1996, Matilda, 1996, The Great White Hype, 1996, Happiness, 1998, The Wedding Singer, 1998. Address: Abrams Artists Agy 9200 W Sunset Blvd Ste 1130 Los Angeles CA 90069-3606

LOVOY, JOSEPH T. investment advisor; b. Birmingham, Ala., Apr. 8, 1932; s. Brace M. and Mary C. (Ciravolo) L.; m. Lynne B. Bass, Feb. 14, 1963; children: Steve, Kenneth, Thomas, Amy, Jon. BS, U. Ala., 1953. CMFC fin. advisor Nat. Endowment for Fin. Edn. Fin. advisor Am. Express Fin. Advisors, Mpls., 1964—. Cons. Escambia County Utility Authority, Pensacola. Chmn. Pensacola (Fla.) Opera Co., 19987-88, Am. Diabetes Assn., Pensacola, 1988-91, Found. Bd. for Pub. TV, Pensacola, 1992—. Recipient Nat. Pub. Broadcasting Svc. award Nat. Pub. Broadcasting, Pensacola, 1998. Office: C-104 744 E Burgess Rd Ste C104 Pensacola FL 32504-6361 Fax: 850-476-0261.

LOVY, ANDREW, osteopathic physician, psychiatrist; b. Budapest, Hungary, Mar. 15, 1935; came to U.S., 1939; s. Joseph and Elza (Kepecs) L.; m. Madeline Rotenberg, Aug. 16, 1959 (div. Sept. 1991); children: Daniel, Jordan, Howard, Jonathan, Elliot, Richard, Mickey. Student, Wayne State U., 1956; BS, Ill. Coll. Optometry, 1957, OD, 1958; DO, Chgo. Coll. Osteopathy, 1962. Diplomate Am. Bd. Psychiatry and Neurology. Intern Mt. Clemens (Mich.) Hosp., 1962—63; resident VA Hosp., Augusta, Ga., 1971—74; prof. psychiatry, chmn. dept. psychiatry Chgo. Coll. Osteo. Medicine, 1981—82; dir. psychiatric tng. program Mich. Osteo. Med. Ctr., Detroit, 1982—86; adj. prof. psychiatry W.Va. Coll. Osteo. Medicine, 1984; clin. prof. psychiatry N.Y. Coll. Osteo. Medicine, 1984; med. dir. Eastwood Clinics, 1987—90; clin. prof. psychiatry N.D. Coll. Medicine, 1990; prof., chmn. dept. psychiatry Chgo. Coll. Osteo. Medicine, 1990—92, 1996; med. dir. behavioral medicine Saginaw Cmty. Hosp., 1992—94; clin. prof. psychiatry Mich. State U., 1995—; dir. psychiatric residency program Midwestern U., 1995—97, prof., chmn. dept. psychiatry, 1996—2001, clin. prof. family medicine, 1999. Forensic med. examiner, 1998—; mem. Nat. Bd. Osteo. Med. Examiners, 1998—. Author: Vietnam Diary, 1971. With M.C., U.S. Army, 1966-68, Vietnam. Decorated Air medal, Purple Heart, Army Commendation medal,

Combat Medic badge, paratrooper wings, Vietnam campaign medal, Vietnam Svc. Expert Rifle, Expert Pistol badge. Fellow Am. Coll. Neurology and Psychiatry (pres. 1984); mem. Am. Osteo. Assn., Am. Heart Assn. (stroke com. 1987-89), Am. Psychiat. Assn., Am. Acad. Pain Mgmt., Assn. Clin. Hypnosis, Am. Osteo. Coll. Neuropsychiatry (pres.-elect 1982-83, pres. 1983-84), Am. Med. Joggers Assn.

LOW, ANDREW M. lawyer; b. N.Y.C., Jan. 1, 1952; s. Martin Laurent and Alice Elizabeth (Bernstein) L.; m. Margaret Mary Stroock, Mar. 31, 1979; children: Roger, Ann. BA, Swarthmore Coll., 1973; JD, Cornell U., 1976. Bar: Colo. 1981, U.S. Dist. Ct. Colo. 1981, U.S. Ct. Appeals (10th cir.) 1986. Assoc. Rogers & Wells, N.Y.C., 1977-81, Davis Graham & Stubbs LLP, Denver, 1981-83, ptnr., 1984—. Editor: Colorado Appellate Handbook, 1984, 94. Pres. Colo. Freedom of Info. Coun., Denver, 1990-92, Colo. Bar Press Com., 1989, appellate practice subcom. Colo. Bar Assn. Litigation Coun., 1994—; bd. dirs. CLE in Colo., Inc., 1993-96; trustee 9 Health Fair, Denver, 1988—; mem. Colo. Sup. Ct. Joint Commn. on Appellate Rules, 1993—. Avocations: skiing, golfing, fly-fishing. Office: Davis Graham & Stubbs LLP Ste 500 1550 17th St Denver CO 80202 E-mail: andrew.low@dgslaw.com.

LOW, ANTHONY, English language educator; b. San Francisco, May 31, 1935; s. Emerson and Clio (Caroli) L.; m. Pauline Iselin Mills, Dec. 28, 1961; children: Louise, Christopher, Georgianna, Elizabeth, Peter, Catherine, Nicholas, Alexandra, Michael, Frances, Jessica, Edward, Charlotte. AB, Harvard U., 1957, MA, 1959, PhD, 1965. Mem. faculty Seattle U., 1965-68; mem. faculty NYU, N.Y.C., 1968—; prof. English lit., 1978—; chmn. dept. English, 1989-95. Vis. scholar Jesus Coll., Cambridge, Eng., 1974-75. Author: Augustine Baker, 1970, The Blaze of Noon, 1974, Love's Architecture, 1978, The Georgic Revolution, 1985, The Reinvention of Love, 1993; editor: Urbane Milton, 1984. Pres. Conf. on Christianity and Lit., 1996-99. Pew Evangelical fellow, 1995; Milton scholar, 1996. Mem. Milton Soc., Donne Soc., MLA, Renaissance Soc., Phi Beta Kappa. Home: 748 Kent Hill Rd East Calais VT 05650 Office: NYU Dept English 19 University Pl New York NY 10003-4556 E-mail: low@compuserve.com.

LOW, ARNOLD KINMAN, systems executive; b. San Francisco, Feb. 22, 1942; s. Howard Y. and Patricia M. (Lee) L.; m. Junko Nerio; 1 child, Sara. AB, Dartmouth Coll., 1963; MBA, San Francisco State U., 1976; Mng. Info. Svcs. Resource, Harvard Bus. Sch., 1984. Sys. assoc. So. Pacific Co., San Francisco, 1965-67; sys. analyst Applied Data Sys. Inc., 1967-68; mgr. data processing I. Magnin & Co., 1968-77; sr. v.p. 1st Nationwide Bank, 1977-86; pres. Low & Assocs., 1986—. Mem. internat. bd. advisors U.S. China Ednl. Inst., San Francisco, 1989—. Mem. adv. bd. San Francisco C.C. Dist., 1974-78; pres. Urban Crossroads Sch., San Francisco, 1975-89; pres. Big Bros.-Big Sisters, San Francisco, 1989-90; foreman San Francisco Civil Grand Jury, 1993-94; trustee Ft. Mason Found., San Francisco, 1996-99. Mem. Data Processing Mgmt. Assn. (pres. 1973-74), Olympic Club. Office: 2915 Baker St San Francisco CA 94123-3209

LOW, BOON CHYE, physicist; b. Singapore, Feb. 13, 1946; came to U.S., 1968; s. Kuei Huat and Ah Tow (Tee) Lau; m. Daphne Nai-Ling Yip, Mar. 31, 1971; 1 child, Yi-Kai. BSc, U. London, Eng., 1968; PhD, U. Chgo., 1972. Scientist High Altitude Observatory Nat. Ctr. for Atmospheric Rsch., Boulder, Colo., 1981-87, sect. head, 1987-90, 97—, acting dir., 1989-90, sr. scientist, 1987—. Mem. mission operation working group for solar physics NASA, 1992-94; vis. sr. scientist Princeton Plasma Physics Lab., 1998-99. Mem. editl. bd. Solar Physics, 1991—. Named Fellow Japan Soc. for Promotion of Sci., U. Tokyo, 1978, Sr. Rsch. Assoc., NASA Marshall Space Flight Ctr., 1980. Mem. Am. Physical Soc., Am. Astron. Soc., Am. Geophysical Union. Office: Nat Ctr for Atmosph Rsch PO Box 3000 Boulder CO 80307-3000 E-mail: low@hao.ucar.edu.

LOW, DENISE LEA, humanities educator; d. William Francis Doson and Dorothy Lea Bruner; m. Thomas Francis Weso; m. Donald Low Low (div. Jan. 10, 1972); children: David Andrew, David Lee. Bachelor Arts, University Kans., Lawrence, Kansas, 1967—71; Master Arts, U. Kans., Lawrence, Kansas, 1971—74; Master Fine Arts, Wichita State U., Wichita, Kansas, 1974—84; PhD, U. Kans., Lawrence, Kansas, 1984—97. Instr. Kans. State U., Manhattan, Kans., 1975—77, U. Kans., Lawrence, 1977—84; prof. Haskell Indian Nations U., 1984—, chair english dept., 2000—. Manuscript committe chair bd. mem. Woodley Press, Topeka, 1985—; rev. editor U. Kans., Lawrence, Kans., 2000—. Contbr. book. Mem. Lawrence Arts Ctr., Lawrence, Kans., 1980—2002; bd. mem. Lied Ctr. Friends, 2002—02. Recipient Roberts Found., Pittsburg, Kans. libr., 1990; fellow Lit. Arts, Kans. Arts Coun., 1991-1993, poetry, Lanna-Newberry, 2001. Mem.: Woodley Press, Writers Pl., Associated Writing Programs (judge 1999—99). Democrat-Npl. Congrgational Kwan Um Zen. Avocation: gardening. Office: Haskell Indian Nations University 155 Indian Avenue Lawrence KS 66044 Office Fax: 785-832-6672.

LOW, DONALD, diplomat, financial investor; b. San Francisco, Sept. 25, 1927; s. Alvin Grant and Annette Violet Low; m. Marion Berman Low, Apr. 7, 1982 (dec. Jan. 1998); children: Mitch, Phillip, Mindy. BA, U. San Francisco, 1952; hon. degree, Chas. Simmons Sch. Human Rels., San Francisco, 1955. Lic. realtor; lic. stock broker. Gen. mgr., developer Villa Roma Hotel, San Francisco, 1972-80; owner Fountain Hotel, Palm Springs, Calif., 1962-72, Hotel Cons., San Francisco, 1980-86; diplomat Republic of Cameroon, 1986—. Vice dean San Francisco Consular Corps; chief fin. officer Am. Arts Soc., San Francisco, 1990—; cons. Internat. Rels. Inc., San Francisco, 1985—. Participant 7 world tennis tours. Lt. USAAC, 1952-54. Mem. World Trade Club, Bankers Club, Commonwealth Club, World Affairs Coun. San Francisco. Avocations: music, opera, tennis, collecting fine watches, symphony. Office: Republic of Cameroon Consulate 147 Terra Vista Ave San Francisco CA 94115-3876

LOW, EMMET FRANCIS, JR. mathematics educator; b. Peoria, Ill., June 10, 1922; s. Charles Walter and Nettie Alys (Baker) Davis; m. Lana Carmen Wiles, Nov. 23, 1974. BS cum laude, Stetson U., 1948; MS, U. Fla., 1950, PhD, 1953. Instr. physics U. Fla., 1950-54; aero. research scientist NACA, Langley Field, Va., 1954-55; asst. prof. math. U. Miami, Coral Gables, Fla., 1955-60, assoc. prof., 1960-67, prof., 1967-72, chmn. dept. math., 1961-66; acting dean U. Miami (Coll. Arts and Scis.), 1966-67, assoc. dean, 1967-68, assoc. dean faculties, 1968-72; prof. math. Coll. at Wise U. Va., 1972-89, dean Coll. at Wise, 1972-86, chmn. dept. math. scis. Coll. at Wise, 1986-89, emeritus prof. math. Coll. at Wise, 1989—. Vis. research scientist Courant Inst. Math. Scis., NYU, 1959-60 Contbr. articles to profl. jours. Mem. Wise County Indsl. Devel. Authority, 1992—, chmn., 1996—. Served with USAAF, 1942-46. Recipient William P. Kanto award for significant contbns. to pub. edn. Forum on Edn., 1998; hon. Ky. Col.; established endowed chair in physics U. Va. Coll. at Wise, 1999. Mem. Am. Math. Soc., Math. Assn. Am., Soc. Indsl. and Applied Math., Nat. Council Tchrs. of Math., Southwest Va. Council Tchrs. of Math. (Outstanding Svc. award 1999), AAUP, AASS, Sigma Xi, Delta Theta Mu, Phi Delta Kappa, Phi Kappa Phi. Clubs: Univ. Yacht (Miami, Fla.); Kiwanis.

LOW, FRANCIS EUGENE, physics educator; b. N.Y.C., Oct. 27, 1921; s. Bela and Eugenia (Ingerman) L.; m. Natalie Sadigur, June 25, 1948; children— Julie, Peter, Margaret. BS, Harvard U., 1942; MA, Columbia U., 1947, PhD, 1949. Mem. Inst. Advanced Study, 1950-52; asst. prof. U. Ill., Urbana, 1952-55, asso. prof., 1955-56; prof. physics MIT, Cambridge, 1957-67, Karl Taylor Compton prof., 1968-85, Inst. prof., 1985-92, Inst. prof. emeritus, 1992—, dir. Center for Theoretical Physics, 1973-76, dir. Lab. for Nuclear Scis., 1979-80, provost, 1980-85. Cons. in field; mem. high energy physics adv. panel Dept. Energy, 1972-76, chmn., 1987-90. Contbr. articles to profl. jours. Served with USAAF, 1942-43; Served with AUS, 1944-46. Mem. NAS (nat. coun. 1986-89), Am. Phys. Soc. (chmn. divsn. particles and fields 1974, councillor-at-large 1979-82), Fedn. Am. Scientists (nat. coun. 1973-77), Am. Acad. Arts and Scis., Internat. Union of Pure and Applied Physics (commn. on particles and fields 1976-82). Home: 28 Adams St Belmont MA 02478-3525 Office: MIT Rm 6-301 Cambridge MA 02139

LOW, FREDERICK EMERSON, English educator; b. Oct. 25, 1943; AA, Am. Coll., Paris, France, 1967; BA, Queens Coll., 1969, MLS, 1976; MA, CUNY, 1972. Prof. La Guardia Comm. Coll., CUNY, Long Island City, N.Y., 1978-95; dir. Asia World Learning Ctr., Inc., Flushing, NY, 1996—2001, Asian-Am. Ctr. for Edn. of N.Y., Inc., Flushing, 1998—2001; pvt. tchr., rschr., 2001—. Home: 221-47 59th Ave Bayside NY 11364-1929 E-mail: fredelow@yahoo.com.

LOW, GEORGE SOLON, business educator, consultant; b. Edmonton, Alta., Can., June 7, 1957; U.S. citizen; s. LeRon and Jeanne Low; m. Colleen Davidson, Aug. 14, 1982; children: Jesse Hinman, Shannon Colleen, Allen George, Margaret Jeanne. BA, Brigham Young U., 1982; MBA, U. Western Ont., London, Can., 1988; PhD, U. Colo., 1994. Media dir. Foster Advt., Winnipeg, Man., Can., 1984-85, MacLaren-McCann Advt., Calgary, Alta., Can., 1984-86, group mgr. media planning Toronto, Can., 1987; lectr. mktg. U. Lethbridge, Can., 1988-94, asst. prof. Can., 1994-96, Tex. Christian U., Ft. Worth, 1996-2000, assoc. prof., 2000—, mem. faculty senate, 1999—. Cons. Exxon Corp., Irving, Tex., 1986-87, Cadillac Fairview Corp., Toronto, Ont., Can., 1988-90, PepsiCo Inc., Purchase, N.Y., 1999-2000. Reviewr Jour. Mktg., 1996—; contbr. articles to profl. jours. Chartered orgn. rep. Boy Scouts Am., Arlington, Tex., 1997—. Rsch. grantee Mktg. Sci. Inst., 1991, 93, 96, 98, Pease Found., 2000; Doctoral fellow Social Sci. and Humanities Rsch. Coun., 1992. Mem. Am. Mktg. Assn. Office: Tex Christian Univ M J Neeley Sch Bus 2800 S University Dr Fort Worth TX 76129-0001

LOW, HARRY WILLIAM, judge; b. Oakdale, Calif., Mar. 12, 1931; s. Tong J. and Ying G. (Gong) L.; m. May Ling, Aug. 24, 1952; children: Larry, Kathy, Allan. AA, Modesto Jr. Coll., 1950; AB Polit. Sci. with honors, U. Calif., Berkeley, 1952, JD, 1955. Bar: Calif. 1955, U.S. Ct. Appeals (9th cir.) 1955. Commr. Workmen's Compensation Commn., 1966; teaching assoc. Boalt Hall, 1955-56; dep. atty. gen. Calif. Dept. Justice, 1956-66; judge Mcpl. Ct., San Francisco, 1966-74, presiding judge, 1972-73; judge Superior Ct., San Francisco, 1974-82; presiding justice Calif. Ct. Appeals, 1st dist., 1982-92; commr. Calif. Ins. Dept., San Francisco, 2000—. Pres. San Francisco Police Commn., 1992-96; pres. San Francisco Human Rights Commn., 1999-2000; mem. Jud. Arbitration and Mediation Svcs., 1992-2000, Commn. on Future of Cts., 1991-94, Commn. on Future of Legal Profession, 1993-95; Calif. Ins. commr., 2000—. Contbr. articles to profl. jours. Chmn. bd. Edn. Ctr. for Chinese, 1969-80, Chinese-Am. Internat. Sch., 1979-99; bd. visitors U.S. Mil. Acad., 1980-83; bd. dirs. Friends of Recreation and Parks, Salesian Boys Club, World Affairs Coun., 1979-85, NCCJ, San Francisco chpt. St. Vincent's Boys Home, Coro Found., 1970-76, San Francisco Zool. Trust, 1987, Union Bank Calif., 1993-2000; pres. San Francisco City Coll. Found., 1977-87, Inst. Chinese Western History U. San Francisco, 1987-89. Mem. ABA (chmn. appellate judges conf. 1990-91, commr. on minorities), San Francisco Bar Assn., Chinese Am. Citizens Alliance (pres. San Francisco chpt. 1976-77, nat. pres. 1989-93), Calif. Judges Assn. (pres. 1978-79), Calif. Jud. Coun., State Bar Calif. (rsch. editor publs. 1958-76, pub. affairs com. 1987-90, exec. bd. 1992-94), Calif. Conf. Judges (editor jour. cts. commentary 1973-76), Calif. Judges Assn. (exec. bd. 1976-79), Asian Bus. League (dir. 1986-93), Nat. Ctr. State Cts. (bd. dirs. 1986-91), San Francisco Bench Bar Media Commn. (chmn. bd. dirs. 1987-92), Boalt Hall Alumni Assn. (Distinguished Svc. award 1992, Judge Lowell Jensen award 2000), Phi Alpha Delta. Office: Calif Dept Ins 45 Fremont St 23r Fl San Francisco CA 94105 *Try to enjoy whatever task you are doing and enjoy the good company of those with whom you associate. Be an active part of the community and try to improve it. Keep busy and try to understand and respect others.*

LOW, JAMES A. physician; b. Toronto, Ont., Can., Sept. 22, 1925; s. Donald M. and Doris V. (Van Duzer) L.; m. Margery Una, Oct. 5, 1952; children: Donald E., Margeret P., Norman I. MD, U. Toronto, 1949. Intern Toronto Gen. Hosp., 1949-50; resident in ob-gyn U. Toronto, 1950-54; fellow ob/gyn Duke U., 1955; clin. instr. dept. ob-gyn U. Toronto, 1955-65; prof. and chmn. dept. ob-gyn Queens U., Kingston, Ont., Can., 1965-85, prof., 1985—. Bd. dirs. Mus. Health Care at Kingston. Mem. editl. bd. Ob-Gyn., 1986-89, Am. Jour. Ob-Gyn., 1995-99. Served with Can. Navy, 1943-45. Fellow: Royal Coll. Physicians and Surgeons Can. (chmn. splty. com. 1976—82, chmn. manpower com. 1984—92); mem.: Am. Acad. Cerebral Palsy, Can. Soc. Clin. Investigation, Soc. Obstetricians and Gynecologists Can., Soc. Gynecol. Investigation, Am. Gynecol. and Obstet. Soc., Assn. Profs. Ob-Gyn. Can. (sec.-treas. 1972—80, pres. 1983—84). Home: 185 Fairway Hills Kingston ON Canada K7M 2B5 Office: Queens U Dept Ob Gyn Kingston ON Canada K7L 3N6

LOW, JOHN WAYLAND, lawyer; b. Denver, Aug. 7, 1923; s. Oscar Wayland and Rachel E. (Stander) L.; m. Merry C. Mullan, July 8, 1979; children: Lucinda A., Jan W. BA, Nebr. Wesleyan U., 1947; JD cum laude, U. Denver, 1951. Bar: Colo. 1951, U.S. Dist. Ct. (Colo. dist.) 1951, U.S. Ct. Appeals (10th cir.), U.S. Supreme Ct. 1960. Ptnr. Sherman & Howard LLC, Denver, 1951-93, counsel, 1993—. Trustee U. Denver, 1987—; chmn. bd. Denver Symphony Assn., 1989-90; vice chmn. Colo. Symphony Assn., 1990-96; pres. Colo. Symphony Found., 1995—, Mesa Verde Found., 1997—; chmn. Colo. Alliance of Bus., Denver, 1983-87. 1st lt. U.S. Army, 1942-46, CBI. Recipient Learned Hand award Am. Jewish Com., 1989, Outstanding Alumni award U. Denver, 1994, Evans Disting. Svc. award U. Denver, 2001.. Mem. ABA, Colo. Bar Assn., Denver Bar Assn., University Club of Denver, Garden of Gods Club (Colorado Springs). Republican. Mem. United Ch. of Christ. Office: Sherman & Howard 633 17th St Ste 3000 Denver CO 80202-3665

LOW, JOSEPH, artist; b. Coraopolis, Pa., Aug. 11, 1911; s. John Routh and Stella (Rent) L.; m. Ruth Hull, Oct. 21, 1940; children: Damaris, Jennifer. Student, U. Ill., 1930-32, Art Students League N.Y., 1935. Founder, 1959; since propr. Eden Hill Press Engaged in printmaking and graphic arts, 1943—; exhbns. include, Princeton, Dartmouth, Williams, U. Ill., Phila. Mus. Art, Brandeis U., Grinnell Coll., Carnegie Inst. Tech., Herron Art Inst., Indpls., U. Ky., others; rep. permanent collections, Princeton, Dartmouth, U. Ky., State Dept., Library of Congress, Chapin Library at Williams Coll., U. Ill., Wesleyan U., Middletown, Conn., Va. Mus. Fine Arts, San Francisco Pub. Library, Boston Atheneum, Boston Mus. Fine Arts, Harvard Coll. Library, Pratt Inst., U. Okla., Newberry Library, Chgo., Met. Mus. Art, Ohio State U.; Bodleian Library, Oxford U., pvt. collections. Home: 29 Fulling Mill Rd Chilmark MA 02535

LOW, LOUISE ANDERSON, consulting company executive; b. Saline, Mich., May 1, 1944; d. Harry Linné and Rose Josephine (Chvala) Anderson; m. James Thomas Low, Dec. 30, 1967; children: James William, Eric Linné, Kari Louise, Antony Anderson. BA in Biology, U. Mich., 1966. Permanent teaching cert., Mich.; cert. master gardener Coop. Ext. Svc. Tchr. secondary sci. Novi (Mich.) Community Schs., 1966-67; rsch. asst. U. Mich. Med. Sch., Ann Arbor, 1967-68; tchr. secondary sci. Livonia (Mich.) Pub. Schs., 1968-72; tax preparer H&R Block, Saline, 1991; sr. exec. asst. Low & Assocs., 1991—. Mem. Saline H.S. PTO, 1995—, Saline Mid. Sch. PTO, 1996; mem. ball com. St. Joseph Hosp., 1994; active Friends of Saline Dist. Libr.; mem. Saline Area Schs. Project, 1997, also mem. bldg. com.; parent advisor; com. mem. Saline H.S. Alumni Assn., 2001—; mem. youth bd. Zion Luth. Ch., Ann Arbor, 1993—98; appt. mem. long-range planning com. Saline Area Schs., 1990—94, appt. mem. gifted and talented com., 1996—. Mem. AAUW (life, bd. dirs., com. chairperson), Washtenaw County Alliance for Gifted Edn. (v.p., bd. dirs. 1988-97), U. Mich. Conger Alumnae Group (bd. dirs., mem. exec. bd.), Alumni Assn. U. Mich. (life), Interlochen Ctr. for Arts Alumni Orgn. (life), Ann Arbor Area Panhellenic Alumnae (pres. 1976-77), Wayne State U. Faculty Wives, Jenny Lind Swedish Cultural Club of Mich. (bd. dirs., program chair), Travis Pointe Country Club, Huron Valley Swim Club, Sigma Kappa (alumnae pres. 1970-72), Alpha Mu Sigma Kappa (mem. corp. bd., mem. found.). Lutheran. Home and Office: Low & Assocs 3431 Surrey Dr Saline MI 48176-9571

LOW, LOUISE O. civic volunteer; b. Monroe, Mich., July 6, 1926; d. Peter Orth and Dora M. Grundman; m. Raymond Low, Aug. 16, 1952 (div. Feb. 1986); children: John D., Scott D. (dec.) Student, Southeastern Univ., Washington D.C. Grants specialist fed. govt., 1946-80. Apptd. Fayette County bd. Care and Treatment of Mentally Deficient Persons, 1991—; bd. dirs FayCo Enterprises workshop for devel. disabled adults, 1998—; bd. dirs., vol. Operation OUTING, 1987-94; bd. dirs., meml. gift officer Friends and Families of Fayette County Hosp., 1988-99; vol. Fayette County Hosp. Aux., 1995—, scholarship com., 1995—, corr. sec., 1998—, v.p., pres, 2000—; mem. So. Ill. Constituency of Vols. Recipient Abe award, Jan. 1997. Mem. Vandalia Women's Club (exec. bd. 1996—. 2d v.p. 1996-98, pres. 1998-2000, del. state convs. 1998, 99, 2000).

LOW, MARY LOUISE (MOLLY LOW), documentary photographer; b. Quakertown, Pa., Jan. 3, 1926; d. James Harry and Dorothy Collyer (Krewson) Thomas; m. Antoine Francois Gagné, Nov. 3, 1945 (div.); children: James L., David W., Stephen J., Jeannie Wolff-Gagné; m. Paul Low, July 11, 1969 (dec. July 1991). Student, Oberlin Conservatory of Music, 1943-44, Oberlin Coll., 1944; cert., Katharine Gibbs Sec. Sch., 1945; degree in psychiat. rehab. work, Einstein Coll. Medicine, 1968-70. Sec. Dept. Store, N.Y.C., 1945; sec., treas. Gagné Assocs., Consulting Engrs., Binghamton, N.Y., 1951-66; psychiat. rsch. asst. Jacobi Hosp., Bronx, 1969-70; asst. to head of sch. Brearley Sch., N.Y.C., 1976-78; pvt. practice documentary photographer San Diego, 1984—. Contbr. articles to profl. jours. Pres., bd. trustees Unitarian-Universalist Ch., 1996-97. Recipient Dir.'s award for excellence Area Agy. on Aging, San Diego, 1993, Citizen Recognition award County of San Diego, Calif., 1993. Avocations: singing, directing church choir, traveling. Office: Molly Low Photography 5576 Caminito Herminia La Jolla CA 92037-7222 E-mail: mlow1926@aol.com.

LOW, MERRY COOK, civic worker; b. Uniontown, Pa., Sept. 3, 1925; d. Howard Vance and Eleanora (Lynch) Mullan; m. William R. Cook, 1947 (div. 1979); m. John Wayland Low, July 8, 1979; children: Karen, Cindy, Bob, Jan. Diploma in nursing, Allegheny Gen. Hosp., Pitts., 1946; BS summa cum laude, Colo. Women's Coll., 1976. RN, Colo. Dir. patient edn. Med. Care and Rsch. Found., Denver, 1976-78. Contbr. chpt. to Pattern for Distribution of Patient Education, 1981. DuArt bd. dirs. U. Denver, 1998—; docent Denver Art Mus., 1979—99, vol. exec. bd., 1988—94, nat. docent symposium com., 1991, chair collectors' choice benefits, 1988; pres. vols., trustee Rocky Mountain Conservation Ctr., 1988—90; co-chair art auction Colo. Alliance Bus., 1992—93, com., 1994—97; founding chair Rocky Mountain Conservation Ctr., 1999; trustee ch. coun., chair invitational art show 1st Plymouth Congl. Ch., Englewood, Colo., 1981—84; bd. dirs. women's libr. assn. U. Denver, 1982—, vice chmn., 1985—86, chair, 1986—87, co-chair spl. event, 1992; bd. dirs. Humanities Inst., 1993—, pres., 1999; bd. dirs. Rocky Mountain Conservation Ctr., 1999—2000, co-chair Founder's Day com., 1994—, chair Culturefest, 1995—96; bd. dirs. Lamont Sch. Music Assocs., 1990—96. Recipient Disting. Svc. award U. Denver Coll. Law, 1988, King Soopers Vol. of Week award, 1989, Citizen of Arts award Fine Arts Found., 1993, Outstanding Vol. Colo. Alliance of Bus., 1994, U. Denver Cmty. Svc. award, 1996. Mem. Am. Assn. Mus. (vol. meeting coord. 1990-91), P.E.O. (pres. Colo. chpt. DX 1982-84), U. Denver Alumni Assn. (bd. dirs., sec. 1996-98), Welcome to Colo., Women for Profit Investment Club (sec. 1999-2002). Republican. Congregationalist. Home: 2552 E Alameda Ave Apt 11 Denver CO 80209-3324

LOW, MORTON DAVID, physician, educator; b. Lethbridge, Alta., Can., Mar. 25, 1935; s. Solon Earl and Alice Fern (Litchfield) L.; m. Cecilia Margaret Comba, Aug. 22, 1959 (div. 1983); children— Cecilia Alice, Sarah Elizabeth, Peter Jon Eric; m. Barbara Joan McLeod, Aug. 25, 1984; 1 child, Kelsey Alexandra MD, C.M., Queen's U., 1960, M.Sc. in Medicine, 1962; PhD with honors, Baylor U., 1966. From instr. to asst. prof. Baylor Coll. Medicine, Houston, 1965-68; assoc. prof. medicine U. B.C., Vancouver, Can., 1968-78, prof. medicine Can., 1978-89, clin. assoc. dean Can., 1974-76, assoc. dean rsch. and grad. studies Can., 1977-78, coord. health scis. Can., 1985-89, creator Health Policy Rsch. Unit, 1987, Alkek-Williams Disting. Prof. and pres. U. Tex. Health Sci. Ctr., Houston, 1989-2000, disting. mem. faculty Grad. Sch. Biomed. Scis., 1989—, dir. Health Policy Inst., 1990—; Rockwell chair in soc. and health, dir. Ctr. Soc./Population U. Tex., 2000—; prof. neurology U. Tex. Med. Sch., 1989—; prof. health policy and mgmt. Sch. Pub. Health U. Tex., 1989—. Cons. in neurology U. Hosp. Shaughnessy site, Vancouver, 1971-89, U. B.C. site, Vancouver, 1970-89; dir. dept. diagnostic neurophysiology Vancouver Gen. Hosp., 1968-87; cons. in EEG, 1987-89; exec. dir. Rsch. Inst., 1981-86; mem. med. sci. adv. com. USIA, 1991-93; adj. prof. Health Informatics Sch. Allied Health Scis.; mem. Premier's Adv. Coun. on Health, Alta., Can., 2000—. Mem. editorial bd. numerous jours.; contbr. articles to profl. jours. Bd. dirs. , Tex. Inst. for Rehab. and Rsch. Found., Greater Houston Ptnrship., 1994-2000, Episcopal Health Charities Found., 1997—; mem. governing bd. Houston Mus. Natural Sci., 1991-97; trustee Kinkaid Sch., Houston, 1991-97, 98—, Meml.-Herman Hosp. Sys., 1997-2000. Med. Rsch. Coun. Can. grantee, 1968-80; recipient Tree of Life award Jewish Nat. Fund, 1995, Caring Spirit award Inst. Religion, 1995. Fellow Am. EEG Soc., Royal Coll. Physicians (Can.), Royal Soc. Medicine (London); mem. AMA, Tex. Med. Assn. (coun. on med. edn. 1990—), Tex. Found. Soc. & Health (founding chmn. 1999), Can. Soc. Clin. Neurophysiology, Internat. Fedn. Socs. for EEG and Clin. Neurophysiology (rules com. 1977-81, sec. 1981-85), Assn. Acad. Health Ctrs. (task force on access to care and orgn. health svcs. 1988-95, chmn. 1992, task force on instnl. values 1989-95), Harris County Med. Soc., Am. Coun. Edn., Forum Club of Houston (governing bd. 1991-96). Avocations: sailing instructing, photography, youth soccer coach, vol. ski-patrol, flying. Office: U Tex-Houston Health Sci PO Box 20036 Houston TX 77225-0036 E-mail: david.low@uth.tmc.edu

LOW, RANDALL, internist, cardiologist; b. San Francisco, June 24, 1949; s. Huet Hee and Betty Tai (Quan) L.; m. Dorothy Fung, May 4, 1975; children: Audrey, Madeleine, Jennifer. AA, City Coll., San Francisco, 1969; BA, U. Calif., Berkeley, 1971; MD, U. Calif., Davis, 1975. Diplomate Am. Bd. Internal Medicine, Nat. Bd. Med. Examiners, Am. Bd. Cardiovascular Diseases. Intern Hosp. of Good Samaritan, L.A., 1975-76, resident, 1976-77, chief med. resident, 1977-78, fellow in cardiology, 1979-81; mem. staff St. Francis Meml. Hosp., San Francisco, 1981—, chmn. dept. cardiology, 1995—; pvt. practice internal medicine and cardiology, 1981—; mem. staff Chinese Hosp., 1981—, chief of medicine, 1991-92; asst. clin. prof. U. Calif., 1994-2000. Mem. courtesy staff St. Mary's Hosp., San Francisco, 1981—, Calif. Pacific Med. Ctr., San Francisco, 1990—; cardiology cons. Laguna Honda Hosp., San Francisco, 1981—. Mem. home health quality assurance com. Self Help for Elderly, San Francisco, 1991—; bd. trustees San Francisco Health Authority, 2000—; bd. dirs. Youth Advocates, San Francisco, 1992-99. Recipient Hearst Pub. Svc. award U. Calif.-Berkeley, 1970, 6th ann. homecare recognition award Self Help for Elderly, 1993. Mem. ACP, Am. Soc. Internal Medicine, Am. Coll. Cardiology, Am. Heart Assn. (bd. govs. 1983-90), Calif. Acad. Medicine, Calif. Med. Soc., San Francisco Med. Soc., bd. dirs., SF Med. Soc., 1999, (bd. dirs. 1999—), Assn. Chinese Cmty. Physicians (sec.-treas. 1986-89), Chinese Cmty. Health Care Assn. (pres. 1991-96, 99—). Office: 909 Hyde St Ste 501 San Francisco CA 94109-4853

LOW, RICHARD H. broadcasting executive, producer; b. Union City, N.J., Feb. 20, 1927; s. Irving and Regina (Krieger) L.; 1 dau., Jennifer Alixe. Student, U. Mich., 1947-49; JD, Columbia U., 1952. With CBS News, 1952-56, CBS-TV Network, 1956-62, dir. contracts, facilities and program sales, 1959-62; with Young & Rubicam, 1962-84, v.p. TV-radio dept., 1970-72, v.p. programming, 1972-73, sr. v.p., 1973-81, responsible for network TV programming and purchasing, 1973-84, includes cable TV, 1980-84, exec. v.p., dir. broadcast programming and purchasing, 1981-84; pres. Manticore Prodns., Inc. 1985—. Pres. Universal Holding Co.; advisor LWV presdl. TV debates, 1980; judge N.Y. World TV Festival, 1979-80, Internat. Emmy awards, 1981-83; panelist Nat. Assn. TV Programming Execs. Conf., 1981; keynote spkr. 25th Anniversary seminar Broadcasters Promotion Assn., 1981; presenter S.I. Newhouse Sch. Pub. Comm., Syracuse U., 1981; discussant Ctr. for Comm., 1982; mem. Task Force on Pub. Broadcasting, 1983. Mem. task force Nat. Coun. Arts, 1977, Aspen Inst., 1973; v.p., trustee Am. Mus. Immigration; trustee Town Hall Found.; bd. dirs. U.S. Comm. 1983 Bicentennial of Air and Space; advisor Ramsey Clark for U.S. Senate, 1970. With U.S. Army, 1945-46. Mem. NATAS (gov. N.Y. 1979-83). Office: 1056 5th Ave New York NY 10028-0112 *In the beginner's mind, there are many possibilities.*

LOW, STEPHEN, foundation executive, educator, former diplomat; b. Cin., Dec. 2, 1927; s. Martin and Margaret (Friend) L.; m. Helen Sue Carpenter, Oct. 9, 1954; children: Diego, Rodman, Jesse. BA, Yale U., 1950; MA, Fletcher Sch. Law and Diplomacy, Tufts U., 1951, PhD, 1956. With Dept. State, various locations, 1956-74; sr. staff mem. NSC, 1974-76; U.S. ambassador to Zambia, 1976-79; U.S. ambassador to Nigeria, 1979-81; dir. Fgn. Service Inst. Dept. State, 1982-87; dir. Bologna (Italy) Ctr. Sch. Advanced Internat. Studies Johns Hopkins U., 1987-92; pres. Assn. Diplomatic Studies and Tng., 1992-97; retired, 1997; pres. Fgn. Affairs Mus. Coun., 2000—. Served with AUS, 1946-47. Address: 2855 Tilden St NW Washington DC 20008-3820

LOW, VICTOR N. historian; b. N.Y.C., Aug. 25, 1931; s. Sol and Rosamond (Trilling) L.; m. Helga Lore Brigitta Paula Frentzel-Beyme, May 10, 1962; children: Joshua David, Gideon Samson. BA, U. Chgo., 1951; MA, Columbia U., 1962; PhD, UCLA, 1967. Edn. officer No. Region Nigera, 1960-61; lectr. Addis Ababa (Ethiopia) U., Addis Ababa, Ethiopia, 1967-69; vis. asst. prof. Mich. State U., East Lansing, 1969-72, acting dir. African Studies Ctr., 1970-71; vis. sr. lectr. The Hebrew U. Jerusalem, 1972-73; sr. lectr. Tel Aviv. U., 1979-80, The Hebrew U. Jerusalem, 1978-80, sr. rsch. fellow, 1978-80; sr. lectr. Ahmadu Bello U., Zaria, Nigeria, 1973-75, chair history divsn., 1973-75; sr. lectr., chair history divsn. U. Ibadan, Jos, Nigeria, 1975-76; vis. assoc. prof. Dartmouth Coll., Hanover, N.H., 1990-91. Chmn. Nigerian Univs. Matriculation Bd. in History, 1974-75; edn. officer no. region Nigeria, 1960-61. Author: (monograph) Three Nigerian Emirates: A Study in Oral History. 1972, (trade book) Lyme Road Letters, 1994; co-editor: (reader) History of Modern Israel, Part I: Zionism, 1979, Part 2: Israel, 1982; tech. editor U.S. Army Corps Engrs., Alexandria, Va., 1985-86; contbr. articles to profl. jours. Chmn. N.Y.C. Students for Stevenson, 1952. With U.S. Army, 1952-54. Fgn. Area Rsch. fellow The Ford Found., England and Nigeria, 1963-65, Nat. Defense Fgn. Lang. fellow, Harvard, 1966, UCLA, 1967. Jewish. Avocations: writing, tennis, classical music, jazz.

LOWDEN, JOHN L. retired corporate executive; b. Yakima, Wash., Oct. 29, 1921; s. Roy Ruben and Hildegarde Annie (Grommesch) L.; m. Janet Katherine Langan, Jan. 21, 1961; children: Susan Elizabeth, Jonathan Roy, Andrew Matthias. BA, U. Nev., 1949. Account supr. Campbell-Ewald Advt., 1951-57, Erwin, Wasey Advt., 1957-59; advt. dir. Gen. Dynamics Corp., 1959-61; account supr. Foote, Cone & Belding, 1961-63; with ITT Corp., 1963-84, v.p. corp. rels. and advt., 1977-84. Author: Silent Wings at War, 1992. Served with USAAF, 1941-45. Decorated 4th deg. knight Order of William (Netherlands); Air medal with oak leaf cluster, Bronze Arrowhead of initial assault troops. Roman Catholic.

LOWDER, MARY KATHERINE, school system administrator; b. Asheville, N.C., Sept. 11, 1943; d. William Robert Jr. and Iris Myrtle (Holden) Sherrill; m. Marcus William Sumner, Oct. 26, 1962 (div. June 1973); 1 child, Marcus Kevin; m. Frank Pearson Robinson, Jr., Oct. 26, 1974 (div. Jan. 1997); m. Charles Douglas Lowder, Aug. 5, 1999. BS in Edn., Western Carolina U., Cullowhee, N.C., 1968, MA in Edn., 1983. Cert. tchr., N.C. Tchr. reading Jackson County Bd. Edn., Sylva, N.C., 1968-69, elem. tchr., 1970-76; instr. reading Western Carolina U., 1968, instr. remedial reading, 1972; Reading Program developer Haywood County Bd. Edn., Waynesville, N.C., 1976-82, Resource and Program developer, 1982—. Cons. divsn. health, safety and phys. edn. N.C. Dept. Pub. Instrn., Raleigh, 1974-75; mem. adv. bd. Haywood Tech. Inst., Clyde, N.C., 1978-79; mem. N.C. Textbook Commn., Raleigh, 1989-93; mem. curriculum rev. com. in mktg. edn., bus. edn. N.C. Dept. Pub. Instrn., 1992, health edn., 1993. Compiler: Robert Lee Holden Family, 1993; contbr. to periodical; creator vocabulary game Jaw Breakers, 1977. Vol. Reading Is Fundamental project Haywood County Libr., 1978-79; treas. PTO, 1971-72; active Haywood County Found. Bd., 1995—. Recipient Gold Key award N.C. State Supt., 1991. Mem. NEA, ASCD, N.C. Assn. Educators (sec. 1977, v.p./pres. elect 1994-95, pres. 1995-96), Internat. Reading Assn. (v.p. 1978-79, pres. 1979-80), Bus. and Profl. Women's Orgn., Friends of Haywood County Libr., Delta Kappa Gamma (corr. sec. 1988-90, v.p. 1990-92, pres. 1992-94), Phi Delta Kappa, Kappa Delta Pi. Democrat. Avocations: genealogy, travel. Home: PO Box 336 Hazelwood NC 28738-0336

LOWE, ALFRED MIFFLIN, III, advertising agency executive, writer; b. Phila., Mar. 18, 1948; s. Alfred Mifflin Jr. and Marian (Higginson) L.; m. Patricia Ann Coppage; 1 child, Alden Mifflin. BA in Art History, Princeton U., 1970. Writer Lansdale & Carr Advt. Agy., Newport Beach, Calif., 1970-72, Asher Gould Advt. Agy., Los Angeles, 1972-73, Wilson, Haight & Welch Advt. Agy., Boston, 1973-74, Creamer, Inc., Providence, 1974-76; owner Loweco Music Co., 1976-80; v.p. Harold Cabot Advt. Agy., Boston, 1980-81; creative dir. Duffy & Shanley Advt. Agy., Providence, 1981-87, Pagano, Schenck & Kay, Providence, 1987—; sr. v.p., creative dir., group head Hill Holliday Connors Cosmopoulos, Boston, 1991—. Author: The Cheapskate's Handbook, 1986, Beasts by the Bunches, 1987, How to be a Celebrity, 1989, I Hate Fun, 1991. Active Redwood Libr. Recipient Clio awards, 1987, Silver Pencil award The One Show, 1988, 2 Bronze Pencil awards, 1991, Silver Cube award N.Y. Art Dirs.' Show, 1995, Silver Lion awards Cannes Film Festival, 1994, 5 Boston Creative Club awards, 3 New Eng. Broadcasting Assn. awards, 48 HATCH awards Boston Advt. Club; winner of 2 radio best awards, 1989. Mem. Newport Casino Lawn Tennis Club, Soc., Newport Preservation Soc., Point Assn. (v.p.). Episcopalian. Avocations: scuba diving, tennis, chess, guitar. Home: 67 Bridge St Newport RI 02840-2425

LOWE, CAMERON ANDERSON, dentist, endodontist, educator; b. Alcester, S.D., Dec. 19, 1932; s. Richard Barrett and Emma Louise (Anderson) L.; m. Doris Teresita Franquez, Dec. 23, 1957; children: Barrett, Steven, Leslie. Student, George Washington U., 1951-53, U. Va., 1955-56; DDS, Georgetown U., 1956-60; cert. residency in endodontics, U.S. Naval Dental Sch., 1967-69. Commd. lt. (j.g.) U.S. Navy Dental Corps, 1960, advanced through grades to capt., 1976, ret., 1978; pvt. practice endodontist Newport News, Va., 1978-81; assoc. prof. dentistry emeritus Old Dominion U., Norfolk, 1991, asst. chair Sch. Dental Hygiene, 1985-89. Adj. asst. prof. Med. Coll. Va.-Va. Commonwealth U. Sch. Dentistry, Richmond, 1979-81. Contbr. articles to profl. jours. and to book: Oral Pathology, 3d edit., 1989. Tutor adult literacy, 1994-99; coord. Neighborhood Watch, 1994-98; pack and troop chmn. Boy Scouts Am., Guam, 1969-72, Virginia Beach, Va., 1972-78. With USN, 1953-55. Mem. Assn. Mil. Surgeons of U.S., Am. Assn. Endodontists, Am. Acad. Oral Medicine, Am. Dental Assn., Va. Acad. Endodontics, USN Assn. Endodontists, Peninsula Dental Soc., Sigma Alpha Epsilon, Delta Sigma Delta, Sigma Phi Alpha (Dental Hygiene Honor Soc.). Methodist. Avocations: tennis, drawing, carving, reading, sculpting. Home: 1497 Wakefield Dr Virginia Beach VA 23455-4541

LOWE, CLAYTON KENT, film critic; b. Endicott, N.Y., July 10, 1936; s. Clayton Edwin and Loretta Arlene (Terry) L.; m. Janet E. Snider, 1957 (div. 1977); children: Steven Scott, Kim Ann Parker, David William, Rebecca Michelle Sobel; m. Robin S. McKell, 1980 (div. 1993). BA, Bethany Coll., 1958; MS, Butler U., 1967; PhD, Ohio State U., 1970; BD, Christian Theol. Sem., Indpls., 1962. Pastor Bellaire (Ohio) Christian Ch., 1957-58, Beallsville (Ohio) Christian Ch., 1958, Russellville (Ind.) Christian Ch., 1958-60, Montclair (Ind.) Christian Ch., 1960-61; youth dir. St. Paul United Ch. of Christ, Columbus, 1967-70; asst. prof. journalism U. Ga., 1970-72; asst. prof. comm. Ohio State U., Columbus, 1972-73, asst. prof. photography and cinema, 1973-74, assoc. prof., 1974—, chairperson photography and cinema, 1974-78, assoc. prof. emeritus, 1992—. Comml. TV prodr., dir., writer Sta. WISH-TV, 1960—66, Sta. WLWI-TV, 1966—67, Sta. WOSU-TV, 1967—70; moderator World Film Classics, Educable TV-25, 1991—97, also bd. dirs.; co-host It's Movie Time, Sta. WCBE-FM; part-time faculty Franklin U., 2000—01; film critic WCBE-FM, 2001—. Editor: The Movies on Media Catalog, 1995, 2000, Movies on Media Video Collection Mem. bd. Columbus Friends of the Libr.; trustee Met. Libr., 1997—. Eli Lilly Found. grantee, 1961-63, Ohio State U. Devel. of Media on Media Study Collection grantee, 1985, Ohio Humanities Coun. grantee 1996-97, 99; recipient Casper award for A Thing Called Hope, Sta. WOSU-TV, 1966, Regional Emmy for A Tribute to Dr. King, 1968, Regional Emmy nominee Lucasville, 1970, High Street, 1975, Leadership award Ohio State U. Outstanding Alumni Soc., 1997. Mem. Univ. Film and Video Assn., Ohio State U. Dept. Photography and Cinema Alumni Assn. (pres. 1994-95, 2001-02, bd. dirs. 1994—), Kiwanis. Home: 68 Walhalla Rd Columbus OH 43202-1441 *If these were my last words, I would write of the beauty that has filled me and that I in turn have filled. I would look past the darkness and pain, toward those radiant spots of light when family and friends were most open and life was at its wondrous best.*

LOWE, DOROTHY ANN, library technician; b. Gibson, N.C., Dec. 20, 1939; d. H. Bruce and Inez Campbell; B.S. in Media Tech., Fed. City Coll., 1975; M.S. in Media Sci., U. D.C., 1979; grad. Foster Inst. Real Estate, 1985; m. John Lowe, Jan. 18, 1958 (div. Dec. 1975); children— Donna, Steven, Inez. Personnel clk. FCC, 1972-76; microfilm photographer Library of Congress, Washington, 1976-77, personnel clk., 1977, library technician, 1977— . Pres., Pentecostal Ch. Missionaries, 1974— . Recipient letter of commendation FCC, 1976. Mem. D.C. Library Assn., U. D.C. Alumni Assn. Democrat. Home: 1208 Gondar Ave Hyattsville MD 20785-4327 Office: Library of Congress 10 1st Ave SW Washington DC 20024-5105

LOWE, DOUGLAS HOWARD, architect; b. Akron, Ohio, Nov. 1, 1952; s. Howard Bernard and Dorothy Rachael (Nowag) L.; m. Mary Louise Folk, Jan. 1, 1975; children: Ashley Marie, Austin Douglas, Andrea Catherine. BA in Pre Architecture with honors, Clemson U., 1974, MArch, 1976. Registered profl. architect, Tex., Va., interior designer, Tex. Archtl. programmer Lockwood, Andrews, Newnam, Houston, 1978-80; sr. assoc. Planning Design Research Corp., 1980-82; v.p., head interior architecture and programming 3D/Internat., San Antonio, 1982-88, exec. v.p., chief ops. officer 3D/M subs., 1988-92; founder, pres. Facility Programming and Consulting, 1992—; co-founder, v.p. Facility Consulting Group, 1994-95. Mem. Design-Build Inst. of Am., First Presbyn. Ch., San Antonio; mem. legis. com. Alamo Heights Ind. Sch. Dist. Mem. AIA, Tex. Soc. Archs., Internat. Facility Mgmt. Assn., Nat. Coun. Archtl. Registration Bds., Nat. Trust Hist. Preservation, Soc. for Coll. and Univ. Planning, Rotary Club San Antonio, Soc. Coll. & Univ. Planning, Town Club San Antonio, Phi Kappa Phi, Tau Sigma Delta. Republican. Presbyterian. Avocations: remodeling homes, golf. Office: Facility Programming & Cons 100 W Houston St Ste 1170 San Antonio TX 78205-1457

LOWE, E(DWIN) NOBLES, lawyer; b. Minturn, Ark., Oct. 4, 1912; s. James A. and Ether (Nobles) L.; m. Catherine McDonald, June 9, 1934 (div. 1959); children: Nancy, Edwin N.; m. Margaret Breece, Dec. 1, 1961; 1 son, James W. AB, U. Ark., 1932, LL.B., 1934; postgrad., Harvard U. Bus. Sch. Advanced Mgmt. Program, 1950. Bar: Ark. 1934, N.Y. 1936, U.S. Ct. Appeals (2d cir.) 1938, D.C. 1975, U.S. Ct. Internat. Trade 1979, U.S. Supreme Ct. 1944. Mem. staff Ark. Bond Refunding Bd., 1934; with legal dept. Electric Bond & Share Co., N.Y.C., 1934-35; assoc. mng. atty., ptnr. Reid & Priest, 1935-43; gen. counsel Westvaco Corp. (formerly W.Va. Pulp & Paper), N.Y.C., 1943-77; dir. pub. rels. Westvaco Corp., 1944-48, dir. govt. affairs, 1947-76, sec., 1947-66, v.p., 1966-77; spl. ptnr. Gadsby & Hannah, N.Y.C., 1978-79; mem. firm Lowe & Knapp, 1979-84; sole practice, 1985-86, Carmel, N.Y., 1986—. Gen. counsel Photography in the Fine Arts, 1957-68; sec., 1974-2000, dir. Fund for Modern Cts., N.Y., 1974—; counsel, dir. Photographic Adminstrs., Inc., 1995-2002. Dir. and counsel, Putnam County Alliance, 1990-99; dir. Putnam County Arts Coun., 1992—; bd. dirs. Putnam Hosp. Ctr. and Found., 1986-98. Recipient Disting. Alumni cert. U. Ark., 1972, 50 Yr. Practice award Fellows of Am. Bar Found., 1985, CLE Spl. award Am. Law Inst.-ABA, 1985, Practice Law Inst. Seligson CLE award, 1986, Disting. Svc. award U. Maine, Pulp and Paper Found., 1990, Disting. Svc. award N.Y. chpt. Am. Corp. Counsel Assn., 1990; Eagle Scout, 1928; decorated Order of the Arrow Boy Scouts Am., 1924. Mem. ABA (bus. law sect., council mem., chmn. 1955-, founder corp. law com. 1955, Life emem. Am. Bar Found., 1969-, emeritus 1979—, hon. mem.,(1999-2003),sr. lawyers divsn. coun. 1992-99, book pub. com. 1990, chmn. 1994-96, Experience mag. editl. bd. 1990-2000, chmn. 1995-96), Am. Arbitration Assn. (exec. com. 1969—, hon. mem. 1977-, chmn. 1972-74, chmn. bd. 1974-77), Am. Law Inst. (life mem.), N.Y. State Bar Assn., 1995-2000, Practicing Law Inst. (trustee 1966-86, pres. 1972-79, chmn. 1979-86, chmn. emeritus 1986—, fin. com. 1974—), Gen. Counsel Assn.,1968-; Dutch Treat Club. (gov., sec. 1993-2000, chmn. 2000-), Assn. Bar City N.Y. (past v.p., exec. chmn.), Am. Soc. of Corp. Sec., Inc.1956-57, nat. dir. 1956-59; World Soc. Ekistics (v.p., exec. com. UN rep. NGO), Univ. Club N.Y. (past v.p. coun., chmn. club activities, charter revision com.), Sigma Nu. Methodist. Home and Office: The Knoll 554 Gypsy Trail Rd Carmel NY 10512

LOWE, GERALD SCOTT, baseball organization executive; b. Silver Spring, Md., Dec. 4, 1969; s. Robert Vernon and Cheryl Ann (Easton) L.; m. Robin S. Cardin, July 3, 1997. BS in Journalism summa cum laude, U. Md., 1991. Sports editor Prince George's Post, Landover, Md., 1990-91; athletic comm. asst. Princeton (N.J.) U., 1991-93; asst. dir. sports info., dir. athletic mktg. and promotions Drexel U., Phila., 1993-95; asst. dir. athletic media rels. Loyola Coll., Balt., 1995-97, dir. athletic publs., media rels. and comms., 1997-98; v.p. Cal Ripken Baseball, 1999—. Rschr. Internat. Lacrosse Fedn., 1996-97; basketball coach The Park Sch., Balt., 1998-98, baseball coach, 1999-99; co-founder "X"tra Bases Sports Camp. Contbr. sports articles to Prince George's Journal, Prince George's Post, Trentonian, Washington County Observer-Reporter, NBA News, Princeton Packet, Princeton Alumni Weekly, Princeton Athletic News, College Hockey Weekly, Loyola Coll. Alumni mag., Princeton Varsity Club News, also others. Vol. baseball coach Bowie (Md.) Babe Ruth Jr. League, 1989-90, Princeton (N.J.) Am. Legion, 1992-93, Bowie H.S., 1988; radio broadcaster Princeton Ice Hockey, 1991-92; Loyola basektball and lacrosse, 1995-98; dir. hockey Md. Youth Hockey Found., 1999-2000. Winner several nat. and regional coll. sports info. publs. and writing awards. Mem. Soc. Profl. Journalists, Golden Key Nat. Honor Soc., Coll. Sports Info. Dirs. Am., Kappa Tau Alpha, Phi Kappa Phi. Avocations: reading, exercise, hockey, computers/desktop publishing, travel, music. Home: 11805 Greenspring Ave Owings Mills MD 21117-1603 Office: 10801 Tony Dr Ste A Lutherville MD 21093 E-mail: scottlowe@riplonbaseball.com.

LOWE, HAROLD GLADSTONE, JR. photojournalist, small business owner, farmer; b. Nashville, Aug. 3, 1933; s. Harold Gladstone and Kathrine (Rice) L.; m. Anne Poteat, Feb. 26, 1957 (div. 1962); 1 child, Harold Guy; m. Linda Susan Brown, Mar. 14, 1976. Student, Vanderbilt U., 1951-52, 53-54, U. of the South, 1952-53. Pres., owner Campus Cameras, Inc., Nashville, 1953-55; photographer Nashville Tennessean Newspaper, 1960-65; photo corr. UP Internat., Nashville, 1961-65; photographer, reporter Sta. WSM TV News, 1965-71; staff photographer, editor Senator Howard Baker, 1971-72; freelance photographer and reporter, 1973-76; photographer, reporter Sta. WTVF-TV News, 1976-78; photograhic supr. State of Tenn., 1978-81; photographer, owner CHSS Newspix-Capitol Press, 1981—. Pres. Campbell-Brown Farms, Inc., Dyersburg, Tenn., 1969—. Photographer Spot News, 1962 (1st Pl. award 1962); photographer, editor (documentary) United Givers Fund, 1970 (Diamond award 1970). Photographer Gov. Lamar Alexander, Nashville, 1979-80, col. aide de camp, 1979, Gov. Ned Ray McWherter, 1986. Mem. Nat. Press Photographers Assn., Tenn. Capitol Press Corps, SDX Soc. Profl. Journalists, Sports Car Club Am., Masons, Sigma Nu. Democrat. Anglican. Avocations: Music, electronics. Home: 1113 Lipscomb Dr Nashville TN 37204-4121 Office: CHSS Newspix Capitol Press 28 Legislative Pla Nashville TN 37219

LOWE, HARRY, museum director; b. Opelika, Ala., Apr. 9, 1922; s. Harry Foster and Lois (Fletcher) L. B.F.A., Auburn U., 1943, M.F.A., 1949; student, Cranbrook Acad., 1951, 53. Prof. art, dir. Art Gallery, Auburn U., 1957-59; dir. Tenn. Fine Arts Center, Nashville, 1959-64; curator exhibits Smithsonian Am. Art Mus, 1964-72; dep. commr. U.S. Exhbn. at Venice Biennale Smithsonian Am. Art Mus. (formerly NAt. Mus. Am. Art), 1966; asst. dir. for ops. Nat. Mus. Am. Art (formerly Nat. Collection Fine Arts), Smithsonian Instn., 1972-74, asst. dir., 1974-81, acting dir., 1981-82, dir., 1983-84, dep. dir. emeritus, 1985—. 1st pres. Tenn. Assn. Museums, 1960 1st pres. Tenn. Assn. Mus., 1960. With F.A. AUS, WWII, ETO. Home: 802 A St SE Washington DC 20003-1340 Office: Smithsonian Am Art Mus Smithsonian Instn Washington DC 20560-0970

LOWE, IDA BRANDWAYN, library administrator, systems administrator; b. Bogota, Colombia, Oct. 5, 1946; came to U.S., 1964; d. Jacobo and Donna (Ghelman) Brandwayn; m. Fredric Robert Lowe, Aug. 16, 1970; children: Evin, Laurence. BA, Cornell U., 1968; MA, New Sch. Social Rsch., 1971; MSLS, Columbia U., 1972; MBA, Baruch Coll., 1988. Cataloger Baruch Coll. Libr., N.Y.C., 1973-80, mgr. info. svcs., 1981-86, asst. dean, 1987, coord. for systems, 1988-94, dep. dir., 1990-97, dir. network techs., 1994-97; mgr. network systems Thomson Fin. Svcs., 1997-2000, dir. ops., user support svcs., 2000—. Cons. UN Ctr. on Transnational Corp., Ethiopia, 1990-91, UN Devel. Prog., N.Y.C., 1989, Telecom & Network Tng., Colombia and Ecuador, 1993, various librs., 1987— various corps., 1986—, UNDP Mozambique, 1993. Contbr. articles to profl. jours. Recipient Baruch/CUNY award for disting. svc., 1993. Home: 45 Strathmore Ln Westport CT 06880-4715 Office: Thomson Fin Svcs 195 Broadway New York NY 10007

LOWE, J. ALLEN, minister; b. Midland, Tex., Dec. 20, 1945; s. Homer Allen and Theresa (Lowry) L.; m. Shirley Christy, Apr. 9, 1965; children: Robert Allen, John David, Steven Scott. BS, Howard Payne U., 1968; MDiv, Tex. Christian U., 1976; postgrad, Princeton Theol., 1990. Cert. secondary tchr.; ordained to the ministry Christian Ch., 1976. Tchr. Bible history Midland (Tex.) Ind. Sch. Dist., 1968-74; assoc. min. First Christian Ch., Denison, Tex., 1974-76; campus min. United Campus Ministries, Warrensburg, Mo., 1976-78; nurture min. Meml. Christian Ch., Midland, Tex., 1978-84; assoc. min. 1st Christian Ch., Corpus Christi, 1984-91; sr. min. South Shore Christian Ch., 1991-2000, First Christian Ch., Richardson, Tex., 2000—. Chmn. Cen. Area Youth Coun., Tex., 1980-84; moderator Youth Ministry Coun. S.W., 1984-87, Bluebonnet Area Youth Coun., 1988-92; advisor Gen. Youth Coun., U.S. and Can., 1985-87; vice moderator Bluebonnet Area of Christian Ch. in S.W., 1994-95; coun. mem. North Tex. Area Youth Ministry, 2001—. Mem. IMPACT, 1974-82, Nat. Peace Acad., 1973-78; coach YMCA basketball, 1980-81, Little League, Youth Flag Football teams, Denison and Midland, 1967-68, 70, 74; mem. ethics commn. City of Corpus Christi, 1994-2000; active City League Youth Basketball, Corpus Christi, 1995-97; mem. com. on the ministry Christian Ch. in the S.W., 1997-2000; mem. North Tex. Area Youth Min. Coun., 2001-03. Recipient Friend of Youth City award, 1989; O.H. Karr Ministerial scholar Tex. Christian U., 1975-76. Mem. Youth Ministry Coun. (moderator 1989-93), Ministerial Alliance. Home: 2722 Laurel Oaks Dr Garland TX 75044 Office: First Christian Ch 601 E Main St Richardson TX 75081-3521 E-mail: jallenlowe@attbi.com. *My guiding principle is that Christianity is a relationship. Therefore, it must be lived as a relationship-we experience the love of God only in relationship to another (others) and thus only in relationship can we teach Christianity. In short, the slogan "Preach the Gospel, use words if necessary.".*

LOWE, JACK, JR. manufacturing executive; Degree magna cum laude, Rice U. CEO, chmn. TDIndustries Ltd., Dallas, 1980—. Bd. dirs. Dallas Citizens Coun., Assoc. Gen. Contractors, United Way Dallas, BBB Met. Dallas, Dallas Zool. Soc., Quality Tex. Found., Tex. Bus. & Edn. Coalition, Sr. Citizens Gt. Dallas. Recipient J. Erik Jonsson Ethics award, SMU Cary M. Maguire Ctr. Ethics & Polit. Responsiblity, 2002, Crystal Achievement award, Nat. Assn. Women in Constrn., Ethics award, Preston Ctr. Rotary Club, SIR award, Assoc. Gen. Contractors, Dallas chpt., Alumni award, Leadership Dallas, Nat. Ernst & Young Entrepreneur of Yr., Franklin Covey Co. Office: TD Industries Corp Hdqs 13850 Diplomat Dr Dallas TX 75234-8849 Office Fax: 972-888-9482.

LOWE, JAMES ALLISON, lawyer, educator; b. Cleve., July 15, 1945; s. Allison S. and Betty B. (Bernstein) L.; m. Jacalyn S. Scholss, June 24, 1967 (div.); children: David, Joseph, Jeremiah; m. Teresa L. DiPuccio, Aug. 13, 1989; 1 child, Alison. BA, U. Pa., 1967; JD cum laude, Cleve. State U., 1972. Bar: Ohio 1972, U.S. Dist. Ct. (no. dist.) Ohio 1973, U.S. Ct. Appeals (6th cir.) 1981, U.S. Supreme Ct. 1979; cert. civic trial adv. Nat. Bd. Trial Advocacy. Assoc. Berkman, Gordon & Kancelbaum, Cleve., 1972—74; sole practice, 1974—76; ptnr. Sindell, Lowe & Guidubaldi Co., L.P.A., 1976—96, Lowe Eklund Wakefield Co., LPA, Cleve., 1996—2000, Lowe Eklund Wakefield & Mulvihill Co., LPA, Cleve., 2000—. Instr. law Cleve. State U., 1974-77, Case Western Res. U., 1979-92. Author: Products Liability Litigation: Pretrial Practice, 1988, Product Liability in Ohio After Tort Reform, 1988. Active Jewish Community Fedn.; fellow Roscoe Pound Found. Fellow Internat. Soc. Barristers, Am. Bd. Trial Advs., Am. Coll. Trial Lawyers; mem. ABA, ATLA (chmn. products liability adv. com., chmn. products liability sect., dir. products liability sect.), Ohio Acad. Trial Attys. (chmn. products liability sect. 1987-89, trustee 1990—), Ohio Bar Assn., Cleve. Acad. Trial Attys. (bd. dirs. 1988—, v.p. 1990—), Greater Cleve. Bar Assn., Attys. Info. Exch. Group, Am. Bd. Trial Advocates. Office: Lowe Eklund Wakefield & Mulvihill Co LPA 610 Skylight Office Tower 1660 W 2nd St # 1660 Cleveland OH 44113-1454 Office Fax: 216-781-2610. Business E-Mail: Jlowe@lewm.com.

LOWE, JAMES EDWARD, JR. plastic and reconstructive surgeon; b. Warsaw, Dec. 5, 1950; s. James Edward and Alice Mae (Gavin) L.; m. Philamina Lucy Lozado, Oct. 7, 1989; children: James III, Jesse, Joseph. BS, Livingstone Coll., 1971; MD, Meharry Med. Coll., 1975. Diplomate Am. Bd. Plastic Surgery. Intern Downstate Med. Ctr., Bklyn., 1975—76, resident in surgery, 1975—78, Luth. Med. Ctr., Bklyn., 1978—82; resident in plastic surgery Lenox Hill Hosp., N.Y.C., 1982—84, pvt. practice, 1984—, assoc. attending surgeon, 1984—99, Good Hope Hosp., Erwin, NC, 1999—. Student mentor Purchase (N.Y.) Coll., 1996—; elder Presbyn. Ch., Scarborough, N.Y., 1998—. Health Career scholar Harvard U. Med. Sch., Boston, 1970. Mem.: NAACP, AMA (Physicians Recognition award 2002), Nat. Med. Soc., Lenox Hill Plastic Surgery Soc., The Morestin Soc., Phi Beta Sigma. Office: 4155 Ferncreek Dr Ste 102 Fayetteville NC 28314 E-mail: j.lowejrmdpc@worldnet.att.net.

LOWE, JOHN, III, consulting civil engineer; b. N.Y.C., Mar. 14, 1916; s. John and Rose Marie (Jahoda) L.; m. Jeanne Wright, June 19, 1943; children: Jonathan Alan, Barbara Jean, Heather Ellen. BS in Engring., CCNY; MSC.E., MIT. Registered profl. engr., N.Y., La., PR., Calif. Instr. U. Md., College Park, 1937-40, MIT, Cambridge, Mass., 1941-44; physicist David Taylor Model Basin, Carderock, Md., 1945; chief soils engr. Tippetts-Abbett-McCarthy-Stratton, N.Y.C., 1945-55, assoc. ptnr., 1956-62, ptnr., 1962-83; pvt. practice geotech. and dam engring., 1984—. Adj. assoc. prof. NYU, 1949-51; lectr. soil mechanics CCNY, 1953-60; 8th Terzaghi lectr., 1971, 4th Nabor Carrillo lectr., 1978, 2d U.S. Com. on Large Dams lectr., 1982, Marty Kapp lectr., 1986; keynote address Roller Compacted Concrete II, 1988, Mueser/Rutledge lectr., 1997; cons. Corps. Engrs., Washington, 1962-80; dam constrn. projects in many countries including U.S., Turkey, Taiwan, Morocco, Pakistan, Greece. Contbr. chpts. to 4 books, 38 articles in field to profl. jours. Decorated comdr. Order of Alouites (Morocco); recipient Townsend Harris medal Alumni CCNY, 1982. Fellow ASCE; mem. NAE, U.S. Com. Large Dam (chmn. 1977-78), Nat. Com. Soil Mechanics and Found. Engring., Moles, Univ. Club, Bronxville Field Club.

LOWE, JOHN BURTON, molecular biology educator, pathologist; b. Sheridan, Wyo., June 13, 1953; s. Burton G. and Eunice D. Lowe. BA, U. Wyo., 1976; MD, U. Utah, 1980. Diplomate Am. Bd. Pathology. Asst. med. dir. Barnes Hosp. Blood Bank, St. Louis, 1985-86; instr. Sch. of Medicine Washington U., 1985, asst. prof. Sch. of Medicine, 1985-86; asst. investigator Howard Hughes Med. Inst., Ann Arbor, Mich., 1986-92, assoc. investigator, 1992-96, investigator, 1997—; asst. prof. Med. Sch. U. Mich., 1986-91, assoc. prof. Med. Sch., 1991-95, prof. Med. Sch., 1995—. Dep. editor Jour. Clin. Investigation, 1997—2002, mem. editl. bd. European Jour. Biochemistry, 2001—; contbr. articles. Fellow: AAAS; mem.: Am. Assn. Physicians, Am. Soc. Clin. Investigation. Office: U Mich Howard Hughes Med 1150 W Medical Center Dr Ann Arbor MI 48109-0726

LOWE, JOHN RAYMOND, JR. mechanical engineer; b. Cleve., May 4, 1922; s. John Raymond Lowe and Mildred Esther (Potter) Grover; m. Doris Jean Woolmington, Mar. 27, 1943; children: David B., Cynthia Ann. BSME, 1949. Registered profl. mech. engr., Ohio; cert. energy mgr. Assn. Energy Engrs. Machinist Warner & Swasey, Cleve., 1940-42; indsl. engr. GM, Elyria, Ohio, 1949-51; mgr. motor design Reliance Electric, Cleve., 1952-70; product mgr. Colt Indsl. Elec. Motors, Beloit, Wis., 1971-73; dir. Lau Industries, Dayton, Ohio, 1974-75; designer Andritz Sprout-Bauer, Muncy, Pa., 1976-97; ret., 1997. Contbr. articles to profl. jours. Pres. Chagrin Falls (Ohio) PTO, 1964-65, Cleve. St. Alumni Assn., 1965-66, Chagrin Falls Bd. of Edn., 1968-70; mem. Jr. Achievement, Cleve., 1966. With U.S. Army, 1944-45. Recipient Purple Heart, Bronze Star, Two Battle Stars, Cert. of Appreciation, 1961. Achievements include design improvements and increased performance that has reduced the cost and broadened the market for double disc pulp refiners that produce the stock for newsprint paper machines; used CAD/CAM for 45 years; wrote many design and manufacturing rules for ISO 9000 registration. Home: 189 James Rd Lewisburg PA 17837-8850

LOWE, JOHN STANLEY, lawyer, educator; b. Marion, Ohio, May 11, 1941; s. John Floyd and Florence (Andrews) L.; m. Jacquelyn Taft, Jan. 15, 1968; children: Sarah Staley, John Taft. BA, Denison U., 1963; LLB, Harvard U.,

1966. Bar: Ohio 1966, Okla. 1980, U.S. Supreme Ct. 1972, Tex. 1989. Adminstrv. officer Govt. of Malawi, Limbe, 1966-69; assoc. Emens, Hurd, Kegler & Ritter, Columbus, Ohio, 1970-75; assoc. prof. law U. Toledo, 1975-78; prof. law U. Tulsa, 1978-87, So. Meth. U., Dallas, 1987—. Vis. prof. U. Tex., Austin, 1983; disting. vis. prof. natural resources law U. Denver, 1987; disting. vis. prof. U. N.Mex., 1996; vis. lectr. U. Dundee, Scotland, 2001- . Author: Oil and Gas Law in a Nutshell, 1983, 4th edit., 2002; editor: Cases and Materials on Oil and Gas Law, 1986, 3d edit., 1998; editor Internat. Petroleum Transactions, 1993, 2d edit., 2000, others. V.p., trustee Rocky Mountain Mineral Law Found. Recipient Outstanding Law Rev. Article award Tex. Bar Found., 1988, 96. Mem. ABA (chair natural resources, energy and environ. law 1992-93), Am. Arbitration Assn., Ctr. Am. and Internat. Law (vice chair, mem. exec. com. adv. bd. Energy Law Inst.), CPR Inst. for Dispute Resolution. Episcopalian. Avocation: sailing. Home: 3526 Greenbrier Dr Dallas TX 75225-5003 Office: So Meth U 3315 Daniel Ave Dallas TX 75275-0001 E-mail: jlowe@mail.smu.edu.

LOWE, LOUIS ROBERT, JR. lawyer; b. Indpls., May 30, 1937; BSCE, Purdue U., 1959; LLD, Ind. U., 1967. Bar: U.S. Dist. Ct. (so. dist.) Ind. 1967, U.S. Tax Ct. 1977; lic. profl. engr. Engr. various cons. and engring. cos., Indpls., 1960-64, Ind. Hwy Needs Study, Indpls., 1966-67; ptnr. Lowe, Gray, Steele & Darko, 1967—. Contbr. articles to profl. jours. Sec. English Speaking Union, Indpls., 1967—; trustee Hanover Coll.; elder Second Presbyn. Ch., trustee. Fellow Indpls. Bar Found.; mem. Ind. Bar Assn., Purdue U. Alumni Assn., Indpls. Purdue Assn. (pres. 1968-69), Contemporary Club (pres. 1986-87), Columbia Club (bd. dirs. 1993-96), Columbia Club Found. (pres. 1995-97), Gyro Club (bd. dirs. 1982-85). Home: 535 Pine Dr Indianapolis IN 46260-1452 Office: Bank One Tower Ste 4600 Indianapolis IN 46204-5146

LOWE, MARY FRANCES, federal government official; b. Ft. Meade, Md., Apr. 15, 1952; d. Benno Powers and Peggy Catherine (Moore) L. BA, Coll. William and Mary, 1972; MA, Fletcher Sch. Law and Diplomacy, 1974, MA Law and Diplomacy in, 1975; diplome, Grad. Inst. Internat. Studies U. Geneva, Switzerland, 1975; M.P.H. in epidemiology, Johns Hopkins Sch. Hygiene and Pub. Health, 1986. External collaborator ILO, Geneva, 1974; legis. asst. to U.S. Senator Richard S. Schweiker Washington, 1975-76; profl. staff mem. health and sci. rsch. subcom. U.S. Senate Com. Labor and Human Resources, 1976-81; exec. sec. U.S. Dept. HHS, 1981-85; sr. asst. to commr. program policy FDA, 1985-89; sr. asst. pesticide programs EPA, 1989-96; Pesticide Ch Comms., 1996-97; asst. Office Environ. Policy U.S. Dept. State, Washington, 1997-99; program advisor pesticide program govt. and internat. svcs. EPA, 1999—. Rep. U.S. delegations 34th and 35th World Health Assemblies, Geneva, 1981, 82, NAFTA and WTO Coms., 1995—; alt. trustee Woodrow Wilson Internat. Ctr. Scholars. Mem. Soc. for Epidemiologic Rsch., Am. Assn. World Health, Exec. Women in Govt., Soc. for Chem. Hazard Comm., Soc. Risk Analysis, Washington World Affairs Coun., Delta Omega. Home: 7920 Spotswood Dr Alexandria VA 22308-1125 Office: US EPA 401 M St SW Washington DC 20460-0001 E-mail: lowe.maryfrances@epa.gov.

LOWE, OARIONA, dentist; b. San Francisco, June 17, 1948; d. Van Lowe and Jenny Lowe-Silva; m. Evangelos Rossopoulos, Dec. 18, 1985; children: Thanos G., Jenny Sophia. BS, U. Nev., Las Vegas, 1971; MA, George Washington U., 1977; DDS, Howard U., 1981; pediatric dental cert., UCLA, 1984. Diplomate Am. Bd. Pediatric Dentists 1991. Instr. Coll. Allied Health Scis. Howard U., Washington, 1974-76, asst. prof., 1976-77; research asst. Howard U. Dental Sch., 1977-81; resident gen. practice Eastman Dental Ctr., Rochester, N.Y., 1981-82; dir. dental services City of Hope Med. Ctr., Duarte, Calif., 1984-86; dental staff Whittier (Calif.) Presbyn. Hosp., 1987—, chief dental staff, 1992-94; asst. prof. Loma Linda (Calif.) U., 1991—. Vis. lectr. pediatric dentistry UCLA; mem. oral cancer task force Am. Cancer Soc., Pasadena, Calif., 1985—; internat. spkr. Europe, Asia. Contbr. articles to profl. jours. Del. People to People Internat. Mem. ADA, Am. Soc. Dentistry for Children (v.p.), Nat. Soc. Autistic Children, Calif. Dental Assn., Am. Acad. Pediatric Dentistry (mem. comm. coun. 1999-2001), San Gabriel Valley Dental Soc. (chmn. 1991—), Tri County Dental Soc. (bd. dirs. 1996—), Calif. Dental Assn., Am. Bd. Pediatric Dentists (bd. cert. 1991), Sigma Xi, Alpha Omega. Republican. Presbyterian. Avocations: cooking, bicycling, walking, aerobic dancing. Office: 8135 Painter Ave Ste 202 Whittier CA 90602-3175 *Personal philosophy: If you tell yourself that you can succeed and really believe you can, you will.*

LOWE, PETER STEPHEN, non-profit company executive; b. Lahore, Pakistan, Oct. 23, 1958; s. Eric and Margaret Winnifred (Bradshaw) L.; m. Tamara Angela Forte, May 9, 1987. BA, Carleton U., Ottawa, Ont., Can., 1986. Pres. Lifemasters Tng. Co., Vancouver, B.C., Can., 1981-87, Global Achievers, New Orleans, 1987-90; pres., chief exec. officer Peter Lowe Internat., Inc., Tampa, Fla., 1990—; CEO LifeWin, Inc., 2002—. Mem. Nat. Spkrs. Assn. Office: 4710 Eisenhower Blvd Ste C4 Tampa FL 33634

LOWE, RALPH EDWARD, lawyer; b. Hinsdale, Ill., Nov. 24, 1931; s. Charles Russell and Eva Eleanor (Schroeder) L.; m. Patricia E. Eichhorst, Aug. 23, 1952; children: John Stuart, Michael Kevin, Timothy Edward. BA, Depauw U., 1953; LLB, U. Ill., 1956. Bar: Ill. 1956, U.S. Dist. Ct. (no. dist.) Ill. 1957, Ga. 1974, U.S. Dist. Ct. (no. dist.) Ga. 1980, S.C. 1990. Assoc. Ruddy & Brown, Aurora, Ill., 1956-58; ptnr. Lowe & Richards, 1959-62, Vincent, Lowe & Richards, Aurora, 1963-71; pvt. practice, Aurora and Atlanta, 1974-85; prin. Lowe & Steinmetz, Ltd., 1985-91; pvt. practice, Aurora, Ill., 1972-74, 92—. Chmn. Inter-Am. Devel. Corp., Ill., 1965-67. Office: 407 W Galena Blvd Aurora IL 60506-3946

LOWE, RANDALL BRIAN, lawyer; b. Englewood, N.J., Nov. 20, 1948; BA, U. R.I., 1970; JD, Washington U., 1973. Bar: Ill. 1973, Conn. 1975, D.C. 1976, U.S. Ct. Appeals (2d and D.C. cirs.) 1976, N.J. 1977, U.S. Dist. Ct. N.J. 1977, U.S. Ct. Appeals (3d cir.) 1977, U.S. Ct. Appeals (9th cir.) 1979, N.Y. 1980, U.S. Dist. Ct. (ea. and so. dists.) N.Y. 1980. Atty. Callis & Filcoff, Granite City, Ill., 1973-75, AT&T, Washington and N.Y.C., 1975-78, ITT Corp, 1978-83, Surrey & Morse, Washington, 1983-86; ptnr. Jones, Day, Reavis & Pogue, 1986-94, Piper & Marbury, Washington, 1994-99, of counsel, 1999-2000; exec. v.p./CLO Prism Comms. Svcs., 1999-2001; ptnr. Davis Wright Tremaine, Washington, 2001—. Office: 1500 K St NW Ste 450 Washington DC 20005-1272

LOWE, ROBERT CHARLES, lawyer, banker; b. Seattle, Jan. 15, 1927; s. Martin M. and Helen (Yaster) L.; m. Hope Lucille Sperstad, Mar. 21, 1952; children: Karen, Karlton, Nelson, Inez. BA, U. Wash., 1953; LL.B., U. Denver, 1959. Bar: Alaska 1961. Accountant Haskins & Sells (C.P.A.s), Los Angeles, 1953-54; agt. Internal Revenue Service, 1954-57; atty. State Alaska, 1960; mem. firm Hughes, Thorsness, Lowe, Gantz & Clark, Anchorage, 1960-75; pres. Safeco Title Agy., Inc., 1975-79; chmn. bd. Peoples Bank & Trust Co., Anchorage. Served with USNR, 1944-46. Mem. Am., Alaska, Anchorage bar assns., Anchorage Estate Planning Council (pres. 1970), Rotary. Home: 17419 N Rainbow Cir Surprise AZ 85374-3594

LOWE, ROBERT CHARLES, lawyer; b. New Orleans, July 3, 1949; s. Carl Randall and Antonia (Morgan) L.; m. Theresa Louise Acree, Feb. 4, 1978; 1 child, Nicholas Strafford. BA, U. New Orleans, 1971; JD, La. State U., 1975. Bar: La. 1975, U.S. Dist. Ct. (ea. dist.) La. 1975, U.S. Ct. Appeals (5th cir.) 1980, U.S. Dist. Ct. (we. dist.) La. 1978, U.S. Supreme Ct. 1982. Assoc. Sessions, Fishman, Rosenson, Boisfontaine, and Nathan, New Orleans, 1975-80, ptnr., 1980-87, Lowe, Stein, Hoffman, Allweiss and Hauver, New Orleans, 1987—. Author: Louisiana Divorce, West Pub. Co., 1984; mem. La. Law Rev., 1974-75; contbr. articles top profl. jours. Named one of Best Lawyers in Am. ann., 1983—. Mem. ABA, La. State Bar Assn. (chmn. family law sect. 1984-85), La. Assn. Def. Counsel, New Orleans Bar Assn. (chmn. family law sect. 1991-92), La. State Law Inst., La. Trial Lawyers Assn., Order of Coif, Phi Kappa Phi. Republican. Home: 9625 Garden Oak Ln New Orleans LA 70123-2005 Office: 701 Poydras St Ste 3600 New Orleans LA 70139-7735

LOWE, ROBERT EDWARD, financial company executive; b. Winnipeg, Man., Can., Oct. 31, 1940; s. Mark Currie and Florence Irene L. Lowe; children: Susan Patricia, Donna Jane, Mark William. MBA, York U., Toronto, 1975. Chartered acct. Ptnr. PricewaterhouseCoopers, Toronto, 1971, dir. insurance, 1996—. Lt. Can. Army Res., 1958-61. Mem. Insolvency Inst. Can., Toronto Golf Club, Nat. Club. Mem. Conservative Party. Presbyterian. Avocations: golf, sailing. Office: PricewaterhouseCoopers Royal Trust Tower Tor-Dom Ctr Ste 3000 PO Box 82 Toronto ON Canada M5K 1G8

LOWE, ROBERT STANLEY, lawyer; b. Herman, Nebr., Apr. 23, 1923; s. Stanley Robert and Ann Marguerite (Feese) L.; m. Anne Kirtland Selden, Dec. 19, 1959; children: Robert James, Margaret Anne. AB, U. Nebr., 1947, JD, 1949. Bar: Wyo. 1949. Ptnr. McAvoy & Lowe, Newcastle, 1949—51, Hickey & Lowe, Rawlins, 1951—55; county and pros. atty., 1955—59; pvt. practice, 1959—67; assoc. dir. Am. Judicature Soc., Chgo., 1967—74; gen. counsel True Oil Co. and affiliates, 1974—98, of counsel, 1998—99. Bd. dirs. Hilltop Nat. Bank, Casper, sec., 1981—; legal adv. divsn. Nat. Ski Patrol Sys., 1975-88; city atty. City of Rawlins, 1963-65; atty., asst. sec. Casper Mountain Ski Patrol, 1988—. Chmn. Casper C. of C. Military Affairs Com., 1995-2000; mem. Wyo. Ho. of Reps., 1952-54; bd. dirs. Vols. in Probation, 1969-82; leader lawyer del. to China, People to People, 1986; mem. Wyo. Vets. Affairs Commn., 1994—, chmn., 1996—; mem. legis. com. United Vets. Coun. Wyo., 1993—; trustee Troopers Found., Inc., 1994—, pres., 1994-99; pres. Casper WWII Commemorative Assn., 1995-96, Navy League Wyo. Coun. (pres. 1997-00); state pres. Wyo., 2000—. Recipient Dedicated Community Worker award Rawlins Jr. C. of C., 1967, Yellow merit star award Nat. Ski Patrol System, 1982, 85, 87, 88, Small Bus. Administrate Vet. Advocate award, 1998, Disting. Svc. award Disabled Am. Vets. Dept., 1994. Fellow Am. Bar Found. (life); mem. VFW (life mem.; post adv. 1991-96, nat. aide-de-camp 1993-94, 98-99, judge adv. dist. 3 Dept. Wyo., 1994—, mil. order of cootie grand judge adv. 1994—), ABA (sec. jud. adminstrn. divsn. lawyers conf., exec. com. 1975-76, chmn. 1977-78, chmn. judicial qualification and selection com. 1986-93, coun. jud. adminstrn. divsn. 1977-78, mem. com. to implement jud. adminstrn. stds. 1978-83, Ho. of Dels. state bar del. 1978-80, 86-87, state del. 1987-93, Assembly del. 1980-83, mem. standing com. on the fed. judiciary 1997-99, ad hoc com. state justice initiatives 1997-99), Am. Judicature Soc. (dir. 1961-67, 85-89, bd. editors 1975-77, Herbert Harley award 1974), Wyo. State Bar (chmn. com. on cts. 1961-67, 77-87), Nebr. State Bar Assn., Ill. State Bar Assn., D.C. Bar, Inter-Am. Bar Assn., Selden Soc., Inst. Jud. Adminstrn., Rocky Mountain Oil and Gas Assn. (legal com. 1976-99, chmn. 1979-82, 90-91), Rocky Mountain Mineral Law Found. (trustee 1980-94), Am. Law Inst. (life), Order of Coif, Delta Theta Phi (dist. chancellor 1982-83, chief justice 1983-93, assoc. justice 1993—; Percy J. Power Meml. award 1983, Gold Medallion award 1990), Casper Rotary Club (pres. 1985-86), Casper Rotary Found. (dir. 1990—, sec. 1990-00). Mem. Ch. of Christ, Scientist. Home and Office: 97 Primrose Casper WY 82604-4018 Office: 5905 Cy Ave Casper WY 82604-4101

LOWELL, BRIANT LINDSAY, policy educator; b. San Francisco, May 19, 1955; s. James and Nada P. Lowell; m. Tammy Jo Tisdal, Aug. 1, 1960 (div. Apr. 1990); m. Michele F. Dandrea, Sept. 20, 1957. BA with honors, U. Utah, 1978, MA, 1980; PhD in Sociology, Brown U., 1985. Postdoctoral rsch. assoc. U. Tex., Austin, 1984—88; rsch. analyst U.S. Dept. Labor, Washington, 1988—95; asst. nat. coord. U.S./Mex. Bi-Nat. Study, 1995—97; dir. policy rsch. U.S. Commn. on Immigration Reform, 1995—97; dir. rsch. Inst. for the Study Internat. Migration, Georgetown U., 1998—2001, Pew Hispanic Ctr., U. So. Calif., Washington, 2002—. Vis. faculty mem. Woodrow Wilson Sch., Princeton U.. Author: (book) Scandinavian Exodus: Demography and Social Development of 19th Century Rural Communities, 1987; editor: Foreign emporary Workers in America: Policies that Benefit America, 1999; co-editor (with Rodolfo de la Garza): Sending Money Home: Hispanic Remittances and Community Development, 2002; contbr. Recipient Coray award for outstanding undergrad., U. Utah, 1978, Dissertation Rsch. award, Brown U., 1982, 1984, Rsch. award, Am.-Scandinavian Found., 1986, Spl. Achievement award, U.S. Dept. Labor, 1989, 1992, 1994, 1995, Exceptional Achievement award, 1991, Spl. Achievement award, U.S. Commn. on Immigration Reform, 1996, 1997, Spl. Recognition award, Georgetown U., 1999, 2000, 2001; fellow Grad. fellow in population studies, NIH, 1981—83. Mem. Population Assn. Am. Avocations: skiing, blading, hiking, playing the saxophone. Office: Pew Hispanic Ctr 1919 M St NW Washington DC 20036

LOWELL, H. BRET, lawyer; b. N.Y., Aug. 5, 1953; s. Stanley and Elaine Lowell; m. Holly Ross, June 20, 1982; 1 child, Michael Stuart. BS in Econs., SUNY, Buffalo, 1975; JD, Georgetown U., 1978. Bar: D.C. 1978, U.S. Dist. Ct. D.C. 1979, U.S. Ct. Appeals (D.C. cir.) 1979. Assoc. Brownstein Zeidman and Lore, Washington, 1978-85; ptnr. Brownstein & Zeidman, 1985-96, Rudnick & Wolfe, Washington, 1996-99, Piper Marbury Rudnick & Wolfe, Washington, 1999—. Author: Regulation of Buying and Selling a Franchise, 1983, 1997, Franchising, 1989, Franchise Sales and Full Agreement Compliance, 1990, Multiple-Unit Franchising: The Key to Rapid System Growth, 1991; coord. (book) Survey of Foreign Laws Affecting International Franchising, 1982; editor Franchise Law Jour., 1984-88, Franchise Law Compliance Manual, 2000. Mem. ABA (forum on franchising, governing com. 1988-97, chair 1992-95, gen. practice sect., co-chair franchise law com. 1989-92), Internat. Bar Assn., N.Am. Securities Adminstrs. Assn. (franchise advisor 1989—). Office: Piper Marbury Rudnick & Wolfe LLP 1200 Nineteenth St Washington DC 20036-2412

LOWELL, HOWARD PARSONS, government records administrator; b. Rockland, Maine, May 10, 1945; s. Chauncey Vernon Lowell and Delia Coffin (Parsons) Morey; m. Marcia Barrell, Feb. 15, 1969 (div. 1980); m. Charlesa Ann Gatson, July 27, 1985, 1 stepson, Garrett Timmons. BA, U. Me., Orono, 1967; MS, Simmons Coll., 1974. Adminstrn. svcs. officer Maine state archives, Augusta, 1968-72; ednl. specialist Mass. bur. libr. ext., Boston, 1974-75; dir. Revere (Mass.) Pub. Libr., 1975-76; freelance cons. Salem, Oreg., 1976-81, Denver, 1976-81; adminstr. Okla. resources br. Okla. Dept. Librs., Oklahoma City, 1981-89; archivist and records administrator State of Del., 1990-2000; dep. asst. archivist for records svcs. (Washington) Nat. Archives and Records Adminstrn., College Park, Md., 2000—. Acting dir. N.E. Document Conservation Ctr., Andover, Mass., 1978. Commr. Nat. Hist. Publs. and Records Commn., 1997-2000. Mem. Acad. Cert. Archivists, Nat. Assn. Govt. Archives and Records Adminstrs. (bd. dirs. 1985-87, 1995-96, pres. 1992-94), Phi Beta Kappa, Phi Kappa Phi, Phi Alpha Theta, Beta Phi Mu. Democrat. Mem. Unitarian Ch. Office: Nat Archives for Records Adminstrn 8601 Adelphi Rd College Park MD 20740-6001

LOWELL, LAURETTA JANE, craftsperson, poet; b. Gunnison, Colo., 1946; d. Howard Milton and Linnia Marie Lowell; m. Robert Bruce Campbell, 1994. Assoc. Gen. Studies, Pikes Peak C.C., 1987; student, Mesa State Coll., 1991, 99. Nurses aide St. Francis Hosp., Colorado Springs, Colo., 1978-85; owner Light in Leather, Delta; owner house cleaning bus. Colorado Springs, 1977-87; ptnr., co-owner Light in Leather/Green Knight Pub., Delta, Colo., 1996—. Author, pub.: Selected Poems of A Religious Nature, 1996, Sample a Poetry Treat, 1997; included in Best Poems of 1998 and numerous other anthologies (editors awards); lyricist Summer Song, 1998. Organizer reunion 1264th Army Engineer Battalion, Delta, 1991-93; leader 4-H, Colorado Springs and Delta, 1984-90; advocate for mental health issues Colo. Health Networks, Colorado Springs, 1996-98; advocate Columbine Group, 1992—. Phi Theta Kappa scholar, 1985, Colo. State Coll. scholarship, 1965. Fellow United Meth. Women; mem. Internat. Soc. Poets (life mem., Poetry Hall of Fame 1996). Avocations: camping, fishing, sewing, cooking, writing. Office: Light in Leather/Green Knight Pub 263 1575 Rd Delta CO 81416-9794

LOWELL, ROLAND M. lawyer; b. Three Rivers, Mich. m. Ruby Ellon Lowell. BA, Kalamazoo Coll., 1969; JD, Vanderbilt U., 1972. Bar: Tenn. 1972, U.S. Ct. Appeals (6th cir.) 1975, U.S. Supreme Ct. 1976, U.S. Dist. Ct. (mid. dist.) Tenn. 1984, U.S. Dist. Ct. (we. dist.) Tenn. 1992. Ptnr. Ludwick & Lowell, Nashville, 1984-87, Lowell & Bradley, Nashville, 1987-91; atty., of counsel Leitner Warner Moffitt Dooley Carpender & Napolitan, 1991-95; atty. Bruce Weathers Corley Dughman & Lyle, 1995—. Mem. Am. Moving and Storage Assn. (agt.), Am. Process Agts. (agt.). Office: Bruce Weathers Corley et al 20th Fl Ste 2075 First American Center Nashville TN 37238

LOWELL, STANLEY EDGAR, accountant; b. N.Y.C., Oct. 12, 1923; s. Benjamin and Valerie (Steinberg) L. Student Tchrs. Coll., Columbia U., 1945; BBA cum laude, CCNY, 1948. CPA, N.Y. Staff acct. S.D. Leidesdorf & Co., Chgo., 1952-54; chief acct. Polyplastex United Inc., Union, N.J., 1955-57; chief auditor Hudson Pulp & Paper Inc., N.Y.C., 1957-62, chief acct., 1962-64; internal audit mgr. Screen Games div. Columbia Picture Industries, 1966-74; chief auditor Alpha Metals, Inc., Jersey City, 1974-77; asst. dir. internal audit CUNY, N.Y.C., 1977-95. Served with USAAF, 1943-44. Mem. Am. Inst. C.P.A.s, N.Y. State Soc. C.P.A.s, Inst. Internal Auditors (cert. internal auditor), Internat. Platform Assn. Home: 302 W 12th St New York NY 10014-6032

LOWELL, STANLEY HERBERT, lawyer; b. Apr. 13, 1919; s. Isidore and Mildred (Cohen) Lowenbraun; m. Vivian Abrams, Mar. 29, 1947 (div. 1973); children: Jeffrey, Darcy, Lauri; m. Leona Schaevitz, June 20, 1974; stepchildren: Barry S., Scott S. BS in Social Sci., CCNY, 1939; LLB, Harvard U., 1942; LLD (hon.), CUNY, 1981. Bar: N.Y. 1942. Asst. U.S. atty., N.Y., 1943-47; ptnr. Lowenbraun & Lowell, N.Y.C., 1947-58, Lowell & Karassik and predecessors, N.Y.C., 1966-78, Fink, Weinberger, Fredman, Berman & Lowell, 1978-93; of counsel Goodkind, Labaton, Rudoff & Sucharow, 1994-99. Former lectr. CCNY; vis. prof. Grad. Sch., CUNY; adj. prof. Fordham U. Sch. Social Svcs. Asst. to borough pres., Manhattan, 1950-53; exec. asst. to mayor, N.Y.C., 1954-58, dep. mayor, 1958; chmn. N.Y.C. Commn. Human Rights, 1960-65; U.S. pub. del. Madrid Conf. Helsinki Final Act, 1979; chmn. N.Y.C. com. Am. Jewish Tercentenary; past chmn. divsn. lawyers; trustee United Jewish Appeal-Fedn. Jewish Philanthropies, bd. dirs., 1962-94; chmn. Nat. Conf. on Soviet Jewry, 1974-76; past chmn. Greater N.Y. Conf. on Soviet Jewry; mem. praesidium Brussels World Conf. on Soviet Jewry; past chmn. Com. for Pub. Higher Edn.; past pres., chmn. Citizens Com. for Children of N.Y.; past vice chmn. Nat. Jewish Coun. Pub. Affairs, Del. Dem. Nat. Conv., 1960, 64, 68; exec. com. Dem. State Com., 1960-68; trustee Jewish Communal Fund N.Y., 1981-91; trustee-at-large, v.p. Jewish Cmty. Rels. Coun., N.Y., 1982-2000; hon. trustee, past pres. N.Y. Shakespeare Festival; spl. counsel pro bono Kings County Hosp. investigation; mem. Mayor's Commn. on Health & Hosp. Corp., 1991; co-chair Friends of City Univ., 1998—. Recipient medal City N.Y., 1965, John F. Kennedy Peace award Jewish Nat. Fund, 1996, Judge Joseph Proskauer award Lawyers United Jewish Appeal-Fedn., John H. Finley medal CCNY Alumni Assn., 1980, Pres.'s medal, 1980; Establishment of Stanley H. Lowell Ann. Humanitarian award N.Y.C. Commn. on Human Rights, 1988. Mem. N.Y. State Bar Assn., Assn. Bar City of N.Y., Harvard Law Sch. Assn. N.Y. (past trustee), Coll. City N.Y. Alumni Assn. (past pres.) Home: 30 Agnew Farm Rd Armonk NY 10504-1371 Office: 700 White Plains Post Rd Scarsdale NY 10583

LOWELL, VIRGINIA LEE, librarian; b. San Jose, Calif., Nov. 21, 1940; d. Earnest S. and Dorothy (Givens) Greene; children: Michael Edward, Christopher Scott. Student, Reed Coll, 1958-61; BA, U. Calif., Berkeley, 1963; MSLS, Western Res. U., 1964. Cataloger Wittenberg U., Springfield, Ohio, 1965-66, John Carroll U., Cleve., 1966-68, Cuyahoga Community Coll., Cleve., 1968-70, cons., instr., 1970; head catalog dept. Cuyahoga County Pub. Library, 1976-78; dir. tech. svcs. Cuyahoga County Pub. Libr., 1979-89; dir. Jackson (Mich.) Dist. Libr., 1989—98; state libr. State of Hawaii, 1998—. Chmn. bd. trustees Ohionet, Columbus, 1987-89. Mem. ALA, Ohio Libr. Assn. (coord. automation and tech. div. 1988—), No. Ohio Tech. Svc. Librs. (chmn. 1988-89), Ohio Women Librs. (treas. 1987-89), Am. Mgmt. Assn., Mich. Libr. Assn. Democrat. Roman Catholic. Avocation: choral singing. Office: 465 S King St Rm B-1 Honolulu HI 96813*

LOWENBERG, GEORGINA GRACE, elementary school educator; b. El Paso, Tex., Feb. 15, 1944; d. Eduardo Antonio and Grace Elizabeth (Fletcher) Orellana; m. Edward Daniel Lowenberg, June 14, 1968, 1968 (div. 1985); 1 child, Jennifer Anne. BSEd, U. Tex., El Paso, 1965, postgrad., 1965-66, U. St. Thomas, 1983. Permanent profl. teaching cert., Tex. Tchr. 5th grade El Paso Pub. Sch. Dist., 1965-70; tchr. 3d grade gifted, talented Ysleta Ind. Sch. Dist., El Paso, 1980—. Mem. com. Tex. State Textbook Selection Com., Austin, 1984-85, Tex. State TEAMS Math Adv. Com., Austin, 1986-87; sci. presentor Silver Burdett, Albuquerque, 1985-86; critic reader Scott-Foresman, Dallas, 1986; pres., v.p. Scotsdale Elem. Sch. PTA, El Paso, 1976-83; v.p. Eastwood Middle Sch. PTA, El Paso, 1984-85; mem. Eastwood Heights Elem. Sch. PTA, 1985-87; sec. Eastwood High Sch. Band Boosters, El Paso, 1985-89, Speech Boosters, 1986-88; life mem. Tex. State PTA, 1981—. Troop leader Brownie and Jr. Girl Scouts Am., El Paso, 1977-82; dir. Eaglette Dance Team, 1994—. Named Tchr. of Yr., Eastwood Heights Elem. Mem. Assn. Tex. Profl. Educators (regional treas. 1987-88). Roman Catholic.

LOWENBERG, LORRAINE LYNETTE, psychiatric and mental health nurse; b. Donnellson, Iowa, Apr. 20, 1940; d. Arnold H. and Frances (Neff) L. BA in Biology, Bluffton (Ohio) Coll., 1962; MBA, Ind. U., South Bend, 1984; ADN, Southwestern Mich. Coll., 1991. RN, Ind.; cert. psychiat. mental health nurse. Adminstrv. sec. Miles Labs., Inc., Elkhart, Ind., 1969-86; exec. sec. Elkhart County Health Dept., 1987-88; asst. to the pres. Goshen (Ind.) Coll., 1988-89; staff nurse Oaklawn Hosp., Goshen, 1991, Elkhart Gen. Hosp., 1991-92; staff nurse inpatient unit Otis R. Bowen Ctr. Human Svcs., Warsaw, 1993-96; staff RN Iowa Dept. Human Svcs., Mental Health Inst., Mt. Pleasant, 2000-01. Mem.: Am. Psychiat. Nurses Assn. Avocations: traveling, hiking, reading. Home: 715 Cleveland Ave Apt 6 Keokuk IA 52632

LOWENBRAUN, SOLOMON MORTIMER, lawyer; b. N.Y.C., Feb. 1, 1921; s. Harry and Mary L.; m. Florence M. Grossman, Aug. 7, 1945; children: Dale Lowenbraun Boyle, Cathy Lowenbraun McKeon, Leslie Lowenbraun Weitzman. BS in Social Sci., CCNY, 1941; JD, Fordham U., 1949. Bar: N.Y. 1950, U.S. Dist. Ct. (so. dist.) N.Y. 1950, U.S. Dist. Ct. (ea. dist.) N.Y. 1953, U.S. Supreme Ct. 1978. Atty. pvt. practice, N.Y.C., 1950—. Lt. comdr. USNR, 1942-45. Mem. N.Y. State Bar Assn., Queens County Bar Assn. Jewish. Home: 16625 Powells Cove Blvd Beechhurst NY 11357-1545 Office: 425 Northern Blvd Ste 27 Great Neck NY 11021

LOWENFELD, ANDREAS FRANK, law educator, arbitrator; b. Berlin, May 30, 1930; s. Henry and Yela (Herschkowitsch) L.; m. Elena Machado, Aug. 11, 1962; children: Julian, Marianna. AB magna cum laude, Harvard U., 1951, LLB magna cum laude, 1955. Bar: N.Y. 1955, U.S. Supreme Ct. 1961. Assoc. Hyde and de Vries, N.Y.C., 1957-61; spl. asst. to legal adv. U.S. State Dept., 1961-63, asst. legal adviser for econ. affairs, 1963-65, dep. legal adviser, 1965-66; fellow John F. Kennedy Inst. Politics Harvard U., Cambridge, Mass., 1966-67; prof. law Sch. Law NYU, N.Y.C., 1967—, Charles L. Denison prof. law, 1981-94, Herbert and Rose Rubin prof. internat. law, 1994—. Arbitrator internat. comml. panels ICC. Author: (with Abram Chayes and Thomas Ehrlich) International Legal Process, 1968-69, Aviation Law, Cases and Materials, 1972, 2d edit., 1981, International Economic Law, vol. I, 1975, 3d edit., 1996, vol. II, 1976, 2d edit., 1982, vol. III, 1977, 2d edit., 1983, vol. IV, 1977, 2d edit., 1984, vol. VI, 1979, 2d edit., 1983, Conflict of Laws, Federal, State and International Perspectives, 1986, 2d edit., 1998, International Litigation and Arbitration, 1993, 2d edit., 2002, International Litigation: The Quest for Reasonableness, 1996, The Role of Government in International Trade: Essays Over Three Decades, 2000; editor, co-author: International Economic Law, 2002, Expropriation in the Americas: A Comparative Law Study, 1971; assoc. reporter Am. Law Inst. Restatement on Foreign Relations Law; co-reporter Am. Law Inst. Project on Internat. Jurisdiction and Judgments; contbr. articles and book revs. on pub. internat. law, internat. econ. law, air law, conflict of laws, arbitration, history and politics to profl. jours. Mem.: ABA, Internat. Acad. Comparative Law, Inst. de Droit Internat., Coun. Fgn. Rels., Am. Law Inst., Am. Arbitration Assn. (arbitrator), Am. Soc. Internat. Law, Assn. of Bar of City of N.Y., Gray's Inn (hon. assoc.). Home: 5776 Palisade Ave Bronx NY 10471-1212 Office: NYU Sch Law Sch Law 40 Washington Sq S New York NY 10012-1005 E-mail: andreas.lowenfeld@NYU.edu.

LOWENFELS, FRED M. lawyer; b. Richmond, Va., Mar. 22, 1944; s. Fred C. and Joan (Weber) L.; m. Joan Roberta Brafman, June 10, 1974; children: Erica Anne, Helene Beth. AB, Harvard U., 1965, JD, 1968; postgrad., Univ. Libre de Bruxelles, 1968-69. Bar: N.Y. 1969. Assoc. Wolf, Haldenstein, Adler, Freeman & Herz, N.Y.C., 1970-74; sr. v.p., gen. counsel Transammonia Inc., 1974—. Trustee Jewish Home and Hosp., N.Y.C., 1974—, chmn. bd. trustees, 2001—. Mem. Assn. Bar. City of N.Y., Am. Corp. Counsel Assn., Harvard Club N.Y.C. Office: Transammonia Inc 350 Park Ave Rm 400 New York NY 10022-6022

LOWENFELS, LEWIS DAVID, lawyer; b. N.Y.C., June 9, 1935; s. Seymour and Jane (Phillips) L.; m. Fern Gelford, Aug. 15, 1965; children: Joshua, Jacqueline. BA magna cum laude, Harvard U., 1957, LLB, 1961. Bar: N.Y. 1961; lic. corp. and securities atty. Ptnr. Tolins & Lowenfels, N.Y.C., 1967—. Adj. prof. Seton Hall U. Law Sch; lectr. Practicing Law Inst., Southwestern Legal Found., U. Minn. Fed. Bar Assn., 1972; pub. gov. Am. Stock Exch.,

1993-96. Co-author: Bromberg and Lowenfels on Securities Fraud and Commodities Fraud, 6 vols., 1999; contbr. articles to profl. jours. With USAR, 1957-63. Mem. ABA (fed. regulation of securities com. 1978—, lectr.), N.Y. County Lawyers Assn. (securities and exchanges com. 1974—), Phi Beta Kappa, Harvard Club. Avocations: reading, writing, athletics. Office: Tolins & Lowenfels 747 3d Ave 19th Fl New York NY 10017-1028 E-mail: Lew@TolinsLowenfels.com.

LOWENHAUPT, CHARLES ABRAHAM, lawyer; b. St. Louis, May 19, 1947; s. Henry Cronbach and Cecile (Koven) L.; m. Rosalyn Lee Sussman, Dec. 28, 1969; children: Elizabeth Anne, Rebecca Jane. BA cum laude, Harvard U., 1969; JD magna cum laude, U. Mich., 1973. Bar: Mo. 1973, U.S. Dist. Ct. (ea. dist.) Mo. 1975, U.S. Ct. Appeals (8th cir.) 1975, U.S. Tax Ct. 1975, U.S. Ct. Claims 1975, U.S. Supreme Ct. 1987. Law clk. to presiding justice U.S. Tax Ct., Washington, 1973-75; ptnr. Lowenhaupt, Chasnoff, Armstrong & Mellitz, St. Louis, 1977-94; mem. adv. faculty Inst. for Pvt. Investors, 1991-93; mem. Lowenhaupt & Chasnoff, LLC, St. Louis, 1994—; emeritus mem. adv. faculty Inst. for Pvt. Investors, 1995—. Spkr. Nat. Assn. Ind. Schs., St. Louis Assn. Legal Assts., Washington U. Bus. Sch., Inst. for Pvt. Investors, numerous others; mem. adv. bd. dirs. Textile Mus., Washington; cmty. outreach adv. coun. St. Louis Coll. Pharmacy, 1998—; lectr. law dept. Fudan U., Shanghai, 1999. Bd. dirs. Ctrl. West End Assn., Inc., St. Louis, 1976-80, Temple Emanuel, St. Louis, 1982-89, Butterfly Ho., St. Louis, sec., 1995—; bd. dirs. Craft Alliance St. Louis, 1987-90, Helicon Found., San Diego, St. Louis Met. Assn. for Philanthropy, St. Louis Regional Med. Ctr. Found., 1993-98, chmn. bd. dirs., 1995-98; bd. dirs. Crown Ctr. St. Louis sect., Nat. Coun. Jewish Women, 1994-96, St. Louis Zoo Found., 1993-99, sec., 1995-98; mem. St. Louis Zool. Subdist. commn., 1989-92; bd. govs. Clements Libr. Assocs., U. Mich., 1997—; mem. St. Louis Cmty. Sch. Assn., 1981-89; pres. Assn. St. Louis U. Librs., Inc., 1982-83; mem. exec. com. U.S.-China C. of C. Midwestern Regional Office; mem. George W. Warren Brown Sch. Social Work nat. coun. Washington U., 2000—; bd. dirs. Found. for Fiduciary Studies, Pitts., 2000—; mem. campaign cabinet Cath. Cmty. Svcs. and Archbishops Commn. on Cmty. Health, 2001. Recipient St. Louis Argus Disting. Citizen award, 2001, Cmty. Svc. award, Young Dems. of St. Louis, 1996. Mem. ABA (tax section, estate and gift section, real property section, probate and trust law, task force legal financial planning, chmn. generation-skipping transfer tax subcom., estate and gift tax com. tax sect. 1995—), Mo. Bar Assn. (tax section, probate and trust section), Bar Assn. of Met. St. Louis (tax section, real property and development sect.), Order of the Coif, St. Louis Estate Planning Coun., Mo. Athletic Club, Harvard Club of N.Y.C., Noonday Club, Harvard Club of St. Louis (pres. 1991-92, chmn. schs. and scholarshop com. 1989-91). Home: 801 S Skinker Blvd Saint Louis MO 63105-3269 Office: Lowenhaupt & Chasnoff LLC 10 S Broadway Ste 600 Saint Louis MO 63102-1733

LOWENKRON, RUTH, lawyer; b. Patchogue, N.Y., Feb. 27, 1960; d. Hans and Irene (Markwald) L. BA, Cornell U., 1981; JD, CUNY, 1986. Bar: N.J. 1986, U.S. Dist. Ct. N.J. 1986, N.Y. 1987, U.S. Dist. Ct. (so. and ea. dists.) N.Y. 1991, U.S. Ct. Appeals (2nd cir.) 1993, U.S. Ct. Appeals (3d cir.) 1999, U.S. Supreme Ct. 1993. Staff atty. Community Health Law Project, East Orange, N.J., 1986-90, N.Y. Lawyers for the Pub. Interest, Inc., N.Y.C., 1990-95, dir. Disability Law Ctr., 1995-99; sr. staff atty. Edn. Law Ctr., Newark, 1999—. Adj. assoc. prof. social work and law, disability law Seton Hall U., 1989—; adj. assoc. prof. disability law Law Sch. CUNY, N.Y.C. Mem. Essex County Bar Assn. (com. on rights of persons with disabilities), ACLU (vol. atty. N.J. chpt.), N.Y. State Bar Assn. (com. on mental and phys. disability). Home: 277 W 10th St Apt 5N New York NY 10014-2552 Office: Edn Law Ctr 155 Washington St Ste 205 Newark NJ 07102 E-mail: lowenkronr@aol.com.

LOWENSTAM, SUSAN GUGGENHEIM, lawyer; b. N.Y.C., Sept. 17, 1942; d. Sig and Ann Ackerman Guggenheim; m. Michael Lowenstam, Oct. 2, 1977; previous marriage Guy Oakes. BA in Polit. Sci., U. Chgo., 1963, postgrad., 1965-66, Free U. Berlin, 1963-64, Cornell U., 1964-65, U. Freiburg, Germany, 1966-67; JD, NYU, 1969; postgrad., Def. Sys. Mgmt. Coll., 1991, Harvard U., 1992. Atty. The Port Authority N.Y. and N.J., N.Y.C., 1969-77; pvt. practice law L.A., 1977-79, 99; v.p., gen. counsel, sec. The Aerospace Corp., 1979-94, OCLC Online Computer Libr. Ctr., Inc., Dublin, 1994-97; v.p., gen. counsel, sec., head human resources Direct Express, L.A., 1998; v.p., gen. counsel, sec. Gen. Atomics, San Diego, 2000—. Reviewer Nat. Tech. Transfer Ctr., 1999—. Fulbright scholar, 1963, Floyd Russell Mechem prize scholar, 1965; German Govt. fellow, 1963, Woodrow Wilson fellow, 1964. Mem. ABA (gen. counsel com. pub. contract law, employment law and internat. law sects.), Army Sci. Bd., Phi Beta Kappa. Office: General Atomics 3550 General Atomics Ct San Diego CA 92121 E-mail: susan.lowenstam@gat.com.

LOWENSTEIN, ALAN VICTOR, lawyer; b. Newark, Aug. 30, 1913; s. Isaac and Florence (Cohen) L.; m. Amy Lieberman, Nov. 23, 1938; children: John, Roger, Jane Lowenstein Forsyth. AB, U. Mich., 1933; MA, U. Chgo., 1935; LLB, Harvard U., 1936. Bar: N.J. 1936. Practiced in Newark and Roseland, 1936—; sr. partner Lowenstein, Sandler, PC, 1961—. Assoc. atty. Temporary Nat. Econ. Com., 1938-39; asst. prof. Rutgers U. Law Sch., 1951-57; chmn. N.J. Corp. Law Revision Commn., 1959-72; spl. hearing officer Dept. Justice, 1961-65; chmn. bd. United Steel & Aluminum Corp., 1976-96. Pres. Jewish Community Council Essex County, 1950-53, United Way Essex and West Hudson, 1953-55; chmn. Newark Charter Commn., 1953, Newark Citizens Com. Mcpl. Govt., 1954-58, Newark Community Survey, 1959-60; v.p. Council Jewish Fedns., 1965-68, assoc. treas., 1981; pres. N.J. Symphony Orch., 1971-73, chmn. bd., 1973-76; mem. adv. council Rutgers U. Sch. Social Work, 1955-64; vice chmn. Liberty State Park Devel. Corp., 1984—; bd. overseers Rutgers U. Found., 1994-2000. Recipient Brotherhood award Nat. Conf. Christians and Jews, 1972, Trustees award for Disting. Community Service, N.J. Inst. Tech., 1984, Equal Justice award Legal Services N.J./N.J. State Bar Assn., 1988. Mem. ABA, N.J. Bar Assn., Essex County Bar Assn. (Pro-Bono Achievement award 1994), Am. Judicature Soc., Order of Coif, Phi Beta Kappa (v.p. N.J. 1951-52), Phi Kappa Phi, Tau Kappa Alpha. Home: 5 Turnberry Ct Maplewood NJ 07040-2423 also: 1872 Arnold Bay Rd Vergennes VT 05491-9152 Office: Lowenstein Sandler PC 65 Livingston Ave Ste 9 Roseland NJ 07068-1725 E-mail: alowenstein@lowenstein.com.

LOWENSTEIN, ALFRED SAMUEL, cardiologist; b. Frankfurt, Germany, Oct. 19, 1931; came to U.S., 1938; s. Ernst and Babette (Stern) L.; m. Mirjam Stern, June, 1957 (div. Feb. 1981); children: Esther, David, Eve; m. Lucy Zilbersweig, Nov. 1, 1981; children: Elie, Daniel, Ariel. BA cum laude with honors in German, NYU, 1953; MD, SUNY, Bklyn., 1957. Intern Montefiore Hosp., Bronx, N.Y., 1957-58, resident, 1959-60, fellow in cardiology, 1960-61; resident Bklyn. VA Hosp., 1958-59; fellow in cardiology St. Vincent's Hosp., N.Y.C., 1970-72; internist Far Rockaway, N.Y., 1963-70; attending cardiologist Beilenson Hosp., Petah Tikva, Israel, 1972-75; pvt. practice Cedarhurst, N.Y., 1975-93, Hewlett, 1993—. Capt. U.S. Army, 1961-63. Fellow Am. Coll. Cardiology; mem. N.Y. State Nassau County Med. Soc., Phi Beta Kappa. Jewish. Office: 1490 Broadway Hewlett NY 11557-1432

LOWENSTEIN, DEREK IRVING, physicist; b. Hampton Court, Eng., Apr. 26, 1943; came to U.S., 1946; s. Siegfried and Ilse (Mildenberg) L.; m. Elaine Hartmann, July 6, 1968; children: Jessica R. Lowenstein-Leif, Peter D. BS, CCNY, 1964; MS, U. Pa., 1965, PhD, 1969. Postdoctoral fellow U. Pa., Phila., 1969-70; research assoc. U. Pitts., 1970-73; asst. physicist Brookhaven Nat. Lab., Upton, N.Y., 1973-75, assoc. physicist, 1975-77, physicist, 1977-83, sr. physicist, 1983—, head Exptl. Planning and Support div., 1977-84, dep. chmn. accelerator dept., 1981-84, chmn. Alternating Gradient Synchrotron dept., 1984-99, chmn. collider accelerator dept., 1999—. Assoc. mem. U.S.-Russia Joint Coordinating Commn. on Fundamental Properties of Matter, 1983—, U.S.-Japan Commn. on High Energy Physics, 1984—; mem. Dept. of Energy High Energy Physics Adv. Panel, 1993-96. Contbr. articles on particle and accelerator physics to profl. jours. Fellow Am. Phys. Soc.; mem. AAAS, N.Y. Acad. Scis., Sigma Xi. Office: Brookhaven Nat Lab AGS Dept Upton NY 11973

LOWENSTEIN, EVE JUDITH, physician, researcher; b. Far Rockaway, N.Y. m. Richard Sidlow; children: Jonathan, Eliana. MS, MD, PhD, NYU. Diplomate Am. Bd. Dermatology. Contbr. articles to profl. jours.; spkr. in field. Office: SUNY Health Sci Ctr Box 46 450 Clarkson Ave Brooklyn NY 11203 Fax: 718-270-2794.

LOWENSTEIN, JAMES GORDON, former diplomat, international consultant; b. Long Branch, N.J., Aug. 6, 1927; s. Melvyn Gordon and Katherine Price (Goldsmith) L.; children: Laurinda Vinson (Douglas), Price Gordon. Grad., Loomis Sch., 1945; BA, Yale U., 1949; postgrad., Harvard Law Sch., 1955-56. With Office Spl. Rep. in Europe, Econ. Cooperation Adminstrn., Paris, 1950-51; mem. U.S. Spl. Mission to Yugoslavia, Sarajevo, 1951; fgn. svc. officer Bur. European Affairs Dept. State, 1957-58; fgn. service officer Am. Embassy, Colombo, Ceylon, 1959-61, Belgrade, Yugoslavia, 1961-64; cons. Fgn. Relations Com., U.S. Senate, Washington, 1965-74; prin. dep. asst. sec. state for European affairs, 1974-77; ambassador to Luxembourg, 1977-81; with Bur. European Affairs, Dept. State, 1981-82; ptnr. IRC Group, Washington, 1982-87; sr. cons. APCO Assocs., 1988-99; sr. advisor Heller and Rosenblatt, 2000—. Mem. internat. observer group Sri Lanka elections, 1993, 94, sr. elections adv. Osce Mission to Bosnia, 1996, 97; chmn. bd. dirs. The Ukraine Fund; past sec. bd. Emerging Eastern European Fund; past chmn. Baltic Investments; co-founder, bd. dirs. French-Am. Found.; bd. dirs., Refugees Internat.; past mem. adv. coun. Sch. Advanced Internat. Studies and Bologna (Italy) Ctr. Johns Hopkins U.; mem. adv. coun. Ctr. on U.S. and France, Brookings Instn. Lt. (j.g.) USNR, 1952-55, staff Naval War Coll., 1954-55. Decorated chevalier Légion d'Honneur (France); Grand Croix de la Couronne de Chene (Luxembourg). Mem. Coun. Fgn. Rels., Internat. Inst. Strategic Studies (London), French Inst. Internat. Rels. Clubs: Metropolitan (Washington); Army-Navy Country (Arlington, Va.); Century Assn., Knickerbocker, Explorers, Yale (N.Y.C.); Harbor (Seal Harbor, Maine); Travellers, Racing Club de France (Paris). Home: 3139 O St NW Washington DC 20007-3117 also: 52 Rue de Varenne 75007 Paris France Office: Heller & Rosenblatt Ste 205 1101 15th St NW Washington DC 20005-5002

LOWENSTEIN, LOUIS, legal educator; b. N.Y.C., June 13, 1925; s. Louis and Ralphina (Steinhardt) L.; m. Helen Libby Udell, Feb. 12, 1953; children: Roger Spector, Jane Ruth, Barbara Ann. BS, Columbia, 1947, LL.B., 1953; M.F.S., U. Md., 1951. Bar: N.Y. 1953. Pvt. practice law, N.Y.C., 1954-78; Assoc. Judge Stanley H. Fuld, N.Y. Ct. Appeals, 1953-54; assoc., then partner Hays, Sklar & Herzberg, 1954-68; partner Nickerson, Kramer, Lowenstein, Nessen, Kamin & Soll, 1968-78; Simon H. Rifkind prof. emeritus law and fin. Columbia U. Law Sch., 1980—, project dir. Instl. Investor Project, 1988-94; pres. Supermarkets Gen. Corp., Woodbridge, N.J., 1978-79. Bd. dirs. Liz Claiborne, Inc. 1988-96; mem. pub. oversight bd. Panel on Audit Effectiveness, 1998-2000. Author: What's Wrong with Wall Street, 1988, Sense and Nonsense in Corporate Finance, 1991; contbr., co-editor: Knights, Raiders and Targets, 1988; editor in chief Columbia Law Rev., 1951-53. V.p., mem. exec. com. Fedn. Jewish Philanthropies N.Y.; pres. Jewish Bd. Family and Children's Svcs. N.Y., 1974—78; trustee Beth Israel Med. Ctr., N.Y.C., 1975—81; dir. Goddard-Riverside Cmty. Ctr., 1996—2002; chmn. bd. dirs. Coalition for the Homeless, 1997—. Mem. ABA, Assn. of Bar of City of N.Y., Am. Law Inst. Home: 5 Oak Ln Larchmont NY 10538-3917 Office: Columbia U Law Sch 435 W 116th St New York NY 10027-7297

LOWENSTEIN, PEDRO RICARDO, gene therapy scientist, educator; b. Buenos Aires; arrived in U.K., 1987,arrived in U.S., 2001; s. Karl Heinz Lowenstein and Eva Sofia Isakowitz; m. Maria Graciela Castro, Jan. 12, 1988; 1 child, Elijah David. BSc, Pestalozzi Schule, Buenos Aires, 1975; MD cum laude, U. Buenos Aires, 1981, PhD summa cum laude, 1984. Postgrad. rsch. fellow neuroendocrine pharmacology divsn. Nat. Rsch. Coun., Buenos Aires, 1982-84; postdoctoral rsch. fellow dept. psychiatry Johns Hopkins Med. Instn., Johns Hopkins U. Sch. Medicine, Balt., 1984-86; vis. fellow lab. neurochemistry NINCDS/NIH, Bethesda, Md., 1987; grade 1 rsch. scientist anat. neuropharmacology unit Dept. Pharmacology, Med. Rsch. Coun., Oxford, Eng., 1987-90; lectr. anatomy dept. anatomy and physiology U. Dundee, Scotland, 1990-92; from lectr. neurosci. dept. physiology to sr. lectr. U. Wales, Coll. Cardiff, 1992-94; Lister Inst. prof. molecular medicine and gene therapy U. Manchester Sch. Medicine, Eng., 1995-2001. Mem. biols. subcom. Medicines Control Agy., U.K., 1999—; advisor, reviewer Gene Therapy Adv. Com., U.K., 1996—; dir. Gene Therapeutics Rsch. Inst., Cedars-Sinai Med. Ctr., L.A., 2001—; prof. medicine dept. medicine UCLA, 2002—. Editor-in-chief Current Gene Therapy, contbr. over 140 articles to profl. jours. Recipient Sir Henry Wellcome Commemorative award for innovative rsch. Wellcome Trust, 1998; rsch. fellow Lister Inst. Preventive Medicine, 1993-2000 rsch. grantee Med. Rsch. Coun., 1998, Biotech. and Biol. Rsch. Coun., 1998. Mem. Neural Disorders Gene Therapy Sci. Com., Am. Soc. Gene Therapy, Soc. for Neurosci., U.S.A., Brit. Neurosci. Assn., Internat. Soc. for NeuroVirology (founding mem.), European Soc. Gene Therapy (chmn., ednl. citee). Jewish. Avocations: human experimentation during the Holocaust, ethics of science, history of science, reading. Office: Cedars-Sinai Medical Ctr Gene Therapeutics Rsch Inst Rsch Pavilion Rm 5093 8700 Beverly Blvd Los Angeles CA 90048 Home: 256 N Clark Dr Beverly Hills CA 90211 Fax: 310-423-0225. E-mail: lowensteinp@cshs.org.

LOWENSTEIN, PETER DAVID, lawyer; b. N.Y.C., Dec. 31, 1935; s. Melvyn Gordon and Katherine Price (Goldsmith) L.; m. Constance Cohen; children from previous marriage: Anthony, Kate E., Christopher. BA, Trinity Coll., 1958; LLB, Georgetown U., 1961. Bar: Conn. 1962, N.Y. 1963. With SEC, Washington, 1961-63; assoc. Whitman & Ransom, N.Y.C., 1963-70, ptnr., 1970-83; sec., gen. counsel Value Line, Inc., 1983-87; v.p., sec., gen. counsel Service Am. Corp., Stamford, Conn., 1988-90; ptnr. O'Connor, Morris & Jones, Greenwich, 1990-92; pvt. practice, 1992—. Legal counsel Value Line Mutual Funds. Bd. dirs. Grand St. Settlement, N.Y.C., 1970-92, Greenwich Health Assn., Conn., 1978-85; bd. dirs. Greenwich chpt. ARC, 1989-94, vice chmn., 1991-93. Mem.: Yale Club of N.Y., Greenwich Field Club, Nantucket Yacht Club. Home: 496 Valley Rd Cos Cob CT 06807-1627 Office: Two Sound View Dr Ste 100 Greenwich CT 06830-5436 E-mail: PDLOW@aol.com.

LOWENSTEIN, RALPH LYNN, university dean emeritus; b. Danville, Va., Mar. 8, 1930; s. Henry and Rachel (Berman) L.; m. Bronia Grace Levenson, Feb. 6, 1955; children: Joan, Henry. BA, Columbia U., 1951, MS in Journalism, 1952; PhD in Journalism, U. Mo., 1967. Reporter Danville (Va.) Register, 1952, El Paso Times, 1954-57; asst. prof. journalism U. Tex. at El Paso, 1956-62, assoc. prof., 1962-65; publs. editor Freedom of Info. Ctr., Columbia, Mo., 1965-67; vis. prof., head journalistic studies Tel Aviv U., 1967-68; assoc. prof. Sch. Journalism, U. Mo., Columbia, 1968-70, prof., 1970-76, chmn. news-editorial dept., 1975-76; press critic CBS Morning News, 1975-76; dean Coll. Journalism and Communications, U. Fla., Gainesville, 1976-94. Author: Bring My Sons from Far, 1966, Pragmatic Fund-Raising, 1997; author: (with John C. Merrill) Media, Messages and Men, 2d edit., 1979; author: Macromedia, 1990; editor (with Paul Fisher): Race and the News Media, 1967. Served with Israeli Army, 1948; AUS, 1952-54. Named to Fla. Freedom of Info. Hall of Fame, 1997; recipient Disting. Svc. award, Columbia Journalism Alumni, 1957, 30th Anniversary award, State of Israel, 1978, Freedom Forum Journalism Adminstr. of Yr. award, 1994. Mem.: Soc. Profl. Journalists (Rsch. in Journalism award 1971), Assn. Edn. in Journalism and Mass Comm. (pres. 1990—91). Home: 1705 NW 22nd Dr Gainesville FL 32605-3953 E-mail: rlowenstein@jou.ufl.edu.

LOWENTHAL, ABRAHAM FREDERIC, international relations educator; b. Hyannis, Mass., Apr. 6, 1941; s. Eric Isaac and Suzanne (Moos) L.; m. Janet Wyzanski, June 24, 1962 (div. 1983); children: Linda Claudina, Michael Francis; m. Jane S. Jaquette, Jan. 20, 1991. AB, Harvard U., 1961, M.P.A., 1964, PhD, 1971; postgrad., Harvard Law Sch., 1961-62. Tng. assoc. Ford Found., Dominican Republic, 1962-64, asst. rep. Peru, 1969-72; asst. dir., then dir. of studies Coun. Fgn. Rels., N.Y.C., 1974-76; dir. Latin Am. program Woodrow Wilson Internat. Ctr. for Scholars, Washington, 1977-83; exec. dir. Inter-Am. Dialogue, 1982-92; prof. Sch. Internat. Rels., U. So. Calif., Los Angeles, 1984—; dir., ctr. internat. studies U. So. Calif., 1992-97; pres. Pacific Coun. Internat. Policy, L.A., 1995—; v.p. Coun. on Foreign Rels., 1995—. Vis. fellow, rsch. assoc. Ctr. Internat. Studies, Princeton U., 1972-74; vis. lectr. polit.. sci. Cath. U. Santiago, Dominican Republic, 1966; lectr. Princeton U., 1974; spl. cons. Commn. U.S.-L.Am. rels., N.Y.C., 1974-76; mem. internat. adv. bd. Ctr. U.S.-Mex. Rels., U. Calif.-San Diego, 1981-94; mem. internat. adv. bd. Helen Kellogg Inst., 1984-95; cons. Ford Found., 1974-90; bd. dirs. InterAm. Dialogue, Fulbright Assn., Pacific Coun. on Internat. Policy. Author: The Dominican Intervention, 1972, 2nd edit., 1995, Partners in Conflict: The United States and Latin America in 1990s, 1991; editor, contbg. author: The Peruvian Experiment: Continuity and Change Under Military Rule, 1975, Armies and Politics in Latin America, 1976, Exporting Democracy: The United States and Latin America, 1991; co-editor, contbg. author: The Peruvian Experiment Reconsidered, 1983, The California-Mexico Connection, 1993; editor Latin Am. and Caribbean Record, vol. IV, 1985-86, vol. V, 1986-87, Latin America in a New World, 1994, Constructing Democratic Governance: Latin America, 1996; mem. editorial bd. Jour. Inter-Am. Studies and World Affairs, 1980-97, New Perspectives Quarterly, 1984—, Hemisphere, Internat. Security, 1977-85, Wilson Quar., 1977-83; contbr. articles to profl. jours. Mem. nat. adv. coun. Amnesty Internat., 1977-83, Ctr. for Nat. Policy, 1986—. Mem. Internat. Inst. Strategic Studies, Am. Polit. Sci. Assn. (coun. 1979-81), Latin Am. Studies (exec. coun. 1979-81), Coun. Fgn. Rels., Overseas Devel. Coun. Democrat. Jewish. Home: 1343 Luna Vis Pacific Palisades CA 90272-2235 Office: Pacific Coun Internat Policy Los Angeles CA 90089-0035

LOWENTHAL, CONSTANCE, art historian, consultant; b. N.Y.C., Aug. 29, 1945; d. Jesse and Helen (Oberstein) L. BA cum laude, Brandeis U., 1967; AM, Inst. Fine Arts, NYU, 1969; PhD, Inst. Fine Arts, NYU, N.Y.C., 1976. Mem. faculty Sarah Lawrence Coll., Bronxville, N.Y., 1975-78; asst. mus. educator Met. Mus. Art, N.Y.C., 1978-85; exec. dir. Internat. Found. Art Research, 1985-98; dir. Commn. for Art Recovery World Jewish Congress, 1998-2001; cons. art ownership disputes, 2001—. Bd. dirs. Ctr. for Edn. Studies, Inc. Regular contbr. Art Crime Update column Wall Street Jour., 1988-97; mem. editl. bd.: The Spoils of War, World War II and Its Aftermath: The Loss, Reappearance and Recovery of Cultural Property, 1997; contbr. articles to Mus. News and other profl. publs.

LOWENTHAL, HENRY, retired greeting card company executive; b. Frankfurt, Germany, Oct. 26, 1931; came to U.S., 1940, naturalized, 1945; s. Adolf and Kella (Suss) L.; m. Miriam Katzenstein, June 29, 1958; children—Sandra, Jeffry, Joan Chana, Benjamin, Avi. BBA cum laude, City U. N.Y., 1952, MBA, 1953; JD, N.Y. U., 1962. CPA. Lectr. acctg. Baruch Coll., N.Y.C., 1952-53; auditor Price Waterhouse & Co., 1955-62; v.p., contr. Am. Greetings Corp., Cleve., 1962-68, contr., 1966-68, sr. v.p., CFO, 1977-95, sr. v.p., 1995-97. V.p. fin., treas. Tremco Inc., Cleve., 1968-77; mem. adv. bd. Case We. Res. U. Dept. Accountancy, 1986-97. Chmn. bd. dirs. Rabbinical Coll. Telshe, 1974-77, v.p., 1977-90; v.p. Hebrew Acad. Cleve., 1977-97; pres. Agudath Israel of Cleve., 1978-95, treas., 1995-97; v.p. Agudath Israel Am., 1989—, chmn. regional v.p.s, 1996—; bd. dirs. Jewish Cmty. Fedn., Cleve., 1979-88, 90-95, chmn. audit com., 1992-95; trustee Mt. Sinai Med. Ctr., Cleve., 1992-96; chmn. citizens rev. com. Cleveland Heights-Univ. Heights Sch., 1972-73, mem. lay fin. com., 1974-79; mem. Cleveland Heights Citizens Adv. Com. for Cmty. Devel., 1976-79; mem. com. Jewish edn. Jewish Cmty. Fedn., Balt., 1997—; bd. advisors job link, 1997—; dir. victim svcs. Northwest Citizens Patrol, 1998-2001; bd. dirs. Beth Medrash Goroha Rabbinical Coll., Lakewood, N.J., Bnos Yisroel Sch., Balt., Shearith Israel Congregation, treas. Mended Hearts Chpt., 2001-2002. With AUS, 1953-55. Mem. AICPA, Assn. of Publicly Traded Cos. (budget & fin. com. 1986-97, bd. dirs. 1987-97, treas. 1990-97), Fin. Execs. Inst. (sec. N.E. Ohio chpt. 1979-80), Ohio Soc. CPA, Greater Cleve. Growth Assn., Beta Gamma Sigma, Beta Alpha Psi. Home: 6115 Biltmore Ave Baltimore MD 21215-3601

LOWENTHAL, SUSAN, artist, designer, retired finance executive; b. Munich, Nov. 30, 1946; came to U.S., 1949; d. Jerry and Gertrude (Wiestreich) L.; m. Alex J. Stolitzka, Oct. 11, 1987. BA, Bklyn. Coll., 1969. Exec. dir. Manhattan Girls Club, N.Y.C., 1969-73; conf. coord. Orton Soc., 1973-77; v.p. Gemtique, 1977-81; broker Prudential Bache, 1981-83, Smith Barney, N.Y.C., 1983-85; pres., chief exec. officer Lowenthal Fin. Svcs., Inc., 1985-89, fin. cons., money mgr., 1990-98; realtor, exclusive buyer agt. March Buyers Realty, 1995—. Designer/artist works sold in museum gift shops and pub. in nat. mags.; guest appearances on cable TV shows; pres. AcScents! Naturally. Artist, designer; designs published in maj. nat. mags. Jewish. Avocations: skiing, reading, bridge. E-mail: susan@acscentsnaturally.com., susan@bysusandesigns.com.

LOWENTROUT, PETER MURRAY, religious studies educator; b. Salinas, Calif., Mar. 14, 1948; m. Christine Ione, Sept. 30, 1980; children: Mary, Brandon. AB, U. Calif., Riverside, 1973; PhD, U. So. Calif., L.A., 1983. Prof. religious studies Calif. State U., Long Beach, 1981—, chair dept. religious studies, 1999—. Contbr. articles to profl. jours. Capt. Orange County Fire Dept., Orange, Calif., 1977-94. Mem. Am. Acad. Religion (regional pres. 1989-90), Ctr. for Theology and Lit. U. Durham (Eng.), Sci. Fi. Rsch. Assoc. (pres. 1991, 92). Office: Calif State U Dept Religious Studies 1250 N Bellflower Blvd Dept Long Beach CA 90840-0001 E-mail: plowentr@csuca.edu. *Though it is the hatred in life that seems most quickly to catch our attention, there is far more love in the world. Learning to see that love and helping others to do so is life's best work.*

LOWER, ROBERT CASSEL, lawyer, educator; b. Oak Park, Ill., Jan. 8, 1947; s. Paul Elton and Doris Thatcher (Heaton) L.; m. Jean Louise Lower, Aug. 24, 1968 (dec. Aug. 1985); children: David Elton, Andrew Bennett, James Philip Thatcher; m. Cheryl Bray, July 26, 1986. AB magna cum laude with highest honors, Harvard U., 1969, JD, 1972. Bar: Ga. 1972. Assoc. Alston & Bird, Atlanta, 1972-78, ptnr., 1978—. Adj. prof. Emory U., 1978-85, 92. Contbr. articles to law jours. Co-founder, pres. Ga. Vol. Lawyers for the Arts, Inc., 1975-79; chmn. Fulton County (Ga.) Arts Coun., 1979-87; trustee Woodruff Arts Ctr., 1988-95, Piedmont Coll., Ga. Found. Ind. Colls. Mem. Ga. Bar Assn., Atlanta Bar Assn., Midtown Bus. Assn. (bd. dirs. 1988-90), Author's Ct. Harvard Club (Ga.), Ansley Golf Club, Phi Beta Kappa. Presbyterian. Avocations: running, music, bonsai. Home: 935 Plymouth Rd NE Atlanta GA 30306-3009 Office: Alston & Bird 1 Atlantic Ctr Atlanta GA 30309-3400 E-mail: rlower@alston.com.

LOWERY, CHARLES DOUGLAS, history educator, academic administrator; b. Greenville, Ala., May 8, 1937; s. Reuben F. and Frances Louise (Jordan) L.; m. Sara Bradford, June 24, 1961; children: Thomas Bradford, Douglas Trenton, Charles Daniel. BA, Huntingdon Coll., 1959; MA, Fla. State U., 1961; PhD, U. Va., 1966. Asst. prof. history Ball State U., Muncie, Ind., 1964-66; from asst. prof. to prof. Miss. State U., Starkville, 1966—, head dept. history, 1985—, asst. dean Coll. Arts and Scis., 1971-74, assoc. dean, 1974-81, dir. Inst. for Humanities, 1981-85. Author: James Barbour: The Biography of A Jeffersonian Republican, 1984, (with others) America: The Middle Period, 1973; Encyclopedia of African-American Civil Rights: From Emancipation to the Present, 1992; contbr. articles to profl. jours. Mem. Citizen's Adv. Coun., Starkville, 1971; mem. Miss. Com. for Humanities, Jackson, 1986-88; vice chmn. Miss. Humanities Coun., Jackson, 1988-89. Grantee NEH, 1980, 81, 84, Miss. Humanities Coun., 1983, 84, 88. Mem. Orgn. Am. Historians, Soc. Historians of Early Am. Rep., So. Hist. Soc., Miss. Hist. Soc. (com. chmn. 1989-90). Democrat. Presbyterian. Avocations: camping, travel, fishing, historical preservation. Home: 609 Sherwood Rd Starkville MS 39759-4009 Office: Miss State U Dept History Drawer H Mississippi State MS 39762 E-mail: cdl2@ra.msstate.edu.

LOWERY, DOUGLAS LANE, retired environmental engineer; b. Ft. Madison, Iowa, Jan. 24, 1939; s. Frank Onel and Buelah Muree (Pechstein) Lowery; m. Sally Ann Giggey, Dec. 23, 1962; children: Lynda Denise, Lori Diane. BCE, Colo. State U., 1962; MS in Sanitary Engring., U. Mo., 1963; postgrad., Calif. Inst. Tech., Pasadena, 1965-66. Registered profl. engr., Calif., Alaska, N.C. Sanitary engring. asst. L.A. Dept. Water and Power, 1963-68; sanitary engring. assoc. L.A. Bur. of Sanitation, 1968-72; environ. conservation mgr. Alaska Dept. Environ. Conservation, Fairbanks, 1972-86, environ. specialist, 1986-94. Various offices Fairbanks Arctic Swim Team, Fairbanks, San Gabriel Valley Orchid Hobbyists, Arcadia, Calif., No. Area Aquatics, N.C. Ctr. Creative Retirement, retirement weekend panelist, 1996, 97, Leadership Asheville Seniors IX planning com., 1996, 97; del. to U.S Swimming Assn. Mem. ASCE (pres. Fairbanks br. 1974-75), Am. Water Works Assn. (life), Am. Pub. Works Assn. (v.p. Alaska 1974-75), Rotary Found. Bequest Soc. (charter), Rotary (Paul Harris fellow, benefactor, past pres., dist. officer, youth exch. chmn.), Sigma Tau, Chi Epsilon, Omicron Delta Kappa, Phi Kappa Tau, Kappa Mu Epsilon. Avocations: travel, hosting friends. Home: 305 Piney Mountain Dr Apt N-2 Asheville NC 28805-1259

LOWERY, F(LOYD) LYNN, JR. insurance executive; b. Milan, Feb. 9, 1940; s. Floyd L. and Seeley (Moore) L.; m. Dale Turner, Jan. 30, 1960; children: Seeley Anne, F. L. III. BBA, U. Memphis, 1962. Regional mgr. Fidelity and Deposit Co. of Md., Memphis, 1963—2000; ret., 2000. Past project chmn. Phoenix Club, Memphis, 1968-75; past commr. Meth. Athletic Assn. of Memphis, 1975-76. Mem. Miss. Surety Assn., Constrn. Fin. Mgmt. Assn., Tenn. Rd. Builders Assn., Miss. Rd. Builders Assn., Associated Builders and Contractors, Mississippi Valley Flood Control ACG. Republican. Office: Fidelity and Deposit Co Md 502 Clark Tower 5100 Poplar Ave Memphis TN 38137-4000

LOWERY, JOANNE, writer, editor; b. Cleve., July 30, 1945; d. Peter Gustav and Julia Lydia (Bede) Witzman; m. Stephen Paul Lowery, June 15, 1968 (div. Oct. 1988); children: Elizabeth Cecilia, Nathan Alexander. AB with distinction, U. Mich., 1967; MA, U. Wis., 1968. Part-time instr. English Elgin (Ill.) C.C., 1986-91, Coll. of DuPage, Glen Ellyn, Ill., 1991-96; mng. editor, copy editor, staff writer Sampler Publs., St. Charles, 1990-92; part-time lectr. English St. Mary's Coll., Notre Dame, Ind., 1997-98. Poetry editor Black Dirt lit. mag., Elgin, 1994-99, feature editor, 1998-99. Author: Coming to This, 1990, Corinth, 1990, Heroics, 1996, Double Feature, 2000; contbr. numerous poems to lit. mags. Mem. Ill. Coalition Against the Death Penalty, Chgo., 1995-96. Recipient lit. award New Letters, 1993. Mem. Amnesty Internat., Nature Conservancy. Home: 412 Evelyn Avenue Kalamazoo MI 49001

LOWERY, LEE LEON, JR. civil engineer; b. Corpus Christi, Tex., Dec. 26, 1938; s. Lee Leon and Blanche Lowery; children: Kelli Lane, Christianne Lindsey. BSCE, Tex. A&M U., 1960, ME, 1961, PhD, 1965. Prof. dept. civil engring. Tex. A&M U., 1960; rsch. engr. Tex. A&M Rsch. Found., 1962—. Pres. Pile Dynamics Found. Engring., Inc., Bryan, Tex., 1962—; pres. Tex. Measurements, Inc., College Station, 1965—; pres. Interface Engring. Assos., Inc., College Station, 1969—; dir. Braver Corp. Bd. dirs. Deep Found. Inst. Recipient Faculty Disting. Achievement Teaching award Tex. A&M U., 1979, Zachary Teaching award, 1989, 91, award of merit Tex. A&M Hon. Soc., 1991; NDEA fellow, 1960-63. Mem. ASCE, NSPE, Tex. Soc. Profl. Engrs., Sigma Xi, Phi Kappa Phi, Tau Beta Pi. Baptist. Achievements include patents in field. Office: Tex A&M U Dept Civil Engring College Station TX 77843-3136 E-mail: Lowery@tamu.edu.

LOWERY, WILLA DEAN, obstetrician, gynecologist; b. Caryville, Fla., Apr. 16, 1927; d. Ernest and Nadine (Fowler) L. BS in Chemistry, Stetson U., 1948; MS in Microbiology, U. Fla., 1952; MD, U. Miami, 1959; MPH, U. Pitts., 1963; MDiv in Theology, Pitt. Theol. Sem., 1995. Diplomate Am. Bd. Ob-Gyn.; ordained to ministry Presbyn. Ch. Microbiologist Fla. Dept. Pub. Health, Jacksonville, 1948-52, pub. health officer, 1959-65; microbiologist U. S. Operation Mission to Brazil, Belém, 1952-55; rotating intern Jackson Meml. Hosp., Miami, Fla., 1959-60; resident in ob-gyn. Magee Women's Hosp., Pitts., 1965-68; asst. prof. ob-gyn. Sch. Medicine, U. Pitts., 1968-69; pvt. practice Pitts., 1970-88; pastor Presbyn. Ch. So. Ind. County Parish, 1995—. Cons. Med. Mission in Brazil, Teresina, 1986-89; mem. Ethics Bd. of Chldns. Hosp U. Pittsburgh, 1998. Contbr. articles to profl. jours. Mem. AMA, ACOG, Pa. State Med. Soc., Allegheny County Med. Soc. Home: 119 Sunnyhill Dr Pittsburgh PA 15237-3666

LOWERY, WILLIAM HERBERT, lawyer; b. Toledo, June 8, 1925; s. Kenneth Alden and Drusilla (Pfanner) L.; m. Carolyn Broadwell, June 27, 1947; children: Kenneth Latham, Marcia Mitchell. PhB, U. Chgo., 1947; JD, U. Mich., 1950. Bar: Pa. 1951, U.S. Supreme Ct. 1955. Assoc. Dechert Price & Rhoads, Phila., 1950-58, ptnr., 1958-89, mng. ptnr., 1970-72; mem. policy com., chmn. litigation dept., 1962-68, 81-84; of counsel Dechert, Phila., 1989—; counsel S.S. Huebner Found. Ins. Edn., 1970-89. Faculty Am. Conf. of Legal Execs., Pa. Bar Inst.; permanent mem. com. of visitors U. Mich. Law Sch. Author: Insurance Litigation Problems, 1972, Insurance Litigation Disputes, 1977. Pres. Strafford Civic Assn., 1958; chmn. Tredyffrin Twp. Zoning Bd., Chester County, Pa., 1959—75; bd. dirs. Paoli Meml. Hosp., 1964—89, chmn., 1972—75; bd. dirs. Main Line Health, Radnor, 1984—89; permanent mem. Jud. Conf. 3d Cir. Ct. 2n lt. USAF, 1943—46. Mem. ABA (chmn. life ins. com. 1984-85, chmn. Nat. Conf. Lawyers and Life Ins. Cos. 1984-88), Order of the Coif, Royal Poinciana Golf Club (bd. dirs. 1997—, sec. 1997-2000, v.p. 2000—), Phi Gamma Delta, Phi Delta Phi. Home: 2777 Gulf Shore Blvd N Apt 4-s Naples FL 34103-4360 Office: Dechert 4000 Bell Atlantic Tower 1717 Arch St Lbby 3 Philadelphia PA 19103-2793

LOWERY, WILLIAM ODELL, personnel services executive; b. Winston-Salem, Aug. 1, 1935; m. Lucienne Lowery, Mar. 3, 1962. BS in Polit. Sci., Trenton State Coll., 1987. Commd. 2d lt. U.S. Army, advanced through grades to maj., 1974, pers. action specialist hdqrs. 24th divsn. Germany, 1962-65, 65-66, pers. mgmt. specialist hdqrs. The Pentagon Washington, 1967-70; instr. engring. OCS U.S. Army, Ft. Belvoir, Va., 1965-67; pers. staff officer to set up operation to deactivate 4th Inf. Divsn., An Khe, Vietnam, 1970-71; pers. hdqrs. DA U.S. Army, Heidelberg, Germany, 1971-74, pers. staff Ft. Ben Harrison, Ind., 1974-79; mail carrier U.S. Postal Svc., New Hope, N.J., 1979-80; pers. specialist Civilian Pers. Office, Ft. Dix, 1980-94; FECA program adminstr. Dept. of Def. Police, N.J., 1996—. Instr. eng. OCS U.S. Army, Ft. Belvoir, Va., 1965-67. Decorated Army Commendation medal (2), Meritorious Svc. medal (2), Bronze Star medal. Home: 37 E Chestnut St Bordentown NJ 08505-2063

LOWES, ALBERT CHARLES, lawyer; b. Oak Ridge, Mo., Dec. 1, 1932; s. Guy Everett and Lillian Bertina (Tuschhoff) L.; m. Peggy Rae Watson, Aug. 27, 1960; children: Danita Rae, Albert Charles II, Kurt Brandon. Student, Cape State Coll., 1954-56; JD, U. Mo., 1959. Bar: Mo. 1959, U.S. Dist. Ct. (ea. dist.) Mo. 1959, U.S. Ct. Appeals (8th cir.) 1971. With Buerkle, Lowes, Beeson & Ludwig, Jackson, Mo., 1959-84; ptnr. Lowes & Drusch, Cape Girardeau, 1984—. Atty. City of Jackson, 1960-62. Staff sgt. USMC, 1950-54, Korea. Mem. Mo. Bar Assn., Internat. Assn. Ins. Counsel, VFW (judge adv. dept. Mo.1962-64, 67-68, state judge adv. 1997-98), Masons, Shriners, Elks. Democrat. Lutheran. Avocations: reading, history, legal fields. Office: Lowes & Drusch 2913 Independence St Cape Girardeau MO 63703-8320

LOWEY, NITA M. congresswoman; b. N.Y., July 5, 1937; m. Stephen Lowey, 1961; children: Dona, Jacqueline, Douglas. BS, Mt. Holyoke Coll., 1959. Community activist, prior to 1975; asst. sec. state State of N.Y., 1975-87; mem. U.S. Congress from 20th N.Y. dist., 1989-92, U.S. Congress from 18th N.Y. dist., 1993—. Mem. appropriations com., 1993—. Democrat. Office: US Ho of Reps 2329 Rayburn Ho Office Bldg Washington DC 20515-0001*

LOWI, ALVIN, JR. mechanical engineer, consultant; b. Gadsden, Ala., July 21, 1929; s. Alvin R. and Janice (Haas) L.; m. Guillermina Gerardo Alverez, May 9, 1953; children: David Arthur, Rosamina, Edna Vivian, Alvin III. BME, Ga. Inst. Tech., 1951, MSME, 1955; PhD in Engring., UCLA, 1956-61. Registered prof. engr., Calif. Design engr. Garrett Corp., Los Angeles, 1956-58; mem. tech. staff TRW, El Segundo, Calif., 1958-60, Aerospace Corp., El Segundo, 1960-66; prin. Alvin Lowi and Assocs., San Pedro, 1966—; pres. Terraqua Inc., Calif., 1968-76; v.p. Daeco Fuels and Engring. Co., Wilmington, 1978—, also bd. dirs.; pres. Lion Engring., Inc. Vis. research prof. U. Pa., Phila., 1972-74; sr. lectr. Free Enterprise Inst., Monterey Park, Calif., 1961-71; bd. dirs. So. Calif. Tissue Bank; research fellow Heather Found., San Pedro, 1966–. Contbr. articles to profl. jours.; patentee in field. Served to lt. USN, 1951-54, Korea. Fellow Inst. Humane Studies; mem. ASME, NSPE, Soc. Automotive Engrs., Soc. Am. Inventors, So. Bay Chamber Music Soc., Scabbard and Blade, Pi Tau Sigma. Jewish. Avocations: chamber music, jazz, photography, classic automobiles, motor sports, philosophy of science. Home and Office: 2146 W Toscanini Dr Palos Verdes Peninsula CA 90275-1420

LOWI, THEODORE J(AY), political science educator; b. Gadsden, Ala., July 9, 1931; s. Alvin R. and Janice (Haas) L.; m. Angele M. Daniel, May 11, 1963; children: Anna Amelie, Jason Daniel. BA, Mich. State U., 1954; MA, Yale U., 1955, PhD, 1961; HLD (hon.), Oakland U., 1972; LittD (hon.), SUNY, Stony Brook, 1988; Doctorate (hon.), Nat. Found. Polit. Scis., Paris, 1992. Mem. faculty dept. govt. Cornell U., 1959-65, 72—, asst. prof., 1961-65, John L. Senior prof. Am. instns., 1972—; assoc. prof. U. Chgo., 1965-69, prof., 1969-72. Fellow Ctr. Advanced Study in Behavioral Scis., 1977-78; chair Am. civilization U. Paris, 1981-82. Author: At the Pleasure of the Mayor, 1964, (with Robert Kennedy) The Pursuit of Justice, 1964, The End of Liberalism, 1969, 2nd edit., 1979, Japanese edit., 1981, French edit., 1987, The Politics of Disorder, 1971, (with others) Poliscide - Big Government, Big Science, Lilliputian Politics, 1976, 90, (with others) Nationalizing Government: Public Policies in America, 1978, Incomplete Conquest: Governing America, 1981, The Personal President: Power Invested, Promise Unfulfilled, 1985, Spanish edit., 1994, (with B. Ginsberg) American Government: Freedom and Power, 1990, 6th edit., 2000, (with B. Ginsberg) Embattled Democracy, 1995, The End of the Republican Era, 1995; (with B. Ginsberg and M. Weir) We the People, 1997, 3rd edit., 2001, (with J. Romance) A Republic of Parties? Debating the Two-Party System, 1998, La Scienza del Politiche, 1999. Chair French-Am. Found., 1981-82. Recipient Richard Neustadt award for Best Book on Presidency, 1986; Social Sci. Rsch. Coun. fellow, 1963-64; Guggenheim Found. fellow, 1967-68; NEH fellow, 1977-78; Ford Found. fellow, 1977-78; Fulbright 40th Anniversary Disting. fellow, 1987. Mem. Am. Polit. Sci. Assn. (v.p. 1985-86, pres. 1991), Am. Acad. Arts and Sci., Policy Studies Orgn. (pres. 1977), Internat. Polit. Sci. Assn. (1st v.p. 1994-97, pres. 1997-2000). Home: 101 Delaware Ave Ithaca NY 14850-4707 E-mail: TJL7@cornell.edu. *If there is a how-to of success it is this: a passion for work, an ethic of workmanship, and an idea of what, in the end, is a good product.*

LOWITT, RICHARD, history educator; b. N.Y.C., Feb. 25, 1922; s. Eugene and Eleanor (Lebowitz) L.; m. Suzanne Catharine Carson, Sept., 1953; children: Peter Carson, Pamela Carson. BSS., CCNY, 1943; MA, Columbia U., 1945, PhD, 1950. Instr. U. Md., College Park, 1948-52; asst. prof. U. R.I., Kingston, 1952-53; faculty mem. Conn. Coll., New London, 1953-66, prof. history, 1966, Fla. State U., Tallahassee, 1966-68, U. Ky., Lexington, 1968-77; prof., chmn. dept. history Iowa State U., Ames, 1977-87, prof., 1987-89, U. Okla., Norman, 1990-97. Mem. Iowa Humanities Bd., 1987-89; mem. Okla. Humanities Bd., 1995-2001; vis. prof. U. Colo., summer 1953, Yale U., 1961-62, Brown U., 1965-66, U. Chattanooga, summer 1965, Emory U., Atlanta; Sutton prof. U. Okla., 1989-90; Regents prof. U. Sci. and Arts of Okla., Chickasha, 1998—. Author: A Merchant Prince of the 19th Century, 1954, George W. Norris, 3 vols., 1963, 71, 78; editor: Nils Olsen and the Bureau of Agricultural Economics, 1980; co-editor: One Third of a Nation-Lorena Hickok Reports on the Great Depression, 1981, The New Deal and the West, 1984, Letters From An American Farmer: The Eastern European and Russian Correspondence by Roswell Garst, 1987, Henry A. Wallace's Irrigation Frontier: On the Trail of the Cornbelt Farmer, 1990, Bronson M. Cutting, Progressive Politican, 1992, Politics in the Postwar American West, 1995, Fred Harris: His Journey From Liberalism to Populism, 2002. Trustee Pub. Library, Lexington, 1973-77. NEH sr. fellow, 1974, John Simon Guggenheim Found. fellow, 1957; grantee Social Sci. Rsch. Coun., 1958, Am. Coun. Learned Socs., 1962, Am. Philos. Soc., 1964, Huntington Libr., 1986; recipient Gaspar Perez de Villagra award Hist. Soc. N.Mex., 1993, Muriel H. Wright award Hist. Soc. Okla., 1995. Fellow Agrl. History Soc. (exec. com. 1973-75, pres. 1991-92); mem. Am. Hist. Assn., So. Hist. Assn. (membership com. 1973, Ramsdell prize com. 1975, program com. 1983, nominating com. 1990), Western History Assn. (bd. editors 1986-88, program com. 1995, merit award 1992), Orgn. Am. Historians (nominating com. 1970, Turner prize com. 1972-76, bd. editors 1985-87). Democrat. Office: Univ Okla Dept History Norman OK 73019-0001

LOWMAN, ROBERT PAUL, psychology educator, academic administrator; b. Lynwood, Calif., Jan. 23, 1947; s. Hubert Alden and Martha Guynn (Howard) L.; m. Kathleen Marie Drew, June 25, 1972; children: Sarah Guynn, Amy Katherine. AB, U. So. Calif., 1967; MA, Claremont U., 1969, PhD, 1973. Asst. prof. U. Wis., Milw., 1972-76; adminstrv. officer APA, Washington, 1976-81; assoc. dean Kans. State U., Manhattan, 1981-86, assoc. dean grad. sch., 1986-90, assoc. vice provost, 1990-91; dir. rsch. svcs. and adj. assoc. prof. psychology U. N.C., Chapel Hill, 1991—, assoc. vice chancellor for rsch., 1994-96, 2001—, assoc. vice provost for rsch., 1996-2001. Editor: APA's Guide to Rsch. Support, 1981; contbr. over 30 articles to profl. jours. Recipient numerous grants. Mem. APA (sec. bd. sci. affairs 1976-81, sec. com. on internat. rels. in psychology 1978-81), AAAS, Am. Psychol. Soc., Soc. for Psychologists in Mgmt. (newsletter editor 1994-96, bd. dirs. 1996-99, pres.-elect 1999, pres. 2000), Nat. Coun. Univ. Rsch. Adminstrs., Soc. Rsch. Adminstrs., Phi Beta Kappa, Phi Kappa Phi, Phi Eta Sigma, Psi Chi. Democrat. Methodist. Home: 104 Chesley Ln Chapel Hill NC 27514-1459 Office: Univ NC Office Rsch Svcs Cb # 4100 Chapel Hill NC 27599-4100 E-mail: lowman@unc.edu.

LOWNDES, DAVID ALAN, programmer analyst; b. Schenectady, N.Y., Oct. 28, 1947; s. John Henry and Iris Anne (Hepburn) L.; m. Peggy Welco, May 3, 1970; children: Diana Justine, Julie Suzanne. AB, U. Calif., Berkeley, 1969, postgrad., 1972-73. Acct., credit mgr. The Daily Californian, Berkeley, 1973-75, bus. mgr., 1975-76; acct. Pacific Union Assurance Co., San Francisco, 1976-77, acctg. mgr., 1977-78; sr. acct. U. Calif., 1978-88, sr. programmer analyst, 1988—. Avocations: genealogy, microcomputing. Home: 1829 Gaspar Dr Oakland CA 94611-2350 Office: U Calif 250 Executive Park Blvd San Francisco CA 94134-3306 E-mail: dlowndes@its.ucsf.edu.

LOWNDES, JEFFREY DENNIS, auto mechanic; b. Lake Syranac, N.Y., May 8, 1970; s. George and Joan (Hyde) L.; m. Janine M. Herbert, Mar. 26, 1996; children: Jeffrey (dec.), Nicholas, Grant, Victoria. Mechanic, owner Lowndes Engine Repair, Orr's Island, Maine, 1987—; investigative asst. Lowndes Investigations, Cundy's Harbor, 1997-98. Avocations: fourwheeling, dirt bikes, snowmobiling, hunting, fishing.

LOWNSDALE, GARY RICHARD, mechanical engineer; b. Poplar Bluff, Mo., Nov. 2, 1946; s. Edward Lee and Margie Lee (Tesreau) Lownsdale; m. Paulette Ann Wermuth, Nov. 30, 1968; children: Charles Edgar, Larissa Renee. BSME, U. Cin., 1970. Registered profl engr, Mich. Trainee engring. mgmt. Chrysler Corp., Highland Park, Mich., 1965-69, contact engr. Hamtramck, 1970-71; prin. design engr. Ford Motor Co., Dearborn, 1971-82; exec. dir. advance programs Schlegel Corp., Madison heights, 1982-86; mgr. automotive design ctr. GE, Pittsfield, Mass., 1986-87, mgr. strategic projects Southfield, Mich., 1990; v.p. design and engring. Autopolymer Design inc., Auburn Hills, 1987-88; chief engr. polymer body Saturn corp., Troy, 1988-90; industry dir. Hercules Incorp., 1990-92; dir. mktg. automotive systems group Johnson Controls, Inc., Plymouth, 1992; dir. comml. bus. APX Internat., Madison Heights, 1993-94; v.p., COO TRANS 2 Corp., Livonia, 1994-96; pres. Mastercraft Boat Co., Vonore, Tenn., 1996-99, Trans Tech Internat., Loudon, 2000—. Presenter int and technology papers. Secy Coventry Gardens Homeowners Asn, Livonia, Mich., 1976—86; dist leader Boy Scouts Am, 1977—; PTA Livonia, 1982—84. Mem.: ASME (sr.), Elfen Soc, Soc Automotive Engrs (co-chmn comt 1991—92), Soc Plastics Engrs, Eng Soc Detroit (vice chmn 1972—82), Soc Naval Architects and Marine Engrs, Am Soc Nautical Engrs, Am Soc Body Engrs, Hadley Hills Homeowners Asn (pres 1990—96), Austin Healy Club Am (pres 1999—), Sports Car Club Am (solo chmn 1972—76, Solo Nat Champion Award 1974). Achievements include patents in field. Avocations: classic car racing and restoration, horse ranching. Home: 417 Shawnee Pl Loudon TN 37774-3164 Office: Trans Tech Internat 417 Shawnee Pl Loudon TN 37774-3164

LOWRANCE, MURIEL EDWARDS, program specialist; b. Ada, Okla., Dec. 28, 1922; d. Warren E. and Mayme E. (Barrick) Edwards; B.S. in Edn., East Central State U., Ada, 1954; 1 dau., Kathy Lynn Lowrance Gutierrez. Accountant, adminstrv. asst. to bus. mgr. East Central State U., 1950-68; grants and contracts specialist U. N.Mex. Sch. Medicine, Albuquerque, 1968-72, program specialist IV, dept. orthopaedics, 1975-86; asst. adminstrv. officer N.Mex. Regional Med. Program, 1972-75. Bd. dirs. Vocat. Rehab. Center, 1980-84. Cert. profl. contract mgr. Nat. Contract Assn. Mem. Am. Bus. Women's Assn. (past pres. El Segundo chpt., Woman of Yr. 1974), AAUW, Amigos de las Americas (dir.). Democrat. Methodist. Club: Pilot (Albuquerque) (pres. 1979-80, dir. 1983-84, dist. treas. 1984-86, treas. S.W. dist., 1984-86, gov.-elect S.W. dist. 1986-87, gov. S.W. dist. 1987-88). Home: 3028 Mackland Ave NE Albuquerque NM 87106-2018

LOWRANCE, PAMELA KAY, medical/surgical nurse; b. Pensacola, Fla., July 17, 1959; d. Carl Boyce and Sara Mae (Wrenn) L. BSN, U. N.C., 1981. RN, N.C.; cert. in chemotherapy adminstrn.; cert. oncology nurse. Staff nurse Charlotte (N.C.) Meml. Hosp. and Med. Ctr.; asst. nurse mgr. Carolinas Med. Ctr. Reviewer continued ednl. material. Mem.: ANA, Soc. Gynecologic Nurse Oncologists, Oncology Nursing Soc., Acad. Med.-Surg. Nurses, Sigma Theta Tau, Zeta Tau Alpha. Home: 6014 Rose Valley Dr Charlotte NC 28210-3830

LOWREY, ANNIE TSUNEE, retired cultural organization administrator; b. Osaka, Japan, Mar. 3, 1929; naturalized U.S. citizen, 1963; d. Shigeru Takahata and Kuniko Takahata Takahashi; m. Lawrence K. Lowrey, Mar. 17, 1953; children: Kristine K. Ricci, Jay. BS in Lit., Wakayama (Japan) Shin-Ai, 1949; BS in Art Edn., Kans. State U., 1967; MA in Indsl. Tech., Wichita State U., 1976. Cert. instr. Wichita-Tchr. Assessment and Assistance Program, 1987. Tchr. Minoshima Elem. Sch., Wakayama, Japan, 1945-46, Wakayama Jr. H.S., 1948-49, Truesdell Jr. H.S., Wichita, Kans., 1967-69; tchr., coord. dept. fine arts Wichita H.S. East, 1969-92, instr. Japanese, 1991-92; lectr. dept. art and indsl. tech. Wichita State U., 1974-88, instr. computer applications in industry, 1990-91; tchr. Woodman Elem. Sch., Wichita, summer 1987; instr. art appreciation Butler County C.C., McConnell and Wichita, 1988-92; dir. edn. and exhbn. Wichita Ctr. for Arts, 1992-95; ret., 1995. Asst. to fine arts photographer Charles Phillips, Wichita, spring 1989; judge Sister City Art Contest, 1991, Wichita Botanica Photography Competition, painting competition Wichita Painter's Guild, design competition Kans. Aviation Mus., 1991-92; instr. art instrnl. strategy to elem. and secondary art tchrs. Ft. Collins and Loveland, Colo. sch. dists., 1989; presenter many profl. confs. and workshops, most Nat. Art Edn. Conf., Phoenix, 1992, Kans. Accessible Arts, 1994, Kans. State U., 1994. Chairperson writing team for Kans. Plan for Indsl. Edn.-TV, 1974-75; co-author tech. edn. curriculum Kans. State Bd. Regents, 1989. Judge Miss Asia contest 10th Ann. Asian Festival, Wichita, 1990; pres. pub. art adv. bd. City of Wichita, 1991—. Carnegie grantee for development of inter-disciplinary program on cultural literacy, 1984, Matsushita Electronic Co. grantee for curriculum devel., 1986; inductee Kans. Tchrs. Hall of Fame, 1994. Mem. NEA (presenter nat. conv. 1985), ASCD, Nat. Art Edn. Assn-.Western Region Secondary Outstanding Educator of Yr. 1988), Kans. Alliance for Arts Edn. (bd. dirs. 1987-89), Phi Delta Kappa (pres. Wichita State U. chpt. 1983-84), Delta Phi Delta. Home: 2727 S Linden St Wichita KS 67210-2423

LOWRIE, ALLEN, geologist, oceanographer; b. Washington, Dec. 30, 1937; s. Allen and Mary (Green) L.; m. Mildred C. McDaniel, Feb. 2, 1985; 1 child from previous marriage, Tanya Anne. BA, Columbia U., 1962. Cert. profl. geologist, Ark., Miss. Geologist Lamont Doherty Geol. Obs., Palisades, N.Y., 1963-68; oceanographer U.S. Naval Oceanographic Office, SSC/NASA, Miss., 1968-81, 84—; geologist Mobil Oil Corp., New Orleans, 1981-84; instr. Tulane U., 1979-82, 90, U. So. Miss., 1984-86, instr. continuing edn., 1985—. Cons. NVII Geofizika, Moscow, Miss. Mineral Resource Inst., U. Miss., Oxford, GAPCO, Inc., Houston, Landscape Studio, Hattiesburg, Miss., Mobil Research & Devel. Corp., Dallas, Sci. Applications Inc., McLean, Va., Geo-Cons Internat., Inc., Kenner, La., Seagull Internat. Exploration Inc., Houston, Planning Systems, Inc., Slidell, La., Corporacion Miners de Cerro Colorado, Republic of Panama, Hotel Drotama, Santa Marta, Colombia, others. Author: Offshore Louisiana Geology, an Offshore Exploration Model, 1988, Gulf of Mexico Salt Tectonics, Associated Processes and Exploration, 1989, Seismic Stratigraphy and Hydrocarbon Traps: Louisiana Onshore and Offshore, Course Notes Series, vol. 5, 1994; contbr. 75 articles to profl. jours. Mem. Am. Assn. Petroleum Geologists (cert., vis. geologists program 1995—, cert. divsn. profl. affairs), Soc. Explor. Geophys., N.Y. Acad. Scis., Am. Geophys. Union, Geol. Soc. Am., Sigma Xi. Episcopalian. Avocations: reading, classical music. Home: 238 F Z Goss Rd Picayune MS 39466-9458 E-mail: alowrie@webtv.net.

LOWRIE, KATHRYN YANACEK, high technology recruiter; b. Midland, Mich., Nov. 23, 1958; d. Frank Joseph and Jacqueline Ann (Sipko) Yanacek; m. David Bruce Lowrie, Mar. 14, 1987; 1 child, Alexandra Yanacek. BA in Psychology, Northea. U., 1980. Psychology technician Rsch. Inst. of Environ. Medicine, U.S. Army, Natick, Mass., 1980-81, computer programmer, 1981-83; assoc. recruiter Mgmt. Adv. Svcs., Burlington, 1983-85, v.p. mgmt. info. sys., 1985-86, exec. v.p., 1986-89; CEO Computer Careers, Raynham, 1989-90; v.p. G.R.S.I. Corp., Middleboro, 1990-94; owner S.B. Industries, Taunton, 1994-96; pres. Enviro-Screen, Inc., 1996-97; sr. assoc. Franklin (Mass.) Key Assocs., 1997-99; contract recruiter, 1999—. Leader Girl Scouts U.S. Roman Catholic. Avocations: dancing, reading, physical fitness, travel, motivational training. E-mail: kylowrie@hotmail.com.

LOWRIE, MICHELE, classics educator; b. New Haven, Apr. 24, 1962; d. Ernest and Joyce (Oliver) L.; m. Seth Fagen, June 12, 1988; 1 child, Lucas Fagen. BA, Yale U., 1984; PhD, Harvard U., 1990. Tchg. fellow Phillips Exeter Acad., Exeter, N.H., 1984-85; instr. Harvard U., Cambridge, Mass., 1989-90; asst. prof. NYU, 1990-96, assoc. prof., 1996—. Mem. Columbia Sem. in Classical Civilization. Author: Horace's Narrative Odes, 1997; contbr. articles to profl. jours. Presdl. fellow NYU, 1994. Mem. Am. Philological Assn. Avocations: gardening. Office: NYU Dept Classics 25 Waverly Pl New York NY 10003-6701

LOWRIE, PAMELA BURT, educator, artist; b. Geneva, May 12, 1937; d. Morris Nathan and Helyn (Beetlestone) B.; children: Edmund Gale, Matthew Burt; m. Michael Hammer, Aug. 14, 1982. BA, U. Mich., 1959; MS in Edn., No. Ill. U., DeKalb, 1970; MA, Claremont Grad. Sch. (Calif.), 1979. Art cons. Sch. Dist. 41, Glen Ellyn, Ill., 1970-72; prof. art Coll. DuPage, 1972-94; ret., 1994; curator Olcott Gallery, Wheaton, Ill., 1994—. Dir., staff Nat. Great Tchrs. Seminars, Williams Bay, Wis., 1976-94; staff Calif. Great Tchrs. Seminar, Santa Barbara, 1979, Hawaii Great Tchrs. Seminar, 1990; vis. prof. Christ Ch. Coll., Canterbury, Eng., 1990. One-woman shows include Loyola U. Gallery, Chgo., U. Ill. Med. Ctr. Gallery, 1978, Elmhurst (Ill.) Coll. Gallery, 1980, Kankakee (Ill.) Coll. Gallery, 1982, The Edge Gallery, Villa Park, Ill., 1984, Gahlberg Gallery Coll. of DuPage, 1986, 87, 92, Elmhurst Art Mus., 1994, Am. Hdqs. of Theosophical Soc., Wheaton, Ill., 1995, 2000, Schafer Gallery, 1995, NICOR, Naperville, Ill., 1996, 97, 2001, Olcott Gallery, Wellness Ctr., 1997, Zurich AM Bldg., Schaumberg, Ill., 1998, DuPage Art League, Wheaton, Ill., 1999, Unilever Corp. Office, Rolling Meadows, Ill., 1999, City Hall, Wheaton, Ill., 2000, Roosevelt U., Schaumberg, Ill, 2001; group shows include Five Women Artists from Ill., Notre Dame U., 1979, Springfield (Ill.) Art Assn. Gallery, 1981, Am. Cultural Ctr., Taipei, Taiwan, 1982, Campanille Gallery, Chgo., 1986, Limelight-Abstract Art, Riverwalk Gallery, Naperville, 1987, David Adler Cultural Ctr., Libertyville, Ill., Norris Gallery, St. Charles, Ill., Gov. State U., Park Forest, Ill., 1982-91, Woman Made Gallery, Gallery Egg, Chgo., Claremont Grad. Sch. Gallery, Calif., 1994, Kohn Turner Gallery, L.A., 1995, N.W. Cultural Coun. Corp. Gallery, 1996-97, Helene Curtis Corp. Ctr., 1997, Unilever Corp., 2000, 2002, Bloomigdale Art Mus., 2001, Roosevelt U., 2001, TLD Design Ctr. and Gallery, 2001, Zurich AM Bldg., 2002, Am. Hdqs. of Theosophical Soc., 2002; represented in permanent collections Coll. DuPage, Glen Ellyn, AT&T, Naperville, Eastman Pharms., Malvern, Pa., Getty Synthetic Fuel, Chgo., Monte Christo Condominiums, Fla., Nara Jr. Coll., Japan, No. Trust Bank, Chgo., Plan Corp., Wheaton, Nat. Hdqs. Theosophical Soc., Wheaton, Zurich-Am. Ins. Co., Schaumberg, Rolling Meadows, Theosophical Soc. in Am., Unilever Corp., Kemper-Zurich. Bd. dirs. Fine Arts Rev. Com., DuPage County, Ill., 1982. Home: 926 N Scott St Wheaton IL 60187-3862 E-mail: pmblowrie@aol.com.

LOWRY, BATES, art historian, museum director; b. Cin., June 21, 1923; s. Bates and Eleanor (Meyer) L.; m. Isabel Barrett, Dec. 7, 1946; children: Anne, Patricia. PhB, U. Chgo., 1944, MA, 1952, PhD, 1955. Asst. prof. U. Calif., Riverside, 1954-57, Inst. Fin. Arts NYU, 1957-59; prof., chmn. dept. art Pomona Coll., Claremont, 1959-63, Brown U., Providence, 1963-68; dir. Mus. Modern Art, N.Y.C., 1968-69; prof., chmn. dept. art U. Mass., Boston, 1971-80; dir. Nat. Bldg. Mus., Washington, 1980-87. Cons. dept. photography Getty Mus., 1992; disting. vis. prof. U. Del. Newark, 1988-89; founder, pres. Com. to Rescue Italian Art, 1966-76; mem. arts coun. MIT, 1974-80. Author: Visual Experience, 1961, Renaissance Architecture, 1962, Muse or Ego, 1963, Building a National Image, 1985, Looking for Leonardo, 1993, The Silver Canvas, 1998; editor: College Art Association Monograph Series, 1957-59, 65-68, Architecture of Washington, D.C., 1977-79, Art Bull., 1965-68; mem.

editorial bd. Smithsonian Instn. Press, 1981-87. Mem. bd. cons. NEH, 1975-81. With U.S. Army, 1942-45. Decorated Grand Officer of Order of Star of Solidarity, Italy, 1967; recipient Gov.'s award for contbn. to art, R.I., 1967; fellow Guggenheim Found., 1972, Inst. for Advanced Study, 1971. Mem. Coll. Art Assn. (bd. dirs. 1962-65), Soc. Archtl. Historians (bd. dirs. 1959-61, 63-65), Dunlap Soc. (pres. 1974-92), Academia del Disegno (hon. mem. Italy). Home: 255 Massachusetts Ave Boston MA 02115-3505

LOWRY, DAVID BURTON, lawyer; b. Bronxville, N.Y., Nov. 6, 1943; s. Burton S. and Virginia Evelyn (Ford) L. BA, U. Ariz., 1966, JD, 1969. Bar: Ariz. 1969, Oreg. 1973. Legal aid atty., Tucson and Coolidge, Ariz. and Hillsboro, Oreg.; asst. atty. gen.; dep. dist. atty. Marion County; dep. pub. defender Mohave County, Ariz.; pvt. practice Portland, Oreg., 1989—. Mem. Oreg. State Bar Assn., Ariz. State Bar Assn., Am. Mgmt. Assn., Assn. Trial Lawyers Am., Alpha Delta Sigma, Phi Alpha Delta, Alpha Sigma Phi. Republican. Home: 13490 SW Genesis Loop Tigard OR 97223-3959

LOWRY, DENNIS MARTIN, computer technician; b. Cleve., Dec. 13, 1953; s. Martin Patrick and Phyllis Ann (Bova) L.; m. Mary Cullinan, Aug. 8, 1973 (div. 1978); 1 child, Matthew Christopher; m. Sylvia Susanne Patterson, Nov. 3, 1979; children: Kevin Thomas, Caitlin Ilene, Danielle Amanda. Student, Cleve. State U., 1971-78. Sr. technician Union Carbide Corp., Cleve., 1973-78; applications analyst Davy McKee Co., Independence, 1978-79; sr. systems programmer Cuyahoga County Hosp., Cleve., 1979-83; regional support specialist Commex Ltd., Rocky River, 1987-88; nat. tech. support mgr. Commex Maintenance Ltd., 1987-89; mgr. Cap Gemini Ernst & Young Tng. Ctr., Middleburg Hts., Ohio, 1989—2000; ops. mgr. Cap Gemini Ernst & Young, Cleve., 2000—. Avocations: theater directing, locksmith. Home: 21144 Mastick Rd Cleveland OH 44126-3056

LOWRY, EDWARD FRANCIS, JR. lawyer; b. L.A., Aug. 13, 1930; s. Edward Francis and Mary Anita (Woodcock) L.; m. Patricia Ann Palmer, Feb. 16, 1963; children: Edward Palmer, Rachael Louise. Student, Ohio State U., 1948-50; AB, Stanford U., 1952, JD, 1954. Bar: Ariz. 1955, D.C. 1970, U.S. Supreme Ct. 1969. Camp dir. Quarter Circle V Bar Ranch, 1954; tchr. Orme Sch., Mayer, Ariz., 1954-56; trust rep. Valley Nat. Bank Ariz., 1958-60; pvt. practice, Phoenix, 1960—; assoc. atty. Cunningham, Carson & Messinger, 1960-64; ptnr. Carson, Messinger, Elliott, Laughlin & Ragan, 1964-69, 70-80, Gray, Plant, Mooty, Mooty & Bennett, 1981-84, Eaton, Lazarus, Dodge & Lowry Ltd., 1985-86; exec. v.p., gen. counsel Bus. Realty Ariz., 1986-93; pvt. practice, Scottsdale, Ariz., 1986-88; ptnr. Lowry & Froeb, 1988-89, Lowry, Froeb & Clements, P.C., Scottsdale, 1989-90, Lowry & Clements P.C., Scottsdale, 1990, Lowry, Clements & Powell, P.C., Scottsdale, 1991—. Asst. legis. counsel Dept. Interior, Washington, 1969-70; mem. Ariz. Commn. Uniform Laws, 1972—, chmn., 1976-88; judge pro tem Ariz. Ct. Appeals, 1986, 92-94; mem. Nat. Conf. Commrs. on Uniform State Laws, 1972-97, life mem., 1997—. Chmn. Coun. of Stanford Law Socs., 1968; bd. dirs. Scottsdale Prevention Inst., 1999—; vice chmn. bd. trustees Orme Sch., 1972-74, treas., 1981-83; trustee Heard Mus., 1965-91, life trustee, 1991—, pres., 1974-75; bd. visitors Stanford Sch. Law; magistrate Town of Paradise Valley, Ariz., 1976-83, town councilman, 1998—, mayor, 1998—; juvenile ct. referee Maricopa County, 1978-83. Capt. USAF, 1956-58. Fellow Ariz. Bar Found. (founder); mem. ABA, Maricopa County Bar Assn., State Bar Ariz. (chmn. com. uniform laws 1979-85), Stanford Law Soc. Ariz. (past pres.), Scottsdale Bar Assn. (bd. dirs. 1991—, v.p. 1991, pres. 1992-95), Ariz. State U. Law Soc. (bd. dirs.), Delta Sigma Rho, Alpha Tau Omega, Phi Delta Phi. Home: 7600 N Moonlight Ln Paradise Valley AZ 85253-2938 Office: Lowry Clements & Powell PC 2901 N Central Ave Ste 1120 Phoenix AZ 85012-2731 also: 6900 E Camelback Rd Ste 1040 Scottsdale AZ 85251-2444

LOWRY, GLENN DAVID, art museum director; b. N.Y.C. s. Warren and Laure (Lynn) L.; m. Susan Chambers, Aug. 24, 1974; children: Nicholas, Alexis, William. BA, Williams Coll., 1976; MA, Harvard U., 1978, PhD, 1982. Asst. curator Fogg Art Mus., Harvard U., Cambridge, Mass., 1978-80; rsch. asst. Archeol. Survey of Mediterranean Town of Amalfi, Italy, 1980; curator Oriental art Mus. Art, R.I. Sch. Design, Providence, 1981-82; dir. Joseph and Margaret Muscarelle Mus. Art, Williamsburg, Va., 1982-84; curator Nr. Ea. art Arthur M. Sackler and the Freer Gallery Art, Smithsonian Instn., Washington, 1984-90, curatorial coord., 1987-89; dir. Art Gallery Ont., Toronto, Can., 1990-95, Mus. Modern Art, N.Y.C., 1995—. Mem. adv. coun. dept. art history and archaeology Columbia U. Co-author: Fatehpur-Sikri: A Source Book, 1985, From Concept to Context: Approaches to Asian and Islamic Calligraphy, 1986, An Annotated Checklist of the Vever Collection, 1988, A Jeweler's Eye: Art of the Book from the Vever Collection, 1988, Timur and the Princely Vision: Persian Art and Culture in the Fifteenth Century, 1989, Europe and the Arts of Islam: The Politics of Taste, 1991. Trustee Metro Toronto Conv. and Visitors Assn. Recipient Inst. Turkish Studies Travel award Smithsonian Instn., 1980, Spl. Exhbns. award, 1987, Scholarly Studies award, 1990. Mem. Assn. Am. Art Mus. Dirs., Coll. Art Assn. Mailing: Mus Modern Art 11 W 53rd St New York NY 10019-5498 : MoMA Queens 33 St at Queens Blvd Long Island City NY 11101*

LOWRY, HAROLD, writer; Tchr. Spkr. in field. Author: 34 Books (Nat. Best Seller list USA Today). Mem.: Romance Writers of Am. (adv., nat. bd. dir., Regional Svc. award 1993, Nat. Svc. award 1993). Office: Romance Writers of America 3707 FM 1960 West Ste 555 Houston TX 77068*

LOWRY, HOUSTON PUTNAM, lawyer; b. N.Y.C., Apr. 1, 1955; s. Thomas Clinton Falls and Jean Allen (Day) L.; m. Kathryn Santoro Curtiss. BA, Pitzer Coll., 1976; MBA, U. Conn., 1980; JD cum laude, Gonzaga U., 1980; LLM in Internat. Law, U. Cambridge, Eng., 1981. Bar: Conn. 1980, U.S. Dist. Ct. Conn. 1981, U.S. Tax Ct. 1982, U.S. Ct. Mil. Appeals 1982, U.S. Ct. Appeals (1st, 2d, 5th, 11th cirs.) 1982, U.S. Ct. Claims 1984, D.C. 1985, U.S. Ct. Appeals (4th, 6th, 7th, 9th, fed., D.C. cirs.) 1985, U.S. Ct. Appeals (3d, 8th, 10th cirs.) 1986, U.S. Supreme Ct., N.Y. 1989. Law clk. to Judge William M. Acker, Jr. U.S. Dist. Ct., Birmingham, Ala., 1982-83; assoc. Tarlow, Levy & Droney, Farmington, Conn., 1983-88; prin. Tarlow, Levy & Droney, P.C., 1989-93, Brown & Welsh P.C., Meriden, 1993—. Mem. adj. faculty internat. trade law and internat. comml. arbitration U. Conn. Law Sch., 1990-95, 99—. Mem. adv. com. on pvt. internat. law Sec. of State, 1996—. Fellow Chartered Inst. Arbitrators; mem. ABA (various coms.), Conn. Bar Assn. (various coms.), Am. Soc. Internat. Law, Internat. Law Assn., Am. Law Inst., Hon. Soc. Gray's Inn, Hartford Club. Office: Brown & Welsh PC PO Box 183 530 Preston Ave Meriden CT 06450-4893 E-mail: hplowry@brownwelsh.com.

LOWRY, JAMES HAMILTON, management consultant; b. Chgo., May 28, 1939; s. William E. and Camille C. Lowry; 1 child, Aisha. BA, Grinnell Coll., 1961; M in Polit. and Instnl. Adminstrn., U. Pitts., 1965; PMD, Harvard U., 1973. Assoc. dir. Peace Corps, Lima, Peru, 1965-67; spl. asst. to pres., project mgr. Bedford-Stuyvesant Restoration Corp., Bklyn., 1967-68; sr. assoc. McKinsey & Co., Chgo., 1968-75; pres. James H. Lowry & Assocs., 1975-2000; v.p. Boston Consulting Group, 2000—. Mem. Small Bus. Adv. Com.; bd. dirs. Johnson Products Co., Burrell Advt. Mem. vis. com. Harvard U.; adv. bd. J.L. Kellogg Grad. Sch. Mgmt., Northwestern U., also adj. prof.; trustee Grinnell Coll.; bd. dirs. Chgo. United, Northwestern Hosp., Chgo. Pub. Libr., Chgo. Fgn. Affairs, African-Am. Inst. Chmn. City of Chgo. Durban/Chgo. Sister City Program; mem. U.S. trade rep. African Trade Adv. Com.; chmn. bd. trustees Sengstacke Enterprises. John Hay Whitney fellow, 1963-65; co-chmn. Chgo. United. Mem. Harvard Alumni Assn. (dir., vis. com.), Inst. Mgmt. Cons., Econ. Club, Monroe Club, Univ. Club, Comml. Club Chgo. Home: 3100 N Sheridan Rd Chicago IL 60657-4954 Office: 211 W Wacker Dr Ste 950 Chicago IL 60606-1241 Fax: 312-223-9575.

LOWRY, JOAN MARIE DONDREA, broadcaster; b. Weirton, W.Va., June 8, 1935; d. Rudolph and Mary (Telmanik) Dondrea; m. Robert William Lowry, June 15, 1957; 1 child, Christopher Scott. BS in Edn., Baldwin-Wallace Coll., 1956; student, Ohio Sch. Broadcasting, 1977-79. Mem. news staff rsch. and mktg. Sta. 3 WE-WWWE, Cleve., 1979-80; gen. mgr., news mgr. Sta. WLRO, Lorain, Ohio, 1980-82; host 35 Live Cinemavidio TV, Elyria, 1980-83; TV show host Continental Cable, Cleve., 1983—; pub. rels. dir. Sta. WZLE, Lorain, 1982-83; broadcaster, cmty. rels. dir. Sta. WRKG, 1983—, news dir., 1988—; broadcaster, host lunchtime radio talk show Sta. WHK, Cleve., 1989-90; corp. affairs and programming mgr. No. Ohio Continental Cablevision, 1991—. Treas. bd. dirs. Better Hearing Inst., Washington, 1992—; spkr. in field. Appeared in motion pictures: Those Lips Those Eyes, 1982, One Trick Pony, 1982; performer comml. Trustee Delta Zeta Found., 1983—95, pres., 1987—95, Woman of Yr., 1995; active Women in Cable, 1993, Lorain Litter Control Bd., 1981—83, Multiple Sclerosis Soc., Am. Cancer Soc., Muscular Dystrophy Assn., Founders Meml. Found., others; mem. cmty. resource coun. Leadership Lorain County, 1988—89, trustee, v.p., active Leadership Coun., 1988—; trustee N.E. affiliate Am. Heart Assn.; v.p. Bay Village PTA Coun., 1973—75; vol. Lorain County Action Bd., 2002; comms. and mktg. com. United Way, 1987—; chair Lorain County Mothers March of Dimes, 1988—2001; trustee Cleve. Hearing and Speech Ctr., 2001; mem. steering com. Nat. Coun. Better Hearing and Speech, 1985—, mem. coun. better hearing and speech month, 1985—, Lorain County coun., 1986—, pres. better hearing and speech month, 1995; bd. dirs. Lorain County Sr. Citizens Assn., 1982—85, Lorain Consumers Coun., 1980—; bd. trustees Clearland Hearing and Speech Ctr., 2001; chmn. adv. bd. Lorain County Heart Assn., 1988; mem. Martin Luther King Steering Com., 1987—; bd. dirs. Lorain County Sr. Citizen's Assn.; grand marshal numerous parades. Named Woman of Achievement, Nat. YWCA and Lorain County Bus. and Industry Assn., 1983, Ohio Delta Zeta Alumnae Woman of Yr., 1995; recipient USAF award, 1982, USN award, 1981, Media award Am. Cancer Soc., 1982, Comm. award Easter Seals Soc., 1981, Cmty. Svc. award Lorain County chpt. Am. Heart Assn., 1981, Service to Mankind award Sertoma Internat., 1988, Baldwin-Wallace Coll. Alumni Merit award, 1996; ofcl. hostess for U.S. Army in Lorain County, 1980-83; Mayor's Proclamation, 1982; hon. recruiter award U.S. Army, 1981; Recognition award Ohio House Reps., Nat. Delta Zeta Woman of Yr. award, 1995, Lorain County Sr. Champion award, 1999. Mem. Bus. and Profl. Women, Lorain County Arts Coun., Leadership Lorain County Alumni Assn. (bd. dirs. 1990—, v.p. 1996—), Baldwin-Wallace Alumni Assn. (nat. pres. 1979-81, Merit award 1996), LWV (chpt. pres. 1966-67), Cleve. Amateur Fencers (pres. 1965-67), Internat. Platform Assn., Rotary (Elyria). Byzantine Catholic. Home: 578 Yarmouth Dr Cleveland OH 44140-1753

LOWRY, KAREN M. biomedical research scientist, pharmacist; b. Stamford, Conn., July 8, 1945; d. Joseph John and Helen Elizabeth (Wykowski) Markovich; m. Atherton Clark Lowry Aug. 17, 1968; children: Atherton Clark Matthew, Suzanne Marie. BS summa cum laude, Fordham U., 1968; MS in Pharmacology, Cornell U., 1971; MA, St. Charles Sem., Wynnewood, Pa., 1983. Registered pharmacist, Pa. Rsch. asst. in biochemistry/molecular biology Thomas Jefferson Med. Sch., Phila., 1971-74; adj. prof. chemistry Holy Family Coll., 1975-76, Arcadia U., Glenside, 1984-87; sr. biochemist, lab. mgr. Beacon Rsch. Inc., 1987-95; pharmacist Abington (Pa.) Meml. Hosp., 2000—, Tenet City Ave. Hosp., Phila., 1998-2000; staff U. Pa. Health System/Presbyn. Med. Ctr., 2000. Asst. sec. Biocoat Inc., Ft. Washington, Pa., 1991-95; mem. sci. adv. bd. UHT, Dobbs Ferry, N.Y., 1987-91. Contbr. articles to profl. jours.; patentee in field. Libr. dir. Immaculate Conception Sch., Jenkintown, Pa., 1980-86; Am. sponsor Vietnamese refugees Cath. Social Svcs., Phila., 1975—. NSF rsch. participant, 1964-68; USPHS grantee, 1968-71. Mem. Am. Chem. Soc., GFWC Everywoman's Club of Glenside (publicity chair 1995-96, pres. 1996-99). Roman Catholic. Avocations: philosophy, growing tomatoes and roses, home repair. Home: 631 Baeder Rd Jenkintown PA 19046-1555

LOWRY, LARRY LORN, management consulting company executive; s. Frank William and Viola Marie L.; m. Jean Carroll Greenbaum, June 23, 1973; 1 child, Alexandra Kristin BSEE, MIT, 1969, MSEE, 1970; MBA, Harvard U., 1972. Mgr. Boston Consulting Group, Menlo Park, Calif., 1972-80; sr. v.p., mng. ptnr. Booz, Allen & Hamilton Inc, San Francisco, 1980-2000, McKinsey & Co., 2001—. Western Electric fellow, 1969, NASA fellow, 1970 Mem. Sigma Xi, Tau Beta Pi, Eta Kappa Nu Presbyterian. Home: 137 Stockbridge Ave Atherton CA 94027-3942

LOWRY, LOIS (LOIS HAMMERSBERG), writer; b. 1937; Author: A Summer to Die, 1977, Find A Stranger, Say Goodbye, 1978, Anastasia Krupnik, 1979, Autumn Street, 1980, Anastasia Again, 1981, Anastasia at Your Service, 1982, The One Hundredth Thing About Caroline, 1983, Taking Care of Terrific, 1983, Anastasia, Ask Your Analyst, 1984, Us and Uncle Fraud, 1984, Anastasia on Her Own, 1985, Switcharound, 1985, Anastasia Has the Answers, 1986, Anastasia's Chosen Career, 1987, Rabbie Starkey, 1987, All About Sam, 1988, Number the Stars, 1989 (John Newbery medal 1990), Your Move, J.P.!, 1990, Anastasia at This Address, 1991, Attaboy, Sam!, 1992, The Giver, 1993 (John Newbery medal 1994), Anastasia Absolutely, 1995, See You Around, Sam!, 1996, Stay! Keeper's Story, 1997, Looking Back, 1998, Zooman Sam, 1999, Gathering Blue, 2000, Gooney Bird Greene, 2002. Address: 205 Brattle St Cambridge MA 02138-3345 Office: care Houghton Mifflin 222 Berkeley St Boston MA 02116-3748

LOWRY, MARILYN JEAN, horticultural retail company executive; b. Greensburg, Pa., Oct. 19, 1932; d. Clifford Henry and Martha McCune (Whitehead) Bushyager; m. John Cathcart Lowry, June 14, 1958; children: Martha Kim Hultberg, John Ryan, Nancy Lynn. BS, Ind. U. of Pa., 1954; MEd, Pa. State U., 1958. Tchr. Jeannette (Pa.) pub. schs., 1954-57; grad. asst. Pa. State U., University Park, 1957-58; demonstration sch. tchr. Towson (Md.) U., 1958-59; sec.-treas. Lowry & Co., Inc., Phoenix, 1964—, 1987—. Master flower show judge Nat. Council State Garden Clubs, Inc., St. Louis, 1987—, landscape design critic, 1985—; master gardener U. Md. Extension Svc., 1984—. Mem. Lutherville Garden Club (pres. 1979—), Am. Assn. Nurserymen Aux. (pres. 1972), Federated Garden Clubs Md. (dir. dist. III 1981-83), Am. Nursery and Landscape Assn. (chmn. wholesale plant sales profls. 1999—). Republican. Presbyterian.

LOWRY, MICHAEL ROY, physician; b. Des Moines, Oct. 5, 1949; s. William L. and Muriel I. (Higdon) L.; m. Candace E. Zadick, June 7, 1980; 1 child, Natalie E. BS, U. Iowa, 1971, MD, 1974. Diplomate Am. Bd. Psychiatry and Neurology. Resident in psychiatry U. Iowa Hosp., Iowa City, 1974-77; instr. dept. psychiatry U. Iowa, 1977-78, asst. prof., 1978-80; asst. prof., dir. residency tng. dept. psychiatry U. Utah, Salt Lake City, 1980-85; med. dir. Wasatch Canyons Hosp., 1985-88; staff psychiatrist LDS Hosp., 1985—2001, Wasatch Canyons Hosp. Ctr. Counseling, Salt Lake City, 1987—2001, U. Utah Neuropsychiat. Inst., 2001—; clin. assoc. prof. dept. psychiatry U. Utah, Salt Lake City, 1985—. Author: Major Depression: Prevention and Treatment, 1984. Mem. AMA, Am. Psychiat. Assn., Alpha Omega Alpha. Congregationalist. Office: 501 Chipeta Way Salt Lake City UT 84108-1222

LOWRY, MONTECUE JUDSON, military historian; b. Ft. Worth, Feb. 23, 1930; s. Mark and Susan Olivia (Hall) Lowry; m. Jo Gail Tuttle, June 4, 1955 (div. Mar. 1985); 1 child Mary ; m. Jennifer Lynn Gunlock, Dec. 27, 1985; children: Jeremy, Montecue J. II. BS, U.S. Mil. Acad., West Point, N.Y., 1953; BA, U. So. Miss., 1958; MS, U.S. Naval Postgrad. Sch., Monterey, Calif., 1965; MA, U. So. Miss., 1967; PhD in Physics, Tex. Christian U., 1977; PhD in History, U. North Tex., 1988. Officer U.S. Army, 1953-73; chief quality control Vinnell Corp., Riyadh, Saudi Arabia, 1982-83; instr. history U. North Tex., Denton, 1983-86; mil. analyst CIA, Washington, 1986-88; assoc. prof. history Liberty U., Lynchburg, Va., 1988-89; assoc. prof. physics Houston Bapt. U., 1990-96; mil. historian, 1996—. Author: (book) Forge of West German Rearmament, 1990, Glasnost, 1991, Great Captains of the Faith, 2002; contbr. articles to profl. jours. Neighborhood commr. Boy Scouts Am., Fulda, Germany, 1960—62; pres. PTA, 1961—62. Mem.: Soc. Mil. History, Am. Hist. Assn. Avocations: bicycling, weightlifting, classical music, reading. Home: 7402 Redding Rd Houston TX 77036-5542

LOWRY, RALPH JAMES, SR. retired history educator; b. Pitts., Dec. 30, 1928; s. Robert William and Elizabeth (Carter) L; 1 son. AB with hons., Lincoln U. of Pa., 1955; MA, Temple U., 1957; PhD, U. N.Mex., 1972; postgrad., Carnegie-Mellon U., 1980. History tchr. William Penn High Sch. for Girls, Phila., 1957-58; asst. prof. dept. history So. Univ., Baton Rouge, 1959-64, Md. State U., Princess Anne, 1965-69; tchr. sixth grade John Marshall Elem. Sch., Albuquerque, 1969-70; assoc. prof. dept. history/geography Va. State U., Petersburg, 1970-78; tchr. English/social studies Schenley High Sch., Pitts., 1978-80; assoc. prof. history and geography Bishop Coll., Dallas, 1980-83; asst. prof. philosophy and history Alcorn State U., Lorman, Miss., 1983-90; assoc. prof. history and geography Lincoln Univ., Pa., 1991; ret. Lincoln Univ. of Pa., 1995. Adj. prof. Black history, John Tyler C.C., Chester, Va., 1971-72, U. Va., Danville, 1972-74; substitute tchr. Dallas Ind. Sch. System, 1983; history scholar U.S. Mil. Acad., West Point, N.Y., summer 1985. Contbr. articles to profl. jours./publs. With USN, 1948-52, Korea. John Hay Whitney fellow, Jessie Smith Noyes scholar, others. Mem. Am. Hist. Soc., Miss. Polit. Sci. Assn., Western Pa. Psychiat. Clinic, Smithsonian Assocs., Western Pa. Rsch. and Hist. Soc., Phi Delta Kappa, Phi Alpha Theta, Alpha Phi Omega, Beta Sigma Tau, Pi Gamma Mu, Alpha Kappa Mu, Alpha Mu Gamma, Shriners. Democrat. Episcopalian. Home: # 424 4511 Walnut St Philadelphia PA 19139-4559

LOWRY, WILLIAM KETCHIN, JR. insurance company executive; b. Columbia, S.C., Oct. 4, 1951; s. William Ketchin and Beverly Hubbard (Frazee) L.; m. Elaine Diana Kent, June 22, 1984; children: Jennifer Lyn, Julia Ann, Samuel Ketchin. BSBA, U. S.C., 1972, M in Acctg., 1973. CPA, S.C. Supr. Ernst & Whinney, Columbia, 1973-81; sr. mgr. Price Waterhouse, Hartford, Conn., 1981-83, Phila., 1983-84; dir. corp. sys. devel. and analysis Am. Can Co., Greenwich, Conn., 1984-86; v.p., treas., CFO Phoenix Re Corp. and Reins. Co., N.Y.C., 1986-90, sr. v.p., treas., CFO, 1990; v.p., treas. Transnat. Ins. Co., 1989-90; bd. dirs., v.p., treas. Nat. Bus. Brokers, Inc., Greenlawn, N.Y., 1989-90; sr. v.p., CFO SCOR U.S. Corp., SCOR Reins. Co. Gen. Security Assurance Corp., N.Y.C., 1990-93, Constn. Reins Corp., 1993-96; exec. v.p. CFO Constn. Reins. Corp., 1996-98; bd. dirs. Constn. Reins Corp., 1994-98, Sirius Reins Corp., 1993-98; pres. CRC Corsair Inc., 1995-98; exec. v.p., COO U.S. RE Cos., Inc., 1998-99, also bd. dirs.; sr. v.p., CFO Swiss Re Am., Armonk, N.Y., 1999-2000; mng. mem. Capital Decision Scis. LLC, 2000—; pres. ICM Ins. Co., 2000—, also bd. dirs. Bd. dirs. U.S. RE Cos., Inc., 1998-99, Sunshine State Ins. Co., 1998-99. Pres., bd. dirs. Groves Homes Assn., Columbia, 1980-81; diaconate West Side Presbyn. Ch., Ridgewood, N.J., 1989-91. Fellow Life Mgmt. Inst.; mem. AICPA, Am. Soc. CLUs, Fin. Execs. Inst., Soc. Ins. Rsch., Soc. Fin. Examiners, Inst. Mgmt. Accts., S.C. Assn. CPAs, The Downtown Assn. (N.Y.C.), Forest Lake Club, Saddle River Valley Swim and Tennis Club, Beta Gamma Sigma, Omicron Delta Kappa, Beta Alpha Psi, Omicron Delta Epsilon, Sigma Phi Epsilon. Methodist. Avocations: golf, tennis. Home: 22 Autumn Ct Upper Saddle River NJ 07458-1853 Office: Capital Decision Scis LLC 22 Autumn Ct Upper Saddle River NJ 07458-1853

LOWSETH, LISA ANNE, veterinarian; b. Rock Springs, Wyo., May 6, 1958; d. Ernest James and Frances Margaret Lowseth. BS with honors, U. Wyo., 1980; DVM, Kans. State U., 1985. Assoc. veterinarian Good Shepherd Animal Clin., Albuquerque, 1986-87; rsch. fellow Lovelace Inhalation Toxicology Rsch. Inst., 1987-89; relief veterinarian, 1990-92; study dir. Internat. Rsch. and Devel. Corp., Mattawan, Mich., 1992-98; sr. toxicologist Alcon Rsch. Ltd., Ft. Worth, 1998—. Contbr. articles and abstracts to profl. jours. Mem. adv. bd. Rock Springs (Wyo.) Humane Soc., 1990-92. Mem. Am. Vet. Med. Assn., Vet. Cancer Soc., Wyo. Vet. Med. Assn., Phi Zeta, Gamma Sigma Delta, Alpha Zeta. Achievements include discovery that serum alpha fetoprotein can be used as a diagnostic tool for canine hepatic tumors. Home: 3720 Lawndale Ave Fort Worth TX 76133-2938 Office: Alcon Rsch 6201 South Fwy Fort Worth TX 76134-2001 E-mail: lisa.lowseth@alconlabs.com.

LOWTHER, FRANK EUGENE, physicist, researcher; b. Orrville, Ohio, Feb. 3, 1929; s. John Finger and Mary Elizabeth (Mackey) Lowther; m. Elizabeth E Koons, Apr. 21, 1951; children: Cynthia E, Victoria J, James A, Frank Eugene. BS Engring. Physics, Ohio State U., Columbus, 1952; postgrad., Boston U., 1952-54. Scientist missile divsn. Raytheon Corp., Boston, 1952-57, GE, Syracuse, N.Y., Daytona Beach, Fla., 1957-65; adv. to pres. Gen. Railway Signal, Rochester, 1965-67; chief sci. Purification Sci., Inc., 1967-72; mgr. ozone R & D W.R. Grace Co., Curtis Bay, Md., 1972-75; sr. engring. assoc. Linde divsn. Union Carbide Corp., Tonawanda, N.Y., 1975-80; scientist Atlantic Richfield-Energy Conversion and Materials Lab., L.A., 1980-93; prin. scientist Atlantic Richfield-Corp. Tech., 1983-85, sci. advisor, 1985-88, rsch. advisor Plano, Tex., 1988-93, cons. tech. advisor, 1993—2001. Advisor Energy Sci Inc, Canandaigua, NY, 1993—, Custom Technology Creations Inc, Canandaigua, NY, 1993—, World Ecol Inc, Geneva, 1999—. Named to Wall of Honor, Nat Aviation and Space Exploration, 2001; recipient Inventor of the Yr Award, Patent Law Assn and Tech Socs Coun, 1976. Fellow: AIAA; mem.: AAAS, IEEE (life), NY Acad Scis, Masons. Achievements include patents in field of ozone technology, plasma generators, solid state power devices, internal combustion engines, electro-desorption, oil field technology, chemical and physical reactors, weapons, others. Home and Office: 4965 Adams Dr Canandaigua NY 14424-4200

LOWTHER, GERALD HALBERT, lawyer; b. Slagle, La., Feb. 18, 1924; s. Fred B. and Beatrice (Halbert) L.; children by previous marriage: Teresa, Craig, Natalie, Lisa. AB, Pepperdine Coll., 1951; JD, U. Mo., 1951. Bar: Mo. 1951. Since practiced in, Springfield; ptnr. firm Lowther, Johnson, Joyner, Lowther, Cully & Housley. Mem. Savs. and Loan Commn. Mo., 1965-68, Commerce and Indsl. Commn. Mo., 1967-73; lectr. U. Tex., 1955-57, Crested Butte, Colo., 1958-59 Contbr. articles law jours. Past pres. Ozarks Regional Heart Assn.; Del., mem. rules com. Democratic Nat. Conv., 1968; treas. Dem. Party Mo., 1968-72, mem. platform com., 1965, 67, mem. bi-partisan commn. to reapportion Mo. senate, 1966; Bd. dirs. Greene County Guidance Clinic, Ozark Christian Counseling Service, Greene County, Mo.; past pres. Cox Med. Center. Served with AUS, 1946-47; Col. staff of Gov. Hearnes 1964, 68, Mo. Mem. ABA, Mo. Bar Assn., Greene County Bar Assn., Def. Orientation Conf. Assn., Internat. Assn. Ins. Counsel, Def. Rsch. Inst., Springfield C. of C. Clubs: Kiwanian (pres. 1962), Quarterback (pres. 1958), Tip Off (pres. 1960). Office: 901 E Saint Louis St Fl 20 Springfield MO 65806-2540 Home: 350 S John Q Hammons Pkwy Springfield MO 65806-2505

LOWTHER, THOMAS EDWARD, lawyer; b. St. Louis, Aug. 14, 1936; s. Noel Edward and Catherine Virginia (Polliham) L.; m. Lois Duggins, Dec. 28, 1963; children: Nancy, Sandra, Patricia, Susan. LLB, Washington U., St. Louis, 1962, MLA, 1999. Bar: Mo. 1962. Assoc. The Stolar Partnership, St. Louis, 1962, ptnr., 1967—, exec. com., 1985—. Chair alumni bd. govs. Washington U., 1999-2000, bd. trustees; pres., St. Joseph's Home for Boys, Marion Hall for Girls, 1997—. Recipient Disting. Alumnus award Washington U. Sch. Law, 1997. Avocations: archaeology, travel, trout fishing. Office: The Stolar Partnership 911 Washington Ave Ste 7 Saint Louis MO 63101-1243 E-mail: tel@stolarlaw.com.

LOWTHIAN, PETRENA, college president; b. Feb. 10, 1931; d. Leslie Irton and Petrena Lowthian; m. Clyde Hennies (div.); children: David L. Hennies, Geoffrey L. Hennies; m. Nisson Mandel, 1987. Grad., Royal Acad. Dramatic Art, London, 1952. Retail career with various orgns., London and Paris, 1949-57; founder, pres. Lowthian Coll. divsn. Lowthian Inc., Mpls., 1964-97. Mem. adv. coun. Minn. State Dept. Edn., Mpls. 1974-82; mem. adv. bd. Mpls. Comty. Devel. Agy., Mpls., 1983-85; mem. Downtown Coun. Mpls., 1972, chmn. retail bd., 1984-92; mem. Bd. Bus. Indsl. Advisors U. Wis.-Stout, Menomonie, 1983-89. Mem. Fashion Group, Inc. (regional bd. dirs. 1980), Rotary (mem. career and econ. edn. 1988—). Home and Office: 10 Creekside Dr Long Lake MN 55356-9431

LOWY, FREDERICK HANS, university president, psychiatrist; b. Grosspetersdorf, Austria, Jan. 1, 1933; arrived in Can., 1944; s. Eugen and Maria (Braun) L.; m. Anne Louise Cloudsley, June 25, 1965 (dec. 1973); children: David, Eric, Adam; m. Mary Kathleen O'Neil, June 1, 1975; 1 dau., Sarah. BA, McGill U., Montreal, 1955, MD, 1959, LLD, 2001, U. Toronto, 1998. Intern, resident in internal medicine Royal Victoria Hosp., Montreal, Que., Can.; resident in psychiatry U. Cin. Hosp., Cin. VA Hosp.; psychoanalytic tng. Montreal Psychoanalytic Inst.; psychiatrist Allan Meml. Inst.-Royal Victoria Hosp., Montreal-McGill U. Faculty Medicine, 1965-70; psychiatrist-in-chief Ottawa Civic Hosp.; also prof. dept. psychiatry U. Ottawa Faculty Medicine, 1971-74; prof. psychiatry, chmn. dept. U. Toronto Faculty Medicine; also dir. Clarke Inst. Psychiatry U. Toronto, 1974-80, dean Sch. Medicine, 1980-87, dir. Ctr. for Bioethics, 1989-95; rector, vice chancellor Concordia U., Montreal, 1995—. Author numerous papers in field; co-editor: A Method of Psychiatry, 1980, Alzheimer's Disease Research, 1991. Officer Order of Can. Fellow Royal Coll. Physicians and Surgeons, Am. Coll. Psychiatrists; mem. Internat. Psychoanalytic Assn., Can. Psychiat. Assn. (editor jour. 1972-76), Am. Psychiat. Assn. Office: Concordia U Office Rector 1455 de Maisonneuve Blvd W Montreal QC Canada H3G 1M8

LOWY, GEORGE THEODORE, lawyer; b. N.Y.C., Oct. 6, 1931; s. Eugene and Elizabeth Lowy; m. Pier M. Foucault, Sept. 7, 1957. BA cum laude, LLB cum laude, NYU. Bar: N.Y. 1955, U.S. Dist. Ct. (so. dist.) N.Y. 1958, U.S. Supreme Ct. 1972, U.S. Ct Appeals (2d cir.) 1975. Assoc. Cravath, Swaine and

Moore, N.Y.C., 1957-65, ptnr., 1965—. Trustee NYU Law Ctr. Found.; bd. dirs. Equitable Life Assurance Soc. U.S., Eramet, Paris, Axa Fin., U.S.; adj. prof. NYU Law Sch., 1983—88; bd. overseers Brandeis U. Grad. Sch. Internat. Econs. and Fin. Fellow ABA; mem. Am. Law Inst., Assn. of Bar of City of N.Y. (chmn. com. on corp. law), Internat. Bar Assn., Union Internat. des Avocats, Cercle Interallie Paris. Home: 580 Park Ave New York NY 10021-7313 Office: Cravath Swaine & Moore World Wide Pla 825 8th Ave Fl 43 New York NY 10019-7416 E-mail: glowy@cravath.com.

LOY, CARL AARON, retired structural design engineer; b. Fort Loramie, Ohio, July 31, 1927; s. Albert Henry and Margaret Viola (Mills) L. B in Aeronautical Engr., Ohio State U., 1955. Engring. draftsman Guided Missile Devel. Divsn., Redstone Arsenal, Ala., 1951-53; assoc. engr. Missile Sect. Bendix Aviation Corp., Mishawaka, Ind., 1955-56; sr. engr. Missile Ops. Sect., Chrysler Corp., Detroit, 1956-59; sr. structural engr. Missile and Space sect. United Aircraft, East Hartford, Conn., 1959-60; aerospace engr. Marshall Space Flight Ctr., Huntsville, Ala., 1960-87, ret., 1988. With U.S. Army, 1950-52. Mem. AIAA, Soc. Automotive Engrs., Auburn-Cord-Duesenberg Mus., Internat. Soc. of Poets. Achievements include co-invention of tank construction for space vehicles.

LOY, FRANK ERNEST, government official; b. Nuremberg, Germany, Dec. 25, 1928; came to U.S., 1939; s. Alfred Loewi and Elizabeth (Loeffler) L.; m. Dale Haven, 1963; children: Lisel, Eric Anthony. BA, UCLA, 1950; LLB, Harvard U., 1953. Bar: D.C. 1953, Calif. 1954. With O'Melveny & Myers, L.A., 1954-65; spl. asst. to adminstr. FAA, 1961-63; spl. cons. to adminstr. AID, 1963-64; dep. asst. sec. state for econ. affairs, 1965-70; sr. v.p. Pan Am. World Airways, Inc., N.Y.C., 1970-73; pres. Pennsylvania Co., Washington, 1974-79, Penn Ctrl. Corp., 1978-79; dir. Bur. Refugee Programs, Dept. State, Washington, 1980-81; pres. German Marshall Fund of U.S., 1981-95; chmn. League Conservation Voters, Washington, 1993-98, pres., 1995-96; chmn. Found. Civil Soc., 1997-98; under sec. of state for Global Affairs U.S. Govt., Washington, 1998—2001. Chmn. U.S. delegation to Climate Change Conf., The Hague, The Netherlands, 2000; dir. Nat. Gallery of Art, 1998—2001; vis. lectr. Yale Law Sch., 1996; dir. Pharm. Product Devel., Inc., 1995—98. Chmn. bd. trustees Goddard Coll., Vt., 1976-78, Environ. Def. Fund, 1983-90, Washington Ballet, 1991-94; U.S. mem. Bd. Regional Environ. Ctr. for Ctrl. and Ea. Europe, Budapest, Hungary, 1990-97. With U.S. Army, 1953-55. Home: 4920 12th St NE Washington DC 20017-2801 E-mail: loyfrank@aol.com.

LOY, RICHARD FRANKLIN, civil engineer; b. Dubuque, Iowa, July 6, 1950; s. Wayne Richard and Evelyn Mae (Dikeman) L.; m. Monica Lou Roberts, Sept. 2, 1972 (div.); children: Taneha Eve, Spencer Charles. BSCE, U. Wis., Platteville, 1973. Registered profl. engr., Wis., Ohio. Engr. aid Wis. Dept. of Transp., Superior, 1969; asst. assayer Am. Lead & Zinc Co., Shullsburg, Wis., 1970; asst. grade foreman Radandt Construction Co., Eau Claire, 1970; air quality technician U. Wis., Platteville, 1972-73; asst. city engr. City of Kaukauna, Wis., 1973-77, City of Fairborn, Ohio, 1977-89, city engr., 1989-93, pub. works dir., 1993—. Bd. dirs. YMCA Fairborn, 1990-95; mem. coun. Trinity United Ch. of Christ, Fairborn, 1989-98; chmn. Chillicothe dist. Tecumseh coun. Boy Scouts Am., 1991-93. Recipient Blue Coat award, 1983; named to Exec. Hall of Fame, N.Y., 1990. Mem. ASCE, NSPE, Am. Pub. Works Assn., Am. Water Works Assn., Inst. Transp. Engrs., Street Maintenance and Sanitation Ofcls. E-mail: GATV10.erinet.com.

LOYA, PRAXEDES, social services administrator; b. Riverside, Calif., Nov. 14, 1938; s. Jose Luz and Guadalupe (Arevalo) Loya. AA, Riverside City Coll., 1958; BA, San Jose State U., 1961; MSW, U. Washington, 1971. Adoptions supr. Riverside County, Riverside, 1972-89; social supr. II Riverside County DPSS, 1989—; social svc. supr. II Riverside County. Sgt. U.S. Army, USAF, 1963-68. Recipient Community Svc. award City of Riverside, 1980, 85. Mem. NASW, CSWO (past pres. and treas.), ERC, OIC (past treas.), CAAA (past nominations com.), LGFR (chmn.), CSSRC (bd. dirs.), CSA. Home: 5510 Magnolia Ave Riverside CA 92506-1819

LOYA, RANALDO, senior physician assistant; b. Whittier, Calif., July 1, 1954; s. Bernard Romero and Nora (Valverde) L. AA in Gen. Edn., Rio Hondo Coll., Whittier, Calif., 1980; BS in Health Sci., Calif. State U., Dominguez Hills, 1982; MHA, U. LaVerne, 1997. Cert. primary care physician asst.; cert. physician's asst.; cert. personal trainer IFPA; cert. sports nutritionist. Emergency med. technician, ambulance driver, attendant Adams Ambulance Co., South Gate, Calif., 1974-75; emergency room technician, clerk Maywood-Bell Cmty. Hosp., Bell, 1975; sr. physician asst. Physician Asst. Svcs., L.A., 1981-94; physician asst. urgent care Ball-Taft Med. Clinic Ctr., Anaheim, Calif., 1984-85; sr. physician asst., corp. v.p., admin. Signal Med. Mgmt., Long Beach, 1985-88; sr. physician asst. U. Calif. Irvine Med. Ctr., Orange, 1988-90, U. So. Calif. Emergency Med. Assoc., L.A., 1989-90, U. Calif. Mt. Zion Med. Ctr., San Francisco, 1990-94, La Clinica Esperanza Mission Neighborhood Health Ctr., San Francisco, 1991-94. Fellow: Am. Acad. Physician Assts., Washington, 1982—; Calif. Acad. Physician Assts., Anaheim, 1982—; past mem. instl. review bd., Project Inform, San Francisco, 1991-92. Contbr. New England Journal of Medicine, 1990; mem. editl. bd. Clinician Reviews. Human rights commr., City of Palm Springs, Calif., 1996—; mem. Long Beach Pride, Inc., 1987-90, past v.p.; mem. Human Rights Campaign Fund, Washington, 1996—; mem. Orange County Gay and Lesbian Comm. Svcs. Ctr., Garden Grove, Calif., 1987-88; mem. adv. bd. The Desert Sun Newspaper Cmty.; mem. Dr. Martin Luther King Commemorative Day Com., Amnesty Internat. With USN, 1975-79, Hawaii. Recipient Meritorious Mast, USN, 1978. Fellow Physicians Assts. Latino Heritage; mem. NAACP, Nat. Assn. Mulitcultural Edn., Calif. Acad. Physician Assts. (minority affairs com.), Calif. Assn. Human Rels. Orgns., Nat. Trust for Hist. Preservation, Internat. AIDS Soc., Drew U. Med. Sch. Alumni Assn., Hispanic C. of C. Democrat. Mem. Unity Ch. Avocations: reading, public speaking, weight lifting. Home: 1179 N Calle Rolph Palm Springs CA 92262-4938

LOYD, PAMELA ANN, academic administrator, educator; b. Detroit, June 18, 1968; d. David Jr. and Deborah Ann (Young) Dail; m. Keith Lamar Loyd, Jan. 19, 1996; children: Keith Lamar, Kristopher Levon. AS, Hawaii Pacific U., 1992; BBA, Detroit Coll. Bus., 1994; MSA, Ctrl. Mich. U., 1995; PhD, Capella U., 2001. Cert. in credit mgmt. Mfg. supr. Ford Motor Co., Livonia, Mich., 1996-97; adj. faculty Baker Coll., Auburn Hills, 1998—, U. Detroit-Mercy, 1998—2001; mem. faculty dept. bus. and corp. svcs., instr. Monroe County C.C., Monroe, Mich., 1998—2002; dir. grad. admissions and student svcs. Marygrove Coll., Detroit, 2002—. Cons., mem. Southfield 2020 Project, City of Southfield, Mich., 1998—. Author: Success. . .Old Testament Truths: A 30-Day Guide to Reaching Your Goals and Objectives, 1998, Newness of Life, Poetry for the Soul, 1998; contbr. articles and poetry to publs. Participant, Sportfishing Facility, Del Mar Beach, Calif., 1987. Sgt. USMC, 1986-95. Decorated Navy Commendation medal; recipient Cert. of Appreciation, Christian Broadcasting Network, 1998. Mem. AAUP, Women Marine Assn., Am. Legion, Nat. Black MBA Assn., Sigma Iota Epsilon. Christian. Avocations: reading, writing, exercise, listening to Christian music. E-mail: ployd53787@hotmail.com.

LOYKE, HUBERT FRANK, internist, cardiologist; b. Cleve., Sept. 9, 1923; s. Frank Alex and Casimer Marie (Malczewski) L.; m. Ellen Marie Eynon, June 16, 1951; children: Thomas F., Christopher J. BS, John Carroll U., 1944; MD, St. Louis U., 1948; postgrad., U. Mich., 1952. Intern St. Alexis Hosp., Cleve., 1948-49; resident St. John Hosp., 1949-51; fellow in hypertension U. Mich., 1951-52; sch. physician Pub. Health Dept., Cleve., 1952-54; chief Hypertension Clinic, 1957-95; dir. Hypertension Lab., 1957-95; internist, cardiologist St. Vincent Charity Hosp., 1957-95; med. examiner FAA, Washington, 1961-63; chief cardiology St. John Hosp., Cleve., 1962-65; chief of staff St. Augustine Manor, 1971-72. Med. advisor ARC, Cleve., 1982-92; physician mem. Sr. Friendship Ctr., Ft. Myers, Fla., 1997-2000. Reviewer 6 med. jours., 1972-95; contbr. over 50 articles to profl. jours. Vol. ARC, Ft. Myers, Fla., 1997—. Capt. USAF, 1955-57. Grantee NIH, 1959-71, Kidney Found., 1977-78, Morison Found., 1980-81. Mem. AMA, Internat. Soc. Hypertension, Coun. High Blood Pressure Rsch. Democrat. Roman Catholic. Achievements include identification of effect of altitude on Sickle Cell disease, liver blood pressure effect, diseases which lower blood pressure, elements which affect blood pressure; demonstrated lowering blood pressure by animal ACE blockade. Avocations: gardening, stamps. Home: 11209 Naomi Dr Parma OH 44130-1557 Office: St Vincent Charity Hosp 2351 E 22d St Cleveland OH 44115-3111

LOZADA, JACOB, federal agency administrator; BS, U. P.R.; MPA, Baylor U.; D in Edn., Walden U. Prin. Global Healthcare Practice Booz Allen and Hamilton; sr. health care planner Sherikon, Inc.; mng. cons. Electronic Data Sys. (EDS) Web Univs. and Tng.; asst. sec. human resources and adminstrn. Dept. Vets. Affairs, Washington, 2001—. Office: US Dept Vets Affairs Human Resources and Adminstrn 810 Vermont Ave NW Washington DC 20420*

LOZANO, JOSE, nephrologist; b. San Vicente, El Salvador, Feb. 11, 1941; came to U.S., 1968; s. Jose E. and Transito Maria (Mendez) L.; m. Hilda Berganza, Jan. 27, 1965; children: Jose E., Claudia Maria. MD, U. El Salvador, 1965. Diplomate Am. Bd. Internal Medicine, Am. Bd. Nephrology. Rotating intern Nat. Med. Ctr., San Salvador, El Salvador, 1963-64; asst. resident in internal medicine Rosales Hosp., 1965-66, resident in internal medicine, 1966-67, chief resident in internal medicine, 1967-68; resident in internal medicine Baylor U. Affiliated Hosps., Houston, 1968-70, fellow in nephrology, 1970-71, 73-74; asst. prof. medicine U. El Salvador, 1971-72; internist and nephrologist Social Security Hosp., San Salvador, 1971-72; instr. in medicine Baylor Coll. Medicine, Houston, 1974-75, asst. prof. medicine in nephrology, 1975-76, clin. asst. prof. medicine, 1976-80; mem. staff internal medicine St. Elizabeth Hosp., Beaumont Med./Surg. Hosp., Bapt. Hosp., Beaumont, Tex., 1976; med. dir. Golden Triangle Dialysis Ctr., 1977-98, BMA Jasper, Jasper, Tex., 1986-98, BMA Orange, Orange, 1987-90. Med. dir. Jasper Dialysis Ctr., 1986-98; mem. Kidney Health Care Adv. Com., 1981-82; pesenter in field. Contbr. articles to profl. publs. Fellow ACP; mem. AMA, Am. Soc. Nephrology, Internat. Soc. Nephrology, Tex. Med. Assn., Harris County Med. Soc., Jefferson County Med. Soc., Physicians for A Nat. Health Plan. Avocations: study of socioeconomic factors in healthcare in U.S., Catholic theologies. Office: Beaumont Nephrology Assocs 2900 North St 410 Beaumont TX 77702-1542 Address: 3150 Medical Center Dr Ste 3 Beaumont TX 77701 E-mail: bmtnp410@aol.com. *In terms of health care we need a system that provides easy, uncomplicated access to primary care services. We urgently need a health care system that provides universal and comprehensive access to health care without considerations given to the ability to pay, race, gender, religion or sexual orientation. We need a system that is independent of employment, in which people with existing conditions are not restricted from free and adequate access to health care. The creation of a universal health care system is in the best interests of all citizens of this country.*

LOZANSKY, EDWARD DMITRY, physicist, author, consultant; b. Kiev, Ukraine, Feb. 10, 1941; came to U.S., 1977; s. Dmitry R. and Dina M. (Chizhik) L.; m. Tatiana I. Yershov, Feb. 27, 1971; 1 child, Tania. MS, Moscow Phys. Engring. Inst., 1966; PhD, Inst. Atomic Energy, Moscow, 1969; LHD, Waynesburg Coll., 1995. Asst. prof. Moscow State U., 1969-71; assoc. prof. Mil. Tank Acad., Moscow, 1971-75; prof. U. Rochester, N.Y., 1977-80, Am. U., Washington, 1981-83, L.I. U., Bklyn., 1983-87; pres. Independent U., Washington, 1987-91. Exec. dir. Andrei Sakharov Inst., Washington, 1981-86; pres. Russia House, Inc., 1991—, Am. U. in Moscow, 1992—, Am. Univs. in Russia, Ukraine and New Independent States, 1994—. Author: Theory of the Spark, 1976, Mathematics, 1976, For Tatiana, 1984, Andrei Sakharov, 1986, Mathematical Competitions, 1988, Democracy: USA-Russia, 1994, Winning Solutions, 1996, Russia: Experience in Democracy, 1997, Foundations of Free Society, 1998, Sociology of Politics: Comparative Study of the American and Russian Realities, 2001. Mem. Russian Acad. Soc. Scis. Avocations: skiing, chess, lecturing on Russia. Office: Russia House 1800 Connecticut Ave NW Washington DC 20009-5731 E-mail: Lozansky@aol.com.

LOZITO, GILDA LELIA, artist, painter; b. N.Y.C., Dec. 20; d. Massimo and Concetta (D'Amico) Greco; m. Rocco Jerome Lozito, Aug. 19, 1941. Student, Bono Hall Acad Fine Arts, 1937-41, Norton Sch. Art, 1949-53, Palm Beach Community Coll., 1960. Art instr. nat. Youth Adminstrn. Art Ctr., N.Y.C., 1939-41; Fed. Civil Svc., Eglin Field, Fla., 1942-45, Morrison Field, 1946; Architect Agnes Ballard, West Palm Beach, 1947-52; art instr. pvt. practice, 1953—; artist Bagatelle Art Shop, Palm Beach, 1960-65; art consignments Gallery Gemini, 1962-69; art judge City of West Palm Beach, 1968; lectr., cons. Fla., 1953—. Cons. in art Pub. Civic Activities, 1970s; dir. exhbns. Nat. League of Am. Pen Women, Palm Beach, 1980s; art instr. in pvt. practice, 1996-99. One woman shows at Norton Mus. Art, West Palm Beach, 1954, Hobbelink Kaastra Art Gallery, Palm Beach, 1955, Upstairs Art Gallery, Palm Beach, 1959, 1st Nat. In Palm Beach, 1970, 71, 72, 73, 74, 76, 90, 91, 92, 93, 94; exhibited in group shows at Palm Beach Coun. Arts, Soc. Four Arts Contemporary Juried Exhbn., Northwood Inst. Art, West Palm Beach, 1997, Palm Beach (Fla.) Garden Gallery Rest., 1998; contbr. illustrations to mags. and jour., art reprodns. for book covers, art revs. in Palm Beach Today, Palm Beach's Pictorial P.B. with photograph, Palm Beach Daily News, Photo. of Paintings; portrait in oil installation wall of City Hall, West Palm Beach, 1995; honored in Heart Ball mag., 2000. Chairperson 20th Anniversary Celebration of Nat. League of Arts & Pen, 1985. Recipient Hon. Diploma awarded in the 2,000 Women of Achievement, 1972, First Prize award Palm Beach Art League Juried Art Exhibition, 1953, First Prize award Lake Worth Art League, 1954, Awards of merit Norton Sch. of Art, 1951, 52, Award of Merit, Palm Beach Nat. League of Art & Pen Women, 1975. Mem. Fla. Artists Group Inc., Soc. Four Arts, Fla. Fedn. Art, Artists Equity Nat., Nat. League Am. Arts and Pen Women (pres.), Palm Beach Quills and Artists, Northwood's Women Aux. in Arts, Nat. Mus. Women Artists, Nat. Mus. Women in the Arts (charter), Fla. Watercolor Soc., Nat. League Am. Women (pres. Palm Beach branch 1985, chairperson anniversary celebration), Norton Mus. Art, Il Circolo Cultural Assn. Avocations: poetry, ceramics, sculpture, calligraphy, gardening. Home and Office: 307 Cordova Rd West Palm Beach FL 33401-7907

LOZOFF, BETSY, pediatrician; b. Milw., Dec. 19, 1943; d. Milton and Marjorie (Morse) L.; 1 child, Claudia Brittenham. BA, Radcliffe Coll., 1965; MD, Case Western Res. U., 1971, MS, 1981. Diplomate Am. Bd. Pediat. From asst. prof. to prof. pediatrics Case Western Res. U., Cleve., 1974-93; prof. pediatrics U. Mich., Ann Arbor, 1993—, dir. Ctr. for Human Growth and Devel., 1993—. Recipient Rsch. Career Devel. award Nat. Inst. Child Health and Human Devel., 1984-88. Fellow Am. Acad. Pediatrics; mem. Soc. for Pediatric Rsch., Soc. Rsch. in Child Devel. (program com. 1991-97), Soc. Behavioral Pediatrics (exec. com. 1985-88), Ambulatory Pediatric Soc. Office: Univ Mich Ctr Human Growth and Devel 300 N Ingalls St Ann Arbor MI 48109-2007

LU, ADOLPH, physicist, researcher; b. Chengdu, Sichuan, China, Feb. 19, 1942; , U.S.1965; s. Frank Chao and Jean Wang Lu; m. Karen Wenfeng Liu, Mar. 10, 1993. BS, Queen's U., Kingston, Can., 1964; MA, U. Toronto, Can., 1965; PhD, U. Calif., Berkeley, 1973. Rsch. physicist U. Paris, 1973—75; rsch. faculty U. Calif., Santa Barbara, 1976—2002, Berkeley, 2002—. Jour. referee IEEE Procs., 1998—. Contbr. articles to more than 400 profl. pubs. Mem.: Am. Phys. Soc. Avocations: skiing, kayaking, calligraphy, guitar. Home: 117 Eagle Trace Dr Half Moon Bay CA 94019 Office: Univ Calif Santa Barbara CA 93106

LU, BAO-YUAN, biochemist, researcher; b. Guichi, China, Dec. 11, 1969; s. Rongfa Lu and Xiaozhen Zheng; m. Wei Liao, May 24, 1971; 1 child, Zean Liao. PhD, Inst. Organic Chemistry, Shanghai, China, 1997. Postdoctoral rschr. Lab. Protein Biochemistry and Tech., Nantes, France, 1998, Inst. Molecular Medicine, Houston, 1999—. Author of many sci. journals. Mem. Am. Chemic Soc., 2001; mem. Sigma Xi. Achievements include patented novel conformational isomers of recombinant murine prion protein. Home: 5606 Bissonnet Apt 67 Houston TX 77081 Office: Inst Molecular Medicine 2121 W Holcombe Houston TX 77030 Fax: (713) 500-2424. E-mail: lubaoyuan@yahoo.com.

LU, CHRISTOPHER DAH-CHENG, nutritionist, educator, university dean; b. Taipei, Taiwan, Aug. 30, 1951; came to U.S., 1976; s. Teh Chiao and Chien Yun (Wu) L.; m. Hsin Huang Lu, June 2, 1979; 1 child, Stephanie Hwan. BS, Nat. Taiwan U., 1974; MS, U. Wis., 1978, PhD, 1981. Cert. mgr., profl. animal scientist. Rsch. asst. U. Wis., Madison, 1976-81; nutritionist Garver Feed & Supply Co., 1980-81; scientist, nutritionist and biochemist Internat. Harvester Co., Elk Grove, Ill., 1981-82; rsch. scientist Prairie View (Tex.) A&M U., 1982-85; prof., dir. Am. Inst. for Goat Rsch., Langston, Okla., 1985-89; prof., dir. internat. programs Langston U., 1989-91; dep. dean Coll. Agr. Sultan Qaboos U., Muscat, Oman, 1992-93, dean Coll. Agr. Oman, 1993-99; dean Sch. Agr. and Natural Sci., SUNY Coll. Agr. and Tech., Morrisville, 1999—2002; vice chancellor acad. affairs U. Hawaii, Hilo, 2002—. Vis. prof. Baylor Coll. Medicine, 1991-92. Author numerous publs. in field. Trustee South-East Consortium for Internat. Devel., Washington, 1985-91. Named hon. prof. U. Autonoma de Zacatecas, 1991, Northwestern Argl. U., China, 1989, U. Autonoma de Nuevo Leon, Mexico, 1988; recipient Outstanding Svc. award Fla. A&M U., 1990, Appreciation award Okla. Goat Producers Assn., 1989; Leadership fellow Nat. Ctr. for Food and Agr. Policy, 1988. Mem. Am. Soc. Animal Sci. (chmn. livestock com. chmn. goat session 1989, 90, 92), Am. Dairy Sci. Assn., Am. Inst. Nutrition, Nutrition Soc., Internat. Goat Assn. (mem. editorial bd., bd. dirs.). Office: U Hawaii at Hilo Office of Vice Chancellor Acad Affairs 200 W Kawili St Hilo HI 96720-4091 E-mail: chrislu@hawaii.edu.

LU, DAN, systems analyst, mathematician, consultant; b. Beijing, Jan. 22, 1960; came to U.S., 1981; s. Yingzhong Lu and Huaiqing Chen; m. Hong Lou, Sept. 28, 1994; children: Katherine H, Isabel. BS in Physics, Beijing U., 1981; MS in Physics, U. Wash., 1983, PhD in Theoretical Physics, 1986. Tchg., rsch. asst. U. Wash., Seattle, 1981-86; postdoctoral rsch. assoc. Washington U., St. Louis, 1986-88; R&D mgr. Yu Feng Internat. Ltd., Hong Kong, 1988-90; sys. cons. Summit Computer Svcs., Charlotte, N.C., 1991-93; sr. sys. cons. Criterion Group, 1993-94; bus. sys. analyst, mathematician INMAR Enterprise, Inc. Info. Tech. (formerly CMS, Inc.), Winston-Salem, N.C., 1994—, sr. technical architect, 1999—. Contbr. articles to profl. pubs. China-U.S. Physics Examination and Application fellow, 1981. Mem. Am. Phys. Soc. Achievements include development of model for market promotion, forecasting system for coupon redemption, set of subroutines to calculate EXAFS electron energy losses. Home: 325 Craver Pointe Dr Clemmons NC 27012-8926 Office: INMAR Enterprises Inc Info Tech 2650 Pilgrim Ct Winston Salem NC 27106-5238

LU, DAVID JOHN, historian, writer; b. Keelung, Taiwan, Sept. 28, 1928; came to U.S., 1950, naturalized, 1960; s. Ming and Yeh (Lai) L.; m. Annabelle Compton, May 29, 1954; children: David John, Daniel Mark, Cynthia King, Stephen Paul. BA in Econs, Nat. Taiwan U., 1950; postgrad., Westminster Theol. Sem., Phila., 1950-52; M. Internat. Affairs, Columbia, 1954; certificate, East Asian Inst., 1954, PhD, 1960. Editor Prentice-Hall, Inc., 1956-60; instr. Rutgers U., 1959; asst. prof. history Bucknell U., Lewisburg, Pa., 1960-64, assoc. prof., 1964-69, prof., 1969-94, prof. emeritus, 1994—, dir. Ctr. for Japanese Studies, 1965-94. Cons. on global edn. Pa. Dept. Edn., 1961-62, 78, U.S. Dept. Edn., 1973-85; resident dir. associated Kyoto program Doshisha U., 1987-88. Author: From the Marco Polo Bridge to Pearl Harbor, 1961, (Japanese edit.) Taiheiyo Senso e no Dotei, 1967, Sources of Japanese History, 2 vols., 1974, Bicentennial History of the United States (in Japanese), 1976, The Life and Times of Matsuoka Yosuke, 1880-1946 (in Japanese), 1981, Inside Corporte Japan: The Art of Fumble-free Management, 1987, Japan: A Documentary History, 1997, Agony of Choice, Matsuoka Yosuke in the Rise and Fall of the Japanese Empire, 2002; translator: The China Quagmire, 1983, What Is Total Quality Control? The Japanese Way, 1985, Kanban, Just-in-Time at Toyota, 1986, Total Quality Control for Management: Strategies and Techniques from Toyota and Toyoda Gosei, 1987 TQC (Total Quality Control), The Wisdom of Japan, 1988; contbr. Sekai to Nippon, weekly, Tokyo. Fulbright-Hays scholar Japan, 1966-67 Presbyterian. Home: 1303 Mazeland Dr Bel Air MD 21015-6358

LU, EDWARD TSANG, astronaut; b. Springfield, Mass., July 1, 1963; s. Charlie and Snowlily Lu. BSE, Cornell U., 1984; DSc in Applied Physics, Stanford U., 1989. Vis. scientist High Altitude Observatory, Boulder, Colo., 1989—92; postdoctoral fellow Inst. Astronomy, Honolulu, 1992—95; mission specialist NASA, Houston, 1995—. Astronaut Space Shuttle Atlantis, 1997, 2000. Fellow, Hughes Aircraft Co.; scholar Presdl. scholar, Cornell U. Mem.: Am. Astronomical Soc., Exptl. Aircraft Assn., Aircraft Owners & Pilots Assn. Avocations: aerobatic flying, coaching wrestling, piano, tennis, surfing. Office: Astronaut Office CB NASA Johnson Space Center Houston TX 77058*

LU, FRANCIS GORDON, psychiatrist; b. San Francisco, Oct. 22, 1949; s. Gordon G. and Jean (Chu) L.; m. Phuong-Thuy Le, July 6, 1996. BA, Columbia U., 1971; MD, Dartmouth U., 1974. Diplomate Am. Bd. Psychiatry and Neurology. Resident in psychiatry Mt. Sinai Med. Sch., 1977; psychiatrist U. Calif., San Francisco, 1977—. Fellow Am. Psychiat. Assn. (Kun-po Soo award 2001), Pacific Rim Coll. Psychiatrists; mem. Phi Beta Kappa. Office: San Francisco Gen Hosp 1001 Potrero Ave San Francisco CA 94110 E-mail: francis.lu@sfdph.org.

LU, GUIYANG, electrical engineer; b. Guiyang, China, May 10, 1946; came to U.S., 1982; s. Wen and Yunqiu Deng; m. Jing Du; 1 child, Jia. Degree in elec. engring., Tsing Hua U., Beijing, 1970; postgrad., South China U. Tech., Guangzhou, 1980-81; MA in Math., Calif. State U., Fresno, 1984; MSEE, Poly. U., N.Y.C., 1986. Instr. in elec. engring. South China U. Tech., Guangzhou, 1973-80; v.p. engring. Kawahara Corp., N.Y.C., 1986-88; H.S. math. tchr. N.Y.C. Bd. Edn., 1988-90; engring. cons. Measurement and Control Sys., N.Y.C., 1989-90; sr. R&D engr. Avid Inc., Norco, Calif., 1991-98; sr. RF engr. Securay Key, Chatsworth, 1998—. U.S. patentee in field. Mem. IEEE. Home: 1718 Eastgate Ave Upland CA 91784-9210 Office: 20447 Nordhoff St Chatsworth CA 91311-6112 E-mail: gylu@aol.com.

LU, HSIN HUANG, radiologist, educator; b. Taichung, Taiwan, July 31, 1954; came to U.S., 1969; d. Hsien-lu and Hui-lien Huang; m. Christopher Dah-Cheng Lu, June 2, 1979; 1 child, Stephanie. BS in Pharmacy, U. Wis., 1977, MD, 1982. Diplomate Am. Bd. Radiology, Am. Bd. Radiation Oncology. Intern Loyola Univ. Med. Ctr., Maywood, 1982-83; resident Baylor Coll. Medicine, Houston, 1983-86; staff radiation oncologist Radiotherapy Assoc., 1986-89, M.H. Radiation Oncology, Houston, 1989—; asst. prof. Baylor U. Coll. Medicine, 1986-95, assoc. prof., 1995—. Sec. M.H. Radiation Oncology Assoc., 1989—; mem. staff Meth. Hosp., Houston, St. Luke Hosp., Tex. Children Hosp. and Harris County Hosp. Dist. Author: Textbook of Sterotactic and Functional Neurosurgery, 1997. Mem. choir West Houston Chinese Ch., 1993—. Mem. AMA, Am. Soc. Clin. Oncology, Am. Coll. Radiology, Am. Soc. Therapeutic Radiology and Oncology, Am. Soc. Breast Disease, Am. Radium Soc. Avocations: tennis, walking, singing, travel. Office: Meth Hosp 6565 Fannin St # Ms121B Houston TX 77030-2707 E-mail: prahhl@netscape.net.

LU, JIN-QIN, electrical engineer; b. July 9, 1957; s. Hanyao Lu and Fengshian Chen; m. Weiqing Wang, Apr. 22, 1985; children: Yijia, Yiyao. MSEE, Yokohama (Japan) Nat. U., 1988, PhD in Elec. Engring., 1991. Rsch. fellow Sony Corp., Tokyo, 1991-95; mgr. Sony Am., San Jose, 1995-97, NEC Electronics, Santa Clara, Calif., 1997—. Contbr. articles to profl. jours. Mem. IEEE (sr.). Achievements include 6 software patents pending. Avocations: traveling, skiing, fishing. E-mail: jin-qin. Home: 818 Wintergreen Way Palo Alto CA 94303-4109 E-mail: lu@el.nec.com.

LU, JOHN KUEW-HSIUNG, physiology educator, endocrinologist; b. Miaoli, Taiwan, Republic of China, Sept. 16, 1937; came to U.S., 1967; s. En-Gie and Jan-Mei (Wu) L.; m. Marianne Mann Wang, Dec. 29, 1969; children: Judith Maria, John Lawrence. BS, Nat. Taiwan Normal U., Taipei, 1961; MS, Nat. Taiwan U. Med. Sch., 1967; PhD, Mich. State U., 1972. Postdoctoral fellow U. Pitts., 1972-74; rsch. assoc. Mich. State U., East Lansing, 1974-75; asst. prof. U. Calif.-San Diego, La Jolla, 1975-77; asst. prof. depts. ob-gyn. and neurobiology UCLA Sch. Med., 1977-82, assoc. prof., 1982-88, prof., 1988—. Mem. biochem. endocrinology study sect. NIH, Bethesda, 1990-94, Health Reviewers Res., NIH, 1994-98. Mem. editl. bd. Procs. Soc. Exptl. Biology and Medicine, N.Y.C., 1987—93, mem. publ. com., 1996—2001; contbr. Recipient Methods to Extend Rsch. in Time award, NIH, 1987—97; grantee Rsch. grantee, Nat. Inst. Aging, 1980—91. Mem. Soc. for Study Reprodn., Endocrine Soc., Am. Physiol. Soc., Soc. for Gynecologic Investigation, Soc. Exptl. Biology and Medicine. Home: 1129 Iliff St Pacific Palisades CA 90272-3830 Office: UCLA Sch Medicine Dept Ob-Gyn 22-172 CHS 10833 Le Conte Ave Los Angeles CA 90095-1740 E-mail: jlu@mednet.ucla.edu.

LU, JUN, biologist; b. Beijing, Jan. 9, 1968; arrived in U.S., 1994; s. Xuchu Lu and Wenmin Wang; m. Xinshi Liu, Aug. 29, 1997; 1 child Rachel J. BS, Wuhan (China) U., 1988, MS, 1991; PhD, Baylor Coll. Medicine, 2001. Rsch. assoc. Cardiovasc. Inst., Chinese Acad. Med. Scis., Beijing, 1991—93, asst. prof., 1993—94; predoctoral rsch. fellow Baylor Coll. Medicine, Houston, 1994—2001; postdoctoral fellow Howard Hughes Inst., Brigham Women Hosp., Boston, 2001—. Contbr. articles to profl. jours. Recipient award of nat. key project, Chinese Nat. Com. Sci. and Tech., Beijing, 1996, Chair's Fund allowance, Gordon Rsch. Conf., N.H., 2000. Mem.: Soc. for Developmental Biology, N.Am. Vascular Biology Orgn., Sigma Xi. Office: Howard Hughes Med Inst Brigham Women Hosp 20 Shattuck St Boston MA 02115

LU, MI, computer engineer, educator; b. Chongqing, Sichuan, China, July 22, 1949; d. Chong Pu Lu and Shu Sheng Fan. MS, Rice U., 1984, PhD, 1987. Registered profl. engr. From asst. prof. to assoc. prof. Tex. A&M U., Coll. Sta., 1987-98, prof., 1998—. Stream chmn. 7th Internat. Conf. Computing and Info., Peterborough, Ont., Can., 1995; conf. chmn. 5th Internat. Conf. Computer Sci. and Informatics, 2000, 6th Internat. Conf., 2002. Assoc. editor Jour. Computing and Info., 1995—, Info. Sci., 1996-97. 2002--; contbr. articles to profl. jours. Mem. Computer Soc. of IEEE (sr.). Office: Tex A&M U Dept Elec Engring College Station TX 77843

LU, MILTON MING-DEH, plastic surgeon, consultant; b. Chengtu, China, Nov. 12, 1919; came to U.S., 1946; naturalized, 1955. s. Yow-Cheng and Su-Cheng (Cheng) L.; m. Hiltrud Marie M. Reineke, Dec. 27, 1963; children: Barbara Ann, Winifred, Rita Doreen, Oliver. DDS, W. China Union U., 1943, MD, 1951; MS, U. Rochester, 1952. Resident Strong Meml. Hosp., Rochester, N.Y., 1947-51; fellow in plastic surgery St. Louis, 1952-56; asst., instr. Strong Meml. Hosp.-Sch. Medicine and Dentistry U. Rochester, 1946-50; asst. plastic surgeon Barnes Hosp.-Wash. U., 1952-56; gen. surgeon VA Hosp., Lebanon, Pa., 1956-58; plastic surgeon St. Joseph's Hosp., Lancaster, Lancaster Gen. Hosp. Cons. Good Samaritan Hosp., Lebanon, Pa. Contbr. articles to profl. jours. Served to maj. Med. Unit, Chinese Army, 1945. Recipient Disting. Svc. award VA Hosp. Fellow Internat. Coll. Dentists, Royal Coll Health, ACS; mem. Robert Ivy Soc. Plastic Surgeons, AMA, Pa. Med. Soc., Lancaster County Med. Soc., Am. Trauma Soc. (founder mem.), Am. Burn Assn. Mem. Soc. Of Friends. Home: 2114 Oregon Pike Lancaster PA 17601-4605

LU, MING LIANG, systems analyst, modeler; b. Xinbin, Liaoning, China, May 13, 1960; s. Chun Jiu and Shang Qing (Wu) L.; m. Wei Lin, Nov. 21, 1985; 1 child, Si. B of Engring., Dalian (China) U. Tech., 1982, M of Engring., 1985, D of Engring, 1989. Asst. lectr. Dalian U. Tech., 1985-86, lectr., 1989-91; rschr. Leeds (Eng.) U., 1991-94; sr. rschr. Tokyo Inst. Tech., 1994-95, assoc. prof., 1995-97; v.p. Aigis Sys., Inc., Newark, 1997-99; product integration mgr. ABB Automation Inc. Intelligent Solution Products, Bloomfield, N.J., 1999-2000; sr. advisor Aspen Tech., Inc., Cambridge, Mass., 2000—. Cons. Japan Energy Corp., Okayama, 1994-97; presenter in field. Contbr. 80 articles to profl. jours., chpts. to books. Mem. Am. Inst. Chem. Engrs., Internat. Soc. Productivity Enhancement, Internat. Soc. for Measurement and Control. Avocations: music, swimming, mountain hiking. E-mail: mingllu@attbi.com.

LU, MING QI, pharmaceutical company executive; b. Qingdao, China, Jan. 26, 1956; came to U.S., 1989; s. Xing Dong Lu and Shu Ying Liu; m. Yen Lee Apr. 13, 1992; children: Lillian, Edbert. MD, Qingdao (China) Med. Coll., 1985; PhD, U. Conn., 1994. Asst. prof. Ocean U. Qingdao, 1986-89; postdoctoral rsch. fellow Mt. Sinai Med. Ctr., N.Y.C., 1989-90, Johns Hopkins U., Balt., 1994-97; scientist West Pharms., Lionville, 1997, sr. scientist, 1998; mgr. pharm. R&D NexMed Inc., Robbinsville, NJ, 1998, asst. dir., 1999—2001, dir., 2002—. Contbr. articles to profl. jours. Johns Hopkins fellow NIH, 1994-95; U. Conn. Rsch. assistantship, 1991-94. Mem. Am. Assn. of Pharm. Sci., Am. Physiology Soc. Avocations: swimming, reading, music. Office: NexMed Inc 350 Corporate Blvd Robbinsville NJ 08691 E-mail: mingqilu@aol.com.

LU, NINGPING, environmental chemist; b. Sichuan, China, June 18, 1941; d. Yiungdi and Jinghua (Liu) L.; m. Li Pin-Fun, July 23, 1964 (div. 1990); children: Ying, Nin. BS in Biophysics, Sichuan U., 1964; MS of Soil Chemistry, Auburn U., 1990, PhD in Environtl. Soil Chemistry, 1993. Dir. Atomic Agrl. Ins., Sichuan, 1983; rsch. assoc. Fertilizer Ins., 1985-86; postdoctoral rsch. assoc. Auburn U., 1993-94, Los Alamos Nat. Lab., 1994-97, tech. staff mem., 1997—. Vis. scientist Purdue U., West Lafayette, Ind., 1983-84, Auburn U., 1984-85; cons. UN Devel. Program in China, Beijing, 1997—. Contbr. over 70 articles to profl. publs. Mem. Agronomy Soc. of Am., Soil Sci. Soc. of Am., Am. Chem. Soc., N.Y. Acad. of Sci., Phi Kappa Phi. Achievements include development of remedial processes of radionuclide (e.g. uranium-238, cesium-137, plutonium-239, strontium-90, Americium-241, american-241, strantium-90) contaminated soils, surface water and ground water; utlization of municipal solid wastes on agricultural land; research in remediation of radionuclide contaminated soil, water and sites; actinide interactions with colloids of metal oxides, clays and silica; transport of radio-colloids in groundwater; stability, solubility and speciation of actinides at nuclear waste repository sites. Office: E-ET Los Alamos Nat Lab Ms J514 Los Alamos NM 87545-0001 E-mail: ningping@lanl.gov.

LU, PAUL HAIHSING, mining engineer, geotechnical consultant; b. Hsinchu, Taiwan, Apr. 6, 1921; came to U.S., 1962; m. Sylvia Chin-Pi Liu, May 5, 1951; children: Emily, Flora. BS in Mining Engring., Hokkaido U., Sapporo, Japan, 1945; PhD in Mining Engring., U. Ill., 1967. Sr. mining engr., br. chief Mining Dept. Taiwan Govt., Taipei, 1946-56; sr. indsl. specialist mining and geology U.S. State Dept./Agy. for Internat. Devel., 1956-62; rsch. mining engr. Denver Rsch. Ctr. Bur. of Mines, U.S. Dept. Interior, 1967-90; geotech. cons. Lakewood, Colo., 1991—. Contbr. over 60 articles to profl. jours. Rsch. fellow Hokkaido U., 1945-46, Ill. Mining Inst., 1966-67. Mem. Internat. Soc. for Rock Mechanics, Am. Rock Mechanics Assn., Mining and Materials Processing Inst. Japan, Chinese Inst. of Mining and Metall. Engrs. (dir., mining com. chair 1960-62, Tech. Achievement award 1962, merit award 1996). Achievements include development of prestressed concrete mine supports; invention of new technologies of rock stress measurement with hydraulic borehole pressure cells and measurement of geomechanical properties of rock masses with borehole pressure cells; invention of integrity factor approach to mine structure design. Home and Office: 1001 S Foothill Dr Lakewood CO 80228-3404

LU, SHIH-PENG, history educator; b. Kao-Yu, Chiang-Su, China, Sept. 16, 1928; s. Ch'un-Tai and Chu-Yin (Chia) L.; m. Wei-Chun Julia Lee; children: Ting Ting, Shin. BA, Nat. Taiwan U., Taipei, 1952. Cert. full prof., Ministry of Edn., Taiwan. Tchg. asst. Taiwan U., Taipei, 1953-55; rsch. asst. Acad. Sinica, 1955-58; lectr. Tunghai U., Taichung, Taiwan, 1958-63, assoc. prof. Taiwan, 1963-67, prof. Taiwan, 1967—. Vis. scholar Harvard U., Cambridge, Mass., 1961-63; rsch. fellow Yale U., New Haven, 1980-81; dir. evening divsn. Tunghai U., 1972-81, chmn. dept. history, 1981-87, dean Coll. Arts, 1988-94; dir. Chinese Culture Monthly, Taichung, 1988—. Author: Vietnam During the Period of Chinese Rule, 1964 (Nat. Sci. Coun. Publ. award 1965), The Modern History of China, 1979 (World Books Co. Authors award 1979), The Contemporary History of China, 1991 (Ministry of Edn. Outstanding Textbook award 1992); editor Chinese Culture Monthly, 1979— (Ministry of Edn. Best Jour. award 1991). 2nd lt. ROTC, Chinese Mil., 1952-53. Named Outstanding Youth, China Youth Corps, Taiwan, 1952, Outstanding Prof., Ministry of Edn., 1992. Mem. Assn. Modern History (chairperson bd. overseers 1994-96), Chinese Hist. Assn. (bd. dirs. 1983-94), Taiwan U. Alumni Assn. (chmn. 1987-89), Assn. for Ming Studies (exec. dir. 1995-97). Avocations: reading, classical music, table tennis, jogging, Chinese opera. Home: 19-8A Tunghai Rd 407 T'aichung Taiwan Office: Tunghai Univ Dept History 407 Taichung Taiwan

LU, SONGWEI, materials scientist; b. Yuyao, Zhejiang, China, Sept. 26, 1965; arrived in U.S., 1998; s. Bingyuan and Xiamei (Chen) L.; m. Jian Yang, Feb. 23, 1994; 1 child, Angela Chang. B, Zhejiang U., Hangzhou, China, 1986; M in Fine Mechanics, Shanghai. Inst. Optics, China, 1989; PhD, U. Saarland, Saarbrücken, Germany, 1998. Asst. dir. optoelectronics divsn. Shanghai CITIC-Jiading Indsl. Co. Ltd., 1989-93; divsn. mgr. Shanghai Guowei Indsl. Co. Ltd., 1994; rschr. Inst. fuer Neue Materialien, Gem. GmbH, U. Saarland, Saarbrücken, Germany, 1995-98; rsch. assoc. Clemson U., 1998-99, Oak Ridge (Tenn.) Nat. Lab., 2000; product engr. Info. Products, Inc., Holland, Mich., 2000-01; devel. project engr. PPG Industries, Inc., Pitts., 2001—. Contbr. articles to profl. jours. Recipient scholarships Zhejiang U., 1984, 85. Mem. Am. Ceramic Soc., Materials Rsch. Soc., Sigma Xi. Avocation: stamp collecting. Office: PPG Industries Inc Glass Tech Ctr PO Box 11472 Pittsburgh PA 15238-0472 E-mail: songweilu@hotmail.com.

LU, TAIJIN, physical chemist, researcher; b. P.R, Jiangsu, China, Aug. 1, 1959; arrived in U.S.A., 1997; s. Tieru Lu and Jizhen Zhou; m. Lian Li; children: Joanna Da. DSc, Tohoku U., Sendai, Japan, 1989. Spl. rschr. Inst. of Physical and Chem. Rsch. (RIKEN), Wako, Japan, 1990—92; rsch. & tchg. fellow Nat. Univ. of Singapore (NUS), Singapore, 1992—96; rsch. scientist Gemological Inst. Am., Carlsbad, Calif., 1997—. Mem.: Optical Engring. Soc. Home: 1913 Triumph Street Vista CA 92083 Office: Gemological Institute of America (GIA) 5355 Armada Drive Carlsbad CA 92008 Fax: 760-598-6959., 760-603-4021. Personal E-mail: taijinlu@hotmail.com. Business E-Mail: tlu@gia.edu.

LU, TSAN FEI, artist; b. Nankang, Kiangsi, China, Mar. 7, 1936; s. Chung Kuan and Ho Yin (Shi) L.; m. Yun Yu Lin, Jan. 1, 1966; children: Chi Lu, San Lu, Bin Lu. BA in Fine Arts, Nat. Normal U., Taipei, Taiwan, 1961; cert. in performing arts, Nat. Motion Picture Inst., Taipei, 1969. Art design mgr. Ocean Advt. Co., Taipei, 1963-69; prodr., actor, asst. dir., playwright Cathay Motion Pictures, Hong Kong, 1969-74; architect designer, v.p. Chevron Asphalt Co., Taipei, 1974-77; chief art dir. Gem Advt. Co., 1979-83; cons., art dir., playwright Sun Motion Pictures, Taipei and Hong Kong, 1984-88; v.p. Fortune Holding Co., Hong Kong, Tailand and, Macau, 1989-92; artist Lu Art Studio, Northport, Ala., 1992—. Chief engr. stadium complex in south east Asia, 1975 (Best Engring. award 1976). Playwright: Uneasy Days, Run for Love, Cobbles; exhbns. at Ferguson Gallery, U. Ala., 1997. Recipient contbr. award Info. Bur. China, 1977, Best Playwright award, 1986, Excellence award NAT Edn. Ctr., 1997. Fellow World Cultural Celebrity Dictionary; mem. West. Ala. Artist Assn., World Chinese Artist Almanac. Avocations: classical music, motion pictures, book reading. E-mail: slu100@hotmail.com.

LU, WEI, engineer, researcher; b. Gejiu, Yunnan, China, July 22, 1974; arrived in U.S., 1997; m. Xuan Huang, Jan. 4, 2001. B in Electronic Engring., Tsinghua U., Beijing, 1997; PhD in Biol. Engring., U. Mo., 2002. Grad. rsch. asst. U. Mo., Columbia, 1997—. Grad. rep. to Grad. Student Assn. U. Mo., Columbia, 1998—2001; treas. Friendship Assn. Chinese Students and Scholars at U. Mo., 2000—01. Mem.: IEEE, Assn. Overseas Chinese Agrl., Biol. and Food Engrs., Am. Soc. Agrl. Engrs., Internat. Soc. for Optical Engring., Alpha Epsilon. Office: Univ Mo - Columbia 161 Agrl Engring Bldg Columbia MO 65211 Business E-Mail: WL17A@mizzou.edu.

LU, YUXIN, historian, linguist; b. Shanghai, China, Oct. 23, 1953; s. Hongbin Lu and Huashen Wang. BA in Japanese Lang. and Lit., Ha'erbin Normal U., 1982; MA in Asian Studies, St. John's U., Queens, N.Y., 1992, ArtsD, 1998. Instr. dept. fgn. langs. Shanghai Med. Coll., 1982-85; rschr. dept. Japanese lang. rsch. Nat. Lang. Rsch. Inst., Tokyo, 1985—; instr. dept. edn. Nat. Ibaragi U., Mito, Japan, 1988-90, rschr. Japan, 1996-99; grad. asst. Asian Studies Inst., St. John's U., 1990-92, grad. asst. history dept., 1992-95; adj. asst. prof. dept. history Dowling Coll., Long Island, N.Y., 1999—. Presenter in field. Author: Formation of Modern Japanese Words, 1987, New York and Tokyo: A Chinese Observations on New York and Tokyo, 1991; co-author: (all with Y. Hida) Dictionary of Japanese-Chinese Homographs, 1987, 4th edit., 1994, Japanese-Chinese Idioms Dictionary, 1989; contbr. articles to profl. jours. Travel grantee Yoshida Shigeru Internat. Found., 1995, Yaching Libr., Harvard U., 1995, Haitian Found., 1995, St. John's U., 1996; grantee Matsushita Internat. Found., 1995, Haitian Found., 1995; doctoral fellow St. John's U., 1992-94; fellow Haitian Found., 1994, 95; Dissertation grantee Sun Yat-Sen Edn. Fund, 1997. Home: PO Box 564094 College Point NY 11356-4094 Office: Dowling Coll Dept History Oakdale NY 11769 E-mail: dowlinghisylu@msn.com.

LUALDI, ROBIN CRAM, clinical social worker, school psychologist; b. Brookline, Mass., May 5, 1938; d. Reginald Maurice and Kathryn Elizabeth (Mosher) Cram; m. Paul Louis Lualdi, Dec. 23, 1961; children: Paul Jr., John, Sarah. BS, Simmons Coll., 1961, MSW, 1970, ABD, 1989. Lic. social worker, Mass.; nat. cert. sch. psychologist; diplomate Nat. Bd. Examiners in Clin. Social Work. Clin. social worker Protestant Social Svc. Bur., Quincy, Mass., 1968-74; sch. social worker, sch. psychologist Marshfield (Mass.) Sch. System, 1974-76, Duxbury (Mass.) Sch. System, 1976—. Pvt. practice, Cohasset, Mass., 1970—; presenter at profl. confs. Contbr. articles to profl. publs. Mem. NASW, NASP, Mass. Assn. Sch. Psychologists, Mass. Asn. Sch. Adjustment Counselors, Duxbury Tchrs. Assn., Mass. Tchrs. Assn. Republican. Episcopalian. Avocations: gardening, sailing, needlepoint. Home: 56 Deep Run Cohasset MA 02025-1102

LUAN, BEN LI, electrochemist, researcher; b. Wendeng, Shandong, China, Nov. 6, 1963; arrived in Can., 1995; s. Yun Fu Luan and Ze Ying Huang; m. Wen Juan Chen, Apr. 1, 1988; 1 child, Bo. B in Engring., Beijing U. Sci. and Tech., 1984, M in Engring., 1987; PhD in Engring., U. Wollongong, Australia, 1996. From asst. prof. to assoc. prof. Tianjin (China) U., 1987-92; rsch. fellow U. Wollongong, 1993-96; vis. fellow Nat. Rsch. Coun., Ottawa, Ont., Can., 1997-98, rsch. officer Can., 1998—. Guest investigator U. Sherbrooke, Can., 1997; cons. Australian Batteries Tech. Pty. Ltd., Wollongong, 1994-96; assoc. dir. Ctr. Energy Storage, Inst. Materials Manu., U. Wollongong, 1995-96. Contbr. papers to profl. jours.; inventor in field. Recipient John Crawford award, 1993, Merit Young Scientist award Sci. and Tech. Acad. China, 1992; NSERC fellow, 1997. Mem. Electrochem. Soc. Avocations: music, sports, bridge. Office: Nat Rsch Coun Canada 800 Collip Cir London ON Canada N6G 4X8 E-mail: bluan@sprint.ca.

LUBAR, JEFFREY STUART, journalist, trade association executive; b. Rockville Centre, N.Y., Apr. 15, 1947; s. Sidney and Rose (Grupsmith) L.; m. Barbara Ruth Bigelman; children— Debra, Adam, Rachel. BA, Am. U., 1969. Dir. Washington News Bur., Susquehanna Broadcasting Co., 1969-86; v.p. pub. affairs Nat. Assn. Realtors, Washington, 1987-99; dir. comms. Mortgage Ins. Cos. of Am., 2000—. Mem. exec. com. of corrs. Radio-TV Assn. (U.S. Congress), 1974-75 Served with AUS, 1969-75. Mem. Burke Racquet Club, Nat. Press Club. Jewish. Home: 6307 Karmich St Fairfax Station VA 22039-1622 Office: 727 15th St NW Washington DC 20005 E-mail: jeff@micadc.org.

LUBAROFF, SCOTT C. music educator; b. Phila., Mar. 2, 1968; s. David Martin and Martha Ida Lubaroff; m. Mary Kristen Van Hemert; children: Andrew, Sarah. MusB in Saxophone/Music Edn., U. Iowa, 1991, MA in Music Edn., MFA in Conducting, U. Iowa, 1999; D Musical Arts in Conducting, Mich. State U., East Lansing, 2001. Cert. music edn. Iowa, 1986. Dir. bands Williamsburg (Kans.) H.S., 1991—97; assoc. dir. bands Kans. State U., Manhattan, 2001—. Mem.: Kans. Bandmasters Assn., Kans. Music Educators Assn., Coll. Band Dirs. Nat. Assn., Music Educators Nat. Conf., Pi Kappa Lambda. Home: 2109 Essex Sq Manhattan KS 66503 Office: Kans State U Dept Music 226a McCain Auditorium Manhattan KS 66506 E-mail: lubaroff@ksu.edu.

LUBATTI, HENRY JOSEPH, physicist, educator; b. Oakland, Calif., Mar. 16, 1937; s. John and Pauline (Massimino) L.; m. Catherine Jeanne Berthe Ledoux, June 29, 1968; children: Karen E., Henry J., Stephen J.C. AA, U. Calif., Berkeley, 1957, AB, 1960; PhD, U. Calif., 1966; MS, U. Ill., 1963. Research assoc. Faculty Scis. U. Paris, Orsay, France, 1966-68; asst. prof. physics MIT, 1968-69; assoc. prof., sci. dir. visual techniques lab. U. Wash., 1969-74, prof., sci. dir. visual Techniques lab., 1974-98. Vis. lectr. Internat. Sch. Physics, Erice, Sicily, 1968, Herceg-Novi, Yugoslavia Internat. Sch., 1969, XII Cracow Sch. Theoretical Physics, Zapokane, Poland, 1972; vis. scientist CERN, Geneva, 1980-81; vis. staff Los Alamos Nat. Lab., 1983-86; guest scientist SSC Lab., 1991-93; mem. physics editorial adv. com. World Sci. Pub. Co. Ltd., 1982-93; guest scientist Fermilab., 1999-2000. Editor: Physics at Fermilab in the 1990's, 1990; contbr. numerous articles on high energy physics to profl. jours. Alfred P. Sloan research fellow, 1971-75 Fellow AAAS, Am. Phys. Soc.; mem. Sigma Xi, Tau Beta Pi. Office: Elem Particle Experiment Group U Wash PO Box 351560 Seattle WA 98195-1560 E-mail: lubatti@phys.washington.edu.

LUBAWSKI, JAMES LAWRENCE, health care consultant; b. Chgo., June 4, 1946; s. Harry James and Stella Agnes (Pokorny) L.; m. Kathleen Felicity Donnellan, June 1, 1974; children: Kathleen N., James Lawrence, Kevin D., Edward H. BA, Northwestern U., 1968, MBA, 1969, MA, 1980. Asst. prof. U. Northern Iowa, Cedar Falls, 1969-72; instr. Loyola U., Chgo., 1974-76; dir., market planning Midwest Stock Exchange, 1976-77; dir. mktg. Gambro Inc., Barrington, 1977-79; mktg. mgr. Travenol Labs., Deerfield, 1979-82; dir. mktg. Hollister Inc., Libertyville, 1982-84; pres., chief exec. officer Neomedica Inc., Chgo., 1984-86; v.p. bus. devel. Evangl. Health Svcs., Oak Brook, 1986-87; pres., chief exec. officer Cath. Health Alliance Met. Chgo., 1987-95; mng. dir. Ward Howell Internat., Chgo., 1995-98; v.p. A.T. Kearney, 1998-2000; pres. Zwell Internat., 2000—02; founder Lubawski & Assocs., Northfield, 2002—. Author: Food and Man, 1974, Food and People, 1979; co-editor: Consumer Behavior in Theory and in Action, 1970. Am. Assn. Advt. Acys. Faculty fellow, 1973. Mem. Evanston Golf Club (pres.), Equestrian Order of Knights of Holy Sepulchre. Avocation: golf, fishing. Office: 1765 Maple St Ste 15 Northfield IL 60093 E-mail: Jim@Lubawski.com.

LUBBERS, ALICE DIANNE, operating room nurse; b. Spokane, Wash., Nov. 10, 1956; d. Donald Lee and Dianne B. (Engstrom) L. BS, U. Idaho, 1979; BSN, Ctr. for Nursing Edn., 1985; MS in Bus. Orgn., 2002. RN, Wash.; CNOR. Commd. U.S. Army, 1988; advanced through grades to maj.; oper. rm. nurse Kootenai Med. Ctr., Coeur d'Alene, Idaho; psychiatric nurse Sacred Heart Med. Ctr., Spokane; neurosurg. head nurse operating room Madigan Med. Ctr., U.S. Army Nurse Corps., Ft. Lewis, Wash., 1988—; head nurse dept. urology Madigan Army Med. Ctr., 1988-2000; head nurse oper. rm. and ctrl. supply Bassett Army Cmty. Hosp., Ft. Wainwright, Alaska, 2000—. Clin. staff perioperative nurse 47th Combat Support Hosp., Operation Desert Shield/Desert Storm, 1991; head nurse OR/CMS 18th MASH, 1991-92; head nurse same day surgery/OR, Bayne-Jones Army Cmty. Hosp., Ft. Polk, La., 1993-96; OR edn. coord./laser safety officer Madigan Army Med. Ctr., Ft. Lewis, Wash., 1997-2000. Decorated Meritorious Svc. medal, South West Asia medal with 3 combat stars, Army Achievement medal, Commendation medals, Kuwait Liberation medal, Nat. Def. Ribbon. Mem. Assn. Oper. Rm. Nurses, Am. Soc. Laser Medicine and Surgery, Laser Inst. Am. Office: Bassett Army Comty Hosp 422 Gaftney Rd Fort Wainwright AK 99703

LUBBERS, AREND DONSELAAR, retired academic administrator; b. Milw., July 23, 1931; s. Irwin Jacob and Margaret (Van Donselaar) L.; m. Eunice L. Mayo, June 19, 1953 (div.); children— Arend Donselaar, John Irwin Darrow, Mary Elizabeth; m. Nancy Vanderpol, Dec. 21, 1968; children— Robert Andrew, Caroline Jayne. AB, Hope Coll., 1953; AM, Rutgers U., 1956; LittD, Central Coll., 1977; DSc, U. Sarajevo, Yugoslavia, 1987; LHD, Hope Coll., 1988; DSc, Akademia Ekonomiczna, Krakow, Poland, 1989, U. Kingston Univ., Eng., 1995. Rsch. asst. Rutgers U., 1954-55; rsch. fellow Reformed Ch. in Am., 1955-56; instr. history and polit. sci. Wittenberg U., 1956-58; v.p. devel. Central Coll., Iowa, 1959-60, pres., 1960-69, Grand Valley State U., Allendale, Mich., 1969-2001; ret., 2001. Mem. Am. Assn. State Colls. and Univs. seminar in India, 1971, Fed. Commn. Orgn. Govt. for Conduct Fgn. Policy, 1972; USIA insp., Netherlands, 1976; mem. pres.'s commn. NCAA, 1984-87, 89—, chmn. pres.'s commn., 1998-2002; bd. dirs. Grand Bank, Grand Rapids, Mich. Sutdent Cmty. amb. from Holland (Mich.) to Yugoslavia, 1951; bd. dirs. Grand Rapids Symphony, 1976-82, 99, Butterworth Hosp., 1988; chmn. divsn. II NCAA Pres.'s Commn., 1992-95, 98-99, mem. pres.'s coun., 1997; mem. Michigan Cmty. Svc. Commn., 2001--. Recipient Golden Plate award San Diego Acad. Achievement, 1962, Golden-Emblem Order of Merit Polish Peoples Republic, 1988, trustee's award cmty. leadership Aquinas Coll., 1998; named 1 of top 100 young men in U.S. Life mag., 1962. Mem. Mich. Coun. State Univs. Pres. (chmn. 1988, 2000—), Grand Rapids World Affairs Council (pres. 1971-73), Phi Alpha Theta, Pi Kappa Delta, Pi Kappa Phi. Home: 4195 N Oak Pointe Ct Grand Rapids MI 49525 E-mail: njdelta@aol.com.

LUBBOCK, JAMES EDWARD, retired writer, photographer, publicity consultant; b. St. Louis, Sept. 12, 1924; s. Winans Fowler and Hildegard Beauregard (Whittemore) L.; m. Charlotte Frances Ferguson, Aug. 24, 1947; children: Daniel Lawrason (dec.), Brian Wade, Kathleen Harper. BA in English, U. Mo., 1949. Asst. editor St. Louis County Observer, 1949-51; staff writer St. Louis Globe-Democrat, 1951-53, state editor, 1954-56; mng. editor Food Merchandising mag., 1956-57; freelance indsl. writer-photographer, cons. St. Louis, 1958-89. Pres. James E. Lubbock, Inc., 1981-89. With Signal Corps, U.S. Army, 1943-46. Mem.: ACLU, Mo. Citizens for the Arts, Common Cause, St. Louis Press Club. Democrat. Home and Office: 10734 Clearwater Dr Saint Louis MO 63123-4911 E-mail: anonynony@mindspring.com.

LUBECK, MARVIN JAY, ophthalmologist; b. Cleve., Mar. 20, 1929; s. Charles D. and Lillian (Jay) L. A.B., U. Mich., 1951, M.D., 1955, M.S., 1959. Diplomate Am. Bd. Opthamology; m. Arlene Sue Bitman, Dec. 28, 1955; children: David Mark, Daniel Jay, Robert Charles. Intern, U. Mich. Med. Ctr., 1955-56, resident ophthalmology, 1956-58, jr. clin. instr. ophthalmology, 1958-59; pvt. practice medicine, specializing in ophthalmology, Denver, 1961—; mem. staff Rose Hosp., Porter Hosp., Presbyn. Hosp., St. Luke's Hosp.; assoc. clin. prof. U. Colo. Med. Ctr. With U.S. Army, 1959-61. Fellow ACS; mem. Am. Acad. Ophthalmology, Denver Med. Soc., Colo. Ophthalmol. Soc. Home: 590 S Harrison Ln Denver CO 80209-3517 Office: 3600 E Alameda Ave Denver CO 80209-3189

LUBELL, ELLEN, writer; b. Bklyn., Apr. 7, 1950; d. Edward and Sonia Lubell. BA in Fine Arts, SUNY, Stony Brook, 1971. Contbg. editor Arts Mag., N.Y.C., 1972-79; editor Womanart Mag., Bklyn., 1976-78; columnist Soho Weekly News, N.Y.C., 1977-79; contbr. Art in Am., 1981-85; dir. pub. rels. Gerstman & Meyers Inc., 1984-89; freelancer, columnist, publicist The Village Voice, 1984-91; dir. comm. Inform, Inc., 1991-95; comm. dir. Child Care Action Campaign, 1995-99; freelance writer Star-Ledger, Newark, 1996-97; dir. pub. rels. The Childrens Aid Soc., N.Y.C., 1999—. Bd. dirs. Kolot Chayeinu. Art Critics fellow Nat. Endowment for the Arts, 1978.

LUBELL, MICHAEL STEPHEN, physicist, researcher, physics educator; b. N.Y.C., Mar. 25, 1943; s. Richard M. and Lillian (Aronoff) L.; 1 child, Karina B. BA, Columbia U., 1963; MS, Yale U., 1965, PhD, 1969. Postdoctoral fellow Yale U., New Haven, 1970, instr., 1971-72, asst. prof., 1972-77, assoc. prof., 1977-80, City Coll., CUNY, N.Y.C., 1980-82, prof., 1983—, chmn. dept. physics, 1999—; dir. pub. affairs Am. Phys. Soc., 1996—. Advisor basic rsch. U.S. Army, 1980-84; mem. exec. com. Internat. Conf. on Physics of Elec. and Atomic Collisions, 1983-91, co-chmn. local organizing com., 1989; vis. scientist Brookhaven Nat. Lab., 1986-87; chmn. com. on atomic and molecular sci. NRC, 1988-90; mem. adv. com. on pub. info. Am. Inst. Physics, 1988-90; vis. lectr. Inst. Theoretical Physics, U. Calif., Santa Barbara, 1990; vis. prof. U. Tex., Austin, 1990, U. Bielefeld, 1993; cons. in field; sci. and tech. policy columnist APS News. Sci. and sci. policy spokesman, radio and TV and print media; contbr. articles to profl. jours. and books. Sci., tech. adv. U.S. Sen. Christopher J. Dodd, Washington, 1980—; chmn. Dem. Town com., Westport, Conn., 1986-91; del. Dem. Nat. Conv., 1984. Rsch. grantee and contracts NSF, Dept. Energy, Dept. Def., 1974—; fellow AEC, 1970, Alfred P. Sloan Found., 1980-84 Fellow AAAS, Am. Phys. Soc. (panel on pub. affairs 1983-84, co-organizer Congl. Day 1991-92, dir. pub. affairs 1995—); mem. N.Y. Acad. Scis., Sigma Xi. Home: PO Box 188 Westport CT 06881-0188 Office: CUNY City Coll Dept Physics Convent Ave New York NY 10031 E-mail: lubell@aps.org.

LUBENSKY, EARL HENRY, diplomat, anthropologist; b. Marshall, Mo., Mar. 31, 1921; s. Henry Carl and Adele Gertrud (Biesemeyer) L.; m. Anita Ruth Price, June 27, 1942 (dec. July 1992); children: Tom, Gerald, John Christopher; m. Margot Truman Patterson, Mar. 26, 1994. BA, Mo. Valley Coll., 1948, LLD (hon.), 1968; BS, Georgetown U., 1949; MS, George Washington U., 1967; diploma, Nat. War Coll., 1967; MA, U. Mo., 1983, PhD, 1991. Mgr. Tavern Supply Co., Marshall, Mo., 1938-42; real estate salesman Mitchell Quick Realtor, Silver Spring, Md., 1948; rsch. analyst Georgetown U., Washington, 1949; reference asst. Libr. of Congress, 1949; fgn. svc. officer Dept. of State, 1949-79, inter-Am. reg. polit. affairs officer, 1956-61, served in Germany, Philippines, Spain, Ecuador, Colombia and El Salvador, 1950—78, officer-in-chg. Antarctic affairs, 1958-59. Diplomat-in-residence, Olivet, Albion and Adrian Colls., Mich., 1973-74; sr. staff mem. internat. affairs Coun.

on Environ. Quality, Washington, 1974-76; spl. amb. to inauguration Pres. Romero, El Salvador, 1977; adj. rsch. assoc. anthropology U. Mo., 1992—. Contbr. articles to profl. jours. Mem. bd. dirs. Columbia Entertainment Co., 1993-99. With Mo. N.G. 1937-40, 48, 2d lt. AUS, 1944, U.S. Army, 1942-45, lt. col. USAR, 1948-81. Eagle Scout Boy Scouts Am., 1939. Mem. Mo. Archaeol. Soc. (charter, v.p.-treas. 1981-90, chmn. bd. trustees 2001—, Appreciation award 1991, 2002), Soc. for Am. Archaeology (Presdl. Recognition award 1991), Inst. Andean Studies, Fgn. Svc. Assn., Diplomatic and Consular Officrs Retired, Boone County Hist. Soc., The Theatre Soc. (treas. 1993-99). Democrat. Avocations: genealogy, gardening, music, ham radio, philately. Home: 1408 Bradford Dr Columbia MO 65203-2302 Office: Dept Anthropology Univ Mo Columbia MO 65211-0001 E-mail: lubenskye@missouri.edu.

LUBERDA, GEORGE JOSEPH, lawyer, educator; b. N.Y.C., Apr. 27, 1930; s. Joseph George and Mary Loretta (Koslowski) L. Bar: D.C. 1959, U.S. Ct. Appeals (D.C. cir.) 1959, Mich. 1970, Mo. 1973. Washington rep. Ford Motor Co., Washington, 1955-59; atty. FTC, 1960-64; trial atty. Antitrust Div. Dept. Justice, 1965-69; sr. atty. Bendix Corp., Mich., 1970-71; assoc. Butzel, Long, Gust, Klein & Van Zile, Detroit, 1972; antitrust counsel Monsanto Co., St. Louis, 1973-88; assoc. Herzog, Crebs and McGhee, 1988-93; ptnr. Luberda & Carp, St. Louis, 1993—2002, Luberda, Gusdorf & Weir, LLC, St. Louis, 2002—. Adj. prof. St. Louis U., 1985-96. Mem. Mo. Bar Assn., Bar Assn. Met. St. Louis. Republican. Roman Catholic. Home: 716 Ridgeview Circle Ln Ballwin MO 63021-7810 Office: Luberda Gusdorf & Weir LLC Ste 1220 225 S Meramec Ave Saint Louis MO 63105-3511

LUBETSKI, EDITH ESTHER, librarian; b. Bklyn., July 16, 1940; d. Dabid and Leah (Aronson) Slomowitz; m. Meir Lubetski, Dec. 23, 1968; children: Shaul, Uriel, Leah. BA, Bklyn. Coll., 1962; MS in L.S., Columbia U., 1965; MA in Jewish Studies, Yeshiva U., 1968. Judaica libr. Stern Coll., N.Y.C., 1965-66, acquisitions libr., 1966-69, head libr., 1969—. Author: The Jewish Woman: Recent Books, 1995, (with Meir Lubetski) Building a Judaica Library Collection, 1983; contbr. articles to profl. jours. Mem. exec. bd. Jewish Book Coun., 1998—. Mem. ALA, ACRL, Assn. Jewish Libr. (corr. sec. 1980-84, pres. N.Y. chpt. 1984-86, nat. v.p. 1984-86, nat. pres. 1986-88, Fanny Goldstein Merit award 1993), N.Y. Libr. Assn. Home: 1219 E 27th St Brooklyn NY 11210-4622 Office: Yeshiva U Hedi Steinberg Libr 245 Lexington Ave New York NY 10016-4605 E-mail: Lubetski@ymail.yu.edu.

LUBIC, ROBERT BENNETT, lawyer, arbitrator, law educator; b. Pitts., Mar. 9, 1929; s. H. Murray and Rose M. (Schwartz) L.; m. Benita Joan Alk, May 18, 1959; children: Wendy, Bret, Robin. AB, U. Pitts., 1950, JD, 1953; LLM in Patent Law, Georgetown U., 1959. Bar: Pa. 1953, U.S. Ct. Appeals (D.C.) cir. 1958, U.S. Supreme Ct. 1958, U.S. Patent Office, 1959, U.S. Dist. Ct. D.C. 1964. Atty., advisor FCC, Washington, 1957-59; pvt. practice, Pitts., 1959-63; asst. prof. law Duquesne U. Law Sch., 1963-65; prof. law Am. U. Law Sch., Washington, 1965-2000, prof. emeritus, 2000—, assoc. dean, 1970-71. Cons. Embassy Republic of Georgia; pres. Stas. WRGI-AM-FM, Naples and Marco Island, Fla., 1974-77; vis. prof. U. P.R. Law Sch., 1993, Internat. Christian U., Tokyo, 1988-89, East China U. Politics and Law, 1994, U. Warsaw, Poland, 1995, U. Turin, Italy, 1997; CEO, gen. counsel GlobalMedArb LLC, 2000—; panel conciliators and arbitrators of Internat. Ctr. of Investment Settlement Disputes of World Bank; permanent panel arbitrator U.S. Postal Sys., Washington, 1978—, U.S. Dept. Labor, Washington, 1982-87; arbitrator Pub. Employee Rels. Bd. D.C., Washington, 1984—, Pub. Employee Rels. Bd. V.I., 1982—, Met. Washington Airports Auth., 2001—; hearing examiner Libr. of congress, 2001—; dir. Labor Disputes Resolution Seminar, Hamilton, Bermuda, 1982-83, Nassau, Bahamas, 1983; labor cons. Govt. of Bermuda, 1985; creator, dir. Ea. European Summer Law Program, Moscow and Warsaw, 1979-81, Chinese Am. Summer Law Program, Beijing, Shanghai and Hong Kong, 1984-86; co-dir. Mid. East Summer Law Program, Jerusalem, 1976, 78. With U.S. Army, 1953-55. Recipient Outstanding Tchr. award Am. U. Student Bar Assn., 1981. Mem. Fed. Comm. Bar Assn., D.C. Bar Assn. Democrat. Jewish. Home: 2813 McKinley Pl NW Washington DC 20015-1104 Office: GlobalMedArb LLC 2813 McKinley Pl NW Washington DC 20015-1104

LUBIC, RUTH WATSON, foundation administrator, nurse midwife; b. Bucks County, Pa., Jan. 18, 1927; d. John Russell and Lillian (Kraft) Watson; m. William James Lubic, May 28, 1955; 1 child Douglas Watson. Diploma, Sch. Nursing Hosp. U. Pa., 1955; BS, Columbia U., 1959, MA, 1961, EdD in Applied Anthropology, 1979; cert. in nurse midwifery, SUNY, Bklyn., 1962; DSc (hon.), 1993; LLD (hon.), U. Pa., 1985; DSc (hon.), U. Medicine and Dentistry, N.J., 1986; LHD (hon.), Coll. New Rochelle, 1992, Pace U., 1994. Staff nurse through head nurse Meml. Hosp. for Cancer and Allied Disease, N.Y.C., 1955-58; clin. assoc. Grad. Sch. Nursing N.Y. Med. Coll., 1962-63; parent educator, cons. Maternity Ctr. Assn., 1963-67, gen. dir., 1970-95, dir. clin. projects, 1995-97; project dir. Nat. Assn. of Childbearing Ctrs., Washington, 1997-99; pres., CEO D.C. Developing Families Ctr., 1998—, also bd. dirs.; pres., CEO D.C. Columbia Birth Ctr., 1998—, also bd. dirs. Cons. in midwifery, nursing and maternal and child health Office Pub. Health and Sci. HHS, 1995—97; adj. prof. divsn. nursing NYU, 1995—; bd. dirs., v.p. Am. Assn. World Health U.S. Com. WHO, 1975—94, pres. Am. Assn. World Health U.S. Com., 1980—81; mem. bd. maternal child and family health NRC, 1974—80; mem. Commn. Grads. Fgn. Nursing Schs., 1979—83, v.p., 1980—81, treas., 1982—83; bd. govs. Frontier Nursing Svc., 1982—92; bd. dirs. Pan Am. Health Edn. Found., pres., 1987—88; vis. prof. King Edward Meml. Hosp., Perth, Australia, 1991; Kate Hanna Harvey vis. prof. cmty. health nursing Frances Payne Bolton Sch. Nursing Case Western Res., 1991; Lansdowne lectr. U. Victoria, B.C., Canada, 1992; adj. prof. Sch. Nursing, Georgetown U., 1997—; Therese Dondero lectr. Am. Coll. Nurse-Midwives Found., 1995; Andrea Printy Meml. lectr. U. Minn., 1998; Kemble lectr. Sch. Nursing, U. N.C., Chapel Hill, 2000. Author (with Gene Hawes): (book) childbearing: A Book of Choices, 1987; contbr. articles to profl. jours. Named Maternal-Child Health Nurse of the Yr., ANA, 1985, Disting. Alumna, U. Pa., 1992; named to Nursing Hall of Fame, 1999; recipient Letitia White award, Florence Nightingale medal, 1955, Nursing Practice award, U. Pa., 1980, Rockefeller Pub. Svc. award, 1981, Hattie Hemschemeyer award, 1983, Alumnae award, Sch. Nursing U. Pa., 1986, McManus medal, Tchrs. Coll. Columbia U., 1992, Disting. Svc. award, Francis Payne Bolton Sch. Nursing, 1993, Hon. Recognition, N.Y. State Nurses Assn., 1993, Nurse-Midwifery Faculty award, Columbia U., 1993, Spirit of Nursing award, Vis. Nurses Svc. N.Y., 1994, Maes-Macinnes award, Divsn. Nursing NYU, 1994, Hon. Recognition, ANA, 1994, Carola Warburg Rothschild award, Maternity Ctr. Assn., 1997, Healthy Babies Project award, 1998, Woman of Distinction award, Nat. Assn. Women in Edn., 1999; fellow MacArthur, 1993; scholar Irving Harris vis., Coll. Nursing U. Ill., 1999. Fellow: AAAS, Soc. for Applied Anthropology, Am. Acad. Nursing (Living Legend award 2001); mem.: APHA (mem. com. on internat. health , sec. maternal and child health coun. 1982, mem. governing coun. 1986—89, mem. nominating com. 1987, mem. action bd. 1988—90), Herman Biggs Soc. (sec.-treas. 1989—90), Am. Assn. Colls. Nursing (McGovern lectr. 1997), Nat. Assn. Childbearing Ctrs. (pres. 1983—91), Inst. of Medicine of NAS (Lienhard award 2001), Am. Coll. Nurse Midwives (v.p. 1964—66, pres.-elect 1969—70), N.Y. Acad. Medicine, Alpha Omega Alpha (hon.). E-mail: Rlubic@aol.com. *As a professional nurse-midwife and public health scientist, the guiding principles of my professional life are to listen carefully to the families to be served and to combine their needs with proven scientific knowledge in constructing models for care. It is my belief that the primary purpose of maternal and child health programs is to assist families to achieve a sense of self-confidence about their ability to bring forth and rear offspring in conjunction with, but not dependent upon, professional guidance.*

LUBICK, DONALD CYRIL, lawyer; b. Buffalo, Apr. 29, 1926; s. Louis and Minna D. (Nabith) L.; m. Susan F. Cohen, June 5, 1960; children: Jonathan, Caroline, Lisa. BA summa cum laude, U. Buffalo, 1945; JD magna cum laude, Harvard U., 1949. Bar: N.Y. 1950, Fla. 1974, D.C. 1981; lic. fgn. law cons. Ont., 1989. Teaching fellow Harvard U. Law Sch., 1949-50; lectr. law U. Buffalo, 1950-61; assoc., then ptnr. Hodgson, Russ, Andrews, Woods & Goodyear, Buffalo and Washington, 1950-61, 64-77, 81-94; tax legis. counsel Treasury Dept., Washington, 1961-64, asst. sec. for tax policy, 1977-81, dir. tax adv. program for countries of Ctrl. and Ea. Europe and former Soviet Union, 1994-96, from acting to asst. sec. for tax policy, 1996-99. Adj. prof. of law Washington Coll. Law, Am. U., 2002—. Author: (with Hussey) Basic World Tax Code and Commentary, 1992, 95. Chmn. Tax Revision Com., City of Buffalo, 1958; mem. adv. com. to select Com. on Election Reform, N.Y. State Legislature, 1974, mem. adv. group to commr. internal revenue, 1976. Served with USAAF, 1945-46. Harvard Internat. Tax Program sr. fellow, 1991—. Mem. ABA, Am. Law Inst., Am. Bar Found., N.Y. State Bar Assn., Fla. Bar Assn., Erie County Bar Assn. Democrat. Jewish. E-mail: donaldlubick@msn.com.

LUBIN, BERNARD, psychologist, educator; b. Washington, Oct. 15, 1923; s. Israel Harry and Anne (Cohen) L.; m. Alice Weisbord, Aug. 5, 1957. BA, George Washington U., 1952, MA, 1953; PhD, Pa. State U., 1958. Diplomate: Am. Bd. Profl. Psychology, Am. Bd. Psychol. Hypnosis; lic. psychologist, Mo., Tex. Intern St. Elizabeths Hosp., 1952-53, Roanoke (Va.) VA Hosp., 1954-55, Wilkes-Barre (Pa.) VA Hosp., 1955; USPHS postdoctoral fellow, postdoctoral residency in psychotherapy U. Wis. Sch. Medicine, 1957-58; staff psychologist, instr. dept. psychiatry Ind. U. Sch. Medicine, Indpls., 1958-59, chief psychologist adult outpatient service, 1960-62, assoc. prof., 1964-67; dir. psychol. services Dept. Mental Health, Indpls., 1962-63, dir. div. research and tng., 1963-67; dir. div. psychology Greater Kansas City (Mo.) Mental Health Found., 1967-74; prof. dept. psychiatry U. Mo. Sch. Medicine, Kansas City, 1967-74, 76—; prof., dir. clin. tng. program dept. psychology U. Houston, 1974-76; prof., chmn. dept. psychology U. Mo. at Kansas City, 1976-83, Curators' prof., 1988; trustees' faculty fellow, 1994. Cons. Am. Nurses Assn., Panhandle Eastern Pipeline Co., Eli Lilly Pharm. Co., U.S. Sprint, Am. Mgmt. Assn., Inst. Psychiat. Research, Ind. U. Med. Center, Ind. U. Sch. Dentistry, Goodwill Industries, USPHS Bur. Health Services, mental retardation div., (univ.-affiliated facilities br.), U.S. VA, Baylor U. Med. Sch., U. Tex. Health Scis. Center, Houston, 1974-76; Mem. tng. staff Nat. Tng. Labs. Inst.; dean or faculty mem. numerous confs., 1960— ; exec. sec. Ind. Assn. for Advancement Mental Health Research and Edn., 1962-67 Author: (with M. Zuckerman) Multiple Affect Adjective Check List: Manual, 1965, 2d edit., 1985, 3d edit., 1999, (with E.E. Levitt) The Clinical Psychologist: Background, Roles and Functions, 1967, Depression: Concepts, Controversies, and Some New Facts, 1975, 2d edit., 1983, Depression Adjective Check Lists: Manual, 1967, rev. edit., 1994, (with L.D. Goodstein and A.W. Lubin) Organizational Development Sourcebooks I and II, 1979; (with W.A. O'Connor) Ecological Approaches to Clinical and Community Psychology, 1984, (with Alice W. Lubin) Comprehensive Index to the Group Psychotherapy Literature: 1906-1980, 1987, (with A.W. Lubin) Family Therapy: A Bibliography, 1937-86, 1988, (with R. Gist) Psychosocial Aspects of Disaster, 1989 (with R.V. Whitlock) Homelessness in America: A Bibliography with Selective Annotations, 1894-1994, 1994, (with D. Wilson, S. Petren and A. Polk) Research on Group Methods of Treatment: 1970-1996, 1996, (with D. Wilson) Annotated Bibliography on Organizational Consultation, 1997, (with P. G. Hanson) Answers to the Most Frequently Asked Questions About Organization Development, 1995, (with R. Gist) Ecological and Community Approaches to Disaster Response, 1999, (with R.V. Whitlock) Mental Health Services in Criminal Justice Settings, 1999, also articles; editorial bd. Jour. Community Psychology; mem. editorial bd. Internat. Jour. Group Psychotherapy, Profl. Psychology: Research and Practice; cons. reader, bd. dirs. Jour. Cons. and Clin. Psychology. Pres. Midwest Group for Human Resources, Inc., 1965-69, trustee, 1965. Recipient N.T. Veatch award for disting. rsch. and creative activity, 1983; faculty fellow U. Kansas City, 1994. Mem. APA (chmn. sponsor approval com., exec. bd. dirs. cons. psychology, coun. rep., Disting. Sr. Contbr. to Counseling Psychology award 1995, Harry Levinson award for excellence in consultation 1996), AAAS, Mo. Psychol. Assn. (exec. bd., Richard Wilkinson Lifetime Achievement award 1997), Am. Group Psychotherapy Assn. (edit. com.); mem. Midwestern Psychol. Assn., Ind. Psychol. Assn. (pres. 1967), World Fedn. for Mental Health, Conf. Psychologist Dirs. and cons. in State, Fed. and Territorial Mental Health Programs (editor conf. procs. 1966-68, Perspective 1966-68, mem. exec. com. 1946-68), Inter-Am. Congress Psychology, Cert. Cons. Internat. (charter), NTL Inst. (bd. dirs. 1986-92), Sigma Xi, Phi Kappa Phi, Psi Chi (v.p. for midwest, mem. nat. coun. 1986-90, pres.-elect 1991-92, pres. 1992-93, past pres. 1993-94). Office: U Mo Kansas City Dept Psychology 5307 Holmes St Kansas City MO 64110-2437

LUBIN, CAROL RIEGELMAN, political scientist; b. Montclair, N.J., Sept. 23, 1909; d. Charles A. and Lilian (Ehrich) Riegelman; m. Isador Lubin, Jan. 30, 1952 (dec. July 1978); 1 child Ann L. Buttenwieser. BA, Smith Coll., 1930; MA, Columbia U., 1933, PhD, 1950. Rschr. Carnegie Endowment for Internat. Peace, N.Y.C., 1930-35; internat. staff Internat. Labour Office, Geneva, Switzerland, 1935-52; asst. to dir. Urban Studies Ctr. Rutgers U., 1960-64; cmty. planner City of Reston, Va., 1964-67; housing assoc., N.Y. Urban Coalition, 1968-70; social policy dir. United Neighborhood Houses, N.Y.C., 1970-80; editl. bd. Unemployment Compensation Commn., Washington, 1979-81; rep. Internat. Fedn. Settlements and Neighborhood Ctrs. at UN, 1982—, also bd. dirs. Co-author: Social Justice for Women: The Internat. Labour Orgn. and Women, 1991. Bd. dirs. Franklin and Eleanor Roosevelt Inst.; bd. dirs., sec. William Hodson Cmty. Ctr.; bd. dirs. Conf. Non-Govt. Orgns. Mem.: Smith Coll. Club N.Y., Women's City Club, Cosmopolitan Club, Nat. Women's Dem. Club, Phi Beta Kappa. Democrat. Home and Office: 1095 Park Ave New York NY 10128-1154

LUBIN, DONALD G. lawyer; b. N.Y.C., Jan. 10, 1934; s. Harry and Edith (Tannenbaum) L.; m. Amy Schwartz, Feb. 2, 1956; children: Peter, Richard, Thomas, Alice Lubin Spahr. BS in Econs., U. Pa., 1954; LLB, Harvard U., 1957. Bar: Ill. 1957. Ptnr. Sonnenschein Nath & Rosenthal, Chgo., 1957—, chmn. exec. com., 1991-96. Bd. dirs., mem. exec. com., sec. audit com., nominating and corp. governance com. McDonald's Corp., Molex, Inc.; chmn. audit com. Daubert Industries Inc., Charles Levy Co., Tennis Corp. Am. Former mem. Navy Pier Redevel. Corp., Highland Park Cultural Arts Commn.; life trustee, former chmn. bd. Highland Park Hosp., Ravinia Festival Assn.; chmn. Chgo. Metropolis 2020, Anchor Cross Soc.; trustee, mem. exec. com. Rush-Presbyn.-St. Luke's Med. Ctr.; life trustee Chgo. Symphony Orch.; bd. dirs., v.p. Ronald McDonald House Charities, Inc., Chgo. Found. for Edn.; former dir. Smithsonian Inst., Washington; pres., bd. dir. The Barr Fund; former bd. dirs., v.p., sec. Ragdale Found.; bd. govs. Art Inst. Chgo.; former mem. Chgo. Lighthouse for the Blind; mem. citizens bd. U. Chgo.; mem. coun. Children's Meml. Hosp.; former bd. overseers Coll. Arts and Sci., U. Pa.; dir. Nat. Mus. Am. History, Washington. Woodrow Wilson vis. fellow Fellow Am. Bar Found., Ill. Bar Found., Chgo. Bar Found.; mem. ABA, Ill. Bar Assn., Chgo. Bar Assn., Lawyers Club Chgo., Chgo. Hort. Soc. (past bd. dirs.), Econ. Club (civic com.), Comml. Club (mem. exec. com.), Std. Club, Lakeshore Club, Beta Gamma Sigma. Home: 2269 Egandale Rd Highland Park IL 60035-2501 Office: Sonnenschein Nath & Rosenthal 233 S Wacker Dr Ste 8000 Chicago IL 60606-6491 E-mail: dlubin@sonnenschein.com.

LUBIN, MICHAEL FREDERICK, physician, educator; b. Phila., Mar. 20, 1947; s. Leonard and Ethel Lubin. BA, Johns Hopkins U., 1969, MD, 1973. Resident Emory U. Affiliated Hosp., Atlanta, 1973-76; asst. prof. medicine Emory U. Sch. Medicine, 1976-82, assoc. prof. medicine, 1982—2001, dir. div. gen. medicine, 1989-95; dir. preoperative clinic Grady Hosp., 1995—; chmn. housestaff evaluation com. Dept. medicine Emory U. Sch. Medicine, 1985—2001, dir. geriatrics assessment clinic, 1998—, prof. medicine, 2001—. Chmn. pharmacy and therapeutics com. Grady Hosp., 1982—, mem. ethics com., 2000—. Editor: Medical Management of the Surgical Patient, 1982; editor: (3d rev. edit.), 1995; editor: Med. Rounds, 1988—90; contbr. Mem. alumni coun. Johns Hopkins U., 1995—2001; mem. Cmty. Supporters of Atlanta Symphony Orch., 1996—98, bd. dirs., 1996—97. Scholar Hartford scholar in Geriatrics, UCLA, 1984—85. Fellow: ACP, Phi Beta Kappa (bd. dirs. Met. Atlanta chpt. 1996—2000, v.p. 2000—, bd. dirs. Nat. fellows 2002—); mem.: Soc. Gen. Internal Medicine, Am. Geriat. Soc., Alpha Omega Alpha, Phi Lambda Upsilon. Office: Emory U Sch Medicine 69 Butler St SE Atlanta GA 30303-3033

LUBIN, STANLEY, lawyer; b. May 7, 1941; children: David Christopher, Jessica Nicole; m. Barbara Ann Lubin. AB, U. Mich., 1963, JD with honors, 1966. Bar: D.C. 1967, U.S. Ct. Appeals (D.C. cir.) 1967, Mich. 1968, U.S. Ct. Appeals (6th cir.) 1968, U.S. Supreme Ct. 1970, Ariz. 1972, U.S. Ct. Appeals (9th cir.) 1976, U.S. Ct. Appeals (fed. cir.) 1985, Tex. 2002, U.S. Ct. Appeals (5th cir.) 2002. Atty. NLRB, Washington, 1966-68; asst. gen. counsel UAW, Detroit, 1968-72; assoc. Harrison, Myers & Singer, Phoenix, 1972-74, McKendree & Tountas, Phoenix, 1975; ptnr. McKendree & Lubin, Phoenix and Denver, 1975-84; shareholder Treon, Warnicke & Roush, P.A., 1984-86; pvt. practice Law Offices Stanley Lubin, Phoenix, 1986-95, The Law Offices of Stanley Lubin, P.C., 1996-98, Lubin & Enoch, P.C., 1999—. Mem. Ariz. Employment Security Adv. Coun., 1975—77. Co-author: Union Fines and Union Discipline Under the National Labor Relations Act, 1971. Active ACLU, dir. Ariz. chpt., 1974-81; mem. Ariz. State Cen. Com. Dem. Party, 1986-91, 93—, sec., 1991-92, mem. state exec. com., 1986-99, Ariz. Dem. Coun., 1987-99, chmn., 1988-93, Thomas Jefferson Forum, 1987-99, chmn., 1988-93. Mem.: ABA, Ariz. Indsl. Rels. Assn. (exec. bd. 1973—, pres. 1979—80, 1984), Indsl. Rels. Rsch. Assn., Maricopa County Bar Assn., State Bar Ariz. Home: 7520 N 9th Pl Phoenix AZ 85020-4138 Office: 349 N 4th Ave Phoenix AZ 85003- E-mail: stanley.lubin@azbar.org.

LUBIN, STEVEN, concert pianist, musicologist; b. N.Y.C., Feb. 22, 1942; s. Jack and Sophie Lubin; m. Wendy Lubin, June 2, 1974; children: Benjamin, Nathaniel. AB in Philosophy, Harvard U., 1963; MS in Piano, Juilliard Sch. Music, 1965; PhD in Musicology, NYU, 1974. Mem. faculty Juilliard Sch. Music, N.Y.C., 1964-65, Aspen (Colo.) Music Sch., 1965; Mem. faculty Vassar Coll., Poughkeepsie, N.Y., 1970-71; coordinator grad. music theory program Cornell U., Ithaca, 1971-75; prof. Conservatory of Music, SUNY, Purchase, 1975—; founding mem. The Mozartean Players, 1978—. Mem., NYU Electronic Composers Workshop, 1967-68; concert pianist tours in U.S. and Europe, 1976— ; appeared as fortepiano soloist and condr. in Authentic-Instrument concert series, N.Y.C., 1981— ; rec. artist Decca, Arabesque Records, Harmonia Mundi; filmed solo performances for Brit. documentary TV in London and Vienna, 1986; soloist in complete Beethoven piano concertos for London/Decca Records, 1987; performed complete cycle Beethoven concertos, London, 1987; solo recordings (new series) Decca including Beethoven Sonatas, 1991; contbr. articles to N.Y. Times, Keyboard Classics, others. Martha Baird Rockefeller grantee, 1968. Mem. Am. Mus. Soc., Soc. Music Theory.

LUBIN, TIMOTHY NORMAN THOMAS, humanities educator; b. Rome, Aug. 15, 1964; s. Richard Michael Lubin and Catherine Porter Vannicola; m. Lori Ann Stevens; children: Leo Stevens-Lubin, Jacob Stevens-Lubin. BA, Columbia U., 1986; MTS, Harvard U., 1989; PhD, Columbia U., 1994. Lectr. Harvard U., Cambridge, Mass., 1994—96, U. Va., Charlottesville, Va., 1996—97; asst. prof. Washington and Lee U., Lexington, 1997—. Contbr. articles to profl. jours. Mem.: Internat. Assn. Vedic Studies, Internat. Assn. Sanskrit Studies, Assn. Asian Studies, Am. Oriental Soc., Am. Acad. Religion. Democrat. Office: Washington and Lee U Dept Religion 23 Newcomb Hall Lexington VA 24450 Office Fax: 540-458-8498. Business E-Mail: lubint@wlu.edu.

LUBINIECKI, GREGORY MICHAEL, physician; b. Pitts., Nov. 18, 1972; s. Anthony Stanley and Robin Lea Lubiniecki. SB, MIT, 1994; MD, Johns Hopkins U., 1998. Diplomate Am. Bd. Internal Medicine. Resident physician Mayo Clinic, Rochester, Minn., 1998-2001; fellow in hematology/oncology U. Pa., Phila., 2001—. Lector Roman Cath. Ch., 1988—. Mem.: ACP, AMA, Am. Soc. Clin. Oncology, Phi Beta Kappa, Alpha Chi Sigma, Sigma Xi. Avocations: cycling, literature, theology. Home: 695 Barton Run Blvd Marlton NJ 08053 Office: Hosp U Pa Divsn Hematology/Oncology 16 Penn Tower 3400 Spruce St Philadelphia PA 19104 E-mail: luber@alum.mit.edu.

LUBINSKY, MENACHEM YECHIEL, communications executive; b. Hanover, Germany, Apr. 13, 1949; arrived in country 1950; s. Chaim P. and Pesa (Lubinsky) L.; m. Hindy Deborah Fink, Jan. 14, 1973; children: Tzipporah, Meiri, Tzviya. BBA, CUNY, 1975, MBA, 1982. Asst. to pres. Agudath Israel of Am., N.Y.C., 1971-72; dir. Boro Park Sr. Citizens Ctr., Bklyn., 1973-74, Project COPE, N.Y.C., 1975-80; dir. gov., pub. affairs Agudath Israel of Am., 1981-84; pres. Lubinsky, Schild Assocs., 1985-86, Lubicom, 1987-90, Integrated Mktg. & Comm. Inc., N.Y.C., 1990—. V.p. Agudath Israel of Am., Inc.; pres. Integrated Mktg. and Comm. Author: Op-Ed-Page, New York Times, 1984, Struggle and Splendor. Bd. dirs. Ohel Children's Home, Jewish Com. Rels. Coun., 1986; pres. Met. N.Y. Coordinating Coun. on Jewish Poverty; v.p. Agudath Israel of Am.; mem. domestic affairs com. United Jewish Appeal, 1992—; mem. Pvt. Industry Coun. City of N.Y. Mem. Pub. Rels. Soc. Am., League of Advt., N.Y.S. Procurement Coun. Avocation: tennis. E-mail: mlubinsky@imcimpact.com.

LUBKER, JOHN WILLIAM, II, manufacturing executive, civil engineer; b. Indpls., Jan. 11, 1943; s. John William and Wilhilmina Jane (Zieglar) L.; m. Kathy Sue Kiel, June 20, 1970; 1 child, John Ryan. BSCE, Purdue U., 1968. Project engr. Amoco Plastics Products, Seymour, Ind., 1968-72, tech. sales rep., 1972-75; project mgr. venture group Amoco Chem. Co., Chgo., 1975-77; so. sales mgr. Amoco Container Co., Norcross, Ga., 1978-79, mgr. mktg. svcs. Atlanta, 1979-80, plant mgr. Worcester, Mass., 1980-83; project devel. mgr. Amoco Foam Products Co., Atlanta, 1983-85, mgr. new technology Smyrna, Ga., 1986-87, mgr. process devel., 1988-90, mgr. cups Atlanta, 1991-92, mgr. venture team, 1992-93, mktg. mgr. indsl. products, 1994-96; mktg. mgr. Pactiv Bldg. Products, 1997-98, mgr. strategic growth and alliances, 1998—. Patentee in field. Mem. Energy Efficient Bldg. Assn., Nat. Home Builders Assn., Soc. Plastics Inc., Insulating Concrete Form Assn., Am. Plastics Coun.-Foam Polystyrene Alliance. Lutheran. Avocations: tennis, golf, sailing. Home: 8895 Willowbrae Ln Roswell GA 30076-3572 Office: Pactiv Bldg Products 2100 Riveredge Pky Ste 175 Atlanta GA 30328 E-mail: thelubkers@prodigy.net., jlubker@pactiv.com.

LUBKIN, GLORIA BECKER, physicist; b. Phila., May 16, 1933; d. Samuel Albert and Anne (Gorrin) B.; m. Yale Jay Lubkin, June 14, 1953 (div. Apr. 1968); children: David Craig, Sharon Rebecca. AB, Temple U., 1953; MA, Boston U., 1957; postgrad., Harvard U., 1974—75. Mathematician Fairchild Stratos Co., Hagerstown, Md., 1954, Letterkenny Ordnance Depot, Chambersburg, Pa., 1955-56; physicist TRG Inc., N.Y.C., 1956-58; acting chmn. dept. physics Sarah Lawrence Coll., Bronxville, N.Y., 1961-62; v.p. Lubkin Assocs., electronic cons., Port Washington, 1962-68; assoc. editor Physics Today Am. Inst. Physics, N.Y.C., 1963-69, sr. editor, 1970-84, editor, 1985-94, editl. dir., 1994-00; editor-at-large, 2001—. Cons. in field; mem. Nieman adv. com. Harvard U., 1978-82; co-chmn. search/adv. com. Theoretical Physics Inst., U. Minn., 1987-89, co-chmn. oversight com. 1989—; mem. mng. com. Westinghouse Sci. Writing Prizes, 1988-91; mem. selection com. Knight Fellowships, 1990. Contbr. articles to profl. publs. Gloria Becker Lubkin Professorship of Theoretical Physics established in her honor U. Minn., 1990; Nieman fellow, 1974-75. Fellow: AAAS (chair nominating com. for sect. B physics 1989), Am. Phys. Soc. (founding mem. com. on status of women in physics 1971—72, exec. com. history of physics divsn. 1983—86, 1992—95, 1998—, exec. com. forum on physics and soc. 1977—78, coun. mem. 1998—, exec. bd. 2000—01, com. on coms. 2000—, chair Lilienfeld prize com. 2002); mem.: Com. Concerned Journalists, DC Sci. Writers Assn., Nat. Assn. Sci. Writers, NY Acad. Scis. (mem. The Scis. pub. com. 1992—93), Sigma Pi Sigma. Jewish. Office: Am Inst Physics One Physics Ellipse College Park MD 20740 E-mail: glubkin@aip.org.

LUBKIN, VIRGINIA LEILA, ophthalmologist; b. N.Y.C., Oct. 26, 1914; d. Joseph and Anna Fredericka (Stern) L.; m. Arnold Malkan, June 6, 1944 (div. 1949); m. Martin Bernstein, Aug. 28, 1949; children: Ellen Henrietta, James Ernst, Roger Joel, John Conrad. BS summa cum laude, NYU, 1933; MD, Columbia Coll. Physicans & Surgeons, 1937. Diplomate Am. Bd. Ophthalmology. Intern Harlem Hosp. Med. Ho., N.Y.C., 1938-40; asst. resident neurology Montefiore Hosp., 1940, asst. resident gen. pathology, 1940-41, fellow in ophthalmology, 1941-42; asst. resident grad. basic sci. P & S Ophthalmology Harkness Eye Inst., 1941-42; resident ophthalmology Kings County Hosp., Bklyn., 1942-43, Mt. Sinai Hosp., N.Y.C., 1943-44; attending ophthalmologist, asst. and assoc. clin. prof. emeritus Mt. Sinai Sch. Medicine, 1944—; also sr. attending ophthalmic surgeon, assoc. plastic surg. N.Y. Eye and Ear Infirmary; pvt. practice N.Y.C., 1945-90; rsch. prof. N.Y. Med. Coll., Valhalla, 1983—. Co-creator, now chief of rsch. bioengineering lab. N.Y. Eye and Ear Infirmary (name now The Aborn), N.Y.C., 1978—; rschr. piezoelectric aspects of ocular tissues; creator first grad. course in oculoplastics and bi-yearly symposia in devel. dyslexia Mt. Sinai Sch. Medicine; educator courses in psychosomatic ophthalmology Am. Acad. Ophthalmology, 1950—60, educator course in complications of blepharoplasty, 1980—90; bd. dirs. Jewish Guild for the Blind; tchr. surg. ophthalmology in French Cameroon Presbyn. Mission, 1951; lectr. in numerous countries including

India, India, 76; lectr. in numerous countries including, India, 92, Pakistan, 76, Pakistan, 84, China, 78, Sri Lanka, 79, South Africa, 82, Singapore, 84, Thailand, 84, Argentina, 86, Peter Island, 87; ednl. dir. Aborn Eye Rsch. Lab. N.Y. Eye and Ear Infirmary, 2001—; hon. attending surgeon N.Y. Eye and Ear Infirmary; rsch. asst. in hematology Mt. Sinai Hosp. with Dr. Nathan Rosenthal, 1937; with Dr. H. Abramson, 37; consulting ophthalmologist Sharon Hosp., Conn.; postgrad. Inst. N.Y. Eye and Ear Infirmary, 1959—71, Am. Acad. Ophthalmology, 1968, 1969—71, N.Y. Eye and Ear Infirmary, 1970, Mt. Sinai Sch. Medicine, 1970; vis. prof. U. San Marco, Lima, Peru, 1967; lectr., co-chmn., chmn., and organizer in field at various meetings, symposiums and confs.; course dir. Mt. Sinai Sch. Medicine, 1971, 73, asst. course dir., 72; dir., founder resident (with Prof. Martin Gersten and Richard Koplin) rsch. fund N.Y. Eye and Ear Infirmary, 1978; edn. dir. dept. biomedical engring. N.Y. Eye and Ear Infirmary, 1978; impartial specialist in ophthamology worker's compensation bd., 1979—. Author (with others): Ophthalmic Plastic and Reconstructive Surgery, 1989, (2d edit.) , 1997; co-author: Tear Osmolarity in Canines; patentee topical estrogen for post-menopausal dry eye; contbr. articles to profl. jours., chapters to books, publs. Bd. dirs. Ctr. fo Environ. Therapeutics, 1995; mem. Jewish Guild for the Blind, 1987—. Grantee Intraocular Lens Implant Mfrs., 1989; recipient Merit award Am. Acad. Ophthalmology and Otolaryngology, 1966, Sr. award, 1989. Fellow ACS, AMA, AAAS, Am. Soc. Ophthalmic Plastic and Reconstructive Surgery (founding), Am. Assn. Ophthalmology and Otolaryngology (instr. 1955-71), Am. Soc. Opthalmic Plastic and Reconstructive Surgery (charter mem., founder 1969), Am. Acad. Facial Plastic and Reconstructive Surgery, N.Y. Acad. Medicine, N.Y. Acad. Scis., Am. Acad. Ophthalmology (Sr. Honor award 1989), Am. Soc. Cataract and Refractive Surgery, PanAm. Soc. Ophthalmology, N.Y. Soc. Clin. Ophthalmology (officer, v.p. 1969-70, pres. 1970-71), Soc. Light Treatment and Biol. Rhythms, Phi Beta Kappa (Mandel chemistry prize), Alpha Omega Alpha. Home: 1 Blackstone Pl Bronx NY 10471-3607 Office: NY Eye and Ear Infirmary 310 E 14th St New York NY 10003-4201 Fax: 718-549-6848; 212-979-4574. E-mail: drvlubkin@aol.com.

LUBKOWSKI, SUZANNE ROSE, spiritual educator; b. Buffalo, Feb. 27, 1955; d. Norman Michael and Alice Mary (Drazek) Takac; m. David John Lubkowski, Oct. 25, 1975; children: Steven David, Kristin Rose. A, No. Va. C.C., 1987; B, George Mason U., 1993, postgrad., 1993—. Cert. spiritual educator, Va. Sec. Nat. Fuel Gas Co., Buffalo, 1973-75, Raytheon Corp., Bedford, Mass., 1975-77; sec., coord. travel and conf. Analytic Scis. Corp., McLean, Va., 1979-85; dir. youth and family ministry Unity of Fairfax, Oakton, 1982-94. Author curriculums. Facilitator Children's Creative Response to Conflict, Va., 1988—; mem. youth and family coun. Unity Life Ctr., Chantilly, Va., 1994, mem. steering com., 1994, pres. bd dirs., 1995—. Recipient Disting. Youth Svc. award Assn. Unity Chs., 1990. Fellow Golden Key Soc.; mem. Phi Betta Kappa. Avocations: reading, nature, fashion. Home: 5724 Pamela Dr Centreville VA 20120-1414

LUBLIN, FRED D. neurologist, researcher; b. Phila., Sept. 28, 1946; s. Paul and Sara Lublin; m. Barbara Hope Swartz, June 11, 1969; children: Alex, Derek. BA magna cum laude, Temple U., 1968; MD summa cum laude, Jefferson Med. Coll., Phila., 1972. Diplomate Am. Bd. Psychiatry and Neurology. Intern, internal medicine Albert Einstein Med. Ctr., N.Y.C., 1972—73; resident, neurology NY Hospital-Cornell Med., 1973—76; neurologist Jefferson Med. Coll., Phila., 1976—96, MCP Hahnemann U., Phila., 1996—2000; prof. Neurology Mt. Sinai Med. Ctr., N.Y.C., 2000—. Dir., Corinne Goldsmith Dickinson Ctr. for multiple sclerosis Mt. Sinai Med. Ctr., New York, NY, 2000—. Contbr. articles to numerous med. jours. Recipient Alumni Prize, Jefferson Med. Coll., 1972, Teacher-Investigator Devel. Award, NIH, 1978-1983. Mem.: Nat. Multiple Sclerosis Soc. (chmn., rsch. programs adv. com. 2000, Hope award, Del. Valley chpt. 1999), Phila. Neurol. Soc. (pres. 1991—92), Am. Assn. of Neurology, Am. Neurol. Assn. Office: Mount Sinai Med Ctr 5 East 98th Street New York NY 10029 Office Fax: 212-423-0440. Business E-Mail: fred.lublin@mssm.edu.

LUBLIN, JOANN SANDRA, journalist; b. Dayton, Ohio, Apr. 8, 1949; d. Irving and Betty Thelma (Friedman) L.; m. Michael Alan Pollock, June 4, 1972; children: Daniel, Abra. BS in Journalism, Northwestern U., 1970; MA in Comm., Stanford U., 1971. Staff reporter Wall Street Journal, San Francisco, 1971-73, Chgo., 1973-79, Washington, 1979-87, bur. news editor London, 1987-89, dep. bur. chief, 1989-90, sr. spl. writer N.Y.C., 1990-92, dep. mgmt. editor, 1992-2000, careers' news editor, 2000—. Keynote spkr. Wharton Sch.'s Inst. of Dirs., Phila., 1997. Ext. publicity chairwoman Sisterhood Temple Beth Or, Washington Twp., N.J., 1992—. Mem. NOW, Soc. Profl. Journalists. Avocations: hiking, biking, swimming, piano playing, gardening. Office: Wall Street Journal 200 Liberty St New York NY 10281

LUBLINER, IRVING, mathematics educator, consultant; b. Oakland, Calif., Aug. 29, 1952; s. Abram and Felicia (Bornstein) L.; m. Joanne C. May Kliejunas. BA, U. Calif., Berkeley, 1974; MA in Teaching, U. Calif., Davis, 1988. Cert. tchr., Calif. Tchr. math. and computer programming, chmn. math. dept. Novato (Calif.) Unified Sch. Dist., 1976-85; program dir., math. specialist Black Pine Circle Sch., Berkeley, 1985-90; math specialist, tchr. Bentley Sch., Oakland, 1990-95, head middle sch., 1995-98, dean of students, 1998—2001, math. splst., 1998—. Instr. U. calif., Davis, 1975-76; dir. Kindercamp, Oakland, 1972-76, Camp Kee Tov, Berkeley, 1980-83; tchr. Marin County Office Edn., San Rafael, Calif., 1982-83; speaker Bur. of Edn. and Rsch., 1992—; speaker, cons., Oakland, 1974—. Contbr. articles to profl. jours. Recipient Hon. Svc. award Calif. Congress Parents and Tchrs., 1985, Spl. Honors award for contbn. to tchg. highly talented youth Johns Hopkins U.*Calif. Tchr. Recognition Program, 1991, 94, 97, 98, 2000; Sarah D. Barton*S. Mark Taper Found. fellow Johns Hopkins U.'s Ctr. for Talented Youth, 1994. Mem. Nat. Coun. Tchrs. Math., Calif. Math. Coun., Alameda and Contra Costa Counties Math. Educators. Avocations: blues harmonica, table tennis. Home: 878 Longridge Rd Oakland CA 94610-2445 Office: Bentley Sch 1 Hiller Dr Oakland CA 94618-2301

LUBLINSKI, MICHAEL, lawyer; b. Eskilstuna, Sweden, Sept. 11, 1951; came to U.S., 1956; s. Walter and Dora L. BA magna cum laude, CCNY, 1972; JD, Georgetown U., 1975. Bar: N.Y. 1976, Calif. 1980, D.C. 2001, Va. 2002, Ct. Internat. Trade 1981, U.S. Dist. Ct. (cen. dist.) Calif. 1981, U.S. Dist. Ct. (so. dist.) N.Y. 1981, U.S. Ct. Appeals (D.C. cir.) 1982. Atty. U.S. Customs Service, Washington, 1975-79, U.S. Dept. Commerce, Washington, 1980; assoc. Mori & Ota, L.A., 1980-84, Kelley Drye & Warren LLP, L.A., 1984-85, ptnr., mem. intellectual property practice group, 1986—. Panel moderator Calif. continuing edn. of bar Competitive Bus. Practices Inst., Los Angeles and San Francisco, 1984. Mem. ABA, Calif. Bar Assn., Los Angeles County Bar Assn. (arbitrator 1981-82, chmn. customs law sect. 1986), N.Y. State Bar Assn., D.C. Bar Assn., Phi Beta Kappa. Avocations: travel, movies. Office: Kelley Drye & Warren LLP 8000 Towers Crescent Drive Ste 1200 Vienna VA 22182 E-mail: mlublinski@kelleydrye.com.

LUBMAN, RICHARD LEVI, physician, educator, research scientist; b. Bklyn., Dec. 10, 1956; m. Sue Ann Feinberg, Dec. 14, 1986; children: Rachel, Louisa. BA, Cornell U., 1977; MD, SUNY, Bklyn., 1981. Diplomate Am. Bd. Internal Medicine, Am. Bd. Pulmonary Diseases; cert. in critical care medicine. Intern, then resident in internal medicine SUNY Downstate Med. Ctr., 1981-84; chief resident SUNY-Bklyn. VA Hosp., 1984-85; fellow in pulmonary and critical care medicine N.Y. Hosp.-Cornell U. Med. Ctr., N.Y.C., 1985-88, instr. medicine, 1988-91; asst. prof. U. So. Calif., L.A., 1991-99, assoc. prof. medicine, 1999—. Expert reviewer Med. Bd. Calif., 1996—. Parker B. Francis fellow Francis Families Found., 1988-91, J. Burns Amberson fellow N.Y. Lung Assn., 1986-88. Fellow ACP, Am. Coll. Chest Physicians; mem. Am. Thoracic Soc., Am. Heart Assn. (initial investigator Greater L.A. affiliate 1993-95), Am. Physiol. Soc., Internat. Union Against Tb and Lung Disease, Western Soc. Clin. Investigation, Am. Soc. Matrix Biology. Office: Hmr 900 2011 Zonal Ave Los Angeles CA 90089-0110 E-mail: rlubman@hsc.usc.edu.

LUBORSKY, FRED EVERETT, research physicist; b. Phila., May 14, 1923; s. Meyer and Cecelia (Miller) L.; m. Florence R. Glass, Aug. 25, 1946; children— Judith, Mark, Rhoda BS, U. Pa., 1947; PhD, Ill. Inst. Tech., 1952. Teaching-research asst. Ill. Inst. Tech., Chgo., 1947-51; research assoc. Gen. Elec. Co., Schnectady, 1951-52, West Lynn, Mass., 1952-58, research physicist Schenectady, 1958-92. Gen. chmn. 2d Joint Internat. Magnetism and Magnetic Materials Conf., 1979; chmn. adv. com. Conf. on Magnetism and Magnetic Materials, 1980 Editor: Amorphous Metallic Alloys, 1984; mem. editorial bd. Internat. Jour. Rapid Solidification, 1984— ; mem. editorial adv. bd. Internat. Jour. Magnetism, 1972— ; contbr. articles to profl. jours.; patentee in field Served with USN, 1944-46 Recipient citation achievement in indsl. sci. AAAS, 1956; Brit. Sci. Research Council fellow, 1977; Coolidge fellow in research and devel. Gen. Elec. Corp., 1978 Fellow IEEE (editorial bd. Transactions on Magnetics jour. 1968— , editor-in-chief 1972-75, editorial bd. Spectrum jour. 1972-73, Centennial medal 1984, mem. Fellows com. 1993—), Am. Inst. Chemists, N.Y. Acad. Scis.; mem. Nat. Acad. Engring., Magnetics Soc. of IEEE (pres. 1975-77, named disting. lectr. 1979, achievement award 1981), Am. Chem. Soc., Materials Research Soc. Home: 137 Glen Eddy Dr Schenectady NY 12309

LUBOVITCH, LAR, dancer, choreographer; b. Chgo. Student, Art Inst. Chgo., U. Iowa, Juilliard Sch. Music, Am. Ballet Theatre Sch., Martha Graham, Anthony Tudor. Dancer debut with Pearl Lang Dance Co., 1962, with modern cos. Glen Tetley, John Butler, Sophie Maslow and Donald McKayle, Manhattan Festival Ballet, Santa Fe Opera, Harkness Ballet, formed Lar Lubovitch Dance Co., 1968; guest choreographer Bat-Dor Dance Co., Gulbenkian Ballet, Dutch Nat. Ballet, Ballet Rambert, Pa. Ballet, Am. Ballet Theatre, Royal Danish Ballet, Bejart Ballet XX Century, Alvin Alley Am. Dance Theater, John Curry Ice Dancing Co., Les Grandes Ballets Canadiens, Stuttgart Ballet, N.Y.C. Ballet, Pacific N.W. Ballet, Paris Opera Ballet, White Oak Dance Project, ballets choreographed include Blue, 1968, Freddie's Bag, 1968, Journey Back, 1968, Greeting Sampler, 1969, Whirligogs, 1969, Unremembered Time-Forgotton Place, 1969, Variations and Theme, 1970, Ecstasy, 1970, Sam Nearlydeadman, 1970, The Teaching, 1970, Some of the Reactions, 1970, The Time Before, 1971, Clear Lake, 1971, Air, 1972, Joy of Man's Desiring, 1972, Chariot Light Night, 1973, Scherzo for Massah Jack, 1973, Three Essays, 1974, Zig Zag, 1974, Avalanche, 1975, Rapid Transit, 1975, Session, 1975, Eight Easy Pieces, 1975, Girl on Fire, 1975, Marimba, 1976, Les Noches, 1976, Scriabin Dances, 1977, Exultate Jubilate, 1977, North Star, 1978, Valley, 1978, Tiltawhirl, 1979, Up Jump, 1979, Mistral, 1980, Cavalcade, 1980, American Gesture, 1981, Beau Danube, 1981, Big Shoulders, 1983, Tabernacle, 1983, Adagio and Rondo, 1984, A Brahms Symphony, 1985, Concerto Six Twenty-Two, 1986, Blood, 1986, Of My Soul, 1987, Musette, 1988, Rhapsody in Blue, 1988, Fandango, 1989, Just Before Jupiter, 1990, Hautbois, 1990, Sinfonia Concertante, 1991, Waiting for the Sunrise, 1991, American Gesture, 1992, So In Love, 1994, Touch Me, 1996, Bach Adagio, 1996, Gershwin Variations, 1996, I'll Be Seeing You, 1996, Othello, 1997, Thus is All, 1998, Yiddish Songs of Love and Wonder, 1999, Meadow, 1999, All Ye Need to Know, 2000, Men's Stories, 2000, My Funny Valentine, 2001, Smile with my Heart, 2002, others; choreographer (TV) Sleeping Beauty (WGBH-TV), 1987, (Broadway plays) Into the Woods, 1987, Salome, 1992, The Red Shoes, 1993, The Planets (A&E-TV), 1994, (Broadway plays) The King and I, 1998, High Society, 1998, The Hunchback of Notre Dame , Berlin, 1999. Guggenheim fellow; CAPS grantee, NEA grantee; nominee Tony award, 1988, Astaire award, 1993-94. Address: care Lubovitch Dance Co 229 W 42d St 8th Fl New York NY 10036

LUBOW, NATHAN MYRON, accountant; b. N.Y.C., Aug. 4, 1929; s. Cornelius W. and Blanche (Igstaedter) L.; m. Joyce S. Litt, Dec. 17, 1955; children: Susan M. Russak, Andrew M. PhB, U. Chgo., 1948; BS in Econs., U. Pa., 1950. CPA, N.Y. Ptnr. Aronson & Oresman, CPAs, 1969-73, Clarence Rainess & Co., N.Y.C., 1973-78, Main Hurdman, N.Y.C., 1978-87, KPMG Peat Marwick, N.Y.C., 1987-90; v.p., mem. Mahoney Cohen & Co., 1990—. Bd. dirs. 465 WEA Owners Corp., N.Y.C., Westmoor Corp., Ft. Worth; mem. adv. bd. Valley Nat. Bank, N.Y. Contbg. editor Secured Lender mag., 1988—. Bd. dirs., treas. Saw Creek Estates Cmty. Assn. Mem. AICPAs, N.Y. State Soc. CPAs, Empire Credit Club, Decorum Credit Club, Friars Club. Home: 465 West End Ave New York NY 10024-4926 Office: Mahoney Cohen & Co CPAs PC 111 W 40th St Rm 1200 New York NY 10018-2506

LUCAK, BASIL KASSIAN, gastroenterologist, educator; b. Prague, Czech Republic, June 9, 1948; came to the U.S., 1954; s. Wasyl Kassian and Pauline Anna (Kozl) L.; children: Natalia A., Peter K. BA magna cum laude, NYU, 1970, MD, 1974. Diplomate Am. Bd. Gastroenterology and Internal Medicine. Intern N.Y. Hosp., N.Y.C., 1974-75, resident in internal medicine, 1975-76; resident in internal medicine, staff SUNY Stony Brook, Northport, N.Y., 1976-77; fellow in gastroenterology Bellevue Hosp., N.Y.C., 1977-79; instr. medicine NYU Sch. Medicine, 1979-86, clin. asst. prof., 1986—; pvt. practice, 1979—. Admissions com. NYU Sch. Medicine, N.Y.C., 1980—, nutrition com., 1996—, clin. study prin. investigator, 1997—. Contbr. articles to profl. jours. Vol. Dvorak Am. Heritage Assn., N.Y.C., 1990—, Bohemian Nat. Hall Restoration Fund, N.Y.C., 1995-96; v.p. Friends of Czech Ctr., N.Y.C., 1995. U. Honors scholar NYU, 1976, U. Honors scholar NYU Sch. Medicine, 1976. Fellow Am. Coll. Gastroenterology; mem. Am. Gastroenterol. Assn., N.Y. Gastroenterol. Assn., N.Y. Soc. for Gastrointestinal Endoscopy, N.Y. Acad. Gastroenterology (pres. 1989), Soc. for Clin. & Exptl. Hypnosis, Phi Beta Kappa, Alpha Omega Alpha. Avocations: Czech music and culture, history, mind and body interaction. Office: 1158 5th Ave New York NY 10029-6917 E-mail: basmed@cyburban.com.

LUCÀ-MORETTI, MAURIZIO, research scientist, nutrition researcher; b. Rome, June 2, 1945; came to U.S., 1995; s. Giuseppe and Elena (Moretti) L.; m. Anna Grandi, Jan. 2, 1974; 1 child, Elena. BS, Ministry of Edn., Caracas, Venezuela, 1969; PhD in Allied Health Scis., DSc in Human Nutrition, Pacific Western U., 1990; MD (hon.), Universidad Santo Tomas, La Paz, Bolivia, 1994; MPH (hon.), Inst. Superiore di Studi Sanitari, Rome, 1995. Rschr. Inst. Italiano di Terapia Fisica e Medicina Interna, Rome, 1974-76, sr. rschr., 1976-78, dir. rsch., 1978-80, Caracas, Venezuela, 1980-88; dir. human nutrition rsch. program and AIDS rsch. program InterAm. Med. and Health Assn., Boca Raton, Fla., 1989—, pres., 1989—; gen. sec. World Acad. Medicine, 1992—; prof. emeritus Pacific Western U., New Orleans, 1992; dir. rsch. Internat. Nutrition Rsch. Ctr., 1995—. Invited prof. Univ. di Chiete, Italy, 1991, Univ. de Asuncion, Paraguay, 1992, Univ. di Roma, Rome, 1995; hon. prof. Univ. de Granada, Spain, 1994, Univ. Nacional Pedro Enrique Ureña, Santo Domingo, Dominican Rep., 1994, Inst. Superiore di Studi Sanitari, 1996, Univ. Catolica Santo Domingo, Dominican Rep., 1996, St. Thomas U., Miami, 1998. Recipient medal Univ. Asuncion, Paraguay, 1992, medal Univ. Granada, Spain, 1993; decorated Cruz de Alfonso X el Sabio, Spani, 1997. Fellow NAS (Dominican Rep.), Royal Nat. Acad. Medicine Spain, Royal Acad. Scis. Spain, Royal Acad. Medicine Salamanca, Royal Acad. Medicine Granada, Royal Acad. Medicine Valencia, Royal Acad. Medicine of Zaragoza, Nat. Acad. Medicine Bolivia, Nat. Acad. Medicine Ecuador, Nat. Acad. Medicine Paraguay, Nat. Acad. Medicine Dominican Rep., Acad. Medicine Maracaibo, Reial Acad. Medicina Catalunya. Achievements: discovery of the Master Amino Pattern (MAP); discovery of the Dietary Protein Engring. (DPE); also patents in nutritional amino acids formulations with extremely high human Net Nitrogen Utilization (NNU). Home: 3025 Saint James Dr Boca Raton FL 33434-3370 Office: Internat Nutrition Rsch Ctr 401 Linton Blvd Delray Beach FL 33444-8157

LUCANDER, HENRY, investment banker; b. Helsingfors, Finland, Dec. 21, 1940; came to U.S., 1965, naturalized, 1974; m. Karen-Jean Olson, Aug. 22, 1981. Student, Gronesche Handelsschule, Hamburg, W.Ger., 1961-62, Pontificia U. Catolica, Rio de Janeiro, 1963-64; diploma, Brazilian Coffee Inst., Rio de Janeiro, 1965; MBA, Columbia U., 1968. With Schenkers Internat. Forwarders, Inc., N.Y.C., 1965-66; coffee merchandizer Anderson Clayton & Co., Inc., 1966-68; with Smith Barney & Co., Inc., 1968-69, Kidder Peabody & Co., Inc., N.Y.C., 1969-70, Lucander & Co., Inc., Investment Bankers, N.Y.C., 1970—, pres., 1972—. Served to lt. Finnish Army, 1960-61. Home: 333 Pearl St New York NY 10038-1609 E-mail: securitiesfutures@yahoo.com.

LUCAS, ALEXANDER RALPH, child psychiatrist, educator, writer; b. Vienna, Austria, July 30, 1931; came to U.S., 1940, naturalized, 1945; s. Eugene Hans and Margaret Ann (Weiss) L.; m. Margaret Alice Thompson, July 6, 1956; children: Thomas Alexander, Nancy Elizabeth Watson, Alexander Eugene, Peter Clayton. BS, Mich. State U., 1953; MD, U. Mich., 1957. Diplomate Am. Bd. Psychiatry and Neurology (psychiatry and child and adolescent psychiatry), Am. Bd. of Med. Specialties. Intern U. Mich. Hosp., 1957-58; resident in child psychiatry Hawthorn Ctr., Northville, Mich., 1958-59, 61-62, staff psychiatrist, 1963-65, sr. psychiatrist, 1965-67; resident in psychiatry Lafayette Clinic, Detroit, 1959-61, rsch. child psychiatrist, 1967-71, rsch. coord., 1969-71; asst. prof. psychiatry Wayne State U., 1967-69, assoc. prof., 1969-71; cons. child and adolescent psychiatry Mayo Clinic, 1971-97; assoc. prof. Mayo Med Sch., 1973-76, prof., 1976-97; emeritus prof., 1998—; head sect. child and adolescent psychiatry Mayo Clinic, Rochester, Minn., 1971-80, emeritus cons., 1998—. Dir. com. on certification in child and adolescent psychiatry Am. Bd. Psychiatry and Neurology, 1997-2001; residency rev. com. Accreditation Coun. for Grad. Med. Edn., 1999-2001. Author: (with C. R. Shaw) The Psychiatric Disorders of Childhood, 1970. Recipient Eating Disorders Scientific Achievement award, 1998. Fellow Am. Acad. Child and Adolescent Psychiatry (life, editl. bd. jour. 1976-82), Am. Orthopsychiat. Assn. (life), Am. Psychiat. Assn. (life); mem. Minn. Soc. Child and Adolescent Psychiatry (pres. 1993-95), Soc. Profs. Child and Adolescent Psychiatry (pres. 2000-2002), Sigma Xi. Achievements include research in biol. aspects of child psychiatry, psychopathology, psychopharmacology, eating disorders, psychiat. treatment of children, adolescents, and young adults. Office: Mayo Clinic 200 1st St SW Rochester MN 55905-0002

LUCAS, AUBREY KEITH, retired university president; b. State Line, Miss., July 12, 1934; s. Keith Caldwell and Audelle Margaret (Robertson) L.; m. Ella Frances Ginn, Dec. 18, 1955; children: Margaret Frances Lucas-Tauchar, Keith Godbold (dec.), Martha Carol Pittman, Alan Douglas, Mark Christopher. BS, U. So. Miss., 1955, MA, 1956; PhD, Fla. State U., 1966; DHL, Miss. Coll., 1997. Instr. Hinds Jr. Coll., Raymond, Miss., 1956-57; pres. Delta State U., Cleveland, 1971-75; asst. dir. reading clinic U. So. Miss., Hattiesburg, 1955-56, dir. admissions, 1957-61, registrar, 1963-69, dean Grad. Sch., 1969-71, pres., 1975-96, pres. emeritus, prof. higher edn., 1997—. Bd. dirs. Miss. Power Co. Author: The Mississippi Legislature and Mississippi Public Higher Education, 1890-1960; contbg. author: A History of Mississippi, 1973. Bd. dirs. Africa U., treas., 1999—; bd. dirs. Pine Burr Area coun. Boy Scouts Am., 1990-2000, Miss. Inst. Tech. Devel., 1984-96, Miss. Power Co., Miss. Assn. Coll., 1979-80, Miss. Arts Commn., 1977-87; bd. dirs. Salvation Army, chmn., 2000—; gen. bd. Global Ministries, United Meth. Ch., 1984-92, gen. bd. higher edn. and ministry, 1992-2000; chmn. Miss. Arts Commn., 1983-85; campaign chmn. Forrest United Way, 1979, So. U. Conf., 1995-96; state chmn. Am. Cancer Soc., 1978; mem. Commn. on Nat. Devel. Postsecondary Edn., 97th Congress; pres. Miss. Econ. Coun., 1982-83; lay leader Miss. Meth. Conf., 1980-88; bd. visitors Air U., 1990-94, chmn., 1991-92; exec. bd. Commn. on Colls. of So. Assn. Colls. and Schs., 1990-93. Mem. Hattiesburg C. of C., Miss. Forestry Assn., Newcomen Soc. N.Am., Am. Assn. State Colls. and Univs. (bd. dirs. 1982-86, chmn. 1984-85), Am. Coun. Edn. (bd. dirs. 1984-86), Miss. Inst. Arts and Letters (pres. 1999-2000), Hattiesburg Cmty. Found., Hattiesburg Conv. Ctr. Commn., Lauren Rogers Mus. Art (pres. bd. trustees, chmn. 2001—), Red Red Rose Club, Sigma Phi Epsilon, Omicron Delta Kappa, Phi Kappa Phi, Pi Gamma Mu, Pi Tau Chi, Kappa Delta Pi, Phi Delta Kappa, Kappa Pi. Home: 3200 Jamestown Rd Hattiesburg MS 39402-2333 Office: U So Miss PO Box 5164 Hattiesburg MS 39406-5164 E-mail: aubrey.lucas@usm.edu.

LUCAS, BERT ALBERT, pastor, social services administrator, consultant; b. Hammond, Ind., Mar. 26, 1933; s. John William and Norma (Gladys) Graham; m. Nanci Dai Hindman, Sept. 10, 1960; children: Bradley Scott, Traci Dai. BA, Wheaton Coll., 1956; BD, No. Bapt. Theol. Sem., 1960, ThM, 1965; MSW, U. Mich., 1971; D in Marriage and Family, Ea. Bapt. Theol. Sem., 1988. Lic. social worker, Ohio; ordained clergyman Am. Baptist Conv.; cert. family life educator. Chaplain Miami Children's Ctr., Maumee, Ohio, 1967-83; assoc. pastor First Bapt. Ch., La Porte, Ind., 1959-62; pastor Maumee Bapt. Ch., 1963-67; adminstrv. social work supr. Lucas County (Ohio) Children Svcs., 1967-97; pastor Holland (Ohio) United Meth. Ch., 1979-90, Broadway United Meth. Ch., 1994-97, Bono Bapt. Ch., Toledo, 1997-99. Adj. prof. Bowling Green (Ohio) State U., 1972-79; family life cons. New Horizon's Acad., Holland, 1984-86, co-dir. family svcs. 1985-86; cons. parenting, marriage enrichment, Toledo, 1986—. Rep. precinct capt., Toledo, 1984. Bert A. Lucas Day proclaimed City of Holland, 1984. Mem. AACD, Am. Assn. Marriage and Family Therapy (assoc.), Assn. for Couples in Marriage Enrichment, Hist. Preservations of Am. (Community Leader and Noteworthy Ams. award 1976-77), Council Family Rels. E-mail: bert.lucas@worldnet.att.net.

LUCAS, C. PAYNE, development organization executive; b. Spring Hope, N.C., Sept. 14, 1933; s. James Russell and Minnie (Hendricks) L; m. Freddie Emily Myra Hill, Aug. 29, 1964; children: Therese Raymonde, C. Payne Jr., Hillary Hendricks. BA in History, U. Md.; LLD (hon.), U. Md., 1975; MA in Govt., Am. U. Asst. dir. Peace Corps, Togo, 1964, dir. Niger, 1965-67, dir. Africa region, 1967-71; pres. Africare, Washington, 1971—. Lectr. in field. Author: (with Kevin Lowther) Keeping Kennedy's Promise--The Peace Corps: Unmet Promise of the New Frontier, 1978; contbr. articles to profl. publs. Bd. dirs. Coun. Fgn. Rels., Overseas Devel. Coun. World Resources Inst., InterAction, Population Action Internat., Kagiso Trust USA, Nat. Planning Assn.; bd. dirs., chmn. Reach & Teach USA; bd. dirs., founding mem. Corp. Coun. on Africa. Recipient Disting. Fed. Svc. award Pres. Lyndon B. Johnson, Presdl. Hunger award for Outstanding Achievement, Pres. Ronald Reagan, 1984, Aggrey medal Phelps-Stokes Fund, 1986, Order of Disting. Svc. award Pres. Kenneth Kaunda of Zambia, 1986, Recognition awards Nat. Order of Rep. Niger, 1988, Zambia, Cote D'Iroire, Senegal, Benin, Disting. Bicentennial award Land Grant Coll., 1990, Hubert H. Humphrey Pub. Svc. award APSA, 1991. Mem. Cosmos Club, Omega Psi Phi. Office: Africare 440 R St NW Washington DC 20001-1935 E-mail: cplucas@africare.org.

LUCAS, CAROL LEE, biomedical engineer; b. Aberdeen, S.D., Feb. 13, 1940; d. Howard Cleveland and Sarah Ivy (Easterby) Nogle; m. Richard Albert Lucas, Feb. 26, 1961; children: Wendy Lee, Sean Richard. BA, Dakota Wesleyan U., 1961; MS, U. Ariz., 1967; PhD, U. N.C., 1973. Tchr. Spanish, Mitchell (S.D.) H.S., 1960-61; tchr. math., English and sci. U.S. Army, Furth, Germany, 1961-62; sys. analyst Cargill Inc., Mpls., 1962-65; rsch. assoc. U. N.C., Chapel Hill, 1973-76, lectr., 1976-77, asst. prof. curriculum in biomed. engring. and math., 1977-84, assoc. prof. dept. surgery, 1984-89, prof., 1989—, acting chmn. curriculum biomed. engring. and math., 1990-92, chmn. biomed. engring., 1992—2001; program dir. NSF, 2001—03. NIH trainee, 1968-73. Contbr. articles to profl. jours. Mem. IEEE, Am. Heart Assn., N.C. Heart Assn., Biomed. Engring. Soc., Cardiovasc. Sys. Dynamics Soc., Am. Inst. Biol. and Med. Engrs. Democrat. Methodist. Home: 2421 Sedgefield Dr Chapel Hill NC 27514-6810 Office: U NC Sch Medicine Dept Biomed Engring 152 Macnider Hall Chapel Hill NC 27599-0001 E-mail: clucas@bme.unc.edu.

LUCAS, CONSTANCE ELAINE, children's librarian; b. Dayton, Ohio, July 8, 1951; d. Kenneth Dunson and Rosa L. (Moon) Persons; m. Mitchell D. Lucas, Nov. 22, 1969 (div. Feb. 1979); children— Mitchell D., Lukinte. B.S. in Polit. Sci., Wright State U., 1980, B.S. in Edn., 1981; M.P.A., Central Mich. U., 1981. Library asst. I, Dayton and Montgomery Counties (Ohio), Dayton, 1969-73, library asst. II, 1973-80, children's librarian, 1981— ; mem. adv. bd. WPTD-TV, 1984—; mem. Nat. Issue Forums, 1984—; trustee Day Break, Inc., sec., 1986-87, nominating chair, 1987, chairperson bd. trustees. Speaker film: What's a Good Book-How to Select a Good Book, 1982. Mem. Republican Nat. Com., Washington, 1980— ; mem. Shiloh Bapt. Ch.; pres. Young Reps. West, Dayton, 1981-83; 1st v.p. Ohio Rep. Council, Columbus, 1981— ; del.-at-large Rep. Nat. Conv., 1984; bd. dirs. Montgomery County Rep. Central and Exec. coms., Dayton, 1977— ; mem. Presdl. Task Force, 1984; del.-at-large Presdl. Library Conf., John Fitzgerald Kennedy Library for Nat. Issue Forum Conf., Boston, 1985; mem. Black Family Coalition, 1984—. Recipient Concordian cert. Nat. Rep. Com., 1980. Mem. ALA, Ohio Library Assn. (chair outreach services to ethnic communities), Dayton and Montgomery Counties Staff Assn. (spl. com., collective bargaining com.). Baptist. Lodge: Athena Chpt. #37 (corr. sec. 1980-81). Home: 2211 Ridge Creek Ct Dayton OH 45426-3139 Office: Madden Hills Libr 2542 Germantown St Dayton OH 45408-1630

LUCAS, CRAIG JOHN, lawyer; b. Ogden, Utah, Mar. 15, 1962; s. Frank James and Joan (Christensen) L. BS, Weber State U., 1985; JD, U. Idaho, 1988. Bar: Nev. 1989, D.C. 1992, U.S. Dist. Ct. Nev. 1990, U.S. Ct. Appeals (9th cir.) 1990. Legis. intern Utah House Majority Leader, Salt Lake City,

1984; Congl. intern U.S. Senate, Washington, 1984; legal intern Idaho Prosecuting Atty. Assn., Boise, 1987; law clk. to Hon. Miriam Shearing 8th Dist. Ct., Las Vegas, 1988-90; from assoc. gen. counsel to chief assoc. counsel State Indsl. Ins. System, 1990-91; pvt. practice, 1992—. Ctrl. com. mem. Rep. Party, Clark County, Nev., 1990-92, conv. del., 1990. Mem. Federalist Soc., Nev. Trial Lawyers Assn. Church of Jesus Christ of Latter-day Saints. Avocations: travel, hiking, skiing. Office: 3634 N Rancho Dr Las Vegas NV 89130 E-mail: clucas@lv.rmci.net.

LUCAS, DALE ADRIAN, landscape company executive, consultant; b. Des Moines, Oct. 23, 1933; s. Cecil Abner and Helga Nancy (Andreasen) L.; m. Margaret Ellen Couts, July 26, 1953 (div. Nov. 1978); children: Katherine, Cheryl, Caryl, James; m. Jary Lea Schjaastad, Mar. 30, 1984; children: Desirée, Quinn, Kelly, Cary, Toni. BS in Zoology, Iowa State U., 1956. Commd. 2d lt. U.S. Army Corps Engrs., 1956, advanced through grades to maj., 1966; ret., 1976; maintenance supr. Staley Corp., Des Moines, 1976-77; tree crew foreman Wright Tree Svc., West Des Moines, 1977-80; grounds worker Drake U., Des Moines, 1980-83, grounds supr., 1983-98; ret., 1998. Cons. in field. Mem. forestry adv. bd. Des Moines Pub. Works, 1996-97; founding mem. 1st pres. Urban Trees, Des Moines, 1986-97. Mem. Iowa State Hort. Soc. (bd. dirs. 1988-97, Merit award 1996), Iowa Arborist Assn. (rep.-at-large 1986-97, v.p. 1985-86, pres. 1986, 98, Outstanding Profl. 1995), Internat. Soc. Arboriculture (cert.) Avocations: travel, gardening, framing, ceramics, swimming, golf. Home: 4305 65th St Urbandale IA 50322-2815 E-mail: dalucas@attglobal.net.

LUCAS, DON JOHN, music educator; b. Alexandria, Va., Dec. 15, 1953; MusB, Tex. Tech. U., 1979, MusM, 1981; postgrad., U. Houston, 1998—; diploma, Guildhall Sch. of Music, London. Dir. bands J.E.B. Stuart High Sch., Falls Church, Va., 1983-85, Cary (N.C.) Sr. High Sch., 1985-87; instr. music Sam Houston State U., Huntsville, Tex., 1991-92, Ea. N.Mex. U., Portales, 1992-93; asst. dir. bands Brenham (Tex.) High Sch., 1993-94; asst. prof. music Tex. Tech. U., Lubbock, 1994—. Founding mem. Am. Classic Trombone Quartet, 1985—; cons. in field. Trombonist St. Paul Chamber Orch., 1989-91; prin. trombonist, soloist Am. Wind Symphony Orch., Pitts., 1980—; performed with San Antonio Symphony, N.Mex. Symphony, Albuquerque, 1999-2000; solo recitals Moscow Conservatory, Conservatoire Superior de Music, Paris, C.B.S.O. Centre Adrian Boult Hall, Birmingham, France, 1999-2000. Mem. Gideons Intenat., Lubbock, 1985—; music ministry Trinity Ch., Lubbock, 1996—. Fulbright scholar, London, 1982-83. Mem. Tex. Music Educators Assn., Internat. Trombone Assn. (life, scholar chair 1998), Brit. Trombone Soc., Pi Kappa Lambda. Avocations: table tennis, arts & crafts. Office: Tex Tech U Sch Music 18th & Boston Lubbock TX 79409 Fax: 806-742-2294.

LUCAS, DONALD LEO, private investor; b. Upland, Calif., Mar. 18, 1930; s. Leo J. and Mary G. (Schwamm) L.; m. Lygia de Soto Harrison, July 15, 1961; children: Nancy Maria Lucas Thibodeau, Alexandra Maria Lucas Ertola, Donald Alexander Lucas. BA, Stanford U., 1951, MBA, 1953. Assoc. corp. fin. dept. Smith, Barney & Co., N.Y.C., 1956-59; gen., ltd. ptnr. Draper, Gaither & Anderson, Palo Alto, Calif., 1959-66; pvt. investor Menlo Park, 1966—. Bd. dirs. Cadence Design Systems, San Jose, Calif., Oracle Corp., Redwood Shores, Calif., Macromedia, San Francisco, PDF Solutions, Inc., TriCord Systems, Inc., Plymouth, Minn., PDF Solutions, San Jose. Mem. bd. regents Bellarmine Coll. Prep., 1977-2002 regent emeritus U. Santa Clara, 1980—. 1st lt. AUS, 1953-55. Mem. Am. Coun. Capital Formation (dir.), Stanford U. Alumni Assn., Stanford Grad. Sch. Bus. Alumni Assn., Order of Malta, Stanford Buck Club, Vintage Club (Indian Wells, Calif.), Menlo Circus Club (Atherton, Calif.), Jackson Hole Golf and Tennis Club, Bighorn Country Club, Calif., Zeta Psi. Home: 224 Park Ln Atherton CA 94027-5411 Office: 3000 Sand Hill Rd Ste 3-210 Menlo Park CA 94025-7119

LUCAS, GEORGE RAMSDELL, JR. philosophy educator; b. San Angelo, Tex., Sept. 8, 1949; s. George Ramsdell and Clare Elizabeth (Baldwin) L.; m. Patricia Cook; children: Jessica, Kimberly, Theresa. BS summa cum laude, Coll. William and Mary, 1971; PhD, Northwestern U., 1978. Asst. prof., chmn. dept. philosophy Randolph-Macon Coll., Ashland, Va., 1978-82; assoc. prof., chmn. dept. philosophy Santa Clara (Calif.) U., 1982-86; assoc. prof. Emory U., Atlanta, 1986-87; prof. philosophy Clemson (S.C.) U., 1987-91; asst. dir. rsch. divsn. NEH, Washington, 1991-95; prof. bus. Georgetown U., 1996—; assoc. dept. chmn., prof. ethics U.S. Naval Acad., 1996—. Exec. dir. Am. Acad. for Liberal Edn., 1998—. Author: The Genesis of Modern Process Thought, 1983, The Rehabilitation of Whitehead, 1989, Perspectives on Humanitarian Military Intervention, 2001; editor: Lifeboat Ethics: Moral Dilemmas of World Hunger, 1976, Poverty, Justice and the Law, 1986; philosophy editor SUNY Press, Albany, 1989—, Ency. Americana; contbr. articles to profl. jours. Am. Coun. Learned Socs. fellow, 1982; Fulbright rsch. fellow, 1989. Mem. Am. Philos. Assn., Metaphys. Soc. Am., Hegel Soc. Am., Omicron Delta Kappa, Phi Beta Kappa. Office: Dept Leadership Ethics & Law MS 7-B US Naval Acad Annapolis MD 21402 E-mail: grlucas@usna.edu.

LUCAS, GEORGE W., JR. film director, producer, screenwriter; b. Modesto, Calif., May 14, 1944; Student, Modesto Jr. Coll.; BA, U. So. Calif., 1966. Chmn. Lucasfilm Ltd., San Rafael, Calif. Creator short film THX-1138, asst. to Francis Ford Coppola The Rain People, dir., co-writer THX-1138, 1970, American Graffiti, 1973, dir., author screenplay Star Wars, 1977; exec. prodr.: More American Graffiti, 1979, The Empire Strikes Back, 1980, Raiders of the Lost Ark, 1981, Indiana Jones and the Temple of Doom, 1984, Labyrinth, 1986, Howard the Duck, 1986, Willow, 1988, Tucker, 1988, Radioland Murders, 1994, (co-author screenplay): Return of the Jedi, 1983; co-exec. prodr. Mishima, 1985; co-author (co-exec. prodr.): Indiana Jones and the Last Crusade, 1989; exec. prodr.(TV series): The Young Indiana Jones Chronicles, 1992—93; author (dir., exec. prodr.): Star Wars: Episode I The Phantom Menace, 1999, Star Wars: Episode II Attack of the Clones, 2002. Office: Lucasfilm Ltd PO Box 2009 San Rafael CA 94912-2009

LUCAS, GEORGES, physicist, researcher; b. Marosvasarhely, Transylvania, Rumania, Dec. 11, 1914; arrived in France, 1933; s. Emeric and Hermine (Grun) Lukacs; m. Irene Weingrow, Jan. 10, 1948. Degree in Chem. Engring., U. Strasbourg, France, 1938; postgrad., Ecole Normale Superieure, Paris, 1938-40; PhD, U. Paris, Sorbonne, 1955. Rsch. assoc. astrophysics Centre Nat. de la Recherche Scientifique Observatory, Meudon, France, 1953-55; with rsch. dept. Tidewater Oil Co., Avon, Calif., 1956-65, Elf-Aquitaine, Paris, 1965-77, ret., 1977. Author: Transfer Theory for Trapped Electromagnetic Energy, 1983; contbr. articles to profl. jours., abstracts to profl. proceedings; patentee in field. Mem. Am. Phys. Soc., Am. Soc. Photobiology, European Photochemistry Assn., European Soc. Photobiology, N.Y. Acad. Scis. Avocation: drawing. Home: 83-85 rue Saint Charles 75015 Paris France

LUCAS, GEORGETTA MARIE SNELL, retired educator, artist; b. Harmony, Ind., July 25, 1920; d. Ernest Clermont and Sarah Ann (McIntyre) Snell; m. Joseph William Lucas, Jan. 29, 1943; children: Carleen Anita Lucas Underwood, Thomas Joseph, Joetta Jeanne Lucas Allgood. BS, Ind. State U., 1942; MS in Edn., Butler U., 1964; postgrad., Herron Sch. of Art, 1961-65, Ind. U., Indpls. and Bloomington, 1960-62, 65. Music, art tchr. Jasonville City Schs., Ind., 1942-43, Van Buren H.S., Brazil, Ind., 1943-46, Plainfield City Schs., Ind., 1946-52, Met. Sch. Dist. Wayne Twp., Indpls., 1952-56, 59-68; art tchr. Met. Sch. Dist. Perry Twp., 1968-81. Lectr. Art Educators Assn. Ind., Ind. U.-Bloomington, 1976. Illustrator: (book) Why So Sad, Little Rag Doll, 1963; artist (painting) Ethereal Season, 1966, (lithograph) Bird of Time, 1965-66; exhibited in group shows Hoosier Salon Art Exhibit, 1954, 56, 60, 62-65, 67, 68, 70, 72, 87, 94, N.Y. Lincoln Ctr., N.Y.C., 1994; represented in permanent collections Ind. State U., Ind.-Purdue U.-Indpls. Jane Voorhees Zimmerli Art Mus., Rutgers U., N.J., Indpls. Pub. Sch. Collection; drummer with Hendricks County Ramblers, 1986—. Mem. NEA (life), Nat. Assn. Women Artist, Ind. Artist Craftsmen, Inc. (hon., pres. 1979-85, 87, 88, scholarship chmn. 1986—, bd. dirs. 1986—), Ind. Fedn. Art Clubs (hon., pres. 1986-87, counselor 1988-91, bd. dirs. 1991—, parliamentarian 1992-94, conv. mgr. 1999, Best of Show 1997), Hoosier Salon, Ind. State U. Mortar Bd., Art Edn. Assn. Ind. (life), Nat. League Am. Pen Women (Ind. state art chmn. 1984-96, Best of Show award 1983, 97, pres. Indpls. br. 1994-96, Ind. State Assn. pres. 1998-2000, front cover drawing Pen Women Nat. Mag. 1994), Fine Art for State Ind. (Internat. Women's Yr. fine art chmn. 1977), Ctrl. Ind. Artists (hon.), Alpha Delta Kappa (life, Ind. state chmn. of art 1973-77, pres. 1972-74, represented by painting in nat. hdqrs.-Kansas City, Mo., Fidelis Delta first v.p.), Retired Educators Sorority (1st v.p., pres. 1997-99), Order of Eastern Star. Republican. Methodist. Avocations: genealogy, travel, numismatics. Home and Office: 3192 E Main St Plainfield IN 46168-2721

LUCAS, HENRY CAMERON, JR. information systems educator, writer, consultant; b. Omaha, Sept. 4, 1944; s. Henry Cameron and Lois (Himes) L.; m. Ellen Kuhbach, June 8, 1968; children: Scott C., Jonathan G. BS in Indsl. Adminstrn. magna cum laude, Yale U., 1966; MS, MIT, 1968, PhD, 1970. Cons. Arthur D. Little, Inc., Cambridge, Mass., 1966-70; asst. prof. computer and info. systems Stanford U., Calif., 1970-74; assoc. prof. computer applications and info. systems NYU, 1974-78, prof., chmn. dept. info. systems, 1978-84; on leave IBM European Systems Research Inst., Belgium, 1981; INSEAD Fontainebleau, France, 1985; prof. info. systems NYU, 1985-2000; Shaw Found. Prof. Nat. Tech. U., Singapore, 1997-98; Robert H. Smith prof. info. sys. Robert H. Smith Sch. Bus. U. Md., 2000—; co-dir. Ctr. for Electronic Markets and Enterprises, 2001—. Author: The T-Form Organization, 1996 Computer-Based Information Systems in Organizations, 1973, The Information Systems Environment, 1980 (with F. Land, T. Lincoln and K. Supper) Casebook for Management Information Systems, 3d edit., 1985, The Analysis, Design and Implementation of Information Systems, 4th edit., 1992, Information Technology for Management 7th edit., 2000, Coping with Computers: A Manager's Guide to Controlling Information Processing, 1982, Introduction to Computers and Information Systems, 1986, Managing Information Services, 1989, Information Technology and Productivity Paradox: Assessing the Value of Investing in IT, 1999, Strategies for Electronic Commerce and the Internet, 2002; editor Indsl. Mgmt., 1967-68; mem. editorial bd. Sloan Mgmt., Rev., 1975-91; assoc. editor MIS Quar., 1977-83; editor in chief Systems, Objectives, Solutions, 1980—, v.p. publications Assn. for Info. Systems, 1996-98; editor-in-chief Jour. and Comms. of AIS, 1998-2001; contbr. articles to profl. jours. Recipient award for excellence in teaching NYU Sch. Bus., 1982 Fellow Assn. Info. Sys.; mem. IEEE, Publs. Assn. for Info. Sys. (v.p. 1995—), Assn. Computing Machinery, Inst. Mgmt. Scis., Phi Beta Kappa, Tau Beta Pi. Home: 871 Coach Way Annapolis MD 21401-6481 Office: Smith Sch Bus U Md 4337 Van Munching Hall College Park MD 20742-1106 E-mail: hlucas@rhsmith.umd.edu.

LUCAS, JAMES E(VANS), operatic director; b. San Antonio, Mar. 15, 1933; s. Mason Harley and Nora Norton (Evans) L. BA, Hiram Coll., 1951; postgrad., Stanford U., 1951-52, Juilliard Sch. Music, 1952-53. Faculty Temple U., 1965-71, Mannes Coll. Music, 1964-70, Manhattan Sch. Music, 1970-78, Carnegie-Mellon U., 1977-79; prof. music, stage dir. Ind. U., 1987-94; vis. prof. Seoul Nat. U., 1996, Dartmouth Coll., 1997. Free-lance operatic stage dir.; worked for opera cos. in U.S., Can. including, Met. Opera, San Francisco Opera, N.Y.C. Opera, Can. Opera Co.; dir. for various summer festivals. Mem. Am. Guild Musical Artists, Am. Fedn. Musicians, Can. Actors Equity. Home and Office: 201 W 85th St New York NY 10024-3907

LUCAS, JAMES RAYMOND, business executive, leadership consultant, author, speaker; b. St. Louis, Mar. 9, 1950; s. James Earl and Anna LaVerne (Ryan) L.; m. Pamela Kay Petersen, June 10, 1972; children: Laura Christine, Peter Barrett, David Christopher, Bethany Gayle. BS in Engring. Mgmt., U. Mo., Rolla, 1972; postgrad., U. Mo., 1978, Regent Coll., Vancouver, B.C., 1999. Registered profl. engr., Mo., Kans. Product analyst The Lee Co., Westwood, Kans., 1971-73; mgr. planning Black & Veatch, Kansas City, Mo., 1973-79; dir. constrn. Hallmark Cards, 1979-81; project mgr. The Pritchard Corp., 1981-83; gen. mgr., pres., CEO EPIC Mfg., 1984-86; pres. Luman Cons. Internat., Prairie Village, Kans., 1983—; exec. dir. Relationship Devel. Ctr., 1992—. Sr. mem. seminar faculty, faculty adv. com. Am. Mgmt. Assn., 1994— (award winner); publisher, pres. Quintessential Books, 1993—. Author: Weeping in Ramah, 1985, The Parenting of Champions, 1989, Noah: Voyage to a New Earth, 1991, Proactive Parenting, 1993, Walking Through the Fire, 1996, Fatal Illusions: Shredding a Dozen Unrealities That Can Keep Your Organization From Success, 1997, Balance of Power: Authority or Empowerment? How to Get the Best of Both in the Interdependent Organization, 1998, The Passionate Organization: Igniting the Fire of Employee Commitment, 1999, 1001 Ways to Connect With Your Kids, 2000, A Perfect Persecution, 2001. Pres. Mother and Unborn Baby Care, Overland Park, 1990; elder Living Faith Ch., 1985-96. Mem. ASTD, Soc. Mfg. Engrs. (sr.), Am. Assn. Christian Counselors (charter), Am. Mgmt. Assn., Class. Avocations: piano, writing music, reading, travel. Home: 7303 Rosewood Shawnee Mission KS 66208-2458 Office: Luman Cons Internat PO Box 2566 Shawnee Mission KS 66201-2566 E-mail: jlucaslc@aol.com.

LUCAS, JAMES WALTER, federal government official; b. Frankfort, Ind., Oct. 20, 1940; s. Walter Kenneth and Hester (Kesterson) L.; m. Sara Sue Stewart, Feb. 17, 1962; 1 dau., Catherine Anne. BS, Ball State U., 1963, MA, 1964; postgrad., Am. U., 1977, Harvard U., 1990; DA, George Mason U., 1995. Asst. dir. intelligence coordination Nat. Security Council, Washington, 1975-76; exec. asst. to dep. dir. CIA, 1976-77, dep. exec. sec., 1977-79; CIA program budget officer Intelligence Community Staff, 1979-81; dep. asst. sec. U.S. Dept. Air Force, 1981-82, prin. dep. asst. sec., 1982-83; dir. crisis mgmt. planning staff Nat. Security Council, 1983-85; Disting. prof., dean Def. Intelligence Coll., Washington, 1985-93; assoc. dir. liaison Def. Intelligence Agy., 1993-96; dep. dir. Open Source Info., CIA, 1996-97; prof. Nat. Def. U., Washington, 1997—. Adj. prof. U. Md.-Far East div., 1970-71, Def. Intelligence Coll., 1974-83; guest lectr. Am. U., Washington, 1971-77; cons. Pres.'s Fgn. Intelligence Adv. Bd. Author: Intelligence and National Security in the Nixon Administration, 1972, Simulation and Strategic Intelligence Analysis, 1973, Information Needs of Presidents, 1989, Organizing the Presidency: The Role of the Director of Central Intelligence, 1995. Pres. Muncie Young Republican's Club, Ind., 1959-64; pres. Muncie Students for Goldwater, 1964; mem. Rep. Nat. Com., Reston Rep. Assn. With USAF, 1965-77, brig. gen. Res., 1977-96. Decorated Legion of Merit, Bronze Star medal, Meritorious Svc. medal, Republic of Vietnam Gallantry Cross with palm. Mem. Am. Polit. Sci. Assn., Internat. Studies Assn., Air Force Assn., Nat. Mil. Intelligence Assn., Res. Officers Assn., Pi Sigma Alpha, Phi Gamma Mu, Sigma Chi Lodges: Masons. Office: CIA Nat Def Univ Washington DC 20319-0001

LUCAS, JANE GARLAND, interior designer, educator; b. Poughkeepsie, N.Y., Aug. 24, 1951. B.A. in Studio Art, Sweet Briar Coll., 1973; M.S. in Interior Design, Drexel U., 1977. Designer, Anderson Notter Finegold Inc., Boston, 1977-81; designer/project mgr. Bennett Assocs., Boston, 1981-82; prin. JGL Interiors, Boston, 1983— ; tchr. Boston Archl. Ctr., 1980— , Chamberlayne Jr. Coll., Boston, 1983— . Mem. Am. Soc. Interior Designers, Inst. Bus. Designers. Office: 75 Broad St Boston MA 02109-4808

LUCAS, KAREN WILLIAMS, controller; b. Ottawa, Can., Nov. 22, 1960; came to U.S., 1981; d. Lloyd George and Irene Katherine Williams; m. Ken W. Lucas, Apr. 18, 1981 (div. Apr. 1999); children: Kennith, James, Nicholas. AA with high honors, Broward C.C., 1990; BBA, Fla. Atlantic U., 1996. Cert. mgmt. acct., fin. mgmt., 2000. Asst. contr. EHP/Carico, Ft. Lauderdale, Fla., 1981-84; staff acct. MAP Builders, Coral Springs, 1984-86; contr. Conviber Co. Inc., Ft. Lauderdale, 1986-89, Commerce Group, Deerfield Beach, Fla., 1991-96, Purofirst Internat. Inc., Ft. Lauderdale, 1996—. Mem. Inst. Mgmt. Acct. (bd. 2000-2001), Beta Gamma Sigma.

LUCAS, LESLEE SUZANNE, artist; b. Eureka, Calif., Mar. 31, 1963; d. Jack Frederick Jr. and Judy Joan (Johnson) Moore; m. Robert Scott Lucas, Feb. 4, 1989; 1 child, Aaron Matthew Lukosh. BS in Drawing with honors, Portland State U., 1986; MFA in Printmaking, U.S.D., 1988. Freelance artist, Portland, Oreg., 1988—. Exhibited in shows at Baird Purviance exhbn. Sonoma Arts Guild, 1993 (Bronze award). Vol. art tchr. Multnomah County Jail, Portland, 1994—; mem. adv. bd. Liturgical and Sacred Arts Ctr., 1993—, founding mem. Sanctuary for the Arts, 1998—. Named Vol. of Yr., Multnomah County Jail, 1996; recipient color publ. award CIVA catalog, 1999. Democrat. Roman Catholic. Office: PO Box 6443 Portland OR 97228-6443

LUCAS, LINDA LUCILLE, dean; b. Stockton, Calif., Apr. 22, 1940; d. Leslie Harold Lucas and Amy Elizabeth (Callow) Farnsworth. BA, San Jose State Coll., 1961, MA, 1969; EdD, U. San Francisco, 1982. Dist. libr. Livermore (Calif.) Elem. Schs., 1962-64; libr. Mission San Jose High Sch., Fremont, Calif., 1964-69; media reference libr. Chabot Coll., Hayward, 1969-75; asst. dean instrn. Chabot-Las Positas Coll., Livermore, 1975-91; assoc. dean instrn. Las Positas Coll., 1991-94, dean acad. svcs., 1994-2000. Participant Nat. Inst. for Leadership Devel., 1991. Bd. dirs. Tri-Valley Community TV, Livermore, 1991-98, Valley Choral Soc., 1993-98, Chabot-Las Positas Colls. Found., Pleasanton, Calif., 1991-94; mem. needs assessment com Performing Arts Coun., Pleasanton. Mem. ALA, Coun. Chief Librs., Assn. Calif. Community Coll. Adminstrs., Calif. Libr. Assn. Avocations: choral music, photography. Home: 4848 Golden Rd Pleasanton CA 94566-6038

LUCAS, LORRAINE J. regulatory affairs professional, clinical research scientist, epidemiologist consultant; b. St. Louis; BS, U. Calif., San Diego, 1981; MSPH, Loma Linda U., 1983; PhD in Epidemiology, U. Tex., Houston, 1988. Corp. mgr. Am. Cyanamid Co., Wayne, N.J., 1988-95; v.p. med. and sci. affairs, clin. trial coord. B. Braun Med. Inc., Bethlehem, Pa., 1996-00; dir. clin. devel. and regulatory affairs LifeCell Corp., Branchburg, NJ, 2000—01; assoc. dir. regulatory affairs BioPharms., Novo Nordisk, Princeton, 2001—. Mem. advising bd. Nat. Death Index., Hyattsville, Md., 1992—; cons., Wayne, 1995-00. Contbr. articles to profl. jours. Mem. CMA, (mem. EO industry coun.), HIMA (mem. NIOSH task force), Regulatory Affairs Profl. Soc., AN Group Inc. Home: 22 Brier Rd Whitehouse Station NJ 08889-3045 Office: Novo Nordisk Pharm Inc One College Rd Princeton NJ 08540 E-mail: lolu@nnpi.com., ljlucas@blast.net.

LUCAS, MARGARET EXNER, housing developer; b. Kweiyang, China, May 13, 1941; d. Wallace and Beatrice (Exner) Liu; m. David Dale Lucas. BA, U. Minn., 1963, MSW, 1977. With Ramsey County Welfare, St. Paul, 1963-64; vol. Peace Corps, Iran, 1965-67; ptnr. M-2 Shelter, Mpls., 1978-80, Brighton Devel. Corp., Mpls., 1980—. V.p. LWVUS, 1990-94; chmn. Minn. Women's Campaign Fund, Mpls.; vice chmn. Minn. Amateur Sports Commn., Blaine, 1986-92; mem. Met. Sports Facilities Commn., Mpls., 1993—; co-chmn. NCAA Women's Final Four, Mpls., 1995; adv. bd. mem. Coll. Arch. and Landscape Arch., U. Minn., 1995-99, chmn. adv. com. women's athletic dept.; mem. bd. regents St. Johns U. Mem. Minn. Women's Econ. Round Table, Internat. Women's Forum. Office: 15 N 12th St Minneapolis MN 55403-1306

LUCAS, MELINDA ANN, pediatrician, educator; b. Maryville, Tenn., June 27, 1953; d. Arthur Baldwin and Dorthy (Shields) L. BA, Maryville Coll., 1975; MS, U. Tenn., 1976, MD, 1981, postgrad., 1992-93, U. Mich., 1995-97. Diplomate Am. Bd. Pediat.; lic. physician, Mich., N.Y., Tenn. Intern U. Rochester, N.Y., 1981-82, resident in pediat., 1982-84; pvt. practice, Maryville, 1984-85; clin. fellow U. Tenn. Genetics Ctr., 1988-89; emergency room pediatrician U. Tenn. Med. Ctr., Knoxville, 1985-90, dir. child abuse clinic, 1985—90, pediat. intensivist, 1985—, 1987—88, acting dir. pediat. ICU, 1987-88, 90-92, faculty, 1988—; fellow in pediat. critical care U. Mich., Ann Arbor, 1995-96; emergency dept. pediatrician U. Tenn. Med. Ctr., Knoxville, 2001—; with ABC Pediatrics, 2000—; adj. asst. prof. U. Tenn. , 2001—. Mem. Pediatric Cons., Inc., Knoxville, 1985—99; physician rep. Project Search Working Symposium, 1990—91, Regional Tenn. Early Intervention Sys., 1992—; adj. asst. prof. dept. theory and practice in tchr. edn. Coll. of Edn., Univ. Tenn., Knoxville. Contbr. articles to profl. jours. Mem. child watch com. Children's Def. Fund, 1977—99; mem. Blount County Foster Care Rev. Bd., Maryville, 1985—93, Blount County Exec. Bd. Maryville Coll. Alumni Assn., 1988—92; mem. adv. bd. Safe Kids of Tenn., 1998—, Knoxville Area Safe Kids, 1998—, ABC Pediat., 2000—; child passenger coord. Am. Acad. Pediats. and U. Tenn Med. Ctr., Knoxville, 1997, child passenger safety techican, 1999—; physician coord. Knoxville Area Project Delivery of Chronic Care. Recipient Spl. Achievement award Am. Acad. Pediatrics/Tenn. Pediatric Soc. TN chpt., 2001, 2002, Spl. Achievement award AAI; United Presbyn. Ch. scholar, 1971, Mary Lou Braly scholar, 1971-74; grantee AAP-Nat. Hwy. Traffic Safety Adminstrn. for Safe Ride Program, 1993. Fellow: Am. Acad. Pediat. (Spl. Achievement award Tenn. chpt.); mem.: Soc. Critical Care Medicine (abstract reviewer 1991, 1992, 1993, 1994, 1995, 1996, 1997, 1998, 1999), Knoxville Area Pediat. Soc., Tenn. Pediat. Soc. (co-chmn. accident and injury prevention com. 1993—95, 1996—97, chmn. accident and injury prevention com. 1997—), Am. Profl. Soc. Abuse of Children, AMA (Physician Recognition award 1984—87, 1988—91, Spl. Achievement award Tenn. chpt. 1991—94, 1994—97, 1997—2000). Methodist. Avocations: basketball, tennis, piano. Home: 1608 Mcilvaine Dr Maryville TN 37803-6230

LUCAS, NANCY BROOME, music educator; b. Greenville, S.C., Apr. 5, 1934; d. Sanford Leroy and Grace Bell (Bounds) Broome; m. John Winston Lucas, June 23, 1956; 1 child, Stephen Winston Lucas. AB in Engl., U. N.C., Greensboro, 1952-56; AB in piano, Limestone Coll., Gaffney. S.C., 1966-69; MM in piano, Converse Coll., Spartanburg, S.C., 1969-72. Com. for local music contests Charlotte (N.C.) Piano Tchrs. Forum, 1969, 73; pres. Queen City Music Club, Charlotte, N.C., 1993; mem. Charlotte (N.C.) Music Club, 1996-97. Mem. bd. Metro. Music Ministries, Charlotte, N.C., 1992. Mem. Monroe (N.C.) Profl. Bus. Women, 1997, Woman Reach, Charlotte, N.C., 1987-97. Mem. Charlotte Piano Tchrs. Forum, Am. Guild of Organists, Charlotte Music Club. United Methodist. Avocations: interior decorating, public speaking.

LUCAS, NORMAN ARTHUR, retired town manager; b. Seymour, Conn., Oct. 11, 1930; s. Rudolph Arthur and Emma Amelia (Haversat) L.; m. Marie Ann Frate, May 24, 1930. BA with high honors, U. Conn., 1952; M in Govtl. Adminstrn., U. Pa., 1954. Asst. to city mgr. City of Concord, N.H., 1953-54; asst. twp. mgr. Parsippany-Troy HIlls (N.J.) Twp., 1954-57; town adminstr. Town of New Canaan, Conn., 1957-69, Town of Darien, 1969-98. Chmn. Darien Health and Safety, 1968-98; sec. Darien Pension Bd., 1971-98. Contbr. articles to profl. jours. Recipient Honor award Noroton Heights Fire Dept., Darien, 1986, Svc. award State of Conn. Gen. Assembly, 1998. Mem. Internat. City Mgmt. Assn. (plaque 1993), Am. Soc. Pub. Adminstrn. (past dir.), Conn. Town and City Mgrs. Assn. (sec.-treas. 1971-72, v.p. 1972-73, pres. 1973-74), Kiwanis (pres. 1968). Lutheran. Avocations: jogging, swimming, photography. Home: 120 Briscoe Rd New Canaan CT 06840-2303

LUCAS, PANOLA, elementary education educator; b. Pikeville, Ky., Nov. 18, 1932; d. Robert Lee and Trulie Ann (Pinson) Fields; m. Kenneth R. Lucas, Dec. 7, 1956 (div. Apr. 1984); 1 child, Nathan Wade. BS in Vocat. Home Econs., Marshall U., 1971; elem. teaching cert., W.Va. State Coll., 1976; cert. prin., W.Va. Coll. Grad. Studies, elem., mid., jr. and sr. high sch. prin., supt., supr. gen. instrn., vocat. admnstr., 1986. Tchr. Buffalo (W.Va.) High Sch., 1972; tchr. homebound Putnam County Bd. Edn., Winfield, W.Va., 1972-86; tchr. Poca (W.Va.) Elem. Sch., 1986-91, Scott Teays Elem. Sch., Scott Depot, W.Va., 1991—. Mem. W.Va. Profl. Educators, Kappa Delta Pi. Democrat. Baptist. Avocations: reading, travel, gardening, bowling, dancing. Home: 205 Hillside Dr # B Nitro WV 25143-2327 E-mail: panolal@msn.com.

LUCAS, PATRICIA LATOURETTE, writer; b. June 27, 1925; m. William Erich Lucas; children: Kathleen, Nancy, Karen, Suzanne, Elizabeth. BA, Whitman Coll., 1947. Author: (books) Overlake, 1979, Historical Highlights of Seattle Tennis Club, 1982, Seattle Children's Home, 1984, Branching Out, History of Laird Norton Families, 1989, Percy, 1990, Sequim Bay Point, 1993, Story of St. Thomas Episcopal Church, 1994, Growing with Seattle, The Story of Sellen Construction Company, 1996, Bridging the Generations, the History of Manson Construction, 2000. Home and Office: PO Box 376 Medina WA 98039-0376

LUCAS, R. ROBERT, finance engineer, corporate tax planner; b. Phila., Feb. 18, 1934; s. Joseph Raphael and Gertrude (Greene) L.; m. Patricia Dwight, Oct. 12, 1954; children: Spencer, Bonnie. AA, New Sch., Edinburgh U., 1966; student, Am. Inst. Tech., Charleston, S.C., 1967. Aide to Hubert Humphrey U.S. Senate, Washington, 1951-57; liaison to CIA USAF, Bolling Field, Washington, 1957-61; tax exec. Tri-State Inst., Washington, 1961-63; CEO Lucas, McDurkin, Edinburgh, 1968-70; v.p. tax accounts Cowan, Hardy, McDurkin, Denver, 1970-85; chmn. bd. Edifice Complex, Charleston, 1985, Monaler0Lucas Kindred Fund, 2001; mgr. Edifice Global Investment Mut. Fund, 2002; pres. Nibuque Pvt. Internat. Banking Group, 2002. Author: Constitution in Conflict, 1970; author articles on taxes and investing. Mem. dist. coms. Boy Scouts Am., Washington and Colo., 44 yrs.; advisor Internat. Ctr. for Law, UN Plz., 1975—, Citizens for a Sound Economy, Washington, 1984—, Cross Current Internat. Inst., Sidney, Ohio, 1990; recruiter Rocky Mountain Tech. Inst., 1961—. Recipient Legion of Honor award Chapel of

Four Chaplains, 1976, Cross of St. Andrew, Greek Army, 1960. Mem. World Future Soc., Am. Astronomy Assn., Boatowners Unltd. Avocations: sailing, camping, cooking, astronomy, archeology. Office: PO Box 894 Mountain Home TN 37684-0894

LUCAS, RHETT ROY, mediator, arbitrator, lawyer, chemical engineer, artist, photographer; b. Columbia, S.C., Nov. 27, 1941; s. Spurgeon LeRoy and Elizabeth (Wells) L.; m. Uta Henkel, Apr. 12, 1967 (div. 1973). BSChemE, U. S.C., 1963; JD, NYU, 1967; postgrad., U. Glasgow, Scotland, 1965-66. Bar: U.S. Supreme Ct., D.C. Rsch. assoc. Twentieth Century Fund, N.Y.C., 1968-69; gen. counsel James Madison Inst., 1969-72, Population Law Ctr., San Francisco, 1972-75; prin. Lucas & Assocs., Washington, 1972-84; artist Beverly Hills (Calif.) Fine Arts, 1984-86, The Rhett Lucas Collection, Santa Fe, and Scottsdale, Ariz., 1988-94; founder The Mediation Practice, 1997. Prin. author U.S. Supreme Ct. briefs in Roe v. Wade, 1972, U.S. vs. Vuitch, 1971, Doe vs. Bolton, 1972 (ACOG amicus), Reno v. Condon, 1999 (amicus), Hill v. Colo., 2000 (amicus), others; contbr. articles to profl jours.; painter approx. 200 nat. and state parks; exhbns. include Oxford U., 1988, Banff Ctr., 1989, Grand Canyon Nat. Park, Ariz., 1991, 92, Capital Reef Nat. Park, Canyonlands Nat. Park, Cumberland Gap Hist. Nat. Park, Death Valley Nat. Pk., John Wesley Powell Meml. Mus., 1992, Powell River History Mus., 1992-93, O'Laurie (Canyonlands) Mus.; also exhbns. in Santa Fe, New Masters Gallery, Taos, N.M., Casa Grande Art Mus., Hubbell's Trading Post Nat. Hist. Pk. Co-founder NARAL, N.Y.C., 1969; founder PRIVATE CITIZEN, 1998, Acad. Population Reproductive Health Counsel, 1998. Root-Tilden scholar NYU Law Sch., 1963-67; Rotary Found. fellow U. Glasgow, 1965-66; population rsch. grantee Rockefeller Found., 1972-74. Mem. ABA (litigation sect.), AIChE, Am. Soc. Marine Artists, Am. Inst. Conservation, Coll. Art Assn., Scottsdale Artist's League, Rockport (Mass.) Art Assn. (life), Wilderness Soc., Can. Alpine Club, Zero Population Growth, Sierra Club (life), Nat. Geog. Soc. (life), Rotary, Order of Coif, Mensa, Nat. Health Lawyers Assn., Am. Trial Lawyers Assn., Materials Info. Soc., Soc. Plastics Industry, Am. Chem. Soc., Order Supreme Ct. Advs. (founder), Acad. Million Dollar Counsel, Mensa, Phi Beta Kappa, Tau Beta Pi, Blue Key (pres.) Avocations: travel, photography, art collecting, golf.

LUCAS, ROBERT FRANK, lawyer; b. Beacon Falls, Conn., Nov. 11, 1935; s. Otto F. and A. Helen (Schuster) L.; m. Regina Abbiati, July 16, 1960; children: Robert Frank Jr., David R., Jennifer J. AB, Bates Coll., Lewiston, Maine, 1956; JD, Boston U., 1959. Bar: Mass. 1960, U.S. Dist. Ct. Mass. 1962, U.S. Supreme Ct. 1973. Trial atty. Boston Legal Aid Soc., 1960-63; prin. Nigro, Pettepit & Lucas, Wakefield, Mass., 1963—. Mem. standing list of masters Mass. Superior Ct., Cambridge, 1979—. Chmn. City of Melrose (Mass.) Bd. of Appeals, 1982—; trustee Melrose High Sch. Permanent Scholarship Fund, 1979—; lay leader 1st United Meth. Ch., Melrose, 1979-82; active Rep. City Com., Melrose, 1980-84. Sgt. USAR, 1959-63. Mem. ABA, Mass. Bar Assn. (bd. dels. 1980-83, exec. com. 1993, chmn. fee arbitration bd. 1983-84, 20th Century Club 1985, Cert. of Appreciation 1988, Community Svc. award 1989), Middlesex County Bar Assn. (bd. dirs. 1986-99), 1st Dist. Ea. Middlesex Bar Assn. (pres. 1987-88), Bellevue Golf Club, Masons (dist. dep. grand master 1982-83). Avocations: music, choral singing, youth sports. Home: 20 Pilgrim Rd Melrose MA 02176-3019 Office: Nigro Pettepit & Lucas 649 Main St Wakefield MA 01880-5216

LUCAS, ROBERT WILLIAM, human resources consultant, writer; b. Balt., Apr. 6, 1951; s. William McKinley and Rosie Lee (Arthur) L.; m. Mary Joy Timmons, Dec. 2, 1988. BS, U. Md., 1985; MA, George Mason U., 1991. Enlisted USMC, 1969, advanced through grades to master sgt., ret., 1991; instr. police firearms NRA, Washington, 1984-87; tng. cons. Encore Mktg. Internat., Lanham, Md., 1987-89; instr. Seminole C.C., Sanford, Fla., 1990-91, Webster U., 1995—; mgr. tng., devel. AAA, Heathrow, Fla., 1991-98; pres. Creative Presentation Resources, Inc., Casselberry, 1995—. Author: Coaching Skills: A Guide for Supervisors, 1994, Training Skills for Supervisors, 1994, Effective Interpersonal Relationships, 1994, Customer Service: Skills and Concepts for Business, 1995, Job Strategies for New Employees, 1996, Communicating One-On-One, 1997, The Big Book of Flip Charts, 1999, Customer Service: Skills and Concepts for Success, 2000, How to be a Great Call Center Representative, 2001, The Creative Training Idea Book, 2002. Mem. com., chair bd. govs., instr. Leadership Seminole, Seminole County, Fla., 1993-97; bd. dirs. Fla. Safety Coun. Mem. Am. Soc. Tng. and Devel. (pres. Ctrl. Fla. chpt. 1995, v.p. profl. devel. 1993-94, v.p. comms. Suncoast chpt. 2000), Nat. Am. Soc. Tng. and Devel. (dir. spl. interest group 1989-90). Avocations: writing, cooking, dancing. Office: Creative Presentation Resources Inc PO Box 180487 Casselberry FL 32718-0487 E-mail: blucas@presentationresources.net.

LUCAS, SHARI, musician, educator; b. Ridgewood, N.J., Sept. 5, 1960; d. Donald and Irene (Van de Veen) L. MusB, Baldwin-Wallace Coll., 1982; MusM, Yale U., 1984. Organist, choir dir. Spring Glen Congrl. Ch., Hamden, Conn., 1983-85; asst. sec. Yale Alumni Fund, New Haven, 1984-86; organist North Haven (Conn.) Congl. Ch., 1985; dir. music First Congl. Ch., Madison, Conn., 1986—. Mem. Am. Guild Organists (dean New Haven chpt. 1996-98), Organ Hist. Soc., Am. Choral Dirs. Assn. Democrat. Avocations: darts, cross stitch, crafts. Office: First Congl Ch 26 Meeting House Ln Madison CT 06443-2660

LUCAS, STANLEY JEROME, retired radiologist, physician; b. Cin., Mar. 23, 1929; s. Morris and Ruby (Schaen) L.; m. Judith Esther Schulzinger, May 14, 1953; children— Barbara Ellen, Daniel Nathan, Betsy Diane, Marvin Howard, Ronna Sue BS, U. Cin., 1948, MD, 1951. Diplomate Am. Bd. Radiology. Intern Cin. Gen Hosp., 1951-52, resident, 1952-53, 55-57; practice medicine specializing in radiology Cin., 1957-2000; mem. staff William Booth Meml. Hosp., 1957-61, Speer Meml. Hosp., 1957-61, Jewish Hosp., Cin., 1961—98. Past chmn. bd. Iona, Inc.; bd. dirs. Physician Ins. Co. Ohio. Chmn. med. div. United Appeal, 1978, Jewish Welfare Fund, 1980; bd. dirs., treas., pres. Midwest Found. Med. Care; founder Choicecare, Inc., 1978-86; mem. policy devel. com. Local Health Planning Agy., 1978-82; trustee Cin. Med. Found., 1995—, also pres., 1999, trustee Health Found. Cin., 1999—. Capt. USAF, 1953-55. Honoree, Jewish Nat. Fund, 1994. Fellow Emeritus Am. Coll. Radiology; mem. Radiol. Soc. N.Am., AMA (alt. del. 1982-87, del. 1987-99), Ohio Med. Assn. (del. 1975-85, 94—, 1st dist. councilor 1985-90, pres.-elect 1991, pres. 1992-93), Cin. Acad. Medicine (pres. 1976-77, co-chmn. 140th anniversary 1997), Radiol. Soc. Cin. (pres. 1967), Ohio State Radiol. Soc. (Silver medal 2000), Am. Roentgen Ray Soc., Phi Beta Kappa, Phi Eta Sigma. Clubs: Losantiville Country. Jewish. Home: 6760 E Beechlands Dr Cincinnati OH 45237-3728

LUCAS, STEVEN MITCHELL, lawyer; b. Ada, Okla., Jan. 19, 1948; s. John Dalton and Cherrye (Smith) L.; m. Lori E. Seeberger; children: Steven Turner, Brooke Elizabeth, Sarah Grace. BA, Yale U., 1970; JD, Vanderbilt U., 1973. Bar: D.C. 1973, U.S. Ct. Mil. Appeals 1974, U.S. Dist. Ct. D.C. 1979, U.S. Ct. Appeals (D.C.) 1979, U.S. Supreme Ct. 1979. Assoc. Shaw, Pittman, Potts & Trowbridge, Washington, 1978-82, ptnr., 1983-92; ptnr., head fin. instns. practice Wiley, Rein & Fielding, 1992-93, Winston & Strawn, Washington, 1993-97; pvt. practice, 1997—. Cons. on internat. rels. Rockefeller Found., N.Y.C., 1978; mem. negotiating team Panama Canal Treaty, Washington, 1975—77; legal advisor Dept. Def. Panama Canal negotiations working group; presdl. appointee (U.S. panelist) Internat. Ctr. for the Settlement of Investment Disputes, ICSID-World Bank, 2002—. Editor in chief Vanderbilt U. Jour. Transnational Law, 1972-73. Capt. JAGC U.S. Army, 1974—77. Mem. ABA, FBA (chmn. internat. law com. 1978-80, Outstanding Com. Chmn. award 1979), Inter-Am. Bar Assn., Am. Soc. Internat. Law, Army-Navy Country Club (Arlington, Va.), Yale Club (N.Y.C.), Army and Navy Club (Washington). Republican. Episcopalian. Home: 1696 Dunstable Green Annapolis MD 21401-6424 Office: 1001 Tigger Ct Annapolis MD 21401 E-mail: smlucas@comcast.net.

LUCAS, SUZANNE, statistician, entrepreneur; b. Baxter Springs, Kans., Jan. 16, 1939; d. Ralph Beaver and Marguerite (Sansocie) L.; children: Patricia Sue Jennings Melrose, Neil Patric Jennings. BA in Math., Calif. State U., Fresno, 1967, MA in Ednl. Theory, 1969; MS in Stats., U. So. Calif., 1979; Exec. Mgmt. Program, UCLA, 2000. Asst. to dir. NSF Inst., Calif. State U., Fresno, 1968; tchr. secondary math. Fresno City Schs., 1968-78; statistician corp. indsl. rels. Hughes Aircraft Co., L.A., 1979-80; pers. adminstr. Hughes Aircraft Co. Space and Comm. Group, 1981-82, mem. tech. staff in math., 1982-85, staff engr., 1986-87; mem. tech. staff cost analysis The Aerospace Corp., 1987-90; sr. staff engr. Hughes Aircraft Co. Electro Optical Sys., 1990-93, scientist engr., 1993-97; scientist, engr. Raytheon Sys. Co., El Segundo, Calif., 1997-98; pres. Lucas Enterprises, Clovis, 1993—. Lectr. in biostats. U. So. Calif., 1979,S.W. Mo. State U. Kiwanis scholar, 1958. Mem. Am. Statis. Assn., Internat. Soc. Parametric Analysts (pres. So. Calif. chpt. 1991-92), Soc. Cost Estimating and Analysis (cert.), U. So. Calif. Alumni Assn. (life), Kappa Mu Epsilon. Office: Lucas Enterprises PO Box 851 Clovis CA 93613 E-mail: suzelucas01@attbi.com.

LUCAS, WAYNE LEE, sociologist, educator; b. Joliet, Ill., Jan. 6, 1947; s. Cecil Elmer and Mabel (Torkelson) L.; m. Nancy Jean Floyd, Aug. 23, 1969; children: Jeffrey, Keri. BS, Ill. State U., 1969, MS, 1972; PhD, Iowa State U., 1976. Assoc. prof. U. Mo. Kansas City, 1976—. Contbr. articles to profl. jours. Mem. Acad. Criminal Justice Scis., Am. Soc. Criminology, Soc. for Study of Social Problems, Midwestern Criminal Justice Assn. Democrat. Presbyterian. Avocations: fishing, guitar, woodworking. E-mail: lucasw@umkc.edu.

LUCAS, WILLIAM MAX, JR. structural engineer, university dean; b. Lamar, Mo., July 23, 1934; s. William Max and Margaret (Jones) L.; children— Jennifer Lynn Lucas Wyatt, Sarah Frances Lucas Whittington, Amy Johanne. BS, U. Kans., 1956, MS, 1962; PhD, Okla. State U., 1970. Registered profl. engr., Kans., Mo. Structural engr. Finney & Turnipseed, Topeka, 1960-62; prof. structural engrng. U. Kans., Lawrence, 1962-74, 78-80, dir. facilities planning, 1974-78, dean Sch. Architecture and Urban Design, 1980-94; prof. arch. and archtl. engrng., 1962-97. Owner W.M. Lucas, Engr., Lawrence, 1964— Author: Matrix Analysis for Structural Engineers, 1968, Structural Analysis for Engineers, 1978; contbr. articles to profl. jours. Mem. Lawrence Bd. Bldg. Code Appeals, 1967-73, Kans. Bldg. Commn., 1982-84; pres. bd. dirs. United Fund, Lawrence, 1976; chmn. Lawrence/Douglas County Planning Commn., 1977-79; mem. consultative coun. Nat. Inst. Bldg. Scis., 1993-99. Mem. Am. Soc. for Engrng. Edn., Assn. Collegiate Schs. Architecture, Nat. Soc. Archtl. Engrs., Sigma Xi, Tau Beta Pi, Tau Sigma Delta. Clubs: Lawrence Country. Home: 2629 Bardith Ct Lawrence KS 66046-4536 Office: U Kans Sch Architecture & Urban Des Lawrence KS 66045-0001

LUCAS, WILLIAM RAY, aerospace consultant; b. Newbern, Tenn., Mar. 1, 1922; married 1948; 3 children. BS, Memphis State U., 1943; MS, Vanderbilt U., 1950, PhD in Chem. Metallurgy, 1952; L.H.D. (hon.), Mobile Coll., 1977; D.Sc. (hon.), Southeastern Inst. Tech., 1980, U. Ala., Huntsville, 1981. Instr. chemistry Memphis State U., 1946-48; chemist guided missile devel. div. Redstone Arsenal, 1952-54, chief chem. sect., 1954-55; chief engr. material sect. Army Ballistic Missile Agy., 1955-56, chief engr. material br., 1956-60; with Marshall Space Flight Center, NASA, 1960—, chief engrng. materials br., 1960-63, material div., 1963-66, dir. propulsion and vehicle engring. lab., 1966-68, dir. program devel., 1968-71, dep. dir., 1971-74, dir., 1974-86; pvt. practice aerospace cons. Hunstville, Ala., 1986—2002. Served as lt. USNR, 1943-46. Recipient Exceptional Sci. Achievement medal NASA, 1964, 2 Exceptional Service medals, 1969, Disting. Service medal, 1972, Disting. Service award, 1981, 86; Presdl. rank Disting. Exec., 1980; Roger W. Jones award for outstanding exec. leadership Am. U., 1981; Space award for outstanding contbns. in field of space VFW, 1983; Disting. Alumni award Memphis State U., 1984; Aubrey D. Green award Lions Club Ala., 1986; named one of Tenn. Outstanding Scientists and Engrs., Tenn. Tech. Found., 1986; named to Ala. Engring. Hall of Fame, 1990. Fellow Am. Soc. Metals, Am. Astronautical Soc. (Space Flight award 1982), AIAA (Oberth award 1965, Holger N. Toftoy award 1976, Elmer A. Sperry group award 1986); mem. Nat. Acad. Engring., Am. Chem. Soc., Sigma Xi, Tau Beta Pi Achievements include research in materials engring. metallurgy, inorganic chemistry, environ. effects on materials, especially space environ. effects.

LUCCA, JOHN JAMES, retired dental educator; b. Bklyn., July 12, 1921; s. Thomas and Marie (Ciancia) L.; m. Mary A. Pascarell, June 22, 1946; children— Diane, Eileen, Denise, Nancy, John, William. AB, NYU, 1941; D.D.S., Columbia, 1947. Diplomate: Am. Bd. Prosthodontics. Research fellow prosthetics Columbia Dental Sch., 1949-52, asst. prof., 1952-57, assoc. prof., 1957-64, head clin. prosthodontics; and postgrad. instr. 1st, 10th Dist. dental socs., 1954-87, prof. dentistry, 1964-87, dir. div. prosthodontics; prof. emeritus Columbia U., 1987—. Cons. Westchester County Med. Ctr.; attending emeritus Presbyn. Hosp.; cons., lectr. U.S. Naval Dental Sch.; mem. examination com. N.E. Regional Bd. Dental Examiners; mem. med. staff Valley Hosp. Contbr. to dental jours., chpts. to various textbooks. Extraordinary minister of the Eucharist, 1974— ; mem. parish council Mt. Carmel Ch., 1985—; hon. police surgeon N.Y.C. Police Dept., 1964— . Served with AUS, 1943-44. Recipient Ella M. Ewell medal Columbia, 1947. Fellow N.Y. Acad. Dentistry, Internat. Coll. Dentists Am. Coll. Dentists, Greater N.Y. Acad. Prosthodontics (pres. 1968), Internat. Coll. Prosthodontists, Am. Acad. Osseo Integration, Am. Coll. Prosthodontics (charter, pres. N.J. state sect. 1979-81); mem. Am. Equilibration Soc., First Dist. Dental Soc. (chmn. prosthodontia sect. 1971), Am. Prosthodontics Soc., William Jarvie Rsch. Soc., Chgo. Acad. Dental Rsch., Knight of Malta, Omicron Kappa Upsilon (pres. Epsilon Epsilon chpt. 1967). Home: 524 Eastgate Rd Ridgewood NJ 07450-2204

LUCCHESI, LIONEL LOUIS, lawyer; b. St. Louis, Sept. 17, 1939; s. Lionel Louis and Theresa Lucchesi; m. Mary Ann Wheeler, July 30, 1966; children: Lionel Louis III, Marisa Pilar. BSEE, Ill. Inst. Tech., 1961; JD, St. Louis U., 1969. Bar: Mo. 1969. With Emerson Electric Co., 1965-69; assoc. Polster, Polster & Lucchesi, St. Louis, 1969-74, ptnr., 1974—. City atty. City of Ballwin, Mo., 1979—85, 1992—. Mem. Zoning Commn., 1971—77; alderman City of Ballwin, 1977—79. Recipient Am. Jurisprudence award, St. Louis U., 1968—69; scholar NROTC, 1957—61. Mem.: ATLA, ABA, Newcomen Soc. N.Am., St. Louis Met. Bar Assn. (exec. com., pres.-elect 1984, pres. 1985—86), Am. Patent Law Assn., Forest Hills Club, Rotary (pres.-elect St. Louis 1991—92, pres. 1992—93). Republican. Roman Catholic. Office: 763 S New Ballas Rd Saint Louis MO 63141-8704 E-mail: llucchesi@patpro.com.

LUCCHETTI, LYNN L. career officer; b. San Francisco, Aug. 21, 1939; d. Dante and Lillian (Bergeron) L. AB, San Jose State U., 1961; MS, San Francisco State U., 1967; grad., U.S. Army Basic Officer Course, 1971, U.S. Army Advanced Officer Course, 1976, U.S. Air Force War Coll., 1983, Sr. Pub. Affairs Officer Course, 1984. Media buyer Batten, Barton, Durstine & Osborn, Inc., San Francisco, 1961-67; producer-dir. Sta. KTVA-TV, Anchorage, 1967-68; media supr. Bennett, Luke and Teawell Advt., Phoenix, 1968-71; commd. 1st lt. U.S. Army, 1971, advanced through grades to lt. col., 1985, col., 1989, brig. gen. nom., 1993, officer, 1971-74, D.C. N.G., 1974-78, U.S. Air Force Res., 1978-99; program advt. mgr. U.S. Navy Recruiting Command, 1974-76; exec. coordinator Joint Advt. Dirs. of Recruiting (JADOR), 1976-79; dir. U.S. Armed Forces Joint Recruiting Advt. Program (JRAP) Dept. Def., Washington, 1979-91, resources mgr. Exec. Leadership Devel. Program, 1991-94. Author: Broadcasting in Alaska, 1942-1966. Active Vols. of ARC. Decorated U.S. Army Meritorious Svc. medal, Nat. Def. medal, U.S. Air Force Longevity Ribbon, U.S. Navy Meritorious Unit Commentation, Dept. Def. Joint Achievement medal, 1984, N.Mex. Legion of Merit, 1999; Sigma Delta Chi journalism scholar, 1960. Mem. Women's Affairs Asn., AF Pub. Affairs Alumni Assn. Home: 11401 Malaguena Ln NE Albuquerque NM 87111-6899 E-mail: lynn_lucchetti@excite.com.

LUCCI, SUSAN, actress; b. Scarsdale, N.Y., Dec. 23, 1946; d. Victor and Jeanette L.; m. Helmut Huber, 1969; children: Liza Victoria, Andreas Martin. BA, Marymount Coll., 1968. Portrays Erica in TV series All My Children, 1970—; appearances in other series include: Fantasy Island, The Love Boat, The Fall Guy; TV films: Invitation to Hell, 1985, Mafia Princess, 1985, Ebbie, 1995, Seduced and Betrayed, 1995, (mini-series) Anastasia: The Mystery of Anna Anderson, 1986, Haunted by Her Past, 1988, Lady Mobster, 1988, The Bride in Black, 1990, The Women Who Sinned, 1991, Double Edge, 1992, Between Love and Hate, 1993, French Silk, 1994, Blood on Her Hands, 1998; host of spl. with Tony Danza 99 Ways to Attract the Right Man. Recipient 20 Emmy nominations and 1 Emmy award for best actress in daytime dramaseries, numerous other awards. Office: All My Children 320 W 66th St New York NY 10023-6397 also: care Sylvia Gold ICM 8942 Wilshire Blvd Beverly Hills CA 90211-1934*

LUCCI, WILLIAM RALPH, JR. school system administrator; b. Great Falls, Mont., Dec. 23, 1956; s. William Ralph and Priscilla (Blake) L.; children: Alexander William, Samuel Christian. BS, North Adams State Coll., 1980; MEd, Bridgewater State Coll., 1982; postgrad., Nova Southeastern U., 1991—. Dir. campus ctr. Xavier U., Cin., 1982-85; asst. dean U. Cin., 1985-87; dean students Coll. of St. Joseph, Rutland, Vt., 1987-94, exec. dir., student support svcs., 1994—2002, asst. prof. comms., 1998-2000; dir. comm. J.A. Russell Corp., 2000—01; curriculum coord. Rutland City Schs., 2001—. Pres. Pinnacle Ednl. Resource Group, 1996—; bd. dirs. Spectrum Youth Svcs., 2001--. Vol. Rutland Open Door Mission, March of Dimes; CAB mem. Vt. Pub. Radio; chair blood drive Hoxworth Blood Ctr.; bd. dirs. Vt. Ct. Diversion, J.T. Bowse Cmty. Health Trust, 1999—; mem. planning commn. Town of Fair Haven, Vt., 1994-97; mem. cmty. adv. bd. Vt. Pub. Radio, 1997-99. Dept. Edn. Title IV grantee, 1991; named Outstanding Young Man in Am., 1988. Mem. NASPA, Am. Coll. Pers. Assn., Vt. Coll. Student Pers. Assn. (bd. dirs. 1988—, pres. 1993-94), Smithsonian Instn. Republican. Baptist. Avocations: antique refinishing, Victorian home renovation, golf, bicycling. Home: PO Box 93 Rutland VT 05702-0093 Office: Stafford Tech Ctr Rutland VT 05701

LUCCO, JAMES PERRY, writer; b. Jamestown, N.Y., Nov. 2, 1946; s. James Perry and Josephine Catherine Lucco; m. Gail Catherine Frazier, July 14, 1986. BA, Columbia U., 1971. Asst. to pres. P&A Ent., Miami, Fla., 1972—74; sr. hearing officer State of N.J., Trenton, 1975—77; comptroller Tiger Mgmt., N.Y.C., 1985—97; asst. to pres. Empire Rubbish & Ash, 1993—96, Moyer Plating, Newark, 1992—95; bus. assoc. T.W. Alexander Esq., Elizabeth, 1995—. Author: (play) A Pagans Wine, 1968, New York City Garbage Wars, 2000. Bd. dirs. South Orange Sr. Citizens, South Orange, NJ, 1992—. Mem.: Lions (dir. pub. rels. 1998—). Roman Catholic. Avocation: golf. Home: 376 Williamson St #8 Elizabeth NJ 07202 Office: T W Alexander Esq 815 Salem Ave Elizabeth NJ 07208

LUCE, CHARLES FRANKLIN, former utilities executive, lawyer; b. Platteville, Wis., Aug. 29, 1917; s. James Oliver and Wilma Fisher (Grindell) L.; m. Helen G. Oden, Oct. 24, 1942; children: James O., Christine Mary, Barbara Anne, Charles Franklin; m. Margaret E. Richmond, Nov. 9, 2002. BA, LL.B., U. Wis., 1941; Sterling fellow, Yale U., 1941-42. Bar: Wis. 1941, Wash. 1946, Oreg. 1945, N.Y. 1981. Law clk. Justice Hugo L. Black, U.S. Supreme Ct., 1943-44; gen. practice law Walla Walla, Wash., 1946-61; adminstr. Bonneville Power Adminstrn., Dept. Interior, Portland, Oreg., 1961-66; under sec. interior Washington, 1966-67; chmn. bd. Consol. Edison Co. of N.Y., Inc., 1967-82, chief exec. officer, 1967-81, chmn. emeritus, 1982—; ptnr. Preston, Thorgrimson, Ellis & Holman, Portland, Oreg., 1982-86; spl. counsel Met. Life Ins. Co., 1987-94. Dir. emeritus UAL and Met. Life Ins. Co.; trustee Henry M. Jackson Found.; trustee emeritus Columbia U., N.Y.C. Mem. Wis. Bar Assn., Phi Beta Kappa, Order of Coif. Episcopalian. Office: Consol Edison 4 Irving Pl New York NY 10003-3502

LUCE, DONALD SANDERS, social worker; b. East Calais, Vt., Sept. 20, 1934; s. Collins Andrew and Margaret Sanders L. BS, U. Vt., 1957; MS, Cornell U., 1959. Vol. Internat. Vol. Svcs., Vietnam, 1958—59, dir. Vietnam, 1960—67; rsch. assoc. Cornell U., Ithaca, NY, 1967—68; rsch. dir. World Coun. Chs., Vietnam, 1969—71; dir. Asia Resource Ctr., Washington, 1971—90; pres., CEO Internat. Vol. Svcs., 1991—96, AIDS prevention coord., 1997—98; dir. deve. Cmty. Missions, Niagara Falls, NY, 1998—. Co-author: Viet Nam: The Unheard Voices, 1968, Hostages of War, 1972. Bd. dirs. Am. Friends Svc. Com., Phila., 1971-91; AIDS prevention activist Western N.Y. Peace Ctr., Buffalo, 1985—. Recipient Peace award War Resistors League, N.Y.C., 1990, Gold medal N.Y. Film Festival, N.Y.C., 1985. Mem. United Ch. of Christ. Avocation: writing poetry.

LUCE, GREGORY M. lawyer; Bar: D.C., Va., Md. With Jones, Day, Reavis & Pogue, Washington. Mem. ABA, Am. Health Lawyers Assn. (bd. dirs. 1996—), Va. State Bar (past chair, mem. bd. govs. health law sect.). Office: Jones Day Reavis & Pogue 51 Louisiana Ave NW Washington DC 20001-2113

LUCE, HENRY, III, foundation executive; b. N.Y.C., Apr. 28, 1925; s. Henry Robinson and Lila Hotz (Tyng) L.; m. Patricia Potter, June 27, 1947 (div. 1954); children: Lila Frances, Henry Christopher; m. Claire McGill, Aug. 6, 1960 (dec. June 1971); stepchildren: Kenneth, William, James; m. Nancy Bryan Cassiday, Aug. 15, 1975 (dec. Mar. 1987); stepchildren: Richard, Bryan (dec.); m. Leila Eliott Burton Hadley, Jan. 5, 1990; stepchildren: Arthur T. Hadley III, Victoria Smitter Barlow, Matthew Smitter Eliott, Caroline Smitter Nicholson. BA, Yale U., 1945; LHD (hon.) , St. Michael's Coll., 1973, LI U., 1986, Pratt Inst., 1991; LLD (hon.) , Coll. of Wooster, 1994; HHD (hon.) , Mapua Inst. of Tech., 2000; DLitt (hon.) , Ctrl. Philippine U., 2002. Commr.'s asst. Hoover Commn. on Orgn. Exec. Br. of Govt., 1948-49; reporter Cleve. Press, 1949-51; Washington corr. Time Inc., 1951-53, Time writer, 1953-55, head new bldg. dept., 1956-60, asst. to pub., 1960-61; circulation dir. Fortune and Archtl. Forum, 1961-64, House & Home, 1962-64; v.p. Time Inc., 1964-80, chief London bur., 1966-68; pub. Fortune, 1968-69, Time, 1969-72, dir. corp. planning, 1972-80; dir. Time, Inc., 1967-89, Time Warner Inc., 1989-96; pres., chmn., CEO Henry Luce Found., Inc., 1958—2002; pres. The New Mus. Contemporary Art, 1977-98. Chmn. Am. Security Systems Inc. Trustee Eisenhower Exch. Fellowships, Ctr. Theol. Inquiry, Christian Ministry in Nat. Pks., N.Y. Hist. Soc., Bklyn. Mus. Art; chmn. Am. coun. UN Univ.; pres. Assn. Am. Corrs. in London, 1968; dir. Nat. Com. on U.S.-China Rels.; chmn. pres.'s coun. Grad. Theol. Union; commr. Nat. Mus. Am. Art; mem. adv. bd. Nat. Acad. Design; mem. adv. coun. Newark Mus. Lt. (j.g.) USNR, 1943-46 2nd Ann. recipient medal for disting. philanthropy Am. Assn. Museums, 1994, Ann. award Assn. N.Y. State Arts Coun., 1995, Frederick Law Olmstead medal Central Park Conservancy, 1996, medal N.Y. Hist. Soc., 1997, St. Nicholas Soc. medal, 1998, Augustine Graham medal Bklyn. Mus. Art, 2000, Conrado Benitez medal Philippine U. for Women, 2000. Mem. Fgn. Policy Assn. (dir., medal 1997), Pilgrims U.S. (pres.), Explorers Club, Fishers Island Club, Hay Harbor Club, Univ. Club, Racquet and Tennis Club, The Brook. Presbyterian (elder). Office: 720 Fifth Ave Ste 1500 New York NY 10019-4107 also: Mill Hill Rd Mill Neck NY 11765

LUCE, Mrs. HENRY See HADLEY, LEILA ELIOTT-BURTON

LUCE, PRISCILLA MARK, public relations executive; b. N.Y.C., Feb. 4, 1947; d. S. Carl and Patricia (Greenfield) Mark; m. Robert Warren Luce, July 19, 1969; children: James Warren, David Mark. BA, U. Pa., 1968. Adminstrv. asst. Phila. Mus. Art, 1968-69; asst. dir. pub. info. Mt. Holyoke Coll., South Hadley, Mass., 1969-71; v.p. Barnes & Roche, Inc., Phila., 1971-82; mgr. civic programs TRW Inc., Cleve., 1982-85, mgr. community relations, 1985-88, mgr. external communications, 1988-90, dir., pub. affairs and advt., 1990-92, v.p. TRW info. sys. and svcs. comms., 1992-94, v.p. mktg. and orgn. comms., 1994—2001, v.p. corp. comm., 2001—. Trustee New Orgn. for the Visual Arts, Cleve., 1983-97, Cmty. Info. Vol. Action Ctr., Cleve., 1984-86, Albert M. Greenfield Found., Phila., 1989—, pres., 1999—; trustee Cleve. State U. Found., 1996—, chmn. devel. com. 1998—, vice-chmn. 1999; trustee Bus. Vols. Unltd., Cleve., 1998—; trustee WCPN Radio, 1997—, chmn. pub. rels. com., 1998-2001; chmn. media and mktg. com. Cleve. Today, 1999-2002; trustee Ohio Chamber Orch., Cleve., 1986-92, chmn. devel. com. 1987-88, chmn., trustee, 1991-92, exec. v.p., 1990-91; pres. New Orgn. for the Visual Arts, Cleve., 1984-86; steering com. Cleve. Art Festival, 1983-84, Mayor's Cultural Arts Planning Task Force, Cleve., 1985-87; trustee Ret. Sr. Vol. Prog., 1991, Western Res. Hist. Soc., 1999-2002; leadership devel. prog. participant United Way Svcs., Cleve., 1983, cons., 1983-85; steering com. Bus. Volunteerism Coun. of Cleve., 1984-92; comm. adv. com. Work in NE Ohio Coun., 1991-94. Recipient Woman of Profl. Excellence award YWCA of Cleve., 1990. Mem.: Cleve. Advt. Club, Pub. Rels. Soc. Am., Nat. Assn. Mfrs. Commns. Coun., Arthur W. Page Soc. Republican. Office: TRW Inc 1900 Richmond Rd Cleveland OH 44124-3760 E-mail: priscilla.luce@trw.com.

LUCE, R(OBERT) DUNCAN, psychology educator; b. Scranton, Pa., May 16, 1925; s. Robert Rennselaer and Ruth Lillian (Downer) L.; m. Gay Gaer, June 6, 1950 (div.); m. Cynthia Newby, Oct. 5, 1968 (div.); m. Carolyn A. Scheer, Feb. 27, 1988; 1 child, Aurora Newby. BS, MIT, 1945, PhD, 1950; MA (hon.), Harvard U., 1976. Mem. staff research lab electronics MIT, 1950-53; asst. prof. Columbia U., 1953-57; lectr. social relations Harvard U., 1957-59; prof. psychology U. Pa., Phila., 1959-69; vis. prof. Inst. Advanced Study, Princeton, 1969-72; prof. Sch. Social Scis., U. Calif., Irvine, 1972-75;

Alfred North Whitehead prof. psychology Harvard U., Cambridge, Mass., 1976-81, prof., 1981-83, Victor S. Thomas prof. psychology, 1983-88, Victor S. Thomas prof. emeritus, 1988, chmn., 1988-94; disting. prof. cognitive sci. U. Calif., Irvine, 1988-94, dir. Irvine Rsch. Unit in math. behavioral sci., 1988-92, disting. rsch. prof. cognitive sci. and rsch. prof. econs., 1994—; dir. Inst. for Math. Behavioral Sci., 1992-98. Chmn. assembly behavioral and social scis. NRC, 1976-79 Author: (with H. Raiffa) Games and Decisions, 1957, Individual Choice Behavior, 1959, (with others) Foundations of Measurement, I, 1971, II, 1989, III, 1990, Response Times, 1986, (with others) Stevens Handbook of Experimental Psychology, I and II, 1988, Sound & Hearing, 1993, Utility of Gains and Losses, 2000. Served with USNR, 1943-46. Ctr. Advanced Study in Behavioral Scis. fellow, 1954-55, 66-67, 87-88, NSF Sr. Postdoctoral fellow, 1966-67, Guggenheim fellow, 1980-81; recipient Disting. award for Rsch. U. Calif., Irvine, 1994, medal, 2001, gold medal award Am. Psychol. Found., 2001. Fellow: Am. Psychol. Soc. (bd. dirs. 1989—91), APA (bd. sci. affairs 1993—95, exec. com. divsn. I 2000, disting. sci. contbn. award 1970, gold medal for lifetime achievement in scientific psychology 2001), AAAS (chair elect psychology sect. 1998—99, chair 1999); mem.: Soc. Math. Psychology (pres. 1979), Psychonomic Soc., Psychometric Soc. (pres. 1976—77), Fedn. Behavioral Psychol. and Cognitive Scis. (pres. 1988—90), Math. Assn. Am., Am. Math. Soc., Nat. Acad. Scis. (chmn. sect. psychology 1980—83, class behavioral and social scis. 1983—86), Am. Philos. Soc., Am. Acad. Arts and Sci., Tau Beta Pi, Phi Beta Kappa, Sigma Xi. Home: 20 Whitman Ct Irvine CA 92612-4057 Office: U Calif Social Sci Plz Irvine CA 92697-5100 E-mail: rdluce@uci.edu.

LUCEK, DONALD WALTER, surgeon; b. Rockford, Ill., Jan. 26, 1945; s. Walter Joseph and Magdalen Mary (Kazunas) L.; m. Mary Philomena Keany, July 6, 1968; children: Patricia, Donald Jr., Michael, Stephen. BA, U. Ill., 1970, MD, 1974. Diplomate Am. Bd. Surgery. Intern, resident in surgery Boston U., 1974-79, clin. instr. surgery, 1980-87, asst. clin. prof. surgery, 1987—; surgeon Milton (Mass.) Hosp., 1979—, pres. med. staff, 1993, chief of surgery, 1993-95, chmn. tissue and transfusion, 1987-93, chmn. operating rm. com., 1993-94; chief of staff, pres. med. staff, chmn. trauma com. Mobridge Regional Hosp., S.D., 1996—. Pres. Milton Office Condo Assn., 1990-94; med. examiner Commonwealth of Mass., Norfolk County, 1989—, Delegate, SD State Med. Assn., 1998, Councilor, SD State Med. Assn., 1999-2000. Fellow ACS, Mass. Med. Soc.; mem. AMA, Boston Surg. Soc., Mass. Medicolegal Soc., S.D. State Med. Assn., Am. Hernia Soc., Am. Soc. Breast Surgeons, Soc. of Am. Gastrointestinal Endoscopic Surgeons. Office: Madelia-Mayo Clinic 155 Drew Ave SE Madelia MN 56062-1841

LUCENTE, ROSEMARY DOLORES, retired educational administrator, consultant; b. Renton, Wash., Jan. 11, 1935; d. Joseph Anthony and Erminia Antoinette (Argano) Lucente. BA, Mt. St. Mary's Coll., 1956, MS, 1963. Tchr. pub. schs., L.A., 1956-65; supr. tchr., 1958-65; asst. prin., 1965-69; prin. elem. sch., 1969-85, 86-99; dir. instrn., 1985-87; ret., 1999. Nat. cons., lectr. Dr. William Glasser's Educator Tng. Ctr., 1968—; nat. workshop leader Nat. Acad. for Sch. Execs.-Am. Assn. Sch. Adminstrs., 1980; L.A. Unified Sch. Dist. rep. for nat. pilot of Getty Inst. for Visual Arts, 1983-85, 92-98, site coord., 1983-86, team leader, mem. supt.'s adv. cabinet, 1987-98. Recipient Golden Apple award Stanford Ave. Sch. PTA, Faculty and Cmty. Adv. Coun., 1976, resolution for outstanding svc. South Gate City Coun., 1976, resolution for commitment to youth L.A. city Coun., 1996; named Woman of Yr., Calif. State Senate, 1997. Mem. NAESP, L.A. Elem. Prins. Orgn. (v.p. 1979-80), Assn. Calif. Sch. Adminstrs. (charter mem.), Assn. Elem. Sch. Adminstrs. (vice chair chpt. 1972-75, 79-80), Assn. Adminstrs. L.A. (charter mem.), Pi Theta Mu, Kappa Delta Pi (v.p. 1982-84, Hon. Educator award 1998), Delta Kappa Gamma, Phi Delta Kappa (Cert. of Recognition of Svc. on Membership Com. 2000). Democrat. Roman Catholic. Home: 6501 Lindenhurst Ave Los Angeles CA 90048-4733

LUCERO, CARLOS, federal judge; b. Antonito, Colo., Nov. 23, 1940; m. Dorothy Stuart; 1 child Carla. BA, Adams State Coll.; JD, George Washington U., 1964. Law clk. to Judge William E. Doyle U.S. Dist. Ct., Colo., 1964—65; pvt. practice Alamosa, 1966—95; sr. ptnr. Lucero, Lester & Sigmund; judge U.S. Ct. Appeals (10th cir.), 1995—. Mem. Pres. Carter's Presdl. Panel on Western State Water Policy. Bd. dirs. Colo. Hist. Soc., Sante Fe Opera Assn. of N.Mex. Recipient Outstanding Young Man of Colo. award, Colo. Jaycees, Disting. Alumnus award, George Washington U.; fellow Paul Harris, Rotary Found. Fellow: Internat. Soc. Barristers, Internat. Acad. Trial Lawyers, Colo. Bar Found. (pres.), Am. Coll. Trial Lawyers, Am. Bar Found.; mem.: ABA (mem. action com. to reduce ct. cost and delay, mem. adv. bd. ABA jour., mem. com. on the availability of legal svcs.), Colo. Rural Legal Svcs. (bd. dirs.), Colo. Hispanic Bar Assn. (profl. svc. award), Nat. Hispanic Bar Assn., San Luis Valley Bar Assn. (pres.), Colo. Bar Assn. (pres. 1977—78, mem. ethics com.), Order of the Coif. Office: US Ct Appeals 1823 Stout St Denver CO 80257*

LUCEY, JEROLD FRANCIS, pediatrician; b. Holyoke, Mass., Mar. 26, 1926; s. Jeremiah F. and Pauline A. (Lally) L.; m. Ingela Barth, Oct. 7, 1972; 1 child, Patrick; children by previous marriage: Colleen, Cathy, David. AB, Dartmouth Coll., 1948; MD, NYU, 1952. Intern Bellevue Hosp., N.Y.C., 1952-53; resident in pediat. Columbia-Presbyn. Med. Ctr., 1953-55; rsch. fellow Harvard-Children's Hosp., 1955-56; rsch. fellow in biochemistry U. Vt., 1956-60, from asst. prof. to prof. pediat., 1961-74, prof., 1974—95, Harry Wallace prof. of neonatology, 1995—. Rsch. fellow in biol. chemistry Harvard Coll., 1960-61; cons. NIH; vis. prof. Royal Soc. Medicine, Eng., 1980. Editor-in-chief Pediatrics, 1974—; contbr. articles on neonatology, phototherapy and transcutaneous oxygen to profl. jours. With USNR, 1944-46. Recipient Humbolt Sr. Scientist award, 1978, United Cerebral Palsy Rsch. award, 1984, McDonald prize, 1991, Apgar award, 1993; Markel scholar, 1960-65, Humbolt scholar, 1978, Univ. scholar, 1991, Columbia Alumnus of the Year award, 1995. Fellow Am. Acad. Pediat. (Grulee award 1988, Lifetime Achievement award 1997); mem. Royal Soc. Medicine, World congress on Perinatal Medicine (pres. 1993), Indian Pediat. Soc. (hon., Gold medal 1994, Perinatal Edn. award 1997), Inst. Medicine. Home: 52 Overlake Park Burlington VT 05401-4012 Office: Mary Fletcher Hosp McClure Rm 718 111 Colchester Ave Burlington VT 05401-1473*

LUCHANSKY, EDWARD, obstetrician-gynecologist, educator; b. Bridgeport, Conn., 1941; MD, U. Med. and Dentistry N.J., 1967. Cert. in ob-gyn. Intern St. Vincents Hosp., Bridgeport, 1967-68, resident in ob-gyn., 1970-73; sr. attending ob-gyn. and sect. chief Ob-Gyn Amb. Svcs. Bridgeport Hosp. Asst. clin. prof. ob-gyn. Yale U. Sch. Medicine. Fellow ACOG; mem. Am. Assn. Gynecol. Laparoscopists, Assn. of Mil. Surgeons of U.S., Aerospace Med. Assn., Civil Aviation Med. Assn.

LUCHOK, JOSEPH ALAN, insurance association communications official; b. Morgantown, W.Va., May 5, 1947; s. John and Anna Luchok; m. Florence Dorsey Carver, Feb. 24, 1979. BA, W.Va. U., 1969, MA, 1971, 73. Dir. debate U. Ga., 1976-83; dir. forensics Mo. Western State Coll., St. Joseph, 1983-94; program instr. CloseUp Found., Alexandria, Va., 1994-97; comm. specialist Am. Accreditation Health Care Commn., Washington, 1998-2000; cmm. mgr. Health Ins. Assn. Am., 2000—. Keynote spkr. CloseUp Found., 2000—; pub. spkr. Mem. Am. Forensic Assn. Avocations: reading, travel. Home: Apt 607 320 23d St S Arlington VA 22202-3832 Office: Health Ins Assn Am 1201 F St NW Ste 500 Washington DC 20004-1204 Fax: 202-824-1614. E-mail: iluchok@hiaa.org., joseph.luchok@verizon.net.

LUCHT, JOHN CHARLES, management consultant, executive recruiter, writer; b. Reedsburg, Wis., June 1, 1933; s. Carl H. and Ruth A. (Shultis) L.; m. Catherine Ann Seyler, Dec. 11, 1965 (div. 1982). BS, U. Wis., 1955, LLB, 1960. News dir. Sta. WISC-AM/FM, Madison, Wis., 1952-55; merchandising dir. The Bartell Group (radio and TV stas.), Milw., 1955-56; instr. U. Wis. Law Sch., 1959-60; TV contracts exec., account exec. J. Walter Thompson Co., N.Y.C., 1960-64; product mgr., new products supr., dir. new product mktg. Bristol-Myers Co., 1964-69; dir. mktg. W.A. Sheaffer Pen Co., Ft. Madison, Iowa, 1969-70; gen. mgr. Tetley Tea div. Squibb Beech-Nut Inc., N.Y.C., 1970-71; v.p. Heidrick & Struggles, 1971-77; pres. The John Lucht Consultancy, Inc., 1977—, The Viceroy Press Inc., 1987—, RiteSite.com, 1998—. Lectr. in field. Author: Rites of Passage at $100,000 to $1 Million Plus, The Insiders's Guide to Executive Job-Changing, Executive Job-Changing Workbook, Insights for the Journey—Navigating to Thrive, Enjoy and Prosper in Senior Management. Mem. Soc. Am. Bus. Editors and Writers, Internat. Assn. Corp. and Profl. Recruiters, State Bar Wis., N.Y. Bd. Trade, Assn. Exec. Search Cons., N.Y. Acad. Scis., Overseas Press Club, Met. Club, Can. Club, Phi Beta Kappa, Phi Eta Sigma, Phi Kappa Phi, Phi Delta Phi, Sigma Alpha Epsilon. Office: Worldwide Plaza West Ste 8-B 350 W 50th St New York NY 10019

LUCHTERHAND, RALPH EDWARD, financial advisor; b. Portland, Oreg., Feb. 9, 1952; s. Otto Charles II and Evelyn Alice (Isaac) L.; children: Anne Michelle, Eric Alexander, Nicholas Andrew, Mistie Rose Beaudoin; m. Victoria Marie Schiffbauer, Nov. 8, 1997. BS, Portland State U., 1974, MBA, 1986. Registered profl. engr., Oreg.; cert. fin. planner; gen. securities broker NYSE/NSAD, registered investment prin. Mech. engr. Hyster Co., Portland, 1971-75, svc. engr., 1975-76; project engr. Lumber Systems Inc., 1976-79; prin. engr. Moore Internat., 1979-81, chief product engr., 1981-83; project engr. Irvington-Moore, 1983, chief engr., 1983-86; ind. cons. engr., 1986; engring. program mgr. Precision Castparts Corp., Portland, 1986-87; personal fin. advisor Am. Express Fin. Advisors, West Linn, Oreg., 1987—94, sr. fin. advisor, 1994—2001; prin. Ralph Luchterhand & Assocs. (a fin. adv. br. of Am. Express Fin. Advisors), 2001—. Ptnr. Bacon, Luchterhand Wilmot & Assocs. (a fin. adv. br. of Am. Express Fin. Advisors), Clackamas, Oreg., 1996-2001, br. mgr., 1999-2000; apptd. to Silver Team, 1991, Gold Team, 1994. Treas., Village Bapt. Ch., Beaverton, Oreg., 1988-91; bd. dirs. Carus Cmty. Planning Orgn., Oregon City, Oreg., 1993-99; active Rolling Hills Cmty. Ch., Tualatin, Oreg., 1995—. Mem. Fin. Planning Assn., Assn. Fin. Planning Profls. Republican. Office: Ralph Luchterhand & Assocs Am Express Fin Advisors 1800 Blankenship Rd Ste 200 West Linn OR 97068 Mailing: PO Box 1216 Mulino OR 97042 Home: PO Box 1216 Mulino OR 97042-1216 E-mail: ralph@bctonline.com.

LUCIA, LUCIAN AMERIGO, chemistry educator; d. Agostino and Maria Lucia; m. Debbie Marie Lentini, May 29, 1993; children: Cecilia, Claudia, Joshua. Bachelor Sci., U. Fla., Gainsville, Florida, 1986—90, Master Sci., 1990—93, PhD, 1993—96. Postdoctoral fellow U. Rochester, Rochester, NY, 1996—97; asst. prof. chemistry Tokyo Met. U., Tokyo, Japan, 1997—97, Inst. Sci. Tech, Atlanta, 1997—97, assoc. prof. chemistry, 2002—. Sec. ACS, Atlanta, 1998—. Tappi Wood Chemistry, Atlanta, 2001—; student advisor tappi, Atlanta, 1998—. Contbr. book. Guardian adv. Tacachale, Gainsville, Fla., 1994—94; mem. Colgia, Atlanta, 1999—99. Mem.: toastmasters. R-Consevative. Achievements include invention of Tandem Fragmentation; Oxygen Delignfication Catalyst. Avocations: pizzles, pizzles, pizzles, pizzles. Office Fax: 404-894-4770. E-mail: lucian.lucia@ipst.edu.

LUCIA, MARILYN REED, physician; b. Boston; m. Salvatore P. Lucia, 1959 (dec. 1984); m. C. Robert Russell; children: Elizabeth, Walter, Salvatore, Darryl. MD, U. Calif., San Francisco, 1956. Intern Stanford U. Hosps., 1956-57; NIMH fellow, resident in psychiatry Langley Porter, U. Calif., San Francisco, 1957-60; NIMH fellow, resident in child psychiatry Mt. Zion Hosp., 1964-66; NIMH fellow, resident in community psychiatry U. Calif., 1966-68, clin. prof. psychiatry, 1982—. Founder, cons. Marilyn Reed Lucia Child Care Study Ctr., U. Calif., San Francisco; cons. Cranio-facial Ctr., U. Calif., San Francisco, No. Calif. Diagnostic Sch. for Neurologically Handicapped Children; dir. children's psychiat. svcs. Contra Costa County Hosp., Martinez. Fellow Am. Psychiat. Assn., Am. Acad. Child Psychiatry; mem. Am. Cleft Palate Assn., San Francisco Med. Soc. Office: 350 Parnassus Ave Ste 602 San Francisco CA 94117-3608

LUCID, ROBERT FRANCIS, English educator; b. Seattle, June 25, 1930; s. Philip Joseph and Nora May (Gorman) L.; m. Joanne K. Tharalson, Sept. 18, 1954; 1 son, John Michael. BA, U. Wash., 1954; MA, U. Chgo., 1955, PhD, 1958. Faculty U. Chgo., 1957-59, Wesleyan U., Middletown, Conn., 1959-64; mem. faculty U. Pa., Phila., 1964—, prof. English, 1975-96, emeritus, 1996—, chmn. dept. English, 1980-85, 90-91, chmn. faculty senate, 1976-77, master Hill Coll. House, 1979-96; master Gregory Coll. House, 1998—. Editor: Journal of Richard Henry Dana, 1968, The Long Patrol, 1971, Norman Mailer, the Man and His Work, 1971. Served with USAF, 1951-53. Recipient Lindback award U. Pa., 1975, Abrams award, 1986; Yaddo fellow, 1970 Mem. MLA, AAUP, PEN (exec. bd. 1987-93), Am. Studies Assn. (exec. sec. 1964-69), Penn Club (N.Y.C.). Office: U Pa Dept English Philadelphia PA 19104 E-mail: rlucid@dept.english.upenn.edu.

LUCIER, P. JEFFREY, publishing consultant; b. Manchester, N.H., June 20, 1941; s. Paul A. and Elaine (Wilson) Fraser L.; m. Judith Margaret Akers, Dec. 21, 1963 (div. 1975); children— Kathryn Elizabeth, Amy Wilson; m. Velma Lee Frye, Nov. 27, 1976 (div. 1981); m. Susan Elizabeth Hess, May 25, 1985; children: Madalyn Antonette, Caitlin Elaine. BA, Union Coll., N.Y., 1963; MA, U. Chgo., 1964. Instr. English, Northwestern U., Evanston and Chgo., 1967-69; registered rep. Paine Webber, Akron, Ohio, 1969-71; asst. to pres. Banks-Baldwin Law Pub., Cleve., 1971-74, v.p. editorial, 1974-76, exec. v.p., 1977-78, pres., editor-in-chief, 1978-96; CEO, Pegasus Techs. Ld., Painesville, Ohio, 1996-98, All-Stater Pub. LLC, Columbus, 1997-2000. Mem. adv. bd. Cleve. Collaborative for Math. Edn.; pres. The Banks-Baldwin Found. Trustee Horizon Montessori Sch.; trustee Cleve. Ctr. Contemporary Art, Cleve. Music Sch. Settlement. Mem.: Cleve. City, Cleve. Playhouse. Democrat. Roman Catholic.

LUCIO, ROSEMARY, retired priest, religious studies educator; b. Jacksonville, Fla., June 25, 1947; d. Alice Mae Robinson; children: Michele Boykins. B in Christian Counseling, St. Thomas Christian Coll., Jacksonville, Fla.; M in Christian Edn., St.Thomas Christian Coll., Jacksonville, Fla.; D of Sacred Theology (hon.) , United Christian Coll., Inc., N.Y.C., 2000. Ordained pastor 1984, ordained apostle 2000. Telephone operator N.Y. Telephone Co., New York, NY, 1970—81; share owner rep. Am. Transtech, Jacksonville , Fla., 1981—85; svc. rep. BellSouth, Jacksonville, 1985—89, bus. svc. rep., 1985—89, learning leader, 1999—2000; customer svc. assoc. BellSouth Bus. Sys., 1989—2000; vicar The Excellent Name of Jesus, Inc., 1985—2001. Motivational speaker, Jacksonville, Fl, —; seminar and workshop facilitator, Jacksonville. Author: Why Fast; contbr. articles. Vol., angel tree coord. Prison Fellowship, Jacksonville; vol. Fla. State Women's Prison; vol. feeding and clothing of homeless Excellent Name Jesus Inc., 1989; pres., CEO Evangelistic Jewish Ctr., 1992—2001. Mem.: BellSouth Pioneers. Avocations: walking, reading, shopping, cooking. Office: The Excellent Name Of Jesus Inc 6557 Leona St Jacksonville FL 32219 Personal E-mail: RLUCIOKINGPRIEST@AOL.COM.

LUCIVERO, LUCRETIA M. lawyer; b. Brooklyn, N.Y., Oct. 9, 1962; d. Luigi and Marta (Amato) L. BA, St. Joseph's Coll., 1984; JD, Touro Law Sch., 1987. Bar: N.Y. 1991, U.S. Dist. Ct. (ea. dist.) N.Y. 1991. Pvt. practice Law Offices of Lucretia M. Lucivero, St. James, NY, 1989—. Mem. Smithtown (N.Y.) Rep. Club, 1995—. Mem. Suffolk County Bar Assn., Columbian Lawyers Assn. Office: 320 Lake Ave Saint James NY 11780

LUCK, ANDREW PETER, federal agency administrator; b. Washington, Aug. 6, 1960; s. Anthony and Olga (Redchuk) L.; m. Susan Marie Walsh, Oct. 21, 1989. BA, U. Md., 1981, profl. devel. cert., 1985; MPA, Am. U., 1991. Adminstrv. asst. Dept. State, Washington, 1979; clk. Fed. Emergency Mgmt. Agy., 1980; adminstr. Internat. Devel. Coop. Agy., 1981; contract specialist U.S. AID, Rosslyn, Va., 1981-92, program analyst West Bank/Gaza Strip program Washington, 1992-95, program analyst Asia and Near East bur., 1995—, sr. program analyst Office Strategic & Econ. Analysis, Regional and Spl. Programs Divsn., 1997-2000, dir. adminstrv. and mgmt. svcs., 2000—. Recipient Svc. award U.S. AID, Rosslyn, 1985, 93, 97, 98, 99, 2000, Meritorious Honor award, 1994, 98. Mem. Washington Group, Montgomery County Coin Club (past pres.), Pi Sigma Alpha. Avocation: numismatics. Home: 1202 Holton Ln Takoma Park MD 20912-7535 Office: USAID Rm 4-09 Ronald Reagan Bldg Washington DC 20523-0001 E-mail: anluck@usaid.gov.

LUCK, GEORG HANS BHAWANI, classics educator; b. Bern, Switzerland, Feb. 17, 1926; came to U.S., 1951; s. Hans and Hanna (Von Ow) L.; m. Harriet Richards Greenough, June 15, 1957; children: Annina, Hans, Stephanie. Student, U. Bern, 1945-49, 50-51, PhD, 1953; student, U. Paris, 1949-50; A.M. (Smith-Mundt fellow), Harvard, 1952. Instr. classics Yale U., 1952-53; instr. classics Brown U., 1953-55, vis. prof., 1969; instr. classics Harvard U., 1955-58; vis. prof. Summer Sch., 1968; lectr. classics U. Mainz, 1958-62; prof. classics U. Bonn, 1962-71; vis. prof. Johns Hopkins U., 1970-71, prof. classics, 1971-90; prof. emeritus, 1990—; chmn. dept. classics Johns Hopkins U., 1973-75. Vis. prof. classics UCLA, 1974, U. Fribourg, 1989; lectr. Smithsonian Institutions, 1992. Author: Der Akademiker Antiochos, 1953, The Latin Love Elegy, 1959, 2d edit., 1969 (German edit. 1961, Spanish edit. 1995), Über einige Interjektionen, d. lat. Umgangssprache, 1964, Ovid, Tristia, text, transl. and commentary, 2 vols., 1967-77, Untersuchungen zur Textgeschichte Ovids, 1969, Eine Schweizerreise: Aus dem Tagebuch des Alfred Miell von Salisbury, 1981, Arcana Mundi: Magic and the Occult in the Greek and Roman World, 1985 (Spanish and Italian edits. 1994, expanded edit., 1997), Lucan, Der Bürgerkrieg, 1985, Der Dichter in der Kutsche, 1986; editor: Tibullus, Carmina, 1987, 2d edit., 1998, Magie und andere Geheimwissenschaften der Antike, 1990, Properz und Tibull, Elegien, 1996, Die Weisheit der Hunde, 1997, Ancient Pathways and Hidden Pursuits, 2000; editor-in-chief Am. Jour. Philology, 1971-81, 86-89; editor Noctes Romanae, 1975-85; contbr. articles to profl. jours. Guggenheim fellow, 1958-59; Swiss Nat. Research Council grantee, 1976-77 Mem. Johns Hopkins Club. Episcopalian. Avocations: gardening, hiking, classical guitar. Home: 1108 Bryn Mawr Rd Baltimore MD 21210-1213 Office: Johns Hopkins U Classics Dept Baltimore MD 21218 *I am not sure I know what success really means, but I do know today that the rewards for your work or your dedication or your experience and skill do not come from outside; they must be found within you, as a gift from God.*

LUCK, JAMES I. foundation executive; b. Akron, Ohio, Aug. 28, 1945; s. Milton William and Gertrude (Winer) L.; children: Andrew Brewer, Edward Aldrich, L. BA, Ohio State U., 1967; MA, U. Ga., 1970. Caseworker Franklin County Welfare Dept., Columbus, Ohio, 1967-69; dir. forensics Tex. Christian U., Ft. Worth, 1970-74; assoc. dir. Bicentennial Youth Debates, Washington, 1974-76; exec. dir. Nat. Congress on Volunteerism and Citizenship, 1976-77; fellow Acad. Contemporary Problems, Columbus, Ohio, 1977-79; exec. dir. Battelle Meml. Inst. Found., 1980-82; pres. Columbus Found., 1981—; exec. dir. Columbus Youth Found. and Ingram-White Castle Funds, 1981—. Co-chmn. Task Force on Citizen Edn., Washington, 1977; mediator Negotiated Investment Strategy, Columbus, 1979; chmn. Ohio Founds. Conf., 1985; cons. HEW, Peace Corps., U. Va. Author: Ohio-The Next 25 Years, 1978, Bicentennial Issue Analysis, 1975; editor: Proceedings of the Nat. Conf. on Argumentation, 1973; contbr. articles to profl. jours. Trustee Godman Guild Settlement House, Columbus, 1979-81, Am. Diabetes Assn., Ohio, 1984-88; chmn. spl. com. on displacement Columbus City Coun., 1978-80; bd. dirs. Commn. on the Future of the Professions in Soc., 1979. Mem. Donors Forum Ohio. Clubs: Capital, Columbus Club, Columbus Met., Kit-Kat. Lodges: Rotary. Avocations: travel, reading. Home: 1318 Hickory Ridge Ln Columbus OH 43235-1131 Office: The Columbus Found 17 S High St Ste 799 Columbus OH 43215

LUCKADOO, THOMAS DAVID, district director; b. Rutherfordton, N.C., Feb. 26, 1963; Reporter, photographer Rutherford County (N.C.) News, 1978-83; owner Photo Finishing Bus., Forest City, N.C., 1983-85; press sec. U.S. Rep. Bill Hendon, Ashville, 1985-86; dist. dir. U.S. Rep. Cass Ballenger, Washington, 1986—. Mailing: PO Box 1830 Hickory NC 28603-1830 Office: Office US Rep Cass Ballenger 361 10th Avenue Dr NE Ste 102 Hickory NC 28601-2610

LUCKE, ROBERT VITO, merger and acquisition executive; b. Kingston, Pa., July 26, 1930; s. Vito Frank and Edith Ann (Adders) L.; m. Jane Ann Rushin, Aug. 16, 1952; children: Thomas, Mark, Carl. BS in Chemistry, Pa. State U., 1952; MS in Mgmt., Rensselaer Polytech Inst., 1960. Polymer chemist Uniroyal Naugatuck (Conn.) Chem. Div., 1954-60; comml. devel. engr. Exxon Enjay Div., Elizabeth, N.J., 1960-66; gen. mgr. Celanese Advanced Composites, Summit, 1966-70; bus. mgr. polymer div. Hooker Chem., Burlington, 1970-74; gen. mgr. Oxy Metal Industries Environ. Equipment. Divs., Warren, Mich., 1974-79; v.p., gen. mgr. Hoover Universal Plastic Machinery Divs., Manchester, 1979-84; pres. Egan Machinery, Somerville, N.J., 1984-87; pres., chief exec. officer Krauss Maffei Corp., Cin., 1987-93; pres. Dubuc, Lucke, Koring Co., Inc., 1990—. Instr., Chem. Market Rsch. Assn., 1974. Author: (with others) Plastics Handbook, 1972; inventor, patentee in field. 1st lt. Corp Engrs., 1952-54, Korea. Senatorial scholar, Pa. State U., 1948-52. Mem. Am. Chem. Soc., Soc. Plastics Engrs. (sect. engr. STDS com. 1969), Tech. Assn. Pulp Paper Industry, Comml. Devel. Assn., Assn. Corp. Growth. Avocations: golf, skiing, travel, gardening. Office: Adventa Global LLC 414 Walnut St Ste 607 Cincinnati OH 45202-3913 E-mail: wiseowl726@aol.net., AdventaGlobal@fuse.net.

LUCKER, JAY K. library science consultant; b. N.Y.C., Feb. 23, 1930; s. Joseph Jerome and Ella (Schwartz) L.; m. Marjorie Stern, Aug. 17, 1952 (dec. Aug. 1997); children— Amy Ellen, Nancy Judith. AB, Bklyn. Coll., City U. N.Y., 1951; MS, Columbia, 1952; postgrad., N.Y. U., 1955-57. Head procurement br., acquisition div. New York Pub. Library, 1954-57, first asst., acting chief, sci. and tech. div., 1957-59; asst. univ. librarian for sci. and tech., asso. prof. Princeton U. Library, 1959-68, asso. univ. librarian, prof., 1968-75; dir. librs. MIT, Cambridge, 1975-95; vis. prof. Grad. Sch. Libr. and Info. Sci. Simmons Coll., Boston, 1995-2001. Chmn. bd. dirs. Captain Libr. Svcs. Corp., 1972-75; vis. lectr. Drexel U. Grad. Sch. Libr. Svc., 1962-67; vice chmn. New Eng. Libr. Info. Network, 1978-79, chmn., 1980-82. Bd. dirs. Boston Libr. Consortium; mem. adv. coms. Brown U., Tufts U., Washington U., St. Louis, Libr. Congress, Engring. Info. Inc. Served with Signal Corps U.S. Army, 1952-54. Council on Library Resources fellow, 1970-71 Fellow AAAS; mem. ALA (council 1978-82), Am. Soc. Info. Sci., N.J. Library Assn. (Distinguished Service award coll. and univ. sect. 1975), Assn. Research Libraries (chmn. interlibrary loan com. 1976-80, dir. 1977-80, pres. 1980-81), Spl. Libraries Assn., Phi Beta Kappa, Alpha Phi Omega, Beta Phi Mu. E-mail: jklucker@mit.edu.

LUCKETT, ESSIE, adult education educator, writer; b. Memphis, Aug. 17, 1928; d. Johnnie and Margaret Pollion; children: Margaret Diane Luckett-Holt, Johnnie Jr. BA, Miss. Indsl. Coll., 1953. Tchr. Hyde Park Sch., Memphis, 1956—71, Treadwell Elem. Sch., Memphis, 1971—88; part-time GED tchr. Memphis City Schs., 1997—. Author: Leaves of Truth, 1990, Gems on Loan from God, 1994. Dir. Watkins Chapel C.M.E. Ch., Memphis, 1996; sec. West Tenn. Ann. Conf., 1975. Mem.: NEA, Tenn. Ednl. Assn., Memphis Ednl. Assn. Home: 2216 Clayton Ave Memphis TN 38108

LUCKEY, ALWYN HALL, lawyer; b. Biloxi, Miss., Oct. 3, 1960; s. Toxie Hall and Joy Evelyn (Smith) L.; m. Jeanne Elaine Carter, Aug. 4, 1984; children: Laurel McKay, Taylor Leah. BA in Zoology, U. Miss., 1982, JD, 1985. Bar: Miss. 1985, U.S. Dist. Ct. (so. and no. dist.) Miss. 1985, U.S. Ct. Appeals (5th cir.) 1985. Assoc. Richard F. Scruggs, Pascagoula, Miss., 1985-88, shareholder, 1988—, Asbestos Group PA, 1988-93; prin. Alwyn H. Luckey, Atty. at Law, Ocean Springs, Miss., 1993—. V.p., bd. dirs. Marine Mgmt., Inc., Ocean Springs, Miss., 1987—. Author: Mississippi Landlord Tenant Law, 1985. Deacon First Presbyn. Ch., Ocean Springs, 1989; chmn. Dole for Pres. com., Jackson County, 1988. Mem. Am. Trial Lawyers Assn., Miss. Bar Assn., Miss. Trial Lawyers Assn., Jackson County Bar Assn., Jackson County Young Lawyers Assn. (v.p.), Ocean Springs Yacht Club, Bienville Club, Treasure Oak Country Club. Avocations: tennis, boating, travel. Office: PO Box 724 Ocean Springs MS 39566-0724

LUCKEY, DORIS WARING, civic volunteer; b. Union City, N.J., Sept. 17, 1929; d. Jay Deloss and Edna May (Ware) Waring; m. George William Luckey, Mar. 29, 1958; children: G. Robert, Jana Elizabeth, John Andrew. AB, U. Rochester, 1950; CLU, Am. Coll., Bryn Mawr, Pa., 1957. With pers. dept., supr. life dept. Travelers Ins. Co., Rochester, N.Y., 1952-58; agt. asst. life underwriting Mass. Mut. Ins. Co., 1958. Chair, various past offices Bd. Coop. Ednl. Svcs. and State Edn. Dept., Vocat. Tech. Adv. Com., Rochester and Albany, 1975—, pres. Rochester, 1975-85, Monroe County Sch. Bds. Assn., Rochester, 1980-81; v.p. Penfield (N.Y.) Schs., 1978-81; various fin. ednl. and speaking engagements LWV, 1983—, chair spkrs. bur. Rochester Metro chpt.; former pres. new investments, trustee ch. coun., pres. ch. coun., chair ch. and min. com., co-chair United Ch. Christ denomination, Genesee Valley; mem., former pres. William Warfield Scholarship Fund Bd.; coord. Young Artist Competition, Penfield Symphony Orch.; former adv. to bd. St. John's Home for Aging, now mem. fin. and pension and pers. com., bd. dirs., exec. com. St. John's home for aging bd.; vol. numerous other civic, cultural, ch. and artistic orgns.; property trustee Trinity South Emanuel United Ch. Christ, chair pastoral search com., 2001--, co-chair investment com.long-range planning com., chair pastoral rels. com.; sec. Leslie Norwood Carter Music Scholarship Fund for Inner City Children. Mem. AAUW (past pres. Greater Rochester br., past bd. dirs., dist. 1 state rep., Greater Rochester br., v.p. for program), LWV (co-chmn. nominating com. Rochester metro, chair of spkr. bur.), Genesee Valley Assn. (response team sexual harrassment in clergy N.Y. conf. United Ch. of Christ). Republican.

LUCKEY, GEORGE WILLIAM, research chemist; b. Dayton, Apr. 17, 1925; s. George Paul and Olive (Lehmer) L.; m. Doris Waring, Mar. 29, 1958; children: Robert, Jana, John. BA in Chemistry, Oberlin Coll., 1947; PhD in Chemistry, U. Rochester, 1950. Rsch. and staff asst. Eastman Kodak Co., Rochester, N.Y., 1950-59, rsch. assoc., 1959-69, lab. mgr., rsch. fellow, 1969-86. Contbr. articles to profl. jours. Mem. Am. Chem. Soc., Am. Phys. Soc., The Electrochem. Soc., Royal Soc. Chemistry, Sigma Xi, Phi Beta Kappa. Achievements include U.S. and fgn. patents; rsch. in diagnostic imaging with x-rays by improvements in intensifying screens, films and processing systems; performance of systems for mammography, other diagnostic uses. Home: 240 Weymouth Dr Rochester NY 14625-1917

LUCKEY, ROBERT REUEL RAPHAEL, retired academic administrator; b. Houghton, N.Y., Nov. 19, 1917; s. James Seymour and Edith Bedell (Curtis) L.; m. Ruth Ida Brooks, Aug. 25, 1945; children: James, John, Linda, Peter, Daniel (dec.), Thomas. BS, BA, Houghton Coll., 1937; MA, N.Y. U., 1939; PhD, Cornell U., 1942; LittD, Houghton Coll., 1980; LLD, Marion Coll., 1987. Secondary tchr. Wilson (N.Y.) Cen. Sch., 1937-39; math. & physics instr. Houghton Coll., 1942, assoc. prof., prof. math. and physics, alumni dir., 1954, dir. devel., v.p. in devel.; pres. Ind. Wesleyan U. (formerly Marion (Ind.) Coll.), 1976-84, 1986-87. Pres. Seneca Council Boy Scouts Am., Olean, N.Y., 1964-65; assessor Township of Caneadea, N.Y., 1951-76. Recipient Silver Beaver award Boy Scouts Am., 1965; named Alumnus of Yr. Houghton Coll., 1976, Disting. Alumnus Houghton Coll., 1984, Sagamore of the Wabash by Gov. of Ind., 1980. Mem. Grant County C. of C. (bd. dirs. 1981-84). Republican. Wesleyan. Avocations: golfing, personal computers. Home: 7363 Campus Heights Rd Houghton NY 14744-8719 also: 22250 Melody Ln Brooksville FL 34601-6705

LUCKIE, ROBERT ERVIN, JR. advertising executive; b. Clanton, Ala., May 3, 1917; s. Robert Ervin and Eliza (Goodwyn) L.; m. Lois Katherine Drolet, May 15, 1942 (dec. May 1987); children: Katherine (Mrs. Andrew J. Shackelford), Robert Ervin III, Anne Claire Luckie Cobb, Thomas George. AB, Birmingham-So. Coll., 1940, LLD (hon.); HHD (hon.), U. Ala. Reporter-columnist Birmingham (Ala.) News, 1940-41, mem. advt. staff, 1945-48; chmn., ptnr. Tucker Wayne/Luckie & Co., Birmingham, 1958-99. Pres. Nat Advt. Agy. Network, 1960, chmn., Luckie/Birmingham, Inc., 1999—. Chmn. for Ala. Radio Free Europe, 1964; co-chmn. Jefferson County United Appeal, 1968; pres. Met. Devel. Bd., 1976; bd. dirs. Blue Cross/Blue Shield, of Ala., Ala. Motorist's Assn.; trustee Birmingham-So. Coll., U. Ala. Birmingham Pres. Coun. Lt. comdr. USNR, 1942-45. Recipient Silver medal award Advt. Fedn. Am. and Printer's Ink, 1963, Disting. Alumni award Birmingham-So. Coll., 1967; named Advt. Man of Yr., Ad Club/Advt. Fedn. Am., 1963; inductee Birmingham Bus. Hall of Fame, U. Ala. Comm. Hall of Fame, 1999. Mem. Birmingham-So. Coll. Alumni Assn. (pres. 1966), Kiwanis (pres. 1964), Downtown Club, The Club (Birmingham) (pres. 1980-81), Birmingham Country Club (pres. 1975), Newcomen Soc., Omicron Delta Kappa, Kappa Alpha. Clubs: Kiwanis (pres. 1964), Birmingham Country (pres. 1975), Relay House (past pres.), Downtown, The Club (Birmingham) (pres. 1980-81). Methodist. Home: 3238 Country Club Rd Birmingham AL 35213-4115 Office: Luckie & Co 600 Luckie Dr Birmingham AL 35223-2429

LUCKMAN, SHARON GERSTEN, arts administrator; b. Sioux City, Iowa, Oct. 10, 1945; d. Robert S. and Libbie (Izen) Gersten; m. Peter Luckman, Nov. 22, 1968 (div. 1979); children: Melissa, Gregory; m. Paul Shapiro, Dec. 13, 1981. BS, U. Wis., 1967; cert. Inst. Not-For-Profit Mgmt., Columbia U., 1982. Dir. 92d St YM/YHA Dance Ctr., N.Y.C., 1978-86; dir. devel. & new ventures Twyla Tharp Dance Found., 1986-87, exec. dir., 1988; dir. Vol. Lawyers for Arts, 1988-92; dir. devel. Alvin Ailey Dance Found., 1992—95, exec. dir., 1995—. Dance tchr. 92nd St. Y, N.Y.C., 1963-78, Nassau C.C., Garden City, N.Y., 1963-78, Long Beach (N.Y.) Pub. Schs., 1963-78; dir. Brant Lake (N.Y.) Dance and Sports Ctr., 1980-86. Chairperson Laban/Bartenieff Inst. Movement Studies, N.Y.C., 1984-87. Democrat. Jewish. Office: Alvin Ailey Dance Found Inc 211 W 61st St 3d Fl New York NY 10023-7832

LUCKNER, HERMAN RICHARD, III, interior designer; b. Newark, Mar. 14, 1933; s. Herman Richard and Helen (Friednour) L. BS, U. Cin., 1957. Cert. interior designer and appraiser. Interior designer Greiwe Inc., Cin., 1957-64; owner, internat. designer Designers Loft Interiors, 1964—; owner Designer Accents, 1991—. Mem. bd. adv. Ohio Valley Organ Procurement Ctr., Cin., 1987—, U. Cin. Fine Arts Collection and Hist. Southwest Ohio, 1987-97; bd. dirs. Cin. Club Travelers, 1997-2000. Mem. Am. Soc. Interior Designers, Appraisers Assn. Am., Metropolitan Club. Republican. Avocations: needlepoint, collecting 18th century Chinese porcelain. Home and Office: 555 Compton Rd Cincinnati OH 45231-5005

LUCKNER, KLEIA RAUBITSCHEK, nursing administrator, lawyer, nurse midwife; b. Princeton, N.J., Jan. 29, 1945; d. Antony Erich and Isabelle (Kelly) Raubitschek; m. Kurt T. Luckner (dec. Nov. 1995); children: Mark Antony, Maia Christina. BSN, Georgetown U., 1967; MSN, Yale U., 1969; JD, U. Toledo, 1990. RN, Ohio, Mich.; Bar: Ohio. Clin. nurse specialist Stanford (Calif.) U. Hosp., 1969-70; instr. parent-child nursing Coll. Nursing U. Mich., Ann Arbor, 1970-71; cons. Perinatal Outreach Project State of Ill., 1970-73; asst. dir. perinatal rsch. Toledo Hosp., 1971-72, clin. dir. ob-gyn. nursing divsn., 1972-85, clin. coord. field svcs., 1985-94, dir. program devel. Ctr. for Women's Health, 1994-98, clin. adminstr. women's health, 1998—; clin. instr. ob-gyn. Med. Coll. Ohio, 1980—. Cons. nurse-midwifery program Georgetown U., Washington, 1994-99; adj. faculty Sch. Nursing U. Mich., Ann Arbor, 1992—; lectr. AWHONN, TAANA, Nashville, 1995, Bowling Green (Ohio) State U., 1996, THSN Alumni Assn., Toledo, 1996, Toledo Pub. Schs., 1996, 97, Am. Bus. Women's Assn., Bowling Green, 1997, N.E. Ohio Dist. Women's Club, Swanton, Ohio, 1997; attendee numerous confs.; guest lectr. U. Mich., Ann Arbor, 1971-73. Contbr. articles to profl. jours. Mem. mng. bd. YMCA Camp Storer, 1987—94, mem. mktg. com., 1987—93; mem. Ohio pub. affairs com. March of Dimes, 1991—94, exec. com., vice chmn. N.W. Ohio chpt., 1991—94, mem. profl. health adv. com., 1988—94; mem. cmty. adv. bd. Asian Mut. Assistance Program, 1993—94; mem. steering com. Toledo Mus. of Art Bus. Coun., 1992—95; bd. dirs. Teen Lines, 1992—96, David's House Compassion, Inc., 1997—98; mem. task force on teenage pregnancy and sch. health Toledo Pub. Schs., 1992—2000; mem. Lucas County Teen Pregnancy Prevention Coalition, 1994—, S.A.N.E. Adv. and Design Com., 1996—, Toledo Mus. Art, 1997—, Lucas County Domestic Violence Task Force, 1996—; med. adv. com. Toledo Pub. Schs., 1998—. Named State of Ohio Nurse of Yr., 1982; recipient recipient Advanced Adminstrv. Cert., ANA, 1984, Silver State award, Toledo Pub. Schs., 1993, Women Making a Difference award, Ohio Dept. Health, 1998, Pres.'s award, ProMedica Health Sys., 1999, Women of Achievement award, Zonta, 2000. Mem.: Am. Coll. Nurse-Midwives, Toledo Women's Bar Assn. (trustee 1993—95, program com. chmn. 1993—95), Toledo Bar Assn. (physician liaison com. 1992—, CLE com. 1992—98), Ohio Women's Bar Assn. Avocations: gardening, gourmet cooking, antique hunting, walking, reading. Home: 3452 Kenwood Blvd Toledo OH 43606-2807 Office: The Toledo Hosp 2142 N Cove Blvd Toledo OH 43606-3896

LUCKNER-SMASSANOW, LUCILLE, school system administrator; b. Corning, N.Y., Oct. 12, 1952; d. Todd and Delores Luckner; m. Lee Smassanow, Feb., 19, 1978; children: Alexi, Alec, Abby. BA, Elmira Coll., 1982; MA, SUNY, Saratoga Springs, 1990; SDA, Coll. New Rochelle, 1991. Cert. sch. adminstr., elem. edn., English 7-12. Tchr. Cedar St. Arts Ctr., Corning, N.Y., 1979-85, CPP Sch. Dist., Corning, 1982-85, Sullivan Co. BOCES, Liberty, 1986-90; dir. cmty. schs. Liberty CSD, NY, 1990—, prin., 1994—; asst supt. SUNY, New Paltz, 1998—, adj. prof., 1995—; ednl. cons., 2000—. Author: Educators Guide to Survival Skills, 1983, Home English Language Program, 1996, My Grandma Saves Things, 2002; developer cmty. schs. summer theatre program White Sulphur Springs Primary Sch., 1999. Legis. com. mem. NYS Cmty. Schs. Assn., 1992—; mem. PTA, Fallsburg, 1985—, Liberty, 1990—. Sgt. USAF, 1971-73. Recipient Promising Practice award White Sulphur Springs Primary Sch., 1999, Cmty. Svc. award Sullivan County Child Care Coun., 1999. Mem. Nat. Social Studies Coun. Avocations: tennis, golf, storytelling. Home: 40 Forest Rd Woodbourne NY 12788-5026 Office: PO 156 School RD White Sulphur Springs NY 12787 E-mail: smassanluc@libertyk12.org.

LUCKTENBERG, JERRIE CADEK, music educator; b. July 19, 1930; d. Ottokar Theodore and Sara (Hitchcock) Č.; m. George Lucktenburg, 1953 (div. 1984); children: Judith, Kathryn, Ted. MusB, Curtis Inst., 1952; MusM, U. Ill., 1953; D of Mus. Arts, U. S.C., 1983. Concertizing as soloist and in chamber groups, Europe, Korea, Australia, U.S., 1954-96; assoc. prof. music Converse Coll., Spartanburg, S.C., 1960-84; artist tchr., chmn. string dept. S.C. Gov.'s Sch. of Arts, Greenville, 1983-97; prof. music, chmn. string dept. U. So. Miss., Hattiesburg, 1984-96; concertmaster Pensacola (Fla.) Symphony, Meridian (Miss.) Symphony, 1986-96, Greater Spartanburg (S.C.) Philharm., 1996—. Author: The Joy of Shifting and Double Stops, a Violinist's Guide to Ease and Artistry, 1991; contbr. articles to profl. jours.; leader numerous workshops and clinics. Fulbright grantee State Acad. Music, Vienna, 1956-57; Ford Found. grantee, 1966-67; recipient Heart of Gold award The Arlington Assisted Living Facility, Hattiesburg, Miss., 1994, Tchr. Recognition award nat. winner Music Tchrs. Nat. Assn., 1974, Excellence in tchg. award, U. Southern Miss., 1990, Alumni Citation Outstanding Achievement as a performer and educator, U.S.C., 1991; citation for Exceptional Leadership and Merit award, 1992. Mem. Am. String Tchrs. Assn. (life; founding pres. Miss. chpt. 1985, jour. reviewer 1987—; Music Tchrs. Nat. Assn. (chmn. S.C. chpt. 1979-82, strings chmn. Miss. chpt. 1987-90), Music Educators Nat. Conf., Suzuki Assn. of Ams., Pi Kappa Lambda. Home: 311 Saranac Dr Spartanburg SC 29307-1141

LUCKY, ROBERT WENDELL, electrical engineer; b. Pitts., Jan. 9, 1936; s. Clyde Arthur and Grace Katherine (Luck) L.; m. Joan Miriam Jackson, Aug. 19, 1961; children: David William, Karen Joan. BSEE, Purdue U., 1957, MS, 1959, PhD, 1961, hon. doctorate, 1988, N.J. Inst. Tech., 1991, Swiss Fed. Inst. Tech., 1999, Monmouth U., 2000. With Bell Telephone Labs., Holmdel, N.J., 1961—, supr. signal theory, 1964-65, head dept. advanced data communications, 1965-76, dir. Electronic and Computer Systems Research Lab., 1977-81, exec. dir. research Communications Scis. Div., 1982-92; corp. v.p. applied rsch. Telcordia Techs., 1992—. Mem. engring. adv. bd. Purdue U., 1973-75; mem. USAF Sci. Adv. Bd., 1979—, vice chmn., 1983-86, chmn., 1986-89; mem. adv. com. NSF, 1983-85; bd. dirs. Engring. Index, 1984-86; mem. engring. adv. bd. Bradley U., 1979-84, U. Calif.-Santa Barbara, 1980—; chmn. tech. adv. coun. FCC, 1999—. Author: Principles of Data Communication, 1968, Silicon Dreams, 1989, Lucky Strike Again, 1993; editor: Proc. of IEEE, 1974-76, Computer Communication, 1975; cons. editor: Plenum Press, 1979—; patentee in field. Bd. dirs. Computer Mus., Boston, 1985— Named Disting. Alumnus Purdue U., 1969; Recipient Marconi Internat. Fellowship prize, 1987. Fellow IEEE (v.p. 1978-79, exec. v.p. 1980-81, publs. bd. 1970-76, bd. govs. info. theory group 1969-74, Thomas A. Edison medal 1995); mem. NAE (computer tech. bd. 1986-90, engring. edn. bd., 1991—, commn. on phys. scis. 1991—), Am. Acad. Arts and Scis., European Acad. Arts and Scis., Communications Soc. (pres. 1977-79, Achievement award 1975), Eta Kappa Nu (nat. dir. 1974-76) Home: 48 Gillespie Ave Fair Haven NJ 07704-3309 Office: Applied Rsch Telcordia Techs Inc 3Z367A 331 Newman Springs Rd # 3z367A Red Bank NJ 07701-5657 Fax: 732-758-4530. E-mail: rlucky@telcordia.com.

LUCY, DENNIS DURWOOD, JR. neurologist, educator; b. Little Rock, July 3, 1934; s. Dennis Durwood and Ann Louise (Besiegel) L.; m. Patricia Wilch, Nov. 26, 1958; children: Stephen H., Vincent A., Denise D., David D. BS, MD, U. Ark., 1959. Diplomate: Am. Bd. Psychiatry and Neurology. Intern U. Ark. Med. Scis., 1959-60, resident in internal medicine, 1960-62, resident in psychiatry, 1962-63; resident in neurology U. Iowa Hosp., 1963-64, 65-66; instr., acting head dept. neurology U. Ark., 1964-65, prof., 1974—, chmn. dept. neurology, 1966-94; mem. exec. com. U. Ark. Coll. Medicine, 1979-83, chmn. council Departmental Chairmen, 1980-81, chair elect acad. senate, 2001—02; chief of staff Univ. Hosp., 1973-76. Bd. dirs. Ark. chpt. Multiple Sclerosis Soc., 1965-78; mem. Ark. Council Devel. Disabilities, 1971-74; bd. dirs. Ark. chpt. Epilepsy Soc., 1972-76; bd. dirs. Holy Souls Cath. Sch., 1974-77, pres. bd., 1976-77. Recipient Golden Apple award U. Ark., 1968-69 Mem. Am. Acad. Neurology, Alpha Omega Alpha. Roman Catholic. Home: 17 Robinwood Dr Little Rock AR 72227-2241 Office: 4301 W Markham St Little Rock AR 72205-7101

LUCY, DLORAH RAE, medical/surgical nurse; b. Big Rapids, Mich., Feb. 24, 1958; d. Raymond V. and Janet C. Lucy. BSN, Ea. Mich. U., 1982; MSN, Madonna U., 1991. RN, Mich. Clin. nurse II U. Mich. Hosp., Ann Arbor, 1982-88; nurse II Catherine McAuley Health Ctr., 1988—92; nursing resource pool U. Mich. Hosp., 1992; adj. faculty Madonna U., Livonia, Mich., 1992; edn. specialist Sinai Hosp., Detroit, 1992-94; home health coord. home care dept. St. Joseph Mercy Health Sys., 1995-97; clin. prof. Madonna U., 1995; drug safety assoc. Parke-Davis Pharm. Rsch., 1997; data coord. STATPROBE, Inc., Ann Arbor, 1997—, med. monitor/drug safety, 2002—. Clin. prof. Madonna U., 1995. Bd. dirs. Condominium Assn., 1998—. Mem. Mich. Nurses Assn. (mem. ho. of dels., mem. continuing edn. adv. com., mem. continuing edn. approval program com., mem. coun. on continuing edn., mem. continuing edn./staff devel. exec. com. 1996-98), Sigma Theta Tau, Kappa Iota. Home: 3067 Forest Creek Ct Ann Arbor MI 48108-5216 E-mail: llucy@comcast.net.

LUCY, ROBERT MEREDITH, lawyer; b. Poplar Bluff, Mo., Apr. 16, 1926; s. James Raymond and Lucile Hargrove (Meredith) L.; m. Mary White George, June 10, 1947; children— Meredith Lucy Knight, Celia Lucy Denton, John Rackley, Robert Meredith Jr. BS, U.S. Naval Acad., 1947; JD, George Washington U., 1954, MS in Internat. Affairs, 1968. Bar: Mo. 1954, D.C. 1954. Commd. 2d lt. USMC, 1947; advanced through grades to col.; student Air War Coll. Maxwell AFB, Montgomery, Ala., 1967-68; staff judge adv. 1st Marine Div., Danang, Vietnam, 1969-70; asst. for legal affairs Office Asst. Sec. Navy for Manpower and Res. Affairs, Washington, 1970-71; legal advisor, legis. asst. to chmn. Joint Chiefs of Staff, 1971-74; ret., 1974; ptnr. Bryan Cave, St. Louis, 1974-96; of counsel, 1997-98; chmn. litigation dept. Bryan, Cave, St. Louis, 1992-94, vice chmn., 1994-95; ret., 1998. Dir. St. Andrew's Episcopal Presbyn. Found., 1995-2001. Decorated Bronze Star, Legion of Merit (3) Mem. ABA (litigation sect.), TechLaw Group, Inc. (pres. 1994-95), Childrens Home Soc. of Mo. (trustee 1989-98). Presbyterian. Home: 38 Picardy Ln Saint Louis MO 63124-1628 E-mail: rmlu@aol.com.

LUCZO, STEPHEN J. computer equipment company executive; Sr. mng. dir. fin., co-head Bear Stearns Global Tech. Group, until 1993; exec. v.p. corp. devel. Seagate Software; sr. mng. dir. fin. Bear Stearns; with Seagate Tech., Inc., Scotts Valley, Calif., 1993—, exec. v.p. corp. devel., pres., 1997-2000, CEO, 2000—. Office: Seagate Tech Inc 920 Disc Dr Scotts Valley CA 95066-4542*

LUDBROOK, PHILIP ALBERT, cardiologist, clinical researcher, educator; b. Adelaide, Australia, Nov. 15, 1940; came to U.S., 1971; s. Albert John and Hilda Alice Maud L.; m. Helen Christine, Jan. 17, 1964; children: Gregory Stewart, Andrew Malcolm, Christopher Jon. MBBS, U. Adelaide, South Australia, 1964. Cert. internal medicine/cardiology, Australia, Eng., U.S. Intern Queen Elizabeth Hosp., Australia, 1964; med. registrar Royal Adelaide Hosp., Australia, 1965—68, cardiology registrar Australia, 1969—70; registrar in cardiology Hammersmith Hosp., Royal Postgrad. Sch., U. London, 1971; dir. cardiac catheterization and intervention Barnes-Jewish Hosp., St. Louis, 1971-96; rsch. fellow U. Calif., San Diego, 1972—73; dir., Ctr. for Adults with congenital heart disease Wash. U. Sch. Medicine, St. Louis, 1995—, assoc. dean Human Studies, chmn. instnl. rev. bd., prof. medicine, radiology. Fellow Royal Australian Coll. Physicians, Am. Coll. Cardiology, Am. Coll. Physicians; mem. Royal Coll. Physicians of Eng. Episcopalian. Avocations: bird watching and breeding, music, reading. Office: Wash U Sch of Medicine Box 8086 660 S Euclid Ave Saint Louis MO 63110-1010

LUDDEN, GEORGE CLEMENS, engineer; b. Washington, Sept. 18, 1945; s. Clemens Pratt and Velma Laverne (Talley) L.; m. Elizabeth Garrett, Aug. 1, 1970; children: Brett Joseph, Jeffrey Clemens, Mark Garrett. BS, Mich. State U., 1967; MBA, Baldwin-Wallace Coll., 1977. Registered profl. engr., Va., Ohio, Calif. Engr. Mare Island Naval Shipyard, Vallejo, Calif., 1967-69, Charleston (S.C.) Naval Shipyard, 1969-73, Davy McKee, Independence, Ohio, 1973-80, proposal mgr., 1980-82; system engr. Va. Power, Richmond, 1982-95; computer specialist St. Mary's Hosp., VA, 1996-97; network mgr. St. Catherine's Sch., 1997—. Utility advisor Electric Power Rsch. Inst., Palo Alto, Calif., 1982-87; lectr. nuclear safety Czechoslovakia, 1987, 89. Contbr. articles on welding design and fabrication to profl. jours. Mem. vol. staff Nat. Air Show, Cleve., 1979, World Cup USA, 1991-94; World Cup amb., 1994; ofcl. Spl. Olympics World Games, 1999; first aid chmn. ARC, Cleve., 1980 mem. Va. Coop. Grad. Engring. Program Adv. Com., Richmond, 1988-90; mem. Elon U. Parents Coun., 1999-2002. Mem. Edison Electric Inst. (task force officer 1985-95), Am. Soc. for Metals Internat.(chpt. chmn. 1971-72), Va. Soc. for Tech. in Edn., Richmond Joint Engrs. Coun. (chmn. 1988-89). Avocations: youth sports, computers. Home: 2914 W Stony Hill Ct Apt 2B Richmond VA 23235 Office: St Catherine's Sch 6001 Grove Ave Richmond VA 23226-2600 E-mail: gludden@st.catherines.org.

LUDDEN, JOHN FRANKLIN, retired financial economist; b. Michigan City, Ind., May 6, 1930; BS in Econs., U. Wis., 1952, MS in Econs., 1955; postgrad., U. Mich., 1955-59. Wage and hour investigator U.S. Dept. Labor, 1960, mgmt. intern, 1960-61, labor economist, 1963; economist, instr. U.S. Bur. of Labor Statis., 1961-63; economist Office of Internat. Ops. IRS, 1963-68, fin. economist Audit div., 1968-86, fin. economist Office of the Asst. Commr. Internat., 1986-95; ret. Office of the Asst. Commr. Internat., 1995. With U.S. Army, 1952-54. Recipient spl. svc. award U.S. Dept. Treasury, 1967, 68, 87, spl. achievement award, 1984, Spl. Act award, 1990, Albert Gallatin award, 1995.

LUDDINGTON, BETTY WALLES, library media specialist; b. Tampa, Fla., May 11, 1936; d. Edward Alvin and Ruby Mae (Hiott) L.; m. Robert Morris Schmidt, Sept. 20, 1957 (div. Dec. 1981); children: Irene Schmidt-Losat, Daniel Carl Schmidt. AA, U. South Fla., 1979, BA in Am. Studies and History, 1980, MA in Libr., Media and Info. Studies, 1982, EdS in Gifted Edn., 1986. Cert. tchr. media and gifted edn., Fla. Media intern Witter Elem. Sch., spring 1982; media specialist Twin Lakes Elem. Sch., 1982-84, Just Elem. Sch., 1984-87, Blake Jr. H.S., 1987-88, Dowdell Jr. H.S. (now Dowdell Mid. Sch.), 1988—. Educator Saturday enrichment program for gifted children U. South Fla., springs 1980, 84, 85; participant pilot summer program in reading and visual arts Just Elem. Sch., 1987; educator gifted edn. program in visual and performing arts Kingswood Elem. Sch., summers 1985, 86, gifted edn. program in video camera Apollo Beach Elem. Sch., summer 1989, Gifted Enrichment Prog. Imagi-lympics 2012, Maniscalco Elem. Sch., 1998, others. Author: (book of poetry) Aaron Tippin: A Hillbilly Knight, 1993; contbr. articles and poems to various books and periodical publs., 1986—. Parent vol. media ctr. Witter Elem. Sch., 1976-78; tchr. sponsor Storytelling Club, Dowdell Jr. H.S., 1994-95; news media liaison, tchr. vol. Dowdell Jr. H.S., 1993-96. Recipient Student Affairs Golden Signet award U. South Fla., 1980, Parent award for continuing support of Fla. chpt. # 39 Am. Indsl. Arts Student Assn., 1987-88, Editor's Choice awards for outstanding achievement in poetry Nat. Libr. of Poetry, 1996; nominee Tchr. of Month, Sta. WTSP-TV, 1994; recognized for contbn. of motivational activity for Sunshine State Young Reader's Award program Fla. Assn. for Media in Edn., Inc., 1985; named to Internat. Poetry Hall of Fame, 1996. Mem. Internat. Soc. Poets (Disting. mem. 1995), Hillsborough Classrm. Tchrs. Assn. (grantee 1988, 90), Hillsborough Assn. Sch. Libr. Media Specialists, Clan Wallace Soc. (life), Phi Kappa Phi, Kappa Delta Pi, Phi Alpha Theta (pres., v.p., rep. to honors coun. 1980, 81, Outstanding Student award), Omicron Delta Kappa (treas., chairperson, del., mem. selection com. 1981, Leslie Lynn Walbolt book award), Pi Gamma Mu. Episcopalian. Avocations: poetry, books, cats, country music. Home: 1032 E Robson St Tampa FL 33604-4344

LÜDECKE, DIETER KONRAD, neurosurgeon; b. Kassel, Germany, Mar. 11, 1943; s. Hans and Lucia (Dux) L.; 3 children. MD, U. Hamburg, Germany, 1975. Researcher U. Hamburg, 1972-84, neurosurgeon, 1984—. Chief neuro endocrine lab. and pituitary surgery unit U. Hamburg, 1980; cons. neurosurgeon Marien Krankenhaus, Hamburg, 1988. Author, editor: Progress Endocrine Research, 1988, 90; contbr. over 150 articles to profl. jours.; patentee microsurgical pressure irrigation suction system. Mem. Internat. Soc. Pituitary Surgeons, Internat. Skull Base Soc., European Neuro Endocrine Assn., German Soc. Endocrinology, German Soc. Neurosurgery, German Skull Base Soc. Office: Univ Hamburg Dept Neurosurgery 20246 Hamburg Germany Fax: 40-42803-5982. E-mail: Ludecke-DK@uke.uni-hamburg.de.

LUDEMANN, CATHIE JANE, lawyer; b. Glen Ridge, N.J., Jan. 30, 1948; d. Blair Edward and Marie Elizabeth (Blum) L. BA in Econs., Douglass Coll., 1970; MBA in Fin., Fairleigh Dickinson U., 1975; JD, Seton Hall Law Sch., 1986. Bar: N.J. 1986. Mgmt. positions Prudential Ins. Co., Newark, 1970-83; rsch. asst. Seton Hall Law Sch., 1983-84; atty. Barry D. Berman, Esq., West Orange, N.J., 1984-87, Sala & Caposela, Esqs., Clifton, 1987-89; sole practitioner Pompton Plains, 1989—. Editor Law Sch. Newspaper, 1985-86. Commr., planning bd., City of Clifton, 1982-86; commr. bd. of adjustment, Twp. of Pequannock, N.J., 1993; v.p., treas. Richfield Village Tenants Assn., Clifton, 1979-82. Mem. N.J. State Bar Assn. Avocations: antiques and collectibles, book collecting, old movies, Big Band music. Home: 105 Newark Pompton Tpke Bldg C Unit 14 D Pequannock NJ 07440-1638 Office: 287 Boulevard Pompton Plains NJ 07444-1726

LUDGIN, CHESTER HALL, baritone, actor; b. N.Y.C., May 20, 1925; s. Michael and Dora Josephine L. Student, Lafayette Coll., 1943, Am. Theatre Wing Profl. Tng. Program, 1948-50. Premiere leading baritone roles in: The Crucible, 1961, The Golem, 1962, Angle of Repose, 1976, A Quiet Place, 1983; appeared in major opera houses throughout the world, including San Francisco Opera Co., N.Y.C. Opera Co., Netherlands Opera, La Scala Opera, Vienna State Opera; singing actor in: musical comedies including Kismet, summer 1972, Most Happy Fella, summer 1977, Shenandoah, summer, 1978, Student Prince, summer 1980, South Pacific, summer 1981, Fanny, summer 1986. Co-chmn. exec. com. Norman Treigle Meml. Fund, 1975— . Served with inf. U.S. Army, 1943-46. Mem. Am. Guild Musical Artists, Actors Equity, AGVA, AFTRA. Home: 205 W End Ave New York NY 10023-4804 Office: care Thea Dispeker Artists Rep 59 E 54th St New York NY 10022-4211 *In observing many of my colleagues in the performing arts as well as those in other walks of life, I long ago came to the conclusion that it is wiser and more personally fulfilling to avoid compromising one's principles in the hope of advancing one's career. If there is truly a talent present, the act of quietly going about one's business with maximum efficiency makes the ultimate statement. Awareness by others of that talent inevitably follows.*

LUDGIN, DONALD HUGH, editor; b. Chgo., Sept. 16, 1929; s. Earle and Mary King (MacDonald) L.; m. Sue Keating Conway, Oct. 26, 1957; children: Sarah, Katherine, Peter. AB, Oberlin Coll., 1951. Asst. editor World Book Ency., Chgo., 1953-56, sr. editor, 1956-62, editl. coord. London and Sydney, Australia, 1962-66, assoc. editor Chgo., 1966-83; pres. Electronic Scribe, Evanston, Ill., 1983-86, Georgetown, Maine, 1986—. Trustee Mus. Contemporary Art, Chgo., 1971-79, sec., 1974-78; mem. awards com. Joseph Jefferson Theatre, Chgo., 1979-81. With U.S. Army, 1951-53. Mem. Graphic Comm. Assn. (editl. bd. jours. 1978). Democrat. Roman Catholic. Home and Office: 661 Indian Point Rd PO Box 367 Georgetown ME 04548-0367

LUDGUS, NANCY LUCKE, lawyer; b. Palo Alto, Calif., Oct. 28, 1953; d. Winston Slover and Betty Jean Lucke; m. Lawrence John Ludgus, Apr. 8, 1983. BA in Polit. Sci. with honors, U. Calif., Berkeley, 1975; JD, U. Calif., Davis, 1978. Bar: Calif. 1978, U.S. Dist. Ct. (no. dist.) Calif. 1978. Staff atty. Crown Zellerbach Corp., San Francisco, 1978-80, Clorox Co., Oakland, Calif., 1980-82, Nat. Semiconductor Corp., Santa Clara, 1982-85, corp. counsel, 1985-92, sr. corp. counsel, asst. sec., 1992-2000, assoc. gen. counsel, asst. sec., 2000—. Contbr. articles to profl. jours. Mem. ABA, Am. Corp. Counsel Assn., Calif. State Bar Assn., Santa Clara County Bar Assn., Phi Beta Kappa. Democrat. Avocations: travel, jogging, opera. Office: Nat Semiconductor Corp 2900 Semiconductor Dr # G3135 Santa Clara CA 95051 E-mail: nancy.lucke.ludgus@nsc.com.

LUDIN, PAMELA S. accountant; b. Camden, N.J., Sept. 13, 1960; d. Edward Nelson and Arlene June Rubenstein Ludin; m. Stewart Neal Abramson, Apr. 17, 1988; children: Matthew, Ethan. BS in Econs., U. Pa., 1981. Cert. mgmt. acct. Asst. staff acct. KPMG Peat Marwick, Phila., 1981-82; contr. Lombard

Med. Assn., 1984-87; staff acct. Scripps Meml. Hosp., La Jolla, Calif., 1987-90; contr./Univ. Womens Healthcare Assocs. U. Pitts. Med. Ctr., 1990-94; dir. ops. Bookminders Inc., Pitts., 1994—2002, treas., 2002—. Fin. com. mem. Three Rivers Cmty. Found., Pitts., 1998—. Mem. Am. Soc. Women Accts. (nat. dir. 1997-99, Women of Achievement award 1999). Home: 522 Glen Arden Dr Pittsburgh PA 15208-2809 Office: Bookminders Inc Ste 100 700 River Ave Pittsburgh PA 15212-5907 E-mail: pludin@bookminders.com.

LUDINGTON, TOWNSEND, English and American studies educator; b. Bryn Mawr, Pa., Jan. 31, 1936; s. Charles Townsend and Constance (Cameron) L.; m. Jane Ross, Feb. 22, 1958; children: David, Charles, James, Sarah. BA, Yale U., 1957; MA, Duke U., 1964; PhD, Duke U, 1967. Tchr. English Ransom Sch., Miami, Fla., 1960-62; from asst. prof. to prof. English U. N.C., Chapel Hill, 1967-78, Cary C. Boshamer prof. English and Am. Studies, 1982—, chair Am. studies curriculum, 1986—2001. Part-time instr. Duke U., 1963-66; resident scholar U.S. Internat. Communication Agy., 1980-81; vis. prof. U.S. Mil. Acad., West Point, N.Y., 1988-89 Author: John Dos Passos, 1980 (Mayflower award 1981), Marsden Hartley, 1992, Seeking the Spiritual: The Paintings of Marsden Hartley, 1998; editor: The Fourteenth Chronicle, 1973, The Devil and Daniel Webster and Other Stories and Poems by Stephen Vincent Benet, 1999, A Modern Mosaic: Art and Modernism in the United States, 2000. Mem. adv. com. Florence Criswold Mus. Capt. USMC, 1957—60. Recipient Outstanding Svc. medal U.S. Army, 1988-89; Fulbright fellow, 1971-72, Nat. Humanities Ctr. fellow, 1985-86, Wurlitzer Found. fellow, 1996, Beinecke Libr. Yale U. fellow, 1998. Mem. Am. Studies Assn., South Atlantic MLA, PEN. Democrat. Avocations: golf, reading. Office: U NC Curriculum in Am Studies Greenlaw Hall Clb # 3520 Chapel Hill NC 27599-0001

LUDLUM, DAVID BLODGETT, pharmacologist, educator; b. N.Y.C., Sept. 30, 1929; s. C. Daniel and Elsie B. (Blodgett) L.; m. Carlene L. Dyke, Dec. 23, 1952; children: Valerie Jean Ludlum Wright, Kenneth David. BA, Cornell U., 1951; PhD, U. Wis., 1954; MD, NYU, 1962. Rsch. scientist Dupont Co., Wilmington, Del., 1954-58; intern Bellevue Hosp., N.Y.C., 1962-63; asst. prof. pharmacology Yale U., New Haven, 1963-68; assoc. prof. U. Md., 1968-70, prof., 1970-76; prof. pharmacology Albany (N.Y.) Med. Coll., 1976-86, chmn. dept. pharmacology, 1976-80, prof. medicine, 1980-86, dir. oncology rsch., 1980-86; prof. pharmacology and medicine U. Mass. Med. Sch., Worcester, 1986-99, prof. emeritus pharmacology and medicine, 1999—. Affiliate prof. chemistry Clark U., Worcester, Mass., 1996-99; adj. prof. chemistry Rensselaer Poly. Inst., Troy, N.Y., 1977-80; vis. prof. oncology Johns Hopkins U., 1973-76; vis. prof. Courtauld Inst., London, 1970. Assoc. editor Cancer Rsch., 1980-87, 89-2000; contbr. articles to profl. jours.; patentee in field. WARF fellow, 1951-52; NSF fellow, 1952-54; Am. Heart Assn. fellow, 1960-62; recipient NIH Rsch. Career Devel. award, 1968; Markle scholar in acad. medicine, 1967-72; lic. physician, N.Y., Conn., Md.; grantee in field. Mem. Am. Soc. Clin. Oncology, Am. Soc. Pharmacology and Exptl. Therapeutics, Am. Assn. Cancer Rsch., Am. Soc. Biochem. and Molecular Biology, Am. Chem. Soc., Phi Beta Kappa, Sigma Xi, Phi Kappa Phi, Alpha Omega Alpha. Home: 24 Linda Ct Delmar NY 12054-3512 Office: U Mass Med Sch Worcester MA 01655-0126 E-mail: david.ludlum@umassmed.edu.

LUDOLF, MARILYN MARIE KEATON, lay worker; b. Morganton, N.C., July 19, 1932; d. Charles Jefferson and Dora Esther (Whitener) Keaton; m. Edwin Forrest Ludolf, Dec. 22, 1957; children: David Forrest, Jonathan Charles. BA, Lenoir Rhyne, 1954. Youth worker Cen. Bapt. Ch., Greenville, S.C., 1964-71, Park Bapt. Ch., Rock Hill, 1958-64; with coll. students Becks Bapt. Ch., Winston Salem, N.C., 1971-89; lay worker singles Calvary Bapt. Ch., 1989—. Youth seminar leader youth activities Park Bapt., Rock Hill, S.C.; youth-Sunday sch. Tng. Union-All areas of Ch. Work, Greenville, S.C. and Winston Salem, N.C.; pub. spkr., sem. leader, Women's Conf. Keynoter. Author: Freed by Faith; contbr. to Guideposts and Bapt. publs. Pres. Old Town Woman's Club, Winston-Salem, 1975-77; chmn. Christian Women's Club Luncheon, Winston Salem, 2000—. Mem. Old Town Woman's Club (pres. 1975-77, Woman of Yr. 1977). Republican. Home: 3745 Whitehaven Rd Winston Salem NC 27106-2530 *Enjoy life. This is Not a Dress Rehearsal. It is a temporary assignment. We each choose our behavior daily. Choose life! The greatest decision I ever made was to let go and let God lead in my life!.*

LUDOVICE, PETER JOHN, chemical engineer; b. Des Plaines, Ill., Apr. 1, 1962; s. William Peter and Mary Jane (Unger) L.; m. Jennifer Davis Clair, May 29, 1993; children: Miranda Claire, Dylan Wright. BSChemE, U. Ill., 1984; PhDChemE, MIT, 1989. Rsch. assoc. ETH-Zurich, Switzerland, 1988-89; vis. scientist IBM Almaden Rsch. Ctr., San Jose, Calif., 1989-91, NASA Ames Lab., Moffett Field, 1989-91; polymer product mgr. Polygen Inc., Waltham, Mass., 1991-92, Molecular Simulations Inc., Burlington, 1992-93; asst. prof. Ga. Inst. Tech., Atlanta, 1993-2000, assoc. prof., 2000—. Tech. cons. Molecular Simulations, Inc., Burlington, Mass., 1992—; faculty mem. Polymer Edn. Rsch. Ctr., Atlanta, 1993—, Ga. Tech Bioengring. Program, Atlanta, 1994—. Mem. editorial bd. Chem. Design Automation News, N.Y.C., 1992-98. Mem. AIChE, Am. Chem. Soc. (Sherwin Williams award 1988). Office: Ga Inst of Technology Sch Of Chem Engring Atlanta GA 30332-0001 E-mail: pete.ludovice@che.gatech.edu.

LUDRICK, BRAD BURTON, science educator; b. Oklahoma City; s. Robert Burton and Harriet Wrynne L.; m. Ardeth Lynn Ainsworth, Aug. 5, 1995; 1 child, Forrest. BS in Human Biology and Chemistry, Southeastern Okla. State U., 1993, MEd in Sci. Edn., 1997; EdD, Tex. A&M U., Commerce, 2001. Grad. asst. Southeastern Okla. State U., Durant, 1994-97, biol. sci. faculty, 1997—; cross-country running coach, 2001—; ranch owner, mgr. One Creek Valley Cattle Ranch, Antlers, Okla., 1990—. Instr. Upward Bound Summer Programs, Durant, 1997—. Music leader and Sunday sch. tchr. Lee Heights Bapt. Ch., Durant, 1995—. With USAR, 1989--. Decorated Army Commendation medal, Army Achievement medal, Armed Forces Res. Achievement medal Nat. Def. medals, Air Force Achievement medal, Air Force Res. Meritorious medals. Republican. Bapt. Avocations: hunting, fishing, riding horses. Office: Southeastern Okla State U PO Box 4014 Durant OK 74701 Office Fax: 580-745-7459. E-mail: bludrick@sosu.edu.

LUDSIN, STEVEN ALAN, investment advisor; b. Passaic, N.J., July 27, 1948; s. Samuel and Sonja (Gottlieb) L. BS, Cornell U., 1970; JD, Fordham U., 1975. Bar: N.Y. 1975. Assoc. Salomon Bros., N.Y.C., 1976-80; dir. instl. sales Ladenburg Thalmann & Co., Inc., 1980-81; v.p. investments Drexel Burnham Lambert, Inc., 1981-83; v.p. Ehrlich Bober Advisors, 1983-84; pres. S.A. Ludsin & Co., 1984—. Pilot program contract and contract to market real estate assets SBA, 1994, 95-97. Mem. Pres.'s Commn. on Holocaust, Washington, 1979, U.S. Holocaust Meml. Coun., Washington, 1980-89, Roundtable Polit. Action Com., N.Y.C., 1968-94; Congl. del. to White Ho. Conf. on Small Bus., 1995; rep. class and founders fund Cornell U., Ithaca, N.Y., 1986, campaign chmn. Class of 1970, 90-95. Mem. N.Y. State Bar Assn., Harmonie Club (forum com. co-chmn. 1986). Avocations: reading, politics, guitar. Office: SA Ludsin & Co PO Box 5050 East Hampton NY 11937-6043

LUDWICK, JACK RYDEL, surgeon; b. Detroit, 1935; MD, U. Mich., 1961. Diplomate Am. Bd. Surgery. Intern St. Joseph Mercy Hosp., Ann Arbor, 1961-62; resident in surgery U. Mich. Med. Ctr., 1962-67, asst. prof. surgery, 1970-71; mem. staff Little Company of Mary Hosp., Torrance, Calif., 1972; clin. prof. surgery UCLA Harbor Med. Ctr., 1972—; pvt. practice Torrance, 1972—. Maj. U.S. Army, 1968-69. Fellow ACS; mem. Soc. Surgery of Alimentary Tract, Alpha Omega Alpha. Office: 4201 Torrance Blvd Ste 550 Torrance CA 90503-4516

LUDWIG, ALLAN IRA, photographer, artist, author; b. N.Y.C., June 9, 1933; s. Daniel and Honey (Fox) L.; m. Janine Lowell, Aug. 1955 (div. 1991); children: Katherine Arabella, Pamela Vanessa, Adam Lowell; m. Gwendolyn Akin, 1992; children: Allan B. Ludwig Jr., Alison Ludwig. BFA, Yale U., 1956, MA, 1962, PhD, 1964. Instr. R.I. Sch. Design, 1956-58; asst. instr. Yale U., 1958-64; asst. prof. Dickinson Coll., 1964-65, assoc. prof., 1965-68, Syracuse U., 1968-69; pres. Automated Communications, Inc., Verona, N.J., 1969-75; dir. Ludwig Portfolios, 1975-90; co-dir. Akin/Ludwig, 1990—. Mem. exec. bd. Alternative Mus. N.Y.C., 1978-88, chmn. bd. dirs., 1982-83; cons. presses U. Mass., U. Ga., Boston Mus. Fine Arts, Smithsonian Instn. Author: Graven Images: New England Stonecarving and its Symbols, 1966, 3d edit., 1999; author exhbn. catalogues; one-person shows include: Silvermine (Conn.) Guild of Art, 1955, Davison Art Ctr., Wesleyan U., Middletown, Conn., 1961, Portland Mus. of Art, Portland, 1962, Mt. Mus. and Arts Ctrs., Miami, Fla., 1976, Jorgenson Art Gallery, U. Conn., Storrs, 1976, Alternative Mus., N.Y.C., 1977, Watson Art Gallery, Norton, Mass., 1978, Alonzo Gallery, N.Y.C., 1978, 79, Cayman Gallery, N.Y.C., 1980, IL Diaframma, Milan, Italy, 1981, Simon Gallery, Montclair, N.J., 1983, art gallery Farleigh Dickinson U., Madison, N.J., 1984, Ctr. for Creative Photography, Tucson, 1986, The Twining Gallery, N.Y.C., 1986, Cepa Gallery, Buffalo, 1986, The Shandai Gallery, Tokyo Inst. of Tech., Tokyo, 1987, White Columns, N.Y.C., 1988, O'Kane Gallery, Houston, 1988, Farideh Cadot Gallery, N.Y.C., 1988, XYZ Gallery, Ghent, Belgium, 1989, Northlight Gallery, 1990, Ariz. State U., Tempe, 1990, Galerie Farideh Cadot, Paris, 1990, Pamela Auchincloss Gallery, N.Y.C., 1991, 92, 94, Gallery 954, Chgo., 1994, Gallery at 777, L.A., 1994, Houston Ctr. for Photography, 1995, Hudson River Mus. Westchester, Yonkers, N.Y., 1995—, The Chrysler Mus., Norfolk, Va., 1995, 2002, CEPA Gallery, Buffalo, 1995, The Kemper Mus. Contemporary Art, Kansas City, Mo., 1997, Galerie Farideh Cadot, Paris, 1999, Ricco Maresca Gallery, N.Y.C., 1999; exhibited in group shows at Bannister Art Gallery, Providence, 1979, Westmoreland County (Pa.) Mus. Art, 1979, Ind. Am. Photography exhbn. Warsaw, Cracow, Katowice, Gdynia, Poland, 1980, Alonzo Gallery, N.Y.C., 1980, Alternative Mus., N.Y.C., 1981, Floating Found. for Photography, N.Y.C., 1981, World Photographic Archive, Parma, Italy, 1984, Diverse Works, Houston, 1985, The State Mus., Trenton, N.J., 1985, San Francisco Mus. Modern Art, 1986, Mus. Photog. Arts, San Diego, 1987, Public Image Gallery, N.Y.C. 1985, Houston Ctr. for Photog., 1988, Catherine Edelman Gall., Chgo., 1989, Univ. Gall., Clark U., Worcester, Mass., 1992, Long Beach (Calif.) Mus. Art, 1992, Preservation House, B.C., Can., 1992, Akin Gall., Boston, 1992, Internatl. Mus. Photography George Eastman House, Rochester, N.Y., 1993, The New Mus., N.Y.C., 1993, Akin Gall., Boston, 1993, Ctr. for Photography at Woodstock, 1993, Montage, Rochester, NY, Parko Gall., Tokyo, 1993, Addison Gall. Am. Art, Andover, Mass., 1994, Mus. Photographic Arts, San Diego, 1995, Mus, Contemporary Art, 1995, The Mercury Gall., Boston, 1995, Calif. Ctr. for the Arts Mus., 1996, Escondido, Calif., Univ. Art Mus., San Diego State U., 1997, Fullerton Mus. Ctr., 1997, The Mus. Modern Art, Oxford, England, 1997, The Julie Dermansky Gall., N.Y.C., 1995, 96,97, Moderna Museet, Stockholm, Sweden, 1998, Finish Mus. Photography, Helsinki, Finland, 1999, Ricco/Maresca Gall., NYC, 1999-2002, Marion Ctr. for Arts, Santa Fe, 2001. Regional chmn. Campaign for Yale Art Sch. Divsn., Met. N.Y.C. area, 1975-76. Bollingen Found. fellow, 1961-63, Am. Philos. Soc. fellow, 1964-66, Am. Coun. Learned Socs. fellow, 1967-68, NEH fellow, 1967; recipient USIS Merit award, 1966, Merit award Assn. State and Local History, 1967-68, Harriette Merrifield Forbes award Assn. Gravestone Studies, U. Conn., Storrs, 1981; Polaroid Found. grantee, 1987-88, Arts grantee N.J. State Coun., 1990, Agfa Corp. grantee, 1990, NEA grantee 1990-91. Democrat.

LUDWIG, CHRISTA, mezzo-soprano; b. Berlin; d. Anton and Eugenie (Besalla) L.; m. Walter Berry, Sept. 29, 1957 (div. 1970); 1 son, Wolfgang; m. Paul-Emile Deiber, Mar. 3, 1972. Ed. German schs. Prof. H.C. Senat, Berlin, 1995. Hon. mem. Vienna Philharm., 1995. Appeared at Staedtische Buehnenm. Frankfurt, W. Ger., 1946-52, Landestheatre, Darmstadt, W. Ger., 1952-54, Hannover, W. Ger., 1954-55, Vienna (Austria) State Opera, 1955—, Medaille, Ville de Paris, 1993, Shibuya-Price, Japan, 1993, others, U.S. appearances include Avery Fisher Hall, N.Y.C., 1978, Lyric Opera, Chgo., 1959-60, 70-71, 73-74, Philharmonic Hall, N.Y.C., 1968, 69, 72, 74, Goldene Ehrennadel Landtstadt, Vienna, 1997, others; guest artist London, Buenos Aires, Munich, Berlin, Tokyo, Salzburg Festival, Athens Festival, Saratoga Festival, Hunter Coll., Met. Mus., Scala Milano, Expo 67, Montreal, and others; rec. artist; author: (biography) In My Own Voice. Decorated Commdr. des Arts et des Lettres, France, 1988, Goldenes Ehren Zeichen Stadt, Salzburg, 1988, Goldene Ehrennadel Stadt und Land, Wien, Austria, 1988, Ordre Pour le Merit, France, 1997; chevalier Legion d'Honneur, France, 1989 ; recipient Mozart medal, Mahler medal, Hugo Wolf medal, Fidelio medal Opera Wien, 1991, Shibuya prize Japan, 1993, Medaille ville Paris, 1993, Medaille Ville de Dijon, 1993. Echo Deutscher Preis, 1994, Karajan preis, Berliner Bär, 1994, Grosses Ehrenzeichen Osterreich, 1994, Ehrenmitglied der Wiener Philharm., Silver Rose, Vienna Philharm., Golden Ring, Vienna Staatsoper, Musician of Yr. award Musical Am., 1994, Cordandeur Pour le Merit France, 1997; named Kammersaengerin, Govt. of Austria, 1962. Mem. NARAS.

LUDWIG, EDWARD J. medical technology company executive; Grad., Holy Cross Coll., Columbia U. Bus. Sch. Mgmt. Becton Dickinson & Co., Franklin Lakes, NJ, 1979—87, corp. planning & devel. mgr., 1987—89, pres. diagnostics divsn. Balt., 1989—94, sr. v.p. fin., CFO Franklin Lakes, NJ, 1995—99, exec. v.p., 1998—99, pres., 1999—, CEO Franklin Lakes , 2000—, chmn. bd., 2002—. Office: Becton Dickinson & Co 1 Becton Dr Franklin Lakes NJ 07417-1815*

LUDWIG, GEORGE HARRY, physicist, electrical engineer; b. Johnson County, Iowa, Nov. 13, 1927; s. George McKinley and Alice (Helm) Ludwig; m. Rosalie F. Vickers, July 21, 1950; children: Barbara Rose, Sharon Lee Taylor, George Vickers, Kathy Ann Ramsay. BA in Physics cum laude, U. Iowa, 1956, MS, 1959, PhD in Elec. Engring., 1960. Head fields and particles instrumentation sect. Goddard Space Flight Center, NASA, 1960-65, chief info. processing div., 1965-71, assoc. dir. for data ops., 1971-72; dir. systems integration Nat. Environ. Satellite Service, NOAA, 1972-75, dir. ops., 1975-80, tech. dir., 1980; sr. scientist Environ. Rsch. Labs., NOAA, Boulder, Colo., 1980-81, dir. Environ. Rsch. Labs., 1981-83; asst. to chief scientist NASA Hdqrs., 1983-84; ind. cons. data mgmt. and space sta. design, 1983-92; sr. rsch. assoc. Lab. for Atmospheric and Space Physics, U. Colo., 1985-91. Vis. sr. scientist NASA hdqrs. Calif. Inst. Tech., 1989—91; prin. designer radiation detection instrumentation for numerous sci. spacecraft including Explorer I, 1956—65; co-discoverer Van Allen radiation belts; expert on NASA sci. and applications rsch. data processing; overseer devel. and operation U.S. Nat. Environ. Satellite Sys. with its GOES and Tiros-N Spacecraft, 1972—80; dir. atmospheric and oceanic rsch. programs NOAA, 1981—83. Served from pvt to capt. USAF, 1946—52, pilot USAF, 1948—52. Named Van Allen scholar, 1958, rsch. fellow, U.S. Steel Found., 1958—60; recipient Exceptional Svc. medal, NASA, 1969, Program Adminstrn. and Mgmt. award, NOAA, 1977, Exceptional Sci. Achievement medal, NASA, 1984. Mem.: Am. Geophys. Union (life), IEEE (sr., life), Torch Club, Eta Kappa Nu, Phi Eta Sigma, Sigma Xi, Phi Beta Kappa. Home: 215 Aspen Trl Winchester VA 22602-1404 E-mail: ludwiggh@visuallink.com.

LUDWIG, GREGORY BRIAN, editor, writer; b. Long Branch, N.J., Dec. 6, 1961; s. Howard Paul and Dorothy Olive (Trehou) Ludwig. BA, George Washington U., 1984; postgrad., Washington U., 1987. Asst. mgr. Cloyd Heck Marvin Ctr., Washington, 1984-85; proofreader, editl. asst. All Am. Crafts, Inc., Newton, NJ, 1990-91; proofreader AB Bookman's Weekly, Clifton, 1992-93; proofreader, asst. editor Clinicians Pub. Group, 1993-94; editl. asst. Reed Reference Pub., New Providence, 1995-96; freelance writer and copy editor, proofreader edn1. pubs. Copy editor: book A Primer of Kleinian Therapy, 1995; contbr. articles to profl. jours. Candidate Charter Study Commn., Vernon Twp., 1995; mem. Vernon Twp. Customer Adv. Coun., 1994—96, Vernon Twp. Environ. Commn., 1996—98, Vernon Twp. Bd. Health, 1997; sec., trustee Vernon (N.J.) Twp. Dem. Club, 1995—; project dir. VISTA/Food Bank Somerset County, Bridgewater, 1986—87. Mem.: N.Y.-N.J. Trail conf. Home: PO Box 289 Highland Lakes NJ 07422-0289 E-mail: grludwig@warwick.net.

LUDWIG, JENS OTTO, social studies educator; b. Frankfurt, Germany, Dec. 24, 1968; s. Almuth Ludwig, Gunter Ludwig. PhD, Duke U., 1994. Assoc. prof. pub. policy Georgetown U., Washington, 1994—; Andrew W. Mellon Fellow in econ. studies The Brookings Instn., 2001—02. Author: Gun Violence: The Real Costs, 2000. Office: Georgetown Univ 3600 N St NW Washington DC 20007 Office Fax: 202-687-5544. Business E-Mail: ludwigj@georgetown.edu.

LUDWIG, KARL DAVID, psychiatrist; b. Johnstown, Pa., June 9, 1930; s. Karl Döring and Kathryn Bride (Palmer) L.; m. Darlene Ann Fisher, July 9, 1959; children: John D., Karl David Jr., Elizabeth Ann Craig, Mark D., Michael D. BA in Biology, St. Vincent Coll., 1952; postgrad., Pa. State U., 1952-53, St. Mary's Sem. & Univ., Balt., 1953-54; MD, U. Pitts., 1960. Intern U.S. Naval Hosp., Phila., 1960-61; resident psychiatry Ea. Pa. Psychiat. Inst., 1961-64; fellow psychiat. rsch. and teaching Jefferson Med. Coll., 1964-66; rsch. psychiatrist, dir alcoholism program Friends Hosp., 1966-73; staff psychiatrist Haverford State Hosp., Haverford, Pa., 1964-71; cons. in psychiatry VA Hosp., Coatesville, 1968-70; chief outpatient svcs. Northeast Community Mental Health Ctr., Phila., 1973, clin. dir., 1973-80; supt. Dixmont State Hosp., Sewickley, Pa., 1980-81; dir. inpatient psychiatry Sewickley Valley Hosp., 1981-95; asst. med. dir. Staunton Clin., 1990-95. Pres. med. staff Friends Hosp., Phila., 1969-71, Northeast Community Mental Health Ctr., Phila., 1974-75. Pres. Phila. Navy chpt. Res. Officers Assn. of U.S., 1975-76, dept. Pa., 1978-79; bd. trustees Valley Care Assn., Sewickley, 1983-93; bd. dirs. Valley Care Nursing Home, Sewickley, 1983-93. Capt. med. corps USNR, ret. Fellow Am. Psychiat. Assn., Psychiat. Physicians Pa. (pres. 1990-91); mem. AMA, Pitts. Psychiat. soc. (pres. 1985-86), Pa. Med. Soc., Allegheny County Med. Soc., Res. Officers Assn. of U.S. (life), Naval Res. Assn. (life), Am. Legion (life), Assn. Mil. Surgeons U.S. (life), Navy League U.S. (life; pres. Pitts. coun. 1998), Mil. Order World Wars (perpetual; comdr. Gen. Matthew B. Ridgway Pitts. chpt. 1997-99). Republican. Roman Catholic. Home and Office: 2168 Reis Run Rd Pittsburgh PA 15237-1425

LUDWIG, KURT JAMES, residence director; b. Bristol, Pa., July 10, 1964; s. Lee Edward Sr. and Pauline Marcella (Stallone) Danis. BA, East Stroudsburg U., 1990; MA, Indiana U. Pa., 1993. Substitute tchr. Montpelier (Vt.) Sch. Dist., 1990-91; residence dir. Thiel Coll., Greenville, Pa., 1991-93; counselor, residence dir. U. Rio Grande, Ohio, 1993-95; residence dir. SUNY, Brockport, 1997-99; coord. residential programs, complex coord. Green Mountain Coll., Poultney, Vt., 1999-2000, dir. residence life, 2000—. Home: 301 Main St Hulmeville PA 19047

LUDWIG, L(OWELL) MARK, social science educator; b. Estevan, Can., Jan. 2, 1933; s. Daniel Robert and Minette Louise (Baue) L.; m. Elizabeth Ann Maimone, Nov. 25, 1968 (div. Oct. 1979); 1 child, Lara Elizabeth; m. Marlyn Ginsburg Josselson, Jan. 6, 1991. AB in Govt., Valparaiso U., 1959; BS in Edn., Kent State U., 1962, MA in History, 1967, PhD in Edn., 1976. Cert. tchr., Ohio. Tchr. social studies Nordonia H.S., Northfield, Ohio, 1959-69; prof. social scis. Cuyahoga Cmty. Coll., Cleve., 1970-86; adj. prof. Cleve. State U., 1987-89; program mgr. U.S. Dept. of Navy, Cleve., 1989-91; quality improvement advisor U.S. Dept. Def., 1991-95; emeritus prof. Cuyahoga Cmty. Coll., 1989—, adj. prof., 1996—. Author: Introduction to Social Science, A Personalized course, Vols. I & II, 1977-78; contbr. articles to sci. and profl. jours. Fulbright fellow U.S. Dept. Edn., 1963, 72, 74. Democrat. Lutheran. Avocations: reading, highpointing, golf, hiking, travel. Home: 3675 Traynham Rd Shaker Heights OH 44122

LUDWIG, RICHARD JOSEPH, ski resort executive; b. Lakewood, Ohio, July 28, 1937; s. Mathew Joseph and Catherine Elizabeth (Sepich) L.; m. Erleen Catherine Halambeck Ramus, July 22, 1977; children: Charleen, Tracey, Charles. Cassandra. Student, Ohio State U., 1955-59; BBA Fenn Coll., Cleve. State U, 1963. C.P.A., Ohio. Sr. acct. Ernst & Whinney, Cleve., 1964-66; supervising acct. Ernst & Young, 1966-70; asst. treas. Midland Ross Corp., Cleve., 1970-71, treas., 1971-76; v.p. fin., treas. U.S. Realty Investments, 1976-78, v.p.-fin., chief fin. officer, 1978-79; owner Boston Mills Ski Resort, Inc., Peninsula, Ohio, 1979—, Brandywine Ski Resort, Inc., Sagamore Hills, 1990—. Mem. Firestone Country Club (Akron, Ohio), Saddlebrook Club (Wesley Chapel, Fla.), Black Diamond Ranch Club (Lecanto, Fla.), Walden Country Club (Aurora, Ohio), Mediterra Country Club (Naples, Fla.), Mayacama Golf Club (Santa Rosa, Calif.), The Club at Mediterra (Naples), Stonewater Golf Club (Highland Heights, Ohio). Home: 15659 Villoresi Way Naples FL 34110 Office: PO Box 175 7100 Riverview Rd Peninsula OH 44264

LUDWIG, WALTHER, classical and neo-Latin studies educator; b. Stuttgart, Fed. Republic Germany, Feb. 9, 1929; s. Paul and Susanna Maria (Morian) L.; m. Karin Adelheid Ruth Fragel, Dec. 28, 1962; children: Carl Friedrich, Ulrike. PhD, U. Tubingen, Fed. Republic Germany, 1954; Habilitation, U. Munich, 1961. Lectr. Free U. Berlin, 1955-58; lectr., reader U. Munich, 1959-64; jr. fellow Ctr. for Hellenic Studies, Washington, 1962-63; prof., dept. chmn. U. Frankfurt am Main, Fed. Republic Germany, 1964-70; mem. Inst. for Advanced Study, Princeton, N.J., 1970; prof., dept. chmn. Columbia U., N.Y.C., 1970-76, U. Hamburg, Hamburg, Fed. Republic Germany, 1976—, dean Germany, 1992-94. Vis. prof. Stanford U., Stanford, Palo Alto, Calif., 1966-67, Tartu U., Estonia, 2002; mem. Fondation Hardt, Geneva Comitee scientifique, 1976-91, Conseil, 1989-92, Deutsche Forschungsgemeinschaft, Kommission fuer Humanismusforschung, 1978-87, internat. com. Wolfenbuetteler Arbeitskreis fuer Renaissanceforschung, 1989—; v.p. Fedn. Internationale des Associations des Etudes Classiques, 1989-94. Author: Litterae Neolatinae, 1989, Vater und Sohn im 16. Jahrhundert, 1999, others; contbr. articles to profl. jours.; mem. editl. bds. various scholarly jours. and series, 1965—. Fellow Am. Coun. Learned Socs., 1974-75. Mem. Akademie der Wissenschaften zu Göttingen, Akademie der Gemeinnützigen Wissenschaften zu Erfurt, Jungius Gesellschaft der Wissenschaften (Hamburg), Acad. Europaea (London), Mommsen-Gesellschaft (pres. 1978-83, v.p. 1983-85), Internat. Assn. for Neo-Latin Studies (v.p. 1982-88, pres. 1988-91), Polish Philological Soc. (hon.). Home: Reventlowstr 19 D-22605 Hamburg Germany Office: U Hamburg Von-Melle-Park 6 D-20146 Hamburg Germany E-mail: walther.ludwig@uni-hamburg.de.

LUDZIK, STEVE, former professional hockey coach; m. Mary Ann Ludzik; children: Stephen, Ryan. Hockey player Niagara Falls Flyers, Ont. Hockey League, 1981-82, Chgo. Blackhawks, NHL, 1982-88, Buffalo Sabres, NHL, 1988-89, Am. Hockey League's Rochester Americans, 1989-92; coach Muskegon Fury, Colonial Hockey League, 1993-94; head coach Detroit Vipers, Internat. Hockey League, 1994-99, Tampa Bay Lightning, NHL, 1999—2001.*

LUEBBERT, KAREN MERRITT, academic administrator; b. St. Louis, Oct. 3, 1942; d. Joseph Henry and Lorene Laura Merritt; m. Jack R. Luebbert, Jan. 27, 1968; 1 child, Katharine. BA, Webster U., 1964; MLS, Case Western Res. U., 1967; PhD, St. Louis U., 1993. Asst. dir. news bur. Washington U., St. Louis, 1964-65; asst. to libr. Webster U., 1965-66, libr., 1967-83; dir. libr. Eden-Webster Libr., 1983-93; v.p. univ. svcs. Webster U., 1988-95, v.p. fin., 1997-98, v.p., exec. asst. to pres., 1995—. Lectr. Washington U., 1977-80; bd. dirs. Mo. Libr. Network Corp., v.p., 1981-83, sec., 1988-89, pres., 1989-92; bd. dirs. Midwest BankCtr., VideoNine; mem. Mo. Higher Edn. Loan Authority, 1994—, v.p., 1995-97, 2001-02, pres., 1997-99; bd. dirs. Higher Edn. Ctr. St. Louis, chair learning resources coun., 1973-75, project dir., 1974-76, v.p., 1997—; pres. St. Louis Regional Libr. Network, 1982-83; bd. dirs., sec. St. Louis Jour. Rev., 1996—. Mem. St. Louis Univ. Club (bd. dirs. 1999—, v.p. 2000—), Beta Phi Mu, Pi Lambda Theta. Office: Webster U 470 E Lockwood Ave Saint Louis MO 63119-3194 E-mail: luebbelkl@webster.edu.

LUEBKE, FREDERICK CARL, retired humanities educator; b. Reedsburg, Wis., Jan. 26, 1927; s. Frederick J. and Martha (Kretzmann) L.; m. Norma Marie Wukasch, Aug. 12, 1951; children: Christina McPhee, John Seikai, David M., Thomas E. BS, Concordia U., 1950; MA, Claremont Grad. U., 1958; PhD, U. Nebr., 1966. Assoc. prof. history Concordia Coll., Seward, Nebr., 1961-68; from assoc. prof. history to prof. history U. Nebr., Lincoln, 1968-86, Charles Mach disting. prof. history, 1986-94, prof. emeritus, 1994—. Author: Bonds of Loyalty, 1974, Germans in Brazil, 1987, Germans in the New World, 1990, A Harmony of the Arts: The Nebraska State Capitol, 1990, Nebraska: An Illustrated History, 1995, European Immigrants in the American West: Community Histories, 1998; editor Great Plains Quar., 1978-84; contbr. articles to profl. jours. Exec. com. Nebr. State Hist. Soc. Found., Lincoln. Rockefeller Found. fellow, 1982, Fulbright rsch. fellow Germany, 1974-75, Newberry Libr. fellow, Chgo., 1977-78; recipient Disting. Career award U. Nebr., 1995. Mem. Orgn. Am. Historians (chmn. nominating bd.), Western History Assn. (chmn. nominating bd., award of Merit 2001), Immigration History Soc. (exec. bd.), Nebr. State Hist. Soc. (bd. dirs., Sheldon award, Sellers award). Avocations: gardening, travel. Home: 3117 Woodsdale Blvd Lincoln NE 68502-5160 E-mail: fcluebke@alltel.net.

LUEBKE, MARTIN FREDERICK, retired curator; b. Concord, Wis., Oct. 2, 1917; s. Frederick John and Martha (Kretzmann) L.; m. Dorothy Lorraine Kutschinski, July 5, 1947 (dec. Mar. 2001); children: Judith, Charles. BS, Concordia Coll., 1941; MA, U. Mich., 1952; PhD, U. Ill., 1966; postdoctoral,

Cambridge U., 1974. Tchr. Our Savior Luth. Sch., Chgo., 1938-45; prin. Immanuel Luth. Sch., Grand Rapids, Mich., 1945-58; prof., dean Concordia Theol. Sem., Springfield, Ill., 1958-76, Ft. Wayne, Ind., 1976-80; curator Saxon Luth. Meml., Frohna, Mo., 1980-86; asst. to pastor Chapel of the Cross Luth., St. Louis, 1987—. Editor: Curriculum in Process, 1963; contbr. articles to profl. jours. Bd. dirs. Mich. Dist. Luth. Ch., Mo. Synod, 1962-75; commr., sec. Perry County Tourism Commn., Perryville, Mo., 1983-86; bd. dirs. River Heritage Assn., Cape Girardeau, Mo., 1984-86. Faculty fellow Aid Assn. Luths., 1963, 73; recipient Outstanding Educators Am. award, 1972, Commendation award Concordia Hist. Inst., St. Louis, 1987. Avocations: music, tour hosting. Home: 6507 Dolphin Cir E Florissant MO 63033-4756 E-mail: mfluebke@aol.com.

LUEBKE, NEIL ROBERT, philosophy educator; b. Pierce, Nebr., Sept. 15, 1936; s. Robert Carl and Cinderetta Amelia (Guthmann) L.; m. Phyllis Jean Madsen, June 15, 1957; children: Anne Elizabeth, Karen Marie. BA, Midland Coll., 1958; MA, Johns Hopkins U., 1962, PhD, 1968. Asst., assoc. then prof. philosophy Okla. State U., Stillwater, 1961-98, head philosophy dept., 1979-85, 89-96, Regents Svc. prof., 1997-98, prof. emeritus, 1998—. Dir. Exxon Critical Thinking Project, 1971-74 Contbr. articles to profl. jours. Woodrow Wilson nat. fellow, 1958-59 Mem. Am. Philos. Assn., Soc. Bus. Ethics, Mountain-Plains Philos. Conf. (chmn. 1971-72, 80-81), Southwestern Philos. Soc. (pres. 1981-82), Phi Kappa Phi (nat. pres. 1998-2001). Democrat. Lutheran. Home: 616 W Harned Ave Stillwater OK 74075-1303 E-mail: nluebke_osu@brightok.net.

LUECKE, ELEANOR VIRGINIA ROHRBACHER, civic volunteer; b. St. Paul, Mar. 10, 1918; d. Adolph and Bertha (Lehman) Rohrbacher; m. Richard William Luecke, Nov. 1, 1941; children: Glenn Richard, Joan Eleanor Ratliff, Ruth Ann (dec.). Student, Macalester Coll., St. Paul, 1936-38, St. Paul Bus. U., 1938-40. Author lit. candidate and ballot issues, 1970—; producer TV local issues, 1981—; contbr. articles to profl. jours. Founder, officer, dir., pres. Liaison for Inter-Neighborhood Coop., Okemos, Mich., 1972—; chair countrywide special edn. millage proposals, 1958, 1969; trustee, v.p., pres. Ingham Intermediate Bd. Edn., 1959-83; sec., dir. Tri-County Cmty. Mental Health Bd., Lansing, 1964-72; founder, treas., pres. Concerned Citizens for Meridian Twp., Okemos, 1970-86; mental health rep. Partners of the Americas, Belize, Brit. Honduras, 1971; trustee Capital Area Comprehensive Health Planning, 1973-76; v.p., dir. Assn. Retarded Citizens Greater Lansing, 1973-83; chair, mem. Cmty. Svcs. for Developmentally Disabled Adv. Coun., 1973-87; dir., founder, treas. Tacoma Hills Homeowners Assn. Bd., 1985-97; facilitator of mergers Lansing Child Guidance Clinic, Clinton and Easton counties Tri-County Cmty. Mental Health Bd., Lansing Adult Mental Health Clinic, founder. Recipient Greater Lansing Cmty. Svcs. Coun. "Oscar," United Way, 1955, state grant Mich. Devel. Disabilities Coun., Lansing, 1983, Disting. award Mich. Assn. Sch. Bds., Lansing, 1983, Pub. Svc. award C.A.R.E.ing, Okemos, 1988, Earth Angel award WKAR-TV 23, Mich. State U., East Lansing, 1990, Cert. for Cmty. Betterment People for Meridian, Okemos, 1990, 2nd pl. video competition East Lansing/Meridian Twp. Cable Comm. Commn., 1990, 1st pl. award video competition, 1992, Outstanding Sr. Citizen award Charter Twp. of Meridian, Okemos, Mich., 2001; Ingham Med. Hosp. Commons Area named in her honor, Lansing, 1971. Mem. Advocacy Orgn. for Patients and Providers (dir. 1994-99). Avocations: reading, interior design, landscaping, gardening. Home: 1893 Birchwood Dr Okemos MI 48864-2766

LUECKE, GREG RICHARD, engineering educator, consultant; b. Orange, Tex., Dec. 2, 1956; m. Jennifer L. Gelwick, Jan. 15, 1956. PhD, Pa. State U., 1992. Profl. engr., Iowa, 1997. Assoc. engr., scientist McDonnel-Douglas Corp., Long Beach, Calif., 1980—81; design engr. Sikorsky Aircraft , Stratford, 1981—88; assoc. prof. Iowa State U., Ames. Co-inventor of hub mounted actuators for blade pitch control, 1984. Grantee Rsch. grant, NSF, 1992—. Mem.: IEEE. Office: Iowa State Univ 1620 Howe Hall Ames IA 50011 Office Fax: 515-294-5530. Business E-Mail: grluecke@iastate.edu.

LUECKE, KENN ROBERT, software engineer; b. St. Charles, Mo., May 12, 1966; s. Robert Clarence and Louise Nora (Meers) L. BS in Computer Sci., U. Mo., St. Louis, 1989; MBA, Washington U., 1999. Programmer-coop McDonnell Douglas, St. Louis, 1988, software engr., 1989—. Mem. Grace Ch. Recipient Tip of the Cop award on Harrier Radar II+ program. Mem. AIAA, Am. Soc. for Quality Control, Am. Assn. Artificial Intelligence, U. Mo.-St. Louis Alumni Assn., Boeing Leadership Soc., Gateway to the West, Forest Park Forever, Am. Polit. Items Collectors. Home: 1005 Olde Coventry Dr Saint Charles MO 63301-1524 Office: McDonnell Douglas PO Box 512 Saint Louis MO 63166-0512

LUECKE, PAMELA, professor, former editor; BA in Philosophy, Carleton Coll., 1974; MA in Journalism, Northwestern U., 1975; MBA, U. Hartford, 1979. Features reporter Hartford Courant , Hartford , Conn., 1975—79; bus. editor The Louisville Times, Louisville, 1981—84; various positions The Courier-Journal , 1981—89; asst. mng. editor/metro Hartford Courant , Hartford , Conn., 1989—95, deputy mng. editor, 1995; editorial page editor Lexington (Ky.) Herald-Leader, 1995—96, editor, v.p., 1996—2000, editor, sr. v.p., 2000—01; prof., Reynolds Chair Dept. Journalism and Mass Comm., Washington and Lee Univ., Va., 2001—. Office: Washington & Lee Univ Lexington VA 24450*

LUEDECKE, WILLIAM HENRY, mechanical engineer; b. Pittsburg, Tex., Apr. 5, 1918; s. Henry Herman and Lula May (Abernathy) L.; m. Mary Anne Copeland, June 3, 1939; children: William Henry, John Copeland. BS, U. Tex., 1940. Registered profl. engr., Tex. Mech. engr. Columbian Gasoline Corp., Monroe, La., 1940-41; supr. shipbldg., mech. engr. USN, Orange, Tex., 1941-42; gen. supr. factory mgrs. N.Am. Aviation Co., Dallas, 1944-46; mech. engr., charge Chrysler Airtemp. div. Chrysler Corp., L.A., 1946-50; owner Luedecke Engrng. Co., Austin, Tex., 1950—; also Luedecke Investment Co. Chmn. bd. dirs. Mut. Savs. Instn., Austin; dir. City Nat. Bank, Austin, 1st Tex. Fin. Corp., Dallas. Bd. dirs. Travis County Heart Fund, Austin YMCA. Named Man of Year, Tex. Barbed Wire Collectors Assn. Mem. Am. Soc. Heating, Refrigerating and Air Conditioning Engrs. (dir., pres. Austin chpt.), Tex., Nat. Socs. Profl. Engrs., C. of C., Econ. Devel. Coun., Better Bus. Bur., Nat. Fedn. Ind. Bus. (nat. adv. coun.), Rotary Club, Austin Club, Westwood Country Club (treas., dir.). Lutheran. Home: 15 Woodstone Sq Austin TX 78703-1159 Office: 1009 W 34th St Austin TX 78705-2008

LUEDER, BARBARA ANN, school psychologist; b. West Union, Iowa, May 3, 1948; d. Carl Andrew and Evalyn Anna (Schlatter) L. AA, Waldorf Coll., Forest City, Iowa, 1968; BA, Luther Coll., Decorah, Iowa, 1970; MA, U. Iowa, 1983, EdS, 1985. Nat. cert. sch. psychologist. Dir. Christian edn. Oak Grove Luth. Ch., Richfield, Minn., 1972-73; secondary resource tchr. Norway (Iowa) Cmty. Schs., 1982-83; sch. psychologist Grand Wood Area Edn. Agy., Cedar Rapids, Iowa, 1985—. Active Zion Luth. Ch., Iowa City, 1985—. Mem.: Internat. Sch. Psychology Assn., Coun. for Learning Disabilities, Coun. for Exceptional Children, Nat. Assn. Sch. Psychologists, Hymn Soc. Am. Avocation: singing. Office: Grant Wood Area Edn Agy 200 Holiday Rd Coralville IA 52241-1178 E-mail: blueder@aea10.k12.ia.us.

LUEDER, DIANNE CAROL, library director; b. Racine, Wis., Aug. 5, 1944; d. James Richard and Margaret Ann Helland; m. Roland Herman Lueder, Aug. 29, 1981 (dec. July 1993); children: Daniel Lee Bertelsen, Barbara Marie Lantz. BA, U. Wis.-Parkside, Kenosha, 1972; MLS, U. Wis., Milw., 1979. Ref./outreach libr. Elk Grove Village (Ill.) Libr., 1979-80; dir. Bartlett (Ill.) Pub. Libr., 1980-84; asst. exec. dir. DuPage Libr. Sys., Geneva, 1984-88; pres. Lueder Enterprises, Inc., Wauconda, 1988—; exec. dir. Roselle (Ill.) Pub. Libr., 1990-01; libr. dir. Menomonie (Wis.) Pub. Libr., 2001—. Author: Administrator's Guide to Library Building Maintenance, 1992. V.p. Roselle Pub. Libr. Found., 1994-2001. Mem. ALA, AAUW, Wis. Libr. Assn., Menomonie Optimist Cub, Rotary Club Menomonie, GFWC Menomonie Woman's Club. Lutheran. Avocations: flying, travel, learning Norwegian language. Home: 343 Red Cedar St Menomonie WI 54751 Office: Menomonie Pub Libr 600 Wolske Bay Rd Menomonie WI 54751 E-mail: dclueder@wwt.net.

LUEDERS, CARL L. finance executive; b. Apr. 15, 1950; BA in econs., Univ. Mass., 1972; MBA, Babason Coll., 1981. Sr. auditor Arthur Andersen & Co., Boston, 1974—78; v.p., contr., treas. Polariod Corp., Cambridge, 1979—, v.p., contr., 1996—2000, v.p., treas., 2000—01, v.p., acting CFO, 2001—02; CFO R.F. Morse & Son, Inc., Westwateham, 2002—; CEO Brine, Inc., Milford, 2002—. Home: 15 Hinkley Rd Newton MA 02468 Office: 784 Memorial Dr Cambridge MA 02139

LUEDERS, WAYNE RICHARD, lawyer; b. Milw., Sept. 23, 1947; s. Warren E. and Marjorie L. (Schramek) L.; m. Patricia L. Rasmus, Aug. 1, 1970 (div. Nov. 1990); children: Laurel, Daniel, Kristin. BBA with honors, U. Wis., 1969; JD, Yale U., 1973, Yale Law Sch. Bar: Wis. 1973. Acct. Arthur Andersen & Co., Milw., 1969-70; atty. Foley & Lardner, 1973-80, ptnr., 1980—. Bd. dirs. numerous cos. Bd. dirs. Riveredge Nature Ctr., Milw., 1983-92, 96-99, Wis. Pro Soccer, 1986—, Milw. Art Mus., 1992-2001, Child Abuse Prevention Fund, Milw., 1989—, Michael Fields Agrl. Inst., 1991—, Florentine Opera Co., 1992—; class agt. Yale Law Sch., 1978—. With U.S. Army, 1969-75. Mem. ABA, AICPA (Wisc.), Wis. Bar Assn., Milw. Bar Assn., Estate Counselors Forum, Univ. Club (Milw.), Phi Kappa Phi. Avocations: theater, racquetball, violin. Office: Foley & Lardner 777 E Wisconsin Ave Ste 3800 Milwaukee WI 53202-5367 E-mail: wlueders@foleylaw.com.

LUEDKE, FREDERICK LEE, manufacturing company executive; b. Milw., Jan. 19, 1938; s. Frederick William and Martha Marie (Widiger) L.; m. Wilma Jeanne Seacat, July 3, 1960; children; Tracy Jeanne, Frederick William II. BSIE, Wichita State U., 1960; MBA, Harvard U., 1966. Mfg. tng. program GE, 1960-64; prodn. gen. supr. Polaroid Corp., Waltham, Mass., 1966-70; mgr. mfg. Millipore Corp., Bedford, 1970-76; dir. mfg. Berol Corp., Danbury, Conn., 1976-87; exec. v.p. Neoperl Inc., Waterbury, 1987-92; pres. Neoperl, Inc., 1992—. Bd. dirs. Nangatuck Valley Devel. Corp., 1994—, v.p., 1996—98; bd. dirs. Platt Bros. and Co., 1996—, Waterbury Partnership 2000, 1999—, Greater Waterbury Workforce Devel. Bd., 2001—; mem. Gov.'s coun. for Econ. Competitiveness and Tech., 1999—, Waterbury City Champion, Inner City Bus. Strategy Initiative, 1999. Founder Waterbury Neighborhood Coun., 1994; pres. Luth. Ch. of Newtons, Mass., 1974—75, 1st Luth. Ch., Waterbury, 1988—89; bd. dirs. Danbury ARC, 1982—84, Easter Seals, 1993—2000, vice chmn., 1994—96, chmn., 1996—98; pres. bd. trustees East Hill Woods Retirement Ctr., Southbury, Conn., 1989—97; mem. Waterbury Found., 1991—; chmn. Incorporators of Waterbury Hosp., 1995—97; trustee Waterbury Hosp., 1997—, vice chmn., 2000—; bd. dirs. Greater Waterbury Health Network, 1999—. Mem. ASME, Am. Soc. Plumbing Engrs., Plumbing Mfrs. Inst. (pres. 1999-2000, bd. dirs. 1995-2000), Am. Soc. Sanitary Engring., Greater Waterbury C. of C. (bd. dirs. 2000—), Rotary (bd. dirs.), Waterbury Club (pres. 1996-98). Republican. Lutheran. Avocations: tennis, mountain hiking. Home: 98 Woodlawn Ter Waterbury CT 06710-1929 Office: Neoperl Inc 171 Mattatuck Heights Rd Waterbury CT 06705-3832

LUEDKE, PATRICIA GEORGIANNE, microbiologist; b. Milw., May 4, 1956; m. Michael Andrew Luedke, July 15, 1978; children: Christopher M., Sean P. BS, Marquette U., 1978, postgrad., 1981-82. Registered med. technologist; registered microbiologist; specialist microbiology; lic. pvt. investigator. Med. technologist Med.-Surgical Clinic, Milw., 1978-79, Milw. County Hosp., 1979, Fort Atkinson (Wis.) Meml. Hosp., 1979-88, Franciscan Shared Lab., Wauwatosa, Wis., 1988—. Cons. Forensic Rsch. Assocs., Oconomowoc, Wis., 1978—. Mem. Am. Soc. Microbiology, Am. Soc. Clin. Pathologists, Anaerobe Soc. Am., N.Y. Acad. Scis. Home: 739 Elizabeth St Oconomowoc WI 53066-3703 E-mail: forensic@execpc.com.

LUEDTKE, ROLAND ALFRED, retired lawyer; b. Lincoln, Nebr., Jan. 4, 1924; s. Alfred C. and Caroline (Senne) L.; m. Helen Snyder, Dec. 1, 1951; children: Larry O., David A. BS, U. Nebr., 1949, JD, 1951. Bar: Nebr. 1951. Since practiced in, Lincoln, 1951—; mem. Luedtke, Radcliffe & Evans (and predecessor), 1973-79; dep. sec. state State of Nebr., 1953-60; spl. legis. liaison Nebr. Dept. State, 1953-60; corps and elections counsel to sec. of state State of Nebr., 1960-65; senator Nebr. Unicameral Legislature, 1967-78, speaker, 1977-78; lt. gov. State of Nebr., 1979-83; mayor City of Lincoln, 1983-87; of counsel McHenry, Haszard, Hansen & Roth, Lincoln, 1987—; ret. Exec. sec. Gov. Nebr. Com. Refugee Relief, 1954-58; del., conferee nat. confs. Past pres. Lancaster County Cancer Soc.; crusade chmn. Nebr. div. Am. Cancer Soc., 1981-82; past dist. v.p., fin. chmn. Boy Scouts Am.; treas. Nebr. Young Republicans, 1953-54; jr. pres. Founders Day, Nebr. Rep. Com., 1958-59; chmn. Lancaster County Rep. Com., 1962-64; bd. dirs. Concordia Coll. Assn., Seward, Nebr., 1962-66, pres., 1965-66; bd. dirs. Lincoln Lutheran Sch. Assn., 1961-65, pres., 1964-65; bd. dirs. Immanuel Health Ctr. Omaha; Tabitha Found., Lincoln, 1986—, v.p., 1990-98; bd. dirs. Nebraska-land Found., Lincoln, 1980-94; pres. 1990-93; bd. dirs. Coords. for Adult Literacy, Nebr., 1984-95, v.p., 1990-92. Served with AUS, 1943-45, ETO. Decorated Bronze Star, Purple Heart; recipient Disting. Service award Concordia Tchrs. Coll., 1965, Disting. Alumni award Lincoln High Sch., 1983 Mem. Am. Bar Assn., Nat. Conf. State Legislators (chmn. criminal justice task force 1975-77, chmn. consumers affairs com. 1975-77, exec. com. 1977-78), Nat. Conf. Lt. Govs. (exec. com. 1981-83), U.S. Conf. Mayors (chmn. human devel. com.), Nat. Conf. Cities (bd. dirs., bd. advisor human devel. com. NLC), Nat. League Cities (bd. dirs.), Nebr. Bar Assn., Lincoln Bar Assn., Am. Legion, DAV, VFW, Lincoln C. of C., Lincoln Gateway Sertoma Club (pres. 1962-63, chmn. bd. 1963-64), Delta Theta Phi. Lutheran.

LUEHRS-KAISER, KAI, writer, scholar, critic; b. Bremen, Germany, July 27, 1961; s. Rudolf and Ute (Kaiser) L. MA, Free U., Berlin, 1992; Dr.phil., Free U. Berlin, 1999. Lectr. Free Univ., Berlin, 1992-96. Author: (book) Excentrische Einsätze, 1998, Flügel und Extreme, 1999, Traditionen und Trabanten, 1999, Schüsse iur Finstere, 2001; contbr. articles to literary mags. and newspapers. Grantee: Free U., Berlin, 1992-94. Mem. Heimito von Doderer Gesellschaft (co-founder, pres. 1995—). Home: Roennebergstr 4 12161 Berlin Germany E-mail: kailuehrskaiser@aol.com.

LUEKE, DONNA MAE, yoga instructor, Reiki practitioner, instructor; b. Toledo, Sept. 18, 1946; d. Herbert Henry and Margery Alberta (Welsh) L. BA, Adrian Coll., 1968. Tchr. Anchor Bay Schs., New Baltimore, Mich., 1968-74; salesperson Jacobson's, Birmingham, 1974-76; sales rep. Stark & Co., Detroit, 1976-80; regional retail supr. Norwich-Eaton Consumer Pharms., Louisville, 1980-83; territory rep. Procter & Gamble, 1983-84; dir. Progressive Retail, Raleigh, N.C., 1984-89; nat. retail mgr. CIBA Consumer Pharms. and CIBA Vision Corp., Wayne, Pa., 1989-92; mem. apprentice program Holistic Options, 1997-98. Student govt. v.p. Adrian Coll., 1966, 67. Mem. Nature Conservancy. Avocations: creative writing, gardening, fishing.

LUENING, ROBERT ADAMI, agricultural economics educator emeritus; b. Milw., Apr. 20, 1924; s. Edwin Garfield and Irma Barbara (Adami) L.; m. Dorothy Ellen Hodgskiss, Aug. 27, 1966. BS, U. Wis., 1961, MS, 1968. Dairy farmer, Hartland, Wis., 1942-58; fieldman Waukesha County Dairy Herd Improvement Assn., Waukesha, 1958; adult agr. instr. Blair Sch. Dist., Wis., 1961-63; extension farm mgmt. agt. U. Wis.-Racine, 1963-69; extension farm record specialist Dept. Agrl. Econs. U. Wis.-Madison, 1969-88; free-lance work, 1988—. Author: (with others) The Farm Management Handbook, 1972, 7th edit., 1991, Teacher's Manual, 1991, Managing Your Financial Future Farm Record Book Series, 1980, 4th edit., 1987, USDA Yearbook of Agriculture, 1989, Beef, Sheep and Forage Production in Northern Wisconsin, 1992, Dairy Farm Business Management, 1996, Poultry Farm Business Management, 1999, 2d edit., 2000; writer mag. column: Agri-Vision, 1970-88. Founder, exec. pres. Lüning Family Orgns. U.S.A., Inc.; bd. dirs. Friends of the Max Kade Inst. for German-Am. Studies. Recipient John S. Donald Excellence in Teaching award U. Wis.-Madison, 1980; recipient Wis. State Farmer award Vocat. Agr. Inst. Wis., 1980, Second Mile award Wis. County Agts. Assn., 1980, Outstanding Svc. to Wis. Agr. award Farm and Industry Short Course, 1989. Mem. Wis. Soc. Farm Mgrs. and Rural Appraisers (coll. v.p. 1976, chmn. editl. com. 1978-80, sec.-treas. 1968-80, pres. 1982, Silver Plow award 1988), Wis. State Geneal. Soc. (pres. S.C. chpt. 1995-96, pres. PAF Users group 1995), Epsilon Sigma Phi (Disting. Service award 1988), Alpha Gamma Rho, Kiwanis. Lodges: Masons. Presbyterian. Home: 5313 Fairway Dr Madison WI 53711-1038 Office: U Wis Dept Agrl and Applied Econs 427 Lorch St Rm 216 Madison WI 53706-1513 E-mail: rluening@facstaff.wisc.edu.

LUEPKER, RUSSELL VINCENT, epidemiology educator; b. Chgo., Oct. 1, 1942; s. Fred Joeseph and Anita Louise (Thornton) L.; m. Ellen Louise Thompson, Dec. 22, 1966; children: Ian, Carl. BA, Grinnell Coll., 1964; MD with distinction, U. Rochester, 1969; MS, Harvard U., 1976; PhD (hon.), U. Lund, Sweden, 1996. Intern U. Calif., San Diego, 1969-70; resident Peter Bent Brigham Hosp., Boston, 1973-74; cardiology fellow Peter Bent Brigham Hosp./Med., 1974-76; asst. prof. divsn. epidemiology med. lab. physiol. hygiene U. Minn., Mpls., 1976-80, assoc. prof., 1980-87, prof. divsn. epidemiology and medicine, 1987—, dir. divsn. epidemiology, 1991—, Mayo prof. pub. health, 2001—. Cons. NIH, Bethesda, Md., 1980—, U. So. Calif., L.A., 1985—, Armed Forces Epidemiology Bd., 1993-97; vis. prof. U. Goteborg, Sweden, 1986, Ninewells Med. Sch., Dundee, Scotland, 1995. With USPHS, 1970-73. Harvard U. fellow, 1974-76, Bush Leadership fellow, 1990; recipient Prize for Med. Rsch. Am. Coll. Chest Physicians, 1970, Nat. Rsch. Svc. award Nat. Heart, Lung and Blood Inst., Bethesda, 1975-77, Disting. Alumni award Grinnell Coll., 1989. Fellow ACP, Am. Coll. Cardiology, Am. Heart Assn. (chmn. coun. on epidemiology 1992-94, chair program com. sci. sessions 1995-97, award of merit 1997), Am. Coll. Epidemiology; mem. Am. Epidemiol. Soc., Am. Soc. Preventive Cardiology (Joseph Stokes award 1999), Delta Omega Soc. (Nat. Merit award 1988). Office: Univ Minn Sch Pub Health Div Epidemiology 1300 S 2nd St Minneapolis MN 55454-1087 E-mail: luepker@epi.umn.edu.

LUEPNITZ, ROY ROBERT, psychologist, consultant, small business owner, entrepreneur; b. Ft. McClellan, Ala., June 3, 1955; s. Carl A. and Helen Elizabeth (Brown) L.; m. Mary Kinloch Bush, Dec. 18, 1981; children: Mary, George, Noel. BA cum laude, Southwestern U., 1979; MS in Counseling Psychology, U. So. Miss., 1981; PhD in Counseling Psychology, Tex. A & M U., 1985. Fellow Am. Bd. Forensic Examiners; cert. health svc. provider in psychology; Internat. Airlines Travel Agt. Network cert. travel agt.; registered treatment provider of sex offenders; bd. cert. forensic examiner; lic. marital and family therapist; lic. psychologist. Intern, vol. Austin (Tex.) State Hosp., 1978-79; counselor Univ. Counseling Psychology Clinic, Hattiesburg, Miss., 1980; master level psychologist Pine Belt Mental Health Ctr., 1981, Tex. Rehab. Commn., Bryan, 1981-82; grad. tchr. Tex. A & M Univ., College Station, 1982-83; psychologist Brazos Valley MHMR Authority, Bryan, 1983-84, mental health dir., 1984-86; pvt. practice psychologist College Station, 1987—. Chmn. bd. for sex abuse Am. Bd. Forensic Psychol. Spltys; cons. Dept. Human Svcs., Bryan, 1987—, Brazos Valley MHRA, Bryan, 1987—, St. Joseph's Hosp., Bryan, The Med. Ctr., College Station, 1991—, Brazos Valley Physicians Orgn., 1997—, various chs., schs., govt. agys.; ptnr. Noel's World of Travel. Sec. Miss. APGA, 1979-81; active sex offender's assessment/treatment program. Mem. Assn. Treatment of Sexual Abuses, Am. Assn. Christian Counselors, Nat. Register Health Svc. Providers in Psychology, Tex. Psychol. Assn., Nat. Criminal Justice Assn. Republican. Methodist. Avocations: teaching Sunday school, travel cruises, fine dining. Home: 1200 Noel Ct College Station TX 77845-8756 Office: Brazos Valley Christian Counseling Ste 160 1700 George Bush Dr East College Station TX 77840 E-mail: drroy3@cox-internet.com.

LUEPTOW, LLOYD BENJAMIN, retired sociologist; b. Columbus, Wis., Aug. 4, 1928; s. Benjamin Walter and Esther Elsie Lueptow; m. Margaret Basilia Guss; children: Diana, Steven. PhD, U. Wis., Madison, 1964. Assoc. prof. Ind. State U., Terre Haute, 1964—67, U. Akron, 1967—74, prof., 1974—88, prof. emeritus, 1989—. Author: (book) Adolescent Sex Roles and Social Change, 1984 (Scholarly Achievement award North Cen. Sociol. Assn., 1985); contbr. book chpts. Ensign USN, 1950—51. Grantee rsch. grantee, NIMH, 1975, Dept. Health, Edn. and Welfare, 1975, Research Grant, NSF, 1967. Mem.: So. Sociol. Soc., Human Behavior and Evolution Soc., Am. Sociol. Assn. Achievements include research that has shown that, contrary to the conventional wisdom regarding reductions in gender differences, there has been stability , even increased differences from the 1970s to the late 1990s. Avocation: sailing.

LUERS, WENDY WILSON WOODS, non-profit foundation executive; b. Ann Arbor, July 16, 1940; d. Ward Wilson and Patricia (Fay) Woods; m. William Turnbull, Jr., Apr. 1, 1967, (div. 1979); children: Connor, Ramsay; m. William Henry, Oct. 18, 1979. Student, U. Madrid, 1961; BA, Stanford U., 1962. Asst. editor San Francisco Mag., 1965-67; asst. prodr. Film Bullett, San Francisco, 1970; stringer Time Mag., 1964-71; commentator KOED TV, 1974-79; dir., spl. project Amnesty Internat.; cultural corr. Venevision TV, Caracas, 1982-83; dir. spl. projects Human Rights Watch, 1987-89; lectr. Nancy Nelson (Agent), N.Y., 1987-89; pres., founder, dir., cons. Found. for a Civil Soc., N.Y.C., 1990—; founder Project Justice in Times Transition Harvard U., 1992—. Mem. steering com. Harvard U., 1999—; bd. dirs. The Ind. Journalism Found., Civic Edn. Project, Fund for Arts and Culture in East and Ctrl. Europe, Olga Havel Found., Vaclav Havel Found., The Annenberg Sch. for Comm./U. So. Calif.; chair White Ho. Fellows N.Y. Regional Selection Panel, Washington, 1993—95; U.S. del. to Orgn. Security & Coop. in Europe Rev. Conf., Budapest, Hungary, 1994; cons. NBC White Paper Series on Urban Crisis. Contbr. articles to mags., newspapers and profl. jours. Founder, pres. Friends of Art & Preservation Embassies, Wash.; bd. dirs. The World Childhood Found.; presdl. apptd. Nat. Coun. on the Arts; mem. Luce Scholars Program, Coun. on Fgn. Rels., Womens Fgn. Policy Group, Leadership Coun. Internat. Rescue; dir. Municipal Advantage Fund Inc. Recipient Gratias Agit award Czech Foreign Ministry, 1997, State Order of the Dual White Cross award Pres. Kovac, Slovakia, 1998. Democrat. Roman Catholic. Avocation: tennis. Home: 254 E 68th St Apt 15A New York NY 10021-6015 Office: Found for Civil Society PO Box 2235 New York NY 10021 Fax: 212-717-5255. E-mail: wluers@fcsny.org.

LUERS, WILLIAM HENRY, foundation administrator, former art museum administrator; b. Springfield, Ill., May 15, 1929; s. Carl U. and Ann L. (Lynd) L.; m. Wendy Woods Turnbull, Oct. 18, 1979; children by previous marriage: Mark B., David L., William F., Amy L. AB, Hamilton Coll., 1951, LLD, 1984; MA, Columbia U., 1958; postgrad., Northwestern U., 1951-52. Commd. fgn. service officer Dept. State, 1957; vice consul Naples, Italy, 1957-59; 2d sec. Am. Embassy, Moscow, 1963-65, polit. counselor Caracas, Venezuela, 1969-73; dep. exec. sec. Dept. State, 1973-75; dep. asst. sec. for inter Am. affairs, Washington, 1975-77; dep. asst. sec. European affairs (Soviet-Eastern Europe), 1977-78; ambassador to Venezuela, Caracas, 1978-82, Czechoslovakia, Prague, 1983-86; pres. Met. Mus. Art, N.Y.C., 1986-99; pres., CEO U.N. Assn. USA, 1999—. Bd. dirs. Wickes Lumber Co., Vernon Hills, Ill., IDEX Corp., Northbook, Ill., Am. On Line L.Am., Fla., The Brazil Fund, Scudder New Asia and Korea Fund, Global High Income Fund; dir.'s visitor Inst. Advanced Study, Princeton, N.J., 1982-83; vis. lectr. Woodrow Wilson Sch., Princeton U., 1983; trustee Rockefeller Bros. Fund, N.Y.C. Mem. adv. bd. Trust for Mut. Understanding, N.Y.C.; trustee adv. coun. Appeal of Conscience Found., N.Y.C.; bd. dirs. Inst. for East West Studies, N.Y.C.; bd. trustees The Howard Gilman Found., N.Y.C. Fellow Am. Acad. Arts and Scis.; mem. Coun. Fgn. Rels., Econ. Club N.Y. (bd. dirs.). Episcopalian. Address: UNA-USA 801 2nd Ave New York NY 10017

LUERSSEN, FRANK WONSON, retired steel company executive; b. Reading, Pa., Aug. 14, 1927; s. George V. and Mary Ann (Swoyer) L.; m. Joan M. Schlosser, June 17, 1950; children: Thomas, Mary Ellen, Catherine, Susan, Ann. BS in Physics, Pa., State U., 1950; MSMetE, Lehigh U., 1951; LLD (hon.), Calumet Coll.; DPS (hon.), Xavier U. Metallurgist research and devel. div. Inland Steel Co., East Chicago, Ind., 1952-54, mgr. various positions, 1954-64, mgr. research, 1964-68, v.p. research, 1968-77, v.p. steel mfg., 1977-78, pres., 1978-85, chmn., 1983-92. Contbr. articles on steelmaking tech. to various publs. Trustee Northwestern U., 1980—; trustee, sec., treas. Munster Sch. Bd., 1957-66; trustee Mus. Sci. & Industry. With USNR, 1945-47. Named disting. alumnus Pa. State U. Fellow Am. Soc. Metals; mem. AIME (Disting. life mem., B.F. Fairless award, Howe meml. lectr. 1988-91), Am. Iron and Steel Inst. (Gary medal, chmn. 1989-90), Nat. Acad. Eng. Home and Office: 8226 Parkview Ave Munster IN 46321-1419

LUERSSEN, THOMAS GEORGE, pediatric neurosurgeon, educator; b. Phila., May 14, 1951; s. Frank Wonson and Joan (Schlosser) L.; m. Norma Jean Schlundt, Aug. 6, 1977; children: John Frank, Brian Thomas, Katharine Rose. BS, Purdue U., 1973; MD, Ind. U., 1976. Diplomate Am. Bd. Neurol. Surgery, Am. Bd. Ped. Neurol. Surgery. Intern Indiana U. Hosp., 1976-77, resident, 1977-81; fellow Children's Hosp. Phila., 1983-84; clin. instr. U. Pa., 1983-84; asst. prof. U. Calif. Med. Ctr., San Diego, 1984-88; assoc. prof., dir. pediatric neurosurgery J.W. Riley Hosp. for Children, Ind. U. Sch. Medicine,

Indpls., 1988-96, prof. neurol. surgery, 1996—. Contbr. over 30 chpts to books, over 80 articles to profl. jours. Office: One Children's Sq JW Riley Hosp for Children Indianapolis IN 46202-5200

LUESCHER, ANDREAS, architecture educator; b. Basel, Switzerland, July 26, 1961; came to U.S., 1990; s. Paul Luescher and Maja Weber; m. Frances Elgood, Dec. 14, 1994; 1 child, Annabelle Drew. AA, Inst. for Tech. Edn., 1986; BArch, Engr. Coll. Cen. Switzerland, Lucerne, 1990; MArch, Phila. Coll. Art and Design, 1993; PhD, Pa. State U., 1998. Draftsman Edmund Jourdan AG, Muttenz, Switzerland, 1978-82, Anton Giess Archtl. Office, Laufenburg, Switzerland, 1983, Andrea Roost Archtl. Office, Berne, Switzerland, 1984; bldg. supr. Straumann Hipp AG, Basel, 1984-90; project mgr. Checkpoint Charlie Bauprojekt GmbH, Berlin, 1993-94; prof. Savannah (Ga.) Coll. Art and Design, 1997-99; asst. prof. Bowling Green (Ohio) State U., 1999—. Invited spkr. Tulane U., New Orleans, 1999; spkr. Am. U., Beirut, 1997; adminstr. Inst. to Study Artifacts of Travel and Tourism, Pa. State U., 1995-97; archtl. cons. Town of Sissach, Switzerland; presenter in field. Contbr. articles to profl. jours., including Cities; Internat. Jour. Urban Policy and Planning, Digital Creativity, Jour. Ednl. Tech. Sys.; drawings and prints exhibited throughout U.S. and Europe, including Hochschule der Bildene Künste, Berlin, 1990, Vitra Design Mus., Weil am Rhein, Germany, 1990, Camera Obscura, Phila., 1992, Sign of the Future, Graz, Austria, 1993, Young Archs., Phila., 1995, Hoyt Nat., New Castle, Pa., 1995, 11th Ann. Grad. Rsch., University Park, Pa., 1996, Non-Sliver: Printing with Light, Phila., 1997, 19th Arts on the River, Savannah, Ga., 1998, 20 North Gallery, Toledo, 2001. Recipient Spirit of Excellence award Toledo 11/The News Channel, 2001; scholar IKEA Found. Switzerland, 1991-93, Swiss Friends of U.S., 1995. Mem. AIA (assoc., scholar 1996), Coll. Art Assn., Assn. Collegiate Schs. of Arch., Design Comm. Assn., Nat. Assn. Indsl. Tech. Office: Bowling Green State U Coll Tech Bowling Green OH 43403-0301 E-mail: aluesch@bgnet.bgsu.edu.

LUESSENHOP, ALFRED JOHN, neurosurgeon, educator; b. Chgo., Feb. 6, 1926; s. Alfred Lewis and Gertrude L.; m. Frances Matthews; children: Cynthia, Constance, John, Charles, Suzanne, Laura. BS, Yale U., 1949; MD, Harvard U., 1952. Intern U. Chgo. Hosps., 1952-53; resident in neurosurgery Mass. Gen. Hosp., Boston, 1953-59; research fellow in surgery Harvard U., Cambridge, 1959; vis. scientist NIH, Bethesda, Md., 1960; prof. surgery Georgetown U. Med. Sch., Washington, 1963—95, prof. emeritus, 1995, chief neurosurgery divsn. Contbr. numerous articles to profl. jours. Served with AUS, 1943-46. Mem. Am. Assn. Neurol. Surgery, Congress Neurosurgery, Am. Acad. Neurosurgery, Soc. Neurosurgery Republican. Presbyterian. Home: 4524 Foxhall Cres NW Washington DC 20007-1055

LUETKEHANS, LARA M. technology educator; b. Chgo., Nov. 23, 1967; d. Joseph Pierri and Joan Loretta Cerceo; m. Peter Gerard Luetkehans, Nov. 2, 1991; children: Joseph Peter, William Anthony. BA, Loyola U. Chgo., 1989; MA, Rosary Coll., 1992; PhD, U. Ga., 1998. Med. libr. Med. Coll. Ga., Augusta, 1992-96; asst. prof. No. Ill. U., DeKalb, 1997—. Contbr. articles and monographs to profl. jours.; also book chpt. Office: No Ill U Etra 219A Gabel Hall Dekalb IL 60115-4317 E-mail: luetke@niu.edu.

LUETKEHOELTER, GOTTLIEB WERNER (LEE LUETKEHOELTER), retired bishop, clergyman; b. Wheatwyn, Sask., Can., Nov. 16, 1929; s. Henry William and Marie Louise (Schlepper) L.; m. Betty Edwards, July 25, 1959; children— David Lee, Jonathan Richard BA, U. Sask., 1952; B.D., Lutheran Coll. and Sem., Saskatoon, Sask., 1955; S.T.M., Vancouver Sch. Theology, 1975; DD, St. John's Coll., U. Manitoba, 1990, Luth. Theol. Sem., Saskatoon, 2000. Ordained to ministry United Luth. Ch. in Am., 1955. Pastor Markinch-Wheatwyn-Cupar Parish, 1955-57; pastor St. Mark's Luth. Ch., Regina, Sask., 1957-61, Erloeser Luth. Ch., Phila., 1961-63, Faith Luth. Ch., Burnaby, B.C., Can., 1963-69, Trinity Luth. Ch., Edmonton, Alta., Can., 1969-76; bishop Central Can. Synod, Luth. Ch. in Am., Winnipeg, Man., Can., 1976-85; bishop Man./Northwestern Ont. Synod, Evang. Luth. Ch. in Can., 1985-94; ret., 1994. Mem. exec. coun. Luth. Ch. in Am., N.Y.C., 1978-85, Anglican-Luth. Dialogue, Can., 1983-95; dir. Can. Luth. World Relief, 1989-98; lectr. Univ. Winnipeg, 1997-98. Bd. govs. Luth. Theol. Sem., Saskatoon, 1976-94, Schmieder resident, 1994-95, lectr. Luth. Theol. Sem., 1995-96. With Royal Can. Navy, 1952-54. Avocations: golf; swimming, writing. E-mail: leelue@gatewest.net.

LUETSCHWAGER, MARY SUSAN, transportation company professional; b. Bloomingdale, Ind., Nov. 19, 1937; d. William Blaine Shade and Goldina VandaVeer (Newlin) Brown; children: Roger, Tisa, Julia, Angela, Robert, William; m. Bruce E. Luetschwager, Sept. 9, 2000. Grad. high sch., Rockville, Ind. Sec., treas. Tri-State Transport, Inc., 1968-73; road driver Roadway Express, Chicago Heights, Ill., 1977—, safety team capt., 1991-92, 94. Completed Passport Tour (Abate), 1990, 94, 2000; mem. Roadway Express Dist. Road Team Dist. 12, 1995-97. Past mem. newsletter com. focus group Roadway Express; mem. focus group Kenworth Driver's Bd., 1992—; active Motorcycle Safety Found., Motorcycle Rider Course; instr. ABATE of Ind., Ind. Dept. of Edn. Recipient truck driving competition awards and motorcycle rally trophies, 3d place 8/48 rally Motorcycle Endurance Rider's Assn., 1996; 1st woman to finish on a Harley-Davidson motorcycle World Famous Iron Butt Rally, 1995, finished 6th place out of 78 starts and 61 finishers in 8th Iron Butt Rally, 1997, placed 3d in twin-trailer truck driving championships in Ill., 2000, 1st, 2001, grand champion, 2001; placed 2nd in competition at Delta Nu Alpha truck driving fraternity in Rockford Ill, 2000, 01, 1st pl. award (grand champion overall) in twin-trailer divsn. of truck driving championships, Ill., 2001; named Ill. TDC Sportsman of the Yr., 1995. Mem. Am. Motorcycle Assn., Am. Bikers Aim Toward Edn., Am. Radio Relay League, Harley Owners Group (newsletter editor Calumet region chpt. 1994-96, Hammond, Ind., asst. dir. Calumet region chpt. 1996-99, 2002, historian, 2000—), Ladies of Harley. Avocations: motorcycle endurance riding, amateur radio. Home and Office: PO Box 316 Griffith IN 46319-0316

LUFFSEY, WALTER STITH, air transportation executive, consultant; b. Richmond, Va., Mar. 15, 1934; s. Roland Emmit and Bernice Irene (Hall) L.; m. Louise Arlington Hicks, Dec. 19, 1956; children: Dennis Glenn, Melinda Denise. Student, U. Richmond, 1952-55, Agrl. Dept. Grad. Sch., 1963-65. With FAA, 1957—, supervisory air traffic control specialist, 1960-63, air traffic control specialist research, 1963-65, sr. air traffic control analyst systems research and devel. service, 1965-71, chief program analysis and reports br., 1971-72, asst. chief program mgmt. staff, 1972-73, spl. asst., assoc. adminstr. for engring. and devel., 1973-74, chief program mgmt. staff system research and devel. service, 1974-75, tech. asst., assoc. adminstr. policy devel. and rev., 1975-78, tech. asst., assoc. adminstr. policy and internat. aviation affairs, tech. asst. to the assoc. adminstr. for aviation standards, 1978-79, dep. assoc. adminstr. for aviation standards, 1979-80, assoc. adminstr. for aviation standards, 1980-85, assoc. adminstr. for air traffic, 1985-86, dir. advanced aviation system design team, 1986-89; sr. v.p. ops. and planning Tech. and Mgmt. Assistance, Washington, 1989-90, exec. v.p., 1990-97; pres. WSL Enterprises, Arlington, 1989—. Author: Air Traffic Control: How to Become an FAA Air Traffic Controller, 1990; contbr. articles to profl. jours. Served with USAF/Va. Air N.G., 1955-58. Recipient Spl. Achievement award FAA, 1970, 78, 85, Disting. Svc. award Aviation Week and Space Tech.-Flight Safety Found., 1982, Laurel award, 2000, Sec.'s award, 1982, Meritorious Exec. award-Presdl. Rank, 1983, Adminstr.'s Superior Achievement award, 1985, others. Mem. AIAA (aero. policy com.), Soc. Sr. Aerospace Execs., Nat. Aero. Assn., Exptl. Aircraft Assn., Aircraft Owners and Pilots Assn., Profl. Women Contrs. Assn., Air Traffic Control Assn. (hon., chair publs. com., Meritorious Achievement award 1965, Tech. Writing 1st pl. award), John Marshall Cadet Alumni Assn., Soc. Airway Pioneers, Va. Aero. Hist. Soc., Order of Quiet Birdmen, Silver Wings Fraternity, Aero Club, Nat. Aviation Club (past pres., gov. emeritus), Kiwanis (past pres. Crystal City). Home and Office: WSL Enterprises 9115 Alexandria Dr Weeki Wachee FL 34613 E-mail: waltluffsey@prodigy.net.

LUFT, ERIC V.D. librarian, educator; b. Woodbury, N.J., Dec. 5, 1952; s. Alexander v.d. and Barbara Elaine (Meeker) L.; m. Jennifer Hamlin, June 23, 1979 (div. Nov. 1993); children: Sarah, Mary Grace. AB magna cum laude, Bowdoin Coll., 1974; MA, Bryn Mawr Coll., 1977, PhD, 1985; student, Columbia U. Rare Book Sch., 1988-89; MLS, Syracuse U., 1993; student, U. Va. Rare Book Sch., 1997. Cataloging asst., libr. asst. Bryn Mawr (Pa.) Coll., 1976-80, 81-82; hist. collections asst. Coll. Physicians Phila., 1980-81; instr. philosophy Villanova (Pa.) U., 1983-85; curator hist. collections SUNY Upstate Med. U. Health Scis. Libr., Syracuse, 1987—; manuscript cataloger, Coll. Environ. Science & Forestry SUNY, 1993; list owner ALHHS-L (online listserve), 1999—. Adj. instr. Humanistic Studies Ctr., Syracuse U., 1986-96, adj. instr. Sch. of Information Studies, Syracuse Univ. , 2002—. cons. rare book cataloging, 1994-96; proprietor Gegensatz Press, North Syracuse, N.Y., 1996—; participant internat. confs., Australia, Eng., Belgium, Can., Germany, Iceland; vis. lectr. U. Iceland, U. Copenhagen; freelance photographer specializing in rare books, 1981-90; facilities planning cons. St. Lawrence County Hist. Assn., N.Y., 1999-2000; adv. bd. World of Genetics, 2001—, World of Anatomy and Physiology, 2001—. Author: Hegel, Hinrichs and Schleiermacher on Feeling and Reason in Religion, 1987; editor: Schopenhauer: New Essays, 1988; contbg. editor: Biographical Dictionary of Literary Influences, the Nineteenth Century, 1800-1914, 2000-01; assoc. editor The Owl of Minerva, 1983-96, Libr. Synapse, 1995—; pronunciation editor: Biographical Ency. of 20th Century World Leaders, 1998-99; contbr. Young Hegelians, 1983, History and System, 1984, Hegel's Philosophy of Spirit, 1987, Existence of God, 1988, Hegel and his Critics, 1989, Dictionary Am. Biography, 1992-96, Scribner Ency. Am. Lives, 1997—, also articles to profl. jours.; contbr. to Magill's Guide to Military History, 2001, International Dictionary of Library Histories, 2001, Science and Its Times, 1999-2001, Ency. of N.Y. State, 2001, Ency. of N.J., 2000, Interdisciplinary Biographical Dictionaries of the Western World's Great Cultural Ideas, 2000-2002, Ency. of the Ancient World, 2002, Ground Warfare, 2002, Biographical Dictionary of Literary Influences, the Twentieth Century, 1914-2000, 2001, World of Genetics, 2001, World of Anatomy and Physiology, 2001, Science in Dispute, 2001—; mem. acad. adv. bds., World of Genetics, 2001, World of Anatomy and Physiology, 2001, World of Microbiology and Immunology, 2002, World of Earth, 2002. Vol. tutor Ethical, Legal and Social Issues in Medicine. Recipient Prologue prize, 1972, Brown Composition prize, 1974, Adèle Mellen prize for excellence in scholarship, 1985, Pres.'s award for excellence in L.S., SUNY Health Sci. Ctr., Syracuse, 1997, Murray Gottlieb prize Med. Libr. Assn., 1999, Links2Go Key Resource award, 2000; Surdna Rsch. fellow, 1973, Whiting fellow in humanities, 1982-83, Francis C. Wood Inst. for History of Medicine fellow, 1984, 99, U.S. Dept. Edn. fellow, 1992-93. Mem. N.Am. Nietzsche Soc., Hume Soc., Am. Philos. Assn. (life mem.), Metaphysical Soc. Am., Hist. Soc. (charter), Hegel Soc. Am. (councillor 1988-92, sec. 1992-94), N.Y. State Assn. European Historians, Interdisciplinary 19th Century Studies, Friends of Book Arts Press, Documentary Heritage Com. Ctrl. N.Y., Internat. Soc. Intellectual History, Soc. for Bioethics and Classical Philosophy, Librs. in History of Health Scis., Am. Phil. Assn. (life), Bowdoin Alumni Club Ctrl. N.Y. (pres. 1985-92). Democrat. Avocations: bridge (life master Am. Contract Bridge League), chess, genealogy, fishing, carpentry. Home: 108 Deborah Ln N Syracuse NY 13212-1931 Office: SUNY Upstate Med Univ Health Scis Libr 766 Irving Ave Syracuse NY 13210-1602 E-mail: gegensatz@alumni.bowdoin.edu.

LUFT, HERBERT, history educator, former dean; b. Frankfurt, Germany, Aug. 17, 1942; came to U.S., 1961; s. Theodor and Hedwig (Theismann) L.; married; children: Sebastian, Rebecca. BA, Pepperdine U., 1965, MA, 1966; PhD, U. So. Calif., 1976. Mem. faculty Pepperdine U., Malibu, Calif., 1967—, prof. history, 1982—, exec. v.p., 1981-83, dean European programs Malibu, London, Heidelberg (Germany) and Florence (Italy), 1983—91. Mem. Kiwanis, Phi Alpha Theta. Mem. Ch. of Christ. Home: 24255 PCH Malibu CA 90263-4225 Office: Pepperdine U Malibu CA 90263-4225 E-mail: herbert.luft@pepperdine.edu.

LUFT, RENE WILFRED, civil engineer; b. Santiago, Chile, Sept. 21, 1943; came to U.S., 1968; s. David and Malwina (Kelmy) L.; m. Monica Acevedo, Aug. 24, 1970; children: Deborah Elaine, Daniel Eduardo, Allegra Filomena; m. Laura J. Gigante, July 11, 1998. CE, U. Chile, 1967; MS, MIT, 1969, DSc, 1971. Registered profl. engr., Alaska, Calif., Wash., Mass., Nev., N.H., R.I., Republic of Chile; registered structural engr., Vt. Asst. prof. civil engring. U. Chile, 1967-68; research asst. MIT, Cambridge, Mass., 1969-71, vis. lectr., 1983-84; staff engr. Simpson, Gumpertz & Heger Inc., Arlington, 1971-74, sr. staff engr., 1975-78, assoc., 1978-83, sr. assoc., 1984-90, prin. San Francisco, 1990—, head design div., 1991-95. Sec. seismic adv. com. Mass. Bldg. Code Commn., 1978-80, chmn., 1981-82; mem. Boston seismic instrumentation com. U.S. Geol. Survey; mem. slabs on ground com. Post-Tensioning Inst., 1994—, also chmn. structural subcom., bd. dirs., 2001—. Contbr. articles to profl. jours. Mem. bldg. seismic safety coun. Earthquake Hazards Reduction Program, 1983-91. Mem. ASCE (outstanding award for paper 1995), Boston Soc. Civil Engrs. (chmn. seismic design adv. com. 1981-86, Clemens Herschel award for tech. paper 1980, pres.'s award for leadership in earthquake engring. 1984), Am. Concrete Inst., Earthquake Engring. Resch. Inst., Structural Engrs. Assn. Calif. (chmn. rsch. com. 2001—), NSPE (Young Engr. of Yr., 1979), Sigma Xi, Chi Epsilon. Home: 206 Windsor Dr Petaluma CA 94952-7516 Office: 222 Sutter St Ste 300 San Francisco CA 94108-4445 E-mail: rluft@sgh.com.

LUFTGLASS, MURRAY ARNOLD, corporate financial executive; b. Bklyn., Jan. 2, 1931; s. Harry and Pauline (Yaged) L.; children by previous marriage: Paula Jean, Bryan Keith, Robert Andrew, Richard Eric; 1 child from 2d marriage: Andrew William. BS, Ill. Inst. Tech., 1952; MS, U. So. Calif., 1959; MBA, U. Conn., 1972. With Shell Chem. Co., Torrance, Calif., 1955-60, 64-66, N.Y.C., 1960-61, 66-69, Wallingford, Conn., 1961-64; asst. gen. mgr. Westchester Plastics div. Ametek, Inc., Mamaroneck, N.Y., 1969-75, dir. corp. devel. N.Y.C., 1975-76, v.p., 1976-83, sr. v.p. corp. devel., 1984-96; mng. dir. M&A London, LLC, 1996—. Contbr. articles to profl. jours., publs.; patentee in field. Lt. (j.g.) USN, 1952-55. Mem. NAM, Soc. Plastics Industry, Assn. Corp. Growth, Soc. Plastics Engrs., Tau Beta Pi, Beta Gamma Sigma, Phi Lambda Upsilon, Univ. Club (N.Y.C.). Office: M&A London LLC PO Box 150 Montclair NJ 07042-0150

LUGAR, RICHARD GREEN, senator; b. Indpls., Apr. 4, 1932; s. Marvin L. and Bertha (Green) L.; m. Charlene Smeltzer, Sept. 8, 1956; children: Mark, Robert, John, David. BA, Denison U., 1954; BA, MA (Rhodes scholar), Oxford (Eng.) U., 1956. Mayor, Indpls., 1968-75; vis. prof. polit. sci. U. Indpls., 1976; mem. from Ind. U.S. Senate, 1977—, chmn. com. fgn. rels., 1985-86, chmn. com. on agr., nutrition and forestry, 1995-2001; chmn. Nat. Rep. Senatorial Com., 1983-84. Pres. Lugar Stock Farm, Inc.; mem. Indpls. Sch. Bd., 1964-67, v.p., 1965-66; vice chmn. Adv. Commn. on Intergovtl. Relations, 1969-75; pres. Nat. League of Cities, 1970-71; mem. Nat. Commn. Standards and Goals of Criminal Justice System, 1971-73; Del., mem. resolutions com. Republican Nat. Conv., 1968, del., mem. resolutions com., 1992, Keynote speaker, 1972, del., speaker, 1980., 88, 92, 96. Author: Letters to the Next President, 1988. Trustee Denison U., U. Indpls., 1970-2002; bd. dirs. Nat. Endowment for Democracy, 1992-2000. Served to lt. (j.g.) USNR, 1957-60. Pembroke Coll., Oxford U. hon. fellow. Mem. Rotary, Blue Key, Phi Beta Kappa, Omicron Delta Kappa, Pi Delta Epsilon, Pi Sigma Alpha, Beta Theta Pi. Methodist. Office: US Senate 306 Hart Senate Bldg Washington DC 20510-0001

LUGBILL, ANN, lawyer; b. P.R., Jan. 9, 1954; BA, Kalamazoo (Mich.) Coll., 1976; JD, U. Va., 1980. Bar: Ohio 1980, D.C. 1999, U.S. Dist. Ct. (so. dist.) Ohio 1981, U.S. Ct. Appeals (6th cir.) 1983, U.S. Supreme Ct. 1997, U.S. Dist. Ct. (no. dist.) Ohio 1998, U.S. Dist. Ct. D.C. 1999. Atty. U.S. Dept. of Labor, Cin., 1980-82, Helmer, Lugbill, Martins & Morgan Co. and predecessor firm, Cin., 1983-98; counsel Manley, Burke & Lipton, 1999—2001. Mem. Ohio Splty. Bd. for Labor and Employment Law Cert., 1997—. Author: (with Helmer) Representing the Terminated Employee in Ohio, 1990, 2d edit., 1997; (with Helmer, Neff) False Claims Act: Whistleblower Litigation, 1994, 2d edit., 1999. Pres. Oakley Residents Assn., Cin., 1982-85; bd. dirs. City of Cin. Cable Communications Bd., 1983-85; trustee Talbert House, Cin., 1983—, v.p., 1987-89, pres., 1989-91; trustee Found. for Talbert House, 2001—; pres. local sch. decision making com. Sands Montessori Sch., 1996-98; bd. dirs. Cin. Parents for Pub. Schs., 1997—. Mem. ABA, AFL-CIO, Lawyers Coordinating Com., ATLA, Ohio Acad. Trial Lawyers, Nat. Employment Lawyers Assn. (Ohio bd. dirs.), Cin. Bar Assn. (grievance com. 1993—), Ohio Acad. Trial Lawyers, Ohio Bar Assn., Fed. Bar Assn., Cincinnatus Assn. (sec. and treas. 1999-2001), Hamilton County Trial Lawyers Assn. (charter), Potter Stewart Am. Inn Ct. (Master Emeritus). Office: 2406 Auburn Ave Cincinnati OH 45219-2702 E-mail: alugbill@choice.net.

LUGENBEEL, EDWARD ELMER, publisher; b. Balt., June 6, 1932; s. Nimrod Augustus and Victoria Elizabeth (Shilling) L.; m. Alice Marie Smith, June 12, 1953; children: Craig Edward, Susan Elizabeth, Douglas Paul, Leslie Jean. BS, U. Md., 1954. With Prentice-Hall, Inc., N.J., 1957-76, exec. editor, asst. v.p., 1972-76; pres. D. Van Nostrand Co., div. Litton Ednl. Pub., Inc. (pubs. coll. textbooks), N.Y.C., 1976-81; v.p. Lynne Palmer Exec. Recruitment, Inc., 1981-83; v.p., editl. dir. W.B. Saunders Med. Pubs., Phila., 1983-85; exec. editor Columbia U. Press, N.Y.C., 1985-98, ret., 1998-99. Cons. Columbia U. Earth Inst. Tchr. Tai Chi, Rockland County, N.Y., 1999—, SUNY-Rockland Cmty. Coll., 2000—, Ramapo, Clarkstown and Nyack Sr. ctrs., Fountainview Sr. Residence, Pomona YM/YWHA. Served as 1st lt. USAF, 1954-57. Mem. AAAS, Am. Inst. Biol. Scis., Am. Geophys. Union, Soc. Vertebrate Paleontology, Internat. Assn. Landscape Ecology, Soc. Conservation Biology, Nyack Tai Chi Acad., Shukokai World Karate Union (Brown Belt), Delta Sigma Pi.

LUGER, DONALD R. engineering company executive; b. May 12, 1938; s. George A. and Elizabeth M. Luger; m. Pat Sanders, Feb. 17, 1968 (dec. 1982); m. Sharon L. Luger, May 14, 1983; children: Christopher Daniel, Morgan Kathleen. BCE, Auburn U., 1962, MSCE, 1964; exec. program, Stanford U., 1979. Registered profl. engr., N.C., Ga., Mich., Va., N.Y. Structural engr. NASA, Huntsville, Ala., summer 1962; area engr. E.I. DuPont Co., Nashville, 1964; structural engr. Hayes Internat. Corp., Huntsville, 1964-65; resident engr. Fibers Industries, Inc., Shelby, N.C. and, Greenville, S.C., 1965-66; project mgr. Lockwood Greene Engrs., Inc., Atlanta, 1967-71, 1971-74, v.p., corp. dir., 1974-78, sr. v.p., corp. dir., 1978-82, pres., 1982-99, CEO, 1983-99, chmn., 1989; pres. D.R. Luger Enterprises, 1999—. Dir. Kliklok Corp., 1999, Qore Inc., 2001; owner Chem. Svcs., 2000; adv. bd. N.Am. br. AMEC, 2001. Mem. ASCE, NSPE, Ga. Soc. Profl. Engrs., Auburn U. Alumni Assn., Auburn Alumni Engring. Coun., Commerce Club, Atlanta Athletic Club. Office: CSP Inc Bldg 8 Ste 1000 3312 N Berkeley Lake Rd NW Duluth GA 30096

LUGER, GEORGE FLETCHER, computer science and psychology educator, consultant; b. Spokane, Wash., Dec. 1, 1940; s. George F. and Loretta C. (Maloney) L.; m. Kathleen Kelly, Aug. 25, 1969; children: Sarah, David, Peter. BS, Gonzaga U., 1963, MS, 1965, Notre Dame U., 1969; PhD, U. Pa., 1973. Rsch. fellow dept. of artificial intelligence U. Edinburgh, Scotland, 1974-79; prof. computer sci. and psychology U. N.Mex., Albuquerque, 1979—. Cons. in field., U.S. and Europe, 1983—. Author: Artificial Intelligence & Design of Expert Systems, 1989, Artificial Intellegence: Structures and Strategies for Complex Problem Solving, 1993, Cognitive Science: The Science of Intelligent Systems, 1994. Grantee NSF, U.S. Dept. Edn., U.S. Dept. Def. Mem. IEEE, Assn. for Computing Machinery, Am. Assn. for Artificial Intelligence, Cognitive Sci. Soc. Avocations: Libros et Liberos. Office: U NMex Dept Of Computer Sci Albuquerque NM 87131-0001

LUGER, STAN, political science educator; b. N.Y.C., Jan. 24, 1956; s. Benjamin and Selma Luger; m. Madeline Milian, Sept. 18, 1999. BA cum laude, SUNY, Oswego, 1978; MA, U. Toronto, Can., 1982; PhD, CUNY, 1988. Asst. prof. polit. sci. Russell Sage Coll., Troy, N.Y., 1987-90; prof., chair polit. sci. U. No. Colo., Greeley, 1990—. Chair faculty senate U. No. Colo., 1997-99. Author: Corporate Power, American Democracy and the Automobile Industry, 2000. Del. Dem. Nat. Conv., N.Y.C., 1992; treas. Universal Health Care Action Network, Boulder, Colo., 1993-96. Recipient Tchg. Excellence award, Mortar Board Honor Soc., 1992, 1994, 1995, 1998, 1999. Mem.: AAUP, Am. Polit. Sci. Assn. (Michael Harrington award 2001). Office: Dept of Polit Sci U No Colo Greeley CO 80639 E-mail: sluger@unco.edu.

LUGG, MARLENE MARTHA, health information systems specialist, health planner; b. Wauwatosa, Wis., Mar. 6, 1938; d. Armand Werner and Elise (Kuehni) Heinrich; m. Richard S.W. Lugg, June 11, 1966 (div. Dec. 1976); children: Jennifer Elsie, William Thomas Armand. BS, U. Wis., 1960; MPH, U. Pitts., 1966, DrPH, 1981. Dep. chair Nat. Com. on Health and Vital Stats., Canberra, Australia, 1973-83; dir. State Ctr. for Health Stats. and Planning Health Dept. Western Australia, Perth, 1966-83; dir. health info. systems program UCLA, 1983-88; vis. prof. pub. health Calif. State U., Northridge, 1987—; health info. systems specialist Kaiser-Permanente-So. Calif., Pasadena, 1988-98; immunization coord./sr. rschr. Kaiser Permanente, Panorama City, Calif., 1998—. Cons. software applications, L.A., 1987—; examiner L.A. Civil Svc. Commn., 1986-88; vis. prof. Pasadena City Coll., 1992—; mem. Calif. State Health Info. Policy Interagy. Com., 1992-94; mem. Calif. Health Data Coordinating Coun., 1995—; bd. dirs. Pub. Health Found. Enterprises, L.A., sec., 1995—; co-chmn. L.A. Immunization Coalition, 2000—; mem. Calif. Coalition for Childhood Immunization, 2000—, Nat. Network Immunization Nurses and Assocs., 2001—. Author: Medical Manpower in Western Australia, 1978; contbg. editor Australian Health Rev., 1998—; contbr. articles on injury, health data systems, immunization, air quality and illness, injury control and Pub. Health Conf. stats./records to profl. jours. Leave No Trace Master Educator, 1998—; Leader, trainer Girl Scouts U.S.A., Milw., Pitts., L.A., 1956—, Australian Girl Guides, Perth, Australia, 1966-82; instr. trainers Girl Scouts U.S.A., 1995—; explorer leader, trainer Boy Scouts Am., Western L.A. and Verdugo Hills, 1983-99; venturer leader/trnr. Boy Scouts Am., Verdugo Hills, 1999—; del. Girl Scouts Nat. Coun., 1996—. Recipient Broughton award Izaak Walton League Am., Wis., 1966, Fisher award Am. Med. Technologists, 1971, Outstanding Young Person award Jaycees, Perth, Australia, 1977, Take Pride in Am. award U.S. Govt., Washington, 1990, Wm. T. Hornaday Gold medal Boy Scouts Am., 1991, Silver Beaver Boy Scouts Am., 1999, Venturer Adult Leadership award, 1999, Thanks Badge Girl Scouts U.S.A., 1990, Thanks Badge II, 2000, Outstanding Family award Girl Scouts San Fernando Valley, 1992, UN Environ. Conservation award, 1992, Wm. Spurgeon award, 1995, Nat. Vohs Quality award Kaiser Permanente, 1995, Spotlight on Leadership award Kaiser Permanente, 1999; named Career Woman of Yr., Daily News, 1983, Woman of the Year San Fernando Valley Girl Scouts, 1995; Nat. Health and Med. Rsch. Coun. pub. health fellow, Australia, 1978, Outstanding Cmty. Svc. Alumni award U. Wis., Milw., 1997. Fellow APHA, Australian Coll. Health Execs. (state bd. dirs. 1977-82), Royal Soc. Health, London; mem. Internat. Epidmiological Assn., So. Calif. Pub. Health Assn. (bd. dirs. 1987-95), N.Y. Acad. Scis. Lutheran. Achievements include research in development of serial section microcinematography, large linked databases, and vaccine safety studies. Office: Kaiser-Permanente So Calif 13652 Cantara St Panorama City CA 91402-5423 E-mail: marlene.m.lugg@kp.org.

LUGINBILL, HEATHER ANN FANGMANN, secondary educator, English; b. Wichita, Kans., Sept. 22, 1973; d. Ronald George and Joice Mary Fangmann. BSE in English, Emporia State U., 1996. Cert. English educator, 5-12. Substitute tchr. USD 394/260, Rose Hill/Derby, Kans., 1996-97; tchr. English USD 490, El Dorado, 1997—. Tchr. Sylvan Learning Ctr., Wichita, 1997-98. Author: (poem) Quivira, 1995. Mem. Assistance League of Wichita, 1995—. English scholar Emporia State U., 1993-96. Mem. Nat. Coun. Tchrs. English. Republican. Avocations: soccer, poetry, running, reading. Home: 1275 S Topeka St El Dorado KS 67042-3791 E-mail: hluginbill@kscable.com., hluginbill@eldoradoschools.org.

LUGINBUHL, BENJAMIN RYAN, music educator; b. Peoria, Ill., Mar. 19, 1976; s. Raymond Gene and Carol Lee Luginbuhl; m. Kristina Chavis Stoller. MusB in Edn., U. of Ill., 1998. Vocal music tchr. Normal Cmty. H.S., Normal, Ill., 1998—. Mem.: Nat. Music Edn. Assn., Am. Choral Dir. Assn., Ill. Music Educators Assn. Home: 19 McCormick Blvd. Normal IL 61761 Office: Normal Community High School 303 Kingsley Normal IL 61761 Fax: 309-454-1845. Business E-Mail: luginbbr@unit5.org.

LUGO, MARK-ELLIOTT, curator; s. Claire Sara Lugo. BA, San Diego State U., 1968—73; MLIS, San Jose State U., 1997—2002. Art critic Union-Tribune Publishing Co., San Diego, 1982—86, San Diego Mag., San Diego, 1987—91; libr. asst., visual arts program coord. San Diego Pub. Libr., 1997—2001, visual arts librarian, curator, 2001—. Libr. curator, visual arts program coord. San Diego Pub. Libr., San Diego, 1997—2002; indep. curator Oceanside Mus. of Art, Oceanside; host profiles city access TV artist interview program. Contbr. articles. Mem.: Combined Orgns. for the Visual Arts (adv. bd. 1992—2002). Office: San Diego Public Library 820 E St San Diego CA 92101 Business E-Mail: mlugo@sandiego.gov.

LUGO, SONIA I. pharmacist, educator; d. Ruben Lugo and Ana Mercedes Lopez; m. Homero A. Monsanto, July 21, 1984. BS of Pharmacy, U. P.R., San Juan, 1982; MS, Purdue U., 1987; PhD, U. Md., 1994. Registered pharmacist. Asst. prof. Sch. of Pharmacy, U. PR.., San Juan, 1993—97; assoc. prof. Sch. of Medicine, 1996—98, Sch. of Pharmacy, U. PR.., San Juan, 1997—. Vis. prof. U. Panama, 2001. Contbr. rsch. articles to profl. jours. Cancer awareness activist Coalicion para prevenir cancer de mama y cervix, San Juan, 1999—2002; coord. fund raising Susan G. Komen, 1997—2002. Recipient Cancer Edn. and Prevention Cert. of Recognition, Cancer Info. Ctr. and P.R. Cancer Ctr., 2000. Master: PRIDCO (scholar 1991—94); fellow: Am. Found. for Pharm. Edn.; mem.: Am. Assn. of Colls. of Pharmacy, Am. Assn. of Pharm. Scientists, Am. Pharm. Assn. (student's chpt. co-advisor 1996—2002). Office: U PR Sch Pharmacy PO Box 365067 San Juan PR 00936-5067 Personal E-mail: slugo@rcm.upr.edu. E-mail: slugo@rcm.upr.edu.

LUH, HOWARD H. aerospace engineer; b. Tainan, Taiwan, Dec. 18, 1936; came to U.S., 1963; BS, Cheng-Kung U., Tainan, 1959; MS, Tex. A&M U., 1964; PhD, U. Calif., Berkeley, 1969. Prin. engr. Radiation Sys., Inc., McLean, Va., 1969-72; sr. tech. Space Sys./Loral, Palo Alto, Calif., 1972—. Contbr. over 37 articles to profl. jours.; patentee (18) in field. Mem. IEEE (chmn. antenna propagation Santa Clara Valley 1984-85). Office: Space Systems/Loral 3825 Fabian Way Palo Alto CA 94303 E-mail: luh.howard@ssd.loral.com.

LUH, JOHN ZENYOUNG, civil engineer; b. Taipei, Taiwan, Aug. 17, 1952; came to U.S., 1985; s. Shen (Chou) Luh; m. Tracy Y. Lo, Oct. 20, 1979; children: Anthony, Daniel. BS, Nat. Chengchi U., Taipei, 1975; MS, Nat. Taiwan U., 1979; PhD, U. Fla., 1989. Registered profl. engr., Fla., N.J., N.Y. Traffic engr. Taiwan Govt., Taipei, 1980-85; grad. rsch. asst. U. Fla., Gainesville, 1985-89; traffic engr. Langan Engring., Inc., Elmwood Park, N.J., 1989-93; sr. traffic engr. Glace & Radcliffe, Inc., Maitland, Fla., 1993-95; sr. transp. engr. IV Post, Buckley, Schuh & Jernigan, Orlando, 1995—. Adj. prof. U. Ctrl. Fla., Orlando, 1994—. Contbr. articles to profl. jours.; reviewer Transp. Rsch. Jour., 1992—. Mem. ASCE, Inst. Transp. Engrs. (tech. advisor 1989—, mem. tech. com. 1990-93, Best Paper award 1987, 88), N.Am. Chinese Transp. Profls. Assn. Home: 1223 Sunshine Tree Blvd Longwood FL 32779-7057 Office: Post Buckley Schuh & Jernigan Inc 482 S Keller Rd Orlando FL 32810-6101

LUHMAN, WILLIAM SIMON, community development administrator; b. Belvidere, Ill., May 15, 1934; s. Donald R. and H. Elizabeth (Rudberg) L. AB, Park Coll., 1956; MA, Fla. State U., 1957. City planner City of Moline, Ill., 1959-64; planning dir. Rock Island County, 1964-66; exec. dir. Bi-State Met. Planning Commn., Rock Island, 1966-71; dir. regional devel. Northeastern Ill. Planning Commn., Chgo., 1971-74, assoc. dir., 1975-76, dep. dir., 1977-79, acting exec. dir., 1979-80, asst. dir., 1980-81; v.p. Pub. Mgmt. Info. Svc., 1981; asst. dir. No. Ill. U. Ctr. Govt. Studies, DeKalb, 1981-91, program coord., 1991; exec. dir. Growth Dimensions for Belvidere-Boone County, Ill., 1991—2001, pres., 1982-86, asst. dir., 2002—. Vis. instr. Augustana Coll., Rock Island, 1967, 69. Bd. dirs. Rockford Area Coun. of 100, 1983-86; Boone County Regional Planning Commn., 1986—, chmn., 1986-90, 2002—; mem. Belvidere-Boone County Regional Planning Commn., 1986—, chmn., 1990-92; bd. dirs. Sch. Dist. 100 Found. for Excellence in Edn., 1992-99; mem. Sch. Dist. 100 Citizens Adv. Coun., 1999—, Sch. Dist. 100 Cmty. Strat. Planning, 1999; bd. dirs. Boone County United Way, 1999—, No. Ill. Cmty. Found.; ; trustee Cmty. Foun. No. Ill., 2002; active Boone County Arts Coun., Friends of Ida Pub. Libr., Belvidere Sister Cities Assn.; Ill. Regional Pub. Libr. Svc. Planning Panelist, 1996. Mem. Am. Soc. Pub. Adminstrn., Am. Planning Assn., Internat. City Mgmt. Assn., Ill. Devel. Coun. Home: 1538 Fremont St Belvidere IL 61008-5939 Office: 200 S State St Belvidere IL 61008-3687 E-mail: bluhman@growthdimensions.org., bluhman@aol.com.

LUHN, ROBERT KENT, writer, magazine editor; b. Oakland, Calif., Nov. 23, 1953; s. Joel Adrian and Norma Jeanne (Arnold) L.; 1 child, Pudge. Student, U. Calif., Davis, 1972-76. Freelance writer, 1968—. Broadcaster, 1979-82; sr. editor PC World mag., San Francisco, 1983-90, contbg. editor, 1990-94; contbg. editor Calif. Republic mag., San Francisco, 1990-94, editor in chief Computer Currents Mag., 1994-2000; exec. editor CNET, 2000—. Author: The Swedish Catfish & Other Tales, 1979, Collected Works, Vol. 3, 1985, Going West, 1988, The Wit is Out, 1993; contbr. fiction, features and poetry to numerous publs., including Harper's, Mother Jones, Omni, Am. Film, Hudson Rev., Nantucket Rev., Christian Sci. Monitor, San Francisco Chronicle, Chgo. Tribune, Phila. Inquirer, PC mag., Computerworld, The Oregonian, Exec. Update, Grapevine Weekly; columnist Computer Currents, 1993-95. Adv. bd. mem. Baykeeper, San Francisco, 1994-96. Mem. ACLU, Amnesty Internat., Greenpeace, Environ. Defense Fund. Avocations: tennis, quoits, writing.

LUHN WOLFE, REBECCA ROSE, career educator, business consultant; b. Houston, Nov. 8, 1951; d. Reynold E. and Rose V. (DiDonna) L. Student, U. Houston, 1971-74; BBA, Rice U., 1982, MBA, 1983; PhD in Comm., U. Houston, 1984. Mgmt. devel. trainer Braniff Airlines Inc., Houston, 1975-77; comm. analyst Continental Airlines Inc., 1977-82; instr. Houston Cmty. Coll., 1982-85; owner Innovative Trng. Acad., Houston, 1982-87; instr. Rice U., 1987-89; owner, pres. Innovative Cons. Svcs., 1987—. Author: Building Business with Communication, 1983; Sales and Service Today, 1981; Careers in Travel, 1980; Management Motivation, 1981. Vol., Assistance League Houston, 1983, Arthritis Found., Houston, 1982-83, Tex. Assn. Pvt. Schs. Recipient Salesmanship award Delta Airlines, Houston, 1976, cert. of merit, 1982; Cert. of Approval, Tex. Edn. Agy., 1983; cert. of merit in mgmt. Rice U., 1983, cert. of merit in sales, mgmt. and tng. devel. Human Dimensions, Houston. Mem. Am. Soc. Tng. and Devel., Nat. Assn. Female Execs., Am. Assn. Women in Community and Jr. Colls., Women in Communication, Women in Edn., Pro Houston (Houston). Home: 7514 Woodridge Pl Houston TX 77055-5079 Office: Innovative Tng Acad 14 Houston TX 77079

LUHRS, CAROL, physician; b. N.Y.C., Dec. 29, 1951; d. Eugene Frederick and Jane Elsie Luhrs; m. David Robert Blumenthal, Apr. 12, 1981; children: Alex Michael, Kelly Anne. BA, Hunter Coll., 1973; MD, SUNY, Bklyn., 1977. Diplomate Am. Bd. Internal Medicine, Am. Bd. Hematology and Med. Oncology, Am. Bd. Palliative Medicine. Intern, resident in internal medicine Kings County Hosp.-Downstate Med. Ctr., Bklyn., 1977-80; fellow in hematology/oncology Bklyn. VA Med. Ctr., 1980-83, staff physician, 1983-84, NIH postdoctoral trainee in hematology, 1984-86, staff physician, 1986-94, chief hematology/oncology sect., 1995—; asst. prof. SUNY Hlth. Scis. Ctr., Bklyn., 1986-94, assoc prof. clin. medicine, 1996—. Contbr. articles to profl. jours. NIH grantee, 1986-91, VA grantee, 1992-95. Mem. Am. Soc. Hematology, Am. Fedn. Clin. Rsch., Am. Soc. Clin. Oncology. Office: Bklyn VA Med Ctr 800 Poly Pl Brooklyn NY 11209-7104

LUHRS, H. RIC, toy manufacturing company executive; b. Chambersburg, Pa., Mar. 22, 1931; s. Henry E. and Pearl (Beistle) L.; m. Grace B. Walke, June 12, 1973; children by previous marriage: Stephen Frederick, Christine Michelle, Terriann, Patricia Denise. BA, Gettysburg Coll., 1953; D of Pub. Svc. (hon.), Shippensburg U., 2000. With The Beistle Co., Shippensburg, Pa., 1948-53, 1959—; pres., gen. mgr. Beistle Co., 1962-90, chmn. bd., 1962—, pres, CEO, 1998—; pres. Lakeside Holding Co. Inc., Boca Raton, Fla., 1996—, A-1 Holdings, Inc., Boca Raton, 1998—. Bd. dirs. The Beistle Co., 1960—, First Nat. Bank of Shippensburg, 1964-80, Commonwealth Nat. Bank, 1980-91, Mellon Bank Commonwealth region, 1991-99, Boca Rsch. Inc., Boca Raton, 1998-2000, Inprimis, Inc., Boca Raton, 2000—; vice chmn. CompuPix Tech. Inc.; pres., 1986-88, gemologist, 1977—; owner Luhrs Gem Testing Lab., 1977—, Luhrs Jewelry, 1976—, Allied Leasing Co., Shippensburg, 1968; pres. South Lac Devel. Co., Boca Raton, Fla., 1986-92; owner Gun Depot, Shippensburg, 1992; chmn. The Walking Quail Sporting Goods Store, Shippensburg, 1994—; chmn. The Meadowlands Mall, Inc., Shippensburg, 1994—, pres., 1998—; chmn. TBHC, Inc., Wilmington, Del., 1994—, pres., 1998—, pres., CEO, 1999—. Chmn. Pub. Libr., 1964-66, 1970-72, 76-78, bd. dirs., 1963-82; chmn. TBHC, Inc., Wilmington, Del., 1994—, pres., 1998—; pres. Community Chest, 1965, bd. dir., 1963-72; pres. Shippensburg Area Devel. Corp., 1966-72; bd. dirs., trustee Carlisle (Pa.) Hosp., 1967-71, Chambersburg Hosp., 1969-75; mem. consumer adv. coun. Capital Blue Cross, 1976-78; bd. dirs. Fla. Atlantic U. Found., 1988-91, Shippensburg U. Found., 1991—. Capt. USAF, 1953-59. Mem. SAR (life), Shippensburg Hist. Soc. (life, bd. dirs. 1968), Shippensburg C. of C. (pres. 1965, bd. dirs. 1964-65), Toy Mfrs. Assn. (bd. dirs. 1969-71), Nat. Sml. Businessmen's Assn., NRA (life, benefactor), NRA Whittington Ctr. Founder's Club, NRA Golden Eagles, Shippensburg Fish and Game Assn. (life, pres. 1963), Carlisle Fish and Game Assn. (life), Pa. Flyers Assn., Am. Legion, VFW (life), Cumberland Valley Indsl. Mgmt. Club, York Printing House Craftsmen, Masons (32 deg.), Shriners, Tall Cedars of Lebanon, Green Jacket Club. Lutheran. Office: 1 Beistle Plz Shippensburg PA 17257

LUHTA, CAROLINE NAUMANN, airport manager, flight educator; b. Cleve., Mar. 26, 1930; d. Karl Henry and Fannie Arletta (Harlan) Naumann; m. Fred Harlan Jones, July 2, 1955 (div. 1961); m. Adolph Jalmer Luhta, Dec. 12, 1968 (dec. 1993); 1 child, Katherine Louise. BA, Ohio Wesleyan U., 1952; BS magna cum laude, Lake Erie Coll., Painesville, Ohio, 1977. Rsch. chemist Standard Oil Co. Ohio, Cleve., 1952-68; office mgr. Adolph J. Luhta Constrn. Co., Painesville, 1968-83; acct. Thomas Y. Ellis, CPA, 1978; bd. dirs. Painesville Flying Svc., Inc., 1968—, flight instr., 1970—, pres., 1993—. Bd. dirs. Concord Air Park, Inc., Painesville, 1968—, pres. 1993—; accident prevention counselor FAA, Cleve., 1975-85. Contbr. articles to profl. jours. Trustee Northeastern Ohio Gen. Hosp., Madison, 1973-83, chmn. bd. 1980-82; trustee Internat. Women's Air and Space Mus., Cleve., 1989—, treas. 1991-95, pres., 1997—; trustee Concord Twp., 1992—. Recipient Aerospace award Cleve. Squadron, Air Force Assn., 1966, Woman of Achievement award Lakeland C.C., 1999, Harvey High Sch. Alumni Assn. Hall Fame, 2001. Mem. Nat. Assn. Flight Instrs., Exptl. Aircraft Assn., Aircraft Owners and Pilots Assn., Ninety-Nines (life, chmn. All-Ohio chpt. 1969-70, Achievement award 1965, Amelia Earhart Meml. scholar 1970), Silver Wings (life), Order Ea. Star, Alpha Delta Pi (life). Avocations: air racing (Powder Puff Derby, All Women's Internat. Air Race). Office: Painesville Flying Svc Inc 12253 Concord Hambden Rd Painesville OH 44077-9566 E-mail: cluhta@iwasm.org.

LUI, ANTHONY TAT YIN, physicist; b. Hong Kong, Dec. 29, 1945; s. Siu Wai and Choi Dai (Chow) L.; m. Theresa Susan Szabo, Nov. 10, 1973; children: Jennifer, Michael, Victoria. BS, Hong Kong U., 1969; MS, U. Calgary, 1971, PhD, 1974. Postdoctoral fellow U. Calgary, 1974-75, U. Alaska, Fairbanks, 1975-76; rsch. assoc. NRC of Can., Ottawa, Ont., 1977-79, The Johns Hopkins U./Applied Physics Lab., Laurel, Md., 1979-83, sr. staff, 1984-85, prin. profl. staff, 1986—. Mem. steering com. of CDAW, NASA, Greenbelt, Md., 1984-90; mem. Grand Tour Cluster SDT, NASA Hdqts., Washington, D.C., 1990-92, mem. Mercury Orbiter SDT, 1996-99; mem. inter-agy. cons. group, NASA, 1993—; cons. Los Alamos Nat. Lab., N.Mex., 1990-95; external examiner for PhD degree, U. Calgary, Can., 1992. Editor: (book) Magnetotail Physics, 1987 (JHU/APL Outstanding Publ. 1987); assoc. editor Geophys. Rsch. Letters, 1997—; contbr. (book) Amazing Mysteries of the World, 1983; contbr. articles to profl. jours. Recipient Linkage grant, NATO, 1993-96. Mem. Am. Geophys. Union (chair student awards com. 1996-98). Home: 10809 Beech Creek Way Columbia MD 21044-1031 Office: Johns Hopkins U/Applied Phy 11100 Johns Hopkins Rd Laurel MD 20723-6005 E-mail: tony.lui@jhuapl.edu.

LUI, ERIC MUN, civil engineering educator, practitioner; b. Hong Kong, Feb. 2, 1958; came to U.S., 1977; s. Kui Leung and Yin Fong Lui. BS in Civil and Environ. Engring., U. Wis., 1980; MS in Civil Engring., Purdue U., 1982, PhD, 1985. Teaching asst. Purdue U., W. Lafayette, Ind., 1981-82, rsch. asst., 1983-85, post-doctoral rsch. asst., 1985-86, lectr., 1985-86; asst. prof. Syracuse (N.Y.) U., 1986-91, assoc. prof., 1992. Engring. cons. in field; advisor ASCE Student Chpt., 1992—, Hong Kong Cultural Assn., 1997—. Co-author: Structural Stability-Theory and Implementation, 1987, Stability Design of Steel Frames, 1991; editor (assoc.): ASCE Jour. Structural Engring., 1994—97; editor: (book), 1997—2000; author: monographs; contbr. more than 60 articles to profl. jours., papers to sci. procs., chapters to books. Recipient Bleyer scholarship U. Wis., 1979, Bates & Rogers Found. scholarship, 1980, David Ross fellowship Purdue U., 1982, 83; recipient Nellie Munsion award 1982, Crouse Hinds award for Excellence in Edn. Syracuse U., 1997. Mem. ASCE, AAUP, Am. Concrete Inst., Am. Acad. Mechanics, Am. Inst. Steel Constrn., Am. Soc. Engring. Edn., Coun. Tall Bldgs. and Urban Habitat, Structural Stability Rsch. Coun., Tau Beta Pi, Phi Kappa Phi, Sigma Xi. Avocations: painting, classical music, piano playing. E-mail: emlui@syr.edu.

LUI, VICTOR KING SHING, pediatrician; b. Hong Kong, Hong Kong, May 19, 1943; Came to the U.S., 1975; s. In Tso and Siu King (Chan) L.; m. Alice Y. Chan Lui, June 1975; children: George, Camillia. BSc, McGill U., Montreal, Canada, 1967, MD, 1971. Diplomate Am. Bd. Pediatrics. Asst. prof. Emory U., Atlanta, 1977-82. Mem. bd. dirs. Dekalb Bd. Health, 1997—. Home: 9 Powers Chase Cir NW Atlanta GA 30327-4625 Office: 3020 Mercer University Dr Atlanta GA 30341-4121 E-mail: viclui@pol.net.

LUIGS, CHARLES RUSSELL, retired gas and oil drilling industry executive; b. Evansville, Ind., Apr. 4, 1933; s. Charles Anthony and Agnes A. (Russell) L.; m. Mary M. McClaine, Sept. 7, 1957; children: Charles Edwin, James Russell, Carol Lynn, Susan Nadine, Michael Alan. BS in Petroleum Engring., U. Tex., 1957; student, St. Edwards U., 1951-52. With U.S. Industries, various locations, 1957-76, v.p., 1969-71, exec. v.p., 1971-74, pres., 1974-76; dir. U.S. Industries, 1971-76; pres., chief exec. officer, dir. Global Marine, Inc., 1977-98, chmn. bd., 1982-99; ret., 1999. Mem. NSPE. Home: PO Box 4577 Houston TX 77210-4577 Office: Global Marine Inc 777 N Eldridge Pkwy Ste 800 Houston TX 77079-4493

LUINE, JEROME ARTHUR, research physicist; b. San Diego, May 6, 1952; s. Arthur and Martha Belle (Bybee) L.; m. Mary Spear, May 28, 1977; children: Carynn Alice, Evan Arthur. BS in physics, Univ. Calif., 1974; PhD in physics, Univ. Colo., 1981. Lectr. Calif. State Univ., Carson, Calif., 1985—; sr. scientist TRW Space & Electronics, Redondo Beach, 1981—. Author: Science Mysteries, 1995; contbr. articles to profl. jours. Mem. com. to choose elem. sch. sci. texts Torrance Unified Sch. Dist., Torrance, Calif., 1993 Avocations: ancient numismatics, astronomy. Office: TRW M5 1075 One Space Park Redondo Beach CA 90278 Fax: 310 812 0542. E-mail: jerome.luine@trw.com.

LUING, GARY ALAN, financial management educator; b. Collins, Iowa, Apr. 24, 1937; s. Dwight Orn and Marjorie Mae (Clemons) L.; m. Sherry Lea Gates, Dec. 19, 1954; 1 child, Heather Sherry-Anne. BS cum laude, Stetson U., 1960; MA, U. Ill., 1961; Dr. Adminstrn. (hon.), Canadian Sch. Mgmt. Auditor Arthur Andersen & Co., Chgo., 1963; prof. Fla. Atlantic U., Boca Raton, 1965—, dean Sch. Bus., 1970-87. Cons. U.S. Treasury; expert witness on valuing closely held corps., 1972— , lectr., U.S., various fgn. countries; dir. Fla. Liquid Assets, Templeton Trust Co.; mem. faculty Internat. Assn. Fin. Planners Editor Fla. C.P.A., 1974; assoc. editor Intellect, 1975-79; tax editor Quick Print, 1988—; contbr. articles to profl. jours. Chmn. Palm Beach County Transp. Com., 1972-75; treas. Ridge Audubon Soc., 1997-98. Served to 1st lt. U.S. Army, 1961-63. Recipient Disting. Service Fla. Accountants Assn., 1991, Alumni Assn. award for Outstanding Svcs., Fla. Atlantic Univ., 1997. Hon. fellow Internat. Soc. Preventive Medicine, Canadian Sch. Mgmt.; mem. AICPA, Am. Acctg. Assn., Acctg. Rsch. Assn., Beta Gamma Sigma, Beta Alpha Psi, Phi Beta Phi (pres. 1974), Phi Kappa Phi. Baptist. Home: 2612 Lake Front Dr Lake Wales FL 33898-7206 E-mail: luing@msn.com., luing@fau.edu. *In the professions, as in life, so much is owed to those who have gone before.*

LUISELLI, JAMES KENNETH, psychologist; b. Malden, Mass., Jan. 12, 1949; s. James Louis and Christine Anne (Santoro) L.; m. Tracy Evans, May 28, 1990; children: Gabrielle Anna, Thomas Payton. BS in Psychology, Tufts U., 1971; MA in Clin. Child Psychology, Goddard Coll., Plainfield, Vt., 1974; EdD in Edn., Boston U., 1979. Lic. psychologist, Mass.; cert. health svc. provider, Mass.; diplomate Am. Bd. Profl. Psychology. Dir. Behavioral Intervention Project, Arlington, Mass., 1974-77; clin. psychologist Perkins sch. for the Blind, Watertown, 1979-89; pvt. practice Sudbury, 1979—; dir. applied rsch. and peer rev. The May Inst., Inc., Norwood, 1996—. Clin. affiliate in psychology McLean Hosp., Belmont, Mass., 1998—; instr. psychology Harvard Med. Sch., Boston, 1997—; adj. instr. spl. edn. Lesley Coll., Boston, 1980; clin. asst. prof. dept. counseling psychology and rehab. and spl. edn. Northeastern U., Boston, 1997—; attending child psychologist Franciscan Children's Hosp., Boston, 1997—, med./dental staff Franciscan Children's Hosp. and Rehab. Ctr., 1997—; cons. in field to pub. schs., various instns.; mem. profl. adv. com. Evergreen Ctr., Milford, Mass., 1991-96; adv. com. on behavioral intervention regulations Disability Law Ctr., Boston, 1994-95; profl. adv. com. Ctr. for Devel. of Human Svcs., Milford, 1994-96. Contbr. over 170 articles to profl. jours.; assoc. editor Edn. and Treatment of Children, 1981-84; bd. editors Edn. and Treatment of Children, 1984-86, Jour. of Developmental and Phys. Disabilities, 1988—, Behavior Modification, 1989—, Jour. Behavioral Edn., 1990—, Behavioral Interventions, 1996—, Mental Health Aspects of Developmental Disabilities, 1997—, Edn. and Treatment of Chidlren, 1999—, Handicap Grave: Ritardo Mentale e Plurimi-norazioni Sensoriali, 1999—; contbg. editor Habilitative Mental Healthcare Newsletter, 1992-96; editl. cons., guest reviewer Jour. of Pediat. Psychology, 1979, 88, Applied Rsch. in Mental Retardation, 1980, 85, Jour. Behavior Therapy and Exptl. Psychiatry, 1982, 85, 86, 89, 96, 97, 98, 2000, Behavior Modification, 1987, 88, Am. Jour. Mental Retardation, 1987, 88, 89, 90, Jour. of Applied Behavior Analysis, 1988, 94, 2000, Rsch. in Developmental Disabilities, 1989, 90, 91, 92, 93, 2000, Behavior Therapy, 1991, Ency. of Human Behavior, 1992; editor: Behavioral Medicine and Developmental Disabilities, 1989; co-editor: Self-Injurious Behavior: Analysis, Assessment and Treatment, 1991, Antecedent control: Innovative Approaches to Behavioral Support, 1998. Tufts U. Alex Elias Meml. Prize scholar, 1971, Boston U. Rsch. scholar, 1977-79, tchg. fellow, 1977-79. Mem. APA, Mass. Psychol. Assn., Berkshire Assn. for Behavior Analysis and Therapy. Avocations: music, athletics, reading. Office: 1 Commerce Way Norwood MA 02062-4628

LUIZZI, RONALD, wholesale distribution executive; b. Neptune, N.J., Apr. 7, 1953; s. Alfredo Luizzi and Mary Kay (Mumford) Figart; m. Kim T. Richardson, May 14, 1994. BA in Psychology, Trenton State Coll., 1975. Pres., chief exec. officer Profl. Divers, Inc., Neptune, 1975-78; nat. dir. projects Nat. Assn. Scuba Diving Schs., Long Beach, Calif., 1978-81; sales mgr. TW Systems, Inc., Honolulu, 1981-85; gen. mgr. TW Systems, Ltd.-Kona, Kailua-Kona, Hawaii, 1985-97, Sobel-Westex, 1998—. East coast regional dir. Nat. Assn. Scuba Diving Schs., Neptune, 1977-78. Contbg. author: (tng. manual) Gold Book, 1977, Safe Scuba, 1977. Scuba advisor YMCA-Kona, Kailua-Kona, 1985—. Mem. Nat. Assn. Instnl. Laundry Mgrs. (cert.), Hawaii Assn. Instnl. Laundry Mgrs. (allied), Nat. Exec. House Keepers Assn. (allied), Hawaii Hotel Assn. (allied), Rotary (sec. 1988-89, v.p. 1989-90, pres. 1990-91), Kona-Kohala C. of C. Avocations: scuba diving, sport fishing, racquetball, jogging, exotic bird collector. Home: 76-6303 Kaheiau St Kailua Kona HI 96740-2275 Office: Sobel-Westex Hawaii 77-6429 Kuakini Hwy Ste C104 Kailua Kona HI 96740-2227

LUJAN, BEN, state representative; Formerly iron worker with Zia Co., Los Alamos, N.Mex.; mem. N.Mex. Ho. of Reps., Dem. Ho. whip under speaker Ray Sanchez, Dem. majority leader under speaker Ray Sanchez, speaker, 2002—. Office: Speaker of the House Rm 104 State Capitol Santa Fe NM 87503*

LUK, TEI LEWIS, financial company executive; b. Shanghai, China, Dec. 5, 1960; arrived in Hong Kong, 1962; s. Chung Lam and Yu Mei (Shu) L.; m. Suk Ting Ng, Jan. 11, 1986; children: Henry, Hayens, Louisa. B in laws (hons.), U. London, London, U.K., 1983; diploma in acctg. and fin., Chartered Assn. of Cert. Accts, London, 1986. Trainee solicitor P.C. Woo & Co., Hong Kong, 1984-86, solicitor, 1986-88, Kenneth W. Leung & Co., Hong Kong, 1988-89; mng. ptnr. Lewis Luk & Co., 1989-91; exec. dir. Harbour Ring Industries Ltd., 1989—. Recipient Young Industrialist Hong Kong award, 1995. Avocations: swimming, table tennis, martial arts, reading.

LUKAC, GEORGE JOSEPH, fundraising executive; b. Garfield, N.J., Mar. 6, 1937; s. Michael and Elizabeth (Gall) L.; m. Alice Louise Osborn, Nov. 8, 1958; children: Mark Robert (dec.), Amy Elizabeth Lowell. BA in Polit. Sci., Rutgers U., 1958. Trainee, systems reviewer Prudential Ins. Co., Newark, 1958-59; asst. editor comm. dept. Johnson & Johnson, New Brunswick, N.J., 1959-61; editor Rutgers Alumni Monthly Rutgers U., 1961-66, asst. dir. alumni rels. and devel., 1966-77; exec. dir. Sangamon State U. Found., Springfield, Ill., 1977-81; dir. devel. and pub. rels. Mo. Hist. Soc., St. Louis, 1981-84; v.p. devel. Rio Grande (Ohio) U., 1984-86; exec. dir. St. Luke's Hosps. Meritcare Found., Fargo, N.D., 1986-90; pres., CEO Venice (Fla.) Hosp. Found., 1990-92; pres. Lehigh Valley Hosp. Trust Fund, Allentown, Pa., 1992-96; exec. dir. Meml. Devel. Found. Rockford (Ill.) Health Sys., 1996-97; dir. devel. Nat. Ctr. Genome Resources, Santa Fe, 1997-98; fin. devel. dir. N.M. and West Texas Am. Red Cross Nat. Headquarters, 1998-2000; exec. cons. resource devel. and mktg., 2000—. Vol. cons. Presbyn. Chs., Fargo, Ballwin, Mo., Venice, Fla., 1978—92, social welfare groups, Fargo, Ballwin, Venice, Allentown, Rockford and Santa Fe, 1978—; ofcl. cons. Ohio Arts Coun., Columbus, 1986; instr., adviser, spkr. univs., groups and confs., 1978—; jury mem. Bread Loaf Writers Conf., 1971, CASE Nat. Awards Contest, 1982; participant survery on globalization processes Duke, George Washington and Rutgers univs., 1999. Editor: Aloud to Alma Mater, 1966, Copyright-The Librarian and the Law, 1972 (Citation N.J. Writers Conf. 1974); contbr.: Big Gifts, 1990; contbr. articles to mags. and profl. jours. Loaned exec. United Way, Fargo, 1987-88, capt., com. mem., 1988-90; bd. dirs. Red. River Dance Co., Fargo, 1989-90; acct. exec. United Way, Rockford, 1997-98; v.p. bd. dirs. Ronald McDonald House, Fargo, 1987-90; mem. Indsl. Devel. Corp. of Lehigh Valley, 1992-96; vol. The Multiple Risk Factor Intervention Trial, Nat. Heart, Lung and Blood Inst, 1975-82; Rep. nat. com. Chmn.'s Campaign Adv. Panel, 1994-2000; vol. N.Mex. Cmty. Health Survey, NCI/U. N.Mex., 1999. Recipient Citation N.J. Writers Conf., 1974, Ashmead award Rutgers Fund, 1968,76, Spl. Recognition award CASE Nat. Alumni Mag. Competition, 1966, award Rutgers Fund, 1961. Mem.: Nat. Conf. Nonprofit Bds., Assn. Hosp. Philanthropy, Inst. on Philanthropy U. Ind. (nstr. cert. exam. 1997, charter assoc., panel of experts), Assn. Fundraising Profls. (cert., found. bd. dirs.), Col. Henry Rutgers Soc. Republican. Congregationalist. Avocations: writing, volunteer consulting, nature, music. Home and Office: 2914 Plaza Blanca Santa Fe NM 87507-5340 E-mail: lukacgj@aol.com.

LUKACH, ARTHUR S., JR. manufacturing executive; b. N.Y.C., Feb. 14, 1935; s. Arthur S. and Marion (Long) L.; 1 child, Justin A. C. BSME, Rensselaer Poly. Inst., 1956; MBA, Harvard U., 1964. V.p. Systemation Inc., Boston, 1967-70; prin. Lukach & Assocs., Cambridge, Mass., 1970-74; mgr. McKinsey & Co. Inc., N.Y.C., 1975-81; chmn., CEO Micromold Products Inc., Yonkers, N.Y., 1982—. Guest lectr. Harvard U., Stanford U., Rensselaer Poly. Inst., Columbia U., Tulane U. Bd. dirs. Vis. Nurse Svc., N.Y.C. Mem. ASME, Soc. Plastics Engrs., Harvard Bus. Sch. Club (N.Y.C.), Harvard Club. Avocations: sailing, windsurfing, skiing, tennis. Home: 36 Northwest Rd East Hampton NY 11937 Office: Micromold Products Inc 200 Corporate Blvd S Yonkers NY 10701-6806 also: 50 W 70th St New York NY 10023-4624

LUKACH, CARL ANDREW, retired chemicals executive; b. Wilkes-Barre, Pa., Dec. 18, 1930; s. John Andrew Lukach and Gabriella Wywiorski; m. Joan Barbara Wojcik; children: Carl John, Theodor, Marianna Lukach Kramer. BS Chemistry, Lehigh U., 1952, MS Chemistry, 1953; PhD, U. Notre Dame, 1956. Rsch. chemist/supervisor Hercules Inc., Wilmington, Del., 1956—73, chem. rsch. manager/dir., 1973—92; dir., oil field svcs. Hercules Aqualon Divsn., Houston, 1987—89, rsch. & devel. dir. Alizay, France, 1990—92. Loaned exec. United Way of Del., Wilmington, 1989—89, allocations com. chmn., 1994—2002. Mem.: Am. Chem. Soc. Roman Catholic. Avocation: travel, investments, real estate. Home: 109 Downs Dr Wilmington DE 19807

LUKACS, JOHN ADALBERT, historian, retired educator; b. Budapest, Hungary, Jan. 31, 1924; came to U.S., 1946, naturalized, 1953; s. Paul and Magdalena Maria L.; m. Helen Schofield, May 29, 1953 (dec. 1970); children: Paul, Annemarie; m. Stephanie Harvey, May 18, 1974. PhD, Palatine Joseph U., Budapest, 1946; fed. doctorate (hon.). Prof. history Chestnut Hill Coll., 1947-94, Chmn. dept. history, 1947-74, ret., 1994; vis. prof. history La Salle Coll., 1949-82, Columbia U., 1954-55, U. Toulouse, France, 1964-65, U. Pa., 1964, 67, 68, Johns Hopkins U., 1970-71, Fletcher Sch. Law, Diplomacy, 1971-72, Princeton U., 1988; vis. prof. U. Budapest, 1991, U. Pa., 1995-97. Author books, including: The Great Powers and Eastern Europe, 1953, A History of the Cold War, 1961, Decline and Rise of Europe, 1965, The Passing of the Modern Age, 1970, Historical Consciousness, 1968, 2d edit., 1985, The Last European War, 1939-41, 1976; 1945, Year Zero, 1978, Philadelphia: Patricians and Philistines, 1900-1950, 1981, Outgrowing Democracy: A historical interpretation of the U.S. in the 20th Century, 1984, Budapest 1900,

1988, Confessions of an Original Sinner, 1990, The Duel (Hitler vs. Churchill 10 May-31 August 1940), 1991, the End of the 20th Century (and the End of the Modern Age), 1993, Destinations Past, 1994, The Hitler of History, 1997, George F. Kennan and the Origins of Containment 1944-46, 1997, A Thread of Years, 1998, Five Days in London, 1999, At the End of an Age, 2002; contbr. numerous articles, essays, revs. to hist. and lit. jours. Mem. Schuylkill Twp. (Pa.) Planning Commn. Recipient Ingersoll prize, 1991, order of merit, Republic Of Hungary, 1994, Matthias Corvinus chair, 2001. Fellow Soc. Am. Historians; mem. Am. Catholic Hist. Assn. (pres. 1977), Am. Philos. Soc. Home: Valley Park Rd Phoenixville PA 19460

LUKACS, MICHAEL EDWARD, communications researcher; b. N.Y.C., Mar. 25, 1946; s. William and Hannah (LeWitter-Wolf) L.; m. Diane Harriet Katz, Oct. 29, 1967. Student, CUNY, Queens, 1965-68; T-3, Radio Corp. Am. Inst. now Tech Careers Inst., N.Y.C., 1968-69. Tech. aide Bell Telephone Labs., Holmdel, N.J., 1969-72, sr. tech. aide, 1972-77, assoc. mem. tech. staff, 1977-81, mem. tech. staff, 1981-83, Bell Communications Rsch., Red Bank, 1983-94, rsch. scientist, 1994-99, Telcordia Techs. (formerly Bell Comms. Rsch.), Red Bank, 1999—. Patentee cathode ray tube dynamic focus apparatus, cathode ray tube electro-optic linearization device, infinitely expandable video conferencing sys., video conf. sys. with multilayer keying of multi video images; (co-inventor) pel recursive motion compensated video coder; (inventor) "Lukacs" coding, disparity corrected predictive coding for 3-D video, "Personal Presence System" advanced multimedia video bridge, multilayer priority video keying, infinitely extensible video conferencing. Recipient Notable Achievement award Bell Labs Research Lab. 113, 1983; R&D 100 award, 1996. Mem. IEEE, Assn. Computing Machinery (Best Paper award 1994), Soc. Motion Picture TV Engrs. Avocations: science fiction, autocross, antique belt buckles. Office: Telcordia Techs 331 Newman Springs Rd Red Bank NJ 07701-5657

LUKASZEWSKI, JAMES EDMUND, communications executive; b. Kewaunee, Wis., Aug. 27, 1942; s. Edmund Ignatius and Virginia Francis Lukaszewski; m. Barbara Ann Bray, Dec. 18, 1964; children: Charles Todd, James Moir. BA, Metropolitan State U., 1974. Asst., press sec. State of Minn., Office of Governor Wendell R. Anderson, St. Paul, 1974-76; deputy commr. Dept. of Econ. Devel., State of Minn., 1976-78; pres. Media Info. Systems Corp., New Brighton, Minn., 1978-83, Brum & Anderson Exec. Tng., Inc., Mpls., 1984-86; ptnr. Chester Burger Co., N.Y.C., 1986-87; sr. v.p., dir. exec. communication programs Georgeson & Co., Inc., 1987-89; pres., chmn. bd. The Lukaszewski Group Inc., White Plains, N.Y., 1989—. Lectr. East Coast Comdr.'s media Tng. Symposium, USMC, 1986—, Nat. Media Conf., N.Y.C., 1986-89; adj. asst. prof. communications NYU Sch. of Continuing and Profl. Studies, 1991—; civilian advisor to the Internat. Disaster Adv. Com., U.S. Dept. State, 1990-94, to USMC, 1986—; commencement spkr. NYU Summer Inst. in Pub. Rels., 1997-2000; lectr. Conf. Bd. of Can., 2000, 01, Chief EH&S Officers' Coun., The Conf. Bd., 2000, Canadian Investor Rels. Inst., 2001, others; nat. lectr., spkr. in field. Author: Executive Television Training Handbook, 1983, The Publicity Handbook, 1984, Having Effective Media Interviews, 1984, Having Effective Media Interviews, 1984, The Tactical Ingenuity Pyramid, 1989, Executive Action Crisis Management Anthology, 1992, Executive Action Crisis Management Workbook, 1992, 93, Executive Action Emergency Media Relations Guide, 1992, 93, Influencing Public Attitudes: Strategies that Reduce the Media's Power, 1992; War Stories and Crisis Communication Strategies, An Anthology, 2000, Crisis Communication Planning Strategies, A Workbook, 2000, Media Relations Strategies During Emergencies, A Guide, 2000, (chpts.) Crisis Response: Inside Stories on Managing Image Under Siege, 1993, Disaster Recovery Testing: Exercising Your Contingency Plan, 1994, Environmental Health and Safety Auditing Handbook, 1994, Practical Public Affairs in an Era of Change: A Cutting Edge Guide for Government, Business and College, 1995; (video cassette) Executive Action Crisis Management System; contbg. editor Pub. Rels. Quar., 1997—; author Strategy quar. supplement to P.R. Reporter, 1998—; guest columnist PR News, 2000—01; editl. bd. Ragan's Pub. Rels. jour., 2000-; editor TRUST newsletter, 2001—; mem. adv. bd. Media Rels. Insider, 2001—. Chmn. Bklyn. Park Tater Daze Celebration, Minn., 1972, Met. State U. Alumni Assn., St. Paul, 1974; chmn. venture fund drive Met. State U., 1990-91; trustee, v.p. Met. State U. Found., St. Paul, 1976-86. Recipient Silver Key award Bklyn. Park Jaycees, Minn., 1973, Drew Middleton award for Disting. Svc. in Support of USMC East Coast Comdrs. Media Tng. Symposium, 1992, award for outstanding svc. Choice in Dying, 1996; named Sound Citizen of Yr. Park Jaycees, 1972. Fellow Pub. Rels. Soc. Am. (accredited; Pres.'s Citation award 1991, 2000, mem bd. ethics and profl. stds., 1990-, active Counselors Acad., corp., employee rels. and pub. affairs/govt. sections, N.Y.C. and Westchester/Fairfield chpts.); mem. Internat. Assn. Bus. Communicators, Pub. Rels. Soc. N.Y., Ctr. for Study of Presidency, Internat. Churchill Soc., The Issue Mgmt. Coun., Fairfield County Pub. Rels. Assn. Avocations: writing, lecturing. Home: 16 Sunset Dr Snug Harbor Danbury CT 06811-3132 Office: Ten Bank St Ste 530 White Plains NY 10606 E-mail: tlg@e911.com.

LUKE, DAVID KEVIN, investment company executive; b. Las Vegas, Nev., Dec. 14, 1960; s. Freddie Allen and Janet Anne (Shelton) L.; Lee-Ann Marie Petryshyn, Apr. 22, 1983; children: Krista Lee-Ann, David Nathan, Spencer Matthew, Ruth Alyssa, Zane Louis-Allan. BA, Brigham Young U., 1984; M of Internat. Mgmt., Am. Grad. Sch. of Internat. Mgmt., 1986. cert. investment broker. Cons. Internat. Small Bus. Inst., Denver, 1985; mgmt. trainee GM Can., Oshawa, Ont., 1986-87; supr. GMAC Can., Toronto, 1987-89; investment broker A.G. Edwards & Sons, Scottsdale, Ariz., 1989-96; portfolio mgr., assoc. v.p. investments Luke Wealth Mgmt. Group of Wachovia Securities, 1996—. Incorporator Protip, Inc., 1991-93. Instr. Ariz. Coun. on Econ. Edn., Tucson, Ariz., 1990-93; treas. Kyrene Schs. Cmty. Found., Tempe, Ariz., 1993-94, appointee Supt. Fin. Com., Advancement Chmn. 1994-95; scoutmaster troop 540 Boy Scouts of Am., 1996-99, com. chair, 1999—. Mem. Ch. Jesus Christ Latter Day Saints. Home: 6135 E Gold Dust Ave Paradise Valley AZ 85253-1242 Office: First Union Securities 20551 N Pima Rd Ste 200 Scottsdale AZ 85255-9154 E-mail: dluke@wachoviasec.com.

LUKE, DAVID LINCOLN, III, retired paper company executive; b. Tyrone, Pa., July 25, 1923; s. David Lincoln and Priscilla Warren Luke; m. Fanny R. Curtis, June 11, 1955. AB, Yale U., 1945; LLD (hon.), Juniata Coll., 1967, Lawrence U., 1976, Salem Coll., 1983, W. Va. U., 1984; DSc. (hon.) , Cold Spring Harbor Lab., 2001. V.p., dir. Westvaco Corp., N.Y.C., 1953-57, exec. v.p., dir., 1957-62, pres., bd. dirs., 1962-80, chief exec. officer, 1963-88, chmn. bd. dirs., 1980-96. Trustee emeritus, past chmn. Cold Spring Harbor Lab.; hon. bd. dirs., former bd. dirs. Josiah Macy Jr. Found.; past chmn., trustee emeritus Hotchkiss Sch. Served from aviation cadet to capt. USMCR., 1942-45. Mem. The River Club, Piping Rock Club, Megantic Fish and Game Corp., John's Island Club.

LUKE, DOUGLAS SIGLER, business executive; b. Middletown, N.Y., Oct. 1, 1941; s. Douglas Sigler Luke and Joanne (Benton) Cowles; m. Anne Sturgis Roosevelt, June 20, 1964 (div. Sept. 1976); m. Sarah Chappell Mullen, Mar. 23, 1991; children: Haven Roosevelt, David Russell, Lindsay Hall. Student, Mexico City Coll., 1961; BA Fgn. Affairs, U. Va., 1964; MBA, The Darden Sch., Charlottesville, Va., 1966. Mem. staff chem. divsn. WestVaco Corp., Covington, Va., 1966-69; dir. corp. planning SCOA Industries, Columbus, Ohio, 1969-71; v.p. fin. Multicon Prop. divsn. Bethlehem Steel Corp., 1971-72; gen. ptnr., CEO, Personal Investments, 1972-79; v.p. Rothschild, Inc. (formerly New Court Securities), N.Y.C., 1979-83, sr. v.p., 1984-87, mng. dir., 1987-90; pres, CEO, WLD Enterprises, Inc., Ft. Lauderdale, Fla., 1991-98; pres., CEO HL Capital, Inc., N.Y.C., 1999—. Bd. dirs. Westvaco Corp., N.Y.C., Regency Realty Corp., Jacksonville, Fla., Orbital Scis. Corp., Fairfax, Va.; mem. adv. bd. Nat. Outdoor Leadership Sch., 1994-99, trustee, 2000—. Founding donor Adopt-a-Class, N.Y.C., 1988;mem. space adv. bd. U. Colo., 1985-89; bd. dirs. condrs. com. Columbus Symphony Orch., 1972-75; trustee The Columbus Acad., Gahanna, Ohio, 1973-77, Girl Scouts U.S., Piedmont Region, Roanoke, Va., 1967-69, Adirondack Coun., 2001—; high tech. com. working group N.Y.C. Partnership Inc., 1988-90. Mem. Ausable Club (St. Huberts, N.Y.), Adirondack Mountain Reserve (St. Huberts, trustee 1985-94, pres. 1988-91, chmn. 1991-94), Va. Club/Yale Club (N.Y.C.), Mashomack Fish and Game Preserve (Pine Plains, N.Y.). Avocations: running, skiing, fly fishing. Office: HL Capital Inc The Chrysler Bldg 48th Fl 405 Lexington Ave Rm 4800 New York NY 10174-4800

LUKE, RANDALL DAN, retired tire and rubber company executive, lawyer; b. New Castle, Pa., June 4, 1935; s. Randall Beamer and Blanche Wilhelmina (Fisher) L.; m. Patricia Arlene Moody, Aug. 4, 1962 (div. Jan. 1977); children: Lisa Elin, Randall Sargent; m. Saralee Frances Krow, Mar. 1, 1979; 1 stepchild, Stephanie Sogg. BA in Econs. with honors, U. Pa., 1957, JD, 1960. Bar: Ohio 1960, Calif. 1962, Ill. 1989. Assoc., ptnr. Daus, Schwenger & Kottler, Cleve., 1965-70; ptnr. Kottler & Danzig, 1970-75, Hahn, Loeser, Freedheim, Dean & Wellman, Cleve., 1975-81; assoc. gen. counsel The Firestone Tire & Rubber Co., Akron, Ohio, 1981-82, v.p., assoc. gen. counsel and sec., 1982-88, Bridgestone/Firestone, Inc., Akron, 1988-91; of counsel Hahn Loeser & Parks, Cleve., 1991-2000. Trustee, Akron Art Mus., 1982-87, Akron Symphony Orch., 1986-87, Cleve. Opera League, 1992-98. Served to Capt. USNR, 1960-81; ret. 1981. Mem.: Ill. Bar Assn., Ohio Bar Assn., Calif. Bar Assn., Union Internat. Avocates (Paris), Union Club (Cleve.)., Mayfield Country Club (S. Euclid, Ohio), Cleve. Skating Club. Republican. Avocations: tennis, jogging, golf, squash, skiing. Home: 13901 Shaker Blvd Cleveland OH 44120-1582

LUKEHART, CHARLES MARTIN, chemistry educator; b. DuBois, Pa., Dec. 21, 1946; s. David Blair and Grace Dorothy L.; m. Marilyn Orleana McKinney, Aug. 4, 1973; children: Mark, Brian, Laura. BS in Chemistry, Pa. State U., 1968; PhD in Inorganic Chemistry, MIT, 1972. Postdoctoral assoc. Tex. A&M U., College Sta., 1972-73; asst. prof. chemistry Vanderbilt U., Nashville, 1973-77, assoc. prof. chemistry, 1977-82, prof., 1982—. Author: Fundamental Transition Metal Organometallic Chemistry, 1985. Rsch. fellow Alfred P. Sloan Found., 1979-81. Mem. Am. Chem. Soc. (chmn. Nashville sect. 1979, 92), Materials Rsch. Soc. Office: Vanderbilt U Dept Chemistry Box 1822 Sta B Nashville TN 37235

LUKENBILL, WILLIS BERNARD, b. Mt. Sylvan, Tex., Mar. 27, 1939; s. Lee Roy Clayton Lukenbill and Tommie Lee McCorkle; m. Shirley Ann Hebert, June 1, 1968; 1 child James Frederick. BS in Edn., U. North Tex., 1961; MLS, U. Okla., 1963; PhD, Ind. U., 1973. Cert. tchr. Tex. Reference libr. Austin Coll., Sherman, Tex., 1963; isntr. La. Poly. U., Ruston, 1964-69; asst. prof. U. Md., College Park, 1973-75; from asst. prof. to assoc. prof. U. Tex., Austin, 1976-96, prof., 1996—. Author: Youth Literature, 1988, AIDS and HIV Programs and Services for Libraries, 1994—2000, Collection Development for the School Medic Library Center in a New Century, 2002; contbr. Bd. dirs. Met. Cmty. Ch., Austin, 1990, archivist cons., 1994—2000. Recipient Libr. Edn. for At-Risk Youth award, U.S. Dept. Edn., 1993—94; fellow Temple tchg. fellow, Grad. Libr. Sch. U. Tex., 1987—88, 1996—97, Commons Tchg. fellow, 2001—; grantee internat. rsch. grant, Policy Rsch. Inst. U. Tex., 1990, policy rsch. grant, 1988. Mem.: ALA (Whitney Carnegie grant 1986), Tex. Libr. Assn., Phi Kappa Phi. Democrat. Avocations: travel, theater , art, music, reading. Home: 1205 Spearson Austin TX 78745 Office: U Tex Austin TX 78712 Office Fax: (512) 471 3971. E-mail: luke@gslis.utexas.edu.

LUKENS, ALAN WOOD, retired ambassador and foreign service officer; b. Phila., Feb. 12, 1924; s. Edward Clark and Frances (Day) L.; m. Susan Atkinson, Dec. 29, 1962; children: Lewis Alan, Susan, Frances Lukens Bennett, Timothy Eric. AB, Princeton U., 1948; postgrad., U. Sorbonne, Paris, 1948, U. Madrid, 1948, Georgetown U., 1951; LLD (hon.), St. Lawrence U., 1987. Tchr. St. Albans Sch., Washington, 1950-51; joined U.S. Fgn. Svc., 1951; vice consul Ankara, Turkey, 1952, Istanbul, Turkey, 1953; pub. affairs officer Martinique, 1954-56; with news divsn. State Dept., 1956-57; U.S. del. 12th UN Gen. Assembly, 1957; mem. internat. staff NATO, Paris, 1958-60; consul Brazzaville, 1960; U.S. rep. to Independence of Congo, Chad, Gabon, Central African Republic, 1961; charge d'affaires Am. Embassy, Bangui, Central African Republic, 1961, Paris, 1961-63, Rabat, Morocco, 1963-65; chief personnel Bur. African Affairs, State Dept., 1965-67; dep. chief mission, counselor embassy Dakar, 1967-70, Nairobi, 1970-72; chief jr. officer div. personnel State Dept., 1973-75; dir. Office Iberian Affairs, 1974-75; counselor, dep. chief mission Am. Embassy, Copenhagen, 1975-78; with Bur. African Affairs, Dept. State, Washington, 1978-79; consul gen. Cape Town, South Africa, 1979-82; dir. office analysis for Western Europe, Bur. Intelligence and Research, Dept. State, Washington, 1982-84; A.E.& P. People's Republic of Congo, 1984-87; cons. on internat. affairs and crisis mgmt. Dept. of State, 1987-93. Washington rep. for Alvensa Corp. and World Water Corp.; lectr. on Africa. Co-chair, Peace Commn. Washington Nat. Cathedral; former trustee Episcopal Acad., Merion, Pa.; coun. mem. Woodrow Wilson House, Washington; v.p. Fgn. Policy Discussion Group, Washington. With AUS, 1943-46. Recipient Commendable Service award State Dept., 1961 Mem. Washington Inst. Fgn. Affairs (pres. DACOR, Diplomatic and Consular Officers Ret.), Princeton Club N.Y.C., Washington Club, Nairobi (pres. Paris chpt. 1961-63), Fgn. Affairs Retirees Md. (pres.), Princeton U. Alumni Coun. (mem. exec. com., pres. Class of 1946), Explorers Club Washington (bd. dirs.), Chevy Chase Club (gov. 1995-2000). Episcopalian. Home: 18 Grafton St Chevy Chase MD 20815-3428

LUKENS, JOHN PATRICK, lawyer; b. Washington, Aug. 10, 1944; s. John F. and Patricia A. Lukens; m. Donna Lukens, Sept. 24, 1987; 4 children. BS, U. Idaho, 1970, JD cum laude, 1973. Public defender Clark County Public Defender, Las Vegas, 1974-76; pvt. practice, 1976-87; chief dep. dist. atty. Clark County Dist. Atty., 1987-97. Contbr. articles to profl. jours. Founder Sexual Abuse Investigation Team Clinic at Child Haven, Clark County Child Death Rev. com. With U.S. Army, 1967-69. Recipient award Com. on Victim's Rights, 1989. Office: 550 E Charleston Blvd Ste B Las Vegas NV 89104-1303

LUKER, RALPH EDLIN, history educator; b. Louisville, Mar. 1, 1940; s. Maurice Sylvester and Beatrice (Edlin) L.; m. Jean Holmes Crawford, May 27, 1966; children: Anne Crawford, Amanda Elizabeth. BA, Duke U., 1962; BD, Drew U., 1966; MA, U. N.C., 1969, PhD, 1973. Asst. prof. of history Allegheny Coll., Meadville, Pa., 1972-79; exec. dir. Del. Humanities Forum, Wilmington, 1980-82; assoc. editor, dir. Martin Luther King Papers Project, Atlanta, 1986-91; assoc. prof. history Antioch Coll., Yellow Springs, Ohio, 1991-94; adj. prof. history Morehouse Coll., Atlanta, 1996-98. Vis. prof. religion Va. Poly. Inst., Blacksburg, 1979-80, 83-84, Lincoln U., Pa., 1985-86; rsch. assoc. R.I. Black Heritage Soc., Providence, 1984; cons. Boston U., 1992, Martin Luther King Papers Project, Stanford, Calif., 1995, Project on Theology and Cmty., Loyola Coll., Md., 1997-99. Author: The Social Gospel in Black and White, 1991, Historical Dictionary of the Civil Rights Movement, 1997; editor: Black and White Sat Down Together, 1995, The Papers of Martin Luther King Jr., 1992, 94. Mem. cmty. adv. bd. Sta. WHYY, pub. radio/TV, Wilmington, Del. and Phila., 1980-86; bd. dirs. Sta. WQLN, pub. radio/TV, Erie, Pa., 1975-79. Grantee NEH, 1978, 84, 85, 86, Pub. Com. for Humanities in Pa., Phila., 1976, Ford Found., N.Y.C., 1970-71, Louisville Inst., 1998, 2002, Va. Found. for the Humanities, 2001. Mem. Am. Hist. Assn., Am. Studies Assn. (Constance Rourke prize com. 1984-86), Orgn. of Am. Historians, So. Hist. Assn. (membership com. 1980-82, 91), St. George Tucker Soc., History News Svc. (steering com. 1997—), Hon. Order Ky. Cols., Hist. Soc. Republican. United Methodist. Avocations: reading, dancing, antiques. Home: 1288 Oakdale Rd NE Atlanta GA 30307-1049

LUKEY, JOAN A. lawyer; b. Malden, Mass., Dec. 28, 1949; d. Philip Edward and Ada Joan (Roberti) L.; m. Philip Davis Stevenson. BA magna cum laude, Smith Coll., 1971; JD cum laude, Boston Coll., 1974. Bar: Mass. 1974, U.S. Dist. Ct. Mass. 1975, U.S. Ct. Appeals (1st cir.) 1976, U.S. Supreme Ct. 1985. Assoc. Hale & Dorr, Boston, 1974-79, jr. ptnr., 1979-83, sr. ptnr., 1983—. Mem. Joint Bar Com. on Judicial Appointments, Mass., 1985-87, steering com. Lawyers' Com. for Civil Rights Under the Law, Boston, 1987-90. Fellow: Am. Coll. Trial Lawyers (mem. state com. 1993—, chair 1997—99, first cir. rules adv. com. 1997, chair 1998—2000); mem.: ABA, Boston Bar Assn. (chair litigation sect. 1990—92, mem. coun. 1987—90, v.p. 1998—99, pres.-elect 1999—2000, pres. 2000—01), Mass. Bar Assn., Boston Club. Office: Hale & Dorr 60 State St Boston MA 02109-1816

LUKOMSKY, VERA, musicologist, pianist, music educator; b. St. Petersburg, Russia, May 30, 1947; came to U.S., 1990; d. Eugene and Sofia (Levin) L.; m. Alexander Lukomsky, Sept. 21, 1966; children: Eva Jane, Daniel. BA in Music, Rimsky-Korsakov Coll. Music, St. Petersburg, 1968; MA in Music, St. Petersburg Conservatory, 1973; postgrad., U. Calif. San Diego, 1992-98. Instr. music State Coll. Music, Novgorod, Russia, 1972-73; instr. Inst. Culture, St. Petersburg, 1972-75, Rachmaninov Sch. Music, St. Petersburg, 1975-89; instr., owner Allegro Piano Studio, Solana Beach, Calif., 1990—; lectr., asst. condr. U. Calif. San Diego, 1997-98; choral dir. San Diego H.S. and Meml. Jr. H.S., 1999-2000. Adj. prof. Nat. U., San Diego, 1999—. Author: The Analysis of Harmony in the Course of Solfeggio and Ear Training, 1985; contbr. articles to profl. jours. Recipient 1st pl. award Third Russian Republic Methodology Competition for Instrs. of Music and Art, 1983, Hendrikson fellowship U. Calif. San Diego, 1994-95. Mem. Am. Assn. Advancement Slavic Studies, Am. Musicological Soc., Coll. Music Soc., Music Tchrs. Nat. Assn., Music Tchrs. Assn. Calif. (cert. of excellence 1999, 2000, 01, 02). Avocations: reading, travel, playing chamber music, theater, movies. Fax: 858-259-7845. E-mail: vlukomsk@ucsd.edu.

LUKS, ALLAN BARRY, executive director; b. N.Y.C., June 27, 1941; s. Joseph Moses and Evelyn (Gropper) L.; m. Karen Greenbaum, Feb. 22, 1969; children: Rachel, David. BA, U. N.C., 1963; JD, Georgetown Law Sch., 1966. Bar: N.Y. Vol. U.S. Peace Corps, Maracay, Venezuela, 1967-69; legal dir. Children's Aid Soc. East Harlem, N.Y.C., 1970-72; asst. dir. Life Ins. Industry Urban Investment Program, 1972-75; sec.-treas. N.Y.C. Rand Inst., 1975-78; exec. dir. Alcoholism Coun. of Greater N.Y., N.Y.C., 1978-88, Inst. for the Advancement of Health, N.Y.C., 1988-90, Big Bros./Big Sisters of N.Y., N.Y.C., 1990—. Author N.Y.C. law, warning posters on drinking during pregnancy, 1983; adj. prof. Fordham U. Grad. Sch. Social Svc., N.Y.C., 1979-88; chmn. legal sect. Internat. Coun. on Alcohol and Addictions, Lausanne, Switzerland, 1980-88; mem. NGO-Crime Prevention and Criminal Justice, UN, N.Y.C., 1982-90. Author: Will America Sober Up?, 1983, The Healing Power of Doing Good, 1991; co-author: You Are What You Drink, 1989; editor Having Been There, 1979. Pres. Cadman Towers Housing, Bklyn., 1971-75; sch. bd. mem. N.Y.C. Sch. Bd. #13, Bklyn., 1975-80; v.p. Brooklyn Heights Assn., N.Y.C., 1982-86; adv. coun. mem. Jr. League N.Y., N.Y.C., 1984-88. Recipient Vol. Leadership award Mayor of N.Y., N.Y.C., 1987, Pub. Svc. award Crains N.Y. Bus. Mag., N.Y.C., 1994. Office: Big Bros/Big Sisters NYC 223 E 30th St New York NY 10016-8203 E-mail: aluks@bigsnyc.org.

LUKSHA, ROSEMARY DOROTHY, art educator; b. Wilkes-Barre, Pa., Jan. 5, 1952; d. William Peter and Julia Catherine (Zavislak) L.; 1 child, Mary Rose. BS in Art Edn., Kutztown (Pa.) U., 1973, MEd, 1991; postgrad., Skidmore Coll., 1978, Marywood Coll., 1975, Wilkes U. Cert. instrnl. II art K-12. Art educator Wyoming Valley West Sch. Dist., Kingston, Pa., 1973-84; co. dancer Wilkes-Barre (Pa.) Ballet Theatre, 1973-80; dance instr. Coll. Misericordia, Dallas, 1980-81; art educator N.W. Area Sch. Dist., Shickshinny, 1988—; co. dancer Scranton (Pa.) Ballet Theatre, 1980-84. Art cons. Wilkes U. Polish Rm. Com., Wilkes-Barre, 1976-92; mem. planning com. Wilkes-Barre Fine Arts Fiesta, 1980-82; illustrator Wilkes-Barre Ballet Theatre, N.E. Ballet, 1977-85, Wyo. Valley Oratorio, Wilkes-Barre, 1979. Choreographer: (dance work) Continue the Balance We Hold, Sisters, Young Choreographer's Performance inN.E. Regional Ballet Festival, 1979. Mem., cantor St. Anthony of Padua Roman Cath. Ch.; advisor St. Anthony of Padua Youth Group, Larksville, Pa. Recipient Dance Scholarship N.E. Regional Ballet Festival, Melissa Hayden Ballet Sch., N.Y.C., 1979. Mem. Nat. Art Edn. Assn., N.W. Area Edn. Assn., Pa. Edn. Assn., Osterhout Libr. Soc., Phi Delta Kappa. Republican. Roman Catholic. Avocations: reading, gardening, travel, bicycling, calligraphy. Office: NW Area Jr/Sr HS RR 2 Box 2271 Shickshinny PA 18655-9201

LUKYANENKO, VALERIY IVANOVICH, physiologist, researcher; b. Alchevsk, Lugansk, Ukraine, June 22, 1961; came to U.S., 1995; s. Ivan Illarionovich and Anna Filippovna Lukyanenko; m. Yevgeniya Olegovna, Feb. 11, 1984; children: Anton, Platon. MS, Leningrad State U., 1987; PhD, Sechenov Inst. Evolutionary Physiology & Biochem., 1991. Rschr. Sechnova Inst. Evolutionary Physiology and Biochem., Leningrad, 1991-95; rsch. assoc. Health Scis. Ctr. Tex. Tech. U., Lubbock, 1995-97, rsch. instr., 1997-99, rsch. asst. prof., 1999—. Contbr. articles to profl. jours. including Jour. Physiology, Biophys. Jour., Pflugers Archive, among others. Lt. USSR Mil., 1979-87. Grantee Am. Heart Assn., 2000. Mem. AAAS, Pavlov Russian Physiol. Soc. (Russia), Biophys. Soc. Avocations: classical music, movies, philosophy. Home: 4314 16th St # 17 Lubbock TX 79416 Office: 3601 4th St Stop 6551 Lubbock TX 79430-6551 E-mail: phyvil@ttuhsc.edu.

LULAY, GAIL C. human resources and corporative outplacement executive, consultant; b. Evanston, Ill., Feb. 13, 1938; d. Earl Albert and Helen Marie (Blackwell) Minnich; m. Wayne L. Lulay, Aug. 15, 1959; children: Michael Brent, Catherine Marie. BS, Elmhurst Coll., 1970; MS, Roosevelt U., 1972. Cert. counselor, Ill. Instr. Dist. #181, Hinsdale, Ill., 1970-74; corp. bus. devel. Continental Bank, Chgo., 1974-79; pres., owner Lulay & Assocs., Inc., Downers Grove, Ill., 1979—. Instr. Elmhurst Coll. Adult Edn., 1982, Coll. of DuPage, Glen Ellyn, Ill., 1983-86; lectr., cons. in field., 1980—. Author: Nelson Eddy, America's Favorite Baratone, Authorized Biographical Tribute, 1992; contbr. articles to profl. jours. Bd. dirs. Crisis Homes, Des Plaines, Ill., 1984-86. Mem. Am. Assn. Counseling and Devel., Am. Soc. Personnel Adminstrn., Assn. Outplacement Cons. Firms, Inc., Human Resources Mgmt. Assn. of Chgo., Roosevelt U. Alumni Assn., Chi Omega. Office: Lulay & Assocs Inc 1431 Opus Pl Ste 535 Downers Grove IL 60515-5724

LULL, ROBERT JOHN, nuclear medicine physician, educator; b. Buffalo, Aug. 23, 1940; s. Joseph J. and Margaret L.; m. Dorothy Lee Murtha, Feb. 2, 1965 (div. 1987); children: Jonathan C., Benjamin D. AB in Biochemistry, Canisius Coll., 1962; MD, Albany Med. Coll., 1966. Diplomate Nat. Bd. Med. Examiners, Am. Bd. Internal Medicine, Am. Bd. Nuclear Medicine; lic. Calif., Tex., N.Y. Commd. U.S. Army, 1966, advanced through ranks to col., 1980; rotating intern Brooke Army Med. Ctr., San Antonio, 1966-67, resident in internal medicine, 1967-70; fellow in nuclear medicine William Beaumont Army Med. Ctr., El Paso, Tex., 1970-72; chief nuclear med. svc. Brooke Army Med. Ctr., San Antonio, 1972-76, Letterman Army Med. Ctr., San Francisco, 1976-90; ret., 1990; assoc. dir. nuclear medicine dept. San Francisco Gen. Hosp., 1990-91; clin. prof. radiology and lab. medicine U. Calif., San Francisco, 1990—, dir. nuclear medicine residency, 1991—; dir. nuclear medicine dept. San Francisco Gen. Hosp., 1991—. Bd. dirs. Calif. Radioactive Materials Mgmt. Forum, Sacramento, Calif., 1986—, chmn., 1989-90; cons., mem. adv. com. FDA, Washington, 1991-97. Editor San Francisco Medicine, 1997-99, mem. editorial bd., 1995—; contbr. 30 peer rev. articles med. jours., chpts. to 7 med. books; reviewer for 8 med. jours.; editor (audio visual med. series) AIMS program, 1987-89. Nuclear medicine cons. Surgeon Gen., U.S. Army, Washington, 1977-90; senate appointee Citizen's Adv. Com. on Nuclear Emergencies, Calif., 1989-92; commr. Calif. Southwestern Low Level Radioactive Waste Compact, 1995—; bd. dirs. Nat. Assn. Cancer Patients, 1995-99. Recipient Boss of Yr. award No. Calif. chpt. Am. Bus. Women's Assn., 1979, Legion of Merit award U.S. Army, Presidio of San Francisco, 1990. Fellow: ACP, Am. Coll. Nuc. Physicians (bd. dirs. 1988—, pres. Calif. chpt. 1990—93, nat. pres. 1992—93, Pres. award 1995); mem.: San Francisco Med. Soc. (bd. dirs. 1996—, editor, chmn. editl. bd. 1998—2000, exec. com. 1998—, sec. 2000—, pres.-elect 2001—02, pres. 2002—), Calif. Med. Assn. (chmn. nuc. medicine sect. 1996—, del. 2000—, nuclear medicine rep. to coun. on scientific affairs 1996—, mem. pres. coun. 2001—, mem. editl. bd. Calif. medicine), Soc. Nuc. Medicine (pres. Calif. chpt. 1986—87, Silver medal 1972—83), Radiol. Soc. N.Am., Am. Coll. Radiology (com. mem. 1990—95). Avocations: trombone, tennis, sailing, horseback riding, skiing. Office: San Francisco Gen Hosp Nuclear Medicine Dept NH 1001 Potrero Ave Rm G100 San Francisco CA 94110-3594

LULL, WILLIAM PAUL, engineering consultant; b. Indpls., Nov. 5, 1954; s. William Roger and Florence Elizabeth (Morris) L.; m. Mary Ann Garrison, Dec. 22, 1989. Student, Ind. State U., 1973-75; BS in Arts & Design, MIT, 1978. Systems designer James Assocs., Architects, Engrs., Indpls., 1978-79; architect TVA, Knoxville, Tenn., 1980; mgr. energy mgmt. div. Dubin-Bloome, Engrs., N.Y.C., 1981; asst. chief of design Syska & Hennessy, Engrs., 1982-83; prin. Garrison/Lull Inc., Princeton Junction, N.J., 1984—. Adj. assoc. prof. NYU, 1983—; lectr., presenter cons. environ. field. Author: Conservation Environment Guidelines for Libraries and Archives, 1990; co-author: Criteria for Storage of Paper-Based Archival Records, 1984; contbr. articles to profl. publs. Mem. ASHRAE (conf. presenter), Illuminating Engrng. Soc. N.Am., Am. Inst. Conservation of Historic and Artistic Works (assoc.), Sigma Pi Sigma. Achievements include pioneering discipline of consulting on conservation environments for preservation of museum library and archival collections. Home: 7 High St Allentown NJ 08501-1914 Office: Garrison/Lull Inc PO Box 459 Princeton Junction NJ 08550-0459

LULLI, BONNIE JEAN, medical group administrator; b. Cin., Jan. 1, 1943; d. Richard Roland and Mary Elizabeth (Kinzer) Lang; m. Arden Darryl Allen, Jan. 30, 1972 (div. Jan. 1988); 1 child, John C.; m. Gordon Agusto Lulli, Sept. 2, 1989. BA in Bus., Calif. State U., Northridge, 1965. Office mgr. Dr. Richard Clancy, Glendale, Calif., 1963-68; bus. mgr. Dr. Vivagene Loop, 1969-75; bus. and office mgr. Dr. Robert B. Gold, Santa Ana, Calif., 1975-87; gen. mgr. So. Calif. Assoc. Plastic Surgeons-Expert Med. Mgmt. Corp., Anaheim, 1987-89; bus. adminstr. Meml. Cardiology Med. Group, Inc., Long Beach, Calif., 1990—. Owner Physicians' Med. Ins. Billing Svc., Huntington Beach, Calif., 1975-90; mem. physicians' office mgrs.' task force Long Beach Meml. Med. Ctr., 1994—. Sec. Fountain Valley (Calif.) Youth Baseball, 1980-86; Stephen min., class instr. Roman Cath. Ch., Huntington Beach. Mem. Med. Group Mgmt. Assn., Profl. Assn. Health Care Office Mgrs. Avocations: snow skiing, working out, reading, travel. Home: 8771 Burlcrest Dr Huntington Beach CA 92646-4618 Office: Meml Cardiol Med Group Inc 2898 Linden Ave Ste 120 Long Beach CA 90806-1627

LUM, JEAN LOUI JIN, nursing educator; b. Honolulu, Sept. 5, 1938; d. Yee Nung and Pui Ki (Young) L. BS, U. Hawaii, Manoa, 1960; MS in Nursing, U. Calif., San Francisco, 1961; MA, U. Wash., 1969, PhD in Sociology, 1972. Registered nurse, Hawaii. From instr. to prof. Sch. Nursing U. Hawaii Manoa, Honolulu, 1961-95, acting dean, 1982, dean, 1982-89, prof. emeritus, 1995—. Project coordinator Analysis and Planning Personnel Svcs., Western Interstate Commn. Higher Edn., 1977; extramural assoc. div. Rsch. Grants NIH, 1978-79; mem. mgmt. adv. com. Honolulu County Hosp., 1982-96; mem. exec. bd. Pacific Health Rsch. Inst., 1980-88; mem. health planning com. East Honolulu, 1978-81; mem. rsch. grants adv. coun. Hawaii Med. Svcs. Assn. Found., Nat. Adv. Coun. for Nursing Rsch., 1990-93. Contbr. articles to profl. jours. Trustee Straub Pacific Health Found., Honolulu; bd. dirs. Friends of the Nat. Inst. of Nursing Rsch., 1994-97. Recipient Nurse of Yr. award Hawaii Nurses Assn., 1982; named Disting. Practitioner in Nursing, Nat. Acads. of Practice, 1986; USPHS grantee, 1967-72 Fellow Am. Acad. Nursing; mem. Am. Nurses Assn., Am. Pacific Nursing Leaders Conf. (pres. 1983-87), Council Nurse Researchers, Nat. League for Nursing (bd. rev. 1981-87), Western Council Higher Edn. for Nurses (chmn. 1984-85), Western Soc. for Research in Nursing, Am. Sociol. Assn., Pacific Sociol. Assn., Assn. for Women in Sci., Hawaii Pub. Health Assn., Hawaii Med. Services Assn. (bd. dirs. 1985-92), Western Inst. Nursing, Mortar Bd., Phi Kappa Phi, Sigma Theta Tau, Alpha Kappa Delta, Delta Kappa Gamma. Episcopalian. Home: 3185 Waialae Ave Honolulu HI 96816-1511 Office: U Hawaii Manoa Sch Nursing Webster Hall 2528 The Mall Honolulu HI 96822

LUM, VIOLA DORIS, music educator, personal financial analyst; b. San Benito, Tex., Apr. 3, 1928; d. Ernest Lee and Jewell Avis (Hughes) Marley; m. S.E. Lum, Dec. 25, 1949; children: Donald Gene, Karen Ann Lum Boer. Tchg. cert., St. Louis Inst. Music, 1947, advanced tchg. cert., 1959. Lic. ins. and securities dealer, Tex. and Okla.; cert. PFA. Instr. music Tarkington Sch., Cleveland, Tex., 1947-53; tchr. piano Cleveland, Pasadena and Conroe, 1953—, Lifestyle Christian Sch., Conroe, 1986-96; newspaper editor Southwestern Gospel Music Assn., Pasadena, 1975-85; fin. analyst Primerica Fin. Svc., Conroe, 1987—. Newspaper pub. Southwestern Gospel Music Assn., Pasadena, 1975-85; beauty cons. Mary Kay Cosmetics, 1982-90; traveled nationwide with Kingdom Seekers, Inc., gospel music ministry, 1970-87. Treas. East Side Assembly of God Ch., Conroe, 1987-94, pianist, Riverside, 1987—. Mem. NASD, Nat. Piano Guild (chmn., hon. tchr. 1993-2001), Music Tchrs. Nat. Assn., Tex. Music Tchrs. Assn. (chmn. Divsn. I, student affiliate coun. 1994—), Conroe Music Tchrs. (pres. 1991-94, Tchr. of Yr. 1994), Cypress Creek Music Tchrs. Assn. (v.p. 1998-2000, Selected Tchr. of the Yr. 1998). Avocations: photography, coin collecting, computers. Home: 13082 Cleveland Rd Conroe TX 77304-4174 Office: Primerica Fin Svcs 1712 N Frazier St Ste 212B Conroe TX 77301-1380 E-mail: selvdl@txucom.net.

LUMB, SANDRA JAYNE, elementary school educator; b. Lawrence, Mass., June 1, 1955; d. William Taylor and Virginia Ruth (Peate) L. BS, U. Lowell, 1977. Cert. tchr., Mass. Instl. asst. Title 1 (Chpt.1), Methuen, Mass., 1978-80; grade 1 tchr. Our Lady of Mt. Carmel Sch., 1980-86, grade 3 tchr., 1986-91, 92-94, tchr. 4th grade, 1994—; asst. adminstr. Our Lady of Mt. Carmel, 1991-92. Mem. Nat. Catholic Edn. Assn. Avocations: bowling, stamp collecting, ch. activities.

LUMB, WILLIAM VALJEAN, veterinarian; b. Sioux City, Iowa, Nov. 26, 1921; m. Lilly Carlson, 1949; 1 child John W. DVM, Kans. State U., 1943; MS, Tex. A&M U., 1953; PhD in Vet. Medicine, U. Minn., 1957; DSc (hon.), Ohio State U., 1999. Intern, resident Angell Meml. Animal Hosp., Boston, 1946—48; from instr. to assoc. prof. medicine and surgery Tex. A&M U., 1949—52; asst. prof. clin. surgery Colo. State U., 1954—58; assoc. prof. surgery and medicine Mich. State U., 1958—60; assoc. prof. medicine Coll. Vet. Medicine, Colo. State U., Ft. Collins, 1960—63, dir. surg. lab., 1963—79, prof. surgery, 1963—81, emeritus prof., 1981—; prof. Ross U., St. Kitts, West Indies, 1986. Pres., CEO The Lubra Co., 1972—99. Author: Small Animal Anesthesia, 1963; author: (with E.W. Jones)) Veterinary Anesthesia, 1973, 1984, Veterinary Anesthesia, Japanese and Spanish translations, 1979; contbr. Named Colo. Vet. of Yr., 1981; recipient Gaines medal, 1965, Ralston Purina Rsch. award, 1980, Jacob Markowitz award, 1986. Mem.: NAS, AAAS, AVMA, Nat. Acads. of Practice, Am. Assn. Vet. Clinicians, N.Y. Acad. Sci., Am. Coll. Vet. Surgeons, Am. Coll. Vet. Anesthesiologists. Address: 1905 Mohawk St Fort Collins CO 80525-1501

LUMBARD, ELIOT HOWLAND, lawyer, educator; b. Fairhaven, Mass., May 6, 1925; s. Ralph E. and Constance Y. L.; m. Jean Ashmore, June 21, 1947 (div.); m. Kirsten Dehner, June 28, 1981 (div.); children: Susan, John, Ann, Joshua Abel, Marah Abel. BS in Marine Transp., U.S. Mcht. Marine Acad., 1943-45; BS in Econs., U. Pa., 1949; JD, Columbia U., 1952. Bar: N.Y. 1953, U.S. Supreme Ct. 1959, Pa. 1983. Assoc. Breed, Abbott and Morgan, N.Y.C., 1952-53; asst. U.S. atty. So. Dist. N.Y., 1953-56; assoc. Chadbourne, Parke, Whiteside & Wolff, N.Y.C., 1956-58; ptnr. Townsend & Lewis, 1961-70, Spear and Hill, N.Y.C., 1970-75, Lumbard and Phelan, P.C., N.Y.C., 1977-82, Saul, Ewing, Remick & Saul, N.Y.C., 1982-84; pvt. practice law, 1984-86; ptnr. Haight, Gardner, Poor & Havens, 1986-88; pvt. practice law, 1988-92; ret. Chief counsel N.Y. State Commn. Investigation, 1958-61; spl. asst. counsel for law enforcement to Gov. N.Y., 1961-67; organizer N.Y. State Identification and Intelligence Sys., 1963-67; chair Oyster Bay Conf. on Organized Crime, 1962-67; criminal justice cons. to Gov. Fla. and other states, 1967; chief criminal justice cons. to N.J. Legis., 1968-69; chmn. com. on organized crime N.Y.C. Criminal Justice Coordinating Coun., 1971-74; organizer schs. of criminal justice at SUNY Albany and Rutgers, Newark; mem. departmental disciplinary com. First Dept., N.Y. Supreme Ct., 1982-88; trustee bankruptcy Universal Money Order Co., Inc., 1977-82, Meritum Corp., 1983-89; spl. master in admiralty Hellenic Lines Ltd., 1984-86; chmn. Palisades Life Ins. Co. (former Equity Funding subs. 1974-75); bd. dir. RMC Industries Corp.; chair Am. Maritime History Project, Inc., Kings Point, N.Y., 1996—; lectr. trial practice NYU Law Sch., 1963-65; mem. vis. com. Sch. Criminal Justice, SUNY-Albany, 1968-75; adj. prof. law and criminal justice John Jay Coll. Criminal Justice, CUNY, 1975-86; arbitrator Am. Arbitration Assn. and N.Y. Civil Ct.-Small Claims Part, N.Y. County; mem. Vol. Master Program U.S. Dist. Ct. (so. dist.) N.Y. Contbr. articles to profl. jours. Bd. dirs. Citizens Crime Commn. N.Y.C., Inc., Big Bros. Movement, Citizens Union; trustee Trinity Sch., 1964-78, N.Y.C. Police Found., Inc., 1971-92, chmn., 1971-74, emeritus. Lt. j.g. USNR, 1943-52. Recipient Disting. Svc. award U.S. Merchant Marine Acad. Alumni, 2000. Mem. Assn. Bar City N.Y., N.Y. County Lawyers Assn., ABA, N.Y. State Bar Assn., Maritime Law Assn., Down Town Assn. Club. Republican. Home: 39B Apple Ln Hollis NH 03049-6311

LUMENG, LAWRENCE, physician, educator; b. Manila, Aug. 10, 1939; came to U.S., 1958; s. Ming and Lucia (Lim) Lu; m. Pauline Lumeng, Nov. 26, 1966; children: Carey, Emily. AB, Ind. U., 1960, MD, 1964, MS, 1969. Intern U. Chgo., 1964-65; resident Ind. U. Hosps., Indpls., 1965-67, fellow, 1967-69, asst. prof. Sch. of Medicine, 1971-73, assoc. prof. Sch. of Medicine, 1974-79, prof. Sch. of Medicine, 1979—, dir. div. gastroenterology and hepatology Sch. of Medieine, 1984—; chief gastroenterology sect. VA Med. Ctr., 1979—. Mem. merit rev. bd. VA. Cen. Office, Washington, 1981-84; mem. alcohol biomed. res. rev. com. NIAAA, Washington, 1982-86; mem. grant rev. panel USDA, Washington, 1985—. Contbr. over 250 articles to profl. jours. Maj. U.S. Army, 1969-71. Fellow ACP; mem. Am. Soc. Clin. Investigation, Am. Soc. Biol. Chemists, Rsch. Soc. on Alcoholism (treas. 1985-87, sec. 1987-89), Am. Gastroenterological Assn., Am. Assn. for the Study of Liver Diseases, Am. Assn. Physicians. Avocations: painting, music. Office: Ind U Med Ctr 975 W Walnut St Indianapolis IN 46202-5181

LUMER, MARK JOSEPH, government executive; b. Bklyn., Sept. 6, 1951; s. Seymour and Bernice (Endlich) L.; m. Beatty Gail Elson, Sept. 7, 1972; children: Michael, Anne, Sarah. BA, SUNY, Buffalo, 1972; MBA, Am. Grad. U., 1984. Cert. assoc. contracts mgr. Contracting officer U.S. Army CECOM, Ft. Monmouth, N.J., 1986, chief compliance, 1986-88, ombudsman, 1988-90; dep. dir. procurement procedures U.S. Army SARDA, Pentagon, Washington, 1990-91, rep. DAR coun., 1991—, mem. army acquisition corps. Adj. prof. Brookdale Community Coll., Lincroft, N.J., 1989-90. Contbr. articles to profl. jours. Ky. col. Hon. Order of Ky. Cols., Louisville, 1990; guest lectr. Nat. Def. U.-Info. Resources Mgmt. Coll., Washington, 1990-91. Recipient Comdr.'s award for Civilian Svc., 1984, Superior Civilian Svc. medal, 1990, Order of Mercury Bronze medal Signal Corps Regimental Assn., 1990; named Top 100 Fed. Employee, 1989-90. Fellow Nat. Contract Mgmt. Assn. (dir. 1991—, functional co-dir. chartering 1991—, mid-atlantic region v.p. 1993-94, nat. v.p. for edn. and cert. 1994—), Contract Mgmt. Inst. (bd. dirs. 1994—), Armed Forces Comm. Electronics Assn., Signal Corps Regimental Assn. Jewish. Avocations: sports, reading. Office: US Army SARDA Pentagon SARD-PP Washington DC 20310-0103

LUMIA, FRANCIS JAMES, internist; b. Trenton, N.J., Apr. 24, 1941; s. Joseph and Rose (Amodio) L.; m. Carolyn King, May 2, 1970; children: Margaret E., Joseph J. BA, U. Chgo., 1963, MD, 1967. Diplomate Am. Bd. Internal Medicine, Am. Bd. Quality Assurance and Utilization Rev. Intern and resident in medicine George Washington U. Hosp., Washington, 1967-70, fellow in cardiology, 1970-72; attending physician Northport VAH, L.I., N.Y., 1972-77; asst. prof. medicine SUNY, Stony Brook, 1972-77; attending physician Deborah Heart and Lung Ctr., Browns Mills, NJ, 1977—, co-dir. sect. of Nvc medicine, 1990—, asst. chair cardiology, 1991—. Physician advisor Peer Rev. Orgn. of N.J., East Brunswick, N.J., 1985—, sanctions com., 1994—; governing coun. Med. Soc. of N.J., Lawrenceville, 1987—. Contbr. articles to profl. jours. Recipient Washington Spl. Clin. fellow Heart Assn., 1971-72. Fellow ACP, Am. Coll. Cardiology, Acad. of Medicine of N.J., Am. Coll. Med. Quality, Am. Coll. of Angiology; mem. Am. Coll. Physician Execs., Med. Soc. N.J. (bd. trustees 1998-2000). Roman Catholic. Avocations: painting, theatre. Office: Deborah Heart & Lung Ctr 200 Trenton Rd Browns Mills NJ 08015-1799

LUMLEY, JOHN LEASK, physicist, educator; b. Detroit, Nov. 4, 1930; s. Charles S. and Jane Anderson Campbell (Leask) L.; m. Jane French, June 20, 1953; children: Katherine Leask, Jennifer French, John Christopher. BA, Harvard, 1952; MS in Engring., Johns Hopkins, 1954, PhD, 1957; Haute Distinction Honoris Causa, Ecole Central de Lyon, France, 1987. Postdoctoral fellow Johns Hopkins, 1957-59; mem. faculty Pa. State U., 1959-77, prof. aerospace engring., 1963-74, Evan Pugh prof. aerospace engring., 1974-77; Willis H. Carrier prof. engring. Cornell U., 1977-2001, prof. emeritus, 2001—. Prof. d'echange U. d'Aix-Marseille, France, 1966-67; Fulbright sr. lectr. U. Liege; vis. prof. U. Louvain-La-Neuve, Belgium; Guggenheim fellow U. Provence and Ecole Centrale de Lyon, France, 1973-74. Author: (with H.A. Panofsky) Structure of Atmospheric Turbulence, 1964, Stochastic Tools for Turbulence, 1970, (with H. Tennekes) A First Course in Turbulence, 1971, (with P. Holmes and G. Berkooz) Turbulence, Coherent Structures, Dynamical Systems and Symmetry, 1996, Engines: An Introduction, 1999; also articles; editor: (with A. Acrivos, L.G. Leal and S. Leibovich) Research Trends in Fluid Dynamics, 1996; tech. editor: Statistical Fluid Mechanics, 1971, 75, Variability of the Oceans, 1977; assoc. editor: Physics of Fluids, 1971-73; assoc. editor Ann. Rev. of Fluid Mechanics, 1976-85, co-editor, 1986-99, editor, 1999—; chmn. tech. editl. bd. Izvestiya: Atmospheric and Oceanic Physics, 1971-96; editorial bd.: Fluid Mechanics: Soviet Research, 1972-94; editor Theoretical and Computational Fluid Dynamics, 1989-98; prin.: films Deformation of Continuous Media, 1963, Eulerian and Lagrangian Frames in Fluid Mechanics, 1968. Recipient medallion U. Liege, Belgium, 1971, Timoshenko medal ASME, 1993. Fellow Am. Acad. Arts and Scis., Am. Acad. Mechanics, Am. Phys. Soc. (exec. com. divsn. fluid dynamics 1972-75, 81-84, chmn. exec. com. divsn. fluid dynamics 1982, 87-89, Fluid Dynamics prize 1990), AIAA (fluid and plasma dynamics award 1982, Hugh L. Dryden rsch. lectureship 1996); mem. NAE, AAAS, N.Y. Acad. Sci., Soc. Natural Philosophy, Am. Geophys. Union, Johns Hopkins Soc. Scholars (charter), Sigma Xi. Home: 743 Snyder Hill Rd Ithaca NY 14850-8708 Office: Cornell U 256 Upson Hall Ithaca NY 14853-7501 E-mail: jll4@cornell.edu.

LUMLEY, THOMAS DEWEY, travel professional, real estate investor; b. Ashland, Ky., Sept. 6, 1944; s. George Francis and Catherine Elanore (Friel) L.; m. Pam Chandler Quinn, Aug. 10, 1996. BS in Acctg., U. Ky., 1969. Lic. real estate sales agt., Ind. Acct. mgr. Trane Co., Lexington, Ky., 1966-69; asst. v.p. fin. Sikes Corp., Lawrenceburg, 1971-74; v.p., co-owner Robert Half & Accountemps, Louisville, 1974-75; exec. v.p., co-owner Fire King Internat., New Albany, Ind., 1975-84; pres., owner Places Travel, Louisville, 1984-94; pres., CEO Carlson Wagonlit Travel/WTS Inc., 1994—; pres. Lumley Enterprises, 1998—. Founder, bd. dirs. Hometown Nat. Bank, New Albany; pres. T&M Homes, New Albany, 1978—. Treas. Hoosier Falls Pvt. Industry Coun., New Albany, 1984—98; chmn. So. 7 Workforce Investment Base. Sgt. U.S. Army, 1969—71. Sgt. U.S. Army, 1969-71. Mem. Soc. Human Resource Execs. (pres. 1985), Kentuckiana World Commerce Coun. (former pres.), So. Ind. C. of C. (pres. 1984). Office: Carlson Wagonlit Travel 845 S 3d St Louisville KY 40203

LUMMUS, CAROL TRAVERS, artist, printmaker; b. Hyannis, Mass., Nov. 2, 1937; d. Frank and Doris (Brown) Travers; m. Bertrand W. Lummus, Jan. 27, 1962; children: Sarah Travers, Jonathan Ames. Student, Walnut Hill Sch., Natick, Mass., 1952-55; AA, Colby-Sawyer Coll., New London, N.H., 1957; student, U. Geneva, 1960-62. Artist, printmaker. Mem. art adv. panel N.H. Commn. on Arts. One-woman shows include Hammerquist, N.Y.C., 1979, La Galeria, San Mateo, Calif., 1980, Alice Bingham, Memphis, 1980, P.S. Gallery, Ogunquit, Maine, 1980, 927 Gallery, New Orleans, Saint Gaudens Nat. Historic Site, Cornish, N.H.; group shows include All New Eng. Show, 1975-76, Currier Mus., Manchester, N.H., 1976, 80, Fitchburg (Mass.) Mus., 1975-76, Instituto Brasil-Estadios Unidos, Brazil, 1978, Hobe Sound (Fla.) Gallery, 1976—, Payson-Waldron, Portland, Maine, 1982, Nat. Assn. Women Artists, 1994, 99, Lund-Wassmer Mus., Utah, 1988, Royal Miniature Art Soc., London, 1995, C.C.C.C. Gallery, Phila., 1999; represented in permanent collections Springfield (Utah) Mus., Snow Coll., Ephraim, Utah, Ogunquit (Maine) Mus. Art; illustrator Cin. mag., Yankee mag. Recipient Rosmond de Kalb award Currier Mus., 1975, 1st prize Fitchburg Mus. Art, 1973, award Miniature Painters and Gravers Soc., Washington, 1996; N.H. Commn. Arts grantee, 1980. Mem. Cape Cod Performing Arts Assn. (bd. dirs.), Conn. League N.H. Craftsmen, Nat. Assn. Women Artists N.Y., Barnstable (Mass.) Yacht Club. Episcopalian. Home (Summer): Box 525 7 Railroad Ave Barnstable MA 02630-1428 Home (Winter): 162 Governor-Wentworth Hwy Mirror Lake NH 03853

LUMPKIN, ANNE CRAIG, retired television and radio company executive; b. DeValls Bluff, Ark., Apr. 3, 1919; d. Claude Cleo and Lou (Craig) L. Student, Little Rock Bus. Sch., 1938-39, Patricia Stevens, 1953. Adminstrv. asst. to pres. Sta. KVLC (S.W. Broadcasting), Little Rock, 1949-52, Sta. KGKO (Lakewood Broadcasting), Dallas, 1952-54, Sta. KTLN, Inc., Denver, 1954-58; asst. mgr. Sta. KLRA, Inc., Little Rock, 1958-83; asst. dir. fin. affairs KLRT-TV, 1983-91; retired, 1991. Mem. Ark. Arts Ctr., Little Rock, Fine Arts Club, Little Rock, Nat Audubon Soc., Ark. Hist. Soc. Mem. Am. Women in Radio-TV, Am. Bus. Women's Assn., Little Rock Club. Baptist. Avocations: interior decorating, porcelain dolls, miniatures, flower gardening.

LUMPKIN, GARY LEONARD, judge; b. Sentinel, Okla. m. Barbara Lumpkin; 1 child. Student, Northwestern State Coll., Alva, Okla., 1964-65; BS, Soutwestern State Coll., Weatherford, Okla., 1968; JD, U. Okla., 1974. Bar: Okla. 1974. Staff atty. Okla. Dept. Consumer Affairs, 1974-75; asst. dist. atty. to 1st asst. dist. atty. Marshall County, Okla., 1976-82, assoc. dist. judge, 1982-85; dist. judge 20th Jud. Dist., Divsn. II, Marshall County, 1985-89; judge Okla. Ct. Criminal Appeals, Oklahoma City, 1989—, vice-presiding judge, 1991-92, 99-00, presiding judge, 1993-94, 2001—; USMC res. judge Navy-Marine Ct. Criminal Appeals, 1994-98. Pres. Okla. Jud. Conf., 1989; past mem. sentencing and release policy com. created by Senate Bill 432 of 42d legislature; rep. Ct. Criminal Appeals on Truth in Sentencing Policy Adv. Commn.; mem. Okla. Supreme Ct. com. on uniform civil jury instrns. and ct. liaison to Ct. of Criminal Appeals uniform criminal jury instrn. com.; bd. dir. Nat. Ctr. for State Cts., Williamsburg, Va. With USMC, 1968-71; col. USMCR, Vietnam, ret. Mem. Okla. Bar Assn. (past chair criminal law com., mem. law related edn. com.), Okla. Bar Found., Okla. County Bar Assn., Marshall County Bar Assn., William J. Holloway Jr. Am. Inns of Ct. (pres.-elect, chair program com. 1992, pres. 1993, William J. Holloway Jr. Professionalism award 1999), VFW, Marine Corps Res. Officers Assn. Baptist. Office: Okla Court Criminal Appeals State Capitol Bldg Rm 230 Oklahoma City OK 73105 Fax: 405-521-4980. E-mail: glumpkin@okcca.net.

LUMPKIN, THOMAS RILEY, physician, educator; b. Tuskegee, Ala., Jan. 4, 1926; s. William Clifford and Harriet Graham (Riley) L.; m. Jean D. Perry, June 10, 1955; children: Leah, Ry, Mary Lyman, Cliff. BS, U. Ala., 1949; DM, Med. Coll. Ala., 1958. Diplomate Am. Bd. Family Physicians. Pvt. practice, Tuskegee, Ala., 1959-65, Enterprise, 1965-74; asst. prof. Coll. of Cmty. Health Scis., Tuscaloosa, 1974-77; assoc. prof. U. Ala., 1977-81, prof. family medicine, 1981-91, prof emeritus, 1991—; interim dean Coll. Cmty. Health Scis. Capstone Med. Ctr., 1979-80. Councilman City of Tuskegee, 1962-64; active Leadership Ala. Class III, 1992-93; bd. dirs. free med. care for under and non-insured Good Samaritan Clinic, 1999. Served with USAAC, 1946, inf. AUS, 1951-52. Mem. Ala. Acad. Family Physicians (pres. 1968-69), Med. Assn. State of Ala. (pres. 1990-91), Rotary Internat. (pres. Enterprise club 1968-69, pres. Tuscaloosa 1993-94, dist. gov. 1997-98), U. Ala. Med. Alumni Assn. (pres. 2001—). Methodist. Avocations: travel, hunting, reading. Home: 2 Ridgeland Tuscaloosa AL 35406-1607

LUMPKIN, VICKI G. minister; b. Denver, Sept. 4, 1950; d. Lester S. and L. Faye (Felton) Gapen; m. Charles D. Lumpkin, Feb. 12, 1971; children: L. David, Michael A., Andrew C. BA, George Mason U., 1973, MA, 1976; MDiv, Bapt. Theol. Seminary, Richmond, Va., 1993; PhD, Union Theol. Sem. in Va., Richmond, 1999. Ordained to ministry Am. Bapt. Ch. Protestant religious edn. coord. U.S. Army, Ft. Dix, N.J., 1984-85; minister of edn. and youth Haymarket (Va.) Bapt. Ch., 1991-95; group facilitator, homiletics Union Theol. Seminary, Richmond, 1995; interim co-pastor Ravensworth Bapt. Ch., Annandale, Va., 1997-98; pastor CityCh., Dallas, 2000—. Adj. prof. Bapt. Theol. Sem., Richmond, 2000, John Leland Ctr. for Theol. Studies, Falls Church, Va.; guest lectr. Bapt. heritage Bapt. Theol. Sem., Richmond, 1996; mem. Leadership Coun., Va. Alliance of Bapts., Richmond, 1995-98. Bd. dirs. Prince William Interfaith Vol. Caregivers, Manassas, Va., 1991-93; co-founder Interdenominal Support Group for Women in Ministry, Bristow, Va., 1992; tchr. of English YMCA, Panama City, 1976-77. Recipient Smyth and Helwys Seminarian award Bapt. Theol. Sem., Richmond, 1993. Mem. N.Am. Acad. of Liturgy, Acad. of Homiletics, Liturgical Conf., Am. Acad. Religion, Soc. Bibl. Lit., Nat. Assn. Bapt. Profs. Religion. Baptist. Avocation: photography. Home: 1409 S Lamar St Apt 523 Dallas TX 75215 Office: Ste 620B 3878 Oak Lawn Ave Dallas TX 75219 E-mail: vglumpkin@2revs.com.

LUMRY, WILLIAM RAYMOND, physician, allergist; b. Coronado, Calif., Feb. 17, 1951; s. Raymond Harley and Evelyn (Bamson) L.; m. Rozalia Nadel, May 18, 1980; children: Ariel Martina, Randall Bamson. BS, Tex. A&M U., 1973; MD, U. Tex., Galveston, 1977. Diplomate Am. Bd. Internal Medicine, Am. Bd. Allergy and Immunology. Intern Jewish Hosp., St. Louis, 1977-78, resident in internal medicine, 1978-80; fellow in allergy/immunology Scripps Clinic and Rsch. Found., La Jolla, Calif., 1980-82; physician Allergy and Asthma Specialists, 1982-98; assoc. clin. prof. Southwestern Med. Sch., U. Tex., Dallas, 1982—; med. dir. AARA Rsch. Ctr., 1988—. Med. dir. Children's Lung Disease, Dallas, 1985—, Better Breathing Club, Med. City, Dallas, 1985—. Contbr. articles to profl. jours. Recipient Alcoa award Alcoa Found., 1976. Fellow Am. Coll. Physicians, Am. Coll. Allergists, Am. Acad. Allergy and Immunology. Republican. Methodist. Avocations: tennis, skiing, photography, sailing. Office: Allergy & Asthma Spec Dallas 9900 N Central Expy Ste 525 Dallas TX 75231-3399

LUMSDEN, IAN GORDON, art gallery director; b. Montreal, Que., Can., June 8, 1945; s. Andrew Mark and Isobel Dallas (Wilson) L.; m. Katherine Elizabeth Carson, July 28, 1979; 1 child, Craig Ian. BA, McGill U., 1968; postgrad., Mus. Mgmt. Inst., U. Calif., Berkeley, 1991. Curator art dept. N.B. Mus., Saint John, 1969; curator Beaverbrook Art Gallery, Fredericton, N.B., 1969-83, dir., 1983-2001. Mem. Cultural Property Export Rev. Bd., 1982-85; mem. program com. 49th Parallel Ctr. for Contemporary Can. Art., 1990-92. Author exhbn. catalogues; contbr. numerous articles to Can. art periodicals. Mem. Can. Museums Assn. (sec.-treas. 1973-75), Can. Art Mus. Dirs. Orgn. (1st v.p. 1977-83, pres. 1983-85, treas. 1998-2001), Atlantic Provinces Art Gallery Assn. (chmn. 1970-72), Am. Assn. Museums, Union Club (St. John, N.B.), Can. Soc. for the Decorative Arts (dir. nat. coun. 1999). Mem. Anglican Ch. of Can. Home: 103 Bliss Carman Dr Fredericton NB Canada E3B 9P2 E-mail: lums@nb.sympatico.ca.

LUMUMBA-KASONGO, TUKUMBI, university educator; b. Nov. 25, 1948; BA, Agrégation, U. Libre du Congo, Kisangani, 1972; M, Harvard U., 1975, U. Chgo., 1980, PhD, 1981. Asst. prof., chmn. dept. polit. sci. U. Liberia, Monrovia, 1982-85; vis. asst. prof. Vassar Coll., Poughkeepsie, N.Y., 1985-91; vis. scholar, sr. fellow Cornell U., Ithaca, 1991—; founder, dir. CEPARRED, Abidjan, Côte d'Ivoire, 1996—. Assoc. prof. polit. sci. Wells Coll., Aurora, N.Y., 1993-98, Herbert J. Charles and Florence Charles Faegre prof. polit. sci., chmn. dept. internat. studies, 1998—. Co-editor Internat. Jour. Comparative Sociology, 1998—; assoc. editor, rschr. Jour. Internat. Rels. and Edn. in Africa, 1998—; edit. bd. Internat. Third World Studies Jour. and Rev., 1999—; contbr. articles to profl. jours. Grantee The World Bank, Washington, 1996, Rockefeller Found., N.Y.C., 1998; recipient Outstanding Tchg. in Polit. Sci. award Am. Polit Sci. Assn. and Pi Sigma Alpha, 1999. Office: Wells Coll PO Box 457 Aurora NY 13026-0457

LUN, LAPMAN, internist; b. Hong Kong, Jan. 28, 1963; MD, Ohio State U., 1989. Diplomate Am. Bd. Internal Medicine, Am. Bd. Hemotology Oncology. Intern Hahnemann U. Hosp., Phila., 1989-90, resident in internal medicine, 1990-92; fellow in hematol. oncology U. Md., Balt., 1992-96; pvt. practice Wooster, Ohio. Mem. staff Wooster Cmty. Hosp., 1996—. Mem. AMA, ACP, Am. Soc. Clin. Oncology, Am. Assn. Cancer Rsch. Office: 1740 Cleveland Rd Wooster OH 44691-2204

LUNA, BARBARA CAROLE, financial analyst, accountant, appraiser; b. N.Y.C., July 23, 1950; d. Edwin A. and Irma S. (Schub) Schlang; m. Dennis Rex Luna, Sept. 1, 1974; children: John S., Katherine E. BA, Wellesley Coll., 1971; MS in Applied Math., Harvard U., 1973, PhD in Applied Math., 1975. CPA; cert. gen. real estate appraiser Calif. Office Real Estate Appraisers; cert. valuation analyst Nat. Assn. Cert. Valuation Analysts; cert. fraud examiner Assn. Cert. Fraud Examiners, mgmt. cons. Inst. Mgmt. Consultants; accredited sr. appraiser Am. Soc. Appraisers; accredited bus. valuation Am. Inst. CPAs. Investment banker Warburg Paribas Becker, L.A., 1975-77; cons., sr. mgr. Price Waterhouse, 1977-83; sr. mgr. litigation Pannell Kerr Forster, 1983-86; nat. dir. litigation cons. Kenneth Leventhal & Co., 1986-88; ptnr. litigation svcs. Coopers & Lybrand, 1988-93; sr. ptnr. litigation svcs. White, Zuckerman, Warsavsky, Luna & Wolf, Sherman Oaks, Calif., 1993—. Expert witness. Mem. Harvard Bus. Sch. Coun. Wellesley scholar, 1971. Mem. AICPA, Assn. Bus. Trial Lawyers (com. on experts), Am. Soc. Appraisers, Assn. Cert. Valuation Analysts, Calif. Office Real Estate Appraisers, Assn. Cert. Real Estate Appraisers, Appraisal Inst., Assn. Cert. Fraud Examiners, Inst. Mgmt. Cons., Calif. Soc. CPAs (econ. damages common interest mem. svcs. com., fraud common interest mem. svcs. com., bus. valuation common interest mem. svcs. com.), Am. Bd. Forensic Accts. and Examiners, Harvard-Radcliffe Club So. Calif. (bd. dirs., membership chair). Avocations: golf, swimming. Home: 18026 Rodarte Way Encino CA 91316-4370 E-mail: bluna@lunala.com., bluna@wzwlw.com.

LUNA, GENE IRVING, academic administrator, education educator; b. Eden, N.C., Sept. 27, 1949; s. Eugene Irving and Martha Elizabeth (Thacker) L.; m. Shelia Jean Bolick, June 5, 1982; children: Rebecca Elizabeth, Emily Katherine. BA, Roanoke Coll., 1971; MA, Appalachian State U., 1981; PhD, U. Fla., 1990; mgmt. devel. program, Harvard U., 1999. Grad. Realtors Inst., N.C.; cert. real estate agt., N.C. Salesperson, realtor Wall, Realtors, Eden, N.C., 1971-73, dir. mktg., v.p., 1974-79; residence life coord. Appalachian State U., Boone, N.C., 1979-83; asst. dir. housing U. Fla., Gainesville, 1983-89, U. Ga., Athens, 1989-92; dir. housing U. S.C., Columbia, 1992—, clin. faculty Coll. Edn., 1994—, assoc. v.p. student devel. and univ. housing, 1997—. Cons. in field, 1990—. Vol. YMCA, Eden, 1972-77, United Way, Athens, 1990-91, Lexington/Richland Dist. Five, Columbia, 1994—, Irmo Recreation Dept., 1997—. Recipient Beene Meml. Svc. award Southeastern Assn. Housing Officers, 1990, Svc. award Southeastern Assn. Housing Officers, 1991, Founder's award, 1998. Mem. World Futurist Soc., Inst. Noetic Sci., Assn. of Coll. and Univ. Housing Officers (Internat. Found. of Excellence award 2002), Omicron Delta Kappa. Avocations: golf, frisbee, racquetball, swimming. Office: U SC 1215 Blossom St Columbia SC 29208-2900 E-mail: genel@sc.edu.

LUNA, MICHAEL DONOVAN, speech language pathologist; b. Panorama City, Calif., Dec. 10, 1968; s. Don Dickerson and Gloria Ruth Luna. BA in Comm. Scis. and Disorders, San Jose (Calif.) State U., 1993, MA in Speech Pathology and Audiology, 1995. Lic. speech-lang. pathologist, Calif. Environ. chemist Animetrix, San Jose, 1989-90; warehouseman, dock worker W. W. Grainger, 1990-95; speech-lang. pathologist San Jose Unified Sch. Dist., 1995-97, 99—; rsch. asst. Ariz. State U., Tempe, 1997-99, instr., 1998. Mem. leadership teams S. Valley Christian Ch., San Jose, 1993-96; sponsor Say No Drugs, San Jose, 1995; asst. scoutmaster Boy Scouts Am., San Jose, 1996. Specialist U.S. Army, 1990-91, Gulf War. Graduate scholar Ariz. State U., 1997. Mem. Am. Speech Lang. and Hearing Assn. Avocations: playing and writing music for piano, synthesizer, organ and guitar, cross-country running, kayaking, snowboarding. Office: San Jose Unified Sch Dist Willow Glen Mid Sch 2105 Cottle Ave San Jose CA 95125-3502 E-mail: mluna@usa.com.

LUNA, PATRICIA ADELE, marketing executive; b. Charleston, S.C., July 22, 1956; d. Benjamin Curtis and Clara Elizabeth (McCrory) L. BS in History, Auburn U., 1978, MEd in History, 1980; MA in Adminstrn., U. Ala., 1981, EdS in Adminstrn., 1984, PhD, ABD in Adminstrn., 1986. Cert. tchr., Ga., Ala. History tchr. Harris County Mid. Sch., Ga., 1978-79, head dept., 1979-81; residence hall dir. univ. housing U. Ala., 1981-83, asst. dir. residence life, 1983-85; intern Cornell U., Ithaca, N.Y., 1983; dir. mktg. Golden Flake Snack Foods, Inc., Birmingham, Ala., 1985-89; sr. v.p. Quest U.S.A., Inc., Atlanta, 1989-90; pres. Promotion Mgmt. Group, Inc., Montgomery, Ala., 1990—. Cons. Capital Campaigns; lectr. in field. Author: Specialization: A Learning Module, 1979, Grantsmanship, 1981, Alcohol Awareness Programs, 1984, University Programming, 1984, Marketing Residential Life, 1985, The History of Golden Flake Snack Foods, 1986, Golden Flake Snack Foods, Inc., A Case Study, 1987, Cases in Strategic Marketing, 1989, Cases in Strategic Management, 1990, Frequency Marketing, 1992. Fundraiser U. Ala. Alumni Scholarship Fund, Tuscaloosa, 1983, Am. Diabetes Assn., Tuscaloosa, 1984, Urban Ministries, Birmingham, 1985-88; fundraiser, com. chmn. Spl. Olympics, Tuscaloosa, 1985; chmn. Greene County Relief Project, 1982-89; bd. dirs. Cerebral Palsy Found., Tuscaloosa, 1985-86; lay rector and com. chm. Kairos Prison Ministry, Tutwiler State Prison, Ala., 1986-92; lobbyist, com. chmn. task force Justice Fellowship, 1988-91; bd. dirs. Internat. Found. Ewha U., Seoul, Korea, 1988-91; chm. bd. dirs. Epiphany Ministries, 1991-98; bd. dirs. Hunting Coll. Fine Arts, chairperson, Coll. Ministries, Whitfield Meml. United Methodist Ch., 1999-2000, chmn. capital fund campaign, 2000—, chmn. stewardship and evangelism com., 2000—; bd. dirs., Whitewater Camp, 1999—, Acad. for Spiritual Formation, 1997-99; com. chmn. Emmaus Ministry, 1985—; chmn. Chrysalis steering com., 1995-97. Recipient nat. award Joint Coun. Econ. Edn., 1979, rsch. award NSF, 1979, Harry Denman Evangelism award, 2001; named to Hon. Order Ky. Cols. Commonwealth of Ky., 1985—, Rep. Senatorial Inner Circle, 1986-96. Mem. Sales and Mktg. Execs. (chmn. com. 1985-86), Leadership Ala. (pres. 1982-83), Am. Mktg. Assn. (Disting. Leadership award 1987, Commemorative Medal of Honor 1988), Assn. Coll. and Univ. Housing Officers (com. chmn. 1983-85), Nat. Assn. Student Personnel Officers, Snack Food Assn. (mem. mktg. com. and conf. presenter), Internat. Coun. Shopping Ctrs. (Merit award 1991, program com.), Commerce Exec. Soc., Omega Rho Sigma (pres. 1983-84), Omicron Delta Kappa, Phi Delta Kappa, Kappa Delta Pi, Phi Alpha Theta. Republican. Methodist. Avocations: skiing, tennis, community/church work, public speaking. E-mail: patluna@charter.net.

LUNA PADILLA, NITZA ENID, photography educator; b. San Juan, P.R., Mar. 13, 1959; d. Luis and Carmen Iris (Padilla) Luna. BFA, Pratt Inst., 1981; MS, Brooks Inst., 1985. Instr. U. P.R., Carolina, 1981-82, Cultural Inst., San Juan, 1988; prof. photography U. Sacred Heart, Santurce, P.R., 1987—; assoc. dir. communication ctr. U. Sagrado Corazon, P.R., 1989-90. Contbr. articles to profl. pubis.; one-woman shows P.R. Inst. Culture, 1988, Art and History Mus., San Juan, 1989, 94, 96, U. P.R., 1989, 90, Brooks Inst. Photootgraphy, Santa Barbara, Calif., 1990, Miriam Walsh Gallery, Glenwood Springs, Colo., 1991, Mus. Ponce, 1991, Spokane (Wash.) C.C., 1994, Centro Europa, San Juan, 1996, Galería de Arte, P.R., 1996; exhibited in group shows Santa Barbara Mus. Art, 1987, Coll. of Santa Fe, N.Mex., 1988, Durango (Colo.) Arts Ctr., 1988, 90, Laband Art Gallery, L.A., 1989, Cultural Ctr., Vercelli, Italy, 1989, Univ. Union Gallery Calif. Poly. State U., 1990, Coconino Ctr. Arts, Flagstaff, Ariz., 1990, Centro Cultural Washington Irving, Madrid, 1991, L.A. County Fair, 1991, Museo del Grabado Latinoamericano, San Juan, 1992, 93, 94, P.R. Inst. Culture, 1994, Hostos Art Gallery, N.Y.C., 1996, The Platinum Gallery, Sante Fe, 1996, Gallería Botello, San Juan, 1996, The Queens Mus., N.Y.C., 1997, The Platinum Gallery, N.Y.C., 1997, Arsenal, San Juan, 1997, Wis. Union Art Gallery, U. Wis., 1998; in permanent collections; juror Fotografia de prensa "Mandin,", 1991-92. MacDowell Colony grantee, Instituto de Cultural Puertorriqueña grantee, 1993, 94, 96. Mem. Soc. Photog. Edn., Friends of Photography. Roman Catholic. Avocations: painting, aerobics. Office: U Sagrado Corazón PO Box 12383 San Juan PR 00914-8505

LUNARDINI, CHRISTINE ANNE, writer, historian, school administrator; b. Holyoke, Mass., Jan. 27, 1941; d. Virgil Joseph and Christine Hildegarde (Cavanaugh) L. AA, Holyoke C.C., 1973; BA, Mt. Holyoke Coll., 1975; MA, Princeton U., 1979, PhD, 1981. Instr. history Princeton (N.J.) U., 1981-85; adminstrv. asst. Refco Inc., N.Y.C., 1985-87; assoc. prof. Pace U., 1987-91; freelance writer, 1991—; exec. asst. to pres. Lynn Chase Designs, Inc., 1999-2000; dir. devel. St. Michael Acad., 2000—. Vis. assoc. prof., Barnard Coll., Columbia U., N.Y.C., 1984-85; project mgr., sr. editor Carlson Pub., Bklyn., 1992-93. Author: From Equal Suffrage to Equal Rights: Alice Paul and the National Women's Party 1910-1928, 1986, The American Peace Movement in the 20th Century, 1994, What Every American Should Know About Women's History, 1996, Women's Rights, 1996; editor, project mgr.: Black Women in America, An Historical Encyclopedia, 2 vols., 1993 (Dartmouth medal 1994), Columbia Guide to American Women: The Nineteenth Century, 1999; mem. editl. adv. bd. Am. Heritage Multi Media, Am. Heritage: Women in Am., 1994—. Princeton U. fellow, 1975-79, Woodrow Wilson nat. fellow, 1980, AAUW nat. fellow, 1980-81. Mem. NOW, Women's Bond Club N.Y., Phi Beta Kappa. Democrat. Episcopalian. Home: 26 Beaver St New York NY 10004-2311 Office: 425 W 33rd St New York NY 10001 E-mail: lunar127@aol.com.

LUND, ARNOLD MILTON, JR. media specialist; b. Seattle, July 21, 1950; s. Arnold Milton and Alice Elizabeth L.; m. Marlene Mildred Meland, Aug. 18, 1973; children: Anna Doribeth, Sonja Faith. BA in Chemistry, U. Chgo., 1972; MA in Exptl. Psychology, Calif. State U., 1977; PhD in Exptl. Psychology, Northwestern U., 1980. Lectr. Calif. State U., Fullerton, 1976-77; rsch. mgr., instr. Northwestern U., Evanston, Ill., 1977-80; mem. tech. staff AT&T Bell Labs., Holmdel, N.J., 1980-85, supr. systems engring. & human factors, 1985-89; sr. dir. human factors & emerging techs. Ameritech, Hoffman Estates, Ill., 1989-97; disting. mem. tech. staff U.S. West Advanced Techs., Boulder, Colo., 1997, dir. new media design & usability, 1997-00; dir. info. architecture and R&D Sapient, Denver, 2000—. Adj. prof. Northwestern U., Evanston, Ill., 1996-97; dir. Infinitec, Inc., Chgo., 1996—. Guest editor IEEE Software, 1997; mem. editl. bd. Internat. Jour. Speech Tech.; contbr. articles to profl. jours.; inventor in field. Elder United Presbyn. Ch., 1986—. Recipient cert. of merit Soc. Motion Picture and TV Engrs., 1993. Fellow Human Factors and Ergonomics Soc. (founder, chair Chgo. Met. chpt. 1990-97, program chair comm. tech. group 1989—, computing syss. tech. group 1996—); mem. Assn. Computing Machinery. Avocations: photography, sports, genealogy. Home: 972 Saint Andrews Ln Louisville CO 80027-9589 Office: Sapient 1899 Wynkoop Ste 500 Denver CO 80202 E-mail: alund@acm.org.

LUND, DARYL BERT, food science educator; b. San Bernardino, Calif., Nov. 4, 1941; married June 15, 1963; children: Kristine, Eric. BS in Math., U. Wis., 1963, MS in food Sci., 1965, PhD in Food Sci., 1968. Rsch. asst. in food sci. U. Wis., Madison, 1963-67, instr., 1967-68, asst. prof., 1968-72, assoc. prof., 1972-77, prof. food sci., 1977-87, chmn. dept. food sci., 1984-87; chmn. dept. food sci., assoc. dir. agrl. experiment sta. Rutgers, the State U., New Brunswick, 1988-89, interim exec. dean agr. and natural resources N.J., 1989-91, exec. dean agr./natural resources, 1991-95, exec. dir. N.J. Agrl. Experiment Sta., dean Cook Coll., 1991-95; Ronald P. Lynch dean of agr. and life scis. Cornell U., Ithaca, N.Y., 1995-2000; exec. dir. North Ctrl. Regional Assn., U. Wis., Madison, 2001—. Vis. engr. Western Regional Rsch. Lab., Berkeley, Calif., 1970-71; advisor for evaluation of food tech. dept. Inst. Agr., Bogor, Indonesia, 1973; mem. four-man evaluation team to review grad. edn. programs Brazilian univs., 1976; vis. prof. food process engring. Agrl. U., Wageningen, The Netherlands, 1979; invited vis. prof. food process engring. Univ. Coll., Dublin, 1982; invited advisor Inter-Univ. Ctr. on Food Sci. and Nutrition, Bogor, 1991; advisor Agrl. U., Bogor, 1992; lectr. in field. Contbr. over 200 articles to profl. jours.; editor 5 books; co-author text book. Recipient Food Engring. award Dairy and Food Industries Supply Assn. and Am. Soc. Agrl. Engring., 1987. Fellow Inst. Food Technologists (Wis. sect. 1968-87, N.Y. sect. 1988-95, ctrl. N.Y. 1995-2000, Travel award as promising young scientist to Internat. Congress on Food Sci. and tech., Madrid 1974, pres. 1990-91, Internat. award 1995), Internat. Union Food Sci. and Tech. (charter fellow); mem. AIChE, Am. Inst. Nutrition, Am. Soc. Agrl. Engrs., Sigma Xi, Gamma Sigma Delta, Phi Tau Sigma. Avocations: golf, travel, wood working. Home: 151 E Reynolds St Cottage Grove WI 53527

LUND, DAVID NATHAN, artist; b. N.Y.C., Oct. 16, 1925; s. Isidore and Mollie (Hirschfield) Lifshitz; m. Sally Harriet Amster, June 17, 1961 (dec. Feb. 1988); children: Andrew Ethan, Giuliana Elizabeth; m. Judith Manelis. BA, Queens Coll., 1948; postgrad., NYU, 1948-50. Adj. asst. prof. painting, drawing, design Cooper Union Art Sch., 1955-57, 59-66, 67-74; instr. painting Cummington (Mass.) Sch. Arts, 1963; instr. in painting Haystack Sch., Deer Isle, Maine, 1963; instr. in drawing and painting Parsons Sch. Design, 1963-66, 67-69; lectr. in drawing Queens Coll., 1964-66; vis. prof. painting Washington U., St. Louis, 1966-67, 85; asst. prof. painting and drawing Columbia U., 1969-82; vis. prof. painting Boston U., 1975-76. Vis. critic; lectr. in field; juror Nat. Selection Com., Fulbright Grants In Art; cons. in painting Creative Artists Public Service, 1979-81; vis. artist Winston-Salem Arts Council and Associated Artists of Winston-Salem, 1975. One-man shows include Grand Central Moderns Gallery, N.Y.C., 1954, Galleria Trastevere, Rome, 1959, Grace Borgenicht Gallery, N.Y.C., 1960, 63, 66, 67, 69, 76, 78, 80, 83, 86, Martin Schweig Gallery, St. Louis, 1966, Kirkland Coll., 1971, Arts Council Winston-Salem, N.C., 1975, Creiger-Seson Gallery, Boston, 1981, Meredith Contemporary Art Gallery, Balt., 1982, U. Alaska, Fairbanks, 1983, Washington U., St. Louis, 1985, Allport Gallery, San Francisco, 1984, A.J. Laderman Fine Arts, Hoboken, N.J., 1990; group shows include Whitney Mus., N.Y.C., 1958, 60, 61, 62, 77, Galleria Schneider, Rome, 1959, Palazzo Venezia, Rome, 1959, Galleria San Marco, Rome, 1959, Washington Gallery Art, 1963, Am. embassy, Athens, Greece, 1966-67, White House, Washington, 1966-67, 67-68, 68-69, Nat. Collection Fine Arts, Washington, 1972-73; represented in permanent collections Whitney Mus., Balt. Mus., Art Gallery Ont., Toronto, Farnsworth Mus., Rockland, Me., Corcoran Gallery Art, Washington, Ft. Worth Art Center, U. Mass., Montclair (N.J.) Mus., Haas Gallery at Bloomsburg State Coll., Kranert Art Gallery, Champagne, Ill., also other public and pvt. collections. Fulbright grantee Rome, 1957-59 Mem. Nat. Acad. Design, Artists Equity. Jewish. Achievements include being subject of numerous profl. pubis.

LUND, DORIS HIBBS, retired dietitian; b. Des Moines, Nov. 10, 1923; d. Loyal Burchard and Catharine Mae (McClymond) Hibbs; m. Richard Bodholdt Lund, Nov. 9, 1946; children: Laurel Anne, Richard Douglas, Kristi Jane Lund Lozier. Student, Duchesne Coll., Omaha, 1941-42; BS, Iowa State U., 1946; postgrad., Grand View Coll., Des Moines, 1965; MS in Mgmt., Iowa State U., 1968. Registered dietitian, lic. dietitian. Clk. Russell Stover Candies, Omaha, 1940-42; chemist Martin Bomber Plant, 1942-43; dietitian Grand Lake (Colo.) Lodge, 1946; tailoring instr. Ottumwa Pub. Schs., 1952-53; cookery instr. Des Moines Pub. Schs., 1958-62; dietitian Calvin Manor, Des Moines, 1963; home economist Am. Wool Coun./Am. Lamb Coun., Denver, 1963-65, The Merchandising Group of N.Y., 1965-68, Thomas Wolff, Pub. Rels., 1968-70; home economist weekly TV program Iowa Power Co., 1968-70; cons. in child nutrition programs Iowa Dept. Edn., Des Moines, 1970-95; ret. Nutritioneering, Ltd., 1995. Mem. Iowa Home Economists in Bus. (pres. 1962-63), PEO. Pres. Callanan Jr. H.S. PTA, 1964, Roosevelt H.S. PTA, 1966; amb. Friendship Force Internat., 1982—; alliance mem. Des Moines Symphony; guild mem. Civic Music Des Moines Met. Opera; mem. Civic Music Guild, Bot. Ctr. Des Moines, Des Moines Art Ctr., Des Moines Civic Ctr.; chmn. Met. Opera Previews; pres. Ctrl. Presbyn. Mariners, Des Moines; ruling elder, clk. of session Ctrl. Presbyn. Session, 1972—78; bd. dirs. Ctrl. Found., Ctrl. Pastor Seeking Nomination Com., 1996; chair cmty. concerns Calvin Cmty. Found., 1998, chair support and edn., 1999—. Duchesne Coll. 4 yr. scholar. Mem. Am. Dietetic Assn., Iowa Home Economists in Bus. (pres. 1962-63), PEO, Pi Beta Phi (pres. 1945-46). Republican. Avocations: international travel, writing, sailing, sewing, cooking. Home: 105 34th St Des Moines IA 50312-4526

LUND, EDWIN HARRISON, business accounting systems executive; b. Erie, Pa., Apr. 4, 1954; s. John Freeman and Shirley (Nick) L.; m. Michele C. Lund, July 9, 1988; children: Christian John Chaffee, Harrison Taylor VonNick, Brett Michael. Student, U. Tex., Dallas, 1981, Pa. State U., 1976. Pres., mgr. Flowerama of Am., Erie, Pa., 1973-79; acctg. mgr. Diversified Human Resources Group, Dallas, 1980-83; acctg. rep. Tex. Dept. Human Resources, 1983-84; mgr. Progressive Bookkeeping Systems, Erie, 1984-85; pres. Presque Isle Group Cos. Inc., 1985—, Rising Star Recordings, Inc., Erie, 1989—. Treas. North Coast Fin. Svcs., Erie, 1989—. Author: How to Value An Accounting Business, 1988. Mem. Leadership Erie Class of 1990. Mem. Nat. Exch. Club (pres. Erie chpt. 1989-91), Nat. Assn. of Accts., Nat. Soc. Pub. Accts., Pa. Notary Soc.; Nat. Red Cross (treas., bd. dirs. Erie chpt.). Office: Lund Acctg Systems 1920 W 8th St Erie PA 16505-4935

LUND, FREDERICK HENRY, aerospace and electrical engineer; b. Seattle, June 2, 1929; s. Henry George and Minnie (Wilbern) L.; m. Joyce Pauline Mon Pleasure, Sept. 8, 1950; children: Frederick Bradley, Christopher Michael, Peter Andrew, Andrea Leslie. BSEE, U. Wash., Seattle, 1951; postgrad., U. Calif., L.A., 1954-56, 57-59; MS in Aeros., MIT, 1957. Registered profl. engr., Fla. Electronics engr. U.S. Naval Air Missile Test Ctr., Point Mugu, Calif., 1951, 53-56; head systems employment br., aero. rsch. engr. U.S. Naval Missile Ctr., 1957-61, head plans and analysis group, gen. engr., 1961-65; sr. rsch. engr. Stanford Rsch. Inst., Menlo Park, Calif., 1965-69; mem. profl. staff Martin Marietta Missile Systems, Orlando, Fla., 1969-93; P.E. cons., 1994-95; electronics engr. Naval Air Dept., Jacksonville, Fla., 1995—. Chmn. com. Ventura area Coun. Boy Scouts Am., Camarillo, Calif., 1962-65, asst. dist. commr., Stanford area coun., Los Altos, Calif., 1967-69, instnl. rep. Cen. Fla. counc., Orlando, 1972-74; mem. pres.'s coun. U. Fla., Gainesville, 1987—. 1st lt. C.E., USAR, 1951-53. USN Bur. Aeros. scholar, 1956-57. Mem. AIAA (sr., missile sys. tech. com. 1987-91), IEEE (life, sect. chmn. 1962-63), Aerospace and Electronics Systems Soc. of IEEE (chpt. chmn. 1972-73), Mil. Ops. Rsch. Soc. (dir. 1962-66), Assn. Old crows (sec. 1973, club dir. 1986-90), Adelphi (sub-chpt. pres. 1948-51), Wesley, Kiwanis, Sigma Xi. Home and Office: 28 Montrano Ave Saint Augustine FL 32080-3819 E-mail: lund@ieee.org., lund@computer.org.

LUND, GEORGE EDWARD, retired electrical engineer; b. Phila., Feb. 17, 1925; s. Harold White and Hannah (Lawford) L.; m. Shirley Bolton Stevens, Sept. 24, 1960; 1 child, Gretchen Lund (Mrs. Kevin J. Collette); step-children: Marsha Stevens (Mrs. Donald Barnett), Roger Stevens, Sharon Stevens (Mrs. David Bailey). BEE, Drexel U., 1952; MEE, U. Pa., 1959; postgrad. in computer sci., Villanova U., 1981-83. Project engr. Burroughs Corp., Paoli, Pa., 1952-86, UNISYS Corp., Paoli, 1986-90, ret., 1990. Assoc. editor, contbr.: Digital Applications of Magnetic Devices, 1960; patentee in field. With USN, 1943-46, ETO. Mem. IEEE (sr.), Eta Kappa Nu. Republican. Methodist. Avocations: photography, amateur radio. Home: 923 Pinecroft Rd Berwyn PA 19312-2123

LUND, JAMES LOUIS, lawyer; b. Long Beach, Calif., Oct. 4, 1926; s. G. Louis and Hazel Eunice (Cochran) L.; m. Jo Alvarez, Aug. 5, 1950; 1 son, Eric James. Student, Stanford U., 1943; BA in Math., U. So. Calif., 1946; postgrad., Grad. Sch. Annapolis, 1949; JD, Southwestern U., 1955; postgrad. Sch. Law, U. So. Calif., 1956. Bar: Calif. 1955, U.S. Dist. Ct. (cen. dist.) Calif. 1955, U.S. Ct. Appeals (9th cir.) 1955, U.S. Tax Ct. 1955, U.S. Supreme Ct. Spl. agt. U.S. Govt., 1950-52; gen. mgr. Pacific ops., gen. counsel Holmes & Narver, Inc., L.A., 1952-66; exec. v.p. Calif. Fabricators, Oakland and Honolulu, 1966-67; sr. ptnr. James Lund Law Firm, Beverly Hills, Tehran, London and Tokyo, 1967-83; pres., founder Fortres Mgmt. Co.; ptnr. Lund & Lund, 1983—. Chmn. bd. Envirotire, 1998—; dir. Superior Vision Svcs., Inc. Lt. comdr. USNR, 1943-46, 48-50. Mem. ABA, SAR, L.A. County Bar Assn., Internat. Bar Assn., Inter-Am. Bar Assn., Asia Pacific Lawyers Assn., Les Ambassadeurs Club (London). Office: Ste 1555 1901 Avenue Of The Stars Los Angeles CA 90067-6052 E-mail: jlundesq@pacbell.net.

LUND, RITA POLLARD, construction executive; b. Vallscreek, W.Va., Aug. 28, 1950; d. Willard Garfield and Faye Ethel (Perry) Pollard. Student, Alexandria Hosp. Sch. Nursing, 1969-70, Columbia Pacific U., 1989-91. Notary pub. Va. Confidential asst. U.S. Ho. of Reps., Washington, 1975-76; exec. asst. White House Domestic Policy Staff, 1977-82; exec. asst. to dep. sci. advisor to pres. White House Sci. Office, 1982-83; asst. to pres. Telecom Futures Inc., 1983-84, v.p. for adminstrn., 1985-86; internat. accounts mgr. TFI Ltd., McLean, Va., 1987-89; ind. cons. telecom. Washington, 1989-90; aerospace cons., 1990—; rep. Scott Sci. & Tech., 1992—; cons. Vanguard Space Corp., 1992—. Exec. dir. Puckett Brothers Corp., 1995—. Marriage commr. State of Va., 2000—. Mem. AIAA, NAFE, Women in Aerospace, Am. Space Transp. Assn., Competitive Alliance Space Enterprise, Fairview Beach Residents Assn. (pres. 1997-2001). Republican. Methodist. Avocations: traveling, genealogy, reading. Home: 5480 Dauphin Landing King George VA 22485

LUND, WENDELL LUTHER, retired lawyer; b. Prentice, Wis., Dec. 31, 1905; s. Rev. Carl A. and Bertha Elizabeth L.; m. Anne Catherine Greve, Nov. 8, 1934 (dec.); children: Judith (Mrs. Barton Biggs), Carole (Mrs. John A. Benning), Mary Wendell; m. Marian Alice Hope, 1981. AB, Augustana Coll., Rock Island, Ill., 1927, DHL, 1968; AM, Columbia U., 1930; JD, Georgetown U., 1938; PhD, Princeton U., 1933. Checker C.&N.W. R.R. (iron ore docks), Escanaba, Mich., 1922-23, worked in tie yard and iron ore docks, summers 1924-27; tchr. Upsala Coll., E. Orange, N.J., 1927-29; asso. prof. English Augustana Coll., 1930-31, exec. sec., 1933-34, Upper Monongahela Valley Com., Washington, 1934; mem. Taylor Act Com., Dept. Interior, 1934; sec. Mich Adminstrv. Bd., Lansing, 1941; exec. dir. Mich. Unemployment Compensation Com., 1941-42; dir. labor prodn. div. WPB, also mem. War Manpower Commn., 1942-43; spl. asst. to chmn. WPB, 1943; practicing atty., mem. firm Lund & O'Brien & predecessor firms, Washington, 1943-96; ret., 1996; chmn., CEO Schonstedt Instrument Co., 1993. Del. World Council of Chs., Evanston, 1954, Uppsala, Sweden, 1968; mem. Bd. Pensions, Lutheran Ch. in Am., 1963-67, 70-79, pres., 1967-68, 74-79; Democratic nominee for Congress, 11th Mich. Dist., 1940; presdl. elector, 1944 Contbr. articles to profl. jours. Bd. dirs. Augustana Coll., 1974-88. Mem. ABA, Bar Assn. D.C., Congl. Country Club (Washington), Burning Tree (Washington), Met. Club (Washington). Home: 3012 Willow Spring Ct Williamsburg VA 23185-3796

LUNDAHL, STEVEN MARK, musician, consultant; b. Bloomington, Minn., Aug. 19, 1955; s. John Miles and Zita Margeurite (Otto) L.; m. Genevieve Catherine Munoz, May 24, 1980 (div.); children: Alexandra Maia, Anders Braeden; m. Kathryn Rose Southworth, Aug. 12, 1995; 1 child, Malia Rose. MusB in Edn., Coll. of St. Scholastica, 1979. Music dir. Utah Shakespearean Festival, Cedar City, Utah, 1979-81; pres. Boston Early Music Ctr., 1980-84; mem. New Eng. Baroque Ensemble, Boston, 1981-86, Waverly Consort, N.Y.C., 1985—; pres. Lundahl Assocs., 1990-97, Lundahl Corp., 1997—. Founding mem. Boston Shawm and Sackbut Ensemble, 1981—99; computer cons., Boston, 1984—. Performer, interpreter of medieval, Renaissance and Baroque instruments; rec. artist Smithsonian Chamber Players, Musical Heritage Soc., Nat. Pub. Radio, Angel/EMI, Harmonia Mundi, Telarc, Erato; guest artist Boston Camerata, 1984—, Calliope: A Renaissance Band, 1985—. Mem. Am. Fedn. Musicians 1974—. Home and Office: 33 Layton Dr Canterbury NH 03224-2017

LUNDBACK, STAFFAN BENGT GUNNAR, lawyer; b. Stockholm, Sweden, Mar. 23, 1947; came to U.S., 1965; s. B. Holger and Ingrid (Fjellstrom) L.; m. Lee Craig, June 14,1969; children: Hadley Elizabeth, Erik Burchfield. Student, U. Stockholm, 1966-67; BA, U. Rochester, 1970; JD, Boston U., 1974. Bar: N.Y. 1975, Fla. 1983. Assoc. Nixon Peabody, LLP, Rochester, N.Y., 1974-83, ptnr., 1983—. Bd. dirs. Scandinavian Seminar, Amherst, Mass.; chmn. Scanamerican Properties, Inc., Atlanta, 1989-99. Mem. Swedish-Am. C. of C. (sec., bd. dirs. 1994—), Country Club of Rochester, Phi Beta Kappa. Avocations: music, literature, sports, current events, photography, golf. Office: Nixon Peabody LLP PO Box 31051 One Clinton First Sq Rochester NY 14603 E-mail: Slundback@NixonPeabody.com., SLundback@aol.com.

LUNDBERG, GEORGE DAVID, II, medical editor in chief, pathologist; b. Pensacola, Fla., Mar. 21, 1933; s. George David and Esther Louise (Johnson) L.; m. Nancy Ware Sharp, Aug. 18, 1956 (div.); children: George David III, Charles William, Carol Jean; m. Patricia Blacklidge Lorimer, Mar. 6, 1983; children: Christopher Leif, Melinda Suzanne AA, North Park Coll., Chgo., 1950; BS, U. Ala., Tuscaloosa, 1952; MS, Baylor U., Waco, Tex., 1963; MD, Med. Coll. Ala., Birmingham, 1957; ScD (hon.), SUNY, Syracuse, 1988, Thomas Jefferson U., 1993, U. Ala., Birmingham, 1994, Med. Coll. Ohio, 1995. Intern Tripler Hosp., Hawaii; resident Brooke Hosp., San Antonio; assoc. prof. pathology U. So. Calif., L.A., 1967-72, prof., 1972-77; assoc. dir. labs. L.A. County-U. So. Calif. Med. Ctr., 1968-77; prof., chmn. dept. pathology U. Calif.-Davis, Sacramento, 1977-82; v.p. scientific info., editor Jour. AMA, Chgo., 1982-99, editor in chief scientific publ., 1991-95; editor in chief AMA Sci. Info. and Multimedia, 1995-99; editor-in-chief Medscape, 1999—2002, editor-in-chief emeritus, 2002—; editor Medscape Gen. Medicine, 1999—; editor-in-chief and exec. v.p. Medicalogic/Medscape, 2000—02; spl. healthcare advisor to CEO WebMD, 2002—. Vis. prof. U. London, 1976, Lund U., Sweden, 1976; prof. clin. pathology Northwestern U., Chgo., 1982—; adj. prof. health policy Harvard U., Boston, 1993—; vis. prof. pathology, 1994-96; sr. fellow Northwestern U., 1999—. Author, editor: Managing the Patient Focused Laboratory, 1975, Using the Clinical Laboratory in Medical Decision Making, 1983, 51 Landmark Articles in Medicine, 1984, AIDS From the Beginning, 1986, Caring for the Uninsured and Underinsured, 1991, Violence, 1992, 100 Years of JAMA Landmark Articles, 1997, Severed Trust: Why American Medicine Hasn't Been Fixed, 2001; contbr. articles to profl. jours. Served to lt. col. M.C., U.S. Army, 1956-67. Fellow Am. Soc. Clin. Pathologists (past pres.), Am. Acad. Forensic Sci.; mem. N.Y. Acad. Scis., Inst. Medicine, Alpha Omega Alpha. Democrat. Episcopalian. Office: Medscape 224 W 30th St New York NY 10001

LUNDBERG, LOIS ANN, political consultant, property manager executive; b. Tulsa, Sept. 21, 1928; d. John T. and Anna M. (Patterson) McQuay; m. Ted W. Lundberg, Sept. 30, 1954; children: Linda Ann, Sharon Lynn. With Pacific Tel., 1950-65; gen. ptnr. McLund Co. Property Mgmt., 1972—; realtor Morgan Realty, 1974—; with Nason, Lundberg and Assoc., Orange, Calif., 1983-85, pres., campaign cons., 1985—. Author: The Big Orange: 50 Year History of the Republican Party in Orange County, 2002. Mem. Rep. State Cen. Com., 1968—; trustee Nixon Law Office Preservation, Inc., 1972-75, Regional Ctr. of Orange County, 1982; bd. dirs. UCI Med. Ctr./Burn Ctr., 1982; apptd. to Coun. on Criminal Justice Com., 1983-91; mem. adv bd. Sta. KOCE-TV, 1976—, La Habra Children's Mus., 1985—; chmn. emeritus Rep. Party Orange County. Recipient Gov. Ronald Reagan award, 1967, Woman of Achievement award City of La Habra, 1979; named Outstanding Rep. of

Orange County, 1978. Mem. NLA (pres.). Lutheran. Home: 1341 Carmela Ln La Habra CA 90631-3311 Office: Nason Lundberg and Assocs 320 W Whittier Blvd Ste 223 La Habra CA 90631-3889

LUNDBERG, SUSAN ONA, musical organization administrator; b. Mandan, N.D., Mar. 15, 1947; d. Robert Henry and Evelyn (Olson) L.; m. Paul R. Wick, July 2, 1972 (div. May 1976); 1 child, Melissa. BA, Stephens Coll., 1969; MLS, Western Mich. U., 1970; MPA, Calif. State U., Fullerton, 1980. Children's and reference libr. Bismarck (N.D.) Pub. Libr., 1970-71; reference libr. U. Tenn., Knoxville, 1971-72; coord. children's svcs. Orange County (Calif.) Pub. Libr., 1972-75; exec. dir. Bismarck-Manda Orch. Assn., 1992—. Exec. dir., founder Sleepy Hollow Summer Theatre, Bismarck, 1990—; trustee Gabriel J. Brown Trust, Bismarck, 1989—. Chair Nat. Music Week N.D., 1990—, Friends of the Belle, 1994—. Named Outstanding Leaders of Yr. Bismarck Tribune, 1995. Mem. Calif. Libr. Assn. (pres. children's svcs. 1971-72), Bismarck Art Assn. (pres. 1982-84), Bismarck Art and Galleries Assn. (bd. dirs. 1985—, pres. 1986-88, Honor Citation award 1992), Jr. Svc. League. Lutheran. Avocations: painting, singing. Home: 112 Ave E W Bismarck ND 58501*

LUNDBLAD, ROGER LAUREN, biotechnology consultant; b. San Francisco, Oct. 31, 1939; s. Lauren Alfred and Doris Ruth (Peterson) L.; m. Susan Hawly Taylor, Oct. 15, 1966 (div. 1985); children: Christina Susan, Cynthia Karin. BSc, Pacific Luth. U., 1961; PhD, U. Wash., 1965. Rsch. assoc. U. Wash., Seattle, 1965-66, Rockefeller U., N.Y.C., 1966-68; asst. prof. U. N.C., Chapel Hill, 1968-71, assoc. prof., 1971-77, prof. pathology and biochemistry, 1977-91; adj. prof., 1991—; dir. sci. tech. devel. Baxter-Hyland/Immuno, Duarte, Calif., 1991-99; biotech. cons., 2000—. Vis. scientist Hyland div. Baxter Healthcare, Glendale, Calif., 1988-89. Author: Chemical Reagents for Protein Modification, 1984, 2d edit., 1990; editor: Chemistry and Biology of Thrombin, 1977, Chemistry and Biology of Heparin, 1980, Techniques in Protein Modification, 1994; editor-in-chief: Biotechnology and Applied Biochemistry, 1996—; contbr. articles to profl. jours. Recipient Career Achievement award U. N.C., 1986. Mem. Am. Soc. Biochem. Molecular Biology, Am. Soc. Microbiology, Am. Heart Assn., Sigma Xi. Office: PO Box 16695 Chapel Hill NC 27514-1587 E-mail: r.lundblad@worldnet.att.net.

LUNDE, ANDERS STEEN, demographer; b. Bridgeport, Conn., Dec. 10, 1914; s. Anders and Cecilia (Steen) L.; m. Eleanor Sheldon, Sept. 9, 1939; children: Erik Sheldon, Peter Steen, Anne Louisa. BA, St. Lawrence U., 1938, MDiv, 1942; MA, Columbia U., 1947, PhD, 1955. Ordained to ministry Unitarian Ch., 1942. Lectr. Rutgers U., New Brunswick, N.J., 1948-51; assoc. prof. St. Lawrence U., Canton, N.Y., 1951-55; prof. Gallaudet Coll., Washington, 1955-58; chief natality statis. br. Nat. Ctr. for Health Statis., 1962-64, asst. dir. nat. vital statis. div., 1964-67, dir. Office of State Svcs. Research Triangle Park, N.C., 1967-74, assoc. dir. Washington, 1974-77; adj. prof. biostatis. Sch. Pub. Health U. N.C., Chapel Hill, 1977—. Cons., author Internat. Inst. Vital Registration and Statis., Bethesda, Md., 1977-80. Author: Whirligigs: Design and Construction, 1982, reprinted (under title Easy-to-Make Whirligigs), 1996, More Whirligigs: Large Scale and Animated Figures, 1984, 2d edit., 1998, reprinted (under title Making Animated Whirligigs), 1998, Whirligigs in Silhouette, 1989, Whirligigs for Children: Young and Old, 1992, reprinted (under title Whimsical Whirligigs and How to Make Them), 2000; contbr. numerous articles to profl. jours. Minister Old Ship Ch., Hingham, Mass., 1941-43, First Unitarian Ch., Phila., 1958-62; mem. adv. com. Ret. Sr. Vol. Program, Chapel Hill, 1983-89; bd. dirs., treas. N.C. Art Soc., 1978-82; bd. dirs., 1st v.p. N.C. Botanical Garden Found., 1984-90. Capt. U.S. Army, 1943-46/ Recipient First award Durham (N.C.) Art Guild, 1982, Hon. Mention, N.C. Mus. History, 1983. Fellow AAAS, APHA, Am. Statis. Assn.; mem. Am. Population Assn. (sec.-treas. 1965-68, bd. dirs. 1968-71). Democrat. Episcopalian. Avocation: wood sculpture. Home: 700 Carolina Mdws Chapel Hill NC 27517-7546

LUNDE, ASBJORN RUDOLPH, lawyer; b. S.I., N.Y., July 17, 1927; s. Karl and Elisa (Andenes) L. AB, Columbia U., 1947, LLB, 1949. Bar: N.Y. 1949. Pvt. practice, N.Y.C., 1950-91; with Kramer, Marx, Greenlee & Backus and predecessors, 1950-68, mem., 1958-68; pvt. practice Columbia County, N.Y., 1991—. Bd. dirs., v.p. Orch. da Camera, Inc., 1964—, Sara Roby Found., 1971—; bd. dirs. Clarion Concerts in Columbia County, 1999—; mem. vis. com. dept. European paintings Met. Mus. Art. Fellow Met. Mus. Art (life); mem. ABA, N.Y. State Bar Assn., Assn. Bar City N.Y., Met. Opera Club, East India Club (London). Avocation: art collecting (donor paintings and sculptures to Met. Mus. Art, N.Y.C., Nat. Gallery Art, Washington, Mus. Fine Arts, Boston, Clark Art Inst., Williamstown, Mass., others). Home and Office: 135 LaBranche Rd Hillsdale NY 12529-5713

LUNDE, DOLORES BENITEZ, retired secondary education educator; b. Honolulu, Apr. 12, 1929; d. Frank Molero and Matilda (Francisco) Benitez; m. Nuell Carlton Lunde, July 6, 1957; 1 child, Laurelle. BA, U. Oreg., 1951, postgrad., 1951-52, U. So. Calif., L.A., 1953-54, Colo. State U., 1957-58, Calif. State U., Fullerton, 1967-68. Cert. gen. secondary tchr., Calif.; cert. lang. devel. specialist. Tchr. Brawley (Calif.) Union High Sch., 1952-55; tchr. Fullerton (Calif.) Union High Sch. Dist., 1955-73; tchrs. aide Placentia (Calif.) Unified Sch. Dist., 1983-85; tchr. continuing edn. Fullerton Union High Sch. Dist., 1985-91; tchr. Fullerton Sch. Dist., 1988, Fullerton Union H.S. Dist., 1989-94. Presenter regional and state convs., so. Calif., 1986-88. Innovator tests, teaching tools, audio-visual aids. Vol. Luth. Social Svcs., Fullerton, 1981-82, Messiah Luth., Yorba Linda, Calif., 1981-88, 91-2001. Recipient Tchr. of Yr. award Fullerton Union High Sch. Dist., 1989. Mem. NEA, AAUW (life, bull. editor 1979-80, corr. sec. 1981-83, program v.p. 1983-84, gift honoree Fullerton br. 1985), Calif. State Tchrs. Assn., Fullerton Secondary Tchrs. Assn., Internat. Club/Spanish Club (advisor La Habra, Calif. 1965-72), Tchrs. English to Speakers Other Langs., Calif. Assn. Tchrs. English to Speakers Other Langs. Avocations: singing, folk and interpretive dance, guitar, reading, travel. Home: 4872 Ohio St Yorba Linda CA 92886-2713

LUNDE, HAROLD IRVING, management educator; b. Austin, Minn., Apr. 18, 1929; s. Peter Oliver and Emma (Stoa) L.; m. Sarah Jeanette Lysne, June 25, 1955; children: Paul, James, John, Thomas. BA, St. Olaf Coll., 1952; MA, U. Minn., 1954, PhD, 1966. Assoc. prof. econs. Macalester Coll., St. Paul, 1957-64; fin. staff economist Gen. Motors Corp., N.Y.C., 1965-67; corp. sec. Dayton Hudson Corp., Mpls., 1967-70; mgr. planning and gen. research May Dept. Stores Co., St. Louis, 1970-72, v.p. planning and research, 1972-78; exec. v.p. adminstrn. Kobacker Stores, Inc., Columbus, Ohio, 1979; prof. mgmt. Bowling Green (Ohio) State U., 1980-98, emeritus, 1998—. Mem. Acad. Mgmt., Am. Econ. Assn., Nat. Assn. Bus. Economists, Decision Scis. Inst., Phi Beta Kappa, Phi Kappa Phi, Omicron Delta Kappa, Beta Gamma Sigma. Home: 880 Country Club Dr Bowling Green OH 43402-1602

LUNDE, KAREN TAMM, real estate broker; b. Chgo., Feb. 21, 1944; d. George Lewis and Margaret D. (Kiesewetter) Tamm; m. Delmar R. Lunde, Dec. 29, 1984. Diploma, Evanston Hosp., 1965; PhB, Northwestern U., 1976; postgrad., Anthony Schs., 1987, 90. Staff, head nurse labor, delivery Evanston (Ill.) Hosp., 1965-67; staff nurse surgery St. Mary's Hosp., Wausau, Wis., 1967-68; staff, head nurse Adams County Meml. Hosp., Friendship, 1968-70; head nurse surg. unit, asst., nursing coord. Evanston (Ill.) Hosp., 1970-72; supr. maternal child nursing Ill. Masonic Med. Ctr., Chgo., 1972-74; adminstr. NAACOG, 1974-79; asst. dir. nursing/nursery, asst. dir. nursing Children's Hosp. Med. Ctr., Oakland, Calif., 1979-84; dir. svcs. Palo Alto Med. Found. Fremont (Calif.) Ctr., 1984-86; cons. Grass Valley, Calif., 1986—; realtor, assoc. ERA Consol. Brokers, 1987-91, broker assoc., 1991—. Contbr. articles to profl. jours. Mem. Chgo. area chpt. March of Dimes, 1975-79, ARC, 1975-79, Nev. County Health Planning Coun., 1990—; mem., sec. bd. dirs. Tri Cities Children's Ctr., 1985-87; bd. dirs. Sierra Nev. Community Svcs. Coun., 1988—. Mem. NAACOG (Ill. sect., chmn. conf. 1972, fin. chmn. conf. 1972, sec. treas. 1972-74, certification corp. item writer neonatal nurses certification exam. 1982-83, Calif. sect., chmn. conf. 1983, mem. nat. com. on devel. 1984-86, Palo Alto chpt., sec.-treas. 1986-87, others), Nat. Osteoporosis Found., Nat. Assn. Realtors, Calif. Assn. Realtors, Northwestern U. Alumnae Club, Evanston Hosp. NursingAlumnae Assn., Nevada County Bd. Realtors (active), Alpha Sigma Lambda. Office: ERA Network Real Estate 167 S Auburn St Grass Valley CA 95945-6531

LUNDE, KATHERINE LAMONTAGNE, educational consultant; b. Kankakee, Ill., May 3, 1947; d. James Armond and Frances Elizabeth (Maas) LaMontagne; children: Lisa Christine, Walter James. BS, No. Ill. U., 1969; postgrad., Jacksonville (Fla.) U., 1972. Cert. elem., secondary and early childhood educator. Tchr. 1st grade Kenwood Elem. Sch., Ft. Walton Beach, Fla., 1970-71; kindergarten tchr., supr. Orange Park (Fla.) Kindergarten, 1972-78; asst. dir. Stoneway Sch., Stoneway Pvt. Sch., Plano, Tex., 1981-82; former dir. Westminster Preschool and Kindergarten, Dallas, 1982-94; exec. dir. edn. TLC Child Devel. Ctr., Plano, Tex., 1997; CEO Katherine Lunde Ednl. Cons., 1994—. Dep. gov. Am. Biog. Rsch. Inst. (life); internat. motivational spkr. spkr.'s bur. Assn. Childhood Edn. Internat.; mem. child care adv. bd. Collin County C.C., 1997—; exec. dir. TLC Child Devel. Ctr., 1997-98. Track coach Spl. Olympics, 1981-83; learning disabilities tutor, 1978-85; bd. dirs. Mi Escuelita Preschs., Inc., 1985-90, v.p. bd. dirs., 1989-90; bd. dirs. Promise Internat., 1998—, Plano Internat. Presch., 2000; children's min. Trinity Episcopal Ch., 1998—. Named Ednl. Rschr. of Yr., ARBI, 2002; recipient, 2002, Christa McAuliffe Outstanding Educator award, 1994; grantee Sewell Fund, Lard Trust. Mem. ASCD, Nat. Assn. Edn. Young Children (life), Kappa Delta Pi. Office: 1415 Halsey Way Ste 320 Carrollton TX 75007-4455

LUNDE, ØIVIND, cultural organization administrator, archaeologist; b. Oslo, Aug. 21, 1943; s. Øivind and Ebba (Hansen) Lunde. PhD, U. Lund, Sweden, 1977. Inspector Riksantikvaren (Ctr. Office of Hist. Monuments and Sites), Oslo, 1968-78, prin. inspector, 1978-88, dir. archaeol. dept., 1989-91; dep. dir. gen. Directorate for Cultural Heritage, 1991, dir. gen., 1991-96. Vis. prof. medieval archaeology, U. Lund, 1984; prof. II medieval archaeology, U. Oslo, 1985—. Author: Trondheim's History in the Archaeological Deposits of the Town, 1977, and other books on medieval archaeology and cultural heritage topics; contbr. papers to profl. jours.; chmn. Norwegian Com. for Urban Historic Studies, 1978-88, mem. 1978-91. Mem. Nat. Coun. Museums, Norwegian Mus. Arch., European Assn. Archaeologists (exec. bd. 1993-96), Norwegian Acad. Sci. and Letters. Home: Schirmersgt 3 A 7012 Trondheim Norway Office: Restoration Workshop Bispegt 11 7012 Trondheim Norway E-mail: oeivind.lunde@kirken.no.

LUNDEBERG, PHILIP KARL BORAAS, curator, consultant; b. Mpls., June 14, 1923; s. Olav Knutson and Vivian Juliet (Boraas) L.; m. Eleanore Lillian Berntson, July 18, 1953; 1 son, Karl Fredrik. BA summa cum laude, Duke U., 1944, MA, 1947; PhD, Harvard U., 1954. Asst. to historian U.S. Naval Ops. in World War II, Navy Dept., 1950-53; asst. prof. history St. Olaf Coll., 1953-55, U.S. Naval Acad., 1955-59; assoc. curator naval history Nat. Mus. History and Tech., Smithsonian Instn., 1959-61, curator of naval history, 1961-84, curator emeritus, 1984—. V.p. Am. Mil. Inst., 1968-71, pres., 1971-73; chmn. Internat. Congress Maritime Museums, 1972-75; v.p. U.S. Commn. on Mil. History, 1975-79, pres., 1980-83; sec. Internat. Commn. Mus. Security, 1975-79; pres. Coun. Am. Maritime Museums, 1976-78. Author: The Continental Gunboat Philadelphia, 1966, 2d edit., 1995, Samuel Colt's Submarine Battery, 1974, American Anti-submarine Operations in the Atlantic, 1943-1945, 1997; co-author: Sea Power: A Naval History, 1960, 81; contbg. author: Guide to the Sources of U.S. Military History, 1975, 93, Seafaring and Society, 1987, To Die Gallantly, 1994, The Battle of the Atlantic (1939-1945), 1994; editor: Bibliographie de L'Histoire des Grandes Routes Maritimes: États-Unis D'Amèrique, 1970; exhibits: Armed Forces of U.S., 1961, By Sea and by Land, 1981. With USNR, 1943-83, 89, comdr. Res. ret., 1992. Decorated Bronze Star, Purple Heart; recipient Bronze medal Internat. Commn. Mil. History, 1975; Austin fellow Harvard U., 1949. Fellow Am. Mil. Inst. (Moncado prize 1964); mem. Coun. Am. Maritime Mus. (hon.), N.Am. Soc. for Oceanic History (K. Jack Bauer award 1998), Naval Hist. Found. (life), Internat. Congress Maritime Mus. (life), Soc. for Mil. History, Phi Beta Kappa. Home: 1107 Croton Dr Alexandria VA 22308-2009

LUNDEEN, ARDELLE ANNE, economist, educator; b. Milbank, S.D., Apr. 16, 1929; d. Louis Peter and Virginia Mary (Kockx) Tuchscherer; m. Kenneth G. Lundeen, Dec. 6, 1948 (dec. Dec. 1985); children: Michael, Jon. BS, S.D. State U., 1970, MS, 1971; PhD, Iowa State U., 1976. Instr. Iowa State U., Ames, 1972—74, rsch. assoc., 1975, S.D. State U., Brookings, 1970—96, from asst. prof. to prof. econs., 1976—96, head dept. econs.; ret., 1997. Contbr. articles to profl. jours. Mem. Brookings City Housing Com., 1980—; com. mem. Brookings Dem. Party, 1985. NSF trainee, 1971. Mem. Am. Agrl. Econ. Assn. (bd. dirs. Found.), Com. on Women in Agrl. Econs. (chmn. 1981-82), Brookings Altrusa Club (pres. 1986-87). Avocations: travel, bridge. Home: 612 6th Ave Brookings SD 57006-1431

LUNDEEN, WILLIAM BRUCE, radiologist; b. Minn., 1928; s. Harry William and Alice Mary (Gessner) L.; m. Letitia Marguerite Hughey, June 6, 1981; 1 child, Letitia Marshall. BS, U. Richmond, 1951; MD, Med. Coll. Va., 1955. Diplomate Am. Bd. Radiology. Intern U. Minn. Hosps., 1955-56, resident, fellow, 1957-61; resident Med. Coll. VA Hosps., 1957-58; fellow radiology therapy U. Minn., 1960-61; radiologist Arlington (Va.) Hosp., 1975—; assoc. clin. prof. radiology Med. Coll. Va., 1961—. Gov.'s ad hoc com. self-referral med. practice Va. State Legis., Richmond, 1991-93; bd. health sys. H.S.A. No. Va., 1980-84. Fellow AMA, Am. Coll. Radiology; mem. Am. Soc. Therapeutic Radiology & Oncology, Med. Soc. Va., Arlington Med. Soc. (bd. dirs. 1979-83), Annapolis Yacht Club, Alpha Omega Alpha. Republican. Episcopalian. Office: Arlington Hosp 1701 N George Mason Dr Arlington VA 22205-3698 Fax: (703) 558-5512.

LUNDERGAN, BARBARA KEOUGH, lawyer; b. Chgo., Nov. 6, 1938; d. Edward E. and Eleanor A. (Erickson) Keough; children: Matthew K., Mary Alice BA, U. Ill., 1960; JD, Loyola U., Chgo., 1964. Bar: Ill. 1964, Ga. 1997, U.S. Dist. Ct. (no. dist.) Ill. 1964, U.S. Tax Ct. 1974. With Seyfarth Shaw, Chgo., 1964—, ptnr., 1971-98, of counsel, 1998—. Fellow Am. Coll. Trust and Estate Counsel; mem. ABA (com. on fed. taxation), Ill. Bar Assn. (coun. sect. on fed. taxation 1983-91, chair 1989, coun. sect. on trusts and estates sect. coun. 1992-97, sec. 1996-97, editl. bd. Ill. Bar Jour. 1993-96), Chgo. Bar Assn. (chmn. trust law com. 1982-83, com. on fed. taxation). Office: Seyfarth Shaw 55 E Monroe St Ste 4200 Chicago IL 60603-5863

LUNDERGAN, CONOR FRANCIS, cardiologist; b. Boston, July 11, 1950; m. Meredith Drapkin, Mar. 10, 1987. BS, Georgetown U., 1972, MS, 1976, MD, 1982. Diplomate Am. Bd. Internal Medicine; bd. cert. interventional cardiology. Resident in medicine Duke U., Durham, N.C., 1982-85, fellow in cardiology, 1985-89; asst. prof. medicine George Washington U., Washington, 1989-94, co-dir. angiographic care lab., 1992—, assoc. prof. medicine, 1994—, dir. basinc sci. rsch. cardiac divsn., dir. fellowship tng., 1994—. Vice-chmn. instnl. rev. bd. for med. rsch. George Washington U. Fellow AHA (bd. dirs. at large Paul White affiliate 1993), Am. Coll. Cardiology. Office: George Washington U Med Ctr 2150 Pennsylvania Ave NW Washington DC 20037-3201 E-mail: clundergan@aol.com.

LUNDERVILLE, GERALD PAUL, bilingual ESL/social studies educator; b. Springfield, Mass., Feb. 22, 1941; s. Leon Albert and Florence Marion (Jolivette) L.; m. Martha Ann Sumner, Mar. 26, 1966 (div. Aug. 1971); m. Bony Lek, June 30, 1984. BA cum laude, U. N.H., 1963; MA, Middlebury Coll., 1969, U. Rochester, 1973, Calif. State U., Long Beach, 1994. Instr. Spanish Berwick Acad., South Berwick, Maine, 1963-64; tchr. French, Spanish Barnstable High Sch., Hyannis, Mass., 1967-68; instr. Spanish Cape Cod Community Coll., West Barnstable, 1968-71; tchr. French, Spanish Stevens High Sch. Annex, Claremont, N.H., 1973-74; tchr. English Centro de Estudios Norteamericanos, Valencia, Spain, 1974-75; dept. head fgn. langs. Merrimack (N.H.) High Sch., 1975-80; tchr. Spanish El Camino Coll., Torrance, Calif., 1980-85; tchr. ESL Wilson High Sch., Long Beach, 1980—, dept. head ESL, 1987-88, tchr. bilingual social studies/Spanish, 1992—, tchr. history/ELD, 1998—. Author: 20th Century Baseball Trivia, 1992; contbr. articles to Am. Atheist Mag. Active Long Beach Area Citizens Peace, 1982—, Animal Protection Inst. Am., Sacramento., 1983—; mem. Civil War Round Table of Long Beach. Served with U.S. Army, 1964-67, Vietnam. Mem. NEA, ACLU, NOW, Modern and Classical Lang. Assn. So. Calif., Tchrs. of English as a 2d Lang., Soc. for Preservation of English Lang. and Lit., VERBATIM, Nat. Humane Edn. Soc., Merrimack Tchrs. Assn. (sec. 1977-80), Lambda Pi. Avocations: cooking, tennis, reading, travel, writing. Home: 1740 Washington St Long Beach CA 90805-5535 Fax: 562-433-2731. E-mail: glunderville@lbusd.k12.ca.us.

LUNDGREN, CARL WILLIAM, JR. physicist; b. Columbus, Sept. 17, 1933; s. Carl William and Anne Katherine (Kuntz) L.; m. Virginia Anne Cullis, Dec. 7, 1963; children: David John, Janet Marie. BEE, U. Cin., 1957, MS, 1959, PhD, 1961. Coop undergrad. engr. govt. products divsn. Avco Corp., Cin. and Evendale, Ohio, 1953-56; asst. supr., rsch. fellow U. Cin. Basic Sci. Rsch. Lab., 1959-61; tech. staff Bell Telephone Labs., Murray Hill, N.J., 1961-66, Holmdel and Middletown, 1966-84; dist. mgr. advanced fiber optics planning Bell Comm. Rsch., Inc., Red Bank, 1984-92; dir. transmission sys. engring. Bellcore, Morristown and Red Bank, 1992-95; dist. mgr., tech. cons. local access architecture AT&T, Holmdel, N.J., 1996-98, Middletown, 1998—. Contbr. articles to profl. jours.; patentee in field. Capt. Signal Corps., U.S. Army, 1961-63. Mem. AAAS, IEEE, N.Y. Acad. Sci., Optical Soc. Am, Nat. Spectrum Mgrs. Assn., Gideons Internat., Sierra Club, Delta Tau Delta, Tau Beta Pi, Eta Kappa Nu, Phi Eta Sigma, Omicron Delta Kappa. Republican. Episcopalian. Home: 60 Woodhollow Rd Colts Neck NJ 07722-1323 Office: AT&T R&D South 200 S Laurel Ave Middletown NJ 07748-1998 E-mail: cwlundgren@att.com., twlxxvcl@optonline.net.

LUNDGREN, CISSI, painter, poet; b. Östersund, Sweden, Jan. 20, 1920; d. Bror Oskar and Julia Erika Lundgren; m. Sven Harry Monvik, Sept. 23, 1939 (dec. Aug. 1996); 1 child, Hans. Student, Konstfack Skola, Stockholm, 1937-39, Coll. Art, pvt. art schs., 1939-44, King Coll., Toronto, 1960-62. One-woman shows include Örebro, 1941; exhibited in group shows at London, 1950-52, Can., 1952-73, Vieneese Biennale, 1963-64, N.Y. State, 1962-70., L.A. and Thousand Oaks, Calif., 1988—; represented in permanent collection Seamens Ch., San Pedro, Calif.; contbr. poetry numerous anthologies, 1988—. Recipient publs. and editors awards, 1990-98. Mem. Am. Scandinavian Found. (life), Internat. Soc. Poets (life), Vasaorden, Sons of Norway, Color and Form, North Valley Art League.

LUNDGREN, GAIL M. lawyer; b. Tacoma, June 14, 1955; d. Arthur Dean and Vera Martha (Grimm) L. AB cum laude, Vassar Coll., 1977; JD cum laude, U. Puget Sound (now Seattle U. Law Sch.), 1980. Bar: Wash. 1981. Legal intern Reed, McClure, Moceri & Thonn, Seattle, 1979, Burges & Kennedy, Tacoma, 1979-80, Lee, Smart, Cook, Martin & Patterson, P.S., Inc., Seattle, 1980-81, assoc., 1981-92; prin. Law Offices Gail L. Weber, Bothell, 1992-95, Tom Chambers & Assocs., 1995-99; lawyer Law Offices of Kirk Bernard, Seattle, 1999; ptnr. Bernard, Lundgren & Assoc., 1999—. Vestry com. Queen Anne Luth. Ch., 1983-86, v.p. congregation, 1988, 89, mem. worship and music com., 1982-83, 84-86, parish edn. com., 1983-84. Recipient Am. Jurisprudence Book award in Criminal Procedure, Corps. and Bus. Planning, 1980. Mem.: ABA, Order of Barristers, Wash. State Trial Lawyers Assn., Fed. Bar Assn., Wash. State Vassar Club (chmn. alumni admissions 1983—85, rep. 1986—92, 2001—, chmn. alumni admissions 2001—). Democrat. Avocations: scuba diving, tennis, classical music, needlepoint, stitchery. Office: Bernard, Lundgren & Assocs PLLC Ste 100 900 Aurora Ave N Ste 100 Seattle WA 98109

LUNDGREN, HARRY R. civil engineer; b. Chgo., May 2, 1928; s. Harry John Lundgren and Edna Isobel (Ferguson) Kohler; m. Joyce Elizbeth Boller, Nov. 19, 1955. BS in Civil Engring, Purdue U., 1950; MS in Structural Engring., Ariz. State U., 1961; PhD in Structural Engring., Okla. State U., 1967. Registered profl. engr., Ariz. Design engr. Kawneer Co., Niles, Mich., 1953-58; chief engr. Fefer Steel, Phoenix, 1958-59; sr. civil engr. Salt River Project, Tempe, Ariz., 1959-61; prof. civil engring. Ariz. State U., 1961-89; prin. Computer Aided Structural Engring., Scottsdale, 1980—. Contbr. articles to Jour. ASCE. Chmn. Bldg. Code Adv. Bd., Tempe, Ariz., 1971-74; mem. C.C. Adv. Bd., Phoenix, 1975-83. With U.S. Army, 1950-52. Named Ariz. Engr. of Yr., Ariz. Soc. Profl. Engrs., 1979. Mem. Am. Soc. Civil Engrs. (life), Structural Engrs. Assn. (bd. dirs., pres., Meritorious Engr.), Chi Epsilon. Avocations: genealogy, reading, golf. Home and Office: 2837 N 76th Pl Scottsdale AZ 85257-1603

LUNDGREN, LEONARD, III, retired secondary education educator; b. San Francisco, June 22, 1933; s. Leonard II and Betty (Bosold) L.; m. Jane Gates, June 12, 1976. AA, City Coll. San Francisco, 1952; AB, San Francisco State U., 1954, MA, 1958, postgrad., 1958-71. Cert. tchr., Calif. Phys. edn. tchr., athletic coach Pelton Jr. High Sch., San Francisco, 1958-59; social studies tchr., dept. chair, phys. edn. tchr., athletic coach Luther Burbank Jr. High Sch., 1959-78; history, govt. econs., geography tchr. George Washington High Sch., 1978-93. Water safety instr. ARC, San Francisco, 1946-61; mem. Calif. Quality Teaching Ctr. Conf. Bd., 1965-67. Author: Guide for Films and Filmstrips, 1966, Teacher's Handbook for Social Studies, 1966, Guide for Minority Studies, 1968. V.p. Lakeside Property Owners Assn., San Francisco, 1986-88, legis. advocate, 1988-95; v.p. West of Twin Peaks Coun., San Francisco, 1986-87; pub. affairs polit. econ. cons., Calif., 1993—; mem. World Affairs Coun. No. Calif. With USN, 1954-56. Fulbright scholar, Greece, 1963; recipient Svc. Pin, ARC, 1961. Mem. NEA (life, del. 1970, 72-76), Calif. Tchrs. Assn. (state coun. rep. 1963-74), Nat. Coun. Social Studies, Calif. Coun. Social Studies (v.p. San Francisco chpt. 1969-70), San Francisco Classroom Tchrs. Assn. (pres. 1972-73, Gavel award 1973), PTA (sch. v.p. 1980-81), Am. Ass.n Ret. Persons (rep. 2001-), Calif. Ret. Tchrs. Assn. (life, legislation chmn. San Francisco divsn. 1995-99, 1st v.p. 1997-99, pres. 1999-2000), Am. Assn. Ret. Persons (cmty. coord. San Francisco 1996-97), San Francisco State U. Alumni Assn. (life, treas. 1959), Calif. Assn. Health, Phys. Edn., Recreation and Dance (life, treas. San Francisco chpt. 1959-60), Nat. Geog. Soc. (life), Phi Delta Kappa (life, pres. chpt. 1965-66). Avocations: travel, swimming, gardening, research, service. *A career in education for me is my life from learning to teaching over and over again. History, government, geography and economics are my major subjects. World travel gives me the chance to see the places I studied and taught.*

LUNDGREN, NILS G.H. economist; b. Skövde, Sweden, July 13, 1936; s. Herman B. and Anna K. (Vestlund) L.; m. Kerstin J. Davidson, Aug. 26, 1959; children: Erik, Irja; m. Eva B. Nisser, July 21, 1985; children: Gustaf, Oskar. BA in Econs., U. Stockholm, 1962, PhD, 1975. Economist EFTA, Geneva, Switzerland, 1963-66; scholar Inst. for Internat. Econ. Studies, Stockholm, 1966-75; vis. scholar U. Reading, U.K., 1975; scholar Govt. Forecasting Inst., Stockholm, 1976-80; chief economist Nordbanken, 1980-96, group chief economist, 1996-99. Chmn. Nat. Assn. Pvt. Schs., Stockholm, 1994-97. Maj. Swedish arty., 1960-94. Mem. Royal Swedish Acad. Engring. Scis., Swedish Econ. Assn. Social Democrat. Office: Nordbanken S-105 71 Stockholm Sweden

LUNDGREN, REGINA ELLEN (REGINA SCOTT), research scientist; b. Tacoma, Oct. 7, 1959; d. Richard Paul and Rosann Marie (Harris) Brown; m. Lawrence Linus Lundgren, Aug. 27, 1988; children: Edward Linus, William Richard. BA, U. Wash., 1985. Dir. Latchkey of U. Place, Tacoma, 1984-86; tech. comms. specialist Battelle, Richland, 1986-95, comms. program mgr., 1995-97, rsch. scientist, 1997-2000; ind. cons., 2000—. Author: Risk Communication: A Handbook for Communicating Environmental, Safety and Health Risks, 1994, (novels) The Unflappable Miss Fairchild, 1998, The Twelve Days of Christmas, 1998, The Bluestocking on His Knee, 1999, Catch of the Season, 1999, A Dangerous Dalliance, 2000, The Marquis' Kiss, 2000, The Incomparable Miss Compton, 2001, The Irredeemable Miss Renfield, 2001, Lord Borin's Secret Love, 2002, Utterly Devoted, 2002; co-editor: Hanford Tank Cleanup: A Guide to Understanding the Technical Issues, 1996.

LUNDGREN, RICHARD JOHN, real estate executive, city planner, preservationist; b. N.Y.C., Dec. 13, 1940; s. John H. and Helen C. (Vetter) L.; m. Nancy Whitin Truslow, Apr. 1, 1972 (dec. 2000); children: Andrew Auchincloss, Elizabeth Whitin. BS, Rensselaer Poly. Inst., 1964; MS, Pratt Inst., 1968; MPA, Harvard U., 1990. Sr. planner Herr Assocs., Boston, 1968-69; project dir. Boston Redevel. Authority, 1969-72; dir. planning Hilgenhurst & Assocs., Boston, 1972-77; v.p. Hunneman Comml. Co., 1977-82, sr. v.p., 1982-94, pres., 1994—. Trustee The Trustees of Reservations, 1985—, Emerald Necklace Conservancy, 1997—, Mass. Farm and Conservation Lands Trust, 1985-92, Boston Local Devel. Corp., 1986-91; dir. Hitoric Mass., 2002--, Initiative for a Competitive Inner City, Boston, 1999—, Vis. Nurse Assn. of Boston, 1972-82; mem. Met. Area Planning Coun., 1978-80, Boston Coord. Com., 1983, Mass. Gov.'s Com. on Pvt. Rental Housing Prodn., 1983-84, Boston Mayor's Com. on Linkage, 1983-84, Center City Task Force, 1983-87, Boston Mayor's Jobs Liaison Com., 1984-90, Park Plz. Civic Adv. Com., 1985-86; Boston Employment Com., 1986-88; chmn. Mass. Realtors

Pub. Policy Com., 1989; adv. com. Boston U. Sch. for Real Estate Studies, 1986-91. With USCGR, 1968-72. Named Greater Boston Realtor of Yr., 1984. Mem.: Greater Boston Bldg. Owners and Mgrs. Assn. (bd. dirs. 1979—88, pres. 1982), Greater Boston Real Estate Bd. (bd. dirs. 1982—89, pres. 1983), Mass. Assn. Realtors, Nat. Assn. Realtors, N.E. Hist. Gen. Soc., Mass. Hist. Soc., Boston Athenaeum, Harvard Faculty Club (Cambridge), The Country Club (Brookline), Somerset Club (Boston). Episcopalian. Home: 48 Centre St Dover MA 02030-2207 Office: Hunneman Comml Co 70-80 Lincoln St Boston MA 02111-2611 E-mail: dlundgren@naihunneman.com.

LUNDIEN, ROBERT GUY, school counselor, band director, educator; b. Joplin, Mo., June 29, 1972; s. Marge Lundien. MS Counseling, SW Mo. State U., Springfield, Missouri, 2002; BS Edn., Mo. So. State Coll., Joplin, Missouri, 1996. Music educator/counselor Diamond R-4 Sch. Dist., Diamond, Mo., 2000—; music educator Nev. R-5 Sch. Dist., Nevada, 1998—2000, Liberal R-2 Sch. Dist., Liberal, 1997—98, Seneca R-7 Sch. Dist., Seneca, 1996—97. Recipient Outstanding Young Man of Am. Award, Young Men of Am., 1998, ODK Nat. Leadership Honor Soc., Mo. So. State Coll., 1996, Spencer Bartlett Respect Award, 1996. Mem.: Mo. State Teachers Assn., Mo. Music Educators Assn. (dist. v.p. 1996—2002), Mo. Bandmasters Assn. Avocations: running, tennis, reading, music. Home: 3902 College View Drive 19C Joplin MO 64801 Office: Diamond High School 401 South Main Diamond MO 64840

LUNDIN, BRUCE THEODORE, engineering and management consultant; b. Alameda, Calif., Dec. 28, 1919; s. Oscar Linus and Elizabeth Ellen (Erickson) L.; m. Barbara Ann Bliss, July 27, 1946 (wid. Feb. 1981); children: Dianne, Robert, Nancy; m. Jean Ann Oberlin, Mar. 22, 1982. BSME, U. Calif.-Berkeley, 1942; D of Engring. (hon.), U. Toledo, 1975. Chief engine research NASA Lewis Ctr., Cleve., 1952-58, asst. dir., 1958-61, assoc. dir., 1961-68, dir., 1969-77; dep. assoc. adminstrn. NASA, Washington, 1968-69. Adv. U.S. Air Force Sci. Adv. Bd., Washington, 1961-77; mem. Aerospace Safety Adv. Bd., Washington, 1961-72; staff dir. Pres.'s Commn. on the Accident at Three Mile Island, 1981; mem. TM1-2 Safety Adv. Bd., 1981-89; chmn. Rockwell Internat. Safety Oversight Panel, 1988-89. Pres. Westshore Unitarian Ch., Rocky River, Ohio, 1967-68; trustee Southwest Gen. Hosp., Berea, Ohio, 1970-75. Recipient Outstanding Leadership medal NASA, 1965, Pub. Service award NASA, 1971, 75, Disting. Service medal NASA, 1971, 77, Engineer of the Year award Nat. Space Club, 1975 Fellow AIAA; mem. Nat. Acad. Engring. Avocations: woodworking; gardening; reading; travel. Home: 5859 Columbia Rd North Olmsted OH 44070-4611

LUNDIN, SHIRLEY MATCOUFF, early childhood and adult educator, consultant; b. Chgo., Feb. 6, 1935; d. William and Emma Martha (Graf) Matcouff; m. Roy Charles Lundin, Sept. 1, 1956; children: Michael Roy, Laura Marie Lundin Simpkiss, Bethel Anne Lundin-Martinez. BA in Liberal Arts, Northwestern U., 1957; M in Adult Continuing Edn., Nat. Louis U., 1981; Myers Briggs Type Indicator Interpreter, Assn. for Psychol. Type, 1995. Dir. HeadStart Ctr. Cmty. Action Program, Evansville, Ind., 1974-76; edn. coord. HeadStart Comty. Action Program in Evansville, 1976-78; asst. program coord. parent edn. program Triton Coll., River Grove, Ill., 1979-80; trainer/field advisor Comty. Econ. Devel. Agt. HeadStart for Child Devel. Assoc. Credential, Chgo., 1981-83; adult devel./program cons. Chgo. Field Ctr. Girl Scouts USA, N.Y.C., 1983-88; coord. vol. svcs. Frank Lloyd Wright Home and Studio Fedn., Oak Park, Ill., 1988-91; adj. faculty, vol. mgmt. curriculum coord. Wm. Rainey Harper Coll., Palatine, 1995—2001; cons., trainer, prin. Lundin & Assocs., Indian Head Park, 1991—. Trainer workshops and seminars in field of vol. program adminstrn.; trainer Heartland Internat. in U.S. and Belarus, 1998-; cons. in field. Co-author (manual) How to Start a Parent Cooperative Preschool, 1980; contbr. articles to profl. jours. Interim dir., bd. pres. Vol. Ctr., Oak Park, 1990—95; Am. vol. for internat. devel. Nat. Forum Fedn., Washington, 1996—97; mem. com. study of infrastructure Village of Oak Park, 1996; internat. trainer Heartland Internat., 1997—; regional chair Unitarian Universalist Svc. Com., Boston, 1977—80; bd. dirs. Sr. Citizens Ctr. , Oak Park and River Forest, 1996—2001, pres., 1998—2001. Mem.: Assn. for Psychol. Type, Chgo. Assn. Psychol. Type, Chgo. Area Tech. Assistance Providers (newsletter editor 1992—94), Assn. Vol. Adminstrn. (bd. dirs., program chair, regional conf. chair Metro Chgo. 1995, profl. devel. com. Metro Chgo. 1993—97), Assn. Vol. Adminstrn. Internat. (mem. regional coun. 1992—95, profl. devel. com., tng. coord. bylaws chair 1995). Avocations: archaeology, choral singing, dream work, travel, family.

LUNDING, CHRISTOPHER HANNA, lawyer; b. Evanston, Ill., June 15, 1946; s. Franklin J. and Virginia (Hanna) L.; children: Elizabeth, Nelson, Alexander, Andrew, Kirsten; m. Barbara J. Fontana, Aug. 19, 1989. BA, Harvard U., 1968; JD, Yale U., 1971. Bar: N.Y. 1972, Fla. 1972, U.S. Supreme Ct. 1975. Law clk. to judge 2d Cir. U.S. Ct. Appeals, N.Y.C., 1971-72; assoc. Cleary, Gottlieb, Steen & Hamilton, 1973-79, ptnr., 1980—. Chmn. Legal Svcs. N.Y.C., 1987-94. Chmn. Belle Haven Tax Dist., Greenwich, Conn., 1986-96, 2001—. Fellow Am. Bar Found. (life); mem. N.Y. County Lawyers Assn. (bd. dirs. 1988-94). Episcopalian. Office: Cleary Gottlieb Steen & Hamilton One Liberty Plz Ste 3800 New York NY 10006 E-mail: CLunding@cgsh.com.

LUNDQUIST, CHARLES ARTHUR, university official; b. Webster, S.D., Mar. 26, 1928; s. Arthur Reynald and Olive Esther (Parks) L.; m. Patricia Jean Richardson, Nov. 28, 1951; children: Clara Lee, Dawn Elizabeth, Frances Johanna, Eric Arthur, Gary Lars. BS, S.D. State U., 1949, DSc, 1979; PhD, U. Kans., 1953. Asst. prof. engring. rsch. Pa. State U., 1953-54; sect. chief U.S. Army Ballistic Missile Agy., Huntsville, Ala., 1956-60; br. chief NASA-Marshall Space Flight Ctr., 1960-62; dir. Space Scis. Lab., 1973-81; asst. dir. sci. Smithsonian Astrophys. Obs., Cambridge, Mass., 1962-73; assoc. Harvard Coll. Obs., 1962-73; dir. rsch. U. Ala., Huntsville, 1982-90, assoc. v.p. for rsch., 1990-96, dir. consortium for materials devel. in space, 1985-98, dir. interactive projects office, 1999—. Editor: (with G. Veis) Smithsonian Institution Standard Earth, 1966, The Physics and Astronomy of Space Science, 1966, Skylab's Astronomy and Space Sciences, 1979. With U.S. Army, 1954-56. Recipient Exceptional Sci. Achievement medal NASA, 1971, Hermann Oberth award AIAA, 1978. Mem. AAAS, Am. Geophys. Union, Am. Astron. Soc., Am. Phys. Soc., Nat. Speleological Soc. Home: 214 Jones Valley Dr SW Huntsville AL 35802-1724 Office: U Ala Research Inst Rm E-37 Huntsville AL 35899-0001 E-mail: lundquc@email.uah.edu., lundquist5@comcast.net.

LUNDQUIST, DANA RICHARD, healthcare executive; b. Mpls., Sept. 12, 1941; s. R. Dana and Mary Jane (Norton) L.; children: Brenda A., Sheila R. BA, Valparaiso U., 1963; postgrad., U. Hawaii, 1963-64, U. Colo., 1963; MBA, U. Chgo., 1966. Adminstrv. asst. U. Chgo. Hosps. and Clinics, 1966—67, asst. supt., 1967—68, asst. dir., 1968—70; officer, bd. dirs. affiliates Hamot Health Systems, Inc., Erie, Pa., 1970—92, pres. parent co., 1981—92, cons., 1992—97; exec. v.p. Hardware Hawaii, 1997—98. Sr. v.p. Highmark Blue Cross Blue Shield, 1993-97; lectr. grad. program in hosp. adminstrn. U. Chgo., 1967-70; mem. Erie County Hosp. Coun., 1978-92, pres., 1982; bd. dirs. Hosp. Coun. Western Pa., 1978-92, vice chmn.; exec. com. Pa. Coun. Teaching Hosps., 1986-90; adv. coun. risk mgmt. Pa. Hosp. Ins. Co., 1982-90, bd. dirs. Vol. Hosps. Am. of Pa., 1985-92, chmn. bd.; bd. visitors The Behrend Coll., Pa. State U., 1990-92; bd. dirs. Pa. Med. Coll., 1991-92, Hardware Hawaii, 1989-98. Mem. Erie Conf. on Community Devel., 1981-92, bd. dirs., 1988-92; bd. dirs. N.W. Pa. Buy Right Coun., 1986-92, United Way Erie County, 1983-92; mem. pres.'s coun. Villa Maria Coll., Erie, 1981-90, bd. incorporators Gannon U., Erie, 1981-92; mem. governing bd. St. Paul's Luth. Ch., Erie, 1973-78, v.p., 1974-78; mem. Erie Down Town Coalition Steering Com., 1990-92, chmn., 1991-92, numerous other activities. Mem. Am. Coll. Healthcare Execs. (former regents adv. coun. Pa.); mem. Am. Hosp. Assn. (governing coun. sect. met. hosps. 1987, alt. ho. of dels. 1988), Hosp. Assn. Pa. (polit. action com. 1981-92), Pa. C. of C., U. Chgo. Hosp. Alumni Assn. (exec. com. 1967-70, 87-92, sec.-treas. 1988, pres. 1990-91), Rotary. Lutheran. Home and Office: PO Box 11889 Merrillville IN 46411-1889 E-mail: dlund13@attbi.com.

LUNDQUIST, GENE ALAN, cotton company executive; b. Bakersfield, Calif., Feb. 25, 1943; s. Felix Waldemar and Elsie Geneva (Bartlett) Lundquist; m. Susan Randour; 1 child Nels Eric. BS, Colo. State U., 1964. Info. specialist Calcot Ltd., Bakersfield, 1969-71, field rep., 1971-74, asst. v.p., 1974-77, asst. v.p., corp. sec., 1977-80, v.p., corp. sec., 1980—. Bd. dirs. Calif. Farm Water Coalition, Water Assn. Kern County; apptd. Calif. Gov.'s Agrl. Summit; bd. dirs., chmn. bd. Agrl. Coun. Calif., 1999-2001. Bd. dirs. Kern County Water Agy., Bakersfield, 1975-91, dir., 1996—; bd. dirs. Bakersfield Salvation Army, 1985-88. With U.S. Army, 1965-67. Decorated Army Commendation medal; Calif. Agr. Leadership Found. fellow, 1973. Mem. Cotton Bd. (alt. dir. 1984-2000), Nat. Cotton Council Am. (del. 1984—), Calif. Cotton Growers Assn. (adv. com. 1976—), Calif. Planting Cotton Seed Distbrs. (adv. com. 1976—). Republican. Avocations: golf, tennis, running, landscaping, reading. Office: Calcot Ltd 1601 E Brundage Ln PO Box 259 Bakersfield CA 93302-0259

LUNDQUIST, JAMES HAROLD, lawyer; b. Chgo., Mar. 24, 1931; s. Harold L. and Beatrice (Anderson) L.; m. Beverly J. Williams, 1955; children: John Redfield, Ann Tecla Walter. AB, Millikin U., 1953; JD, John Marshall Law Sch., 1955. Bar: Ill. 1954, N.Y. 1961, D.C. 1961, U.S. Supreme Ct. 1966. Pvt. practice, Chgo., 1954-55; with Barnes, Richardson & Colburn, N.Y.C., Washington, Chgo., 1957-98, sr. ptnr., 1990-98; adj. asst. prof. Bklyn. Law Sch., 1981-86; counsel Pavia & Harcourt, N.Y.C., 1999—. Bd. dirs. YKK Corp. of Am. Author: Europe and the New U.S. Bloc Politik, 1992. Pres., trustee East Hampton Hist. Soc., 1995-98; mem. Nassau County Mental Health Bd., 1965-70; corp. mem. Community Svc. Soc. N.Y.C., 1970-78; bd. dirs. NCCJ, Nassau County-N.Y., 1965-79; GATT-USTR dispute panelist, 1980-81. Served U.S. Army, 1955-56. Decorated Chevalier de l'ordre National du Merite Francais, 1980, Cavaliere Ordine al Merito della Repubblica Italia, 1994. Mem. ABA (chmn. standing com. on customs law 1968-73), Assn. of Bar of City of N.Y., Customs and Internat. Trade Bar Assn. (pres. 1978-80), Italy-Am. C. of C. (pres. 1985-87, 96-98), Union League Club (N.Y.C.), Country Club Naples (Fla.). Democrat. Methodist.

LUNDQUIST, WEYMAN IVAN, lawyer; b. Worcester, Mass., July 27, 1930; s. Hilding Ivan and Florence Cecilia (Westerholm) L.; m. Joan Durrell, Sept. 15, 1956 (div. July 1977); children— Weyman, Erica, Jettora, Kirk; m. Kathryn E. Taylor, Dec. 28, 1978; 1 child, Derek. BA magna cum laude, Dartmouth Coll., 1952; LLB, Harvard U., 1955. Bar: Mass. 1955, Alaska 1961, Calif. 1963, Vt. 1994. Assoc. Thayer, Smith & Gaskill, Worcester, 1957-60; atty. U.S. Attys. Office, Mass. and Alaska, 1960-62; assoc. Heller, Ehrman, White & McAuliffe, San Francisco, 1963-65, ptnr., 1967—; counsel, v.p. State Mut. Life Ins. Co., Worcester, 1965-67. Vis. prof. environ. studies Dartmouth Coll., Hanover, N.H., 1980, 84, bus. sch., 1997, vis. scholar, 1994-97, adj. prof. Amos Tuck Bus. Sch., Dartmouth Coll., 1997-99; program chmn. 1990 Moscow Conf. on Law and Bilateral Econs. Rels.; mem. U.S. adv. com. Alaska/Can./Soviet No. Justice Conf., 1993-94, N.Y., San Francisco Cutting Edge Lawyer Liability Programs, 1989; assoc. dir. Inst. Arctic Studies, Dartmouth Coll., 1999—; bd. dirs. U. Press New Eng., 1997, West Coast Magnetics, Stockton, Calif, Environmental Careers Orgn., ECO, Boston, 2001. Author: (fiction) The Promised Land, 1987, (nonfiction) The Art of Shaping the Case, 1999; contbr. articles to profl. jours. Trustee Natural Resources Def. Coun., 1982-91. Recipient CPR Significant Achievement award, 1987. Fellow ABA (founder and chmn. litigation sect. 1978-79, chmn. Soviet Bar Assn. liaison com. 1986, co-chmn. spl. com. for study discovery abuse 1976-83, spl. com. on tort liability sys. 1981-84, superfund 301e study group advisor to U.S. Congress, 1983), Am. Coll. Trial Lawyers; mem. Dartmouth Lawyer's Assn. (founding mem.), Am. Antiquarian Soc. (councillor), Assn. Life Ins. Coun., U.S. Supreme Ct. Hist. Soc., No. Dist. Hist. Soc., Dartmouth Lawyers Assn., Swedish Am. C. of C. (pres., bd. dirs. western U.S. 1982-89). Avocations: squash, skiing, writing. Home: 16 Occum Rdg Hanover NH 03755-1410 Office: PO Box 5527 53 S Main St Ste 313 Hanover NH 03755-2022 Fax: 603-543-8615. E-mail: wey@dartmouth.edu.

LUNDREGAN, WILLIAM JOSEPH, lawyer; b. Peabody, Mass., Nov. 8, 1940; s. William J. and Suzanne G. (Hichens) L.; m. Jane T. Lundregan, July 15, 1967; children: Catherine S., William J., Anne T. BS in BA, Boston Coll., 1962, LLB, 1967. With office of tax counsel United Shoe Machinery Corp., Boston, 1967; atty. tax dept. Arthur Young & Co., 1967-69; first asst. clk. magistrate First Dist. Ct. of Essex, Salem, Mass., 1969-74; ptnr. Welch & Lundregan, 1974-88, Lundregan Law Offices, Salem, 1974—. Corporator, trustee, bd. investment Salem Five Cents Savs. Bank; gen. counsel Essex County Retirement Bd., treas.; gen. counsel Salem Contributory Retirement Bd., Salem Housing Authority, Beverly Housing Authority, 1988—. Bd. dirs. North Shore Cath. Charities, Peabody; trustee, pres. Salem Atheneum; pres., dir. Boys and Girls Club, Salem; city solicitor City Salem, 1999-2001. 1st lt. U.S. Army, 1962-64. Mem. Mass. Bar Assn., Salem Bar Assn., Essex County Bar Assn. (exec. com.), Rotary (bd. dirs., pres. 1985-86), Corinthian Yacht Club (membership com.). Roman Catholic. Home: 11 Faye Cir Marblehead MA 01945-3714 E-mail: wjl@lundreganlaw.com.

LUNDSAGER, CHRISTIAN BENT, retired mechanical engineer, consultant; b. Holbaek, Denmark, Feb. 27, 1925; came to U.S., 1952; s. Hans Christian and Marta (Nielsen) L.; m. Else Tork, July 10, 1947; children: Soren, Margrethe, Hanne, Eva. MSME, Tech. U., Denmark, 1950. Lic. profl. engr., Md. Lab. asst. Tech. U., Denmark, 1947-52; rsch. engr. DuPont Co., Buffalo, N.Y. and Wilmington, Del., 1952-62; rsch. assoc. W.R. Grace & Co., Columbia, Md., 1962-90; pvt. practice Ashton, 1990—. Inventor over 30 patents. Mem. Soc. Plastics Engrs. (sr. emeritus, councilor 1967-68), Balt.-Washington Soc. Plastics Engrs. (pres. 1966), Fedn. Materials Socs. (trustee 1969). Avocations: sailing, woodworking. Home and Office: 1308 Patuxent Dr Ashton MD 20861-9759

LUNDSTEDT, SVEN BERTIL, behavioral and social scientist, educator; b. N.Y.C., May 6, 1926; s. Sven David and Edith Maria L.; m. Jean Elizabeth Sanford, June 16, 1951; children: Margaret, Peter, Janet. AB, U. Chgo., 1952, PhD, 1955; SM, Harvard U., 1960. Lic. in psychology, N.Y., Ohio; cert. Council for Nat. Register of Health Services. Asst. dir. Found. for Research on Human Behavior, 1960-62; asst. prof. Case-Western Res. U., Cleve., 1962-64, assoc. prof., 1964-68; assoc. prof. adminstrv. sci. Ohio State U., Columbus, 1968-69, prof. pub. policy and mgmt., 1969—, Ameritech Research prof., 1987-89, prof. internat. bus. and pub. policy, 1988—, prof. mgmt. and human resources, 1990—, mem. John Glenn Inst. for Pub. Svc. and Pub. Policy, 1999—. Affiliate scientist Battelle PNL, 1994—; chmn. Battelle endowment program for tech. and human affairs, 1976-80, mem. Univ. Senate; dir. project on edn. of chief exec. officer Aspen Inst., 1978-80; advisor Task Force on Innovation, U.S. Ho. of Reps., 1983-84, Citizens Network for Fgn. Affairs, 1988—; mem. Am. Com. on U.S. Soviet Relations, 1985—, chair trade and negotiation project; cons. E.I. duPont de Nemours & Co., B.F. Goodrich Co., Bell Telephone Labs., Battelle Meml. Inst., Nat. Fulbright Award Com.; invited speaker Royal Swedish Acad. Scis., 1989. Author: Higher Education in Social Psychology, 1968; co-author: Managing Innovation, 1982, Managing Innovation and Change, 1989; author, editor: Telecommunications, Values and the Public Interest, 1990; contbr. articles to profl. jours. Pres., Cleve. Mental Health Assn., 1966-68; mem. Ohio Citizen's Task Force on Corrections, 1971-72. Served with U.S. Army, 1944-46 Harvard U. fellow, 1960; grantee Bell Telephone Labs., 1964-65, NSF, 1965-67, Kettering Found., 1978-80, Atlantic Richfield Found., 1980-82, German Marshall Fund of U.S. to conduct internat. ednl. joint ventures on econ. negotiations, Budapest, Hungary, 1990; recipient Ohio Ho. of Reps. award, 1986. Mem.: Internat. Soc. Panetics (mem., sec. bd. govs., founding mem.), Am. Soc. for Pub. Adminstrn. (pres. Central Ohio chpt. 1975—77, founder, chmn. com. on bus. govt. relations 1977—79, editl. bd. Pub. Adminstrn. Rev. 1978—82), Am. Acad. Arts and Scis. (chmn. PIN com. on east/west trade negotiation), Internat. Inst. for Applied Systems Analysis (innovation task force, nat. adv. com. project. internat. negotiation with AAAS, founder, chmn. U.S. Midwest Assn. for IIASA 1986—, sr. social sci. advisor 1994—), Am. Psychol. Assn. Unitarian Universalist. Home: 197 Riverview Park Dr Columbus OH 43214-2023 Office: Ohio State U Sch Pub Policy and Mgmt 2100 Neil Ave Columbus OH 43210-1144 E-mail: lundstedt.1@osu.edu.

LUNDSTROM, GILBERT GENE, banker, lawyer; b. Sept. 27, 1941; s. Vernon G. and Imogene (Jackett) L.; m. Joyce Elaine Ronin, June 26, 1965; children: Trevor A., Gregory G. BS, U. Nebr., 1964, JD, 1969; MBA, Wayne State U., 1966. Bar: U.S. Dist. Ct. (1st dist.) Nebr. 1969, Nebr. 1969, U.S. Ct. Appeals (5th cir.) 1970, U.S. Ct. Appeals (10th cir.) 1971, U.S. Ct. Appeals (8th cir.) 1974, U.S. Ct. Appeals (3d cir.) 1986. Ptnr. Woods & Aitken Law Firm, Lincoln, Nebr., 1969-93; pres., CEO, chmn. bd. Tier One Bank, 1994—. Pres., CEO Tier One Bank, a Delaware Corp.; part-time faculty law sch. U. Nebr.-Lincoln, 1970-74; dir. First Fed. Lincoln Bank, TMS Corp. of Ams., First Fin. Corp.; bd. dirs. Sahara Enterprises, Inc., Sahara Coal Co., Chgo.; dir., vice chmn. Fed. Home Loan Bank Topeka, 1996-98, 99-2002, dir. City of Lincoln C. of C. Bd. dirs. Folsom Children's Zoo, Lincoln, 1979-83, St. Elizabeth Hosp. Found.; dir. Nat. Coun. Fed. Home Loan Banks, Lincoln C. of C. Fellow Nebr. State Bar Assn.; mem. ABA, ATLA, Lincoln Bar Assn., Nebr. Bar Assn., Newcomer Soc. U.S., Heartland Cmty. Bankers Assn. (bd. dirs.), Lincoln C. of C., Country Club of Lincoln, Firethorn County Club, Masons, Scottish Rite (33 degree), Lincoln C. of C. (bd. dirs.) Republican. Methodist. Home: 9519 Firethorn Ln Lincoln NE 68520-1459 Office: First Fed Lincoln 1235 N St Lincoln NE 68508-2083

LUNDSTROM, MARJIE, newspaper editor and columnist; Grad., U. Nebr. Columnist, editor, nat. corr. The Denver Post, 1981-89; with The Sacramento Bee, 1989-90, 91—; nat. corr. Gannett News Svc., Washington, 1990-91. Recipient Pulitzer Prize for nat. reporting, 1991. Office: The Sacramento Bee PO Box 15779 Sacramento CA 95852-0779

LUNDT, ERIC L. lawyer; b. N.Y.C., July 20, 1965; s. Rudy Oscar and Susan Robin (Cagan) L. BBA cum laude, U. Miami, Coral Gables, Fla., 1987, JD, 1990. Bar: Fla. 1990, U.S. Ct. Appeals (11th cir.) 1994, U.S. Dist. Ct. (so. dist.) Fla. 1994, U.S. Dist. Ct. (mid. dist.) 1995, U.S. Supreme Ct. 1995, U.S. Dist. Ct. (no. dist.) Fla. 1997. Summer assoc. Daniels & Hicks P.A., Miami, 1988-90; law clk. 3d Dist. Ct. of Appeals of Fla., 1990-92; adj. prof. Miami-Dade C.C., 1991-92; assoc. Kelly, Black, Black, Byrne & Beasley, P.A., Miami, 1992—96; shareholder Heinrich Gordon Hargrove Weihe & James, P.A., Ft. Lauderdale, 1996—. Cons., rev. editor West Ednl. Pub., St. Paul, 1992-93. Vol. coord. Health Crisis Network, Miami, 1995. Mem. ABA, Def. Rsch. Inst. (drug and med. device com. 1999—), Dade County Bar Assn. (dir. young lawyers sect. 1994-97, cert. of merit 1994), Fla. Bar (exec. com. on eminent domain 1993-96, appellate practice and advocacy sect. 1994—), Broward County Bar Assn. (young lawyers exec. com. 1997-98). Avocations: tennis, travel, oenology. Office: Heinrich Gordon Hargrove Weihe & James PA 500 E Broward Blvd Ste 1000 Fort Lauderdale FL 33394-3087

LUNDY, ANSTIS BURWELL, artist; b. Plainfield, N.J., Aug. 28, 1924; d. William Russell and Aubrey (Eaton) Burwell; m. William Ames Atchley, Apr, 14, 1945 (div. 1955); 1 child Mark Ames Atchley; m. Victor Alfred Lundy, Sept. 19, 1960; 1 child, Nicholas Burwell Lundy. Student, Cours Fenelon, Paris, 1938, Cleve. Inst. Art, 1940-42, Boston Mus. Sch. Fine Arts, 1942-43, Glassell Sch. Art, 1977-81. Draftsmans Harvard U., Cambridge, Mass., 1943-46, various archtl. and engring. cos., 1946-58, Fritz Benedict, Architect, FAIA, Aspen, Colo., 1958-59; art tchr. Anderson Ranch Art Ctr., 1984-88, 90-93, Southwest Craft Ctr., San Antonio, 1985, Beaumont (Tex.) Art League, 1981, Spring Island, S.C., 1998; and yrly. workshops Aspen, 1993-2000. One-woman shows include Patricia Moore Gallery, Aspen, 1970, 82, 85, 90, 94, 96, Silvermine Guild Artists, New Canaan, Conn., 1972, Moody Gallery, Houston, 1984, 87, 92, Katharina Rich Perlow Gallery, N.Y.C., 1988, Evelyn Siegel Gallery, Ft. Worth, 1992, 95, Adelson Gallery, Aspen, 1996; exhibited in group shows at Silvermine Guild Artists, 1969, Guilford Art League, 1969, Creative Arts Workshop, New Haven, Conn., 1969, Moody Gallery, 1980, 85, Houston Art League, 1980, 81, Glassell Sch., Houston, 1981, Springfield Art Mus., Mo., 1981, Watercolor Art Soc., Houston, 1981, 82, 83, 84, 85, Art Ctr., Waco, Tex., 1982, Houston Festival, 1982, McNay Mus., San Antonio, 1983, Toni Jones Gallery, Houston, 1984, Transco Tower Gallery, Houston, 1985, 87, 88, Perception Gallery, Houston, 1986, Cullen Ctr., Houston, 1986, Sheraton Gallery, Dallas, 1986, 1401 W. Gray Gallery, Houston, 1988, Zan's, 1990, Aries Gallery, 1990, Butera's Cafe, Houston, 1991, Galveston Arts Ctr., Tex., 1991, Barney Wykoff Gallery, Aspen, 1995, Lobby Gallery, Houston, 1996, Cloister Gallery, Houston, 1997; represented in permanent collections Transco Energy, Tex. Commerce Banks, U. Houston, 1010 Lamar Restaurant, Moody-Rambin, Baylor Coll. Medicine, Wilson Industries, CBS, Gerald Hines Galleria, Enron, Continental Airlines, St. Luke's Tower, The Little Nell Hotel. Nat. coun. bd. Anderson Ranch Arts Ctr., Aspen, 1997-2000; sponsor Mus. Fine Arts, Houston, 1997-2000, Contemporary Arts Mus., Houston, 1997-2000; donor Aspen Art Mus., 1990-2000. Studio: Anstis Lundy Studio 701 Mulberry Ln Bellaire TX 77401-3805

LUNDY, AUDIE LEE, JR. lawyer; b. Columbus, Ga., Mar. 10, 1943; s. Audie Lee and Mary Blanche (Snipes) L.; m. Ann Porter, June 11, 1966; children: Travis Stuart, Katherine Porter. BA, Yale U., 1965; LLB magna cum laude, Columbia U., 1968. Bar: N.Y. 1968, D.C. 1976, Pa. 1988, Md. 1990. Assoc. firm White & Case, N.Y.C., 1968-71, 74-75, London, 1971-74, Washington, 1975-78; asst. gen. counsel Campbell Soup Co., Camden, N.J., 1978, gen. counsel, 1979-88, v.p., gen. counsel, 1988-89; ptnr. Tydings & Rosenberg LLP, Balt., 1989—. Bd. mgrs. St. Christopher's Hosp. for Children, Phila., 1980-89, vice-chmn. 1986-89; trustee Food and Drug Law Inst., Washington, 1982-91, The Children's Guild, Inc., Balt., 1992—, chmn. 1997-99. Mem. ABA, Am. Soc. Internat. Law, Assn. Gen. Counsel (emeritus). Republican. Presbyterian. Clubs: Merion Cricket Home: 203 Goodwood Gdns Baltimore MD 21210-2531 Office: Tydings & Rosenberg LLP 100 E Pratt St Baltimore MD 21202-1009 E-mail: llundy@tydingslaw.com.

LUNDY, BARBARA JEAN, training executive; b. Chgo., Feb. 2, 1950; Tchr., facilitator Red Rocks C.C., Golden, Colo., 1986-90, AMI, St. Lukes Hosp., Denver, 1986-90; tchr. Arapaho C.C., 1991-95; tng. mgr. Denver Options, 1995—. Mediator U. Denver. Author, poet, editor Market Mountain Writers, 1978-81; co-author: You Can Collect Child Support, 1989. Profl. vol. VIDA Vols., Pueblo, Colo., 1971-73; vol. dir. Legal Aid Soc., Denver, 1980-85; bd. mem., editl. bd. Colo. Women's Polit. Caucus, Denver, 1980-81; state commn. mem. Colo. Child Support Commn., Denver, 1984-85; co-founder Kids in Need Support (KINS), Denver, 1986-87; com. mem. Denver Dist. Ct.: Bench, Bar, Cmty. Rels. Com., Denver, 1987-89. Mem. Assn. Persons Supported Employment (spkr. nat. conv. 1998), Hayna Writers. Avocations: science, history and philosophy reading, piano, writing. Office: Denver Options 5250 Leetsdale Dr Ste 200 Denver CO 80246-1451 E-mail: blundy@denveroptions.org.

LUNDY, JANET CECILE, histotechnologist; b. Laverty, Okla., May 20, 1942; d. Cecil LeRoy and Grace (Arnold) Parish; student pub. schs., Chickasha, Okla.; m. J. W. Lundy, Oct. 20, 1963. Histology technician Presbyn. Hosp., Oklahoma City, 1960-68; supr. histotech. Okla. Health Scis. Ctr., Oklahoma City, 1968-71; supr. histotech. Hillcrest Osteo. Hosp., Oklahoma City, 1972-75; supr., histotechnologist Bapt. Med. Center Okla., Oklahoma City, 1975-83; founder, operator Precision Histology Lab Inc., 1983—; mem. adj. faculty Oscar Rose Jr. Coll. (now Rose State Coll.), 1978-83; founding officer Post Burn Support Group Okla., Inc., 1989. Mem. steering com. Linwood Pl. Neighborhood Assn., 1980-82. Mem. Okla. Soc. Histotechnologists, Nat. Soc. Histotech., Am. Soc. Clin. Pathologists (assoc.). Mem. Ch. Nazarene. Home: 3132 NW 22nd St Oklahoma City OK 73107-3018

LUNDY, J(OSEPH) EDWARD, retired automobile company executive; b. Iowa, Jan. 6, 1915; s. Vern E. and Mary L. (Chambers) L. BA, U. Iowa, 1936. Fellow Princeton U., 1936-39, mem. econs. faculty, 1940-42, beginning as planning ofcl.; with Ford Motor Co., Dearborn, Mich., 1946-85, successively dir. fin. planning and analysis, gen. asst. contr., 1946-57, treas., 1957-61, v.p., contr., 1961-62, v.p. fin., 1962-67, exec. v.p., 1967-79, dir. and vice-chmn. fin. com., 1979-85. Dir. research and analysis Office Statis. Control, Hdqrs. USAAF, 1945 Served from pvt. to maj. USAAF, 1943-45. Decorated Legion of Merit. Mem. Dearborn Country Club, Phi Beta Kappa, Delta Upsilon. Clubs: Detroit Princeton. Roman Catholic. Home: 7 Brookwood Ln Dearborn MI 48120-1302

LUNDY, MARILYNN FRANCES, designer, consultant; b. Washington, June 16, 1939; d. Kenneth Merle and Julia (Tassey) L. BA, Pa. State U., 1961. Asst. buyer Abraham & Straus, Bklyn., 1961-63; buyer J.C. Penney Co., Inc., N.Y.C., 1963-73; merchandise man Family Fashions by Avon, 1973-74; product merchandise Federated Dept. Stores, 1975-80; prin. Lundy Ltd., 1981-82; dir. mktg. Lincoln Ctr. Performing Arts, 1982-83; prin. Interior and Exterior Life Design, Environ. Images, Art and More, 1984—. Avocations: arts, athletics. Office: Interior & Exterior Life Design Suite 30 S One Lincoln Plaza New York NY 10023-7136 E-mail: intextlifedesign@aol.com.

LUNDY, ROBERT FIELDEN, minister; b. Stilesboro, Georgia, Mar. 29, 1920; s. Clyde Enoch and Elisabeth Marion (Teilmann) L.; m. Elizabeth Frances Hall, June 15, 1944; children: Robert Fielden, Jr., Allen Francis, Carolyn Elisa Lundy Crowe. BA cum laude, Emory and Henry Coll., 1941, DD, 1961; MDiv, Emory U., 1944; postgrad. Chinese lang., Yale U., 1948-50. Ordained to ministry The Meth. Ch., 1946. Pastor First Meth. Ch., Oak Ridge, Tenn., 1944-48; missionary The Meth. Ch., Malaysia and Singapore, 1950-64, bishop Malaysia and Singapore, 1964-68; mem. staff world divsn. bd. of missions United Meth. Ch., N.Y.C., 1968-71, exec. sec. southeastern jurisdiction Atlanta, 1971-76; sr. pastor Broad St. Ch., Cleveland, Tenn., 1976-81; dist. supt. Knoxville (Tenn.) Dist., 1981-85; pastor Norris, Tenn., 1985-90. Pres. Coun. of Chs., Malaysia and Singapore, 1966-67; chmn. Laymen Abroad Nat. Coun. Chs., N.Y.C., 1970-71; chmn. Appalachian devel. com. Commn. on Religion in Appalachia, 1974-77. Editor: Malaysia Message, 1952-55, 58-60, 62-64, World Divsn. Newsletter, 1968-71, Forward, 1991-97; contbr. to biography Prophetic Evangelist, 1993. Chmn. Haywood County Craft Coop., Waynesville, NC, 1991, Haywood County Com. for Peace, Waynesville, 1995; chmn. com. on religious life Hiwassee Coll., 1996—; chmn. commn. on congrl. care Long's Chapel UMC, 1998—2000; mem. adv. coun. Found. for Evangelism, 1994—; trustee Paine Coll., 1976—81, Hiwassee Coll., 1996—2003. Mem. Kiwanis (chmn. internat. understanding Waynesville, N.C. 1993-96, 98—) Democrat. Avocations: biographical trivia on U.S. Presidents, yard and garden care. Home: 97 Lundy Ln Waynesville NC 28786-6686

LUNDY, SADIE ALLEN, retired small business owner; b. Milton, Fla., Mar. 29, 1918; d. Stephen Grover and Martha Ellen (Harter) Allen; m. Wilson Tate Lundy, May 17, 1939 (dec. 1962); children: Wilson Tate Jr., Houston Allen, Michael David, Robert Douglas, Martha Jo-Ellen. Degree in acctg., Graceland Coll., 1938. Acct. Powers Furniture Co., Milton, Fla., 1939-40, Lundy Oil Co., Milton, 1941-52; controller First Fed. Savs. & Loan, Kansas City, Mo., 1953-55, Herald Pub. Co., Indepenence, 1956-58; mgr. Baird & Son Toy Co., Kansas City, 1959-62; regional mgr. Emmons Jewelers of N.Y., 1963-65; owner, pres. Lundy Tax Service, Independence, 1965-85; corporate sec. and treas., purchasing mgr. Optimation, Inc., 1974-85, mgr., 1985—, ret., 2001—. V.p. Lundy Oil Co., Milton, 1941-52. Contbr. articles to profl. jours. Mem. com. Neighborhood Council, Independence, 1985. Mem. Am. Bus. Women's Assn., Independence C. of C. (mem. com. 1965-85). Republican. Mem. Reorganized Ch. of Jesus Christ of Latter Day Saints. Club: Independence Women's. Avocations: counseling, swimming, bicycling. Home and Office: PO Box 520238 Independence MO 64052-0238 E-mail: slundy@optinest.com.

LUNDY, SHERMAN PERRY, secondary school educator; b. Kansas City, Mo., July 26, 1939; s. Loren F. and O. Metta (Brown) L.; m. Beverly J., Feb. 25, 1960; children: Paul, Carolyn. BA, U. Okla., 1963; MA, So. Meth. U., 1966; EdS, U. Iowa, 1975. Cert. tchr., Iowa. Tchr. Platte Canyon High Sch., Bailey, Colo., 1964-65, Lone Grove (Okla.) High Sch., 1966-68, Ardmore (Okla.) High Sch., 1968-69; tchr., sci. dept. chair Burlington (Iowa) High Sch., 1969—. Geologist Basic Materials Corp., Waterloo, Iowa, 1983—, Raid Quarries, Burlington, 1975-80. Contbr. articles to profl. jours.; author curriculum guide: Environmental Activities, 1975. Mem., commr. Regional Solid Waste Commn., Des Moines County, 1990—; mem., pres. Conservation Bd., Des Moines County, 1978-88; bd. dirs. Iowa Conservation Bd. Assn., 1984-85; mem. Civil Rights Commn., City of Burlington, 1970-76; pres. Burlington Trees Forever, 1998-99. With USMC, 1960-64. Recipient Silver Beaver Boy Scouts Am., 1975, Service Recognition, Des Moines County Conservation Bd., 1988, Project ESTEEM agt., Harvard/Smithsonian, 1992, Soil Conservation Water Shed Achievement award State of Iowa, 1998, DAR Award for Conservation, 1998, Environ. Educator of Yr. award U.S. EPA, Region 7, Iowa, 1998. Mem. Geol. Soc. Am. (North Cen. edn. com. 1989—), Iowa Acad. Sci. (edn. com. 1990-91, chair earth sci. tchrs. sect. 1993-94, exec. bd. 1992-94), Nat. Assn. Geology Tchrs. (Outstanding Earth Sci. Tchr. 1992, v.p. ctrl. sect. 1994-95, pres. ctrl. sect. 1996-98), Soc. Econ. and Sedimentary Geology, Geol. Soc. Iowa, Am. Chem. Soc. (Excellence in Sci. Tchg. award consortiums 1996, Chem. Cos. award), Unitarian Fellowship, Sons of Confederate Vets. (comdr. Camp 1759 1998—), SE Iowa Civil War Round Table (chair 1992-94). Unitarian Universalist. Avocations: civil war, stamp collecting, fossil collecting. Home: 4668 Summer St Burlington IA 52601-8985

LUNDY, VICTOR ALFRED, architect, educator; b. N.Y.C., Feb. 1, 1923; s. Alfred Henry and Rachel Lundy; m. Shirley Corwin, 1947 (div. 1959); children: Christopher Mark, Jennifer Alison; m. Anstis Manton Burwell, Sept. 19, 1960; 1 child, Nicholas Burwell. BArch, Harvard U., 1947, MArch, 1948. Registered architect, Tex., N.Y., Calif. Pvt. practice architecture, Sarasota, Fla., 1951-59, N.Y.C., 1960-75; prin. Victor A. Lundy & Assocs., Inc., Houston, 1976-84; design. prin., v.p. HKS Inc., Dallas, 1984-90. Vis. prof. Grad. Sch. Design, Harvard U., Sch. Architecture, Yale U., Columbia U., U. Calif., Berkeley, Calif. Poly. State U. San Luis Obispo, U. Houston, U. Rome, others; U.S. specialist-architect in U.S.I.A. exhibit, USSR, 1965. Responsible for design St. Paul's Luth. Ch., Sarasota, 1959, new sanctuary, 1970, 1st Unitarian Ch. of Fairfield County, Westport, Conn., 1961, 1st Unitarian Congl. Soc., Hartford, Conn., 1964, Ch. of Resurrection, East Harlem Protestant Parish, N.Y.C., 1966, exhbn. bldg. and exhibit for AEC in S.Am. (Buenos Aires, Rio de Janeiro, Bogota, Santiago), 1967 (Silver medal for exhbn. Archtl. League N.Y. 1965), recreation shelters for Nat. Mus. History and tech., Smithsonian Instn., Washington, 1967, U.S. States Tax Ct. bldg. and pla., Washington, 1976, U.S. Embassy, Colombo, Sri Lanka, for Office of Fgn. Bldgs., Dept. State, 1983 (U.S. Presdl. Design Awards Program 1988, Fed. Design Achievement award), Austin Centre-Omni Hotel, Austin, Tex., 1984, One Congress Pla., Austin, Tex., 1984, Walnut Glen Tower, Dallas, 1985, Mack Ctr. II, Tampa, Fla., 1990, Greyhound Corp. Ctr., Phoenix, 1991, GTE Telephone Ops. World Hdqrs., Irving, Tex., 1991, Tex. A&M Found Hdqs., 1999, others; archtl. work represented in Berlin Internat. Archtl. Exposition, 1957, Sao Paulo Internat. Biennial Exposition, 1957, 5th Congress Union Internat. Des Architectes, Moscow, 1958, Expo '70 Exhbn., Osaka, Japan, 1970, travelling exhbn. of architecture in S.Am. Sgt. inf. U.S. Army, 1943-46, ETO. Decorated Purple Heart; recipient Gold medal award Buenos Aires Sesquicentennial Internat. Exhbn., 1960, Gold medal award Buenos Aires Sesquicentennial Internt.Exhbn., 1960; Silver medal Archtl. League N.Y., 1965; Charles Hayden Meml. Scholastic scholar, 1939-43, Edward H. Kendall scholar Harvard U., 1947-48, Rotch travelling scholar Boston Soc. Architects, 1948-50; travelling fellow Harvard U., 1948-50; Dept. State grantee, 1965. Fellow AIA. Avocations: painting, sculpture. Home: 701 Mulberry Ln Bellaire TX 77401-3805

LUNDY, WALKER, newspaper editor; b. St. Petersburg, Fla. m. Saralyn Lundy; 2 children. BSJ, U. Fla. Reporter Atlanta Jour.-Constitution; reporter, city editor Detroit Free Press; mng. editor, exec. editor Tallahassee Democrat; mng. editor Ft. Worth Star-Telegram; editor Arkansas Gazette, Little Rock; exec. editor, sr. v.p. St. Paul Pioneer Press, 1990—2001; editor Philadelphia Inquirer, 2001—. Office: Philadelphia Inquirer PO Box 8263 Philadelphia PA 19130*

LUNDY-SLADE, BETTIE B. retired electronics professional; b. Marinette, Wis., Feb. 16, 1924; d. Adolph Gustav and Bertha Julian (Keller) Limberg; m. George Wesley Lundy II, Nov. 11, 1951 (div. 1956); children: George Wesley III, Genise Wynell, Charles Edward; m. Jim Donovan Slade, July 20, 1973. Lic. vocat. nurse, psychiat. technician, Calif. With Allis Chalmers, Milw., 1942-44, Gen. Dynamics, San Diego, 1959-65, Tetedyne Ryan, San Diego, 1966-76, Cubic, San Diego, 1976-86; ret., 1986. Author: (poetry) Do You Have a Minute, 1991, (biography) Growing Up on a Farm During the Depression, 1995, Book III Wistful Wanterings, 1992; artist over 100 paintings, 1986—. Den mother Boy Scouts Am., San Diego; Sunday sch. tchr. Luth. Ch., San Diego. With USN Waves, 1944-50. Recipient Sen. Cashman award Marinette, Wis., 1937, Letter of Appreciation Mother Teresa, 1992, Gen. Norman Schwarzkoph, 1993, Queen Elizabeth, 1993. Mem. Internat. Soc. Poets (life), Nat. Parks & Conservation, Smithsonian Assocs., Peal Ctr. Christian Living, Nat. Audubon Soc., Nat. Mus. Women in Arts. Republican. Avocations: soft sculpture, crocheting, short stories and poetry, , oil, acrylic and water color painting. Home: 6315 Thorn St San Diego CA 92115-6908

LUNGREN, JOHN HOWARD, law educator, oil and gas consultant, author; b. Chgo., Feb. 11, 1925; s. Charles Howard and Edna Hughes (Edwards) L.; m. Phyllis Joan Jolidon, Dec. 12, 1953 (div.); 1 son, John Eric; m. Susan Jeanette Whitfield, Sept. 22, 1984. B.A., Beloit Coll., 1948; J.D., Marquette U., 1952; M.A., U. Wis.-Milw., 1974. Bar: Wis. 1952, Ill. 1975, Kans. 1980. Assoc. gen. counsel A. O. Smith Corp., 1964-74; gen. atty. Clark Oil & Refining Corp., 1954-64; prof. law Lewis U., Glen Ellyn, Ill., 1975-80; assoc. prof. law Washburn U. Sch. Law, Topeka, 1980-85; practice, Chgo., from 1977; with Turner & Boisseau Ltd., Wichita, Kans., 1985-88; of counsel Lungren and Whitfield-Lungren, Wichita, 1987—; cons. oil and gas; Kans. rep. legal com. Interstate Oil Compact. Chmn., Milwaukee County Republican Party, 1966-70; justice of peace, Wauwatosa, Wis., 1964-68. Served with USN, 1943-46. Mem. ABA, Ill. Bar Assn., Wis. Bar Assn., Kans. Bar Assn., Wichita Bar Assn.

LUNGSTRUM, JOHN W. federal judge; b. Topeka, Nov. 2, 1945; s. Jack Edward and Helen Alice (Watson) L.; m. Linda Eileen Ewing, June 21, 1969; children: Justin Matthew, Jordan Elizabeth, Alison Paige. BA magna cum laude, Yale Coll., 1967; JD, U. Kans., 1970. Bar: Kans. 1970, Calif. 1970, U.S. Dist. Ct. (ctrl. dist.) Calif., U.S. Ct. Appeals (10th crct.). Assoc. Latham & Watkins, L.A., 1970-71; ptnr. Stevens, Brand, Lungstrum, Golden & Winter, Lawrence, Kans., 1972-91; U.S. Dist. judge Dist. of Kans., Kansas City, 1991—, chief judge, 2001—. Lectr. law U. Kans. Law Sch., 1973—; mem. faculty Kans. Bar Assn. Coll. Advocacy , Trial Tactics and Techniques Inst., 1983-86; chmn. Douglas County Rep. Ctrl. Com., 1975-81; mem. Rep. State Com.; del. State Rep. Convention, 1968, 76, 80; chair com. on ct. adminstrn. and case mgmt. Jud. Conf. of the U.S., 2000—. Chmn. bd. dirs. Lawrence C. of C., 1990-91; pres. Lawrence United Fund, 1979; pres. Independence Days Lawrence, Inc., 1984, 85, Seem-to-be-Players, Inc., Lawrence Rotary Club, 1978-79; bd. dirs. Lawrence Soc. Chamber Music, Swarthout Soc. (corp. fund-raising chmn.); mem. Lawrence Art Commn., Williams Scholarship Fund, Lawrence League Women Voters, Douglas County Hist. Soc.; bd. trustees, stewardship chmn. Plymouth Congl. Ch.; pres. Lawrence Round Ball Club; coach Lawrence Summertime Basketball; Vice chmn. U. Kans. Disciplinary Bd.; bd. govs. Kans Sch. Religion; bd. dirs. Kans. Day Club, 1980, 81. National Merit scholar, Yale Nat. scholar. Fellow Am. Bar Found.; mem. ABA (past mem. litigation and ins. sect.), Douglas County Bar Assn., Johnson County Bar Assn., Wyandotte County Bar Assn., Kans. Bar Assn. (vice chair legislative com., subcom. litigation, mem. continuing legal edn. com.), U Kans. Alumni Assn. (life), Phi Beta Kappa, Phi Gamma Delta, Phi Delta Phi. Avocations: basketball, hiking, skiing. Office: Robt J Dole US Courthouse Ste 517 500 State Ave Rm 517 Kansas City KS 66101-2400

LUNINE, JONATHAN IRVING, planetary scientist, educator; b. N.Y.C., June 26, 1959; BS magna cum laude, U. Rochester, 1980; MS, Calif. Inst. Tech., 1983, PhD, 1985. Rsch. assoc. U. Ariz., Tucson, 1984-86, asst. prof. planetary scis., 1986-90; vis. asst. prof. UCLA, 1986, assoc. prof., 1990-95, prof., 1995—, faculty mem. program in applied math., 1992—, chair theoretical astrophys. program, 2000. Interdisciplinary scientist on joint U.S.-European Cassini mission to Saturn; mem. com. planetary and lunar exploration space sci. bd. NAS, 1986-90; chmn. NASA Solar Sys. Exploration subcom., 1990-95; chmn. Pluto Express Sci. Definition Team, 1995; disting. vis. scientist Jet Propulsion Lab., 1997—; mem. exec. com. space studies bd. NRC, 1998—, chmn. com. on origin and evolution of life in the universe of space studies bd., 2000—; mem. sci. coun. NASA Astrobiology Inst., 2001—. Author: Earth: Evolution of, 1999; contbr. articles to profl. jours.; co-editor: Protostars and Planets III, 1993. Mem. Internat. Mars Exploration Adv. Panel NASA, 1993-94, space sci. adv. com., 1990-95; exec. com. NRC Space Studies bd., 1998—. Named one of 50 Emerging Leaders, Time Mag., 1994; recipient Cospar Zeldovich prize, Soviet Intercosmos and Inst. for Space Rsch., 1990, Arthur Adel award sci. achievement, No. Ariz. U., 2000. Fellow: Am. Geophys. Union (Macelwane medal 1995); mem.: NAS (nat. assoc.), European Geophys. Soc., Internat. Coun. Sci. Unions, Internat. Acad. Astronautics, Am. Astron. Soc. (Harold C. Urey prize 1988), Sigma Xi. Avocation: hiking. Office: U Ariz Dept Planetary Scis PO Box 210092 Tucson AZ 85721-0092 E-mail: jlunine@lpl.arizona.edu.

LUNN, KITTY ELIZABETH, actress; b. New Orleans, Aug. 5, 1950; d. Hugh I. Morrison and Beatrice (McClung) Farrell; m. Andrew Macmillan, Dec. 21, 1989. Student, Washington Sch. Ballet, 1965-68, Neighborhood Playhouse Sch., 1968-70; degree summa cum laude, CUNY, 1995. Dancer Washington Ballet, 1965-68; radio producer WOR Radio, N.Y.C., 1983-85, WABC Talk Radio, N.Y.C., 1985-87; performer CBS TV, 1990-93. Founder, artistic dir. Infinity Dance Theatre, 1995. Prin. works include Agnes of God, 1992-95, Edinburgh Festival, Fan's False Face Soc., 1990, The Waiting, 1990, Sand Dragons, 1990, As the World Turns, 1990-92, Awakenings, 1990, Eyes of a Stranger, 1979, Loving, 1995, Monograms, 1996-97, numerous TV appearances, 1978-86; dancer Cleve. Ballet, Dancing Wheels. Bd. dirs. Hosp. Audiences, Inc., N.Y.C., 1990—; dir. svcs. people with disabilities Actors' Work Program, N.Y.C., 1991—; mentor networking project YWCA, N.Y.C., 1991-95; mem. White House Conf. on Libr. and Info. Svcs., Washington, 1991; N.Y. State Libr. regent advisor; del. Dem. Nat. Conv., 1992. Named Belle Zeller scholar, CUNY, 1993, Woman of Excellence, 1994. Mem. SAG, AFTRA (nat. bd. dirs.), Nat. Alliance Broadcast Engrs. and Technicians, Actor's Equity Assn. (councillor Eastern Regional adv. bd. 1990—, chair performers with disabilities com. 1990—). Roman Catholic. Office: Actors' Equity Assn 165 W 46th St Fl 15 New York NY 10036-2500

LUNNEY, DANIEL THOMAS, chaplain; b. Green Bay, Wis., Apr. 18, 1967; s. James Kitrick and Maureen Margaret (Kadletz) L. BA in Global Peace & Social Justice, St. Norbert Coll., 1990, M Theol. Studies, 1996; cert. in healthcare ethics, Rush U., 2002. Pastoral min. St. Bernadette Parish, Appleton, Wis., 1990-94; chaplain resident Rush-Presbyn.-St. Luke's Med. Ctr., Chgo., 1994-95; coord. vol. svcs. AIDS Pastoral Care Network, 1995-98; chaplain cons. Fourier Pastoral Svcs., 1996—; chaplain, bereavement coord. Hospice of West Suburban Hosp., Oak Park, 1999-2000; coord. mission and spiritual care dept. Advocate Ravenswood Med. Ctr., Chgo., 2000—02; chaplain mission and spiritual care dept. Advocate Ill. Masonic Med. Ctr., 2002—. Spkr. in field; workshop presenter Nat. Cath. AIDS Network Min. Conf., 1996, 97, 98; mem. nat. conf. planning staff Nat. Cath. AIDS Network, 1998—; respondent to plenary Nat. Assn. Cath. Chaplains Symposium, 2002. Editor: Communities of Care, 1996, Nat. Cath. AIDS Network Website, 2001—. Chmn. AIDS Vol. Edn. Consortium, Chgo., 1996-98. Conf. scholar U.S. Conf. on AIDS, 1996, 98; recipient Young Alumni award St. Norbert Coll., 1999, Ann. Value Leader for Equality award Advocate Ravenswood Med. Ctr., 2000. Mem. Nat. Assn. Cath. Chaplains (cert.). Democrat. Home: 918 W Winona St Unit 505 Chicago IL 60640-6347 Office: Advocate Ill Masonic Med Ctr Mission & Spiritual Care 836 W Wellington Chicago IL 60657 E-mail: dan41867@attbi.com., daniel.lunney@advocatehealth.com.

LUNSFORD, L. DADE, neurosurgeon; b. Roanoke, Va., July 25, 1948; s. Lita Lunsford; m. Julianne M. Lunsford; children: Stephanie, Andrew. BS with high hons., U. Va., 1970; MD, Columbia U., 1974. Intern U. Va., Charlottesville, 1974-75; resident U. Pitts., 1975-80; fellow Karolinska Inst., Stockholm, 1980-81; instr. dept. neurol. surgery U. Pitts., 1979-80, asst. prof., 1980-85, assoc. prof., 1985-90, prof., 1990—, asst. prof. dept. radiology, 1982-85, assoc. prof., 1985-90, prof. dept. radiology and dept. radiation oncology, 1990—, Lars Leksell prof. neurol. surgery, 1998—, chmn. dept. neurol. surgery, 1997—. Chmn. sci. bd. Accuray Oncology, 1999; mem. Elekta Sci. Coun., 2000. Editor: Youmans, 2001—, Yourdoctor.com, 2001—; editor: Modern Stereotatic Neurosurgery, 1988, Stereotactic Radiosurgery: Neurosurgery Clinics of North America, 1992, Stereotactic Radiosurgery Update, 1992, Stereotactic Radiosurgery, 1993, Gamma Knife Brain Surgery, 1998. Recipient Internat. Stereotactic Radiosurgery Jacob Fabrikant award, 1997, U. Pitts. Med. Sch. McElroy award, 1997, Faculty Tchg. award Dept. Neurosurgery, 1997, 99, 2000; named Lars Leksell Provost Lecture; William P. Van Wagenen fellow, 1980. Mem. Pitts. Neurosci. Soc. (v.p. 1987-88, pres. 1989-90), Am. Soc. for Stereotactic and Functional Neurosurgery (bd. dirs. 1986—, v.p. 1993, pres. 1995-97, mem. joint sect. for stereotactic and functional neurosurgery 1986—, chmn. 1995-97), Internat. Assn. for Study of Pain, Am. Pain Soc., Internat. Stereotactic Radiosurgery Soc. (pres. 1991-94, bd. dirs. 1995), Pitts. Neurosci. Soc., Phi Sigma, Phi Beta Kappa. Avocations: tennis, golf, skiing, swimming, piano. Office: Univ of Pittsburgh Med Ctr Dept Neurol Surgery 200 Lothrop St #B-400 Pittsburgh PA 15213 E-mail: pschmitt@neuronet.pitt.edu.

LUNSFORD, THOMAS RAY, orthotist, mechanical engineer; b. Clayton, N.Mex., Oct. 31, 1940; s. Roy McCall and Ola Oran (Jackson) L.; m. Brenda Rae Quortrup, Feb. 12, 1966. BSEE, U. Tex., El Paso, 1962; MS in Nuclear Engring., UCLA, 1969. Bd. cert. orthotics Am. Bd. for Cert. in Orthotics and Prosthetics. Sr. engr. N.Am. Aviation, Inc., L.A., 1963-69; engring. mgr. Nat. Cash Register, Hawthorne, Calif., 1969-76; chief orthotist Rancho Los Amigos Med. Ctr., L.A., 1976-93, The Inst. for Rehab. and Rsch., Houston, 1993-96; pres. Lone Star Orthotics, Inc., 1996—. Clin. dir. orthotics and prosthetics Calif. State U. Dominguez Hill, Carson, Calif., 1978-93; dir. orthotic rsch. Rehab. Engring. Ctr., Downey, Calif., 1990-93; asst. prof. Baylor Coll. Medicine, Houston, 1993—; pres. Kit Sys., Houston, 1980—, Am. Acad. Orthotists and Prosthetists, Alexandria, Va., 1993; commr., exec. bd. Commn. on Accreditation of Allied Health Profs., Chgo., 1994—; chmn. long range orthotics cert. exam. Am. Bd. for Cert. Orthotics and Prosthetics, Alexandria, 1995—. Author: Strength & Materials in Orthotics and Prosthetics, 1996; rsch. editor Jour. Prosthetics and Orthotics, 1987—. Active Toastmasters Internat., Hawthorne, Calif., 1974-85. Recipient Article of the Yr. awards Am. Acad. Orthotics and Prosthetics, 1987, 93, 94, 95; grantee Nat. Inst. for Disability and Rehab. Rsch., Bethesda, Md., 1990-93, NASA, Houston, 1995-98. Home: 2218 Sendera Ranch Dr Magnolia TX 77354-6800 Office: Lone Star Orthotics Inc 8399 Almeda Rd Ste L Houston TX 77054-7105

LUNSFORD, W. BRUCE, health facility administrator, health and medical products executive; b. Nov. 11, 1947; m. Becky Lunsford, Aug. 29, 1970; children: Amy, Cindy, Brandy. BA, U. Ky., 1969; JD, Salmon P. Chase Coll. Law, 1974. CPA Ky., Ohio; bar: Ky. 1974, Ohio 1974. With Alexander Grant & Co., CPA, Cin., 1969—74, Keating, Muething and Klekamp Attys., Cin., 1974—79; dep. sec. Ky. Devel. Cabinet and Gov.'s Legis. Liaison, 1980—81; sec. Ky. Commerce Cabinet, 1981—83; of counsel, atty. Greenebaum Doll & McDonald, Louisville, 1984—91; chmn., pres., CEO Vencor Inc., 1985—99; pres., CEO Ventas Inc., 1998, chmn., 1998—. Bd. trustees U. Ky., 1983—87, Centre Coll., 1992—97, Shakertown at Pleasant Hill, Ky., Inc., 1992—; bd. trustees., sec. Bellarmine Coll., 1991—97; bd. govs. Salmon P. Chase Coll. Law, 1983—87; bd. dirs. Greater Louisville Fund for the Arts, 1990—97, Ky. Ctr. for the Arts Endowment Fund, Inc., 1992—97, Ky. Econs. Devel. Corp., 1989—, chmn., 1996—; bd. dirs., exec. com. Nat. City Bank, Ky., 1991—; bd. dirs. Res-Care, Inc., 1992—, Churchill Downs, Inc., 1995—, Nat. City Corp., 1995—; Fedn. Am. Health Sys., 1996—; bd. dirs. exec. com. Greater Louisville Econ. Devel. Partnership, 1992—. Named Entrepreneur of the Yr., Ky. and So. Ind., 1988, U. Ky. Bus. Leader of Yr., 1994; named to Kentuckiana Bus. Hall of Fame, 1993. Mem.: AICPA (Outstanding CPA in bus. and Ind. 1996), Omicron Delta Kappa. Office: Ventas Inc 4360 Brownsboro Rd Ste 115 Louisville KY 40207-1642*

LUNT, ALAN NICHOLAS, psychiatric rehabilitation counselor; b. Pitts., Dec. 11, 1955; s. Harry Edward and Carmela Lunt. BA, Rutgers U., 1979; AS, U. Medicine and Dentistry N.J., 1995, MS, 2001. Peer advocate mental Health Assn. of Morris Co., Madison, 1995—96, Bridgeway, Elizabeth, N.J., 1995—. Contbr. articles to profl. jours. Mem. Internat. Assn. Psychosocial Rehab. Svc., Nat. Alliance for Mentally Ill, Mental Health Assn. of Morris county, N.J. Psychiat. Rehab. Assn. (bd. dirs. 1997—). Avocation: piano. Home: 32 Koster Blvd Apt 4A Edison NJ 08837 Office: Bridgeway Pact 615 North Broad St Elizabeth NJ 07208

LUNT, HARRY EDWARD, metallurgist, consultant; b. N.Y.C., Apr. 30, 1924; m. Carmela (Tamburri) Lunt, June 19, 1950; children: Teresa, Alan, Diana, Linda, Steven. AB, Syracuse U., 1948, postgrad., 1948-50; MS, Iowa State U., 1953. Registered profl. engr., Del., Calif. Rsch. asst. Ames (Iowa) Lab., U.S. AEC, 1950-53; devel. metallurgist U.S. Steel Corp. Applied Rsch. Labs., Monroeville and Homestead, Pa., 1953-63; sr. engr. Westinghouse Rsch. Labs., Churchill, 1963-66; corp. metallurgist Worthington Corp., Harrison, N.J., 1967-74; corp. cons. engr. Burns & Roe Enterprises, Inc., Oradell, 1974-94; cons. metallurgist Mendham, 1995—. Mem. tech. adv. com. Materials Properties Coun., N.Y.C., 1980—. Author tech. papers and conf. proceedings in field. Fellow ASTM (chmn. com. on steel, stainless steel and related alloys 1986-92, bd. dirs. 1990-92, Merit award 1981), Standards Engring. Soc. (Robert J. Painter Meml. award 1989), Am. Soc. Metals (life; chmn. N.J. chpt. 1976-77); mem. Am. Welding Soc., Nat. Assn. Corrosion Engrs. (accredited corrosion specialist), Phi Beta Kappa. Home and Office: 13 Brockden Dr Mendham NJ 07945-3010

LUNT, HORACE GRAY, linguist, educator; b. Colorado Springs, Colo., Sept. 12, 1918; s. Horace Fletcher and Irene (Jewett) L.; m. Sally Herman, June 2, 1963; children: Elizabeth, Catherine. AB, Harvard U., 1941; MA, U. Calif., Berkeley, 1942; postgrad., Charles U., Prague, Czechoslovakia, 1946-47; PhD (Rockefeller fellow), Columbia U., 1950. Lectr. in Serbo-Croatian Columbia U., 1948-49; asst. prof. Slavic langs. and lit. Harvard U., 1949-54, asso. prof., 1954-60, prof., 1960—, Samuel H. Cross prof. Slavic langs. and lits., 1965-89, Samuel H. Cross prof. Slavic langs. and lits., emeritus, 1989—, chmn. dept. Slavic langs. and lits., 1959-73, 75-76, 82-83; chmn. Slavic and East European Lang. and Area Ctr., 1983-89; mem. exec. com. Russian Rsch. Ctr., 1970-91, fellow, 1991—; mem. exec. com. Harvard Ukrainian Research Inst., 1974-91, fellow, 1991—. Author: Grammar of the Macedonian Literary Language, 1952, Old Church Slavonic Grammar, 1955, 7th rev. edit., 2001, Fundamentals of Russian, 1958, 2d rev. ed., 1968, Progressive Palatalization of Common Slavic, 1981, (with M. Taube) The Slavonic Book of Esther: Text, Lexicon, Linguistic Analysis, Problems of Translation, 1998; editor: Harvard Slavic Studies, 1953-70. Served with U.S. Army, 1942-45. Guggenheim fellow, 1960-61 Mem. Macedonian Acad. Arts and Scis. (corr.). Home: Apt 11C 1105 Massachusetts Ave Cambridge MA 02138-5223 Office: Harvard U Barker Ctr Cambridge MA 02138

LUNT, LORA G. international education educator, language educator; b. Princeton, NJ, Mar. 21, 1940; m. C. Richard K. Lunt; children: Emily Garland, Mary. PhD in French, McGill University, Montreal, Canada, 2001; PhD in Arabic, Indiana University, Bloomington, IN, 1978; MAT. in French, The Johns Hopkins University, Baltimore, MD, 1963; BA in French Honors, Swarthmore College, Swarthmore, PA, 1962. French instructor University of Maine, Orono, ME, 1963—64; ESL teacher Peace Corps, Sfax, Tunisia, 1964—66; French instructor Canton Agricultural and Technical College, Canton, NY, 1963—63; French teacher Potsdam High School, Potsdam, 1963—80; French instructor, adjunct St. Lawrence University, Canton, 1981—81; Associate Dean of Arts and Sciences SUNY Potsdam, Potsdam, 1981—86, Interim Chair of Modern Languages, 1987—88, French instructor, 1989—90, Director of International Education, 1990—. Editor: (book) The Potsdam Reader , 1982 (SUNY Potsdam President's Award Excellence Acad. Svc. , 2000); contbr. articles newsletter N.E. Conf. Tchg. Fgn. Langs., articles including Institut des Belles Lettres Arabes; dir.: (grant project US Dept. Edn.) Potsdam College Foreign Language Project, 1985, Potsdam College Collaborative Project, 1989, (grant project US Dept. State) Tunisia-SUNY Potsdam Bus. Edn. Partnership , 2002—. Host Mother AFS, Potsdam, NY, 1977—78, 1983—84, 1987—88; Clerk St. Lawrence Valley Friends Meeting, 2000—01; Organizer of Bus Stop AFS, 1987; Member World in Potsdam Diversity Festival, 1998—2002. Recipient Dictée Ameriques, Quebec, Can., 2002. Mem.: Northeast Modern Language Association, Conseil International des Etudes Francophones, NAFSA Organization of International Educators. Office: SUNY Potsdam 44 Pierrepont Ave. Potsdam NY Office Fax: 315-267-2656.

LUNTE, CRAIG EDWARD, science educator, department chairman; b. St. Louis, Aug. 6, 1957; s. Edward August Lunte, Lois Margaret Lunte; m. Susan Marie Hommel; children: Alyson, Kathryn. BS, U. Mo., Rolla, 1979; PhD, Purdue U., 1984. Asst. prof. U. Kans., Lawrence, 1987—93, assoc. prof., 1993—97, prof., 1997—. Editor: Jour. Pharm. and Biomed. Analysis, 1999. Fellow: Am. Assn. Pharm. Scientists; mem.: AAAS, Soc. Electroanalytical Chemistry, Am. Chem. Soc., Sigma Xi. Office: Department of Chemistry Univ Kans Lawrence KS 66045 Office Fax: 785-864-5396. Business E-Mail: clunte@ku.edu.

LUNTZ, MAURICE HAROLD, ophthalmologist; b. Capetown, South Africa, July 27, 1930; came to U.S., 1978; s. Montague Bernard and Sarah Miriam (Friedman) L.; m. Angela June Myerson, June 21, 1956; children: Melvyn Howard, Caryn Susan, David Sean. B Medicine B Surgery, Capetown U., 1952; MD, U. Witwatersrand, Johannesburg, South Africa, 1974. Diplomate Am. Bd. Ophthalmology. Lectr. ophthalmology Oxford (Eng.) U., 1960-62; prof., chmn. ophthalmology U. Witwatersrand, 1964-78; dir. ophthalmology Beth Israel Med. Ctr., N.Y.C., 1978-88; chief glaucoma svc. Manhattan Eye, Ear & Throat Hosp., 1992—, pres., bd. surgeon dirs., 1993-95; prof. Mt. Sinai Sch. Medicine, N.Y.C., 1978—; clin. prof. NYU, 2000—. Cons. Merck, Sharp & Dohme, N.J., 1980-82; chmn. Internat. Com. Ophthalmic Edn., 1974-90; clin. prof. NYU, 2000—. Author: Uveitis, 1983, Glaucoma Surgery, 1984, 2d edit., 1995, Innovations in Diagnosis and Management of the Glaucomas, 2002; mem. editl. bd. Highlights Ophthalmology, Panama, 1970—; contbr. articles to profl. jours.; prodr. film Glaucoma Surveys, 1970. Fellow Royal Coll. Surgeons (Edinburgh), Coll. Surgeons South Africa (hon.); mem. Academia Ophthalmologica Internationalis. Office: 115 E 61st New York NY 10021 E-mail: Juneboy193@aol.com.

LUO, HONG YUAN, biomedical scientist, educator; b. Shengyang, Liaoning, China, June 29, 1951; d. Xin Luo and Rong K. Ren; children: Patrick Yj, Michael Yl. MD, Zhongshan Med. Sch., Guangzhou, China, 1976; M Medicine, Chinese Acad. Med. Scis., Beijing, 1982; PhD, McMaster U., 1993. Tchg. asst. Zhongshan Med. U., 1976-78; rsch. assoc. Beijing Nutrition, 1982-85; vis. scholar McMaster U., Hamilton, Ont., Can., 1985-87; postdoctoral fellow U. Tex. Med. Br., Galveston, 1993-95, instr. biomed. scis., 1995-99; rsch. specialist U. Pa., Phila., 2000—. Mem. Am. Soc. Hematology. Achievements include development of 2 monoclonal antibodies for human embryonic hemoglobin zeta chain, which have been used for identifying Alpha-thalassemia (Southeast Asian deletion) carriers in population; this deletion causes hydrops fetalis syndrome that leads to fetal death; these antibodies have also been used to identify the fetal cells in maternal blood for non-invasive prenatal diagnosis. Avocations: swimming, movies, music, photography. Home: 8480 Limekiln Pike # 1212 Wyncote PA 19095-2801

LUO, NIANZHU, mechanical engineer; b. Chengdu, China, Aug. 1, 1951; s. Qianhe and Jiqin (Feng) L.; m. Shufang Ye, Jan. 1, 1979; two children. BS, Southwest Jiaotong U., 1976; MS, U. Wis., 1986, PhD, 1989. Lectr. Southwest Jiaotong U., Sichuan, China, 1977-82; rsch. fellow U. Wis., Madison, 1983-85; from sr. engr. to tech. specialist Case Corp., Chgo., 1990-95; fluid power specialist Sauer-Sundstrand, Newtown, Pa., 1995-99; engring. mgr. Sauer-Danfoss Inc., 2000—. Mem. Soc. Automotive Engrs., Assn. Chinese Scientists & Engrs. Home: 261 Sassafras Dr Easley SC 29642-8264

LUO, QINGZHENG, physics researcher; b. Chongqing, Sichuan, People's Republic of China, Mar. 12, 1967; came to U.S., 1995; s. Xianyin and Yuangui (Liu) L.; m. Qi Wang, June 28, 1993; children: Landi, Kevin. BS, Sichun U., Chengdu, 1989; MS in Physics, Academia Sinica, Lanzhou, 1992; PhD, U. Iowa, 2000. Rsch. asst. Inst. Modern Physics Academia Sinica, 1989-92, engr., rsch. assoc., 1992-95; rsch. asst. U. Iowa, Iowa City, 1995-00; sr. mem. tech. staff Cadence Design Sys., San Jose, 2000—. Contbr. articles to profl. jours. including Physics of Plasmas, Nuclear Physics A, Phys. Rev C. Mem. Am. Phys. Soc. Home: 7060 Via Pacifica San Jose CA 95139 Office: Bldg # 11 2655 Seely Ave San Jose CA 95134

LUO, SHAWN HAISHENG, retail company executive; b. Shantou, Guangdong, China, Apr. 4, 1961; came to U.S., 1990; s. Xu Luo and Shaofen Wu; m. Crystal Xiaoping Zheng, May 8, 1990. BS, Zhongshan U., Guangzhou, China, 1983; MS, Capital Normal U., Beijing, 1987; PhD, Claremont Grad. U., 1995. Mem. cons. team Info. Inst., U. So. Calif., Santa Monica, 1990-91, Chevron Oil Field Rsch. Co., La Habra, Calif., 1991-92; statis. analyst Pharmavite Corp., Mission Hills, 1996-98, mgr. prodn. planning San Fernando, 1998-2000; dir. supply chain cons. Quevera (formerly Millennia Vision Corp.), San Jose, 2000-01; dir. inventory productivity Circuit City Stores, Inc., Richmond, Va., 2001—. Contbr. articles to sci. jours., including Jour. Math. and Computer Modeling, Math. Engring. in Industry, Jour. Math. Physics. Dissertation grantee Claremont Grad. U., 1993. Mem. Am. Prodn. and Inventory Control Soc. Home: 273 Hartman Ct San Dimas CA 91773 Office: Circuit City Stores Inc 9954 Mayland Dr Richmond VA 23233 E-mail: shawn_luo@circuitcity.com.

LUO, WEI, electronics engineer; b. Wuhan, Hubei, China, 1973; s. Qifang Jin and Yongmei Luo; m. Wen Tian, July 4, 2001. BS, Tsinghua U., Beijing, China, 1995; MS, U. Md., 1997, PhD, 1999. Engr. and scientist Lucent Techs., Bell Labs., Holmdel, NJ, 1999—. Reviewer: ; contbr. articles to profl. jours. Mem.: IEEE. Achievements include patents in field. Office: Lucent Techs/Bell Labs 101 Crawfords Corner Rd Holmdel NJ 07733

LUO, XIAOCHUAN, power system engineer; b. Liang Ping, Si Chuan province, China, Nov. 9, 1971; s. Yaoqiang Luo and Zhenqu Lam; m. Jin Hua Thian. Ph.D, Texas A&M University, College Station, 2000. Engr. East China Elec. Power Design Inst., Shang Hai, China, 1995—97; rsch. asst. Tex. A&M U., College Station, 1997—2000; engr. ISO New England Inc., Holyoke, Mass., 2000—. Reviewer and panel chair Fifth Multi-Conf. on Systemics, Cybernetics and Informatics., 2001; mem. Inter-Area Dynamic Analysis Working Group of Northeast Power Coord. Coun., 2000—; mem. Transmission Task Force and Stability Task Force of New Eng. Power Pool., 2000—. Contbr. articles to profl. jours. papers to confs. including: author: (Paper presentation at IEEE PES 1999) Summer Meeting, 1999 (Honorable Mention, 1999), 34th Ann. Hawaii Internat.Conf. on System Sci. Mem.: IEEE, IEEE Power Engring. Soc., IEEE-PES Power System Dynamic Modeling Subcom., IEEE-PES Risk, Reliability and Probability Application Subcom. Avocations: music, sports, travel.

LUOMA, GARY A. accounting educator; b. Pequaming, Mich., June 14, 1936; s. Otto Samuel and Ruth Eleanor (Braeger) L.; m. Evelyn Marie Gervais, July 7, 1956; children: Gary Jr., Valerie, Steven, Patricia. BA, Northern Mich. U., 1958; MA, Western Mich. U., 1959; D of Bus. Adminstrn., Washington U. St. Louis, 1966. CPA, CMA, CFM. Lectr., instr., asst. to dean Washington U., St. Louis, 1959-64; asst. prof., assoc. prof., prof., dir. BBA program Emory U., Atlanta, 1964-77; dir. sch. acctg., prof. Ga. State U., 1977-86, U. S.C., Columbia, 1986—. Cons. in field. Author: Financial Aspects of Contract Negotiation and Administration, 1972, Fund Accounting for Colleges and Universities, 1973, Accounting and Record Keeping for Small Business, 1982, Cases on Business Ethics, 1988; contbr. articles to profl. jours. With USNR, 1954-58. Office: U SC Sch Bus Columbia SC 29208-0001

LUONG, KHANH VINH QUOC, nephrologist, researcher; b. Cantho, Vietnam, Oct. 20, 1952; s. Hien Vinh Luong and Lieu Thi Huynh; m. Lan Thi Hoang Nguyen, Oct. 15, 1981. MD, U. Kans., 1981. Diplomate Am. Bd. Internal Medicine, Am. Bd. Nephrology, Nat. Bd. Med. Examiners. Intern in internal medicine St. Elizabeth Med. Ctr., Northeastern Ohio U., Youngstown, 1981; resident internal medicine Tulane U. Hosp. Program, New Orleans, 1982-83, City of Faith Med. and Rsch. Ctr., Oral Roberts U., Tulsa, Okla., 1986-87; fellow in nephrology Cedars-Sinai Med. Ctr., UCLA Program in Nephrology, L.A., 1987-90; pvt. practice Westminster, Calif., 1990—. Vis. asst. prof. medicine UCLA Sch. Medicine, 1989-90; presenter at nat. and internat. meetings; contbr. articles to profl. jours. Contbr. articles to profl. jours. Nat. Kidney Found. So. Calif. fellow, 1989-90. Fellow ACP, Am. Coll. Endocrinology, Am. Coll. Allergy, Asthma and Immunology, Am. Coll. Nutrition; mem. Am. Soc. Nephrology, Internat. Soc. Nephrology, Am. Assn. Clin. Endocrinologists, Endocrine Soc., Am. Soc. Bone and Mineral Rsch., Assn. Vietnamese Physicians of the Free World, Vietnamese Med. Assn. in U.S., Vietnamese Am. Med. Rsch. Found. (pres.). Office: 9188 Bolsa Ave Westminster CA 92683-5556

LUONGO, C. PAUL, public relations executive; b. Winchester, Mass., Dec. 31, 1930; s. Carmine and Carmela (Gilberti) L. Grad., Cambridge Sch. Radio-TV, 1955; diploma, Bentley Coll., 1951; BSBA, Suffolk U., 1955; MBA, Babson Coll., 1956; AAS (hon.), Grahm Jr. Coll., 1970. Jr. exec. Raytheon Co., Lexington, Mass., 1956-59; account exec. Young & Rubicam, Inc., 1959-62; v.p. Copley Advt. Agy., Boston, 1962-64; pres. C. Paul Luongo Co., 1964—. Guest appearances include: (TV programs) Today Show, NBC-TV, 1984-89, Tomorrow Show, NBC-TV; TV-radio programs, Can.; author: America's Best!, 1980; contbr. syndicated newspaper-mag. features to Pub. Rels. Today; contbg. editor Travel Smart, N.Y., mo. newsletter. Founder Anthony Spinazzola Meml. Scholarship Found., Boston U., 1986-88; vol. U.S.S. Constn. Mus., Boston, Sta. WGBH-TV, Boston, TV Auctions, 1991-2000; mem. WORLDBOSTON, Boston, Mus. Fine Arts, Black Ships Festival, Inc., Newport, R.I.; pub. rels. dir. centennial ba.. Belcourt Castle, Newport, 1994. With AUS, 1952-54. Mem. Boston Stockbrokers Club, Boston Advt. Club, Newcomen Soc. N.Am., Am. Inst. Wine and Food, Japan-Am. Soc. R.I., Neighborhood Assn. of Back Bay, Inc., Back Bay Assn., Suffolk U. Gen. Alumni Assn. (bd. dirs. 1994-98), James Beard Found., Friends of the Boston Pops. Office: 441 Stuart St Boston MA 02116-5019 *I believe in the work ethic, integrity and the maximum utilization of time for work and recreational activities. I loathe prejudice in any form, dishonesty and indolent people.*

LUONGO, JANET DUFFY, art educator, writer, artist, speaker, trainer; b. N.Y.C., Mar. 2, 1949; d. Edmund John Duffy and Frances Barbara (Beyer) Savin; m. James Paul Luongo, 1976. BA, Adelphi U., 1972; MS, CUNY, 1977. Cert. art tchr., Conn. Tchr. art Acad. St. Joseph's, Brentwood, NY, 1975-78; tchr. art, chmn. Internat. Sch. Geneva, Chataigneraie, Switzerland, 1981-86; tchr. art Wilton (Conn.) Pub. Schs., 1988-92, tchr. adult edn., 1974—; art history and comms. tchr. Sacred Heart U., Fairfield, Conn., 1992—; curator art edn. Discovery Mus., Bridgeport, 1993—, v.p. edn., 1996—; prin. Open Minds Open Doors, LLC, Norwalk, 1991—; master tchg. artist Conn. Commn. Arts, 2001—. Founder, pres. Conn. chpt. Women's Caucus for Art, 1990-94, nat. bd. mem., 1991-94, 98-2000; judge art shows, Fairfield County, Conn. One-woman shows include Galerie Motte, Geneva, 1986; exhibited in group shows at HarperCollins Pubs., 1996, galleries in Soho and Paris, Aldrich Mus. Contempoary Art, Ridgefield, Conn.; pub. works in The World, Sept., 1989, Fairfield County Woman, Feb. 1995; performances at Ticknor Gallery/Harvard U., 1996, Writers' Voice, Fairfield, Conn., 1996; curator art exhibit Oddfellows Playhouse, Middletown, Conn., 1997; author: How I Got to Paris Despite Stupid Bureaucrats. Mem. Unitarian Universalist Svc. Com., Boston, 1988—. Recipient Human Rels. award Dale Carnegie Sch., Conn., 1987, Disting. Adv. for Arts award Conn. Commn. on Arts, 1999, Publs. award New Eng. Mus. Assn., 1999, Leadership award Urban Artists Initiative, 1999, Outstanding Mus. Educator of Conn. Conn. Art Educators Assn., 1999; Gen. Electric fellow Nat. Gallery of Art, 1997. Mem. Nat. Art Educators Assn., Conn. Alliance for Art Edn., Nat. Spkrs. Assn.(co-pres. 2002-03), Womens Caucus for Art (regional v.p. 1998—, advb. bd.), Mensa, Nat. Spkrs. Assn. N.Y. Tri-Statechpt. (co-pres. elect 2002-). Avocations: painting, public speaking, photography, creative writing. Home and Office: 49 Creeping Hemlock Dr Norwalk CT 06851-1017

LUPASH, LAWRENCE OVIDIU, computer analyst, researcher; b. Bucharest, Romania, May 29, 1942; came to U.S., 1980; s. Ovidiu Dumitru and Stefania Maria (Lebu) L. BS, Polytechnic Inst. of Bucharest, 1964; MS, Polytechnic Inst. Bucharest, Romania, 1965, PhD, 1972. Sr. engr., researcher Inst. Automation, Bucharest, 1971-72; sr. analyst, researcher, computing ctr. U. Bucharest, 1972-79; sr. analyst Intermetrics, Inc., Huntington Beach, Calif., 1980-94, LL Consulting, Fullerton, 1994—, Trimble Navigation Ltd., 1997—. Asst. prof. Polytechnic Inst. Bucharest, 1966-67, 67-68, 71-72; lectr. U. Bucharest, 1973-78; vis. prof. U. Tirana, Albania, 1973. Co-author: Numerical Methods in Systems Theory, 1974; contbr. numerous articles to profile pubs. Recipient Rep. award Polytechnic Inst. Bucharest, 1962; grantee Case Western Reserve U., 1968, Romanian Acad. Scis., 1968. Mem. IEEE, Soc. Indsl. and Applied Math., Assn. Computing Machinery, Am. Philatelic Soc., Orange County Philatelic Soc. Mem. Greek Orthodox Ch. Office: LL Cons 2625 Monterey Pl Fullerton CA 92833-2084

LUPERT, LESLIE ALLAN, lawyer; b. Syracuse, N.Y., May 24, 1946; s. Reuben and Miriam (Kaufman) L.; m. Roberta Gail Fellner, May 19, 1968; children: Jocelyn, Rachel, Susannah. BA, U. Buffalo, 1967; JD, Columbia U., 1971. Bar: N.Y. 1971. Ptnr. Orans Elsen & Lupert, N.Y.C., 1971—. Contbr. articles to profl. jours. Mem. ABA, N.Y. State Bar Assn. (trial lawyers sect.), Assn. of Bar of City of N.Y. (com. fed. legislation 1977-80, profl. and jud. ethics com. 1983-86, com. on fed. cts. 1986-89, 95-96), Phi Beta Kappa. Office: Orans Elsen & Lupert 1 Rockefeller Plz New York NY 10020-2102 E-mail: llupert@oelaw.com.

LUPIA, DAVID THOMAS, corporate financial advisor, management consultant; b. Flandreau, S.D., Mar. 18, 1950; s. Archy L. and Carol L. (Cherney) L; children: Allison, Nathan. AB, Rutgers Coll., New Brunswick, N.J., 1972; MBA, U. Pa., 1974. Cert. mgmt. cons. Fin. analyst Exxon Corp., N.Y.C., 1974-76; sr. fin. analyst Esso Inter-Am., Inc., Coral Gables, Fla., 1976-78; treas. Esso Caribbean, 1978-80; fin. mgr. Esso Australia, Ltd., Sydney, 1980-83; sr. fin. advisor Exxon Co., U.S.A., Houston, 1983-85, Exxon Corp., N.Y.C., 1985-87; sr. v.p. Lehman Bros., 1987-92; prin. David T. Lupia, Inc., Corp. Fin. Adv. Svcs., 1992—. Mem. Phi Beta Kappa, Omicron Delta Epsilon, Beta Gamma Sigma. Home and Office: 190 High Ridge Rd Ridgefield CT 06877

LUPIANI, DONALD ANTHONY, psychologist; b. N.Y.C., June 7, 1946; s. Louis and Josephine (Boccia) L.; m. Linda Moyik, June 20, 1970; 1 child, Jennifer. BA, Iona Coll., 1968; MA, Columbia U., 1971, PhD, 1973; post-doctoral, Behavior Therapy Inst., White Plains, N.Y., 1976. Lic. psychologist, N.Y.; diplomat Am. Bd. Profl. Psychology, Am. Bd. Psychotherapy, Am. Acad. Behavioral Medicine, Intenat. Acad. Behavioral Medicine, Internat. Acad. Behavioral Medicine. Clin. assoc. Columbia U., N.Y.C., 1974-85, Fordham U., Bronx, N.Y., 1979-81; dir. psychology and spl. edn. svcs. Riverdale Country Sch., 1973-87; chief psychologist Franciscan Order of Priests, N.Y.C., 1983—; pvt. practice Yonkers, N.Y., 1975—. Dir. spl. svcs. Riverdale Country Sch., Bronx., 1973-87; bd. dirs. St. Ursula Learning Ctr., Mt. Vernon, N.Y. Contbr. articles to profl. jours. Bd. dirs., mem. The St. Ursula Learning Ctr. Fellow Am. Orthopsychiat. Assn., Am. Coll. Psychology, Am. Acad. Sch. Psychology; mem. APA, N.Y. State Psychol. Assn., Westchester County Psychol. Assn. (chmn. ethics com. 1980-87). Roman Catholic. Avocations: woodworking, painting, drawing. Home and Office: 227 Mile Square Rd Yonkers NY 10701-5369

LUPIEN, R. M. military officer; b. Ste-Seraphine, Que., Can. Naval fire controlman Can. Forces, Montreal, 1970—71, HMCS Gatineau, 1971, HMC St. Croix, HMC Terra Nova, HMC Saskatchewan, HMC Mackenzie, HMC Kootenay; instr., then sr. instr. Can. Forces Fleet Sch. Esquimalt, 1983—88; with 201 tech. svc. detachment Can. Forces, Montreal, 1988—90; sr. combat systems engring. chief petty officer Fleet Sch. Esquimalt, 1990—94; coxswain HMCS Kootenay, 1994; sr. chief petty officer Can. Forces Fleet Sch. Esquimalt, 1994—97; chief warrant officer Can. Forces Leadership and Recruit Sch., St.-Jean-sur-Richelieu, 1997—99, Can. Forces, 2001—. Office: Dept of National Def 101 Colonel By Dr Ottawa ON Canada K1A 0K2*

LUPIN, FREDA MERLIN, civic leader; b. New Orleans, Aug. 19, 1932; d. Jacob and Molly (Friedman) Merlin; m. E. Ralph Lupin, Mar. 18, 1951; children: Jay Stephen, Michael. Grad. high sch., New Orleans. Chmn. numerous coms. Children's Hosp., New Orleans, 1973-82, mem. hon. bd. 1976, 84—; co.-chmn. numerous coms. Sta. WYES-TV, 1973—, trustee, 1986—, WYES-PBS, 1987—, New Orleans Mus. Art, 1988—; chmn. tour of homes Ladies Leukemia League, 1974, co-chmn. LLL luncheon, 1978-79, v.p., 1979-80, pres., 1981, mem. adv. bd., 1982-84; chmn. big gifts luncheon Jewish Welfare Fund Campaign, 1976, mem. new gifts div., 1984; bd. dirs. women's com. New Orleans Symphony, 1977-80; chmn. gourmet gala March of Dimes, New Orleans, 1983, mem. gourmet gala com., 1987; mem. adv. bd. Ridgewood Prep. Sch., 1983—; mem. Sun King Nat. Com. La. State Mus., 1983-84; mem. mayor's host com. La. World Expn., 1984; bd. dirs. Speech and Hearing Ctr., 1984—; mem. Odyssey Ball com. New Orleans Mus. Art, 1985-87, mem. bd. advisors 1986—; v.p. New Orleans City Ballet, 1986—; mem. Vieux Carre Property Owners, Mayor's Bicentennial Constn. Commn., 1987, Gov.'s Commn. on Internat. Trade, Industry and Tourism, 1987; chmn. Overture to the Cultural Season, 1979. Named one of Women in Forefront, 1985; recipient Living Giving award Juvenile Diabetes Found., 1988, Vol. Activist award, 1988. Mem. Nat. Trust for Hist. Preservation, Aux. Tulane Med. Ctr. (charter mem.), New Orleans Mus. Art (women's aux.), Met. Mus. Art, The Smithsonian, La. Hist. Soc., La. Heart Assn. (wine and cheese festival 1970), Contemporary Arts Ctr., Preservation Resource Ctr. New Orleans, Council of Jewish Women (chmn. com. 1971), Am. Israel Cultural Found. (chmn. reservations 1974, bd. dirs. 1974-76), New Orleans C. of C. (women's aux.) Clubs: Patio Planters, Piroutte. Lodges: Sertoma (Service to Mankind award New Orleans chpt. 1984). Democrat. Avocations: symphony, ballet, political campaigns, reading.

LUPINI, CHRISTOPHER ALBERT, computer engineer, consultant; b. Dearborn, Mich., Apr. 22, 1965; s. Albert Dante and Cynthia Grace (Zyla) L.; m. Carrie Melissa-Olivia Toler, June 6, 1987; children: Anthony Christopher, Olivia Maria, Gabriel Albert, Nicholas James Wallace, Joseph Dominic. BS in Computer Engring., U. Mich., 1987; student, U. Colo., 1988; MSEE, Purdue U., 1992. Registered profl. engr., Ind.; cert. master technician Automotive Svc. Excellence. Assoc. software engr. Martin Marietta I&CS, Denver, 1987-88, elec. engr. Washington, 1988-89; sr. project engr. Delphi Delco Electronics Sys., Kokomo, Ind., 1989—. Gen. mgr. Lupini Engring. Co., Kokomo, 1992—; educator Univ. Consortium Continuing Edn., L.A., 1993—. Author: Vehicle Multiplex Communication; contbr. articles to Automotive Engring., IEE Automotive Electronics, SAE Transactions. Recipient quality performance awards GM, 1991, 92, 93, 95, 97. Mem. Soc. Automotive Engrs. and Svc. Technicians Soc. (Excellence in Oral Presentation 1992). Republican. Roman Catholic. Achievements include discovery of equations relating clock tolerance, propagation delay, and wire length for the CAN data bus; co-development of GM' J1850 class 2 serial data bus; rsch. in future transp. tech. Home: 390 S Hickory Ln Kokomo IN 46901-3995 Office: 1 Corporate Ctr Kokomo IN 46902-4000 E-mail: christopher.a.lupini@delphiauto.com.

LUPKIN, JONATHAN DANIEL, lawyer; b. N.Y.C., Feb. 6, 1968; s. Stanley Neil and Anne Rachel Lupkin; m. Michelle Ilene Gitlitz, June 10, 1990; children: Shira, Arielle, Leora, Ilana. BA, Columbia U., 1989, JD, 1992. Bar: N.Y. Law clk. hon. Edward R. Korman U.S. Dist. Judge Ea. Dist. N.Y., Bklyn., 1992-93; assoc. Kramer Levin Naftalis & Frankel, N.Y.C., 1993-96, Solomon, Zauderer, Ellenhorn, Frischer & Sharp, N.Y.C., 1996—. Staff mem. Columbia Law Rev., 1990-91, notes and comments editor, 1991-92. Harlan Fiske Stone scholar Columbia U. Sch. Law, N.Y.C., 1990, 92. Mem. Assn. of the Bar of the City of N.Y. (sec. com. on criminal advocacy 1995-97, com. on the judiciary 1998—), Soc. Sachems (sr.). Jewish. Avocations: reading, tropical fish. Office: Solomon Zauderer Ellenhorn Frischer & Sharp 45 Rockefeller Plz Ste 730 New York NY 10111-0064 Fax: 212-956-4068. E-mail: jlupkin@szefs.com.

LUPKIN, STANLEY NEIL, lawyer; b. Bklyn., Mar. 27, 1941; s. David B. and Sylvia (Strassman) L.; m. Anne Rachel Fischler, June 3, 1962; children: Jonathan Daniel, Deborah Eve. BA, Columbia Coll., 1962; LLB, NYU, 1966. Bar: N.Y. 1966, U.S. Dist. Ct. (so. and ea. dists.) N.Y. 1970, U.S. Ct. Appeals (2d cir.) 1970, U.S. Supreme Ct. 1971. Asst. dist. atty., sr. trial atty., chief indictment bur. N.Y. County Dist. Atty.'s Office, N.Y.C., 1966-71; asst. commr. City of N.Y., 1966-71; 1st dep. commr., commr. Dept. Investigation, N.Y.C., 1978-82; ptnr. Litman, Asche, Lupkin, Gioiella & Bassin, 1982-96; sr. v.p., office pres. Decision Strategies LLC, 1996—. Mem. faculty Nat. Coll. Dist. Attys., Houston, 1974—75, FBI Nat. Acad., Quantico, Va., 1980—82. Co-author book: Anatomy of A Municipal Franchise: N.Y.C. Bus Shelter Program, 1973-79, 4 vols., 1981. Trustee, counsel Solomon Schechter Sch. of Queens, Flushing, N.Y., 1974—; mem. secondary schs. com. admissions office Columbia Coll., N.Y.C., 1987-99. With USAR, 1963-69. Mem.: NACDL, Internat. Assn. Ind. Pvt. Sector Insps. Gen., Am. Corp. Counsel Assn., N.Y. Criminal Bar Assn., N.Y. State Assn. Criminal Def. Lawyers, Assn. Bar City N.Y. (chmn. com. on criminal justice ops. 1982—85, com. on criminal cts. 2001—), N.Y. State Bar Assn. (chmn. com. on def. 1985—2000, chmn. com. on prosecution 1977—85, exec. com. criminal justice sect. 1977—2000, Prosecutor of Yr. award 1981), Soc. Columbia Grads. (v.p. 1989—98, dir. 1989—). Avocations: classical music, Talmudic law. Office: 33 E 33d St New York NY 10016

LUPO, DAVID EMORY, computer scientist; b. Charleston, S.C., Dec. 17, 1953; s. Clinton Jones, Jr. and Vera Gwendolyn (Canaday) L.; m. Terry Bean, Apr. 7, 1979; children: Nathan Andrew, Timothy David. BS in Computer Scis./Math., Duke U., 1976, MDiv, 1983. Ordained deacon and elder S.C. Conf. The United Meth. Ch. Computer programmer Duke U. Med. Ctr., Durham, N.C., 1976-80; pastor The United Meth. Ch., S.C., 1983-94; computer programmer Automated Trading Desk, Mt. Pleasant, 1994-98, v.p. of rsch. and devel., 1999—. Part-time instr. in computer sci. Duke U., 1979-81. Pres. Beaufort Ministerial Assn., 1987-88. Mem. Assn. for Computing Machinery, Phi Beta Kappa. Democrat. Avocations: Boys Scouts of Am., walk to Emmaus. Office: Automated Trading Desk Inc 11 Ewall St Mount Pleasant SC 29464

LUPO, RAPHAEL V. lawyer; b. Washington, Oct. 15, 1941; BSEE, George Washington U., 1963, JD, 1968. Bar: Va. 1968, D.C. 1968, U.S. Dist. Ct. D.C. 1968, U.S. Dist. Ct. (ea. dist.) Va. 1969, U.S. Patent and Trademark Office, U.S. Claims Ct. 1969, U.S. Ct. Appeals ((D.C. cir.) 1968, U.S. Ct. Appeals (4th cir.) 1969, U.S. Ct. Appeals (fed. cir.) 1982, U.S. Ct. Customs and Patent Appeals 1969, U.S. Supreme Ct. 1969, U.S. Ct. Appeals 1982. Assoc. solicitor U.S. Patent and Trademark Office, 1969-77; dep. asst. gen. counsel for patents Dept. Energy, 1977-80; atty. Spencer & Kaye, Washington, 1980-82, Lupo Lipman & Lever, Washington, 1982-89, Willian Brinks Olds Hofer Gilson & Lione, P.C., Washington. Adj. prof. George Washington U. Law Sch., 1992; speaker 6th Annual Jud. Conf. U.S. Ct. Appeals (Fed. cir.), 1988, 10th Annual Jud. Conf. U.S. Ct. Appeals (Fed. cir.), 1992. Co-author: Patent Litigation and Strategy, 1999. Mem. ABA (amicus com., contbr. Patent Litigation Strategies Handbook section of Intellectual Property BNA 2000), D.C. Bar, Va. State Bar, Am. Intellectual Property Law Assn. Office: McDermott Will & Emery 600 13th St NW Fl 12-8 Washington DC 20005-3005

LUPO, ROBERT EDWARD SMITH, real estate developer and investor; b. New Orleans, May 27, 1953; s. Thomas Joseph and Alvena Florence (Smith) L.; m. Mary Lynn Puissegur, June 16, 1980; children: Robert Thomas Smith, Francesca Marfese Smith. BArch, Tulane U., 1977. Owner Robert Edward Smith Lupo Properties, New Orleans, 1976—; cons. various firms, 1977—; COO Commodore Thomas J. Lupo Enterprises, Williams-Lupo, Smith-Lupo, 1981—; pres. Hedwig, Inc., Zephyr, Inc., Noroaltom Devel. Co., Inc., 1981—. Cons. Mrs. Thomas J. Lupo properties. Grad. Met. Area Leadership Forum, New Orleans, 1980; bd. dirs., pres. New Orleans Mcpl. Yacht Harbor, 1989-93; life mem. Friends Audubon Zoo, 1983—; bd. dirs. New Orleans Met. Area Com., 1985-90; guardian mem. Boy Scouts Am., 1991—; mem. capital projects oversight com. Orleans Parish Sch. Bd., 1995—; mem. bd. commrs. Orleans Levee Dist., 1996—. Recipient Gov.'s award State of La., 1980, Tulane Assocs. award Tulane U., 1986; named One of 10 Best Dress Men, Men of Fashion, 1983, named to Hall of Fame, 1991. Mem. Aquarium Ams. (life), Assn. Naval Aviation (charter), Sigma Alpha Epsilon (founding). Clubs: Semreh. Republican. Roman Catholic. Office: 145 Robert E Lee Blvd New Orleans LA 70124-2552

LUPPENS, CARL HENRY, real estate broker and developer; b. Long Beach, Calif., Aug. 25, 1952; s. Charles Louis and Marguerite Mae (Schmidt) L.; m. Diane Hagnaur Muckerman, Sept. 15, 1979; children: Laura Marguerite, Carolyn Leigh. BA, Claremont McKenna Coll., 1974; JD, U. Colo., 1978. Bar: Mo. 1978, Co. 1981. Field engr. Alaskan Resource Sci. Corp., Fairbanks, 1974-75; jr. ptnr. Bryan, Cave, McPheeters & Roberts, St. Louis, 1978-80; atty. Manville Corp., Denver, 1980-81; sr. v.p. Vantage Properties, Inc., Aurora, Colo., 1981-84; v.p. Riva Cos., Denver, 1984-86; ptnr. Argus Real Estate Ptnrs., Inc., 1986-88; v.p. Cushman Realty, 1989—. Lectr. real estate Grad. Sch. Bus. Adminstrn. U. Denver. Developer Country Club Towers, 1987, Washington Ctr., 1988. Mem. 50 for Colo., Denver, 1988—, task force Downtown Denver Plan, 1986-87. Recipient Merit award Am. Soc. Landscape Architects, 1987. Mem. Urban Land Inst., Denver Bar Assn., Denver Athletic Club. Republican. Presbyterian. Avocations: skiing, mountaineering, scuba diving, bicycling, photography. Office: Cushman Realty Corp 370 17th St Ste 3600 Denver CO 80202-5686

LUPTON, JONATHAN JARMAN, urban planner, educator; b. Raleigh, N.C., Nov. 2, 1960; s. James Harold and Eliza Jarman Lupton; m. Cynthia Buckelew Lupton, June 3, 1995. BA in History, Kalamazoo Coll., 1982; MA in Geography, U. Chgo., 1987; MS in Cmty. and Regional Planning, U. Tex., 1990. Rsch. asst. U. Chgo., 1982-83; libr. clk. Austin (Tex.) Pub. Libr., 1983-90; planner Pueblo County, Colo., 1990-91; worksite coord. Literacy Coun. Arkansas County, Stuttgart, 1991-93; planner, statistician Metroplan, Little Rock, 1993-99; rsch. assoc. U. Ark., 1999; rsch. planner Metroplan, 2000—. Adj. instr. Ark. State U., Beebe, 1997—; forecaster Population and Employment Projection for Little Rock area, Metro 2025 Plan, 2000. Author: (newsletters) Metroplan Economic Rev. and Outlook, 1996-2000, Metroplan Demographic Rev. and Outlook, 1995-2000. Mem. Am. Inst. for Cert.

Planners (cert.), Am. Planning Assn. Democrat. Episcopalian. Avocations: amateur weather forecasting, hiking, religious studies, geography studies. Home: 3729 Loch Ln North Little Rock AR 72116 Office: Metroplan 501-B W Markham St Little Rock AR 72201 E-mail: jlupton@metroplan.org.

LUPTON, MARY HOSMER, retired small business owner; b. Olympia, Wash., Jan. 2, 1914; d. Kenneth Winthrop and Mary Louise (Wheeler) Hosmer; m. Keith Brahe-Wiley, Oct. 12, 1940 (dec. Apr. 1955); children: Sarah Hosmer, Wiley Guise, Victoria Brahe-Wiley; m. Thomas George Lupton, Nov. 27, 1965 (dec. Feb. 1989); 1 stepson, Andrew Henshaw Lupton. Student, Gunston Hall Jr. Coll., 1932-33; BS in Edn., U. Va., 1940. Ptnr. Wakefield Press, Earlysville, Va., 1940-55; owner, operator Wakefield Forest Bookshop, 1955-65, Forest Bookshop, Charlottesville, 1965-85, Wakefield Forest Tree Farm, 1955-85. Contbr. articles to profl. mags. Corr. sec. Charlottesville-Albemarle Civic League, 1963-64; sec. Instructive Vis. Nurses Assn., Charlottesville, 1961-62; chmn. pub. info. Charlottesville chpt. Va. Mus. Fine Arts, 1970-77; mem. Albemarle County Forestry Com., 1961-62; bd. dirs. Charlottesville-Albemarle Mental Health Assn., 1980-82, 89-91. Mem. AAUW, DAR (Am. Heritage com. chmn. 1983-85, 89-91), Assns. of U. Va. Libr., New Eng. Hist. Geneal. Soc., Conn. Soc. Genealogists, Geneal. Soc. Va. Hist. Soc., Albemarle County Hist. Soc., Va. Soc. Mayflower Descs. (asst. state historian 1979-82), LWV, Soc. Mayflower Descs., Am. Soc. Psychical Rsch., Brit. Soc. Psychical Rsch., Nature Conservancy, Charlottesville Soc. of Friends, Jefferson Soc., Cornerstone Soc. (charter), Lawn Soc. (charter), Chi Omega. Address: 2610 Barracks Rd Rm H252 Charlottesville VA 22901-2121

LUPU, RADU, pianist; b. Galati, Romania, Nov. 30, 1945; s. Meyer and Ana (Gabor) L. Attended Conservatoire, Moscow, USSR, 1961-69. London debut, 1969, Berlin, 1972, U.S. debut with Cleve. Orch. in N.Y.C., appearances with worldwide maj. orchs., including Berlin Philharmonic, Vienna Philharmonic, Israel Philharmonic, Orch. de Paris, Concertgebouw, N.Y. Philharmonic, Phila. Symphony Orch., Chgo. Symphony Orch., Cleve. Symphony Orch.; recs. include Beethoven cycle with Israel Philharmonic and Zubin Mehta, Schubert Sonatas, Beethoven Sonatas, Mozart Sonatas for Violin and Piano with Szymon Goldberg, Schubert Lieder with Barbara Hendricks, Mozart and Schubert duets and Mozart Concerto for 2 pianos, both with Murray Perahia, Brahms Piano Concerto #1 Mozart and Beethoven Quintets in E Flat, Schubert Piano Duets with Daniel Barenboim. Recipient 1st prize Van Cliburn Internat. Piano Competition, 1966, Enescu Competition, 1967, Leeds Internat. Piano Competition, 1969, Edison award for Schumann Kinderszenen, Kreisleriana, 1995, Grammy award for Schubert D960 and D664 record, 1995. E-mail: artists@terryharrison.force9.co.uk.

LUPULESCU, AUREL PETER, medical educator, researcher, physician; b. Manastiur, Banat, Romania, Jan. 1, 1923; came to U.S., 1967, naturalized, 1973; s. Peter Vichentie and Maria Ann (Dragan) L. MD magna cum laude, Sch. Medicine, Bucharest, Romania, 1950; MS in Endocrinology, U. Bucharest, 1965; PhD in Biology, U. Windsor, Ont., Can., 1976. Diplomate Am. Bd. Internal Medicine. Chief lab. investigations Inst. Endocrinology, Bucharest, 1950-67; rsch. assoc. SUNY Downstate Med. Ctr., 1968-69; asst. prof. medicine Wayne State U., 1969-72, assoc. prof., 1973—. Vis. prof. Inst. Med. Pathology, Rome, 1967; cons. VA Hosp., Allen Park, Mich., 1971-73. Author: Steroid Hormones, 1958, Advances in Endocrinology and Metabolism, 1962, Experimental Pathophysiology of Thyroid Gland, 1963, Ultrastructure of Thyroid Gland, 1968, Effect of Calcitonin on Epidermal Cells and Collagen Synthesis in Experimental Wounds As Revealed by Electron Microscopy Autoradiography and Scanning Electron Microscopy, 1976, Hormones and Carcinogenesis, 1983, Hormones and Vitamins in Cancer Treatment, 1990, Cancer Cell Metabolism and Cancer Treatment, 2001; reviewer various sci. jours.; contbr. chpts., numerous articles to profl. publs. Fellow Fedn. Am. Socs. for Exptl. Biology; mem. AMA, AAAS, Electron Microscopy Soc. Am., Soc. for Investigative Dermatology, N.Y. Acad. Scis., Am. Soc. Cell Biology, Soc. Exptl. Biology and Medicine. Republican. Achievements include research on hormones and tumor biology; studies regarding role of hormones and vitamins in carcinogenesis. Home: 21480 Mahon Dr Southfield MI 48075-7525 Office: Wayne State U Sch Medicine 540 E Canfield St Detroit MI 48201-1928

LURENSKY, MARCIA ADELE, lawyer; b. Newton, Mass., May 4, 1948; BA magna cum laude, Wheaton Coll., 1970; JD, Boston Coll. Law Sch., 1973. Bar: Mass. 1973, D.C. 1990, U.S. Dist. Ct. (we. dist.) Wis. 1978, U.S. Dist. Ct. Mass. 1974, U.S. Ct. Appeals (1st cir.) 1974, U.S. Ct. Appeals (3d cir.) 1982, U.S. Ct. Appeals (4th cir.) 1984, U.S. Ct. Appeals (5th cir.) 1995, U.S. Ct. Appeals (8th cir.) 1985, U.S. Ct. Appeals (9th cir.) 1976, U.S. Ct. Appeals (10th cir.) 1995, U.S. Ct. Appeals (11th cir.) 1982, U.S. Ct. Appeals (fed. cir.) 1989, U.S. Claims Ct. 1989, U.S. Supreme Ct. 1979. Atty. U.S. Dept. Labor, Washington, 1974-90, Fed. Energy Regulatory Commn., U.S. Dept. Energy, Washington, 1990—. Mem. Phi Beta Kappa. Office: Fed Energy Regulatory Commn 888 1st St NE Washington DC 20426-0002

LURENSKY, ROBERT LEE, economist, educator; b. Roxbury, Mass., May 5, 1928; s. Abraham and Celia (Kamm) L.; m. Eleanor Vivian Goldman, Oct. 15, 1961; children: Harriet Claire, Steven Michael. BA, Syracuse U., 1950; MBA, Wharton Sch. U. Pa., 1952; MA, Harvard U., 1954. Economist, loan officer Export-Import Bank of U.S., Washington, 1961-67; internat. fin. economist Office Internat. Fin., U.S. Dept. Commerce, 1967-84, Office of Internat. Major Projects, Washington, 1984-93, Office of Energy, Environment and Infrastructure, Washington, 1993—94; ret., 1994. Assoc. prof. fin. Southeastern U., Washington, 1966-91, dir. dept. fin. and banking, 1966-88, asst. to acad. v.p., 1988-89. Comdr. USNR, 1953-73. Mem. Am. Econ. Assn., Phi Beta Kappa. Jewish.

LURIA, MARY MERCER, lawyer; b. Boston, Dec. 29, 1942; d. Albert and Mabel (Jacomb) Mercer; m. Nelson J. Luria, June 19, 1967. AB, Radcliffe Coll., 1964; LLB, Yale U., 1967. Bar: N.Y. 1968. Assoc. Simpson, Thacher & Bartlett, N.Y.C., 1967-68, Hale & Dorr, Boston, 1968-69, Satterlee & Stephens, N.Y.C., 1969-74, ptnr., 1974-86, Patterson, Belknap, Webb & Tyler, N.Y.C., 1986-97, Davis & Gilbert, N.Y.C., 1997—. Mem. ABA, N.Y. State Bar Assn., Assn. Bar City N.Y. Avocations: gardening, photography. Office: Davis & Gilbert 1740 Broadway Fl 3 New York NY 10019-4379 E-mail: mluria@dglaw.com.

LURIE, ABRAHAM, social worker, educator; b. N.Y.C., Oct. 18, 1917; s. Isidore and Celia (Kulak) L.; m. Nettie Manheim, June 14, 1948; children: Susan, Debra. BS, CCNY, 1941; ML, Ohio State U., 1943; MS, Columbia U., 1948; PhD, NYU, 1964. Psychiat. social worker Mannhattan State Hosp., N.Y.C., 1947-48, Project Follow-Up, Bellevue Hosp., N.Y.C., 1948-50; dir. social work Hillside Hosp., Queens, N.Y., 1950-73, L.I. Jewish Hillside Hosp., Queens, 1973-84; prof. Adelphi U., Garden City, N.Y., 1984-89; prof. social work SUNY, Stony Brook, 1977—. Cons. VA Northport (N.Y.) Hosp., 1970—, Nassau County Mental Health Assn., Mineola, N.Y., 1984—. Editor: Social Work in Mental Health, 1976; co-editor: Social Work with Group Health, 1982, Social Work Administration, 1985, Critical Social Welfare Issues, 1997. Bd. dirs. Nassau County Mental Health Assn., 1984-87; now bd. dirs. Variety Pre-Schoolers, Syosset, N.Y. Named Social Worker of Yr. Israel Cummings Found., 1966; recipient Ida M. Cannon award Am. Hosp. Assn., 1978, Hy Wiener Lecture award Soc. Hosp. Social Workers, 1985, Sy Silverberg award L.I. Jewish/Hillside Hosp., 1986; Brookdale Found. exch. fellow, 1978. Fellow Am. Orthopsychiat. Assn.; mem. Nat. Assn. Social Worker, Acad. Cert. Social Workers, Am. Assn. Marriage and Family Therapy, Am. Assn. Psychiat. Social Work (nat. v.p. 1955-56), Soc. Hosp. Social Work (nat. pres. 1978-79), Nat. Acad. Practice (Disting. Practitioner). Office: Health Scis Ctr Suny Sch Social Welfar Ctr Stony Brook NY 11794-0001

LURIE, ALISON, writer; b. Chgo., Sept. 3, 1926; children: John, Jeremy, Joshua. AB, Radcliffe Coll., 1947. Lectr. English Cornell U., 1968-73, adj. assoc. prof. English NY, 1973-76, assoc. prof., 1976-79, prof., 1979—98. Author: V.R. Lang: A Memoir, 1959, Love and Friendship, 1962, The Nowhere City, 1965, Imaginary Friends, 1967, Real People, 1969, The War Between the Tates, 1974, Only Children, 1979, The Language of Clothes, 1981, Foreign Affairs, 1984, The Truth About Lorin Jones, 1988, Don't Tell the Grownups, 1990, Women and Ghosts, 1994, The Last Resort, 1998, Familiar Spirits, 2001. Recipient award in lit. Am. Acad. Arts and Letters, 1978, Pulitzer prize in fiction, 1985; fellow Yaddo Found., 1963-64, 66, Guggenheim Found., 1965, Rockefeller Found., 1967, Prix Femina Etranger, 1989. Home: 1409 Hanshaw Rd Ithaca NY 14850 E-mail: al28@cornell.edu.*

LURIE, ALVIN DAVID, lawyer; b. N.Y.C., Apr. 16, 1923; s. Samuel and Rose L.; m. Marian Weinberg, Aug. 21, 1944; children: James, Jeanne, Margery, Jonathan. AB, Cornell U., 1943, LLB, 1944. Bar: N.Y. 1944, D.C. 1978. Ptnr. Lurie & Rubin, N.Y.C., 1961-68, Aranow, Brodsky, Bohlinger & Einhorn, N.Y.C., 1968-74; asst. commr. for employee plans and exempt orgns. IRS, Washington, 1974-78; ptnr. Chadbourne, Parke, Whiteside & Wolff, N.Y.C., 1978-84, Meyers, Tersigni, Lurie, Feldman & Gray, N.Y.C., 1984-94; atty. Alvin D. Lurie, 1994-96; ptnr. Lurie & Gelband, Larchmont, N.Y., 1996; pres. Alvin D. Lurie, PC, New Rochelle, 1996—; dir. N.Y. Ctr. Fin. Studies, 1980—. Mem. adv. bd. NYU Tax Inst., 1978-90; mem. adv. bd.Tax Mgmt., 1978—; mem. adv. bd. Tax Analysts and Advocates, 1995—; spl. counsel Small Bus. Coun. Am., 1978—. Coun. N.Y. Society Financial Sources Profl. 1978-,. Author: Lurie's Commentaries on Pension Design, 1980, Lurie's Guide to VEBAs, 1983, Collected Commentaries on Pensions, 1984, ESOPs Made Easy, 1985; editor: Employee Benefits and Executive Compensation (NYU review), 1998—; contbr. articles to profl. jours.; co-editor-in-chief Cornell Law Quar., 1943-44. editor-in-chief: Pension & Benefit Power, 2002. Mem. ABA, N.Y. State Bar Assn. (chmn. spl. com. pension simplification 1986—), Assn. Bar City N.Y., Am. Coll. Tax Counsel, Am. Coll. Employee Benefits Counsel (charter), N.Y. Bar Found. Office: 145 Huguenot St New Rochelle NY 10801-5200 *Hard work, in intensive spurts, is my formula. The work must be varied, permitting application of different skills in constantly changing, creative ways. But one thing more is needed: carpe diem.*

LURIE, DAPHNE, clinical psychologist, lecturer, educator; b. Tel Aviv, May 31, 1965; came to U.S. 1966. d. Ranan and Tamar R.; m. Stephen Daniel Sprinkle, Aug. 17, 1999; 1 child: Samuel David. Grad. degree in psychology, Williams Coll., 1987; PhD, U. S.C., 1996. Psycholo. rschr. with Vietnam vets. Seattle Va. Med. Ctr., Nat. Ctr. Post-Traumatic Stress Disorder, 1988-89; predoctoral internship Seattle Va. Med. Ctr., 1994-96; counselor psychol. svcs., therapist, spvr. students Clemson U., 1997-01; pvt. practice, specializing in couples' counseling Clemson. Doctoral work and tchg., U. S.C., 1989-93. Mem. APA, S.C. Psychol. Assn.

LURIE, JEFFREY, professional sports team executive; b. Sept. 8, 1951; married; 2 children. BA, Clark U.; MA in Psychology, Boston U.; PhD in Social Policy, Brandeis U. Pres., CEO Chestnut Hills Prodn., L.A.; dir. Harcourt Gen. Inc.; owner Phila. Eagles, 1994—. Mem. NFL expansion com., fin. com. Former trustee Clark U.; dir. Nat. Alliance for Autism Rsch., Boston; active local charitable cmty., Phila. Mem. Phila. C. of C. (exec. com.). Office: Philadelphia Eagles 3501 S Broad St Ste 4A Philadelphia PA 19148-5298*

LURIE, KONSTANTIN ANATOLY, mathematician, educator; b. St. Petersburg, Russia, Nov. 15, 1935; came to U.S., 1989, naturalized, 1994; s. Anatoly Isakovich and Berta Yakovlevna Lurie; m. Ella Sergeevna Zhuravleva, Dec. 27, 1967 (dec. Feb. 1986); 1 child, Dmitri; m. Sofya Yankelevna Fedorovich, Aug. 22, 1989; 1 child, Aleksandra Fedorovich. Engr.-rschr., Leningrad (USSR) Poly. Inst., 1959; PhD in Physics and Math., A.F. Ioffe Phys.-Tech. Inst., Leningrad, 1964; DSc in Physics and Math., Acad. of Sci. USSR, 1972. Sr. rsch. scientist A.F. Ioffe Phys.-Tech. Inst., Leningrad, 1953-88; rsch. scientist, leading rsch. scientist Acad. Sci. USSR, 1988; prof. Leningrad Shipbuilding Inst., 1986-87; Goebel vis. prof. U. Mich., Ann Arbor, 1989; prof. math. Worcester (Mass.) Poly. Inst., 1989—. Vis. prof. Tech. U. Denmark, Lyngby, 1981, vis. prof. math., 1999; vis. prof.-lectr. U. Yerevan, Armenia, 1984. Author: (books) Optimal Control in Problems of Mathematical Physics, 1975, Applied Optimal Control of Distributed Systems, 1993, (book chpts.) Topics in Optimization, 1967, Recent Trends in Optimization Theory and Applications, 1995, Homogenization, 1999, (with. A. V. Cherkaev) Material Instabilities in Continuum Mechanics and Related Math. Problems, 1988, Topics in the Mathematical Modelling of Composite Materials, 1997; editor: (books) Applications of the Theory of Optimal Control to Structural Optimization, 1977, (with A. V. Cherkaev) Optimal Design of Elastic Contstruction Elements, 1981; contbr. papers in field to profl. jours. Rsch. grantee Dept. of Def., 1990-92, NSF, 1993-96, 98-2001, 2002-2005; Fulbright fellow, 1999. Office: Worcester Poly Inst 100 Institute Rd Worcester MA 01609-2247 E-mail: klurie@wpi.edu.

LURIE, NICOLE, former health science association administrator; BA, U. Pa., 1975, MD, 1979; MSPH, UCLA, 1982. Resident UCLA, 1982; cons. RAND Corp., Santa Monica, Calif.; asst. prof. medicine UCLA; asst. to assoc. prof. U. Minn., prof. medicine and pub. health, 1985-98, dir. primary care rsch. and edn., dir. divsn. gen. and internal medicine; prin. dep. asst. sec. for health Office Pub. Health and Science, Washington, 1998—2001; senior researcher Rand Corp., 2002—. Former sr. assoc. editor Health Svcs. Rsch. Recipient Henry J. Kaiser Found. Faculty Scholar award, 1987, Nellie Westerman Prize for Rsch. in Ethics, 1987, Young Investigator award Assn. Health Svcs., 1990, Heroine in Health Care award Minn. Women's Consotium, 1994, award Am. Soc. Clin. Investigation, 1995, Article of Yr. Assn. Health Svcs., 1996, spl. recognition for Physical-Led Rsch. Minn. Physicians, 1997. Mem.: Soc. Gen. Internal Medicine (coun., treas., pres.), Inst. of Medicine. Office: Rand Corp 1200 South Hayes St Arlington VA 22202-5050*

LURIE, RANAN RAYMOND, political cartoonist, political analyst, artist, lecturer; b. Port Said, Egypt, May 26, 1932; came to U.S., 1968, naturalized, 1974; s. Joseph and Rose (Sam) L. (parents Israeli citizens); m. Tamar Fletcher, Feb. 25, 1959; children: Rod, Barak, Daphne, Danielle. Student, Herzelia High Sch., Tel Aviv, Israel, 1949; student, Jerusalem Art Coll., 1951. Corr. Maariv Daily, 1950-52; features editor Hador Daily, 1953-54; editor-in-chief Tevel mag., 1954-55; staff polit. cartoonist Yedioth Aharonot Daily, 1955-66, Honolulu Advertiser, 1979; lectr. polit. cartooning U. Hawaii; univ. lectr. in fine arts, polit. cartoon and polit. analysis Am. Program Bur., Boston.; polit. cartoonist Time Internat. mag., 1994-97. Inventor 1st electronically syndicated bus.-news cartoon Lurie's Business World; 101 million readers of 1105 newspapers in 102 countries; 1999 Guiness Book of World Records; chief judge Internat. Cartoon Comp., Seoul, Korea, 1996, 97; sr. assoc. Ctr. Strategic and Internat. Studies, Washington. Author: Among the Suns, 1952, Lurie's Best Cartoons, 1961, Nixon Rated Cartoons, 1973, Pardon Me, Mr. President, 1974, Lurie's Worlds, 1980, So sieht es Lurie, 1981, Fed. Republic Germany, Lurie's Almanac (U.K.), 1982, (U.S.A.), 1983, Taro's International Politics, Japan, 1984, Lurie's Middle East, Israel, 1986; creator: The Expandable Painting, 1969; Cartoons used as guidelines in several encys., polit. sci. books.; 22 shows, Israel, Can., U.S., 1960-75, including, Expo 67, Can., Dominion Gallery, Montreal, Que., Can., Lim Gallery, Tel Aviv, 1965, Overseas Press Club, N.Y.C., 1962, 64, 75, U.S. Senate, Washington, Honolulu Acad. Fine Arts, 1979; represented by Circle Gallery, 1988-93; exhibited numerous group shows including, Smithsonian Instn., 1972, Circle Gallery, Washington, 1989; creator Japan's nat. cartoon symbol Taro-San, Taiwan's nat. cartoon symbol Cousin Lee; polit. cartoonist, Life Mag., N.Y.C., 1968-73, polit. cartoonist, interviewer, Die Welt, Bonn, W. Ger., 1980-81; contbr.: N.Y. Times, 1952—; contbg. editor, polit. cartoonist, Newsweek Internat., 1973-76, editor, polit. cartoonist, Vision Mag. of South Am., 1974-76, syndicated, United Features Syndicate, 1971-73; syndicated nationally by Los Angeles Times, also internationally by, N.Y. Times to over 260 newspapers, 1973-75, internationally by Editors Press Syndicate (345 newspapers), King Features Syndicate, 1975-83; syndicated in U.S. by Universal Press Syndicate, 1982-86, Cartoonews Internat. Syndicat, 1986—; polit. cartoonist, The Times of London, 1981-83, ABC's Nightline, 1991—, World News Show, 1993; sr. polit. analyst, editorial cartoonist Asahi Shimbun, Japan's largest daily newspaper, 1983-84; sr. analyst and polit. cartoonist U.S. News & World Report, 1984-85; chief editorial dir. Editors Press Service, 1985; joined staff MacNeil/Lehrer News Hour (PBS).as daily polit. cartoonist, analyst; editl. bd. Mid. East Quarterly, 1994—; creator, editor-in-chief Cartoon News, The Current Events Ednl. Mag., 1996—; polit. cartoonist Fgn. Affairs Mag., 2000—. Chief judge Seoul (Republic of Korea) Internat. Cartoon Competition, 1996, 97. Served as maj. Combat Paratroop, Israeli Army Res., 1950-67. Recipient highest Israeli journalism award, 1954; U.S. Headliners award, 1972; named Outstanding Editorial Cartoonist of Nat. Cartoonist Soc., 1971-78; Salon award Montreal Cartoon, 1971; N.Y. Front Page award, 1972, 74, 77; cert. merit U.S. Publ. Designers, 1974; award Overseas Press Club, 1979; John Fischetti polit. cartoon award, 1982, 86; Ranan R. Lurie Internat. Polit. Cartoon ann. award created in his honor by Nat. Fedn. Hispanic Owned Newspapers, 1994, Ranan R. Lurie Internat. award for Polit. Cartooning created by U.N. Soc. of Writers, 1995, Annual Ranan Lurie Polit. Cartoon award created in his honor by U.N., 2000; recip. 1996 Hubert Humphrey 1st Amendment and Freedom of the Press Award, 1996; UN Corrs. Assn. ranan Lurie Polit. Cartoon award created in his honor, 1999; nominated for Nobel Peace Prize, 2002. Mem. Soc. Profl. Journalists, Nat. Cartoonists Soc. Am., Assn. Editorial Cartoonists, Mensa, Overseas Press Club, Friars Club. Inventor 1st electronically animated TV news cartoon; creator 1st syndicated bus.-news cartoon Lurie's Business World; 104 million readers of 1,105 newspapers in 104 countries; 1999 Guiness Book of World Records. Office: Cartoonews Internat 375 Park Ave Ste 1301 New York NY 10152-1399 E-mail: cartoonews@aol.com., luriehonor@aol.com. *The moment of truth will come when the cartoonist gauges the margin of time from the day he drew the cartoon. Then he can see how correctly he has evaluated the situation through his work. Eventually, the simple facts and reality always win. Then it becomes apparent that wishful thinking is meaningless and the capacity to evaluate the project and even predict the events that are happening will eventually cement the professional status and integrity of the political cartoonist.*

LURIX, PAUL LESLIE, JR. chemist; b. Bridgeport, Conn., Apr. 6, 1949; s. Paul Leslie and Shirley Laurel (Ludwig) L.; m. Cynthia Ann Owens, May 30, 1970; children: Paul Christopher, Alexander Tristan, Einar Gabrielson. BA, Drew U., 1971; MS, postgrad., Purdue U., 1973. Tech. dir. Analysts, Inc., Linden, N.J., 1976-77; chief chemist Caleb Brett USA, Inc., 1977-80; v.p. Tex. Labs., Inc., Houston, 1980-82; pres. Lurix Corp., Fulshear, Tex., 1982—. Cons. LanData, Inc., Houston, 1980-88, Nat. Cellulose Corp., Houston, 1981-88, Met. Transit Authority, Houston, 1981—, Phillips 66, Houston, 1986—, Conoco, Inc., Houston, 1988—, Caronia Corp., Houston, 1988-98, WBC Holdings, Inc., 1989-96, M&H Engring., 1994-00, Compaq Computer, 1996—, Baylor Coll. Medicine, 2000—; dir. rsch. and devel. Stockbridge Software, Inc., Houston, 1986-88; v.p. Diesel King Corp., Houston, 1980-82. Contbr. articles to profl. jours. Fellow Am. Inst. Chemists; mem. AAAS, ASTM, Am. Chem. Soc., Soc. Applied Spectroscopy, N.Y. Acad. Sci., Kiwanis (pres. 1970-71), Phi Kappa Phi, Phi Lambda Upsilon, Sigma Pi Sigma. Republican. Methodist. Achievements include patents for distillate fuel additives and e-commerce; research on infrared spectroscopy, data base programming for science and industrial applications; subspecialities in infrared spectroscopy, information systems, storage, and retrieval (computer science). Avocations: tennis, golf, piano.

LURTON, HORACE VANDEVENTER, brokerage house executive; b. Washington, Oct. 16, 1941; s. Horace Harmon III and Eleaner (Pentz) L.; m. Nancy Taylor Mackall, Aug. 30, 1964 (dec. 1992); children: Bowie VanDeventer, Sallie Taylor. Student, Gettysburg U., 1962; BS, Am. U., 1965. Registered prin. SEC. Stockbroker Thomson, McKinnon & Auchincloss, Washington, 1966-76, Dean Witter Reynolds, Chevy Chase, Md., 1977-79; stockbroker, branch mgr., dir. Johnston, Lemon & Co., Inc., Bethesda, 1979-89, stockbroker, br. mgr., dir. Washington, 1989-90; v.p., branch mgr. Janney, Montgomery, Scott, 1990—. Active various orgns. and charities, Washington, Md. Episcopalian. Avocation: biking. Home: 5004 Scarsdale Rd Bethesda MD 20816-2438 Office: Janney Montgomery Scott 1225 23rd St NW Washington DC 20037-1102

LURYE, HELEN, artist; b. Kemerovo, Siberia, Russia, Aug. 27, 1961; came to U.S., 1989; d. Anasi Holland and Ludmila Tkalina; m. Michael Lurye, Apr. 23, 1988; 1 child, Karina Victoria. BA, Inst. Culture, Moscow, 1983; postgrad., Winchester Sch. Art, Eng., 1991; AA, Fashion Inst. Tech., N.Y.C., 1992. Represented by Ward-Nasse Gallery, N.Y.C. Exhibited in group shows at Alumni Exhbn. Fashion Inst. Tech., 1992, Ward-Nasse Gallery, 1997, Internat. Film and Video Festival, 1998, A.I.R. Gallery, N.Y.C., 1998, Ctr. for Visual Art, Oakland, Calif., 1998, Glen Eure's Ghost Fleet Gallery, Nags Head, N.C., 1999, Stupino, Russia, 1999, Sharjah Arts Mus., United Arab Emirates, 2000, Jazz Gallery, N.Y.C., 2000, Multicultural Ctr., Bloomsburg U., Pa., PaintingsDirect.com, 2000, Open Space Gallery, Saratoga Springs, N.Y., 2001, WorldArtistRegistry.com, 2001, works. Mem. Colored Pencil Soc. Am., Ward-Nasse Gallery, Nat. Soc. Painters, Nat. Acrylic Soc. Avocations: travel, meditation, swimming with dolphins. E-mail: Helenlurye@yahoo.com.

LUSAS, EDMUND WILLIAM, food processing research executive; b. Woodbury, Conn., Nov. 25, 1931; s. Anton Frank and Damicele Nellie (Kasputis) L.; m. Jeannine Marie Muller, Feb. 2, 1957; children: Daniel, Ann, Paul. BS, U. Conn., 1954; MS, Iowa State U., 1955; PhD, U. Wis., 1958; MBA, U. Chgo., 1972. Project leader Quaker Oats Rsch. Labs., Barrington, Ill., 1958-61, mgr. canned pet foods rsch., 1961-67, mgr. sci. svcs., 1972-77; assoc. dir. Food Protein R&D Ctr., Tex. A&M U., College Station, 1977-78, dir., 1978-93, head fats, oils and extrusion programs, 1993-97; pres. Ed Lusas, Problem Sovlers, Inc., Bryan, Tex., 1997—. Author more than 175 publs.; editor Jour. Am. Oil Chem. Soc., 1980-88; patentee in field. Fund raiser YMCA, Crystal Lake, Ill., 1970-77, chmn. fin. com., 1977. Recipient F.N. Peters rsch. award Quaker Oats Co., 1968; Gen. Foods rsch. fellow, 1956, 57. Mem. Am. Oil Chemists Soc., Inst. Food Technologists, Am. Chem. Soc., Am. Assn. Cereal Chemists, Am. Soc. Agrl. Engrs., R&D Assocs., Guayule Soc. Am., Sigma Xi, Phi Tau Sigma. Home and Office: 3604 Old Oaks Dr Bryan TX 77802-4743

LUSCH, CHARLES JACK, oncologist; b. Lehighton, Pa., Feb. 15, 1936; s. Charles Norman and Loretta (Gaumer) L.; m. Carole Faye Eckart, Aug. 17, 1957; children: Marjorie, Susan, Stephen, Robert. AB in Biology magna cum laude, Lafayette Coll., Easton, Pa., 1957; MD, Temple U., 1961. Diplomate in med. oncology, hematology, internal medicine, forensic medicine; diplomate Am. Bd. Forensic Medicine. Pres. Berks Hematology-Oncology Assocs., Reading, Pa., 1968—; chief sect. of med. oncology & hematology Reading Hosp. & Med. Ctr., 1970—; dir. Pa. State Hemophilia Ctr., Reading Hosp. & Med. Ctr., 1973—; v.p. Lusch Motor Parts, Lehighton, Pa., 1975—; chief sect. med. oncology & hematology Community Gen. Hosp., Reading, 1980—; asst. chief medicine Reading Hosp. and Med. Ctr., 1986—; med. dir. Pocono Internat. Raceway, 1980-85; chmn. institutional rev. bd. Reading Hosp. and Med. Ctr., 1986—, dir. continuing med. edn., 1987—; med. dir. Berks County Hospice, Berks County Vis. Nurse Assn., Reading, 1987—; dir. oncology svcs. Reading Hosp. and Med. Ctr., 1990—. Med. adv. com. Pa. Blue Shield, Camp Hill, Pa., 1987—; bd. dirs. Berks Home Health Car, Reading Cancer Ctr., Reading Hosp.; malpractice cons. Med. Protective Ins. Co., Ft. Wayne, Ind., 1985—; cons. in hematology and oncology Pottsville (Pa.) Hosp. and Good Samaritan Hosp., 1975—; clin. asst. prof. medicine Pa. Med. Sch., 1984—, Pa. State Med. Sch., 1981—, Temple U. Med. Sch., clin. assoc. prof. 1990; sr. clin. instr. Mahnemann U. Med. Sch., 1968—; prin. investigator Ea. Coop Oncology Group, 1975-90, Nat. Surg. Adj. & Breast Project, 1986—. Contbr. articles to profl. jours.; editor The Med. Record (regional med. jour.), 1970-71. Advisor Future Physicians Am., Reading, 1965; bd. dirs. Berks County unit Am. Cancer Soc., Reading, 1968-78, Keystone Cmty. Blood Bank, Reading, 1970-80; adv. com. The Women's Ctr., Reading Hosp., 1987-88; mem. bd. divsn. ch. soc. Evang. Luth. Ch. Am., Chgo.; pres. ch. coun. Atonement Luth. Ch., Wyomissing, Pa. Lt. comdr. USPHS, 1965-67. Fellow ACP; mem. Pa. Soc. Hematology-Oncology (sec.-treas. 1986-87), Am. Soc. Clin. Oncology, Am. Soc. Hematology, Am. Fedn. Clin. Rsch., Acad. Hospice Physicians (publs. com. 1989—), U.S. Amateur Ballroom Dance Assn. (past pres. Reading chpt.), Sports Car Club Am., Phi Beta Kappa, Alpha Omega Alpha. Republican. Lutheran. Avocations: competition ballroom dancing, tennis, motor racing. Home: 1617 Meadowlark Rd Wyomissing PA 19610-2820 Office: Berks Hematology Oncology Assoc 301 S 7th Ave Reading PA 19611-1410

LÜSCHEN, GÜNTHER RUDOLF FRIEDO, sociology educator; b. Oldenburg, Germany, Jan. 21, 1930; s. Gustav Hermann Anton and Elsa Pauline Elisabeth (Magnus) L.; m. Klara Maria Mertens, Dec. 22, 1958 (div. Aug. 1989); children: Birgit, Gerhard; m. Leila Antoun Sfeir, Nov. 18, 1989; 1 child, Gerlinde. PhD, U. Graz, Austria, 1959; MA, U. Bonn, Germany, 1960; D (hon.), U. Jyvaskyla, Finland, 1990. Rsch. assoc. U. Cologne, Germany, 1961-64; assoc. prof. U. Bremen, Germany, 1965-72; prof. U. Ill., 1966-90, prof. emeritus, 1990—; prof. Tech. U. Aachen, Germany, 1982-89, U. Düsseldorf, Germany, 1990-95, 2001—, U. Ala., Birmingham, 1995-2001. Pres. Internat. Com. Sociology of Sport/UNESCO, 1967-80, Rene-König-Gesellschaft, Cologne, Germany, 1993-96; mem. Rsch. Coun. Internat. Soc.

Assn., 1966-74, 82. Author: Sociology of Sport, 1967, Health Systems in the European Union, 1995; co-author: Health Promotion Policy in Euope, 1999; editor: Deutsche Soziologie seit 1945, 1979, Das Moralische in der Soziologie, 1998, Sportpolitik, 1996; co-editor: Soziologie der Familie, 1970, Handbook of Social Science of Sport, 1981. Founder Polit. Action Group, Oldenburg, 1969. Recipient Fed. Merit Cross, German Pres., 1989, citation Internat. Com. Sociology of Sport, 1993, Nat. citation N.Am. Assn. Sociology Sport. Mem. Internat. Sociol. Assn. (life), Midwest Sociol. Soc., Am. Sociol. Assn., German Sociol. Assn. Avocations: tennis, guitar. Home: Sodenstich 35a 26131 Oldenburg Germany Office: U Duesseldorf Detp Sociology Duesseldorf Germany

LUSCHER, ROBERT MICHAEL, English educator, department chair; b. San Diego, Sept. 10, 1954; s. Joseph R. and Claire F. (Radomile) L.; m. Diana Lynn Raab, Sept. 6, 1975; children: Aurora Nicole, Julia Christine. BA in Lit., U. Calif. San Diego, La Jolla, 1976; MA in English, Duke U., 1978, PhD in English, 1984. Instr. dept. English La. State U., Baton Rouge, 1984-86; asst. prof. dept. English Catawba Coll., Salisbury, N.C., 1986-90, honors dir., prof. dept. English, 1990-93, prof., chair dept. English, 1993-95; prof., chair English dept. U. Nebr., Kearney, 1995—. Lectr. N.C. Humanities Coun./Duke U. Continuing Edn., 1993-95. Author: John Updike: A Study of the Short Fiction, 1993; criticism editor Short Story, Studies in Short Fiction, 1990—; contbr. essays and articles to profl. jours. Summer Study grantee NEH, 1993; grantee U. Nebr. Kearney Rsch. Svcs. Coun., 1995. Mem. MLA, Midwest MLA, Soc. for the Study of the Short Story, Phi Eta Sigma. Democrat. Avocations: reading, running, outdoor activities. Office: Univ Nebr Kearney Dept English 905 W 25th St Dept English Kearney NE 68849-1320

LUSHER, JEANNE MARIE, pediatric hematologist, educator; b. Toledo, June 9, 1935; d. Arnold Christian and Violet Cecilia (French) L. BS summa cum laude, U. Cin., 1956, MD, 1960. Resident in pediat. Tulane divsn. Charity Hosp. La., New Orleans, 1961-64; fellow in pediat. hematology-oncology Child Rsch. Ctr. Mich., Detroit, 1964-65, St. Louis Children's Hosp./Washington U., 1965-66; instr. pediat. Washington U., St. Louis, 1965-66; from instr. to assoc. prof. Sch. Medicine Wayne State U., Detroit, 1966-74, prof., 1974-97, disting. prof., 1997—; dir. divsn. hematology-oncology Children's Hosp. Mich., 1976—. Marion I. Barnhart prof. hemostasis rsch. Sch. Medicine Wayne State U., Detroit, 1989—; med. dir. Nat. Hemophilia Found., N.Y.C., 1987—94, chmn. med. and sci. adv. coun., 1994—2001, bd. dirs., 1997—2001, co-chmn. gene therapy working group, 2000—. Author, editor: Treatment of Bleeding Disorders with Blood Components, 1980, Sickle Cell, 1974, 76, 81, Hemophilia and von Willebrand Disease in the 1990's, 1991, Acquired Bleeding Disorders in Children, 1981, F VIII/von Willebrand Factor and Platelets in Health and Disease, 1987, Inhibitors to Factor VIII, 1994, Blood Coaqulation Innhibitors, 1996. Mem. Citizens Info. Com., Pontiac Township, Mich., 1980-82; apptd. mem. Hazardous Waste Incinerator Commn., Oakland County, Mich., 1981. Recipient Disting. Alumnus award U. Cin. Alumni Assn., 1990, Lawrence Weiner award Wayne State U. Sch. Medicine Alumni Assn., 1991. Mem. Am. Bd. Pediat. (chmn. sub-bd. on hematology-oncology 1988-90), Am. Soc. Hematology (chmn. sci. com. pediat. 1991-92, sci. com. hemostasis 1998—), Am. Pediat. Soc., Soc. Pediat. Rsch., Internat. Soc. Thrombosis-Hemostasis (chmn. factor VIII/IX subcom. 1985-90, chmn. sci. and standardization com. 1996-98), Mich. Humane Soc. Avocations: nature, wildlife. Office: Children's Hosp Mich 3901 Beaubien Blvd Detroit MI 48201-2119 E-mail: jlusher@med.wayne.edu.

LUSK, CHARLES MICHAEL, III, real estate professional; b. Houston, Apr. 7, 1948; s. Charles Michael and Ursula Josephine (Guseman) L.; m. Kathleen Frances Carroll, Nov. 24, 1973; children: Andrew Stephen, Lauren Carroll. AA, Schreiner Inst., 1969; BA in English, Baylor U., 1971. Cert. real estate broker, Tex. Broker, salesman Coldwell Banker Company, Houston, 1971-74; owner, operator Lusk Properties, 1975—; v.p. Mortgage & Trust, Inc. (subs. Mellon Bank N.A.), 1977-86; exec. v.p. Commonwealth Fed. Savs. Assn., 1986-89; prin., pres. Realty Adv. Group, Inc., 1990—. Trustee J & J Drilling Co., Lulling, Tex., 1989-95; contractor Resolution Trust Corp., Houston, 1990-95; trustee Gen. Homes Liquidating Trust, Houston, 1991-2000; v.p., bd. dirs. Houston Housing Fin. Corp. Active Houston Livestock Show & Rodeo, Houston, 1989—; exec. com. West Univ. Party, Houston, 1989-93. Mem. CCIM, Am. Soc. Real Estate Counselors, Tex. Bd. Realtors, Houston Bd. Realtors, Urban Land Inst., The Briar Club (various offices, 1984—), Tex. Corinthian Yacht Club, Breakfast Assn. Republican. Methodist. Avocations: sailing, travel. Home: 3718 Chevy Chase Dr Houston TX 77019-3012 Office: Realty Adv Group, Inc One W Loop South Ste 690 Houston TX 77027 E-mail: cmlusk@prodigy.net.

LUSK, GLENNA RAE KNIGHT (MRS. EDWIN BRUCE LUSK), librarian; b. Franklinton, La., Aug. 16, 1935; d. Otis Harvey and Lou Zelle Knight; m. John Earle Uhler, Jr., May 26, 1956; children: Anne Knight, Camille Allana; m. 2d, Edwin Bruce Lusk, Nov. 28, 1970. BS, La. State U., 1956, MS, 1963. Asst. librarian Iberville Parish Library, Plaquemine, La., 1956-57, 1962-68; tchr. Iberville Parish Pub. Schs., Plaquemine, 1957-59, Plaquemines Parish Pub. Schs., Buras, La., 1959-61; dir. Iberville Parish Library, Plaquemine, 1969-89; chmn. La. State Bd. Library Examiners, 1979-89; pres. Camille Navarre Gallery, Ltd., Zachary, La., 1989-94. Mem. Iberville Parish Econ. Devel. Council, Plaquemine, 1970-71; sec. Iberville Parish Bicentennial Commn., 1973—; mem. La. Bicentennial Commn., 1974; bd dirs. McHugh House Mus., 1991-92. Named Outstanding Young Woman Plaquemine, La. Jr. C. of C., 1970. Mem. La. (sect. chmn. 1967-68), Riverland (sec. 1973-74) libraries assns., Capital Area Libraries (chmn. com. 1972-74). Republican. Episcopalian. Author: (with John E. Uhler, Jr.) Cajun Country Cookin', 1966, Rochester Clarke Bibliography of Louisiana Cookery, 1966, Royal Recipes from the Cajun Country, 1969, Iberville Parish, 1970. Home: 13291 Legacy Ct Baton Rouge LA 70816-7936

LUSK, HARLAN GILBERT, national park superintendent, business executive; b. Jersey City, June 22, 1943; s. Harlan H. and Mary M. (Kuhl) L.; m. Catherine L. Rutherford, Oct. 11, 1986. BA in History, Gettysburg Coll., 1965, D of Pub. Svc. (hon.), 2001. Supervisory historian Cape Hatteras Nat. Seashore, Manteo, N.C., 1968; historian Nat. Pk. Svc., Washington, 1968-69; programs specialist So. Utah Group, Cedar City, 1968-70; pk. supt. Wolf Trap Farm Pk., Vienna, 1970-72; supervisory pk. ranger Blue Ridge Pkwy., Roanoke, 1972-74; pk. supt. Appomattox (Va.) Courthouse, Nat. Hist. Pk., 1974-76, Valley Forge (Pa.), Nat. Hist. Pk., 1976-81, Big Bend (Tex.) Nat. Pk., 1981-86, Glacier Nat. Pk., West Glacier, Mont., 1986-94; pk. supt. Albright Tng. Ctr. Grand Canyon Nat. Pk., Ariz., 1994-95; chief, Divsn. Tng. and Employee Nat. Park Svc., Washington, 1995-97; retired from park svc., 1997; chmn. Gil Lusk Assocs., 1997—; group mgr. The Cholla Group, 1997—. Organizer 1st regional conf. Rio Grande Border, States on Pks. and Wildlife, Laredo, Tex., 1985 Bd. dirs. Tech. Com. on Pks. and Recreation Cen. Va. Planning Dist., 1972-74, Fed. Exec. Assn. Roanoke Valley, 1972-74, Flathead Basin Commn., 1986-94, Flathead Conv. and Visitor Assn., 1986-94, Sonoran Inst., 1995-2001; prin. founder, 1st pres., Appomattox County Hist. Soc., 1974-76; trustee Sci. Mus. Assn. Roanoke Valley, 1972-74, Nature Conservancy Mont., 1994—; ex-officio Friends of Valley Forge, 1977-81; founder, ex-officio, bd. dirs. Valley Forge Pk. Interpretive Assn., 1977-81; founder Big Bend Area Travel Assn., chmn., 1984-86. Recipient Meritorious Svc. award. Dept. Interior, 1986, Disting. Svc. award, 1999. Mem. Glacier Natural History Assn. (ex officio 1986-94), Glacier Nat. Pk. Assocs. (founder, ex-officio 1989-94), George Wright Soc., Lions, Rotary. Avocations: golf, antiques, computers, collecting artwork, hiking. E-mail: hglusk@msn.com., gil@rancholajoya.com.

LUSK, MARY MARGARET, music educator; b. Athens County, Ohio, Mar. 17, 1936; d. Raymond Edward and Clara Grace (Johnston) Sanborn; m. Harold Waldo Mowery, Jan. 3, 1953 (div. Apr. 1961); children: Margaret Maria Barnhill, Harold Waldo 2nd; m. Ned Eugene Lusk, June 22, 1961; children: Bonita Jean Denig, Amy Beth Noykos, Melissa Kae Pfenning. Student, Ashland Jr. Coll., Russell, Ky., 1955-56, Ohio No. U., 1957. Apprentice music tchr., Nelsonville, Ohio, 1951-53; pvt. music tchr., 1951—. Traveling pianist Princeton Sem. Summer Mission Tour, summers 1949-52; ch. and youth camp music instr., 1953-60; adjudicator Teen Talent Contests, Ctrl. and Northwestern Ohio, 1968—; organist Patrick Heinl Funeral Home, 1976-88, Bayliff and Eley Funeral Home, 1988—. Columnist Wapakoneta Daily News, 1987-90; author of poetry. Dir., leader The Singing Lusk Family, 1975—; mem. Ohio Alliance for Arts Edn., 2002—; min. music Ch. of the Nazarene, Wapakoneta, Ohio, 1968—76, Cridersville, 1976—83, First Presbyn. Ch., St. Marys, 1984—85, United Meth. Ch., Botkins, 1986—88, Salem United Meth. Ch., Wapakoneta, 1988—99; organist Byron Ch. , Fairborn, Ohio, 2000—. Mem. Music Tchrs. Nat. Assn., Ohio Music Tchrs. Assn., Northwestern Ohio Music Tchrs. Assn. Republican. Avocations: reading, writing, traveling, collecting miniature pianos, collecting Precious Moments figurines. Home: 920 Springwood Ln Wapakoneta OH 45895-9236

LUSK, WILLIAM EDWARD, real estate and oil company executive; b. Medicine Lodge, Kans., May 16, 1916; s. William Edward and Teresa (Rhoades) L.; m. Anita Ballard, Feb. 1, 1942; children— William Edward, Janet Kathryn and James Raymond (twins). BS in Edn; AB in Econs., Ft. Hays State Coll., 1939; student, Washburn U., 1936; postgrad., Kans. U., 1940-41. Tchr. Protection (Kans.) High Sch., 1939-41; mgr. real estate dept. Wheeler, Kelly & Hagny Investment Co., Wichita, Kans., 1946-63; co-founder, exec. v.p., treas., dir. Clinton Oil Co., 1963-73; pres. Lusk Real Estate Co., 1963—, Lusk Investment Co., 1973—. Pres. Wichita Real Estate Bd., 1961 Founder Lusk Found., 1968, William E. Lusk Scholarship, Ft. Hays State Coll., 1969; bd. dirs. Jr. Achievement Wichita. Served with USNR, 1942-46; comdr. Res. Named Kans. Realtor of Year Kans. Assn. Real Estate Bds., 1962; recipient Alumni Achievement award Ft. Hays Kan. State Coll., 1971 Mem. VFW, Sojourners, Res. Officers Assn., Naval Res. Officers Assn., Navy League, Phi Alpha Delta, Alpha Kappa Psi (hon.) Methodist (bd. dirs. 1965-70, fin. chmn. 1969—). Clubs: Wichita Country, Wichita (bd. dirs. 1969-72, pres. 1972), McConnell AFB Officers. Lodge: Masons (32 degree). Home: 6 West Pkwy N Wichita KS 67206-2446 Office: 1608 E Lewis St Wichita KS 67211-1823 E-mail: William.lusksr@gte.net. *In business and personal relationships I have found strength in times of adversity and self-control in times of success by forming the habit of calling to mind this guideline: Things are never as good as they seem to be on the day they look good--nor are things as bad as they seem to be on the day they appear bad.*

LUSS, DAN, chemical engineering educator; b. Tel Aviv, May 5, 1938; came to U.S., 1963, naturalized, 1973; s. Manfred and Gertrude (Weinstein) L.; m. Amalia Rubin, Sept. 4, 1966; children: Noya, Limor. BS, Technion Inst. Tech., Haifa, Israel, 1960, MSc, 1963; PhD, U. Minn., 1966. Registered profl. engr., Tex. Asst. prof. chem. engring. U. Minn., Mpls., 1966-67, U. Houston, 1967-69, assoc. prof., 1969-72, prof., 1972—, chmn. dept., 1975-95, 99-00; assoc. dir. Tex. Ctr. for Superconductivity, 1988-92. Cons. to several chem. cos. Editor: Revs. in Chem. Engring.; mem. editorial bd. Sci. and Engring, Catalysis Rev. Fellow Am. Inst. Chem. Engrs. (Allan P. Colburn award 1973, Profl. Progress award 1979, Wilhelm award 1986, chmn. awards com., former mem. editorial bd. jour.,former dir.), Am. Chem. Soc. (Honor scroll award of Indsl. Engring. Chemistry div. 1967); mem. NAE, Am. Soc. Engring. Edn. (Curtis McGraw award 1977 3M-Chem. Engring. lectureship award 1985) Home: 6242 Paisley St Houston TX 77096-3727 Office: U Houston Dept Chem Engring Houston TX 77204-4004

LUSSEN, JOHN FREDERICK, pharmaceutical laboratory executive; b. N.Y.C., Jan. 5, 1942; s. Frederick Maurice and Kathleen (Herlihy) L.; m. Kathleen Elizabeth Sheppard; children: Tara, Eric, Gregory. BS in Fin., Fordham U., 1963, JD, 1967; LLM in Tax, NYU, 1971. Bar: N.Y. 1967. Tax atty. Pfizer Inc., N.Y.C., 1971-74; mgr. taxes SCM Corp., 1974-79; v.p. taxes Abbott Labs., Abbott Park, Ill., 1979—. PhRMA tax com. Fin. Execs. Inst. Capt. U.S. Army, 1968-70. Mem. ABA, Tax Execs. Inst., Bus. Roundtable (mem. tax subcom.), P.R. USA Found. (pres.). Avocations: tennis, golf. Home: 1055 Westleigh Rd Lake Forest IL 60045 Office: Abbott Labs D367 AP6D 100 Abbott Park Rd Abbott Park IL 60064-6057 E-mail: john.lussen@Abbott.com.

LUSSI, CAROLINE FRANCES DRAPER, resort executive; b. Glen Falls, N.Y., Apr. 5, 1939; d. Arthur Gibb and Lili Caroline (Gadeke) Draper; m. Serge Gail Lussi, Feb. 7, 1960; children: Arthur, Cristina, Katrina. Student, U. Colo., 1957-58; AAS, Paul Smith's Coll., 1960; grad., Holiday Inn U., 1969. Profl. ski instr., 1960—; mgr. Holiday Motor Motel, Wilmington, N.Y., 1961-62, owner, 1962-69; owner, innkeeper Holiday Inn, Lake Placid, 1969—; sec. Lake Placid Vacation Corp., 1969—. Co-owner Lake Placid Resort, 1996—; co-owner, treas. Lake Placid Marina Corp. Mem. adv. bd. Alpine 1980 Olympics; bd. dirs. Lake Placid Meml. Hosp., 1975-81, also mem. aux.; trustee Paul Smiths Coll., 1984-88, 98—. Named Top 10% Innkeeper Holiday Inns, 1972-75. Mem. Lake Placid C. of C., Profl. Ski Instrs. Am. (cert.), Essex County Adirondack Garden (pres. 1991-92), Shoreowner's Assn. (mem. bd. dirs. 1994-2001), Nature Conservancy (mem. bd. dirs. Adirondack chpt. 1993-2001). Episcopalian. Office: Lake Placid Resort Holiday Inn Lake Placid NY 12946

LUSSKY, WARREN ALFRED, librarian, educator, consultant; b. Chgo., Apr. 16, 1919; s. Arthur W. and Alma (Proegler) L.; m. Mildred Joann Island, June 12, 1948. Student, U. Ill., 1941-42; BA, U. Colo., 1946; MA, U. Denver, 1948. Asst. libr. Pacific Luth. Coll., Parkland, Wash., 1948-49; libr. Hopkins Transp. Libr., Stanford, 1950, Rocky Mountain Coll., Billings, Mont., 1950-55; head libr. Nebr. Wesleyan U., Lincoln, 1955-56; dir. libr., assoc. prof. Tex. Luth. Coll., Sequin, 1956-85. Libr. cons.; mem. accrediting team Tex. Edn. Agy., 1961, 84. Prin. contbr. to design new Tex. Luth. Coll. Libr.; rsch. and publs. on design and functions coll. libr. bldgs. Mem. Am. Libr. Assn., Tex. Libr. Assn. (dist. vice chmn. 1965, chmn. 1966), S.W. Libr. Assn., Coun. Rsch. and Acad. Librs. (bd. dirs. 1968-85, pres. 1976-78). Home: 357 Irvington Dr San Antonio TX 78209-4221

LUST, ELENORE, artist; b. Chgo. d. Herbert and Dora (Koumas) Lust; m. Robert Eising, Jan. 7, 1932 (div.). Student, Smith Coll., 1929-30; BA, NYU, 1935, MA, 1957. Cert. tchr., N.Y., N.J. Dir., co-founder Norlyst Art Gallery, N.Y.C., 1940-49; art tchr. Cape of Good Hope Sem., Capetown, South Africa, 1952-55, St. Siprian's Sch., Capetown, 1952-55, N.J. High Schs., 1957-79. Art lectr. Herald Tribune N.Y.C., 1944-49, art tchr. Little Red Sch. House, N.Y.C., 1944-49, Bklyn. Mus. Art Sch., 1947-50, Rancocas Valley Region High Sch., 1959-68; spl. edn. tchr. Lenape High Sch. System, 1970-79. Exhibited in one-woman shows at Norlyst Art Gallery, 1944, Stuttaford's Gallery, Capetown, 1952, Cafe Gallery, Burlington, N.J., 1988, Ft. Dix, Pemberton, N.J., 1988; represented in permanent collections at Ft. Dix, Mus. Women in Arts, Washington, and 74 other pvt. and corp. collections. Vol. art asst. tchr. Walter Elem. Sch., Lumber, N.J.; vol. Meml. Hosp., Mt. Holly, N.J. Mem. AAUW, Burlington County Art Guild (pres. 1983-85, v.p. 1989), Atlantic City Art Ctr., Trenton Artists' Workshop Assn., So. N. J. Advocates for Arts, Artworks/Princeton. Democrat. Episcopalian. Studio: PO Box D Mount Holly NJ 08060

LUST, HERBERT COHNFELDT, II, finance executive; b. Chgo., Oct. 31, 1926; s. Herbert Cohnfeldt and Jennie (Friedman) L.; m. Virginia Wertheimer; children: Herbert Cohnfeldt III, Conrad. MA, U. Chgo., 1948. Pres. Pvt. Water Supply, Inc. Greenwich Assocs., N.Y.C., 1961—, co-owner, dir. Gallery Bernard, 1969-87; dir. First Va. Real Estate Trust, Washington, 1981-83; chmn. bd. BRT, Great Neck, N.Y., 1983-85; chmn. United Mchts. & Mfg., Teaneck, N.J., 1991-93; owner Herbert Lust Gallery, N.Y.C., 1995—. Lectr. comparative lit. U. Chgo., 1956-59; bd. dirs. Prime Hospitality, BRT. Author: 12 Principals of Art Investment, 1969, Alberto Giacometti, 1970, Enrico Baj, 1972, Violence and Defiance, 1983. Served in USN, 1944-46. Named Fulbright scholar, 1949-51. Jewish. Office: 1356 Madison Ave New York NY 10128-0826

LUST, HERBERT COHNFELDT, III, securities trader; b. Chgo., Jan. 15, 1957; s. Herbert Cohnfeldt Lust II and Frances Ratcliffe Hutchins; m. Melani D'amore Espinosa, May 17, 1997; 1 child, Terry Grosvenor Hutchins. BA, NYU, 1976, MBA, 1986. Account rep., ltd. ptnr. Herzfeld & Stern, N.Y.C., 1978-88; portfolio mgr. distressed investments Halcyon Investments, 1988-89; head distressed rsch. Bear Stearns & Co., 1990-94; co-head high yield dept. Furman Selz, 1994-95; head distressed rsch. Lehman Bros., 1995-97; bus. mgr. distressed securities Smith Barney, 1997-98, J.P. Morgan, N.Y.C., 1998—. Author: Alexandera Finds Out. Home: 7609 Stonewood Ct Minneapolis MN 55439-2640

LÜST, REIMAR, foundation president; b. Wuppertal, Germany, 1923; BS Physics, U. Frankfurt, Germany, 1949; Ph. D., Max-Planck Inst., Göttingen, Germany, 1955; Fulbright fellow, Enrico Fermi Inst. U. Chgo., Germany, 1955-56; Habilitation, U. Munich TH, Germany, 1959. Vis. prof. NYU, N.Y.C., 1959-60; mem. Max-Planck-Inst. f. Physik u. Astrophysik, Munich, Germany, 1960; vis. prof. MIT, Cambridge, 1961, Cal. Tech., Pasadena, 1962; dir. ESRO (European Space Research Organization), 1962-64, Inst. f. Extraterrestr. Physik, Max-Planck-Inst. f. Physik u. Astrophysik, Garching b. Munich, Germany, 1963; aus. ord. prof. U. Munich, Germany, 1963-72; hon. prof. U. Munich TH, Germany, 1963-72; v.p. ESRO, Germany, 1968-70; chmn. Wissenschaftsrat, Germany, 1969-72; pres. Max-Planck-Gesellschaft zur Förderung der Wissenschaften, 1972-84; gen. dir. Europäische Weltraumorganisation, Paris, France, 1984-90; pres. Alexander von Humboldt-Stiftung, Bonn, Germany, 1989-99, hon. pres. Germany, 1999—; prof. U. Hamburg, Germany, 1992. Max-Planck-Inst., Göttingen, Physics, 1951-55, Fulbright Fellow, Enrico Fermi Inst., U. Chicago, 1955-56; chmn. bd. Internat. U. Bremen, 1999—. Office: Humboldt Found Max Planck Inst Bundesstraße 55 D-20146 Hamburg Germany

LUSTED, DONA SANDERS, music educator, consultant, organist; b. Washington, Oct. 2, 1951; d. Troy Harry and Rosemarie (Klemann) Sanders; m. Barry Emile Lusted, Nov. 7, 1982; children: Lori Marie, Luke Alan. Degree in ch. music, Evang. Landeskirchen Musik., Dusseldorf, Germany, 1969; BS in Music Edn. and German, Jacksonville State U., 1973; MM in Piano Performance, La. State U., 1975, PhD in Music, 1984. Instr. Northeastern Okla. State U., Tahlequah, 1975-76, Baker (La.) Mid. Sch., 1976-77; organist First United Meth Ch., Tahlequah, 1975-76; assoc. dir. music, organist Broadmoor United Meth. Ch., Baton Rouge, 1977—; pvt. music instr. Okla., Ala., La., 1969—; instr. La. State U., Baton Rouge, 1978-79. Dir. Summer Music and Arts/Theater Camp, Baton Rouge, 1987—; adjudicator Okla. Fedn. Music Clubs, Muskogee, 1976, Bayouland Choral Festival, Nichols State U., Thibadoux, 1994, 2000, Baton Rouge Choral Soc., 1978-79; co-founder/codir. South La. chpt. Choristers Guild, 1994-2000. Mem. Am. Guild Organists, Music Tchrs. Nat. Assn., La. Fedn. Music Clubs, Baton Rouge Piano Tchrs. Methodist. Avocations: swimming, reading, traveling. Home: 10709 Waverland Dr Baton Rouge LA 70815-5056 Office: Broadmoor United Meth Ch 10230 Mollylea Dr Baton Rouge LA 70815-4698

LUSTENADER, BARBARA DIANE, human resources executive; b. Albany, N.Y., Nov. 26, 1953; d. Charles Elmer and Janet Barbara (Bergh) Setzer; m. Robert Alan Lustenader, May 20, 1972. BA in English, Coll. St. Rose, Albany, 1974; MA in English, SUNY, Oswego, 1979. Cert. sr. profl. human resources (SPHR); cert. tgn. generalist; cert. instrnl. designer; cert. tng. facilitator; cert. master trainer; cert. acad. cert. diplomate. Tchr. English Port Byron (N.Y.) Cen. Schs., 1974-79; saleswoman Miller/Hahn, Auburn, N.Y., 1979-80; exec. asst. to v.p. devel. Wells Coll., Aurora, 1980-83, adminstrv. asst. to pres., 1983-85, assoc. dir. admissions, 1985-87; asst. div. mgr. human resources Yaskawa Electric Am., Inc., Northbrook, Ill., 1987-89, div. mgr. corp. adminstrn. and human resources, 1989-90, dir. adminstrn. and human resources, br. mgr., 1990-94; pres. Lake Assocs., Inc., Albany, 1994—. Adj. instr. Coll. St. Rose, 2002-; spkr. in field, 1994—. Bd. dirs., co-chair student chpts. CRHRA, 2001-2002, v.p., 2002—; Lake County (Ill.) Youth Conservation Corps, 1993-96, chmn. 501(3) (c) com., 1993-94; bd. dirs., vol., co-chmn. Friends Schweinfurth Meml. Art Ctr., Auburn, 1983; bd. dirs., sec., chmn. human resource com., nominating com. YWCA Lake and McHenry Counties, 1995-97. Mem.: LWV (bd. dirs., fin. chmn. Cayuga County, N.Y. chpt. 1984—86, Mundelein chpt. 1988—90, 1996—97), ASTD, Am. Acad. Cert. Consultants and Experts, Capital Region Human Resource Assn. (bd. dirs. 2001—02, v.p. bd. dirs. 2002—), Conn. Bus. and Industry Assn., Bus. Coun. N.Y. State, Lake County Women in Mgmt. (awards com. 1991, 1994, 1995, chair 1996, chair program com. 1994—96, Women of Achievement award 1996), Am. Soc. Healthcare Human Resource Adminstrs., Worldat-Work, No. Ill. Bus. Assn. (co-chmn. pers. generalists roundtable 1987—97, compensation com. 1989—2000, human resources policies and practices com. 1989—2000, Outstanding Individual Contbr. award 1995), No. Ill. Soc. Human Resource Mgmt. (fin. com. 1990, cert. com. 1995—96, program com. 1996—97, Profl. Excellence award 1995), Nat. Women in Mgmt. Orgn. (Charlotte Danstrom award 1996), Basically Bach (devel. com. 1991). Office: Lake Assocs Inc 18 Thatcher St Albany NY 12207-3009

LUSTGARTEN, CELIA SOPHIE, freelance consultant, writer; b. N.Y.C., Oct. 24, 1941; d. Benjamin and Sarah Goldie (Marcus) L. Contbr. short stories and poetry to lit. publs., including Shameless Hussy Rev., Cow in Road, Egad!, Apocalypse 3, Grasslands Rev., New Canadian Rev., Herspectives, Perceptions, Spokes, T.O.P.S. No. 69. Recipient 1st prize for short story Alt. Realities Soc. and Imaginative Fiction Soc., Victoria, B.C., Can., 1986. Mem. Internat. Women's Writing Guild, Poets and Writers. Avocation: travel. Home: 317 3rd Ave San Francisco CA 94118-2402 E-mail: cswildfire@earthlink.net.

LUSTIG, DAVID CARL, III, lawyer; b. Walden, N.Y., July 6, 1954; s. David Carl, Jr. and Violet (Rosenblum) L.; m. Debra Silver, Aug. 13, 1977; children: David, Evan. BS magna cum laude, Syracuse U., 1975; JD, Hofstra U., 1978. Bar: N.Y. 1979, U.S. Dist. Ct. (so. dist.) N.Y. 1979, U.S. Dist. Ct. (ea. dist.) N.Y. 1979, U.S. Ct. Appeals (2d cir.) 1986, U.S. Supreme Ct. 1993. Assoc. Esau J. Mishkin, Garden City, N.Y., 1978-79, Arye & Kors, P.C., N.Y.C., 1979-84; ptnr. Arye, Kors, Lustig & Sassower, 1984—. Lectr. in field. Mem. ATLA, ACLU, N.Y. State Trial Lawyers Assn. (bd. dirs.), N.Y. County Lawyers Assn., Am. Bd. Trial Advocates, Jewish Lawyers Guild, Am. Civil Liberties Union. Office: Arye Lustig & Sassower PC 20 Vesey St New York NY 10007-2913

LUSTIG, DOUGLAS JAMES, lawyer; b. Rochester, N.Y., July 19, 1949; s. Abraham and Ilene (Liberman) L.; m. Karen Ann Schiff, Aug. 17, 1975; children: Benjamin, JoEllen, Lindsay. BS, Syracuse (N.Y.) U., 1971; JD, Bklyn. Law Sch., 1974. Bar: N.Y. 1975, U.S. Dist. Ct. (we. dist.) N.Y. 1975, U.S. Supreme Ct. 1984. Assoc. Laverne, Sortino & Hanks, Rochester, 1975-79; ptnr. Laverne, Sortino, Hanks & Lustig, 1979-84; sole practice, 1984-94; ptnr. Saperston & Day PC, 1997—2001, Chamberlain, D'Amanda, Oppenheimer & Greenfield, 2001—. Mem. U.S. panel of trustees We. Dist. N.Y., Bankruptcy Ct., 1983—; lectr. N.Y. State Bar Assn., Monroe County Bar Assn., Nat. Bus. Inst. Past pres. Jewish Family Svc. of Rochester, Inc.; v.p. Helping People With AIDS. Mem. ABA, N.Y. State Bar Assn., Monroe County Bar Assn., Yates County Bar Assn., Nat. Assn. Bankruptcy Trustees, Comml. Law League, Am. Bankruptcy Inst. (pres.), Irondequoit Country Club. Republican. Jewish. Home: 17 S Pittsford Hill Ln Pittsford NY 14534-2896 Office: 800 First Federal Plz Rochester NY 14614-1916 also: 100 E Main St Penn Yan NY 14527-1668 Fax: 585-232-3882. E-mail: djl@dog.com.

LUSTIG, GRAHAM, artistic director; b. London; Student, Royal Ballet. Joined Dutch Nat. Ballet, prin. dancer; co-founder Dance Advance; joined Sadler's Wells Royal Ballet (now Birmingham Royal Ballet), 1980, prin. dancer. Choreographer-in-residence Washington Ballet. Choreographer Thanatos Instinct (Dutch Ministry on Culture award), Evening; commd. works include Peter Pan for Scottish Ballet, Uncertain Stages, George's Day Out and The Shrew for Introdans, D'Ensemble for No. Ballet Theatre, Appassionato for Singapore Dance Theatre, A Far Cry for Hartford Ballet, Borderlines for BalletMet. Office: Am Repertory Ballet Co 301 N Harrison St Princeton NJ 08540-3512

LUSTIG, JOANNE, librarian; b. Newark, July 22, 1952; d. Melvin and Grace Ann (Kertsmar) L.; m. Glenn Seggel, Mar. 26, 1988. BA summa cum laude, Montclair State Coll., 1975; MLS, Rutgers U., 1978. Asst. libr. Sterling Drug Inc., N.Y.C., 1979-80, sr. editor, 1980; info. specialist Knoll Pharms., Whippany, N.J., 1980-82, sr. info. specialist, 1982-84, mgr. med. and sci. info., 1984-96, assoc. dir. med. and sci. info., 1996—. Bd. dirs. Highlands Regional Libr. Coop., Chester, N.J., 1990-94, pres. 1991-92; mem. N.J. Libr. Network Strategic Planning Com., 1990-91. Mem. NAFE, Spl. Librs. Assn. (N.J. chpt. pres. 1987-88, v.p. 1986-87, editor bull. 1984-86, Pharm. Divsn. archivist 1989-90, chair regional program planning com. 1985-86), Soc. for Competitive Intelligence Profls., Drug Info. Assn. Jewish. Office: Knoll Pharms 3000 Continental Dr N Budd Lake NJ 07828-1234

LUSTIG, ROBERT ALLAN, radiation oncologist; b. Newark, Mar. 28, 1944; s. Seymour and Gertrude (Clarin) L.; m. Susie Jo Birenbaum; children: Julia, Alexa. BS, Franklin and Marshall Coll., 1966; MD, Jefferson Med. Coll., 1969. Diplomate Am. Bd. Radiology. Intern Met. Hosp., N.Y.C., 1969-70, resident, 1970-71; resident in radiation oncology Thomas Jefferson U. Hosp., Phila., 1973-76; asst. radiation oncologist Cooper Hosp., Univ. Med. Ctr.,

Camden, N.J., 1976-79, attending radiation oncologist, 1979-80, 81—, acting chief dept. radiation oncology, 1980-81; instr. Jefferson Med. Coll., Phila., 1976-80, asst. prof., 1980—; clin. asst. prof. U. Medicine and Dentistry N.J./Robert Wood Johnson Med. Sch., Camden, 1985-89, clin. assoc. prof., 1989-98; clin. assoc. prof., assoc. chmn. clin. rsch. dept. radiation oncology Hosp. U. Pa., Phila., 1998—. Cons. in radiation oncology Our Lady of Lourdes Hosp., Camden, West Jersey Hosp. Sys., Camden, Univ. Med. Ctr., Stratford, NJ; presenter in field. Contbr. articles to profl. publs. Med. officer USN, 1971-73. Am. Cancer Soc. fellow, 1974-75, 83-84, 84-85. Fellow Am. Coll. Radiology (mem. various coms., prin. investigator, chmn. data accession com.); mem. AMA, AAAS, Am. Soc. Therapeutic Radiology and Oncology, Radiol. Soc. N.Am., N.J. Med. Soc., Am. Soc. Clin. Oncology. Office: Hosp U Pa Dept Radiation Oncology 3400 Spruce St Philadelphia PA 19104-4206

LUSTIG, SUSAN GARDNER, occupational therapist; b. Beloit, Wis., Apr. 27, 1942; d. James and Sally Howell; m. Karl Lustig, Aug. 16, 1969 (div. 1997); children: Kurt, Daniel, Benjamin, David, Amy, Richard, Lauren. BS with distinction, U. Minn., 1965. Lic. occupl. therapist. Occupl. therapist Minn. State Hosp., Hastings, 1965-66; occupl. therapy cons. Hawaii Divsn. Vocat. Rehab., Honolulu, 1966-67; occupl. therapist Kaneohe (Hawaii) State Hosp., 1967, Minn. VA Hosp., Mpls., 1967-68, unit supervisor, 1968-70; chief occupl. therapist, occupl. therapy dept. mgr. Avery Health Care Sys., Newland, N.C., 1997-2000; established occupational therapy depts. Rehab Works/Autumn Care Marion.Autumn Care Drexel, 2000—01; occupl. therapist RehabWorks/Autumn Care, Marion, Drexel, 2000—. Pres. LaSalle County (Ill.) Med. Aux., 1976—78; pianist, Sunday sch. tchr. Long Ridge Bapt. Ch.; bd. dirs. Harrison County Sheltered Workshop, 1971—72, Ottawa (Ill.) Pub. Health Nursing, 1976—78, Cooking for Christ, 1998—, Heartland Christian Acad. Sch., 1986—88, Diversified Industries, Port Angeles, Wash., 1980—82. Mem.: N.C. Occupl. Therapy Assn., Nat. Bd. for Cert. of Occupl. Therapists, Am. Occupl. Therapy Assn. Republican. Baptist. Avocations: organ, antiques, woodcarving, ice skating, reading. Home: 15 Little Cow Camp Rd Newland NC 28657-8704

LUSTIK, BORIS, pediatrician; b. Nov. 23, 1939; MD, Nat. U. Mex., Mexico City, 1965. Attending physician J.T. Mather Hosp., Port Jefferson, N.Y., 1971—, St. Charles Hosp., Port Jefferson, 1971—, SUNY, Stony Brook, 1980—; clin. assoc. prof. pediatrics Univ. Hosp., SUNY, 1997—. Address: 239 Boyle Rd Selden NY 11784-1955

LUSZTIG, PETER ALFRED, university dean, educator; b. Budapest, Hungary, May 12, 1930; s. Alfred Peter and Susan (Szabo) L.; m. Penny Bicknell, Aug. 26, 1961; children: Michael, Cameron, Carrie. B in Com., U. B.C., Vancouver, Can., 1954; MBA, U. Western Ont., London, Can., 1955; PhD, Stanford U., 1964. Asst. to comptroller B.C. Electric, Vancouver, 1955-57; instr. fin. U. B.C., 1957-60, asst. prof. fin., 1962-64, assoc. prof., 1968-95, Killam sr. research fellow, 1968-69, prof., 1965-68, dean faculty commerce, 1977-91, dean emeritus, 1995—. Chair, bd. trustees BC Health Benefit Trust; bd. dirs. Canfor Corp., Royal Sun Alliance (Can.) Western Assurance, Que. Assurance, Roins Fin. Holdings; fed. commr. BC Treaty Commn., 1995—; vis. prof. IMEDE, Switzerland, 1973-74, London Grad. Sch. Bur. Studies, 1968-69, Pacific Coast Banking Sch., 1977—; sr. advisor B.C. Ministry of Econ. Devel., Small Bus. and Trade, 1991. Author: Report of the Royal Commission on Automobile Insurance, 2 vols., 1968, Financial Management in a Canadian Setting, 6th rev. edit., 2001, Report of the Commission on the B.C. Tree Fruit Industry, 1990. Ford Found. faculty dissertation fellow, Stanford U., 1964. Lutheran. Office: BC Treaty Commn 203 1155 W Pender St Vancouver BC Canada V6E 2Z2 E-mail: p.lusztig@shaw.ca.

LUTER, JOSEPH WILLIAMSON, III, meat packing and processing company executive; b. Smithfield, Va., 1940; married BBA, Wake Forest Coll., 1962. Pres. Smithfield Packing Co., Arlington, Va., 1964-69, Bryce Mountain Resort Inc., 1969-75; with Smithfield Foods Inc., Arlington, 1975—, pres., 1975-86, 89—, chief exec. officer, 1975—, chmn., 1977—. Office: Smithfield Foods Inc 200 Commerce St Smithfield VA 23430-1204*

LUTES, DONALD HENRY, architect; b. San Diego, Mar. 7, 1926; s. Charles McKinley and Helen (Bjoraker) L.; m. Donnie Wageman, Aug. 14, 1949; children: Laura Jo, Gail Eileen, Dana Charles. B.Arch., U. Oreg., 1950. Pvt. archtl. practice, Springfield, Oreg., 1956-58; ptnr. John Amundson, 1958-70; pres. Lutes & Amundson, 1970-72; ptnr. Lutes/Sanetel, 1973-86. Adj. assoc. prof. architecture U. Oreg., 1964-66, 89-2000; chmn. Springfield Planning Commn., 1954-65, 93-99, Urban Design and Devel. Corp., 1968-70, Eugene Non-Profit Housing, Inc., 1970 Architect: Springfield Pub. Library, 1957, Mt. Hood Community Coll., 1965-79, Shoppers Paradise Expt. in Downtown Revitalization, 1957. Chmn. Springfield United Appeal, 1959. Served to 1st lt. AUS, 1943-46, 51-52. Decorate Bronze Star; named Jr. 1st Citizen, Springfield C. of C., 1957, 1st Citizen, 1968, Disting. Citizen, 1995. Fellow AIA (bd. dirs. 1987-90, v.p. 1991, doc. com. 1993-2000); mem. Rotary, Theta Chi. Home: 778 Crest Ln Springfield OR 97477-3601

LUTES, TODD OAKLEY, political science educator; b. Dearborn, Mich., Aug. 29, 1965; s. Oakley S. and Karen D. (Johnson) L.; m. Elaine K. Drees, Mar. 15, 1993 (div. 1996); 1 child, Lydia K. BA, Tex. Luth. Coll., 1987; MA, U. Ariz., 1989, PhD, 1995. Tchg. asst. grad. dept. U. Ariz., Tucson, 1987-91; assoc. mem. faculty Pima C.C, 1990-92; instr. polit. sci. U. Ariz., Sierra Vista, 1991-95, asst. prof., 1995—. Mem. Am. Polit. Sci. Assn. Lutheran. Office: U Ariz 1140 Colombo Ave Sierra Vista AZ 85635-2390

LUTEY, JOYCE LOUISE, real estate broker; b. Canton, Ohio, Jan. 11, 1946; d. William Clayton and Virginia Ruth (Wilgus) Sommers; m. Paul E. Lutey (dec. Feb. 2002); children: David Michael Calhoun, Traci Lyn Calhoun Tedrick. Student, U. Chattanooga, 1963-65, Mansfield Bus. Coll., Canton, Ohio, 1991-93, Assoc in Bus. Adminstrn., 1993. Cert. property mgr. Property mgr. Niebel Realty, North Canton, Ohio, 1981-85, Century 21 Americana Properties, St. Petersburg, Fla., 1987, Royal Estate Mgmt. Corp., Canton, 1989-90; pres., broker Greystone Group, 1989-99, Ostendorf-Morris Co., Canton, 1993-96; office leasing cons. Remax/Sedona, Ariz., 1999-2000; receptionist, asst. property mgr. Coldwell Banker First Affiliate, Sedona, 2000—01; asst. property mgr. Coldwell Banker, Mabery-Cottonwood, 2001—02; office supr. Lake Clarke Gardens Condominium, Inc., 2002—. Office supr. Lake Clarke Gardens Condominium, Inc. Mem. AARP, Nat. Assn. Realtors, Ariz. Assn. Realtors, Sedona, Verde Valley Assn. Realtors, Inst. Real Estate Mgmt. (Phoenix chpt. # 47), Women's Coun. Realtors (phone chmn. 1982, publicity chmn. 1983, treas. 1984, pres.-elect 1985, phone com. 1990), Canton/Massilon-St. Petersburg Bd. Realtors (program com. 1982-85, bldg. com. 1985, equal opportunity in housing com. 1990), Nazir Caldron Supreme Caldron (past Mighty Chosen One), Order Ea. Star (Delta chpt. # 539), VFW Auxiliary. Avocations: music, reading. Home: 3408 Cypress Trail # A103 West Palm Beach FL 33461

LUTGEN, ROBERT RAYMOND, newspaper editor; b. Fairmont, Minn., Oct. 27, 1949; s. William J. and Barbara Estella (Sanger) L.; m. Teresa L. Palm, July 17, 1971; children: Mark, Kyle, Laura. BA, Ctrl. Wash. State Coll., 1971. Reporter, asst. city editor Yakima (Wash.) Herald Republic, 1970-77; city editor Bryan (Tex.) Eagle, 1977-81, Texarkana (Tex.) Gazette, 1981-83, mng. editor, 1983-87; asst. mng. editor Ark. Dem., 1987-91; mng. editor Ark. Dem.-Gazette, 1991-99, Chattanooga Times Free Press, 1999—. Recipient Best News Story award, Editorial Writing award, Headline Writing award AP Mng. Editors Assn., 1985. Mem. Ark. AP (pres. 1989-90), Mng. Editors Assn. (bd. dirs. 1986-91). Avocations: travel, golf, reading. Home: 141 S Brent Dr Ringgold GA 30736-8243 Office: Chattanooga Times Free Press 400 E 11th St Chattanooga TN 37403-4203 E-mail: lutgen1@aol.com.

LUTH, JAMES CURTIS, systems consultant; b. Fairmont, Minn., May 19, 1961; s. Richard H. and Doris M. (Shockley) L.; m. Susan Marie Euteneuer, Aug. 6, 1994; children: Jacqueline Briann, Kevin James. BA, Wartburg Coll., Waverly, Iowa, 1983; MBA, U. Minn., 1992. Programmer, analyst Grinnell (Iowa) Mut. Reins Co., 1984-86; systems cons., Analyst Internat. Corp., Rochester, Minn., 1986-88; analyst Internat. Corp., Mpls., 1988-89; systems cons. Analytical Techs., Inc., St. Paul, 1989-94; sys. cons. AstroTek Inc., Savage, Minn., 1994-95; ind. sys. cons., 1995—. George A. Hormel Co. merit scholar, 1979; Wartburg Coll. scholar, 1979. Methodist. Avocations: sports, personal computing, investing. Home: 15038 Monterey Ave S Savage MN 55378-4642

LUTH, WILLIAM CLAIR, retired research manager; b. Winterset, IA, June 28, 1934; s. William Henry Luth and Ora Anna (Klingaman) Sorenson; m. Betty L. Heubrock, Aug. 23, 1953; children: Linda Diane, Robert William, Sharon Jean. BA in Geology, U. of Iowa, 1958, MS in Geology, 1960; PhD in Geochemistry, Penn State U., 1963. Research assoc. in geochemistry Pa. State U., University Park, Pa., 1963-65; asst. prof. geochemistry MIT, Cambridge, Mass., 1965-68; assoc. prof. geology Stanford U., 1968-77, prof. of geology, 1977-79; supr. geophysics div. Sandia Nat. Labs, Albuquerque, 1979-82, mgr. geosciences dept., 1982-90; mgr. geoscis. rsch. program U.S. Dept. Energy, Washington, 1990-95, acting dir. divsn. engring. & geosci., 1994-95, dir. divsn. engring and geosci., 1996; ret., 1996. Geoscientist US ERDA/DOE Washington, 1976-78; faculty sabbatical Sandia Laboratories, Albuquerque, N. Mex., 1975, visiting staff mem. Los Alamos Nat. Lab, 1978. Contbr. articles to profl. jours. Served with U.S. Army, 1953-56. Grantee NSF, 1964-78. Avocations: photography, travel. Home: 653 N 63d Pl Mesa AZ 85205-6745 E-mail: wluth@cox.net.

LUTHER, AMANDA LISA, producer; b. La Mesa, Calif., Apr. 27, 1959; d. Edward Earl Jr. and Hilda (Bender) Marsh; m. Jeffrey Henry Luther, June 18, 1994; children: April Wilhelmina, Carly Julietta. Student, UCLA, 1977-79; BA in Fine Arts, Columbia Coll., 1981. Freelance prodn. mgr., L.A., 1980-90; Coordinating prodr. Telepictures, Burbank, Calif., 1991-94, Saban Entertainment, Valencia, 1995-98; freelance prodr., 1999—. Host Antelope Valley Home & Garden Show, The Official Fair Show; contbg. author: Cooking at the Library. Mem. Earth Comms. Office, Mom's Club of East Palmdale. Avocations: dance, camping, films, crafts, cooking. Home: 37402 Harrow Ct Palmdale CA 93550-7742

LUTHER, BRUCE CHARLES, sound technician; b. Pequannock, N.J., Mar. 20, 1964; s. Bruce Frederick Luther and Diane Mae Thompson Neubert; m. Jacquelyn Anne D'Amico, May 22, 1992. Cert. Audio Rsch., W. Milford, N.J., 1983. Recording engr. Twain Recording Studio, W. Milford, 1982-86; ops. mgr. Rabsons of 57th St., N.Y.C., 1986-90; sound engr. Sound Stage Corp., 1990; a/v cons. Harvey Electronics, 1990-91, Sound City, N.Y.C., 1991-92; tech. v.p. Sound Sight Technologies Corp., 1992—. DBS cons. Sundance, Aspen, Colo., 1996, NFL, N.Y.C., 1995; DBS cons/technician WNBC, N.Y.C., 1994; DBS mgmt. 1st Brokers Corp., N.Y.C., 1995; sound tech., audio/video expert for pvt. home sys.; audio cons. WNBC News, Internat. longevity Ctr. of Columbia U., NFA., SEC. Regional dir. Jerry Brown for Pres., N.Y.C., 1992. Mem. CBGB & OmFug Engring. Democrat. Buddhist. Office: Sound Sight Technologies Corp 124 W 30th St Ste 208 New York NY 10001-4013

LUTHER, DAVID BYRON, management consultant; b. Utica, N.Y., May 26, 1936; s. Everett David and Mary (Brown) L.; m. Geraldine Frost; children: Leslie, Gregory, Valorie. BS, Syracuse U., 1958, MBA, 1961. Mfg. mgr. Corning Glass Works, 1962-74, dir. pers. resources, 1974-76, asst. corp. contr., 1976-78, dir. corp. planning, 1978-79, dir. info. svcs., 1979-80, v.p. pers., 1980-83, v.p. quality, 1983-85, sr. v.p., corp. dir. quality, 1985-94; founder, prin. Luther Quality Assocs., Corning, then Fairfield, Conn., 1994—. V.p. ops. Green Mountain Energy Resources, South Burlington, Vt., 1998-99; exec. in residence Syracuse U. Sch. Bus., 1994-96; mem. exec. session on pub. sector mgmt. Harvard U. Kennedy Sch., 1998-2000; mem. conf. bd. steering com. Global Ctr. for Performance Excellence; nat. chmn. Koalaty Kid Edn. Project; judge Malcolm Baldrige Nat. Quality award, 1988-91. Fellow Am. Soc. Quality (chmn. 1995-96, pres. 1994-95); mem. Internat. Acad. of Quality. Home: 157 Greenfield Hill Rd Fairfield CT 06828 Office: Luther Quality Assoc PO Box 320185 Fairfield CT 06432-0185 E-mail: dbluther@compuserve.com.

LUTHER, GEORGE ALBERT, truck brokerage executive; b. Pulaski, N.Y., Feb. 16, 1926; s. Leslie Leon and Bertha Adelaide (Kind) L.; m. Lucile Pauline Lane, May 26, 1945; children: John Paul, Roger Lane. Grad., Ithaca (N.Y.) High Sch., 1943. Driver Mayflower Van Lines, Ithaca, 1946-47, Red Star Express, Auburn, N.Y., 1947-52; owner, operator B&L Trucking, Locke, 1952-56; transport broker Cross Country Truck Svc. Inc., Lakeland, Fla., 1956-61, Horne Distbrs., Inc., Sanford, 1961-62; office mgr., broker Cross Country Truck Svc., Inc., Lakeland, 1962-67, Haines City (Fla.) Truck Brokers, Inc., 1967-84, co-owner, 1984-88. Pres. Nat. Agrl. Transp. League, Tavares and Leesburg, Fla., 1966-67, 75-77; v.p. Fla. Watermelon Growers & Distbrs. Assn., Lakeland, 1972-74, Nat. Watermelon Growers & Distbrs. Assn., Morven, Ga., 1974-75. Editor, writer Luther Family newsletter, 1986—; pub. Luther Family in Am., 1976, Luther Genealogy, 2001; contbr. articles to mags. Sec., chief exec. officer, genealogist Luther Family Assn., Lakeland, 1986—. Avocations: history, genealogy. Home: 2027 Spyglass Ct Lakeland FL 33810-6737 E-mail: luthergen@juno.com.

LUTHER, JOHN STAFFORD, biology educator, consultant; b. Apr. 5, 1943; s. John Andrew and Marcia (Stafford) L.; div.; 1 child, David. BA, Beloit (Wis.) Coll., 1965; MA, Calif. State Coll., Hayward, 1968. Mem. faculty dept. biology Merritt Coll., Oakland, Calif., 1968-70; mem. faculty Coll. of Alameda, 1970—. Chmn. sci. and math. div., Coll. of Alameda, 1973-75; cons. Environ. Impacts Reports, 1972—; leader natural history trips, 1978—; mem. Ednl. Use Adv. Com., East Bay Regional Park Dist., 1981-90. Contbr. articles to Western Birds; mem. editl. bd. Western Birds. Tchr. natural sci. docent program Oakland Mus., 1987-2000. Mem. Western Field Ornithologists (pres. 1978-81, dir. 1975-91), Calif. Bird Records Com. (sec. 1976-81), Sierra Club, Am. Birding Assn., Golden Gate Audubon Soc. (bd. dirs., 2002-), Nature Conservancy, Point Reyes Bird Obs., Alameda County Breeding Bird Atlas (bd. dirs.), Oakland Zoo-East Bay Zool. Soc., Calif. Acad. Scis., San Francisco Bay Bird Obs. Home: 6511 Exeter Dr Oakland CA 94611-1641 Office: Coll of Alameda 555 Atlantic Ave Alameda CA 94501-2109

LUTHER, MICHAEL R. federal agency administrator; BS in Math., Birmingham-So. Coll.; MS in Applied Math., Auburn U. Rschr. pvt. industry; various tech., mgmt. and exec. positions NASA, Washington, dep. assoc. adminstr. Office Earth Sci., 1998—. Sr. fellow Harvard U. John F. Kennedy Sch. Mgmt., 1990. Avocations: music, sports, travel. Office: NASA Hdqrs Mail Code Y 300 E St SW Washington DC 20546

LUTHER, RICHARD S. music educator; b. Placerville, Calif., Nov. 21, 1951; s. Emerald R. and Barbara R. Luther; m. Kathleen H. Luther; 1 child Erin 1 child Ben 1 child Sam. BA, Calif. State U., Chico, 1974. Cert. tchr. Calif., 1974. Dir. music Vacaville (Calif.) HS, 1983—. Dir. honor band No. Counties HS. Dir.: (Honor Band) Northern Counties High School Honor Band. Mem.: Nat. Music Educators Conf. Avocation: golf. Home: 370 Camellia Way Vacaville CA 95688 Office: Vacaville Unified Sch Dist 751 School St Vacaville CA 95688 Home Fax: 707-447-5607; Office Fax: 707-447-5607. Personal E-mail: Rloo@aol.com. Business E-Mail: RickL@VUSD.SolanoCOE.K12.CA.US.

LUTHER, THOMAS WILLIAM, retired physician; b. Milw., Feb. 27, 1925; s. Elmer Charles and Ida Martha (Sohrweide) L.; m. Warrene E. Luther; children: Brian Thomas, Siri Karen Luther Witt. BS, U. Wis., 1947, MD, 1950. Diplomat Am. Bd. Dermatology. Intern West Suburban Hosp., Oak Park, Ill., 1950-51; resident VA Hosps., 1951-52, 55-56, U. Pa., 1954-55. Lt. USN, 1943-54. Fellow Am. Acad. Dermatology; mem. AMA, Wis. Med. Soc., Wis. Dermatologic Soc., Appleton Rotary. Avocations: archaeology, genealogy. Home: 1936 Palisades Dr Appleton WI 54915-1023

LUTHER, WILLIAM P. congressman; b. Fergus Falls, Minn., June 27, 1945; s. Leonard and Eleanor L.; m. Darlene Luther, Dec. 16, 1967; children: Alexander, Alicia. BS in Elec. Engring. with high distinction, U. Minn., 1967; JD cum laude, U. Minn. Law Sch., 1970. Judicial clerkship 8th cir. U.S. Ct. Appeals, 1970-71; atty. Dorsey & Whitney Law Firm, Mpls., 1971-74, William P. Luther Law Office, Mpls., 1974-83; founder, sr. ptnr. Luther, Ballenthin & Carruthers Law Firm, 1983-92; state sen. 47th dist. State of Minn., 1977-94, asst. maj. leader, 1983-94; mem. U.S. Congress from 6th Minn. dist., 1995—; mem. commerce com., telecomm., trade & consumer protection , fin., hazardous materials subcoms. Home: 6375 Saint Croix Trl N Apt 147 Stillwater MN 55082-6932 Office: US House Reps 117 Cannon House Office Bldg Washington DC 20515-2306 also: 1811 Weir Dr Ste 150 Woodbury MN 55125-2291*

LUTHER-LEMMON, CAROL LEN, elementary school educator; b. Waverly, N.Y., May 8, 1955; d. Carl Ross and Mary Edith (Auge) Luther; m. Mark Kevin Lemmon, June 21, 1986; children: Matthew C., Cathryn M. BS, Ithaca Coll., 1976; MS in Edn., Elmira Coll., 1982. Cert. elem. and secondary tchr., Pa., N.Y. Reading aide Waverly (N.Y.) Central Schs., 1978-80; tchr. reading N.Y. State Div. for Youth, Lansing, 1981-82; tchr. title I reading, mem. student assistance program and instructional support team Rowe Mid. Sch., Athens (Pa.) Area Sch. Dist., 1982-94; tchr. Title I reading Lynch Elem. Sch., 1995—. Basketball coach Youth Activities Dept., Athens, 1982-85, asst. softball coach, 1990-91; mem. ad hoc com. Waverly Sch. Dist., 1990-91; mem. Goal G parents & edn. Mid. Sch. Implementation Team for WINGS-Waverly in a Global Soc. for Waverly Ctr. Sch. Dist. Strategic Plan; bd. dirs. SACC, 1995-96, Waverly Cmty. Ch., 1976-78; active Girls' Softball League Waverly, 1978-80, 99, commr., 1980; choir mem. Meth. Ch., Wverly, 1976-90, 97—, adminstrv. bd., trustee, chmn. bd. trustees, 1995, 96, 2001—; mem. Valley Chorus, Pa. and N.Y., 1983-86, 98—; mem. Village of Waverly Recreation Commn., 1999—. With USAR, 1977-83. Mem. ASCD, AAUW (v.p. Waverly br. 1982-83, pres. Waverly br. 1992-97), Am. Legion Aux. (girl's state rep. 1972, girl's state chmn. 1976-80 Waverly post, counselor 1977), Chemung Area Reading Coun., N.Y. State Reading Assn. Republican. Home: 490 Waverly St Waverly NY 14892-1102 Office: Athens Area Sch Dist Pennsylvania Ave Athens PA 18810-1440 E-mail: ccmml@stny.rr.com.

LUTHEY, GRAYDON DEAN, JR. lawyer, educator; b. Topeka, Sept. 18, 1955; s. Graydon Dean Sr. and S. Anne (Murphy) L.; m. Deborah Denise McCullough, May 26, 1979; children: Sarah Elizabeth, Katherine Alexandra. BA in Letters with highest honors, U. Okla., 1976, JD, 1979; Fellow in Theology, Oxford (Eng.) U., 1976. Bar: Okla. 1979, U.S. Ct. Appeals (10th cir.) 1979, U.S. Dist. Ct. (no., we. and ea. dists.) Okla. 1980, U.S. Supreme Ct. 1982. Assoc. Jones, Givens, Gotcher, Bogan & Hilborne, Tulsa, 1979-84, ptnr., 1984-92, also bd. dirs.; ptnr. Hall, Estill, Hardwick, Gable, Golden & Nelson, 1992—, also bd. dirs. Adj. assoc. prof. U. Tulsa, 1985-87, adj. prof., 1987—; vis. fellow in theology Keble Coll., Oxford (Eng.) U., 1976; presiding judge Okla. Temporary Ct. Appeals, 1992-93; mem. Okla. Supreme Ct. Rules Com., 1992—. Bd. dirs. Tulsa Ballet, 1987-2000; chmn. Tulsa Pub. facilties Authority, 1990-93; tustee Episcopal Theol. Sem. of S.W., 1991-99, exec. com., 1992-99; vice chmn. Univ. Hosps. Authority, 1993-94, chmn. 1994-98, sec., 1998-99; chancellor Episcopal Diocese Okla., 1986-99; mem. bd. visitors Okla. Coll. Arts and Scis., 1997—; mem. State of Okla. Futures Auth., 1998-2002, chmn., 1999-2002. Nat. Merit scholar U. Okla., 1973. Fellow Am. Bar Found.; mem. ABA, Okla. Bar Assn. (chmn. continuing legal edn. com. 1989-91), Tulsa County Bar Assn. (bd. dirs. 1983-89, Disting. Svc. award 1988), Am. Law Inst., Am. Inns of Ct., Summit Club, So. Hills Country Club, Beta Theta Pi, Phi Beta Kappa, Omicron Delta Kappa. Office: Hall Estill Hardwick Gable Golden & Nelson 320 S Boston Ave Ste 400 Tulsa OK 74103-3704 E-mail: dluthey@hallestill.com.

LUTHRA, GURINDER KUMAR, osteopath; b. Jullundur, Punjab, India, June 18, 1964; s. Satya Pal and Suraksha (Kumari) L.; m. Bhawna Narang, Mar. 20, 1989. BS in Biology with honors, U. Tex., Arlington, 1987; DO with honors, Tex. Coll. Osteo. Medicine, 1991. Rsch. technician U. Tex. Health Sci. Ctr., Houston, 1982-84, Tex. Coll. Osteo. Medicine, Ft. Worth, 1987; resident in internal medicine U. Tex. Med. Br., Galveston, 1991-94, acad. faculty in dept. internal medicine, 1994-95, fellow in gastroenterology, 1995-97, asst. prof. divsn. gastroenterology dept. internal medicine, 1997—, assoc. dir. gastroenterology fellowship program, 1997-98, dir. gastroenterology fellowship program, 1998—. Houston Osteo. Found. scholar, 1988-91, Acad. scholar U. Tex., Arlington, 1985-87. Mem. Tex. Osteo. Med. Assn., Am. Osteo. Assn., Student Osteo. Med. Assn., Psi Sigma Alpha (Membership award 1988-91). Avocations: table tennis, photography, jogging, computers. Home: 17010 Sailors Moon Ct Friendswood TX 77546-3447 Office: U Tex Med Br 301 University Blvd Galveston TX 77555-5302

LUTHRA, HARVINDER S. rheumatologist, researcher; b. Amritsar, Punjab, India, Mar. 14, 1945; arrived in U.S., 1979; s. Kishan Chand and Harbans Kaur (Nagpal) L.; m. Annu Duggal, Mar. 15, 1975; children: Payal, Gauri, Sonaar. Grad., St. Peter's Coll., 1960, St. John's Coll., Agra, UP, 1962; MBBS, Christian Med. Coll., Ludhiana, India, 1967. Rotating intern. CMC, Ludhiana, 1967, residency 1968; intern. Middlesex Gen. Hosp., New Brunswick, N.J., 1969; resident in internal med. Mt. Sinai Hosp., Chgo., 1970-72; trainee, rheumatology Mayo Clinic, Rochester, Minn., 1972-74, cons., 1975—; John Finn prof. med. Mayo Med. Sch., 1989—, chmn., divsn. rheumatology, 1996. Bd. dirs. Am. Bd. Internal Medicine, chair subsplty. rheumatology, 1998-2002. Contbr. articles to profl. jours. Achievements include research in collagen induced arthritis in mice, HLA-B27 molecule's role in arthritis. Office: Mayo Clinic 200 1st St SW Rochester MN 55905-0002 E-mail: luthra@mayo.edu.

LUTHRA, VEENA, psychiatrist; b. Pune, India, Jan. 4, 1958; came to U.S., 1995; d. Narshinghdas and Sheel K. Mehndiratta; m. Bharat B. Luthra, Jan. 19, 1986; children: Prateek, Ria. MBBS, Topiwala Nat. Med. Coll., 1980; MD, G.S. Med. Coll., 1984. Bd. cert. Am. Bd. Psychiatry and Neurology. Lectr. psychiatry G.S. Med. Coll., Bombay, India, 1985-86; cons. psychiatrist Purohit Clinic, Sharjah, United Arab Emirates, 1987-89, New Delhi, 1990-92, Psychol. Medicine Hosp., Kuwait, 1992-95; resident psychiatrist Med. Coll. Pa., Phila., 1995-98; fellow in child/adolescent psychiatry MCP-Hahnemann U., 1998—; asst. prof. dept. psychiatry Med. Coll. Pa.-Hahnemann U., 2000—. Co-owner Khajuraho Restaurant, Phila. Recipient Best of Philly award, 1999, 2001. Mem. Am. Psychiat. Assn., Am. Acad. Child & Adolescent Psychiatry, Pa. Med. Soc., South Asia Forum. Avocations: swimming, traveling, cooking, photography. Home: 311 Countryview Dr Bryn Mawr PA 19010-2036 Office: Eastern Pa Psychiat Inst 3200 Henry Ave Philadelphia PA 19129-1137 E-mail: veena.luthra@drexel.edu.

LUTHRINGSHAUSER, DANIEL RENE, manufacturing company executive; b. Fontainebleau, France, July 23, 1935; came to U.S., 1937; s. Ernest Henri and Jeanne (Guerville) L.; m. Carol King; children: Mark Ernest, Heidi Elizabeth. BS, NYU, 1956, MBA, 1970. With exec. tng. program, internat. pub. relations Merck & Co. Inc., Rahway, N.J. and N.Y.C., 1962-65; dep. mktg. dir. Merck Sharp & Dohme Internat., Brussels, 1965-66; mktg. service dir. Paris, 1966-69; gen. mgr. Merck Sharp & Dohme/Chibret, 1970-74; v.p. mktg. Merrell (France), 1974-78; v.p. gen. mgr. Revlon Devel. Corp., 1978-82, Medtronic Europe, Paris, Africa, Middle East, 1982-86; v.p. internat. Medtronic Inc., Mpls., 1986-98; prin. DRL Internat. Cons., 1998—. Bd. dirs. Medtronic Found., Mpls., 1986-91; chmn. Internat. Assn. of Prosthesis Mfrs., Paris, 1983-85. Bd. dirs. Am. Hosp. Paris, 1983-86, 94-95, Minn. Internat. Ctr., 1990—; mem. Am. Club Paris, 1970-80, Medtronic Found., Mpls., 1986-91. Served to capt. USAF, 1956-62. Recipient Gold medal Am. Mktg. Assn., 1956. Mem.: Ausable (Keene Valley, N.Y.). Avocations: gardening, golf, squash, skiing. Home: 480 Peavey Rd Wayzata MN 55391-1529 Office: PO Box 286 Wayzata MN 55391

LUTHY, RICHARD GODFREY, environmental engineering educator; b. June 11, 1945; s. Robert Godfrey Luthy and Marian Ruth (Ireland) Haines; m. Mary Frances Sullivan, Nov. 22, 1967; children: Matthew Robert, Mara Catherine, Jessica Bethlin. BSChemE, U. Calif., Berkeley, 1967; MS in Ocean Engring., U. Hawaii, 1969; MSCE, U. Calif., Berkeley, 1974, PhDCE, 1976. Registered profl. engr., Pa.; diplomate Am. Acad. Environ. Engrs. Rsch. asst. dept. civil engring. U. Hawaii, Honolulu, 1968-69; rsch. asst. div. san. and hydraulic engring. U. Calif., Berkeley, 1973-75; asst. prof. civil engring. Carnegie Mellon U., Pitts., 1975-80, assoc. prof., 1980-83, prof., 1983—, assoc. dean Carnegie Inst. Tech., 1986-89, head dept. civil and environ. engring., 1989-96, Lord prof. environ. engring., 1996-2000; Silas H. Palmer prof. dept. civil and environ. engring. Stanford (Calif.) U., 2000—. Shimizu Corp. vis. prof. dept. civil engring. Stanford U., 1996-97; cons. sci. adv. bd. U.S. EPA, 1983—, Bioremediation Action com., 1990-92; cons. U.S. Dept. Energy, 1978—, various pvt. industries; del. water sci. and tech. bd. NAE, Washington and Beijing, 1988; mem. tech. adv. bd. Remediation Techs., Inc., Concord, Mass., 1989-94, Fostin Capital, Pitts., 1991-94, Balt. Gas & Elec., 1992-95, Pa. Dept. Environ. Protection, 1994-96; mem. sci. adv. com.

Hazardous Substance Rsch. Ctr. Stanford U., 1994-99; chair Gordon Rsch. Conf. Environ. Scis., 1994; Nat. Rsch. Coun. Commn. on Innovative Remediation Tech., Com. on Intrinsic Remediation, Com. on Bioavailabilty, Water Sci. and Tech. Bd., 1997—, chair, 2000—. Contbr. articles to tech. and sci. jours. Chmn. NSF/Assn. Environ. Engring. Prof. Conf. on Fundamental Rsch. Directions in Environ. Engring, Washington, 1988. Lt. C.E. Corps, USN, 1969-72. Recipient George Tallman Ladd award Carnegie Inst. Tech., 1977. Mem. ASCE (Pitts. sect. Prof. of Yr. award 1987), Nat. Acad. Engring., Assn. Environ. Engring. Sci. Profs. (pres. 1987-88, Nalco award 1978, 82, Engring. Sci. award 1988, Svc. award 1999), Water Environ. Fedn. (rsch. com. 1982-86, awards com. 1981-84, 89-94, std. methods com. 1977—, groundwater com. 1989-90, editor jour. 1989-92, Eddy medal 1980, McKee medal 2000), Internat. Assn. on Water Quality (Foudners award U.S. Nat. Com. 1986, 93, orgnl. com. 16th Biennial Conf. Washington 1992), Am. Chem. Soc. (divsn. environ. chemistry, mem. editl. adv. bd. Environ. Sci. Tech. 1992-95). Presbyterian.

LUTKENHOUSE, ANNE, non-profit executive; b. S.I., N.Y., Feb. 18, 1957; d. Emile Anthony and Jane Anne Lutkenhouse. BA magna cum laude, Wagner Coll., 1979; cert. Goethe Inst., N.Y.C., 1981. Supr. Credit Suisse, N.Y.C., 1979-85; dist. office adminstr. N.Y. City Council, 1985-86; asst. dir., Appalachian Trail Field asst., N.Y.-N.J. Trail Conf., N.Y.C., 1986—; dir. N.J. Appalachian Trail Ridge Runner Program; contbg. cons. Wagner Coll. Study Program, Bregenz, Austria, 1978-92. Photographer, producer photography show, 1984. instr. safety program ARC, S.I., 1977; campaign aide council member Fossella, N.Y. City Council, S.I., 1985; sec., bd. dirs. South Shore Swimming Club, Inc.; pres., bd. dirs. S.I. Chamber Music Players, 1984-86; co-chmn. Flag Day Parade, Tottenville Improvement Council, Inc., 1986; vol. Am.-Scandinavian Found.; producer Appalachian Trail 50th Anniversary Celebration, N.Y., 1987; alumni agt. telefund/ann. fund Wagner Coll., 1992. Contbr. travel articles to mags; contbg. writer Appalachian Trailway News, 1987—, Appalachian Trail Guide to N.Y., N.J., 11th and 12th edits. Mem. NAFE, Am.-Scandinavian Found., Protectors of Pine Oak Woods, Norwegian-Am. C. of C. Democrat. Roman Catholic. Avocations: needlecrafts, ballet, skiing, travel. Home: 1100 Clove Rd Apt 9J Staten Island NY 10301-3633 Office: NY-NJ Trail Conf 232 Madison Ave New York NY 10016-2901

LUTRINGER, RICHARD EMIL, lawyer; b. N.Y.C., Feb. 4, 1943; s. Emil Vincent Lutringer and Alice Hamilton Rich; m. Dagmar Bonitz, May 1, 1970 (div. 1980); m. Clarinda Higgins, Oct. 11, 1980 (div. 1999); children: Emily, Eric. AB, Coll. of William and Mary, 1964; JD in Internat. Affairs, Cornell U., 1967; MCL, U. Chgo., 1969. Bar: N.Y. 1972, U.S. Dist. Ct. (so. dist.) N.Y. 1972. Assoc. Whitman & Ransom, N.Y.C., 1971-80, ptnr., 1980-94, Morgan, Lewis & Bockius LLP, N.Y.C., 1994—. V.p. N.Y.-N.J. Trail Conf., N.Y.C., 1976-80; pres. German-Am. Roundtable, Inc., 1998—. Mem. ABA, Internat. Bar Assn., Assn. of Bar of City of N.Y. (chmn. com. fgn. and comparative law 1990-93), Am. Fgn. Law Assn. (pres. 1989-93, treas. 1986-89), European-Am. C. of C. (vice-chair trade com. 1992-98), German-Amer. C of C, Inc., Philadelphia (bd. dirs., 1999—, v.p., sec. 2001—), German Am. Law Assn. (bd. dirs. 2000—). Avocations: sailing, hiking, skiing. Home: 32 Bridge St Westport CT 06880-6033 Office: Morgan Lewis & Bockius LLP 101 Park Ave New York NY 10178-0060 E-mail: rlutringer@morganlewis.com.

LUTSEP, HELMI LIIA, neurologist, educator; b. St. Paul, Mar. 31, 1962; d. Helmut and Ligita Lutsep; m. David W. Robinson, Apr. 18, 1998. BA, St. Olaf Coll., 1984; MD, Mayo Med. Sch., 1988. Diplomate Am. Bd. Psychiatry and Neurology. Neurology resident Mayo Grad. Sch. Medicine, Rochester, Minn., 1988-92; behavioral neurology fellow and attending U. Calif., Davis, 1992-95; cerebrovascular disease fellow, clin. instr. Stanford (Calif.) U., 1995-96; asst. prof. Oreg. Health Scis. U., Portland, 1996—2001, assoc. prof., 2001—. Cons. Endovasix, Inc., Belmont, Calif., 1996—; mem. spkrs. bur. Genentech, Inc., 1996—, Bristol-Myers Squibb, 1998—, Sanofi, 1998—, Boehringer Ingelheim, 1998—. Editor-in-chief: Neurology-Emedicine, 1999; contbr. chpts. to books. Grantee Small Bus. Innovation Rsch. Program, 1999, Med. Rsch. Found., Portland, 1999. Mem. Am. Acad. Neurology, Am. Heart Assn. (stroke divsn., abstract com.), Soc. for Neurosci., Estonian Cmty. Portland, Phi Beta Kappa. Avocations: volleyball, hiking, skiing, Estonian activities. Office: Oreg Stroke Ctr OHSU CR 131 3181 SW Sam Jackson Park Rd Portland OR 97201-3011 E-mail: lutseph@ohsu.edu.

LUTSKY, SHELDON JAY, financial and marketing consultant, writer; b. New Kensington, Pa., Jan. 13, 1943; s. Hyman I. and Rose S. (Schwartz) L. BS, Kent State U., 1967; postgrad., U. Colo., 1969-70. Chemist B.F. Goodrich, Akron, Ohio, 1966; with United Bank of Denver, 1968-75; founder Mountain States Ski Assn., pub. Mountain States Recreation, Denver, 1976-81; pres. Dolphin Assocs., 1981—; sec.-treas. Millennium Ballast, L.L.C., 2000—. Pres. Eagle Venture Acquisitions, Inc., 1986-90; pres. Sunburst Acquisitions I, Inc., 1997—. Co-patent developer (patent) power factor correction circuit for power supplies and electronic ballasts, 2001. Recipient Burr Photog. Achievement award Kent State U., 1965. Mem. Nat. Ski Writers Assn. Achievements include development of Slope Scope, ski slope evaluation system; patent for control cir. for poller factor correction, 2001. Home: 4807 S Zang Way Morrison CO 80465-1630 Office: Dolphin Assocs 2124 S Dayton St Denver CO 80231-3425

LUTTER, CHARLES WILLIAM, JR. lawyer; b. Kenosha, Wis., July 12, 1944; s. Charles William and Eva (Kuyawa) L.; m. Carol Hamilton Ewing, July 13, 1974; children: Charles William III, Scott. BS, U. Wis., 1966; postgrad., U. Tex., 1972; JD, St. Mary's U., 1976. Bar: Tex. 1976, U.S. Dist. Ct. (no. dist.) 1977, U.S. Dist. Ct. (so. dist.) 1981, U.S. Dist. Ct. (we. dist.) 1985, U.S. Ct. Appeals (5th and 11th cir.) 1981. Gen. atty. fin. SEC, Atlanta, 1976-80, chief regulations br. Houston, 1980-83; ptnr. Byrnes & Martin, 1983-84, Martin, Shannon & Drought, Inc., San Antonio, 1984-87; sr. corp. atty. LaQuinta Motor Inns, Inc., 1987-90; v.p., assoc. gen. counsel, sec. United Svcs. Advisors, Inc., 1991-93, v.p., spl. counsel, sec., 1993-95, legal/operational cons., 1995—; counsel to trust and ind. trustees ICON Funds, 1996—, Lindbergh Funds, 1999—, AmeriSen Funds, 2001—; of counsel MGL Cons. Corp., Houston, 2000—. Mem. planning com. Ann. Securities Regulation Conf., SEC, Tex. Securities Bd., State Bar Tex., U. Tex. Law Sch., 1986—; mem. initial exec. com. San Antonio Tech. Adv. Group, 1985-87; mem. target '90 Goals for San Antonio Sci. and Tech. Venture Task Force, 1985-90, exec. com. for forum on entrepreneurship, 1985-87; mem. estate planning coun. Southwest Found. Biomed. Rsch., San Antonio, 1987—; mem. U. Tex. Health Sci. Ctr. Estate Planning Coun., 1998—; arbitrator Nat. Assn. Securities Dealers, N.Y. Stock Exch., Mcpl. Securities Rulemaking Bd. Contbr. articles to profl. jours. Bd. dirs. Boysville, San Antonio, 1989—, mem. exec. com., 1995-99, pres., 1999; scout leader Alamo Area coun. Boy Scouts Am., 1988—. Capt. USAF, 1966-71. Decorated Air medal (6). Mem. ABA, State Bar Tex. (securities and investment banking com. 1984—, ad hoc subcom. on securities activities of banks 1987-89, subcom. on rules of fair practce for Tex. broker-dealers 1990), Internat. Assn. for Fin. Planning (bd. dirs. and regulatory coord. San Antonio chpt. 1987-98), Investment Co. Inst. (SEC rules com. 1993-95), San Antonio Bar Assn., San Antonio Bar Found., U. Wis. Alumni Assn., Air Force Assn., John M. Harlan Soc., Kiwanis, Phi Delta Phi. Office: 103 Canyon Oaks Dr San Antonio TX 78232-1305 also: care US Global Investors 7900 Callaghan Rd San Antonio TX 78229-2327 also: care MGL Cons Ste 300 100 Grogan's Mill Rd The Woodlands TX 77380

LUTTER, PAUL ALLEN, lawyer; b. Chgo., Feb. 28, 1946; s. Herbert W. and Lois (Muller) L. BA, Carleton Coll., 1968; JD, Yale U., 1971. Bar: Ill. 1971, U.S. Tax Ct. 1986. Assoc. Ross & Hardies, Chgo., 1971-77, ptnr., 1978—. Co-author: Illinois Estate Administration, 1993. Dir. Howard Brown Health Ctr.; chmn.'s coun. Design Industries Found. Fighting AIDS, Chgo. Mem. ABA, Chgo. Bar Assn. Home: 2214 N Magnolia Ave Chicago IL 60614-3104 Office: Ross & Hardies 150 N Michigan Ave Ste 2500 Chicago IL 60601-7567

LUTTERODT, CLEMENT H. mathematician, educator; b. Nsawam, Ghana, Aug. 17, 1943; arrived in U.S., 1979; s. Samuel Augustus and Olaonipekuh Lutterodt; m. Sarah Anne French, Sept. 25, 1971; children: Tobias, Isabelle, Justine. BSc, U. Ghana, Legon, 1967, MSc, 1972; PhD, U. Birmingham, Eng., 1974. Lectr. U. Cape Coast, Ghana, 1973—78, sr. lectr. Ghana, 1978—80; vis. asst. prof. U. South Fla., Tampa, 1980; asst. prof. Howard U., Washington, 1980—84, assoc. prof., 1984—90, prof., 1990—. Contbr. articles to profl. jours. Fellow, Internat. Ctr. for Theoretical Physics, Miramare, Italy, 1975, 1977, 1980, 1981, others. Mem.: N.Y. Acad. Scis., Am. Math. Soc. Achievements include creator the field of rational approximants in several complex variables. Avocations: ping-pong, walking. Office: Howard Univ Dept Math 6th St NW Washington DC 20059

LUTTIG, J. MICHAEL, federal judge; b. Tyler, TX, 1954; BA, Washington and Lee U., 1976; JD, U. Va., 1981. Asst. counsel The White House, 1981—82; law clk. to Judge Antonin Scalia U.S. Ct. of Appeals D.C. Cir., 1982—83; law clerk to chief justice Warren Burger Supreme Ct. of U.S., 1983—84, spl. asst. to chief justice Warren Burger, 1984—85; assoc. Davis Polk & Wardwell, 1985—89; prin. dep. asst. atty. gen., office of legal counsel U.S. Dept. of Justice, 1989—90, asst. atty. gen., office of legal counsel, counselor to atty. gen., 1990—91; judge U.S. Cir. Ct. (4th cir.), McLean, Va., 1991—. Mem. Nat. Adv. Com. of Lawyers for Bush, 1988, Lawyers for Bush Com., 1988. Mem.: ABA, D.C. Bar Assn., Va. Bar Assn. Office: US Ct of Appeals 4th Cir US Courthouse 401 Courthouse Sq Fl 9 Alexandria VA 22314-5704 also: US Ct Appeals 11th Cir 56 Forsyth St NW Atlanta GA 30303*

LUTTINGER, AMY LORE, secondary education educator, researcher; b. Stamford, Conn. d. Lionel and Lenore Luttinger; m. Philip Kaaret, June 7, 1992; children: Alexander Kaaret, Maija-Liisa Luttinger. BS in Physics, MIT, 1981; PhD in Molecular Biology, Princeton U., 1992. Post-doctorate Pub. Health Rsch. Inst., N.Y.C., 1992-96; prof. N.Y. Inst. Tech., 1996-98, Salem (Mass.) State Coll., 1998—. Contbr. articles to profl. jours. Office: Salem State Coll Dept Biology 352 Lafayette St Salem MA 01970-5348

LUTTNER, EDWARD F. consulting company executive; b. Cleve., Feb. 16, 1942; s. John J. and Angela (Haberbosch) L.; m. Nancy E., July 15, 1977; children: Amy, Mark. BA, Loyola U., 1966, MDiv, 1974; MA, U. Detroit, 1970. Cert. NASD. Dir. standards-devel. Bernard Haldane Assocs., Boston, Internat. Career Consulting Corp., Waltham, Mass.; v.p. career mgmt. svcs. Bernard Haldane Assocs., Cleve.; dir. profl. svcs. Right Assocs., Phila.; pres. Elby Career Group, Inc., Cleve. V.p. Rotary, Fairview Park, 1988-89. Mem. AACD, Nat. Career Devel. Assn.

LUTTON, SUZANNE RODKEY, cardiologist; b. Nov. 22, 1964; BS, Northwestern U., 1986; MD, Wayne State U., 1990. From resident in cardiology to mem. staff Cleve. Clin., 1990—97; staff cardiologist sect. heart failure/cardiac transplant Cleve. Clinic Found., 1997—2001; pvt. practice Diagnostic Cardiology Assoc., Youngstown, Ohio, 2001—. Contbr. numerous articles to profl. jours., chpts. to books. Address: 1325 Fiftrh Ave Youngstown OH 44504

LUTTRELL, GEORGIA BENA, musician; b. Carbondale, Ill., Oct. 24, 1927; d. George Newton and Phyllis Bena (Gent) Gher; m. Claude Edward Luttrell, Mar. 25, 1964 (dec. Aug. 1987). BA, So. Ill. U., 1947; MusM, Northwestern U., Evanston, Ill., 1948; postgrad., various univs. Asst. prof. music Huntingdon Coll., Montgomery, Ala., 1948-50; music supr. Community Unit Dist. 2 Williamson County, Marion, Ill., 1950-53; music tchr. Dubois Grade Sch., Springfield, 1953-55; dir. choral music Feitshas High Sch., 1955-67; chairperson music dept. Springfield S.E. High Sch., 1967-83; ind. music coord./pianist Springfield, 1983—. Accompanist various soloists and choirs, 1944—; accompanist Ill. Music Educators Assn., 1956-66; talent adjudicator Ill. High Sch. Assn., 1957-89, Ill. Elem. Sch. Assn., 1957-89. Pianist Springfield Symphony Orch., 1954-55; author (poet): American Poetry Anthology, 1988, Love's Greatest Treasures, 1989. Dir. choirs Douglas United Meth. Ch., Springfield, 1964-72; choir dir. Unity Ch., Springfield, 1981-85; vol. vocalist Ill. Symphony Chorus, formerly Springfield Symphony Chorus, 1986—. Grantee Carnegie Rsch. Found., 1949, State of Ill., Evanston Twp. High Sch., 1968. Mem. Internat. Platform Assn. (gov., music dir., pianist), Ill. Ret. Tchrs. Assn. Avocations: swimming, writing, sewing, dancing, crafts, travelling.

LUTTRELL, MARY LOU, elementary educator; b. Monroe County, Iowa, June 22, 1929; d. Forrest Charles and Catherine Cecilia (Stone) Sutcliffe; m. John Joseph, June 24, 1950; children: John S. (dec.), William A., Mary Elizabeth. AA, Ottumwa Heights Coll., 1949; BS in Elem. Edn., No. Ariz. U., 1969. Cert. tchr., N.Mex. 5th grade tchr. Albia (Iowa) Pub. Schs., 1949-51; 6th grade tchr. Chariton (Iowa) Pub. Schs., 1953-59, Cortez (Colo.) Pub. Schs., 1959-61, Cathedral Elem. Sch., Gallup, N.Mex., 1962-69; 5th grade tchr. Farmington (N.Mex.) Pub. Schs., 1969-90, sci.-math. advisor, 1994—; prin. Sacred Heart Sch., Farmington, 1990-92. Mem. N.Mex. history curriculum writing com. Farmington Pub. Schs., 1978-79. Pres. Lucas County Iowa Edn. Assn., 1957-58. Recipient Robert H. Taft Inst. Govt. award Robert H. Taft Found., 1976. Mem. N.Mex. Assn. Edn. Retirees, San Juan County Assn. Edn. Retirees (v.p. 1997, pres. 1998). Roman Catholic. Avocations: travel, reading, bridge. Home: 600 W 20th St Farmington NM 87401-3994

LUTTRULL, SHIRLEY JOANN, protective services official; b. Fordland, Mo., Feb. 26, 1937; d. Thomas Marion and Pauline (Sherrow) Pirtle; m. Leslie Allen Luttrull, June 3, 1956 (div. May 1978); children: Vicki Lynn, Ricki Allen; m. Orben Lowell Clark, Dec. 31, 1982 (div. Oct. 1987); m. Barry Mabe, June 1992 (div. Oct. 1994). Student, Southwest Mo. State U., 1979. Checker Lea's Market, Fordland, Mo., 1955-56; plant supr. Mellers Photo Lab., Springfield, 1968-82; shopper Hopper and Hawkins, Dallas, 1982-83; crew leader Sentinal Security, Okla. City; from crew leader to sales mgr. Shrink Control Corp., Houston, 1984-88; owner Internal Theft Control, Springfield, 1988—. Mem. Mo. Retail Grocers Assn., Pilot Internat., Springfield C. of C. Republican. Avocations: water skiing, scuba diving, ballrooom dancing. Home and Office: 1347 S Airwood Dr Springfield MO 65804-0520

LUTTS, RALPH HERBERT, scholar, educator, museum administrator; b. Quincy, Mass., Jan. 7, 1944; s. Herbert Warren Lutts and Jean May (MacKenzie) Easton. BA in Biology, Trinity U., San Antonio, 1967; EdD, U. Mass., 1978. Curator, educator Mus. Sci., Boston, 1967-73; naturalist Hampshire Coll., Amherst, Mass., 1973-80, mem. natural sci. faculty, 1976-84; dir. Blue Hills Trailside Mus., Mass. Audubon Soc., Milton, 1980-90; dir. edn. Va. Mus. Natural History, Martinsville, 1990-92, dir. outreach divsn., 1992-94, rsch. assoc., 1994-97; mem. faculty Goddard Coll., Plainfield, Vt., 1995—; mem. adj. faculty U. Va., Charlottesville, 1995—; mem. adj. history faculty Va. Tech., 1998—. Pres. Alliance for Environ. Edn., 1988-89; founding pres. New Eng. Environ. Edn. Alliance, 1980-84; assoc. Ctr. for Animals and Pub. Policy, Tufts U. Sch. Vet. Medicine, North Grafton, Mass., 1989-90; dept. dir. mid-atlantic region Global Network of Environ. Edn. Ctrs., 1993-95, bd. dirs., 1994-96. Author: The Nature Fakers: Wildlife, Science and Sentiment, 1990; editor: The Wild Animal Story, 1998; founding editor New Eng. Jour. Environ. Edn., 1985-88; contbr. articles to profl. jours. Pres. Hitchcock Ctr. for Environ., Amherst, Mass., 1977-79; treas. Mass. Environ. Edn. Soc., 1982-84; mem. Blue Hills citizens' adv. com. Met. Dist. Commn., 1988-89, mgmt. adv. com., 1989-90; mem. sec.'s adv. group on environ. edn. Mass. Exec. Office for Environ. Affairs, 1989-90; mem. exec. com. Patrick Environ. Awareness Group, 1998-99; assoc. dir. Patrick Soil and Water Conservation Dist., 2001-2002. Recipient New Eng. award for achievement New Eng. Environ. Edn. Alliance, 1989; Paul Harris fellow Rotary Internat. Mem. Am. Soc. Environ. History, Assn. for Study of Lit. and Environ., Internat. Soc. Environ. Ethics, Forest History Soc. (Ralph W. Hidy award 1993), N.Am. Assn. Environ. Edn., Am. Nature Study Soc. (bd. dirs. 1990-98, pres. 1995-97), Authors Guild, Popular Culture Assn. (area chair 1993-95), Nat. Writers Union.

LUTTWAK, EDWARD NICOLAE, academic administrator, educator, policy and business consultant; b. Arad, Transylvania, Nov. 4, 1942; came to U.S., 1972, naturalized, 1981; s. Josif Menashe and Clara (Baruch) L.; m. Dalya Iaari, Dec. 14, 1970; children: Yael Rachel, Joseph Emannuel. B.Sc. with honors, London Sch. Econs., 1964; PhD (Univ. fellow), Johns Hopkins U., 1975. Vis. prof. polit. sci. Johns Hopkins U., 1973-78; sr. fellow Georgetown U. Center Strategic and Internat. Studies, 1978-87, research prof. internat. security affairs, 1978-82, Burke chair in strategy, 1987—, dir. geo-econs., 1991-94, sr. fellow, 1994—; sr. fellow in preventive diplomacy Office of Sec. of Def., Nat. Security Coun. and Dept. State. Cons. Office of Sec. of Def., Nat. Security Coun., Dept. of Def. Army, Navy and U.S. Air Force, Fgn. (allied) Govs. and U.S., overseas bus. entities. Author: Coup d'Etat, 19 edits. including 12 for lang. translations, 1968-79, Dictionary of Modern War, 1971 (also Spanish edit.), The Political Uses of Sea Power, 1975 (also Japanese edit.), The Israeli Army, 1975, 85, (also Chinese edit.), The Grand Strategy of the Roman Empire, 1976 (also Hebrew, Italian and French edits.), Strategy and Politics: Collected Essays, 1980, The Grand Strategy of the Soviet Union, 1983 (also Italian and French edits.),The Pentagon and the Art of War: The Question of Military Reform, 1985 (also Italian, Japanese and Korean edits.), Strategy and History: Collected Essays, On the Meaning of Victory, 1986 (also Italian edit.), Strategy: The Logic of War and Peace, 1987 (also Chinese, French and Italian edits.), revised edit., 2001, (with Stuart Koehl) Dictionary of Modern War, 1991 (also Italian edit.), The Endangered American Dream, 1993 (also French, Italian, German and Japanese edits.), (with G. Tremonti, Carlo Palanda) Il Fantasma della Poverta, 1995, (with Susanna Creperio) Cose e Davvero La Democrazia, 1996, Turbo Capitalism, U.K. edit., 1998, Turbo-Capitalism: Winners and Losers in the Global Economy, U.S. edit., 1999, French edit., 1999, Italian edit., 1999, Portuguese edit., 1999, Polish edit., 1999, German edit., 1999, Dutch edit., 1999, Japanese edit., 1999, Chinese edit., 1999, Taiwan edit., 1999, Spanish edit., 1999, La Renaissance De La Puissance Aerienne Strategique, 1999, Il Libro Della Liberta 2000 (with Susanna Creporop Verraiti); contbr. articles to Fgn. Affairs, London Rev. of Books, Times Lit. Supplement, Commentary National Interest. Republican. Jewish. Office: CSIS 1800 K St NW Washington DC 20006-2294

LUTVAK, MARK ALLEN, computer company executive; b. Chgo., Feb. 9, 1939; s. Joseph Issac and Jeanette Nettie (Pollock) L.; m. Gayle Helene Rotofsky, May 24, 1964; children: Jeffrey, Eric. BSEE, U. Mich., 1962; MBA, Wayne State U., Detroit, 1969. Sales rep. IBM Corp., 1962-64; from sales rep. to corp. product mgr. Burroughs Corp., Detroit, 1964-76; mgr. product mktg. Memorex Corp., Santa Clara, Calif., 1976-80, product program gen. mgr., 1980-81; dir. product mktg. Personal Computer divsn. Atari, Inc., Sunnyvale, 1981-83; dir. mktg., v.p. Durango Sys., San Jose, 1983-85; dir. mktg. ITTQUME Corp., 1985-87; v.p. mktg. Optimem, Mountain View, Calif., 1987-88; dir. mktg. Priam Corp., San Jose, 1988-91; dir. Memorex, Santa Clara, 1991-94; pres. Synergistic Mktg., 1994—. Prof. Applied Mgmt. Center, Wayne State U., 1967-72, Walsh U., Troy, Mich., 1974-76, West Valley Coll., Saratoga, Calif., 1977-78. Trustee, pres. brotherhood Temple Emanuel, San Jose, 1979-80. Mem. IEEE, Soc. Applied Math., Alpha Epsilon Pi. Home: 899 Balboa Ln Foster City CA 94404-2931 E-mail: mlutvak@ihot.com.

LUTWAK, ERWIN, mathematician, educator; b. Chernovtsy, USSR, Feb. 9, 1946; came to U.S., 1956, naturalized, 1961; s. Herman and Anna (Halpern) L.; m. Nancy Ruth Selwyn, Mar. 7, 1968. BS, Poly. Inst. N.Y., Bklyn., 1968, MS, 1972; PhD, 1974. Instr. math. Poly. Inst. N.Y., Bklyn., 1975-77, asst. prof., 1977-81, assoc. prof., 1981-86, prof. 1986—, dept. head 1999—. Mem. editorial bd.: Advances in Math., Ency. of Math. and its Applications; co-editor: N.Y. Acad. Sci. publ., 1985; contbr. articles to sci. jours. Named Disting. Prof. of Yr., Student Govt., Poly. Univ., Bklyn., 1980. Mem. Am. Math. Soc., London Math. Soc., Math. Assn. Am., N.Y. Acad. Scis.(chmn. math. sect. 1988-91), Sigma Xi. Home: 1623 3rd Ave Apt 11C New York NY 10128-3639 Office: Poly U 333 Jay St Brooklyn NY 11201-2907

LUTZ, CHARLES BRADLEY, university bookstore administrator; b. Tiffin, Ohio, Oct. 22, 1962; s. James Ward and Karen Joan (Emerine) L.; m. Christina Louise Boes, Nov. 18, 1989; children: Derek Charles, Emily Christine. BBA, Tiffin U., 1986, MBA, 1994. Asst. mgr. Consolidated Stores, Findlay, 1986-88, 90-91; sales rep. Harold Printers, New Washington, Ohio, 1988-90; dir. bookstore Tiffin (Ohio) U., 1991—. Mem. Phi Theta Pi (v.p. 1987—). Office: Tiffin U 155 Miami St Tiffin OH 44883-2161

LUTZ, FRANCIS CHARLES, university dean, civil engineering educator; b. Pottsville, Pa., Apr. 5, 1944; s. Charles Henry and Pauline Anna (Weislo) L.; m. Evelyn Florence Zommer, Apr. 29, 1972; 1 child, Stephanie Diane BSCE, N.J. Inst. Tech., 1966; MSCE, NYU, 1967, PhD, 1971. Assoc. M. Disko Assocs., West Orange, N.J., 1970-72; asst. prof. civil engring. Worcester Poly. Inst., Mass., 1972-76, prof., 1980-96, assoc. dean, 1980-90, dean undergrad. studies, 1990-95; dean sch. sci., tech. & engring. Monmouth U., West Long Branch, N.J., 1996—. Cons. Council on Environ. Quality, Washington, 1974-75; reviewer NSF Co-editor: Studies in Science, Technology and Culture, Worcester Poly. Inst.; contbr. articles to profl. jours. Trustee Worcester Ctr. for Crafts, 1992—; mem. Boston Fed. Exec. Bd., 1972-74, Cen. Mass. Regional Planning Commn., Worcester, 1975-77. Am. Council on Edn. fellow, 1988-89; honors scholar NYU. Mem. ASCE, Am. Soc. Engring. Edn., Boynton Assn. (pres. 1982, 83), JETS (bd. dirs.), Sigma Xi, Chi Epsilon. Office: Monmouth U Office of Dean Sch Sci Tech & Engring West Long Branch NJ 07764-1898

LUTZ, FRANK WENZEL, education administration educator; b. St. Louis, Sept. 24, 1928; s. Vincent J. and Helen M. (Scrivens) L.; m. Susan Virginia Bleikamp, July 12, 1958; children: Paul E., Andrew C., Lynn S. AA, Harris Tchrs. Coll., 1948; BS, Washington U., 1950, MS, 1954, EdD, 1962. Instr. Washington U., St. Louis, 1961-62; from asst. to assoc. prof. NYU, N.Y.C., 1964-68; dir. divsn. policy studies Pa. State U., State College, 1968-73, prof. edn. adminstrn., 1974-80; dean Sch. Edn. Eastern Ill. U., 1980-82, asst. to v.p., 1982-83; prof., dir. Ctr. Policy Studies Tex. A&M-Commerce (formerly East State U.), Commerce, Tex., 1983-91, prof. edn. adminstrn., 1983-98, prof. emeritus, 1998; sr. nat. lectr. Nova S.E. U., Ft. Lauderdale, Fla., 1991-98; prof. edn. adminstrn. U. Tex.-Pan-Am., Edinburg, 1998—2002. Mem. adv. com. Opportunities Acad. Mgmt. Tng., Phila., 1975—90; mem., pres. Pattonville (Mo.) Sch. Bd., 1960—62; adv. bd. Nederland Columbine Clinic, 2001—. Author seven books, numerous book chpts. in field; contbr. over 100 articles to profl. jours. Chair Nederland Cmty. Ctr. Bd., 1998-2000; deacon 1st Presbyn. Ch., Commerce, Tex., 1989-91. Doctoral fellow Washington U., 1960-61; grantee U.S. Office Edn., OEO. Mem. Am. Ednl. Rsch. Assn. (sec. Divsn. A 1970-72, dir. rsch. pre-session 1969, program com. 1970), Commerce Rotary (dist. 5810, pres. 1991-92, chair internat. svc. 1994-96, Found. award 1994, Paul Harris fellow), Peak-to-Peak Rotary (int. chair 2000—, Dist. 5450 world cmty. svc. and youth exch. com. 1999—), Phi Delta Kappa (life, pres. Washington U. chpt. 1960, 1st v.p. East Tex. State U. chpt. 1985, Lafferty Faculty Senate Disting. scholarship award 1996). Avocations: appaloosa horses, opera, classical music. Home: PO Box 51 Nederland CO 80466-0051 Office: U Tex-Pan Am 1201 W University Dr Edinburg TX 78539-2909

LUTZ, GRETCHEN KAY, English language educator; b. Ft. Worth, Jan. 6, 1948; BA, Tex. Christian U., 1970; MA, U. Houston, 1974, Rice U., 1995, PhD, 1998; postgrad., Dartmouth Coll., 1994; PhD, Rice U., 1998. High sch. and mid. sch. tchr. English Galveston and Deer Park (Tex.) Sch. Dists., 1970-77; instr. ESL and English, Schreiner Coll., Kerrville, Tex., 1979-80; instr. English, San Jacinto Coll. Ctr., Pasadena, 1981-93; testing coord. Am. Acad. of Excellence Charter H.S., Houston, 2001—. Contbr. articles to profl. jours. Mem. MLA, Nat. Symposium for Coherence in Liberal Arts, C.C. Humanities Assn., Am. Culture and Popular Culture Assn., U.S. European Command Mil. to Mil. Program Conf., Am. Studies Assn. Tex., South Ctrl. MLA, Conf. Coll. Tchrs. English (exec. coun.), S.W. Conf. Christianity and Lit., Western Soc. 18th Century Studies, Tex. Folklore Soc., S.W. Regional Conf. English in Two-Year Colls., Tex. Voices Sesquicentennial Series, Rice English Symposium, San Jacinto Coll. Faculty Symposium. Home: 8100 Cambridge # 151 Houston TX 77054

LUTZ, JAMES GURNEY, lawyer; b. Cin., Sept. 18, 1933; s. Arthur Harold and Frances (Gurney) L.; children: Monica, Susan. JD, U. Cin., 1960. Bar: Ohio 1960, U.S. Dist. Ct. (so. dist.) Ohio 1961, U.S. Ct. Appeals (6th cir.) 1961, U.S. Tax Ct. 1975, U.S. Supreme Ct. 1975. Ptnr. Barbour, Kinpel & Allen, Cin., 1960-68; chief counsel E.C. Industries Inc., 1968-71; sr. ptnr. Lutz Cornetet & Albrinck, 1971—. Pres., mem. bd. dirs. Motivation Dynamics Inc., Cin., 1978-85. Advisor, staff Hamilton County Vocat. Schs., Cin., 1968; advisor U. Cin. Coll., 1970-75; mem. adv. counsel Wyoming (Ohio) Bd. Edn., 1972-75; mem. bd. Ohio Pvt. Industry Coun., Columbus, 1975; gen. counsel S.W. Ohio Autistic Assn., Cin., 1980—. Mem. ABA, ATLA, Ohio Acad. Trial Lawyers, Ohio State Bar Assn., Cin. Bar Assn. Avocations: psychology, computer science. Office: Lutz Cornetet & Albrinck 130 Tri County Pkwy Cincinnati OH 45246-3289 E-mail: jlutz@lcalaw.com.

LUTZ, JOHN THOMAS, author; b. Dallas, Sept. 11, 1939; s. John Peter and Esther Jane (Gundelfinger) L.; m. Barbara Jean Bradley, Mar. 15, 1958; children: Steven, Jennifer, Wendy. Student, Meramec C.C., 1965. Author: The Truth of the Matter, 1971, Buyer Beware, 1976, Bonegrinder, 1977, Lazarus

Man, 1979, Jericho Man, 1980, The Shadow Man, 1981; (with Steven Greene) Exiled, 1982; (with Bill Pronzini) The Eye, 1984, Nightlines, 1984, The Right to Sing the Blues, 1986, Tropical Heat, 1986, Ride the Lightning, 1987, Scorcher, 1987, Dancers Debt, 1988, Shadowtown, 1988, Kiss, 1988, Better Mousetraps (short story collection), 1988, Time Exposure, 1989, Flame, 1990, Diamond Eyes, 1990, SWF Seeks Same (Single White Female), 1990, Bloodfire, 1991, Hot, 1992, Dancing with the Dead, 1992, Spark, 1993, Thicker than Blood, 1993, (short story collection) Shadows Everywhere, 1994, Torch, 1994, Death by Jury, 1995, Burn, 1995, Lightning, 1996; (novel and screenplay) The Ex, 1996, Oops!, 1998; (with David August) Final Seconds, 1998; (short stories) Until You Are Dead, 1998, The Nudget Dilemmas, 2001, The Night Caller, 2001, The Night Watcher, 2002; contbr. short stories and articles to mystery and private-eye mags. Mem. Mystery Writers Am. (Scroll 1981, Edgar award 1986), Pvt.-Eye Writers Am. (Shamus award 1982, 88, Life Achievement award 1995, Short Mystery Fiction Soc. Golden Derringer Life Achievement award 2001). Democrat. Home and Office: 880 Providence Ave Saint Louis MO 63119-2072

LUTZ, MATTHEW CHARLES, oil company executive, geologist; b. Bunkie, La., Mar. 28, 1934; s. John Matthew and Maxie Mae (Andrus) L.; m. Patricia Dawnn Feazel, Apr. 11, 1953; children: Matt Jr., Cyndy, Tracey, Clay. BS, U. Southwestern La., 1956. Various geol. profl. positions Tidewater-Getty Oil Co., 1956-71; asst. dist. geologist Getty Oil Co., Houston, 1971-73, dist. geologist Midland, Tex., 1973-78, ctrl. divsn. geologist Tulsa, 1978-80, offshore dist. exploration mgr. Houston, 1980, so. divsn. exploration mgr., 1980-82, gen. mgr. offshore exploration and prodn., 1982-83, exploration mgr. so. divsn., 1983-84; sr. v.p. exploration Enserch Exploration, Inc., Dallas, 1984-92; also bd. dirs. Enwserch Exploration, Inc.; vice chmn. and bus. devel. mgr. Hunter Resources, Inc., Irving, Tex., 1993-95, also bd. dirs.; vice chmn. exploration and bus. dvel. mgr. Magnum Hunter Resources, Inc., 1995-97, chmn., exec. v.p., 1997—. Mem. Am. Assn. Petroleum Geologists, Houston Geol. Soc., Dallas Geol. Soc., Dallas Petroleum Club. Republican. Baptist. Avocations: travel, golf, hunting. Office: Magnum Hunter Resources Inc 600 Las Colinas Blvd E Ste 1100 Irving TX 75039-5635

LUTZ, MYRON HOWARD, obstetrician, gynecologist, surgeon, educator; b. N.Y.C., June 26, 1938; s. Morris David and Rose (Greenblatt) L.; m. Judy Cohen, Aug. 6, 1963; children: Mark Steven, Sheri Lutz Barnett, Kenneth Ian. BA, Columbia U., 1960; MD, NYU, 1964. Diplomate Am. Bd. Ob-Gyn., Am. Bd. Gynecologic Oncology. Intern Phila., Gen. Hosp., 1964-65; resident in ob-gyn. Albert Einstein Coll. Medicine, Bronx, N.Y., 1965-69; fellow M.D. Anderson Hosp., Houston, 1971-72, U. Miami (Fla.) Sch. Medicine, 1972-73; asst. prof. ob-gyn. Med. U. S.C., Charleston, 1973-76, co-dir. gynecology oncology, 1973-77, clin. assoc. prof. ob-gyn., 1977—, clin. assoc. prof. surgery, 1986—; pvt. practice, 1973—. Mem. cancer adv. bd. Roper Hosp., Charleston, 1993—; star TV mid-day talk show, 1990—. Mem. editl. bd. House Calls mag., 1992—. Bd. dirs. Am. Cancer Soc., Charleston, 1974-75, v.p., 1975-76, pres., 1976-78; bd. dirs. Trident Acad., Charleston, 1982-86, Hospice, Charleston, 1984-86. Maj. M.C., U.S. Army, 1969-71. Fellow ACOG, ACS; mem. AMA, Am. Radium Soc., Am. Soc. Clin. Oncology, Soc. Gynecologic Oncologists, Felix Rutledge Soc., S.C. Med. Soc., S.C. Oncology Soc., Charleston Med. Soc. Avocations: water and snow skiing, archery, biking. Home: 1205 Wisteria Rd Charleston SC 29407 Office: 1205 Wisteria Dr Charleston SC 29407-5902 E-mail: jmlutz@home.com.

LUTZ, RANDALL MATTHEW, lawyer; b. New Brunswick, N.J., June 1, 1945; s. Ralph P. and Gertrude (Goodman) L. BS with high honors, U. Md., 1967, JD, 1970. Bar: Md. 1970, U.S. Dist. Ct. Md. 1970, U.S. Ct. Appeals (4th cir.) 1970, U.S. Supreme Ct. 1975. Assoc. Burke, Gerber & Wilen, Balt., 1970-75; asst. atty. gen. State of Md., 1975-84; dir. criminal enforcement U.S. EPA, Washington, 1984-87; ptnr. Kaplan, Heyman, Greenberg, Engleman & Belgrade, Balt., 1987-90, Smith, Somerville & Case, LLC, Balt., 1990-98, Hodes, Ulman, Pessin & Katz, PA, Towson, Md., 1998—. Lectr. in field. Author: (column) Environmental Law jour.,1987-88. Mem. dist. cabinet Balt. area coun. Boy Scouts Am., 1974-75. Mem: ABA, Md. Bar Assn., Nat. Health Lawyers Assn. Office: Hodes Ulman Pessin & Katz PA 901 Dulaney Valley Rd Towson MD 21204-2600 E-mail: rlutz@hupk.com.

LUTZ, RAYMOND PRICE, retired industrial engineer, educator; b. Oak Park, Ill., Feb. 27, 1935; s. Raymond Price and Sibyl Elizabeth (Haralson) L.; m. Nancy Marie Cole, Aug. 23, 1958. BSME, U. N.Mex., 1958, MBA, 1962; PhD, Iowa State U., 1964. Registered profl. engr., N.Mex., Okla. With Sandia Corp., Albuquerque, summers 1958-63; instr. mech. engring. U. N.Mex., 1958-62; from asst. to assoc. prof. indsl. engring. N.Mex. State U., 1964-68; prof. head indsl. engring. U. Okla., 1968-73; prof., acting dean U. Tex. Sch. Mgmt., Dallas, 1973-76, dean, 1976-78, exec. dean grad. studies and rsch., 1979-92, prof. ops. mgmt., 1992-2001, ret., 2001. Cons. Bell Telephone Labs., Tex. Instruments, Kennecott Corp., Bath Iron Works, Sabre, Inc., City of Dallas, Oklahoma City; cons. U.S. Army, USAF, U.S. Dept. Transp., Los Angeles and Seattle public schs.; mem. shipbldg. productivity panel NRC Editor: The Engring. Economist, 1973-77, Indsl. Mgmt., 1983-87. Pres., bd. dirs. United Cerebral Palsy, Dallas, 1978, treas., 1984-88; bd. dirs., treas. Amigos Bibliographic Network, Dallas, 1984-90; chmn., bd. dirs. S.W. Police Inst., Dallas, 1980—; v.p., bd. dirs. Santa Fe Opera, 1988—; bd. dirs. Dallas Opera, 1989-2001, Santa Fe Opera Found., 1993-2000. Fellow AAAS, Am. Inst. Indsl. Engrs. (v.p. industry and mgmt. divsns., trustee, dir. engring. economy divsn., systems engring. group); mem. Am. Soc. Engring. Edn. (chmn. engring. economy divsn., Eugene L. Grant award 1972), INFORMS, Dallas Classic Guitar Soc. (bd. dirs. 1993-96, v.p. 1994-96), Ops. Mgmt. Assn. (bd. dirs. 1994-98), Sigma Xi (bd. dirs. 1990-98, 99—, chmn. capital campaign 1992—, exec. com. 1992-95). Avocation: jogging. Home: 1230 Turquoise Trl Cerrillos NM 87010-9716 E-mail: rplutz@worldnet.att.net.

LUTZ, REINHART, English language educator, writer; b. Taipei, Taiwan, Feb. 28, 1960; BA, Free U. Berlin, 1983; MA, U. Calif., Santa Barbara, 1985, PhD, 1991. Asst. prof. U. of the Pacific, Stockton, Calif., 1991-96, assoc. prof. dept. english and film studies, 1996—. Mem. MLA, Soc. for Cinema Studies. Office: U Pacific Dept English Stockton CA 95211-0001 E-mail: rlutz@uop.edu.

LUTZ, WILLIAM LAN, lawyer; b. Chgo., May 18, 1944; s. Raymond Price and Sibyl (McCright) L.; m. Jeanne M. McAlister, Dec. 27, 1969; children: William Lan, David Price. BS, U. Tex., 1965, JD, 1969. Bar: Tex. 1969, N.Mex. 1970. Assoc. Martin, Lutz, Cresswell & Hubert and predecessor firms, Las Cruces, N.Mex., 1969-82; former U.S. atty. dist. N.Mex. U.S. Dept. Justice, Albuquerque, 1982-91; ptnr. Martin, Lutz, Roggow, Hosford & Eubanks, P.C., Las Cruces, 1991—. Mem. ABA, N.Mex. Bar Assn. (mem. bd. bar commrs. 1995-97); Aggie Sports Assn. (bd.dirs.) N.Mex. State U. Methodist. Office: Martin Lutz Roggow Hosford & Eubanks PC 2100 N Main St Ste 2 Las Cruces NM 88001-1183

LUTZE, RUTH LOUISE, retired textbook editor, public relations executive; b. Boston, Apr. 19, 1917; d. Frederick Clemons and Louise (Rausch) L. BA with honors, Radcliffe Coll., 1938; postgrad., Boston U., 1938-39. Tchr. Winthrop (Mass.) Pub. Schs., 1938-39; with pub. rels. dept. Boston City Club, 1939-42; sr. projects editor D.C. Heath & Co., Lexington, Mass., 1942-82. Book reviewer, lectr., cons. on pub. rels., lectr. textbook publ. Bd. dirs. Winthrop Improvement and Hist. Assn., 1980—; vol. tchr. Boston Pub. Schs., 1967-77; mem. Winthrop Rep. Town Com., 1970—; v.p. 1st Luth. Ch. Boston, 1986, deacon, 1980—. Recipient cert. appreciation for vol. in edn., Kiwanis Club of East Boston, 1972. Mem. Radcliffe Club Boston. Avocations: volunteer work, theatre, birdwatching, reading, art exhibits. Home: 110 Circuit Rd Winthrop MA 02152-2819

LUTZKER, ELLIOT HOWARD, lawyer; b. Flushing, N.Y., Feb. 22, 1953; s. Stanley Lawrence and Mildred Lutzker; m. Jill Leslie Simon, Aug. 24, 1975; children: Stacey, Amanda. BA, SUNY, Stony Brook, 1974; JD, N.Y. Law Sch., 1978. Bar: N.Y. 1979, Fla. 1979, U.S. Dist. Ct. (so. and ea. dists.) N.Y. 1979. Atty. SEC, N.Y.C., 1978-81; assoc. Bachner, Tally, Polevoy, Misher & Brinberg, 1981-85; ptnr. Snow Becker Krauss P.C., 1985—. Mem. ABA (corp., banking law div.). Jewish. Avocations: reading, sports. Home: 15 Kevin Ct Jericho NY 11753-1308 Office: Snow Becker Krauss PC 605 3rd Ave Fl 25 New York NY 10158-0125 E-mail: elutzker@sbklaw.com.

LUVISI, LEE, concert pianist; b. Louisville, Dec. 12, 1937; m. Nina Hussey, June 20, 1959; 1 son, Brian. Student, Curtis Inst. Music, 1952-57. Mem. faculty Curtis Inst. Music, 1957-62; artist in residence U. Louisville Sch. Music., 1963—2001. Artist-mem., Chamber Music soc. Lincoln Ctr. Address: Michal Schmidt Artists Int 59 E 54th St New York NY 10022-4211

LUXEMBURG, JACK ALAN, rabbi; b. Feb. 16, 1949; s. Milton Irwin and Bernice Esther (Adler) L.; m. Barbara Elaine Etkind, June 15, 1975; children: Daniel, Michael. BA, Trinity Coll., 1970; MA in Hebrew Letters, Hebrew Union Coll., 1973; D of Ministry, Wesley Theol. Sem., 1987; DDiv, Hewbre Union Coll., 2001. Ordained rabbi, 1976. Rabbi intern B'nai B'rith Hillel at Ohio State U., Columbus, Ohio, 1973-74; regional dir. Hashachar/Young Judaea, Cin., 1972-75; student rabbi Temple Ahavat Shalom, Coriopolis, Pa., 1975-76; assoc. rabbi Main Line Reform Temple, Wynnewood, 1976-81; rabbi Temple Beth Ami, Rockville, Md., 1981—. Bd. dirs. Jewish Social Svc. Agy., Rockville, United Jewish Appeal Fedn., Greater Washington Charles E. Smith Jewish Day Sch., Rockville; exec. com. mem. Jewish Community Coun. of Greater Washington, 1985-87, 92—, v.p., 1994-2000, pres., 2000—. Mem. Montgomery County (Md.) Civil Rights Monitoring Group, 1988, Inter-Religious Com. on Drug Abuse, Montgomery County, 1989; bd. dirs. Washington Area Community Investment Fund, Washington, 1988-89; mem. Citizens Adv. Coun. Montgomery County (Md.) Sch. Bd., 1981-83; nat. coord. synagogue campaign U.S. Holocaust Meml. Mus. Recipient Leadership award Am. Jewish Congress, 1988, 92, Rabbinic award Coun. of Jewish Fedns., 1991. Mem. Nat. Rabbinical Cabinet of United Jewish Appeal (exec. com. 1986—), Am. Jewish Congress (regional pres. 1987-92, nat. governing coun. 1987-92), Cen. Conf. Am. Rabbis (regional pres. 1990-92, nat. exec. com. 1990-92), Washington Bd. Rabbis (v.p. 1989-93, pres. 1993-95). Office: Temple Beth Ami 14330 Travilah Rd Rockville MD 20850-3527 *Few things are complete in themselves. Words require deeds; action requires purpose. Knowledge requires understanding; intellect requires soul. Individuality requires community; life requires love. Only in the service of the sacred do all things find Shalom—wholeness and peace.*

LUXENBERG, ALISA LYNN, art historian; b. Cleve., June 23, 1960; d. Herbert and Marianna (Dunchack) L. BA in Art History/French Lit., Duke U., 1982; MA in Art History, Boston U., 1984; PhD in Art History, NYU, 1990. Instr. Am. U. in Paris, 1990; Gould Found. fellow Princeton (N.J.) U., 1991-92; vis. asst. prof. Washington U., St. Louis, 1992-93, Ohio State U., Columbus, 1993-94, Case Western Reserve U., Cleve., 1996, U. Ky., Lexington, 1997-99; asst. prof. art history U. Ga., Athens, 1999—. Contbg. author: (exhbn. catalog) Spain, Espagne, Spanien, 1993, Painting in Spain in Age of Enlightenment, 1997, Mehr Licht, 1999, La Commune Photgraphi+248e, 2000. Kress summer travel grantee Boston U., Austin, Tex., 1984, grantee program for cultural cooperation Spanish Ministry and Am. Univs., 1999; Model/Gould fellow Nat. Gallery Can., 1995, CHA fellow U Ga., 2002-. Mem.: Assn. Historians Spanish and Hispanic Art Hist. Studies, Assn. Historians of 19th Century Art, Coll. Art Assn. (co-chair session at ann. conf. 1995). Office: U Ga Dept Art Visual Arts Bldg Athens GA 30602-4102

LUXENBERG, MALCOLM NEUWAHL, ophthalmologist, educator; b. Philipsburg, Pa., July 29, 1935; s. Maurice and Henrietta (Neuwahl) L.; m. Sandra Diane Rosen, June 16, 1957; children: Steven Neuwahl, Cathy Ann. Student, Tulane U., 1953-56; MD, U. Miami, Fla., 1960. Diplomate: Am. Bd. Ophthalmology. Intern Cin. Gen. Hosp., 1960-61; resident in neurology U. Vt. Affiliated Hosps., Burlington, 1961-63; resident in ophthalmology Bascom Palmer Eye Inst., U. Miami-Jackson Meml. Hosp., Miami, Fla., 1963-66; asst. prof. ophthalmology Coll. Medicine, U. Iowa, Iowa City, 1968-70; chief ophthalmology service VA Hosp., 1968-70; practice medicine specializing in ophthalmology West Palm Beach, Fla., 1970-72; clin. asst. prof. ophthalmology Bascom Palmer Eye Inst., Sch. Medicine, U. Miami, 1971-72; prof., chmn. dept. ophthalmology Med. Coll. Ga., Augusta, 1972-2000. Cons. ophthalmology VA Hosp., Augusta, 1972—; sr. surgeon USPHS, 1966-68. Mem. editl. bd.: Archives of Ophthalmology, 1986-94. Recipient Outstanding Civilian Service Medal Dept. of Army, 1986. Mem. AMA, Am. Acad. Ophthalmology (hon. award 1986), Am. Ophthalmol. Soc., Assn. Univ. Profs. in Ophthalmology (pres. 1982-83), Ga. Soc. Ophthalmology, Med. Assn. Ga., Richmond County Med. Soc. Home: 512 Scotts Way Augusta GA 30909-3238 Office: Med Coll Ga Dept Ophthalmology Augusta GA 30912 E-mail: mlux@knology.net., mluxenbe@mail.mcg.edu.

LUXENBERG, STEVEN MARC, newspaper editor; b. Detroit, July 25, 1952; s. Julius Sam and Beth (Cohen) L.; m. Mary Jo Kirschman, June 28, 1981; children: Joshua K., Jill K. AB magna cum laude, Harvard U., 1974. Reporter Balt. Sun, 1974-79, 81-82, city editor, 1979-81, met. editor, 1982-84; dep. asst. mng. editor The Washington Post, 1985-91, asst. mng. editor investigative news/spl. projects, 1991-96; asst. mng. editor Outlook, 1996—. Recipient Outstanding News Reporting award Nat. Headliners, 1975, award for state govt. reporting Md.-Del.-D.C. Press Assn., 1982, Feature Writing award, 1988. Office: Washington Post 1150 15th St NW Washington DC 20071-0002 E-mail: outlook@washpost.com.

LUXMOORE, ROBERT JOHN, soil and plant scientist; b. Adelaide, South Australia, Australia, Nov. 7, 1940; came to U.S., 1966; s. John Alexander and Mary Elinor (Martin) L.; Annetta Paule Watson, Oct. 18, 1975. B of Agrl. Sci., U. Adelaide, 1962, B of Agrl. Sci. with honors, 1963; PhD, U. Calif., Riverside, 1969. Cert. profl. soil scientist. Agronomist Dept. Agr., Adelaide, 1963-66; rsch. assoc. U. Ill., Champaign-Urbana, 1969-70; soil physicist U. Calif., Riverside, 1970-71; rsch. assoc. U. Wis., Madison, 1971-72; rsch. scientist Oak Ridge (Tenn.) Nat. Lab., 1973-86, sr. rsch. scientist, 1986-2000; dir. RJL Cons. Svcs., Harriman, Tenn., 2001—. Cons. Ctr. for Law and Social Policy, Washington, 1979; com. mem. NRC, Washington, 1989-90. Editor: Coupling of Carbon, Water and Nutrient, 1986; contbr. articles to profl. jours. and chpts. to books. Com. mem. Rural Abandoned Mines Program, Morgan County, Tenn., 1979-81; bd. dirs. Tenn. Citizens for Wilderness Planning, Oak Ridge, 1988-91; bd. dirs. Save Our Cumberland Mountains, Lake City, Tenn., 1995-2000. Recipient Tech. Achievement award Martin Marietta Energy Systems, 1987; Australian Cattle & Beef Rsch. scholar, 1962. Fellow AAAS, Soil Sci. Soc. Am. (tech. editor 1988-90, editor-in-chief 1991-93, bd. dirs. 1994-97, exec. com. 1999-2002); mem. Internat. Union Forestry Rsch. Orgns. (chmn. working party 1983-90, coord. dep. subject group 1991-95, exec. bd. 1996—), Am. Geophys. Union. Home: 295 Solomon Hollow Rd Harriman TN 37748-3634 Office: Oak Ridge Nat Lab PO Box 2008 Oak Ridge TN 37831-2008 E-mail: awrl@juno.com.

LUYENDYK, BRUCE PETER, geophysicist, educator, institution administrator; b. Freeport, N.Y., Feb. 23, 1943; s. Pieter Johannes and Frances Marie (Blakeney) L.; 1 child, Loren Taylor Luyendyk. BS Geophysics, San Diego State Coll., 1965; PhD Marine Geophysics, Scripps Inst. Oceanography, 1969. Geophysicist Arctic Sci. and Tech. Lab. USN Electronics Lab. Ctr., 1965; lectr. San Diego State Coll., 1967-68; postgrad rsch. geologist Scripps Inst. Oceanography, 1969; postdoctoral fellow dept. geology and geophysics Woods Hole Oceanographic Instn., 1969-70, asst. scientist dept. geology and geophysics, 1970-73; asst. prof. U. Calif., Santa Barbara, 1973-75, assoc. prof., 1975-81, prof. dept. geol. scis., 1981—, acting dir. Inst. Crustal Studies, 1987-88, dir. Inst. Crustal Studies, 1988-97, chair dept. geol. scis., 1997—. Participant, chief sci. oceanographic cruises, geol. expdns.; coord. bd. So. Calif. Integrated GPS Network, 1997-2000. Editorial bd. Geology, 1975-79, Marine Geophysical Rschs., 1976-92, Jour. Geophysical Rsch., 1982-84, Tectonophysics, 1988-92, Pageoph, 1988-95; contbr. articles to profl. jours., chpts. to books, encys. Co-recipient Newcomb Cleveland prize AAAS, 1980; recipient Antarctic Svc. medal U.S. NSF, Dept. Navy, 1990, Disting. Alumni award San Diego State U., 1983, numerous rsch. grants, 1971—. Fellow Geol. Soc. Am., Am. Geophys. Union. Office: U Calif Santa Barbara Dept Geol Scis Santa Barbara CA 93106 E-mail: luyendyk@geol.ucsb.edu.

LUZA, RADOMIR VACLAV, historian, educator; b. Prague, Czechoslovakia, Oct. 17, 1922; s. Vojtech V. and Milada (Vecera) L.; m. Libuse Ladislava Podhrazska, Feb. 5, 1949; children: Radomir V., Sabrina. JuDr, U. Brno, Czechoslovakia, 1948; MA, NYU, 1958, PhD, 1959. Assoc. prof. modern European history La. State U., New Orleans, 1966-67; prof. history Tulane U., 1967—. Scholar-in-residence Rockefeller Found., Bellagio Study Ctr., 1988; prof. gen. history Masaryk U., Brno, 1993—. Author: The Transfer of the Sudeten Germans, 1964, History of the International Socialist Youth Movement, 1970, (with V. Mamatey) A History of the Czechoslovak Republic, 1918-1948, 1973, Austro-German Relations in the Anschluss Era, 1975, Österreich und die Grossdeutsche Idee in der NS-Zeit, 1977, Geschichte der Tschechoslowakischen Republik 1918-1948, 1980, A History of the Resistance in Austria, 1938-1945, 1984, Der Widerstand in Österreich, 1938-1945, 1985, La Rèpublique Tchècoslovaque 1918-1948, 1987, The Czechoslovak Social Democracy Abroad, 1948-1989, 2001, The Hitler Kiss: A Memoir of the Czech Resistance, 2002; mem. editl. bd. East European Quar., Contemporary Austrian Studies. With Czechoslovak Resistance, 1939-45. Recipient all Czechoslovak mil. decorations; prize Theodor Körner Found., Vienna, 1965, J. Hlavka Hon. medal Czechoslovak Acad. Arts and Scis., 1992, T.G. Masaryk medal Pres. of Czech Rep., 1996, Austrian Cross of Honor Sci. and Art I. Class, 1997, Meml. medal Czech Rep., 2000; grantee Social Rsch. Coun., Am. Philos. Soc., Coun. Learned Socs., Fulbright Com., NEH. Mem. Am. Hist. Assn., Czechoslovak History Conf., So. Conf. Slavic Studies, Am. Assn. Advancement Slavic Studies. Home: 3316 Twin Silo Dr Blue Bell PA 19422-3286 Office: Tulane U Dept History New Orleans LA 70118

LUZA, RADOMIR VOJTECH, JR. poet, film producer; b. Vienna, Dec. 7, 1963; s. Radomir Vaclav and Libusc Podhraska Luza; m. Monica Ann Leininger, Aug. 13, 1999. BA in English, Tulane U., New Orleans, 1985. Staff writer Goodwill Games, Atlanta, 1985; freelance journalist/reporter Jersey City, 1981—; prodr., owner Radman Prodns., 1994—. Co-host performance night Alliteration Alley, 2002. Editor (pubr.): Voices in the Libr. jour., 2002, Dancing Sprite Pubs., 2002—. 2d vice chair 132d Assembly Dist., Bucks County, Pa., 1997—98; auditor cand. Dem. Party of Middletown, 1997, parliamentarian, 1996—97; chmn. Young Dems. of Bucks County, 1995—98; bd. rep. CYO, Harahan, La., 1983—84. Recipient Disting. Award of Recognition, Dem. Party of Middletown, 1996, Award of Poetic Excellence, Sparrowgrass Poetry Forum, 1995. Mem.: Screen Actors Guild, Actors Equity Assn. (EEOC com. 2001—), Am. Acad. Poets. Avocations: tennis, basketball, bowling, doubloon collecting. Home and Office: Radman Productions 36 Liberty Ave #2 Jersey City NJ 07306

LUZHANSKY, DMITRY M. chemical engineer, researcher; b. Tashkent, Uzbekistan, Nov. 29, 1957; s. Moshe S. Luzhansky and Polina B. Polinkovskaya; m. Maria N. Zisman; children: Igor, Leah. BS in Thermal Engring., Tech. U., Tashkent, 1979, PhD in Chem. Engring., 1985. Jr. scientist Tech. U., Tashkent, Uzbekistan, sr. scientist Uzbekistan, 1985—93; unit ops. lab mgr. U. Pa., Phila., 1994—98; sr. engr. Donaldson Co., Inc., Mpls., 1998—. Co-author: (book) Wastefree Technology of Polymer Processing, 1989. Mem.: AIChE, Am. Fiber Soc., Am. Chem. Soc. Office: Donaldson Co Inc PO Box 1299 Minneapolis MN 55440 Office Fax: 952-887-3937. Business E-Mail: dmitryl@corptech.donaldson.com.

LUZIO, TIMOTHY JOSEPH, protective services official; b. St. Louis, Dec. 25, 1956; s. Kenneth F. and Genevieve J. (Ford) L.; m. Mary Dale Leitze, Nov. 12, 1977; children: Glenn J. Smith, Christopher Alan, Nathan Scott. Cert., Forest Park C.C., 1977. Lic. paramedic, Mo.; Certified firefighter, fire officer; ACLS provider, pre-hosp. trauma life support provider. Nurse asst. Belleville (Ill.) Meml. Hosp., 1974-78; paramedic City of St. Louis, 1978; paramedic, fire fighter Creve Coeur (Mo.) Fire Protection Dist., 1979—, paramedic capt., 1996—. Coord. emergency med. svcs. week Creve Coeur Fire Protection Dist., 1994—, vial of life coord., 1994—, internet web page designer, 1996—, citizen's CPR officer, 1996—, emergency med. svcs. pub. rels. and fire prevention liaison officer, 1996—, ice rescue specialist 2000—. Webelos leader, com. mem. Boy Scouts Am., Belleville, 1979-82; Bible studies leader, deacon, elder, tchr. 1st Christian Ch., Belleville, 1990-95, chmn. bd. 1999-2001. Named Emergency Med. Svcs. Provider of Yr. St. John's Mercy Med. Ctr., 1995, Emergency Med. Svcs. Officer of Yr. Creve Coeur-Olivette C. of C., 1995-96; recipient Honor Mo. Ho. of Reps., 1996. Mem. Am. Heart Assn. (instr. BLS 1980—). Avocations: computers, boating, horseback riding, R.V.ing, designing web page. Home: 1319 Terrace Green Ln O'Fallon IL 62269-7213 Office: Creve Coeur Fire Protection Dist 11221 Olive Blvd Creve Coeur MO 63141-7652 E-mail: medictim1@yahoo.com.

LUZKOW, JACK LAWRENCE, history educator, writer, consultant; b. Detroit, Dec. 18, 1941; s. Irving and Sally (Eagle) Farber; m. Susan Frankel, Mar. 27, 1964 (div. Dec. 1973); 1 child, Catherine Alexis; m. Virginia Ann Trieglaff, May 15, 1976 (div. May 1998); 1 child, Frank Jason; m. Yelena Vardzigoulova, July 23, 1998. BA, Wayne State Univ., 1966; MA, St. Louis Univ., 1975, PhD, 1981. Bibliographic specialist Southern Ill. Univ., Carbondale, 1979-81; history prof. Union Coll., Barbourville, Ky., 1981-84, Marycrest Coll., Davenport, Iowa, 1984-90, Teikyo-Marycrest Univ., Davenport, 1990—. Pres. Cons. Global Learning, Davenport, 1992-2000; v.p. Lonetree Enterprises, Davenport, 1991-99; pres., Parma House, Ltd., 2000—; v.p. Marycrest Acad. Senate, Davenport, 1990-91; past pres. Inst. Ednl. Seninars, Davenport, 1988; speaker Vis. Artists Series, Davenport, 1985. Author: (novels) The Birthday Present, 2001, Armageddon International University, 2001; contbr. articles to profl. jours. V.p. Latin Am. Human Rights Action Ctr., Iowa City, Iowa, 1988-90. Recipient Mellon-James Still fellowship, Univ. Ky., 1982, 84, rsch. grant Ky. Humanities Coun., Barbourville, 1984, dean's grant Marycrest Coll., 1986, 89, 90, Teikyo Marycrest Univ., 1991. Mem. Nat. Soc. Sci. Assn. (nat. governing & edn. bd. 1990-98), European Studies Assn., Radical Historians of Am., Mo. Valley Hist. Assn., Western Ill. Humanities Coun. Home: 1012 N Summit Apt C Iowa City IA 52245 Office: Teikyo Marycrest Internat U 1607 W 12th St Davenport IA 52804-4034 E-mail: jlluzkow@hotmail.com.

LUZKY, LEONARD, law enforcement official, national guard officer, educator; b. Nuremberg, Germany, Apr. 2, 1946; s. Igor Sergeavich and Feride Ablajkimova-Dorosh; m. Michele Pengitore, Nov. 26, 1998; 1 child Dana Lyn Piscal ;children from previous marriage: Alayna Dorso, Garrett Bayard. M in Human Resources, Pepperdine U., 1977. Cert. police tng. commn., 1967. Infantryman/rigger U.S. Army, 1963-66; sgt. Haledon (N.J.) Police Dept., 1967-73; officer, detective Dover Twp. Police, Toms River, N.J., 1973-95; col., dir. civilian pers. N.J. Army N.G., Ft. Dix, 1977—; safety officer Toms River Bd. Edn., 1999—. Adj. prof. Ocean County Coll., Toms River, 1990—; cons. 1st Response Protective Svcs., Bayville, N.J., 1995—. Mem. Mcpl. Alliance, Twp. of Dover, Toms River, 1993—. Named Policeman of Yr./Crime Prevention Practitioner, State of N.J., 1975, 89. Mem. N.J. Crime Prevention Officer's Assn. (life, pres. 1990-93, Practitioner of Yr. 1985, 90). Republican. Russian Orthodox. Avocation: singing. Home: 962 Riverbrook Ct Toms River NJ 08753-4490 Fax: (732) 573-1252. E-mail: lluzky@adelphia.net.

LVOVSKY, YURI, physicist, applied superconductivity engineer; b. Dnepropetrovsk, Ukraine, Apr. 9, 1952; came to the U.S., 1991; s. Mikhail and Genya (Kuperman) L.; m. Eugenia A. Pekker, July 6, 1974; 1 child, Marianna. BS in Physics and Applied Math., Novosibirsk (Russia) U., 1974; PhD in Physics, Inst. Thermal Physics, Novosibirsk, 1981. Jr. rsch. fellow Inst. Thermal Physics, Soviet Acad. Scis., Novosibirsk, 1974-83; sr. rsch. fellow Ukrainian Acad. Sci., Dnepropetrovsk, 1983-91; prin. engr. Babcock & Wilcox Co., Lynchburg, Va., 1992-97; sr. magnet analyst Intermagnetics Gen. Corp., Latham, N.Y., 1997-99, lead engr., 1999—. Contbr. articles to profl. jours. Achievements include research on thermal stability and quench in a.c. and d.c. superconductors; contributed to the theory of self-sustained oscillations and autowaves in nonlinear dissipative media and applied results to the analysis of superconducting systems; performed key analysis of superconducting magnets for accelerators, fusion and superconducting magnetic energy storage. Office: Intermagnetics Gen Corp Magnet Bus Unit PO Box 461 450 Old Niskayuna Rd Latham NY 12110-1500

LYALL, KATHARINE C(ULBERT), academic administrator, economics educator; b. Lancaster, Pa., Apr. 26, 1941; d. John D. and Eleanor G. Lyall. BA in Econs., Cornell U., 1963, PhD in Econs., 1969; MBA, NYU, 1965. Economist Chase Manhattan Bank, N.Y.C., 1963-65; asst. prof. econs. Syracuse U., 1969-72; prof. econs. Johns Hopkins U., Balt., 1972-77, dir. grad. program in pub. policy, 1979-81; dep. asst. sec. for econs. Office Econ. Affairs, HUD, Washington, 1977-79; v.p. acad. affairs U. Wis. Sys., 1981-85; prof. of econ. U. Wis., Madison, 1982—; acting pres. U. Wis. Sys., 1985-86, 91-92, exec. v.p., 1986-91, pres., 1992—. Bd. dirs. Kemper Ins. Cos., Marshall & Ilsley Bank, Wis. Power & Light, Alliant; pres., bd. dirs. Carnegie Found. for Advancement of Teaching. Author: Reforming Public Welfare, 1976, Microeconomic Issues of the 70s, 1978. Mem. Mcpl. Securities Rulemaking Bd.,

Washington, 1990-93. Mem. Am. Econ. Assn., Assn. Am. Univs., Phi Beta Kappa. Home: 6021 S Highlands Ave Madison WI 53705-1110 Office: U Wis Sys Office of Pres 1720 Van Hise Hall 1220 Linden Dr Madison WI 53706-1559

LYBARGER, JEFFREY ALLEN, epidemiology research administrator; b. Granite, Ill., 1951; MD, So. Ill. U., 1976. Diplomate Am. Bd. Preventive Medicine in Pub. Health, Preventive Medicine and Occupl. Medicine. Intern in pediat. St. Louis U. Glennon Hosp., 1976-77; resident in occupl. medicine U. Cin., 1979-81; resident in pub. health, pub. medicine Ctrs. for Disease Control, Atlanta, 1982-84; dir. divsn. health studies Agy. for Toxic Substances and Disease Registry, 1989—. Mem. Soc. for Epidemiol. Rsch., Soc. for Occupl. and Environ. Health, Internat. Soc. for Environ. Epidemiology. Office: Agy Toxic Subs/Disease Reg 1600 Clifton Rd NE Stop E28 Atlanta GA 30329-4018

LYBARGER, JOHN STEVEN, human resources development consultant, trainer; b. Yuba City, Calif., June 13, 1956; s. Rodger Lee and Phyllis Ruth (Roseman) L.; m. Marjorie Kathryn Den Uyl, Aug. 22, 1981; children: Ashley Ann, Ryan Christopher. AA, Yuba Community Coll., 1977; BS in Christian Edn., Biola U., La Mirada, Calif., 1980; MS in Counseling, Calif. State U., Fullerton, 1984; PhD in Psychology, Calif. Coast U., 1985, MBA in Bus. Adminstrn., 1999. Lic. marriage family and child counselor; cert. alternative dispute resolution educator/practitioner. Assoc. dir. Concept 7 Family Svcs., Tustin, Calif., 1981-85; exec. dir. Family Life Ctr., 1984-86; pres. Marriage & Family Counseling, La Habra, Calif., 1985-89; clin. dir. New Life Treatment Ctrs., Inc., Laguna Beach, 1988-89; faculty Loma Linda (Calif.) U. Sch. Medicine, 1990; dir. partial hospitalization programs CPC Brea Canyon Hosp., 1991-93; clin. dir. Oasis Counseling Ctr., Denver, 1993-95; pres. Lybarger & Assocs., Westminster, Colo., 1995—. Tng. cons. Dale Carnegie Tng., Denver, 1995-96; pres., CEO Nat. Coun. on Sexual Addiction, Atlanta, 1990-94. Mem. Am. Assn. for Marriage and Family Therapy (clin.). Republican. Avocations: skiing, tennis, racquetball. Home: 8489 W 95th Dr Broomfield CO 80021-5330 Office: 9975 Wadsworth Pkwy Ste K2-414 Broomfield CO 80021-4296

LYBARGER, MARJORIE KATHRYN, nurse; b. Holland, Mich., Apr. 23, 1956; d. Richard Simon and Mary Kathryn (Homan) Den Uyl; m. John Steven Lybarger, Aug. 22, 1981; children: Ashley Ann, Ryan Christopher. BA in Psychology, Biola U., Calif., 1979, BS in Nursing, 1984. RN, Calif. Staff nurse Presbyn. Intercommunity Hosp., Whittier, Calif, 1985-86, Healthcare Med. Ctr., Tustin, Calif., 1986-88; staff nurse med.-telemetry unit Friendly Hills Regional Med. Ctr., La Habra, 1988-90; staff nurse telemetry unit Riverside (Calif.) Community Hosp., 1990-93; staff nurse med. telemetry unit St. Anthony's Ctrl. Hosp., Denver, 1993-94; clin. RN 1 cardiovascular intermediate care unit St. Anthony's Ctr., 1994-98, staff RN, 1998—. case mgr., 1999—. Mem. Gamma Phi Beta. Republican. Avocations: snowskiing, swimming, tennis. Home: 8489 W 95th Dr Broomfield CO 80021-5330 E-mail: mklyb@aol.com.

LYBECKER, MARTIN EARL, lawyer; b. Lincoln, Nebr., Feb. 11, 1945; s. Earl Edward and Jeanette Frances (Kiefer) L.; m. Andrea Kristine Tollefson, Dec. 27, 1969; children: Carl Martin, Neil Anders. BBA, U. Wash., 1967, JD, 1970; LLM in Taxation, NYU, 1971; LLM, U. Pa., 1973. Bar: Wash. 1970, D.C. 1972, Pa. 1982. Atty. investment mgmt. div. SEC, Washington, 1972-75, assoc. dir. div., 1978-81; assoc. prof. SUNY, Buffalo, 1975-78; ptnr. Drinker Biddle & Reath, Washington, 1981-87, Ropes & Gray, Washington, 1987—2002, Wilmer, Cuther & Pickering, Washington, 2002—. Adj. prof. Georgetown U., Washington, 1974-75, 80-81; vis. assoc. prof. Duke U., Durham, N.C., 1977-78, sr. lecturing fellow in law, 2000—. Contbr. articles to law revs. Fellow U. Pa. Ctr. for Study of Fin. Instns., 1971-72. Mem. ABA (mem. subcom. on investment cos. and investment advisers, mem. subcom. on securities activities of banks, mem. com. on fed. regulation of securities bus. law sect., mem. com. on devels. in investment svcs. bus. law sect., chair com. of banking bus. law sect.), Am. Law Inst., Univ. Club Washington. Home: 2806 Daniel Rd Bethesda MD 20815-3149 Office: Wilmer Cuther & Pickering 2445 M St NW Washington DC 20037-1420 E-mail: mlybecker@wilmer.com.

LYBERATOS, ANDREAS, physicist, researcher; b. Pireas, Greece, June 2, 1960; arrived in England, 1979; s. Nicholas and Eugenia (Benetatou) L.; m. Hara Papadaki, 1996; 1 child, Eugenia. BSc in Physics with honors, U. London, 1982, PhD in Physics, 1986. Chartered physicist. Rsch. fellow Lancashire Poly., Preston, Eng., 1989-90, Manchester (Eng.) U., 1990-91, Keele (Eng.) U., 1991-96, Crete U., Iraklion, Greece, 1996-2001, Seagate Technology Inc., Pitts., 2001—. Vis. rschr. IBM, San Jose, Calif., 1984-85. Contbr. articles on theoretical ferromagnetism to profl. jours. With Greek Mil., 1986-88. Mem. Magnetics Soc. of IEEE, Inst. Physics. Address: Seagate Rsch 1251 Waterfront Pl Pittsburgh PA 15222 E-mail: andreas.lyberatos@seagate.com.

LYCETT, SARA See FINNEGAN, SARA ANNE

LYDER, COURTNEY HARVEY, nursing educator, consultant; b. Port of Spain, Trinidad a, June 8, 1966; came to U.S., 1981; s. Ormond and Jean Peters. BA, Beloit (Wis.), 1989; BS, Rush U., Chgo., 1989; MS, Rush U., 1990, D in Nursing, 1991. Asst. prof. St. Xavier U. Sch. Nursing, Chgo., 1991-94; from asst. to assoc. prof. Yale U. Sch. Nursing, 1994-97; assoc. prof., 1997—. Cons. U.S. Health Care Financing Adminstrn., Washington, 1997—; bd. dirs. Nat. Pressure Ulcer Adv. Bd., Washington, 1997. Mem. Gerontol. Soc. Am., Ea. Nursing Rsch. Soc., Sigma Theta Tau. Avocations: traveling, reading, scuba diving. Office: Yale U Sch Nursing 100 Church St S New Haven CT 06519-1703

LYDING, JOHN FREDERICK, retired government administrator, editor; b. Paterson, N.J., May 8, 1930; s. Peter and Francis (Krampert) L.; m. Evelyn Margaret Telford, June 5, 1954; children: Karen E., Leslie A., Kimberly K. BS, U.S. Naval Acad., 1954; BS in Elec. Engring., U.S. Naval Postgrad. Sch., Monterey, Calif., 1962; MPA, Am. U., 1972. Commd. ensign U.S. Navy, 1954, advanced through grades to lt. comdr., 1963, ret., 1971; systems analyst Leulejian Assocs., Roslyn, Va., 1972-76; sr. analyst Info. Spectrum Inc., Alexandria, 1976-77; divsn. dir. Santa Fe Corp., Falls Church, 1977-87; dir. driver licensing State of Md., Glen Burnie, 1988-95. Editor periodical The Perfins Bull., 1982-98. Recipient Navy Achievement medal, Armed Forces Expeditional medal. Mem. Am. Philatelic Soc., The Balt. Philatelic Soc. (bd. govs., 1998-2002, periodical assoc. editor 2000—02), Perfins Soc. (periodical editor 1982-98), Perfins Club, Naval Acad. Alumni Assn., U.S. Submarine Vets., Precancel Stamp Soc. Avocations: stamp collecting, woodworking.

LYE, WILLIAM FRANK, history educator; b. Kimberley, B.C., Can., Feb. 19, 1930; came to U.S., 1955, naturalized, 1981; s. Arthur Percy and Jessie Loretta (Prince) L.; m. Velda Campbell, Oct. 16, 1953; children: William Mark, Matthew Campbell, David Arthur, Victoria, Regina. Student, Ricks Coll., 1953-55, Duke U., 1963; BS, Utah State U., 1959; MA, U. Calif., Berkeley, 1959; PhD, UCLA, 1969. Instr. polit. sci. Ricks Coll., Rexburg, Idaho, 1959-63, 67-68, head dept. polit. sci., 1959-63; tchg. asst. dept. history UCLA, 1964-65; asst. prof. Utah State U., Logan, 1968-69, acting head dept. history and geography, 1969-70, assoc. prof., head dept. history and geography, 1970-73, prof., head dept. history and geography, 1973-76, dean Coll. Humanities, Arts and Social Scis., 1976-83, v.p. for univ. rels., prof. dept. history and geography, 1983-91, prof. history, 1991-95, emeritus, 1996—. Vis. lectr. dept. history Brigham Young U., Provo, Utah, 1970; temporary lectr. dept. history U. Cape Town, Republic of South Africa, 1974; social cons. for project design teams in land conservation, U.S. Agy. for Internat. Devel., Khartoum, Sudan, 1978, Maseru, Lesotho, 1979; mem. higher edn. taskforce on telecom., Utah, 1977-82; chmn. State of Utah Telecom. Coop., 1987, Regents' Com. on Credit by Exam., Utah, 1976; mem. adv. com. Sta. KULC-TV, State Ednl. Telecom. Operating Ctr., 1976-80; bd. dirs., exec. com. Children's Aid Soc. Utah, 1985-89, pres., 1990-91; mem. Utah Statehood Centennial Commn., 1989-96, Utah Christopher Columbus Quincentenary Commn., 1990-91. Author: (with Colin Murray) Transformations on the Highveld: The Tswana and Southern Sotho, 1980, paperback edit., 1985; editor: Andrew Smith's Journal of His Expeditiion into the Interior of South Africa, 1834-36, 1975; prodr. (TV series) Out of Africa, 1977, The God Seekers, 1978; contbr. articles and book revs. to profl. publs. Chmn. State Day celebration, Logan, Utah, 1973, univ. drive for new Logan Regional Hosp.; bishop LDS Ch., 1993-96; chair bd. Nora Eccles Harrison Mus. of Art, 1996—; pres. Friends of USU Librs., 1997—; project dir. Cache Valley Habitat for Humanity, 1999—. Recipient Leadership award Standard of Calif., 1957, Idea of Yr. award Utah State U., 1971, Faculty Svc. award Associated Students, Utah State U., 1977-78, Nicholas and Mary Kay Leone Leadership award, 1991, Caring for Children award Children's Aid Soc. Utah, 1994, Disting. Svc. award Utah State U., 1999, Disting. Emeritus Svc. award Ricks Coll., 2001; Woodrow Wilson Nat. fellow, 1958, Fgn. Area fellow Social Sci. Rsch. Coun., Republic of South Africa, Eng., 1966-67, 67-68; faculty devel. grantee Utah State U., 1972, Human Sci. Rsch. Coun. of South Africa publ. grantee, 1975, Mauerberger Trust grantee, 1976. Mem. African Studies Assn., Royal African Soc., Western Assn. Africanists (program chmn. 1972-74, pres. 1974-76), Am. Soc. Landscape Archs. (accreditation bd. 1976-93), Phi Kappa Phi, Phi Alpha Theta. Home: 60 Raymond Ct Logan UT 84321-4259 Office: Utah State U Dept History 650 N 1100 E Logan UT 84322-0001 E-mail: wlye@pcu.net.

LYERLA, BRADFORD PETER, lawyer; b. Savanna, Ill., Aug. 2, 1954; s. Ralph Herbert and Nancy Lee (Nelson) L.; m. Marilyn Wyse, Aug. 18, 1979; 3 children. BA, U. Ill., 1976, JD, 1980. Bar: Ill. 1980, U.S. Dist. Ct. (no. dist.) Ill. 1980, U.S. Dist. Ct. (no. dist.) Ind. 1982, U.S. Dist. Ct. (no. dist.) Calif. 1991, U.S. Dist. Ct. (ctrl. dist.) Ill. 1991, U.S. Dist. Ct. (ea. dist.) Wis. 2000, U.S. Dist. Ct. Nebr. 1998, U.S. Ct. Appeals (7th cir.) 1983, U.S. Ct. Appeals (fed. cir.) 1991, U.S. Ct. Appeals (2d cir.) 2002, U.S. Supreme Ct. 1995. Former ptnr. Jenner & Block, Chgo.; trial lawyer; ptnr. Wallenstein & Wagner Ltd. Lectr. on litigation and intellectual property law. Author publications in field; editor U. Ill. Law Rev., 1978-80. Bd. dirs. North Suburban Bd. of the Heartland Alliance, Wilmette, Ill., 1987-96, pres. 1993-94; bd. dirs. Traveler's and Immigrant's Aid, Chgo., 1991-95; bd. dirs., sec. Youth Svcs. Project, Inc., Chgo., 1987-91; mem. U. Ill. Pres.'s Coun.; founding mem. Cribbett Soc., U. Ill. Coll. Law; mem. Saints Faith Hope and Charity, Winnetka, Ill. Recipient John Powers Crowley Justice award People's Uptown Law Ctr., 1989. Fellow Am. Bar Found.; mem. ABA (editor litigation sect. intellectual properties litigation quar. 1990—, intellectual property sect. com. on unfair competition litigation), Ill. Bar Assn. (sect. coun. gen. practice sect. 1984-85, intellectual property sect. 1989—, co-editor intellectual property newsletter 1989-95, chair 1996-97), Chgo. Bar Assn. (legal ethics), Am. Intellectual Property Law Assn. (antitrust and fed. lit. com.), Intellectual Property Law Assn. Chgo. (patent litigation), Michigan Shores Club, Phi Beta Kappa, Phi Kappa Phi. Office: Wallenstein & Wagner 53rd Fl 311 S Wacker Dr Chicago IL 60606

LYERLY, ELAINE MYRICK, advertising executive; b. Charlotte, N.C., Nov. 26, 1951; d. J.M. and Annie Mary (Myrick) L.; m. Marc Rauch, Jan. 17, 1987. AA in Advt. and Comml. Design, Cen. Piedmont Community Coll., 1972. Freelance designer Sta. WBTV, Charlotte, N.C., 1972; fashion illustrator Matthews Belk, Gastonia, 1972-73; designer Monte Curry Mktg. and Communication Svcs., Charlotte, 1973-74, exec. v.p., 1974-77; pres. Repro/Graphics, 1975-77, Lyerly Agy. Inc., Charlotte, 1977—. Organizing dir. First Trust Bank. Illustrator: Mister Cookie Breakfast Cookbook, 1985. Former chmn. regional blood com. Greater Carolinas chpt. ARC, 1990-93, mem. nat. implementation com., 1991, chair nat. conv., 2001, mem. nat. bd. govs., 2002--; bd. dirs. United Way, 1996, Child Care Resources, Inc., YMCA. Named Bus. Woman of Yr., Shearson Lehman Hutton/Queens Coll., 1989, N.C. Young Careerist Bus. and Profl. Women's Club, 1981; recipient ACE award Women in Comms., 1993, CPCC Hagemeyer award, 1996, Schley Lyons Leadership Charlotte award, 1999, Bus. Jour. Top 25 Women of Achievement award 2001. Mem. Women Execs., Women Bus. Owners (adv. coun., Leadership award 1990, Woman Bus. Owner of Yr. award 1994), Pub. Rels. Soc. Am. (Counselors Acad. 1985—), Charlotte C. of C. (bd. dirs., diversity coun., long-range planning com., Bus. Woman of Yr. award 1985), Hadassah. Republican. Jewish. Office: Lyerly Agy Inc 4819 Park Rd Charlotte NC 28209-3274 E-mail: elyerly@lyerly.com.

LYERLY, HERBERT KIM, oncology researcher, surgery educator; b. San Diego, Aug. 26, 1958; s. Albert Elliot and Mitsu (Kinoshita) L.; m. Anne Drapkin. BS, U. Calif., Riverside, 1980; MD, UCLA, 1983. Diplomate Am. Bd. Surgery. Intern Duke U., Durham, N.C., 1983, resident in surgery, 1990-94, from asst. prof. to assoc. prof. surgery, 1990-97, asst. prof. pathology, 1991-98, clin. dir. molecular therapeutics, 1993-97, asst. prof. immunology, 1995-97, prof. surgery, 1997—, clin. dir. Ctr. for Molecular and Cellular Therapy, 1997-98, assoc. prof. pathology, 1998—. Editor: Surgical Intensive Care, 2d edit., 1989, co-editor: Surgical Intensive Care, 3d edit., 1991, Companion Textbook of Surgery, 1992, Essentials of Surgery, 1994; co-editor Textbook of Surgery, 15th edit., 1997, Companion Textbook of Surgery, 2d edit., 1997. Mem. ACS, Assn. Acad. Surgery, Soc. Surg. Oncology, Soc. Univ. Surgeons, Am. Soc. Clin. Oncology, Am. Assn. Cancer Rsch. Office: Duke U Hosp PO Box 2606 Durham NC 27715-2606

LYEW, MICHAEL ANDREW, physician, anesthesiologist; b. London, Nov. 27, 1955; came to U.S., 1990; s. Thomas George and Cynthia Veronica (Lai) L. MB, BChir, U. West Indies, Kingston, Jamaica, 1980; MSc in Bioengineering, Dundee (Scotland) U., 1983. Diplomate Am. Bd. Anesthesiology. Registrar in anesthesia U. Dundee Hosp., 1985-88; sr. resident, fellow dept. anesthesia McGill U., Montreal, Que. Can., 1988-89; fellow cardiac anesthesiology Emory U., Atlanta, 1990-92; asst. prof., staff anesthesiologist V.A. Med. Ctr., Dublin, 1992-94, Buffalo (N.Y.) U., 1994-96; asst. prof., staff anesthesiologist dept. anesthesia Mercer U. Med. Ctr. Ctrl. Ga., Macon, 1997-99; dir. pediat. cardiol. anesthesia Children's Med. Ctr., Augusta, Ga., 1999—; assoc. prof. Med. Coll. Ga., 1999—. Dir. Cardiac anesthesia, V.A. Med. Ctr., Buffalo, mem. Liaison com. Blood Bank; co-dir. perfusion svc., Med. Ctr. Ctrl. Ga. Contbr. articles to prof. jours. Asst. March of Dimes Walk America, Macon, 1998; contbr. Republican Party, 1998. Recipient Excellence In Perioperative Care award Med. Ctr. Found., 1997. Fellow Royal Coll. Anesthetists; mem. Soc. Cardiovasc. Anesthesia, Internat. Anesthesia Rsch. Soc., Soc. Pediat. Anesthesia, Am. Soc. Anesthesiologists. Achievements include discovery of device for measuring carbon dioxide during artificial ventilation, 1983, monitoring neuromuscular blockade, 1989, reading thrombelastograms, 1992, reading sonoclot signatures, 1997, investigation of air-oxygen entrainment by verturi masks, 1990. Avocations: photography, scuba diving, skiing. Office: Childrens Med Ctr Dept of Anesthesiology 1446 Harper St Augusta GA 30901-5114 E-mail: mlyew@mail.mdg.edu.

LYFORD, CABOT, sculptor; b. Sayre, Pa., May 22, 1925; s. Frederic Eugene and Eleanor (Cabot) L.; m. Joan Ardyth Richmond, June 22, 1953; children: Matthew, Julia, Thaddeus. BFA, Cornell U., 1950. Exec. trainee NBC, N.Y.C., 1952-54; producer and dir. J. Walter Thompson, 1954-57, Sta. WGBH-TV, Boston, 1957-59; program mgr. Sta. WENH-TV, Durham, N.H., 1959-63; chmn. Dept. Art The Phillips Exeter (N.H.) Acad., 1963-86. Prin. sculptures include pub. monuments in Portland, Maine and Portsmouth, N.H., Berwick, Maine; represented in permanent collections at Portland Mus., Chattanooga Mus., Indpls. Mus., Wichita (Kans.) Mus., Ogunquit (Maine) Mus., Currier Gallery, Manchester, N.H., Addison Gallery, Andover, Mass., Theme sculpture New Bedford (Mass.) Whaling Mus.e With inf. U.S. Army, 1943-46, PTO. Recipient Sculpture prize Nat. Design Acad., 1990. Home: 4 Fish Point Rd New Harbor ME 04554-4606

LYJAK CHORAZY, ANNA JULIA, pediatrician, medical administrator, educator; b. Braddock, Pa., Feb. 25, 1936; d. Walter and Cecilia (Swiatkowski) Lyjak; m. Chester John Chorazy, May 6, 1961; children: Paula Ann Chorazy, Mary Ellen Chorazy-Cuccaro, Mark Edward Chorazy. BS, Waynesburg Coll., 1958; MD, Women's Med. Coll. Pa., 1960. Diplomate Am. Bd. Pediats. Intern St. Francis Gen. Hosp., Pitts., 1960-61; resident in pediats., tchg. fellow Children's Hosp. of Pitts., 1961-63, pediatrician, devel. clinic, 1966-75; pediat. house physician Western Pa. Hosp., Pitts., 1963-66; med. dir. Rehab. Instn. Pitts., 1975-98, Children's Inst., Pitts., 1998—2001; ret., 2001. Clin. asst. prof. pediats. Children's Hosp. Pitts. and U. Pitts. Sch. Medicine, 1971-94, clin. assoc. prof. pediats., 1994-2001; pediat. cons. Children's Home Pitts., 1985-2001. Author chpts. to books. Co-chmn. EACH Joint Planning and Assessment, Pitts., 1980-85; mem. adv. com. 10th Nat. Conf. on Child Abuse, Pitts., 1993. Recipient Miracle Maker award Children's Miracle Network, 1995. Fellow Am. Acad. Pediats.; mem. Pitts. Pediat. Soc. Avocations: reading, comedy, theatre, music, opera. Home: 131 Washington Rd Pittsburgh PA 15221-4437 E-mail: ajccjc@attbi.com.

LYKES, JOSEPH T., III, investments manager; b. Galveston, Tex., Mar. 6, 1948; BA, Washington and Lee U., 1970. Ind. investment mgmt., Tampa, Fla. Office: 1304 DeSoto Ave Ste 303 Tampa FL 33606

LYLE, JAMES ARTHUR, real estate broker; b. Charlottesville, Va., Mar. 9, 1945; s. James Aaron and Sallie (Tuthill) Lyle; m. Martha Lee Gale, Jan. 28, 1978 (dec. June 2, 2000); children: Cory Jackson, Martha Jessica. BS in Indsl. Mgmt., Ga. Inst. Tech., 1968. Cert. comml. investment mem. Mktg. rep. IBM, Atlanta, 1970-71; investment cons. La Salle Ptnrs., El Paso, Tex., 1971-76; owner James Arthur Lyle and Assocs., 1976—. Bd. dirs. Hueco Mountain Estates, Inc., pres., 1983—; bd. dirs. Remington Oil and Gas Corp. Chmn., vice-chmn. El Paso City Plan Commn., 1978-82; vice-chmn. Internat. Airport Bd., 1982; adv. bd. El Paso Bikeway, 1986-88; active El Paso County Planning Commn., 1986-98; bd. dirs. NCCJ, 1978-82, Southwestern Gen. Hosp., 1979-83, El Paso Econ. Devel. Bd., 1980-82; bd. dirs. Am. Heart Assn., 1989-93; mem. Leadership El Paso, 1981-82 1st lt. U.S. Army, 1968-70. Named Bus. Assoc. of Yr., Am. Bus. Womens Assn., 1984, S.W. Challenge Series Champion, 1991-2002, Ironman World Triathlon Championship, 1992, N.Mex. State Triathlon champion, 1999, El Paso Sr. Games Hall of Fame, 2000, Tuscon Triathlon Series Champion, 2001, Tex. Sr. Games Triatholon Champion. Mem. SAR (dist. v.p., Bronze Good Citizenship medal 1996, Cert. of Disting. Svc.), Nat. Assn. Realtors, Realtors Nat. Mktg. Inst., Nat. Assn. Indsl. and Office Parks, Tex. Property Exchangors (Best Exch. 1979), Tex. Assn. Realtors, Tex. Real Estate Polit. Action Com. (life), El Paso Bd. Realtors (bd. dirs. 1975-88, cert. comml. investment mem. 1975—, El Paso-West Tex. cert. comml. investment mem., pres., sec.-treas. 1975—, comml.-investment real estate coun. 1971—), El Paso Indsl. Devel. Bd., El Paso Investment Exch. Svc., Sons Confederate Vets, Sunturians (life), Half Fast Track Club (v.p. multisports), USA Triathlon (bd. dirs. 1995-2001), Team El Paso, Delta Sigma Pi (life), Sigma Alpha Epsilon (life). Republican. Episcopalian. Avocation: triathlons. Home: 811 Rim Rd El Paso TX 79902 Office: James Arthur Lyle & Assocs 720 Arizona Ave El Paso TX 79902-4402

LYLE, JOHN WILLIAM, JR. former state senator, high school principal; b. Providence, May 19, 1950; s. John William and Lois (Smith) L.; m. Lori A. Lyle, Feb. 16. 1992. BA, Barrington Coll., 1973; MEd, Providence Coll., 1978; JD, Suffolk U., 1992. Tchr. Lincoln (R.I.) Sch. Dept., 1974-95, adminstr., 1995-97; senator State of R.I., Dist. 34, 1981-86, 91-94, minority whip, 1993-94; asst. prin. Lincoln H.S., 1995-97; prin. Central Falls (R.I.) H.S., 1997—. Mem. adj. faculty R.I. Coll., Providence, 1990-97, C.C. R.I., Lincoln, 1991-97. Contbr. articles to profl. jour. Trustee Cumb-Line Boys and Girls Club, Cumberland, R.I., 1982; rep. candidate for Sec. of State of R.I., 1986; tennis umpire USTA, N.Y.C., 1985-95; 1st v.p. New Eng. Tennis Umpires Assn.; chair Lincoln Substance Abuse Prevention Coun., 1998-99, R.I. Water Resources Bd., 1987-89; mem. adv. bd. Central Falls Sch., 1997—, SCOPE, 1997—; bd. dirs. R.I. Interscholastic League, 1998—. Robert A. Taft Inst. fellow, 1975, 79, Johns Hopkins U. Close Up fellow; recipient Oustanding Alumnus award Barrington Coll., 1982, Disting. Alumnus award, 1984, Appreciation award No. R.I. Sr. Svcs., 1983, John E. Fogarty award, 1995. Mem. R.I. Bar Assn., R.I. Assn. Social Studies Tchrs., Lincoln Fraternal Order Police, R.I. Assn. Secondary Sch. Prins. (Outstanding First Yr. Prin. 1998), Lincoln Tchrs. Assn. (exec. bd. 1987-90). Avocations: travel, reading, running, cooking. Office: Central Falls HS 24 Summer St Central Falls RI 02863-2142

LYLE, ROBERT EDWARD, chemist; b. Atlanta, Jan. 26, 1926; s. Robert Edward and Adaline (Cason) L.; m. Gloria Gilbert, Aug. 28, 1947 (dec. Dec. 1996); m. Anne Carroll Kohl, Aug. 1, 1997. BA, Emory U., 1945, MS, 1946; PhD, U. Wis., Madison, 1949. Asst. prof. Oberlin Coll., Ohio, 1949-51; asst. prof. U. N.H., Durham, 1951-53, assoc. prof., 1953-57, prof., 1957-76; prof., chmn. dept. chemistry U. North Tex., Denton, 1977-79; v.p. chemistry, chem. engr. S.W Rsch. Inst., San Antonio, 1979-91; v.p. GRL Cons., 1992-97, pres., 1997—. Vis. prof. U. Va., Charlottesville, 1973-74, U. Grenoble, France, 1976; adj. prof. Bowdoin Coll., Brunswick, Maine, 1975-79, U. Tex., San Antonio, 1985—. Mem. editl. bd. Index Chemicus, 1976—. USPHS fellow Oxford U., Eng., 1965; recipient honor scroll award Mass. chpt. Am. Inst. Chemistry, 1971; Harry and Carol Mosher co-awardee, 1986. Fellow AAAS; mem. Am. Chem. Soc. (councilor 1965-84, 86-92, medicinal chemistry divsn.), Royal Soc. Chemistry, Alpha Chi Sigma (editor Hexagon 1992-99, Kuebler award 1998). Methodist. Office: GRL Cons 12814 Kings Forest Dr San Antonio TX 78230-1511 E-mail: geegeel@aol.com.

LYLES, ADELE HEMPHILL, secondary school educator; b. Toccoa, Ga., May 3, 1948; d. Horace and Ruth Boyette Hemphill; m. Samuel Clair Lyles; children: Heath. MA in Edn., North Ga. Coll. and State U., 1985. Cert. secondary English tchr. Secondary English tchr. Stephens County H.S., Toccoa, 1981—. Participant Yonah Cmty. Chorus, Toccoa, 1974—99. Recipient Blue Ridge Leadership award, Blue Ridge Leadership Conf., 2000. Mem.: Nat. Coun. Tchrs. English. Methodist. Avocations: swimming, singing, piano. Office: Stephens County HS 6438 White Pine Rd Toccoa GA 30577

LYLES, MARK BRADLEY, advanced technology company executive, dentist; b. Paducah, Ky., Dec. 3, 1957; s. Kendall Smith Lyles and Charlotte Dean (Ruley) Martell; m. Catherine Lynn Gregg, Mar. 17, 1984 (div. 1995); children: Austin Bradley, Dahlon Patrick. AS, BS, BA in Biology and Chemistry, Murray (Ky.) State U., 1978, MS, EdS, 1981; DMD, U. Louisville, 1986; PhD in Cellular and Structural Biology, U. Tex., San Antonio, 2001. Resident in oral and maxillofacial surgery U. Tex. Health Sci. Ctr., 1991-95; founder, chief exec. officer, pres. Talis Techs., Inc., San Antonio, 1992—; founder, pres., chief sci. officer Materials Evolution and Devel. U.S.A., Inc. (M.E.D. USA), 1993—. Presenter in field. Contbr. articles to profl. jours.; inventor use of ultra-low density fused fibrous ceramics for indsl. applications, use of fused fibrous ceramics in dental materials, implantable sys. for cell growth control, filters for polynuclear aromatic hydrocarbon containing smoke. Comdr. USNR, 1983—. Recipient Dentist-Scientist award Nat. Inst. Dental Rsch., 1991-98; Dept. Chemistry and Bd. Regents scholar Murray State U., 1975-77, Imagineer of Yr. award Mind Sci. Found., 1997; Grad. Coop. Edn. fellow Nat. Ctr. Toxicol. Rsch., EPA, FDA, 1979-80, Grad. fellow U. Louisville, 1981-82. Mem. Am. Coll. Oral and Maxillofacial Surgeons (Walter Lorenz Residents Rsch. award 1994), Acad. Osseointegration, Acad. Gen. Dentistry, Navy Inst., Assn. Mil. Surgeons U.S., Hon. Order Ky. Cols., Naval Res. Officers Assn., Phi Delta Kappa. Republican. Avocations: rifle and pistol marksmanship, weight training, sailing, travel, Harley's. Home: 9127 Cap Mountain Dr San Antonio TX 78255-2057 E-mail: jawbrkr@texas.net.

LYLISTON, WILLIAM PHILLIP, writer, poet; b. Hampton, Va., Apr. 14, 1955; s. William D. and Aurelia M. LyL. Student, U. Richmond, 1973, Christopher Newport U., 1977-79, 84-86. Dept. store, grocery store clk., shipyard laborer; freelance writer, 1975—. Author: (sci. fiction) All Living Things, 1982, Live Wires, 1985, A Time for Caring, 1986, A Voyage to the Stars and Beyond, 1989, A World United in Endeavor, 1990, Writing Poetry for the Fun of It, 1990, Concert on a Far Planet, 1991, The Example of Jesus Christ, 1992, Scenes From the American Blue Ridge, 1992, Lament of an Artificial Intelligence, 1994, Reflections, 1996. Mem. Va. Democratic Orgn., poll-worker, office worker, poll-organizer, state conv. del., 1992 Mem. Internat. Soc. Poets. Methodist. Avocations: walking, guitar, playing games, computers.

LYMAN, ARTHUR JOSEPH, financial executive; b. Evergreen Park, Ill., May 18, 1953; s. Arthur Edward and Margaret (O'Conner) L.; m. Janet Lee Wenzel, Sept. 9, 1984; children: Christina Lee, Alissa Mary, Arthur Joseph Jr. BA, Knox Coll., 1975; M in Mgmt., Northwestern U., 1977. CPA, Ill.; CFP. Audit supr. Arthur Andersen & Co., Chgo., 1977-83; fin. planning analyst Montgomery Ward & Co., 1983-84; dir. fin. and adminstrn. ctrl. region Pricewaterhouse Coopers LLP, 1984-88, CFO Midwest region, 1989-93, nat. dir. fin. field ops., 1993—2001; v.p. finance Med. Rsch. Labs., Buffalo Grove, 2001—. Nation chief YMCA Indian Guides, 1994, 95, 96, 98, fedn. chief, 1997. Mem. AICPA, Fin. Execs. Inst. (bd. dirs. Chgo. chpt. 1992—, pres. 1997-98), Ill. Inst. CPA's, Pi Sigma Alpha, Tau Kappa Epsilon (honor award 1988, chmn. bd. trustees 1988-93). Roman Catholic. Home: 3 Cornell Dr Lincolnshire IL 60069-3222 Office: Med Rsch Labs 1000 Asbury Dr Buffalo Grove IL 60089

LYMAN, CHARLES EDSON, materials scientist, educator; b. Willimantic, Conn., Mar. 7, 1946; s. Edson Hunt and Sylvia (Hill) L.; m. Valerie Ann Livingston, Aug. 30, 1984. BS, Cornell U., 1968; PhD, MIT, 1974. Postdoctoral fellow dept. metallurgy Oxford (England) U., 1974-76; asst. prof. Rensselaer Poly. Inst., Troy, N.Y., 1976-80; staff scientist E.I. DuPont de Nemours, Wilmington, Del., 1980-84; assoc. prof. Lehigh U., Bethlehem, Pa., 1984-90, prof., 1990—. Electron microscopy steering com. Argonne (Ill.) Nat. Lab., 1984—. Author, editor: Scanning Electron Microscopy, X-Ray Microanalysis, and Analytical Electron Microscopy: A Laboratory Workbook, 1990; editor-in-chief: Microscopy and Microanalysis; contbr. articles to profl. jours. Mem. Microscopy Soc. Am. (pres. 1991), Microbeam Analysis Soc. (bd. dirs. 1993-95, pres. 2000), Am. Soc. Materials Internat., Am. Chem. Soc., Burnside Plantation Inc. (pres. 1993), Historic Bethlehem, Inc. (pres. 1996-98). Home: 444 N New St Bethlehem PA 18018-5814 Office: Lehigh U Whitaker Lab 5 E Packer Ave Bethlehem PA 18015-3102 E-mail: charles.lyman@lehigh.edu.

LYMAN, GARY HERBERT, epidemiologist, cancer researcher, educator; b. Buffalo, Feb. 24, 1946; s. Leonard Samuel and Beatrice Louise Lyman; children: Stephen Leonard, Christopher Henry. BA, SUNY, Buffalo, 1968, MD, 1972; MPH, Harvard U., 1982. Diplomate Am. Bd. Internal Medicine, Am. Bd. Oncology and Hematology. Resident in medicine U. N.C., Chapel Hill, 1972-74; fellow in oncology Roswell Park Meml. Inst., Buffalo, 1974-77; rsch. instr. medicine SUNY Med. Sch., 1974-77; mem. faculty U. South Fla. Coll. Medicine, Tampa, 1977-2000, assoc. prof. medicine, 1980-86, prof. medicine, 1986-2000, dir. divsn. med. oncology, 1979-93, chief medicine H. Lee Moffitt Cancer and Rsch. Inst., 1988-2000, prof. epidemiology and biostates., 1988-2000; Thomas Ordway prof. medicine divsn. hematology and oncology Albany (N.Y.) Med. Coll., Union U., 2000—02, dir. Cancer Ctr., 2000—02; prof. biometry and stats. SUNY Sch. Pub. Health, 2000—02; prof. medicine, dept. medicine U. Rochester (N.Y.) Sch. Medicine and Dentistry, 2002—; dir. biostats., assoc. dir. for health svcs. and outcomees rsch. James P. Wilmot Cancer Ctr., 2002—. Vis. prof. med. stats. London Sch. Hygiene and Tropical Medicine, 1997—98. Co-author: Geriatric Oncology, 1998, Comprehensive Geriatric Oncology, 1997; contbr. chpts. to books, articles to profl. jours. Spl. fellow Leukemia Soc. Am., 1976-77; postdoctoral fellow biostats Harvard U., 1981-82; spl. clin. rellow Roswell Park Meml. Inst., 1975-76. Fellow ACP, Am. Coll. Preventive Medicine, Am. Coll. Clin. Pharmacology, Royal Coll. Physicians (Edinburgh); mem. Am. Soc. Clin. Oncology. Achievements include work in cancer clinical trials, biostatistics, epidemiology, clinical decision analysis. Office: U Rochester Med Ctr Box 704 601 Elmwood Ave Rochester NY 14642 Office Fax: 585-273-1043. E-mail: gary_lyman@urmc.rochester.edu.

LYMAN, HELEN HUGUENOR, library science educator; b. Hornell, N.Y., Mar. 16, 1910; d. Leon C. and Lora M. (Hamilton) Huguenor; m. Vreelandt B. Lyman Jr., Apr. 29, 1939 (Dec. Feb. 1946). BA, U. Buffalo, 1932, BSLS, 1940; postgrad., U. Chgo., 1955-56. Libr. Buffalo Pub. Libr., 1932-52, head adult edn. dept., 1943-52; dir. adult edn. survey ALA, Chgo., 1952-53; adult svcs. librarian Hild regional br. Chgo. Pub. Libr., 1953-59; specialist in adult svcs., pub. libr. cons. Wis. Free Libr. Commn., Madison, 1959-63; dir. reference dept., assoc. prof. Lockwood Meml. Libr., SUNY, Buffalo, 1964-65; pub. libr. specialist adult svcs. Office Edn., Dept. HEW, Washington, 1965-67; dir., prin. investigator rsch. project Libr. Sch. U. Wis., Madison, 1967-72, asst. prof., 1966-72, assoc. prof., 1973-76, prof., 1976-77, prof. emerita Sch. Libr. and Info. Studies, 1978—; adj. prof. Sch. Info. and Libr. Studies SUNY, Buffalo, 1978-99. Instr. Great Books course Millard Fillmore Coll., U. Buffalo, 1950-51; dir., cons. Reading Guidance Inst., Libr. Sch., U. Wis., 1965; vis. lectr. SUNY-Buffalo, 1966; lectr. in field. Author: Adult Education Activities in Public Libraries, 1954, Library Materials in Service to Adult New Reader, 1973, Reading the Adult New Reader, 1976, Literacy and the Nations Libraries, 1977; editor issue Libr. Trends, 1971; spl. editor Wis. Libr. Bull., 1969, cons. editor, 1963; contbr. numerous articles to profl. publs.; numerous consultations, presentations and com. assignments. Mem. nat. adv. bd. Ctr. for the Book in the Libr. Congress, 1978-84; mem. com. on profl. devel. Chgo. Pub. Libr. Staff Assn., 1958-59; bd. dirs. Univ. Book Store, Madison, 1973-77, chmn. awards com., 1974-76, sec., 1976-77. Recipient Disting. Achievement in Librarianship, Buffalo & Erie Co. Pub. Libr., 1999. Mem. ALA (Joseph W. Lippincott for Disting. Librarianship award 1979, Margaret E. Monroe Libr. Adult Svcs. award 1986, mem. various coms., v.p. 1968-69, pres. adult svcs. divsn. 1969-70, chmn. publs. adv. com. 1971-73, mem. coun. 1962-65, 68-70, advisor to yearbook editors 1976-85, mem. nominating com. 1977-78), N.Y. Libr. Assn. (adult edn. com. 1947), U. Buffalo Alumni Assn. (disting. alumni award 1987). Democrat. Avocations: gardening, reading.

LYMAN, HENRY, retired publisher, marine fisheries consultant; b. Boston, Oct. 30, 1915; s. Henry and Elizabeth (Cabot) L.; m. Marjorie Borum, June 27, 1953 (dec. Mar. 1996). AB cum laude, Harvard Coll., 1937. Reporter Cape Cod Colonial, Hyannis, Mass., 1937-38; reporter Athol Daily News, 1938-40; editor Open Road Pub. Co., Boston, 1946-48; publisher Salt Water Sportsman, 1948-85, pub. emeritus, 1985—. Advisor Internat. Conv. Conservation of Atlantic Tunas, Washington, 1976-86, New England Fishery Mgmt. Coun., Saugus, Mass., 1980-84; bd. dirs. Atlantic Salmon Fedn., N.Y.C., Nat. Coalition for Marine Conservation, Savannah, Ga., Environ. League Mass., Boston; mem. U.S. sect. North Atlantic Salmon Conservation Orgn., Edinburgh, Scotland, 1983-92. Author: Bluefishing, 1953, rev. edit., 1987, Successful Bluefishing, 1974, (with others) The Complete Book of Striped Bass Fishing, 1954, The Complete Book of Weakfishing, 1959, Tackle Talk, 1971, Bottom Fishing, 1984; contbr. articles on marine fisheries matters. Trustee New England Aquarium, Boston, 1973-88, life trustee, 1988—; founding. trustee Coldwater Conservation Fund, Vienna, Va., 1993—; trustee Manomet Obs., Mass., 1978-90, hon. trustee, 1990—; bd. dirs. Samual Cabot, Inc., Boston, 1974-91, Fund for Preservation of Wildlife and Natural Areas, Boston, 1979-89; incorporator Harvard Mag., Cambridge, Mass., 1979—. Comdr. USNR, 1940-46, 52-53. Mem. Nat. Wildlife Fedn. (bd. dirs. 1983-89), New England Outdoor Writers Assn. (life., bd. dirs. 1960-62), Outdoor Writers Assn. Am., Tavern Club (sec. 1980-83, pres. 1983-84), Harvard Club, Phi Beta Kappa. Avocations: angling; hunting. Home: 10 Longwood Dr Westwood MA 02090-1123 Office: Salt Water Sportsman 263 Summer St Boston MA 02210-1506

LYMAN, JOHN LESLIE, emergency physician; b. Berkeley, Calif., Dec. 3, 1946; BS in Psychology, U. Calif., Davis, 1969; MD, Wright State U., 1980. Diplomate Am. Bd. Emergency Medicine. Intern Miami Valley Hosp., Dayton, Ohio, 1980-81; resident in emergency medicine Wright State U., 1981-83, asst. prof., 1983-86, assoc. prof., 1996—; pvt. practice Panama City, Fla., 1986-92; med. dir. emergency dept. U. Ala., 1992-94; regional med. dir. InPhyNet, Ft. Lauderdale, Fla., 1994-97, Premier Health Care, Dayton, 1997-2000, v.p. emergency medicine, 2000-01; chief med. officer, chief clin. officer, CEO New Century Physicians Premier Health Care, 2001—. Assoc. prof. Wright State U. Sch. Medicine. Mem. Am. Coll. Emergency Physicians, Am. Coll. Physician Execs., Aerospace Med. Assn. Office: 332 Congress Park Dr Dayton OH 45458 E-mail: jlyman@phcsday.com.

LYMAN, PEGGY, artistic director, dancer, choreographer, educator; b. Cin., June 28, 1950; d. James Louis and Anne Earlene (Weeks) Morner; m. David Stanley Lyman, Aug. 29, 1970 (div. 1979); m. Timothy Scott Lynch, June 21, 1982 (div. 1997); 1 child, Kevin Kynch. Grad. h.s., Cin. Solo dancer Cin. Ballet Co., 1964-68, Contemporary Dance Theater, 1970-71; chorus dancer N.Y.C. Opera, 1969-70; Radio City Music Hall Ballet Co., 1970; chorus singer, dancer Sugar, Broadway musical, N.Y.C., 1971-73; prin. dancer Martha Graham Dance Co., 1973-88, rehersal dir., 1989-90; artistic dir. Martha Graham Ensemble, 1990-91; faculty Martha Graham Sch., 1975—; co-artistic dir. Dance Conn., Hartford, 1998-2000. Head dance divns. No. Ky. U., 1977—78; artistic dir. Peggy Lyman Dance Co., N.Y.C., 1978—89; asst. prof. dance, guest choreographer Fla. State U., Tallahassee, 1982—89; guest choreographer So. Meth. U., Dallas, 1986; adjudicator Nat. Coll. Dance Festival Assn., 1983—; co-host To Make a Dance, QUBE cable TV, 1979; mem. guest faculty Am. Dance Festival , Durham, NC, 1984; site adjudicator NEA, 1982—84; tchr. Sch. Dance Conn., 1992—, East Conn. Concert Ballet, 1992—94; guest faculty Wesleyan U. , Middletown , Conn., 1992; guest artist Conn. Coll., 1993; chair dance divsn. Hartt Sch., U. Hartford , Conn., 1994—2001; dir. dance divsn. Hartt Sch., U. Hartford, Conn., 2002—; freelance master tchr. internat. univs. Prin. dancer (TV spls.) Dance in America, 1976, 79, 84; guest with Rudolph Nureyev (CBS-TV) Invitation to the Dance, 1980; guest artist Theatre Choreographique Rennes, Paris, 1981, Rennes, France, 1983; Adelaide U., 1991; site dir. Martha Graham's Diversion of Angels for student concert U. Mich., 1992, Martha Graham's Panorama, U. Ill., Champaign-Urbana, 1993, Towson State U., 1997, Martha Graham's Diversion of Angels for Dutch Nat. Ballet, 1995, Diversion of Angels and Acts of Light for Dance Conn., 1998, Ballet Argentino, 1999; choreographer: Conundrum (solo), 1982, Mantid (group), 1984, Roll, Spin, Draw, or Fold (group), 1984, Chope Dance (solo), 1985, Mirror's Edge (group), 1986, No Gavotte Bach (group), 1995, Interior Landscapes (group), 1997, Family Portrait (group), 1999. Founding mem. Cin. Arts Coun., 1976-78. Mem. Am. Guild Mus. Artists. Office: Dance Conn 224 Farmington Ave Hartford CT 06105-3501 E-mail: dancectplyman@snet.net.

LYMAN, RICHARD WALL, foundation and university executive, historian; b. Phila., Oct. 18, 1923; s. Charles M. and Aglae (Wall) L.; m. Elizabeth D. Schauffler, Aug. 20, 1947; children: Jennifer P., Holly Lyman Antolini, Christopher M., Timothy R. BA, Swarthmore Coll., 1947, LLD (hon.), 1974; MA, Harvard U., 1948, PhD, 1954, LLD (hon.), 1980, Washington U., St. Louis, 1971, Mills Coll., 1972, Yale U., 1975; LHD (hon.), U. Rochester, 1975, Coll. of Idaho, 1989. Teaching fellow, tutor, Harvard U., 1949-51; instr. Swarthmore Coll., 1952-53; instr., then asst. prof. Washington U., St. Louis, 1953-58; mem. faculty Stanford U., 1958-80, 88-91, prof. history, 1962-80, 88-91, Sterling prof. emeritus, 1980-91, assoc. dean Sch Humanities and Scis., 1964-66, v.p., provost, 1967-70, pres., 1970-80, pres. emeritus, 1980—, dir. Inst. Internat. Studies, 1988-91; pres. Rockefeller Found., 1980-88. Spl. corr. The Economist, London, 1953-66; bd. dirs. Coun. on Founds., 1982-88, Independent Sector, 1980-88, chair, 1983-86, Nat. Com. on U.S.-China Rels., 1986-92; dir. IBM, 1978-92, Chase Manhattan Corp., 1981-91. Author: The First Labour Government, 1957; editor: (with Lewis W. Spitz) Major Crises in Western Civilization, 1965, (with Virginia A. Hodgkinson) The Future of the Nonprofit Sector, 1989; editorial bd. Jour. Modern History, 1958-61. Mem. Nat. Coun. on Humanities, 1976-82, vice chmn., 1980-82; chmn. Commn. on Humanities, 1978-80; trustee Rockefeller Found., 1976-88, Carnegie Found. Advancement of Tchg., 1976-82, World Affairs Coun. of No. Calif., 1992-98; bd. dirs. Nat. Assn. Ind. Colls. and Univs., 1976-77, Assn. of Governing Bds. of Univs. and Colls., 1994-97, Am. Alliance for Rights and Responsiblities, 1993—; chmn. Assn. Am. Univs., 1978-79. With USAAF, 1943-46. Decorated officier Legion of Honor; recipient Clark Kerr award U. Calif., Berkeley, 1981; Fulbright fellow London Sch. Econs., 1951-52, hon. fellow, 1978— ; Guggenheim fellow, 1959-60 Fellow Royal Hist. Soc.; mem. Am. Acad. Arts and Scis., Am. Hist. Assn., Council on Fgn. Relations, Am. Philos. Soc., Conf. Brit. Studies, Phi Beta Kappa. Office: Stanford U Sch Edn Stanford CA 94305

LYMAN, WILLIAM WELLES, JR. retired architect; b. New London, Conn., Aug. 31, 1916; s. William Welles and Gladys Estelle (Latimer) L.; m. Margaret Helen Whittemore, July 12, 1941 (div. Sept. 1970); children: Cheryl, Steven, Philip, Susan, Donna, Patricia; m. Joan Evelyn Dalrymple, Sept. 26, 1970. BArch, U. Mich., 1939; MArch, Harvard U., 1940. Architect various orgns., Boston, 1941-42; pvt. practice Cambridge, Mass., 1947-53; chief designer Smith, Hinchman & Grylls, Detroit, 1953-56; architect Swanson Assocs., Bloomfield Hills, Mich., 1956-59, Smith & Smith Assocs., Royal Oak, 1959-62, Jickling Lyman & Powell Assocs., Inc., Birmingham, 1962-81, ret., 1981. Mem. faculty Harvard U., Cambridge, Mass., 1947-53; lectr. on early Am. furniture, 1975—. Pres. Cambridge Coun. PTAs, 1950-52, Harlan Sch. PTA, 1960-61; treas. Mass. Coun. for Better Schs., 1950-52; chmn. Citizens Elem. Curriculum Study Birmingham Pub. Schs., 1962-63; bd. dirs. South Oakland Symphony Soc., 1960-63, Birmingham Teen. Ctr., 1965-67, Birmingham Cmty. House, 1967-70, Profl. Skills Alliance, Detroit, 1973-75, Birmingham Hist. Bd., 1969-73, chmn., 1972-73; chmn. Birmingham Hist. Dist. Study Com., 1975-77, Cmty. Devel. Svcs., Portsmouth, N.H., 1993-96; pres. Birmingham Hist. Soc., 1980-81, bd. dirs. 1967-70; chmn. acquisitions com. John W. Hunter House, 1974-82; bd. govs. Warner House Assn., Portsmouth, N.H., 1983-91, chmn., 1986-88. U.S. Coast Guard, 1942-46. Fellow: AIA; mem.: York Pub. Libr. Assn. (trustee 1999—2002), Mich. Soc. Architects (pres. 1970). Unitarian Universalist. Home: 15 Victoria Ct York ME 03909-1454

LYNCH, AMANDA KATHRYN, writer; b. Pitts., July 20, 1970; d. Calvin Stewart and Audrey Clark Lynch; m. Craig Eric Morris, Jan. 24, 1998. BA, Point Pk. Coll., 1996. Author: (book) Sane Living, 1997; contbr. column; dir.: (plays) for Seton Pioneers; contbr. flash fiction, articles. Recipient One Month Writer residency, Vt. Studio Ctr., 1998. Mem.: Pitts. Profl. Women Writers, Assn. Women in Comm., Soc. Profl. Journalists. Conservative. Avocations: fishing, hiking, movies, computer games, community theatre. Personal E-mail: amandawriter@yahoo.com.

LYNCH, BENJAMIN LEO, oral surgeon educator; b. Omaha, Dec. 29, 1923; s. William Patrick and Mary (Rauber) L.; m. Colleen D. Cook, Nov. 10, 1956; children: Kathleen Ann, Mary Elizabeth, Patrick, George, Martha, Estelle. BSD, Creighton U., 1945, DDS, 1947, MA, 1953; fellow, U. Tex., 1947-48; MSD, Northwestern U., 1954. Diplomate Am. Bd. Oral and Maxillofacial Surgery. Asst. instr. oral surgery Creighton U., 1948-50, instr., 1950-52, asst. prof., 1952-53; dean Creighton U. (Sch. Dentistry), 1954-61, assoc. prof. oral surgery, 1954—57, prof. oral surgery, 1957-86, prof. emeritus, 1986—, dir. oral surgery dept., 1954-67; also coordinator grad. and postgrad. programs; chief oral surgeon Douglas County Hosp., Omaha, 1951-63; pres. dental staff Children's Meml. Hosp., 1952, 59, co-founder cleft palate team, 1959; chmn. dept. dentistry Bergan-Mercy Hosp., Omaha, 1963-68; mem. exec. com., head dental staff Luth. Hosp., 1963-66; bd. dirs. Nebr. Dental Service Corp., 1972-78, pres., 1974-78; treas. Children's Meml. Hosp. Med.-dental staff, 1979-81. Guest lectr. Walter Reed Grad. Sch. Medicine, 1957-58. Mem. Omaha-Douglas County Health Bd., 1966-68, v.p., 1967, pres., 1968; exec. com. Nebr. divsn. Am. Cancer Soc., 1963-67; bd. dirs. Nebr. Blue Cross, 1968-89, Creighton U. Alumni Coun., Omaha chpt., 1989-91, Cath. Acad., Omaha, 2000—; trustee United Cath. Social Svcs., 1989-95; adv. bd. to dean Creighton U. Dental Sch., 1984—, vice chmn., 1992-93, chmn., 1993-94; pres. Creighton U. Graybackers, 1991-94. Served at Walter Reed U.S. Army Med. Ctr., 1955-57. Recipient Alumni merit award Creighton U., 1978; named one of Ten Outstanding Young Omahans, 1952, 53, 58; inducted into Nebr. Dental Hall of Fame, 1981 Fellow Am. Coll. Dentists (pres. Nebr. chpt. 1973-74); mem. Am. Soc. Oral Surgeons, Midwest Soc. Oral Surgeons, Nebr. Soc. Oral Surgeons (founder 1957, pres. 1961), Nebr. Dental Soc. (trustee 1964-66), Omaha Dist. Dent Soc. (pres. 1963-64), Am. Coll. Oral-Maxillofacial Surgeons (founding mem.), Nebr. Soc. Dental Anesthesiology (founder, 1st pres.), Alpha Sigma Nu, Omicron Kappa Epsilon, Delta Sigma Delta. Home: 509 S Happy Hollow Blvd Omaha NE 68106-1224

LYNCH, BEVERLY PFEIFER, education and information studies educator; b. Moorhead, Minn. d. Joseph B. and Nellie K. (Bailey) Pfeifer; m. John A. Lynch, Aug. 24, 1968. BS, N.D. State U., 1957, L.H.D. (hon.); MS, U. Ill., 1959; PhD, U. Wis., 1972. Librarian Marquette U., 1959-60, 62-63; exchange librarian Plymouth (Eng.) Pub. Library, 1960-61; asst. head serials div. Yale U. Library, 1963-65, head, 1965-68; vis. lectr. U. Wis., Madison, 1970-71, U. Chgo., 1975; exec. sec. Assn. Coll. and Research Libraries, 1972-76; univ. librarian U. Ill.-Chgo., 1977-89; dean Grad. Sch. Libr. and Info. Sci. UCLA, 1989-94, prof. Grad. Sch. Edn. and Info. Studies, 1989—; interim pres. Ctr. for Rsch. Librs., Chgo., 2000-01. Author: (with Thomas J. Galvin) Priorities for Academic Libraries, 1982, Management Strategies for Libraries, 1985, Academic Library in Transition, 1989, Information Technology and the Remaking of the University Library, 1995. Named Acad. Libr. of Yr., 1982, one of top sixteen libr. leaders in Am., 1990; fellow Indo-U.S. Subcommn. on Edn. and Culture, 1992-93. Mem. ALA (pres. 1985-86, coun. 1998—, com. on accreditation 1999—, chair 1999—), Nat. Info. Stds. Orgn. (bd. dirs. 1996—, vice chair 1999-2001, chair 2001—),Rare Book Sch. U. Va.(bd. dir.), Acad. Mgmt., Am. Sociol. Assn., Assn. for the Study of Higher Edn., Bibliog. Soc. Am., Caxton Club, Grolier Club, Book Club Calif., Phi Kappa Phi. Office: UCLA Grad Sch Edn Info Mailbox 951521 Los Angeles CA 90095-0001

LYNCH, BRIDGET, artist; b. June 6, 1953; Student, Colo. U., Kyoto, Japan, 1973-74; BA, U. Kans., 1975; student, Sch. Mus. Fine Arts, Boston, 1983-85. Works include solo installations Simmons Coll., Boston, 1996, U. Mass., Lowell, 1997, Montserrat Coll. Art, Beverly, Mass., 1998, Multi-Media, Art Complex Mus., Duxbury, Mass., 1999, Gallery X-New Bedford (Mass.) Film and Video Festival, 2001. Recipient award St. Botolph Club Found., 1995, Puffin Found., 1996, others. Avocations: cooking, gardening, walking. Studio: 52A Hall St Jamaica Plain MA 02130-3220

LYNCH, CATHERINE GORES, social work administrator; b. Waynesboro, Pa., Nov. 23, 1943; d. Landis and Pamela (Whitmarsh) Gores; m. Joseph C. Keefe, Nov. 29, 1981; children; Shannon Maria, Lisa Alison, Gregory T. Keefe, Michael D. Keefe. BA magna cum laude with honors, Bryn Mawr Coll., 1965; postgrad., Cornell U., 1966-67. Cert. police instr. Mayor's intern Human Resources Adminstrn., N.Y.C., 1967; rsch. asst. Orgn. for Social and Tech. Innovation, Cambridge, Mass., 1967-69; cons. Ford Found., Bogota, Columbia, 1970; staff Nat. Housing Census, Nat. Bur. Statistics, 1971; evaluator Foster Parent Plan, 1973; rsch. staff FEDESARROLLO, 1973-74; dir. Dade County Advocates for Victims, Miami, Fla., 1974-86; asst. to dep. dir. Dept. Human Resouces, 1986-87, computer liaison, 1987-88, asst. adminstr. placement svcs. program, 1988-89; exec. dir. Health Crisis Network, 1989-96; liaison HIV cmty. svc. State of Fla. Health and Rehab. Svcs., 1996-97; program ops. adminstr. adult protective svcs. Fla. Dept. Children and Families, 1997-2000; dir. grants mgmt. U. Miami Sch. Nursing, 2000—. Guest lectr. local univs. Participant, co-chmn. various task forces rape, child abuse, incest, family violence, elderly victims of crime, nat. state, local levels, 1974-86, 99—; developer workshops in field; participant, chair, co-chair task forces on HIV/AIDS impact; long term care, children and AIDS, AIDS orgnl. issues, 1991-96; mem. gov.'s task force on victims and witnesses, gov.'s task force on sex offenders and their victims, gov.'s Red Ribbon panel on AIDS, 1992-93, gov.'s interdepartmental work group, 1993-96; mem. ednl. rev. com. Am. Found AIDS Rsch., 1991-96; vice chair Metro-Dade HIV Svcs. Planning Coun., 1991-93; active Fla. HIV Svcs. Adv. Coun., 1991-94; rev. panel Fed. Spl. Projects of Nat. Significance; adv. coun. Metro Dade Social Svcs., 1995-96; cert. expert witness on battered women syndrome in civil and criminal cts. Contbr. writings to field to publs. Recipient various pub. svcs. awards including WINZ Citizen of Day, 1979, Outstanding Achievement award Fla. Network Victim Witness Svcs., 1982, Pioneer award Metro-Dade Women's Assn., 1989; Fulbright scholar U. Central de Venezuela, Caracas, 1965-66; Lehman fellow Cornell U. Mem. NASW, Nat. Orgn. of Victim Assistance Programs (bd. dirs. 1977-83, Outstanding Program award 1984), Fla. Network of Victim/Witness Programs (bd. dirs., treas. 1980-81), Am. Soc. Pub. Adminstrs., Dade County Fedn. Health and Welfare Workers, Fla. Assn. Health and Social Svcs. (Dade county chpt., treas., 1979-80), LWV (bd. dirs. Dade County chpt. 1988-92), Fla. Consortium Sch.-Based Health Ctrs. (sec. 2001—). Office: U Miami Sch Nursing 5801 Red Rd Coral Gables FL 33143 E-mail: clynch@miami.edu.

LYNCH, CHARLES ALLEN, investment executive, corporate director; b. Denver, Sept. 7, 1927; s. Laurence J. and Louanna (Robertson) L.; divorced; children: Charles A., Tara O'Hara, Casey Alexander; m. Justine Bailey, Dec. 27, 1992. BS, Yale U., 1950. With E.I. duPont de Nemours & Co., Inc., Wilmington, Del., 1950—69, dir. mktg., 1965—69; corp. v.p. SCOA Industries, Columbus, Ohio, 1969—72; corp. exec. v.p., also mem. rotating bd. W.R. Grace & Co., N.Y.C., 1972—78; chmn. bd., chief exec. officer Saga Corp., Menlo Park, Calif., 1978—86, also dir.; chmn., chief exec. officer DHL Airways, Inc., Redwood City, 1986—88; also dir.; pres., CEO Levolor Corp., 1988—89, also bd. dir., chmn. exec. com. of bd., 1989—90; chmn. Market Value Ptnrs. Co., Menlo Park, Calif., 1990—95; chmn., dir. Fresh Choice, Inc., Santa Clara, 1995—; also bd. dirs.; chmn. Market Value Ptnrs. Co., 1999—; chmn., CEO Food Platform, The Shansby Group, 2001—; CEO food platform The Shansby Group, 2001—; chmn. adv. bd. Clark/Bardes Cons., 2000—. Bd. dirs. Spectrum Organic Products, Inc., SRI Internat., Cloudsource, Inc. Bd. dirs. United Way, 1990-92, past chmn. Bay Area campaign, 1987; vice chmn., dir. Bay Area Coun.; past chmn. Calif. Bus. Roundtable; mem. adv. bd. U. Calif.-Berkeley Bus. Sch., Governance Bd.; chmn. bd. trustees Palo Alto Med. Found. Mem. Yale Club (N.Y.C.), Internat. Lawn Tennis Club, Menlo Country Club (Calif.), Pacific Union Club (San Francisco), Coral Beach and Tennis Club (Bermuda), Vintage Club (Indian Wells, Calif.), Menlo Circus Club. Republican. Home: 96 Ridge View Dr Atherton CA 94027-6464 Office: 333 Ravenswood Ave Ste Ag320 Menlo Park CA 94025-3453

LYNCH, CHARLES ANDREW, chemical industry consultant; b. Bklyn., Jan. 6, 1935; s. Charles Andrew and Mary Martina (McEvoy) L.; m. Marilyn Anne Monaco, July 30, 1960; children: Nancy Callan, Cara Martina. BS, Manhattan Coll., 1956; PhD, U. Notre Dame, 1960. Rsch. chemist Esso Rsch. & Engring. Co., Linden, N.J., 1960-65; rsch. supr. organic chemistry divsn. FMC Corp., Balt., 1965-72, rsch. mgr. indsl. chemistry divsn. Princeton, N.J., 1972-74; exec. v.p. Am. Oil & Supply Co., Newark, 1974-80; tech. dir., dir. sales & mktg., dir. rsch. & bus. devel., v.p. tech. Hatco Corp., Fords, N.J., 1981-95; with Calivera Cons., 1995—; account exec. N.J. Commerce and Econ. Growth Commn., 1997—. Contbr. articles to profl. jours.; patentee in field (U.S. and foreign). Mem. Am. Chem. Soc., Soc. Tribologists and Lubrication Engrs. (chmn. N.Y. sect. 1980-81, 97-98), Ind. Lubricant Mfrs. Assn. (bd. dirs. 1985-88).

LYNCH, CHARLES THEODORE, SR. materials science engineering researcher, consultant, educator; b. Lima, Ohio, May 17, 1932; s. John Richard and Helen (Dunn) L.; m. Betty Ann Korkolis, Feb. 3, 1956; children: Karen Elaine Ostdiek, Charles Theodore Jr., Richard Anthony, Thomas Edward. BS, George Washington U., 1955; MS, U. Ill., 1957, PhD in Analytical Chemistry, 1960. Group leader ceramics div. Air Force Materials Lab., Wright-Patterson AFB, Ohio, 1962-66; lectr. in chemistry Wright State U., Dayton, 1964-66; chief advanced metall. studies br. Air Force Materials Lab., Wright-Patterson AFB, 1966-74, sr. scientist, 1974-81; head materials div. Office of Naval Rsch., Arlington, Va., 1981-85; pvt. practice cons. Washington, 1985-88; sr. engr. space ops. Vitro Corp., 1988-95, 96-98; cons. Burke, Va., 1996—; sr. cons. space ops. Marconi Systems Techs., Washington, 1998-99; v.p. RSC&L,Inc., Grayling, Mich., 1996—. USAF liaison mem. NMAB Panels on Solids Processing, Ion Implantation and Environ. Cracking, Washington, 1975-76, 78, 81; U.S. rep. AGARD structures and materials panel NATO, 1983-85. Co-author: Metal Matrix Composites, 1972; editor, author: Practical Handbook of Materials Science, 1989; editor: (series) Handbook of Materials Science, vol. I, 1974, vol. II, 1975, vol. III, 1975; vice chmn. editorial bd. Vitro Corp. Tech. Jour., 1989-92, chmn., 1993; contbr. articles to profl. jours. including Jour. Am. Ceramics Soc., Analytical Chemistry, Sci., Transactions AIME, Corr. Jour., Jour. Inorganic Chemistry, SAMPE, Jour. Less Common Metals. Mem., soloist George Washington U. Traveling Troubadours, Washington, 1950-55; choir dir. Trinity United Ch. of Christ, Fairborn, Ohio, 1966-81, Univ. Bapt. Ch., Champaign, Ill., 1957-60, Chapel II, Wright-Patterson AFB, Ohio, 1960-64; pres. Pub. Sch. PTO, 1967-69. 1st lt. USAF, 1960-62. Bailey scholar U. Ill., 1958-60; recipient Commendation medal USAF, 1962, Outstanding Achievement cert. NASA, 1992, award Soc. for Tech. Comm. Publ., 1993. Mem. Am. Chem. Soc. (treas. 1966-67, chmn. audit sect. 1967-68), ASM Internat. (sec. oxidation and corrosion com. 1980-81, chmn. 1981-82). Presbyterian. Achievements include patents for new corrosion inhibitors including encapsulated types, and for alkoxides and oxides; co-development of the refractory ceramic Zytrite, the first high density translucent zirconia made from thermal or hydrolytic decomposition of mixed alkoxides followed by hot pressing; pioneered general approach of organometallic compounds as precursors of high purity, fine particulate, materials. Office: 5629 Kemp Ln Burke VA 22015-2041

LYNCH, CHARLOTTE ANDREWS, retired communications executive; b. Fall River, Mass., Mar. 25, 1928; d. Alan Hall and Florence (Worthen) Andrews; m. Francis Bradley Lynch, June 7, 1952; children: Sarah Faldetta, Richard, Stephen, William. AB in Philosophy, Radcliffe Coll., 1950; postgrad., U. Bridgeport, 1969-71. Adminstrv. asst. Mass. Congl. Confs. and Missionary Soc., Boston, 1951-52; journalist Town Crier newspaper, Westport, Conn., 1968; asst. dir. devel. Cape Cod Hosp., Hyannis, Mass., 1975-76; parish adminstr. S. Congl. Ch., Centerville, 1976-83; cons. to ethnic advt. agy. Loiminchay, Inc., N.Y.C., 1992-98; ret. Mem. Radcliffe Club Cape Cod (v.p. 1990-97, pres. 1997-2000, exec. com. 1990-2000), Harvard Club of Boston. Republican. Roman Catholic. Avocation: travel.

LYNCH, CRAIG TAYLOR, lawyer; b. Miami, Fla., Apr. 26, 1959; s. Glenn James and Faith Rowland (Folsom) L. BS, Fla. State U., 1981; JD, U. N.C., Chapel Hill, 1986. Bar: N.C. 1986, U.S. Dist. Ct. (we. dist.) N.C. 1986, U.S. Ct. Appeals (4th cir.) 1992. Analyst Ford Motor Co., Charlotte, N.C., 1981-82, zone mgr., 1982-83; assoc. Parker, Poe, Adams & Bernstein, 1986-93, ptnr., 1994—, chmn. recruiting com., 1996—. Author: A Marketing Plan for Basketball, 1981. Vol. Lawyers Program, Charlotte, 1986—. Named to Charlotte Bus. Jour. Forty Under Forty, 1995. Mem. ABA (real property sect.), Nat. Multiple Sclerosis Soc. (co-chair Nat. Chmn.'s Adv. Coun. 2000—, fundraising com. chmn. Mid-Atlantic chpt. 1992-93, bd. dirs. 1993—, chmn. 1995-98, Young Profl. Vol. of Yr. 1993), N.C. State Bar Assn., N.C. Bar Assn., Mecklenburg County Bar Assn., Fla. State U. Alumni Assn. (bd. dirs. 1987—), Fla. State U. Alumni Club Charlotte (pres. 1990-93, mem. comml. bd. realtors local region 1997—), Charlotte Chamber Leadership Sch. (Land Use com., Tower Club Charlotte, Beta Gamma Sigma, Phi Delta Phi. Avocations: photography, running, golf, sports, travel. Office: Parker Poe Adams & Bernstein LLP Three First Union Ctr 401 S Tryon St Ste 3000 Charlotte NC 28202

LYNCH, DAVID WILLIAM, physicist, educator; b. Rochester, N.Y., July 14, 1932; s. William J. and Eleanor (Fouratt) L.; m. Joan N. Hill, Aug. 29, 1954 (dec. Nov. 1989); children: Jean Louise, Richard William, David Allan; m. Glenys R. Bittick, Nov. 14, 1992. BS, Rensselaer Poly. Inst., 1954; MS, U. Ill., 1955, PhD, 1958. Asst. prof. physics Iowa State U., 1959-63, assoc. prof., 1963-66, prof., 1966—, chmn. dept., 1985-90, disting. prof. liberal arts and scis., 1985—; on leave at U. Hamburg, Germany; and U. Rome, Italy, 1968-69; sr. physicist Ames Lab. of Dept. of Energy; acting assoc. dir. Synchrotron Radiation Ctr., Stoughton, Wis., 1984. Vis. prof. U. Hamburg, summer 1974; dir. Microelectronics Rsch. Ctr., Iowa State U., 1995-99. Fulbright scholar U. Pavia, Italy, 1958-59. Fellow Am. Phys. Soc.; mem. AAAS, Optical Soc. Am. Achievements include research on solid state physics. Home: 2020 Elm Cir West Des Moines IA 50265-4294 E-mail: dwl@ameslab.gov.

LYNCH, DENIS PATRICK, dentist, educator; b. Kansas City, Kans., Oct. 5, 1951; s. Patrick Edward and Helen Mary Lynch; m. Monica Colosimo, June 29, 1973; children: Sydney Alexis, Shannon Meredith. DDS, U. Calif., San Francisco, 1976; PhD, U. Ala., Birmingham, 1985. Asst. prof. U. Tex. Dental Br., Houston, 1981-88, assoc. dean acad. affairs, 1987-89, assoc. prof., 1989-93, exec. assoc. dean, 1988-92, U. Tenn., Memphis, 1993-97, prof. medicine, 1994—, prof. grad. health scis., 1998—, prof. biologic and diagnostic scis., 1993—. Cons. Commn. on Dental Accreditation, Chgo., 1990—. Author: The Mouth: Diagnosis and Treatment, 1998; author (chpt.): Development of a Houston Community-Based Dental Health Care Clinic for Indigent HIV-Positive Patients, 1994, Diseases of the Mouth, 1996, Stomatitis: Diagnosis and Treatment, 1998; reviewer Jour. Am. Dental Assn., 1988—. Instr. Confraternity of Christian Doctrine, Our Lady of Sorrow Ch., Birmingham, 1976-81; cons. Bering Dental Clinic, Houston, 1988-93; chair expert review panel for HIV/Hepatitis B Infected Dental Health Care Workers, Tex. State Bd. Dental Examiners, Houston, 1992-93; HIV/AIDS educator ARC, Houston, 1991-93. Fellow Am. Acad. Oral and Maxillofacial Pathology (chair parameters of care com. 1995-98); mem. ADA (spkr.'s bur. 1991-94), Internat. Assn. Dental Rsch. (pres. exptl. pathology group 1992-93), Am. Assn. Dental Schs. (del. exec. com. 1977-79). Roman Catholic. Avocations: golf, bridge, reading, travel. Home: 1924 Kilbirnie Dr Germantown TN 38139-3420 Office: Univ Tenn 875 Union Ave Memphis TN 38163-0001 Fax: 901-448-2671. E-mail: dlynch@utmem.edu.

LYNCH, DENISE RENEE, music educator; b. Florence, S.C., July 21, 1963; d. D.J. and Eve G. Lynch. BA, Coker Coll., 1985; M Music Edn., Fla. State U., 1987. Music tchr., choral dir. Guinyard Butler Mid. Sch., Barnwell, S.C., 1988-90, J. C. Lynch Elem. Sch., Coward, 1990-91, Colleton Elem. Sch., Walterboro, 1991-95; choral dir. Pleasant Hill (S.C.) Sch., 1995—. Mem. Music Educators Nat. Conf. Home: 204 Middleton Place Dr Piedmont SC 29673-7789 Address: 204 Middleton Place Dr Piedmont SC 29673-7789

LYNCH, DENNIS JAMES, plastic surgeon; b. Bayonne, N.J., Aug. 5, 1939; s. Dennis J. Lynch and Eileen Mallon; m. Mary; children: Dennis, David, Sarah. BS, Villanova U., 1961; MD, Georgetown U. Med. Ctr., 1965. Diplomate Am. Bd. Surgery, Am. Bd. Plastic Surgery. Resident U. Pa., Phila., 1965-74; plastic surgeon Scott & White Clinic, Temple, Tex., 1974—. Dir. divsn. plastic surgery Tex. A&M Med. Sch., Temple, 1974-87, chair dept. surgery, 1990—; bd. dirs. Scott & White Clinic, 1981-95. Mem. AMA, Am. Coll. Surgeons, Am. Cleft Palate Assn., Am. Assn. Plastic Surgeons, Tex. Soc. Plastic Surgeons, Am. Soc. Plastic & Reconstructive Surgeons (pres. elect 1996—, pres. 1997), Am. Bd. Plastic Surgery. Roman Catholic. Avocations: tennis, sailing. Office: Scott & White Meml Hosp 2401 S 31st St Temple TX 76508-0001

LYNCH, EDWARD PHILIP, management consultant; b. Bedford, Eng., Nov. 14, 1948; s. Eddie Joseph and Margaret Elizabeth Lynch; m. Carole Ann Blundell, Sept. 25, 1976; 1 child, Philip. BSc with 1st class honors, Salford U., Lancashire, Eng., 1972; PhD, Nottingham (Eng.) U., 1978; MBA, Open U., Buckinghamshire, Eng., 2002. Product planner Roussel Phams., London, 1977-79; mktg. mgr. Courtaulds, NewCastle, Eng., 1979-83; comml. mgr. Cambridge (Eng.) Life Scis., 1983-88; European sales and mktg. mgr. Pfizer, Sandwich, Eng., 1988-97, bus. devel. dir. Canterbury, Eng., 1997-98; cons., 1998—. Mem. Assn. MBAs. Avocations: flyfishing, walking, theatre, sports. Home and Office: 16 Cherry Garden Rd Canterbury CT2 8EL England

LYNCH, FRAN JACKIE, investment advisory company executive; b. Bklyn., Dec. 15, 1948; d. William R. and Ruth (Slaiman) Diamondstein; m. James P. Lynch, Jan. 8, 1969; children: Cheryl Ann, Christopher, Kevin. BA, Bklyn. Coll., 1969; student, Suffolk Community Coll., Brentwood, N.Y., 1980-82; postgrad, L.I. U., 1983. V.p. Castle Capital Corp., N.Y.C., 1971-74; agt. Jerome Castle Found., 1970-74; dir. office services Penn-Dixie Industries, 1970-74; exec. asst. Med. Fin. Advisor, 1974; v.p. Sept. Capital Corp., Glen Cove, N.Y., 1977-80; controller Bobgar Inc., Wallweaves Inc. and N.Y. Twine, Syosset, 1980-86, The Kapson Group, Commack, 1987-91, Westbury Transport ETAL, Astoria, 1991-93; ptnr. Econometric Capital Advisors Inc., Miami, Fla., 1992—; bus. mgr. Am-Pro Protective Agy., Columbia, S.C., 1994-96; pres. Carolina Sr. Devel., Rock Hill, 1996—; dir. devel. Kapson Sr. Quarters Corp., 1998-99. Cons. Women's Times, Queens, N.Y., 1987; dir. devel. Kapson Sr. Quarters, 1998—. Sec. Elwood Booster Club, East Northport, N.Y., 1987; mem. Harley Ave. PTA, 1980-87; coach Northport Youth Soccer, 1982; tchr. Confraternity Christian Doctrine Project St. Elizabeth's Ch., 1972-80, bd. dirs. Parish council, S. Huntington, N.Y., 1978-80. Home: 1817 Cavendale Dr Rock Hill SC 29732-9358 E-mail: csdcorp@aol.com.

LYNCH, FRANK THOMAS, aeronautical engineer, consultant; b. Binghamton, N.Y., Oct. 19, 1933; s. John Francis and Irene Elizabeth L.; m. Blanca Lynch, Dec. 10, 1966; children: Fernando, Maria, Monica, Manuel, Jose. BS in Aero. Engring., U. Notre Dame, 1955; postgrad., Cornell U., 1955-56. Propulsion airframe integration specialist Douglas/McDonnell Douglas, Calif., 1956-65, drag predicition specialist, 1956-65, chief aerodynamics configuration design br., 1965-76, program mgr. aerodynamics R&D, 1976-89, tech. program mgr. exptl. and computational aerodynamics, 1976-89, mgr. aerodynamics tech., 1989-93, program and technical mgr. integrated wing design, 1993-99; sr. mgr. subsonic aerodynamics tech. devel. Douglas/McDonnell Douglas (now The Boeing Co.), Long Beach, 1993-99; pvt. practice Lynch Aerodyn Cons., Yorba Linda, 1999—. Chmn. NASA Aerodynamics adv. group, 1995-97, Airframe Sys. adv. group, 1997-2000, Aerospace Tech. adv. group, 1998-2000. Contbr. numerous articles to profl. publs., including Jour. of Aircraft, Aero. Jour., Prog. Aero. Sci., others; presenter in field. Vol. Corazon Charities, 1998—; coach youth football, Santa Monica, 1956-62. Recipient Disting. Pub. Svc. medal NASA, 1994; technical fellow McDonnell Douglas/Boeing Corp., 1992. Mem. AIAA (aerodynamics award 1999). Roman Catholic. Avocations: writing, golf, tennis. Home and Office: 5370 Via Mira Yorba Linda CA 92886-5014 Fax: 714-779-3541. E-mail: aerofrank@aol.com.

LYNCH, FRANK P. pediatric surgeon; b. Denver, Oct. 4, 1940; MD, U. Colo., 1965. Diplomate Am. Bd. Surgery; cert. in pediat. Intern Yale-New Haven Hosp., 1965-66; resident in surgery U. Colo. Med. Ctr., 1966-70; resident in pediat. surgery Childrens Hosp., L.A., 1972-74; asst. surgeon U. So. Calif. Sch. Medicine, 1972; from asst. clin. prof. to clin. prof. surgery U. Calif., San Diego, 1974-95, chief dept. pediat., 1981-95; pvt. practice. Mem. ACS, Am. Acad. Pediat., Am. Assn. Surgery of Trauma, Am. Pediat. Surg. Assn., PAPS. Office: San Diego Chldns Surg 3030 Childrens Way Ste 403 San Diego CA 92123-4228

LYNCH, GERALD WELDON, academic administrator, psychologist; b. N.Y.C., Mar. 24, 1937; s. Edward Dewey and Alice Margaret (Weldon) L.; m. Eleanor Gay Sherry, Dec. 5, 1970; children: Timothy, Elizabeth. BS, Fordham Coll., 1958; PhD, N.Y. U., 1968. Tech. employment rep. Bell Telephone Labs., N.Y.C., 1958-63; psychologist VA Hosp., N.Y., Palo Alto, Calif., 1964-68; asst. prof. psychology John Jay Coll. Criminal Justice, N.Y.C., 1967-71, dir. student activities, 1968-70, asso. prof., 1971-74, prof., 1974—, dean students, 1968-71, v.p., 1971-76, pres., 1976—. Chmn. Use of Force in Jails, N.Y.C., 1987—; mem. internat. curriculum com. Internat. Law Enforcement Acad., Budapest, Hungary, 1996—; mem. Ind. Commn. on Policing No. Ireland, 1998-2000; coord., co-chair Biennial Conf. Series, St. Petersburg, 1992, N.Y., 1994, Dublin, Ireland, 1996, Budapest, 1998, Bologna, 2000. Editor: Humaw Dignity and the Police, 1999; contbr. articles to profl. jours. Chmn. N.Y.C. Police Found., 1979-92; chmn. N.Y. State Casino Gambling Study Panel, 1979, N.Y. State Fire Fighting Pers. Edn. and Stds. Com., 1980—, Westchester County Spl. Task Force on Dept. Pub. Safety Svcs.; mem. N.Y. State Fire Safety Task Force, 1981, N.Y. State Crime Control Planning Bd., 1979-86; chmn. bd. advisors Channel 13, 1984-87; chmn. N.Y.C. Fire Safety Found., 1984—; vice chmn. U.S. Marshals Found., 1987—; pres. Cath. Interracial Coun., 1990—; chmn. Mayoral Search Com. for Police and Fire Commn. Recipient Criminal Justice award N.Y. State Bar Assn., 1977; Disting. Alumni award in edn. Fordham Coll. Alumni Assn., 1978; Brotherhood award NCCJ, 1985; named Person of Yr., N.Y.C. chpt. Indsl. Security Soc., 1987, N.Y.C. Police Dept. Patrolwomen's Endowment Assn., 1987, Man of Yr., Police Self Support Group, 1989. Mem. Acad. Criminal Justice Scis., Am. Soc. Criminology, Am. Assn. State Colls. and Univs., AAAS, Am. Psychol. Assn. Democrat. Roman Catholic. Office: CUNY John Jay Coll Criminal Justice 899 10th Ave New York NY 10019-1069 E-mail: president@jjay.cuny.edu.

LYNCH, HARRY JAMES, retired biologist; b. Glenfield, Pa., Jan. 18, 1929; s. Harry James and Rachel (McComb) L.; m. Pokum Lee Lynch. BS, Geneva Coll., Beaver Falls, Pa., 1957; PhD, U. Pitts., 1971; postgrad. Bio-Space Tech. Tng. Program, NASA and U. Va., 1970. Clin. chemist West Penn Hosp., Pitts., 1955-56; grad. teaching asst. U. Pitts., 1966-71, sr. teaching fellow, 1971; postdoctoral fellow MIT, Cambridge, 1973-75, rsch. assoc. dept. nutrition, lab. neuroendocrine regulation, 1973-75, lectr., 1976-81, rsch. scientist dept. brain and cognitive sci., 1982-92; ret., 1992. Contbr. more than 60 articles on the pineal gland to profl. jours. and books; patentee on implantable programmed microinfusion apparatus, 1981. With USN, 1950-54. NIH postdoctoral fellow 1971-73. Democrat. Avocation: study of animal behavior. Office: MIT E25-615 77 Mass Ave Cambridge MA 02139-4307

LYNCH, JAMES WALTER, mathematician, educator; b. Cornelia, Ga., Mar. 28, 1930; s. Ulysses Samuel and Ida Dell (Woodall) Lynch; m. Monika Antonie Fehrmann, May 2, 1959; children: Steve, David, Judith. AB, U. Ga., 1952, MA, 1956. Math. statistician Proving Ground, Aberdeen, Md., 1956-61; asst. prof. math. Ga. So. U., Statesboro, 1961-92, prof. emeritus math., 1992—; ret. prof. emeritus of math. Contbr. articles to profl. jours. Grantee, NSF, 1964. Mem.: AAAS, Can. Math. Soc., Ga. Coalition for Excellence in Tchg. Math., Ga. Coun. Tchrs. Math. (life), Sigma Xi (life). Lutheran. Achievements include discovery of that American Indians designed their projectile points to conform to the golden section ratio. Avocations: coin collecting, gardening, shooting. Home and Office: 172 Thornhill Dr Athens GA 30607-1743 E-mail: jamwallyn@aol.com.

LYNCH, JOHN A. lawyer, state legislator; b. Oct. 21, 1938; s. John A. Lynch; m. Deborah A. Lynch; children: Patricia, John P., Matthew J. L. Grad., Holy Cross Coll., 1960; LLB, Georgetown U., 1963. Bar: N.J. 1963. Ptnr. Lynch, Martin, Kroll, North Brunswick; mayor New Brunswick, 1978-90; mem. N.J. Senate, Dist. 17, Trenton, 1982—; minority leader, 1992-98; senate pres., 1990-91; majority leader, 1986-89. Mem. judiciary com. N.J. Senate, 1998—, pres., 1990—92, minority leader, 1992—98. Mem. Gov.'s Commn. on Sci. and Tech. Mem. Middlesex County Trial Lawyers Assn. (past pres.). Home: 11 Cotter Dr New Brunswick NJ 08901-1506 Office: 1368 How Lane North Brunswick NJ 08902

LYNCH, JOHN BROWN, plastic surgeon, educator; b. Akron, Ohio, Feb. 5, 1929; s. John A. and Eloise L.; student Vanderbilt U., 1946-49; M.D., U. Tenn., 1952; children: John Brown, Margaret Frances Lynch Callihan; m. Mary Joyce Burrus, Dec. 1, 1994. Rotating intern John Gaston Hosp., Memphis, Tenn., 1953-54; resident in gen. surgery U. Tex. Med. Br., Galveston, 1956-59, resident in plastic surgery, 1959-62, instr., 1962, asst. prof. surgery, 1962-67, asso. prof., 1967-72, prof., 1972-73; prof., plastic surgery, chmn. dept. plastic surgery Vanderbilt U. Med. Center, 1973—. Served as capt. USAF, 1954-56. Diplomate Am. Bd. Plastic Surgery (chmn.). Fellow ACS; mem. Singleton Surg. Soc. (pres. 1982-83), AMA, Am. Soc. Plastic and Reconstructive Surgeons (pres. 1983-84), Am. Assn. Plastic Surgeons, Plastic Surgery Research Council, Am. Cleft Palate Assn., Am. Burn Assn., Soc. Head and Neck Surgeons, Internat. Burn Assn., Pan Am. Med. Assn., Am. Cancer Soc. (pres. Galveston County, Tex., Chpt. 1968), So. Med. Assn. (pres.-elect 1983-84), Tenn. med. Assn., Nashville Acad. Medicine, Tenn. Soc. Plastic Surgeons, Southeastern Soc. Plastic Surgeons, Southeastern Surg. Soc., H. William Scott, Jr. Soc., Nashville Surg. Soc., Am. Soc. Maxillofacial Surgeons, So. Surg. Assn., Am. Surg. Assn., Sigma Xi. Contbr. numerous articles to med. publs.; editor: (with S.R. Lewis) Symposium on the Treatment of Burns, 1973. Home: 5810 Hillsboro Pike Nashville TN 37215-4602 Office: Vanderbilt Hospital Nashville TN 37232-0001

LYNCH, JOHN EDWARD, JR. lawyer; b. Lansing, Mich., May 3, 1952; s. John Edward and Miriam Ann (Hyland) L.; m. Brenda Jayne Clark, Nov. 16, 1984; children: John E. III, Robert C., David B., Patrick D., Jacqueline E. AB, Hamilton Coll., 1974; JD, Case Western Res. U., 1977. Bar: Conn. 1978, Ohio 1980, U.S. Dist. Ct. (no. dist.) Ohio 1980, U.S. Ct. Appeals (6th cir.) 1980, Tex. 2000. Assoc. Thompson, Weir & Barclay, 1977-78; law clk. U.S. Dist. Judge, Cleve., 1978-80; assoc. Squire, Sanders and Dempsey, 1980-86, ptnr., 1986-96; v.p., gen. counsel, sec. Caliber System, Inc., Akron, Ohio, 1996-98; sr. v.p. gen. couns. BP America, Inc., 1998-99; assoc. gen. counsel Upstream Western Hemisphere BP, 1999—. Master bencher Am. Inns of Ct. Found., 1987-98; mem. civil justice reform act adv. group U.S. Dist. Ct. (no. dist.) Ohio. Del. Hamilton Coll. Alumni Coun., 1992-97, regional chair alumni admissions, 1993—; trustee The Cath. Charities Corp., 1995-97; mem. Cuyahoga County Rep. Exec. Com., Cleve., 1984—; mem. Seton Soc. St. Vincent Hosp. Fund. Roman Catholic. Avocations: golf, jogging. Home: 918 Peachwood Bend Dr Houston TX 77077-1555 Office: BP 200 Westlake Park Blvd Houston TX 77079-2604 E-mail: lynchjl@bp.com.

LYNCH, JOHN JAMES, lawyer; b. Evergreen Park, Ill., Aug. 22, 1945; s. John J. and Agnes (Daly) L.; m. Kathleen Russell, Aug. 15, 1970; children: Kerry, Elizabeth, Erin. BA, St. Mary of the Lake Sem., 1967; MA in Philosophy, DePaul U., 1970, JD, 1973. Bar: Ill. 1973, U.S. Dist. Ct. (no. dist.) Ill. 1973, U.S. Ct. Appeals (7th cir.) 1976. Assoc. McKenna, Storer, Rowe, White & Haskell, Chgo., 1973-75, Haskell & Perrin, Chgo., 1975-77, ptnr., 1977-2000, Figliulo & Silverman, Chgo., 2000—. Mem. ABA, Ill. State Bar Assn., Chgo. Bar Assn., Fedn. Ins. & Corp. Counsel. Office: Figliulo & Silverman Ten S LaSalle St Ste 3600 Chicago IL 60603 E-mail: jlynch@fslegal.com.

LYNCH, JOHN JOSEPH, lawyer; b. Mt. Pleasant, Mich., Jan. 31, 1936; s. Edward N. Lynch and Dorothy K. Botsford; m. Sandra Claire Nunneley, Feb. 4, 1941; children: James, Michael, Patrick, Katherine. BS, John Carroll U., 1960; JD, U. Mich., 1963. Ptnr. Lynch Gallagher Lynch & Martineau, Mt. Pleasant, Mich., 1963—. Arbitrator Am. Arbitration Assn., U.S. Dist. Ct. (we. dist.) Mich., 1980; referee Cir. Ct., Mt. Pleasant, 1963-68. Bd. dir. C.M. Cmty. Hosp., Mt. Pleasant, 1965-80, Broomfield Fund., Mt. Pleasant, 1968-75. With USN, 1955-57. Recipient Plaque Am. Arbitration Assn., 1983, C.M. Cmty. Hosp., 1996. Mem. Mich. Oil and Gas Assn. (legal com.), Assn. Irish Am. Attys. Avocations: fly fishing, hunting, fishing, diving. Office: Lynch Gallagher Lynch & Martineau 555 N Main St Mount Pleasant MI 48858-1651

LYNCH, JOHN PETER, lawyer; b. Chgo., June 5, 1942; s. Charles Joseph and Anne Mae (Loughlin) L.; m. Judy Godvin, Sept. 21, 1968; children: Julie, Jennifer. AB, Marquette U., 1964; JD, Northwestern U., 1967. Bar: Ill. 1967, U.S. Ct. Appeals (7th cir.) 1979, U.S. Ct. Appeals (5th cir.) 1976, U.S. Supreme Ct. 1979. Ptnr. Kirkland & Ellis, Chgo., 1973-76, Hedlund, Hunter & Lynch, Chgo., 1976-82, Latham, Watkins, Hedlund, Hunter & Lynch, Chgo., 1982-85, Latham & Watkins, Chgo., 1985—. Mem. vis. com. Northwestern U. Law Sch. Served as lt. USN, 1968-71. Mem. ABA, Ill. Bar Assn., Assn. Trial Lawyers Am., Order of Coif, City Club, Exec. Club, Met. Club. Notes and Comments editor Northwestern U. Law Rev., 1967. Home: 439 Sheridan Rd Kenilworth IL 60043-1220 Office: Latham & Watkins Ste 5800 Sears Tower Chicago IL 60606

LYNCH, JOHN TERRENCE, football player; b. Hinsdale, Ill., Sept. 25, 1971; m. Linda; 1 child, Jake. Student, Stanford U. Safety Tampa Bay Buccaneers. Active San Diguieto Boys Club; creator Lynch's Safety Zone; founder Lynch Family Legacy Scholarship. Office: Tampa Bay Buccaneers 1 W Buccaneer Pl Tampa FL 33607-5797*

LYNCH, JOHN THOMAS, retired science foundation administrator, physicist; b. Washington, Mar. 21, 1938; s. John Thomas and Mary Ellen (Kaye) L.; m. Leslie Gray, June 22, 1959 (div. June 1972); children: John Thomas III, Michael Gray; m. Carol Rollins, July 5, 1980. BS in Physics, Va. Poly. Inst., 1963; MS in Physics, U. Wis., 1965, PhD, 1972. Lab. technician Nat. Bur. Standards, Washington, 1957-60; rsch. scientist U. Wis., Madison, 1965-78; staff Los Alamos (N.Mex.) Nat. Labs., 1978-81; program scientist NASA Hdqs., Washington, 1981-85; program dir. aeronomy and astrophysics Polar programs NSF, 1985-2000; ret., 2000. Contbr. articles to sci. jours. Recipient Antarctic svc. medal USN, 1986; a mountain in Antarctica is named in his honor. Mem. AAAS, Am. Geophys. Union, Astron. Soc. Pacific. Avocations: music, sailing. E-mail: JLynch137@home.com.

LYNCH, JOSEPH JAMES, philosopher; b. Decatur, Ala., Aug. 28, 1953; s. Joseph James Lynch and Edith Todd; life ptnr. Regina Dawn Hudachek; 1 child Kane. BA, Va. Commonwealth U., 1982; MA, Claremont Grad. U., 1986, PhD, 1992. Lectr. philosophy Calif. State U., Fullerton, 1987—89, Calif. Poly. State U., San Luis Obispo, 1990—2001, assoc. prof. philosophy, 2001—. Editor: (academic jour.) Between the Species, 1998; contbr. articles and revs. to profl. jours. Chair Coll. of Liberal Arts Caucus, Acad. Senate, San Luis Obispo, 2001—; lectr. rep. Calif. Faculty Assn., 1995—2001. Recipient Oustanding Lectr. award, San Luis Obispo chpt. Calif. Faculty Assn., 2001, President's award, 2001. Mem.: Soc. for Study of Philosophy and Martial Arts (founder, chair 1997—2002), Soc. for Study of Ethics and Animals (Pacific coord. 1997—2002), Soc. for Study of Philosophy and Psychology, Am. Philos. Assn., Calif. Faculty Assn. (lectr. rep. 1995—2001), White Heron Sangha (bd. dirs. 2001—02). Green Party. Buddhist. Avocations: 2nd degree black belt in Hawaiian kempo, Taijiquan. Office: Calif Poly State U One Grand Ave San Luis Obispo CA 93407 Home Fax: 805-756-7028; Office Fax: 805-756-7028. Personal E-mail: jlynch@calpoly.edu. E-mail: jlynch@calpoly.edu.

LYNCH, JOSEPH MICHAEL, engineer, consultant; b. West New York, N.J., July 12, 1922; s. Peter Lawrence and Catherine Anne (Dritschel) L.; m. Anna Marie Lewandoski, June 8, 1943; children: Joan, Laurie, Peter, Joseph, Anna, Grace. ME in Engring., Stevens Inst. Tech., 1948; postgrad., Vanderbilt U., Pratt Grad. Sch. Planning, NYU. Registered profl. engr. and land surveyor, N.Y., N.J.; cert. profl. planner, N.J. Engr., supr. O'Kane Marine Repair Co., Hoboken, N.J., 1948-50; engr. Madison Contractors, Weehaken, 1950-53; engr., owner Mayo, Lynch & Assocs., Secaucus, 1953—. Chmn. bd. Plaza Nat. Bank, Secaucus, 1960-61; mcpl. engr. Towns of Weehawken, Secaucus, Hoboken, Bethel & Callicoon, N.Y. and N.J.; mem. adv. bd. New Jersey Bank, Passaic, 1970-80. Chmn. Secaucus Planning Bd., 1960; adv. bd. mem. Passaic (N.J.) Planning Bd., 1970, N.J. Bank, Passaic; trustee Stevens Acad., Hoboken, N.J. Tech. sgt. U.S. Army, 1942-46. Fellow Soc. Civil Engrs. (various coms.); mem. NSPE (various coms.), Soc. Mcpl. Engrs. (various coms.), Profl. Land Surveyors. Roman Catholic. Achievements include U.S. patents for screening apparatus and treatment process; U.K. patent for apparatus. Avocations: golfing, woodworking, clock building and repair. Home: 717 John St Secaucus NJ 07094-3207 Office: Mayo Lynch & Assocs Inc 333 Meadowlands Pkwy Secaucus NJ 07094-1814

LYNCH, KEVIN J. publishing executive, media planner; BA in English and Comm., Kean U., 1978. Sales rep. McCall, 1981-83, So. Living, 1983-86, ea. regional mgr., 1986, nat. sales mgr., 1992, nat. advt. dir., 1994-95, v.p., pub., 1995—. Office: P O Box 2581 Birmingham AL 35209*

LYNCH, LAURA ELLEN, elementary education educator; b. Chgo., June 25, 1965; d. Edgar Lewis and Loretta Ann (Sheehar) Hield; m. Terrence Michael Lynch, June 22, 1991; children: Dennis Edgar, Ellen Rose. BA in Edn., St. Xavier U., 1987. Cert. tchr., Ill. Tchr. Queen of Martyrs Sch., Chgo., 1987-92; tutor, 1992—; co-owner Histories for Kids, 2002—.

LYNCH, LINDA LOU, reading and language arts specialist, educator; b. L.A., Feb. 9, 1941; d. Alexander Alfred and Gizella Mary (Bajus) Laszloffy; m. John Joseph Lynch, June 13, 1964; children: Valerie Ann, Colinda Lee, Lee Anne Ellen. BS, Calif. State U., Northridge, 1964; MEd, Loyola Marymount U., L.A., 1990; EdD, Pepperdine U., 1995. Cert. tchr., Calif. Computer programmer Union Bank, L.A., 1962-64; substitute tchr. various sch. dists. Calif., 1964-68, 79-80; tchr. Richard H. Dana Mid. Sch., Hawthorne, 1980-88; reading specialist Wiseburn Sch. Dist., 1988-91; elem. sch. tchr. Juan de Anza Elem. Sch., 1991-93; reading specialist Wiseburn Sch. Dist., 1994-99; tchr. 1st grede Juan de Anza Elem. Sch., Hawthorne, 1999—. Adj. faculty mem. Loyola Marymount U., L.A., 1991—, dir. reading program Grad. Sch., 1992; rsch. asst. Pepperdine U., L.A., 1992-94, teaching asst., 1993, asst. dir. student tchrs., 1993, adj. prof., 1994—; adj. prof. Chapman U., L.A., 1995—. Mem. NEA, AAUW, ASCD, Am. Edn. Rsch. Assn., Internat. Reading Assn., Calif. Reading Assn., Ventura County Reading Assn., Calif. Tchrs. Assn., Wiseburn Faculty Assn., Phi Delta Kappa. Democrat. Roman Catholic.

LYNCH, MILTON TERRENCE, retired advertising agency executive; b. Denver, Feb. 27, 1931; s. Thomas Lillis and Pauline Regina (Yaeger) L.; m. Katherine Marie Stamey, July 19, 1958; children— Carrie Elizabeth, Michael Thomas, Brian Wilson B.F.A., Washington State U., Pullman, 1953. Promotion mgr. Gen. Mills, Inc., Palo Alto, Calif., 1956-62; v.p. Robert Ebey Co., 1962-66; exec. v.p. Steedman, Cooper & Busse, San Francisco, 1966-74; owner, prin. Lynch & Assocs., 1974-78; exec. v.p. Lynch & Rockey Advt., 1978-84; pres., chief exec. officer Evans/Lynch Rockey, Inc., 1984-87; chmn., chief exec. officer Evans/San Francisco, 1987-90. Dir. Evans Communications, Salt Lake City Vol. cons. Internat. Exec. Svc. Corps., 1991—. Served to capt. Inf. U.S. Army, 1953-55. Mem. San Francisco Advt. Golf Assn. (pres. 1982-83). Republican. Roman Catholic. Avocations: golf; tennis; gardening; writing. Home: 12779 Homes Dr Saratoga CA 95070-4016

LYNCH, NANCY ANN, computer scientist, educator; b. Bklyn., Jan. 19, 1948; d. Roland David and Marie Catherine (Adinolfi) Evraets; m. Dennis Christopher Lynch, June 14, 1969; children: Patrick, Kathleen (dec.), Mary. BS, Bklyn. Coll., 1968; PhD, MIT, 1972. Asst. prof. math. Tufts U., Medford, Mass., 1972-73, U. So. Calif., Los Angeles, 1973-76, Fla. Internat. U., Miami, 1976-77; assoc. prof. computer sci. Ga. Tech. U., Atlanta, 1977-82, MIT, Cambridge, 1982-86, prof. computer sci., 1986—, NEC prof. software sci. and engring., 1996—. Ellen Swallow Richards chair MIT, 1982-87, Cecil H. Green chair, 1994-96. Contbr. numerous articles to profl. jours. Fellow Assn. Computing Machinery. Roman Catholic. Office: MIT NE43-365 Lab for Computer Sci Cambridge MA 02139

LYNCH, NEIL L(AWRENCE), retired state supreme court justice; b. Holyoke, Mass., June 26, 1930; AB sum laude, Harvard U., 1952, LL.B., 1957. Bar: Mass. 1952. Assoc. firm. Hale Sanderson Byrnes & Morton, Boston, 1957-65; gen. counsel Mass. Port Authority, 1965-76; assoc. Herilhy and O'Brien, Boston, 1976-79; chief legal counsel to gov. State of Mass., 1979-81; assoc. justice Supreme Jud. Ct. Mass., 1981—2000, retired assoc. justice Mass., 2000. Mem. Airport Operators Council Internat., 1965-76, chmn., 1974-75; adj. prof. law, legal writing and environ. law New Eng. Law

Sch., 1968-74, assoc. prof. corp. law and evidence, 1974-76 Served to 1st lt. USAF, 1952-54. Mem. ABA (pub. contracts com. pub. contract law sect. 1975-76), Boston Bar Assn., Mass. Bar Assn.*

LYNCH, PATRICK, lawyer; b. Pitts., Nov. 11, 1941; s. Thomas Patrick and Helen Mary (Grimes) L.; m. M. Linda Maturo, June 20, 1964; children: Megan, Kevin, Colin, Brendan, Erin, Brian, Liam, Eamonn, Kilian, Caitlin, Ryan, Declan, Cristin, Mairin, Sean. BA in Philosophy, Loyola U., L.A., 1964, LLB, 1966. Bar: Calif. 1967, U.S. Dist. Ct. (cen., so., no. and ea. dists.) Calif., U.S. Ct. Appeals (9th cir.), U.S. Supreme Ct. Ptnr. O'Melveny & Myers, Los Angeles, 1966—. Panelist PLI Annual Antitrust Law Inst., 1982-2000. Bd. editors Matthew Bender Fed. Litigation Guide Reporter. Fellow Am. Coll. Trial Lawyers; mem. L.A. County Bar Assn. Office: OMelveny & Myers 400 S Hope St Los Angeles CA 90071-2899

LYNCH, PETER, biology educator; b. Cambridge, Mass., Jan. 10, 1957; s. Kevin Andrew and Anne (Borders) L.; m. Jessica Maria Jansen, June 16, 1984; children: Ian Jacob, Micah William. BS in Zoology with honors, U. N.C., 1981; postgrad. U. Md., 1981; MS in Zoology, U. R.I., 1985; EdM in Curriculum and Instrn., U. Lowell, 1986. Spl. seminar tchr. biology Cambridge (Mass.) Friends Sch., 1975-76; grad. lab. instr. gen. biology U. Md., College Park, 1981; chemistry & algebra tchr., ice hockey coach, dormitory dir. Concord (Mass.) Acad., 1983; dir. Living World Summer Program Beauvoir Elem. Sch., Washington, 1983; grad. lab. instr. U. R.I., Kingston, 1983-84; sci. tchr. Haverhill (Mass.) H.S., 1986-88, Fair Haven (Vt.) Union High Sch., 1988-95, chair dept. math. and sci., 1995-96; chair dept. sci. The Gailer Sch., Vt., 1996-2001; sci. tchr. Rutland Sr. H.S., 2001—. Technician dept. environ. medicine NYU, Sterling Forest, 1976; summer tchr. Beauvoir Elem. Sch., 1976-80, 82; co-chair Joint Tchrs. Assn./Sch. Bd. com. to investigate health ins. alternatives Fair Haven Union H.S., 1989-90, chair Tchrs. Assn. contract negotiation team, 1990-91, mem. search com. for vice prin., 1991, mem. search com. for prin., 1995, 98; bd. dirs. The Gailer Sch., 1997-98; founder, exec. dir. Green Across the Pacific, 1997—; founder, chmn. Undergrad. Zoology Colloquium, U. N.C., Chapel Hill; seminar presenter. Recipient Coker award for excellence in undergrad. rsch. U. N.C., 1981, award for excellence in teaching Addison-Rutland Supervisory Union Bd., 1994. Mem. NSTA, Tanglefoot Cloggers (Winchester, Mass.), Cub Hill Cloggers (Balt.), Cane Creek Cloggers (Carrboro, N.C.), Stony Creek Cloggers (Durham, N.C.), The Christmas Revels (chorus mem.), Pi Lambda Theta. Office: Green Across the Pacific 1594 N Orwell Rd Shoreham VT 05770-9565

LYNCH, PETER JOHN, former dermatologist; b. Mpls., Oct. 22, 1936; s. Francis Watson and Viola Adeline (White) L.; m. Barbara Ann Lanzi, Jan. 18, 1964; children: Deborah, Timothy. Student, St. Thomas Coll., 1954-57; BS, U. Minn., 1958, MD, 1961. Intern U. Mich. Med. Ctr., 1961-62, resident in dermatology, 1962-65, asst. prof., then assoc. prof. dermatology, 1968-73; clin. instr. U. Minn., 1965; chief dermatology and venereal disease Martin Army Hosp., Columbus, Ga., 1966-68; asso. prof. to prof. dermatology U. Ariz., Tucson, 1973-86, chief sect. dermatology, 1973-86, asso. head dept. internal medicine, 1977-86; prof., head dermatology U. Minn. Med. Sch., Mpls., 1986-95; med. dir. ambulatory care U. Minn. Health Sys., 1993-95; prof., chmn. dept. dermatology U. Calif., Davis, 1995-2000, prof. emeritus, 2000—. Author: (with S. Epstein) Burckhardt's Atlas and Manual of Dermatology and Venereology, 1977, Dermatology for the House Officer, 1982, 3rd edit., 1994, (with W.M. Sams) Principles and Practice of Dermatology, 1992, 2nd edit., 1996, (with I.E. Edwards) Genital Dermatology, 1994. With AUS, 1966-68. Decorated Army Commendation Medal; recipient Disting. Service award for faculty U. Mich., 1970, Disting. Faculty award U. Ariz., 1981 Mem. Am. Acad. Dermatology (bd. dirs. 1974-78, v.p. 1991-92), Assn. Profs. Dermatology (bd. dirs. 1976-80, pres. 1994-96), Internat. Soc. Study of Vulvar Disease (bd. dirs. 1976-79, pres. 1983), Soc. Investigative Dermatology, Am. Bd. Dermatology (bd. dirs. 1984-89), Gougerot Soc. (Bronze medal award), Alpha Omega Alpha. Democrat. Roman Catholic. Home: 332 Sandpiper Dr Davis CA 95616-7536 Office: U Calif 4860 Y St # 3400 Sacramento CA 95817-2307

LYNCH, PRISCILLA A. nursing educator, therapist; b. Joliet, Ill., Jan. 8, 1949; d. LaVerne L. and Ann M. (Zamkovitz) L. BS, U. Wyo., 1973; MS, St. Xavier Coll., Coll., 1981. RN, Ill. Staff nurse Rush-Presbyn.-St. Luke's Med. Ctr., Chgo., 1977-81, psychiat.-liaison cons., 1981-83, asst. prof. nursing, unit dir., 1985—. Mgr. and therapist Oakside Clinic, Kankakee, Ill., 1987—; mem. adv. bd. Depressive and Manic Depression Assn., Chgo., 1986—; mem. consultation and mental health unit Riverside Med. Ctr., Kankakee, 1987—; speaker numerous nat. orgns. Contbr. numerous abstracts to profl. jours., chpts. to books. Bd. dirs. Cornerstone Svcs., ARC of Ill. Recipient total quality mgmt. award Rush-Presbyn.-St. Luke's Med. Ctr., 1991, named mgr. of the quarter, 1997, Wayne Lerner Leadership award, 1998. Mem. ANA, Ill. Nurses Assn. (coms.), Coun. Clin. Nurse Specialists, Profl. Nursing Staff (sec. 1985-87, mem. coms.). Presbyterian. Home: 606 Darcy Ave Joliet IL 60436-1673

LYNCH, REINHARDT, chef, restaurant owner; BA French, MBA, Ind. U. Co-owner The Inn at Little Washington, Washington, 1978—. Office: PO Box 300 Washington VA 22747*

LYNCH, RICHARD ANTHONY, philosopher, educator; b. Portsmouth, Va., Aug. 26, 1967; s. Vincent Michael Lynch and Evelyn Watson Pope. BA, U. Tex., 1991; MA, Northwestern U., 1993; postgrad., Boston Coll., 1993—2000. Tchg. fellow Boston Coll., Chestnut Hill, Mass., 1998—2000; vis. instr. philosophy Wabash Coll., Crawfordsville, Ind., 2000—. Dir. N.Am. Students of Cooperation, Ann Arbor, Mich., 1989—92; pres. Inter-Cooperative Coun. Inc., Austin, 1989—90. Contbr. articles to profl. jours. Fellow, Woodrow Wilson Found., 1991. Mem.: Soc. for Phenomenology and Existential Philosophy, Am. Philos. Assn., Foucault Cir.

LYNCH, ROBERT BERGER, lawyer; b. LaCrosse, Wis., June 10, 1931; s. Jan P. and Eve (Berger) Lynch; m. Iris D. Healy; 1 child Jan Fredrick. BS, U.S. Merchant Marine Acad., 1955; JD, U. of the Pacific, 1967. Bar: Calif. 1969, U.S. Supreme Ct. 1972. Engr. Aerojet Gen. Corp., Sacramento, 1955-61, proposal mgr., 1961-63, asst. contract adminstrn. mgr., 1963-66, contract adminstrn. mgr., 1967-70; pvt. practice, Rancho Cordova, 1969—. Instr. bus. law Solano C.C., 1977—79, San Joaquin Delta Coll., 1978—79; mediator family law panel Sacramento Superior Ct.; traffic and small claims pro tem judge Sacramento, 1997—2001; appointed presiding judge Mcpl. Ct., Bisbee, Ariz., 2001—. Active various charity fund-raising campaigns in Sacramento, 1966-68; mem. mission com. St. Clements Episcopal Ch., Rancho Cordova, Calif., 1967-68; trustee Los Rios C.C. Dist., Calif., 1971-79; vestryman, reader St. Mark's Anglican Ch., Loomis, Calif., 2000-01, St. John the Divine Ch., Hereford, Ariz., 2002-. With USCG, 1949-51, USNR, 1951-80, N.G., 1988-91, maj. AUS, ret. Mem. IEEE, Calif. Wildlife Fedn., Internat. Turtle Club, Marines Meml. Assn., Am. Legion, Mensa. Office: 8752 E Mustang Trl Hereford AZ 85615-9298 E-mail: rblynch@starband.net.

LYNCH, ROBERT EMMETT, mathematics educator; b. Chgo., Feb. 5, 1932; s. Joseph Burke and Mildred Cecilia (Bildhauser) L.; m. Martha Bolling Hacker, Oct. 8, 1955; children: Barbara Ann, William Robert, Pamela Elizabeth. B Engring. Physics, Cornell U., 1954; MS, Harvard, 1959, PhD, 1963. Sr. rsch. mathematician Gen. Motors Rsch. Lab., Warren, Mich, 1961-64; assoc. prof. computer sci. and math. U. Tex., Austin, 1964-67, Purdue U., West Lafayette, Ind., 1967-85, prof., 1985—; prof. emeritus, 1998—. Author: (with Garrett Birkhoff) Numerical Solution of Elliptic Problems, 1984; (with John R. Rice) Computers, Their Impact and Use/with Basic, 1975, Computers, Their Impact and Use/With Fortran, 1977, Computers, Their Impact and Use/with PL/1, 1978. Lt. USAF, 1955-57.

LYNCH, ROBERT L. art association administrator; Former exec. dir. arts ext. svc. divsn. continuing edn. U. Mass., Amherst, 1974-84; former pres., CEO Nat. Assembly Local Arts Agys., 1984-96; pres., CEO Ams. for Arts, Washington, 1996—. Spkr., trainer in field. Past bd. dirs. Ireland Am. Arts Exchange, Craft Emergency Relief Fund, State Arts Advocacy League Am., Kennedy Ctr.'s Alliance Arts Edn., edn. adv. coun. Nat. Endowment Arts, Nat. Coalition Edn. and Arts; founding mem., bd. dirs. Nat. Cultural Alliance; past vice chmn. advcacy team Mass. State Arts Coun.; original sponsor Nat. Arts and Humanities Month. Recipient 4 Top Innovative Programming awards in continuing edn. Nat. U. Continuing Edn. Assn. Office: Americans for the Arts 1000 Vermont Ave NW Fl 12 Washington DC 20005-4903 E-mail: rlynch@artsusa.org.

LYNCH, ROBERT MARTIN, lawyer, educator; b. St. Louis, Mar. 28, 1950; s. Raymond Burns and Nancy Winn (Roeder) L.; m. Cynthia Kay Allmeyer, June 7, 1974; children: Christopher, Kelly, Stephanie. AB, St. Louis U., 1972, JD, 1975. Bar: Mo. 1975, D.C. 1985, Tex. 1992. Law clk. to presiding justice Mo. Ct. Appeals, St. Louis, 1975-76; atty. Southwestern Bell Telephone Corp., 1976-79, atty. network, 1979-83, gen. atty., 1983-88, v.p., asst. gen. counsel, 1988-91; v.p., gen. counsel Tex. office Southwestern Bell Telephone Co., Dallas, 1991-93, v.p., gen. counsel external affairs San Antonio, 1993-98; sr. v.p., gen. counsel external affairs SBC Comm., Inc., 1998—, sr. v.p., gen. counsel bus. and consumer markets, 1999-2000; sr. v.p. gen. counsel SBC Ops., Inc., 2000—. Instr. paralegal studies St. Louis Community Coll., 1977—. Mem. ABA, Tex. Bar, Dallas Bar Assn., Mo. Bar Assn. (adminstrv. law com. coun.), St. Louis Bar Assn. (chmn. adminstrv. law com. 1981-82), Am. Corp. Counsel Assn. (chmn. communications com. St. Louis chpt., chmn. law dept. mgmt. com. 1997-98, bd. dirs. 1999—). Republican. Avocations: racquetball, writing. E-mail: rlynch@corp.sbc.com.

LYNCH, ROBERT STEPHEN, JR. electrical engineer, researcher and developer; b. Albany, N.Y., May 18, 1960; s. Robert Stephen Lynch and Venna (Downs) Gleason; m. Cheryl Ann Fear; children: Robert Stephen III, Ryan Joseph. AA, Hudson Valley C.C., Troy, N.Y., 1980, AS, 1982; BSEE, Union Coll., 1984, MSEE, 1991; PhD, U. Conn., 1999. Elec. engr. IBM, Kingston, N.Y., 1984-86; sr. electronics engr. Naval Undersea Warfare Ctr., Newport, 1991—. Contbr. articles. Mem. IEEE (sensor array and multichannel processing com.), Planetary Soc., Nat. Geog. Soc., Internat. Soc. of Info. Fusion. Avocations: amateur astronomy, hist./mil. simulation gaming, youth football league. Home: 866 North Rd Groton CT 06340-3276 Office: Naval Undersea Warfare Ctr 1176 Howell St Newport RI 02841-1703

LYNCH, SAMUEL CURLEE, JR. (SIR SAMI LYNCH), painter; b. Salisbury, N.C., July 31, 1953; s. Samuel and Mae (Alexander) L. Student, Windsor (Ont., Can.) U., 1970-73, Acad. for Arts, N.Y.C., 1978, Raymond Duncan Acad., Paris, 1981, Writers Inst., Mamaroneck, N.Y., 1991-92. Registered Soc. N.Am. Artists, diamond banking account cons., DeBeers. Artist Windsor Sun, 1973-74; artist, editor asst. Akwesasne Notes, St. Regis, Que., Can., 1974; graphic artist Art Leadley, Windsor, 1974; counseling asst. S.W. Regional Centre, Cedar Springs, Ont., 1974-76; art dir., set. designer Video Variety, N.Y.C., 1977-79; instr. painting and sculpture Waterworks, Salisbury, 1980; artist, fashion designer DHR/555 Import-Export, N.Y.C. and Montreal, 1985-86; artist, writer, inventor, designer Fine Arts Restoration/Preservation Svc., Landis, N.C., 1986—; coml. product designer, 1998—. Ptnr. Royal Whispers Note Card Co., prin. artist; v.p. Native Cultural Centre, Windsor, 1974; mem. Rowan Art Guild, Salisbury, 1980. Inventor art material Wings Easel, 1983; illustrator/editor The Oracle, 1985-87; works include Wedding Party/On a Summer's Night, Storm Shelter, (oils) Legends of the Firebird, 2002, Celestial Symphony, 2002, mini-pastels, 1985-86, watercolor, oils; commemorative art of Princess Grace for Royal Family of Monaco/Consul de Monaco; exhibited in numerous shows in U.S. and abroad; paintings in Royal Collection of Hutt River Principality (1-3); works in Royal Collection of Hutt River Principality. Artist, Landis Heritage Day Com., 1987-94; mem. Met. Soc. des Amis de la Fondation and Fondation Maeght. Decorated knight Royal Order (Hutt River Principality); recipient Bronze Medallion of Paris, Acad. Raymond Duncan, 1981, Prix du Centennaire, Musèo Duncan, 1981, Salon d'Aout award, 1981, certificate Vintner, Sursum Corda, Brussels, 2001, Archtl./Landscape Design Outstanding Artistic Ability award, 1966, Art award, 1970, Comte de Lyon-Satolas, 2000, Outstanding Achievement in arts medal, Princess Li Chieu-Hoang, Vietnam, 2001, Outstanding Artist citation Ordern Soverèin de Lichtenstein, 2001, Royal medal for Arts HM Volodar nad Volodarme of Ukraine, 2001, Duc de l'Iled' Oléron, 2001; Royal Patronage, Hutt River Province Principality, 1994, others; named His Royal Highness Prince of Trabzon, 2001, grand master Knights Order of St. John of Jerusalem. Mem. Societe des Amis de la Fondation Maeght. Avocations: horticulture, wine making, art and antiques collecting, music, architecture. Office: Sami Lynch PO Box 331 Landis NC 28088-0331 E-mail: royalwhispers@hotmail.com.

LYNCH, SANDRA LEA, federal judge; b. Oak Park, Ill., July 31, 1946; d. Bernard Francis and Eugenia Tyus (Shepherd) Lynch; married; 1 child. AB in Philosophy, Wellesley Coll., 1968; JD cum laude, Boston U., 1971. Bar: Mass. 1971, U.S. Supreme Ct. 1974. Law clk. to Hon. Raymond J. Pettine U.S. Dist. Ct., Providence; asst. atty. gen. Commonwealth of Mass., Boston, 1974; gen. counsel Mass. Dept. Edn., 1974—78; ptnr. Foley, Hoag & Eliot, 1978—95; judge 1st cir. U.S. Ct. Appeals, 1995—. Contbr. articles to profl. jours. Past co-chair leading industries com. Greater Boston C. of C. Recipient Disting. Alumnae award, Boston U. Law Sch., 1993, Wellesley Coll., 1997, Disting. Svc. award, Planned Parenthood, 1991. Mem.: ABA, Boston Bar Assn. (pres. 1992—93, Jud. Excellence award 2001), Mass. Bar Assn., Nat. Assn. Women Judges, Women's Forum. Office: US Ct Appeals One Courthouse Way Ste 8710 Boston MA 02210-3010*

LYNCH, STEPHEN F. state legislator; BS, Wentworth Inst.; JD, Boston Coll. Law Sch. Mem. Mass. Ho. of Reps., Boston, 1995-96, Mass. Senate, Boston, 1996—. Home: 55 G St South Boston MA 02127-2954 Office: 235 Cannon HOB Washington DC 20515*

LYNCH, THOMAS GERALD, surgeon, educator; b. Cedar Rapids, Iowa, Oct. 7, 1947; s. Harvey Edward Lynch; m. Jane Marie Waldvogel; children: Thomas, Ryan. BS, John Carroll U., Cleve., 1969; MD, Georgetown U., 1973. Cert. Am. Bd. of Surgery, gen. vascular surgery. Prof. of surgery U. of Nebr. Med. Ctr., Omaha, 1999—2002, vice-chmn. dept. of surgery, 2001—. Office: U Nebr Med Ctr Dept Surgery 983280 Nebr Med Ctr Omaha NE 68198-3280 Office Fax: (402) 559-6749. Personal E-mail: tlynch@unmc.edu. Business E-Mail: tlynch@unmc.edu.

LYNCH, THOMAS J. telecommunications industry executive; married; 4 children. B, Rider U. Joined Gen. Instrument, 1982, controller cable set-top unit, CFO cable set-top unit, v.p. mktg. distbn. sys., v.p., gne. mgr. transmission network sys. strategic bus. unit Pa., sr. v.p., gne. mgr. satellite and broadcast network sys. strategic bus. unit San Diego; corp. v.p., gen. mgr. satellite and broadcast network sys. broadband comms. sector (formerly Gen. Instrument Corp.) Comms. Enterprise Motorola, Inc., exec. v.p., pres. integrated electronic sys. sector Ill. Office: Motorola 1303 Algonquin Schaumburg IL 60196*

LYNCH, THOMAS JOSEPH, museum and historic house manager; b. Omaha, Feb. 15, 1960; s. James Humphery and Patricia Mae (Gaughan) L. BA in History, U. Nebr., 1984. Mus. asst. Father Flanagan's Boys' Home, Boys Town, Nebr., 1986-88, mus. assoc., 1988-93; CEO, mgr. Boys Town Hall of History and Fr. Flanagan's House, 1993—. Bd. dirs. Union Pacific R.R. Mus. Mem. Am. Assn. for State and Local History, Am. Mus. Assn., Nebr. Mus. Assn. (bd. dirs., v.p.), Nat. Hist. Landmark Stewards Assn. Office: Boys Town Hall of History 14057 Flanagan Blvd Boys Town NE 68010-7509

LYNCH, THOMAS PETER, securities executive; b. N.Y.C., May 3, 1924; s. Michael Joseph and Margaret Mary (Fitzgerald) L.; m. Madeleine D'Eufemia, June 3, 1950; children: Francine, Richard. Student, Syracuse U., 1943-44; BBA, Baruch Coll., 1947. Acct. Deloitte, Haskins & Sells, N.Y.C., 1947-56; partner Bache & Co., 1956-61; v.p. E.F. Hutton Co. Inc., 1962-67; sr. v.p. E.F. Hutton Group Inc., 1967-72, exec. v.p., 1972-83, pres., dir., 1983-85; ret., 1985. Pres., dir. Cash Res. Mgmt. Inc., 1976-85 Served with U.S. Army, 1943-46. Decorated Bronze Star. Mem. AICPA, Fin. Execs. Inst., Canoe Brook Country Club, Baltusrol Golf Club, Johns Island Club, Morris County Golf Club.

LYNCH, TIMOTHY P. science administrator; Grad., Harvard Bus. Sch., Colgate U. With investment banking divsn. Chase Securities, Inc., Goldman, Sachs & Co.; dir. strategic planning Elan Corp., plc, Dublin, 1999; CFO, v.p. fin. adminstrn. InterMune, Inc., Brisbane, Calif., 1999—. Office: InterMune Inc 3280 Bayshore Blvd Brisbane CA 94005*

LYNCH, TIMOTHY CRONIN, lawyer; b. Washington, Mar. 14, 1969; BA cum laude, Loyola Coll., Balt., 1991; JD, U. Md., 1995. Bar: Md. 1995, Va. 1996, DC 1999, U.S. Dist. Ct. (ea. and we. dists.) Va., U.S. Dist. Ct. Md., U.S. Ct. Appeals (4th cir.). Law clk. to hon. J. James McKenna Cir. Ct. for Montgomery County Md., Rockville, 1995-96; assoc. Shulman, Rogers, Gandal, Vorday & Ecker, 1996-97, Shar, Rosen & Warshaw, Balt., 1997-00. Office: Shar Rosen & Warshaw LLC 26 South St Baltimore MD 21202-3215 E-mail: TLynch@triallaw.com.

LYNCH, TIMOTHY JEREMIAH-MAHONEY, lawyer, educator, theologian, realtor, writer; b. June 10, 1952; s. Joseph David and Margaret Mary (Mahoney) L. MS, JD in Taxation, Golden Gate U., 1981; MA, PhD in Modern European History, U. San Francisco, 1983; Licentiate, Inter-Am. Acad., Rio de Janeiro, 1988; PhD in Classics and Divinity/Theology, Harvard U., 1988; JSD in Constl. Law, Hastings Law Ctr., 1990. Bar: D.C. 1989, Calif., U.S. Ct. Appeals (2d cir.) 1989, U.S. Ct. Appeals (4th cir.) 1990; mem. Bar/Outer Temple/Comml. Bar of U.K.; European Econ. Ct. of 1st Instance. Legal bus., tax, counsel Lynch Real Estate, San Francisco, 1981-85; researcher, writer Kolb, Roche & Sullivan, 1986-88; chmn. internat. law dept. Timothy J.M. Lynch & Assocs., 1987-88, chmn., mng. dir. law dept., 1988—. Chmn., pres., CEO Lynch Real Estate Investment Corp., San Francisco, 1989—; ptnr. Lynch Investment Corp.; bd. lawyer/arbitrators Pacific Coast Stock Exch., NASD, 1994—; chmn. bd. Lynch Holdings Corp. Group; corp. counsel, sr. ptnr. L.A. Ctr. Internat. Comml. Arbitration, 1991—; vis. fellow classics, Inst. of Classical Studies, U. London; rsch. prof. Canon law and ecumenical ch. history grad. Theological Union U. Calif. Berkeley, 1992—; vis. scholar Patristic theology and classical philosophy of ecumenical doctrines, U. Laval, Quebec, Can., 1993—; vis. scholar Medieval ch. history U. Leeds, Eng., 1993-95; del. lectr. 24th Internat. Congress Arts Comms., Kreble Coll., Oxford U., 1997; arbitrator Iran-U.S. Claims Tribunal, The Hague, 1993; mem. internat. corp. adv. bd. J.P. Morgan and Co., N.Y.C.; bd. dirs. Morgan-Stanley Corp., N.Y.C.; chmn. Latin Am., African and Middle East Corp. Groups J.P. Morgan Internat., Corp.; adv. bd. Morgan Stanley Corp., N.Y.C.; mem. Orgn. Econ. Cooperation and Devel., mem. adv. com. Internat. Labor Orgn.; participant Forum/A Group of Internat. Leaders, Calif., 1995, mem. adv. bd. U.S.-Saudi Arabia Bus. Coun., OECD on Industry and Fin., Paris, 1995, others; apptd. U.S. amb. Spl. Del. to Commn. Security/Coop. in Europe on Econ. and Pub. Reforms in Russian Republics; participant World Outlook Conf. on 21st Century, 1995; mem. Nat. Planning Assns., Washington, Brit.-North Am. Com. on Econ. and Pub. Policy Planning, Global Econ. Coun.; mem. adv. bd. Nat. Bus. Leadership Coun., Washington; mem. Arbitration Tribunal, Geneva; judge World Intellectual Property Orgns.; selected arbitrator, mem. tribunal; mem. arbitration bd., panel of arbitrators NAFTA Trade Policy; mem. adv. com. on private internat. law U.S. State Dept., Washington; mem. Dead Sea Scrolls Rsch. Project, 1998; mem. author and writers group on multi-vol. transl. series classical works from late Roman, medieval near eastern, patristic and early Christian ch. periods Princeton U., 1998, Cath. U. Am., 1998, U. Calif., Berkely, 1998; rsch. prof. Old and New Testament bibl. lit. commentary, 1998. Author: (10 vol. manuscript) History of Ecumenical Doctrines and Canon Law of Church; editorial bd. Internat. Tax Jour., 1993; author: Publishers National Endowment for Arts and Humanities Classical Translations: Latin, Greek, and Byzantine Literary Texts for Modern Theological-Philosophical Analysis of Social Issues; Essays on Issues of Religious Ethics and Social, Public Policy Issues, 1995, 96, others; editorial bd. Internat. Tax Jour., 1993, Melrose Press: Internat. Firm; contbr. articles to profl. jours. Dir., vice chmn. Downtown Assn. San Francisco; councillor, dir. Atlantic Coun. U.S., 1984—; corp. counsel, chmn. spl. arbitrator's tribunal on U.S.-Brazil trade, fin. and banking rels. Inter-Am. Comml. Arbitration Commn., Washington; chmn. nat. adv. com. U.S.-Mid. East rels. U.S. Mid. East Policy Coun., U.S. State Dept., Washington, 1989—; mem. Pres. Bush's Adv. Commn. on Econ. and Public Policy Priorities, Washington, 1989; mem. conf. bd. Mid. East Policy Coun., U.S. State Dept., Washington, 1994—; elected mem. Coun. of Scholars U.S. Libr. Congress, Washington; bd. dirs. Internat. Diplomacy Coun., San Francisco Opera, Ballet, Symphony Assns. Recipient Cmty. Svc. honors Mayor Dianne Feinstein, San Francisco, 1987, Leadership awards St. Ignatius Coll. Prep., 1984, Calif.'s Gold State award, 1990, AU-ABA Achievement award, 1990, Medal of Honor Order Internat. Ambs. Com. U.S. State Dept. and Foreign Svc. Inst., Washington D.C., World Lifetime Achievement award, Induction 20th Century Millenium Hall Fame and Dist. Leadership Hall Fame Am. Acad. Achievement, 1998, award Superior Talent in Bus. and Arts, Century Dist. Acheivement award, Am. Acad. Achievement, 1998, Internat. Cultural award, 1997, Presdl. Seal Honor, 1997, Decree Internat. Cultural Letters, 1997; named Civic Leader of Yr., Nat. Trust for Hist. Preservation, 1988, 89; named to Presdl. Order of Merit, 1991., Induction U.S. Lib. Congress 500 Leaders of Influence Hall Fame, 1998, Noble Installation Orders of Knighthood Royal British Legions by Queen Elizabeth II, 1998. Fellow World Jurist Assn., World Assn. Judges (Washington); mem. ATLA, Internat. Bar Assn. (various coms., internat. litigation, taxation, labor issue), Am. Arbitration Assn. (panelist, internat. decree), Am. Fgn. Law Assn. (various coms.), Am. Soc. Ch. History, Am. Inst. Archaeology (Boston), Pontifical Inst. Medieval Studies (Toronto, Can.), Am. Hist. Assn., Am. Philol. Assn., Inst. European Law, Medieval Acad. Am., U.S. Supreme Ct. Hist. Soc. (presdl. seal of honor, cultural diploma honor), J Canon Law Soc. U.S., Nat. Planning Assn., Nat. Assn. Scholars (Eminent Scholar of Yr. 1993), Netherlands Arbitration Inst. (mem. Gen. Panels of Arbitrators, mem. Permanent Ct. Arbitration), Calif. Coun. Internat. Trade (GATT com., tax com., legis. com.), Practicing Law Inst., Am. Fgn. Law Assn. (mem. editl. bd. Working Groups on Rsch. Jour. for Legal systems of Africa, Mid. East, Latin Am., EEC and Soviet Union), U.S.-China Bus. Coun. (export com., GATT com., banking and fin. com., import com.), Bay Area Coun. (corp. mem.), Nat. Acad. Conciliators (Spl. award), Internat. Bar (mem. U.S. Group on Model on Insolvency Corp. Acts), Ctr. Internat. Comml. Arbitration, Comml. Club (various positions), Am. Venture Capital Assn., Pacific Venture Capital Assn., Am. Soc. Internat. Law, Washington Fgn. Law Soc., Asia-Pacific Lawyers Assn., Soc. Profls. in Dispute Resolution, British Inst. Internat. and Comparative Law, Internat. Law Assn. (U.S. br.), Commercial Bar Assn. of United Kingdom (London), Inter-Pacific Bar Assn. (Tokyo; mem. arbitration intellectual property, consitutional taxation, labor, legal groups), Inst. European Law Faculty of Laws (United Kingdom), Urban Land Inst. Internat., Mid. East Inst. (Am.-Arab Affairs Coun.), Inter-Am. Bar Assn., 1987—, Calif. Trial Lawyers Assn., Ctr. Reformation Rsch. (co-chmn. Calif. State Com. on U.S-Mid. East Econ. and Polit. Rels.), Soc. Biblical Lit., Am. Acad. Arts and Letters, Am. Acad. Religion, World Lit. Acad., Coun. Scholars, Am. Com. on U.S.-Japan Rels., Japan Soc. No. Calif., Pan-Am. Assn. San Francisco, Soc. Indsl./Office Realtors, Assn. Entertainment Lawyers London, Royal Chartered Inst. Arbitrators (London), Soc. Indsl. and Office Realtors, Urban Land Inst., San Francisco Realtors Assn., Calif. Realtors Assn., Coun. Fgn. Rels., Chgo. Coun. Fgn. Rels., Conf. Bd., San Francisco Urban and Planning Assn., U.S. Trade Facilitation Coun., Asia Soc., Am. Petroleum Inst., Internat. Platform Assn., San Francisco C. of C. (bus. policy com., pub. policy com., co-chmn. congl. issues study group), Am. Inst. Diplomacy, Overseas Devel. Coun. (Mid. East, Russian Republics, Latin Am. studies group), Internat. Vis. Ctr. (adv. bd.), Fin. Execs. Inst., Nat. Assn. Corp. Dirs., Heritage Found. (bd. dirs.), Archaeological Inst. Am. (fellow coun. near east studies, Egyptology), Am. Literature Judicature Soc., Soc. of Biblical, Nat. Assn. Indsl. and Office Properties, World Literary Acad. (Cambridge, Eng.), Am. Acad. Arts & Letters, Am. Acad. Religion, Pres. Club, Nat. Assn. Bus. Economists, Villa Taverna Club, Palm Beach Yacht Club, Pebble Beach Tennis Club, Calif. Yacht Club, Commonwealth Club, City Club San Francisco, British Bankers Club, London, San Diego Track Club (registered athlete), Crow Canyon Country Club (bd. dirs.), Western Venture Capital Assn., Am. Venture Capital Assn., Authors Guild, Internat. Pen Soc., diplomate-delegate World Econ. Summit Conf., Paris, 1998, IOSECC Conf. Internat. Org. Securities Conf., Paris, 1998. Republican. Roman Catholic; Clubs: Crow Canyon Country Club, The Players. Avocations: theater, social entertainment events, opera, ballet, fine arts. Home: 501 Forest Ave Palo Alto CA 94301-2631 Office: 540 Jones St Ste 201 San Francisco CA 94102-2008

LYNCH, VICTOR K. lawyer; b. Latrobe, Pa., Sept. 9, 1929; s. Victor E. and Helen (Kamerer) L.; m. Jane Louise Sutherland, June 11, 1951 (div. 1970); children: G. Michael, Janet L. Mutschler, Steven J., David J., Thomas S., Victoria A. BS in Sanitary Engring., Pa. State U., 1951; LLD, Duquesne U., 1958. Bar: Pa. 1959. Design engr., constrn. insp. The Chester Engrs., Pitts.,

1953-54, project engr., 1954-58; assoc. Burgwin, Ruffin, Perry & Pohl, 1958-62; ptnr. Ruffin, Perry, Springer, Hazlett & Lynch, 1962-70; assoc. Litman, Litman, Harris & Specter, P.A., 1971-74, Lynch, Lynch, Carr & Kabala, Pitts., 1974-78; ptnr. Lynch and Lynch, 1978—. 1st lt. USAF, 1951-53. Recipient Bedell award Water Pollution Control Fedn., 1973. Mem. Water Pollution Control Assn. of Pa. (pres. 1972-73, Sludge Shoveler's award 1970, Johnny Clearwater award 1971), Pa. Soc. Profl. Engrs. Home: 1000 Grandview Ave Pittsburgh PA 15211-1362 Office: 403 Times Bldg 336 4th Ave Pittsburgh PA 15222-2004 Fax: (412) 391-8603.

LYNCH, WILLIAM FRANCIS, JR. secondary mathematics educator; b. Sharon Hill, Pa., July 9, 1956; s. William Francis Sr. and Patricia Claire Marie (Kilpatrick) L.; m. Marian Grace Geiger, Nov. 11, 1985. BS in Social Studies Edn., Temple U., 1978, postgrad., 1980-81; MA in Edn. in Math., Beaver Coll., 1984; postgrad., U. of the Arts, Phila., 1992-93. Social studies tchr. Ben Franklin H.S., Phila., 1978-79; math., English, reading, TV tchr. William Penn H.S., 1979; math., English, reading, social studies tchr. Stetson Jr. H.S., 1980-84; secondary sch. math. tchr. CAPA, 1984-85, Phila. H.S. for Girls, 1985, Kensington H.S., Phila., 1985, Edison H.S., Phila., 1985-86; math., sci., reading tchr. Jones Mid. Sch., 1986-90; math. tchr., head dept. LaBrum Mid. Sch., 1990-96, Phila. H.S. Girls, 1996—2001; math., social sci. tchr., asst. disciplinarian, acad. tutor Central H.S., 2001—. Acad. tutor, student advisor Phila. Sch. Dist., 1978—. Author curriculum in field. Mem. Phila. Fedn. Tchrs. Avocations: woodwork, music, sports, art, reading.

LYNCH, WILLIAM REDINGTON, lawyer; b. N.Y.C., Nov. 17, 1928; s. Francis Russell Vincent and Helen Adams (Barrett) L.; m. Mary Pomeroy Grant, Aug. 22, 1958; children: Melissa L. Woolford, Elizabeth Barrett, Cynthia Pomeroy, Kimberly Townsend, Sarah Phillips. Student, Phillips Exeter Acad., 1944-47; BA, Yale U., 1951; JD, Columbia U., 1958. Bar: N.Y. 1959, Conn. 1963. Assoc. Milbank Tweed Hadley & McCloy, N.Y.C., 1958-62, Cummings & Lockwood, Stamford, Conn., 1962-66, ptnr., 1966—, ptnr. in charge Greenwich office, 1978-88. Bd. dirs. Greenwich Plaza Inc., 1970-74, Harrison & Ellis Inc., Cairo, Ga., 1985-87, Greenwich News Inc., 1986-90; chmn. ADM Mgmt. Corp., 1989-91. Chmn. Pub. Works Com., Greenwich, 1974-77, Greenwich United Way Campaign, 1975-76; vice chmn. Greenwich Bd. Edn., 1977-81, Rep. Town Meeting, 1967-77, dir., sec. Forum World Affairs, 1992-95. Lt. USNR, 1952-56. Mem. ABA, Conn. Bar Assn., Greenwich Bar Assn. (pres. 1979-80), Greenwich Field Club (pres. 1973-75), Round Hill Club (dir., sec. 1993-96). Congregationalist. Home: 100 Bedford Rd Greenwich CT 06831-2535 Office: Cummings & Lockwood 2 Greenwich Plz Ste 5 Greenwich CT 06830-6390

LYNCH, WILLIAM THOMAS, JR. advertising agency executive; b. Evergreen Park, Ill., Dec. 3, 1942; s. William T. and Loretta J. L.; children: Kelly, Maureen, Kim, Meagan, Molly. BA, Loras Coll., 1964; MBA, U. Iowa, 1966. Media trainee Leo Burnett Co. Inc., chgo., 1966-68, asst. account exec., 1968-76, v.p., 1976-79, sr. v.p., 1979-82, exec. v.p., 1981-85; vice chmn. Leo Burnett USA, 1985-89, chmn., CEO Chgo., 1987-91; pres. Leo Burnett Co., Inc., 1992-93; pres., CEO Leo Burnett Worldwide, 1993; CEO, pres. Leo Burnett Worldwide, Leo Burnett Co. Inc., 1993-97; pres., CEO Liam Holdings, Prospect Heights, Ill., 1997—. Bd. dirs. Pella Corp., Krispy Creme Doughnut Corp., SEI Info. Tech. Mem. coun. U. Chgo. Grad. Sch. Bus.; bd. dirs. Northwestern Meml. Found., Northwestern Meml. Hosp., Chgo.; bd. dirs., exec. com. Big Shoulders Archdiocese of Chgo.; bd. regents Loras Coll. Mem. Econ. Club Chgo., Comml. Club Chgo. Roman Catholic. Avocations: running, skiing, gardening, golf. Office: Liam Holdings 206 N Pine St Prospect Heights IL 60070-1524

LYNCH, WILLIAM WALKER, banker; b. Washington, Sept. 18, 1926; s. Talbott and Gertrude (Farrell) L.; m. Barbara Van Sant, Apr. 21, 1951; children: John S., William Walker, Franklin P., Mark F. BA, George Washington U., 1950. Vice pres., treas., dir. Met. Mortgage Co., Washington, 1950-55; dir., mem. exec. com. Prog. Fed. Savs. & Loan Assn., 1953-58; v.p., treas., dir. Anderson & Co., Inc., 1953-59; with First Bank of Fla., West Palm Beach, Fla., 1959-98, exec. v.p., 1966-89, pres., chief exec. officer, 1989-94, chmn. bd., 1994-98. Chmn. 1st Palm Beach Bancorp., 1994-98; mem. tournament com. 53d PGA Championship, 1971; mem. tournament com. 19th World Cup, Internat. Golf Assn., 1971, 69th PGA Championship, 1987; dist. dir. Fla. League Fin. Instns., 1991; dir. Fed. Home Loan Bank of Atlanta, 1991-94; bd. dirs. Fla. Bankers Assn., 1994. Treas. Herbert Hoover Dike Dedication com., 1960; Asst. treas. Fla. Kennedy-Johnson campaign, 1960; bd. dirs. Am. Cancer Soc., 1967-69, 79—, hon. life dir. local United Way, 1962-64. With USNR, 1944-46. Recipient Free Enterprise Companion medal Palm Beach Atlantic Coll., 1989. Mem. West Palm Beach C. of C. (bd. dirs. 1970), Kiwanis (bd. dirs. West Palm Beach club 1961, v.p. 1970-71, pres. 1971-72), No. Palm Beach Country Club, Pi Kappa Alpha. Republican. Roman Catholic. Home: 1032 Country Club Dr North Palm Beach FL 33408-3716

LYNCH, WILLIAM WRIGHT, JR. investment executive, engineer; b. Dallas, Aug. 26, 1936; s. William Wright Sr. and Alma Martha (Hirsch) L.; m. June 11, 1960; children: Mary Margaret, Katherine. BSEE, U. Ariz., 1959; MBA, Stanford U., 1962. Pres. Ins. Bldg. Corp., Dallas, 1965-84; ptnr. Estacado Ptnrs., 1985—, Encino Co., Dallas, 1970—, Cimarron Properties Co., Tucson, 1972-83. Pres., bd. dirs. Argus Realty Corp., Dallas, 1972—; bd. dirs. Lynch Properties Inc., Dallas, Lynch Investment Co., Dallas, Fleetwood Transp. Svcs., Inc., Dallas; adv. dir. Sun Valley Fruit Co., Albuquerque, LTD Enersyst Devel. Ctr., Inc., Dallas, 1995-98, TEWA Mouldings, Albuquerque, Hacienda Packing, Albuquerque, Belle Vista Homes, Dallas, 1998—. Bd. dirs. Dallas Symphony Orch., 1966-74, Dallas Civic Music, 1970-77, Ednl. Opportunities Inc., Dallas, 1973-90, Dallas Coun. World Affairs, 1990-96; trustee W. W. Lynch Found., Dallas, 1968—. Capt. U.S. Army, 1959-60. Mem. Brook Hollow Club, Verandah Club, M.O. Club (Tuscon). Republican. Episcopalian. Office: Lynch Investment Co Ste 1600 LB-16 1845 Woodall Rodgers Fwy Dallas TX 75201-2295 E-mail: w.w.lynch@sbcglobal.net.

LYNDALL, JANICE THOMPSON, vocational counselor; b. Mobile, Ala., Feb. 13, 1945; d. Sam M. and Julia H. Thompson; 1 child, Daniel T. Lyndall. BA in Psychology, U. South Ala., 1989, MS in Counseling, 1991. Cert. rehab. counselor, lic. profl. counselor, lic. bachelor social worker. Rehab. counselor Dept. Rehab. Svcs., Mobile, 1989-98; program mgr. Goodwill Easter Seals, 1998—. Recipient Svc. award, Ind. Living Ctr., Mobile, 1994, 95. Mem. Nat. Rehab. Assn. (counselor divsn.), Ala. Rehab. Assn. (counselor divsn.), Mobile Lic. Profl. Counselor Assn., Friends of the Libr., Tillman's Corner Area C. of C. (bd. mem. 2000—), West Mobile Kiwanis. Baptist. Avocations: painting, writing poetry and fiction, arts and crafts, collectibles.

LYNDE, MYRON STAN, cartoonist; b. Billings, Mont., Sept. 23, 1931; s. Myron Wayne and Eleanor Della Lynde; m. Lynda Brown Lynde, Nov. 25, 1989; children: Shannon, Casey, Matt, Mark, Mark, Rich, Taylor. None, U. of Mont., Missoula, MT, 1949—51, Sch. of Visual Arts, New York, NY, 1967—58. Comic strip artist Rick O' Shay, Latigo; author: (novels) The Bodacious Kid, Careless Creek, Vigilante Moon. Pn3 USN, 1951—55, Pto. Recipient The Inkpot Award, San Diego Comic Conv., 1977, Governor's Award for the Arts, Montant Arts Coun., 1983. Mem.: Nat. Cartoonists Soc., Western Writers of Am. Lutheran (Alc). Avocation: big game hunting. Office: Cottonwood Publishing Inc 120 Greenwood Drive Helena MT 59601 Home Fax: 406-495-1380. Personal E-mail: oldmt@mt.net.

LYNDRUP, PEGGY B. lawyer; b. Winnipeg, Can., Mar. 27, 1949; BS in Edn. magna cum laude, U. N.D., 1969; MEd, Kent State U., 1971; JD summa cum laude, U. Louisville, 1979. Bar: Ky. 1979, U.S. Dist. Ct. (we. dist.) Ky. 1979, U.S. Dist. Ct. (ea. dist.) Ky. 1981. Atty. Greenebaum Doll & McDonald, PLLC, Louisville, 1979—. Recipient Disting. Alumnus award U. Louisville Sch. Law, 1989; Brandeis scholar. Mem. ABA, Louisville Bar Assn. (pres. 1989). Office: Greenbaum Doll & McDonald PLLC 3300 National City Tower Louisville KY 40202 E-mail: pbl@gdm.com.

LYNDS, BEVERLY TURNER, retired astronomer; b. Shreveport, La., Aug. 19, 1929; d. Homer Emory and Nettie Lee (Robertson) Turner; m. Clarence Roger Lynds, June 19, 1954 (div. Oct. 1986); 1 dau., Susan Elizabeth; m. Leo Goldberg, Jan. 2, 1987 (dec. Nov. 1987). BS, Centenary Coll., 1949; postgrad., Tulane U., 1949-50; PhD, U. Calif., Berkeley, 1955. Rsch. assoc. U. Calif., 1955-58, Nat. Radio Astronomy Obs., Green Bank, W.Va., 1959-60; asst. prof. astronomy U. Ariz., 1961-65, assoc. prof., 1965-71; assoc. astronomer, asst. to dir. Kitt Peak Nat. Obs., Tucson, 1971-75, astronomer, asst. dir., 1976-77, astronomer, 1977-86; cons. Assn. Univs. for Rsch. in Astronomy, 1986-87; assoc. Ctr. for Astrophysics and Space Astronomy U. Colo., Boulder, 1987—; Sky Math liaison Unidata, UCAR, 1991—; adj. prof. physics Portland State U., 1999—. Author: (with others) Elementary Astronomy, 1959; editor: (with others) Dark Nebulae, 1971. Mem. AAAS (chmn. sect. D), Internat. Astron. Union, Am. Astron. Soc. (councillor), Nat. Coun. Tchrs. Math., Am. Indian Sci. and Engring. Soc. *Knowing that there are many ways of making a contribution to the world we live in and choosing to use the opportunities available can result in a personal satisfaction which is the best form of success.*

LYNDS, LUCINDA, music educator; b. Taunton, Mass., Sept. 12, 1953; d. Charles Francis and Wilma Ruth (Simmons) MacDonald; m. Warren Eugene Lynds, Oct. 7, 1978; children: Matthew Warren, Victoria Leigh. MusB, Lowell State Coll., 1975; MEd, Lesley Coll., 1989; cert. in Advanced Grad. Study, Fitchburg State Coll., 1997. Cert. music tchr., Mass., supr./dir. Elem. music specialist Fall River (Mass.) Pub. Sch., 1975—. Co-founder, co-dir. Fall River Elem. Select Chorus, 1994-96. Choir, soloist, asst. organist Memorial United Meth., Taunton, Mass., organ restoration com., music com., chmn. scholarship com., Christian edn. com., trustee. Mem. Am. Fedn. Musicians (bd. dirs. 1981-91), Music Educators Nat. Conf., ASCD, Mass. ASCD, Mass. Music Educators Assn., Mass. Tchrs. Assn., Fall River Educators Assn. Avocations: sewing, crafts, organ playing. Office: Fall River Music Dept 615 Tucker St Fall River MA 02721-3348

LYNE, DOROTHY-ARDEN, educator; b. Orangeburg, N.Y., Mar. 9, 1928; d. William Henry and Janet More (Freston) Dean; m. Thomas Delmar Lyne, Aug. 16, 1952 (div. June 1982); children: James Delmar, Peter Freston, Jennifer Dean. BA, Ursinus Coll., 1949; MA, Fletcher Sch. Law and Diplomacy, 1950. Assoc. editor World Peace Found., Boston, 1950-51; editorial assoc. Carnegie Endowment Internat. Peace, N.Y.C., 1951-52; dir. Assoc. of Internat. Rels. Clubs, 1952-53; editor The Town Crier, Westport, Conn., 1966-68; editorial assoc. Machinery Allied Products Inst., Wash., 1959-63; tchr. Helen Keller Mid. Sch., Easton, Conn., 1967-89. Vice chmn. Cooperative Ednl. Svcs., Fairfield, 1983-85. Editor: Documents in American Foreign Rels., 1950, Current Rsch. in Internat. Affairs, 1951. Chmn. Westport Zoning Bd. of Appeals, 1976-80, Westport Bd. of Edn., 1985-87; vice chmn. Westport Bd. of Edn., 1980-85; mem. Westport Charter Revision Commn., 1966-67. Republican. Episcopalian.

LYNETT, WILLIAM RUDDY, publishing, broadcasting company executive; b. Scranton, Pa., Jan. 18, 1947; s. Edward James and Jean O'Hara Lynett; m. Mary Jean Foley; children: Scott, Jennifer, Christopher P., Brigid P., Jean O. BS, U. Scranton, 1972. Pub. Scranton Times, 1966—; pres., chief exec. officer Shamrock Communications, Inc., 1971—; pres. Towanda Daily Rev., 1977-81, Owego Pennysaver Press, Inc., 1977-81. Owner, Pres. Mgmt. Program, Harvard U., 1990; vice-chmn. bd. dirs. WVIA TV. Bd. dirs. Cmty. Med. Ctr., Scranton, 1974—96; pres. Scranton Cultural Ctr.; chmn. Mayor's Libr. Fund Drive, 1974; chmn. spl. gifts divsn. Heart Fund, 1975; bd. govs. Scranton Area Found., chmn., 1996—97; trustee U. Scranton, 1990—96; chmn. Steamtown Nat. Pk. Grand Opening Com.; mem. exec. com. N.E. coun. Boy Scouts Am. Mem. Nat. Assn. Broadcasters, Pa. Assn. Broadcasters, Am. Newspaper Pubs. Assn., Pa. Newspaper Pubs. Assn., Greater Scranton C. of C. (chmn. membership drive 1980-81) Clubs: Scranton Country, Elks, K.C. Democrat. Roman Catholic. Office: 149 Penn Ave Scranton PA 18503-2022

LYNGBYE, JØRGEN, hospital administrator, researcher; b. Andst, Denmark, July 23, 1929; arrived in Norway, 1988; s. Knud and Estrid Marie Schou (Nielsen) L.; m. Ulla von Holstein, July 15, 1967 (div. 1982); 1 child, Rie; m. Jintana Detwilaiphong, Jan. 3, 1994. MD, U. Copenhagen, 1956; PhD, U. Arhus, Denmark, 1969. Asst. U. Arhus, 1957-65; asst. prof. U. Copenhagen, 1966-72; sr. cons. Regional Hosp., Frederiksborg, Denmark, 1973-83, Førde, Norway, 1984; assoc. prof. molecular biology U.S., 1985-86; prof. U. Thailand, 1986-88; dir. Regional Hosp., Molde, Norway, 1988-98; sci. advisor Copenhagen, 1999—. Author: (novels) Clinical Biochemistry, 1986, Twins -- A Unique World Scenario, 1995, Norwegian Handbook of Laboratory Medicine, 1999, Danish textbook of Laboratory Medicine, 2001, From Terror to Wisdom: An Autobiography, 2002; contbr. articles. Sec. Danish Polit. Orgn., Copenhagen, 1977-81. Lt. Danish Army, 1951-66. Decorated WEO Order (Thailand); recipient prize Danish Sci. Soc., 1978, Prix Scientifique, France, 1980, prize Danish Soc. for Protection of Animals, 1987, Applied Physics award, 1993. Fellow N.Y. Acad. Scis.; mem. Danish Med. Assn. (rep. 1978-83). Avocations: world ecology, philosophy, mathematics, nuclear physics, music.

LYNHAM, C(HARLES) RICHARD, foundry company executive; b. Easton, Md., Feb. 24, 1942; s. John Cameron and Anna Louise (Lynch) L.; m. Elizabeth Joy Card, Sept. 19, 1964; children: Jennifer Beth, Thomas Richard. BME, Cornell U., 1965; MBA with distinction, Harvard U., 1969. Sales mgr. Nat. Carbide Die Co., McKeesport, Pa., 1969-71; v.p. sales Sinter-Met Corp., North Brunswick, N.J., 1971-72; sr. mgmt. analyst Am. Cyanamid Co., Wayne, 1972-74; gen. mgr. ceramics and additives div. Foseco Inc., Cleve., 1974-77, dir. mktg. steel mill products group, 1977-79; pres., chief exec. officer Exomet, Inc. subs. Foseco, Inc., Conneaut, Ohio, 1979-81, Fosbel Inc. subs. Foseco, Inc., Cleve., 1981-82; gen. mgr. splty. ceramics group Ferro Corp., 1982-84, group v.p. splty. ceramics, 1984-92; owner, pres. Harbor Castings, Inc., North Canton, Ohio, 1992—, Island Castings, Inc., Muskegan, Mich., 2000—; owner, CEO Blue Ridge Castings, Inc., Piney Flats, Tenn., 2000—. Bd. dirs. Corrpro Cos., Inc., Western Res. Bancorp., Inc. Patentee foundry casting ladle, desulphurization of metals. Past pres. bd. trustees Hospice of Medina County; treas., past pres. bd. trustees BridgesHome Health Care. Capt. C.E., U.S. Army, 1965-67. Decorated Bronze Star with one oak leaf cluster; recipient Frank H.T. Rhodes Exemplary Alumni Svc. award, Cornell U., 1999. Mem. Am. Foundrymen's Soc., Cornell U. Alumni Coun., Cornell U. Alumni Class 1963 (past v.p., past pres.), Cornell U. Alumni Fedn. (past pres., bd. dirs., past v.p.), Chippewa Yacht Club (commodore 1982), Cornell Club of N.E. Ohio (past pres., bd. dirs.), Harbor Bay Yacht Club. Republican. Congregationalist. Avocations: sailing, genealogy. bus. Home: 970 Hickory Grove Ave Medina OH 44256-1616 Office: Harbor Castings Inc 4321 Strausser St NW North Canton OH 44720-7144 E-mail: lynhamcr@ohio.net., harborci@raex.com.

LYNKER, JOHN PAUL, newscaster; b. Bklyn., Aug. 30, 1927; s. Paul Warren and Evelyn Foland (Briggs) L.; m. Linda Ann Cairrao, Sept. 26, 1992; children: Roger John, Denise Suzanne Lynker Duclos, John Paul Jr., Whitney Ellen Lynker Trifiletti. Student, Steven's Inst. Tech., 1944, 46, Columbia U., 1946-49. News anchor WPAT Radio, Paterson, N.J., 1951-52, Sta. WVNJ, Newark, 1952-56, WWJ Radio, Detroit, 1960-65, KGO Radio (ABC), San Francisco, 1971-75, WEEI Radio (CBS), Boston, 1975-80, WTOP Radio, Washington, 1980—; pres., gen. mgr. WSKN (now WGHQ), Kingston, N.Y., 1956-60; freelance newscaster N.Y.C., 1965-71. Pres. The Programmers, N.Y.C., 1965-71. Bd. dirs. Arthritis Found., Washington; pres. Res. Officers' Assn., Boston, 1973, Washington, 1982; deacon Reformed Ch. of Am. Capt. USCGR, 1959-85. Recipient Legend award Washington Area Broadcasters Assn., 1992. Mem. VFW, Washington Automotive Press Assn. (pres. 1990-91), Internat. Motor Press Assn., Aircraft Owner and Pilots Assn., Radio and TV Corrs. Assn., Nat. Press Club, White House Corrs. Assn. Avocations: flying, boating, old cars. Office: WTOP Radio 3400 Idaho Ave NW Ste B Washington DC 20016-3046 Home: Apt D 20 Nob Hill Rd New London CT 06320-3239

LYNN, ANNE MARIE, anesthesiologist, pediatrician; b. Scranton, Pa. AB, Cornell U., 1971; MD, Stanford U. Sch. Medicine, 1975. Diplomate Am. Bd. Pediatrics, Am. Bd. Anesthesiology. Intern U. Wash., Seattle, 1975-76, resident pediatrician, 1976-78, resident anesthesiologist, 1978-80; fellow pediatric intensive care Hosp. Sick Children, Toronto, 1980-81; active staff U. Wash. Affiliated Hosp., Children's Hosp.; profl anesthesiology and pediatrics U. Wash., 1996—. Mem. Am. Acad. Pediatrics, Am. Soc. Anesthesiologists, Wash. State Soc. Anesthesiologists, Soc. Pediatric Anesthesia. Office: Dept Anesthesiology CH-05 Children's Hosp Med Ctr Seattle WA 98105

LYNN, ARTHUR DELLERT, JR. economist, educator; b. Portsmouth, Ohio, Nov. 12, 1921; s. Arthur Dellert and Helen B. (Willis) L.; m. Pauline Judith Wardlow, Dec. 29, 1943 (dec. 1995); children: Pamela Wardlow, Constance Karen, Deborah Joanne, Patricia Diane. Student, Va. Mil. Inst., 1938-39, U.S. Naval Acad., 1939-40; BA, Ohio State U., 1941, MA in Econs., 1943, JD, 1948, PhD in Econs., 1951; postgrad. in law, U. Mich., 1968-70. Bar: Ohio 1948, U.S. Supreme Ct. 1966. Upper Ohio Valley corr. Cin. Enquirer, 1937-38; ptnr. Lynn & Lynn, Columbus, 1948-49; chief clk. to dir. Ohio Dept. Hwys., 1957; mem. faculty Ohio State U., Columbus, 1941-86, prof. econs., 1961-86, asst. dean, 1959-62, assoc. dean Coll. Commerce and Adminstrn., 1962-65, assoc. dean faculties, assoc. provost, 1965-70, assoc. dean Coll. Adminstrv. Sci., 1984-86, assoc. dean emeritus Coll. Bus., 1986—, lectr. Coll. Law, 1961-67, adj. prof. law, 1967-86, prof. pub. adminstrn., 1969-86, prof. emeritus pub. policy and mgmt., 1986—, lectr. exec. devel. program, 1958-71, acting dir. divsn. pub. adminstrn., summers 1973, 74, acting dir. Sch. Pub. Adminstrn., summer 1975, 84-86. Vis. prof. econs. Ohio Wesleyan U., 1958-59, U. Calif., Berkeley, summer 1972; vis. lectr. USAF Inst. Tech., Wright-Patterson AFB, Ohio, 1959-60; mem. Ohio Gov.'s Econ. Rsch. Coun., 1966-70; mem. assoc. faculty Lincoln Inst. Land Policy, Cambridge, Mass., 1989-97. Author: Building the House: The Ohio State University School of Public Administration, 1969-89; editor: The Property Tax and Its Administration, 1970, Property Taxation, Land Use and Public Policy, 1976, Land Value Taxation, 1982; editorial adv. bd.: Tax Bramble Bush, 1959-70; assoc. editor: Nat. Tax Jour., 1971-88; bd. editors: Am. Jour. Econs. and Sociology, 1981-2002. Trustee Griffith Meml. Found. Ins. Edn.; chmn. external econs. adv. com. Marietta Coll., 1975-79; assoc. Nat. Regulatory Rsch. Inst., 1980-98; mem. Alcohol, Drug Addiction and Mental Health Svcs. Bd., Franklin County, Ohio, 1990-2000; bd. dirs. NAMI-Ohio Alliance for Mentally Ill, 1992-95, hon., 1995—; bd. dirs. Metro Behavioral Health Care Network, 1996-98, Planned Lifetime Assistance Network of Ctrl. Ohio, 1999-. 1st lt. F.A. AUS, 1942-46, PTO and Japan. Rsch. fellow Ohio Dept. Mental Health, 1991-92. Mem. ABA (chmn. com. state and local taxes sect. taxation 1961-63), Ohio Bar Assn., Columbus Bar Assn., Am. Econ. Assn., Royal Econ. Assn., Nat. Tax Assn. (chmn. com. model property tax assessment and equalization methods and procedures 1961-65, mem. exec. com. 1965-73, v.p., pres. 1969-70), Tax Inst. (adv. coun. 1960-63), Nat. Tax Assn.-Tax Inst. Am. (sec. 1975-84, treas. 1984-88, bd. dirs. 1975-88, counselor 1988-98, hon. 1988—), Am. Arbitration Assn. (nat. panel), Ohio Coun. Econ. Edn. (bd. dirs. 1964-74), Com. on Taxation, Resources, and Econ. Devel. (co-chmn. 1979-87), Internat. Fiscal Assn., Internat. Assn. Assessing Officers (edn. adv. com.), Columbus Athletic Club, Torch Club, Faculty Club, Rotary, Ohio State U. Pres.' Club, Omicron Delta Epsilon, Beta Theta Pi, Phi Delta Phi, Beta Gamma Sigma, Pi Sigma Alpha, Pi Alpha Alpha. Republican. Episcopalian. Home: 1301 La Rochelle Dr Columbus OH 43221-1531

LYNN, BONNIE JANE, music educator; b. Richmond, Va., Jan. 30, 1953; d. Edson Myron and Margaret Amy (Dudley) L. B in Music, U. Md., 1978. Owner/mgr., tchr. Lynn's Music Svc., Bowie, Md., 1974—; pvt. tchr., class piano tchr. Prince George's C.C., Largo, 1980-86; tchr. Suitland Sch. Performing Arts Prince George's County Sch. Sys., Upper Marlboro, 1997—2000. Mem. Am. Coll. Musicians, Am. Guild Organists (Scholarship award 1997), Music Tchrs. Nat. Assn. (Bowie chpt.), Bowie C. of C. Avocation: ballroom dancing.

LYNN, CHRISTOPHER KENNETH, internist, educator; b. Seattle, Dec. 18, 1956; s. Kenneth Clyde and Bettylu (Hines) L.; m. Elloise Carol Gard, Oct. 1990. BS, Duke U., 1978; MD, Med. Coll. of Ohio, 1983. Diplomate Am. Bd. Internal Medicine. Intern Med. Coll. Ohio, Toledo, 1983-84, resident, 1984-86, asst. prof. internal medicine, 1986-91, assoc. prof., 1992—, clerkship dir. internal medicine, 1987—, co-chief divsn. gen. internal medicine, 1995—. Dir. phys. exam course Med. Coll. Ohio, 1988—, curriculum com., 1990-2000, chmn. subcom. on 3d and 4th yr. curriculum, 1990-2000. Mem. ACP, Soc. of Gen. Internal Medicine, Clerkship Dirs. Internal Medicine. Office: Med Coll Ohio Dept Medicine Box #10008 3000 Arlington Ave Toledo OH 43699

LYNN, D. JOANNE, physician, ethicist, health services researcher; b. Oakland, Md., July 2, 1951; d. John B. and Mary Dorcas (Clark) Harley; m. Barry W. Lynn; children: Christina, Nicholas. BS summa cum laude, Dickinson Coll., 1970; MD cum laude, Boston U., 1974; MA in Philosophy and Social Policy, George Washington U., 1981; MS Clin. Evaluative Scis., Dartmouth Coll., 1995. Diplomate Am. Bd. Internal Medicine. Resident internal Medicine The George Washington U. Med. Ctr., 1974-77; emergency rm. physician, triage physician Washington VA Hosp., 1977-78; faculty assoc. for medicine and humanities divsn. experimental programs George Washington U., Washington, 1978-81, dir. divsn. aging studies, 1988-92, prof. health care scis. and medicine, 1991-92, assoc. chairperson dept. health care scis., 1990-92, dir of the Ctr. to Improve the Care of the Dying, 1995-2000; prof. medicine, cmty. and family medicine, sr. assoc. Ctr. Evaluative Clin. Scis. Dartmouth-Hitchcock Med. Ctr., Hanover, N.H., 1992-95, assoc. dir. Ctr. for Aging, 1992-95; dir. RAND Ctr. for Improve Care of the Dying, Arlington, Va., 2000—; pres. Ams. for Better Care of the Dying, 1995—. Robert Wood Johnson clin. scholar George Washington U., 1977-78, sr. fellow Ctr. Health Policy Rsch., 1991-92; asst. dir. med. studies The Pres. Commn. for Study of Ethical Problems in Medicine and Biomed. and Behavioral Rsch., 1981-83; med. dir. The Washington Home, 1983-89, Hospice of Washington, 1979-91, George Washington Cancer Home Care Program and Home Health Svcs. of The Washington Home, 1990-92, staff physician, 1979-92; fellow Hastings Ctr., 1984—; mem. working group on guidelines for care of terminally ill, 1985-87, rsch. project on ethical issues in care and treatment of chronically ill, 1985-87, working group on new physician-patient relationship, 1991-94, v.p., 1987, chair fellows nominating com., 1991; mem. coordinating coun. on life-sustaining med. treatment decision making by cts. Nat. Ctr. State Cts., 1989-93; fellow Kennedy Inst., 1991; mem. geriat. and gerontology adv. com. Dept. Vet. Affairs, 1991-97; mem. bioethics com. Vets. Health Adminstrn., 1991-93; active Washington Area Seminar on Sci., Tech., and Ethics, 1982-92, Nat. Clin. Panel on High-Cost Hospice Care, Washington, 1991; presenter in field. Author: (with J. Harrold) Handbook for Mortals: Guidance for People Facing Serious Illness, 1999, (with A. Kabamell and J. Lynch Schuster) Improving Care for the End of Life: A Sourcebook for Health Care Managers and Clinicians, 2000; author chpts. to books; mem. editl. bd. The Ency. of Bioethics, 1994-95; mem. adv. editl. bd. Biolaw, 1983, The Hospice Jour., 1984—, Med. Ethics for the Physician, 1985-92, Med. Humanities Rev., 1986—, Cambridge Quar., 1991-95; contbr. articles, revs. to profl. jours. Peter Jeffries and Jeanne Arnold scholar, 1973; recipient Wellington Parlin Sci. Scholarship award, 1979, Dr. Bertha Curtis prize Boston U. Med. Sch., 1974, Nat. Bd. award Med. Coll. Pa., 1992. Fellow ACP (mem. subcom. on aging 1986-91), Am. Geriatrics Soc. (mem. com. public policy 1983-98, mem. ethics com. 1988, chair subcom. on ethics and policy 1986, chair ethics com. 1991-98, bd. dirs. 1991-97); mem. AAAS, APHA, Am. Fedn. Clin. Rsch., Am. Health Care Assn. (mem. task force on AIDS 1987-89), Am. Hosp. Assn. (mem. spl. com. on biomedical ethics 1983-85, 89-94), Am. Med. Dirs. Assn., Am. Soc. Law and Medicine, Am. Coll. Health Care Adminstrs. (mem. nat. adv. com. wandering patients 1987-88), Nat. Inst. on Aging (mem. senile dementia of Alzheimer's type, mem. rsch. ethics task force 1981-82, Am. Geriatrics Soc. rep. 1984-86), Soc. Health and Human Values (mem. gov. coun. 1981-84), Inst. Medicine (mem. com. on future issues in med. tech. devel. 1992-94), N.H. Med. Soc., Soc. Health and Human Values (mem. gov. coun. 1981-84), Internat. Hospice Inst. (mem. physician's adv. com. 1984-86), Med. Soc. D.C. (mem. legis. affairs com. 1985-92, vice chairperson 1991-92), Soc. Gen. Internal Medicine (mem. editl. adv. bd. Jour. 1988-91), Inst. of Medicine, Americans for Better Care of the Dying (pres.). Office: RAND 1200 S Hayes St Arlington VA 22202-5050 E-mail: JLynn@medicaring.org.

LYNN, DALE See SWEENEY, DALE M.

LYNN, EMERSON ELWOOD, JR. retired newspaper editor/publisher; b. Boulder, Colo., Aug. 18, 1924; s. Emerson Elwood and Ruth Merriman (Scott) L.; m. Mickey June Killough, Jan. 27, 1950; children: Emerson Killough, Michael Jay, Angelo Scott, Susan. BS, U. Chgo., 1947. Editor/pub. The Humboldt (Kans.) Union, 1951-58, The Bowie (Tex.) News, 1958-65, The Iola (Kans.) Register, 1965-2001. Chmn. Iola Industries, Inc.; mem. SEK, Inc.; chmn. bd. dirs. Huck Boyd Found., Manhattan, Kans., 2001—. Chmn. Allen County Hosp. Bd., Iola, 1970-77, adv. bd. Kans. Dept. Transp., Topeka,

1992-93; mem. panels on reform of probate code, Kans. Jud. Coun., others; mem. Pulitzer Prize Nominating Jury, 2000-20001. Sgt. USAF, 1942-46. Rotary Internat. fellow U. Melbourne, 1948-49. Mem. Rotary Internat. (pres.), Kans. Press Assn. (pres. 1979, Clyde Reed Master Editor award 1995), William Allen White Found. (pres. 1978). Republican. Presbyterian. Home: 821 S Buckeye St Iola KS 66749-3807 Office: The Iola Register 302 S Washington St Iola KS 66749-3255

LYNN, EVADNA SAYWELL, investment analyst; b. Oakland, Calif., June 16, 1935; d. Lawrence G. Saywell; m. Richard Keppie Lynn, Dec. 28, 1962; children: Douglas, Melisa. BA, MA in Econs., U. Calif., Berkeley. CFA. With Dean Witter, San Francisco, 1958-61, 70-71, Dodge & Cox, San Francisco, 1961-69; fin. analyst, v.p. Clark, Dodge & Co., 1971-73, Wainwright Securities, N.Y.C., 1977-78; 1st v.p. Merrill Lynch Capital markets, 1978-90; sr. v.p. Dean Witter Reynolds, 1990-97; forest products cons., San Francisco, 1997—. Mem. Assn. for Investment Mgmt. and Rsch., San Francisco Security Analysts (treas. 1973-74), Fin. Women's Club San Francisco (pres. 1967). Office: Apt F 1824 Jackson St San Francisco CA 94109-2873

LYNN, GENEVIEVE, artist; b. Balt. d. Yen-Mow and Helen Lynn. BA, Oberlin Coll., 1991; cert. in drawing and painting, Corcoran Sch. Art, 1997; student, Art League, Alexandria, Va.; studied master brush painting, with Diana Kan, 2001, with Ning Yeh, 2002. Graphics artist USA Today, Arlington, Va., 1995-2000. Exhibited in group shows at Design Ctr., Washington, 1998, Photo 98 Ellipse Arts Ctr., Arlington, 1998, Art League Gallery, Alexandria, 1999, 2000, Wilson Gallery, Washington, 2000, 2001, Springfield Art Guild, Alexandria, 2000, Arts Coun. Fairfax County Open Exhbn., Annandale, Va., 2000, Rock Creek Gallery, Washington, 2000, Courthouse Galleries, Portsmouth, Va., 2001, Chalres Sumner Sch. Mus. Archives, Washington, 2001, Dumbarton Concerts Gallery, 2002, one-woman shows include Artscape, Balt., 2000, 2001, 2002, Arlington Ctrl. Libr., 2000, Art-o-Matic, Washington, 2000, 2002, Barnes and Noble, Falls Church, Va., 2001, Arlington, VA., 2002, Kennedy Ctr., Washington, 2001, Bethesda (Md.) Row Arts Festival, 2001, Dumbarton Concerts, Washington, 2002. Recipient Equal Merit award, Springfield Art Guild Fall Show, 2000, others. Mem.: Washington Project Arts/Corcoran, Arts Coun. Fairfax County, Illustrators Club, Nat. Geog. Soc., Sumi-e Soc. Am., Corcoran Gallery Art. E-mail: projects@jaderiverstudio.com.

LYNN, GEORGE GAMBRILL, lawyer; b. Birmingham, Ala., Mar. 3, 1946; s. Henry Sharpe and Fariss (Gambrill) L.; m. Gabriella Hulsey, Aug. 30, 1969 (div. Aug. 1980); children: Gabriella Hansell, George Gambrill Jr. AB, Princeton U., 1968; JD, U. Va., 1974. Bar: Ala. 1974. Law clk. to Hon. Walter P. Gewin U.S. Ct. Appeals 5th Cir., Tuscaloosa, Ala., 1974-75; assoc., ptnr. Cabaniss, Johnston, Gardner, Dumas & O'Neal, Birmingham, 1975-84; ptnr. Maynard, Cooper & Gale, 1984—, mng. ptnr., 2000—. Mem. Ala. com. U.S. Civil Rights Commn., Birmingham, 1988-92; chmn. State of Ala. Ballet, Birmingham, 1989-95. Lt. (j.g.) USN, 1968-71, Vietnam. Mem. ABA, Ala. State Bar Assn. (chmn. sect. on antitrust and bus. torts 1988-89), Birmingham Bar Assn., Birmingham Rotary (trustee 1999—). Republican. Episcopalian. Avocations: tennis, travel. Home: 2712 Lockerbie Cir Birmingham AL 35223-2904 Office: Maynard Cooper & Gale 2400 Amsouth/Harbert Pla 1901 6th Ave N Birmingham AL 35203-2618 E-mail: glynn@mcglaw.com.

LYNN, JONATHAN ADAM, film director, writer, actor; b. Bath, England, Apr. 3, 1943; s. Robin and Ruth (Eban) L.; m. Rita Merkelis, Aug. 1, 1967; 1 child. MA, Pembroke Coll., 1964; MA (hon.), Sheffield U. Actor Cambridge Circus, N.Y.C., 1964, The Ed Sullivan Show, 1964; repertory actor Leicester, Edinburgh, Bristol Old Vic, London; artistic dir. Cambridge Theatre Co., 1977-81. Author: A Proper Man, 1976, Mayday, 1993; co-author: (with Anthony Jay) The Complete Yes Minister, 1984, Yes, Prime Minister, the Diaries of the Rt. Hon. James Hacker, vol. I, 1986, vol. II, 1987; performed in: (plays) Green Julia, 1965, Fiddler on the Roof, 1967-68, Blue Comedy, 1968, The Comedy of the Changing Years, 1969, When We are Married, 1970, (TV movies) Barmitzvah Boy, 1975, The Knowledge, 1979, Outside Edge, 1982, Diana, 1984; dir.: (London) The Plotters of Cabbage Patch Corner, 1970, The Glass Managerie, 1977, The Gingerbread Man, 1977, 78, The Unvarnished Truth, 1978, The Matchmaker, 1978, Songbook, 1979 (SWET award 1979), Tonight at 8:30, 1981, Arms and the Man, 1981, Pass the Butler, 1982, Loot'nt, 1984, A Little Hotel on the Side, 1984, Jacobowski and the Colonel, 1986, Three Men on a Horse, 1987 (Olivier award), RSC: Anna Christie, 1980, (Broadway) The Moony Shapiro Songbook, 1981, (short film) Mick's People, 1982; TV scriptwriter situation comedies, including: My Brother's Keeper, 1974-75 (also co-starred), Yes, Minister (also radio scripts), 1980-82, (Broadcasting Press Guild award 1980, Pye TV Writers award 1981), Yes, Prime Minister, 1986-87 (Pye TV Writers award 1986, Broadcasting Press Guild award 1986, ACE award 1988); film scriptwriter: The Internecine Proect, 1974; film scriptwriter, dir.: Clue, 1986, Nuns on the Run, 1990, My Cousin Vinny, 1991; film dir. The Distinguished Gentleman, 1992, Greedy, 1995, Sgt. Bilko, 1996, Trial and Error, 1997. Recipient Writer's award BAFTA, 1987. Address: Peters Fraser & Dunlop c/o Ken Kamins ICM 8942 Wilshire Blvd Beverly Hills CA 90211-1934

LYNN, JUDITH, opera singer, artist, voice teacher; b. Chgo. d. Louis Leo and Mollie (Rudman) Cogan; m. Filippo Joseph DeStefano, Dec. 26, 1965. Student, L.A. Conservatory Music & Art, 1959-62, U. Vienna, 1964; Hon. Tchg. Degree, Conservatorio de Musica, Maracay, Venezuela, 1987; student, Fashion Inst. Tech., 1987-91; pvt. student music and voice, Filippo De Stefano; coaching, Giuseppe Pais, Lina Pagliughi, Felix Popper, Ruth and Mario Chamlee, Richard Hageman; student art, Albert & Yolanda Pels. V.p., mus. adminstr. Opera Lirica De Stefano, Caracas, 1983-87; sec., treas. De Stefano Presents, Inc., N.Y.C., 1991—. Sang lead roles in: Don Giovanni, sang lead roles in: Rigoletto, sang lead roles in: La Bohème, sang lead roles in: Magic Flute, sang lead roles in: La Traviata, sang lead roles in: Les Pêcheurs de Perles, sang lead roles in: Lucia di Lammermoor, sang lead roles in: I Lombardi, sang lead roles in: Die Entführung aus dem Serail, sang lead roles in: Showboat, sang lead roles in: Lakmé, sang lead roles in: Carmen, sang lead roles in: others, appeared with: Phila. Grand Opera Co., appeared with: N.Y.C. Opera, appeared with: Israel Nat. Opera, appeared with: Stichting Haagse Volksopera, appeared with: Teatro alla pergola, appeared with: Teatro de la Opera de Maracay, appeared with: Riverside Opera Assn., appeared with: Redlands Bowl Assn., appeared with: Conn. Grand Opera, appeared with: Group Opera of N.Y.C., appeared with: others; TV appearances include Teleprompter Cable TV--Opera at the Cloisters and La Traviata, (solo concert) Juventud Musical Venezolana, Caracas; recordings include: The Messiah, G.F. Handel; Exhibited in group shows at Casa de la Cultura, Maracay, Galeria EuroAmericano, Caracas, Ateneo de Los Teques, Venezuela, Landmark Edn. Corp., N.Y.C., Bayside (N.Y.) Hist. Soc., Ho. of George, N.Y.C., N.Y. Hilton and Towers, The Pen and Brush Club, poster, children's books. Recipient 1st prize (voice) Ebell of L.A., 1960, winner Am. Opera Auditions, 1963 (debut in Milan, Italy), 3d prize painting Salon Imagen and Grumbacher, Venezuela, 1984. Mem. Am. Watercolor Soc. (assoc.). Office: The Ansonia/Studio 14-40 2109 Broadway New York NY 10023-2106 E-mail: jlynnart@mindspring.com., destefanopresent@mindspring.com.

LYNN, KATHERINE LYN, quality engineer, chemist; b. Nagoya, Japan, June 25, 1954; (parents Am. citizens); d. Jimmie Frank and Barbara Sue (Whiteside) Sutton; m. Richard Shelly Lynn, Feb. 28, 1981. BS in Chemistry cum laude, Calif. State U., Fullerton, 1979. Cert. quality engr. Am. Soc. Quality, cert. quality auditor, cert. quality mgr. Technician U.S. Borax Corp., Anaheim, Calif., 1974-79; chemist Armstrong World Industries, Southgate, 1979-82; project engr. Hydril Co., Whittier, 1982-84; sr. quality engr. So. Calif. Gas Co., L.A., 1984—. Patentee fluorspar flotation. Bd. dirs. East Side Christian Ch., 1987-89. Mem. Soc. Plastic Engrs., Am. Soc. for Quality, Am. Soc. for Quality Cert. (bd. dirs.), Am. Chem. Soc., Sierra Club. Mem. Christian Ch. Avocations: outdoor activities, backpacking, Nordic and Alpine skiing. Home: 5120 Faust Ave Lakewood CA 90713-1924 Office: So Calif Gas Co PO Box 3249 Los Angeles CA 90051-1249 E-mail: klynn@socalgas.com.

LYNN, LARRY (VERNE LAURISTON LYNN), engineering executive; b. Seattle, Sept. 5, 1930; s. Eldin Verne and Irma (Tuell) Lynn; m. Emily Jean Badger, Oct. 4, 1952 (div. 1988); m. Shirley Marie Pieczynski, Sept. 27, 1988. BS in Physics, Tufts U., 1951. Assoc. divsn. head, mem. steering com. Lincoln Lab. M.I.T., Lexington, Mass., 1953-79; dir. defensive systems Office of the Undersecretary of Defense, Washington, 1979-81; dep. dir. Adv. Rsch. Project Agy., 1981-85; v.p., COO Atlantic Aerospace Electronics, Greenbelt, Md., 1985-93; dep. under sec. defense Office Sec. Defense, Washington, 1993-95, dir. def. adv. rsch. project agy., 1995-98; pres., owner, cons. Larry Lynn Assocs., Williamsburg, Va., 1998—. Contbr. numerous articles to profl. jours. Lt. JG USNR, 1951-53. Fellow IEEE (life). Home: 400 Flagship Dr # 1105 Naples FL 34108 Office: Larry Lynn Assocs 124 The Green Williamsburg VA 23185-8252

LYNN, LAURENCE EDWIN, JR. university administrator, educator; b. Long Beach, Calif., June 10, 1937; s. Laurence Edwin and Marjorie Louise (Hart) L.; m. Patricia Ramsey Lynn; 1 dau., Katherine Bell; children from previous marriage— Stephen Louis, Daniel Laurence, Diana Jane, Julia Suzanne. AB, U. Calif., 1959; PhD (Ford Found. fellow), Yale, 1966. Dir., dep. asst. sec. def. (OASD/SA) Dept. Def., Washington, 1965-69; asst. for program analysis NSC, 1969-70; assoc. prof. bus. Grad. Sch. Bus., Stanford (Calif.) U., 1970-71, vis. prof. pub. policy, 1982-83; asst. sec. planning and evaluation HEW, Washington, 1971-73; asst. sec. program devel. and budget U.S. Dept. Interior, 1973-74; sr. fellow Brookings Instn., 1974-75; prof. pub. policy John Fitzgerald Kennedy Sch. Govt. Harvard U., Cambridge, Mass., 1975-83; dean Sch. Social Service Adminstrn. U. Chgo., 1983-88, prof., sch. of social svc. adminstrn. and Harris grad. sch. pub. policy studies, 1983—, dir. Ctr. for Urban Rsch. and Policy Studies, 1986—; dir. Mgmt. Inst., 1992-99; Sydney Stein, Jr. prof., 1997—2002; Buch chair and prof. Bush Sch. Govt. and Pub. Svc. , Tex A&M U., 2002—. Author: Designing Public Policy, 1980, The State and Human Services, 1980, Managing the Public's Business, 1981, Managing Public Policy, 1987, Public Management as Art, Science and Profession, 1996, Teaching and Learning with Cases: A Guide; co-author: The President as Policymaker, 1981, Improving Governance: A New Logic for Empirical Research, 2001; contbr. articles to profl. jours. Bd. dirs. Chgo. Met. Planning Coun., 1984-89, Leadership Greater Chgo., 1989-92; mem. coun. of scholars Libr. of Congress, 1989-93. 1st lt. AUS, 1963-65. Recipient Sec. Def. Meritorious Civilian Svc. medal, Presdl. Cert. of Disting. Achievment, Vernon prize, best book award Acad. Mgmt., 1996. Fellow Nat. Acad. Public Adminstrn.; mem. ASPA, U. Calif. Alumni Assn., Coun. on Fgn. Rels., Assn. Pub. Policy Analysis and Mgmt. (past pres.), Phi Beta Kappa. Office: 22129 Academic West 4220 TAMU Coll College Station TX 77843-4220 E-mail: llynn@bushschool.tamu.edu.

LYNN, LEONARD HARVEY, business educator; b. Portland, Oreg., Sept. 28, 1942; s. Roy Leonard and Eunice Evelyn Lynn; m. Kuniko Yamada, Oct. 25, 1969; children: Kenneth Roy, Clifford Masami. MA, U. Oreg., 1967, U. Mich., 1976, PhD, 1980. Advt. copy supr. Asia Advt., Tokyo, 1968-73; asst. prof. Carnegie-Mellon U., Pitts., 1979-87; assoc. prof. mgmt. policy Case Western Res. U., Cleve., 1987-95, prof. mgmt. policy, chair dept. mktg. and policy, 1995—. Mem. am. adv. com. Japan Found., N.Y.C., 1999—. Author: How Japan Innovates, 1982, Organizing Business, 1988. With U.S. Army, 1961-64. Mem. IEEE, Acad. Mgmt., Acad. Internat. Bus., Assn. Japanese Bus. Studies (treas. 1988-96, pres. 1995-97). Home: 23220 Shaker Blvd Shaker Heights OH 44122-2660 Office: Case Western Res Univ 10900 Euclid Ave Cleveland OH 44106-4901 Fax: 216-368-4785. E-mail: lhl@po.cwru.edu.

LYNN, LINDA BROWN, business educator; b. Chgo., July 15, 1943; d. Kenneth Herbert Brown and Velma Margaret Graves; m. W. Lee Lynn, Aug. 12, 1967 (div. Sept. 1976). BA in Edn., BS in Edn., U. Ariz., 1965; MA in English Lit., Ind. U., 1967; MBA, U. Ariz., 1978. Tchr. secondary sch. English various schs., Calif., Ind., Oreg., 1965-71; owner, contractor Lynn Constrn. Co., Bend, Oreg., 1972-75; asst. constrn. mgr. Arieb Enterprises, Riyadh, Saudi Arabia, 1981-82; constrn. supr. U.S. Home, Tucson, 1978-80, 83-85; real estate developer The JNC Cos., 1985-87; mem. faculty, chair dept. bus. Pima C.C., 1988—. Adj. prof. U. San Francisco, 1990-92. Avocations: travel, sailing, movies, walking, reading. Office: 1255 N Stone Ave Tucson AZ 85709-3002

LYNN, MICHAEL A. historic site director; BA with High Distinction, U. Va., 1974; MA in History Mus. Adminstrn., SUNY, Oneonta, 1980. Curatorial intern Fenimore House/N.Y. State Hist. Assn., Cooperstown, N.Y., 1978-79; curator of collections Lynchburg (Va.) Mus. System, 1979-81; dir. Stonewall Jackson House, Lexington, Va., 1981-94; exec. dir. Stonewall Jackson House/Found., 1994—. Mem. Mus. and Hist. Sites Working Group Va. History Initiative, 1996—98; Va. state dir. Southeastern Mus. Conf., 1993—99; bd. dirs. Assn. for the Preservation of Civil War Sites, 1990—95, officer Va. Assn. of Mus.; others; mem. Rockbridge Area Tourism Devel. Bd., 2000—02, Lexington Archtl. Rev. Bd., 1999—; coun. mem.-at-large Southeastern Mus. Conf., 2000—; spkr. in field. Vol. VISTA, Charlottesville, Va., 1975-77; mem. tourism adv. coun. Lexington, Rockbridge County, Buena Vista, 1996-99; founding bd. dirs. Lexington Downtown Devel. Assn., 1985-87, 89-95; elder Lexington Presbyn. Ch.; mem. task force Project Horizon: Alternatives for Abused Adults, 1983-84, founding bd. dirs., 1984-86, others. Office: Stonewall Jackson House 8 E Washington St Lexington VA 24450-2529

LYNN, MIDGE, artist; b. N.Y.C., Dec. 04; d. Seymour and Lillian Dribben; m. Laurence L. Lynn, Feb. 18, 1989; 1 child, Kelly. BA, Calif. State U., Northridge, 1982; MFA, Otis Art Inst., 1984. Pres., bd. dirs. L.A. Art Assn., 1998—2002. Exhbns. include Brand Libr. Gallery, Pasadena, Glendale 1996 (Brand Assocs. award), San Bernardino County Mus. 1997 (1st Place), Barnsdall Mcpl. Gallery. Mem. World Affairs Coun., Group Nine. Home: PO Box 861657 Los Angeles CA 90086 E-mail: lynnlm@earthlink.net.

LYNN, MORTON DANIEL, orthopedist; b. Paterson, N.J., Apr. 4, 1939; s. Allan A. and Sophie (Schwartz) L.; m. Susan Z. Zeller, July 3, 1966; children: Allison, Elizabeth, Sarah, Geoffrey (dec.). AB, Dartmouth Coll., 1961; MD, Cornell U., 1965. Diplomate Nat. Bd. Med. Examiners, Am. Bd. Orthopedic Surgeons. Intern, resident in surgery U. Hosp., Cleve., 1965-67; resident in orthopedics Vanderbilt U. Hosp., Nashville, 1967-70; pvt. practice New Eng. Orthopedic Surgeons, Springfield, Mass., 1972—. Active staff Baystate Med. Ctr., Springfield, 1972—, Mercy Hosp., Springfield, 1982—, Shriners Hosp., Springfield, 1973—; asst. clin. instr. orthopedics N.Y. Med. Coll., N.Y.C., 1970-72, Boston U. Med. Sch., 1972-82, clin. asst. prof. orthopedics, 82—; v.p. med. staff Baystate Med. Ctr., 1989, 90, pres., 1991, 92. Contbr. articles to profl. jours. Lt. comdr. USPHS, 1970-72. Named Triplane Ankle Fracture, 1972. Fellow Am. Acad. Orthopedic Surgeons; mem. Mass. Med. Soc., AMA, New Eng. Orthopedic Soc., Eastern Orthopedic Soc., Am. Acad. Cerebral Palsy, Am. Orthopedic Foot and Ankle Soc. Avocations: tennis, piano, fishing, skiing, golf. Office: New Eng Orthopedic Surgeons 300 Carew St Springfield MA 01104-2316

LYNN, NAOMI B. academic administrator; b. N.Y.C., Apr. 16, 1933; d. Carmelo Burgos and Maria (Lebron) Berly; m. Robert A. Lynn, Aug. 28, 1954; children: Mary Louise, Nancy Lynn Francis, Judy Lynn Chance, Jo-An Lynn Cooper. BA, Maryville (Tenn.) Coll., 1954; MA, U. Ill., 1958; PhD, U. Kans., 1970. Instr. polit. sci. Cen. Mo. State Coll., Warrensburg, Mo., 1966-68; asst. prof. Kans. State U., Manhattan, 1970-75, assoc. prof., 1975-80, acting dept. head, prof., 1980-81, head polit. sci. dept., prof., 1982-84; dean Coll. Pub. and Urban Affairs, prof. Ga. State U., Atlanta, 1984-91; chancellor U. Ill., Springfield, 1991-2001, chancellor emerita, 2001—. Cons. fed., state and local govts., Manhattan, Topeka, Altanta, 1981-91; bd. dirs. Bank One Springfield. Author: The Fulbright Premise, 1973; editor: Public Administration, The State of Discipline, 1990, Women, Politics and the Constitution, 1990; contbr. articles and textbook chpts. to profl. pubs. Bd. dirs. United Way of Sangamon County, 1991—, Ill. Symphony Orch., 1992-95; bd. dirs. Urban League, 1993—. Recipient Disting. Alumni award Maryville Coll., 1986; fellow Nat. Acad. Pub. Adminstrn. Mem. Nat. Assn. Schs. Pub. Affairs and Adminstrn. (nat. pres.), Am. Soc. Pub. Adminstrn. (nat. pres. 1985-86), Am. Polit. Sci. Assn. (mem. exec. coun. 1981-83, trustee 1993—), Am. Assn. State Colls. and Univs. (bd. dirs.), Midwest Polit. Sci. Assn. (mem. exec. coun. 1976-79), Women's Caucus Polit. Sci. (pres. 1975-76), Greater Springfield C. of C. (bd. dirs. 1991—, accreditation task force 1992), Cosmos Club, Pi Sigma Alpha (nat. pres.). Presbyterian.

LYNN, PATRICIA ANNE, student services representative; b. Newton, Iowa, Sept. 9, 1950; d. Harold Clifford (dec.) and Alice Marie (Uhlig) Johnson; divorced. AA in Psychology, Trinidad (Colo.) Jr. Coll., 1970; BS in Psychology, Ft. Lewis Coll., Durango, Colo., 1972; AA in Vet. Tech., Internat. Sch., Scranton, Pa., 1980. Customer svc. agt. Waco Scaffolding & Equipment, Denver, 1980-83; leasing agt. Look Ltd. Realty, Federal Heights, Colo., 1983-84; sales assoc. Lynn & Assocs., Aurora, 1991—; customer svc. team leader EBSCO Industries, Golden, 1984-96; student svcs. rep. Coll. for Fin. Planning, Denver, 1997—. Political aide Dem. Party, Denver; docent Denver Zoo; vol. ARC, Aurora. Mem. Rocky Mountain Midget Racing Assn., Vintage Motor Racing Assn. Jehovah'S Witness. Avocations: auto racing, restoring antique cars. Home: 19013 E Carmel Cir Aurora CO 80011-3621 Office: Coll for Fin Planning 6161 S Syracuse Way Greenwood Village CO 80111 E-mail: trishia268@consultant.com.

LYNN, ROBERT WILLIAM, strategic planning consultant; b. Jan. 27, 1943; s. William Ernest and Jeannette (Reardon) Lynn; m. Sara E. Davis, Aug. 26, 1961 (dec. Nov. 1980); children: Robert, John, William, David, Michelle; m. Karen Gross, Mar. 3, 2001. AAS in Supervision, Purdue U., 1974, BS in Indsl. Engring., 1976; MBA, Ind.-Wesleyan U., 1991. Engr. No. Ind. Pub. Svc. Co., Crown Point, 1968-77, engring. supr. Gary, 1977-79, sr. cons. Hammond, 1979-82, mgr., 1982-89, asst. to sr. v.p. and gen. mgr. energy distbn., 1989-90, mgr. strategic planning, 1990-96, lectr., 1992-93; exec. dir. Nesi Integrated Energy Resources, Inc., 1997-2000; ind. strategic planning cons. Omaha, 2000—. Advisor Purdue U.-Hammond, 1979-2000. With USN, 1960-67. Mem. Inst. Indsl. Engrs. (sr. project award 1976). Avocations: woodcarving, sculpture. Home: 3020 NW 76th Ave Ankeny IA 50021 Office: Strategy Play Book 3020 NW 76th Ave Ankeny IA 50021 E-mail: lynnlink@earthlink.net.

LYNN, ROBERT PATRICK, JR. lawyer; b. N.Y.C., Nov. 17, 1943; s. Robert P. and Marie (Madeo) L.; m. Maria T. Zeccola, Nov. 18, 1967; children— Robert P. III, Stephanie M., Kerry Elizabeth. B.A., Villanova U., 1965; J.D., St. John's U., Bklyn., 1968. Bar: N.Y. 1969, U.S. Dist. Ct. (ea. dist.) N.Y. 1975, U.S. Ct. Appeals (1st cir.) 1978, U.S. Ct. Appeals (2d cir.) 1975, U.S. Supreme Ct. 1978. Clk., then assoc. Leboeuf, Lamb & Leiby, N.Y.C., 1966-69; dep. town atty. Town of North Hempstead, Manhasset, N.Y., 1969-71; assoc. Sprague Dwyer Aspland & Tobin, Mineola, N.Y., 1971-75, ptnr., 1975-76; ptnr. Lynn & Ledwith, Garden City, N.Y., 1976-92; spl. prosecutor Inc. Village of Bayville, 1975-76. Bd. dirs. Cath. Charities, 1971-89, chmn., 1982; vice chmn. Diocese of Rockville Centre Family Life Ctr., 1978-82. Mem. Nassau County Bar Assn., Suffolk County Bar Assn., N.Y. State Bar Assn. Roman Catholic. Clubs: Wheatley Hills Golf Club (East Williston, N.Y.); Lloyd Neck Bath (Lloyd Harbor, N.Y.), La Romana Country Club (Dominican Rep.). Office: 330 Old Country Rd Ste 103 Mineola NY 11501-4143 also: GV269 Casade Campo La Romana Dominican Republic Home: 6 Richard Ln Huntington NY 11743-2354

LYNN, SHARON, artist; b. Bethesda, Md., Apr. 1, 1952; d. Jean Doris (McDermott) Jacobs; m. Necdet Senhart, Oct. 24, 1976; 1 child, Ben. BA, SUNY, N.Y.C., 1994. Art dir. Pompeii Prodns., N.Y.C.; v.p. Bliss Street, Inc. Solo exhibitions at Pierce Coll., Athens, Greece, Beachcomber, Jacksonville Beach, Fla., Halstead's, N.Y.C., Bot. Gardens, N.Y.C.

LYNN, THEODORE STANLEY, lawyer; b. N.Y.C., Aug. 2, 1937; s. Irving and Sydell (Gorlie) Lynn; m. Linda Isabel Freeman, July 21, 1968; children: Jessica, Douglas. AB, Columbia U., 1958; LLB, Harvard U., 1961; LLM, NYU, 1962; SJD, George Washington U., 1972. Law clk. to Hon. Bruce M. Forrester U.S. Tax Ct., Washington, 1962-64; tchg. fellow in law George Washington U., 1963-64; ptnr. Webster & Sheffield, N.Y.C., 1964-90, Stroock & Stroock & Lavan, N.Y.C., 1991—. Consult Admin Conf US, Washington, 1974—75; founding counsel Pension Real Estate Asn, Washington, 1981—84. Author: Real Estate Limited Partnerships, 3d ed, 1991, Real Estate Investment Trusts (supplemented annually), 1994; contbr. articles to profl jours. Secy Manhattan Sch Dance, 1974—93; trustee Birch Wathen Lenox Sch, New York, NY, 1975—93; bd dirs Citizens Union, 1991—, vice-chair, 2001—; dir Sutton Area Community Inc, 1995—; treas, trustee Citizens Union Found, 2000—; spec asst Mayor John V Lindsay, New York, NY, 1966—69; bd dirs Manhattan Community Bd # 6, 1977—. Mem.: ABA, Asn Bar City NY, Fed Bar Coun, Harvard Club, Univ Club. Office: Stroock & Stroock & Lavan 180 Maiden Ln Fl 17 New York NY 10038-4937 E-mail: tlynn@stroock.com.

LYNN, WALTER ROYAL, civil engineering educator, university administrator; b. N.Y.C., Oct. 1, 1928; s. Norman and Gussie (Gdalin) L.; m. Barbara Lee Campbell, June 3, 1960; children: Michael Drew. BS, U. Miami, 1950; MS, U. N.C., 1955; PhD, Northwestern U., 1963. Registered profl. engr., N.Y. State registered land surveyor, Fla. Land surveyor Ehly Constrn. Co., Miami, Fla., 1950-51; chief party Rader Engring. Co., 1951; supt. sewage treatment, lectr. civil engring. U. Miami, 1951-53, asst. prof. mech. engring., 1954-55, asst. prof. civil engring., 1955-57, research asst. prof. marine lab., 1957-58, assoc. prof. civil and indsl. engring., 1959-61; dir. research Ralph B. Carter Co., 1957-58; assoc. prof. san. engring. Cornell U., Ithaca, N.Y., 1961-64, prof. civil and environ. engring., 1964—, dir. Center Environ. Quality Mgmt., 1966-76, dir. Sch. Civil and Environ. Engring., 1970-78, dir. Program on Sci., Tech. and Society, 1980-88, dean univ. faculty, 1988-93; sr. fellow Ctr. for the Environ., 1992-97, 2000—, dir., 1996-97, univ. ombudsman, 1998—; adj. prof. pub. health Med. Coll. Cornell U., 1971-80. Mem. spl. adv. commn. on solid wastes NRC, 1968-76, mem. com. to rev. Washington met. water supply, 1976-84, chmn., 1980-84, mem. bd. water sci. and tech., 1982-86, chmn., 1982-85, mem. com. on water resources rsch., 1987-90, chmn., 1988-90; mem. U.S. Nat. Com. for the Decade on Nat. Disaster Reduction, 1991-96, chmn., 1991-96; cons. WHO, 1969—, Rockefeller Found., 1976-81, SEARO, 1978; chmn. N.Y. State Water Resources Planning Coun., 1986—, NRC Bd. on Nat. Disasters, 1992-96 (chmn. 1992-96). Editor: (with A. Charnes) Mathematical Analysis of Decision Problems in Ecology, 1975; assoc. editor: Jour. Ops. Research, 1968-76, Jour. Environ. Econs. and Mgmt, 1972-88; contbr.: chpt. to Human Ecology and Public Health, 1969; author articles. Chmn. Ithaca Mayor's Citizens Adv. Com., 1964-65, Ithaca Urban Renewal Agy., 1965-68; trustee Cornell U., 1980-85, Village of Cayuga Heights, 2000—; bd. dirs. Cornell Research Found., 1978-96; commr. So. Cayuga Lake Intergovtl. Water Commn., 1997—. Served with AUS, 1946-48. Recipient Disting. Alumnus award U. Miami, 1985, U. N.C., 1996, Pub. Svc. award Universities Coun. on Water Resources, 1991, Conservation Svc. award U.S. Dept. Interior, 1994. Fellow ASCE (life), AAAS; mem. Nat. Acad. Engrs. Mex. (corr.), Sigma Xi, Phi Kappa Phi., Chi Epsilon Home: 102 Iroquois Pl Ithaca NY 14850-2221 E-mail: WRL1@cornell.edu.

LYNNE, JUDITH, interior designer; b. Beaver Falls, Pa. d. Clinton Axel August and Irene Lucille (Williams) Stromberg; 1 child, Mark Jonathan Enlow. Student, UCLA, 1979-80. Cert. interior designer, Calif. Owner Judith Lynne Interior Design, Palm Springs, Calif., 1977—. Mem. Am. Soc. Interior Designers (bd. dirs. 1994-95, 97—, pres.-elect 1998—, Disting. Svc. award 1997, Design Excellence award 1998), Ptnrs. Edn., Fashion Group Internat. Office: Judith Lynne Interior Design PO Box 4998 Palm Springs CA 92263-4998

LYNNE-O'BRIEN, VINCENT, stage manager, director, actor; b. East Orange, N.J., Dec. 11, 1935; s. Patrick A. and Mary (Gallagher) O'B. BBA, Seton Hall U., 1957. Artistic dir. Shoreline Youth Theatre, Madison, Conn., 1978-85, Shubert Acad., Shubert Theatre, New Haven, 1990-95; dir. Alliance Theatre, New Haven, 1977-88, Stratford Cmty. Svcs., 1986-88, Jewish Cmty. Svcs., New Haven, 1986-87. Appearances include (on Broadway) The Boy Friend, No Time for Sargeants, Fiorello, Golden Boy, Best Laid Plans, Sweet Charity, Billy, (regional theaters) West Side Story, Mass Appeal, Tribute, Odd Couple, You Can't Take It with You, Diary of Ann Frank, The Sea Gull, Cape Cod-Wellfleet, 1999, You Can't Take It with You, Cape Cod-Orleans, 1999, On Golden Pond, (TV shows) Studio One, U.S. Steel, I Remember Mama, Voice of Firestone, Lucy Arnaz Show, I Bonino, Search for Tomorrow; (TV movies) Princess Daisey, Prisoner without a Name, Cell without a Number; theatrical films include The Long Grey Line, Ragtime, Ghost Busters, Godfather III, Other Peoples Money, Amistad; dir. Life With Father, Broadway Bound. Dir. Daniel Hand Drama Soc., 1975-85; bd. dirs. ABC Program, 1984-86, Madison Arts and Sci. Council, 1985-86; commr. conservation com. Town of Eastham, Mass. Mem. Actors Equity Assn., Screen Actors Guild, Am. Fedn. TV and Radio Artists, Madison C. of C. (bd. dirs. 1979-85), Eastham Conservation Commn. Roman Catholic. Avocations: tennis, travel. Home: 488 1st NH Turnpike Northwood NH 03261 E-mail: vinmort@metrocast.net.

LYNT, RICHARD KING, microbiologist; b. Washington, Feb. 25, 1917; s. Richard King and Elsie Ackerman (King) L.; m. Elizabeth Mackenzie Cissel, Nov. 17, 1944; children: Richard, Margaret, David. BS in Bacteriology, U. Md., 1939, MS in Bacteriology and Food Technology, 1942. Grad. asst. bacteriology U. Md., College Pk., Md., 1939-40; food inspector, bacteriologist D.C. Health Dept., Washington, 1940-42; lab officer, hosp. corps, med. svc. corps USNR, Bethesda, Md., Oceanside, Calif., 1942-46; bacteriologist E.R. Squibb & Sons, New Brunswick, N.J., 1946-48; rsch. fellow Rutgers U., 1948-49; bacteriologist NIH Nat. Inst. Allergy and Infectious Disease, Bethesda, 1951-63; microbiologist U.S. FDA Div. Microbiology, Washington, 1963-83; microbiologist cons., retired Silver Spring, Md., 1983—. Mem. interagy. botulism rsch. coordinating com., Washington, 1968-83; faculty mem. Am. Soc. for Microbiology Continuing Edn. Com., Dallas, 1981; mem. People to People Enzymology Del. to People's Republic of China, 1985. Author: (with others) Clostridium Botulinum, 1970-84; contbr. chpts to books, articles to profl. jours. Mem. Pinecrest Citizens Assn., Silver Spring, 1960-98; adminstrv. bd. Marvin Meml. United Meth. Ch., Silver Spring, 1985—; judge of elections Bd. Suprs. Elections, Montgomery County, Md., 1988-92. Served to lt. Med. Svc. Corps, USNR, 1942-46. Recipient Awards of Merit, U.S. FDA, 1974. Mem. N.Y. Acad. Sci., Inst. Food Technologists, Naval Res. Assn., Am. Soc. for Microbiology, AAAS. Republican. Methodist. Achievements include isolation of type B Influenza Virus in monkey kidney tissue culture; antigenicity and heat resistance of Clostridium Botulinum, grouping proteolytic type A,B, and F strains and nonproteolytic types B,E,F strains in homogeneous gr. Home: 14619 Deerhurst Ter Silver Spring MD 20906-1831

LYON, ANDREW BENNET, economics educator; b. Chgo. s. Richard M. and Rhee Lyon; m. Jennifer A. Sour, May 1987; 2 children. AB, Stanford U., 1980; PhD, Princeton U., 1986. Economist Jt. Com. on Taxation, U.S. Congress, Washington, 1985-87; asst. prof., dept. econ. U. Md., College Park, 1987-93, assoc. prof., dept. econ., 1993—; vis. fellow Brookings Inst., 1994-95. Cons. and expert witness, 1987—; dir. Unisys Credit Corp., Detroit, 1991-92; sr. econ. Coun. Econ. Advisers, 1992-93; dep. asst. sec. tax analysis U.S. Treasury Dept., 2001–. Author: Cracking the Code: Making Sense of the Corporate Alternative Minimum Tax, 1997; contbr. numerous articles to profl. jours. Nat. Bur. Econs. fellow, 1987-94. Mem. Am. Econ. Assn., Nat. Tax Assn. (Outstanding Doctoral Dissertation award 1986, Fed. Tax Com. 1991), Phi Beta Kappa. Office: U Md Dept Econs College Park MD 20742-0001

LYON, BRUCE ARNOLD, lawyer, educator; b. Sacramento, Sept. 24, 1951; s. Arnold E. and Arlene R. (Cox) L.; m. Patricia J. Gibson, Dec. 14, 1974; children: Barrett, Andrew. AB with honors, U. Pacific, 1974; JD, U. Calif.-Hastings Coll. Law, 1977. Bar: Calif. 1977, U.S. Dist. Ct. (ea. and no. dists.) Calif. 1977. Ptnr. Ingoglia, Marskey, Kearney & Lyon, Sacramento, 1977-84; sole practice Auburn, Calif., 1984-91; ptnr. Robinson, Robinson & Lyon, 1991-98, Robinson, Lyon & Springford LLP, Auburn, 1999—. Instr. in law Sierra Coll., Rocklin, Calif., 1983-98. Mng. editor Comment, A Jour. of Comm. and Entertainment Law, 1974; contbr. articles to trade publs. Bd. dirs. Auburn Cmty. Found., Gold Country Sci. and Tech. Found. Mem.: ABA, Thurston Soc., Placer County Bar Assn., State Bar Calif., Native Sons of the Golden West, Internat. Platform Assn., Mensa, Order of Coif. Office: Robinson Lyon & Springford LLP One California St Auburn CA 95603

LYON, CARL FRANCIS, JR. lawyer; b. Sumter, S.C., May 9, 1943; s. Carl Francis and Sophie (Goldstrum) L.; m. Maryann Mercier; children— Barbara Ruth, Sarah Frances, Carl Francis, III. AB, Duke U., 1965, JD with honors, 1968. Bar: N.Y. 1969, D.C. 1977. Assoc., then ptnr. Mudge Rose Guthrie Alexander & Ferdon, N.Y.C., 1968-95, mem. exec. com., 1986-87, 94-95; ptnr. Orrick Herrington & Sutcliffe, 1995—, mem. exec. com., 1998-2000. Contbr. articles to profl. publs. Mem. ABA (vice-chmn. spl. com. on energy fin. 1988-91), N.Y. State Bar Assn., D.C. Bar Assn., Am. Pub. Power Assn., Duke U. Law Alumni Coun., Order of Coif, Phi Alpha Delta. Office: Orrick Herrington Sutcliffe 666 5th Ave Rm 203 New York NY 10103-1798

LYON, DAVID WILLIAM, research executive; b. Lansing, Mich., Mar. 26, 1941; s. Herbert Reid and Mary Kathleen (Slack) L.; m. Catherine McHugh Dillon, July 8, 1967. BS, Mich. State U., 1963; M in City and Regional Planning, U. Calif., Berkeley, 1966, PhD, 1972. Regional economist Fed. Res. Bank Phila., 1969-71; rsch. dir. human and econ. resources The N.Y.C.-Rand Inst., 1972-75, v.p., 1975; sr. economist The Rand Corp., Santa Monica, Calif., 1975-77, dep. v.p., 1977-79, v.p. domestic rsch. divsn., 1979-93, v.p. external affairs, 1993-94; pres., CEO Pub. Policy Inst. Calif., 1994—. Adj. prof. U. Pa., 1975; mem. adv. bd. Inst. for Civil Justice, 1987-93, Rand-Urban Inst. Program for Rsch. on Immigration Policy, 1988-91, Drug Policy Rsch. Ctr., 1989-93, So. Calif. Health Policy Rsch. Consortium, 1989-94, Rand Ctr. for U.S.-Japan Rels., 1989-93, Rand Ctr. for Asia-Pacific Policy, 1993-95; dir. Coll. Environ. Design Coun., U. Calif., Berkeley, 1979-90. Mem. publs. com. Rand Jour. Econs., 1984-94; contbr. articles to profl. jours. Bd. dirs. Ctr. for Healthy Aging, Santa Monica, Calif., 1985-94, pres., 1989-91; mem. adv. coun. Coll. Environ. Design, U. Calif., Berkeley, 2000—. Mellon fellow in city planning, 1966-68; Econ. Devel. Adminstrn. grad. fellow, 1966 Mem. Coun. on Fgn. Rels., World Affairs Coun. No. Calif. (trustee 1999—), Japan Am. Soc. So. Calif. (bd. dirs. 1990-94), Japan Soc. No. Calif. (bd. dirs. 2000-), Asia Soc. So. Calif. Ctr. (mem. adv. coun. 1988-), Pacific Coun. on Internat. Policy, Delta Phi Epsilon, Lambda Alpha Internat. Office: Pub Policy Inst Calif 500 Washington St Ste 800 San Francisco CA 94111-2919 E-mail: lyon@ppic.org.

LYON, GORDON WILLIAM, philosophy educator; b. Durban, South Africa, Nov. 9, 1966; s. William and Jean Margaret (Colinese) L.; m. Eileen Lesley Groth, July 26, 1997; 1 child, James William. BA, U. Natal, Durban, 1988, BA Hons., 1989; MPh, U. Cambridge, Eng., 1991, PhD, 1994. Lectr. in philosophy Rhodes U., Grahamstown, South Africa, 1994-97; vis. asst. prof. philosophy Fla. State U., Tallahassee, 1997-2001, SUNY, Fredonia NY, 2001—. Chmn. Natal U. Film Soc., Durban, S. Africa, 1986-87. Mem. editl. com. Jour. Social Theory and Practice; contbr. articles to profl. jours. Pres. Cambridge U. Ramblers Hiking Club, 1992-93. Recipient U. Natal scholarships, Durban, South Africa, 1986, 87, 88, 89, South African Nat. Scholarship, 1989, Doctoral Merit scholarship Human Scis. Rsch. Coun., Ctr. for Sci. Devel., 1991-93, Overseas Rsch. Students Scheme award, Com. Vice Chancellors and Prins., London, 1989-92. Cambridge Overseas Trust, 1989-92, Trinity Coll. Overseas Students award, 1989-92. Mem. Am. Philos. Assn., So. Soc. for Philosophy and Psychology, Fla. Philos. Assn. Office: Dept Philosophy SUNY Fredonia Fredonia NY 14063 E-mail: gordon.lyon@fredonia.edu.

LYON, HENRY CLARENCE, artist; b. Ithaca, N.Y., Jan. 25, 1930; s. Clarence William Lyon and Katherine Elizabeth Rothermich; m. Bettie Ann Buell, June 14, 1952; children: Jeffery, Christine, Sandra. BS, Cornell U., 1952. Mgr. Young & Halstead Co., Mt. Kisco, N.Y., 1955-65; sales cons. Upjohn Co., Kalamazoo, 1965-78; hotel mgr. Continental Devel. Co., Honolulu, 1978-80; condo. mgr. Waikoloa (Hawaii) Villas, 1980-90; regional acct. exec. Hyatt Resorts, Waikoloa, 1990-92; artist Henry C. Lyon Artist, 1992—. Executed portraits of 42 U.S. presidents; represented in pvt. collections. 1st lt. U.S. Army, 1952-54. Mem. Waimea Arts Coun. Avocations: reading, research, nature and health walks, travel, botany. Home: PO Box 383133 Waikoloa HI 96738-3133 E-mail: alohalyon@aol.com.

LYON, HOWARD P. musician, educator; b. Middleburgh, N.Y., Apr. 22, 1940; s. Donald Rich and Alice Louise (Rushmer) Lyon; m. Mary Katherine Alexander, June 17, 1962 (div. Mar. 1978); children: Katherine E., Naida-Ann M., Meredith L., Rebekkah L.; m. Mary Ann Saylor, July 13, 1979 (div. Mar. 2001); children: Elizabeth R., Miranda S. MusB in Applied Violin, Mich. State U., 1962. Cert. music tchr. Pa. Inspector Retail Credit Co., Lansing, Mich., 1962—69; freelance musician, 1962—; head console dept. Organ Supply Industries, Erie, Pa., 1969—91; asst. concert master violin sect. Erie Philharm., 1969—; concert master Erie Chamber Orch., 1977—; adj. music instr. Edinboro U. Pa., 1982—; tchr. music Erie Sch. Dist., 1997—2000. Solo violin and harpsichord appearances Erie area, 1962—; rschr. Hubisz Report on Phys. Sci. Textbooks, 2000; spkr. Am. Assn. Physics Tchrs. Nat. Conf., Rochester, NY, 2001. Contbr. articles to profl. jours. Dir. The Textbook League, Sausalito, Calif., 2001—. Achievements include research on the number of errors in science textbooks, which has resulted in coverage from Boston Globe, Baltimore Sun, N.Y. Observer, Reader's Digest and ABC's 20-20. Avocations: reading, canoeing, swimming, chess. Home: 1029 Washington Pl Erie PA 16502 E-mail: aintlyin@juno.com.

LYON, JAMES A. clinical pharmacist, researcher; b. Mpls., June 24, 1949; s. James A. and Jeanne E. Lyon; m. Carol A. Nowicki, July 31, 1973; children: Julie, Amy. BS in Pharmacy, U. Pitts., 1972; PharmD, U. Mich., 1974. Registered pharmacist, Ohio. Asst. prof. pharmacy U. Pitts., 1974-82; v.p. clin. rsch. Biodecision Labs., Pitts., 1982-88, PPD, Wilmington, N.C., 1988-94; sr. dir. phase I AAI, 1994—. Adj. assoc. prof. pharmacy U. N.C. Sch. Pharmacy, Chapel Hill, 1995—. Avocation: golf. Home: 16 Robert E Lee Dr Wilmington NC 28412-6724 Office: AAI 2320 Scientific Park Dr Wilmington NC 28405-1800 Fax: (910) 815-2313. E-mail: jim.lyon@AAIIntl.com.

LYON, JAMES BURROUGHS, lawyer; b. N.Y.C., May 11, 1930; s. Francis Murray and Edith May (Strong) L. BA, Amherst Coll., 1952; LLB, Yale U., 1955. Bar: Conn. 1955, U.S. Tax Ct. 1970. Asst. football coach Yale U., 1953-55; assoc. Murtha, Cullina LLP (and predecessor), Hartford, Conn., 1956-61, ptnr., 1961-96, counsel, 1996—. Adv. com., lectr. and session leader NYU Inst. on Fed. Taxation, 1973-86; mem. IRS Northeast Key Dist.'s Exempt Orgns. Liaison Group, Bklyn., 1993—. Mem. editl. bd. Conn. Law Tribune, 1988—. Chmn. 13th Conf. Charitable Orgn. N.Y.U. Inst. on Fed. Taxation, 1982; trustee Kingswood-Oxford Sch., West Hartford, Conn., 1961—91, hon. trustee, 1991—, chmn. bd. trustees, 1975—78; exec. com., chmn. Amherst Coll. Alumni Coun., 1963—69; trustee Old Sturbridge Village, Mass., 1974—2001, chmn. bd. trustees, 1991—93; trustee Ella Burr McManus Trust, Hartford, 1980—99; hon. trustee Old Sturbridge Village, 2001—; trustee Ellen Battell Stoeckel Trust, Norfolk, Conn., 1994—, Hartford YMCA, 1985—, St. Francis Hosp. Found., 1991—, Watkinson Libr., 1990—, pres., 2001—; trustee Wadsworth Atheneum, Hartford, 1968—93, pres., 1981—84, hon. trustee, 1993—; trustee Horace Bushnell Meml. Hall, 1993—, sec., 1996—; corporator Inst. Living, 1981—, Hartford Hosp., 1975—, St. Francis Hosp., Hartford, 1976—, Hartford Pub. Libr., 1979—; bd. dirs. Conn. Policy and Econ. Com., Inc., 1991—98; mem. Conn. adv. com. New Eng. Legal Found., 1991—; mem. adv. com. Florence Griswold Mus., Old Lyme, 1991—; bd. vis. Hartford Art Sch., 1995—; trustee Conn. Hist. Soc., 2000—, Conn. Jr. Republic, Litchfield, 2000—; mem. N.E. regional coun. Nat. Club Assn., 1998—. Recipient Eminent Svc. medal Amherst Coll., 1967, Nathan Hale award Yale Club Hartford, 1982, Disting. Am. award No. Conn. chpt. Nat. Football Found. Hall of Fame, 1983, Community Svc. award United Way of the Capital Area, 1986; honored as a direct descendant of its founder Mary Lyon, Mt. Holyoke Coll., South Hadley, Mass. 1997. Fellow: ABA (exempt orgn. com., co-chmn. subcom. on mus. and other cultural orgns. sect. of taxation 1988—), Am. Coll. Tax Counsel, Phi Beta Kappa; mem.: Am. Law Inst., Conn. State Srs. Golf Assn., Univ. Club Hartford (pres. 1976—77), Limestone Trout Club (East Canaan, Conn.), Yale Golf Club, Mory's Assn. (New Haven), Wianno Club (Osterville, Mass.), Dauntless Club (Essex, Conn.), Union Club N.Y.C., Yale Club, Hartford Golf Club. Office: 185 Asylum St Hartford CT 06103-3408 E-mail: jlyon@murthalaw.com.

LYON, JAMES HUGH, education specialist, legislative consultant; b. Clarksburg, W.Va., Apr. 17, 1936; s. James M. and Mildred E. Lyon; m. Marilyn Jean Lyon. BA in English, Salem Internat. U., 1960; MA, W.Va. U., 1967. Cert. English tchr., Ohio. Tchr. coll. preparatory English Harrison County (W.Va.) Schs., 1960-64, Urbana (Ohio) City Schs., 1964-70; edn. cons., lobbyist Ohio Edn. Assn., Columbus, 1970-93; edn. cons. Lyon Assocs., Canton, Ohio, 1993—. Mem. Nat. Assn. Lobbyists for Sch. Employees, Ohio Edn. Assn. (edn. specialist in Ohio state legislature 1981-93, Outstanding Svc. award 1986), Elks. Home and Office: 6627 Avalon St NW Canton OH 44708-1084

LYON, JAMES KARL, German language educator; b. Rotterdam, Holland, Feb. 17, 1934; came to U.S., 1937; s. T. Edgar and Hermana (Forsberg) L.; m. Dorothy Ann Burton, Dec. 22, 1959; children: James, John, Elizabeth, Sarah, Christina, Rebecca, Matthew, Melissa. BA, U. Utah, 1958, MA, 1959; PhD, Harvard U., 1963. Instr. German Harvard U., Cambridge, Mass., 1962-63, asst. prof., 1966-71; assoc. prof. U. Fla., Gainesville, 1971-74; prof. U. Calif. San Diego, La Jolla, 1974-94, provost Eleanor Roosevelt Coll., 1987-94; prof. dept. Germanic and Slavic langs. Brigham Young U., Provo, Utah, 1994—. Vis. prof. U. Augsburg, Germany, 1993. Author: Konkordanz zur Lyrik Gottfried Benns, 1971, Bertolt Brecht and Rudyard Kipling, 1975, Brecht's American Cicerone, 1978, Bertolt Brecht in America, 1980, Brecht in den USA, 1994. Capt. M.I., U.S. Army, 1963-66. NEH fellow, 1970, Guggenheim Found. fellow, 1974; Ford Found. grantee, 1988, 91. Mem. MLA, Am. Assn. Tchrs. German, Internat. Brecht. Soc., Phi Beta Kappa. Democrat. Mem. Lds Ch. Avocations: back-packing, fishing. Office: Brigham Young U Dept Germanic & Slavic Lang 4094 Jesse Knight Human Bld Provo UT 84602-6120 E-mail: james_lyon@byu.edu.

LYON, JERRY D. school psychologist; b. Seattle, Nov. 29, 1944; s. John D. and Estelle G. Lyon; m. Kathleen A. L., Sept. 30, 1967 (div. 1994). BS in Psychology and Sociology, U. Wis., Superior, 1969, MS in Edn., 1970. Cert. sch. psychologist, Wash. School psychologist Coop. Ednl. Svc. Agy., Gillette, Wis., 1970-73, Ednl. Svc. Dist., Bremerton, Wash., 1973-77, Quillayute Valley Sch. Dist., Forks, 1977-86, Port Angeles (Wash.) Sch. Dist., 1986—. Adv. bd. West End Outreach Svcs. Mental Health Bd., Forks, 1974-82. Vista vol. Phila., 1966; vocalist Logos Musical, Port Angeles, 1995-96. Mem. Nat. Assn. Sch. Psychologists, Wash. State Assn. Sch. Psychologists (adv. bd. 1995-97). Avocations: fly fishing, music, reading, photography. Office: Port Angeles Sch Dist 216 E 4th St Port Angeles WA 98362-3200 E-mail: jerry-d-lyon@pasd.wednet.edu.

LYON, JOANNE B. psychologist; b. Little Rock, June 2, 1943; d. F. Ike and Marie (Graham) Beyer; m. James S. Lyon, Dec. 1971 (div. Sept. 1975), m. John M. Lofton, May 22, 1983 (dec. Feb. 1990). BA, Webster U., 1966; MEd, U. Mo., St. Louis, 1976, PhD, 1986. Lic. psychologist, Kans. Reading specialist Rockwood Sch. Dist., St. Louis, 1976-79; psychology cons. handicapped component St. Louis Head Start, 1982-83; intern Topeka State Hosp., 1983-84; dir. partial hosp. programs Family Svc. & Guidance Ctr., Topeka, 1985-89; pvt. practitioner and joint owner Shadow Wood Clin. Assocs., 1989—, adminstr., 1999-2000. Clin. supr. Family Svc. and Guidance Ctr., Topeka, 1989-93; psychology adv. bd. Behavioral Scis. Regulatory Bd., 1996-98. Mem. exec. bd. Interfaith of Topeka, 1995-99, I Have a Dream Coalition, 1994-98; bd. dirs. Temple Beth Sholom Sisterhood, 1997-2000, Temple Beth Sholom, 1997-2000, Torah Learning Ctr., 2000—. Sherman scholar U. Mo., St. Louis, 1982. Mem. APA, Kans. Psychol. Assn., Am. Orthopsychiat. Assn., Soc. for Personality Assessment. Jewish. Home: 9630 Hardy St Overland Park KS 66212-3350 Office: 8340 Mission Rd Prairie Village KS 66206-1355 also: 2933 SW Woodside Dr Topeka KS 66614

LYON, LOUISE MINOR, music educator; b. Atlanta, Jan. 28, 1951; d. Harold Whitfield and Louise Lallande (Hoyt) Minor; m. Silas Tarpley Lyon, Feb. 12, 1977; children: Jennifer, Heather. BA, Agnes Scott Coll., 1973; MFA, U. Ga., 1976. Cert. music tchr. Pvt. piano tchr., Marietta, Ga., 1976—. Press Found. scholar in music, 1970-73. Mem. Cobb County Music Tchrs. Assn. (sec. 1981-83, bd. dirs. 1981-95), Greater Atlanta Music Alliance (sec. 1990-92), Ga. Music Tchrs. Assn. (IMTF chmn. 1992-94, chmn. pub. rels. 1994-96), So. Divsn. Music Tchrs. (zoning com. 1992-94), Pi Kappa Lambda. Republican. Presbyterian. Avocations: gardening, reading, sewing, crafts. Home: 5573 Woodberry Cir Marietta GA 30068-1843

LYON, MARTHA SUE, research engineer, retired military officer; b. Oct. 3, 1935; d. Harry Bowman and Erma Louise (Moreland) Lyon. BA in Chemistry, U. Louisville, 1959; MEd in Math., Northeastern Ill. U., 1974; postgrad., McGeorge Sch. Law, 1981-82, Northwestern Calif. U., 1999—, George Washington U., 1995—96. Cert. tchr. Ill., Ky. Rsch. assoc. U. Louisville Med. Sch., 1959-61, 62-63; commd. ensign USNR, 1965; advanced through grades to commr. USN, 1983; instr. instrumentation chemistry Northwestern U., Evanston, Ill., 1968-70; tchr. sci., chemistry, gifted math. Waukegan (Ill.) pub. schs., 1970-75; phys. scientist Libr. of Congress, Washington, 1975-76; rsch. engr. Lockheed Missiles & Space Co., Sunnyvale, Calif., 1976-77; instr., assoc. chmn. dept. physics U.S. Naval Acad., Annapolis, Md., 1977-80; analyst sys. analysis divsn. Office of Chief of Naval Ops. Staff, Washington, 1980-81; comdg. officer Naval Rsch. Ctr., Stockton, Calif., 1981-83; mem. faculty Def. Intelligence Coll., 1983-85; program mgr. Space and Naval Warfare Sys. Command, 1985-86; commdg. officer PERSUPPACT Memphis, 1986-88; program mgr. Space and Naval Warfare Sys. Command, 1988-91; sect. chief Def. Intelligence Agy., 1991-95. Chief marching divsn. Nat. Homecoming Parade and N.Y.C. Regional Parade Task Force Desert Storm, 1991—95; contractor mgr. supporting officer spl. asst. to Sec. of Def. for Gulf War Illnesses Investigations, 1997—98; pro bono work for Class Act Group; Fla. chpt. svc. officer, comdr. dist. 4 DAV. Mem. citizen rev. panel Fla. Foster Care Project Marion County, 1999; mem. exec. com. Marioun County Dem. Grantee, Am. Heart Assn., 1960—62, 1997—98, NSF, 1971, 1982. Mem.: Pvt. Investigators Assn. Va., Evidence Photographers' Internat. Coun., Internat. Soc. Bassists, Internat. Conf. Women in Sci. Engring. (protocol chair), Am. Soc. Photogrammetry, Am. Statis. Assn., Am. Fedn. Musicians, Soc. Women Engrs., Am. Chem. Soc., Mensa, Order Eastern Star, Delta Phi Alpha, Zeta Tau Alpha. Achievements include development of of processes used in archival photography. E-mail: mslyon@att.net.

LYON, MARY KUEHLEWIND, nurse; b. Buffalo, Oct. 20, 1963; d. Charles Benjamin and Clara Ann (Kraus) Kuehlewind; m. Robert Gordon Lyon, July 19, 1986; children: Garnet Rexford II, Graham Pierce. BS in Nursing cum laude, SUNY, Buffalo, 1985. Supr. Home Care, Kenmore, N.Y., 1977-82; student lab. instr. SUNY, Buffalo, 1982; RN charge night shift Kenmore Mercy Hosp., 1985-88; dental asst. Dr. Arthur Miller DDS PC, Elmira, N.Y., 1988-90; prepared childbirth instr., sibling preparation educator Arnot Ogden Med. Ctr., 1989-2000; breast health specialist Ogden Med. Ctr., 2000—01. Recipient Gabriel award for children's stories, 1995, Telly award, 1997, Cert. of Merit for Proclaim award, 1995. Mem. Sigma Theta Tau. Avocations: children, animals, writing children's stories.

LYON, RICHARD, mayor emeritus, retired naval officer; b. Pasadena, Calif., July 14, 1923; s. Norman Morais and Ruth (Hollis) L.; m. Cynthia Gisslin, Aug. 8, 1975; children: Patricia, Michael, Sean; children by previous marriage: Mary, Edward, Sally, Kathryn, Patrick (dec.), Susan. B.E., Yale U., 1944; MBA, Stanford U., 1953. Commd. ensign USN, 1944; advanced through grades to rear adm. SEAL, 1974; served in Pacific and China, World War II; with Underwater Demolition Team Korea; recalled to active duty as dep. chief Naval Res. New Orleans, 1978-81. Mem. Chief Naval Ops. Res. Affairs Adv. Bd., 1978-81; exec. v.p. Nat. Assn. Employee Benefits, Newport Beach, Calif., 1981-90; mem. Bd. Control, U.S. Naval Inst., 1978-81; pres. Civil Svc. Commn., San Diego County, 1990, Oceanside Unified Sch. Bd., 1991; mayor City of Oceanside, 1992-2000. Pres. bd. trustees Children's Hosp. Orange County, 1965, 72. Decorated Legion of Merit. Mem. Nat. Assn. Securities Dealers (registered prin.), Newport Harbor Yacht Club, Oceanside Yacht Club, Rotary (Anaheim, Calif. pres. 1966). Republican. Episcopalian. Home: 600 S The Strand Oceanside CA 92054-3902 E-mail: lyonclan@aol.com.

LYON, RICHARD HAROLD, physicist educator; b. Evansville, Ind., Aug. 24, 1929; s. Chester Clyde and Gertrude Lyon; m. Jean Wheaton; children: Katherine Lyon Davis, Geoffrey Cleveland, Suzanne Marie Riggle. AB, Evansville Coll., 1952; PhD in Physics (Owens-Corning fellow), MIT, 1955; DEng, U. Evansville, 1976. Asst. prof. elec. engring. U. Minn., Mpls., 1956-59; Mem. research staff Mass. Inst. Tech., 1955-56, lectr. mech. engring., 1963-69, prof. mech. engring., 1970-95, prof. emeritus, 1995—, head mechanics and materials div., 1981-86. NSF postdoctoral fellow U. Manchester, Eng., 1959-60; sr. scientist Bolt Beranek & Newman, Cambridge, 1960-66, v.p., 1966-70; chmn. Cambridge Collaborative, Inc., 1972-90; v.p. Grozier Pub., Inc., 1972; pres. Grozier Tech. Systems, 1976-82, RH Lyon Corp., 1976—. Author: Transportation Noise, 1974, Theory and Applications of Statistical Energy Analysis, 1975, 2d edit. (with R. DeJong), 1994, Machinery Noise and Diagnostics, 1987, Designing for Product Sound Quality, 2000; mem. editl. bd. Acoustical Soc. Japan, 1996—. Bd. dirs. Boston Light Opera, Ltd., 1975; mem. alumni bd. U. Evansville, 1988-94, trustee, 1995-98, chmn. ann. fund, 1996-97. Recipient Rayleigh medal Brit. Inst. Acoustics, 1995, Nat. Acad. Engring. award 1995, Disting. Alumni award U. Evansville, 1997, medal of Hon., 2002. Fellow: AAAS, Acoustical Soc. Am. (assoc. editor jour. 1967—74, exec. coun. 1976—79, v.p. 1989—90, pres. 1993—94, Silver medal in engring. acoustics 1998), Internat. Inst. Acoustics and Vibrations (hon.); mem.: Brit. Inst. Acoustics (Rayleigh medal 1995), Nat. Acad. Engring., Sigma Xi, Sigma Pi Sigma. Achievements include research, publs. in fields of nonlinear random oscillations, energy transfer in complex structures, sound transmission in marine and aerospace vehicles, building acoustics, environmental noise, machinery diagnostics, home theater audio systems. Home: 60 Prentiss Ln Belmont MA 02478-2021 Office: RH Lyon Corp 691 Concord Ave Cambridge MA 02138-1002 E-mail: rhlyon@lyoncorp.com.

LYON, RICK (RICHARD WOODWARD), water transportation professional, poet; b. San Juan, P.R., Oct. 24, 1953; s. Basil Woodward Richard and Nancy Walko L. BA, Boston U., 1980; MFA, Columbia U., 1982. Ferryboat operator Essex (Conn.) Island Marina, 1986-95; launch operator Essex Yacht Club, 1995—. Guest lectr. Naugatuck Valley Cmty. Tech. Coll., Waterbury, Conn., 1994-96. Author: Bell 8, 1994; asst. editor Parnassus: Poetry in Rev., 1980-82; author poems. Recipient The Nation award Poetry Ctr. of 92d St. Y and Nation mag., 1989; fellow Conn. Commn. on the Arts, 1990, Camargo Found., 1995. Episcopalian. Avocations: motorcycling, sailing. Home: 65 Main St Unit 17 Ivoryton CT 06442 Office: Essex Yacht Club 13 Novelty Ln Essex CT 06426

LYON, ROBERT, ballet dancer; b. Heidelberg, West Germany; Student, Guilerland Youth Commn. Ballet Program, New Sch. Ballet, Schenectady, NY, Sch. Am. Ballet. Mem. corps de ballet N.Y.C. Ballet, 1987—98, soloist, 1998—. Dancer (ballets) The Bounding Line, Slonimsky's Earbox, Brahms-Schoenberg Quartet, The Four Temperaments, A Midsummer Night's Dream, The Nutcracker, Delight of the Muses, Fearful Symmetries, The Waltz Project, numerous others, guest artist Chgo. City Ballet prodn. of Cinderella. Office: NYC Ballet NY State Theatre 20 Lincoln Ctr Plz New York NY 10023-6913*

LYON, ROBERT CHARLES, lawyer; b. Southampton, N.Y., July 2, 1953; s. Charles and Harriet L.; m. Maureen Griffin, Sept. 1, 1979; children: Christopher Charles, Sean Robert, Katherine Joy. BBA with highest hons., Hofstra U., 1976; JD, So. Meth. U., 1979. Bar: Tex. 1980, U.S. Dist. Ct. (no. dist.) Tex. 1982, U.S. Ct. Appeals (5th cir.) 1984, U.S. Supreme Ct. 1992; bd. cert. personal injury trial law, Tex. Bd. Legal Specialization. Assoc. Lyon & Smith, Mesquite, Tex., 1979-83; ptnr. Lyon & Lyon, Mesquite and Rowlett, 1983-91; pvt. practice Rowlett, 1991—. Sec. Starlight Candles, Ltd., Bloomington, Minn., 1996-2000, TPR Ltd., Edina, 1996-98. Coach soccer, T-ball, baseball Rockwall YMCA, 1987-94; den leader Cub Scouts, Rockwall, 1990-91. Mem. ABA, ATLA, Tex. Trial Lawyers Assn. (assoc. dir. and dir. 1991—), State Bar Tex. (adminstrn. of the rules of evidence com. 1998—), Dallas Trial Lawyers Assn. (bd. dirs. 1990-92, treas. 1992-93, sec. 1993-94, v.p. 1994-95, pres. elect 1995-96, pres. 96-97), Dallas Bar Assn. (judiciary com. and fee dispute com. 1998-2001, legal ethics com. 2000—), Mesquite Bar Assn., Rockwall County Bar Assn. (pres. 1990-91), Patron Ducks Unltd. Democrat. Office: 3301 Century Dr # A Rowlett TX 75088-7511 Fax: 972-475-5804. E-mail: attybob@msn.com.

LYON, RONALD EDWARD, management consultant, computer consultant; b. Kansas City, Kans., Apr. 13, 1936; s. William Edward and Lillian (Gee) L.; m. Josette Paula Larré, July 24, 1959; children: Michael Alan, Mark Alexander, Matthew Adam, Collette Allison. Owner Hansler Outboard & Austin Aqua Sports, Austin, Tex., 1959-63; gen. mgr. Wayne Green Ent.-73 Mag., Peterboro, N.H., 1963-65; with Computer Control Corp., 1965-71; sales person Radio Shack (Tandy) & Sterling Elec. Co., Maine, N.H., Vt. areas, 1971-82; sales engr. Pall Corp./Russell Assocs., Inc., Watertown, Mass., 1982-87; mgr. eastern region Fansteel/Wellman Dynamics, 1984-87; CEO, COO Laryon Assocs., Inc., Keene, N.H., 1987—. With USAF, 1955-59. Mem. U.S. Power Squadron, Soc. for Preservation and Encouragement of Barber Shop Quartet Singing in Am. Avocations: sailing, ham radio, computers, skiing, square dancing. Home: McIntire Rd Munsonville NH 03457

LYON, THOMAS L. agricultural organization administrator; b. Toledo, Sept. 12, 1940; m. Barbara Lyon; children: Jeff, Melissa, Scott. BS in Dairy Sci., Iowa State U., 1962. Exec. sec. Iowa State Dairy Assn.; with 21st Century Genetics, gen. mgr., 1976-93; pres. Coop. Resources Internat., Shawano, Wis.,

1993—, now CEO. Bd. dirs. Am. Farmland Trust, Coop. Bus. Internat., Coop. Devel. Found.; chmn. Nat. Coop. Bus. Assn.; mem. Nat. Rural Devel. Task Force & Coop. 2000 com., Dairy Shrine Club, steering com. Wis. Dairy Inititative 2020, Kellogg Found. Food Systems; bd. advisors U. Wis., Eau Claire; bd. visitors U. Wis., Madison; trustee Grad. Inst. Coop. Leadership, Coop. Found.; cons. U. Wis. Bus. Schs. Review. Recipient Friend of Extension award U. Wis., 1981, Wis. Friend of County Agents award, 1984, Dairy Industry Person of Yr. award World Dairy Expo, 1985, Nat. Coop. Pub. Svc. award, 1991, Disting. Citizen Shawano award, 1993, Agribus. award Iowa State U. Coll. Agr. Alumni Soc., 1995. Office: Coop Resources Internat 100 NBC Dr PO Boox 469 Shawano WI 54166

LYON, WAYNE BARTON, manufacturing company executive; b. Dayton, Oct. 26, 1932; m. Maryann L., 1961; children: Karyn, Craig, Blair. BSChemE, U. Cin., 1955; MBA in Mktg., U. Chgo., 1969. Registered profl. engr., Mich. Tech. rep. Union Carbide, Chgo., 1955-62; product devel. mgr., v.p. bus. devel. Ill. Tool Works, 1962-72; group v.p., exec. v.p. Masco Corp., Taylor, Mich., 1972-85, pres., coo, 1985-96, also bd. dirs.; chmn., pres., chief exec. officer Lifestyle Furnishings, High Point, N.C., 1996-2000; chmn. Lifestyle Furniture Internat., 2000—02; ret., 2002. Bd. dirs. Masco Corp., Taylor, Mich.; lectr. AMA. Patentee in field. Bd. govs., trustee Cranbrook Ednl. Cmty., Bloomfield Hills, Mich., 1984—. Capt. U.S. Army, 1955—63. Mem.: Bloomfield Hills Country Club, Orchard Lake Country Club (trustee 1985—90). Address: Lifestyle Furnishings 4000 Lifestyle Ct High Point NC 27265-9432

LYON, WILFORD CHARLES, JR. insurance executive; b. Blackfoot, Idaho, June 1, 1935; s. Wilford Charles and Nellie Anna (Estenson) L.; m. Eleanor Perkins, Aug. 23, 1957; children: Katherine Ann, Wilford Charles III. BS, Ga. Inst. Tech., 1958; MA in Actuarial Sci., Ga. State Coll., 1962. Asst. v.p. Ind. Life and Accident Ins. Co., Jacksonville, Fla., 1963-69, asst. v.p., dir. methods and planning dept., 1969-70, v.p., home office coordinator, 1970-79, pres., chief adminstrv. officer, 1979-84, chmn. bd., chief exec. officer, 1984-96; bd. dir., mem. exec. and audit com. Fla. Bank Inc. Trustee, mem. exec. com. Edward Waters Coll., Jacksonville, 1983-96, chmn., bd. visitors, 1993-96, 2001-02. Trustee Gator Bowl Assn., Jacksonville, 1981—, pres., 1981; pres. Jacksonville C. of C., 1984; trustee Cmty. TV, Inc., Jacksonville, 1980-93, chmn., 1991-92, mem. exec. com., 2001-02; trustee Univ. Hosp., Jacksonville, Inc., 1985-86, Jacksonville Cmty. Found., 1999--; bd. dirs. YMCA Fla.'s First Coast, 1985—, sec., 1986, vice chmn., 1987, chmn., 1988 (Svc. to Youth award 1991); chmn. 1991 Nat. Vol. Week, Vol. Jacksonville, Inc.; pres. bd. Cypress Village, Inc., 1998-99; deacon, elder, clk., trustee Presbyn. Ch. Recipient Disting Svc. award Jacksonville Jaycees, 1972, Jack Donnell award Outstanding Businessman of the Year, 1983, Dick Hutchinson award Sertoma Club South Jacksonville, 1972, Svc. to Mankind award, 1972, Boss of Yr. award Profl. Secs. Internat., 1972-73, Victory Crusade award Fla. Cancer Soc., 1969, Ins. Industry Community Svc. award Jacksonville Assn. Life Underwriters, 1986, C.G. Snead Meml. award Jacksonville Assn. of Life Underwriters, 1991, Top Mgmt. award Sales and Mktg. Execs. of Jacksonville, 1990, Clanzel T. Brown award Jacksonville Urban League, 1991, Svc. to Youth award YMCA of Fla.'s First Coast, 1991, Humanitarian award NCCJ, 1994. Mem. Life Insurers Conf. (exec. com. 1981-91, chmn. membership com. 1981-86, sec. 1984-85, vice chmn. 1985-86, chmn. 1986-87), Am. Coun. Life Ins. (Fla. state v.p. 1981-96, bd. dirs. 1987-88, bd. dirs. Polit. Action Com. 1988-94), Southeastern Actuaries Club, Rotary Club Jacksonville (pres. Mandarin club 1977-78, Paul Harris fellow, dist. gov. 697 1985-86), Masons (33 deg.), York Rite, Scottish Rite Bodies, Shriners (potentate Morocco Temple 1973, emeritus rep.). Republican. Home: 1915 Epping Forest Way S Jacksonville FL 32217

LYON, WILLIAM CARL, sports columnist; b. Carmi, Ill., Feb. 10, 1938; s. Clyde William and Harriet Kathryn (Murphy) L.; m. Ethel Gay Slade, Nov. 6, 1964; children— James Charles, John William. Student, Western Mil. Acad., Alton, Ill., 1956; BS in Liberal Arts, U. Ill., Champaign, 1961. Feature writer, sports writer, police reporter Champaign-Urbana News-Gazette, 1956-66; sports writer, gen. columnist Evansville (Ind.) Courier & Press, 1966-69; mng. editor East St. Louis (Ill.) Metro-East Jour., 1969-71, Champaign-Urbana News-Gazette, 1971-72; bus. editor Phila. Inquirer, 1972-73, sports writer, syndicated columnist, 1973—. Author: It's All in the Game, 1982, We Owed You One, 1983, When the Clock Runs Out, 1999, 110%, 2001; contbr. numerous articles to mags. in U.S. and Can. With inf. U.S. Army, 1961. Named Sportswriter of the Yr., State of Pa., 1977, 79-85; recipient 76 state and nat. awards for writing, Best Newspaper Writing award Am. Soc. Newspaper Editors, 1980, Nat. Headliner award, 1988; 6-time nominee for Pulitzer Prize for disting. commentary; inducted into Pa. Sports Hall of Fame, 1989. Methodist. Home: 89 Cherry Hill Ln Broomall PA 19008-1508 Office: Phila Inquirer 400 N Broad St Philadelphia PA 19130-4099 E-mail: blyon@phillynews.com.

LYON, WILLIAM JAMES, sociology educator; b. El Paso, Tex., Feb. 22, 1957; s. James William and Ana (Mendez) L.; m. Brandi A. Ferrari; children: Kim, Aaron. BA, U. Tex., El Paso, 1982, MA, 1984. Therapist Cath. Soc. Svc., Phoenix, 1989-99; tchr. sociology, social work, adminstrn. of justice Paradise Valley C.C., 1992—. Mem. adj. faculty Lewis-Clark State Coll., Lewiston, Idaho, 1989. Nat. Hispanic Fund scholar Wash. State, 1985-86, 87-88. Office: Paradise Valley CC 32nd St and Union Hills Phoenix AZ 85032

LYONS, BERYL BARTON ANFINDSEN, sales professional; b. Jersey City, Dec. 12, 1925; d. Edward I. and Beatrice (Means) Anfindsen; m. Robert Lyons, Dec. 18, 1954; children: Susan E.L. Paglia, Robert Jr., Christopher B. Student, Traphagen Sch. Fashion Illustration, summer 1943-44, St. Elizabeth Coll., N.J., 1945-46; BA, Coll. N.Y.U., 1949. With Lord & Taylor, N.Y.C., 1949-52; jr. exec. Hahne & Co., Newark, 1952; hostess Statler Hotel, L.A., 1952; model Powers Modeling Agency, N.Y.C., 1952; mdse. demonstration REH, Wayne, N.J., 1978-94, Prestige Promotion, Wayne, 1978-94, McKenzie Assoc., Cape Cod, Mass., 1994-97; with promotional advt. dept. Checkers Product Servicing, Hopkinton, 1997-2001, Promotional Advt., Saco, Maine, 1997—2002, Fraser & Wagner, Scituate, Mass., 1997—2002, Suray Promotions, 2000—02. With Avon, 1971-2001, team leader, asst. mgr., 1971-78. Author numerous poems. Juror Newark, 1991; election worker Livingston, N.J., 1991, 92, 93. Scholar Phoenix Art Sch., 1944. Mem. Lunenburg Women's Club. Republican. Presbyterian. Avocations: art illustration, poetry, aerobic and aqua exercies, reading, grandchildren. Home: 500 Pennsylvania Ave Apt 208 Leominster MA 01453-7413

LYONS, CHAMP, JR. state supreme court justice; b. Boston, Dec. 6, 1940; m. Emily Lee Oswalt, 1967; children— Emily Olive, Champ III. AB, Harvard U., 1962; LL.B., U. Ala., 1965. Bar: Ala. 1965, U.S. Supreme Ct. 1973. Law clk. U.S. Dist. Ct., Mobile, Ala., 1965-67; assoc. Capell, Howard, Knabe & Cobbs, Montgomery, 1967-70, ptnr., 1970-76, Helmsing, Lyons, Sims & Leach, Mobile, 1976-98; legal advisor Hon. Fob James, Jr. Gov. State Ala., 1998; assoc. justice Supreme Ct. of Ala., Montgomery, 1998—. Mem. adv. commn. on civil procedure Ala. Supreme Ct., 1971-98, chmn., 1985-98. Author: Alabama Practice, 1973, 3d edit., 1996; contbr. articles to law jours. Mem. ABA, Ala. Bar Assn., Mobile Bar Assn. (pres. 1991), Am. Law Inst., Ala. Law Inst., Farrah Law Soc., Harvard U. Alumni Assn. (S.E. regional dir. 1988-91, v.p.-at-large 1992-94, 1st v.p. 1994-95, pres. 1995-96). Home: PO Box 1033 Point Clear AL 36564-1033 Office: Supreme Ct of Ala 300 Dexter Ave Montgomery AL 36104-3741*

LYONS, CHARLES M. academic administrator; Pres. Univ. Maine; vice chancellor, univ. coll. Univ. Maine Sys. Office: U Maine Robinson Hall 46 U Dr Augusta ME 04330-9410*

LYONS, CHERIE ANN, researcher, writer; b. Denver, Dec. 15, 1948; d. Clair Leroy and Mary Margaret (Benner) Case; m. David Greer Lyons, Aug. 22, 1970; children: Michael Greer, Andrea Christine. BS, U. Colo., 1971, MA, 1975, PhD, 1992. Profl. tchr. cert., adminstr., cert. Colo. Dept. Edn. Tchr. English Cherry Creek Schs., 1971—76; tchr. English, health edn. Jefferson County Schs., Lakewood, Colo., 1971—76, curriculum writer, 1975—78, project dir., career edn., 1976—81, staff devel. specialist, 1981—87, jr. h.s. prin., 1987—88, coord. prevention program, 1989—90; exec. dir., dir. grants devel. Jefferson Found., 1990—; cons. Region VII Tng. Ctr., U.S. Dept. Edn., Ctr. Substance Abuse Prevention; dir. Sch. Team Approach to Substance Abuse Prevention Jefferson County; coord. Jefferson County Prevention Task Force; exec. dir. rsch. and resource devel. Jefferson County Schs., 1995—96; exec. dir. planning, rsch. and resource devel. Jefferson County Sch. Dist., 1996—2001; prof. ednl. adminstrn. U. Colo., Denver, 2001—; rsch. assoc. RMC Rsch. Corp., 2002—. Author: The Writing Process: A Program of Composition and Applied Grammar, Book 12, 1982. Mem.: Nat. Soc. for Study of Edn., Assn. Supervision and Curriculum Devel., Am. Soc. for Quality, Jefferson County Adminstrs. Assn., Phi Delta Kappa. Home: 7584 Taft Ct Arvada CO 80005-3294 Office: RMC Rsch Corp 1512 Larimer St Ste 540 Denver CO 80202 E-mail: lyons@rmcdenver.com.

LYONS, DAVID BARRY, philosophy and law educator; b. N.Y.C., Feb. 6, 1935; s. Joseph and Betty (Janower) L.; m. Sandra Yetta Nemiroff, Dec. 18, 1955; children— Matthew, Emily, Jeremy. Student, Cooper Union, 1952-54, 56-57; BA, Bklyn. Coll., 1960; MA (Gen. Electric Found. fellow), PhD (Woodrow Wilson dissertation fellow), Harvard U., 1963; postgrad., Oxford (Eng.) U., 1963-64. Asst. prof. Philosophy Cornell U., Ithaca, N.Y., 1964-67, assoc. prof., 1967-71, prof., 1971-90, Susan Linn Sage prof. Philosophy, 1990-95; chmn. dept. Philosophy, 1978-84; prof. Law, 1979-95, Boston U., 1995—, prof. philosophy, 1998—. Author: Forms and Limits of Utilitarianism, 1965, In the Interest of the Governed, 1973, Ethics and the Rule of Law, 1984, Moral Aspects of Legal Theory, 1993, Rights, Welfare, and Mill's Moral Theory, 1994; editor: Philos Rev., 1968-70, 73-75. Recipient Clark award Cornell U., 1976; Woodrow Wilson hon. fellow, 1960-61, Knox travelling fellow, 1963-64; Guggenheim fellow, 1970-71, Soc. for Humanities fellow, 1972-73, Nat. Endowment for Humanities fellow, 1977-78, 84-85, 93-94. Mem. Am. Philos. Assn., Am. Soc. Polit. and Legal Philosophy, Soc. Philosophy and Pub. Affairs. Office: Boston U Law Sch 765 Commonwealth Ave Boston MA 02215-1401 E-mail: dbl@bu.edu.

LYONS, DENNIS GERALD, lawyer; b. Passaic, N.J., Nov. 20, 1931; s. Denis A.G. and Agnes C. (Dyt) L.; m. Anna Maria Nuñez, 1983; 1 child, Alexandra; children by previous marriage: Andrew, Sarah, Tessa. AB, Holy Cross Coll., 1952; JD, Harvard U., 1955. Bar: D.C. 1955, N.Y. 1956, U.S. Supreme Ct 1960. Law clk. U.S. Supreme Ct., Washington, 1958-60; assoc. firm Arnold & Porter, 1960-62, ptnr., 1963—; v.p., gen. counsel, dir. Gulf United Corp., Jacksonville, Fla., 1968-80; asst. sec. Braniff Airways, Dallas, 1966-77; trustee GMR Properties, Boston, 1971-81; dir. Gulf Broadcast Co., Dallas, 1983-86; vis. prof. law U. Va., Charlottesville, 1982-83. Pres. Harvard Law Rev., 1954-55 Served with USAF, 1955-58. Mem. ABA, Am. Law Inst. Office: Arnold & Porter 555 12th St NW Washington DC 20004-1206 E-mail: lyonsden@erols.com., dennis_lyons@aporter.com.

LYONS, DOROTHY SCHILL, retired accountant; b. Toledo, July 21, 1928; d. Edwin G. and Mae E. (Fraser) Schill; m. Roger G. Lyons, Aug. 16, 1952; children: Roger E., Barbara J., Bruce G. BS, Ohio State U., 1950. Bookkeeper McKay Industries, Jackson, Mich., 1973-78; sr. acct. Temec Trading Co., Farmington Hills, 1978-92; ret. Active Foote Hosp. Aux.; past pres. Jackson Dist. Dental Aux.; past treas. Mich. State Dental Aux., Jackson Jr. Welfare League; past chmn. women's div. United Found.; solicitor Am. Cancer Soc., March of Dimes; mem. women div. Jackson Symphony Orch. Mem. Nat. Assn. Accts., Jackson Country Club. Home: 1024 Eagle Point Rd Clarklake MI 49234-9012 Office: Tremec Trading Co 23382 Commerce Dr Farmington MI 48335-2726

LYONS, FRANCIS XAVIER, lawyer; b. Evanston, Ill., Apr. 1, 1962; s. Thomas George and Ruth Frances (Tobin) L.; m. Mary Patricia Rotunno, Apr. 25, 1992; children: Caroline Marie, Elizabeth Lahey. BA in History, U. Minn., 1984; JD, Loyola U., Chgo., 1988. Bar: Ill. 1988, U.S. Dist. Ct. (no. dist.) Ill. 1989, U.S. Dist. Ct. (ctrl. dist.) Ill. 1990, U.S. Ct. Appeals (D.C. cir.) 1994. Asst. atty. gen., gen. law divsn. Ill. Atty. Gen.'s Office, Chgo., 1988-93, asst. atty. gen. environ. control divsn., 1993-94; trial atty. environ. and natural resources divsn. Environ. Enforcement Sect., U.S. Dept. Justice, Washington, 1994-99; regional adminstr. U.S. EPA Region 5, Chgo., 1999-2001; ptnr. Gardner, Carton & Douglas, 2001—. Mem. 45th Ward Regular Dem. Orgn., Chgo., 1988-94; mem. Young Dems. Cook County, Chgo., 1990-91; mem. steering com. Dem. Leadership for 21st Century, Chgo., 1992-93; bd. dirs. Lake Michigan Fedn. Capt. USAR. ret. Recipient Special Achievement and Commendation award U.S. Dept. Justice; named one of 40 Ill. Attys. Under 40 to Watch, Law Bull. Pub. Co., 2000. Mem. ABA, Ill. Bar Assn. Chgo. Bar Assn., Cath. Lawyers Guild Chgo., Delta Tau Delta, Phi Alpha Delta. Office: Gardner Carton & Douglas 321 N Clark St Chicago IL 60610-4795 E-mail: flyons@gcd.com.

LYONS, GENE MARTIN, political scientist, educator; b. Revere, Mass., Feb. 29, 1924; s. Abraham M. and Mary (Karger) L.; m. Micheline Pohl, Sept. 5, 1951; children— Catherine Anne, Daniel Eugene, Mark Lucien. BA, Tufts Coll., 1947; license en Scis. Politiques, Grad. Inst. Internat. Studies, Geneva, Switzerland, 1949; PhD, Columbia, 1958. Mgmt. officer Internat. Refugee Orgn., Geneva, 1948-52; budget and adminstrv. officer UN Korean Reconstrn. Agy., 1952-56; mem. faculty Dartmouth Coll., 1957-94, prof. govt., 1965-94, dir. Pub. Affairs Center, 1961-66, 73-75, asso. dean faculty social scis., 1974-78; rsch. fellow Dickey Ctr. Dartmouth Coll., Hanover, N.H., 1994—. Vis. lectr. Sch. Mgmt. MIT, 1961-70; exec. sec. adv. com. govt. program behavioral scis. Nat. Acad. Scis., 1966-68; dir. dept. social scis. UNESCO, 1970-72; mem. U.S. Nat. Commn. for UNESCO, 1975-80, vice chmn., 1977-78; adv. U.S. del. UNESCO 19th Gen. Conf., 1976, 20th Gen. Conf., 1978; U.S. rep. to UNESCO European Conf., 1977; prof. associé U. Paris I, 1986; exec. dir. acad. council on the UN system, 1987-92. Author: Military Policy and Economic Aid: The Korean Case, 1961; co-author: (with J.W. Masland) Education and Military Leadership, 1959, (with L. Morton) Schools for Strategy, 1965, The Uneasy Partnrship, 1969; Editor: Social Research and Public Policies, 1975; editor, contbr. America: Purpose and Power, 1965, Social Science and the Federal Government, 1971; co-editor, contbr. Beyond Westphalia?, 1995, The United Nations System: The Policies of Member States, 1995. Served with AUS, 1943-46. Mem. Acad. Coun. on UN System, Internat. Studies Assn., Coun. on Fgn. Rels. Home: Main St Norwich VT 05055 Office: Dartmouth Coll Dickey Ctr Hanover NH 03755 E-mail: Gene.Lyons@Dartmouth.edu.

LYONS, HARVEY ISAAC, mechanical engineering educator; b. N.Y.C., Sept. 26, 1931; s. Joseph and Betty L.; m. Rebecca Anne Szeman, June 10, 1978; children: Neal Joshua, Leslie Eve. Cert. in indsl. design, Pratt Inst., 1952; BSME, The Cooper Union, 1962, MS in Mech. Engring., 1971; PhD in Mech. Engring., Ohio State U., 1978. Registered profl. engr., N.Y., Ohio, Wis., Wash., Mont., N.H., Mich. From design engr. to sr. mech. engr. various orgns., N.Y.C., 1954-72; assoc. prof. mech. engring. Mont. State U., Bozeman, 1978-79, U. Wis.-Parkside, Kenosha, 1979-81, U. N.H., Durham, 1981-84, Seattle U., 1984-85; chmn. dept. mech. engring. Alfred (N.Y.) U., 1985-88; assoc. prof. mech. engring. Union Coll., Schenectady, 1988-92, Ind. Inst. Tech., Ft. Wayne, 1992-95; cons. engr. in pvt. practice Ind., 1995-98; assoc. prof. mech. engring. Ea. Mich. U., 1998—. Contbr. articles to profl. jours. Sgt. 2d inf. divsn. U.S. Army, 1952-54, Korea. Mem. ASME, NSPE, Nat. Assn. Indsl. Tech., Am. Soc. Engring. Edn., Soc. Mfg. Engrs. Achievements include development of methods to investigate tribological phenomenon of Fretting-Wear in-situ, towards development of failure prediction criteria, development of mechanical engineering departments in industry and academe. Avocations: skiing, flying, karate, tennis, backpacking. Home: 1330 W Stadium Blvd Apt 5 Ann Arbor MI 48103-5363 E-mail: harvey.lyons@emich.edu.

LYONS, JAMES ALOYSIUS, JR. naval officer; b. Jersey City, Sept. 28, 1927; s. James Aloysius and Marion F. (Bach) L.; m. Renee Wilcox Chevalier, Apr. 10, 1954; children— Michele, Yvonne, James Aloysius, III BS, U.S. Naval Acad., 1952; BS command and staff course, Naval War Coll., 1963-64; MS, Nat. War Coll., 1970-71. Commd. ensign U.S. Navy, 1952, advanced through grades to Four Star Admiral, 1985; served at sea aboard sixth fleet flagship U.S.S. Salem, 1952—59; exec. officer U.S.S. Miller, 1959-61; anti-submarine warfare and weapons officer cruiser-destroyer Flottilla Four, 1961—63; dir. Navy plans, strategic plans div. Office of Chief of Naval Ops. Washington, 1964-66; comdr. USS Charles S. Sperry, 1966-68; exec. asst. and sr. aide to dep. chief naval ops. for plans and policy, 1971-74; comdr. guided missile cruiser USS Richmond K. Turner, 1974-75; chief of staff Carrier Group Four, 1975-76; sr. asst. on Joint Chiefs of Staff Matters, div. strategy, plans and policy, Office Chief Naval Ops. Washington, 1976-78; dep. dir. strategic plans and policy div., 1978; asst. dep. for polit. mil. affairs Directorate Orgn. Joint Chiefs of Staff U.S. Navy, Washington, 1978-79, dir. polit.-mil. affairs Directorate Orgn. Joint Chiefs of Staff, 1979-80, comdr. Task Force 72, also comdr. Naval Surface Group Western Pacific, 1980-81, comdr. U.S. 2d Fleet, Joint Task Force 120 and NATO Command Striking Fleet Atlantic, 1981-83, dep. chief naval ops. Office of Chief Naval Ops., 1983—85, comdr.-in-chief US Pacific Fleet, 1985—87. Sr. U.S. rep. arms limitation talks with USSR, Helsinki, 1978, Mexico City, 1978; sr. U.S. rep. Incidents at Sea Talks with USSR, Moscow, 1984; sr. Navy mem. U.S. Del., UN Mil. Staff Com., 1983—85. Decorated Legion of Merit, Meritorious Service medal with gold star, Navy Commendation medal with gold star, Navy Achievement medal, DSM with two gold stars, Def. Superior Svc. medal, DSM govs. of Korea, Phillipines, Thailand, France. Mem. U.S. Naval Acad. Alumni Assn., U.S. Naval Acad. Athletic Assn. Roman Catholic. Home: 9481 Piney Mountain Rd Warrenton VA 20186-7441 Office: Lion Associates 8653 Richmond Hwy Alexandria VA 22309 Home Fax: 540-349-8757; Office Fax: 703-619-1409.

LYONS, JAMES EDWARD, publishing executive; b. N.Y.C., Feb. 7, 1952; s. James Vincent and Audrey Lucille (Garbers) L.; m. Blythe Mitchell Jones, June 6, 1981; children: James Edward Jr., Michael Davidson. BA cum laude, Bowdoin Coll., 1974. Advanceman and legis. asst. to Congressman William S. Cohen of Maine, Washington, 1972-75; pub. U. Press Am., Lanham, Md., 1975—, also bd. dirs.; pres. Madison Books, Inc., 1986—, U. Pub. Assocs. Inc., 1986—, Rowman and Littlefield Pubs., Inc., 1988—, Barnes and Noble Books, 1988—, Littlefield, Adams Quality Paperbacks, 1988—, Nat. Book Network, Inc., 1986—, Scarecrow Press, Inc., 1995—, Vestal Press, 1997—, New Amsterdam Books, 1998—, Ivan R. Dee, 1998—, Lexington Books, Inc., 1998—. Nat. adv. com. to sec. HEW, 1974, The Derrydale Press, Inc., 1999—, Ardsley House, Pubs., 1999—, AltaMira Press, 1999—, Roberts Rinehart, 2000—, General Hall, 2000—, Madison House, 2000—, Sheed & Ward, 2002; panelist U.S. Dept. Edn., 1986-87; mem. USIA book and libr. adv. com., 1981-93. Mem. Statue of Liberty-Ellis Island Centennial Commn., 1986-89; Presdl. appointee Nat. Commn. on Librs. and Info. Sci., 1991-93; trustee Georgetown U. Libr., 1981-92. Mem. Assn. Am. Pubs. (exec. coun. profl. and scholarly pub. div. 1990-93, coll. div. faculty rels. com.), Soc. Scholarly Pubs. (chmn. publs. com. 1979-80), Coun. on Fgn. Rels., Young Pres. Orgn. (bd. dirs. 1994-99), Rolling Rock Club (Ligonier, Pa.), Chevy Chase Club, N.Y. Anglers Club, Psi Upsilon. Presbyterian. Office: Rowman & Littlefield Pub Group 4720 Boston Way Lanham Seabrook MD 20706-4310

LYONS, JERRY LEE, mechanical engineer; b. St. Louis, Apr. 2, 1939; s. Ferd H. and Edna T. Lyons Diploma in Mech. Engring., Okla. Inst. Tech., 1964; MSME, S.W. U., 1983; PhD in Engring. Mgmt., Southwest U., 1984. Registered profl. engr., Calif.; diplomate Am. Bd. Forensic Engring. and Tech., Am. Coll. Forensic Examiners in forensic engring. and tech. (life). Project engr. Harris Mfg. Co., St. Louis, 1965-70, Essex Cryogenics Industries, St. Louis, 1963-65, 70-73; mgr. engring. rsch. Chemetron Corp., 1973-77; cons. fluid controls Wis. U., 1977—; pres., chief exec. Yankee Ingenuity, Inc., St. Louis, 1974—; v.p., gen. mgr. engring. R & D Essex Fluid Controls divsn. Essex Industries, Inc., 1977-90; pres. Lyons Pub. Co., 1983—; pres., CEO Innovative Controls subs. Yankee Ingenuity, Inc., Ft. Wayne, Ind., 1991—. Chmn. exec. bd. continuing engring. edn. in St. Louis for U. Mo., Columbia, 1980-81; bd. dirs. Intertech., Inc., Houston; cons. fluid power dept. Bradley U., Peoria, 1977-84. Author: Home Study Series Course on Actuators and Accessories, 1977, The Valve Designers Handbook, 1983, The Lyons' Encyclopedia of Valves, 1975, 93, The Designers Handbook of Pressure Sensing Devices, 1980, Special Process Applications, 1980; co-author: Handbook of Product Liability, 1991; contbr. articles to profl. jours.; patentee in field. With USAF, 1957-62. Recipient Winston Churchill medal, 1988, Dwight D. Eisenhower Achievement award of honor, 1990; named Businessman of Week (KEZK radio), Eminent Churchill fellow Winston Churchill Wisdom Soc. Fellow ASME; mem. N.Y. Acad. Scis., Soc. Mfg. Engrs. (life mem., cert. product design, chmn. Mo. registration com. 1975-90, chmn. St. Louis chpt. 1979-80, internat. dir. 1982-84, 85-87, engr. of yr. 1984, internat. award of merit 1985), Nat. Soc. Profl. Engrs., Mo. Soc. Profl. Engrs., St. Louis Soc. Mfg. Engrs. (chmn. profl. devel., registration and cert. com. 1975-79), Instrument Soc. Am. (sr. life mem., control valve stability com. 1978-84), Computer and Automated Sys. Assn. (1st chmn. St. Louis chpt. 1980-81), St. Louis Engrs. Club (award of merit 1977, Wisdom award of honor 1987, Wisdom Hall of Fame 1987), Am. Security Coun. (committeeman 1976—), Nat. Fluid Power Assn. (com. on pressure ratings 1975-77), Am. Legion. Lutheran. Achievements include patentee in field. Home: 1719 Wisteria Pl Fort Wayne IN 46818-8812 Office: Innovative Controls Inc 2705 Camino Court Fort Wayne IN 46808 Fax: 260-471-3153. E-mail: a1yankee@aol.com.

LYONS, JOHN DAVID, French, Italian and comparative literature educator; b. Springfield, Mass., Oct. 14, 1946; s. John Joseph and Loretta Francis (Feighery) L.; m. Patricia Stuart, July 31, 1971; 1 dau., Jennifer Catherine. AB, Brown U., 1967; MA, Yale U., 1968, PhD, 1972. Asst. prof. French, Italian and comparative lit. Dartmouth Coll., Hanover, NH, 1972-78, assoc. prof., 1978-82, prof. N.H., 1982-87, chmn. comparative lit. program, 1981-84, chmn., prof. dept. French and Italian, 1987; dir. Am. Univ. Ctr. for Film and Critical Studies, Paris, 1984-85; prof. French U. Va., Charlottesville, 1987-92, Commonwealth prof. French, 1993—, chmn. dept., 1989-92, 98-99. Author: A Theatre of Disguise, 1978, The Listening Voice, 1982, Exemplum, 1989, The Tragedy of Origins, 1996, Kingdom of Disorder, 1999; co-editor: Mimesis: Mirror to Method, 1982, Dialectic of Discovery, 1983, Critical Tales, 1993; editor: Art, Architecture, Text: The Late Renaissance, 1985; assoc. editor Continuum, 1987-93; editor Academe, 1994-97; editl. adv. bd. Philosophy and Literature, 1992-2002, French Forum. Recipient Robert Fish award for teaching Dartmouth Coll., 1978, Outstanding Tchr. award U. Va., 1996; Woodrow Wilson fellow, 1967, ACLS study fellow, 1978, NEH fellow, 1985-89, 92-93, ACLS contemplative practice fellow, 2002, J.S. Guggenheim fellow, 2002-, Ctr. for Advanced Studies U. Va. fellow, 1987-89. Office: U Va Dept French Lang & Lit Charlottesville VA 22903

LYONS, JOHN W(INSHIP), retired government official, chemist, consultant; b. Reading, Mass., Nov. 5, 1930; AB in Chemistry, Harvard U., 1952; AM in Phys. Chemistry, Washington U., St. Louis, 1963, PhD in Phys. Chemistry, 1964. With Monsanto Co., 1955-73, group leader, sect. mgr. research dept., inorganic chems. div., 1962-69, mgr. comml. devel., head fire safety center, 1969-73; mem. ad hoc panel on fire research Nat. Bur. Standards, Washington, 1971-73; dir. Center for Fire Research, 1973-77, Inst. Applied Tech., 1977-78, Nat. Engring. Lab., 1978-89; acting dep. dir. Nat. Bur. Standards, 1983; dir. Nat. Inst. Standards and Tech., Gaithersburg, Md., 1990-93, Army Rsch. Lab., Adelphi, 1993-98; ret., 1998. Chmn. Products Rsch. Com. (trust which adminstrs. fire rsch. fund), 1974-79; vis. lectr. various univs.; co-chmn. U.S.-Japan Natural Resources Panel on Fire Rsch., 1975-78; mem. adv. com. on engring NSF, 1981-90; mem. bd. visitors Coll. Engring., U. Md., 1980-90, 99—, mem. bd. visitors Biotech. Inst., 1999—; mem. adv. com. Naval Rsch. Lab., 1985; mem. com. on fed. labs. Office Sci. and Tech. Policy. Author: Viscosity and Flow Measurement, 1963, The Chemistry and Uses of Fire Retardants, 1970; Fire, 1985; contbr. numerous articles to profl. publs. Chmn. blue ribbon com. on rsch. and pub. svc. U. Md., 1993. Recipient gold medal Dept. Commerce, 1977, President's Mgmt. Improvement award White House, 1977, President's Disting. Exec. Rank award, 1981, E.U. Condon award, 1986; Disting. Svc. award U. Md. Coll. Engring., 1990, Centennial medal, 1994; 1st ann. Outstanding Achievement award Fire Retardant Chem. Assn., 1994. Fellow AAAS, Washington Acad. Sci.; mem. Am. Chem. Soc. (chmn. St. Louis sect. 1971-72), Nat. Fire Protection Assn. (bd. dirs. 1978-84), ASTM (bd. dirs. 1985-87), Nat. Acad. Engring., Sigma Xi. E-mail: jlyons@frederickmd.com.

LYONS, MOIRA K. state legislator; b. Trenton, N.J. BA, Georgian Ct. Coll.; student, Miami U. Mem. Conn. Ho. of Reps., mem. appropriations com., chmn. transp. com., 1985—92, appt. dep. ho. spkr., 1993-95, majority leader, 1995—99, deputy spkr., 1993—94, spkr., 1999—. Bd. dirs. Conn. Women's Hall of Fame, Hartford, Workplace, Inc., Bridgeport, CTE (anti-poverty agency), the Women's Business Devel. Ctr., Jackie Robinson Hall of Fame, SoundWaters Community Ctr. for Environ. Edn.; Curriculum Adv., Leadership Fairfield Co. program, SACIA. Good Housekeeping magazine award for Women in Govt., 2000, Conn. Assoc. of Public Schools Superintendents Disting. Svc. award, 2000, Conn. Coalition for Land Preservation, 2000, Conn. Coalition of Police and Corrections Officers of Conn. Legis. Leadership award, 2000, Junior League of Stamford-Norwalk Cmty. Leadership award,

Greenways Coun. Recognition award, Nat. Assoc. of Women Business Owners, Hartford Coll. for Women's Pioneer Woman of the Year award, 1999, Conn. Fedn. of Business and Professional Women's Clubs President's Courage award, 1999, Henry Toll Fellowship, Bice Clemow award, Conn. Coun. on Freedom of Information, March 2002, Conn. Nurturing award, April, 2002. Mem., Gov.'s Coun. on Econ. Competitiveness and Tech., Drugs Don't Work Sch., Campus, Cmty. and Youth Com. Democrat. Office: Legislative Office Bldg Rm 4105 Capital Ave Hartford CT 06106-1591 E-mail: Moira.Lyons@po.state.ct.us.*

LYONS, NANCE, lawyer; b. Boston, Mar. 8, 1943; d. Dr. Timothy F.P. and Ann (Doherty) Lyons. BA, Boston Coll., Newton, Mass., 1964; JD cum laude, Suffolk U., 1977. Bar: Mass. 1977, U.S. Dist Ct. Mass. 1977. Legis. and adminstrv. asst. to Sen. Edward M. Kennedy, Washington, 1967-70; sole practice Boston, 1977-86; atty. Comras & Jackman, 1986-90; sole practice, 1990—. With Bar Overseers Disciplinary Hearing Panel, 1987-93; active Joint Bar Com. on Jud. Appts., 1991-93; lectr. in field. Contbr. articles to profl. jours. Spl. corp. counsel City of Boston, 1977-82; asst. commr. Addiction Svcs. Agy., N.Y.C., 1972-73. Mem. Am. Trial Lawyers Assn., Mass. Acad. Trial Attys. (gov. 1987—, legislation com. 1990-96, mem. exec. com. 1994-2000, chair employment rights com. 1994-2000, women's com. 1994—), Mass. Assn. Women Lawyers (dir. 1983-89, 91-94, chair legis. com. 1984-89), Mass. Bar Assn. (legis. subcom. civil litigation sect. 1985-87, alt. dispute resolution com. 1988), Boston Bar Assn. (vol. lawyers project 1977—). Democrat. Office: 5th Fl 132 Boylston St Boston MA 02116 *Notable cases include: Drinkwater vs. School Committee of Boston, 550 NE 2nd 385 Mass., 1990, which resulted in a unanimous decision of the highest court that a valid affirmative action plan is not an affirmative defense to a charge of reverse discrimination.*

LYONS, NATALIE BELLER, family counselor; b. Havana, Cuba, Apr. 3, 1926; d. Herman Lawrence and Jennie (Engler) B.; widowed, Apr. 18, 1986; children: Anne, Sara. Degree in Surveying and Land Appraising, BS, Inst. Vedado, Havana, 1943; BA, U. Mich., 1946; MEd, U. Miami, Fla., 1967. Family counselor, mem. staff furniture design and mfg. co. George B. Bent Co., Gardner, Mass., 1953-58; tchr. H.S., Winchendon, Hollywood, Fla., 1962, parochial sch., Ft. Lauderdale, 1963-64; family counselor Miami, 1967—; project dir. Cen. Am. fisheries program Peace Corps, 1972-74. Counselor Svc. Corp. of Ret. Execs., Miami, 1993, bd. dirs., 1994—; bd. dirs. mem. Com. for Accuracy in Mid-East Reporting in Am., 1990—. Pres. Miami region Hadassah, 1989—91; mem. cmty. rels. coun. Greater Miami Jewish Fedn., 1985—; bd. dirs. Miami Civic Music Assn., 1985—; nat. women's divsn. Am. Soc. for Technion, 1991—, pres., 2000—; co-chmn. Pro-Israel Rally, Tri County, 1991; co-chmn Joint Action Com., Miami, 1989—91; founder, dir. Cmty. Inst. Jewish Studies, Hollywood, 1962—64; tng. dir. Los Amigos de las Ams., 1975—. Recipient Leadership award Hadassah, 1987, honoree Am. Soc. for Technion Scholarship Fund, 1991; named Woman of Yr., Hadassah, 1991. Mem.: Am. Inst. Tech. (nat. pres. women's divsn.), Israel Inst. Tech. (pres. so. region 1996—2000), Am. Soc. for Technion (nat. pres. 2001—), Svc. Corps. of Ret. Execs. (bd. dirs. 1997—). Democrat. Avocations: travel, reading, antiques, family, performing arts. E-mail: Lyons.den@mindspring.com.

LYONS, NICK, publishing executive; b. N.Y.C., June 5, 1932; s. Nathan and Rose (Bernstein) Ress; m. Mari Blumenau, Sept. 1, 1957; children: Paul, Charles, Jennifer, Anthony. BS in Econs., U. Pa., 1953; MA in Am. Lit., U. Mich., 1961, PhD in Am. Lit., 1963. Prof. English Hunter Coll., N.Y.C., 1961-88; exec. editor Crown Pubs., Inc., 1963-78; pres. Nick Lyons Books, 1979-84, Lyons & Burford, Pubs., N.Y.C., 1984-98; chmn. bd. dirs. The Lyons Press, 1999—2001. Author: The Sony Vision, 1975, The Seasonable Angler, 1970, Bright Rivers, 1978, Confessions of a Fly Fishing Addict, 1988, Spring Creek, 1991, Full Creel, 2000. With U.S. Army, 1954-55. Avocation: fly fishing. Home: 342 W 84th St New York NY 10024-4202

LYONS, PATRICE ANN, lawyer; b. Albany, N.Y., Feb. 16, 1942; d. James Sarsfield and Mary (O'Brien) L.; m. Robert E. Kahn, Sept. 13, 1980. BA, Pace U., 1963; MA, Syracuse U., 1966; JD, Georgetown U., 1969. Bar: N.Y. 1970, D.C. 1988, U.S. Supreme Ct. 1978. Examiner U.S. Copyright Office Libr. of Congress, Washington, 1969-71, sr. atty., 1976-87; asst. legal officer UN Ednl. Sci. and Cultural Orgn., Paris, 1971-76; ptnr. Haley, Bader & Potts, Washington, 1987-90; pvt. practice, 1991—. Mem. ABA, N.Y. Bar Assn., Computer Law Assn., Copyright Soc. of the USA, Fed. Bar Assn. E-mail: palyons@bellatlantic.net.

LYONS, PATRICK JOSEPH, management educator; b. N.Y.C., Dec. 12, 1943; s. Joseph Raphael and Catherine (Albrecht) L.; m. Georgette Marie Tumasonis, June 27, 1970; children: Michael, Theresa, George. BEE, Manhattan Coll., 1965; MS in Applied Math., Case Western Res. U., 1967; PhD in Applied Math., Adelphi U., 1973. Systems analyst Grumman Aerospace, Bethpage, N.Y., 1967-75, asst. mgr., 1975-76; prof. mgmt. St. John's U., Jamaica, 1976—. Cons. mgmt. sci., 1978—. Contbr. articles to profl. jours. Adult edn. instr. Sacred Heart Ch., Bayside, N.Y., 1983—. Mem. IEEE, Inst. Ops. Rsch. and Mgmt. Sci., N.Y. Acad. Scis. Roman Catholic. Avocations: photography, jogging. Office: St John's U Coll Bus Jamaica NY 11439-0001

LYONS, PAUL VINCENT, lawyer; b. Boston, July 19, 1939; s. Joseph Vincent and Doris Irene (Griffin) L.; m. Elaine Marie Hurley, July 13, 1968; children: Judith Marie, Maureen Patricia, Paula Anne, Joseph Hurley BS cum laude, Boston Coll., 1960; MBA, NYU, 1962; JD, Suffolk U., Boston, 1968. Bar: Mass. 1968, U.S. Cir. Ct. (1st cir.) 1969, U.S. Supreme Ct. 1991. Div. adminstrn. mgr. Pepsi-Cola Co., N.Y.C., 1962-64; mem. bus. faculty Burdett Coll., Boston, 1964-68; atty. NLRB, 1968-73; assoc. Foley, Hoag & Eliot, 1973-77, ptnr., 1978—. Mem. faculty Boston U., 1972-74. Mem. Town Meeting, Milton, Mass., 1986—2002, Pers. Bd., Milton, 1994—. Lt. U.S. Army, 1960—62. Mem. ABA, Mass. Bar Assn., Boston Bar Assn. Office: Foley Hoag & Eliot LLP 1 Post Office Sq Ste 1700 Boston MA 02109-2175 E-mail: plyons@foleyhoag.com.

LYONS, PHILLIP MICHAEL, SR. insurance accounting and real estate executive; b. Gueydan, La., Nov. 22, 1941; s. Joseph Bosman and Elder (Richard) L.; children from previous marriage: Phillip M., Wilton J.; m. Regina Zoe (Malloy) Johnson, Aug. 15, 1991; stepchildren: Jennifer R. Johnson, Tracey L. Johnson. Student, McNeese State Coll., 1959-62, Alvin Jr. Coll., 1964, Coll. of Mainland, 1974; BBA, U. Houston, 1977, postgrad., 1984. CPA; cert. in employee benefit law; assoc. in risk mgmt; FLM I. Adminstrv. trainee Am. Nat. Ins. Co., Galveston, Tex., 1965, asst. mgr., acting mgr. policy issue dept., 1966-67, mgr., 1967-71, mgr. pre-issue dept., sys. analyst, 1971-72, divsn. mgr., policyholder's svc. divsn., 1972-74, dir. ordinary policyholder's svc., 1974-76, dir. combination policy records, 1976-77; supervising acct. materials acctg. comptr.'s dept. Aramco Svcs. Co., Houston, 1977-79, ins. adviser treas.'s dept., 1979-80, adminstr. risk mgmt. and ins. divsn., treas.'s dept., 1980-87, sr. ins. advisor, 1988-98; sr. employee benefits cons. Equiva Svcs., 1998-99, adminstr. employee benefits fin. and contracts, 1999—. Ptnr. Lyons Real Estate, Sulphur, La., 1966—; bd. dirs. Studio B, Inc., Houston. Solicitor United Fund, 1966-69; pres. Alvin Youth Baseball Tex. League, 1982. Fellow Life Mgmt. Inst.; mem. AICPA, TSCPA, Risk and Ins. Mgmt. Soc. (assoc. in risk mgmt.), Jr. C. of C. (bd. dirs. 1972, state bd. dirs. 1972-74, Sparkplug of Yr. 1972-73, Roadrunner of Yr. 1972-73), Masons, Order of Ea. Star, Shriners, KC. Home: 223 W Sherwood Dr Alvin TX 77511-5109 also: 1012 S Stanford St Sulphur LA 70663-4824 Office: 1100 Louisiana St Ste 2200 Houston TX 77002-5220 E-mail: pmlyons@equiva.com., pmlyons@ev1.net.

LYONS, RICHARD KENT, economics educator; b. Palo Alto, Calif., Feb. 10, 1961; s. J. Richard and Ida (Primavera) L. BS in Bus. with highest honors, U. Calif., Berkeley, 1982; PhD, MIT, 1987. Rsch. analyst SRI Internat., Menlo Park, Calif., 1983-84; summer intern Orgn. for Econ. Cooperation & Devel., Paris, 1985, Bd. Govs., Fed. Res. System, Washington, 1986; asst. prof. Columbia U., N.Y.C., 1987-91; assoc. prof., 1991-93; asst. prof. U. Calif., Berkeley, 1993-96, assoc. prof., 1996—2000, prof., 2000—. Rsch. assoc. Nat. Bur. Econ. Rsch., Cambridge, Mass., 1989—; chmn., dir. Matthews Asian Funds, iShares Inc., Barclays Gloval Investors Funds. Assoc. editor Calif. Mfmt. Rev.; contbr. articles to profl. jours. NSF grad. fellow, 1984. Mem. Am. Econ. Assn., Coun. on Fgn. Rels., Phi Beta Kappa, Beta Gamma Sigma, Sigma Alpha Epsilon. Democrat. Avocations: squash, guitar, French. Office: U Calif Haas Sch Bus Berkeley CA 94720-1900

LYONS, ROBERT WILLIAM, medical educator, infectious disease consultant; b. Westmont, N.J., June 23, 1937; s. William John and Anna Agnes (Sullivan) L.; m. Constance Cryer, June 18, 1966 (div. 1974); m. Virginia Palmer Riggs, Aug. 29, 1981. BS, Georgetown U., 1960; MD, Yale U., 1964. Diplomate Am. Bd. Internal Medicine, Am. Bd. Infectious Disease. From asst. prof. to asst. clin. prof. medicine Yale U., New Haven, 1970-79, assoc. clin. prof. medicine, 1979—; from asst. prof. to assoc. prof. medicine U. Conn. Med. Sch., Farmington, 1972-87, prof. medicine, 1988—. Acting chief infectious diseases U. Conn. Med. Sch., Farmington, 1975-81; chief infectious diseases St. Francis Hosp., Hartford, Conn., 1972—, Mt. Sinai Hosp., Hartford, 1990—. Contbr. articles to profl. jours. Pres. Conn. Infectious Disease Soc.; past pres. Hartford Med. Soc.; patron Yale Art Gallery, New Haven, 1991—, China Inst. N.Y., N.Y.C., 1992—. Lt. USNR, 1965-67. Fellow ACP, Infectious Disease Soc. Am., Jonathan Edwards Coll., Yale U.; mem. Internat. AIDS Soc., Asia Soc. (pres. cir. 1993—), Yale Club N.Y.C., Town and County Club, Hartford Club. Avocation: collecting Asian art especially Japanese prints. Office: St Francis Hosp 114 Woodland St Ste 1 Hartford CT 06105-1299

LYONS, TERRENCE ALLAN, merchant banking, investment company executive; b. Grand Prairie, Alta., Can., Aug. 1, 1949; s. Allan Lynnwood and Mildred Helen (Smith) L. B in Applied Sci., U. B.C., 1972; MBA, U. Western Ont., 1974. Registered profl. engr., B.C. Gen. mgr. Southwestern Drug Co., Vancouver, B.C., Can., 1975-76; mgr. planning Versatile Corp., 1976-83, asst. v.p., 1983-86, v.p., dir., 1986-88; pres., mng. ptnr. B.C. Pacific Capital Corp., 1988—; mng. ptnr. Brascan Fin. Corp. Bd. dirs. Internat. Utility Structures, Persona Inc.; pres., chief exec. officer FT Capital Ltd., 1990—; chmn. Northgate Exploration Ltd. Author articles on mfg. tech. Office: Brascan Fin Corp Royal Ctr PO Box 11179 2050 1055 W Georgia St Vancouver BC Canada V6E 3R5 E-mail: tlyons@bcpacific.com.

LYONS, THOMAS PATRICK, economics educator; b. Groton, Conn., Sept. 8, 1953; BA in Asian Studies, Cornell U., 1979, MA in Econs., 1982, PhD in Econs., 1983. Asst. prof. econs. Dartmouth Coll., Hanover, N.H., 1983-87; vis. asst. prof. Cornell U., Ithaca, N.Y., 1986-88, asst. prof., 1988-91; assoc. prof., 1991-2000; dir. East Asia program Cornell U., Ithaca, N.Y., 1991-94, dir. undergrad. studies, econs., 1995—, prof., 2000—. Author: Economic Integration and Planning in Maoist China, 1987, China's War on Poverty, 1992, Economic Geography of Fujian: A Sourcebook, vols. 1 and 2, 1995, 97; contbr. numerous articles to profl. jours. With USN, 1972-76. Rsch. grantee Ford Found., 1987. Mem. Am. Econ. Assn., Assn. for Asian Studies, Assn. Am. Geographers. Office: Cornell U Dept Econs Uris Hall Ithaca NY 14853-7601 E-mail: tpl4@cornell.edu.

LYONS, WILLIAM HARRY, law educator; b. Fitchburg, Mass., Mar. 5, 1947; s. William Earl and Jeanette Underwood (Weed) L.; m. Karen Virginia Knapp, June 27, 1970; children: Virginia Lynne, Kevin Michael. BA, Colby Coll., Waterville, Maine, 1969; JD, Boston Coll., 1973. Bar: Maine 1973, Mass. 1973, Nebr. 1985, U.S. Dist. Ct. Maine 1974, U.S. Dist. Ct. Nebr. 1986, U.S. Tax Ct. 1986. Assoc. Vafiades, Brountas & Kominsky, Bangor, Maine, 1973-80, ptnr., 1980-81; prof. law U. Nebr., Lincoln, 1981—. Vis. prof. Boston Coll. Law Sch., 1997-98, Vt. Law Sch., spring 2001; planning com. Gt. Plains Fed. Tax Inst., Lincoln, 1982—, program chmn., 1992, pres., 1993; adv. com. Gt. Plains Studies, Lincoln, 1983; prof. in residence IRS, 1987-88. Articles editor The Tax Lawyer, 1982-85; contbr. articles to profl. jours. Tax adviser Lincoln Nonprofit Devel. Corp., Lincoln, 1983—. Recipient Disting. Tchg. award Nebr. U. Found., Lincoln, 1984, Student Bar Assn. U. Nebr.-Lincoln Coll. Law, 1984-85, 97, 99. Fellow Am. Coll. Tax Counsel; mem. ABA (group editor sect. of taxation newsletter 1986-88, chmn. individual investments and workouts com. 1995-97, chmn. important devel. subcom. 2001—), Maine State Bar Assn., Nebr. State Bar Assn., Am. Judicature Soc., Delta Theta Phi. Democrat. Home: 5232 S Bristolwood Ln Lincoln NE 68516-1676 Office: U Nebr Coll Law PO Box 830902 Lincoln NE 68583-0902 E-mail: wlyons2@unl.edu.

LYONS, III, PHILIP ADAM, music educator; b. Louisville, Apr. 18, 1976; s. Philip Adam Lyons, Jr. and Esmena Oxales Lyons; m. Rachel Dawn Wilkerson, Dec. 23, 1998; children: Jack Benjamin Lyons. Bachelors in Music in Music Edn., U. o f Fla., Gainesville, Florida, 1999. Band dir./ wrestling coach U. of Fla., Gainesville, Fla., 1999—2002. Se dist. pres. Kappa Kappa Psi, Gainesville, Fla., 1994—98; first chair clarinet / condr. Clay County Cmty. Band, Orange Park, Fla., 1999—99; mem. Coll. Music Educators Nat. Conf., Atlanta, 1999—, Ga. Music Educators Assn., Ashburn, Ga., 1999—. Contbr. articles to newspapers. Mem. Charecter Ednl. Partnership, Ga., 1999—99; min. of music and youth Harmony Bapt. Ch., Ashburn, 1999—99; jr. deacon Sycamore Lodge No. 210 of Free and Accepted Masons, 2001—01. Democrat-Npl. Southern Baptist. Avocations: coaching wrestling, coaching wrestling, coaching wrestling, coaching wrestling, coaching wrestling. Home: GA Office: Turner County Middle/High School 316 Lamer Street Ashburn GA 31714 E-mail: phil.lyons.iii@att.net.

LYSACK, CATHERINE L. medical educator; b. St. Boniface, Man., Can., Feb. 23, 1963; d. Allan and Shirley Helen Lysack; m. Stewart Wayne Neufeld, Sept. 5, 1992. BA, U. Man., Winnipeg, Can., 1984, BMR, 1988, PhD, 1997; MSc, Queen's U., Kingston, Can., 1992. Asst. prof. Wayne State U., Detroit, 1997—. Mem. editl. bd.: Am. Jour. Occupl. Therapy, 2001—03, Mem. editl. bd.: Occupl. Therapy Jour. Rsch., 2002—04; contbr. Recipient NHRDP fellow, Health Can., 1993—97, Aging Women and Well-Being award, NIH, 2000—01. Mem.: Gerontol. Soc. Am., Am. Anthropology Assn., Can. Assn. Occupl. Therapists, Am. Occupl. Therapy Assn. Avocations: squash, skiing, rollerblading, bicycling. Office: Wayne State U 87 E Ferry St Detroit MI 48202 Fax: 313-875-0127. E-mail: c.lysack@wayne.edu.

LYSAKER, EARL C., JR. internist; b. Snohomish, Wash., Dec. 11, 1948; s. Earl C. and Elvera Lysaker; m. Helen Katherine Conneran, July 22, 1972; 1 child, Megan. BS in Biology, Moorhead State U., 1970; MD, U. Minn., 1979. Diplomate Am. Bd. Internal Medicine. Instr. dept. medicine U. Minn. Med. Sch., Mpls., 1982-83; pvt. practice, 1983-85, Lake Worth, Fla., 1985-95; dir. Med. Specialists of Palm Beaches, 1995—, physician internal medicine, 1995—. Chmn., bd. dirs. Palms West Hosp., Loxahatchee, Fla., 1992-97; chief dept. medicine Palm Beach Regional Hosp., Lake Worth, 1987-88. Dir. Palm Beach County Sch. Arts, West Palm Beach, 1998-2001. With USN, 1971-73. Named Best Physician, Readers of Palm Beach Life Mag., 1988, Best Physicians in South Fla., Miami Metro Mag., 1998, 99, Best Primary Care Physicians in U.S., Town and Country Mag., 2000. Fellow ACP; mem. Alpha Omega Alpha. Avocations: tennis, snow skiing. Office: Med Specialists of Palm Beaches Ste 205 5503 S Congress Ave Atlantis FL 33462

LYSEN, LUCINDA KATHERINE, nutrition support nurse, dietitian; b. Blue Island, Ill. d. Walter Herbert and Margaret D. (Long) Lysen. BSN, Northwestern U., 1983; BA, St. Xavier Coll., 1976. Clin. nutrition intern Luth. Gen. Hosp., Park Ridge, Ill., 1977; registered dietitian Christ Hosp., Oak Lawn, 1978-85; rsch. assoc. Northwestern Meml. Hosp., Chgo., 1980-85; exec. dir. Ctr. for Nutritional Rsch., Port St. Lucie, Fla., 1987-94. Cons. in nutrition and health care issues, Stuart, Fla., 1994—, Chgo., 1994—; med. editor S.W. Messenger Press Newspapers, Chgo., 1997—. Author: Quick Reference to Clinical Dietetics, 1997. Mem. Am. Dietetic Assn. (past dir. quality assurance and legis. coms., chmn. dietitians in nutrition support practice group 1991-92, joint commn. accreditation of healthcare orgns., clin. indicator task force, rep. to joint comm. accreditation of healthcare orgns. nutritional care hosp. and home care task forces 1993, mem. com. to develop acuity based standards for registered dietitians), ASPEN (nurse counselor Fla. chpt. 1991, dietitian counselor 1992, sec. 1993, pres.-elect 1994, pres. 1995, past pres. 1996). Home: 7820 Arquilla Palos Heights IL 60463 E-mail: dietdown@aol.com.

LYSHAK-STELZER, FRANCES, artist; b. Detroit, June 3, 1948; d. Peter Paul and Frances Ellen (Harrington) Lyshak; m. Stephen Stelzer, Oct. 10, 1994. BFA, Wayne State U., 1970; MPS, Pratt Inst., 1978. Art therapist Creative Women's Collective, N.Y.C., 1978-79; creative arts therapy coord./dir. art therapy internship tng Bronx Children's Psychiat. Ctr., 1979—. One-woman shows include La Mama La Galleria, N.Y.C., 1993, 96, 98, Claire Dunphy's Studio, N.Y.C., 1985, Wow Theatre/Gallery, N.Y.C., 1983, Bill Rice Studio, N.Y.C., 1984, 88; group shows include Provincetown (Mass.) Art Assn. and Mus., 1983, Art Quest 86, L.A., Mus. of the Hudson Highlands, N.Y., 1985, Interart de St. Armand Gallery, 1983, Park Ave. Atrium, 1984, Cash/Newhouse Gallery, 1985, Marymount Manhattan Coll. Gallery, 1989, La Mama La Galleria, N.Y.C., 1985, 86, 92, Denise Bibro Fine Art, N.Y.C., 1996, RC Fine Art, N.J., 1999, Barbara Ann Levy Gallery, N.Y.C., 1999; author: The Secret: Art and Healing from Sexual Abuse, 1999. Mem. Am. Art Therapy Assn. (bd. cert. art therapist registered), Nat. Registry Cert. Group Psychotherapists (cert. group psychotherapist), cert. alcohol and substance abuse counselor).

LYSNE, ALLEN BRUCE, laboratory director; b. Owen, Wis. s. Almond P. and Helen A. (Childs) L.; children: Michael, Bruce, Brooke. BS, U. N.D., 1960. Lic. med. technologist, N.D. Bd. Clin. Lab. Practice; cert. clin. lab. scientist, Nat. Cert. Agy. Clin. lab. dir USPHS Indian Hosp., Fort Yates, N.D., 1961-62; asst. dir. biochemistry Dr. Salsbury's Lab., Charles City, Iowa, 1963-63; clin. lab. dir Lake Region Clinic, Devils Lake, N.D., 1963-69; CEO Meml. Hosp. Assn., Maddock, 1969-75; asst. exec. dir. ops. N.D. Health Care Rev., Minot, 1976-80; regional mgr. Colo. Found. Med. Care, Pueblo, Denver, Colo., 1980-87; dir. diagnositc svcs. Cmty. Hosp., Hillsboro, N.D., 1988-92; clin. lab. dir. Carroll County Meml. Hosp., Carrollton, Mo., 1992—. Chmn. Coun. on Aging, Pueblo, 1980-87. Mem. Am. Chem. Soc., Am. Assn. Clin. Lab. Sci., Am. Assn. Clin. Chemistry, Sci. Pub. Interest, Mo. Assn. Clin. Lab. Sci., N.Y. Acad. Scis. Achievements include research in effectiveness, toxicity and safety of 2 new drugs for coccidioidomycosis. Office: Carroll County Meml Hosp 1502 N Jefferson St Carrollton MO 64633-1948

LYSON, THOMAS A. sociologist, educator; b. Oak Park, Ill., Jan. 30, 1948; s. Helen P. Lyson, Stanley H. Lyson; m. Loretta Carrillo; children: Mercedes, Helena. BA, W.Va. U., 1970, MA, 1972; PhD, Mich. State U., East Lansing, 1976. Prof. Clemson (S.C.) U., 1977—86; Liberty Hyde Bailey prof. Cornell U., Ithaca, NY, 1987—. Editor Rural Sociology, Ithaca, 1996—2000; dir. Cmty., Food and Agriculture Program, Ithaca, 1992—. Mayor Village of Freeville, NY, 2000—. Mem.: So. Sociol. Soc., Rural Sociol. Soc. (Outstanding rschr. 2001), Am. Sociol. Assn. Roman Catholic. Home: 1 Union St Freeville NY 13068 Office: Cornell Univ Dept Rural Sociology Ithaca NY 14853 Office Fax: 607-254-2896. Business E-Mail: tal2@cornell.edu.

LYST, JOHN HENRY, former newspaper editor; b. Princeton, Ind., Mar. 28, 1933; s. John Henry and Marguerite (McQuinn) L.; m. Sharon Long, Dec. 29, 1956; children: Shannon M., Bettina A., Audrey K., Ellen K. AB, Ind. U., 1955. Reporter Indpls. Star, 1956-67, bus. columnist, from 1967, editor editl. page, 1979—2000. Corr. N.Y. Times, from 1964. Served with AUS, 1956-59. Mem. Indpls. Press Club (pres. 1968, bd. dirs. 1969), Sigma Delta Chi. Office: Indpls Newspapers Inc PO Box 145 Indianapolis IN 46206-0145*

LYSTAD, MARY HANEMANN (MRS. ROBERT LYSTAD), sociologist, author; b. New Orleans, Apr. 11, 1928; d. James and Mary (Douglass) Hanemann; m. Robert Lystad, June 20, 1953; children: Lisa Douglass, Anne Hanemann, Mary Lunde, Robert Douglass, James Hanemann. AB cum laude, Newcomb Coll., 1949; MA, Columbia U., 1951; PhD, Tulane U., 1955. Postdoctoral fellow social psychology S.E. La. Hosp., Mandeville, 1955-57; field rsch. social psychology Ghana, 1957-58, South Africa and Swaziland, 1968, Peoples Republic of China, 1986; chief sociologist Collaborative Child Devel. Project, Charity Hosp. La., New Orleans, 1958-61; feature writer African div. Voice Am., Washington, 1964-73; program analyst NIMH, 1968-78, asso. dir. for planning and coordination div. spl. mental health programs, 1978-80; chief Nat. Ctr. for Prevention and Control of Rape, 1980-83, Ctr. Mental Health Studies of Emergencies, 1983-89; pvt. cons. specializing on mental health implications social and econ. problems Bethesda, Md., 1990—. Cons. on youth Nat. Goals Research Staff, White House, Washington, 1969-70. Author: (nonfiction) Social Aspects of Alienation, 1969, As They See It: Changing Values of College Youth, 1972, Violence at Home, 1974, A Child's World As Seen in His Stories and Drawings, 1974, From Dr. Mather to Dr. Seuss: 200 Years of American Books for Chidlren, 1980, At Home in America, 1983; (fiction for children) Millicent the Monster, 1968, James the Jaguar, 1972, Jennifer Takes Over P.S. 94, 1972, Halloween Parade, 1973, That New Boy, 1973, Play Ball, 1997; editor: Innovations in Mental Health Services to Disaster Victims, 1985, Violence in the Home: Interdisciplinary Perspectives, 1986, Mental Health Response to Mass Emergencies: Theory and Practice, 1988. Recipient Spl. Recognition award USPHS, 1983, Alumna Centennial award Newcomb Coll., 1986. Home and Office: 4900 Scarsdale Rd Bethesda MD 20816-2440

LYSYK, KENNETH MARTIN, judge; b. Weyburn, Sask., Can., July 1, 1934; s. Michael and Anna (Maradyn) L.; m. Patricia Kinnon, Oct. 2, 1959; children: Joanne, Karen (dec.), Stephanie. BA, McGill U., 1954; LL.B., U. Sask., 1957; B.C.L., Oxford U., 1960. Bar: Sask., B.C., Yukon, apptd. Queen's counsel 1973. Lectr. U. B.C., 1960-62, asst. prof., 1962-65, assoc. prof., 1965-68, prof., 1968-69; adviser Constl. Rev. sect. Privy Council Office, Govt. of Can., Ottawa, 1969-70; prof. Faculty of Law U. Toronto, 1970-72; dep. atty. gen. Govt. of Sask., Regina, 1972-76; dean Law Sch., U. B.C., Vancouver, 1976-82; judge Supreme Ct. of B.C., 1983—. Dep. judge Supreme Ct. Yukon, 1991—, N.W. Territories, 1991—; judge Ct. Martial Appeal Ct. Can., 1995—; assoc. dir. Nat. Jud. Inst., 1996-98; chmn. Alaska Hwy. Pipeline Inquiry, 1977; sole commr. Yukon Electoral Boundaries Commn., 1991. Mem. Can. Bar Assn., Internat. Commn. Jurists (Can. sect.; v.p. for B.C. 1992-2002), Can. Inst. for Adminstrn. of Justice (pres. 1989-91). Office: Law Ct 800 Smithe St Vancouver BC Canada V6Z 2E1 E-mail: kenneth.lysyk@courts.gov.bc.ca.

LYTAL, PATRICIA LOU, art educator; b. Ft. Wayne, Ind., Sept. 11, 1936; d. George F. and Geraldine (Beck) Heingartner; m. Wayne Earl Lytal; Sept. 16, 1956; children: Michael Wayne, Patrick Allen (dec.), Terry Lee, Shawn David. Tchr. oil painting Ft. Wayne Park Sch. Bd, 1980-83, Ind. U.- Purdue U. Continuing Edn., Ft. Wayne, 1986-90; ind. tchr. oil painting, 1976-95. Instr. Ft. Wayne Sr. Ctr., Decatur (Ind.) Park Bd., Ft. Wayne Park and Recreation Dept.; tchr. oil painting for Chpt. 2 through St. Joseph Med. Ctr.; tchr. South Bay Adult Sch., 1996-97, 98; judge art contest Ft. Wayne Women's Club, 1989-90, 94. Artist: (murals) Diehm Mus. Natural History, 1981, Grace United Meth. Ch. Home, 1983, La Margarita Restaurant. Recipient 3d pl. china painting State of Ind., Best of Show award Ft. Wayne Woman's Club Ind. Artist Show, award Montpelier Brass Latch Art Show, 1993, 94, 95, Judges award Huntington Coll. Arts Contest, 1993. Mem. Brown Country Art Soc., Park County Art Soc., Ft. Wayne Artist Guild, Torrence Artist Guild, Niguel Art Assn., San Clemente Arts and Crafts Club. Democrat. Avocations: China painting, silverpoint drawing, fishing, swimming, traveling. Home and Office: 25507 S Western Ave Apt 6 Lomita CA 90717-2733

LYTLE, CHARLES FRANKLIN, biology educator; b. Crawfordsville, Ind., May 13, 1932; s. Robert Earl and Rose May (Caplinger) L.; m. Carol Helen Cottingham, Jan. 22, 1955; children: Charles G., Eric, Stephen, Victoria Lytle Utesch, Thomas; m. Brenda Sue Evans, Oct. 9, 1999. AB, Wabash Coll., 1953; MA, Ind. U., 1958, PhD, 1959. Rsch. assoc. Ind. U., Bloomington, 1959-60; asst. prof. zoology Tulane U., New Orleans, 1960-62; rsch. analyst U.S. Army, Washington, 1962-64; assoc. prof. Pa. State U., State College, 1964-69; prof. biology, coord. biol. scis. N.C. State U., Raleigh, 1969-93, coord. biology outreach programs, 1994—. Vis. prof. Duke U., Durham, N.C., 1972, 76, 88, mem. adv. com., 1971-84; vis. prof. Fla. Atlantic U., 1988, U. Ala., summers, 1988-98, Jacksonville U., summers, 1990-2000, The Bolles Sch., Jacksonville, Fla., summers, 1990-2000, Millsaps Coll., summer, 1992, Thammasat U., Thailand, summer, 1996; cons. Coll. Bd., Atlanta, 1980—, N.C. Wildlife Resources Commn., Raleigh, 1980-87, Ednl. Testing Svc., 1977—, Carolina Biol. Supply Co., Burlington, N.C., 1988—; mem. N.C. Sci. and Math. Adv. Coun., 1997-99; mem. adv. bd. N.C. Math. and Sci. Network, 1999-2002; mem. N.C. Sci. Framework Com., 2000; bd. dirs. Quantum Rsch. Svcs., Inc. Author: A Laboratory Guide to Biology, 1987, General Zoology Laboratory Guide, 13th edit., 2000; co-author: Laboratory Investigations in Biology, 1995, (videodisc) The Biology Encyclopedia; author, dir. 40 instrnl. programs on videotape and film; contbr. articles to profl. jours. Recipient Pub. Svc. award N.C. Optometric Soc., 1975, Outstanding Tchr. award N.C. State U., 1982, Disting. Svc. award N.C. Acad. Sci., 1991, Disting. Svc. in Sci. Edn. award N.C. Sci. Tchrs. Assn., 1991, Disting. Svc. award Nat. Assn. Acads. Sci., 1995, Sci. Star award SCIENCE: N.C., 1995, Outstanding Svc. award

The College Bd. So. Region, 1995, Outstanding Ext. and Outreach award N.C. State U. Alumni, 2000. Fellow AAAS; mem. NSTA, Nat. Assn. Biology Tchrs. (cons.), Am. Inst. Biol. Scis., Nat. Assn. Acad. Sci., Nat. Sci. Leadership Assn., Nat. Speakers Assn., Text and Acad. Authors Assn. (McGuffey Outstanding Textbook award 1997), Sigma Xi. Home: 2708 Townedge Ct Raleigh NC 27612-4301 Office: NC State Univ Biol Scis Outreach Programs PO Box 7532 Raleigh NC 27695-7532

LYTLE, L(ARRY) BEN, insurance company executive, lawyer; b. Greenville, Tex., Sept. 30, 1946; children: Hugh, Larry. BS in Mgmt. Sci. and Indsl. Psychology, East Tex. State U., 1970; JD, Ind. U., 1980. Computer operator/programmer U.S. Govt., Ft. Smith, Ark., 1964-65; customer engr. Olivetti Corp., San Antonio, 1965-66; mgr. computer ops. and computer software LTV Electrosystems, Greenville, 1966-70; project mgr. electronic fin. system, dir. systems planning Assocs. Corp. N.Am., South Bend, Ind., 1970-75; asst. v.p. systems Am. Fletcher Nat. Bank, Indpls., 1975-76; with Anaheim Ins. Cos., Inc., 1976-99; pres. Assoc. Ins. Cos., Inc., 1987-99, COO, 1987-89, CEO, 1989-99. Chmn. bd. dirs. Anthem Cos., Inc., Acordia, Inc.; chmn. bd. dirs. AdminaStar, Inc., Health Networks Am., Inc., Novalis, Inc., Robinson-Conner Nev., Inc.; bd. dirs. The Shelby Ins. Group, Raffensperger, Hughes & Co., Inc., Indpls. Power and Light Co. Enterprises; mem. adv. bd. CID Venture Ptnrs., Ltd. Partnership; rschr., cons. state and fed. govt. orgns., including, Adv. Coun. on Social Security, Pepper Commn. of U.S. Congress, others. Chmn. health policy commn. State of Ind., Indpls., 1990-92; active various civic orgns., including United Negro Coll. Fund, Indpls. Mus. Art. Mem. ABA, Ind. Bar Assn., Indpls. Bar Assn., Ind. State C. of C. (bd. dirs.), Indpls. C. of C. (bd. dirs.). Home: PO Box 441830 Indianapolis IN 46244-1830 Office: Anthem Ins Cos Inc 120 Monument Cir Indianapolis IN 46204-4906*

LYTLE, MICHAEL ALLEN, criminologist, consultant; b. Salina, Kansas, Oct. 22, 1946; s. Milton Earl and Geraldine Faye (Young) L.; div.; 1 child, Eric Alexander. BA, Ind. U., 1973; grad. cert., Sam Houston State U., Huntsville, Tex., 1977; MEd, Tex. A&M U., 1978; postgrad., 1978-80; student, Nat. Def. U., 1988. Substitute high sch. tchr., Butler Cty., KS, 1969; instr. criminal justice Cleaveland State C.C., Tenn., 1974-77; adj. instr. criminal justice U. Tenn., Chattanooga, 1975-76; tchg. asst. Tex. A&M U. Sys., 1977-80, intern adminstrv. asst. Office Vice Chancellor Legal Affairs and Gen. Counsel, 1980, staff assoc. Office Chancellor, 1980-81, asst. to chancellor, 1981-83, asst. dir. govt. rels., 1983-84, spl. asst. to chancellor for fed. rels., 1984-87; dir. rsch. devel. and spl. asst. to v.p. for rsch. and grad. studies Syracuse U., N.Y., 1987, exec. dir. govt. rels., 1987-89, sr. rsch. assoc. tech. and info. policy prog. Maxwell Sch. Citizenship and Pub. Affairs, 1987-92, dir. fed. rels., 1989-92, adj. prof. internatl. bus. studies NY, 1990-92; prin. and sr. couns. The Erik Alexander Group, 1992-93; exec. dir. instl. devel. U. Tex., Brownsville, 1993-95, sr. lectr. criminal justice, 1995-97; rsch. fellow Office Undersec. Def., 1997; sr. rsch. assoc. Sci. Applications Internat. Corp., 1997-99; adj. prof. criminal justice Marymount U. and Lutheran Colls., Wash. Consortiums, 1999—; dep. mgr. tech. svcs. divsn. Sci. Applications Internat. Corp., 2000—. Rep., Coun. on Fed. Rels., Assn. Am. Univs.; instl. rep. Rsch. Univs. Network; exec. dir. Tex. Com. for Employer Support of the Guard and Res., 1982-86; mem. US Mexico Com. Philanthropy and the Border, 1994-95, militarily critical techs. adv. com. US Internat. Bus. Studies, Tex. A&M Univ., 1986-87; res. asst. army attache to Rep. of Ireland, 1986-87; mem. exec. com. N.E. Parallel Architectures Ctr.; mem. Sec. of Army's adv. panel in ROTC affairs, 1988-92; cons. Nat. Inst. Justice, 2000--, Office of Victims of Crime, 2002--. Mem. editl. bd., Jour. Tech. Transfer, 1987-95, contbr. articles to profl. jours. Served with USAR, Vietnam and Bosnia. Trustee, Brownsville Hist. Mus. Assn., 1994-96. Decorated Legion of Merit, Bronze Star, Purple Heart, Meritorious Svc. medal with 2 oak leaf clusters, Joint Svc. Commendation medal, Army Commendation medal with 4 oak leaf clusters. Inter-Univ. Seminar Armed Forces and Soc. fellow, 1979; assoc. Ctr. NATO Studies, Kent State Univ. Fellow Am. Coll. Forensic Examiners (life); mem. AAAS (bd. advs. nat. security and sci. comm. proj. mem. awd. sel. panel. sci. freedom and responsiblity), Nat. Assn. State Univs. and Land-Grant Colls. (vet. affairs and nat. svc. com.), Am. Soc. for Pub. Adminstrn. (exec. com. sect., past chair on Nat. Security and Def. Analysis), Atlantic Counc. U.S. (councilor), Forensic Sci. Soc., Acad. Criminal Justice Scis., Internatl. Assn. Law Enforcement Intelligence Analysts, Internatl. Assn. Chief's Police, mem., US Attorney's Law Enforcement Coordinating Com., southern dist., Tex., 1995-97. Mem. Army and Navy Club, Capitol Hill Club, Sigma Xi, Phi Delta Kappa. Republican. Episcopalian. Address: 260 S Reynolds St Apt 403 Alexandria VA 22304-4430

LYTLE, STEPHEN CHARLES, music educator; b. Nashville, Dec. 24, 1968; s. James Charles Lytle and Frances Eloise Edney. BM, U NC, Chapel Hill, NJ, 1991; MM, Northwestern U, Evanston, IL, 2001. Teaching Certificate NC, 1991. Band dir. H J McDonald Mid. Sch., New Bern, NC, 1994—95; band and orch. dir. Erwin Mid. Sch. and Triton H.S., Erwin, 1995—96, East Chapel Hill H.S., Chapel Hill, 1996—. Chairman-band festival Southeastern Band Assn, NC, 1996—96; sec. NC Orch. Directors Div, NC, 1998—; chairman-clinic band Ctrl. Dist. Band Assn, NC, 2001—01. Mem.: Internat. Assn of Jazz Edn., Nat. Assn for Music Edn., NC Music Educators Assn. Avocation: freelance musician. Office: East Chapel Hill High School 500 Weaver Dairy Rd Chapel Hill NC 27514 Office Fax: 919-969-2492. E-mail: slytle@chccs.k12.nc.us.

LYTTLE, CHRISTOPHER SHERMAN, medical sociologist; b. Chgo., Apr. 12, 1951; s. David Janes and Eulene (Sherman) L.; m. Holly Douglas Mackley, Aug. 8, 1987; children: Zachary Douglas, Maxwell Clifford. BA, U. N.H., 1976; MA, U. Chgo., 1983. Rsch. specialist Ctr. for Health Adminstrn. Studies, Chgo., 1983-96; sr. rsch. assoc. Rush Primary Care Inst., 1996-2000; rsch. faculty Ctr. for Healthcare Studies, Northwestern U. Sch. Medicine, 2000—. Avocations: sailing, music, genealogy. Home: 18358 Dundee Ave Homewood IL 60430-3108

LYTTON, BERNARD, urology educator; b. London, June 28, 1926; came to U.S., 1962; s. Morris and Pearl (Zuckerberg) L.; m. Norma M. Mendle, Oct. 28, 1963; children: Sharon, Simon, Timothy, Jennifer. MB, BS, U. London, 1948. House officer, sr. registrar Royal London Hosp., 1948-50, 58-61; prof., chief urology Yale Univ. Sch. Medicine, New Haven, 1967-87, Donald Gultrie prof. surgery, 1987—; Master Jonathan Edwards Coll. Yale U., 1987-97. Squadron leader Royal Airforce Med. Br., Eng., 1950-52. Fellow ACS, Royal Coll. Surgeons Eng.; mem. Am. Urol. Assn. (Hugh Hampton Young award 1985, pres. New Eng. sect. 1974), Am. Assn. Genio-Urinary Surgeons, Clin. Soc. Genio-Urinary Surgeons (pres. 2000-01), Soc. Pelvic Surgeons. Avocations: tennis, skiing, history, hiking. Home: 21 Autumn St New Haven CT 06511-2220 Office: Yale U Sch Medicine Sect Urology PO Box 208041 New Haven CT 06520-8041

LYTTON, LINDA ROUNTREE, marriage and family therapist, test consultant; b. Suffolk, Va., Mar. 30, 1951; d. John Thomas and Anne Carolyn (Edwards) Rountree; m. Daniel Michael Lytton, June 23, 1973; 1 child, Seth Daniel. BS, Radford U., 1973; MS, Va. Poly. Inst. and State U., 1992. Collegiate profl. cert.; lic. profl. counselor, Va., 1995; lic. marriage and family therapist, 1997. Tchr., cons. Fauquier County Pub. Schs., Warrenton, Va., 1973-74, Chesterfield County Pub. Schs., Richmond, 1974-78, Williamsburg (Va.)-James City Pub. Schs., 1979-83, Prince William County Pub. Schs., Manassas, Va., 1983-89; hist. area interpreter Colonial Williamsburg Found., 1978-79; outpatient therapist Prince William County Community Svcs. Bd., 1989-91, emergency svcs. therapist, therapist cons., 1991-93; marriage and family therapist Menninger Care Sys., Inc., Manassas, 1993-99; pvt. practice Ashton Profl. Ctr., 1996—. Cons. Horizons for Learning, Inc., Richmond, 1989—. Great Books Leader, 1993—. Mem. Am. Assn. Marriage and Family Therapy, Va. Assn. Marriage and Family Therapy, Internat. Assn., Marriage and Family Counselors, Sigma Kappa (life). Avocations: tennis, biking, boating, water skiing. Home: 12046 Market Square Ct Manassas VA 20112-3214 also: Fairfield Office Pk 12890 Harbor Dr Woodbridge VA 22192-2921 E-mail: llytton796@aol.com.

LYTTON, ROBERT LEONARD, civil engineer, educator; b. Port Arthur, Tex., Oct. 23, 1937; m. Robert Odell and Nora Mae (Verrett) L.; m. Eleanor Marilyn Anderson, Sept. 9, 1961; children: Lynn Elizabeth, Robert Douglas, John Kirby. BSCE, U. Tex., 1960, MSCE, 1961, PhD, 1967. Registered profl. engr., Tex., La., land surveyor, La. Cowhand Slaughter Ranch, Douglas , Ariz., 1963; assoc. Dannenbaum and Assocs., Cons. Engrs., Houston, 1963-65; U.S. NSF fellow U. Tex., Austin, 1965-67, asst. prof., 1967-68; NSF fellow Australian Commonwealth Sci. & Indsl. Rsch. Orgn., Melbourne, Australia, 1969-70; assoc. prof. Tex. A&M U., College Station, 1971-76, prof., 1976-90, Wiley chair prof., 1990-95; dir. ctr. for infrastructure engring. Tex. A&M U. , 1991—; Benson chair prof. Tex. A&M U., 1995—; divsn. head Tex. Transp. Inst., 1982-91, head infrastructure and transp. divsn. civil engring. dept., 1993-95. Bd. dirs. MLA Labs., Inc., Austin, Lyric Tech., Llc., Houston; v.p. bd. dirs. MLAW Cons., Inc., Austin, 1980—, ERES Cons., Inc., Champaign, Ill., 1981-95, Geostructural Tool Kit, Inc., 1995--, Lyrical Analytical Svcs., Inc., 2002; prin. investigator strategic hwy. rsch. program A005 rsch. project, 1990-93; Disting. lectr. Transp. Rsch. Bd., 2000. Patentee sys. identification and analysis of subsurface radar signals. Active St. Vincent de Paul Soc., Houston, 1963-65, Redemptorist Lay Mission Soc., Melbourne, Australia, 1969-70. Capt. U.S. Army, 1961-63. Recipient SAR medal of honor St. Mary's U., 1957, Soc. Am. Mil. Engrs. Outstanding Sr. cadet U. Tex., 1959, Disting. Mil. grad. award, 1960, Hamilton Watch award Coll. Engring., 1960, Everite Bursary award Coun. for Sci. and Indsl. Rsch., South Africa, 1984, Disting. Achievement award Tex. A&M U. Assn. Former Students, 1996, Zachry Sr. Rschr. award Tex. Transp. Inst., 1996. Fellow ASCE (John B. Hawley award Tex. sect. 1966); mem. NSPE, Transp. Rsch. Bd. (chmn. com. A2LO6 1987-93), Internat. Soc. for Soil Mechanics and Geotech. Engring. (U.S. rep. tech. com. TC-6 1987—, keynote address 7th internat. conf. on expansive soils 1992, keynote address 1st internat. conf. on unsaturated soils 1995), Assn. Asphalt Paving Technologists, Post-Tensioning Inst. (adv. bd.), Tex. Soc. Profl. Engrs., Internat. Soc. Asphalt Pavements, Sigma Xi, Phi Kappa Delta, Chi Epsilon, Tau Beta Pi, Phi Kappa Phi. Roman Catholic. Office: Tex A&M U 503A CE Tex Transp Inst Bldg College Station TX 77843-0001 E-mail: rllytton@mail.com.

LYU, SEUNG WON, metallurgical engineer, environmental scientist; b. Seoul, Korea, May 15, 1934; came to U.S., 1958; naturalized, 1968; s. Yohan and Kyun Shin (Kim) L.; m. Yun O. Chung; children: John A., Lori K. BS in Chem. Engring., Ind. Inst. Tech., Ft. Wayne, 1961; BS in Metall. Engring., Ill. Inst. Tech., Chgo., 1975; MAS in Environ. Sci., Governors State U., University Park, Ill., 1981. Registered profl. engr. Ill., Calif.; cert. ind. wastewater treatment operator, Ill. Metallurgist Verson Allsteel Press Co., Chgo., 1962-65; metall. engr. Am. Std.-ARI, Franklin Park, Ill., 1965-67; sr. rsch. metallurgist Continental Group, Oak Brook, 1967-70; sr. prin. engr. Am. Nat. Can Co., Chgo., 1970-83; asst. prof. Ill. Inst. Tech., Glen Ellyn, Ill., 1983-88; pres., chief engr. Prospect Testing Labs., Des Plaines, 1985—. Tech. cons. Korean Small and Medium Indsl. Promotion Corp., Seoul, 1983; metall. cons. Verson Allsteel Press Co., Chgo., 1985—. Bd. dirs. Korean-Am. Cmty. Svc., Chgo., 1989-95, Niles (Ill.) Korean Sch., 1990—. Mem. ASTM. Republican. Presbyterian. Achievements include 6 patents in metallurgy, tooling and container application; method of making tin-layered stock material; die and method of assembly and application; split punch design and wall/bottom profile for containers. Office: Prospect Testing Labs Inc 1245 E Forest Ave Des Plaines IL 60018-1564 Home: 1819 Krowka Dr Des Plaines IL 60018-2976

LYYTINEN, KALLE JUHANI, computer scientist, educator; b. Helsinki, Aug. 19, 1953; s. Veli Kaarlo and Raili Annikki (Lehto) Lyytinen; m. Pirjo-Riitta Taipale, Sept. 6, 1974; children: Joonas, Juho, Markus. BA, U. Jyväskylä (Finland), 1976, MA, 1977, PhD, 1986. Rschr. U. Stockholm, 1981-82; prin. rschr. Acad. Finland, Jyväskylä, 1983-85; vis. rschr. London Sch. Econs., 1986; prof. U. Jyväskylä, 1987—, Hong Kong U. Sci. and Tech., 1993-94; G.E. Smith vis. prof. Ga. State U., 1997, dean, mem. faculty info. tech., 1998-2000; prof. Case Western Res. U., Cleve., 2001—. Editor: several profl. and acad. jours.; contbr. articles to profl. jours. Served to 3d st. inf. Finnish Army, 1972—73. Mem.: Internat. Fedn. Info. Processing (tech. com. 8, 2d chair 1991—93, chair ICIS com. 1998—99). Avocation: literature. Home: 2926 Torrington Rd Shaker Heights OH 44122 Office: Dept Info Sys Weatherhead Sch Mgmt Western Res U 10000 Euclid Ave Cleveland OH 44106-7235 E-mail: kalle@po.cwru.edu.

MA, ALAN WAI-CHUEN, lawyer; b. Hong Kong, Apr. 20, 1951; s. Pak Ping and Qi Quon (Hung) Ma. BBA, U. Hawaii, 1975; MBA, Chaminade U., 1981; JD, Golden Gate U., 1983. Bar: Hawaii 1984, U.S. Dist. Ct. Hawaii 1984, U.S. Ct. Appeals (9th cir.) 1986, U.S. Supreme Ct. 1989. Ptnr. Oldenberg & Ma, Honolulu, 1984—90; prin. Law Offices Alan W.C. Ma, 1990—95, 1999—; counsel Goodsill Anderson Quinn & Stifel, 1995—99. Adj. prof. law U. Hawaii, Honolulu, 1988-95. Co-editor: New Waves for Foreign Investors, 1990. Recipient Outstanding Vol. award Hawaii Cmty. Svc. Coun., 1990. Mem. ABA, Am. Immigration Lawyers Assn. (chpt. chair 1993-94), Internat. Bar Assn., Inter-Pacific Bar Assn., U.S. Japan Vols. Assn. (bd. dirs. 1989—), Overseas Chinese Am. Assn. (bd. dirs. 1993-94). Avocation: tennis. Office: PO Box 23014 Honolulu HI 96823 E-mail: lawyer.ma@verizon.net.

MA, CHUNG-PEI MICHELLE, astronomer, educator; BS, PhD, MIT, 1993. From asst. prof. to assoc. prof. physics and astronomy U. Pa., Phila., 1996—2001; assoc. prof. astronomy U. Calif., Berkeley, 2001—. Contbr. articles to profl. jours. Recipient Annie J. Cannon award, 1997, 1st prize Taiwan Nat. Violin Competition, 1983, Cottrell Scholars award Rsch. Corp., 1999, Lindback award for Disting. Tchg., U. Pa., 1999; Alfred P. Sloan fellow, 1999; Sherman Fairchild fellow, 1993. Mem. Phi Beta Kappa. Achievements include research in the formation and evolution of galaxies and large scale structure in the Universe; performed numerical simulations of the clustering of dark matter in various cosmological models of structure formation from the Early Universe until the present day; computation of the temperature variations imprinted on the cosmic microwave background radiation which provides a snapshot of the infant Universe. Avocation: classical violin. Office: U Calif Berkeley Dept Astronomy 601 Campbell Hall 94720

MA, FENGCHOW CLARENCE, agricultural engineering consultant; b. Kaifeng, Honan, China, Sept. 4, 1919; came to U.S., 1972; s. Chao-Hsiang and Wen-Chieh (Yang) Ma; m. Fanny Luisa Corvera-Achá, Jan. 20, 1963; 1 child, Fernando. BS in Agr., Nat. Chekiang U., Maytan, Kweichow, China, 1942; postgrad. in agrl. engring., Iowa State U., 1945-46. Cert. profl. agronomist, Republic of China, 1944; registered profl. agrl. engr., Calif. Chief dept. ops. Agrl. Machinery Operation and Mgmt. Office, Shanghai, China, 1946-49; sr. farm machinery specialist Sino-Am. Joint Commn. on Rural Reconstrn., Taipei, Taiwan, Republic of China, 1950-62; agrl. engring. adviser in Bolivia, Peru, Chile, Ecuador, Liberia, Honduras, Grenada, Bangladesh FAO, Rome, 1962-80; consulting agrl. engr. to USAID projects in Guyana & Peru IRI Rsch. Inst., Inc., Stamford, Conn., 1981-82, 83, 85; chief adviser Com. Internat. Tech. Coop., Taipei, 1984-85; pres. FCM Assocs., Inc., 1962—. Short consulting missions to Paraguay, Saudi Arabia, Indonesia, Malawi, Swaziland, Barbados, Dominica, Ivory Coast, Vietnam, Philippines, Nicaragua and others. Author papers, studies; contbr. articles to profl. publs. Mem. Am. Soc. Agrl. Engrs. Avocations: reading, stamp and coin collecting. Home: 1004 Azalea Dr Sunnyvale CA 94086-6747 Office: PO Box 70096 Sunnyvale CA 94086-0096

MA, HAI-FEI, research scientist; b. Qingdao, Shandong, China, May 7, 1957; came to U.S., 1997; BS, Ocean U. Qingdao, 1982; PhD, Hokkaido (Japan) U., 1989. Postdoctoral fellow Mitsubishi Kasei Inst. Life Scis., Tokyo, 1989-91; rsch. asst. prof. Inst. Devel. Biology Chinese Acad. Scis., Beijing, 1991-92, rsch. assoc. prof. Inst. Devel. Biology, 1992-97; postdoctoral fellow Baylor Coll. Medicine, Houston, 1997-99, rsch. assoc., 1999-2001; mgr. transgenic facility MCB, Harvard U., Cambridge, Mass., 2001—. Editor: Advances in Developmental Biology, 1994; contbr. articles to profl. jours. Honored Grad. Student fellow Ministry Edn., 1982-89; rsch. grantee Presdl. Fund Chinese Acad. Scis., 1993-95, Nat. Natural Sci. Found. China, 1996-99. Achievements include patents for photography aid for reducing shadows and reflections; invention of mouse embryo freezing kit. Office: MCB Harvard U Genome Manipulations Facility 16 Divinity Ave Cambridge MA 02138 Fax: 713-798-3175.

MA, HONG, plant molecular biologist, educator; b. Shanghai, People's Republic of China, Oct. 19, 1960; came to U.S., 1980; s. Zhe and Linsun (Hu) M.; m. Yi Hu, Aug. 10, 1987; children: Jason J., Julia C. BA summa cum laude, Temple U., 1983; PhD, MIT, 1988. Tchg. asst. MIT, Cambridge, 1983—84, rsch. asst., 1984—88; postdoctoral fellow Calif. Inst. Tech., Pasadena, 1988—90; staff investigator Cold Spring Harbor (N.Y.) Lab., 1990—91, sr. staff investigator, 1992—96, assoc. investigator, 1996—98; assoc. prof. biology and life scis. consortium Pa. State U., State College, 1998—2002, prof. biology and life scis. consortium, 2002—. Adj. faculty SUNY, Stony Brook, 1991-98; mem. faculty SUNY-Cold Spring Harbor Lab.-Brookhaven Joint, 1991-98; adviser undergrad. rsch. program Cold Spring Harbor Lab., 1991-98; mem. panel NIH Biol. Study Sect., 1995, 96-99; spkr. in field; competitive grants review panelist USDA, 1997; lectr. Cold Spring Harbor Lab., 1993-98; advisor undergrad. rsch. program Pa. State U., 1998—. Assoc. editor for Plant Molecular Biology, 1996—; reviewer articles for Sci., Genetics, Molecular Cellular Biology, Molecular Gen. Genetics Devel., Devel. Genetics, Proc. Nat. Acad. Sci., USA, Plant Cell, Plant Jour., Plant Molecular Biology, Plant Physiology, Plant & Cell Physiology, Plant Soc., Sci., Am. Jour. Botany, Current Biology, Current Opinion Cell Biology, Gene Devel., Gene; contbr. articles to profl. jours. Mem. selection com. Ptnrs. for Future High Sch. Students, Cold Spring Harbor Lab., N.Y., 1991-98; mentor high sch. student rsch. project Westinghouse Talent Competition, 1993, 97-98. Recipient jr. rsch. award, Am. Cancer Soc., 1994; fellow, MIT, 1983, Helen H. Whitney Found., 1988; grantee, NSF, 1990, 1991, 1994, 1998, 2000, 2001, USDA, 1991, 1992, 1994, 1995, 1996, 2001, Am. Cancer Soc., 1995, NIH, 2001, Dept. Energy, 2002. Mem. AAAS, Am. Assn. Plant Biologists, Genetic Soc. Am., Am. Soc. Microbiology, Internat. Soc. Plant Molecular Biologists, Assn. Chinese Students and Scholars in Life Scis., Soc. Chinese Bioscientists Am., N.Y. Acad. Scis. Avocations: reading, stamp collecting, gardening. Office: Pa State U Dept Biol Life Scis Consort 504 Wartik Lab University Park PA 16802-5807

MA, JINPENG, economics and business educator; b. Xishui, Hubei, China, Apr. 10, 1962; came to U.S., 1989; s. Degui and Yongjun (Li) M.; m. Mei Han, July 18, 1987; 1 child, Lynn. BA in Engring., Huzhong Agrl. U., Wuhan, China, 1984; MSc in Engring., Beijing Agrl. Engring. U., 1987; PhD in Econs., SUNY, Stony Brook, 1993. Postdoctoral fellow Hebrew U., Jerusalem, Israel, 1994; assoc. prof. econs. and bus. Rutgers U., Camden, N.J., 1994—. Contbr. articles to profl. jours. Mem. Am. Econ. Assn., Econometric Soc. Home: 21 Corbin Dr Exton PA 19341

MA, KUO CHUN, neuropathologist; b. Beijing, Nov. 1, 1923; s. Chih Dao and Xiao Zhang (Chien) M.; m. Wen Hua Deng, Feb. 22, 1953; children: Ma Xiang, Deng Yuan. MD, Cheeloo U., Tsinan, China, 1951. Asst. resident in pediats. Shanghai Infectious Hosp., 1951-52; asst. resident, resident and lectr. pathology Shanghai Med. U., 1952-57; lectr. pathology Chongqing (China) Med. Coll., 1957-80; assoc. prof., prof. pathology Shanghai Med. U., 1980-89; ret.; vis. prof. pathology Loma Linda (Calif.) U., 1982; vis. prof. neuropathology Lab. Neuropathology, Uppsala (Sweden) U., 1990-94. Dir. nat. tng. courses neuropathology Chinese Min. Health, Shaghai Med. U., 1980-85; cons. Lab. Neuropathology, Dept. Neurology, Huashan Hosp., Shanghai Med. U., 1978-80; lectr. dept. clin. neurology Cath. U., Rome, 1989-90, Neurol. Inst., U. Vienna, Austria, 1990. Contbr. articles to profl. jours. Recipient Hon. Award for best med. student U.S. Ednl. Found. in China, 1949; grantee Stiftelsen Gamla Tjänarinnor, Uppsala, 1992, The Werner-Gren Found., Uppsala, 1993. Mem. Chinese Assn. Neuropathology (exec. com.), Internat. Soc. Neuropathology, Scandinavian Soc. Neuropathology. Avocations: figure skating, Peking opera, swimming, photography, Chinese painting. Home: West Nanjing rd 1191-5C Shanghai 200040 China

MA, NAIYANG, metallurgical engineer, researcher; b. Huaiyin, Jiangsu, China, May 11, 1959; s. Chengfu Ma, Yanchi Hu; m. Shuhua Liu; children: Mary. BS, Chongqinh (China) U., 1982; MS, U. Sci. and Tech. Beijing, 0985; PhD, U. Utah, 2000. Lectr. East China Inst. Metallurgy, MaanShan, China, 1985—94, assoc. prof. China, 1994—95; rsch. asst. U. Utah, Salt Lake City, 1996—99, tchg. asst., 1998—99, rsch. fellow, 1999—. Programmer ProPay, USA, Orem, Utah, 2000—02. Contbr. articles to profl. jours. Recipient Outstanding Paper award, MaanShan Assn. Sci. and Tech., 1988, "Ironmaking " Editl., 1991, Excellent Paper award, China Ministry of Metall. Industry, 1992. Mem.: MSE, TMS. Avocation: QiGong. Home: 657E Candlelite Ln Midvale UT 84047 Office: U Utah 135S 1460E Rm 412 Salt Lake City UT 84112 Personal E-mail: naiyangm@yahoo.com. Business E-Mail: nma@mines.utah.edu.

MA, QINGLI, environmental hydrologist; b. Chengwu, Shandong, China, Sept. 3, 1964; came to U.S., 1991; s. Hanying Ma and Meiliang Feng; m. Qun Zhang, Oct. 24, 1991; children: Yan, David. BSc, Shandong U., Jinan, 1985; MSc, Zhejiang U., Hangzhou, Zhejiang, China, 1988; PhD, U. Ga., 1998. Vis. scientist USDA Agrl. Rsch. Svcs., Ft. Collins, Colo., 1991-94; rsch. scientist U. Ga., Athens, 1995-98; vis. scientist AgResearch, Hamilton, New Zealand, 1998-99; soil scientist USDA-Agrl. Rsch. Svcs.-U.S. Salinity Labs./U. Calif.-Riverside, 1999—2000; sr. environ. hydrologist, cons. Environ. and Turf Svc., Inc., Wheaton, Md., 2000—. Author: (book) Root Zone Water Quality Model, 1992; contbr. articles to periodicals. USDA-Office of Internat. Corp. and Devel. Rsch. fellow, 1991, U. Ga. fellow, 1995, AgResearch rsch. fellow, 1998, U.S. Salinity Lab. rsch. fellow USDA-Agrl. Rsch. Svcs., 1999. Mem. AAAS, Am. Soc. Agronomy, Soil Sci. Am., New Zealand Plant Protection Soc. Office: Environ and Turf Svc Inc # 208 11144 Georgia Ave Wheaton MD 20902 E-mail: qinglima@aol.com.

MA, TSU SHENG, chemist, educator, consultant; b. Guangdong, China, Oct. 15, 1911; came to U.S., 1934, naturalized 1956; s. Shao-ching and Sze (Mai) M.; m. Gioh-Fang Dju, Aug. 27, 1942; children: Chopo, Mei-Mei. BS, Tsinghua U., Peking, 1931; PhD, U. Chgo., 1938. Faculty U. Chgo., 1938-46; prof. Peking U., 1946-49; sr. lectr. U. Otago, New Zealand, 1949-51; mem. faculty NYU, 1951-54, CUNY, 1954—, prof. chemistry, 1958—, prof. emeritus, 1980—. Vis. prof. Tsinghua U., 1947, Lingnan, 1949, NYU, 1954-60, Taiwan U., 1961, Chiangmei U., 1968, Singapore U., 1975; hon. prof. Hangzhou Tchrs. Coll., 1998—; specialist Bur. Ednl. and Cultural Affairs State Dept., 1964, Hong Kong, Philippines, Burma, Sri Lanka; Fulbright lectr., 1961-62, 68-69. Author: Small-Scale Experiments in Chemistry, 1962, Organic Functional Group Analysis, 1964, Microscale Manipulations in Chemistry, 1976, Organic Functional Group Analysis by Gas Chromatography, 1976, Quantitative Analysis of Organic Mixtures, 1979, Modern Organic Elemental Analysis, 1979, Organic Analysis Using Ion-Selective Electrodes, 1982, Trace Element Determination in Organic Materials, 1988; editor: Mikrochimica Acta, 1965-89; contbr. articles to profl. jours., chpts. to 10 books. Recipient Benedetti-Pichler award in microchemistry, 1976. Fellow N.Y. Acad. Sci., AAAS, Royal Soc. Chemistry, Am. Inst. Chemists; mem. Am. Chem. Soc., Soc. Applied Spectroscopy, Am. Microchem. Soc., Sigma Xi. Achievements include 1 patent; research in trace element analysis, microchemical investigation of medicinal plants, organic analysis and synthesis in the milligram to microgram range, and the use of small-scale, inexpensive equipment to teach chemistry. Home: 7 Banbury Ln Chapel Hill NC 27517-2500 Office: CUNY Dept Chemistry Brooklyn NY 11210

MA, XIAOLIANG, research scientist; b. Fuzhou, Fujian, China, Mar. 18, 1957; s. Hongxiang Ma and Xuan Lin; m. Xi ana Jiang; children: Ruilong, Toby. B in Engring. Sci., Zhejiang U., Hangzhou, China, 1982; M in Engring. Sci., China Coal Rsch. Inst., Beijing, 1987; D in Engring. Sci., Kyushu U., Fukuoka, Japan, 1995. Asst. engr. China Coal Rsch. Inst., Beijing, 1982—84, engr., 1987—91; vis. rschr. Nat. Inst. for Resources and Environment, Tsukuba, Japan, 1991—92; rsch. assoc. Energy Inst., Pa. State U., University Park, 1995—, group leader, 2000—. Contbr. chapters to books, articles. Mem.: Am. Chem. Soc. (reviewer 1996—, mem. divsn. fuel chemistry 1995—, mem. divsn. petroleum chemistry 1995—). Avocation: photography. Office: The Energy Inst 409 Academic Activities Building University Park PA 16802-2308 Office Fax: 814-863-8892. Business E-Mail: mxx2@psu.edu.

MA, XING, optical engineer; b. Jianjin, People's Republic of China, Dec. 15, 1954; d. Tai and Suwen (Yu) M.; m. Tianxiang Liu, Sept. 28, 1984; children: Patrick, Alex. BS in Physics, Normal U. Tianjin, China, 1980; PhD in Elec. Engring., U. New South Wales, Sydney, Australia, 1995. Optical engr. Electronic Material Co., Tianjin, China, 1981-86; rsch. asst. U. New South Wales, Sydney, Australia, 1987-94; rsch. engr. Dept. Comm. RMIT, Melbourne, Australia, 1994-97; sr. fiber optics engr. E-TEK Dynamics, San Jose, Calif., 1998—. Chief tech leader for design of new products: CADM and

5-part WDM device. Mem. IEEE. Avocations: coin collecting, shell collecting, swimming, volleyball. Office: E-TEK Dynamics 1865 Lundy Ave San Jose CA 95131-1834 E-mail: xing.ma@etek.com.

MA, XIN-LIANG, biomedical researcher, educator; b. Taiyuan, China, Aug. 21, 1957; came to U.S., 1989; s. Ren-Chen Ma and Yu-Lang Wang; m. Yaping Guo, Jan. 28, 1986; children: Jeffrey, Joanna. MMed, Shangxi Med. U., Taiyuan, China, 1982; PhD, 4th Mil. Med. U., Xian, China, 1988. Asst. prof. Thomas Jefferson U., Phila., 1993-97, rsch. dir. emergency medicine, 1993—, assoc. prof. surgery, 1997—2002, prof. surgery, 2002—. Presenter over 100 abstracts at nat. and internat. confs. Rschr. in myocardial apoptosis after reprefusion, opposite role of nitric oxide and nitroxyl in myocardial reprefusion injury; contbr. over 100 articles to profl. jours. Fellow Soc. for Acad. Emergency Medicine (Best Basic Sci. award 1998, 2000); mem. Am. Heart Assn. Home: 12 Kyle Ct Mount Laurel NJ 08054 Office: Thomas Jefferson U 1020 Sansom St Philadelphia PA 19107 Fax: (215) 923-6225. E-mail: Xin.Ma@mail.tju.edu.

MA, YO-YO, cellist; b. Paris, 1955; m. Jill; children: Nicholas, Emily. Studied with Janos Scholz; studied with Leonard Rose, Juilliard Sch. Music, N.Y.C., 1962; AB, Harvard U., 1976, MusD (hon.), 1991. Debut at age 9, Carnegie Hall, N.Y.C.; appeared with Pablo Casals, Isaac Stern, Leonard Bernstein, Emanuel Ax, Jaime Laredo, performs throughout world with maj. orchs.; rec. artist Sony Classical; recs. include Portrait of Yo-Yo Ma, Japanese Melodies, Anything Goes (with Stephanie Grapelli), Hush (with Bobby McFerrin), Yo-Yo Ma at Tanglewood, The New York Album, Cello Suites Inspired By Bach, Great Cello Concertos, Made in America, Portrait of Cello Works, Premieres, Simply Baroque, Simply Baroque 2, Solo, Soul of The Tango, Tavener-Protecting Veil/Wake Up. Recipient Avery Fisher prize, 1978, 14-time Grammy award winning artist. Office: ICM Artists 40 W 57th St Fl 16 New York NY 10019

MA, ZHENKUI, remote sensing applications scientist, consultant; b. Shenyang, Liaoning, China, Nov. 4, 1955; arrived in U.S., 1983; s. Deshan Ma and Shuxuan Zhang; m. Shufang Zhao; children: Bin, Jeanne. BS, Beijing Forestry Coll., 1982; MS, U. Mich., 1985, PhD, 1990. Sr. specialist Weyerhaeuser, Federal Way, Wash., 1996—2002, info. tech. cons., 2002—. Internat. cons. UN, Beijing, 1994—96. Mem.: Am. Soc. for Photogrammetry and Remote Sensing (bd. dirs. Seattle 2001, Puget Sound region). Achievements include research in mapping large geographic areas biodiversity protection. Home: 21745 113th Place SE Kent WA 98031 Office: Weyerhaeuser 33405 Eighth Ave South Federal Way WA 98003 Office Fax: 253-924-2301. Personal E-mail: zhenkui_ma@yahoo.com. Business E-Mail: zhenkui.ma@weyerhaeuser.com.

MA, ZHONGGUO (JOHN MA), engineering educator, researcher; s. Kun Ma and Zhi Yuan; m. Michelle Liao; 1 child Ding. BSCE, Shijiazhuang (China) Rlwy. Inst., 1984; MSCE, S.W. Jiaotong U., Chengdu, China, 1987; PhD, U. Nebr., 1998. Cert. profl. structural engr. Nebr. Rsch. asst. prof. U. Nebr., Lincoln, 1998—99; asst. prof. U. Alaska, Fairbanks, 1999—. Mem.: ASCE (T. Y. Lin award 2002), Precast/Prestressed Concrete Inst. (Martin P. Korn award 2001), Am. Concrete Inst. Office: U Alaska Fairbanks PO Box 755900 Fairbanks AK 99775 Office Fax: 907-474-6087. E-mail: ffzm@uaf.edu.

MAAG, URS RICHARD, statistics educator; b. Winterthur, Switzerland, Jan. 20, 1938; m. Tannis Yvonne Arbuckle, July 31, 1965; children: Liane, Karin, Eric Diploma in Math, Swiss Fed. Inst. Tech., Zurich, 1961; M.Sc., U. Toronto, Can., 1962, PhD, 1965. Asst. prof. U. Montreal, Canada, 1965—72, assoc. prof. Canada, 1972-78, prof. Canada, 1978—2001, adj. prof. Canada, 2001. Contbr. articles to profl. jours. Mem. Statis. Soc. Can. (sec. 1973-77, pres. 1980, Founder Recognition award 1998), Am. Statis. Assn. (pres. Montreal chpt. 1975-77), Internat. Statis. Inst., Can. Assn. Rd. Safety Profls., Inst. Math. Stats. Home: 3484 Marlowe Ave Montreal QC Canada H4A 3L7 Office: U Montreal Dept Math and Stats CP 6128 Succ Centre-ville Montreal QC Canada H3C 3J7

MAARBJERG, MARY PENZOLD, office equipment company executive; b. Oct. 2, 1943; d. Edmund Theodore and Lucy Adelaide (Singleton) Penzold; m. John Peder Maarbjerg, Oct. 20, 1966; 1 child, Martin Peder. AB, Hollins Coll., 1965; MBA, Wharton Sch., Pa., 1969. Cons. bus. and fin., Stamford, Conn., 1977-78; corp. staff analyst Pitney Bowes, Inc., 1978-80, mgr. pension and benefit fin., 1980-81, dir. investor rels., 1981-85; v.p. planning and devel. Pitney Bowes Credit Corp., Norwalk, Conn., 1985-86, treas., v.p. planning, 1986-94; v.p. mktg. devel. and mng. dir. Asia Pacific Bowes Fin. Svcs., 1994-95, v.p. ops. and mng. dir., 1995-97; v.p. corp. svcs. Pitney Bowes, Inc., Stamford, 1997-99, v.p. real estate and adminstrn., 1999-2001, v.p. adminstrn. and process integration, 2001—. Mem. adv. com. City of Stamford Mcpl. Employees Retirement Fund, 1980-85; mem. fin. adv. com. YWCA, Stamford, 1982-86; bd. dirs. Stamford Symphony, 1985-95, Vis. Nurses Assn., 1984-86, Am. Recorder Soc., 1986-98, Am. Classical Orch., 1999—; bd. dirs. Stamford Partnership, 1998—, chmn., 2000—; bd. dirs., treas. Amherst Early Music, 2000—. Fellow Royal Statis. Soc.; mem. Fin. Execs. Inst., Phi Beta Kappa. Office: Pitney Bowes Inc 1 Elmcroft Rd Stamford CT 06926-0700 E-mail: mary.maarbjerg@pb.com.

MAAS, ANTHONY ERNST, retired pathologist; b. Utrecht, The Netherlands, May 6, 1926; came to U.S., 1959; s. Willem A. and Tono Clara (Bonebakker) M.; m. Julia Margaret Lampley, July 7, 1962; children: Willem Fulton, Julie Estelle, Anthony Ernst Jr. BS, U. Utrecht, 1948, MD, 1953. MD, Pa.; cert. anatomical and clin. pathologist. Asst. pathologist United Hosp., Port Chester, N.Y., 1965-66; assoc. pathologist Polyclinic Hosp., Harrisburg, Pa., 1966-74, Holy Spirit Hosp., Camp Hill, 1974-90, dir. labs., 1990-96, Harrisburg State Hosp., Harrisburg, 1990-96. Contbr. articles to profl. jours. Fellow Coll. Am. Pathologists, Am. Soc. Clin. Pathologists; mem. AMA, Pa. Med. Soc., Dauphin County Med. Soc., Torch Club of Harrisburg (pres. 1983). Republican. Presbyterian. Avocations: reading, traveling, gardening, walking.

MAAS, DUANE HARRIS, distilling company executive; b. Tilleda, Wis., Aug. 26, 1927; s. John William and Adela (Giessel) M.; m. Sonja Johnson, Mar. 11, 1950; children: Jon Kermit, Duane Arthur, Thomas Ervin. BS, U. Wis., 1951. With Shell Chem. Corp., 1951-59; plant mgr. Fleischmann Distilling Corp., Owensboro, Ky., 1959-63, Plainfield, Ill., 1963-65; asst. to v.p. Barton Distilling Co., Chgo., 1965-68, exec. asst. to pres., 1968, v.p. adminstrn., 1968; v.p., gen. mgr. Barton Brands, Inc., Chgo., 1968— 72; pres. Leaf Confectionery div. W.R. Grace, 1972-74; v.p., gen. mgr. Romano Bros., 1974-79; v.p., sec.-treas. Marketing Directions Inc., 1974-77; pres. Associated Wine Producers, Inc., 1979-80; exec. v.p., chief exec. officer Mohawk Liqueur, Detroit, 1980-86; v.p. McKesson Wine & Spirits Group of N.Y., 1982-86; pres. Mgmt. Cons. Services Co., Chgo., 1986—, U.S. Distilled Products Co., Princeton, Minn., 1996-99, Am. Distilled Products Corp., 2001—. Chmn. Qingdao Johnson Distiller Co. Ltd., Qingdao, China, 1996-99; past pres. Bart on Distilling (Can.), Ltd.; past mng. dir. Barton Distilling (Scotland), Ltd.; past dir. Barton Distillers Europe, Barton Internat., Ltd. Sec.-treas. Plainfield Twp. Park Dist., 1967-70; chmn. Plainfield Planning and Zoning Commn., 1965-70. Served with USAAF, 1945-47. Mem.: Wis. Alumni Assn. Lutheran. Home and Office: 13264 W Highway 29 Bowler WI 54416 E-mail: dhm@mcservices.com.

MAAS, FRANK, judge; b. N.Y.C., June 10, 1950; s. Herbert N. and Vera (Neu) M.; m. Sidney L. Maas, June 22, 1980; children: Edward, Arthur. BA, Harpur Coll./SUNY, Binghamton, 1972; JD, NYU, 1976. Assoc. Curtis, Mallet-Prevost, Coit & Mosle, N.Y.C., 1976-78; asst. U.S. atty. So. Dist. N.Y., 1980-86; ptnr. Phillips, Lytle, Hitchcock, Blaine & Huber, 1986-95; 1st dep. commr. N.Y.C. Dept. Investigation, 1995-99; U.S. magistrate judge So. Dist. N.Y., N.Y.C., 1999—. Dep. commr., spl. counsel N.Y.C. Dept. Bus. Svcs., 1995-99. Mem. Coun. on Jud. Adminstrn. (assoc. of the bar 1997—), N.Y. State Bar Assn. (comml. and fed. litigation sect. 1984—), Fed. Bar Coun. Office: US Courthouse 500 Pearl St Rm 740 New York NY 10007-1502

MAAS, JANE BROWN, advertising executive; b. Jersey City; d. Charles E and Margaret (Beck) Brown; m. Michael Maas, Aug. 30, 1957; children: Katherine, Jennifer. BA, Bucknell U., 1953; postgrad., U. Dijon, France, 1954; MA, Cornell U., 1955; LittD, Ramapo Coll., 1986, St. John's U., 1988. Assoc. producer Name That Tune TV Program, N.Y.C., 1957-64; v.p. Ogilvy and Mather Inc., 1964-76; sr. v.p. Wells, Rich, Greene, Inc., 1976-82; pres. Muller Jordan Weiss Inc., 1982-89, Earle Palmer Brown Cos., N.Y.C., 1989-92, chmn., 1992-94, chmn. emeritus, 1994—. Co-author: (book) How to Advertise, 1975, Better Brochures, 1981, Adventures of a Advertising Woman, 1986, The New How to Advertise, 1992, Christmas in Wales: A Homecoming, 1994. Bd govs comt Scholastic Achievement, 1985—92; active Girl Scouts US, NY, 1970—76; mem adv bd William E Simon Grad Sch Bus, Univ Rochester, 1989—; pub dir AIA, 1993—95; trustee Bucknell Univ, Lewisburg, 1976—86, Fordham Univ, NY, 1983—91. Named Woman of the Yr, NY Advert, 1986; recipient Matrix Award, Women in Communications, 1980. Mem.: AIA (hon.), Am Asn Advert Agencies (bd govs), Am Archit Found (regent 1993—2000), Phi Beta Kappa. Avocations: creative writing, jogging. Home: PO Box 1109 Westhampton Beach NY 11978-7109 E-mail: janemaas@worldnet.att.net.

MAAS, JOE (MELVIN JOSEPH MAAS), retired federal agency administrator; b. Washington, Feb. 29, 1940; s. Melvin Joseph and Katherine (Endress) M.; m. Constance Mary Haile, June 13, 1965; children: Christine, Michael, Kevin. BS, U. Md., 1965; postgrad., Stanford U., 1972-73. Dir. career edn. U.S. Dept. Labor, Washington, 1969-73; dep. dir. pers. SBA, 1973-76, dir. pers., 1976-82, asst. adminstr., 1982-95. Sr. v.p. Crave Entertainment Group, Inc., 2000; mem. Internat. Pers. Assn., 1981-83, chairperson, 1982. Bd. dirs., treas. Snowden Mill Assn., Silver Spring, Md., 1991-99, 2001-02, pres. 2002—; Wash. rep. Ind. Charities of Am., 1995-96; bd. dirs. Amen Found., 1998—. With USMCR, 1957-64. Mem. Fed. Exec. Adminstrs. Assn., Sr. Exec. Assn., Pub. Employee Roundtable (bd. dirs. 1994—, chair Pub. Svc. Excellence awards 1996-98, treas. 1998-2002), Coun. Former Fed. Execs. (pres., bd. dirs. 1995—), Nat. Assn. Ret. Fed. Employees (chpt. pres. 1996-98, v.p. 1998-2000, state tng. officer 1997-01), Volkswagen Club (pres. Washington club 1988-95). Roman Catholic. Home: 2213 Aventurine Way Silver Spring MD 20904-5253

MAAS, WERNER KARL, microbiology educator; b. Kaiserslautern, Germany, Apr. 27, 1921; came to U.S., 1936, naturalized, 1945; s. Albert and Esther (Meyer) M.; m. Renata Diringer, Oct. 15, 1960; children— Peter, Andrew, Helen. AB, Harvard U., 1943; PhD, Columbia U., 1948. Postdoctoral fellow Calif. Inst. Tech., Pasadena, 1946-48; commd. officer USPHS, Tb Research Lab., Cornell U. Sch., N.Y.C., 1948-54; asst. prof. pharmacology NYU, 1954-57, assoc. prof. microbiology, 1957-63, prof., 1963-94, prof. emeritus, 1994—, chmn. dept. basic med. scis., 1974-81. Career grantee USPHS, 1962-94. Mem. Am. Soc. Biol. Chemists, Genetics Soc. Am., Am. Soc. Microbiology. Home: 86 Villard Ave Hastings On Hudson NY 10706-1821 Office: 550 1st Ave New York NY 10016-6402 E-mail: maasw01@med.nyu.edu.

MAASS, ARTHUR, political science and environmental studies educator; b. Balt., July 24, 1917; s. Arthur Leopold and Selma (Rosenheim) M. AB, Johns Hopkins, 1939; M.P.A., Harvard, 1941, PhD, 1949. Adminstrv. asst. Bur. Budget, 1939-40; intern Nat. Inst. Pub. Affairs, 1939-40; research technician Nat. Resources Planning Bd., 1941-42; budget analyst Dept. Navy, 1946; water resources analyst Natural Resources Task Force, Hoover Commn., 1948; faculty Harvard, 1949—, prof. govt., 1959-67, Frank G. Thomson prof. govt., 1967-84, prof. emeritus, 1984—, chmn. dept., 1963-67. Cons. Office Dir. Budget, 1949, Office Sec. Interior, 1950-52, Pres.'s Materials Policy Commn., 1951-52, TVA, 1952, C.E., 1961—, Bur. Reclamation, 1971, Ministry Water Conservancy, People's Republic China, 1980—; vis. prof. polit. sci. U. Calif. at Berkeley, 1951, U. P.R., 1955, El Colegio de México, 1986, U. Internat. Menendez y Pelayo, Valencia, Spain, 1990. Author: Muddy Waters, The Army Engineers and the Nation's Rivers, 1951, Congress and the Common Good, 1983, Water Law and Institutions in the Western U.S.: Comparisons with Early Developments in California and Australia, Contemporary Developments in Australia and Recent Legislation Worldwide, 1990; co-author: Area and Power, 1959, Design of Water-Resource Systems: New Techniques for Relating Economic Objectives, Engineering Analysis and Governmental Planning, 1962, A Simulation of Irrigation Systems, 1971, rev., 1974, 78, 87, Chinese edit., 1980, . . . and the Desert Shall Rejoice: Conflict, Growth and Justice in Arid Environments, 1978, rev. edit., 1986, Un Modelo de Simulacion Para Sistemas de Regadio, 1985; contbr. articles to profl. jours. Served to lt. comdr. USNR, 1942-46. Guggenheim fellow, 1955; Fulbright research fellow Spain, 1960-61; Faculty research fellow Social Sci. Research Council, 1961 Mem.: Harvard (N.Y.C.). Home: 63 Atlantic Ave Boston MA 02110-3722 Office: Harvard U Littauer Ctr Cambridge MA 02138

MAATMAN, GERALD LEONARD, insurance company executive; b. Chgo., Mar. 11, 1930; s. Leonard Raymond and Cora Mae (Van Der Laag) M.; children: Gerald L. Jr., Mary Ellen; m. Bernice Catherine Brummer, June 3, 1971. BS, Ill. Inst. Tech., 1951. Asst. chief engineer Ill. Inspection & Rating Bur., Chgo., 1951-58; prof., dept. chmn. Ill. Inst. Tech., 1959-65; v.p. engrng. Kemper Group, 1966-68, pres. Nat. Loss Control Svc. Corp., 1969-74, v.p. corp. planning Long Grove, Ill., 1974-79, sr. v.p. info. svcs. group, 1979-85, exec. v.p. ins. ops., 1985-87; pres. Kemper Nat. Ins. Co., 1987-92, CEO, 1989-95, also bd. dirs., chmn. bd. dirs., 1991-95. Bd. dirs. Advs. for Auto and Hwy. Safety, 1992-98; chmn. bd. trustees Underwriters Labs., 1991-2002. Lt. (j.g.) USCGR, 1952-54. Mem. Knollwood Golf Club, Springs Club, Tau Beta Pi. Republican. Roman Catholic.

MAATSCH, DEBORAH JOAN, financial company executive, tax advisor; b. Lincoln, Nebr., Mar. 26, 1950; d. Leon F. Forst and Jarolyn J. Hoffman Forst Conrad; m. Gordon F. Maatsch, Mar. 14, 1969; children: Jason, Diana. BS, U. Nebr., 1976; MBA, U. Phoenix, 1997. Accredited tax advisor; IRS enrolled agt. Acct., supr. U.S. Civil Svc., Heidelberg, Germany, 1971—73; paralegal Mattson Rickets Davies et al, Lincoln, Nebr., 1976—87; tax cons., 1981—, Denver, 1981—; paralegal Wade Ash Woods & Hill, P.C., 1986—94; sr. trust adminstr. Investment Trust Co., 1994—96; compliance officer Nelson, Benson and Zellmer, Inc., 1995—96; pres. DGJD Inc., 1993—; contr. Arena Devel., Inc., 1996—2000; pres. Boyd Industries, Inc., 2001—; dir., pres. JCCA, 2001—. Mem. Park County Sr. Wellness Team, 1999—; mem. bus. adv. bd. Ponderosa H.S., 1994-98. Contbr. articles to profl. jours. Event chmn., vol. Jefferson Cmty. Ctr., 1999—; bd. dirs. JCCA, 2001–, pres., 2002–; bd. dirs. Kids Roundup, 2002–; coord. Jefferson Hist. Preservation Fund. Mem. Doane Coll. Alumni Assn. (dir. 1989-93). Avocations: travel, outdoor activities. Office: DGJD Inc PO Box 267 Jefferson CO 80456-0267 also: Boyd Industries Inc PO Box 315 Boyd TX 76023 E-mail: dgjdinc@bemail.com.

MABASA, TERESA ALBAR, social welfare association administrator; b. Roxas City, Capiz, The Philippines, Oct. 2, 1935; d. Catalino Reyes Mabasa and Antonia Andrada Albar. BE, U. The Philippines, Diliman, Quezon City, 1956; MA in Social Work, St. Louis U., 1968; PhD in Orgn. & Devel. and Planning Inst., S.E. Asia Interdisciplinary Devel., Antipolo, The Philippines, 1981. Registered social worker. Acad. dean La. Salette U., Santiago City, The Philippines, 1982-85; pres., superior Coll. of Sacred Heart, Iloilo City, The Philippines, 1985-88; dir. Devel. Ctr. of Nazareth, Aklan, The Philippines, 1988-91; ministry coord. for social svcs. Daus. of Charity of St. Vincent de Paul, Paranaque, The Philippines, 1991-94, asst. visitatrix The Philippines, 1994-97, visitatrix, provincial superior The Philippines, 1997—. Program dir. CARITAS Manila, 1978-81; cons. planning Manila Archdiocese, 1996-97. Vol. Nat. Movement Free Election, Indonesia and The Philippines, co-chair Parañaque chpt., 1996—; mem. Konsyensyang Pilipino, 1996—. Recipient Most Outstanding Adminstr. in Western Visayas Region award Dept. of Edn., Iloilo, 1987, Most Outstanding Profl. Social Worker award Profl. Regulation Com., Manila, 2000; scholar U. The Philippines, 1952. Mem. AMRSP (bd. dirs. 1999—), Philippine Assn. Social Workers Inc. (life, pres. Iloilo chpt. 1987-88, cons. 1998-99) Roman Catholic. Avocations: reading, swimming, museums, plays. Home and Office: Daus of Charity St Vincent 8486 E Service Rd Km 18S NCR Paranaque 1700 MM Philippines Fax: 63.2.838.8987. E-mail: secoff@compass.com.ph.

MABEE, CARLETON, historian, educator; b. Shanghai, China, Dec. 25, 1914; s. Fred Carleton and Miriam (Bentley) M.; m. Norma Dierking, Dec. 20, 1945; children: Timothy I., Susan (Mrs. Paul Newhouse). AB, Bates Coll., 1936; MA (Perkins scholar), Columbia U., 1938, PhD, 1942. With Civilian Pub. Svc., 1941-45; Instr. history Swarthmore (Pa.) Coll., 1944; tutor Olivet (Mich.) Coll., 1947-49; asst. prof. liberal studies Clarkson Coll. Tech., Potsdam, N.Y., 1949-51, asso. prof., 1951-55; prof., 1955-61; dir. social studies div. Delta Coll., University Center, Mich., 1961-64; prof., chmn. dept. humanities and social scis. Rose Poly. Inst., Terre Haute, Ind., 1964-65; prof. history State U. Coll. at New Paltz, N.Y., 1965-80, prof. emeritus, 1980—. Participant in projects for Am. Friends Service Com., 1941-47, 53, 63; Fulbright prof. Keio U., Tokyo, 1953-54 Author: The American Leonardo, A Life of Samuel F.B. Morse, 1943, The Seaway Story, 1961, Black Freedom: The Nonviolent Abolitionists from 1830 through the Civil War, 1970, Black Education in New York State: From Colonial to Modern Times, 1979; author: (with Susan Mabee Newhouse) Sojourner Truth: Slave, Prophet, Legend, 1993; Listen to the Whistle: An Ancedotal History of the Wallkill Valley Railroad in Ulster and Orange Counties, N.Y., 1995; also articles: editor: (With James A. Fletcher) A Quaker Speaks from the Black Experience: The Life and Selected Writings of Barrington Dunbar, 1979, Bridging the Hudson: The Poughkeepsie Railroad Bridge and its Connecting Rail Lines, a Many-Faceted History, 2001. Trustee Young-Morse Hist. Site, Poughkeepsie, N.Y.; ofcl. town historian, Gardiner, N.Y. Recipient Pulitzer prize in biography, 1944, Bergstein award for excellence in teaching Delta Coll., 1963, Anisfield-Wolf award race rels., 1971, Gustavus Myers award for outstanding book on human rights, 1994; rsch. grantee Rsch. Found. SUNY, 1965, 67, 68, 80, Am. Philos. Soc., 1970, Nat. Inst. Edn., 1973-76, NSF, 1982-83. Mem. N.Y. State Hist. Assn., Phi Beta Kappa, Delta Sigma Rho. Methodist. Home: 2121 Route 44-55 Gardiner NY 12525-5808

MABEE, JOHN RICHARD, physician assistant, educator; b. San Francisco, Sept. 18, 1956; s. Robert John and Mary Sachiko (Nose) M.; m. Cheryl Ann Saxton, June 24, 1978 (div. Aug. 1995); children: Jonathan, Alan; m. Carol Mendez, 1998. BS, Regents Coll., 1981; MS, Calif. State U., L.A., 1991; PhD, Union Inst., Cin., 2001. Cert. physician asst., Nat. Commn. Cert. Physician Assts. Physician asst. resident dept. emergency medicine LA County/U. So. Calif. Med. Ctr., 1984-85, emergency medicine physician asst., 1985—. Rsch. asst. dept. biology Calif. State U., L.A., 1987—88, lectr., 1988—91, physician asst., 1992; rsch. physician asst. U. So. Calif. Emergency Medicine Assocs., L.A., 1993—95, clin. instr. dept. emergency medicine, 1994—, conscious sedation adv. com., 1995—, lectr. sch. medicine, 1995—2000, asst. prof. clin. family medicine, 2001—. Contbr. articles to profl. jours. Named Alumnus of Yr., Emergency Medicine Physician Asst. Residency, 1994. Fellow Am. Acad. Physician Assts., Calif. Acad. Physician Assts. (Educator of Yr. 1998); mem. AAAS, N.Y. Acad. Scis., Soc. Emergency Medicine Physician Assts. (founding, election com., 1988—). Democrat. Avocations: reading, watching videos, horseback riding, chess, cooking, tae kwon do. Home: 302 Pamela Kay Ln La Puente CA 91746-2726 Office: U So Calif Keck Sch Medicine 1000 S Fremont Ave Bldg 6 Alhambra CA 91803

MABEE, KEITH V. communications/investor relations executive; BS in Journalism, Bowling Green State U., 1969; MEd in Sociology, Wayne State U., 1972; MBA, Pepperdine U., 1980. Comm. specialist Internat. Paper Co., N.Y.C., 1969-70, 73; pub. affairs officer, U.S. Army NATO, Europe, 1970-72; sr. lectr. Coll. Mgmt., Queensland U. Tech., Australia, 1973-77; organizational/effectiveness officer U.S. Army, Pacific, 1978-80; sr. v.p., corp. comm. AMFAC, Inc., San Francisco, 1980-89; v.p. comm. Indsl. Indemnity, 1989-93; v.p. corp. rels. Figgie Internat. Inc., 1993-98; sr. exec. v.p. Dix & Eaton, 1997-98, pres., 1998—2001, pres., COO, 2001—. Former pres. San Francisco chpt. Nat. Investor Rels. Inst., former officer, former dir. nat. bd., mem. sr. roundtable steering com.; founding trustee, lectr. San Francisco Acad.; bd. dirs. Ohio Tuition Trust Authority. Mem. Pub. Rels. Soc. Am. Office: The Galleria and Tower at Erieview 1301 E 9th St Ste 1300 Cleveland OH 44114-1882 Fax: 216-241-3070.

MABEE, SANDRA IVONNE, timpanist, percussionist, educator, clergyman; b. Hato Rey, P.R., Jan. 13, 1955; d. Nelson Custudio Noriega and Norma Ruth (Eiseman) Lee; m. Carl Mabee, 1980; 1 child, Rebecca Lee. BA in Bibl. Studies summa cum laude, Patten Coll., 1977; BM magna cum laude, San Francisco Conservatory, 1983; MA in Music cum laude, Calif. State U., Hayward, 1985; PhD in Religion, Christian Bible Coll., N.C., 2000. Ordained min. Evang. Ch. Alliance, 1991, Unveiled Christ Ministries, 1997; cert. Evangelical Tchr.'s Tng. Assn. Prin. timpanist Bay Area Women's Philharm., San Francisco, 1980—; prof. music Patten Coll., Oakland, Calif., 1983-89, chairperson profl. studies divsn., 1986-88; min. of music El Cerrito (Calif.) Christian Ctr., 1988-91; prof. music Hayward Christian Sch., 1988-91; intern pastor, dir. music ministry Trinity Ch., Oakland, Calif., 1991-92; pastor, dir. music ministries Unveiled Christ Ministries, 1992—; prof. music Las Positas Coll., 1996—. Tympanist, percussionist various orchs., Bay Area, Calif., 1977—; pvt. tchr. music lessons, Bay Area, 1977—; percussion ensemble Patten Coll., Oakland, 1983-84; producer sing-it-yourself Messiah Patten Coll., Oakland, 1986; guest dir. choral Landmark Ministries, Oakland, 1990; seminar instr., Landmark Sch. Ministries, Oakland, 1990, Internat. Radio Broadcast, 1998. Prison ministry vol. Alameda County Jail, Oakland, 1990, Vacaville Fed. Prison, Follow-up Ministries; vol. rest home, Oakland, 1985—, Assn. of Christian Schs. Inc./Song Shop; founder Tracy Percussion Ensemble, 1999—. San Francisco Conservatory scholar, 1980-83; named Outstanding Young Woman of Am., 1986, 87, winner concerto soloist Redwood Symphony, 1988, for Outstanding Svc. to Teaching Profession A.B.I. Mem. Percussive Arts Soc., Hymn Soc. of Am., Sarasota Acad. Christian Counseling, Am. Assn. Christian Counselors. E-mail: sandymabee@thevision.net.

MABEY, RALPH R. lawyer; b. Salt Lake City, May 20, 1944; s. Rendell Noel and Rachel (Wilson) M.; m. Sylvia States, June 5, 1968; children: Rachel, Elizabeth, Emily, Sara. BA, U. Utah, 1968; JD, Columbia U., 1972. Bar: Utah 1972, U.S. Dist. Ct. Utah 1972, U.S. Ct. Appeals (10th cir.) 1976, N.Y. 1985, U.S. Supreme Ct. 1988, U.S. Ct. Appeals (4th cir.) 1988, U.S. Ct. Appeals (3d cir.) 1993. Law clk. Atty. Gen., Salt Lake City, 1970, U.S. Dist. Ct., Salt Lake City, 1972-73; ptnr. Irvine, Smith & Mabey, 1973-79; U.S. bankruptcy judge U.S. Ct., 1979-83; ptnr. LeBoeuf, Lamb, Greene & MacRae, Salt Lake City and N.Y.C., 1983—. Sr. lectr. Brigham Young U. Sch. Law, Provo, Utah, 1983—, U. Utah Coll. Law, Salt Lake City, 1983-85. Mng. editor Norton Bankruptcy Law Adviser, 1983-85; contbg. author: Collier Bankruptcy Manual, 1986—, Collier on Bankruptcy, 15th Edition. With USAR, 1968-74. Mem. ABA (bus. bankruptcy com., joint task force bankruptcy court structure and insolvency processes), Nat. Bankruptcy Conf., Am. Law Inst., Am. Bankruptcy Inst., Am. Coll. Bankruptcy (pres.). Republican. Mem. Lds Ch. Avocations: running, fly fishing. Home: 253 S 1550 E Bountiful UT 84010-1350 Office: LeBoeuf Lamb Greene & MacRae 1000 Kearns Bldg 136 S Main St Salt Lake City UT 84101-1601 also: 125 W 55th St New York NY 10019-5369 E-mail: mabey@LLGM.com.

MABILANGAN, FELIPE HUGO, JR. Philippine diplomat; b. Manila, Feb. 15, 1936; s. Felipe and Felisa (Hugo) M.; m. Ada Ledesma, Dec. 8, 1943; children: Jose Antonio, Anne Marie, Lisa. BA, Balliol Coll., U. Oxford, Eng., 1959; MA, Balliol Coll., U. Oxford, 1964; diploma in internat. rels., U. Geneva, 1965. Fgn. svc. officer Philippines Ministry Fgn. Affairs, 1962-75, dir. gen., 1975-79, permanent del. to UNESCO, 1980-82, amb. to France and Portugal, 1979; amb. to People's Republic of China, 1990-94; permanent rep. of The Philippines to the UN N.Y.C., 1994—. Mem. adv. com. on adminstrv. and budgetary questions UN. Recipient Outstanding Young Men award for govt. svc. Manila Jaycees, 1975, Order Diplomate Merit, Govt. Republic of Korea, 1976, Nat. Order Merit, France, 1987; Carnegie fellow U. Geneva, 1964-65. Mem. Manila Polo Club, Racing Club France (Paris). Office: Perm Mission of Philippines to UN 556 5th Ave Fl 5 New York NY 10036-5002

MABLEY, JACK, newspaper columnist, communications consultant; b. Binghamton, N.Y., Oct. 26, 1915; s. Clarence Ware and Mabelle (Howe) M.; m. Frances Habeck, Aug. 29, 1940; children: Mike, Jill, Ann, Pat, Robert. BS, U. Ill., 1938. With Chgo. Daily News, 1938-61, reporter, writer, columnist, 1957-61; columnist Chgo.'s Am., 1961-69, asst. mng. editor, 1966-69; asso. editor Chgo. Today, 1969-73; columnist Chgo. Today, Chgo. Tribune, 1973-74, Chgo. Tribune, 1974-82; pres. Mabley & Assocs., Corp. Communications, Glenview, Ill., 1982; columnist Daily Herald, Arlington Heights, 1987—. Lectr. journalism Northwestern U., 1949-50 Pres. Village of Glenview, Ill., 1957-61, Skokie Valley Community Hosp., Skokie, Ill., 1977-79. Served from ensign to lt. USNR, 1941-45. Recipient Media award Nat. Assn. for Retarded Citizens, 1977 Home and Office: 2275 Winnetka Rd Glenview IL 60025-1825 E-mail: jmabley@dailyherald.com.

MABREY, VICKI, news correspondent, anchor; b. St. Louis; BA in Polit. Sci. cum laude, Howard U., 1977. AFTRA tng. reporter Sta. WUSA-TV, Washington, 1982-84; gen. assignment reporter Sta. WBAL-TV, Balt., 1984-92; corr. CBS News, Dallas, 1992-95, London, 1995-98, 60 Minutes II, N.Y.C., 1998—. Recipient 2 Emmy awards, 1996, 2 Emmy awards, 1997. Office: c/o 60 Minutes II 524 W 57th St New York NY 10019-2902*

MABROUK, SARAH LOU, mathematician, educator; b. Peoria, Ill., Mar. 3, 1962; d. Ahmed Fahmy and Barbara Elaine (Ford) M. AB in Math. and Physics, Wheaton Coll., Norton, Mass., 1984; MA in Math., Boston U., 1988, PhD in Math., 1994. Tchg. fellow math. dept. Boston U., 1984-88, lectr. summer term, 1986-94, lectr. math. dept. Coll. Arts and Scis., 1988-95, summer orientation faculty advisor Coll. Arts and Scis., 1989-92, asst. prof. divsn. sci. and math., mem. Coll. Gen. Studies, 1995—2000, summer orientation faculty advisor Coll. Arts and Sciences, 1989—99, summer orientation faculty advisor Coll. Gen. Studies, 1998-99; asst. prof. dept. math. Framingham (Mass.) State Coll., 2000—, coord. gen. math., dept. math., 2000—, vis. asst. prof. grad. and continuing edn., 2000—02. Lectr. sci. and engring. program Met. Coll., Boston U., 1986, 94-95; lectr. Met. Coll., Boston U., 1987-88; faculty advisor Coll. Arts and Scis. Boston U., summer 1996; moderator paper session 6th Conf. on Tching. of Math., 1997; co-organizer, moderator contributed paper sessions joint math. meetings AMS, MAA, 2001--; chair program com. NES, MAA spring meeting, 1999, 2000; chair program com. and local arrangements com. NES, MAA fall meeting, 2002; presenter in field at various workshops; reviewer 9 textbooks; mem. Student Life Task Force U. com. Boston U., 1996-2000; coord. math. Coll. Gen. Studies, 1999-2000; student asst., preceptor Wheaton Coll. in math., computer sci., physics., 1981-84, 1982-83; presenter in field. Boston U. scholar, 1988-89, 92-94, Phi Beta Kappa Grace Shepard scholar, 1984. Mem. AAUP, Am. Math. Soc., Assn. for Women in Math., Math. Assn. Am. (co-chair prog. com. short course com. northeast sect. spring meeting, 1999, organizer, moderator paper session Mathfest, 1999, 2000), Nat. Coun. Tchrs. Math, Assn. Rsch. in Undergrad. Math. Edn., Mass. Tchrs. Assn. Avocations: clarinet, computer, sewing, tennis, music. Home: PO Box 2752 Framingham MA 01703-2752 Office: Framingham State Coll 100 State St PO Box 9101 Framingham MA 01701-9107 E-mail: smabrouk@frc.mass.edu.

MABRY, BOBBY SCOTT, lawyer; b. Houston, Oct. 2, 1958; s. Alvin Irwin and Cathryn Scott M.; m. Denise Brown Patrick (div.); m. Edith Bess Premazon, June 26, 1994; 1 child, Joseph Samuel. BA, Austin Coll., 1982; JD, South Tex. Coll., 1990. Tchr. Saint Thomas H.S., Houston, 1982-87; law clk. George W. Wilhite & Assocs., Inc., 1987-90; proprietor Law Offices of Bob Mabry, 1990—; assoc. atty. Kenneth L. Rothey & Assocs., P.C., 1997-99, of counsel, 1999—2001. Mock trial sr. judge South Tex. Coll. Law, Houston, 1998; republican primary precinct judge Harris County, Houston, 1996; probar vol. lawyer, McAllen, Tex., 1995; campaign mgr. Fitzpatrick for City Coun. Campaign, Sherman, Tex., 1980. With USMCR, 1981. Mem. State Bar Tex., Federalist Soc. Houston Lawyers Chpt. Unitarian Universalist. Avocations: reading, walking.

MABRY, DONALD JOSEPH, university administrator, history educator; b. Atlanta, Apr. 21, 1941; s. Jerry Leon and Eunice Leigh (Harris) M.; m. Susan Strong Johnston, July 28, 1962 (div. Oct. 1986); children: Scott, Mark; m. Paula Ann Crockett, Dec. 18, 1992. BA, Kenyon Coll., Gambier, Ohio, 1963; MEd, Bowling Green State U., 1964; PhD, Syracuse U., 1970. Instr. St. Johns River Community Coll., Palatka, Fla., 1964—67; rsch. asst. fin. aid Syracuse U., NY, 1967—68, teaching fellow in history, 1968—69, Maxwell fellow, 1969—70, vis. lectr. dept. history, 1969—70; asst. to chancellor U. Kans., Lawrence, 1978—79; from. asst. prof. to prof. dept. history Miss. State U., Mississippi State, 1970—, asst. to pres., 1979—81, assoc. dean for budget and rsch., 1991—2001; now dir., assoc. dean Biol. Physical Sciences Rsch. Inst. Sr. fellow Ctr. for Internat. Security and Strategic Studies, Miss. State U., 1981-91. Author: Mexico's Accion Nacional, 1973, The Mexican University and the State, 1982, (with others) Neighbors--Mexico and the United States, 1981; editor: The Latin American Narcotics Trade and U.S. National Security, 1989; contbr. articles to profl. jours. Mem. Am. Coun. on Edn. (exec. com. Coun. of Fellows 1980-83), South Ea. Coun. on Latin Am. Studies, The hist. Text Archive (founding editor). Avocation: computer telecommunications. Home: 206 Hiwassee Dr Starkville MS 39759-2105 Office: Miss State U Drawer H Mississippi State MS 39762 E-mail: djm1@ra.msstate.edu.

MABRY, PAUL DAVIS, psychobiologist, educator, researcher; b. Meridian, Miss., Sept. 28, 1943; s. Paul Davis and Frances Elizabeth (Thigpen) M.; m. Celia Elaine Hales, 1986. BS, Millsaps Coll., Jackson, Miss., 1965; MS, U. Miss., 1967, PhD, 1970. Rsch. trainee dept. neurosurgery U. Miss. Med. Ctr., 1966, predoctoral rsch. fellow, 1969-70; rsch. assoc. neurosci. and behavior program Princeton U., N.J., 1970-76; chair dept. psychology, head div. behavioral & natural scis. Sacred Heart Coll., Belmont, N.C., 1976-86; chair dept. Psychology U. St. Thomas, St. Paul, 1986-91, assoc. prof., 1986—, dir. behavioral neurosci. program, 1991—. Contbr. articles to profl. jours. NIMH fellow, 1969. Mem. AAAS, Soc. for Neurosci., Am. Psychol. Assn., Internat. Brain Rsch. Orgn., Sigma Xi. Home: 28 Mississippi River Blvd N Saint Paul MN 55104-5713 Office: Dept Psychology U St Thomas 2115 Summit Ave Saint Paul MN 55105-1048 E-mail: pdmabry@stthomas.edu.

MABRY, PHILIP T. marketing professional; b. Spartanburg, SC, Feb. 29, 1940; s. Roy T. and Eleanor Eva (Waddell) Mabry; m. Mary E. Byars, July 3, 1961 (div. Mar. 1980); children: Tammy Kay Waldrop, Phyllis Dianne Gibbons, Sonya Kowalski; m. Amy D. Mabry, June 18. Founder Ams. for Human Rights, Greenville, SC, 1975—79; pres. Western Rsch. Cons., Euless, Tex., 1982—; sales/mktg. rep. D.F.W. Mktg., 1998—. Cons. U.S. Dept. State, Washington, 1982—87. Contbr. news articles, interviews on Iran/Contra and Iran hostage af. Polit. activist Rep. Party, Washington, 1962—. Recipient Cert. of Appreciation, Nat. Rep. Party, 2001, Cert. of Membership, Acad. Polit. Sci., 2001. Republican. Avocations: golf, coins, reading, American history. Home: 605 Del Paso St Apt 416 Euless TX 76040 Office: Western Rsch Cons 605 Del Paso St 76040

MABRY, SONDRA B. nurse educator and practitioner; children: Kristin, Elin M. BSN, U. Pa., 1962; MEd in Health Edn., Temple U., 1981; MSN, Widener U., 1988; postmaster's cert., Gwynedd-Mercy Coll. RN, Pa.; cert. RN practitioner, Pa. Staff nurse Lankenau Hosp., Wynnewood, Pa., instr. Sch. Nursing; sch. nurse Norristown (Pa.) Ares Sch. Dist.; resident nurse ACTS, Inc., retirement cmty., Spring House, Pa.; instr. Abington (Pa.) Meml. Hosp. Sch. Nursing, 1981—2000. Contbg. author: Community and Home Care Health Plans, 1990, American Nursing Review for NCLEX-PN, 1992. Co-chmn. blood drives APC, 1991-97. Recipient Lois Ryan Allen publ. award Nurses Assn. for Tchr. Edn., Award for Excellence in Tchg. Northeast Coalition, 1999. Mem. Am. Acad. Nurse Practitioners, Oncology Nursing Soc., Sigma Theta Tau. Home: 1035 Kingsdown Ct Ambler PA 19002-1833 Office: Abington Meml Hosp 1200 Old York Rd Abington PA 19001-

MABUNDA, GLADYS, nursing educator; b. Bushbuckridge, South Africa; arrived in U.S., 1984; d. Jossie and Thema Mabunda; 1 child Shane. BSN, U. South Africa, Pretoria, 1983; MSN, St. Louis U., 1988, PhD, 1996. RN. RN Dept. Health South Africa, Pretoria, 1978—84, St. Louis U., 1986—88; pub. health nurse II St. Louis City Health Dept., 1989—91; nursing instr. Mo. Bapt. Med. Ctr., St. Louis, 1992—96; asst. prof. So. Ill. U., Edwardsville, 1996—2002, assoc. prof., 2002—. Contbr. articles to profl. jours. Vol. trainer St. Louis Effort AIDS, 1993—. Mem.: APHA, Sigma Theta Tau (Martha Welch Rsch. grantee 1997, Marilyn Rsch. award 1997, Writing Pub. award 1997, 2001). Avocation: traveling. Office: So Ill U Edwardsville Saint Louis MO 63126 Business E-Mail: gmabund@siue.edu.

MACAFEE, NORMAN, writer, translator; b. Phila., Mar. 18, 1943; s. Norman Stanley Stewart MacAfee and Thelma Evelyn Dietz; ptnr. Miguel Cervantes-Cervantes. BA, U. Pa., 1965; MFA in English, U. Iowa, 1967. Author: (ballet libretto) The Re-Creation of the New World, 1984, (poetry) A New Requiem, 1988, (opera) The Death of the Forest, 1998; translator: (with Luciano Martinengo) Poems (Pier Paolo Pasolini), 1982, rev. edit., 1996, (with Lee Fahnestock) Les Misérables (Victor Hugo), 1986, Witness to My Life (Jean-Paul Sartre), 1992, Quiet Moments in a War (Jean-Paul Sartre), 1993, (with Luigi Fontanella) Lines of Light (Daniele del Giudice), 1988, Heroines (Claude Cahun), 1999; creator: (performance work) Pier Paolo Pasolini: The Eyes of a Poet, a Reading of His Poetry, 1990; featured poet Words-Music-Words, N.Y.C. and Bklyn., 1985; contbr. poetry, fiction, drawings and transls. to jours. Fellow Nat. Endowment for the Arts, 1992; grantee Wheatland Found., 1992; recipient Renato Poggioli award PEN Am. Ctr., 1980, Disting. Transl. award Am. Lit. Translators Assn., 1994. Democrat. Home: 55 W 11th St New York NY 10011 E-mail: nsmacafee@earthlink.net.

MACAFEE, SUSAN DIANE, reporter; b. Feb. 1944; Attended, Foothill Coll. Disc jockey with news, pub. affairs; engr., editor, prodr. Sta. KZSU-Stanford U., Calif., 1975-80; freelance reporter, broadcast journalist, 1975—. Writer, prodr., engr. editor, narrator 25 original nationwide news stories and furnished story material for numerous radio stas. and networks, TV stas. including NPR, Pacifica, ABC, NBC and CBS networks, BBC radio and TV, Channel 9 Australia, numerous newspapers and magazines; rschr., documentor and author: Agent Orange Pilot Nutritional Detox Program, 1986, (5-part series) Food-Diet-Crime, Behavior and Learning Disability Connection, 1986; author, prodr., engr., editor and narrator: Treatment of Refractory Eosinophilia Myalgia Syndrome Associated with the Injestion of L-Tryptophan Containing Products, Parts I and II, 1990; interviewer, recorder, transcriber: A Historical Prospective of Vitamin C With Linus Pauling, 1991; researcher, documentor, writer Postscipt: Interactions of Glutathione, Ascorbic Acid HIV and AIDS, 1992, Neural Tube Defects and Folic Acid, 1995, Chromium - A New Treatment for Adult Type II (Maturity Onset) Diabetes, 1996. The Legality and Use of Bone Wax, 1997, 1999. V.p. Calif. Coll. Young Reps., 1967; sec., asst. to Nat. Field Dir. Coll. Young Reps., Rep. Nat. Com., Washington, 1968; dir. precinct orgn. Calif. State Assembly Campaign, San Francisco Rep. Ctrl. Com., 1968. Recipient 3 Nat. awards Young Rep. Nat. Com., 1967-68. Home and Office: 334 Paseo De Golf Green Valley AZ 85614-3319

MACALISTER, ROBERT STUART, oil company executive; b. L.A., May 22, 1924; s. Robert Stuart and Iris Grace (Doman) MacA.; m. Catherine Vera Willby, Nov. 15, 1947 (dec. 1994); children: Rodney James, Sara Marjorie Pfirrmann; m. Grace V. LeClerc, Dec. 2, 1995. *Grandfather Alexander MacAlister was a noted physician in Camden, New Jersey, a member of the state medical board and personal doctor to Walt Whitman. Uncle Paul R. MacAlister was a famous architect, interior designer, and regular guest on the Today Show. Son Rodney J. is a government relations representative for Europe, Africa and the Middle East for Conoco based in London, England. His purview covers Europe, Africa, and the Middle East. He has masters degrees from Redlands University and completed one year of international studies in French at the Sorbonne. He has an English wife and two children. Daughter Sara Pfirrmann has a masters degree from the University of Denver and taught elementary school prior to having two sons. She tutors all ages in reading and math, and is an elder in her Presbyterian church. All four grandchildren are outstanding scholars in private schools.* Student, Brighton Coll., Sussex, Eng., 1945; BSME, Calif. Inst. Tech., 1947. Registered profl. engr., Tex. Petroleum engr. Shell Oil Co., 1947-56; mgmt. trainee Royal Dutch Shell, The Hague, Netherlands, 1956-57; with exec. staff, mgr. Shell Oil Co., U.S.A., 1957-68; v.p., ops. mgr. Occidental Petroleum Corp., Tripoli, Libya, 1968-71; mng. dir.various subs. London, 1971-76; mng. dir., pres. Occidental Internat. Oil, Inc., 1976-78; pres., chmn. bd. Can. Occidental Petroleum Ltd., Calgary Alberta, 1978-81; mng. dir. Australian Occidental Petroleum Ltd., Sydney, 1982-83, Hamilton Bros. Oil & Gas Ltd., London, 1983-86; petroleum cons. Camarillo, Calif., 1986—. Exec. U.K. Offshore Operators, London, 1972-78, 83-86. Cubmaster Boy Scouts Am., Larchmont, N.Y., 1964-65, scoutmaster, Houston, 1965-68. Sgt. U.S. Army, 1944-45, ETO. Mem. Am. Assn. Petroleum Geologists, Soc. Petroleum Engrs., Can. Petroleum Assn. (bd. govs. 1978-81), Las Posas Country Club, Gold Coast Srs., Caltech Torchbearer. Republican. Episcopalian. Avocations: carpentry, crafts, watercolor painting, golfing, gardening. Home and Office: 78 Lopaco Ct Camarillo CA 93010-8846

MACALPINE, MICHELLE LEWIS, neuroscientist; b. Colorado Springs, Colo., Dec. 19, 1954; d. Arthur and Erma Lewis; m. J. David MacAlpine; children: Kira, Caylan. BA, Colo. State U., 1976; MA, U. Colo., 1983; PhD, U. Tex.-Dallas, Richardson, 1998. Owner Lariat, Ft. Collins, Colo., 1983-87, Brain Tng., Plano, Tex., 1995—; trainer Lectra, Richardson, 1987-89. Author: Word Master, 1996, Treating Developmental Delays and Autistic Spectrum Disorders, 1997, 2d edit., 1998. Mem. APA, Am. Psychol. Soc. Democrat. Achievements include obtaining of 100% recovery rate in group of autistic children by promoting their cognitive development. Avocations: quilting, art. Office: Brain Tng 6913 K Ave Ste 309 Plano TX 75074 E-mail: braintrain@aol.com.

MACALUSO, FRANK AUGUSTUS, oil company executive, banker; b. Cheyenne, Wyo., May 27, 1931; s. Frank R. and Thelma Elizabeth (Speight) M.; m. Margaret Ann Lynch, Oct. 14, 1950; children: Anne Marie Macaluso Foust, Elizabeth Mary Macaluso Nance, Margaret Mary Macaluso Walters, Teresa Marie Macaluso Fleming, Frank A. Jr. BA, Regis Coll., 1950. Asst. cashier Merchants Bank, Gallup, N.Mex., 1950-52, Citizens Bank, Aztec, 1952-56; v.p. 1st Nat. Bank, Farmington, 1957-59; founder, chmn., CEO Macaluso Oil Co., 1959-2000; dir. Four Corners Savings Bank, 1969-85; organizer, chmn. bd. dirs. Sunwest Bank, 1974-97; dir. Sunwest Fin. Svcs., Albuquerque, 1988-92. Chmn. Amigo Petroleum Co., Albuquerque, 1988—; chmn. Texaco Wholesale Coun., 1994; pres., dir. Star Makers Acceptance Corp., 1994-97; founder, dir., chmn. bd. Four Corners Cmty. Bank, Farmington, N.Mex., 2000—. Mem. Gov's. Bus. Adv. Coun., N.Mex. State Bd. Fin., Santa Fe, 1970-82, 91-95, N.Mex. Energy Conversation Comm., N.Mex. 1st, Albuquerque, 1986—; bd. dirs. U. N.Mex. Found., Albuquerque, 1988-98. Named Boss of Yr. by Jaycees, 1971, Top 100 Powerbrokers N.Mex. Bus. Weekly, 2000. Mem. N.Mex. Petroleum Marketers Assn. (pres. 1974-75), N.Mex. Amigos, San Juan Country Club (pres. 1980-82), Farmington C. of C., KC, Elks. Democrat. Roman Catholic. Avocation: golf. Office: PO Box 90 2501 E Main St Farmington NM 87401-7723

MACAN, WILLIAM ALEXANDER, IV, lawyer; b. Boston, Nov. 21, 1942; s. William A. and Carol (Whitten) M.; m. Jane Mitchell Ahern, Sept. 3, 1965; children: Sandra Jane, William Andrew. BS, Haverford Coll., 1964; LLB, U. Pa., 1967. Bar: Pa. 1968, U.S. Tax Ct. 1970, N.Y. 1999. Law clk. to judge U.S. Tax Ct., Washington, 1967-69; assoc. firm Morgan, Lewis & Bockius, Phila., 1969-76; ptnr. Morgan, Lewis & Bockius L.L.P., 1976-2000, Allen & Overy, N.Y.C., 2000—. Lectr. legal instns., seminars. Author publs. on tax-oriented equipment leasing, other tax subjects. Mem. ABA. Presbyterian. Office: Allen & Overy 1221 Ave of the Americas New York NY 10020 E-mail: william.macan@newyork.adlerovery.com.

MACARIN-MARA, LYNN, psychotherapist, consultant; b. Queens, N.Y., Feb. 27, 1948; d. David and Grace Macarin; m. Marvin Weingast, Sept. 2, 2000; 1 child, Leah Mara. MA, NYU, 1972; MSW, Hunter Sch. Social Work, 1980. Cert. psychoanalytic psychotherapy, hypnotherapy and hypnoanalysis. With Greenwich Inst. Psychotherapy and Psychoanalysis, 1984-87; pvt. practice, 1987—; pres. Face to Face Psychotherapy Svcs., Metuchen, N.J., 1987—; dir. family and children svcs. Ednl. Alliance, Inc., N.Y.C., 1990-95. Adj. prof. SUNY, Staten Island, N.Y., 1972-73, New Sch. for Social Rsch., N.Y.C., 1980-81. Contbr. articles to profl. jours. Chairperson membership com. Temple Emanu-El, Edison, N.J., 1998-2001. Mem. N.J. Soc. for Clin. Social Work (newsletter editor 1997-99). Democrat. Jewish. Avocations: traveling, dancing, writing, painting. Office: Face to Face Psychotherapy Svcs 2 Blair Ave Metuchen NJ 08840

MACARIO, ALBERTO JUAN LORENZO, physician; b. Naschel, Argentina, Dec. 1, 1935; came to the U.S., 1974, naturalized, 1980; s. Alberto Carlos and Maria Elena (Giraudi) M.; m. Everly Conway, Mar. 16, 1963; children: Alex, Everly. MD, Nat. U. Buenos Aires, 1961. Intern Ramos Mejia Hosp., Buenos Aires, 1958-60, resident, 1960, Rivadavia Hosp., Buenos Aires, 1961-62, physician-hematologist, 1962-64; fellow NRC Argentina, 1964-69; head dept. radioactive isotopes Inst. Hematol. Investigations, Nat. Acad. Medicine, 1967-69; Eleanor Roosevelt fellow Internat. Union Against Cancer, Dept. Tumorbiology, Karolinska Inst., Stockholm, 1969-71; mem. sci. staff Lab. Cell Biology NRC Italy, Rome, 1971-73; head lab. immunology Internat. Agy. Rsch. on Cancer, WHO, Lyons, France, 1973-74; rsch. scientist Brown U., Providence, 1974-76; rsch. scientist divsn. labs. and rsch. N.Y. State Dept. Health, Albany, 1976-79, chief hematology clin. lab. cr., 1979-81; dir. clin. and exptl. immunology sect. Lab. Medicine Inst., 1981-83, rsch. physician, 1981—, Wadsworth Ctr. N.Y. State Dept. Health. Prof. dept. biomed. scis. Sch. Pub. Health, SUNY, Albany, 1985—, mem. senate, 1989-94; adj. prof. pathology and lab. medicine Albany Med. Coll., 1991—; mem. structural and cell biology program Albany Univs. and Colls.; grant reviewer for nat. and internat. agys.; manuscript reviewer for sci. jours. Editor multivolume treatise Monoclonal Antibodies Against Bacteria and treatise Gene Probes for Bacteria; contbr. chpts. to books and encys. and articles to profl. jours. Recipient Diploma de Honor prize Nat. U. Buenos Aires, 1961, Bernardino Rivadavia prize Nat. Acad. Medicine Argentina, 1967, Ciencia e Investigation prize Argentinian Soc. Advancement Sci., 1967; Ford Found.-NAS travel fellow, 1968, Eleanor Roosevelt fellow, 1969. Mem. Internat. Soc. Microbial Ecology, Cell Stress Soc. Internat., Scandinavian Soc. Immunology, Italian Assn. Immunologists, French Soc. Immunology, Am. Assn. Immunologists, Am. Soc. Microbiology (sect. editor Manual of Clin. Lab. Immunology 4th and 5th edits. 1989-97), Am. Soc. Investigative Pathology, Assn. Internat. Union Against Cancer. Achievements include patents in field; discovered primary myeloperoxydase deficiency in leucocytes, and oscillations of antibody affinity during maturation of immune responses; developed method for immunologic identification of bacteria (archaea) that produce methane gas; discovered antigenic diversity of these microbes in natural and manufactured ecosystems; described structural topography of methanogenic archaea and population dynamics in granular microbial consortia; found novel multicellular forms of archaea; isolated for the first time ABC-transporter genes and the genes in the hsp70(dnak) locus from an archaebacterium (archaeon); devised and constructed the first integration vector for genetically engineering a methanogen useful for waste bioconversion; discovered a uni-celled organism with the main four chaperoning systems in its cytosol. Office: Empire State Pla Dept Health Wadsworth Ctr PO Box 509 Albany NY 12201-0509 E-mail: macario@wadsworth.org. *I am capable of walking alone, but with my wife by me, I fly. We can both ascend toward the sky and together we reach the stars. Separately, alone, who knows, we might never have been able to rise above the mountains, perhaps not even the hills, we have conquered, flapping our wings in unison.*

MACAROV, DAVID, former social work educator; b. Savannah, Ga., Nov. 20, 1918; s. Isaac and Fannie (Schoenberg) M.; m. Frieda Dee Rabinowitz, Dec. 5, 1946; children: Varda, Frances, Raanan, Annette. BSc, U. Pitts., 1951; MS, Western Res. U., 1954; PhD, Brandeis U., 1968. Dir. youth dept. Am. Zionest Coun., 1954-58; lectr. Paul Baerwald Sch. of Social Work, Hebrew U., Jersualem, 1958-65, assoc. prof., 1965-84, prof., 1984—, prof. emeritus. Author: Incentives to Work, 1970, The Short Course in Development, 1974, Work and Welfare, 1978, Quitting Time, 1982, Certain Change, 1988, Social Welfare, 1991; editor: Persistent Unemployment, 1991, Computers in the Human Services, 1990; co-editor: Social Welfare in Socialist Countries, 1992; contbr. articles to profl. jours. Founder, chmn. Joseph J. Schwartz Grad. Program for Tng. Cmty. Ctr. Dirs. and Sr. Staff, 1969-74. Sgt. USAAF, 1942-45; lt. col. Israeli Airforce, 1947-49. Mem. NASW, Internat. Assn. Sch. of Social Work, Soc. for Reduction of Human Labor (founder, chmn.). Avocations: lawn bowling, opera, folk dancing, gardening. Home: Nayot 8 93704 Jerusalem Israel E-mail: davidmacarov@huji.ac.il.

MACARTHUR, CAROL JEANNE, pediatric otolaryngology educator; b. Glendale, Calif., Aug. 23, 1957; d. Seth Gerald and Barbara Jeanne (Shaw) MacA.; m. Geoffery Buncke, Dec. 14, 1990; children: Keith Davis, Michelle Jeanne. BS, Occidental Coll., 1979; MD, UCLA, 1984. Diplomate Am. Bd. Otolaryngology. Intern U. Calif., Davis, 1984-85, resident in otolaryngology, 1985-90; fellow in pediatric otolaryngology Boston Children's Hosp., 1990-91; instr. dept. otolaryngology U. Calif.-Davis, Sacramemto, 1989-90; clin. fellow in otology and laryngology Harvard U. Med. Sch., Boston, 1990-91; asst. prof. U. Calif., Irvine, 1991—2002, asst. prof. dept. pediatrics, 1993-98, program dir. dept. otolaryngology-head and neck surgery, 1992-95; staff dept. otolaryngology Oreg. Health Scis. U., Portland, 2002—. Recipient investigator devel. award Am. Acad. Facial Plastic and Reconstructive Surgery, 1993. Fellow ACS, Am. Acad. Pediatrics; mem. Am. Soc. Pediat. Otolaryngology, Soc. for Ear, Nose and Throat Advances in Children, Am. Acad. Otorhinolaryngology-Head and Neck Surgery, Alpha Omega Alpha. Home: 4018 Canal Woods Ct Lake Oswego OR 97034 Office: Oreg Health Scis U Dept Otolaryngology 3131 SW Sam Jackson Park Rd Portland OR 97201-3011

MACARTHUR, DIANA TAYLOR, advanced technology executive; b. Santa Fe, July 7, 1933; widowed; children: Elizabeth Tschursin, Alexander Tschursin. BA, Vassar Coll., 1955. Cons. economist Checchi & Co., 1957-61; v.p., dir. Thomas J. Deegan Co., 1961-62; dep. chief West Africa Peace Corps, 1963, reg. program officer for North Africa, Near East, South Asia, 1964, dir. divsn. pvt. and internat. orgns., 1965-66; pvt. cons., 1966-74; program mgr. Aerospace Divsn. Gen Elec. Co., 1974-76; pres. Consumer Dynamics, 1977-80; v.p., dir. Dynamac Internat. Inc., 1980-88, chmn., pres., CEO, 1988—; chmn., CEO Rsch. Analysis and Mgmt. Corp., 1988-92. Pres. Fgn. Traders, Inc., 1980-86. Trustee Menninger Found., Topeka, 1972—, Lady Bird Johnson Wildflower Ctr., 1985-2001; mem. Pres.'s Com. of adv. on Sci. and Tech., 1994-01; citizens adv. bd. to the Pres. Coun. on Youth Opportunity, 1966-70; served on CSIS Strengthening of Amer. Com., 1992, The Nat. Benefits from Nat. Lab. Com., 1993, The Sr. Policy on Nat. Challenges, 1996, Geopolitics of Energy Com.; mem. The Chancellor's Adv. Coun. U. System of Md.; bd. visitors U. Md. Biotech. Inst.; adv. com. Ctr. Strategic & Internat. Studies; bd. dirs. Atlantic Coun. U.S.A.; mem. bus. adv. coun. Ctr. for China-U.S. Coop., U. Denver. Mem. Coun. on Competitiveness, Business-Higher Edn. Forum (mem. exec. com.), Tech. Coun. Md. (mem. exec. com.), Phi Beta Kappa. Office: Dynamac Internat Inc 2275 Research Blvd Rockville MD 20850-3268 E-mail: dmacarthur@dynamac.com.

MACARTNEY, NORMAN SCARBOROUGH, retired middle school educator; b. Pt. Washington, N.Y., Oct. 29, 1938; s. Horace Bramwell Macartney and Jean Sheila MacPhail; m. Armena Virginia Dolloff, June 15, 1968; children: Lisa Kimberly, Jennifer Lynn, David Cameron. Bachelor's, Colby Coll., 1961. Field geologist Core Labs., Bogota, Colombia, 1964-65; asst. geophysicist Atlantic Refining Co., Dallas, 1965-66; tchr. sci. and math. Cardigan Mountain Sch., Canaan, N.H., 1966-68, Selwyn Sch., Denton, Tex., 1968-69, Cistercian Prep. Sch., Irving, 1969-71, Rippowam Cisqua Sch., Bedford, N.Y., 1971-81, head sci. dept., 1974-81; pres., owner Dalijen Landscaping Design, Katonah, 1985-94; ret. Author: Probing the Heart, 2000. With USN, 1961-63. Mem. U.S. Master's Swimming (Top 10, 1998, nat.). Avocations: motorcycling, swimmng, writing. Home: 729 Comet Dr Beaufort NC 28516

MACAULAY, LAWRENCE A. Canadian government official; b. St. Peters Bay, Sept. 9, 1946; s. Archibald and Bernadette MacAulay; m. Frances Elaine O'Connell, Aug. 16, 1972; children: Carolyn, Rita, Lynn. Mem. House of Commons, 1988—, apptd. assoc. critic for fisheries and oceans, 1989, apptd. critic for srs. and assoc. critic for fisheries, 1990; sec. of state for vets. Govt. of Can., 1993—, min. labour, solicitor gen. of Can., 1998—. Mem. standing com. on forestry and fisheries, caucus com. on health and social devel.; acclaimed chair Atlantic Caucus, 1992. Roman Catholic. Office: House of Commons 556 Confederation Bldg Ottawa ON Canada K1A OA6*

MACAULAY, LINDA LOUISE, medical/surgical nurse, department chairman; b. Barberton, Ohio, June 16, 1949; d. Eugene Pratt and Sarah Louise (Seiler) Sines; m. Thomas II Macaulay, Mar. 19, 1945; children: Thomas III, Ann Marie. Assoc. Degree, Goldenwest Coll., Huntington Beach, Calif., 1985. RN Calif. Bd. Registered Nursing. Claims examiner Prudential Ins., Akron, Ohio, 1969—75; staff nurse Santa Anna (Calif.) Hosp., 1985—89; nurse mgr. St. Jude Mens Ctr., Fullerton, Calif., patient rep., 2001—. Mem.: Sisters in Crime (v.p. 2000—01). Democrat. Roman Catholic. Avocations: bicycling, hiking, travel, writing. Home: 5862 Lynnbrook Plz Yorba Linda CA 92886 Office: St Jude Med Ctr 108 E Valencia Mesa Dr Fullerton CA 92635 E-mail: lumac616@aol.com.

MACAULAY, RONALD KERR STEVEN, linguistics educator, former college dean; b. West Kilbride, Ayrshire, Scotland, Nov. 3, 1927; came to U.S., 1965; s. Robert Wilson and Mary Robb (McDermid) M.; m. Janet Grey, July 25, 1956; children: Harvey, Anna. MA, U. St. Andrews, 1955; PhD, UCLA, 1971. Lectr. Brit. Inst., Lisbon, Portugal, 1955-60, Brit Council, Buenos Aires, Argentina, 1960-64; asst. prof. linguistics Pitzer Coll., Claremont, Calif., 1965-67, assoc. prof., 1967-73, prof., 1973-99, dean faculty, 1980-86, prof.

emeritus, 2000—. Author: Language, Social Class and Education, 1977, Generally Speaking: How Children Learn Language, 1980, Locating Dialect in Disourse: The Language of Honest Men and Bonnie Lasses in Ayr, 1991, The Social Art: Language and Its Uses, 1994, Standards and Variation in Urban Speech: Some Examples From Lowland Scots, 1997; editor: (with R.P. Stockwell) Linguistic Change and Generative Theory, 1972, (with D. Brenneis) The Matrix of Language: Contemporary Linguistic Anthropology, 1996. Home: 317 W 7th St Claremont CA 91711-4312 Office: Pitzer Coll 1050 N Mills Ave Claremont CA 91711-6901

MACAULEY, WILLIAM FRANCIS, lawyer; b. Boston, Sept. 12, 1943; s. Bernard Joseph and Mary Louise (Dolan) M.; m. Sheila Rose Hubbard, June 29, 1968; children: Jennifer, Douglas, Leiha, Brian. AB, U. Wash., 1966; JD, Boston U., 1969. Bar: Mass. 1969, U.S. Dist. Ct. Mass. 1970, U.S. Ct. Appeals (1st cir.) 1977, U.S. Dist. Ct. R.I. 1979, U.S. Tax Ct. 1982, U.S. Dist. Ct. Conn. 1983. Assoc. Craig & Craig, Boston, 1970-74; prin. Tyler, Reynolds & Craig, 1975-78; pres. Craig and Macauley, 1979—. Contbr. articles to profl. jours. Trustee Boston U., The Raymond Found., Boston; bd. dirs. YMCA Greater Boston. Mem. ABA, Mass. Bar Assn., Boston Bar Assn. Home: 55 Buttricks Hill Rd Concord MA 01742-5314 Office: Craig and Macauley Profl Corp 600 Atlantic Ave Ste 2900 Boston MA 02210-2215 E-mail: macauley@craigmacauley.com.

MACAVOY, PAUL WEBSTER, economics, management educator, university dean; b. Haverhill, Mass., Apr. 21, 1934; s. Paul Everett and Louise Madeline (Webster) MacA.; m. Katherine Ann Manning, June 13, 1955; children: Libby, Matthew. AB, Bates Coll., 1955, LL.D., 1976; MA, Yale, 1956, PhD, 1960. Asst. to full prof. MIT, Cambridge, Mass., 1963-74, Henry R. Luce prof. pub. policy, 1974-75; mem. Pres.'s Coun. Econ. Advisers, 1975-76; prof. econs. and mgmt. Yale U., 1976-81, Beinecke prof. econs., 1981-83; dean W.E. Simon Grad. Sch. Bus. Admin. U. Rochester, 1983-91; Williams Bros. prof. Yale Sch. Mgmt. Yale U., 1992—, dean Yale Sch. Mgmt., 1992-94. Bd. dirs. Lafarge Corp. Author: Price Formation in Natural Gas Fields, 1962, (with Stephen Breyer) Energy Regulation by the Federal Power Commission, 1974, (with R. Pindyck) The Economics of the Natural Gas Shortage, 1975, The Regulated Industries and the Economy, 1979, World Crude Oil Prices, 1981, Energy Policy, 1983, Explaining Metals Prices, 1988, Industry Regulation and the Performance of the American Economy, 1992, The Failure of Antitrust and Regulation to Establish Competition in Long Distance Telephone Service Markets, 1996, The Natural Gas Market: Sixty Years of Regulation and Deregulation, 2000; editor: Ford Administration Papers on Regulatory Reform, 8 vols., 1977-78, Privatization and State-Owned Enterprise: Assessment for the United Kingdom, Canada and the United States, 1988. Home: 420 Humphrey St New Haven CT 06511-3711 Office: Yale Sch Mgmt PO Box 208200 New Haven CT 06520-8200 E-mail: paul.macavoy@yale.edu.

MACAVOY, THOMAS COLEMAN, glass manufacturing executive, educator; b. Jamaica, N.Y., Apr. 24, 1928; s. Joseph V. and Edna M. Mac A.; m. Margaret M. Walsh, Dec. 27, 1952; children: Moira Mac Avoy Brown, Ellen Mac Avoy Jennings, Christopher, Neil. BS in Chemistry, Queens Coll., 1950; MS in Chemistry, St. John's U., 1952, DSc (hon), 1973; PhD in Chemistry, U. Cin., 1952. Chemist, Charles Pfizer & Co., Bklyn., 1957-60; mgr. electronics rsch. Corning Glass Works, N.Y., 1960-64, dir. phys. rsch., 1964-66, v.p. electronic products divsn., 1966-69, v.p. tech. products divsn., 1969-71, pres., 1971-83, vice-chmn., 1983-87; prof. mgmt. grad. sch. U. Va., 1988—. Patentee in field; contbr. articles to tech. jours. Trustee Corning Mus. Glass; past pres. Boy Scouts Am. With USN, 1946; with USAF, 1952-53. Recipient Silver Antelope award Boy Scouts Am., 1976, Silver Beaver award, 1975, Silver Buffalo award, 1982, Bronze Wolf award, 1988. Roman Catholic. E-mail: tcm2m@virginia.edu.

MACBAIN, WILLIAM HALLEY, minister, theology educator, seminary chancellor; b. Cambridge, Ont., Can., Aug. 12, 1916; s. George Alexander and Grace Ann (Wilkins) MacB.; m. Mary Ann Munday, Aug. 20, 1941; children: Grace Elizabeth MacBain Silvester, Constance Marilyn MacBain Parker. Licentiate in Theology, Toronto Baptist Sem., Ont., 1939; DD (hon.), Cen. Bapt. Sem., Toronto, 1962. Ordained to ministry Bapt. Ch., 1940. Pastor, founder Temple Bapt. Ch., Sarnia, Ont., 1937-64; pastor Forward Bapt. Ch., Toronto, 1964-73; dir., gen. sec. Fellowship Fgn. Missions, 1973-81; chancellor Cen. Bapt. Sem., 1981-93, Heritage Bapt. Bible Coll. and Theol. Sem., Cambridge, Ont., Can., 1993—. Pastor emeritus Forward Bapt. Ch., Toronto, 1994—; chmn. Can. Bd. Greater Europe Mission, 1963-73. Mem. Fellowship Evang. Bapt. Chs. in Can. (pres. 1953-54, 83-84) Conservative. Home: 35 Wynford Heights Cres Apt 2603 Don Mills ON Canada M3C 1L1 Office: Heritage Bapt Bible Coll and Theol Sem 175 Holiday Inn Dr Cambridge ON Canada N3C 3T2

MACBETH, ANGUS, lawyer; b. L.A., May 9, 1942; BA, Yale U., 1964, LLB, 1969. Bar: N.Y. 1970, D.C. 1981. Law clk. to Hon. Harold R. Tyler, Jr. U.S. Dist. Ct. (so. dist.) N.Y., 1969-70, asst. U.S. atty. criminal divsn., 1975-77; chief pollution control sect. Land and Natural Resources Divsn., U.S. Dept. Justice, 1977-79, dep. asst. atty. gen., 1979-81; ptnr. Sidley, Austin, Brown & Wood, Washington. Adj. prof. law N.Y. Law Sch., 1985—; spl. counsel Wartime Relocation and Internment Civilians Commn., 1981-83. Mem. D.C. Bar (steering com. energy and natural resources divsn. 1982-84), N.Y. State Bar Assn. (exec. com. sect. environ. law 1981—), Phi Beta Kappa. Office: Sidley Austin Brown & Wood 1501 K St Washington DC 20005

MACBETH, LYNN ELLEN, lawyer; b. Bethlehem, Pa., Mar. 21, 1955; d. James Bart MacBeth and Dolores Lucille (Baab) Fredericks; m. Stephen J. Scholze, June 3, 1978 (div. Oct. 1983); 1 child, Zachary; m. James M. Kelly, Jan. 15, 1988; children: Barney, Toby. BA in English, Chatham Coll., 1977; JD, U. Pitts., 1982. Bar: Pa. 1983, U.S. Dist. Ct. (we. dist.) Pa. 1983. Assoc. Koegler & Tomlinson, Pitts., 1983-88, Weiler & Weiler, Pitts., 1989-92, Pillar Mulroy & Ferber, Pitts., 1992-97. Law clk. Ct. Common Pleas Allegheny County, Pitts., 1986-88; mediator Family Mediation Coun. We. Pa., Pitts., 1993—, bd. dirs., sec., 1997—. Author: (manuals) Effective Family Law Practice, 1996, Child Custody in Pennsylvania: the Substantive Law for Mediators, 1997, Paralegals in Family Law Practice, 1997, Probate: Beyond the Basics, 1997, (workshop) The Attorney's Role in Mediation, 1998, Who's Ready for Mediation? Assessment and Intervention for Client Readiness, 1999; contbr. articles to profl. jours. Vol. Children's Hosp. Pitts., 1995-96. Mem. ABA, Allegheny County Bar Assn. Avocations: French language and culture, cooking. Home: 211 Highland Rd Pittsburgh PA 15235-3010 Office: Ste 1301 310 Grant St Pittsburgh PA 15219-2207

MACCALLUM, LORENE (EDYTHE MACCALLUM), pharmacist; b. Monte Vista, Colo., Nov. 29, 1928; d. Francis Whittier and Berniece Viola (Martin) Scott; m. David Robertson MacCallum, June 12, 1952; children: Suzanne Rae MacCallum Barslund and Roxanne Kay MacCallum Batezel (twins), Tracy Scott, Tamara Lee MacCallum Johnson, Shauna Marie MacCallum Bost. BS in Pharmacy U. Colo., 1950. Registered pharmacist, Colo. Pharmacist Presbyn. Hosp., Denver, 1950, Corner Pharmacy, Lamar, Colo., 1950-53; rsch. pharmacist Nat. Chlorophyll Co., Lamar, 1953; relief pharmacist, various stores, Delta, Colo., 1957-59, Farmington, N.Mex., 1960-62, 71-79, Aztec, N.Mex., 1971-79; mgr. Med. Arts Pharmacy, Farmington, 1966-67; cons. pharmacist Navajo Hosp., Brethren in Christ Mission, Farmington, 1967-77; sales agt. Norris Realty, Farmington, 1977-78; pharmacist, owner, mgr. Lorene's Pharmacy, Farmington, 1979-88; tax cons. H&R Block, Farmington, 1968; cons. Pub. Svc. Co., N.Mex. Intermediate Clinic, Planned Parenthood, Farmington; first woman registered pharmacist apptd. N.Mex. Bd. Pharm., 1982-92. Author numerous poems for mag. Advisor Order Rainbow for Girls, Farmington, 1975-78. Mem. Nat. Assn. Bds. Pharmacy (com. on internship tng., com. edn., sec., treas. dist. 8, mem. impaired pharmacists adv. com., chmn. impaired pharmacists program N.Mex., 1987—, mem. law enforcement legis. com., chmn. nominating com. 1992), Nat. Assn. Retail Druggists, N.Mex. Pharm. Assn. (mem. exec. coun. 1977-81), Order Eastern Star (Farmington). Methodist. Home and Office: 75 Trew Creek Rd Durango CO 81301-8307 *Personal philosophy: Live life to the fullest, make every minute count. Enjoy yourself--it's later than you think.*

MACCARIO, MAURICE MALCOLM, oral and maxillofacial surgeon, consultant; b. Newark, Jan. 17, 1942; s. Melchiorre Malcolm and Susan (Bocchino) M.; m. Rosemarie Agnes Nocera; children: Lenora, Marcus. BA, Villanova U., 1964; DDMedicine, Fairleigh Dickinson U., 1968. Diplomate Am. Bd. Oral and Maxillo Facial Surgery. Intern Bklyn. Jewish Hosp., 1969; resident Bklyn. Vets. Hosp., 1970; chief resident Bklyn. Cumberland Med. Ctr., 1971; sr. registrar North Staffordshire Royal Infirmary, Eng., 1971-72; tchr. oral surgery Bklyn. Hosp., 1972-82; pvt. practice, Oakland, N.J., 1972—; mem. staff Valley Hosp., Ridgewood, 1971—, dir. oral surgery NJ, 1980—87, chief and dir. oral surgery, 1999—. Cons. St. Joseph Hosp., Paterson, N.J., 1971—. Contbr. articles to profl. jours. V.p. Oakland (N.J.) Rep. Club., 1986-88. Fellow Am. Assn. Oral and Maxillofacial Surgeons, Oral Surgery Soc. N.J., Am. Mensa Soc. Roman Catholic. Avocation: private pilot. Home: 160 Long Hill Rd Oakland NJ 07436-3113 Office: 180 Ramapo Valley Rd Oakland NJ 07436-2524 Address: 103 St Martin Dr Palm Beach Gardens FL

MACCARONE, FRANCES MARY, publishing executive; b. Bklyn., June 20, 1945; d. Cosmo Mitrano and Mary Theresa Coraggio; m. Joseph Maccarone, Jan. 8, 1966; children: Jolene, Anthony. Grad. H.S., Babylon (N.Y.) H.S., Babylon, N.Y., 1963. Telemarketer Daily News, Holtsville, N.Y., 1975-76; subscriptions Ronkonkoma (N.Y.) Review, 1976-78, advtsg. sales rep., 1978-89; advtsg. sales mgr. Fire Island Tide, Bohemia, N.Y., 1984-89; advtsg. sales rep. Smithtown (N.Y.) Messenger, 1988-89; pub. Our Place Newspapers, Ronkonkoma, 1989—. Fundraiser Lake Nutrition Meals on Wheels, Ronkonkoma, 1991—. Recipient Cert. Appreciation Lake Rep. Club, 1992, Brookhaven Town Bd., 1992, Edward Romaine County Clk., 1992, Proclamation Steve Levy county legislator, 1996, Ronkonkoma C. of C. Heart and Soul awards plaque, 1997. Mem. Ronkonkoma C. of C. (bd. dirs. 1989—, publicity, head com. Easter, Halloween, Memorial Day, Christmas, Labor Day, Cert. Appreciation 1994, 97, Heart & Soul award 1997), Holbrook C. of C. (pres. 1995-96, plaque 1996, bd. dirs. 1991—, publicity, head com. Easter, Halloween, Memorial Day, Heart and Soul Dinner Dance, Little Mr. and Miss awards; Mem. of Yr. award), Brookhaven Coalition C. of C. (Mem. of Yr. award 1999). Roman Catholic. Avocations: chess, baseball, football. Office: Our Place Newspapers PO Box 346 Bohemia NY 11716-0346 E-mail: ourplace20@aol.com.

MACCARTHY, TALBOT LELAND, civic volunteer; b. St. Louis, Jan. 28, 1936; d. Austin Porter Leland and Dorothy (Lund) Follansbee; m. John Peters MacCarthy, June 21, 1958; children: John Leland MacCarthy, Talbot MacCarthy Payne. BA, Vassar Coll., 1958. Sec., treas. Station List Pub. Co., St. Louis, 1975-85, pres., 1985-90. Hon. trustee Robert E. Lee Meml. Assn., Arts and Edn. Coun. Greater St. Louis, pres., 1978-80, emerita; past vestry mem. St. Michael and St. George Ch., 1997-00; past trustee St. Louis Art Mus., St. Louis Merc. Libr. Assn., Family & Children's Svc. Greater St. Louis, Health and Welfare Coun., Greater St. Louis, Jr. Kindergarten St. Louis Page Park YMCA, Scholarship Found. St. Louis, Friends St. Louis Art Mus. Bd., Ch. St. Michael and St. George Sch. Bd., Mid-Am. Arts Alliance; chmn. Mo. Arts Coun., 1980-85; past chmn. Vol. Action Ctr. Greater St. Louis; past vice chmn. bd. dirs. Mary Inst.; past pres. Jr. League St. Louis; mem. Nat. Coun. Arts, 1985-91; mem. nat. coun. for Sch. of Art Washington U. Recipient Woman of Achievement citation St. Louis Globe Democrat, 1979, Mo. Citizens for Arts/Arts Advocacy award, 1987, Mo. Arts Award, 1993. Mem. Vassar Club St. Louis (past pres.), Mary Inst. Alumnae Assn. (past pres.), Colonial Dames Am., Garden Club St. Louis. Republican. Episcopalian. Avocations: tennis, visual arts, performing arts.

MACCARTHY, TERENCE FRANCIS, lawyer; b. Chgo., Feb. 5, 1934; s. Frank E. and Catherine (McIntyre) MacC.; m. Marian Fulton, Nov. 25, 1961; children— Daniel Fulton, Sean Patrick, Terence Fulton, Megan Catherine BA in Philosophy, St. Joseph's Coll., 1955; JD, DePaul U., 1960. Bar: Ill. 1960, U.S. Dist. Ct. (no. dist.) Ill. 1961, U.S. Ct. Appeals (7th cir.) 1961, U.S. Supreme Ct. 1966. Assoc. prof. law Chase Coll. Law, Cin., 1960-61; law clk. to chief judge U.S. Dist. Ct., 1961-66; spl. asst. atty. gen. Ill., 1965-67; exec. dir. Fed. Defender Program, U.S. Dist. Ct. (no. dist.) Ill., Chgo., 1966—. Mem. nat. adv. com. on criminal rules; 7th cir. criminal jury instrn. com.; chmn. Nat. Defender Com.; chmn. bd. regents Nat. Coll. Criminal Def.; faculty Fed. Jud. Ctr., Nat. Coll. Criminal Def., Nat. Inst. Trial Advocacy, U. Va. Trial Advocacy Inst., Harvard Law Sch. Trial Advocacy Program, Western Trial Advocacy Inst., Northwestern U., U. Ill. Defender Trial Advocacy course, Nat. Criminal Def. Coll., Loyola U. Trial Advocacy Program; lectr. in field Contbr. articles on criminal law to profl. jours. Bd. dirs. U.S.O. Served as 1st lt. USMC, 1955-57 Recipient Nat. Legal Aid and Defender Assn./ABA Reginald Heber Smith award, 1986, Alumni Merit award St. Joseph Coll., 1970, Cert. of Distinction USO, 1977, Harrison Tweed Spl. Merit award Am. Law Inst./ABA, 1987, Bill of Rights award Ga. chpt. ACLU, 1986, William J. Brennan award U. Va., 1989, Alumni Svc. award DePaul U. Coll. Law, 1994, Ann. Significant Contbns. award Calif. Attys. for Criminal Justice, Defender of the Century Fed. Defenders Assn., Inns of Ct. and Ct. of Appeals (7th cir.) Professionalism award; named to Outstanding Young Men of Am., 1970. Mem. ABA (past chmn. criminal justice sect., ho. of dels., bd. govs., Charles English award criminal justice sect.), Ill. Bar Assn., Chgo. Bar Assn., 7th Cir. Bar Assn., Nat. Assn. Criminal Def. Lawyers (Disting. Svc. award 1993), Nat. Legal Aid and Defender Assn., Nat. Coll. Criminal Def. (chair), Union League of Chgo. (pres.). Democrat. Roman Catholic. Office: US Dist Ct No Dist Ill 55 E Monroe St Ste 2800 Chicago IL 60603-5802

MACCARTHY, TIMOTHY CHARLES, association executive; b. Washington, Jan. 19, 1945; s. Shane and Anna M. MacC.; m. Marilu Elsbernd, June 7, 1969; children: Katherine Anna, Brendan Shane, Brian Timothy. BA in Polit. Sci., Wheeling Jesuit U., 1967; MS in Pub. Rels., Am. U., 1975. Legis. asst. U.S. Senator Ed Gurney, Washington, 1970-71; minority counsel govt. ops. commn. U.S. Senate, 1971-72; spl. programs coord. Nat. Park Svc., 1972-74; dir., mgr. Fed. Liaison dept. Motor Vehicle Mfrs. Assn., 1974-90; v.p., dir. Nissan N.Am., 1990-99; pres., CEO Assn. of Internat. Automobile Mfrs., Arlington, Va., 2000—. Guest lectr. Am. U. Lobbying Inst., Washington, 1995-2000, Harvard U., John F. Kennedy Sch. of Govt., 1998. Bd. trustees Cystic Fibrosis Found., Bethesda, Md., 1980—; bd. dirs. Japan-Am. Soc. of Washington, 1992-99, The Alliance of Auto Mfrs., 1999, Calif. Automotive Ind. Alliance, L.A., 1997-99; active Ams. for Free Internat. Trade Polit. Action com., Alexandria, 1992—. Lt. j.g. USN, 1967-69. Roman Catholic. Avocations: tennis, golf, jogging. Office: Assn of Internat Auto Mfrs 1001 19th St N Ste 1200 Arlington VA 22209

MACCAULEY, HUGH BOURNONVILLE, banker; b. Mt. Vernon, N.Y., Mar. 12, 1922; s. Morris Baker and Alma (Gardiner) MacC.; m. Rachael Gleaton, Aug. 30, 1943 (div. May 1980); m. Felice Cooper, Dec. 2, 1980. Student, Rutgers U., 1939-41, Tex. Christian U., 1948-50, U. Omaha, 1957-59. With 102nd Cavalry, Essex Troop N.J. Nat. Guard, 1940-42; commd. 2d lt. U.S. Army, 1943; advanced through grades to col. U.S. Army, USAF, Washington, 1943-73; v.p. Great Am. Securities, San Bernardino, Calif., 1979-94; founder., chmn. bd. Desert Cmty. Bank, Victorville, 1980-95, chmn. emeritus, 1995; account exec. Gorian Thornes, Inc., San Bernardino, 1995-96. Bd. dirs. Desert Cmty. Bank. Bd. dirs. Air Force Village West, 1986-88; chmn. bd. and CEO Gen. and Mrs. Curtis E. Lemay Found., 1987-99, chmn. emeritus, dir., 1999—. Decorated Air medal, Legion of Merit. Mem.: Daedalian Soc., Balboa Bay Club. Republican. Presbyterian. Avocation: golf. Home: 214 Golden West St Huntington Beach CA 92648 *Personal philosophy: Whatever the game play by the rules.*

MACCHIA, ANTHONY FRANCIS, economist, management consultant; b. N.Y.C., Dec. 21, 1952; s. Frank and Stella M.; m. Irene Leung, Sept. 11, 1982. BA in Econs., SUNY-Stony Brook, 1973, B Engring., 1973; PhD, U. Pa., 1979. Economist, Office of Sec., Dept. Interior, Washington, 1976; instr. Wharton Sch.-Fels Ctr., U. Pa., Phila., 1977-78; sr. economist, antitrust div. Dept. Justice, Washington, 1979-81; mem. Atty. Gen.'s AT&T Relief Task Force, Washington, 1980-81; sr. assoc. Mgmt. Analysis Ctr., Washington, 1981-83; pres. Macchia & Co., Phila., 1983— ; chief cons. mergers, acquisitions and bus. disputes Japanese and U.S. cos. Author: The Hospital and the Industrial Organization of the Hospital Market, 1979, The Challenges of a New Era: Competitive Strategy, Value Creation and Securitization, 1987, The Securitization of Real Estate: Strategies for Investment Banking, 1987; mem. bd. contbg. editors The Real Estate Fin. Jour., 1987—. Wharton-Fels fellow U. Pa., 1973-77; recipient U.S. Atty. Gen.'s Spl. Achievement award Dept. Justice, 1980. Fellow Tau Beta Pi; mem. Am. Econ. Assn., Am. Fin. Assn., Omicron Delta Epsilon. Roman Catholic. Home: 1520 Spruce St Apt 602 Philadelphia PA 19102-4507 Office: Macchia & Co 1411 Walnut St Ste 200 Philadelphia PA 19102-3129

MACCHIA, FRANK JOHN, composer, musician; b. San Francisco, Oct. 12, 1958; s. Frank John Macchia and Dolores Catherine Gardner; m. Tracy Stuperus London, Sept. 26, 1993; 1 child Charles Stephen ; m. Ruth Berit Vaage. MusB in Composition, Berklee Coll. Music, 1980. Instrumeentalist/woodwinds Brian Wilson, Van Dyke Parks, L.A., 1993—99; orchestrator Mark Isham, Larry Groupe, 1997—2001, George S. Clinton, John Ottman, L.A., 1997—2001; condr., arranger World St. Awards/ABC TV, 2001; film and TV composer various networks and studios, 1992—. Author, composer, prodr.: audio books Little Evil Things, Vols. 1-5, 1997—2001, composer, prodr.: music CD Introducing Freddie Maximum, 1989, composer, prodr.: music CD Frankie Maximum Goes Way Out West, 1991. Recipient Mercer Elllington award, Berklee Coll. Music, 1979, DB Composer award, Down Beat mag., 1979; grantee, Nat. Endowment for Arts, 1980. Avocations: technology, horror fiction, animation. Home and Office: 1801 N Lima St Burbank CA 91505-1527

MACCHIA, VINCENT MICHAEL, lawyer; b. Bklyn., Dec. 30, 1933; s. Vincent and Lina Rose (Cewli) M.; m. Irene Janet Audino, Feb. 27, 1965; children: Lauren, Michele, Michael. BS, Fordham U., 1955, LLB, 1958; LLM, NYU, 1967. Bar: N.Y. 1958. Assoc. Bernard Remsen Millham & Bowdish, N.Y.C., 1959-60; atty. Equity Corp., 1961-63, Pfizer Inc., N.Y.C., 1964, TWA, N.Y.C., 1964-66; mem. Gifford, Woody, Palmer & Serles, 1966-85, Townley & Updike, N.Y.C., 1985-90; of counsel Smith, Don, Alampi, Scala & D'Argenio, Ft. Lee, N.J., 1990-91; counsel Tenzer, Greenblatt, LLP, N.Y.C., 1991-2000, Diamant, Katz Kahn & Co. LLP, N.Y.C., 2000—. Dir. Hudson Rev., Inc. Mem. editl. staff Fordham Law Rev., 1956-58. With USAR, 1958-64. Mem. ABA, N.Y. State Bar Assn. Republican. Roman Catholic. Home: 4 Greentree Dr Scarsdale NY 10583-7014

MACCHIAROLA, FRANK JOSEPH, academic administrator, educator; b. N.Y.C., Apr. 7, 1941; s. Joseph John and Lucy (Bernardo) M.; m. Mary Teresa Collins, June 13, 1970; children: Joseph John, Michael Collins, Frank Joseph. BA, St. Francis Coll., 1962, L.H.D. (hon.), 1981; LL.B., Columbia U., 1965, PhD, 1970; L.H.D. (hon.), Coll. S.I., 1983; LL.D. (hon.), Dominican Coll., 1983, Manhattan Coll., 1983, St. Joseph's Coll., Molloy Coll., 1999. From fellow to prof. polit. sci. CUNY, 1964-83, v.p., 1977-78; asst. v.p. Columbia U., N.Y.C., 1973-74; dep. dir. N.Y. State Emergency Fin. Control Bd. for N.Y.C., 1976-77; chancellor of schs. N.Y.C. Public Sch. System, 1978-83; pres., chief exec. officer N.Y.C. Partnership, Inc., 1983-87; pres. Acad. of Polit. Sci., 1987-91; prof. bus. Columbia U., N.Y.C., 1987-91; dean Benjamin N. Cardozo Sch. of Law, Yeshiva U., 1991-96; of counsel Tannenbaum, Helpern, Syracuse and Hirschtritt, 1991—; pres. St. Francis Coll., N.Y., 1996—. Bd. dirs. Jeffries Group Inc.; trustee Manville Personal Injury Settlement Trust. Mem., pres. Community Sch. Bd. 22, N.Y.C., 1973-78. Decorated cavalieri Order of Merit Italy; recipient cert. of merit Dirigible Soc. Am., 1976 Democrat. Roman Catholic. Office: 900 3rd Ave New York NY 10022-4728 also: 180 Remsen St Brooklyn NY 11201-4305 E-mail: fmacchia@stfranciscollege.edu.

MACCINI, LOUIS JOHN, economic educator; b. Cambirdge, Mass., Aug. 3, 1942; s. Joseph and Jennie (Leccacorvi) M.; m. Carol Monterisi, June 25, 1965; children: Michael S., Sharon L. BS in Economics, Boston Coll., 1965; PhD in Economics, Northwestern U., 1970. From asst. prof. to assoc. prof. economics The Johns Hopkins U., Balt., 1969-86, prof., 1986—, chair, 1992—. Ad hoc com. mem. graduate fin. aid, Johns Hopkins U., editorial bd., public interest investment adv. com., law sch. com., med. sch. com., and other coms.; mem. recruting chair dept. grad. student advisor dept., and other depts. Referee Am. Econ. Review, Jour. Econ. Dynamics and Control, Oxford Econ. Papers, and others; contbr. articles to profl. jours. Grantee NSF. Mem. Am. Econ. Assn., The Econometric Soc., Internat Soc. Inventory Rsch. Office: Johns Hopkins U 3400 N Charles St Baltimore MD 21218-2680 E-mail: maccini@jhu.edu.

MACCLEAN, WALTER LEE, dentist; b. Sheridan, Wyo., July 10, 1935; s. Edward Satterlee and Eleanor Elizabeth (Weir) Mac.; m. Nancy Lee Strale, Sept. 4, 1965 (div. 1975); children: David Satterlee, Carrie Lynn. BS with honors, U. Wyo., 1957, postgrad., 1958; DMD, U. Oreg., Portland, 1962. Mil. dental adv. Korean Mil. Adv. Group, Wonju, 1962-63; chief dental svc. Dugway Chem. Testing Ctr., Utah, 1965-68; pvt. dental practice Cheyenne, Wyo., 1968-70; assoc. prof. Sheridan Coll., 1970-76; staff dentist VA Hosp. Med. Ctr., Ft. Meade, S.D., 1976-93; ret., 1993. Cons., lectr. Health Edn. Program Svc., Ft. Meade, 1984-93. With U.S. Army 1962-68. Mem. ADA. Seventh-Day Adventist. Home: PO Box 450 Hardin MT 59034-0450 also: Highbourne House 13 15 Marylebone High St London W1M 3PE England

MACCOBY, ELEANOR EMMONS, psychology educator; b. Tacoma, May 15, 1917; d. Harry Eugene and Viva May (Johnson) Emmons; m. Nathan Maccoby, Sept. 16, 1938 (dec. Apr. 1992); children: Janice Carmichael, Sarah Maccoby Blunt, Mark. BS, U Wash., 1939; MA, U. Mich., 1949, PhD, 1950. Study dir. div. program surveys USDA, Washington, 1942-46; study dir. Survey Rsch. Ctr. U. Mich., Ann Arbor, 1946-48; lectr., rsch. assoc. dept. social rels. Harvard U., Cambridge, Mass., 1950-58; from assoc. to full prof. Stanford (Calif.) U., 1958-87, chmn. dept. psychology, 1973-76, prof. emeritus, 1987—. Author: (with R. Sears and H. Levin) Patterns of Child-Rearing, 1957, (with Carol Jacklin) Psychology of Sex Differences, 1974, Social Development, 1980, (with R.H. Mnookin) Dividing the Child: Social and Legal Dilemmas of Custody, 1992, (with Buchanan and Dombusch) Adolescents after Divorce, 1996, The Two Sexes: Growing Up Apart, Coming Together, 1998; editor: (with Newcomb and Hartley) Readings in Social Psychology, 1957, The Development of Sex Differences, 1966. Recipient Gores award for Excellence in Teaching Stanford U., 1981, Disting. Contbn. to Ednl. Research award Am. Ednl. Research Assn., 1984, Disting. Sci. Contbn. to Child Devel. award Soc. for Research in Child Devel., 1987, Disting. Sci. Contbns. award Am. Psychol. Assn., 1988; named to Barbara Kimball Browning professorship Stanford U., 1979—. Fellow APA (pres. Divsn. 7, 1971-72, G. Stanley Hall award 1982), Soc. for Rsch. in Child Devel. (pres. 1981-83, mem. governing coun. 1963-66, Am. Psychol. Soc.; mem. NAS, AAAS, Am. Acad. Arts and Scis., Inst. Medicine, Western Psychol. Assn. (pres. 1974-75), Inst. for Rsch. on Women and Gender, Social Sci. Rsch. Coun. (chmn. 1984-85), Consortium of Social Sci. Assns. (pres. 1997-98), Am. Psychol. Found. (Life Achievement award 1996). Democrat. Home: 729 Mayfield Ave Palo Alto CA 94305-1016 Office: Stanford U Dept Psychology Stanford CA 94305-2130

MACCOLL, J. A. lawyer; b. Evanston, Ill., July 29, 1948; BA, Princeton U., 1970; JD, Georgetown U., 1973. Bar: Md. 1974, U.S. Dist. Ct. Md. 1974, U.S. Ct. Appeals (4th cir.) 1974. Asst. U.S. atty. Dist. Md., 1978—81; ptnr. Piper & Marbury; v.p., gen. counsel U.S. Fidelity & Guaranty Corp., Balt., 1987—91, sr. v.p., gen. counsel, 1991—95, exec. v.p. dept. human resource, gen. counsel, 1995—98; exec. v.p., gen. counsel The St. Paul Cos., Inc., 1998—2002, vice chmn., gen. counsel, 2002—. Editor-in-chief Georgetown Law Jour., 1972-73. Office: The St Paul Cos Inc 5801 Smith Ave Baltimore MD 21209-3611

MACCOLL, ROBERT, research scientist, biomedical educator; b. Bklyn., Mar. 27, 1942; s. Robert and Mildred P. (Lanigan) MacC.; children from previous marriage: Robert Michael, Daniel, Laurie Claire; m. Charlotte V. MacColl, 1992. BA, Queens Coll., 1963; MS, U. Miss., University, 1967; PhD, Adelphi U., 1969. Postdoctoral work Wadsworth Ctr. N.Y. State Dept. Health, Albany, N.Y., 1969-70; rsch. scientist Wadsworth Ctr., N.Y. State Dept. Health, 1970—, chief lab. biophysics, 1986-91, dir. biochemistry core, 1991—. Prof. biomed. scis. SUNY, Albany, 1989-2001. Author: Phycobiliproteins, 1987; contbr. articles to profl. jours. Mem. Am. Chem. Soc. Republican. Roman Catholic. Avocations: reading, baseball. Home: 682 Myrtle Ave Albany NY 12208-3331 Office: NY State Dept Health Wadsworth Ctr Empire State Plz PO Box 509 Albany NY 12201-0509

MAC CORMAC, EARL RONALD, retired education educator; b. N.Y.C., Apr. 26, 1935; s. Earl Copeland and Katherine Kissel MacC.; m. Nancy Hamilton, Aug. 23, 1958; children: Ann F., Susan H. B Engring., Yale U., 1955, MA, 1959, PhD, 1961. Adminstrv. asst. Hazen Found., New Haven,

1958-61; Charles A. Dana Prof. of Philosophy Davidson (N.C.) Coll., 1961-86; Fulbright Prof. U. Madras, India, 1985-86; sci. advisor to gov. Gov.'s Office, Raleigh, N.C., 1986-92; pres. N.C. Quality Leadership Found., 1992-94; cons. prof. of radiology Duke U. med. Ctr., Durham, N.C., 1994—. Adj. prof. indsl. engring. N.C. State U., Raleigh, 1986-92; exec. dir. N.C. Bd. Sci. and Technology, Raleigh, 1986-92; mem. kuratorium Wissenschaftszentrum, North-Rhine Westphalia, 1991—; nat. Fulbright selection com. Inst. of Internat. Edn., N.Y., 1984-87. Author: (books) Metaphor and Myth in Science and Religion, 1976, A Cognitive Theory of Metaphor, 1985, Myths of Science and Technology, 1986; co-author: Decision Analysis Applied to Electrical Rate Design, 1985; co-editor: (book) Fractals in Brain, Fractals in Mind, 1995; editl. bd. John Benjamins Pubs., 1998—. Bd. dirs. Alt. Energy Corp., N.C., 1989-92; adv. bd. N.C. Solar Ctr., Raleigh. Named Outstanding Engring. Student, ASME, 1955; recipient Jefferson award for Tchg., McConnell Found., Davidson, 1971. Mem. N.C. Soc. for Electron Microscopy and Microbeam Analysis (hon.), Tau Beta Pi, Sigma Xi. Presbyterian. Avocations: tennis, golf. Home: 4413 Keswick Dr Raleigh NC 27609-6325 E-mail: emaccormac@aol.com.

MACCORMACK, GEORGE F. pharmaceutical executive; b. Mass., 1943; m. Deborah MacCormack. BS, Northeastern U., 1966, MS in Chem. Engring., 1968; MBA, U. Del., 1973. Dir. ops. for Specialty Chemicals DuPont, 1995—96; v.p., gen. mgr. DuPont Specialty Chemicals, 1996—98, DuPont White Pigment & Mineral Products, 1998—99; group v.p. polyester enterprise DuPont, 1999—2000, group v.p. chemicals and polyester, 2000—02; group v.p. DuPont Textiles & Interiors, 2002—. Office: DuPont Corp Info Ctr Barley Mill Plz PIO Wilmington DE 19880-0010*

MAC CREADY, PAUL BEATTIE, aeronautical engineer; b. New Haven, Sept. 29, 1925; BS in Physics, Yale U., 1947; MS, Calif. Inst. Tech., 1948, PhD in Aeros. cum laude, 1952. Founder, pres. Meteorology Rsch. Inc., 1955—70, Atmospheric Rsch. Group, 1958—70; founder AeroVironment Inc., Pasadena, Calif., 1971, CEO, chmn., 1994, chmn., 1994—. Leader team that developed Gossamer Albatross for human-powered flight across English Channel, 1979; leader devel. team Solar Challenger, ultralight aircraft powered by solar cells, 1981, GM-Sunraycer, 1987, GM-Impact, 1990; cons. in field, 1951—; mem. numerous govt. tech. adv. coms. Contbr. articles to profl. jours. Named Aerospace laureate, Aviation Week and Space Tech.; named one of 20th Century's Greatest Minds, Time Mag.; named to Aviation Week Hall of Fame; recipient Collier trophy, Nat. Aero. Assn., 1979, Edward Longsreth medal, Franklin Inst., 1979, Engr. of Century gold medal, ASME, 1980, Ralph Coats Roe medal, 1998, Gold Air medal, Fedn. Aero. Internat., 1981, Inventor of Yr. award, Assn. Advancement Innovation and Invention, 1981, Blue Sky merit award, CALSTART, 1998, Howard Hughes Meml. award, Aviation Club So. Calif., 1999, Spl. Achievement award, Design News, 1999. Mem.: NAE, AIAA (Reed Aero. award 1979), Am. Meteorol. Soc. (chmn. com. atmospheric measurements 1968—69, councillor 1971—74), Am. Acad. Arts and Scis. Office: Aerovironment Inc PO Box 5031 1610 S Magnolia Dr Monrovia CA 91016 Office Fax: 626-357-9628.*

MACCULLAGH, BRUCE SCOTT, fund raiser, software designer; b. Zumbrota, Minn. BA, Marietta Coll., 1984. Transp. coord. NCAA Divsn. III Baseball World Series, 1983-86; coord. dev. gifts and records Andover Newton Theol. Sch., Newton Center, Mass., 1987-89; software trainer Deaconess Health Sys., St. Louis, 1994-96; database mgr., grants rschr. Deaconess Found., 1996-97; fundal analyst Quodata Corp., Hartford, Conn., 1997-2000; data svcs. programmer Jenzabar Corp., 2001—. Corp. bd. dirs. United Ch. Bd. World Ministries, Cleve., 1994-2000; mem. fin. com. Silver Lake Conf. Ctr. Conn. Conf. United Ch. of Christ, Hartford, 1999-2002; treas. Litchfield N. Assn. Conn. Conf. United Ch. of Christ, 2000-2002; vol. Conn. Pub. TV, Hartford, 1997—; guide dog foster Fidelco Guide Dog Found., Bloomfield, Conn., 2000—. Mem. Assn. Fund Raising Profls.

MACDIARMID, ALAN GRAHAM, metallurgist, educator; b. Masterton, New Zealand, Apr. 14, 1927; married, 1954; 4 children. BSc, U. New Zealand, 1948, MSc, 1950; MS, U. Wis., 1952, PhD in Chemistry, 1953, Cambridge U., 1955. Asst. lectr. in chemistry St. Andrews U., 1955; from instr. to assoc. prof. U. Pa., Phila., 1955-64, Sloan fellowship, 1959-63, prof. chemistry, 1964—, Blanchard prof. chemistry. Recipient Francis J. Clamer medal, Franklin Inst., 1993, Nobel Prize in Chemistry, 2000. Mem.: Royal Soc. Chemistry, Am. Chem. Soc. Achievements include preparation and characterization of organosilicon compounds; preparation and charachterization of derivatives of sulfur nitrides and quasi one-dimensional semiconducting and metallic covalent polymers such as polyacetylene and its derivatives. Office: U Pa Dept Chemistry 231 S 34th St Philadelphia PA 19104-3803

MACDONALD, ALAN HUGH, librarian, university administrator; b. Ottawa, Ont., Can., Mar. 3, 1943; s. Vincent C. and Hilda C. (Durney) MacD.; children: Eric Paul Henry, Nigel Alan Christopher. BA, Dalhousie U., Halifax N.S., 1963; BLS, U. Toronto, Ont., 1964. With Dalhousie U., 1964-78, law librarian, 1965-67, 69-71, asst. univ. librarian, 1970-72, health sci. librarian, 1972-78, lectr. Sch. Libr. Svcs., 1969-78; with U. Calgary, Canada, 1979—, sr. advisor Info. Resources Canada, 1999—, asst. to provost Canada, 1999—, adj. prof. faculty comm. and culture, dir. info. svcs. Canada, 2000—, dir. Info Svcs. Canada, 1988—99, dir. librs. Canada, 1979-92, univ. orator Canada, 1989—; dir. U. Calgary Press, 1984—90. Chair editl. Bd. U. Calgary Press, 2001—; librarian N.S. Barristers Soc., 1969-74; mem. adv. bd. Nat. Libr. Can., 1972-76, Health Scis. Resource Ctr., Can. Inst. Sci. and Tech. Info., 1977-79; mem. Coun. of Prairie Univ. Librs., 1979-92, 97-98, chair, 1984-85, 89, 91; Bassam lectr. U. Toronto Faculty Info. Studies, 1994, Lorne MacRae lectr. Libr. Assn. Alta., 1996; mem. steering com. Alta. Libr. Knowledge Network, 1999—, steering. com. Can. Digital Libr. Rsch. Inst. Initiative, 1999-2000. Mem. editorial bd. America: History and Life (ABC-CLIO), 1985-93. Pres. TELED Cmty. Media Access Orgn., Halifax, 1972—74; mem. Minister's Com. on Univ. Affairs, Alta., 1979—83; bd. dirs. Alta. Found. for Can. Music Ctr., 1985—92, Can. Inst. for Hist. Microreprodn., 1990—98, pres., 1996—97; bd. mem. Calgary Learning Ctr., 1997—, vice-chair, 2000—. Council Library Resources fellow, 1975; exec. fellow Univ. Microfilms Internat., 1986; recipient Disting. Acad. Librarian award Can. Assn. of Coll. and Univ. Libraries, 1988, U. Toronto Faculty of Info. Studies Alumni Jubilee award, 1999. Mem.: Order of U. Calgary, Calgary Cmty. Network Assn. (bd. dirs. 1994—99, chair 1996—99), Can. Assn. Rsch. Librs. (bd. dirs. 1981—86, v.p. 1985—86), Can. Assn. Info. Sci. (pres. 1979—80), Foothills Libr. Assn., Libr. Assn. Alta. (v.p. 1988—89, Pres.' award 1992), Atlantic Provinces Libr. Assn. (pres. 1977—78), Can. Libr. Assn. (treas. 1977—79, pres. 1980—81, Award for Outstanding Svc. to Librarianship 1997), Australian Libr. and Info. Assn. (assoc.), Can. Health Libr. Assn. (life; treas. 1977—79). Office: U Calgary MLT750 2500 University Dr NW Calgary AB Canada T2N 1N4 E-mail: ahmacdon@ucalgary.ca.

MACDONALD, ALEXANDER EDWARD, meteorologist; b. Fort Snelling, Minn., Mar. 29, 1945; s. Alexander Colin and Marie Christine (Peterson) MacD.; m. Susan Hayes, June 17, 1969; children: Lee Alexander, Ann Elizabeth, Michael Hayes. BS, Mont. State U., 1967; MS, U. Utah, 1973, PhD, 1975. Meteorologist Nat. Weather Svc., Salt Lake City, 1973-80, NOAA/Forecast Systems Lab., Boulder, Colo., 1980—. Dir. NOAA Forecast Systems Lab., 1988—. Capt. USAF, 1967-71. Fellow Am. Meteorol. Soc. (exec. com. 1993-96). Home: 8554 Thunderhead Dr Boulder CO 80302-9381 Office: NOAA/ERL 325 S Broadway St Boulder CO 80305-3464 E-mail: macdonald@fsl.noaa.gov.

MACDONALD, ANDREW, entrepreneur; b. Waterbury, Conn., Apr. 14, 1958; s. James and Martha Rose (Siebert) M.; m. Diane Marie Nodine, Dec. 29, 1989; children: Duncan Andrew, Cameron Lewis, Gavin John. BA in Econ., Drew U., 1980; postgrad., Heriot-Watt U., 1996. Internal auditor, mgmt. cons. Insilco Corp., Meriden, Conn., 1982-85; product mgr., asst. contr. Stewart Stamping Corp., Yonkers, N.Y., 1985-87; dir. mktg. Stewart Connector Systems, Glen Rock, Pa., 1988-89, mng. dir. Konigstein, Germany, 1990-96; v.p. European ops. Stewart Connector Sytems, 1996; pres. Intelcap Resources, Inc., Newtown Square, Pa., 1997-99; dir. sales Amphenol CNP, Danbury, Conn., 1999—2001; v.p. Internat. Renaissance Learning, Wisconsin Rapids, Wis., 2002—. Avocations: writing, tennis, skiing, travel, astronomy. Home: 3630 Richland Hills Rd Wisconsin Rapids WI 54494

MACDONALD, CAROLYN ANN, physicist, educator; b. Santa Monica, Calif., Sept. 15, 1958; d. Harry Edward and Betty Jean (Rutter) MacDonald; m. Ross, Jr. Stewart, Aug. 18, 2001. BS, Calif. Inst. Tech., Pasadena, 1979; MS, Harvard U., 1982, PhD, 1986. Sr. programmer Abacus Computer/Rockwell Internat., Downey, Calif., 1980-81; postdoctoral fellow Harvard U., Cambridge, Mass., 1986; asst. prof. physics SUNY, Albany, 1986-94, assoc. prof., 1994-98, prof., 1998—, assoc. dir. Ctr. for X-ray Optics, 1991—. Cons. Mech. Tech., Inc., Albany, 1990-91, X-Ray Optical Sys., Inc., 1992-94; mem. adv. bd. Hudson Valley C.C., Troy, 1986-91; lectr. in field. Contbr. articles to profl. jours. IBM fellow for Women, 1979; Calif. Inst. Tech. prize scholar, 1978, others; recipient U. Faculty Rsch. award, 1993, Materials Rsch. Soc. Grad. Student award, 1986. Mem. Am. Phys. Soc. (sect. chair 1997-99), Optical Soc. Am. (chpt. v.p. 1990-91), Materials Rsch. Soc. (session chmn. 1990), Bohmische Phys. Soc., Am. Assn. Physicists in Medicine, Soc. Photo-instrumentation Engrs. (conf. chmn. 1999-2002). Achievements include establishment that crystallization in metals is not diffusion-limited by producing picosecond time-resolved crystallization measurements in metals; development of capillary x-ray optics for medical and materials analysis applications. Office: Physics Dept Suny Albany NY 12222-0001 E-mail: c.macdonald@albany.edu.

MACDONALD, DAVID RICHARD, industrial psychologist; b. Dowagiac, Mich., May 20, 1953; s. Jerrold Brewster and Shirley Ann (Shaffer) MacD.; m. Mary Elizabeth Olson, Dec. 20, 1975 (div. Sept. 5, 1995); 1 child, Sarah Ann; m. Cathleen Jean Carlson, July 25, 1996. AS, Southwestern Mich. Coll., 1973; BBA, Western Mich. U., 1975, MA, 1976, EdS, 1979; PhD, Mich. State U., 1986. Cert. Birkman Method cons. Announcer, boardman WDOW AM/FM, Dowagiac, Mich., 1969-72; mgmt. devel. specialist Interstate Motor Freight System, Grand Rapids, 1977-79; sr. mgmt. tng. instr. GTE Gen. Telephone Co. Mich., Muskegon, 1979-82; cons. human resources devel. Steelcase, Inc., Grand Rapids, 1982-86, mgr. performance devel., 1986-96, mgr. assessment process, 1996—; pres. Plectrum, Mich., 1997—. Cons., speaker in field; facilitator, program dir. Devel. Dimensions Internat., Pitts., 1981; facilitator Alamo Learning Systems, Southfield, Mich., 1983, 86, Wilson Learning Corp., Eden Prairie, Minn., 1983; job analysis program mgr. Barry M. Cohen & Assocs., Largo, Fla., 1985; asst. prof. grad. mgmt. Aquinas Coll., Grand Rapids, 1983—; asst. prof. Coll. Bus., Western Mich. U., Kalamazoo, 2001—; co-chair Internat. Congress on Assessment Ctr. Methods, 1998, mem. planning com., 1998, chair Internat. Task Force on Assessment Ctr. Guidelines, 1999—. Prodr. CD: The Historical Harpsichord, 1997. Co-chair United Way Steelcase campaign, Grand Rapids, 1986; bd. dirs. human resource com., Thresholds, Grand Rapids, Mich., 2001-04; mentor lang. skills, Madison Park Elem. Sch., Grand Rapids, 1997—. Mem. ASTD (sec. W. Mich. chpt. 1977-79), Soc. Indsl.-Orgnl. Psychology, Am. Psychol. Assn., Nat. Soc. for Performance and Instrn., Mensa, Phi Kappa Phi. Republican. Avocations: building harpsichords, stained glass, brewing, gardening, early music. Home: 2306 Prospect Ave SE Grand Rapids MI 49507-3159 Office: PO Box 1967 Grand Rapids MI 49501-1967

MACDONALD, DAVID ROBERT, lawyer, fund administrator; b. Chgo., Nov. 1, 1930; s. James Wear and Frances Esther (Wine) M.; m. Verna Joy Odell, Feb. 17, 1962; children: Martha, Emily, David, Rachel, Rebecca. BS, Cornell U., 1952; JD, U. Mich., 1955. Bar: Ill. 1955, Mich. 1955, D.C. 1983. Practiced in Chgo., 1957-74; mem. firm Kirkland, Ellis, Hodson, Chaffetz & Masters, Chgo., 1957-62, ptnr., 1962, Baker & McKenzie, Chgo., 1962-74, 77-81; asst. sec. of Treasury for enforcement, ops. and tariff affairs Dept. Treasury, Washington, 1974-76; undersec. of Navy, 1976-77; dep. U.S. Trade Rep., 1981-83; ptnr. Baker & McKenzie, Chgo., 1983-96. Bd. dirs. Mestek, Inc. (N.Y. Stock Exch.). Pres. David R. Macdonald Found., 1996—. Mem. ABA, D.C. Bar Assn., Chgo. Assn. Commerce and Industry (bd. dirs. 1977-81), Order of Coif, Econ. Club (Chgo.), Cosmos Club (Washington), Grolier Club (N.Y.C.). Home: 6605 Radnor Rd Bethesda MD 20817-6324 Office: 815 Connecticut Ave NW Washington DC 20006-4004

MACDONALD, DONALD ARTHUR, publishing executive; b. Union City, N.J., Nov. 30, 1919; s. Richard A. and Marie (McDonald) M.; m. Ruth Moran, Dec. 21, 1942; children: Ronald A., Martha J., Marie C., Donald A., Charles A. BS cum laude, NYU, 1948, MBA, 1950. Advt. sales rep. Wall St. Jour., Dow Jones & Co., Inc., N.Y.C., 1953-55, mgr. New Eng. and Can. ter., 1955-58, ea. advt. mgr., 1958-61, exec. advt. mgr., 1961-63, advt. dir. sales promotion and prodn. depts., 1963-67, v.p. advt. sales, 1970-74, sr. v.p., 1974—, also dir.; vice chmn. Dow Jones & Co. Inc., 1979—, also dir.; dir. Far Ea. Econ. Rev., Hong Kong. Chmn. coun. judges Advt. Hall of Fame, 1972-78. Author: An Arrow for Your Quiver, 1994. Capt. AUS, 1942-46, World War II. Named to Advt. Hall of Fame, 1985. Mem. Am. Advt. Fedn. (dir. 1962— , past chmn., Barton A. Cummings Gold Medal award, 1995), Advt. Fedn. Am. (past gov. 2d dist., past chmn. joint commn., past chmn.), Advt. Council (dir.), N.Y. Advt. Club (past dir., Silver medal award 1965), Beta Gamma Sigma. Clubs: Downtown Athletic (N.Y.C.), Yale (N.Y.C.); Rumson Country (N.J.). Home: 15 Buttonwood Ln Rumson NJ 07760-1045

MACDONALD, DONALD ARTHUR, JR. physician, surgeon; b. Englewood, N.J., May 9, 1955; s. Donald Arthur and Ruth Moran M.; m. Florence Twombly Childs, June 14, 1980; children: Donald, Alexandra, Margaret, Ian. BA with highest honors, Williams Coll., 1977; MD, Dartmouth U., 1980. Diplomate Am. Bd. Ophthalmology. Intern Mary Imogene Bassett Hosp., Cooperstown, N.Y., 1980-81; resident Manhattan Eye Ear & Throat Hosp., N.Y.C., 1981-84, attending physician, 1985—; fellow N.Y. Eye Ear & Throat Hosp., 1984-85; attending physician Riverview Med. Ctr., Red Bank, N.J., 1985—, chief dept. ophthalmology, 1995-97. Trustee Rumson (N.J.) Country Day Sch., 1990-96, Monmouth County Vol. Ctr., 1996-98, Horizons Program, Rumson, 1996—; trustee, bd. dirs. ALS Assn. Greater N.Y. chpt.; bd. dirs. Burden Ctr. for the Aging, 2000—. Mem. Lions, Rumson Country Club (commodore 1998—), Seabright Lawn Tennis and Cricket Club, St. Andrews Soc. N.Y. Roman Catholic. Office: 43 N Gilbert St Red Bank NJ 07701-4913 E-mail: Drdonaldmadonald@mac.com.

MACDONALD, DONALD STOVEL, corporate director; b. Ottawa, Ont., Can., Mar. 1, 1932; s. Donald Angus and Marjorie (Stovel) M.; m. Ruth Hutchison, Mar. 4, 1961 (dec.); children: Leigh, Nikki, Althea, Sonja; m. Adrian Merchant Lang, Sept. 10, 1988; stepchildren: Maria (dec.), Timothy, Gregory, Andrew, Elisabeth, Amanda, Adrian. Student, Ashbury Coll., Ottawa; BA, U. Toronto, Ont., 1951; LLB, Osgoode Hall Law Sch., 1955; LLM, Harvard, 1956; diploma internat. law, Cambridge U., 1957; LLD, St. Lawrence U., U N.B. Saint John, 1990; DEng, Colo. Sch. Mines; LLD, U. Toronto, 2000. Bar: Called to Ont. bar 1955. Assoc. McCarthy & McCarthy, Toronto, 1957-62; M.P. for Toronto-Rosedale, 1962; reelected, 1963, 65, 68, 72, 74; parliamentary sec. to Min. of Justice, 1963-65, to Min. of Finance, 1965, to Sec. of State for External Affairs, 1966-68, to Min. of Industry, 1968; pres. Privy Coun. and Govt. House Leader, 1968-70; min. of nat. def., 1970-72; min. energy, mines and resources, 1972-75; min. of fin., 1975-77; ptnr. firm McCarthy & McCarthy, Toronto, 1977-88; high commr. for Can. to U.K., 1988-91; counsel McCarthy Tetrault, Toronto, 1991-2000. Sr. advisor UBS Bunting Warburg, Toronto, 2000—; spl. lectr. U. Toronto Law Sch., 1978-82, 86-88; chmn. Royal Commn. on Econ. Union and Devel. Prospects for Can., 1982-85; chmn. adv. com. competition Ont. Electricity Sys., 1995-96; chmn. Inst. for Rsch. on Pub. Policy, Montreal, 1991-97, Siemens Can. Inc., 1991—, Atlantic Coun. of Can., 1998—; bd. dirs. Aber Diamond Corp., Boise (Idaho) Cascade Corp., The Clan Donald Lands Trust, Skye, Scotland, 1991—; chmn., trustee IPC US Income Comml. REIT, 2001--; trustee Clean Power Income Fund, 2001--. Named Freeman of the City of London, 1990, hon. fellow Trinity Hall, Cambridge U., 1994, Companion of the Order of Can., 1994. Mem. Queen's Privy Coun. Can., Delta Kappa Epsilon. Liberal. Baptist. Personal E-mail: hondon@merchantmac.com . Business E-mail: conald.macdonald@ubsw.com.

MACDONALD, ELEANOR JOSEPHINE, epidemiology educator, cancer epidemiology consultant; b. Boston, Mar. 4, 1906; d. Angus Alexander and Catharine Pauline (Boland) M. AB, Radcliffe Coll., 1928; postgrad., Harvard, 1930-36. Epidemiologist divsn. cancer Mass. Dept. Pub. Health, Boston, 1930-41; tchr. Tufts Coll. Sch. Dentistry, 1930-45, Harvard Sch. Pub. Health, 1936; epidemiologist in cancer Conn. State Dept. Health, 1941-48; epidemiologist, prof., head dept. epidemiology M.D. Anderson Cancer Hosp. and Tumor Inst. U. Tex., Houston, 1948-74, emeritus epidemiologist, 1974-82. Cons. Meml. Sloan Kettering, 1944-48, Nat. Adv. Cancer Coun., 1946-48; cancer epidemiology cons., 1982—. Co-author: (with Evelyn Heinze) The Epidemiology of Cancer in Texas 1944-1966, 1978, (with Wellington and Wolf) Cancer Mortality: Environmental and Ethnic Factors, 1979; contbr. 220 articles to profl. jours. Recipient Myron Gordon award for work on melanoma Pigment Cell Growth Assn., 1971, Disting. Alumna award Radcliffe Coll., 1973. Fellow APHA, Pub. Health Cancer Assn. (sec. 1954-64, pres. 1964-64), Am. Radium Soc.; mem. Am. Assn. for Cancer Rsch. Roman Catholic. Achievements include development of initial statewide cancer regulatory and follow-up program in Connecticut. Avocation: playing cello. Home: 2107 University Blvd Houston TX 77030-1218 E-mail: ejmacdonald@mindspring.com.

MACDONALD, ELIZABETH HELEN, bassoonist, educator; b. Lancaster, Pa., July 5, 1942; d. Joseph Harold and Verna Elizabeth (Schaeffer) Bishop; B.Mus. in Music Edn., Eastman Sch. Music, Rochester, N.Y., 1964, M.Mus. in Music Lit. and Performance, 1966; m. William Dallas MacDonald, Aug. 17, 1968. Bassoonist, Music in Maine Woodwind Quintet, Bangor, 1966-67; dir. jr. high sch. band and elem. instrumental music, Brewer, Maine, 1967-69; instr. music history, woodwind class and bassoon No. Conservatory Music, Bangor, 1967-69; tchr. jr. high sch. gen. and instrumental music, Orono, Maine, 1969-72; tutor bassoon and oboe Colby Coll., Waterville, Maine, 1972-75; instr. bassoon, woodwind ensemble coach U. Maine, Orono, 1977—; prin. bassoonist Portland (Maine) Symphony Orch., 1967-91; pvt. woodwind instr., 1972— ; recitalist, soloist, music adjudicator, 1966— . Mem. Internat. Double Reed Soc. Republican. Methodist. Home: 48 Dillingham St Bangor ME 04401-6804 Office: U Maine Lord Hall Orono ME 04473

MACDONALD, FLORA ISABEL, Canadian government official; b. North Sydney, N.S., Can., June 3, 1926; d. George Frederick and Mary Isabel (Royle) MacD. Attended Empire Bus. Coll.; grad., Nat. Def. Coll., 1972; DHL (hon.), Mt. St. Vincent U., 1979, various univs., Can., U.S. and U.K. Exec. dir. Progressive Conservative Party Hdqs., Ottawa, Ont., Can., 1957-66; adminstrv. officer, tutor dept. polit. studies Queen's U., 1966-72; mem. Can. Parliament for Kingston and the Islands, Ont., 1972-88; Progressive Conservative spokesman for Indian affairs and no. devel. Can. Parliament, 1972; for housing and urban devel., 1974; chmn. Progressive Conservative Caucus Com. on Fed.-Provincial Relations, 1976; sec. of state for external affairs, 1979-80; minister employment and immigration, 1984-86; min. comms., 1986-89; chairperson Internat. Developmental Rsch. Ctr., 1992-97; spl. adv. Commonwealth of Learning, 1990-91. Vis. fellow Ctr. for Can. Studies, U. Edinburgh, 1989; host T.V. series North South Vision T.V., 1990-94. Bd. dirs. Carnegie Commn. Re-preventing Deadly Conflict, 1994-99, Friends of the Nat. Libr., Shashtri Indo-Can. Adv. Coun.; program advisor CARE Can.; Future Generations, Franklin, W.Va., Helpage Internat., London, 1996-2001, Partnership Africa-Can., Ottawa, Can.; co-chair Can Coord. Com. UN Yr. of Older Persons, 1999; active C.O.D.E.; hon. pres. Assn. Can. Clubs, World Federalists, Can.; patron Commonwealth Human Rights Initiative. Decorated Companion Order of Can., Order of Ont. Mem. Nat. Mus. Scotland (hon. patron Can.), UN (Eminent Persons to study Trans-Nat. Corps. in South Africa 1989). Mem. United Ch. of Canada. Office: Ste 1103 350 Queen Elizabeth Drivewy Ottawa ON Canada K1S 3N1 E-mail: flora@intlanet.ca.

MACDONALD, GARY BRUCE, communications executive; b. Spokane, Wash., Apr. 17, 1950; s. William and Thelma (Wilhelm) MacD.; m. Joy Bea Fukumoto, June 1973 (div. Dec. 1980). BA, Fairhaven Coll., 1973. Fgn. svc. officer U.S. Info. Agy., Washington, 1976-84; asst. cultural attache U.S. Embassy, Rabat, Morocco, 1977-78; dir. Am. Cultural Ctr., Damascus, Syria, 1978-82; planning officer Office Acad. Programs, Washington, 1982-83; country affairs officer Office of N. African Near Eastern and South Asian Affairs, 1983-84; exec. dir. AIDS Action Coun., 1984-87; coord. Asia/Near East programs AIDSCOM Acad. Ednl. Devel., 1987-91; dep. dir. Acad. Ednl. Devel. AIDS Communication Support, 1991-93; sr. program officer social devel. programs Acad. Ednl. Devel., 1993-95, Midwest rep. Indpls., 1995—. Cons. World Bank, India, 1992—, U.S. Agy. for Internat. Devel., Washington, 1987-89, WHO, Geneva, 1987, Pan Am. Health Orgn., Mexico City, 1987, govts. of Philippines, Thailand, Indonesia, 1987-89. Editor: Five Experimental Colleges, 1973; contbr. articles to profl. jours. Clark county coord. Youth for McCarthy, Vancouver, Washington, 1968; v.p. Gay Activists Alliance, Washington, 1983-84; chmn. com. on human rels. Met. Police, Washington, 1985; pres. Indiana Youth Group, 1997-2000. Recipient Pub. Svc. award Franklin E. Kameny, 1985, Cert. of Honor City and County of San Francisco, 1986, Harvey Milk Pub. Svc. award Nat. Gay and Lesbian Health Found., 1987, Alumni Fellow award Fairhaven Coll., 1991. Office: Acad Ednl Devel 902 N Meridian St Apt 314 Indianapolis IN 46204-4047 E-mail: gmacdonald1@indy.rr.com.

MACDONALD, GORDON CHALMERS, management consultant; b. Boston, Sept. 27, 1928; s. Frank C. and Anna E. (MacLean) MacD.; m. Eileen T. Harkins, May 25, 1952; children: Brian P., Peter G., Keith A., Audrey A. AA, Boston U., 1950, BBA, 1952; grad. advanced mgmt. program, Harvard U., 1979. Grad. tng. program Westinghouse Electric Corp., Pitts., 1952-64, regional/zone mgr., 1953-60, nat. mdse. mgr. Metuchen, N.J., 1960-64; asst. to v.p. sales mgr. Magnavox Co., N.Y.C., 1964-68; v.p. mktg. GTE Corp., Batavia, N.Y., 1968-69; dir. mktg. Mitsubishi Internat. Corp., Lincolnwood, Ill., 1969-75, v.p. N.Y.C., 1975-88, sec., 1984-88, advisor, 1989-91, bd. dirs., 1976-88; prin., mgmt. cons. G.C. MacDonald & Assocs., Greenwich, Conn., 1988—. Chmn. Sea Explorers com. Boy Scouts Am., Greenwich, 1976-81. With U.S. Army, 1946-48. Mem.: U.S. Power Squadron (comdr. 1981-82, exec. com. 1987—) (Greenwich). Avocations: sailing, skiing, bridge. Home: 11 Highgate Rd Riverside CT 06878-2610 E-mail: Grampymac@snet.net.

MACDONALD, GUY ALLEN, telecommunications company executive; b. Mineola, N.Y., July 25, 1956; s. Howard Dewey and Patricia Ann Macdonald. BBA, Grove City Coll., 1978; MBA, U. Md., 1997. Arza mgr. Goodyear, Lubbock, Tex., 1978-80; store mgr. D&L Sporting Goods, 1980, silk screen mgr. Odessa, Tex., 1980-81; commd. ensign USN, 1981, advanced through grades to lt. comdr., 1992, bailer officer, drainage control officer USS Gridley, 1981-85, asst. ops. officer USS Denver, 1985-87, scheduling officer Comnansurfpac, 1987-90, ops. officer USS Fort McHenry, 1990-92, 1st lt., lt. comdr. USS Tripoli, 1992-93, staff ops. intelligence NATO Italy, 1993-98; territory mgr. GTE, Stockbridge, Mich., 1998-2000; terr. mgr. Vrerizon, Ft. Wayne, Ind., 21000—. Home: 9811 Red Twig Pl Fort Wayne IN 46804 Office: Verizon 4027 Beckwith Dr Fort Wayne IN 46808 E-mail: guy.macdonald@verizon.com.

MACDONALD, HUGH IAN, university president emeritus, economist, educator; b. Toronto, Ont., Can., June 27, 1929; s. Hugh and Winnifred (Mitchell) M.; m. Dorothy Marion Vernon, June 4, 1960; 5 children. B.Com., U. Toronto, 1952; MA, Oxford (Eng.) U., 1954, B.Phil., 1955; LLD (hon.), U. Toronto, 1974; D Univ. (hon.), The Open U. of the U.K., 1998; DLitt (hon.), The Open U. of Sri Lanka, 1999. Lectr. U. Toronto, 1955-62, asst. prof., 1962-65; dean of men U. Toronto (Univ. Coll.), 1956-65; chief economist Govt. Ont., Toronto, 1965-67, dep. treas., 1967, dep. treas., dep. minister econs., 1968, dep. treas., dep. minister econs. and intergovtl. affairs, 1972; pres. York U., Toronto, Ont., 1974-84; prof., dir. York Internat., 1984-94, prof., pres. emeritus, 1984—. Past pres. World U., Univ. Svc. Can.; past chmn. Hockey Can.; chmn. The Commonwealth of Learning. Rhodes scholar, 1952; recipient Can. Centennial medal, 1967, Queen's Silver Jubilee medal, 1977, Officer, Order Can., 1977, Commemorative medal 125th Anniv. Can. Confederation, 1992, Vanier medal for Distinction in Pub. Svc. and Excellence in Pub. Adminstrn., 2000. Office: York U Rm 226R SSB 4700 Keele St Toronto ON Canada M3J 1P3 E-mail: yorkmpa@yorku.ca.

MACDONALD, HUGH JOHN, music educator, writer; b. Newbury, U.K., Jan. 31, 1940; came to the U.S., 1987; s. Staurt Hugh and Dorothea Margaret Macdonald; m. Naomi Jane Butterworth Le Fleming, Sept. 14, 1963 (div. 1973); children: Myditsa Lucy Herz, Polly Alice Jane, Felix, Phoebe; m. Mary Elizabeth Babb, Sept. 15, 1979; 1 child, John Paxton. BA, Cambridge (Eng.) U., 1961, MA, 1966, PhD, 1969. Lectr. music Cambridge U., 1966-71, Oxford (Eng.) U., 1971-80; Gardiner prof. music Glasgow (Scotland) U., 1980-87; Avis Blewett prof. music Washington U., St. Louis, 1987—. Vis. prof. music Ind. U., Bloomington, 1979, Melbourne (Australia) U., 1995, U. Ill., Urbana,

1996. Author: Skryabin, 1978, Berlioz, 1982; editor: Selected Letters of Berlioz, 1995. Recipient Szymanowski medal Poland, 1983; fellow Royal Coll. Music, London, 1992. Office: Dept Music Washington Univ Saint Louis MO 63130

MACDONALD, J. RANDALL, information technology executive; B in Polit. Sci., M in Indsl. Rels., St. Francis Coll. Human resources position Ingersoll-Rand Co., Sterling Drug Inc.; various human resources positions GTE, 1983—2000; exec. v.p. human resources and adminstrn. Verizon Comms. (formerly GTE); sr. v.p. human resouces IBM, 2000—. Bd. dirs. Covance (formerly Corning Pharm. Svcs.); mem. Cornell U. Ctr. for Advanced Human Resources Study, chmn. exec. bd. Bd. trustees St. Francis Coll., Pa. Fellow: Nat. Acad. Human Resources (bd. dirs. 2000—); mem.: Labor Policy Assn. (vice chmn. bd. dirs.), Pers. Roundtable, Cowdrick Group. Office: IBM 1133 Westchester Ave White Plains NY 10604*

MACDONALD, JAMES KENNEDY, JR. executive search consultant; b. Providence, Mar. 6, 1956; s. James Kennedy and Virginia (Spargo) M.; m. Julie Ann Kuhn, Jan. 2, 1988. BA, Yale U., 1978; MBA, Cornell U., 1984; postgrad., N.Y. Law Sch., 1986. Tchr. Westminster Sch., Simsbury, Conn., 1978-79; systems support analyst The New Eng., Boston, 1979-82; pers./labor rels. adminstr. Nat. Broadcasting Co., Inc., N.Y.C., 1984-87; cons./assoc. Russell Reynolds Assocs., Inc., 1987-90, chief of staff, 1990-93; dir. human resources/exec. recruitment U.S. HomeCare Corp., Hartsdale, N.Y., 1993-94; v.p. Halbrecht Lieberman Assocs., Inc., Stamford, Conn., 1994-95; v.p. recruiting Primedia, Inc. (formerly K-III Comm. Corp.), N.Y.C., 1995-97; v.p. human resources Goldman Sachs & Co., 1997-99; mng. dir. Ross & Co., Southport, Conn., 2000—. Mem. dean's alumni exec. coun. The Johnson Sch.-Cornell U., 1987-89, class officer, 1989—; mem. devel. com. Stamford (Conn.) Ctr. for the Arts, 1989-91; active United Way, 1982-90, mem. chmn.'s campaign cabinet, Stamford, 1987; mem. alumni schs. com. Yale U., 1988-92; chmn. Yale Hockey Assn., 1997-99. Francis Ouimette Caddie scholar, 1974-77; The Johnson Sch.-Cornell U. scholar, 1982-84. Mem. Southwestern Conn. Area Conf. of Ind. Assns. (pres. search com. 1990, pub. policy task force 1990), Yale Club of N.Y.C. (admissions com. 1985-87). Avocations: jazz, sports, biographies.

MACDONALD, JAMES ROSS, physicist, educator; b. Savannah, Ga., Feb. 27, 1923; s. John Elwood and Antonina Jones (Hansell) M.; m. Margaret Milward Taylor, Aug. 3, 1946; children: Antonina Hansell, James Ross IV, William Taylor. BA, Williams Coll., 1944; SB, MIT, 1944, SM, 1947; PhD, Oxford (Eng.) U., 1950, DSc, 1967. Staff Digital Computer Lab., MIT, 1946-47; physicist Armour Rsch. Found., Chgo., 1950-52; assoc. physicist Argonne Nat. Lab., 1952-53; with Tex. Instruments Inc., Dallas, 1953-74, v.p. corp. rsch. and engring., 1968-73, v.p. corp. R & D, 1973-74; cons., 1974—; dir. Simmonds Precision Products Inc., 1979-83; William Rand Kenan Jr. prof. physics U. N.C., Chapel Hill, 1974-91, prof. emeritus, 1991—. Adj. prof. biophysics U. Tex. Med. Sch., Dallas, 1954-74; solid state scis. panel NRC, 1965-73; adv. com. for sci. edn. NSF, 1971-73; vis. com. physics MIT, 1971-74; external adv. com. Engring. Expt. Sta., Ga. Inst. Tech., 1976-79 Editor, contbr.: Impedance Spectroscopy-Emphasizing Solid Materials and Systems, 1987; mem. editl. bd. Jour. Applied Physics, 1984-86; contbr. over 220 articles to profl. jours. Mem. Dallas Radio Commn., 1967-71; mem. sci. adv. coun. Callier Hearing and Speech Ctr., Dallas, 1974-78; bd. dirs. League for Ednl. Advancement in Dallas, 1965-70; adv. com. Weber Rsch. Inst., 1985-90. Rhodes scholar Oxford U., 1948-50. Fellow Am. Phys. Soc. (mem. com. on edn. 1973-75, mem. com. on applications of physics 1975-78, George E. Pake prize 1985), IEEE (awards 1962, 74, assoc. editor Transactions of Profl. Group on Audio 1961-66, Transactions on Audio and Electroacoustics 1966-73, Edison Gold medal 1988), AAAS; mem. NAE (exec. com. assembly of engring. 1975-78, coun. 1971-74), NAS (chmn. numerical data adv. bd. 1970-74, mem. com. on motor vehicle emissions 1971-74, chmn. com. on motor vehicle emissions 1973-74, mem. com. on satellite power sys. 1979-81, mem. com. on sci., engring., and pub. policy 1981-83, mem. commn. on phys. scis., math., and applications 1985-88, mem. report rev. com. 1990-97), Am. Inst. Physics (mem. governing bd. 1975-78, chmn. com. on profl. concerns 1976-78), Electrochem. Soc., Audio Engring. Soc., Phi Beta Kappa, Sigma Xi, Tau Beta Pi. Achievements include 10 patents in field. Office: Univ NC Dept Physics And Astronomy Chapel Hill NC 27599-3255 E-mail: macd@email.unc.edu.

MACDONALD, JOHN THOMAS, educational administrator; b. Utica, N.Y., Nov. 21, 1932; s. Gerald Clement and Mildred (Hayes) MacD.; m. Marcia Sprague Gallup; children: Terrence (dec.), Anthony, Elizabeth, Michele, Elise, Denise. BS, Northeastern U., 1958, MEd, 1960; PhD, U. Conn., 1970. Cert. elem. and secondary sch. tchr., prin., supt., Mass., Conn. Supervising prin. Noank, Ft. Hill. and Poquonnock Elem. Schs., Groton, Conn., 1962-66, Robert E. Fitch Jr. High Sch., Groton, 1966-70; rsch. asst. Ednl. Resources and Devel. Ctr. U. Conn., Storrs, 1969-70; supt. schs. Wallingford (Conn.) Pub. Schs., 1970-73, Walpole (Mass.) Pub. Schs., 1973-78, Dartmouth (Mass.) Pub. Schs., 1978-86; commr. edn. State Dept. Edn., Concord, N.H., 1986-90; asst. sec. for elem. and secondary edn. U.S. Dept. Edn., Washington, 1990-93; dir. state leadership ctr. Coun. of Chief State Sch. Officers, 1993-99, sr. advisor, 2000-01; prof. of ednl. policy and leadership Neag Sch. Edn., U. Conn., 2001—; dir. NE Ctr. for Ednl. Policy and Leadership. Mem. Postsecondary Edn. Commn., Concord, 1986-90, Coun. for Tchr. Edn., Concord, 1986-90, Profl. Standards Bd., Concord, 1986-90; trustee Univ. System of N.H., Durham, 1986-90; mem. Surgeon Gen's Task Force, 1990-93; mem. White House Conf. on Indian Edn., 1990-93; mem. Interagy. Com. on Sch. Health, 1990-93, others; mem. dean's adv. coun. U. Conn., 1999—, Coll. Arts and Scis., Northeastern U., 1999—; mem. adv. coun. Va. Edn. Policy Inst., Va. Commonwealth U., 2000—; mem. adv. bd. ERIC, Washington, 1998—. Contbr. articles to profl. jours. Co-chmn. Emergency Sch.-Aide Proposals, U.S. Office Edn., 1973—75; mem. adv. com. external program rev. CDC, 1992—; mem. nat. adv. bd. ERIC Clearinghouse, 1999—; mem. Mass. Adv. Commn. for Ednl. TV, 1983—86, N.H. Task Force on Child Abuse, 1987—90; mem. nat. adv. coun. Northeastern U., 1990—; mem. Galaxy Classroom Nat. Adv. Coun. Galaxy Inst. for Edn., 1992—; mem. sch. health policy initiative Ctr. for Population & Family Health Columbia U., 1992—; mem. Packard roundtable to children Ctr. for Health Policy George Washington U., 1992—; mem. adv. bd. Va. Commonwealth Policy Inst., 1999—; mem. Dean's adv. council Neag Sch. Edn. U. Conn., 1999—, Coll. Arts & Scis. Northeastern U., 1999—. Recipient Sears B. Condit award, 1958, Alumni award Northwestern U., 1973, Recognition award Coun. of Chief State Sch. Officers, 1990. Fellow Phi Delta Kappa, Phi Alpha Theta; mem. N.H. Sch. Bldg. Authority, Mass. Assn. Sch. Supts. (pres. 1985-86). Office: U Conn Neag Sch Edn Dept Ednl Leadership 249 Glenbrook Rd Box U-2093 Storrs Mansfield CT 06269-2064 E-mail: macmarjack@aol.com.

MACDONALD, KAREN CRANE, occupational therapist, geriatric counselor; b. Denville, N.J., Feb. 24, 1955; d. Robert William and Jeanette Wilcox (Crane) M.; m. Geno Piacentini, Oct. 22, 1993. BS, Quinnipiac Coll., 1977; MS, U. Bridgeport, 1982; PhD, NYU, 1998. Cert. occupational therapist. Occupational therapist, coord. of spl. care unit Jewish Home for the Elderly, Conn., 1987-92, N.Y. Inst., N.Y.C., 1984-86; pvt. practice Fairfield County, Conn., 1977-88; occupl. therapist Rehab. Assocs., Fairfield, 1993-96. Instr. NYU, 1985-89, Quinnipiac Coll., 1986-92; lectr., cons. in field. Contbr. articles to profl. jours. Youth leader, deacon Union Meml. Ch., Stamford, Conn., 1980-88; deacon Southport Congl. Ch., 1992-94; chair consumer com. Alzheimer's Coalition of Conn., 1991-92. Teaching fellow NYU, 1983-86. Mem. World Fedn. Occupl. Therapy, Am. Occupl. Therapy Assn. (scholar 1985, coun. edn.), Conn. Occupl. Therapy Assn. (gerontology liaison 1980-83), NY Acad. Scis., Amer. Assn. for Advancement of Scis., Pi Lambda Theta. Avocations: poetry writing, quilting. Home: 1 Davenport St Norwalk CT 06851-4601

MACDONALD, KEN CRAIG, geophysicist; b. San Francisco, Oct. 14, 1947; m. Rachel Haymon, 1984. BS in Engring. Geoscis., U. Calif., Berkeley, 1970; PhD in Marine Geophysics, MIT/Woods Hole, 1975. Cecil H. and Ida Green postdoctoral scholar Scripps Instn. of Oceanography, 1975-76, asst. rsch. geophysicist, lectr., 1976-80; assoc. prof. U. Calif., Santa Barbara, 1980-83, prof., 1983—. Chief scientist on over 30 deep sea expeditions; prin. ALVIN diver on over 40 dives to the mid-ocean ridge. Assoc. editor Jour. of Geophys. Rsch., 1979-82, Earth and Planetary Sci. Letters, 1978-88; mem. editorial bd. Marine Sci. Revs., 1986—; editor Marine Geophys. Rschs., 1986-90; contbr. over 100 articles to profl. jours. Mem. ALVIN Rev. Com., 1979-82; mem. Ocean Sci. Bd. of NAS, 1980-83, Lithosphere Panel Advanced Ocean Drilling Project, 1983-85, Ocean Scis. Panel, NSF, 1984-86, COSOD II planning com.; mem. various RIDGE coms., RIDGE steering com., 1987-90; mem. NSF Ocean Scis. Strategic Plan for Rsch. and Edn. Com., 1993-94, U.S. Geodynamics Comm., 1997—. Regents scholar U. Calif., Berkeley, 1966-70, Mineral Tech. scholar, 1967-70, Cecil H. and Ida Green scholar Inst. Geophysics and Planetary Physics/U. Calif., San Diego, 1975-76; NSF Grad. fellow, 1970-73;recipient AAAS Newcomb-Cleveland prize, 1980, Robert L. and Bettie P. Cody prize and medal Scripps Instn. Oceanography, 1994; named U. Hawaii SOEST Disting. lectr., 1990. Fellow Am. Geophys. Union, Geol. Soc. Am.; mem. Phi Beta Kappa, Sigma Psi. Avocations: windsurfing, fly fishing. Office: U Calif Santa Barbara Dept Geol Sci Santa Barbara CA 93106 E-mail: macdonald@geol.ucsb.edu.

MACDONALD, KENNETH GORDON, JR. surgeon; b. Charleston, W.Va., Sept. 6, 1954; s. Kenneth Gordon and Ellen Nora (Cook) M.; m. Jane Ethel Miller, May 19, 1979; children: Gloria Jane, Clara Ellen, Elizabeth Jeanne. BS in Biology cum laude, Washington and Lee U., Lexington, Va., 1976; MD, W.Va. U., 1981. Diplomate Am. Bd. Surgery, Nat. Bd. Med. Examiners; lic. physician N.C.; cert. ATLS, ATLS instr. Intern in internal medicine N.C. Bapt. Hosp., Bowman-Gray Sch. Medicine, Winston-Salem, 1981-82, resident in gen. surgery, 1982-84, Pitt County Meml. Hosp./East Carolina U. Sch. Medicine, Greenville, 1984-86, chief resident in gen. surgery, 1986-87; clin. instr. surgery East Carolina U. Sch. Medicine, 1987-88, asst. prof. surgery, 1988-93, assoc. prof. surgery, 1993-2000, prof. surgery, 2000—, chief gastrointestinal surgery and surg. endoscopy, 1989—, dir. dept. surgery obesity rsch. prog., 1997—. Primary investigator FDA trial of laparoscopic adjustable silicon gastric band Bioenterics Corp., Carpinteria, Calif., 1996—; lectr. in field. Assoc. editor Current Surgery, 1990—; contbr. articles to profl. jours., chpts. to books. Mem. exec. bd. East Carolina coun. Boy Scouts Am., 1988-93, chmn. health and safety com., 1988—; participant 3d ann. corp. spelling bee Literacy Vols. of America/Pitt County, 1993. Ciba-Geigy Corp. grantee, 1993, Roerig/Pfizer Pharms. grantee. Fellow ACS (1st prize for presentation 1986), Southeastern Surg. Congress; mem. AMA, Am. Soc. Bariatric Surgery (chmn. program com., ex-officio mem. exec. coun. 1991, 92, exec. coun. 1992-95, fin. com. 1995—, pres.-elect 1995-96, pres. 1996-97), Assn. Acad. Surgery, Assn. for Surg. Edn., N.C. Med. Soc., Pitt County Med. Soc., Soc. Am. Gastrointestinal Endoscopic Surgeons, Soc. for Surgery of Alimentary Tract, Walter J. Pories Soc. (founding mem.), Sigma Xi. Avocations: golf, tennis, skiing. Office: Brody Sch Medicine East Carolina U 600 Moye Blvd Greenville NC 27858-4300 E-mail: macdonaldk@mail.ecu.edu.

MACDONALD, KENNETH R., JR. author, artist; b. N.Y.C., Apr. 14, 1944; s. Kenneth R. and Wilma Christine (Lange) M. BA, Lehigh U., 1967; MA, W.Va. U., 1970, PhD, 1976. Instr. W.Va. U., Morgantown, 1980-81. Author: (books) The Destiny of Man, 1978, The Gods, 1993, The Palace of Time: The Proof of God and Immortality, 1999, Henry Lange: Master Painter, 2001. Home and Office: PO Box 1027 Middlebury VT 05753-5027

MACDONALD, KIRK STEWART, lawyer; b. Glendale, Calif., Oct. 24, 1948; s. Bruce Mace and Phyllis Jeanne MacDonald. BSCE, U. So. Calif., 1970; JD, Western State U., 1982. Bar: Calif. 1982, U.S. Dist. Ct. (cen. dist.) Calif. 1982, U.S. Ct. Appeals (9th cir.) 1982, U.S. Dist. Ct. (no. dist.) Calif. 1984, U.S. Dist. Ct. (so. dist.) Calif. 1985, U.S. Dist. Ct. (ea. dist.) Calif. 1987. Dist. engr. Pacific Clay Products, Corona, Calif., 1971-76, Nat. Clay Pipe Inst., La Mirada, 1976-82; ptnr. Gill and Baldwin, Glendale, 1982—. Mem. ABA, L.A. County Bar Assn., Water Environ. Assn., Calif. Water Environ. Assn. Avocations: travel, woodworking. Office: Gill & Baldwin Ste 405 130 N Brand Blvd Glendale CA 91203-2646 E-mail: kirk@gillandbaldwin.com.

MAC DONALD, MARGARET CLARK, retired real estate agent; b. Lewiston, Maine, Dec. 20, 1929; d. Arthur Bailey and Blanche (Plummer) Clark; m. John Edward Mac Donald, June 16, 1951 (dec. July 1988); children: Cornelia Ann Roberts (dec.), Edward Clark, Susan Mac Donald Moynahan. BS, Skidmore Coll., 1951. Bus. rep. N.Y. Bell Co., N.Y.C., 1951-52; show room mgr. Bonnie Doone, 1952-53; interior decorator Susan Wang, 1953-54; designer Maggie Mac Donald Interiors, Miami, Fla., 1960-64; owner, sec. Atlantic Millwork, Inc., 1964-88; assoc. realtor Keyes Co. Realtors, 1995-98. Pres. Homemaker Svc. Dade County, Cmty. Vol. Svc. Bur., 1967-68; pres. Jr. League Miami, Inc., 1969-70, chmn. sustaining mems., 1982; pres. Vis. Nurse Assn. Dade County, Fla., Inc., 1975-77; pres., past treas. Metropolitans, 1983-84; second v.p., spl. events chmn. The Vizcayans, 1984-85; pres. Dade County Nat. Soc. Colonial Dame Am., 1988-89; pres. Colonial Dame of Am. XVII, 1989-90, rec. sec., 1998-99. Mem. Nat. DAR (Biscayne chpt., del. conf. Washington, corr. 1998-99), Daus. Colonial Wars, Founders and Patriots (v.p. 2000). Avocations: reading, tennis. Home: 13480 Wansteadt Pl Bristow VA 20136-5728

MACDONALD, MARTHA FRANCES, clarinetist, music educator; b. Shreveport, La., Dec. 27, 1938; d. Charles Clayton and Mary Elizabeth (Fitzgerald) Varnell; m. Robert Claude MacDonald, Sept. 7, 1962; children: Robert Scott, Richard Charles. B Music Edn., Baylor U., 1961; MusM, U. Mich., 1963; D Music Arts, U. Tex., 1985. Tchr. music Clawson (Mich.) Pub. Schs., 1971-72, Houston Pub. Schs., 1972-75; instr. clarinet Am. Sch., The Hague, The Netherlands, 1976-78, U. Tex., Austin, 1982-85; pvt. tchr. music, 1978—; exec. dir., clarinetist Austin Chamber Ensemble, 1985—; pres. Mu Phi Epsilon Found., 1993—. Bd. dirs. Music Umbrella, Austin, 1989-94. Clarinetist Cantilena Chamber Soloists, Austin, 1981-86, Trio Contraste, Austin, 1992—. Pres. Austin Young Artists Concert, 2001—. Mem. Music Tchrs. Nat. Assn. (cert., pres. Austin 1989-91), Internat. Clarinet Assn., Nat. Fedn. Music Clubs (v.p. Austin 1991-92), Austin Dist. Music Tchrs. Assn. (pres. 1989-91), Mu Phi Epsilon (pres. Austin alumni 1993-97). Avocations: travel, reading, cooking, cross-stitch. Home and Office: 8909 Wildridge Dr Austin TX 78759-7355

MACDONALD, MICHAEL JOSEPH, physician, administrator; b. Lafayette, Ind., Aug. 22, 1962; s. Hugh Joseph and Joan Evelyn (Ruel) MacD. AA, Brevard C.C., 1982; BS, Fla. State U., 1984, BA, 1986; DO, Southeastern U., 1990; MPH, Harvard U., 1995. Intern family practice USN, Jacksonville, Fla., 1990-91, flight surgeon candidate Pensacola, 1991-92, flight surgeon South Weymouth, Mass., 1992-94; occupl. medicine resident Harvard U., Boston, 1994-96; occupational med. specialist Health First Physicians, Melbourne, Fla., 1996—, co-dir., 1996—. Contbr. articles to profl. jours. Active Make-a-Wish Found., Boston, 1994-96. Lt. USN, 1990-94; lt. comdr. USNR, 1995—. Mem. AMA, Am. Osteo. Assn., Harvard Club, Fla. State Alumni Assn. Republican. Roman Catholic. Avocations: running, golf, swimming, volleyball, skiing. Home: 365 Ocean Oaks Dr Indialantic FL 32903-2748 Office: Health First Physicians Inc 1051 S Hickory St Melbourne FL 32901-1962

MACDONALD, NORVAL (NORVAL WOODROW MACDONALD), safety engineer; b. Medford, Oreg., Dec. 8, 1913; s. Orion and Edith (Anderson) MacD.; m. Elizabeth Ann Clifford, Dec. 8, 1937; children: Linda (Mrs. Bob Comings), Peggy (Mrs. Don Lake), Kathleen (Mrs. Michael Nissenberg). Student, U. So. Calif., 1932-34. Registered profl. safety engr., Calif. Safety engr. Todd Shipyards, San Pedro, Calif., 1942-44, Pacific Indemnity Ins. Co., San Francisco, 1944-50; area safety engring. chief safety engr. Indsl. Ind., 1950-76; supervising safety engr. Beaver Ins. Co., 1976-82, v.p. loss control, 1982-88; cons. safety engr. MacDonald and Assocs., 1988-99. Tchr. adult evening classes U. San Francisco, 1960-63, Golden Gate U., 1969-76. Contbr. articles to profl. jours.; producer safety training films. Mem. ASME, Am. Soc. Safety Engrs. (pres. San Francisco chpt. 1958, 59), Las Posas Country Club, Masons, Shriners. Methodist. Home: 1710 E Shoreline St Camarillo CA 93010-6018 E-mail: nmacd@aol.com.

MACDONALD, PAMELYN MARIE, psychology educator; b. Washington; d. Paul J. and Donna M. MacD.; m. William Albert Stallworth, Dec. 26, 1998. BA in Psychology, U. Ala., 1991, MA in Psychology, 1992; PhD in Devel. Psychology, U. Houston, 1998. Asst. prof. psychology Washburn U., Topeka, 1998—. Contbr. articles to profl. jours. Rschr. Equine Facilitated Mental Health. Teaching fellow U. Houston, 1993-98. Mem. APA, Soc. Rsch. Child Devel., Soc. Teaching Psychology. Office: Washburn U 1700 SW College Ave Topeka KS 66621 E-mail: zzmacd@washburn.edu.

MACDONALD, PAUL EDWARD, electrical engineer; b. Syracuse, N.Y., Nov. 2, 1954; s. Cornelius J. and Virginia F. (Vassallo) MacD.; m. Linda Marie Fredrick, Aug. 20, 1983; children: Maeghen Leigh, Charles Fredrick. B Archtl. Engring., Pa. State U., 1977. Registered profl. engr., Va., Md., D.C., Conn., W.Va., Del., Ill. Engring. in tng. Syska & Hennessy, Washington, 1977-78, jr. engr., 1978-79, project engr., 1979-80, Meta Engrs. P.C., Washington, 1980-82, dir. elec. engring., 1982-88, chief elec. engring., 1988-91, v.p., chief elec. engring., 1991-99, pres., 1999—. Den leader Cub Scouts, Boy Scouts Am., Alexandria, Va., 1994-99, asst. scoutmaster Troop 993, Alexandria, 1999—; mem. consortium for the advancement of bldg. scis. Pa. State U., 1995—. Mem. NSPE, Nat. Soc. Archtl. Engrs., D.C. Soc. Profl. Engrs. (pres. 1991-92, bd. dirs. 1986—, Outstanding Svc. award 1987, 88), Sierra Club (life), Appalachian Trail Conf. Roman Catholic. Avocations: woodworking, making stringed musical instruments, playing guitar, banjo and dulcimer, hiking. Home: 8801 Lukens Ln Alexandria VA 22309-4105 Office: Meta Engrs PC 1220 L St NW Washington DC 20005-4018 E-mail: pmacdonald@metaengineers.com.

MACDONALD, PETER DAVID, lawyer; b. Ft. Snelling, Minn., Aug. 30, 1946; s. Alexander Colin and Marie (Peterson) MacD.; m. Kathleen Bourke, Dec. 27, 1969; children: Bourke, Evan. BA in Econs., U. Mont., 1969; MS in Urban Planning, U. Ariz., 1972, JD, 1975. Bar: Ariz. 1976. Planning counsel, dep. city atty. City of Salinas, Calif., 1977-82; city atty. City of Gonzales, 1980-82, City of Pleasanton, 1982-88; pvt. practice, Pleasanton, 1988—. Chmn. bd. dirs. Valley Cmty. Bank, 2001. Mem. Calif. Bar Assn., Bay Area City Attys. Assn. (pres. 1984), Ea. Alameda County Bar Assn. (pres. 1997), U.S. C. of C., Pleasanton C. of C. (pres. 1992), Rotary (Pleasanton chpt., pres. 1998). Home: 5258 Crestline Way Pleasanton CA 94566-5470 Office: 400 Main St Ste 210 Pleasanton CA 94566-7371 E-mail: petemacd@ix.netcom.com.

MACDONALD, R. FULTON, venture developer, business educator; b. Monmouth County, N.J., Dec. 24, 1940; s. James Fleming Smith Macdonald and Jane Macfarlane Barnes Abbott; m. Carol Jean Archer (div.); 1 child, Paige Brubaker Smith; m. Laura Boswell; children: George Dewey Boswell, James Fleming Smith Macdonald II. AB, U. Pa., 1963, MBA, 1969; postgrad. sr. mktg. mgmt., Stanford U., 1979. Systems mgr., mcht. John Wanamaker, Inc., Phila., 1969-74; prin. Booz, Allen & Hamilton, N.Y.C., 1974-79; pres. Irwill Industries, 1979-82, Internat. Bus. Devel. Corp., N.Y.C., 1982—; chmn. IBEX Mktg. Corp., 1988—. Pres. Simfer Operational Internat., Inc., N.Y.C., 1984; vice chmn. Neusteter Co., Denver, 1984-85; dir. Fragrances Selective, Inc., 1985-87; mng. dir. Stuyvesant Group Internat., Dutch Am. Bus. Advisors, N.Y.C. and Amsterdam, 1987-88; chmn. Am. Bus. Media, Inc., 1989-90, One Ams., Inc., Washington, 1990—; mng. dir. Synoptics Devel. Corp., N.Y.C., 1992—; dir. C4SI, Inc., Ill., 1998—, First Fin. M&A, Fla., 1998—; vice chmn., dir. CloseOutNow.com, N.Y., 1999-2001; adj. prof. Grad. Bus. Sch., Columbia U., N.Y.C., 1984-85, Mgmt. Inst. NYU, 1992-98, chmn. Globalization Adv. Bd., 1993-94; vice chmn., dir. World Brand Management.com, Jacksonville, Fla.; pres., CEO, dir., Asia Am. Investments.com, Holdings Ltd., N.Y., 2000—; co-CEO First Fin. Corp., Invescorp, Miami, Fla., 2001—. Designer Manpower Mgmt. Concepts computer system, 1972—; author, pub. The IBD Quarterly Report, 1996—; contbr. articles to bus. publs. Capt. inf. U.S. Army, 1963-67, Vietnam. Decorated Bronze Star Mem. Inst. Mgmt. Consultants (cert. mgmt. cons. 1989), Global Econ. Action Inst., Soc. Mayflower Descendants, Soc. Coll. Alumni U. Pa. (pres. 1973-74, bd. mgrs. 1975—), Ripon Soc. (Washington), Penn Club (N.Y.). Republican. Christian Scientist. Avocation: squash. Home: 40 Central Park S Ph A New York NY 10019-1633 Office: Internat Bus Devel Corp 730 5th Ave Ste 900 New York NY 10019-4105 E-mail: fultonm@aol.com., ibdcorpny@aol.com.

MACDONALD, ROBERT LOUGHLIN, neurosurgeon, educator; b. Eugene, Oreg., June 30, 1961; came to U.S., 1993; MD, U. B.C., 1985; PhD, U. Alberta, 1991. Diplomate Am. Bd. Neurosurgery. Intern St. Michael's Hosp.-U. Toronto, 1985-86; resident U. Toronto, 1986-93; attending in neurosurgery U. Chgo. Med. Ctr., 1993—; assoc. prof. Pritzker Sch. Medicine-U. Chgo., 1993—. Office: U Chgo Med Ctr Sect NS MC3026 5841 S Maryland Ave Chicago IL 60637-1463 E-mail: lmacdona@surgery.bsd.uchicago.edu.

MACDONALD, ROBERT RIGG, JR. museum director; b. Pitts., May 11, 1942; s. Robert Rigg and Ruth (Johnson) M.; m. Catherine Ronan, Nov. 27, 1965; children: Matthew, Robert, Catherine. BA, U. Notre Dame, 1964, MA, 1965, U. Pa., 1970. Asst. curator Smithsonian Instn., Washington, 1965; curator Mercer Mus., Doylestown, Pa., 1966-70; dir. New Haven Colony Hist. Soc., 1970-74, La. State Mus., New Orleans, 1974-85; dir., CEO Mus. of City of N.Y., 1985—. Adj. prof. mus. studies NYU, 1989—; mem. Commn. on Mus. for a New Century. Editor: Editor: New Haven Colony Furniture, 1973, Louisiana Images 1880-1920, 1975, Louisiana Black Heritage, 1977 Louisiana Portraitures, 1979, Louisiana Legal Heritage, 1981, The Sun King: Louis XIV and the New World, On Being Homeless , A Community of Many Worlds: Arab American New Society, 2002. Decorated chevalier de l'Ordre des Arts et des Lettres (France), cruz de Caballero de la Orde de Isabel La Catolica (Spain); assoc. fellow Berkeley Coll., Yale U., 1978; Hagley fellow U. Del., 1970-71; Univ. scholar U. Notre Dame, 1964-65 Mem. Am. Assn. State and Local History (coun.), Am. Assn. Mus. (pres. 1985-88, chmn. ethics task force 1988-91), Century Assn. Roman Catholic. Home: 35 Edgewood Ln Bronxville NY 10708-1946 Office: Mus NYC 1220 5th Ave New York NY 10029-5221 E-mail: rrmacdonald@mcny.org., robertrm2@aol.com.

MACDONALD, RONALD FRANCIS, financial services company executive; b. Detroit, July 23, 1946; s. Alfred and Marianne Dorothy (Paddock) Mac.; m. Harriet Pratt Higgins, Dec. 18, 1982 (div. 1997); children: John Higgins, Peter Brewer. BS, U. Detroit, 1968; MBA, Mich. State U., 1970. V.p. Northern Trust Co., Chgo., 1970-84, Bankers Trust Co., N.Y.C., 1984-89; mng. dir. CapMAC Holdings, Inc., 1989-97, MBIA Ins. Corp., Armonk, N.Y., 1998-2000, Chubb Fin. Solutions Inc., N.Y.C., 2001—. Mem. Ins. Industry Planning Forum, N.Y. Athletic Club, Royal Oak Soc. Roman Catholic. Avocations: skiing, running, art history, reading. Home: # 5-E 64 E 94th St New York NY 10128-0773

MACDONALD, R(ONALD) NEIL (RONALD ANGUS NEIL MACDONALD), physician, educator; b. Calgary, Alta., Can., Jan. 6, 1935; s. Angus Neil and Florence Mary (Macdonald) MacD.; m. Mary Jane Whiting, June 30, 1962; children: Cynthia, David, James, Gavin. BA, U. Toronto, 1955; MD, CM, McGill U., Montreal, 1959; LLD (hon.), U. Calgary, Can., 1996. Demonstrator, lectr. McGill U., 1965-67, assoc. dean, faculty of medicine, 1967-70; assoc. dir., dir. Oncology Day Ctr., Royal Victoria Hosp., Montreal, 1967-71; exec. dir. Provincial Cancer Hosps. Bd., Edmonton, Alta., Can., 1971-75; prof. medicine U. Alta., 1971-94; dir. Cross Cancer Inst., 1971—80, 1981-87; assoc. dir., prof. palliative care Royal Victoria Hosp., Montreal, 1980-81; prof. palliative medicine Alta. Cancer Found., Edmonton, 1987-94; dir. cancer ethics program Inst. Recherches Cliniques Montreal, 1994—2002; prof. oncology McGill U., 1994—. Mem. cancer expert adv. panel WHO, Geneva, 1986—. Co-editor: Oxford Textbook of Palliative Medicine, 1993, 2d edit., 1998; editor: Palliative Medicine: A Case Based Manual, 1998; contbr. articles on treatment of cancer pain and other topics to profl. jours. Recipient Queen's Jubilee medal, 1977, Alta. Achievement award, 1980, Blair award Nat. Cancer Inst., 1980, Edmonton Achievement award, 1994. Fellow Coll. Physicians and Surgeons Can., Royal Coll. Physicians Edinburgh (hon.); mem. Order of Can., Can. Cancer Soc. (nat. bd. dirs. 1981-87), Can. Oncology Soc. (pres. 1977-78), Am. Soc. Clin. Oncology (sec.-treas. 1980-82), Can. Soc. Palliative Care Physicians (pres. 1993-94). Roman Catholic. Avocation: history.

MACDONALD, SANDY, writer; b. N.Y.C., Feb. 13, 1949; d. William G. and Margaret (Sweeney) MacD.; m. John Goodwin Devaney, Dec. 19, 1981; 1 child, Laurel. Asst. editor TDR, N.Y.C., 1969-70; editor Scripts, 1970-72; co-editor Aphra, 1972-77; sr. editor New Age Jour., Boston, 1977-84; submissions coord. Houghton Mifflin, 1986-92; freelance writer, Cambridge, Mass., 1980—. Author: The Toys R Us Guide to Choosing the Right Toys, 1996, Quick Escapes from Boston, 2000, 02. Recipient fellowship in lit. transl. NEA, 1989, Benjamin Fine journalism award Nat. Assn. Secondary Sch.

Prins., 1995. Mem. Am. Soc. Journalists and Authors, Nat. Book Critics Cir., Soc. Am. Travel Writers, Nat. Assn. Snowsports Journalists. Democrat. Avocations: acting, singing. Home: 421 Broadway Cambridge MA 02138-4278 E-mail: smacd@aol.com.

MACDONALD, SHARON ETHEL, dancer, choreographer, administrator; b. Pittsfield, Mass., Mar. 24, 1952; d. Harry and Angeline (Saracco) MacD. BA, Skidmore Coll., 1974; MA, Smith Coll., 1992. Faculty Smith Coll., Northampton, Mass., 1974-76; dancer, tchr. Berkshire Ballet, Pittsfield, 1976-77; dance dir. Becket (Mass.) Arts Ctr., Mass., 1977-80; faculty mem. Williams Coll., Williamstown, 1979-80; co-artistic dir., owner N.E. Am. Ballet, Northampton, 1980-85; devel. dir., tchr. Berkshire Ballet, Pittsfield, 1984-85; adminstr., tchr. Hartford (Conn.) Ballet, Inc., 1985-90; artistic dir., exec. dir. Am. Dance Inst., 1995—; freelance dir., choreographer, master tchr. Asst. choreographer Easthampton Mass. Community Theatre Assn., 1981-83, Project Opera, 1982; bd. dirs. Jacob's Pillow Dance Festival, Becket, 1978-81; bd. trustees Becket Arts Ctr., 1979-80; tchr. Trinity Coll., Hartford, Conn., 1990-96, Hartford Conservatory, 1996—; dance specialist Pittsfield (Mass.) Pub. Schs., 1996-99; dir. mktg., bus. cons. Limelight Prodns., Inc., 1990-2002; guest artist numerous pub schs., pvt. studios, colls., and univs. Pres. Friends of Jacob's Pillow, Becket, 1978-81, Friends of The Hartford Ballet, 1988-91, Jacob's Pillow Alumnae/Archives Com., 1988-96, Dance History Scholars, 1976-78, 91—; chmn. Lee (Mass.) Cultural Coun., 1995—. Mass. Arts Lottery Grantee Mass. Arts Coun., 1984, Arts Lottery Grantee Northampton Arts Coun., 1984; Smith Coll. Fellow. Mem. Smith Coll. Club. Democrat. Baptist. Avocations: writing, antiques, collecting dance and theatre memorabilia. Home: PO Box 697 Stockbridge MA 01262-0697

MACDONALD, SHEILA DE MARILLAC, company executive; MBA, Harvard U. Prin. Tex. Transaction Mgmt. Co., Fair Winds Corp., Houston, 1990—. Chpt. 11 trustee, 1997-99; pres., CEO Bristol Resources Corp., 2000. Mem. Harvard Club N.Y., Met. Club, Petroleum Club. E-mail: sheilamacdonald@msn.com.

MACDONALD, STEPHEN HUGH, physician, reserve naval officer; b. Lafayette, Ind., Aug. 22, 1962; s. Hugh Joseph and Joan Ruth (Ruel) MacD. AA, Brevard Community Coll., 1982; BS, Fla. State U., 1984, BA, 1986; DO, Southeastern U. Health Scis., 1990; MPH, Harvard U., 1995. Diplomate Am. Bd. Occupl. Medicine, Am. Bd. Forensic Medicine, Am. Bd. Aerospace Medicine, Am. Bd. Managed Care Medicine, Am. Bd. Pain Mgmt., Am. Bd. Healthcare Quality and Mgmt., Am. Bd. Healthcare Execs.; ind. med. examiner, med. rev. officer, sr. aviation med. examiner. Commd. lt. USN, 1990; intern in family practice Naval Hosp., Pensacola, Fla., 1990-91; flight surgeon USNR, Beaufort, S.C., 1992-94; resident occupl. medicine Harvard U., Cambridge, Mass., 1994-96; co-med. dir. Health First Occupational Medicine, Melbourne, Fla., 1996—. Lt. comdr. USNR, 1996, USNR, 2002. Republican. Roman Catholic. Avocations: athletics, drawing, painting. Home: 834 Brookside Dr Indialantic FL 32903-3605

MACDONALD, THOMAS COOK, JR. lawyer, mediator; b. Atlanta, Oct. 11, 1929; s. Thomas Cook and Mary (Morgan) MacD.; m. Gay Anne Everiss, June 30, 1956; children: Margaret Anne, Thomas William. BS with high honors, U. Fla., 1951, LL.B. with high honors, 1953. Bar: Fla. 1953; cert. mediator Supreme Ct. Fla. and U.S. Dist. Ct. (mid. dist.) Fla. Practice law, Tampa, 1953—; mem. firm Shackleford, Farrior, Stallings & Evans, 1953-97; mem. Cook & MacDonald, Tampa, 1997—. Spl. counsel Gov. of Fla., 1963, U. Fla., 1972-98; del. 5th cir. Jud. Conf., 1970-81; mem. adv. com. U.S. Ct. Appeals (5th cir.), 1975-78, (11th cir.), 1988-93; mem. Fla. Jud. Qualifications Commn., 1983-88, vice chmn., 1987, chmn., 1988, gen. counsel, 1997—; mem. judicial nominating com. Fla. Supreme Ct., 1995-99. Mem. Fla. Student Scholarship and Loan Commn., 1963-67; bd. dirs. Univ. Cmty. Hosp., Tampa, 1968-78, Fla. West Coast Sports Assn., 1965-80, Hall of Fame Bowl (now Outback Bowl) Assn., 1989-93, Jim Walter Corp., 1979-87; mem. Hillsborough County Pub. Edn. Study Commn., 1965; lic. lay eucharistic min. Episcopal Ch., 1961—; chancellor Episcopal Diocese of S.W. Fla., 1990-93, 2000—, ch. atty. for ecclesiastical ct., 1998-2000; bd. dirs. U. Fla. Found., 1978-86, Shands Tchg. Hosp., U. Fla., 1981-95; counsel Tampa Sports Authority, 1983-94. Recipient George Carr award FBA, 1991, Herbert Goldburg award Hillsborough County Bar Assn., 1995. Fellow Am. Coll. Trial Lawyers (chmn. state com. 1990-91), Am. Bar Found., Fla. Bar (chmn. com. profl. ethics 1966-70, bd. govs. 1970-74, bar mem. Supreme Ct. com. on stds. conduct governing judges 1976, Presdl. award of merit 1995); mem. ABA (com. on ethics and profl. responsibility 1970-76), Am. Law Inst. (life), 11th Cir. Hist. Soc. (trustee 1982-95, pres. 1989-95), U. Fla. Nat. Alumni Assn. (pres. 1973), Phi Kappa Phi, Phi Delta Phi, Fla. Blue Key, Kappa Alpha. Episcopalian. Home: 1904 S Holly Ln Tampa FL 33629-7004 Office: 100 N Tampa St Ste 2100 Tampa FL 33602-5809

MACDONELL, HERBERT LEON, criminalist, consultant, educator; b. Wellsville, N.Y., July 23, 1928; s. Leon John Duncan MacDonell and Catherine Winifred Williams; m. Phyllis Barbara Austin, Aug. 19, 1950; adopted children: Candy, Cindy, Wendie, Wendy, Cathy, Joanne, Mark, David, Debra, John, Karen, Paul. BA in Chemistry, Alfred U., 1950; MS in Chemistry, U. R.I., 1956. Cert. sr. crime scene analyst. Prof. Milton (Wis.) Coll., 1951-54, Corning (N.Y.) C.C., 1960-92; cons. Lab. Forensic Sci., Corning, 1970—; prof. Elmira (N.Y.) Coll., 1972-83. Fellow Am. Acad. Forensic Sci. (chmn. 1969-70); mem. Internat. Assn. for Identification (various coms., Dondaro award 1974), Internat. Assn. Bloodstain Analysts (dist. mem., historian 1983—), Can. and English Forensic Sci. Socs., Rotary. Democrat. Episcopalian. Achievements include inventor/patentee for MAGNA Brush for fingerprints. Avocations: model trains, stamps, glass, woodworking, firearms. Home and Office: PO Box 1111 Corning NY 14830-0911 E-mail: forensic@localnet.com.

MACDONNELL, JOANNE CAPELLA, writer, editor, editorial consultant; b. Santa Rosa, Calif., Jan. 26, 1937; d. Joseph Lawrence and Mabel Alida (Strome) Capella; m. S.J. Cogliandro, Feb. 23, 1957 (div. 1963); 1 child, Cory; m. Ignacio Plancarte Lopez, June 2, 1964 (dec. 1971); children: Kenneth Lopez, Lauren Lopez; m. John Faust MacDonnell, Sept. 6, 1981. Student, U. Calif., Berkeley, 1955-56, San Jose (Calif.) State U., 1956-57. Advt. Palo Alto Times, Calif., 1960-62; columnist San Jose Mercury News, 1962-83; clk. Santa Clara County Superior Ct., San Jose, 1984-99; ret.; writer, columnist thecolumnists.com, 1999—. Author six-part series on unsafe toys, 1968; humor columnist San Jose Mercury News, 1977-81. Writer fund-raising brochure Valley Med. Ctr., San Jose, 1964; vol. Alexian Bros. Hosp., San Jose, 1967; TV appearances local pub. TV, San Jose, 1967-70. Recipient 2nd Place feature series award San Francisco Press Club 1968 series entered into congl. record by Rep. Don Edwards, 1969, Achievement in writing award Santa Clara County Pen Women Los Gatos Calif. 1965, Santa Clara County Family Law award for excellence, 1995. Mem. San Francisco Press Club, San Jose Newspaper Guild. Democratic. Roman Catholic. Avocations: gourmet cooking, reading. Home: 3514 El Grande Dr San Jose CA 95132-3110

MACDONOUGH, ROBERT HOWARD, consulting engineer; b. Chgo., Jan. 24, 1941; s. John Haaf and Helen Margaret (McWilliams) MacD.; m. Joan Carol Rosecrants, Dec. 28, 1963 (div. Nov. 1975); children: John Haaf, Thomas William, Mark Peter; m. Barbara Jean Barone, Apr. 18, 2001. BS in Engring. Ops., Iowa State U., 1962; MA in Econ., Drake U., 1966. Registered profl. engr., Iowa; enrolled agent. Assoc. Mgmt. Sci. Am., Palo Alto, Calif., 1969; mng. assoc. Theo. Barry & Assoc., Los Angeles, 1970-72; mgr. indsl. engring. Advanced Memory Systems, Sunnyvale, Calif., 1972-73; mgr. planning and engring. Signetics, 1973-75; pres. Facilities Cons., Mountain View, Calif., 1976-96. Instr. H&R Block; cons. assoc. Shumaker Tax Cons., 1996-01. Mem. Nat. Assn. Enrolled Agts., Calif. Soc. Enrolled Agts., Ctrl. Coast Soc. Enrolled Agts., Phi Gamma Delta. Republican.

MACDOUGAL, GARY EDWARD, corporate director, foundation trustee; b. Chgo., July 3, 1936; s. Thomas William and Lorna Lee (McDougall) MacD.; children: Gary Edward, Michael Scott; m. Charlene Gehm, June 15, 1992. BS in Engring., UCLA, 1958; MBA with distinction, Harvard U., 1962. Cons. McKinsey & Co., L.A., 1963-68, ptnr., 1968-69; chmn. bd., chief exec. officer Mark Controls Corp. (formerly Clayton Mark & Co.), Evanston, Ill., 1969-87; gen. dir. N.Y.C. Ballet, 1993-94; chmn. Gov. Task Force on Human Svcs. Reform State of Ill., 1993-97. Sr. advisor and asst. campaign mgr. George Bush for Pres., Washington, 1988; chmn. Bulgarian-Am. Enterprise Fund, Chgo. and Sophia, Bulgaria, 1991-93, bd. dirs., 1991—; apptd. to U.S. Commn. on Effectiveness of UN, 1992-93; bd. dirs. United Parcel Svc. Am., Inc., Atlanta; adv. dir. Saratoga Ptnrs., N.Y.; instr. UCLA, 1969. Author: Make a Difference: How One Man Helped Solve America's Poverty Problem, 2000; contbr. articles to Harvard Bus. Rev., Wall St. Jour., N.Y. Times, Chgo. Tribune, other publs., chpts. to books. Trustee Annie E. Casey Found., UCLA Found., 1973-79, W.T. Grant Found., 1992-94, Russell Sage Found., 1981-91, chair, 1987-90; apptd. by Pres. Bush as pub. del., alt. rep., U.S. Del. UN 44th Gen. Assembly, 1989-90; commr. Sec. Labor's Commn. on Workforce Quality and Productivity, Washington, 1988-89; chmn. Ill. Rep. Party, 2002-. Lt. USN, 1958-61. Mem. Coun. Fgn. Rels., Author's Guild, Harvard Club, Kappa Sigma. Episcopalian. Home: 505 N Lake Shore Dr Apt 2711 Chicago IL 60611-3406

MACDOUGALL, SIR DONALD (SIR GEORGE DONALD ALASTAIR MACDOUGALL), economist; b. Glasgow, Scotland, Oct. 26, 1912; s. Daniel Douglas and Beatrice Amy (Miller) MacD.; m. Bridget Christabel Bartrum, 1937 (dissolved 1977); children: John Douglas, Mary Jean; m. Laura Margaret Hall, 1977 (dec. 1995). MA, Oxford U., 1938; LLD (hon.), U. Strathclyde, 1968; LittD (hon.), U. Leeds, 1971; DSc (hon.), U. Aston, 1979. Asst. lectr., then lectr. econs. U. Leeds, 1936-39; with statis. br. Office First Lord Admiralty, 1939-40, Office Prime Min., 1940-45; ofcl. fellow Wadham Coll. Oxford U., 1945-50, domestic bursar, 1946-48, hon. fellow, 1964—, faculty fellow Nuffield Coll., 1947-50, professorial fellow, 1950-52, ofcl. fellow, 1952-64, first bursar, 1958-64, hon. fellow, 1967—, univ. Nuffield reader internat. econs., 1950-52; hon. fellow Balliol Coll., Oxford U., 1992—. Econ. dir. Orgn. European Econ. Cooperation, Paris, 1948-49; chief adv. statis. br. Office Prime Min., 1951-53; vis. prof. Australian Nat. U., Canberra, 1959, MIT Ctr. Internat. STudies, New Delhi, 1961; econ. dir. Nat. Econ. Devel. Office, 1962-64; mem. Turnover Tax Com., 1963-64; dir. gen. Dept. Econ. Affairs, 1964-68; head govt. econ. svc., chief econ. adv. Treasury, 1969-73; chief econ. adv. Confedn. Brit. Industry, 1973-84. Author: The World Dollar Problem, 1957, The Dollar Problem: A Reappraisal, 1960, Studies in Political Economy, 2 vols., 1975, Don and Mandarin: Memoirs of an Economist, 1987; co-author: Measures for International Economic Stability, 1951, The Fiscal System of Venezuela, 1959; chmn. EEC Report of Study Group on Role of Public Finance in European Integration, 1977; contbr. articles to profl. publs. Decorated Knight, Officer Order Brit. Empire, commdr.; scholar George Webb Medley Jr., 1934, George Webb Medley Sr., 1935. Fellow Brit. Acad.; mem. Coun. Royal Econ. Soc. (pres. 1972-74), Nat. Inst. Econ. and Social Rsch. (chmn. exec. com. 1974-87), Soc. Strategic and Long-Range Planning (pres. 1977-85), Soc. Bus. Eocnomists (v.p. 1978—), Reform Club (London). E-mail: donald.mac@virgin.net.

MACDOUGALL, GORDON PIER, lawyer; b. Bethlehem, Pa., May 31, 1930; s. Curtis Daniel and Elizabeth (Pier) MacD. AB, U. Mich., 1952; postgrad., Columbia U., 1952-55. Bar: Wis. 1955, N.Y. 1958, D.C. 1960. Atty. N.Y. Cen. R.R. Co., N.Y.C., 1957-59; assoc. LaRoe, Winn & Moerman, Washington, 1959-66; pvt. practice, 1966—. Spl. asst. atty. gen. Commonwealth Pa., Washington, 1971-78; asst. counsel Pa. Pub. Utility Commn., Washington, 1975-80. Named Disting. Hoosier Gov. Edgar D. Whitcomb, Inpls., 1972. Mem. Assn. Transp. Law, Logistics and Policy, Transp. Lawyers Assn., Maritime Adminstrv. Bar Assn., Transp. Research Forum (gen. counsel). Office: 1025 Connecticut Ave NW Washington DC 20036-5405 Home: 2000 N St NW Washington DC 20036-2349

MACDOUGALL, HARTLAND MOLSON, corporate director, retired bank executive; b. Montreal, Que., Can., Jan. 28, 1931; s. Hartland Campbell and Dorothy (Molson) MacD.; m. Eve Gordon, Oct. 29, 1954; children: Cynthia, Wendy, Keith, Willa, Tania. Ed., LeRosey, Switzerland, 1947-48, McGill U., 1949-53, Advanced Mgmt. Program, Harvard U., 1976. With Bank Montreal, various locations, 1953-84, dir., 1974, vice chmn., 1981; chmn., dir. Royal Trustco Ltd., Toronto, 1984-93. Dep. chmn. London Ins. Group, Inc., London Life Ins. Co., 1985-97, Robert T. JOnes Jr. Can. Scholarship Found.; dir. Conros Corp. Founding chmn. Heritage Can., St. Michael's Hosp. Found., The Japan Soc.; past chmn. Can.-Japan Bus. Com.; gov., past pres. Coun. Can. Unity; dir. Friends of the Youth Awards Inc., U.S.; past pres. Royal Agrl. Winter Fair; mem. Internat. Coun. Music Ctr. L.A., Can. Sports Hall of Fame; bd. govs. Can. Olympic Found.; bd. dirs. Can. Soc. for Weismann Inst., Empire Club Found.; sen. Stratford Shakespearean Found.; former chmn. The Duke of Edinburgh Awards Internat. Coun. Decorated Order of Can., comdr. Royal Victorian Order, Order of the Rising Sun, Gold and Silver Star (Japan); recipient Gabrielle Leger medal, 1978. Avocations: golf, gardening, skiing, tennis, farming. Home: 16978 Shaws Creek Rd Belfountain ON Canada L0N 1B0 Office: BCE Place 181 Bay St Ste 4420 PO Box 771 Toronto ON Canada M5J 2T3 Office Fax: 416-369-9495.

MACDOUGALL, INGEBORG REIBLING, mental health nurse; b. Orange, N.J., June 3, 1927; d. August Gottlieb and Heidi Ericka (Muller) Reibling; m. Hollis Blenus MacDougall, Apr. 1, 1950; children: Linda D., Jo Ann, Glen D. BA in Nursing Edn., Bates Coll., 1950; MS, Boston U., 1980. RN, Mass.; cert. psychiat. clin. specialist. Psychiat. clin. specialist VA, Mass., 1971-96, coord. employee assistance program, 1991-96; pvt. practice psychotherapy and consultation Lexington, 1984—. Chem. dependency educator, adj. clin. faculty Boston Coll., U. Mass., Lowell; lectr. on impaired practice, addictions, leadership devel., employee assistance, psychopharmacology in addictions; cons. in field. Contbg. author: A Faculty Guide to Impaired Student Practice, 1995; contbr. articles to jours. Fellow Am. Orthopsychiat. Assn.; mem. ANA, Mass. Nurses Assn. (Staff Devel. award, co-chair addictions coun., peer assistance com., chair com. on interstate licensure), Mass. Assn. RNs, Am. Psychiat. Nurses Assn., Soc. for Family Therapy, Nat. Nurses Soc. on Addiction, Sigma Theta Tau.

MACDOUGALL, JOHN DUNCAN, surgeon; b. Indpls., Mar. 4, 1925; s. Duncan Campbell and Beulah Stewart (Ward) MacD.; m. Inga Margaretha Tranberg, Oct. 6, 1951 (div. 1980); children: Duncan Campbell, Stewart Andrew, Eric Matthew, Victoria Suzanne MacDougall Oehmen; m. Barbara Lee Mayse, Nov. 1, 1980; children: Katherine Jane, James William. BS, Ind. U., 1948; MD, Ind. U., Indpl., 1951. Diplomate Am. Bd. Surgery, Am. Bd. Thoracic Surgery. Pvt. practice, Indpls., 1957-93; pres. med. staff St. Francis Hosp., Beech Grove, 1975, pres. adv. bd., 1993-95, chmn. governing bd. trustees, 1995—. Chmn. bd. dirs. Med. Assurance of Ind., Indpls., 1987-2000, med. cons., 1993-. Exec. com. dean's coun. Ind. U. Sch. Medicine, Indpls., 1988—, mem. adv. com., 1989-96, pres. dean's coun., 1992-95; mem. Ind. Govs. Task Force on Organ Transplantation, Indpls., 1986-89; pres. Ind. Med. Polit. Action Com., Indpls., 1992-98; bd. dirs. Ind. Med. History Mus., 1989-2000; mem. Ind. Hist. Soc., Indpls. Mus. Art; pres. Indpls. English Speaking Union, 1997—. With U.S. Army, 1943-46, ETO. Decorated Bronze Star medal. Fellow ACS; mem. AMA (del., chmn. Ind. delegation), Ind. State Med. Assn. (pres. 1987-88), Indpls. Med. Soc. (pres. 1978-79), Orgn. State Med. Assn. Pres. (pres. 1994-95), Nat. Med. Vets. Assn. (bd. dirs. 1992—), Am. Legion (comdr. Paul Coble Post # 26 1999-2001), Masons, Indpls. Lit. Club, Contemporary Club, Meridian Hills Country Club. Republican. Episcopalian. Avocations: woodworking, golf, fishing. Home: 7202 Dean Rd Indianapolis IN 46240-3628 Office: Med Assurance of Ind Ste 300 8425 Woodfield Crossing Blvd Indianapolis IN 46240-2495 E-mail: jmacdougall@maih.com.

MACDOUGALL, MALCOLM EDWARD, lawyer; b. Denver, Jan. 26, 1938; s. Malcolm W. and Helen (Harlow) MacD.; m. Phyllis R. Pomrenke, Dec. 20, 1959; children: Barry Malcolm, Christopher Scott (dec.). BS, Colo. State U., 1959; LLD, U. Colo., 1962. Bar: Colo. 1962, U.S. Dist. Ct. Colo. 1962. Law clk. to judge U.S. Ct. Appeals (10th cir.), Denver, 1962-63; atty. Denver Water Bd., 1963-65; assoc. Saunders, Snyder and Ross, Denver, 1965-68; gen. counsel Golden Cycle Corp., Colorado Springs, Colo., 1968-71; ptnr. Geddes, MacDougall and Worley, P.C., 1971-91; sole practitioner MacDougall Law Office, 1991-99; shareholder MacDougall, Woodridge & Worley, PC, 1999—. Bd. dirs. Park State Bank. Mem. Colo. Bar Assn. Republican. Office: Ste 204 530 Communication Cir Colorado Springs CO 80905 E-mail: sandy@waterlaw.tr.

MACDOUGALL, PETER, lawyer; b. Boston, Sept. 22, 1937; s. Duncan Peck and Hildegard (Moebius) MacD. AB, Harvard U., 1958, LLB, 1963. Assoc. Ropes & Gray, Boston, 1964-73, ptnr., 1973-97, ret., 1997—. Sheldon fellow Harvard U., 1963-64. Mem.: Harvard (Boston). Avocations: concert and opera going, gardening, reading, travel. Home: 1720 Washington St Key West FL 33040-4916 also: 542 River Rd Westport MA 02790-5161 E-mail: pmacdougall@earthlink.net.

MACDOUGALL, PRESTON JOHN, chemistry educator; b. Toronto, June 14, 1961; s. William David and Donalda May (Mazur) MacD.; m. Tara Ann McConnell, Aug. 21, 1982; children: Byron, Devon, Aurora. BSc with honors, McMaster U., Hamilton, Ont., 1983, PhD in Chemistry, 1989. Rsch. and tchg. asst. McMaster U., 1983-88; postdoctoral fellow Tex. A&M U., College Station, 1989-92, rsch. assoc., 1991-92; postdoctoral fellow Los Alamos Nat. Lab., 1992-94; asst. prof. Middle Tenn. State U., Murfreesboro, 1994-99, assoc. prof., 1999—. Cons. NASA Ames Res. Ctr., 1997—. Contbr. articles to profl. jours. Mem. Am. Chem. Soc. Presbyterian. Achievements include research in theories of chemical reactivity and electron transport based on the topological properties of the electron density in position and momentum space, respectively. Office: Middle Tenn State U 1301 E Main St # X101 Murfreesboro TN 37132-0001

MACDOUGALL, RUTH DOAN, writer; b. Laconia, N.H., Mar. 19, 1939; d. Daniel and Ernestine Elizabeth Doan; m. Donald Keith MacDougall, Oct. 9, 1957. Student, Bennington Coll., 1957-59; BEd, Keene State Coll., 1961. Mem. coun. advisors N.H. Mag., Manchester, 1999—. Author: The Cheerleader, 1973, Snowy, 1993, 50 Hikes in the White Mountains, 1997, 50 More Hikes in New Hampshire, 1998. Mem. Nat. Writers Union, N.H. Writers Project. Democrat. Avocation: hiking. Home: 285 Range Rd Center Sandwich NH 03227

MACDOUGALL, WILLIAM LOWELL, magazine editor; b. Des Moines, July 24, 1931; s. David Gregory and Elizabeth Jeanette (Dugan) MacD. AB, Willamette U., Salem, Oreg., 1952; M.J. in Journalism (Pulitzer scholar 1953-54), Columbia U., 1953. Reporter Washington Star, 1958-62; corr. Los Angeles Times, 1962-63; asso. editor, then London corr. U.S. News & World Report, 1964-68, asst. mng. editor, 1978-86; mng. editor Artsreview mag. NEA, 1987; pres. Atlantic Media Co., Arlington, Va., 1989—. Author: American Revolutionary: A Biography of General Alexander McDougall, 1977. Served with USAF, 1954-57. Recipient George Washington medal Freedoms Found., 1978, citation U.S. Bicentennial Commn., 1976 Methodist. Office: Atlantic Media Co 5000 37th St N Arlington VA 22207-1823

MACDOWELL, RICHARD T. surgeon, educator; b. Albany, N.Y., Jan. 23, 1948; s. Robert L. and Madah (Taylor) M.; m. Geraldin Roberta Goetchis, Aug. 25, 1973 (dec.); children: Shannon T., Katherine F., Jennifer R. BS, Rensselaer Poly. Inst., 1968; MD, Albany Med. Coll., 1972. Diplomate Am. Bd. Surgery. Intern Albany Med. Coll., 1972-73, resident in surgery, 1973-76; practice medicine specializing in surgery Albany, 1976—. Mem. faculty Albany Med. Coll., 1972—, assoc. prof., 1980—, pres. Faculty Orgn., 1984-88, chmn. accelerated admissions com. 1982-88; cons. VA Hosp., 1976—, N.Y. State Health Care Consortium, 1983—, St. Peter's Hosp., 1986, vice chmn. med. staff Albany Med. Ctr. Hosp., 1999—. Contbr. articles to profl. jours. Bd. dirs. Mental Health Assn. Albany, 1978-82. Fellow ACS (coun. 1983—, field liaison, cancer com. 1986, pres. Upstate chpt. 1994, gov. 1999—); mem. Assn. Acad. Surgeons, East Coop. Oncology Group, Soc. Oncology Edn. Avocations: tennis, skiing, running, diving. Office: 319 S Manning Blvd Albany NY 12208-1742

MACE, JERILEE MARIE, opera company executive; BA in Speech Comm. and Mgmt. magna cum l, Simpson Coll., 1991. Mem. adminstrv. staff Des Moines Metro Opera, 1976, dir. mktg., exec. dir., 1988—. Developer OPERA Iowa, Des Moines Metro Opera; cons. various opera cos. On-site evaluator NEA; grad., bd. dirs. Greater Des Moines Leadership Inst.; founding mem. Warren County Leadership Com. Named Iowa Arts Orgn. of Yr., 2000; recipient Outstanding Achiever award, Ft. Dodge C. of C., 1994, Best Kept Secret award for bus. excellence, Greater Des Moines Partnership 2001, Women of Influence award, Des Moines Bus. Record, 2001; fellow exec., OPERA Am., 1993. Office: Des Moines Metro Opera 106 W Boston Ave Indianola IA 50125-1836 E-mail: jerimace@aol.com.

MACE, JOHN WELDON, pediatrician; b. Buena Vista, Va., July 9, 1938; s. John Henry and Gladys Elizabeth (Edwards) M.; m. Janice Mace, Jan. 28, 1962; children: Karin E., John E., James E. BA, Columbia Union Coll., 1960; MD, Loma Linda U., 1964. Diplomate: Am. Bd. Pediatrics, Sub-bd. Pediatric Endocrinology. Intern U.S. Naval Hosp., San Diego, 1964-65, resident in pediatrics, 1966-68; fellow in endocrinology and metabolism U. Colo., 1970-72; asst. prof. pediatrics Loma Linda (Calif.) U. Med. Center, 1972-75, prof., chmn. dept., 1975—. Med. dir. Loma Linda U. Children's Hosp., 1990-92, physician-in-chief, 1992—. Contbr. articles to profl. jours. Treas. Found. for Med. Care San Bernardino County, 1979-80, pres., 1980-82; mem. Congl. Adv. Bd., 1984-87; pres. So. Calif. affiliate Am. Diabetes Assn., 1985-86, dir., 1987-89; chmn. adv. bd. State Calif. Children's Svcs., 1986—; bd. dirs. So. Calif. Children's Cancer Svcs., 1993-94, Loma Linda Ronald McDonald House, 1991—. Aetna Health Plans of Calif., 1993-95; bd. dirs. Loma Linda U. Health Care, 1995—. Named Alumnist of Yr., Loma Linda U. Sch. Medicine, 1994; recipient Shirley N. Pettis award, 2002. Mem. AAAS, N.Y. Acad. Sci., Calif. Med. Soc. (adv. panel genetic diseases State Calif., 1975—, chmn. acad. practice forum 1997—), Western Soc. Pediatric Rsch., Lawson Wilkens Pediatric Endocrine Soc., Assn. Med. Pediatric Dept. Chmn., Am. Acad. Pediatrics, Sigma Xi, Alpha Omega Alpha. Office: Loma Linda U Childrens Hosp 11234 Anderson St Loma Linda CA 92354-2870

MACE, STEPHEN ALAN, investment advisor; b. Springfield, Mo., Dec. 30, 1957; s. Leslie Jasper and Virginia Sue (Dunaway) M.; m. Deborah Marie Smith, Dec. 3, 1983; children: Andrew Stephen, Ashley Marie, Alexander Edward. BA, William Jewell Coll., 1979; JD, U. Mo., 1982. Bar: Mo. 1982; CPA, Mo.; CFP; CFA Assn. Investment Mgmt. and Rsch. Tax specialist Coopers & Lybrand, St. Louis, 1982-85; atty. Blumenfeld, Sandweiss, et al, 1985-86; sr. trust officer Boatmen's Nat. Bank, 1986-89; prin. Moneta Group, Inc., 1989-94; portfolio cons. Templeton Portfolio Adv., Carmel, Calif., 1994-2000; mng. dir., gen. counsel Centurion Alliance, Inc., 2000—. Mem. Mo. Bar, Bar Assn. Met. St. Louis, Fin. Planning Assn. (nat. bd. dirs., chair audit com. 1993, mem. practitioner adv. coun. 1991-93), Kiwanis Internat. (charter pres. chpt. 1982-83, Disting. Club Pres. 1983). Republican. Baptist. Avocations: scuba diving, big-game hunting, fly fishing, skiing, tae kwon do (2d degree black belt).

MACE, SUSAN LIDGATE, comparative literature educator, researcher; b. San Francisco, Apr. 24, 1945; d. Anthony William and Pauline Kathryn (Quirk) Lidgate; m. Gerald Norman Mace, 1970. AB in Comparative Lit., U. Calif., Berkeley, 1967, PhD in Comparative Lit., 1991; MA in Comparative Lit., San Francisco State U., 1970. Tchg. asst. in comparative Lit. San Francisco State U., 1968-70, vis. asst. prof., 1992-93; lectr. lit. U. Calif., Santa Cruz, 1986-87; lectr. European lit. Ea. Mich. U., Europe, 1988-89; sr. lectr. lit. Maria Curie-Sklodowska U., Lublin, Poland, 1991-92, lectr. (IREX) Internat. Rsch. and Exch. Bd. Poland, 1996; Fulbright prof. Am. studies and lit. U. Zagreb, Croatia, 1993-95; assoc. in comparative lit. U. Calif., Berkeley, 1973-75, 78-79, acting instr., 1980-83, 85-86, vis. scholar, 1995-97, 2000—; Fulbright prof. Am. Lit. and studies Tallinn Pedagogical U., Estonia, 1998-99. Dir. Florence Howe award for Feminist Literary Criticism (MLA), 1980; panel chmn. 20th Century Lit. Conf., U. Louisville, 1986, 89, 91, 93, 96-98, 2000; performance cons. Teatre Neu, Barcelona, Spain, 1995; judge Nat. Jr. Classical League Essay Contest, Am. Classical League, 1985-87; conf. presenter and participant in field, including Internat. Conf. on Am. Culture, Opatia, Croatia, 1994, 20th Century Lit. Conf., Louisville, 1997, 2000, Internat. Tartu Conf. on No. Am. Studies, Estonia, 1999; various TV, radio and press interviews; seminar dir. Estonian Nat. Conf. on Tching. Postmodern Am. Lit., Pärnu, 1999. Assoc. editor, prin. writer Polish lit. Ency. of Women's Lit., 1998; contbr. articles to profl. jours. Grantee U. Calif., Berkeley, 1973-82, humanities rsch., 1981-83; rsch. grantee Newhouse Found., 1981-82, Heller Fund, 1987, 89, 90, Internat. Rsch. and Exch. Bd., 1996; Fulbright sr. scholar Croatia, 1993-95, Estonia, 1998-99. Mem. MLA, AAUP, Am. Soc. for Theatre Rsch., Women's Caucus for Modern Langs. (western regional dir. 1980-82), Pacific Ancient and MLA (presiding officer slavic and East European lit. 1987), Am. Studies Assn., Am. Comparative Lit. Assn., Internat. Comparative Assn., MELUS:

Soc. for Study Multi-Ethnic Lit. U.S., N.Am. Conf. on Brit. Studies, Fulbright Assn. Democrat. Home: 1698 San Lorenzo Ave Berkeley CA 94707-1848 Office: U Calif Dept Comparative Lit Berkeley CA 94720-0001

MACEDONIA, MICHAEL RAYMOND, computer scientist; b. Ft. Meaded, Md., June 26, 1957; s. Raymond Melvin and Madonna Maria M.; m. Theresa Marine Stein, Dec. 30, 1982; children: Robert Rebecca. PhD in Computer Sci., Naval Postgrad. Sch., Monterey, CA, 1995. Cert. modeling and simulation profl. NTSA, 2001. Commd. U.S. Army, 1979; v.p. rsch. Fraunhofer CRCG, Providence, 1995—97; chief scientist US STRICOM, Orlando, Fla., 1998—2002; advanced through grades to maj. U.S. Army. Editor: (column) Entertainment Computing, IEEE Computer, 2002. Roman Catholic. Home: 226 Chestnut Ridge St Winter Springs FL 32708 Office: STRICOM 12350 Research Pkwy Orlando FL Personal E-mail: macedonia@computer.org. Business E-Mail: michael_macedonia@stricom.army.mil.

MACELVAINE, WILLIAM STEPHEN, rancher, consultant; b. Topeka, Sept. 27, 1944; s. Robert Capps and Gretchen (Swatszel) MacE.; m. Susan Lynn Allison, June 14, 1968; children: Dianna, LeeAnn, Steve Jr., Brian. BS in Farm Mgmt., Calif. Poly. State Coll., San Luis Obispo, 1969. Water treatment plant operator I, waste water treatment plant operator II; comml. pilot. Owner, operator Souza Ranch, Morro Bay, Calif., 1965—, Rancho Colina Mobile Home Cmty., Morro Bay, 1971—. Owner MacElvaine Consulting, Morro Bay, 1992—; dir. Mid State Fair Bd., Paso Robles, Calif., 1996—. County supr. dist. 2, Bd. Suprs. San Luis Obispo County, 1979-83; regional commr. So. Ctrl. Region Coastal Commn., San Luis Obispo, Santa Barbara and Ventura Counties, Calif., 1979-81; mem. Calif. Coastal Commn., 1983-92; Rep. nominee from dist. 18, Calif. Sentate, 1994. With Calif. N.G., 1963-69. Mem. San Luis Obispo County Farm Bur., Flying Samaritans (pilot 1990—), Calif. C. of C. Republican. Protestant. Avocations: flying, genealogy, chess, swimming. Home: 1325 Atascadero Rd Morro Bay CA 93442-1803 Office: Rancho Colina Mobile Home Cmty 1045 Atascadero Rd Morro Bay CA 93442-1800

MACER, DAN JOHNSTONE, retired hospital administrator; b. Evansville, Ind., May 25, 1917; s. Clarence Guy and Ann (Johnstone) M.; m. Eugenia Loretta Andrews, June 1, 1943; children: Eugenia Ann, Dan James. BS, Northwestern U., 1939, MS in Hosp. Adminstrn. with distinction, 1959. Chief hosp. ops. VA br. office, St. Paul, 1947-50; asst. mgr. VA hosps., Ft. Wayne, Ind., 1951, Kerrville, Tex., 1952, Augusta, Ga., 1952-56; mgr. VA Hosp., Sunmount, N.Y., 1956-58; dir. Va Research Hosp., Chgo., 1958-62; mem. hosp. adminstrn. faculty Northwestern U., 1959-61; dir. VA Hosps., Pitts., 1962-67; asst. vice chancellor health professions U. Pitts., 1968-71; prof. med. and hosp. adminstrn. U. Pitts. Grad. Sch. Pub. Health, 1962-71; prof. Coll. Health and Coll. Medicine, U. Okla., 1971-89, retired, 1989; dir. VA Hosps. and Clinics, Oklahoma City, 1971-76, VA Med. Dist. 20 (Okla.-Ark.), 1971-76. Lectr. George Washington U., 1961-71; v.p. Hosp. Casualty Co., Oklahoma City, 1978-89; pres. Dan J. Macer & Assos., Inc.; cons. to health field; cons. nat. health profl. assns., indsl. corps., archtl. corps, health planners; cons. Health Services and Mental Health Adminstrn., HEW, 1968 Mem. editorial bd.: Nursing and Health Care, 1980-88; author articles in field. Coordinator civil def. and disaster planning all hosps., Chgo. nr. North Side, 1961; chmn. welfare and planning council Savannah River Community Chest, Augusta, 1954-56; chmn. group 17 fed. sect., govt. div. United Fund Allegheny County, 1964-65; mem. Fed. Interagy. Bd. Dirs., 1964-68; sec. U. Pitts. Health Center, 1969-71; chmn. health com. Health and Welfare Assn. Alleghany County, 1970-71; chmn. devel. com. Northwestern U. Alumni Program in Hosp. Adminstrn., 1962-63; chmn. adv. com. Regional Med. Program Western Pa., 1966-71; mem. steering com. Comprehensive Health Planning Western Pa.; dir. Am. States Regional Conf., 1971; vice chmn. procedures com., mem.-at-large exec. com. Okla. Regional Med. Program, 1971-78; mem. Gov's Adv. Com. Comprehensive Health Planning, 1971-80, Gov's Com. Employment of Handicapped, 1972, Pres.'s Com. Employment of Handicapped, 1962; chmn. VA chief med. dir.'s com. for evaluation and reorgn. VA health care delivery services, 1974-76; chmn. planning com. for constrn. New Children's Meml. Hosp., 1974-78; chmn. Gov.'s Ad Hoc Com on Fed.-State Planning, 1973-78; mem. Gov.'s Health Scis. Center planning and adv. com., 1973-78, State Health Planning Council, 1973-78; chmn. Okla. Health Goals and Planning Priorities Com., 1973-80; bd. dirs. Comprehensive Health Planning Agy., Western Pa.; bd. dirs. Health Services Corp., 1969-71, Okla. affiliate Am. Heart Assn., 1980-89; trustee Okla. Council Health Careers and Manpower, 1976-80; examiner Am. Coll. Hosp. Adminstrs. Lt. col. Med. Adminstrv. Corps, AUS, 1941-46. Decorated Bronze Star, Purple Heart; recipient citations VFW, 1959, citations Am. Legion, 1956, 58, citations DAV, 1964, citations Okla. Regional Med. Program, 1976, citations Okla. Gov.'s Office Health Planning, 1976, Laura G. Jackson award in recognition exceptional service in field of hosp. adminstrn., 1971, Disting. Service award Coll. Pub. Health U. Okla., 1987, Disting. Dedicated Service award Okla. Hosp. Assn., 1987; Leadership programs established in his honor Coll. Pub. Health, U. Okla. Fellow Am. Pub. Health Assn., Am. Coll. Health Care Execs. (life); mem. Am. Hosp. Assn. (life, mem. council med. edn. 1976-79), Hosp. Assn. Pa. (vice chmn. med. relations 1965-66, chmn. rehab. com. 1965-66, vice chmn. council on profl. practices, dir.), Hosp. Council Western Pa., Assn. Am. Med. Colls. (exec. com. council teaching hosps.), Oklahoma City C. of C. (vice chmn. research and edn. div. 1975-80), Northwestern U. Alumni Assn. (pres. Acacia chpt. 1961, hosp. adminstrn. chpt. 1962) Clubs: Kiwanian (Chgo.), University (Pitts.), Petroleum, Twin Hills Golf and Country (Oklahoma City), Faculty House (Oklahoma City). Home: Ste 450 6305 Waterford Blvd Oklahoma City OK 73118-1120

MACER, GEORGE ARMEN, JR. orthopedic hand surgeon; b. Pasadena, Calif., Oct. 17, 1948; s. George A. and Nevart Akullian M.; m. Celeste Angelle Lyons, Mar. 26, 1983; children: Christiana Marilu, Marina Lynn, Emily Sue. BA, U. So. Calif., 1971, MD, 1976. Diplomate Am. Bd. Med. Examiners; diplomate in orthop. surgery and hand surgery Am. Bd. Orthop. Surgery. Intern Meml. Hosp. Med. Ctr., Long Beach, Calif., 1976; resident Orthop. Hosp./U. So. Calif., 1977-81; pvt. practice hand surgery Long Beach, 1983—; asst. clin. prof. orthops. U. So. Calif., L.A., 1983-89, 90—; cons. hand surgery svc. Rancho Los Amigos Hosp. Downey, 1990—. Cons. Harbor UCLA Med. Ctr., Torrance, 1983—. Joseph Boyes Hand fellow, 1982; mem. AMA, Calif. Med. Assn., Los Angeles County Med. Assn., Calif. Orthop. Assn., Western Orthop. Assn., Am. Soc. for Surgery of Hand, Am. Acad. Orthop. Surgery. Republican. Avocations: boating, skiing, scuba diving, carpentry. Office: 3550 Linden Ave Ste 2 Long Beach CA 90807-4577

MACER-STORY, EUGENIA ANN, writer, artist; b. Mpls., Jan. 20, 1945; d. Dan Johnstone and Eugenia Loretta (Andrews) Macer; divorced; 1 child, Ezra Arthur Story. BS in Speech, Northwestern U., 1965; MFA, Columbia U., 1968. Writing instr. Polyarts, Boston, 1970-72; theater instr. Joy of Movement, 1972-75; artistic dir. Magik Mirror, Salem, Mass., 1975-76, Magick Mirror Comm., 1977—. Author: Congratulations: The UFO Reality, 1978, Angels of Time, 1982, Project Midas, 1986, Dr. Fu Man Chu Meets the Lonesome Cowboy: Sorcery and the UFO Experience, 1991, 3d edit., 1994, Gypsy Fair, 1991, The Strawberry Man, 1991, Sea Condor/Dusty Sun, 1994, Awakening to the Light-After the Longest Night, 1995, (short stories) Battles with Dragons: Certain Tales of Political Yoga, 1993, 2d edit., 1994, Legacy of Daedulus, 1995, The Dark Frontier, 1997, Troll and Other Interdimensional Invasions (short stories), 1999, Congratulations: The UFO Reality (ebook), 2000, Vanishing Questions (poetry), 2000, Carrying Thunder (poetry), 2002: Crossing Jungle River, 1998, Doing Business in Adirondacks; Unexplained and Anomalous Events, 2002; (plays) Fetching the Tree, Archaeological Politics, 2002, Strange Inquiries, Divine Appliance, 1989, The Zig Zag Wall, 1990, The Only Qualified Huntress, 1990, Telephone Taps Written Up for Tabloids, 1991, Wars with Pigeons, 1992, Conquest of the Asteroids, 1993, Commander Galacticon, 1993, Meister Hemmelin, 1994, Six Way Time Play, 1994, Radish, 1996, Setting Up for the World Trade Centaur, 1996, Mister Shooting Star, 1998, Wild Dog Casino, 1999, Magic Mirror Space Installation at 515 Greenwich Street, 1999-2001, The Old Gaffer From Boise (at Gallery 113), 2000, The Redecoration According to Currier (at Gallery 113), 2001, (play) Ayr Chronicon Sylvestre (at Theatre for the New City), 2002, others; philosophy writer; contbr. articles to profl. jours.; author poetry in Woodstock Times, Lamia Ink!, Manhattan Poetry Rev., Sensations, Kore, The Rift mag., Poet's House, Poetry Publ. Showcase, Poetry.com Anthology, 2000, Theatre for the New City Festivals, 1997—, others; feature writer Newspeak Pubs., 1995, Paranoia Mag., 2002; editor Yankee Oracle Gazette, 1999; personal appearance as profl. clairvoyant (TV documentary) Haunted Houses, 1996, UFO Desk, Sta. WBAI radio shows, 1996-2001, Star People Confs., 1998—; interviewer Interview and Occult Investigations, Magonia Mag. Online, 1998, Paranoia Mag., 2000, Infinity Factory: exhbn. paintings Barcelona, Spain, 1999, 2000, Magick Mirror Comm. Installation, 1999-2001, 515 Greenwich Gallery, So-Ho, N.Y., 1999, City Art Gallery, Stockholm, 2000, Gam'Art Diffusion, Port Frejus, France, 2002, Kelikian Gallery, Beirut, 2002. Shubert fellow, 1968. Mem. Am. Soc. Dowsers, Dramatists Guild (spkr., interviewer on radio shows and internet confs.), Theosophical Soc. Democrat. Avocations: swimming, outdoor activities, hiking. Office: Magick Mirror Comm PO Box 741 New York NY 10116-0741

MACESICH, GEORGE, econmomics professor; b. Cleve., May 27, 1927; m. Susana Sonja Svorkovich, Feb. 16, 1955; children: Maja, Milena, George M.P. AA, George Washington U., 1951, BA, 1953, MA, 1954; PhD, U. Chgo., 1958. Tchg. and rsch. positions while completing graduate study, 1953-58; rsch. economist U.S. C. of C., Washington, 1958-59; asst. prof. Econs. Fla. State U., Tallahassee, 1959-61, assoc. prof. Econs., 1961-63, prof. Econs. Tallhassee, 1963—, U. Belgrade, Yugoslavia, 1972—. Mem. Editorial Bd. So. Econ. Jour., 1961-63; cons. U.S. Dept. Commerce, 1961-65; vis. economist Nat. Bank of Yugoslavia, 1965; founding dir. Ctr. for Yugoslav-Am. Studies, Rsch. and Exchanges, Fla. State U., 1961—, Inst. Comparative Policy Studies Rsch. and Exchanges, 1992—; cons. Jour. of Political Economy, U. Chgo., 1968-81, The Coun. of Grad. Schs. in U.S., Washington, 1971-82, Jour. of Money, Credit and Banking, 1977-89; editorial bd. Foreign Trade and Cycles, 1970-76, So. Economic Jour., 1972-76; and numerous other roles related to economics. Author, co-author or editor of 30 published books and over 100 articles including The International Monetary Economy and the Third World, 1981, Politics of Monetarism: Its Historical and Institutional Development, 1984, Monetary Reform and Cooperation Theory, 1989, Money and Democracy, 1990, (with D. Dimitrijevic) The Money Supply Process: A Comparative Analysis, 1990, World Debt and Stability, 1990, Reform and Market Democracy, 1991, Yugoslavia in the Age of Democracy: Essays on Economic and Political Reform, 1992, Monetary Policy and Politics: RulesVersus Discretion, 1992, Successor States and Cooperation Theory, 1994, Monetary Reform in Former Socialist Countries, 1995, Integration and Stabilization: A Monetary View, 1995, Transformation and Emerging Markets, 1996, The U.S. in a Changing Global Economy: Policy Implications and Issues, 1997, World Economy at the Cross Roads, 1997, Money, Systems and Growth, 1998, Political Economy of Money: The Emerging Fiat Monetary Regime, 1999, Issues in Money and Banking, 2000, Money and Monetary Regimes, 2002; contbr. numerous articles to profl. jours. Bd. dirs. Coun. Econ. Devel., Tallahassee, Fla., 1961-63, Nikola Tesla Meml. Soc., 1980-81; mem. U.S. - Yugoslav Economic Coun., 1987—, Inst. for Internat. Edn. Screening Com. 1984-87. With U.S. Navy 1944-53. Recipient Ford Found. fellowship, 1959-60, Fulbright fellowship, 1965, Order of Yugoslav Star with Gold Wreath, Yugoslav Govt., 1983, award of Merit, U. Zagreb, 1989. Mem. Am. Acad. Polit. and Social Sci., Am. Econ. Assn., Am. Foreign Svc. Assn., Am. Statis. Assn., So. Economic Assn., U.S. Naval Inst., Pi Gamma Mu. Home: 2401 Delgado Dr Tallahassee FL 32304-1303 Office: Inst Comparative Policy and Dept Economics Fla State U Tallahassee FL 32306

MACEWAN, NIGEL SAVAGE, merchant banker; b. Balt., Mar. 21, 1933; s. Nigel Savage and Ellen (Wharton) MacE.; children: Alison, Nigel, Pamela, Elizabeth; m. Judith Sperry, Sept. 2, 1995. BA, Yale U., 1955; MBA, Harvard U., 1959. Assoc. Morgan Stanley & Co., N.Y.C., 1959-62, White, Weld & Co., N.Y.C., 1962-63; v.p. R.S. Dickson & Co., Charlotte, N.C., 1963-68; chmn. Fin. Cons. Internat. Ltd., Brussels, 1965-68; successively gen. ptnr., exec. v.p., pres., dir. White, Weld & Co., N.Y.C., 1968-78; sr. v.p., dir. Merrill Lynch, Pierce, Fenner & Smith, 1978-87; chmn. Merrill Lynch Capital Ptnrs., 1985-87; pres., CEO Kleinwort Benson, N.Am. Inc., 1987-93, also bd. dirs. Chmn. Kleinwort Benson North Am., Inc., Kleinworth Benson Holdings, Inc., Alex Brown Kleinwort Benson Realty Advs.; bd. dirs. Kleinwort Benson Group plc, Kleinwort Benson Ltd., 1987-93, Kleinworth Benson Australian Income Fund, 1992-99; adj. prof. bus. adminstrn. NYU, 1973-75. Pres. Tokeneke Tax Dist., Darien, 1978-80, later treas.; bd. dirs. Islesboro (Maine) Health Ctr., 1994—, Sailors Mus. and Lighthouse, Islesboro, 1993-2000; trustee coun. Island Inst., 1997—; adv. coun. Islesboro Island Trust, 1997-2000, Conservation Law Found., 1998—. Served with USN, 1955-57. Mem. Securities Industry Assn. (chmn. N.Y. group 1975-76), N.Y. Yacht Club, Yale Club N.Y., Wee Burn Country Club, Tokeneke Club, Tarrantine Club (Dark Harbor, Maine), Cruising Club Am., Clyde Cruising Club (Scotland). Republican. Episcopalian. Home: 153 Oenoke Ln New Canaan CT 06840-4518 E-mail: nsmace@email.msn.com.

MACEY, JONATHAN R. law educator; b. 1955; BA, Harvard U., 1977; JD, Yale U., 1982; PhD (hon.), Stockholm Sch. Econs., 1996. Bar: Ga. 1986. Law clk. to Hon. Henry J. Friendly U.S. Ct. Appeals (2nd cir.), N.Y.C., 1982-83; asst. prof. Emory U., 1983-86, assoc. prof., 1986-87; vis. assoc. prof. U. Va., 1986-87; prof. Cornell U., 1987-90; vis. prof. U. Chgo., fall 1989, prof., 1990-92; J. Dupratt White prof. law Cornell U., Ithaca, N.Y., 1993—; dir. John M. Olin program in law and econs. Cornell U. Law Sch., 1992—. Vis. prof. Harvard U., 1999, Bocconi, Milan, 2000. Recipient Paul M. Bator prize Federalist Soc. for Law and Pub. Policy, 1995, D.P. Jacobs prize. Mem. ABA (bus. assn. and corp. gov.), Am. Law and Econs. Assn. (bd. dirs.), Am. Law Inst., N.Y. Stock Exchange (mem. legal adv. bd.). Office: Cornell U Law Sch Myron Taylor Hall Ithaca NY 14853 E-mail: Jonathan-Macey@postoffice.law.cornell.edu.

MACEY, WILLIAM BLACKMORE, oil company executive; b. Buffalo, Aug. 1, 1920; s. Richard Charles and Doris (Bourne) M.; m. Jean Olive Mullins, Oct. 6, 1945; 1 dau., Barbara Jean. BS in Petroleum Engring, N.Mex. Sch. Mines, 1942; D.Engring. (hon.), N.Mex. Inst. Mining and Tech., 1984. Dist. engr. N.Mex. Oil Conservation Commn., 1946-48; dist. supt. Am. Republics Corp., 1948-52; chief engr. N.Mex. Oil Conservation Commn., 1952-54, state geologist, dir., 1954-56; v.p. Internat. Oil & Gas Corp. (and predecessor co., developers mineral properties), Denver, 1956-60, then pres., 1960-67; pres. Nielson Enterprises Inc., oil and gas prodn. and pipelines, livestock ranching, 1967-74; v.p., dir. Y-Tex Corp. (mfr. livestock identification tags), 1972-73; pres. GEN Oil Inc. (oil and gas prodn.), 1972-75, Col. Cody Inn (real estate and golf course devel.), 1970-73; pres., dir. Macey & Mershon Oil, Inc., 1974-93; dir. Juniper Oil and Gas Corp., Denver, 1981-83, Ruidoso (N.Mex.) State Bank Holding Co., 1987—; pres. The Macey Corp., Denver, 1985—. Chmn. Pres.'s N.Mex. Inst. Mines and Tech., 1980-82; mem. adv. bd. U. Ariz. Heart Ctr., 1997—; mem. Pres.'s U. Ariz. Found. Served from 2d lt. to capt. USAAF, 1942-45. Mem.: N.Mex. Oil and Gas Assn. (exec. com. 1949—52, 1960—61), Popejoy & Pres.'s Club (U. N.Mex.), N.Mex. Jockey Club (bd. dirs. 1985—88, 1991—93, pres. 1993), Ruidoso, Tucson Country Club, Altolakes Golf and Country Club, Skyline Country Club (Tucson) (dir., treas. 1980—82, pres. 1982—83), Garden of the Gods. Episcopalian. Home: 7010 N Javelina Dr Tucson AZ 85718-1850 also: 10153 Masters Dr NE Albuquerque NM 87111-5894 Office: PO Box 2210 Denver CO 80201-2210

MACFADYEN, JOHN ARCHIBALD, III, lawyer; b. Bethleham, Pa., Dec. 7, 1948; s. John Archibald Jr. and Nancy (Gerrish) MacF.; children: James C., Alexander L., Christopher G.; m. B. Jean Rosiello. AB, Harvard Coll., 1970; JD, Boston U., 1974. Bar: R.I. 1974, Mass. 1974, U.S. Dist. Ct. R.I. 1975, U.S. Supreme Ct. 1978, U.S. Ct. Appeals (1st cir.) 1983. Staff atty. Office of Pub. Defender, Providence, 1975-81; assoc. Vetter & White, 1981-83; sole practitioner, 1983—. Lectr. Law Seminars Internat., Seattle, 1991. Co-author: R.I. Criminal Procedure, 1988. Fellow Am. Coll. Trial Lawyers, Am. Acad. Appellate Lawyers; mem. R.I. Bar Assn. (lectr. 1989—), R.I. Bd. Bar Examiners, Barrister, Am. Inns. of Ct. Office: The Remington Bldg 91 Friendship St Providence RI 02903-3837

MACFARLAND, MIRIAM KATHERINE (MIMI MACFARLAND), computer science consultant, writer; b. Trenton, N.J., June 21, 1949; d. James and Merrianne (Collins) MacF.; children: Bridget Lorraine MacFarland, Chloe Merrianne Griffin. Student, Rutgers U., 1976-78, U. Pa., 1981-83; B in Liberal Studies with distinction, U. Okla., 2000; student in lit., Oxford U., Eng., 1988, Fine Arts Work Ctr., Provincetown, Mass., 1999; postgrad., L.I. U., 2000—. Programmer-analyst R&D Computer Scis. Corp., Warminster, Pa., 1977-81; programmer-analyst NASA/Ames Rsch. Ctr., Moffett Field, Calif., 1978; staff writer, computer graphics engring. Aydin Controls, Inc., Ft. Washington, Pa., 1981-82; writer BancTec, Inc., Oklahoma City and Dallas, 1983-95; cons. engr. MCI Comm. Internat., Rye Brook, N.Y., 1984-86, Western Union Internat., N.Y.C., 1984, RCA Global Comm., Fort Lee, N.J., 1985; cons. engr., writer Siemens Med. Sys., Iselin, 1988-98; adj. assoc. prof. English, Southampton Coll. L.I. U., 2001—. Guest spkr. Okla. State U., Edmond, 1994, Americorps, Oklahoma City, 1995; mem. dean's student adv. com. U. Okla., 1999-2000. Author poetry, plays, numerous lit. revs., CONTACT/II, The Bloomsbury Rev., Another Chgo. Mag., Renovated Lighthouse; author: 14 books and numerous shorter works pertaining to computer scis.; contbr. articles and poetry to jours., books and mags. Mem. Dem. Nat. Com. L.I. U. fellow in writing, 2000—, GAPA awardee, 2000—. Mem. ACLU, Associated Writing Programs, Phi Kappa Phi. Protestant. Office: 2323 Blue Creek Ct Norman OK 73026 E-mail: mimimac621@aol.com.

MACFARLANE, ALASTAIR IAIN ROBERT, business executive; b. Sydney, Australia, Mar. 7, 1940; came to U.S., 1978; s. Alexander Dunlop and Margaret Elizabeth (Swan) M.; m. Madge McCleary, Sept. 24, 1966; children: Douglas, Dennis, Robert, Jeffrey. B in Econs. with honours, U. Sydney, 1961; MBA, U. Hawaii, 1964; postgrad., Columbia U., 1964; AMP, Harvard U., 1977. Comml. cadet B.H.P. Ltd., Australia, 1958-62; product mgr. H.J. Heinz Co., Pitts., 1965-66, gen. mgr. new products div. Melbourne, Australia, 1967-72; ptnr., dir., gen. mgr. Singleton, Palmer & Strauss McAllan Pty. Ltd., Sydney, 1972-73; dir., gen. mgr. successor co. Doyle Dane Bernbach Internat. Inc., 1973-77, group sr. v.p. N.Y.C., 1978-84; pres., chief exec. officer PowerBase Systems, Inc., 1984-85, Productivity Software Internat. L.P., N.Y.C., 1985-86; div. pres., pub. Whittle Comm. L.P., Knoxville, Tenn., 1987-88; chmn., CEO Phyton Techs. Inc., 1988-94; pres., CEO Knox Internat. Corp., 1988-94; chmn., CEO Mich. Bulb Co., Grand Rapids, 1988-94; dir. Univ. of Sydney USA Found., 1994—; chmn., CEO Creative Pub. Internat., Inc., Minnetonka, Minn., 1997-99; sr. v.p. Pleasant Co., Middleton, Wis., 2000-2001; CEO Centric Strategies Internat., Inc., Mpls., 2001—. Chmn., CEO Lansinoh, Labs., Inc., Oak Ridge, Tenn., 1994—96; lectr. Monash U., Melbourne, 1970—71; ind. mgmt. cons., Melbourne, 1970—72. Author papers in field. V.p. Waverley Dist. Cricket Club, 1975-77. East-West Ctr. fellow, 1962-64; Australian Commonwealth scholar, Australian Steel Industry scholar, 1958-61. Fellow Australian Inst. Mgmt. (assoc.); mem. Australian Soc. Accts. (assoc.), Harvard Club N.Y.C., Blackhawk Country Club (Madison). Home and Office: Centric Strategies Internat Inc 6219 S Highlands Ave Madison WI 53705

MACFARLANE, ANDREW WALKER, media specialist, educatorm, actor; b. Toronto, Ont., Can., Feb. 18, 1928; s. Joseph Arthur and Marguerite (Walker) MacF.; m. Betty Doris Wright Seldon; 1 stepchild, Elizabeth Seldon; children by previous marriage: Jeanie Andreas, Catriona Flora. Student, U. Sask., Can., 1945-46; BA, U. Toronto, 1949; M.L.S., U. Western Ont., 1977. With Canadian Press, Toronto, 1949; reporter Halifax (N.S., Can.) Chronicle Herald, 1949-51, Scottish Daily Express, Glasgow, 1951-53; subeditor London Evening Standard, 1953-55; copy editor, night editor, feature editor, gen. reporter, daily columnist, asst. to pub. Telegram, Toronto, 1955-64, mng. editor, corporate dir., 1964-69, dir. research and devel., 1969-71, exec. editor, 1971—; dir. Citizen's Inquiry br. Ministry Govt. Services, Province of Ont., 1971-72; chmn. dept., dean Grad. Sch. Journalism, U. Western Ont., 1973-80, prof., 1981-93; prof. emeritus U. Western Ont., 1993—; chair mass media studies, dir. Ctr. in Mass Media Studies Grad. Sch. Journalism, U. Western Ont., 1990-93. Co-chmn. Ont.-Que. Journalist Exchange. Author: The Neverland of the Neglected Child, 1957, It Seemed Like a Good Idea at the Time, 1983, Local Flavor, 1990; editor: Byline, 1983, Byline Canada, 1984. Bd. dirs. Canadian Medic-Alert, 1959; past bd. dirs. Met. Toronto Children's Aid Soc.; chmn. advisory council Province of Ont. Medal Good Citizenship. Recipient Bowater award, 1960, Nat. Newspaper award, 1958, 59, Nat. Teaching award Poynter Inst. for Media Studies, 1987, Province Ont. Bicentennial medal; Southam fellow, 1961. Mem. Assn. for Edn. in Journalism and Mass Comm., Can. Comm. Assn., Alliance of Can. Cinema TV and Radio Artists, Commonwealth Assn. for Edn. in Journalism and Comm. (founding pres.), Can. Actors Equity Assn. (apprentice mem.), Toronto Press Club.

MACFARLANE, JOHN ALEXANDER, former federal housing agency administrator; b. Winnipeg, Man., Can., Sept. 6, 1916; s. John MacKay and Annie Catherine (Smith) MacF.; m. Gladys Valda Church, Dec. 20, 1941; children: John Lane, Elizabeth Ann, Janet Christine. BA with honours, U. Man., Winnipeg, 1939. With stats. br. Wartime Prices and Trade Bd., Ottawa, Ont., Can., 1940-46; supr. stats. dept. Cn. Mortgage and Housing Corp., 1946-65, asst. dir. econs. and stats. div., 1965-69, asst. dir. secretariat div., 1969-78; ret., 1978; treas. Caribbean and N.Am. area coun. World Alliance Ref. Chs., 1984—. Treas. Ottawa Valley Cricket Coun., 1946-70, 73-80, pres., 1970-73, 83-88; moderator Presbytery of Ottawa, Presbyn. Ch. Can., 1994-96, rep. elder, 1961-97. Recipient Long Svc. medal Boy Scouts Assn., 1945, Centennial medal Govt. of Can., 1967, spl. achievement award for amateur sport Govt. of Ont., 1991; mem. choir St. Andrew's Presbyn. Ch. Mem. Def. Cricket Club (sec.-treas. 1944-46, pres. 1951-76, 78-92). Avocation: stamp collecting. Address: 1216 Foxborough Private Gloucester ON Canada K1J 1E2 E-mail: JAMacF@aol.com. *I have touched many people as the years have passed; if I have helped one for the better I shall rest content.*

MACFARLANE, JOHN CHARLES, utility company executive; b. Hallock, Minn., Nov. 8, 1939; s. Ernest Edward and Mary Bell (Yates) MacF.; m. Eunice Darlene Axvig, Apr. 13, 1963; children: Charles, James, William. BSEE, U. N.D., 1961. Staff engr. Otter Tail Power Co., Fergus Falls, Mn., 1961-64, div. engr. Jamestown, N.D., 1964-71, div. mgr. Langdon, 1972-78, v.p. planning and control Fergus Falls, 1978-80, exec. v.p., 1981-82, pres. and chief exec. officer, 1982—, also bd. dirs., now chmn. Bd. dirs. Wells Fargo, Fergus Falls, Pioneer Mut. Ins. Co. Pres. Langdon City Commn., 1974-78; chmn. Fergus Falls Port Authority, 1985-86; bd. dirs. Minn. Assn. Commerce and Industry, Minn. Safety Coun., Edison Electric Inst., Village Family Svcs., Fargo; bd. dirs. U. N.D. Energy Rsch. Adv. Coun. Served with U.S. Army, 1962-64. Mem. Am. Mgmt. Assn., IEEE (chmn. Red River chpt.), U. N.D. Alumni Assn., Fergus Falls C. of C. Lodges: Rotary, Masons. Republican. Presbyterian. Office: Otter Tail Power Co 215 S Cascade St Fergus Falls MN 56537-2897

MACFARLANE, MAUREEN ANNE, lawyer; b. Boston, May 19, 1965; d. Joseph Alexander and Lorraine Anne (Walsh) MacF. BA magna cum laude, Boston Coll., 1986, MA in English, 1999; JD, Boston U., 1989, MS in Journalism, 1990. Bar: Mass. 1989, U.S. Dist. Ct. Mass. 1990, U.S. Ct. Appeals (D.C. and 1st cirs.) 1990, U.S. Supreme Ct. 1993. Law clk. to presiding justice Mass. Ct. Appeals, Boston, 1989-90; assoc. Widett Slater & Goldman P.C., 1990-92, Hutchins, Wheeler & Dittmar, P.C., Boston, 1992-95; atty. Lucash, Gesmer & Updegrove, LLP, 1995-98, Boston Pub. Sch. Dept., Office Legal Advisor, 1998-2001; legal counsel Cambridge (Mass.) Pub. Sch. Dept., 2001—. Writer Mass. Lawyers Weekly, Boston, 1988-89. Sec. Boston Liturgical Dance Ensemble, Chestnut Hill, Mass., 1989—; mem. Boston Mayor's Youth Leadership Corp., Boston, 1991-92; exec. com. Boston U. Sch. Law Alumni, 1993—; spl. events chair McMullen Mus. Coun., 1997-99. Mem. ABA, Mass. Bar Assn., Boston Bar Assn. (YLS steering com. 1991-94, children's outreach task force 2000-2002), Mass. Coun. Sch. Attys. Office: 159 Thorndike St Cambridge MA 02141-1528

MACGINN, NOELA PATRICIA, family nurse practitioner; b. Mar. 17, 1961; BSN, SUNY, Stony Brook, 1983, MS, Nurse Practitioner, 1989. RN, N.Y., 1983; cert. family nurse practitioner, N.Y., 1989, Am. Bd. Occupl. Health Nurse, 1994, Am. Acad. Nurse Practitioners, 1995, ANA family nurse practitioner, 1993. Occupl. health nurse practitioner L.I. Jewish Med. Ctr., Lake Success, NY, 1989-93; clin. mgr. for employee health NYU Med. Ctr., 1993-96; dir. Sound Shore Health Sys., New Rochelle, NY, 1996-99; nurse practitioner, officer J.P. Morgan Chase, N.Y., 1999—2002; cosmetic nurse practitioner Dr. Andrew Kleinman Plastic Surgery, Westchester, NY, 1998—; skincare practitioner SkinKlinic, N.Y.C., 2002. Home: 100 Beekman St Apt 20C New York NY 10038-1815

MACGOWAN, EUGENIA, lawyer; b. Turlock, Calif., Aug. 4, 1928; d. William Ray and Mary Bolling (Gilbert) Kern; m. Gordon Scott Millar, Jan. 2, 1970 (dec. Jan. 1997); 1 dau., Heather Mary. AB, U. Calif., Berkeley, 1950;

JD, U. Calif., San Francisco, 1953. Bar: Calif. 1953; cert. family law specialist Calif. State Bar Bd. Legal Specialization. Research atty. Supreme Ct. Calif., 1954, Calif. Ct. Appeals, 1955; partner firm MacGowan & MacGowan, Calif., 1956-68; pvt. practice, San Francisco, 1968-99. Bd. dirs. San Francisco Speech and Hearing Center, San Francisco Legal Aid Soc., J.A.C.K.I.E. Mem. Am., Calif., San Francisco bar assns., Queen's Bench. Clubs: San Francisco Lawyers, Forest Hill Garden. Office: 236 W Portal Ave San Francisco CA 94127-1423

MACGOWAN, SANDRA FIRELLI, publishing executive, publishing educator; b. Phila., Nov. 9, 1951; d. William Firelli and Barbara (Gimbel) Kapalcik. BS in Biology, BA in English, Pa. State U., 1973, MA in English Lit., 1978. Cert. supervisory analyst N.Y. Stock Exchange. Editor McGraw-Hill Pub. Co., N.Y.C., 1979-81; sr. acquisitions editor Harcourt Brace Jovanovich, Inc., 1981-82; sr. editor The Coll. Bd., 1982-88; v.p., head editorial CS First Boston Corp., 1988-94; v.p. supervisory analyst internat. rsch. SBC Warburg, 1994-96; v.p., supervisory analyst internat. rsch. Arnhold and S. Bleichroeder, 1996—. Part time assoc. prof. pub. NYU Sch. Continuing Edn., N.Y.C., 1985—. Author: 50 College Admission Directors Speak to Parents, 1988. Democrat. Avocations: art, reading, travel. Office: Arnhold and S Bleichroeder Fl 44 1345 Avenue Of The Americas New York NY 10105-4300

MACGREGOR, DAVID LEE, lawyer; b. Cedar Rapids, Iowa, Sept. 17, 1932; s. John H. and Beulah A. (Morris) MacG.; m. Helen Jean Kolberg, Aug. 7, 1954; children— Scott J., William M., Brian K., Thomas D. BBA, U. Wis., 1954, LL.B., 1956. Assoc. Quarles & Brady and predecessor firms, Milw., 1959-64, ptnr., 1964-99, retired, 1999—. Pres. Nat. Assn. Estate Planning Coun., 1979-80, pres. Milw. chpt. 1972-73; mem. adv. bd. CCH Fin. and Estate Planning, N.Y.C., 1982-87 Mem. State Bar Wis. (chmn. taxation sect. 1977-78), Regency House Condominium Assn. (treas., dir.), Stackner Family Found. Inc. (asst. sec., dir.). Home: 929 N Astor St Unit 1608 Milwaukee WI 53202-3486 Office: Quarles & Brady 411 E Wisconsin Ave Ste 2550 Milwaukee WI 53202-4497

MACGREGOR, GEORGE LESCHER, JR. freelance writer; b. Dallas, Sept. 15, 1936; s. George Lescher and Jean (Edge) MacG.; divorced; children: George Lescher III, Michael Fordtran. BBA, U. Tex., 1958. Asst. cashier First Nat. Bank in Dallas, 1960-64, asst. v.p., 1964-68; v.p. Nat. Bank of Commerce of Dallas, 1968-70, sr. v.p., 1970-73, exec. v.p., 1973-74; pres., chief exec. officer Mountain Banks Ltd., Colorado Springs, 1974-77; chief exec. officer Highfield Fin. (U.S.A.) Ltd., 1978-83; chmn. bd., chief exec. officer, dir. Dominion Nat. Bank, Denver, 1981-84; chmn. bd., chief exec. officer Royal Dominion Ltd.; chmn. bd., chief exec. officer, dir. Market Bank of Denver, 1983-84; vice chmn., dir. Bank of Aurora, Denver, 1983-84; chmn., pres., chief exec. officer Alamosa Bancorp. of Colo., 1983-84; pres., chief exec. officer Am. Interstate Bancorp., 1984-88; pres. Banco, Inc., 1984-89; sr. mng. ptnr. Scotland Co., Denver, London, 1988-91; free-lance writer, 1992—. Served with M.C. AUS, 1958-60. Mem. Am. Inst. Banking (hon.), Young Pres.'s Orgn., Koon Kreek Club, Broadmoore Golf Club, Oxford Club, Phi Gamma Delta. Anglican Catholic. Home and Office: 1736 Blake St Denver CO 80202-1226 Fax: 303-292-9794.

MACGREGOR, GLENDA SUE, b. Harlingen, Tex., Mar. 2, 1943; d. Nolan Edgar and Helen Doris (Hays) Wilborn; children: Matthew Chandler, Heather Joan; m. John MacGregor. BS, U. Ill., 1965. Rsch. asst. Ill. Geol. Survey, Urbana, 1965-67; tchr. Arcola (Ill.) Jr. High Sch., 1967-69; geology text author O'Fallon (Ill.) High Sch., 1976-82; compliance officer St. Clair County Grants Dept., Belleville, Ill., 1983-87; dir. job tng. McKendree Coll., Lebanon, 1987-88, dean of admissions and fin. aid, 1988—2001; cons. coll. enrollment mgmt. Co-author: (high sch. text) Geology Is, 1977. Bd. dirs. bootstrap program St. Clair County Housing Authority, 1991—. Mem. Nat. Assn. Coll. Admissions Counseling, Nat. Assn. Collegiate Registrars and Admissions Officers, Ill. Assn. Collegiate Registrars and Admissions Officers, Ill. Assn. Coll. Admissions Counselors, Avocations: walking, cycling, arts and crafts, reading, music. Home and Office: 2715 Ridgeview Way Marion IA 52302 Office: McKendree Coll 701 College Rd Lebanon IL 62254-1212 E-mail: smacgregorgl@hotmail.com.

MACGREGOR, JAMES THOMAS, toxicologist; b. N.Y.C., Jan. 14, 1944; s. James and Phyllis (Bowman) MacG.; m. Judith Anne Anello, July 12, 1969; 1 child, Jennifer Lee. BS in Chemistry, Union Coll., Schenectady, N.Y., 1965; PhD in Toxicology, U. Rochester, 1971. Diplomate Am. Bd. Toxicology. Postdoctoral fellow U. Calif., San Francisco, 1970-72; dir. food safety rsch. USDA, Berkeley, Calif., 1972-88; assoc. prof. U. Calif., 1978-88; pres. Toxicology Consulting Svcs., Danville, Calif., 1988-90; dir. toxicology and metabolism lab. SRI Internat., Menlo Park, 1990-97; dir. Office of Testing and Rsch. FDA Ctr. for Drug Evaluation and Rsch., Rockville, Md., 1997-2001; dep. dir. Washington ops. FDA Nat. Ctr. for Toxicological Rsch., 2001—. Mem. numerous nat. and internat. profl. coms. and working groups. Mem. editorial bd.: Environ. Molecular Mutagenesis, N.Y.C., 1986-88, Mutation Res., Amsterdam, 1989-91, 97—, Mutagenesis, Oxford, 1989-93. Recipient Alexander Hollender award, 1995. Mem. Am. Assn. Cancer Rsch., Assn. Govt. Toxicologists (pres.-elect, 2002—), Soc. Toxicology, Environ. Mutagen Soc. (treas. 1986-89, pres. 1992-93), Genetic Environ. Toxicology Assn. No. Calif. (pres. 1982). Office: FDA Nat Ctr for Toxicological Rsch HFT-10 16-53 5600 Fishers Ln Rockville MD 20857-0001 E-mail: jmacgregor@nctr.fda.gov.

MACGREGOR, MEICHELLE ROSE, lawyer; b. Bronx, N.Y., May 23, 1967; BA in Gen. Lit., SUNY, Binghamton, 1989; JD, Bklyn. Law Sch., 1994. Bar: N.Y., N.J., U.S. Dist. Ct. (so. dist.) N.Y., U.S. Dist. Ct. (ea. dist.) N.Y. Law clk. to hon. Bernard J. Fried Supreme Ct., State of N.Y., 1994-96; assoc. Cowan Liebowitz and Latman, P.C., N.Y.C., 1994—. Assoc. mng. editor Bklyn. Jour. Internat. Law, 1993-94. Scholarship Bklyn. Law Sch., 1992-93, 93-94. Office: Cowan Liebowitz Latman PC 1133 Avenue Of The Americas New York NY 10036-6710 Home: 111-113 Montague St 6D Brooklyn NY 11201

MACGUNNIGLE, BRUCE CAMPBELL, manufacturing company executive; b. Providence, Mar. 18, 1947; s. Douglas Campbell and Dorothy Stewart (Greene) McGunigle; m. Kathleen Marie Walsh, Aug. 4, 1973; children: Douglas Campbell II, Alison Campbell. BS, U. R.I., 1970. From export credit mgr. to export sales mgr. Brown & Sharpe Mfg. Co., North Kingstown, R.I., 1982-89; bus. mgr. W.R. Cobb Co., Cranston, 1989—. Dir. Varnum House Mus., East Greenwich, R.I., 1990—. Author: Rhode Island Freemen 1747-1755: A Census of Registered Voters, 1976, Docents' Guide to the James Mitchell Varnum House Museum, 1989, Mayflower Families, Vol. 4, 1990, 2d edit., 1995, Edward Fuller and His Descendants for Five Generations, East greenwich Rhode Island Historical Cemetery Inscriptions, 1991, Children's Walking Tour of Historic East Greenwich, R.I., 1994, 3d edit., 1999; editor: New England's Victory at Lousburg in 1745, 1986, Rhode Islanders Misbehave at Surinam in 1744: A Complaint Against the Captain and Crew of the Prince Charles of Loraine of Bristol, Rhode Island, 1976, Carnage at Cartagena: Captain William Hopkins and His Rhode Island Recruits in the Campaign Against Cartagena and Cuba 1741, 1988, John Brown of Providence and His Chariot, 1989, Delenda est Canada--Canada Must be Conquered, 1990, Red Coats and Yellow Fever: Rhode Island Troops at the Siege of Havana 1762, 1991, The Game Cock Readies to Strike: Abraham Whipple, Commander of the Schooner Game Cock, Receives Letters of Marque from Governor Stephen Hopkins, 1759, 1993. Bd. dirs. East Greenwich Preservation Soc., 1984-96; vestryman St. Martin's Episcopal Ch., Providence, 1973-76, St. Luke's Episcopal Ch., East Greenwich, 1984-86; comdg. officer Varnum Continentals, East Greenwich, 1993—; mem. com. troop 2 Boy Scouts Am., East Greenwich, 1988—; mem. East Greenwich Hist. Dist. Commn., 1982—. Col. R.I. Militia. Recipient John Nicholas Brown award League R.I. Hist. Socs., 1993, cert. of commendation Am. Assn. for State and Local History, 1994, Meritorious Svc. medal R.I. Militia, 1993, Marion Fry Hist. Preservation award Town of East Greenwich, 1995. Mem. Soc. Mayflower Descendants (gov. 1986-89, capt. gen. 1987-90, asst. gov. gen. 1996-99, cert. commendation 1987, 91, 93, 96), New Eng. Hist. and Geneal. Soc., R.I. Soc. Colonial Wars (historian 1984-2000), R.I. Geneal. Soc. (pres. 1980-83, Doane-Farnum award 1993), R.I. Hist. Soc., Huguenot Soc. R.I. (pres. 1989—), East Greenwich Vet. Firemen's Assn., Univ. Club Providence. Avocations: genealogy, reading. Home: 80 Rector St East Greenwich RI 02818-3313 Office: WR Cobb Co 850 Wellington Ave Cranston RI 02910-3729 E-mail: k8bcm@cux.com.

MACH, RACHEL, accountant; b. Toledo, Nov. 26, 1968; d. Terry Richard and Susan (Starks) Hayes; m. Gregory Alexander Mach, Dec. 25, 1992; children: Alexander, Heidi. BS in Acctg., Alderson-Broaddus Coll., 1990. Acct. Davis Trust Co., Elkins, W.Va., 1990—98, contr., 1998—; client support rep. Profitstar, Inc., Omaha, 1996—97. Contr. Friends of Ft. Liberte, Elkins, W.Va., 1993—.

MACHADO, CAROLYN FRANCES, political consultant; b. Providence, Mar. 13, 1967; d. Edward Steven and Patricia Ann Machado; m. Eugene Christopher Ulm, Feb. 14, 1998. BA in Polit. Sci., Boston U., 1990; postgrad., Georgetown U. Legis. rschr. Environ. and Energy Study Inst., Washington, 1988; fin. dir. Rep. Claudine Schneider Senate Campaign, Providence, 1990, Steve Duprey Congl. Campaign, Concord, N.H., 1992, Rep. Bill Zeliff Congl. Campaign, Manchester, 1992; media dir. Renew Am., Washington, 1991-92; dir. Am. Cons. Engrs./Polit. Action Com. and grassroots programs Am. Cons. Engrs. Coun., 1992-95; prin., founder Machado & Co., 1994—; Washington corr. to overseas radio stas. Australia, New Zealand, 1996—. Vol. cons./trainer Internat. Rep. inst., Washington, 1998—, Women's Campaign Fund, Washington, 1997—; mem. polit. adv. bd. Voter.com, Boston, 1999—. Named Rising Star of Politics, Campaigns and Elections mag., 1996. Mem. Am. Assn. Polit. Cons., U.S. House and Senate Press Gallery, New Zealand Nat. Press Club (hon.). Republican. Roman Catholic. Avocations: travel, photography, writing. Office: Machado & Co 6111 Newman Rd Fairfax VA 22030-5918 Fax: 703-266-5873.

MACHALOW, ROBERT ALLEN, librarian; b. Queens, N.Y., Oct. 22, 1951; s. Leonard S. M. and Roslyn Miller; m. Rosalie D. Slifkin, Nov. 23, 1975; children: Deborah Penney, Charles Scott. BA in English, SUNY, Stony Brook, 1973; MA in English, Ind. U., 1974; MLS, Rutgers U., 1975; postgrad., Adelphi U., 1981-82. Cert. pub. libr., N.Y. Libr. H.W. Wilson Co., Bronx, N.Y., 1975-76, Children's TV Workshop, N.Y.C., 1976-78; program assoc. Found. Ctr., 1978-79; faculty libr. cons. Hudson County C.C., Jersey City, 1979-81; instr. Brandeis Sch., Lawrence, N.Y., 1981-82; prof. libr., chief libr. York Coll. CUNY, Jamaica, 1982—. Evening reference libr. Poly. Inst. N.Y., Bklyn., 1976-78; instr. Malcolm-King: Harlem Coll. Ext., N.Y.C. and Coll. Mt. St. Vincent, Riverdale, N.Y., 1979-80; vol. basic skills instr., cons. Queens Day Ctr. L.I. Jewish Med. Ctr., Jamaica, 1980; instr. Hudson County C.C., Jersey City, 1979-81, libr., 1980-81; instr. Poly. Inst. N.Y., Bklyn., 1982; tutor Writing Skills Ctr. York Coll. CUNY, Jamaica, 1983-84; instr. writing Rsch. Found. CUNY, N.Y.C., 1985—. Contbr. articles to profl. jours. Avocations: writing, reading, computers. Office: York Coll Libr 94-20 Guy R Brewer Blvd Jamaica NY 11451-0001

MACHANN, CLINTON JOHN, English educator; b. Bryan, Tex., July 18, 1947; s. J.W. and Sophie E. Machann; m. Virginia Brown; children: Alena, Theresie, Sarah. BA, Tex. A&M U., 1969; PhD, U. Tex., 1976. Tchr. Tex. Pub. Schs., Houston, 1969-71; tchg. asst. U. Tex., Austin, 1971-76; prof. English Tex. A&M U., College Station, 1976—. Chmn. bd. dirs. Czech Ednl. Found. Tex., 1995—; Fulbright lectr. Charles U., Prague, Czech Republic, 1990. Author: The Genre of Autobiography in Victorian Literature, 1994, Matthew Arnold: A Literary Life, 1998, Jason Jackson, 1993; editor: Czech-Americans in Transition, 1999. Mem. MLA. Avocations: writing novels and poems, songwriting. Home: 1029 Walton Dr College Station TX 77840-2310 Office: Tex A&M U Dept English College Station TX 77843-4227

MACHASKEE, ALEX, newspaper publishing company executive; b. Warren, Ohio; m. Carol Machaskee. BA in Mktg., Cleve. State U., 1972, LHD (hon.), 1995, U. Akron, 1998. Sports reporter The Warren (Ohio) Tribune; promo dir. to dir. labor rels. & pers. to v.p., gen. mgr. The Plain Dealer, Cleve., 1985-90, pres., pub., 1990—. V.p. Mus. Arts Assn. (Cleve. Orch.); chmn. United Way Campaign; mem. bd. governance, fin. and adminstrn. com. Cleve. Found.; bd. dirs. Ohio Arts Coun., Univ. Cir. Inc., Greater Cleve. Growth Assn., Cleve. Tomorrow, Gt. Lakes Sci. Mus., United Way Svcs., Mus. Coun. of Cleve. Mus. Art, St. Vladimir's Orthodox Theol. Sem.; vis. com. Weatherhead Sch. Mgmt., Case Western Res. U.; adv. com. Newspaper Mgmt. Ctr., Northwestern U.; trustee WVIZ/PBS and 90.3 WCPN ideastream; nat. bd. dirs. IOCC. Mem. Newspaper Assn. Am. (mem. labor rels. subcom.), Am. Soc. Newspaper Editors, Greater Cleve. Roundtable (past chmn.). Office: Plain Dealer Pub Co 1801 Superior Ave E Cleveland OH 44114-2198

MACHE, ULRICH, German language educator; b. M. Friedland, Germany, Nov. 24, 1928; came to U.S., 1961; s. Walter T. and Hertha J. Kolbow; m. Britta Maria Runge, Aug. 18, 1963; 1 child, Sasi. BA, U. B.C., Vancouver, Can., 1959, MA, 1961; PhD, Princeton U., 1963. Lectr. Harvard U., Cambridge, Mass., 1963-64; asst. prof. Princeton (N.J.) U., 1964-67; assoc. prof. SUNY, Albany, 1967-70, prof., 1970-94; retired, 1994. Editor works by A. H. Bucholtz and Philipp von Zesen; contbr.: Dictionary of Literary Biography, 1996, Deutsche Biogrphische Enzyklopaedie, 1995, Literaturlexikon, 1988-93; contbr. numerous articles to scholarly publs. Home: 206 Forest Ln Bellingham WA 98225-5804 Fax: (360) 738-3563. E-mail: ulma3@home.com.

MACHELL, IAIN HUGH, artist educator; b. Dundee, Scotland, Feb. 2, 1954; s. Roger Keys and Elizabeth Margaret M. Diploma in Art, Grays Sch. of Art, Aberdeen, Scotland, 1977, postgrad. diploma in Art, 1978; MFA, U. Albany, N.Y., 1988. Sculpture instr. Newark Tech. Coll., Nottingham, Eng., 1982-84; adjunct faculty in sculpture Mansfield Coll. of Art., Eng., 1983; sculpture instr. Ulster County C.C., Stone Ridge, N.Y., 1984-86; instr., teaching asst. in sculpture and 3D design U. Albany, 1986-88; adjunct faculty in sculpture Rensselaer Polytech. Inst., Troy, 1988; adjunct faculty in 3D design/drawing Berkshire C.C., Pittsfield, Mass., 1989-90; faculty in drawing Bennington (Vt.) Coll., 1989—2001, sculpture studio mgr., teaching asst., 1988-90; adjunct faculty in drawing and painting C.C. of Vt., Bennington, 1989; vis. artist and lectr. Ind. U. Pa., 1991, Shepherd Coll., Shepherdstown, W.Va., 1993; faculty in 3D media and concepts, sculpture & installation Carnegie-Mellon U., Pitts., 1993; vis. asst. prof. in 3D foundations W.Va. U., Morgantown, 1990-92, asst. prof. in 3D foundations and sculpture, 1992-98; vis. artist, lectr. U. Mass., Amherst, 1999. Chair, assoc. prof. sculpture Montserrat Coll. Art, 1998-2000; vis. lectr. Ind. U. Pa., 1996; curator and panelist Laura Mesaros Gallery, Morgantown, W.Va., 1994; panelist CAA Conf., St. Louis, 1995, Toronto, Can., 1998; panel chair FATE Conf., Richmond, Va., 1997; faculty Eugene Lang Coll. New School U., N.Y.C., 2001. Recipient numerous grants in art. Mem. Coll. Art Assn., U.S. Scotland Consotrium. Office: 1002 Manhattan Ave 2nd Fl Brooklyn NY 11222-1314 E-mail: machelli@newschool.edu.

MACHEN, ETHEL LOUISE LYNCH, retired academic administrator; b. Chgo., July 16, 1938; d. Samuel Thomas and Louise (Brown) Lynch; m. Robert Caldwell Jr., Sept. 7, 1957 (div. 1968); m. Ronald C. Machen, July 27, 1997. BS in Bus. Edn., DePaul U., 1976; MS in Counseling Psychology, MS in Adminstrn., George Williams Coll., Downers Grove, Ill., 1979. Lic. tchr., Ill. Sec. Inland Steel Co., Chgo., 1957-68; adminstrv. asst. 1st Nat. City Bank, St. Thomas, V.I., 1968-71; pers./purchasing mgr. Peoples Bank of V.I., 1971-73; bus. edn. tchr. Ctrl. YMCA Coll., Chgo., 1976, Chgo. Profl. Coll., 1976-78; rsch. asst. U. Ill., Chgo., 1978-79, rsch. assoc., 1980-81, asst. dir. early outreach, 1981-83, dir. early outreach, 1983-98; ret. Pres. Lynch Enterprises, Summit, Ill., 1987—; cons. Chgo. Pub. Schs. Monitoring Commn. for Desegregation Implementation, 1996-97; mem. adv. bd. Ctr. for Ednl. R&D U. Ill., Chgo., 1989-98, Project Canal, Chgo. Pub. Schs., 1990-92; mem. exec. bd. Chgo. Coun. Postsecondary Edn., 1989-91; lectr. African-Am. Studies Ctr., Smithsonian Inst., Washington, 1992; mem. counselor articulation bd. DePaul U., 1993-97; field reader U.S. Dept. Edn., 1993—, U.S. Dept. Energy, 1995; mem. adv. coun. Greater Chgo. Youth Behavior Project, 1993-97. Active Chgo. Urban League, Lulac Coun. 5201, 1988-91, Ill. Com. on Black Concerns in Higher Edn., 1989-98. Recipient Health Careers Opportunity Program award U.S. Dept. HHS, 1987-80, 93-95, Dept. HHS Pub. Health Svcs., 1994, 95, Disting. Alumna award Argo Community High Sch., 1993, Dean's Merit award Coll. of Edn., 1998, Early Outreach Eagle award, 1998. Mem. Am. Assn. for Higher Edn. (Achievement award 1991), Nat. Assn. for Coll. Admissions Counselors, Assn. Black Women in Higher Edn. (founding mem. Chgo. chpt.). Baptist. Avocations: horticulture, reading, walking, travel.

MACHEN, J. BERNARD, academic administrator; m. Chris; children: Maggie, Michael, Lee. DDS, St. Louis U., 1968; MS, U. Iowa, 1972, PhD in Edn. Psychology, 1974. Prof., assoc. dean U. N.C., 1983-89; pres. Am. Assn. Dental Schs., 1987; dean U. Mich. Sch. Dentistry, 1989-95; provost, exec. v.p. acad. affairs U. Mich., 1995-97; pres. U. Utah, 1998—. Mem. Inst. Medicine Com. in Future Dental Edn. Nat. Acad. Scis., 1993-95. Office: U of Utah 201 Presidents Cir Rm 203 Salt Lake City UT 84112-9008*

MACHIDA, CURTIS A. research molecular neurobiologist, educator; b. San Francisco, Apr. 1, 1954; AB, U. Calif., Berkeley, 1976; PhD, Oreg. Health Scis. U., 1982. Postdoctoral scientist Oreg. Health Scis. U., Portland, 1982-88; asst. scientist div. neurosci. Oreg. Regional Primate Research Ctr., Beaverton, 1988-95; assoc. scientist divsn. neuroscience Oreg. Regional Primate Rsch. Ctr., 1995—2002; assoc. rsch prof. oral molecular biology Sch. Dentistry Oreg. Health Sci. U., 2002—. Rsch. asst. prof. biochemistry and molecular biology Oreg. Health Sci. U., 1989-95, mem. faculty neurosci. and molecular and cell biology grad. programs, 1989—, adj. assoc. prof. biochemistry and molecular biology, 1995—; mem. grad. faculty biochemistry and biophysics Oreg. State U., Corvallis, 1997—; mem. Institutional Ethics oversight com., Institutional Bisafety com., Instnl. Animal Care and Use com.; mem. biotech. program adv. com. Portland C.C. Editl. cons. Oreg. Health Scis. U. News, 1984-87; editor Adrenergic Receptor Protocols, 1997-99, Viral Vectors for Gene Therapy: Methods and Protocols, 2000—; ad-hoc reviewer Endocrinology, Molecular Pharmacology, Biochimica et Biophysica Acta, Am. Jour. Physiology, Lab. Animal Sci., NSF; contbr. articles, revs., and abstracts to profl. jours. and internat. confs. Recipient Leukemia Assn. award, 1981, Tartar award Med. Rsch. Found. Oreg., 1980; NIH fellow, 1980-82, 85-87, grantee, 1989, 95, 98; rsch. grantee Med. Rsch. Found. Oreg., Wills Found., Nat. Parkinson Found., Collins Med. Trust, Murdock Charitable Trust and Rsch. Corp. Mem. AAAS, Am. Soc. Biochemistry and Molecular Biology, Am. Soc. Microbiology, Soc. Neurosci., Am. Heart Assn. (basic scis. coun., established investigator 1994-99), Am. Soc. Gene Therapy, U.S.-Israel Binational Sci. Found. (reviewer). Achievements include patent on dopamine receptor and genes; cloning of several adrenergic receptor genes and simian retroviral infectious genomes; depositor, nucleotide sequence to EMBL and GenBank databases, and clones to American Type Culture Collection. Office: Oreg Health Sci U Sch Dentistry Dept Oral Molecular Biology 611 SW Campus Dr Portland OR 97201-3097 Fax: 503-494-8772. E-mail: machidac@ohsu.edu.

MACHLE, EDWARD JOHNSTONE, theology educator, retired; b. Canton, China, Sept. 29, 1918; s. Edward Charles and Jean (Mawson) M.; m. Neva Hull, Aug. 29, 1942; children— Stewart, Douglas, Kathi; m. Mary Lou Reynolds, Dec. 15, 1970; 1 child, Michelle; stepchildren— Rebecca, Richard, Harvey, Robin. Student, Pacific Lutheran Jr. Coll., 1937; BA, Whitworth Coll., 1939; B.D., San Francisco Theol. Sem., 1942, MA, 1944; PhD, Columbia U., 1952. Ordained to ministry Presbyn. Ch., 1942; minister Concrete, Wash., 1942-43; asst. minister San Francisco, 1943-44, Mineola, N.Y., 1944-46; instr. Columbia, 1946-47; asst. prof. U. Colo., 1947-53, asso. prof., 1953-63, prof., 1963-80, emeritus, 1981—, chmn. dept., 1951-52, 56-58, 66-69. Vis. lectr. U. Alta., summer 1960, Iliff Sch. Theology, 1962, Evergreen State, 1981, Peninsula Coll., 1985-86; in-parish research dir. San Francisco Theol. Sem.; dir. music St. Andrew Presbyn. Ch., Boulder, Colo., 1961-70; guest lectr. ch. music U. Colo. Sch. Music, 1950-65; disting. faculty fellow Sheldon Jackson Coll., 1986-88. Author: Nature and Heaven in the Xunzi, 1993. Mem. Am. Phil. Assn., Soc. Asian and Comparative Philosophy, Acad. Religion. Presbyterian. Home: 11 Silver Canyon Place The Woodlands TX 77381 E-mail: machle@wt.net. *Faith is largely willingness to learn of what can destroy us. Idolatry feeds on our fear of having faith. Research methods spring from the soil of our cultured idolatries. Thus, to learn, faith must at times be a traitor to "learning.".*

MACHLEIDT, RUPRECHT, physicist; b. Kiel, Germany, Dec. 18, 1943; came to U.S., 1985; s. Dietrich and Erika (Eber) M.; m. Francessca Sammarruca; children: Dario Alexander, Helga Julia. MS in Physics, U. Bonn, Germany, 1971, PhD in Physics, 1973. Postdoctoral rsch. assoc. U. Bonn, Germany, 1974-75, SUNY, Stony Brook, 1976-77; asst. prof. U. Bonn, Germany, 1978-83; vis. sr. scientist Triumf, Vancouver, Can., 1983-85; vis. rsch. physicist LAMPF, Los Alamos, N.Mex., 1986-88; adj. assoc. prof. UCLA, 1986-88; assoc. prof. U. Idaho, Moscow, 1988-91, prof. physics, 1991—. Cons. Los Alamos (N.Mex.) Nat. Lab., 1986-88. Author: (chpt. book) The Meson Theory of Nuclear Forces and Nuclear Structure; contbr. numerous articles to profl. jours. Recipient Fellowship Deutsche Forschungs-Gemeinschaft, 1976-77, 83-85. Mem. Am. Phys. Soc. Achievements include co-development of Bonn Meson-Exchange Model for the Nucleon-Nucleon Interaction; research on nuclear matter theory with subnuclear degrees of freedom and relativity, relativistic few-nucleon physics. Office: U Idaho Dept Physics Moscow ID 83843

MACHOVER, CARL, computer graphics consultant; b. Bklyn., Mar. 26, 1927; s. John Herman and Rose (Alter) M.; m. Wilma Doris Simon, June 18, 1950; children: Tod, Julie, Linda. BEE, Rensselaer Poly. Inst., 1951; postgrad., NYU, 1953-56. Mgr. applied engring. Norden div. United A/C Corp., 1951-59; mgr. sales Skiatron Electronics & TV, N.Y.C., 1959-60; v.p. mktg., dir. Info. Displays, Inc., Mount Kisco, N.Y., 1960-73, v.p., gen. mgr., 1973-76; pres. Machover Assocs. Corp., White Plains, N.Y., 1976—. Adj. prof. Rensselaer Poly. Inst.; mem. RPI H&SS adv. bd. Bradford EIMC Indsl. Adv. Bd. Author: Gyro Primer, 1957, Basics of Gyroscopes, 1958; mem. editl. bd. IEEE Computer Graphics and Applications, Computers and Graphics, Spectrum; editor C4 Handbook, 1989, 2d edit., 1995, The CAD/CAM Handbook, 1996; co-editor Computer Graphics Rev.; co-exec. prodr. The Story of Computer Graphics, 1999; contbr. articles to profl. jours. Mem. adv. bd. Pratt Ctr. for Computer Graphics in Design. With USNR, 1945-46. Recipient Frank Oppenheimer award Am. Soc. for Engring. Edn., 1971, Orthagonal award N.C. State U., 1988, Vanguard award Nat. Comp. Graphics Assn., 1993; named to Computer Graphics Hall of Fame Fine Arts Mus. of L.I., Hempstead, N.Y., 1988. Fellow Soc. for Info. Display (pres. 1968-70), Eurographics Assn.; mem. IEEE, Assn. for Computing Machinery, Am. Inst. Design and Drafting, Soc. Mfg. Engrs., Nat. Computer Graphics Assn. (bd. dir., pres. 1989-90), Computer Graphics Pioneer, Art and Sci. Collaborators Inc. (pres. 1995—), Sigma Xi, Tau Beta Pi, Eta Kappa Nu. Home: 152 Longview Ave White Plains NY 10605-2314 Office: Machover Assocs Corp PO Box 308 152A Longview Ave White Plains NY 10605-2314 E-mail: cmachover@aol.com.

MACHOVER, WILMA SIMON, musician; b. Troy, N.Y., Mar. 4, 1929; d. Morris and Estelle (Greenspan) Simon; m. Carl Machover, June 18, 1950; children: Tod, Julie, Linda. BS in Music, Juilliard Sch., 1952. Nat. cert. tchr. of music. Pianist, ind. music tchr., Westchester County, N.Y., 1961—; dir. adult music ctr. Westchester Conservatory, White Plains, 1982-86; dir. artistic programs Hoff-Barthelson Music Sch., Scarsdale, NY, 1987—. Author: Improvising/Composing in a Changing World, 1988, Sound Choices: Guiding Your Child's Musical Experiences, 1996. Bd. dirs. White Plains Youth Bur., 1992-99. Mem. Music Tchrs. Nat. Assn. (state pres. 1982-86), Music Tchrs. Coun. (Westchester pres. 1972-76), Westchester Musicians Guild. Avocations: reading, art, travel. Office: Hoff-Barthelson Music Sch 25 School Ln Scarsdale NY 10583 Office Fax: 513-946-9142.

MACHTIGER, HARRIET GORDON, retired psychoanalyst; b. N.Y.C., July 27, 1927; d. Michael J. and Miriam D. (Rand) Gordon; m. Sidney Machtiger, Feb. 7, 1948; children: Avram Coleman, Marcia Gordon, Bennett Rand. BA, Bklyn. Coll., 1947; diploma with distinction, U. London, 1966, PhD, 1974. Cert. psychologist, Pa. Tchr. Phila. Pub. Schs., 1962-64; ednl. therapist Child Guidance Tng. Ctr., London, 1966-68, Sch. Psychol. Svc./Inner London Edn. Authority, 1968-70; therapist Paddington Day Hosp., London, 1970-71, London Ctr. for Psychotherapy, 1971-74, Staunton Clinic U. Pitts., 1974-78; pvt. practice Pitts., 1976-2000; ret., 2000. Pres. C.G. Jung Ctr., Pitts., 1976-81; cons. in field. Active S.W. Pitts. Cmty. Mental Health, 1976-78; dir. Pitts. program Inter-Regional Soc. Jungian Analysts, 1975-85. Recipient Pa. Dept. Edn. award for disting. contributions to advancement in edn., 1962,

Social Sci. Rsch. Coun. award, 1973. Mem. Pa. Psychol. Assn., Brit. Psychol. Soc., Brit. Assn. Psychotherapists. Home: 6562 Jog Palm Dr Boynton Beach FL 33437-3925 E-mail: hmachtiger@aol.com.

MACHUCA, CARLOS R. financial, management consultant; b. Santiago, Chile, May 25, 1948; came to U.S., 1969; s. Carlos Enrique Machuca and Maria Luisa Canales; m. Omelia M. Jones, Nov. 2001; children from previous marriage: Russel Marcus, Jorge, Carlos, Jennifer. BFA magna cum laude, N.Y. Inst. Tech., 1974; MBA in Mktg. and Internat. Bus., NYU, 1981. Lic. ins. agt., real estate agt., securities, N.C.; cert. mgmt. cons. Ptnr. M-Graphic Co., Santiago, 1966-69; exec. v.p. Alexander Proudfoot Co., West Palm Beach, Fla., 1976-96; pres. L.Am. Inst. Mgmt. Resources, Las Vegas, Nev., 1996-98; pres. CRM Internat., LLC, Raleigh, N.C., 1998—, Global Bus. Ptnrs., LLC, Wilmington, Del., 1998-99; fin. cons. Merrill Lynch, Raleigh, 1999—2001; exec. v.p. Prondfoot Consulting, West Palm Beach, Fla., 2001—. Haskins ptnr. mem. NYU, N.Y.C., 1986—. Author: Completeness Management Sys., 1998; patent publishing Confederate Treasure, 1998. Life mem. Rep. Nat. Com. Mem. Inst. Mgmt. Cons., N.C. Mus. History, Person's House Preservation Assn. Roman Catholic. Avocations: soccer, camping, history, teaching, travel. Office: 1 Libeertas Rd Bryanston 2021 PO Box 752 Rivonia 27601-2933 2128 South Africa

MACHULAK, EDWARD LEON, real estate, mining and advertising company executive; b. Milw., July 14, 1926; s. Frank and Mary (Sokolowski) M.; m. Sylvia Mary Jablonski, Sept. 2, 1950; children: Edward A., John E., Lauren A., Christine M., Paul E. BS in Acctg., U. Wis., 1949. Chmn. bd., pres. Commerce Group Corp., Milw., 1962—, San Luis Estates, Inc., Milw., 1973—; Homespan Realty Co., Inc. Universal Developers, Inc., 1972—, Ecomm Group, Inc., 1974—; chmn. bd., CEO Gen. Lumber & Supply Co., Inc., 1949—. Bd. dirs., v.p. San Sebastian Gold Mines, Inc., 1969—73, chmn. bd., pres., 1973—; bd. dirs., sec. Landpak, Inc., 1985—, Edjo Ltd., 1976—; ptnr. Weem Assocs., 1974—; designee Comseb Joint Venture Woodcreek Devel. Corp., 1987. Nat. adv. coun. SBA, 1972-74, co-chmn., 1973, 74; active Pres.' Coun. Marmion Mil. Acad., Aurora, Ill., 1966-79, lay life trustee, 1972, fin. advisor, 1964-71, chmn. spl. fund raising com., 1966-67, planning com., 1972-79; chmn. adv. bd. Jesuit Retreat House, Oshkosh, Wis., 1966-68; chmn., bd. dirs. Spencerian Coll. Bus., 1973-74; chmn. St. John Cathedral Symphony Concert Com., Milw., 1978; sustaining mem. Met. Mus. Art, 1974—; Reorganized bus. leader Congl. Rec., 1976. With AUS, 1945-46. Recipient Recognition award U.S. SBA, 1975, Am. Womens Assn. in El Salvador award, 1990, Recognition award San Sebastian Cmty., 1992, Santa Rose de Lima, 1994, El Salvador, 1991, La Asciacion de Desarrollo Comunal San Sebastian, 1997, Sebastian Cmty. El Salvador award, 1992, El Salvador Ministry Edn. award, 1992; Edward L. Machulak Day proclaimed by students of Canton San Sebastian, El Salvador, May 9, 1992; named Hon. Life Mem. Mid-Continental Railway, 1963. Mem. Nat. Assn. Small Bus. Investment Co.'s (nat. chmn. legis. com. 1968-73, bd. govs. 1970-74, exec. com. 1971-74, sec. 1972-74, Disting. Svc. award Am. Small Bus. 1970), Midwest Regional Assn. Small Bus. Investment Cos. (bd. dirs. 1968-74, v.p. 1970-71, pres. 1971-72, Outstanding Svcs. award 1972), State of Wis. Coun. Small Bus. Investment (chmn. 1973-74), Wis. Bd. Realtors (various coms. 1955-88), Milw. Bd. Realtors (com. mem. 1955-88), Tripoli Country Club (Milw.), KC (4th degree, Recognition award 1989). Home: 903 W Green Tree Rd Milwaukee WI 53217-3716 Office: 6001 N 91st St Milwaukee WI 53225-1721 E-mail: info@commercegroupcorp.com.

MACIAS, EDWARD S. chemistry educator, university official and dean; b. Milw., Feb. 21, 1944; s. Arturo C. Macias and Minette (Schwenger) Wiederhold; m. Paula Wiederhold, June 17, 1967; children: Matthew Edward, Julia Katherine. AB, Colgate U., 1966; PhD, MIT, 1970. Asst. prof. Washington U., St. Louis, 1970-76, assoc. prof., 1976-84, prof. chemistry, 1984—, chmn. dept., 1984-88, provost, 1988-95, interim dean Faculty Arts and Scis., 1994-95, exec. vice chancellor and dean Faculty Arts and Scis., 1995—. Cons. Meteorology Rsch., Inc., Altadina, Calif., 1978-81, Salt River Project, Phoenix, 1980-83, Santa Fe Rsch., Bloomington, Minn., 1985-88, AeroVironment, Inc., Monrovia, Calif., 1986-88. Author: Nuclear and Radiochemistry, 1981; editor: Atmospheric Aerosol, 1981; contbr. numerous articles to profl. jours. Bd. dirs. Mark Twain Summer Inst., St. Louis, 1984-87, 88-90, The Coll. Sch., St. Louis, 1984-88, Colgate U., 1997—. Grantee NSF, EPA, Electric Power Rsch. Inst., So. Calif. Edison Co., Dept. Energy, AEC. Mem. Am. Chem. Soc., Am. Assn. Aerosol Rsch. (editorial bd.), Am. Phys. Soc., AAAS. Home: 6907 Waterman Ave Saint Louis MO 63130-4333 Office: Washington U Campus Box 1094 One Brookings Dr Saint Louis MO 63130

MACIEL, PATRICIA ANN, development professional; b. Providence, Jan. 13, 1940; d. Raymond Wallace Sr. and Elizabeth Josephine (Kelly) Ross; m. John Maciel Jr., July 24, 1963; children: Kelly Patricia, Christopher John. EdB, R.I. Coll., 1961, MA in Tchg., 1976. Cert. tchr., R.I. Tchr. 3rd tchr. Pawtucket (R.I.) Pub. Schs., 1961-62; tchr. 5th and 6th grades Providence Pub. Schs., 1962-63; tchr. Pawtucket and Providence Pub. Schs., 1963-72; tchr., curriculum coord. Holy Name Sch., Providence, 1972-80; dir. ednl. programming Basic Skills, Inc., 1980-83; dir. devel./pub. rels. IN-SIGHT, Warwick, R.I., 1983-88; coord. ann. giving and spl. events St. Joseph Health Svcs. R.I., North Providence, 1988-2000; pvt. fundraising cons., 2000—. Editor, author newsletter IN-SIGHT News, 1980-83. Sec. exec. bd. Holy Name Sch., 1972-80; pres. employee activities com. St. Joseph Health Svcs. R.I., 1991-93; founding mem., pres. Friends of the Pawtucket Pub. Libr., 1966; pres. Pawtucket Jr. Woman's Club, 1965; publicity chair Middlebridge Assn., South Kingstown, R.I., 1989-90; mem. Narrow River Preservation Assn., South Kingstown, 1976—; mem. Save the Bay, State of R.I., 1987—; ex officio mem. R.I. Coll. Found., 1992-94, corporate bd. dirs., 1996-97, sec., 1997-99, v.p., 1999-2001, pres., 2001—, chair ad hoc com. capital campaign, 2000-01, vice chair alumni capital campaign, 2001—; rev. com. United Way S.E. New England, 1999; mem. adv. bd. Villa at St. Antoine, 2002—. Recipient Alumna of Yr award Rhode Island Coll., 1992. Mem. R.I. Coll. Alumni Assn. (treas. exec. bd. 1990-92, chair ann. fund dr. 1990-92, chair class reunion 1981, 86, 91, class news sec. 1972-78, pres. 1992-94). Roman Catholic. Avocations: swimming, boating, walking, bicycling. Home: 3 Hunters Run North Providence RI 02904 E-mail: jmjpam@aol.com.

MACIEROWSKI, EDWARD MICHAEL, philosopher; b. Springfield, Mass., Nov. 1, 1948; s. Edward Macierowski, Lenore Lilian (Kiesnowski) Macierowski; m. Carol Marie Krowel Nitz, Dec. 31, 1994; children: Jacob, Jeremiah, Janea, David, Hailey. BA magna cum laude, St. John's Coll., 1970; MA, U. Toronto, 1973; MSL magna cum laude, Pontifical Inst. Medieval Studies, Can., 1976; PhD, U. Toronto, 1979. Lectr., asst. prof. U. St. Thomas, Houston, 1979—83; vis. asst. prof. Cath. U. Am., Washington, 1983—86, scholar in residence, 1986—87; assoc. prof. Christendom Coll., Front Royal, Va., 1987—93; assoc. prof. Philosophy Benedictine Coll., Atchison, Kans., 1993—. Translator: Apollonius of Perga On Cutting Off a Ratio, 1987, Medieval Exegesis, vol. 2, 2000. Chmn. instrn. com. Archdiocesan Bd. Edn., Washington, 1984—87. Recipient Award, Imperial Iranian Acad. Philosophy, 1976—77. Mem.: Fellowship of Cath. Scholars (life), Am. Philos. Assn. (life; Pres. Kansas City chpt. 1997—98), Am. Cath. Philos. Assn. (life). Roman Catholic. Achievements include research in Greek and Arabic sources of medieval Latin scholastic philosophy; Dialogue between Christian and Islamic civilizations, especially St. Thomas Aquinas and the Iranian philosopher Arienna. Avocations: historical geography, mneumonics. Office: Benedictine College 1020 N 2d St Atchison KS 66002

MACILVAINE, CHALMERS ACHESON, retired financial executive, former association executive; b. Bklyn., Oct. 25, 1921; s. James Andrew and Helen Marguerite (Acheson) MacI.; m. Elizabeth Jean Babcock, Mar. 26, 1943; children: Judith Anne, Joseph Chad, Martha Elizabeth. AB, Stanford U., 1943. With Kaiser Steel Corp., 1946-73, asst. controller, 1953-62, treas., 1962-70, v.p., 1967-70, v.p. finance and planning, 1970-73; also v.p., dir. subsidiaries; v.p. project financing group Bank of Am., San Francisco, 1973-74, sr. v.p., dep. head Asia div., 1974-77; sr. v.p.-fin. Peabody Coal Co., St. Louis, 1978-80; sr. v.p., dir. Stifel, Nicolaus & Co., Inc., 1980-83; exec. dir. Japan Am. Soc. of St. Louis, 1983-85. Pres. Bamerical Internat. Fin. Corp., 1973-74 Served to lt. (j.g.) USNR, 1943-46. Mem. Phi Beta Kappa, Sigma Chi. Clubs: Tokyo Lawn Tennis, Burns Club of St. Louis. Home: PO Box 332 Friendship ME 04547-0332

MACILWAINE, MARY JARRATT, public relations executive; b. Clifton Forge, Va., Oct. 29, 1942; d. Robert Bell and Mary Louise (Wood) J. BA, Mary Baldwin Coll., Staunton, Va., 1964; cert. bus., Katharine Gibbs Sch., Boston, 1965. Staff asst. com. on agr. U.S. Ho. of Reps., 1975-81; asst. sec. food and consumer services Dept. Agr., 1981-85; v.p. Wampler & Assocs. Inc., Washington, 1985-86; pres. Jarratt & Assocs., Inc., 1986-90; asst. to pres and CEO Va. Nat. Bank, Charlottesville, 2000—. Editor various legis. reports. Republican. Episcopalian. Home: 1149 Marion Dr Charlottesville VA 22903-4649 E-mail: mmacilwaine@virginianb.com.

MAC INNES, VIRGINIA LEWIS, real estate broker; b. Bklyn., Oct. 14, 1921; d. James Parker and Daisy Emerson (Larom) Lewis; m. David Mac Innes, Aug. 31, 1940; children: Suzanne Larom, David Bruce, Janet Elizabeth, Diane Emerson. BS in Econs. and Bus. Mgmt., Empire State Coll. SUNY, Albany, 1992. Lic. real estate broker, N.Y. Broker Terrace Realty, Forest Hills, N.Y., 1967—. Pres. Women's Guild St. Luke's Episcopal Ch., Forest Hills, 1963-65; v.p. Citizens Inquiry on World Trade Ctr., N.Y.C., 1965-68; pres. Oquaga Lake Improvement Assn., Deposit, N.Y., 1965-66; chmn. Bicentennial Commn., Cmty. Bd. # 6, Queens, N.Y., 1976-77; pres. Am. Legion Aux. Unit # 630, Forest Hills, 1976-77; v.p. Forest Hills C. of C., 1982-83, bd. dirs. 1978-79; organizing pres. Remsen Family Revolutionary Cemetery Coalition, Forest Hills, 1983. Mem. AAUW, Benjamine Romaine Soc. NSDAR (regent 1960-62), Nat. Soc. Children Am. Revolution (organizing pres. 1954, dir. N.Y. State 1957-60), Daus. of Brit. Empire, Colonial Dames XVII Century, Moorings Club, Women's Club of forest Hills, Inc. (past pres. 1968-70). Republican. Avocations: writing, photography. Home: 2205 N Southwinds Blvd Apt 207 Vero Beach FL 32963-4324 Office: Terrace Realty 16 Station Sq Forest Hills NY 11375-5234

MACINNIS, AL, professional hockey player; b. Inverness, N.S., Can., July 11, 1963; Hockey player Calgary (Can.) Flames, 1981-94, St. Louis Blues, 1994—. Recipient Max Kaminsky trophy, 1982-83, Conn Smythe trophy, 1988-89; played in NHL All-Star Game, 1985, 88, 90-92, 94; named to The Sporting News All-Star first team, 1989-90, 90-91, NHL All-Star first team, 1989-90, 90-91, Stanley Cup championship team, 1989. Office: care St Louis Blues Kiel Ctr 1401 Clark Ave Saint Louis MO 63103-2700*

MACIOCE, FRANK MICHAEL, lawyer, financial services company executive; b. N.Y.C., Oct. 3, 1945; s. Frank Michael and Sylvia Maria (Morea) M.; children: Michael Peter, Lauren Decker, Theodore Kenneth; m. Helen Latourette Duffin, July 9, 1988. BS, Purdue U., 1967; JD, Vanderbilt U., 1972. Bar: N.Y. 1973, U.S. Dist. Ct. (so. dist.) N.Y. 1973, U.S. Ct. Appeals (2d cir.) 1975, U.S. Supreme Ct. 1976. Mem. law dept. Merrill Lynch, Pierce, Fenner & Smith Inc., N.Y.C., 1972-80, v.p., 1978-88, 1st v.p., 1988-2000, Merrill Lynch Investment Mgrs., N.Y.C., 2000—. Mgr. corp. law dept. Merrill Lynch & Co., Inc., N.Y.C., 1980-93, asst. gen. counsel, 1982—; gen. counsel investment banking group, 1993-95, ops., svcs. and tech. counsel, 1995-2000, sec. of audit, compensation and nominating coms. bd. dirs., 1978-83, sec. exec. com., 1981-83; mng. dir. Merrill Lynch Overseas Capital, N.V., Netherlands Antilles, 1980-85; sec., dir. Merrill Lynch Employees Fed. Credit Union, N.Y.C., 1978-82; dir. Merrill Lynch Pvt. Capital Inc., N.Y.C., 1981-87, Teleport Comm. Group Inc., N.Y.C., 1987-92, Enhance Fin. Services Inc, N.Y.C., 1988-92; fin. planning adv. bd. Purdue U., 1996-2000. Served with U.S. Army, 1969-70. Mem. ABA, Assn. of Bar of City of N.Y. Home: 22 Essex Rd Summit NJ 07901-2802 Office: Merrill Lynch Investment Mgrs 800 Scudders Mill Rd Plainsboro NJ 08536 E-mail: frank_macioce@ml.com.

MACIOCE, MARIE ELIZABETH (MARIE TOMAS), writer; b. Bklyn., June 15, 1948; d. Mary Antonette Cirabisi, Sam Tomasino; m. Patrick Francis Macioce, Oct. 16, 1983; children: Debra Nyhus, Dawn Slosberg. Journalist Courier Life Pubs., Bklyn., 1973—78; freelance writer, humorist United Feature Syndicate, N.Y.C., 1976—78, screenplay writer, 1977—78; ghost writer Katherine Falk, Bklyn., 1975—76; TV and radio commericals writer Milton Kapulus Advt. Agy., Westchester, 1978—79; sitcom writer (for hire) Rosa Colosemo, Australian Producer, Melbourne, Australia, 1984—86; humorist Frontporch4news, Tex., 2001. Author: (columnist) Of That & This, 1975 (Coney Island Feature Writer of the Year, 1976), (biographical) Rachel, 1980, (screenwriter (work for hire) Rockula, 1978, (work for hire)sitcom) Bindy , 1986, (optioned screenplay) Bungle of Joy, 1989, (novel) I'm Here and I'm Fine, 1998, Naughty Business, 2001, Don Juan and the Perfect Woman, 2001. Roman Catholic. Avocations: dancing, cooking, antiquing. Personal E-mail: misshotdog15.

MACIOCH, JAMES EDWARD, investment consultant, financial planner; b. Cleve., Mar. 30, 1947; Cert. fin. planner, Coll. for Fin. Planning, Denver, 1992; BS, U. Dayton, 1969; MBA, Olivet Nazarene U., 1997. Lic. series 7, Nat. Assn. Securities Dealers. Registered floor broker Mid-Am. Commodity Exch., 1988-90; registered floor broker, mem. Chgo. Bd. Trade, 1990-2000; investment cons. Montano Securities Corp., Chgo., 1993-94, Dickinson & Co., Rosemont, Ill., 1995-96, Rosemont Investment Corp., 1996—. Mem. Fin. Planning Assn. Office: Rosemont Investment Corp 5600 N River Rd Ste 180 Rosemont IL 60018-5184

MACIONE, JOE, television station executive; b. Arcola, Miss., Mar. 30, 1937; s. Joe and Pauline (Nabers) M.; m. Annette P. Pritchette, Apr. 30, 1960; children: Kimberly Caldwell, Kyle P. BSBA, U. Miss., 1958. CPA Miss., Ark., La. Ptnr. Sayle & Macione, Greenville, Miss., 1969-84; gen. mgr. WXVT-TV, 1983-90; exec. v.p., gen. mgr. WCYB-TV, Bristol, Va., 1990—. Chmn. bd. dirs. Wellmont Health Sys., Bristol Regional Med. Ctr., Hawkins County Hosp.; trustee cert. program Estes Park Health Care Inst.; bd. dirs. Bristol Surgery Ctr., Bristol Regional Med. Ctr., Beaver Creek Walk, Bristol, Bristol Train Sta. Found., Bristol VA/TN Rotary Club, Greater Tri-Cities Bus. Alliance; mem. jr. league of Bristol's Cmty. Adv. Bd.; mem. indsl. commn. Sullivan County, Tenn. Trustee King Coll., Speedway Children's Charities; found. mem. East Tenn. State U.; bd. dirs. Va. Coalition for Open Govt. Bd., Kingsport C. of C., Nat. Ctr. for Quality, N.E. Tenn./S.W. Va. C. of C. Coalition, U. Miss. Alumni Assn.; bd. dirs., vice chmn. govt. rels. com. Greenville, Miss. Planning Com.; mem. adv. bd. U. Miss. Acctg. Sch., Greenville Jr. Achievement, Allied Enterprises, Greenville, Divsn. Miss. Dept. Rehab. Svcs.; bd. trustees Greenville Found.; chmn. visitor and conv. bur., tour DuPont chmn. Bristol C. of C.; v.p. mktg. divsn. Greenville C. of C.; pres. Leland, Miss. C. of C., Leland Rotary, Leland Acad. Named Health Care Hero, Bus. Jour. of the TriCities, 2001. Mem. AICPA, Va. Assn. Broadcasting (bd. dirs., pres.), Nat. Assn. Broadcasting, Tenn. Assn. Broadcasters (bd. dirs.), Miss. Soc. CPAs. Avocations: travel, civic involvement. Office: WCYB-TV 101 Lee St Bristol VA 24201-4355

MACIONE, KYLE PRITCHETT, pharmaceutical company executive, lawyer; b. Jackson, Miss., Dec. 28, 1963; s. Joe and Annette (Pritchett) M.; m. Beatriz Huarte, Sept. 17, 1993; children: Robert huarte Macione, Alexandra Huarte Macione. BA in Accountancy, U. Miss., 1986; MA in Accountancy, U. Ala., 1987; JD, Washington & Lee U., 1991. Bar: Tenn., 1991, Va., 1992, U.S. Dist. Ct. (we. dist.) Va., U.S. Dist. Ct. (ea. dist.) Tenn., 1992, U.S. Dist. Ct. Appeals (6th cir.), 1992; CPA, Miss. CPA tax dept. KPMG Peat Marwick, Jackson, 1988; assoc. atty. Elliott Lawson & Pomrenke, Bristol, Va., 1992-96; corp. counsel King Pharm., Inc., Tenn., 1996—, exec. v.p. corp. affairs, 1998—. Bd. dirs. Bristol Ballet Company Bristol Va.-Tenn., 1993-99, treas., 1994-95; bd. dirs. Main St. Bristol, 1997-98, Wellmont Found., 2001—; bd. trustees Barter Theatre, 2001—. Mem. Va. State Bar, Va. Bar Assn., Tenn. Bar Assn., Miss. Soc. CPAs, Bristol Va. Bar Assn. (sec., treas. 1993-94), Bristol Tenn. Bar Assn., Beta Alpha Psi, Beta Gamma Sigma. Home: 142 E Main St Abingdon VA 24210-2835 Office: King Pharm Inc 501 5th St Bristol TN 37620-2304 E-mail: kmacione@aol.com.

MACIONIS, JOHN JOHNSTON, sociologist, educator, writer; b. Phila., Oct. 19, 1947; s. John Joseph and May (Johnston) M.; m. Amy Marsh Macionis, June 6, 1987; children: McLean, Whitney. BA, Cornell U., 1970; MA, U. Penn., 1971, PhD, 1975. Prof., Prentice Hall disting. scholar sociology Kenyon Col., Gambier, Ohio, 1978—. Author: Sociology, 1987, Sociology, Can. edit., 1994, Hebrew edit., 1999, Asian edit., 1998, Spanish translation, 1999, Internat. English edit., 1998, Society: The Basics, 1992, Can. edit., 1999, Cities and Urban Life, 1998, (with others) Seeing Ourselves: Classic, Contemporary and Cross-Cultural Readings in Sociology, 1989, Sociology: A Global Introduction, 1998, Sociology: International English Edit., 1998, Sociologia, 1999, Social Problems, 2001. Recipient award for Disting. Contbn. to Tchg., North Ctrl. Sociol. Assn., 1998. Home: 1300 Park Rd Mount Vernon OH 43050-3855 Office: Kenyon Col Dept Sociology Gambier OH 43022 E-mail: macionis@kenyon.edu.

MACIORA, JOSEPH GERARD VINCENT, reference librarian; b. New London, June 18, 1959; s. Joseph George and Mary Agnes (Mik) M. BA in History-Am. Studies, Ctrl. Conn. State U., New Britain, 1982; MLS, SUNY, Albany, 1984. Reference libr. social sci. dept. Boston Pub. Libr., Boston, 1984—2000, libr. sci. reference dept., 2000—. Compiler: Maciora and Mik Families Genealogy, 1982, Polish American Genealogical Articles, 1989, Polish Cemetery Inscriptions-New Hampshire, 1991. Mem. Polish Geneal. Soc. Am., Polish Geneal. Soc. Mass., Polish Geneal. Soc. N.E. (v.p. 1984), New Eng. Historic and Geneal. Soc., Berkshire Family Hist. and Geneal. Soc., Cath. Libr. Assn. Roman Catholic. Avocations: philately, photography, reading, movies, travel to Europe. Office: Boston Pub Libr Sci Ref Dept 700 Boylston St Boston MA 02116-4795 E-mail: jmaciora@bpl.org.

MACISAAC, JOHN ANTHONY, retired municipal official; b. Albany, N.Y., Feb. 16, 1935; s. Joseph Leonard and Josephine MacIsaac. Grad. high sch., Schenectady, N.Y. Cert. assessor profl., assessor advanced, real estate appraiser, N.Y. Real property appraisal technician trainer dept. assessment City of Schenectady, 1979-81, real property appraisal, 1981-91, sole assessor, 1991-97; ret., 1997-98; town assessor Town of Rotterdam, 1998—2001, ret., 2001. Active Rep. polit. campaign. With U.S. Army, 1957, 61-62. Named on Ronald Reagan Eternal Flame of Freedom, Washington, 1994; represented in Nat. Rep. Victory Monument, Washington, 1995; recipient Rep. Presdl. award, 1994, Rep. Congl. Order of Freedom, 1995, Presdl. Order of Merit, Nat. Rep. Senatorial Com.; inducted into Presdl. Legion of Merit Honor Roll. Mem. Inst. Assessing Officers (cert. profl. assessor), Albany-Schenectady Assessors Assn., N.Y. State Assessors Assn., Schoharie County Hist. Soc. (life), Clan Donald U.S.A. (life), Am. Legion. Avocations: stamps and coins, antiques, gardening, wood walks, Acadian genealogy.

MACIUSZKO, KATHLEEN LYNN, librarian, educator; b. Nogales, Ariz., Apr. 8, 1947; d. Thomas and Stephanie (Horowski) Mart; m. Jerzy Janusz Maciuszko, Dec. 11, 1976; 1 child, Christinia Alexsandra. BA, Ea. Mich. U., 1969; MLS, Kent State U., 1974; PhD, Case Western Res. U., 1987. Reference libr. Baldwin-Wallace Coll. Libr., Berea, Ohio, 1974-77, dir. Conservatory of Music Libr., 1977-85; dir. bus. info. svcs. Harcourt Brace Jovanovich, Inc., Cleve., 1985-89; staff asst. to exec. dir. Cuyahoga County Pub. Libr., 1989-90; dir. Cleve. Area Met. Library System, Beachwood, Ohio, 1990; media specialist Cleve. Pub. Schs., 1991-93, Berea (Ohio) City Sch. Dist., 1993—. Author: OCLC: A Decade of Development, 1967-77, 1984; contbr. articles to profl. jours. Named Plenum Pub. scholar, 1986. Mem. Spl. Librs. Assn. (pres. Cleve. chpt. 1989-90, v.p. 1988-89, editor newsletter 1988-89), Baldwin-Wallace Coll. Faculty Women's Club (pres. 1975), Avocation: piano. Office: Midpark HS 7000 Paula Dr Middleburg Heights OH 44130

MACIVER, JOHN KENNETH, lawyer; b. Milw., Mar. 22, 1931; s. Wallace and Elizabeth (MacRae) MacI.; m. Margaret J. Vail, Sept. 4, 1954; children: Douglas B., Carolyn V., Kenneth D., Laura E. BS, U. Wisc., 1953, LLB, 1955; D Laws & Econ. Devel. (hon.), Milw. Sch. Engring., 1997. Bar: Wisc. 1955. Sr. ptnr. Michael Best & Friedrich LLP, Milw., 1955—. Mem. various bds. dirs. Chmn. Thompson for Gov. steering coms., 1986, 90, 94, 98; state chmn. Wisc. Bush for Pres. coms., 1980, 88, 92; chmn. Wis. Nixon for Pres. com., 1968, 72, Olson for Gov. com., 1970; co-chmn. Wis. George W. Bush for Pres., state co-chair, 2000; vice chmn. Knowles for Gov. com., 1964, 66; bd. dirs. Milw. Symphony Orch., 1968-96, pres. 1981-82; trustee Milw. Symphony Endowment Trust, 1988—; chmn. exec. com., bd. govs. East-West Ctr., 1970-76 (Disting. svc. award Honolulu 1976); pres., chmn. bd. dirs. Nat. Coun. Alcoholism, 1974-77, bd. dirs. 1968-78 (Silver Key award N.Y. 1975); pres., campaign co-chmn. United Performing Arts Fund Greater Milw., 1974-76 (Stiemke award Arts 1988); bd. dirs., exec. com. Greater Milw. Edn. Trust, 1988-97, Project New Hope, 1991—; sec., gen. counsel Wisc. Mfrs. and Commerce, 1980—; regent, sec., gen. counsel Milw. Sch. Engring., 1987—; bd. dirs., sec. Pettit Nat. Ice Tng. Ctr., 1992—; bd. dirs. Milw. Nat. Heart Project; bd. dirs., exec. com., founding mem., sec. Competitive Wisc. Inc., 1982—; bd. dirs., vice-chair Met. Milw. Assn. Commerce, 1987—; mem. Greater Milw. Com. 1985—; trustee Milw. County Pub. Mus., 1989-92. Recipient Wisc. Gov.'s awards in Support of Arts, 1989, cmty. svc. award Assoc. Gen. Contractors of Greater Milw. Mem. Wis. Bar Assn. (chmn. commn. litigation costs and delay, past chmn. labor law sect., commn. on jud. elections and ethics), Milw. Bar Assn. (chmn. jud. selection and qualifications com.), Milw. Club, Town Club. Republican. Avocations: Am. history, tennis, charities, politics. Home: 959 E Circle Dr Milwaukee WI 53217-5362 Office: Michael Best & Friedich 100 E Wisconsin Ave Ste 3300 Milwaukee WI 53202-4108

MACIVOR, CATHERINE J. lawyer; b. Royal Oak, Mich., Aug. 17, 1960; d. Angus Stewart and Hazel (Arnold) M. BA magna cum laude, Boston U., 1983; JD, U. Miami, 1989. Bar: Fla. 1992. Atty. Richard & Richard, P.A., Miami, 1990-94; pvt. practice, 1994-96, Franklin & Marbin, P.A., North Miami Beach, 1996—. Tem. Fla. Bar (family law sect., appellate law sec.), DAR. Episcopal. Avocations: swimming. Office: Franklin and Marbin Citicentre Ph 2 290 NW 165th St North Miami Beach FL 33169-6457

MACK, ALAN WAYNE, interior designer; b. Cleve., Oct. 30, 1947; s. Edmund B. and Florence I. (Oleksa) M. BS in Interior Design, Case Western Res. U., 1969. Designer interior design dept. Halle's, Cleve., 1969, 71-73; designer Nahan Co., New Orleans, 1973-75, Hemenway's Contract Design, New Orleans, 1975-76; ptnr. Hewlett-Mack Design Assocs., 1976-85; prin., dir. interior design HLM Design, Inc., 1985—2001; prin., ptnr. Proteus Group, Chgo., 2001—. Mem. adv. com. interior design dept. Delgado Jr. Coll., New Orlean s; mktg./merchandising adv. coun. St. Mary's Dominican Coll., New Orleans; mem. friends devel. coun. U. Iowa Mus. Art, 1986-91, chair, 1990-91; chmn. adv. com. interior design program Iowa State U., 1991-96; mem. design review com., City of Iowa City, 1992-93. Co-author: audiovisual presentation Nat. Home Improvement COun. Conf., 1981. Bd. dirs. Johnson County United Way, 1991-96. Served with U.S. Army, 1969-71. Mem. ASID (profl. mem., presdl. citation 1980, treas. La. dist. chpt. 1984), Vis. Nurses Assn. (bd. dirs. 1991-96), Found. for Interior Design Edn. Rsch. (standards com. 1972-76, bd. visitors 1977-80, accreditation com. 1981-95, trustee 1996-99, chmn. bd. dirs. 1998, pres. 1999). Home: 3800 N Lake Shore Dr Ste 2G Chicago IL 60613-3313 E-mail: amack@proteusgroup.net.

MACK, ARTHUR NEAL, emergency medicine and family practice physician; b. Abiline, Tex., Dec. 3, 1955; s. Alonzo Vandeveer and Mary Elizabeth (Milner) M.; m. Teresa Ann Wehrheim, Nov. 29, 1987; children: Aaron Matthew, Andrew Nathan, Abram Daniel, Hannah Michele, Abby Lynn. BS in Biology, Graceland Coll., 1978; MD, U. Ill., 1983. Pvt. practice family medicine Richland Meml. Hosp., Olney, Ill., 1986-90; dir. emergency svcs. Harrisburg (Ill.) Med. Ctr., 1990-91; staff emergency physician St. Mary's Med. Ctr., Evansville, Ind., 1991-94; assoc. dir. Family Practice Residency, 1995-96; dir. St. Mary's Med. Ctr., 1996-98; clin. asst. prof. of family medicine Ind. U., 1995-98; preceptor of family nurse practitioners U. So. Ind., 1996-98; dir. TPI Ctr. for Med. Studies, 1996—. Contbr. articles to profl. jours. Mem. Am. Acad. of Family Physicians (grad. nat. inst. for program dir. devel. 1996), Ind. Acad. of Family Physicians. Avocations: God, family, medicine, fishing. Office: 119 Oakfield Dr Brandon FL 33594 Home: 5206 Culusaja Cir Valrico FL 33594-8265

MACK, CHARLES DANIEL, III, labor union executive; b. Oakland, Calif., Apr. 16, 1942; s. Marlene Helen Fagundes, Oct. 15, 1960; children: Tammy, Kelly, Kerry, Shannon. BA, San Francisco State Coll., 1964. Truck driver Garrett Freight Lines, Emeryville, Calif., 1962-66; bus. agt. Teamsters Local No. 70, Oakland, 1966-70, sec.-treas., 1972—. Legis. rep. Calif. Teamsters Pub. Affairs Coun., Sacramento, 1970-71; trustee Western Conf. Teamsters Pension Trust Fund, 1980—, pres. Teamsters' Joint Coun., San Francisco, 1982—, v.p. western region, 1998—; mem. Calif. Inst. for Fed. Policy Rsch., 1993—. Bd. dirs. Econ. Devel. Corp. Oakland, 1980-90, Calif. Compensation Ins. Fund, San Francisco, 1980-86, Calif. Coun. Econ. and Environ. Balance, Calif. Found. on Environ. and the Economy. E-mail: wrvpmack@aol.com., ibt70@aol.com.

MACK, CONNIE, III (CORNELIUS MACK), former senator; b. Phila., Oct. 29, 1940; s. Cornelius Mack and Susan (Sheppard) McGillicuddy; children: Debra Lynn, Cornelius Harvey. Degree in bus., U. Fla., 1966. Mgmt. tng. Sun Bank, Cape Coral, Fla., 1966-68; v.p. bus. devel. First Nat. Bank, Ft. Myers, 1968-71; sr. v.p., dir. Sun Bank, Cape Coral, Fla., 1971-75; pres., dir. Fla. Nat. Bank, 1975-82; mem. U.S. Ho. of Reps. from 13th Dist. Fla., Washington, 1983-89; former Senator from Fla U.S. Senate , 1989-2001; sr. policy advisor Shaw Pittman LLP, 2001—. Former chmn. joint econ. com.; former mem. com. on fin., com. on banking, housing and urban affairs, former chmn. subcom. on econ. policy; bd. dirs LNR Property Corp. Bd. dirs., chmn. Palmer Drug Abuse Program, Cape Coral; bd. dirs. Cape Coral Hosp. Mem. Exact Scis. Corp. (dir. 2001-), Met. Ft. Myers C. of C., Cape Coral C. of C. Republican. Roman Catholic. Office: Shaw Pittman LLP 2300 N St NW Washington DC 20037*

MACK, DANIEL RICHARD, furniture designer; b. Rochester, N.Y., Dec. 23, 1947; s. Richard Cornelius and Virginia Anne Mack; m. Theresa Marie Husted, May 31, 1969; children: Kendra, Jessica, Eliza. BA, U. Toronto, Ont., Can., 1969; MA, New Sch. for Social Rsch., 1975. Journalist Sta. WRVR-FM, N.Y.C., 1971-73; spl. journalist NBC Radio, 1973-75; journalist NBC TV, 1981-83; asst. prof. Fordham U., Bronx, N.Y., 1975-81; pres. Daniel Mack Rustic Furnishings, Inc., Warwick, 1983—. Treework cons. Centerbrook Architects, Essex, Conn., 1990-91. Author: Making Rustic Furniture, 1992, The Rustic Furniture Companion, 1996, Simple Rustic Furniture, 1999, Log Cabin Living, 1999; represented in permanent collections at Cooper Hewitt Mus., Mus. of Fine Arts, Houston, Mus. of Fine Arts, Boston, Am. Craft Mus., The Hechinger Collection. Fellow N.Y. Found. for Arts, 1985-86, 90-91, Mid-Atlantic Arts Found., 1989-90. Home: 14 Welling Ave Warwick NY 10990-1514

MACK, DENNIS WAYNE, lawyer; b. Chgo., Sept. 11, 1943; s. Walter Andrew and Betty Jane (Klimek) M. BA, Yale U., 1965; JD, Harvard U., 1969. Bar: N.Y. 1970. Assoc. firm Curtis Mallet-Prevost Colt & Mosle, N.Y.C. and Paris, 1969-78; sec., gen. counsel Dominion Textile (USA) Inc., N.Y.C., 1978-91, v.p., 1986-91; pvt. practice, 1991—; gen. counsel Knoa Corp., 2000—. Alt. rep. Internat. Lesbian and Gay Assn. at ECOSOC of UN, 1994. Mem. dept. fin. Presbytery N.Y., 1978-83. Mem. ABA, N.Y. State Bar Assn., Bar Assn. City N.Y. (spl. com. on AIDS and the law 1996-2001). Home: 180 Riverside Dr New York NY 10024-1021

MACK, DIANA TRIMBLE, interior designer; b. Nampa, Idaho, Apr. 24, 1953; d. Shelley Dell and Iris Joaquine Trimble; B.F.A., U. Idaho, 1976; m. John Frederick Mack, Aug. 30, 1978. Interior designer Showroom One, Boise, Idaho, 1976-77, Don Gile Architects and Planners, Boise, 1977; pres. Trimble & Assocs., Boise, Idaho, 1977-83, Dundas Office Interiors, Boise, 1983; mgr. interior design dept. Lombard-Conrad Architects, Boise, 1983— . Mem. Sales Mktg. Execs., Kappa Kappa Gamma. Republican. Roman Catholic. Club: Crane Creek Country. Office: 1221 Shoreline Ln Boise ID 83702-6870

MACK, EDWARD GIBSON, retired business executive; b. Toronto, Ont., Can., Dec. 4, 1917; s. Edward Gibson and Marion Margaret (Ward) M.; m. Ruth Harriet Davies, Aug. 3, 1940 (dec.); children: Edward Davies Mack, Carol Mack Fuller, Susan Mack Vassel; m. Isolde Maderson, Sept. 30, 1978. Grad., Pickering Coll., 1938; student, Syracuse U., 1938-40, U. Pa., 1945-46. Investment analyst trust dept. Syracuse (N.Y.) Trust Co., 1939-43; acct. Hurdman & Cranstoun CPA's, Syracuse, 1943-44; from dist. sales mgr. to dir. mktg. and product research Easy Washing Machine Corp., 1948-55; dir. research Avco Corp., Connersville, Ind., 1955-58; exec. sec. planning and policy bd. Aeronca Mfg. Corp., Middletown, Ohio, 1958-60; pres. E.D.I., State College, Pa., 1960-62; pres., dir. Sherman Indsl. Electronics Inc., Eutectics Inc.; exec. Richards Musical Instruments, Inc., Elkhart, Ind., 1962-65; mgr. supply and distbn. plastic products Union Carbide Ltd., Lindsay, Ont., 1965-68; corp. sec. Dominion Dairies Ltd., Toronto, 1968-73, v.p., sec., 1973-81. Sec., dir. Sealtest (Can.) Ltd., 1968-81 Bd. mgmt. Pickering Coll., 1980-88. Served with U.S. Army, World War II. Mem. Inst. Chartered Secs. and Adminstrs. (assoc.), Pickering Coll. Alumni Assn. (chmn. 1981-86), Am. Legion, Elks, Sigma Chi. Democrat. Home: 217-5 Selby Ranch Rd American River Dr Sacramento CA 95864-5826

MACK, FRANCIS MARION, lawyer, engineer; b. Columbia, S.C., Sept. 13, 1949; s. Frank Cebron and Leila (Redmon) M.; m. Nina Graham Reid, May 5, 1979; children: James, Catherine. BS in Engring., U. S.C., 1970, M in Engring., 1974, JD, 1982. Bar: S.C. 1982, U.S. Dist. Ct. S.C. 1982, U.S. Ct. Appeals (4th cir.) 1983; registered profl. engr., S.C. Engr. U.S. Army C.E., Savannah, Ga., 1970-79; atty. Richardson, Plowden, Carpenter & Robinson, Columbia, 1982—. Lectr. in field. Supt. Sunday sch. Mt. Zion United Meth. Ch., Sandy Run, S.C., 1988—. Named to Best Lawyers in Am., 2000-01. Mem. ABA, Am. Arbitration Assn. (arbitrator, Dist. Svs. award, 1991), Nat. Soc. Profl. Engrs., Am. Soc. Mech. Engrs., Phi Beta Kappa. Republican. Office: Richardson Plowden Carpenter & Robinson 1600 Marion St Columbia SC 29201-2913 E-mail: fmack@rpcrlaw.com.

MACK, GAYE FERRIS, health care educator, flower essence practitioner; b. Elkhorn, Wis., May 22, 1948; d. Robert Gaye and Barbara Davis Ferris; m. Stephen Barry Mack, Aug. 26, 1972; 1 child, Robert Lakin. Student, U. Iowa, 1966-68; BA, Monmouth Coll., 1971; MA, DePaul U., 1999. Cert. travel counselor Inst. Cert. Travel Agts., Mass. Exec. asst. Wesley-Jessen, Inc., Chgo., 1973-78; tour mgr. Roberta Fisher Travel, Elk Grove, 1983-84, Travel House, Barrington, 1984-86; supr. custom touring Abercrombie & Kent, Internat., Oak Brook, 1986-90; staff Ctr. for Holistic Medicine, Northbrook, 1994-95; lectr., trainer Nelson-Bach, USA, Ltd., Wilmington, Mass., 1997—; educator Spectrum Organics, Inc., Peta Luma, Calif., 2001—; cons. Allied Clin. Psychologists, Arlington Heights, Ill., 2001—. Mem. internat. register Bach practitioners Dr. Edward Bach Found., U.K. Mem.: Chgo. Area Holistic Arts and Health Alliance, Dr. Edward Bach Found. (registered practitioner), White Eagle Lodge (UK). Avocations: traveling, medieval history, cultural medicine. E-mail: naturesbridge@aol.com.

MACK, GREGORY JOHN, financial executive and consultant; b. Buffalo, Oct. 11, 1954; s. Henry and Dorothy Catherine (Boone) M.; m. Rosemary Lynn Testa, Aug. 17, 1979; children: Lindsey Marie, Stephanie Kaitlyn. BS in Polit. Sci., SUNY, Buffalo, 1978. Cert. tchr., N.Y. Police officer Town of Amherst, N.Y., 1978-81; fin. cons., regional v.p. Cigna Individual Fin. Advisors, Amherst, 1981-94; dir. new bus. devel. Manulife Fin., U.S., Williamsville, N.Y., 1997—. Host radio show Fin. Forum, Sta. WXBX; speaker in field. Host daily radio show Fin. Forum, Sta. WWWS. Mem. Buffalo Life Underwriters Assn., Buffalo C. of C., Gen. Agts. and Mgrs. Assn. (Agt. of Yr. award 1987-92), Cigna's President's Club (life, pres. 1990-91), Cigna's Honor Table (pres. 1987-89), Cigna's Gold Key (chmn. 1988), Cigna's Excalibur (life). Republican. Roman Catholic. Avocations: hockey, golf, tennis, baseball, skiing. Home: 241 Halston Pky East Amherst NY 14051-1856 Office: Manulife Fin 6225 Sheridan Dr Ste 203 Williamsville NY 14221-4800

MACK, J. CURTIS, II, civic organization administrator; b. Los Angeles, Dec. 22, 1944; s. James Curtis and Ahli Christina (Youngren) M.; m. Tamara Jo Kriner, Jan. 23, 1988; children: James Curtis III, Robert Lee, Edward Albert. BA cum laude, U. So. Calif., 1967, M in Pub. Adminstrn., 1969, MA, 1976. Asst. to regional dir. VA, Los Angeles, 1973-79; exec. dir. Citizens for the Republic, Santa Monica, Calif., 1979-85; asst. sec. oceans and atmosphere U.S. Dept. Commerce, Washington, 1985-88; pres. Los Angeles World Affairs Coun., 1988—. Adj. prof. Pepperdine U. Grad. Sch. Pub. Policy, 1999—; bd. dirs. Brentwood Bank of Calif. Mem. Pres.'s Commn. on White House Fellowships, 1984-85; mem. exec. adv. bd. European Union Ctr. Calif. Col. USAFR, 1969-99. Mem. Coun. Fgn. Rels., Nat. Space Club (bd. dirs. 1987-88). Republican. Episcopalian. Avocation: philatelist. Office: LA World Affairs Coun 345 S Figueroa St Ste 313 Los Angeles CA 90071-1002

MACK, JAMES A. health products executive; BSChemE, Mich. Tech. U.; MBMA, Western New Eng. Coll. V.p. Olin Corp., 1985—90; exec. v.p. Oakite Products., Inc., 1982—84; various positions, most recently pres., gen. mgr. chem. divisn. The Sherwin-Williams Co., 1977—81; pres. Cambrex Corp., East Rutherford, NJ, 1990—, CEO, 1995—, chmn. bd., 1999—. Bd. trustees Mich. Tech Alumni Fund. Mem.: Synthetic Organic Chem. Mfg. Assn. (past chmn. bd. govs.). Office: Cambrex Corp 1 Meadowlands Plz East Rutherford NJ 07073 Office Fax: 201-804-9853. E-mail: communications@cambrex.com.*

MACK, JAMES WILLARD, artist, educator; b. Kingsburg, Calif., Sept. 9, 1924; s. Richard Artemus and Edna Rae (Baldwin) M.; m. Frances Joy Sarver, June 13, 1947; children: James Willard Jr., Gretchen Lorraine Mack Beale. BA, San Jose State Coll., 1949, MA, 1959. Cert. secondary tchr., Calif. Art tchr. Corcoran (Calif.) H.S., 1950-53, North H.S., Bakersfield, Calif., 1953-56, Los Altos (Calif.0 H.S., 1956-64; asst. prof. art Foothill Coll., Los Altos Hills, Calif., 1964-69; art tchr. Kamehameha Schs., Honolulu, 1969-71; instr. art U. Hawaii/Leeward C.C., Leeward Oahu, Hawaii, 1972-74; artist profl. studio, Kailuo, 1969-84, Taos, N.Mex., 1984-92, San Miguel de Allende, Mex., 1992-93, LaConner, Wash., 1996—. Bd. dirs. Contemporary Art Ctr., Honolulu, 1978-80. Exhibited in shows at Senate Rotunda, Washington, Oakland (Calif.) Art Mus., Honolulu Acad. Art, Hawaii Watercolor Soc., Wailea Arts Ctr., Maui, Hawaii, Elaine Horwitch Galleries, Sedona, Ariz., Suzanne Brown Gallery, Scottsdale, Ariz., Philip Bareiss Fine Art, Taos, N.Mex., Colorado Springs Fine Arts Ctr., Stables Art Ctr., Taos, U. Colo., Colorado Springs, Stewart's Fine Art, Taos, Scott-Milo Gallery, Anacortes, Wash., N.Mex. Arts, others. Lectr. to civic groups, 1964-69. Sgt. U.S. Army, 1943-46, ETO. Mem.: Phi Delta Kappa, Theta Delta Phi. Avocations: fishing, hiking, travel. Home: PO Box 926 1002 B Ave Carrizozo NM 88301 E-mail: MackJ3@Tularosa.com.

MACK, JIM, advertising executive; With Frankel & Co., Chgo., 1979-89, pres., 1989-98, pres., CEO, 1998—2002, Chmn., 2002—. Office: Frankel and Co 111 E Wacker Dr Chicago IL 60601-3713*

MACK, JUDITH COLE SCHRIM, political science educator; b. Cin., Aug. 9, 1938; d. James Douglass and Cathleen (Cole) Schrim; m. Thomas H. Mack, Jan. 3, 1968; children: Robert Michael, Cathleen Cole. AB with high distinction, U. Ky., 1960; AM, Radcliffe Grad. Sch., 1962; MPhil, Columbia U., 1988, postgrad., 1986—. Tchr. The Lexington (Ky.) Sch., 1962-63; instr. Russian Emory U., Atlanta, 1963-64, Kent (Ohio) State U., 1964-65; instr. Hunter Coll., N.Y.C., 1988-90; adj. lectr. Barnard Coll., spring 1991, 92; instr. Douglass Coll. Rutgers U., 1992-93. Rsch. asst. sociology dept. U. Ky., summer 1961; rsch. asst. Russian and East European Studies Ctr., UCLA, 1965-67; rsch. asst. security studies ctr. UCLA, 1967-68; adj. lectr. Hunter Coll., N.Y.C., spring 1988; presenter in field. Chmn. State Pub. Affairs Com., N.J. Jr. Leagues, 1979-80; bd. dirs. Children's Aide Adoption Soc., Hackensack, N.J., 1979-90, v.p. 1985-90; bd. dirs. Assn. for Children N.J., Newark, 1982—, v.p. 1983-88, chair special events 1999; trustee Divsn. Youth and Family Svcs., Trenton, 1982-91, v.p. 1983-88, others; mem. Millburn-Short Hills County Com. Rep. Party, 1994—, corr. sec., 1994-96, chmn. 1996-98. Recipient Woodrow Wilson fellowship Radcliffe Coll., 1960-61, Nat. Def. fellowship Radcliffe Coll., 1961-62. Mem. Nat. Soc. Colonial Dames Am. (N.J. treas. 1995—), Mortar Board, Phi Beta Kappa, Phi Sigma Iota. Episcopalian. Avocations: bridge, cooking, ballet, theater, movies. Home: 47 Knollwood Rd Short Hills NJ 07078-2821

MACK, JULIA COOPER, retired judge; b. Fayetteville, N.C., July 17, 1920; d. Dallas L. and Emily (McKay) Perry; m. Jerry S. Cooper, July 30, 1943; 1 dau., Cheryl; m. Clifford S. Mack, Nov. 21, 1957. BS, Hampton Inst., 1940; LL.B., Howard U., 1951; JD (hon.), U. D.C., 1999. Bar: D.C. 1952. Legal cons. OPS, Washington, 1952-53; atty.-advisor office gen. counsel Gen. Svcs. Adminstrn., 1953-54; trial appellate atty. criminal div. Dept. Justice, 1954-68; civil rights atty. Office Gen. Counsel, Equal Employment Opportunity Commn., 1968-75; assoc. judge Ct. Appeals, 1975-89; sr. judge DC Ct. of Appeals, 1989—2001. Mem. Am., Fed., Washington, Nat. Bar Assns., Nat. Assn. Women Judges. Home: 1610 Varnum St NW Washington DC 20011-4206

MACK, MARK PHILIP, chemical company executive; b. Buffalo, Jan. 14, 1950; s. Stanley Joseph and Florence M. (Kopacz) M.; m. Jean Ann Merrick, June 2, 1984; 1 child, Hannah Elizabeth. BS in Chemistry, Buffalo State Coll., 1971; PhD in Chemistry, SUNY, Buffalo, 1976. Rsch. assoc. Duke U., Durham, N.C., 1975-77; rsch. chemist Conoco Inc., Ponca City, Okla., 1977-80, group supr., 1980-81; group leader Conoco/DuPont, 1982-85; sr. supr. DuPont Polymer Products, Wilmington, Del., 1985-89; rsch. mgr. OxyChem, Houston, 1989-90; dir. tech. Occidental Chem. Corp., 1990-95, Lyondell Petrochem. Co., Houston, 1995-97, v.p. licensing, 1996-97; dir. R&D Equistar Chems., LP, 1997-99, dir. catalyst R&D, analytical chemistry and polymer sci., 1999—2002; chief scientist Lyondell/Equistar, Cin., 2002—. Patentee in field; contbr. articles to profl. jours. Mem. Am. Indian Relief Coun.; mem. adv. bd. Black Am. PAC; mem. World Affairs Coun. Greater Cin., Ctr. for Sci. in the Pub. Interest. Recipient Linus Pauling award SUNY-Buffalo, 1971, Outstanding Student in Chemistry award Western N.Y. Sect. Am. Chem. Soc., 1971, Samuel B. Silbert Fellowship SUNY-Buffalo, 1974-75, Conoco Patent award, 1983, Equistar/Lyondell Inventor award, 2001 Mem. AAAS, Am. Chem. Soc., Soc. Plastics Engrs., N.Y. Acad. Sci., Am. Mgmt. Assn., Product Devel. and Mgmt. Assn., Sigma Xi. Home: 8483 Beckett Pointe Dr West Chester OH 45069-6440 Fax: 513-530-4267. E-mail: mark.mack@equistarchem.com.

MACK, MICHAEL J. engineer, consultant; b. Viola, Ill., July 3, 1925; s. Thomas Edward and Elizabeth Bernidette Mack; children: Kathleen, Carol, Patrick, Michele, Michael, Marybeth, Christi, Timothy. BS in Aero. Engring., U. Notre Dame, 1946; MS in Mech. Engring., U. Iowa, 1949. Engr. John Deere, Moline, Ill., 1946—47, Dubuque, Iowa, 1949—56, Waterloo, 1956—87. Dir. Deere Product Engring. Ctr. John Deere, Waterloo, 1971—87; cons. Blount Mfg. , Waterloo, 1990—93. Bd. mem. Covenant Health Sys., Waterloo, 1980—2001, bd. chair, 1996—2001; bd. mem. Wheaton (Ill.) Franciscan Svcs., 2001—02. Ensign USN, 1946. Fellow: Soc. Automotive Engrs. (chair fellow com. 1995); mem.: Iowa State Mech. Engring. Adv. Coun. (past pres.), Coordinating Rsch. Coun. (pres.). Roman Catholic. Home: 1433 Olympic Dr Waterloo IA 50701-4640

MACK, ROBERT WHITING, computer consultant; b. Cambridge, Mass., June 7, 1949; s. Robert Anthony and Caroline Mack. BA, Harvard U., 1971, JD, 1974. Bar: Mass. 1974. Assoc. Hale and Dorr, Boston, 1974-79, jr. ptnr., 1979-83, sr. ptnr., 1983-88, of counsel, 1988-89; computer cons., 1990-99; co-dir. info. technology, 2000—. Bd. dirs. Cambridge Cmty. Television, Inc., 1996-2000, treas. 1997-2000; bd. dirs., chief tech. officer FreshAddress, Inc., 1999—, Votemaker, Inc., 1999-2002. Mem. Conservation Commn., Lincoln, Mass., 1981-91; bd. dirs. Harvard Gay and Lesbian Rev., 1994-97; bd. dirs. Lincoln Homes Corp., 1991-95, pres., 1992-94; bd. dirs. Greater Boston coun. Am. Youth Hostels, 1990-92, pres., 1991-92. Mem.: Harvard Gay and Lesbian Caucus (bd. dirs. 1994—2001, co-chair 1994—97), Chiltern Mountain Club (bd. dirs. 1992—95, co-chair 1993—95). Home: 10 Magazine St Apt 805 Cambridge MA 02139-3330

MACK, STEPHEN W. financial planner; b. Chgo., Mar. 4, 1954; s. Walter M. and Suzanne (Charbonneau) M.; m. Dayle A. Rothermel, Nov. 19, 1983; children: Michael, Veronica, Kevin. BBA in Fin., U. Mich., 1976; cert., Coll. Fin. Planning, Denver, 1987. NASD Lic. Series 63 Uniform Securities Agent State Law Exam., Series 7 Gen. Securities Rep., Series 5 Interest Rate Options, Series 8 Gen. Securities Sales Supr., Series 15 Fgn. Currency Options, Series 24 Gen. Securities Prin., Series 4 Registered Options Prin., Series 53 Municipal Securities Prin. Gen. sales mgr. Mack Cadillac Corp., Mt. Prospect, Ill., 1976-81; sales rep. Merrill Lynch Co., Chgo., 1981-84, resident mgr. Rockford, Ill., 1984-85, asst. v.p. Skokie, 1985-86; pres., chief exec. officer Mack Investment Securities, Inc., Glenview, 1986—. Editor, distributor Mack Tracks (trademark), monthly newsletter; creator, developer Money Mgrs. Plus Program and Website. Bdi. dirs. Glenview Youth Baseball, 1994-99, pres., 1999-2001. Mem. Inst. Cert. Fin. Planners, Internat. Assn. registered Fin. Planners, Nat. Assn. Securities Dealers, Internat. Assn. Fin. Planners, Am. Assn. Cert. Fin. Planners, Am. Assn. Registered Fin. Planners, Am. Assn. Registered Investment Advisers, Soc. Asset Allocation and Fund Timers, Mensa. Avocations: skiing, tennis, running. Office: Mack Investment Securities Inc 1939 Waukegan Rd Glenview IL 60025-1715

MACK, SUSAN PRESCOTT, practical nursing educator; b. Milton, Fla., Apr. 12, 1957; d. John Hansel and Dorothy Lawrence (Wise) Prescott; 1 child from previous marriage, Heather Denise Phillips; m. Willie Mack; children: Dakota Suzanne, Cheyenne Noel. Cert. of practical nursing with honors, Pensacola Jr. Coll., 1976; ADN, Jefferson Davis Jr. Coll., 1980; BSN, U. South Ala., 1989, MSN, 1999. RN, Fla. Jay Hosp., 1976-80; Santa Rosa Med. Ctr., 1980-92; relief staff nurse Am. Nurses Svcs., Inc., Pensacola, Fla., 1992-97; ICU staff Atmore Cmty. Hosp., 1994-2000; home health nurse Advance Home Health, 1996-98. Adj. in nursing Pensacola Jr. Coll., 1992—96, asst. prof. of pratical nursing, 1997—. Mem. Fla. Nurses Assn., Assn. Practical Nurse Educators Fla., Sigma Theta Tau, Alpha Theta Chi. Home: 4949 Horace Lunsford Rd Milton FL 32570-8500

MACK, THEODORE, lawyer; b. Ft. Worth, Mar. 5, 1936; s. Henry and Norma (Harris) M.; m. Ellen Feinknopf, June 19, 1960; children: Katherine Norma, Elizabeth Ellen, Alexandra. AB cum laude, Harvard U., 1958, JD, 1961. Bar: Tex. 1961, U.S. Supreme Ct. 1971, U.S. Ct. Appeals (5th cir.) 1967, U.S. Ct. Appeals (11th cir.) 1981, U.S. Dist. Ct. (no. dist.) Tex. 1961, U.S. Dist. Ct. (we. dist.) Tex. 1968, U.S. Dist. Ct. (so. dist.) Tex. 1968, U.S. Dist. Ct. (ea. dist.) Tex. 1999. Assoc. Mack & Mack, Ft. Worth, 1961-62, ptnr., 1963-70; dir., pres., v.p., treas., ptnr. Renfro, Mack and Hudman, P.C. and predecessors, 1970-93; spl. counsel Brackett & Ellis, P.C. and predecessors, 1993—. Trustee Ft. Worth Country Day Sch., 1976-82; bd. dirs. Beth-El Congregation, 1964-73, 75-78, pres. 1975-77; bd. dirs. Jewish Fedn. Ft. Worth, 1965-72; mem. Leadership Ft. Worth, 1973-74; bd. dirs. Sr. Citizens Ctrs., Inc., 1969-81, Family and Individual Svcs., 1981-84, Presbyn. Night Shelter Tarrant County, Inc., 1992-97; pres. Harvard Law Sch. Assn. Tex., 1976-77. Fellow Tex. Bar Found. (life); mem. Tex. Bar Assn., ABA, Am. Inn Ct. (master of the bench John C. Ford Inn), Tarrant County Bar Assn., Bar Assn. 5th Cir. Ct., Colonial Country Club, Ft. Worth Club, City Club, Harvard Club (N.Y.C., Boston). Democrat. Jewish. Home: 2817 Harlanwood Dr Fort Worth TX 76109-1226 Office: 100 Main St Fort Worth TX 76102-3090 Office Fax: 817-870-2265. E-mail: tmack@belaw.com.

MACK, THOMAS RUSSELL, foundation administrator, management consultant; b. Independence, Iowa, May 22, 1955; s. Russell John and A. Catherine M.; children: Christopher E., Stephen A. BA, Morningside Coll., 1978; MBA, U. S.D., 1988. CEO, dir. Whitestone Found. Rsch., Inc., Sioux City, Iowa, 1981—; tax splst. Commerce Clearing House, 1991-95; v.p., controller Grand Prairie Cos., 1996-98; pres. Greenway-Infinity Internat., Inc., 1998—. Staff instr. Upper Iowa U., 1989-90; vis. prof. Mont. Coll. Mineral Sci. & Tech., 1988-89, auditor, examiner Iowa Dept. Revenue. Bd. dirs. The Exodus Counseling Ctr., Lombard, Ill., 1998—, Iowa Bapt. Mission Inc, West Des Moines, 1998—, Shepherd Ministries, Milo, Iowa, 1981—. Home: 1513 S Rustin St Sioux City IA 51106-2240

MACK, WILLIAM JOSEPH, psychotherapist, rehabilitation specialist; b. Evergreen Park, Ill., Mar. 5, 1943; s. Arol Ruth (Tallut) M.; m. Margaret Grace McCullom, Jan. 8, 1966 (div. Aug. 1979); children: William, Amy; m. Joan Kinnon, May 22, 1987; stepchildren: Margaret, Wendy, Douglas, Suzanne. BA, U. Dayton, 1965; cert., Ind. State U., Terre Haute, 1980; MA, Ball State U., 1983; M Health Scis., Governors State U., 1994; Doctorate, Am. Inst. Hypnotherapy, 1995. Lic. social worker, Ill.; cert. addictions counselor, clin. hypnotherapist, Ill.; nat. cert. master addictions counselor; lic. clin. profl. counselor, Ill. Mktg. rep. Texaco Inc., Lockport, Ill., 1969-73; med. rep. Merrell-Dow, Kokomo, Ind., 1973-82; program coordinator Pilsen Vocat., Chgo., 1983-85; dir. sheltered workshop Edgewater Community Mental Health Ctr., 1985-88; mem. staff Edgewater Uptown Community Mental Health Ctr., 1988-92; program dir. Community Counseling Ctrs. Chgo., 1992-96; mgr. adult health ctr. Chgo. Commons, 1996-97; psychiat. social worker S. Mary of Nazareth Hosp., Chgo., 1997—; program therapist River Edge Hosp., Forest Park, Ill., 2000—. Adj. faculty mem. Kendall Coll.; therapist Vet. Ctr., Chicago Heights, Ill., 1984-85. Instr. first aid ARC, Chgo., 1986. Served with U.S. Army, 1965-68; Res. ret. Mem NASW, Internat. Assn. PsychoSocial Profls., Am. Assn. Profl. Hypnotherapists, Mktg. Execs. for Sheltered Workshops, Chgo. Soc. Clin. Hypnosis, Am. Legion, Ret. Officers Assn. Democrat. Roman Catholic. Avocations: flying, photography. Home: 1640 Barnsdale Rd #201 La Grange Park IL 60526 Office: River Edge Hosp 8311 Roosevelt Rd Forest Park IL 60130 E-mail: wjmack9@cs.com.

MACKAIG, JANET BROWNLEE, artist, printmaker, educator; b. Santa Monica, Calif., July 16, 1931; d. Roy Edward and Lorna (Feckler) Murphy; m. Richard Allaire Mackaig, Dec. 15, 1950; children: Janet (Mrs. William Chadwick), Steven Richard. AA, Pasadena City Coll., 1964; BA, Calif. State U., Los Angeles, 1969, MA, 1971, postgrad., 1975, UCLA, 1975. Tchr. Creative Arts Group, Sierra Madre, Calif., 1965-75, Duarte (Calif.) Unified Sch. Dist., 1973-76, Otis Art Inst., Los Angeles, 1975-76, Saddleback Coll., Mission Viejo, Calif., 1976-78, Laguna Beach Sch. Art, 1980—. One-man shows: Upstairs Gallery, Claremont, Calif., 1969, U. Oreg., 1976, Fine Arts Gallery, Laguna Beach, Calif., 1981, Minot (N.D.) State Coll., 1981; group shows include: Colorprint U.S.A., Tex. Tech. U., 1975, U. Ala., 1975, Pioneer Press Traveling Print Show, Africa, 1975-76, Art-A-Multi-Cultural Show, Calif. Mus. Sci. and Industry, 1978, Contemporary Korean Printmakers Assn. Print Show, 1978, Coos Art Mus., Coos Bay, Oreg., 1979, La Grange (Ga.) Coll., 1980, Trenton (N.J.) State Coll., 1980, Internat. Print Biennial, Miami, Fla., 1982, Nat. Printmaking Invitational, San Bernardino, Calif., 1983, Angeles Gate Cultural Ctr., San Pedro, Calif.; represented in permanent collections. Bd. dirs. Womanspace, 1974—. Recipient Calif. Purchase awards Santa Monical Coll., 1973, Calif. State U., Los Angeles, 1976, Calif. Poly. U., Pomona, 1979. Mem. Laguna Beach Art Assn., Calif. Soc. Printmakers, Los Angeles Printmaking Soc. (pres. 1977-78), Los Angeles Inst. Contemporary Art, Print Club Phila., Pasadena Artists Concern. Club: Pioneer Press. Home: 23821 Salvador Bay Monarch Beach CA 92629-4207

MACKALL, HENRY CLINTON, lawyer; b. Ft. Lauderdale, Fla., Apr. 6, 1927; s. Douglass Sorrel and Mildred (Parker) M.; m. Mary Margaret Sullivan, June 21, 1952; children: Caroline Clark, Nancy Sorrel, Lucy Parker. BA, U. Va., 1950, LLB, 1952. Bar: Va. 1951. Ptnr. Mackall, Mackall & Gibb, P.C. and predecessors, Fairfax, Va., 1952—. Asst. commr. accounts Fairfax County (Va.), 1963—; spl. commr. in chancery for audit functions for Cir. Ct. Fairfax County, 1976—; substitute judge Fairfax County Ct., Juvenile and Domestic Relations Ct. Fairfax County, 1964-69. Trustee Fairfax Hosp. Assn., 1966-75; with Va. State Bar Client Security Fund Bd., 1976-88, chmn., 1977-78; bd. dirs. F&M Bank, No. Va. Served with AUS, 1945-46. Fellow Am. Coll. Trusts & Estate Counsel, Am. Coll. Real Estate Lawyers, Va. Law Found.; mem. ABA, Va. Bar Assn. (regional v.p. 1963-64), Fairfax County Bar Assn. (pres. 1966-67), Hist. Soc. Fairfax County (pres. 1970-72), Jamestowne Soc. (gov. 1995-97), River Bend Country (pres. 1967-68) (Gt. Falls, Va.), Georgetown Assembly (Washington). Democrat. Episcopalian. Home: 1032 Towlston Rd Mc Lean VA 22102-1111 Office: 4031 Chain Bridge Rd Fairfax VA 22030-4103 E-mail: mackmarhen@aol.com., mackgibb@aol.com.

MACKALL, LAIDLER BOWIE, lawyer; b. Washington, Aug. 8, 1916; s. Laidler and Evelyn (Bowie) M.; m. Nancy M. Taylor, Aug. 28, 1942; children: Nancy Taylor Mackall Lurton (dec.), Christie Beall Mackall Connard, Susan Somervell Mackall Smythe, Bruce Bowie Mackall McConihe; m. Prudence Robertson Colbert, July 26, 1978. AB, Princeton U., 1938; postgrad., Georgetown U., 1938-40, JD, 1947. Bar: D.C. bar 1947, ICC bar 1951, U.S. Supreme Ct. bar 1958. Law clk. to chief judge of predecessor to D.C. Ct. Appeals, 1946-47; assoc. Minor, Gatley & Drury, Washington, 1947-49, Steptoe & Johnson, Washington, 1949-51, ptnr., 1952-86, of counsel, 1986-98. Mem. D.C. Ct. Appeals Com. on Admissions, 1974-78, D.C. Circuit Jud. Conf., 1983, 85, 86; bd. mgrs. Nat. Conf. Bar Examiners, 1974-77 Served to col. USAAF, 1940-46, 51. Decorated Silver Star, 2 D.F.C.s, 5 Air medals, 3 Presdl. unit citations. Fellow Am. Coll. Trial Lawyers (emeritus); mem. ABA (past vice chmn. standing com. aviation ins. law), D.C. Bar, Bar Assn. D.C. (past chmn. com. on negligence, motor vehicle and compensation law), Barristers Club (v.p. 1964), Chevy Chase Country Club, Met. Club, Hawk's Nest Golf Club of Fla. Episcopalian. Home (Summer): 3809 Village Park Dr Chevy Chase MD 20815-5746 Home: 151 Passage Island Vero Beach FL 32963-4265 E-mail: lbmackall@webtv.net.

MACKAMAN, DONALD HAYES, lawyer; b. Des Moines, Oct. 29, 1912; s. Frank Hindes and Eva (Hayes) M.; children: Linda, Bert, Donald Jr. BA, Drake U., 1933, JD, 1935. Sec., v.p., gen. counsel Campbell Taggart, Inc., Dallas, 1933-77; of counsel Gardere Wynne Sewell LLP, 1977—. Mem. Order of Coif, Phi Beta Kappa. Bus. Office: Gardere Wynne Sewell LLP 1601 Elm St Ste 3000 Dallas TX 75201-4761 E-mail: dmackaman@gardere.com, macdo2@airmail.net.

MACKANESS, GEORGE BELLAMY, retired pharmaceutical company executive; b. Sydney, Australia, Aug. 20, 1922; came to U.S., 1965, naturalized, 1978; s. James Vincent and Eleanor Frances (Bellamy) M.; m. Gwyneth Patterson, May 5, 1945; 1 son, Miles Philip. M.B. BS with honors, U. Sydney, 1945; D.C.P., London U., 1949; MA with honors, U. Oxford, 1949, D.Phil., 1953. Demonstrator, tutor in pathology Sir William Dunn Sch. Pathology, Oxford, 1949-53; sr. fellow Australian Nat. U., 1954-58, asso. prof., 1958-60, professorial fellow, 1960-63; prof. microbiology U. Adelaide, 1963-65; dir. Trudeau Inst., 1965-76; pres. The Squibb Inst. for Med. Research, Princeton, N.J., 1976-88. Clin. prof. dept. medicine Coll. of Medicine and Dentistry of N.J.; adj. prof. pathology N.Y. U. Author articles in field. Recipient Paul Ehrlich-Ludwig Darmstaedter prize, 1975 Fellow Royal Soc. London. Home: 677 Lake Frances Dr Charleston SC 29412-4345

MACKAUF, STEPHEN HENRY, lawyer; b. Gulfport, Miss., Mar. 7, 1945; s. Walter Scott and Rose Evelyn (Berkowitz) Mackauf. AB cum laude, U. Miami, Coral Gables, Fla., 1965; JD, Columbia Law Sch., 1968. Bar: Fla. 1969, N.Y. 1970, U.S. Dist. Ct. (so. dist.) N.Y. 1970. Assoc. Kelley Drye & Warren, N.Y., 1968-70, Gair, Gair & Conason, N.Y., 1970-78, ptnr, 1978-90; ptnr. Gair, Gair, Conason, Steigman & Mackauf, 1990—. Co-author: Obstetrical-Neonatal Malpractice, 1984, Failures in Anesthesia Care, 1985; editor: Hospital Liability, 1986, Advanced Medical Malpractice Trial Techniques, 2000, Trial of an Obstetrical Malpractice Case; co-author: Failure to Diagnose Fetal Distress, 2001. Mem.: ATLA, Assn. of Bar of City of N.Y., N.Y. State Trial Lawyers Assn. Office: 80 Pine St Fl 34 New York NY 10005-1702

MACKAY, ALFRED F. dean, philosophy educator; b. Ocala, Fla., Oct. 1, 1938; s. Kenneth Hood and Julia Horsey (Farnum) MacK.; m. Ann Nadine Wilson, Feb. 4, 1962; children: Douglas Kevin, Robert Wilson. AB, Davidson Coll., 1960; PhD, U. N.C., 1967. Prof. philosophy Oberlin (Ohio) Coll., 1967-84, 96—, dean Coll. Arts and Scis., 1984-95, acting pres., 1991. Vis. asst. prof. philosophy dept. U. Ill., Urbana/Champaign, 1970-71; vis. prof. philosophy dept. Wayne State U., Detroit, 1983. Author: Arrow's Theorem: The Paradox of Social Choice, 1980; editor: Society: Revolution and Reform, 1971, Issues in the Philosophy of Language, 1976. Campaign cons. Buddy MacKay for U.S. Senate, Fla., 1988. 1st lt. U.S. Army, Airborne, 1961-63. Fellow Woodrow Wilson Found., 1963-66, Am. Coun. of Learned Socs., 1973, Humanities fellow Rockefeller Found., 1981. Democrat. Avocations: choral singing, automobiles. Office: Oberlin Coll Dept Philosophy King Bldg Oberlin OH 44074

MACKAY, CYNTHIA JEAN, music educator; b. Kane, Pa., Apr. 30, 1943; d. Theodore Elmer and Frances Agnes (Bertch) Johnson; m. Angus James Mackay, Dec. 30, 1972; children: Shannon Leslie, Brendan Douglas. BS, Mansfield (Pa.) State Coll., 1965; cert., U. Calif., San Diego, 1972. Cert. basic tchg., Oreg.; std. life tchg. credential, Calif; cert. music educator K-12, Tex. Instr. vocal music Camp Curtin Jr. H.S., Harrisburg, Pa., 1965-69, Lincoln Jr. H.S., Oceanside, Calif., 1969-73, Poynter Jr. H.S., Hillsboro, Oreg., 1973-75; tchr. piano Collingswood, N.J., 1976-94, Spring, Tex., 1976-94; tchr. music Holmsley Elem. Sch., Houston, 1995—. Organist 1st Meth. Ch., Kane, 1958-61; part-time organist 1st Presbyn. Ch., Mansfield, 1961-65; piano accompanist, 1958—. Ednl. docent Houston Symphony League, 1985-92, creator Alice Flores Scholarship Competition, 1988; dist. vol. music coord., Klein, Tex., 1987-88; mem. Cypress Woodlands Jr. Forum, North Houston, Tex., 1988-94; pres. PTO Haude Elem., Spring, Tex., 1988-89, Strack Intermediate, Spring, 1991-92; 1st v.p. Klein Oak Strutters Booster Club, 1992-93. Mem. Tex. Music Educators Assn., Cypress Creek Music Tchrs. Assn. (corr. sec.). Republican. Presbyterian. Avocation: travel. Home: 3419 Blue Cypress Dr Spring TX 77388-5808

MACKAY, DAVID B. b. Yonkers, N.Y., May 1, 1944; s. Norman A. and Katherine D. MacK.; m. Carole E. Bartlett, Aug. 9, 1945; children: Deborah, Jonathan. PhD, Northwestern U., Evanston, Ill., 1971. Mktg. educator Ind. U., Bloomington, Ind., 1971—. Pres. PROSCAL, Bloomington, 2000—; vis. prof. Norwegian Sch. Econs., Bergen, Norway, 1987—88. Contbr. articles (Dow Technology tchg. award, 1997). Grantee Probabilistic Scaling, NSF, 1976-1995. Mem.: Psychometric Soc., Assn. Computing Machinery, Am. Statistical Assn., Am. Mktg. Assn. Office: Ind U 1309 E 10th St Bloomington IN 47405 Office Fax: 812 855 6440. Business E-Mail: mackay@indiana.edu.

MACKAY, GAIL, librarian; b. New Castle, Ind., Nov. 13, 1948; d. Frederick Earl and Rosemary (Garvey) Brown; children: Heather E., Douglas F. BA in English, Purdue U., 1971; MLS, Ball State U., 1973. Cert. tchr., libr., Ind. English tchr. Taylor H.S., Kokomo, Ind., 1977-84; libr. Ind. U., 1992—. Author and presenter. Pres., Tribal Trails coun. Girl Scouts U.S.A., 1995—, nat. cert. instr. of trainers, 1992—. Recipient Tchg. Excellence Recognition award Ind. U. Kokomo, 1998, Faculty Colloquium on Excellence in Tchg., 1999, Thank Badge, Girl Scouts, 1989. Mem. ALA, Ind. U. Librs. Assn. (chair profl. devel. 1994), Ind. Libr. Fedn. (co-chair instrn. sect. 1994—). Roman Catholic. Office: Ind U Kokomo PO Box 9003 Kokomo IN 46904-9003

MACKAY, GLADYS GODFREY, adult education educator; b. Buffalo, Sept. 17, 1915; d. Joseph Edwin and Hazel Winifred (Brown) Godfrey; m. James Albert MacKay, July 11, 1944 (wid. June 1997); children: Michael Paul, Cynthia Louise. BS, Cornell U., 1936; MA, Columbia U., 1940; postgrad., Case Western Res. U., Cleve., 1948-50. Cert. tchr. N.Y. Asst. home demonstration agt. Cornell U., N.Y., 1936-38; tchr. rural vocat. home econs. Consolidated Schs., Gilbertsville, 1938-39; jr./sr. h.s. home econs. tchr. City Pub. Sch., Peekskill, 1940-42; home econs. instr. Mather Coll./Cleve. Coll., Western Res. U., Cleve., 1946-48; marriage counselor/probation officer Lucas County Ct of Domestic Rels., Toledo, 1950-51; tchr./psychologist, spkr.'s bur. Family Health Assn. and Cen. Sch. of Practical Nursing, Cleve., 1951-54. Rep. to nat. consumer-retailer coun. for AAUW, Am. Stds. Assn., N.Y.C., 1940-42; mem. com. setting textile color-fastness stds. for FTC, Am. Stds. Assn., 1941; mem. task force to develop health edn. curriculum, Cleve. Heights Bd. of Edn., Ohio, 1967-69; mem. adv. bd. Children's Svcs., Cleve., 1963-65; mem. mental health com. Fedn. for Cmty. Planning, Cleve., 1977-78, others. Active Coun. on World Affairs, Cleve., 1960-76; presenter Cleve. Growth Assn., 1964, Ohio Citizen's Coun., Columbus, 1974-77, others; presenter Met. Health Planning Corp., Cleve., 1978, chair Health Edn. Conf., 1978. Lt. USNR, 1942-46, WWII. Recipient Navy Commendation; named to Nat. Inst. of Pub. Affairs Conf. on Met. Problems, AAUW, Washington, 1968. Mem. AAUW (life, honoree Ohio Wall of Fame 2000), Case Western Res. Univ. Women's Club (bd. mem. Sch. Medicine), Cleve. Acad. of Medicine Aux., Pi Lambda Theta. Presbyterian. Avocations: travel, reading, creative thinking. Achievements include being one of first 2 women to fly Navy antisubmarine Patrol NAS, Norfolk, Va., 1943. Home: 162 Kendal Dr Oberlin OH 44074-1907

MACKAY, HAROLD HUGH, lawyer; b. Regina, Sask., Can., Aug. 1, 1940; s. John Royden and Grace Madeliene (Irwin) MacK.; m. Jean Elizabeth Hutchison, Dec. 27, 1963; children: Carol, Donald. BA, U. Sask., 1960; LLB, Dalhousie U., Halifax, N.S., 1963. Bar: Sask. 1964, Queen's Counsel 1981. Assoc. MacPherson Leslie & Tyerman, Regina, 1963-69, ptnr., 1969-75, 76—, mng. ptnr., 1989-96, chmn., 1997—. Bd. dirs. IMC Global Inc.; chmn. task force Future of the Can. Fin. Svcs. Sector, 1997-98; chair Saskatchewan Inst. Pub. Policy. Trustee Found. for Legal Rsch. Mem. Internat. Bar Assn., Can. Bar Assn., Law Soc. Sask. Mem. United Ch. Office: 1500 1874 Scarth St Regina SK Canada S4P 4E9 E-mail: hmackay@mlt.com.

MACKAY, JACK WHITING, civil engineer; b. Asheville, N.C., Jan. 24, 1910; s. Daniel MacNeill and Emily Whiting (Walters) M.; m. Gweneth Moxley, Sept. 24, 1938; children: Jack W., Marian MacKay Pfeiffer, Richard MacNeill. BS in aeronautical engr., U. Ala., 1935, BS in civil engr., 1936, Profl. Degree Civil Engring., 1956. Registered profl. engr., Ala. Instr. U. Ala., Tuscaloosa, 1933-36, Birmingham, Ala., 1936-45; engr. trainee Am. Cast Iron Pipe Co., 1936-40, sales engr., 1947-50, asst. southern sales mgr., 1951-53, asst. gen. sales mgr., 1953-56, v.p., gen. sales mgr., 1956-75, bd. mgmt., 1956-75, bd. mgmt., sec., 1956-75. Chmn. pub. rels. com. Cast Iron Pipe Rsch. Assn., Chgo., 1965-75; pres. Alloy Cast Inst., N.Y., 1960-61; cons. engr. Caldwell MacKay Co., Birmingham, 1983-95. Author: American Pipe Manual, 1951; contbr. articles to profl. jours. Pres. Anti-Tuberculosis Soc., 1957-58. Named Birmingham Civil Engr. Yr., Ala. Soc. Am. Soc. Civil Engrs., 1969. Fellow ASCE (life, chmn. pub. com. pipe 1973); mem. Am. Water Works Assn. (Nat. Distribution award, 1956, life), Ala. Soc. Profl. Engrs., St. Andrews Soc. Sons of Revolution, Birmingham Kiwanis Club (chmn. coms.), Birmingham Country Club, Tau Beta Pi. Presbyterian. Achievements include invention of fastite pipe joint; co-inventor pipejoint conductive gasket and boltless river crossing pipe joint; led company as first U.S. producer of Ductile Iron Pipe and acquisition of steel pipe mill and valve and hydrant business. Home: 225 University Park Dr Birmingham AL 35209-6772

MACKAY, JAMES ROBERT, psychiatric social worker, mayor, educator; b. Medford, Mass., May 8, 1930; s. James Alexander and Julia (MacNaught) MacK. BA, Tufts U., 1952, MA, 1954; MSW, Boston U., 1958; PhD, Union Inst., 1987. Social worker Peter Bent Brigham Hosp., Boston, 1958-60; dir. alcoholism N.H. Dept. Health and Welfare, Concord, 1960-63; dir. cmty. mental health State of N.H., 1963-64; pvt. practice psychotherapy, 1964-97; exec. dir. Merrimack Valley Assistance Program, 2002—; adj. faculty U. N.H., Durham, 1995—. Mem. bd. examiners mental health practice State of N.H., 1995-97; mayor City of Concord, N.H., 1986-88, 90-91; sr. lectr. psychotherapy Franklin Pierce Law Center, Concord, 1978; lectr. U. Conn. Grad. Sch. Social Work, 1981-88; adv. com. City of Concord Airport, 1992—. Contbr. articles on alcoholism, addiction, and juvenile delinquency to profl. jours. Chmn. N.H. Coun. Aging, 1969-83; chmn. Merrimack Valley AIDS Program, 2000-2002; pres. N.H. Social Welfare Coun.; chmn. N.H. del. to White House Conf. Aging, 1974, 80; chmn. N.H. Com. Older Am. Act, 1968-69; mem. Concord City Coun., 1980-91; chmn. Concord Pub. Transp. Adv. Bd., 1982-86; del. N.H. Rep. Conv., 1982; del. N.H. Constl. Conv., 1984; N.H. State Rep., 1995-96, 2001—; chmn. City of Concord Rep. Com.; mem. exec. com. Rep. State Rep. Com.; pres. Concord Outright Inc., 2000-; commr. Christa McAuliffe Planetarium, 2001-. Recipient Ann. award N.H. Social Welfare Coun., 1970, Vaughn award Activities in Aging, N.H., 1974; named Social Worker of Yr., State of N.H., 1997. Mem. NASW (pres. N.H. chpt. 1995-97), AAUP, Nat. League Cities (human devel. policy com. 1986). Office: 139 N State St Concord NH 03301-6414

MACKAY, LEO SIDNEY, JR. federal agency administrator; b. San Antonio, Aug. 15, 1961; s. Leo Sidney Sr. and Barbara Jean (Hodge) MacK.; m. Heather Lee Deebel, Jan. 9, 1993; children: Sarah Bley, Josiah Edward Earl. BS, U.S. Naval Acad., 1983; M Pub. Policy, J.F. Kennedy Sch. Govt., 1991; PhD, Harvard U., 1993. Commd. ensign USN, 1983, advanced through grades to lt. comdr., 1993; flight student Naval Aviation Tng. Comd., Pensacola, Fla., 1983-85; F-14 fighter pilot U.S. Navy, Virginia Beach, Va., 1985-89; grad./doctoral student Harvard U., Cambridge, Mass., 1989-92; instr. history dept. U.S. Naval Acad., Annapolis, Md., 1992-93; mil. asst. office of sec. of def. Dept. of Def., Washington, 1993-95; ret., 1995; dir. market devel. Lockheed Martin Corp., Bethesda, Md., 1995-97; v.p. bus. devel. and strategic planning Bell Helicopter Textron, Inc., Ft. Worth, 1997—2001; dep. secy. U.S. Dept. Veterans Affairs, Washington, 2001—. Contbr. articles to profl. jours.; article reviewer Internat. Security Jour., Cambridge, Mass., 1991-94. Pres. congregation St. Martin's Luth. Ch., Annapolis, 1996-97. Kennedy fellow J.F. Kennedy Sch. Govt., Cambridge, 1989-90, guest fellow Brookings Inst., Washington, 1992-93, Internat. Affairs fellow Coun. Fgn. Rels., N.Y.C., 1995-96; MacArthur scholar MacArthur Found., Cambridge, 1991-92. Mem. Internat. Inst. Strategic Studies, U.S. Naval Inst., Coun. Fgn. Rels., Arlington C. of C. (bd. dirs.), U.S. Naval Acad. Alumni Assn. (nat. trustee 1995-98), Army and Navy Club. Republican. Lutheran. Avocations: tennis, sailing, golf. Office: US Dept Veterans Affairs Off of the Secy 810 Vermont Ave NW Washington DC 20420-0001 Office Fax: 202-273-4877.*

MACKAY, MALCOLM, executive search consultant; b. Bklyn., Nov. 6, 1940; s. John F. and Helen (Pflug) MacK.; m. Cynthia Johnson, Aug. 29, 1964; children: Robert Livingston, Hope Winthrop. AB cum laude, Princeton U., 1963; JD, Harvard U., 1966. Bar: N.Y. 1967. Assoc. Milbank, Tweed, Hadley and McCloy, N.Y.C., 1966-69; dep. supt. N.Y. State Ins. Dept., 1969-71, 1st dep. supt., 1971-73; vice chancellor L.I. U., Greenvale, N.Y., 1973-75; sr. v.p. Blue Cross & Blue Shield of Greater New York, 1975-77, N.Y. Life Ins. Co., N.Y.C., 1977-89; mng. dir. Russell Reynolds Assocs., 1989—. Bd. dirs. Independence Savs. Bank, Bklyn., Empire Fidelity Investments Life Ins. Co. Trustee Independence Found. Mem. Century Assn., Piping Rock Club. Home: 2 Montague Ter Brooklyn NY 11201-4105 Office: Russell Reynolds Assocs 200 Park Ave New York NY 10166-0005

MACKAY, NANCY, librarian, oral historian; b. Boston, May 7, 1945; m. Feb. 14, 1970 (div. July, 1982); children: Michael Siano, Christiaan Siano. BA, U. Calif., 1967, M in Libr. Info. Sci., 1983. Head tech. svcs. and electronic resources Mills Coll., Oakland, Calif., 1989—. Adv. bd. Legacy Oral History Project, San Francisco, 1996—; exec. com. Bay Area Oral Historians; project dir. Slavonic Oral History Project, 1998—; archivist Oakland Living History Program, 2002—. Dancer, Slavonijo Dance Ensemble, San Francisco, 1985-91. Mem. Dance Heritage Coalition, Oral History Assn. Avocations: dance, gardening, yoga, Balkan culture. Office: Mills Coll 5000 MacArthur Blvd Oakland CA 94613-1301 E-mail: dancing@alum.berkeley.edu.

MACKAY, NEIL DUNCAN, plastics company executive; b. Chelsea, Mass., Nov. 5, 1931; s. Allan Foster and Helen May (Smith) MacK.; m. Marcia Ann McCarthy, Aug. 22, 1953 (dec. 1979); children: Duncan, Jerry, Alan, Neil, Bonnie; m. Beverly J. Burke, May 31, 1991. BS, BA, Northeastern U., Boston, 1954. Gen. mgr. Plastic Molding Corp., Newtown, Conn., 1954-67; market specialist Chem. div. Uniroyal, N.Y.C., 1967-70; project mgr. Colt Ind. Korean Project, 1970-76; pres. Automatic Injection Molding Corp., Berkeley Heights, N.J., 1976-87, Diamond Mgmt. Cons., Inc., Winchester, N.H., 1988—. Bd. dirs. Frazier & Son, Inc., Clifton, N.J., 1987—, Lor-Tech Plastics, Inc., Berkeley Heights, N.J. Author: Korean Plastics, 1973. Mem. Rep. Nat. Com., Washington, 1986-92. Recipient Outstanding Performance award Ministry Nat. Def. Republic of Korea, 1974. Mem. Am. Profl. Capt.'s Assn., Soc. Plastics Engrs. (sec. 1963-70, treas. 1983-86), Scottish-Am. Cultural Soc., St. Andrews Soc. N.Y., Plastic Pioneers Assn., Stuyvesant Yacht Club, Am. Yacht Club. Republican. Presbyterian. Avocation: sailing. Home: 19 Lovely Ln Winchester NH 03470-2916 Office: Diamond Mgmt Cons Inc PO Box 40 Winchester NH 03470-0040

MACKAY, RAYMOND ARTHUR, chemist; b. N.Y.C., Oct. 30, 1939; s. Theodore Henry and Helen Marie (Cusack) M.; m. Mary Dilberian, Aug. 13, 1966; 1 child, Chelsea Christine; children by previous marriage: Brett, Edward. BS in Chemistry, Rensselaer Poly. Inst., 1961; PhD in Chemistry, SUNY-Stony Brook, 1966. Rsch. assoc. Brookhaven Nat. Lab., Upton, N.Y., 1966-67; prof. Drexel U., Phila., 1969-83; chief chem. div. Chem. Research and Devel. Ctr., Aberdeen Proving Ground, Md., 1983-91; prof. chemistry, dir. ctr. advanced materials processing Clarkson U., Potsdam, N.Y., 1991—, currently on leave as dir. of Rsch. & Tech., U.S. Army Edgewood Chem. Biological Ctr. Contbr. articles to profl. jours. Served to capt. U.S. Army, 1967-69. Grantee U.S. Army, Dept. Energy, Army Rsch. Office, NSF, Acad. Applied Scis., 1972-83, 95—, NATO, 1982-86, NYSSTF, 1991—. Mem. Am. Chem. Soc., Am. Oil Chemists Soc. (assoc. editor), Sigma Xi. Office: Clarkson U PO Box 5665 Potsdam NY 13699-0001

MACKAY, ROBERT BATTIN, museum director; b. Bklyn., Jan. 24, 1945; s. John French and Helen (Pflug) Mack; m. Anna V.; 1 child, Hale V. BS, Boston U., 1968, PhD in Am. Studies, 1980; MEd, Harvard U., 1972. With Archtl. Heritage, Inc., Boston, 1967-71; dir. Soc. Preservation of L.I. Antiquities, Cold Spring Harbor, NY, 1974—. Chmn. N.Y. State Bd. Hist. Preservation; mem. N.Y. State Coun. Parks, N.Y. State Heritage Areas. Editor: Long Island: An Illustrated History, 2000, AIA Architectural Guide of L.I., L.I. Country Houses and Their Architects, 1997. Treas. St. Giles Found.; v.p. Homeland Found.; adv. Gerry Found.; trustee Seatuck Enrivon. Assn., I.Y.R.S. Mem. N.Y. Yacht Club (chmn. fine arts com.). Home: 59 Midland St Cold Spring Harbor NY 11724-1805 Office: Soc Preservation of LI Antiquities PO Box 148 Cold Spring Harbor NY 11724-0148

MACKAY, WILLIAM ANDREW, judge; b. Halifax, N.S., Can., Mar. 20, 1929; s. Robert Alexander and Mary Kathleen (Junkin) MacK.; m. Alexa Eaton Wright, July 7, 1954; 1 dau., Margaret Kathleen. BA, Dalhousie U., 1950, LL.B., 1953, LL.M., 1954, Harvard U., 1970; LL.D. (hon.), Meml. U. Nfld., St. F.X. Univ., N.S. Bar: N.S.; Named queen's counsel. Fgn. service officer Dept. External Affairs, Ottawa, Ont., Can., 1954-57; asst. sec. Royal Com., 1955-57; sucessively asst. prof., assoc. prof., prof. law, dean Faculty of law Dalhousie U. (Halifax), N.S., Can., 1957-69, v.p., 1969-80, pres., vice-chancellor, 1980-86; ombudsman N.S., 1986-88; judge Fed. Ct. Can., trial div., Ottawa, Ont., Can., 1988—. Chmn. Assn. Atlantic Univs., Halifax, 1981-83; v.p.. Assn. Univs. and Colls. Can., 1982-83, pres., 1983-85; pres. Conf. Gov. Bodies Legal Profession Can., 1968-69, Assn. Can. Law Tchrs., 1964-65 Chmn. N.S. Human Rights Com., Halifax, 1967-86; chmn. N.S. Commns. on Salary and Allowances of Elected Provincial Ofcls., 1974, 78, 81, 83, 84, 85; chmn. N.S. Task Force on AIDS, 1987-88. Mem. Can. Bar Assn. Home: 4-433 Besserer St Ottawa ON Canada K1N 6B9 Office: Fed Ct of Canada Ottawa ON Canada K1A 0H9

MACKELLAR, JAMES MARSH, minister; b. Wilkes-Barre, Pa., June 23, 1931; s. Gordon and Anita Ferous (Cornelius) MacK.; m. A. Eugenia Orthey, Aug. 20, 1955; children: Ian James, Margaret Alice, Bruce William. BA, Cornell U., 1952; MDiv, Princeton Theol Sem., 1955. Ordained to ministry Presbyn. Ch., 1955. Pastor 1st Presbyn. Ch., Dryden, N.Y., 1955-59, Waverly, 1959-65, Stirling, N.J., 1965-76, Forest Presbyn. Ch., Lyons Falls, N.Y., 1976-85; stated clk. Presbytery, Newton, N.J., 1970-75, Synod of the N.E., 1975-96, Presbytery of No. New Eng., 1987-92. Capt. Twp. Long Hill, N.J., First Aid Squad, 1974-76; permanent jud. commn. Gen. Assembly Presbyn. Ch., 1991-97; moderator Town of Newport, Vt., 1993—; mem. adv. com. on the Constn. of the Gen. Assembly, Presbyn. Ch. in U.S.A., 1998—, moderator, 2001—. Mem. Nat. Assn. Parliamentarians (registered parliamentarian), Vt. Ecumenical Coun. and Bible Soc. (v.p. 1990-91, pres. 1991-92), Border Area Clergy Assn. (treas. 1992-2001). Home and Office: 5006 Lake Rd Newport Center VT 05857-9494

MACKEN, DANIEL LOOS, physician, educator; b. Rochester, N.Y., May 7, 1933; s. Daniel Edward and Mary Frances (Loos) M.; children: Elizabeth Redford, Diana Loos; m. Maria Luisa Medina de Palma, Nov. 16, 1979. AB, Holy Cross Coll., Worcester, Mass., 1955; postgrad., Yale U., 1956-57; MD, Boston U., 1960. Resident Roosevelt & Columbia-Presbyn. Hosps., N.Y.C., 1960-63; fellow Am. Heart Assn., 1964-65; dir. coronary care unit Walter Reed Gen. Hosp., Washington, 1968; staff rsch. physician Walter Reed Army Inst. of Rsch., 1970; instr. Columbia U., N.Y.C., 1966-78, asst. clin. prof., 1979—. Pres. Medica Found., Inc., N.Y.C., 1971—; bd. dirs. Medica Endowment Fund, N.Y.C.; vis. lectr. U. saigon, Vietnam, 1969. Contbr. chpts. in book and articles to profl. jours.; student editor Jour. of History of Medicine and Allied Scis., 1956-57. Lt. Col. U.S. Army, Med. Corp, 1967-70, Vietnam. Decorated Bronze Star, Vietnam Cross. Fellow Am. Coll. Cardiology, Royal Soc. Medicine, N.Y. Acad. Medicine, Harvey Soc.; mem. AMA, Assn. Mil. Surgeons of U.S., Am. Heart Assn., Met. Govs. Island Officers Club. Republican. Roman Catholic. Home: 570 Park Ave New York NY 10021-7370 Office: Columbia-Presbyn Med Ctr 161 Fort Washington Ave New York NY 10032-3713 E-mail: DLM1@columbia.edu.

MACKENBACH, FREDERICK W. welding products manufacturing company executive; b. St. Marys, Ohio, Mar. 10, 1931; s. Frederick Jacob and Mabel (Tangeman) M.; m. Jo Ann Dietrich, Oct. 21, 1953; children: John Frederick, David Dietrich. BS in Econs., Wharton Sch. Fin. & Commerce, 1953. Various sales engr. positions The Lincoln Electric Co., Indpls., Ft. Wayne, L.A., 1956-64, asst. dist. mgr. L.A., 1973-76, dist. mgr., 1976-88; pres. Lincoln Electric Mexicana, 1988-91, Lincoln Electric Latin Am., 1991-92; pres., COO The Lincoln Electric Co., Cleve., 1992-96, ret., 1996. Mem. Com. on Fgn. Rels.; bd. dirs. Torrance Meml. Med. Ctr. Health Care Found., Goodwill Industries So. Calif. Coun. mem. City of Palos Verdes Estates (Calif.) City Coun. With U.S. Army 1953-55. Mem. Econ. Roundtable in L.A., Am. Welding Soc. Office: Lincoln Electric Co 732 Via Somonte Palos Verdes Estates CA 90274-1629 E-mail: mackenbach@aol.com.

MACKENZIE, ANN HALEY, science educator; b. Centerville, Ind., Jan. 29, 1957; d. William Howard and Shirley Anne (Wilson) Haley; children; Kristen Rae, Matthew Adler. MEd, U. Cin., 1987, EdD, 1989. Sci. tchr. Hazelwood West Jr.-Sr. H.S., Mo., 1979—81, Kings Mills Schs., Ohio, 1987—92; instnl. coord. Mo. Botanical Garden, St. Louis, 1981—82; grad. rsch. asst. U. Cin., 1983—87, adj. instr., 1986, Miami U., Oxford, 1986, vis. asst. prof., 1992—95; project dir. Miami U., Ohio's NSF State Systemic Inst. in Math. and Sci., 1993—94; asst. prof. Miami U., 1995—2002, assoc. prof., 2002—. Chair secondary sci. Nat. Bd. Profl. Tchg. Stds., 1991-98; evaluator, cons. GE Aircraft Engines, Evendale, Ohio, 1987-91; cons. Biol. Sci. Curriculum Study, Colorado Springs, 1990—, cons. Am. Physiol. Soc., 1994—, Nat. Geog., 1997-99, Harvard/Smithsonian Astrophys. Rsch. Group, 2001-; internat. rschr., Australia; instr./leader Dragonfly Workshops, 2000; evaluator NSTA Sci-Links Project, 2000. Recipient Ohio Tchr. of Yr. award Chief State Bd. Supts., 1990, Presdl. award for excellence in math. and sci. teaching NSF/NSTA, 1991. Mem. AAAS (evaluator, author), Nat. Assn. Rsch. in Sci. Teaching, Am. Edn. Rsch. Assn., Nat. Sci. Tchrs. Assn., Nat. Assn. Biology Tchrs. (dir.-at-large 2000—). Home: 8397 Sailboat Ln Maineville OH 45039-8858 Office: Miami U 467 McGuffey Hall Oxford OH 45056-2076 E-mail: drannhm@aol.com.

MACKENZIE, CHARLES ALFRED, lawyer; b. Houston, Sept. 20, 1965; s. Charles Lester and Glenda Faye M.; m. Gretchen Hartberg, Aug. 5, 1989; children: Katherine Ann, James Andrew. BA, Baylor U., 1987, MA, 1988, JD, 1991. Bar: Tex. 1991; bd. cert. civil appellate law Tex. Bd. Legal Specialization. Atty. 10th Ct. Appeals, Waco, Tex., 1991-94; assoc. Haley & Davis, 1994—. Grader Tex. Bd. Law Examiners, Waco, 1996-99; lectr. law Baylor U., Waco, 1991-92, 2000; mem. civil appellate law adv. commn. Tex. Bd. Legal Specialization. Mem. Waco-McLennan County Young Lawyers Assn. (pres. 2000-01, Outstanding Young Lawyer award 1999), State Bar Tex. (mem. appellate sect. coun.), Abner V. McCall Am. Inn of Ct. (sec.-treas. 2000-01). Baptist. Avocation: photography. Office: Haley & Davis 510 N Valley Mills Dr Ste 600 Waco TX 76710-6078 Fax: 254-776-6823. E-mail: AMackenzie@HaleyDavis.com.

MACKENZIE, CHARLES RUDD, lawyer; b. Boston, Dec. 19, 1964; s. Alan Eno Mackenzie and Susan Taylor Menges; m. Jessica Stretton, Sept. 2, 2000. BA, Bowdoin Coll., 1987; JD, Western New Eng. Coll., 1993; M of Studies in Environ. Law cum laude, Vt. Law Sch., 1994. Rsch. dir. Senator Chafee Com., Cranston, R.I., 1988; fgn. policy aide U.S. Senator John Chafee, Washington, 1989-90; pvt. practice law Hastings on Hudson, N.Y., 1995—. Bd. dirs. Vols. for Peace Internat. Vol. Svc., Belmont, Vt. Pres. Historic Properties, Inc., Hanover, Pa. Mem. N.Y. State Bar Assn., 1995, U.S. Dist. Court (so. and ea. dist. of N.Y. 1995), Westchester County Bar Assn., Yonkers Lawyers Assn., Estate Planning Coun. Westchester, Delta Kappa Epsilon (v.p. chpt. 1985, 86). Office: 422 E 83rd St New York NY 10028

MACKENZIE, CHARLES SHERRARD, academic administrator; b. Quincy, Mass., Aug. 21, 1924; s. Charles Sherrard and Dorothy (Eaton) MacK.; m. Florence Evelyn Phelps Meyer, Aug. 28, 1964 (dec. 1981); 1 child, Robert Walter Meyer; m. Lavonne Rudolph Gaiser, Mar. 30, 1985. Student, Boston U., 1942-43; BA, Gordon Coll., 1946; M.Div., Princeton Theol. Sem., 1949, Th.D., 1955, PhD, 1957; LHD, Grove City Coll., 1997; postgrad., U. Paris, 1953. Ordained to ministry Congl. Christian Ch., 1949. Pastor Carversville (Pa.) Christian Ch., 1948-51; fellow faculty Princeton Theol. Sem., 1949-51, 53-54, Princeton U., 1954-64; pastor First Presbyn. Ch., Avenel, N.J., 1954-64, Broadway Presbyn. Ch., Columbia U., N.Y.C., 1964-67, First Presbyn. Ch., Stanford U., San Mateo, Calif., 1967-71; pres. Grove City (Pa.) Coll., 1971-91, chancellor, 1991-92; advisor to pres., prof. philosophy Reformed Seminary, Orlando, Fla., 1992—; sr. min. Eastminster Presbyn. Ch., Wichita, Kans., 1993. Bd. dirs. Covenant Life Ins. Co., C.S. Lewis Inst.; cons. Oxford Project, 1992—, Provident Mutual Ins. Co.; lectr. Oxford U., 1965, U. Hamburg, 1968, Columbia U., 1964-67, Stanford U., 1967-71, U. Pitts., 1990-93; adv. Provident Mutual Ins. Co. Author: The Anguish and Joy of Pascal, 1973, Freedom, Equality, Justice, 1980, The Trinity and Culture, 1985. Bd. dirs. Knox Fellowship, Frontline, Orlando; mem. Human Relations Commn., San Mateo, 1968-70; mem. Indsl. Devel. Council, Grove City,

1972-75. Served with USAF, 1951-53. Mem. Presbyn. Coll. Union, Am. Assn. Pres.'s Ind. Colls. and Univs. (dir., pres.), Nat. Assn. Ind. Colls. and Univs. (mem. secretariat 1985-91), Freedoms Found. (nat. jury), Soc. Christian Philosphers, Duquesne Club (Pitts.), Univ. Club Boston, Citrus Club (Orlando), Evangelical initiative Notre Dame U., Rockford Inst. Main St. com. (De Toqueville award 1998). Republican. Address: 1231 Reformation Dr Oviedo FL 32765-7197

MACKENZIE, DONALD ANGUS, sociology educator; b. Inverness, Scotland, May 3, 1950; s. Angus Donald and Anne (Paterson) MacK.; children: Alice MacKenzie Bamford, Iain Angus MacKenzie Bamford. BSc, U. Edinburgh, 1972, PhD, 1978. Lectr. in sociology U. Edinburgh, 1975-88, reader in sociology, 1988-92, prof. sociology, 1992—. Vis. prof. Harvard U., 1997. Author: Statistics in Britain, 1981, Inventing Accuracy, 1990 (Ludwik Fleck prize 1993, co-winner Merton award 1993), Knowing Machines, 1996. Recipient Usher prize Soc. for History of Tech., 1986, U.S. Navy prize in Naval History, 1989, Life Mems. prize in Elec. History IEEE, 1992. Fellow Royal Soc. Edinburgh. Avocations: cycling, walking, chess. Office: U Edinburgh 18 Buccleuch Pl Edinburgh EH8 9LN Scotland

MACKENZIE, DONALD MATTHEW, JR. minister; b. Chgo., Mar. 25, 1944; s. Donald Matthew Sr. and Ruth Vicory (Yoakum) M.; m. Judith Joy Petterson, May 31, 1966; children: Mary Hye Won, Alice Eun Ah. AB, Macalester Coll., 1966; MDiv, Princeton (N.J.) Sem., 1970, ThM, 1971; PhD, NYU, 1978. Assoc. dir. field edn. Princeton Sem., 1971-80; assoc. pastor Nassau Presbyn. Ch., Princeton, 1980-83; pastor The Ch. of Christ at Dartmouth Coll., Hanover, N.H., 1983-95; examiner D in Ministry program Princeton Sem., 1980—; min. and head of staff U. Congl. United Ch. of Christ, Seattle, 1995—. Adj. prof. practical theology Bangor (Maine) Theol. Sem., 1991-95. Contbr. articles to profl. jours. Bd. dirs. Trenton (N.J.) Ecumenical Area Ministry, 1977-83, Wesley-Westminster Found., Princeton U., 1981-83; trustee N.H. Conf., United Ch. of Christ, 1990-92. Mem. Assn. Profs. and Researchers in Religious Edn., United Ch. of Christ, Washington, North Idaho, Conf. United Ch. of Christ, Phi Delta Kappa. Democrat. Home: 16011 36th Ave NE Seattle WA 98155-6623 Office: U Congl United Ch of Christ 16th Ave NE Seattle WA 98105

MACKENZIE, DONALD MURRAY, hospital administrator; b. Toronto, Ont., Can., June 5, 1947; s. Donald Alexander and June Cameron MacKenzie; m. Marilyn Adele McNaughton, Jan. 3, 1970; children: Jennifer, Katherine, Kenneth. BA in Econs., U. Toronto, 1968, MA in Polit. Sci., 1970, D Health Adminstr., 1974. Exec. asst. Mt. Sinai Hosp., Toronto, 1974-76, successively asst. exec. dir., assoc. exec. dir., v.p., 1974-89; pres. North York Gen. Hosp., 1989—; asst. prof. U. Toronto, 1989—. Chair Cardiac Care Network Ontario, 2001—; bd. dirs. Neuchâtel Jr. Coll. Editor: History of Canadian Hospitals, 1972; contbr. articles to profl. jours. Bd. dirs. Cancer Care Ontario. Mem. Can. Coll. Health Svc. Execs. (cert., various coms.), Can. Cancer Soc. (hon. life, pres. Ont. div. 1989-91, award of merit 1988), Ont. Hosp. Assn. (chmn. 1999-2000), York Club, Toronto Bd. Trade, Parkview Golf Club (bd. dirs.). Anglican. Avocations: golf, tennis, canoe tripping. Office: North York Gen Hosp 4001 Leslie St North York ON Canada M2K 1E1

MACKENZIE, ELIZABETH ANN, music educator; b. Oak Park, Ill., Feb. 11, 1948; d. William Faraar and Mary Eilene (Spahr) Moore; m. Paul Blanchard Mackenzie, Jan. 1, 1973; children: Rachel Elizabeth, Katherine Ann, David Alexander. BA, Wheaton Coll., 1969. Accompanist, companion Compassion, Inc., Ill., 1972; tchr. Busy Bee Nursery Sch., Urbana, 1973-75; homebound tchr. Urbana Schs., 1973-75; head tchr. Head Start Program, Tompkins County, N.Y., 1976-81; tchr. piano pvt. practice, 1993—. Mem. Glen Ellyn Hist. Soc., 1993—, LWV, 1994—, PTA, 1986—. Mem.: Music Edn. Found. (co-chair Musical Mayhem fundraiser 1999—2000), Ill. State Music Tchrs. Assn. (pres. west suburban chpt. 1999—2001). Avocations: travel, reading, gardening. Home: 605 Pleasant Ave Glen Ellyn IL 60137-4031

MACKENZIE, GEORGE ALLAN, diversified company executive; b. Kingston, Jamaica, Dec. 15, 1931; s. George Adam and Annette Louise (Maduro) MacK.; m. Valerie Ann Marchand, June 30, 1971; children from previous marriage: Richard Michael, Barbara Wynne. Student, Jamaica Coll., Kingston, 1944-48. Commd. flying officer Canadian Air Force, 1951, advanced through grades to lt. gen., 1978; comdr. Canadian Forces Air Command, Winnipeg, Man., 1978-80, resigned, 1980; exec. v.p., COO Gendis Inc., 1980-89, pres., COO, 1989-99, pres., CEO, 1999—, also bd. dirs.; bd. dirs. Sony of Can. Ltd., Willowdale, Ont., Can.; chmn., CEO SAAN Stores Ltd., 1999—. Chmn. exec. com. SAAN Stores Ltd.; bd. dirs. Gendis Inc., Boltons Capital Corp., Fort Chicago Energy Mgmt. Ltd., Gendis Realty, Inc. Mem. regional adv. bd. Carleton U.; mem. jud. coun. Province of Manitoba; mem. Bus. Coun. Manitoba; bd. trustees Victoria Gen. Hosp. Decorated comdr. Order of Mil. Merit, Order St. Johns, Can. Decoration, Knight of St. Lazarus of Jerusalem. Mem. United Services Inst. Can. (hon. v.p.), Canadian Corps Commissionaires (gov.), Police Chiefs Research Found. (co-chmn.), Lakewood Country Club (Delta), Manitoba Club, St. Charles Golf and Country Club. Home: 383 Christie Rd Winnipeg MB Canada R2N 4A5 Office: Gendis Inc 1370 Sony Pl Winnipeg MB Canada R3T 1N5

MACKENZIE, JAMES, fire protection and industrial safety executive; b. Camden, N.J., Sept. 1, 1933; s. Murdo James and Pearl (Mickle) M.; m. Sally Ann Park, July 22, 1960 (dec. Mar. 2001); m. Margaret A. Rush, Jan. 8, 2002. BS in Sci., Muhlenberg Coll., 1957; MA in Chemistry, The Coll. of N.J., 1969. Cert. safety profl., hazardous material supr., fire ofcl., environ. insp., forensics examiner, vocat. edn. educator, N.J., level II fire svc. instr., marine firefighting technician. Project leader ESB, Inc., Yardley, Pa., 1959-70; supr. process engring. CBS Records, Pitman, N.J., 1970-71; quality assurance supr. C and D Batteries, Canshohoken, Pa., 1971-72; ptnr. MacWell Enterprises, Medford, N.J., 1972-73; fire protection engr. Merck and Co., Inc., Rahway, 1973-88; pres. Teaberry Assocs., Beaufort, N.C., 1988—. Instr. fire sci. Coastal Carolina C.C., 1999; mem. Tng. and Edn. Adv. Coun., N.J. Fire Com., Trenton, 1986-98; mem. hazardous materials tng. adv. com. N.J. State Police, Trenton, 1988-98; chmn. Occupl. Safety Conf., Cranford, N.J., 1984-88; mem. N.J. State Safety Com., Delaware River Marine Firefighting Task Force. Pub. Haz-Mat Tech., 1986-95, Haz Packs, 1989-94; author: Firefighter Guide Sheets, 1978. Safety officer Taunton Vol. Fire Co., Medford, 1961-98 (Chief's award 1991); vol. instr. Burlington County Girl Scouts, Westhampton, N.J., 1989; instr. Burlington County Fire Acad., Mt. Holly, N.J., 1962-98; mem. N.J. State Safety Com., South River-Merrimon Fire Dept. Recipient Disting. Svc. award N.J. State Safety Coun., Cranford, 1988, Dedicated Svc. award Taunton Vol. Fire Co., 1989. Mem. ASTM (F23 com. 1976—, E34 com. 1990—), Nat. Fire Protection Assn., Am. Soc. Safety Engrs. (editor 1973-89), Internat. Soc. Fire Svc. Instrs., Internat. Assn. Fire Chiefs, Environ. Assessment Assn., Am. Coll. Forensic Examiners (diplomate), N.C. Maritime Mus., Core Sound Decoy Mus., N.C. Fossil Club, Carteret County Wildlife Club, Carteret County Model R.R. Club. Republican. Methodist. Avocations: model railroading, camping, birdwatching. Office: Teaberry Assocs 963 Osprey Point Rd Beaufort NC 28516-6660 E-mail: jmackenzie@clis.com.

MAC KENZIE, JAMES DONALD, clergyman; b. Detroit, Nov. 17, 1924; s. James and Ida Catherine (Conklin) M.; m. Elsie Joan Kerr, May 7, 1960; children: Janet Eileen, Kayly Kathleen, Christy Carol, Kenneth Kerr. Student, Moody Bible Inst., 1946-49, Union Theol. Sem., 1952. Ordained to ministry Presbyn. Ch., 1953. Pastor Calvary Ch., Swan Quarter, N.C., Edenton (N.C.) Presbyn. Ch., 1952-60, Kirkwood Ch., Kannapolis, N.C., 1960-64, Barbecue and Olivia Ch., Olivia, 1964-71, Elise Ch., Robbins, 1971-92, Horseshoe Presbyn. Ch., Carbonton, 1971—. Co-founder, Rehoboth Gospel Fellowship, Chicago, 1949. tchr. North Moore High School, 1977-87.; instr. Sandhills Comm Coll., 1986. Columnist The Chowan Herald, Edenton, N.C., 1952-60, The Robbins (N.C.) Record, 1971-86, The Pilot, Southern Pines, N.C., 1987—. Historian Fayetteville Presbytery, 1975—, chmn. hist. com., 1983—, moderator, 1978. Founder Conf. on Celtic Studies, Campbell Coll. (now Campbell U.), Buies Creek, N.C., 1972—; councillor Conf. on Scottish Studies (Can.), 1968-75; co-founder Rehoboth Gospel Fellowship, Chgo., 1949. With AUS, 1943-45, ETO. Decorated Purple Heart, Bronze Star, Combat Inf. Badge; recipient Disting. Citizen award, Robbins, 1983, Disting. Pastor award, 1988, Scottish Heritage Ctr. award St. Andrews Presbyn. Coll., Laurinburg, N.C., 1999. Mem. N.C. Presbyn. Hist. Soc. (pres. 1972-74, Author's award 1970, 75, Cert. Merit 1975), Harnett Hist. Soc. (pres. 1968-71, Distinguished Service award 1970, Scottish Heritage award 1999), Irish Uillean Pipers Soc., Gaelic Soc. of Inverness, An Comunn Gaidhelach (life). Author: Colorful Heritage, 1970; editor: The Uilleann Piper, 1974—; contbr. articles to profl. jours. Home and Office: PO Box 867 Robbins NC 27325-0867

MACKENZIE, JOHN, retired oil industry executive; b. 1919; BS, N.Y. U., 1948. Accountant S.Am. Devel. Co., N.Y.C., 1938-41; financial comptroller French Oil Ind. Agy.-Groupment D'Achat des Carburants, N.Y., 1946-53; v.p., treas. George Hall Corp., 1954-56; asst. treas. Am. Petrofina, Inc., 1956-61, sec., 1961-64, v.p., sec., 1964-68, sr. v.p., sec., 1968-84; ret., 1984. Decorated comdr. Order of Crown (Belgium) Address: 3861 Frio Way Frisco TX 75034-8469

MACKENZIE, JOHN ANDERSON ROSS, historian, educator; b. Edinburgh, Scotland, Aug. 26, 1927; came to U.S., 1959; s. Donald Ross and Edith Agnes (Anderson) M.; m. Flora Margaret Duncan, July 14, 1951; children: Sheena, Donald, Alasdair. MA with honors, Edinburgh U., 1949, BD with Distinction, 1952, PhD, 1962; Teol. Lic., U. Lund, Sweden, 1964; D Humanities, Shenandoah U., 1994. Ordained to ministry Ch. of Scotland, 1953; ordained to priesthood Episcopal Diocese Western N.Y., 1998. Min. St. Andrew's Clermiston, Edinburgh, 1954-59, Westminster Presbyn. Ch., Richmond, Va., 1959-64; prof. ch. history Union Theol. Sem., 1964-81; sr. min. 1st Presbyn. Ch., Gainesville, Fla., 1981-89; dir. dept. religion Chautauqua (N.Y.) Instn., 1989-99; historian Chautauqua, 1999—; priest assoc. St. Luke's Episc. Ch., Jamestown, NY, 2001—. Adj. prof. Cath. U., Washington, 1965-71; vis. prof. Orthodox Theol. Sem., Kottayam, India, 1972-73. Author: Trying New Sandals, 3d edit., 1977; co-author (with Elaine Kaye): William Edwin Orchard: A Study in Christian Exploration, 1990; co-editor (with Marcus Borg): God at 2000; author: Threads, A Book of Prayers and Stories, 2001. Mem. Downtown Redevel. Agy., Gainesville, 1983—89; bd. dir. North Fla. Retirement Village, 1984—89, chmn., 1987—89; bd. dir. Samaritan Ctr., 1987—89, Hospice Chautauqua County, 1998—2001, Saging Ctr., 2001—. Recipient Patronal medal Cath. U. Am., Washington, 1977. Democrat. Home: 65 W Summit Ave Lakewood NY 14750-1127 Office: Chautauqua Instn Archives Chautauqua NY 14722

MACKENZIE, JOHN DOUGLAS, engineering educator; b. Hong Kong, Feb. 18, 1926; came to U.S., 1954, naturalized, 1963; s. John and Hannah (Wong) MacK.; m. Jennifer Russell, Oct. 2, 1954; children: Timothy John, Andrea Louise, Peter Neil. BS, U. London, 1952, PhD, 1954. Research asst., lectr. Princeton U., 1954-56; ICI fellow Cambridge (Eng.) U., 1956-57; research scientist Gen. Electric Research Ctr., N.Y.C., 1957-63; prof. materials sci. Rensselaer Poly. Inst., 1963-69; prof. engring. U. Calif., Los Angeles, 1969—. U.S. rep. Internat. Glass Commn., 1964-71 Author books in field (6); editor: Jour. Non-Crystalline Solids, 1968—; contbr. articles to profl. jours.; patentee in field. Fellow Am. Ceramic Soc., Royal Inst. Chemistry; mem. Nat. Acad. Engring., Am. Phys. Soc., Electrochem. Soc., ASTM, Am. Chem. Soc., Soc. Glass Tech. Office: U Calif 6532 Boelter Hall Los Angeles CA 90095-1595

MACKENZIE, KENNETH DONALD, management consultant, educator; b. Salem, Oreg., Dec. 20, 1937; s. Kenneth Victor and Dorothy Vernon (Minaker) M.; m. Sally Jane McHenry, June 16, 1957; children: Dorothy Jane Rivette, Carolyn M. McFarland, Susan M. Treber, Nancy M. Murphy. AB in Math, U. Calif., Berkeley, 1960, PhD in Bus. Adminstrn, 1964. Cert. mgmt. cons. Asst. prof. indsl. adminstrn. Carnegie Mellon U., 1964-67; assoc. prof. industry Wharton Sch. U. Pa., 1967-71; prof. mgmt. scis. U. Waterloo, Ont., 1969-72; Edmund P. Learned disting. prof. Sch. Bus. U. Kans., Lawrence, 1971—; pres. Organizational Systems, Inc., 1976-84; founder, pres. Mackenzie And Co. Inc., 1983—, e-MAC Cons., Inc., Lawrence, 2000—. Author: An Introduction to Continuous Probability, 1969, A Theory of Group Structures, 2 vols., 1976, Basic Theory, 1976, A Theory of Group Structures, vol. II: Empirical Tests, 1976, Organizational Structures, 1978, Organizational Design: The Organizational Audit and Analysis Technology, 1986, The Organizational Hologram: The Effective Management of Organizational Change, 1991, Practitioner's Guide for Improving an Organization, 1995; co-editor: Current Topics in Management, Vol. IV, 1999, Vol. V, 2000; editor: Organizations Behavior series; mem. editorial bd. of profl. jours. Served with USMCR, 1957-60, with Army N.G., 1960-64. Fellow AAAS; mem. APA, Acad. Mgmt., Inst. Mgmt. Scis. (chmn. coll. on orgns. 1983-93), Orgnl. Design, Meso Orgnl. Studies Group. Republican. Home: 502 Millstone Dr Lawrence KS 66049-2350 Office: Mackenzie and Co Inc 3d Fl 700 Massachusetts St Fl 3D Lawrence KS 66044-2344 also: U Kans Sch Bus Lawrence KS 66045-0001 E-mail: hologram@orgdesign.com., survey@e-macconsulting.com. *While the pursuit of a better theory of organizations has led me from the classroom to the laboratory and then into the boardrooms of corporations, the thrust of all these many activities has been to develop the science of organizations.*

MACKENZIE, LEWIS WHARTON, military officer; b. Truro, N.S., Can., Apr. 30, 1940; s. Eugene Murdock and Shirley Helena (Wharton) MacK.; m. Dora Rosalie McKinnon; 1 child, Kimm Katheryn. Student, NATO Def. Coll., Rome, 1977; BA in Polit. Sci., U. Man., Winnipeg, Can., 1988; PhD (hon.), St. Francis Xavier U., 1993; LLB (hon.), St. Mary's U., 1993, Acadia U., 1993, U. Calgary, 2000. Commd. 2d lt. Can. Armed Forces, 1960, advanced through grades to major gen., 1992; teamsite comdr. Internat. Commn. Control and Supervision, Vietnam, 1972; co. comdr. UN Emergency Peace Keeping Force, Cairo, 1973; exec. asst. to comdr. Can. Forces Europe, Lahr, Fed. Republic Germany, 1974-77; comdr. Nicosia dist. UN Peacekeeping Force, Cyprus, 1978; commdg. officer 1st bn. Princess Patricia's Can. Light Infantry, Calgary, 1977-79; faculty mem. Can. Forces Staff Coll., Toronto, 1979-82; dep. chief staff for tng. Can. Army, Montreal, 1983-85; dir. pers. careers officers Can. Armed Forces, Ottawa, 1985-87; dir. Combar Related Employment of Women, 1987-88; comdr. combat tng. ctr. Can. Armed Forces, Gagetown Can. Forces Base, N.B., 1988-1990; pres., mgr. Gen. MacKenzie Enterprises Inc., Gen. MacKenzie Comms. Inc. Comdr. UN Peacekeeping Force, Ctrl. Am., 1990-91, chief staff Unprotection force, Yugoslavia, 1992, comdr. UN forces to open Sarajevo airport for humanitarian relief, 1992; host TV documentary "A Soldier's Peace." Author: Peacekeeper, Road to Sarajevo, 1993. Mem. bd. advisors Can. Fedn. for AIDS Rsch., Can. Spl. Olympics, Computer Devices Can.; patron Saving Our Mil. Heritage, The Normandy Project, Internat. Comty. for Relief of Starvation and Suffering, Can.; bd. dirs. Magnifoam Internat. Decorated Meritorious Svc. Cross (2) (Can.); invested Order of Ont.; recipient Birks gold medal Xavier Jr. Coll., Sydney, N.S., Can., 1960, Vimy award, 1993, medal of honour UN Assn., 1994, World Peace award, 1993; named Canadian of Yr., Tourism Industry Assn. of Can., 1992; Internat. fellow U.S. Army War Coll., 1982-83; Nat. Sports Car champion, 1981; Nat. Formula Ford B Class champion, 1995, 96; named to McLean's Honor Roll., 1993. Avocation: motor racing. E-mail. Home and Office: 580 Manitoba Street Bracebridge ON Canada P1L 1W9 E-mail: lewmack@muskoka.com.

MACKENZIE, LINDA ALICE, natural health and awareness company executive, radio host, educator, hypnotherapist, motivational speaker, publishing executive; b. Bronx, N.Y., June 24, 1949; d. Gino Joseph and Mary J. (Damon) Arale; m. John Michael Lassourreille, Aug. 7, 1968 (div. 1975); 1 child, Lisa Marie Lassourreille; m. Donald John Mackenzie, July 2, 1978 (div. 1982). Student, Richmond Coll., 1967-68, West L.A. C.C., 1978-81. Spl. rep. N.Y. Telephone Co., White Plains, 1968-71; asst. mgr. Paul Holmes Real Estate Inc., Richmond, N.Y., 1974-77; telcom applications specialist engring. Continental Airlines, L.A., 1977-83; data transmission specialist Western Airlines, 1983-87; owner Computers on Consignment, El Segundo, Calif., 1984-94. Cons. Caleb Feb. Credit Union, Las Vegas, Nev., 1985, Nat. Dissemenators, Las Vegas, Nev., 1985, Vega & Assocs. Prodn. Divsn., 1987, Uptech/Downtech, 1986, Dollar Rent-a-Car, 1987, Advanced Digital Networks, 1987, Pomona Sch. Dist., 1987, State Senate, 1988, Nordstroms, 1988, Flying Tigers, 1988, Fed. Express, 1989, Sita/ITS, 1990—92, Neutrogena, 1991, B & B Computers, 1992; mktg. cons. AT&T, L.A., Calif., 1984—85, Radio KPSL, 1995—97, Carter Broadcasting Talk Am., 1995—97, WDRC, 1995, WXLW, 1995, CRN, Pax, 1995—2002, chsr, 2002—; mktg. cons. CHSR Healthylife.net Creative Health & Spirit Show, 1995—; owner Creative Health & Spirit, Manhattan Beach, Calif., 1995—; pres. Creative Health and Spirit Products, Inc., 1997—2001. Author: The World Within, 1983, Inner Insights-The Book of Charts, 1997, The Total Mind-Body-Spirit Weight Loss Program Audiovisualization Tapes, 1998, How to Self-Publish Your Personal Growth Book, 1999, Help Yourself Heal-Menopause (audio tape), 1999, Help Yourself Health With Self-Hypnosis, 2000; contbr. Am. Anthology Poetry, 1987, 88, Poetic Voices of Am., 1988, Sparrowgrass: 10 Years of Excellence, 1998. Recipient Alexander award, Met. Mus. Art, N.Y.C., 1967, Covr Best Metaphys. Book, 2nd place, 1998, Covr Best Spoken World Audio, 2nd place, 1999. Mem. Am. Bd. Hypnotherapists, Am. Inst. Hypnotherapy, Nat. Assn. Alt. Health Care Providers. Republican. Avocations: painting, creative writing, golf, skiing, travel.

MACKENZIE, MALCOLM ROBERT, personnel management consultant; b. Revere, Mass., Oct. 12, 1924; s. Malcolm John and Helen Margaret (Pelrine) Mack.; m. Chieko Yoshida, Nov. 4, 1954; 1 child, Kenneth Andrew. BA, Tufts U., 1945; Japanese Lang. cert., Sophia U., Tokyo, 1951; Advanced Mgmt. Program, U. Hawaii, 1966. Dep. civilian pers. dir. U.S. Army, Camp Zama, Japan, 1959-63, civilian pers. dir. Fort Shafter Honolulu, 1963-65; chief employee mgmt. U.S. Army Pacific Headquarters, 1965-69; civilian pers. dir. electronics command Fort Monmouth, N.J., 1969-76; command civilian pers. mgr. Naval Edn. and Tng., Naval Air sta. Pensacola, Fla., 1976-81; pers. mgmt. cons. Gulf Breeze, 1981—. Mem. Human Rights Advocacy Com., Dist. I, Pensacola, 1982-84; asst. dist. dir. Fla. Spl. Olympics, Pensacola, 1982-86; bd. dirs. Pensacola Penwheels, Employ the Handicapped, Pensacola, 1983—; pres. Pensacola Spl. Steppers retarded dancers, 1983; mem. Fla. gov.'s Com. on Employment of Handicapped, 1983; chmn. com. for handicapable dancers United Square Dancers Am., 1984-2000; active Handicapped Boy Scouts, Pensacola; pres. Assn. retarded Citizens-Escambia, Pensacola, 1985-87, Fla. State Assn. for Retarded Citizens, 1987-90; mem. Fla. Developmental Disbility Coun., 1992-2000; state bd. dirs. Fla. Blueprint for Sch. To Community Transitions, 1993-96, Aging & Devel. Disabilities Effort, 1994-2000. With USNR, 1943-45, PTO. Recipient Commemorative medallion Tokyo Met. Govt., 1963, cert. appreciation, Chief of Staff, Ground Office, Defense Agy., Japan, 1963, dir. fgn. affairs. Kanagawa Prefecture, Japan, 1963, dir. fgn. affairs, Saitama Prefecture, Japan, 1963. Mem. Internat. Pers. Mgmt. Assn. (pres. far east chpt. 1960-63, Honolulu chpt. 1964-65, N.J. chpt. 1973-74), Am. Soc. Pub. Adminstrn., Fed. Pers. Coun. Pacific (chmn. 1965-66), Fed. Pers. Coun. N.J. (chmn. 1972-73), Gulf State Fed. Pers. Coun. (vice-chmn. 1980-81), Indsl. Rels. Rsch. Assn., Am. Soc. Tng. and Devel., Fla. Pub. Pers. Assn., Eastern Regional Orgn. for Pub. Adminstrn., Am. Arbitration Assn. (mem. comml. and trade panels), Northwest Fla. Area Agy. on Aging (adv. coun. 1990-92), Parent Edn. Network (cert. trainer 1989-92). Republican. Roman Catholic. Avocations: bowling, golf. Home and Office: 2652 Venetian Way Gulf Breeze FL 32563-3038

MAC KENZIE, NORMAN HUGH, retired English educator, writer; b. Salisbury, Rhodesia, Mar. 8, 1915; s. Thomas Hugh and Ruth Blanche (Huskisson) MacK.; m. Rita Mavis Hofmann, Aug. 14, 1948; children: Catherine, Ronald. BA, Rhodes U., South Africa, 1934, MA, 1935, Diploma in Edn., 1936; PhD (Union scholar), U. London, 1940; DLitt (hon.), St. Joseph's U., Phila., 1989. Lectr. in English Rhodes U., South Africa, 1937, U. Hong Kong, 1940-41, U. Melbourne, Australia, 1946-48; sr. lectr.-in-charge U. Natal, Durban, 1949-55; prof., head English dept. U. Coll., Rhodesia, 1955-65, dean Faculty Arts and Edn., 1957-60, 63-64; prof., head English dept. Laurentian U., Ont., Can., 1965-66; prof. English Queen's U., Kingston, 1966-80, emeritus prof., 1980—, dir. grad. studies in English, 1967-73, chmn. council grad. studies, 1971-73, chmn. editorial bd. Yeats Studies, 1972-74. Exec. Central Africa Drama League, 1959-65; mem. exec. com. Can. Assn. Irish Studies, 1968-73 Author: South African Travel Literature in the 17th Century, 1955, The Outlook for English in Central Africa, 1960, Hopkins, 1968, A Reader's Guide to G.M. Hopkins, 1981; editor: (with W.H. Gardner) The Poems of Gerard Manley Hopkins, 1967, rev. edit., 1970; Poems by Hopkins, 1974, U. Natal Gazette, 1954-55, The Early Poetic Manuscripts and Notebooks of Gerard Manley Hopkins in Facsimile, 1989, The Poetical Works of Gerard Manley Hopkins, 1990, rev. 1992, The Later Poetic Manuscripts of G.M. Hopkins in Facsimile, 1991; contbr.: chpts. to Testing the English Proficiency of Foreign Students, 1961, English Studies Today-Third Series, 1963, Sphere History of English Literature, Vol. VI, 1970, rev. edit., 1987, Readings of the Wreck of the Deutschland, 1976, Festschrift for E.R. Seary, 1975, British and American Literature 1880-1920, 1976, Myth and Reality in Irish Literature, 1977, Dispersal and Renewal: Hong Kong University during the War Years, 1998; articles to Internat. Rev. Edn., Bull. Inst. Hist. Research, Times Lit. Supplement, Modern Lang. Quar., Queen's Quar., others. Served with Hong Kong Vol. Def. Corps, 1940-45; prisoner of war, China and Japan 1941-45. Brit. Council scholar, 1954; Killam sr. fellow, 1979-81; Martin D'Arcy lectr. Oxford U., 1988-89. Fellow Royal Soc. Can.; mem. English Assn. Rhodesia (pres. 1957-65), So. Rhodesia Drama Assn. (vice chmn. 1957-65), Hopkins Soc. (pres. 1972-75), Yeats Soc. (life), MLA (life), Internat. Hopkins Assn. (bd. scholars 1979—), Queen's U. Saturday Club (sec. 1977-97). Home: 416 Windward Pl Kingston ON Canada K7M 4E4

MACKENZIE, RONALD ALEXANDER, anesthesiologist; b. Detroit, Mar. 31, 1938; s. James and Elizabeth Mackenzie; m. Nancy Lee Vogan, Aug. 25, 1962; children: Margaret, James. BS, Alma Coll., 1961; DO, Kansas City Coll., 1967. Diplomate Am. Bd. Anesthesiology. Resident in anesthesiology Detroit Osteo. Hosp., 1970-72, Cleve. Clinic, 1972-73, Mayo Clinic, Rochester, Minn., 1973-74, cons. in anesthesia, 1974—; pres. ceo Am. Soc. Anesthesiologists. Vice-chmn. dept. anesthesiology Mayo Clinic, 1988-98. Pres. Minn. Orch., Rochester, 1987-89. Fellow Am. Coll. Anesthesiologists; mem. Am. Soc. Anesthesiologists (bd. dirs. 1983-87, sec. 1991-97, 1st v.p. 1998, pres.-elect 1999), Sigma Xi. Avocations: sailing, photography. Office: Mayo Clinic 200 1st St SW Rochester MN 55905-0002*

MACKENZIE-WOOD, MELODY, entrepreneur; b. Portsmouth, Va., Dec. 13, 1955; d. Herbert Marion and Carolyn (Tarkenton) Criswell; m. David Mackenzie-Wood. BS in English & Speech Edn. with honors, U. Tenn., 1977. Pub. rels. Reliance Group Holdings, N.Y.C., 1981-85; human rels./employee rels. Broad Inc./SunAmerica, L.A., 1985-92; CEO, founder, coach, entrepreneur, corp. trainer, spkr. Lifeworks Resources. Motivational spkr., tchr. in field. Office: Lifeworks Resources 534 Beau Chene Dr Mandeville LA 70471-1777

MACKERODT, FRED, public relations specialist; b. Bklyn., Sept. 17, 1938; s. Leroy and Margaret (Murphy) M.; m. Christy Woods, June 7, 1987. Student, NYU, 1958-59. Freelance writer, photographer, N.Y.C. and Barcelona, Spain, 1968-73; editor Cars Mag., Popular Publs. Inc., N.Y.C., 1973-76; pres. Fred Mackerodt, Inc. (pub. relations and publicity), 1976—, Stone House Farm, Inc., 2001—. Contbr. articles to popular mags.; contbg. editor, sci. and tech.: Popular Mechanics, 1987—. Spl. dep. sheriff Indian River County, Fla., 1994—2001. Mem. Aviation and Space Writers Am., Internat. Motor Press Assn., Publicity Club N.Y., Wings Club, N.Y. Zool. Soc. (aquarium field assoc. 1971—) Home: 940 Craigville Rd Chester NY 10918 Office: Apt 612 205 W 86th St New York NY 10024-3362 E-mail: fmackerodt@fredmackerodt.com.

MACKERRAS, SIR CHARLES (SIR ALAN CHARLES MACLAURIN MACKERRAS), conductor; b. Schenectady, N.Y., Nov. 17, 1925; s. Alan Patrick and Catherine Mackerras; m. Helena Judith Wilkins, 1947; 2 children. Student, Sydney Conservatorium Music, Australia, 1938-42; student with Vaclav Talich, Prague Acad. Music, 1947-48; DMus (hon.), U. Hull, 1990, U. Nottingham, 1991, U. Brno, Czech Republic, 1994, York (Eng.) U., 1994, Griffith U., Brisbane, Australia, 1994, Oxford (Eng.) U., 1997, Prague Acad. Music, 1999, Napier U., Scotland, 2000. Prin. oboist Sydney (Australia) Symphony Orch., 1943-46; staff condr. English Nat. Opera (formerly Sadler's Wells Opera), London, England, 1948-54, musical dir. England, 1970-77; prin. condr. BBC Concert Orch., 1954-56; first condr. Hamburg Opera, 1966-69; chief guest condr. BBC Symphony Orch., 1976-79; chief condr. Sydney Symphony Orch., Australian Broadcasting Commn., 1982-85; prin. guest condr. Royal Liverpool Philharm. Orch., 1986-88, Scottish Chamber Orch., 1992-95, condr. laureate, 1995—; music dir. Orch. of St. Luke's, 1998-2001; pres. Trinity Coll. Music, London, England, 2000. Freelance condr. with most Brit. and many continental orchs., concert tours USSR, South Africa, N.Am., Australia, 1957-66, U.S. coast-to-coast, 1983; prin. guest condr. San Francisco Opera, 1993-96, prin. guest condr. emeritus, 1996—; prin. guest condr. Royal Philharm. Orch., 1993-96, Czech Philharm. Orch., 1997—; mus. dir. Welsh Nat. Opera, 1987-92, condr. emeritus, 1993—; appearances at internat. festivals and opera houses; frequent radio and TV broadcasts; comml. recordings, notably Handel, Mozart operas and symphonies, Janácek, Brahms, Beethoven and Schubert. Published ballet arrangements Pineapple Poll (Sullivan), Lady and the Fool (Verdi), reconstrn. Sullivan's lost Cello Concerto; contbr. appendices to book: A Musicians' Musician, articles to Opera Mag., Music and Musicians, other jours. Hon. fellow Royal Coll. Music, Royal Acad. Music, Trinity Coll. Music (London), Royal No. Coll. Music, St. Peter's Coll., Oxford, 1999; recipient Evening Standard award for opera, 1977, Janáček medal, 1978, Gramophone Record of Yr. award, 1977, 80, 99, Grammy award for best opera recording, 1981, Gramophone Best Opera Recording award, 1983, 84, 94, 99, prix Fondation Jacques Ibert, 1983, Record of Yr. award Stereo Rev., 1983, Chocs de l'Année award, 1998, Edison award, Preis der Deutschen Schallplattenkritik, Prix Caecilia, 1999, Royal Philharmonic Soc. Conducting award, 1999; Chopin prize and lifetime achievement award, Cannes Classical, awards at Midem, 2000; decorated comdr. Order Brit. Empire, 1974; created knight, 1979, Companion, Order of Australia, 1997, Medal of Merit Czech Republic, 1996. Office: Askonas Holt Ltd Lonsdale Chambers 27 Chancery Ln London WC2A 1PF England

MACKEY, BETTY BARR, writer; b. Hartley, Del., Apr. 14, 1945; d. Irwin R. and Florence Lenore (Skliar) B.; m. Thomas E. Mackey, July 20, 1968; children: Edward Leland, Alan Thomas. BS, Drexel U., 1967. Copy editor W.B. Saunders Publishers, Phila., 1967-68; writer, 1977—; photographer Wayne, Pa., 1993—; pub. B.B. Mackey Books, 1986—. Cons., Wayne, Longwood, Fla., 1984—; lectr. in field. Author: The Gardener's Home Companion, 1991, Cutting Gardens, 1993, A Cutting Garden for Florida, 1986, 1992, 2001; editor: Creating and Planting Garden Troughs, 1999; contbr. articles to profl. jours. Mem. LWV, N.J., Fla., Pa., 1971—; bd. dirs. Greater Mercer Comprehensive Planning Coun., 1981-83. Mem. Garden Writers Assn. of Am., Pa. Horticultural Soc. (cookbook com. 1992), Hardy Plant Soc. (membership chair 1990-93), Mid-Atlantic Publishers Assn. (sec. 2000-2001). Office: BB Mackey Books PO Box 475 Wayne PA 19087-0475 E-mail: bbmackey@prodigy.net.

MACKEY, CHARLES RALPH, benefits firm executive; b. Belvidere, Ill., Dec. 24, 1947; s. Ralph Winfield and Anne Patricia (Belmont) M.; children: Stuart, Shaun; m. Janice L. Kalsted, May 17, 1991; children: Sarah C., Steven C. BS in Urban Studies, BS in Polit. Sci., Elmhurst (Ill.) Coll., 1980. CFP, Life Underwriters Tng. Coun. I and II; registered rep. Nat. Assn. Securities Dealers; cert. employee benefit cons. Agt. Occidental/Transam. Life, Oakbrook, Ill., 1973-78; owner Key Fin., Carol Stream, 1978-83; broker, mgr. Brodsky Agy., Palatine, 1983-89; pres. Mackey Benefits Group, Inc., 1983—. Pres. Heritage Lake Estates Assn., Wheaton, Ill., 1976-78. Mem. Internat. Found. Employee Benefit Plans, Nat. Assn. Life Underwriters, Nat. Assn. Health Underwriters, Internat. Assn. Fin. Planners. Presbyterian. Avocations: martial arts, music. Home: 2216 Spyglass Hill Cir Valrico FL 33594-5231 Office: 865 E Wilmette Rd Ste G Palatine IL 60074-6493

MACKEY, DIANE STOAKES, lawyer; b. Laverne, Minn., Mar. 28, 1937; d. Homer R. and Astrid Stoakes; children: Benjamin, Stuart, Sarah. BS, Northwestern U., 1958; JD, U. Ark., 1978. Bar: Ark. 1978, U.S. Dist. Ct. (ea. dist.) Ark. 1978, U.S. Ct. Appeals (8th cir.) 1978. Law clk. to Chief Judge G. Thomas Eisele U.S. Dist. Ct. (ea. dist.) Ark., Little Rock, 1978-80, asst. U.S. atty., 1980-83; ptnr. Friday Eldredge & Clark, 1983—. Adj. prof. U. Ark. Sch. Law, Little Rock; co-chair fed. practice com., ea. dist. Ark. Author: Review of Year's Cases, 1978, Stone V. Powell, Not As We Like It, 1977, The Emergency Medical Treatment and Active Labor Act: An Act Undergoing Judicial Development, 1997; editor-in-chief U. Ark.-Little Rock Law Jour. Trustee, past pres., bd. trustees Ark. Children's Hosp., Little Rock, 1992-96; chair Good Shepherd Retirement Ctr., Little Rock; mem. commn. on ministry Diocese of Ark., 1987-99; mem., officer Jr. League, Little Rock; bd. dirs. United Way, 1996—, chmn. bd. 2000-02; bd. dirs. U. Ark.-Little Rock Found., 1997—. Fellow Ark. Bar Found., Am. Bar Found.; mem. ABA, Ark. Bar (chair environ. com. 1991-93, health law com. 1995—), Ark. Bar Assn., Pulaski County Bar Assn., Am. Law Inst. Home: 3404 Cedar Hill Rd #3 Little Rock AR 72202-1913 Office: Friday Eldredge & Clark 400 W Capitol Ave Little Rock AR 72201-3436 E-mail: mackey@fec.net.

MACKEY, GEORGE WHITELAW, mathematician, educator; b. St. Louis, Feb. 1, 1916; s. William Sturges and Dorothy Frances (Allison) M.; m. Alice Willard, Dec. 9, 1960; 1 child, Ann Sturges Mackey. BA, Rice Inst., 1938; A.M., Harvard U., 1939, PhD, 1942; MA, Oxford, 1966. Instr. math. Ill. Inst. Tech., 1942-43; faculty instr. math. Harvard U., 1943-46, asst. prof., 1946-48, assoc. prof., 1948-56, prof. math., 1956-69, Landon T. Clay prof. math. and theoretical sci., 1969-85, prof. emeritus, 1985—. Vis. prof. U. Chgo., summer, 1955, UCLA, Summer, 1959, Tata Inst. Fundamental Rsch., Bombay, 1970-71, U. Calif., Berkeley, 1984; Walker Ames vis. prof. U. Wash., summer, 1961; Eastman vis. prof. Oxford (Eng.) U., 1966-67; assoc. prof. U. Paris, 1978; vis. rschr. Math. Sci. Inst., Berkeley, 1983; lectr. U. Heidelberg, Germany, 1988, CUNY, 1987, U. Iowa, 1988, Kings Coll. of U. London, 1991; invited lectr. U. Munich, Germany, 1994, U. Heidelberg, 1995; vis. lectr. U. Tainjin, U. Beijing, U. Shanghai,. U. Hong Kong, 19911 mem. Inst. Advanced Study Princeton U., 1978. Author: Mathematical Foundations of Quantum Mechanics, 1963, Lectures on the Theory of Functions of a Complex Variable, 1967, Induced Representations and Quantum Mechanics, 1968, The Theory of Unitary Group Representations, 1976, Unitary Group Representations in Physics, Probability and Number Theory, 1978, The Scope and History of Commutative and Noncommutative Harmonic Analysis, 1992; contbr. articles math. jours. Served as civilian, operational research sect. 8th Air Force, 1944; applied math. panel NDRC, 1945. Recipient Humboldt prize Max Planck Inst., Bonn, Fed. Republic of Germany, 1985-86; Guggenheim fellow, 1949-50, 61-62, 70-71; Vis. scholar Catalan U., Bellaterra, Spain, 2002. Mem. Am. Math. Soc. (v.p. 1964-65, Steele prize 1974), Nat. Acad. Scis., Am. Philos. Soc., Am. Acad. Arts and Scis., Phi Beta Kappa, Sigma Xi. Office: Harvard U Dept Math 1 Oxford St Cambridge MA 02138-2901

MACKEY, JEFFREY ALLEN, priest; b. Kingston, N.Y., July 12, 1952; s. Allen William and Vivian Mathilda (Hornbeck) M.; m. Martha LaVonne Webster, Dec. 18, 1971; children: Guy Linwood, Kenyon Paul, Geoffrey Joel. BS, Nyack Coll., 1974; D of Sacred Lit., Ridgedale Theol. Sem., 1975; MDiv, Macon (Ga.) Bible Inst., 1976, DHL, 1978; D Ministry, Mansfield Sch. Div., 1985, Grad. Theol. Found., 1990; cert. of theol. studies, Gen. Theol. Sem., 1993; postgrad., Grad. Theol. Found., 1991—, U. of the South; DHL, St. Paul Theol. Sem., 2000. Ordained to ministry Congl. Christian Ch., 1974; ordained priest Episcopal Ch., 1993. Min. music Neversink Valley Bapt. Ch., Huguenot, N.Y., 1969-70; pastor Ponckhockie Congl. Ch., Kingston, 1971-74, The Alliance Ch., Andover, 1974-76; acad. dean Macon (Ga.) Bible Inst., 1976-78; min. Oak Grove Gospel Tabernacle, Williamsport, Pa., 1977-80, 69th St. Alliance Ch., Phila., 1980-83; sr. min. Vestavia Alliance Ch., Birmingham, Ala., 1983-87, Hope Alliance Ch., New Hartford, N.Y., 1987-91; assoc. rector Grace Ch., Utica, N.Y, 1991-96, vicar Waterville, N.Y., 1995-96; rector Trinity Episcopal Ch., DeRidder, La., 1996-97; vicar Polk Meml. Episcopal Ch., Leesville, 1996-97; rector St. Mark the Evangelist Ch., North Bellmore, N.Y., 1997-99; registrar/Bible faculty Nyack Coll., Manhattan Campus, N.Y.C., 1999-2000, assoc. dean for acad. affairs, 2000-2001, acad. dean, 2001—. Adj. prof. Cranmer Theol. House, Sheveort, La., 1997, Nyack (N.Y.) Coll., 1998-99; assisting priest St. John's Episcoal Ch., Kingston, N.Y., 2000—02; interim rector St. John's Ch., Kingston, N.Y., 2002-. Author: A Worship Manifesto, 1986, Indicatives and Imperatives, 1987, Christ's Centripetal Cross, 1990; co-author: Where Love and People Are, 1990; contbg. author: Prophet of Justice, Prophet of Life: Essays on William Stringfellow, 1997, A Diary of Three Decades: Grace Church, Utica, N.Y. 1963-96, 1999, And Jesus Everything: Conversations with A.B. Simpson, 2000; contbr. numerous articles to profl. jours. Mem. Alcohol and Drug Abuse Prevention Treatment Program, Birmingham, 1987-88; chaplain N. Bellmore Vol. Fire Dept., 1998-99. Mem. Fellowship Christian Sch. Adminstrs., Evang. Theol. Soc., Am. Assn. Sch. Adminstrs., Am. Guild Organists, Anglican Assn. of Biblical Scholars, Order of Preachers (Anglican), Inst. for Advanced Theology, Soc. Biblical Lit. Avocations: organ and piano playing, collecting art and statues, hymn writing, walking, restoring antique automobiles. Home: PO Box 111 West Shokan NY 12494-0111 E-mail: mackeyj@ncmc.nyack.edu.

MACKEY, LOUIS HENRY, philosophy educator; b. Sidney, Ohio, Sept. 24, 1926; s. Louis Henry and Clara Emma (Maurer) M.; children: Stephen Louis, Thomas Adam, Jacob Louis, Eva Maria. BA, Capital U., 1948; student, Duke, 1948-50; MA, Yale, 1953, PhD, 1954. Instr. philosophy Yale U., 1953-55, asst. prof., Morse fellow, 1955-59; assoc. prof. philosophy Rice U., Houston, 1959-65, prof., 1965-67, U. Tex., Austin, 1967—2002. Author: Kierkegaard: A Kind of Poet, 1971, Points of View: Readings of Kierkegaard, 1986, Fact, Fiction, and Representation, 1997, Peregrinations of the Word: Essays on Medieval Philosophy, 1997, An Ancient Quarrel Continued: The Troubled Marriage of Philosophy and Literature; contbr. articles to profl. jours. Recipient Harry Ransom award for Tchng. Excellence, 1987, Pres.'s Assocs. award for Tchng. Excellence, 1991, Grad. Tchng. award 1994; NEH fellow, 1976-77. Episcopalian. Home: 4105 Victory Dr Apt A108 Austin TX 78704-7552 Office: Univ Texas 316 WAG Austin TX 78712

MACKEY, MARGARET EMMIE, library media specialist; b. Lancaster, S.C., Aug. 2, 1947; d. Furman Robert and Margaret Edna (Stogner) M. BA, Winthrop Coll., 1968; MAT, U. S.C., 1975; MEd, Winthrop Coll., 1980. Tchr. English, social studies Alexander Graham Jr. High Sch., Charlotte, N.C., 1968-69; grad. teaching asst. U. S.C., Columbia, 1969-71; tchr. English, chemistry Andrew Jackson High Sch., Kershaw, S.C., 1971-82; libr. media specialist Heath Springs (S.C.) Elem. Sch., 1982-86, Andrew Jackson High Sch., 1986—. Mem. ALA, S.C. Assn. Sch. Librs. (treas. 1989-91), Lancaster County Librs. Assn. (pres. 1991-93), Libr. Media Specialist Network (pres. 1987-88), Assn. Sch. Librs., Young Adult Libr. Svcs. Assn. Presbyterian. Avocations: reading, computers, travel. Office: Andrew Jackson High Sch 6925 Kershaw Camden Hwy Kershaw SC 29067-9572

MACKEY, MAUREEN ANN, nutrition scientist; b. San Francisco, May 22, 1955; d. John McBurney and Gloria Regina (Holsten) M.; divorced; 1 child, Patrick Mackey Yee. BS, U. Calif., Davis, 1978; MS, U. Minn., 1981, PhD, 1985. Registered dietitian; cert. nutrition specialist. Nutritionist Kellogg Co., Battle Creek, Mich., 1985-90; from assoc. dir. nutritional sci. to dir. nutritional sci. NutraSweet Co., Deerfield, Ill., 1990-97; dir. applied nutrition Monsanto Co., Skokie, 1992-2000, global leader nutritional sci. affairs, 2000—. Editor: Nutritional Toxicology, 1994, 2002, Nutrition in th 90s, Vols. 1 and 2, 1992, 1995; contbr. articles. Fellow: Am. Coll. Nutrition (bd. dirs.); mem.: Inst. Food Technologists, Am. Diabetes Assn. Republican. Roman Catholic. Office: Monsanto Co 800 N Lindbergh Saint Louis MO 63167 E-mail: maureen.a.mackey@monsanto.com.

MACKEY, PATRICIA ELAINE, university librarian; b. Balt., July 29, 1941; d. Timothy and Hazel Mozelle (Davis) M. BA in Anthropology, CUNY, 1978; MLS, Columbia U., 1981. Asst. libr. I, European Exch. Sys., Mainz-Kastel, Germany, 1966-68; interlibr. loan asst. Poly. U., Bklyn., 1968-72, Rockefeller U., N.Y.C., 1972-73, sr. libr. asst., 1974-80, libr., 1981-91, univ. libr., 1991—. Mem. various libr. coms., N.Y.C., 1991—. Chair pub. svc. scholars program Hunter Coll. CUNY, 1992—; bd. trustees Met. N.Y. Libr. Coun., 2000—. Named to, Hunter Coll. Hall of Fame, 2002. Mem. ALA, N.Y. State Libr. Assn., Assn. Coll. and Rsch. Librs., Alumni Assn. Hunter Coll. (bd. dirs. 1998—, 2d v.p.). Democrat. Roman Catholic. Avocations: reading, chess, gardening. Office: Rockefeller U Libr RU Box 263 1230 York Ave New York NY 10021-6307 E-mail: mackey@rockefeller.edu.

MACKEY, PHILIP ENGLISH, non-profit organization consultant; b. Phila., Dec. 6, 1938; s. Charles David and Mary Alice (Meehan) M. BA, U. Pa., 1960, MA, 1965, PhD, 1969. Asst. prof. history Rutgers U., Camden, N.J., 1969-76; lobbyist N.J. Sch. Bds. Assn., Trenton, 1976-79, dir. mgmt. info., 1979-87; pvt. practice cons. to non-profit orgns. Lambertville, N.J., 1987—. Author: Voices Against Death: Two Centuries of American Appeals Against Capital Punishment, 1976, The Givers Guide: Making Your Charity Dollars County, 1990, (with Barbara J. Hansen) Your Public Schools: What You Can Do to Help Them, 1993; editor: A Gentleman of Much Promise: The Diary of Isaac Mickle, 1837-1845, 2 vols., 1977; editor Family Life Matters, Rutgers U., 1992-2001 (Journalism award for editl. excellence Newsletter Pubs. Found. 1996); contbr. articles to profl. publs. Bd. dirs. Lambertville Edn. Found., 1992—. Lt. (j.g.) USN, 1960-63. Avocations: mountain climbing, hiking, cooking. Home and Office: 47 Lambert Ln # 9 Lambertville NJ 08530-1915 E-mail: pmackey@voicenet.com.

MACKIE, RICHARD H. orchestra executive; married; 3 children. Grad., Tulane U.; M in Arts Adminstrn., U. Wis., Madison. Jazz musician New Hyperion Oriental Foxtrot Orch.; pres. Friends of WHA-TV; dir. devel. Edgewood Coll.; exec. dir. Madison (Wis.) Symphony Orch., 1999—. Office: Madison Symphony Orch 6314 Odana Rd Madison WI 53719*

MACKIE-MASON, JEFFREY KING, economics and information technology educator; b. N.Y.C., Aug. 22, 1959; s. John Huey and Janice Ruth (Auman) Mason; m. Jane Lillian MacKie, Aug. 23, 1980; children: Brian Alexander, Andrew Reid. AB, Dartmouth Coll., 1980; MPP, U. Mich., 1982; PhD, MIT, 1986. Cons., lobbyist Nat. Audubon Soc., Washington, 1979; rsch. resident Dept. of Energy, 1981; spl. cons. Nat. Econ. Rsch. Assocs., Cambridge, Mass., 1984-87; asst. prof. econs. U. Mich., Ann Arbor, 1986-92, assoc. prof. econs. and pub. policy, 1992—, assoc. prof. info., 1996-98, prof. info., 1998—. Antitrust cons. TVA, 1982-84, Bristol Myers, 1986, Pacific Telesis, 1986, Intel, 1988, Virtual Maintenance, Inc., 1989-90, Grumman System Support Corp., 1990, Systemcare Inc., 1991, Comm-Tract, Inc., 1991, Datastat Co., 1992, ITS, 1994-95, Sun Microsystems, 1995, AT&T, 1995, Am. Online, 1995, EDS, 1995, ASI, 1996, Bell Atlantic, 1996, Disc Mfg. Inc., 1996, GTE, 1997, Am. Online, 1998. Mem. editl. bd. RAND Jour. of Econs., 1996—, Telecomm. Sys., 1996—, Netnomics, 1996—; referee Jour. Polit. Economy, Am. Econ. Rev., Jour. Fin., others; contbr. articles to profl. jours. Paul R. Richter fellow, 1979-80, Andrew W. Mellon Nat. Resource Econs. fellow, 1980, Phoenix Meml. Lab. Energy Rsch. fellow, 1982-82, NSF, 1982-85, Alfred P. Sloan Found. fellow, 1985-86, Collegiate Coun. fellow, 1987-88, Nat. fellow Hoover Instn., Stanford U., 1990-91, faculty rsch. fellow Nat. Bur. Econ. Rsch., 1987-93, rsch. assoc., 1993—, IBM U. Partnership fellow, 1998—; Joseph A. Livingston Rsch. scholar, 1989-90; Rackham Faculty Rsch. grantee, 1987-88, 89-99, Rsch. Partnership grantee U. Mich., 1988-90, Faculty Recognition Fund grantee, 1990—, NSF grantee, 1990-91, 91-93, 93-97, DARPA grantee, 1997—. Mem. Econometric Soc., Am. Fin. Assn., Am. Econs. Assn. Office: U Mich Dept Econs 462 Lorch Hall Ann Arbor MI 48109

MACKIEWICZ, EDWARD ROBERT, lawyer; b. Jersey City, July 2, 1951; s. Edward John and Irene Helen (Rakowicz) H. BA, Yale U., 1973; JD, Columbia U., 1976. Bar: N.J. 1976, U.S. Dist. Ct. N.J. 1976, N.Y. 1977, U.S. Dist. Ct. (so. and ea. dist.) N.Y. 1977, D.C. 1978, U.S. Dist. Ct. D.C. 1978, U.S. Ct. Appeals (D.C. cir.) 1978, U.S. Ct. Appeals (3d cir.) 1980, U.S. Supreme Ct. 1980, Md. 1984, U.S. Ct. Claims 1984, U.S. Ct. Appeals (4th cir.) 1986, U.S. Dist. Ct. Md. 1990. Assoc. Carter, Ledyard & Milburn, N.Y.C., 1976-77, Covington & Burling, Washington, 1977-82; counsel for civil rights litigation solicitor's office U.S. Dept. Labor, 1982-83; sr. assoc. Jones, Day, Reavis & Pogue, 1983-85; gen. counsel Pension Benefit Guaranty Corp., 1985-87; of counsel Pierson, Ball & Dowd, 1987-89; ptnr. Reed Smith Shaw & McClay, 1989; gen. counsel Masters, Mates & Pilots Benefit Plans, Linthicum Heights, Md., 1989-92; of counsel Steptoe & Johnson, L.L.P., Washington, 1992-98, ptnr., 1999—. Mem. adv. coun. Sec. of Labor's ERISA, 1991-93; prof. lectr. in law Nat. Law Ctr., George Washington U., 1993—. Mem. Am. Coun. Young Polit. Leaders (del. to Australia 1985), Univ. Club, Yale Club. Home: 3001 Veazey Ter NW Apt 1032 Washington DC 20008-5406 Office: 1330 Connecticut Ave NW Washington DC 20036-1704 E-mail: emackiew@steptoe.com.

MACKILLOP, JAMES JOHN, English language educator, journalist, critic; b. Pontiac, Mich., May 31, 1939; s. Colin and Margaret Ann (Gillis) MacK.; m. Patricia MacKillop, Aug. 29, 1964; children: Molly Elizabeth, Colin Kahan. AB, Wayne State U., 1962, MA, 1968; PhD, Syracuse U., 1975. Instr. English Mich. Technol. U., Houghton, 1963-66; prof. Onondaga Cmty. Coll., Syracuse, N.Y., 1967-99. Vis. fellow Harvard U., Cambridge, Mass., 1975; vis. prof. U. Rennes, France, 1994. Contbg. editor Syracuse New Times, 1984—; author: Dictionary of Celtic Myth, 1998; editor (anthology): Irish Literature: A Read, 1987, Contemporary Irish Cinema, 1999. Mem. Syracuse Press Club. Avocation: travel. Home: 108 Limestone Ln Syracuse NY 13219-2144

MACKIN, CHARLES PHILIP, JR. lawyer; b. Boston, Dec. 13, 1947; s. Charles Philip and Mary Patricia (Sparkes) M.; m. Deborah Ann Huey, Oct. 18, 1980; children: Emily K., Claire E.S. BA, St. Anselm Coll., 1969; JD, Loyola U., New Orleans, 1972; MGA, U. Pa., 1987; grad., U.S. Army War Coll., 1990. Bar: Pa. 1972, U.S. Ct. Mil. Appeals 1973, U.S. Ct. Appeals (D.C. cir.) 1977, U.S. Supreme Ct. 1977, U.S. Ct. Appeals (3rd cir.) 1985. Asst. dist. atty., Coudersport, Pa., 1978-81; sr. dep. atty. gen. Office of Atty. Gen. of Pa., Harrisburg, 1982-86, chief dep. atty. gen., 1986-89; dep. chief counsel for investigations Dept. Auditor Gen. of Pa., 1989-91, dep. auditor gen., 1991-96. Capt. USMC, 1972-77. Mem. Pa. Bar Assn., Army Navy Club (Washington). Office: 3300 Trindle Rd Camp Hill PA 17011-4432

MACKIN, JEANNE ANN, writer, educator; b. Waterloo, N.Y., June 9, 1948; d. Richard J. and Helen (Campfield) M.; m. Stephen Poleskie. BA in English, Ithaca Coll., 1970; MFA in Creative Writing, Bennington Coll., 1986. Columnist Ithaca (N.Y.) Times, 1974—; sci. writer Cornell U., Ithaca, 1979—; writing instr. Ithaca Coll., 1991—; MFA faculty mem. Goddard Coll., 2001—. Cons. Strong Mus., Rochester, 1994; cons., auditor N.Y. State Coun. on Arts, N.Y.C., 1984—; writing tchr. State Coun. on Arts, Hawaii, 1992; spkr. in field. Author: The Frenchwoman, 1989, The Queen's War, 1991, Dreams of Empire, 1996, The Sweet By and By, 2001, The Cornell Book of Herbs, 1993; editor: Book of Love, 1998. Recipient Excellence in Newswriting award Coun. for Advancement and Support of Edn., 1986, Writing Scholarship award Wesleyan U., 1989; rsch. fellow Am. Antiquarian Soc., 1999. Mem. Author's Guild. Avocations: gardening, travel, textile arts. Home: PO Box 849 Ithaca NY 14851-0849

MACKINNEY, ARCHIE ALLEN, JR. physician; b. St. Paul, Aug. 16, 1929; s. Archie Allen and Doris (Hoops) MacK.; m. Shirley Schaefer, Apr. 9, 1955; children— Julianne, Theodore, John. BA, Wheaton (Ill.) Coll., 1951; MD, U. Rochester, 1955. Intern, resident in medicine U. Wis. Hosp., 1955-59; clin. assoc. NIH, 1959-61; clin. investigator VA, 1961-64; asst. prof. medicine U. Wis., Madison, 1964-68, assoc. prof., 1968-74, prof., 1974-98, med. alumni prof., 1987. Mentor class of '03 U. Wis. Med. Sch.; chief hematology VA Hosp., Madison, 1964-98, chief nuclear medicine, 1964-73, 78-79 Author (editor): Pathophysiology of Blood, 1984, Hematology for Students, 2002; contbr. Trustee Intervarsity Christian Fellowship, 1985-88. Served with USPHS, 1959-61. Danforth assoc., 1962 Mem. Am. Soc. Hematology, Am. Fedn. Clin. Research, Central Soc. Clin. Research. Republican. Baptist. Home: 190 N Prospect Ave Madison WI 53705-4071 Office: 2500 Overlook Ter Madison WI 53705-2254

MACKINNIS, ANN PHELPS, municipal government and land use management; b. Hartford, Conn., Sept. 3, 1936; d. George Henry and Margaret Louise (Stewart) Phelps; m. Frank Reader MacKinnis, March 15, 1957 (div. Dec. 1980); children: Robert Phelps, John Stewart. AS in Retailing Summa cum laude, Lasell Jr. Coll., 1956; BSBA summa cum laude, Coll. of St. Elizabeth, 1988. Acctg. clerk Washington Aluminum Co., Balt., 1975—78; adminstrv. aide Town of Morristown, N.J., 1975-78, adminstrv. officer planning and zoning bd. NJ, 1986—, mgr. divsn. land use adminstrn. N.J., 1986—. Trustee Christmas on the Green, Morristown, 1978-86; adj. prof. Rutgers U. Editor: Morristown Master Plan, 1978-79; also author of ordinances and pamplets. Mem. Morris County Bldg. Ofcls. Assn., Dover, N.J., 1995—, Rutgers Club, New Brunswick, 1998—, Calvert Marine Mus., Solomons Island, Md., 1997—; mem. Mayor's Design Rev. Com., Morristown, N.J., 2001—. Recipient Women of Accomplishment, Outstanding Acad. Achievement, Coll. of St. Elizabeth, 1985, Scholastic Achievement award, 1988. Mem. N.J. Planning Ofcls. (Achievement in Planning award 1997), N.J. Assn. Planning and Zoning Adminstrs. (pres. 1996-99, bd. dirs. 1992—, chmn. edn. and cert. commn. 1999—), Morristown Town Coun. (Achievement in Planning award 1997), Rutgers Club, Calvert Marine Mus. Republican. Protestant. Avocations: sailing, travel, reading, jigsaw and word puzzles. Home: 14 Cromwell Dr Morristown NJ 07960-4602 Office: Town of Morristown 200 South St Morristown NJ 07960-0914 E-mail: A.Mackinnis@TownofMorristown.org.

MACKINNON, JAMES GORDON, economist, educator; b. Charlottetown, P.E.I., Can., Jan. 4, 1951; s. James William and Marion Elizabeth (Smith) MacK; m. Susan Gentleman, Nov. 23, 1985. B.A. with honors, York U., 1971; M.A., Princeton U., 1974, Ph.D., 1975. Asst. prof. Queen's U., Kingston, Ont., Can., 1975-78, assoc. prof., 1978-82, prof., 1982— . Mem. editorial bd. Can. Jour. Econs., 1984— . Contbr. articles to profl. jours. Doctoral fellow Can. Council, 1972-75; leave fellow Soc. Scis. and Humanities Research Council of Can., 1981-82. Mem. Can. Econs. Assn., Am. Econs. Assn., Econometric Soc. Mem. United Ch. of Can. Avocation: sailing. Office: Queen's U Dept Econs Kingston ON Canada K7L 3N6

MACKINNON, JOHN ALEXANDER, lawyer; b. Glen Ridge, N.J., Feb. 5, 1949; s. John and Carol McNeir (Cox) M.; m. Anne Rider Patterson, Aug. 19, 1972; children: Lindsay Rider, John William. BA, Williams Coll., 1971; JD, U. Va., Charlottesville, 1974. Assoc. Brown & Wood, N.Y.C., 1974-82, ptnr., 1983-2001, Sidley Austin Brown & Wood, N.Y.C., 2001—. Trustee, Tuxedo Park Libr., N.Y., 1982-89; mem. chmn., bd. zoning appeals, Tuxedo Park, 1987-89. Mem. The Tuxedo Club.

MACKINNON, JOHN JEFFERSON, archaeologist, anthropology and history educator; b. Flint, Mich., Dec. 26, 1943; s. Henry John and Amanda Wood (Lifsey) MacK.; m. Virginia Maud Sherwood, June 28, 1968 (div. Aug. 1983); 1 child, Ian Jefferson; m. Carol Jane Key, Mar. 18, 1994. BA in Ancient History, U. Mich., 1965; postgrad. summer sch. in history, Oxford (Eng.) U., 1967; MA in History and Edn., U. Wis., 1967, MS in Anthropology, 1980, PhD in Anthropology, 1989. Tchr. LaFollette H.S., Madison, Wis., 1967-78; tchg. asst. U. Wis., 1979-87; instr. Coll. Lake County, Grayslake, Ill., 1987-90; lectr. U. Wis., Madison, 1987, Whitewater, 1988-90; adj. prof. Lakeland Coll., Sheboygan, Wis., 1979-85; mem. faculty Shimer Coll., Waukegan, Ill., 1987-90; lectr. U. Md. European Divsn., College Park, 1990-93; prof. anthropology and history, coord. anthropology program Collin County C.C., Plano, Tex., 1993—. Prin investigator Point Placencia (Belize) Archaeology Project, 1983—; discoverer, excavator 88 ancient Maya sites on coast and cays of Belize. Contbr. articles to profl. archaeology and history jours., encys., and books. Advisor Collin Co. Archaeological Soc., 1997—, Faculty advisor Amnesty Internat., Collin County C.C., 1993—; Eagle scout, 1968. Named Outstanding Wis. Humanities Tchr., English Spkg. Union, Milw., 1969; field rsch. grantee Earthwatch, Cambridge, Mass., 1983-87; radiocarbon rsch. grantee NSF, 1986, Innovative Tchg. of Field Courses Awd. Grantee Am. Anthropology Assn., 1998. Fellow Am. Anthrop. Assn.; mem. Soc. Am. Archaeology, Soc. Primitive Tech., Soc. Anthropology in Cmty. Colls., Tex. Archaeol. Soc. Mem. Green Party. Avocations: bagpipes, Scottish country dancing, Egyptian hieroglyphic translation. Home: 948 Goodwin Dr Plano TX 75023-4905 Office: Collin County Cmty Coll 2800 E Spring Creek Pkwy Plano TX 75074-3300

MAC KINNON, LEITA KECK, real estate broker; b. Ralls, Tex., May 4, 1939; d. Clarence D. and Vergie (Russell) Mc Candless; student Tex. Inst. Tech., 1961-62, U. Houston, 1970-74; m. Robert L. Mac Kinnon, Feb. 4, 1974; children— Rhonda Dixon, Brenda Nicholson. Salesperson, Century 21 N.W. Properties Co., Houston, 1970-76, Century 21 Regional Properties Co., Houston, 1976-79; owner, mgr. Century 21 Pin Oak Properties, Houston, 1979— ; dir. bus. devel. Guardian Title Co. of Houston, 1983— ; tchr. real estate. Cert. broker, Tex. Mem. Women's Council Houston Bd. Realtors Houston C. of C., Nat. Assn. Realtors. Democrat. Baptist. Office: 4120 Southwest Fwy Ste 100 Houston TX 77027-7309

MACKINNON, MALCOLM D(AVID), retired insurance company executive; b. Guelph, Ont., Can., Mar. 9, 1931; came to U.S., 1955; s. A.L. and Jean (Butchart) MacK.; m. Betty Campbell, June 18, 1955; children: Sandra, Katherine, Donald. BA, U. Toronto, 1953. CLU; chartered fin. analyst. With Prudential Ins. Co., 1954-94, v.p., 1979-81, sr. v.p., 1981-82, Roseland, N.J., 1982-94; ret., 1994. Commentator pub. radio. Trustee Kean Coll., Union, N.J., 1990-93, Millburn Free Pub. Libr., 1996—, pres., 1997-2000; chmn. Milburn Short Hills chpt. ARC, 1992-94. Fellow Soc. Actuaries; mem. Canoe Brook Country Club (Summit, N.J.). Home: 23 Grosvenor Rd Short Hills NJ 07078-1639

MACKINNON, PEGGY LOUISE, public relations executive; b. Florence, Ariz., June 18, 1945; d. Lacy Donald Gay and Goldie Louise (Trotter) Martin; m. Ian Dixon Mackinnon, Oct. 20, 1973. BA, San Jose State U., 1967, postgrad., 1968. Cert. secondary tchr., Calif. Tchr. Las Lomas H.S., Walnut Creek, Calif., 1968-69; edn. officer Ormond Sch., Sydney, Australia, 1970-72; tchr. Belconnen H.S., Canberra, Australia, 1972-73; temp. exec. sec. various orgns., London, 1973-75; mktg. mgr. Roadtown Wholesale, Tortola, British Virgin Islands, 1975-80; sr. v.p., gen. mgr. Hill & Knowlton Inc., Denver, 1981-96; pres. Peggy Mackinnon Inc., 1996—. Bd. dirs. Rocky Mountain Poison and Drug Found., Denver, 1984-87, Denver C. of C., Boy Scouts Am., Denver coun. Avocations: tennis, skiing, fishing, travel. Home and Office: Apt 21 9200 Cherry Creek South Dr Denver CO 80231-4018

MACKINNON, ROGER ALAN, psychiatrist, educator; b. Attleboro, Mass., Feb. 13, 1927; s. Irville Herbert and Helen (Junk) MacK.; m. Florence Lundgren, Apr. 8, 1949 (div. 1970); children: Carol Louise, Stuart Alan; m. Nadine Trasenster, May 28, 1971. Student, Princeton U., 1944-46; MD, Columbia U., 1950, cert. in psycoanalytic medicine, 1957. Diplomate Am. Bd. Psychiatry and Neurology. Intern E.W. Sparrow Hosp., Lansing, Mich., 1950-51; resident in psychiatry N.Y. State Psychiatric Inst., N.Y.C., 1951-52, 52-54; chief psychiatry Vanderbilt Clinic, Presbyn. Hosp., 1959-77; prof. clin. psychiatry Coll. Physicians & Surgeons, Columbia U., 1986-97, prof. emeritus, 1997—; tng., supervising analyst Columbia U. Psychoanalytic Ctr., 1970—, asst. dir. for selection, 1981-91, dir., 1991-97; attending psychiatrist Presbyn. Hosp., N.Y.C., 1972—, N.Y. State Psychiatric Inst., N.Y.C., 1972—. Asst. examiner Am. Bd. Psychiatry and Neurology, 1960-70; cons., lectr. in field. Co-author textbook: The Psychiatric Interview, 1971, The Psychiatric Evaluation, 1986; contbr. articles to profl. jours., chpts. to books. Lt. USNR, 1952-54. Fellow Am. Psychiat. Assn. (life), N.Y. Acad. Medicine; mem. Am. Psychoanalytic Assn., Assn. Psychoanalytic Medicine (George E. Daniels Merit award 1995), N.Y. Psychiat. Soc. (pres. 1987-88), N.Y. Psychiat. Inst. (Centennial award 1996). Avocations: woodworking, boating, hiking. Home: 11 Edgewood St Tenafly NJ 07670-2909 Office: 11 E 87th St New York NY 10128-0527

MACKINNON, SALLY ANNE, retired fast food company executive; b. Chgo., Apr. 20, 1938; d. Eugene and Anne Elizabeth (Jones) MacK. BA, Smith Coll., 1960; postgrad., U. Ark., 1961-62. Brand mgr. Speidel div. of Textron, Providence, 1967-70; mktg. mgr. Candy Corp. Am., Bklyn., 1970-72; v.p. account service William Esty Advt., N.Y.C., 1972-76; mktg. mgr. R.J. Reynolds Tobacco, Winston-Salem, N.C., 1976-84, v.p. new brands, 1984-86; v.p. new products mktg. Ky. Fried Chicken, Louisville, 1986-88; ret., 1988. Democrat. Episcopalian. Avocations: photography, travel. Home: 7500 E Boulders Pkwy # 20 Scottsdale AZ 85262

MACKINNON, STEPHEN R. Asian studies administrator, educator; b. Columbus, Nebr., Dec. 2, 1940; s. Cyrus Leland and Helen (Wigglesworth) MacK.; m. Janice Carolyn Rachie, July 15, 1967 (dec. Sept. 1999); children: Rebecca, Cyrus R. BA, Yale U., 1963, MA, 1964; PhD, U. Calif., Davis, 1971. Acting instr. Chinese U., Hong Kong, 1968-69; dir. Asian Studies, prof. history Ariz. State U., Tempe, 1971—; vis. assoc. Chinese Acad. Social Sci., Beijing, 1979-81, 85. Mem. U.S. State Dept. Selection Bd., Washington, 1991, Nat. Com. on U.S.-China Rels., N.Y.C., 1991—; cons. PBS film documentary "Dragon and Eagle" on U.S.-China rels., San Francisco, 1986—. Author: (book) Power/Politics China, 1980; co-author: (books) Agnes Smedley, 1988, China Reporting, 1987; co-editor: (book) Chinese Women Revolution, 1976 (ALA notable book 1976), Scars of War, 2001; lectr. on China to local orgns. and TV, 1981—. Commr. Phoenix Sister Cities, 1986-91; bd. dirs. Com. on Fgn. Rels., Phoenix, 1988—; bd. dirs. Marshall Fund Ariz., 1995—. Rsch. fellow Am. Coun. Learned Socs., Hong Kong, 1978, Fulbright Found., India, 1977-78; rsch. sr. Com. on Scholarly Com. People's Republic China, Washington-Beijing, 1992. Mem. Assn. Asian Studies (bd. dirs. 1990-91), Am. Hist. Assn. (program com. 1990-91). Avocations: tennis, hiking, jazz. Office: Ariz State U History Dept Ctr Asian Studies Tempe AZ 85287-2501 E-mail: stephen.mackinnon@asu.edu.

MACKINTOSH, CAMERON, musical theater producer; b. Enfield, Middlesex, Eng., Oct. 17, 1946; s. Ian Robert and Diana Gladys (Tonna) M. Student, Prior Pk. Coll., Somerset, Eng., Cen. Sch. for Speech and Drama. §st. stage mgr. Oliver! tour, British cities, 1965; N.Y. debut as producer, deviser Tomfoolery, Top of the Gate, 1981; London debut producer Little Women, Jeanetta Cochrane, 1967; producer, deviser musicals Anything Goes, Saville, London, 1969, Trelawney, Sadler Wells, Prince of Wales, 1972, The Card, Queens, 1973, Winnie the Pooh, Phoenix, 1974, 75, Owl and the Pussycat Went To See, Westminster, 1975, Side By Side By Sondheim, Wyndhams and Garrick, 1976, Oliver!, Albery, 1977-80, Aldwych, 1983, Godspell, Phoenix, 1975, Her Majesty's P.O.W., Shaftsbury, 1977, Duke of York, 1978, Diary of a Madam, Phoenix, 1977, After Shave, Apollo, 1977, Out On a Limb, Vaudeville, 1977, Gingerbread Man, Old Vic, 1978, 79, Royalty, 1980, Westminster, 1981, My Fair Lady, Adelphi, 1979, Tomfoolery, Criterion, 1980, Jeeves Takes Charge, Fortune, 1981, Cats, New London, 1981, Song and Dance, Palace, 1982, Blondel, Old Vic, Aldwych, 1983, Little Shop of Horrors, Comedy, 1983, Abbacadabra, Lyric Hammersmith, 1983, The Boyfriend, Old Vic, and Albery, 1985, Les Misérables, 1985, The Phantom of the Opera, 1987, Follies, 1989, Miss Saigon, 1989, Five Guys Named Moe, 1990, Moby Dick: Putting It Together, 1992, Carousel, 1993 (Tony award, 1994), Oliver!, 1994, Martin Guerre, 1996, Oklahoma, 1999, The Witches of Eastwick, 2000, My Fair Lady, 2001; major tours in Britian include Little Women, 1967, Murder at the Vicarage, 1969, Rebecca, 1969, At Home with the Dales, 1970, Salad Days, 1972, Butley, 1973, Winnie the Pooh, 1973-74, Time and Time Again, 1974, Godspell, 1974-80, The Owl and The Pussycat Went To See, 1974, 75, 76, Relatively Speaking, 1974-75, An Inspector Calls, 1974, Private Lives, 1974, Bell, Book and Candle, 1974, A Merry Whiff of Windsor, 1975, So Who Needs Marriage. 1975, John, Paul, George and Ringo, 1975-76, Rock Nativity, 1975-76, Touch of Spring, 1976, Virginia Woolf, 1976, Lauder, 1976, Oliver!, 1977, 83, Side By Side By Sondheim, 1978-79, My Fair Lady, 1978, 81-82, Rocky Horror Show, 1979-80, Gingerbread Man, 1979, Oklahoma, 1980; also tours various shows to Can., Republic S. Africa, Ireland, Scandinavia, Australia, U.S.A. Decorated knight of the Brit. Empire. Fellow St. Catherine's Coll. (hon., Oxford); mem. Soc. West End Theatres (exec. officer), Dramatists League, League Am. Theaters, Am. Dramatists Guild. Address: 1 Bedford Sq London England WC1B 3RA also: 1650 Broadway Ste 800 New York NY 10019-6833

MACKINTOSH, FREDERICK ROY, oncologist; b. Miami, Fla., Oct. 4, 1943; s. John Harris and Mary Carlotta (King) MacK.; m. Judith Jane Parnell, Oct. 2, 1961 (div. Aug. 1977); children: Lisa Lynn, Wendy Sue; m. Claudia Lizanne Flournoy, Jan. 7, 1984; 1 child, Gregory Warren. BS, MIT, 1964, PhD, 1968; MD, U. Miami, 1976. Intern then resident in gen. medicine Stanford (Calif.) U., 1976-78, fellow in oncology, 1978-81; asst. prof. med. U. Nev., Reno, 1981-85, assoc. prof., 1985-92, prof. medicine, 1992—. Contbr. articles to profl. jours. Fellow ACP; mem. Am. Soc. Clin. Oncology, Am. Cancer Soc. (pres. Nev. chpt. 1987-89, Washoe chpt. 1988-90), No. Nev. Cancer Coun. (bd. dirs. 1981-92), No. Calif. Cancer Program (bd. dirs. alt. 1983-87, bd. dirs. 1987-91). Avocation: bicycling. Office: Med Sch Assocs North Ste 302 1500 E 2nd St Reno NV 89502

MACKLE, ELLIOTT, writer; b. Miami, Fla., Mar. 11, 1940; s. Elliott James Mackle and Milbrew Ewing Wright; life ptnr. George Robert Mende. BA, U. Miami, Coral Gables, FL, 1962, MA, 1971; PhD, Emory U., Atlanta, GA, 1972—77. Pub. info. specialist GA Dept. of Edn., Atlanta, 1979—82; columnist Atlanta Mag., 1985—87, Creative Loafing, Atlanta, 1985—87; dining critic Atlanta Journal-Constitution, 1987—97; writing tchr. Ga. State U., 1997—99; chief restaurant critic Creative Loafing, 1997—. Restaurant awards com. mem. James Beard Found., New York, 1992—97. Author: (television drama) High Tide at Hunting Island, 1997; contbr. television cooking series, guidebook. Capt. USAF, 1963—67, Calif., Libya, Italy. Mem.: Phi Kappa Phi. Avocations: raising and showing miniature schnauzer dogs, travel.

MACKLEM, MICHAEL KIRKPATRICK, publisher; b. Toronto, Ont., Can., July 12, 1928; s. Hedley Clark and Mary Eileen (Kirkpatrick) M.; m. Anne Woodburne Hardy, Dec. 30, 1950; children— Timothy Street, Nicholas Hardy. BA, U. Toronto, 1950; AM (Charles Scribner fellow), Princeton U., 1952, PhD (Porter Ogden Jacobus fellow, Royal Soc. Can. fellow), 1954. Instr., English Yale U., New Haven, 1954-55; staff editor Ency. Canadiana, 1955-58; asst. to dir. Humanities Research Council of Can., 1958-60; gen. mgr. Oberon Press, Ottawa, Ont., 1966-85. Pres. Michael, Hardy, Ltd., Ottawa, 1972— Author: The Anatomy of the World: Relations Between Natural and Moral Law from Donne to Pope, 1958, God Have Mercy: The Life of John Fisher of Rochester, 1967, Cinderella, 1969, Voyages to New France 1615-1618, 1970, Voyages to New France 1599-1603, 1971, The Sleeping Beauty, 1973, Jacques the Woodcutter, 1977, Liberty and the Holy City, 1978, The Oberon Reader, 1991, The Oberon Poetry Collection, 1992. Can. Council fellow, 1964-65 Home: 555 Maple Ln Ottawa ON Canada K1M 0N7 Office: Oberon Press 400-350 Sparks St Ottawa ON Canada K1R 7S8 E-mail: oberon@sympatico.ca.

MACKLER, TINA, artist; b. London; d. Leon and Ethel Mackler; 1 dau., Leonore. Student, Arts Students League, N.Y.C., Indsl. Sch. Design, New Sch. Tchr. art Nat. Acad. Ballet, N.Y.C., 1966-69; tchr. adults West Side YMCA. Asst. studio instr. Met. Mus. Art, N.Y.C., vol. program, 1990—. Illustrator: Informal Dictionary of Ballet, 1966; co-author, illustrator: To Dance, To Live; pub. Dance Horizons, 1977; one-persons shows include Alfred Valente Gallery, N.Y.C., 1967, Mus. Performing Arts, N.Y.C., 1973, Adelphi U., L.I., 1975, Phila. Art Alliance, 1976, Jackson (Miss.) Mus. Art, 1978, Northeastern U., Boston, 1980; exhibited in group and solo shows Alfredo Gallery, N.Y.C., 1964, 66, Dutchess Hall Gallery, Poughkeepsie, N.Y., 1969, Wright/Hepburn/Webster Gallery, N.Y.C., 1960, 70, N.Y. Pub. Libr., 1973, O'Keefe Ctr., Ont., Can., 1974, Ball State U., 1974, N.A.D. annual, 1974, Audubon Artists Annual, 1975, Nat. Pastel Show, 1975, Commedia Dell Art Adelphi U., 1974, Guild Gallery, N.Y.C., 1978, Met. Mus. of Art, 1987-88; works represented in permanent collections Nat. Coll. Fine Prints, Smithsonian Instn., Washington, Israel Mus., Jerusalem, La Jolla (Calif.) Mus., U. Wis. Mus., Circus World Mus., Baraboo, Wis., Fairleigh Dickinson U., Circus Hall of Fame Mus., Sarasota, Fla., Adelphi U., Creative Dance Found. for Negro Arts, Tuskegee, Ala., Mus. Performing Arts Lincoln Ctr., N.Y.C., Jackson (Miss.) Mus. Art, Original Print Collectors Group Ltd., Northeastern U., also pvt. collections. Home: 25 Central Park W Apt 7C New York NY 10023-7253 *I have long felt the influence which the arts exert on the minds and hearts of mankind. Believing, as I do, that the world today stands in need of spiritual truths, ideals and moral standards, it is my desire to reach out and set before the public some of the beauty and grandeur which reside in the human soul and expresses itself through that most primal art - the dance.*

MACKLIN, ANTHONY P. foundation administrator; b. Indpls., Apr. 18, 1967; s. Larry D. and Janet E. M.; m. Alexius Smith, Mar. 18, 2000. MA, Manchester Coll., 1989; M in Music Composition, Butler U., 1995. Cert. econ. devel. fin. Program asst. Ind. Main St. Program, Indpls., 1989-93; state grants mgr. Ind. Dept. Commerce, 1993-95; program officer Ctrl. Ind. Cmty. Found., 1996-99, dir. cmty. initiatives, 2000—. Bd. dirs. The Old Centrum, Indpls. Composer (musical work) Catharsis; musician (cassette) Surging Generals, 1992. Deacon Northminster Presbyn. Ch., Indpls., 1996-98; co-coord. Interfaith Hospitality Network, Indpls., 1996-99; treas., newsletter editor Keystone Monon Neighborhood Partnership, Indpls., 2000. Mem. Ind. Assn. Cmty. Econ. Devel., Ind. Advs. for Arts (bd. dirs. 1998—), Historic Landmarks Found. Ind. Episcopal. Home: Ctrl Ind Cmty Found 615 N Alabama Ste 119 Indianapolis IN 46204-1498 Fax: 317-637-6402. E-mail: tonym@cicf.org.

MACKLIN, CROFFORD JOHNSON, JR. lawyer; b. Columbus, Ohio, Sept. 10, 1947; S. Crofford Johnson, Sr. and Dorothy Ann (Stevens) M.; m. Mary Carole Ward, July 5, 1969; children: Carrie E., David J. BA, Ohio State U., 1969; BA summa cum laude, U. West Fla., 1974; JD cum laude, Ohio State U., 1976. Bar: Ohio 1977, U.S. Tax Ct. 1978. Acct. Touche Ross, Columbus, 1976-77; assoc. Smith & Schnacke, Dayton, 1977-81; ptnr. Porter, Wright, Morris & Arthur, 1983-88; shareholder Smith & Schnacke, 1988-89; ptnr. Thompson, Hine LLP, 1989—; practice group leader personnel and succession planning Thompson, Hine & Flory, 2001—; sole practice Dayton, 1981-82. Adj. faculty Franklin U., 1977; adj. prof. U. Dayton Law Sch., 1981. Contbr. articles to profl. jours. Bd. dirs. Great Lakes Nat. Bank Ohio, 1997, Easter Seals, 1984-86. Served to capt. USMCR, 1969-74. Fellow Am. Coll. Trust and Estate Counsel; mem. ABA, Dayton Bar Assn. (chmn. probate com. 1981-83), Dayton Trust & Estate Planning (pres. 1983-84), Ohio Bar Assn. Presbyterian. Home: 3 Forest Pl Glendale OH 45246-4407 Office: Thompson Hine LLP 2000 Courthouse Pla NE PO Box 8801 Dayton OH 45401-8801

MACKLIN, MARTIN RODBELL, psychiatrist; b. Raleigh, N.C., Aug. 27, 1934; s. Albert A. and Mitzi (Robdell) M.; m. Ruth Chimacoff (div.); children: Meryl, Shelley; m. Anne Elizabet Warren, May 25; children: Alicia, Aaron. BME, Cornell U., 1957, M in Indsl. Engring., 1958; PhD in Biomed. Engring., Case Western Res. U., 1967, MD, 1977. Diplomate Am. Bd. Psychiatry and Neurology; cert. in alcoholism and other drug dependencies Am. Soc. Addiction Medicine. Investigator Am. Heart Assn., Cleve., 1969-74; vis. fellow U. Sussex, Brighton, England, 1970; assoc. prof. biomed. engring. Case Western Res. U., 1972-81, asst. prof. psychiatry, 1981—; clin. dir. Horizon Ctr. Hosp., Warrensville Township, Ohio, 1981-83; adminstrv. dir. Riverview Psychiat. Assocs., 1983-94; med. dir. Woodside Hosp., 1989-94; v.p. med. affairs UHHS Geauga Regional Hosp., Chardon, Ohio, 1994—; 27. Psychiat. cons. Glenbeigh Hosp., Ohio and Fla.; cons. various indsl. cos.; chair quality intervention panel Ohio State Med. Bd. Contbr. articles to profl. jours; patentee in field. NIH rsch. grantee Kellogg Found., Cleve., 1967-81; Laughlin fellow Am. Coll. Psychiatry, 1980. Mem. Am. Psychiat. Assn., Am. Coll. Physician Execs., Cleve. Acad. Medicine, Cleve. Psychiat. Soc. Avocations: woodworking, gardening. Home: 348 N Chestnut St Jefferson OH 44047-1103 E-mail: martin.macklin@uhhs.com.

MACKLIN, PHILIP ALAN, physics educator; b. Richmond Hill, N.Y., Apr. 13, 1925; s. Egbert Chalmer and Margaret Griswold (Collins) M.; m. Cora Baldwin Galindo, Sept. 5, 1953; children: Susan, Steven, Peter. BS cum laude, Yale U., 1944; MA, Columbia U., 1949, PhD, 1956. Physicist Carbide & Carbon Chems. Corp., Oak Ridge, 1946-47; research scientist AEC, Columbia U., 1949-51; instr. physics Middlebury Coll., Vt., 1951-54, acting chmn. dept., 1953-54; mem. faculty Miami U., Oxford, Ohio, 1954—, prof. physics, 1961-93, chmn. dept., 1972-85, prof. emeritus, 1993—. Research scientist Armco Steel Co., summers 1955-56; vis. prof. U. N.Mex., summers 1957-68, Boston U., fall 1985-86; physicist Los Alamos Sci. Labs., summers 1960-62; participant NSF summer insts., 1970-71; vis. scientist MIT, 1985-86 Author publs. in field; patentee in field. Vestryman Holy Trinity Episcopal Ch., Oxford , 1959-61, 67, 71-73, 75-77, mem. fin. com., chmn. blood assurance program, 1980—, lector, 1989—; active PTO. With USN, 1944-46. Mem. AAAS, AAUP, LWV of Oxford (treas. 1986-88, dir. governance 1997—), Am. Phys. soc., Forum Physics and Soc., Am. Assn. Physics Tchrs., Kiwanis (bd. dirs. 1994-97), Torch Club of Butler County (pres. 1982-83, 96-97, mem. editl. adv. com. The Torch), 1809 Club (pres. 1964-65), Campus Ministry Ctr. (trustee 1994-2002), Union of Concerned Scientists, Ctr. for Voting and Democracy (charter), Membership Assn. Miami U. Art Mus. (exec. com. 1999-2002), Phi Beta Kappa (pres. Iota of Ohio chpt. 1987-88), Sigma Xi, Sigma Pi Sigma, Omicron Delta Kappa. Democrat. Home: 211 Oakhill Dr Oxford OH 45056-2710 Office: Culler Hall Miami Univ Oxford OH 45056 E-mail: macklipa@muohio.edu.

MACKLIN, RUTH, bioethics educator; b. Newark, Mar. 27, 1938; d . Hyman and Frieda (Yaruss) Chimacoff; m. Martin Macklin, Sept. 1, 1957 (div. June 1969): children: Meryl, Shelley Macklin Taylor. BA with distinction, Cornell U., 1958; MA in Philosophy, Case Western Res. U., 1966, PhD in Philosophy, 1968. Instr. in philosophy Case Western Res. U., Cleve., 1967-68, asst. prof., 1968-71, assoc. prof., 1971-76; assoc. for behavioral studies The Hastings Ctr., Hastings-on-Hudson, N.Y., 1976-80; vis. assoc. prof. Albert Einstein Coll. Medicine, Bronx, 1977-78, assoc. prof., 1978-84, prof. dept. epidemiology and social medicine, 1984—. Cons. NIH, 1986—; advisor WHO, Geneva, 1989—; mem. White House Adv. Com. on Human Radiation Experiments, Washington1994; chair ethical rev. com. UNAIDS, Geneva, 1996—2001. Author: Man, Mind and Morality, 1982, Mortal Choices, 1987, Enemies of Patients, 1993, Surrogates and Other Mothers, 1994, Against Relativism, 1999; contbr. articles to ethics, law and med. jours. Fellow: APHA, Am. Soc. Law, Medicine and Ethics, Inst. Medicine NAS, The Hastings Ctr., Am. Philis. Assn. (life); mem.: Am. Soc. Bioethics and Humanities (bd. dirs. 1997—99), Internat. Assn. Bioethics (bd. dirs., pres. 1999—2001). Democrat. Office: A Einstein Coll Medicine Dept Epidemiology & Social Medicine 1300 Morris Park Ave Bronx NY 10461-1926

MACKLIS, ROGER MITON, physician, educator, researcher; b. Stratford, Conn., Mar. 12, 1956; m. Carol Clark, July 25, 1987; children: Andrew Clark, Paul Clark. BS, MS, Yale U., 1978; MD, Harvard U., 1983. Diplomate Am Bd Radiation Oncology. Instr. Harvard Med. Sch., Boston, 1988-89, asst. prof. radiation oncology, 1989-93; dep. div. chief Children's Hosp., 1990-93; chmn. dept. radiation oncology Cleve. Clinic Found., 1993—. Biomedical consult, Boston, 1989—; prof radiology/radiation oncology Ohio State Univ, 1995—; assoc prof hist med Case Western Res Univ, 1995—. Author: (book) Manual of Introductory Clinical Medicine, 1984; contbr. articles to profl jours. Recipient Resident Research Award, ASTRO, 1988, Jr Faculty Research Award, Am Cancer Soc, 1990. Mem.: Soc Chairs of Acad Radiation Oncology Programs (treas, vpres, pres), Am Soc Therapeutic Radiology and Oncology, Am Soc Clin Oncology (Young Investigator Award 1987), Radiation Research Soc. Achievements include research in research on new approaches to cancer treatment involving radioactively labeled molecules and novel technologies for minimizing medical errors in oncology. Office: Cleve Clinic Found Dept Radiation Oncology 9500 Euclid Ave Cleveland OH 44195-0001 Business E-Mail: macklis@radonc.ccf.org.

MACKNIGHT, CAROL BERNIER, educational administrator; b. Quincy, Mass., Apr. 12, 1938; d. Harold Nelson and Marguerite (Norris) Bernier; m. William J. MacKnight, Aug. 19, 1967. BS, Ithaca Coll., N.Y., 1960; MM, Manhattan Sch. Mus., N.Y.C., 1961; Dipl., Fontainebleau Sch. Music/Art, France, 1963; EdD, U. Mass., 1973. Asst. to supt. Falmouth (Mass.) pub. schs., 1975-76; dir. bus., mgmt., engring. prog. Sch. Bus. Adminstrn. U. Mass., Amherst, 1976-79, assoc. dir. continuing edn., 1979-82, dir. Office Instructional Tech., 1982—. Trustee New Eng. Regional Computer Program, Inc., 1986—92; bd. dirs. Info. Sys. and Bus. Exch., 1992—93; keynote spkr. Australian Soc. for Computers in Learning In Tertiary Edn. Conf., Adelaide, 1996; conf. chair Transforming Practice with Tech., 2002. Editor: Jour. Computing in Higher Edn., 1988—, Jour. Info. Sys. for Mgrs., 1992—93; mem. editl. rev. bd.: Jour. of Computer-Based Instrn., 1988—2002, author/editor: computer progs.; contbr. articles to profl. jours. CDC grantee, 1986, Regents of Boston grantee, 1988, Lilly Fellow Mentor, 1991-92. Mem. ACM, Assn. for Computing Machinery, Educom, bd. dirs. Soc. Applied Learning Tech., New England Regional Computer Program. Avocations: music, photography, tennis, hiking, skiing. Office: Norris Consulting and Pub PO Box 2593 Amherst MA 01004

MACKNIGHT, DAVID LAURENCE, dentist; b. Cin., May 24, 1947; s. Clifford Charles and Lucille W. MacKnight; children: Andrea Steiner, Eric Thomas. BS cum laude, Ohio U., 1970; DDS summa cum laude, Ohio State U., 1974. Clin. instr. dentistry Ohio State U., 1974; resident in gen. dentistry Denver Gen. Hosp., 1974-75; gen. practice dentistry Cin., 1976—. Internat. author and lectr. on dental practice and personal mgmt. Fellow Acad. Gen. Dentistry; mem. ADA, Am. Acad. Oral Medicine, Ohio Dental Assn., Cin. Dental Soc. Avocation: skiing, guitar, woodworking, tennis, photography. Home: 7726 Twelve Oaks Dr Cincinnati OH 45255-4317 Office: 473 Cininnati Batavia Pike Cincinnati OH 45244

MACKNIGHT, WILLIAM JOHN, chemist, educator; b. N.Y.C., May 5, 1936; s. William John and Margaret Ann (Stuart) M.; m. Carol Marie Bernier, Aug. 19, 1967 BS, Rochester U., N.Y., 1958; MA, Princeton U., N.J., 1963, PhD, 1964. Research assoc. Princeton U., N.J., 1964-65; asst. prof. chemistry U. Mass., Amherst, 1965-69, assoc. prof. chemistry, 1969-74, prof. chemistry, 1974-76, dept. head polymer sci., 1976-85, prof. polymer sci. and engring., 1985-88, 95-96, head dept. polymer sci. & engring., 1988-95, disting. univ. prof., 1996-98, Wilmer D. Barret disting. prof., 1998-99, Wilmer D. Barret Disting. prof. emeritus, 1999—. Mem. sci. and tech. adv. bd. Alcoa, Pitts., 1984-86, Diversitech Gen., Akron, Ohio, 1985-89; mem. panel for materials sci. Nat. Bur. Standards, Washington, 1983-89. Author: Polymeric Sulfur and Related Polymers, 1965; Introduction to Polymer Viscoelasticity, 2d edit., 1983 Served to lt. USN, 1958-61 Recipient Ford prize in high polymer physics Am. Phys. Soc., 1984, award for disting. svc. in the advancement of polymer sci. Japan Soc. for Polymer Sci., 1998; Guggenheim fellow, 1985 Fellow: AAAS, Am. Phys. Soc. (exec. com. 1975—76); mem.: Am. Chem. Soc. (award in polymer chemistry 1997, Herman F. Mark award polymers chemistry divsn. 2002), Nat. Acad. Engring., Cosmos Club. Avocations: music, sports. Home: 127 Sunset Ave Amherst MA 01002-2019 Office: U Mass Polymer Sci & Engring Dept Conte Bldg Amherst MA 01003 E-mail: wmacknight@polysci.umass.edu.

MACKO, DAVID, retired bank adjustor; b. Cleve., Apr. 20, 1942; s. Michael and Anna (Ratica) M. BA, Adelbert Coll. (now Western Res. Case Western Res.), 1964. Author: (pamphlet) The Plot to Abolish Marriage, 1982. Candidate for state rep. Am. Party, Cuyahoga County, Ohio, 1972; treas. Am. Party of Cuyahoga County, 1974-77; treas. Am. Party of Ohio, 1977-80; sec. Libertarian Party of Ohio, 1989-92, N.E. Ohio regional rep., 1988—. With U.S. Army, 1966-68. Mem. The John Birch Soc. (life), Am. Legion. Russian Orthodox. Avocations: vacations to battlefields and historic sites, reading, chess, movies. Home: 28810 Cannon Rd Solon OH 44139

MACKO, JOHN, lawyer, farmer; b. Franklin, N.J., Apr. 2, 1947; s. John S. and Dorothy (Kruppa) M.; m. Anna Elin Kjartansson, July 12, 1975; 1 child, John H. BSEE, BS in Mgmt., MIT, 1965-70, MS in Mgmt., 1970; MS in Acctg., JD summa cum laude, Syracuse U., 1978. Bar: N.Y. 1979, Fla. 1979, D.C. 1980. Fin. analyst Xerox Corp., Rochester, N.Y., 1970-72, mkt. planning mgr., 1972-74, fin. mgr., 1974-76; assoc. Harris, Beach, Wilcox, Rubin & Levey, Rochester, 1978-82; ptnr. Githler, Samloff, 1982-86, Githler, Samloff, Macko & Githler, Rochester, 1986-87; mng. ptnr. Githler, Macko, Reichert & Clawson, 1987-91; owner Barrister Farms, Geneseo, N.Y., 1983—, Macko Apartments, Rochester, 1972—; pvt. practice, 1992—. Vice-pres., treas bd. Southeast Area Coalition, Rochester, 1978-82; treas. bd. Rochester Housing Coun., 1978-82; chmn. Rochester Sch. Budget Com., 1981, 12th Ward Rep. Com.; scoutmaster Troop 70 and 75 Boy Scouts Am., Geneseo, N.Y., 1991-97, commr. Iroquois Trail Coun., 1997—. Mem. Jaycees (chmn. Xerox chpt.), Order of Coif, Law Rev., Justinian Soc., MIT Club, Beta Alpha Psi. Home: 42 Second St Geneseo NY 14454-1223 Office: 42 2nd St Geneseo NY 14454-1223

MACKOWSKI, JOHN JOSEPH, retired insurance company executive; b. Westport, Mass., Feb. 1, 1926; s. John J. and Victoria K. (Skript) Mieczkowski; m. Ruth Williams, Feb. 3, 1951; children: Martha, John Matthew, Daniel, Joan. AB, Duke U., 1948; student, Harvard Advanced Mgmt. Program, 1970, 71. With Ins. Co. of N.Am., Boston, Phila., Chgo., 1948-51; with Atlantic Mut. Ins. Co., N.Y.C., 1951-88, chmn., CEO, to 1988. Bd. dirs. Transatlantic Holdings, Inc. 1st lt. USMCR, 1943-46. Mem. Sawgrass Club (Ponte Vedra Beach, Fla.), Acoaxet Country Club (Westport Harbor, Mass.), Spindle Rock Yacht Club, Sigma Chi, Beta Lambda. Episcopalian. Home: 1506 Birkdale Ln Ponte Vedra Beach FL 32082-3500 also: 33 Widgeon Ln Little Compton RI 02837-1960 E-mail: jmackowski@aol.com.

MACLACHLAN, DOUGLAS LEE, marketing educator; b. Hollywood, Calif., Aug. 27, 1940; s. Alexander D. and Patricia E. (Culver) MacL.; m. Natalie Bowditch Knauth, July 23, 1966; children: Heather Bowditch, Trevor Douglas. AB in Physics, U. Calif., Berkeley, 1962, MBA, 1965, MA in Stats., 1970, PhD in Bus. Adminstrn, 1971; student, Hastings Sch. Law, 1965-66. Instr. bus. adminstrn. U. Calif., Berkeley, 1969-70; v.p. Hartec Corp., Newport Beach, Calif., 1965-70; acting asst. prof. U. Wash., Seattle, 1970-71, asst. prof., 1971-74, asso. prof., 1974-78, prof., chmn. dept. mktg. and internat. bus., 1978-86, prof., acting chair dept. mktg. and internat. bus., 1993-94, Affiliate Program Disting. prof. mktg. and internat. bus., 1986-88, Nordstrom prof. retail mktg., 1988-89, Ford Motor Co. prof. mktg., 1989-90, assoc. dean Sch. Bus., 1995-99. Vis. prof. bus. adminstrn. U. Calif., Berkeley, 1974; vis. prof. Institut Europeen des Affaires, Fontainebleau, France, 1982—83, Cath. U. Leuven, Belgium, 1991—92, Koc U., Istanbul, 2001; dir. Univ. Book Store, 1985—2002. Contbr. articles profl. jours.; editorial bd.: Jour. Mktg. Research, 1975-81. Mem. Am. Mktg. Assn. (dir. Puget Sound chpt. 1975-77, 90-91, pres. 1978-79), Informs, Am. Statis. Assn., Decision Scis. Inst., Assn. Consumer Research, Clan MacLachlan Soc. (pres. n.w. br. 1995—), Alpha Kappa Psi, Kappa Delta Rho. Home: 16305 Inglewood Rd NE Kenmore WA 98028-3908 Office: U Washington Box 353200 Seattle WA 98195-3200 E-mail: macl@u.washington.edu.

MACLACHLAN, GORDON ALISTAIR, biology educator, researcher; b. Saskatoon, Sask., Can., June 30, 1930; s. Hector Ross and Nellie (Glass) M.; m. Sarah Dangerfield, June 26, 1959; children: Mary, Anna. BA, U. Sask., 1952, MA, 1954; PhD, U. Man., 1956. NRC postdoctoral fellow Imperial

WHO'S WHO IN AMERICA

Coll., London, 1956-59; asst. prof. U. Alta., Edmonton, 1960-62; assoc. prof biology McGill U., Montreal, 1962-69, prof., 1970-98, emeritus prof., 1998 chmn. dept., 1970-75, 95, dean. grad. studies, vice prin. rsch., 198 Commonwealth prof. Australia, 1975 Home: #2104 1088 Quebec St ver BC Canada V6A 4H2 E-mail: gmaclachlan@shaw.ca. ...62; ...tt Jr. ...mpton, ...t Time, ...n, Stars,

MACLACHLAN, PATRICIA, author; b. Cheyenne, Wyo., ... Binegar, Philo and Madonna (Moss) Pritzkau; m. Robert MacLach... Seven Kisses children: John, Jamie, Emily. BA, U. Conn., 1962. Tc... Book award High Sch., Manchester, Conn., 1963-79. Vis. lectr. ... Scott O'Dell Mass., 1986—. Author: The Sick Day, 1979, Arth... Jefferson Cup 1980 (Golden Kite award Soc. Children's Bo... State Children's Frogs, and Friends, 1980, Through Grandp... ns of Minna Pratt, 1982, Mama One, Mama Two, 1982, Tom... 988), Three Names, in a Row, 1983, Unclaimed Treasures, ... 1993, Skylark, 1994, 1984), Sarah, Plain and Tall, 1985 ...ah Plain and Tall, 1988, Historical Fiction award 1985, ... Aid Family Svc. Agency, award Va. Libr. Assn. 1986, C...n's fiction. Office: Curts Book award N.J. Libr. Ass... New York NY 10003-6935* 1988 (Parent's Choice ... 1991, Journey, 1991 ... What You Know ... Skylark, 1992 ... 1970-80. R... Brown ...

...acturing corporation executive, ... Sergeant and Theadora Beidler ... Carolyn. AB in Econs., Miami U., ... Inc., Cleve., 1967—; founder, chmn. ...-78; founder, pres., chmn. bd. Fluid ...der, chmn. bd., pres. T&M Co., Cleve., ...966—; chmn. bd., pres. Sergeant Realty, ...ustries, Cleve., 1975-77, MWL Systems, ...Nat. Sanitation Found., Ann Arbor, Mich., ...Rep. State Cen. Com., 1968-72; bd. dirs. ...0. Served with arty. AUS, 1964-66. Fellow ... mem. Nat. Environ. Health Assn., Am. Pub. ...lution Control Fedn., Cen. Taekwondo Assn. (2d ... Belt Fedn. (black belt instr.), Mercedes Benz Club ... Leadership Soc. (sch. headmaster soc., devel. com. ...ayflower Descendants, Delta Kappa Epsilon (nat. bd. ...pa chpt. 1969—), Mentor Harbor Yachting Club, The ...ion Soc., Union League Club (N.Y.C.), Yale Club ... (N.Y.C.), N.Y. Acad. Scis. Office: Jet Inc 750 Alpha Dr ...43-2167

MAC... ...

..., ROY, business executive, former government official; b. Vancouver, B.C., Can., Oct. 26, 1934; s. Wilbur and Anne (Graham) MacL.; m. Alethea Mitchell, June 25, 1959; children: Ian, Vanessa, Malcolm. BA, U. B.C., 1955; MA, U. Cambridge, Eng., 1957; postgrad., Harvard U., 1974; MDiv, U. Toronto, 1991, DCL (hon.), 1996; DHL (hon.), U. North Ala. Fgn. service officer Can. Diplomatic Service, Vietnam, Czechoslovakia, Switzerland, UN, 1957-69; dir. corporate pub. affairs Massey-Ferguson Ltd., Toronto, Ont., 1969-74; chmn., chief exec. officer Ogilvy & Mather, Can., Toronto, 1974-76; chmn. C.B. Media Ltd., 1976-93; mem. Parliament of Can., 1979-84, 88-96, parliamentary sec. to minister energy, mines and resources, 1980-82, minister of state (fin.), 1983-84, minister of nat. revenue, 1984, minister of internat. trade, 1993-96; high commr. for Can. to U.K. of Gt. Britain and No. Ireland, 1996-2000. Dir. Standard Life, 2000—, Brascan, 2000—, Can. Tire, 2000—, Patheon Algonna Ctrl., 2000—. Author: Canadians in Russia, 1918-19, 1976, Canadians on the Nile, 1882-1898, 1978, Canadians Behind Enemy Lines, 1939-1945, 1981, Honourable Mentions, 1986, African Exploits: The Diaries of William Stairs, 1998; contbr. articles to jours. Hon. col. 7th Toronto Regt., Royal Can. Arty. Fellow: Royal Soc. Arts; mem.: White's and Pratt's and Athenaeum (London), Rideau Club (Ottawa), Toronto Club, Royal Can. Yacht Club. Address: 425 Russell Hill Rd Toronto Canada M5P 2S4

MACLAREN, WILLIAM GEORGE, JR. engineering executive; b. Chgo., May 6, 1928; s. William George Sr. and Dorothy Pauline (Costello) MacL.; m. Marie Lorraine Logan, Sept. 15, 1951 (div. Dec. 1977); children: Vanessa Ann MacLaren-Wray, Jon Mark, Scott William; m. Mary Patricia Loftus, Dec. 22, 1977 (div. Oct. 1995); m. Brigitte Hildegard Krakau, Apr. 19, 1997. BS in Indsl. Engring., U. Pitts., 1951; MS in Indsl. Engring., Syracuse U., 1958; PhD in Indsl. Mgmt., Columbia Pacific U., 1989. Commd. 2nd lt. USAF, 1951, advanced through grades to major gen., 1974; comdr. 5BW Minot AFB, N.D., 1972-74; chief of staff 15 AF, 1975; comdr. Pacific Comm. Area, 1975-78; vice comdr. Air Force Comm. Command, 1978-79; dir. Command Control and Comm. Hdqs. USAF, 1979-81; dir. Comm. and Info. Sys. NATO, 1981-84; ret. USAF, 1984; v.p. Gia, Inc., Arlington, Va., 1984-90, 93-95; dir. gen. NATO/NATO Air Command and Control Mgmt. Agy., Brussels, 1990-93; v.p. BEI, Inc., Alexandria, Va., 1995—. Contbr. articles to profl. jours. Regional bd. dirs. Boy Scout Am., Minot, N.D., 1972-74. Named Disting. Engring. Alumnus U. Pitts., 1986. Mem. AIAA, Inst. Indsl. Engrs., Air Force Assn., Armed Forces Comm. and Electronics Assn. (regional v.p. 1975-78, Gold medal 1983), Am. Def. Preparedness Assn., Order of Daedalians (chpt. pres. 1976-78, merit award 1979), Rotary. Republican. Avocations: golf, long distance bicycling, private flying. Home: 438 N Park Dr Arlington VA 22203-2344 Office: SAIC 1800 Diagonal Rd Ste 510 Alexandria VA 22314-2840

MACLAUCHLIN, ROBERT KERWIN, communications artist, educator; b. Framingham, Mass., Oct. 8, 1931; s. Charles Lewis and Elinor Frances (Kerwin) MacL.; m. Elizabeth D'Ann Willson, June 13, 1964. BA in Sociology, U. Mass., Amherst, 1954; MEd, Bridgewater State Coll., 1958; MS in Radio and TV, Syracuse U., 1959; PhD in Speech, Radio, TV, Mich. State U., 1969. Personnel trainee Nat. Security Agy., Washington, 1954-55; elem. sch. tchr. Mattapoisett (Mass.) Pub. Schs., 1957-58; asst. prof., dir. programming Maine Ednl. TV Network, Orono, 1959-66; assoc. prof. speech communications, dir. TV-Radio instrn. Colo. State U., Ft. Collins, 1969-76, prof., dir. TV-Radio instrn., 1976-98, prof. emeritus, 1998—. Cons. U. Maine, Orono, 1968, Ft. Collins Presbyn. Ch., 1976-78, Sta. KCOL-AM-FM Ft. Collins, 1978, Pub. Health Assn., Ft. Collins, 1985; archives program guest Maine Pub. Broadcast, Orono, 1983; adv. team NASA, 2000; invited lectr. Met. State Coll., Denver, 2001, Metro State Coll., Denver, 2001, 02. Festival luncheon spkr. dist. convention Rotary Club, 1998; layman's Sunday spkr. First Presbyn. Ch., Ft. Collins, 2002. Served with inf. U.S. Army, 1955-57. Recipient Excellence in Teaching award Mich. State U., 1969, Friend of Broadcasting award Colo. Broadcasters Assn., 1985, Resolution award Colo. Broadcasters Assn., 1997, Oliver P. Pennock Disting. Svc. award Colo. State U., 1997; named Disting. Vis. Prof. U. Vt., Burlington, 1983, A Teacher Who Makes A Difference Denver's Rocky Mountain News, KCNC-TV, 1987; endowed scholarship named in his honor, Colo. State U., 2000. Mem. NATA (panel Colo. chpt. 1989—), Broadcast Edn. Assn. (Industry State chmn. 1981-86, panel 1991—, chmn. faculty internship com. 1991—), Colo. Broadcasters Assn. (edn. com. 1972—, Hall of Fame com. 1980—, human resources com. 1991, Friend of Broadcast award 1985, panelist summer conv. 1994, panelist summer conv. 1995), Broadcast Pioneers (charter mem. Colo. chpt.), Kiwanis (Disting. past pres. 1979-80, Legion of Honor award 2000). Republican. Avocations: outdoor activities. Home: 1407 Country Club Rd Fort Collins CO 80524-1907 E-mail: bobmacl@lamar.colostate.edu. *Personal philosophy: Set high goals, enjoy people and laughter, and always seek to give back more to society than you take from it.*

MACLAURY, ROBERT E(THAN), language educator; b. Oceanside, Calif., May 24, 1944; s. Richard Joyce and Margaret Christensen MacLaury; m. Maria Isabel MacLaury. BA, U. of the Ams., Mexico City, 1967, MA, 1970; PhD, U. Calif., Berkeley, 1986. Vis. prof. U. Ariz., Tucson, 1988—90, U. Regina, Canada, 1993, George Washington U., Washington, 1993—95; de Carle lectr. U. Otago, Dunedin, New Zealand, 1998. Author: (book) Color and Cognition in Mesoamerica, 1997; co-editor: (book anthology) Language and the Cognitive Construal of the World, 1995; editor: (spl. jour. issue) Vantage Theory, 2002. Fellow Fulbright fellow, 1978, Wenner Gren fellow, 1990. Achievements include research in Mesoamerican color survey; Zopotec language description; vantage theory. Avocation: hiking.

MACLAY, DONALD MERLE, retired lawyer; b. Belleville, Pa., Feb. 16, 1934; s. Robert Barr and Grace Virginia (Royer) M.; m. Nancy Margaret Hixenbaugh, Sept. 13, 1958; children: Susan Jo (dec.), Timothy Dean. AB magna cum laude, Grove City Coll., 1956; LLB, U. Pa., 1961. Bar: D.C. 1968, Pa. 1970. Commd. fgn. svc. officer U.S. Dept. State, 1961; assigned Am. embassy, Cotonou, Dahomey (Benin), 1962-64, Am. Consulate Gen., Frankfurt, Fed. Republic Germany, 1964-66, U.S. Dept. State, Washington, 1966-69; dir. courses of study Am. Law Inst.-ABA Com. on Continuing Profl. Edn., Phila., 1969-87, dep. exec. dir., 1987-99, ret., 1999. Served with U.S. Army, 1956-58. Mem. Am. Law Inst. Democrat. Presbyterian. Home: 936 Church Rd Springfield PA 19064-3935

MACLEAN, BABCOCK, lawyer; b. N.Y.C., Jan. 26, 1946; s. Charles Chalmers and Lee Selden (Howe) MacL.; m. Cynthia Gannon, Feb. 15, 1983. BA, Yale U., 1967; MA, Columbia U., 1970; JD, Case Western Res. U., 1975; LLM in Taxation, NYU, 1987. Bar: Ohio 1975, N.Y. 1983. Assoc. Hadley, Matia, Mills & MacLean, Cleve., 1976-77, mem., 1977-83; tax editor Rsch. Inst. Am., N.Y.C., 1983-85; assoc. Robinson Brog, 1985-86, mem., 1987—. Adj. asst. prof. taxation Pace U., N.Y.C., 1983-84; adv. bd. Rsch. Inst. Am., 1992-97. Mem. ABA (sect. taxation), N.Y. State Bar Assn. (sect. taxation), Assn. Bar City N.Y., Yale Club, St. Anthony Club, N.Y. Yacht Club, Seawanhaka Corinthian Yacht Club, St. Andrew's Soc. N.Y., Pilgrims of the U.S. Republican. Episcopalian. Home: 77 W 55th St New York NY 10019-4910 Office: Robinson Brog 1345 Avenue Of The Americas New York NY 10105-0144

MACLEAN, BARBARA HUTMACHER, author, retired journalist, writer; b. Toledo, Dec. 16, 1926; d. Norman Eugene and Betty Lucille Price; div. 1971; m. E. Fraser MacLean, Aug. 30, 1977; children: Beth, Jessica, Cary, David, Clay. Student, Rockford Coll., 1945, Western Mich. Coll., 1946. Reporter News-Leader, Richmond, Va., 1962; editor-writer News-Chronicle, Thousand Oaks, Calif., 1963-70, Star-Free Press, Ventura, 1971-75, Daily Dispatch, East London, South Africa, 1974-78, Wenatchee (Wash.) World, 1980-92, ret., 1992. Exchange journalist The Examiner, Huddersfield, Eng., 1983, China Daily, Beijing, 1988, The Times, Windhoek, Namibia, 1991. Author: In Black and White: Voices of Apartheid, 1980 (Eng.), 1983, I Can't Do What? Voices of Pathfinding Women, 1997. Named Woman of Achievement AAUW, 1997; recipient Nat. Headliners award, 1968, 1st Social Issues Reporting award Soc. of Profl. Journalists, 1989. Home: 40 Hemlock Ct Port Townsend WA 98368-9446

MACLEAN, DAVID BAILEY, chemistry educator, researcher; b. Summerside, P.E.I., Can., July 15, 1923; s. William and Lulu Adelaide (Stewart) McL.; m. Helen Shirley Canning, Dec. 28, 1945 (dec. 1950); 1 child, Susan; m. Regina Lane, Sept. 21, 1951; children— David, Richard, Robert, Gillian, stepchildren— Gary Hutton, Dariel Hutton B.Sc., Acadia U., 1942; PhD, McGill U., 1946. Research chemist Dominion Rubber Co., Guelph, Ont., Can., 1946-49; assoc. prof. chemistry N.S. Tech. Coll., Halifax, Can., 1949-54, McMaster U., Hamilton, Ont., 1954-60, prof., 1960-89, prof. emeritus, 1989—. Mem. Council of Ont. Univs., Toronto, 1982-84 Fellow Royal Soc. Can., Chem. Inst. Can.; mem. Am. Chem. Soc., Am. Soc. Mass Spectroscopy Home: 394 Queen St S Hamilton ON Canada L8P 3T9 Office: McMaster U Dept Chemistry Main St W Hamilton ON Canada L8S 4M1 E-mail: david.maclean@sympatico.ca.

MACLEAN, IAIN STEWART, religion educator; b. Bellville, South Africa, Jan. 6, 1956; s. William Mathie and Elizabeth Sutherland (Symes) MacL.; m. Jennifer Kay Berenson, Nov. 16, 1991; children: Rachel Meghan, Duncan Berenson. BA, U. Cape Town, S. Africa, 1976; BD, Rhodes U., Grahamstown, S. Africa, 1980; BA with honors, U. S.Africa, Pretoria, 1981; ThM, Princeton Theol. Seminary, 1985; ThB with honors, U. S.Africa, 1986; ThD, Harvard U., 1996. Ordained Presbytery of Cape Town, Presbyn. Ch. of So. Africa. Chaplain Presbyn. Ch. of So. Africa, Namibia, 1979-81, min. Heidelberg, 1981-84; youth min. 1st Parish in Lincoln, Mass., 1985-87; religious edn. dir. 1st Congregational Ch., W. Boylston, 1987-90; tchg. fellow Harvard U., Cambridge, 1987-95; supply min. Allston (Mass.) Congregational Ch., 1992-95; min.-at-large Presbytery of the Peaks (Presbyn. Ch. USA), 1996—. Vis. asst. prof. religion and philosophy Roanoke Coll., Salem, Va., 1995—97, Washington and Lee U., Lexington, Va., 1997—98; asst. prof. western religious thought, philosophy and religion dept. James Madison U., Harrisonburg, Va., 1998—2001, assoc. prof., , 2001—. Translator: Reformed Reader Vol. 1, 1993, Opting for Democracy: Liberation Ideology and the Struggle for Democracy in Brazil, 1999, God, Meaning & Morality, 1998; co-editor: Encyclopedia of Religion in American Politics, 1999; editor (assoc.): Encyclopedia of Religion and War; contbr. articles to profl. jours. Recipient medal Internat. Philatelic Exhibit, 1973; writing fellow Bok Teaching Ctr., Harvard U., 1991, teaching award 1993. Mem. Royal Philatelic Soc., Presbytery of Cape Town, Am. Acad. Religion, Mass. Bay Assn. of United Ch. of Christ, Karl Barth Soc. Avocations: philately, book collecting, amateur archaeology, geology. Home: 1013 Barrens Village Ct Roanoke VA 24019-2344 E-mail: macleaix@jmu.edu. *Human beings are called to responsible living and (re) creating of life. This will involve struggle and conflict, but its reward will be in a life well lived for others.*

MACLEAN, JUDITH E. writer, editor; b. L.A., May 13, 1946; d. Fred M. and Dorothy C. (Schmidt) MacL. BA, Rice U., 1969; postgrad., Duquesne U., 1970-71; postgrad. lang. study, Sorbonne U., 1966. Family therapist Families Together, Pitts., 1974-76; reporter In These Times, Chgo., 1976-77; co-chmn. New Am. Movement, 1977-79; editor Am. Soc. on Aging, San Francisco, 1980-85; freelance writer, editor, 1986—. Instr. U. Calif. Berkeley ext., San Francisco, 1994-95, Support Ctr., San Francisco, 1992-93. Co-author: (book) Women Take Care, 1986; contbr. articles/stories to publs. Newsletter editor: Harvey Milk Lesbian and Gay Dem. Club, San Francisco, 1982-85, polit. action chmn., 1986-87; mem. nat. com. New Am. Movement, Pitts., 1972-76; mem. Nicaragua Solidarity Brigarde, Leon, Nicaragua, 1986. Named Vol. of Yr. Harvey Milk Lesbian and Gay Dem. Club, San Francisco, 1986. Avocations: cross-country skiing, backpacking, mini-triathlons, hiking, sea kayaking.

MAC LEAN, LLOYD DOUGLAS, surgeon; b. Calgary, Alta., Can., June 15, 1924; s. Fred Hugh and Azilda (Trudel) MacL.; m. Eleanor Colle, June 30, 1954; children— Hugh, Charles, Ian, James, Martha. B.Sc. (Viscount Bennett scholar), U. Alta., 1947, MD (Viscount Bennett scholar), 1949; PhD, U. Minn., 1957. Resident U. Minn. Hosp., Mpls., 1950-56; instr. dept. surgery U. Minn., 1956-58, asst. prof. surgery, 1958-59, asso. prof., 1959-62; prof. McGill U., Montreal, Que., Can., 1962—, chmn. dept. surgery Can., 1968-73, 77-82, 87-88. Surgeon-in-chief Ancker Hosp., St. Paul, 1957-62, Royal Victoria Hosp., Montreal, 1962-88; Edward Archibald prof. surgery McGill U., 1988-93, prof. surgery 1993—. Contbr. numerous articles on surgery, shock, host resistance and transplantation to profl. jours. Decorated officer Order Can. Fellow Royal Soc. Can.; mem. Am. Surg. Assn. (pres. 1992-93), A.C.S. (pres. 1993-94), Central Surg. Assn. (pres. 1985), Am. Physiol. Soc., Am. Assn. Thoracic and Cardiovascular Surgery, Soc. Surgery of Alimentary Tract. Home: # 1402-80 Berlioz Montreal QC Canada H3E 1N9 Office: McGill Univ 687 Pine Ave W Montreal QC Canada H3A 1A1 E-mail: lloydm@citenet.net.

MACLEAN, NEIL V. forensic psychologist; b. Bangor, Maine, June 2, 1935; m. Martha Robinson, June 17, 1962; children: Bethany, Christopher. EdD, U. Maine, Orono, 1973. Sr. clin. psychologist Augusta Mental Health Inst., 1973-86; chief forensic psychologist State of Maine, Augusta, 1986-98. Former chmn. State of Maine Bd. Examiners of Psychologists. Fellow Maine Soc. Forensic Psychologists (chmn. 1995-97—); mem. Maine Psychol. Assn. (pres. 1997-98). Avocation, U.S. history re-enactments. Office: 22 Summer St Hallowell ME 04347-1121

MACLEAN, PAUL DONALD, government institute medical research official; b. Phelps, N.Y., May 1, 1913; s. Charles Chalmers and Elizabeth (Dreyfus) MacL.; m. Alison Stokes, July 16, 1942; children— Paul, David, Alexander, James, Alison. BA, Yale U., 1935; postgrad., U. Edinburgh, Scotland, 1935-36; MD cum laude, Yale U., 1940; DSci (hon.), SUNY, Binghamton, 1986. Intern in medicine Johns Hopkins U., 1940-41; asst. resident medicine New Haven Hosp., Yale Sch. Medicine, 1941-42, research asst. pathology, 1942, asst. prof. physiology, 1949-51, asst. prof. psychiatry, physiology and neurology, 1951-53, assoc. prof. physiology, 1956-57; clin. instr. medicine U. Wash. Med. Sch., Seattle, 1946-47; USPHS research fellow Harvard U. Med. Sch., also Mass. Gen. Hosp., 1947-49; dir. EEG lab. New Haven Hosp., 1951-52; assoc. prof. psychiatry, physiology and neurology, attending physician Grace-New Haven Hosp., 1953-56; sr. postdoctoral fellow NSF dept. physiology U. Zurich, 1956-57; chief sect. limbic integration and behavior Lab. Neurophysiology Intramural Research, NIMH, USPHS, Dept. Health and Human Services, Bethesda, Md., 1957-71; chief lab. brain evolution and behavior Intramural Research, 1971-85; sr. research scientist Intramural Research Program, NIMH, 1985—. Author: The Triune Brain in Evolution, 1990; mem. editorial bd.: Jour. Nervous and Mental Disease. Emeritus trustee L.S.B. Leakey Found. Served to maj. M.C. AUS, 1942-46, PTO. Recipient award for disting. research Assn. for Research in Nervous and Mental Disease, 1964; Salmon medal and Lectureship award, 1966; Superior Service award HEW, 1967; Hincks Meml. lectr. Ont.; Spl. award Am. Psychopathol. Assn., 1971; G. Burroughs Mider NIH Lectureship award, 1972; Karl Spencer Lashley award Am. Philos. Soc., 1972; Adolph Meyer Lectureship award Am. Psychiat. Assn., 1982, Anokhin medal P.K. Anokhin Inst. Normal Physiology USSR Acad. Med. Scis., 1986; hon. Fulton fellow Yale U. Med. Sch., 1990. Mem. Am. Neurol. Assn., Am. Physiol. Soc., Am. Assn. Electroencephalographers, Am. Assn. Neurol. Surgeons, Soc. Neurosci., Am. Assn. Anatomists, Sigma Xi, Alpha Omega Alpha. Home: 10450 Lottsford Rd Apt 1218 Mitchellville MD 20721-2746 Office: NIMH Intramural Rsch Prog 9000 Rockville Pike Bethesda MD 20892-0001

MACLEAN, STEVE(N) G. astronaut; b. Ottawa, Ont., Can., Dec. 14, 1954; m. Nadine Wielgopolski; 3 children. BS in Physics with honors, York U., Toronto, Ont., 1977, PhD, 1983. Sports adminstr., pub. rels. York U., Toronto, 1974—76; mem. Can. Nat. Gymnastics Team, 1976—77; astronaut Can. Space Agy., 1983—88, program mgr. advanced space vision sys., 1987—93, astronaut advisor to strategic techs. in automation and robotics program, 1988—91, program mgr. orbiter space vision sys., sci. advisor to internat. space sta., 1993—94; acting dir.-gen. Can. Astronaut Program, 1994—96; astronaut NASA, Johnson Space Ctr., Houston, 1996—. Adj. instr. York U., Toronto, 1980—83; adj. prof. Inst. Aerospace Studies U. Toronto, 1993. Achievements include research in electro-optics, laser-induced fluorescence of particles and crystals and multi-photon laser spectroscopy. Avocations: hiking, canoeing, flying, parachuting, gymnastics. Office: Astronaut Office/CB NASA Johnson Space Ctr Houston TX 77058*

MACLEAN, WALTER MARCUS, engineering educator, retired; s. Donald Marcus and Zelpha Eleanor (Young) Maclean; m. Doris Hansen, June 19, 1954; children: Walter II, Pamela. BSME, U. Calif., Berkeley, 1956, M in Engr. Naval Arch., 1957, D in Engr. Naval Arch., 1967. Registered profl. engr., Calif. Engr. Morris Guralnick Assn., San Francisco, 1955-59, Inst. Engring. Rsch., Berkeley, 1959-65; prof. Webb Inst. Naval Arch., Glen Cove, N.Y., 1965-72, U.S. Merchant Marine Acad., Kings Point, 1972-75, 87-95, prof. emeritus, 1995—; mgr. Nat. Maritime Rsch. Ctr., 1975-87. Contbr. articles to profl. jours., meetings and symposiums. Fellow ASME, Soc. Naval Arch. & Marine Engrs. (various tech. com. 1960—); mem. Am. Soc. Naval Engrs., N.Y. Acad. Scis., Sigma Xi. Republican. Protestant. Avocations: small boat sailing, travelling. Home: 24 Harbor Way Sea Cliff NY 11579-2114 Office: US Merchant Marine Acad Steamboat Rd Kings Point NY 11024-1699 E-mail: macleanwalter@aol.com.

MACLEISH, ARCHIBALD BRUCE, museum administrator; b. White Plains, N.Y., May 6, 1947; s. Kenneth and Carolyn Elizabeth (de Chadenedes) MacL.; m. Patricia Ann McCue, Aug. 10, 1974; children: Kenneth Thomas, Padraic Andrew. BA, Johns Hopkins U., 1969; MA, SUNY, Oneonta, 1972. Asst. curator N.Y. State Hist. Assn., The Farmers' Mus., Cooperstown, 1972-73; assoc. curator N.Y. State Hist. Assn., 1980-83, curator of collections, 1984-93, dir. collections, 1993-99; curator of collections The Farmers' Mus., 1984-93, dir. collections, 1993-99; curator The Ky. Mus., Bowling Green, 1973-80; collections mgr. Newport Restoration Found., 1999—. Mem. adj. tchg. faculty Cooperstown Grad. Program, 1980-99. Author: Care of Antiques and Historical Collections, 1985; editor K.A.M. News, 1975-80. Former bd. dirs. Gallery 53, Cooperstown, Hanford Mills Mus.; mem. Ad Hoc Citizen's Com., Cooperstown, 1987-99. Mem. Am. Assn. Mus., Am. Assn. for State and Local History, Am. Inst. Conservation, Cooperstown Grad. Assn., New England Mus. Assn. Democrat. Avocations: road running, gardening, guitar, fishing, cross-country skiing. Office: Newport Restoration Found 51 Touro St Newport RI 02840-2932 E-mail: BMacNRF@aol.com.

MACLEISH, RODERICK, novelist, screenwriter, television producer; b. Bryn Mawr, Pa., Jan. 15, 1926; s. Norman Hillard and Lenore (McCall) MacL.; m. Diana S. Chapin, May 1, 1950 (div. June 1971); children: Cynthia Sumner, Roderick Jr. Student, U. Chgo., 1944-45; DHL (hon.), Washington-Jefferson Coll., 1958. Copy boy, TV script editor ABC, N.Y.C., 1945-51; news dir. WBZ-Westinghouse Broadcasting Co., Boston, 1951-57; Washington bur. chief Westinghouse Broadcasting Co., 1957-59, chief fgn. corr., 1959-66, sr. commentator Washington, 1966-71; commentator CBS, 1971-76, NPR, Washington, 1976-90; commentator, TV prodr. Monitor Radio-TV, 1990-97; ret., 1997. Writer, narrator (PBS 3-hr. spl.) The Hermitage, 1994-95; author: The First Book of Eppe, 1985, Prince Ombra, 1987, Crossing At Ivalo, 1989. Pres. Assn. Am. Corrs. in London, 1964. Mem. Cosmos Club (Washington). Episcopalian. Home: 4000 Cathedral Ave NW Washington DC 20016-5249

MACLENNAN, BERYCE WINIFRED, psychologist; b. Aberdeen, Scotland, Mar. 14, 1920; came to U.S., 1949, naturalized, 1965; d. William and Beatrice (MacCrae) Mellis; m. John Duncan MacLennan, Nov. 29, 1944. BSc with honors, London Sch. Econs., 1947; PhD, London U., 1960. Diplomate Am. Bd. Clin. Psychology; cert. group therapist, trauma specialist. Group psychotherapist, youth specialist cons., N.Y.C. and Washington, 1949-63; dir. Ctr. for Prevention Juvenile Delinquency and New Careers, Washington, 1963-66; sect. chief NIMH, Mental Health Study Ctr., Adelphi, Md., 1967-70, chief, 1971-74; regional adminstr. Mass. Dept. Mental Health, Springfield, 1974-75; sr. mental health adv. GAO, Washington, 1976-90; pvt. practice, specialist psychotherapy Bethesda, Md., 1990—. Clin. prof. George Washington U., 1970—; group therapy cons. D.C. Mental Health Svcs., 1993—, Washington Assessement and Therapy Svcs., 1992—; lectr. Montgomery C.C., 1988-91, Washington Sch. Psychiatry Geropsychiatric Program, 1997—; mem. tech. adv. com. Prince George's County Mental Health Assn., 1968-84; cons. Washington Bus. Group on Health, 1990-91, KOBA, 1991; mem. Trauma Psychotherapy Groups, 2002, Hebrew Home Rsch. Inst. Elder Housing Socialization and Memory Improvement Groups, 2000-2002. Mem. NIMH Prevention Intervention Rsch. Task Force, 1990-91, Montgomery County Victims Assistance Programs, 1990-95; v.p. Compliance, Federally Employed Women, 1979-81; pres. Glenecho chpt. Older Women's League, 1993-94. Fellow APA, Am. Orthopsychiat. Assn.; disting. fellow Am. Group Psychotherapy Assn.; mem. Washington Mushroom Club. Democrat.

MACLENNAN, DAVID HERMAN, research scientist, educator; b. Swan River, Man., Can., July 3, 1937; s. Douglas Henry and Sigridur (Sigurdson) MacL.; m. Linda Carol Vass, Aug. 18, 1965; children: Jessica Lynn (dec.), Jeremy Douglas, Jonathan David. BSA, U. Man., 1959; MS, Purdue U., 1961, PhD, 1963; DSc (hon.), U. Man., 2001. Postdoctoral fellow Inst. Enzyme Research, U. Wis., Madison, 1963-64; asst. prof. U. Wis., 1964-68; assoc. prof. U. Toronto, 1969-74, prof., 1974-93, J.W. Billes prof. med. rsch., 1987—, Univ. prof., 1993—, acting chmn., 1978-80, chmn., 1980-90; prin. investigator Can. Genetic Diseases Network of Ctrs. of Excellence, 1991—. Mem. med. adv. bd. Muscular Dystrophy Assn. Can., 1976-87; mem. scientists' rev. panel Med. Rsch. Coun. Can., 1988-90; chmn. molecular biology and pathology grants com. Heart and Stroke Found. Can., 1995-99; mem. rsch. rev. panel U. Ottawa Heart Inst., 1991-95; cons. Merck, Sharp and Dohme, West Point, Pa., 1992-98; mem. med. rev. panel Gairdner Found., 1999-2001; mem. med. adv. bd., 2001—. Assoc. editor Can. Jour. Biochemistry, 1972-76; mem. editl. bd. Jour. Biol. Chemistry, 1975-80, 82-87; contbr. articles on muscle membrane biochemistry to profl. jours. Decorated Officer Order of Can.; recipient Gairdner Found. Internat. award, 1991; Can. Med. Rsch. Coun. scholar, 1969-71, I.W. Killam Meml. scholar, 1977-78, I.W. Killam Meml. prize Health Scis., 1997, Jonas Salk award Ont. March of Dimes, 1998. Fellow Royal Soc. Can., Royal Soc. London (Glaxo-Wellcome prize 2000), NAS (fgn. assoc.); mem. Can. Biochem. Soc. (Ayerst award 1974), Am. Soc. Biol. Chemists, Biophys. Soc. (Nat. Lectr. award 1990). Home: 293 Lytton Blvd Toronto ON Canada M5N 1R7 Office: U Toronto-Banting & Best Med Rsch 112 College St Toronto ON Canada M5G 1L6 E-mail: david.maclennan@utoronto.ca.

MACLEOD, ANGUS, internist; b. Romford, Essex, U.K., Apr. 24, 1943; came to U.S., 1967; s. Malcolm Macleod and Jean (Littlefair) McKean; m. Gwynne Louise Grellner, May 23, 1969 (div. Aug. 1987); children: Kenneth, Anne, Stephen. MB, ChB, Glasgow (Scotland) U., 1967. Diplomate Am. Bd. Internal Medicine. Intern Lutheran Hosp., St. Louis, 1967-68; resident in internal medicine St. Louis U., 1969, 71-73, fellow in cardiology, 1973-74; physician Grandel Med. Group, St. Louis, 1974—2000. Instr., then asst. prof. medicine St. Louis U.; chmn. dept. medicine Lutheran Hosp., St. Louis; pres. Grandel Med. Group, St. Louis. Capt. U.S. Army, 1969-71. Decorated Bronze Star. Mem. ACP, Mo. State Med. Soc., St. Louis Met. Med. Soc. E-mail: corvus24@aol.com.

MACLEOD, DONALD MARTIN, corporate professional; b. N.Y.C., May 21, 1929; s. John and Annie Campbell (Martin) MacL.; m. Beverly Ann Thomson, Feb. 16, 1952 (div. Nov. 18, 1979); children: James Donald, Terry Ann; m. Harriet Elaine Hoff, Feb. 17, 1989 (dec. Mar. 1993). BS in Mech. Engring., Rensselaer Poly. Inst., 1951. Engr. IBM Corp., Endicott & Kingston, N.Y., 1951-54; supr. quality control Ronson Corp., East Stroudsburg, Pa., 1954-55; pres. Manco Specialties, Apalachin, N.Y., 1955-58; engring. supr. Link Aviation, Binghamton, 1958-59; sales mgr. Universal Instruments Corp., 1959-61; mktg. mgr. Xerox Corp., Rochester, N.Y., 1961-71; pres. Industry Search Inc., 1971-83; gen. mgr. Consler Sci. Design, Inc., Tampa, Fla., 1983-88; pres. Industry Tech, Oldsmar, 1989—. Home: 110 Lesley Ln Oldsmar FL 34677-2090 Office: Industry Tech 188 Scarlet Blvd Oldsmar FL 34677-3002 E-mail: industrytech@ij.net.

MACLEOD, DONALD WILLIAM, secondary school educator; b. Stornoway, Scotland, Oct. 3, 1935; s. Angus and Mary (MacArthur) MacL.; m. Theresa Plaskon, Aug. 25, 1973; children: Heather Anne, Robert Angus. BS, Fairleigh Dickinson U., 1964; MA, Seton Hall U., 1968, Kean U., 1977. Tchr. English and pub. speaking Hawthorne (N.J.) H.S., 1964-97, head soccer coach, 1977-79, asst. soccer coach, 1988-94, tchr. English and pub. spkg., 1995-98. Adj. prof. comms. Ramapo Coll. of N.J., Mahwah, N.J., 1981-84; tchr. English Englewood (N.J.) Adult H.S., 1987-94; adj. prof. English Ramapo Coll. N.J., 1998. With U.S. Army, 1958-60. Mem. NEA, N.J. Edn. Assn., Hawthorne Tchrs. Assn. (past v.p.). Presbyterian. Avocations: soccer, Scottish Gaelic lang., bagpipe music, jogging.

MACLEOD, GLEN GARY, English language educator; b. Berea, Ohio, Oct. 10, 1948; s. William and Laura (Hall) MacL. BA, Wesleyan U., 1971; MA, Princeton U., 1978, PhD, 1981. From instr. to asst. prof. English Southampton Coll. L.I. Univ., Southampton, N.Y., 1980-83; from asst. prof. to prof. English U. Conn., Waterbury, 1983—. Author: Wallace Stevens and Company, 1983, Wallace Stevens and Modern Art, 1993. NEH fellow, 1983; Huntington Libr. fellow, San Marino, Calif., 1984; Getty fellow, 1987-88. Mem. MLA, AAUP, Am. Lit. Assn., Wallace Stevens Soc., William Carlos Williams Soc. Office: U Conn 32 Hillside Ave Waterbury CT 06710-2217

MACLEOD, GORDON C. surgeon; b. Quincy, Mass., July 12, 1930; AB, Harvard U., 1952, MD, 1956. Diplomate Am. Bd. Surgery. Intern Madigan Army Hosp., Tacoma, 1956-57; resident Brigham-Childrens Hosps., Boston, 1957-59; surg. resident Boston Univ. Hosps., 1959-61; staff surgeon USAF Hosp., Tachi-Kawa AB, Japan, 1961-64, surgeon Westover AFB, Mass., 1964-68, David Grant USAF Med. Ctr., Calif., 1968-74; chmn. surgery USAF Med. Ctr., Scott AFB, Ill., 1974-76; active staff Washington Hosp., Fremont, Calif., 1976—2002, med. dir. oper. rm., 1998-2000. Instr. surgery Boston U., 1960-61; instr. U. Calif., Davis, 1969-71, asst. clin. prof. surgery, 1971-74. Mem. ACS, AMA. E-mail: gcmacleod@attbi.com.

MACLEOD, GORDON KENNETH, physician, educator; b. Boston, Jan. 30, 1929; s. Gordon Kenneth and Margaret J. MacL.; m. Janet B., Aug. 17, 1957; children— Gordon K. III, Alexander B. AB, Blackburn Coll., 1954; MD, U. Cin., 1960. Indsl. engr. Procter & Gamble Co., Cin., 1954-56; intern Boston City Hosp., 1960-61; resident, clin. fellow Mass. Gen. Hosp., Boston, 1961-64; rsch. fellow Harvard U., 1962-64; sr. resident, sr. physician Boston VA hosp., 1964-66; asst. clin. prof. medicine Yale U., 1966-69, assoc. clin. prof. medicine and pub. health, 1969-71; dir. HMO Svc., HEW, 1971-73; prof. dept. health svcs. adminstrn. Grad. Sch. Pub. Health, U. Pitts., 1974—, chmn. dept., 1974-83, assoc. clin. prof. medicine, 1976-86, clin. prof. medicine, 1986—; pres. senate U. Pitts., 1997-98. Sec. health, State of Pa., 1979; academic dean Semester at Sea, 1999, interim dir. MD/MPH program, 2000—; mem. staff W. Penn Hosp.; mem. nat. adv. coun. divsn. rsch. resources NIH, 1983-87; cons. Shadyside Hosp.; cons. in field. Editor: (with Mark Perlman) Health Care Capital: Competition and Control, 1978; contbr. articles to profl. jours. Served with U.S. Army, 1948-49. Ford Found. travel grantee, 1973 Fellow ACP; mem. Allegheny County Med. Soc., AMA (editorial bd. jour. 1989-94), Am. Pub. Health Assn., Med. Adminstrs. Conf., Pa. Pub. Health Assn., Pa. State Med. Soc. (pres.), Pitts. Acad. Medicine. Office: 130 Desoto St Pittsburgh PA 15213-2535 *My first job was an industrial engineer with later training in internal medicine; it uniquely prepared me for an academic career in health management with intervals as a government executive at federal and state levels. My most challenging assignments were in initiating the Health Maintenance Organization program nationally, in managing the health aspects of the nuclear accident at Three Mile Island, and in training young persons for careers in internal medicine and health management.*

MACLEOD, HUGH ANGUS MCINTOSH, optical science educator, physicist, consultant; b. Glasgow, Scotland, June 20, 1933; came to U.S., 1979; s. John and Agnes (Maclure) M.; m. Ann Turner, May 25, 1957; children: Hugh, Ivor, Charles, Eleanor, Alexander. BSc with honors, U. Glasgow, 1954; D of Tech., Coun. for Nat. Acad. Awards, 1979; D honoris causa, U. Aix-Marseille, 1997. Chartered physicist. Grad. apprentice Sperry Gyroscope Co. Ltd., Brentford, Eng., 1954-56, engr., 1956-60; chief engr. Williamson Mfg. Co. Ltd., London, 1961-62; sr. physicist Mervyn Instruments Ltd., Woking, Eng., 1963; tech. mgr. Sir Howard Grubb Parsons & Co. Ltd., Newcastle upon Tyne, 1964-70; reader in thin-film physics Newcastle upon Tyne Poly., 1971-79; assoc. prof. U. Aix-Marseille III, France, 1979; prof. optical scis. U. Ariz., Tucson, 1979-95, prof. emeritus, 1995—; pres. Thin Film Ctr., Inc., 1992—; dir. Precision Optics Corp., Inc., 1997—2002. Author: Thin-Film Optical Filters, 2001; editor Jour. Modern Optics, London, 1988-93; contbr. over 200 articles to profl. jours., chpts. to books. Fellow Inst. Physics (London), Optical Soc. Am. (dir.-at-large 1987-89, Esther Hoffman Beller award 1997), SPIE-Internat. Soc. Optical Engring. (Gold medal 1987), Am. Vacuum Soc., Soc. Vacuum Coaters (Nathaniel H. Sugerman Meml. award 2002), French Vacuum Soc. (John Matteucci award 2000, Internat. Conf. on Vacuum Web Coating). Anglican. Avocation: piano. Home: 2745 E Via Rotunda Tucson AZ 85716-5227 Office: Thin Film Ctr Inc 2745 E Via Rotunda Tucson AZ 85716-5227 E-mail: angus@thinfilmcenter.com.

MACLEOD, JAMES L. minister, finance executive, gallery owner; b. Oakdale, La., Apr. 27, 1937; s. William Lasater and Sara Louise (Macaulay) MacL. BA, Washington and Lee U., 1959; MA, BD, Emory U., 1968; D. Miss. State U., 1972. Minister U.S.-So. Presbyn. Ch., 1963-85, minister assoc. reform synod, 1985—; educator Ga. State Schs., 1972-91; pres. Brunswick (Ga.) Fin., 1991—, Brunswick Gallery, 1993—; min. First Assoc. Reformed Pres. Ch., Augusta, Ga., 1988—99. Author: Great Dr. Waddel, 1985, A Season of Grace, 1974, Presbyterian Tradition in the South, 1978. Mem. Soc. of the Cin., Washington, 1970; councilman City of Brunswick, 1994—, mayor pro tem, 1996—. Scholar Fulbright Commn., Calcutta, India, 1980, NEH, Sarasota, Fla., 1986. Fellow Soc. of Antiquaries Scotland; mem. NEA, Ga. Assn. Edn., Pinnacle Club, Phi Delta Kappa. Democrat. Presbyterian. Office: 304 Singleton Ave Sylvania GA 30467-1847 Home: 304 Singleton Ave Sylvania GA 30467-1847

MACLEOD, JOHN AMEND, lawyer; b. Manila, June 5, 1942; s. Anthony Macaulay and Dorothy Lillian (Amend) M.; m. Ann Klee; children: Kerry, Jack. BBA, U. Notre Dame, 1963, JD, 1969. Bar: D.C. 1969, U.S. Supreme Ct. 1980. Assoc. Jones, Day, Reavis & Pogue, Washington, 1969-73, ptnr., 1974-79, Crowell & Moring, Washington, 1979—. Mem. mgmt. [illegible] 1979-82, 83-86, 91-94, 99-2000, chmn., 1984-85, 93-94. mem. mgmt. bd. [illegible] exec. com., 2000—, chmn. of the firm, 2000—. Editor-in-chief Notre Dame Law Rev., 1968-69; contbr. articles to profl. jours. Trustee Energy Mineral and Law Found., 1979—; bd. dirs. St. Francis Ctr., 1982—91; C&M Internat., 1991—94, 1999—. Served to lt. U.S. Army, 1963—65. Recipient disting. mining lawyer award Nat. Mining Assn., 1995, forest industry victory of yr. award Am. Forest and Paper Assn., 1994. Mem. ABA, D.C. Bar Assn., Notre Dame Law Assn. (dir., exec. bd.), Ptnrs. Leadership Forum, Metro. Club (Washington). Home: 4040 Swartz Rd Maurertown VA 22644-2320 Office: Crowell & Moring 1000 Pennsylvania Ave NW Washington DC 20004-2595

MACLEOD, NORMAJEAN, writer; b. Logansport, Ind., Feb. 27, 1929; d. Norman and Mabel (Clark) Ulery; m. John Charles MacLeod, Sept. 13, 1947; 1 child, Ian. Asst. mgr. Village Theatre, Bloomington, Ind., 1969-71; mgr. Motel 6 Corp., Santa Barbara, Calif., 1972-73; data sys. coord. Ind. U., Bloomington, 1973-90, editor edn. comm., 1990-95. Lectr., workshop dir., 1981-93. Author: Womanclature: The Queen Bee Syndrome, 1984, Poetica Erotica, 1988; pub. in anthologies. Mem. Internat. Women's Writing Guild, Nat. Fed. State Poetry Socs., Ind. State Fedn. Poetry Clubs, United Poets Laureate Internat., Internat. Lawrence Durrell Soc. E-mail: redshadstudia@hotmail.com.

MACLEOD, ROBERT ANGUS, microbiology educator, researcher; b. Athabasca, Alta., Can., July 13, 1921; s. Norman John and Eleonora Pauline Bertha (Westerhoff) MacL.; m. Patricia Rosemarie Robertson, Sept. 1, 1948; children— Douglas John, Alexander Robert, Kathleen Mary, David Gordon, Michael Norman, Susan Joan BA with honors in Chemistry, U. B.C., Vancouver, Can., 1943, MA in Chemistry and Biology, 1945; PhD in Biochemistry, U. Wis., Madison, 1949. Asst. prof. Queen's U., Kingston, Ont., Can., 1949-52; sr. biochemist Fisheries Research Bd. Can., Vancouver, B.C., 1952-60; assoc. prof. to prof., chmn. dept. microbiology Macdonald Coll., McGill U., Ste. Anne de Bellevue, Que., Can., 1960-86, prof. emeritus Can., 1986—. Cons. Def. Research Bd., Ottawa, Ont., 1965-75; assoc. editor Can. Jour. Microbiology, Ottawa, 1965-70 Author tech. papers Recipient Harrison prize Royal Soc. Can., 1960; Can. Soc. Microbiologists award, 1973 Fellow Royal Soc. Can.; mem. Can. Soc. Microbiologists (pres. 1976-77, hon. mem. 1993), Am. Soc. Microbiology (hon. mem. 1992). Avocations: swimming, fishing. Home: 10 Slate St Stittsville ON Canada K2S 1Y5 E-mail: ramacl@sympatico.ca.

MACLEOD, ROBERT FREDRIC, editor, publisher; b. Chgo., Oct. 15, 1917; s. Ernest F. and Martha W. (Ruzicka) MacL.; children— Merrill, Robert Fredric, E. Jay, Ian. BA, Dartmouth Coll., 1939. Advt. mgr. Town & Country mag., N.Y.C., 1949; v.p., pub. Harper's Bazaar, 1950-55, 55-60; v.p., advt. dir. Hearst Mags., 1960-62; pub. Seventeen mag., 1962-63; v.p., dir. mktg. Subscription TV Inc., Santa Monica, Calif., 1963-64; editor, pub. 'Teen Mag., Los Angeles, 1965—, now editorial dir., exec. pub.; sr. v.p. Petersen Pub. Co., L.A., 1976-95; ret., 1995; pub. cons., 1995—. Served to maj. USMC, 1941-46. Named to Football Hall of Fame, 1977 Mem.: Bel Air Country. Home: 110 Colony Dr Malibu CA 90265

MACLEOD, STUART MAXWELL, health science administrator, educator, pharmacologist, physician; b. Toronto, Ont., Can., June 20, 1943; s. Ellis Maxwell and Irene Constance (Howlett) M.; m. Patricia Ann Marontate, 1967 (div. 1986); children: Andrew, Virginia; m. Helen Nancy McCullough, 1987. BSc, MD, U. Toronto, 1967; PhD, McGill U., 1972. Clinician, scientist Addiction Rsch. Found. Ont., Toronto, 1973-78; sr. scientist Rsch Inst. Hosp. for Sick Children, 1979-86; prof. medicine, pediat., pharmacology, clin. biochemistry U. Toronto, 1984-86; prof. medicine, pediats., clin. epidemiology and biostats. McMaster U., Hamilton, Ont., 1987—, dean faculty health scis., 1987-92; dir. Father Sean O'Sullivan Rsch. Ctr., 1992—, Ctr. for Evaluation of Medicines, 1992-97; v.p. med. affairs Innovus Rsch. Inc., Burlington, Ont., Can., 1996—. Mem. Premier's Coun. on Health Strategy, Ont., 1987-91; chmn. Coun. Ont. Faculties Medicine, Ont., 1989-91; vice chair sci. adv. bd. Health Can., 2000—. Bd. dirs. Ont. Mental Health Found., 1998—. Clin. rsch. scholar Ont. Ministry of Health, 1978-83; recipient sr. investigator award Can. Soc. Clin. Pharmacology, 1987, Disting. Svc. award, 2001. Fellow Royal Coll. Physicians (Can., Edinburgh, Glasgow); mem. European Soc. Devel. Pharmacology Therapy, Am. Soc. for Clin. Pharmacology and Therapeutics, Can. Soc. for Clin. Investigation (pres. 1984-85, Disting. Svc. award 1999), Can. Pharmacol. Soc., Am. Soc. for Pharmacology and Exptl. Therapeutics, Soc. for Pediat. Rsch., Assn. Can. Med. Colls. (exec. com. 1988-91), Alpha Omega Alpha. Office: Innovus Rsch Inc 1016-A Sutton Dr Burlington ON Canada L7L 6B8 Fax: 905-331-9912. E-mail: smacleod@innovus.com.

MACLEOD, WILLIAM BENTLEY, economics and law educator; b. Iserlohn, Germany, 1954; came to U.S., 1995; m. Raisa Nones (div.); children: Raisa, Gabriela; m. Janet Marion Currie, May 18, 1997; children: Joana, Daniel. BA magna cum laude, Queen's U., Kingston, Ont., Can., 1975, MSc in Math., 1979; PhD in Econs., U. B.C., Vancouver, Can., 1984. From asst. prof. to assoc. prof. Queen's U., 1982-90; assoc. prof. U. Montreal, 1990-92, prof. econs., 1992-96, Boston Coll., 1996-97; prof. econs. and law U. So. Calif., L.A., 1997—, dir. Ctr. for Law, Econs. and Orgn., 1997—, chair sr. recruiting, 2000—. Cons. Ind. Power Producers Ont., Toronto, 1990-92, Human Resources Can., Ottawa, Ont., 1993-95; Harold Innis Meml. lectr., 1996; vis. prof. econs. and law Calif. Inst. Tech., 2002. Contbr. articles to profl. jours. NSF grantee, 1997—. Mem. AAAS, Am. Econs. Assn., Econometric Soc., Soc. Labor Economists (H. Gregg Lewis prize 2002), Assn. for Comparative Systems, Econ. Sci. Assn. Office: U So Calif 3620 S Vermont Ave Los Angeles CA 90089-0082

MACLIN, ALAN HALL, lawyer; b. DuQuoin, Ill., Dec. 22, 1949; s. John E. and Nora (Hall) M.; m. Joan Davidson (div. Dec. 1981); children: Molly, Tess, Anne; m. Jeanne Sittlow, Nov. 17, 1984. BA magna cum laude, Vanderbilt U., 1971; JD, U. Chgo., 1974. Bar: Minn. 1974, U.S. Dist. Ct. Minn. 1974, U.S. Ct. Appeals (8th cir.) 1974, U.S. Ct. Appeals (5th cir.) 1975. U.S. Supreme Ct. 1978. Asst. atty. gen. Minn. Atty. Gen., St. Paul, 1974-80; chief anti-trust divsn. Briggs & Morgan, 1980—, mem. bd. dirs., 1993-96. Mem. Minn. State Bar Assn. (treas. anti-trust sect. 1978-80, 96-98, chair 1998—), Ramsey County Bar Assn. (sec. jud. com. 1980-82), Phi Beta Kappa. Unitarian Universalist. Office: Briggs & Morgan 2200 1st St N Saint Paul MN 55109-3210 E-mail: amaclin@briggs.com.

MACLIN, ERNEST, biomedical diagnostics company executive; b. N.Y.C., Jan. 25, 1931; s. Samuel and Dora (Sonsky) M.; m. Edith Samuel, Feb. 18, 1956; children: Alan David, Deborah Ellen, Julie Anne. BME, CCNY, 1952, M Engring., 1969. Registered profl. engr., N.Y., N.J. Engr. Reeves Instrument Corp., N.Y.C., 1952-54, Adrian Wilson Assocs., Nagoya, Japan, 1956-57, Ford Instrument Co., L.I., N.Y., 1957-58, Technicon, Tarrytown, 1968-69; engr., unit head Kearfott divsn. Singer Corp., Little Falls, N.J., 1958-68; v.p. R & D, Electro-Nucleonics Inc., Fairfield, 1969-90; pres. The Product Devel. Group, Paramus, 1990—. Bd. dirs. Nat. Com. for Clin. Lab. Stds., Villanova, Pa., 1981-87. Contbr. articles to profl. jours.; patentee various instruments. Capt. USAF, 1954-57; mem. USAFR ret. Fellow ASME; mem. Am. Assn. Clin. Chemistry. Jewish. Home and Office: 659 Rutgers Pl Paramus NJ 07652-4207

MACMAHON, THOMAS P. health products executive; V.p. public affairs and planning, 1982-1983, Roche Diagnostic Svcs., 1982—83, v.p. and gen. mgr. diagnostics, 1983; sr. v.p. Hoffman-La Roche Inc., 1993—97; chmn., CEO, pres. Lab. Corp. Am. Holdings, Burlington, NC, 1997—. Office: Lab Corp Am Holdings 358 S Main St Burlington NC 27215*

MACMANUS, SUSAN ANN, political science educator, researcher; b. Tampa, Fla., Aug. 22, 1947; d. Harold Cameron and Elizabeth (Riegler) MacM. BA cum laude, Fla. State U., 1968, PhD, 1975; MA, U. Mich., 1969. Instr. Valencia C.C., Orlando, Fla., 1969-73; rsch. asst. Fla. State U., 1973-75; asst. prof. U. Houston, 1975-79, assoc. prof., 1979-85, dir. MPA program, 1983-85; rsch. assoc. Ctr. Pub. Policy, 1982-85; prof., dir. PhD progam Cleve. State U., 1985-87; prof. pub. adminstrn. and polit. sci. U. South Fla., Tampa, 1987—, chair dept. govt. and internat. affairs, 1987-93, disting. univ. prof., 1999. Vis. prof. U. Okla., Norman, 1981—; field rsch. assoc. Brookings Inst., Washington, 1977-82, Columbia U., summer, 1979, Princeton (N.J.) U., 1979—, Nat. Acad. Pub. Adminstrn., Washington, summer, 1980, Cleve. State [illegible] auth[illegible] Instit[illegible] Comm[illegible] Historica[illegible] Local and [illegible] Public Instit[illegible] Century, 1996[illegible] Critters & Crac[illegible] author: Targeting [illegible] The Lutz Depot, 20[illegible] Changing Art and Polit[illegible] manuals in field, mem. ed[illegible] to books. Bd. dirs. Housto[illegible] treas.; mem. LWV, Gov.'s [illegible] (Tex.) Women's Polit. Caucus, [illegible] chair Fla. Elections Commn., [illegible] Advisers, 2000—. Recipient U. Ho[illegible] award, 1977, Herbert J. Simon award [illegible] Pub. Adminstrn., 1981, Theodore &[illegible] Scholar award U. South Fla., 1991, Disting[illegible] Excellence award, 1999; Ford Found. fellow[illegible] Faculty, 1972, U. Houston, 1976-77, 79, 83; [illegible] 1989; Choice mag. award, 1996; named Dist[illegible] fellow Fla. Inst. of Govt., 2000—. Mem. Am. Poli[illegible] 1983-84, chair sect. intergovtl. rels., award 1989, [illegible] pres.-elect sec. urban politics 1994-95, pres. sect. urba[illegible] Polit. Sci. Assn. (v.p. 1990-91, pres.-elect 1992-93, pre[illegible] award com. 1983-84, best paper on women and politics [illegible] award 2001), Midwest Polit. Sci. Assn., Western Polit. Sci. A[illegible] ern Polit. Sci. Assn. (local arrangements com. 1982-83, pr[illegible] 1977-80), ASPA (nominating com. Houston chpt. 1983, bd. me[illegible] chpt., pres.-elect 1991, Lilly award 1992), Policy Studies Orgn. ([illegible] bd. jour. 1981—, exec. coun. 1983-85), Women's Caucus Polit. Sci. ([illegible] pre-decision rev. com. 1982-83, projects and programs com. 1981, fin.-[illegible] com. 1980-81), Fla. Polit. Sci. Assn. (pres. 1997-98, Manning Dauer Dis[illegible] Fla. Polit. Sci. award 2001), Acad. Polit. Sci., Mcpl. Fin. Officers Assn., P[illegible] Kappa Phi (Artist/Scholar award U. South Fla. 1997), Phi Beta Kappa, Pi Sigma Alpha (mem. exec. coun. 1994-96, pres. 2000—), Pi Alpha Alpha. Methodist. Home: 2506 Collier Pky Land O'Lakes FL 34639-5228 Office: U South Fla Dept Polit Sci Tampa FL 33620 E-mail: samacmanus@aol.com.

1982-83, Westat, Inc., Washington, 1983—. Author: Revenue Patterns in [illegible]es and Suburbs: A Comparative Analysis, 1978, Federal Aid to [illegible]93; author: (with others) Governing A Changing America, 1984; [illegible]ncis T. Borkowski) Visions for the Future: Creating New [illegible]ships Among Academia, Business, Government, and [illegible] Reapportionment and Representation in Florida: A [illegible]oing Business with Government: Federal, State, [illegible]urchasing Practices for Every Business and [illegible]Old: Generational Combat in the 21st [illegible] R. MacManus) Citrus, Sawmills, [illegible]d Central Pasco County, 1998; [illegible]ith Elizabeth R. MacManus) [illegible]olitical Landscape: The [illegible]ricting, 2002; writer: [illegible] to jours., chpts. [illegible]es., v.p. fin., [illegible] County [illegible] Inc.;

MACMASTER, DANIEL MILLER, retired museum official; b. Chgo., Feb. 11, 1913; s. Daniel Howard and Charlotte Louise (Miller) MacM.; m. Sylvia Jane Hill, Feb. 22, 1935; children— Daniel Miller, Jane Irene (Mrs. Robert W. Lightell). Student, Lakeside Press Tng. Sch., 1930-31, U. Chgo., 1931-34; L.H.D., Lincoln Coll., 1970; D.H.L., DePaul U., 1978. Mem. staff Mus. Sci. and Industry, Chgo., 1933—, acting dir., 1950, dir., 1951-72, pres., 1968-78, pres. emeritus, 1978—, life trustee, 1968—. Gen. mgr. Chgo. R.R. Fair, 1948-49 Author: (with others) Exploring the Mysteries of Physics and Chemistry, 1938; book reviewer; contbr. to newspapers, mags., encys. Mem. Homewood (Ill.) Bd. Edn., 1945-49, pres., 1948-49; mem. U. Ill. Citizen' Adv. Com., 1945—; sec. Higher Edn. Commn. Ill., 1955-59; dir. Hyde Park Bank and Trust Co., 1965-86; U.S. State Dept. Specialist to Ireland, Germany, Sweden, 1963; dir. Floating Seminar to Greece, 1960; guest mus. cons. Fed. Republic Germany, 1961, Iran, 1973, 74, 76, Hong Kong, 1978, 89, 90, 91, Singapore, Chili and Peru, 1978, Poland, Czechoslovakia and Hungary, 1979, Mexico, 1980, 81, Saudi Arabia, 1981, 82, 84, Columbia, Ecuador and Bolivia, 1983, Taiwan 1986-90, 92, 94; mem. Nat. 4-H Svc. Com.; hon. dir. Chgo. Chamber Orch. Soc., pres., 1969-70; bd. dirs. Sears Roebuck Found., 1970-73, Internat. Coll. Surgeons Hall of Fame; mem. Lincoln Acad. Ill.; hon. trustee U. Chgo. Cancer Rsch. Found.; life trustee Adler Planetarium; dir. emeritus Monmouth Coll.; bd. govs. Chgo. Heart Assn., vice chmn., 1972-73; founder Scotish Heritage Libr., 1999. Decorated Golden Cross Royal Order Phoenix Greece; Officer's Cross Polonia Restituta Poland; Grand Badge of Honor Austria; Grand Badge of Honor of Burgenland Austria; Golden Badge of Honor Vienna; Officer's Cross 1st class Order of Merit Germany; Officer Order of Merit Luxembourg; Order Cultural Merit Poland; Royal Swedish Order North Star; recipient Patriotic Civilian Service award U.S. Army, St. Andrews Soc. Citizen of Yr. award, 1978 Fellow Assn. Sci. and Tech. Centers; mem. Kappa Sigma. Clubs: Tavern, Quadrangle, Commercial. Home: 2311 183rd St Apt 209 Homewood IL 60430-3146

MACMASTER, ROBERT ELLSWORTH, historian, educator; b. Winthrop, Mass., Oct. 10, 1919; s. Joseph Oscar and Ruby (Slocomb) MacM.; m. Ann Elizabeth Lynch, Apr. 28, 1942; children— Angus Michael, Martha Ann, David Joseph. AB, Harvard, 1941, A.M., 1948, PhD, 1952. Mem. faculty MIT, 1952-90, prof. history and lit., 1967-90, prof. emeritus, 1990—, chmn. history faculty, 1970-72. Author: Danilevsky: A Russian Totalitarian Philosopher, 1967; contbr. articles on L.N. Tolstoi to publs. Served with AUS, 1941-46. Mem. Am. Assn. Advancement Slavic Studies. Home: 461 Main St Hingham MA 02043-4701 Office: MIT Dept History Cambridge MA 02139

MACMEEKEN, JOHN PEEBLES, foundation executive, educator; b. Aug. 15, 1924; s. John West and Esther (Strong) M.; m. Mary Swanberg, Nov. 26, 1949; children: Carol B. Macmeeken Luther, John W., Susan G. Student, U. Calif., Berkeley, 1941-43, Ind. U., 1943-44; JD, Harvard U., 1948. Bar: Calif. 1948. Assoc. Chickering & Gregory, San Francisco, 1948-60, ptnr., 1960-82, Pettit & Martin, San Francisco, 1982-93; v.p. Zynk Indsl. Corp., 1995-98; pres. Found. for Books to China, 1993—, SOAR Bus. Inst., 1998—. Bd. dirs. Lanark West Corp.; pres. Clinton U., San Francisco, 1995-97; lectr. law Fudan U., Shanghai, China, East China Normal U., Shanghai, Nanking U., China, Zhongshan U., Guangzhou. Sgt. U.S. Army, 1943-45. Mem. ABA, Calif. Bar Assn., San Francisco Bar Assn., World Affairs Coun., Outlook Club Calif., World Trade Club. Republican. Congregationalist. Home: 5708 Glenbrook Dr Oakland CA 94618-1724 E-mail: jmacmeeken@aol.com.

MACMILLAN, DAVID PAUL, retired oil company executive; b. East Orange, N.J., Nov. 16, 1943; s. Hugh Dame and Marie Ann (Hahn) MacM.; m. Rosemary Longo, Nov. 16, 1969; children: Melanie, Hugh. With Exxon Rsch. and Engring. Co., various locations, 1969-85, sect. head Florham Park, N.J., 1978-80, project mgr. Denver, 1980-82, spl. assignment to sr. gen. mgr. Florham Park, 1982-83, project mgr.-Belgium, 1983-85, engring. mgr. U.K., 1993-95, mgr. spl. projects divsn. U.K., 1996-97, mgr. project mgmt. divsn. U.K., 1996-97, project dir. Japan, 1997-99. Staff advisor controllers dept., Exxon Co. Internat., Florham Park, N.J., 1986-88, sr. advisor materials dept., 1991-93; materials mgr. Exxon Cen. Svcs., Florham Park, 1989-91. Served with USMC, 1961-65. Mem. Nat. Assn. Purchasing Mgrs., Am. Soc. Quality Control, Tokyo Am. Club, Kyokawa Country Club, Tau Beta Pi, Pi Tau Sigma. Republican. Presbyterian. Home: PO Box 101 Florham Park NJ 07932-0101

MACMILLAN, FRANCIS PHILIP, physician; b. Everett, Mass., June 19, 1937; s. Edward Joseph and Katherine H. (Hogan) M.; m. Nancy Marie Mirabello, May 18, 1963; children: Frank, Edward, Paul, John, Kerry. BS, Boston Coll., 1959; MD, N.Y. Med. Coll., 1964. Diplomate Am. Bd. Internal Medicine, Am. Bd. Gastroenterology. Intern Boston City Hosp., 1964-65, resident in internal med., 1965-66; resident Boston VA Hosp., Jamaica Plains, Mass., 1966-68; practice medicine specializing in gastroenterology Pentucket Med. Assn., Inc., Haverhill, 1968—. Pres. med. staff Hale Hosp., Haverhill, 1975-78, chief of medicine, 1980-82; cons. in gastroenterology Lawrence (Mass.) Gen. Hosp., Holy Family Hosp., Methuen, Mass., Anna Jaques Hosp., Newburyport, Mass. Contbr. articles to profl. jours. Served to maj. USAR, 1968-71. Fellow Am. Coll. Physicians. Fellow Am. Coll. Gastroenterology; mem. Am. Med. Assn., Mass. Med. Assn., Am. Soc. Internal Med., Am. Gastroent. Assn., New England Endoscopy Soc. (pres. 1996-97), Bd. Health Physicians (chmn. 1997-98), Bd. Health (No. Andover chpt.). Clubs: Haverhill Golf and Country (bd. dirs. 1983-86). Roman Catholic. Avocations: golf, tennis. Office: One Parkway Haverhill MA 01830 also: 203 Turnpike St North Andover MA 01845-5042 E-mail: fpmmd@mediaone.net.

MACMILLAN, HOKE, state attorney general; m. Becky Klemt; children: Ryan Klemt, Christopher Klemt. BA, U. Wyo., 1967, JD, 1970. Bar: Wyo., Colo., Nebr., U.S. Ct. Appeals (10th cir.), U.S. Ct. Mil. Appeals, U.S. Supreme Ct. Capt. U.S. Army JAG, 1970—74; mem. Pence and Millett, Laramie, Wyo., 1974—2001, sr. ptnr., 1982—2001; atty. gen. State of Wyo., 2001—. Fellow: Am. Bar Found.; mem.: Albany County Bar Assn., Nebr. State Bar, Wyo. State Bar (pres. 1996—97). Office: Atty Gens Office 123 Capitol Bldg 200 W 24th St Cheyenne WY 82002*

MACMILLAN, KIP VAN METRE, foundation executive; b. Evanston, Ill., Dec. 18, 1937; s. Charles Daniel and Janet Marvia (Van Metre) M.; m. Linda Jean Griesbach, Dec. 22, 1962; children: Christopher, Julia. Sgt., lt., div. comdr. Evanston Police Dept., 1961-88; supr. Polio Plus campaign Rotary Found., Evanston, 1988-90, ret., 1990. Bd. dirs. Youth Orgn. Umbrella, Evanston, 1974, McGaw YMCA, Evanston, 1976-89, Shore Cmty. Svcs. for Retarded Citizens, Evanston, 1986-90, Teton County Crime Stoppers; pres. Teton Youth & Family Svcs.; chmn. Evanston March of Dimes, 1987; mem. adv. com. Cook County Dept. Children and Family Svcs., Chgo., 1987-90; mem. Ill. Coord. System Response Project-Mass Abuse of Children, Springfield, 1987-89; dir., treas. Evanston Sister City Found., 1989-90; vol. Grand Teton Music Festival. Recipient Top Vol. of Yr. award North Shore mag., 1987, Jay Moore award Youth Orgn. Umbrella, 1988, William Harper award McGaw YMCA, 1975. Mem. Nat. Soc. Fundraising Execs., Rotary (bd. dirs. Evanston club 1986-89, bd. dirs. Jackson Hole club, pres. Jackson Hole club 1994-95, Outstanding Rotarian Evanston club 1988), Am. Soc. Indsl. Security, Am. Legion. Republican. Episcopalian.

MACMILLAN, PETER ALAN, lawyer; b. Mpls., Apr. 10, 1955; s. John Louis and Celeste Caroline (Eggers) MacM.; m. Karen Christine Johnson, Mar. 19, 1988. BS, Mankato State U., 1977; JD, Hamline U., 1980; postgrad., Sch. Law U. San Deigo, 1980. Bar: Minn. 1980, U.S. Tax Ct. 1980, U.S. Dist. Ct. Minn. 1981, U.S. Dist. Ct. (no. dist.) Tex. 1992, U.S. Ct. Appeals (5th cir.) 1993, U.S. Ct. Appeals (8th cir.) 1995, U.S. Supreme Ct. 1992. Pvt. practice, Robbinsdale, Minn., 1981-84; assoc. Rosenthal & Rondoni, Ltd., Mpls., 1984-85; ptnr. Rosenthal, Rondoni & MacMillan, Ltd., 1985-96, Rondoni, MacMillan & Schneider Ltd., Mpls., 1996—. Chmn. Minn. Jaycees Found. 1987-88, trustee, 1988-92. Mem. ABA, Minn. State Bar Assn., Hennepin County Bar Assn., Assn. Trial Lawyers Am., Am. Judicature Soc., Minn. Trial Lawyers Assn., Min. Def. Lawyers Assn., Def. Rsch. Inst., Jaycees (pres. Robbinsdale chpt. 1986, Jr. chamber internat. senate). Lutheran. Home: 11282 71st Ave N Osseo MN 55369-7621 Office: MacMillan & Wallace PLLP 9955 59th Ave N Ste 125 Minneapolis MN 55442-1071 Office Fax: 763-559-1064.

MACMILLAN, ROBERT FRANCIS, director university service; b. Easton, Pa., Oct. 3, 1925; s. William F. and Margaret (Woodruff) M.; m. Dolores G., June 7, 1952; 1 child, R. David. BS in Elec. Engring., Lafayette Coll., 1949; BD, Southern Bapt. Theol. Sem., 1952, ThM and MRE, 1954, 56; PhD, Am. U., 1969. Lic. psychologist, Pa. Assoc. pastor 1st Bapt. Ch., Washington, 1955-69; dir. psychol. svcs. U. Pa., East Stroudsburg, 1969—. Pres., Assn. Pa. State Coll. U Faculty, 1980—. Chmn. Monroe County Planning Commn., Stroudsburg, 1974-85. Sgt. U.S. Army, 1943-46. Mem. Am. Psychol. Assn. Home: 32 Club Ct Stroudsburg PA 18360-1548 Office: East Stroudsburg U Dept of Psychol Stroudsburg PA 18301

MACMILLAN, ROBERT SMITH, electronics engineer; b. L.A., Aug. 28, 1924; s. Andrew James and Moneta (Smith) M.; m. Barbara Macmillan, Aug. 18, 1962; 1 child, Robert G. BS in Physics, Calif. Inst. Tech., 1948, MS in Elec. Engring., 1949, PhD in Elec. Engring./Physics cum laude, 1954. Rsch. engr. Jet Propulsion Lab., Calif. Inst. Tech., Pasadena, 1951-55, asst. prof. elec. engring., 1955-58; assoc. prof. elec. engring. U. So. Calif., L.A., 1958-70; mem. sr. tech. staff Litton Sys., Inc., Van nuys, Calif., 1969-79; dir. sys. engring. Litton Data Command Sys., Agoura Hills, 1979-89; pres. The Macmillan Group, Tarzana, 1989—. Treas., v.p. Video Color Corp., Inglewood, 1965-66; cons. fgn. tech. div. USAF, Wright-Patterson AFB, Ohio, 1957-74, Space Tech. Labs., Inglewood, Calif., 1956-60, Space Gen. Corp., El Monte, Calif., 1960-63. With USAAF, 1943-46. Mem. IEEE, Am. Inst. Physics, Am. Phys. Soc., Sigma Xi, Tau Beta Pi, Eta Kappa Nu. Achievements include research in ionospheric, radio-wave, propagation; very low frequency radio-transmitting antennas; optical coherence and statistical optics. Home: 350 Starlight Crest Dr La Canada Flintridge CA 91011-2839 Office: The Macmillan Group 5700 Etiwanda Ave Unit 260 Tarzana CA 91356-2546 E-mail: rsmacmillan@aol.com.

MACMILLAN, WILLIAM HOOPER, university dean, educator; b. Boston, Oct. 21, 1923; s. Alexander Stewart and Leslie (Hooper) M.; m. Anne Stearns, May 29, 1948; children: Leslie Jean, Robert Bruce, William Ian. BA, McGill U., 1948; PhD, Yale U., 1954. Instr. pharmacology U. Vt. Coll. Medicine, 1954-55, asst. prof., 1955-59, asso. prof., 1959-64, chmn. dept. pharmacology, 1962-63, prof. pharmacology, 1964-76, dean Grad. Coll., 1963-69, 71-76; rsch. fellow USPHS, U. Oxford, Eng., 1958-59; cons. New Eng. Assn. Schs. and Colls., 1967-76; Ford Found. project specialist, sci. adv. to Haile Sellassie U., Addis Ababa., Ethiopia, 1969-71; prof. biology, dean Grad. Sch. U. Ala., 1976-91, prof. biology, dean emeritus, 1991—; cons. So. Assn. Colls. and Schs., 1976-91. Exec. com. African grad. Fellowship Program, African-Am. Inst., N.Y.C., 1971-92; chmn. com. biomed. scis. Coun. of Grad. Schs., Washington, 1973-77, bd. dirs., 1985-88; exec. com. N.E. Assn. Grad. Schs., 1975-76; v.p. Conf. So. Grad. Schs., 1981, pres., 1982; pres., v.p. New Eng. Assn. Grad. Schs., 1971; bd. dirs. Oak Ridge Associated Univs., 1987-93. Cmty. activator, chair, bd. dirs. regional non-profit agencies, 1992—. With USNR, 1944—46. Mem. Am. Soc. Pharmacology and Exptl. Therapeutics, AAAS, N.Y. Acad. Sci., AAUP, Sigma Xi.

MACMILLEN, RICHARD EDWARD, biological sciences educator, researcher; b. Upland, Calif., Apr. 19, 1932; s. Hesper Nichols and Ruth Henrietta (Golder) MacM.; m. Ann Gray, June 12, 1953 (div. 1975); children: Jennifer Kathleen, Douglas Michael; m. Barbara Jean Morgan, Oct. 23, 1980; 1 child, Ian Richard. BA, Pomona Coll., 1954; MS, U. Mich., 1956; PhD, UCLA, 1961. From instr. to assoc. prof. Pomona Coll., Claremont, Calif., 1960-68. Wig Disting. prof., 1965; assoc. prof., then prof. U. Calif., Irvine, 1968—, chair dept. population and environ. biology, 1972-74, chair dept. ecology and evolutionary biology, 1984-90; prof. emeritus, 1993—. Mem. award panel NSF, Washington, 1976-80; coord. U. Calif. Multi-Campus Supercourse in Environ. Biology, White Mountain Rsch. Sta., spring 1996, 97, tchg. participant, 1998—; mem. STAR fellowhip panel EPA; mem. rev. panel, EPA Star grad. fellowship prgm., 2002. Contbr. numerous articles to profl. jours. Chair sci. adv. bd. Endangered Habitats League, 1991-93. Recipient rsch. awards NSF, 1961-83; Fulbright-Hays advanced rsch. fellow Monash U., Australia, 1966-67. Fellow AAAS; mem. Am. Soc. Mammalogists (life), Ecol. Soc. Am. (cert. sr. ecologist), Am. Ornithologists Union, Cooper Ornithol. Soc. (life, bd. dirs. 1982-84). Democrat. Avocations: fly fishing, camping, hiking, nature photography. Home: 705 Foss Rd Talent OR 97540-9758 E-mail: bidmac@jeffnet.org. *As world human populations continue to increase, our natural world continues to degrade. It is incumbent upon all of us to accept the responsibility of stewarding our land and its biota as precious and renewable resources.*

MACMINN, PAMELA LEE See KOPACK, PAMELA LEE

MACMULLEN, JEAN ALEXANDRIA STEWART, nurse, administrator; b. N.Y.C., Feb. 21, 1945; d. John Douglas and Isabella Stewart (Park) MacM. Diploma in nursing, Lenox Hill Hosp., N.Y.C., 1965; BSN, Adelphi U., 1969, MSN, 1971; MA in Anthropology, U. South Fla., 1978. Nurse renal disease unit N.Y. Hosp., N.Y.C., 1971-72; clin. nurse specialist VA Hosp., Tampa, Fla., 1972-76, med.-surg. coord., 1976-82; assoc. chief nurse VA Med. Ctr., Gainesville, 1982-93, assoc. med. ctr. dir. patient support svcs. Montgomery, Ala., 1993-98; pvt. practice Inverness, Fla., 1998—. Editor Am. Assn. Nephrology Nurses, Pitman, N.J., 1980-82, referee, adviser, 1983—; contbr. articles to profl. jours. Mem.: Fla. Nurses Assn., Am. Nephrology Nurses Assn., Order Eastern Star. Republican. Episcopalian. Avocations: gardening, raising orchids.

MACMULLEN, RAMSAY, retired history educator; b. N.Y.C., Mar. 3, 1928; s. Charles William and Margaret (Richmond) MacM.; m. Edith Merriman Nye, Aug. 7, 1954 (div. 1991); children: John A., Priscilla N., William R., Lucinda S.; m. Margaret McNeill, Aug. 1, 1992. AB, Harvard U., 1950, AM, 1953, PhD, 1957. Instr., asst. prof. U. Oreg., 1956-61; asso. prof., prof. Brandeis U., 1961-67, chmn. dept. classics, 1965-66; prof. Yale U., 1967-93, Dunham prof. history and classics, 1979-93, chmn. dept. history, 1970-72, master Calhoun Coll., 1984-90. Author: Soldier and Civilian in the Later Roman Empire, 1963, Enemies of the Roman Order, 1966, Constantine, 1969, Roman Social Relations, 1974, Roman Government's Response to Crisis, 1976, Paganism in the Roman Empire, 1981, Christianizing the Roman Empire, 1984, Corruption and the Decline of Rome, 1988, Changes in the Roman Empire, 1990; (with E.N. Lane) Paganism and Christianity, 1992, Sisters of the Brush, 1997, Christianity and Paganism, 1997, Romanization in Augustus' Time, 2000, Sarah's Choice, 2001. Recipient Porter prize Coll. Art Assn., 1964; Fulbright fellow, 1960-61; Guggenheim fellow, 1964; Princeton Inst. for Advanced Study fellow, 1964-65; Nat. Endowment for Humanities sr. fellow, 1974-75; Lifetime award Scholarly Distinction, Am. Historical Assn., 2001. Mem. Soc. for Promotion Roman Studies, Assn. Ancient Historians (pres. 1978-81) Home: 25 Temple Ct New Haven CT 06511 Office: Yale U Dept History New Haven CT 06520 E-mail: ramsay.macmullen@yale.edu.

MACMURRAY-SCHMELTER, KRISTIN ANN, marketing professional; b. Chicago Heights, Ill., Apr. 20, 1960; d. Charles Gaylord and Shirley Joan (Westphal) MacMurray; m. George Robert Schmelter, May 31, 1986; children: Samantha Marie, Alexander Charles. BA, Western Mich. U., 1981; MBA, Lake Forest Grad. Sch. Mgmt., 2000. Mgr. advt. Washington Nat. Ins. Co., Evanston, Ill., 1982-87; creative dir., asst. v.p. S & H Citadel, Hillside, 1987-94; mtkg. mgr. Abbott Labs., Abbott Park, 1994-2000, nat. mktg. mgr., 1999—, sales ops. mgr., 2000—. Designer flexographic calendar. Bd. dirs. Evanston Drug Treatment Ctr., 1985; assoc. leader Girl Scouts U.S.A., Lake Villa, Ill., 1998-00, leader, 2001-02. Office: Abbott Labs D353 AP 30 Abbott Park IL 60064-3501

MACMURREN, HAROLD HENRY, JR. psychologist, lawyer; b. Jersey City, Sept. 18, 1942; s. Harold Sr. and Evelyn (Almone) MacM.; m. Margaret Bartro, Nov. 21, 1970. BA, William Paterson Coll., Wayne, N.J., 1965; MA, Jersey City Coll., 1973; EdD, St. Johns U., N.Y.C., 1985; JD, Rutgers U., 1989. Cert. secondary tchr., N.J.; Bar: N.J. 1989. Instr. Wanaque (N.J.) Bd. Edn., 1965-66, cons. psychologist, 1983-84; instr. Elmwood Park (N.J.) Bd. Edn., 1967-70; coll. faculty mem., psychologist Assoc. Clinic, Jersey City, 1971-72; cons. psychologist Rockaway (N.J.) Bd. Edn., 1972-83; intern lawyer Environ. Law Clinic, Newark, 1988-89; cons. psychologist Pequannock (N.J.) Bd. Edn., 1984—; pvt. practice law, 2000—. Coord. of child study team Sandyston Walpack Sch. System; adj. prof. William Paterson Coll.; spkr. and writer in field. Mem. ABA, NEA, N.J. Edn. Assn., N.J. Psychologist Assn., N.J. Bar Assn., Sierra Club, Phi Delta Kappa. Avocations: reading, travel, skiing, hiking. Home: 4 Systema Pl Sussex NJ 07461-2833

MACMURREN, MARGARET PATRICIA, secondary education educator, consultant; b. Newark, Nov. 4, 1947; d. Kenneth F. and Doris E. (Lounsberry) Bartro; m. Harold MacMurren, Nov. 21, 1970. BA, Paterson State U., 1969; MA, William Paterson Coll., 1976; postgrad., Jersey City State Coll., 1976—. Tchr. Byram (N.J.) Twp. Schs., 1969-77; learning cons., child study team coord. Andover Regional Schs., Newton, N.J., 1977—. Mem. NEA, N.J. Edn. Assn., N.J. Assn. Learning Cons., Sussex Coutny Assn. Learning Cons. (pres. 1982-83, 93-94, sec.-treas. 1991-92, v.p. 1992-93), Andover Regional Edn. Assn. (pres. 1986-87). Avocations: skiing, dancing, weight training, travel, reading. Home: 4 Systema Pl Sussex NJ 07461-2833 Office: Andover Regional Schs 707 Limecrest Rd Newton NJ 07860-8801

MACNAIR, WILMER EVERETT, sociologist, educator, minister; b. Niagra Falls, Ny, Oct. 15, 1932; s. Everett Wilmer MacNair and Dora Irene Taylor; m. Sarah Redd Callaway, Aug. 6, 1971; m. Dorothy Lois Kelso, May 29, 1953 (div. Dec. 6, 1971); children: Rachel, Daniel. BA, Pk. Coll., Kansas City, MO, 1953; BD, Chgo. Theol. Sem., Chicago, IL, 1956; PhD, U. Wis., Madison, WI, 1965. Ordained United Ch. Christ. Instr. Elmhurst Coll., Elmhurst, Ill., 1961—64; asst. prof. West Tex. State U., Canyon, Tex., 1964—66; assoc. prof. Memphis State U., Memphis, 1966—70, West Tex. State U., Canyon, Tex., 1970—73, U. La. Lafayette, Lafayette, La., 1973—. Supply preacher Luth. Presbyn. Congl., 2002—02; exec. officer Faculty Senate U. La. Lafayette, Lafayette, La., 2001—. Author: (book) Basic Thinking, Ten Commandment and The Forthcoming Crisis in Community in America. Participant Witness Peace, Nicaragua, 1989—92. Socialist. United Church Christ. Avocation: jogging. Home: 149 Memory Lane Lafayette LA 70506 Office: University Louisiana Lafayette PO Box 4-0198 Lafayette LA 70504

MACNALLY, ROBERT FALCONER, II, retired sports equipment company executive; b. Evanston, Ill., Apr. 28, 1932; s. Maxwell Falconer and Dorothy Hosmer (Nelson) MacN.; m. Elizabeth Weeks, June 30, 1956; children: Robert F. III, Susan E., Anne M. Goto, William N. AB in Chemistry, Dartmouth Coll., 1953; MBA, Harvard Bus. Sch., 1958. With W.R. Grace & Co., Cambridge, Mass., 1958-69, Ideal Roller Co., Chgo., 1969-73, pres., 1973-74; v.p., gen. mgr. Sta-Hi Sys., Nashua, N.H., 1974-76; pres. chem. group Kinark Corp., Hinsdale, Ill., 1976-79; pres., CEO Tommy Armour Golf Co., Morton Grove, 1979-95, chmn., 1995-97; ret., 1997. Bd. dir. Adams Golf Co., Plano, Tex. Patentee weight-balanced golf clubs. Bd. dirs. emeritus, chmn. Nat. Golf Found., Jupiter, Fla., 1979—; chmn. The Cmty. House, Hinsdale, 1985-86, Midwest Indsl. Mgmt. Assn., Westchester, 1988-89; bd. dirs., treas. Chgo. Boys & Girls Clubs, 1971—; sr. warden Grace Episcopal Ch., Hinsdale, 1996-99. Lt. (j.g.) USN, 1953-56, Korea. Recipient Herb Graffis award Nat. Golf Found., 1992, John F. Atkinson award Chgo. Boys & Girls Clubs, 1989, Ernie Sabayrac award PGA of Am., Palm Beach Gardens, Fla., 1997; named to Ill. PGA Hall of Fame, 1991, Golf Father of Yr., Golfweek Mag., Orlando, 1992. Mem. Hinsdale Golf Club (bd. dirs. 1978-2000). Republican. Episcopalian. Avocations: golf, travel, photography. Home: 750 Wilson Ln Hinsdale IL 60521-4842 E-mail: rfmacnally@aol.com.

MACNAUGHTON, ANGUS ATHOLE, finance company executive; b. Montreal, July 15, 1931; s. Athole Austin and Emily Kidder (MacLean) MacN.; children: Gillian Heather, Angus Andrew. Student, Lakefield Coll. Sch., 1941-47, McGill U., 1949-54. Auditor Coopers & Lybrand, Montreal, 1949-55; acct. Genstar Ltd., 1955, asst. treas., 1956-61, treas., 1961-64, v.p., 1964-70, exec. v.p., 1970-73, pres., 1973-76, vice chmn., chief exec. officer, 1976-81, chmn. or pres., chief exec. officer, 1981-86; pres. Genstar Investment Corp., 1987—. Vice chmn., bd. dirs. Barrick Gold Corp.; bd. dirs. Clarica Life Ins. Co., Diversified Collection Svcs., Inc., Fairmont Hotels & Resorts Inc., Genstar Investment Corp., Ind. Life and Annuity Co.; bd. dirs. Keyport Benefit Life Ins. Co.; bd. dirs. Keyport Life Ins. Co., Sun Life Assurance Co. Can. (U.S.), Sun Life Ins. and Annuity Co. Can. (N.Y.), Varian Semicondr. Assocs., Inc.; past pres. Montreal chpt. Tax Execs. Inst. Bd. govs. Lakefield Coll. Sch.; past chmn. San Francisco Bay Area coun. Boy Scouts Am.; bd. dirs. San Francisco Opera; trustee World Affairs Coun. of No. Calif. Mem. Pacific Union Club, World Trade Club, Villa Taverna (San Francisco), Mt. Royal Club (Montreal), Toronto Club. Address: Barrick Gold Corp 200 Bay St Ste 2700 Toronto ON Canada M5J 2J3 Office: 555 California St Fl 48 San Francisco CA 94104-1502

MACNEAL, EDWARD ARTHUR, economic consultant; b. Winona Lake, Ind., Apr. 19, 1925; s. Kenneth Forsythe and Marguerite Josephine (Giroud) MacN.; m. Priscilla Creed Perry, Dec. 27, 1952; children: Catherine Wright, Madeleine Creed. Student, Harvard, 1943; BA, U. Chgo., 1948, MA, 1951. Exec. sec. Internat. Soc. Gen. Semantics, Chgo., 1947-50; staff cons. James C. Buckley, Inc., N.Y.C., 1951-55; market researcher Socony Mobil Oil Co., 1955-58; research dir. O.E. McIntyre, Inc., 1958-61; econ. cons. N.Y., 1956-66, Wayne, Pa., 1966—. Adv. local govt. agys. Author: The Semantics of Air Passenger Transportation, 1981, MacNeal's Master Atlas of Decision Making, 1988, Mathsemantics: Making Numbers Talk Sense, 1994. Served with AUS, 1943-46, ETO. Mem. ABA, Am. Statis. Assn., Am. Econ. Assn., Am. Math. Soc., Internat. Soc. Gen. Semantics (dir.), Inst. Gen. Semantics (dir.), Am. Sociol. Assn., Am. Assn. Airport Execs., Travel and Tourism Rsch. Assn., Travel Rsch. Forum, Nat. Aviation Club, Harvard Club (Phila.), Wings Club. Home: 348 Louella Ave Wayne PA 19087-4855 Office: PO Box 249 Wayne PA 19087-0249 E-mail: macneal@erols.com.

MACNEIL, IAN RODERICK, lawyer, educator; b. N.Y.C., June 20, 1929; s. Robert Lister and Kathleen Gertrude (Metcalf) Macneil; m. Nancy Carol Wilson, Mar. 29, 1952; children: Roderick, Jennifer, Duncan (dec.), Andrew. BA magna cum laude, U. Vt., 1950; LLB magna cum laude, Harvard U., 1955. Bar: N.H. 1956. Law clk. Hon. Peter Woodbury, 1955-56; asso. Sulloway Hollis Godfrey & Soden, Concord, N.H., 1956-59; mem. faculty Cornell U. Law Sch., Ithaca, N.Y., 1959-72, 74-80, Ingersoll prof. law, 1976-80; Wigmore prof. law Northwestern U. Sch. Law, Chgo., 1980-99, prof. emeritus, 1999—. Vis. prof. U. East Africa, 1965-67, Duke U., 1971-72; prof. law, mem. Inst. Advanced Studies, U. Va., 1972-74; vis. fellow Centre for Socio-legal Studies and Wolfson Coll., Oxford U., 1979; hon. vis. fellow faculty law U. Edinburgh, 1979, 87; Rosenthal lectr. Northwestern U. Sch. Law, 1979; Braucher vis. prof. Harvard U., 1988-89. Author: Bankruptcy Law in East Africa, 1966, Contracts: Exchange Transactions and Relations, 2d edit., 1978, The New Social Contract, 1980, American Arbitration Law: Reformation Nationalization Internationalization, 1992; co-author: Federal Arbitration Law, 1994. Served with U.S. Army, 1951-53. Guggenheim fellow, 1978-79. Fellow Royal Soc. Antiquaries (Scotland); mem. ABA, Am. Law Inst., N.H. Bar Assn., Am. Acad. Arts and Scis., Standing Coun. Scottish Chiefs. Home: 95/6 Grange Loan Edinburgh EH9 2ED Scotland

MAC NEIL, JOSEPH NEIL, archbishop; b. Sydney, N.S., Can., Apr. 15, 1924; s. John Martin and Kate (Mac Lean) Mac N. BA, St. Francis Xavier U., Antigonish, N.S., 1944; postgrad., Holy Heart Sem., Halifax, N.S., 1944-48, U. Perugia, 1956, U. Chgo., 1964; JCD, U. St. Thomas, Rome, 1958. Ordained priest Roman Cath. Ch., 1948. Pastor parishes in, N.S., 1948-55; officialis Chancery Office, Antigonish, 1958-59; adminstrn. Diocese of Antigonish, 1959-60; rector Cathedral Antigonish, 1961; dir. extension dept. St. Francis Xavier U., Antigonish, 1961-69, v.p., 1962-69; bishop St. John, N.B., Can., 1969-73; chancellor U. St. Thomas, Fredericton, 1969-73; archbishop of Edmonton, Alta., 1973-99; ret., 1999. Chmn. Alta Bishops' Conf., 1973-99; chmn. bd. Newman Theol. Coll., Edmonton, 1973-99, St. Joseph's Coll. U. Alta., Edmonton, 1973-99. Vice chmn. N.S. Voluntary Econ. Planning Bd., 1965-69; bd. dirs. Program and Planning Agy., Govt. of N.S., 1969; exec. Atlantic Provinces Econ. Coun., 1968-73, Can. Coun. Rural Devel., 1965-75; bd. dirs. Futures Secretariat, 1981, Ctr. for Human Devel., Toronto, Ont., Can., 1985-95; mem. bd. mgmt. Edmonton Gen. Hosp., 1983-92, Edmonton Caritas Health Group, 1992-99; mem. Nat. Com. for Can. Participation in Habitat, 1976. Mem. Can. Assn. Adult Edn. (past pres. N.S.), Can. Assn. Dirs. Univ. Extension and Summer Schs. (past pres.), Inst. Rsch. on Pub. Policy (founding mem.), Can. Conf. Cath. Bishops (pres. 1979-81, mem. com. on ecumenism 1985-91, com. on missions 1991-96, mem. permanent coun. 1993-95). Office: Archbishop Emeritus Edmonton 8421 101st Ave Edmonton AB Canada T6A 0L1

MACNEIL, ROBERT BRECKENRIDGE WARE, retired broadcast journalist, writer; b. Montreal, Que., Can., Jan. 19, 1931; came to U.S., 1963; s. Robert A.S. and Margaret Virginia (Oxner) MacN.; m. Rosemarie Anne Copland, 1956 (div. 1964); children: Catherine Anne, Ian B.; m. Jane J. Doherty, May 29, 1965 (div. 1983); children: Alison N., William H.; m. Donna P. Richards, Oct. 20, 1984. Student, Dalhousie U., 1949-51; BA, Carleton U., 1955; LHD (hon.), William Patterson Coll., 1977, Beaver Coll., Bates Coll., 1979, Lawrence U., 1980, Bucknell U., 1982, George Washington U., Kings Coll., Trinity Coll., U. Maine, 1983, Brown U., 1984, Colby Coll., Carleton Coll., U. S.C., 1985, Franklin and Marshall Coll., 1987, Nazareth Coll., Washington Coll., 1988, Kenyon Coll., 1990, U. Western Ont., 1992, U. Miami, Clark U., 1994, U. L.I., 1995, Columbia U., 1995, Princeton U., 1995, The Cooper Union, 1996, U. Toronto, 1997, Mt. Allison U., 1998; LHD (hon.), Dalhousie U., 2000. Radio actor CBC, Halifax, N.S., Can., 1950-52, radio/TV announcer, 1954-55; announcer Sta.-CJCH, Halifax, 1951-52; announcer, news writer Sta. CFRA, Ottawa, Ont., Can., 1952-54; sub-editor to filing editor Reuters News Agy., London, 1955-60; news corr. NBC, 1960-63, Washington, 1963-65, N.Y.C., 1965-67; corr. Panorama program BBC, London, 1967-71, 73-75; sr. corr. Nat. Public Affairs Center for TV, Washington, 1971-73; exec. editor, co-anchor MacNeil/Lehrer Report, Sta. -WNET-TV, N.Y.C., 1975—, MacNeil/Lehrer News Hour, PBS, 1983-95, ret., 1995. Author: The People Machine, The Influence of Television on American Politics, 1968, The Right Place at the Right Time, 1982, Wordstruck, 1989, Burden of Desire, 1992, The Voyage, 1995, Breaking News, 1998; co-author: The Story of English, 1986; editor The Way We Were 1963, 1988. Trustee Freedom Forum Newseum. Decorated Officer Order of Can., 1998; inductee TV Acad. Hall of Fame, 1999; recipient Lifetime Achievement award Overseas Press Club, 1995, Broadcaster of Yr. Internat. Radio and TV Soc., 1991, Paul White award Radio TV News Dirs. Assn., 1990, Medal of Honor U. Mo. Sch. Journalism, 1980; Catto fellow The Aspen Inst. Fellow AAAS, The MacDowell Colony (chmn. 1993); mem. AFTRA, Assn. Radio and TV News Analysts, Japan Soc. (trustee), Writers Guild Am., Century Club (N.Y.C.). Office: c/o MacNeil-Lehrer Prodns 2700 S Quincy St Ste 240 Arlington VA 22206-2226

MACNEILL, JAMES WILLIAM, international environment consultant; b. Sask., Can., Apr. 22, 1928; s. Leslie William and Helga Ingeborg (Nohlgren) MacN.; m. Phyllis Beryl Ferguson, Nov. 30, 1953; children: Catherine Anne, Robin Lynne. BA, U. Sask., 1949, BE Mech., 1958, LLD (hon.), 1988; Diplome, U. Stockholm, 1951; DSc (hon.), McGill U., 1992; D of Environ. Studies (hon.), U. Waterloo, 1993; LHD (hon.), Lakehead U., 1994. Spl. adv. on constl. rev. Privy Council Office, Govt. Can., Ottawa, Ont., 1969-70; asst. sec. Can. Ministry of State for Urban Affairs, 1970-73, permanent sec., 1973-76; Can. AEP, Can. commr.-gen. UN Human Settlements Conf., Vancouver, B.C., 1975-78; dir. environ. directorate OECD, Paris, 1978-84; sec. gen. World Commn. Environment and Devel., Geneva, 1984-87; sr. fellow Inst. Research Pub. Policy, Ottawa, 1987-93; pres. J.W. MacNeill and Assocs., 1987-98; chmn. Internat. Inst. for Sustainable Devel., 1994-99. Spl. advisor to adminstrn. UN Devel. Program, 1994-97; chmn. ind. insp. panel World Bank, 1997—. Author: Environmental Management, 1971, Beyond Interdependence, 1991. Apptd. officer Order of Can., 1995. Recipient Saskatchewan Achievement award, 1985, Silver medal City of Paris, 1984, Climate Inst. award, 1991, Swedish WASA award, 1991, Lifetime Achievement award Govt. of Can., 1993. Mem. Assn. Profl. Engrs. Ont., Assn. Profl. Engrs. Sask. E-mail: jwmacneill@attglobal.net., jmacneill@worldbank.org.

MACNEILL, JOHN HARMON, mechanical engineer; b. Honolulu, Oct. 27, 1919; s. John Pehrson and Harriett Thelma (Harmon) MacN.; m. Margaret Elizabeth Benedict, Sept. 16, 1947; children: Jean Benedict, John Benedict. BS, U. Calif., Berkeley, 1942. Registered profl. engr., Calif. Mech. engr. Fairchild Engine & Airplane Corp., Oak Ridge, 1947-48, Raytheon Mfg. Co., Waltham, Mass., 1948-50; sr. engr. Air Force Missile Test Ctr., Patrick AFB, Fla., 1950-54; v.p. engring. Soroban Engring., Inc., Melbourne and Palm Bay, 1954-70, Optical Bus. Machines, Melbourne, 1970-82; sr. engr. Fla. Data Corp., 1982-88, Technoogy Svc. Group Inc., Melbourne, 1988-93; owner MacNeill Engring., 1995—. Careers Day presenter various schs., 1980-94; judge state sci. and engring. fairs Fla. Found. Future Scientists, 1980-2000. Sponsor, organizer internat. sailing regatta, 1969-94. 1st lt. Ordnance, U.S. Army, 1942-46, PTO. Mem. ASME, Space Coast Personal Computer Users Group, Phi Beta Kappa, Sigma Xi, Tau Beta Pi. Republican. Achievements include patents for rack and pinion differential printer, high speed tape punch, high speed dot matrix printer, optical character reader. Avocations: restoring and repairing autos, sailing, listening to music. Home: 1320 S Riverside Dr Indialantic FL 32903-3553

MACNEILL, JOHN SEARS, JR. civil engineer; b. Weehawken, N.J., Jan. 24, 1927; s. John Sears and Margaret (Stalee) MacN.; m. Elizabeth Frances Hazzard, July 15, 1950; children: Allen Donald, Billie Jean, Claudia Lynn. BCE, Cornell U., 1950. Registered profl. engr., Maine, Md., Mass., Mont., N.H., N.J., N.Y., Pa., Vt., W. Va.; land surveyor, Maine, N.H., N.Y., Pa. Field engr. Lasker Goldman, Cortland, N.Y., 1950-51; asst. supt. John Kinner & Assocs., Corning, 1951-53; field engr. Roger & McKay Inc., 1953-54; archtl. draftsman Allegheny Homes Corp., Homer, N.Y., 1954-57; pvt. practice, 1957-76; pres. John S. MacNeill, Jr., P.C., 1976—. Past pres. Consulting Engring. Coun., N.Y. Past chmn. Cortland County Econ. Devel. Commn.; past pres. Cortland County Lic. Land Surveyors Assn.; past dist. chmn. Rotary Youth Exch., 1988-90; past pres. Baden-Powell Coun. Boy Scouts Am. Recipient Silver Beaver award Boy Scouts Am. Fellow ASCE; mem. N.Y. State Soc. Profl. Engrs. (Engr. Yr., past pres.), Cortland Coll. Devel. Found. (treas. 1985—); mem. Ctrl. N.Y. Scottish Games Assn. (pres. 1990-93), Cortland Rotary Club (Paul Harris fellow, pres. 1992-93), Crown City

Toastmasters (past pres.), Cortland County C. of C. (past pres., v.p.). Avocations: wilderness hiking, world travel, fishing. Home: 10 Balmoral Way Homer NY 13077-9417 Office: John S MacNeill Jr P C 74 N West St PO Box 320 Homer NY 13077-0320

MACNICHOL, EDWARD FORD, JR. biophysicist, educator, consultant; b. Toledo, Oct. 24, 1918; s. Edward Ford and Adelaide (Foster) MacN.; m. Anne Proctor Ayer, Sept. 7, 1940; (dec. Nov. 1996); children: Edward Ford III, Anne (Mrs. David A. Brownell); m. Dorothy B. Thorne, Apr. 5, 1998. AB, Princeton, 1941; student, U. Pa., 1946-48; PhD, Johns Hopkins, 1952. Staff mem. radiation lab. Mass. Inst. Tech., 1941-46; from instr. to prof. biophysics Johns Hopkins, 1952-68; research biophysicist, asst. dir. Marine Biol. Lab., Woods Hole, Mass., 1972-76; dir. Lab. Sensory Physiology, 1973-84. Prof. physiology Boston U. Med. Sch., 1973-2001, prof. emeritus, 2001—; dir. Nat. Inst. Neurol. Diseases and Stroke, 1968-72; acting dir. Nat. Eye Inst., NIH, 1968-69; Mem. visual scis. study sect. NIH, 1963-66; mem. bd. sci. counsellors Nat. Inst. Neurol. Disease, and Blindness, 1965-68, chmn., 1968— ; mem. U.S. Nat. Com. Photobiology, 1966-68, U.S. Nat. Com. Pure and Applied Biophysics, 1966 Co-editor: Sensory Processes, 1978-82. Bd. dirs. Deafness Research Found., 1973-83, sec., 1976-78. Recipient certificate of appreciation War Dept.-Navy Dept., 1947 Fellow IEEE (life, Engring. in Biology and Medicine prize award 1965, Centennial medal 1984, editor trans. biomed. engring. 1963-65); mem. AAAS (life), Am. Phys. Soc., Am. Physiol. Soc., Biophys. Soc., Soc. for Neurosci., Assn. Rsch. Vision and Ophthalmology (hon. life), Corp. Bermuda Biol. Sta. Rsch. (life trustee 2001). Achievements include research in neurophysiology of vision; design instrumentation biol. research. Home: RR 1 Box 65A 11 5 Bold Meadow Cir Edgartown MA 02539 E-mail: tedmacn@aol.com. *I have found a career, which has involved research, administration, engineering and teaching, to be both rewarding and challenging. I would regret not having had all these experiences; particularly the contact with different kinds of people having different ways of thinking. I would urge young people, above all, to understand thoroughly the basic principles involved in what they are doing, then work out the details, instead of just learning by rote the details of a narrow specialty.*

MACO, PAUL STEPHEN, securities and exchange administrator; s. Paul and Rose Mary (McFadden) M.; m. Lisa M. Griglack, Aug. 23, 1997; 1 child, Claire Fiona. BA, Lehigh U., 1974; JD, NYU, 1977. Ptnr. Mintz, Levin, Cohn, Ferris, Glovesky & Popeo, Boston, 1988-94; faculty law Morin Ctr. for Internat. Banking Law Boston U., 1992-96, 99—; atty. fellow Office of Gen. Counsel SEC, Washington, 1994, dir. Office of Mcpl. Securities, 1995—. Adj. assoc. prof. Washington Coll. Law Am. U., 1999. Author: (with others) Bond Markets, Law and Regulation, 1999; bd. editors Jour. of Mcpl. Fin. Dir. Traditions for Tomorrow, Inc. Mem. ABA (co-reporter disclosure rules of counsel 1994), Nat. Assn. Bond Lawyers (dir. 1989-92, chair spl. com. on securities laws and disclosure 1987-89). Office: Office of Mcpl Securities SEC 450 5th St NW Washington DC 20549-0001

MACO, TERI REGAN, accountant, engineer; b. Allentown, Pa., Nov. 4, 1953; d. Francis M. and Jacqueline K. (Becker) Regan; m. Bruce F. Maco, Oct. 1, 1983; children: Adam S., Alex M. BSChemE with honors, Lehigh U., 1975; MBA with distinction, U. New Haven, 1979; cert. in sci., West Chester U., 1994. Supr. Ivory, Procter & Gamble Mfg. Co., S.I., N.Y., 1975-77; asst. mgr. processing Chesebrough-Ponds, Inc., Clinton, Conn., 1977-81, sec. and bd. dirs. credit union, 1980; group supr. McNeil Consumer Products, Ft. Washington, Pa., 1981-83; mgr. processing Johnson & Johnson, 1983-84, mgr. nat. planning, 1984-87, group mgr. acctg., 1987-93; pres. Child Placement Network, Inc., Norristown, Pa., 1989-93; tchr. Phoenixville (Pa.) H.S., 1993-94; treas. Borough of Collegeville, 1995-97; pres. T. Maco & Assocs. LLC, Collegeville, 1996—. Treas. United Fund Collegeville-Trappe, Inc., 1996-2000; developer computer-based tng. program. Author: Capital Asset Pricing Model: Capital Budgeting Applications (NAA Manuscript award 1979). Recipient Johnson & Johnson Achievement awards, 1989, 92. Democrat. Roman Catholic. Home and Office: T Maco & Assoc 4183 Ironbridge Dr Collegeville PA 19426-1189 E-mail: tmaco@tmaco.net.

MACOMBER, JOHN D. investment company executive; b. Rochester, N.Y., Jan. 13, 1928; s. William Butts and Elizabeth Currie (Ranlet) M.; m. Caroline Morgan, Oct. 21, 1955; children: Janet Morgan, Elizabeth Currie, William Butts II. BA, Yale U., 1950; MBA, Harvard U., 1952. Mng. dir. McKinsey & Co., N.Y.C., France and Switzerland, 1954-73; chmn., CEO Celanese Corp., 1973-87; chmn. J.D. Macomber & Co., 1987-89; pres., chmn. Export-Import Bank of U.S., Washington, 1989-92; prin. JDM Investment Group, 1992—. 1st lt. USAF, 1952-54. Mem. Links (N.Y.C.), River Club (N.Y.C.), Union Club (N.Y.C.), Metropolitan (Washington). Office: JDM Investment Group 2806 N St NW Washington DC 20007-3339

MACON, CAROL ANN GLOECKLER, micro-computer data base management company executive; b. Milw., Mar. 25, 1942; d. William Theodore and Gwendolyn Martha (Rice) Gloeckler; m. Jerry Lyn Macon, Aug. 28, 1981; children: Christian, Marie. BS in Edn. cum laude, U. Wis., Milw., 1969; postgrad., Midwestern State U., Wichita Falls, Tex., 1977, U. Tex., San Antonio, 1978, U. Colo., Colorado Springs. Tchr., Lubbock, Tex.; patient affairs coord. Cardiac Assocs., Colorado Springs; co-founder, CFO Macon Systems, Inc. Artist, Australia, Tex., Colo. Founding mem. Pikes Peak Botanic Gardens Com. Mem.: Pikes Peak Rose Soc., Colorado Springs Fine Arts Ctr., Ikebana Internat. (chpt. 95), Kissing Camels Garden Club, Colo. Mountain Club, Psi Chi, Sigma Tau Delta, Kappa Delta Pi, Phi Kappa Phi.

MACON, IRENE ELIZABETH, interior designer, consultant; b. East St. Louis, Ill., May 11, 1935; d. David and Thelma (Eastlen) Dunn; m. Robert Teco Macon, Feb. 12, 1954; children: Leland Sean, Walter Edwin, Gary Keith, Jill Renee Macon Martin, Robin Jeffrey, Lamont. Student Forest Park Coll., Washington U., St. Louis, 1970, Bailey Tech. Coll., 1975, Lindenwood Coll., 1981. Office mgr. Cardinal Glennon Hosp., St. Louis, 1965-72; interior designer J.C. Penney Co., Jennings, Mo., 1972-73; entrepreneur Irene Designs Unltd., St. Louis, 1974—; vol. liaison Pub. Sch. System, St. Louis, 1980-82; cons. in field. Inventor venetian blinds for autos, 1981, T-blouse and diaper wrap, 1986, owner, partner, mgr., Black Ball Inc., St. Louis, 1996—; cons., bus. mgr. Anything and Everything Store, St. Louis; Author 26th Word newsletter, 1986, (songs) My God's Child Teach Free Will, God is Hiring Now, 1993. Committeewoman Republican party, St. Louis, 1984; vice chair 4th Senatorial Dist. of Mo., 1984, vol. St. Louis Assn. Community Orgns., 1983; instr. first aid Bi-State chpt. ARC, St. Louis, 1984, mem. speakers bur., 1991; cubmaster pack #80 Keystone dist. Boy Scouts Am.; block capt. Operation Brightside, St. Louis, 1984; co-chair status and role of women Union Meml. United Meth. Ch., 1986—, program resource sec., 1990—; trustee Wofit Found., 1989; spokesperson Minority Affairs Initiative Program Am. Assn. Retired Persons, 1991; sec. to block Fedn. Block Units St. Louis Urban League, 1994; mem. Notary Pub. Commn., 1994—; Rep. election judge 26.8 pct Ward, 1994; pub. speaker, story teller prayer breakfast Grace Chapel Ministries, 1994; gospel radio program host Sta. KSTL Radio; transl. bible stories Old Testament and New Testament, It's Gospel Time; volunteer Northside Preservation Commission 1996; speaker at Black Alcoholic/Drug Svc. Info. Center, 1996. Composer religious music, The Ball Point, monthly newsletter and weekly talk radio prog., WGNU Radio, 1998, special guest and player relations, Old Negro Sports Hist. Biographies. Named One of Top Ladies of Distinction St. Louis, 1983. Mem. NAACP, Am. Soc. Interior Designers (assoc.), Nat. Mus. Women in the Arts (charter), Nat. Stroke Assn., Internat. Platform Assn., Nat. Coun. Negro Women (1st v.p. 1984), Invention Assn. of St. Louis (subcom. head 1985), Coalition of 100 Black Women, St. Louis Assn. Fashion Designers, Pres. Club. Methodist. Achievements include invention of Irene's Autoshade, an accordian type of pleated material designed to adhere to automobile windows for the purpose of protecting it from the sun. Avocations: reading, designing personal wardrobe, modeling, horseback riding, boating.

MACON, JERRY LYN, software company owner, software publisher; b. Okla., Jan. 10, 1941; s. James Westwood and Mary Isabelle (Hankins) M.; m. Carol Ann Gloeckler, Aug. 28, 1981; children: Heather, Scott, Karla. BS in Physics magna cum laude, Colo. Coll., 1963; MS in Physics, MIT, 1966; MBA in Fin., U. Colo., 1980. Physics instr. U.S. Naval Acad., Annapolis, Md., 1966-69; stockbroker Merrill Lynch, Colorado Springs, 1969-71; dir. systems analysis and programming Colorado Springs Pub. Schs., 1971-80; co-founder, pres. Alpine Software, Inc., Colorado Springs, 1980-82, Macon Systems Inc., Colorado Springs, 1981—. Author: (software) DB Master, 1980, Advanced DB Master, 1981, Advanced DB Master for Windows Version 6.11, 1999, Version 6.3a6, 2001. Mem. Colorado Springs Fine Arts Ctr., 1982—. Cmdr. U&SN, 1966-69. Boettcher Found. scholar, 1959; Woodrow Wilson fellow, 1963; MIT rsch. assistantship, 1964. Mem. Nat. Fedn. Ind. Bus., Pikes Peak Rose Soc., Colo. Mountain Club, Phi Beta Kappa. Avocations: mountain climbing, hiking, travel, reading history, growing roses.

MACON, MYRA FAYE, retired library director; b. Slate Springs, Miss., Sept. 29, 1937; d. Thomas Howard and Reba Elizabeth (Edwards) M. BS in Edn., Delta State U., 1959; MLS, La. State U., 1965; postgrad., U. Akron, Ohio; EdD, Miss. State U., 1977. Librarian Greenwood (Miss.) Jr. High Sch., 1959-62, Greenwood High Sch., 1962-63, Grenada (Miss.) High Sch., 1963-64; library supr. Cuyahoga Falls (Ohio) City Schs., 1964-71; assoc. prof. U. Miss., Oxford, 1971-83; dir. libraries Delta State U., Cleve., 1983-95. Editor: School Library Media Services for Handicapped; editor: ANRT Newsletter, Miss. Libraries; contbr. articles to profl. jours. Mem. ALA, Southeastern Library Assn., Miss. Library Assn., Exch. Club, Phi Delta Kappa, Beta Phi Mu, Delta Kappa Gamma, Omicron Delta Kappa. Home: RR 3 Box 215A Calhoun City MS 38916-9323

MACOVSKI, ALBERT, b. N.Y.C., May 2, 1929; s. Philip and Rose (Winogr) Macovski; m. Adelaide Paris, Aug. 5, 1950; children: Michael, Nancy. BEE, City Coll. N.Y., 1950; MEE, Poly. Inst. Bklyn., 1953; PhD, Stanford U., 1968. Mem. tech. staff RCA Labs., Princeton, NJ, 1950—57; asst. prof., then assoc. prof. Poly. Inst. Bklyn., 1957—60; staff scientist Stanford Rsch. Inst., Menlo Park, Calif., 1960—71; fellow U. Calif. Med. Center San Francisco, 1971—72; prof. elec. engring. and radiology Stanford U., 1972—, endowed chair, Canon USA prof. engring., 1991—. Dir. Magnetic Resonance Sys. Rsch. Lab.; cons. to industry. Author. Recipient award for color TV cirs., Inst. Radio Engrs., 1958; fellow spl., NIH, 1971. Fellow: IEEE (Zworykin award 1973), Internat. Soc. Magnetic Resonance in Medicine (trustee 1991—94, gold medal 1997), Optical Soc. Am., Am. Inst. Med. Biol. Engring.; mem.: NAE, Am. Assn. Physicists in Medicine, Inst. Medicine, Eta Kappa Nu, Sigma Xi. Jewish. Achievements include patents in field. Home: 2505 Alpine Rd Menlo Park CA 94025-6314 Office: Stanford U Dept Elec Engring Stanford CA 94305 E-mail: macovski@stanford.edu.

MACPHEE, CRAIG ROBERT, economist, educator; b. Annapolis Royal, N.S., Can., July 10, 1944; came to U.S., 1950; s. Craig and Dorothy (Seney) MacP.; m. Kathleen Gray McCown, Feb. 6, 1966 (div. 1981); children: Paul, Heather, Rob; m. Andrea Joy Sime, June 26, 1983. BS, U. Idaho, 1966; MA, Mich. State U., 1968, PhD, 1970. Asst. prof., then assoc. prof. econs. U. Nebr., Lincoln, 1969-89, prof., 1989—, chmn. econs. dept., 1980—83, 1989—98. Econ. affairs officer UN, Geneva, 1975-77; internat. economist U.S. Dept. Labor, Washington, 1983-84; cons. in field. Author: Economics of Medical Equipment and Supply, 1973, Restrictions on International Trade in Steel, 1974. Mem. Am. Econ. Assn., Midwest Econ. Assn., Nebr. Econ. and Bus. Assn., Delta Sigma Pi (faculty adviser 1982-95), Phi Eta Sigma, Omicron Delta Epsilon. Avocations: running, skiing, sailing, reading. Home: 631 Hazelwood Dr Lincoln NE 68510-4325 Office: U Nebr Coll Bus Dept Econs Lincoln NE 68588-0489

MACPHERSON, COLIN R(OBERTSON), pathologist, educator; b. Aberdeen, Scotland, Sept. 2, 1924; came to U.S., 1956; s. Donald J.R. and Nora (Tait) M.; m. Margaret E. Mitchell, Dec. 21, 1949; children: Shelagh, Catherine, Janet, Mary. MBChB, U. Cape Town, Union South Africa, 1946, M.Med., MD in Pathology, 1954. Diplomate Anatomic and Clinical Pathology, Blood Banking. Resident, instr. U. Cape Town, 1948-54; fellow Postgrad. Med. Sch., London, 1955-56; asst., assoc. then prof. pathology Ohio State U., Columbus, 1956-75, vice chmn. lab. med., 1961-75; dir. lab. medicine U. Cin., 1975-87, dep. dir. Hoxworth Blood Ctr., 1988-90, prof. dept. pathology and lab. medicine, 1991-95, prof. emeritus, 1995—. Contbr. articles to profl. jours. Chmn. bd. schs., rev. bd. Nat. Accrediting Agy. for Clin. Lab. Scis., 1968-74. Mem. Am. Assn. Blood Banks. Presbyterian. Avocations: music, color photography. Office: U Cin Med Ctr Goodman St Cincinnati OH 45267-0714

MACPHERSON, ROBERT DUNCAN, mathematician, educator; b. Lakewood, Ohio, May 25, 1944; s. Herbert G. and Jeanette (Wolfenden) MacP. BA, Swarthmore Coll., 1966; MA, PhD, Harvard U., 1970; DSc (hon.), Brown U., 1994, U. Lille (France), 1993. Instr. Brown U., Providence, 1970-72, asst. prof., 1972-74, assoc. prof., 1974-77, prof., 1977-85, Florence Pirce Grant prof., 1985-87; prof. MIT, Cambridge, Mass., 1987-94, Inst. Advanced Study, 1994—. Mem. Inst. des Hautes Etudes Sci., Paris, France, 1974-75, 76-77, 80-81, Steklov Math Inst., Moscow, USSR, 1980; vis. prof. U. Rome, 1985, 2000, U. Chgo., 1991, Max-Planck Inst. for Math, 1992; chmn. NRC Bd. Math. Scis., 1997-2000. Co-author: Stratified Morse Theory, 1988, Nilpotent Orbits, 1989; contbr. numerous articles to profl. jours. Chmn. Former Soviet Union Aid Fund, 1991-96. Recipient Steele prize, 2002. Mem.: NAS (Math award 1992), Nat. Orgn. of Gay and Lesbian Sci. and Tech. Profs., Soc. for Applied and Indsl. Math., Am. Math. Soc., Am. Philos. Soc., Am. Acad. Arts and Scis., Moscow Math. Soc. (hon.), Phi Beta Kappa. Home: 19 Haslet Ave Princeton NJ 08540-4913 Office: Inst for Advanced Study Princeton NJ 08540 E-mail: rdm@ias.edu.

MACPHERSON, SHIRLEY, clinical therapist; b. Bayonne, N.J., June 16, 1934; d. Alexander Phillip and Milldred (Gurstelle) Gottlieb; m. Duncan MacPherson, Jan. 2, 1981; children from previous marriage: Suzanne Pugsley, Brett Barber. BS, Columbia U., NYU, 1951; MS, Juilliard Sch. Music, 1955; MEd, Calif. State U., Northridge, 1967; MA in Psychology, Pepperdine U., 1992; PhD in Psychology, Pacific Western U., 1998. Concert pianist Norman Seman Prodns., N.Y.C., 1952-61; indsl. health educator Am. Med. Internat., L.A., 1968-70; cons., lectr. Hosp. Mgmt. Corp., 1970-80; regional dir. Control Data Corp., 1980-86; outplacement specialist Ind. Cons., 1986-90; psychologist, intern Airport Marina Counseling Svcs., 1990-93; staff psychologist Forensic Psychology Assocs., Sherman Oaks, Calif., 1993-94; staff clin. psychologist Pacific Psychologist Assocs., L.A., 1992-94; clin. therapist employee profiling and crisis intervention MacPherson Relationship Counseling, 1993—. Author: Rx for Brides, 1990, Understanding Your Man, 1998. Vol. Cmty. Alliance to Support and Empower, L.A., 1994-96, South Bay Free Clinic, L.A., 1995-97; mem. Town and Gown Scholarship program, U. So. Calif., L.A. Mem. AAUW, APA, Calif. Psychol. Assn., L.A. Psychol. Assn., L.A. World Affairs Coun., Am. Bd. Hypnotherapy, Am. Assn. Humanistic Psychology, Am. Assn. Suidiology, Juilliard Alumni Assn., Pepperdine Alumni Assn., Internat. Wound Ballistics Assn. Avocations: French and Italian, piano, studies. E-mail: Shirlmac@ix.netcom.com.

MACQUEEN, CHER, retired newscaster, sportscaster, interior designer; b. Kansas City, Mo., Mar. 20, 1952; d. Ira Raymond and Peggy Estelle (Turner) Milks. AA in Liberal Arts, L.A. Valley Coll., 1982; BS in Liberal Studies, Excelsior Coll., Albany, N.Y., 1993; grad., Barbizon Sch. Modeling, 1996; postgrad., Calif. State U., San Bernardino, 1998—; cert. in Interior Design, U. Calif., Riverside, 2002. Lic. radio-TV operator. Personnel specialist U.S. Army, Honolulu, 1973-75, adminstrv. specialist San Francisco, 1975-77, broadcast journalist Vicenza, Italy, 1977-80; radio traffic specialist Armed Forces Radio and TV, L.A., 1980-84, radio prodn. specialist, 1984-86, supr. broadcast support specialist Sun Valley, Calif., 1986-90, broadcast support mgr, 1990-91, internal info. mgr., 1991-94, news and sports specialist, 1994-99. Mem.: DAV (life), Am. Soc. Interior Designers, Pacific Pioneer Broadcasters, Women in Mil. Svc. for Am. (charter), Armed Forces Broadcasters Assn. (v.p. L.A. chpt. 1991—93). Avocations: crafts, crocheting. Home: PO Box 276 Highland CA 92346-0276

MAC RAE, ALFRED URQUHART, physicist, electrical engineer; b. N.Y.C., Apr. 14, 1932; s. Farquhar and Eliza J. (Urquhart) Mac R.; m. Peggy M. Hazard, May 13, 1967; children: Susan, Pamela. BS in Physics, Syracuse U., 1954, PhD in Physics, 1960. Dir. integrated circuit devel. Bell Labs., Murray Hill, N.J., 1979-83, dir. satellite communications systems Homdel, 1983-95; pres. Mac Tech., Berkeley Heights, 1995—. Chair NASA Internat. Technology Studies, 1997-98; mem. adv. com. to bd. trustees N.J. Inst. Tech., 1981-85. Bd. editor: Vacuum Sci. and Tech, 1965-67, Rev. Sci. Instruments, 1969-71; contbr. articles to jours.; patentee in field. Bd. dirs. Summit Area ARC, 1996—, chmn., 2001-02. Fellow IEEE, Am. Phys. Soc.; mem. Bohmische Phys. Soc., IEEE Electron Devices Soc. (pres. 1986-87, chmn. field awards 1989-93, Ebers award 1994). Office: 72 Sherbrook Dr Berkeley Heights NJ 07922-2346

MACRAE, CAMERON FARQUHAR, III, lawyer; b. N.Y.C., Mar. 21, 1942; s. Cameron F. and Jane B. (Miller) MacR.; m. Ann Wooster Bedell, Nov. 30, 1974; children: Catherine Fairfax, Ann Cameron. AB, Princeton U., 1963; LLB, Yale U., 1966. Bar: N.Y. 1966, D.C. 1967, U.S. Dist. Ct. (so. dist.) N.Y. 1975. Atty.-advisor Office of Gen. Counsel to Sec. Air Force, Washington, 1966-69; assoc. Davis, Polk & Wardell, N.Y.C., 1970-72; dep. supt. and counsel N.Y. State Banking Dept., 1972-74; sr. ptnr. LeBeoug, Lamb, Greene & MacRae, 1975—. Dir. Nat. Integrity Life Ins. Co., 2000—. Note and comment editor Yale Law Jour., 1965-66. Trustee, sec. St. Andrew's Dune Ch., 1982—; hon. chmn. Clear Pool Inc., 1990-94. Capt. USAF, 1966-69. Mem. Assn. of Bar of City of N.Y. (past mem. securities regulation com., banking law com.), D.C. Bar Assn., Racquet and Tennis Club, Union Club (N.Y.C.), Meadow Club (v.p., bd. govs.), Bathing Corp. Southampton, Shinnecock Hills Golf Club (Southampton), Cottage Club (Princeton, N.J.), Jupiter Island Club. Republican. Episcopalian. Office: LeBoeuf Lamb Greene & MacRae 125 W 55th St New York NY 10019-5369 E-mail: c.f.macrae@llgm.com.

MAC RAE, HERBERT FARQUHAR, retired college president; b. Middle River, N.S., Can., Mar. 30, 1926; s. Murdoch John and Jessie MacLennon; m. Mary Ruth Finlayson, Sept. 24, 1955; children— Roderick John, Elizabeth Anne, Christy Margaret, Mary Jean. Diploma NS, Agrl. Coll., 1952; BSc, McGill U., 1954, MSc, 1956, PhD, 1960, DSc (hon.), 1987; LLD (hon.), Dalhousie U., 2000. Chemist, food and drug directorate Dept. Nat. Health and Welfare, Ottawa, Ont., 1960-61; mem. faulty Macdonald Coll. McGill U., 1961-72, assoc. prof. animal sci. Macdonald Coll., 1967-70, prof. animal sci. dept. Macdonald Coll., 1970-72; prin. N.S. Agrl. Coll., Truro, 1972-89, ret., 1989. Named to Can. Agrl. Hall of Fame, 1994. Fellow: Agrl. Inst. Can.; mem.: Can. Soc. Animal Sci., Rotary Internat. (Four Aves. of Svc. citation 2002), Order of Can. Home: 7 Hickman Dr Truro NS Canada B2N 2Z2 E-mail: herbmac@ns.sympatico.ca.

MACRI, THEODORE WILLIAM, book publisher; b. N.Y.C. s. Francis Carl and Emma Julia (Fantini) M.; m. Joan Michele Damato; children: Alicia, Theodore William AB, Villanova U.; MA, NYU. With Doubleday & Co. Inc., N.Y.C., dir. domestic rights, 1978-82, editorial group dir., 1982-83, asst. to pres., 1983; v.p., pub. R.R. Bowker Co., 1983-85; v.p., dir. subs. rights Contemporary Books, Inc., 1985-90; v.p. Carol Pub. Group, Inc., N.Y.C., 1990-94; pres. Ted Macri Assocs., 1994—. Bd. dirs. CUNY Ctr. for Pub., Nat. Book Awards Mem. N.Y. County Republican Com.; mem. men's com. Mus. Natural History, N.Y.C. Served to lt. (j.g.) USNR. Named Disting. Alumnus Villanova U. Mem. Assn. Am. Pubs. (edn. com.), Am. Bookseller's Assn. Clubs: N.Y. Athletic (N.Y.C.). Republican. Roman Catholic. Office: 180 Central Park S Ste 441 New York NY 10019-1562 E-mail: papatwm@aol.com.

MACRIS, MICHAEL, lawyer; b. Jackson Heights, N.Y., July 12, 1949; Student, Cornell U.; BA with distinction, Stanford U., 1971; JD, Columbia U., 1974. Bar: N.Y. 1975, Conn. 1976. Mem. Cahill Gordon & Reindel, N.Y.C. Bd. editors Columbia Law Rev., 1973-74; co-editor ERISA & Benefits Law Jour., 1992-99. Harlan Fiske Stone scholar. Fellow Am. Coll. Employee Benefits Counsel (charter); mem. ABA (chmn. com. on fiduciary responsibility, real property, probate and trust law sect. 1993—), Phi Beta Kappa. Office: Cahill Gordon & Reindel 80 Pine St Fl 19 New York NY 10005-1790

MACRIS, NICHOLAS THEODORE, allergist; b. Bklyn., Oct. 27, 1931; MD, SUNY, Bklyn., 1958. Diplomate Am. Bd. Allergy and Immunology. Intern Lenox Hill Hosp., N.Y.C., 1958-59, resident in internal medicine, 1961-63; fellow in allergy and immunology Rockefeller U. Lab. Immunology, 1963-65; fellow in allergy N.Y. Hosp.; chief allergy and immunology Lenox Hill Hosp.; clin. prof. medicine, co-dir. allergy and immunology tng. Cornell U. Med. Sch., N.Y.C. Fellow Am. Acad. Allergy and Immunology, Am. Coll. Allergy and Immunology; mem. AMA, Am. Assn. Immunology, N.Y. Acad. Medicine, Clin. Immunology Soc. Office: 1430 2nd Ave Rm 102 New York NY 10021-3313

MACRURY, KING, management counselor; b. Manchester, N.H., Oct. 14, 1915; s. Colin H. and Lauretta C. (Shea) MacR.; 1 son, Colin C. AB, Rollins Coll., 1938; postgrad., St. Anselms Coll., L.I. Coll. Medicine, Princeton. Asst. personnel dir. Lily-Tulip Cup Corp., 1939; asst. dir. market research Ward Baking Co., 1940-41; staff mem. Nat. Indsl. Conf. Bd., 1941-43; cons. indsl. relations and orgn. planning McKinsey & Co., 1946-48; internal cons. Oxford Paper Co., 1949-50; installer, dir. indsl. relations Champion Internat. Co., 1950-51; pvt. practice mgmt. counselor, 1951—. Lectr. Indsl. Edn. Inst., 1962-68, Mgmt. Center, Cambridge, 1968-71, Dun & Bradstreet, 1979— ; extension div. U. N.H., 1968— ; extension program U. Maine, 1978— ; also U. Bridgeport, extension program U. Conn.; coordinator mgmt. edn. extension div. U. Conn., 1964-68, Philippine Council Mgmt., 1969— , Econ. Devel. Found. Philippines, 1969— , Am. Metal Stamping Assn., 1969— ; condr. mgmt. seminars for Asian Assn. Mgmt. Orgns. C.I.O.S., 1972; Mem. Indsl. Devel. Commn. Andover, 1957-58; manpower com. U.S. Dept. Labor Bus. Adv. Council, 1958-61. Author: Developing Your People Potential; Contbr. numerous articles in field to profl. jours. Served to lt. USNR, 1943-46. Mem. N.H. Dental Soc. (hon.), Smaller Bus. Assn. N.E., Res. Officers Assn. Office: PO Box 215 Rye NH 03870-0215 *As individuals or as corporations, we derive our vitality from the responsiveness of those to whom we are bound in interest or effort. So it becomes, necessarily, our primary goal to inspire and to nurture this elemental source of strength.*

MACSAI, JOHN, architect; b. Budapest, Hungary, May 20, 1926; came to U.S., 1947, naturalized, 1954; s. Ferenc and Margit (Rosenfeld) Lusztig; m. Geraldine Marcus, May 7, 1950; children: Pamela, Aaron, Marian, Gwen. Baccalaureate summa cum laude, Kolcsey Gimnasium, Budapest, 1944; student, Atelier Art Sch., Budapest, 1941-43, Poly. U., 1945-47; BArch magna cum laude, Miami U., Oxford, Ohio, 1949. Archtl. designer Skidmore, Owings & Merrill, Chgo., Pace Assos., Chgo., Raymond Loewy Assos., Chgo., 1949-55; ptnr. Hausner & Macsai, 1955-71, Campbell & Macsai, Chgo., 1971-74; prin. John Macsai & Assocs. Architects, Inc., 1975-90, O'Donnell Wicklund Pigozzi & Peterson, Chgo., 1991-2000, ret., 2000. Prof. architecture U. Ill., Chgo., 1970-76, prof. emeritus, 1997—. Author: High Rise Apartment Buildings: A Design Primer, 1972, Housing, 1976, Housing, 2d edit., 1982, Housing, Russian edit., 1980, Housing, Mexican edit., 1984; co-author: Designing Environments for the Aged, 1977, Housing for a Maturing Population, 1983, (ency.) Highrise Apartment Buildings, 1988, East European Modernism, 1996;prin. works include Nat. Opinion Rsch. Ctr., U.Chgo., 1967, High Energy Physics Bldg., 1968, Social Svcs. Ctr., 1970, Harbor House, 1965, Malibu East, 1972, Waterford apt. bldg., 1976, U. Chgo. faculty townhouses, 1986, Fairfield Ct. housing for the elderly, 1988, Evanston Pl. apt. bldg and city garage, 1991, 2960 N. Lake Shore Dr. Housing for the Elderly, 1991, exhibitions include watercolors at Gallery 1756, Chgo., 1991—2002, Chgo. Cultural Ctr., 2000, Cliffdwellers Club, 2002. Fellow AIA (13 design award citations Chgo. chpt.). Jewish. Home: 1501 Hinman Ave Apt 3B Evanston IL 60201-4675 E-mail: jgmacsai@uic.edu.

MACTAGGART, BARRY, retired corporate executive; b. Kandos, Australia, Dec. 29, 1931; came to U.S., 1972; s. Malcolm Ian and Dorothy (Schroder) MacT.; m. Robin Margaret Wilson, Nov. 24, 1962; children: Susan, Ian, Cameron. Cert. acct., Inst. Chartered Accts., Australia, 1954. Audit mgr. Peat, Marwick, Mitchell, Sydney, Australia, 1950-58; auditor, controller eastern area Pfizer Internat., Hong Kong, 1959-64; controller Pfizer Asia, Tokyo, 1964-65, dir. adminstrn., 1966-67; mgr. country Pfizer Australia, 1967-68; pres. Pfizer Asia, Hong Kong, 1968-72; exec. v.p. Pfizer Internat., N.Y.C., 1972-80, pres., 1980-81, pres., chmn. bd. dirs., dir., 1981-91. Mem. Indian Harbor Yacht Club, Hong Kong Club, The Pilgrims Club, John's Island Club, Riomar Bay Yacht Club, Univ. and Schs. Club. Home: 180 N Shore Pt Vero Beach FL 32963-3726

MACTAGGART, TERRENCE JOSEPH, professor, former university chancellor; b. Buffalo, Sept. 20, 1946; s. Joseph Carol and Genieve Mary (Quinn) MacT. BA in English and Philosophy, Canisius Coll., Buffalo, 1967; MA in Lit., St. Louis U., 1971, PhD in Lit., 1976; MBA, St. Cloud (Minn.)

State U., 1986. Prof. Blackburn Coll., Carlinville, Ill., 1973-74; dir. Webster U., St. Louis, 1974-77; acting dean U. Alaska, Fairbanks, 1977-79; dean St. Cloud (Minn.) State U., 1979-83; v.p. Met. State U., St. Paul, 1983-86; vice chancellor Minn. State U. System, 1986-87; chancellor U. Wis., Superior, 1987-91, Minn. State U. System, Saint Paul, 1991-95; prof. English Minn. State U., 1991-95; chancellor U. Maine System, Bangor, 1996—2001; prof. Univ. of Maine, 2002—. Fulbright Scholar in Thailand, 1996. Editor: Cost Effective Assessment of Prior Learning, 1983; contbr. articles on higher edn. to profl. jours. Sgt. U.S. Army, 1969-71, Viet Nam. NDEA fellow, 1968-72. Mem. Phi Beta Kappa. Avocations: cross country skiing, sailing. Office: Univ Maine System Office 107 Maine Ave Bangor ME 04401-4380*

MACTIER, ANN DICKINSON, school system administrator; b. Ravenna, Nebr., June 29, 1922; d. Robert Smith and Carrie (Clark) Dickinson; m. James Allan Mactier, Feb. 26, 1944; children: James Allan II, Judith Ann, Robert Dickinson. BS, Northwestern U., 1944; BA, U. Nebr., Omaha, 1963, MA, 1969. Owner, mgr. Ponca Hills Riding Acad., Omaha, 1966-73; cmty. coord. Coll. Fine Arts, U. Nebr., 1974-75. Mem. Omaha Jr. League, 1944—57; mem. exec. com. Riverfront Devel. Corp., Omaha, 1973—79; founder, pres. Florence Arts Coun., 1975—79; mem. Omaha Pub. Schs. Bd. Edn., 1983—98; mem. Nebr. State Bd. Edn., 1996—, v.p., 2001—02; mem. steering com. Coun. Urban Bds. Edn., 1996—98; bd. dirs. Coun. Great City Schs., 1984—89. Home: 3811 N Post Rd Omaha NE 68112-1209 E-mail: mactier@starband.net.

MACUMBER, JOHN PAUL, insurance company executive; b. Macon, Mo., Jan. 21, 1940; s. Rolland Deardorf and Althea Villa (Cason) M.; m. Marilyn Sue Ashe, Nov. 10, 1962; children: Leanne, Cheryl. BA, Cen. Meth. Coll., Fayette, Mo., 1962; Assoc. in Risk Mgmt., Ins. Inst. Am., 1978. Casualty underwriter U.S. Fidelity & Guaranty Co., St. Louis, 1962-66; automobile underwriter Am. Indemnity Co., Galveston, Tex., 1966-69; auto casualty underwriter St. Paul Cos., New Orleans, 1969-73; sr. comml. casualty underwriter Chubb/Pacific Indemnity, Portland, Oreg., 1973-75; casualty underwriter Interstate Nat. Corp., L.A., 1975-76, underwriting supr., 1976-78, v.p., br. mgr. Mpls., 1978-82, also v.p. subs. Chgo. Ins. Co.; umbrella/spl. risk supr. Guaranty Nat. Ins. Co., Englewood, Colo., 1982-85; br. mgr. Burns & Wilcox Ltd.-West, Salt Lake City, 1985-96; v.p. M.J. Kelly Ins. Brokers of Utah, Sandy, 1997—. With USAF, 1962-68. Nat. Methodist scholar, 1958; named Co. Person of Yr. Profl. Ins. Agts. Utah, 1991, Ind. Ins. Agts. of Utah, 1996. Mem. Ins. Assn. Utah (sec.-treas. 1992-93, v.p. 1993-94, pres. 1994-95), Ind. Ins. Agts. Utah, Surplus Line Assn. Utah (bd. dirs. 1994-97, 1999—, sec.-treas. 2000-2001, v.p. 2001-02, pres. 2002—), Nat. Assn. Profl. Surplus Lines Offices, Utah Rock Art Rsch. Assn. (v.p. 2000-01, pres. 2002—), Optimists (charter pres. 1968), Kiwanis (charter pres. 1979), Insurance Club, Blue Goose Club (Salt Lake City). Mem. Unity Ch. of Salt Lake City (v.p., bd. dirs. 1988). Home and Office: 9683 Buttonwood Dr Sandy UT 84092-3245

MACUR, PATRICIA ALICE, senior system analyst, programmer; b. Chgo. d. Alexander J. and Alice Mary (Styburski) Mackiewicz; m. George J. Macur; children: Alexander, Cindy Macur Conti. BS, SUNY, 1978; MS, Thomas J. Watson Sch. of Engring., 1984. System control analyst IBM Corp., Endicott, N.Y., 1977; programmer trainee intelligent systems NCR, Ithaca, 1978-79, assoc. programmer software integration, 1980, assoc. programmer I gen. purpose systems, 1980-81, programmer, analyst terminal software div., 1981-84; applications analyst material mgmt. systems Eastman Kodak Co., Rochester, 1984-86, applications analyst planning and control systems, 1986-88; sr. programmer, analyst mfg. systems Ingersoll-Rand Systems, Athens, Pa., 1989-91; sr. assoc. programmer copics packing applications system IBM, Atlanta, 1991-94, customer svc. rep. S.E. region, 1991-94; fin. analyst People Soft/Oracle Fins., 1995; sr. sys. analyst PPL, 1996—. Avocations: horseback riding. Home: 3441 Alexander Pl Smyrna GA 30082-3065 Office: 945 E Paces Ferry Rd PO Box 18616 Atlanta GA 31126-0616 E-mail: macur@plantation-ppl.com.

MACURDY, JOHN EDWARD, basso; b. Detroit, Mar. 18, 1929; s. Blanchard Archibald and Dorathea Rosalie (Radtke) Mc Curdy; m. Justine May Votypka, Apr. 12, 1958; children— Allison Anne, John Blanchard. Student, Wayne State U., 1947; student of Avery Crew, Detroit, 1946. Mem. N.Y.C. Opera, 1959-62, Met. Opera, 1962—. Appeared in U.S., Europe, including San Francisco Opera, La Scala; performances include world premieres Mourning Becomes Electra, Met. Opera, 1967, opening night Anthony and Cleopatra, Met. Opera, 1966, Wuthering Heights, Santa Fe Opera, 1958, Six Characters in Search of an Author, N.Y.C. Opera, 1959, Griffalkin, Tanglewood Festival, 1957; Am. premieres Capriccio, Santa Fe Opera, 1958, Murder in the Cathedral, Empire State Music Festival, Bear Mountain Park, N.Y., 1959, Inspector General, N.Y.C. Opera, 1960; appeared with numerous orchs.; film Don Giovanni, 1979; participant 40th Anniversary Sud-Deutsche Rundfunk, 100th Anniversary Gala Met. Opera, 1983. Served with USAF, 1950-54. Recipient medal for artistic merit during Mich. Week City of Detroit, 1969; inducted into Acad. Vocal Hall of Fame, 1985. Mem.: Bohemian Club of San Francisco. Presbyterian. Office: Met Opera Lincoln Ctr New York NY 10023

MAC WHINNIE, JOHN VINCENT, artist; b. Rockville Centre, N.Y., Apr. 22, 1945; s. Milton Joseph and Inez Genevieve (LaFlamme) Mac W.; m. Virginia Gail Gettling, June, 1985; children: Milton John, Emma Katherine. B.A. magna cum laude, Southampton Coll., 1972. Artist, painter Water Mill, N.Y. Exhibited in group shows: Met. Mus. Art, 1979, Guggenheim Mus., 1979, Lehigh U., 1979, Bklyn. Mus., 1981, Am. Acad. and Inst. Arts and Letters, 1981, New Orleans Mus. Contemporary Art, Guild Hall, Easthampton, N.Y.; one-man shows include: Marlborough Gallery, N.Y., Andre Emmerich Gallery, N.Y.; represented in permanent collections: Guggenheim Mus., Bklyn. Mus., Phillips Collection, Walker Art Ctr., Parrish Art Mus., Guild Hall, numerous others. Recipient First prize in painting Parrish Art Mus., 1971, Excellence in Painting award Heckscher Mus., 1974. Avocations: metaphysics, gardening, antique collecting. Home: Deerfield Rd Water Mill NY 11976

MACWILLIAMS, KENNETH EDWARD, investment banker; b. Newburyport, Mass., Aug. 21, 1936; s. Harold Freeman and Helen (Melia) MacW.; m. Angelyn Wishnack, July 16, 1960 (div. 1975); children: Robert Hovey, James Stuart. BA, Harvard U., 1958, MBA, 1962. V.p. Morgan Guaranty Trust Co., N.Y.C., 1962-71; sr. assoc. Goldman Sachs & Co., 1971-74; mng. dir., domestic merchant banking group Manfacturers Hanover Trust Co., 1975-82; chmn., chief exec. officer Prudential Capital Corp. subs. Prudential Ins. Co. Am., Newark, 1982-90; pres. Prudential Equity Mgmt. Assn. subs. Prudential Ins. Co. Am., 1990-92; founder, pres. Woodrow Wilson Assocs., Chapel Hill, NC, 1993—. Office: PO Box 3119 Chapel Hill NC 27515-3119

MACY, JOHN PATRICK, lawyer; b. Menomonee Falls, Wis., June 26, 1955; s. Leland Francis and Joan Marie (LaValle) M. BA, Carroll Coll., 1977; JD, Marquette U., 1980. Bar: Wis. 1980, U.S. Dist. Ct. (we. and ea. dists.) Wis. 1980, U. S. Ct. Appeals (7th cir.) 1980. Assoc. Hippenmeyer Reilly Arenz Molter Bode & Gross, Waukesha, Wis., 1980-83; ptnr. Arenz Molter Macy & Riffle, S.C., 1983--. Lectr. in field. Mem. ABA, Waukesha County Bar Assn. (chair 1995-96). Republican. Roman Catholic. Home: 4839 Hewitts Point Rd Oconomowoc WI 53066-3320 Office: Arenz Molter Macy & Riffle SC 720 N East Ave Waukesha WI 53186-4800

MACY, STEVEN C. real estate investor; b. Dayton, Ohio, July 6, 1949; s. Charles Arthur and Anne Cecelia Macy; m. Lauralynn Macy, May 20, 1977 (div. Sept. 1999); children: Christopher B., Tiffany L.; m. Robin Ashford, Dec. 15, 1999; 1 child, Alexa A. Assoc. Bus. Mgmt., Sinclair Coll., Dayton, 1970. Cert. property mgr. Regional mgr. WM Properties Inc., N.Y.C., 1970-73; 1st v.p. Smith Barney Haris Upham Inc., 1974-84, Security Capital Corp., N.Y.C., 1984-87; sr. v.p. Integrated Resources Inc., 1987-91; co-founder TGM Assocs. LP, 1991—; exec. v.p. TGM Realty Corps. I II III IV V VI XX XXX, 1993—, TGM Investment Corp. No. I, 1993—. Dir. Showplace Inc., Beach Haven, N.J., J.P. Hayes Inc. Mem. Rep. Nat. Com., Washington, 1983—; mem. Colonial Debutante Ball Com., N.Y.C., 1997, Internat. Debutante Ball Com., N.Y.C., 1998. Mem. Inst. Real Estate Mgmt., Nat. Multi Housing Coun., Pension Real Estate Assn., N.Y. SAR, N.J. Children of Am. Revolution, KC (3rd degree), Little Egg Harbor Yacht Club. Roman Catholic. Avocations: sailing, travel. Office: TGM Assocs LP 650 5th Ave New York NY 10019-6108 E-mail: smacy@tgmassociates.com.

MACY, TERRENCE WILLIAM, social services administrator; b. Springfield, Mass., Apr. 13, 1946; s. Thomas William and Bertha (Johnson) M.; m. Linda Kautz, Aug. 28, 1971; children: Arianne, Tyler. BA, Assumption Coll., 1970; MA, Ohio State U., 1977, PhD, 1980. Instr. Hartford Regional Ctr., Newington, Conn., 1970-73, residential program supr., 1973-74; adminstrv. asst. to supt. Orient (Ohio) Developmental Ctr., 1974-77, dir. transition office, 1977-79; supt. SW Ohio Developmental Ctr., Fairfield, 1979-83; dir. residential svcs. DATAHR, Inc., Brookfield, Conn., 1983-86, dir. residential and vocat. svcs., 1986-89, dir. vocat. svcs., 1989-90; exec. dir. SARAH TUXIS Residential and Cmty. Resources, Inc., Guilford, 1990—. Adj. prof. non-profit mgmt. grad. program U. Conn., 1996-99; cons. Fla. Dept. Mental Retardation, 1982; mem. Regional Human Rights Commn., 1991-97, chmn., 1993-96. Author: A Resource Manual on Transition Shock, 1985. V.p. Bethel (Conn.) Coop. Ext. Svc. Coun., 1987-91; vice-chmn. Brookfield Dem. Town Com., 1989-90, mem. Brookfield Planning Commn., 1989-91; mem. Madison Inland Wetlands Commn., 1993-94; mem. Madison Planning and Zoning Commn., 1994—, Legis. Citation Conn. Gen. Assembly, 1966; mem. Madison Dem. Town Com., 1996—, vice chair, 1998-2002, chair, 2002-. Recipient commendation Ohio Legislature, 1983, Statesman award Conn. Jaycees, 1989. Fellow Am. Assn. Mental Retardation (sec. Ohio chpt., 1977-81, chmn. adminstrv. divsn. 1982, pres. 1983-84, chmn. Conn. chpt. resdl. divsn. 1991, 2d v.p. 1992, pres. 1994); mem. U.S. Jaycees (Gov.'s civic leadership award 1985, 89), Conn., Coun. Execs., vice-chmn. 1991-92, chmn. 1992-95), Conn. Assn. Resdl. Facilities (bd. dirs. 1995-97), Conn. Assn. Non-Profits (v.p. 1997-99, pres. 1999—). Roman Catholic. Office: SARAH TUXIS Residential and Cmty Resources Inc 45 Boston St Guilford CT 06437-2816 E-mail: tuxis@cshore.com., mace4@prodigy.net.

MACZULSKI, MARGARET LOUISE, event marketing professional, meeting manager; b. Detroit, Apr. 01; d. Bohdan Alexander and Olga Louise (Martinuick) M. BS, Mich. State U.; cert. E-Commerce Mgmt., DePaul U., 2000. Cert. meeting mgr. Mgr. meetings Nat. Assn. Realtors, Mktg. Inst., Chgo., 1977-82, mgr. mktg., 1982-83; regional sales mgr. Fairmont Hotels, 1982; dir., mgr. trade shows and confs. Capital Cities Am. Broadcasting Co./Pub. Div., Wheaton, 1983-85; mgr. meeting and conf. planning Soc. Human Resource Mgmt., Alexandria, Va., 1985-90; mgr. meeting and conv. planning Kraft Foods, Glenview, Ill., 1990-95; cons. meetings and spl. events Chgo., 1996-98; sr. mgr. meeting and travel svcs. Coll. Am. Pathologists, Northfield, 1998-2000; conv. mgr. Common, A User Group, 2001—02, cons. meetings and spl. events, 2002—. Mem. Meeting Planners Internat., Greater Washington Soc. Assn. Execs. (past chmn. site inspection com.), Soc. Corporate Meeting Planners, Am. Soc. Assn. Execs., Mich. State U. Alumni Assn. (treas. D.C. chpt. 1987-90), Soc. for Corp. Mtg. Planners, Assn. Forum, Profl. Conf. Mgmt. Assn. Republican. Roman Catholic. Avocations: piano, swimming, skiing. Home: 849 W Lakeside Pl 3 East Chicago IL 60640-6693 E-mail: gwenraz@aol.com.

MADAN, DEEPAK SHEELMOHAN, engineer; b. Bombay, India, Dec. 5, 1959; came to U.S., 1982; s. Sheel Mohan and Koushala S. (Ghai) M.; m. Anuradha P., July 3, 1989; 1 child, Nikhil S. B Technology/Metall. Engr., Indian Inst. Technology, Kanpur, India, 1982; MS Materials Engr., Rensselaer Polytechnic Inst., 1986, PhD Materials Engr., 1988. Industry rsch. cons. Rensselaer Polytechnic Inst., Troy, N.Y., 1982-87; sr. materials engr. Elkem Metals Co., Pitts., 1987-95; dir. technology & new bus. devel. F.W. Winter, Inc. & Co., Camden, N.J., 1995—. Patentee in field; contbr. tech. papers to profl. publs. Mem. Am. Soc. Metals, The Minerlas, Metals and Materials Soc., Am. Powder Metallurgy Inst., Alpha Sigma Mu. Avocations: photography, travel, computers. Office: FW Winter Inc & Co Delaware Ave and Elm St Camden NJ 08102

MADANSKY, ALBERT, statistics educator; b. Chgo., May 16, 1934; s. Harry and Anna (Meidenberg) M.; m. Paula Barkan, June 10, 1990; children from previous marriage: Susan, Cynthia, Noreen, Michele. AB, U. Chgo., 1952, MS, 1955, PhD, 1958. Mathematician Rand Corp., Santa Monica, Calif., 1957-65; sr. v.p. Interpub. Group of Companies, N.Y.C., 1965-68; pres. Dataplan Inc, 1968-70; prof. computer scis. CCNY, 1970-74; prof. bus. adminstrn. grad. sch. U. Chgo., 1974—, assoc. dean, 1985-90, dep. dean, 1990-93, H.G.B. Alexander prof. bus. adminstrn., 1996-99, H.G.B. Alexander emeritus bus. adminstrn., 1999—. Bd. dirs. Analytic Services, Washington, 1975—. Author: Foundations of Econometrics, 1975, Prescriptions for Working Statisticians, 1988. Fellow: Ctr. for Advanced Study in Behavioral Scis., Am. Statis. Assn., Inst. Math. Stats., Econometric Soc. Home: 200 E Delaware Pl Apt 23F Chicago IL 60611-5799 Office: U of Chicago Grad Sch Business Chicago IL 60637 E-mail: albert.madansky@gsb.uchicago.edu.

MADARA, JAMES LEE, dean, epitheliologist, pathologist, educator; b. Altoona, Pa., Sept. 16, 1950; s. Daniel Rodman and Margaret Jane (Hauser) M.; m. Victoria Mollenkopf, May 14, 1975; children: J. Maxwell, Alexis Lindsy. BA, Juniata Coll., 1971; MD, Hahnemann Med., 1975. Cert. anatomic and clin. pathology. Instr. pathology Harvard Med. Sch., Boston, 1980-81, asst. prof. pathology, 1981-85, assoc. prof. pathology, 1985-91; assoc. prof. of health scis. and tech. Harvard-M.I.T., 1986-91; prof. pathology Harvard U. Med. Sch., 1993-97; Timmie prof., chmn. dept. pathology & lab. medicine Emory U. Sch. Medicine, Atlanta, 1997—2002; dean, v.p. for medical affairs Pritzker Sch. of Med. and Div. of Biological Sciences, U. of Chicago, Chicago, Ill., 2002—. Assoc. editor Gastroenterology, 1986-91; mem. editl. bd. Jour. Clin. Investigation, 1987—; editor-in-chief Am. Jour. Pathology, 2000; contbr. over 160 articles to profl. jours. Grantee NIH, 1980—. Mem. Am. Soc. for Clin. Investigation (elected), Am. Soc. for Cell Biology, Am. Gastroenterological Assn. (rsch. coun. 1988-90, Ross Rsch. scholar award 1982), Am. Physiol. Soc., Am. Assn. Pathology (Parke/Davis award 1990), Assn. Am. Physicians. Achievements include description of functional sequellae of neutrophil-epithelial cell interactions; recognition that tight junctions between epithelial cells are regulated under physiological conditions. Office: Pritzker Sch of Med U of Chicago 5841 S Maryland Ave Chicago IL 60637 E-mail: james_madara@emory.org.*

MADARAS, MARCEL BRADUT, research scientist; b. Cluj-Napoca, Romania, Mar. 20, 1966; came to U.S., 1991; s. Ioan and Letitia Madaras; m. Mihaela Luminita Bojin, Aug. 25, 1996; children: Nora Simina, Alexandra Iulia. BS, Babes-Bolyai U., Cluj-Napoca, 1990; PhD, U. N.C., 1996. Asst. prof. Babes-Bolyai U., Cluj-Napoca, 1990-91; rsch. asst. U. N.C., Chapel Hill, 1992-96; rsch. scientist YSI, Inc., Yellow Springs, Ohio, 1996-2000; sr. rsch. scientist Eastman Kodak Co., Rochester, N.Y., 2001—. Contbr. articles to Jour. Electroanalytical Chemistry, Electroanalysis, Analytica Chimica Acta, Analytical Chemistry. Recipient third place student poster competition Am. Soc. for Biomed. Engring., Chapel Hill, 1995. Mem. Am. Chem. Soc., Romanian Soc. for Analytical Chemistry. Avocations: history, soccer, classical music, piano. Home: 587 Morning Glory Dr Webster NY 14580 Office: Eastman Kodak Co Rsch Labs 1999 Lake Ave Rochester NY 14650 E-mail: mmarcel_madaras@kodak.com.

MADAWICK, PAULA CHRISTIAN, artist, educator; b. Ft. Worth, Feb. 14, 1945; d. Tucker Paul Madawick and Lois (Percy) Long; m. Thomas J. Huggins III, Jan. 23, 1965 (div. Jan. 1981); children: Jonathan, James. Student, Sch. Visual Arts, N.Y.C., 1962-92, SUNY, Purchase, 1989-90; B in Visual Studies, Empire State Coll., 1992. Artist asst. Jasper Johns, A. Warhol, Robert Rauschenberg, N.Y.C., 1962-65; asst. art dir. Flair Display Co., Bronx, N.Y., 1980-83; real estate broker Jan Connor, Realtor, N.Y.C., 1983-92; instr. drawing Rockland Ctr. for Art, West Nyack, 1993, 94, 99-2001; gallery dir. Edward Hopper House Art Ctr., Nyack, N.Y., 1993-98, exec. dir., 1996-99; gallery dir. O.C.C. Art Ctr., Demarest, N.J., 2000—. Adj. prof. SUNY Empire Coll. and Rockland Coll., Hartsdale, N.Y., 1994-2001; mem. panel Snug Harbor Cultural Ctr., S.I., 1997; artist-in-residence Blue Hill Cultural Ctr., Pearl River, N.Y., 1994. Contbr. Creative Colored Pencil Landscape, 1996, Realist Painting After Edward Hooper, 1996, The Best of Colored Pencil #2 and #3, 1993, 94; represented in collections at Snake Island Rsch., Toronto, Chase Manhattan Bank, N.A., Bergen Mus. Art and Sci. Mem. Arts Coun. Rockland County, 1990—, Rockland Ctr. for the Arts, 1977—. Recipient Ted and Carol Shen drawing award Silvermine Guild Arts Ctr., 1999, Rockland County Exec. award for visual art, 2002; grant Vt. Studio Ctr., 1998. Mem. Colored Pencil Soc. Am. (signature mem., nat. workshop instr. 1999). Avocations: cycling, hiking. Studio: 159 Piermont Ave Piermont NY 10968-1259 E-mail: clpencil@prodigy.net.

MADAY, CLIFFORD RONALD, insurance professional; b. Cin., Mar. 15, 1947; s. John J. and Betty (Kucha) M.; m. Ellen Doolittle, Aug. 31, 1968; children: Michael, Brian, Christina, Andrew. BS, Northeastern U., 1976. Cert. protection profl. With The Hartford Ins., 1977—, loss control mgr. N.H., 1981-83, Charlotte, N.C., 1983—. Bd. dirs., soccer commr. and coach Matthews (N.C.) Athletic and Recreation Assn., 1983-91; select coach Charlotte United Soccer, 1991-95. 1st lt. U.S. Army, 1965-69, Vietnam. Decorated Bronze Star. Mem. Am. Soc. for Indsl. Security, Am. Soc. Safety Engrs. Avocations: soccer coach, gourmet cooking. Home: 321 W 7th St Charlotte NC 28202-1607 Office: Hartford Ins Co 8711 University East Dr Charlotte NC 28213-4204

MADDALENA, LUCILLE ANN, management consultant; b. Plainfield, N.J., Nov. 8, 1948; d. Mario Anthony and Josephine Dorothy (Longo) M.; m. James Samonte Hohn, Sept. 7, 1975; children: Vincent, Nicholas, Mitchell. AA, Rider U., 1968; BS, Monmouth U., 1971; EdD, Rutgers U., 1978. Newscaster, dir. pub. rels. Sta. WBRW, Bridgewater, N.J., 1971-73; editor-in-chief Commerce mag., New Brunswick, 1973-74; dir. pub. rels. Raritan Valley Regional C. of C., 1973-74; aide pub. relations to mayor City of New Brunswick, 1974; dir. comm. United Way Cen. Jersey, New Brunswick, 1974-77; mgmt. cons. United Way Am., Alexandria, Va., 1977-78; pres., owner Maddalena Assocs., Chester, N.J., 1978—; sr. cons. United Rsch. Co., Morristown, 1980-81; sr. ptnr., dir. OCD Group, Parsippany, 1984-87; chmn. bd. dirs. OCD Group (subs. Xicom Inc.), Morristown, 1988; pres. Morris Bus. Group, Chester, 1989—. Adj. faculty Somerset County Coll., Bridgewater, N.J., 1970, Fairleigh Dickinson U., 1980; guest lectr. Rutgers U., New Brunswick, N.J., 1975-80; designer publicly offered seminars for Bell Atlantic, 1992-98; cons. change Howmet, Alloy, Dover, N.J., 1993-98; consortium trainer Johnson & Johnson, 1988—; developer redesign program Howmet Alloy Divsn., 1994; instr. on-line worldwide grad. mgmt. program Seton Hall U., 1999-2001; profl. mentor to execs. in maj. firms, 1990—. Author: A Communications Manual for Non-Profit Organizations, 1980; editor New Directions for Instl. Advancement, 1980-81. Chmn. pers. com., police com. Chester Borough Coun., 1984-87; pres. Chester Consolidation Study Commn., 1990. Recipient Mayor's Commendation City of New Brunswick, 1973, Chester Borough, N.J., 1988. Mem. AAUW, LWV, Nat. Assn. Press Women, N.J. Elected Women Officials, Kappa Delta Pi. Clubs: N.J. Sled Dog Assn. Republican. Roman Catholic. Avocation: writing, working with non-profits. Home: 75 Melrose Dr Chester NJ 07930-2321 Office: Morris Bus Group PO Box 641 Chester NJ 07930-2920 E-mail: lucille@morrisbusinessgroup.com.

MADDALON, GLENN O. health facility administrator, consultant; b. Redondo Beach, Calif., Apr. 10, 1967; s. Glenn Ottavio and Linda Mary Jane (Mulliken) M. BA in Pub. Rels., San Jose State U., 1990. Acct. coord. Creative Impact Pub. Rels., Costa Mesa, Calif., 1995, Stevenson Systems Inc., Irvine, 1995-96; mgr. field svcs. Am. Cancer Soc., Mission Viejo, 1996-97, sr. mgr. field svcs. Downey, 1997-98, dir. cancer control Pasadena, 1998-99; v.p. devel. Am. Health Mgmt. Inc., Downey, 1999—, Rancho los Amigos Found., Downey, 1999—. Bd. dirs. So. Calif. Cancer Pain Inst.; with Drugs, Alcohol, Tobacco Adv. com., 1997-98, Pasadena Health Advisory Com., 1999-2000; trainer diversity Am. Cancer Soc., 1999—. Coord Spl. Olympics, 1985-87; active Norwalk (Calif.) Coord. Coun., 1997-98, Downey Coord. Com., 1997-98. Recipient gold award United Way, L.A., 1994, 99, 2000. Mem. Nat. Soc. Fundraising Execs. (mem. com. 1999—), Assn. Healthcare Philanthropy, So. Calif. Cancer Pain Inst., Downey Rotary. Republican. Avocations: running, skiing, swimming, marathons. Home: 2322 Ternberry Ct Tustin CA 92782 Office: Rancho los Amigos Found 76106 Imperial Hwy # 601 Downey CA 90242 E-mail: gmaddalon@oclung.org.

MADDALONI, BETTY, elementary education educator; b. Waterbury, Conn., Aug. 17, 1951; d. Vincent P. and Bertha T. (Yanny) M. BS, So. Conn. State U., 1973, MS, 1976; postgrad., St. Joseph Coll., 1988. Cert. profl. educator, pre-K-6, Conn. Tchr. elem. Norton Sch., Cheshire, Conn., 1973-74, Darcey Sch., Cheshire, 1974-77, Highland Sch., Cheshire, 1977—. Mem. prin.'s adv. coun. Highland Sch., 1995-98, mem. PTA; mem. Cheshire Technology Coun., Highland Tech. Com., Highland Interdisciplinary Com. Mem. NEA, Conn. Edn. Assn., Edn. Assn. Cheshire, So. Conn. State U. Alumni Assn. Avocations: reading, gardening, nature study, bowling. Office: Highland Sch 490 Highland Ave Cheshire CT 06410-2582

MADDEN, BARTLEY JOSEPH, economist; b. N.Y.C., Nov. 3, 1943; s. Bartley Joseph and Genevieve Helen (Ghegan) Madden; m. Maricela Elizondo, 1995; children: Lucinda, Miranda, Jeffrey, Gregory. BS in Mech. Engring., U. So. Calif., Los Angeles, 1965; MBA, U. Calif., Berkeley, 1970. V.p. Callard, Madden & Assocs., Chgo., 1970—83; sr. v.p. Harbor Capital Advisors, 1983—92; ptnr. Holt Value Assocs., 1993—2001; mng. dir. CSFB Holt, 2002—. Author: CFROI Valuation: A Total System Approach to Valuing the Firm, 1999. With U.S. Army, 1966-68. Mem. Tau Beta Pi, Beta Gamma Sigma. Office: CSFB Holt 300 S Riverside Plz Ste 1400N Chicago IL 60606-6737 Address: 28 S Loomis St Naperville IL 60540-4937

MADDEN, CYNTHIA ANN, pediatric and family nurse practitioner, educator; b. Sharon, Pa., Dec. 6, 1957; d. Edward A. and Mary Ann (Mc Williams) M. BA, Salisbury (Md.) State U., 1979, BS, 1980; MS in Nursing, U. Pitts., 1982; post masters cert. family nurse practitioner, Wilmington Coll., 1997. Charge nurse pediatrics Peninsula Gen. Hosp. Med. Ctr., Salisbury, 1980-81, 83; instr. nursing Salisbury State U., 1984-86, 96; pediatric nurse practitioner Johns Hopkins Hosp., Balt., 1986-94; asst. prof. nursing Cath. U. Am., Washington, 1988; pediat. nurse practitioner A.I. du Pont Inst., Wilmington, Del., 1994-97, Delmar (Del.) Jr./Sr. H.S., 1996—. Mem. ANA, Nat. Assn. Pediatric Nurse Practitioners and Assocs., Am. Acad. Pediatrics, Sigma Theta Tau, Psi Chi. Home: 8774 Mar Lynn Dr Delmar MD 21875-2442 Office: Delmar High Wellness Ctr 200 N 8th St Delmar DE 19940-1374 E-mail: cmadden@fastol.com.

MADDEN, DAVID, author; b. Knoxville, Tenn., July 25, 1933; s. James Helvy and Emile (Merritt) M.; m. Roberta Margaret Young, Sept. 6, 1956; 1 son, Blake Dana. BS, U. Tenn., 1957; MA, San Francisco State Coll., 1958; postgrad., Yale Drama Sch., 1959-60. Faculty Appalachian State Tchrs. Coll., Boone, N.C., 1957-58, Centre Coll., Danville, Ky., 1960-62, U. Louisville, 1962-64, Kenyon Coll., Gambier, O., 1964-66, Ohio U., Athens, 1966-68; writer-in-residence La. State U., Baton Rouge, 1968-92, dir. creative writing program, 1992-94, dir. U.S. Civil War Ctr., 1992-99, Donald and Velvia Crumbley prof. creative writing, 1999—. Alumni prof. La. State U., 1994. Author: (novels) Cassandra Singing, 1969, Bijou, 1974, The Suicide's Wife, 1978, Pleasure Dome, 1979, On the Big Wind, 1980, Sharpshooter: A Novel of the Civil War, 1996, (stories) The Shadow Knows (Nat. Coun. on Arts selection), 1970, The New Orleans of Possibilities (lit. criticism) Wright Morris, 1964, Poetic Image in Six Genres, 1969, James M. Cain, 1970, A Primer of the Novel, 1980, Writers' Revisions, 1981, Cain's Craft, 1985, Revising Fiction, 1988, Rediscoveries II, 1988; asst. editor: The Kenyon Rev., 1964-66; editor: Remembering James Agee, 1974; co-editor: (with P. Bach) Classics of Civil War Fiction, 1991, Beyond the Battlefield, 2000, The Legacy of Robert Penn Warren, 2000. Served with AUS, 1953-55. Recipient Rockefeller grant in fiction, 1969; John Golden fellow in playwriting, 1959 Mem. Authors League, Associated Writing Programs (bd). Democrat. Office: La State U Dept English Baton Rouge LA 70803-0001

MADDEN, EDWARD HARRY, philosopher, educator, retired; b. Gary, Ind., May 18, 1925; s. Harry Albert and Amelia Dorothy (Schepper) M.; m. Marian Sue Canaday, Sept. 15, 1946; children: Kerry Arthur, Dennis William. AB, Oberlin Coll., 1946, A.M., 1947; PhD, U. Iowa, 1950. Prof. philosophy U. Conn., 1950-59, San Jose State Coll., 1959-64, SUNY, Buffalo, 1964-80, prof. emeritus, 1980, U. Ky., 1982-95, ret., 1995. Vis. prof. Brown U., 1954-55, Amherst Coll., 1962, U. Toronto, 1967, Am. U. Beirut, Lebanon, 1969-70; sr. research fellow Linacre Coll., Oxford U., 1978, Inst. Advanced Study, Princeton, 1980-81. Author: Philosophical Problems of Psychology, 1962, Chauncey Wright and the Foundations of Pragmatism, 1963, Evil and the Concept of God, 1968, Civil Disobedience and Moral Law, 1968, The Structure of Scientific Thought, 1960, Causal Powers, 1975, Causing, Perceiving and Believing, 1975, Freedom and Grace, 1982; co-author, editor: Theories of Scientific Method, 1960, Philosophical Perspectives on Punishment, 1968, The Idea of God, 1968; gen. editor: Harvard U. Press Source Books in History Sci.; mem. editl. bd.: The Works of William James, Thoreau

Quar., History of Philosophy Quar., Philosophy of Sci., 1960-76; mem. adv. bd.: A Critical Edition of the Correspondence of William James (Am. Coun. Learned Socs.). Served with USNR, 1943-45. Recipient Am. Philos. Soc. research grant, 1961, Fulbright-Hays award, 1969-70, Herbert W. Schneider award Soc. for Advancement Am. Philosophy, 1991. Fellow Asa Mahan Soc.; mem. C.S. Peirce Soc. (pres. 1962-63, sec.-treas., editorial bd. Transactions of Soc.), Am. Council Learned Socs. (selection com.), Am. Philos. Assn. (co-chmn. com. publs. 1960-77), Phi Kappa Phi. Home: 4 Sanctuary Cir White River Junction VT 05001-2960

MADDEN, HEATHER ANN, aluminum company executive; b. Sharon, Pa., Dec. 20, 1967; d. Edward Arthur and Mary Ann (McWilliams) M. BS in Bus., Salisbury (Md.) State U., 1991; MS in Bus., Johns Hopkins U., 1994. With Delmarva Aluminum Co., Inc., Delmar, Del., 1984-95, exec.'s asst., 1987-95, also dir., 1990—; instr. office sys. tech. Del. Tech. & C.C., Georgetown, 1995—. Owner, operator software consulting and tng. firm, 1997—. Vol. The Holly Ctr., Salisbury, 1992-94. Recipient Holly Svc. award The Holly Found., Salisbury, 1994. Avocations: women's softball, personal computers, dogs, swimming, gardening. Home: 8300 Robin Hood Dr Salisbury MD 21804-2216

MADDEN, JAMES COOPER, V, management consultant; b. Glen Cove, N.Y., June 18, 1961; s. James Cooper IV and Linda Marie (Lizza) M.; m. Heather Madden; 1 child, Jennifer Louise. Student, Webb Inst. Naval Architecture, Glen Cove, 1979-80; BA cum laude, BBA magna cum laude, So. Meth. U., 1983. Cert. Soc. Naval Architects and Marine Engrs. Cons. Andersen Cons./Arthur Andersen, Houston, 1983-85, sr. cons., 1985-87, mgr. L.A., 1987-90, sr. mgr., 1990-91; prin. Booz-Allen & Hamilton, 1991-93; v.p. mng. dir. MCI Systemhouse, 1993-95, pres. U.S. and Mexico ops., 1995-97, CFO, 1997-98; chmn., pres. Exult, Inc., Irvine, Calif., 1998—. Contbr. articles to profl. jours. Bd. dirs. Exolt. Webb Inst. Naval Architecture scholar, 1979-80. Avocations: sailing, snow skiing, travel, reading. Office: Exult Inc 4 Park Plz Ste 1000 Irvine CA 92614-2552

MADDEN, JAMES D. forensic engineer; b. Jersey City; s. Louis A. and Ann Madden. BSChemE, U. S.C., 1963, ME, 1966. Lic. profl. engr., Ohio; cert. diplomate forensic engr. Process engr. Monsanto Co., Alvin, Tex., 1966-67; process and project engr. Union Carbide Corp., Houston, 1967-70; systems engr. M.W. Kellogg Co., 1970-73, prin. systems engr., 1974-77; sr. process engr. Litwin Co., 1973-74; sr. project engr. Davy Powergas, 1977-78, supervising project engr., 1978-79; mgr. equipment engring. DM Internat., 1979-80, project engring. mgr., 1980-83; owner, forensic engr. Madden Forensic Engring., Parma, Parma Heights and Brecksville, Ohio, 1983—. Pres. Houston Young Adult Rep. Club, 1970-73; chmn. Tex. Young Adult Rep. Clubs, 1973. NSF rsch. grantee, 1963; NASA fellow, 1963-65; named to Outstanding Young Men Am., 1973. Mem. ASME, NSPE, AIChE, Soc. Automotive Engrs., Nat. Fire Protection Assn., Inst. Transp. Engrs., Am. Soc. Agrl. Engrs., Bldg. Ofcls. and Code Adminstrs. Internat., Nat. Acad. Forensic Engrs., Sigma Xi, Sigma Pi Sigma, Tau Beta Pi, Omicron Delta Kappa. Office: 10175 Brecksville Rd Cleveland OH 44141-3205

MADDEN, JEROME ANTHONY, lawyer; b. Memphis, Aug. 24, 1948; s. Bernard Clark and Virginia Ann (Golas) M.; m. Cynthia S. Madden, June 27, 1992; 1 child, Clark John. BA, The Franciscan U. Steubenville, Ohio, 1971; JD summa cum laude, U. Dayton, 1978. Bar: Ohio 1978, D.C. 1979, U.S. Dist. Ct. D.C. 1979, U.S. Ct. Appeals (D.C. cir.) 1980, U.S. Ct. Claims 1984, U.S. Ct. Appeals (Fed. cir.) 1984, U.S. Supreme Ct. 1984, U.S. Ct. Appeals (7th and 11th cirs.) 1987, U.S. Ct. Appeals (4th and 5th cirs.) 1988, U.S. Ct. Appeals (9th cir.) 1991, U.S. Ct. Appeals (2d & 10th cirs.) 1992, U.S. Ct. Appeals (1st cir.) 1993. Law clk. to chief justices O'Neill and Leach Ohio Supreme Ct., Columbus, 1978-79; assoc. Cadwalader, Wickersham & Taft, Washington, 1979-85; sr. trial counsel U.S. Dept. Justice, 1985-91; counsel, then acting sr. counsel, then supervisory counsel FDIC Appellate Litigation Sect., Comml. Litigation Unit, 1991-98; trial atty. U.S. Dept. Justice, Comml. Litigation Br., 1998—. Adj. prof. George Washington U. Sch. Law, Washington, 2000—. Editor-in-chief U. Dayton Law Rev., 1977-78. Served with USMCR, 1970-76. Mem. D.C. Bar Assn. Roman Catholic. Avocation: golf. E-mial. Home: 1502 Powells Tavern Pl Herndon VA 20170-2831 Office: US Dept of Justice 1100 L St NW Washington DC 20005-4035 E-mail: Jerome.Madden@usdoj.gov.

MADDEN, JOHN FRANCIS, fundraising executive; b. New Brunswick, N.J., Apr. 13, 1964; s. John Francis and Helen Madden; m. Cynthia Madden, Apr. 22, 1990; children: Kateri, Paige. BA, U. Dayton, 1986. Tchr. St. Joseph H.S., Metuchen, N.J., 1987-91, chmn. religious studies dept., 1991-97, dir. campus ministry, 1997-99, dir. alumni rels., 1999-2000, dir. devel., 2000—. Office: St Joseph HS 145 Plainfield Ave Metuchen NJ 08840 E-mail: maddkap@optonline.net.

MADDEN, JOHN PATRICK, lawyer; b. N.Y.C., Sept. 9, 1945; s. Eugene Patrick and Eileen Mary (Gaughan) M.; m. Sally Williams, Apr. 21, 1984; children: Samuel, Christopher. BCE, Manhattan Coll., 1967; MSCE, NYU, 1969; JD, St. John's U., 1978. Bar: U.S. Patent Office 1978, N.Y. 1979, N.J. 1982, U.S. Dist. Ct. (so. and ea. dists.) N.Y. 1982, U.S. Dist. Ct. N.J. 1982, U.S. Supreme Ct. 1985; cert. internat. arbitrator, constrn. panelist, comml. mediator, D.O.D. instr. Law clk., assoc. Buckley, Treacy, Shaffel Mackey & Abbate, N.Y.C., 1977-80; cons. Contractors Consulting Svcs. Inc., Greatneck, N.Y., 1980-81; ptnr. Madden, Sciarra & Muirhead, N.Y., N.J., 1981-82, Canfield, Venusti, Madden & Rossi, Manhattan, N.Y., 1983—. Lectr. in field. Contbr. articles to profl. jours. V.p. N.Y.C. Jaycees, 1975-95. ROTC USAF, 1963-65. Mem. ABA (pub. contract law sect., forum com. on constrn. industry), London Ct. Internat. Arbitration, Swiss Arbitration Assn., Am. Trial Lawyers Assn., N.Y. State Bar Assn., N.Y. State Trial Lawyers Assn., Assn. of Bar of City of N.Y., Nat. Arts Club. Office: Canfield Venusti Madden & Rossi 230 Park Ave Rm 2525 New York NY 10169-2599

MADDEN, JOSEPH DANIEL, trade association executive; b. N.Y.C., Dec. 25, 1921; s. Thomas A. and Margaret (McFadden) M.; m. Eileen M. MacDonnell, Sept. 8, 1951; children: Joseph Daniel, Jr., Maureen A. BS, Fordham U., 1951; MBA, N.Y. U., 1956. Credit investigator Dun & Bradstreet, N.Y.C., 1947-48; credit mgr. Devoe & Raynolds Co., 1948-50; accounts supr. credit dept. Admiral Corp., 1950-51; nat. credit mgr. Standard Toch Chems., Inc., S.I., N.Y., 1951-52; with chems. and plastics div. Union Carbide Corp., Danbury, Conn., 1952-62; mgr. Detroit sales office, 1958-60; sr. staff adminstr. Soc. Plastics Industry, Washington, 1962-69; exec. v.p. Drug, Chem. and Allied Trades Assn., East Windsor, N.J., 1969-88, cons. assn. mgmt., 1988—. With U.S. Army, 1942-43. Mem. Am. Soc. Assn. Execs. (cert.), N.Y. Soc. Assn. Execs. (past bd. dirs., Exec. of Yr. award 1988), Soc. Friendly Sons of St. Patrick, Kiwanis (past pres. Bayside, sec.), Am. Legion, Am. Assn. Ret. Persons (past pres. local chpt.), Toastmasters Internat. (past pres. local club). Home: 201-26 38th Ave Flushing NY 11361-1849 E-mail: josephdmaddensr@att.net.

MADDEN, MARIE FRANCES, marketing professional; b. Weatherby, Mo., Sept. 27, 1928; d. Truman E. and Hazel (Tiller) Wilford; m. Mertice A. Madden, July 20, 1974. Grad. high sch., Cameron, Mo. Cert. personnel cons. Office mgr. Bechtel Corp., San Francisco, Lawrence, Kans., 1948-52; adminstrn. asst. Milton P. Allen, Atty., 1952-56, Philip T. Sharples, Entrepreneur, Phila., 1956-74; corp. sec. Madden Aircraft Sales Corp., Dallas, 1974-81; pres., owner Madden Co., Inc. of Dallas, 1981-89; exec. dir. TPC Madden Mktg. Group, 1989-91; owner, pres. Madden Mktg. and Design Group, 1991—; ptnr. Madden-Otterbine Tng., 1994-99. Pres. Innovative Sign Group, 1999—. Mem. Metroplex Assn. Pers. Cons. (bd. dirs. 1986-87), Tex. Assn. Pers. Cons. (bd. dirs. 1987-89), Apt. Assn. Greater Dallas, Nat. Apt. Assn., Nat. Assn. Home Builders, Tex. Apt. Assn. Avocations: reading, golfing. Home: 606 Laredo Cir Allen TX 75013-5441 Office: 1819 Firman Dr Ste 145 Richardson TX 75081-1868 E-mail: mmadden@madden-otterbine.com.

MADDEN, MARTIN GERARD, former state legislator; b. Washington, May 24, 1949; s. Anthony M. and Catherine W. Madden; m. Julia Gatewood Spangler, July 29, 1988; children: Donald Gerard, Thomas Martin, Christina Lynne, Marguerite Allen Spangler. BA in Econs., Iona Coll., 1971. Mem. Md. Ho. of Dels., Annapolis, 1991-94; mem. Md. Senate, 1995—2002; senate minority leader State of Md. Gen. Assembly, 1999—2001, mem. senate budget and taxation com. Mem. budget and tax com.; co-chmn. joint com. on welfare reform. Republican. Roman Catholic. Avocation: folk art collector. Office: 420 Miller Senate Bldg Annapolis MD 21401-1991 E-mail: themaddens@hotmail.com.

MADDEN, MICHAEL DANIEL, finance company executive; b. Buffalo, Feb. 16, 1949; s. Daniel Francis and Miriam (Catron) M.; m. Mary Madden, May 1, 1976; children: Daniel, Kristina, Megan, Michael. BA in Econs. magna cum laude, Le Moyne Coll., 1971; MBA with distinction, U. Pa., 1973. Assoc. Kidder, Peabody & Co., N.Y.C., 1973-77, v.p., 1977-80, mng. dir., 1980-85, head investment banking, 1985-88, Lehman Bros., N.Y.C., 1989-93; exec. mng. dir. Global Capital Markets Kidder, Peabody Co., 1993-94; vice chmn., chief origination officer Paine Webber Inc., 1995-96; chmn., CEO Hanover Capital LLC, 1996—; ptnr. Beacon Group; sr. ptnr. Questor Mgmt., 1999—. Bd. dirs. Gruntal & Co., Comforce Corp., Transonic Sys. Inc. Bd. dirs. Freeport Properties, Inc., Immedient Corp., Cath. TV Ctr., N.Y.C., 1981-85, Canisius Prep. Sch., Buffalo, 1992—; chmn. bd. trustees LeMoyne Coll., Syracuse, N.Y., 1987—. Mem. Am. Petroleum Inst., MBA Assn., Univ. Club, The Creek, Longboat Key Club. Republican. Roman Catholic. Avocations: boxing, hunting, tennis, coin collecting, fishing. Office: Questor Mgmt 9 W 57th St New York NY 10019 E-mail: mmadden@questorfund.com.

MADDEN, MURDAUGH STUART, lawyer; b. Morgantown, W.Va., Feb. 26, 1922; s. Joseph Warren and Margaret (Liddell) M.; m. Constance Viens McKenna, May 12, 1999; children by previous marriage: Liddell Louise, Murdaugh Stuart Jr., Michael Mann. Student, Oberlin Coll., 1939-40; BA, George Washington U., 1942; JD, Harvard U., 1948. Bar: D.C. 1948, Va. 1948, U.S. Supreme Ct. 1953. Asst. counsel Bur. Aero., Washington, 1948-50; sole practice, 1950-61, 71—; sr. ptnr. Shaw, Pittman, Potts, Trowbridge & Madden, 1961-71. Sr. counsel Humane Soc. U.S., Atlantic Devel. Co. and related corps. Author: (with Sherman L. Cohn) The Legal Status and Problems of the American Abroad, 1966. Trustee Inst. for Study Nat. Behavior, Princeton, N.J., Friends of India Com., Washington; pres. World Fedn. for Protection Animals, The Netherlands; v.p. World Soc. forProtection Animals, London. With USAAF, 1942-45, ETO. Mem. ABA (past chmn. internat. and comparative law com. internat. transp., chmn. subcom. on charitable orgns. internat. law sect. 1985—), D.C. Bar Assn., (past dir., past chmn. com. bar ethics), Va. Bar Assn., The Barristers, Am. Soc. Internat. Law, Harvard Law Sch. Assn., Oberlin Alumni Assn., Metropolitan Club, Harvard Club N.Y., Internat. Lawn Tennis Club U.S., Chevy Chase Club, Phi Sigma Kappa. Episcopalian. Home: 2530 Queen Annes Ln NW Washington DC 20037-2148 Office: 2100 L St NW Washington DC 20037-1525

MADDEN, NANCY A. systems analyst; b. St. Cloud, Minn., Dec. 21, 1951; d. Keith Warren and Norma Louise (Hoglund) M. BS in Bus. Mgmt., St. Cloud State U., 1975; MBA, U. Minn., 1990. Bus. analyst Dun & Bradstreet, Inc., Mpls., 1975-77; sales rep. Gourmet Foods, St. Paul, 1977-79; regional mgr. Estee Lauder, Inc., N.Y.C., 1979-81, regional mktg. dir., 1981-84, regional account mgr., 1984-90, systems analyst, 1990—. Mem. MN100, Bloomington, Minn., 1991-92. Mem. Cornerstone (bd. dirs. 1992—), Jr. League Mpls. (bd. dirs., mgmt. bd. 1990-91, sec. 1991-92, v.p. adminstrn. 1992-93).

MADDEN, PALMER BROWN, lawyer; b. Milw., Sept. 19, 1945; m. Susan L. Paulus, Mar. 31, 1984. BA, Stanford U., 1968; JD, U. Calif., Berkeley, 1973. Bar: Calif. 1973, U.S. Dist. Ct. (no. dist.) Calif. 1973, U.S. Supreme Ct. 1982. Ptnr. McCutchen, Doyle Brown & Enersen, Walnut Creek, 1985-98; prin. ADR Svcs., Alamo, Calif., 1999—. Pres. State Bar Bd. Govs., 2000-2001. Chair bd. govs. Continuing Edn. of the Bar, 1997; judge pro tem Contra Costa Superior Ct., 1991-98; pres. Contra Costa Coun., 1995, Kennedy-King Found., 1994; bd. dirs. Episcopal Homes Found., 2001. Mem. Contra Costa County Bar Assn. (pres. 1996-97). Democrat. Episcopalian. Office: ADR Svcs 3000 Danville Blvd # 543 Alamo CA 94507

MADDEN, PAUL ROBERT, lawyer, director; b. St. Paul, Nov. 13, 1926; s. Ray Joseph and Margaret (Meyer) Madden; m. Rosemary R. Sorel, Aug. 7, 1974; children: Margaret Jane, James Patrick, Derek R. Sorel, Lisa T. Schoutsen. Student, St. Thomas Coll., 1944; AB, U. Minn., 1948; JD, Georgetown U., 1951. Bar: Ariz. 1957, Minn. 1951, D.C. 1951. Assoc. Hamilton & Hamilton, Washington, 1951-55; legal asst. to commr. SEC, 1955-56; assoc. Lewis and Roca, Phoenix, 1957-59, ptnr., 1959-90, Beus, Gilbert & Morrill, Phoenix, 1991-94, Chapman and Cutler, Phoenix, 1994-97; of counsel Gallagher & Kennedy, 1997—. Sec. Minn. Fedn. Coll. Rep. Clubs, 1947-48; chmn. 4th dist. Minn. Young Rep. Club, 1948; nat. co-chmn. Youth for Eisenhower, 1951-52; mem. Ariz. Rep. Com., 1960-62; bd. dirs. Found. Jr. Achievement Ctrl. Ariz., Cath. Community Found., Phoenix, St. Joseph the Worker, Prescott People Who Care, 2001—; past bd. dirs., past chmn. Mesa Air Group, Inc., Camelback Charitable Trust, Found. for Sr. Living; past bd. dirs. The Samaritan Found., Phoenix, Ariz. Club, Phoenix, 1990-93; past bd. dirs., vice chmn. Cen. Ariz. chpt. ARC; past bd. dirs., past pres. Jr. Achievement Cen. Ariz., Inc.; mem. nat. bd. visitors U. Ariz. Law Sch.; corp. counsel, inst. bd. Georgetown U. Sch. Law, 1998—; dir. Cath. Social Svcs., Prescott, 2002—, The Indsl. Devel. Authority of the City of Prescott. With USNR, 1946-48. Mem. ABA, Ariz. Bar Assn., Maricopa County Bar Assn., Fed. Bar Assn., Yavapai County Bar Assn., The Barristers Club (Washington), Arizona Club, Phi Delta Phi. Home: 1565 Range Rd Prescott AZ 86303 Office: Gallagher & Kennedy PA 101 E Gurley Ste 214 Prescott AZ 86301 Office Fax: 928-445-5804. E-mail: prm@gknet.com.

MADDEN, RICHARD BLAINE, forest products executive; b. Short Hills, N.J., Apr. 27, 1929; s. James L. and Irma (Twining) M.; m. Joan Fairbairn, May 24, 1958; children: John Richard, Lynne Marie, Kathryn Ann, Andrew Twining. BS, Princeton U., 1951; JD, U. Mich., 1956; MBA, NYU, 1959; PhD (hon.), St. Scholastica Coll., 1994. Bar: Mich. 1956, N.Y. 1958. Gen. asst. treas.'s dept. Socony Mobil Oil Corp., N.Y.C., 1956-57, spl. asst., 1958-59, fin. rep., 1960; asst. to pres. Mobil Chem. Co.; also dir. Mobil Chems. Ltd. of Eng., 1960-63; exec. v.p., gen. mgr. Kordite Corp.; also v.p. Mobil Plastics, 1963-66; v.p. Mobil Chem. Co., N.Y.C., 1966-68, group v.p., 1968-70; asst. treas. Mobil Oil Corp., 1970-71; chmn. Mobil Oil Estates Ltd., 1970-71; pres., chief exec. Potlatch Corp., San Francisco, 1971-77, chmn. chief exec. officer, 1977-94; ret., 1994. Bd. dirs. CNF Inc., URS Corp.; former bd. dirs. Potlatch Corp., PG&E Corp., Del Monte Corp., AMFAC Inc., Bank Calif. N.A. and BankCal Tri-State Corp.; from lectr. to adj. assoc. prof. fin. NYU, 1960-63; bd. dirs. Hospitaller; Order of Malta, Western Assn.; bd. govs., mem. adminstrv. compensation, audit & labor rels. com. San Francisco Symphony. Bd. dirs. Smith-Kettlewell Eye Rsch. Inst., trustee emeritus, former chmn. Am. Enterprise Inst.; former mem. bd. Nat. Park Found.; hon. trustee Com. for Econ. Devel. Lt. (j.g.) USNR, 1951-54. Mem. N.Y. Bar Assn., Mich. Bar Assn. Clubs: Bohemian (San Francisco); Lagunitas (Ross, Calif.); Metropolitan (Washington). Roman Catholic.

MADDEN, ROBERT EDWARD, surgeon, educator; b. Oak Park, Ill., Sept. 16, 1925; s. Joseph Edward and Gertrude Celelia (McGowan) M.; m. Susan Ann Hale, May 24, 1958; children: Robert Joseph, Lisa Marie, Karen Louise, Kevin Francis. BS in Medicine, U. Ill., Chgo., 1950, MS in Biochemistry, MD, U. Ill., Chgo., 1952. Diplomate Am. Bd. Surgery, Bd. Thoracic Surgery. Assoc. in surgery U. Ill. Coll. Medicine, Chgo., 1957-58; sr. surgeon Nat. Cancer Inst., Bethesda, Md., 1959-60; asst. prof. surgery N.Y. Med. Coll., N.Y.C., 1961-66, assoc. prof., 1966-71, prof. Valahlla, 1971—. Mem. N.Y. State Health Rsch. Coun., Albany, 1976—; med. coord. N.Y. State Dept. Health, 1998—. Author: (with Lippincott) Problems In General Surgery, 1988; editor: Gastrointestinal Bleeding, 1987; editor-in-chief N.Y. Med. Quarterly, 1979-90; contbr. articles to profl. jours. With U.S. Army, 1943-46. Recipient Borden Undergrad. Rsch. award Borden Corp., 1952; postdoctoral fellow Am. Cancer Soc., 1958-59. Fellow ACS (com. on cancer 1993-97); mem. Am. Soc. for Vascular Surgery, Soc. Internat. Chirurgie, Am. Assn. Cancer Edn. (pres. 1979), N.Y. Cancer Soc. (pres. 1975-76), N.Y. State Cancer Programs Assn. (pres. 1975-76), Knights of Holy Sepulchre, Knights of the Order of Malta, Pi Gamma Mu. Republican. Roman Catholic. Home: 6 Crows Nest Rd Bronxville NY 10708-4802 Office: NY Med Coll Munger Pavilion Valhalla NY 10595 E-mail: remadden@bellatlantic.net.

MADDEN, TERESA DARLEEN, insurance agency owner; b. Dallas, Aug. 4, 1960; d. Tommy Joe Frederick Dodd and Mary Helen (Sterner) Smith; m. Kim Ashley Madden, June 2, 1989. Student, Tex. Tech U., 1978-81. Cert. ins. counselor. With personal lines svc. Charles R. Ervin Ins., Midland, Tex., 1981, Bryant Scalf Ins., Richardson, 1981-82; with comml. ins. svc. Street & Assocs. Inc., Dallas, 1982-84; with comml. ins. sales/svc. Hotchkiss Ins., 1984-85; mgr. sales Abbott-Rose Ins. Agy., 1985-89; owner Glenn-Madden & Assocs. Ins., 1990—. Methodist. Office: Glenn Madden & Assocs Inc 13601 Preston Rd Ste 106E Dallas TX 75240-4906 E-mail: dmadden@glenn-maddeninsurance.com.

MADDEN, THERESA MARIE, elementary education educator; b. Phila., Feb. 12, 1950; d. James Anthony and Marie Margaret (Clark) Madden. BA in Social Sci., Neumann Coll., 1977; postgrad., Beaver Coll., Immaculata Coll. Cert. tchr. Pa., prin. Pa. Tchr. elem. grades St. Anthony Sch., Balt., 1971-73, St. Mary-St. Patrick Sch., Wilmington, Del., 1973-74, Queen of Heaven Sch., Cherry Hill, N.J., 1974-77, St. Bonaventure Sch., Phila., 1977-78, 79-83, St. Stanislaus Sch., Lansdale, Pa., 1978-79; substitute tchr. various schs. Phila., 1983-84; tchr. 8th grade math. St. Cecilia Sch., 1984-94; tchr. math., vice prin. Corpus Christi Sch., Lansdale, Pa., 1994-99; tchr. grades 6-8 St. Maria Goretti Sch., Hatfield, 1999—. Mem. vis. team Mid. States Assn., Phila., 1992, Phila., 97, Phila., 99, Phila., 2000, Phila., 02; presenter workshops. Mem.: Assn. Tchrs. Math. Phila. and Vicinity, Pa. Coun. Tchrs. Math., Nat. Coun. Tchrs. Math. Roman Catholic. Avocations: crocheting, cross stitch, baking, walking. Office: St Maria Goretti Sch Cowpath Rd Hatfield PA 19440

MADDEN, THOMAS F. medieval history eductor, author; b. Phoenix, June 10, 1960; s. Thomas J. and Joyce L. (Parsons) M.; m. Page A. Ettle, Oct. 15, 1994; children: Helena, Melinda. BA, U. N.Mex., 1986; MA, U. Ill., 1990, PhD, 1993. Asst. prof. history St. Louis U., 1992-96, assoc. prof., 1996—, chmn. dept., 1996-98, 2001—. Cons. on crusade topics Ency. Brit., Chgo., 1999—. Co-author: The Fourth Crusade: The Conquest of Constantinople, 1997 (History Book Club selection 1998); author: A Concise History of the Crusades, 1999 (Washington Post Book World Raves selection 2000); co-editor: Medieval and Renaissance Venice, 1999. Rsch. grantee Gladys Krieble Delmas Found., 1990, 98. Mem. Medieval Acad. Am., The Hist. Soc., Cath. Hist. Assn., Soc. for Study Crusades and Latin East, Midwest Medieval History Conf. (pres. 1999-2000). Roman Catholic. Office: 3800 Lindell Blvd Saint Louis MO 63108-3414 Fax: 314-977-1603. E-mail: maddentf@slu.edu.

MADDEN, WALES HENDRIX, JR. lawyer, director; b. Amarillo, Tex., Sept. 1, 1927; s. Wales Hendrix and Kathryn (Nash) M.; m. Alma Faye Cowden, Nov. 8, 1952; children: Wales Hendrix III, Straughn. BA, U. Tex., 1950, LL.B., 1952. Bar: Tex. 1952. Practiced in Amarillo. Mem. Tex. Constnl. Revision Commn., 1973. Mem. Tex. Coll. and Univ. System Coord. Bd., 1964—69, Amarillo Area Found.; Cal Farley's Boys Ranch; Pres.'s Export Coun., 1981; mem. Select Com. Higher Edn., 1985, 1987; chmn. SWST Regional Panel, Pres.'s Commn. on White House Fellowships, 1989—90, Tex. Water Devel. Bd., 2002; mem. Gov.'s Com. on Ad Valorem Taxes, 1996; bd. regents Amarillo Coll., 1958—59, U. Tex., 1959—65; trustee Trinity U., San Antonio; chmn. bd. Internat. Food and Agrl. Devel., 1990—94. Served with USNR. Named Outstanding Man of Amarillo, 1972; Disting. Alumnus U. Tex., 1979, U. Tex. Law Sch., 1986. Mem. ABA, Amarillo Bar Assn. (pres. 1956), Tex. Philos. Soc., Amarillo C. of C. (pres. 1968), State Bar Tex., State Jr. Bar Tex. (pres. 1956), Friar Soc., Phi Alpha Delta, Phi Delta Theta, Phi Eta Sigma, Pi Sigma Alpha. Presbyterian (elder). Home and Office: PO Box 15288 Amarillo TX 79105-5288

MADDEN, WANDA LOIS, nurse; b. Augusta, Kans., Apr. 26, 1929; d. George W. and Lillian B. (Dobyns) Provost; m. Laurence R. Madden, June 3, 1947 (div. 1961); children: Matthew, Mark, Luke, John, Michele. ADN, Pasadena City Coll., 1970; postgrad., Calif. State U. Consortium, 1986. RN, Calif.; ordained to ministry Am. Fellowship Ch., 1995. CCU nurse Huntington Meml. Hosp., Pasadena, Calif., 1970-71; ICU Community Hosp., Pico Rivera, 1971-72; CCU nurse Queen of the Valley Hosp., West Covina, 1973-74; ICU supr. Visalia (Calif.) Community Hosp., 1974-77, 89-90, ICU nurse, 1978, San Miguel Hosp. Assn., San Diego, 1978-79; supr. Casa Blanca Corp., 1979-80; dir. nursing Visalia Convalescence Hosp., 1981-89, Westgate Gardens Convalescent Ctr., Visalia, 1990; psychiat. staff nurse Mill Creek Hosp., 1990-91; AIDS case mgr. Tulare County Health Svcs., 1993-95; assoc. lay pastor Met. Cmty. Ch. of Sequoias, Visalia, 1994-95; pastor Tulare County Rainbow Cmty. Ch., 1995—. Mem. Tulare County HIV Care Consortium, Tulare County HIV-AIDS Edn. and Prevention Planning Com.; gay and AIDS activist, Tulare County; mem. AIDS Outreach Ministry in Home & Hosp. and Outreach to Gay/Lesbian and Transgender Cmty. Home and Office: 2725 N Canary Dr Visalia CA 93291-1719

MADDEN, WILLIAM LEE, JR. lawyer; b. Hastings, Nebr., Mar. 13, 1948; BA with distinction, Stanford U., 1970; JD, Cornell U., 1973. Bar: Mont. 1974, U.S. Dist. Ct. Mont. 1974, U.S. Ct. Appeals (9th cir.) 1975. Assoc. Towe, Neely & Ball, Billings, Mont., 1973-75; ptnr. Goetz & Madden, Bozeman, 1975—81, Goetz Madden & Dunn, P.C., Bozeman, 1981—98; pvt. practice William Madden, Jr., P.C., 1998—. Bd. dirs. Cinnabar Found., Bozeman. Mem. ABA, ATLA, Am. Arbitration Assn., Mont. Trial Lawyers Assn., Mont. State Bar Assn., Gallatin County Bar Assn. Office: William Madden Jr PC 2066 Stadium Dr Ste 104 Bozeman MT 59715-0616

MADDERN, DAVID, artist; b. Gill, Mass., Oct. 23, 1933; BM, U. Miami, 1973, MM, 1974. Music instr. Barry U., Miami, 1977—. Contbr. The Best of Watercolor, 1995, vol. III, 1999, The Best of Flowers, 1996, The Best of Watercolor Painting Color, 1997, Floral Inspirations, 1997, The Best of Watercolors Vol. III, 1999, The One-Hour Watercolorist, 2002; exhibited in shows at Ft. Lauderdale (Fla.) Festival of Arts, Artists' Showcase Bapt. Hosp., Banyan Festival, Coconut Grove, Fla., South Miami Art Festival, Key Biscayne (Fla.) Art Festival, Mus. Sci., Miami, Riveria Country Club, Miami; featured in The One Hour Watercolorist, 2001. Named Best in Flora Cultural Coun., Inc., Miami, 1991, Best in Show, Ft. Lauderdale Festival of Arts, 1993, Miami Watercolor Soc., 1993, Goldcoast Watercolor Soc., Ft. Lauderdale, 1995, 97, Fla. Flora Art Exhibit, Miami, 1996; First Place Watercolor, Key Biscayne Art Festival, 1995, Baptist Hosp. Artists Showcase, Miami, 1995; Best of Show, 58th Anniversary Juried Exhibit Fla. Artists, 1999, 1st pl. Miami Watercolor Soc. 26th ann. fall exhibit, 1999, 1st Place Watercolor Pembroke Pines (Fla.) Fine Arts, 2000, Best of Show Cauley Square (Fla.) Fine and Arts Show, 2000, 1st Pl. Internat. Watercolor Biennial, Miami, 2000. Mem.: Miami Watercolor Soc. (1st v.p. 1993—95), Fla. Watercolor Soc. (signature), La. Watercolor Soc. (signature), Watercolor West (signature), N.W. Watercolor Soc. (signature). Home: 6492 SW 22nd St Miami FL 33155-1945

MADDIN, ROBERT, metallurgist educator; b. Hartford, Conn., Oct. 20, 1918; s. Isadore I. and Mae (Jacobs) Levine; married, July 8, 1945; children: Leslie, Jill. BS in Metall. Engring., Purdue U., 1942; DEng., Yale U., 1948. Registered profl. engr., Pa. Asst., assoc. prof. Johns Hopkins U., Balt., 1949-55; prof. U. Pa., phila., 1955-73, univ. prof., 1973-83; vis. prof. Harvard U., Cambridge, Mass., 1983-87, curator, 1987—; vis. prof. Oxford (Eng.) U., 1970, vis. fellow Wolfson Coll., 1987. Vis. prof. U. Birmingham, Eng., 1953-54; vis. scholar Hebrew U., Jerusalem, 1976; hon. prof. Beijing Sci. and Engring. U., 1986; hon. mem. Japan Metals. Editor-in-chief Math., Sci., and Engring, 1965-82; contbr. more than 250 publs. to profl. jours. 1st Lt. USAF, 1942-45. Disting. Sr. Sci. fellow A. von Humboldt Found., Germany, 1989-90, Disting. Alumnus Purdue U., 1974; recipient Pomerance award Archaeol. Inst. Am., 1994, medal of merit U. Pa. Fellow Am. Soc. Metallurgists, TMS. Avocations: history early metallurgy. E-mail: bobmaddin@cstone.net.

MADDING, CLAUDIA, agricultural products executive; b. Detroit, Dec. 27, 1950; d. Clarence Irving and Theresa Flemming; m. John Eldon Madding, Apr. 4, 1979; children: Jonathan, Bryan, Collin. Student, Millikin U., 1969, Richland C.C., Decatur, Ill., 1979-80. Stenographer State of Ill., Springfield, 1968-74; adminstrv. asst. Archer Daniels Midland Co., Decatur, 1979-93, asst. sec., 1993—2001, exec. asst. to chmn. bd., 1994—2001, pres. ADM found., asst. sec., 1997—, exec. asst. to chmn. emeritus, exec. asst. to chmn. bd., 1999—, sec. to exec. com., 1999—2001. Bd. dirs. United Way of Decatur, Decatur Club, Decatur, St. Teresa H.S. Ednl. Found.; past bd. dirs. Jr. Achievement Decatur, Holy Family Sch.; adv. bd. The Parent Project for Duchenne, Muscular Dystrophy Rsch., Inc., Middletown, Ohio. Mem.: Country Decatur. Roman Catholic. Avocations: reading biographies, watching 1930-40's movies, foreign stamp collecting. Home: 16 Oakridge Dr Decatur IL 62521-4600 Office: Archer Daniels Midland Co 4666 E Faries Pkwy Decatur IL 62526-5666

MADDOCK, JEROME TORRENCE, information services specialist; b. Darby, Pa., Feb. 7, 1940; s. Richard Cotton and Isobel Louise (Mezger) M.; m. Karen Rhueama Weygand, Oct. 2, 1965. BS in Biology, Muhlenberg Coll., 1961; MS in Info. Sci., Drexel U., 1968. Editorial assoc. Biol. Abstracts, Phila., 1962—63; mgr. rsch. info. Merck & Co., West Point, 1963—72; sr. cons. Auerbach Assocs., Inc., Phila., 1972—79; mgr. libr. and info. svcs. Solar Energy Rsch. Inst., Golden, Colo., 1979—88; mgr. info. svcs. Transp. Rsch. Bd., Washington, 1988—89; project mgr. IHS Enterprise, Boulder, Colo., 1999—2001; ind. cons., 2002—. Del. Gov.'s Conf. on Libr. and Info. Svc., Pa., 1978; mem. blue ribbon panel to select archivist of U.S., Washington, 1979; U.S. del. to ops. com. on transp. rsch. info. Orgn. for Econ. Cooperation and Devel., 1988-99. Bd. dirs. Paoli (Pa.) Pub. Libr., 1976-77; bd. trustees Louisville County Pub. Libr., 2002-; With USAFR, 1962-68. Mem. AAAS, Am. Soc. Info. Sci. (chmn. 1974-75), Elks, Beta Phi Mu, Pi Delta Epsilon. Republican. Episcopalian. Achievements include projection of information science operations 10 years into the future. Home: 545 W Laurel Ct Louisville CO 80027-1116 Office: IHS Enterprise # C303 15 Inverness Way E Englewood CO 80112-5710

MADDOCK, LAWRENCE HILL, retired language educator; b. Ogden, Utah, July 14, 1923; s. Lawrence J. and Nellie (Hill) M. Student, U. Fla., 1941-42; BA, George Peabody Coll., 1946, PhD, 1965; MA, U. So. Calif., 1949. Tchr. pub. schs., Jacksonville, Fla., 1949-52; instr. U. Fla., Gainesville, 1952-53; asst. prof. California (Pa.) State Coll., 1955-56, assoc. prof., 1956-64, N.E. La. State Coll., Monroe, 1964-67, U. West Fla., Pensacola, 1967-90. Author: The Door of Memory, 1974, John Maddock: Mormon Pioneer, 1996; contbr. chpts. to books and articles to profl. jours. Mem. MLA (bibliographer 1978-93), Thomas Wolfe Soc., Mormon History Assn. Republican. Mem. Lds Ch. Home: 1012 Gerhardt Dr Pensacola FL 32503-3222

MADDOCKS, ROBERT ALLEN, lawyer, manufacturing company executive; b. Missouri Valley, Ia., Dec. 25, 1933; s. Clarence A. and Helen Louise (Unger) M.; m. JoAnn Skaggs, June 2, 1956; children— Todd Duncan, Susan Colette, Amy Annette. BS, Drake U., 1956, JD, 1958. Bar: Iowa 1958, U.S. Supreme Ct. 1969, Ohio 1970, Mo. 1972, Colo. 1992. Pvt. practice law, Clarion, Ia., 1958-67; atty. Massey Ferguson, Inc., Des Moines, 1967-68; div. gen. counsel Akron, Ohio, 1968-69; asst. sec., gen. counsel, dir. corp. relations Kellwood Co., St. Louis, 1970-73, sec., gen. counsel, 1973-90, v.p., 1978-90, also bd. dirs. subs. cos. Dep. chmn., dir. Smart Shirts Ltd., Hong Kong, 1980-90; sec. Midwest Credit Corp.; Wright County atty., Clarion, 1961-65; chmn., dir. Appt. Zone., 1998-99. Trustee Maryville Coll., St. Louis, 1975-78, Drake U., 1987-94; bd. dirs. Kellwood Found., 1975-90. Mem. Am. Bar Assn., Inter-Am., Ia., Ohio, Mo., Colo. bar assns., Am. Trial Lawyers Assn., Nat. Corporate Secs. Assn., Comml. Law League, Licensing Execs. Soc., Am. Apparel Mfrs. Assn. (legal com. 1972-90). Home: 5605 Southern Hills Ct Flower Mound TX 75022-9738 Fax: 817-430-8539. E-mail: bmadox@earthlink.net.

MADDOX, ALVA HUGH, retired state supreme court justice; b. Andalusia, Ala., Apr. 17, 1930; s. Christopher Columbus and Audie Lodella Maddox; m. Virginia Roberts, June 14, 1958; children: Robert Hugh, Jane Maddox. AB in Journalism, U. Ala., Tuscaloosa, 1952, JD, 1957. Bar: Ala. 1957. Law clk. to Judge Aubrey Cates, Ala. Ct. Appeals, Montgomery, 1957-58; field examiner Chief Atty.'s Office, VA, 1958-59; law clk. to Judge Frank M. Johnson, U.S. Dist. Ct., 1959-61; pvt. practice, 1961-65; cir. judge, spl. cir. judge Montgomery Cir. Ct., 1963, asst. dist. atty., 1964; legal advisor to govs. including George C. Wallace, Lurleen B. Wallace, Albert P. Brewer, State of Ala., Montgomery, 1965-69; assoc. justice Supreme Ct. Ala., 1969-2001; ret., 2001. Adv. bd. JUSTEC Rsch. Author: Alabama Rules of Criminal Procedure, 1991, supplements, 1992—. Founder youth jud. program YMCA, Montgomery, 1979, also mem. metro. bd. dirs. 2d lt. USAF, 1952-54, col. USAF Res. ret. Recipient Man of Yr. award YMCA, 1988, Disting. Program Svc. award, 1989, Srs. of Achievement award Montgomery Coun. on Aging, 1999. Mem. ABA, Ala. Bar Assn. (Jud. award of merit 1997), Inst. Jud. Adminstrn., Christian Legal Soc. (bd. dirs.), Federalist Soc. (bd. dirs.), Hugh Maddox Inn of Ct. Montgomery (charter, founding mem.), Am. Jud. Soc., Kiwanis (past bd. dirs. Montgomery), Am. Inns of Ct. (trustee), Order of Samaritan/U. Ala. Law Sch. Democrat. Baptist. Office: Supreme Ct Ala 300 Dexter Ave Montgomery AL 36104-3741 E-mail: HMaddox@alalinc.net.

MADDOX, JOHN EARL, minister, educator; b. Clayton, Ala., Sept. 14, 1935; s. John and Eddie Mae (Jarrett) M.; m. Bennie Lee Farrior, Mar. 12, 1955; children: Dondee Earl, John S., Tammie Gail. ThB, St. Stevens Bible Coll., 1971; MRE, Washington Saturday Coll., Howard U. Campus, 1982, D Ministry, 1985. Ordained to ministry Bapt. Ch., 1981. Lay minister Mt. Zion Bapt. Ch., Havre D'Grace, Md., 1955-56; Sunday sch. tchr. Post Chapel, Ft. George G. Meade, 1959-60; deacon 1st Bapt. Ch., Landover, 1973-80, assoc. minister, 1980-81; pastor Gethsemane Bapt. Ch., Mitchellville, 1981—. Co-host Holy Land Tour, Jerusalem, 1983; instr. Washington Saturday Coll., Sch. Religious Edn., Howard U. Campus, Washington. Editor-in-chief GBC Herald, 1989—. Commr. Marlton Control Commn., Upper Marlboro, Md., 1976-79; mem. project evaluation group on elderly abuse Prince Georges County, Upper Marlboro, 1985-90. Warrant officer U.S. Army, 1953-73. Decorated Bronze Star, Commendation medal, others. Recipient cert. of appreciation Pres. Richard M. Nixon, 1973, others. Mem. Bapt. Ministers Conf. of Washington D.C. and Vicinity, Bapt. Assn. and Auxiliaries of So. md. and Vicinity. Democrat.

MADDOX, NANCY MCCRAINE, lawyer; b. Greenwood, Miss., Apr. 3, 1950; d. Bill F. and Helen M. Maddox; m. John Kenneth Pieralisi, Sept. 25, 1976 (div. Aug. 1989). BA, U. Memphis, 1972; JD, U. Miss., 1991. Bar: Miss. 1991, U.S. Ct. Appeals (5th cir.) 1991, U.S. Dist. Ct. (no. and so. dists.) Miss. 1991, Tenn. 1998. Assoc. Holcomb Dunbar, Southaven, Miss., 1991-98, Myers & Assocs., Hernando, 1999-2000; pvt. practice Olive Branch, 2000—. Bd. dirs. Miss. Coun. Sch. Bd. Attys., 1998-2000. Methodist. Office: Atty at Law 9356 Goodman Rd Ste 109 Olive Branch MS 38654 E-mail: nmmaddox@aol.com.

MADDREY, WILLIS CROCKER, medical educator, internist, academic administrator, consultant, researcher; b. Roanoke Rapids, N.C., Mar. 29, 1939; s. Milner Crocker and Sara Jean (Willis) M.; m. Ann Marie Matt; children: Jeffrey, Gregory, Thomas. BS, Wake Forest U., 1960; MD, Johns Hopkins U., 1964. Diplomate: Am. Bd. Internal Medicine. Intern Osler Med. Service Johns Hopkins Hosp., Balt., 1964-65, asst. resident, 1965-66, 68-69, chief resident, 1969-70; fellow in liver disease Yale U., 1970-71; asst. prof. medicine Johns Hopkins U., Balt., 1971-75, assoc. prof., 1975-79, prof., 1980-81, asst. dean Sch. Medicine, 1975-79, assoc. dir. dept. medicine Baltimore, 1979-82; prof., chmn. dept. medicine Jefferson Med. Coll., Phila., 1982-90; v.p. clin. affairs U. Tex. Southwestern Med. Ctr., Dallas, 1990-93, exec. v.p. clin. affairs, 1994—. Assoc. editor: Medicine, 1972-82, Hepatology, 1988-95, mem. editl. bd., 1981-84, 86-87, Gastroenterology, 1982-87, Am. Jour. Medicine, 1978-87; contbr. articles to profl. jours. Bd. dirs. Am. Liver Found., 1976-80, Dallas County Med. Soc., 1996-98; trustee Magee Rehab. Hosp., Phila., 1982-87. With USPHS, 1966-68. Mem. ACP (bd. regents 1984-94, pres. 92-93), Am. Soc. Clin. Investigation, Am. Gastroenterol. Assn., Am. Assn. Study Liver Disease (pres. 1982). Republican. Office: U Tex Southwestern Med Ctr 5323 Harry Hines Blvd Dallas TX 75390-8570

MADDULAPALLI, KUMAR ANIL, information scientist; s. Somasekhara Sarma and Ranganayaki Maddulapalli. B in Tech., Indian Inst. of Tech., 1999. Grad. tchg. asst. SUNY, Binghamton, NY, 1999—2000; grad. rsch. asst. U. of Md., Coll. Pk., Md., 2000—. Sec. of student amenities ctr. Indian Inst. of Tech., Madras, India, 1993—94. Mem.: ASME, Inst. for Ops. Rsch. and Mgmt. Sci. Home: 120 Westway Apt 201 Greenbelt MD 20770 Office: University of Maryland Department of Mechanical Engineering College Park MD 20742 E-mail: makumar@wam.umd.edu.

MADDUX, GREGORY (GREGORY ALAN MADDUX), professional baseball player; b. San Angelo, Tex., Apr. 14, 1966; Grad. high sch., Las Vegas. Baseball player Chicago Cubs, 1986—92, Atlanta Braves, 1992—. Recipient Cy Young award Baseball Writers' Assn. Am., 1992, 93, 94, 95; named to All-Star team, 1988, 92, 94-5; recipient Gold Glove Award, 1990-96; Sporting News All-Star Team, 1992-94; named Nat. League Pitcher of Yr., Sporting News, 1993; Nat. League Innings Pitched Leader, 1991-92, earned run avg., 1995, fielding percentage, 1990-95. Achievements include being a mem. World Series championship team, 1995. Office: Atlanta Braves Turner Field PO Box 4064 Atlanta GA 30302-4064*

MADDUX, JOHN ARTHUR, humanities educator, poet; b. Cincinnati, Ohio, Oct. 25, 1949; s. John William and Mary Lucille Maddux. AA, Raymond Walters Coll., Cincinnati, OH, 1969; BA, Univ. Cin., Cincinnati, OH, 1971, MA Ed., 1984, Doctorate Ed., 1988. Dir. edn. Cin. Bd. of Edn., Cincinnati, Ohio, 1973—75; social worker/abuse specialist Dept. Human Services, Hamilton County, 1977—81; adjuct instr. (english) Univ. Cin., Cincinnati, 1986—; dir. edn. Coll. of Art Advt., 1989—. Cons. Marion-Merril Dow, Cincinnati, Ohio, 1984—85, IBM, Boca Raton, Fla., 1985—86, Procter & Gamble, Cincinnati, Ohio, 1989. Author: (book) A Thousand Tomorrows, The Classic Star Trek Trivia Book, On Being Gay: Essays for the Real World. Pres./founder Gay/Lesbian Alliance of Ohio, Ohio, 1987—89; bd. mem. Stonewall Human Rights Org., Cincinnati, 1987—91; pres. Gay/Lesbian Coalition, 1989—92; cons. Gay/Lesbian Pride Festival, 1999. Recipient Vol. Award of Exception, Action/Vista, Wash., 1972, Wash. Vol. Award, Pacific County, Raymond, Wash., 1972, Promotion of Racial Harmony, Brother to Brother, Cin., OH, 1990. Mem.: Nat. Coun. of Teachers of English. Independent. Unitarian Universalist. Avocations: camping, hiking, gardening, coin collecting. Office: Univ Cincinnati PO Box 210069 Cincinnati OH 45221-0069

MADDY, DUANE KEITH, management consultant; b. Washington, Oct. 6, 1964; s. Keith Thomas and Colleen Jo-Anne (Barlow) M.; m. Valerie Ann Dawley, Mar. 17, 1990. BS in Bus. Adminstrn., U. Phoenix, San Jose, 1987; MBA in Mgmt., Southwest U., Kenner, La., 1989, PhD in Venture Mgmt., 1994. Equities analyst Dean Witter Reynolds, Sacramento, 1985-87; separate acct. analyst Am. Gen. Life Ins. Co., 1987-88; corp. trust analyst Tex. Commerce Bank, Houston, 1988-90; tax compliance analyst IRS, Seattle, 1991-93; acct. compliance analyst Western Wireless, Bellevue, Wash., 1994; sr. sales cons. Princess Cruises, Seattle, 1994-97; sr. merger cons. David Stone & Assocs., San Francisco, 1997-99; chmn. bd. Maddy Consulting, Milford, Ohio, 1986—. Pub. spking. Readers Digest Assn., Fair Oaks, Calif., 1980. Author: The Maddy Report, 1986-91, Finite Stock Selection, 1987. Life Scout Boy Scouts, Davis, Calif., 1980; reserve Police Officer Davis (Calif.) Police Dept., 1982. Mem. Am. Mgmt. Assn., Am. Heart Assn. Republican. Methodist. Avocations: photography, travel, model railroading, car restoration. E-mail address. Office: 1001 Lillies Ln Ellicott City MD 21043-4755 Fax: 513-722-0074. E-mail: maddyconsulting@yahoo.com.

MADDY, PENELOPE JO, philosopher, educator; b. Tulsa, July 4, 1950; d. Richard and Suzanne (Lorimer) Parsons. BA in Math., U. Calif., Berkeley, 1972; PhD in Philosophy, Princeton U., 1979. Asst. prof. U. Notre Dame (Ind.), 1978-83; assoc. prof. U. Ill., Chgo., 1983-87, U. Calif., Irvine, 1987-89, prof., 1989—, chair philosophy dept., 1991-95, chair logic and philosophy of sci., 1998-2001. Author: Realism in Mathematics, 1990, Naturalism in Mathematics, 1997; editor Notre Dame Jour. Formal Logic, 1979-84, editl. bd., 1984—; editl. bd. Jour. Philos. Logic, 1985—, Jour. Symbolic Logic, 1995-2000, Philosophia Mathematica, 1993—. Fellow AAUW, 1982-83, U. Calif., 1988-89; NSF grantee, 1986, 88-89, 90-91, 94-95, Marshall scholar, 1982-83, Westinghouse Sci. scholar, 1968-72. Mem. Assn. Symbolic Logic (mem. exec. com. 1993-96, v.p. 2001—), Am. Philos. Assn. (mem. exec. com. 1993-95), Philosophy of Sci. Assn. (mem. governing bd. 1993-95), Am. Acad. Arts and Scis. Office: Dept Logic and Philosophy of Sci U Calif at Irvine Irvine CA 92697-5100 E-mail: pjmaddy@uci.edu.

MADE GOWDA, NETKAL M. chemistry educator; b. Netkal, India, Apr. 10, 1947; came to U.S., 1979; s. Made Gowda and Ningamma Made Gowda; m. Bharathi B. Made Gowda; children: Nindini, Pavithra, Pallavi. BS, Mysore (India) U., 1969, MS, 1971, PhD, 1978. Asst. prof. chemistry We. Ill. U., Macomb, 1987-88, 89-92, U. Virgin Islands, St. Thomas, 1988-89; assoc. prof. chemistry We. Ill. U., Macomb, 1992-96, prof. chemistry, 1996—, acting chair chemistry dept., 1998, chair chemistry dept., 1999—. Vis. prof. chemistry, U. Mysore, fall 1998. Mem. editl. adv. bd., Internat. Jour. Chem. Kinetics, 1993-99. Mem. Am. Chem. Soc., Am. Inst. Chemists, Internat. Union Pure and Applied Chemistry, Ill. Acad. Scis., Sigma Xi, Phi Kappa Phi. Office: Western Ill U Dept Chemistry 214 Currens Hall Macomb IL 61455 E-mail: GN-Made@wiu.edu.

MADEIRA, EDWARD W(ALTER), JR. lawyer; b. Phila., Feb. 10, 1928; s. Edward W. and Alice T. (Thompson) M.; m. Grace Luquer, Oct. 13, 1956; children: Martha L., Melissa P., Amanda T. AB, U. Pa., 1949, LL.B., 1952. Bar: Pa. 1953. Law clk. Justice John C. Bell, Jr., Phila., 1952-53; ptnr. Pepper, Hamilton & Scheetz, 1961—; co-chmn. Pepper, Hamilton LLP, 1992-94; chmn. emeritus Pepper, Hamilton & Scheetz, 1994—. Lectr. law Villanova Law Sch., 1992-99; dir. PA Futures Commn. on Justice in the 21st Century. Assoc. trustee U. Pa. 1989—. Fellow Am. Coll. Trial Lawyers, Internat. Acad. Trial Lawyers; mem. ABA (ho. of dels. 1989-92, chmn. com. on fed. jud. improvements 1991-96, chmn. com. on separation of powers, jud. independence 1997, chmn. com. on jud. selection standards 1999), Jud. Conf. 3d Cir., Phila. Bar Assn., Pa. Bar Assn., Internat. Assn. Ins. Counsel, Defender Assn. Phila. Republican. Episcopalian. Home: 227 Atlee Rd Wayne PA 19087-3835 Office: Pepper Hamilton LLP 3000 Two Logan Sq 18th Arch St Philadelphia PA 19103

MADEIRA, FRANCIS KING CAREY, conductor, educator; b. Jenkintown, Pa., Feb. 21, 1917; s. Percy Childs and Margaret (Carey) M.; m. Jean E. Browning, June 17, 1947. Grad., Avon Old Farms, 1934; student, Julliard Grad. Sch., 1937-43; DFA (hon.), Providence Coll., 1966; DHL, R.I. Coll., 1969; MusD (hon.), Brown U., 1976. Instr. music Brown U., 1943-46, asst. prof. music, 1946-56, assoc. prof. music, 1956-66. Founder, condr. R.I. Philharm. Orch., 1945-78; concert pianist recitals and condr. concerts, U.S. and Europe; also guest condr. U.S. and fgn. orchs. World premiere Trilogy (JFK-MLK-RFK) (by Ron Nelson), R.I. Philharmonic Orch., 1969. Mem. music panel Maine State Arts Commn., 1987-90; bd. trustees Saco River Festival Assn., 1988-94; mem. adv. bd., trustee Portland (Maine) Symphony Orch., 1996—. Recipient Gov.'s award for excellence in arts, 1972; John F. Kennedy award for svc. to cmty., 1978, Maestro award R.I. Philharm. Orch., 1998, Millennium Reflections award R.I. Philharm. Orch., 1999.

MADEIRA, ROBERT LEHMAN, professional society administrator; b. Elizabethtown, Pa., Aug. 30, 1915; s. Isaac Titus and Elsie Hernley (Lehman) M.; m. Mary Elizabeth Evans, Feb. 5, 1938; children: Terry Madeira Harsney, Chase Landre. Student, Juniata Coll., 1933-34; BS in Econs, Elizabethtown Coll., 1937; postgrad., Mpls. Honeywell Sch. Aero. Engring., U. Minn., 1945. Pianist, tchr., Elizabethtown, 1935-41; automobile salesman Packard Lancaster Co., Lancaster, Pa., 1937; owner, mgr. Conewago Foods, Elizabethtown, 1938-39; aircraft technician U.S. Air Force Middletown, Pa. and Columbia, S.C., 1941-42; project engr. Mpls. Honeywell, Chgo. and Mpls., 1942-45; mgr. Iceland, Inc., Elizabethtown, 1945-51; exec. sec. Nat. Frozen Food Locker Inst., 1951-55; exec. dir. Nat. Inst. Locker and Freezer Provisioners, 1955-73, Am. Assn. Meat Processors, Elizabethtown, 1973-80, exec. dir. emeritus, 1980-85. Tchr. course in assn. mgmt. Yale U., Mich. State U., Syracuse U., ,966-70; condr. internat. meat processing seminars, Europe, S.Am., Australia, New Zealand, The Orient, Africa, 1962-85. Chmn. Elizabethtown ARC, 1948-49, Elizabethtown Community Chest, 1952-53, Elizabethtown Park Dr., 1950; bd. dirs. Lancaster Com. of 100, 1953-57, Elizabethtown Music Found., 1951-57; bd. dirs. Norlanco Med. Center, Elizabethtown, 1972-75, chmn. fund dr., 1972-73. Recipient Man of Yr. award Nat. Inst. Locker and Freezer Provisioners, 1955; honor cert. Freedoms Found. at Valley Forge, 1976 Mem. Am. Soc. Assn. Execs. (Key award 1971, chartered assn. exec.), C. of C. U.S., Nat. Assn. Exhbn. Mgrs., Nat. Fedn. Ind. Bus., Gideons Internat., Nat. Right-to-Work Com. Republican. Presbyterian. Home: 660 Willow Valley Sq Apt M102 Lancaster PA 17602-4874 Office: Am Assn Meat Processors PO Box 269 Elizabethtown PA 17022-0269 E-mail: bobmadeira@webtv.net.

MADEJ, HENRY MARK, legislative counselor; b. Bellingham, Wash., Jan. 17, 1945; s. Henry Andrew and Sylvia (Kingma) M. BA, U. Albany SUNY, 1967, MPA, 1968. Project mgr. N.Y. State Urban Devel. Corp., Albany, 1969-72; dir. minority staff assistance program N.Y. State Senate, 1974; program assoc. to lt. gov. Mary Anne Krupsak, 1975-76; dep. dir./dir. Assembly Rsch. Svc., 1976-93; spl. asst. to assemblyman Kevin Cahill, 1993-94; legis. dir. to Roberto Ramirez N.Y. State Assembly, 1995—2000; legis. rep. Poswein N.Y., 2001—. Staff mem. N.Y. State del. 1984 Dem. Nat. Conv., San Francisco. V.p. Pine Hills Neighborhood Assn., Albany, 1982-95, pres., 1995—; pres. West Hill Improvement Corp., Albany, 1976-83; reg. vice chair N.Y. State New Dem. Coalition, Upstate N.Y./Albany, 1972-82; mem. Albany Charter Revision Commn., 1996-98. Mem. State Acad. Pub. Adminstrn. (elected), R.F. Kennedy Dem. Club (treas. 1995-97). Home: 194 Western Ave Albany NY 12203-1227

MADEJSKI, ROSE MARY, pharmacist, educator; b. May 1, 1937; BS cum laude, U. Buffalo, 1959. Lic. pharmacist, N.Y. Staff pharmacist VA Hosp., Buffalo, 1959-60, Pritchard Pharmacy, Buffalo, 1967-69, Niagara Falls (N.Y.) Meml. Ctr., 1969-70, Columbus Hosp., Buffalo, 1970-73; enterostomal therapist, orthopedic fitter, pharmacist Stalls Health Svcs., 1973-90; cons. enterostomal therapist Kenmore (N.Y.) Mercy Hosp., 1988-90; pres. M&R Pharmacy Cons., Grand Island, N.Y., 1975-90; v.p. Stalls Pharmacy and Health Svcs., Buffalo, 1980-90; clin. asst. prof. pharmacy SUNY, 1990—. Contbr. articles to profl. jours. including Am. Pharmacist, U.S. Pharmacist, N.Y. State Pharmacist, among others. Grantee Marion Merrell Dow, Merck, Sharp & Dohme, and the Upjohn Co.; recipient Leadership award Bristol Myers Squibb, Inc., 1990, award Am. Cancer Soc., 1978, Outstanding Pharmacist award Indo-Am. Pharm. Soc., 1991, Bowl of Hygeia, 1995, Susan B. Anthony award, 1996; named Outstanding Alumnus U. Buffalo, 1992. Mem. Pharmacists Soc. State N.Y. (pres. 1989-90, chmn. 1990-91), Pharmacists Assn. Western N.Y. (bd. dirs. 1975-78, 94-99, Hall of Fame 2002), Health Sys. Agy. Erie County (vice chair 1975). E-mail: madejski@acsu.buffalo.edu.

MADELL, SAMUEL H. radiologist; b. N.Y.C., 1925; AB, U. Ill., 1947; MD, Columbia U., 1951. Diplomate Am. Bd. Radiology. Intern Mt. Sinai Hosp., N.Y.C., 1951-52; resident in radiology Columbia-Presbyn. Med. Ctr., 1952-55; asst. radiologist Columbia U. Physicians and Surgeons, N.Y.C., 1955-57; assoc. vis. radiologist Bronx Mcpl. Hosp. Ctr., 1957-68, attending radiologist, 1968-80; asst. attending radiologist Mt. Sinai Hosp., N.Y.C., 1961-81; cons. radiologist St. Lukes Hosp., 1974-81; attending radiologist Lenox Hill Hosp., 1977-85, cons. radiologist, 1985-96, cons. physician ob-gyn, 1985-92, hon. cons. radiology, hon. cons. physician, 1996-97, emeritus cons. physician, 1997—. Mem. N.Y. State Bd. for Profl. Med. Conduct, 1988—; bd. dirs. Med. Liability Mut. Ins. Co.; instr. radiology Columbia U. Physicians and Surgeons, 1955-57; asst. clin. prof. radiology to assoc. clin. prof. radiology Albert Einstein Coll. Medicine, 1957-80; asst. clin. prof. radiology, Mt. Sinai Med. Sch., 1966-68, lectr. radiology, 1968-81. Fellow Am. Coll. Radiology (bd. chancellors 1978-84); mem. AMA, Am. Roentgen Ray Soc., N.Y. Roentgen Soc. (past pres.), N.Y. County Med. Soc. (past pres.), N.Y. State Med. Soc. E-mail: smadell@carroll.com.

MADER, CHARLES LAVERN, chemist; b. Dewey, Okla., Aug. 8, 1930; s. George Edgar and Naomia Jane (Harer) M.; m. Emma Jean Sinclair, June 12, 1960; 1 child, Charles L. II. BS, Okla. State U., 1952, MS, 1954; PhD, Pacific Western U., 1980. Fellow Los Alamos (N.Mex.) Nat. Lab., 1955—; JIMAR sr. fellow U. Hawaii, Honolulu, 1985-94; pres. Mader Cons. Co., 1985—. Author: Numerical Modeling of Detonation, 1979, Numerical Modeling of Water Waves, 1988, Numerical Modeling of Explosives and Propellants, 1997; editor: Los Alamos Explosives Performance Data, 1982, LASL Phermex Data, vol. 1, 1980, vol. 2, 1980, vol. 3, 1981; contbr. numerous articles to profl. jours.; author 70 reports. Scoutmaster Boys Scouts Am., Los Alamos, 1971-85. Fellow Am. Inst. Chemists; mem. Am. Chem. Soc., Combustion Inst., Tsunami Soc. (editor 1985—), Marine Tech. Soc., Sigma Xi, Pi Mu Epsilon, Phi Lambda Upsilon. Methodist. Achievements include development and definition of field of numerical modeling of explosives and water waves. Office: Mader Cons Co 1049 Kamehame Dr Honolulu HI 96825-2860 also: 214 Barranca Rd Los Alamos NM 87544-2410 also: PO Box 5930 Avon CO 81620-5930 E-mail: mccohi@aol.com.

MADER, DAVID, federal agency administrator; b. Jersey City; BS in polit. sci., Mt. St. Mary's Coll., Emmitsburg, Md., 1970, Syracuse U., 1983. Mgmt. analyst IRS, N.Y.C., 1970, various mgmt. positions; selected for IRS exec. devel. program, 1986; asst. dir., Detroit Computing Ctr.; asst. dir. N.J. dist. Newark; dep. asst. commr. (planning and rsch.) Washington; asst. commr. (human resources); chief mgmt. and finance, 1994-2000; asst. dept. commr., 2000—. Office: Dept Treasury IRS 1111 Constitution Ave NW Washington DC 20224-0001

MADER, DOUGLAS PAUL, research administrator; b. Brookings, S.D., May 16, 1963; s. Lawrence Harold Mader Jr. and Susan Margaret (Littleton) Burk; m. Darla Sue Hower, Dec. 30, 1991; children: Alyssa, Megan, Matthew. BS in Engring. Physics, S.D. State U., 1985; MS in Math., Colo. Sch. of Mines, 1990; PhD in Mech. Engring., Colo. State U., 1994. Cert. quality engr. Am. Soc. Quality Control, 1990-93. Quality control engr. Govt. Electronics Group, Motorola, Scottsdale, Ariz., 1985-87; integrated circuit test engr. Semiconductor Products sector, Motorola, Mesa, 1987-88; sr. staff engr. Six Sigma Rsch. Inst., Motorola, Schaumburg, Ill., 1990-92, prin. staff scientist, 1992; cons. Rockwell Internat., Cedar Rapids, Iowa, 1992-93; quality engring. mgr. Advanced Energy Industries, Ft. Collins, Colo., 1993-95; instr. stats. and mech. engring. Colo. State U., 1993-94; statistician Hewlett-Packard Co., Greeley, Colo., 1995-96, sr. quality cons., 1996-97, quality engring. mgr., 1997; mfg. mgr. Hewlett-Packard Corporate Quality, Palo Alto, Calif., 1997-99, quality program mgr., 1999; dir. Seagate Technology, Longmont, Colo., 1999-2000; v.p. Six Sigma Acad., 2000—; pres., CEO SigmaPro Inc., Ft. Collins, 2001—. Author: Process Control Methods, 1993 (videotapes) Concurrent Engineering - The Foundation of Six Sigma Quality, 1992; mem. editorial bd. Internat. Jour. of Ops. and Quantitative Mgmt., 1994—. Mem. Am. Statis. Assn., Inst. Indsl. Engrs., Am. Soc. Quality Control (mem. standing rev. and mix media rev. bd. 1992—, mem. editl. bd. for quality engring. 1994—), Inst. Ops. Rsch. and Mgmt. Sci., Decision Scis. Inc. Office: SigmaPro Inc 3131 S College Ave Ste 2A Fort Collins CO 80525

MADER, JON TERRY, physician, educator; b. Madison, Wis., Mar. 21, 1944; s. John Henry and Louise E. (Hancock) M.; m. Donna Belinda Milner, May 7, 1994; children: Travis Jon, Amy Eileen, Bret Mark, Jason Darrel Samuel, Jon Henry. BA, Wabash Coll., 1966; MD, Ind. U., 1970. Diplomate Am. Bd. Internal Medicine; cert. Am. Bd. Infectious Diseases. Intern U. Tex. Med. Br., Galveston, 1970-71; resident in internal medicine, 1971-73; fellow in infectious disease, 1973-74, 76-77; asst. prof. dept. internal medicine div. infectious disease, 1978-82; assoc. prof. internal medicine div. infectious diseases, 1982-89; prof., 1989—; acting chief div. infectious diseases, 1990-94; mem. med. staff, 1977—; prof. pathology, 1992—. Adj. prof. orthopaedics, 1993—; chief hyperbaric medicine, dept. orthopaedic surgery and Rehab., Galveston, 1979-2001, divsn. hyperbaric medicine and wound healing dept. orthopaedic surgery and rehab., Galveston, 2001—; trainee in hyperbaric oxygenation therapy NASA Manned Spacecraft Ctr., Houston, 1973; bd. advisors Ocean Corp., Houston. Served with M.C., USN, 1974-76; capt. USNR, 1990. Recipient numerous fellowships and grants. Fellow Am. Bd. Internal Medicine; mem. ACP, Am. Soc. Microbiology, Undersea and Hyperbaric Med. Soc. (exec. com., past pres.), Am. Coll. Hyperbaric Medicine (past pres.), Am. Fedn. Clin. Rsch., Infectious Disease Soc. Am., Musculoskeletal Infection Soc. (past pres.). Presbyterian. Home: 5139 Oak Ct Dickinson TX 77539-7528 also: 5129 Oak Ct Dickinson TX 77539-7528 Office: U Tex Med Br Div Hyperbar Med/Wound Care 301 University Blvd Galveston TX 77555-5302 E-mail: jtmader@utmb.edu.

MADGETT, NAOMI LONG, poet, editor, publisher, educator; b. Norfolk, Va., July 5, 1923; d. Clarence Marcellus and Maude Selena (Hilton) Long; m. Julian F. Witherspoon, Mar. 31, 1946 (div. Apr. 1949); 1 child, Jill Witherspoon Boyer; m. William H. Madgett, July 29, 1954 (div. Dec. 1960); m. Leonard P. Andrews, Mar. 31, 1972 (dec. May 1996). BA, Va. State Coll., 1945; MEd, Wayne State U., 1956; PhD, Internat. Inst. for Advanced Studies, 1980; LHD (hon.), Siena Heights Coll., 1991, Loyola U., 1993; DFA (hon.), Mich. State U., 1994. Reporter, copyreader Mich. Chronicle, Detroit, 1946; svc. rep. Mich. Bell Telephone Co., 1948-54; tchr. English pub. high schs., 1955-65, 66-68; rsch. assoc. Oakland U., Rochester, Mich., 1965-66; mem. staff Detroit Women Writers Conf. Ann. Writers Conf., 1968—; lectr. English U. Mich., 1970-71; assoc. prof. English Eastern Mich. U., Ypsilanti, 1968-73, prof., 1973-84, prof. emeritus, 1984—; editor-pub. Lotus Press, 1974—. Editor Lotus Poetry Series, Mich. State U. Press, 1993-98. Author: (poetry)

Songs to a Phantom Nightingale (under name Naomi Cornelia Long), 1941, One and the Many, 1956, Star by Star, 1965, 70, Pink Ladies in the Afternoon, 1972, 90, Exits and Entrances, 1978, Phantom Nightingale: Juvenilia, 1981, Octavia and other Poems (Creative Achievement award Coll. Lang. Assn.), 1988, Remembrances of Spring: Collected Early Poems, 1993; Octavia: Guthrie and Beyond, 2002 (textbook) (with Ethel Tincher and Henry B. Maloney) Success in Language and Literature B, 1967, A Student's Guide to Creative Writing, 1980; editor: (anthology) A Milestone Sampler: 15th Anniversary Anthology, 1988, Adam of Ife: Black Women in Praise of Black Men, 1992; In Her Lifetime tribute Afrikan Poets Theatre, 1989. Participant Creative Writers in Schs. program. Recipient Esther R. Beer Poetry award Nat. Writers Club, 1957, Disting. English Tchr. of Yr. award, 1967; Josephine Nevins Keal award, 1979; Mott fellow in English, 1965, Robert Hayden Runagate award, 1985, Creative Artist award Mich. Coun. for the Arts, 1987, award Nat. Coalition 100 Black Women, 1984, award Nat. Coun. Tchrs. English Black Caucus, 1984, award Chesapeake/Virginia Beach chpt. Links, Inc., 1981, Arts Found. Mich. award, 1990, Creative Achievement award Coll. Lang. Assn., 1988; Arts Achievement award Wayne State U., 1985, The Black Scholar Award of Excellence, 1992; Am. Book award, 1993, Mich. Artist award, 1993; Creative Contbrs. award Gwendolyn Brooks Ctr. Black Lit. and Creative Writing Chgo. State U., 1993, George Kent award, 1995; Naomi Long Madgett Poetry award named for her, 1993—; inducted Sumner H.S. Hall of Fame, St. Louis, 1997, Nat. Lit. Hall Fame for Writers African Descent, Chgo. State U., 1999, Mich. Women's Hall of Fame, 2002; named Poet Laureate, City of Detroit, 2001—. Mem. NAACP, Coll. Lang. Assn., So. Poetry Law Ctr., Langston Hughes Soc., Detroit Women Writers, Charles H. Wright Mus. African Am. History, Fred Hart Williams Geneal. Soc., Alpha Kappa Alpha. Congregationalist. Home: 18080 Santa Barbara Dr Detroit MI 48221-2531 Office: PO Box 21607 Detroit MI 48221-0607 E-mail: nlmadgett@aol.com. *I have tried to set an example of excellence in the use of language, especially the language of poetry. If I can leave behind some enduring work—my own words and the words of others I have published—I will consider myself amply rewarded for my labors. The truly great people I have known have given a great deal of themselves in the service of others, have not been puffed up by their own importance, and have maintained integrity in their personal and professional lives. They have been my models.*

MADHAVAN, MURUGAPPA CHETTIAR, economics educator, international consultant; b. Kandramanickam, Tamilnadu, India, Dec. 17, 1932; came to U.S., 1960; s. L. Murugappa Chettiar and Adaikkammai Achi (Meyyappan) M.; m. Nachammai Manickam, May 3, 1953; children: Nachiappa, Nataraj. BA with honors, Annamalai U., India, 1955, MA, 1958; MS, U. Wis., 1963, PhD, 1969. Lectr. in econs. Annamalai U., 1955-60; economist Europe and Mid. East World Bank, Washington, 1963-66, asst. sec. econ. com., 1966-68; dir. Ctr. for Rsch. in Econ. Devel. San Diego State U., 1969-85, prof. econs., 1974—, dir. Asian Studies, 1991-2000, chmn. dept. Asian Studies, 1999-2000. Prof. econs. Nat. Inst. Bank Mgmt., Bombay, 1971-72; vis. prof. econs. Indian Inst. Tech., Madras, 1979-80, U. Putra, Malaysia, 2002; Father Carty Meml. lectr. U. Madras, 1980; vis. Fulbright prof. U. of the Philippines, 1987-88; cons. UN Devel. Program, N.Y.C., 1987-88, Gen. Atomics, San Diego, 1993-99; advisor Gov. Sim Grinio, The Philippines, 1988; vis. scholar Internat. Monetary Fund Inst., Washington, D.C., 2002; Fulbright sr. specialist Faculty of Law and Econ. Svcs., Phnom Penh, Cambodia, summer 2001. Co-author: The Transfer of Knowledge Through Expatriate Nationals, 1988. Chmn. World Affairs Coun. San Diego, 1991-93; pres. Tamil Nadu Found., Inc., Chgo., 1985-87, life mem.; advisor Mingei Internat. Mus., San Diego, 1985—; pres. San Diego Indian Am. Soc., 1984-99. Fulbright fellow, 1960; recipient Hon. Am. award Ams. by Choice, 1987, Leadership and Contbn. award Tamil Nadu Found., 1994; Fulbright sr. scholar Fulbright Program in Ho Chi Minh City, U. Econs., 2000, U. Putra Malaysia, 2000. Mem. Am. Econ. Assn., Indian Econ. Assn. (life), Assn. Indian Econ. Studies (life). Democrat. Avocations: reading, walking, organizational activities. Home: 8727 Verlane Dr San Diego CA 92119-2033 Office: San Diego State U Coll Arts & Letters Ctr Asian Studies San Diego CA 92182 E-mail: madhavan@mail.sdsu.edu.

MADHUSOODANAN, SUBRAMONIAM, psychiatrist, educator; b. Trivandrum, India, Sept. 7, 1947; came to U.S., 1976; s. Subramoniam Pillai and Leelavathi K. Amma; m. Rama Sivathanu, Feb. 5, 1976 (div. Feb. 1991); children: Leena, Deepa; m. Gunjan Jain, Sept. 12, 1991; 1 child, Neha. MBBS, Trivandrum Med. Coll., 1971; Diploma in Otorhinolaryngology, Kurnool (India) Med. Coll., 1975; MD, SUNY, 1992. Diplomate in psychiatry and geriatric psychiatry Am. Bd. Psychiatry and Neurology, Am. Bd. Quality Assurance and Utilization Physicians, Am. Soc. clin. Psychopharmacology, Inc. Instr. Mt. Sinai Sch. Medicine, CUNY, 1978-82; asst. attending psychiatrist Mt. Sinai Svcs., City Hosp. Ctr. at Elmhurst, N.Y., 1979-81; med. dir. outpatient alcohol program St. John's Episcopal Hosp., Far Rockaway, 1981-83, acting dir. psychiatry, 1984-86, assoc. chair psychiatry, 1986—, program dir. geriatric psychiatry fellowship program, 1993—; dir. psychiatry Peninsula Hosp., 1983—; with SUNY Downstate Med. Ctr., Bklyn., clin. instr., 1993, clin. assoc. prof. dept. psychiatry, 1997—2002, clin. prof., 2002—. Cons. psychiatrist St. John's Nursing Home, Peninsula Nurses Home, Far Rockaway Nursing Home, Brookhaven Nursing Home Haven Manor, 1981—. Mem. Am. Psychiat. Assn., Am. Geriatric Psychiatry Assn., World Fedn. Mental Health, Am. Geriatric Soc., Queens County Psychiat. Soc., Lawrence Assn. Democrat. Hindu. Avocations: gardening, photography, travel. Home: 249 Broadway Lawrence NY 11559-1511 Office: St John's Episcopal Hosp 327 B 19th St Far Rockaway NY 11691

MADIAN, ALAN LEONARD, economist, management consultant; b. N.Y.C., May 25, 1938; s. Sydney and Anna (Lieber) M.; m. Susan R. Kneller, Apr. 20, 1986; children: Nicholas James Kneller, Antonia Chloe Kneller. AB, U. Calif., Berkeley, 1959; MA, Yale U., 1961; postgrad., Oxford (Eng.) U., 1963-65. Sr. rsch. scientist econs. Columbia U., 1963; asst. prof. U. Rochester, N.Y., 1964-65; from asst. prof. to assoc. prof. London Sch. Econs., 1965-70; sr. economist Inst. Pub. Adminstrn., N.Y.C., 1971-74; pres. Econ. Strategies, Inc., 1975, 78; econ. advisor to gov. State of N.Y., 1976-77; prin. assoc. Robert R. Nathan Assocs., Washington, 1979-80; cons. U.S. Senate Antitrust Subcom., 1980; dir. econ. studies Hamilton, Rabinovitz & Szanton, Inc., Washington, 1981; pres. Madian Econ. Assocs., 1981-97; mng. dir. Erb & Madian, Inc., 1984-97; CEO Lafayette Capital Corp., 1987—; from prin. to sr. v.p. Hagler Bailly Inc., 1997-2000, v.p., 1997-99, sr. v.p., 1999-2000; mem. mgmt. group PA Consulting Group, 2000—. Cons. World Bank, Goldman Sachs, others. Contbr. to books, articles to profl. jours. Exec. com. Young Dems. Calif., 1958-59; dir. Children's Found., 1985-96; No.-Calif./gov. campaign mgr. Edmund G. Brown, 1962. Served with AUS, 1955. Woodrow Wilson fellow, 1959-60, Falk Found. fellow, 1960. Mem. Am. Econ. Assn., Royal Econ. Soc., Internat. Assn. Energy Economists, Nat. Assn. Bus. Economists, Phi Beta Kappa. Office: 1776 Eye St NW Washington DC 20006-3700 Home: 1919 Franklin Ave Mc Lean VA 22101-5309 E-mail: alan.madian@paconsulting.com.

MADICH, BERNADINE MARIE HOFF, savings and loan executive; b. Duluth, Minn., Mar. 4, 1934; d. Palmer and Esther (Anderson) Hoff; m. Michael Madich, May 23, 1955 (div. 1986); children: Michael R.H., Tina B. Watts, Rory G. (dec.). Student, Inst. Fin. Edn., 1972, 73, 77-78, 83-84, 86-87, cert. real estate law, 1984. Operator Northwestern Bell Telephone, 1952-53; bookkeeper Riveria Hotel, Daytona Beach, Fla., 1953-54; with N.Y. Life Ins. Co., Duluth, Minn., 1954-55; telephone operator St. Lukes Hosp., 1968-72; teller St. Louis County Fed. Savs. and Loan, 1972-73, sec., ins. mortgage counselor, 1973-83, loan servicing specialist, 1983-86, asst. mgr. loan servicing dept., 1986-97, retired, 1997. Pack leader Boy Scouts Am., Duluth, 1964-68; leader Girl Scouts U.S., Duluth, 1972-74; chmn. Duluth Hall of Fame, 1983—; doscent Glensheen U. Minn., 1979-85; vol. St. Luke's Hosp., Duluth, 1968-72; asst. treas. Port Cities Luncheon, Duluth, 1984-86, treas., 1987—, co-chair, 1989—, chmn., 1989-90; chairperson Duluth East High Sch. All-Sch. Reunion, 1986, Duluth Ice Follies Reunion, 1998, co-chairperson reunion 1924-98; active Lakeside Presbyn. Ch.; vol. Miller Dwan Hosp., 2001. Named Port Cities Women of Yr., 1996. Mem. Duluth Area Ins. Women (treas. 1977-79, v.p. 1979-80, pres. 1985, advisor 1991-92), Duluth Bus. and Profl. Women (treas. 1976-88, 2d v.p. 1986, 1st v.p. 1987, pres. 1988—), Ambassadors of Duluth, Duluth C. of C. (Twin Ports Woman of Yr. 1995), Duluth Curling Club, Duluth Figure Skating Club, Altrusa Internat. Home: 1902 Saint Louis Ave Apt 119 Duluth MN 55802-2487 E-mail: bmadich@aol.com.

MADIGAN, JANET A. psychiatrist, child psychiatrist, educator; b. Summit, N.J., July 22, 1952; d. James D. Madigan and Edna U. Hiltz; m. robert J. harrity Jr., June 24, 1978; children: Ryan, Sean. AB, Mt. Holyoke Coll., 1974; MD, N.Y. Med. coll., 1977. Diplomate Am. Bd. Psychiatry, Am. Bd. Child Psychiatry. Fellow in psychiatry Yale U. Sch. Medicine, New Haven, 1977-81, fellow in child psychiatry, 1981-83; fellow Zero to Three Nat. Ctr. Clin. Infant Programs, Washington, 1983-85; clin. assoc. Western New Eng. Inst. for Psychoanalysis, New Haven, 1989—; asst. clin. prof. Yale U. Child Study Ctr., 1989—; pvt. practice child psychiatry. Cons. New Haven Edn. and Childcare Cons., 1995—, Pediat. Psychiat. Collaborative, New Haven, 1993—; supr. Yale Long Trm Psychotherapy Program, New haven, 1996—, yale Child Devel. Unit, 1985—; mem. pvt. practice com. Conn. Coun. Child Psychiatry, New Haven, 1995—. Mem. APA, Am. Acad. Child and Adolescent Psychiatry, Am. Psychoanalytic Assn. (affil.), Nat. Ctr. Clin. Infant Psychiatry (past fellow), Conn. Coun. child Psychiatry, Western New Eng. Inst. for Psychoanalysis (clin. assoc.). Avocations: tennis, skiing, gardening, loomwork. Office: 240 Bradley St New Haven CT 06510-1103 Fax: 203 776-0071.

MADIGAN, JOHN WILLIAM, publishing executive; b. Chgo., June 7, 1937; s. Edward P. and Olive D. Madigan; m. Holly Williams, Nov. 24, 1962; children: Mark W., Griffith E., Melanie L. BBA, U. Mich., 1958, MBA, 1959. Fin. analyst Duff & Phelps, Chgo., 1960-62; audit mgr. Arthur Andersen & Co., 1962-67; v.p. investment banking Paine, Webber, Jackson & Curtis, 1967-69; v.p. corp. fin. Salomon Bros., Chgo., 1969-74; v.p., CFO, dir. Tribune Co., Chgo., 1975-81, exec. v.p., 1981-91; pub. Chgo. Tribune, 1990-94; pres., CEO Tribune Pub. Co., Chgo., 1991-94; pres., COO Tribune Co., 1994-5, pres., CEO, 1995—, chmn., pres., CEO, 1996—. Bd. dirs. AP, Morgan Stanley, AT&T Wireless Svcs. Trustee Rush-Presbyn.-St. Luke's Med. Ctr., Mus. TV and Radio in N.Y., Northwestern U., Ill. Inst. Tech.; mem. bd. overseers Hoover Instn. Mem. Chgo. Coun. on Fgn. Rels. (chmn.), Robert R. McCormick Tribune Found. Office: Tribune Co 435 N Michigan Ave Chicago IL 60611-4066

MADIGAN, JOSEPH EDWARD, financial executive, consultant, director; b. Bklyn., June 26, 1932; s. James Peter and Mary (Goldman) M.; m. Catherine Cashman, July 26, 1980; children: Kerri Ann, Kimberly Ann Burquest, Elizabeth Ann Laginess. BBA cum laude, Baruch Coll., CUNY, 1958; MBA, NYU, 1963. Adminstrv. asst. Assoc. Metals & Minerals Corp., 1961-63; fin. analyst, fgn. exch. trader, corp. portfolio trader AMAX, Inc., 1963-65; mgr. corp. portfolio, dir. cash mgmt., asst. treas. TWA, Inc., 1965-68; treas. Borden, Inc., 1968-76, v.p., treas., 1976-80; exec. v.p., chief fin. officer, dir. Wendy's Internat., Inc., Dublin, 1980-87. Bd. dirs Frank Gates Holding, Columbus Show Case Co., Scioto Properties LLC. With USN, 1951-55. Mem. Fin. Execs. Inst., Nat. Investor Rels. Inst., Baruch Coll.-CUNY Alumni Assn., NYU Alumni Assn., Country Club at Muirfield Village, Imperial Golf Club (Naples, Fla.), Beta Gamma Sigma. Republican. Roman Catholic. Home: 5555 Heron Point Dr # 2102 Naples FL 34108

MADIGAN, MICHAEL JOSEPH, state legislator; b. Chgo., Apr. 19, 1942; m. Shirley Roumagoux; children: Lisa, Tiffany, Nicole, Andrew. Ed., U. Notre Dame, Loyola U., Chgo. Mem. Ill. Ho. of Reps., 1971—, majority leader, 1977-80, minority leader, 1981-82, house spkr., 1983-94, Dem. leader, 1995-96, ho. spkr., 1997—; lawyer. Sec. to Alderman David W. Healey; hearing officer Ill. Commerce Commn.; del. 6th Ill. Constnl. Conv.; trustee Holy Cross Hosp.; ex officio mem. adv. com. to pres. Richard J. Daley Coll.; adv. com. Fernley Harris Sch. for Handicapped; committeeman 13th Ward Democratic Orgn.; chmn. Ill. Dem. Party, 1998-. Mem. Council Fgn. Relations, City Club Chgo. Office: House Reps 300 State Capital Bldg Springfield IL 62706-0001*

MADISON, ANNE CONWAY, public relations and marketing professional; b. Balt., Mar. 13, 1963; d. Earl Cranston Jr. and Nancy (Schucker) C.; 1 child, Ryan Douglas. BS in Comm., Wittenberg U., 1985. Pub. rels. specialist Springfield (Ohio) Met. Housing Authority, 1984-85; account rep. CT Corp. System, Washington, 1985-86; pub. rels. asst. Ryland, Columbia, Md., 1986-88, comm. coord., 1988-90, mgr. mktg. comm., 1990-92, dir. mktg. comm., 1992-94, v.p. comms., 1994—; pres. Madison Mktg. Comms., 2001—. Bd. dirs., officer Domestic Violence Cr. of Howard County, Columbia, 1987-96; bd. dirs. Children of Separation and Divorce. Named Vol. of Yr. Domestic Violence Ctr., 1988, recipient Spirit award, 1992; named one of Top 100 Women in Md., Warfields mag., 1996. Mem. Pub. Rels. Soc. Am., Nat. Investor Rels. Inst. Republican. Roman Catholic. Office: 6885 Caravan Ct Columbia MD 21044 E-mail: acmadison@home.com.

MADISON, EDDIE LAWRENCE, JR. public relations consultant, editor, writer; b. Tulsa, Sept. 8, 1930; s. Eddie Lawrence Sr. and Laverta (Pyle) M.; m. Davetta Jayn Cooksey, Nov. 17, 1956; children: Eddie Lawrence III, Karyn Devette, David Cooksey. B in Journalism, Lincoln U., Jefferson City, Mo., 1952; MA, U. Tulsa, 1959. Editor-in-chief Okla. Eagle, Tulsa, 1954-59; assoc. editor Chgo. Daily Defender, 1959-61; dep. editor Assoc. Negro Press, Chgo., 1961-63; sect. editor Chgo. Tribune, 1963-65; dep. dir. publs. divsn. Domestic and Internat. Bus., U.S. Dept. Commerce, Washington, 1965-69; mgr. cmty. svcs. Evening Star Broadcasting Co., 1969-78; asst. editor Bus. Am. Mag., 1978-81; press asst. Ho. of Reps., 1981-82; pub. affairs specialist U.S. Dept. HHS, 1982-92, mgr. HHS radio, 1991-92; asst. prof., chmn. dept. comm. Lincoln U., 1992-99; exec. editor Okla. Eagle, Tulsa, 2001—; pres., CEO Three Elms & Assoc., Inc., 2001—. Founder Nat. Broadcast Assn. for Cmty. Affairs, Washington, 1974, 1st pres., 1974-77; adj. prof. Tulsa C.C. Corres. Native Am. Times. Pres. Brightwood Civic Assn., Washington, 1969-72; mem. media adv. com. Mo. Arts Coun., 1996-99; mem. tobacco coalition and assist coms. Am. Cancer Soc., 1993-99; Hist. Preservation Commn., 1997-99; bd. dirs. Opportunities Industrialization Ctr., Washington, 1971-77, D.C. United Way, 1972-77, Boy Scouts Am., Washington, 1972-77. With U.S. Army, 1952-54; corr., Army Times, columnits, Recon Observer, Ellsworth AFB, S.D. Mem. Alpha Phi Alpha (pres. Washington chpt. 1969-72, nat. dir. pub. rels. 1985-91, co-chair nat. pub. policy com. 1973, v.p. Montgomery County chpt. 1987-89, pres. Jefferson City Beta Zeta Lambda chpt. 1993, assoc. editor Sphinx mag., award of merit Ea. region 1992). Methodist. Avocations: photography, aerobics, jogging. Home: 4355 S Braden Ave Tulsa OK 74135-6337 Office: The Okla Eagle 624 E Archer St Tulsa OK 74120-1000 Address: Native Am Times 12833 E 41st St Tulsa OK 74146 also: Three Elms & Assocs PO Box 161 Tulsa OK 74101-0161 Fax: 918-852-8905. E-mail: emadsept@aol.com., threeelms1@aol.com.

MADISON, JACQUELINE EDWINA, librarian; b. Darlington, S.C., July 16, 1951; d. John Brown and Lula M. (Mack) McLeod; m. Calvin Lee Madison, Aug. 18, 1975; children: Jaquenette M., Calexandria J. BS, Fayetteville State U., 1972; MLS, Emporia State U., 1991. Insp. FDA, Orlando, Fla., 1972-73; supr. appt. clk. U.S. Army Hdqrs., Nurnberg, Germany, 1975-78; tchr. ESL Big Bend Coll., Ft. Lewis, Wash., 1980-82; libr. tech. Ft. Riley (Kans.) Libr., 1987-90; info. specialist Battelle Pacific N.W. Nat. Lab., Richland, Wash., 1991-97; sr. libr. Wyeth Rsch., Chazy, NY, 1997—. Owner, cons. Jaqcal's, Pasco, Wash., 1995—; mem. Wash. Com. for Student Learning, Olympia, 1994-97. Author: Jaqcal's Infophone Parent/Teacher Communication Line, 1995. Bd. dirs. Girl Scouts USA North Country, 1998—; mem. Friends of Mid-Columbia Libr., Kennewick, Wash., 1992—; mem. Multi-Cultural Affairs, Pasco, Wash., 1994—; v.p. Parent/Tchr. Group, Pasco, 1991—. With U.S. Army, 1974-77, Germany. Mem. NAFE, AAUW (sec. 1991), Spl. Libr. Assn., Am. Chem. Soc., Phi Beta Kappa. Avocations: computers, reading, cooking, museums, animals. Office: Battelle Pacific NW Nat Lab PO Box 999 Richland WA 99352-0999 also: Wyeth Ayerst Rsch Drug Safety Info Ctr 641 Ridge Rd Chazy NY 12921-2420

MADISON, JAMES RAYMOND, lawyer; b. White Plains, N.Y., Apr. 27, 1931; s. Raymond S. and Katherine (Sherwin) M.; m. Mary Massey, Sept. 19, 1953; children: Michael, Matthew, Molly. BS, Stanford U., 1953, LLB, 1959. Bar: Calif. 1960, U.S. Dist. Ct. (no. dist.) Calif. 1960, U.S. Ct. Appeals (9th cir.) 1960, U.S. Dist. Ct. (ctrl. dist.) Calif. 1970, U.S. Supreme Ct. 1973, U.S. Dist. Ct. (ea. dist.) Calif. 1981, U.S. Dist. Ct. (so. dist.) Calif. 1988. Assoc. Orrick, Herrington & Sutcliffe, San Francisco, 1959-67, ptnr., 1968-95; pvt. practice Menlo Park, Calif., 1996—. Trustee Antioch U., Yellow Springs, Ohio, 1980-87; bd. dirs. Planned Parenthood Alameda/San Francisco, 1984-89; pres. Calif. Dispute Resolution Coun., 2001. Lt. (j.g.) USN, 1953-56. Mem. ABA, ASCE, State Bar Calif., Bar Assn. San Francisco, San Mateo County Bar Assn., Am. Arbitration Assn. (large complex case panel arbitrators and mediators, No. Calif. regional adv. coun.). Democrat. Episcopalian. Avocation: soccer. Office: 750 Menlo Ave Ste 250 Menlo Park CA 94025-4758 E-mail: jrmcoach@aol.com.

MADISON, ROBERT PRINCE, architect; b. Cleve., July 28, 1923; s. Robert J. and Nettie (Brown) M.; m. Leatrice L. Branch, Apr. 16, 1949; children: Jeanne Marie, Juliette Branch. Student, Howard U., 1940-43, HHD, 1987; B.Arch., Western Res. U., 1946-48; M.Arch., Harvard, 1952; DFA (hon.), Cleveland State U., 2000. Mem. various archtl. firms, 1948-52; instr. Howard U., Washington, 1952-54; chmn., CEO Robert P. Madison Internat., architects, engrs. and planners, Cleve., 1954—. Trustee Am. Automobile Assn.; vis. prof. Howard U., 1961-62; lectr. Western Res. U., 1964-65; mem. U.S. architects del. Peoples Repub. China, 1974 Prin. works include U.S. Embassy Dakar, Senegal, West Africa, 1966, State of Ohio Computer Ctr., 1988, Cuyahoga County Jail, 1990, Continental Airlines Hub Concourse, Cleve. Internat. Airport, 1991. Mem. tech. adv. com. Cleve. Bd. Edn., 1960—; mem. adv. com. Cleve. Urban Renewal, 1963—; mem. fine arts adv. com. to mayor, Cleve.; mem. archtl. adv. coun. Cornell U.; trustee Case Western Res. U., Cleve. Opera, 1990, NCCJ, 1990, Commn. on Higher Edn., 1990; bd. dirs. Jr. Achievement Greater Cleve.; trustee Cuyahoga County Hosp. Found., 1983—, Univ. Circle Inc., Midtown Corridor Inc.; mem. Ohio Bd. Bldg. Standards, 1986, Cleveland Heights City Planning Commn., 1987. 1st lt., inf. AUS, 1943-46. Decorated Purple Heart; Fulbright fellow, 1952-53; recipient Disting. Svc. award Case Western Res. U., 1989, Disting. Archtl. Firm award Howard U., 1989, Entrepreneur of Yt. award Ernst Young, Inc., Merrill Lynch, 1991, Arch. of Yr. Nat. Tech. Assn., 1996, Martin Luther King Jr. Corp. award African-Am. Archives Aux. Western Res. Hist. Soc., 1997, Disting. Alumni award Case We. Res. U., 1997; named to Corp. Hall of Fame, Ohio Assembly of Couns., 1991, Pres. award Kent State U., 1999. Fellow AIA (chpt. pres., nat. task force for creative econs. 1976, mem. jury of fellows 1983-85, mem. nat. judicial coun. 1993, Gold Medal Firm award Ohio 1994, Gold Medal award Ohio 1997); mem. Architects Soc. Ohio, Epsilon Delta Rho, Alpha Phi Alpha, Sigma Pi Phi. Home: 13600 Shaker Blvd Apt 206 Cleveland OH 44120-1591 Office: Robert P Madison Internat Inc 2930 Euclid Ave Cleveland OH 44115-2416

MADISON, SAM A., JR. football player; b. Thomasville, Ga., Apr. 23, 1974; Student, Louisville. Cornerback Miami Dolphins, 1997—. Active Habitat for Humanity, Prudential/No Passing Zone. Named first-team All-Pro, Sports Illustrated, 1998, second-team AP All-Pro, 1998, first-team All-AFC selection Football News, 1998, second-team All-Pro Choice, Football Digest, 1998, first-team All-Pro selection AP, USA Today, Sports Illustrated, The Sporting News, Pro Football Weekly, Football Digest, 1999, NFL Alumni Assn. Defensive Back of Yr., 1999, Dolphins' MVP, 1999; named to AFC Pro Bowl squad, 1999. Office: Miami Dolphins Tng Facility 7500 SW 30th St Davie FL 33314*

MADISON, T. JEROME, business executive; b. N.Y.C., June 2, 1940; s. Theodore H. and Eleanor E. (Eveland) M.; m. Marsha A. Heeb, Sept. 26, 1964 (dec.); children: Jillian, Kimberly, Ryan. BS, U. Pa., 1962; MBA, Monmouth U., 1975. CPA, N.J. Mgr. KPMG, Newark and Princeton, N.J., 1970-75, Abbott Labs., North Chicago, Ill., 1976; asst. corp. contr. Rhone-Poulenc Rorer (now Aventis), Ft. Washington, Pa., 1977-78; corp. contr. Aventis, 1979-82; v.p. fin. Cytogen Corp., Princeton, N.J., 1982-86; pres., CEO, dir. Outwater & Wells Ventures, Inc., 1981-85, Atlantic Capital Resources Group, Inc., 1985-87, Founders Court Investors Inc., Princeton, N.J., 1986-91, Montgomery Ptnrs., 1991—. Chmn., CEO Pilling Co., 1986-91, AxCell Bioscis. Corp, 1996-97, Trinity Tech. Ptnrs., 1997—; chmn. Cytonautics, Somerset Ctrl. Corp.; bd. dirs. SynteciQ, MedicaMetrix, ProTech., DiscoveReactor, ProMed Systems. Flight Officer USN, 1962-66.

MADIX, ROBERT JAMES, chemical engineer, educator; b. Beach Grove, Ind., June 22, 1938; s. James L. and Marjorie A. (Strohl) M.; children: Bradley Alan, David Eric, Micella Lynn, Evan Scott. BS, U. Ill., 1961; PhD, U. Calif., 1964. NSF postdoctoral fellow Max Planck Inst., Göttingen, Fed. Republic of Germany, 1964-65; asst. prof. chem. engr. Stanford (Calif.) U., 1965-72, assoc. prof., chem. engr., 1972-77; prof. chem. engring. Stanford U., 1977—, chmn., chem. engr., 1983-87, prof. chemistry, 1981—. Cons. Monsanto Chem., St. Louis, 1975-84, Shell Oil Co., Houston, 1985-86; Peter Debye lectureship Cornell U., 1985; Eyring lectr. chemistry Ariz. State U., 1990; Barnett Dodge lectr. Yale U., 1996; disting. prof. lectr. U. Tex., Austin, 1980; Walter Robb Disting. lectr. Penn State U., 1996; chmn. Gordon Rsch. Conf. on Reactions on Surfaces, 1995. Assoc. editor Catalysis Rev., 1986—, Catalysis Letters, 1992—, Rsch. on Chem. Intermediates, 1994—; contbr. articles to profl. jours. Recipient Alpha Chi Sigma award AIChemE, 1990, Paul Emmett award Catalysis Soc. N.Am., 1984, Humboldt U.S. Sr. Scientist prize, 1978; Ford Found. fellow, 1969-72. Mem. AIChE, Internat. Precious Metal Inst. (Henry J. Alber award 1997), Am. Chem. Soc. (Irving Langmuir Disting. Lectr. award 1981, Arthur Adamson award 1997, Am. Phys. Soc., Am. Vacuum Soc., Calif. Catalysis Soc. Office: Stanford Univ Dept Chemical Engring Stanford CA 94305-5025

MADLANG, RODOLFO MOJICA, retired urologic surgeon; b. Indang, Cavite, The Philippines, Apr. 9, 1918; came to U.S., 1953; s. Simeon Fajardo and Eugenia R. (Mojica) Madlangsacay; m. Lourdes Recto Gregorio, Dec. 8, 1946; children: Cesar, Rodolfo G., Mercy Lynn. AA, U. Philippines, Manila, 1939, MD, 1945. Diplomate Am. Bd. Urology. Resident in gen. surgery Philippine Gen. Hosp., Manila, 1946-49; resident in urology St. Francis Hosp., Peoria, Ill., 1953-55; asst. prof. physiology Far Ea. U. Inst. Medicine, Manila, 1956-58, cons. in urology, 1956-58; attending urologist St. Catherine Hosp., East Chicago, Ind., 1958-81, chief surgery, 1977-79; attending urologist St. Margaret Hosp., Hammond, 1960-81; chief urology U.S. VA Outpatient Clinic, L.A., 1982-98. Fellow ACS; mem. AMA, Am. Urol. Assn., Pan Pacific Surg. Assn., Assn. Mil. Surgeons of the U.S., Ind. State Med. Assn., N.Y. Acad. Scis. Republican. Roman Catholic.

MADNI, ASAD MOHAMED, engineering executive; b. Bombay, Sept. 8, 1947; came to U.S., 1966; s. Mohamed Taher and Sara Taher (Wadiwalla) M.; Gowhartaj Shahnawaz, Nov. 11, 1976; 1 child, Jamal Asad. Gen. cert. edn., U. Cambridge, Eng., 1964; AAS in Electronics, RCA Insts., Inc., 1968; BS in Engring., UCLA, 1969, MS in Engring., 1972; postgrad. exec. inst., Stanford U., 1984; cert. in engring. mgmt., Calif. Inst. Tech., 1987; PhD in Engring., Calif. Coast U., 1987; sr. exec. program, MIT, 1990. Chartered elec. engr., U.K.; chartered engr. Engring. Coun., U.K. Sr. instr. Pacific States U., L.A., 1969-71; sr. electronics auditor Pertec Corp., Chatsworth, Calif., 1973-75; project engr., sr. engr., prog. mgr., dir. advanced programs Microwave div. Systron Donner, Van Nuys, 1975-82, dir. engring., 1982-92; gen. mgr. Microwave and Instrument div. Systron Donner, 1985-90; chmn., pres., chief exec. officer Systron Donner Corp., 1990-92; pres., CEO Sensors and Controls Group BEI Electronics, Inc., 1992-93, BEI Sensors & Sys. Co., 1993—; pres., COO BEI Techs. Inc., 2000—. Vice-chmn. IEEE-MTTS, San Fernando Valley chpt., 1991-92, chmn., 1992-94; tech. advisor Test and Measurement World, Boston, 1982-90; adv. Calif. State U. Northridge. Recipient Joseph F. Engelberger Best Paper award, World Automation Congress, 2000, Disting. Alumni award, Calif. Coast U., 2001, Profl. Achievement award, UCLA, 2002. Fellow: IEEE (adv. bd. MTT-S San Fernando Valley chpt. 1993—, tech. review com. aerospace conf. 1994—, 3d Millennium medal), Internat. Biog. Assn., N.Y. Acad. Scis., Inst. Advancement Engring., Instn. Elec. Engrs. (U.K.); mem.: AAAS, NRA (life), AIAA (sr. life) (vice chair honors and awards L.A. sect. 2000—01), Soc. Automotive Engrs., MIT Soc. Sr. Execs. (life), Assn. Old Crows (life gold cert. of merit 1992), MIT Alumni Assn. (life), UCLA Alumni Assn. (life), Calif. Rifle and Pistol Assn. (life). Home: 3281 Woodbine St Los Angeles CA 90064-4836 Office: BEI Techs Inc 13100 Telfair Ave Sylmar CA 91342-3576 E-mail: bei1madni@aol.com. *Personal philosophy: There is no substitute for talent and vision complemented by perseverance, dedication and integrity.*

MADNI, IMTIAZ K. mechanical engineer; b. Bombay, India, June 28, 1948; s. Ahmad K. and Zulaikha K. Madni; m. Neelofar I. Malik; children: Nishaat, Sabeeha, Asim. PhD, Iowa State U., 1975. Mech. engr., scientist Brookhaven

Nat. Lab., Upton, NY, 1975—80, scientist, 1987—98; assoc. prof. King Fahd U. Petroleum and Minerals, Dhahran, Saudi Arabia, 1980—86; prin. engr. Framatome ANP, Inc., Richland, Wash., 1998—. Cons. Energy Rsch. Inc., Rockville, Md., 1989—98. Contbr. articles to profl. jours. Office: Framatome ANP Inc 2101 Horn Rapids Rd Richland WA 99352 Business E-Mail: Imtiaz_Madni@nfuel.com.

MADONIA, VINCENT V. cardiologist, medical educator; b. Bklyn., Nov. 1, 1926; s. Vincent and Lillian Madonia; m. Ann Susan Madonia, July 5, 1959; children: Susan Carol, William James, Ann Carol. BA, Columbia Coll., 1947; MD, NYU, 1950. Diplomate Am. Bd. Internal Medicine. Med.-surg. intern St. Vincent's Hosp., N.Y., 1950-51; resident medicine and cardiology Bklyn. Vets. Hosp., 1951-54; pvt. practice cardiologist Garden City, N.Y., 1954—; attending physician Winthrop U. Hosp., Mineola, 1957—; asst. prof. clin. medicine SUNY, Stony Brook, 1975—. Bd. dirs. Nassau Cancer Soc., Mineola, 1960-66, Nassau Heart Assn., Mineola, 1967-70; sec., chmn. pub. rels. com. Nassau County Med. Soc., Garden City, N.Y., 1966-68. Maj. USAR, 1944—; ships surgeon U.S. Merchant Marines, 1952—. Fellow ACP; mem. Am. Coll. Cardiology (N.Y. chpt.). Office: 520 Franklin Ave Garden City NY 11530

MADONNA, (MADONNA LOUISE VERONICA CICCONE), singer, actress, producer; b. Bay City, Mich., Aug. 16, 1958; d. Sylvio and Madonna Ciccone; m. Sean Penn, Aug. 16, 1985 (div. 1989); m. Guy Ritchie, 2000; 2 children, Lourdes, Rocco. Student, U. Mich., 1976-78. Dancer Alvin Ailey Dance Co., N.Y.C., 1979; CEO Maverick Records, L.A. Albums include Madonna, 1983, Like a Virgin, 1985, True Blue, 1986,(soundtrack)Who's That Girl, 1987, (with others) Vision Quest Soundtrack, 1983, You Can Dance, 1987, Like a Prayer, 1989, I'm Breathless: Music From and Inspired by the Film Dick Tracy. 1990, The Immaculate Collection, 1990, Erotica, 1992, Bedtime Stories, 1994, Something to Remember, 1995, (soundtrack) Evita, 1996, Ray of Light, 1998 (Grammy award for Best Pop Album 1999), (with others) Austin Powers, The Spy Who Shagged Me soundtrack, 1999, Music, 2000; film appearances include A Certain Sacrifice, 1980, Vision Quest, 1985, Desperately Seeking Susan, 1985, Shanghai Surprise, 1986, Who's That Girl, 1987, Bloodhounds of Broadway, 1989, Dick Tracy, 1990, Truth or Dare, 1991, Madonna, 1992, Body of Evidence, 1992, A League of Their Own, 1992, Dangerous Game, 1993, Blue in the Face, 1995, Four Rooms, 1996, Girl 6, 1996, Evita, 1996 (Golden Globe, 1997); Broadway theater debut in Speed-the-Plow, 1987; TV Happy Birthday Elizabeth: A Celebration of a Life, 1997, The Next Best Thing, 2000, Swept Away, 2002; author: Sex, 1992; stage appearance in Up for Grabs, 2002. Roman Catholic. Office: 8491 W Sunset Blvd Ste 485 West Hollywood CA 90069-1911 Address: Maverick Recording Co 9348 Civic Center Dr Ste 100 Beverly Hills CA 90210-3606*

MADORE, JOYCE LOUISE, gerontology nurse; b. Madison, Kans., Dec. 15, 1936; d. Lionel Wiedmer and Mary Elizabeth (Piley) Murphy; m. Robert Madore, Aug. 15, 1969; children: Carl, Clay. BS, Emporia State U., 1980; diploma, Newman Hosp., 1981, Southwest Mo. State U., 1988. RN, Kans., Mo.; cert. gerontol. nurse, non profit adminstr.; cert. and lic. nursing home adminstr. Med. charge nurse St. Mary's Hosp., Emporia, Kans., 1971-72; dir. nursing Madison (Kans.) Manor, 1974-81, 82-83; staff nurse Newman Meml. Hosp., Emporia, 1981-82; dir. Daybreak Adult Day Svcs., dir. HELP program Springfield (Mo.) Area Coun. of Chs., 1983-99; asst. dir. nursing Emporia Presbyterian Manor, Kans., 1999—. Mem. Gov.'s Com. to Establish Rules and Regulations on Adult Day Care Patients State of Mo.; cons. U. Mo. Coop. Extension Svc. Program Guides on Adult Day Care; bd. dirs. S.W. Alzheimers Assn., 1998—. Contbr. (video) Understanding Aging Program; developer Home Guide for the Homebound, 1996. Named one of Outstanding Nurses in Mo., St. Louis U., 1989; recipient Salute to Health Care award Springfield C. of C., 1998. Mem. NAFE, Adult Day Care Assn. (past sec., exec. past v.p. 1989-91), Mo. Nurses Assn., Mo. Adult Day Care Assn. (pres. 1991-95, Exec. award 1995), Mo. League Nursing. Home: 714 Exchange St Emporia KS 66801-3010

MADORY, JAMES RICHARD, hospital administrator, former air force officer; b. Staten Island, N.Y., June 11, 1940; s. Eugene and Agnes (Gerner) M.; m. Karen James Clifford, Sept. 26, 1964; children: James E., Lynn Anne, Scott J., Elizabeth Anne, Joseph M. (dec.). BS, Syracuse U., 1964; MHA, Med. Coll. Va., 1971. Enlisted USAF, 1958; x-ray technician Keesler Area Med. Ctr., Biloxi, Miss., 1959-62; commd. 2d lt. USAF, 1964, advanced through grades to maj., 1979—; x-ray technician Keesler Area Med. Ctr., Biloxi, Miss., 1959-62; adminstr. Charleston (S.C.) Clinic, 1971-74, Beale Hosp., Calif., 1974-77; assoc. adminstr. Shaw Regional Hosp., S.C., 1977-79; ret. USAF, 1979; asst. adminstr. Raleigh Gen. Hosp., Beckley, W.Va., 1979-81; adminstr., dir., sec. bd. Chesterfield Gen. Hosp., Cheraw, S.C., 1981-87; pres., CEO Grand Strand Hosp., Myrtle Beach, 1987-95, trustee, 1987-95; elected vice chairman Horry County Planning Commn., 1996-98; cons. Healthcare Adminstrn., 1995—. Adv. bd. Cheraw Nursing Home, 1984-85. Contbr. articles to profl. jours. Chmn. bd. W.Va. Kidney Found., Charleston, 1980-81; chmn. youth bd. S.C. TB and Respiratory Disease Assn., Charleston, 1972-73; county chmn. Easter Seal Soc., Chesterfield County, S.C., 1984-85; campaign crusade chmn. Am. Cancer Soc., Chesterfield County, 1985-86; chmn. dist. advancement com. Boy Scouts Am., 1987-90; bd. dirs. Horry County United Way, 1989-95, Horry County Access Care, 1989-91; trustee Cheraw Acad., 1982-85, Grand Strand Gen. Hosp., 1987-94, Coastal Acad., 1988-90; commr. Horry County Planning Commn., 1995-97, vice chmn., 1996-97; mem. Myrtle Beach AFB Redevel. Authority, 1997—; chmn. Horry County Boys & Girls Clubs Am., 1998-99, bd. dirs., 1998-2000; apptd. Myrtle Beach Air Base Redevel. Authority, 1998, Waccamaw Regional Workforce Investment Bd., 1998, vice-chmn., 1998—; vice-chmn. Horry County Republican Party, 1998-99; S.C. fin. steering com.; campaign chmn. McCain 2000 for Pres., 1999-2000, Harry County. Decorated Bronze Star, Vietnamese Cross of Gallantry, Vietnamese Medal of Honor; named to S.C. Order of Palmetto Gov. David Beasley, 1995. Fellow Am. Coll. Hosp. Adminstrs., Am. Coll. Health Care Execs; mem. S.C. Hosp. Assn. (com on legislation 1984-86, trustee 1989-94), Am. Acad. Healthcare Adminstrs., Cheraw C. of C. (bd. dirs. 1982-83), Rotary (pres. 1984-85). Republican. Roman Catholic. Home and Office: 341 Implement Dr Aiken SC 29803-6293 E-mail: jmadory@yahoo.com.

MADORY, RICHARD EUGENE, lawyer; b. Kenton, Ohio, May 14, 1931; s. Harold Richard and Hilda (Strictland) M.; m. Barbara Jean Madory, Sept. 25, 1955; children— Richard Eugene, Terry Dean, Michael Wesly. B.S. in Edn., Ohio State U., 1952; J.D., Southwestern U., 1961. Bar: Calif., 1961, U.S. Ct. Mil. Appeals, U.S. Supreme Ct., U.S. Dist. Ct. (cen. dist.) Calif. With firm Madory, Booth, Zell & Pleiss, Santa Ana, Calif., 1962— , now pres., v.p., sec.-treas. lectr. Continuing Edn. of Bar State of Calif. Served to col. USMC. Fellow Am. Coll. Trial Lawyers; mem. ABA, Orange County Bar Assn., Los Angeles County Bar Assn., So. Calif. Def. Counsel Assn., Am. Bd. Trial Advs., Nat. Bd. Trial Advocacy. Office: 17822 17th St Ste 205 Tustin CA 92780-2152

MADOW, LEO, psychiatrist, educator; b. Cleve., Oct. 18, 1915; s. Solomon Martin and Anna (Meyers) Madow; m. Jean Antoinette Weisman, Apr. 16, 1942 (dec.); children: Michael, Robert; m. Barbara N. Young, Dec. 26, 2000. AB, Western Res. U., 1937, MD, 1942; MA, Ohio State U., 1938. Diplomate Am. Bd. Psychiatry and Neurology. Intern Phila. Gen. Hosp., 1942-43; resident Phila. Gen. Hosp., Jefferson Hosp., Inst. Pa. Hosp., 1943-46; practice medicine specializing in psychiatry Phila., 1948—; prof., chmn. dept. neurology Med. Coll. Pa., 1958-65, prof., chmn. dept. psychiatry and neurology, 1965-70, prof., chmn. dept. psychiatry, 1970-81, clin. prof. psychiatry Hershey Med. Ctr., 1982—; sr. cons. psychiatry Inst. Pa. Hosp., Phila., 1975—. Tng. analyst, past pres. Phila. Psychoanalytic Inst.; past pres., mem. med. staff Inst. Pa. Hosp. Author: Anger, 1972, Love, 1983, Guilt, 1989; editor: Dreams, 1970, Sensory Deprivation, 1970, Psychomimetic Drugs, 1971, Integration of Child Psychiatry with Basic Resident Program, 1975. Served to capt. AUS, 1944-46. Named Outstanding Educator of Am. Med. Coll. Pa., 1972. Fellow ACP, Am. Psychiat. Assn. (life), Phila. Psychiat. Soc. (Lifetime Achievement award 1991) (past pres.), Am. Coll. Psychiatrists, Am. Coll. Psychoanalysts (pres. 1989-90, Laughlin award 1990); mem. Am. Psychoanalytic Assn., Am. Neurol. Assn., Phila. Psychoanalytic Soc. (past pres.), Alpha Omega Alpha, Phi Soc. Home: 135 Sibley Ave Narberth PA 19072-1318 Office: 135 Sibley Ave Narberth PA 19072-1318 Fax: 610-664-1102. E-mail: leomadow@aol.com.

MADRAS, BERTHA KALIFON, neuroscientist, educator, consultant; b. Montreal, Quebec, Canada, Dec. 9, 1942; m. Peter Madras, June 21, 1964; children: Cynthia Gumbert, Claudine D. BSc, McGill U., 1963, PhD, 1967. Postdoctoral fellow Tufts U., Boston, 1966-67; postdoctoral fellow rsch. assoc. MIT, Cambridge, 1967-69, 72-74; asst. prof. U. Toronto, 1979—80, Harvard Med. Sch., Boston, 1986-90, assoc. prof., 1990-99, prof., 1999—, assoc. dir. pub. edn. divsn. addictions, 1998—. Mem. sci. adv. com. Brookhaven Nat. Lab., Upton, N.Y., 1998—; pub. info. animal com. Soc. Neurosci., Washington, 1992-96; rev. com., cons. Nat. Inst. Drug Abuse, chair B study sect., 1998-99; MDCN-5 rev. com.; cons. Ont. Mental Health Found., 1984-90, chmn. fellowships and awards com., 1988-90; chmn. radiation safety Harvard U., 1987-99, acting dir. Primate Ctr., 1998-99; mem. Dana Alliance for Brain Initiatives; bd. dirs., Coll. on Problems Drug Dependence, 1998—. Author: (book chpt.) Dopamine, 1984; editor: Neurosci.; mem. editl. bd. Synapse, 1991—; sci. fair judge; contbr. articles to profl. jours. Sci. fair judge. Recipient Rsch. grants Nat. Inst. Drug Abuse, 1992—, 94—, Sci. Edn. Partnership award grant, 1992-94, Parkinson's Disease Found., 1990-91, Nat. Inst. Neurol. Disease and Stroke, 1994, 99—, NIMH, Dana Alliance for Brain Initiatives. Mem. Soc. for Neuroscience, Coll. Probs. Drug Dependence. Achievements include development of a marker for Parkinson's disease and attention deficit hyperactivity disorder, a probe for cocaine binding sites in brain; mapped cocaine binding sites in the brain, relevant to the behavioral effects of cocaine; developed a PET imaging SPECT for living brain; developed a PET and SPECT imaging drug to monitor Parkinsonism and ADND in brain; program director museum project to teach public how drugs work in brain; development with Dr. Luke Sato of CD-ROM on how drugs affect brain. Office: Harvard Medical Sch 1 Pine Hill Rd Southborough MA 01772-1312 E-mail: bertha-madras@hms.harvard.edu.

MADRIA, SANJAY, computer scientist, educator; b. India, Aug. 14, 1965; s. M. L. and Geeta Madria; m. Ninu Porwal; children: Priyank, Pranal. Ph.D, Indian Inst. of Tech., Delhi, India, 1993. Asst. prof. U. Sains Malaysia, Penang, Malaysia, 1996—98; vis. asst. prof. Purdue U., West Lafayette, Ind., 1999—2000; asst. prof. U. Mo., Rolla-Rolla, 2000—. Contbr. articles to profl. jours. Mem.: ACM, IEEE (sr.). Home: 1809 Ashwood Dr Rolla MO 65401 Office: Univ Missouri Rolla Rolla MO 65401

MADRICK, JEFFREY G. writer, editor, economic consultant; b. N.Y.C., July 15, 1947; s. Milton and Corazon (De Arego) M.; m. Gloria Jean Adrian, June 29, 1969 (div. 1975); 1 child, Matina. BS salutatorian, NYU, 1969; MBA, Harvard U., 1971. Writer, columnist Money Mag., N.Y.C., 1972-75; fin. editor, columnist Bus. Week, 1975-78; exec. asst. to pres. Columbia Pictures, 1979-80; writer, cons., 1980-82; TV corr., commentator ESPN, 1982-85, NBC News, N.Y.C., 1985-93; writer, 1993—. Adj. prof. social sci. Cooper Union, N.Y.; sr. fellow World Policy Inst., N.Y.; fellow Shrevestein Ctr. for Peace, Politics and Policy, Harvard U. Author: Taking America, 1987 (Bus. Week award 1987), The End of Affluence, 1995 (N.Y. Times Notable Book award); editor Challenge Mag., 1995—. Recipient Emmy award, 1986, Page One award Newspaper Guild, 1979. Mem. Beta Gamma Sigma.

MADRID, OLGA HILDA GONZALEZ, retired elementary education educator, association executive; b. San Antonio, May 4, 1928; d. Victor A. and Elvira Ardilla Gonzalez; m. Sam Madrid, Jr., June 29, 1952; children: Ninette Marie, Samuel James. Student, U. Mex., San Antonio, St. Mary's U.; BA, Our Lady of Lake U., 1956, MEd, 1963. Cert. bilingual tchr., adminstr., Tex. Sec. Lanier High Sch. San Antonio Ind. Sch. Dist., 1945-52, tchr. Collins Garden Elem. Sch., Storm Elem. Sch., 1963-92; tutor Dayton, Ohio, 1952-54. Bd. dirs., sch. rep. San Antonio Tchr.'s Coun., 1970-90; chair various coms. Collins Garden Elem., 1970-92. Elected dep. precinct, senatorial and state Dem. Convs., San Antonio, 1968—; apptd. commr. Keep San Antonio Beautiful, 1985; life mem., past pres. San Antonio YWCA; bd. dirs. Luth. Gen. Hosp., Nat. Conf. Christians and Jews, Cath. Family and Children's Svcs., St. Luke's Luth. Hosp.; nat. bd. dirs. YWCA, 1985-96, also mem. exec. com.; mem. edn. commn. Holy Rosary Parish, 1994—; mem. bus. assocs. com. Our Lady of the Lake U., 1995—. Recipient Outstanding Our Lady Lake Alumni award Our Lady Lake U., 1975, Guadalupana medal San Antonio Cath. Archdiocese, 1975, Yellow Rose Tex. citation Gov. Briscoe, 1977; Olga H. Madrid Ctr. named in her honor, YWCA San Antonio and San Antonio City Coun., 1983; Lo Mejor De Lo Nuestro honoree San Antonio Light, 1991, honoree San Antonio Women's History Month Coalition, 1996; named Our Lady of Lake Outstanding Alumna, 1999. Mem. San Antonio Bus. and Profl. Women, Inc. (mem. exec. com.), Salute Quality Edn. (honoree 1993), Delta Kappa Gamma (Theta Beta chpt., mem. exec. com.). Avocations: reading, gardening. Home: 2726 Benrus Blvd San Antonio TX 78228-2319

MADRID, PATRICIA A. state attorney general; BA in English and Philosophy, U. N.Mex., 1969, JD, 1973; cert., Nat. Jud. Coll., U. Nev., 1978. Bar: N.Mex. Dist. judge N.Mex. State Dist. Judge, 1978—84; atty. gen. State of N.Mex., 1999—. Named Latina Atty. of Yr., Nat. Hispanic Bar Assn., 2001. Office: Atty Gens Office PO Drawer 1508 Santa Fe NM 87504-1508

MADRY-TAYLOR, JACQUELYN YVONNE, educational administrator; d. Arthur Chester and Janie (Cowart) Madry; 1 child, Jana LeMadry. BA, Fisk U., 1966; MA, Ohio State U., 1969; EdD, U. Fla., 1975. Cert. Inst. for Ednl. Mgmt., Harvard U., 1981. Tchr. Spanish Terry Parker Sr. High Sch., Jacksonville, 1967-72; instr. U. Fla., Gainesville, 1972-75; asst. to v.p. for acad. affairs. Morris Brown Coll., Atlanta, 1975-76; dean for instructional svcs. No. Va. Community Coll., Annandale, Va., 1976-83; dean undergrad. studies Bridgewater (Mass.) State Coll., 1983-92, exec. asst. to acting pres., 1988, acting v.p. acad. affairs, 1988-90; dir. Acad. Leadership Acad. Am. Assn. State Coll. and Univs., Washington, 1992-94; dir. ednl. programs and svcs. United Negro Coll. Fund Hdqs., 1994-97; pres. JYM Assocs., 1999—. Cons. to colls., univs. and orgns., 1997-99; cons. W.K. Kellog Found., 1993-97; bd. dirs. Bridgewater State Coll. Early Learning Ctr., 1984-88; evaluator U.S. Dept. State/Fgn. Svc., Washington, 1982—, U.S. Dept. Edn., 1989—; pres. JYM Assocs., 1999—. Vice chmn. No. Va. Manpower Planning Coun., Fairfax County, Va., 1981. Recipient Cert. Achievement Bridgewater State Coll. Black Alumni, 1988, Women Helping Women award Soroptimist Internat., 1983, Outstanding Young Women Am. award, 1976, 78; named Personalities of South, 1977; recipient Outstanding Tchr./Student Rels. Humanitarian award B'nai B'rith, 1972. Mem. Pub. Mem. Assn. U.S. Fgn. Svc., Soroptimist Internat., Boston Club (v.p. 1986-88), Jack and Jill of Am., Inc., Pi Lambda Theta, Phi Delta Kappa, Alpha Kappa Alpha, Links Inc. (Reston, Va. chpt.). Methodist. Avocations: playing piano, bike riding. Home and Office: 12274 Angel Wing Ct Reston VA 20191-1119 Fax: 703-716-4364. E-mail: jkemt@aol.com.

MADSEN, BARBARA A, state supreme court justice; BA, U. Wash., 1974; JD, Gonzaga U., 1977. Pub. defender King and Snohomish Counties, 1977—82; staff atty. Seattle City Atty.'s Office, 1982—84, spl. prosecutor, 1984—88; judge Seattle Mcpl. Ct., 1988—92; justice Washington Supreme Ct., Olympia, 1993—. Office: Wash Supreme Ct PO Box 40929 Olympia WA 98504-0929*

MADSEN, DOROTHY LOUISE (MEG MADSEN), writer; b. Rochester, N.Y. d. Charles Robert and Louise Anna Agnes Meyer; m. Frederick George Madsen, Feb. 17, 1945 (dec.). BA, Mundelein Coll., Chgo., 1978; grad., US Army Command and Genl. Staff Coll., 1960. Feature writer Gannett Newspapers, Rochester Democrat & Chronicle, 1939-41; pub. rels. rep. Rochester Tel. Corp., 1941-42; exec. dir. LaPorte (Ind.) chpt. ARC, 1964; dir. adminstrv. svcs. Bank Mktg. Assn., Chgo., 1971-74; exec. dir. Eleanor Women's Found., 1974-84; founder Meg Madsen Assocs., 1984-88, women's career counselor; founder Clearinghouse Internat. Newsletter, Eleanor Women's Forum, Clearinghouse Internat., Eleanor Intern Program Coll. Students and Returning Women. Chief top secret global encrypted radio telephone conf. Pentagon, Washington, 1945; conf. aide to Pres. Harry S Truman, Washington, 45. Chief Overseas Classified Conf. Svc., War Dept. Gen. Staff, 1944-46. Lt. col. WAC, 1942-47, 67-70. Lt. col. WAC, 1942—47. Decorated Legion of Merit, Meritorious Svc. award. Mem.: Res. Officers Assn., Mundelein Alumnae Assn., Ret. Officers Assn., Phi Sigma Tau (charter mem. Ill. Kappa chpt.). Home and Office: 1030 N State St Apt 25H Chicago IL 60610-2831

MADSEN, GEORGE FRANK, lawyer; b. Sioux City, Iowa, Mar. 24, 1933; s. Frank O. and Agnes (Cuhel) M.; m. Magnhild Norstog; 1 child, Michelle Marie. BA, St. Olaf Coll., 1954; LLB, Harvard U., 1959. Bar: Ohio 1960, Iowa 1961, U.S. Dist. Ct. (no. and so. dists.) Iowa, U.S. Ct. Appeals (8th cir.), U.S. Supreme Ct. 1991. Trainee Cargill, Inc., Mpls., 1954; assoc. Durfey, Martin, Browne & Hull, Springfield, Ohio, 1959-61; assoc., then ptnr. Shull, Marshall & Marks, Sioux City, 1961-85; ptnr. Marks & Madsen, 1985-97, Marks, Madsen & Hirschbach, Sioux City, 1998-99, Mayne, Marks, Madsen & Hirschbach, LLP, Sioux City, 1999-2001. Author, editor: Iowa Title Opinions and Standards, 1978; contbg. author: The American Law of Real Property, 1991. Sec., bd.dirs. Sioux City Boys Club, 1969-76; mem. Sioux City Zoning Bd. Adjustment, 1963-65; active Iowa Mo. River Preservation and Land Use Authority, 1992-2001, pres., 1997-2001. Lt. USAF, 1954-56. Fellow Iowa State Bar Found.; mem. ABA, Iowa Bar Assn., Woodbury County Bar Assn., Nat. Wildlife Assn., Mont. Wildlife Assn., Pheasants Forever, Phi Beta Kappa (past pres. Siouxland chpt.), Rotary Internat. Avocations: skiing, hunting, swimming, reading. Office: PO Box 3661 Sioux City IA 51102-3661

MADSEN, H(ENRY) STEPHEN, retired lawyer; b. Momence, Ill., Feb. 5, 1924; s. Frederick and Christine (Landgren) Madsen; m. Carol Ruth Olmstead, Dec. 30, 1967; children: Stephen Stewart, Christie Morgan, Kelly Ann. MBA, U. Chgo., 1948; LLB, Yale U., 1951. Bar: Wash. 1951, Ohio 1953, U.S. Supreme Ct. 1975. Rsch. asst. Wash. Water Power Co., Spokane, 1951; assoc. Baker, Hostetler & Paterson, Cleve., 1952-59, ptnr., 1960-88, sr. ptnr., 1989-92; ret., 1992. Danish consul for Ohio, 1973—98. Active Bus. Advisers Cleve.; trustee Breckenridge Ret. Cmty., Ohio Presbyn. Ret. Svcs. With AC U.S. Army, 1943—46. Decorated Knight Queen of Denmark. Fellow: ABA (life); mem.: Cleve. Bar Assn., Am. Law Inst., Am. Coll. Trial Lawyers (life), Country Club Cleve.

MADSEN, LOREN WAKEFIELD, sculptor; b. Oakland, Calif., Mar. 29, 1943; s. Roy Sondergaard and Kathryn O. (Finerty) M.; m. Libbe Hurvitz, June 30, 1968; children: Anne Lea, Nora Karin. Student, Reed Coll., Portland, 1961-63; BA, UCLA, 1966, MA, 1970. One-man shows include Riko Mizuno Gallery, L.A., 1973, 74, McKee Gallery, N.Y.C., 1976, 77, 82, 84, 86, 90, 92, 96, 98, L.A. Louver Gallery, Venice, Calif., 1976, 78, Hansen Fuller Goldeen Gallery, San Francisco, 1980, Wright State U., Dayton, 1980, U. Mass., 1981, Cheryl Haines Gallery, San Francisco, 1991, Art First Gallery, London, 1998, Mus. Contemporary Art, San Diego, 2000; group shows include Los Angeles County Mus. Art, 1974, 76, 83, Hayward Gallery, London, 1975, Walker Art Ctr., Mpls., 1976, Biennale of Sculpture, Sydney, Australia, 1976, Ft. Worth Mus. Art, 1977, Joslyn Art Mus., Omaha, 1979, Hirshhorn Mus., Washington, 1979, Newport Harbor Art Mus., 1982, Freedman Gallery, Albright Coll., 1987, Art First Gallery, London, 1998, SUNY, Stony Brook, 1999, Drury Coll., Mo., 1999, MCA, San Diego, 2000, others. Nat. Endowment for Arts grantee, 1975-76, 80-81 Office: 426 Broome St New York NY 10013-3251 E-mail: lmadsen@bellatlantic.net.

MADSEN, STEPHEN STEWART, lawyer; b. Spokane, Wash., Oct. 13, 1951; s. H. Stephen Madsen and Sarah Pope (Stewart) Ruth; m. Rebecca Wetherill Howard, July 28, 1984; children: Stephen Stewart Jr., Lawrence Washington, Christina Wetherill, Benton Howard. BA, Harvard U., 1973; JD, Columbia U., 1980. Bar: N.Y. 1981, U.S. Dist. Ct. (so. dist.) N.Y. 1981, U.S. Ct. Appeals (6th cir.) 1983, U.S. Ct. Appeals (8th cir.) 1985, U.S. Ct. Appeals (2d, 7th and D.C. cirs.) 1994, U.S. Supreme Ct. 1996. Law clk. to presiding judge U.S. Ct. Appeals 2d cir., N.Y.C., 1980-81; assoc. Cravath, Swaine & Moore, 1981-88, ptnr., 1988—. Bd. visitors Columbia U. Sch. Law, 1991—; bd. govs. Hill-Stead Mus., 1995-2002; mem. vestry St. Bartholomew's Ch., 1995—. Mem. ABA, N.Y. State Bar Assn. (exec. com. antitrust law sect. 1998—), New York County Lawyers Assn., London Ct. Internat. Arbitration, Fedn. Bar Coun. Office: Cravath Swaine & Moore Worldwide Pla 825 8th Ave Fl 38 New York NY 10019-7475

MADSON, DAVID JOHN, fundraising executive; b. Mpls., 1955; s. John Richard and K. Rae Madson; m. Helen M. DeMichiel; 1 child, Antonia. BS in Comm. magna cum laude, U. Minn., Mpls., 1979; postgrad., U. Minn., 1986-87. Advanced cert. fund raiser exec. Media arts instr. ACTION Cmty. Outreach Program, 1976-77; photography instr. Inver Hills C.C. Program, 1978-84; assoc. dir. devel. Film in the Cities, St. Paul, 1981-84; exec. dir. Boston Film/Video Found., 1984-85; assoc. devel. officer propsect rsch. U. Minn. Found., 1985-86; chief devel. officer Coll. Edn. U. Minn., Mpls., 1987-93, chief devel. officer Cancer Ctr., 1993-95; dir. devel. Sch. Nursing U. Calif., San Francisco, 1995-98, dir. devel. Sch. Dentistry, 1998-00, sr. devel. dir. Univ. rels. Berkeley, 2000—. Mem. adv. panels Minn. State Arts Bd., St. Paul, 1993-95, Nat. Endowment Arts, Washington, 1991, 93-94; cons. Jerome Hill Theatre Devel., 1985; panelist photography fellowships Minn. State Arts Bd., 1985, NEA, 1994; cons. Media Arts Ctr. Project, Artspace, Mpls., 1985-86; cons. nat. satellite distbn. project Deep Dish Pub. Access TV, N.Y.C., 1985-87; panelist McKnight Found./Mpls. Arts Commn., 1986-88; devel. cons. Mgmt. Assistance Project, 1991; media grants rev. panelist Minn. Humanities Commn., 1991; program com. Minn. Coun. on Planned Giving Conf., 1992. Exhibited in group photography shows at St. Paul Sci. and Art Ctr., 1974, Kennedy Ctr. for Arts, Washington, 1975, Nash Gallery, 1976, 81, Coffman Union Gallery, 1977-78, Film in the Cities, 1977, Hunt Gallery. Treas. Univ. Film Soc., Mpls., 1981-84, 89-95, KFAI Cmty. Radio, Mpls., 1989-92; pres. Seward Cmty. Coop., Mpls., 1993-95, United Cerebral Palsy, San Francisco, 1996-99, Red Eye Collaboration Theater, Mpls., 1986-91; bd. dirs. Lowertown Cmty. Coun., 1981-83, Palace Theater Co., 1982-84, So. Theater, 1986-89, Minn. Span Assn., 1988-93; arts adv. com. City of St. Paul Planning Dept., 1982-84; mem. Chain of Lakes planning com. City of Mpls. Park Bd., 1989; bd. dirs. Powderhorn Cmty. Coun., 1985-90, treas., 1986-88; co-founder, treas. Lowertown Lofts Artist Housing Coop., 1982-90; facilities com. Minn. chpt. Am. Youth Hostels, 1990-93; devel. com. Headwaters Fund, 1990-93, sec. Film in the Cities, 1993-95; pres. Berkeley Montessori Sch., 1998-2000; bd. dirs., co-pres. Friends of Photography, Ansel Adams Ctr., San Francisco, 1999-2002; bd. dirs. Golden Gate Coun. Am. Youth Hostels, 2002—, Mechanics' Inst. Libr., 1999— Mem. Assn. Fundraising Profls. (v.p. Golden Gate chpt. 1996-99, bd. dirs. Minn. chpt. 1993-95, v.p. external affairs 1999-2001, nat. govt. rels. com. 2000—, nat. edn. com. 2001—), U. Minn. Alumni Assn. (nat. bd. 1996-2002, pres. San Francisco charter 1995-98). Avocations: cross country skiing, bicycling. Office: U Calif Berkeley 2440 Bancroft Way Berkeley CA 94720-4200 E-mail: djm1@urel.berkeley.edu.

MADU, LEONARD EKWUGHA, lawyer, human rights officer, newspaper columnist, politician, business executive; b. Ibadan, Nigeria, Mar. 17, 1953; came to U.S., 1977; s. Luke E. and Grace (Dureke) M.; m. Jaculine Stephanie Turner, June 4, 1980; children: Christine, Oscar. BA, Marshall U., 1980; JD, U. Tenn., 1988; MA, Am. U. Rsch. assoc. Lamberts Publs., Washington, 1980-82; data specialist Govt. Employees Ins. Co., 1982-85; law intern Knoxville (Tenn.) Urban League, 1986-88; cons. Morris Brown Coll., Atlanta, 1988; staff atty. East Carolina Legal Svc., Wilson, N.C., 1989-90; cons. youth devel. Nat. Crime Prevention Coun., Washington, 1990; contract compliance officer Walters State C.C., Morristown, Tenn., 1990; examiner Dept. of Human Svc., Nashville, 1990-93; human rights officer Human Rights Commn., 1993—; pres. Panafrica, 1994—; CEO Madu and Assoc. Internat. Bus. Cons., 1996—; with Bus. Forum & Banquet, 1994—; 1st v.p. Nashville Multicultural Partnership, Inc., 2000—. Polit. cons. Embassy of Nigeria, Washington, 1995; cons. Embassy of Sierra Leone, Washington, 1995, Healthcare Internat. Mgmt. Co., 1996—, Embassy of Mozambique, 2000—, Embassy of Togo, 2001—; bd. dirs. Peace and Justice Ctr., Nashville; pres. African Conglomerates Internat., Inc. Editor: African Nations Handbook, 1994, Directory of African Universities and Colleges, 1994; editor-in-chief Panafrican Digest, 1994, Panafrican Jour. of World Affairs, 1994; columnist Met. Times, Nashville, 1991—, The African Herald, Dallas, 1995—, U.S./African Voice, Balt., 1995—, African Sun Times, 1995—, The Nigerian and African, 1995—, The African Press, N.Y. Co-chmn. Clergy and Laity Concerned, Nashville, 1992-95; mem. curriculum and character com. Met. Sch. Bd., Nashville, 1994-97; co-coordinator The Haitian Project, 1991-94; vice-chmn. Nigerian Network Leadership awards N.Y., 1996; chmn. Internat. Women's Expo, Knoxville, 1996; co-chair Miss Nigeria Internat. Beauty Pageant, Washington, 1995, Miss Africa Internat. Beauty Pageant, Nashville, 1996, Igbo Union Chieftaincy Coronation Ceremony, Nashville, 1995; chmn. Nigerian Patriotic Front, 1997—; coord. United Nigeria Congress Party, 1997-98, Southeast U.S.; recruiter internat. students Tenn. State U., 1998-99; chmn. bd. dirs. Africa Found., Washington, 2001—. Recipient World Hunger Devel. Program award Marshall U., 1978-79, Hall of Nations scholar Am. U., 1980, 82, Mary Strohbel award United Way, 1994-95, Non-profit Vol. award Nat. Conf. of

Christians and Jews, 1994. Mem. NAACP, U.S. Com. on Fgn. Rels., Soc. Profl. Journalists, UN Assn., Orgn. African Natonals (pres. 1994), African C. of C. (pres. 2000—). Avocations: reading, travel, soccer, ping-pong, tennis. Office: Panafrica 1016 18th Ave S Nashville TN 37212-2105

MADURA, JAMES ANTHONY, surgical educator; b. Campbell, Ohio, June 10, 1938; s. Anthony Peter and Margaret Ethel (Sebest) M.; m. Loretta Jayne Sovak, Aug. 8, 1959; children: Debra Jean, James Anthony II, Vikki Sue. BA, Cogate U., 1959; MD, Western Res. U., 1963. Diplomate Am. Bd. Surgery. Intern in surgery Ohio State U., Columbus, 1963—64, resident in surgery, 1966—71; asst. prof. surgery Ind. U., Indpls., 1971—76, assoc. prof. Surgery, 1976—80, prof. Surgery, 1980—, J.S. Battersby prof. surgery, 2001—. Dir. gen. surgery Ind. U. Sch. Medicine, Indpls., 1985—, vice-chmn., 1985—. Contbr. articles to profl. jours. Capt. U.S. Army, 1964-66, Vietnam. Fellow Am. Coll. Surgeons; mem. Cen. Surg. Assn., Western Surg. Assn., Soc. Surgery Alimentary Tract, Midwest Surg. Assn., Internal Biliary Assn., Assn. Acad. Surgeons, The Columbia Club. Republican. Roman Catholic. Home: 9525 Copley Dr Indianapolis IN 46260-1422 Office: Ind U Dept of Surgery 545 Barnhill Dr # 244 Indianapolis IN 46202-5112 Personal E-mail: jmadura1@comcast.net. Business E-Mail: jmadura@iupui.edu.

MADURGA, GONZALO F. artistic director, actor, singer; b. Havana, Cuba, Jan. 21, 1932; arrived in U.S., 1953; s. Bernabé Madurga and Matilda Barrena. MS, L.I. U., 1977. Cert. bilingual tchr., NY. Artistic dir. Counterpoint Theatre, N.Y.C., 1972-75, Operatic, Concert & Theatre Artists, Inc., Miami, Fla., 1996—. Acting appearances include Carmelina, N.Y.C., 1979, La Verbena de la Paloma, Queens, NY, 1985 (Best Actor, Assn. Cronistas de Espectaculos 1985), Romeo and Juliet, NYC, 1994, Coimbra, Miami, 1994 (Best Actor Assn. Críticos y Cronistas de las Artes 1994), The Fantasticks, Miami, 1996, Macbeth, NY, 1997, The Merchant of Venice, 1997, NY, Drama, Death and the Maiden, Coconut Grove, Fla., 1999, Praying with the Enemy, Coconut Grove, 2000, Hamlet, Fla., 2000, Anna in the Tropics, Fla., 2000, The Man of La Mancha, NJ, The Most Happy Fella. With U.S. Army, infantry, 1956-58. Mem. Actors' Equity, Screen Actors' Guild, Am. Fed. T.V. Radio Artists, Nat. Acad. T.V. & Sciences, Home and Office: Operatic Concert & Theatre Artists Inc 1315 SW 21st St Miami FL 33145 Fax: (305) 858-0365. E-mail: gonzalomadurga@msn.com.

MADVA, STEPHEN ALAN, lawyer; b. Pitts., July 27, 1948; s. Joseph Edward and Mary (Zulick) M.; m. Bernadette A. McKeon; children: Alexander, Elizabeth. BA cum laude, Yale U., 1970; JD, U. Pa., 1973. Bar: Pa. 1973, U.S. Dist. Ct. (ea. dist.) Pa. 1975, U.S. Ct. Appeals (3d cir.) 1976, U.S. Ct. Appeals (11th cir.) 1987, U.S. Supreme Ct. 1985, N.Y. 1990. Asst. defender Defender Assn. Phila., 1973-75, fed. defender, 1975-77, also bd. dirs., 1985—; assoc. Montgomery, McCracken, Walker & Rhoads, Phila., 1977-81, ptnr., 1981—, mem. mgmt. com., 1993—, chmn. litigation sect., 1993—2002, vice chmn., 2002—. Bd. dirs. Ferag-Ams., LLC, WRH Mktg. Ams., LLC. Bd. dirs. Ctrl. Phila. Devel. Corp., 1995—, Opera Co. of Phila., 2000—, St. Christopher's Hosp. for Children, 2001—. Fellow Internat. Soc. Barristers, Am. Coll. Trial Lawyers; mem. ABA, Internat. Assn. Def. Counsel, Pa. Bar Assn. (mem. ho. of dels.), Phila. Bar Assn. (bd. govs. 2002--, fed. cts. com., chmn. commn. on jud. selection and retention.), Def. Rsch. Inst., Hist. Soc. Pa., Yale Alumni Assn. (schs. com.), Yale Rowing Assn., Union League of Phila. Democrat. Avocations: tennis, distance running, opera, classical music. Home: 2055 Lombard St Philadelphia PA 19146-1314 Office: Montgomery McCracken Walker & Rhoads 123 S Broad St Fl 24 Philadelphia PA 19109-1099 E-mail: smadva@mmwr.com.

MADY, BEATRICE M. artist; b. N.Y.C., Dec. 30, 1953; d. Raymond J. and Beatrice A. Mady; m. David W. Cummings, Oct. 2, 1982. Student, Bklyn. Mus. Art Sch., 1971-72; BFA, U. Dayton, 1976; MFA, Pratt Inst., 1978. One-woman shows include Rockville Centre (N.Y.) Pub. Gallery, 1976, Jersey City (N.J.) Visual Art Gallery, 1988, Caldwell (N.J.) Coll., 1991, Johnson & Johnson Gallery, New Brunswick, N.J., 1992, Johnson & Johnson Consumer Products Divns., Skillman, N.J., 1993, Rabbet Gallery, New Brunswick, 1996, Maurice M. Pine Gallery, Fair Lawn, N.J., 1997; exhibited in group shows at Newark Mus., 1982, Summit (N.J.) Art Ctr., 1985, Gallery Jupiter, Little Silver, N.J., 1986, Morris Mus., Morristown, N.J., 1987, Yuma (Ariz.) Art Ctr., 1989, Van Vorst Gallery, Jersey City, 1990, City Without Walls Gallery, Newark, 1993, Rabbet Gallery, New Brunwick, 1995, Watchung (N.J.) Arts Ctr., 1996, Seton Hall U. Law Sch., Newark, 1996, 00, Merck Corp. Hdqs., White House, N.J., 1997, Ben Shahn Gallery, Wayne, N.J., 1998, City Without Walls Gallery, Newark, 1998, Seton Hall Law Sch., Newark, 2000; works in pub. collections at Ortho Dermatological, Skillman, N.J., Janssen Pharmaceutia, Titusville, N.J., Bristol-Meyers Squibb, Plainsboro and Lawrenceville, N.J., Johnson & Johnson, New Brunswick, Sydney & Francis Lewis Found., Richmond, Va., Drew U. Mus., Madison, N.J., Arenol Chem. Corp., N.Y.C., Goetz and Mady-Grove, Jericho, N.Y. Painting fellow Pratt Inst., Bklyn., 1977-78, N.J. State Coun. on the Arts, 1985; grantee Ford Found., 1978. Mem. Coll. Art Assn.

MAECHLING, CHARLES, JR. lawyer, diplomat, educator, writer; b. N.Y.C., Apr. 18, 1920; s. Charles and Eugenie H. M.; m. Janet Leighton, Sept. 2, 1944; children: Philip Leighton and Eugenie Elisabeth (Mrs. David Buchan). Attended, Birch Wathen Sch., N.Y.C., 1924-37; BA with honors, Yale U., 1941; JD, U. Va., 1949. Bar: N.Y. 1949, D.C. 1957. Assoc. Sullivan & Cromwell, N.Y.C., 1949-51; atty. Office Sec. Air Force, 1951-52; counsel Electronics Industries Assn., Washington, 1953-56; founding ptnr. Shaw, Pittman, Potts & Maechling, 1956-61; dir. for internal def. Dept. State, Washington, 1961-63; spl. asst. to undersec. and amb.-at-large Averell Harriman, 1963-66; dep. gen. counsel NSF, 1966-71, spl. asst. to dir., 1972-74; prof. law U. Va., 1974-76; spl. counsel N.Y. law firms, 1976-81; sr. assoc. Carnegie Endowment for Internat. Peace, 1981-85; vis. fellow, mem. law faculty Cambridge U. (Wolfson Coll.), Eng., 1985-88; guest scholar internat. law Brookings Inst., Washington, 1989-93; internat. cons., 1993—. Legal adviser internat. matters NAS, 1970-73, mem. ocean policy com.; mem. law-of-sea and other adv. coms. Dept. State; gen. counsel Fairways Corp., 1959-61; adj. prof. Georgetown Law Sch., Sch. Internat. Svc., Am. U.; mem. adv. bd. Internat. Peace Acad.; lectr. U.S. Def. Schs., also Hague Acad. Internat. Law; arbitrator complex internat. cases; chair U.S.-IIASA Planning Group, 1981-83. Editor-in-chief Va. Law Rev., 1948-49; contbr. articles to N.Y. Times, Internat. Herald Tribune, Boston Globe, L.A. Times, Miami Herald, profl. and lit. jours. Bd. dirs. Coun. for Ocean Law, Washington Inst. Fgn. Affairs; mem. U.S. Com. for IIASA; outside counsel to CIA, 1957-60. From ensign to lt. comdr. USNR, 1941-47, at sea and secretariat Joint Chiefs Staff, 1943-44, del. 1943 Cairo Conf., UN Law of Sea Conf., 1971-82; asst. naval attache Peru, 1945-47. Mem.: ABA, Am. Soc. Internat. Law, Colonnade Club (Charlottesville), Yale Club (Washington), Cosmos Club (Washington), City Tavern Club (Washington). Avocation: languages. Home: 3403 Lowell St NW Washington DC 20016-5024 Home (Summer): 367 Bar Rd Saint Andrews NB Canada E5B 2P7

MAEDA, J. A. data processing executive, consultant; b. Mansfield, Ohio, Aug. 24, 1940; d. James Shunso and Doris Lucille Maeda; m. Robert Lee Hayes; 1 child Brian Sentaro Hayes. BS in Math., Purdue U., 1962, postgrad., 1962-63, Calif. State U., Northridge, 1968-75; cert. profl. designation in tech. of computer operating systems and tech. of info. processing, UCLA, 1971. Cons., rsch. asst. computer ctr. Purdue U., West Lafayette, Ind., 1962-63; computer operator, sr. tab operator, mem. faculty Calif. State U., Northridge, 1969, programmer cons., tech. asst. II, 1969-70, supr. acad. applicatons, EDP supr. II, 1970-72, project tech. support coord. programmer II, office of the chancellor, 1972-73, tech. support coord. statewide timesharing tech. support, programmer II, 1973-74, acad. coord., tech. support coord. instrn., computer cons. III, 1974-83; coord. user svcs. info. ctr., mem. tech. staff IV CADAM INC subs. Lockheed Corp., Burbank, Calif., 1983-86, coord. user svcs., tech. specialist computing dept., 1986-87; v.p., bd. dirs. Rainbow Computing, Inc., Northridge, 1976-85; dir. Aki Tech/Design, 1976—. Mgr. mktg. thaumaturge Taro Quipu Cons., Northridge, 1987—; tech. cons. Digital Computer Cons., Chatsworth, Calif., 1988; computer tech., fin. and bus. mgmt., sys. integration, 1988—90; tech. customer software support Collection Data Sys., Westlake, Calif., 1991; sr. tech. writer Sterling Software, 1992—2000; info. mgmt. divsn. Computer Assocs. Internat., Inc., 2000—. Contbr. Mem.: DECUS (ednl. spl. interest group 1977—83, ednl. steering com. RSTS/E 1979—82), SHARE, IEEE, Soc. for Tech. Comm. Avocations: photography, photojournalism, vintage automobiles. Office: Computer Assocs Internat Inc 8511 Fallbrook Ave Ste 200 West Hills CA 91304

MAEDA, KENJI, medical educator, educator; b. Tsu-City, Japan, Apr. 1, 1939; s. Tamotsu and Sumi (Kubo) M.; m. Mayuko Matsunaga, Mar. 30, 1975; children: Kayaho, Mayuho. MD, Nagoya U., 1965, PhD, 1978. Intern Nagoya U. Br. Hosp., 1965-66, asst., 1973-79, assoc. prof., 1979-91, prof. dept. medicine, 1991—, dir., 1992-96; prof. medicine Daiko-Med. Ctr. Nagoya U. Editor: Contributions to Nephrology, 1993, 94; contbr. articles to profl. jours. Recipient Jinkenkyukai award Japan Kidney Found., Tokyo, 1993. Mem. N.Y. Acad. Sci., AAAS, Am. Soc. Nephrology. Home: 20-1 5 chome Fujimidai Chikusa-ku Nagoya Aichi 464-0015 Japan Office: Nagoya U Daiko Med Ctr 20-1-1 Daiko Higashi-Ku Nagoya 461-0047 Japan E-mail: kmaeda@tsuru.med.nagoya-u.ac.jp.

MAEDA, KOICHI, pathologist; b. Tokyo, Aug. 30, 1942; s. Toyoji and Umeko (Goto) M.; m. Kimiko Sugiyama, Oct. 23, 1967; children: Yuko, Hayato, Chiaki. MD, Shinshu U., Matsumoto, Japan, 1967. Diplomate Am. Bd. Pathology, Clin., Anatomic and Hematology. Hematopathologist dept. pathology Henry Ford Hosp., Detroit, 1976—. Cons. Mercy Hosp., Detroit, 1997—. Fellow Coll. Am. Pathologists, Am. Soc. Clin. Pathologists. Achievements include study of pathogenesis in familial crystalline dystrophy of retina with co-workers.

MAEDA, NOBUYO, pathology and laboratory medicine educator; b. Japan, Apr. 4, 1949; came to U.S., 1978; m. Oliver Smithies, Feb. 22, 1992. BSc, Tohuku U., Japan, 1972, MSc, 1974, PhD, 1977. Rschr. chemistry Tohoku U., 1977-78; rsch. assoc. physiol. chemistry U. Wis., Madison, 1978-81, rsch. assoc. genetics, 1981-83, asst. scientist, 1983-86, assoc. scientist, 1986-88; assoc. prof. pathology U. N.C., Chapel Hill, 1988-96, prof., 1996—. Contbr. articles to profl. jours. Rsch. grantee NIH, 1989—, rsch. grantee in aid Am. Heart Assn., 1993-95, 97—. Home: 318 Umstead Dr Chapel Hill NC 27516-1809 Office: U NC Chapel Hill CB 7525 710 Brinkhous Bullitt Bldg Chapel Hill NC 27599-0001

MAEDER, GARY WILLIAM, lawyer; b. L.A., Dec. 21, 1949; s. Clarence Wilbur and Norma Jean (Buckbee) M.; m. Sue Ellen; children: Stephen Gregory, Charlene Michelle. BA, UCLA, 1971, JD, 1975; student, Fuller Seminary, 1971-72. Bar: Calif. 1975. Assoc. Kindel & Anderson, L.A., 1975-82, ptnr., 1982-96; shareholder Heller Ehrman White & McAuliffe LLP, 1996—. Author: God's Will for Your Life, 1973, 76, 91. In elder adult edn. St. John's Presbyn. Ch., L.A., 1981—86, 1994—96; bd. dirs. Christian Legal Soc. L.A., 1975—, Christian Conciliation Svcs. L.A., 1983—88. Mem. Los Angeles County Bar Assn. (state and local tax com.), Christian Legal Soc. (bd. dirs. 1989-92), Order of Coif, Phi Beta Kappa. Office: 601 S Figueroa St 40th Fl Los Angeles CA 90017 E-mail: gmaeder@hewm.com.

MAEHL, JANE CECILIA, social worker, administrator; b. Summit, N.J., Nov. 2, 1967; d. Donald Kenneth and Ruth Louise Maehl. BA, BSW, Juniata Coll., 1989; MSW, Marywood Coll., 1992. Lic. social worker, Pa. Social worker Cornell Hall Convalescent Ctr., Union, N.J., 1989-91, Presbyn. Children's Village, Rosemont, Pa., 1992-94, social worker II, 1994-95, supr., 1995-97, supr. II, 1997-98, dir. clin. svcs., 1998-2000, dir. residential treatment, 2000—. Adj. instr. Widener U., Chester, Pa., 2000—, Edn. Consortium, Phila., 2000—; adj. musician, 1997—. Head cook homeless project St. Paul's Luth. Ch., Ardmore, Pa., 1999—. Mem. NASW, NAWCC, AMC. Avocations: playing flute, music, hiking, bicycling, sports. Office: Presbyn Childrens Village 452 S Roberts Rd Bryn Mawr PA 19010 Home: 803 Andover Ct West Chester PA 19382-6662

MAEHL, WILLIAM HARVEY, historian, educator; b. Bklyn., May 28, 1915; s. William Henry and Antoinette Rose (Salamone) M.; m. Josephine Scholl McAllister, Dec. 29, 1941; children: Madeleine, Kathleen. BSc, Northwestern U., 1937, MA, 1939; PhD, U. Chgo., 1946. Asst. prof. history St. Louis U., 1941-42, Tex. A&M U., College Sta., 1943, De Paul U., Chgo., 1944-49; historian Dept. of Def., Karlsruhe, Stuttgart, Fed. Rep. Germany, 1950-52; chief briefing office U.S. hdqrs. U.S. Hdqs. European Command, Frankfurt, Germany, 1952-53; chief historian Arty. Sch., Okla., 1954; with War Plans Office, Hdqs. No. Air Materiel Area for Europe, Burtonwood, Eng., 1954-55; assoc. prof. European history Nebr. Wesleyan U., Lincoln, 1955-57, prof., 1958-62, 65-68; prof. German history Auburn (Ala.) U., 1968-81, prof. emeritus, 1981—. Vis. prof. U. Nebr., 1962, U. Auckland, New Zealand, 1963-64, Midwestern U., Wichita Falls, Tex., 1965. Author: German Militarism and Socialism, 1968, History of Germany in Western Civilization, 1979, A World History Syllabus, 3 vols., 1980, August Bebel, Shadow Emperor of the German Workers, 1980, The German Socialist Party: Champion of the First Republic, 1918-33, 1986; author monographs for U.S. Army in Europe, chpts. in books, atomic, biol. and emergency war plans for No. Air Materiel Area for Europe; contbr. poetry to Question of Balance, Tears of Fire, Disting. Poets Am., Best Poems of 1995, Journey of Mind; contbr. articles to profl. jours. Grantee Nebr. Wesleyan U., 1959, Auburn U., 1969-73, 79-80, Am. Philosophical Soc., 1973-74, Deutscher Akademischer Austauschdienst, 1978. Mem. Am. Hist. Assn., Phi Kappa Phi, Phi Alpha Theta.

MAEHL, WILLIAM HENRY, historian, university administrator, educational consultant; b. Chicago Heights, Ill., June 13, 1930; s. William Henry and Marvel Lillian (Carlson) M.; m. Audrey Mae Ellsworth, Aug. 25, 1962; 1 child, Christine Amanda. BA, U. Minn., 1950, MA, 1951; postgrad (Fulbright fellow), King's Coll., U. Durham, Eng., 1955-56; PhD, U. Chgo., 1957; LHD (hon.), Fielding Inst., 1993. Asst. prof. Montclair (N.J.) State Coll., 1957-58; asst. prof. Washington Coll., Chestertown, Md., 1958-59, U. Okla., Norman, 1959-64, asso. prof., 1964-70, prof. English history, 1970-86; dean Coll. Liberal Studies, 1976-86, vice provost for continuing edn. and public service, 1979-86; pres. The Fielding Inst., Santa Barbara, Calif., 1987-93, pres. emeritus, 1993—. Prin. investigator Project for a Nation of Lifelong Learners, Regents Coll., Albany, N.Y., 1994-97; vis. prof. U. Nebr., summer 1965; vis. fellow Wolfson Coll. Oxford (Eng.) U., spring 1975; fellow Salzburg Seminar in Am. Studies, 1976. Author: The Reform Bill of 1832, 1967, Lifelong Learning at Its Best: Innovative Practices in Adult Credit Programs, 2000; editor: R.G. Gammage, Chartist Reminiscences, 1981, Continuum: Jour. of the Nat. Continuing Edn. Assn., 1980-83, also articles. Mem. coun. Nat. Ctr. for Adult Learning, 1990—2001; bd. dirs. Alliance for Alternative Degree Programs, 1988—90; trustee Coun. for Adult and Exptl. Learning, 1990—94, Southwestern Coll., 2000—02. Leverhulme Research fellow, 1961-62; grantee Am. Philos. Soc., 1961-62, 67-68, 71, 76 Fellow: Assn. Grad. Liberal Studies Programs, Royal Hist. Soc.; mem.: Adult Higher Edn. Alliance, Conf. on Brit. Studies. Office: PO Box 23565 Santa Fe NM 87502 E-mail: wmaehl2@cs.com.

MAEHR, MARTIN LOUIS, psychology educator; b. Guthrie, Okla., June 25, 1932; s. Martin J. and Regina (Meier) M.; m. Jane M. Pfeil, Aug. 9, 1959; children— Martin, Michael, Katherine BA, Concordia Coll., 1953, MA, 1959; PhD, U. Nebr., 1960. Counselor U. Nebr., Lincoln, 1959-60; asst. prof. to assoc. prof. Concordia Sr. Coll., Fort Wayne, Ind., 1960-67; assoc. prof. ednl. psychology U. Ill., Urbana, 1967-70, prof., 1970—, chmn. dept. ednl. psychology, 1970-75, assoc. dean grad. and internat. programs prof., 1975-77, research prof., dir. Inst. Research on Human Devel., prof. ednl. psychology, 1977-88, assoc. dir. Office Gerontology and Aging Studies, 1980-82; prof. edn. and psychology U. Mich., Ann Arbor, 1988—, chair combined program edn. and psychology, 1988-92. Vis. prof. U. Queensland, Australia, 1981; vis. prof., cons. to dean Faculty Edn. U. Tehran, Iran, 1973-74 Author: Sociocultural Origins of Achievement, 1974, (with Jane Maehr) Being a Parent in Today's World, 1980, (with L.A. Braskamp) The Motivation Factor, 1986, (with Carol Midgley) Transforming School Cultures, 1996; editor: Advancement in Motivation and Achievement series; contbr. articles to profl. jours. Lutheran.

MAEKAWA, KOJI OGURA, technology company administrator; b. Fukui, Japan, Sept. 11, 1954; s. Eiji and Toshiko M.; m. Yukiko Ogura, Nov. 30, 1995. BSChemE, Tokyo U. of Agr. & Tech., 1979; MBA, U. St. Thomas, St. Paul, 1992. Analytical engr., Analytical Lab. Sumitomo 3M, Sagamihara, Japan, 1979-81, chem. engr., Corporate Lab. Japan, 1982-87; process engr., Optical Storage Divsn. Minn. Mining Mfg., St. Paul, 1988-92, sr. process devel. engr., 1993-96; technical team leader Imation Corp. Adv. Imaging Technology, 1997-98, bus. devel. mgr., 1998-99, program mgr., 1999—. Intellectual property translator (English/Japanese), language soc. Minn. Mining Mfg., 1993—; cons. Expert Magnetics Corp., Chiba, Japan, 1993—. Patentee in field. Mem. Am. Japanese Soc. Avocations: golf, gardening. Office: Imation Corp Advanced Imaging Tech Mercury Bldg 1 Imation Pl Oakdale MN 55128-3414 Home: Apt 3309 4515 Carlyle Ct Santa Clara CA 95054-3962 Fax: 651-704-5840. E-mail: kjom1@mn.mediaone.net., kmaekawa@imation.com.

MAELAND, ARNULF JULIUS, research scientist; b. Aakrehamn, Norway, Apr. 21, 1933; came to U.S., 1952; s. Erling Magnus and Dagny Marie M.; m. Gunhild Olaug, June 18, 1955; children: Lynn Solveig, David Erling, Kerry Brynhild. BS, Augsburg Coll., 1955; MS, Tufts U., 1959; PhD, U. Vt., 1965. NATO postdoctoral fellow NRC Inst. Atomic Energy, Kjeller, Norway, 1965-66; NAS-NRC postdoctoral rsch. assoc. NRC Army Materials Rsch. Ctr., Watertown, Mass., 1966-68; prof. Worcester (Mass.) Polytechnic Inst., 1968-75; sr. rsch. assoc. Allied Corp., Morristown, N.J., 1975-90; vis. sr. rsch. fellow Inst. Energy Tech., Lillesrom, Norway, 1992—. Chmn. Gordon Rsch. Confs., Kingston, R.I., 1999; advisor Internat. Sci. and Tech. Ctr., Moscow, 1998—; program evaluator Norwegian Rsch. Coun., Oslo, Norway, 1998-99; cons. Norsk Hydro, Oslo, 2000—. Editor: Hydrides for Energy Storage, 1977; patentee in field; contbr. articles to profl. jours. Rsch. grantee Aluminum Assn., 1969-75. Lutheran. Avocations: stamp collecting, traveling, classical music. Home: 305 Cactus Hill Ct Royal Palm Beach FL 33411 Office: Inst Energy Tech Kjeller N-2027 Norway

MAERKER, GERHARD, food science consultant; b. Bernburg, Germany, Nov. 4, 1923; came to U.S., 1938; s. William and Else (Behr) M.; m. Roselle Kosack, Aug. 26, 1951; children: Wendy Ellen Maerker Harris, Heidi Ann Maerker Zod. BS in Chemistry, Phila. Coll. of Pharmacy and Sci., now U. Scis. in Phila., 1951; MA in Chemistry, Temple U., 1952, PhD in Organic Chemistry, 1957. Rsch. chemist USDA, Wyndmoor, Pa., 1958-66, head lubricants investigations, 1966-70, chief animal fat lab., 1970-80, lead scientist, 1980-92, ret., 1992. Author book chpts.; contbr. articles to profl. jours.; patentee in field. Mem. AAAS, Am. Chem. Soc., Am. Oil Chemists Soc. (past pres., chmn. nat. coms. 1960-90, chmn. nat. meetings 1971, 74, 85, 90). Home: 206 Haws Ln Oreland PA 19075-2426

MAEROFF, GENE I. academic administrator, journalist; b. Cleve., Jan. 8, 1939; s. Harry B. and Charlotte (Szabo) M.; children: Janine Amanda, Adam Jonathan, Rachel Judith. BS, Ohio U., 1961; MS, Boston U., 1962. Teaching fellow Boston U., 1961-62; news bur. dir. R.I. Coll., 1962-64; religion editor Akron (Ohio) Beacon Jour., 1964-65; with Cleve. Plain Dealer, 1965-71, assoc. editor, 1969-71; edn. writer N.Y. Times, N.Y.C., 1971-86; sr. fellow Carnegie Found. for the Advancement of Teaching, Princeton, N.J., 1986-97; dir. Hechinger Inst. Tchr.'s Coll. Columbia U., N.Y.C., 1997—. Contbr. mags. Author: Don't Blame the Kids, 1981, School and College, 1983, The Empowerment of Teachers, 1988, The School-Smart Parent, 1989, Sources of Inspiration, 1992, Team Building for School Change, 1993, Altered Destinies, 1998, Imaging Education, 1998, The Learning Connection, 2001; (with others) The New York Times Guide to Suburban Public Schools, 1976, Scholarship Assessed, 1997, Imaging education, 1998; contbr. The Human Encounter: Readings in Education, 1976, Human Dynamics in Psychology and Education, 1977, Social Problems, 1978, Education Reform in the '90's, 1992, Teachers As Leaders, 1994. Trustee Guild-Times Scholarship Fund, Ed Bang Journalism Scholarship Found.; mem. adv. bd. Inst. Ednl. Mgmt., Harvard U., Ednl. Resources Info. Ctr., U.S. Dept. Edn., Nat. Ctr. for Postsecondary Governance. Recipient writing awards Press Club Cleve., A.P. Soc. Ohio, Edn. Writers Assn., AAUP, Internat. Reading Assn. Mem. Blue Key, Omicron Delta Kappa, Kappa Tau Alpha, Phi Sigma Delta. Office: 23 Carriage Pl Edison NJ 08820-4023

MAERSCH, NANCY KAY, health facility administrator; b. Norfolk, Nebr., May 11, 1942; d. Ambrose Pryor and Angela Gertrude (Goergen) Jordan; m. Frank C. Maersch, May 11, 1968; 1 child, Todd F. BS in Med. Tech., Mt. Marty Coll., 1963; MA in Health Care Adminstrn., Cen. Mich. U., 1981. Diplomate in lab mgmt.; cert. med. technologist, cert. hematology specialist. From med. technologist to mgr. adminstrv. svc. and mktg. Madison (Wis.) Gen. Hosp. Lab., 1963-85; from mgr. mobile diagnostics to mgr. lab. ops. Meriter Gen. Med. Labs., Madison, 1985-96; dir. regional devel. Meriter Hosp., 1997—. Bd. dirs. Dane County Cytology Ctr., Madison, Wis. chpt. of Clin. Lab. Mgmt. Assn. Chair Edgefest event Edgewood H.S. Aux., 1987—92; vol. Ronald McDonald House, mem. house adv. com., 2001—; mem. RMH Gala Planning Com., 2001—, Bus. Forum, Madison, 1989—95; bd. dirs. parents assn. Marquette U., 1993—97. Mem. Am. Soc. Clin. Lab. Sci., Wis. Soc. Clin. Lab. Sci. (sec. 1967-70, 76-80), Clin. Lab. Mgmt. Assn. (Wis. chpt. bd. dirs., pres. 1997-98, chair bi-state conf. 1999, 2001, chair CLMA-WI/WMGMA Joint Conf. 2000), Women in Healthcare Mgmt., Med. Group Mgmt. Assn., Madison Area Lab. Suprs., Madison Civics Club. Roman Catholic. Avocations: sailing, cross-country skiing, reading, walking. Home: 6413 Keelson Dr Madison WI 53705-4370 Office: Meriter Hosp McConnell Hall 1010 Mound St Madison WI 53715-1532 E-mail: nmaersch@meriter.com.

MAERTIN, JAMES LEE, accountant; b. Berkeley, Calif., Dec. 18, 1960; s. Donald Lee Maertin and Liberty (Wegener) Goodwin. BA, Portland State U., 1986. CPA, Oreg. Acct. Portland (Oreg.) Opera Assn., 1984-87; sr. acct. Weisbarth Altman & Michaelson CPAs, N.Y.C., 1987-89; corp. tax acct. Mfrs. Hanover, 1989-90; internat. tax acct. James Maertin CPA, 1991—; tax acct. John Fredenberger Esq., Paris, 1993. Dir., founder Hopa Dance Ensemble, 1985-91. Mem. Internat. House, 1992—. Mem.: Internat. Ho. Avocations: dance (Ballroom, ballet, Capoeira...), travel. Office: Rm 208 110 W 40th St New York NY 10018-8584

MAES, JOHN LEOPOLD, theologian, psychologist, educator; b. Watertown, Mich., Aug. 6, 1923; s. John and Mary (Cornwell) M; m. Mary M. Johnson, Aug. 28, 1942; children: Barbara (dec.), John David. BTh, Owosso Coll., 1948; AB, Mich. State U., 1954, MA, 1957, PhD, 1963. Ordained to ministry United Meth. Ch., 1963, United Ch. Christ, 1976; lic. health care provider in psychology Nat. Registry Health Care Providers in Psychology, Mass., Maine, lic. psychologist, Mass., Maine. Pastor, Houghton Lake, Mich., 1948-52, Francestown, N.H., 1977-80; assoc. prof. Sch. Theology Boston U., 1963-72, adj. prof. Colls. Liberal Arts, Edn. and Theology, exec. dir. Danielsen Inst., 1982-89, prof. emeritus, cons., 1989—; prof., acad. dean Franklin Pierce Coll., Rindge, N.H., 1972-75; cons., pvt. practice, 1975-82; bd. govs. Danielsen Inst., 1967-82; min. couns. 1st Congl. United Ch. Christ, Bradenton, Fla., 1999—. Dir. counseling ctr. Boston U., 1967—72, acting assoc. dean student affairs, 1970—72; writer pastoral counselor's licensure exam. State of Maine, 1991; guest lectr., vis. prof. Caribbean Grad. Sch. Theology, 2001. Author: Suffering: A Caregiver's Guide, 1990; (with others) Fathering: Fact or Fable, 1977, Maturity and the Quest for Spiritual Meaning, 1988, Psychological Perspectives and the Religious Quest, 1999; contbr. articles to profl. jours. John L. Maes grad. scholar established in honor Boston U., 2001. Mem. APA, Am. Assn. Pastoral Counselors (diplomate, bd. govs. 1966-71, chmn. ctrs. and tng. com. 1967-71, mem. pastoral counselors exam. bd. 1994-98), Am. Mental Health Counselors Assn. Democrat. Home: 391 Main Rd Islesboro ME 04848-4503 also: 4419 56th St W Bradenton FL 34210-2715 *In the long run it doesn't matter what the causes of suffering are; the unavoidable personal task is to put life back together, making meaning of the environment in which it is lived, and to go on from there.*

MAES, PETRA JIMENEZ, state supreme court justice; widowed; 4 children. BA, U. N.Mex., 1970, JD, 1973. Bar: N.Mex. 1973. Pvt. pratice law, Albuquerque, 1973-75; rep., then office mgr. No. N.Mex. Legal Svcs., 1975-81; dist. judge 1st Jud. Dist. Ct., Santa Fe, Los Alamos, 1981-98; chief judge, 1984-87, 92-95; justice Supreme Ct. N.Mex., 1998—. Active S.W. coun. Boy Scouts Am., mem. dist. coms.; presenter pre cana St. John's Cath. Ch.; bd. dirs. Nat. Ctr. on Women and Family Law; chairperson Tri-County Gang Task Force; mem. Gov.'s Task Force on Children and Families, 1991-92; mem. adv. com. Santa Fe County Jail, 1996. Mem. N.Mex. Bar Assn. (elderly law com. 1980-81, alternative dispute resolution com. 1987-92, code of jud. conduct com. 1992—, juvenile cmty. corrections svcs. com. chairperson), Hispanic Women's Coun. (charter). Office: Supreme Court NMex PO Box 848 Santa Fe NM 87504-0848*

MAESTRONE, FRANK EUSEBIO, diplomat; b. Springfield, Mass., Dec. 20, 1922; s. John Battista and Margaret Carlotta (Villanova) M.; m. Jo Colwell, Jan. 20, 1951; chilren: Mark, Anne. BA, Yale U., 1943; grad., Naval War Coll., 1963. With Fgn. Svc., Dept. State, 1948-84; assigned to Vienna and Salzburg, Austria, 1948, 54, Hamburg, Germany, 1949, Khorramshahr, Iran, 1960; with NATO, Paris, 1963, Brussels, 1968-71; counselor of embassy for polit. affairs Am. Embassy, Manila, 1971-73; Dept. State adviser to pres. Naval War Coll., 1973; min.-counselor Am. Embassy, Cairo, 1974, amb. to Kuwait, 1976-79; diplomat-in-residence U. Calif., San Diego, 1979; spl. rep. of Pres., dir. U.S. Sinai Support Mission, 1980; exec. dir. World Affairs Coun., San Diego, 1984-86; adj. prof. internat. rels., amb.-in-residence U.S. Internat. U., 1986-90. Mem. adv. bd. Hansen Inst. for World Peace, San Diego State U. Found. With AUS, 1943-46. Decorated chevalier du Merite Agricole (France). Mem. Internat. Inst. Strategic Studies. E-mail: fmaestrone@juno.com.

MAEV, ROMAN GRIGORIEVICH, physicist, educator; b. Moscow, May 23, 1945; arrived in Can., 1993; s. Grigorii Romanovich and Miriam Benetelievna (Kompaneetz) M.; m. Elena Yuryevna Topchieva, Sept. 23, 1994. BSc, MSc, Moscow Phys. Engring. Inst., 1969; PhD, USSR Acad. Scis., Moscow, 1973. Asst. prof., assoc. prof. applied Physics and Biophysics Moscow Phys. Tech. U., 1983-94; head lab. biophys. introscopy Inst. Chem. Physics, USSR Acad. Scis., Russia, 1984-87; dir. Acoustic Microscopy Ctr. Russian Acad. Scis., 1987-97, dir. Internat. Advanced Material Study Ctr., 1997—; prof. physics, dir. Ultrasonic Rsch. Lab. U. Windsor, Ont., Can., 1996—; dir. Daimler Chrysler-U. Windsor Ctr. Imaging Rsch. and Advanced Materials Characterization, Can., 1997—. Guest rschr. Nat. Inst. Stds. and Tech., Washington, 1993; vis. prof. U. Munich, 1990, Oxford U., 1988; sci. cons. Daimler-Benz AG, Siemens AG, German-Russian Non-Profit Mktg. Venture Project, 1991-94, Can.-Russia Intergovtl. Advanced Tech. Working Group, 1995—. Co-author: Sound and Light: Interaction in the Media, 1981 (award 1984); co-editor, author: Microscope Photometry and Acoustic Microscopy in Science, 1985 (award Leitz Corp. Germany 1986); co-inventor method of investigation of internal structure of objects in transmission acoustic, 1986 (gold medal Russian Nat. Exhbn. 1987). Fellow gen. counsel All Soviet Union Orgn. Young Scientists and Specialists, 1975-84; mem. UNESCO Commn. Men and the Biosphere, 1980-96; chief commn. Young Scientists in Nat. Russian Chem. Soc., 1988—; mem. program com. All Soviet Union Regular Sch. Actual Problems of Physics, 1974-84. Recipient Pioneer award World Fedn. Ultrasound in Medicine and Biology, 1988, Internat. Sci. Found. award Am. Inst. Ultrasound in Medicine, 1988, Centenary Ernst Abbe medal World Microscopical Soc., 1987. Fellow Can. Phys. Soc., Russian Acad. Scis. (sci. acoustic coun. 1982—); mem. IEEE (sr.). Avocations: skiing, music, art. Office: U Windsor Dept Physics 401 Sunset Ave Windsor ON Canada E-mail: maev@uwindsor.ca.

MAFFEI, STEPHEN ROGER, medical products executive, treasurer; b. N.Y.C, July 24, 1939; s. Roger S. and Catherine E. (Premo) M.; m. Barbara A. Tomek, Apr. 15, 1961; children: Stephen, Matthew, Joseph. BS, U. Bridgeport, 1960; MBA, Pace U., 1976. Analyst Dun & Bradstreet, N.Y.C., 1961-63; sr. analyst Burlington Industries, 1963-66; asst. treas. U.S. Mineral, Stanhope, N.J., 1966-71; sec.-treas. Mueller Group, Alpha, 1971-73; chief fin. officer, v.p., sec.-treas. Landis & Gyr Inc., Elmsford, N.Y., 1973-84; chief fin. officer, v.p. fin., treas. Meadox Meds. Inc., Oakland, N.J., 1984-92. Bd. dirs. Ramco Inc., Dumont, N.J., Watershed Inc., Englishtown, N.J. Home: 2 Trenton Ave Lavallette NJ 08735-2717 Office: Maffei Inc PO Box 487 Marlboro NJ 07746-0487

MAFFEO, ALPHONSE A. anesthesiologist; b. 1947; MD, SUNY Syracuse, 1972. Diplomate Am. Bd. Anesthesiology. Intern Harrisburg Hosp., 1972-73; res. anesthesiology Mass Gen. Hosp., Boston, 1973-75; physician Lehigh Valley Hosp., Allentown, Pa., 1977—, chmn. anesthesiology, 1990-2001. Clin. assoc. prof., assoc. chmn. anesthesiology Pa. St. U. Hershey Med. Ctr., 1994—2001. Fellow ABA, Am. Coll. Anesthesiologists, mem. Am. Soc. Anesthesiologists. Office: Allentown Anesthes Assn Inc 1245 S Cedar Crest Blvd Ste 301 Allentown PA 18103-6258

MAFFEO, VINCENT ANTHONY, lawyer, executive; b. Jan. 22, 1951; s. Michael Anthony and Marie Maffeo; m. Debra Maffeo, Dec. 16, 1972. BA summa cum laude, Bklyn. Coll., 1971; JD, Harvard U., 1974. Bar: NY 1975, Calif. 1982, Va. 1988, DC 1988, Mich. 1994. Assoc. Simpson Thacher & Bartlett, N.Y.C., NY, 1974—77; legal counsel Comms. Sys. divsn. ITT, Hartford, Conn., 1977—79; v.p., gen. counsel Bus. Comms. divsn. ITT, Des Plaines, Ill., 1979—80; asst. counsel western region ITT, 1980—83; group counsel ITT Europe, Inc., 1983—86; v.p. gen. coun. ITT Defense Inc., 1987—91; v.p., gen. coun. ITT Automotive, Inc., 1992—95; sr. v.p., gen. counsel ITT Industries, Inc., 1995—. Lt. Judge Adv. Gen. Corps. USNR, 1975. Mem.: ABA, N.Y.State Bar Assn., Calif. State Bar, Phi Beta Kappa. Office: ITT Industries Inc 4 W Red Oak Ln Ste 2 White Plains NY 10604-3617

MAFFITT, JAMES STRAWBRIDGE, lawyer; b. Raleigh, N.C., Oct. 29, 1942; s. James Strawbridge III and Lois (Handy) M.; children: Amy Maffitt Barkley, Margaret Maffitt Kramer; m. Frances Holton, Aug. 15, 1981. BA, Washington and Lee U., 1964, LLB, 1966. Bar: Va. 1966, Md. 1969. Assoc. Apostolou, Place & Thomas, Roanoke, Va., 1966-67; trust officer Mercantile-Safe Deposit & Trust Co., Balt., 1967-71; from assoc. to ptnr. Cable, McDaniel, Bowie & Bond, 1971-82; ptnr. Maffit & Rothschild, 1982-85, Anderson, Coe & King, Balt., 1986-90, Miles & Stockbridge , Easton, Balt., 1990—. Chmn. Acad. Art Mus., 1994—97, bd. dirs., 1993—99; trustee Grayce B. Kerr Fund, Inc., 1998—; bd. dirs. Chesapeake Coll., 2002—, Leadership Md., 2002—, United Fund of Talbot County, 1994—98, pres., 1997—98. Fellow Md. Bar Found.; mem. ABA (ho. dels. 1986-88), Md. Bar Assn. (bd. govs. 1989-91), Va. Bar. Assn., Balt. City Bar Assn. (pres. 1985-86), Wednesday Law Club, Talbot Country Club, Harbourtowne Country Club. Republican. Episcopal. Avocations: waterfowl hunting, golf. Home: 9498 Martingham Cir Saint Michaels MD 21663-2238 Office: Miles & Stockbridge 101 Bay St Easton MD 21601-2748 also: Miles & Stockbridge 10 Light St Baltimore MD 21202-1407 E-mail: jmaffitt@milesstockbridge.com.

MAFFLY, ROY HERRICK, medical educator, retired; b. Berkeley, Calif., Nov. 26, 1927; s. Alfred Emil and Frances Elizabeth (Henderson) M.; m. Marilyn Miles, Feb. 2, 1952; children: Robert, Nancy, Laurie. AB, U. Calif.-Berkeley, 1949; MD, U. Calif.-San Francisco, 1952. Intern U. Calif.-San Francisco, 1952-53, resident in medicine, 1953-54, research fellow in medicine, 1959-61; resident in medicine Herrick Meml. Hosp., Berkeley, 1954-55; research fellow in medicine Mass. Gen. Hosp., Boston, 1957-59; asst. prof. medicine Stanford U., Palo Alto, Calif., 1961-65, assoc. prof., 1965-70, prof., 1970-92, assoc. dean students Sch. Medicine, 1983-92, chmn. dept. physiology, 1986-88; ret., 1992. Chief renal service VA Med. Ctr., Palo Alto, Calif., 1968-83; mem. adv. com. on renal dialysis ctrs. State of Calif., 1966-70; mem. gen. med. B study sect. NIH, 1967-71; dir. Health Edn. Network, 1980-83; mem. medicine test com. Nat. Bd. Med. Examiners, 1981-88, chmn. medicine test com., 1983-88, mem. com. for comprehensive part II exam., 1987-89; established investigator Am. Heart Assn., 1961-66, mem. rsch. study com., 1972-82, rsch. com., 1976-82. Served to lt. USNR, 1955-57, PTO. Recipient Kaiser award for teaching Stanford U. Sch. Medicine, 1970, 72, 77, 79, 86, 87; recipient Bloomfield award for teaching Stanford U. Sch. Medicine, 1977, Gores award for teaching Stanford U., 1982; Disting. Achievement award Am. Heart Assn. Sci. Council, 1984; Gift of Life award Nat. Kidney Found. No. Calif., 1985. Mem. Am. Heart Assn., Am. Physiol. Soc., Am. Soc. Clin. Investigation (editorial com. 1970-75), Nat. Kidney Found. (sci. adv. bd. 1970-77). Home: 1401 Webster St Palo Alto CA 94301-3649 E-mail: rmaffly@stanford.edu.

MAFI, MOHAMMAD, civil engineer, educator; BS, Sharif U. Tech., Tehran, Iran, 1977; MS, Pa. State U., 1980, PhD, 1985. Registered profl. engr. N.Y., Pa. Asst. prof. dept. civil engring. Union Coll., Schenectady, N.Y., 1985-90, assoc. prof., chmn. dept., 1990-94. Pres. SAFE Cons. Bridge Inspection, Design and Rehab., Schenectady, 1985—. Contbr. articles to sci. and engring. publs. Mem. ASCE, Am. Soc. Engring. Edn. (Dow Outstanding Young Faculty award 1989), Am. Concrete Inst., Concrete Reinforcing Steel Inst., Chi Epsilon, Tau Beta Pi. Office: Union Coll Dept Civil Engring Schenectady NY 12308

MAGADAN, DAVID JOSEPH, professional baseball player; b. Tampa, Fla., Sept. 30, 1962; m. Monique Magadan; children: Jordan, Christian. Student, U. Ala. 1st baseman-3d baseman N.Y. Mets, N.Y.C., 1986-92, Fla. Marlins, Miami, 1993; 1st-baseman-3d-baseman-designated hitter Seattle Mariners, 1993; 1st baseman-3d baseman Fla. Marlins, 1994, Houston Astros, 1995; 1st baseman-3d baseman-designated hitter Oakland (Calif.) Athletics, 1997-99, San Diego Padres, 1999—. Drafted Boston Red Sox, 1980, declined; led U. Ala. to championship game 1983 Coll. World Series, 1983, led NCAA Divsn. 1 with .525 batting average, 1983. Chmn. No Small Affair-South. Recipient Payson award for humanitarian svc., N.Y. chpt. Baseball Writers' Assn. Am.; recipient USA Baseball Golden Spikes award, 1983, named Coll. Player of Yr., Baseball Am., 1983, named All-Southeast Conf. Office: c/o San Diego Padres PO Box 2000 San Diego CA 92112-2000

MAGAFAS-KUFTA, DIANIA LEE, geriatric nurse consultant, administrator; b. Chgo., Oct. 17, 1963; d. Alec and Jacqueline Magafas; m. David Kufta, May. 27, 2001; 1 child, Jason. BS, St. Xavier Coll., Chgo., 1986, MSN, 1991. Staff nurse Ingalls Meml. Hosp., Harvey, Ill., 1986—88; asst. DON Wedgewood Nursing Pavilion, Chgo., 1988—90; nursing cons. long term care Dynamic Healthcare Cons., Inc., Skokie, 1990—. Mem. Sigma Theta Tau. E-mail: dmagafas@aol.com.

MAGARGEE, W(ILLIAM) SCOTT, III, lawyer; b. Abington, Pa., Sept. 3, 1940; m. Annette Bruno, July 6, 1963; children: Scott, Todd, Ashley. AB, Princeton U., 1962; LLB, Yale U., 1966. Bar: Pa. 1966, U.S. Dist. Ct. (ea. dist.) Pa. 1966, U.S. Tax Ct. 1973. Assoc. Dechert Price & Rhoads, Phila., 1966-75, ptnr., 1975—. Mem. citizens adv. com. Southeastern Pa. Transp. Authority, 1988—; bd. dirs. United Way Southeastern Pa., 1994—, C.C. Phila. Found., pres., 2000—. Fellow Am. Coll. Employee Benefits Counsel; mem. ABA (sect. taxation, real estate, probate, trust law, bus. law), Phila. Bar Assn., Princeton Club Phila., Princeton Univ. Alumni Coun. (chmn. 1985-87). Office: Dechert Price & Rhoads 4000 Bell Atlantic Tower 1717 Arch St Philadelphia PA 19103-2793

MAGARIAN, ROBERT ARMEN, medicinal chemist, researcher, educator , author, inventor; b. East St. Louis, Ill., July 27, 1930; s. Leon and Pauline Mary (Struel) M.; m. Charmaine Virginia Kugler, June 24, 1950; children: Paula, Cindy, Leslie, Robert. Student, Washington U., St. Louis, 1951-52, Bellville Jr. Coll., 1948—50; BA, U. Miss., 1956, BS in Pharmacy with highest honors, 1960, PhD, 1966. Registered pharmacist, Miss., Ill. Am. Found. for Pharm. Edn. fellow, 1961-66; NIH postdoctoral research fellow U. Kans., Lawrence, 1966-67; asst. prof. St. Louis Coll. Pharmacy, 1966-70; assoc. prof. U. Okla. Coll. Pharmacy, Norman, 1970-76; prof. U. Okla., Oklahoma City, 1978-96, prof. emeritus, 1996—. Exec. dir. Kappa Psi, pharm. frat., 1980-2000. Assoc. editor Current Medicinal Chemistry, 1995-97; patentee in field. Served with U.S. Army, 1952-54, Korea. Recipient teaching awards Coll. Pharmacy, U. Okla., 1974, 78, 86, 89, Excellence in Rsch. and Svc. award, 1985, Baldwin study-travel award, 1978, Assocs. Disting. Lectureship award, 1988; named Outstanding Prof. Okla. Soc. Hosp. Pharmacists, 1987, Alumni Teaching Excellence award, 1989, Outstanding Teaching award Gamma Omicron, 1990, 91, 92; Mead-Johnson grantee Am. Assn. Colls. Pharmacy, 1968, NSF grantee, 1968-70, Nat. Cancer Inst. grantee, 1987-93. Mem. Am. Assn. Colls. Pharmacy, Am. chem. soc., Sigma Xi, Phi Kappa Phi, Kappa Psi (Tchr. Excellence award 1990, 92), Rho Chi (chpt. Rsch. award 1981). Episcopalian. Office: 311 N Mercedes Dr Norman OK 73069-6447

MAGARO, PETER ANTHONY, psychology educator; b. Harrisburg, Pa., Jan. 24, 1935; s. Peter A. and Mildred (Alexis) M.; m. Geneva L. Watts, Aug. 22, 1964; children— Lisa, Jennie, Elizabeth, Peter BS, Pa. State U., 1959; PhD, U. Ill., 1965. Mem. faculty No. Ill. U., DeKalb, 1965-68; mem. faculty U. Main, Orono, 1968-80, prof., until 1980; prof. psychology Ohio State U., Columbus, 1980—. Cons. State of Maine, U.S. Govt. Author: Construction of Madness, 1976, The Mental Health Industry, 1978, Cognition in Schizophrenia and Paranoia, 1980 Fulbright fellow, Florence, Italy, 1976; Inst. for Indian Studies scholar, India, 1982 Fellow Am. Psychol. Assn. Office: Ohio State U Dept Psychology Columbus OH 43210

MAGASANIK, BORIS, microbiology educator; b. Kharkoff, U.S.S.R., Dec. 19, 1919; came to U.S., 1938; s. Naum and Charlotte (Schreiber) M. BS, CCNY, 1941; PhD, Columbia U., 1948; MS (hon.), Harvard U., 1958. Tech. asst. Mt. Sinai Hosp., N.Y.C., 1939-41; rsch. asst. Columbia U., 1948-49; Ernst fellow Harvard U. Med. Sch., Boston, 1949-51, assoc. to assoc. prof., 1951-59; prof. microbiology MIT, Cambridge, 1960-77, Jacques Monod prof., 1977—, head dept. biology, 1967-77. Tutor in biochem. scis. Harvard U., 1951—. Contbr. over 250 sci. articles and revs. to profl. publs. With M.C., U.S. Army, 1942-45, ETO. Guggenheim fellow, 1959; Markle scholar in med. scis., 1951-56; recipient SelmanA. Waksman Award in Microbiology Nat. Acad. of Sciences, 1994, Lifetime Achievement award Abbott-ASM, 2000. Mem. NAS, Am. Acad. Arts and Scis., Am. Soc. Microbiology, Am. Soc. Biol. Chemists. Home: 54 Garfield St Cambridge MA 02138-1802 Office: MIT Dept Biology Rm 68625 77 Massachusetts Ave Cambridge MA 02139-4301 E-mail: bmag@mit.edu.

MAGAW, JOHN W. federal agency administrator; b. Columbus, Ohio; m. Helen Mahley; 5 children. BA in Edn., Otterbein Coll., 1957. Patrolman State of Ohio, Columbus, 1958-66; joined U.S. Secret Svc., 1967, spl. agt., 1967, former head protection for U.S. President and First Lady Washington, until 1992, 17th dir., 1992-93; dir. Bur. Alcohol, Tobacco & Firearms, 1993—99; spl. advisor to Dir. FEMA, 1999—2001; under secy. security U.S. Dept. Transp., 2002. Bd. trustees Otterbein Coll., Westerville, Ohio. Recipient Presdl. Rank Meritorious award, 1991. Mem. Fed. Investigators Assn., Internat. Assn. Chiefs of Police (exec. com. adv. com. for internat. policy). Office: US Dept Transp Transp Security Admin 400 7th St SW Washington DC 20590*

MAGAZINE, ALAN HARRISON, association executive, consultant; b. Cambridge, Mass., May 16, 1944; s. Arnold Lloyd and Ruth Magazine; m. June Ann O'Donohue, June 20, 1971 (div. Feb. 1984); children: Sarah Elizabeth, David Michael; m. Cynthia Louise Cordiner, Aug. 30, 1984. BA, Monmouth Coll., 1966; MPA, Kent State U., 1968; PhD, U. Md., 1976. Sr. cons. Real Estate Rsch. Corp., Washington, 1969-72; exec. dir. Nat. Ctr. for Pub. Svc. Internships, 1972-75; nat. policy coord. Internat. City Mgmt. Assn., 1973-76; dep. asst. dir. U.S. Commn. on Fed. Paperwork, 1976-78; dir. office of intergovernmental rels. EPA, 1978-81; dir. Bus.-Higher Edn. Forum, 1981-86; pres. coun. on competitiveness adv. com. Congl. Tech. Policy Task Force, 1986-89; adv. bd. George Mason U. Ctr. Conflict Resolution, 1986-89; pres. Health Industry Mfgs. Assn., 1990-99; cons. in field, 1999—2001; sr. advisor Coun. on Competitiveness, 2000—. Bd. dirs. Dickinson Coll., Clark Ctr. Pub. Policy, Congrl. Econ. Leadership Inst., Healthcare Tech. Inst. Bd. Advisors, Sunrise Techs. Internat., Inc., Eyetel Corp., PLC Med. Inc., Innotech, USA; adv. bd. George Mason U. Ctr. Conflict Resolution, 1986-89, Brookings Inst. Ctr. Econ. Progress and Employment, 1986-89; mem. U.S. China Joint Commn. on Commerce and Trade, 1996-97 Author: Environmental Management in Local Government, 1977. Bd. dirs. Met. Washington Coun. of Govts., 1972-79; mem. Fairfax County Bd. Suprs., Va., 1972-79; chmn. No. Va. Transp. Commn., 1974-75; mem. No. Va. Planning Dist. Commn., Fairfax, 1976-79; mem. Dickinson Coll. Parents Coun., 1994-98, bd. dirs. Clark Ctr. for the Study of Contemporary Issues. With USAFR, 1968-71. Ford Found. fellow, 1970-71. Democrat. Jewish. Avocations: jogging, reading. Home: 322 S Fayette St Alexandria VA 22314-5903 E-mail: penrosemagazine@comcast.net.

MAGAZINE, MICHAEL, management science educator; b. N.Y.C. s. Abraham and Ethel Magazine; children: Roger Eric, Jill Lara. BS, CCNY, 1964; MS, NYU, 1966; PhD, U. Fla., 1969. Profl. Engr., Ont. Can. Asst. prof. N.C. State U., Raleigh, 1969-75; orgn. of am. states prof. Pontifica Universidad Catolica, Rio de Janeiro, 1972; assoc. prof., prof., dept. head U. Waterloo, Ont., 1975-95; prof., Ohio eminent scholar, assoc. dean faculty and rsch. U. Cin., 1995—. Vis. scientist INRIA, Roquencourt, France, 1982; vis. prof. MIT, Cambridge, 1992. Editor: (book) Quantitative Models for Supply Chain Management, 1999; mem. editl. bd. Mgmt. Sci., 1986-96; contbr. articles to profl. jours. Vol. Am. Tennis Prof., Cin., 1997, 98, 99. Mem. Inst. Ops. Rsch. and mgmt. Sci. (v.p. 1997-99), Mfg. and Svc. Ops. Mgmt. (pres. 1996, editl. bd., sr. editor 1998—, Svc . award 1998), Internat. Jour. Prodn. Rsch. (editl. bd. 1999). Avocation: tennis. Office: U Cin Dept QAOM PO Box 210130 Cincinnati OH 45221-0130 E-mail: mike.magazine@uc.edu.

MAGAZINER, ELLIOT ALBERT, musician, conductor, educator; b. Springfield, Mass., Dec. 25, 1921; m. Sari Fromkin; 2 children. Student, Nat. Orch. Assn., 1937-40, Princeton U., 1943, Juilliard School of Music, 1946-50. Music dir., prof. music Manhattanville Coll., Purchase, N.Y., 1970—. Faculty Westchester Conservatory Music, Summit Music Festival, 2001. Debut: Town Hall, N.Y.C., 1952; staff artist, concertmaster CBS-TV and Radio; Networks: condrs. Reiner, Ansermet, Beecham, Stokowski; condr. and sr. violin instr. Westchester Conservatory of Music; vis. condr. Dubuque Symphony; soloist N.Y. Philharm. Symphony, Symphony of the Air, Kol Visrael, symphonies in Chgo., Ft. Myers, Dubuque, York, St. Petersburg, Lincoln Ctr., N.Y.C., 2002; recitals in N.Y.C., Washington, Detroit, Amsterdam, Paris, Jerusalem; star of CBS-TV, The Violin. Recs.: Charles Ives Sonata #2, Charles Ives Trio (with Frank Glazer and David Weber); Vivaldi Concerto in C and Concerto in B (with orchestre Symphonique de Paris); conductor Westchester All County Festival Orch. Mem. AAUP, N.Y. TV Musicians (pres.), CBS Musicians Fund (sec.) Avocations: collecting unique and ancient instruments. Home: 250 Garth Rd Apt 2b3 Scarsdale NY 10583-3954 Office: Manhattanville Coll 2900 Purchase St Purchase NY 10577-2131

MAGAZINER, FRED THOMAS, lawyer; b. Phila., July 4, 1947; s. Henry Jonas and Reba (Henken) M.; m. Phyllis Heller, June 28, 1970; children: Daniel, Andrew. BA, Columbia U., 1969, JD, 1976. Bar: Pa., U.S. Dist. Ct. (ea. dist.) Pa., U.S. Ct. Appeals (3rd cir.), U.S. Claims Ct. Law clk. to judge Max Rosenn U.S. Ct. Appeals (3rd cir.), Phila., 1976-77; assoc. Dechert, Price & Rhoads, 1977-84, ptnr., 1984—. Mem. ABA, Pa. Bar Assn., Phila. Bar Assn., Am. Law Inst. Democrat. Jewish. Home: 1021 W Cliveden St Philadelphia PA 19119-3702 Office: Dechert Price & Rhoads 4000 Bell Atlantic Tower 1717 Arch St Lbby 3 Philadelphia PA 19103-2713 E-mail: fred.magaziner@dechert.com.

MAGAZINER, HENRY JONAS, architect, writer; b. Phila., Sept. 13, 1911; s. Louis and Selma (Jonas) M.; m. Reba Henken, June 19, 1938; children: Ellen Louise (Mrs. Alan I. Widiss), Fred Thomas. BArch, U. Pa., 1936. Cert. Nat. Coun. Arch. and Registration Bds. Draftsman Phila. City Planning Project, 1936-37; draftsman Louis Magaziner (Architect), Phila., 1937-39, architect, 1946-48; chief Architects' Squad, Day & Zimmermann, Inc., Burlington, Iowa, 1940-41; architect Albert Kahn (Architect), Detroit, 1942; designer Wright Aero. Corp., Wood Ridge, N.J., 1943-45; ptnr. Louis & Henry Magaziner, Phila., 1948-56; architect, planner pvt. practice, 1956-72; regional hist. architect, archtl. historian Mid-Atlantic region Nat. Pk. Svc., Phila., 1972-87; pvt. practice architecture, 1987—. Archtl. adviser Phila. Hist. Commn., 1970-75, mem. archtl. com., 1979-85, chmn. archtl. com., 1972-75. Author: The Golden Age of Ironwork, 2000. Mem. Carpenters' Co. of City and County of Phila., mem. mng. com. historic Carpenters' Hall, 2000—; v.p. Phila. Health and Welfare Coun., 1957-61, Phila. chpt. Victorian Soc. Am., 1975; v.p. city planning Germantown Comty. Coun., 1957-62; bd. dirs. Downtown Children's (day care) Ctr., 1956-73, v.p., 1960-61; bd. dirs. Allens Ln. Art Ctr., 1945-67, Neighborhood Ctr. Phila., 1956-74, Hist. Soc. Pa., 1970-74, Chestnut Hill Hist. Soc., 1970-80, Phila. chpt. Assn. for Preservation Tech., 1991-98, Clean Air Coun., 1980-92, Center City Residents Assn., 1995-96, Rittenhouse Plz., Inc., 1995-96; bd. dirs. Maxwell Mansion Mus., pres., 1964-67; trustee Stewardsom Meml. Fellowship in Arch., 1958-90. Recipient Presdl. award for Excellence in Design for the Govt., 1988, James Biddle award Preservation Alliance for Greater Phila., 1999; named to Germantown Hall of Fame, 1994. Fellow AIA (mem. com. on hist. resources, John Harbeson award 2000); mem. ASTM (mem. com. on hist. preservation stds. 1981-90), Am. Inst. Conservation, Assn. for Preservation Tech., Ea. Nat. Pk. and Monument Assn., Fellows in Am. Studies (pres. 1983-84), Nat. Trust for Hist. Preservation, Soc. Archtl. Historians (bd. dirs. 1977-80, mem. editl. bd. 58 vol. Buildings of the United States 1992-98), Bldg. Conservation Internat., Victorian Soc. Am., T-Square Atelier (pres. 1963-65), Pa. Soc. Architects, Pa. Acad. Fine Arts, Libr. Co. Phila., Sierra Club, Athenaeum of Phila., Preservation Action. Home: 2 Franklin Town Blvd Apt 2404 Philadelphia PA 19103-1237 Fax: 215-545-8397. *I do hope that we can pass on to future generations a prejudice-free America having a natural environment without pollution and a man-made environment with its best elements both preserved and appreciated. Achieving these objectives is an unending struggle but one certainly worth winning. God willing, I expect to continue to fight for these ends.*

MAGDOL, MICHAEL ORIN, bank executive; b. N.Y.C., May 18, 1937; s. David Aaron and Ruth (Wein) M.; m. Alice Jane Gates, Aug. 29, 1940 (div. Sept. 1974); 1 child, David; m. Patricia Elizabeth Marshall, Feb. 1, 1943; 1 child, Jennifer. BSE, U. Pa., 1959. Internat. officer Mfrs. Hanover Trust Co., N.Y.C., 1959-65; exec. v.p. J. Henry Schroder Bank, 1965-87; vice chmn., chief fin. officer, dir. Fiduciary Trust Co. Internat., 1987—. Bd. dirs. Arch Chems. Inc. Bd. dirs. Boy Scouts Am., N.Y.C., 1975—, Children Oncology Soc. N.Y., Lingnan Found. Mem. Am. Bankers Assn. (internat. bd. dirs. 1980-83), N.Y. State Bankers Assn. (chmn. internat. com. 1982-95), Univ. Econs. Club, Onteora Club (Tannersville, N.Y.). Office: Fiduciary Trust Co Internat 600 5th Ave New York NY 10020 E-mail: mmagdol@ftci.com.

MAGDOVITZ, ETHAN H. information architect; b. Chgo., Apr. 14, 1970; s. Bernard A. and Abby (Schaffer) M. BS in Computer Sci., Rensselaer Poly. Inst., 1992; postgrad., London Bus. Sch. Software engr. Amdahl Corp., Sunnyvale, Calif., 1991; experienced sr. cons. Andersen Cons. (Emerging Tech. Solutions Group), Chgo., 1992-95; sr. mgr. Technology Enablers, Inc., Dallas, 1995-2000. Author: Computer Language/PIE, 1992. Mem. Assn. for Info. and Image Mgmt. Avocations: singer/songwriter, fitness, reading. Home: 901 Harbor Dr Belleair Beach FL 33786-3261

MAGDOVITZ, LAWRENCE MAYNARD, real estate executive, lawyer; b. Clarksdale, Miss., Aug. 21, 1937; s. Harry David and Lenabel (May) M.; m. Kerin Coffey, June 25, 1972 (dec. Apr. 1994); children: Beth, Larry. BA, Vanderbilt U., 1959, JD, 1961. Bar: Tenn. 1961, Miss. 1961, Ky. 1962. Trust officer First Nat. Bank, Mayfield, Ky., 1961-62; sole practice law Clarksdale, 1962—; br. office Collierville, Tenn., 1984-95; realtor Valley Realty Co., Clarksdale, 1962—, Magdovitz Agy., Inc., Clarksdale, 1972—, First, Inc., Clarksdale, 1973—; ins. exec. Mid-Am. Ins. Agy., 1985—. Mem. Miss. State Bar Assn., Ky. State Bar Assn., Tenn. State Bar Assn., Memphis Bar Assn., Clarksdale Bd. Realtors. Lodges: B'nai Brith (pres. Clarksdale br. 1979-82), Elks. Republican. Jewish. Office: 112 E 2nd St Clarksdale MS 38614-4206 Fax: 662-624-4821.

MAGEE, A. ALAN, artist; b. Newtown, Pa., May 26, 1947; s. Richard Forrest and Rena (Cook) M.; m. Monika Gabriele Ruth Siekmann, Jan. 4, 1969. Student, Tyler Sch. of Art, 1965-66, Phila. Coll. Art, 1967-69. Contbr. articles to profl. jours.; one-person shows include Allport Assocs. Gallery, Larkspur, Calif., 1978, 81, Clark Gallery, Lincoln, Mass., 1979, Staempfli Gallery, N.Y.C., 1980, 82, Staempfli one-person show, 1990, FIAC Grand Palais, Paris, 1983, Norton Gallery and Sch. of Art, West Palm Beach, Fla., 1983, San Jose Mus. of Art, 1983, Newport Art Mus., 1984, Farnsworth Art Mus., Rockland, Maine, 1984, Arkansas Art Ctr., Columbus Mus. of Art, Ohio Chicago Art Inst.,U. Maine, 1985, Fresno Art Ctr., 1985, Los Angeles, 1986, Schmidt-Bingham Gallery, N.Y.C., 1986, 88, 89, Allport Assocs. Gallery, San Francisco, 1986, Joan Whitney Payson Gallery at Westbrook Coll., Portland, Maine, 1990, Farnsworth Art Mus., 1991, James A. Michener Art Mus., Doylestown, Pa., 1991, Ringling Sch. Art & Design, Sarasota, Fla., 1992, Fine Arts Ctr. at Cheekwood, Nashville, 1992, Edith Caldwell Gallery, San Francisco, 1992, 93, 95, 96, 97, Edith Lambert Gallery, Santa Fe, 1995, Hollis Taggart Gallery, N.Y.C., 2000, San Francisco, 2000, Berlin Philharmonic Hall, 2000, Forum Gallery, Los Angeles, 2001, 02; group shows include Farnsworth Art Mus., Rockland, Maine, 1985, Akron (Ohio) Mus. of Art, 1985, Maine Coast Artists, Rockport, 1985, Ark. Art Ctr, Little Rock, 1985, Smithsonian Instn., Nat. Air and Space Mus., Washington, 1985, Wunderlich & Co., N.Y.C., 1986, Light Gallery, N.Y.C., 1986, Schmidt-Bingham Gallery, N.Y.C., 1986, 88, Mus. Fine Arts, Springfield, 1986, Butler Inst. Am. Art, Youngstown, Ohio, 1987, Am. Acad. and Inst. of Arts and Letters, N.Y.C., 1987, Nat. Invitational Drawing Exhbn., 1989, Staempfli Gallery, N.Y.C., 1990, Albrecht Art Mus., St. Joseph, 1990, Nat. Acad. of Design, N.Y.C., 1990, Edith

Caldwell Gallery, San Francisco, 1993, 94, 95, 96, Nora Eccles Harrison Mus. of Art, Logan Utah, 1992, Portland Mus. of Art, 1993, Creiger Dane Gallery, Boston, Mass., 1995, Phila. Art Mus., 1995, Forum Gallery, N.Y.C, 1996, Nat. Mus. Am. Art, Washington, 1997, Hollis Taggart Gallery, N.Y., 1998, Hackett, Feedman Gallery, San Francisco, 1998, Portland Mus. Art, 1998, Farnsworth Art Mus., 1998, Art Inst. Chgo., 1999, Katonah Mus. Art, 1999, U. Rochester, 1999, O.P. FotoGalery, Hong Kong, 1999, others; pub. collections include Farnsworth Art Mus., Rockland, Arco Collection, Lucasfilm, Bank of Japan, Mobil Oil, Janss Collection, Los Angeles, Achenbach Collection, Palace of the Legion of Honour, San Francisco, Art Inst. Chgo., Portland (Maine) Mus. of Art, Rutgers U. Art Mus., and others; commns. include mural U. Maine, 1997, Maine State House, 1999; author: Stones and Other Works, 1987, Alan Magee 1981-91, Archive, Monotypes, Alan Magee, 2000; TV: Visions of Darkness and Light, 1988. Recipient Richard and Hinda Rosenthal Found. award N.Y.C., Am. Book award, Nevelson award, 1982; The Leo Meissner Prize, Nat. Acad. of Design, 1990. Home: 476 Pleasant Point Rd Cushing ME 04563-3422

MAGEE, BERNARD DALE, obstetrician, gynecologist; b. Niagara Falls, N.Y., June 8, 1950; s. Bernard Dale and Rose (Roffle) M.; m. Melanie Ann Ciszek, Aug. 31, 1974; 1 child, Ryan. Student, SUNY, Buffalo, 1968-71; MD, SUNY, Syracuse, 1975; MS, Dartmouth Coll., 1998. Diplomate Am. Bd. Ob-Gyn, Am. Bd. Med. Examiners. Obstetrician-gynecologist Fallon Clinic, Worcester, Mass., 1979-83; pvt. practice Shrewsbury, 1983-96, U. Mass. Cmty. Physicians, 1996—2001, Mass., 2001—. Chmn. ob-gyn com. Ctrl. Mass. Health Care, Worcester, 1990-97, trustee, 1993-95. Fellow Am. Coll. Ob-Gyn.; mem. AMA, Mass. Med. Soc. (chmn. com. on quality in med practice), Worcester Dist. Med. Soc. (treas. 1988-94, pres. 1995-96), Maddox Soc. (pres. 1992-94). Avocations: medical history, antique medical books and instruments, skiing. Office: 604 Main St Shrewsbury MA 01545-5639 E-mail: bdalemagee@townisp.com.

MAGEE, CHARLES THOMAS, international consultant, retired diplomat; b. Clifton Forge, Va., Mar. 6, 1932; s. Charles Thomas and Dorothy Elizabeth (McPherson) M.; m. Maideh Mazda, May 30, 1959; 1 child, Maya. BA, Harvard U., 1953. Vice consul Am. Consulate, Windsor, Can., 1961-63; polit.-mil. affairs officer Am. Emb., Paris, 1964-66; polit. officer Soviet desk Dept. State, 1966-68; polit. officer Am. Embassy, Moscow, 1969-71; dep. dir. for ops. Exec. Secretariat Dept. State, Washington, 1971-72, officer-in-charge French desk, 1972-74; polit. officer, exec. asst. to amb. Am. Embassy, Paris, 1974-77, dep. chief mission Sofia, Bulgaria, 1977-80; chief jr. officer div. Bur. Pers. Dept. State, 1980-82, fgn. svc. insp., 1982-83; cons. gen. U.S Consulate Gen., Leningrad, USSR, 1984-86; spl. asst. to mayor City of San Francisco, 1986-87; dir. Russian lang. ops. U.S. Del. to Negotiations on Nuclear and Space Arms with USSR, Geneva, 1988-91; sr. program officer Citizens Democracy Corps, Washington, 1992-93; amb. mission to Latvia Orgn. Security and Coop. Europe, 1994-97, amb. mission to Ukraine, 1998-99. Ofcl. election observer, Ukraine, 1998, 2002, Russia, 2000; polling supr., Bosnia and Herzegovina, 2000; head Orgn. for Security and Coop. in Europe election observation mission to Former Yugoslav Republic of Macedonia, Azerbaijan, 2000, Moldova, Bulgaria, 2001; cons. Acad. Arrangements Abroad, N.Y.C., 1987—, Dept. of State, 1989—, Seabourn Cruise Line, San Francisco, 1989-92, Acad. Travel Abroad, Washington, 1995; asst. prof. Dept Navy, 1959-61. Lt. USN, 1953-59. Mem. Am. Fgn. Svc. Assn., Harvard Club. Home and Office: 4518 Albemarle St NW Washington DC 20016-2016 E-mail: ctmagee32@aol.com.

MAGEE, DONALD EDWARD, retired national park service administrator; b. Trenton, N.J., Sept. 24, 1937; s. Donald A. and Anna C. (Bocskowics) M.; m. Linda Kimball, June 27, 1964; children: Kevin, Bonnie Magee Burch, Gale. BS in Forestry Mgmt., U. Mass., 1964. Pk. ranger Bryce Canyon (Utah) Nat. Pk., 1966-68; area mgr. Sunset Crater Nat. Monument, Flagstaff, Ariz., 1968-73; mgmt. analyst Nat. Capital Region, Washington, 1973-80; supt. Stones River Nat. Battlefield, Murfreesboro, Tenn., 1980-89, USS Ariz. Meml., Pearl Harbor, Hawaii, 1989-95; ret., 1995. With USN, 1956-58. Recipient Excellence of Svc. award Dept. of Interior, 1991. Home: 95-457 Kaukoe St Mililani HI 96789-1865

MAGEE, ELIZABETH SHERRARD, civic organization volunteer; b. Rock Island, Ill., Sept. 11, 1922; d. Benjamin Harrison and Helen Lucile (Williams) Sherrard; m. Harber Homer Hall, June 15, 1944 (div. 1949); 1 child, John Sherrard Hall; m. Curtis Lyness Johnson, Dec. 18, 1951 (dec. July 1957); children: Peter Hays Johnson, Julie Jaye Johnson Kimball; m. Robert Milton Magee, Sept. 21, 1963 (dec. 1988); 1 child, Robert Decker (dec. 1983). Student, Augustana Coll., Rock Island, 1940-42. Office mgr., sec. Chgo. Motor Club, Rock Island, 1942-44; personal shopper M.L. Parker Co., Davenport, Iowa, 1945-46. Mem. Jr. Bd. Rock Island, 1944—65, ARC nursing duties, Rock Island, 1971—75, Presbyn. Women Rock Island, 1960—99; clerk of session Broadway Presbyn. Ch., 1990—93, 1995—98, 2002. Mem. DAR (state rec. sec. 1995-97, divsn. I dir. 1997-99, editor Biennial Procs. Ill. State Orgn. 1995-97, state vice regent 2000-02), Internat. Order Kings Daus. and Sons, P.E.O. Sisterhood (past pres., sec., treas.). Republican. Presbyterian. Avocations: computers, stamps, coins. Home: 17575 Warner Castle Rd Orion IL 61273-9181

MAGEE, J. MARVIN, electronics executive; BSME, U. New Brunswick; MBA, McMaster U. Exec. staff IBM, Canada, 1979—97; exec. v.p. Celestica Worldwide Ops., Toronto, Canada, 1999—2001; sr. v.p. Canadian ops. Celestica, Inc., Canada, 1997—99, pres., COO Canada, 2001—. Office: Celestica Inc 12 Concorde Pl Toronto M3C 3R8 Canada

MAGEE, JOHN FRANCIS, research company executive; b. Bangor, Maine, Dec. 3, 1926; s. John Henry and Marie (Frawley) M.; m. Dorothy Elma Hundley, Nov. 19, 1949; children: Catherine Anne, John Hundley, Andrew Stephen. AB, Bowdoin Coll., 1947; MS, U. Maine, 1952; MBA, Harvard U., 1948; LLD, Bowdoin Coll., 1996. With Arthur D. Little, Inc., Cambridge, Mass., 1950-98, v.p., 1961-72, pres., 1972-86, chief exec. officer, 1974-88, chmn., 1986-98, also dir., 1968-98. Author: Physical Distribution Systems, 1967, Industrial Logistics: Analysis and Management of Physical Supply and Distribution Systems, 1968, (with D. M. Boodman) Production Planning and Inventory Control, 1968; (with W. Capacino and W. Rosenfield) Modern Logistics Management, 1985. Trustee Emerson Hosp., Thompson Island Outward Bound Edn. Ctr., chair, 1995—2000; emeritus trustee Bowdoin Coll.; hon. trustee Woods Hole Oceanographic Instn.; mem. dean's coun. Harvard U. Grad. Sch. Edn.; chmn. Bowdoin Coll., 1990—93. Fellow Phi Beta Kappa (life); mem. Ops. Research Soc. Am. (pres. 1966-67), Inst. Mgmt. Scis. (pres. 1971-72), Phi Kappa Psi. Clubs: Concord (Mass.) Country (gov. 1971-74); The Country (Brookline, Mass.); Somerset (Boston). Comml. (pres.). Office: Arthur D Little Inc 25 Acorn Park Cambridge MA 02140-2301 E-mail: magjfmagee@netscape.net.

MAGEE, KAREN STROPE, nurse, health facility administrator; b. Washington, Mar. 9, 1944; d. Orval M. and Esther E. (Roberts) Strope; m. J. Kenneth Magee, Jan. 15, 1966; children: James Kenneth, Kelly Janean. Diploma, Washington Hosp. Sch. Nursing, 1965; BSN summa cum laude, SUNY, New Paltz, 1985; MS in Nursing, Columbia U., 1990; postmasters cert. in nursing, Villanova U., 2000. Cert. community health nurse. Staff nurse Westmoreland Hosp., Greensburg, Pa., 1966; asst. head nurse Comanche County Meml. Hosp., Lawton, Okla., 1967-68; staff nurse Washington (Pa.) Hosp., 1965-66, 68-77; cmty. health nurse Good Samaritan Hosp./Cert. Home Health Agy., Suffern, N.Y., 1985-90, supervising cmty. health nurse, 1990-97, asst. dir. patient svcs., 1997-2000; dir. patient svcs. Cert. Home Health Agy., 2000—. Mem. Washington Hosp. Sch. Nursing Alumni Assn., Columbia U. Sch. Nursing Alumni Assn., SUNY New Paltz Nursing Alumni Assn., Sigma Theta Tau. E-mail: karensmagee@hotmail.com.

MAGEE, PAUL TERRY, geneticist and molecular biologist, educator; b. Los Angeles, Oct. 26, 1937; s. John Paul and Lois Lorene (Cowgill) M.; m. Beatrice Buten, Aug. 6, 1964; children: Alexander John, Amos Hart. BS, Yale U., 1959; PhD, U. Calif., Berkeley, 1964. Am. Cancer Soc. postdoctoral fellow Lab. Enzymologie, Gif-sur-Yvette, France, 1964-66; mem. faculty Yale U., 1966-77, asst. prof. microbiology, 1966-72, assoc. prof. microbiology and human genetics, 1972-75, assoc. prof. human genetics, 1975-77; dean Trumbull Coll., 1969-72; prof. microbiology, chmn. dept. microbiology and pub. health Mich. State U., East Lansing, 1977-87, dir. Biotech. Research Ctr., 1985-87; dean Coll. Biol. Scis. U. Minn., 1987-95, prof. genetics and cell biology, 1987—. Mem. genetics adv. panel NSF, 1978-83, mem. adv. com. biology directorate, 1992-97, chair, 1995-96; chmn. BBS task force looking to 21st century, 1991; cons. Corning Glass Works, 1978-80, Pillsbury Rsch., 1990-96; mem. pers. com. Am. Cancer Soc., 1983-87; mem. microbial genetics and physiology study sect. NIH, 1984-88; co-chmn. com. grad. record exam. biochemistry cell and molecular biology Ednl. Testing Svc., 1988-98; co-chair Gordon Rsch. Conf. on Cellular and Molecular Mycology, 1996; mem. microbiology and infectious disease rsch. com. NIH, 1994-99, chair, 1996-99; chair Burroughs Wellcome Fund Award Com. in Molecular Pathogenic Mycology, 1995-2001; traveling fellow Japanese Soc. for Promotion of Sci., 1995—; divsn. F lectr. annual meeting Am. Soc. Microbiology, 1998; found. lectr. Brit. Soc. for Med. Mycology, 2002. Mem. editorial bd. Jour. Bacteriology, 1975-80, Molecular and Cell Biology, 1981-92, Fungal Genetics and Biology, 1996—. Named Mich. champion masters swimming, 1978-84, 86, Minn. champion masters swimming, 1988, 89, 91-99, nat. YMCA swimming champion, 1990, nat. Can. swimming champion, 1999. Mem. AAAS, Am. Soc. Microbiologists, Am. Acad. for Microgiology, Genetics Soc. Am. Jewish. Office: U Minn Coll Biol Scis Dept Genetics and Cell Biol Minneapolis MN 55455

MAGEE, THOMAS ESTON, JR. minister; b. DeRidder, La., Aug. 9, 1947; s. Thomas Eston and Doris Maxine (Gallion) M.; m. Linda Ruth Lewis, Nov. 9, 1967. Student, McNeese State U., 1966-69; BTh, Tex. Bible Coll., 1972. Ordained to ministry United Pentecostal Ch., 1973. Asst. pastor United Pentecostal Ch., Pasadena, Tex., 1969-72; instr. Tex. Bible Coll., Houston, 1970-72, dean of women, 1970-71; evangelist United Pentecostal Ch., various locations, U.S., 1972-77; pastor 1st United Pentecostal Ch., Ragley, La., 1977-97, Beth-El Pentecostal Ch., DeRidder, 1997-99, Pentecostal Worship Ctr., DeRidder, 1999—. Sect. youth dir. La. dist. United Pentecostal Ch., 1979-83, sect. Sunday sch. dir., 1984-86, sec. sec.-treas. 1989-97. Named col., La. Gov., 1975. Democrat. Home: 711 S Texas St Deridder LA 70634-4715 Office: Pentecostal Worship Ctr PO Box 697 Deridder LA 70634-0697 *As a minister, I am looked upon as the one who has all the "right" answers to life's problems. I have discovered that life is not always fair but God is always just.*

MAGEE, THOMAS HUGH, lawyer; b. Rochester, N.Y., Aug. 15, 1943; s. Edward Charles and Jane Kathleen (Cranmer) M.; m. Judith Joy Stone, Oct. 2, 1982; 1 child, Michael Julian. BSME, U. Rochester, N.Y., 1965; JD, Syracuse U., 1973. Bar: N.J. 1974, U.S. Dist. Ct. N.J. 1974, U.S. Ct. Appeals (D.C. cir.) 1975, N.Y. 1981, U.S. Supreme Ct. 1978, U.S. Patent and Trademark Office. Sr. patent counsel RCA Corp., Princeton, N.J., 1973-86, GE/RCA Licensing Operation, Princeton, 1986-88; corp. counsel E.I. duPont de Nemours & Co., Wilmington, Del., 1988—. Lt. USN, 1965-70, Capt. USNR (ret.), 1991. Navy commendation medal with combat V, Vietnam, 1969. Mem. Am. Intellectual Property Law Assn. (com. chair 1974—), Phila. Intellectual Property Law Assn. (com. chmn. 1974—), N.J. Patent Law Assn., Justinian hon. law soc., Phi Alpha Delta. Republican. Presbyterian. Avocations: tennis, handball, coin-collecting. Home: 721 Severn Rd Wilmington DE 19803-1724 Office: E I duPont de Nemours & Co Barley Mill Plz BMP 25-1372 Wilmington DE 19880 E-mail: thomas.h.magee@usa.dupont.com.

MAGEE, WAYNE EDWARD, biochemistry educator, researcher; b. Big Rapids, Mich., Apr. 11, 1929; s. William Fredrick and Elsie E. (Gifford) M.; m. Nannette A. Pierce, June 11, 1951; children: Lawrence, William, John. BA magna cum laude in Chemistry, Kalamazoo Coll., 1951; MS in Biochemistry, U. Wis., 1953, PhD in Biochemistry, 1955. Sci., then sr. sci. Upjohn Co., Kalamazoo, 1955-71; prof. life sci. Ind. State U., 1971-74; prof. biology, head divsn. allied health and life sci. U. Tex., San Antonio, 1975-80; prof. biochemistry, head dept. bacteriology and biochemistry U. Idaho, 1981-85; dir. divsn. Life. Scis., prof., head dept. biosci./biotech. Drexel U., Phila., 1985-92, prof. biosci., 1985-95, W.R. Nes prof. bioscience, 1995-99; prof. emeritus, 1999—. Adj. prof. biology Western Mich. U., 1970-71; adj. prof. molecular and cellular biology U. Ariz., 2000—. Contbr. articles and abstracts to profl. jours., chpts. in books. Wis. Alumni Found. Grad. fellow, 1951-52; Predoctoral fellow NSF, 1952-55. Fellow AAAS, Am. Chem. Soc., Am. Inst. Biol. Sci., Am. Soc. Biochemistry and Molecular Biology, Am. Soc. Microbiology. Achievements include research on phospholipid membranes, liposomes as drug carriers, immune modulation, monoclonal antibodies. Home: 7672 S Galileo Ln Tucson AZ 85747 Office: U of Ariz Dept Molec and Cell Biology PO Box 210106 Tucson AZ 85721-0106 E-mail: mageewe@aol.com.

MAGEE, WILLIAM, state legislator; m. Jeanette Magee. Ed., Cornell U. Mem. N.Y. State Assembly, 1991—, chmn. assembly subcom. of vol. fire fighters com., 1999—, chmn. agrl. com., 1999—. Mem. joint legis. com. on dairy industry devel., mem. aging com., agr. com., higher edn. com., banking com., local govt. com. Office: 214 Farrier Ave Oneida NY 13421-1611 E-mail: mageew@assembly.state.ny.us.

MAGEE-EGAN, PAULINE CECILIA, psychology and management educator; b. N.Y.C., Feb. 27, 1934; d. John Joseph and Rosina (Sweeney) Magee; m. Patrick Joseph Egan, Aug. 5, 1967; children: Anne, Patrick, Deirdre, John. BS, Fordham U., 1956, MS, 1957, PhD, 1963. Cert. psychologist, N.Y. Rsch. asst. Fordham U., N.Y.C., 1956-58; asst. dir. Bur. Testing and Guidance St. John's U., Jamaica, N.Y., 1958-62, asst. prof. psychology, 1962-78, assoc. prof. mgmt., 1978-98, prof., 1998—, assoc. dean external rels. Coll. Bus. Adminstrn., 1997-2000. Cons. in field, 1962—. Contbr. articles to profl. publs. Bd. dirs. Winston Pres. Sch., N.Y.C., 1989—, St. Vincent's Hosp., Harrison, N.Y. Mem. APA, N.Y. State Psychol. Assn. (past pres. pers., indsl. and orgnl. div.). Avocations: gourmet cooking, trap shooting, tennis. Home: 321 Avenue C New York NY 10009-1628

MAGEN, MYRON SHIMIN, osteopathic physician, educator, university dean; b. Bklyn., Mar. 1, 1926; s. Barney and Gertrude Beatrice (Cohen) M.; m. Ruth Sherman, July 6, 1952; children— Jed, Ned, Randy D.O., Coll. Osteo. Medicine and Surgery, 1951; Sc.D. (hon.), U. Osteo. Medicine and Health Scis., Des Moines, 1981. Rotating intern Coll. Hosp., Des Moines, 1951-52, resident in pediatrics, 1953-54; chmn. dept. pediatrics Coll. Osteo. Medicine and Surgery, 1958-62, Riverside Osteo. Hosp., Trenton, Mich., 1962-68, Detroit Osteo. Hosp., 1965-67; med. dir., dir. med. edn. Zieger-Botsford Hosps., Farmington, Mich., 1968-70; prof. pediatrics Mich. State Coll. Osteo. Medicine, East Lansing, 1970—, dean, 1970-98, dean emeritus, 1998—. Mem. spl. med. adv. group to chief med. dir. VA, 1973-77; mem. grad med. edn. nat. div. com. HHS, Washington, 1978-80; James Watson disting. lectr. Ohio Ostio Assn., 1974, Grad. Med. Edn. Nat. Adv. Com.; Watson Meml. lectr. Am. Coll. Osteo. Pediatricians, 1987; chair Mich. Med. Schs. Coun. Deans, 1979-84, 90-91; mem. PEW Health Professions Com., 1991—. Contbr. articles to profl. jours. Served with USN, 1943-45 Recipient Disting. Service award Okla. Coll. Osteo. Medicine and Surgery, 1975; Founder's medal Tex. Coll. Osteo. Medicine, 1978 Mem. NAS, Am. Assn. Colls. Osteo. Medicine (pres. 1977), Am. Osteo. Assn. (com. edn., chair com. on colls. 1987-90, La. Burns lectr. 1977, chair bur. profl. edn. 1990-92), Am. Coll. Osteo. Pediats. (pres. 1965-66), Inst. of Medicine, Mich. Assn. Osteo. Physicians and Surgeons. Home: 1251 Farwood Dr East Lansing MI 48823-1831 Office: Mich State Univ Coll Osteopathic Medicine 541 W Fee Hall East Lansing MI 48824-1315

MAGENHEIM, MARK JOSEPH, physician, epidemiologist, educator; b. Deland, Fla., Nov. 1, 1947; s. Milton David and Dolores Ella (Raithel) M. BA cum laude, Wash. U., 1969; MPH, Yale U., 1971; MD with honors, McMaster U., 1974. Diplomate Am. Bd. Preventive Medicine, Am. Bd. Pub. Health, Am. Bd. Family Medicine. Health officer, prof. Oreg. State U., Corvallis, 1976-78; prof. cmty. health U. Sierra Leone, Freetown, West Africa, 1978-81; asst. prof. McMaster U., Hamilton, Ont., Can., 1978-83; asst. state health officer State of Fla., Tallahassee, 1989-91; health officer, dir. Sarasota (Fla.) County Health Dept., 1984—; med. dir. Hospice of S.W. Fla., Sarasota, 1994-99. Adj. prof. U. South Fla., Tampa, 1985—; mem. staff Doctor's Hosp. Sarasota; adv. com. for HIV and STD Prevention CDC, ACHSP chair, 1996-2000. Author, editor Clinics in Geriatric Medicine, 1986, (with others) Practice of Geriatrics, 1986; contbr. articles to profl. jours. Vice-chmn. instnl. rev. bd. Sarasota Meml. Hosp., 1992—. Recipient Surgeon Gen.'s medallion of excellence USPHS, 1989, award of commendation, 1989, Leadership award Ctrs. for Disease Control, 1991-92; recipient numerous grants. Fellow Royal Soc. Tropical Medicine and Hygiene; mem. Pub. Health Leadership Soc. (chair 1993-95), Fla. Pub. Health Leadership Inst., Fla. Pub. Health Assn., Fla. Med. Assn. (Roy Baker Leadership award 2000), Fla. Soc. for Preventive Medicine, Sarasota County Med. Soc. (chair pub. health com. 1987—). Avocations: tennis, music, bicycling, international travel. Home: 4571 Robin Hood Trail W Sarasota FL 34232 Office: Sarasota County Health Dept PO Box 2658 Sarasota FL 34230-2658 E-mail: mark_magenheim@doh.state.fl.us., markomag@comcast.net.

MAGER, ARTUR, retired aerospace company executive, consultant; b. Nieglowice, Poland, Sept. 21, 1919; arrived in U.S., 1939, naturalized, 1944; s. Herman and Ella (Kornbluh) M.; m. Phyllis R. Weisman, Aug. 19, 1942; 1 child Ilana Gail. BS, U. Mich., 1943; MS, Case Inst. Tech., 1951; PhD in Aeros., Calif. Inst. Tech., 1953. Aero. rsch. scientist NASA Lewis Labs., Cleve., 1946-51; rsch. scientist Marquardt Corp., Van Nuys, Calif., 1954-60; dir. Nat. Engrng. Sic. Co., Pasadena, 1960-61; dir. spacecraft scis. Aerospace Corp., El Segundo, 1961-64, gen. mgr. applied mechanics divsn., 1964-68, v.p., gen. mgr. engrng. sci. ops., 1968-78, v.p. engrng. group, 1978-82, cons., 1982—. Mem. BSD Re-entry Panel, 1961—63; mem. NASA com. missile and space vehicle aerodynamics, 1963—65; mem. adv. com. AFML, 1971—72; mem. NASA Adv. Coun., 1982—86; chmn. NASA Space Applications Adv. Com., 1982—86; mem. Aeros. and Space Engrng. Bd. NRC, 1982—87; mem. Space Sta. Task Force NRC, 1983—87, mem. Shuttle Critically and Hazard Analysts Rev. Bd., 1986—88; mem. DSB NASP Task Force, 1987—88, AFSB Hypersonic Task Force, 1987—88. Contbr. articles to profl. jours. Mem. alumni fund coun. Calif. Inst. Tech., 1972—74; trustee West Coast U., 1980—92; mem. devel. disabilities bd. Area X, 1976—80, chmn., 1976—78; 1st v.p. Calif. Assn. Retarded, 1983—85; pres. Exceptional Children's Found., 1970—72; bd. councilors U. So. Calif. Sch. Engrng., 1976—86. Recipient Disting. Alumni award, U. Mich., 1969, Golden Rule award, Calif. Assn. Retarded, 1977, 1989. Fellow: AAAS, AIAA (chmn. L.A. sect. 1967—68, bd. dirs. 1975—77, pres. 1980—81), Inst. Advanced Engrng.; mem.: Nat. Acad. Engrng., Technion Soc., Sigma Xi. Home and Office: 1353 Woodruff Ave Los Angeles CA 90024-5129 E-mail: ap.mager@verizon.net.

MAGER, EZRA PASCAL, investment management company executive; b. N.Y.C., Nov. 1, 1941; s. Harold and Naomi (Levinson) M.; m. Sarah Johnson, Mar. 25, 1964 9div.); 1 child, Emma Rachel; m. Reeva Starkman, May 14, 1972; children: Camilla Elizabeth, Michael Johanon. BA, Cornell U., 1963; MBA, Harvard, 1966. Successively v.p., sr. v.p., exec. v.p. and dir. Seiden & DeCuevas, Inc., N.Y.C., 1966-73; exec. v.p., dir. Furman Selz Mager Dietz & Birney, Inc., 1973-90; vice chmn. United Auto Group, Inc., 1990-96, Cross Continent Auto Retailers, Inc., N.Y.C., 1996-97, First Team Auto Corp., N.Y.C., 1997-98; pres. Torrey Funds Mgmt., 1998—. Trustee Baron de Hirsch Fund. Mem. N.Y. Soc. Security Analysts, Alpha Delta Phi. Clubs: Harvard (N.Y.C.). Democrat. Home: 141 E 72d St New York NY 10021-4315 Office: Torrey Funds Mgmt 505 Park Ave New York NY 10022

MAGER, MARGARET JULIA ECKSTEIN, special education educator; b. Belleville, Ill., May 4, 1954; d. Wilbert Frank and Therese Rose (Holdmeyer) Eckstein; m. Stephen Charles Mager, Oct. 1, 1983; children: Julia, Therese, Elizabeth. BA summa cum laude, St. Louis U., 1976; MEd in Spl. Edn. summa cum laude, U. Mo., St. Louis, 1983. Cert. tchr., spl. edn. tchr., Mo. Tchr. spl. edn. Cen. Sch.-Francis Howell Dist., St. Charles, Mo., 1975-85, Castlio Sch.-Francis Howell Dist., St. Charles, 1985-95, John Weldon Elem. Sch. Francis Howell Dist., St. Charles, 1995—. Troop leader St. Charles area coun. Girl Scouts U.S.; coach St. Charles Spl. Olympics, 1976-85; bd. dirs. Willows Way, bd. dirs. St. Monica Sch. Recipient St. Anne award Cath. Girl Scouting, 2001. Mem. Coun. Exceptional Children, Learning Disabilities Assn., St. Charles Assn. Retarded Citizens (recording sec. 1982-83, Vol. of Yr. 1983), Am. Guild English Handbell Ringers, Choristers Guild, Mo. Citizens for Life, Bread for the World, Right to Life, Am. Assn. on Mental Retardation, Phi Beta Kappa. Roman Catholic. Avocations: music, photography, gardening. Home: 767 Montmartre Dr Saint Louis MO 63141-6121 Office: John Weldon Elem Sch 7370 Weldon Springs Rd Saint Charles MO 63304-8618

MAGFORD, MARY, investment company executive; BA with honors, U. Wales, 1966. Ptnr. Mogford Campbell Inc.; com. chair bd. dirs. Ont. SuperBuild Corp., Toronto, Canada, 2000—. Bd. dirs. Falconbridge Ltd., MDS Inc., Potash Corp. Saskatchewan, Sears Can., Teranet Inc., Altamira Adv. Coun.; hon. gov. Trent U.; assoc. mem. Bd. Can. Policy Rsch. Network; former dep. minister of fin., Ont.; former minister natural resources. Vol. Hosp. Sick Children Foun., Toronto Symphony Found.; former vice chair Hosp. Sick Children; former mem. Econ. Coun. Can., Bd. Nature Conservancy Can., Premier's Jobs and Investment Bd. Scholar Lady Astor scholar, Coll. William and Mary. Office: Ont SuperBuild Corp 6th Flr Frost Bldg S 7 Queen's Park Crescent Toronto ON M7A 1Y7 Canada Office Fax: 416-325-8851. E-mail: Info@SuperBuild.gov.on.ca.*

MAGGARD, WOODROW WILSON, JR. management consultant; b. Quincy, Ill., Feb. 5, 1947; s. Woodrow Wilson and Claire Lorraine (Lyons) M.; m. Linda Margaret Davis, Dec. 30, 1967; children: Jared Isaac, Erin Leigh-Taylor, Solveig Kirsten, Christian Heinrich, Anica May, Kayla Margaret. BA, Brigham Young U., 1971; postgrad., Ventura Coll. Law, 1975; MPA, Consortium of Calif. State U., 1978. Cert. rev. appraiser; registered mortgage underwriter. Divsn. mgr. Sears, Roebuck & Co., Provo, Utah and Ventura, Calif., 1967-74; adminstrv. officer County of Ventura, 1974-78; founding ptnr. Maggard, Maughan, Gress and Assocs., Ventura, 1976-83; founder Intermountain Property Svcs., 1974—; pres., CEO Ariz. Tech. Incubator, Inc., 2000—. Bd. dirs. EmisCo Internat. Corp., Phoenix, Qameleon, Inc., Scottsdale, Ariz.; v.p. econ./bus. devel. Dineh Coops., Inc., Chinle, Navaho Nation Ariz., 1978-80; dir. econ. devel. City of Scottsdale, Ariz., 1980-81; exec. dir., CEO Fairbanks (Alaska) Devel. Authority, 1981-87; co-founder Pacific Rim Inst., 1984—; founder Maggard & Maggard, Fairbanks and Orlando, 1983—; pres., co-founder So. Global Trading Co., Tex. and Orlando, 1991-98; sr. v.p. Cookies N' Cream, Inc., Tex. and Fla., 1990-91; exec. dir., CEO Reichenbach Techs, Provo, Utah, 1975—, pres., 1999—; exec. dir., CEO Ctrl. Fla. Rsch. Park, Orlando, 1988-91, Reichenbach Maegert Internat., Provo, 1997—; chmn. NETeXc, Inc., Wilmington, Del. and Provo, 1998-2000, bd. dirs. 1998—; co-founder LearnDaily.com, Provo, 1999—; pres., CEO Del. Tech. Park, Inc., Newark, 1993-98; chmn. Calif. Mission Days Food, Altaloma, Calif., 1996-99, Ariz. Mfg. Ext. Partnership, Scottsdale, 2000-02, Rural Incubator Bd. Ariz., 2000—; exec. dir., CEO Inst. Applied Composites Tech., Newark, 1993-98; instr. real estate econs./appraisal Oxnard (Calif.) Coll., 1975-78; instr. bus. Utah Tech. Coll., Provo, 1978. Contbr. articles to profl. jours. and books. Active Boy Scouts Am.; high priest Ch. of LDS; econ. dir. City of Dover, N.H., 1988; exec. dir. Dover Indsl. Devel. Authority; exec. dir. Del. Tech. Park and Inst. for Applied Composites Tech.; office of vice provost U. Del., Newark, 1993-98; bd. dirs. WMFE-TV, Fla. Hosp. Found.; bd. dirs. Next Level Found., 2002—; interim dir., Miller Bus. Innovation Ctr., Salt Lake City, 2002—. Recipient Nat. Merit award for excellence in comml. devel., 1987, Dixwell Pierce award, 1975, Alaska Environ. Enhancement award, 1983; one of Top 10 Sci. Parks in the World Cen. Fla. Rsch. Park, 1991. Mem. Nat. Assn. Seed and Venture Funds (sec.), Am. Soc. Pub. Adminstrn., Internat. Right-of-Way Assn. (internat. property mgmt. com.), Nat. Assn. Rev. Appraisers and Mortgage Underwriters (sr.), Nat. Coun. on Urban Econ. Devel., Am. Econ. Devel. Coun. (internat. com.), Nat. Bus. Incubation Assn., So. Indsl. Devel. Coun., Assn. Univ.-Related Rsch. Parks (bd. dirs.), Del. Innovation Fund (bd. dirs.), Urban Land Inst., Nat. Assn. Indsl. and Office Parks, Am. C. of C. Rschrs. Assn., Acad. Polit. Sci., United Indian Planners, Japan-Am. Soc. Cen Fla. (bd. dirs.), Inst. Internal Auditors, Assn. U. Tech. Mgrs., Sci. and Tech. Coun. of the States, Soc. Profl. Composite Engrs. (charter), Suppliers Advanced Composite Materials Assn., Soc. for Advancement of Materials and Process Engrng., Assn. Tech. Transfer Soc., Licensing Execs. Soc., Rotary, Phi Alpha Theta. Independent. Home: 4006 N Canyon Rd Provo UT 84604-5018 Office: 1435 N Hayden Rd Scottsdale AZ 85257-3773

MAGGIOLO, ALLISON JOSEPH, lawyer; b. New River, N.C., Aug. 29, 1943; s. Allison and Florence Celeste (Vago) M. Cert., U. Paris-Sorbonne, 1965; AB, Brown U., 1966; JD, U. Louisville, 1975. Bar: Ky. 1976, U.S. Dist. Ct. (we. dist.) Ky. 1981. Ops. mgr., stockbroker Bache & Co., Louisville, 1970-73; ptnr. Reisz, Blackburn, Manly & Treitz, 1976-78, Greenebaum Boone Treitz Maggiolo & Brown, Louisville, 1978-91, Wyatt, Tarrant & Combs, Louisville, 1991—. Workshop panelist Fin. Adv. Coun., 1994; panelist Seminar on Defaulted Bond Issues, 1987-89, Bond Counsel and the Corp.

Trustee, 1990-92, Defaults and Workouts, 1993. Author: Indenture Trustee Liability and Defaulted Bond Issues, 1987, Minimizing Indenture Trustee Liability and Defaulted Bond Issues, 1991, Bond Default Resolution, 1993; co-author: The legal Aspects of Doing International Business in Kentucky, 1990. Mem. exec. com. St. Louis Com. Fgn. Rels., 1979—, chmn., 1991—96; bd. dirs. Ky. Show, Louisville, 1978—91, Ky. Opera, Louisville, 1978—91, mem. hon. coun., 1991—; bd. dirs. Glassworks Found., 2002—. Decorated Bronze Star. Mem. Internat. Bar Assn., Nat. Assn. Bond Lawyers, Bond Attys. Workshop (planning com. 1991-93), Pendennis Club, Wynn Stay Club, Jefferson Club. Office: Wyatt Tarrant & Combs Citizens Plz Louisville KY 40202-2823

MAGGIPINTO, V. ANTHONY, lawyer; b. Tucson, Apr. 15, 1943; s. William Vito and Elizabeth Maria (Rice) M.; m. Maria Teresa Zequeira, Aug. 31, 1976; children: Marshall Albert Nicholas, Spencer William Jonathan. AB cum laude, Southampton Coll., 1970; JD, Fordham U., 1976. Bar: Fla. 1977, N.Y. 1978, U.S. Dist. Ct. (ea. and so. dists.) N.Y. 1979, U.S. Ct. Appeals (2d cir.) 1980. Asst. to pres. Interpub. Group of Cos., N.Y.C., 1965-66; asst. dean of admission Southampton (N.Y.) Coll., 1971-73; investigative aide N.Y. State Com. on Jud. Conduct, N.Y.C., 1974-76; asst. state atty. Dade County State Atty., Miami, Fla., 1977-78; asst. dist. atty. Suffolk Dist. Atty., Hauppauge, N.Y., 1978-80; asst. county atty. Suffolk County Atty., Hauppauge, 1980-84; sole practice Riverhead and St. James, N.Y., 1982—. Mem. spl. coms. on discovery, civil litigation U.S. Dist. Ct. (ea. dist.) N.Y., Bklyn., 1983-90, 95—, arbitrator, 1986—, Civil Justice Reform Act adv. group, 1990-95, chair jury task force, 1993—, commendation U.S. Dist. Ct., 1997. Mem. appeals bd. SSS, 1982—2001, vice chmn., 1986—97, chmn., 1997—2001. Served with submarine svc. USN, 1961—65. Recipient Disting. Alumni award L.I. U., 1990. Mem.: Southampton Coll. Alumni Assn. (exec. com. 1997, pres. 2001—02, bd. dirs.), Navy League (judge adv. L.I. coun. 1992—), U.S. Naval Inst., Fla. Bar Assn., Suffolk County Bar Assn., N.Y. State Bar Assn. (exec. com. real property sect. 1997—2002), Golf Club (counsel 1980—, bd. govs.), Nissequogue Club. Republican. Roman Catholic. Avocations: hiking, horseback riding. Office: 1212 Roanoke Ave Riverhead NY 11901-2740

MAGGS, PETER BLOUNT, lawyer, educator; b. Durham, N.C., July 24, 1936; s. Douglas Blount and Dorothy (Mackay) M.; m. Barbara Ann Widenor, Feb. 27, 1960; children: Bruce MacDowell, Gregory Eaton, Stephanie Ann, Katherine Ellen. AB, Harvard U., 1957, JD, 1961; postgrad. (exchange student), Leningrad (USSR) State U., 1961-62. Bar: D.C. 1962. Research assoc. Law Sch. Harvard U., 1963-64; asst. prof. law U. Ill., 1964-67, assoc. prof., 1967-69, prof., 1969-88, William and Marie Corman prof., 1988-98, Peer & Sarah Pedersen prof., 1998—2002, acting dean, 1990, Clifford M. and Bette A. Carney chair in law, 2002—; dir. Rule of Law program Washington, 1994. Fulbright lectr. Moscow State U., 1977; reporter Uniform Simplification of Land Transfers Act.; vis. prof. George Washington U., 1998. Author: (with others) The Mandelstam File, 1996; translator: Civil Code of the Russian Federation, 1998, Civil Code of the Republic of Armenia, 1999, (in Russian) Intellectual Property, 2000, Internet and Computer Law, 2001, Trademark and Unfair Competition, 2002; designer talking computers for the blind. Fulbright rsch. scholar, Yugoslavia, 1967; Fulbright disting. chair, Trento, 2002; East-West Ctr. fellow, 1972, Guggenheim fellow, 1979. Mem. ABA, D.C. Bar, Am. Assn. Advancement Slavic Studies, Assn. Am. Law Schs., Am. Law Inst. (consultative group, UCC Article 2), Internat. Acad. Comparative Law. Office: U Ill Coll Law 504 E Pennsylvania Ave Champaign IL 61820-6909 E-mail: p-maggs@uiuc.edu.

MAGID, LEE, video and recording producer, manager, composer, lyricist; b. N.Y.C., Apr. 6, 1926; s. Abraham and Clara Magid; divorced; children: Diane, Deborah, Adam, Andrea. Grad. high sch., Bronx, N.Y., 1944. Produced for Decca, Jubilee, RCA, ABC, Bluesway, Dawn, LMI, others, 1946-2000; artist, repetoire Nat. Records, N.Y.C., 1947-49, Savoy Records, Newark, 1950-53; pres. Lee Magid Inc., Malibu, Calif., 1967-99. Theatrical mgr., N.Y.C. and Calif., 1952—; music bus. cons., L.A., 1963-97; video and record producer, N.Y.C., 1944-97; developer careers of Della Reese, Lou Rawls, O.C. Smith, Al Hibbler, Tramaine Hawkins, Earl Grant, others. Prodr.: (video) Tramaine Hawkins Live, 1990 (Grammy and Dove awards 1991), Joy That Floods My Soul (Grammy and Dove awards 1989), Sparrow Records, LMI, Grass Roots Records; author, prodr. (theatre play): I Sing Because I'm Happy, the Devil, The Blues and The Gospel Queen; prodr. film based on life of Mahalia Jackson; writer: Top 1953 R&B Song Hit, "I Played The Fool". Mem. ASCAP, BMI, SESAC. Fax: 310-457-8891.

MAGIDSOHN, HERMAN EDWARD, lawyer; b. Detroit, Dec. 7, 1936; s. Harry and Barbara M.; m. Leslie Marcia Krimton, July 12, 1970; children: Blair H., Heather B., Allison A. BA, U. Mich., 1959; BBA, U. Miami, 1961; JD, Southwestern U., 1970. Bar: U.S. Dist. Ct. (ctrl. dist.) Calif. 1971, U.S. Ct. Appeals (9th cir.) 1971. Assoc. Mansell & Giddens, L.A., 1971-73, Coleman & Coleman, L.A., 1973-75; pvt. practice Encino, Calif., 1975—. Office: Law Offices of Herman E Magdsohn 15720 Ventura Blvd Ste 418 Encino CA 91436-4709

MAGIDSON, JAY, statistician; b. Chgo., Mar. 18, 1947; s. Samuel and Shirley Arlene (Weininger) M.; m. Elizabeth Katherine Morgan, Oct. 26, 1976; children: Jeremy, Jenna. BA, U. Ill., 1969; MS in Bus., U. Wis., 1971; PhD in Mgmt., Northwestern U., 1976. Sr. analyst Ill. Bell Telephone Co., Chgo., 1971-72; sr. statistician Abt Assocs., Inc., Cambridge, Mass., 1976-81; founder, pres. Statis. Innovations, Inc., Belmont, 1981—. Presenter seminars; cons. A.C. Nielsen Co., Chgo., Nat. Geographic Soc., Washington, 1984—, Beneficial Mgmt. Corp., Peapack, N.J., 1989—; instr. Boston U., Tufts U.; mem. govt. adv. panel USDA, 1984; expert reviewer govt. panel NIH, Washington, 1989, 91, NSF, Washington, 1982, 87. Author: Reforming Schools, 1980, SPSS PC+ CHAID version 5.0 for DOS and 6.0 for Windows Computer Manual; editor: Analyzing Qualitative/Categorical Data, 1978, Advances in Factor Analysis and Structural Equation Models, 1979; designer CHAID market segmentation computer package, GOLDMINER (graphical ordinal logit displays based on monotonic regression) computer package, latent gold program for latent class modeling, TYPE-O-GRAPHIC profiler statistical modeling program; contbr. articles to profl jours.; mem. editl. rev. bd. Jour. Direct Mktg., Evanston, Ill., 1988—, Jour. Targeting, Measurement and Analysis for Mktg.; computer sect. editor Jour. Mktg. Rsch., 1983-85. Coach youth basketball, baseball and soccer teams. Mem. Am. Statis. Assn., Assn. for Psychol. Type. Achievements include patent for Apparatus and Method for Graphical Display of Statistical Effects in Categorical and Continuous Outcome Data. Office: Statis Innovations Inc 375 Concord Ave Belmont MA 02478-3048

MAGIE, GREGORY ALDEN, music educator; b. Bukidnon, Mindenau, Philippines, Nov. 27, 1967; s. Allan Rupert Magie and Louane Audrey Anderson; m. Michelle Alice Bower, Jan. 4, 1992; children: Andrew, Elizabeth; children: David. MusB, Eastman Sch. of Music, 1990; MusM, U. of Redlands, 1993; D in Musical Arts, UCLA, 1996. Vis. asst. prof. Pomona Coll., Claremont, Calif., 1999; asst. prof., dir. of orch. Graceland U., Lamoni, Iowa, 2000—01, San Francisco State U., San Francisco, 2001—. Music dir. Arrowbear Music Camp Orch., Arrowbear, Calif., 1996—98; dir. of music Moorpark Presbyn. Ch., Moorpark, Calif., 1996—2000; asst. dir. Pasadena Lyric Opera, Pasadena, Calif., 1998—2000. Music director (opera) George Bizet's Carmen, 1999. Fellow: Pi Kappa Lambda. Conservative. Presbyterian. Avocation: golf. Home: 1557 1st Ave Walnut Creek CA 94597 Office: San Francisco State University 1600 Holloway Ave San Francisco CA 94132 E-mail: magie@sfsu.edu.

MAGIELNICKI, ROBERT L. lawyer; b. Perth Amboy, N.J., Mar. 28, 1947; s. Leon C. and Dorothy M. (Hudanish) M.; m. Kathleen J. Urban, June 14, 1969; children: Robert Jr., Kimberly, Peter, Matthew. AB with honors, Rutgers U., 1967; JD with distinction, Cornell U., 1970. Bar: N.Y. 1971, U.S. Supreme Ct. 1974, D.C. 1990. Commd. lt. USN, 1968; assoc. Donovan Leisure Newton & Irvine, N.Y.C., 1970-71, 74-80; asst. staff judge advocate U.S. Naval Base Subic Bay, Republic of Philippines, 1971-73; asst. prof. law U.S. Naval Acad., Annapolis, Md., 1973-74; assoc. litigation and antitrust counsel Gen. Electric Co. Hdqrs., Fairfield, Conn., 1980-83, counsel, 1989-90; divsn. gen. counsel Gen. Electric Factory Automation Products, Charlottesville, Va., 1983-88; ptnr. Kutak Rock, Washington, 1990-2000, Schnader Harrison Segal & Lewis LLP, Washington, 2000—. Avocations: tennis, golf, swimming, reading. Office: Schnader Harrison Segal & Lewis LLP 11th Fl East 1300 I St NW Washington DC 20005-3314

MAGILL, FRANK JOHN, federal judge; b. Verona, N.D., June 3, 1927; s. Thomas Charles and Viola Magill; m. Mary Louise Timlin, Nov. 22, 1955; children: Frank Jr., Marguerite Connolly, R. Daniel, Mary Elizabeth, Robert, John. BS in Fgn. Svc., Georgetown U., 1951, LLB, 1955; MA, Columbia U., 1952. Ptnr. Nilles, Hansen, Magill & Davies, Ltd., Fargo, ND, 1955—86; judge U.S. Ct. Appeals (8th cir.), 1986—. Chmn. fin. disclosure com. U.S. Jud. Conf., 1993—98. Fellow: Am. Coll. Trial Lawyers; mem.: Cass County Bar Assn. (Pres. 1970). Republican. Avocations: tennis, sailing, skiing. Home: 501 7th St S Apt 301 Fargo ND 58103-2761 Office: Quentin N Burdick US Courthouse 655 1st Ave N Ste 320 Fargo ND 58102-4932 Fax: 701 297-7255. E-mail: frank_magill@ca8.uscourts.gov.

MAGILL, SAMUEL HAYS, academic administrator, higher education consultant; b. Decatur, Ga., July 19, 1928; s. Orrin Rankin and Ellen Howe (Bell) M.; children: Samuel Hays Jr., Katherine Magill Walters, Suzanne Magill Weintraub. AB, U. N.C., 1950; BD, Yale U., 1953; PhD, Duke U., 1962; LHD (hon.), Stockton State Coll., 1990. Ordained to ministry Congl. Christian Ch., 1953; gen. sec. Davidson Coll. YMCA, 1953-55; dir. student activities U. N.C., Chapel Hill, 1955-58, asst. dean student affairs, 1958-59; chaplain Dickinson Coll., 1962-63, asst. prof. religion, 1962-66, asso. prof. religion, 1966-68, dean coll., 1963-68; pres. Council Protestant Colls. and Univs., Washington, 1968-70; exec. asso., chief office acad. affairs Assn. Am. Colls., 1971-76; pres. Simon's Rock Early Coll., Great Barrington, Mass., 1976-79, Monmouth U., West Long Branch, N.J., 1980-93, pres. emeritus, 1993—; higher edn. cons., 1993-98; assoc. dir. gift planning U. N.C., 1999—. Adj. prof. Duke U., 1996. Trustee Jersey Shore Med. Ctr., 1985-93; bd. overseers N.J. Gov.'s Schs., 1986-93. Guerney Harris Kearns fellow in religion, 1960-61; Danforth Found. spl. grad. fellow, 1959-61. Fellow Soc. Values in Higher Edn. (dir. 1969-81); mem. Am. Assembly Collegiate Sch. Bus. (accreditation task force 1989-90), NCAA (pres.'s commn. 1990-93), Am. Coun. Edn. (commn. leadership devel. 1982-85, commn. on minority affairs 1986-89), Harvard Inst. Ednl. Mgmt., Assn. Ind. Colls. and Univs. N.J. (dir. 1980-93, exec. com. 1983—, chair 1987-89), Order of Golden Fleece U. N.C., Fearrington Dem. Club (co-chair 1997-98), Rotary Club. Home: 1 Weybridge Pl Chapel Hill NC 27517-8938 E-mail: Smagill@mindspring.com.

MAGILL, SAMUEL WALLACE, international relations specialist; b. Ashtabula, Ohio, Oct. 8, 1919; s. William Joseph and Lucia (Ackerman) M.; m. Edna Merle Stinson, Oct. 24, 1942 (div. 1961; children: Samuel Wallace Jr., Merle Lynn; m. Bertha Lefkowitz, May 15, 1962. BSc, U. Md., Frankfurt, Germany, 1961; MA, Boston U., Heidelberg, Germany, 1965; cert., Newspaper Inst. Am., 1979. Commd. 2nd lt. U.S. Army, 1940; advanced through grades to lt. col. 513 Mil. Intelligence Group, 1963; adminstrv. officer Adjutant Gen., Columbus, Ohio, 1949-51; ops. officer 137th Tank Battalion, Ft. Polk, La., 1951-53; dep. chief 5th Strategic Intelligence Det., Stuttgart, Germany, 1954-57; asst. chief security Fourth U.S. Army, San Antonio, 1957-59; dir. ops. 513 Mil. Intelligence Group, Oberursel, Germany, 1959-61; exec. officer Electronic R&D Activity, White Sands, N.Mex., 1961-63; chief collection U.S. Army Europe, Heidelberg, 1963-68; ret. U.S. Army, 1968; program analyst U.S. AAFES-Europe, Munich, 1968-75; pres. German-Am. Men's Club, 1978—. Tech. advisor, dialog coach, prodn. asst. Bavaria Film Studio, MGM, ABC Circle Films, Lorimar Prodns., 20th Century Fox, and others, Munich, 1978-89; asst. mgr. M.C. Robinson, Co., Ashtabula, 1946-49. Author numerous poems; contbr. articles to profl. jours. Decorated Bronze Star (4), Legion of Merit (2), French Croix de Guerre, German Cross of Merit, Bavarian Order of Merit (Germany); recipient Presdl. citation U.S. Govt., 1945. Mem. Internat. Platform Assn., Nat. Geographic Soc., Fedn. German Am. Clubs (v.p. 1987-94, Spl. award 1989). Avocations: geology, archeology, photography, fishing. Home: Elektrastrasse 11 81925 Munich 81 Germany Fax: 49 89911463.

MAGILL, SHERRY, foundation administrator; m. Robert J. Willis. BA, U. Ala., 1974, MA, 1976; PhD, Syracuse U., 1984. V.p., dep. to pres. Washington Coll., Md.; program officer for edn. Jessie Ball duPont Fund, Jacksonville, Fla., 1991-93, exec. dir., 1993-2000, pres., 2000—. Sr. moderator Aspen Inst.; founding exec. dir. Wye Faculty Seminar. Former chair Fla. Funders Group, state bd. dirs. P.A.C.E. Ctr. for Girls; former bd. dirs. Leadership Jacksonville; former chair jud. nominating commn. Fla. State Supreme Ct. Mem. Southeastern Coun. Founds. (bd. dirs.), Jacksonville Women's Network (bd. dirs.). Office: Jessie Ball DuPont Fund One Independent Dr Ste 1400 Jacksonville FL 32202-5011 E-mail: smagill@dupontfund.org.

MAGISON, DEBORAH HELEN, elementary education educator; b. Abington, Pa., Aug. 9, 1969; d. Ernest C. and Doris K. (Ko) M. BS in Elem. Edn./Early Childhood, Kutztown (Pa.) U., 1991; postgrad, Bloomsburg U., 1997—. Cert. tchr. instrnl. I, Pa. Tchr. asst. summer camp Ardsley (Pa.) Day Care Ctr., 1989-91, tchr. summer camp, summer 1991, tchr., supr., 1991-98; long-term sub. tchr. Abington (Pa.) Sch. Dist., 1998—. Jr. ch. tchr., Bible Sch. tchr. Faith Cmty. Ch., Roslyn, Pa., 1996—; strategic planner Abington Sch. Dist., 1995. Mem. Del. Valley Assocs. Edn. Young Children. Avocations: art, crafts, writing, fitness. Home: 2131 Curtis Ave Abington PA 19001-2523 Office: Overlook Elem Sch 2001 Old Welsh Rd Abington PA 19001-1215

MAGLACAS, A. MANGAY, nursing researcher, educator; BSN, Vanderbilt U.; MPH, U. Minn.; DPH, Johns Hopkins U.; DSc (hon.), U. Ill. Former chief sci. for nursing devel. health manpower divsn. WHO, Geneva, Switzerland, 1976-89, regional nurse adviser Southeast Asia Office Delhi, India, 1972-75. Internat. health/nursing cons., 1989—; adj. prof. Coll. Nursing, U. Ill., Chgo., 1990—; various vis. prof. positions in several countries, 1990—. Former mem., bd. dirs. Internat. Coun. Nurses, 1989-93; fgn. assoc. NAS Inst. Medicine, 1988—. Rockefeller fellow, 1964-67; Fulbright-Smith-Mundt scholar, 1952-54; recipient Outstanding alumni award Vanderbilt U., 1986, Internat. Pub. Health Leadership award Johns Hopkins U., 1992, Outstanding Profl. award for Nursing, Profl. Regulation Commn. of Philippines, 2000, Profl. Recognition award U. Philippines, 1989, Disting. Achievement award Philippine Nurses Assn., 1989, Outstanding Alumni award U. Philippines Sch. Nursing, 1987, Disting. Leadership award USA Commn. on Grads. of Fgn. Nursing Schs., 2002; named Woman of Yr. Am. Rsch. Inst. Bd. Internat. Rsch., 1988. Fellow Royal Coll. U.K. (hon.). Office: 59 Chemin de Planta CH-1223 Cologny Switzerland

MAGLEBY, FLORENCE DEMING, special education educator; b. Porterville, Utah, Apr. 15, 1912; d. Vernon and Lydia (Florence) Deming; m. McRay Magleby, June 1, 1938; children: McRay, Jr., Susan D., Tom D. BS in Elem. and Secondary Edn., U. Utah, 1954, MS in Ednl. Psychology, 1969; EdD in Ednl. Psychology, Western Colo. U., 1977. Cert. early childhood edn., elem., secondary, spl. edn. and learning disabilities tchr., Utah, adminstr./supr., Utah, Orton-Gillingham therapist. Psychoednl. diagnosis, therapy practice, Salt Lake City, 1980-83, 88-00; psychol. evaluator Wash. County Sch. Dist, 1984-88; postdoctoral U. Utah; state specialist learning disabilities Utah State Office Edn., 1969-77; grant proposal field reader U.S. Office Edn.; dir. Utah State Learning Disability Ctr., 1971-73; clinic coord., demonstration tchr. Exemplary Ctr. Reading Instrn., 1967-69. Mem. Internat. Learning Disabilities Assn., Learning Disabilities Assn. Utah, (profl. adv. bd.), Internat. Reading Assn., Utah Coun Internat. Reading Assn., Orton Dyslexia Soc. (life), Coun. Exceptional Children (life), Delta Kappa Gamma, Utah Reading Resource Network Ctr. (adv. bd.). Home: 109 E South Temple Apt 3G Salt Lake City UT 84111-1106

MAGLIATO, HENRY J. orthopedic surgeon; b. N.Y.C., June 8, 1933; s. E. Henry and Anna (Carillo) M. BS cum laude, Fordham U., 1954; MD, SUNY, 1958. Diplomate Am. Bd. Orthopedic Surgery. Intern L.I. Coll. Hosp., Bklyn., 1958-59; resident surgery Manhattan Hosp., 1959-60; resident orthopedic surgery St. Lukes Hosp., N.Y.C., 1960-63; attending orthopedic surgeon St. Luke's-Roosevelt, Beth Israel and Columbia U., 1963—, pvt. practice, 1963—. Police surgeon N.Y.C. Police Dept., 1981—; asst. prof. orthopedic surgery emeritus N.Y. Med. Coll., Valhalla, N.Y.; impartial cons. U.S.D.O.L., 1964—, acting med. dir., 2000—. Fellow ACS, Am. Acad. Orthopedic Surgeons, Internat. Assn. Chiefs of Police, N.Y. State Med. Soc., New York County Med. Soc., N.Y. Shields Republican. Roman Catholic. Avocations: travel, swimming, cruising, gourmet dining, medical law. Office: PO Box 2326 New York NY 10021-0056

MAGLICH, BOGDAN CASTLE, physicist; b. Yugoslavia; came to U.S., 1956, naturalized, 1972; s. Cveta and Ivanka (Bingulac) M.; children: Marko Castle, Ivanka Taylor, Roberta Cveta, Angelica Dara, Aleksandra Mara Nadine. Diploma physics, U. Belgrade, 1951; MS, U. Liverpool, Eng., 1955; PhD, MIT, 1959. Staff mem. Lawrence Berkeley Lab., 1959-62; dep. group leader Brit. group, 1962-63; leader Swiss group CERN European Orgn. Nuclear Rsch., 1964-67; vis. prof., joint faculty mem. Princeton U.-U. Pa. accelerator U. Pa., 1967-69; prof. physics, prin. investigator high energy physics Rutgers U., 1969-74; pres., chmn. Fusion Energy Corp., Princeton, N.J., 1972-81, Aneutronix, Inc., 1982-83, Sci. Transfer Assocs., Inc., 1981-84, United Scis., Inc., 1984-87, AE Labs Aneutronic Energy Lab., Inc., 1986-88; pres. Advanced Physics Corp., 1988-94; chmn. Advanced Projects Group, Inc., 1994—, HiEnergy Microdevices, Ltd., 1995—. Chmn. The Tesla Found., 1985—; resident scientist UN-ILO Seminar Econ. Devel. East Africa, Kenya, 1967; lectr. Postdoctoral Sch. Physics, Yerevan, USSR, 1965, Internat. Sch. Majorana, Italy, 1969; mem. U.S. delegation Internat. Conf. High Energy Physics, Vienna, 1968, Kiev, 1970; spl. rep. of U.S. Pres. to Yugoslavia, 1976; sci. project dir. Univ. Research Ctr., King Abdulaziz U., Saudi Arabia, 1981-82; prin. investigator for aneutronic energy USAF Weapons Lab., 1985-87, USAF Space Tech. Ctr., 1988-89. Editor: Adventures in Exptl. Physics, 1972-80. Chmn. Yugoslav-Am. Bicentennial Com., 1975-76; co-chmn. Serbian-Am. Com. for a Dem. Yugoslavia, 1989-92; pres. World Serbian Union, Geneva, 1990-92. Recipient White House citation, 1961; Bourgeois d'honneur de Lens Switzerland, 1973; UNESCO fellow, 1957-58 Fellow Am. Phys. Soc.; mem. Serbian Acad. Scis. and Arts (Yugoslavia), Ripon Soc. (bd. govs.), Nassau Club, MIT Club, Sigma Xi. Mem. Serbian Orthodox Ch. Achievements include discovering omega-meson, sonic spark chamber, missing-mass spectrometer, delta-meson, g-meson, S, T and U-mesons, precetron, self collider migma, aneutronic energy process, supersenzor and microsenzor atometry, and neutron microscope; patentee in field. E-mail: maglich2@aol.com.

MAGLIO, CHRISTOPHER JOHN, psychologist, educator; b. Dover, N.H., May 19, 1965; s. Alphonse Gustavo Sr. and Claire Elizabeth Maglio; m. Tjitske Gay Tubbergen, Aug. 7, 1992; 1 child, Alexander Nickolai Tubbergen-Maglio. BS in Psychology, Ariz. State U., 1987, M of Counseling, 1989, PhD in Counseling Psychology, 1992. Lic. psychologist, Mo.; lic. profl. counselor, Mo. Crisis therapist Scottsdale (Ariz.) Camelback Hosp., 1988-91; counseling psychology intern Tex. A&M U., College Station, 1991-92; pvt. practice Kirksville, Mo., 1994—; asst. prof. counseling Truman State U., 1992-93, asst. prof. counseling, program dir., 1993-97, assoc. prof. counseling, program dir., 1997—. Bd. dirs., chmn. Mo. State Com. Psychologists, Jefferson City. Bd. dirs. Hospice 2000, Kirksville, 1993-99. Mem. APA (divsn. 17 program com. 1997-2000), ACA (sec. divsn. Assn. for Counselor Edn. and Supervision 1988-99). Democrat. Avocations: music, cooking. Home: PO Box 360 Kirksville MO 63501-0360 Office: Truman State U Divsn Social Sci 100 E Normal St Kirksville MO 63501-4200 Fax: 660-785-4181. E-mail: cjmaglio@truman.edu.

MAGLIOCCA, LARRY ANTHONY, education educator; b. New Castle, Pa., Sept. 3, 1943; s. Anthony Norman Magliocca and Madeline Rose Ross; m. Judie Alene Kerr, Sept. 1, 1964 (div.); children: Jeannine Marie, Seth Bryan; m. Phyllis Marion Gentry, May 9, 1981 (div.); 1 child, Nicholas Rossi; m. Karen Elizabeth Sanders, Jan. 23, 1996. BSEd, Slippery Rock State Coll., 1967; MEd, U. Pitts., 1970; PhD, Ohio State U., 1978. Dir. Youth Devel. Ctr. of Pa., New Castle, 1967-70; state cons. S.D. Dept. Pub. Inst., Pierre, S.D., 1970-73; coord. Balt. City Pub. Schs., 1973-76; exec. dir. Ctr. for Spl. Needs Population, Columbus, Ohio, 1979—; assoc. prof. Ohio State U., 1988—, charter faculty Primary Care Inst., 2000—; adj. faculty Saybrook Grad. Sch., San Francisco, 2000—. Charter faculty Ohio Primary Care Inst., 2000—; vis. lectr. Melbourne (Australia) State Coll., 1978-79; adj. faculty Johns Hopkins U., Balt., 1974-76, Saybrook Grad. Sch., San Francisco, 2000—; blue ribbon task force, Chgo. City Pub. Schs., 1985; sr. ptnr. The Compact. Author Teaching Mainstreamed Students, 1982, 2d edit., 1988, Strategic Teaching, 1991; contbr. articles to profl. jours.; editor The Directive Teacher jour., 1976-84; author/designer instructional materials in math. problem solving, 1992. Founder Young Scientists Club, Westerville, Ohio, 1990-92; rsch. fellow Internat. Sys. Inst., 1994-96. Mem.: Internat. Soc. Systems Sci. (v.p. 2002—), Coun. for Exceptional Children, Am. Assn. for Artificial Intelligence, Soc. for Gen. Systems Rsch. Democrat. Unitarian-Universalist. Avocations: poetry, travel, fly fishing. Office: Ctr Spl Needs Populations 700 Ackerman Rd Ste 440 Columbus OH 43202-1559 E-mail: magliocca.1@osu.edu.

MAGLIOCCO, PETER ANTHONY, editor, writer; b. Glendale, Calif., Oct. 26, 1948; s. George Peter and Viola Julia (Pazzelli) M. BA in Fine Arts, Calif. State U., Northridge, 1975. Artist, Northridge, Calif., 1975-82; editor, writer Limited Editions Press, 1982-85, Las Vegas, 1985—. Author: Among a Godly Few, 1982, Poetica Rex., 1994, In a Land of Techno-Rave, 1994, Non-Parables, 1996, Kiss of Space, 1997, The Anomalies: (Hardly Working in Sin City), 1998, The Movie President (& Other Poems), 1999, Veteran's Day at Midnight, 2000; editor Art: Mag, 1984—. With U.S. Army, 1967-70. Hon. mem. Internat. Biog. Ctr. (mem. adv. coun. 1999-2001). Avocations: art, reading, music, sports. Office: Limited Editions Press PO Box 70896 Las Vegas NV 89170-0896 E-mail: magman1@mindspring.com.

MAGLIOCHETTI, JOSEPH M. automotive executive; BA, U. Ill. With Victor Mfg. Co. subs. Dana Corp., Chgo., 1967-78; gen. mgr. spicer clutch divsn. Dana Corp., Toledo, 1978-80, pres. London, 1980-85, group v.p. N.Am. ops. Toledo, 1985-90, pres. automotive N.Am. ops., 1990-92, pres. N.Am. ops., 1992-96, pres., 1996-97, pres., COO, 1997-99, pres., CEO & chmn., 1999—. Office: Dana Corp PO Box 1000 Toledo OH 43697-1000*

MAGLIONE, LILI, fine artist, art consultant; b. Manhasset, N.Y., Jan. 30, 1929; d. Angelo and Mary (Marciano) M.; m. Bernhart H. Rumphorst, June 1, 1957; children: Catherine, Douglas. AD, Traphagen Sch., N.Y.C., 1950; student, Art Students League, N.Y.C., 1950-52. Fashion artist Butterick Pattern Co., N.Y.C., 1952-53; fashion art cons. Miss. America Inc., 1953-54; dept. head fashion art office Simplicity Pattern Co., 1953-58, fashion art cons., 1958-62; art dept. cons. Nassau County Mus., Roslyn, N.Y., 1984-86; dir. decorative affairs Harbor Acres Assn., Port Washington, 1987-89, Sands Point (N.Y.) Mus., 1989-91; art cons. Horst Design Assocs., Huntington, N.Y., 1992—. One-woman shows include Palm Gallery, Southampton, N.Y., 1980, Art Internat., Chgo., 1985, Isis Gallery, Port Washington, 1987, Gallery 84, N.Y.C., 1989, 1991, 1993; artist (one-woman retrospective shows include) Harkness Gallery, 1978, James Hunt Barker Gallery , 1984, Sands Point Mus., 1988, Fairfield U., 1995;exhibitions include Nat. Arts Club, N.Y.C., 1997; contbr. poetry Nat. Libr. Poets, Artists Mag., Am. Artist Mag., Internat. Artist Mag. (Master Painter of the World). Hon. trustee Parents TV Coun., 2000—. Recipient Winner Art Expo 98, B.J. Spoke Gallery, N.Y.C., 1998, Manhattan Arts Internat. Critics Choice award, 1998, Artists Mag. Ann. Competition finalist, 2001, Best in Show award ann. exhibit, Pen and Brush Club, N.Y.C., 2001, Liquetex Purchase award, 1998, Amsterdam award of excellence, 1998, award for acrylic painting, Nat. Arts Club, N.Y.C., 1998, Art Calendar Centerfold award, 1998, award of merit, Allied Artists of Am., 1999, cert. of merit, Art Calendar mag., 1999, Award of Excellence, Manhattan Arts Internat., 2000, award, Nat. Assn. Women Artists, 2000. Mem.: Nat. Soc. Painters in Acrylic and Casein (Meml. award 2001, best in show award Pen and Brush 2001, finalist Artists Mag. ann. competition 2001), Portrait Soc. Am. Inc., Internat. Soc. Poets, Nat. Mus. Women in the Arts, Nat. Assn. Women Artists (Meml. award 2001, Salmagundi Meml. award 2001). Roman Catholic. Avocations: horticulture, flower arrangement, nutrition, music, child care. Home: 7 Harmony Rd Huntington NY 11743-2315 E-mail: maglione@optonline.net.

MAGNABOSCO, LOUIS MARIO, chemical engineer, researcher, consultant; b. Glarus, Switzerland, Nov. 29, 1938; s. Josef and Maria (Schlittler) M.; m. Vreni S. Zentner, Mar. 18, 1966 (div. Sept. 1985); 1 child, Henry Louis; m. D'Ella P. Phelon, Apr. 25, 1990; 1 child, Deon M. BSChemE, Swiss Fed. Inst. Tech., Zurich, 1961, MSChemE, 1963, ScD, 1967. Sr. scientist FMC Corp.,

Santa Clara, Calif., 1967-68; from engr. to project engr. Shell Devel. Co., Emeryville, 1968-72, sr. engr. Houston, 1972-74, staff engr., 1974-76; processing specialist ARCO, Harvey, Ill., 1976-79, mgr. process devel., 1979-85; cons. Magna Assocs., Olympia Fields, Ill., 1985-87; mgr. processes and catalysis Enimont, Zurich, 1987-90; pres. Chem. Enging. Ptnrs., Newport Beach, Calif., 1990-93; v.p. R&D Intercat, Sea Girt, N.J., 1993-94; cons. Magna Assocs., 1994—. Cons. to maj. corps. Contbr. articles to internat. profl. jours.; conducted seminars and gave lectures on hydroprocessing internationally in petroleum field. Mem. AIChE, AAAS, Am. Chem. Soc. Catalysis Club. Achievements include: invention and development of Fluid Catalytic Cracking Sulfur Oxide Reduction Tech. (DESOX and NOSOX technologies); developer of math. models for: hydrotreating, hydrocracking, other petroleum processes, recycling tech. used motor oils, semi-synthetic lube oil process (H-H process). Avocations: reading, tennis, travels. E-mail: LouisMag@aol.com.

MAGNABOSCO-BOWER, JENNIFER LYNN, mental health professional; b. Champaign-Urbana, Ill., Aug. 14, 1963; d. Peter Thomas and Gail Gwendolyn Magnabosco; m. Anthony G. Bower, July 12, 1997. BA, MA, U. Chgo., 1985; MPhil, Columbia U., 1995, PhD, 2001. Staff therapist Postgrad. Ctr. for Mental Health, N.Y.C., 1988-90; rsch. assoc. Grad. Sch. Bus. Decision Rsch. Lab., U. Chgo., 1986, 1993—94, Ctr. for Psychiat. Rehab., U. Chgo., 1994; adminstr., rsch. assoc. Ctr. for the Study of Social Work Practice, N.Y.C., 1991-92, project mgr., 1995-96, dir. adminstrn. and ops., 1994-97; mental health cons. Wayne, Pa., Redwood City and L.A., Calif., 1998—2001; assoc. policy rschr. RAND, Santa Monica. Ad hoc tech. rev. com. Dept. of Health and Human Svcs., Substance Abuse and Mental Health Svcs. Adminstrn., Ctr. for Mental Health Svcs., Rockville, 1997-99. Author, co-editor: Outcomes Measurement in the Human Services: Cross Cutting Issues and Methods (NASW Press Best Seller 1997-98); co-author: Cultural Contingencies: Behavior Analytic Perspectives, 1997. Mem. AAAS, Am. Psychol. Assn., Am. Pub. Health Assn., U. Chgo. Alumni Assn. (bd. govs., v.p., Young Alumni Citation 1997, Vol. Leadership All Univ. award). Democrat. Avocations: tennis, piano playing, doll and fan collecting, fundraising, history ancient civilizations. Home: 1107 Princeton St TH #103 Santa Monica CA 90403 Office: PO Box 2138 Santa Monica CA 90407-2138

MAGNANI, RICHARD ANTHONY, music educator; b. Framingham, Mass., Dec. 6, 1955; s. Louis John Magnani, Angie Franchi; m. Diane Carol Miller, Sept. 5, 1994; 1 child Julia Jeanne. BA in Music Edn., Berklee Coll. Music, Boston, 1978; MA, SUNY-Stony Brook. Cert. Music educator N.Y. Saxophonist Smokin Joe Frazier Revue, Phila., 1978—82; mgr. health club Nautilus of Ashland, Ashland, Mass., 1982—91; dir. band and orch. Meadow Sch., Baldwin, NY, 1991—. Mem.: PTA (life), Nassau Music Educators Assn., N.Y. State Sch. Music Assn., Music Educators Nat. Conf. Democrat. Roman Catholic. Avocations: hockey, physical fitness. Home: 145 Lorraine Cir West Sayville NY 11796 Office: Meadow School 880 Jackson St Baldwin NY 11510

MAGNANO, SALVATORE PAUL, retired financial executive, treasurer; b. Portland, Conn., Jan. 10, 1934; s. Salvatore and Lucy (Dimodica) M.; m. Lois Jewel Johnson, July 16, 1955; children: Paul C., Mark J., Peter E. B.Metall. Enging., Rensselaer Poly. Inst., Troy, N.Y., 1955; MBA, Northwestern U., Chgo., 1959. Div. controller Sanders Assocs., Inc., Nashua, N.H., 1962-73; v.p., controller Teledyne Mec, Palo Alto, Calif., 1973-75; div. controller Sanders Assocs., Inc., Nashua, 1975-79, grp. controller, 1979-81, grp. v.p., controller, 1981-86, v.p. fin. and treas., 1986-96; ind. fin. and adminstrv. cons., 1996—. Pres. Boys and Girls Club of Greater Nashua, 1988-89, bd. dirs., 1981—; bd. dirs. Boys and Girls Club of Greater Nashua Charitable Found., 1991—; trustee Daniel Webster Coll., Nashua, 1993—, Congl. Ch. of Hollis, 2002-. Lt. USN, 1955-57. Mem. Fin. Execs. Inst., Beta Gamma Sigma (award for excellence 1959).

MAGNEE, TOM, federal agency administrator; Various tech., mgmt. and exec. positions NASA, dir. program planning and devel. Office Earth Sci., 2000—. Office: NASA Hdqrs Mail Code Y 300 E St SW Washington DC 20546

MAGNER, JEROME ALLEN, entertainment company executive; b. Bklyn., Mar. 14, 1929; s. Herman and Evelyn I. (Wolfe) M.; m. Frances Ogens, Mar. 22, 1953; children: Merrill, Steven. BBA cum laude, CCNY, 1951. Asst. to treas., chief acct. Grayson-Robinson Stores, Inc., S. Klein Dept. Stores, Inc., N.Y.C., 1951-59; contr. Food Fair Properties, 1959-61; v.p., contr. Am. Leisure Products Corp., N.Y.C. and Providence, 1961-69; sr. v.p. fin., treas., CFO, Nat. Amusements Inc., NE Theatre Corp., Dedham, Mass., 1969—. Mem. Nat. Assn. Theatre Owners (bd. dirs.), CCNY Alumni Assn. Office: Nat Amusements Inc 200 Elm St Dedham MA 02026-4536 E-mail: JMagner@nationalamusements.com.

MAGNER, MARTHA MARY, education educator, consultant; b. Yonkers, N.Y., June 5, 1932; d. John Joseph and Lena (Doyle) Hunt; m. Thomas Kevin Magner, Oct. 2, 1954; children: Lee Ann, Myra, Megan, John. BS in Acctg., Fordham U., 1953, MS in Reading, 1978, PhD in Curriculum and Tchg., 1991. Cert. elementary and secondary tchr., N.Y. Pub. acct. Arthur Young & Co., N.Y.S., 1953-56; kindergarten tchr. Nanuet (N.Y.) Pubs. Schs., 1970-75, tchr. 3d grade, 1975-78, reading specialist, 1978—, district testing coord., 1986—. Pvt. practice acct., N.Y.C., 1953—; adj. prof. grad. edn. Coll. Mt. St. Vincent, Riverdale, N.Y., 1995—, Fordham U., N.Y.C. Vol., treas. West Nyack (N.Y.) Swim Club, 1970-83; vol., scorer Ramapo (N.Y.) football and basketball, 1968-72. Mem. ASCD (assoc.), Nat. Middle Sch. Assn., Nat. Coun. Tchrs. English (chair jr. high/middle sch. assembly), Internat. Reading Assn. (adolescent literacy commn.), N.Y. State Middle Sch. Assn., N.Y. State Reading Assn., N.Y. State English Assn., Phi Delta Kappa, Nanuet PTA (life), Delta Kappa Gamma. Republican. Roman Catholic. Avocations: travel, family, reading. Home: 44 Forest Ridge Rd Nyack NY 10960-1754 Office: A MacArthur Barr Middle Sch 143 Church St Nanuet NY 10954-3030

MAGNES, HARRY ALAN, physician; b. Orange, N.J., Dec. 3, 1948; s. Sam and Shirley (Daniels) M.; m. Patricia Bruce, Mar. 25, 1989; 1 child, Carlos Fontiveros. AB in Biology magna cum laude, Brown U., 1970; MD, Yale U., 1974; M in Med. Mgmt., Tulane U., 1998; cert. in med. mgmt., Am. Coll. Physician Execs., 1997. Diplomate Am. Bd. Internal Medicine, Am. Bd. Med. Mgmt. Intern, resident internal medicine U. Iowa Hosps. and Clinics, 1974-77; ptnr., med. dir., pres., CEO Gallatin Med. Clinic, Downey, Calif., 1977-2001; pres., CEO Gallatin Med. Corp., 1992-94; med. dir., bd. dirs. Gallatin Med. Found., 1993-2001; chief med. officer Gallatin Med. Group, 2000-2001, Physician Assocs of Greater San Gabriel Valley, Pasadena, Calif., 2001—. Staff physician Downey Cmty. Hosp., 1977—96, Presbyn. Intercmty. Hosp., 1992—2001; clin. instr. Rancho Los Amigos Hosp., Downey, 1981—83; chairperson bd. dirs. Primehealth of So. Calif., 1997—99; bd. dirs. Calif. Health Network, sec.-treas., 1998—99; project adv. bd. VA/UCLA/RAND Calif. Med. Group, IPA Governance Project, 1997—98. Author: Rheumatic Fever in Connecticut, 1974. James Manning scholar Brown U., 1968. Mem.: Med. Group Mgmt. Assn., Am. Med. Group Assn. (policy com. 1994—98, legis. com. 1997—2000), Calif. Assn. Physician Orgns., Healthcare Assn. So. Calif. (chmn. med. dirs. forum 1997—98), Am. Coll. Physician Execs., Delta Omega, Sigma Xi, Phi Beta Kappa. Avocation: racquetball. Office: Physician Assocs 199 S Los Robles Ave Ste 300 Pasadena CA 91101

MAGNESS, NAN JEAN, social services administrator; b. Austin, Tex., May 12, 1953; d. Kenneth W. and Shirley J. (Bowen) Frazier; m. Randal E. Magness, Aug. 12, 1971; children: Dana, Megan. BS, La. State U., Shreveport, 1976; MA, La. Tech. U., 1979. Cert. vocational rehab. counselor La., 2001. Asst. trainer Southwestern Electric Power Co., Shreveport, 1979-80; adminstrv. asst. Magness Electric, 1980-87; with Caddo Parish Schs., 1989-91; exec. dir. Ark.-La.-Tex. Crisis Ctr., Shreveport, Bossier, 1992—, Ark-La-Tex Crisis Pregnancy Ctr., Shreveport, Bossier, 1992—; counselor vocat. rehab. State of La., 2001—. Adj. instr. Bossier C.C., 1987-88. Judge Mrs. Louisiana Contest, 1998, Mrs. Mississippi Contest, 1998; mem. adv. bd. Bethesda Med. Clinic, 1998. Fellow Plantation Club. Avocations: walking, movies, redecorating, water sports. Office: Ark-La-Tex Crisis Pregnancy Ctr 4048 Youree Dr Shreveport LA 71105-2936

MAGNESS, RHONDA ANN, microbiologist; b. Stockton, Calif., Jan. 30, 1946; d. John Pershing and Dorothy Waneta (Kelley) Wetter; m. Barney LeRoy Bender, Aug. 26, 1965 (div. Jan. 1977); m. Gary D. Magness, Mar. 5, 1977; children: Jay D.(dec.) , Troy D. BS, Calif. State U., 1977. Lic. clin. lab. scientist Nat. Cert. Agy., Calif., cert. med. technologist, clin. lab. scientist. Med. asst. C. Fred Wilcox, MD, Stockton, 1965-66; clk. typist Dept. of U.S. Army, Ft. Eustis, Va., 1967, Def. Supply Agy., New Orleans, 1967-68; med. asst. James G. Cross, MD, Lodi, Calif., 1969, Arthur A. Kemalyan, MD, Lodi, 1969-71, 72-77; med. sec. Lodi Meml. Hosp., 1972; lab. aide Calif. State U., Sacramento, 1977; phlebotomist St. Joseph's Hosp., Stockton, 1978-79; supr. microbiology Dameron Hosp. Assn., 1980—. Active Concerned Women Am., Washington, 1987—. Mem.: San Joaquin County Med. Assts. Assn., Calif. Assn. Clin. Lab. Technologists, San Francisco Offshore, Nat. Geog. Soc., Nat. Audubon Soc., Jobs. Daus. (chaplain 1962—63). Baptist. Avocations: boating, birdwatching, sewing, reading. Home: 9627 Knight Ln Stockton CA 95209-1961 Office: Dameron Hosp Lab 525 W Acacia St Stockton CA 95203-2405 E-mail: gnrmagness@aol.com.

MAGNO, GIL D. music educator; b. Funchal, Madeira Island, Portugal, June 14, 1934; s. Americo J. and Maria Franca DeJesus; life ptnr. Terezinha D. Dos Santos; children: Derek DeJesus , Lygeia DeJesus, Nydia DeJesus, Elyssia DeJesus. BA in Music Edn., Boston Conservatory of Music, 1959. Bassoonist Birmingham Symphony, Ala., 1959—62; band dir. Warrior H.S. Band, Warrior, 1959—61; classical guitar instr. U. Ala. Student Union, Tuscaloosa, 1961—62, New Eng. Conservatory of Music Prep Dept., Boston, 1964—65; vocal coach Magnoart Studio and Pubs., Coconut Grove, Fla., 1967—, personal devel. cons., author, 1985—. Author: (Book) Developing Confidence & Personal Magnetism, 2000, (Video) Magno Vocal Course #1, 2000; composer: (CD) A Tapestry of Love, 1998; author: (Cassette Book) Magno Vocal Technique, 2001, (Book) The Secret, 1999, (Cassettes) Personal Magnetism - Creating a Successful Life in a Confused World, 2001; editor: (Book) How to Find Your Purpose in Life, 1986; author: How to Attract Your Love-Life-Partner, 1987; LP Album. With USAR, 1954—62, Boston. Mem.: ASCAP, Music Tchr. Nat. Assn., Fla. Music Tchrs. Assn. Libertarian. Avocation: gardening. Personal E-mail: Gmagno5@cs.com. Business E-Mail: Gmagno5@cs.com.

MAGNUS, SANDRA H, astronaut; b. Belleville, Ill., Oct. 30, 1964; BS in Physics, U. Mo., Rolla, 1986, MS in Elec. Enging., 1990; PhD, Ga. Inst. Tech., 1996. Stealth engr. McDonnell Douglas Aircraft, 1986—91; fellow Inst. Tech. Ga., 1991—96; astronaut NASA Johnson Space Ctr., Houston, 1996—. Avocations: reading, soccer, travel, water-skiing. Office: Astronaut Office Johnson Space Ctr Houston TX 77058

MAGNUSON, DENNIS DUANE, secondary education educator; b. Dickinson, N.D., Oct. 21, 1946; s. Clarence Severin and Edith Rosella (Wick) M.; m. Susan Lee Urban, June 15, 1969; children: Jerry Paul, Douglas Duane. BA, Black Hills State U., 1968, BS, 1970; MEd, U. Wyo., 1990. Tchr. Harding County Sch. Dist., Buffalo, 1968-72, Sweetwater Sch. Dist. # 1, Rock Springs, Wyo., 1973—. Mem. NEA, Sweetwater Edn. Assn., Wyo. Edn. Assn. (chmn. polit. action com. 1984-87, chmn. resolutions 1985-87). Democrat. Lutheran. Office: East Jr High Sch PO Box 1089 Rock Springs WY 82902-1089

MAGNUSON, JON ALLAN, research engineer; b. Albert Lea, Minn., Dec. 10, 1951; s. Erick Joel and Evelyn Arlene (Iams) M.; m. Cheryl Anne Anderson, July 17, 1981. BS in Physics, Idaho State U., 1979; PhD in Physics, Dartmouth Coll., 1985, M Enging., 1986. Journeyman carpenter Mitchell Constrn. Co., Pocatello, Idaho, 1970-75; health physicist Idaho Nat. Engring. Lab., summer 1978; tchrs. asst., rsch. asst. Dartmouth Coll., Hanover, N.H., 1980-86; assoc. fellow Nichols Rsch. Corp., Newport Beach, Calif., 1986—. Editor interface control document various cos., El Segundo, Calif., 1992—; cons. IR surveillance sys. L.A. AFB/Space Divsn., El Segundo, 1986—. Dartmouth fellow, Hanover, 1980-86. Mem. IEEE, Am. Def. Preparedness Assn., Internat. Soc. Optical Engrs., Mensa. Lutheran. Avocations: computer programming, amateur geologist, eco-tourist. Office: Nichols Rsch Corp 3919 Westerly Pl Newport Beach CA 92660-2308

MAGNUSON, NANCY, librarian; b. Seattle, Aug. 15, 1944; d. James Leslie and Jeanette (Thomas) M.; 2 sons, Daniel Johnson, Erik Johnson. BA in History, 1977; MLS, U. Wash., 1978. With. King County Libr. System, Seattle, 1973-80; rsch. asst. Free Libr. Phila., 1980-81; asst. libr. Haverford (Pa.) Coll., 1981-87; libr. dir. Goucher Coll., Balt., 1987—. Contbr. to profl. publs. Mem. ALA (com. on status of women in librarianship, various others), Online Computer Libr. Ctr. Users Coun., Md. Libr. Assn., Congress Acad. Libr. Dirs., NOW, Women's Internat. League for Peace and Freedom, Balt. Bibliophiles, Jane Austen Soc. N.Am. Democrat. Office: Goucher Coll Julia Rogers Libr 1021 Dulaney Valley Rd Baltimore MD 21204-2753

MAGNUSON, PAUL ARTHUR, federal judge; b. Carthage, S.D., Feb. 9, 1937; s. Arthur and Emma Elleda (Paulson) Magnuson; m. Sharon Schultz Magnuson, Dec. 21, 1959; children: Marlene Peterson, Margaret(dec.) , Kevin, Kara Berger. BA, Gustavus Adolphus Coll, 1959; JD, William Mitchell Coll., 1963; DLL (hon.), Wm. Mitchell Coll., 1991. Bar: Minn. 1963, U.S. Dist. Ct. Minn. 1968. Asst. registrar William Mitchell Coll. of Law, 1959-60; claim adjuster Agrl. Ins. Co., 1960-62; clk. Bertie & Bettenberg, 1962-63; ptnr. LeVander, Gillen, Miller & Magnuson, South St. Paul, Minn., 1963-81; judge U.S. Dist. Ct. Minn., St. Paul, 1981—, chief judge, 1994—2001. Jurist-in-residence Hamline U., 1985, Augsberg Coll., 1986, Bethel Coll., 1986, Concordia Coll., St. Paul, 1987, U. Minn., Morris, 1987; instr. William Mitchell Coll. Law, 1984-92, Corcordia Coll., Moorhead, 1988, St. John's U., 1988, Coll. of St. Benedict, 1988; mem. judicial conf. com. on adminstrn. of Bankruptcy System, 1987-96, chmn. 1993-96; mem. judicial conf. com. on Internat. Judicial Rels., 1996—, chair, 1999—; mem. com. on dist. judges edn. Fed. Judicial Ctr., 1998—. Mem. Met. Health Bd., St. Paul, 1970-72; legal counsel Ind. Republican Party Minn., St. Paul, 1979-81 Recipient Disting. Alumnus award Gustavus Adolphus Coll., 1982, First Disting. Svc. award William Mitchell Coll. Law, 1999. Mem. Minn. State Bar Assn., 1st Dist. Bar Assn. (pres. 1974-75), Dakota County Bar Assn., Am. Judicature Soc., Fed. Judges Assn. (bd. dirs. 1993—, treas. 1997-2001, v.p. 2001—). E-mail: PAMagnuson@mnd.uscourts.gov.

MAGNUSON, ROBERT MARTIN, retired hospital administrator; b. Chgo., June 28, 1927; s. Martin David and Adena Marie (Hallberg) M.; m. Patricia Ann McNaughton, Dec. 30, 1960; children: Thomas Martin, Dana Caroline. BS cum laude, Lake Forest (Ill.) Coll., 1951; MBA, Harvard U., 1955. Factory budget mgr., asst. budget dir. Zenith Radio Corp., Chgo., 1955-57; asst. adminstr., controller Elmhurst Meml. Hosp., (Ill.), 1957-64, asso. adminstr., 1964-66, pres., 1966-92. Officer, dir. Chgo. Hosp. Council, 1972-79, chmn. bd. dirs., 1983; mem. hosp. adv. council Ill. Dept. Pub. Health, 1972-76; faculty preceptor U. Chgo. Program in Hosp. Adminstrn., 1971-92, Northwestern U. Program in Hosp. and Health Sci. Adminstrn., 1972-92; dir. DuPage County Community Nursing Service, 1964-67, Health Chgo. HMO, 1984-92, Elmhurst Fed. Savs. & Loan Assn., 1971-92; pres. Meml. Health Services, Inc., 1980-92. Pres. Elmhurst Meml. Hosp. Found., 1980-92. Served with USN, 1945-48, 51-52. Mem. Am. Coll. Health Care Execs., Ill. Hosp. Assn. (dist. pres. 1967-69, bd. dirs. 1985-90), Inter-Hosp. Planning Assn. of Western Suburbs (pres., dir.) Clubs: Medinah (Ill.) Country. Republican.

MAGNUSON, ROGER JAMES, lawyer; b. St. Paul, Jan. 25, 1945; s. Roy Gustaf and Ruth Lily (Edlund) M.; m. Elizabeth Cunningham Shaw, Sept. 11, 1982; children: James Roger, Peter Cunningham, Mary Kerstin, Sarah Ruth, Elizabeth Camilla, Anna Clara, John Edlund, Britta Kristina. BA, Stanford U., 1967; JD, Harvard U., 1971; BCL, Oxford U., 1972. Bar: Minn. 1973, U.S. Dist. Ct. Minn. 1973, U.S Ct. Appeals (8th, 9th, 10th cirs.) 1974, U.S. Supreme Ct. 1978. Chief pub. defender Hennepin County Pub. Defender's Office, Mpls., 1973; ptnr. Dorsey & Whitney, 1972—. Dean Oak Brook Coll. of Law and Govt. Policy, 1995—; chancellor Magdalen Coll., 1999—. Author: Shareholder Litigation, 1981, Are Gay Rights Right, The White-Collar Crime Explosion, 1992, Informed Answers to Gay Rights Questions, 1994; contbr. articles to profl. jours. Elder, Straitgate Ch., Mpls., 1980—. Mem. Christian Legal Soc., The Am. Soc. Writers of Legal Subjects, Mpls. Club, White Bear Yacht Club. Republican. Home: 625 Park Ave Saint Paul MN 55115-1663 Office: Dorsey & Whitney LLP 50 S 6th St Ste 1500 Minneapolis MN 55402-1498 Business E-Mail: magnuson.roger@dorseylaw.com.

MAGNUSON, ROY WILLIAM, secondary school educator; b. St. Paul, July 30, 1954; s. Osgood Teofil and Ethel Sylvia Magnuson; m. Mary Patricia Drew, July 15, 1989. BA in History, Augsburg Coll., 1991. Cert. tchr. social studies, grades 7-12. Dir. Langford Park recreation ctr. St. Paul Pks. and Recreation, 1974-78; youth worker Wilder Found., St. Paul, 1985-91; ednl. asst. St. Paul Pub. Schs., 1980-85, coach football, wrestling, track Como Sr. H.S., 1979—, tchr. U.S., African Am., Asian Am. history Como. Sr. H.S., 1992—. Mem. exec. bd. St. Paul Trades and Labor Assembly, 1997—, Progressive Minn., 2000—. Mem. St. Paul Fedn. Tchrs. (chair COPE com. 1996—, mem. exec. bd. 1996—). Democrat. Avocations: reading, golf, horseshoes, travel. Home: 727 Wheelock Pkwy W Saint Paul MN 55117-4110 Office: Como Pk Sr HS 740 Rose Ave W Saint Paul MN 55117-4042 E-mail: roymagnuson@spps.org.

MAGNUSON, VALERIE, poet, artist, export consultant; b. Detroit, Feb. 14, 1957; BA, Wayne State U., 1978; MS in Bus. Adminstrn., Ctrl. Mich. U., 1992. Internat. dir. H O Trerice Co., Oak Park, Mich., 1984—2000. Bi-lateral trade team Can. mem. State Mich.-Office of Gov., Lansing, 1992—. Author: Destiny, 2000, In the Midst, 2002; co-author: Five Gates of Poetry, 2001, Baloney, 2002, author numerous poems;exhibitions include Royal Ont. Mus. Exhbn., 1985, Corning Mus. Glass, 1986. Pres. Royal Oak Arts Coun., 1983—85, Madison Heights Art Assn., 1993—95; active Stained Glass Assn. Am., St. Louis, 1985—98. Mem.: Sigma Iota Epsilon. Home: 830 Holly Bush Dr Holly MI 48442 Personal E-mail: valmag@hotmail.com.

MAGNUSSEN, CARL RICHARD, medical educator; b. Balt., Sept. 11, 1944; s. Carl Christian and Lucille Beatrice (Stratton) M.; m. Ellen Jean Furney, Sept. 22, 1973; children: Eric Joseph, Ann Elizabeth. AB, Northwestern U., Evanston, Ill., 1967; MD, Johns Hopkins U., 1971. Asst. prof. medicine Sch. Medicine, U. Rochester, N.Y., 1977-83, assoc. prof., 1983—; head infectious diseases unit St. Mary's Hosp., Rochester, 1977-96, chmn. medicine, 1996-2000; assoc. med. dir. Highland Hosp., N.Y., 2000—. Fellow Am. Coll. Physicians, Infectious Diseases Soc. Am.; mem. Soc. Hosp. Epidemiologist Am. Office: Highland Hosp 1000 South Ave Rochester NY 14620-2782

MAGNUSSON, M(ARYLIN) SUE SHIREY, real estate executive; b. Ft. Wayne, Ind., Nov. 24, 1934; d. Charles Dwight and Gertrude Lavon (Fletcher) Shirey; m. Robert Alfred Magnusson, Aug. 25, 1956 (div. 1978); children: Maryrose Lavon Magnusson, Norman Alfred II. BA, U. Ill., 1956. Med. asst. Dr. Anson Perina, Ophthalmologist, Morristown, N.J., 1964-70; real estate agt. Coutts Realtors, 1968-70, Comey & Shepherd Realtors, Cin., 1971-77, Herron, Hansen & Rebhun Realtors, Cin., 1977-82, Sherman Realtors, Cin., 1982-85; real estate agt., pres., owner Indian Hill Properties Realtors, 1985—. Pres. Am. Field Svc., Cin., 1973-75; pres. Hamilton County Spl. Olympics, Cin., 1976, pres., chmn. bd., 1977; chmn. bd. Samaritan Counseling Ctr., Cin., 1986-88. Republican. Methodist. Avocations: painting, birding, theater, travel, mystery/courtcase novels. Home: PO Box 43269 Cincinnati OH 45243-0269

MAGONI, DESPO, artist; b. Feb. 17, 1943; MFA, Polytechnion of Athens, 1967. One-person shows include Henry-Hicks Gallery, Bklyn., 1976, Nonson Gallery, N.Y.C., 1976, 78, Ora Gallery, Athens, 1978, 81, 83, Kouros GAllery, N.Y.C., 1984, Alternative Mus., N.Y.C., 1986, New Forms Gallery, Athens, 1988, 99, Bklyn. Coll. Art Gallery, 1994, Robeson Gallery, Rutgers U., Newark, 1994, André Zarre Gallery, N.Y.C., 1997, Parsons Sch. of Design, N.Y.C., 1999, John Jay Coll. Art Gallery, N.Y.C., 1999; exhibited in group shows at Kouros Gallery, 1983, Mint Mus., Charlotte, N.C., 1989, Mitchell Mus., Mt. Vernon, Ill., 1989, Haggerty Mus. Art, Marquette U., Milw., 1990, Pratt Inst. Gallery, N.Y.C., 1990, André Zarre Gallery, 1997, Islip Mus., Oakdale, N.Y., 1997; pub. collections include Vorres Mus., Paiania, Greece, Mus. Modern Art, Guadalajara, Mexico, Mint Mus., Charlotte, N.C., Alternative Mus., N.Y.C., Pratt Inst. Libr., N.Y.C.

MAGOON, DONALD W. retired business educator; b. Big Rapids, Mich., Mar. 1, 1910; s. Elbert Elvin Magoon and Edith Marie Whitsey; widowed, 1994; children: Elbert, Louise Libii, Carol Feakins. BSME, U. Mich., 1932, MS, 1934, MBA, 1941. Grad. gemologist Gemological Inst. Am. Instr. Findlay (Ohio) Coll., 1932-33, asst. prof., 1934-37; rschr. L.A. Examiner, 1938-39; asst. prof. bus. La. State U., Baton Rouge, 1940-41; treas. Meijer Supermkts., Grand Rapids, Mich., 1946-60; cons. U.S. State Dept., Israel, Mex., 1961-64; prof. bus. Ea. Mich. U., Ypsilanti, 1965-80; prof. emeritus, 1980—. Tutor, Canton (Ohio) City Schs., 1996—. Capt., statis. officer, U.S. Army Signal Corps, 1941-46. Mem. Rotary Club Canton (various coms. 1995-2001). Avocation: gemology.

MAGOON, NANCY AMELIA, art association administrator, philanthropist; b. N.Y.C., Apr. 19, 1941; d. Jack and Norma Harriet (Hirschl) Parker; m. Robert Cornelius Magoon, Mar. 16, 1978; children: Adam Glick, Peri Curnin. Student, Cornell U., 1958-59. Gallerist Hokin Gallery, Miami, 1986-89; sec. Nat. Found. Advancement in Arts, 1989-94; nat. coun. mem. Aspen Art Mus., 1985—, Aspen Ballet, 1985—. V.p. Ctr. for Fine Arts, Miami, 1984-94, Miami City Ballet, 1990-94. Bd. dirs. Cmty. Alliance Against AIDS, 1990-92; coun. mem. Susan Komen Breast Cancer, Aspen, 1994—; hon. trustee Ctr. for Fine Arts, Miami Beach, 1996; trustee Site Santa Fe, 1996; mem. nat. coun. Jazz Aspen, 1999—; mem. collectors com. Nat. Gallery, Washington, 2000; bd. dirs. Aspen Cmty. Found., 2000. Named one of Outstanding Women in Miami, 1992; NEA grantee, 1995. Avocations: skiing, golf, fly fishing, skeet and clay target shooting.

MAGOON, PATRICK M. healthcare executive; MS, U. Ill., 1978. Pres., CEO Children's, 1998. Mem. Nat. Assn. of Children Hosp., Ill. Hosp. Assn., Met. Chgo. Healthcare Coun. (bd. dirs.), Comml. Club, Econ. Club, Exec. Club, City Club Chgo. Office: 2300 N Childrens Plz Chicago IL 60614-3363

MAGOR, LOUIS ROLAND, conductor; b. Auburn, Nebr., May 16, 1945; s. John William and Eleanor Lucille (Niemann) M. B.Mus. Edn., Northwestern U., 1967, Mus.M., 1974. Choral dir. Avoca Jr. High Sch., Wilmette, Ill., 1968-70; choral dir. Niles North High Sch., Skokie, 1970-73; dir. San Francisco Symphony Chorus, 1974-82, Schola Cantorum, 1982-85, San Francisco Boys Chorus, 1985-88; artistic dir. Seattle Bach Choir, 1990—2001. Founder The Louis Magor Singers; mem. faculty San Francisco Conservatory of Music, 1976-78, San Francisco State U., 1979-80 Founder West Seattle Children's Chorus, 1990—; condr. Sing-It-Yourself Messiah, 1979-91, Calif. Symphony Chorus, 1990-92; exec. prodr. Sandy Bradley's Potluck, 1995-96; co-founder, mng. dir. Hokum Hall, 1993—. Mem. Pi Kappa Lambda. E-mail: louis@magor.com.

MAGORIAN, JAMES, writer, poet; b. Palisade, Nebr., Apr. 24, 1942; s. Jack and Dorothy (Gorthey) M. BS, U. Nebr., 1965; MS, Ill. State U., 1969; postgrad., Oxford U., 1972, Harvard U., 1973. Author children's books: School Daze, 1978, 17%, 1978, The Magic Pretzel, 1979, Ketchup Bottles, 1979, Imaginary Radishes, 1980, Plucked Chickens, 1980, Fimperings and Torples, 1981, The Witches' Olympics, 1983, At the City Limits, 1987, The Beautiful Music, 1988, Magic Spell #207, 1988; author numerous books of poetry, including: Ideas for a Bridal Shower, 1980, The Edge of the Forest, 1980, Spiritual Rodeo, 1980, Tap Dancing on a Tight Rope, 1981, Training at Home to Be A Locksmith, 1981, The Emily Dickinson Jogging Book, 1984, Keeper of Fire, 1984, Weighing the Sun's Light, 1985, Summer Snow, 1985, The Magician's Handbook, 1986, Squall Line, 1986, The Hideout of the Sigmund Freud Gang, 1987, Haymarket Square, 1998, Dragon Bones, 1999, Millennial Journal, 2000, (novels) America First, 1992, Hearts of Gold, 1996; contbr. poems and stories to numerous publs. Home and Office: 1225 N 46th St Lincoln NE 68503-2308

MAGOWAN, PETER ALDEN, professional baseball team executive, grocery chain executive; b. N.Y.C., Apr. 5, 1942; s. Robert Anderson and Doris (Merrill) M.; m. Jill Tarlau (div. July 1982); children: Kimberley, Margot, Hilary; m. Deborah Johnston, Aug. 14, 1982 BA, Stanford U., 1964; MA, Oxford U., Eng., 1966; postgrad., Johns Hopkins U., 1967-68. Store mgr. Safeway Stores Inc., Washington, 1968-70, dist. mgr. Houston, 1970-71, retail ops. mgr. Phoenix, 1971-72, divsn. mgr. Tulsa, 1973-76, mgr. internat. divsn. Toronto, Ont., Can., 1976-78, mgr. western region San Francisco, 1978-79, CEO Oakland, Calif., 1980-93, chmn. bd. dirs., 1980-98; pres., mng. gen. ptnr. San Francisco Giants, 1993—. Bd. dirs. Daimler Chrysler Corp., Caterpillar, Safeway Inc. Office: San Francisco Giants 24 Willie Mays Plz San Francisco CA 94107-2199

MAGOWAN, ROBIN, writer; b. San Francisco, Sept. 4, 1936; d. Robert A. and Doris Merrill M.; m. Juliet Ily Mattila, Sept. 4, 2001; children: Samantha, Colin. BA, Harvard U., 1955; MA, Columbia, 1960; PhD, Yale U., 1964.

Lectr., asst. prof. U. Wash., Seattle, 1962—65; asst. prof. U. Calif., Berkeley, Calif., 1965—70. Author: Lilac Cigarette in a Wish Cathedral, 1998, Memoirs of a Minotaur, 1999, Improbable Journeys, 2002. Avocations: alpine gardening, birdwatching, cycling. Home: PO Box 511 Salisbury CT 06068-0511

MAGRASS, YALE ROBERT, sociology educator, writer; b. Boston, Jan. 15, 1950; s. Harold B. and Evelyn P. (Sandler) M.; m. Ana M. Matos, Aug. 13, 1989; children: Jose, Miguel, David. BA magna cum laude, Brandeis U., 1971; postgrad., Columbia U., 1971-72; PhD in Sociology, U. Calif., Santa Barbara, 1978. Instr. U. Calif., Santa Barbara, 1975-77, U. Lowell, Mass., 1977-78; prof. U. Mass., North Dartmouth, 1978—. Cons. Profl. as Workers NIMH Grant, Boston, 1982-90; dir. Holocaust Oral History Project, New Bedford, 1980-84. Author: Thus Spake the Moguls, 1982, Power in the Highest Degree, 1990; mem. editl. bd. Humanity and Soc., 1983—, Quar. Jour. of Ideology, 1992—. Del. New Jewish Agenda, Israel, 1983, Cultural Exch. Program, China, 1986, Economist Tour of Eastern Europe, USSR, Hungary, Bulgaria, 1987, North Am. & Cuban Philosophers, Havana, 1995, Congress on Human Co-Existence, 2000. Columbia U. fellow, 1972, U. Calif. fellow, 1973. Mem. Am. Sociol. Assn., Assn. Humanist Sociologists, Radical Philosophers Assn., New Mobilization for Survival, Mass Pirg. Avocations: computers, hiking, video, travel. Office: U Mass North Dartmouth MA 02747

MAGRATH, C. PETER, educational association executive; b. N.Y.C., Apr. 23, 1933; s. Laurence Wilfrid and Giulia Maria (Dentice) M.; m. Deborah C. Howell, 1988; children: Valerie Ruth, Monette Fay. BA summa cum laude, U. N.H., 1955; PhD, Cornell U., 1962. Faculty Brown U., Providence, 1961-68, prof. polit. sci., 1967-68, assoc. dean grad. sch., 1965-66; dean Coll. Arts and Scis. U. Nebr., Lincoln, 1968-69, dean faculties Coll. Arts and Scis., 1969-72, interim chancellor, 1971-72, prof. polit. sci., 1968-72, vice-chancellor for acad. affairs, 1972; pres. SUNY, Binghamton, 1972-74, prof. polit. sci., 1972-74; pres. U. Minn., Mpls., 1974-84, U. Mo. System, 1985-91, Nat. Assn. State Univs. and Land Grant Colls., Washington, 1991—. Bd. dirs. Salzburg Seminar. Author: The Triumph of Character, 1963, Yazoo: Law and Politics in the New Republic, The Case of Fletcher v. Peck, 1966, Constitutionalism and Politics: Conflict and Consensus, 1968, Issues and Perspectives in American Government, 1971; (with others) The American Democracy, 2d edit., 1973; (with Robert L. Egbert) Strengthening Teacher Education, 1987; contbr. articles to profl. jours. Served with AUS, 1955—57. Mem. Assn. Am. Univs. (chmn. 1985-86), Phi Beta Kappa, Phi Kappa Phi, Pi Gamma Mu, Pi Sigma Alpha, Kappa Tau Alpha. Office: Nat Assn State U and Land Grant Colls 1307 New York Ave NW Ste 400 Washington DC 20005-4722 E-mail: cmagrath@nasulgc.org. *True personal success cannot be measured by public acclaim, recognition, or status. It grows out of an ability to recognize right from wrong, and to maintain principles of fairness and understanding in all human relationships - regardless of one's role in life. In my case I have tried to fulfill this ideal; I have been willing to exercise leadership by asserting my judgements and views openly and directly on the educational and human issues that came my way.*

MAGRATH, JANE, music educator; b. Conway, SC, Dec. 27, 1949; MusB, Wesleyan Coll., 1972; MusM, U. N.C., 1974; MusD, Northwestern U., 1982. Prof. U. Okla., Norman, 1981—; author, editor Alfred Publishing, Inc., Van Nuys, Calif., 1985—. Lectr. in field. Author: Pianist's Guide to Standard Literature, 1995; editor (music series) Masterwork Classics, 1988, 89, 92, 2000, Encore, 1990; editl. bd. Piano Forum; Masterpieces with Flair, 1993, Melodious Masterpieces, 1993. Office: Univ Okla Sch Music 500 W Boyd St Norman OK 73019-2070 E-mail: jmagrath@ou.edu.

MAGRAW, RICHARD SHANNON, security consultant; b. St. Paul, Nov. 7, 1951; s. Richard Mueller Magraw and Shirley Edna Shannon; m. Kathy Ann Shollenberger, May 14, 1986. Student, Sidwell Friends Sch., Washington, 1967-69, George Washington U., 1969-71, Columbia U., 1972-73. Security cons. EIR News Svc. Inc., Leesburg, Va., 1979—. Democrat. Office: EIR News Svc Inc 60 Sycolin Rd SE Leesburg VA 20175

MAGRILL, JOE RICHARD, JR. religious organization administrator, minister; b. Marshall, Tex., Aug. 7, 1946; s. Joe Richard and Mary Belle (Chadwick) M. BA summa cum laude, East Tex. State U., 1967; MDiv, Princeton Theol. Sem., 1970, MTh, 1972; MLS, Rutgers U., 1971. Ordained to ministry Cumberland Presbyn. Ch., 1970. Stated supply min. Newsome (Tex.) Cumberland Presbyn. Ch., 1966-67; Christian edn. asst. United Presbyn. Ch., Carlstadt, N.J., 1967-70; order libr. Princeton (N.J.) Theol. Sem., 1969-72; head libr., prof. Memphis Theol. Sem., 1972-79; pastor Brookhaven Cumberland Presbyn. Ch., Nashville, 1987-89; asst. to stated clk. Gen. Assembly Office, Cumberland Presbyn. Ch., Memphis, 1979-83, supr. ctrl. acctg. div., 1980-87, editor The Cumberland Presbyn., 1984-87, chief exec. bd. stewardship, 1989—, mem. Gen. Assembly Coun., 1993—. Mem. Trinity Presbytery of Cumberland Presbyn. Ch., 1970—; sec.-treas. Hist. Found. Cumberland Presbyn. Ch., Memphis, 1974—; bd. dirs. Hist. Found. Presbyn. Ch. U.S., Montreat, N.C., 1980-83. Editor: In the Valley of the Cauca, 1981, One Family Under God, 1982, Family of Faith, 1998. Recipient achievement award Hist. Found. Cumberland Presbyn. Ch., 1980; scholar Phi Alpha Theta, 1967, Am. Theol. Libr. Assn., 1970. Democrat. Avocations: computers, historical research. Office: Cumberland Presbyn Ch 1978 Union Ave Memphis TN 38104-4134 E-mail: jrm@cumberland.org.

MAGRILL, ROSE MARY, library director; b. Marshall, Tex., June 8, 1939; d. Joe Richard and Mary Belle (Chadwick) M. BS, E. Tex. State U., 1960, MA, 1961; MS, U. Ill., 1964, PhD, 1969. Asst. to dean women E. Tex. State U., Commerce, 1960-61, librarian II, 1961-63; teaching asst. U. Ill., Urbana, 1963-64; instr. to asst. prof. E. Tex. State U., Commerce, 1964-67; asst. prof. Ball State U., Muncie, 1969-70; asst. prof. to prof. U. Mich., Ann Arbor, 1970-81; prof. U. N. Tex., Denton, 1981-99; dir. libr. E. Tex. Bapt. U., Marshall, 1987-2001. Accreditation site visitor ALA, Chgo., 1975—; cons. in field. Co-author: Building Library Collections, 4th edit. 1974, Library Technical Services, 1977, Building Library Collections, 5th edit. 1979, Acquisition Management and Collection Development in Libraries, 2d edit. 1989; author: Family of Faith, 1998. Trustee Memphis Theol. Sem., 1988-98; treas. Mission Synod of Cumberland Presbyn. Ch., 1989—; mem. bd. fin. Trinity Presbytery, 1989—; sec.-treas. Harrison County Hist. Commn., 1995—; trustee Hist. Found., 1999—; sec. Nat. Conv. Cumberland Presbyn. Women, 2000—. Recipient award Cumberland Presbyn. History, 1995. Mem. ALA (RTSD Resources Sect. pub. award 1978), Tex. Libr. Assn. Home: 804 Caddo St Marshall TX 75672-2414

MAGRUDER, JAMES HAMPTON, trade association executive; b. Balt., Mar. 3, 1965; s. Alexander Clarke and Marcella (Lawson) M.; m. Lora Ann Dunn, Oct. 19, 1996. BA, Pfeiffer U., 1988; MPA, Va. Tech., 1996. Rsch. asst. ICF Kaiser, Fairfax, Va., 1990-96; electronic data interchange project mgr. Animal Health Inst., Alexandria, 1997-98; Y2K project specialist AAMVA-Net, Inc., Arlington, 1998-99, bus. analyst, 2000—. Mem. Am. Soc. Assn. Execs., Ju Jitsu Am., Soc. Cinn., Sons Colonial Wars. Republican. Avocations: scuba diving, Ju Jitsu, wine collecting, fly fishing. Office: AAMVANet Inc 4301 Wilson Blvd Ste 400 Arlington VA 22203-1867 Fax: (703) 522-1553. E-mail: jmagruder@aamva.org.

MAGRUDER, JAMES RICHARD, writer, translator; b. Washington, Oct. 8, 1960; s. Frederick Elliott Magruder and Carolyn Ann Schroen. BA in French Lit., Cornell U., 1982; MA in French Lit., Yale U., 1984, MFA and DFA in Dramaturgy, 1992. Literary mgr. La Jolla (Calif.) Playhouse, 1990-91; dramaturg Ctr. Stage, Balt., 1991—. Vis. lectr. Yale Sch. Drama, New Haven, 1997—, Johns Hopkins U., Balt., 1999-2000; cons. Nat. Endowment for the Arts, Washington, 1997—. Translator: Three French Comedies, 1996; author (adaptation): The Imaginary Invalid, 1999; author: (play) Bad Beans, 2000; librettist: Broadway musical Triumph of Love, 1997. Recipient John Gassner prize Yale Theater Mag., New Haven, 1987, 88; named Outstanding Literary Translation of the Yr., Am. Literary Translators Assn., 1997, writer-in-residence New Harmony (Ind.) Project, 2000; Jerome fellow Am. Theatre Mag., N.Y.C., 1992. Home: #A-4 3024 N Calvert St Baltimore MD 21218

MAGSIG, JUDITH ANNE, early childhood education educator, retired; b. Saginaw, Mich., Nov. 9, 1939; d. Harold Howard and Catherine Louise (Barstow) Gay; m. George Arthur Magsig, June 22, 1963; children: Amy Catherine, Karl Joseph. BA, Alma Coll., 1961. Cert. tchr., early childhood tchr., Mich. 1st grade tchr. Gaylord (Mich.) Schs., 1961-64, spl. edn. tchr., 1965-67, kindergarten tchr., 1968-99, ret., 1999. Instr. Suzuki violin method; second violinist Traverse (Mich.) Symphony Orch., 1985-92, Cadillac (Mich.) Symphony Orch., 1999—, Gaylord Chamber Orch., 2001—. Mem. ASCD, NEA, Mich. Edn. Assn., Gaylord Edn. Assn. (historian 1997-99), Assn. for the Edn. of Young Children, Assn. for Childhood Edn. Internat., Suzuki Assn. Am., Am. String Tchrs. Assn., Music Tchrs. Nat. Assn., Order Eastern Star (chaplain 1997-98, warder 1999-2000, electa 2000—), Spirits of the North, Alpha Delta Kappa (pres. Beta Rho chpt. 1980-82, 84-86, treas. 1996-2000, music chmn. Mich., v.p. Beta Rho chpt. 2000-01). Methodist. Avocations: cross-stitch, camping, canoeing, sewing. Home: 2130 Evergreen Dr Gaylord MI 49735-9165 Office: Musik Haus 2300 S Otsego Ave Gaylord MI 49735-1869 E-mail: gjmagsig@avci.net.

MAGUIRE, BLANCHE JOAN (MAGGIE MAGUIRE), watercolorist; b. N.Y.C., July 5, 1922; m. Joseph Thomas Maguire; children: Thomas Joseph, Kathleen Julie. BA, U. Tex., El Paso, 1971, postgrad., 1972-73. Cert. art teacher. Chmn. Allied Military Host Family Program, Ft. Bliss, Tex., 1970-73. Named Woman Yr. El Paso Herald Post, 1971; recipient honor Allied Military Host Family Program Post Gen., 1970-73. Mem. ARC, Nat. Soc. Arts Letters (chmn. El Paso chpt. 1970-72), El Paso Art Assn., Discover El Paso (bd. dirs.), C. of C. Home: 5120 Camino De La Vista Dr El Paso TX 79932-2202

MAGUIRE, CHARLOTTE EDWARDS, retired physician; b. Richmond, Ind., Sept. 1, 1918; d. Joel Blaine and Lydia (Betscher) Edwards; m. Raymer Francis Maguire, Sept. 1, 1948 (dec.); children: Barbara, Thomas Clair II (dec.). Student, Stetson U., 1936-38, U. Wichita, 1938-39; BS, Memphis Tchrs. Coll., 1940; MD, U. Ark., 1944; LHD (hon.) , Fla. State U., 2002. Intern, resident Orange Meml. Hosp., Orlando, Fla., 1944-46; resident Bellevue Hosp. and Med. Ctr., NYU, N.Y.C., 1954, 55; instr. nurses Orange Meml. Hosp., 1947-57, staff mem., 1946-68, Fla. Santarium and Hosp., Orlando, 1946-56, Holiday House and Hosp., Orlando, 1950-62; mem. courtesy and cons. staff West Orange Meml. Hosp., Winter Garden, Fla., 1952-67; active staff, chief dept. pediat. Mercy Hosp., Orlando, 1965-68; med. dir. med. svcs. and basic care Fla. Dept. Health and Rehab. Svcs., 1975-84; med. exec. dir., med. svcs. divsn. worker's compensation Fla. Dept. Labor, Tallahassee, 1984-87; chief of staff physicians and dentists Ctrl. Fla. divsn. Children's Home Soc. Fla., 1947-56; dir. Orlando Child Health Clinic, 1949-58; pvt. practice medicine Orlando, 1946-68; asst. regional dir. HEW, 1970-72. Pediat. cons. Fla. Crippled Children's Commn., 1952-70, dir., 1968-70; med. dir. Office Med. Svcs. and Basic Care, sr. physician Office of Asst. Sec. Ops., Fla. Dept. Health and Rehab. Svcs.; clin. prof. dept. pediat. U. Fla. Coll. Medicine, Gainesville, 1980-87; mem. Fla. Drug Utilization Rev., 1983-87; real estate salesperson Investors Realty, 1982—; bd. dirs. Stavros Econ. Ctr. Fla. State U., Tallahassee; mem. pres.'s coun. Fla. State U., U. Fla., Gainesville; Charlotte Edwards Maguire eminent scholar chair and scholarships for qualified students, 1999. Mem. profl. adv. com. Fla. Center for Clin. Services at U. Fla., 1952-60; del. to Mid-century White House Conf. on Children and Youth, 1950; U.S. del from Nat. Soc. for Crippled Children to World Congress for Welfare of Cripples, Inc., London, 1957; pres of corp. Eccleston-Callahan Hosp. for Colored Crippled Children, 1956-58; sec. Fla. chpt. Nat. Doctor's Com. for Improved Med. Svcs., 1951-52; med. adv. com. Gateway Sch. for Mentally Retarded, 1959-62; bd. dirs. Forest Park Sch. for Spl. Edn. Crippled Children, 1949-54, mem. med. adv. com., 1955-68, chmn., 1957-68; mem. Fla. Adv. Coun. for Mentally Retarded, 1965-70; dir. ctrl. Fla. poison control Orange Meml. Hosp.; mem. orgn. com., chmn. com. for admissions and selection policies Camp Challenge; participant 12th session Fed. Exec. Inst., 1971; del. White House Conf. on Aging, 1980; dir. Stavros Econ. Ctr. Fla. State U.; trustee Fla. State U. Found., 1998—, mem. campaign com. Charlotte Edwards Maguire Eminent Scholarship named in hon. Fla. State U., Outstanding Woman in Our Comty. AAUW, Tallahassee. Mem. AMA (life), Nat. Rehab. Assn., Am. Congress Phys. Medicine and Rehab., Fla. Soc. Crippled Children and Adults, Ctrl. Fla. Soc. Crippled Children and Adults (dir. 1949-58, pres. 1956-57), Am. Assn. Cleft Palate, Fla. Soc. Crippled Children (trustee 1951-57, v.p. 1956-57, profl. adv. com. 1957-68), Mental Health Assn. Orange County (charter mem.; pres. 1949-50, dir. 1947-52, chmn. exec. com. 1950-52, dir. 1963-65), Fla. Orange County Heart Assn., Am. Med. Women's Assn., Am. Acad. Med. Dirs., Fla. Med. Assn. (life, chmn. com. on mental retardation), Orange County Med. Assn., Orange Med. Soc. (life), Fla. Pediat. Soc. (pres. 1952-53), Fla. Cleft Palate Assn. (counselor-at-large, sec.), Nat. Inst. Geneal. Rsch., Nat. Geneal. Soc., Assn. Profl. Genealogists, Tallahassee Geneal. Soc., Fla. State U. Found. Inc. (bd. dirs. Stavoris Ctr. for Econ. Edn.), Capital City Tiger Bay Club, Fla. Econs. Club, Francis Eppes Soc. Fla. State U., Econ. Club Fla. Clubs: Governors. Home: 4158 Covenant Ln Tallahassee FL 32308-5765

MAGUIRE, FRANK EDWARD, retired non-commissioned military officer; b. Phila., Oct. 2, 1930; s. Frank Joseph and Clara Martha (Veit) Maguire; m. Frances Marie Devlin, Sept. 19, 1956 (dec.); children: Frank L., Michael T.(dec.) , Kevin M.(dec.) , Patricia K. Dawson. BA in History, Chapman Coll., 1969, MA in Edn., 1972; AA in Resource Mgmt., C.C. of Air Force, 1984. Enlisted USAF, 1951, promoted to chief master sgt., 1977, ret., 1983, prodn. analysis tech. Del., 1955-61, Hickam AFB, Hawaii, 1961-64, Pease AFB, N.H., 1964-66, prodn. analysis supt. Vandenberg AFB, Calif., 1966-68, Utapao AFB, Thailand, 1968-69, March AFB, Calif., 1969-72, Bitberg AFB, Germany, 1972-76, data system mgr. Wright Patterson AFB, 1976-89, acquisition program mgr., 1989—. Warranty cons. Soc. of Logistical Engrs., 1995, A.F. Inst. Tech., Wright Patterson AFB, 1996-97. Pres. Base Enlisted Affairs Com., Wright Patterson AFB, 1977-82; chair Kevin M. Maguire Meml. Scholarship, 1992—. Decorated Bronze Star, Commendation medal, Meritorious Svc. medals (2 times); named to Order Ky. Cols.; invested Wright State U. Stanley Heritage Soc., 2000. Mem. Air Force Assn., Air Force Sgts. Assn., The Ret. Enlisted Assn., Air Force Mus. Found., Smithsonian Assocs., Nat. Geographic Assn. Republican. Roman Catholic. Avocations: singing, social contbns. Home: 7315 Montague Rd Huber Heights OH 45424-3048 Office: F-22 Special Program Office 2725 C St Bldg 553 Wright Patterson AFB OH 45433-7424

MAGUIRE, JAMES HARVEY, physician; b. Easton, Pa., Nov. 25, 1948; s. James I and Elizabeth C (Updegrove) Maguire. AB, Princeton U., 1970; MD, Harvard U., 1974, MPH, 1978. Cert. internal med, infectious disease. Rsch. assoc. Harvard Sch. Pub. Health, Boston, 1978-81; instr. in medicine Harvard Med. Sch. Pub. Health, 1982-85; asst. prof. Medicine Tropical Pub. Health, Boston, 1985-92, assoc. prof. medicine, 1992-2001; physician, clin. dir. infectious disease Brigham Womens Hosp., 1992-2001; chief parasitic disease epidemiology br. divsn. parasitic Ctrs. for Disease Control & Prevention, Atlanta, 2001—. Editor: Parasitic Diseases, 1993; sect. editor: Am. Jour. Tropical Medicine and Hygiene, 2002—. Recipient Ben Kean medal, 2001. Mem.: Infectious Disease Soc Am, Am Soc Tropical Med and Hygiene (councillor 2000—). Avocation: tennis. E-mail: jmaguire@cdc.gov.

MAGUIRE, JOHN DAVID, academic administrator, educator, writer; b. Montgomery, Ala., Aug. 7, 1932; s. John Henry and Clyde (Merrill) M.; m. Lillian Louise Parrish, Aug. 29, 1953; children: Catherine Merrill, Mary Elizabeth, Anne King. AB magna cum laude, Washington and Lee U., 1953, Litt.D. (hon.), 1979; Fulbright scholar, Edinburgh (Scotland) U., 1953-54; B.D. summa cum laude, Yale, 1956, PhD, 1960; postdoctoral research, Yale U. and U. Tübingen, Germany, 1964-65, U. Calif., Berkeley, 1968-69, Silliman U., Philippines, 1976-77; HLD (hon.), Transylvania U., 1990. Dir. Internat. Student Ctr., New Haven, 1956-58; mem. faculty Wesleyan U., Middletown, Conn., 1960-70, asso. provost, 1967-68; vis. lectr. Pacific Sch. Religion and Grad. Theol. Union, Berkeley, 1968-69; pres. SUNY Coll. at Old Westbury, 1970-81, Claremont (Calif.) Grad. U., 1981-98. Sr. fellow Claremont Grad. U. Sch. Politics and Econs.; dir. nat. project Renewing Democracy through Interracial/Multicultural Comty. Bldg., 1998—. Author: The Dance of the Pilgrim: A Christian Style of Life for Today, 1967; also numerous articles. Mem. Conn. adv. comt. US Comn. Civil Rights , 1961—70; participant White House Conf. on Civil Rights, 1966; advisor Martin Luther King Cent. Social Change, Atlanta, 1968—, permanent trustee, 1968—, 1st chmn. bd. dirs., 1968—; bd. dirs. Nassau County Health and Welfare Coun. , 1971—81, pres., 1974—76; trustee United Bd. Christian Higher Ed in Asia, 1975—81, Inst. Int. Ed. , 1980—86; charter trustee Tomas Rivera Policy Inst., Claremont, Calif., 1984—, vice chmn., 1987—94, treas., 1995—; with Asn. Ind. Calif. Cols. and Univs. , 1985—98; chmn. Asn. Ind. Calif. Cols. and Univs., 1990—92, mem. exec. comt., 1992—98; with Calif. Achievement Coun., 1985—94, chmn., 1990—94; with Transylvania Univ. Bingham Trust, 1987—, Lincoln Found. and Lincoln Inst. Land Policy, Inc., 1987—94; The JL Found., 1988—; with Bus. Enterprise Trust, 1989—99; with Educ. Found. African Ams., 1991—99; bd. dirs. Asn. Am. Cols. and Univs., 1981—86, chmn., 1984—85; bd. dirs. Legal Def. and Edu. Fund NAACP, 1991—, west coast div., 1981—91, Thacher Sch. , Ojai, Calif., 1982—94, vice chmn., 1986—90; with Salzburg Seminar, 1992—96; charter mem. Pacific Coun. Int. Policy , 1995—; mem. Am. Comt. US-Soviet Rels., 1981—92, Blue Ribbon Calif. Comn. Teaching Profession , 1984—86; mem. gov. coun. Aspen Inst. Wye Faculty Seminar, 1984—94; mem. Coun. Fgn. Rels., 1983—; mem. adv. bd. RAND Cent. Research Immigration Policy, 1994—97, Peter F. Drucker Found. Non-Profit Mgt , 1990—, Andrew Young Sch. Policy Ga. State Univ., 1999—, The Eureka Communities , 1998—; mem. Pres.'s Adv. Coun. Comn. on Calif. Master Plan Higher Educ. , 1986—87, Los Angeles Educ. Alliance Restructuring Now, 1992—98, Calif. Bus. Higher Educ. Forum, 1992—98; leader Idyllwild Sch. Summer Poetry Festival, 1998—. Recipient Julia A. Archibald High Scholarship award Yale Div. Sch., 1956; Day fellow Yale Grad. Sch., 1956-57; Kent fellow, 1957-60; Howard Found. postdoctoral fellow Brown U. Grad. Sch., 1964-65; Fenn lectr., 7 Asian countries, 1976-77; recipient Conn. Prince Hall Masons' award outstanding contbns. human rights in Conn., 1965; E. Harris Harbison Gt. Tchr. prize Danforth Found., 1968 Fellow Soc. Values Higher Edn. (pres. 1974-81, bd. dirs. 1972-88); mem. Phi Beta Kappa, Omicron Delta Kappa Democrat. Office: Claremont Grad U Inst for Dem Renewal 170 E 10th St Claremont CA 91711-5909

MAGUIRE, JOHN PATRICK, investment company executive; b. New Britain, Conn., Apr. 1, 1917; s. John Patrick and Edna Frances (Cashen) M.; m. Mary-Emily Jones, Sept. 8, 1945; children: Peter Dunbar (dec.), Joan Guilford. Student, Holy Cross Coll., 1933-34; degree in bus. adminstrn. with distinction, Babson Inst., 1936; AB cum laude, Princeton U., 1941; BS (hon.), Babson Inst., 1995, Babson Coll., 1995; JD, Yale U., 1943; PhD (hon.), St. Bonaventure U., 1965. Bar: Conn. 1943, N.Y. 1944. Assoc. Cravath, Swaine & Moore (and predecessor), N.Y.C., 1943-50, 52-54; v.p., dir. Forbes, Inc.; also mng. editor Investors Adv. Inst., 1951-52; asst. counsel Gen. Dynamics Corp., 1954-60, sec., 1962-87, v.p., 1981-87; sec., gen. counsel Tex. Butadiene and Chem. Corp., 1960-62; with J.P. Maguire Investment Advisors, 1987-95; exec. v.p. Fiduciary Asset Mgmt. Co., 1995—2002. Mem. bd. govs. N.Y. Young Rep. Club, 1951-52; chmn. fin. and investment coms. St. Louis Art Mus., 1984-94; trustee St. Bonaventure U., 1965-71, Webster U., 1983-85, John Burroughs Sch. (chmn. investment com.) 1976-85. Mem. ABA. Clubs: Piping Rock (Locust Valley, L.I.); Yale (St. Louis); St. Louis Country; Princeton (St. Louis); Tiger Inn (Princeton). Home: PO Box 1088 Boca Grande FL 33921-1088 E-mail: jmaguire@sbcglobal.net.

MAGUIRE, KEVIN, travel management consultant; b. Austin, Tex., Dec. 27, 1951; parents Jack R. and Pat (Horton) M.; m. Jimmy Gay Freeze, June 15, 1974; children: Christopher, Shannon. BA, BJ in Pub. Rels., U. Tex., 1974. Sr. rep. for youth and student sales Pan Am. World Airways, Houston, 1970-74; asst. v.p. United Bank of Tex., Austin, 1974-76; sr. program developer State Bar of Tex. Comprehensive Offender Manpower Program, 1976-79; pres. Travel Place of Austin, Inc., 1979-83; gen. mgr. Tex. br. IVI Travel, Inc., Chgo., 1983-86; owner, mgr. KM Travel Mgmt. Co., Austin, 1976—; pres., CEO The Expedition Devel. Co. Internat. Bus. & Resource Group, 1991—; exec. dir. sales S.W. region Total Travel Mgmt. Inc., Austin, 1994-95; travel mgr. Tokyo Electron Am., Inc., 1995—. Travel and mktg. cons. IBM Tex. Employees Fed. Credit Union, Austin, 1982-88; travel cons. to compt. pub. accts. State of Tex., 1986—, U. Tex. Med. Ctr., San Antonio, 1986-87. Contbr. articles to mags. Sustaining mem. Salvation Army, Austin, 1980; mem. Austin Cultural and Bus. Exch., 1987. Recipient Disting. Svc. award Tex. Corrections Assn., 1976. Mem. Nat. Bus. Travel Assn. (bd. dirs. 2000-01, pres. NBTA chpt. Pres. Coun., 2000—), Austin Bus. Travelers Assn. (Bus. Travel Profl. award 1999, Founders award 2000), Ex-Students Assn. (life). Avocations: travel, racquetball, piano playing, reading, photography. Home: 7010 Narrow Oak Trail Austin TX 78759-4625 Office: 2400 Grove Blvd Austin TX 78741-6500 E-mail: kmaguire@aus.telusa.com.

MAGUIRE, LAMBERT, social worker, educator; b. Chgo., Oct. 26, 1946; s. Lambert and Mary Ann (Murphy) Maguire; m. Barbara Ann Magnusson, June 11, 1971; children: Amy, Mandy. BS, Loyola U., Chgo., 1968; AM, U. Chgo., 1971; MA, U. Mich., 1976, PhD, 1979. Lic. social worker Pa. Dir. Treatment Outcome Rsch., Ann Arbor, Mich., 1976—78; chmn. direct practice U. Pitts., 1979—, asst. prof., 1979—84, assoc. prof., 1984—90, prof., 1990—. Chair direct practice U. Pitts. Sch. Social Work, 1980—; prin. investigator NIMH, Pitts., 1980—81, 1981—83. Author: Understanding Social Networks, 1983, Il Lavoro Sociale Di Rete, 1991, Social Support Systems in Practice, 1991, Japanese edit., 1995, Clinical Social Work, 2002. Capt. USPHS U.S. Army, 1971—74. Fellow, U. Chgo., NIMH, 1969—71. Mem.: NASW, Soc. Social Work Rsch., Acad. Cert. Social Workers. Roman Catholic. Avocations: swimming, travel, opera. Office: U Pitts Sch Social Work 2331 C of L Pittsburgh PA 15260

MAGUIRE, ROBERT FRANCIS, III, real estate investor; b. Portland, Oreg., Apr. 18, 1935; s. Robert Francis Jr. and Jean (Shepard) M. BA, UCLA, 1960. Vice pres. Security Pacific Nat. Bank, L.A., 1960-64; chmn. Maguire Thomas Ptnrs., 1964—. Exec. bd. med. scis. UCLA. Bd. dirs. Los Angeles County Mus. Art; trustee UCLA Found., Bard Coll.; bd. dirs. St. John's Hosp., Music Ctr. Bd. Govs., Calif. Mem.: California (Los Angeles); Valley (Montecito, Calif.), L.A. Country. E-mail: robert.maguire@maguirepartners.com.

MAGUIRE, ROBERT O. musician, consultant; b. Portland, Maine, Jan. 31, 1948; s. Robert O. and Shirley S. Maguire; m. Maureen Kelley, May 16, 1981; children: Shannon L., Megan E. AA, Seminole CC, Sanford, Florida, 1971—72; MusB Edn., Fla. State U., Tallahassee, Florida, 1972—75; MusM Edn., Rollins Coll., Winter Park, Florida, 1976—78. Department of Education D.O.E., Fla., 1975. Choral dir. Seminole H.S., Sanford, Fla., 1975—; adj. faculty Seminole CC, 1977—81; jazz band dir. Seminole H.S., 1982—2001, marching band dir., 1982—87; bass player Altamonte Springs Jazz Ensemble, Altamonte Springs, 1995—98. Wdw cast choir dir. Walt Disney World, Buena Vista, Fla., 1979—79; bass player Sea World, Orlando, Fla., 1985—85, Walt Disney World, Orlando, Fla., 1986—86. Dir.(arranger): (entertainment/convention work) Performing Ensemble (6-16 pieces) (Outstanding Educator of the Yr., 1981). Staff sgt. U.S. Air Force, 1966—70, Edwards AFB. Scholar, Fla. State U., 1974-75. Master: Masonic Lodge #239; mem.: Internat. Ass'n of Jazz Educators, Am. Choral Director's Ass'n, Music Educator's Nat. Conf., Fla. Vocal Assn. (dist. chair 2001—). Democrat-Npl. Christian. Avocations: computers, midi. Home: 4214 Shades Crest Lane Sanford FL 32773-8191 Office: Seminole High School 2701 Ridgewood Avenue Sanford FL 32773 Home Fax: 407-320-7009; Office Fax: 407-320-5024. Personal E-mail: rmaguire@cfl.rr.com. E-mail: bob_maguire@scps.k12.fl.us.

MAGUIRE, TOBEY, actor; b. Santa Monica, Calif., June 27, 1975; Actor: Revenge of the Red Baron, 1994, Joyride, 1997, The Ice Storm, 1997, Deconstructing Harry, 1997, Pleasantville, 1998, Fear and Loathing in Las Vegas, 1998, Ride with the Devil, 1999, The Cider House Rules, 1999, Wonder Boys, 2000, Cats & Dogs, 2001, Spider-Man, 2002. Recipient Best Supporting Actor, Toronto Film Critics Assn., 2000. Office: c/o SFM 1122 S Robertson Blvd Los Angeles CA 90036 also: PO Box 5617 Beverly Hills CA 90210*

MAGUIRE-ZINNI, DEIRDRE, federal community development management analyst; b. Bklyn., Oct. 21, 1954; d. James Michael and Dorothy Ursula (Gronske) Maguire; m. Nicholas A. Zinni, Aug. 27, 1977; 1 child, Miles Angelo. BA with honors, SUNY, Stony Brook, 1976; MS, Fla. State U., 1981. Housing specialist Suffolk Community Devel. Corp., Coram, N.Y., 1977-78; planner Palm Beach County Housing and Community Devel., West Palm Beach, Fla., 1980-83, sr. planner, 1983-84, mgr. adminstrn. and ops., 1984-87; fed. community planning and devel. rep. HUD, Jacksonville, 1987-88, community planning and devel. specialist, Entitlement Cmtys. Divsn. Washington, 1988-91, asst. dir. entitlement communities, 1991-94, dir. entitlement communities divsn., 1994-99, mgmt. analyst office of CFO, 1999—2001; sr. mgmt. analyst Office of Cmty. Planning and Devel. Comptroller, 2001—. Staff liaison

Affordable Housing Task Force, West Palm Beach, 1985-86, Fla. Community Devel. Assn., 1985-87. Democrat. Roman Catholic. Avocations: reading, baking. E-mail: Deirdre_Maguire-Zinni@hud.gov.

MAGURNO, RICHARD PETER, lawyer; b. Suffern, N.Y., June 29, 1943; s. Eugene and Rose (Foresta) M. BS, Georgetown U., 1964; MS, U. Wis., 1965; JD, Fordham U., 1968. Bar: N.Y. 1970, Fla. 1982, U.S. Supreme Ct. 1974, U.S. Ct. Appeals (2d, 5th, 11th cirs.) 1976, U.S. Dist. Ct. (so. and ea. dists.) N.Y. 1979. Atty. Eastern Air Lines, N.Y.C., 1970-73, sr. atty., 1973-76, gen. atty., 1976-79, dir. legal Miami, Fla., 1980, v.p. legal, asst. sec., 1980-84, gen. counsel, sr. v.p. legal, sec., 1984-88; ptnr. Lord Day & Lord, Barrett Smith, 1989-94; gen. counsel, sr. v.p. legal Trans World Airlines, St. Louis, 1994-98; aviation cons., 1998-2000; gen. counsel, sr. v.p., sec. Airtran Airways, 2000—. Author: Romantic Suffern, 1773-1973, 1973. Served in Peace Corps, 1968-69. Mem. ABA, Bar Assn. City of N.Y., Fla. Bar Assn. Democrat. Roman Catholic.

MAG WALZ, GÜNTHER, artist; b. Graz, Styria, Austria, Feb. 19, 1939; s. Rudolf and Anna (Arnsek) W.; m. Elisabeth Walz-Babor, Oct. 9, 1979. Diploma in Painting and Graphics, U. of Applied Art Vienna, 1961. Cert. graphic artist. Artist numerous exhibition. Individual exhbns.: Gallery Carneri, Graz, 1975, Culture Ctr. Minorites, Graz, 1978, Kleine Galerie, Vienna, 1986, Gallery at Fliederlich, Nuremberg, Germany, 1996, Magnus Hirschfeld Ctr., Hamburg, Germany, 1997, Limner Gallery, N.Y., 1994, Galerie Im Sonntags-Club, Berlin, 1996, Gallery "Y", Johannesburg, South Africa, 1983, Gallery Prisma, Vienna, 1993. Home: Sedlitzkygasse 20 A-1110 Vienna Austria E-mail: walzwerk@aon.at.

MAH, TINA LILY, science administrator; b. San Francisco, July 27, 1967; d. William and Nancy Mah. BA, U. Calif., Berkeley, 1989; doctorate, U. Calif., Santa Cruz, 1997. Tech. writer Data Base Architects, Alameda, Calif., 1989-90; chemist Pacific Environ. Lab., San Francisco, 1990-91; applications devel. chemist Rosemount Analytical Dohrmann Divsn., Santa Clara, 1991-92; grad. tchg. asst. U. Calif., Santa Cruz, 1992-93, grad. rsch. asst., 1993-97; postdoctoral fellow U. Calif. Berkeley, 1998—99; product specialist Varian Inc., NMR Sys., Palo Alto, 1999-2001; product line mgr. semicondr. divsn. Coherent Inc., Santa Clara, 2001; tech. support mgr. Ciphergen Biosys. Inc., Fremont, 2002—. Contbr. articles to profl. jours. Mem. ACS, Assn. Women in Sci., Biophys. Soc., Sigma Xi. Avocations: swimming, cycling, creative writing, music, hiking. Home: 1425 Bellevue Ave Apt 18 Burlingame CA 94010-3917 Office: Ciphergen Biosys Inc 6611 Dumbarton Cir Fremont CA 94555 E-mail: tlmah@alum.berkeley.edu.

MAHA, CALLEN DALE, civil engineer; b. San Antonio, July 18, 1959; s. John J. and Lorraine D. (Moczygemba) M.; m. Debora J. Moczygemba, Feb. 26, 1983; children: Ross, Kristi. BSCE, Tex. A&M U., 1981, MCE, 1984. Registered profl. engr., Tex., N.Mex., Ariz., Okla., Pa., La., Wyo., S.C.; cert. project mgmt. profl. Project engr. Marathon Pipe Line Co., Houston, 1981-83; grad. teaching asst. Tex. A&M U., College Station, 1983-84; project engr. Exxon Co. U.S.A., Midland, Tex., 1984-90; project mgr. Ref-Chem Engring. & Constrn. Corp., Odessa, 1990—. Author: Concrete Laboratory Manual, 1984. Mem. ASCE, NSPE. Home: 2005 Centerview Midland TX 79707-9760

MAHADESHWAR, SANJAY SAKHARAM, marine consultant; b. Bombay, Nov. 10, 1956; came to U.S., 1989; s. S.B. Mahadeshwar and Manorama (Tara) Parker; m. Sonal Sanjay, Jan. 31, 1982; children: Teja, Pooja. Master Mariner, L.B.S. Nautical & Engr. Coll., Bombay, 1983; BBA, Internat. U., Independence, Mo., 1989, MBA, 1990. Officer cadet shipping cos., 1974-77, 2nd officer, 1977-80; chief officer Oil/Shipping Cos. Lines, Oslo and Solli, Norway, 1980-84; capt. supertankers Barber Internat. Wilhelmsen, Norway, 1984-89; marine cons. Internat. Marine Svcs., Queens, N.Y., 1989-90; v.p. Edex Corp., Bklyn., 1990-92; pres. Sanson Marine Inc., Roselle, N.J., 1992—. Cons., marine loss control expediter P & I Clubs, Shipowners, Bear Stearns, N.Y., Houston, 1992-97; cons., port capt. IMC, Citgo Petroleum, N.Y., U.S.A. East Coast, 1992-97; cons., adviser PSA, Vitol S.A., Houston, Argosy, U.K., 1997-98; marine cons. Exxon, Exxon Chems. Seariver Maritime, N.J., N.Y., 1997-98; course dir. Internat. U., Independence, mo., 1990-97. Recipient outstanding merit award Internat. U., Independence, 1990-97. Mem. Marine Soc., Exxon Seariver Maritime (N.Y., N.J. coord. marine cons., lead cons. 1997-98). Avocations: writing, reading, table tennis, swimming, yoga. Home and Office: 1 Peru St Edison NJ 08820-2625

MAHADEVA, MANORANJAN, financial executive, accountant; b. Colombo, Sri Lanka, Feb. 12, 1955; came to U.S., 1977; s. Kandiah and Rupavathy (Ponniah) M.; m. Donna Sue Martin, May 12, 1986; 1 child, Danielle. BBA, U. Tex., 1981; MBA, N. Tex. State U., 1985. Notary pub., Tex.; lic. real estate broker, Tex.; CPA, Tex.; cert. mgmt. acct. and cert. fin. mgmt. Inst. Mgmt. Accts.; cert. fraud examiner, cash mgr.; profl. Acad. Healthcare Mgmt.; accredited in bus. valuation AICPA. Asst. contr. Presbyn. Village North, Dallas, 1981-84; CFO Dallas Meml. Hosp., 1984-86; exec. dir. Associated Orthopedics & Sports Medicine, Plano, Tex., 1986-95; CFO Access Med. Supply Inc., 1988-95; mng. dir. YNM Corp., 1987-95; practice adminstr. Tex. Orthopaedic Assocs., Dallas, 1995-96; dir. project mgmt. Physician Reliance Network, 1996-99; dir. valuations, bus. devel. US Oncology, Houston, 1999—2001, dirp. fin. planning, 2001—. Chief fin. officer Access Med. Supply, Inc., 1988-96. Mem. editl. rev. bd. Jour. Accountancy and Strategic Fin., Today's CPA. Mem. Leadership Plano Class 8, 1990-91, bd. dirs., mem. exec. bd., 1991-97, chmn. exec. bd., 1992-93; mem. Mental Health Assn. Collin County; bd. dirs. Nat. Assn. Cmty. Leadership, vice chair, 1995-97, chair-elect, 1997-98, chair, 1998-99; bd. dirs. Am. Heart Assn.; bd. dirs., treas. Crisis Ctr. of Collin County; chmn. emergency svcs. Coalition of Collin County; steering com. Leadership USA, 1996-97. Recipient Nat. Disting. Leadership award, 1994; Presdl. scholar Wayne (Nebr.) State U., 1977-78; Mano Mahadeva Day proclaimed in his honor Mayor of Plano, 1999. Mem. Nat. Assn. Accts. (bd. dirs. North Dallas chpt. 1985-86), Am. Hosp. Assn., Internat. Students Assn., Plano C. of C. (chmn. cmty. edn. com.), Leadership Plano Alumni Assn. (bd. dirs.), Toastmasters, Lions (past pres. Plano, Lion of Yr. award 1993), Rotary (sec., program chmn., pres. Plano 1996-97, Rotarian of Yr. award 1995, Paul Harris fellow 1998), Delta Sigma Pi, Beta Gamma Sigma. Avocations: reading, tennis, playing drums, jogging, cooking. Home: 23 Indian Summer Pl Spring TX 77381-6236 Office: US Oncology 16825 Northchase Dr Ste 1300 Houston TX 77060-6005

MAHADEVAN, KUMAR, marine laboratory director, researcher; b. Madras, Tamilnadu, India, Sept. 29, 1948; came to U.S., 1971; s. Sockalingam Ponnusamy and Pankajam (Nadar) M.; m. Linda Claire Goggin, Sept. 27, 1980; children: Andrew, Alexander, Chad, Vijayan. BS, Madras U., 1967; MS, Annamalai U., Chidambaram, India, 1971; PhD, Fla. State U., 1977. Instr. Chingleput (India) Med. Coll., 1967-68, Lakshman's Coll., Madras, 1968-69; rsch. asst. Fla. State U., Tallahassee, 1971-75; staff scientist Conservation Cons., Inc., Palmetto, Fla., 1975-78; sr. scientist Mote Marine Lab., Sarasota, 1978-79, dir. div., 1979-86, interim co-dir., 1984, exec. dir., 1986—. Mem. Coun. on Ocean Affairs, Washington, 1989-91, steering com. Gulf of Mex. Program, Atlanta, 1988-96; mem. South Atlantic and Gulf States Coastal Protection Commn., 1990-93; vice chmn. NOAA Marine Rsch. Bd., Gulf of Mex., 1992-96. Contbr. articles to profl. publs. Mem. sch. adv. bd., Sarasota, 1988-89; mem. tech. adv. bd. Myakka River, Sarasota, 1987-90; legis. liason Parents Assn. of Sarasota Schs., 1988-89; bd. dirs. Jason Found. for Edn., 1991—, Health Care Sarasota, 1997-98; vice chmn. Fla. Ocean Alliance, 2000—; mem. Fla. Gov.'s Ocean Com., 1997-98. Nat. Merit scholar Univ. Grants Commn., India, 1969-71. Mem. N. Am. Benthological Soc., Oceanographic Soc., World Aquaculture Soc., Deep Sea Biol. Soc. (hon.), Fla. Acad. Scis. (councillor 1975), So. Assn. Marine Labs (pres. 1990, exec. bd. 1986-91, treas. 1995—), Assn. Marine Labs Caribbean (pres. 1987-88, exec. bd. 1984—), Nat. Assn. Marine Labs. (pres. 1994-95), Sigma Xi. Republican. Avocations: racquetball, fishing, gardening. Office: Mote Marine Lab 1600 Ken Thompson Pkwy Sarasota FL 34236-1096 E-mail: kumar@mote.org.

MAHAFFEY, JOHN CHRISTOPHER, association executive; b. Jefferson City, Mo., July 20, 1953; s. Fred Turner and Betty Cord (Woodfill) M.; children: Michael, Katherine. BA, Western Ill. U., Macomb, 1975; MS, DePaul U., 1999. Legis. aide Congressman Harold R. Collier, Washington, 1972-73; legis. asst. Nat. Assn. Retail Druggists, 1975-76; dir. Commn. and Meetings Nat. Assn. Bds. of Pharmacy, Chgo., 1976-80; pres., CEO Association Forum, 1980—. Mem. Assn. Com. of 100, U.S. C. of C., 1995—. Commr. City of Park Ridge Econ. Devel. Commn., Park Ridge, Ill., 1990-94, 96-2000; mem. exec. com. Chgo. Conv. and Tourism Bur., 1993—. Recipient Disting. Alumni award Western Ill. U., Macomb, 1993. Fellow Am. Soc. Assn. Execs. (mem. cert. commn. 1989-91, Key award 1994); mem. The Tower Club, Univ. Club Chgo. Presbyterian. Office: Association Forum 20 N Wacker Dr Ste 3000 Chicago IL 60606-3101 E-mail: Mahaffey@associationforum.org.

MAHAFFEY, KATHRYN ROSE, risk assessor; b. Johnstown, Pa., Dec. 24, 1943; d. William T. and Harriet L. Mahaffey; m. Samuel Nelson Kramer, June 1977 (div. 1984); children: Harriet Mahaffey Kramer, Charles Herbert Kramer; m. David Ernst Jacobs, Oct. 13, 1996. BS, Pa. State U., 1965; PhD, Rutgers U., 1968. Sr. environ. scientist Nat. Inst. Environ. Health Sci., Research Triangle Park, N.C., 1987-93, Nat. Ctr. for Environ. Assessment, U.S. EPA, Cin., 1993-99, br. chief, 1983-87; dir. divsn. exposure assessment Office of Prevention, Pesticides, Toxic Substances, U.S. EPA, Washington, 1999—. Asst. prof. dept. pathology U. N.C. Sch. Medicine, Chapel Hill, 1969-71. Editor: Dietary and Environmental Lead: Human Health Effects, 1985, (with others) Clinical Effects of Environmental Chemicals, 1989; contbg. author books and reports; author articles. Mem. Am. Soc. for Nutritional Scis., Am. Soc. for Clin. Nutrition, Soc. for Internat. Nutrition Rsch. Office: 1200 Pennsylvania Ave NW MC 7203 Washington DC 20460 E-mail: mahaffey.kate@.epa.gov.

MAHAFFEY, KAY P. artist, interior designer; b. Cin., Oct. 16, 1936; d. Frederick and Eva Nell (Cricher) Pfiester; m. Virgil B. Mahaffey (dec.); children: Lynn Elizabeth, Margaret Kay. BS in Edn., BA in Design, U.Cin., 1958; MA in Art Edn., U. Washington, Seattle, 1972. Art tchr. Various Pub. Schs., Ohio, Wis., Wash., 1958-62; art mobile designer Bucks County C.C., Pa., 1975-76; cons. to legislators N.J. Commn. on the Arts, Trenton, N.J., 1975-78; facilities planning, constrn. Bank Am. S.W., Phoenix, 1980-86; asst. prof. Ariz. State U., Coll. Arch. and Design, Tempe, 1987-89; chair interior design N.W. Coll. of Art, Poulsbo, Wash., 1992-97; supr. relocation Puget Sound Energy, Facilities, Bellevue, 1997-99; architectural interior designer, 1999—. Chair comty. peer outreach com. Ariz. State U. Coll. of Design, Tempe, 1987-89; mem. adv. bd. interior design Northwest Coll. Art, Poulseo, Wash., 1992—; bd. dirs. Edmunds Wash. Pub. Facilities Dist.; bd. trustees West Sound Acad. Artist: works exhibited in juried exhbns. Bellevue, Wash., Colo., Ariz., Pa., Ohio; collections in U.S., Japan and Germany; author: (curricula) Tune in to Where You Live, 1972, Facilities Planning, 1986-87. Organizer Speakers' Bur., N.W. Kidney Ctr., Seattle, 1969-75; co-chair Kappa Kappa Gamma Scottsdale Chpt. Alumni Art Show, 1983, 84; corp. rep. to steering com. Phoenix Ariz. Core Devel., 1984-85; designer, planner Women's Crisis Ctr., Scottsdale, 1986-87 Recipient scholarship Nat. Oceanic Atmospheric Assn., Seattle,1970, grad. fellowship Kappa Kappa Gamma, 1970, Award of Excellence, N.W. Kidney Ctr., 1972. Mem. Internat. Facility Mgmt. Assn., Am. Soc. Interior Design, Internat. Interior Design Assn. Avocations: skiing, tennis, kayaking, gardening, cross-country skiing. Home and Office: 18730 94th Ave W Edmonds WA 98020-2320

MAHAFFEY, REDGE ALLAN, movie producer, director, writer, actor, scientist; b. Bethesda, Md., Dec. 15, 1949; s. George Newton and Lila Katherine (Drum) M.; m. Ellen Cecilia Cranston, May 30, 1973 (div. Dec. 1980); m. Patricia Jane Guy, Apr. 29, 1984 (div. Sept. 1994); children: Travis Guy, Morgan Nicole; m. Veronica Bird, Sept. 24, 1994; children: Ryan Alexander, Ramsey Blake. BS, U. Md., 1971, MS, 1973, PhD, 1976. NRC postdoctoral fellow Nat. Acad. of Scis., Washington, 1976-77; research physicist Naval Research Lab., 1977-78; sr. research physicist Sachs/Freeman Assocs., Bladensburg, Md., 1978-79, dir. research Bowie, 1979-81, exec. v.p., chief scientist Largo, 1981-91, also bd. dirs. Landover, 1985—; mng. ptnr. Ramsway Pictures, 1991—; pres. WHOH, Largo, Md., 1993—. Instr. George Washington U., Washington, 1979-80, Prince George's Coll., 1987; pres. Capitol Contracts, Bowie, 1981-83. Author: A Higher Education, 1989, Me, Myself and I, 1992, Deadly Rivals, 1992; exec. prodr., writer Deadly Rivals, 1992, Quest of the Delta Knight, 1993; prodr., actor, writer, dir. Life 101, 1995 (hon. mention Atlantic City Film Festival 1997), First Encounter, 1997; prodr., actor, dir., writer She's Too Tall, 1998 (Best Comedy award Atlantic City Film Festival 1998); contbr. articles on lasers and particle beams to sci. jours., also short stories, essays and poems to mags.; patentee laser, x-rays and particle beams. Recipient Research Publ. award Naval Research Lab., 1978, 1st Place Novel Internat. Lit. Awards, 1988, award of merit Internat. Soc. for Advancement of Poetry, 1990. Mem. IEEE, Am. Phys. Soc., Mensa, Intertel, Nat. Writer's Club, Internat. Platform Assn., Internat. Soc. Phil. Enquiry, Writer's Assn. Anne Arundel County, Bethesda Writer's Ctr., Inst. Noetic Scis. Clubs: Sea Dragons Martial Arts(Washington) (treas. 1984-85, instr. 1987-91). Republican. Avocations: martial arts, softball, basketball. Office: SFA Inc 9315 Largo Dr W Largo MD 20774-4755

MAHAFFY, TELFAIR, safety scientist; b. Jacksonville, Fla., Jan. 26, 1936; s. Conrad Brickwedel and Mary Willard (Telfair) M.; m. Nancy A. Scheurer, Oct. 23, 1959 (div.); children: Anne, Michael. AB in English, U. N.C., 1958; postgrad., Yale U., 1958-60. Mortgage broker The Travelers, Jacksonville, Fla., 1960-64, Norton Realty, Jacksonville, 1964-68; v.p. Haughton & Co., 1968-72; pres., onwer Fla. Mortgage Exch., 1972-87; safety dir. Holmes Lumber Co., 1987-99. Bd. dirs. Jacksonville Athletic Charities, 1988-93, v.p. Mem. Fla. Hunter-Jumper Assn. (pres. 1978), North Fla. Hunter-Jumper Assn. (pres. 1976), Osprey Club (bd. dirs. 1998—). Republican. Episcopalian. Avocations: swimming, horse show jumping. Home: 4944 Arapahoe Ave Jacksonville FL 32210-8336 Office: Builders First Source 6550 Roosevelt Blvd Jacksonville FL 32244-4098

MAHAJAN, SANJIV RAI, entrepreneur; b. Delhi, India; s. Swaran and Amrit Rai M.; m. Pratima Kaushik, Jan. 22, 1980; children: Payal, Sushaen. BA in Econs. with honors, Shri Ram Coll. Commerce, Delhi, 1978. Mktg. dir. SanSun Electronics P. Ltd., Madras, India, 1984-85; pres. MARRS Inc., New Delhi, 1985-90; mng. dir. SPSS South Asia, 1993-96; internat. dir. SPSS Internat., Woking, 1996-98; dir. SPSS Inc., Chgo., 1998-2000; CEO IGPartner.Net Corp., North Brunswick, N.J., 2000—. Pres. Fedn. of Asian Am. Tech. Cos., Woodbridge, N.J., 2000—; chmn. STATSIG, New Delhi, 1993-96; co-founder 6 cos.; expert worldwide markets for tech. products and svcs. Contbr. articles to profl. jours. Mem. Am. Mktg. Assn., Himalayan Mountaineering Assn. Office: IGPartner Net Corp 64 Timber Ridge Rd North Brunswick NJ 08902-5515 E-mail: srmahajan@igpartner.net.

MAHAJAN, SUBHASH, electronic materials educator; b. Gurdaspur, India; m. Sushma Sondhi, Sept. 3, 1965; children: Sanjoy, Sunit, Ashish. BS with highest honors, Panjab U., India, 1959; BE in Metallyrgy with highest honors, Indian Inst. Sci., 1961; PhD in Materials Sci. and Engring., U. Calif., 1965. Rsch. asst. U. Calif., Berkeley, 1961-65; rsch. metallurgist U. Denver, 1965-68; Harwell fellow Atomic Energy Rsch. Establishment, Harwell, Eng., 1968-71; mem. tech. staff AT&T Bell Labs., Murray Hill, N.J., 1971-83, rsch. mgr., 1981-83; prof. electronic materials dept. material sci. and engring. Carnegie Mellon U., Pitts., 1983-97; prof. electronic materials Ariz. State U., Tempe, 1997—, assoc. chair, 1999, interim chair and chair dept. chem. and materials engring., 2000—. Mem. site panel Materials Rsch. Lab., 1993; vis. prof. U. Antwerp, Belgium, 1991, Ecole Ctrl. Lyon, Ecully, France, 1993; lectr., spkr., patentee, cons. in field. Editor (with V.G. Keramidas): Electrochemical Society Symposium Volume, 1983; editor: (with L.C. Kimerling) The Concise Encyclopedia of Semiconducting Materials and Related Technologies, 1992; editor: Handbook on Semiconductors, vol. 3, 1994; editor: (with D. Bloor, R.J. Brook and M.C. Flemings) The Encyclopedia of Advanced Materials, 1994; editor: (with K.H. Jurgen Buschow, Robert W. Cahn et al) Encyclopedia of Materials: Science and Technology, 2001; more than 190 articles to profl. jours. Mem. materials rsch. adv. com. divsn. materials rsch. NSF, 1989-92. Fellow TMS, Am. Soc. Metals Internat. (Albert Sauveur Achievement award), Minerals, Metals and Materials Soc.; mem. Materials Rsch. Soc. (editor symposium volume 1983, organizer symposium Am. Assn. Crystal Growers), Electrochem. Soc. (mem. electronics divsn. 1973-86, divisional editor 1976-86), Minerals, Metals and Materials Soc. (mem. phys. metallurgy com. 1976-83, vice chmn. mech. metallurgy com. 1978-79, mem. 1975-80, mem. electronic materials com. 1990-94, chmn. electronic, magnetic and photonic materials com. 1984-86, tech. dir. bd., John Bardeen award), Sigma Xi. Home: 8824 S Poplar St Tempe AZ 85284-4521 Office: Ariz State U Dept Chem and Materials Engring Tempe AZ 85287-6006 E-mail: smahajan@asu.edu.

MAHAN, CHARLES SAMUEL, public health educator; b. Pitts., Nov. 4, 1938; AB, W.Va. U., 1960; MD, Northwestern U., 1964. Diplomate Am. Bd. Ob-Gyn. Intern Hennepin County Gen. Hosp., Mpls., 1964-65; med. fellow in obstetrics and gynecology U. Minn. Hosp., 1965-68; staff physician Shands Teaching Hosp., Coll. Medicine U. Fla., Gainesville, 1974-95, dir. divsn. ambulatory svcs. women, 1974-87, assoc. prof. dept. obstetrics and gynecology, 1974-80, prof., 1980—, acting chmn. dept. obstetrics and gynecology, 1978-79; asst. and assoc. prof. dept. obstetrics and gynecology med. sch. U. Minn., Mpls., 1970-74; dir. maternal and child health State of Fla., 1982-86; dep. sec. health, state health officer Fla. Dept. Health and Rehabilitative Svcs., 1988-95; prof. dept. cmty. and family health, maternal health program U. South Fla. Coll. Pub. Health, Tampa, 1995—, dean, 1995—2002. Sr. assoc. physician ob-gyn. Pilot City Health Ctr., Mpls., 1970-74; med. dir. Red Door Venereal Disease Clinic, Mpls., 1972-74; dir. North Ctrl. Fla. Maternity and Infant Care, Family Planning, Teen-Age Pregnancy Team Projects, and WIC Program, 1974-87; assoc. dir. Tech. Assistance Health Rsch. Group, Gainesville, 1975-82; chmn. med. care evaluation com. Shands Teaching Hosp., 1976-80; mem. faculty senate U. Fla., 1976-78, 79-80, 87-88, mem. outpatient clinics com., 1978-86, mem. health policy task force, 1992—, mem. promotion and tenure com. coll. medicine, 1978-81, dir. undergrad. edn. dept. ob-gyn., 1980-85, pres. faculty, 1982-83, mem. faculty coun., 1982-85, dir. Fla. midwifery resource ctr., 1992—, mem. nurse-midwife tng. program adv. com. coll. nursing, 1982—, mem. adv. com. inst. HIV rsch. and edn., 1992—; mem. State of Fla. Family Planning Coun., 1976-79; chmn. 1st ann. med. alumni sci. seminar Hennepin County Med. Ctr., Minn., 1976; mem. Alachua County Child Advocacy Coun., 1977-79; mem. adv. bd. Rape Info. and Counseling Ctr., 1977-79; mem. nat. adv. coun. maternal, fetal and infant nutrition USDA, 1978-81; chmn. health com. Alachua County Human Svcs. Planning Coun., 1980-82, acting pres. coun., 1982; mem. adv. bd. Nat. Cesarean/Support, Edn. and Concern, 1984-89; gov.'s rep. Healthy Mothers/Healthy Babies Steering Com., 1985—; chmn. rsch. adv. com. nat. study freestanding birth ctrs. Nat. Assn. Childbearing Ctrs., 1986-88; chmn. Gov.'s Task Force AIDS, 1988-90; mem. child health initiative nat. adv. com. Robert Wood Johnson Found., 1992—, dir. healthy futures: a program to imporve maternal and infant care in the South, 1987-92; mem. adv. com. to dir. Ctrs. Disease Control and Prevention, 1994—, chair, 1995--; mem. secy. adv. com. on Infant Mortality Health and Human Svcs., 1996--, Bright Futures for Women Commn., 2000--; vis. prof. various instns.; lectr. in field. Editor: Generally Funny: A Monograph of Medical Ancedotes and Cartoons, 1976; contbr. chpts. and revs. to books and articles to profl. jours. Active Nat. Found.-Mar. Dimes, 1978-88, chmn. edn. adv. com., 1978-82, 85-87; active Leadership Gainesville, 1978; mem. ob-gyn. alumni coun. med. sch. Northwestern U., 1986—; mem. Gov.'s Adv. Coun. Farmworkers Affairs, 1988—; mem. innovation coun. Ounce Prevention Fund Fla., 1994—. With USN, 1957-70, res. Recipient Cmty. Svc. award Gainesville Women's Health Ctr., 1976, Spl. MCH award Fla. Coun. Primary Care, 1984, Spl. Award for Mother-Infant Health, Coalition Fla. Childbirth Educators, 1984, Award for MCH Leadership, So. Health Assn., 1991, Mary E. Switzer award Assn. Schs. Applied Health Professions, 1992, State of Fla. Cabinet Disting. Svc. award, 1992; Rsch. fellow USN, Aviation Med. Acceleration Lab., 1961. Mem. AMA, APHA (mem. coun. maternal and child health 1985-88), Am. Coll. Ob-Gyn. (chmn. spl. interest group ambulatory reproductive health care 1978-80, chmn. dist. IV maternity mortality com. 1979-81, mem. com. health care underserved women 1988—, chmn. 1992, chmn. nat. fetal-infant mortality rev. steering com. 1990—), Nat. Assn. Childbearing Ctrs. (bd. dirs. 1983—), Nat. Perinatal Assn. (bd. dirs. 1996—), Fla. Ctr. Children and Youth, Fla. Healthy Mothers/Healthy Babies Coalition (Spl. Award for MCH Leadership 1985), Fla. Med. Assn. (mem. com. pub. health 1988—, mem. com. AIDS 1988-96), Fla. Obstet. and Gynecol. Soc., Fla. Perinatal Assn. (bd. dirs. 1993—), Fla. Pub. Health Assn. (chmn. maternal and child health sect. 1987-88, mem. jour. editl. bd. 1987—), Fla. Soc. Childbirth Educators, Assn. State and Territorial Health Ofcls. (mem. exec. com. 1991—, pres. 1993-94), Inst. Women's Health (founding mem.), W.Va. U. Alumni Assn. (life), Rotary Club Tallahassee (bd. dirs. 1989-90). Home: 1001 N Riverhills Dr Tampa FL 33617-4241 Office: MDC 056 13201 Bruce B Downs Blvd Tampa FL 33612-3805

MAHAN, CLARENCE, retired govenment official, writer; b. Dayton, Ohio, Jan. 1, 1939; s. Clarence Mahan and Elsie (Crouch) Dlitz; m. Suky Mahan, May 27, 1962; children: Sean M., Christiane Elizabeth. BA, U. Md., 1963; MA, Am. U., 1968; MBA, Syracuse U., 1969. Dep. comptroller U.S. Army, Japan, 1974-76; dep. chief program and budget Defense Commn. Agy., Arlington, Va., 1976; aide Asst. Sec. Army, Washington, 1976-77; chief operating appropriations Dept. AF, 1979-80; dir. fin. and acctg. Dept. Energy, 1980-81, dep. comptroller, 1981-82; dir. fiscal and contracts mgmt. EPA, 1982-83, dep. comptroller, 1983-85, dir. Rsch. Program Mgmt. Office, 1985-95. Instr., lectr. in field. Contbr. articles to profl. jours. and hort. mags. With U.S. Army, 1959-62, Korea. Mem. Am. Iris Soc. (bd. dirs., 2d v.p. 1991-95, 1st v.p. 1995-98, pres. 1998-2001), Hist. Iris Preservation Soc. (pres. 1991-93), Soc. Japanese Irises (pres. 1989-92), Reblooming Iris Soc. (bd. dirs. 1986-94, pres. 2002--). Democrat. Home and Office: 7311 Churchill Rd Mc Lean VA 22101-2001 E-mail: cemahan@aol.com.

MAHAN, DAVID JAMES, retired university official; b. St. Louis, May 29, 1934; s. John William and Eleanor (Johnson) M.; m. Jane E. Pyle, Nov. 28, 1957; children: Elizabeth Mahan-Shaw, Kathryn Goodman. BA, Okla. Baptist Coll., 1956; MA, Washington U., St. Louis, 1962, EdD, 1968. Cert. elem., secondary English tchr., Mo., cert. elem. prin., Mo., cert. supt., Mo. Adminstr., tchr. St. Louis Pub. Schs., 1958-90, supt., 1990-96; supt. in residence U. Mo., St. Louis, 1996-99. Co-author: The Faculty Team: School Organization for Results, 1971. Bd. dirs. Commerce and Growth Assn., St. Louis, 1990—, Asthma and Allergy Found. Am., St. Louis, 1990—, St. Louis Symphony Soc., 1992—, Boy Scouts Am., 1992—. Home: 5 Portland Ct Saint Louis MO 63108-1293

MAHAN, GERALD DENNIS, physics educator, researcher; b. Portland, Oreg., Nov. 24, 1937; s. Thomas Finley and Julia Kay (Swails) M.; m. Sally Ann Spaugh, Feb. 20, 1965; children— Christopher Parker, Susan Thayer, Roy Finley AB, Harvard U., 1959; PhD in Physics, U. Calif.-Berkeley, 1964. Rsch. physicist GE, Schenectady, 1963-67, part-time, 1967-84; assoc. prof. physics U. Oreg., Eugene, 1967-73; prof. physics Ind. U., Bloomington, 1973-82, disting. prof., 1982-84; disting. prof. physics U. Tenn., Knoxville, 1984—2001, Penn State U. , University Park. Guest prof. Niels Bohr Inst., Copenhagen, 1977-78 Author: Many-Particle Physics, 1981; contbr. numerous articles on physics to profl. jours. Alfred Sloan fellow, 1968-70. Fellow Am. Phys. Soc.; mem. NAS. Office: Penn State U 104 Davey Lab University Park PA 16802 E-mail: gmahan@psu.edu.

MAHAN, JAMES CAMERON, judge; b. El Paso, Tex., Dec. 16, 1943; m. Eileen Agnes Casale, Jan. 13, 1968; 1 child, James Cameron Jr. BA, U. Charleston, 1965; JD, Vanderbilt U., 1973. Bar: Nev. 1974, U.S. Dist. Ct. Nev. 1974, U.S. Ct. Appeals (9th cir.) 1975, U.S. Tax Ct. 1980, U.S. Supreme Ct. 1980. Assoc. Lee & Beasey, Las Vegas, Nev., 1974-75; mem. firm John Peter Lee Ltd., 1975-82; sr. ptnr. Mahan & Ellis, Chartered, 1982-99; dist. ct. judge 8th Jud. Dist. Nev., 1999—2002; U.S. dist. judge, 2002—. With USN, 1966-69. Office: 333 Las Vegas Blvd S Las Vegas NV 89101 E-mail: james_mahan@nvd.uscourts.gov.

MAHAN, JAMES S. communications company executive; BA in Econs., Washington & Lee U. V.p. Wachovia Bank & Trust Co., Winston-Salem, N.C.; co-founder Cardinal Bancshares, Lexington, Ky.; pres., COO, vice chmn. Citizens Union Nat. Bank & Trust Co.; CEO Security First Techs, Atlanta, 1995-99, S1 Corp., Atlanta, 1999—. Office: S1 Corp 3500 Lenox Rd Ste 200 Atlanta GA 30326

MAHAN, SHIRLEY JEAN, nursing educator; b. Corbin, Ky., July 19, 1937; d. Jacob Monroe and Geneva Samantha (Pennington) Lloyd; m. Clarence Edward Mahan, Mar. 28, 1954; children: Clarence Sandy, Randall Barry. AS in Nursing, Ea. Ky. U., 1985, BSN, 1989; MSN, Bellarmine Coll., 1999. Staff nurse Knox County Gen. Hosp., Barbourville, Ky., 1983-87, Bapt. Regional Med. Ctr., Corbin, 1987-93; mem. faculty Lincoln Meml. U., Harrogate, Tenn., 1989—. Mem. ANA, Ky. Nurse Assn., Nazarene Health Care Fellowship, Pinnacle Honor Soc., Sigma Theta Tau. Home: PO Box 8 Corbin KY 40702-0008

MAHANES, DAVID JAMES, JR. retired distillery executive; b. Lexington, Ky., June 19, 1923; s. David James and Ethel (Brock) M.; m. Dorothy Jean Richardson, Oct. 28, 1950; 1 child, David James III. BS, U. Ky., 1947; MBA, Harvard U., 1950. Regional mgr. Jack Daniel Distillery, Nashville, 1960-65, v.p., 1965-70, sr. v.p., 1970-71, exec. v.p., 1971-85, pres., 1985-88, chmn. bd. dirs. Chmn. bd. dirs. Early Times Distillery Co., Can. Mist Distilling Co., Thoroughbred Plastics Co. Lt. inf. AUS, 1943-46, ETO; lt. col. AG ret. Recipient Bronze Star; Runnerup as outstanding sales exec. Gallagher Report, 1982. Mem. SAR (pres. Andrew Jackson chpt.), Soc. Colonial Wars in Tenn. (gov., dep. gov. gen., sec.), English Speaking Union (dir.), Res. Officers Assn., The 200 Club, Belle Meade Country Club, Beaver Creek Club, Exch. Club, Tenn. Profl. Golfers Assn. (hon.), Nashville Srs. Golf Assn., Kappa Alpha, Beta Gamma Sigma. Republican. Presbyterian. Home: Apt 256 11 Burton Hills Blvd Nashville TN 37215-6141 E-mail: djmandot@aol.com.

MAHANES, MICHAEL WAYNE, organizational development executive; b. Fulton, Mo., Jan. 18, 1956; s. Paul W. and Betty Catherine (Kelsey) M.; m. Cynthia Anne Ward, June 13, 1981; children: Catherine Anne, Michael Wayne Jr., Ian Ward. BFA, Westminister Coll., 1977. Tchr. William Woods Coll., Fulton, 1978-79; dir. audio-visual studio Daniel/Flour Internat., 1979-81; dir. audio-visual dept. and Lifelong Learning Ctr., tng. coord. MEMC Electronics Materials Co., Spartanburg, S.C., 1981-98; corp. dir. orgnl. devel. Lockwood Greene, 1998—. Mem. com. Malcolm Baldrige Nat. Quality Award; dir. Skills Enhancement Ctr., Next Step Program, Life-Long Learning Ctr.; master trainer Zenger Miller; cons. in field, 1982—. Writer, dir., cameraman (video) Collective Works of Michael Mahanes, 1979—; writer, editor over 500 videos; co-inventor electronic data gathering indsl. problem solving method, 1981. Pre-sch. tchr. Southside Bapt. Ch., Spartanburg, 1982—; pre-sch. tchr. Southside Bapt. Ch., Spartanburg, 1986—, deacon, chmn. broadcast sound; active ARC; mem. Edn. Consensus Project, 1992—; cubmaster Cub Scout Pack 3. Mem. Am. Soc. Tng. and Devel., Internat. TV Assn., Carolina Soc. Tng. and Devel. Republican. Avocations: old movies, family outings to the beach and mountains. Office: Lockwood Greene 1500 Internat Dr Spartanburg SC 29304 E-mail: mmahanes@lg.com.

MAHANTHAPPA, KALYANA THIPPERUDRAIAH, physicist, educator; b. Hirehalli, Mysore, India, Oct. 29, 1934; s. Kalyana and Thippamma (Maddanappa) T.; m. Prameela Talkerappa, Oct. 30, 1961; children: Nagesh, Rudresh, Mahesh. BSc, Central Coll. Bangalore, India, 1954; MSc, Delhi U., 1956; PhD (Faculty Arts and Scis. fellow), Harvard, 1961. Research assoc. U. Cal. at Los Angeles, 1961-63; asst. prof. U. Pa., Phila., 1963-66; mem. Inst. Advanced Study, Princeton, N.J., 1964-65; assoc. prof. physics U. Colo., Boulder, 1966-69, prof., 1969—, faculty research fellow, 1970-71, 76-77, 83-84, 93-94. Vis. prof./scientist U. Rome, 1970, Internat. Ctr. for Theoretical Physics, 1971, Cambridge U., 1976-77; cons. Aerojet-Gen., L.A., 1962-63; dir. Summer Inst. Theoretical Physics, Boulder, 1968-69, NATO Advanced Study Inst. in Elem. Particles, 1979, NATO Advanced Rsch. Workshop on Superstrings, 1987; gen. dir. Theoretical Advanced Study Inst. in Particle Physics, 1989—; sr. vis. rsch. fellow Imperial Coll., London, 1983-84. Contbr. articles to profl. jours. Fellow Am. Phys. Soc.; mem. AAAS, Sigma Xi. Achievements include research theoretical high energy and elementary particle physics. Home: 4760 Lee Cir Boulder CO 80303-1111 E-mail: ktm@verb.colorado.edu.

MAHAR, ELLEN PATRICIA, law librarian; b. Washington, Jan. 15, 1938; d. Richard A. and Lina Mahar. BA, St. Joseph Coll., Emmitsburg, Md., 1959; MLS, U. Md., 1968. Asst. librarian Covington & Burling, Washington, 1971-73, libr. dir., 1978-92; librarian Shea & Gardner, 1974-78; mgr. info. ctr. Assn. Comml. Real Estate, Herndon, Va., 1992-94; head libr. Caplin & Drysdale Chtd., Washington, 1994—. Co-editor: Legislative History of the Securities Act of 1933 and the Securities Act of 1934, 11 vols., 1973. Mem. Am. Assn. Law Libraries, Spl. Libraries Assn., Law Librarians' Soc. Washington. Office: Caplin & Drysdale Chtd 1 Thomas Cir NW Fl 11 Washington DC 20005-5802

MAHAR, LAWRENCE WILLIAM, publisher, writer; b. Saratoga Springs, N.Y., July 18, 1928; s. John P. and Edna P. (Krajewski) M.; m. Hazel C. Holmwood, May 7, 1955; children: Michael, Laura, Monica, William, Frances, Daniel, Lawrence, Patrick. BA in English, Siena Coll., 1951. Advt. and pub. rels. dir. Stewart's Ice Cream Corp., Saratoga, 1953-56; mktg. communications mgr. GE, Waterford (N.Y.), Pittsfield, Mass., 1956-71; v.p. Ross Roy/Compton, Inc. Advt., N.Y.C., 1971-81; pres. L & H Mahar Art Publishers, Middle Grove, N.Y., 1981—. Cons. Ross Roy/Compton, Inc., N.Y.C., 1981-82. Contbr. articles to mags. and profl. jours. Mem. Bd. Edn., Saratoga Springs, 1968-69; publicity chmn. Saratoga County Am. Cancer Soc., Saratoga Springs, 1964-69; adv. com. N.Y. State Legis. Cpl. U.S. Army, 1951-53. Republican. Roman Catholic. Avocations: cross-country skiing, hiking. Home: 945 Murray Rd Middle Grove NY 12850-1141 Office: L&H Mahar Art Publishers 945 Murray Rd Middle Grove NY 12850-1141 E-mail: larrywmahar1@juno.com.

MAHARAM, LEWIS GARY, sports medicine physician; b. Bklyn., Feb. 2, 1955; s. Robert Donald and Jane Barbara (Lowy) M.; divorced; 1 child, Edward Raymond. BA in Biology with honors, Lafayette Coll., 1977; MD, Emory U., 1985. Cert. in sports medicine. Surg. intern Columbia-Presbyn. Med. Ctr., N.Y.C., 1985-86; med. intern Danbury (Conn.) Hosp., 1986-87; med. resident N.Y. Infirmary/Beekman Downtown Hosp., 1987-89; sports medicine fellow Pascack Valley Hosp., Westwood, N.J., 1989-90, dir. sports medicine fellowship program, 1990-91; med. dir. Met. Athletics Congress, N.Y.C., 1991—96. Med. dir. Nat. Scholastic Track and Field Championship, N.Y.C., 1989-96; vol. med. capt. N.Y.C. Marathon, 1987-99; med. cons. Am. Acad. Sports Dentistry, Maywood, N.J., 1990—; team physician Emerson (N.J.) High Sch. Football, 1989-90. Author: Maharam's Curve: The Exercise High—How to Get It, How to Keep It, 1992, A Healthy Body, 1998; contbr. articles to profl. jours.; med. advisor MasterSports newsletter. Fellow Am. Coll. Sports Medicine (pres. N.Y. chpt., med. dir. various marathons including N.Y.C. Marathon and Country Music Marathon); mem. ACP, Internat. Med. Dirs. Assn. (chmn. bd. govs.), Am. Running and Fitness Assn., Am. Bd. Sports Medicine (chmn. bd. examiners), Nat. Athletic Trainers Assn. (assoc.), Nat. Strength & Conditioning Assn., Downtown Athletic Club (chmn. sports medicine 1993—). Avocations: swimming, painting, writing. Home: 800A 5th Ave Ste 302 New York NY 10021-7215 Office: 800A 5th Ave Ste 302 New York NY 10021-7215

MAHARIDGE, DALE DIMITRO, journalist, educator; b. Cleve., Oct. 24, 1956; s. Steve and Joan (Kopfstein) M. Student, Cleve. State U., 1974-75. Free-lance reporter various publs., Cleve., 1976; reporter The Gazette, Medina, Ohio, 1977-78; free-lance reporter Cleve. Plain Dealer, 1978-80; reporter The Sacramento Bee, 1980-91; lectr. Stanford U., Palo Alto, Calif., 1992—. Author: Journey to Nowhere: The Saga of the New Underclass, 1985, repub. with introduction by Bruce Springsteen, 1996, And Their Children After Them, 1989 (Pulitzer Prize for gen. nonfiction 1990), The Last Great American Hobo, 1993, The Coming White Minority: California's Eruptions and the Nation's Future, 1996, Vintage Books edit., 1999; contbr. articles to profl. jours. Nieman fellow Harvard U., 1988; grantee Pope Found., 1994, Freedom Forum, 1995. Democrat. Office: Stanford U Dept Comm Bldg 120 Stanford CA 94305 E-mail: maharidg@leland.stanford.edu.

MAHDAVI, KAMAL B. writer, researcher; b. Esfahan, Iran, Sept. 1, 1933; came to U.S., 1958, naturalized. s. Ebrahim B. and Ghamar (Jalilian) M. BA, U. Calif., Berkeley, 1964; MA, U Toronto, 1965; postgrad., U. Cambridge, Eng., 1965-69. Cert. coll. tchr., Calif. R&D rschr. U. Stockholm, 1969-71; freelance rschr., writer self-employed, San Francisco, San Diego, 1972—. Ind. legal rschr. San Francisco, San Diego, 1980—. *Kamal B. Mahdavi's two discoveries that the socionatural problems are the scientific and technological problems unsolvable through the methodologies of the pseudosciences, such as the social and the behavioral sciences and the philosophical motions. Also, the United State of the North America is a de facto police state, not a genuine democracy. These are the subjects of the two future books respectively entitled, "The Solution of the Socionatural Problems" and "The De Facto Police State."* Author (as K.M.B. Writer): Technological Innovation: An Efficiency Investigation, 1972; contbr. articles to profl. jours. Civil rights litigant. Avocations: swimming, chess. Office: PO Box 121164 San Diego CA 92112-1164

MAHER, BRENDAN ARNOLD, psychology educator, editor; b. Widnes, Eng., Oct. 31, 1924; came to U.S., 1955; s. Thomas F. and Agnes (Power) M.; m. Winifred Barbara Brown, Aug. 27, 1952; children: Rebecca, Thomas, Nicholas, Liam, Niall. BA with honours, U. Manchester, Eng., 1950; MA, Ohio State U., 1951, PhD, 1954; student, U. Ill. Med. Sch., 1952-53; AM (hon.), Harvard, 1972; DPhil (hon.), U. Copenhagen, 1998. Diplomate Am. Bd. Examiners in Profl. Psychology. Psychologist Her Majesty's Prison, Wakefield, Eng., 1954-55; instr. Ohio State U., 1955-56; asst. prof. Northwestern U., 1956-58; asso. prof. La. State U., 1958-60; lectr. Harvard, 1960-64; chmn. Center Research Personality, 1962-64; prof. U. Wis., 1964-67, 71-72; vis. fellow U. Copenhagen, 1966-67, vis. fellow and rsch. scientist, 1979, 96-98; prof. psychology Brandeis U., 1967-72; dean Brandeis U. (Grad. Sch.), 1969-71, dean faculty, 1971-72; E. C. Henderson prof. psychology Harvard U., 1983-99, E.C. Henderson rsch. prof., 1999—, prof., 1972—, chmn. dept. psychology and social relations, 1973-78, chmn. dept. psychology, 1987-89, dean Grad. Sch. Arts and Scis., 1989-92; assoc. psychologist McLean Hosp., Belmont, Mass., 1968-77, psychologist, 1977-84. Cons. in medicine Peter Bent Brigham Hosp., Boston, 1977-85; cons. in psychology Mass. Gen. Hosp., 1977—. Author: Principles of Psychopathology, 1966, Introduction to Research in Psychopathology, 1970, A Passage to Sword Beach, 1996; co-editor: National Research Council: Research Doctorate Programs in the United States, 1995; editor Progress in Exptl. Personality Rsch., 1964-87, Jour. Cons. and Clin. Psychology, 1972-78; cons. editor Rev. Personality and Social Psychology, Clin. Psychology Rev. Served with Brit. Royal Navy, 1943-47. Recipient Zubin award for rsch. in psychopathology, 1998. Fellow AAAS, Am. Psychol. Soc.; mem. Brit. Psychol. Assn. (chartered psychologist U.K.), Soc. Rsch. in Psychopathology (pres. 1985-87), Phi Beta Kappa. Office: Harvard U William James Hall Cambridge MA 02138 also: Giffords Island Mahone Bay NS Canada E-mail: bam@wjh.harvard.edu.

MAHER, CORNELIUS CREEDON , III, neurologist, toxicologist, army officer; b. N.Y.C., Jan. 30, 1949; s. Cornelius Creedon Jr. and Hester (Sullivan) M.; m. Lynn Marie Elliott, July 15, 1972; children: Christa, Cornelius IV, Kimberley. BS in Chemistry, Boston Coll., 1969; MS in Chemistry, U. Mich., 1973, PhD in Chemistry and Environ. Health, 1976; MD, St. Louis U., 1986. Diplomate Am. Bd. Psychiatry and Neurology. Rsch. fellow Brookhaven Nat. Lab., Upton, N.Y., 1969; rsch. fellow then lectr. U. Mich., Ann Arbor, 1969-76; rsch. assoc. Children's Hosp. Med. Ctr., Boston, 1976-77; indsl. toxicologist West Allis (Wis.) Meml. Hosp., 1977-82; commd. 2d lt. U.S. Army, 1982, advanced through grades to col., 2001; intern in neurology Letterman Army Med. Ctr., San Francisco, 1986-87, resident in neurology, 1987-90; staff neurologist William Beaumont Army Med. Ctr., El Paso, 1990-94; asst. chief neurology dept. Walter Reed Army Med. Ctr., Washington, 1994-98; chief operational neurology Madigan Army Med. Ctr., Tacoma, 1998—2001; staff dir. Joint Readiness Clin. Adv. Bd., Ft. Detrick, Md., 2001—. Mem. neurology faculty Tex. Tech. U., 1991—, Uniformed Svcs. U. of Health Scis., 1995—, U. Wash., 1999—. Contbr. articles to profl. jours. Mem. AMA, Am. Acad. Neurology, Am. Chem. Soc., Assn. Mil. Surgeons, N.Y. Acad. Scis., Sigma Xi, Phi Lambda Upsilon, Alpha Chi Sigma. Office: JRCAB 1423 Sultan Dr Fort Detrick MD 21702 Business E-Mail: cornelius.maher@det.amedd.army.mil.

MAHER, DANA FITZGERALD, composer, musician; b. Tulsa, Okla., Aug. 8, 1969; d. Michael Thomas and Judith Welham Fitzgerald; m. Brian William Maher, Nov. 21, 1992; children: Quinn Christopher, Liam Joseph Godfrey. BA, U. Tulsa, 1991, MusM, 1996. Accompanist, choir dir. Trinity Presbyn. Ch., Tulsa, 1991-97; accompanist Tulsa Pub. Schs., 1995-98; pianist Goodwin/Maher Duo, Tulsa, 1995—; artistic dir. Amadeus Piano Festival, 1995—. Composer A Dwelling Place, 1997, Four Fables for Piano, 1999, Nocturne, 1999, An Artists Palette, 1999, Rustic Songs & Dances for piano solo (2000). Mem. Music Tchrs. Nat. Assn. (profl. cert. piano and theory), Okla. Music Tchrs. Assn. (adjudicator 1997—, jr. audition chair 1998—), Tulsa Music Tchrs. Assn. (bd. mem. 1996—), Hyechka Club (bd. mem. 1998—), Piano Study Club (pres. 1997-98). Avocations: reading, cooking. E-mail: edmaher@gbronline.com.

MAHER, DAVID WILLARD, lawyer; b. Chgo., Aug. 14, 1934; s. Chauncey Carter and Martha (Peppers) M.; m. Jill Waid Armagnac, Dec. 20, 1954; children: Philip Armagnac, Julia Armagnac. BA, Harvard, 1955, LLB, 1959. Bar: N.Y. 1960, Ill. 1961, Wis. 1996, U.S. Patent Office 1961. Pvt. practice, Boston, N.Y.C., 1958-60; assoc. Kirkland & Ellis, and predecessor firm, 1960-65, ptnr., 1966-78, Reuben & Proctor, 1978-86, Isham, Lincoln and Beale, 1986-88, Sonnenschein, Nath & Rosenthal, Chgo., 1988—. Gen. counsel BBB Chgo. and No. Ill.; lectr. DePaul U. Sch. Law, 1973—79, Loyola U. Law Sch., Chgo., 1980—84. Vis. com. U. Chgo. Div. Sch., 1986—. 2d lt. USAF, 1955-56. Fellow Am. Bar Found. (life); mem. ABA, Am. Law Inst., Ill. Bar Assn., Wis. State Bar, Chgo. Bar Assn., Internet Soc. (v.p. pub. policy), Chgo. Lit. Club, Union League Club, Tavern Club. Roman Catholic. Home: 501 N Clinton St Apt 1503 Chicago IL 60610-8886 Office: Sonnenschein Nath & Rosenthal 233 S Wacker Dr Ste 8000 Chicago IL 60606-6491 E-mail: dmaher@sonnenschein.com.

MAHER, E. J. retired priest; b. N.Y.C., Jan. 1, 1929; s. Bernard Joseph and Evelyn Marie (Feeney) Maher. Student, Niagara, N.Y., 1948—50; Bachelor's Degree, LaSalle U., 1953; Master's Degree, Temple U., 1958. Cert. secondary history Pa. History tchr. Archdiocese Phila., 1950—51; social studies tchr. Sch. Dist. Phila., 1953—82; priest Archdiocese of Phila., 1988—2000, ret., 2000—. Chaplain Blind Guild, Phila., 1999—, pres., 2001. Polit. campaigner Dem. Party, Phila., 1966. Mem.: KC (chancellor 1987—2001, Man of Yr. 1980). Democrat. Roman Catholic. Avocation: piloting small planes. Home and Office: St William Ch 6200 Rising Sun Ave Philadelphia PA 19111-5621

MAHER, FRANK ALOYSIUS, research and development executive, psychologist; b. Jamaica, N.Y., Mar. 31, 1941; s. Frank A. and Gertrude F. (Peterson) M.; m. Barbara A. Eggers, Aug. 14, 1965 (div. 1978); children: B. Kelly, F. Scott, Erin K.; m. Karen S. Adcock, June 28, 1980. BA, U. Dayton, 1966, MS, 1971. Lic. psychologist, Ohio. Research psychologist Ritchie Inc., Dayton, Ohio, 1965-68, Bunker Ramo, Dayton, 1968-70; lectr., research assoc. Wright State U., 1970-71; research psychologist USAF, Wright Patterson AFB, Ohio, 1971-84; dir. Perceptronics, Inc., Dayton, 1984-87; rsch. and devel. exec. Unisys, 1987-92, bus. devel. cons., 1992-94; dir. Gibson Fisher Ltd, 1997—. Counseling psychologist Eastway Mental Health Ctr., Dayton, 1974-75, Good Samaritan Mental Health Ctr., Dayton, 1979. Conbtg. author: Perceptions in Information Sciences; editor: Developmental Learning Handbook. Bd. dirs. Miami Valley Mental Health Assn., Dayton, 1974-77, Greene Mental Health Assn., Xenia, Ohio, 1977. Roman Catholic. Avocations: tennis, skiing, sailing, sports car racing. Office: Gibson Fisher 3070 Riverside Dr Columbus OH 43221 E-mail: frankamaher@aol.com.

MAHER, GARY LAURENCE, lawyer; b. Summit, N.J., Dec. 19, 1965; s. William J. and Eileen B. (Galen) M.; m. Dana V. Dombroski, Nov. 11, 1994; 2 children. BA in Psychology, U. Pa., 1988; JD, Rutgers U., Camden, 1992. Bar: N.J. 1992, Pa. 1992, U.S. Dist. Ct. N.J. 1992. Law clk. to Hon. Ross R. Anzaldi and Hon. Edward J. Toy, Superior Ct. of N.J., Elizabeth, 1993-94; assoc. Mandell & Selesner P.C., Red Bank, N.J., 1994-95; sr. litigation assoc. Shain, Schaffer & Rafanello, P.C., Bernardsville, 1995-2001; ptnr. Maher & Maher LLC, Scotch Plains, 2001—. Mem. Geneal. Soc. West Fields; trustee Geneal. Soc. N.J., 1995—. Avocations: music, inline skating, genealogy. Office: Maher & Maher LLC 106 Center St PO Box 983 Garwood NJ 07027-0983 E-mail: maherlaw@juno.com.

MAHER, L. JAMES, III, molecular biologist; b. Mpls., Nov. 28, 1960; s. Louis James and Elizabeth Jane (Crawford) M.; m. Laura Lee Moseng, July 2, 1983; children: Elizabeth Lillian, Christina Ailene. BS in Molecular Biology, U. Wis., 1983, PhD in Molecular Biology, 1988. Fellow U. Wis., Madison, 1983-84, rsch. asst., 1984-88; postdoctoral fellow Calif. Inst. Tech., Pasadena, 1988-91; asst. prof. molecular biology Eppley Inst., U. Nebr. Med. Ctr., Omaha, 1991-95; assoc. prof. biochem. molecular biology Mayo Found., Rochester, Minn., 1995-2000, prof., 2000—. Editorial bd. Antisense and Nuclear Acid Drug Design, 1991—, Nucleic Acids Rsch. Jour., 1988—; contbr. articles to profl. jours. Musician, Madison Symphony Orch., 1983-88, Calif. Inst. Tech. Symphony Orch., L.A., 1988-91. Gosney fellow, 1988; Am. Cancer Soc. postdoctoral fellow, 1988. Mem. AAAS, Phi Beta Kappa. Evangelical Christian Ch. Achievements include research in chemical and biochemical agents designed to artificially regulate the flow of genetic information in biological systems. Office: Mayo Found Dept Biochem and Molec Biol 200 1st St SW Rochester MN 55905-0001

MAHER, LISA KRUG, editor; b. N.Y.C., Nov. 11, 1952; d. George William and Rita (Earle) Krug; m. Barney Rosset, Nov. 5, 1980 (div. Dec. 1990); 1 child, Chantal; m. Richard Maher, July 29, 2000. BA magna cum laude, Smith Coll., 1974; MA, Columbia U., 1976. Editor Latin Am. Series, N.Y.C., 1976-86; gen. editor Grove Press, 1987-89; mng. editor Aperture, 1987-90; pvt. practice, 1990—. Writer and editor UNICEF, N.Y.C., 1995—. Author: James Baldwin, 1989, Thurgood Marshall, 1993 (Outstanding Book For Teenagers award 1994). Mem. Phi Beta Kappa

MAHER, LOUIS JAMES, JR. geologist, educator; b. Iowa City, Dec. 18, 1933; s. Louis James and Edith Marie (Ham) M.; m. Elizabeth Jane Crawford, June 7, 1956; children: Louis James, Robert Crawford, Barbara Ruth. BA, U. Iowa, 1955, MS, 1959; PhD, U. Minn., 1961. Mem. faculty dept. geology and geophysics U. Wis.-Madison, 1962—, prof., 1970—, chmn. dept., 1980-84. Contbr. articles to profl. jours. Served with U.S. Army, 1956-58. Danforth fellow, 1955-61; NSF fellow, 1959-61; NATO fellow, 1961-62 Fellow AAAS, Geol. Soc. Am.; mem. Am. Quaternary Assn., Ecol. Soc. Am., Wis. Acad. Sci., Arts and Letters, Sigma Xi. Episcopalian. Office: U Wis Dept Geology and Geoph 1215 W Dayton St Madison WI 53706-1600 E-mail: maher@geology.wisc.edu.

MAHER, PATRICIA MARIE, lawyer; b. Bklyn., June 26, 1954; d. Joseph Francis and Margaret (O'Keefe) M.; m. Charles A. Arcodia; children: Marybeth, Nicole, Juliette. BA, Siena Coll., 1976; JD, St. John's U., 1983. Bar: Mass. 1983, N.Y. 1984, Md. 1991, Va. 1992, D.C. 1992. Social worker Charlton Sch., Burnt Hills, N.Y., 1977-79; ptnr. Maher & Lawrence, N.Y.C., 1983-93; sr. trial atty. PMA Ins., 1993-96; mng. ptnr. Maher & Assocs., Towson, Md., 1996—. Mem. ABA, N.Y. State Bar Assn. Avocations: jogging, golf, tennis.

MAHER, PATRICK JOSEPH, retired utility company executive; b. Dublin, Ireland, Apr. 20, 1936; came to U.S., 1946, naturalized, 1955; s. Pierce Albeus and Mary (Brady) M.; children: Kathy, Kevin, Erin, Megan. BBA, Iona Coll., 1959; MBA, N.Y. U., 1965. With spl. devel. program Chase Manhattan Bank, N.Y.C., 1961-64, 2d v.p. fiduciary dept., 1964-68; asst. v.p. Nat. Comml. Bank, Albany, N.Y., 1968-70; chief sect. utility fin. N.Y. State Pub. Svc. Commn., 1970-74; v.p., chief fin. officer Washington Gas Light Co., 1974-80, exec. v.p. fin. and adminstrn., 1980-87, pres., 1987-92, 1992-99, chmn. bd. dirs., CEO, 1993-98, chmn. bd. dirs., 1998-99. Served with USAR, 1960-61. Mem. Am. Gas Assn., Nat. Soc. Rate of Return Analysts, Natural Gas Men's Roundtable, Inst. Gas Tech., Associated Electric and Gas Ins. Svcs., U.S. C. of C., Rotary, N.Y. Athletic Club, Washington City Club. Roman Catholic.

MAHER, ROBERT RAYMOND, JR. music educator; b. Providence, Oct. 11, 1969; s. Robert Raymond, Sr. and Virginia Sharon (DeFusco) Maher; m. Patricia Ann Lill, June 26, 1999. MusB, R.I. Coll., 1993; cert. in tchg., U. R.I., 1998. Provisional cert. R.I. State Dept. Edn., profl. cert. R.I. State Dept. Edn. Choral/gen. music tchr. Cranston (R.I.) Pub. Sch. Sys., 1992—98; studio tchr. guitar Chris B's Music, 1992—98; band, gen. music tchr. Smithfield Pub. Sch. Sys., 1999; studio tchr. guitar Votta Music, Johnston, 1999—2002; choral/gen. music tchr. Providence Pub. Sch. Sys., 1999—. Treas. Harry Kizirian Elem. Sch. PTO, Providence, 2001—. Mem.: R.I. Music Educator's Assn., Music Educator's Nat. Conf. Avocations: bicycling, composing, golf, performing, reading.

MAHER, STEPHEN TRIVETT, lawyer, educator; b. N.Y.C., Nov. 21, 1949; s. William John and Jean Dorothy (Trivett) M.; m. Sharon Leslie Wolfe, Nov. 22, 1981 (dec.); children: Meaghan Wolfe, Caitlin Wolfe. BA, NYU, 1971; JD, U. Miami, Coral Gables, Fla., 1975. Bar: Fla. 1975, U.S. Dist. Ct. (so. dist.) Fla. 1976, D.C. 1979, U.S. Dist. Ct. (no. dist.) Fla. 1979, U.S. Supreme Ct. 1980, U.S. Ct. Appeals (5th and 11th cirs.) 1981, U.S. Dist. Ct. (so. dist.) Fla. 1982, U.S. Dist. Ct. (mid. dist.) Fla. 1983. Assoc. Chonin & Levey, Miami, 1975; staff atty. Legal Svcs. of Greater Miami, Inc., 1975-81; assoc. Finley, Kumble, Wagner et al, Miami, 1981-84; dir. clin. program Sch. of Law U. Miami, Coral Gables, 1984-90, assoc. prof. law Sch. of Law, 1984-92; pvt. practice Stephen T. Maher, P.A., Miami, Fla., 1992—. Mem. Fla. Bar/Fla. Bar Found. Joint Commn. on Delivery Legal Svcs. to the Indigent, Tallahassee, 1990-91, chair, organizer Seventh Adminstrv. Law Conf., Tallahassee, 1990, Conf. on the Fla. Constn., 1995; cons. on in-house legal edn. Contbr. articles to profl. jours. Fellow Fla. Bar Found. (life, bd. dirs. 1984-91); mem. ABA, Fla. Bar (chair adminstrv. law sect. 1993-94, chair coun. of sects. 1996-97), Dade County Bar Assn. Home: 1015 Sevilla Ave Miami FL 33134-6328 Office: 1500 Miami Ctr 201 S Biscayne Blvd Miami FL 33131-4332

MAHER, TERRY MARINA, religious organization administrator; b. Phila., Oct. 13, 1955; d. Thomas Michael and Marion Teresa (Corbett) M. BA in History and Religious Studies, U. San Diego, 1977; M in Theol. Studies, Cath. Theol. U., Chgo., 1989. Cert. bereavement facilitator. Dir. religious edn. Diocese of San Diego, 1977-80, Archdiocese of Cin., 1982-84, assoc. dir. youth ministry, 1984-87; pastoral assoc. Diocese of Toledo, 1989-95, Good Shepherd Catholic Ch., Cin., 1997—. State chancellor Internat. Educators for Peace Edn. Contbr. poetry to mags. Sec. social concerns bd. Met. Chs. United, Dayton; mem. justice com. Sisters of the Precious Blood; active tour to explore conditions in Nicaragua, New Orleans, 1983, 10-day tour of Guatemala, 1991, tour of Mexico City, 1992, Grenada, 1997; founder, v.p., bd. dirs. Care and Share Ctr. City of Sandusky, Ohio, 1991-95; Ohio state chancellor Internat. Educators for World Peace; v.p. Care and Share, Inc. of Erie County, 1993-95, Refugee Resettlement, 2001. Mem. Sanctuary, Pledge of Resistance, Internat. Assn. Educators for Peace (state chancellor), Am. Acad. Bereavement. Democrat. Avocations: racquetball, biking, non-violent sports, roller blading. Home: 7033 Windword Way Apt 235 Cincinnati OH 45241-4547

MAHER, THOMAS GEORGE, producer, media educator; b. St. Louis, Feb. 18, 1947; s. Dale Russel and Dorothy Leone (Levzow) M.; m. (div.). BA, St. Louis U., 1969, AM, 1971; PhD, U. So. Calif., 1985. Cert. C.C. tchr. and supr., Calif. Tchg. fellow St. Louis U., 1969-71; assoc. prof. Chaffey Coll., Rancho Cucamonga, Calif., 1974-79, media dir., 1980-84; assoc. producer Corp. for C.C. TV, Orange, 1979-80; assoc. dir. instrnl. tech. Calif. State Poly. U., Pomona, 1984-89; dir. office media svcs. U. Ill., Chgo., 1989-94; dir. office instrnl. svcs. Colo. State U., Ft. Collins, 1994—, interim v.p. divsn. ednl. outreach, 2000—02. Cons. Rsch. Comm., Ltd., Boston, 1984—; book reviewer Focal Press, Inc., Boston, 1985—. Writer: (TV series) Project: Universe, 1978 (Emmy award nomination 1979), The Business of Management, 1981; assoc. producer, dir., writer (TV series) Oceanus: The Marine Environment, 1979 (Emmy award 1980); exec. producer (TV program) For the People: Local Gov. Budget Making, 1992 (Cert. Merit, Chgo. Internat. Film/Video Festival 1992); producer, dir. numerous ednl. TV shows, 1974—. 1st lt. USAF, 1971-74. Mary Clemens scholar St. Louis U., 1965-67, Educare scholar U. So. Calif., 1983-84. Mem. Acad. TV Arts and Scis., Am. Ednl. Research Assn., Assn. for Ednl. Comm. and Tech. Democrat. Roman Catholic. Avocations: reading spy novels, computers, running, theatre. Office: Colo State U A 71 Clark Bldg Fort Collins CO 80523-0001 E-mail: tmaher@colostate.edu.

MAHER, TIMOTHY JOHN, pharmacologist, educator; b. Boston, Nov. 24, 1953; s. Robert Daniel and Veronica Irene (Cody) M.; m. Barbara Jean Walz, Aug. 20, 1977; children: Andrew Michael, Matthew Edward, Elizabeth Irene, Jonathan Daniel. BS, Boston State Coll., 1976; PhD, Mass. Coll. Pharmacy, 1980. Asst. prof. Mass. Coll. Pharmacy, Boston, 1980-83, assoc. prof., 1983-87, prof., 1987—, chmn., 1987-93, dir. pharm. scis., 1994-99, Sawyer prof. pharm. scis., 1994—; exec. dir., dean rsch. and grad. studies Longwood Pharm. Rsch., Inc. Postdoctoral fellow MIT, Cambridge, 1983-88, lectr., 1988—; bd. dirs. Mass. Soc. Med. Rsch., Chelmsford, 1985—; adv. bd. Mass. Poison Control System, Boston, 1990—. Contbr. over 150 articles to profl. jours. Roman Catholic. Achievements include 4 patents, involving the use of L-Tyrosine to enhance/supplement the pharmacological activity of various sympathomimetic amine drugs. Office: Mass Coll Pharmacy 179 Longwood Ave Boston MA 02115-5804 E-mail: tmaher@mcp.edu.

MAHER, WILLIAM JAMES, investment executive; b. Chgo., Feb. 23, 1937; s. Alexander E. and Merle G. Maher. BBA, Marquette U., 1961. Merchandising exec. Montgomery Ward & Co., Inc., Chgo., 1962-68; mgmt. cons. Cresap, McCormack & Paget, N.Y.C., 1968-69; v.p., treas. Solar Prodns., Inc., L.A., 1969-72; v.p., sec., treas. Creative Mgmt. Assocs., 1972-74; v.p., dir. Josephson Internat., Inc., 1975-83; pres. Tipperary Prodns., Inc., Beverly Hills, Calif., 1983-88, Winter Park Capital Assets, Inc., 1989-98; investment cons. L.A., 1999—. Office: 10354 Wilshire Blvd Ste 40 Los Angeles CA 90024-4726

MAHESH, VIRENDRA BHUSHAN, endocrinologist; b. India, Apr. 25, 1932; came to U.S., 1958, naturalized, 1968; s. Narinjan Prasad and Sobhagyawati; m. Sushila Kumari Aggarwal, June 29, 1955; children: Anita Rani, Vinit Kumar. BSc with honors, Patna U., India, 1951; MSc in Chemistry, Delhi U., India, 1953, PhD, 1955; DPhil in Biol. Sci, Oxford U., 1958. James Hudson Brown Meml. fellow Yale U., 1958-59; asst. rsch. prof. endocrinology Med. Coll. Ga., Augusta, 1959-63, assoc. rsch. prof., 1963-66, prof., 1966-70, Regents prof., 1970-86, Robert B. Greenblatt prof., 1979-99, chmn. endocrinology, 1972-86, chmn., Regents prof. physiology and endocrinology, 1986-99, chmn. physiology and endocrinology, 1986-99, regents prof., chmn. emeritus physiology and endocrinology, 1999—, Robert B. Greenblatt prof. emeritus endocrinology, 1999—. Dir. Ctr. for Population Studies, 1971-99; mem. reproductive biology study sect. NIH, 1977-81, mem. human embryology and devel. study sect. NIH, 1982-86, 90-93, chmn., 1991-93. Contbr. articles to profl. jours., chpts. to books; editor: The Pituitary, a Current Review, Functional Correlates of Hormone Receptors in Reproduction, Recent Advances in Fertility Research, Hirsuitism and Virilism, Regulation of Ovarian and Testicular Function, Excitatory Amino Acids: Their Role in Neuroendocrine Function; mem. editl. bd. Steroids, 1963—, Jour. of Clin. Endocrinology and Metabolism, 1976-81, Jour. Steroid Biochemistry and Molecular Biology, 1991—, Assisted Reproductive Tech./Andrology, 1993—, Endocrinology, 1999—; mem. adv. bd. Maturitas, 1977-81; editor-in-chief Biology of Reprodn., 1999—. Recipient Rubin award Am. Soc. Study Sterility, 1962, Billings Silver medal, 1965, Best Tchr. award freshman class Sch. Medicine, Med. Coll. Ga., 1969, Outstanding Faculty award Sch. Medicine, 1992, Outstanding Faculty award Sch. Grad. Studies, 1981, 94, Disting. Teaching award, 1988, Excellence in Rsch. award Grad. Faculty Assembly, 1987-91, 93-95, Disting. Scientist award Assn. Scientist Indian Origin in Am., 1989, Lifetime Achievement award Sch. Medicine, 1997; rsch. grantee NIH, 1960—. Mem. Chem. Soc. (Eng.), Soc. Biochem. and Molecular Biol., Soc. Neurosci., Endocrine Soc., Soc. for Gynecologic Investigation, Internat. Soc. Neuroendocrinology, Soc. for Study Reproduction (Carl G. Hartman award 1996), Am. Physiol. Soc., Internat. Soc. Reproductive Medicine (pres. 1980-82), Soc. Exptl. Biology and Medicine, Am. Fertility Soc., Am. Assn. Lab. Animal Sci., N.Y. Acad. Scis., AAUP, Sigma Xi. Office: Med Coll of Ga Dept Physiology & Endocrinology Augusta GA 30912-3000 E-mail: vmahesh@mail.mcg.edu.

MAHEU, SHIRLEY, Canadian legislator; b. Montreal, Que., Can., Oct. 7, 1931; d. George William Johnson and Bertha Hunt; m. Renè Albert Maheu, Sept. 5, 1953; children: Ronadl, Richard, Daniel, Marc. Diploma, O'Sullivan Bus. Coll. Cert. ins. broker. Ins. broker; mcpl. councillor City of Saint-Laurent, Canada, 1982-88; mem. City of Saint-Laurent Mcpl. Coun., 1982—86; mem. from Saint-Laurent Cartierville Ho. of Commons, Canada, 1988-96; mem. Can. Senate, Ottawa, Canada, 1996—. Pres. Saint-Laurent br. Red Cross Soc. Mem.: Saint-Laurent C. of C. Roman Catholic. Office: Canadian Senate Wellington St EB Rm 263 Ottawa ON Canada K1A 0A4

MAHEY, JOHN ANDREW, retired museum director; b. DuBois, Pa., Mar. 30, 1932; s. Manasseh A. and Bernyce (Holdar) M. Student, Columbia U., 1950-52; BA, Pa. State U., 1959, MA, 1962. Asst. dir. Peale Mus., Balt., 1964-69; dir. E.B. Crocker Art Gallery, 1969-72, Cummer Gallery of Art, 1972-75, Meml. Art Gallery of U. Rochester, 1975-79; chief curator Philbrook Art Center, Tulsa, 1979-84; dir. San Antonio Mus. Art, 1984-89, Flint (Mich.) Inst. of Arts, 1989-96. Contbr. articles on artists to art his. jours.; author exhbn. catalogs. Fulbright scholar, 1962 Mem. Phi Beta Kappa, Phi Alpha Theta. Home: 6212 Spring Knoll Dr Harrisburg PA 17111-6861 E-mail: mahey@aol.com.

MAHFOOD, STEPHEN MICHAEL, governmental agency executive; b. Evansville, Ind., Feb. 12, 1949; s. George Mahfood and Bonnie Short Morse; m. Kathleen Kas; children: Nadia Joan, Leila Emma, Toni Henzler. BS, Rutgers U., 1971; grad. environ. leadership program, Yale U., 1992. Environ. dir. Project Hope, Tunisia, 1975-77; dir. prin. asst. Dept. of Health Mo. State Health Planning and Devel. Agy., Jefferson City, 1977-78, dir., 1978-81; gen. mgr. Chimney Rock (N.C.) Co., 1982-84; dir. Mo. Environ. Improvement and Energy Resources Authority, Jefferson City, 1984-97, Mo. Dept. Natural Resources, Jefferson City, 1998—. Vol. YMCA, Beirut, Lebanon, 1974; past pres. Coun. of Pollution Control Fin. Agys., environ. fin. adv. bd. EPA; appointed Congressman Anthony's Ho. Ways and Means Task Force on Pub. Fin.; past pres. Mo. Waste Control Coalition; mem., co-founder Coun. Infrastructure Fin. Authorities; mem. Environ. Coun. of States, Govs. Task Force on Compensation, Govs. Adv. Com. on Chip Mills. Recipient Achievement award Mo. Waste Control Coalition, 1986, 88, Presdl. Environ. Challenge award, 1992. Mem. Am. Mgmt. Assn., Am. Planning Assn., Nat. Assn. Environ. Profls., Missouri River Basin Assn. (bd. dirs.), Upper Miss. Rural Basin Assn. (bd. dirs.), Mo. Soil and Water Commn. Avocations: canoeing, cross country skiing, hiking, motorcycling, horseback riding. Home: 7311 North Shore Dr Hartsburg MO 65039-9211 Office: Mo Dept Natural Resources PO Box 176 Jefferson City MO 65102-0176

MAHFOUZ, ILHAM BADREDDINE, artist; b. Damascus, Syria, Jan. 2, 1956; came to U.S., 1972; d. Abdul Rahman Badreddine and Zabia Zebian Keilani; m. Abdul Razak Mahfouz, Aug. 27, 1972; children: Ruba, Rodwan. BFA in Painting, Ea. Mich. U., 1992; cert. interior design, La Salle U., 1979. Mem. Student Artist Gallery/Ea. Mich. U., Ypsilanti, 1991-92, Access, Dearborn, Mich., 1990-93; tchr. ceramic, painting, mixed media Pontiac (Mich.) Art Ctr., 1997-2001; tchr. ceramic, mixed media Birmingham Bloomfield (Mich.) Art Ctr., 1999—; Arabic lang. instr. U. Detroit Mercy, 2001—; tchr. Pontiac Art Ctr., 1997—. Ceramics and mixed media tchr. Pontiac Creative Art Ctr., Mich., 1997-2000; tchr. art Internat. Sch., Farmington Hill, Mich., 1997; co-founder Alternative Artists Group, 1994—; tchr. Lake Orion Sch. Author: poetry;one-woman shows include The Cultural Assn., Franklin, Mich., 1989, Islamic Cultural Inst., Auburn Hills, Mich., 1989, M.Y.N.A. Art Show, Franklin, 1991—92, Alternative Artist Space Gallery, Southfield, Mich., 1997, Trapper Alley Gallery, Detroit, 1998, Urban Park Gallery, 1998, Pontiac Creative Art Ctr., 2000, exhibited in group shows at Common Ground Gallery, Windsor, Ont., Can., 1994, Arab World Festival, Detroit, 1994, Agora Gallery, N.Y.C., 1994, 1998, Mich. Sci. and Rsch. Devel., Dearborn, 1995, Pontiac Artists Studio Tour, 1996, Arab/Latino Art Show, Detroit, 1996, Oak Park Libr., Mich., 1997, Pontiac Art Ctr., 1997, Friendship Fedn., El-Cajon, Calif., 1997, Contemporary Mus., 1999—2000, Pontiac Creative Art Ctr., 1999—2000, Farmington Hills (Mich.) Festival of Art, 2000, Dream of Humanity, Southfield, 2000, Swedish-Am. Mus. Ctr., Chgo., 2001, Bagly House, Detroit, 2001, numerous others; contbr. articles to profl. jours. including Arab Am. Jour., Al-Dar Al Arabi; subject of articles Al-Dar Al Arabi mag., Manhattan Arts Internat., 1993, New Art Internat., 2000. Recipient Merit award Manhattan Arts Internat., N.Y., 1993, 1st prize McKenny Union's Art Show, Ea. Mich. U., 1991, Earth and Art Gallery, Milford, Mich., 1990. Mem. Internat. Muslimah Women Artists Group (pres. 1997-98), Golden Key. Islamic. Avocations: Arabic and conversational Spanish languages. E-mail: ilhamart@hotmail.com.

MAHL, GEORGE FRANKLIN, psychoanalyst, psychologist, educator; b. Akron, Ohio, Nov. 27, 1917; s. Floyd Alexander and Margaret (Strecker) M.; m. Martha Jane Fenn, Jan. 10, 1944; 1 dau., Barbara Jessica. A. B., Oberlin Coll., 1939, MA, 1941; PhD, Yale U., 1948; certificate, Western New Eng. Inst. Psychoanalysis, 1962. Asst. psychology Oberlin Coll., 1939-41; rsch. asst. in psychology Yale U., New Haven, 1941-42, mem. faculty, 1947—, prof. psychiatry and psychology, 1964-88, prof. emeritus, 1988—; tchr. Western New Eng. Inst. Psychoanalysis, 1961-85, pres., 1972-74. Served to 1st lt. AUS, 1942-46. Fellow AAAS, APA; mem. Ea. Psychol. Assn., Western New Eng. Inst. Psychoanalysis, Western New Eng. Psychoanalytic Soc., Internat. Psychoanalytical Assn., Inst. Psychoanalytic Tng. and Rsch. (N.Y.). Home: 106 Bayard Ave North Haven CT 06473-4303

MAHLA, MICHAEL E. anesthesiologist, educator; b. Wilmington, Del., Mar. 8, 1953; s. Elbert Myron and Mary Pauline (Tice) M.; m. Sno Ellen White, June 8, 1979; 1 child, Melody Joy. BS in Chemistry, Davidson Coll., 1975; MD, Jefferson Med. Coll., 1979. Diplomate Am. Bd. Anesthesiology. Intern Walter Reed AMC, Washington, 1979-80, resident in anesthesiology, 1980-83; fellow in neuroanesthesiology Johns Hopkins Med. Inst., Balt., 1983; mem. staff Shands Teaching Hosp., Gainesville, Fla.; assoc. prof. anesthesiology/neurosurgery U. Fla. Coll. Medicine. Program dir. anesthesiology residency Walter Reed AMC, Washington, 1986-88; assoc. prof., assoc. chair edn. dept. anesthesiology U. Fla. Coll. Medicine, Gainesville, 1995—. Author: (with others) Clinical Anesthesiology Practice, 1994, Clinical Neuroanesthesia, 1997. Fellow Am. Soc. Neurologic Monitoring; mem. AMA, Am. Soc. Anesthesiologists, Soc. Neurosurg. Anesthesia and Critical Care. Office: Box 100254 Dept Anesthesiology Gainesville FL 32610-0254

MAHLBURG, NORINE ELIZABETH, retired nurse; b. Onawa, Iowa, June 16, 1917; d. James Erve and Florence Elizabeth (Larson) Zortman; m. Milton William Mahlburg, Mar. 4, 1946; children: Suzanne, William, Marie, Robert. RN, St. Joseph Coll. Nursing, 1945; BSN, St. Francis Coll., 1975. RN, Iowa, Ill. Pvt. duty nurse Third Dist., Sioux City, Iowa, 1945-46, Rockford, Ill., 1947-61; polio nurse ARC, Rockford (Ill.) Hosps., 1945; new born nursery Swedish-Am. Hosp., Rockford, 1962; shop nurse Giant Photos, 1963-67; with Staff Relief Health Care Instns., 1967-76; staff nurse of devel. disabilities Singer Zone Ctr., Ill. Dept. Mental Health, 1976-91, ret., 1991. Author: (booklet) Birding in Rockford, 1952, (book) Larson-Fors History, 1993. Donor, advisor Rockford Peace and Justice, 1985—. Recipient Life Pin Nat. PTA, 1963, Scouter's Key Cub Scouts Am., 1967, Disaster pin ARC. Mem. ANA (50 Yr. mem.), Rockford Woman's Club (sec. 1994), North Ctrl. Ill. (life, pres. 1975-85), Ornithol. Soc. (bd. dirs. 1991-94), DAR (bd. dirs. 1987-89), Swedish Hist. Soc. (sec. 1993—), Moose Club (com. 1984—), Rock River Gem and Mineral Soc., Burpee Natural History Assn. (life). Democrat. Roman Catholic. Avocations: Great book club, travel, gardening, nature study, bridge. Home: 6 Johns Woods Dr Rockford IL 61103-1680

MAHLE, CHRISTOPH ERHARD, electrical engineer; b. Stuttgart, Germany, Mar. 7, 1938; came to U.S., 1968; s. Ernst Johannes and Else (Wurth) M.; m. Mary Heavenrich, Mar. 23, 1975; children: Lisa, Charles. Diploma engring., Swiss Fed. Inst. Polytech., Zurich, 1961, D of Sci. Tech., 1966. Rsch. asst. Swiss Fed. Inst. Tech., Zurich, Switzerland, 1961-67; with tech. staff Comsat Labs., Clarksburg, Md., 1968-71, sect. head, 1971-73, dept. mgr., 1973-81, dir., 1981-83, exec. dir., 1983-94, v.p., 1995-96; ret., 1996. Patentee in field; contbr. articles to profl. jours. Fellow IEEE. Avocations: music, mountain climbing. E-mail: chrismahle@usa.net.

MAHLER, EDWARD L. engineer, consultant; b. Waynesboro, Va., May 16, 1957; s. Marvin C. Mahler; m. Susan C. Cunningham, July 15, 2000; children: Laura, Rachael, Audra Snyder. BS, Va. Inst. Tech. and State U., 1979. Cert. energy mgr., indoor air quality profl. Maj. account exec. Am. Electric Power, Christiansburg, Va., 1996—98; owner, team leader Mahlertech Svcs., Roanoke, 1999—. Mem.: AEE, ASHRAE, Chamber of Commerce. Office: Mahlertech Svcs P O Box 7925 Roanoke VA 24019 Office Fax: 1-888-677-6838. E-mail: mahlertechservices@cox.net.

MAHLER, HALFDAN THEODOR, physician, health organization executive; b. Vivild, Denmark, Apr. 21, 1923; s. Magnus and Benedicte (Suadicani) M.; m. Ebba Fischer-Simonsen, Aug. 31, 1957; children: Per Bo, Finn. MD, U. Copenhagen, 1948, postgrad. degree in pub. health; LLD (hon.), U. Nottingham, Eng., 1975; MD (hon.), Karolinska Inst., Stockholm, 1977; Docteur, de l'Universite des Scis. Sociales de Toulouse, France, 1977; DPH (hon.), Seoul Nat. U., 1979; ScD (hon.), U. Lagos, Nigeria, 1979, Emory U., 1989; MD (hon.), Warsaw Med. Acad., 1980; LHD, U. Nacional Federico Villareal, Lima, Peru, 1980; LHD (hon.), U. Gand, Belgium, 1983, CUNY, 1989; MD (hon.), Charles U., Prague, 1982, Mahidol U., Bangkok, Thailand, 1982, Aarhus U., Denmark, 1988, U. Copenhagen, 1988, Aga Khan U., Pakistan, 1989; LHD (hon.), U. Nacional Autonoma de Nicaragua, 1983; PhD (hon.), The Semmelweis U., Budapest, Hungary, 1987; LLD (hon.), McMaster U., Can., 1989; DSc (hon.), SUNY, 1990; MD (hon.), U. Newcastle Upon Tyne, 1990; LLD (hon.), U. Exeter, 1990, U. Toronto, 1990. Specialized tng. in TB; active field of internat. pub. health work; planning officer mass Tb campaign Ecuador, 1950-51; sr. officer nat. Tb program WHO, India, 1951-61, chief Tb unit, Hdqrs., 1962-69, sec. to expert adv. panel on Tb, 1962-69, dir. project systems analysis, 1969-70, asst. dir.-gen. div. health services and div. family health, 1970-73, dir.-gen., 1973-88, dir. gen. emeritus, 1988; sec. gen. Internat. Planned Parenthood Fedn., 1989-95. Contbr. articles on epidemiology and control of Tb, polit., social, econ, and technol. priorities in health sector, application of systems analysis to health care problems to profl. jours. Decorated Grand Officier de l'Ordre Nat. du Benin, 1975, Grand Officier de l'Ordre Nat. du. Voltaique, Upper Volta, 1978, comdr. de l'Ordre Nat. du Mali, 1982, Grand Officer de l'Ordre du Merite de la Rep. du Senegal, 1982, comdr. 1st class Order White Rose (Finland), Grand Officier de l'Ordre nat. malgache, Madagascar, 1987, Grand Cross Icelandic Order of the Falcon, 1988, Grand Cordon of Order Sacred Treasure, Japan, 1988, Bourgeoisie d'Honneur, Geneva, Switzererland, Grand Croix De L'Ordre De Merite, Luxenbourg, 1990; recipient Jana Evangelisty Purkyne medal (Presdl. award) Prague, 1974, Comenius U. gold medal Bratislava, 1974, Carlo Forlanini gold medal Federazione Italiana contro la Tubercolosi et le Malattie Polmonari Sociali Rome, 1975, Ernest Carlsens Found. Prize Copenhagen, 1980, Georg Barfred-Pedersen prize Copenhagen, 1982, Hagedorn medal and prize Denmark, 1986, Freedom From Want medal Roosevelt Inst., 1988, Storkors Af Dannebrogsordenen, Denmark, 1988; hon. prof. U. Nacional Mayor de San Marcos, Lima, Peru, U. Chile Faculty of Medicine, Beijing Med. Coll., Rep. of China, Shanghai Med. U.; Bartel World Affairs fellow Cornell U., 1988; U.N. Population award, 1995, Andrija Stampar award, 1995. Fellow Royal Coll. Physicians (London), Faculty Community Medicine of Royal Colls. Physicians U.K. (hon.), Indian Soc. for Malaria and other Communicable Diseases (hon.), Royal Soc. Medicine (London) (hon., U.K.-U.S. Hewitt award 1992), London Sch. Hygiene and Tropical Medicine (hon.); mem. Med. Assn. Argentina (hon.), Latin Am. Med. Assn. (hon.), Italian Soc. Tropical Medicine (hon.), Belgium Soc. Tropical Medicine (assoc.), Societe medicale de Geneve (hon.), Union internationale contre la Tuberculose (hon.), Societe francaise d'Hygiene, de Medecine sociale et de Genie sanitaire (hon.), Uganda Med. Assn. (hon. life), Coll. Physicians and Surgeons, Bangladesh Royal Coll. Gen. Practitioners (ad eundem), List of Honour of the Internat. Dental Fedn., Am. Pub. Health Assn. (hon.), Nat. Acad. Medicine Mex. (hon.), Nat. Acad. Buenos Aires (hon.), Swedish Soc. Medicine (hon.), Brit. Medal Assn. (hon. fgn. corr. 1990), Inst. Medicine (NAS U.S.A.). Home and Office: Chemin de Pont-Céard 12 CH-1290 Versoix Switzerland Fax: 022-755 26 10. E-mail: halfdan.mahler@bluewin.ch.

MAHLER, PHILIP HENRY, mathematics educator; b. Boston, Aug. 27, 1946; s. Henry Siever and Anne Elizabeth (McInerny) M.; m. Marguerite Aline St. Jean, Sept. 27, 1969. BA, Assumption Coll., 1968; MA in Teaching, U. Fla., 1976. Instr. Henry Ford C.C., Dearborn, Mich., 1977-81; computer programmer Pub. Svc. Co. N.H., Manchester, 1981-82; prof. Middlesex C.C., Bedford, Mass., 1982—. Author: Trigonometry, 1994, College Algebra and Trigonometry, 1994, Precalculus, 1995. With USN, 1968-72. Mem. Math. Assn. Am., Am. Math. Assn. Two-Yr. Colls. (v.p. 1996-99, pres. 2001--), New Eng. Math. Assn. Two-Yr. Colls. (pres. 1992-93), Mass. C.C. Coun. (bd. dirs. 1984-96, Jon Butler award 1993, v.p. 1996-00, pres. 2000-02). Democrat. Avocations: flying, astronomy, traveling. Office: Middlesex C C Springs Rd Bedford MA 01730 E-mail: mahlerp@middlesex.cc.ma.us.

MAHLER, RICHARD JOSEPH, internist; b. N.Y.C., Mar. 4, 1934; s. Jacob and Naomi (Feder) M.; m. Ida May Adler, Aug. 23, 1960; children: Susan Toba, Jonathan David. BA, NYU, 1955; MD, N.Y. Med. Coll., 1959. Diplomate Am. Bd. Internal Medicine. Intern New Rochelle (N.Y.) Hosp., 1960; resident in internal medicine N.Y. Med. Coll., N.Y.C., 1960-63, metabolic rsch. fellow, 1962-63, instr. medicine, 1964-67, asst. prof., 1967-70, assoc. prof., 1970-71; traveling fellow N.Y. Acad. Medicine, 1963-64; practice medicine specializing in internal medicine N.Y.C., 1964-71; chief sect. diabetes Met. Hosp., 1968-71; assoc. dir. dept. metabolism and endocrinology City Hope Med. Ctr., 1971-73; dir. dept. metabolism and endocrinology Eisenhower Med. Ctr., Palm Desert, Calif., 1973-88, mem. med. staff, 1973-88, pres., 1976-79; clin. assoc. prof. medicine Cornell U. Med. Coll. Dept. Medicine, Section Endocrinology, 1988—; assoc. attending physician N.Y. Hosp., 1988—. Med. cons. to Merck and Co., Rahway, N.J., 1971-74, U.S. Vitamin Corp., N.Y.C., 1973-76; spl. cons. to FDA, 1972. Assoc. editor Hormone and Metabolic Rsch., 1969-76, co-editor, 1976—; assoc. editor Jour. Clin. Endocrinology and Metabolism, 1997—; contbr. articles on metabolic rsch. and diabetes to profl. jours., chpts. to med. books. Fellow ACP; mem. Endocrine Soc., Am. Diabetes Assn. (Devel. award 1966-67), Am. Fedn. Clin. Research, Diabetes Assn. So. Calif., Western Soc. Clin. Research, Am. Physiol. Soc., N.Y. Acad. Scis., Royal Soc. Medicine, Assn. Am. Med. Colls., Alpha Omega Alpha. Jewish. Home: 165 E 72d St New York NY 10021-4335 Office: 220 E 69th St New York NY 10021

MAHLER, RICHARD TERENCE, finance executive; b. Galt, Ont., Can., May 15, 1943; s. Lawrence Herman and Therese (Trepanier) M.; m. Susan Jane Campbell, May 25, 1968; children: Stephen, Katherine. BSc, U. Waterloo, 1966; MBA, McMaster U., Hamilton, 1975. Asst. contr. Ford Motor Can., Oakville, Ont., 1967-81; v.p. fin., chief fin. officer Amdahl Can. Ltd., Toronto, 1981-90; exec. v.p., CFO Finning Internat. Inc., Vancouver, B.C., 1990—. Chmn. Oakville Galleries, Ont., 1971-79; pres. U. Waterloo Adv. Coun., 1984-90; bd. dirs. Nat. Ballet Sch., Toronto; dir. Vancouver Bd. Trade; past chmn. coop. coun. Simon Fraser U., 1993-95; mem. bus. coun. B.C. Econ. Policy Adv. Group, 1994. Mem. Fin. Execs. Inst., Coun. Fin. Execs. Conf. Bd. Can., Hollyburn Country Club, Seymour Golf Club, Canadian Club Vancouver. Office: Finning Internat Inc Ste 1000 Park Pl 666 Burrard St Vancouver BC Canada V6C 2X8

MAHLER, STEPHANIE IRENE, retired administrative manager; b. Bennington, Vt., Jan. 29, 1952; d. Guenther Alexander and Barbara Irene (Overlock) M.; m. Kirby B. Schuller, Apr. 28, 1990. BA in Speech with honors, Allegheny Coll., 1973. Customer service rep. Albany (N.Y.) Felt Co., 1974-77; order systems analyst Miller Brewing Co., Milw., 1977-78, area mgr., 1978-80, regional adminstr., 1980-83, price promotions mgr., 1983-85, asst. brand mgr., 1985-88, mgr. mktg. projects, 1988-90; market mgr. Johnson Controls, Inc., 1990-92; sr. agt. AMEX Life Assurance Co., 1992-93; asst. to the pres. Performance Enhancement Psychol. and Phys. Therapy Svcs., Brookfield, Wis., 1994-95, mktg. dir., 1994-95; asst. to gen. mgr. SPI Comms., 1996, human resources adminstr., 1996-97, acct., 1996-97, systems adminstr., 1997; regional adminstrv. mgr. STS Cons., Ltd., Milw., 1997-2000; ret., 2000. Mem. pres.'s club Albany Area C. of C., Albany, 1975-76; mgmt. advisor Jr. Achievment, 1973-74. Named One of Outstanding Young Women of Am., Montgomery, Ala., 1983; Presdl. scholar, 1969, Alden scholar Allegheny Coll., Meadville, Pa., 1970-73. Mem. AAUW, NOW (at-large), Phi Beta Kappa. Home: 8325 N Links Way Milwaukee WI 53217-2821

MAHLMAN, JERRY DAVID, research meteorologist; b. Crawford, Nebr., Feb. 21, 1940; s. Earl Lewis and Ruth Margaret (Callendar) M.; m. Janet Kay Hilgenberg, June 10, 1962; children: Gary Martin, Julie Kay AB, Chadron State Coll., Nebr., 1962; MS, Colo. State U., 1964, PhD, 1967; LHD (hon.), Chadron State Coll., 2000. Instr. Colo. State U., Fort Collins, 1964-67; from asst. prof. to assoc. prof. Naval Postgrad. Sch., Monterey, Calif., 1967-70; rsch. meteorologist NOAA Geophys. Fluid Dynamics Lab., Princeton, NJ, 1970-84, lab. dir., 1984-2000; lectr. with rank of prof. Princeton U., 1980—2002; sr. rsch. fellow Nat. Ctr. for Atmospheric Rsch., Boulder, Colo., 2001—. Chmn. panel on mid-atmosphere program NAS-NRC, 1982-84, mem. climate rsch. com., 1986-89, mem. panel on dynamic extended range forecasting, 1987-90; mem. U.S.-USSR Commn. on Global Ecology, 1989-92; mem. Bd. on Global Change, 1991-95, Bd. on Sustainable Devel., 1995-2000; U.S. rep. world climate rsch. program Joint Sci. Commn., 1991-96. Contbr. over 100 articles to profl. jours. Bd. dirs. Lawrence Non-Profit Housing Inc., 1978-88. Recipient Disting. Authorship award Dept. Commerce, 1980, 81, Gold medal, 1986, Disting. Svc. award Chadron State Coll., 1984, Presdl. Rank award disting. exec. 1994, Honor Alumnus award Colo. State U. 1995, Climate Protection award EPA, 2000. Fellow Am. Geophys. Union (Jule Charney lectr. 1993), Am. Meterol. Soc. (awards com. 1984, 95, chmn. 2000, chmn. upper atmosphere com. 1979, assoc. editor Jour. Atmospheric Sci. 1979-86, councilor 1991-94, Editor's award 1978, Carl-Gustaf Rossby Rsch. medal 1994, disting. lectr. 1999). Home: 460 Golden Ln Longmont CO 80501 Office: Nat Ctr for Atmospheric Rsch PO Box 300 Boulder CO 80307-3000 E-mail: jmahlman@ucar.edu.

MAHMOOD, AAMER, computer system architect; b. Lahore, Pakistan, Jan. 27, 1956; came to U.S., 1979; s. Muhammad Iftikhar Quereshi and Farakh (Sultana) Iftikhar; m. Samira Aftab, June 28, 1985; children: Muhammad Bilal, Umer Ali. BSEE with honors, U. Engring. & Tech., Lahore, 1979; MSEE, Stanford U., 1980, PhD in Elec. Engring., 1986. Lectr. U. Egnring. & Tech., 1979; teaching asst. Stanford (Calif.) U., 1980-82, rsch. asst., 1983-85; mem. tech. staff Rolm Milspec Computers, San Jose, Calif., 1986-88; mgr., tech. leader CPU and memory systems Amdahl/Advanced Systems, Sunnyvale, 1988-93; sr. engring. architect network hardware Cisco Systems, San Jose, 1994—. Contbr. articles to profl. jours. Bd. of Secondary Edn. merit scholar, Lahore, 1971, Bd. of Intermediate Edn. talent scholar, Lahore, 1973. Mem. IEEE (sr.), Assn. Computing Machinery, Stanford Alumni Assn. (life). Home: 1098 Cardinal Way Palo Alto CA 94303-3540 E-mail: amahmood@cisco.com.

MAHMOOD, AKHTAR HASAN, physicist, educator, researcher; b. Dhaka, Bangladesh, Mar. 26, 1969; s. Mohammad Ahsan Ali and Selima Akhtar; m. Sitara Swati Zaman, Jan. 12, 1997. BSc with honors, Edinboro U. Pa., 1992; MSc, SUNY, Albany, 1994, PhD, 1998. Rsch. asst. SUNY, Albany, 1994-98, lab. instr., 1994-97, rsch. scientist high energy physics lab., 1998-99; lectr. U. Tex. Pan Am., Edinburg, 1998-99, asst. prof., dir. Ctr. High Energy Physics, 1999—. Grant reviewer NASA, 1999, NSF, 2000, 02. Contbr. over 200 articles to profl. jours. Recipient Provost Scholar Awd, 2000, Rsch. Coll. Sci. & Engring 2000, Outstanding Faculty award, 2000, Cos&E Rsch. Excellence award, 2000; Rsch. grantee Tex. Higher Edn. Coord. Bd., 1999, Rsch. grantee U. Tex. Pan Am., 1999, Faculty Rsch. grantee, 1999, 2000, 01. Mem. AAAS, CLEO, Am. Phys. Soc., N.Y. Acad. Scis., Sigma Xi, Pi Mu Epsilon, Phi Kappa Phi. Moslem. Achievements include discovery of several new subatomic particles. Home: 917 Stonehaven Blvd Apt 3 Edinburg TX 78539-7576 Office: U Tex Pan Am Dept Physics 1201 W University Dr Edinburg TX 78539-2909 E-mail: mahmooda@panam.edu.

MAHMOOD, ASIM, neurosurgeon; b. Lahore, Punjab, Pakistan, Dec. 4, 1957; came to U.S., 1984; s. Mohammed Iftikhar Qureshi and Farakh (Sultana) Iftikhar; m. Noor-Ul-Ain Farooqi, Dec. 29, 1989; children: Selina, Nijah, Aamal. MBBS, King Edward Med. Coll., Lahore, Pakistan, 1982. Resident in gen. surgery Easton (Pa.) Hosp., 1986-88; resident in neurosurgery Henry Ford Hosp., Detroit, 1989-93, sr. staff neurosurgery, 1994—. Contbr. articles to profl. jours. Mem. Islamic Assn. Greater Detroit, 1995. Recipient Dr. Rahim Khan Gold medal U. Punjab, Lahore, 1982. Fellow Royal Coll. Surgeons (Scotland); mem. North Am. Skull Base Soc., Am. Assn. Neurol. Surgeons, Mich. Med. Soc., Wayne County Med. Soc. Islamic. Avocations: reading, movies. Home: 4317 Ramsgate Ln Bloomfield Hills MI 48302-1639 Office: Henry Ford Hosp 2799 W Grand Blvd Detroit MI 48202-2689 E-mail: nsaam@neuro.hfh.edu.

MAHMOOD, ISMAIL ALI, artist, systems analyst; b. Cairo, May 18, 1946; came to U.S., 1986; children: Self, Ramy. BA in Commerce, Ein-Shams U., Cairo, 1969, MS in Computer Sci., 1985; postgrad., North Light Art Sch., 1991. Mainframes computer analyst programmer Egypt Air, Cairo, 1971-86, Am. Airlines, Dallas, 1986-94, Contact Network, Dallas, 1994-95, Compupros, Inc., Dallas, 1995-97, Sabre, Dallas, 1997—2002; ret., 2002. Exhibited in group shows at Eastside Creative Arts Club, 1992 (2d pl.), Trinity Arts Guild, 1994 (1st pl.), Irving Art Assn., 1996 (2d pl.). Mem. Assoc. Creative Artists, Irving Art Assn. Home: 2516 Chinaberry Dr Bedford TX 76021-5214 E-mail: ismmahmood@aol.com.

MAHMOOD, KHALID, physician; b. Gujranwala, Pakistan, Feb. 15, 1938; came to U.S., 1971, naturalized, 1977; s. Muhammad Saied and Mumtaz Begum (M. Ataullah) Mazharie; m. Patricia Hope Ashleman, June 15, 1975 (div. 1996); children: Farrah Renee, Tarik Adam, Anissa Natalia. F.Sc., Govt.

Coll., Abbottabad, Pakistan, 1956; B.Sc., U. Punjab, 1960; MB, BS, King Edward Med. Coll., 1962. Intern Danbury (Conn.) Hosp., 1963-64; resident in surgery Lewis Gale Hosp., Roanoke, Va., 1964-65; resident in otolaryngology Albert Einstein Coll. Medicine and Bronx Mcpl. Hosp. Ctr., N.Y.C., 1965—68; instr., fellow Bronx Municipal Hosp., 1968-69; research fellow otolaryngology U. Toronto, Ontario, Can., 1969-70; practice medicine specializing in otolaryngology Toronto, 1971, Sandusky, Ohio, 1972—; mem. cons. staff, chief otolaryngologist Good Samaritan Hosp., 1972-85; mem. staff, cons., chief div. otolaryngology Providence Hosp., 1974—2001, chief of staff, 1995-96; mem. cons. staff St. Francis Rehab. Hosp., Greensprings, 1980-88; mem. active and cons. staff Firelands Regional Med. Ctr., Sandusky, 1985—. Clin. asst. prof. dept. surgery (otolaryngology), Med. Coll. Ohio, Toledo, 1984—. Fellow ACS, Royal Coll. Physicians and Surgeons (Can.), Am. Acad. Otolaryngology and Head and Neck Surgery; mem. Erie County Med. Soc. (pres.-elect 2000-01), Ohio Med. Assn. Avocation: research on tritiated thymidine study of irradiated cancer larynx, 1968-69. Home: 18 Sawmill Creek Dr W Huron OH 44839-1029 Office: 1221 Hayes Ave Sandusky OH 44870-3345 E-mail: khalidmdus@yahoo.com.

MAHMOOD, M. F. research scientist, educator; s. Abdul Wahab and Mehrun Nisa (Begum) M.; m. Ghazala Mahmood; children: Fahad, Zafar, Asad and Sara. MS in mathematics, Allahabad Univ., Allahabad, India, 1966; MS in physics, Aligarh Univ., Aligarh, India, 1968; PhD in physics, Howard Univ., Wash., D.C., 1988. Tchr. in physics & mathematics Schs./Colls./Univs., India and Abroad, 1970-82; adj. prof. in mathematics & physics Univ. of Dist. of Columbia, Wash., D.C., 1983-88; rsch. scientist Howard Univ., 1988—; adj. assoc. prof. Div. of Theoretical Physics, Molise, Italy, 1995—; asst. prof. of mathematics Howard Univ., Wash., D.C., 1999—. Contbr. articles to profl. jours., contbr. rsch. papers in field, contbr. in scientific experimentation. Recipient rsch. grants, Air Force Office of Scientific rsch. and Dept. of Army, Wash. D.C., 1994-97, 1995-00. Mem. Am. Physical Soc., Optical Soc. of Amer., Inst. of Elec. and Electronics Engrs., SPIE (The Internat. Soc. for Optical Engrg.), Optical Soc. of Amer., Hon. Soc., Sigma Pi Sigma Physics. Avocations: reading, listening to classical music, drawing, badminton, chess. Office: Howard U 2400 6th St NW MSC 590048 Washington DC 20059 E-mail: mmahmood@howard.edu.

MAHMOUD, ADEL A. infectious diseases, tropical medicine physician, pharmaceutical executive; b. Cairo, Egypt, Aug. 24, 1941; arrived in U.S., 1972; s. Abdel Fattah and Fathia (Osman) Mahmoud; m. Sally L. Hodder, Jan. 31, 1993. Grad., Cairo U., 1958, MD, 1963; PhD, U. London, 1971. Lic. Ohio. Asst. lectr. Ain Shams U., Cairo, 1965—68; WHO fellow U. London, 1969—72; rsch. assoc., prof. Case Western Res. U., Cleve., 1973—87; physician-in-chief Univ. Hosps., 1987—98; prof., chmn. dept. medicine Case Western Res. U., 1987—98; pres. vaccines Merck & Co. Inc., Whitehouse Sta., NJ, 1998—. Mem. adv. bd. Nat. Allergy and Infectious Diseases, Forgarty Internat. Ctr., Bethesda, Md.; chmn. forum on emerging infections Inst. Medicine. Editor: The Eosinophil in Health and Disease, 1979, Tropical and Geographical Medicine, 1990, Schistosomaisis, Tropical Medicine Sci. and Practice, Vol. 1, 2001, Biological Threats and Terrorism: Assessing the Science and Response Capabilities, 2002. Fellow: Infectious Diseases Soc. Am.; mem.: Inst. Medicine, Assn. Am. Physicians, Am. Soc. Clin. Investigations. Office: Merck & Co One Merck Dr Whitehouse Station NJ 08889

MAHMOUD, AHMED MOHAMED, information technology executive; b. Tripoli, Libya, June 6, 1964; s. Mohamed R. and Nadia A. (El Boury) M.; m. Michele A. Mobley, May 26, 1990; children: Maryam, Adam, Sami. BS, Tex. A&M U., 1987, MS, 1990. Rsch. asst. Tex. A&M U., College Station, 1986-90; computational programmer U. Houston, 1990-91; database analyst Eastman Kodak Co., Rochester, N.Y., 1991-95; sr. mgr. corp. info. tech. Dell Computer Corp., Austin, Tex., 1995-99, dir. corp. info. tech., 1999—. E-mail: ahmed_mahmoud@dell.com.

MAHMOUD, HOSAM M. statistics educator, academic administrator; b. Cairo, Apr. 16, 1954; came to U.S., 1979; s. M. Mahmoud and M. Shafi; m. Fatemeh Rahnavard, Sept. 14, 1984. BS, Cairo U., 1976; MS, Ohio State U., 1981, PhD, 1983. Prof. George Washington U., 1983—, chmn. stats. dept., 1998—2001. Vis. prof. Waterloo U., Ont., Can., 1990, Princeton (N.J.) U., 1998; vis. scholar Ctr. Math. Rsch., Spain, 1996, Int. Nat. Rsch., France, 1997. Author books; contbr. articles to profl. jours. Office: George Washington U Dept Stats 2201 G St # 315 Washington DC 20052-0001

MAHMOUDI, MASSOUD, b. Tehran, June 2, 1957; s. Mohammad Hossein and Zohreh Mahmoudi. BS, Insts. of Paramed. Scis., Tehran, 1978; MS, Ea. N.Mex. U., 1980; PhD, U. North Tex., 1986; DO, Kirksville Coll. Osteo. Med., 1994. Registered microbiologist; lic. physician, N.J., Calif.; DEA; bd. cert. internal medicine, allergy & immunology; diplomate Am. Osteo. Bd. Internal Medicine. Rsch. asst. dept. biol. scis. U. North Tex., Denton, 1981; postdoctoral fellow dept. cell biology and neurosci. U. Tex. Southwestern Med. Ctr., Dallas, 1986-87, postdoctoral rsch. fellow dept. microbiology, 1987-89, rsch. assoc., 1989, rsch. assoc. dept. biochemistry, 1989-90; intern in primary care internal medicine Yale U. Sch. Medicine, 1994-95; resident in internal medicine U. Medicine and Dentistry of N.J., 1995-98; clin. fellow in allergy and clin. immunology U. Calif., Davis, 1998-00; pres., CEO Western Allied Med. Group, Sacramento, 1999-2000; pvt. practice allergy and clin. immunology, 2000—; clin. asst. prof. dept. internal medicine Coll. Osteo. Med. U. Medicine and Dentistry of N.J., 2000—; mem. clin. faculty San Fracisco Coll. Osteo. Medicine Touro U., 2000—. Presenter in field. Contbr. numerous articles and abstracts to profl. jours., including Jour. Cellular and Molecular Biology, Allergy, Jour. Cell Biology. Mem. AMA (Physician Recognition award), ACP, Am. Acad. Allergy Asthma and Immunology, Am. Coll. Allergy, Asthma and Immunology, Am. Coll. Osteo. Internists, Am. Osteo. Assn., Allergy Assn. No. Calif., Am. Osteo. Coll. Allergy and Immunology (3rd v.p.), Nat. Registry of Microbiologists, Tex. Assn. Osteo. Physicians, N.J. Assn. Osteopathic Physicians and Surgeons. Avocations: tennis, swimming. Office: 221 Almendra Ave Los Gatos CA 95030 E-mail: ma0003@dnamail.com.

MAHMUD, SHIREEN DIANNE, photographer; b. Chittagong, Pakistan, Oct. 4, 1949; came to U.S., 1974; d. Mohammed Mazhurul Qudus and Mumtaz Mahal Begum; m. Abdul Wazed Mahmud, Apr. 10, 1966 (div. 1996); children: Sharmin, Anita. BA in Mass Comm., U. Hartford, 1982. Part-time med. sec., Middletown, Conn., 1979-82; freelance photographer, 1985—; typist Aetna Ins. Co., 1991; freelance photographer Conn. Post. Prodr. feature program Storer Cable Comm., Clinton, Conn., 1991-95; freelance photojournalist Middletown Press, Durham Gazette, Middletown, 1991-95; mem. Bridgeport Regional Bus. Coun., 1997. Literacy vol. Russell Libr., Middletown, Conn. Mem. AAUW, Nat. League Am. Pen Women, Internat. Soc. Poets (Hall of Fame award 1997), Conn. Soc. Poets, Conn. Songwriter's Assn., Internat. Platform Assn. Home: 2612 North Ave Unit G-4 Bridgeport CT 06604-2324

MAHNKE, KURT LUTHER, psychotherapist, clergyman; b. Milw., Feb. 18, 1945; s. Jonathan Henry and Lydia Ann (Pickron) M.; m. Dana Moore, Mar. 19, 1971; children: Rachel Lee, Timothy Kurt, Jonathan Roy. BA, Northwestern Coll., Watertown, Wis., 1967; MDiv, Wis. Luth. Sem., 1971; MA, No. Ariz. U., 1984. Cert. profl. counselor, marriage and family therapist, ind. clin. social worker, trauma counselor. Pastor Redeemer/Grace Luth. Chs., Phoenix & Casa Grande, Ariz., 1971-75, St. Philips Luth. Ch., Milw., 1975-78, 1st Luth. Ch., Prescott, Ariz., 1978-82; counselor NAU Counseling/Testing Ctr., Flagstaff, 1983-84, Wis. Luth. Child & Family Svc., Wausau, Wis., 1984-86, area adminstr. Appleton, 1986-89; founder, psychotherapist Family Therapy & Anxiety Ctr., Menasha, 1989—. Part-time min. St. Paul Luth. Ch., Appleton, 1993-94; presenter Nat. Police Week, Washington, 1995—, 13th Nat. Conf. on Anxiety Disorders, Charleston, S,C., 1993; cons. editor Northwestern Pub. House, Milw., 1990—; adj. faculty Fox Valley Tech. Coll., Appleton, 1993—; on-call critical incident stress debriefer, U.S. Marshall's Svc., 1999—; critical incident stress cons., Appleton Police Dept., Bri Ilion Police Dept., Menasha Police Dept., Neenah Police Dept., Two Rivers Police Dept., Outagamie County Sheriff's Dept., 1999—, New London Police Dept., Winnebago County Sheriff's Dept., 2000—. Cons. editor Counseling at the Cross, 1990; contbr. articles to profl. publs. Cons. Wis. Evang. Luth. Synod, Milw., 1986—; cons. crisis counselor Fox Valley Luth. H.S., Appleton, Appleton Police Dept., Menasha Police Dept., Brillion Police Dept. Outagamie County Sheriff's Dept., 1998—, New London Police Dept., Winnegago County Sheriff's Dept., U.S. Marshall's Office, 1999—; crisis counselor, clin. dir. Critical Incident Stress Debriefing Team, Fox Cities, 1991—, U.S. Atty.'s Office, 1995-99; victim crisis response coord. Appleton Police Dept., 1996-99, Neenah Police Dept., Menasha Police Dept., Town of Menasha Police Dept., 1997-99. Mem. Internat. Critical Stress Found., Nat. Anxiety Found., Obsessive Compulsive Found. Republican. Lutheran. Office: Family Therapy/Anxiety Ctr 1477 Kenwood Ctr Menasha WI 54952-1160 E-mail: klmahnke@aol.com.

MAHOMED, YOUSUF, physician, cardiothoracic surgeon; b. Pretoria, South Africa, Dec. 23, 1945; s. Moosa Kara and Fatima Mahomed (Ahmed) M.; m. Lorraine S. Mahomed, Jan. 26, 1980; children: Julie M., Adam J. MD, Royal Coll. Surgeons Ireland, 1970. Diplomate Am. Bd. Thoracic Surgery. Resident in surgery St. Joseph Hosp./U. Mich., Ann Arbor, 1971-75; staff surgeon U. Calif., Davis, 1975-76; resident in plastic surgery Case Western Res. U., Cleve., 1976-78, staff in plastic surgery/oncology, 1978-79; resident in cardiothoracic surgery Ind. U., Indpls., 1979-81, staff cardiothoracic surgeon, 1981—, prof. surgery, 1991—, dir. adult cardiac surgery, 1995—. Cons. Ethicon; prin. investigator Cardiogenesis; mem. cardiothoracic core team Clarian Health. Contbr. chpts. to books, articles to profl. jours. Bd. dirs. Park Tudor Sch., Indpls., 1992—. Fellow ACS, Am. Coll. Cardiology, Am. Coll. Chest Physicians, Internat. Coll. Surgeons; mem. Am. Assn. Thoracic Surgery, Internat. Soc. Minimally Invasive Cardiac Surgery, Soc. Vascular Surgery, Soc. Thoracic Surgeons, Am. Heart Assn., Internat. Soc. for Heart and Lung Transplantation, Internat. Soc. of Cardiovascular Surgery. Islamic. Office: Ind U Sch Medicine Clarion Cardiovascular Ctr 1801 N Senate Blvd MPC 2 Ste 3550 Indianapolis IN 46202-5112

MAHON, ARTHUR J. lawyer; b. N.Y.C., Jan. 13, 1934; s. Arthur Logan and Mary Agnes (Craine) M.; m. Myra E. Murphy, Aug. 10, 1957; children: Maura, Madonna, Arthur, Nancy. BA, Manhattan Coll., 1955; JD, NYU, 1958. Bar: N.Y., Fla., D.C. Adj. prof. law NYU Sch. of Law, N.Y.C., 1964-78; ptnr. Mudge, Rose, Guthrie, Alexander & Ferdon, 1970-94; counsel Donovan Leisure Newton & Irvine, 1994-98, McDermott, Will & Emery, 1998—. Trustee Manhattan Coll., N.Y., 1988—, Adrian and Jesse Archbold Charitable Trust, N.Y.C., 1976—, N.Y. Presbyn. Hosp., N.Y.C., 1994—; mem. joint bd. N.Y. Hosp.-Cornell Med. Ctr., N.Y.C., 1990-98; com. on trust and estate gift plans Rockefeller U., N.Y.C., 1984—; bd. dirs. United Way Internat., 1988-94, Alexandria, Va., chmn. planned giving and endowments com. Archdiocese, N.Y.C., 1982-97; bd. overseers Cornell Med. Coll., N.Y.C., 1986—, chmn., 1992-95; dir. Am. Skin Assn., N.Y.C., 1989—; counsel Ira W. De Camp Found., 1994—; v.p., dir. Cath. Communal Fund, Archdiocese of N.Y., 1997—, trustee Inner City Scholarship Fund, 1998—. Served to capt. USAF, 1958-60. Root-Tilden scholar NYU. Mem. N.Y. State Bar Assn., Bar Assn. City of N.Y., Fla. Bar Assn., D.C. Bar Assn. Home: 16 Cambridge Dr Madison CT 06443-3016 Office: McDermott Will & Emery 50 Rockefeller Plz Fl 12 New York NY 10020-1600

MAHON, JOHN FRANCIS, management policy educator; b. Phila., June 25, 1948; s. Joseph A. and Mary J. (Mclaughlin) M.; m. Julia M. Weiss, Oct. 18, 1969; 1 child, Elizabeth. BS in Econs., U. Pa., 1970; MBA with honors, Bryant Coll., Smithfield, R.I., 1976; D in Bus. Adminstr., Boston U., 1982. Instr. mgmt. Southeastern Mass. U., 1977-80; instr., rsch. asst. Boston U., 1977-80, from asst. prof. to prof. mgmt. policy, 1980—, interim dir. exec. edn. programs, 1984, assoc. dean sch. mgmt., 1987-88. Speaker and presenter in field. Author: (with others) Management: Functions and Responsibilities, 1990, Management Instructors's Handbook, vols. I and II, 1990, Management Student's Handbook, 1990, Management Test Bank, 1990, Management Video Handbook, 1990; assoc. editor Internat. Jour. Orgnl. Analysis, 1991-92; mem. editorial bd. Case Rsch. Jour., 1988—; contbr. articles to profl. jours. Mem. Zoning Bd. Rev., Newport, R.I., 1981-84; bd. dirs. Issue Exch., Washington, 1990-95; apptd. mem. Social Issues in Mgmt. divsn. Governance Com., 1990-91; town moderator Town of Tiverton, R.I., 1993—. Lt. USN, 1970-77. Recipient Community Svc. award Mayor of Phila., 1977; Richard D. Irwin fellow, 1980, Lifetime Achievement award Boston U. SMG alumni, 1995. Mem. Acad. of Mgmt. (chair SIM divsn. 1994-95), Internat. Assn. Bus. Soc. (program chair annual meeting 1991, v.p. 1991-92, pres. 1992-93), Acad. Internat. Bus., Issues Mgmt. Assn., Beta Gamma Sigma. Avocations: cross-country skiing, traveling, reading. Office: Boston U Sch Mgmt 621 Commonwealth Ave Boston MA 02215-1605

MAHON, MALACHY THOMAS, SR. lawyer, educator; b. N.Y.C., Jan. 4, 1934; s. James and Alice (Rooney) M.; m. Margaret Phyllis Kirwan, Jan. 25, 1958 (dec. 1993); children: Veronica Mahon Grover, Laura Mahon Chandonnet, Malachy. BA, Manhattan Coll., 1954; JD, Fordham U., 1960. Bar: N.Y. 1960. Law clk. to chief magistrate John M. Murtagh, N.Y.C., 1959-60; law clk. to justice Tom C. Clark U.S. Supreme Ct., 1960-61; assoc. Hale Russell & Stentzel, N.Y.C., 1961-62, Mudge Rose Guthrie & Alexander, N.Y.C., 1979-80; of counsel Farrell, Fritz, Caemmerer, Cleary, Barnosky & Armentano, Mineola, NY, 1982-83, Havens & Lombard, Flushing, N.Y., 1994-95; prof. Fordham U. Law Sch., 1962-68; prof. law Hofstra U. Law Sch., 1968—, founding dean, 1968-73, S.B. Wilzig disting. prof. banking, 1985—. Vis. prof. U. Tex. Law Sch., 1973-74; exec. dir., spl. N.Y. State asst. atty. gen. Meyer Investigation of Coverup Charges Against the Spl. Attica Prison Riot Prosecutor's Office, 1975; Chief counsel N.Y. Gov.'s Spl. Com. on Criminal Offenders, 1966; mem. Nassau County Bd. Ethics, 1983-96, chmn., 1989-96; chmn. merit selection com. EDNY Bankruptcy Judges, 1985-88. Staff author: Mental Illness, Due Process and the Criminal Defendant, 1968; monthly comml. law columnist: N.Y. Law Jour, 1976-78. Served with U.S. Army, 1954-56. Mem. ABA, N.Y. State Bar Assn., Assn. Bar City N.Y., Am. Law Inst. Home: 14 Duke Of Gloucester Manhasset NY 11030-3210 Office: Hofstra U Law Sch Hempstead NY 11550

MAHON, ROBERT, photographer; b. Wilmington, Del., Dec. 28, 1949; s. Clifton and Mary Veronica (Figash) M.; m. Carol Joyce, Apr. 24, 1983. BA in Am. Studies, U. Del., 1971. One-man shows include Twining Gallery, N.Y.C., 1985, Mercer Coll., Trenton, N.J., 1993, Anne Reid Gallery, Princeton, 1996, N.J. State Mus., 1997, Dana Libr. Rutgers U., Newark, 1998, RVC Coll., N.J., 2001, exhibited in group shows at Whitney Mus. Am. Art, 1982, Phila. Mus. Art, 1982, 1995, Am. Ctr., Paris, 1982, Mus. Modern Art, N.Y.C., 1983, 1984—85, 1993, Kolnischer Kunstverein, 1983, Art Inst., Chgo., 1985, Twining Gallery, 1985—86, 1988, 1989, N.J. State Mus., 1990, 1997, 1999, Guggenheim Soho, 1994, Sandra Gering Gallery, N.Y.C., 1996, Newark Mus., 1997, Korn Gallery Drew U., Madison, N.J., 1999, N.Y. Pub. Libr., 1999, Guild Hall, East Hampton, N.Y., 1999, also others, Represented in permanent collections Phila. Mus. Art, Mus. Modern Art, Met. Mus. Art, N.Y. Pub. Libr., Humanities Rsch. Ctr., U. Tex., Austin, Princeton U. Libr., Princeton U. Art Mus., Harvard U. Art Mus., N.J. State Mus., Newark Mus., Montclair Art Mus., Rutgers U., Dana Libr., Zimmerli Mus., Noyes Mus., also pvt. collections. Guggenheim grantee, 1985; RCIP Printmaking fellow, 1996. Home: PO Box Q Stockton NJ 08559-0390 E-mail: robtmahon@aol.com.

MAHON, THOMAS JAMES, management consultant; b. Camden, N.J., Jan. 9, 1946; s. Edward Leo and Helen (Dalanni) M.; m. Donna Mae Hastings, Mar. 27, 1976; 1 child, Hilarie M. Hastings-Mahon. BA in Polit. Sci., LaSalle Coll., 1968; MPA, U. N.H., 1975. Spl. rsch. analyst Dep. of Def., Ft. Meade, Md., 1968-74; labor market analyst Dept. of Employment Sec., Concord, 1976-78; adminstrv. asst. to selectmen Town of Pelham, N.H., 1978-82; mem. svcs. rep. Compensation Fund of N.H., Concord, 1982-88, mem. svcs. cons., 1988-92, sr. cons., 1992—. Contbr. articles to profl. jours. Chmn. Sch. Space Needs, Merrimack, N.H., 1978, 95, 98, Mcpl. Budget Com., Merrimack, 1985, 92-98, 99-2002, Sch. Bd., Merrimack, 1986-88, 4th of July Com., 1997—; mem. Libr. Bldg. Rev. com., 1999-. With U.S. Army, 1968-70, Vietnam. Mem. Exch. Club of Merrimack (treas. 1990-92, pres. 1998), Jaycees (internal v.p. Dover club 1974-75, pres. College Park club 1974), N.H. Mcpl. Mgmt. Assn., Internat. Assn. Continuing Edn. and Tng., Internat. City Mgmt. Assn. Avocations: model railroading, photography, crossword puzzles, mil. history. Home: 31 Naticook Rd Merrimack NH 03054-4227 Office: NHPRIMEX3 46 Donovan St Concord NH 03301-2624 E-mail: tmahon@nhprimex.com.

MAHONE, BARBARA JEAN, automotive company executive; b. Notasulga, Ala., Apr. 19, 1946; BS, Ohio State U., 1968; MBA, U. Mich., 1972; program for mgmt. devel., Harvard U., 1981. Sys. analyst GM, Detroit, 1968-71, sr. staff asst., 1972-74, mgr. career planning, 1975-78, dir. pers. adminstrn. Rochester, N.Y., 1979-81, mgr. indsl. rels. Warren, Ohio, 1982-83, dir. human resources mgmt. Chevrolet-Pontiac-Can. group, 1984-86, dir. gen. pers. and pub. affairs Inland divsn. Ohio, 1986-88, gen. dir. pers. Indland Fisher Guide divsn. Detroit, 1989-91, gen. dir. employee benefits, 1991-93, dir. human resources truck group Pontiac, 1994—2000, exec. dir. human resources, 2001—. Chmn. Fed. Labor Rels. Authority, Washington, 1983-84, Spl. Panel on Appeals; dir. Metro Youth; mem. bd. govs. U. Mich. Alumni. Bd. dirs. ARC, Rochester, 1979-82, Urban League Rochester, 1979-82, Rochester Aea Multiple Sclerosis; mem. human resources com. YMCA, Rochester, 1980-82; mem. exec. bd. Nat. Coun. Negro Women; mem. allocations com. United Way Greater Rochester. Recipient Pub. Rels. award Nat. Assn. Bus. and Profl. Women, 1976, Mary McLeod Bethune award Nat. Coun. Negro Women, 1977, Senate resolution Mich. State Legislature, 1980; named Outstanding Woman, Mich. Chronicle, 1975, Woman of Yr., Nat. Assn. Bus. and Profl. Women, 1978, Disting. Bus. Person, U. Mich., 1978, one of 11 Mich. Women, Redbook mag., 1978. Mem. Nat. Black MBA Assn. (bd. dirs., nat. pres. Disting. Svc. award, bd. dirs., nat. pres. Outstanding MBA), Women Econ. Club (bd. dirs.), Indsl. Rels. Rsch. Assn., Internat. Assn. for Pers. Women, Engring. Soc. Detroit. Republican. Home: 175 Kirkwood Ct Bloomfield Hills MI 48304-2927 Office: MC 483-585-227 585 South Blvd Pontiac MI 48341-3146

'MAHONE, GLENN, federal agency administrator; B Commn. and Speeck, U. Ctrl. Ark. Mgmt. cons. to pres., CEO Stephens Engring. Co., Inc., Lanham, Md.; cons. employment and tng. U.S. Dept. Labor, Washington; v.p., dir. sales tng. and devel. FirstSouth Savs. and Loan, Little Rock; dir. info. svcs., press sec. Office Ark. Sec. of State; comml. sales and mktg. mgr. ADT Security Svcs., Balt.; key advisor U.S. EEOC, 1999—2000; sr. advisor, press sec. NASA, Washington, 2000, acting assoc. adminstr. pub. affairs, 2001—02, asst. adminstr. pub. affairs, 2002—. Office: NASA Hdqrs Mail Code P 300 E St SW Washington DC 20546

MAHONEY, ANN DICKINSON, fundraiser; b. Topeka, Sept. 12, 1961; d. Jacob Alan II and Ruth (Curd) Dickinson; m. Michael James Mahoney, May 29, 1993; children: James Junius Castle, Catherine Lane, Grace Dickinson. AB in History, Grinnell Coll., 1983; postgrad., McGill U., Montreal, Quebec, Can., 1985. Analyst, corp. fin. dept. E.F. Hutton & Co., Inc., N.Y.C., 1983-85; pres., owner The Dark Side, 1985-87; asst. dir. individual giving Meml. Sloan-Kettering Cancer Ctr., 1987-88, dir. spl. gifts, 1988-91; assoc. dir. devel. Sch. Humanities and Scis. Stanford (Calif.) U., 1991-96; ind. fundraising cons., 1996—. Devel. asst. regional office Brandeis U., N.Y.C., 1987. Vol. interviewer Grinnell Coll., N.Y.C., San Francisco, 1983—; chair No. Calif. adv. bd. Nat. Found. for Tchg. Entrepreneurship, 2000—. Mem. Nat. Soc. Fund Raising Execs., Jr. League San Francisco (com. chmn. 1996-98), Pacific Rsch. Inst. for Pub. Policy, Hist. Topeka (Kans.) Assn., Friends of Filoli (Woodside, Calif.), Peninsula Assn. Retarded Children & Adults Aux. (bd. dirs. 1998-2002, pres. 2000), (San Mateo, Calif.), San Francisco Ballet Auxiliary, , Villa Taverna San Francisco, Spokane Club (Wash.), Hayden Lake (Idaho) Country Club. Republican. Episcopalian. E-mail: admahone@pacbell.net.

MAHONEY, CATHERINE ANN, artist, educator; b. Macon, Mo., Nov. 18, 1948; d. Joe H. and Berniece Joyce (Garnett) Dickson; m. Michael W. Mahoney, July 19, 1969; children: Karin Lynn Mahoney Broeker, Ryan Michael. BS in Edn. with honors, Truman U., Kirksville, 1969. Mo. state life cert. for tchg. art. Elem./secondary art instr. Bucklin (Mo.) R-I Schs., 1970-74; pvt. art instr. Groom (Tex.) Artist's Assn., 1974-75; substitute tchr. Gasconade R-I Schs., Hermann, Mo., 1977-89; pvt. art instr. Colorful Brushes Studio, 1987—; elem./secondary art instr. Crosspoint Christian Schs., Union, 1994-98. Pres. City of Hermann Arts Coun., 1983-87, membership chmn., 1980-82; dir. Summertime Children's Watercolor Workshops, Colorful Brushes, Hermann, 1987—. One-woman shows at N.E. Mo. State U., Kirksville, 1969, Capitol City Art Guild, Jefferson City, Mo., 1983, Kolbe Gallery of Art, Hermann, 1984, Colorful Brushes Studio, Hermann, 1987-94; designer Sister Cities Emblem City of Hermann/Arolsen, Germany, 1989; works published in: Best of Watercolor: Texture, 1998. Pres. Hermann Parent-Tchr. Orgn., 1985—87; leader 4-H, Girl and Boy Scouts, Hermann, 1982—95; organist, pianist, tchr. Hermann Cath. and Bapt. Chs., 1977—97, E. Free Ch., 1997—2002. Named Outstanding Young Woman of Yr., Hermann Jaycees, 1984, 1st place award Mo. Artists Collection, Mo. Pub. Svc., Sedalia, Mo., 1992, 3d place award and purchase prize Watercolor USA, Springfield (Mo.) Art Mus., 1995, 1st place award Arts Rolla Art Show, 1999. Mem.: Oil Painters Am., St. Louis Artist Guild (mem. art sect., Hon. Mention 1993, 1998, 2002), Watercolor USA Honor Soc. (hon. Art Show award 1995), Okla. Watercolor Assn. (assoc. included Art Show 1989), Nat. Watercolor Soc. (assoc. included Nat. Art Show 1995). Avocations: piano, reading, embroidery, sewing, knitting. Home: 1058 Old Stonehill Hermann MO 65041 Office: Colorful Brushes Studio 126 E 4th St Hermann MO 65041-1130 E-mail: camahoney@ktis.net.

MAHONEY, DAVID L. pharmaceutical wholesale and healthcare management company executive; b. Brighton, Mass., June 24, 1954; s. Thomas H.D. and K. Phyllis (Norton) M.; m. Winn Canning Ellis, Sept. 26, 1992. AB in English, Princeton U., 1975; MBA, Harvard U., 1981. Asst. gen. mgr. Ogden Food Svc. Corp., L.A., 1975-76, concessions mgr. East Boston, Mass., 1976-77, gen. mgr., 1977-78, ops. analyst, 1978-79; assoc. McKinsey & Co., San Francisco, 1981-86, prin., 1986-90; v.p. strategic planning McKesson Corp., 1990-94, pres. HDS, Inc., 1994-95, pres. pharm. svcs., 1995-97, group pres. pharm svcs. & internat. group, 1997-99; exec. v.p., CEO pharm. svcs. bus. McKesson HBOC, 1999, co-CEO, 1999-2001; CEO iMcKesson, 2000-01. Mem. City Club of San Francisco, San Francisco C. of C., Young Pres. Orgn. Avocations: outdoor activities, photography. Office: McKesson Corp 235 Montgomery St Ste 820 San Francisco CA 94104-5292

MAHONEY, DONNA MARIE, psychotherapist; b. Oak Park, Ill., Mar. 13, 1961; d. Thomas Joseph and Eileen Mary Mahoney. MA, Loyola U., 1989; PhD, Inst. Clin. Social Work, 2000. Acad. advisor Triton Coll., River Grove, Ill., 1984-87; psychotherapist Centrum Clinic, Oak Park, 1989-97; psychotherapist, case mgr. Kenneth Young Ctrs., Elk Grove, Ill., 1989-96; psychotherapist Anxiety and Stress Ctr., Orland Park, 1996—. Pvt. cons. Anxiety and Stress Ctr., Orland Park, Ill., 2000—; adj. faculty mem. Argosy U., Rolling Meadows, Ill. Contbr. articles to profl. jours. Mem. Anxiety Disorders Assn. Am., Obsessive Compulsive Fedn., Ill. Soc. Clin. Social Work, Chgo. Assn. Psychoanalytic Psychology. Democrat. Avocations: aerobics, music. Home: 712 Bell Ave La Grange IL 60525

MAHONEY, F. STEVEN, accountant, lawyer; b. Dover, N.J., Sept. 20, 1958; s. Frank and Margaret M.; m. Lucinda Olsen; children: Ryan, Tyler, Kyle, Sean. BS, Pa. State U., 1979; JD, U. San Francisco, 1985. Bar: Calif. 1985, Tex. 1986, Alaska 1991, U.S. Tax Ct. 1985. Mgr. collection control Zilog Inc., San Jose, Calif., 1983-86; dir. taxes Advanced Nuc. Fuels Inc., Seattle, 1986-88; sr. tax Exxon Corp., Houston, 1988-89; tax compliance mgr. Lyondell Corp., 1989-90; mng. tax counsel Atlantic Richfield Co., L.A., 1990-96; v.p. tax, gen. tax officer ARCO Alaska Inc., Anchorage, 1996-98; v.p. tax ARCO Pipeline, 1998-2000; of counsel Hughes Thorsness Powell Huddleston & Bauman, 2000—. Bd. dirs. Performing Arts Ctr., Anchorage, 1995—; mem. exec. bd. western area coun. Boy Scouts Am. Mem. ABA, Calif. Bar Assn., Tex. Bar Assn., Alaska Bar Assn., Assn. Fundraising Profls. (bd. dirs.). Home: PO Box 200429 Anchorage AK 99520-0429 Office: 701 W 8th St Ste 230 Anchorage AK 99501 E-mail: fsm@htlaw.com.

MAHONEY, GERALD FRANCIS, manufacturing company executive; b. Bklyn., July 31, 1943; s. Francis B. and Leona (Gray) M.; m. JoAnne A. Maselli, May 2, 1971; children: G. Scott, Ryan J. BA, Adelphi U., 1965; MBA, Northeastern U., 1966. CPA, N.Y. Mgr. Arthur Andersen & Co., N.Y.C., 1966-73; asst. contr. Bairnco Corp., 1973-78, v.p. fin., 1980-81, gen. mgr. Pensauken, N.J., 1979-80, v.p., div. pres. Union, 1981-83; sr. v.p. fin. and adminstrn. Polychrome Corp., Yonkers, N.Y., 1984-87; pres. Transcrit Corp., Brewster, 1987-90, Pavey Envelope & Tag Corp., Jersey City, 1991-94; chmn., CEO Mail-Well, Inc., Englewood, Colo., 1994—. Mem. AICPA, N.Y. State Soc. CPA's, Noyac Country Club (Sag Harbor, N.Y., bd. dirs. 1980-83), Glenmoor Country Club (Englewood, Colo.), Ridgewood Country Club (N.J.). Republican. Roman Catholic. Avocations: golf, tennis. Office: Mail Well Inc 8310 S Valley Hwy # 400 Englewood CO 80112 Home: 266 Cook St Denver CO 80206

MAHONEY, JAMES R. federal agency administrator; b. Syracuse, N.Y. D in Meteorology, MIT. Faculty pub. health Harvard U.; co-founder Environ. Rsch. and Tech., Inc.; sr. exec. Bechtel Group, San Francisco, Internat. Tech. Corp., L.A., Washington; dir. Nat. Acid Precipitation Assessement Program, 1988; asst. adminstrv. for oceanic and atmospheric rsch. Dept. Commerce, Silver Springs, Md., 2001—; pres. Consulting and Ventures Group. Mem.: NAS (com. mem., co-chmn. bd. on atmospheric sci. and climate), Am. Meteorol. Soc. (pres. 1990—91). Office: Dept Commerce Oceanic and Atmospheric Rsch 1315 East-West Hwy Silver Spring MD 20910-3279*

MAHONEY, JOËLLE KATHERINE, astrological consultant, communications educator; b. Amiens, France, Jan. 6, 1948; came to U.S., 1953; d. Louis James and Regine (LeClercq) Dennis; m. John William Christopher Mahoney, Aug. 14, 1971. AA, Boro Manhattan C.C., 1971; BA, Adelphi U., 1982; postgrad., Hofstra U., 1989—. Profl. cert. in astrology; cert. master practitioner neurolinguistic programming; cert. neurolinguistics programming. Trilingual translator N.A. Bogdan Co., N.Y.C., 1967-71; practicing astrologer Long Island, N.Y., 1971-74; founding pres. Astrological Rsch. Centre and Tng. Inst. Ltd., Mineola, 1974-84; internat. astrological cons. Brewster, 1984—. Pres. French Regional Alliance for Nat. Costume Edn., 1999—. Author: Concept I, II and III, 1974, In Search of Time, 1989. Vol. fund raiser Americares, New Canaan, Conn., 1991-94, Silver Hill Hosp., New Canaan, 1992-94, City Harvest, N.Y.C., 1995-97; amb. All Nations Universal Pageant Orgn., 1998-99. Named Mrs. France, 1996, Mrs. All Nations Universal, 1997; named amb.-at-large All Nations Universal Orgn., 1998. Mem. Astrologers Guild Am. (pres. 1980-83), Congress of Astrological Orgns. (v.p. 1981-84). Avocations: equitation, oil painting, writing, fitness, animal welfare. Home: 5 Fair Meadow Dr Brewster NY 10509-4617

MAHONEY, JOHN JOSEPH, business executive, educator; b. Chattanooga, Nov. 9, 1921; s. John J. and Helen M. (Armstrong) M.; m. Elizabeth DuBose Porcher, June 25, 1949. BS in Commerce, The Citadel, 1946; MS in Indsl. Mgmt., Ga. Inst. Tech., 1967. Ordained deacon Roman Cath. Ch., 1979. Instr. dept. bus. adminstrn. The Citadel, Charleston, S.C., 1947-50, asst. prof., 1967-92; founder, pres., gen. mgr. Carolinga Vending Inc., 1947-67, Shamrock Sys., Inc., 1960-67. Dir. Charles F. Cates & Sons, Inc. Pickle Co., Faison, N.C., also mem. exec. com.; v.p., treas., dir. Cons. to Bus., Inc. (formerly Mahoney Cons., Inc.); dir., pres. Associated Distbrs., Inc., Metro Stylists, Inc.; dir. Aunt Jane Foods, Inc.; S.C. editor Diaconal Quar.; founder, bd. dirs. Isnt. Organizational Excellence, Charleston. S.C., 1998—. Procurator, advocate diocesan tribunal Diocese of Charleston; mem. Bishop's Com. on Vocations: pres. Cath. Charities, 1958-60; bd. dirs. Charleston Devel. Bd., 1957-60, Charleston C. of C., United Fund, Charleston, 1955-57, Family Agy., Charleston, 1956-60; chmn. Pres.'s Export Expansion Coun. Atlanta Region; initiator, planner Ctr. for Entrepreneurship, Charleston Coll. Served to lt. AUS, 1943-46, capt. Res. Recipient Disting. Svc. award Jaycees, 1956. Mem. So. Mgmt. Assn., Fellowship Cath. Scholars, Hibernian Soc. (life), Confederate Hist. Assn., SCV (former mem. gen. staff, chaplain-in-the-field S.C. divsn.), O'Mahoney Records Soc., Assn. Pvt. Enterprise Edn. (former mem. exec. com.), Fund for Conservative Majority (bd. dirs.), Irish Am. Cultural Inst. (life). Home: 1602 Porchers Bluff Rd Mount Pleasant SC 29466-8942 Office: 276 E Bay St Charleston SC 29401-2600

MAHONEY, JOHN L. English literature educator; b. Somerville, Mass., Feb. 4, 1928; AB, Boston Coll., 1950, AM, 1952; PhD, Harvard U., 1957. Instr. of English Boston Coll., 1955-59, asst. prof. of English, 1959-62, assoc. prof., 1962-65, prof., 1965—, Rattigan prof. English, 1994—2002, Rattigan prof. English emeritus, 2002—, chmn. dept., 1962-67, 69-70, dir. PhD program in English, 1970-75, 82-85, mem. ednl. policy com. Grad. Sch. Arts and Scis., 1985-87. Vis. prof. of English Harvard U. summer sch., 1963, 65, 67, 71, 80, 83, 86; cons. for self-study Weston Coll. Schs. of Philosophy and Theology, Boston Coll., 1965; sem. leader programs for women, Boston Coll., Newton Coll., 1976, 78, 79; mem. numerous acad. coms. and couns.; cons., mem. English adv. com. Commonwealth of Mass., 1968-70; mem. acad. coun. Coll. of Advancing Studies, Boston Coll., 1969—, univ. core curriculum devel. com., 1991-97; bd. trustees St. John's Sem., Brighton, Mass., com. on acad. affairs, 1980-86; sec. bd. trustees Katharine Gibbs Sch., Boston, 1982-90; mem. adv. bd. Jesuit Inst., Boston Coll., 1987—; mem. Boston Coll. Coun. the Arts, 1997—. Author: The Whole Internal Universe: Imitation and the New Defense of Literature in British Criticism, 1660-1830, 1985, The Persistence of Tragedy: Episodes in the History of Drama, 1985, The Logic of Passion: The Literary Criticism of William Hazlitt, rev. edit., 1981, Wordsworth: A Poetic Life, 1997, Wordsworth and the Critics, 2001; editor, author intro. and notes: The Enlightenment and English Literature, 1980, The English Romantics: Major Poetry and Critical Theory, 1978, An Essay of Dramatic Poetry and Other Critical Writings by John Dryden, 1965, William Duff's Essay on Original Genius, 1964; contbr. Imagination and the Ways of Genius (in Approaches to Hazlitt), 1986, Teaching the Immortality Ode with Coleridge's Dejection: An Ode (in Approaches to Teaching Wordsworth's Poetry), 1986, Teaching Shelley's Skylark and the Defence of Poetry (in Approaches to Teaching Shelley's Poetry), 1990, and others; editor: (with J. Robert Barth, S.J.) Coleridge, Keats, and the Imagination: Romanticism and Adam's Dream, 1990, Seeing Into the Life of Things: Essays on Literature and Religion, 1998; mem. editl. bd. Boston Coll. Mag., 1981-90; author articles, papers delivered at profl. confs.; reviewer for Studies in Romanticism, The Wordsworth Circle, Nineteenth Century Contexts, So. Humanities Rev., Coll. Lit.; series editor Fordham U. Press Series on Religion and Lit., 1997—. Active Sacred Heart Parish, Lexington, Mass., del. to Lexington Coun. Chs., 1968, chmn. parish coun., 1969-72, mem. parish coun., 1995-98, vice chmn., 1996-98, mem. religious edn. commn., 1974-79, 90-93, sem. leader Christian Youth Edn., 1969-73, lector, 1972—; mem. Archdiocese of Boston Commn. for Promotion of Parish Couns., 1969-74, Benjamin Mays Mentor Ahana program, 1993—. Boston Coll. Grad. Sch. fellow, 1950-52; Boston Coll. Faculty rsch. grantee, 1964, 68, 86, 92, 96, 97, 98, Mellon Found. grantee for rsch. and faculty devel., 1981-82; grantee rsch. Am. Philos. Soc., 1987; recipient Boston Coll. Campus Coun. Tchr. of Yr. award, 1966, Boston Coll. alumni award for excellence in edn., 1978, Andrè Favat award Mass. Coun. Tchrs. English, 1988, Prof. of Yr. award Coun. for Advancement and Support of Edn. Mass., 1989. Mem. AAUP (pres. Boston Coll. chpt. 1962), MLA, Am. Soc. Eighteenth Century Studies, N.E. Soc. Eighteenth Century Studies, Wordsworth-Coleridge Assn. Am., Keats-Shelley Assn. Am., The Johnsonians, Alpha Sigma Nu, Phi Beta Kappa (Tchg. award Boston Coll. 1994). E0-mail. E-mail: mahoneyj@bc.edu.

MAHONEY, KATHLEEN MARY, lawyer; b. Methuen, Mass., Oct. 24, 1954; d. Joseph Patrick and Beatrice Evelyn (Blackington) M.; m. Mark Dennis Schmitt, May 26, 1979; children: Alexis Anne Schmitt, Brynne Elizabeth Schmitt. BA, Keene (N.H.) State Coll., 1976; JD, Syracuse (N.Y.) U., 1979. Bar: Minn. 1979, U.S. Dist. Ct. Minn. 1980, U.S. Ct. Appeals (8th cir.) 1985, U.S. Supreme Ct. 1988. Instr. Sch. of Law Hamline U., St. Paul, 1979-80; law clk. to hon. justice Douglas K. Amdahl Minn. Supreme Ct., 1980-81; law clk. to hon. judge Neal P. McCurn U.S. Dist. Ct. (no. dist.) N.Y., Syracuse, 1981-83; spl. asst. atty. gen. Atty. Gen.'s Office State of Minn., St. Paul, 1983-89; assoc. Oppenheimer, Wolff & Donnelly, 1989-91, sr. assoc., 1991-93, ptnr., 1994—2002, chair labor and employment practice group, 1995-97, mng. ptnr., 1997-2000; ptnr. Larson-King, 2002—. Cons. George Banzhaf Co., Milw., 1979-80; adj. prof. Hamline U. Sch. of Law, 1987-89. Mem. Dist. 621 Study Adv. Com., Shoreview, Minn., 1989-91, chair, 1991-93; mem. Turtle Lake Sch. Adv. Com., Shoreview, 1988-96; mem. exec. com., bd. dirs. Voyageurs Regional Nat. Park Assn., 1993-95; mem. Class of '93; bd. dirs. St. Paul Vol. Ctr., 1994-99; leader Girl Scouts Am., 1993-99; mem. Leadership St. Paul.; bd. dirs. Girl Scout Council St. Croix Valley, 2001—. Mem. ABA, Minn. Bar Assn., Ramsey County Bar Assn. Office: Oppenheimer Wolff & Donnelly Plz VII 45 S 7th St Ste 3300 Minneapolis MN 55402

MAHONEY, LINDA KAY, mathematics educator; b. Bay Shore, N.Y., June 8, 1951; d. James Nathaniel and Katherine Pauline (Booth) Palmer Jr.; m. Peter Allan Mahoney, Jr., June 5, 1976; children: Matthew J., Michael J., Patrick A. BS, U. Md., 1972; MEd, 1979; postgrad., R.I. Coll., 1988-89, Providence Coll., 1989-90. Tchr. math. Prince George's County Pub. Schs., Benjamin Tasker Jr. High, Bowie, Md., 1973-76; tchr. substitute Warwick (R.I.) Pub. Schs., 1987-90, tchr. math., 1990-91; instr. math. Ctrl. Tex. Coll., P.R., 1992-96, U. Tenn., Knoxville, 1996—. Vol. Sherman Elem. Sch., Warwick, 1989-90, Rohr Elem. Sch., Chula Vista, Calif., 1985-87. Mem. Nat. Coun. Tchrs. Math., Math. Assn. Am. Republican. Lutheran. Avocations: gardening, baking. E-mail: mahoney@math.utk.edu.

MAHONEY, MARGARET ELLIS, accountant; b. Detroit, Mar. 17, 1929; d. Seth Wiley and Mildred Elizabeth (Hill) Ellis; m. Stephen Bedell Smith, Mar. 15, 1956 (div. Oct. 1962); 1 child, Laura Elizabeth; m. Patrick John Mahoney, Sept. 1, 1972 (dec.). BA, Butler U., 1953. Copywriter Hook Drugs Inc., Indpls., 1953; continuity dir. Sta. WXLW, 1954-57; ptnr. Steve Smith and Assocs. Advt., 1956-62; account mgr. Sive Advt., Cin., 1963-64, Associated Advt., Cin., 1964-65; copywriter SuperRX Drugs Inc., 1965-72; promotion writer U.S. News and World Report, Washington, 1974; asst. mgr. advt. Drug Fair, Alexandria, Va., 1975-82; dir. advt. Cosmetic and Fragrance Concepts Inc./DBA Cosmetic Ctrs., Beltsville, Md., 1982-89; advt., prodn. cons. Nat. Red Cross, Galladet U., Washington, 1989-94; asst. to real estate agt. Carmel, Ind., 1994-96; editl. cons., mem. svc. rep., acctg. clk. Angie's List, 1996—. Vestrywoman St. Matthews Episcopal Ch., Cin., 1969-71; hosp. chmn. Sleepy Hollow Citizens Assn., Falls Church, Va., 1973; vol. resident assoc. program Smithsonian Instn., Washington, 1989-94; chmn. membership and pub. rels. Friends Chinn Park Regional Libr., Woodbridge, Va., 1991-94; vol. Indpls. Art Ctr. Gift Shop, 1997—, Prince William Symphony Orch., Prince William County Voter Registration Bd. Mem. Potomac Valley Aquarium Soc. (past treas., past sec., editor jour.), Am. Cichlid Assn. (nat. pub. rels. chair 1985-90), Delta Delta Delta. Avocations: swimming, reading, needlework, travel, computers. Home: 9850 Greentree Dr Carmel IN 46032-9099 E-mail: mmah317@aol.com.

MAHONEY, MARGARET A. federal judge; b. 1949; BA, Coll. St. Catherine, 1971; JD, U. Minn., 1974. Bankruptcy judge U.S. Bankruptcy Ct. Dist. Minn., 1984-87, U.S. Bankruptcy Ct. (so. dist.) Tex., 1987-89; ptnr. Weil, Gotshal & Manges, 1989-93; chief bankruptcy judge U.S. Bankruptcy Ct. (so. dist.) Ala., Mobile, 1993—. Office: 201 Saint Louis St Mobile AL 36602-2919 Fax: 251-441-5612. E-mail: margaret_mahoney@alsb.uscourts.gov.

MAHONEY, MARGARET ELLERBE, foundation executive; d. Charles Hallam and Leslie Nelson (Savage) M. BS magna cum laude, Vanderbilt U., 1946; LHD (hon.), Meharry Med. Coll., 1977, U. Fla., 1980, Med. Coll. Pa., 1982, Williams Coll., 1983, Smith Coll., 1985, Beaver Coll., 1985, Brandeis U., 1989, Marymount Coll., 1990, Mt. Sinai Sch. Medicine, 1992, Rush U., 1993, SUNY, Bklyn., 1994, N.Y. Med. Coll., 1995. Fgn. affairs officer State Dept., Washington, 1946-53; exec. assoc., assoc. sec. Carnegie Corp., N.Y.C., 1953-72; v.p. Robert Wood Johnson Found., Princeton, N.J., 1972-80; pres. Commonwealth Fund, N.Y.C., 1980-94, MEM Assocs., Inc., N.Y.C., 1995—. Contbr. articles to profl. jours.; spkr. in field. Trustee John D. and Catherine T. MacArthur Found., 1985—2002, Smith Coll., 1988—93, Columbia U., 1991—96, Carnegie Found. Advancement of Tchg., 1963—2001, Arthur Ashe Found., 1997—; vis. fellow Sch. Arch. and Urban Planning, Princeton U., 1973—80; bd. dirs. Coun. on Found., 1982—88; mem. N.Y.C. Commn. on the Yr. 2000, 1985—87, MIT Corp., 1984—89; bd. govs. Am. Stock Exch., 1987—92, Skillbuilders Fund, 1993—, Am. Skin Assn., 1994—, Classroom Inc., 1996—; mem. adv. bd. Office of Med. Examiner, N.Y.C., 1987—; vice chmn. N.Y.C. Mayor's Com. for Pub./Pvt. Partnerships, 1990—93; bd. dirs. Alliance for Aging Rsch., 1987—, Overseas Devel. Coun., 1988—2001, Nat. Found. Ctrs. for Disease Control and Prevention, Inc., 1994—, chmn., 1996—98; mem. vestry Parish of Trinity Ch., 1982—89, 1991—95. Recipient Frank H. Lahey Meml. award, 1984, Women's Forum award, 1989, Walsh McDermott award, 1992, Disting. Grantmaker award Coun. Founds., 1993, Edward R. Loveland award ACP, 1994, Spl. Recognition award AAMC, 1994, Merit medal Lotos Club, 1994, Terrance Keenan Leadership award in health philanthropy Grantmakers in health, 1995, Distinction award Am. Skin Assn., 1998, Rsch. Am. award, 1999, Hon. Classmate Class of 1976 award Princeton U., 2001. Mem. AAAS, Inst. Medicine of NAS, Am. Acad. Arts and Scis., Am. Philos. Soc., Coun. Fgn. Rels., Fin. Women's Assn. N.Y., N.Y. Acad. Medicine, N.Y. Acad. Scis., Alpha Omega Alpha. Office: MEM Assocs Inc 521 5th Ave Rm 1801 New York NY 10175-0088

MAHONEY, MAUREEN E. retired secondary education educator; b. Jersey City, Aug. 24, 1940; d. Michael J. and Margaret M. (Lynch) M. BA, Montclair State Coll., Upper Montclair, N.J., 1962, MA, 1964; postgrad., NYU, Fairleigh Dickinson U. Tchr. English Teaneck (N.J.) High Sch., Northern Highlands Regional High Sch., Allendale, N.J., 1994. N.J. state judge Nat. Coun. Tchrs. English Achievement awards in writing; critiquer in creative writing Bergen County Teen Arts Festival; supr. M.A. in Tchg. candidates Fairleigh Dickinson U. Dir. children's theater prodns., dramatic prodns. 2d lt. USAF, 1962. Mem. NEA, N.J. Edn. Assn., Bergen County Edn. Assn., Northern Highlands Edn. Assn., Nat. Coun. Tchrs. English, Bergen County Tchrs. English, N.J. Coun. Tchrs. English, N.J. Reading Coun./N.J. Reading Assn., Bergen County Ret. Tchrs. Assn., Affiliate of Internat. Reading Assn., Soc. Women Educators, Delta Kappa Gamma. Home: 115 Sherman Ave Teaneck NJ 07666-4120

MAHONEY, MICHAEL AUGUSTINE, minister; b. Long Island City, N.Y., July 20, 1941; s. Thomas Ffrancis and Helen Marie Mahoney; m. Anne Marie Cirello, June 3, 1972; children: Michael, Bryan, Megan. BS, U. Dayton, 1962; MS, L.I. U., 1975, PhD, 1986; MA, Sem. Immaculate Conception, 2000—00. Ordained deacon Diocese of Rockville Ctr., N.Y.; cert. tchr. N.Y. Tchr. Cathedral Latin HS, Cleveland, 1960—62, Most Holy Trinity HS, Bklyn., 1962—63, St. James Sch., Chester, Pa., 1963—67; regional quality contr. TWA, N.Y.C., 1967—73; biology, earth sci., Latin tchr. Bay Shore Sch., 1977—84, chairperson world lang., 1983—2002; dir. religious edn., youth min. St. Patrick Ch., 2001. Chairperson gen. gifts YMCA Gt. South Bay, Bay Shore, 1989—91. Recipient Man of Yr., Bay Shore Athletic Sponsors, 1985, Bonaventure award, Capuchin Youth and Family Ministry, 2000, Officer Jantzen award, Suffolk Coalition, 2002. Mem.: Bay Shore Clergy Assn., Nat. Assn. Secondary Sch. Principals, N.Y. Classical Assn., Nat. Honor Soc. (first faculty mem. inducted 1986). Roman Catholic. Avocations: gardening, reading. Home: 475 Peters Blvd Brightwaters NY 11718 Office: St. Patrick Cath Ch 9 N Clinton Ave Bay Shore NY 11706 Home Fax: 631-665-9009. Personal E-mail: deac20@msn.com.

MAHONEY, MICHAEL JAMES, investment and software executive; b. Spokane, Wash., July 18, 1960; s. James Lyle and Frances Edith (Castle) M.; m. Ann Dickinson, May 29, 1993; children: James Junius Castle, Catherine Lane, Grace Dickinson. BA in History cum laude, Whitman Coll., 1982; MBA, Stanford U., 1991. Analyst corp. fin. dept. E.F. Hutton & Co., Inc., N.Y.C., 1982-85; assoc. cons. Bain & Co., Inc., Boston, 1985-87, cons., 1987-89; summer assoc. Goldman, Sachs & Co., N.Y.C., 1990; investment analyst G.T. Global (acquired by AIM Funds), San Francisco, 1991-93; portfolio mgr., lead mgr. G.T. Global Telecom. Fund, 1993-99; sr. portfolio mgr. AIM Funds, San Francisco, 1998-99; founding ptnr. J&M Investments, Menlo Park, 1996—; sr. analyst, portfolio mgr., dir. Dresdner RCM Global Investors, San Francisco, 1999-2000; chief strategy officer Neon Yoyo, Inc. (acquired by Interwoven, Inc.), 2000; dir. Interwoven, Inc., Sunnyvale, 2000—01; mng. dir., sr. portfolio mgr., bd. dirs. EGM Capital, Inc., San Francisco, 2001—. Guest lectr. in investments Stanford Grad. Sch. of Bus., 1994—; frequent print and TV commentator on the telecomms. industry and investing, 1993—. Pres. Spokane County Young Reps., 1976-78; campaign mgr. Malone for U.S. Senate, Boston, 1988; bd. overseers Whitman Coll., investment com. 1999—. Recipient Pete Reid award Whitman Coll., 1997. Mem. O'Mahony Records Soc., Ea. Wash. Geneal. Soc., Pacific Rsch. Inst. for Pub. Policy (mem. tech. adv. bd.), Stanford Alumni Assn. (life), Guardsmen, Villa Taverna (San Francisco), Spokane Club (Washington), Lincoln Club of No. Calif., Hayden Lake Country Club (Idaho), Phi Beta Kappa, Sigma Chi (com. chmn. 1979-80). Office: EGM Capital Inc Two Embarcadero Ctr Ste 1300 San Francisco CA 94111 E-mail: mmahoney@egm.com.

MAHONEY, MICHAEL ROBERT TAYLOR, art historian, educator; b. Worcester, Mass., Jan. 24, 1935; s. Michael J. and Mary (Taylor) M. Grad., Phillips Acad., 1953; BA, Yale U., 1959; PhD, Courtauld Inst., U. London, 1965. Finley fellow Nat. Gallery Art, 1962-64; fellow Harvard Center Italian Studies, Villa I Tatti, 1963; museum curator Nat. Gallery Art, 1964-69; prof. fine arts, chmn. dept. Trinity Coll., Hartford, Conn., 1969-86, Genevieve Harlow Goodwin prof. fine arts, 1974-99. Incorporator Hartford Pub. Library, 1970-99; elector Wadsworth Atheneum, Hartford, 1974-85 Author: The Drawings of Salvator Rosa, 1977, (with Jean Cadogan) Wadsworth Atheneum Paintings II: Italy and Spain; editor: National Gallery of Art Report and Studies in the History of Art, 1968-69. Trustee Cesare Barbieri Found., Trinity Coll., 1977-99, Watkinson Libr., Trinity Coll., 1985-99, Somerset House Art History Found., N.Y.C., 1985—; bd. govs. Hill-Stead Mus., Farmington, Conn., 1992-95; mem. adv. coun. Am. Friends of Georgian Group, 1996—.

MAHONEY, THOMAS HENRY, IV, finance executive; b. Cambridge, Mass., May 27, 1952; s. Thomas Henry Donald and Kathrine Phyllis (Norton) M.; m. Emily A. Chien, Nov . 11, 1989. AB, Harvard Coll., 1973; MBA, U. Pa., 1976. Assoc. corp. fin. Dillon, Read & Co. Inc., N.Y.C., 1976-80, v.p. corp. fin., 1981-84, Oppenheimer & Co., Inc., N.Y.C., 1984-86; v.p. debt fin. Merrill Lynch Capital Markets, 1986-87, dir. product devel., 1988-89, mng. dir., 1989-96; mng. dir. global pvt. capital Deutsche Morgan Grenfell, 1996-98; mng. dir., group head Pvt. Equity Group, PaineWebber Inc., 1998-2000; v.p. fin., CFO Molecular OptoElectronics Corp., Watervliet, N.Y., 2000—. Bd. dirs. Molecular Optoelectronics Corp., Notifact Corp. Bd. dirs. New Eng. Soc. in City N.Y., N.Y.C. Opera. Mem. Coun. Fgn. Rels., Doubles Club, Harvard Club (N.Y.C.), Harvard Club (Boston), Univ. Club, Meadow Club Southampton. Republican. Home: 21 E 87th St Apt 8C New York NY 10128-0506 Office: Molecular OptoElectronics Corp 877 25th St Watervliet NY 12189 E-mail: mahoney@moec.com.

MAHONEY, TIM J. utility company executive; b. Rochester, N.Y. s. William F. and Phyllis M. M.; m. Myra A. Mahoney, 1978; children: Mark, Kevin. AS, City Coll., Santa Barbara, 1975; BA, U. Calif., Santa Barbara, 1977. With govt. affairs Santa Barbara C. of C., 1980-85; with pub. rels.-mktg. Santa Barbara Med., 1986-89; exec. dir. Santa Barbara Taxpayers, 1986-97, Santa Barabara Indsl., 1985-97, United Against Crime, Santa Barbara, 1990-97, Cachuna R&D, Santa Barbara, 1993-97; dist. mgr. So. Calif. Gas Co., Santa Barbara and San Lius Obispo, 1998—. Office: So Calif Gas Co 134 E Victoria St Santa Barbara CA 93101-2019

MAHONEY, TIMOTHY JAMES, marketing professional; b. Ogdensburg, N.Y., July 19, 1956; s. James Joseph and Elsie Jane (Connard) M.; m. Christina Lynn Penland, May 4, 1985; children: Mary Catherine, Samuel Wells. Student, U. Vienna, Austria, 1976; BA in Fgn. Langs. and Internat. Studies, Newberry Coll., 1978; MBA in Mktg. Mgmt., Drexel U., 1984. Mktg. rep. Sara Lee Foods-PYA/Monarch Food Svc. Divsn., Greenville, S.C., 1978-81; analyst mktg. rsch. Subaru of Am., Cherry Hill, N.J., 1984-85, mgr. info. sys., 1985-87, mgr. advt. and merchandising, 1987-89, mgr. mktg. rsch., 1989-91, mgr. product planning and rsch., 1991-94, dir. mktg., 1995-99; v.p. gen. mgr. mktg. Porsche Cars North Am., Atlanta, 1999—. Bd. mem. Rainbow Card Found., Phila.; mktg. trustee Franklin Inst. Sci. Mus., 1996-99. Chairperson for ednl. grants Subaru of Am. Found., Cherry Hill, 1986-87. Recipient Cert. of Excellence, Art Dirs. Club N.J., 1989, First Place award Excellence, Advt. Club N.J., 1989; named to Advt. Age's Mktg. 100, 1996. Mem. Am. Mktg. Assn. (exec. mem.), Soc. Automotive Analysts, World Future Soc., Beta Gamma Sigma. Presbyterian. Avocations: reading, swimming, foreign language study, travel, computers. Home: 3664 Blakeford Way Marietta GA 30062-5392

MAHONEY, WILLIAM FRANCIS, editor/author; b. Joliet, Ill., Jan. 24, 1935; s. Cletus George and Mildred Marie (Ochs) Mahoney; m. Carroll Frances Johnson, June 28, 1958; children: Erin Michele Alderfer, Kevin William, Megan Ann, Sheila Marie Startup, Nora Aileen Petchkofski. BS in Journalism, Marquette U., 1957. Reporter Ft. Wayne (Ind.) News Sentinel, 1958-59; pub. rels. mgr. Motorola, Inc., Franklin Park, Ill., 1959-66; sr. acct. exec. Young & Rubicam, Inc., Chgo., 1966-68; pub. info. dir. ABA, 1969-71; investor rels. mgr. Chemetron Corp., 1971-76; corp. comm. dir. Scott Paper Co., Phila., 1976-80; pub. rels. dir. Esmark Inc., Chgo., 1980-81; prin. Mahoney & Mitchell Incorp., Phila., 1981-89, Investor Rels. Ptnrs., Livingston, N.J., 1993—. Author: Investor Relations: The Professional's Guide to Financial and Marketing Communications, 1991, The Active Shareholder, 1993, The Strategy and Practice of Investor Relations, 1997; author, editor: The Investor Relations Guide, 1999; exec. editor Shareholder Value Mag., Investor Rels. Update, 1981-99, Valuation Issues. Mem. Nat. Investor Rels. Inst., Vesper Club. Republican. Roman Catholic. Office: 716 S Brandywine St West Chester PA 19382-3511 E-mail: wfmahoney@csi.com.

MAHONY, ROGER MICHAEL, archbishop; b. Hollywood, Calif., Feb. 27, 1936; s. Victor James and Loretta Marie (Baron) M. AA, Our Lady Queen of Angels Sem., 1956; BA, St. John's Sem. Coll., 1958, BST, 1962; MSW, Cath. U. Am., 1964. Ordained priest Roman Cath. Ch., 1962, ordained bishop, 1975, created cardinal priest, 1991. Asst. pastor St. John's Cathedral, Fresno, Calif., 1962, 68-73, rector, 1973-80; residence St. Genevieve's Parish, 1964—, adminstr., 1964-67, pastor, 1967-68; titular bishop of Tamascani, aux. bishop of Fresno, 1975-80; chancellor Diocese of Fresno, 1970-77, vicar gen., 1975-80; bishop Diocese of Stockton (Calif.), 1980-85; archbishop Archdiocese of L.A., 1985—, cardinal priest, 1991—; diocesan dir. Cath. Charities and Social Svc. Fresno, 1964-70; exec. dir. Infant of Prague Adoption Svc., Cath. Welfare Bur., Fresno, 1964-70. Chaplain St. Vincent de Paul Soc., Fresno, 1964-70; named chaplain to Pope Paul VI, 1967; mem. faculty extension div. Fresno State U., 1965-67; sec. U.S. Cath. bishops ad hoc com. on farm labor Nat. Conf. Bishops, 1970-75; chmn. com. on pub. welfare and income maintenance Nat. Conf. Cath. Charities, 1969-70; bd. dirs. West Coast Regional Office Bishops Com. for Spanish-Speaking, 1967-70; chmn. Calif. Assn. Cath. Charities Dirs., 1965-69; trustee St. Patrick's Sem., Archdiocese of San Francisco, 1974-75; mem. adminstrv. com. Nat. conf. Cath. Bishops, 1976-79, 82-85, 87-90, 92-95, 98—, com. migration and refugees, 1976-95, chmn. com. farm labor, 1981-92, com. moral evaluation of deterrence, 1986-88; cons. com., chmn. for ProLife Activities, 1990-95; mem. com. social devel. and world peace U.S. Cath. Conf., 1985-93, chmn. internat. policy sect., 1987-93; com. justice and peace, Pontifical Couns., 1984-89, 90-98, chmn. com. domestic policy, 1998—, pastoral care of migrants and itinerant people, 1986-91, social comms., 1989—. Mem. Urban Coalition of Fresno, 1968-72, Fresno County Econ. Opportunities Commn., 1964-65, Fresno County Alcoholic Rehab. Com., 1966-67, Fresno City Charter Rev. Com., 1968-70, Mexican-Am. Council for Better Housing, 1968-72, Fresno Redevel. Agy., 1970-75, L.A. 2000 Com., 1985-88, Fed. Commn. Agrl. Workers, 1987-93, Blue Ribbon Com. Affordable Housing City of L.A., 1988; mem. commn. to Draft an Ethics Code for L.A. City Govt., 1989-90; bd. dirs. Fresno Cmty. Workshop, 1965-67, Rebuild L.A., 1992-95; trustee St. Agnes Hosp., Fresno, 1969-73, Cath. U. Am., 1984-88, 98—. Named Young Man of Yr. Fresno Jr. C. of C., 1967 Mem. Canon Law Soc. Home: 555 W Temple St Los Angeles CA 90012-2707 Office: Archdiocese LA 3424 Wilshire Blvd Los Angeles CA 90010-2241

MAHONY, SHEILA ANNE, cable television executive; b. Yonkers, N.Y., Jan. 30, 1942; d. Paul Ambrose and Grace (Sullivan) M.; m. Charles A. Riggs, July 7, 1983; stepchildren: Charles Riggs, Julia Riggs. BA, Newton Coll. Sacred Heart, Mass., 1963; JD, Fordham U., 1967. Asst. corp. counsel Law Dept. City of N.Y., N.Y.C., 1967-72; regional dir. Cable TV Info. Ctr., The Urban Inst., Washington, 1972-74, gen. counsel, 1974-75, exec. dir., 1976-77, Carnegie Commn. on Future of Pub. Broadcasting, N.Y.C., 1977-79; v.p. govt. rels. Cablevision Systems Corp., Woodbury, N.Y., 1980-95, sr. v.p. comm. and pub. affairs, 1995-99, exec. v.p. comm., govt. and pub. affairs, 1999—, dir. N.Y., 1988—. Mem. exec. com. CSPAN, 2000—. Author: Keeping PACE With the New Television, 1979. Dir. C-SPAN, Washington, 1990—. Found. for Minority Interests in Media, N.Y.C., 1992—; bd. dirs. Lustgarten found., 2000—, Legal Aid Soc. of N.Y., 2000—. Mem.: Legal Aid Soc. (bd. dirs. 2000—), Cable TV and Telecom. Assn. N.Y. (dir. 1995—, 1st vice chair 1997—2001, chair 2001—), Cable TV Pub. Affairs Assn. (dir. 1994—98), Lustgarten Found. for Pancreatic Cancer Rsch. (bd. dirs. 1999—). Office: Cablevision Systems Corp 1111 Stewart Ave Bethpage NY 11714-3581

MAHOOD, JAMES EDWARD, lawyer; b. Sewickley, Pa., Feb. 2, 1948; s. James Calvin and Pauline (DeShields) M.; m. Beth Ann Leuenberger, July 12, 1985. BA, Bard Coll., 1971; JD, U. Pitts., 1974. Bar: Pa. 1974. Atty. Neighborhood Legal Svcs., Pitts., 1974-76, mng. atty., 1976-80; assoc. Wilder & Miller, P.C., 1980-83, ptnr., 1983-87, Wilder & Mahood, P.C., Pitts., 1987-92, Wilder, Mahood & Crenney, Pitts., 1992-99, Wilder & Mahood, Pitts., 2000—. Co-author: Pennsylvania Family Law Practice and Procedure Handbook, 1986, 2nd edit., 1989. Fellow Am. Acad. Matrimonial Lawyers (cert. matrimonial arbitrator and mediator); mem. ABA, Pa. Bar Assn. (coun., family law sect. 1989-92, treas. 1993-94, sec. 1994-95, 2nd vice chair 1995-96, chair elect 1997-98, chair 1998-99, mem. code of evidence com.,1997—), Allegheny County Bar Assn. (coun., family law sect. 1986-89, 90-93, 94-97, civil rules com., pub. svc. com.), Joint Family Law Coun. Pa. (adv. com. to jt. state gov. commn. on adoption law 1997—), Neighborhood Legal Svcs. Assn. (bd. dirs. 1993—, treas. 1994-95, pres. 1996-98, equal justice campaign com. 1993-2000, co-chair 2000—). Avocation: American and world history. Office: Wilder & Mahood 10th Fl Koppers Bldg 436 7th Ave Pittsburgh PA 15219-1826 E-mail: jmahood@wildermahood.com.

MAHOOD, JAMES HERBERT, writer; b. Mineola, N.Y., Mar. 22, 1937; s. Cecil Heber Mahood, Mayme (Revere) Mahood; m. Kristine Elizabeth Wenburg, July 2, 1989. BA in English Lit., U. Mass., 1961; MA in east-West Psychology, Calif. Inst. Integral Studies, San Francisco, 1984; PhD of Psychology and English, Union Inst., 1988. Registered counselor Wash., 1999. Reporter The Record, Hackensack, NJ; staff writer Time Inc., N.Y.C.,; assoc. editor Newsweek Books; dir. pub. dept. Inst. Humane Studies, Menlo Park, Calif.; instr. writing Calif. Inst. Integral Studies, San Francisco; asst. prof. Catawba Coll., Salisbury, NC; ind. editor, writer Harcourt, Holt, etc., 2000—. Cons. various pubs. Sp4 U.S. Army, 1957—59. Republican. Episcopalian. Home: 2711 24th Ave SE Olympia WA 98501

MAHORNER, JAMES M. engineer; b. DeLand, Fla., Jan. 28, 1932; s. James Glennon and Sue Mahorner; m. Brenda Johnson (div. May 0, 1992); children: John G., James G., Mary Christine Gore, Amy Caprice, Ted G. JD, Stetson U., DeLand, FL; BS, US Naval Acad., Annapolis, MD. Bar: Fla. Atty. Pvt. Practice, Fla., 1975—; gen. counsel Dept. of HRS, 1970—74; trial counsel Dept. of Agr., 1965; ptnr. Dickens, Linn, and Mahorner, Tallahassee, 1967—70, White, Phipps, Linn, Furnell and Mahorner, Tallahassee, 1965—67; atty. State Attorney's Gen. Office, 1960—65. Democrat-Npl. Avocations: chess, bridge, tennis. Home: 1221 Sunapree Avenue North Atlantic Beach FL 32233 Office: 234 9th Avenue South Jacksonville Beach FL 32250 Office Fax: 904-249-0851. E-mail: jgmahorner@netzero.net.

MAHORSKY, JODY, massage therapist, educator; b. Fountain Hill, Pa., Nov. 3, 1952; d. Frank William and Edith Claire (Beers); children: Benjamin Hugo, Natalie Elmer, Samantha Elmer. BS, Kutztown (Pa.) U., 1974. Cert. Therapeutic Massage and Reflexology, Pa. Author: (poetry) Literary mags., 1986—. Mem. Assn. Bodyworkers and Massage Profls.

MAHOWALD, ANTHONY PETER, geneticist, developmental biologist, educator; b. Albany, Minn., Nov. 24, 1932; s. Aloys and Cecilia (Maus) Mahowald; m. Mary Lou Briody, Apr. 11, 1971; children: Maureen, Lisa, Michael. BS, Spring Hill Coll., 1958; PhD, Johns Hopkins U., 1962. Asst. prof. Marquette U., Milw., 1966-70; asst. staff mem. Inst. Cancer Rsch., Phila., 1970-72; assoc. prof. Ind. U., Bloomington, 1972-76, prof., 1976-82; Henry Willson Payne prof. Case Western Res. U., Cleve., 1982-90, chmn. dept. anatomy, 1982-88, chmn. dept. genetics, 1988-90; Louis Block prof., chmn. dept molecular genetics and cell biology U. Chgo., 1990—2002, Louis Block prof. emeritus, 2002—. Chmn. Com. Devel. Biology U. Chgo., 1991-99. Woodrow Wilson Found. fellow, 1958, NSF fellow, 1958-62. Fellow AAAS, Am. Acad. Arts and Scis., Soc. Scholars Johns Hopkins U.; mem. Nat. Acad. Scis., Genetics Soc. Am. (sec. 1986-88), Soc. Devel. Biology (pres. 1989, editor-in-chief jour. 1980-85), Am. Soc. Cell Biology (coun. mem. 1996-98). Office: U Chgo Dept Molec Genet/Cell Biol 920 E 58th St Chicago IL 60637-5415

MAHR, AARON LEE, retired government executive; b. Canton, Ill., Jan. 4, 1947; s. Ivan Lee and Nina Berniece Mahr; m. Nicole Adrienne Bourque, June 30, 1987; children: Jennifer Ward, David Abba, Timothy. BA, Emory U., 1969; Sr. Ofcls. in Nat. Security, Harvard U., 1991. Cert. Army Acquisitions Corps. Inventory mgmt. specialist U.S. Army Weapons Command, Rock Island, Ill., 1969-70; supply sys. analyst Frankford Arsenal, Phila., 1970-71, U.S. Army Gen. Materiel & Petroleum Ctr., New Cumberland, Pa., 1971-74; Jordan/Kuwait country desk officer U.S. Army Internat. Logistics Command, Alexandria, Va., 1974-76; Mid-East program mgr. U.S. Army Security Assistance Command, 1976-82; Mid-East program mgr. Office Dep. Chief Staff for Logistics Hdqs. Dept. of the Army, Pentagon, Washington, 1982-83; chief Israel and Turkey divsn. U.S. Army Security Assistance Command, Alexandria, 1983-85; dir. Internat. Coop. Programs Activity, 1986—. Diabetes hotline cons. Inst. for Peripheral Nerve Surgery, Balt., 2000—. Chmn. fund raising Children's House by the Sea, Grant-A-Wish Found. Mem. Assn. U.S. Army (assoc.), Am. Def. Preparedness Assn. (internat. subcom. 1987-97), Kiwanis Internat., Order of DeMolay, Delta Tau Delta. Avocations: videography, photography, travel, fishing. Home: 100 Tail of the Fox Dr Ocean Pines MD 21811 E-mail: aruba4us@mchsi.com.

MAHSMAN, DAVID LAWRENCE, religious publications editor; b. Quincy, Ill., Aug. 16, 1950; s. Alvin Henry and Dorothy Marie (Schnack) M.; m. Lois Jean Mohn, July 27, 1975. BS in Journalism, So. Ill. U., 1972; MDiv, Concordia Theol. Seminary, Fort Wayne, Ind., 1983; STM, Concordia Sem., St. Louis, 1995. Staff writer Paddock Publs., Arlington Heights, Ill., 1972-73, Decatur (Ill.) Herald & Rev., 1973-76; press asst. Hon. Tom Railsback U.S. Ho. Reps., Washington, 1976-79, campaign press sec. Hon. Dan Coats Ft. Wayne, Ind., 1979-80, 82; pastor Trinity Luth. Ch., Glen Cove, N.Y., 1983-85; dir. news and info. Luth. Ch.-Mo. Synod, St. Louis, 1985—; exec. editor, contbr. Luth. Witness, 1985—; exec. editor Reporter, 1985—. Mem. Inter-Luth. task force on pornography Luth. Coun. U.S.A., 1986; mem. Washington adv. coun. Mo. Synod, Office of Govt. Info., Washington, 1987-2000. Editor: Augsburg Today: This We Believe, Teach and Confess, 1997. Recipient Jacob Scher Investigative Reporting award Women in Comm., 1974, Commendation award Concordia Hist. Inst., 1988, 98. Mem. Concordia Hist. Inst. (life). Republican. Avocations: travel, photography. Office: Luth Ch-Mo Synod 1333 S Kirkwood Rd Saint Louis MO 63122-7226 E-mail: david.mahsman@lcms.org.

MAHVI, DAVID M. surgeon, educator; b. Oklahoma City, Dec. 30, 1955; m. Christine C. Cox, Sept. 29, 1984; children: David, Allison, Jonathan. Student, U. Okla., 1978—81; MD, Med. U. S.C., 1981. From asst. prof. to assoc. prof. surgery U. Wis., Madison, 1989-2001, prof., 2001—. Fellow ACS, Soc. Surg. Oncology; mem. Soc. Univ. Surgeons, Madison Surg. Soc. (pres. 1997). Avocations: windsurfing, skiing, golf. Office: U Wis 600 Highland Ave H4-726 Madison WI 53792

MAI, CHAO CHEN, engineer; b. Kwangchow, Canton, China, Feb. 26, 1936; came to U.S., 1962, naturalized, 1973; m. Shao Shen Yam; children: Glenn, Kenneth. MSEE, Oreg. State U., 1964; PhD in Elec. Engring., Utah State U., 1968. Project engr. Sylvania Electric Co., Woburn, Mass., 1967-70; mgr. R&D Mostek Corp., Carrollton, Tex., 1970-76, v.p. R&D, 1976-84; founder, sr. v.p. Dallas Semiconductor Corp., 1984-2000, pres. and COO, 2000—. Mem. IEEE, Electrochem. Soc. Achievements include patent for Silicon gate combined with depletion load process, method for making a semiconductor device, MOSFET Fabrication Process; research advanced processing technology in integrated circuits; subspecialty integrated circuits, microchip technology.

MAI, WILLIAM FREDERICK, plant nematologist, educator; b. Greenwood, Del., July 23, 1916; s. William Frederick and Laurana (Owens) M.; m. Barbara Lee Morrell, June 2, 1941; children: Virginia Mai Abrams, William Howard, Eliabeth Hardy. BS, U. Del., 1939; PhD, Cornell U., 1945. Asst. prof. Cornell U., Ithaca, N.Y., 1946-49, assoc. prof., 1949-52, prof., 1952-81, Liberty Hyde prof. plant pathology, 1981-83, prof. emeritus, 1983—. Cons. Nat. Acad. Scis., Internat. Potato Ctr., Brands Co., AID Author (with H.H. Lyon), Pictoral Key to Genera of Plant Parasitic Nemtodes, 1960, 5th edit. 1993, Plant Parasitic Nematodes, 1971; editor: Control of Plant Parasitic Nematodes, 1968. Coach Little League Baseball and Football, Ithaca, 1955-60; chmn. Community Orgn., 1960-65. Recipient award of distinction Internat. Plant Protection Conf., 1979; Paul Harris fellow Rotary Found., 1997. Fellow Am. Phytopath. Soc. (pres. Northeastern div. 1968-69 award of merit Northeastern div); mem. AAAS, Soc. Nematologists (pres. 1969 hon. life), Helminthological Soc. Washington, Soc. European Nematologists, Potato Assn. Am. Lodges: Rotary. Home: 613 E Shore Dr Ithaca NY 14850-2135 Office: Cornell U Dept Plant Pathology Ithaca NY 14853

MAIBACH, BEN C., JR. service executive; b. Bay City, Mich., 1920; With Barton-Malow Co., Detroit, 1938—, v.p., dir.-in-charge field ops., 1949-53, exec. v.p., 1953-60, pres., 1960-76, chmn. bd., 1976; chmn. and dir. Barton-Malow Ent.; chmn. bd. Cloverdale Equipment Co. Trustee Barton-Malow Found, Maibach Found., 1967—; chmn. Apostolic Christian Woodhaven, Detroit; bishop Apostolic Christian Ch., Mich., Ont., Fla.; bd. dirs. S.E. Mich. chpt. ARC, Rural Gospel and Med. Missions of India. Home: 29711 Wentworth St Apt 207 Livonia MI 48154-3887 also: 5525 Azure Way Sarasota FL 34242-1857

MAIBACH, HOWARD I. dermatologist; b. N.Y.C., July 18, 1929; s. Jack Louis and Sidonia (Fink) M.; m. Siesel Wile, July 8, 1953; children— Lisa, Ed, Todd. AB, Tulane U., 1950, MD, 1955. Diplomate: Am. Bd. Dermatology. Intern William Beaumont Army Hosp., El Paso, Tex., 1955-56; resident, fellow in dermatology USPHS, Hosp. of U. Pa., 1959-61; asst. instr. U. Pa., 1958-61, lectr., 1960-61; practice medicine specializing in dermatology U. Calif. Hosps., San Francisco, 1961—; asst. prof. dermatology U. Calif. Sch. Medicine, 1961-63, asso. prof., 1967-73; research asso. Cancer Research Inst., 1967—; mem. staff U. Calif.-H.C. Moffitt Hosps., 1961—. Cons. Laguna Honda Hosp., 1962-66, chief dermatology service, 1963-67; cons. Letterman Gen. Hosp., Calif. Med. Facility, Vacaville, San Francisco Gen. Hosp., Sonoma State Hosp., Eldridge, Calif., Stanford Research Inst., Menlo Park, Calif., Calif. Dept. Public Health, Berkeley, VA Hosp., Research Inst. Fragrance Materials, Inc., David Grant USAF Hosp. of Travis AFB, Naval Hosp., San Diego, Wilford Hall AFB, Tex., Army Environ. Health Agy., Md.; mem. Internat. Contact Dermatitis Research Com. Editor: Animal Models in Dermatology, 1965; co-editor: Dermatotoxicology and Pharmacology, 1977, Skin Microbiology, 1981; bd. editors: Internat. Jour. Dermatology, 1974—; editorial bd.: Contact Dermatitis: Environ. Dermatology, 1974—, Clin. Toxicology, 1976—; internat. editorial bd.: Excerpta Media, 1976—; author, coauthor, editor of over 30 books and 750 publs. Served to capt. M.C. U.S. Army, 1955-58. Recipient awards Soc. Cosmetic Chemists, 1970, 71, 73 Fellow A.C.P.; mem. Am. Acad. Dermatology (award for essay 1961), San Francisco Dermatol. Soc. (pres. 1970-71), Pacific Dermatol. Assn., Soc. Investigative Dermatology, N.Y. Acad. Scis., Calif. Med. Assn., Am. Fedn. Clin. Research, AMA, San Francisco Med. Soc., Am. Dermatol. Assn., Internat. Soc. Tropical Dermatology, Am. Soc. Clin. Pharmacology and Therapeutics, Am. Coll. Toxicology; hon. mem. Swedish Dermatol. Soc., Am. Vet. Dermatol. Assn., Am. Acad. Vet. Dermatology, Danish Dermatol. Soc., German Dermatol. Soc. Office: U Calif Hosp San Francisco CA 94143-0989

MAICKEL, ROGER PHILIP, pharmacologist, educator; b. Floral Park, N.Y., Sept. 8, 1933; s. Philip Vincent and Margaret Mary (Rose) M.; m. Lois Louise Pivonka, Sept. 8, 1956; children: Nancy Ellen Maickel Ward, Carolyn Sue Maickel Anderson. BS, Manhattan (N.Y.) Coll., 1954; postgrad., Poly. Inst. Bklyn., 1954-55; MS, Georgetown U., 1957, PhD, 1960. Biochemist Nat. Heart Inst., Bethesda, Md., 1955-65; asso. prof. pharmacology Ind. U., 1965-69, prof., 1969—, head sect. pharmacology med. scis. program, 1971-77; prof. pharmacology and toxicology, head dept. Sch. Pharmacy and Pharmacal Scis. Purdue U., West Lafayette, Ind., 1977-83; dir. lab. animal program Purdue U., 1988-98, emeritus prof., 1999—; acting v.p. product acquisition and devel. BetaMED Pharms., Inc., Indpls., 1983-84. Adv. editor: Pergamon Press, 1970-88; adv. editorial bd.: Neuropharmacology, 1974-88. Bd. dirs. TEAMS, Inc., 1981-87, Am. Coun. on Sci. and Health, 1993-2000; trustee AAALAC, 1992—. Recipient Alumni award in medicine Manhattan Coll., 1972 Fellow: AAAS, Collegium Internat. de Neuro-Psychopharmacologicum, Royal Soc. Chemistry, Am. Coll. Neuropsychopharmacology, Am. Inst. Chemists (bd. dirs. 1989—92, 2001—, pres.-elect 1992—94, pres. 1994—96, chmn. 1996—98); mem.: ASTM, Soc. Toxicology, Soc. Neurosci., N.Y. Acad. Scis., Internat. Soc. Psychoneuroendocrinology, Internat. Assn. Chiefs Police, Soc. Forensic Toxicologists, Am. Soc. Clin. Pharmacology and Therapeutics, Am. Soc. Pharmacology and Exptl. Therapeutics, Am. Chem. Soc., Rho Chi, Sigma Xi. Home: 3567 Canterbury Dr Lafayette IN 47909-3714 E-mail: maickel@pharmacy.purdue.edu. *As a human being, I hope to be able to do my best in the roles of scientist, teacher, and citizen by fulfilling the academic criteria of teaching, research, and service to the utmost degree humanly possible.*

MAICKI, G. CAROL, former state senator, consultant; b. Holden, Mass., July 16, 1936; d. John Arne and Mary Emily (Bumpus) Mannisto; m. Henry J. Maicki, May 4, 1957; children: Henry III, Matthew, Scott, Julia, Mary. BA, U. Mich., 1978. Exec. dir. Sweetwater County Task Force/Sexual Assault, Rocksprings, Wyo., 1978-81; program mgr. Family Violence/Sexual Assault, Cheyenne, 1981-85; coord. S.D. Coalition Against Domestic Violence and Sexual Assault, Black Hawk, 1985-90; state senator S.D. Legislature, Pierre, 1990-92. Cons. Black Hawk, 1990—, Nat. Coalition Against Domestic Violence, 1987; spkr. Nat. Coalition Against Sexual Assault, Portland, Oreg., 1987, 96, Rutger Ctr. for Women in Politics, San Diego, 1991, Gov.'s Conf., Las Vegas, Nev., 1997; mem. planning com. Office for Victims of Crime, U.S. Justice, Phoenix, 1989; expert witness state and fed. cts., 1990—. Author: (manuals) Operating Standards, 1984, Rules and Regulations, 1986, Shelter Procedures, 1987, Administrative Procedures, 1995, Responders to Rope, 1996, Cultural Competency, 2001. Com. mem. Health and Human Svc. State Legislature, Pierre, 1990-92, local govt., 1990-92; commn. mem. local govt. study commn., Pierre, 1990-92; bd. dirs. Crisis Intervention Svcs., 1991-99, Dakotah territory, 1996—; apptd. def. adv. com. on women in svcs. Sec. of Def., 1995-97; apptd. exec. com. def. adv. com. on women in the svcs., 1996-97; founder Women's Connection, Inc., 1996; mem. Dacotah Terr. Youth Devel., Inc. Recipient award Gov. Wyo., 1985, Spirit of Peace award Women Against Violence, Rapid City, 1993, U.S. Dept. of Justice award, 1994, fellowship Share Our Strength, 1996-98, Equity award S.D. chpt. AAUW, 1996, Failure is Impossible award Rapid City, 1998. Mem. S.D. Alliance for Mentally Ill, Rapid City Womens Network, S.D. Advocacy Network for Women. Democrat. Avocations: reading, crosswords, gardening. Home: PO Box 375 Black Hawk SD 57718-0375 E-mail: gcarol@starband.net.

MAIDA, CARL ALBERT, anthropologist; b. Trenton, N.J., Nov. 3, 1947; s. Nicholas Charles and Concetta Virginia Maida; m. Gail Lucille Gulick, June 27, 1976 (div. Mar. 1987); children: Vanessa Claire, Alexandra Nicole; m. Barbara Lynn Yablon, June 17, 1990. BA, Syracuse U., 1969; MA, New Sch. Social Rsch., 1972; PhD, U. Calif., L.A., 1981. Lectr. CUNY, 1974-75; rsch. assoc. Charles R. Drew U. Sci. and Medicine, L.A., 1979-81; postdoctoral rsch. assoc. UCLA, 1981-84, asst. rsch. anthropologist, 1984-94; lectr. Calif. State U., Northridge, 1984—; assoc. rsch. anthropologist UCLA, 1995-99, assoc. adj. prof., 1999—. Cons. Pub. Health Found., L.A., 1985-94, RAND, Santa Monica, Calif., 1994-99. Author: Black Networks of Care: Culture, Health and Learning in an Urban Community, 1981, The Crisis of Competence: Transitional Stress and the Displaced Worker, 1989, Children and Disasters, 1999. Recipient grants Helena Rubinstein Found., 1982-84, John D. and Catherine T. MacArthur Found., 1984-86, Joan B. Kroc Found., 1985-86, Robert Wood Johnson Found., 1996-98, NIH, 2000—. Fellow Am. Anthrop. Assn., Soc. Applied Anthropology; mem. AAAS (Pacific divsn. chair social, polit. and econ. scis. sect. 1986-2000, chair health scis. 2001—). Home: 3042 Westridge Cir Thousand Oaks CA 91360-1051 Office: Univ Calif 10833 Le Conte Ave Los Angeles CA 90095-3075 Fax: 805-492-7067. E-mail: cmaida@ucla.edu.

MAIDMAN, RICHARD HARVEY MORTIMER, lawyer; b. N.Y.C., Nov. 17, 1933; s. William and Ada (Seegle) M.; m. Lynne Rochelle Lateiner, Apr. 3, 1960 (div. Sept. 1987); m. Gail Lowe Haymes, Sept. 27, 1998; children: Patrick, Mitchel, Dagny. BA, Williams Coll., 1955; JD, Yale U., 1959; postgrad., NYU Grad. Sch. Bus., 1957, NYU Grad. Sch. Law, 1960, 77. Bar: N.Y. 1961, Fla. 1961, U.S. Dist. Ct. 1962, 79, U.S. Ct. Appeals 1966, U.S. Supreme Ct. 1978. Assoc. Saxe, Bacon & O'Shea, N.Y.C., 1962-64; ptnr. Weiner, Maidman & Goldman, 1964-67; pvt. practice N.Y.C. and Fla., 1968—. Of counsel Shwal, Thompson & Bloch, N.Y.C. and Geneva, 1976-87, Maidman and Mittelman, LLP, 1996—; pres. MBS Equities, Inc., 1970-88, Fashion Wear Realty Co., Inc., N.Y.C., 1975—; mng. gen. ptnr. Richard and David Maidman, N.Y.C., 1972—, Barcelona Hotel Ltd., Miami Beach, Fla., 1975-84, New Haven Projects Co., 1987—; dir. The Farr Companies, Washington, 1990-92; legis. counsel Theodore R. Kupferman, 17th Congl. Dist. N.Y., 1966-68; receiver Halloran House Hotel, N.Y.C., 1981; chmn. Townhouse Mgmt. Co., 1998—. Contbr. articles to profl. jours. Mem. ABA, N.Y. State Bar Assn., Fla. Bar Assn., Assn. of the Bar of the City of N.Y., Bankruptcy Lawyers Assn., N.Y.C. Real Estate Bd. N.Y. Home: Stamboat Landing 27 Astor Ln Sands Point NY 11050-2602 also: 9 E 79th St New York NY 10021-0123 Office: 70 E 55th St New York NY 10022-3222 E-mail: rhmm59@aya.yale.edu., richard@maidman.org.

MAIDMAN, STEPHEN PAUL, lawyer; b. Hartford, Conn., Feb. 8, 1954; s. Harry and Roslyn (Mandell) M.; m. Mari Rosenberg, Oct. 13, 1996. AB summa cum laude, Bowdoin Coll., 1976; MBA, U. Pa., 1979, JD, 1980. Bar: Pa. 1980, Mass. 1996, U.S. Dist. Ct. (ea. dist.) Pa. 1980, U.S. Ct. Appeals (3d cir.) 1980, U.S. Dist. Ct. Mass. 1996, U.S. Ct. Appeals (1st cir.) 1996, U.S. Supreme Ct. 1997. Assoc. Drinker, Biddle & Reath, Phila., 1980-81; atty. IBM, Boca Raton, Fla., 1981-84, N.Y.C., 1984-85, staff atty., 1985-87, Rye Brook, N.Y., 1987-88, lab. counsel Poughkeepsie, 1988-92, site counsel Hopewell Junction, 1992-95; pvt. practice, Springfield, Mass., 1996—. Adj. faculty U. Conn Law Sch., 2001—. Co-class agt. Bowdoin Coll. Alumni Fund. Mem. Nat. Assn. Criminal Def. Lawyers, Mass. Bar Assn., Mass. Assn. Criminal Def. Lawyers, Hampden County Bar Assn. Avocations: running, black Labradors. E-mail: maidman@!prodigy.net. Office: 1145 Main St Ste 417 Springfield MA 01103-2123

MAIDON, CAROLYN HOWSER, teacher education director; b. Chgo., May 13, 1946; d. Lloyd Earl and Esther Lillian (Beck) Howser; m. Charles Randall Maidon, Nov. 21, 1970; children: Randall Scott, April Janel. BS in Edn., Okla. State U., 1968; MS in Edn., N.C. State U., 1984, postgrad., 1987—. Tchr. biology and English Cary (N.C.) High Sch., 1968-71; grad. instr. N.C. State U., Raleigh, 1984-85, asst. affirmative action officer, 1985-89, asst. dir. univ. undesignated program, 1989-95; dir. tchr. edn., 1995-99; coord. MentorNet N.C. State U., Raleigh, 2000—; chief, tchr. edn. sect. N.C. Dept. Pub. Instrn., 1999-2000. Home: 4204 Belnap Dr Apex NC 27502-5378 Office: NC State U PO Box 7632 Raleigh NC 27695-7632

MAIENSCHEIN, FRED C. retired physicist; b. Belleville, Ill., Oct. 28, 1925; s. Fred and Ethel (Forsythe) M.; m. Joyce Kylander, Aug. 14, 1948; children: Jane, Jon. BS in Chem. Engring, Rose Hulman Inst. Tech., 1945; MS in Physics, Ind. U., 1948, PhD in Physics, 1949. Physicist Oak Ridge Nat. Lab., 1951-60, assoc. dir. engring. physics div., 1960-66; co-dir. Oak Ridge Electron Linear Accelerator, 1965-74, dir. engring. physics div., 1966-90, ret., 1990. Current neurosci. scholar; mem. com. reactor physics Nuclear Energy Agy., 1962-89; mem. adv. com. radiation aspects of SST, FAA, 1969-74; mem. subcoms. Nat. Com. Radiation Protection, 1959-71. Contbr. articles profl. jours., chpts. in books. Fellow Am. Nuclear Soc.; mem. Am. Phys. Soc., AAAS, Soc. Neurosci., Tau Beta Pi. Home: 838 W Outer Dr Oak Ridge TN 37830-8402

MAIER, CHARLES STEVEN, history educator; b. N.Y.C., Feb. 23, 1939; s. Louis and Muriel (Krailsheimer) M.; m. Pauline Alice Rubbelke, June 17, 1961; children— Andrea Nicole, Nicholas Winterer, Jessica Elizabeth Heine. AB, Harvard U., 1960; postgrad., St. Anthony's Coll., Oxford, Eng., 1960-61; PhD, Harvard U., 1967. Instr. history Harvard U., Cambridge, Mass., 1967-69, asst. prof., 1969-73, lectr., 1973-75; vis. prof. U. Bielefeld, Fed. Republic Germany, 1976; assoc. prof. history Duke U., Durham, N.C., 1976-79, prof., 1979-81; prof. history Harvard U., Cambridge, Mass., 1981-91, Krupp Found. prof. European studies, 1991—2002; Leverett Saltonstall prof. history, 2002; dir. Ctr. for European Studies, 1994-2001. Rsch. fellow Lehrman Inst., N.Y.C., 1975-76; mem. assoc. staff Brookings Instn., Washington, 1978-84; mem. coun. Fondation Jean Monnet pour l'Europe, Lausanne, Switzerland; mem. joint comm. on We. Europe Social Sci. Rsch. Coun. and Am. Coun. Learned Socs., 1978-84, chmn., 1979-81; mem. German Am. Acad. Coun., Bonn, Germany and Washington, 1998-2001. Author: Recasting Bourgeois Europe, 1975 (Am. Hist. Assn. George Louis Beer award 1976, Herbert Baxter Adams award 1977), In Search of Stability, 1987, The Unmasterable Past, 1988, Dissolution: The Crisis of Communism and the End of East Germany, 1997; editor: The Origins of the Cold War and Contemporary Europe, 1978, rev. edit., 1990, (with Dan S. White) The Thirteenth of May and the Advent of de Gaulle's Republic, 1967, (with Leon Lindberg) The Politics of Inflation and Economic Stagnation, 1985, Changing Boundaries of the Political, 1987, The Marshall Plan and Germany, 1991. Decorated Commdr.'s Cross, Order of Merit (German Fed. Rep.); fellow NEH, 1977-78, German Marshall Fund, 1980-81, Guggenheim Found., 1984-85; rsch. grantee MacArthur Found., 1988-89. Fellow Woodrow Wilson Ctr. for Scholars (Washington); mem. Council on Fgn. Relations, Am. Hist. Assn., Soc. Italian Hist. Studies, Soc. Historians of Am. Fgn. Rels., Am. Acad. Arts and Scis., Phi Beta Kappa Home: 60 Larchwood Dr Cambridge MA 02138-4639 Office: Harvard U Ctr for European Studies Cambridge MA 02138 E-mail: csmaier@fas.harvard.edu.

MAIER, GERALD JAMES, corporate executive; b. Regina, Sask., Can., Sept. 22, 1928; s. John Joseph and Mary (Passler) M. Student, Notre Dame Coll. (Wilcox), U. Man., U. Alta., U. Western Ont.; LLD (hon.), U. Alberta, 1999, U Alta. With petroleum and mining industries, Can., U.S., Australia, U.K.; responsible for petroleum ops. Africa, United Arab Emirates, S.E. Asia; past chmn., pres., CEO TransCan. PipeLines, Calgary, 1985-99; vice-chmn. NOVA Chems. Corp., 1998-2000. Bd. dirs. Stream-Flo Industries, Ltd., Vintage Petroleum, Inc.; past chmn. Can. Nat. Com. for World Petroleum Congresses; past chmn. Van Horne Inst. for Internat. Transp. Chmn. bd. dirs. Notre Dame Coll. Named Hon. Col. (ret.) King's Own Calgary Rgt., Resource Man of Yr. Alta. Chamber of Resources, 1990; recipient Can. Engr.'s Gold medal Can. Coun. Profl. Engrs., 1990, Disting. Alumni award U. Alta., 1992, Mgmt. award McGill U., 1993, Centennial award Alta Assn. Engrs., Geologists and Geophysicists, Hal Godwin award for excellence in internat. bus. U. Calgary, 1999, Can. Bus. Leader award U. Alberta, 1999; inductee Can. Petroleum Hall of Fame, 1999. Fellow Can. Acad. Engring.; mem. Assn. Profl. Engrs., Geologists and Geophysicists Alta. (past pres.), Can. Inst. Mining and Metallurgy (Past Pres.'s Meml. medal 1971). Avocations: golf, downhill skiing, shooting, fishing. Office: Granmar Investments Ltd 400 3rd Ave SW Ste 3300 Calgary AB Canada T2P 4H2

MAIER, HAROLD GEISTWEIT, law educator, lawyer; b. Cin., Mar. 25, 1937; s. Alfred F. and Alberta (Wilmes) M.; divorced; children: Marc L., Kurt S. BA in English Lit., U. Cin., 1959, JD, 1963; postgrad., Free U., Berlin, 1959-60; LLM, U. Mich., 1964; postgrad., U. Munich, 1964-65. Bar: Ohio 1963. Mem. faculty laws Vanderbilt U., Nashville, 1965—, prof., 1970—, David Daniels Allen prof. law, 1988—, dir. Transnat. Legal Studies program, 1973-99. Faculty San Diego Internat and Comparative Law Inst., King's Coll., U. London, 1986, 87, Regent's Coll., 1989, 91, 96; vis. prof. law U. Pa., 1985, U. N.C., Chapel Hill, 1987; vis. Lyle T. Alverson prof. law George Washington U., Washington, 1987-88; vis. Woodruff prof. internat. law U. Ga., Atlanta, 1995; prof. law summer program LSU, Aix-en-Provence, France, 1995; vis. Straus disting. prof. law Pepperdine U., Malibu, Calif., 2000-01; cons. Office of Sec. Army, Panama Canal Treaty Negotiations, 1976; guest scholar Brookings Instn., Washington, 1976-77; dir. PDS Patrons, Inc. (Univ. Sch. of Nashville), 1975-87, pres., 1978-79; counselor on internat. law Office of Legal Adviser, U.S. Dept. State, 1983-84; Blain Sloan disting. lectr. internat. law Pace U. Sch. Law, White Plains, N.Y., 2001 Bd. editors Am. Jour. Internat. Law, 1984-88, Academic Coun., Inst. Transnational Arbitration, 1996—; bd. editors Am. Jour. Comparative Law, 1997—; U.S. Assoc. Constitutional Law, 1997—, Am. Br. Internat. Law Assn.; author: (with T. Buergenthal) Public International Law in a Nutshell, 1985, 2d edit., 1989, (with T. Buergenthal, K. Doehring, J. Kokott) Grundzüge des Völkerrechts, 1987, Manual de Derecho Internacional Publico, 1994; contbr. numerous articles in field to profl. jours. Recipient Luftbrucke Dankstipendium, Free U. Berlin, 1959-60; Ford internat. studies fellow U. Mich., 1964-65, Vanderbilt U. faculty fellow, 1976-77. Mem. Am. Soc. Internat. Law (exec. coun. 1974-78, 84-87), Am. Soc. Comparative Law (bd. dirs. 1984-2001), Am. Law Inst., Order of Coif, Omicron Delta Kappa, Phi Alpha Delta, Tau Kappa Alpha, Pi Delta Epsilon. Office: Vanderbilt U Law School 131 21st Ave S Nashville TN 37203

MAIER, HENRY B. environmental engineer; b. Yonkers, N.Y., July 11, 1925; s. Henry and Adelaide (Boyce) M.; m. Elizabeth A. Maier, May 4, 1968. BA, Columbia U., 1947; postgrad., Adelphi U., Hofstra U. Prin. Maier Solar Developments, Hempstead, N.Y. Author: Techniques for Seascape Painting. Mem. AIAA, Am. Chem. Soc., N.Y. Acad. Scis. Achievements include patents for elapsed time indicator, multiple reflecting solar collecting system, electro-responsive coatings, fusion power pellets, and fusion power; design of initial stage of work for aerospace vehicle, comet flyby study; development of rapid method for perspective visualizations, for views of engineering and design concepts; definition of geometrics for placement of measuring points by approximation; research on inorganic sulfur and chlorine pollutants from combustion of fossil fuels and from incinerator processes, and their interactive roles in the progressive deterioration of the stratospheric ozone shield previously blocking frequencies in the infrared, far infrared and microwave frequencies, with particular regard to the prediction and pattern formation of major North Atlantic storm systems; study for a comet detecting telescope; design study for single span, steel beam highway bridge for enhanced safety from emerging situations of high-speed trucks, severe weather conditions and limited maintenance; study of architectural modern design, Y2K study. Home: 6 Sealey Ave Apt 3K Hempstead NY 11550-1232

MAIER, HOWARD ROBERT, urban planner, government agency administrator; b. Cleve., Oct. 10, 1944; s. Ernest and Florence B. Maier; m. Sue A. Maier, February 4, 1973; children: Matthew A., Abigail F., Michael C. BA in Econs., Ohio State U., Columbus, 1966, M in City Planning, 1972; MS in Pub. Mgmt., Case Western Res. U., 1974. Assoc. planner Met. Health Planning Corp., Cleve., 1970-71; prin. planner Cuyahoga County Regional Planning Commn., 1971-75; dir. planning and devel., asst. dir., cmty. planner City of Cleveland Heights, 1975-85; exec. staff Jewish Cmty. Fedn., Cleve., 1985-88; dir. spl. projects N.E. Ohio Areawide Coord. Agy., 1988-89; acting exec. dir. Northea. Ohio Areawide Coord. Agy., 1989-91; exec. dir. Northea. Ohio Area Wide Coord. Agy., 1991—. Mem. adj. faculty and adv. coms. Cleve. State U., 1974—. Editl. cartoonist Sun Newspapers, 1975-77. Active Leadership Cleve., Gov. Regional Econ. Devel. Adv. Bd., Build Up Greater Cleve., Greater Cleve. Growth Assn., Ohio Canal Corridor Adv. Bd.; v.p. bd. dirs. Planned Lifetime Assistance Network N.E. Ohio; mem. adv. bd. No. Ohio divsn. March of Dimes; mem. Ohio State U. Advocates. Mem. Am. Planning Assn. (Excellence in Planning Leadership award), Am. Inst. Cert. Planners (cert.), Nat. Assn. Regional Councils (exec. dirs. com.), Ohio Planning Conf., Assn. Met. Planning Orgns. Avocations: family activities, art, cartooning. Office: NE Ohio Areawide Coord Agy 1299 Superior Ave Cleveland OH 44114 E-mail: hmaier@mpo.noaca.org.

MAIER, KURT SALOMON, historian, librarian; b. Kippenheim, Germany, May 4, 1930; came to U.S., 1941; s. Siegfried and Charlotte (Auerbacher) M.; m. Margery Teal, Apr. 20, 1967. BA, Hunter Coll., N.Y.C., 1960; MA, Columbia U., N.Y.C., 1962, PhD, 1969, MLS, 1975. Asst. prof. Columbia U., N.Y.C., 1965-75, Iona Coll., New Rochelle, N.Y., 1968-75; libr. Leo Baeck Inst., N.Y.C., 1975-78, Libr. Congress, Washington, 1978—. Contbr. articles to profl. jours. Woodrow Wilson fellow Ford Found., 1962. Jewish. Avocations: military history, printing history, Judaica, German exile studies, documentary photography. Office: Libr Congress 1 Independence Ave SE Washington DC 20540 E-mail: kmai@loc.gov.

MAIER, PAUL VICTOR, pharmaceutical executive; b. Seattle, Nov. 6, 1947; s. Norman Alvin and Rosalie (Godek) M.; m. Shirley Diehl, Aug. 11, 1979. BS, Pa. State U., 1969; MBA, Harvard U., 1975. Fin. analyst Greyhound Corp, Phoenix, 1975-76; asst. mgr. Wells Service Wells Fargo Bank, San Francisco, 1976-78; v.p. Fin. Cummins Service and Sales, Los Angeles, 1978-84; v.p., treas. ICN Pharms, Inc., Costa Mesa, Calif., 1984-90; v.p. fin. DFS West, 1990-92; sr. v.p., CFO Ligand Pharmaceuticals, Inc., San Diego, 1992—. Chmn. audit com. Entropin Inc., 2000—, also bd. dirs. Chmn. hosp. div. United Way Region V, L.A., 1983-84; bd. dirs. The Wellness Community, San Diego, 1993—. Served with USNR, 1969-95. Mem. Fin. Execs. Inst., The Athletic Congress, Pa. State Club of S.D., Harvard Bus. Sch. Assn. So. Calif., Ctr. for Non-Profit Mgmt., Vis. Nurse Assn. L.A. (bd. dirs. 1979-92, chmn.), Protection Mut. Inst. (West Coast adv. bd. 1985-90). Republican. Roman Catholic. Office: Ligand Pharmaceuticals 10275 Science Center Dr San Diego CA 92121-1117 E-mail: pmaier@ligand.com.

MAIER, PAULINE, history educator; b. Apr. 27, 1938; d. Irvin Louis and Charlotte (Winterer) Rubbelke; m. charles Steven Maier, June 17, 1961; children: andrea Nicole, Nicholas Winterer, Jessica Elizabeth Heine. AB, Radcliffe Coll., 1960; postgrad., London Sch. Econs., 1960-61; PhD in History, Harvard U., 1968; LLD (hon.), Regis Coll., 1987; DHL (hon.), Williams Coll., 1993. Asst. prof. then assoc. prof. history U. Mass., Boston, 1968-77; Robinson-Edwards prof. history U. Wis., Madison, 1977-78; prof. history MIT, Cambridge, Mass., 1978—, William R. Kenan Jr. prof. history, 1990—. Dept. head, MIT, 1979-88, mem. coun. Inst. Early Am. History, 1982-84; trustee Regis Coll., 1988-93; trustee Commonwealth Sch., 1991-96; bd. mgrs. Old South Meeting House, 1987-97. Author: From Resistance to Revolution: Colonial Radicals and the Development of American Opposition to Britain, 1765-1766, 1972, The Old Revolutionaries: Political Lives in the Age of Samuel Adams, 1980, The American People: A History, 1986, American Scripture: Making the Declaration of Independence, 1997. Recipient Douglass Adair award Claremont Grad. Sch.-Inst. Early Am. History, 1976, Kidger award New Eng. History Tchrs. Assn., 1981; fellow Nat. Endowment Humanities, 1974-75, 88-89, Charles Warren fellow, 1974-75, Guggenheim fellow, 1990. Mem. Orgn. Am. Historians (mem. exec. bd. 1978-82), Am. Hist. Assn. (mem. nominations com. 1983-85, chmn. 1985), Soc. Am. Historians, Am. Antiquarian Soc. (mem. exec. coun. 1984-89), Colonial Soc. Mass. (mem. exec. coun. 1990-93), Mass. Hist. Soc., Am. Acad. Arts and Scis. Home: 60 Larchwood Dr Cambridge MA 02138-4639 Office: MIT E51-279 77 Massachusetts Ave Cambridge MA 02139-4307 E-mail: pmaier@mit.edu.

MAIER, PETER KLAUS, lawyer, business executive; b. Wurzburg, Germany, Nov. 20, 1929; came to U.S., 1939, naturalized, 1945; s. Bernard and Joan (Sonder) M.; m. Melanie L. Stoff, Dec. 15, 1963; children: Michele Margaret, Diana Lynn. BA cum laude, Claremont McKenna Coll., 1949; JD, U. Calif., Berkeley, 1952; LLM in Taxation, NYU, 1953. Bar: Calif. 1953, U.S. Supreme Ct. 1957; cert. specialist in taxation law, Calif. Atty. tax div. U.S. Dept Justice, Washington, 1956-59; pvt. practice tax law San Francisco, 1959-81. Prof. law Hastings Coll. Law, U. Calif., San Francisco, 1967-95; vis. prof. U. Calif. Boalt Sch. Law, Berkeley, 1988-98, Stanford U. Sch. Law, 1996-98; chmn. Maier & Siebel, Inc., Larkspur, Calif., 1981—; mng. dir. U.S. Trust Co. NA, San Francisco, 1998—; chmn. Fromm Inst. for Lifelong Learning, U. San Francisco, 1997—; pres. John B. Huntington Found., 1996—. Author books on taxation; contbr. articles to profl. jours. Chmn. Property Resources Inc., San Jose, Calif., 1968-77; pres. Calif. Property Devel. Corp., San Francisco, 1974-81. Capt. USAF, 1953-56. Mem. San Francisco Bar Assn. (chmn. sect. taxation 1970-71), Order of Coif. Home: 2559 Clay St San Francisco CA 94115 Office: Maier & Siebel Inc 1 Embarcadero Ctr 20th Fl San Francisco CA 94111 E-mail: pmaier@ustrust.com.

MAIER, ROBERT HENRY, real estate executive; b. Greenville, Tex., Nov. 19, 1932; s. William Lokey and Charlsie Lorraine (Nation) M.; m. Ruth Jean Chapman, Mar. 1, 1968; children: Alice, Joy Kupp. BA, So. Meth. U., 1964. Pers. dir. Atlantic Richfield Co., Dallas, 1954-69; v.p. adminstrn. ETMF Freight System, 1969-78; chief pers. officer Varo, Inc., Garland, Tex., 1978-80; corp. v.p. adminstrn. Comml. Metals Co., Dallas, 1980-88; pres., COO The Staubach Co., 1988-93; pres., CEO, bd. dirs. Cornerstone Mgmt. Co., 1993-96; pres., CEO ProblemSolvers, Inc., 1996—. Mem. Rotary, Masons. Republican.

MAIER, ROMULUS, journalist; b. Bucharest, Romania, May 5, 1961; arrived in U.S., 1998; s. Romulus and Victoria Maier; m. Irena Maier, Jan. 20, 1990. BSc in Engring., Polytech. Inst., Bucharest, Romania, 1987; Grad. degree in Journalism, Superior Sch. Journalism, Bucharest, Romania, 1993; MA in Polit. Sci., U.Conn., Storrs, 2001. Reporter Romanian Reality, Bucharest, Romania, 1991—92, chief editor, 1992—93; econ. chief editor Free Romania, 1993—97, dep. chief editor, 1997, press corr., 1997—; grad. asst. U. Conn. T. Dodd Rsch. Ctr., Storrs, 2000—. Exec. prod. mgr. Rsch. Eqipment Factory, Bucharest, 1990—91; polit. and econ. advisor CDR Campaign 1996, Bucharest, 1995—96; vis. prof. Superior Sch. Journalism, Bucharest, 1994—95. Mem.: Internat. Orgn. Journalists, Acad. Polit. Sci., Am. Polit. Sci. Assn. Eastern Orthodox. Home: 1250 Farmington Ave Apt B8 Hartford CT 06107 Office: Univ Conn 541 Mansfield Rd Storrs Mansfield CT 06269 E-mail: irerom@msn.com.

MAIER, VINCENT BAINES, radiation physicist; b. Glenside, Pa., Dec. 14, 1937; s. Vincent and Edna F. (Firman) M.; m. Barbara Anne Pisano, June 5, 1971. BS in Physics, Drexel U., Phila., 1962; MS in Physics, U. N.H., 1966. Cert. in diagnostic and therapeutic radiol. physics Am. Bd. Radiology. Asst. prof. Coll. Misericordia, Dallas, 1965-76; assoc. radiation physicist Geisinger Med. Ctr., Danville, 1976—. Chmn. ann. blood dr. ARC, St. Columba Ch., Bloomsburg, Pa., 1978-88. Mem. Am. Assn. Physicists in Medicine, Am. Assn. Physics Tchrs., Frosty Valley Country Club. Avocations: woodworking, golf, reading, classical music. Home: 108 Charlene Dr Danville PA 17821-9157 Office: Geisinger Med Ctr 100 N Academy Ave Danville PA 17822-2900 E-mail: vmaier@geisinger.edu.

MAIER, WILLIAM OTTO, martial arts, yoga and pilates instructor, author, seminar leader, consultant; b. Newark, July 15, 1949; s. Emil William Maier and Elizabeth Muriel Flader; children: William Wyatt, Kami Elizabeth. BA, Marietta (Ohio) Coll., 1971; MA, Coll. of Wooster (Ohio), 1973; grad., Citizens Police Acad., 1995. Lic. sr. mastr ninjutsu Interant. Bujinkan Dojo, Noda City, Japan, cert. lic. tactical master instr. CDT Non-Lethal Force Tng. Tchr. Howard County (Md.) Pub. Schs., 1975-78; dean Martial Arts Am., Columbia, Md., 1975—2002. Mem. faculty martial arts Am. Bus. Coll., Irvine, Calif., 1995. Author: Modern Ninjutsu; featured on (TV) on CNN, ABC, NBC and CBS. Named Sch. of Month Black Belt Mag., Sept. 1992, Master Instr. of Yr., Internat. Hall of Fame, 2000; recipient State Md. Govs. citation, 1992, Nat. Sch. of Yr. award U.S. Martial Arts Assn., 1992, 93, Cmty. Svc. award, 1993, Excellence award Martial Arts Bus. Info. Mag., 1996, recognition Md. Senate, 1995, County Exec. Proclamation, 1999. Mem. U.S. Marital Arts Assn. (cons., bd. dirs. 1986-95, named Man of Yr. 1991, recipient award for best student retention 1988-93, Top Sch. award 1994), Martial Arts Am. (cons., bd. dirs. 1995-2001, award Excellence 1997, 99, 2000). Office: Fitness Plus Inc PO Box 2275 Columbia MD 21045-1275 E-mail: willmaier@connext.net.

MAIER, WILLIAM ERNST, JR. railroad executive; b. Neptune, N.J., Aug. 11, 1953; s. William Ernst and Gloria M. BSEE, Lehigh U., 1975; MBA, Ind. U., 1981. Supr. elec. equipment Consolidated Rail Corp., N.Y.C., 1976-77, program coord. Plainfield, Ind., 1977-78, gen. foreman-locomotive, 1978-79, mgr. motive power-western Indpls., 1979-81, asst. shop mgr. Cleve., 1981-82, electronic engr. track geometry car Phila., 1983-86, engr. electronic measuring systems, 1986-99; engr., track analysis and scheduling CSX Transp., Jacksonville, Fla., 1999—. Unit commr. Burlington County Coun., Boy Scouts Am., 1990-99. Mem. IEEE, Locomotive Maintenance Officers Assn., Am. Railway Engring. and Maintenance of Way Assn. Home: 4550 Princess Labeth Ct Jacksonville FL 32258-4199 Office: CSX Transp 4901 Belfort Rd Ste 130 Jacksonville FL 32256-6020 E-mail: william_maier_notes@csx.com.

MAIERHAUSER, JOSEPH GEORGE, entrepreneur; b. Yankton, S.D., Mar. 23, 1927; s. Joseph and Angela M. (Jung) M.; m. Reta Mae Brockelsby, Nov. 25, 1948 (div. 1965); 1 child, Joe; m. Martha Helen Kuehn, Dec. 10, 1965. Student, U. S.D., Vermillion, 1946, S.D. Sch. Mines and Tech., Rapid City, 1947. Sales mgr. Black Hills Reptile Gardens, Rapid City, S.D., 1949-54; operator Colossal Cave Park, Vail, Ariz., 1956—; ptnr. Sta. KRNR, Roseburg, Oreg., 1961—. Mem. adv. bd. Salvation Army, Tucson, 1979-86; govs. appointee San Pedro Rparian Nat. Cons. Area Adv. Com., 1989—; past pres. So. Ariz. Internat. Livestock Assn., 1987-88; bd. dirs. Friends of Western Art., Tucson; co-founder Pima County Parklands Found.. With U.S. Navy Air Corps., 1944-45. Mem. Mountain Oyster Club (pres. 1989-91, bd. dirs. 1980-83). Republican. Avocation: conservation. Home: Bear Paw Vail AZ 85641 Office: Colossal Cave Mountain Park PO Box D70 Vail AZ 85641-0070

MAIERLE, BETTE JEAN, director nursery school; b. Greenville, Mich., Sept. 8, 1933; d. Clinton and Bonnie (Briggs) Peckham; m. Ronald Matthew Maierle, Aug. 27, 1960; children: Steven, Suzanne, Peter, AnneMarie Maierle Krepela, Laura. AD in Secretarial Sci., Davenport Univ., 1952; BA in Speech Pathology, Mich. State U., 1956; MA in Human Devel. and Resources, Wayne State U., 1976. Speech pathologist Ferndale (Mich.) Schs., 1956-60; tchr. of deaf Walled Lake (Mich.) Schs., 1960-61; tchr. spl. edn. Troy (Mich.) Schs., 1961-69; part time theme reader Detroit Pub. Schs., 1964—74; speech pathologist Birmingham (Mich.) Schs., 1967-68; tchr. spl. edn. Avondale Schs., Auburn Hills, Mich., 1968—89; owner, dir. Meadowbrook Nursery Sch., Troy, 1968—; speech pathologist Mich. Sch. for Deaf and Blind, Flint, Mich., 1991-97. Fruit and vegetable insp. USDA, Traverse City, Mich., summers 1990-95. Vol. St. Daniel's Cath. Ch., Clarkston; vol. Rep. Party, Clarkston. Republican. Roman Catholic. Avocations: travel, antiques. Home: 8220 Reese Rd Clarkston MI 48348-2742 Office: Meadowbrook Nursery 6995 Livernois Rd Troy MI 48098-1572 E-mail: betty_ron@hotmail.com.

MAIER-LORENTZ, MADELINE MARIE, nurse educator; b. Boulder City, Nev., Oct. 7, 1952; d. William J. and Madeline A. (Menegus) Maier; m. John F. Lorentz, May 22, 1982; 1 child, William Charles Lorentz. BA in Psychology, U. San Francisco, 1974, BSN, 1979; MSN, U. Phoenix, 1998; postgrad., Grad. Sch. Am., 1998—. RN, Calif.; cert. pub. health nurse, Calif. Nurse Davies Med. Ctr., San Francisco, 1979-81; nurse to pvt. practice plastic reconstructive surgeon, 1979-81; nurse Richland Meml. Hosp., Columbia, S.C., 1981-82; dir. clin. svcs. OccuPoint Med. Corp., 2000—. Vol. election dist. congressman, San Diego, 1993-98. Mem. ANA, ACA, Nat. League Nursing, Am. Acad. Bereavement, Calif. Advocates Nursing Home Reform, Psi Chi, Sigma Theta Tau. Republican. Roman Catholic. Avocations: reading. Home: 11539 Keisha Cv San Diego CA 92126-6604 E-mail: mlorentzrn@aol.com., cupoint@earthlink.net.

MAIESE, KENNETH, neurologist; b. Audubon, N.J., Dec. 5, 1958; s. Charles and Margaret (Fioretti) M. BA summa cum laude, U. Pa., 1981; MD, Cornell U., 1985. Intern N.Y. Hosp., 1985-86, resident in neurology, 1986-89, asst. attending physician, 1989-94; asst. prof. Cornell U. Med. Coll., N.Y.C., 1989-94; assoc. prof. dept. neurology, anatomy and cell biology Wayne State U. Ctr. for Molecular Toxicology & Medicine, Detroit, 1994—; dir. lab. molecular and cellular cerebral ischemia Wayne State U. Ctr. for Molecular Toxicology, 1994—, prof. dept. neurology, anatomy, cell biology, 1999—. Dir. neurol. diagnosis N.Y. Hosp., 1991-94. Author: Neurology and General Medicine, 1989, Neurological and Neurosurgical ICU Medicine, 1988; contbr. articles to Neurology, Jour. Cerebral Blood Flow and Metabolism, Jour. Intensive Care Medicine, Jour. Neurosci., Jour. Neurosci. Rsch., Neurosci. Lett., Jour. Brain Rsch., Jour. Neurochem. Circulation. Joseph Collins scholar, 1981-85, Grupe Found. scholar, 1985; grantee NIH, 1990—, Nat. Stroke Assn., 1992-94, Alzheimer's Assn., 1994—, Am. Heart Assn., 1995—, United Cerebral Palsy Found., 1995—, Janssen Found., 1995—; recipient Young Scientist award Jours. Cerebral Blood Flow, 1991, Hoechst Investigator award, 1993, Robert G. Siekert award in stroke, 1994, Johnson and Johnson Disting. Investigator award, 1996-98, Maiese Lab. Neurosci. Tng. award J & J/Janssen, 1998, Boehringer Investigator award, 1999, NIH/NIEHS award. Mem. Am. Acad. Neurology, N.Y. Acad. Scis., Assn. for Rsch. in Nervous and Mental Diseases, Am. Neurol. Assn. (elected), Soc. Neurosci. Roman Catholic. Achievements include rsch. in imidazole receptors, cerebral ischemia, nitric oxide toxicity, growth factor neuroprotection, signal cellular transduction mechanisms, metabotropic glutamate receptors, gene regulation, and gene therapy. Office: Wayne State U Sch Medicine 8C-1 U Health Ctr Dept Neur 4201 Saint Antoine St Detroit MI 48201-2153

MAIESE, MARIO LOUIS, cardiologist, educator; b. Camden, N.J., May 17, 1943; s. Oreste Maiese and Catherine Rosello; m. Audrey Anne Bonomo, June 15, 1968; children: John, Diane, Michelle, Anthony. DO, Coll. Osteopathic Med. & Surg., Des Moines, 1969; BS, St. Joseph's U., 1965. Cert. internal medicine, cardiology. Physician, Sewell, NJ, 1973-96; clin. assoc. prof. N.J. Sch. Osteo. Medicine & Dentistry, 1980—; physician, med. dir. S. Jersey Heart Group, Sewell, 1996—; pres. Group III S. Jersey Heart, 1997-98. Dir. critical care Washington Twp. divsn. Kennedy Health Sys., Turnersville, N.J., 1976-95, subsection chief cardiology, 1983—, med. dir., 1985-95. Editor, contbr. Heartbeat, 1995—. Fellow Am. Coll. Cardiology; mem. Am. Heart Assn., Am. Coll. Ostepathic Internists. Avocations: cooking, tennis, bicycling. Office: S Jersey Heart Group 539 Egg Harbor Rd Ste 1 Sewell NJ 08080-2371 E-mail: maiese@dnamail.com.

MAIL, PATRICIA DAVISON, public health specialist; b. Kamloops, B.C., Can., Dec. 10, 1940; d. George Allen and Constance (Davison) M. BS, U. Ariz., 1963, MA, 1970; MS, Smith Coll., 1965; MPH, Yale U., 1967; postgrad., Seattle U., 1974; PhD, U. Md., 1996. Cert. health edn. specialist. Commd. officer USPHS, 1970-97; chief health edn. br. Portland Indian Health Svc., 1979-86; dep. chief field ops. Nat. Health Svc. Corps., 1986-87, dep. chief clin., prof. activities bd., 1987-88, br. chief Health Resources and Svcs. Adminstrn., 1988; dep. staff dir. Office Pub. Health Svc. Surgeon Gen., 1989; officer pers. specialist, chief profl. edn. Alcohol, Drug Abuse and Mental Health Adminstrn., 1990-92; chief evaluation sect., divsn. clin. and prevention rsch. Nat. Inst. Alcohol Abuse and Alcoholism, 1991—93, extramural sci. adminstr., 1993-97; faculty Medicine Creek Tribal Coll., 1998—99. Mem. faculty Seattle U., 1974-78; commr. Nat. Commn. Health Edn. Credentialing, chair, 1993-94; accreditation site visitor Coun. on Edn. in Pub. Health, 1996—; vis. scientist Addictive Behaviors Rsch. Ctr., U. Wash., 1998-99, rsch. scientist, 1999—; pres. Dragon-Archer Cons., 1997—; asst. prof. Oreg. Health Scis. U., 1998-99. Author: (with D.R. McDonald) Tulapai to Tokay, 1980; editor Soc. for Pub. Health Edn. Sounds, 1976-86; assoc. editor Health Promotion Practice; contbr. articles to profl. jours. USPHS traineeship, 1965-67; grantee NDEA, 1968-70. Fellow Am. Sch. Health Assn., Soc. Applied Anthropology; mem. AAAS (life), APHA (chair pub. health edn. sect. 1995-96, chmn. continuing profl. edn. com. 1997, 98, exec. bd. 2001—, Early Career award Pub. Health Edn. sect. 1979, Judith Miller award 1998, Exec. Dir.'s citation 1999), Commd. Officers Assn. USPHS (life), Am. Assn. Health Edn. (life), Am. Acad. Health Behavior (bd. dirs.), Soc. Pub. Health Edn., Med. Anthropology Soc., Assn. Mil. Surgeons U.S. (life), Res. Officers Assn. (life), Smith Coll. Alumnae Assn., Delta Psi Kappa, Eta Sigma Gamma. Episcopalian. Home: 35214 28th Ave S Federal Way WA 98003-7120 E-mail: pmail@sprynet.com.

MAILACHALAM, BABU, research scientist; b. Nellikuppam, Tamlnadu, India, July 27, 1966; s. Rangasamy and Chandra)3 Mailachalam; m. Priya Natarajan, Dec. 6, 1998. BE, Annamalai U., Chidambaram, India, 1987; ME, Birla Inst. Tech. & Sci., Pilani, India, 1989; PhD, Indian Inst. Tech., Madras, 1997. Customer engr. HCL Ltd., New Delhi, 1987-88; project assoc. Indian Inst. Tech., Madras, 1989-90, 95-97; cons. Sigma Tech Electronics, India, 1994-95; sr. systems analyst Ramco Systems, India, 1997-99; rsch. fellow Ctr. High Performance Embdded Systems, Nanyang Tech. U., Singapore, 1999—2000; prin. engr. Integrated Intellectual Property, Inc., Santa Clara, Calif., 2000—01; staff engr. Lattice Semicondr. Corp., San Jose, 2001—. Cons. Micro Time Systems, Madras, 1990-94. Contbr. articles to profl. jours. Sec. Brahmaputra Hostel Coun., Indian Inst. Tech., Madras, 1992-93, mem. bd. adad. rsch., 1993-94. Mem. IEEE. Avocations: reading, amateur radio. Home: 1235 Wildwood Ave # 127 Sunnyvale CA 94089 Office: 2680 Zanker Rd San Jose CA 95134 E-mail: babumchalam@yahoo.com.

MAILANDER, WILLIAM STEPHEN, lawyer; b. Dover, N.J., July 25, 1958; s. William Stephen and Doris Elizabeth (Post) M.; m. Judith Gay Burrows, May 20, 1989 (div. 1993); m. Rosalind Eager, Dec. 15, 1999. BA, NYU, 1984; JD, Temple U., 1988; MBA, Johns Hopkins U., 2001. Bar: Pa. 1988, N.J. 1991, D.C. 1996; U.S. Ct. Vets. Appeals 1991, U.S. Ct. Appeals (fed. cir.) 1993, U.S. Supreme Ct. 1994. Staff atty. Bd. Vets. Appeals, Washington, 1988-90, Coast Guard Chief Counsel, Washington, 1990-91, VA Gen. Counsel, Washington, 1991-93; asst. gen. counsel Paralyzed Vets. Am., 1993—2001; dep. gen. counsel Paralyzed Vets. of Am., 2001—. Faculty continuing legal edn. seminars, 1993—. Contbr. articles to profl. jours. With USMC, 1976-79. Decorated Navy Achievement medal. Mem. FBA (chair membership vets. law sect. 1993-94, editor newsletter 1996—). Avocations: reading, running. Office: Paralyzed Vets Am 801 18th St NW Washington DC 20006-3517

MAILER-HOWAT, PATRICK LINDSAY MACALPINE, investment banker; b. Edinburgh, Scotland, Feb. 4, 1955; came to U.S., 1985, naturalized 1993. s. George Maxton Macalpine and Margaret Lorrain (Guild) M.; m. Rebecca Lynn Clifford, Mar. 30, 1985; children: Brodie Clifford, Lindsay Angevine. Grad. in Sovereign's Platoon, Royal Mil. Acad. Sandhurst, 1974. Lt. Scots Guards; futures trader J.H. Rayners Ltd., London, 1977-80; ptnr. investment mgr. Mailer Walker Internat. Ltd., 1980-85; mgr. trade fin. svcs. Equator Bank Ltd., Hartford, Conn., 1985-88; v.p. Brazil sales First Nat. Bank Boston, N.Y.C., N.Y., 1989-93, dir. internat. banking, 1993-95; sr. v.p. equity sales ING Baring Securities, N.Y.C., N.Y., 1995-96; dir. internat. equity sales Instinet Corp., 1996-99; v.p. for S.Am., Internat. Planning Group Ltd., Boston, 1999—. Lt. Brit. Army, 1974-77. Mem. Inst. CFPs (cert.), Longwood Cricket Club (Boston), Union Club (N.Y.), Union Boat Club (Boston), Duxbury Yacht Club (Mass.), Somerset Club (Boston). Home: 41 Edgehill Rd Brookline MA 02445-7702 Office: Internat Planning Group Ltd 62 Walnut St Wellesley MA 02481-2113 E-mail: pmhowat@ipgltd.com.

MAILLET, MARTIN JOSEPH, SR. retired police captain; b. Lynn, Mass., Jan. 2, 1933; s. Joseph Maximum and Mary Agnes (Deveau) M.; m. Elizabeth Ann Kasprzyk, June 16, 1957; children: Martin Joseph Jr., Lawrence James, Jayne Marie. Student, Bloomberg's Sch. Law, Boston, 1958-63, Boston U., 1970, North Shore Community Coll., 1974-76; grad., Linotype Sch., Boston, 1954. Cert. secondary tchr., Mass. Linotype operator Willimantic (Conn.) Chronicle, 1954-55; police officer Saugus (Mass.) Police Dept., 1957-64, police sergeant, 1964-73, police capt., exec. officer to chief, 1973-95; ret., 1995. Dep. sheriff Essex County Sheriffs, 1987—, Mass Police Assn., 1957—. Cpl. U.S. Army, 1950-52, Korea. Democrat. Roman Catholic. Avocations: health club fitness, jogging, swimming, travel. Home: PO Box 1471 Saugus MA 01906-0771

MAILLOUX, ROBERT JOSEPH, physicist; b. Lynn, Mass., June 20, 1938; s. Joseph H. and Nora S. M.; m. Marlene Schirf, Jan. 14, 1967; children: Patrice, Julie, Denise. BS, Northeastern U., 1961; SM, Harvard U., 1962, PhD, 1965. Physicist NASA Electronics Rsch. Ctr., Cambridge, Mass., 1965-70, Air Force Cambridge Rsch. Labs., Bedford, 1970-77, Rome Air Devel. Ctr., Bedford, 1977-80, chief antennas and components div., electromagnetic directorate, 1980-91; sr. scientist Air Force Rsch. Lab., 1992—. Lectr. Tufts U., Boston, 1985—. Author: Phased Array Antenna Handbook; guest editor IEEE/AP-S Transactions Spl. Issue on Phased Array Antennas, 1999; contbr. chpts. to 8 textbooks, articles to sci. jours. Served with C.E. U.S. Army, 1966-68. Recipient Air Force Marcus O'Day paper award, 1971, Engineer of Yr. award RADC, 1988; RADC fellow, 1988. Fellow IEEE (chmn. tech. com. 1997 phased array symposium, spl. achievement award 1969, 76, nat. lectr., assoc. editor Transactions on Antennas and Propagation 1984-92, Harry Diamond award 1991, Fred Diamond award 1997, IEEE Third Millenium medal, 2000); mem. Antenna and Propagation Soc. (chmn. Boston chpt. 1968, nat. meetings chmn. 1977-80, adcom mem. 1977-80, v.p. 1982, pres. 1983), Internat. Sci. Radio Union (Commn. B. tech. activities chmn. 1980—), Sigma Xi (pres. Hanscom chpt. 1980-81), Eta Kappa Nu, Tau Beta Pi. Achievements include 11 patents in field. Office: AFRL/SNH 31 Grenier St Hanscom AFB MA 01731-3008

MAIMAN, DENNIS JAY, neurosurgeon; b. Milw., July 26, 1953; s. Irwin and Belle Maiman; m. Donnalyn Ziger, Apr. 4, 1976; children: Nechama, Shoshana, Yehudit, Moshe. BS, U. Wis., Milw., 1973; MD, Med. Coll. Wis., Milw., 1977; PhD, Marquette U., 1986. Cert. Am. Bd. Neurol. Surgery. Resident in neurosurgery Med. Coll. Wis., Milw., 1977-82, asst. prof. neurosurgery, 1982-86, assoc. prof., 1986-92; prof., 1992—; chief spinal cord injury programs VA Med. Ctr., Milw., 1984-96; dir. Spinal Cord Injury Ctr., Milw. Regional Med. Ctr., 1984—. Fellow ACS; mem. Am. Assn. Neurosurgeons, Am. Parapalegia Soc. (bd. dirs.), Soc. Neurosci., Cervical Spine Research Soc. Jewish. Office: Med Coll Wis Dept Neurosurgery 9200 W Wisconsin Ave Milwaukee WI 53226-3522

MAIMAN, GEORGE, accountant, finance consultant; b. Hungary, Aug. 30, 1939; s. Al and Anna (Stern) M.; B.A., Concordia U., 1965, Bernard Baruch Coll., City U. N.Y., 1975; m. Edith Schwartz, Nov. 13, 1966; children—Ronald E., Andrew D. Controller, Unimet Corp., N.Y.C., 1973-75, Pickwick Internat. Inc., Woodbury, N.Y., 1975-77; prin. Maiman & Co., C.P.A.'s, N.Y.C., 1977— ; cons. C.P.A., N.Y. State. Mem. Am. Inst. C.P.A.'s. Office: 250 W 57th St New York NY 10107

MAIMON, ELAINE PLASKOW, English educator, university provost, campus chief executive officer; b. Phila., July 28, 1944; d. Louis J. and Gertrude (Canter) Plaskow; m. Morton A. Maimon, Sept. 30, 1967; children: Gillian Blanche, Alan Marcus. AB, U. Pa., 1966, MA, 1967, PhD, 1970. Asst. prof. Haverford (Pa.) Coll., 1971-73; lectr. Arcadia U., Glenside, Pa., 1973-75, asst. prof., dir. writing, 1975-77, assoc. prof., 1977-83, assoc. dean, 1980-84, assoc. v.p., prof. English, 1984-86; adj. assoc. prof. U. Pa., Phila., 1982-83; assoc. dean of coll. Brown U., Providence, 1986-88; dean, prof. English Queens Coll. CUNY, Flushing, N.Y., 1988-96; campus CEO, provost Ariz. State U. West, Phoenix, 1996—; v.p. Ariz. State U., 1996—. Nat. bd. cons. NEH, 1977-81; mem. adv. bd. Cox Comms., 1997-2001—; bd. dirs. Arrowhed Cmty. Bank. Co-author: Writing in the Arts and Sciences, 1981, A Writer's Resource, 2002; co-editor: Readings in the Arts and Sciences, 1984, Thinking, Reasoning and Writing, 1989. Trustee Heard Mus., Phoenix, 1999—. Recipient Golden Heart award, Today's Ariz. Woman, 2000, Women of Distinction award, YMCA, Maricopa County, 2001, YWCA award in Edn., 2002; grantee Elaine Maimon award for Excellence in Writing named in her honor, Arcadia U., 1994. Mem.: MLA (exec. com.), Am. Assn. Colls. and Univs. (exec. bd. 2002—), Assn. Am. Colls., Conf. on Coll. Composition Comm. (exec. com. 1985—87), ACE Nat. Commn. Women, Nat. Coun. Tchrs. English (nominating com. 1986—87, teaching of writing divsn. 1991), Phi Beta Kappa. Home: 20726 N 55th Ave Glendale AZ 85308-9342 Office: Ariz State U W PO Box 37100 4701 E Thunderbird Rd Phoenix AZ 85069-7100 E-mail: elaine.maimon@asu.edu.

MAIN, EDNA DEWEY (JUNE MAIN), education educator; b. Hyannis, Mass., Sept. 1, 1940; d. Seth Bradford and Edna Wilhelmina (Wright) Dewey; m. Donald John Main, Sept. 9, 1961 (div. Dec. 1989); children: Alison Teresa Main Ronzon, Susan Christine Main Leddy, Steven Donald Main. Degree in merchandising, Tobe-Coburn Sch., 1960; BA in Edn., U. North Fla., 1974, MA in Edn., 1979, M in Adminstrn. and Supervision, 1983; PhD in Curriculum and Instrn., U. Fla., 1990. Asst. buyer Abraham & Straus, Bklyn., 1960-61; asst. mdse. mgr. Interstate Dept. Stores, N.Y.C., 1962-63; tchr. Holiday Hill Elem. Sch., Jacksonville, Fla., 1974-86; instr. summer sci. inst., 1984-92; prof. edn. Jacksonville U., 1992—. Also coord. masters program in integrated learning and ednl. tech.; instr. U. Fla., 1987-90, U. North Fla., 1990-92; cons. Assn. Internat. Schs. in Africa, 1994-97. Co-author: Developing Critical Thinking Through Science, 2001. Rep. United Way, 1981-86; tchr. rep., chpt. leader White House Young Astronaut Program, 1984-85; team leader NSF Shells Elem. Sci. Project. Recipient Innovative Excellence in Tchg., Learning and Tech. award Internat. Coll. Conf., 1999, Outstanding Alumni award U. North Fla., 1999, Eve award for Edn., 2001; named Carnegie Found. Fla. Prof. of Yr., 2002, Jacksonville U. Prof. of Yr., 2002. Mem. ASCD, ISTE, Nat. Sci. Tchrs. Assn. (sci. tchrs. achievement recognition award 1983), Phi Kappa Phi, Phi Delta Kappa, Delta Kappa Gamma, Kappa Delta Pi. Republican. Episcopalian. Office: Jacksonville U 2800 University Blvd N Jacksonville FL 32211-3394 E-mail: jmain@ju.edu.

MAIN, LAURIE (LAURENCE GEORGE MAIN), actor; b. Melbourne, Victoria, Australia, Nov. 29, 1922; came to U.S., 1960; Tchr. Agnes Moorehead Sch., L.A., 1968-72. Appeared in English repertory and Diary of a Nobody, My Wife's Lodger, Waltz of the Torreadors, On The West End Stage; broadway plays First Impressions, Jolly's Progress, Camelot, Lord Pengo, 13 Rue de Lamour for 15 yrs.; host, narrator Welcome to Pooh's Corner (Disney Channel); also appeared in numerous TV plays and series and over 25 films. Recipient 3 gold records for narration, Disney Records. Avocations: swimming, traveling, walking. Home: 532 N La Jolla Ave Los Angeles CA 90048-2235

MAIN, MICHAEL DEE, information developer; b. Anderson, Ind., Oct. 12, 1956; s. John Dyson and Marilyn Anne (Miller) M.; m. Deborah Lee Holland, Oct. 19, 1996. BA in English, Ind. U., 1979, MLS, 1981. System svcs. libr. Ind. U. Librs., Bloomington, 1981-85, acquisitions libr., 1985-96, info. technologist, 1996-98; br. libr. mgr. Ind. U. Journalism Libr., 1985; info. developer CDI Info. Svcs./IBM, Beaverton, Oreg., 1998—, Waite Group, Inc., 2002—. Entrepreneurial cons. Star Thrower Pub., 1996—. Author: (electronic novel) Apollo: An American Life, 1997. Writer's fellow Nat. Endowment for Arts and Ind. Arts Commn., 1992-93. Mem. Soc. Tech. Comm., Ind. Arts Commn. (contbg. artist, advisor 1993—), Sierra Club, Audubon Soc., Japanese Garden Soc. Oreg., Nature Conservancy, Amnesty Internat. Buddhist (ordained Karma Kagyu Lineage Holder 2000). Avocations: collecting music, music criticism, Web consulting and design, health and wellness technologies and distribution networks. Home: 19483 SW Jaylee St Aloha OR 97007 Office: IBM Beaverton MS RHE2-501 15450 SW Koll Pkwy Beaverton OR 97006 E-mail: michael.main@star-thrower.com.

MAIN, MYRNA JOAN, retired mathematics educator; b. Kirksville, Mo., Oct. 31, 1947; d. Stanford H. and Jennie Vee (Nuhn) Morris; m. Carl Donet Main, Feb. 22, 1968; children: D. Christopher, Laura S. BSE, Northeast Mo. State U., 1968, MA, 1970. Instr. math. Callao (Mo.) Sch., 1968-73; tchr., chair dept. math. Macon (Mo.) R-I Schs., 1973—; regional dir. math. Mo. Middle Sch.; math. leadership coord. U. Mo., Columbia, Mo. math. leadership project coord., 1999—. Ext. staff Moberly (Mo.) Area C.C., 1983—, Cen. Meth. Coll., 1994; adj. faculty N.E. Mo. State U., Kirksville, 1987-93; mentor Mo. Math. Mentoring Project, Moberly, 1989-96; trainer Mo. Show-Me Stds. and Frame Works, 1997; Mo. Math. Leadership Project dir. U. Mo., Columbia; mgr. Midwest Bone & Joint Ctr. PC, Macon, Mo. Organist, UBS tchr. Crossroads Christian Ch., Macon, 1981—; mem. Macon County Watershed Adv. Bd., Long Br. Recipient Presdl. award for excellence in math., 1989; named Outstanding Secondary Tchr., Sigma Xi Truman State Univ. Chpt., 1999; semi-finalist The Disney Co. Presents the Am. Tchr., 1991. Mem. AAUW (chpt. pres. 1980-81), Nat. Coun. Tchrs. Math., Mo. Coun. Tchrs. Math. (treas. 1978-79, v.p. 1976), Mo. Alliance for Sci., Math. and Tech. Edn. (bd. dirs. 1988-92, mem. Mo. Framework writing team), Macon R-I Christian Club (co-sponsor). Democrat. E-mail: mainfarms@yahoo.com.

MAIN, PATRICIA ENGLANDER, investor; b. London, Apr. 8, 1931; d. Harry Norman and Eve (Roth) Englander; m. Frank Graham Main, Apr. 30, 1966 (div. Apr. 1981); m. Franklin Walter Mohney, Aug. 10, 1981 (dec. May 2, 1991); children: Lisa Nicole Kelly, Susan Jennifer Kerschner, Jacqueline Eve Singer. Student, Mt. Holyoke Coll., 1948-50. Dir. pub. rels. Contemporary Arts Mus., Houston, 1962-64; relocation sales assoc. Paul Reinke Corp., Cherry Hill, N.J., 1964-69; account exec. Relocation Realty Svc. Corp., N.Y.C., 1972-76, v.p. ops., 1976-79; owner Patricia Mohney Gallery, Reading, Pa., 1981-84; v.p. Venture Components Corp., N.Y.C., 1984-92; pvt. investor, 1992—. Trustee, bd. mem. Reading Art Mus., 1980-83; mem. bus. and profl. com. N.Y.C. Ballet, 1985-95; mem. com. denominational affairs All Souls Ch., N.Y.C., 1998—. Mem. Mt. Holyoke Coll. Alumnae Club (bd. dirs. 1969-77, pres. 1977-79). Office: 65 E 76th St Ste 3B New York NY 10021-1844

MAIN, PHILIP DAVID, lawyer, probate judge; b. New Britain, Conn., Apr. 10, 1936; s. George Lawrence Main and Nancy Elia; m. Patricia Ann Baker, Sept. 10, 1960; children: Linda S. Erwin, William G. BA in History, Bates Coll., 1958; LLB, George Washington U., 1961. Bar: Conn. 1962. Staff atty. CIGNA, Bloomfield, Conn., 1961-63; ptnr. Pease & Main, Simsbury, 1963—. Judge Granby (Conn.) Probate Ct., 1990—. Town com. chmn., Granby. Mem. Granby Lions Club (pres. 1966-68). Office: Pease & Main PO Box 544 Simsbury CT 06070-0544 E-mail: peasemain@netzero.net.

MAIN, ROBERT GAIL, communications educator, training consultant, television and film producer, former army officer; b. Bucklin, Mo., Sept. 30, 1932; s. Raymond M. and Inez L. (Olinger) M.; m. Anita Sue Thoroughman, Jan. 31, 1955; children: Robert Bruce, David Keith, Leslie Lorraine. BS magna cum laude, U. Mo., 1954; grad. with honors, Army Commd. Gen. Staff Coll., 1967; MA magna cum laude in Comm., Stanford U., 1968; PhD, U. Md., 1978. Commd. 2d lt. U.S. Army, 1954, advanced through grades to lt. col., 1968; mem. faculty Army Commd. Gen. Staff Coll., 1968-70; chief speechwriting and info. materials divsn. U.S. Army Info. Office, 1971, chief broadcast and film divsn., 1972-73; dir. def. audiovisual activities Office of Info. for Armed Forces, 1973-76; ret., 1976; prof. instrnl. tech. Calif. State U., Chico, 1976—, dept. chair, 1993-98. Cons. in field. Author: Rogues, Saints and Ordinary People, 1988; prodr. (TV documentary) Walking Wounded, 1983, Army Info. Films, Army Radio Series, 1972-73; contbr. articles on computer based tng. and telecoms. to scientific and profl. jours. Decorated Legion of Merit, Meritorious Svc. medal, Commendation medal with oak leaf cluster, combat Inf. Badge; Vietnamese Cross of Gallantry; recipient Freedom Found. awards, 1972, 73, 74; Bronze medal Atlanta Film Festival, 1972; Best of Show award Balt. Film Festival, 1973; Creativity award Chgo. Indsl. Film Festival, 1973; Cine gold award Internat. Film Prodrs. Assn., 1974; named an Outstanding Prof. Calif. State U., 1987-88. Mem. Phi Eta Sigma, Alpha Zeta, Phi Delta Gamma, Omicron Delta Kappa, Alpha Gamma Rho.

MAINELLA, FRANCES P. federal agency administrator; b. Groton, Conn. Student, U. Conn.; M in Counseling, Ctrl. Conn. State Coll. H.S. phys. edn. tchr.; staff Southington Conn. Park and Recreation Dept.; exec. dir. Fla. Recreation and Park Assn.; dir. Fla. State Parks; dir. Nat. Park Svc., U.S. Dept. Interior, Washington, 2001—. Office: US Dept Interior Nat Park Svc 1849 C St NW Washington DC 20240*

MAINES, LEAH, writer, poet; b. Cin., Feb. 15, 1962; d. William Murrell and Mary Elizabeth (Jackson) Dungan; m. Kevin Murphy Maines, Apr. 9, 1990; children: Christen Jo, Elizabeth Ann Cordell. Student, King's Coll., London, 1993, Marino Inst., Dublin, Ireland, 1994, Gifu (Japan) U., 1994-95; BA, No. Ky. U., 1996; MDiv, Cin. Bible Sem., 2000—. Office asst. Finishing Touches Secretarial Sch., Cin., 1979—, asst. dir., 1996—. Poet-in-residence No. Ky. U. Author: Looking to the East with Western Eyes, 1998; contbr. articles to profl. publs. Radio reader for the blind Radio Reading Svcs., Cin., 1997. M.F. Zalla Found. grantee No. Ky. U., London, 1993, Mazak scholar No. Ky. U., Gifu, 1994-95, U. Honors scholar No. Ky. U., Highland Heights, 1996. Mem. Ky. Writers Coalition, Ky. Poetry Soc., Verse Writers' Guild Ohio, Ky. Col. (col. 1992—), No. Ky. U. Alumni Assn. (bd. mem. 1997—), Cin. Writers Project, Sigma Tau Delta (chpt. pres. 1995-96), Alpha Chi, Omicron Delta Kappa, Golden Key. Democrat. Avocation: international travel. Home: 130 The Masters Highland Heights KY 40324 E-mail: leahmaines@aol.com.

MAINOR, ROBERT PEREZ, computer software and management executive, marketing consultant; b. Washington, Apr. 5, 1953; s. Jesse Brownard and Andreita Ramos (Perez) M. BA, Auburn U., 1975, MS, 1977; postgrad., U. Calif., Berkeley, 1978-79. Cert. systems profl. Systems engr. Electronic Data Systems, Dallas, 1977-79; systems analyst Compuware Corp., Southfield, Mich., 1979-81, dist. sales mgr. Washington, 1981-83; pres., CEO SEARA Info. Strategy Corp., McLean, Va., 1983—91; v.p., gen. mgr. CompuServe Systems Integration Group, Columbus, Ohio, 1991-96; v.p. Bell Atlantic Internet Solutions, Inc., Reston, Va., 1996-99; pres., mng. dir. COLT Internet, plc, London, 1999—2002; pres., CEO Xpedite, Inc., Tinton Falls, NJ, 2002—. Cons. Triangle Software, San Jose, Calif., 1982-84, Empact Software, Stone Mountain, Ga., 1984, Data Kinetics, Ottawa, Ont., Can., 1986-89; instr. George Washington U., 1986-91. Contbr. articles to profl. jours. Assoc. mem. Arlington Hosp. Found., 1985. Mem. ABA (chmn. computers and mktg. com. econs. law practice sect. 1987-89), Data Processing Mgmt. Assn., Assn. Systems Mgmt., Washington Systems Users Group (chmn.), Burke Jaycees., Sporting Club. Roman Catholic. Avocations: racquetball, travel, golf, real estate investing, scuba, writing articles and fiction.

MAINOUS, ARCH G., III, medical educator; b. Lexington, Ky., Oct. 31, 1960; s. Arch G. Jr. and Rosalie R. Mainous; m. Amy V. Blue, May 29, 1993; 1 child, Ryan. BA in Psychology cum laude, U. Ky., 1982; MA in Sociology, U. Tex., 1985, PhD in Sociology, 1988. Cons. CME Rsch., Inc., Lexington, 1984-90; asst. prof. family medicine U. Ky., 1990-96, asst. prof. internal medicine and family medicine, 1993-96, assoc. prof. family medicine, psychiatry, internal medicine, 1996-98; assoc. prof. family medicine, biometry and epidemiology Med. U. S.C., Charleston, 1998-2001, prof. family medicine, biometry and epidemiology, 2001—. Mem. rev. panel Small Bus. Innovation, NIH, Washington, 1999—, Rural Health Outreach, HRSA, Washington, 1995-97; chair grant review panel Nat. Inst. Child Health and Human Devel., 2000-01; vis. prof. U. Leicester, U.K., 1999, U. Auckland, New Zealand, 2001. Meml. editl. bd. Archives of Family Medicine, AMA, 1995-2000, Family Medicine, 2001—; contbr. over 115 articles to profl. jours. Mem. Soc. Tchrs. Family Medicine (rsch. com. 1997-2001), Sigma Xi, Psi Chi. Avocations: art, movies, basketball. Office: Med U SC Dept Family Medicine PO Box 250192 295 Calhoun St Charleston SC 29425

MAINPRIZE, DONALD CHARLES, minister, writer; b. Coleman, Mich., Aug. 28, 1930; s. James Raymond and Ople Belle Mainprize; m. Doris Olive Humphrey, July 27, 1952; children: Daniel Andrew, Debra Ann, Susan Lynn, Edward Raymond. Pastor's diploma, Grand Rapids Sch. Bible & Music, 1953; student, Dallas Theol. Sem., 1957; BA in Profl. Writing, U. Okla., Norman, 1960; MA in English and Am. Lit., Ctrl. Mich. U., 1967. Pastor Dildine Comty. Ch., Ionia, Mich., 1953—56; pastor First Presbyn. Ch. , Minco, Okla., 1958—60; mng. editor Scripture Press, Wheaton, Ill., 1960—64; freelance writer Houghton Lake, Mich., 1965; 5th grade tchr. Houghton Lake Elem. Sch., 1965—66; grad. asst. Ctrl. Mich. U., Mt. Pleasant, 1966—67, instr. journalism, advt., composition, 1967—68; English tchr. Houghton Lake Schs., 1965—94. Writing cons. Writing Doctor, Roscommon, Mich., 1994—2002; supply pastor various denominations, Mich., 1965—2001. Author: Enjoy The Christian Life, 1966, 2d edit., 1971, Meditations for Teachers, 1974 (1st prize humorous poetry, Poetry Soc. Mich.), (poetry) ABC's for Tchrs. Mem. Kiwanis, Minco, Okla., 1958—60. Republican. Episcopalian. Achievements include first to introduce rollercoaster poems in Language Arts and the English Jour. Avocations: travel, writing, walking, reading. Home: 519 W Higgins Lake Dr Roscommon MI 48653

MAINS, RONDA M. music educator, musician; b. American Fork, Utah, Oct. 11, 1955; d. Donn Rollo and June Moubray Miller; m. Robert Edward Mains, Apr. 28, 1989. MusB, Boise State U., 1978, MA, 1980; D in Musical Arts, U. Oreg., 1993. Elem. music specialist Kuna (Idaho) Pub. Schs., 1980-81, Salem (Oreg.) Pub. Schs., 1981-86; from asst. prof. music to prof. U. Ark., Fayetteville, Ark., 1987—2002, prof. music, 2002—. Vis. fellow Lucy Cavendish Coll., Cambridge (Eng.) U., 1997-98; prin. flutist North Ark. Symphony, Fayetteville, 1987—, Music Festival Ark., Fayetteville, 1990-97; flutist Lyrique Quintet, Fayetteville, 1990—, Novaria, Fayetteville, 1990—; adv. bd. mem. Walton Arts Ctr., Fayetteville, 1999—. Performer (CD) Novaria, 1996. Fulbright Faculty Cambridge fellow Fulbright Coll., U. Ark., 1997. Mem. ASCD, Nat. Flute Assn., Brit. Flute Soc., Music Tchrs. Nat. Assn., Music Educators Nat. Conf. (collegiate advisor), Coll. Music Soc. Avocations: sailing, raising tropical fish and Old English Sheepdogs, gardening. Office: Dept Music Univ Ark Fayetteville AR 72701

MAINWARING, SCOTT PATTERSON, political scientist, educator; b. July 18, 1954; s. William Thomas and Camille Brent Mainwaring; m. Susan M. Elfin, Aug. 9, 1986; children: Benjamin E., Grace E. BA in Polit. Sci., MA in Polit. Sci. magna cum laude, Yale U., 1976; PhD in Polit. Sci., Stanford U., 1983. Asst. prof. govt. U. Notre Dame, Ind., 1983—88, assoc. prof. govt., 1988—93, prof. govt., 1993—96, chair dept. govt., 1996—97, Eugene Conley prof. govt., 1996—; dir. Kellogg Inst. Internat. Studies, 1997—. Mem. Coun. on Fgn. Rels., 1986-91; mem. rsch. coun. Internat. Fourm for Dem. Studies, Nat. Endowment for Democracy, Washington, 1994—; cons. The Ford Found., N.Y., Inter-Am. Dialogue, Washington, MacArthur Found., Chgo., Woodrow Wilson Ctr. for Scholars, Washington. Author: The Catholic Church and Politics in Brazil, 1916-1985, 1986, Rethinking Party Systems in the Third Wave of Democratization: The Case of Brazil, 1999; co-editor: Building Democratic Institutions: Party Systems in Latin America, 1995, Presidentialism and Democracy in Latin America, 1997. Recipient Hubert Herring prize Pacific Coast Coun. on Lat. Am. Studies, 1983-84; fellow Woodrow Wilson Ctr., 1995-96, Guggenheim, 2000. Mem. Am. Polit. Sci. Assn., Latin Am. Studies Assn. (treas. 1997-2000), Phi Beta Kappa. Office: Kellogg Inst 205 Hesburgh Ctr Notre Dame IN 46556-5677 E-mail: Mainwaring.1@nd.edu.

MAINWARING, THOMAS LLOYD, motor freight company executive; b. Cleve., Aug. 25, 1928; s. Hugh Trevor and Mary Beatrice (Ottman) M.; m. Gladys Fraser Mehr, June 10, 1983; children by previous marriage— Kevin, James, Eileen, Scott, Bruce BA, Albion Coll., 1950; MBA, Western Res. U., 1958. C.P.A., Ohio. Controller Cleve. Cartage Co., 1959-61, v.p., treas., 1961-64; controller Associated Truck Lines, Inc., Vandenberg Ctr., Grand Rapids, Mich., 1964-69; v.p. fin. Associated Transport, Inc., N.Y.C., 1969-70, exec. v.p. fin. and adminstrn., 1970-72; pres. Ryder Truck Lines Inc., Jacksonville, Fla., 1972-78, exec. v.p., chief operating officer, 1978-81, chief exec. officer, 1981-84; pres. Freight System div. Ryder System Inc., Miami, 1984-86; cons. trucking industry affairs Arlington, Va., 1986-88; pres., chief oper. officer H & M Internat. Transp., Inc., 1989-91, vice chmn., 1991-92; transp. cons., 1992-93; pres., gen. mgr. E.I. Kane Intermodal Transport, Inc., Balt., 1993-95, vice chmn., 1995, transp. cons., 1996—. Bd. dirs. Trucking Mgmt., Inc. Mem. exec. com. United Way Jacksonville, 1981-84; trustee Albion Coll., 1977; bd. dirs. Goodwill Industries North Fla. Served with AUS, 1950-53. Mem. Am. Trucking Assn. (nat. acctg. and fin. council 1964, pres. 1971, chmn. ATA Found. 1986-88, exec. com. 1985-88), Fla. Trucking Assn. (bd. dirs. 1973, pres. 1979), Am. Mgmt. Assn. (lectr. seminars), Jacksonville Area C. of C. (bd. govs., com. of 100, v.p. internat. 1984), Cen. and So. Motor Freight Tariff Assn. (bd. dirs. 1981-84, pres. 1983, exec. com. transp. rsch. bd. 1987-89), Sigma Nu. Home and Office: PO Box 1232 Middleburg VA 20118-1232

MAINZER, FRANCIS KIRKWOOD, neurosurgeon, health facility consultant; b. Clearfield, Pa., May 16, 1930; s. Francis Stanislaus and Dorothy (Kirkwood) M.; m. Joan Elizabeth Heydon, Sept. 19, 1964; children: Karen Elizabeth, Kristen Ann Mainzer Gillespie, Kathleen Patricia Mainzer Neumuller, Carole Jenifer Mainzer Bower. BA in Biology and Psychology, Amherst Coll., 1952; MD, George Washington U., 1959. Cert. Am. Bd. Neurol. Surgery. Attending neurosurgeon St. Vincent Health Ctr., Erie, Pa., 1965-92, chief of neurosurgery, 1992, asst. chief surgery, 1992; attending neurosurgeon Hamot Med. Ctr., 1965-84, chief neurosurgery, 1974; cons. neurosurgery VA Med. Ctr., 1965-80, Metro Health Ctr., Erie, 1965-92; physician surveyor Joint Commn. on Accreditation of Healthcare Orgns., Oakbrook Terrace, Ill., 1992-98; survey team leader J.C.A.H.O., 1994-98; cons. in hosp. quality improvement, 1998—2002. Mem. spinal cord injury adv. com. Pa. Dept. Health, Harrisburg, 1973-78; mem. stds. com. Pa. Trauma Systems Found., Harrisburg, 1985-92; reviewer Keystone Peer Rev., Harrisburg, 1986-89. Mem. Erie Philharm. Bd., 1967-71. Capt. USMCR, 1952-63, Korea. Mem. Am. Assn. Neurol. Surgeons, Congress Neurol. Surgeons, Pa. Neurosurg. Soc. (sec.-treas. 1981-84, pres. 1985, dir. 1975—), Mid-Atlantic Neurosurg. Soc. (dir. 1980—). Episcopalian. Avocations: radio-controlled model aeronautics, woodworking, skiing.

MAIOCCHI, CHRISTINE, lawyer; b. N.Y.C., Dec. 24, 1949; d. George and Andreina (Toneatto) M.; m. John Charles Kerecz, Aug. 16, 1980; children: Charles George, Joan Christine. BA in Polit. Sci., MA in Polit. Sci., Fordham U., 1971, JD, 1974; postgrad., NYU, 1977—. Bar: N.Y. 1975, U.S. Dist. Ct. (so. and ea. dists.), N.Y. 1975, U.S. Ct. Appeals (2nd cir) 1975. Law clk. to magistrate U.S. Dist. Ct. (so. dist.) N.Y., N.Y.C., 1973-74; atty. corp. legal dept. The Home Ins. Co., 1974-76; asst. house counsel corp. legal dept. Allied Maintenance Corp., 1976; atty. corp. legal dept. Getty Oil Co., 1976-77; v.p., mgr. real estate Paine, Webber, Jackson & Curtis, Inc., 1977-81; real estate mgr. GK Techs., Inc., Greenwich, Conn., 1981-85; real estate mgr., sr. atty. MCI Telecom. Corp., Rye Brook, N.Y., 1985-93; real estate and legal cons. Wallace Law Registry, 1994-96; sr. assoc. counsel Met. Transp. Authority, 1996-99, dep. gen. counsel, 1999—. Mem.: ABA, Indsl. Devel. Rsch. Coun. (program v.p. 1985, Profl. award 1987), Nat. Assn. Corp. Real Estate Execs. (pres. 1983—84, treas. 1984—86, bd. dirs. 1995—, exec. v.p. N.Y. chpt. 2000—01), The Corp. Bar (sec. real estate divsn. 1987—89, chmn. 1990—92), Women's Bar Assn. Manhattan, NY. Bar Assn., Dobbs Ferry Women's Club (program dir. 1981—92, 1994—96, publicity dir. 1992—94), Jr. League Club. Avocations: sports, theatre, gardening. Home: 84 Clinton Ave Dobbs Ferry NY 10522-3004 E-mail: cmaiocch@mtahq.org.

MAIORIELLO, RICHARD PATRICK, retired otolaryngologist; b. Mar. 17, 1936; s. Gesumino Theodore and Angelina (Del Rossi) M.; m. Susan Hemenway, Mar. 6, 1979; children: Gabriel, Angela, Richard. AB, U. Pa., 1960; MD, Jefferson Med. Coll., 1964; MS, Thomas Jefferson U., 1972. Diplomate Nat. Bd. Med. Examiners, Am. Bd. Otolaryngology. Commd. 2d lt. USAF, 1963, advanced through grades to col., 1977, ret., 1979; intern Keesler Hosp., 1965-67; chief flight medicine USAF Base, Bitburg, Fed. Republic Germany, 1965-68; resident in otolaryngology Thomas Jefferson Hosp., Phila., 1968-71, 72-73; dir. med. edn. Andrews AFB, 1974-78; assoc. prof. uniformed svcs. Univ. Health Scis., 1978-79; assoc. prof. Northeastern Ohio U. of Medicine, 1983—; mem. staff Aultman Hosp., 1979—; assoc. staff Timken Mercy Med. Ctr., 1981—, Union Hosp., 1988—; retired, 2001. Cons. otolaryngology to Surgeon Gen., 1977—; pres. Mid-Ohio Dressage Assn. With USNR, 1954-58. Decorated Air Force Commendation medal. Fellow ACS, Am. Soc. Head and Neck Surgery; mem. Am. Acad. Otolaryngology, Am. Acad. Facial Plastic and Reconstructive Surgery, Am. Assn. Cosmetic Surgery, Vail Cosmetic Surg. Soc., Hanoverian Soc. (exec. v.p.), U.S. Dressage Fedn. (chmn. all-breeds coun.), Centurion Club. Republican. Roman Catholic.

MAIOTTI, DENNIS PAUL, travel company executive; b. Cleve., Oct. 14, 1950; s. Raymond Joseph and Shirley Mae (Lang) M.; m. Rebecca Mueller, Aug. 11, 1973; children: Jennifer, David. BA, Baldwin-Wallace Coll., 1972; postgrad., Ohio U., 1972-73, Northwestern U., 1974. Cert. secondary tchr. Asst. employee relations Eaton Corp., Cleve., 1973-74, mgr. prodn., 1974-76, v.p. mktg., 1976-84, exec. v.p., 1984-86; pres. Lennon Wallpaper Co., Joliet, Ill., 1986-88, Mokena (Ill.) Mills Inc., 1988-99, Group Travel, Inc., Joliet, 2000—. Editor, columnist South Life met. newspapers, Cleve., 1968-72. Mem. Wallcovering Mfgrs. Assn., Kappa Delta Pi, Delta Phi Alpha. Republican. Lutheran. Avocations: golf, tennis, boating, travel. E-mail: dmaiotti@grouptravelinc.com.

MAIR, DOUGLAS DEAN, medical educator, consultant; b. Mpls., May 29, 1937; s. Lester Alexander and Irene Clare (Fisher) M.; m. Joanne Mary Elliott, Aug. 18, 1963; children: Scott, Michele, Todd. BA, U. Minn., 1959, MD, 1962. Bd. cert. pediats. and pediat. cardiology. Cons. Mayo Clinic, Rochester, Minn., 1971—; from asst. prof. pediats. to assoc. prof. pediats. Mayo Med. Sch., 1972-80, prof. pediats., 1980—, assoc. prof. internal medicine, 1978—. Contbr. numerous articles and book chpts. to profl. publs. Capt. USAF, 1966-67.

MAIR, VICTOR HENRY, language and literature educator; b. East Canton, Ohio, Mar. 25, 1943; s. Joseph Charles and Esther Frieda Louise (Boyce) M.; m. Li-ching Chang, Dec. 15, 1969; 1 child, Thomas Krishna. BA, Dartmouth Coll., 1965; postgrad., U. Wash., 1967; BA in Chinese and Sanskrit with honors, U. London, 1972, MPhil in Chinese, 1984; MA in Chinese Lit., Harvard U., 1973, PhD in Chinese Lit., 1976; MA (hon.), U. Pa., 1985. Vol. Peace Corps, Nepal, 1965-67; lectr. English lang. and lit. Tunghai U., Taichung, Taiwan, 1970-72; tchg. fellow and lectr. Chinese religion and lit. Harvard U., Cambridge, Mass., 1973-77; asst. prof. Chinese religion and lit., 1977-79; asst. prof. Chinese U. Pa., Phila., 1977-79, assoc. prof. Chinese, 1984—88, prof. Chinese, 1989—, cons. scholar Mus. Archaeology and Anthropology; concurrent prof. dept. Chinese Sichuan U., Chengdu, China, 1997—, Peking U., China, 1998—. Vis. prof. dept. Asian and African studies Duke U., 1993-94, vis. rsch. prof., fellow Inst. Rsch. in Humanities Kyoto (Japan) U., 1995-96; mem. Sch. Hist. Studies Inst. Advanced Study, Princeton, N.J., 1998-99; humanities PhD nat. fellowship selection com. NEH, 1992-95, nat. fellowships for univ. tchrs. selection com.; Chinese studies fellowship selection com. Am. Soc. Learned Socs., 1993-97; mem. Inter-Univ. Bd. Chinese Lang. Studies, 1997—; disting. vis. prof. dept. Chinese U. Hong Kong, 2002-; presenter, cons. in field. Co-author: The Tarim Mummies, 2000; editor: The Columbia Anthology of Traditional Chinese Literature, 1994, The Bronze Age and Early Iron Age Peoples of Eastern Central Asia, 2 Vols., 1998, others; co-editor: A Reader of Chinese Folk and Popular Literature; assoc. editor: Han-Ying cidian (ABC Chinese-English Dictionary), 1997; editor, founder: Xin Tang (Jour. Romanized Mandarin, 1982—, Sino-Platonic Papers, 1986—; contbr. articles to profl. jours., chpts. to books; translator, cotranslator numerous books; appeared in documentary on mummies of Ctrl. Asia NOVA, 1997, (film) Riddle of the Desert Mummies Discovery Channel, 1998; prin. investigator rsch. project on Bronze Age and Iron Age desiccated mummies of the Tarim Basin and surrounding areas, 1991—. Woodrow Wilson fellow, 1967-68, fellow Nat. Def. Fgn. Lang., 1968, 70, 72-75, Marshall fellow Sch. Oriental and African Studies U. London, 1968, Arthur Lehman fellow, 1974, Whiting fellow, 1975, Nat. Humanities Ctr., 1991-92; grantee Alfred P. Sloan Found., 1992, U. Pa. Rsch. Found., 1994-95, Luce Found., 1994-97, Lang. Consortium, 1997-98, Freeman Found., 1997—, Dept. Edn., 2000-02. Mem. Am. Comparative Lit. Assn., Am. Oriental Soc., AAUP, Assn. Asian Studies, Soc. Study Chinese Religion, T'ang Studies Soc. (dir. 1987—), Chinese Lang. Soc. Hong Kong, Oriental Club Phila., Assn. Am. for Promotion Chinese Lang. Reform, Linguistic Soc. Am., World History Assn., Permanent Internat. Altaistic Conf., Inst. Ancient Equestrian Studies. Avocations: running, learning languages, playing French horn. Office: Dept Asian and Middle Eastern Studies University of Pa Philadelphia PA 19104-6305 Office Fax: 215-573-9617 .

MAIRE, BARBARA JEAN, volunteer; b. Chgo., Feb. 23, 1932; d. Eldee W. and Emilie (Gadecki) Sayre; m. L. Thomas Maire, July 25, 1953. Student, Art Inst., Chgo., 1946-50. Officer mgr., asst. sec., cost acct. Buchen Advt., Inc., Chgo., 1952-72; with pub. rels. dept. Sebring (Fla.) Internat. Raceway, 1986—. Bd. mem. Sebring Internat. Raceway Adv. Coun., 1986—; bd. dirs. Lake Briarwood Homeowners Assn., Arlington Heights, Ill., 1976-80; active Citizens for Utility Rate Equity, Sebring,, 1989-92, SE div. Adminstr. Race Control, Sports Car Club Am., 1989-96; coord. Highlands County, Fla. Lakewatch, 1991—; mem. code enforcement bd. City of Sebring, 1993—. Mem. Fla. Steinmetz Alumni Assn., Sports Car Club Am. (bd. govs. 1985-92, chmn. race ofcl. licensing 1986-91, Race Ofcl. of Yr. 1988), MG Car Club Am. (officer 1962-67, Mem. of Yr. 1966), Am. Model Yachting Assn. (exec. sec. 1977-87), Sebring Country Club. Democrat. Home and Office: 104 W Lake Drive Blvd Sebring FL 33875-5021 E-mail: maire@strato.net.

MAIROSE, PAUL TIMOTHY, mechanical engineer, consultant; b. Mitchell, S.D., Aug. 4, 1956; s. Joseph E. and Phyllis R. (Glissendorf) M.; m. Connie L. Nickell, Apr. 1, 1989 (dec. June 8, 1992); m. Donna M. Ward, Sept. 10, 1993; children: Carly J., Kevin P., Sydney S. BSME, S.D. Sch. Mines and Tech., 1978; postgrad., Tulane U., 1986. Registered profl. engr., Wash. Mech. engr. UNC Nuclear Industries, Richland, Wash., 1979-80, Wash. Pub. Power Supply System, Richland, 1980-85, 89; cons. La. Power & Light Co., New Orleans, 1985-86, Erin Engrng. & Rsch. Inc., Walnut Creek, Calif., 1986-87, Sacramento Mcpl. Utility Dist., 1987-89; mech. engr. GE, Portland, Oreg., 1989-90; sr. cons. Rocky Flats Project Cygna Energy Svcs., 1990-91; v.p. mktg. Data Max, 1991—; pvt. practice cons. engr. Vancouver, Wash., 1991—; project engr. Mactec, Inc., Richland, 1990-91; pres. Project Tech. Mgmt., 1990—; chief engr. Southwest Clean Air Agy., Vancouver, Wash., 1992—; owner M-n-M Distributing, 1998—. Mem. Wash. State Title V Permit Writers Subcom., 1994—, Wash. State New Source Rev. Subcom., 1994—; v.p. M-n-M Distbg., 1998—. Co-author: Topical Report on Extreme Erosion at Yucca Mountain, Nevada, 1993, RACT Evaluation for the Centralia Plant, Centralia, Washington. Mem. ASME (assoc.), ASHRAE (assoc.), Air and Waste Mgmt. Assn., Aircraft Owners and Pilots Assn., Profl. Assn. Diving Instrs., Air & Waste Mgmt. Assn., Sierra Club, Bards of Bohemia. Republican. Roman Catholic. Avocations: foreign travel, hiking, bicycling, private piloting, scuba diving. Home: 4606 NW 387th St Woodland WA 98674-3423 E-mail: Paul@swcleanair.org.

MAISANO, PHILLIP NICHOLAS, investment company executive; b. Newark, May 15, 1947; s. Salvatore and Mary (Vella) M.; m. Mary-Alice Yanch, Aug. 10, 1968; children: Phillip, Matthew. BA, Belmont (N.C.) Abbey Coll., 1969; MBA, Iona Coll., 1976; postgrad., NYU Law Sch., 1972-73, Columbia U., summer 1987; LLD (hon.), Belmont Abbey Coll., 1999. CLU. Asst. v.p. The Equitable, N.Y.C., 1969-79; v.p. Manhattan Life Ins. Co., 1979-81, MONY Fin. Svcs., Purchase, N.Y., 1981-88, sr. v.p., 1989—; pres. Evaluation Assocs. Inc., Norwalk, Conn., 1988—, chmn., CEO, 1996; incorporator New Dartmouth Bank, Hanover, N.H., 1991—. Trustee Belmont Abbey Coll., 1992—; bd. advisors Hagan Sch. of Bus. Iona Coll. Contbr. articles to profl. publs. 1st lt. USAR. Mem. Investment Mgmt. Cons. Assn. (chmn. adv. bd. 2000—). Roman Catholic. Avocations: football coaching, softball, running, golf, skiing. Home: 6 Charlotte Ct Montvale NJ 07645-1005 Office: 200 Connecticut Ave Norwalk CT 06854-1940

MAISEL, HERBERT, computer science educator; b. N.Y.C., Sept. 22, 1930; s. Hyman and Dora (Goldstein) M.; m. Millicent Sherry Kushner, Apr. 13, 1957; children— Scott Alan, Raymond Bruce. B.S., CCNY, 1951; M.S., NYU, 1952; Ph.D., Catholic U. Am., 1964. Mathematician, statistician Dept. Army, Aberdeen, Md., Washington, 1954-63; dir. acad. computer ctr. Georgetown U., Washington, 1963-76, prof. computer sci., 1963— ; systems advisor Social Security Adminstrn., Balt., 1976-84; cons. Nat. Bur. Standards, Gaithersburg, Md., 1968-72, Balt. Housing Authority, 1972-73, Social Security Adminstrn., Balt., 1966-73; mem. study group HHS, Washington, 1975-76. Author: An Introduction to Electronic Digital Computers, 1969; Simulation of Discrete Stochastic Systems, 1972; Computers for Social and Economic Development, 1974; Computers: Programming and Applications, 1975; also others. Contbr. articles to profl. jours. Mem. Community Housing Resources Bd., Montgomery County, Md., 1975. Recipient spl. service award Internat. Assn. Parents of Deaf, 1982. Fellow Assn. Computing Machinery (chmn. external activities bd. 1981-86, chmn. mems. and chpts. bd. 1978-80, chmn. nominating com. 1983-84, mem. council, chmn. Washington chpt. 1971-73, Outstanding Contribution award 1986); mem. Phi Beta Kappa (chmn. Georgetown chpt. 1974-76), Sigma Xi. Jewish. E-mail: HMaisel999@aol.com

MAISEL, SHERMAN JOSEPH, economist, educator; b. Buffalo, July 8, 1918; s. Louis and Sophia (Beck) M.; m. Lucy Cowdin, Sept. 26, 1942; children: Lawrence C., Margaret L. AB, Harvard U., 1939, M.P.A., 1947, PhD, 1949. Mem. bd. govs. FRS, 1965-72; economist, fgn. service res. officer Dept. State, 1945-46; teaching fellow Harvard U., 1947-48; asst. prof., assoc. prof., prof. bus. adminstrn. U. Calif. at Berkeley, 1948-65, 72-86; sr. economist Nat. Bur. Econ. Research-West, 1973-78; chmn., bd. dirs. Farmers Savings & Loan, 1986-88; pres. Sherman J. Maisel & Asscs. Inc., 1986—. Fellow Fund For Advancement Edn., 1952-53, Inst. Basic Math. with Application to Bus., 1959-60, Center for Advanced Study in Behavioral Scis., 1972; mem. adv. coms. to Bur. Census, FHA, State of Calif., Ford Found., Social Sci. Research Council; mem. bldg. research adv. bd. NRC. Author: Housebuilding in Transition, 1953, Fluctuations, Growth, and Forecasting, 1957, Managing the Dollar, 1973, Real Estate Investment and Finance, 1976, Risk and Capital Adequacy in Commercial Banks, 1981, Macroeconomics: Theories and Policies, 1982, Real Estate Finance, 1987, 2d edit., 1992. Bd. dirs. Berkeley Unified Sch. Dist., 1962-65. Served to capt. AUS, 1941-45. Mem. Am. Fin. Assn. (pres. 1973), Am. Econ. Assn. Home: 2164 Hyde St San Francisco CA 94109-1788 Office: U Calif Haas Bus Sch Berkeley CA 94720-1900

MAISLIN, ISIDORE, hospital administrator; b. N.Y.C., Aug. 4, 1919; s. Solomon and Rose (Baruch) M.; m. Frances Mussman, Jan. 18, 1948; children— Wendy Sue (Mrs. Neil Robbins), Steven William. BS, Columbia, 1950, MS, 1951. Asso. dir. Albert Einstein Med. Center, Phila., 1950-59; asso. dir. Mt. Sinai Hosp. Greater Miami, Mimai Beach, Fla., 1959-63; adminstr. Scranton (Pa.) Gen. Hosp., 1963-64; exec. dir. Jewish Home of Eastern Pa., Scranton, 1964-67; adminstr. South Mountain (Pa.) Restoration Center, 1967—. Served with AUS, 1943-46. Fellow Am. Coll. Hosp. Adminstrs., Am. Pub. Health Assn., Royal Soc. Health. Home and Office: 535 Colfax Ave Scranton PA 18510-2364

MAISSEL, LEON ISRAEL, physicist, engineer; b. Cape Town, South Africa, May 31, 1930; came to U.S., 1956; s. Charles and Emily (Cohen) M.; m. Raina Eve Corren, Jan. 26, 1956; children: Simon, Gerda, Joseph. B.Sc., U. Cape Town, 1949, M.Sc., 1951; PhD, U. London, 1955. Staff scientist Philco Corp., Phila., 1956-60; adv. physicist IBM Corp., Poughkeepsie, N.Y., 1960-63, sr. engr., 1963-81, sr. tech. staff mem., 1981-93; patent writer, 1994—. Author, editor: Handbook of Thin Film Technology, 1969, An Introduction to Thin Films, 1970; contbr. articles profl. jours.; patentee in field. Recipient Outstanding Invention award IBM Corp., 1968; recipient Outstanding Contbn. award IBM Corp., 1969 Fellow IEEE; mem. Am. Vacuum Soc. (Dir. 1966-68) Lodges: B'nai B'rith. Democrat. Jewish. Home: 16 Smoke Rise Ln Wappingers Falls NY 12590-1240 *Most people, properly trained, can solve well-defined problems. The ability to deal with poorly-defined problems is much rarer and is the key to success in science.*

MAISTO, JOHN F. ambassador; b. Braddock, Pa., Aug. 28, 1938; married; 3 children. BSFS, Georgetown U., 1961; MA, San Carlos Coll., Guatemala, 1962. With BiNational Ctr., Cordoba, Argentina, 1963-66; asst. cultural affairs officer USIA, Cochabamba, Bolivia, 1966-68; with Fgn. Svc., 1968—; adminstrv. asst. Fgn. Svc. Inst. Dept. State, 1968-69; econ. and comml. officer U.S. Embassy, La Paz, Bolivia, 1969-71; internat. rels. officer Ops. Ctr., 1971-72; spl. asst. Office of Counselor, 1972-73; internat. rels. officer office Andean affairs, bur. inter-Am. affairs Dept. State, 1973-75; polit. officer U.S. Embassy, San Jose, Costa Rica, 1975-78, Manila, 1978-82; dep. dir. office Philippine affairs, bur. East Asian and Pacific affairs Dept. State, 1982-84, dir., 1984-86; dep. chief of mission and charge d'affaires Am. Embassy, Panama, 1986-89; dep. permanent U.S. rep. to OAS, 1989-92; dep. asst. sec. state for Ctrl. Am. and Panama Dept. State, 1992-93; U.S. amb. to Nicaragua, 1993-96; U.S. amb. to Venezuela, 1997—2000; spl. asst. to Pres., sr. dir. for western hemisphere affairs Nat. Security Coun., 2001—.

MAITLAND, GUY EDISON CLAY, lawyer; b. London, Dec. 28, 1942; (mother Am. citizen); s. Paul and Virginia Francesca (Carver) M. BA, Columbia U., 1964; JD, N.Y. Law Sch., 1968. Bar: N.Y. 1969, U.S. Dist. Ct. (so. and ea. dists.) N.Y. 1969, U.S. Ct. Appeals (2d and D.C. cirs.) 1969. Assoc. Burlingham, Underwood & Lord, N.Y.C., 1969-74; admiralty counsel Union Carbide Corp., 1974-76; exec. v.p., gen. counsel, officer Liberian Svcs., Inc., N.Y.C. and Reston, Va., 1976-99; pres. Trust Co. of the Marshall Islands, Inc., 1990—; mng. ptnr. Internat. Registries, Inc., 2000—. Del. UN Conf. on Trade and Devel., Manila, 1979, Belgrade, 1983; participant London Conf. on Limitation of Maritime Liability, 1976; mem. legal com. Internat. Maritime Orgn. (UN) London, 1980—; del. UN Conf. on Law of the Sea, 1976-82, London UN Maritime Law Conf., 1984; co-founder The Admiralty-Fin. Forum, N.Y.C., 1986; mng. ptnr. Internat. Registries, Inc. Contbr. articles on maritime law, U.S. shipping policy. Mem. N.Y. Rep. State Exec. Com., 1974-76; del. Rep. Nat. Conv., Kansas City, 1976; sec. N.Y. Rep. County Com., 1976-87, vice chmn., 1988—, mem. exec. com., 1974-76; co-chmn. Citizens for Reagan, N.Y. State, 1979-80; trustee Am. Mcht. Marine Mus. Found. at U.S. Mcht. Marine Acad., King's Point, Nat. Maritime Hist. Soc., chmn., 2000-01; trustee N.Y. Maritime Coll. at Ft. Schuyler Found., Inc.; bd. dirs. Coast Guard Found.; del. UN Geneva Conf. on Arrest of Vessels, 1999; bd. dirs. Seamen's Ch. Inst., N.Y.C., Ctr. for Seafarers Rights; mem. adv. com. Am. Maritime History Project. Named Outstanding Young Man of Am. U.S. Jaycees, 1975; hon. del Rep. Nat. Conv., Dallas, 1984. Mem. ABA, Assn. of Bar of City of N.Y. (chmn. admiralty com. 1982-85), Maritime Law Assn. U.S. (chmn. com. on intergovtl. orgns. 1987-95), Ctr. for Seafarer's Rights Seamen's Ch. Inst. (bd. dirs. 1995—), Maritime Assn. Port of N.Y. (dir. 1984-87, 98—, pres. 1999-2001). Office: Internat Registries Inc 11495 Commerce Park Dr Reston VA 20191-1507

MAITRA, SUBIR RANJAN, medical educator; b. Calcutta, India, Oct. 2, 1943; came to U.S., 1983; s. Sudhir R. and Nilima (Sanyal) M.; m. Sakti Sanyal, July 6, 1975; 1 child, Soma. BS, Calcutta U., 1964, MS, 1966, PhD, 1971, DSc, 1990. Lectr. in Physiology Banaras U., Varanasi, India, 1973-78, 81-83; sr. Fulbright rsch. scholar Henry Ford Hosp., Detroit, 1979-80, rsch. assoc. in hypertension, 1983-85; rsch. assoc. in physiology Loyola U., Chgo., 1985-86, asst. prof. physiology, 1987-88; dir. trauma rsch. surgery SUNY, Stony Brook, 1988-90, asst. prof., dir. trauma rsch. emergency medicine, surgery, 1990-93, assoc. prof., dir. rsch. emergency medicine, 1993—. Recipient Gold medal Calcutta U., 1966; prin. investigator Indian Coun. Med. Rsch., 1981, Univ. Grants Commn., 1983; grantee NIH, 1993-96, 96-99, 1999-2003. Mem. AAAS, Am. Physiol. Soc., Shock Soc., Soc. for Acad. Emergency Medicine. Avocations: travel, community activities, sports.

MAIWURM, JAMES JOHN, lawyer; b. Wooster, Ohio, Dec. 5, 1948; s. James Frederick and Virginia Anne (Jones) M.; m. Wendy S. Leeper, July 31, 1971; children: James G., Michelle K. BA, Coll. Wooster, 1971; JD, U. Mich., 1974. Bar: Ohio 1974, D.C. 1986, Md. 1987, N.Y., 1987. Ptnr. Squire, Sanders & Dempsey, Cleve. and Washington, 1974-90; ptnr., group head Crowell & Moring, Washington, 1990-98; ptnr. Squire, Sanders & Dempsey, 1998-99; chmn., CEO Kaiser Group Internat., Inc., Fairfax, Va., 1999-2000; mng. ptnr. Squire, Sanders & Dempsey, Washington, 2001—. Bd. dirs. Workflow Mgmt., Inc., Cortez III Svc. Corp., Kaiser-Hill Co., LLC, Kaiser Group Holdings Inc. Contbr. articles to profl. jours. Bd. trustees Davis Meml. Goodwill Industries, 1996—. Mem. ABA, D.C. Bar Assn., Leadership Washington. Home: 9419 Brian Jac Ln Great Falls VA 22066-2002 Office: Squire Sanders & Dempsey LLP 14th fl 8000 Towers Crescent Vienna VA 22182

MAIZE, JOHN CHRISTOPHER, dermatology educator; b. Elizabeth, N.J., July 23, 1943; s. Donald Adam and Caroline Marie (Costanzo) Maize; m. Janice Lee Bentley, May 21, 1966; children: Sandra Kristine Tolly, John C. Jr., Jennifer Lee. MD, U. Mich., 1968. Cert. Am. Bd. Dermatology. Intern U. Mich., Ann Arbor, 1968—69, residency in dermatology, 1968—72; asst. prof. dermatology SUNY, Buffalo, 1972—77, assoc. prof., 1977—80, Med. U. of S.C., Charleston, 1980—83, prof., 1983—89, prof., chmn. dept. dermatology, 1989—. Author: Pigmented Lesions of the Skin, 1987, Cutaneous Pathology, 1998. Fellow: Am. Soc. Dermapathology (pres. 1995), Am. Acad. Dermatology; mem.: Am. Bd. Dermatology (dir. 1990—99, pres. 1999), S.C. Dermatol. Assn. (pres. 2001), S.C. Med. Assn., Internat. Soc. Dermatopathology (sec. 1987—89, pres. 1989—91), Am. Dermatol. Assn. Roman Catholic. Avocations: fishing, golf, travelling. Office: Med U SC 171 Ashley Ave Charleston SC 29425-0001

MAIZE, LINDA LOU, elementary education educator; b. Hazen, N.D., Aug. 30, 1952; d. F. Robert and Mary (Keller) Oestreich; m. Kirk Edward Maize, Aug. 10, 1974; 1 child, Allen Edward. BS in Elem. and Spl. Edn., U. Nebr., 1974; MS, Minot State U., 1998. Tchr. Naughton Sch., Bismarck, N.D., 1974-75; elem. tchr. Golden Valley (N.D.) Pub. Sch., 1975-78, Beulah (N.D.) Pub. Schs., 1978—. Tchr. Bible sch. Concordia Luth. Ch., Beulah, 1976-77, Wednesday sch. tchr., 1994—; vol. campaign for U.S. senator, Beulah, 1982, 84; past sec. Dist. 33 Dem. Com., Beulah; leader Boy Scouts Am.; leader 4-H, 1999; sec. Beulah Area Dollars for Scholars, Mercer County 4-H Coun. Mem. ASCD, Internat. Reading Assn., Nat. Coun. Tchrs. Math., Nat. Coun. Tchrs. English, N.D. Edn. Assn. (dist. 33 govt. rels. contact 1982-88, 93—), Beulah Edn. Assn. (treas. 1979-80, v.p. 1981-82, pres. 1982-83), Am. Quarter Horse Assn., Delta Kappa Gamma. Avocations: reading, riding, stamp art, photo albums, quarter horses. Office: Beulah Elem Sch 200 7th St NW Beulah ND 58523

MAIZEL, ROY, federal agency administrator; BA in Polit. Sci., U. Rochester, 1979, MS in Pub. Policy Analysis, 1981. Dir. resource mgmt. divsn. Office of Space Sci. NASA, Washington, 1997—, presdl. mgmt. intern Office Space Flight, 1981, various program analyst positions, 1981—87, various mgmt. positions space shuttle, space sta. and mission to planet earth programs, 1988—97. Office: NASA Hdqrs Mail Code S 300 E St SW Washington DC 20546

MAIZEL, SAMUEL RUVEN, lawyer; b. Paterson, N.J., Apr. 9, 1955; s. Solomon S. and Anita M. Maizel; 1 child, Andrew Chapin. BS, U.S. Mil. Acad., 1977; MA, Georgetown U., 1983; JD, George Washington U., 1985. Commd. 2d lt. U.S. Army, 1977, advanced through grades to lt. col., 1996, infantry officer, 1977-82, criminal trial lawyer Frankfort, Germany, 1986-90, Dhahran, Saudi Arabia, 1990—91; trial atty. U.S. Dept. Justice, Washington, 1991-96; of counsel Pachulski, Stang, Ziehl, Young & Jones P.C., L.A., 1997—. Mem. editl. bd. Calif. Bankruptcy Jour.; contbr. articles to profl. jours. Decorated Bronze Star, Meritorious Svc. medal with oak leaf cluster, Army Commendation medal with oak leaf cluster, Army Achievement medal, S.W. Asia Svc. medal, Nat. Def. Svc. medal with bronze svc. star, Army Svc. ribbon, Overseas Svc. ribbon, Kingdom of Saudi Arabia Liberation of Kuwait medal Kingdom of Saudi Arabia, 1991, Liberation of Kuwait medal Govt. Kuwait, 1992. Mem. ABA (chair), Am. Bankruptcy Inst. (vice chair health care solving issues com.), Am. Health Lawyers Assn. Office: Pachulski Stang Ziehl Young & Jones PC Ste 1100 10100 Santa Monica Blvd Los Angeles CA 90067-4100

MAJD, MASSOUD, radiology and nuclear medicine educator; b. Yazd, Iran, July 23, 1935; came to U.S., 1961; s. Jalil and Khadijeh Majd; m. Fereshteh H.S. Javadi, June 23, 1968; children: Kurosh, Katayoon. MD, Tehran U., 1960. Diplomate Am. Bd. Radiology, Am. Bd. Nuclear Medicine. Intern Deaconess Hosp., Buffalo, 1961-62; resident Georgetown U., Washington, 1962-66, instr. radiology, 1965-66, 68-70; asst. prof. Pahlavi U., Shiraz, Iran, 1966-68, George Washington U., 1970-72, assoc. prof., 1972-79, prof. radiology and pediatrics, 1979—; radiologist, dir. pediatric nuclear medicine Children's Nat. Med. Ctr., Washington, 1968—. Adj. prof. radiology Georgetown U., 1981—; staff radiologist Georgetown U. Hosp., 1965-66; radiologist Pahlavi U. Hosps, Shiraz, 1966-68; assoc. staff radiology Children's Med. Ctr., 1968-72, sr. attending staff radiology, 1972—, founder dir. sect. nuclear medicine, 1969—; presenter in field. Contbr. chpts. to books and articles to profl. jours. Fellow Soc. Uroradiology, Am. Coll. Radiology, Am. Coll. Nuclear Physicians, Am. Acad. Pediatrics; mem. Am. Roetgen Ray Soc., Radiologic Soc. N.Am., European Soc. Pediatric Radiology (affiliate), European Assn. Nuclear Medicine, Soc. Pediatric Radiology, Soc. Nuclear Medicine, Pediatric Imaging Coun., John Caffey Soc. Home: 8605 Stirrup Ct Potomac MD 20854-4843 Office: Childrens Nat Med Ctr 111 Michigan Ave NW Washington DC 20010-2916 E-mail: mmajd@cnmc.org.

MAJERUS, PHILIP WARREN, physician; b. Chgo., July 10, 1936; s. Clarence Nicholas and Helen Louise (Mathis) Majerus; m. Janet Sue Brakensiek, Dec. 28, 1957; children: Suzanne, David, Juliet, Karen; m. Elaine Michelle Flansburg, 1996. BS, Notre Dame U., 1958; MD, Washington U., 1961. Resident in Medicine Mass. Gen. Hosp., Boston, 1961—63; research assoc. NIH, Bethesda, Md., 1963—66; asst. prof. biochemistry Washington U., St. Louis, 1966—75, asst. prof. medicine, 1966—69, assoc. prof. medicine, 1969—71, prof. medicine, 1971—, dir. div. hematology, 1973—, prof. biochemistry, 1976—. Mem. editl. bd. numerous jours. and profl. mags.; contbr. articles. Recipient Faculty Rsch. Assoc. award, Am. Cancer Soc., 1966—75, Disting. Career award for contbns. to hemastasis, Internat. Soc. for Thrombosis and Hemostasis, 1985, Alumni Faculty award, Washington U. Sch. Medicine, 1986, The Robert J.. and Claire Pasarow Found. award, 1994, Bristol-Myers Squibb prize for cardiovascular rsch., 1998, numerous others. Fellow: ACP; mem.: Inst. of Medicine of NAS, Am. Soc. Clin. Investigation (pres. 1981—82), Am. Soc. Biol. Chemists, Am. Fedn. Clin. Rsch., Am. Soc. Hematology (pres. 1991), Assn. Am. Physicians, Am. Acad. Arts and Scis., Alpha Omega Alpha, Sigma Xi. Home: 7220 Pershing Ave Saint Louis MO 63130-4248 Office: Wash Univ Sch of Med Dept Int Med Saint Louis MO 63110

MAJESTÉ, RICHARD MICHAEL, pathologist; b. New Orleans, Oct. 24, 1957; BA in Biology, U. New Orleans, 1978; MD, La State U., Shreveport, La., 1983. Staff pathologist Armed Forces Inst. Pathology, Washington, 1987-90, Meth. Med. Ctr., Peoria, Ill., 1991-92, Atlanta Med. Ctr., Atlanta, 1992—. Lt. comdr. USNR, 1987-89. Fellow Coll. Am. Pathologists; mem. Am. Soc. Clin. Pathologists, Calif. Soc. Pathologists, Internat. Soc. Gyn. Pathologists, Internat. Acad. Pathology. Office: Atlanta Med Ctr Dept Pathology 300 Boulevard NE Atlanta GA 30312-1206

MAJESTY, MELVIN SIDNEY, psychologist, consultant; b. New Orleans, June 6, 1928; s. Sidney Joseph and Marcella Cecilia (Kieffer) M.; m. Bettye Newanda Gordon, Dec. 18, 1955; 1 child, Diana Sue. BA, La. State U., 1949; MS, Western Res. U., 1951; PhD (USAF Inst. Tech. fellow), Case-Western Res. U., 1967. Commd. 2d lt. USAF, 1951, advanced through grades to lt. col., 1968; program mgr., asst. dir. tng. rsch. Air Force Human Resources Lab., 1967-69; dir. faculty and profl. ednl. rsch. USAF Acad., 1969-72; dir. plot tng. candidate selection program Officer Tng. Sch., Air Tng.Command, 1972-76; ret. USAF, 1976; personnel selection cons. to Calif. State Pers. Bd., Sacramento, 1976-92. Patentee listening center; founded pers. testing for ballistic missile and space systems; directed largest study of fighter pilot selection since World War II; pioneered use of phys. testing as replacement for the maximum age requirement in law enforcement jobs; developed phys. fitness tests and established psychol. screening standards for state highway patrol officer and police officers; contbr. numerous articles to profl. publs. With U.S. Army, WWII, 1944-46, Korea, Vietnam, USAF, 1951-76. Decorated Commendation medal (2), Meritorious Svc. medal (2), Am. Campaign medal, WWII Victory medal, WWII Overseas Occupation medal, Ballistic Missile badge, numerous others. Mem.: DAV, VFW, Am. Psychol. Assn., Military Officers Assn. Am., Mil. Order Fgn. Wars, Amvets, Nat. Assn. Uniformed Svc., Vietnam Vets. Am., Am. Bible Soc., Am. Family Assn., Am. Legion. Avocation: being a grandfather. Office: 801 Capitol Mall Sacramento CA 95814-4806

MAJETE, CLAYTON AARON, sociology educator; b. Woodland, N.C., Apr. 19, 1941; s. Barnabus and Doreather (Jefferson) M.; 1 child from previous marriage— Lisa. BA, Morgan State U., 1965; MA, NYU, 1967, PhD, 1984. Lectr., Nassau Community Coll., L.I., N.Y., 1967-69; lectr. Baruch Coll. CUNY, N.Y.C., 1970-84, prof. sociology and anthropology, 1984—. Mem. Gov. Harry Hughes' internal staff for 1986 Gubernatorial campaign; researcher for N.Y. Times and WCBS-TV and published on front page of N.Y. Times a study on Race Rels. in N.Y.C., 1985; exec. dir. Bedford Stuyvesant Community Corp., Bklyn., on leave, 1977-78; cons. Okla. U. Med. Sch., Norman. Assoc. editor Jour. Intergroup Rels.; contbr. articles to The Western Jour. of Black Studies and other black studies jours. Commr., Boy Scouts Am., Bklyn., 1980-83. NIMH fellow Johns Hopkins Med. Sch., 1969; Wharton Sch. fellow U. Pa., 1981. Mem. AAUP, NACCP, Morgan State U. Alumni Assn. (chmn. scholarship and recruitment com.), Inst. Urban Affairs (chmn. bd. dirs.), Am. Sociol. Assn. Democrat. Home: 35 Hampton Pl Brooklyn NY 11213-2612 Office: CUNY Baruch Coll 17 Lexington Ave New York NY 10010-5518

MAJEV, HOWARD RUDOLPH, lawyer; b. N.Y.C., Dec. 10, 1952; s. Benny and Hela (Wolnowicz) M.; m. Janet Brandt; children: Brendan Joshua, Collin Campbell. BA, Johns Hopkins U., 1973; JD, U. Md., 1976. Bar: Md. 1978, D.C. 1995. Exec. asst. to city coun. pres. City of Balt., Balt., 1976-79; assoc. Weinberg and Green, 1979-84; ptnr. Weinberg & Green, 1985-94, Piper Marbury Rudnick & Wolfe LLP (formerly Rudnick & Wolfe), Washington, 1994-2001, Winston & Strawn, Washington, 2001—. Author: (with K.S. Koenig) How to be a Legal Eagle: A Checklist for Remodelers, 1988; dir. Lex Mundi, 1992-94. Dir. Citizens Planning and Housing Assn., Balt., 1985-95, pres., 1990-92; bd. dirs. Md. Food Bank, Inc., 1988-92, Florence Crittenton Svcs. Balt., 1986-87, Sinai Hosp. Balt., 1990-92, Levindale Hebrew Geriat. Home and Hosp., 1991; devel. coun. The Kennedy Krieger Inst., 1988-92; participant Leadership-Greater Balt. Com., 1986. Mem. ABA, D.C. Bar Assn., Md. State Bar Assn. Avocations: tennis, reading. Office: Winston & Strawn 1400 L St NW Washington DC 20005 E-mail: hmajev@winston.com.

MAJEWSKI, THEODORE EUGENE, chemist; b. Boonton, N.J., July 5, 1925; s. Witold Charles and Felixa (Tkacz) M.; m. Cynthia Ann Davis, Sept. 26, 1953; children: Andrea, Theodore, Steven, Felicia, Cynthia, Melissa. BA, Syracuse U., 1951; MS, U. Del., 1953, PhD, 1960. Chemist Dow Chem. Co., Midland, Mich., 1957-69; rsch. chemist Philip Morris USA, Richmond, Va., 1969-92; ret., 1992. Cons. Herald Pharmacal, Richmond, 1979-81. Contbr. articles to profl. jours.; patentee in field. Bd. dirs. Boy Scouts Am., Richmond, 1957-91. With USN, 1943-46, PTO. Recipient Silver Beaver award Boy Scouts Am., 1980. Mem. Am. Chem. Soc., AAAS, Alpha Ci Sigma. Avocations: travel, fishing, reading, camping. Home: PO Box 8117 Kitty Hawk NC 27949-8117

MAJLESSI, HOJABR FAZEL, health facility administrator; b. Sept. 1, 1936; MD, Shiraz (Iran) U., 1960. Diplomate Am. Bd. Anatomic Pathology, Am. Bd. Clin. Pathology, Am. Bd. Family Medicine, Am. Bd. Bioanalysis, Am. Bd. Cytopathology, Am. Bd. Forensic Medicine, Internat. Bd. Cytopathology, Am. Bd. Forensic examiners. Med. dir. Ajman (United Arab Emirates) Hosp., 1961-65; intern Prince Georges Hosp., 1966-67; resident Miss. U. Med. Ctr., 1967-68; resident in pathology Boston Hosp. for Women, Harvard Med. Sch., Peter Bent Brigham Hosp.; tchg. fellow Harvard Med. Sch., 1968-71; resident in pediatric pathology Harvard Med. Sch., Peter Bent Brigham Hosp., 1969-70, resident in clin. pathology, 1970-71; fellow in nuclear medicine, endocrinology and toxicology Kans. U. Med. Ctr., 1971-72; fellow in immunohematology Hosp. of U. Pa., 1981-82; dir. labs., chair dept. pathology Kessler Meml. Hosp., Hammonton, N.J., 1974—, pres. med. and dental staff, 1985-86, dir. med. edn., 1986—. Asst. clin. prof. pathology Coll. of Medicine N.J., 1972-90; instr. pathology U. Pa. Med. Sch., 1975-79. Fellow ACP, Am. Coll. Pathologists, Am. Soc. Clin. Pathologists, Internat. Acad. Pathology, Am. Coll. Forensic Medicine, Royal Soc. Health, Internat. Acad. Cytopathology, Nat. Acad. Clin. Biochemistry; mem. AMA (del. hosp. med. staff sect. 1985—), Am. Coll. Forensic Examiners, N.J. Med. Soc., N.J. Pathology Soc., Atlantic County Med. Soc. Address: 1955 Philadelphia Ave Egg Harbor City NJ 08215-1631

MAJMUDAR, BHAGIRATH, medical educator; b. Nadiad, India, Jan. 29, 1938; came to U.S., 1967; s. Nanubhai and Pramilaben (Trivedi) M.; m. Uma Mehta, May 24, 1962; children: Nija, Sangini. MB BS, B.J. Med. Coll., Ahmedabad, India, 1962, MD, 1966. Diplomate Am. Bd. Pathology; ordained Hindu priest, 1976. Asst. prof. pathology B.J. Med. Coll., 1966-67; chief resident in pathology Salem (Mass.) Hosp., 1967-69; instr. in pathology Ohio State U., Columbus, 1971-75; asst. prof. pathology Emory U., Atlanta, 1971-75, assoc. prof. pathology, 1975-85, assoc. prof. ob-gyn, 1978—, prof. pathology, 1985—. Lectr., trainer S.E. Regional Tng. Ctr., Atlanta, 1988-; lectr. in field. Contbr. articles to profl. publs. Mem. Interfaith Com., State of

Ga., 1991-94, Interfaith Com. for Olympic Games, Atlanta, 1992-96; pres. India Am. Cultural Assn., Atlanta, 1976, chmn. bd. dirs., 1979. Recipient Outstanding Cmty. Svc. award India-Am. Cultural Assn., 1982. Fellow Coll. Am. Pathology, Internat. Acad. Pathology; mem. Soc. Med. Assn. (sec., chmn. 1992-95), Internat. Soc. for Study of Vulvovaginal Diseases, Arthur P. Soc. Surg. Pathologists, Internat. Soc. Gynecol. Pathology, Alpha Omega Alpha. Avocations: acting, directing and writing plays; writing, interfaith spirituality, global travel. Home: 3220 Olde Dekalb Way Atlanta GA 30340-4531 Office: Grady Health Sys Pathology Dept 80 Butler St SE Atlanta GA 30303-3031 E-mail: bmajmud@emory.edu.

MAJOR, CLARENCE LEE, novelist, poet, educator, artist; b. Atlanta, Dec. 31, 1936; s. Clarence and Inez (Huff) M.; m. Pamela Ritter, May 8, 1980. BS, SUNY, Albany; PhD, Union Inst. Prof. U. Colo., Boulder, 1977-89, U. Calif., Davis, 1989—. Author: All-Night Visitors, 1969, 2d version, 1998, Dictionary of Afro-American Slang, 1970, No, 1973, Reflex and Bone Structure, 1975, rev. edit., 1996, Emergency Exit, 1979, My Amputations, 1986, Such Was the Season, 1987, Painted Turtle: Woman with Guitar, 1987, Fun and Games, 1990, Calling the Wind, 1993, Juba to Jive: A Dictionary of African American Slang, 1994, Dirty Bird Blues, 1996; poetry: Swallow the Lake, 1970, Symptoms & Madness, 1971, Private Line, 1971, The Cotton Club, 1972, Inside Diameter: The France Poems, 1985, Painted Turtle, 1988, Surfaces and Masks, 1988, Some Observations of a Stranger at Zuni in the Latter Part of the Century, 1989, Parking Lots, 1992, The Garden Thrives, 1996, Configurations: New and Selected Poems, 1958-1998, 1998 (Nat. Book Award finalist 1999), Clarence Major and His Art: Portraits of an African American Postmodernist, 2001, Necessary Distance, 2001, Come By Here: My Mother's Life, 2002, Waiting for Sweet Betty, 2002, Conversations with Clarence Major, 2002; group shows include Kresge Mus., Mich., 2001; contbr. articles to Washington Post Book World, L.A. Times Book Rev., N.Y. Times Book Rev. Recipient Nat. Council on Arts award, Washington, 1970; Western States Book award, Western States Found., Santa Fe, 1986; Fulbright grantee, 1981-83. Office: U Calif Dept English 281 Voorhies Hall Davis CA 95616

MAJOR, COLEMAN JOSEPH, chemical engineer; b. Detroit, Sept. 7, 1915; s. Coleman I. and Anna (Galik) M.; m. Marjorie Lois Shenk, Nov. 21, 1941; children: Roy Coleman, Marilyn M. Phillips Bever. BS, U. Ill., 1937; PhD, Cornell U., 1941. Chief prodn. engr., supt. services Sharples Chems., Inc., Wyandotte, Mich., 1941-50; asso. prof. chem. engring. U. Iowa, 1950-56; head high energy chems. Am. Potash & Chem. Corp., Whittier, Calif. and Henderson, Nev., 1956-59; prof. chem. engring. U. Iowa, 1959-64; prof., head dept. chem. engring. U. Akron, 1964-70; dean Coll. Engring., also dir. Inst. Technol. Assistance, 1970-80; dir. Inst. Biomed. Engring. Rsch., 1979-80; cons. computers. Contbr. articles to tech. jours.; patentee in field. Named Chem. Engr. of Yr., 1979; C.J. Major Scholarship award established in his honor, 1990; recipient Disting. Svc. award U. Akron, 1993. Fellow Am. Inst. Chem. Engrs.; mem. Am. Chem. Soc., Sigma Xi, Tau Beta Pi. Home: 7838 Jaymes St Dublin OH 43017-8812 *A few guidelines that I have used: 1. Work very hard but find time to relax. 2. Push yourself ahead, but don't hold anyone else back. 3. When gathering facts, be rigorous and unrelenting but when making decisions involving people, use the art of compromise.*

MAJOR, JOHN CHARLES, judge; b. Mattawa, Ont., Can., Feb. 20, 1931; s. William and Elsie (Thompson) M.; m. Hélène Provencher, 1959; children: Suzan, Peter, Paul, Steven. BComm, Loyola Coll., Montreal, 1953; LLB, U. Toronto, 1957. Bar: Alta. 1958, Queen's Counsel, 1972. With Bennett, Jones & Verchere, Calgary, 1957-91, sr. ptnr., 1967; sr. counsel City of Calgary Police Svc., 1975-85; counsel McDonald Commn., 1978-82; sr. counsel Province of Alta., 1987, Alta. Ct. Appeal, 1991; mem. Supreme Ct. of Can., Ottawa, Ont., 1992—. Fellow Am. Coll. Trial Lawyers; mem. Can. Bar Assn., Can. Inst. of the Adminstrn. of Justice, Can. Judges Conf., The Glencoe Club (Calgary), Calgary Golf and Country Club, Ottawa Hunt and Golf Club. Avocation: golf. Office: Supreme Court of Can Wellington St Ottawa ON Canada K1A 0J1

MAJOR, JOHN KEENE, radio broadcasting executive; b. Kansas City, Mo., Aug. 3, 1924; s. Ralph Hermon and Margaret Norman (Jackson) M.; m. Gracemary Somers Westing, Apr. 9, 1950 (div.); children: John Westing, Ann Somers, Richard Jackson; m. Lee Adair Jordan, June 25, 1970. Student, U. Kansas City, 1940-41; BS, Yale U., 1943; MS, 1947; DSc, U. Paris, 1951. Lab. asst. physics Yale U., 1943-44, instr., research asst. physics, 1952-55; sci. staff spl. studies group, div. war research Columbia U., 1944; instr. physics and chemistry Am. Community Sch., Paris, 1948-49; research fellow Centre National de la Recherche Scientifique, Laboratoire de Chimie Nucleaire, Coll. de France, 1951; Carnegie Found. fellow Laboratoire Curie, Institut du Radium, 1951; assoc. prof. physics Western Res. U., 1955-57, chmn. dept., 1955-60, 61-64, Perkins prof. physics, 1957-66; staff assoc. univ. sci. devel. sect. div. instl. programs NSF, 1964-68; prof. physics, dean Grad. Sch. Arts and Scis., U. Cin., 1968-71; prof. physics NYU, 1971-74, dean Grad. Sch. Arts and Scis., 1971-73; vis. scholar Alfred P. Sloan Sch. Mgmt., MIT, 1973-74; prof. physics Northeastern Ill. U., Chgo., 1974-77, v.p. acad. affairs, 1974-75; cons. NSF, 1968-69; sci. cons. Sonar Analysis Group, 1946-47; gen. mgr. Sta. WONO, Syracuse, N.Y., 1977; dir. research and mktg. Sta. WFMT, Chgo., 1978-81; chmn. bd., pres. KCMA, Inc., 1980—; gen. mgr. Sta. KCMA, 1981-88. Mem. exec. com. radio project Ctr. for Pub. Resources, 1980-81; vis. prof. U. Mysore, 1967, Sardar Patel U., 1968; sci. eq. specialist U. Tunis, 1968. Contbr. articles to profl. jours. Bd. dirs. Concertime, 1985—, prs. 1993-95; bd. dirs. Tulsa Opera, 1984-95, Tulsa Philharm. Soc., 1988-95; vol. exec. Internat. Exec. Svc. Corps, Bulgaria, 1993, Armenia 1995, Ga. 1996. Fellow at Lab. für Technische Physik, Technische Hochschule Munich, 1960-61; Fulbright fellow U. Paris, 1949-50. Mem. Classical Music Broadcasters Assn. (exec. v.p., 1979-80, bd. dir. 1979-82, 85-87, 89-93, pres. 1980-81, 90-91, Walter Neiman award 1998), Cosmos Club (Washington), Sigma Xi. Home: 3701 N Cincinnati Ave Tulsa OK 74106-1533 E-mail: jkmajor2@juno.com.

MAJOR, MARY JO, dance school artistic director; b. Joliet, Ill., Dec. 5, 1955; d. George Francis and Lucille Mae (Ballun) Schmidberger; m. Perry Rex Major, June 9, 1979. AA, Joliet Jr. Coll., 1976; BA, Lewis U., 1978; MS, Ill. State U., 1983; postgrad., No. Ill. U., Nat. Louis U., Gov.'s State U., Olivet Nazarene U., Aurora U. Cert. tchr., Ill. Tchr., softball coach St. Rose Grade Sch., Wilmington, Ill., 1977-78; tchr., coach volleyball, basketball, softball Reed Custer High Sch., Braidwood, 1978-79; pvt. tutor, 1979; tchr. Coal City (Ill.) Middle Sch., 1980—, basketball coach, 1980-84; owner, dir., choreographer Major Sch. Dance, Inc., Coal City, 1984—; owner Technique Boutique, 1991—. Aerobics instr. Wilmington Park Dist., 1977-82, Coal City Shape Shoppe, 1980-82; cheerleading sponsor Joliet Jr. Coll., 1976-77, aerobics instr., 1980-81; pvt. dance instr., Coal City, 1981; dancer, choreographer Coal City Bi-Centennial Celebration, 1981, Coal City Community Celebration, 1982; founder Major Motion Dancers, 1984—; tchr., Russia, 1990; dancer, choreographer various performances for ch. and civic orgns.; televised half-time performance and tour Citrus Bowl. Commd. to choreograph and appear in video prodn.: Jacinta, Not an Ordinary Love, The Patty Waszak Show A Bit of Branson, 1995—; performer on televised Easter Seals Telethon from the Empress Casino, Joliet. Mem. Arts Coun. Co-op. Recipient Proclamation of Achievement award Dance Olympus, Chgo., 1986-99, Best Choreographer award 1990, Merit award Tremaine Dance Conv., 1991-92; named Best Actress, Joliet Kiwanis, 1989, Best Musician, 1990. Mem. NEA, Ill. Edn. Assn., Coal City Cmty. Unit Edn. Assn. Office: Major Sch Dance Inc 545 E 1st St Coal City IL 60416-1643

MAJOR, PATRICK WEBB, III, principal; b. Wai, Maharastra, India, Mar. 12, 1947; s. Patrick W. Jr. and Alice (Seeland) M.; m. Daphnelynn Jantz, June 26, 1971; children: Mindy Joy, Matthew Patrick Webb. BA in BE, Columbia Internat. U., 1969; BA, Biola U., 1972; MA, Point Loma Nazarene U., 1979; postgrad., U. Calif., Irvine. Cert. secondary tchr., adminstr., Calif. Prin. Omega High Sch., Bakersfield, Calif., 1980-84; headmaster Bakersfield Christian Life Schs., 1984-86; prin. North Kern Christian Sch., Wasco, Calif., 1986-88; prin., adminstr. Yucaipa (Calif.) Christian Schs., 1988-2000; prin. Christian H.S., El Cajon, Calif., 2000—. Chmn. ACSI So. Calif. Accreditation Comm., 1998—. Mem. ASCD, Assn. Christian Schs. Internat. (former dist. rep., exec. bd. 1992—), Ctrl. Redwood League (pres. 1985-86), CIF Ctrl Sect., Internat. Fellowship Christian Sch. Adminstrs. E-mail: patmajor@aol.com., pmajor@christianunified.com.

MAJOR, ROY COLEMAN, language educator; b. Wyandotte, Mich., June 29, 1945; s. Coleman Joseph and Marjorie Lois (Shenk) M.; m. Elza Arientie de Magalhães, June 12, 1970 (div. Jan. 1993); children: Sylvia Magalhães, Alexander Christopher; m. Ann Oakason, June 2, 2000. BA, U. Akron, 1967; MA, U. Ariz., 1970, Ohio State U., 1976, PhD, 1979. Instr. English Curso Oxford, Rio de Janeiro, 1971-73, Inst. Brasil-Estados Unidos, Rio de Janeiro, 1971-74; instr. linguistics, English Tchr.'s Tng. Course, 1971-74; instr. linguistics Pontifícia U. Cath., 1972-73; instr. English U. Gama Filho, 1973-74; grad. tchg. asst. Ohio State U., Columbus, 1975-79; lectr. San Diego State U., 1979-81; asst. prof. Wash. State U., Pullman, 1981-87, assoc. prof., 1987-92, dir. TESOL, 1981-92; assoc. prof. Ariz. State U., Tempe, 1992-99, prof., 1999—. Dir. programs in linguistics and TESL, Ariz. State U., Tempe, 1997-2002; 1st acad. coord. Intensive Am. Lang. Ctr., Wash. State U., 1983-85, acting dir. undergrad. program linguistics, 1989-90; vis. assoc. prof. U. Hawaii, Honolulu, 1990; vis. assoc. prof. No. Ariz. U., Flagstaff, 1993; internat. lectr. in field. Author: Foreign Accent: The Ontology and Phylogeny of Second Language Phonology, 2001; guest editor: Studies in Second Language Acquisition, 1998; reviewer numerous jours.; rschr. second lang. phonology The Ontogeny Phylogeny Model, The Similarity Differential Rate Hypothesis; contbr. chpts. to books and articles to profl. jours. Doris Duke Found. grantee, 1969; Fulbright Found. scholar, 1982-83; Postdoctoral fellow NIH, 1985. Mem. Linguistics Soc. Am., Am. Assn. Applied Linguistics, TESOL, Ariz. TESOL. Democrat. Avocations: hiking, camping, running, concerts, plays. Office: Ariz State Univ Dept English Tempe AZ 85287-0302

MAJORS, BETTY-JOYCE MOORE, genealogist, writer; b. Tullahoma, Tenn., Nov. 22, 1930; d. Frank Russell and Willie Eveline (Cope) Moore; m. Charles Anderton Majors, June 19, 1953; children: Robert Cope Majors, Carolyn Lynn (Majors) Diehl. Student, Israel Conservatory of Music, Jerusalem, 1951; BS, Mid. Tenn. State U., 1952. Pub. sch. music tchr., Lynchburg, Tenn., 1953-54; computer programmer AEDC, Arnold Air Force Station, 1954-86; genealogist, author, lectr., 1986—. Author: DeKalb County, Tennessee Genealogy from Settlement Books, 1992, Warren County, Tennessee Deed Book A, 1992, Warren County, Tennessee Will Books, 3 vols., 1992-95; co-author: Warren County, Tennessee Annotated Cemetery Books, 4 vols., 1994-99. Chmn. Coffee County Tenn. Records Commn., Manchester, Tenn., 1990—, also archivist, Coffee County Tenn., 1997—. Mem.: DAR (state chmn. 1980—82), Colonial Order of Crown, Ams. of Royal Descent, Magna Charta Dames (state chmn. 1972—73), Sons and Daus. of Pilgrims (state officer 1981—82), USD1812 (chpt. officer 2000—), Colonial Dames XVII Century (nat. officer 1979—83). Avocations: reading, cooking. Home: 111 Oak Park Dr Tullahoma TN 37388-4677

MAJORS, NELDA FAYE, physical therapist; b. Houston, Aug. 3, 1938; d. Columbus Edward and Mary (Mills) M. Cert. in Phys. Therapy, Hermann Sch. Phys. Therapy, Houston, 1960; BS, U. Houston, 1963. Lic. phys. therapist, Tex. Staff therapist Tex. Med. Ctr. Hermann Hosp., Houston, 1960-61; phys. therapist Chelsea Orthopedic Clinic, 1961-63; dir. phys. therapy Meml. Hosp. Southwest, 1963-75; owner, pres. Nelda Majors, Inc., 1975—. Mem. profl. adv. bd. Logos Home Health Agy., Houston, 1985-86; adv. dir. Prime Bank, Houston; sec.-treas., bd. dirs. Dominion Media Corp. Ptnr. Houston Proud Ptnr., 1986—; founder, pres. Instnl. Safety Advs. Inc., 1994—; bd. dirs. Texans for the Improvement of Long Term Care Facilities, 1995—; active St. Stephens Episcopal Ch., 2001—; trustee St. Stephen's Episc. Sch., Houston. Named All Am. Softball Pitcher, Amateur Softball Assn., 1964, All-Regional and All-State Pitcher, Tex. Amateur Softball Assn., 1954-70; named to Houston Amateur Softball Assn. Softball Hall of Fame, 1994. Mem. Am. Phys. Therapy Assn. (pvt. practice sect.), Ams. for Separation of Ch. and State, Tex. Phys. Therapy Assn., U. Houston Alumni Assn., E. Cullen Soc. (U. Houston), Rotary Club (Houston, Meml. Spring br.), Phi Kappa Phi. Clubs: U. Houston Cougar. Republican. Avocations: softball, bicycling, traveling, golf, reading.

MAJORS, RICHARD GEORGE, psychology educator; b. Ithaca, N.Y. s. Richard G. II and Fannie Sue Majors; 1 child Lillian A. McGill. AA, Auburn (N.Y.) Community Coll., 1974; BA in History, Plattsburgh State Coll., 1977; PhD in Ednl. Psychology, U. Ill., 1987. Various social svc. positions, 1976-79; probation officer, ct. investigator Plattsburgh, 1979; clin. intern McKinley Health Ctr., Urbana, Ill., 1981; rsch. asst. U. Minn., Mpls., 1981, U. Ill., Urbana, 1981-84; instr. Parkland C.C., Champaign, Ill., 1985; rsch. asst. U. Ill., 1985-86; postdoctoral fellow U. Kans., Lawrence, 1987-89; postdoctoral fellow, clin. fellow Harvard Med. Sch., Boston, 1989-90; asst. prof. psychology U. Wis. Sys., 1990-93; sr. rsch. assoc. The Urban Inst., Washington, 1993-95; sr. fellow David Walker Rsch. Inst., Mich. State U., East Lansing, 1995—. Hon. vis. scholar Georgetown U., 1996-97; Leverhulme vis. fellow for rsch. in Eng., 1996-97; sr. fellow Manchester U., England, 1997—. Co-author: Coolpose: The Dilemmas of Black Manhood in America, 1992, The American Black Male: His Present Status and Future, 1994, Educating Our Children: New Directions and Radical Approaches, 2001; founder Jour. of African Am. Men. Named one of Outstanding Young Men of Am., 1987; Canterbury fellow U. Christchurch, New Zealand, 2000. Fellow: APA (predoctoral minority fellow 1984, Minority Achievement award for Rsch. in Psychology 1995); mem.: Soc. Psychol. Study of Ethnic Minority Issues, Nat. Coun. African Am. Men (chmn., co-founder), Greenpeace, Phi Delta Kappa, Kappa Delta Pi. Avocations: reading, traveling, cycling. Office: 17 Regency Wharf Hooten Ln, Leigh Lancashire WN7 3BF England

MAJUMDAR, MUKUL KUMAR, economist, educator; b. Krishnagar, India, Dec. 6, 1944; came to U.S., 1965, naturalized, 1971; s. Nirmal Kanti and Sita (Mitra) M.; m. Malabika Dutta, Aug. 8, 1969. BA in Econs. with honors 1st class, Calcutta (India) U., 1966; PhD in Econs, U. Calif., Berkeley, 1970. Asst. prof. econs. Stanford U., 1969-72; lectr. London Sch. Econs., 1972-73; assoc. prof. Cornell U., 1973-77, prof., chmn. dept. econs., 1977—, Warshow prof. econs., 1983—. Ford rotating research prof. U. Calif., Berkeley, 1976-77 Coordinating editor: The Rev. Econ. Studies, 1976— ; asso. editor: Jour. Math. Econs, 1974— , Jour. Econ. Theory, 1977— . Recipient Coll. de France medal, 1989; Guggenheim fellow, 1976-77. Fellow Econometric Soc. Office: Cornell U Dept Econs Uris Hall Ithaca NY 14850

MAK, BEN BOHDAN, engineer; b. Chortkiw, Ukraine, June 11, 1926; s. Iwan and Antonya (Smerechynská) M. Student, U. Cracow (Poland) Poly., Friburg U., Ukrainian Tech. Husbandry Inst, U. Miami, War Coll.; MSME, MS in Mgmt. Engring., MS in Ordnance Engring., MBA, N.J. Inst. Tech. Registered profl. engr.; cert. plant engr. Design engr., engring. mgr. Bernard & Burk-Huston Corp., Miami, Fla., 1956-60; instr. value engring. U. Miami, Fla., 1959-60; prof. ordnance engring., logistic armament Air Force Inst. Tech.; gen. engr., mgr. Wiz Kids; engring. mgr. Sec. Def. Office Dept. Def., 1961-69; v.p. engring. Metal Improvement Co. and Valiant Metal Products Co., 1969-78; engring. mgr. Coll. Medicine and Dentistry N.J., 1978-82; dean facilities, engr., arch. Dutchess C.C., 1982-89; pvt. practice cons. mgmt., engring., mktg., 1970—. Author: Value Engineering, 1963, Bomb Fragmentation, 1964, Value Analysis for Industry, 1965, Sydor-Shelest, 1996, UPA Officer School, 1998; contbr. articles to profl. jours. 1st lt. army USSR, WWII, Ukrainian Insurgent Army, 1945-48. Recipient awards and merit citations U.S. Army, USN, USAF, Sec. of Def., Pres.'s office, univs. Mem. NSPE, ASME, Assn. Phys. Plant Adminstrs. of Univs., Soc. Cert. Plant Engrs., Ukrainian Engrs. Soc. Am., Assn. Energy Engrs., Ordnance Assn., APPA, others. Avocations: architecture, history.

MAK, CONNIE YIN HING, accountant; b. Hong Kong, Nov. 17, 1966; came to U.S., 1989; d. Wing Tim Mak and Lai Chun Chow. BS, Brigham Young U., Laie, Hawaii, 1993; M Accountancy, U. Hawaii, 1994; MBA in Internat. Bus. and Fin., Hawaii Pacific U., 1998. Sr. sec. State Bank of India, Hong Kong, 1986-89; dir.'s student asst. Brigham Young U., 1991-93; fiscal clk. U. Hawaii, Honolulu, 1993-94; acct. Y. Hata Co., 1994-95; sr. acct. Urban Mgmt. Corp., 1995—. Exec. sec. Hong Kong Club, Honolulu, 1992; treas. Internat. Indian Soc., Honolulu, 1993; vol. River of Lie Missin, Honolulu, 1997; treas. for rep. State of Hawaii. Mem. Am. Acctg. Assn., Inst. Mgmt. Accts., Am. Soc. Women Accts., Honolulu Chinese Jaycees (dir. cmty. devel. 1996, asst. treas. 1997—, Outstanding New Mem. award 1996, Cmty. Svc. award 1997), Social Dance Sports Club, Delta mu Delta, Mu Kappa Tau, Beta Gamma Sigma, Phi Beta Lambda. Avocations: volunteering, cycling, reading, ballroom dancing, swimming. Office: Urban Mgmt Corp 850 Richards St Ste 603 Honolulu HI 96813-4799

MAK, KEN PING, brokerage executive; b. Stamford, Conn., June 20, 1972; s. Ty Tse-Fai and Susan Pui-San Mak. AB, Brown U., 1994; MBA, Columbia U., 1999. Fin. analyst Kidder, Peabody & Co., N.Y.C., 1994; sr. analyst TD Securities (USA) Inc., 1995-97; equity rsch. analyst Putnam Investments, Boston, 1998; v.p. product devel. CSFB Direct, Inc., Jersey City, 1999—. Avocations: reading, investing, cooking, playing tennis, traveling. Home: 7 E 14th St Apt 1019 New York NY 10003-3130 Office: CSFB Direct Inc Harborside Fin Ctr 501 Plaza II Jersey City NJ 07311 E-mail: kenpmak@hotmail.com.

MAK, SIOE THO, retired engineer; b. Medan, Indonesia, Sept. 3, 1932; came to the U.S., 1967; s. Boen Kit Mak and Tjioe Nio Tjoa; m. Giok Nio Njoo, June 10, 1959; children: Sharleen Aylien, Shanta Aylan. Diploma in elec. engring., U. Indonesia, 1958; MSc in Elec. Engring., Ill. Inst. Tech., 1961, PhD in Elec. Engring., 1970. Sr. lectr. Bandung Inst. Tech., Bandung, Indonesia, 1961-67; rsch. project mgr. Joslyn Rsch. Ctr., Woodstock, Ill., 1970-78; sr. staff scientist ESCO & Emerson Electric Co., St. Louis, 1978-96; ret., 1996; power quality specialist Advantage Engring., Chesterfield, Mo., 1996—. Part-time sr. staff scientist Distbn. Control Sys., Inc., St. Louis, 1996—. Contbr. articles to profl. jours. Fellow IEEE. Achievements include patents in communication technology. Avocations: reading, listening to classical music, home improvement, travel, research. Home: 15268 Kempwood Dr Chesterfield MO 63017-7411 E-mail: sioetmak@aol.com.

MAK, WING KWONG TONY, life insurance executive, training consultant; b. Hong Kong, Mar. 2, 1952; s. Man Mak and Jun Poon; m. Kam Amy Tse, Dec. 25, 1979; children: Emily Sui Wo, Fiona Sui Wah. B of Social Sci. (hon.), Chinese U. of Hong Kong, 1976. Tchr. St. Joannes Coll., Hong Kong, 1976-77; dist. dir. Am. Internat. Assurance (Bermuda) Ltd., 1977—. Chmn. Tony Cons. Ltd., Hong Kong, 1994—; bd. dirs. Faith Asia Cons. Ltd.; cons. Consultancy De Excel, Kuala Lumpur, Malaysia, 1992—; hon. advisor Elite Children Tng. Ctr., Kuala Lumpur, 1997—. Chmn. Ins. Tng. Bd. of Hong Kong Govt., 1992—; vice chmn. Hong Kong Amateur Handball Assn., 1984-88, Lion's Club of Hong Kong, 1987; mem. adv. com. Humanities Program Hong Kong Baptist U., 2000—. Mem. Life Underwriters Assn. of Hong Kong (pres. 1988-89), Life Underwriters Assn. Charitable Found. (vice chmn.), 4th Asia Pacific Life Ins. Congress (chmn. 1997). Office: 701 Island Pl Tower 510 King's Rd Hong Kong Hong Kong

MAKADOK, STANLEY, management consultant; b. N.Y.C., Mar. 30, 1941; s. Jack and Pauline (Speciner) M.; BME, CCNY, 1962; MS in Mgmt. Sci., Rutgers U., 1964; m. Neilia A. David, Nov. 12, 1989; 1 child from previous marriage, Richard. Bus. systems analyst Westinghouse Electric Corp., Balt., 1964-65; project engr., corp. cons. Am. Cyanamid Corp., Pearl River, N.Y., Wayne, N.J., 1965-68; v.p., bus. devel. and planning Pepsico Inc. and affiliates, Purchase, N.Y., Miami, Fla., 1968-75; mgr. fin. and planning cons. Coopers & Lybrand, N.Y.C., 1975-77; pres. Century Mgmt. Cons., Inc., Princeton, N.J., 1977—. Contbr. articles to profl. jours. Office: Century Mgmt Cons Inc 32 Nassau St Princeton NJ 08542-4503

MAKALOU, OUMAR, economic advisor; b. Kita, Mali, 1934; s. Sambou and Coumba (Tounkara) M.; m. Morimoussou Koite, July 30, 1944; children: Modibo Mao, Kalle, Mamaye, Sambou, Coumba. BA in Law (Polit. Economy), Paris U., 1960, MA in Econs., 1968; PhD in Econs., U. Paris-Sorbonne, 1970. Insp. Fin. Services, Paris, 1956-60; pres. Devel. Bank, Bamako, Mali, 1961-63; state controller Office of Pres., Koulouba, Mali, 1963-68; dir. gen. Treasury Banks and Ins., 1968-71, Internat. Coop., Koulouba, 1971-73; chmn. bd. dirs. Cen. Bank, Bamako, Mali, 1973-77; chief of staff Office of Pres.; dep. dir. African dept. IMF, Washington, 1977-84; sr. advisor IMF Inst., 1984—. Vis. prof. U. Montreal, Que., Can., 1983. Author: Budget Equilibrium in Developing Countries, 1970. Named Grand Officer of the Cross of Merit, Fed. Republic of Germany, Officer of Merit Order of France, Knight of the Nat. Order of Mali. Mem. Soc. for Internat. Devel. (bd. dirs. 1986-90), Internat. Profl. Bankers' Assn., Nat. Economists Club (Washington). Avocations: reading, music, the arts. Home: 5915 Bradley Blvd Bethesda MD 20814-1106 Office: IMF 700 19th St NW Washington DC 20431-0001

MAKAR, JIMMY, race car driver; b. Cedar Knolls, N.J., Mar. 24, 1956; m. Patti Makar; children: Alex, Dillon. Crew chief Joe Gibbs Racing, Huntersville, NC, 1995—. Office: Joe Gibbs Racing 13415 Reese Blvd W Huntersville NC 28078

MAKAR, NADIA EISSA, secondary education educator, educational administrator; b. Cairo, Oct. 7, 1938; came to U.S., 1966. d. Michel and Yvonne (Bitar) Issa; m. Boshra Halim Makar, Jan. 1, 1960; children: Ralph, Roger. Cert., Moscow U., 1964; BA, St. Peter's Coll., 1969, MA, 1981; postgrad., Hope Coll. and Brown U., 1972, 1973. Cert. tchr., supr., prin., N.J. Tchr. Hudson Cath. H.S., Jersey City, 1970-72, sci. dept. chairperson, 1972-79; coord. Convocation Model Project Union City N.J. Bd. Edn., 1979-81, tchr., coord. industry and coll. rels., 1989-96, sci. supr., 1996—. Mem. Bd. Edn., Jersey City; cons. Stevens Inst. Tech. Hughes Grant, Hoboken, N.J., 1989-94; cons./advisor Project RISE. Author: Health; Space; Environment, 1980; co-editor NSSA mag., 1974-76; contbr. articles to profl. jours. Co-founder N.J. Bus./Industry/Sci. Edn. Consortium, 1981; pres. Bus./Profl. Women, Jersey City, 1984-86, sec. N.J., 1985, dir. dist. III, 1995—; treas. Mental Health Assn., Hudson County, 1977-80; bd. dirs. N.J. Math. Coalition; U.S. del. 1st U.S./Russian Meeting for Math. Educators. Recipient Outstanding Secondary Educator Am. award U.S. Sec. Edn., 1973, award Mfg. Chemists Assn., 1975, recognition award Gov. State of N.J., 1988, Presdl. award for excellence in math. and sci. teaching, 1989, Sigma Xi award of encouraging rsch. at pre-coll. level, award parents Assn., 2001; named to Hall of Fame Hudson County Sci. Fair, 2001. Mem. Am. Chem. Soc. (chmn. Hudson-Bergen sect. 1980-82, sec. N.Y. sect. 1994—, reviewer for Chem. Edn. Jour., bd. dirs. Home PC Mag., Nicol award 1975, Outstanding Achievement award New Eng. region 1976), St. Peter's Coll. Alumni Assn. (v.p. 1982-88, treas.), Nat. Coun. Tchrs. Math (reviewer). Office: Union Hill High Sch 3808 Hudson Ave Union City NJ 07087-6020 E-mail: nmakar@union-city.k12.nj.us.

MAKAROV, YURI VIKTOROVICH, electrical engineering educator, researcher; b. Samarkand, Uzbekistan, USSR, May 22, 1956; came to U.S., 1997; s. Viktor Fedorovich and Zoya Grigorievna (Shishko) M.; m. Yulia Anatolievna Yulusova, May 7, 1976 (div. Dec. 1993); 1 child, Makarova Anna; m. Tamara Sergeevna Sotnikova, June 20, 1996. PhD in Elec. Engring., Leningrad (Russia) Poly. Inst., 1984. Sr. rsch. fellow Leningrad Poly. Inst., 1986-87, lectr., 1987-90; assoc. prof. St. Petersburg Tech. U., 1990-97; rsch. assoc. U. Newcastle, Australia, 1993-95; rsch. assoc., sr. rsch. assoc. U. Sydney, N.S.W., Australia, 1995-97; sr. rsch. assoc. Howard U., Washington, 1997-98; sr. engr. So. Co. Svcs., Inc., Birmingham, Ala., 1998—2001, Calif. ISO, Folsom, 2001—. Co-author: Methods for Stability Margin Computations in Complicated Power Systems, 1988, Equivalencing of Complicated Power Systems in Control Problems, 1989, Fast Methods for Power System Load Flow Computation, 1990. Mem. IEEE (sr.). Russian Orthodox. Avocations: walking, reading, cooking. Home: 250 McAdoo Dr Apt 1311 Folsom CA 95630 Office: Calif ISO 151 Blue Ravine Rd Folsom CA 95630 E-mail: ymakarov@caiso.com., yuri_makarov@hotmail.com.

MAKARUK, HANNA EWA, theoretical physicist; b. Warsaw, Poland; d. Leszek Henryk and Halina (Wojnowska) M.; m. Robert Michal Owczarek. MSc, U. Warsaw, 1989; PhD summa cum laude, Polish Acad. Scis., 1994. Rsch. asst. Polish Acad. of Scis. Inst. of Fundamental Technol. Rsch., Warsaw, 1989-94, assoc. prof., 1994—; postdoctoral fellow Los Alamos Nat. Lab., 1996-98, tech. staff mem., 1999—. Lecturing prof. Polish Acad. of Scis., 1995-96. Referee Classical and Quantum Gravity, Jour. of Physics, Jour. of Tech. Physics, Reports on Math. Physics; reviewer Math. Revs.; contbr. articles to profl. jours. Fellowship Kosciuszko Found., N.Y.C., 1996, Japanese Soc. for the Promotion of Sci., 1995; rsch. grant Polish State Com. for Sci., Warsaw, 1995. Mem.: IEEE Computer Soc., IEEE, Inst. of Physics U.K., Am. Math. Soc., Polish Phys. Soc., Soc. for Indsl. and Applied Math., Polish Soc. for Applied Electromagnetics, Internat. Soc. for Interaction between Math. and Mechanics. Roman Catholic. Achievements include research in the description of conductivity in conducting polymers by multidimensional Dirac equation, spinor structure methods; new algebraic methods in strongly nonlinear problems and field theory; math. methods in theory of neural networks. Office: Los Alamos Nat Lab E-ET M 319 Los Alamos NM 87545-0001

MAKARY, ADEL ZAKI, hematologist; b. July 26, 1937; MB BCh, Cairo U., 1960. Straight med. intern Balt. City Hosps./Johns Hopkins U., 1971-72, asst. resident in medicine, 1972-73, fellow in hematology, 1973-74; chief sect. hematology Geisinger Med. Ctr., Danville, pa., 1986-99; clin. prof. medicine Jefferson Med. Coll., Phila., 1989—. Fellow in hematology Baltimore City Hosps., Johns Hopkins U., 1973—74. Contbr. numerous articles to profl. publs. Fellow ACP; mem. Ea. Coop. Oncology Group. Office: Geisinger Med Ctr 100 N Academy Ave Danville PA 17822-2001

MAKAU, JOHN, artist; b. Amsterdam, Jan. 27, 1927; s. Victor and Elisabeth (van Gyzelen) M.; m. Corry Saakes, 1962 (div. 1967); children: Desiree, Sandra, Petra; m. Lydia Catharina Amman, Apr. 1977. Owner Lyra Art Gallery & Studio, Sarasota, Fla., 1977—. Home: 5216 Creekside Trail Sarasota FL 34243

MAKEL, DENNIS MICHAEL, lawyer; b. Waynesburg, Pa., Mar. 3, 1956; s. John Joseph and Lucille Eleanor (Buday) M.; m. Donna Annette Martin, Oct. 2, 1992; children: Lea Celene Bentz, Dennae Leanne. BA, Washington and Jefferson Coll., 1978; JD, Duquesne U., 1982. Bar: Pa. 1984, U.S. Dist. Ct. (we. dist.) Pa. 1997, U.S. Ct. Appeals (3d cir.) 1997. Law clk. to J. David L. Gilmore Washington County Ct. Common Pleas, Washington, 1984-86, asst. dist. atty., 1986-93; sch. dist. and mcpl. solicitor Washington and Greene Counties, 1993—. Bd. dirs. Law Libr. Com., Washington County, 1986-90; trustee Fredericktown (Pa.) Area Pub. Libr., 1986-89, Bethlehem-Ctr. Edn. Found., Fredericktown, 1995-97; mem. Centerville Borough Bicentennial Com., Centerville, Pa., 1995-96. Mem. Pa. State Assn. Twp. Solicitors, Pa. Sch. Bd. Solicitors Assn., Pa. Borough Solicitors Assn., Masons, Scottish Rite. Democrat. Roman Catholic. Avocations: travel, coin collecting, military history reading. Home: 163 Clare Dr Washington PA 15301-6639 Office: PO Box 4193 Washington PA 15301-1117

MAKEPEACE, DARRYL LEE, consulting company executive; b. Pitts., Oct. 24, 1941; s. Thomas Henry Makepeace and Nevada Ruth (Wagener) Desin. BS in Indsl. Engring., Pa. State U., 1969; MBA, Pepperdine U., 1982. Dept. mgr. Procter & Gamble, Cin., 1969-72; plant mgr. CBS Mus. Instruments, Fullerton, Calif., 1972-76; dir. mfg. Frigid Coil/Wolf Range, Whittier, 1977-79; mgr. materials mgmt. Nat. Supply, Los Nietos, 1979-85; assoc. prof. mgmt. Calif. State U., Fullerton, 1982-86; mgr. mfg. Nat. Supply, Los Nietos, Calif., 1985-86; program mgr. Armco Cumberland Group, Middletown, Ohio, 1986, ptnr., cons. Mason, 1986-87; prin., owner Cumberland Group, Cin., 1988—; owner Phoenix Cons., Inc., 1991-96; owner, pres. D.L. Makepeace & Assocs., Poway, Calif., 1991—. Assoc. prof. mgmt. Wright State U., Dayton, Ohio, 1987-88, Miami U., Oxford, Ohio, 1988-89; bd. dirs. rlogic, Inc. Author: The System, American Iron and Steel Institute, Steel Body Panel Performance Characteristics, 1991; contbr. articles to profl. jours. Served with U.S. Army, 1960-61. Named to Honorable Order of Ky. Cols. Mem. Am. Prodn. and Inventory Control Soc., Inst. Indsl. Engrs., Alpha Pi Mu, Tau Beta Pi, Sigma Tau. Avocations: reading, chess, traveling. E-mail: DARRYLMAKEPEACE@ad.com.

MAKEPEACE, MARY LOU, mayor; 2 children. BA in Journalism, U. N.D.; MPA, U. Colo., Colorado Springs. Tchr. Am. Sch., Tananarive, Madagascar; asst. to Def. Attaché Am. Embassy, Prague, Czechoslavakia; adult edn. officer Ramstein AFB, Germany; case worker, adminstr. El Paso County Dept. Social Svcs., 1974-82; exec. dir. Cmty. Coun. Pikes Peak Region, 1982-84; dist. 1 rep. City Colorado Springs, 1985-97, vice mayor, 1997, mayor, 1997—. Exofficio mem. Econ. Devel. Coun. Bd. Dirs.; chair Econ. Devel. Com., Task Force City Svcs. to Srs., urban affairs com. Pikes Peak Area Coun. Govts.; apptd. Colo. Space Adv. Coun.; adj. prof. U. Colo.; ex-dir. leadership Pikes Peak Mem. steering com. Imagination Celebration; sr. advisor Palmer Found., Pikes Peak Partnership; mem. Nat. League Cities Leadership Tng. Coun.; past mem. Colo. Mcpl. League Exec. Bd., 1st United Meth. Ch. Gates Found. fellow, 1992; recipient Svc. Mankind award Centennial Sertoma Club, 1985, Mary Jean Larson Cmty. Svc. award Girl Scouts Wagon Wheel Coun., 2002, Spence Vanderlin Pub. Ofcl. award Am. Pub. Power Assn., 2002; named Super Woman Women's Health Ctr., 1988, Best City Councilmem. Springs Mag., 1991; honored Women in Your Life dinner Women's Found. Colo., 2002. Mem. Am. Soc. Pub. Adminstrn., Pi Alpha Alpha. Office: City Colo Springs Ste 300 107 N Nevada Ave Colorado Springs CO 80903-1898

MAKER, JANET ANNE, author, lecturer; b. Woburn, Mass., Feb. 13, 1942; d. George Walter and Margaret Anna (Kopasz); children: Thomas Walter, Jane McKinley. BA, UCLA, 1963; MS, Columbia U., 1967; PhD, U. So. Calif., 1978. Prof. L.A. Trade Tech. Coll., 1991—. Author: Get It All Together, 1979, Interpretive Reading Comprehension, 1984, Keys to a Powerful Vocabulary, Level I, 1981, 88, 94, Level II, 1983, 90, 94, Keys to College Success, 1980, 85, 90, 98, College Reading, Book 1, 1984, 88, 91, 96, 00, Book 2, 1982, 86, 89, 92, 96, 00, Book 3, 1985, Academic Reading with Active Critical Thinking, 1995. Avocation: blues music. Home and Office: 925 Malcolm Ave Los Angeles CA 90024-3113 E-mail: jamaker2001@hotmail.com., makerja@trade.laccd.edu.

MAKHADMI, JAMIL ABDULLAH, academic director; b. Makkah, Saudi Arabia, Oct. 8, 1956; s. Abdullah A. Makhadmi and Khadijah A. Faiead; m. Tracey J. Murphy, May. 11, 1985; children: Mohammed, Mashael, Ibrahim, Sulman, Khadijah. AS in Aerospace Engring., Pima C.C., Tucson, 1982; BS in Mech. Engring., U. Miami, 1986; MS in Mech. Engring., San Jose State U., 1987; PhD in Mech. Engring., U. Leeds (Eng.), 1995. Maintenance engr. Petromin Mobile Refinery, Pemr-Ef, Yanbu Al, Saudi Arabia, 1988-89; maintenance engr. internat. airport project Ministry Def. and Aviation, Jeddah, Saudi Arabia, 1989-90; asst. prof. dept. mech. engring. Umm Al-Qura U., Makkah, Saudi Arabia, 1990-99, chmn. mech. engring. dept., 1990-99, dir. registration com. 5th Saudi Engring. Conf., 1998, dir. acad. suprs. and registration dept. students; grad. student advisor, cons. Saudi Arabia Cutlural Attache, Washington, 2000—. Contbr. articles to profl. jours. Home: PO Box 15898 Jeddah Saudi Arabia 34470 Office: Umm Al-Qura U Mech Engring PO Box 715 Makkah Saudi Arabia E-mail: makhadmi@yahoo.com.

MAKHIJA, MOHAN, nuclear medicine physician; b. Bombay, Oct. 1, 1941; came to U.S., 1969; m. Arlene Zambito, Nov. 11, 1978. MD, Bombay U., 1965. Diplomate Am. Bd. Nuclear Medicine, Am. Bd. Radiology; cert. spl. competence in nuclear radiology. Resident in radiology Morristown (N.J.) Meml. Hosp., 1972—75; resident in nuclear medicine Yale-New Haven Hosp., 1975—75; fellow Yale U. Sch. Medicine, New Haven, 1976—77; jr. attending physician Helene Fuld Med. Ctr., Trenton, NJ, 1977—78; acting dir. dept. nuclear medicine Monmouth Med. Ctr., Long Branch, N.J., 1978, dir. nuclear medicine sect. NJ, 1979—, asst. attending radiology, 1978—80, assoc. attending radiology, 1980—83, attending radiologist, 1983—2000, St. Peter's U. Hosp., New Brunswick, 2001—, Robert Wood Johnson Univ. Hosp., New Brunswick, 2001—. Sr. instr. Hahneman U., Phila., 1978-80, clin. asst. prof., 1980-83, clin. assoc. prof., 1983-91, clin. prof., 1991-94, clin. prof. radiologic scis. Med. Coll. Pa. and Hahnemann U., 1994-2000; clin. prof. radiology U. Medicine and Dentistry NJ-Robert Wood Johnson Med. Sch., 2002—; radiol. cons. to N.J. State Bd. Med. Examiners., 1994. Contbr. articles to profl. jours. Fellow: ACP (spkr. ho. of dels. 1992—93), Am. Coll. Radiology, Am. Coll. Nuclear Phsyicians; mem.: Assn. Med. Specialties N.J. (sec. 2001—02, pres.-elect 2002—), Soc. Nuclear Medicine (bd. govs. Gt. N.Y. chpt. 1992—98), Indo-Am. Soc. Nuclear Medicine (pres. 1992—92), Radio Soc. N.J. (chmn. nuclear medicine 1988—94, treas. 1994—95, sec. 1995—96, v.p. 1996—97, pres.-elect 1997—98, pres. 1998—99, chmn. nominting com. 2001—02, chmn. fellowship com. 2002—), Monmouth County Med. Soc. (pres. 1991—92). Home: 5 High Ridge Rd Ocean NJ 07712-3460 Office: St Peter's U Hosp 254 Easton Ave New Brunswick NJ 08901

MAKHOV, ALEXANDER MIKHAILOVICH, medical educator, molecular biology researcher; b. Kaduy, Vologda, Russia, Sept. 24, 1951; came to U.S., 1991; s. Mikhail Nikolaevich and Alexandra Ivanovna M.; m. Natalia Nikolaevna, Dec. 21, 1996; 1 child, Nikolai A. BS, Polytech. Inst., St. Petersburg, Russia, 1976; PhD, Inst. Virology, Moscow, 1983. Engr. Inst. of Electronics, Moscow, 1976-79; rsch. scientist Inst. Virology, 1984-86, sr. rsch. scientist, 1987-90; visitor scientist NIH, Bethesda, Md., 1991-92; postdoctoral fellow U. N.C., Chapel Hill, 1993-96, rsch. assoc., 1997—99, asst. prof., 2000—. Contbr. articles to profl. jours.; patentee in field. Grantee Com. of Molecular Virology, 1990, Fogarty Internat. Ctr., 1991, Com. on Molecular Virology, 1993, Internat. Sci. Found., 1993. Mem. Russian Biochem. Soc., Microscopic Soc. of Am., Am. Soc. for Microbiology, Coun. for Molecular Virology. Avocations: classical music, tennis, traveling. E-mail: makhov@med.unc.edu.

MAKHZOUMI, ZIAD, management consultant, consultant; b. Beirut, Jan. 20, 1955; s. Mustapha and Aicha (Zeidan) M.; m. Zeina Takieddine; children: Hala, Tarek. BS in Engring., U. Manchester, 1978, MBA, 1981. Assoc. Booz Allen & Hamilton, N.Y.C., 1981-85; founder, dir. City of London Investment Group PLC, London, 1987—2000; sr. v.p. Future Pipe Industries BV, 1987—2000; master practitioner Neuro-Linguistic Programming. Contbr. Am.-Arab Affairs Council, Washington, 1987. Moslem. Avocations: marathon running, tennis, music. Office: Bus Resources Cons Ltd 58 Grosvenor St London W1K 3JB England

MAKI, ATSUSHI, economics educator; b. Kanagawa, Japan, Jan. 14, 1948; s. Sadao and Eiko (Yamaguchi) M.; m. Michie Yabu, Feb. 28, 1975; children: Chiori, Hisashi. BA, Keio U., 1971, MA, 1973, PhD, 1993. Asst. prof. Keio U., Tokyo, 1973-79, assoc. prof., 1979-87, prof., 1987—. Guest rsch. officer Ministry Posts and Telecom., 1988-90; vis. scholar Harvard U., Cambridge, Mass., 1982-84, 2001; vis. prof. Osaka (Japan) U., 1989, Ecole Superieure des Scis. Econs. et Cmmls., France, 1994; vis. fellow Australian Nat. U., Canberra, 1990, Massey U., New Zealand, 1991, U. Western Australia, Perth, 1993, Victoria U., Wellington, New Zealand, 1997, Bur. Labor Stats., Washington, 2001. Author: Consumer Preferences and Measurement of Demand, 1983, Japanese Consumer Behavior, 1998, Applied Econometrics, 2001. Recipient award Japan Found., 1996; Abe fellow SSRC, 2001; Ministry of Edn. grant-in-aid, 1997-99. Mem. Am. Econ. Assn., Econometric Soc., Japanese Econ. Assn., Japan Assn. Stats., Japan Soc. Household Econs., Royal Econ. Soc. Home: 107-8 Terao Kawagoe-shi Saitama 350-1141 Japan Office: Keio U 2-15-45 Mita Minato-ku Tokyo 108-8345 Japan E-mail: maki@fbc.keio.ac.jp.

MAKI, DANIEL DAWSON, radiologist, researcher; b. Atlanta, Jan. 27, 1970; s. Dennis G. Maki and Gail D. Dawson. MD, U. Minn., 1996. Cert. bd. cert. diagnostic radiology. Radiologist, rschr. U. Pa., Phila., 1996—2000; attending radiologist Scottsdale (Ariz.) Meml. Hosps., 2000—. Recipient Contrast Rsch. award, Soc. of CT & MRI, 1998. Mem.: Am. Roentgen Ray Soc. (life), Am. Coll. of Radiology (life), Radiologic Soc. N.Am. (life Rsch. award 1998, Roentgen Rsch. Fellow award 2000). Avocations: aviation, scuba diving, volleyball. Office: Scottsdale Med Imaging PO Box 1573 Scottsdale AZ 85252 Business E-Mail: cactusrad@hotmail.com.

MAKI, DENNIS G. medical educator, researcher, clinician; b. River Falls, Wis., May 8, 1940; m. Gail Dawson, 1962; children: Kimberly, Sarah, Daniel. BS in Physics with honors, U. Wis., 1962, MS in Physics, 1964, MD, 1967. Diplomate Am. Bd. Internal Medicine, Am. Bd. Infectious Diseases, Am. Bd. Critical Care Medicine. Physicist, computer programmer Lawrence Radiation Lab., AEC, Livermore, Calif., 1962; intern, asst. resident Harvard Med. unit Boston City Hosp., 1967-69, chief resident, 1972-73; with Hosp. Infections sect. Ctrs. for Disease Control, USPHS, Atlanta, 1969-71; acting chief nat. nosocomial infections study Ctr. for Disease Control, USPHS, 1970-71; sr. resident dept. medicine Mass. Gen. Hosp., 1971-72, clin. and research fellow infectious disease unit, 1973-74; asst. prof. medicine U. Wis., Madison, 1974-78, assoc. prof., 1978-82, prof., 1982—; hosp. epidemiologist, U. Wis. Hosp. and Clinic, 1974—; Ovid O. Meyer chair in medicine U. Wis., 1975—, head sec. infectious diseases, 1979—, attending physician Ctr. for Trauma and Life Support, 1976—. Clinician, rschr., educator in field; mem. program com. Intersci. Conf. on Antimicrobial Agts. and Chemotherapy, 1987-94; mem. Am. Bd. Critical Care Medicine, 1989-95. Sr. assoc. editor Infection Control and Hosp. Epidemiology, 1979-93; mem. editl. bd. Jour. Lab. and Clin. Investigation, 1980-86, Jour. Critical Care, 1985-96, Jour. Infectious Diseases, 1988-90, Critical Care Medicine, 1989-94, 97—; contbr. articles to med. jours. Recipient 1st award for disting. rsch. in Antibiotic Rev., 1980, Internat. CIPI award, 1994, SHEA lectr., 1999, numerous tchg. awards and hon. lectrs. Master ACP; fellow Infectious Diseases Soc. Am. (coun. 1993-96), Am. Acad. Microbiology, Soc. for Critical Care Medicine, Surg. Infection Soc.; mem. Soc. Hosp. Epidemiologists Am. (pres. 1990), Ctrl. Soc. for Clin. Rsch., Am. Soc. Microbiology, Am. Fedn. Clin. Rsch., Alpha Omega Alpha (nat. bd. dirs. 1983-89). Office: U Wis Hosp and Clinics H4/574 Madison WI 53792 Fax: 608-231-3896. E-mail: dgmaki@facstaff.wisc.edu.

MAKI, HOPE MARIE, artist, sculptor, illustrator, poet, educator; b. St. Joseph, Mo., Jan. 14, 1938; d. William Edward Duncan and Myrle Marie Howard; 3 children. Host TV art show Channel 6, Fort Walton Beach, Fla.; owner art sch., gallery; art tchr., 1957—. Exhibited in shows at Arts-Inter-Salon Int des Sekneurs de L'Art, Chateauneuf du Pape, France, 1994, Salon Int des Seigneurs de L'Art, Palais des Congres Marseille, 1994, Mountserrat Gallery, N.Y.; represented in permanent pvt. and pub. collections; created art for the blind, 1963—; Author and illustrator: Trader Joni His Life, 2001. Named One of Best New Poets Am. Poetry Assn., 1987, 88, 89; recipient Award of Poetic Achievement, Amherst Soc., recognition of outstanding achievements in art edn. Cox Comm., 2000; poem placed in spl. collection Statue of Liberty Nat. Monument, 1992. Mem. Nat. Mus. of Women in the Arts. Avocation: poetry. Home: 3985 Langley Ave Pensacola FL 32504-8371

MAKI, KAZUMI, physicist, educator; b. Takamatsu, Japan, Jan. 27, 1936; s. Toshio and Hideko M.; m. Masako Tanaka, Sept. 21, 1969. BS, Kyoto U., 1959, PhD, 1964. Research asso. Inst. for Math. Scis., Kyoto U., 1964; research asso. Fermi Inst., U. Chgo., 1964-65; asst. prof. physics U. Calif., San Diego, 1965-67; prof. Tohoku U., Sendai, Japan, 1967-74; vis. prof. Universite Paris-Sud, Orsay, France, 1969-70; prof. physics U. So. Calif., Los Angeles, 1974—. Vis. prof. Inst. Laue-Langevin, U. Paris-Sud, France, 1979-80, Max Planck Inst. fur Festkorper Forschung, Stuttgart, Germany, 1986-87, U. Paris-7, 1990, Hokkaido U., Sapporo, Japan, 1993, Centre de Recherche sur Tres Basses Temperatures, Grenoble, France, 1993-94, Instituto de Ciencia de Materiales, Madrid, Spain, 1994, Max Planck Inst. Phys. Complex Sys., Dresden, Germany, 2001-02. Assoc. editor Jour. Low Temperature Physics, 1969-91; contbr. articles to profl. jours. Guggenheim fellow, 1979-80, Japan Soc. Promotion of Sci. fellow, 1993; Fulbright scholar, 1964-65; recipient Nishina prize, 1972, Alexander von Humboldt award, 1986-87. Fellow Japan Soc. Promotion of Sci., Am. Phys. Soc.; mem. AAAS, Phys. Soc. Japan. Office: U So Calif Dept Physics and Astronomy Los Angeles CA 90089-0484 E-mail: kmaki@usc.edu.

MAKIHARA, MINORU, diversified corporation executive; b. London, Jan. 12, 1930; BA, Harvard U., 1954. With Mitsubishi Corp., Tokyo, 1956-59, London, 1959-67, with Marine Products dept. Tokyo, 1967-70, dep. gen. mgr., 1976-80, gen. mgr. Marine Products dept., 1980-83, gen. mgr. mktg. and coordination dept., 1983-85, bd. dirs., 1986-88, mng. dir., 1988-90, sr. mng. dir., 1990-92, pres., chmn., 1992-98, 1998—; with, then gen. mgr. Mitsubishi Internat. Corp., Seattle, 1970-71, v.p., gen. mgr., 1980-83, gen. mgr. Washington, 1971-76, exec. v.p., gen. mgr., 1985-86, pres. N.Y.C., 1987-90, chmn., 1990-92; pres. Mitsubishi Corp., Tokyo, 1992—98, chmn., 1998—. Vice chmn. the Keidanren (Japan Fedn. of Econ. Orgns.); mem. exec. com. Trilateral Comm. (Japan, NAm., Europe); vice chmn. Japan U.S. Bus. Coun. Office: Mitsubishi Corp Office of the Chmn 6-3 Marunouchi 2-chome Chiyoda-ku Tokyo 100 8086 Japan Office Fax: +81-3-3210-8935.

MAKINEN, MARVIN WILLIAM, biophysicist, educator; b. Chassell, Mich., Aug. 19, 1939; s. William John and Milga Katarina (Myllyla) M.; m. Michele de Groot, July 30, 1966; children: Eric William, Stephen Matthew. AB, U. Pa., 1961; postgrad., Free U. Berlin, 1960-61; MD, U. Pa., 1968; DPhil, U. Oxford, Eng., 1976. Diplomate Am. Bd. Med. Examiners. Intern Columbia-Presbyn. Med. Ctr., N.Y.C., 1968-69; rsch. assoc. NIH, Bethesda, Md., 1969-71; vis. fellow U. Oxford, Eng., 1971-74; asst. prof. biophysics U. Chgo., 1974-80, assoc. prof., 1980-86, prof. biochemistry and molecular biology, 1986—, chmn. dept., 1988-93. Established investigator Am. Heart Assn., 1975-80; lectr. in field. Contbr. numerous articles to profl. jours. Sr. surgeon USPHS, 1969-71. John Simon Guggenheim fellow 1997-98, John E. Fogarty Sr. Internat. fellow, 1984-85, European Molecular Biology Orgn. sr. fellow, 1984-85, NIH spl. fellow, 1971-74, Berquist fellow Am. Scandinavian Found., 1970. Fellow Am. Inst. Chemists; mem. Am. Chem. Soc., Biophys. Soc., Am. Soc. Biochemistry and Molecular Biology, The Protein Soc., AAAS. Office: U Chgo Dept Biochemistry/Mol Biol 920 E 58th St Chicago IL 60637-5415 E-mail: makinen@uchicago.edu.

MAKINS, CHRISTOPHER JAMES, foreign policy institute administrator; b. Southampton, N.Y., July 23, 1942; s. Roger Mellor and Alice Brooks (Davis) M.; m. Wendy Whitney, July 26, 1975; 1 child, Marian Whitney. BA, Oxford U., Eng., 1963; MA, Oxford U., 1971. From 3rd to 1st sec. Her Majesty Diplomatic Svc., London, Paris, Washington, 1964-75; dep. dir. Trilateral Commn., N.Y.C., 1975-76; sr. assoc. Carnegie Endowment for Internat. Peace, Washington, 1977-79; sr. scientist, asst. v.p. Sci. Applications Internat. Corp., 1979-89; dir. internat. security programs Roosevelt Ctr. Am. Policy Studies, 1985-89; v.p., exec. v.p. Aspen Inst., 1989-97; pres. Atlantic Coun. U.S., 1999—. Sr. adviser German Marshall Fund U.S., Washington, 1997—99; mem. internat. adv. bd. ICL Ltd., London, 1999—2000; bd. dirs. New Star Enhanced Income Trust, 2001—. Contbr. articles to profl. jours. Mem. coun. Non-Profit Sector Rsch. Fund, Washington, 1997—2001; bd. dirs. Washington Concert Opera, 1987—, chmn., 1993—97; trustee The Phillips Collection, Washington, 1991—98, Greater Washington Ednl. Telecomms. Assn., 1980—88. Fellow All Souls Coll., Oxford, 1963-70; mem. Coun. Fgn. Rels., Internat. Inst. Strategic Studies, Pratts Club, Met. Club. Avocations: tennis, squash, boating, opera. Home: 3034 P St NW Washington DC 20007-3052 Office: 1024 29th St NW Washington DC 20007-3831

MÄKITALO, ASKO, engineer; b. Loimaa, Finland, Mar. 23, 1962; s. Erkki and Airi (Nakkila) M. MS, Tampere (Finland) U. Tech., 1987. CAM engr. Valmet Paper Machinery Oy, Jyväskylä, Finland, 1986-88; sales rep. cadcam sys. Wärtsilä Info. Technologies, Turku, Finland, 1988-90; sr. engr. Raisio Group Raisio (Finland) Engring., Finland, 1990-95; specialist Elomatic Oy, Raisio, 1995—. Mem. IEEE, ASM.

MAKKAY, ALBERT, broadcast executive; b. Carteret, N.J., Apr. 13, 1934; s. John E., and Helen (Fetyko) M.; Maureen Monaghan, Oct. 29, 1962; children: Allison, Albert, Colleen. BS in Mktg., U. Ariz., 1961. Gen. sales mgr. Sta. KTAN, Tucson, 1961-66; gen. mgr. Sta. WPST, Trenton, 1966-70; v.p. gen. mgr. Sta. WLKW, Providence, 1970-75; v.p., gen. mgr. Sta. WEZE, Boston, 1975-79; owner Sta. WKPE, Orleans, Mass., 1979-83, Sta. WKFM, Syracuse, N.Y., 1983-86, Stas. WPXC, WRZE, WCIB, Hyannis, Mass., 1986—; pres. Makkay Group Broadcasting. Dep. sheriff (hon.) Barnstable County Sheriff's Office. Sgt. U.S. Army, 1953-56. Mem. KC, Nat. Assn. Broadcasters, New Eng. Broadcasters Assn., Mass. Broadcasters Assn., Korean Vets. Assn., Korean War Vets., Nam Vets of Cape Cod (Mass.) Assn. (hon.), Otis (mem. adv. bd.), Knights Columbus. Roman Catholic. Avocations: travel, golf, swimming. Home: 306 Captain Lijahs Rd Centerville MA 02632-1614 Office: 154 Barnstable Rd Hyannis MA 02601-2930 E-mail: capemo@aol.com.

MAKKAY, MAUREEN ANN, broadcast executive; b. Chgo. d. John Paul and Bernice Ann (Williams) Monaghan; m. Albert Makkay, Oct. 20, 1962; children: Allison, Albert Jr., Colleen. BA, U. R.I., 1974. Cert. secondary sch. tchr., Mass. Adminstr. Ednl. Records Bur., Wellesley, Mass., 1979-81; local sales mgr. Sta. WKZE, Orleans, 1981-83; nat. sales mgr. Sta. WKFM, Syracuse, N.Y., 1983-85; pres. Sta. WPXC-FM, Hyannis, Mass., 1987—; v.p. Sta. WRZE, Nantucket, Sta. WCIB-FM, Falmouth. Corporator Cape Code Five Cents Savings Bank, 1998—. Pres. Cape and Islands unit Am. Cancer Soc., 1988-91, bd. dirs., 1989-95; mem. pers. bd. Town of Barnstable, Mass., 1989-94, chmn., 1990-91; bd. dirs. Cape Cod Alcoholism Intervention and Rehab., Inc., 1995—. Mem. Bus. and Profl. Women Cape Cod (bd. dirs. 1989—), Am. Women in Radio and TV, Nat. Assn. Braodcasters. Office: Sta WPXC-FM Radio 154 Barnstable Rd Hyannis MA 02601-2930

MAKOUS, BRUCE B. fundraiser; b. Phila., June 24, 1953; s. Norman and Dorothy Makous; m. Barbara H. Makous, Oct. 17, 1981; children: Dyani, Kacie. BA in Lit., Oberlin Coll., 1976; MA in Cultural Adminstrn., NYU, 1986. CLU. Gen. mgr. 78th Street Theatre Lab., N.Y.C., 1979-81; comm. cons. Price Waterhouse Nat. Offices, 1981-84; dir. info. svcs. Theatre Comm. Group, 1984-86; mng. dir. Attic Theatre, Detroit, 1986-89, Players Theatre Columbus, Ohio, 1989-90; founder, pres. Makous Mktg. & Fundraising, Phila., 1990-93; dir. devel. Am. Coll., Bryn Mawr, 1993-98, dir. planned giving, 1998-99; dir. major and planned gifts Drexel U., Phila., 1999-2000, asst. v.p. for major and planned gifts, 2000—01; maj. gifts and planned giving officer Am. Assn. for Cancer Rsch., 2001—. Lectr. Wayne State U., Detroit, 1998-89, Assn. Fundraising Profls.-Villanova (Pa.) U., 1998—. Co-prodr. Back in the World, 1987 (award for best play outside N.Y. Nat. Theatre Critics Assn. 1987); assoc. editor Boulevard lit. mag., 1991—. Grad. Leadership, Inc. Class of 1992, 1991-92; co-chmn. bd. dirs. Prints in Progress, Phila., 1993-95. Mgmt. for Arts Rev. scholar NYU, 1983-86. Mem. Assn. Fundraising Profls. (cert., pres. Greater Phila. chpt. 2001-02), Nat. Com. on Planned Giving. Democrat. Roman Catholic. Avocation: writing novels. Home: 7905 Cadillac Ln Philadelphia PA 19128 Office: Am Assn Cancer Rsch Ste 826 150 S Independence Hall W Philadelphia PA 19106-3483 Fax: 215-895-4966. E-mail: makous@aacr.org., bmakous@aol.com.

MAKOUS, NORMAN, internist, cardiologist, educator; b. Chgo., July 22, 1924; s. Lawrence Alonzo and Ruth (Luehring) M.; m. Dorothy Murl Bowlin, Sept. 25, 1948; children: David, Bruce, Catherine, Monte, Joseph, Martin, John, Virginia, Dorothy, Margaret. BS, U. Wis., 1945, MD, 1947. Diplomate in internal medicine and cardiovascular diseases Am. Bd. Internal Medicine. Mixed intern Rsch. Hosp., Kansas City, Mo., 1947-48, resident in internal medicine, 1948-50; fellow in cardiovasc. disease U. Vt., Burlington, 1950-51; resident in internal medicine U.S. Naval Hosp., Camp Lejeune, N.C., 1951-52; dir. cardiac catheterization lab. Kansas City, Mo., 1955-56; fellow in cardiovasc. disease Pa. Hosp., Phila., 1953-54, assoc. cardiologist, assoc. physician to hosp., 1960-72, cardiologist, physician to hosp., 1972-2000, cons., 2000—01; pvt. practice Kansas City and Independence, Mo., 1956-59, Phila., 1959-2001; assoc. in medicine U. Pa., 1959-71, asst. prof. clin. medicine, 1971-74, clin. asst. prof. medicine, 1974—, Thomas Jefferson U., Phila., 1994—. Physician advisor Keystone Profl. Rev. Orgn., 1986-93; mem. cons. Pa. Bur. Disability Determination, 1981-2001; cardiology cons. Phila. City Solicitor's Office, 1986-; mem. peer rev. panel Jour. Cardiopulmonary Rehab., 1990; mem. adv. group Greater Delaware Valley Regional Med. Program, 1971-75. Contbr. articles to med. jours., chpts. to books. Founder, acting chmn. Southeastern Pa. Regional High Blood Pressure Control Program, 1978-80; mem. interim bd. Health Sys. Agy. Southeastern Pa., 1975-77, chmn. adv. coun., 1979-80; trustee Edna B. Kynett Meml. Found., Phila., 1963—, v.p., 1994-96, pres., 1997—; pres. Home and Sch. Assn., Our Lady of Lourdes Parish, Phila., 1972-73, mem. parish pastoral coun., 1991-95, co-chmn., 1993-95; trustee Vis. Nurse Assn. Greater Phila., 1997-2000. Lt. USNR, 1943-45, 50-52, Res., 1952-62. Recipient Legion of Honor, Chapel of Four Chaplains, 1980, Spl. Achievement award Southeastern Pa. Regional High Blood Pressure Control Program. Fellow ACP, Am. Coll. Cardiology, Am. Soc. Internal Medicine; mem. AMA, Pa. Med. Soc. (chmn. profl. liability ins. appeals com. 1986-91), Phila. County Med. Soc. (standing com. Med. Econs., 1979-86, pres. Center City br. 1980-81, sec. 1990-91, chmn. membership and orgn. com. 1991-2000, Cristol award 1994), Am. Heart Assn. (fellow coun. clin. cardiology, pres. Southeastern Pa. affiliate 1988-89, bd. govs., program chmn. 1988-92, pres. Pa. affiliate 1981-82, Disting. Svc. award Pa. affiliate 1982, Disting. Achievement award Pa. affiliate, 1986, Disting. Achievement award Southeastern Pa. affiliate 1988, Vol. of Yr. award Southeastern Pa. affiliate 1988), Pa. Soc. Internal Medicine (pres. 1983-84). Avocations: tennis, cinematography. Office: 829 Spruce St Ste 304 Philadelphia PA 19107-5752 E-mail: drnmakous@aol.com.

MAKOUS, WALTER LEON, visual scientist, educator; s. Lawrence and Ruth Lorraine (Luehring) Makous; m. Marilyn Ann Carlson, Feb. 2, 1958 (div. 1981); children: Ann, James, Matthew; m. Joyce Brown Menconi, 1974 (div. 1981); m. Barbara Anne Duggins, Apr. 29, 1982. BS, U. Wis., 1958; M.Sc., Brown U., 1961, PhD, 1964. Mem. staff IBM, Yorktown Heights, N.Y., 1963-66; asst. prof. psychology U. Wash., 1966-69, lectr. in physiology and biophysics, 1966-69, assoc. prof. psychology, 1969-74, prof. psychology, 1974-79; prof. psychology, ophthalmology and visual sci. U. Rochester, 1979-95; prof. brain and cognitive sci., ophthalmology & visual sci., 1995—; dir. Ctr. for Visual Sci. U. Rochester, 1979-90. Northwest rep, charter mem steering comt West Coast Regional Consortium Univs in Neurosciences, 1976—79; mem coun on energy saving through more efficient lighting NAS-NRC, 1978—79, night vision coun, 1985—86; chmn ctr symp Univ Rochester, 1981—82; sensory processes panelist NSF, Washington, 1977—82, mem adv comt applied sci and research applicaitons policy, 1978—81; rev comt Presidential Young Investigator Award Program, 1984; vis scientist IBM

Research, 1970—71. Editor (consult ed): Sensory Processes, 1977—79, Jour of the Optical Soc Am, 1982—86; contbr. articles to profl jours. With USNR, 1953—55. Grantee, Nat Eye Inst, 1969—, NSF, 1959—62, 1981—82. Fellow: AAAS, Optical Soc Am (mem coord vision and physiological optics comt 1983—89, coord vision and med optics comt 1983—89, publs comt 1985—89, chmn fellows and hon mems comt 1986, ed vision and color 1982—86, feature ed applied vision 1989—90), Am Psychol Soc; mem.: Am Nat Standards Inst/Human Factor & Ergonomics Soc-100 (rev comt 1992—), Human Factors and Ergonomics, Psychonomic Soc, Soc Neuroscience, Asn Research in Vision and Ophthalmology (chmn sect psycho-physics 1977). Office: U Rochester Ctr for Visual Sci Rochester NY 14627 E-mail: walt@cvs.rochester.edu.

MAKOWSKI, EDGAR LEONARD, obstetrician and gynecologist; b. Milw., Oct. 27, 1927; s. Adam and Ernestine (Horn) M.; m. Patricia M. Nock, Nov. 1, 1952; children: Peter, James, Ann, Mary, Thomas, Paul. BS, Marquette U., 1951, MD, 1954. Intern Deaconess Hosp., Milw., 1954-55; resident in Ob/Gyn U. Minn., Mpls., 1955-59, asst. prof., 1959-66, asso. prof., 1966; asso. prof. Ob/Gyn U. Colo., Denver, 1966-69, prof., 1969-93, chmn. dept., 1976-88, prof. emeritus, 1993—. Contbr. articles to sci. jours., chpts. to books. Served with AUS, 1946-47. NIH spl. fellow in physiology Yale U., 1963 Mem. Am. Gynecol. and Obstet. Soc. (pres.), Am. Coll. Obstetricians and Gynecologists, Soc. Gynecol. Investigators, Central Assn. Obstetricians and Gynecologists, Colo. Soc. Ob/Gyn., Perinatal Research Soc. (pres.). Roman Catholic. Achievements include radioactive microsphere technique for determination of organ blood flow. E-mail: EdPat124@msn.com.

MAKRI, NANCY, chemistry educator; b. Athens, Greece, Sept. 5, 1962; came to the U.S., 1985; d. John and Vallie (Tsakona) M.; m. Martin Gruebele, July 9, 1992; children: Alexander Makris Gruebele, Valerie Gruebele Makri. BS, U. Athens, 1985; PhD, U. Calif., Berkeley, 1989. Jr. fellow Harvard U., Cambridge, Mass., 1989-91; from asst. prof. to assoc. prof. U. Ill., Urbana, 1992-99, prof., 1999—. Recipient Beckman Young Investigator award Arnold & Mabel Beckman Found., 1993, Ann. medal Internat. Acad. Quantum Molecular Sci., 1995, Camille Dreyfus Tchr.-Scholar award The Camille and Henry Dreyfus Found., 1997, Agnes Fay Morgan award Iota Sigma Pi, 1999, physics prize Bodossaki Found., 1999; named NSF Young Investigator, 1993; Packard fellow for sci. and engring. David and Lucile Packard Found., 1993, Sloan Rsch. fellow Alfred Sloan Found., 1994, Cottrell scholar Rsch. Corp., 1994; univ. scholar U. Ill., 1999. Fellow: AAAS, Am. Phys. Soc. Home: 2722 Valley Brook Dr Champaign IL 61822-7634 Office: U Ill Urbana Dept Chem 601 S Goodwin Ave Urbana IL 61801-3709 E-mail: nancy@makri.scs.uiuc.edu.

MAKRIDIS, ODYSSEUS, education educator, writer; b. Athens, Sept. 8, 1962; arrived in U.S., 1986; s. Konstantine and Styliani Makridis; m. Carol Crosby, Sept. 22, 1999. DLA, Anatolia Coll., Thessalonika, Greece, 1986; BA, Middlebury Coll., 1988; PhD, Brandeis U., 1999, postgrad., 2001. Tchg. fellow, lectr. Brandeis U., Waltham, Mass., 1996—2001; faculty Fairleigh-Dickinson U., Madison, NJ, 2002—. Lectr. Bentley Coll., Waltham, 1999—2000; tchg. fellow Kennedy Sch. Govt., Cambridge, Mass., 1999—2001; vis. faculty Hellenic Coll., Brookline, Mass., 2001; dissertation adv. Ignatius U., Staten Island, NY, 1998—; cons., tutor Greek Inst., Cambridge, 1998—. Mem.: Phi Beta Kappa. Greek Orthodox. Avocations: reading, walking, translating, soccer, bodybuilding. Office: Fairleigh-Dickinson Univ Dept Philosophy 285 Madison Ave Madison NJ 07940 E-mail: omakridis@aol.com.

MAKRIS, ANDREAS, composer; b. Salonica, Greece, Mar. 7, 1930; came to U.S., 1950, naturalized, 1962; s. Christos and Kallitza (Andreou) M.; m. Margaret Lubbe, June 12, 1959; children: Christos, Myron. Grad. with highest honors, Nat. Conservatory, Salonica, 1950; postgrad., Kansas City (Mo.) Conservatory, 1953, Mannes Coll. Music, 1956, Aspen Music Festival, 1956-57, Fontainbleau (France) Sch., 1958; pupil of Nadia Boulanger. Adv. to Maestro Rostropovich for new music, 1979-90. Compositions premiered and performed in U.S., Can., S.Am., Europe, Japan, USSR; composer-in-residence Nat. Symphony Orch., 1979-90; prin. works include Scherzo for Violins, 1966, Concerto for Strings, 1966, Aegean Festival, 1967, Anamnesis, 1970, Viola Concerto, 1970, Concertino for Trombone, 1970, Efthymia, 1972, Five Miniatures, 1972, Mediterranean Holiday, 1974, Fantasy and Dance for Saxaphone and Piano, 1974, Saxaphone and Concert Band or Saxaphone Strings and Harp, 1974, Chromatokinesis, 1978, In Memory, 1979, Variations and Song for Orchestra, 1979, Fanfare Alexander 1980, Fourth of July March, 1982, Violin Concerto, 1983, Nature-Life Symphonic Poem, 1983, Caprice "Tonatonal", 1986, Intrigues for Solo Clarinet and Wind Ensemble, 1987, Concertante for Violin, Cello, Clarinet, French Horn, Percussion and Orchestra, 1988, Sonata for Cello and Piano, 1989, Symphony to Youth for Full Orchestra, 1989, Trilogy for Orchestra, 1990, Polychornion Chorus and Orchestra, 1990, Procession Chorus and Brass Quintet, 1990, Intrigues for Solo Clarinet, Strings, Brass and Percussion, 1991, Concertino for Organ, Flute and Strings, 1992, A Symphony for Soprano and Strings, 1992, Woodwind Quintet, 1993, Decalog (ten songs for young students), 1995, Antithesis for Orch., 1995, J.F.K. Commemorative Fanfare for Strings and Snare Drum, 1995, Concerto for Violin and Strings, 1996, Introduction and Kalamatianos for solo trumpet, strings, snare and bass drums, 1997, Sonatina for Solo Violin, 1997, Sextet for Woodwind Quintet and Piano in 3 Movements, 1999, Concertino for Flute or Violin and Piano, 1999, Serenade for Voice and Violin, 2001; also works for violin, string quartets, voice quintets, duets and arrangements of Paganini, Bach, Corelli and Fiorillo. Recipient citation Greek Govt., 1980; Student Program grantee Phillips U., Enid, Okla., 1950, grantee Nat. Endowment Arts, 1967, grantee Martha Baird Rockefeller Fund, 1970, grantee Damrosh Found., 1958 Mem. ASCAP (ann. awards 1980-2000), Internat. Platform Assn. Greek Orthodox. Home: 11204 Oak Leaf Dr Silver Spring MD 20901-1313 Office: Nat Symphony Orch Kennedy Ctr Washington DC 20566-0001 *Two important elements have contributed tremendously to my composing: As a child I was in the midst of war in Greece, and, while all wars are terrible, it taught me both self-discipline and an appreciation for simplicity. Just being alive and able to compose makes me very happy. As a student I was not able to have a piano, the most valuable instrument for a composer. I learned to write with only a pencil and paper for full orchestra, and this liberated me both musically and practically.*

MAKRIS, CONSTANTINE JOHN, infosystems engineer; b. Chalkis, Greece, Nov. 16, 1927; s. John Constantine and Chryso M.; came to U.S., 1952, naturalized, 1960; radio engring. diploma Inst. Electronic Tech., Athens, Greece, 1951; BEE, N.Y. U., 1958, MEE, 1962; m. Helen Loukaides, 1956; children: John, Nicholas, Dorothy. Research scientist NYU, N.Y.C., 1958-62; product mgr. computer research and devel. Mergenthaler div. Eltra, Plainview, N.Y., 1962-69; mgr. advt. devel. Harris-Intertype, Watchung, N.J., 1969-73; pres. Orthodata Inc., Glen Cove, N.Y., 1973-75; sr. staff mem., project mgr. Network Analysis Corp., Gt. Neck, N.Y., 1976-78; sr. systems engr., asst. sec. Mfrs. Hanover Trust Co., N.Y.C., 1978-88; sr. communications planner networks and telecommunications Grumman Data Systems div. Grumman Corp., Bethpage, N.Y., 1988-92, comm. cons., Glen Cove, N.Y., 1993—; lectr., cons. Vice pres. High Elms Civic Assn., 1968-69, Ch. Council, 1976-77. Served with Greek Air Force, 1949-51. Mem. IEEE, Computer Soc., Communications Soc. Club: Krikos Inc. (v.p. bd. dirs. 1983-86, chmn. L.I. chpt. 1981-83). Contbr. articles to profl. orgns. Home and Office: 42 Old Tappan Rd Glen Cove NY 11542-1248

MAKSI, GREGORY EARL, engineering educator; b. Wilkes-Barre, Pa., May 9, 1939; s. Stephen Cedric and Laura Victoria (Pytell) M.; children: Sabrina, Jared, Joshua. BSME, Ga. Inst. Tech., 1961, MS in Indsl. Mgmt., 1964; PhD in Edn. Adminstrn., U. Miss., 1983. Registered profl. engr., Tenn. Mech. engr. Ellicott Machine Corp., Balt., 1961-62; project engr. Celanese Corp., Rock Hill, S.C., 1964-67; assoc. prof. State Tech. Inst., Memphis, 1967-71, prof., 1971-73, program chmn. of indsl. engring., 1973-90, dept. chmn. mech. engring./indsl. engring., 1990—. Cons. Tenn. Ednl. Alliance, Nashville, 1994—, U. Ark., Millington, Tenn., 1988, instr., 1988—; curriculum coord. Memphis City H.S., 1993—; quality-productivity adv., 1990—; CAD/CAM cons., 1995—. Hon. sheriff Shelby County Sheriff's Office, 1991; hon. state legis. Tenn. Ho. Reps., Nashville, 1992. Named Disting. Engr. Memphis Engrs. Coun., 1986, Outstanding Tech. Tchr. Am. Tech. Edn. Assn., 1998, Leadership Excellence award Nat. Inst. of Staff and Orgnl. Devel., 1997. Mem. Soc. Mfg. Engrs. (Outstanding Engr. 1998), Inst. of Indsl. Engrs., World Future Soc., Tenn. Profl. Engrs. Soc., Epsilon Pi Tau. Avocations: computers, tennis, racquetball, fishing. Office: State Tech Inst Memphis 5983 Macon Cv Memphis TN 38134-7642

MAKSIMENTSEV, MAKSYM GENNADIYOVYCH, economist, educator; b. Kiev, USSR, July 2, 1976; s. Gennadiy Oleksandrovych Maksimentsev and Svitlana Sergiyivna Maksimentseva. MA in Internat. Economy, T. Shevchenko Nat. U., Kiev, 1998, PhD in Internat. Economy, 2000; MA in Applied Econ., Northeastern U., 2002. Cert. translator, interpreter. Asst. prof. Inst. Internat. Rels. T. Shevchenko Nat. U., Kiev, 1998—; project mgr., office mgr. Ctr. European Studies T. Schevchenko Nat. U., 1998—. Co-author: World Economy, 2000 (Philip Morris Best Book in Economics awards 1999). Mem. Inst. Internat. Rels. Alumni Assn. Avocations: reading, tennis, soccer. Home: Apt 16 24 Lunacharskogo str. 02002 Kiev Ukraine Address: 36 Briggs Street Wollaston MA 02170 E-mail: maksiments@hotmail.com.

MAKTOUF, SAMIR, education company executive; b. Sousse, Tunisia, June 25, 1957; s. Salem Bechir and Douja (Zaabouri) M.; m. Raja Khabcheche, Apr. 3, 1995 (div. Feb. 1997); 1 child, Ameen. grad., pilot cert., Tunisian Air Force Acad. Pilot Tunisian Air Force, Bizerta, 1979-83; sales mgr. Sorena, Tunis, Tunisia, 1983-84; pilot Aeroclub Herault, Montpellier, France, 1984-86; asst. chief flight instr. Pro-flite, Vero Beach, Fla., 1986-89; pres., owner Fla. Pilot Sch. Inc., Fort Pierce, 1990—; tchr. Indian River Cmty. Coll., 1992—. Cons. aviation degree Palm Beach Cmty. Coll., 1997-99; cons. Training Piper Aircraft Corp., Pratt & Whitney and Sikorsky Aircraft; aviation safety counsellor, FAA, 1997—. Author: Radio Communication, 1989, Economic Growth of General Aviation in South Fla., 1989. Mem. Aircraft Owner & Pilot Assn., Nat. Assn. Flight Instr. Avocations: reading, boating, traveling. Office: Florida Pilot Sch Inc PO Box 258 Stuart FL 34995-0258 Home: PO Box 258 Stuart FL 34995-0258

MALA, THEODORE ANTHONY, physician, consultant; b. Santa Monica, Calif., Feb. 3, 1946; s. Ray and Galina (Liss) M.; children: Theodore S., Galina T.; 1 adopted child, Christine A. Lindholm. BA in Philosophy, DePaul U., 1972; MD, Autonomous U., Guadalajara, Mex., 1976; MPH, Harvard U., 1980. Spl. asst. for health affairs Alaska Fedn. Natives, Anchorage, 1977-78; chief health svcs. Alaska State Divsn. Corrections, 1978-79; assoc. prof., founder, dir. Inst. for Circumpolar Health Studies, U. Alaska, 1982-90; founder Siberian med. rsch. program U. Alaska, 1982, founder Magadan (USSR) med. rsch. program, 1988; commr. Health and Social Svcs. State of Alaska, Juneau, 1990-93; pres., CEO Ted Mala, Inc., Anchorage, 1993-97; pres., ptnr. Mexican-Siberian Trading Co., Monterrey, Mex., 1994-96; CEO, Confederated Tribes of Grand Ronde, Oreg., 1998-99; dir. tribal rels. Southcentral Found., Anchorage, 1999—, 2000—. Traditional healing dir. Southcentral Found., Anchorage, 2000—; Alaska rsch. and publs. com. Indian Health Svc., USPHS, 1987-90; advisor Nordic Com. Meeting, WHO, Greenland, 1985; mem. Internat. Organizing Com., Circumpolar Health Congress, Iceland, 1992-93; chmn. bd. govs. Alaska Psychiat. Inst., Anchorage, 1990-93; cabinet mem. Gov. Walter J. Hickel, Juneau, 1990-93; advisor humanitarian aid to Russian Far East U.S. Dept. State, 1992-96; cons. USAID on U.S.-Russian Health Programs, 1994; apptd. adv. com. Sec. of Health and Human Svc. on Minority Health for the U.S., 2000—. Past columnist Tundra Times; contbr. articles to profl. jours. Trustee United Way Anchorage, 1978-79; chmn. bd. trustees Alaska Native Coll., 1993-96. Recipient Gov.'s award, 1988, Outstanding Svc. award Alaska Commr. Health, 1979, Ministry of Health citation USSR Govt., 1989, Citation award Alaska State Legislature, 1989-90, 94, Commendation award State of Alaska, 1990, Alaska State Legislature, 1994, Honor Kempton Svc. to Humanity award, 1989, citation Med. Comty. of Magadan region, USSR, 1989; Nat. Indian fellow U.S. Dept. Edn., 1979. Mem. Assn. Am. Indian Physicians (pres.), N.Y. Acad. Scis., Internat. Union for Circumpolar Health (permanent sec.-gen. 1987-90, organizing com. 8th Internat. Congress on Circumpolar Health 1987-90), Russian Acad. Polar Medicine (elected). Avocations: cross-country skiing, hiking, photography, travel. E-mail: tmala@post.harvard.edu. *Personal philosophy: Progress in the North will come only when circumpolar countries put aside their geopolitical thinking and work together as one northern family.*

MALACH, MONTE, physician; b. Jersey City, Aug. 15, 1926; s. Charles and Yetta (Pascher) M.; m. Ann Elaine Glazer, June 15, 1952 (dec. June 1989); children: Barbara Sandra, Cathie Tara, Matthew David; m. Barbara Meryl Lipstein, Dec. 24, 1994; stepchildren: Heather Ilene, Jennifer Beth, Matthew Howard. BA, MD, U. Mich., 1949. Diplomate Am. Bd. Internal Medicine, Nat. Bd. Med. Examiners. Intern Beth Israel Hosp., Boston, 1949-50, resident, 1950-51, chief resident, 1951-52, Kings County Hosp., Bklyn., 1954-55; practice medicine specializing in internal medicine and cardiology, 1955-97; dir. CCU Bklyn. Hosp., 1965-91, dir. emeritus CCU, 1991—; med. dir., clin. coord. Medicare IPRO Downstate N.Y., 1990—. Pres. profl. staff Bklyn. Hosp., 1966-69, chmn. med. bd., 1971-72; attending staff Caledonian Hosp., pres. profl. staff, 1984-85; pres. profl. staff Bklyn. Hosp.-Caledonian Hosp., 1987-89, chmn. med. bd., 1988-89; cons. Kings County Hosp.; tchg. fellow Tufts U. Med. Sch., 1951-52; instr. medicine Downstate Med. Ctr., Bklyn., 1955-59, clin. asst. prof. medicine, 1959-68, clin. assoc. prof., 1969-76, clin. prof., 1976—; clin. prof. medicine NYU Med. Ctr., 1994—; bd. dirs. Bay St. Landing One Owners Corp., 1985-87; v.p. Ocean View Condos, 1989-90, pres., 1990-95; med. dir. IPRO Medicare Rev., N.Y. State, 1990—, IPRO N.Y. State Peer Rev., 1990—. Kings County committeeman Democratic Party, 1964, 65. Served with USNR, 1944-46, to 1st lt. M.C. U.S. Army, 1952-54. Recipient 1st Prize for Crisis Mgmt. Habitat Mag., 1987. Fellow Am. Coll. Chest Physicians, ACP (master, Laureate award 2000), Am. Coll. Cardiology (task force Health Care Quality Improvement Initiative 1996—); mem. AMA (chmn. sect. coun. internal medicine 1980), N.Y. Heart Assn., Am. Soc. Internal Medicine (master, trustee 1975-79, sec.-treas. 1979—, pres. elect 1981, pres. 1982-83, chmn. investment com. 1985-93), N.Y. State Soc. Internal Medicine (pres. 1973-74, dir. 1966-84, chmn. Bklyn. chpt., v.p. 1971, award of merit 1978), Bklyn. Soc. Internal Medicine (mem. council 1965, pres. 1969-72), Med. Soc. State of N.Y. (chmn. sect. internal medicine 1976, chmn. med. care ins. com. 1988-93), Federated Council for Internal Medicine (chmn. 1979-80), Med. Soc. County Kings (censor 1985-91). *There is a place for hard work, scrupulous ethics and pride of accomplishment. A great marriage and a fine close family are buffers against adversity.*

MALADKAR, MADAN ANANDA RAO, internist; b. Davanagere, Karnataka, India, July 22, 1965; came to U.S., 1989; s. Ananda Rao and Kamala Anand (Gaddale) M.; m. Vandana Chennuru, Feb. 12, 1988; children: Nikita, Rhea. Student, Dharmapravartha Rajanahalli Madduravappa Sci. Coll., Davanagere, India, 1983; MBBS, Jagathguru Jayadeva Murugarajendra Med. Coll., Davanagere, 1988. Diplomate Am. Bd. Internal Medicine. Resident St. Joseph Mercy-Oakland, Pontiac, Mich., 1994-97; internist Family Wellness Ctr., Silver Spring, Md., 1997—2001; chief, Internal Medicine Clinic Fox Army Health Ctr., Redstone Arsenal, Ala., 2001—. Mem.: AMA. Avocations: tennis, computers. Home: 105 Camden Circle Madison AL 35758 E-mail: mmaladkar@hotmail.com.

MALAFA, MOKENGE PETER, surgeon; b. Lagos, Nigeria, Oct. 10, 1958; came to U.S., 1978; Grad., U. Wis., MD, 1986. Intern Med. Ctr. Ohio, Toledo, 1986-87, resident, 1987-91; with Meml. Med. Ctr., St. Johns Hosp., 1994—. Surg.-Oncology fellow City of Hope, Duarte, Calif., 1991-94. Mem. AMA, AAAS, Am. Coll. Surgeons, Soc. Surg. Oncology, Am. Soc. of Clin. Oncology. Office: SIU Sch Medicine PO Box 19638 Springfield IL 62794-9638

MALAFRONTE, DONALD, health executive; b. Bklyn., Dec. 16, 1931; s. Pasquale and Amalia (Castaldo) M.; m. Diane Freedenberg, Jan. 7, 1960 (dec. Nov. 14, 1970); children: Philip, Victor.; m. Hillary Demby, Oct. 30, 1982. BS, NYU, 1954. Reporter L.I. Daily Press, 1956-58; reporter, editor Newark Star-Ledger, 1958-65, art columnist, 1963-70; adminstrv. asst. to mayor of Newark, 1965-70; dir. Newark Model Cities Program, 1967-70, Newark Community Devel. Adminstrn., 1968-70; chief urban field operations N.J. Regional Med. Program, 1970-73; pres. Urban Health Inst., Roseland, N.J., 1973—. Cons. to hosps., local govts., 1970— Author articles in field. Served with AUS, 1954-56. Recipient Joyce Kilmer fiction prize NYU, 1953 Office: Urban Health Inst 101 Eisenhower Pky Roseland NJ 07068-1028 Home: 1056 5th Ave New York NY 10028-0112

MALAGA, STANLEY, accounting educator; b. Bronx, N.Y., Dec. 16, 1942; s. Benjamin and Rita Malaga; m. Leda Malaga, June 7, 1964; children: Ross, Meredith, Mitchell. BS, L.I. U., 1964; MBA, Bernard Baruch Coll., 1971. CPA, N.Y.; cert. valuation analyst. Acct. Stanley Katz & Co., N.Y.C., 1964-68, Hurdman and Cranston, N.Y.C., 1968-71; prof. acctg. and taxation L.I. U., Brookville, N.Y., 1971—. Ptnr. Bertucelli & Malaga LLP, Hauppauge, N.Y., 1994—, Malaga & Malaga PC, Hauppauge, 1984-94; lectr. in field. Author: Automatic Tax Planner, 1984. Active Hauppauge Indsl. Assn., 1989; bd. dirs. Suffolk County Girl Scouts, Hauppauge, 1989. Mem. AICPA, Am. Acctg. Assn., N.Y. State Soc. CPAs, C.W. Post Tax Inst. (dir.), Acad. Mktg. Sci., Nassau/Suffolk Soc. CPAs (chmn. fed. tax com.). Avocations: golf, swimming, bridge. Office: Bertucelli & Malaga LLP 3033 Expressway Dr N Farmingville NY 11749-5309

MALAGUTI, ANDREA, Italianist; b. Bondeno, Italy, Dec. 8, 1964; came to U.S., 1993; Laurea, U. Padua, Italy, 1989; PhD, Harvard U., 1999; postgrad., U. Calif., Berkeley, 1990-91. Free-lance editor/journalist, Ferrare, Italy, 1989—90; translator, editor, 1991—93; tchg. fellow Harvard U., Cambridge, Mass., 1993—99, tchg. asst., 1999—2001; lectr. in Italian Bennington (Vt.) Coll., 2000; asst. prof. dept. Italian Columbia U., N.Y.C., 2001—. Contbr. articles to profl. jours. Mem. MLA, Am. Assn. Italian Studies, Am. Assn. Tchrs. Italian. Office: 512 Hamilton Hall New York NY 10027 E-mail: am2057@columbia.edu.

MALAMED, SEYMOUR H. motion picture company executive; b. N.Y.C., June 17, 1921; s. Abraham and Bess (Kaisin) M.; m. Doris Raphael, May 19, 1946; children— Margery, Susan, Nancy. BBA, City Coll. N.Y., 1942. Engaged in entertainment field, 1954—; asst. to v.p., treas. Screen Gems Co., 1956-62; treas. parent co. Columbia Pictures Corp., 1962—, v.p., 1963-73, exec. v.p., 1973—. Served with AUS, World War II. Mem. Motion Picture Acad. Arts and Scis. Clubs: Friars (N.Y.C.); Metropolis Country (Westchester County); High Ridge Country (Palm Beach, Fla.), Metropolis Country Club. Home: 135 Central Park W Apt 9nc New York NY 10023-2465 Office: 301 W 57th St Ste 336 New York NY 10019-3114

MALAMUD, ALEXANDER, lawyer, consultant; b. Beltz, Moldova, Jan. 4, 1971; came to U.S. s. Yafim and Haya Urman M. BS in Criminal Justice, U. Ariz., 1996; postgrad., UCLA, 1996-2000. CEO, pres. Orient Express, Inc., Bklyn., 1995—. Bus. cons. N.Y. Transporters Assn., 1994; mem. adv. bd. Metro, Inc., Phoenix, 1994-96; cons. Mass. Transp. Mem. N.Y. Transp. Assn. Republican. Avocations: reading books, basketball, practicing law. Home: 29 Park View Pl Fair Lawn NJ 07410-4353 Office: 177 Sargeant Ave Clifton NJ 07013-1934

MALAMUD, DANIEL, biochemistry educator; b. Detroit, June 5, 1939; s. Jack and Jennie (Ashe) M.; m. Judith Disner, Mar. 7, 1961; children: Randy, Lisa. BS, U. Mich., 1961; MA, Western Mich. U., 1962; PhD, U. Cin., 1965; MA, U. Pa., 1983. Postdoctoral fellow Temple U., Phila., 1966-68, asst. prof. pathology, 1968-69; asst. biologist Mass. Gen. Hosp., Boston, 1969-72, assoc. biologist, 1972-77; assoc. prof. biochemistry Sch. Dental Medicine, U. Pa., Phila., 1977-84, prof. biochemistry, 1984—, chmn. dept., 1985-92. Asst. prof. pathology Harvard U., Boston, 1970-77; vis. assoc. prof., Fulbright lectr. U. Philippines, Manila, 1975; vis. scientist Wistar Inst., Phila., 1985; affiliated scientist Monell Chem. Senses Ctr., Phila., 1985—; exch. scientist Hebrew U., Jerusalem, 1982. Author: Autoradiography, 1969, Saliva As a Diagnostic Fluid, 1993; contbr. over 90 articles to profl. jours., chpts. to books. Recipient Career Devel. award NIH, 1972-77. Mem. Am. Soc. Biol. Chemists, Am. Soc. Cell Biologists, Am. Soc. Microbiologists, Am. Soc. Biochem. Molecular Biology, N.Y. Acad. Scis. Office: U Pa Sch Dental Medicine 4001 Spruce St Philadelphia PA 19104-4118 E-mail: malamud@pobox.upenn.edu.

MALAMUTH, NEIL MOSHE, psychology and communication educator; BA in Psychology summa cum laude, MA in Psychology, UCLA, 1972, PhD in Social Psychology and Personality, 1975. Lectr. dept. psychology, UCLA and postdoctoral fellow Ctr. for Behavioral Therapy, Beverly Hills, Calif., 1975-77; asst. prof. psychology U. Man., Winnipeg, Can., 1977-80, assoc. prof. Can., 1980-82; prof. comm. and psychology, chairperson dept. comm. U. Mich., Ann Arbor, 1991-94; tchg. asst. dept. psychology UCLA, 1971-73, rsch. assoc. Ctr. for Computer-Based Behavioral Studies, 1973-75, assoc. prof., 1982-86, assoc. dir. Ctr. for Study of Women, 1986-87, prof. comm. and psychology, 1982-91, 94—, chairperson comm. studies program and speech dept., 1984-91, 94—. Vis. scholar Stanford (Calif.) U., fall 1988; mem. rev. com. on violence and stress NIMH, 1989-93; Lady Davis sr. fellow Hebrew U. Jerusalem, spring 1995; participant leadership inst. Freedom Forum, Columbia U., summer 1992; participant workshop for deans and chairpersons Annenberg Programs, Washington, winter 1993; presenter various profl. and ednl. confs., most recently Oakland (Mich.) U., 1994, Nat. Assn. for Devel. of Work with Sex Offenders, Durham (Eng.) U., 1994, Soc. for Sci. Study of Sex., Miami, Fla., 1994, Ctr. for Study of Evolution and Origins of Life, UCLA, 1994, Ctr. for Evolutionary Psychology, Santa Barbara, Calif., 1995, Tel Aviv U., 1995, Bar-Ilan U., Israel, 1995, Hebrew U. Jerusalem, 1995, NRC, Washington, 1995, Soc. Exptl. Social Psychology, Washington, 1995, Nat. Assn. for Treatment of Sexual Aggression, New Orleans, 1995, Polish Nat. Acad. Sci., Warsaw U., 1995. Co-author: An Instructor's Manual and Guide for Teaching a Course in Social Psychology, 1976, Pornography, 1993; co-editor Sites and Insights in Psychology, 1976; co-editor, contbr. chpt. to: Pornography and Sexual Aggression, 1984, Sex, Power, Conflict: Evolutionary Feminist Perspectives, 1996; contbr. chpt. to: Aggression in Children and Youth, 1984, Handbook of Research on Rape and Sexual Assault, 1984, Media Violence and Pornography: An International Perspective, 1984, The psychology of Women: Ongoing Debates, 1987, Public Communication and Behavior, Vol. 2, 1989; contbr. or co-contbr. various chpts., also numerous articles; mem. editl. bd. Motivation and Emotion, 1983-89, Comm. Rsch., 1986-92, Jour. Sex Rsch., 1982-99, Sexual Abuse: A Jour. and Treatment, 1995-99; assoc. editor Comm. Concepts Series, 1989-98, Jour. Rsch. in Personality, 1990-93; co-editor issue Jour. Social Issues, 1986. Recipient John Kendall award for Outstanding Contbns. to Psychology, Gustavus Coll., Minn., 1987; rsch. grantee Social Sci. and Humanities Rsch. Coun. Can., 1979-81, NIMH, 1986-89, 89-91, 91-92; named one of 7 scholars among top 100 rschrs. in 4 categories of eminence Personality and Social Psychology Bull., 1992. Fellow APA, Am. Psychol. Soc.; mem. Internat. Comm. Assn. (presenter 1994, Top 5 Conf. Paper award mass comm. divsn. 1987), Internat. Soc. for Rsch. on Aggression, Soc. for Psychol. Study of Social Issues, Soc. for Sci. Study of Sex, Phi Beta Kappa. Office: UCLA Comm Studies Program 334 Kinsey Hall Los Angeles CA 90095-0001

MALANCA, ALBERT ROBERT, lawyer, mediator; b. Tacoma, Apr. 25, 1927; s. Albert and Caroline (Mencarelli) M.; m. Jeannine Marian O'Halloran, June 13, 1952 (dec. Sept. 1993); children: Rand (dec.), Gina M., Warren A.; m. Glenna Lee Bradley-House, Jan. 1, 1994; 1 child, Chaise. BA, U. Wash., 1949, JD, 1950. Bar: Wash., U.S. Dist. Ct. (we. and ea. dists.) Wash., U.S. Supreme Ct. Assoc. Goodwin Eastvold & Hicks, Tacoma, 1951-54; ptnr. Goodwin Hicks & Malanca, 1954-55, Goodwin Hicks Malanca & Hager, Tacoma, 1955-57, Carnahan Gordon & Goodwin, Tacoma, 1957-60, Gordon Goodwin Sager Hicks & Thomas, Tacoma, 1960-62, Gordon Goodwin Sager & Thomas, Tacoma, 1962-66, Gordon Sager Honeywell Malanca & Peterson, Tacoma, 1966-68, Gordon Honeywell Malanca Peterson & Johnson, Tacoma, 1968-70, Gordon Thomas Honeywell Malanca Peterson O'Hern & Johnson, Tacoma, 1970-76, Gordon Thomas Honeywell Malanca Peterson & O'Hern, Tacoma, 1976-85; sr. ptnr. Gordon Thomas Honeywell Malanca Peterson & Daheim, 1985—. Mediator and arbitrator, Tacoma/Seattle, 1985—. Author, speaker legal seminars. Patron, Tacoma Art Mus., 1998. Fellow Am. Coll. Trial Lawyers (state chmn. 1985-86), Am. Bar Found. (life); mem. ABA, Wash. State Bar Assn., Fed. Bar Assn. (pres. 1980-81), Tacoma-Pierce County Bar Assn. (trustee 1975-77). Episcopalian. Avocations: boating, skiing, fishing, hunting, golf. Home: 8915 N Harborview Dr Unit 101 Gig Harbor WA 98332-2179 Office: Gordon Thomas Honeywell Malanca Peterson & Daheim 1201 Pacific Ave Ste 2200 Tacoma WA 98402-4314 E-mail: malaa@gth.com.

MALANI, NARENDRA, physician; b. San Ramon, Calif., Aug. 28, 1958; s. Udaychand and Sarawati M.; m. Hina Malani, Jan. 17, 1982; 1 child, Neilkanth. MBBS, U. Calcutta, India, 1982. Diplomate Am. Bd. Internal Medicine, Pulmonary Disease, Critical Care Medicine, Geriatric Medicine. Acting chief pulmonary/critical care VA Med. Ctr., Livermore, Calif., 1989-91; chair dept. medicine San Ramon Regional Med. Ctr., Calif., 1998-99. Bd. mem. Gardian Rehabilitation Hosp., San Ramon, 1999. Fellow Am. coll. Physicians, Am. Coll. Chest Physicians. Avocations: wind surfing, trekking, moutain climbing. Office: 5401 Norris Canyon Rd Ste 308 San Ramon CA 94583-5408

MALANY, LE GRAND LYNN, lawyer, engineer, bank executive; b. May 14, 1941; s. LeGrand Franklin and Marion (Jaynes) M.; m. Barbara Bumgarner, June 26, 1965; children: LeGrand Karl, Siobhan, Carleen. BS in Engring. Physics, U. Ill., 1964, JD, 1970. Registered profl. engr., Ill.; bar: Ill. 1970, U.S. Dist. Ct. (cen. dist.) Ill. 1970, Ill. Supreme Ct. 1970, U.S. Ct. Mil. Appeals 1971, U.S. Ct. Appeals (7th cir.) 1972, U.S. Dist. Ct. (so. dist.) Ill. 1974, U.S. Supreme Ct. 1975, U.S. Dist. Ct. (no. dist.) Ill. 1982; lic. real estate broker, bldg. inspector, mgmt. planner, and asbestos project designer Ill. Asst. astonomer Adler Planetarium, Chgo., 1960-63; rsch. asst. Portland Cement Rsch. Assn., Skokie, 1964; instr. dept. gen. engring. U. Ill., 1965-70; instr. Office Instrn. Resources, 1967-68; lectr. Police Tng. Inst., Urbana, Ill., 1969-70; project dir. driver control program U.S. Dept. Transp., 1971-73, project dir., author driver license examiner tng. curriculum, 1973; assoc. drivers license adminstr. State of Ill., Springfield, 1973-74, asst. auditor gen., 1977-83, asst. atty. gen., dir. policy, planning and tech., 1983-85, chief internal auditor office of atty. gen., 1985-86, spl. asst. atty. gen., 1986—, spl. asst. auditor gen. and gen. counsel office auditor gen., 1986-92, gen. counsel state comptroller Cusas II project, 1986-88; ptnr. Kabumoto and Malany, 1986—97. Commr. Williamsville-Sherman Water Commn., 1997—; pres. Microgeneral Ltd., 1983—, assoc. ptnr. Johnson & Assoc., 1990-93, Mgmt. Control Sys., Inc., 1986; chmn. bd. Flowers LaGrand Ltd., 1985—; founder, dir. Foster Bank, Chgo., 1988-90; expert U.S. Fed. Energy Adminstrn., 1974; counsel juvenile divsn. Cir. Ct., Sangamon County, Ill., 1973-75; chief counsel Ill. Dept. Motor Vehicles, Springfield, 1974; trustee Meret Ctr., Inc., 1973-75; internat. dir. construction Shelter Now Internat., HQ Oshkosh, Wis., 1999—. Dem. candidate for States Atty., Sangamon County, Ill., 1980; program dir. sch. renovation projects, Macedonia, 2000, Housing Renovations for Refugees, Macedonia, 1999; bd. dirs. J. Keil Braid Leadership Found., Villagrove, Colo., 1997—, Home Ownership Program for Equity, Springfield, Ill., 1998-2001, Springfield Heritage Found., 1999—; country dir. Macedonia for Shelter Now Internat., 2000—. Recipient Midwest Intergovtl. Audit Forum Recognition award, 1981. Mem. ABA, Am. Phys. Soc., Nat. Soc. Profl. Engrs., Ill. Socs. Profl. Engrs., Ill. Farm Bur., Ill. Christmas Tree Growers Assn., Ill. Foster parents Assn., Rotary (Springfield chpt. sec. 1983-85, pres. 1986-87, trustee Rotary South Found. 1986-93), Habitat for Humanity-Sangamon County (bd. dirs. 1996-2001, dir. constr. 1998-2000). Achievements include development statewide motorcycle driver licensing program. Home: 600 S Rose Hill Ave Springfield IL 62704-1560 Office: 631 E Adams St Springfield IL 62701-1947

MALASANOS, LOIS JULANNE FOSSE, nursing educator; b. LaPorte City, Iowa, Sept. 1, 1928; d. Lewis Reginald and Henrietta Marie Fosse; widowed; children: John, Toree. BSN, U. Tex., 1948; BA in Gen. Sci., U. Iowa, 1952; MA in Nursing Edn., U. Chgo., 1959; PhD in Physiology, U. Ill., 1973. Assoc. dir. nursing U. Iowa Hosps., Iowa City, 1950-51, staff charge nurse, 1951; instr. operating room Sch. Nursing, Michael Reese Hosp., Chgo., 1951-58; charge nurse, med.-surg. U. Chgo., Billings Hosp., 1952-59; pvt. duty nurse Ill., 1959-63; charge nurse, maternal-infant nursing Weiss Meml. Hosp., Chgo., 1963-66; asst. prof. Loyola U., 1966-69; teaching asst. in physiology U. Ill., 1969-73, assoc. prof., assoc. head gen. nursing dept. Coll. Nursing, 1973-76, prof., assoc. head gen. nursing dept., 1976-80; prof., dean Coll. Nursing U. Fla., Gainesville, 1980-95, Disting. Svc. prof., 1995—. Instr. anatomy and physiology Cook County Hosp., Chgo., 1973; lectr. endocrinology Chgo. Coll. Osteopathic Medicine, 1973-80; active Pres. Clinton's Task Force on Health Care, 1993; cons. Am. Assn. Med. Colls., 1977-78, Am. Heart Assn., 1977-94, Am. Jour. Nursing, 1978-79, Gainesville (Fla.) Vets. Ctr., 1980-95, Lake Butler Receiving Ctr., 1980—; presenter papers in field; cons. to numerous colls. and univs. regarding curriculum, nursing care and endocrinology; chair Deans and Dirs. of Fla. Colls. Nursing, 1981-89; chair edn. com. State Bd. Nursing, 1983-87, chair probable course com., 1984-95, 96--; vis. prof. Dokuz Eylul U., Izmir, Turkey, 1995-96; cons. curriculum and evaluation to more than 50 programs in U.S., P.R., Iceland, Turkey, Lebanon, Japan, Thailand, Philippines. Co-author, editor: Manual of Medical Surgical Nursing, 1983, Translating Comitment to Reality, 1986, Health Assessment, 1977 (Am. Jour. Nursing Book of Yr. award 1977), 4th edit., 1989; editor: Vital Signs, 1981-90, Fla. Cancer Nursing News, 1983-84; co-editor: Fla. Nursing Rev., 1986-90; mem. editl. rev. bd. Image, 1980-96; editl. cons. Nursing, 1982-94; manuscript referee Rsch. in Nursing and Health, 1980-94, Jour. Profl. Nursing, 1985-94, Turkish Jour. Nurse Rshc.; chairperson adv. com. Nursing Outlook, 1986-91, Peer Rev., 1986-94; contbr. more than 100 articles, revs. to profl. jours. Mem. nursing com., scholarship com. and rsch. rev. com. Am. Cancer Soc., Tampa, Fla., 1980-94. Recipient Bronze medal Fla. Heart Assn., 1986, Silver medal Fla. Heart Assn., 1989, 93; named Disting. Alumnus U. Tex. Med. Br., 1985; named to Disting. Faculty, Albany State U., 1988, Hall of Fame, U. Tex. Med. Br., 1992; NEH fellow, 1981; Fulbright awardee to Turkey, 1995-96, 2001. Mem. ANA (mem. coun. nurse rschrs.), AACN, AAAS, AAUP, Am. Acad. Nursing (mem. pub. com. 1986-89) Am. Assn. Higher Edn., Am. Assn. Colls. Nursing, Fla. Nurses Assn. (mem. dist. 10), N.Y. Acad. Sci., Fla. League Nursing, Nat. League Nursing (chairperson, mem. coun. baccalaureate and higher degree program, Dirs. award 1995, site visitor for program rev. 1980—, bd. rev. for accreditation 1993-2002), State Bd. Nursing (mem. probable cause com.), So. Regional Edn. Bd., Sigma Xi, Sigma Theta Tau, Phi Kappa Phi (pres. 1987-88). Office: U Fla Coll Nursing PO Box 100187 Gainesville FL 32610-0187 E-mail: malaslj@nursing.ufl.edu.

MALASKY, ELLEN WEISBERG, human resource development executive; b. Stamford, Conn., June 28, 1947; d. Benjamin Robert and Marion (Sharlach) Weisberg; m. Gary A. Malasky, Apr. 3, 1982; children: Mitchell Weisberg, Cynthia Weisberg. BA, Boston U., 1969; MEd, George Washington U., 1978. Asst. bank examiner Fed. Res. Bank of N.Y., N.Y.C., 1969-73; tng. coord. Consol. Edison N.Y., 1973-74; prin. Arthur Young, Reston, Va., 1974-83; sr. mgr. Ernst & Young, Washington, 1990—. Co-chair parent svc. assn. Georgetown Day Sch., 1999—. Contbr. chapters to books. Chair women's com. Arena Stage, Washington, 1984—87; v.p. Art Barn, 1987—88; bd. dirs. Jewish Cmty. Ctr., 1988—99, chair youth and family divsn., 1990—94. Recipient Pres. award, D.C. Jewish Cmty. Ctr., 1993. Mem.: AICPA (com. chair 1982—84), ASTD. Avocations: theater , sports. Home: 3036 44th St NW Washington DC 20016-3514 Office: Ernst & Young 1225 Connecticut Ave NW Washington DC 20036 E-mail: ellen.malasky@ey.com.

MALATESTA, MARY ANNE, lawyer; b. Wapakoneta, Ohio, Aug. 7, 1954; d. Leo J. Jr. and Ellen E. Malatesta. BA in English, Ohio State U., 1976; JD, U. Colo., 1979. Bar: Colo. 1979, U.S. Dist. Ct. Colo. 1979, U.S. Ct. Appeals (9th cir.) 1989, U.S. Ct. Appeals (10th cir.) 1990, U.S. Dist. Ct. Ariz. 1992. Dep. dist. atty. 1st Jud. Dist., Golden, Colo., 1979-84; assoc. Tilly & Graves, P.C., Denver, 1985-88, shareholder, 1988-93; asst. atty. gen. Office Atty. Gen. State of Colo., 1994—. Mem. faculty Nat. Inst. Trial Advocacy, South Bend, Ind., 1989-90, asst. team leader, 1990-93, team leader, 1994—; lectr. U. Denver, 1990, 91, 97—; guest faculty U. Colo., 1992—; organizer Victims of Violence seminar; mem. faculty Am. Bd. Trial Advocates seminar, 1992, Domestic Violence Prosecution Tng. Course, 1994, Child Advocates Tng. Course, 1996; master Am. Inns of Ct. Judge William E. Doyle Inn, 1994—, Women's Leadership Forum, 1996—. Founder, mem. Facio ut Des, Denver, 1987-94. Mem. Colo. Bar Assn., Denver Bar Assn. (professionalism com. 1990—, co-chair professionalism com. 1994-99, professionalism conciliation panel mem. 1999—), Colo. Women's Bar Assn. Avocations: hiking, horseback riding, spectator sports. Office: Office of Atty Gen 1525 Sherman St Fl 5 Denver CO 80203-1700

MALAVE, ANDRES, pharmacologist, educator; b. San Juan, Puerto Rico, Nov. 18, 1949; s. Andres Malave, Adela Nevarez; m. Lillian Arce, July 28, 1972; children: Jose A., Jaime E., Josue I., Jessica H. BS in Pharmacy, U. P.R., 1972; MS, Purdue U., 1981, PhD of Pharmacology, 1983. Registered pharmacist P.R. Instr. U. P.R., San Juan, 1975—78, asst. prof., assoc. prof., 1984—91; prof., chmn. Nova Southeastern U., Ft. Lauderdale, Fla., 1992—2001, assoc. dean, 2001—. CEO MCSI, Ft. Lauderdale, 2001—. Malave Consulting Svcs., Inc., Ft. Lauderdale, 2001—. Recipient Bristol Meyers/Squibb Faculty Devel. award, 1991—92; scholar, Fulbright, 2001. Mem.: N.Y. Acad. Sci., Soc. Neurosci., Am. Assn. Coll. Pharmacy. Achievements include development of simple non-radioactive assay for estimating protein kinase C and protein phosphatase-1. Avocations: sports, racquetball, basketball, music, guitar. Home: 224 La Costa Way Weston FL 33326

MALAYERY, NASRIN, educator, consultant; b. Tehran, Iran, Jan. 27, 1943; U.S. citizen, 1990; d. Mahmoud Malayery and Ghamar Narjis Kia. BA with spl. honors in history, George Washington U., 1964; EdM in Edn. and Social Studies, Boston U., 1967, EdM in Media and Tech., 1977, EdD in Media Tech., 1986. Editor in-house mgmt. jour. Oil Consortium, Employee Comm., Tehran, 1970-74; mgr. documents and publs. Iran-UNESCO Adult Literacy Program, 1974-76; instr., instrnl. designer Shiraz (Iran) U. Med. Sch., 1977-81; ednl. cons. WHO Eastern Mediterranean Regional Orgn., Alexandria, Egypt, 1981-87; sr. ednl. cons. Compaq Computer Corp., Littleton, Mass., 1987—. Mem. Internat. Soc. for Performance Improvement, Nat. Mus. of Women in the Arts (assoc.), Libr. of Congress Assocs., Phi Beta Kappa. Avocations: writing, reading, gardening, ballet, yoga. Home: 7 Millstone Ct Cold Spring KY 41076-1861

MALBON, CRAIG CURTIS, pharmacology educator, university official; b. Providence, June 1, 1950; s. Elroy Willis and Edith Roberta (Curtis) M.; children: Lindsey Gei Sook, Hailey Sook Yee; m. Hsien-yu Wang, June 26, 1993. BA, Mass. State Coll., Worcester, 1972; PhD, Case Western Reserve U., 1976. NIH postdoctoral fellow sect. physiological chemistry Brown U., Providence, 1976-77, research assoc. sect. physiological chemistry, 1977, asst. prof. research sect. physiological chemistry, 1978; asst. prof. dept. pharmacology SUNY Sch. Medicine, Stony Brook, 1978-83, assoc. prof., 1983-90, prof., 1990—; leading univ. prof. Sch. Medicine SUNY, 1993—, vice chmn. dept. pharmacology, 1988-89, prof. dept. pharmacology, 1990—, assoc. dean biomed. scis. Sch. Medicine, 1989-93, v.p. rsch., 1993-97; vice dean Univ. Hosp. and Med. Ctr. SUNY, 1993—. Bd. dir. diabetes & metabolic diseases rsch. program NIH, Stony Brook, NY, mem. cell biology & physiology study sect., Bethesda, Md., 1981—86; bd. dir. LI High Tech. Incubator; mem. sci. adv. bd. Brookhaven Nat. Lab. DOE, 1998—. Mem. editl. bd. Am. Jour. Physiology, 1985—, assoc. editor, 1993-99; mem. editl. bd. Jour. Biol. Chemistry, 1988-93; contbr. articles to profl. jours. Mem. Marine Biol. Lab., Inc., Woods Hole, Mass., 1986; bd. dirs. Faculty/Student Assn., Inc., Stony Brook, 1979-82. Recipient nat. rsch. Svc. award NIH, 1976-80, career devel. award, 1981-86; rsch. award Am. Cancer Soc., 1998. Mem. Biophys. Soc., N.Y. Acad. Scis., Am. Physiol. Soc. (editl. bd. 1986, assoc. editor 1990), Am. Soc. for Biochemistry and Molecular Biology (editl. bd. 1988), Biochem. Soc. (U.K.) (hon.), Sigma Xi. Home: PO Box 2726 East Setauket NY 11733-0852 E-mail: craig@pharm.sunysb.edu.

MALBON, LOUISE, registered, nurse, hypnotherapist writer, publisher; b. Fayetteville, N.C., Feb. 13, 1956; d. Margaret Bess and John Bullard, Fletcher Bess (Stepfather); children: Lessel Malbon, III, Lawrence A., Leslie. Assoc. Applied Scis., Excelsior Coll., 1987. Cert. CPR instr., ACLS instr.; RN; cert. clin. hypnotherapist. Clin. resource nurse educator DC Gen. Hosp., Washington, 2001—02; ambulatory svs. coord. Wash. Hosp. Ctr., 2002. ACLS instr. Wash. Adventist Hosp. Tng. Ctr., Takoma Park, 2002—. Author: Caring Enough to Change, 2002. Cmty. activist 8th Precinct Civic Assn., Chillum, 1987—2002. Named 100 Extra Ordinary Nurses, Sigma Theta Tau Internat. Honor Soc. Nursing, 2001. Mem.: Emergency Nurses Assn. Democrat. Baptist. Home and Office: Fresh Start Hypnotherapy and Pub 5405 13th Avenue Chillum MD 20783 Home Fax: 301-559-5720. Personal E-mail: LSMLB@AOL.COM. Business E-Mail: Freshstarthypnotherapy.com.*

MALBURG, DAVID MATHEW, civil and transportation engineer; b. Corning, N.Y., June 13, 1967; s. Philip Duane and June (Wilson) M.; m. Jeanne Marlene Matteson, July 4, 1998. A in Occupl. Studies, SUNY, Alfred, 1987; AAS, Corning (N.Y.) C.C., 1994; BS, Clarkson U., 1996. Constrn. mgr. Streeter Assocs., Inc., Elmira, N.Y., 1996-98; civil engr. N.Y. State Dept. Transp., Coopers Plains, 1999—. Asst. scoutmaster Boy Scouts Am., Canisteo, N.Y., 1998—. Specialist U.S. Army, 1987-90, 91, Desert Storm. Decorated Army Achievement medal, Nat. Defense medal. Mem. ASCE, Order of the Engr. Methodist. Avocations: hiking, camping, design, karate, biking. Home: PO Box 969 Corning NY 14830

MALCHIODI, JOANNE MARIE, elementary education educator, reading consultant; b. New Haven, Mar. 23, 1947; d. Joseph Foster and Ethel Augusta Bertha (Kuss) Grady; m. George Louis Malchiodi, Aug. 9, 1969; children: Dawn Marie, Laura Ann, Karen Lynn. BS, So. Conn. State Coll., New Haven, 1969; MS, Eastern Conn. State Coll., Willimantic; 6th yr. degree, U. Conn., Storrs, 1999. Cert. elem. tchr., remedial reading and lang. arts tchr., reading recovery tchr. Conn.; cert. reading cons., Conn. 2nd grade tchr. East Haddam (Conn.) Elem., 1969-70; nursery sch. tchr. St. Stephen's, East Haddam, 1971-72; remedial reading tchr. Lebanon (Conn.) Elem. Sch., 1986-96; reading tchr. Horace Porter Sch., Columbia, Conn., 1996-98; reading recovery tchr. Jack Jackter Elem. Sch., Colchester; K-1 reading cons., 1998-2000; reading cons. North Windham Elem. Sch., Windham, Conn., 2000—. Pvt. tutor; summer sch. tchr., 1986, 94. Chair scheduling Conntrek IV, Lebanon, 1991; co-chair Alcohol Free After Graduation Party, 1991-92. Mem. Eastern Conn. Reading Coun. (newspaper liaison 1989-90, rec. sec. 1990-93, treas. 1993-95), Nat. Coun. Tchrs. of English, Conn. Reading Assn., Internat. Reading Assn., Reading Recovery Coun. N.Am., Phi Lambda Theta, Phi Delta Kappa. Avocations: sewing, crafts, walking, reading. Home: 64 Kick Hill Rd Lebanon CT 06249-1224 Office: N Windham Elem Sch 112 Jordan Ln North Windham CT 06256

MALCOLM, DAVID JOHN, structural engineer, researcher; b. Dunedin, New Zealand, Apr. 27, 1943; came to U.S., 1992; s. J. Laurence and Sylvia B. (Hooper) M.; m. Megan A. Whittingham, May 15, 1976; children: John A.S., Peter J.S., Thomas D.W. BSc in Civil Engring., U. Bristol, Eng., 1965; M of Engring. (Structural), McGill U., Montreal, Can., 1969; PhD in Solid Mechanics, U. Calgary, Alberta, Can., 1973. Asst. engr. W. S. Atkins & Ptnrs., Epsom, Eng., 1965-67; asst. prof. Lakehead U., Thunder Bay, Ontario, Can., 1973-76; assoc. prof. U. Calgary, 1976-80; sr. engr. Indal Tech., Inc., Mississauga, Ont., 1981-89, Lavalin Engrs., Toronto, 1989-91; sr. scientist R. Lynette & Assocs. Advanced Wind Turbines, Seattle, 1992—99. Contbr. about 50 articles to profl. jours. Recipient Best Paper award, ASME Wind Energy Symposium, 1984. Mem. ASCE (Moiseiff prize 1984), Profl. Engrs. of Ontario (registered profl. engr.), Internat. Assn. Shell Structures, Canadian Wind Energy Assn. (v.p. 1988-91). Avocations: skiing, mountaineering, photography. Home: 714-17 Ave Kirkland WA 98033 Office: Global Energy Concepts LLC 5729 Lakeview Dr NE # 100 Kirkland WA 98033

MALCOLM, JOYCE LEE, historian, educator; b. Glen Falls, N.Y. d. Jacob N. and Florence R. Sitrin; m. Lawrence M. Johnson; children: Mark S., Lisa A.; m. Neil Law Malcolm, Jan. 1, 1977; 1 child, George Law. BA, Barnard Coll., 1963; MA, Brandeis U., 1972, PhD, 1977. Assoc. prof. history Bentley Coll., Waltham, Mass., 1988-92, prof. history, 1992—. Sr. fellow MIT Security Studies Program, Cambridge, 1998—; dir. New Eng. Heritage Ctr., Waltham, 1986—2001; cons. Legal and Constl. History, 1994—, Mass. Dept. Edn., 1996—. Author: Caesar's Due: Loyalty and King Charles, 1984, To Keep and Bear Arms, 1994; editor: The Struggle for Sovereignty, 2 vols. , 1999, Guns and Violence: The English Experience, 2002. Grantee NEH, 1979-80, Huntington Libr., 1991, Howe Rsch. Harvard Law Sch., 1980-81; rsch. fellow Earhart Found., 1996-97. Fellow Royal Hist. Soc.; mem. Am. Hist. Assn., Nat. Assn. Scholars, Am. Soc. Legal History, Conf. on Brit. Studies, Hist. Soc. Avocations: horseback riding, hiking, rare books. Office: 175 Forest St Waltham MA 02452-4713 E-mail: jmalcolm@bentley.edu.

MALCOLM, KENNETH W. former state legislator, banker; b. Albany, N.Y., Dec. 30, 1920; m. Dorothy Malcolm, 1948; 3 children. BS in Advt., Bryant Coll., 1950; postgrad., Russell Sage Coll. Mem. budget com. Town of Hampton, N.H., 1973-89, chmn., 1981, mem. police study commn., 1983, mem. exec. com., 1990-91; chmn. Hampton Rep. Com.; vice chmn. Rock City Maintenance Com., 1982-86. Dist. mgr., market dir. Skil Corp.; mem. from dist. 17 N.H. State Ho. of Reps., 1983-93, mem. from dist. 22, 1993—, mem. transp. com., mem. state inst. housing com., mem. econ. com., clk. legis. adminstrn. com. Mem. solid waste com. Coun. State Govts., 1985-86, mem. intergovts. com. Recipient Scouter's Key Svc. award Boy Scouts Am. Mem. Am. Legion, United Spanish War Vets, Order DeMolay (award 1940), Masons (50-Yr. medal 1993). Address: 8 Bourn Ave Hampton NH 03842-1136

MALCOLM, MOLLY BETH, political party official, counselor; BAS in Elem. Edn. with high honors, So. Meth. U., 1976; MS in Counseling and Guidance, Tex. A&M U.-Texarkana, 1988. Lic. profl. counselor, lic. chem. dependency counselor, Tex. Tchr. pub. schs., Ark., Tex., Okla., 1977-87; elem. counselor Texarkana (Ark.) Schs., 1987-89; drug. abuse prevention and counseling specialist Region VII Edn. Svc. Ctr., Kilgore, Tex., 1989-90; drug free schs. student assistance coord. Longview (Tex.) Ind. Sch. Dist., 1990-92; counseling and student svcs. coord. Texarkana (Tex.) Ind. Schs., 1992-93; owner, counselor Malcolm Cons., 1993—; field dir. Max Sandlin for Congress Campaign, 1996; dist. cmty. outreach coord. Congress Max Sandlin, Tex. 1st Dist., 1997-98; state chair Tex. Dem. Party, 1998—. Contbr. publs. and curricula. Active Dem. Nat. Com., 1998—, mem. exec. com., 2000—; active Presbytery of the Pines, Synod of the Sun Presbyn. Ch. USA, Pine Street Middle Sch. PTA; pres. Texarkana Ind. Sch. Dist., 1993-94; deacon First Presbyn. Ch., Texarkana; mem. Jr. League Texarkana; advisor for career devel. U. Tex. Chi Omega; Texarkana bd. dirs. Susan G. Komen Race for the Cure. Recipient Rising Stars in Politics Class of 2000 award Tex. Lyceum Assn. Campaigns and Elections Mag., Pres.' award Ark. Counseling Assn., 1989, Hon. Bill Clinton Gov. Ark. Traveler award, 1989, Texarkana Alumni Achievement award Tex. A&M U., 1989. Mem. Tex. Counseling Assn. (Disting. Svc. award 1993, 96), Tex. Mental Health Counselors Assn., Tex. Sch. Counselors Assn., Tex. Assn. for Multicultural Counseling and Devel. (chair awards com. 1994), N.E. Tex. Counseling Assn., Assn. State Dem. Chairs (co-chair resolution com. 1999—, exec. com. 2001-, treas. 2001-), Tex. Dem. Women (pres. 1997-99, Mem. of Yr. 1998), Leadership Texarkana Alumi Assn. (adv. bd. 1996-99), Jr. League Texarkana, Texarkana C. of C. (mil. affairs com.), Leadership Tex. Alumnae Assn. (life, adv. bd. 1996-99), Ark. PTA (life), DAR, Tex. A&M U. at Texarkana Alumni Assn. (life, Achievement award 1989), So. Meth. U. Alumni Assn. (life), NAACP, Rotary Internat. (Texarkana Oaklawn chpt.), Psi Chi (v.p. 1987-89), Delta Kappa Gamma (pres. chpt. 1988-89), Chi Omega (pres. chpt. alumni assn. 1998-99), Dem. Nat. Com., Texarkana C. of C. Mil. Affairs Com., Tex. Lyceum Assn. (bd. dirs.). Office: Tex Dem Party 701 Rio Grande Austin TX 78701

MALCOLM, RICHARD WARD, academic administrator, consultant; b. Columbus, Ohio, July 27, 1933; s. Ralph James and Beatrice (Ward) M.; 1 child, Gwynn Malcolm Socolich. BS, U. Findlay (Ohio), 1956; MA, Ariz. State U., 1960; MEd, U. So. Calif., 1965, EdD, 1966. Acad. dean Martin Coll., Pulaski, Tenn., 1965-67; dean instrn. Arapahoe C.C., Littleton, Colo., 1967-71; chair edn. divsn. Chapman U., Orange, Calif., 1971-80; assoc. prof. U. So. Calif., 1976-77; dean instrn. Mesa (Ariz.) C.C., 1980-91; asst. to provost Chandler (Ariz.)/Gilbert C.C., 1991-92, chair divsn. social and behavioral scis., 1993-96; dir. R & D Williams campus Maricopa C.C., 1998-97; coord. Phoenix Ctr. U. Findlay, 1997—. Author: Mental Measurement Yearbook, 1972. Pres. Ariz. Rail Pasenger Assn., Phoenix, 1984-93. Mem. Am. Assn. Higher Edn., Ariz. Acad. Adminstrv. Assn. (treas. 1991—), Rotary. Methodist. Avocations: reading, travel, hiking, railroading, music. E-mail: pultolic@aol.com.

MALDE, HAROLD EDWIN, retired federal government geologist; b. Reedsport, Oreg., July 9, 1923; s. Emil and Bessie May (Alspaugh) M.; m. Caroline Elizabeth Rose, Dec. 21, 1954; children; Margaret Jean, Melissa Ruth. AB, Willamette U., 1947; postgrad., Harvard U., 1947-48, U. Colo., 1948-51. Geologist U.S. Geol. Survey, Denver, 1951-87, emeritus, 1987—. Mem. Colo. com. for Nat. Register Hist. Places, 1972-80; vol. photographer Nature Conservancy, 1987—; mem. paleoanthropology del. to Peoples Republic China, Nat. Acad. Scis., 1975, mem. various coms. for study surface mining; mem. oil shale environ. adv. panel U.S. Dept. Interior, 1976-80. Contbr. numerous sci. papers to profl. lit. Served to ensign USNR, 1942-44. Recipient Meritorious Service award U.S. Dept. Interior, 1979, Oak Leaf award Nature Conservancy, 1993. Fellow Geol. Soc. Am. (Kirk Bryan award 1970, assoc. editor 1982-88), AAAS, Ariz.-Nev. Acad. Sci.; mem. Am. Quaternary Assn., Explorers Club. Democrat. Unitarian Universalist. Home: 842 Grant Pl Boulder CO 80302-7415 E-mail: halmalde@msn.com.

MALDEN, KARL (MALDEN SEKULOVICH), actor; b. Chgo., Mar. 22, 1914; s. Peter and Minnie (Sebera) Sekulovich; m. Mona Graham, Dec. 18, 1938; children— Mila, Carla. Student, Goodman Theatre, Chgo., 1935-38. Pres. Acad. of Motion Arts and Scis., 1989-92; mem. Citizens Stamp Com., U.S. Govt., Washington. Actor, 1935— ; stage plays include Golden Boy, 1938, Gentle People, 1939, Key Largo, 1940, Flight to the West, 1942, Uncle Harry, 1940, All My Sons, 1949, A Streetcar Named Desire, 1950, Desire Under the Elms, 1952, Desperate Hours, 1954; in motion pictures, 1940— , films include: Boomerang, Gunfighter, 1945, Halls of Montezuma, 1950, A Streetcar Named Desire (Acad. award for best supporting actor), 1951, Ruby Gentry, 1952, I Confess, 1953, On the Waterfront, 1954, Baby Doll, 1956, Desperate Hours, 1957, Fear Strikes Out, 1957, The Hanging Tree, 1959, Pollyanna, 1960, One Eyed Jacks, 1961, Parrish, The Adventures of Bullwhip Griffin, 1967, Patton, 1970, Beyond the Poseidon Affair, 1978, Meteor, 1979, Sting II, 1982, Twilight Time, 1982, Billy Galvin, 1987, Nuts, 1987; TV films include: Word of Honor, 1981, Miracle on Ice, 1981, Intent to Kill, 1983, Fatal Vision, 1984 (Emmy award), My Father My Son, 1988, The Hijacking of the Achille Lauro, 1989, Call Me Anna, 1990, Absolute Strangers, 1991, Back to the Streets of San Francisco, 1992; dir.: Time Limit, 1957, Billion Dollar Brain, 1967, Hot Millions, 1968, Hotel, Cat O'Nine Tails, 1971, Wild Rovers, 1971, Summertime Killer, 1973, Nuts, 1987; star TV series Streets of San Francisco, 1972-77, Skag, 1980. Recipient Donaldson award, 1950, Critic's award, 1950. Address: 1845 Mandeville Canyon Rd Los Angeles CA 90049-2222

MALDONADO, CARLOS MANUEL, surgeon; b. Barcelona, Spain, Sept. 25, 1938; came to U.S., 1964. MD, U. Barcelona, 1964. Diplomate Am. Bd. Surgery. Intern Columbia Hosp., Milw., 1964-65; resident in gen. surgery Marquette Affiliatee Hosps., 1966-68; fellow in thoracic cardiac surgery Newark Beth Israel Med. Ctr., 1969-70, resident in gen. surgery, 1972-75. Mem. staff Martin Meml. Hosp., Stuart, Fla., Martin Meml. Hosp. South, Ft. Salerno, Fla., 1975—, chief of surgery, 1983-85, chmn. quality coun., 1994—. Fellow ACS; mem. AMA, Fla. Med. Assn., Internat. Soc. Cardiovascular Surgery, Southeastern Surg. Congress, Martin County Med. Soc. (pres. 1999). Address: 421 SE Osceola St Stuart FL 34994-2505 E-mail: carlosmmaldonado@compuserv.com.

MALDONADO, F. CÉSAR, priest, educator; b. Itapaya-Cochabamba, Bolivia, Jan. 6, 1962; arrived in U.S., 1998; s. Benigno Maldonado, Pastora Sanabria. Philosophy Licenciatura, Faculty Latin Am. Social Sci., Cochabamba, 1986; B. Theology, U. Catolica, 1990; M.Anthropology, FLACSO, Quito, Ecuador, 1992; postgrad., Georgetown U., Washington, 1999—. Ordained priest, Roman Cath. Ch.; entered Soc. of Jesus. Tchr. Juan XXIII H.S., Cochabamba, Bolivia, 1987—88; prof. Pontificia U. Catòlica, Quito, Ecuador, 1991—92; cons. Acciõn Cultural Loyola, Sucre, Bolivia, 1993—95; prof. U. Catolica, Colhambamba, Bolivia, 1995—97; prin. Juan XXIII H.S., 1996—97; cons. Centro de Investigacion y Promociõn Campesinado, Santa Cruz, Bolivia, 1997—98; prof. U. Gabriel Renẽ Moreno, 1997—98. Contbr. Mem.: Spanish Masses Arlington. Roman Catholic. Avocations: sports, meditation, writing poetry. Mailing: 37th and O Sts NW Washington DC 20057-0001 E-mail: fcm@georgetown.edu.

MALDONADO, JUDITH ANN BATORSKI, art association administrator; b. Eden, N.Y., Oct. 8, 1949; d. John Michael and Ethel (Owens) B.; m. Michael J. Rocco (div. Oct. 1980); 1 child, Flora; m. Maximino Maldonado Jr., Oct. 13, 1997. Student, Colo. Springs Coll. Bus., 1981; AS in Fine Arts, Suffolk C.C., 1983; BA, SUNY, Stonybrook, 1985, MA, 1987; postgrad., Columbia Coll. Chgo. Film Sch., 1985. Caretaker, asst. mgr. Farmer's Shared Home, Danbury, N.H., 1979-80; cert. educator Assn. for Childbirth at Home, Internat., L.A., 1980; accts. payable clk. Pikes Peak C.C., Colorado Springs, Colo., 1981-82; office mgr. Three Village Meals-on-Wheels, Stonybrook, 1984; grad. sec. art dept. SUNY, 1986-87, art gallery intern Fine Arts Ctr.,

1987; dir. ops., dir. master classes and free concerts Islip Arts Coun., East Islip, N.Y., 1987-89; cons. N.Y. State Coun. on the Arts, N.Y.C., 1989—; co-owner, cons. Fire and Earth Designers and Feng Shui Consultants, Patchogue, N.Y., 1999—. Participant Arts in Bus. Mgmt. seminar Citibank/ABC, N.Y.C., 1987, cmty. leaders luncheon Fox Channel 5, N.Y.C., 1987; asst. to dir. Newsday's L.I. Summer Arts Festival Cmty. Affairs Dept., 1989, Suffolk County Motion Picture and TV Commn., Hauppauge, N.Y., 1988—, Summer Film Festival, 1988-90; cons. N.Y. State Coun. Arts, 1989-90, cons., 1990-91; interior decorator Trans-Designs, 1992; ind. contractor KM-Matol Corp, Que., Can., 1993; intern Nat. Inst. Inner Healing, Rich in Mercy Inst.; Feng Shui cons., 1998; interior design cons. Black Hat Sect. Tibetan Buddhism Feng Shui, 1999. Photographs included in Photography Forum's Coll. Photography Ann., 1985. Campaign dir. Food for Poland, Colorado Springs, 1982; organizer Granite State Alliance, Portsmouth, N.H., 1979, Safe 'n' Sound anti-nuclear campaign, Shoreham, N.Y., 1979; grad. rep. Sch. Continuing Edn. SUNY Stonybrook, judicial com. on acad. standing, SUNY Stonybrook, 1986-87; vol. Vietnam Vets. Theatre Ensemble, 1988, New Community Cinema, Huntington, N.Y., 1988; active exec. com. Dowling Coll. Spring Tribute Concert, Oakdale, N.Y., 1989; asst. to dir. Newsday Community Rels. Dept. L.I. Arts 89, 1989; founding mem. com. corr. L.I. Green Party, Brookhaven Twp., 1990—; participant Life in the Spirit seminar Cath. Charismatic Renewal, N.Y., 1992; tchr. Our Lady of Mt. Carmel Ch., N.Y., 1991—; active Pastoral Coun., 1992—. Mem. Internat. Platform Soc., Contemporary Hispanic Artists of L.I. (advisor to bd. dirs. Ctrl. Islip 1988-89). Roman Catholic. Avocations: screen-writing, poetry, photography, interior design and decoration, therapeutic touch healing. Home: 40 W 4th St Patchogue NY 11772-2171 also: 1075 Bay Shore Ave Bay Shore NY 11706-2738

MALDONADO, RAUL ROBERT, writer, poet, playwright; b. N.Y.C., May 14, 1956; s. Angel Louis Maldonado, Gloria Martinez; m. Donna Victoria Tellone, Sept. 20, 1975 (dec. Mar. 1998); children: Cristi-Ann, Michelle-Lee, Toni; m. Claire Furber. AS, Mercy Coll., Dobbs Ferry, N.Y., 1986; student, Hollywood Film Sch., N.Y.C., 2000. Poet Yonkers Pub. Libr., NY; CEO Speec Inc., N.Y.C., Filmworks, 2002—. Poetry readings the Point, Hunts Point, NY, The Orange Bear, Manhattan, NY, The Revival, Manhattan, NY, Knitting Factory, Manhattan, NY, Washington Jefferson Meml., DC, Edwin's Cafe, N.Y.C., NY, Cup and Chaucer, Montclair, NJ, Moroccan Star Cafe, Bklyn., WVOX Radio Westchester County, NY, Howland Cmty. Ctr., Beacon, NY, Famous Nuyorican Poets Cafe, N.Y.C., Mercy Coll. 2000 Tri-State Coll. Slam, numerous others; host poetry and music venues Wayne Pub. Libr., NJ; host Young Peoples Poetry Slam; motivational speaker. Author: This Ain't No Pocket Diary, 2001; prodr.(and playwright): Poet Warriors, 2002; playwright A Cautionary Tale; contbr. articles to profl. jours. and publs.; author: Blue Angels, 2000, (cassette) Catching Angels, 1999, World Healing Book. Vol. Literacy Vols. of Am., Westchester, NY, 1998—2001. Sgt. USMC, 1976—82. Mem.: Poets and Writers. Avocations: chess, reading, walking. Mailing: 155 Linden Rd Wayne NJ 07470 Office: Speec Inc 7 Jones Pl Yonkers NY 10703

MALDONADO-BEAR, RITA MARINITA, economist, educator; b. Vega Alta, P.R., June 14, 1938; d. Victor and Marina (Davila) Maldonado; m. Larry Alan Bear, Mar. 29, 1975. BA, Auburn U., 1960; PhD, NYU, 1969. With Min. Wage Bd. & Econ. Devel. Adminstr., Govt. of P.R., 1969-70; asst. prof. econs. Manhattan Coll., 1970-72; assoc. prof. econs. Bklyn. Coll., 1972-75; assoc. prof. fin. & econs., undergrad./grad. divsn. Stern Sch. Bus. NYU, 1975-81, prof., 1981—. Vis. assoc. prof. fin. Stanford (Calif.), Grad. Bus. Sch., 1973-74; acting dir. markets, ethics & law, NYU, 1993-94; cons. Morgan Guaranty Trust Co., N.Y.C., 1972-77, Bank of Am., N.Y.C., 1982-84, Res. City Bankers, N.Y.C., 1978-87, Swedish Inst. Mgmt., Stockholm, 1982-91, Empresas Master of P.R., 1985-90. Author: Role of the Financial Sector in the Economic Development of Puerto Rico, 1970; co-author: Free Markets, Finance, Ethics and Law, 1994; contbr. artiles to profl. jours. Bd. dirs. Medallion Funding Corp., 1985-87; mem. NYU Senate and Faculty Coun., 1995—, chair fin. com., 1996—; apptd. adv. bd. dirs. equity & diversity in ednl. environs. Mod. States Commn. Higher Edn., 1991—; trustee Securities Industry Assn., N.Y. Dist. Econ. Edn. Found., 1994—; chair NSF, Nat. Vis. Com. Curriculum Devel. Project Networked Fin. Simulation, 1995—; econ. cons. Inst. Women of Color, NAt. Coun. Black Women Cmty. Svcs. Fund, 2000—; trustee Bd. Edn., Twp. Mahwah, N.J., 1991-92. P.R. Econ. Devel. Adminstrn. fellow, 1960-65, Marcus Nadler fellow, NYU, 1966-67, Phillips Lods Dissertation fellow, 1967-68. Mem. Am. Econs. Assn., Am. Fin. Assn., Metro. Econ. Assn. N.Y., Assn. Social Econs. (trustee exec. coun. 1994-96). Home: 95 Tam O Shanter Dr Mahwah NJ 07430-1526 Office: Mgmt Edn Ctr 44 W 4th St Ste 9-190 New York NY 10012-1106

MALE, ALAN THOMAS, engineering educator, association executive; b. Birmingham, England, Sept. 3, 1937; came to U.S., 1968; s. Albert Leslie and Olive (Caddel) M.; m. Beryl Glover, Sept. 20, 1958; children: Andrew James, Christopher John. BSc, U. Birmingham, 1958, PhD, 1962. Registered profl. engr. Pa., Ky.; chartered engr. U.K. Lectr. U. Birmingham, 1960-67; supr. Westinghouse Astronuclear Lab., Pitts., 1968-70; from mgr. metals processing to mgr. processing rsch. Westinghouse Rsch. Labs., 1970-83; mgr. advanced processing Westinghouse Sci. & Tech. Ctr., 1990-91; prin., tech. mgr. Concurrent Techs. Corp., Johnstown, Pa., 1992-96; dir. Ctr. for Robotics and Mfg. Systems U. Ky., assoc. dean rsch. and grad. studies College of Engring., 1996—, prof. mech. engring. Holder 16 patents in field. Fellow Inst. Materials (award 1977), Soc. Mfg. Engrs. (life mem., internat. dir. 1991-99, pres. N.Am. mfg. rsch. inst. 1988-89, Frederick W. Taylor Rsch. medal 1989, internat. pres. 1997-98), ASM Internat.; mem. ASME, AWS. Republican. Methodist. Avocations: freemasonry, carpentry, fishing. Home: 3390 Mantilla Dr Lexington KY 40513-1039

MALE, ROY RAYMOND, English language educator; b. Bklyn., Mar. 15, 1919; s. Roy Raymond and Mary Edwards (Brooks) M.; m. Carolyn Kate Conlisk, Aug. 19, 1944; children: Marilyn, Frank. BS, Hamilton Coll., 1939; MA, Columbia U., 1940; PhD, U. Tex., 1950. Instr. English U. Tex., 1946-50; asst. prof. Tex. Tech. Coll., 1950-55; mem. faculty U. Okla., 1955-84, Boyd prof. English emeritus. Vis. prof. Bowling Green U., 1962, U. Wash., 1968, U. Tex. at Arlington, 1971 Author: Hawthorne's Tragic Vision, 1957, Enter, Mysterious Stranger, 1979; editor: Types of Short Fiction, 2d edit, 1970, Money Talks, 1981; co-editor: Am. Literary Masters, 1974. Served with AUS, 1940-45. Ford Found. fellow, 1954-55; Recipient Regents award excellence teaching U. Okla., 1968 Mem. Modern Lang. Assn., South Central Modern Lang. Assn. (pres. 1968) Home: Hilton Head Plantation 40 Field Sparrow Rd Hilton Head Island SC 29926-1813

MALEC, WILLIAM FRANK, utilities company executive; b. Broadalbin, N.Y., June 22, 1940; s. Henry and Anna Frances M.; m. Sarah Powell, Sept. 11, 1965; children: Charles A., Mariah E. BS cum laude, Niagara U., 1962; MBA, Ind. U., 1967; AMP, Harvard U., 1987. Mgmt. trainee Marine Midland Bank, Buffalo, 1962-63; project budget analyst Cleve. Electric Illuminating Co., 1967-68; asst. treas. Mid-Continent Telephone Co., Hudson, Ohio, 1968-75; v.p., treas. Gulf States Utilities, Beaumont, Tex., 1975-78; treas. Cen. and S.W. Corp., C&W Leasing Inc., CSW Energy Inc., CSW Fin., Inc., Dallas; v.p., treas. Cen. and S.W. Services, Inc., 1978-89; pres. C&W Credit, Inc., 1985-89; exec. v.p., CFO TVA, Knoxville, 1989-95. Pres. Paradise Ranch Homeowners Assn.; founder Fredericksburg New Comers Club. Served with U.S. Army, 1963-65. Mem. Nat. Mgmt. Assn., Leading Chief Fin. Officers. Republican. Roman Catholic. Office: 110 N Nilam St No PMB 123 Fredericksburg TX 78624

MALECKI, EDWARD STANLEY, JR. political science educator; b. Chgo., Nov. 16, 1938; s. Edward Stanley and Lucille Clara (May) M.; m. Judith Evelyn Sobczak, Aug. 24, 1962; children: Stephen, Robert. BA, U. Ill., 1961, LL.B., 1963, MA, 1965, PhD (Charles Merriam fellow), 1969. Bar: Ill. 1963. Asst. prof. polit. sci. Calif. State U., L.A., 1967-71, assoc. prof., 1971-76, prof., 1976—, chair dept. Polit. Sci., 1993-99, acting dir. curriculum and instrn., 1998-99, dir. curriculum and instrn., 1999, acting assoc. dean, 1999—2002; dean Coll. Arts and Scis., Met. State U., Mpls./St. Paul, 2002—. Author: (with H.R. Mahood) Group Politics: A New Emphasis, 1972; contbr. articles to profl. jours.; patentee in field for kneading paddle extraction device. Chmn. Caucus for a New Polit. Sci., 1970-71; ednl. cons. Foothill Urban League, 1969-70; bd. dirs. Pasadena Area Democratic Council, 1974. Calif. State U. Los Angeles Found. grantee, 1971-72, 84-85; HEW-Urban League grantee, 1969-70; NEH fellow, 1987. Mem. Ill. Bar Assn., Am. Polit. Sci. Assn. (Outstanding Tchg. in Polit. Sci. award with Pi Sigma Alpha 1998), Am. Sociol. Assn., United Profs. Calif. (chpt. sec. 1974), ACLU (chpt. pres. 1974, 85-86, bd. dirs. So. Calif. 1981), Phi Kappa Phi. Home: 2225 Midwick Dr Altadena CA 91001-2828 Office: 5151 State University Dr Los Angeles CA 90032-4226

MALEE, THOMAS MICHAEL, lawyer; b. Omaha, May 25, 1947; BA, Carroll Coll., 1970; JD, U. Mont., 1975. Bar: Mont. 1975, U.S. Dist. Ct. Mont. 1975, U.S. Ct. Appeals (9th cir.) 1986, U.S. Supreme Ct. 1988. Staff atty. State of Mont. Legis. Counsel, Helena, Mont., 1975-76; asst. atty. gen. State of Mont., 1976; pvt. practice Seattle, Tacoma area, Wash., 1977-78, Helena, 1979-82, Billings, Mont., 1982—. Mem. State Bar of Mont. (ins. com. 1988—). Roman Catholic. Avocations: skiing, fitness. Office: 1109 N 22nd St Ste 103A Billings MT 59101-0253

MALEFAKIS, EDWARD E. history educator; b. Springfield, Mass., Jan. 2, 1932; s. Emmanuel A. and Despina (Sophoulakis) M.; m. Cali Doxiadis, 1988; children from previous marriage: Michael, Laura. AB, Bates Coll., 1953; MA, Johns Hopkins U., 1955; PhD, Columbia U., 1965. Instr. Northwestern U., 1962-63, assoc. prof., 1968-71; asst. prof. Wayne State U., Detroit, 1963-64; asst. prof. modern European history Columbia U., 1964-67, prof., 1975—, U. Mich., Ann Arbor, 1971-74. Author: Agrarian Reform and Peasant Revolution in Spain, 1970, Southern Europe in the 19th and 20th Centuries, 1992; editor: Indalecio Prieto, 1975, La guerra de España, 1936-39, 1996, Franquismo: El juicio de la historia, 2000. Recipient Herbert Baxter Adams award Am. Hist. Assn., 1971, Faculty Teaching award Northwestern U., 1971, medal of honor U. Internacional Menendez Pelayo, 1982, Orden de Mérito Civico (Spain), 1988, Nebrija prize U. Salamanca, 2000; Social Scis. Rsch. Coun. grantee, 1967, NEH grantee, 1977; Guggenheim fellow, 1974, Inst. Juan March fellow, 1991. Mem. Modern Greek Studies Assn. (exec. com. 1981-87), Soc. for Spanish and Portuguese Hist. Studies (exec. council 1969-72), Spanish Inst. N.Y.C. (bd. dirs. 1982—). Democrat. Greek Orthodox. Home: 380 Riverside Dr New York NY 10025-1858 Office: Columbia Univ 524 Fayerweather Hall New York NY 10027

MALEK, FREDERIC VINCENT, finance company executive; b. Oak Park, Ill., Dec. 22, 1936; s. Fred W. and Martha (Smickilas) M.; m. Marlene A. McArthur, Aug. 5, 1961; children: Fred W., Michelle A. BS, U.S. Mil. Acad., 1959; MBA, Harvard U., 1964; D of Humanities (hon.), St. Leo Coll., St. Petersburg, Fla., 1970. Assoc. McKinsey & Co., Inc., L.A., 1964-67; chmn. exec. com. Triangle Corp., Columbia, S.C., 1967-69; dep. under sec. HEW, Washington, 1969-70; spl. asst. to Pres. U.S., 1970-73; dep. dir. U.S. Office of Mgmt. and Budget, 1973-75; with Marriott Corp., 1975-88, sr. v.p., 1975-77, exec. v.p., 1978-88; pres. Marriott Hotels and Resorts, 1981-88, Northwest Airlines, Mpls., 1989-90, vice chmn., 1990-91, also bd. dirs.; campaign mgr. Bush-Quayle '92, 1991-92; co-chmn. CB Comml. Real Estate Group, 1989-96; chmn. Lodging Opportunities Fund, 1991—, Thayer Capital Ptnrs., 1992—, Thayer Hotel Investors, 1994—. Chmn. 1996 Rep. Presdl. Trust, 1995-96; bd. dirs. Automated Data Processing Corp., Am. Mgmt. Sys. Inc., Fed. Nat. Mortgage Assn., N.W. Airlines, FPL Group Inc., UBS Brinson Funds, Manor Care Inc.; dir. with rank of amb., 1990 Econ. Summit, 1989—; adj. prof. U. S.C., 1986-89; lectr. Kennedy Sch. Govt., Harvard U., 1976. Mem. Pres.'s Commn. on White House Fellows, 1971-75, White House Domestic Coun., 1974-75, Pres.'s Commn. on Pers. Interchange, 1974-76; dep. dir. com. for Re-election of Pres., 1972; Pres.'s Commn. on Pvt. Sector Initiatives, 1982-85, dir. conv. Bush for Pres., 1988; mem. Nat. Coun. on Surface Transp. Rsch., 1993-95; nat. adv. bd. Nat. Ctr. Econ. Edn. of Children, 1980-82; mem. Pres.'s Coun. on Phys. Fitness and Sports, 1986-91. Named Bus. Statesman of Yr. Harvard Bus. Sch. Club Washington, 2000, Citizen of Yr. Boy Scouts Am. Nat. Capitol Coun., 2000. Mem. Am.-Israel Friendship League (bd. trustees 1991—), Aspen Inst. (bd. trustees 1996—). Episcopalian. Avocations: bicycling, skiing. Office: 1455 Pennsylvania Ave NW Washington DC 20004-1008

MALEK, MARLENE ANNE, cultural organization, foundation executive; b. Oakland, Calif., June 22, 1939; d. William Alexander and Yolanda Katherine (Stella) McArthur; m. Frederic Vincent Malek; children: Frederic William, Michelle Anne. Student, Armstrong U., 1959, Marymount U., 1979. Mem. women's bd. Am. Heart Assn., 1973—. Vice chmn. bd. dirs. Marymount U., Arlington, Va.; mem. cmty. bd. and nat. com. for the performing arts Kennedy Ctr.; mem. adv. bd. Second Genesis, Bethesda, Md.; bd. dirs. Nat. Mus. Women in Arts; mem. Nat. Dialogue on Cancer; pres. Friends of Cancer Rsch.; presdl. appointment to Nat. Cancer Adv. Bd., 1991-96; mem. bd. overseers Duke U. Cancer Ctr. Episcopalian. Avocations: cross country skiing, road biking.

MALEK, REZA SAID, urological surgeon; b. Aug. 22, 1940; s. Said and Banoo (Rais) M.; m. Haleh F. Rassa, Feb. 9, 1980. MB, BS, U. London, 1964; MS in Urology, U. Minn., 1971. Diplomate Am. Bd. Urology. Intern St. Mary's Hosp., Eastbourne, Eng., 1964-65, Lister Hosp., Hitchin, Eng., 1964-65; resident, sr. house officer St. Thomas's Hosp., U. London, 1965-66, Mayo Grad. Sch. Medicine, Rochester, Minn., 1967-71; rsch. fellow in calculous disease of urinary tract, vis. clin. surgeon Bowman-Gray Sch. Medicine, Winston-Salem, N.C., 1971-72; instr. urology Mayo Clinic, Rochester, 1972-74, asst. prof., 1974-76, assoc. prof., 1976-91, prof., 1991—. Adviser to regional dir. WHO, 1972; cons. urology Mayo Clinic, 1972—; mem. Am. Bd. Urology Examiners commn., 1978-81. Mem. editl. bd. Mayo Clin. Proceedings, 1994-96. Fellow ACS, Royal Coll. Physicians and Surgeons of Can., Am. Soc. for Laser Medicine and Surgery; mem. AMA, Am. Urological Assn. Home: 1523 Camelback Ct NE Rochester MN 55906-8960 Office: Mayo Clinic 200 1st St SW Rochester MN 55905-0002

MALENA, J(AMES) ROBERT, mathematics educator; b. Monongahela, Pa., Nov. 30, 1942; s. Vincent James Jr. and Hazel Joan (Gori) M.; m. Julia Ann Duda, July 4, 1968; children: Jay Robert, Rebecca Rae. BS, California U. Pa., 1965, MEd, 1970. Cert. tchr., Pa. Tchr. Belle Vernon (Pa.) Area High Sch., 1965-67, Monongahela (Pa.) Valley Cath. H.S., 1967-74, Pleasant Hills (Pa.) Middle Sch., 1974-78; prof. math. Community Coll. Allegheny County-South Campus, West Mifflin, Pa., 1978—, chmn. math. dept., 1999—. Adj. faculty Calif. U. Pa., 1986-92; mem. adv. bd. Restructuring the Math. Bridge Project, 1994-95. Mem. Rostraver Twp. (Pa.) Recreation Commn., 1973—, pres., 1979-82; bd. dirs. Amaty C. Found., 1999-2001. Mem. Am. Math. Assn. Two-Yr. Colls. (chair devel. math. com. 1987-91, chair edn. com. 1991-93, mem. strategic planning com. 1992, steering com. 1993, treas. 1993-99), Nat. Coun. Tchrs. Math., Pa. State Math. Assn. Two-Yr. Colls. (pres. 1989-91). Home: 361 Markle Rd Belle Vernon PA 15012-3112 Office: Community Coll Allegheny County South Campus 1750 Clairton Rd West Mifflin PA 15122-3029

MALENG, NORM, prosecutor; b. Acme, Wash., 1938; m. Judy Maleng; 1 child. BS in Econs., U. Wash., 1960, JD, 1966. Bar: Wash. State 1967, U.S. Supreme Ct. 1983, USOC Wash. 1973. Staff atty. U.S. Senate Com. on Commerce; pvt. practice Seattle; chief dep. civil divsn. King County, prosecutor, 1978—. Chair Gov.'s Task Force on Cmty. Protection, 1989; vice chair Wash. Sentencing Guidelines Commn. Named Outstanding Pub. Ofcl. in King County, Mcpl. League, 1986. Mem. Wash. Assn. Pros. Attys. (pres.), Nat. Dist. Attys. Assn. (v.p., mem. exec. bd.), Wash. Assn. County Ofcls. (pres.). Office: W554 KC Courthouse 516 3d Ave Seattle WA 98104

MALENKA, BERTRAM JULIAN, physicist, educator; b. N.Y.C., June 8, 1923; s. Morris and Mollie (Wichtel) M.; m. Ruth D. Stolper, Mar. 28, 1948; children: David Jonathan, Robert Charles. AB, Columbia, 1947; MA, Harvard, 1949, PhD, 1951. Research fellow Harvard, 1951-54; asst. prof. physics Washington U., St. Louis, 1954-56; asso. prof. Tufts U., Medford, Mass., 1956-60; faculty Northeastern U., Boston, 1960—, prof. physics, 1962-93, prof. emeritus, 1993—. Mem. sci. adv. group Harvard-Mass. Inst. Tech. Cambridge Electron Accelerator, 1956— Mem. vis. com. dept. conservation Mus. Fine Arts, Boston, 1997—. Mem. Am., Italian phys. socs., N.Y. Acad. Scis., Phi Beta Kappa, Sigma Xi. Achievements include research and publs. on theory of nuclear forces and structure of nucleus, explanation polarization phenomena in high-energy scattering, gamma radiation, electric polarization deuteron, accelerator design. Home: 16 Rutledge Rd Belmont MA 02478-3323 Office: Northeastern Univ Dept Of Physics Boston MA 02115

MALERNEE, JAMES KENT, JR. management consultant; b. Durango, Colo., June 15, 1947; s. James Kent and Norma Virginia (Calhoon) M.; m. Charlean Ann Born, Aug. 21, 1971 (div. May 1, 1992). BS in Engring., U. Tex., Austin, 1970; PhD in Bus. Adminstrn., U. Tex., 1977; MBA, So. Meth. U., 1972. Petroleum engr. Tex. R.R. Commn., 1970-71; instr. fin. U. Tex., 1973-75; lectr. fin. U. Tulsa, 1975-76; assoc. Mgmt. Analysis Ctr., Northbrook, Ill., 1977-80, v.p. and Palo Alto, Calif., 1980—; sr. v.p. The MAC Group, 1987-89; also dir. MAC Rsch.; CEO, mng. dir. Cornerstone Rsch., N.Y.C., 1989-2000, pres., CEO, 2000—. Lectr. mgmt. Stanford U., 1983; leader seminars on mergers and acquisitions and corp. strategy; guest speaker in field of strategy; speaker on damages in securities litigation P.L.I. and ABA; expert witness in securities and fin. Contbr. articles to profl. jours. Named one of Outstanding Young Men Am. U.S. Jaycees, 1977. Mem. Fin. Mgmt. Assn. (v.p. 1981-82, bd. dirs. 1983-85), Assn. Corp. Growth. Home: 208 E 51st St # 123 New York NY 10022-6557 Office: Cornerstone Rsch 599 Lexington Ave New York NY 10022-6030

MALERSTEIN, ABRAHAM JOSEPH, psychiatrist, researcher; b. Cin., Nov. 2, 1924; s. Leo and Rhea (Goldstein) M.; m. Evelyn Mae Cohen (div. 1958); m. Jean Elizabeth Hayward, Dec. 6, 1958; children: Barbara, Sarah, Julia, David. AB, U. Calif., Berkeley, 1949; MD, Chgo. Med. Sch., 1954. Diplomate Am. Bd. Psychiatry. Intern Cook County, Chgo., 1954-55; resident Langley Porter Clinic, San Francisco, 1955-58; assoc. clin. prof. U. Calif., 1967—, assoc. clin. prof. Davis Med. Ctr. Sacramento, 1987-88; pvt. practice San Francisco, 1958-86; staff psychiatrist Atascadero (Calif.) State Hosp., 1985-87; pvt. rschr. San Francisco, 1988—; owner Cole Valley Press, 1993—. Vis. scholar U. Calif., Berkeley, 1998—. Author: The Conscious Mind, 1986; co-author: A Piagetian Model of Character Structure, 1982, Psychotherapy and Character Structure, 1989; contbr. articles to profl. jours. Pfc. U.S. Army, 1943-46. Fellow Am. Psychiatric Assn. (life). E-mail: ajmalerstein@earthlink.net.

MALEY, PATRICIA ANN, preservation planner; b. Wilmington, Del., Dec. 25, 1955; d. James Alfred and Frances Louise (Fenimore) M.; m. Scott A. Stone, Dec. 7, 1991 (div. June 1994). AA, Cecil C.C., 1973; BA, U. Del., 1975, MA, 1981. Cert. secondary tchr., Del. Analyst econ. devel. City of Wilmington, 1977-78, evaluation specialist, 1978-80, planner II mayor's office, 1980-86, cons. preservation, 1986-87; dir. Belle Meade Mansion, Nashville, 1987-88; dir. planning, devel. Children's Bur. of Del., Wilmington, 1988; prin. preservation planner Environ. Mgmt. Ctr., Brandywine Conservancy, Chadds Ford, Pa., 1988-92; planning cons., 1992-95; design review and preservation commn. coord. Wilmington Dept. Planning, 1995—, code enforcement constable, 1997—. Cons. cultural resources M.A.A.R. Inc., Newark, Del., 1987, ITC Cons., Wilmington, 1985-86; mem. Planned Approach to Comty. Health, Wilmington, task force for Wilmington Enterprise Comty. Health Benchmarking Project. Contbg. photographer America's City Halls, 1984; author numerous Nat. Register nominations, 1980-86; 88—. Pres., founder Haynes Park Civic Assn., Wilmington, 1977-80; photographer Biden U.S. Senate Campaign, New Castle County, Del., 1984; sec. parish coun. Our Lady Fatima Roman Cath. Ch., 1985-86, choir dir., 1983-87; mem. com. on design & renovation of worship spaces Diocese of Wilmington, also mem. Diocesan com. on music; bd. dirs. Del. Children's Theatre; music dir. St. Elizabeth Ann Seton parish, Bear, Del., 1988—, mem. long range planning com./demographics. U. Del. fellow, 1976-77. Mem.: New Castle County (Del.) Bd. Realtors, Am. Planning Assn. (exec. com. Del. chpt. 1997, elected state chpt. treas. 1997, 1999, 2001), Am. Inst. Cert. Planners (cert. planner), Nat. Trust Hist. Preservation, Del. Hist. Soc., Nat. Pastoral Musicians Assn., Pi Sigma Alpha. Democrat. Avocations: photography; choral, piano, organ music. Office: City of Wilmington Dept Planning 800 N French St Fl 7 Wilmington DE 19801-3590 E-mail: trish1225@aol.com.

MALEY, WAYNE ALLEN, engineering consultant; b. Stanley, Iowa, Mar. 9, 1927; s. Neil Gordon and Flossie Amelia (Wharram) M.; m. Marianne Nelson, Aug. 2, 1959; children: James G., Mary E., Mark A. BS in Agrl. Engring., Iowa State U., 1949; postgrad., Purdue U., Ga. Tech., IIT. Cert. mediator. Power use advisor Southwestern Electric, Greenville, Ill., 1949-53; field agt. Am. Zinc Inst., Lafayette, Ind., 1953-59; mktg. devel. specialist U.S. Steel, Des Moines, 1959-65, mktg. rep. Pitts., 1965-71, bar products rep., 1972-76; assoc. Taylor Equipment, 1977-81; mgr. pub. rels. Am. Soc. Agrl. Engrs., St. Joseph, Mich., 1981-84, dir. mem. svcs., 1984-92; cons. Tech. Tours, 1992—. Author: Iowa Really Isn't Boring, 1993, (textbook) Farm Structures, 1957, (computer program/workbook) Rim Lift Material Handling, 1970 (Blue Ribbon award 1971); editor: Agriculture's Contract with Society, 1991. Pres. Ednl. Concerns for Hunger Orgn., Ft. Myers, Fla., 1979-81; dist. activity dir. Boy Scouts Am., Moon Twp., 1969-70. With USN, 1945-46. Named Hon. Star Farmer, FFA Ill., 1958. Fellow Am. Soc. Agrl. Engrs. (bd. dirs. 1979-81 hon. for forum leadership 1991); mem. Agrl. Editors Assn., Coun. Engring. Soc. Execs. (bd. dirs. 1984-85), Sigma Xi (pres./del. Whirlpool chpt. 1993-94). Presbyterian. Achievements include patents for fence building machine, for material handling system; design of cable fences; design and installation of steel beverage can recycling center. Home and Office: Tech Tours 2592 Stratford Dr Saint Joseph MI 49085-2714 E-mail: wamaley@juno.com.

MALGIERI, NICK, chef, author, educator; b. Newark, Sept. 30, 1947; s. Nufre and Antoinette (LoConte) M. BA in French, Seton Hall U., 1970; AOS in Culinary Arts, Culinary Inst., Hyde Park, N.Y., 1973. Pastrycook Seehotel Meierhof, Zurich, 1973-74, Hotel de Paris, Monte Carlo, 1974, Sporting Club, Monte Carlo, 1974-76, Hotel la Reserve, Beaulieu, France, 1974; pastry chef Windows on the World, N.Y.C., 1976-79; asst. pastry chef Hotel Waldorf Astoria, 1979; chmn. baking dept. N.Y. Restaurant Sch., 1979-83; dir. baking program Inst. of Culinary Edn., 1984—; founder, owner Total Heaven Baking Co. Exec. chef Paine Webber; pastry chef Board Room; cons. Inhilco, Inc.; guest lectr. Smithsonian Instn.; Am. spokesperson for Switzerland tourism. Author: Nick Malgieri's Perfect Pastry, 1989, Great Italian Desserts, 1990, How to Bake, 1995 (James Beard Found. Cookbook award/Best Book on Baking/Desserts of 1995), Chocolate, 1998 (IACP/Julia Child cookbook award 1998, Salon Internat. du Livre award), Cookies Unlimited, 2000, Perfect Cakes, 2002; contbr. articles and recipes to newspapers and profl. jours. Named One of 10 Best Pastry Chefs in USA, Pastry Art & Design Mag., 1998, 99. Mem. Internat. Assn. Culinary Profls. (cert. culinary profl., chmn. certification 1989-91), Amicale Culinaire de Monaco, Societe Culinaire Philanthropique N.Y., Federazione Italiana dei Cuochi, James Beard Found. (coord. competitions 1991-95), N.Y. Assn. Cooking Tchrs. (former bd. dirs., Ann. honor 2000), Cooking Advancement, Rsch. and Edn. Found. (former trustee), Bakers Dozen East (founding mem.). Home: 277 W 10th St New York NY 10014-2562 Office: Inst of Culinary Education 50 W 23d St New York NY 10010

MALGUARNERA, SALVATORE CHRIS, mechanical engineer; b. Bklyn., Dec. 31, 1946; s. Christopher Joseph and May Malguarnera; m. Linda Ann Skinner, Dec. 5, 1971; children: Maria Julie Lynn, Michael Wayne. BS, U.S. Mil. Acad., 1969; MSME, MIT, 1976, PhD in Mech. Engring., 1978. Registered profl. engr., Tex., Ohio. Commd. 2d lt. U.S. Army, 1969, advanced through grades to dapt.; combat engr. unit comdr. U.S. Army Corps Engrs., Ft. Bragg, NC, 1969—74, Vietnam; asst. prof. mech. engring. Tex. A&M U., College Station, 1978—81; sr. drilling engr. Superior Oil Co., Lafayette, La., 1982—89; R&D mgr. NL Industries, Houston, 1984—86, dir. North Sea MWD Aberdeen, Scotland, 1986; tech. cons. S.E.A., Inc., Columbus, Ohio, 1987—. Contbr. articles to profl. jours. Fellow, NSF, 1975—78, Swope Found., 1974—75; grantee, NASA, Dept. Transp., 1980—81. Mem.: Soc. Automotive Entrs., Soc. Petroleum Entrs. Roman Catholic. Achievements include patents for fluid delivery and mixing system; method and apparatus for treatment of particulate materials; flowmeter. Avocations: fitness, keyboard. Home: 256 E Granville Rd Columbus OH 43085 Office: FTI/SEA Cons 7349 Worthington-Galena Rd Columbus OH 43085 Office Fax: 614-884-8014.

MALHERBE, ABRAHAM JOHANNES, VI, religion educator, writer; b. Pretoria, South Africa, May 15, 1930; arrived in US, 1951; s. Abraham Johannes and Cornelia Aletta (Meyer) Malherbe; m. Phyllis Melton, May 28, 1953; children: Selina, Cornelia, Abraham Johannes VII. BA, Abilene Christian U., 1954; STB, Harvard U., 1957; student, U. Utrecht, The Netherlands, 1960-61; ThD, Harvard U., 1963; LLD (hon.), Pepperdine U., 1981; LHD (hon.), Centre Coll., 1990; STD (hon.), Providence Coll., 1994; DD (hon.), U. Pretoria, 2000. Minister Ch. of Christ, Lexington, Mass., 1956-63; asst. and assoc. prof. Abilene (Tex.) Christian U., 1963-67; vis. scholar Harvard Divinity Sch., Cambridge, Mass., 1967-68; assoc. prof. Abilene Christian U., 1968-69, Dartmouth Coll., Hanover, N.H., 1969-70, Yale Divinity Sch., New Haven, 1970-77, prof., 1977-81, Buckingham prof., 1981-94, assoc. dean acad. affairs, 1987-89, prof. emeritus, 1994—. Guest prof. U. Pretoria, South Africa, 1989, 98. Author: (book) Social Aspects of Early Christianity, 1983, Moral Exhortation, 1986, Paul and the Thessalonians, 1987, Ancient Epistolary Theorists, 1988, Paul and the Popular Philosophers, 1989, Commentary on Thessalonian Letters, 2000; mem ed bd: Bible Rev, 1986—, consult: Anchor Bible Dictionary, 1992; contbr. articles to profl jours; inspiration for book: Greeks, Romans and Christians: Essays in Honor of Abraham J Malherbe, 1990. Recipient Teaching Award, Abilene Christian U., 1965, 1967, Outstanding Alumni Citation, 1996, NEH award, 1973. Mem.: Novum Testamentum (mem edtl. bd. 1991—), Religious Studies Rev (mem edtl. bd. 1980—), Studiorum Novi Testamenti Soc., N Am Patristic Soc. (co-founder Restoration Qtrly. 1957), Soc Biblical Literature, South African New Testament Soc (hon.). Ch Of Christ. Home: 71 Spring Garden St Hamden CT 06517-1913 Office: Yale Divinity Sch 409 Prospect St New Haven CT 06511-2167 E-mail: abraham.malherbe@yale.edu.

MALHI, GURBAX SINGH, legislator; b. India; m. Devinder Brar, Mar. 16, 1976; children: Gurinder, Harinder. BA in Polit. Sci., English, History, Punjab U., India; BA in Polit. Sci., English and History. Prior com. appts. Ho. of Commons Standing Com. for Govt. Ops., Standing Com. on Procedure and Ho. Affairs, Spl. Com. on Code of Conduct for MPs and Senators, Subcom. on Bus. of Supply, Pearson Airport Subcom., Limousine Subcom.; assoc. mem. Com. for Fgn. Affairs, 0000—00; mem. Ho. of Commons Standing Com. for Human Resources, 0000—00; with Justice, Legal Affairs, Human Rights, Industry Coms.; mem. Scrutiny of Regulations Com.; chmn. Ho. of Commons Standing Com. for Libr. of Parliament; former pres. Bramalea-Gore-Malton Fed. Liberal Assn.; elected Ho. of Commons, 1993, re-elected, 1997, 2000, apptd. parliamentary sec. to min. of labour, 2001—; current mem. Standing Com. on Human Resources Devel. Founder, chair Canada-South Asia Parliamentary Friendship Group. Active Toronto Real Estate Bd., Canadian Real Estate Assn.; former dir. Malton Neighborhood Svcs. Office: Unit 4-2565 Steeles Ave E Brampton ON L6T 4L6 Canada E-mail: malhig@parl.gc.ca.

MALHOTRA, ASHOK KUMAR, philosophy educator; b. Ferozepur, India, 1940; came to the U.S., 1963, naturalized, 1977. s. Nihal Chand and Vidya (Wanti) M.; m. Nina Judith Finestone, Oct. 24, 1966 (dec.); children: Raj Kumar, Ravi Kumar. BA, U. Rajasthan, 1961, MA, 1963; PhD, U. Hawaii, 1969. Asst. prof. SUNY, Oneonta, 1967-70, assoc. prof., 1970-80, prof., 1980—, chmn. philosophy dept., 1975-80. Vis. prof. SUNY-Buffalo, summer 1970, Kurukshetra U. and Birla Inst., Pilani, India, spring 1980; grants reviewer NEH, 1978—; bd. dirs. SUNY Press editorial, 1989-93, dir. SUNY study abroad, program to India, 1980—; cons. TV series Kung Fu: The Legend Continues., 1992. Author: Sartre's Existentialism in Nausea and Being and Nothingness, 1978, Sartre's Existentialsim as Literature and Philosophy, 1995, Pathways to Philosophy: A Multidisciplinary Approach, 1996, Culture and Self, 1997, Transcreation of the Bhagavad Gita, 1998, Instant Nirvana, 1999, An Introduction to Yoga Philosophy, 2001; TV appearances include ABC World News Now, NBC News, JAIN TV, Doordarshan TV, ZEE TV (India), Natraj TV (Holland), All India Radio. Founder Ninash Found. Oneonta; established Indo-Internat. Sch., Dundlod, Rajasthan, India. Recipient Excellence in Tchg. award United Univ. Profession; East-West Ctr. fellow, 1963-65, 66-67, Friend of Ednl. award City of Oneonta, 1998, Disting. Alumni award East West Ctr., 2000; N.Y. State Dept. Edn. grantee, 1967-68, 68-69, summer 1969, NEH grantee, summer 1979. Mem. Am. Philos. Assn., Soc. Asian and Comparative Philosophy, Assn. Asian Studies, N.Y. State Asian Studies Soc., Internat. Phenomenol. Soc. Home: 17 Center St Oneonta NY 13820-1445 E-mail: malhotak@oneonta.edu.

MALHOTRA, DEEPAK KUMAR, nephrologist; b. Amritsar, India, Mar. 7, 1956; came to the U.S., 1958; s. Om Parkash and Bimla (Vijh) M.; m. Judith Maria Konfal, Apr. 20, 1989; children: Kristin, Nathan. BS, Case Western Res. U., 1978, PhD, 1984, MD, 1985. Resident Cleve. Clinic Found., 1985-88; fellow U. Colo. Health Scis. Ctr., Denver, 1988-91; asst. prof. U. N.Mex., Albuquerque, 1991-97; assoc. prof. Med. Coll. Ohio, Toledo, 1997—. Staff physician VA Med. Ctr., Albuquerque, 1991-93, 96—; cons. pharmacy and therapeutics U. N.Mex., 1994—. Contbr. articles to profl. jours. Grantee Am. Heart Assn., 1994. Mem. Internat. Soc. Nephrology, Am. Soc. Nephrology, Am. Soc. Transplant Physicians Internat., Soc. Magnetic Resonance in Medicine, ACP. Avocations: woodworking, photography, home and automotive repair. Home: 7238 Saint Thomas Ct Toledo OH 43617-2244 Office: Med Coll Ohio Dept Medicine Divsn Nephrology 3000 Arlington Ave PO Box 10008 Toledo OH 43699-0008

MALHOTRA, HARISH K. psychiatrist, educator; b. Lahore, Pakistan, Dec. 4, 1945; came to U.S., 1973; s. Sohan Lal and Krishna M.; m. Mahamaya Malhotra, Oct. 29, 1972; children: Gautam, Rahul. MBBS, Glancy Med. Coll., Amritsar, India, 1967; MD in Psychiatry, Postgrad. Inst. Med. Edn. & Rsch., Chandigarh, India, 1972. Diplomate Am. Bd. Psychiatry and Neurology. Rotating intern Victoria Jubilee Hosp., Amritsar, 1968; resident in psychiatry Postgrad. Inst. Med. Edn. and Rsch., Chandigarh, 1970-72, acting registrar in psychiatry, 1972; resident in psychiatry, assoc. dept. psychiatry N.J. Med. Sch., Newark, 1973-75, instr. dept. preventive medicine, 1976-77, asst. prof. dept. psychiatry, 1977, clin. asst. prof. dept. psychiatry, 1977-84, 91—; pvt. practice Elizabeth, N.J., 1977-82, New Providence, 1982-84, Springfield, 1985-93, Summit, 1993—; assoc. attending dept. psychiatry Elizabeth Gen. Hosp., 1977-82; staff psychiatrist Overlook Hosp., Summit, 1982—. Sabbatical leave, India, 1984-85; med. advisor to judges in bur. hearing and appeals, divsn. disability determinations Social Security Adminstrn., 1978-96; med. dir. psychiat. day care ctr., div. drug abuse, dept. preventive medicine and cmty. health N.J. Med. Sch., Newark, 1976-77; chmn. med. audit com. Elizabeth Gen. Hosp., 1979-82; chmn. dept. psychiatry Overlook Hosp., 1999—; psychiat. cons. Alexian Bros. Hosp., Elizabeth, 1977-82. Creator numerous profl. audiocassettes; contbr. articles to profl. jours.; presenter in field. Bd. advisors Internat. Soc. Korean Studies in Ams., 1996—. Recipient Silver medal Proficiency in Physiology. Mem. Am. Psychiat. Assn. Avocation: numismatics. Office: 33 Overlook Rd Ste 212 Summit NJ 07901-3563 Fax: 908-277-1439. E-mail: nanabhai@pol.net.

MALHOTRA, INDU, research scientist, researcher; b. Amritsar, Punjab, India; came to U.S., 1970; d. Jaichand and Pushpa (Khanna) Mehra; m. Girish K. Malhotra; children: Rohit, Malvika. BS, U. Bombay, 1965, MS, 1968. Microbiologist Greystone Hosp., Greystone Park, N.J., 1970-71; rsch. asst. U. Cin., 1978-81; rsch. scientist Interferon Scis. Inc., New Brunswick, N.J., 1982-85; lab. mgr. Case Western Res. U., Cleve., 1987—. Dir. Epcot Internat. Cleve., 1996—. Contbr. articles to profl. jours. including Am. Jour. Tropical Medicine and Hygiene, Analytical Biochemistry, and Jour. Immunology. V.p. Asian Am. Indian Women's Orgn., Cleve., 1995. Mem. Am. Soc. Tropical Medicine and Hygiene. Avocations: community services, cooking, travel, table tennis. Office: Case Western Res U 2109 Adelbert Rd Cleveland OH 44106-2624

MALHOTRA, MAHAMAYA, psychiatrist; b. Patiala, India, Feb. 10, 1948; d. Bharat Chand and Manorma (Khosla) Khanna; m. Harish Kumar Malhotra, Oct. 26, 1972; children: Gautam, Rahul. MBBS, Gandhi Med. Coll., 1970; degree in psychiatry, U. Med. Dentistry N.J., 1977. Diplomate Am. Bd. Psychiatry and Neurology. Intern Gandhi Hosp., India, 1970-71, Niloufer Hosp., India, 1971-72; resident U. Medicine and Dentistry of N.J., 1975-77, Bergen Pines County Hosp., Paramus, N.J., 1977-78; cons. Elizabeth (N.J.) Gen. Hosp., 1978-81, St. Elizabeth Hosp., Elizabeth, 1978-81, Alexian Bros. Hosp., Elizabeth, 1978-81, Overlook Hosp., Summit, N.J., 1981—. Cons. Youth and Family Counseling Svcs., Westfield, N.J., 1979-84, Family and Children's Soc., Elizabeth, 1980-84; pvt. practice, Elizabeth, 1978-81, New Providence, Springfield, N.J., 1983-93, Summit, N.J., 1993—. Contbr. articles to newspapers. Mem. AMA, Am. Psychiat Assn., Am. Med. Women's Assn., N.J. Psychiat. Assn., N.J. Med. Women's Assn. Home: 20 Grove Ter Summit NJ 07901-4102 Office: 33 Overlook Rd Ste 212 Summit NJ 07901-3563 Fax: (908) 277-1439. E-mail: maya07901@yahoo.com.

MALHOTRA, NARESH KUMAR, management educator; b. Ambala, Punjab, India, Nov. 23, 1949; came to U.S., 1975; s. Har Narian and Satya (Kakkar) M.; m. Veena Bahl, Aug. 13, 1980; children: Ruth Veena, Paul Naresh. *Dr. Malhorta converted from Hinduism to Christianity on March 19, 1978. He is a Bible preacher, teacher, and evangelist. He has preached the Gospel in 24 countries and has been blessed to see more than 100,000 people pray to accept the Lord Jesus Christ as their personal Savior. He frequently travels overseas to share his faith in the Lord Jesus Christ. He is a Deacon and member of the First Baptist Church, Atlanta. He has been married to Veena for over 22 years and they have two children, Ruth and Paul.* BTech with honors, Indian Inst. Tech., Bombay, 1971; MBA, I.I.M., Ahmedabad, India, 1973; MS, SUNY, Buffalo, 1978, PhD, 1979. Mgmt. cons. ASCI, Hyderabad, India, 1971-73; asst. prof. Ga. Tech. Inst., Atlanta, 1979—, assoc. prof. mgmt., coord. mktg., 1982-87, 89—, prof., 1988, Regents' prof., 1992—. Organizer several nat. and internat. mktg. mgmt. confs. *Malhotra is ranked the number one researcher in the country based on four different rankings; articles published in: Journal of Marketing Research, 1980-1985; Journal of Health Care Marketing, Journal of the Academy of Marketing Science,since 1986-1995, Journal of the Academy of Marketing Science since inception through volume 23, 1995.* Author: Marketing Research: An Applied Orientation (N.Am., European, Internat., Australia and New Zealand, Spanish edits.); contbr. articles to profl. jours. Lay preacher of the Gospel. Fellow Acad. Mktg. Sci. (disting., program chmn. 1984-85, 85-86, v.p. programs 1988-90, chmn. bd. 1990-92, pres. 1994-96, chmn. found. 1996—, Top Rsch. Jour., Jour. Mktg. Rsch., Jour. Acad. Mktg. Sci., Jour. Healthcare Mktg.), Decision Scis. Inst. (track chmn. 1984-86); mem. Am. Mktg. Assn. (track chmn. 1983-84), Am. Statis. Assn. Republican. Baptist. Avocations: reading, writing, ch. activities, outdoor activities. Home: 1956 Lenox Rd NE Atlanta GA 30306-3035 Office: Ga Tech Inst Sch Mgmt Atlanta GA 30332-0001 E-mail: naresh.malhotra@mgt.gatech.edu.

MALHOTRA, RIPUDAMAN, chemist, researcher; b. Dehradoon, India, July 25, 1950; s. Madan Kishore and Shakuntala M.; m. Ellen R. Dunn, May 15, 1979; children: Asha. PhD, U. So. Calif., 1979. Chemist SRI Internat., Menlo Park, Calif., 1979-96, dept. dir., 1996—. Chair Gordon Rsch. Conf. Hydrocarbon Resources, Ventura, Calif., 2001—. Co-author: Nitration: Methods and Mechanisms, 1989; editor: Combinatorial Materials Development, 2002; co-editor Synthesis and Characterization of Advanced Materials, 1997. Recipient Cleve. Newcombe medal AAAS, 1998. Office: SRI Internat 333 Ravenswood Ave Menlo Park CA 94025 Fax: 650-859-6196. E-mail: ripu@sri.com.

MALHOTRA, YOGESH, former computer scientist, consultant, entrepeneur, former computer engineer; b. India, Jan. 11, 1964; B in Engring. with distinction, U. Delhi, India, 1984; MBA Phi Kappa Phi and Beta Gamma Sigma honors, U. Nev., Las Vegas, 1993; PhD in Bus. Adminstrn./Info. Sys. and Knowledge Mgmt. with honors, U. Pitts., 1998. Cert. computing profl.; chartered engr. Exec. engr. Suzuki Maruti Udyog Ltd., Gurgaon, India, 1984-87; sys. analyst Tata Unisys Ltd., New Delhi, 1987-89; sr. sys. analyst JK Technosoft, Neepz, India, 1989; sr. cons. info. sys. Bank Am., Nev., 1990-91; prin. founder, knowledge architect @BRINT.COM, The Biztech Network, Pitts., 1994—; founder, chmn., chief knowledge officer Brint.com L.L.C., 1998, Fla. Atlantic U. Prof. bus. adminstrn. Northwestern U., Carnegie Mellon U., U. Pitts., Fla. Atlantic U., 1998; cons. info. sys. Unisys Corp., Atlanta, 1987-89, Banque Indo Suez, Hong Kong, 1989; coun. ptnr. U.S. Fed. Govt. Best Practices Coun., 1996—; reviewer Acad. Mgmt., 1997; mem. adv. panel knowledge mgmt. Govt. The Netherlands, Amsterdam, 1998, Arthur Andersen, Chgo., 1998; founding mem., contbg. editor Ziff Davis Standard for Internet Commerce; lectr. U. Pitts., 1993-98; founder Knowledge Mgmt. Think Tank and WWW Virtual Libr. on Knowledge Mgmt., 1997—; prof., spkr. in field. Lead author, editor: Knowledge Management and Virtual Organizations, 2000; assoc. editor: e-Service Quarterly, Information Strategy: The Executive's Jour. of Expert Systems, Jour. of Global Information Management; editor-in-chief: Knowledge Management; mem. internat. editl. rev. bd. Info. Resources Mgmt. Jour., contbr.rschd. articles to profl. jours.; reviewer info. tech. publs. and e-commerce and knowledge mgmt. books; contbr. pub. interviews to profl. jours including CIO Enterprise, Information Week, Wall Street Jour., Inc., others; contbr. citations of work to worldwide bus. and tech. trade press, govt. and corp. reports, confs., others. Expert interviews analyses featured in Business Week, Wall Street Journal, Forbes, Fortune, Inc., CIO Magazine, Information Week, Computerworld, etc. BRINT Institute, Syracuse, NY, 1998—2001, As thought leader, advice and opinion quoted in strategy and policy documents of pre-eminent worldwide governments, corporations, and institutions. Recipient Kaizen Quality Improvement awards Japanese Car Mfg. Co., 1984-87, Japanese Lang. award Larget Car Mfr. India, Gurgaon, 1984-87, Online Achievement award Industry.Net, 1996, Top Rank cert. Am. Inst. Banking; Doctoral Consortium fellow Acad. Mgmt., 1997, doctoral fellow & scholar U. Pitts., 1993-96. Mem. Inst. Engrs. (life). Avocations: information systems, e-business, knowledge management. Office: School of Management Syracuse University Syracuse NY 13244 Home and Office: Apt 53D 5100 Highbridge St Fayetteville NY 13066-2467 E-mail: yogesh.malhotra@brint.com.

MALI, PAUL, publisher, retired minister; b. Hartford, Conn., July 6, 1926; BS in Engring., U. Conn., 1953, MS, 1962, PhD in Mgmt. and Engring., 1967. Cert. mgmt. cons. Inst. Mgmt. Cons. Elec. engr. Gen. Dynamics, Groton, Conn., 1953—67, dir., 1961—67; prof. of mgmt. Entrepreneurial, New London, Conn., 1961—67; prof. mgmt. U. Conn., Hartford, 1967—94; minister/co-pastor Bible Student ch., New London, Conn., 1994—. Author: (book) various profl. books, including Writing and Word Processing for Scientists and Engineers, 1981, MBO Updated, 1986, (ministerial books) The Bible as a Rising Civilization, 1998, Ten Bad Mistakes About God, 2000, Terrorism and the Permission of Evil, 2002, Biblical View on Human Cloning, others, 2002. Pres. Good Samaritan Fund, New London, Conn., 1994—; bd. dirs. 12 state cmty. colls., 1981—88. Mem.: Am. Mgmt. Assn., Phi Delta Kappa, Etta Kappa Nu, Tau Beta Pi.

MALIA, GERALD ALOYSIUS, lawyer; b. Blakeley, Pa., Aug. 6, 1933; s. Anthony Francis and Mary Agnes (Kelly) M.; m. Mary Catherine Carolan, June 27, 1959; children: Mary Catherine Malia Higgins, Carolan Elizabeth Malia Taylor, Elizabeth Kelly, Gerald Anthony. BS, St. Peter's Coll., Jersey City, 1954; JD, Georgetown U., 1958, LLM, 1959. Bar: D.C. 1959, U.S. Ct. Appeals (D.C. cir.) 1959, U.S. Supreme Ct. 1964. Law clk. Chief Judge A. Hood D.C. Ct. Appeals, Washington, 1959-60; from assoc. to ptnr. Ragan & Mason, 1961-92; counsel Kirlin, Campbell & Keating, 1993—2000; pvt. practice, 2000—. Adj. prof. Georgetown U. Law Ctr., Washington, 1973—; Disting. lectr. Cath. U. Law Sch., Washington, 1979—; vis. prof. World Maritime U., Malmo, Sweden, 1992—; del. Jud. Conf., Washington, 1994—; industry prof. Webb Inst., N.Y.C., 1996—. Author: Maritime Law: The Need for a Comprehensive Maritime Code, 1983; editor Georgetown Law Jour., 1958. 1st lt. U.S. Army, 1954-56. Mem. ABA, Maritime Adminstrv. Bar Assn. (pres.), Maritime Law Assn., Cosmos Club, Congressional Country Club. Roman Catholic. Avocation: golf. Office: Law Office of Gerald A Malia 1660 L St NW Washington DC 20036-5603

MALICAY, MANUEL ALABAN, physician; b. Zamboonga City, The Philippines, Aug. 13, 1947; arrived in US, 1973; s. Bernardino Malicay Agan and Juliana (Alaban) Malicay; m. Lourdes V Manzano, Jan. 20, 1974; children: Mark, Marlo, Brian, Michael, Margaret. BS, Far Eastern U., Manila, 1967, MD, 1972. Rsch. and tchg. fellow Far Eastern U., Manila, 1972-73; intern St. Francis Hosp., Evanston, Ill., 1973-74; resident in internal medicine Vets. Hosp., Hines, 1974-76; pvt. practice Bolingbrook, 1976—; physician Hinsdale (Ill.) Hosp., 1976-97, Hindsdale (Ill.) Hosp., 1976—, Good Samaritan Hosp., Downers Grove, Ill., 1977—, vice chmn. dept. medicine, 1998—2001, chmn. Clin. Quality Coun., 1999-2001. Chmn continuing med educ comt IPMS, 1998—. Editor: IPMS Today, 1989—91. Trustee Far Ea. Univ. Sch. Med. Alumni Found., 1993—2001; pres. Class of 1972, Far Ea. Univ. Dr. N. Reyes Med. Alumni Found.; v.p. Far Ea. Univ. Sch. Med. Alumni Found., 2002—. Named Most Outstanding Silver Jubilarian, Far Eastern Univ Dr N Reyes Med Alumni Found, 1997. Fellow: ACP; mem.: AMA, Far Eastern Univ Med Alumni Asn Ill (pres. 1991—93, co-chair conv. ann. reunion and sci. seminar 1993, Oustanding Alumnus 1995), Assn. Philippine Physicians Am. (co-chair 25th ann. conv. and sci. seminar 1996, gov. 1996—2001), Ill Med Soc (del. 1990—), DuPage County Med Soc (bd. dirs. 1986—2002), Ill Philippine Med Soc (seminar program dir. 1994, pres. 1994—96, chmn CME comt 1998—, program dir. Primary Care Update 1999, 2001, Disting Leadership Award 1996, Disting Physician Award Organized Med 1999, Disting Serv Award 2001). Avocations: tennis, dancing. Home: 2 S 676th Ave Vendome Oak Brook IL 60521 Office: 402 W Boughton Rd Bolingbrook IL 60440-1872 also: 47 6th Ave La Grange IL 60525-2499

MALICK, ELDON ROY, music educator, musician; b. Ft. Wayne, Ind., July 27, 1951; s. Roy Harrison and Loretta Matlick; m. Pamela Ann Shepherd, June 16, 1974; 1 child Jeremy Matlick. B Music Edn., Ea. Ky. U., 1973; MusM in Horn Performance, Ind. U., 1980, MusD, 1997. Dir. bands Crittenden County Pub. Schs., Marion, Ky., 1973—78; hornist, assoc. prifn. Owensboro (Ky.) Symphony, 1974—83, Evansville (Ind.) Philharm., 1982—83; music prof. Murray (Ky.) State U., 1980—83; assoc. prof. music U. Okla., Norman, 1983—; prin. hornist Oklahoma City Philharm., 1989—. Pres. orch. com. Oklahoma City Philharm., Oklahoma City, 1998; soloist Owensboro Symphony, 1982, Paducah (Ky.) Symphony, 1983, Oklahoma City Symphony, Oklahoma City, 1998, Oklahoma City Philharmonic, Oklahoma City, 2002. Musician: (CD) Horn Concert, 2002, (solo CD) Horn Konzert, Bavarian Horn, (solo performances) Internat. Horn Symposia. Mem.: Internat. Horn Soc. (state rep. 1986—), Music Tchrs. Nat. Assn., Am. Fedn. Musicians, Phi Kappa Lambda (chpt. pres. 1999—). Home: 1217 Willow Rock Ct Norman OK 73072

MALICK, TERRENCE (DAVID WHITNEY II), film director; b. Waco, Tex., Nov. 30, 1943; Motion picture director, writer, prodr. Films include Dirty Harry, 1971, Pocket Money, 1972, Deadhead Miles, 1972, Badlands, 1973 (Golden Seashell award 1974), The Gravy Train, 1974, Days of Heaven, 1978 (Best Dir. award Cannes Film Festival 1979, nominee Golden Globe award 1979, N.Y. Film Critics Circle award 1978), The Thin Red Line, 1998 (nominee Best Dir. Oscar 1999, nominee Best Writing Oscar 1999, Golden Berlin Bear award 1999, Chgo. Film Critics Assn. award 1999, Golden Satellite award 1999, others). Office: c/o DGA 7920 W Sunset Blvd Los Angeles CA 90046-3300 also: c/o Harley Williams 1900 Ave of the Stars Fl 17 Los Angeles CA 90067*

MALICKI, GREGG HILLARD, agricultural equipment manufacturing executive; b. Chgo., Feb. 13, 1947; s. Hillard Lawrence and Virginia Valerie (Vosen) M.; 1 child, James Michael. BSBA, U. Ill., Champaign, 1975; MBA, U. Iowa, 1985; student, Coll. DuPage, Glen Ellyn, Ill., 1972-73, Ill. Inst. Technol., 1965-68. First lt. U.S. Army, 1969-72; sr. engring. analyst Deere & Co., Moline, Ill., 1975-87, sr. cons. engr., 1987-94; regional mgr. Internat. Supply Mgmt. Svcs., Moline, 1994-97, mgr., 1997-2000, Enterprise Supply Mgmt., Deere & Co., 2000—. Pres. Inst. Indsl. Engrs., Moline Ill., 1987—. Col. Army N.G., 1975-2000. Recipient Letter of Commendation Nat. Merit 1965 Mem. Inst. Indsl. Engrs. (sr.; pres. 1987—), Inst. for Supply Mgmt., Soc. Automotive Engring., Am. Prodn. and Inventory Control Soc., Phi Theta Kappa, Chi Gamma Iota. Roman Catholic. Avocation: conversational in German. Home: 3418 49th St Moline IL 61265-6614

MALIGAS, MANUEL NICK, metallurgical engineer; b. Thimena, Greece, May 9, 1943; came to U.S., 1950; s. Nick and Jane M.; children: James Paul, John Michael. BE, Youngstown U., 1966; MS, Youngstown State U., 1974. Sr. material engr. Goodyear Aerospace, Akron, Ohio, 1966-76; plant metallurgist Tex. Bolt, Houston, 1976-81; sr. material engr. N.L. Shaffer, 1981-83; ind. cons. M&M Metall., 1983; materials engring. specialist FMC Corp., 1983—. Engring. material specialist, instr. materials U. Houston; presenter symposia. Contbr. articles to profl. publs.; editl. com. Advanced Materials and Processes. Fellow ASM Internat. (past officer); mem. Am. Petroleum Inst. (chmn. material and welding coms.), Nat. Assn. Corrosion Engrs. (chmn.). Achievements include development of of carbon composite materials for aircraft brakes; use of laser and HVOF process for hard facing; patents for for hardface coating for gate valves; for high strength weld overlay material for corrosion resistance. Home: 9721 Cypresswood # 913 Houston TX 77070 Office: FMC Corp PO Box 3091 Houston TX 77253-3091 E-mail: mmmal@pdq.net.

MALIK, GHAUS MUHAMMAD, neurosurgeon; b. Mar. 1, 1946; MD, King Edward Med. Coll., Lahore, Pakistan, 1968. Sr. staff neurosurgeon Henry Ford Hosp., Detroit, 1975—; vice chmn. dept. neurosurgery Henry Ford Health Sys., 1983—; chair divsn. neurosurgery William Beaumont Hosp., Royal Oak, 2000—. Office: 2799 W Grand Blvd Detroit MI 48202-2608

MALIK, JOHN STEPHEN, lawyer; b. Bryn Mawr, Pa., Sept. 15, 1958; s. John and Mary M. (Pisko) M. BA, St. Joseph's U., 1980; JD, Del. Law Sch., 1983. Bar: Del. 1984, Pa. 1984, U.S. Dist. Ct. Del. 1984, N.J. 1985, U.S. Ct. Appeals (3d cir.) 1990, U.S. Supreme Ct. 1989. Adj. faculty Widener U., Wilmington, 1984-86; sole practice, 1985—. Mem. ATLA, Am. Judicature Soc., Nat. Assn. Criminal Def. Lawyers, Del. Assn. Criminal Def. Lawyers, Del. Bar Asns. Democrat. Roman Catholic. Office: 100 E 14th St Wilmington DE 19801-3210

MALIK, OM PARKASH, electrical engineering educator, researcher; b. Sargodha, Punjab, India, Apr. 20, 1932; arrived in Can., 1966; s. Arjan Dass and Kesar Bai (Ahuja) M.; m. Margareta Fagerstrom, Dec. 22, 1968; children: Ola Parkash, Mira, Maya. Nat. Diploma in Elec. Engring., Delhi (India) Poly., 1952; M in Engring., Roorkee (India) U., 1962; PhD, London U., 1965; D.I.C., Imperial Coll., London, 1966. Registered profl. engr., Ont., Alta. Asst. engr. Punjab State Elec. Bd., 1953-61, asst. to chief engr., 1957-59; rsch. engr. English Elec. Co., Eng., 1965-66; asst. prof. U. Windsor, Ont., Can., 1966-68; assoc. prof. U. Calgary, Alta., Can., 1968-74, prof. Can., 1974-97, faculty prof. Canada, 1997—2000, assoc. dean student affairs, faculty engring. Can., 1995-98, assoc. acad. dean faculty engring. Alta., Can., 1979-90, acting dean Can., 1981, prof. emeritus Canada, 1997—. Cons. prof. Huazhong U. Sci. and Tech., Wuhan, People's Republic China, 1986—. Assoc. editor Can. Elec. and Computer Engring. Jour., 1988-97, mng. editor, 1998—; contbr. 400 articles to profl. jours. Indsl. tng. scholar Govt. India, 1952-53, sr. indsl. tng. scholar Confedn. Brit. Industries, 1959-60; recipient Can. Pacific Rwy. engring. medal Engring. Inst. Can., 1997, Alberta Ingenuity Fund Rsch. Excellence award, 2002. Fellow IEEE (life, chmn. Western Can. coun. 1983-84, chmn. student activities Can. region 1979-82, Centenniel medal 1984, Merit award 1986, Third Millennium medal 2000, A.G.L. McNaughton award 2001), EIC, Inst. Elec. Engrs., Can. Acad. Engring.; mem. IEEE Power Engring. Soc. (machine theory subcom. 1979—, excitation sys. subcom. 1988—, sys. dynamic performance com. 1988—, energy devel. and power generation com. 1990—), Assn. Profl. Engrs., Geologists and Geophysicists Alta. (Vol. Svc. award 1990, Alberta Ingenuity Rsch. Excellence award), Assn. Profl. Engrs. Ont., Am. Soc. Engring. Edn., Can. Elec. Assn. (assoc., controls com. 1977-92, chmn. digital control com. 1977-85, chmn. edn. com. 1983-85, mem. expert sys. com. 1989-94), Confederacion Panamericana de Ingenieria Mecanica, Electica y Ramas Afines (v.p. 1987-2000, bd. dirs. region I, 1991-93). Hindu. Home: 4 6841 Coach Hill Rd SW Calgary AB Canada T3H 3T9 Office: U Calgary Dept Elec & Computer Engring 2500 University Dr NW Calgary AB Canada T2N 1N4 E-mail: maliko@ieee.org.

MALIN, HOWARD GERALD, podiatrist; b. Providence, Dec. 2, 1941; s. Leon Nathan and Rena Rose (Shapiro) M. AB, U. R.I., 1964; MA, Brigham Young U., 1969; BSc, Calif. Coll. Podiatric Medicine, 1969, DPM, 1972; MSC, Pepperdine U., 1978; MD (hon.) , Internat. U. Sch. Medicine, Winnipeg, Man., Can., 2001; MD (hon.) , Internat. U. Sch. Medicine, 2001. Diplomate Am. Bd. Podiatric Pub. Health, Am. Bd. Podiatric Orthopedics, Am. Acad. of Wound Care Mgmt. Extern in podiatry VA Med. Ctr., Wadsworth, Kans., 1971-72, Marine Corps Res. Dept., San Diego, 1972; resident in podiatric medicine and surgery N.Y. Coll. Podiatric-Medicine, N.Y.C., 1972-73; resident in podiatric surgery, instr. in podiatric surgery N.Y. Coll. Podiatric Medicine, 1973-74; pvt. practitioner in podiatric medicine and surgery Bklyn., 1974-77; mem. staff Prospect Hosp., Bronx, N.Y., 1974-77; chief podiatry service, mem. staff, cons. sports medicine David Grant U.S. Air Force Med. Ctr., Travis AFB, Calif., 1977-80; chief podiatric sect., mem. staff VA Med. Ctr., Martinsburg, W.Va., 1980—. Instr. ednl. devel. program VA Med. Ctr., Martinsburg, W.Va., 1980—; clin. prof. med. sci. Alderson-Broaddus Coll., U. Osteopathic Medicine and Health Scis.; adj. prof. Barry U. Sch. Podiatric Medicine; dir. extern program Pa. Coll. Podiatric Medicine. Editorial rev. bd. Jour. Contemporary Podiatric Physician, 1991—. Lt. Col. USAFR, 1977-2001. Fellow Am. Soc. Podiatric Dermatology, Am. Coll. Foot Orthopedics, Am. Coll. Podiatric Physicians, Am. Coll. Podiatric Radiology (archivist, past pres.), Am. Soc. Podiatric Medicine (past pres., archivist), Am. Coll. Foot and Ankle Pediatrics (pres. archivist, historian), Am. Profl. Wound Care Assn., Royal Soc. Health; mem. Am. Acad. Podiatric Sports Medicine (assoc.), Assn. Mil. Surgeons U.S. (life), Am. Coll. Podiatric Surgery (assoc.), Am. Assn. Podiatric Med. Writers (pres., archivist), Phi Kappa Theta, Phi Kappa Psi. Home: 118 Trooper Drive Apt 2D Martinsburg WV 25401-3723 Office: VA Med Ctr Dept Podiatry Martinsburg WV 25401 Fax: 304-262-7446.

MALIN, IRVING, English literature educator, literary critic; b. N.Y.C., Mar. 18, 1934; s. Morris and Bertha (Silverman) M.; m. Ruth Lief, Dec. 18, 1955; 1 child, Mark. BA, Queens Coll., 1955; PhD, Stanford U., 1958. Acting instr. English Stanford U., 1955-58; instr. Ind. U., 1958-60; from instr. to prof. CCNY, 1960-72, prof., 1972—. Cons. Jewish Publ. Soc., 1964, Am. Quar., 1964, NEH, 1972, 79, 80, 81, 82, B'nai B'rith, 1974-75, Yaddo, 1975-77, Jewish Book Coun., 1976, 79, PEN, 1978-82, Princeton U. Press, 1979, Fairleigh Dickinson Press, 1980, Wayne State U. Press, 1980, Internat. Coun. Exch. of Scholars, 1980-81, Duke U. Press, 1981, Jewish Daily Forward, 1981, U. Pitts. Press, 1981, Papers on Lang. and Lit., 1981, U. Ga. Press, 1983, UMI Rsch., 1989, Gordian Press, 1990, Ctr. for Study of Higher Edn., 1990, Mosiac, 1991, MacArthur Found., 1996, U. of S.C. Press, 1998, Purdue U. Press, Lafayette, Ind., 1999. Author: William Faulkner: An Interpretation, 1957, New American Gothic, 1962, Jews and Americans, 1965, Saul Bellow's Fiction, 1969, Nathanael West's Novels, 1972, Isaac Bashevis Singer, 1972; co-editor: Breakthrough: A Treasury of Contemporary American Jewish Literature, 1964, William Styron's The Confessions of Nat Turner: A Critical Handbook, 1970, The Achievement of William Styron, 1975, William Goyen, 1997, Into the Tunnel, 1998, Garrett's Elizabethan Trilogy, 1998; editor: Psychoanalysis and American Fiction, 1965, Saul Bellow and the Critics, 1967, Truman Capote's in Cold Blood: A Critical Handbook, 1968, Critical Views of Isaac Bashevis Singer, 1969, Contemporary American-Jewish Literature: Critical Essays, 1973, Conrad Alken's Prose, 1982; co-editor: Underwords: Perspectives on Der DeLillo's Underworld, 2002; adv. editor: Studies in American Jewish Literature, Jour. Modern Literature, Review of Contemporary Fiction, Saul Bellow Jour., 20th Century Literature; reviewer: Hollins Critic, So. Quar.; co-editor Paul Bowles, 1986, Spl. Issue of 20th Century Lit., James Dickey Spl. Issue of S.C. Rev., 1994, Pynchon and Mason and Dixon, 2000, So. Novelists on Stage and Screen So. Quar., 1995, James Dickey's Fiction Spl. Tex. Rev., 1996, Leslie Fiedler and American Culture, 1999, Torpid Smoke: The Stories of Vladimir Nabokov, 2000. Fellow Yaddo, 1963, Nat. Found. for Jewish Culture, 1963-64, Huntington Libr., 1978. Mem. MLA, AAUP, Am. Studies Assn., Am. Jewish Hist. Soc., Melville Soc., Authors League Am., Soc. Study of So. Lit., Poe Studies Assn., English Inst., Nathaniel Hawthorne Soc., N.Y. Acad. Scis., Poetry Soc. Am., Popular Culture Assn., Nat. Book Critics Circle, Sherwood Anderson Soc., Internat. Assn. Univ. Prof. English, Kafka Soc., English-Speaking Union, Multi-Ethnic Lit. U.S. Soc., Hastings Ctr., Am. Jewish Congress, Assoc. Writing Programs, Nat. Coun. Tchrs. of English, Vladimir Nabokov Soc., Phi Beta Kappa. Jewish. Home: 96-13 68th Ave Forest Hills NY 11375-5039 Office: CCNY Dept English New York NY 10031

MALIN, ROBERT ABERNETHY, investment management executive; b. Mt. Vernon, N.Y., Dec. 13, 1931; s. Patrick Murphy and Caroline Cooper (Biddle) M.; m. Gail Lassiter, Nov. 5, 1960; children: Alison Campbell, Robert Lassiter. AB, Dartmouth Coll., 1953, MBA, 1954. Asst. to comptroller Biddle Purchasing Co., N.Y.C., 1958-59; with Blyth & Co., Inc., 1960-71, v.p., 1965-71, dir., 1968-71, sr. v.p., mem. exec. com., 1971-72; sr. v.p. corp. fin. Reynolds Securities Inc., N.Y.C., 1972-74, dir., 1973-74; mng. dir. First Boston Corp., N.Y.C., 1974-90; gen. ptnr. Tiedemann Investment Group, 1991-96; mng. dir. SeaBridge Investment Advisors, Summit, N.J., 1997—. Mem. adv. council Fin. Acctg. Standards Bd., 1973-78. Served as lt. (j.g.) USNR, 1954-57. Mem.: Securities Industry Assn. (acctg. com.), Investment Bankers Assn. Am., The Moorings Club, Morris County Club, Beacon Hill Club, Links Club. Republican. Home: 105 Whittredge Rd Summit NJ 07901-3709 Office: SeaBridge Investment Advisors 450 Springfield Ave Ste 301 Summit NJ 07901-2610 E-mail: malinrobta@aol.com., bobmalin@seabridge.com.

MALIN, SETH ARNOLD, surgeon, educator; b. Bridgeport, Conn., 1942; MD, Jefferson Med. Coll., 1970. Diplomate Am. Bd. Surgery. Intern N.Y. Hosp.-Cornell Med. Ctr., 1970-71; resident in surgery Yale-New Haven Hosp., 1971-73, U. Cin. Hosp. Group, 1973-77; staff surgeon U.S. Army, Ft. Sill, Okla., 1977-79; chief gen. surgery, dir. surgery Delaware County Meml. Hosp., Drexel Hill, Pa.; mem. staff Fitzgerald-Mercy Hosp.; pvt. practice. Clin. asst. prof. surgery Jefferson Med. Coll., 1979—. Fellow ACS. Office: Med Conf Ctr/Delaware County Meml Hosp 2100 Keystone Ave Drexel Hill PA 19026-1129

MALINA, CAROL JOY, clinical social worker; b. July 2, 1959; AB, Washington U., St. Louis, 1981; MSW, Boston U., 1986. Program dir., family therapist Family Continuity Programs Inc., Framingham, Mass., 1986-91, dist. clin. dir. Beverly, 1991-93; clin. coord. New Eng. Home for Little Wanderers, Watertown, 1993-97; psychotherapist Stoney Brook Counseling Ctr., Billerica, 1998—2000; tng. dir., clin. coord. Concord Family and Youth Svcs., Acton, 2000—. Bd. dirs. Dance New Eng., Cambridge, Mass., 1994-96, 98-2000. Mem. NASW, Phi Beta Kappa.

MALINDZAK, GEORGE STEVE, JR. cardiopulmonary physiology, toxicologist, biomedical engineer; b. Cleve., Jan. 3, 1933; s. George Steve Sr. and Mary (Zemancik) M.; m. Marianne Beamer, June 27, 1959; children: Katherine, Scott, Edward, Eric. AB cum laude in Chemistry and Biology, Western Res. U., 1956; MSc in Physiology and Biophysics, Ohio State U., 1959, PhD in Physiology and Biophysics, 1961; postgrad., MIT, 1963-65, Stanford U., 1969. Metallurgist Thompson & Co., Cleve., 1956-57; from instr. to asst. prof. dept. physiology Bowman Gray Sch. Medicine, Winston-Salem, N.C., 1962-68, assoc. prof., 1968-73; rsch. physiologist U. N.C.-EPA, Chapel Hill, 1973-76; prof., chmn. dept. physiology N.E. Ohio U. Coll. Medicine, Rootstown, 1976-85; prof., chmn. dept. biomed. engring. La. Tech. U., Ruston, 1985-88; health sci. adminstr. NIH, Nat. Inst. Environ. Health Scis., Rsch. Triangle Park, NC, 1988—96, branch chief, 1996—99, ret., 1996. Cons. Internat. Chelation Rsch. Found., 1982—, Tech. Adv. Svc. for Attys., 1979—. Contbr. articles to profl. publs. Mem. U.S. Power Squadron (boating), 1967—. With U.S. Army, 1950-53. Grantee NIH, 1961-73, N.C. Heart Assn., 1962-73, EPA, 1973-76, Am. Heart Assn., 1977-85. Mem. AAAS, Am. Soc. Engring. Edn., Am. Physiol. Soc., Am. Soc. Pharmacology and Exptl. Therapeutics, Assn. Chmn. Depts. Physiology, IEEE Engring. in Medicine and Biology Group, Biomed. Engring. Soc., Am. Heart Assn. (basic sci. coun.), Assn. Computing Machinery, AAUP, Biophys. Soc., La. Engring. Soc., Sigma Xi, Beta, Beta, Beta, Alpha Eta Mu. Achievements include research in environmental toxicology, asthma intervention, cardiopulmonary toxicology, coronary and cerebral vascular reactivity and spasm, coronary and cerebral ischemia and hypoxia and vascular control, carbon monoxide toxicity, autonomic and receptor physiology and pharmacology, control of blood flow in health and disease, microcirculation of the heart, cardiopulmonary function and environmental toxicology, hypoxia, ischemia and circulatory function, pathophysiology of coronary and peripheral vascular atherosclerosis, echocardiography and ventricular function, spinal cord trauma, cardiac function and rehabilitation of alcoholics, peripheral vascular disease, medical electronics and medical engineering, cardiovascular modeling, indicator-dilution techniques and analyses, mathematical and computer analyses of biological systems. Home: 10009 Bushveld Ln Raleigh NC 27613-6145

MALING, GEORGE CROSWELL, JR. physicist; b. Boston, Feb. 24, 1931; s. George Croswell and Marjory (Bell) M.; m. Norah J. Horsfield, Dec. 29, 1960; children: Ellen P., Barbara J., Jeffrey C. AB, Bowdoin Coll., 1954; S.B., S.M., MIT, 1954, Elec. Engr., 1958, PhD in Physics, 1963. Rsch. asst., postdoctoral fellow MIT, 1957-65; adv. physicist IBM Corp., 1965-71, sr. physicist N.Y., 1971-92; pres. Empire State Software Systems, Ltd., 1992-93; dir. Noise Control Found., Inc., Poughkeepsie, 1975—; chmn. com. Sl-acoustics Am. Nat. Standards Com., 1976-79; dir. INCE Found., Inc., 1993—; mng. dir. Inst. of Noise Control Engring., 1994—. Pres. INCE Found., 1999—. Editor: Noise/News, 1972-92; mng. editor: Noise/News Internat., 1993—; assoc. editor Jour. Acoustical Soc. Am., 1976-83; editor tech. proc.; contbr. numerous articles to profl. jours. Served with U.S. Army, 1955-57. Recipient Rayleigh medal Inst. Acoustics U.K., 1999. Fellow IEEE, AAAS, Acoustical Soc. Am. (exec. coun. 1980-83, Silver medal in noise 1992), Audio Engring. Soc.; mem. Inst. Noise Control Engring. (bd. dirs. 1972-77, pres. 1975), Internat. Inst. Noise Control Engring. (bd. dirs. 1980-86, 90—, v.p. comms. 1997—), Nat. Acad. of Engring. E-mail: maling@alum.mit.edu.

MALININ, THEODORE, medical educator, researcher; b. Krasnodar, Russia, Sept. 13, 1933; came to U.S., 1949; s. Ivan M. and Olga A. (Senitzkaya) M.; m. Dorothy Rearick, Sept. 4, 1960; children: Ellen T., Alexander T., Catherine T., Michael T. BS, Concord Coll., 1955; MS, U. Va., 1958, MD, 1960; DSc (hon.), U. Scranton, 1990. Asst. prof. Georgetown U., Washington, 1964-68, assoc. prof., 1968-70; prof. surgery U. Miami, Fla., 1970-79, prof. orthopaedics, 1979—. Author: Surgery and Life, 1978; editor 3 books; contbr. over 200 articles to profl. jours. Active Nat. Rep. Com., Washington, 1964—; treas. Mannheimer Found., sec. ACMS, Inc., 1999—, sec. Sumter Recycling and Solid Waste Disposal, 1999—. Surgeon USPHS, 1962-64. Recipient Orden, U. Javeriana, 1992. Mem. AMA, Am. Acad. Orthopaedic Surgeons, Am. Soc. Invest. Pathology, Royal Soc. Medicine, Rotary (Disting. Rotarian 1994). Achievements include patents in field; research on latent injury in cryopreservation of cartilage, cartilage structure, and tissue banking; definition of behavior of transplanted cartilage and bone. Office: U Miami Dept Orthopaedics R-12 PO Box 16960 Miami FL 33101-6960

MALINKOVSKAJA, SOFIJA SERGEJ, library director; b. Volodarsk, Ukraine, Russia, Feb. 10, 1930; d. Sergej and Lidija (Lutchko) Titov; m. Albert Malinkovskij, 1952 (div. Sept. 1972); children: Sergej, Vladimir. Logic lectr. Riga State Pedagogical Inst., 1953-58; sch. prin. Riga H.S., 1958-62; dir. libr., pensioner U. Latvia, Riga, 1992—. Contbr. articles to profl. jours. Dep. Regional Soviet, Riga, 1959-62. Recipient three medals for Disting. Govt. Labor, Ministry of Edn., 1967-90, achievement medals, 1992; hon. Culture Figure of Latvia, 1979. Mem. Coun. Rsch. Librs., Coun. Librs. Latvia Ministry of Edn. (chairwoman 1962-92). Avocations: reading, music, philosophy of religion. Office: Latvian State U Libr Bul'var Rajnisa 19 Riga Latvia

MALINOSKI, FRANK JOSEPH, general practice physician; b. Troy, N.Y., Sept. 4, 1954; s. Frank and Ruth Elizabeth (Martin) M.; m. Judith Ann Sanders, May 23, 1981; children: Wayne D. Peschel, Matthew C. BA, Colby Coll., Waterville, Maine, 1976; PhD, Rutgers U., 1981; MD, Albany (N.Y.) Med. Sch., 1985. Commd. U.S. Army, 1981, advanced through grades to lt. col.; intern Brooke Army Med. Ctr., San Antonio, 1985-86; physician U.S. Army Med. Research Inst. Infectious Diseases, Frederick, Md., 1986-92; reservist U.S. Army, 1992—; dir. clin. rsch. Lederle-Praxis Biols., Rochester, N.Y., 1992-96; sr. v.p. med. affairs NABI, Rockville, Md., 1996-99; asst. v.p. clin. affairs-vaccines Wyeth-Ayerst Global Pharms., 2000—02, v.p. clin. affairs, 2002—. Cons. Frederick Med. Ctr. Clinic, Walkersville, Md., 1987-92; affiliate staff Frederick Meml. Hosp., 1987-92. Contbr. articles to profl. jours. Mem. Frederick County Substance Abuse Coun., 1988-92, Drug Utilization Rev. Bd. of Md., Balt., 1989-92, Instn. Biosafety Com., 1988-92. Nat. Cancer Inst. fellow, 1978-81; Cystic Fibrosis Found. fellow, 1979-80; N.Y. State Health Research Council fellow, 1981-82. Mem. AMA, Am. Soc. Microbiology, Am. Soc. Virology, Am. Soc. Torpical Medicine and Hygiene, Am. Assn. Family Physicians, Infectious Disease Soc. of Am. Republican. Home: 115 Valley Park Rd Phoenixville PA 19460-5734 Office: Wyeth 555 E Lancaster Ave Saint Davids PA 19087

MALINOWSKI, ARTHUR ANTHONY, lawyer, labor arbitrator; b. Chgo., Apr. 4, 1929; s. Ignatius and Sophie (Data) M. BS in Econs., DePaul U., 1956, JD, 1960; MS in Indsl. Rels., Loyola U., 1958; PhD, Ill. Inst. Tech., 1972; LLM in Labor Law, Chgo. Kent Coll. Law, 1981. Bar: Ill. 1960. Instr. indsl. rels. Loyola U., Chgo., 1963-69, prof., 1969-94; prof. emeritus, 1994—; mem. Ill. Office Collective Bargaining, Chgo., 1973-83. Lectr. dept. econs. Ill. Inst. Tech., Chgo., 1965-68. Mem. Ill. Bar Assn., Indsl. Rels. Rsch. Assn., Nat. Acad. Arbitrators, Knights Malta, Phi Alpha Delta, Alpha Sigma Nu, Pi Gamma Mu, Iota Sigma Epsilon, Beta Gamma Epsilon. Home: 9240 Major Ave Morton Grove IL 60053-1552 Office: Loyola U of Chgo 25 E Pearson Ste 1250 Chicago IL 60611-2147

MALINOWSKI, DENNIS EDMUND, government consultant; b. Sheboygan, Wis., Mar. 18, 1948; s. Edmund Thomas and Delores Rose (Zientarski) M.; m. Linda Ann Paulinski, June 15, 1968; children: Patrick, Melanie, Anne. BBA, U. Notre Dame, 1970. Analyst Dun & Bradstreet, Chgo., 1970-72; prodn. supr. Ball Brothers Corp., Mundelein, Ill., 1972-74; adjudicator, specialist, personnel dir. State of Wis., Madison, 1974-81; asst. mgr. claims Wis. Physicians Svc., 1981-84; fin. dir. Walworth County, Elkhorn, Wis., 1984-90; state mgr. MAXIMUS, Inc., Madison, 1990—. Instr. Madison Area Tech. Coll., 1973-89. Cubmaster Boy Scouts Am., Madison, 1978; basketball coach St. Dennis Parish and YMCA, Madison, 1979-81; active local ch. groups. Nelson Mufflen scholar, 1966. Mem. Wis. Counties Fin. Officers Assn. (v.p. 1984-85), Notre Dame Alumni Assn. South Ctrl. Wis. (pres. 1979-82, exec. bd. 1990-93), Nat. Notre Dame Alumni Assn. (senate rep. 1981-82, 87). Roman Catholic. Avocations: photography, music, sports. Home: 4323 Sprecher Rd Madison WI 53718-6537 Office: MAXIMUS Inc 2702 International Ln Ste 204 Madison WI 53704-3117 E-mail: denlinda68@cs.com.

MALINOWSKI, MARYELLEN, photographer, artist; b. Oak Park, Ill., Oct. 10, 1961; d. Richard A. and Mary Jo (Curran) Lamz; m. Preston Malinowski; children: Nicole, Brielle, Demi. Student, Internat. Acad. Merch./Design, Chgo., 1985, Maine Photog. Workshops, Rockport, 1996, Elgin (Ill.) C.C., 1993-94. Owner Visual Elements, Dundee, Ill., 1992-94; owner, dir. The Infrared Light Gallery, Houston, 1994—; represented by Fraser Gallery, Washington. Spkr. in field. Author: The Sacred Light, 1999; exhibited infrared photography in shows. Founder, bd. dirs. The Sacred Light Found. Recipient awards for photography; People's Choice award Women's Work Exhbn., Woodstock, 1995, 1st place Georgetown Internat. Fine Art Exhbn., Washington, 1997; recipient Ill. Women's Works Scholarship, 1996. Mem. Kodak Profl. Network, Luminos Printmakers Guild, Nat. Mus. Women in Arts. Office: The Infrared Light Gallery PO Box 218542 Houston TX 77218 E-mail: maryellen@infraredlight.com.

MALINOWSKI, PATRICIA A. community college educator; b. Buffalo, Jan. 19, 1950; d. Raymond J. and Emily M. (Ferek) Cybulski; m. Leonard T. Malinowski, July 12, 1975; children: Adam, Christopher. BA, SUNY, Fredonia, 1971; MEd, Bowling Green State U., 1972. Prof. devel. studies Finger Lakes C.C., Canandaigua, N.Y., 1987-92, assoc. prof., 1992-96, prof. devel. studies, 1996—, chair devel. studies dept., 1991—. Editor: Rsch. and Tchg. in Devel. Edn., 1990—; contbr. Sch. bd. mem. St. Mary's Sch., Canandaigua, 1993—99; active Literacy Vols., 1994—2000; counselor Boy Scouts Am., 1998—; active Canandaigua PTO, 1998—; mem. Ontario County Arts Coun., 2001—. Recipient Excellence in Profl. Svc. award, N.Y. State Chancellor, 1993, Disting. Svc. award, Finger Lakes C.C., 1988, 2000, Pelican award, Boy Scouts Am., 2002. Mem.: NADE (edn. bd. 1994—, Outstanding Publ. award 1995), N.Y. Coll. Learning Skills Assn. (v.p., sec., conf. chair 1987—, Outstanding Profl. Svc. award 1995), N.Y. State English Coun., N.Y. State Reading Assn., Nat. Coun. Tchrs. English, Internat. Reading Assn. (editl. bd. 1994—), Nat. C.C. Chair Acad. (editl. bd. 1992—), Phi Delta Kappa. Avocation: Avocations: family, reading, travel, walking. Office: Finger Lakes CC 4355 Lakeshore Dr Canandaigua NY 14424-8347 E-mail: malinopa@flcc.edu.

MALINS, DONALD CLIVE, biochemistry, researcher; b. Lima, Peru, May 19, 1931; came to U.S., 1947; s. Richard Henry and Mabel (Madeline) M.; m. Mary Louise Leiren, 1962; children: Christopher W., Gregory S., Timothy J. BA, U. Washington, 1953; BS in Chemistry, Seattle U., 1954; PhD in Biochemistry, U. Aberdeen, 1967, DSc, 1976. Dir. environ. conservation div. Nat. Marine Fisheries Svc., Seattle, 1974-87; sr. scientific cons. U.S. Dept. Justice, Washington, 1989-91; sci. cons. NOAA, 1990-92; prin. scientist, dir. molecular epidemiology program Pacific N.W. Rsch. Inst., Seattle, 1992—; rsch. prof. dept. chemistry Seattle U., 1972-95. Affiliate prof. dept. environ. health U. Washington, 1984—, Coll. Ocean & Fishery Scis. U. Washington, 1974-91; editor-in-chief Aquatic Toxicology, 1980-95; lectr., speaker in field. Contbr. articles to profl. jours.; inventor in field. Bd. dirs. Am. Oceans Campaign, 1989-91; adv. bd. Internat. Jt. Commn., 1990-91. Recipient U.S. Dept. Commerce Gold medal, 1982. Mem. NAS, Am. Soc. Biochemistry and Molecular Biology, Am. Assn. for Cancer Rsch. Office: Pacific Northwest Rsch Inst Biochem Oncology Program 720 Broadway Seattle WA 98122-4302 E-mail: dmalins@puni.org.

MALIS, ANDREW GARY, telecommunications company executive; b. Boston, Aug. 20, 1953; s. Irving and Nora Malis; m. Leslie Seaton, July 30, 1978; 1 child, Jonathan. ScB in Computer Sci., Brown U., 1975; ScM in Applied Math. and Computer Sci., Harvard U., 1979. Mem. tech. staff Mitre Corp., Bedford, Mass., 1975-78; divsn. engr. Bolt Beranek and Newman, Cambridge, 1979-93; cons. engr. Ascom Nexion, Acton, 1993-96; sr. cons. engr. Cascade Comm./Ascend Comm./Lucent Techs., Westford, 1996-2000; chief technologist Vivace Networks, Inc., San Jose, Calif., 2000—. Chmn. working group Internet Engring. Task Force, Reston, Va., 1993—, ATM Forum, St. Louis, 1998-2000; mem. tech. adv. bd. Megisto Sys., Inc., Germantown, Md., 2000—; cons. Coun. Tech. Advisors, Gerson Lehrman Group, N.Y.C., 2000—; chmn. tech. com. Multi-Protocol Label Switching Forum, Fremont, Calif., 2000—; spkr., chmn. numerous telecom.-related confs. Contbr. articles to sci. jours., including Proces. IEEE, IEEE Comm.; author telecom. stds. documents, 1981—. Bd. dirs., past pres. Temple Emanuel, Andover, Mass., 1986—. Recipient spl. tech. achievement award Frame Relay Forum, 1994, Disting. Svc. award, 1999; Spotlight award ATM Forum, 2000. Mem. IEEE, Internet Soc., Sigma Xi. Democrat. Jewish. Achievements include patent for method and apparatus for enabling flow control over multiple networks having disparate flow control capability. Avocation: travel. Office: Vivace Networks Inc 2730 Orchard Pky San Jose CA 95134 E-mail: andy.malis@vivacenetworks.com.

MALIS, LEONARD IRVING, neurosurgeon; b. Phila., Nov. 23, 1919; s. Morris Melvin and Dorothy (Brodsky) M.; m. Ruth Gornstein, June 24, 1942; children: Larry Alan, Lynne Paula. MD, U. Va., 1943. Intern Phila. Gen. Hosp., 1943-44; resident in neurology Mt. Sinai Hosp., N.Y.C., 1947, resident in neurosurgery, 1948-50, neurosurgeon in chief, dir. dept. neurol. surgery, 1970-92; prof., chmn. dept. neurosurgery Mt. Sinai Sch. Medicine, CUNY, 1970-92, prof. emeritus dept. neurosurgery, 1993—; fellow in neurophysiology Med. Sch., Yale U., 1951; practice medicine specializing in neurosurgery N.Y.C., 1951-95. Cons. in field. Contbr. numerous articles to profl. jours.; developer various surg. and electronic instruments. Capt. M.C., U.S. Army, World War II. Mem. ACS, Am. Assn. Neurol. Surgery, Congress Neurol. Surgeons, Am. Physiol. Soc., Soc. Neuroscis., Am. Acad. Neurol. Surgery, Soc. Neurol. Surgeons, Alpha Omega Alpha. Home: 219-44 Peck Ave Hollis NY 11423 E-mail: nsdoclen@aol.com.

MALISHENKO, TIMOTHY PETER, business executive; b. Reading, England, Nov. 4, 1944; s. John and Myra Phillys (Morris) M.; m. Jane Baxter, Mar. 17, 1968; 1 child, Andrew. BSBA, Ohio State U., 1968; MBA in Supply Chain Mgmt., Mich. State U., 1969; MS in Sys. Mgmt., U. So. Calif., 1972; postgrad., Squadron Officer Sch., Maxwell AFB, Ala., 1973, Armed Forces Staff Coll., Norfolk, Va., 1979, Nat. War Coll., Washington, 1986. Commd. 2d lt. USAF, 1968, advanced through grades to maj. gen., 1998, adminstrv. contracting officer, rep. Hughes Aircraft Co. Calif., 1969-73, procurement staff mgmt. officer, Air Staff Tng. Program Washington, 1973-74, from dep. plant rep. to plant rep. Sec. Air Force Spl. Proj. Sunnyvale, Calif., 1974-76, chief contracts and acquisition NATO E-3A Early Warning Sy. Brunssum, The Netherlands, 1979-82, dep. dir. R&D contracting Aero. Sys. Divsn. Wright-Patterson AFB, Ohio, 1982-84, dir. contracting, dep. aero. equipment, 1984-86, chief contract support divsn. Office Asst. Sec. Washington, 1987-88, chief, sys. and logistics contracting divsn., 1988-89, asst. dep. asst. sec. for contracting, 1989-90, dir. contracting Electronic Sys. Ctr. Hanscom AFB, Mass., 1990-93, dep. dir. contracting Hdqrs. Air Force Materiel Command Wright-Patterson AFB, Ohio, 1993-94, dir. contracting Hdqrs. Air Force Materiel Command, 1994-95; dep. asst. sec. for contracting USAF, Pentagon, Washington, 1995-97, dir. def. contract mgmt. agy., 1997-2001; v.p., contracts and pricing, space and comm. group The Boeing Co., Seal Beach, Calif., 2001—. Maj. gen. USAF. Contbr. articles to profl. jours. Decorated Legion of Merit with oak leaf cluster, Def. Meritorious Svc. medal, Meritorious Svc. medal with two oak leaf clusters. E-mail: malishenko.tj@verizon.net., timothy.p.malishenko@boeing.com.

MALIT, LEE ARNALL, physician; b. Phila., Dec. 21, 1946; MD, Jefferson Med. Coll., 1969. Diplomate Am. Bd. Anesthesiology. Intern Thomas Jefferson U. Hosp., Phila., 1969-70; resident in anethesiology Hosp. U. Pa., 1970-72; fellow in pediat. anesthesiology rsch. Hosp. U. Pa.-Children's Hosp., 1972-73; clin. assoc. anesthesia NIH, Bethesda, Md., 1973-75; asst. prof. dept. anesthesia Pa. State U., Hershey, 1976-78; staff Lankenau Hosp., Phila., 1979—2002; clin. asst. prof. Thomas Jefferson U., 1979—2002. Lt. comdr. USPHS, 1973-75. Mem. AMA, Internat. Anesthesia Rsch. Soc., Am. Soc. Anesthesiology, Soc. Cardiovasc. Anesthesiologists, Pa. Soc. Anesthesiology, Pa. Med. Soc., Montgomery County Med. Soc., Phila. Soc. Anesthesiology.

MALIZZIO, DONNA MARIE, social worker; b. Chgo., Sept. 24, 1959; d. Nicholas Michael and Marion Josephine (Pecora) M.; m. Michael Lynn Ruebensam, June 5, 1993. BS in Social Work, Ill. State U., 1981; MSW, U. Ill., 1983. Lic. clin. social worker Ind., diplomate clin. social work, diplomate clin. forensic counseling. Mental health technician Chgo. Heights (Ill.) Terrace, 1979-83; intern in social work Ill. State Psychiat. Inst., Chgo., 1982-83; clin. social worker The Hammond Clinic, Munster, Ind., 1984—. Divorce mediator trainer Mediation and Consultation Inst., Chgo., 1994, advanced divorce mediator trainer, 1995. Mem.: NASW (qualified clin. social worker), Social Work Alumni Network. Avocations: painting, drawing, interior decorating, exercising, cooking.

MALKANI, PRAKASH, medical educator, neuroradiologist; b. New Delhi, July 16, 1956; came to the U.S., 1990; s. Kotumal D. and Parpati K. (Abichandani) M.; m. Sonia N. Jiandani, Sept. 15, 1986; children: Natasha, Alisha. Student, U. Delhi, 1973; MB, BChir, All India Inst. Med. Sci., Delhi, 1979, MD, 1983. Diplomate Am. Bd. Radiology, Am. Bd. Neuroradiology. Intern All India Inst. Med. Sci., 1978; resident in radiology N.Y. Med. Coll., 1990-93, fellow in neuroradiology, 1990-91; head dept. imaging Hinduja Hosp., Bombay, 1985-90; clin. asst. prof. Mich. State U., East Lansing, 1993—2001; pres. Advanced Diagnostic Imaging, Saginaw, Mich., 2001—. Mem. MRI adv. bd. GE Asia Pacific, Singapore, 1986-90; chmn. radiology Covenant Health Sys., 1998-2001; pres. Advanced Diagnostic Imaging, 2001-02. Merit scholar Bd. Secondary Edn., New Delhi, 1972. Mem. Am. Soc. Neuroradiology, Saginaw Med. Radiology (treas. 1994-98, pres.), Saginaw County Med. Soc. (pres. 2002--). Home: 8348 Circlewood Dr N Saginaw MI 48609-8521 Office: Advanced Diagnostic Imaging 100 S Jefferson Saginaw MI 48603-2171 E-mail: malkani@aol.com.

MALKASIAN, GEORGE DURAND, JR. physician, educator; b. Springfield, Mass., Oct. 26, 1927; s. George Dur and Gladys Mildred (Trombley) M.; m. Mary Ellen Koch, Oct. 16, 1954; children: Linda Jeanne, Karen Diane, Martha Ellen. AB, Yale U., 1950; MD, Boston U., 1954; MS, U. Minn., 1963. Diplomate Am. Bd. Ob-Gyn. Intern Worcester (Mass.) City Hosp., 1954-55; resident in ob-gyn Mayo Grad. Sch. Hosp., Rochester, Minn., 1955-58, 60-61; mem. faculty Mayo Med. Sch., 1962—, prof. ob-gyn, 1976—, chmn. dept. ob-gyn, 1976-86. Author articles in field. Served to lt. comdr. M.C., USNR, 1958-60. Named Tchr. of Yr., Mayo Grad. Sch. Medicine, 1973, 77, Alumnus of Yr., Boston U. Sch. Med., 1990. Fellow Royal Coll. Obstetricians and Gynecologists (ad eundum); mem. ACS, Am. Coll. Ob-Gyn (pres. 1989-90), Am. Ob-Gyn Soc., Am. Radium Soc., Soc. Ob-Gyn, Assn. Profs. Ob-Gyn., N.Am. Ob-Gyn. Soc., Ctrl. Assn. Ob-Gyn, Minn. Soc. Ob-Gyn, Internat. Fedn. Ob-Gyn (v.p. 1997—), Zumbro Valley Med. Soc. (exec. dir. 1996—). Home: 1750 11th Ave NE Rochester MN 55906-4215 Office: Mayo Clinic 200 1st St SW Rochester MN 55905-0001

MALKAWI, ALI MAHMOUD, architecture educator, researcher; b. Irbid, Jordan, Feb. 12, 1967; came to U.S., 1989; s. Mahmoud Ahmed and Safia (Khatib) M. BS in Archtl. Engring. with honors, Jordan U. Sci. and Tech., Irbid, 1989; MArch, U. Colo., Denver, 1990; PhD with honors, Ga. Inst. Tech., 1994. Project designer Malkawi Cons. Engrs., Amman, Jordan, 1989; instr. Ga. Inst. Tech., Atlanta, 1992-94, doctoral fellow, 1991-94, project coord., 1994; asst. prof. architecture U. Mich., Ann Arbor, 1994—; coord., asst. prof., 1994—; postdoctoral/Oberdick fellow U. Mich., Ann Arbor, 1994-95; assoc. prof. U. Pa., Phila., 2001—. Vis. prof. Harvard Grad. Sch., 2001—; pres.

Intelligenet Energy Optimization Cons., Ann Arbor, 1995—. Mem. ASHRAE, Acoustical Soc. Am., Illumination Engring. Soc., Am. Solar Energy Soc. Achievements include copyrighted theory development and implementation of intelligent CAD software. Office: U Pa Dept Arch 207 Meyerson Hall Philadelphia PA 19104-6311 E-mail: malkawi@pobox.upenn.edu.

MALKIEL, BURTON GORDON, economist, educator; b. Boston, Aug. 28, 1932; s. Sol and Celia (Gordon) Malkiel; m. Judith Ann Atherton, July 16, 1954 (dec. 1987); 1 child Jonathan ; m. Nancy Weiss, July 31, 1988. BA, Harvard, 1953, MBA, 1955; PhD, Princeton, 1964. Assoc. Smith Barney & Co., N.Y.C., 1958—60; asst. prof. dept. econs. Princeton U., 1964—66, assoc. prof., 1966—68, prof., 1968—81, Rentschler prof. econs., 1969—81, chmn. dept. econs., 1974—75, 1977—81, Chem. Bank chmn.'s prof. econs., 1988—; dean Sch. Orgn. and Mgmt., Yale U., 1981—87. Mem. Pres.'s Coun. Econ. Advisors, 1975—77; dir. Jeffrey Co., Prudential Life Ins. Co. Am., BKF Capital, Vanguard Group, Neuvis Corp. Author: The Term Structure of Interest Rates, 1966; author: (with others) Strategies and Rational Decisions in the Securities Options Market, 1969; author: A Random Walk Down Wall Street, 1973, A Random Walk Down Wall Street, 7th edit., 1999, The Inflation-Beater's Investment Guide, 1980, Global Bargain Hunting, 1998; author: (with others) The Index Fund Solution, 1999. 1st lt. U.S. Army, 1955—58. Mem.: Am. Fin. Assn. (dir., pres. 1978). Home: 76 North Rd Princeton NJ 08540-2430 Office: Princeton U Dept Econs Princeton NJ 08544-0001 E-mail: bmalkiel@princeton.edu.

MALKIEL, NANCY WEISS, college dean, history educator; b. Newark, Feb. 14, 1944; d. William and Ruth Sylvia (Puder) W.; m. Burton G. Malkiel, July 31, 1988. BA summa cum laude, Smith Coll., 1965; MA, Harvard U., 1966, PhD, 1970. From asst. to assoc. prof. history Princeton (N.J.) U., 1969-82, prof., 1982—; master Dean Mathey Coll., 1982-86, dean of coll., 1987—. Author (as Nancy J. Weiss): Charles Francis Murphy, 1858-1924: Respectability and Responsibility in Tammany Politics, 1968, (with others) Blacks in America: Bibliographical Essays, 1971, The National Urban League, 1910-1940, 1974, Farewell to the Party of Lincoln: Black Politics in the Age of FDR, 1983 (Berkshire Conf. of Women Historians prize 1984), Whitney M. Young Jr., and the Struggle for Civil Rights, 1989. Trustee Smith Coll., Northampton, Mass., 1984-94; trustee Woodrow Wilson Nat. Fellowship Found., 1975—, chmn. bd. trustees, 1999—. Fellow Woodrow Wilson Found., 1965, Charles Warren Ctr. for Studies in Am. History, 1976-77, Radcliffe Inst., 1976-77, Ctr. for Advanced Studies in Behavioral Scis., 1986-87. Mem. Am. Hist. Assn., Orgn. Am. Historians (chmn. status women hist. profession 1972-75), So. Hist. Assn., Phi Beta Kappa. Democrat. Jewish. Office: Princeton U Office Dean Of College Princeton NJ 08544-0001

MALKIN, BARRY, film editor, consultant; b. N.Y.C., Oct. 26, 1938; s. Richard and Helen (Kandix) M.; m. Stephanie Byer, Apr. 5, 1971; 1 child, Sacha Janine. BA, Adelphi U., 1960. Freelance film editor Sacha Prodns., Inc., N.Y.C., 1964—. Editor: (films) The Rain People, 1969, They Might Be Giants, 1971, Who is Harry Kellerman and Why Is He Saying All Those Terrible Things About Me?, 1971, Cops and Robbers, 1973, One Summer Love, 1976, Somebody Killed Her Husband, 1978, Last Embrace, 1979, (with Edward Beyer and David Ray) One Trick Pony, 1980, Windows, 1980, (with Mark Laub) Four Friends, 1981, (with Laub, Robert Q. Lovett and Randy Roberts) Hammett, 1982, Rumble Fish, 1983, (with Lovett) The Cotton Club, 1984 (Acad. award nominee for best film editing 1984), Peggy Sue Got Married, 1986, Gardens of Stone, 1987, Big, 1988, New York Stories ("Life Without Zoe"), 1989, The Freshman, 1990, (with Lisa Fruchtman and Walter Murch) The Godfather Part III, 1990 (Acad. award nominee for best film editing 1990), Honeymoon in Vegas, 1992, It Could Happen to You, 1994, Jack, 1996, The Rainmaker, 1997, Isn't She Great, 1999, Lucky Numbers, 2000. Mem. Acad. Motion Picture Arts and Scis., Motion Picture Editors Guild, Am. Cinema Editors. Home and Office: 275 Central Park W New York NY 10024-3015 E-mail: cpwblackie@aol.com.

MALKIN, CARY JAY, lawyer; b. Chgo., Oct. 6, 1949; s. Arthur D. and Perle (Slavin) M.; m. Lisa Klimley, Oct. 27, 1976; children: Dorothy R., Victoria S., Lydia R. BA, George Washington U., 1971; JD, Northwestern U., 1974. Bar: Ill. 1974, U.S. Dist. Ct. (no. dist.) Ill. 1974, N.Y. 2001. Assoc. Mayer, Brown & Platt, Chgo., 1974-80, ptnr., 1991—2002, Mayer, Brown, Rowe & Maw, Chgo., 2002—. Chmn. spl. events com. Mental Health Assn., 1984-85; mem. steering com. Endowment Campaign of the Latin Sch. of Chgo., 1990-91, trustee, 1991-2000, v.p., 1992-98, chmn. capital campaign, 1995-98, nat. trustee, 2000-2002, sr. trustee, 2002—; mem. exec. com. Friends of Prentice Women's Hosp., 1991-92; bd. dirs. SOS Children's Village Ill., 1992-96; mem. M.S. Weiss fund bd. Children's Meml. Hosp., 1989-93; mem. Graziano Fund bd. Children's Meml. Hosp., 1993-96; mem. steering com. Founder's Coun. Field Mus., 1995—, chmn. steering com., 1999—, trustee, 1999—. Mem. Chgo. Club, Saddle and Cycle Club, Arts Club, Standard Club, Order of the Coif, Phi Beta Kappa. Home: 233 E Walton St Chicago IL 60611-1526 Office: Mayer Brown Rowe & Maw 190 S La Salle St Ste 3100 Chicago IL 60603-3441

MALKIN, HAROLD MARSHALL, medical researcher; b. San Francisco, Oct. 9, 1923; s. Charles Herman and Dorothy Levin Malkin; m. Joanne Clark (div.); m. Sonja Sandeman (div.); children: Alison Walkin, Dinah Walkin, Aaron Walkin, Miriam Walkin, Richard Walkin. AB, U. Calif., Berkeley, 1947, MA, 1949; MD, U. Chgo., Chicago, 1951. Dir. MML Diagnostic Labs, Palo Alto, Calif., 1954—72, Solano Clin. Labs, Berkeley, 1972—78, Gslerwelch Laboratories, San Leandro, 1978—86; cons. Smith Kline Laboratories, Dublin, 1986—93, Quest Diagnostic Labs, Dublin, 1993—. Instr. Stanford U. Sch. Medicine, Palo Alto, Calif., 1954—60, intern in pathology, Calif., 1960—62. Author: (pathology book) Out of the Mist; contbr. articles to profl. jours. Sgt. Army Med. Dept., 1943—46, Pto. Fellow fellowship, Nat. Found. Infantile Paralysis, 1951-1953, Am. Cancer Soc., 1953-1954. D-Liberal. Achievements include research in Protein and Nucleic Acid Metabolism. Avocation: medical history. Home: 9 Rio Porto Court Sacramento CA 95831

MALKIN, MICHAEL M. lawyer; b. New Haven, Nov. 1, 1944; s. Eli B. and Gladys (Pollak) M.; children: Andrea, Lisa, Daniel. BA, U. N.Mex., 1966; JD, NYU, 1969. Bar: N.Y. 1970, U.S. Dist. Ct. (so. dist.) N.Y. 1971, U.S. Dist. Ct. (ea. dist.) N.Y. 1971, U.S. Ct. Appeals (2d cir.) 1972, U.S. Supreme Ct. 1984. Assoc. Weil, Lee & Bergin, N.Y.C., 1970-76, Weil, Guttman & Davis, N.Y.C., 1976-77, ptnr., 1977-82, Weil, Guttman, Davis & Malkin, N.Y.C., 1982-86, Weil, Guttman & Malkin, N.Y.C., 1986-95, Weil, Guttman & Malkin, LLP, N.Y.C., 1995—. Judge Giles Sutherland Rich Moot Ct. Competition, N.Y.C., 1982; arbitrator Civil Ct. of City N.Y., 1984-88. Mem. editl. bd. Trademark Reporter, 1973-75, 88-90, contbg. editor, 1974-75. Mem. N.Y. State Bar Assn., U.S. Trademark Assn., Phi Delta Phi, Alpha Epsilon Pi. Office: Weil Guttman & Malkin LLP 60 E 42nd St Rm 4210 New York NY 10165-4299 Business E-Mail: mmalkin@e-wgmlaw.com.

MALKIN, MOSES MONTEFIORE, employee benefits administration company executive; b. Revere, Mass., Sept. 18, 1919; s. Irving and Annie (Helfant) M.; m. Hannah Lacob, Oct. 11, 1941. AB, U. N.C., 1941; BSME, Columbia U., 1948. Enrolled actuary; CLU. Engr. GE, Schenectady, N.Y., 1948-50; engr. Gen. Bronze, Inc., Jersey City, 1950-51; v.p. Malkin Warehouse, Inc., New Haven, 1951-57; pvt. practice actuary, 1957-72; chmn., actuary Profl. Pensions, Inc., Middletown, 1972-99; ret., 1999. Presenter pension issues at numerous confs., 1970-80. Pres., founder Milford, Conn., 1962, Milford Child Guidance Clinic, 1966; pres. Clifford Beers Child Guidance, New Haven, 1971, Jewish Family Svc., New Haven, 1973. With U.S. Army, 1941-45, ETO. Mem. Am. Acad. Actuaries, Am. Soc. Pension Actuaries (instr. 1984), Am. Soc. CLUs, Phi Beta Kappa, Tau Beta Pi. Jewish. Office: Profl Pensions Inc 245 Long Hill Rd Middletown CT 06457 Address: 1514 Heron Dr Sun City Center FL 33573-4707

MALKIN, PETER LAURENCE, lawyer, real estate investor; b. N.Y.C., Jan. 14, 1934; s. Samuel and Gertrude (Greenberger) Malkin; m. Isabel L. Wien, July 10, 1955. Grad. cum laude, Poly. Prep. Country Day Sch., 1951; AB summa cum laude, Harvard Coll., 1955; LLB magna cum laude, Harvard U., 1958. Bar: N.Y. 1958, Conn. 1976, Fla. 1977. Sr. ptnr., chmn. Wien & Malkin LLP, N.Y.C., 1958—; mng. Empire State Bldg. Assocs. L.L.C., 1961—; chmn. W & M Properties, Inc., N.Y.C., 1965—. Bd. dirs. U.S. Trust Corp.; ptnr. N.Y.C. Partnership and C. of C., 2001—; founding chmn. Grand Ctrl. Partnership Inc. & 34th Street Partnership, Inc.; dir., sec. Fashion Ctr. Bus. Improvement Dist.; dir. Realty Found. N.Y., 1981—, v.p., 1995—; mem. adv. com. Greenwich (Conn.) Japanese Sch., 1992—; mem. N.Y.C. Mayor's Bus. Adv. Coun., 1997—2002; gov. Real Estate Bd., N.Y.C., 1993—2000, N.Y.C., 2001—; co-founder, hon. co-chmn. Com. to Encourage Corp. Philanthropy, 1998—. Nat. vice-chmn. Harvard Law Sch. Fund, 1967-71, chmn. nat. scholarship com., 1975-76, chmn. N.Y.C. com., 1981-83; founder, bd. dirs. Urban League Southwestern Fairfield County, 1969-73, treas., 1969-71; bd. dirs., mem. exec. com. Lincoln Ctr. for Performing Arts, 1979—; bd. dirs. Inst. Internat. Edn., 1983-89, hon. 1994—; trustee Nat. Trust for Hist. Preservation, 1988-91, mem. adv. coun., 1997—; founding chmn. Greenwich (Conn.) Green & Clean, Inc., 1986—, Greenwich Adopt-A-Road, 1996-; v.p., mem. exec. com. Greenwich chpt. NAACP, 1967-69; trustee Citizens Budget Commn., N.Y.C., 1971-91, Jewish Communal Fund, N.Y., 1976-81; dean's coun., Harvard U., 1987-95; chmn. capital campaign and chmn. dean's coun., 1995—, mem. overseers com. to visit Kennedy Sch. Govt., 1976-82, 83-89, 90—, to visit Harvard Law Sch. 1977-83; exec. com. Program for Ctr. for Jewish Studies, 1974-80; bd. overseers Harvard Coll., 1989-95, overseers com. univ resources, 1972—, exec. com., 1985—; dean's adv. com., Harvard Law Sch., 1988-90; elected dir. Harvard Alumni Assn., 1981-83; chmn. schs. and scholarship com. Harvard U., Greenwich, 1973-79; exec. com. Assn. Better N.Y., 1972—. Recipient Nat. Preservation Honor award Nat. Trust Hist. Preservation, 1987, President's award Grad. Sch. and Univ. Ctr. CCNY, 1989, Crain's All-Star award, 1994, Nacore Disting. Man of Yr. award, 1995; named Outstanding Young Man, N.Y.C. Jaycees, 1969, fellow Brandeis U., 1970—, Man of Yr., Hist. Soc. Greenwich, Conn., 1993. Mem. Harvard Law Sch. Assn. N.Y.C. (trustee 1968-70, v.p. 1973-74), Assn. Bar City N.Y., Century Assn., The Links N.Y., The Hasty Pudding Inst. 1770, AD Hon., Harvard Varsity Club (Cambridge), Harvard Club N.Y.C. (bd. mgrs. 1979-81), Harvard Club (Fairfield County, Conn., v.p. 1974-75, bd. dirs. 1976-80), Bailwick Club (hon. life mem., founding pres.), Blind Brook Club, Conn. Golf Club, Phi Beta Kappa. Office: 60 E 42d St New York NY 10165-0015 Office Fax: 212-850-2780. E-mail: plmalkin@wienmalkinllp.com.

MALKIN, STANLEY LEE, neurologist; b. Pitts., Nov. 11, 1942; s. Maurice and Bessie Beatrice (Serbin) M.; children: Justin Ross, Keith Richard. BA with honors, U. Pa., 1964; MD, U. Pitts., 1968. Diplomate Am. Bd. Psychiatry and Neurology, Nat. Bd. Med. Examiners. Intern Montefiore Hosp., Pitts., 1968-69; resident in neurology Columbia-Presbyn. Med. Ctr., N.Y.C., 1969-72; chief neurology svc., Wright-Patterson AFB, Dayton, 1972-74; practice medicine specializing in neurology N.Y.C.; attending staff Mt. Sinai Hosp.; former dir. Neuro-Diagnostic Lab., Englewood; asst. clin. prof. neurology Mt. Sinai Sch. Medicine; founder Bergen-Passaic Tomography Ctr., Fairlawn, N.J. Neurology cons. Regent Hosp.; med. dir. Pain Suppression Labs., Inc.; med. dir. Efficient Health Systems, Inc.-N.Y.C. Healthline; founder, med. dir., exec. v.p. Hosp. Diagnostic Equipment Corp., 1987—; pres. Cancer Treatment Holdings, Inc, 1993-95, dir. 1993-94, sr. med. dir. 1995-97; founder Montvale Med. Imaging Assocs. (N.J.), N.Y. Med. Imaging, N.Y.C., Hosp. Diagnostic Equipment Corp. Co-mcpl. coord. Ft. Lee Citizens for McGovern, 1972; ptnr. Sall/Myers Med. Assocs., prin. 1995—; mem. Edgewater Rent Control Bd., 1978. Maj. M.C. USAF, 1972-74. Recipient Comdr.'s Recognition award for care of repatriated prisoners of war, 1973. Fellow Royal Soc. Medicine; mem. Am. Acad. Neurology, Am. Assn. Electrodiagnostic Medicine, Am. Soc. Neuro-Imaging (charter), EEG and Clin. Neurosci. Soc., Am. Assn. Study Headache, Nat. Headache Found., Internat. Headache Soc., Nat. Neurotrauma Soc., N.Y. Acad. Scis., NYU Bellevue Psychiat. Soc., European Fedn. Neurol. Socs. Office: 120 W 44th St Ste 601 New York NY 10036-4011 also: 136 E 57th St Ste 600 New York NY 10022-2707

MALKINE-FALVEY, FERN SYLVIE, writer, journalist, painter; b. Brooklyn, Ny, Apr. 11, 1950; d. Georges Alexandre and Sonia May Malkine; m. Peter Anthony Falvey, June 20, 1992. MS Spl. Edn., Fordham U., New York, New York, 1976; BS History/English Lit., NYU, New York, New York, 1974; AA History/English, Ulster County CC, Stone Ridge, New York, 1972. Rschr./writer Editions de la Difference, Paris, France (incl. Monaco), 1976—78; copy editor Elle Mag., France (incl. Monaco), 1983—85; painter/freelance journalist self-employed, Woodstock, NY, 1985—89; gallery dir. Isidore Ducasse Fine Arts, Manhattan, 1989—92; art cons. Pavillion des Arts Mus., Paris, France (incl. Monaco), 1998—99; copy editor Look Mag., New York, NY, 1978—79; curator On-line Gallery, Woodstock, 2001—; painter The Art Gallery - Western New Eng. Coll., Springfield, Mass., 2002—; fgn. correspondant Paris Match, New York, NY, 1979—81. Author: (book) Georges Malkine: An Arbitrary Destiny, Georges Malkine; Le Vagabond du Surrealism. Vol. Congressman Matt McHugh, Kingston, NY, 1981, Justice of the Peace Sid Slayton, Wood stock, 1982. Mem.: Hist. Soc. of Woodstock. Avocations: guitar, lute, historical post cards, designing moccasins, designing tapestries. Home: PO Box 261 Shady NY 12409 Personal E-mail: fpfalvey@rcn.com.

MALKINSON, FREDERICK DAVID, dermatologist, educator; b. Hartford, Conn., Feb. 26, 1924; s. John Walter and Rose Malkinson; m. Una Zwick, June 15, 1979; children by previous marriage: Philip, Carol, John. Student, Loomis Inst., 1937-41; 3 yr. cert. cum laude, Harvard U., 1943, DMD, 1947, MD, 1949. Intern Harvard-Beth Israel Hosp., Boston, 1949-50; resident in dermatology U. Chgo., 1950-54, from instr. to assoc. prof. dept. dermatology, 1954-68; prof. medicine and dermatology U. Ill., Chgo., 1968-71; chmn. dept. dermatology Rush Med. Coll. and Rush-Presbyn.-St. Luke's Med. Ctr., 1968-92, Clark W. Finnerud, M.D. prof. dept. dermatology, 1981-95, 95—; trustee Sulzberger Inst. Dermatol. Comm. and Edn., 1976-96; pres. Sulzberger Inst. Dermatol. Communication and Edn., 1983-88, 93-96; prof. emeritus Rush Presbyn.-St. Luke's Med. Ctr., Chgo., 1995—. Editor: Year Book of Dermatology, 1971-78; chief editor: AMA Archives of Dermatology, 1979-83; bd. editors, 1976-84, Jour. AMA, 1979-83; editorial cons. World Book Medical Encyclopedia, 1991—; contbr. articles and abstracts to profl. jours., chpts. to books. Active Evanston (Ill.) Libr. Bd., 1988-94, pres., 1993-94. With M.C. USN, 1950-52. Grantee U.S. Army, 1955-61, USPHS, 1962-73 Fellow AAAS; mem. Am. Acad. Dermatology (v.p. 1987-89, dir. 1964-67), Am. Dermatol. Assn., Soc. Investigative Dermatology (v.p. 1978-79, dir. 1963-68), Am. Fedn. Med. Rsch., Cen. Soc. Clin. Rsch., Radiation Rsch. Soc., Assn. Profs. of Dermatology (dir. 1982-85), Dermatology Found. (trustee 1980-93, pres. 1983-85), Nat. Coun. on Radiation Protection and Measurements (mem. com. on cutaneous radiobiology 1986-92), Chgo. Dermatol. Soc. (pres. 1964-65, Gold Medal award 1992), Chgo. Lit. Club (v.p. 1997-99, pres. 1999-2000, v.p. 2000-02). Office: Rush-Presbyn-St Luke's Med Ctr Kidston 507b 1653 Congress Street Pkwy Chicago IL 60612 Office Fax: (312) 942-7778.

MALKOFF, MARC DAVID, neurologist; b. Youngstown, Ohio, Aug. 6, 1960; s. Solomon and Shirley Malkoff. BS, Kent (Ohio) State U., 1980; MD, Northeastern Ohio U., 1984. Diplomate Am. Bd. Psychiatry and Neurology. Intern Cleve. Clinic Found., 1984-85; resident in neurology Emory U., Atlanta, 1985-88, chief resident in neurology, 1987-88; fellow in neurocritical care Johns Hopkins U., Balt., 1988-90; asst. prof. neurology and anesthesiology Saint Louis U., 1990-95; assoc. prof. neurology and anesthesiology Ind. U., Indpls., 1995-98, U. Tex., Houston, 1998—. Reviewer Jour. Stroke, Jour. Annals of Pharmacology Therapy. Fellowship Charles A. Dana Found., 1988-90. Fellow Am. Stroke Assn., Am. Heart Assn., Am. Acad. Neurology (exec. com. critical care/emergency neurology and interventional sects.), Soc. of Critical Care Medicine (pres. neurosci. sect.), Am. Soc. of Neuroimaging (program and exec. com.), Argentinian Coun. of Cardiology (corr. mem.). Office: U Tex Houston Health Sci Ctr MSB 7044 6431 Fannin St Houston TX 77030-1501 E-mail: marc.d.malkoff@uth.tmc.edu.

MALKOVICH, JOHN, actor; b. Christopher, Ill., Dec. 9, 1953; m. Glenne Headley, 1982 (div.); children: Amandine and Loewy, with Nicoletta Peyran. Student, Eastern Ill. U., Ill. State U. Co-founder Steppenwolf Theatre, Chgo., 1976 Made N.Y.C. theatrical debut in True West, 1982 (Obie award, Clarence Derwent award); other theatrical appearances include: Death of a Salesman, 1984, Burn This, 1987, States of Shock; dir. Balm in Gilead, 1984-85, Arms and the Man, 1985, The Caretaker, 1986, Coyote Ugly, (Chgo., Kennedy Ctr. for Performing Arts, Washington) 1985, Libra, 1994, Steppenwolf, 1994; appeared in films Places in the Heart, 1984, The Killing Fields, 1984, Eleni, 1985, Making Mr. Right, 1987, Glass Menagerie, 1987, Empire of the Sun, 1987, Miles From Home, 1988, Dangerous Liaisons, 1988, The Sheltering Sky, 1990, Queen's Logic, 1991, The Object of Beauty, 1991, Shadows and Fog, 1992, Jennifer 8, 1992, Of Mice and Men, 1992, In The Line Of Fire, 1993 (Academy award nomination best supporting actor 1993), Alive, 1993, Touchstone, 1994, Para De La Nuages, 1994, Mary Reilly, 1994, Mulholland Falls, 1996, Der Unhold, 1996, The Portrait of a Lady, 1996, Primary Colors, 1997, Con Air, 1997, The Man in the Iron Mask, 1998, Rounders, 1998, Le Temps retrouvé, 1999, The Libertine, 1999, Ladies Room, 1999, Joan of Arc, 1999, Being John Malkovich, 1999 (American Comedy Award, 2000), Shadow of the Vampire, 2000, Les Ames Forte, 2001, Knockaround Guys, 2001, Je rentre a la Maison, 2001, Ripley's Game, 2002; co-exec. prodr. The Accidental Tourist, 1988; dir. Danler Upstairs, 1998, The Libertine, 1999; appeared in TV films Word of Honor, 1981, American Dream, 1981, Death of a Salesman, 1985 (Emmy award 1986), Heart of Darkness, 1994, RKO 281, 1999, Les Miserables, 2000, Napoleon, 2002. Office: William Morris Agency One William Morris Place Beverly Hills CA 90212*

MALKOVICH, MARK PAUL, III, musician, artistic director, scientist, sports agent; b. Eveleth, Minn., July 10, 1930; s. Mark II and Mary Frances (Greben) M.; m. Joan Shewring, Feb. 7, 1959; children: Mark IV, Erik, Kent, Kara. BS in Chemistry, Columbia U., 1952, MS, 1953; studied piano with Dorothy Crost Bourgin, Chgo. Mus. Coll., 1947-50; William Beller ch. Piano Dept., Columbia U., 1951-54; Adele Marcus, Juilliard Sch., 1959-62; MusD (hon.), Salve Regina, 1993; DFA, U. R.I., 1994; MusD, Cath. U. Am., 1999. Pres. Gum Industries, Ltd., N.Y.C., 1964-69. Artistic and gen. dir. Newport Music Festival, 1975—; exec. dir. Palm Beach Festival, Fla., 1984-86; guest lectr. TV and radio appearances and adjudicator at music competitions; pres. Chopin Found. of U.S., Miami, Fla., 1985; presented N.Am. debuts of Bella Davidovich, Jean-Philippe Collard, Dmitry Sitkoveksky, Andrei Gavrilov, others; founder Sports US—A—SR; negotiator/agt. for USSR leading hockey players Fetisov, Krutov, Larionov, Makarov, 1989. Recipient Individual Achievement award Bus. Vols. for the Arts, R.I., 1998; named to R.I. Heritage Hall of Fame, 2000. Mem. Harvard Mus. Assn., Newport Reading Rm., Spouting Rock Beach Assn. Office: care Newport Music Festival PO Box 3300 Newport RI 02840-0992

MALKOWICZ, STANLEY BRUCE, urologist; b. Passaic, N.J. s. Stanley Jacob and Jeanne (iracki) M.; m. Denise Elaine Ewald, Sept. 22, 1985. BA, U. Vt., 1977; MD, U. Pa., Phila., 1981. Intern in surgery Hosp. U. Pa., Phila., 1981-82, resident in surgery, 1982-83, resident in urology, 1983-86, chief resident in urology, 1986-87; fellow in urologic oncology U. So. Calif., L.A., 1987-88, Hosp. U. Pa., Phila., 1988-90, asst. prof. surgery, 1990-95, assoc. prof., 1995—; chief urology Phila. VA Med. Ctr. Assoc. scientist Wistar Inst. Anatomy and Biology, Phila., 1988—; Nat. Kidney Found. rsch. fellow, 1983-84; Am. Found. Urologic Disease rsch. scholar, 1988-90. Contbr. articles to profl. jours. Mem. AAAS, Am. Urologic Assn., Am. Soc. Clin. Oncology, Soc. Univ. Urologists, Urodynamics Soc., Assn. Academic Surgeons, Soc. Pelvic Surgeons, Soc. Urologic Oncology, Urol. Rsch. Soc., Phila. Urol. Soc. (pres.), S.E. Pa. Am. Cancer Soc. (pres.), Sigma Xi. Presbyterian. Avocations: camping, reading, cooking. Office: Hosp U Pa 3400 Spruce St Philadelphia PA 19104-4206

MALKUS, DAVID STARR, mechanics educator, applied mathematician; b. Chgo., June 30, 1945; s. Willem V.R. Malkus and Joanne (Gerould) Simpson; m. Evelyn R. (div.); children: Christopher, Annelise, Byron, Renata. AB, Yale U., 1968; PhD, Boston U., 1976. Mathematician U.S. Nat. Bur. Standards, Gaithersburg, Md., 1975-77; asst. prof. math. Ill. Inst. Tech., Chgo., 1977-83, assoc. prof., 1983-84; assoc. prof. mechanics U. Wis., Madison, 1984-87, prof., 1987—, chmn. Rheology Rsch. Ctr., 1991-94. Chair prof. Nanjing (People's Republic China) Aero. Inst., 1986. Co-author: Concepts and Applications of Finite Element Analysis, 1989; contbr. articles to Computer Methods Applied Mech. Engring., Jour. Computational Physics. Mem. Soc. Rheology. Achievements include research on finite element methods--reduced and selective integration techniques, a unification of concepts. Home: 2710 Mason St Madison WI 53705-3716 Office: U Wis Dept Engring Physics 1500 Engineering Dr Madison WI 53706-1609 E-mail: malkus@cms.wisc.edu.

MALL, WILLIAM JOHN, JR. aerospace executive, retired Air Force general; b. Pitts., Jan. 13, 1933; s. William John and Margaret (Henry) M.; m. Vivian Lea Fenton; children— Michele, William, Catherine BBA, U. Pitts., 1954; MBA, George Washington U., 1966; sr. mgrs. in govt. program, Harvard U., 1980. Commd. officer USAF, 1954, advanced through grades to maj. gen., 1981; insp. gen. Mil. Airlift Command., Scott AFB, Ill., 1978, comdr. 436 wing Dover AFB, Del., 1979; DCS personnel Mil. Airlift Command, Scott AFB, Ill., 1979-81; comdr. Air Rescue Service, 1981-83, 23d AF/MAC, Scott AFB, 1983-85; assigned to Hdqrs USAF, Bolling AFB, D.C., 1985-86; ret.; dir. integrated logistics support div. Douglas Aircraft Co., Long Beach, Calif., 1987-89, gen. mgr. human resources, 1989-91; exec. dir. LAX Two Corp., L.A., 1991-99. Decorated Legion of Merit, Bronze Star, Air medal Mem. Airlift Assn., Daedalians, Jolly Green Pilots Assn. Avocations: tennis, sailing. Office: LAX Two Corp 200 World Way Los Angeles CA 90045-5859

MALLARD, STEPHEN ANTHONY, retired utility company executive; b. Jersey City, Sept. 15, 1924; s. Stephen F. and Gertrude V. (Donahue) M.; m. Winifred Anne Carey, June 7, 1947; children: Stephen Kevin, Catherine Anne, Eileen Rosemary Mallard McClenahan. M.E., Stevens Inst. Tech, Hoboken, N.J., 1948, MSE.E., 1951. Registered profl. engr. With elec. distbn., system planning and devel. Pub. Service Electric and Gas Co., Newark, 1951-77, v.p. system planning, 1977-80, sr. v.p. planning and research, 1980-88, sr. v.p. transmission systems, 1989; pvt. practice engring. Nutley, N.J., 1990—. Advisor Brookhave Nat. Lab.; cons. Manhattan Coll. Bd. dirs. Met. chpt. ARC, Fairfield, N.J., 1985—, bd. dirs. No. N.J. chpt., 1988—; bd. dirs. Essex County Grand Jury Assn., 1978-87. With USN, 1944-46, PTO. Fellow IEEE; mem. Nat. Soc. Profl. Engrs., , Conf. Internationale des Grands Reseaux Electriques a Haute Tension, Eta Kappa Nu, Tau Beta Pi Roman Catholic. Home and Office: 68 High St Nutley NJ 07110-1134 E-mail: samallardnj@aol.com.

MALLEIN, DARLA J. educator; BS in Secondary Edn., Emporia State U., 1980, MS, 1994. Tchr. Americus Elem. Sch., 1981-83; 8-12th grade lang. arts, yearbook LeRoy H.S., 1983-87; 9-11th grade lang. arts Emporia H.S., 1987-88; 8th grade social studies Emporia Mid. Sch., 1988—2001; social studies edn. specialist Emporia State U., 2001—. Adj. faculty Emporia State U. Coll. Liberal Arts and Scis., 1998. Contbr. articles to profl. jours. Named Outstanding Young Educator Kans. Jaycees, 1996, Wal-Mar Tchr. of Yr. 1998, Kans. Tchr. of Yr. 1998; grantee Emporia Middle Sch. PTO, 1992, Southeastern Kans. Edn. Found., 1995, 7 grants Southwestern Bell Excellence in Edn., 1991-95, Emporia Schs. Found., 1998, 99, Michael Jordan Found. grant, 2000. Mem. NEA (chair comms. com. 1997-99, bd. edn. liaison 1995-99, others), Kans. Coun. for the Social Studies (state bd. mem. 1994—, others), Nat. Coun. for the Social Studies, Kans. Assn. for Middle Level Edn., Phi Kappa Phi, Phi Delta Kappa. Home: 1901 Meadowlark Ln Emporia KS 66801-6125

MALLER, OWEN, clinical psychologist; b. Bklyn., Jan. 27, 1930; s. Randolph Guggenheim and Edith M.; m. Alma Maller, Aug., 1974. BS, U. Ill., 1952, PhD, 1964; MA, So. Meth. U., Dallas, 1955. Cert. Nat. Register Health Svc. Providers in Psychology. Rsch. psychologist VA Hosp. and U. Pa., Phila., 1966-76; assoc. chief rsch. Dept. Army U.S. Army Lab, Natick, Mass., 1976-90; head edn. Am. Cancer Soc., Bryn Mawr, Pa., 1990-94; therapist Psych Resource Assn., Bala Cynwyd, 1994-99; clin. psychologist Cummings & Tannenbaum & Assocs., Narbeth, 1999—. 1st lt. U.S. Army, 1952-54. USPHS post doctoral fellow U. N.C.--Raleigh, 1964-66; post doctoral fellow Duke U., 1966-67. Mem. APA, Pa. Psychol, Sigma Xi (chair 1985, award 1987). Home: 100 Grays Ln Apt 205 Haverford PA 19041-1753 E-mail: owenm@worldnet.att.net.

MALLERY, DAVID, education association executive, consultant; b. Sugar Hill, N.H., Aug. 3, 1923; s. Otto Tod and Louise Marshall Mallery; m. Judith Chappell Mallery, June 15, 1956; children: Roger, Diane Mallery Cusick. BA, Haverford (Pa.) Coll., 1945, PhD (hon.), 1995; MA, Middlebury (Vt.) Coll., 1950. Tchr. English Germantown Friends Sch., Phila., 1946-58; seminar leader Friends Coun. on Edn., 1959-94; dir. profl. devel. Nat. Assn. Ind. Schs., Washington, 1959—. Edn. cons., 1959—; tchr. Bell Tel./U. Pa. Inst. for Humanistic Studies for Execs., 1960's. Author: High School Students Speak Out, 1960's, Ferment on the Campus, 1960's. Edn. advisor Tracy S. Voorhees, Pres. Eisenhower's rep. on Cuban refugee crisis, 1959-60; founding trustee Am. Film Inst., 1967-79. Lt. (j.g.) USNR, 1943-46, WW II. Recipient

Klingenstein award Columbia U. Tchrs. Coll., 1996. Avocations: film, theater, music, international networking. Home: 9006 Crefeld St Philadelphia PA 19118-3607 Office: Nat Assn Ind Schs Sugar Loaf Conf Ctr 9230 Germantown Ave Philadelphia PA 19118-2603

MALLET, ALEXIS, JR. construction company executive; b. New Iberia, La., Nov. 9, 1951; s. Alexis Sr. and Adelia Maria (Comeaux) M.; m. Brenda King (div.); children: Lorphy, Devlin, Casey, Reagan; m. Sarah Elizabeth Roach, Oct. 24, 1987 (div.); children: Thomas Wilson, Alexis III, Joseph Taylor. BA, U. S.W. La., 1975. Bookkeeper A & A Home Supplies, New Iberia, 1969-71; sales staff Voorhies Supply Co., 1972-74; CEO Royal Constrn. Co., 1974—. Bd. dirs. 1st Gen. Enterprises, Ft. Lauderdale, Fla.; CEO First Gen. Svcs., South La., 1990; legal constrn. cons. in field. Prodr. (album) Fourth Hour, 1982. Cert. restorer Nat. Inst. Disaster Restoration; past v.p., bd. dirs. Iberia Bldg. Assn. Recipient Sales Achievement award Southern Structures, La., 1987, Superior Performance award Southern Structures, 1984, Facility award U.S. Tennis Assn., 1982. Mem. Inst. Inspection Cleaning and Restoration, Assn. Specialists in Cleaning and Restoration (cert. fire restoration specialist), Nat. Inst. Disaster Repair (Phoenix award for innovation in reconstruction 1999, Chrysalis Design Build award 1999). Republican. Roman Catholic. Avocations: fishing, hunting, golf. Office: 103 Bradbury Xing Lafayette LA 70508-6640

MALLET, JACQUES ROBERT, art dealer; b. Paris, Feb. 19, 1945; came to U.S., 1972; s. Jean-Pierre Theodore and Christiane Claire (De Watteville-Berckheim) M.; m. Laurie Helene Belhassen, May 30, 1973 (div. 1985); children: Clementine, Arthur. B in Maths., Lycee Louis-Le-Grand, Paris, 1966; M in Econs., U. Paris, 1971; MBA, Columbia U., 1973. Salesman mut. funds Banque De Neuflize, Schlumberger, Mallet, Paris, 1969; asst. v.p. Kuhn Loeb & Co. Inc., N.Y.C., 1973-78; sr. assoc. corp. fin. ABD Securities Corp., 1978-80; pres. Mallet Fine Art Ltd., 1982—. Mem.: Nat. Arts (N.Y.C.); Brooks's (London). Office: Mallet Fine Art Ltd 220 Park Ave S Apt 9B New York NY 10003-1519

MALLETT, DEBORAH GLENN, gifted talented education educator, coordinator; b. Beaumont, Tex., May 20, 1951; d. Gerald Gordon and Mildred (Long) Mallett; m. Eric Lee Newman, Aug. 10, 1985 (dec. Sept. 1987). BA in Elem. Edn., Baylor U., 1973; cert. in ins. mktg., U. Houston, 1983; MEd summa cum laude, U. Oreg., 1991. Cert. gifted edn. educator, Tex.; cert. tchr., Tex., N.Mex., Ala. Women's ministry coord. Campus Crusade for Christ, San Bernardino, Calif., 1973-79; tchr. Spring Br. Ind. Sch. Dist., Houston, 1979-81; paralegal Butler, Binion, Rice, Cook, Knapp, 1081-83, Fouts and Moore, 1983-84; owner fashion cons. bus. Design for Beauty, Houston, 1983-85, fashion cons., 1984-85; tchr. The Kinkaid Sch., 1985-89, Beaumont (Tex.) Ind. Sch. Dist., 1989-90; talented/gifted facilitator and coord. Alamogordo (N.Mex.) Pub. Sch. Sys., 1992-94. Ednl. cons., Houston, 1990-92; mem. adv. bd. Marrs Hill Prodns., Houston, 1991-92, South Ctrl. Aviation Ministries, Houston, 1985-87; cons. Gifted Edn. Task Force, Albuquerque; owner Ednl. Cons. Svcs. Author numerous short stories. Named one of Notable Women of Tex., State of Tex., 1984-85. Mem. NEA, ASCD, Nat. Assn. for Gifted Child, U.S. Water Fitness Assn. (cert. instr.), State Bar Tex. Legal Assts. Divsn. (charter mem.), Baylor Alumni Assn; Tex. Assn. for Gifted and Talented. Republican. Baptist. Avocations: writing, painting, aerobics, skiing, fashion.

MALLETT, JEFF, information technology executive; Founder, dir. IPT Corp., 1987; v.p., founding exec. team mem. Reference Software; founder consumer divsn. WordPerfect Corp., 1993; v.p., gen. mgr. Novell; joined Yahoo!, Sunnyvale, Calif., 1995, pres., COO, also bd. dirs. Office: Yahoo! 701 1st Ave Sunnyvale CA 94089

MALLETTE, DAVID, performing company executive; Exec. dir. Ft. Worth Ballet, Ft. Worth/Dallas Ballet, 1990—. Office: Ft Worth Dallas Ballet 6845 Green Oaks Rd Fort Worth TX 76116*

MALLETTE, MALCOLM FRANCIS, newspaper editor, educator; b. Syracuse, N.Y., Jan. 30, 1922; s. Ralph Joseph and Hermia Ruth (Barry) M.; m. Eleanor Christine Ingram, Sept. 21, 1946; children: Gary, Bruce, David. BS magna cum laude, Syracuse U., 1947. Profl. baseball pitcher, Norfolk, Va., Newark, Kansas City, Memphis, Sacramento, Bklyn., Montreal, 1946-52; sports reporter Asheville (N.C.) Times, 1951-54; sports editor Asheville Citizen, 1954-56; sports dir. Winston-Salem (N.C.) Jour. & Sentinel, 1956-59; mng. editor Winston-Salem Jour., 1959-66; assoc. dir. Am. Press Inst., Reston, Va., 1966-69, mng. dir., 1969-75, sec., dir., 1975-79, dir. devel., 1979-87; dir. projects World Press Freedom Com., 1987-96. Guest lectr. Grad. Sch. Journalism, Columbia, 1969-71, Am. Press. Inst., Columbia, 1961-66, U. N.C. Sch. Journalism, 1964; Def. Info. Sch. Ft. Benjamin Harrison, Ind., 1987. Author (with others), editor: Handbook for Journalists of Central and Eastern Europe, 1990, transl. to Polish, Czechoslovakian, Hungarian, Romanian, Bulgarian, Albanian, Russian; author (Seminar) The Story of the American Press Institute, 1992; contbr. articles to various mags. Served to capt. Signal Corps, AC AUS, 1943-46. Named to N.C. Journalism Hall of Fame. Mem. AP Mng. Editors Assn. (dir. 1961-66, regent 1976—), AP News Coun. (pres. N.C. 1964), Assn. Profl. Baseball Players (life) Clubs: Rotarian. Baptist. Home: 15 Barratts Chapel Ct Durham NC 27705-1311

MALLETTE, PHYLLIS SPENCER COOPER, medical/surgical nurse; b. Chestertown, Md., Nov. 18, 1944; d. Charles P. and Elma (Brown) Spencer; m. Arthur E. Mallete, June 5, 1982; m. Winsor A. Cooper, Jr., Feb. 10, 1966 (dec. 1982); children: Winsor A. Cooper III, Elma Cooper Henderson. ASN, Rutgers U., 1965; BSN cum laude, Coll. of N.J., 1978. Cert. critical care, IV therapy, acute respiratory care, OSHA regulations, advanced coronary care, med. office mgmt., case mgmt., utilization rev.; RN, Md., N.J., Pa. Nurse delivery room St. Francis Med. Ctr., Trenton, N.J., 1971-73; nurse ICU Delaware Valley Med. Ctr., Langhorne, Pa., 1973-74; coord. nights Robert Wood Johnson U. Hosp., New Brunswick, N.J., 1974-75; occupational health RN Warner-Lambert/Parke-Davis Co., Morris Plains, 1977-79; sr. profl. rep. hosp., coord. sales tng. Merck Human Health Svcs. Divsn., Phila., 1979-89; co-coord. 400 trainee field force expansion Merck Sharp & Dohme, Denver, 1989; pharm. specialist, 1997; clin. nurse Johns Hopkins Hosp., Balt., 1989-90; office mgr. Arthur E. Mallette, M.D., Pikesville, 1990-94; quality mgmt. analyst United Health Care, Inc., Balt., 1994-96, United Health Care of Fla., 1996-97; pharm. specialist AstraZeneca, LP, Tampa, Fla., 1997—2000, dist. sales mgr., 2000—. Med. cons. N.J. Pub. TV, Trenton, 1974. Mem. Nat. Assn. Healthcare Quality, Sigma Theta Tau. Independent. Methodist. Avocations: computer, mystery and adventure novels, walking, movies. Home: 24837 Cranes Roost Cir Leesburg FL 34748 Office: AstraZeneca LP Ste 600 6200 W Courtney Campbell Cswy 600 Tampa FL 33607-7215

MALLEY, J. WALLACE, JR. lawyer; b. Washington, Nov. 1, 1947; m. Margaret Allen, July 29, 1972; children: Sean, Colin, Brian. BA, Duke U., 1969; JD, Georgetown U. Law Ctr., 1972. Bar: D.C. 1973, U.S. Ct. Mil. Appeals 1973, Vt. 1976, U.S. Dist. Ct. Vt. 1976, U.S. Ct. Appeals (D.C. cir.) 1985, U.S. Ct. Appeals (8th cir.) 1986, U.S. Ct. Appeals (2d cir.) 1981, U.S. Supreme Ct. 1985. Staff judge advocate USN, Washington, 1972-76; dept. state's atty. Bennington County, Bennington, Vt., 1976; from asst. atty. gen. to chief dep. atty. gen. Office of the Atty. Gen., Montpelier, 1976—, acting atty. gen., 1997; Toll fellow Coun. of State Govts., 1997. Mem. sound sci. com. Coun. of State Govts., 1999; model rules of profl. conduct com. Vt. Supreme Ct. Com., Montpelier, 1995-96; chair Legis. Solid Waste Commn. Pres. Montpelier PTO, 1982-84; bd. dirs. Montpelier Little League, 1990. Lt. USNR, 1972-76. Mem. Vt. Bar Assn. Avocations: singing, gospel music, acting, sailing, railroads. Office: Office of Atty Gen 109 State St Montpelier VT 05609-1001

MALLEY, JAMES HENRY MICHAEL, industrial engineer; b. Providence, Oct. 15, 1940; s. Leo Henry and Gladys Elizabeth (Canning) M.; children: James Michael, Julie Michele; m. Joyce Sue Marie Greenwell, Aug. 28, 1993. BS in Engring., U.S. Mil. Acad., 1962; MS in Indsl. Engring., U. R.I., 1977. Commd. U.S. Army, 1962-84, advanced through grades to lt. col., ret., 1984, milt. advisor Rep. of Vietnam, 1964-65; co. comdr. Army Tng. Ctr., Ft. Benning, Ga., 1965-67; ops. and exec. officer First Air Cavalry Divsn., Vietnam, 1968-69; asst. prof. U. R.I., Kingston, 1969-73; asst. inspector gen. U.S. Army Criminal Investigation Command, Washington, 1973-76; ops. rsch. analyst and study dir. U.S. Army Concepts Analysis Agy., Bethesda, Md., 1977-80; dir. tng. U.S. 7th Army Combined Arms Tng. Ctr., Vilseck, Germany, 1980-81; chief of ops. rsch. and sys. analysis U.S. Army Europe, Heidelberg, Germany, 1981-84; mgr. engring. svcs. Orion Internat. Tech., Inc., Albuquerque, 1985-90; temp. recall, Ops. Desert Shield/Desert Storm U.S. Army, 1991; army after action report integrator ODCSOPS-HQDA, Washington, 1991; prin. analyst Gen. Rsch. Corp., 1992; ops. rsch. and analysis exec. Lockheed-Sanders, Merrimack, N.H., 1992-98; ops. rsch. exec. Textron Sys., Wilmington, Mass., 1998—. Mgmt. advisor to chmn./CEO PC Support, Inc., Albuquerque, 1986—; presenter numerous symposia, U.S. and Europe. Decorated Silver Stars (2), Legion of Merit, Bronze Stars (3), Air medals (4), Purple Heart, Vietnamese Cross of Gallantry with Gold Star (1) with Palm (2). Mem. Ops. Rsch. Soc. Am., Assn. of U.S. Army, U.S. Naval Inst., Internat. Test & Evaluation Assn. Home: PO Box 746 Merrimack NH 03054-0746

MALLEY, RAYMOND CHARLES, retired foreign service officer, industrial executive; b. Cambridge, Mass., Dec. 22, 1930; s. William and Evangeline (Vautour) M.; m. Rita Ann Masse, May 26, 1951 (dec. June 1989); children: Keith, Bruce, Gregory; m. Josette Lucile Vidril Murphy, Aug. 11, 1995. AA, Boston U., 1950, BS, 1952; MA Equivalent, U. Geneva, Switzerland, 1955; MA and PhD ABD., Fletcher Sch. Law & Diplomacy (Tufts U. and Harvard U.), Mass., 1956. Economist, fin. analyst Texaco, Inc., N.Y.C., 1957-61; fgn. svc. officer U.S. Dept. State/A.I.D., Washington & fgn. posts, 1961-82; dir. U.S. Trade and Devel. Program, Washington, 1980; v.p. Silopress, Inc., Sioux City, Iowa, 1982-87; pres. Silopress Can., 1985—87; cons., advisor Labat-Anderson Internat., Arlington, Va., 1988-93; sr. group advisor, N. & S. Am. rep. Halla Bus. Group, Seoul (Korea), N.Y.C., Washington, 1991—. Chmn. Halla Am. Inc., 1996-2001. Mem. exec. bd. Coll. of Mgmt., Long Island U., Brookville, N.Y., 1994—. 2nd Lt., 1st Lt., Capt. then Major U.S. Air Force Res. Recipient Nat. Def. Svc. medal during Korean War. Mem. Acadian Cultural Soc., Am. Fgn. Svc. Assn., Diplomatic and Consular Officers Ret., U.S. Profl. Tennis Registry, Harvard Club. Roman Catholic. Avocation: tennis (ranked sr. player, cert. tennis instr.). Home: 10 Berrill Farms Ln Hanover NH 03755-3205 Office: Halla America Inc 6224 Loch Raven Dr Mc Lean VA 22101-3133 E-mail: Rcmalley@aol.com.

MALLIK, MUHAMMAD ABDUL-BARI, soil microbiologist; b. Pabna, Bangladesh, Mar. 15, 1927; s. Monsur Ali and Ataharun-Nisa Mallik; m. Rowshan Jahan Hamida, Sept. 24, 1966; 1 child, Abds-Sami. BSc, Rajshahi (Bangladesh) Coll., 1949; MSc, Dhaka (Bangladesh) U., 1952; MS, Minn. U., 1961; PhD, Okla. U., 1964. Lectr. botany U. Karachi, Pakistan, 1956-59, asst. prof. Pakistan, 1964-68, 69-72; vis. scholar dept. botany Baghdad (Iraq) U., 1968-69; asst. prof. Dhaka (Bangladesh) U., 1973-74; rsch. assoc. dept. botany and microbiology u. Okla., Norman, 1974-75; assoc. rsch. prof. agrl. rsch. program Langston (Okla.) U., 1975-82, rsch. prof. agrl. rsch. program, 1982—. Author: Introduction to Fungi, 1973; contbr. articles to profl. and popular publs. Fulbright scholar Minn. U., St. Paul, 1961; rsch. grantee Pakistan Agrl. Rsch. Coun., Karachi, 1968-69, USDA, Langston, 1982—. Mem. Am. Soc. Agronomy, Internat. Allelopathy Soc., Okla. Acad. Sci., Bangladesh Bot. Soc. Democrat. Moslem. Avocation: gardening. Home: 2611 S Oxford Dr Stillwater OK 74074-2276 Office: Langston Univ Agrl Rsch Program PO Box 730 Langston OK 73050-0730

MALLING, HEINRICH VALDEMAR, geneticist; b. Copenhagen, Apr. 21, 1931; came to U.S., 1963; s. Henry August Valdemar and Jenny Bolette (Hansen) M.; m. Bodil Jensen, June 15, 1955 (div. June 1968); children: Tove, Soren, Jakob, Mikael; m. Martha Hale Shackford, July 18, 1969; children: Richard, Kevin, Kirsten. PhD, U. Copenhagen, 1957, Lic. Sci., 1962. Rsch. staff Leo Pharm., Copenhagen, 1957-58; postdoctoral fellow Inst. Genetics U. Copenhagen, 1958-61, assoc. prof., 1961-63; rsch. staff mem. Oak Ridge (Tenn.) Nat. Lab., 1963-72; sect. head Nat. Inst. Environ. Health Sci., Research Triangle Park, N.C., 1972-76, 82—, lab. chief, 1976-82. Adj. prof. N.C. State U., Raleigh, 1972-78, U. N.C., Chapel Hill, 1976—; dir. Environ. Mutagen Info. Ctr., Oak Ridge, 1968-72. Editorial bd. Environ. and Molecular Mutagenesis, 1989—, Mutation Rsch., 1971—; contbr. articles to profl. jours. Nation chief YMCA Indian Guides, Knoxville, Tenn, 1970, Raleigh, 1974. Recipient Sci. award Environ. Mut. Soc., Washington, 1980; Grad. fellow U. Copenhagen, 1953-57, postdoctoral fellow NSF, 1958-61. Mem. Environ. Mutagen Soc. (com. 1989—), Med. Rsch. Coun. (Can., grant revs. 1987—). Democrat. Lutheran. Achievements include patent in transgenic mice for study of mammalian mutagenesis; first to demonstrate mammalian liver microsomes can active non-mutagenic carcinogens to mutagens, others achievements. Home: 3200 Winged Elm Ln Chapel Hill NC 27514-9530 Office: Nat Inst Environ Health Sci PO Box 12233 Durham NC 27709-2233 E-mail: mmalling@bellsouth.net., malling@niehs.nih.gov.

MALLING, MARTHA HALE SHACKFORD, social worker, educator; b. Atlanta, Aug. 20, 1944; d. James Atkins and Ada Vernon (Morrow) Shackford; m. Heinrich Valdemar Malling, July 18, 1969; children: Richard, Kevin, Kirsten. Student, U. Tenn., 1968-70; BA in Psychology, U. N.C., 1978, MSW, 1983; postgrad., Tavistock Clinic, London, 1987-88. LCSW N.C. Lab. technician in genetics N.C. State U., Raleigh, 1964-66, Oak Ridge (Tenn.) Nat. Lab., 1966-67; spl. edn. tchr. Hill Learning Ctr. Durham (N.C.) Acad., 1978-81; social worker II IDTU Children's Inst. John Umstead Hosp., Butner, N.C., 1983-84; clin. social worker Duke U. Med. Ctr., Durham, 1985-87, U. N.C. Hosps., Chapel Hill, 1989-90; social work clin. specialist Child-Outpatient Clinic Dorothea Dix Hosp., Raleigh, N.C., 1990—; pvt. practice Chapel Hill and Durham, 1990—. Peer counselor Office Continuing Edn. Duke U., Durham, 1976—77; crisis counselor and tng. team mem. Orange-Person-Chatham Mental Health Ctr., Chapel Hill, 1979—82; workshop leader N.C. State Tchrs. Duke U. Med. Ctr., Durham, 1986, diabetes day workshop leader, 87; adj. instr. U. N.C. Sch. Social Work, 1996—2001, mem. adv. com. on field edn., 1999—, adj. asst. prof., 2001—. Co-chair PTA Carolina Friends Sch., Durham, 1978—79, chmn. children's sect. art festival, 1978—81. Scholar VA, State of N.C., 1964. Mem.: C. G. Jung Soc. (mem.-at-large 1989—90), Assn. Cert. Social Workers, NC Soc. Clin. Social Work (treas.-sec., co-chair com. psychoanalysis 1995—97, exec. bd. dirs., treas. 1990—94). Democrat. Presbyterian. Avocations: hiking, design, music, reading. Home: 3200 Winged Elm Ln Chapel Hill NC 27514-9530 Office: Dix Hosp Child Outpatient Clinic 820 S Boylan Ave Raleigh NC 27603-2246

MALLINSON, JAMES A., JR. student health services administrator; b. Lancaster, Pa., Aug. 19, 1952; s. James A. and Barbara M. Mallinson; m. Carla A. Mallinson, Aug. 24, 1973; children: Christine, Stephen. BA, Catawba Coll., Salisbury, N.C., 1973; MA, Western Carolina U., Cullowhee, N.C., 1975. Cert. clin. addictions specialist, clin, supr., master addiction counselor. Addictions counselor Tri-County Mental Health, Salisbury, 1976-80, coord. ct. svcs., 1980-81, dir. substance abuse svcs., 1981-93; substance abuse specialist Brocker Health Ctr. U. N.C., Charlotte, 1993-94, dir. student health svcs., 1994—. Cons. and trainer on addictions and ethics, Salisbury, 1981—; adj. lectr. U. N.C., Charlotte, 1994—. Troop leader Boy Scouts Am., Salisbury, 1987—. Mem. Nat. Assn. Alcoholism and Drug Abuse Counselors, Addiction Profls. N.C., Am. Coll. Health Assn., So. Coll. Health Assn. Democrat. Lutheran. Office: Brocker Health Ctr U NC Charlotte 9201 University City Blvd Charlotte NC 28223-0001 E-mail: jamallin@email.uncc.edu.

MALLINSON, RICHARD GREGORY, chemical engineering educator; b. Indpls., Apr. 9, 1954; s. Harry and Susan Louise (Keckler) M. BSChemE, BS in Biomed. Engring., Tulane U., 1977; MSChemE, Purdue U., 1979, PhD, 1983. Rsch. asst. Purdue U., West Lafayette, Ind., 1977-83, Argonne Nat. Lab., Chgo., 1978; asst. prof. chem. engring. U. Okla., Norman, 1983-89, assoc. prof., 1989-99, dir. Inst. for Gas Utilization Techs., 1995—, prof., 1999—. Faculty fellow Lawrence Livermore Nat. Lab., Livermore, Calif., 1990; vis. prof. Tianjin (China) U., 1994—, Chulalongkorn U., Bangkok, 1994—; ptnr. OKKINETICS, Norman, 1996-2000; prin. investigator Univ. Technologists, Inc., Norman, 1988-91; Kerr McGee Disting. lectr. Kerr-McGee Found./U. Okla., 1989-94. Contbr. many articles on Energy. Bd. dirs. C.D. Mallory Found., Inc., Ala., 1994-99, Heartland Found., Inc., Okla., 1995—; mem. Okla. Found. for Excellence, 1993—. 1st lt. USAR, 1977-85. Mem. AIChE (dir. local sect. 1989, symposia organizer 1986-89), Am. Chem. Soc. (symposia organizer 1985-91), Am. Soc. Engring. Edn., Sigma Xi. Achievements include patents pending and patents in field for high density natural gas storage at high temperature, and chemical conversion of natural gas at low temperatures; other areas of exoertise such as natural gas utilization, clean production of N204, emulsion polymerization modeling, alkane cracking modeling, coal conversion modeling. Avocations: competitive sailing, sailing race management, sail cruising, scuba, swimming. Home: 4631 Ridgeline Dr Norman OK 73072-1700 Office: U Okla 100 E Boyd St Rm T335 Norman OK 73019-1028 E-mail: mallinson@on.edn.

MALLINSON, SARAH JANE, volunteer civic activities; b. Independence, Mo., Jan. 26, 1923; d. Ellis, Jr. and Mabel Oleta (Tandberg) Short; m. John William Mallinson, Jr., Aug. 13, 1944; children: Dana, Anne, Laura Buchanan, John William, III, Matthew, Donald. Student, Kansas City Jr. Coll., Kansas City, Mo., 1941-43, U. Mo., 1961-62. Quality control inspector Lake City Remington Arms, Inc., Independence, 1943; clk., def. contract Ford Motor, Co., Kansas City, 1943-44. Cons. Nat. Geographic mag., 1991. Prodr. video Petticoat Pioneers; contbr. articles to hist. jours. and beef promotion mags. Established Bess Truman's birthday celebration ann. event, 1988—; organized fundraising drive for funds to restore Statue of Liberty; chair marking of historic Wayne City Landing site, 1983; first pres. Freinds of the Nat. Frontier Trails Ctr., Independence, 1987, Jackson County, Mo. Geneal. Soc., 1979; organized local chpt. Mo. River Outfitters, Nat. Santa Fe Trail Assn., 1991; vol. in edn. Kansas City Schs., 1982-83. Recipient Cmty. Leadership award Pres. George Bush, Washington, 1991, Gold award Hist. Preservation award U.S. Dept. Interior, Washington, 1996, Nat. DAR, Washington, 1996, award for effort to increase literacy State of Mo., Jefferson City, 1989, 20-Yr. Leadership award 4-H Coun., Jackson County, 1980, others. Mem. Oreg./Calif. Trail Assn. (charter), Santa Fe Trail Assn. (charter), DAR (regent Independence Pioneers chpt. 1984-86), Victorian Soc. Vaile Mansion (charter), Colonial Dames XVIII, Nat. Huguenot Soc., Nat. Trust for Hist. Preservation, Friends of Univ. Women, The Smithsonian Assocs., others. Home: PO Box 8604 Independence MO 64054-0604

MALLO-GARRIDO, JOSEPHINE ANN, advertising agency owner; b. Agana, Guam, Mar. 20, 1955; d. Benjamin Corneja and Salvacion (Lacuesta) Mallo; m. John Marco Haniu Garrido, Feb. 16, 1980; children: Josiah Michael (dec.), Jordan Thaddeus. Student, U. Guam, Agana, 1972-74; BA in Journalism, Seattle U., 1976; MBA, Pepperdine U., 1982. Reporter Pacific Daily News, Agana, 1976, features editor, 1977-78, asst. city editor, 1978-79; copy editor features Honolulu Star-Bull., 1979-81; advt. copywriter Advt. Factors, Honolulu, 1981-83; communications specialist Liberty House, 1983-84; editor, advt. copywriter Safeway Stores Inc., Oakland, Calif., 1984-88; features writer Tracy (Calif.) Press, 1988-91; mktg. mgr. ComputerLand of Guam, Maite, 1992-93; mktg. officer Citibank, Agana, 1993-94; owner JMG Advt., 1994—. Newspaper graphics cons. Pacific Daily News, 1984. Editor/writer Foods Unltd., 1984-88, Tracy Community Hosp. Health Beat and Update, 1988-91; editor Pacific Voice, 1977-78; contbr. articles to profl. jours. Vol. Engaged Encounter, Honolulu, 1989, Trans-Pacific Yacht Race, Honolulu, 1983, United Way, Oakland, 1986; advt. coord. Easter Seals, 1987; organist St. Patrick's Ch., Honolulu, 1980—84, Immaculate Heart of Mary Ch., Toto, Guam, 1994—; mem. adv. bd. Cath. Social Svcs., Agana, Guam, 1993—97, bd. dirs., 1997—, bd. trustees, 2002—. Recipient Cert. Achievement award Advt. Age Mag., 1985, Cert Appreciation award Am. Heart Food Festival, 1985, Best in the West award Am. Advt. Fedn., 1986, Retail Nutrition award Nat. Potato Promotion Bd., 1986, Spl. Achievement award Newspaper Spl. Sect. Mother's Day/Father's Day Coun., 1989, 90, Best Feature Story 2d place Calif. Newspaper Pubs. Assn., 1989, 1st place Classified Advt. Assn., 1989, 1st place appetizer Spam Food Festival, 1991. Mem. Guam C. of C. (media coord. 1993-95), Citiclub (exec. sec. 1994-95). Roman Catholic. Avocations: piano, travel.

MALLORY, ARTHUR LEE, university dean, retired state official; b. Springfield, Mo., Dec. 26, 1932; s. Dillard A. and Ferrell (Claxton) M.; m. Joann Peters, June 6, 1954; children: Dennis Arthur (dec.), Christopher Lee, Stephanie Ann, Jennifer Lyn. BS, S.W. Mo. State Coll., 1954; MEd, U. Mo., 1957, EdD, 1959; HHD, S.W. Bapt. Coll., Mo., 1972. History supr. U. Mo. Lab. Sch., Columbia, 1956-57; asst. to supt. schs. Columbia, 1957-59; asst. supt. schs. Parkway Sch. Dist., St. Louis County, Mo., 1959-64; dean evening div. U. Mo., St. Louis, 1964; pres. S.W. Mo. State U., Springfield, 1964-70, dean Coll. Edn., 1991-94; commr. edn. Mo. Dept. Edn., Jefferson City, 1971-87. Dir. Internat. House, U. Mo., Columbia, 1956-59; chmn. bd. Mo. Coun. on Econ. Edn., 2000—. V.p. Ozarks coun. Boy Scouts Am., 1967, pres. Gt. Rivers coun., 1972-73, Greene County Assn. for Retarded Citizens, 1989—, pres., 1991-96, mem. north ctrl. region exec. bd., 1984—; bd. dirs. Meml. Cmty. Hosp., Mid-Continent Regional Ednl. Lab., Ozark Pub. Telecoms. Inc., 1989—; chmn. bd. Mo. Coun. on Econ. Edn.; bd. regents Mo. State Univs.; trustee Pub. Sch. Retirement, William Jewell Coll., 1972-74; chmn. com. bds. So. Bapt. Conv., 1972-73, mem. com. or bds., 1981—; mem .exec. bd. Mo. Bapt. Conv., 1972-75, 77-80, 2d v.p., 1995-96, pres., 1996-97; trustee Southwestern Bapt. Theol. Sem., Fort Worth, 1995—; mem. adv. com. Young Audiences, Inc., 1986, ARC Bd., Greene County, 1986, Children's Svcs. Commn., chmn., 1986—, Edn. Commn. U.S.; bd. dirs. Ozark Pub. TV; chmn. bd. advisors Windemere Bapt. Assembly, 1992—, chmn. bd. trustees, 2000--; pres. Gt. River coun. Boy Scouts Am., 1972, 73; chmn. Mo. Coun. for Econ. Edn., 2000--. With U.S. Army, 1954-56. Recipient Disting. Service award Mo. Jr. C. of C., 1966; Distinguished Service award U. Mo., 1976; Faculty/Alumni award U. Mo., 1976; Silver Beaver award Boy Scouts Am., 1983, Good Shepherd and Cross, 1986, Disting. Citizen award, 1986; hon. life mem. Mo. Congress Parents and Tchrs.; named Springfield's Outstanding Young Man of Yr., 1965; Champion of Excellence PUSH, 1978 Mem. Am. Assn. State Colls. and Univs., N. Central Assn. Colls. and Secondary Schs., Council Chief State Sch. Officers, Mo. Assn. Sch. Adminstrs., NEA, Mo. Tchrs. Assn. So. Baptist (deacon). Clubs: Masons (33 deg.), Rotary.

MALLORY, DORIS ANN BOURGEOIS, social worker, counselor; b. Jeanerette, La., Aug. 12, 1946; d. Leroy (dec.) and Earlean (Bradley) Bourgeois (dec.); m. Booker Tony Mallory, Oct. 25, 1975 (div.); children: Vincent, Lieta Lynette, Kimberly Denise. BA, Grambling U., 1968; MSW, SUNY, Albany, 1971; MS in Counseling, L.I. U., 1983. Cert. social worker, N.Y.; nat. cert. counselor; diplomate Am. Register Clin. Social Workers. Substitute tchr. St. Mary Parish Sch. Bd., Franklin, La., 1968-69; chief social worker St. John's Day Care Ctr., Albany, 1971; coord. family care O.D. Heck Devel. Ctr., Valatie, N.Y., 1971-80; consent decree specialist Office Mental Retardation and Devel. Disabilities, Albany, 1980-85, coord. consent decree, 1985-86, statewide family care coord., 1986—. Family therapist D.A.M. Counseling, Albany, 1982-87, Project Hope Albany, 1988-90; mem. adj. faculty SUNY Sch. Social Welfare, 1978-87, Empire State Coll., Albany, 1987-88. Trustee, treas. choir, deaconess min., chmn. renovation com. Morning Star Missionary Bapt. Ch., Albany, 1969—, chmn. bd. trustees, 1994—. Recipient Gold plaque award Outstanding Svc. Morning Star Missionary Bapt. ch., 1998, plaque Black Women's Assn. Albany, 1977, Family Care Providers Assn., 1977, 80, 94, Hope House, 1990, cert. for outstanding svc. YWCA, Albany, 1982; cert. of appreciation S. Colonie Sch. Dist., 1998. Mem. NASW (bd. cert. diplomate in clin. soc. work, 1988—), AACD, Am. Assn. U. Women, 1998—, Assn. Multicultural Devel., Nat. Coun. Negro Women, N.Y. State Assn. Counseling Devel., Order Ea. Star (past mastron Albany 1983), Delta Sigma Theta (rec. sec. 1982, pres. Albany alumnae chpt. 1991-94, 91-95), NAACP, Nat. Adult Family Care Orgn. (bd. dirs. 1996—), key communicator S. Colonie Sch. dist., 1994—. Avocations: jogging, cooking, flower gardening, meditating. Home: PO Box 5776 Colonie NY 12205-0776

MALLORY, ELGIN ALBERT, business educator, management consultant; b. Lake Arthur, N.Mex., Aug. 7, 1938; s. Albert Edgar and Thelma Ann (McCulley) M.; m. Shirley Jo Robberson, June 12, 1959 (dec. Oct. 1990); children: Brenda Sue Mallory Gottlieb, Linda Jo Mallory Rose; m. Sarah Ann Appel, Aug. 1, 1992; children: Lynn Janette Appel, Karen Kay Appel Olson. BS, Ea. N.Mex. U., Portales, 1964; MEd, Ea. N.Mex. State U., Portales, 1969; PhD, Colo. State U., 1990. Cert. supt. schs., h.s. prin., math. and chemistry tchr., N.Mex., Colo. Tchr. h.s. math. Clovis (N.Mex.) Mcpl. Sch., 1964-71; jr. h.s. prin. Grants (N.Mex.) Mcpl. Sch., 1971-73; h.s. prin. Silver Consol. Sch., Silver City, N.Mex., 1973-75, Roswell (N.Mex.) Ind. Sch. Dist., 1975-78; dir. secondary edn. Mesa County Sch. Dist., Grand Junction, Colo., 1978-80, asst. supt., 1980-83; owner, mgr. House of Sleep, 1983-87; prof. Mesa State Coll., 1986-95. Mgmt. cons. to small businesses, Colo. and N.Mex., 1985—. Bd. dirs. Mesa County Econ. Coun., Grand Junction, 1983-87; pres. bd. Western Colo. coun. Boy Scouts Am., 1982-90; bd. dirs., campaign chair United Way, Grand Junction, 1980—. Recipient Silver Beaver award Boy Scouts Am.,

1983. Mem. Am. Statis. Assn., Mountain Plains Mgmt. ASsn., Coop. Edn. Assn., Western Mgmt. and Mktg. Assn. Republican. Presbyterian. Avocations: golf, fishing, hunting, motorcycle riding, boating. Home: 2098 Hodesha Ct Grand Junction CO 81503-1049 E-mail: malloryeanda@aol.com.

MALLORY, FRANK BRYANT, chemistry educator; b. Omaha, Mar. 17, 1933; s. Deane Havercroft and Helen (Bryant) M.; m. Patricia Ann Livingston, June 30, 1951; children— Mary Susan, Paul Deane, Philip Howard (dec.), Michele; m. Clelia Sara Wood, Nov. 26, 1965. BS, Yale U., 1954; PhD, Calif. Inst. Tech., 1958. Asst. prof. Bryn Mawr (Pa.) Coll., 1957-63, assoc. prof., 1963-69; prof. chemistry Bryn Mawr Coll. (Pa.), 1969—, W. Alton Jones prof. chemistry, 1985—, chmn. dept., 1982-92; acad. dep. to pres. Bryn Mawr (Pa.) Coll., 1978-81. Vis. assoc. Calif. Inst. Tech., 1963-64; vis. prof. Yale U., 1968, 78-79, lectr., 1977-78; vis. prof. SUNY-Albany, summer 1967; vis. fellow Cornell U., 1970-71; vis. prof. U. Pa., 1988-89. Mem. adv. bd. Jour. Organic Chemistry, 1988-93; contbr. articles to profl. jours. Mem. sci. and arts com. Franklin Inst., Phila. Recipient Bond award Am. Oil Chemists Soc., 1970, Lindback award for disting. tchg., 1992; John Simon Guggenheim fellow, 1963-64, Alfred P. Sloan rsch. fellow, 1964-68, NSF sr. postdoctoral fellow, 1970-71. Mem. Am. Chem. Soc. (exec. com. of organic divsn. 1986-95, symposium officer 1989-95, award Phila. sect. 1989), Phila. Organic Chemists Club (past sec., chmn.). Home: 321 Caversham Rd Bryn Mawr PA 19010-2927 Office: Bryn Mawr Coll Dept Chemistry Bryn Mawr PA 19010

MALLORY, FRANK LINUS, lawyer; b. Calgary, Alta., Can., May 5, 1920; s. Frank Louis and Anna Amy (Allstrum) M.; m. Jean Ellen Lindsey, Jan. 29, 1944; children: Susan Mallory Remund, Ann, Bruce R. AB with distinction, Stanford U., 1941, LLB, 1947. Bar: Calif. 1948. Assoc. Gibson, Dunn & Crutcher, L.A., 1947-54; ptnr. L.A. and Orange County, Calif., 1955-88. Cert. specialist taxation law Calif. Bd. Legal Specialization, 1973-89. Pres. Town Hall of Calif., L.A., 1970, Boys Republic, Chino, Calif., 1962-64; pres. Braille Inst. Am., L.A., 1988-92. Lt. (j.g.) USNR, 1942-46. Mem. ABA, Calif. Bar Assn., Los Angeles County Bar Assn., Orange County Bar Assn., Newport Harbor Yacht Club, Big Canyon Country Club, Transpacific Yacht Club (staff commodore), Order of the Coif, Phi Beta Kappa. Republican. Home: 633 Bayside Dr Newport Beach CA 92660-7213 E-mail: flmallory@CS.com.

MALLORY, JOAN MATEY, music educator, composer; b. Bridgeport, Conn., Mar. 25, 1937; d. Andrew and Anna Matey; m. Daniel Payne Oppenheim, Aug. 2, 1958; 1 child Vicki Oppenheim Michalica ; m. Franklin Bernard Mallory, Feb. 14, 1982; stepchildren: Frank B. Mallory Jr, Jennifer E. Mallory McBee. MusB, Yale U., 1959. Pvt. piano tchr., 1972—82; piano performance, 1990—. Composer: (CD) Joan Plays...#1 Piano, 1999, Joan Plays...#2 Piano, 2001. Avocations: interior decorating, feeding wildlife, making jewel boxes. Office: Box 4181 Silver Spring MD 20914

MALLORY, LATASHA TENE, mental health therapist; b. Melrose Park, Ill., Aug. 2, 1972; d. Joe Lee Brown and Linda Diane Mallory. BA in Psychology, So. Ill. U., 1995, MSEd in Ednl. Psychology, 1999. Nat. cert. counselor, LCSW profl. counselor. Counselor intern Delta Ctr. Inc., Cairo, 1998-99; therapist ProCare Ctrs., Melrose Park, 1999—. Mem. ACA. Home: 1047 S 32nd Ave Bellwood IL 60104 E-mail: LMALL96454@aol.com.

MALLORY, ROBERT MARK, controller, finance executive; b. Mattoon, Ill., Apr. 15, 1950; s. Robert Monroe and Betty Ann (Mudd) M.; m. Diana Marie Burde, Aug. 19, 1972; 1 child, Laura Elizabeth. BS in Accountancy, U. Ill., 1972; MBA, Northwestern U., 1985. CPA, Ill. Staff acct. Price Waterhouse, Chgo., 1972-74, sr. acct., 1974-77, mgr., 1977-79; dir. internal audit Mark Controls Corp., Skokie, Ill., 1979-81, corp. contr., 1981-86, v.p., contr., 1986-88; contr., dir. planning Tribune Co., Chgo., 1988-91, v.p., contr., 1991—. Bd. dirs. Met. Family Svcs. Mem. AICPA (Elijah Watts Sells award 1972), Ill. CPA Soc., Fin. Execs. Inst., Internat. Newspaper Fin. Execs. (bd. dirs.), Beta Gamma Sigma. Methodist. Home: 3312 Lakewood Ct Glenview IL 60025-2505 Office: Tribune Co 435 N Michigan Ave Chicago IL 60611-4066 E-mail: mallory435@aol.com.

MALLORY, STEVEN REECE, software engineering executive; b. Lynwood, Calif., Nov. 23, 1947; s. Joseph William and Edith Pauline (Robertson) M.; m. Kelly Kay Walsh, Jan. 2, 1977 (div. June 1980); m. Elizabeth Margaret Kuntz, Sept. 1, 1990; 1 child, Lauren Beth. BS in Applied Math., Calif. State Poly. Coll., 1971, MS in Computer Sci., 1976. Mem. tech. staff Hi-Shear Corp., Torrance, Calif., 1971, 73-74, Sci. Applications, Inc., San Diego, 1971-72, Planning Rsch. Corp., San Diego, 1972-73, Universal Analytics, Inc., Westchester, Calif., 1976-77; mgr. tng. applications divsn. Sci. Applications Inc., San Diego, 1977-84; mgr. computer and sys. applications group Photon Rsch. Inc., 1984-86; dep. v.p., mgr. engring. ops. Titan Sys. Inc., 1986-88; mgr. software devel. engring. IVAC Corp., 1988-95; sys. verification mgr. Cardiac Pathways Corp., Sunnyvale, Calif., 1996-97; sr. software specialist 3M Health Care, Ann Arbor, Mich., 1997-98; dir. software engring. Aastrom Bioscis. Inc., 1998—. Cons. and presenter in field. Author: Software Development and Quality Assurance for the Healthcare Manufacturing Industries, 2d edit., 1996, Software Quality Assurance SOPs for Healthcare Manufacturers, 1997; mem. editl. bd. Med. Device and Diagnostic Industry; contbr. articles to profl. jours. Mem. IEEE, Nat. Assn. Watch and Clock Collectors, Assn. for Advancement of Med. Instrumentation, Assn. for Computer Machinery, Soc. for Computer Simulation, Soc. Indsl. and Applied Math., Am. Soc. Quality Control. Republican. Avocation: antique clock restoration, clock company historical research. Home: 11545 Windcrest Ln Apt 194 San Diego CA 92128-4241 Office: 24 Frank Lloyd Wright Dr Ann Arbor MI 48105-9755

MALLORY, TROY L. accountant; b. Sesser, Ill., July 30, 1923; s. Theodore E. and Alice (Mitchell) M.; m. Magdalene Richter, Jan. 26, 1963. Student, So. Ill. U., 1941-43, Washington and Jefferson Coll., 1943-44; BS, U. Ill., 1947, MS, 1948. Staff sr. supr. Scovell, Wellington & Co., CPAs, Chgo., 1948-58; mgr. Gray Hunter Stenn CPAs, Quincy, Ill., 1959-62, ptnr., 1962-99. Mem. fin. com. United Fund, Adams County, 1961-64; bd. dirs. Woodland Home for Orphans and Friendless, 1970—, pres., 1981-84, 87-90. Served with 84th Inf. Divsn. AUS, 1942-45. Decorated Purple Heart, Bronze Star. Mem. AICPA, Ill. CPA Soc., Quincy C. of C. (bd. dirs. 1970-76), Rotary (bd. dirs. Quincy 1967-70, pres. 1978-79), Shriners (bd. dirs. Quincy 1982-85, pres. 1988), Royal Order Jesters (Ct. 20 dir. 1997), Railsplitters Soc. (pres. 1993). Home: 2229 Jersey St Quincy IL 62301-4341

MALLORY, WILLIAM BARTON, III, lawyer; b. New River, N.C., June 8, 1944; s. William B. and Marion (Lucas) M.; m. Margaret Mary Milnor; children: Barton, Bennett, Brian, Allison. BA, U. Va., 1966; JD, U. Tenn., 1969. Bar: Tenn. 1969. Assoc. Heiskell, Donelson, Adams, Williams & Wall, Memphis, 1969; gen. counsel Guardsmark Inc., N.Y.C., 1969-73; v.p., gen. counsel The Crump Cos. Inc., Memphis, 1973-86; vice chmn., gen. counsel Guardsmark Inc., 1986-93; v.p., gen. counsel Terminix Internat., 1994—. Mem.: ABA, Yale Club of N.Y.C.

MALLOUH, CAMILLE, urologist, medical educator; b. Beirut, June 13, 1930; came to U.S., 1958; s. Said and Laura (Majdalani) M.; m. Vivian R. McGrath, June 3, 1961; children: Catherine M., Stacy A. BS, French Lycee Higher Math., Beirut, 1951; MD, St. Joseph U., Beirut, 1957. Diplomate Am. Bd. Pathology, Am. Bd. Urology. Intern Elizabeth (N.J.) Gen. Hosp., 1958-59; resident in urology N.Y. Med. Coll., N.Y.C., 1959—65, instr., 1965-72, asst. prof., 1972-82, assoc. prof. Valhalla, 1982-93, prof., chmn. dept. urology, 1993—2000, prof. emeritus, 2000—; pvt. practice, 1965—. Chief urology Bird S. Coler Hosp., Roosevelt Island, N.Y., 1968-71, Met. Hosp., N.Y.C., 1972—. Fellow ACS, N.Y. Acad. Medicine; mem. AMA, Am. Urol. Assn. Presbyterian. Office: New York Medical College Dept Urology Valhalla NY 10595

MALLOW, KATHLEEN KELLY, accountant; b. Chgo., Dec. 27, 1946; d. Robert Henry Kelly and Irene Alice Smith Kelly; m. Kenneth R. Mallow, July 9, 1983; children: Heather K. Peet, Christopher C. Mallow, Daniel S. Peet. BSc in Acctg., De Paul U., 1971; MBA, Keller Grad. Sch., 1986. Asst. supr. Dept. Fin. Instns. State of Ill., Chgo., 1994—, review examiner, 1994—. Mem. working group of edn. and tng. Commn. of Status of Women, Ill. Mem. AAUW (bd. dirs., past pres. 1971—), Home of the Sparrow. Home: 1219 E Plate Dr Palatine IL 60074-7260 Office: State of Ill Dept Fin Instns 100 W Randolph St Ste 15-700 Chicago IL 60601-3234

MALLOY, DANNEL PATRICK, mayor; m. Cathy Malloy; children: Dan, Ben, Sam. LLB, Boston Coll. Bar: Conn., Mass., N.Y., U.S. Dist. Ct. Conn., U.S. Dist. Ct. (ea. and so. dists.) N.Y. Asst. dist. atty. Bklyn., N.Y. Dist. Atty.'s Office, 1980-84; ptnr. Abate & Fox, Stamford, Conn., 1984-95; mayor City of Stamford, 1995—. Mem. bd. fin. City of Stamford, 1983-94, Stamford Bd. Edn., 1994-95; spl. master Conn. Superior Ct.; lectr. Family Law Tng. Seminar. Past bd. dirs. Teen Life Ctr., Liberation Programs, Inc., CTE; treas. Conn. Conf. Municipalities, 1997-98, v.p.; vice chair mayors and pub. schs. task force U.S. Conf. Mayors; mem. fair policy steering com. Nat. League of Cities, 1997-98, mem. task force on youth and edn; chmn. Dem. Mcpl. Ofcls. Orgn.; mem. Dem. Nat. Com., mem. exec. com.; mem. adv. bd. U.S. Conf. Mayors. Mem. ABA, ATLA, Nat. Trial Lawyers Assn., Conn. Bar Assn., Conn. Trial Lawyers Assn. Office: Office of Mayor PO Box 10152 Stamford CT 06904-2152*

MALLOY, EDWARD ALOYSIUS, priest, university administrator, educator; b. Washington, May 3, 1941; s. Edward Aloysius and Elizabeth (Clark) M. BA, U. Notre Dame, 1963, MA, 1967, ThM, 1969; PhD, Vanderbilt U., 1975. Joine Congregation Holy Cross, 1963, ordained priest Roman Cath. Ch., 1970. Instr. U. Notre Dame, Ind., 1974-75, asst. prof., 1975-81, assoc. prof., 1981-88, prof. theology, 1988—, assoc. provost, 1982-86, pres. elect, 1986, pres., 1987—. Bd. regents U. Portland, Oreg., 1985—. Author: Homosexuality and the Christian Way of Life, 1981, The Ethics of Law Enforcement and Criminal Punishment, 1982, Culture and Commitment: The Challenge of Today's University, 1992, Monk's Reflections: A View from the Dome, 1999; co-author: Colleges and Universities as Citizens, 1999; contbr. articles to profl. jours. Chmn. Am. Coun. on Edn.; bd. dirs. NCAA Found., 1989—; mem. Bishops and Pres.' com. Assn. Cath. Colls. and Univs., 1988—; bd. dirs. Internat. Fedn. Cath. Univs., 1988—; mem. Pres.'s Adv. Coun. on Drugs, 1989—; mem. adv. bd. AmeriCorps and Nat. Civilian Community Corps, 1994-97; interim chmn. Ind. Commn. on Community Svc., 1994-97; mem. Boys and Girls Clubs Am., 1997—; trustee St. Thomas U., 1997—, Vanderbilt U., 1999; bd. advisors Bernardin Ctr., 1997—; bd. dirs. Points of Light; past chmn. Campus Compact. Established chair Cath. Studies in the name of Edward A. Malloy, Vanderbilt U., 1997. Mem. Cath. Theol. Soc., Am. Soc. Christian Ethics, Bus.-Higher Edn. Forum, Assn. Governing Bds. of Univs. and Colls. (vice chair 1996—), The Conf. Bd., Nat. Assn. of Ind. Colls. and Univs. (bd. dirs. 1997). Office: U Notre Dame Office Pres Notre Dame IN 46556

MALLOY, JAMES MATTHEW, health management executive, healthcare consultant; b. N.Y.C., Aug. 26, 1939; s. Peter Joseph and Catherine (Cunningham) M.; m. Joan Elizabeth Wagner, Sept. 9, 1967; children— Stephen, Christopher BS, Manhattan Coll., 1961; MPH, Yale U., 1967. Asst. to dir. Yale New Haven Hosp., New Haven, 1967-69; assoc. adminstr. Waterbury Hosp., 1969-75; exec. dir., CEO Jersey City Med. Ctr., N.J., 1975-77; dir., CEO U. Conn. Hosp., Farmington, 1977-82; CEO U. Ill. Hosp. and Clinics, Chgo., 1982-87; exec. v.p. Our Lady of the Resurrection Med. Ctr., 1988-89; pres., CEO, St. Dominic Jackson Meml. Hosp., Jackson, Miss., 1989-91; sr. v.p. health affairs Miss. and La. Blue Cross/Blue Shield, 1991-92; health care cons., pres. Malloy Assocs., 1992—; pres., CEO S.E. Managed Care Orgn., 1993-95. Cons. NIH, Bethesda, Md., 1976-84; dir. Univ. Health Consortium; chmn. Compass Health Plan, Chgo., 1983-87; dir. Hosp. Fund, Inc., New Haven; lectr. Yale U. Sch. Medicine; asst. prof. U. Miss. Sch. Nursing; assoc. prof. U. Ill. Sch. Pub. Health Contbr. articles to profl. jours. Past chmn. Miss. chpt. Nat. Multiple Sclerosis Assn.; mem. Wilson Rsch. Found. (chmn. 1999—). Fellow: Am. Coll. Healthcare Execs.; mem.: Am. Assn. Healthcare Cons., Pub. Health Alumni Assn., Yale U. Assoc. Pub. Health Alumni Assn. (dir. 1996—), Yale Club (pres. Miss. chpt.). Avocations: golf, jogging. Home and Office: 177 Saint Andrews Dr Jackson MS 39211-2532 E-mail: jmalloy@son.unsmed.edu.

MALLOY, JOHN RICHARD, lawyer, chemical company executive; b. Boston, Nov. 26, 1932; s. Thomas Francis and Mary (Field) M.; m. Maraleta Ellerson, May 24, 1960; children: Maureen, John, Megan, Elizabeth. BA, St. John's Sem., Brighton, Mass., 1954; LLB, Boston Coll., 1957. Bar: Mass. 1957. V.p., dir. fin. Remington Arms Co., Inc., Bridgeport, Conn., 1975-78; chief counsel, energy and raw materials E. I. du Pont de Nemours and Co., Wilmington, Del., 1978-79, asst. gen. counsel legal, 1979-83, dir. pub. affairs, 1983-85, v.p. pub. affairs, 1983-85, sr. v.p. external affairs, 1985-92, v.p., spl. counsel to chmn. bd., 1992-93; ret., 1993. Chmn. Jobs for Del. Grads, Wilmington, 1985-97, Del. Compensation Commn., 1988-96; trustee Med. Ctr. of Del., Christiana, 1985—, Del. Pension Fund, 1993-99; bd. dirs. Del. Cmty. Found., 1996-2000, Children's Beach House, 1993-2000; mem. Minner Commn., Del., 1993-96; chmn. Del. Coun. on Transp., 1994-2001, Riverfront Devel. Corp., 2002—; trustee Archmere Acad., 2001—. Mem. ABA, Fed. Bar Assn. Democrat. Roman Catholic. Avocations: tennis, golf, skiing.

MALLOY, JOHNN EDWARD, media artist, writer; b. Superior, Wis., Jan. 1, 1940; s. Robert Francis and Celestine Marie (Evenson) M. BS, U. Wis., LaCrosse, 1962; MS, Winona (Minn.) State U., 1967; MEd, Chgo. State U., 1970; EdS, Ea. Ill. U., 1977; D Arts, U. No. Colo., 1982. Cert. K-14 tchr., Ill., Wis., Colo. Tchr. speech and English Merrill (Wis.) Pub. Schs., 1962-65; tchr. radio and TV Harvey (Ill.) Sch. Dist., 1965-94; instr. speech and theatre, set designer So. Suburban Coll., South Holland, Ill., 1968-70, 75-77, 85; media lectr. Chgo. State U., 1970-72; supr. media lab. U. No. Colo., Greeley, 1980-82; news anchor Colo. Radio Info. Svc., 1981-82. Actor College Street Players, LaCrosse, 1964, Summer Theatre Co., Charleston, Ill., 1974-78; actor, dir. Theatre 21 Co., South Holland, 1974-78; scene painter Sedona (Ariz.) Art Ctr. Theatre, 1996; tech. asst. Red Barn Playhouse, Saugatuck, Mich., 1996—; theater mgr. Thornton Auditorium, Harvey, Ill., 1976-96; art assoc. You'nique Internat. Gallery, Douglas, Mich., 1999—, Art Assoc. Discovery Art Ctr., Saugatuck, Mich., 2000—. Author: Communication in the High School: Speaking and Listening, 1972, Instructional Guides to Media Communication, 1982; prodr. TV mag. series Getting Around, 1981-94. Active, CAP, Chgo., 1965—; participant in tchr.-in-space program NASA, 1985-86; charter sponsor, USAF Meml., Washington. Recipient degree of Diamond Key Coach, Nat. Forensic League, Ripon, Wis., 1994, Silver Medalist Canon USA Photo Contest, 1985, Publ. award Internat. Libr. Photography, 1999; Cert. of Recognition in CBS TV Worth Teaching Program, 1987. Mem. NEA, Ill. Speech and Theatre Assn., Ill. Edn. Assn., Am. Air Mus. Britain (founding mem.), Challenger Ctr. (founding mem.), Air Force Assn., Nat. Air & Space Soc. (founding mem.), Libr. of Congress Assocs. (founding mem.), Saugatuck-Douglas Hist. Soc. (Mich. chpt.), Brit. Interplanetary Soc. Lutheran.

MALLOY, MICHAEL JOSEPH, lawyer; b. Dec. 31, 1950; s. Martin Joseph and Mary Rita (Hannigan) M. ; m. Rosemary Elizabeth Dilworth, Aug. 30, 1975; children: Caroline Rose, Michael David, Brian Patrick, Sean Martin. BS, Villanova U., 1972; JD, Widener Coll., 1976. Bar: pa. 1976, U.D. Ct. Appeals (3d cir.) 1983, U.S. Supreme Ct. 1986. Sole practice, Media, Pa., 1976—. Minor trial atty. Office of Pub. Defender, Media, 1976-79, maj. trial atty., 1979-81, chief maj. trial unit, 1981-90, Solicitor, Irish Ctr., Phila.; lectr. law Del. County Community Coll., 1977-80. Recipient award for outstanding commitment, Del. County Assn. Criminal Def. Lawyers, 2000, Green Jacket Man of Yr. award, Friendly Sons of St. Patrick of Del. County, 2001. Mem. ATLA, Pa. Bar Assn., Del. County Bar Assn., Fed. bar Assn., Pa. Criminal Def. Assn., Del. County Criminal Lawyers Assn., Nat. Criminal Def. Lawyers Assn., Brehon Irish Law Soc. (NAACP Robert A. Wright Freedom award 2000, named Lawyer Yr. 2000). Republican. Roman Catholic. Home: 100 Maple Ave Narberth PA 19072-2413 Office: 10 Veterans Sq Media PA 19063-3103 E-mail: burrcat@msn.com.

MALLOY, MICHAEL PATRICK, law educator, writer, consultant; b. Haddon Heights, N.J., Sept. 23, 1951; s. Francis Edward and Marie Grace (Nardi) M.; divorced; 1 child, Elizabeth; m. Susie Pieratos, Jan., 1992; children: Michael Emil, Nicholas Charles, Edward Francis, Theodora Marie. BA magna cum laude (scholar), Georgetown U., 1973, PhD, 1983; JD (scholar), U. Pa., 1976. Bar: N.J. 1976, U.S. Supreme Ct. 1991. Rsch. assoc. Inst. Internat. Law and Econ. Devel., Washington, 1976-77; atty. advisor Office Fgn. Assets Control Dept. Treasury, 1977-80, Office of Comptroller of Currency, Washington, 1981; spl. counsel SEC, 1981-82; asst. prof. N.Y. Law Sch., N.Y.C., 1982-83; spl. asst. Office of Gen. Counsel U.S. Dept. Treasury, Washington, 1985; assoc. prof. Seton Hall U. Sch. Law, Newark, 1983-86, prof., assoc. dean, 1986-87; prof. Fordham U. Sch. Law, N.Y.C., 1987-96, dir. grad. studies, 1990-94; prof. U. of Pacific McGeorge Law Sch., 1996—, dir. JD concentration in internat. legal studies, 1999—2001. Law lectr. Morin Ctr. Banking and Fin. Law Studies Boston U. Sch. Law, 1986-90, 95-96, 2001; vis. prof. U. Salzburg, Austria, 2000, Suffolk U. Sch. Law, 2001-2002; cons. bank regulation and pvt. internat. law matters. Author: Corporate Law of Banks, 2 vols. , 1988, Economic Sanctions and U.S. Trade, 1990, The Regulation of Banking, 1992, Banking Law and Regulation, 3 vols., 1994, Fundamentals of Banking Regulation, 1998, International Banking, 1998, Banking and Financial Services Law, 1999, Hornbook on Bank Regulation, 1999, 2d edit., 2002, U.S. Economic Sanctions: Theory and Practice, 2001; contbr. articles and revs. and comments to profl. jours. Recipient Spl. Achievement award Dept. Treasury, 1982. Mem.: L'Association des Auditeurs et Anciens Auditeurs de l'Academie de Droit International de la Haye, Hegel Soc. Am., Assn. Am. Law Schs. (chair-elect and program chair 2001—02, chair sect. fin. insts. and consumer fin. execs. 2002—), Internat. Law Assn. (com. chair Am. br. 1995—97), Am. Soc. Internat. Law (exec. coun. 1986—89), Phi Beta Kappa. Office: U of Pacific McGeorge Sch Law 3200 5th Ave Sacramento CA 95817-2705 E-mail: mmalloympm@aol.com.

MALLOY, MICHAEL TERRENCE, journalist, newspaper editor; b. Chgo., Feb. 26, 1936; s. Medard Valentine and Lucille (Zehrol)M.; m. Ruth Gwendolyn Lor, June 5, 1965; children: Linda Jo, Terrence. Student, Reed Coll., 1953-54, Columbia U., 1966-67. Police reporter City News Bur. Chgo., 1956-58; reporter, then bur. chief and chief corr. S.E. Asia UPI, Japan, Laos, India, Vietnam and Thailand, 1960-66; reporter Nat. Observer, Washington, 1968-76, mng. editor, 1976-77; reporter Asian Wall St. Jour., Manila, 1977-80, mng. editor, Hong Kong, 1980-84; mng. editor Dow Jones Can., Toronto, Ont., 1984-94; chief corr. Dow Jones India Report, 1995-97. Author: Racing Today, 1967, The Art of Retirement, 1967. With U.S. Army, 1958-60. E-mail: mikemalloy@idirect.ca.

MALLUCHE, HARTMUT HORST, nephrologist, medical educator; b. Jan. 1, 1943; arrived in U.S., 1975, naturalized, 1985; s. Harald E. and Renate (Muenzberg) M.; m. Gisela Gleich, Dec. 19, 1975; children: Nadine, Danielle, Tiffany. Abitur, Albertus Magnus Coll., Koenigstein, Germany, 1963; postgrad., Phillips U., Marburg/Lahn, Fed. Republic Germany, 1963—65, U. Innsbruck, Austria, 1965—66, U. Vienna, 1966; MD, J.W. Goethe U., Frankfurt, Fed. Republic Germany, 1969. Diplomate German Bd. Internal Medicine. Intern County Hosp., Aichach, Germany, 1969—70; resident in internal medicine, fellow in nephrology Cen. Internal Medicine, Univ. Hosp., Frankfurt Am Main, Germany, 1970—75; asst. prof. medicine U. So. Calif., Calif., 1975—78, assoc. prof., 1978—81; prof., dir. divsn. nephrology, bone and mineral metabolism U. Ky. Med. Ctr., Lexington, 1981—. Cons. NIH, FDA; mem. Va. Merit Rev. Bd. Nephrology; program dir. Gen. Clin. Rsch. Ctr. Author: (monograph) Atlas of Mineralized Bone Histology, 1986; editor: Clinical Nephrology; contbr. articles to profl. jours. and books. Grantee, NIH, 1982—, Shriner's Hosp. for Crippled Children, 0192—. Fellow: ACP; mem.: AAAS, Internat. Soc. Bone Morphometry (founder), Internat. Soc. Nephrology, Am. Fedn. Clin. Rsch., European Dialysis and Transplantation Assns., Am. Soc. Physiol. endocrinology, Am. Soc. Bone and Mineral Rsch., Am. Soc. Clin. Investigation, Am. Soc. Nephrology.

MALM, RITA H. securities executive; d. George Peter and Helen Marie (Woodward) Pellegrini; m. Robert J. Malm, Apr. 19, 1970. Student, Packard Jr. Coll., 1950-52, N.Y. Inst. Fin., 1954, N.Y. Inst. Fin. , 1958, Wagner Coll., 1955. Sales asst. Dean Witter & Co., N.Y.C., 1959-63, asst. v.p., compliance dir., 1964-74; v.p., dir. Securities Ind. Assocs., 1969-72; CEO Muriel Siebert & Co., Inc., 1981-83; pres., founder Madison-Chapin Assocs., 1984-89; pres. Hayward Malm Securities, Ltd., 1989-93; pres., founder Concord Stuart, Inc., 1993—. Art mktg. cons. Author: Dying On Wall Street, 1996; author NASD Series 63 Blue Sky Uniform Securities Agent State Law Exam for Potential Stock Brokers, NASD Stockbroker Examination, NASD Series 6 primer. Bd. dirs. Head Start, 1996—. Mem. NAFE (bd. dirs.), Am. Caner Soc. (bd. dirs. Jupiter/Tequesta chpt. 1992-95), Profl. Women's Network (founder Palm Beach and Martin Counties 1991), Women's Bond Club N.Y. (dir., v.p. program chmn., pres. 1980-82), Cornell U. Club Ea. Fla. (bd. dirs. 1995). Address: PO Box 8603 Jupiter FL 33468-8603

MALM, ROGER CHARLES, lawyer; b. Hot Springs, S.D., July 8, 1949; s. Harry Milton and Angeline Mae (Johnson) M.; m. Sandra M. Metz, July 15, 1972; children: Andrew, Elliott, Nicholas. BA, St. Olaf Coll., 1971; JD, U. N.D., 1974. Bar: N.D. 1974, Ariz. 1975, Minn. 1980, U.S. Dist. Ct. N.D. 1974, U.S. Dist. Ct. Ariz. 1976, U.S. Ct. Appeals (9th cir.) 1981, U.S. Supreme Ct. 1981, U.S. Ct. Appeals (8th cir) 1982, U.S. Dist. Ct. Minn. 1985, U.S. Claims Ct. 1985, U.S. Tax Ct. 1988. Ptnr. Brink, Sobolik, Severson, Malm & Albrecht, P.A., Hallock, Minn., 1980—; county atty. Kittson County, 1995—. Pres. N.W. Minn. County Atty.'s Coun. Hospice dir. Kittson County Hospice, Inc., 1984—; bd. dirs. Cmty. Theatre, Hallock, 1987—, Greater Grand Forks Cmty. Theater, 1991-95. Mem. ABA, Ariz. Bar Assn., N.D. Bar Assn., Minn. Bar Assn. (mem. bd. govs. 1993-2000), Am. Acad. Hosp. Attys., Norwest Minn. Atty.'s Coun. (pres.). Lutheran. Avocations: skiing, sailing. Office: Brink Sobolik Severson Malm & Albrecht PO Box 790 Hallock MN 56728-0790

MALME, JANE HAMLETT, lawyer, educator, advisor; b. N.Y.C., Dec. 2, 1934; d. Robert T. and Minnie (Means) Hamlett; m. Charles I. Malme, June 17, 1961; children: Robert H., Karen I. AB, Brown U., 1956; cert., U. Kobenhavn, Copenhagen, Denmark, 1959; JD, Northeastern U., 1977. Bar: Mass., 1977. Counsel Mass. Tax Commn., Boston, 1978-79; chief bur. local assessment Mass. Dept. Revenue, 1978-90; prin. Mcpl. Mgmt. and Taxation Cons. Svcs., Hingham, 1990—; fellow Lincoln Inst. Land Policy, Inc., Cambridge, 1993—. Faculty Lincoln Inst. Land Policy, Inc., Cambridge, 1989—; adv. property tax OECD, Paris, 1993-97; legal adv. property tax USAID, Russia, 1995-99, Poland, 1998-99, Slovenia, 2001-02, Korea Tax Inst., 1995-96. Author: (with Joan Youngman) Internat. Survey of Taxes on Land and Buildings, 1994, Development of Property Taxation in Countries in Transition, 2001; contbr. articles profl. jours. Trustee Old Ship Ch., Hingham, 1992-97; treas. Betty Taymor Scholarship Fund, Boston, 1992—; pres. Network for Women in Politics and Govt., McCormack Inst., Boston, 1992-94, mem. adv. com. Ctr. for Women in Politics and Pub. Policy, U. Mass., Boston, 1998—. Mem. Internat Assn. Assessing Officers (founder, state and prov. adminstrv. sect., legal com. 1997-, Presidential citation 1983), Mass. Assn. Assessing Officers (hon. lifetime), Mass. Bar Assn., Nat. Tax Assn. (program com. 1998-99), Nat. Assn. Tax Adminstrs. (chair property tax sect. 1988). Unitarian Universalist. Avocations: community service, women in politics, travel.

MALMGREN, HARALD BERNARD, economist; b. Boston, July 13, 1935; s. Berndt Birger and Magda Helena (Nilsson) M.; m. Patricia A. Malmgren, 1959 (div. 1975); children: Karen Philippa, Britt Patricia, Erika Nina; m. Linda V. Einberg, Oct. 3, 1987; children: Markus Harald, Liivia Linda, Viivianne Vaike. BA summa cum laude, Yale U., 1957; postgrad., Harvard U., 1959; PhD, Oxford U., 1961. Asst. prof. dept. engring. and econs. Cornell U., Ithaca, N.Y., 1961-62; head, econ. group Inst. for Def. Analyses, Washington, 1962-64; asst. U.S. trade rep. Exec. Office Pres. The White House, 1964-69; sr. fellow Overseas Devel. Coun., 1969-71; ambassador, dep. U.S. trade rep., 1972-75; sr. fellow Woodrow Wilson Internat. Ctr. for Scholars, Washington, 1975-76; prof. George Washington U., 1976-77; pres. Malmgren, Inc., 1977—; mng. dir. Malmgren, Golt, Kingston, Ltd., London, 1979-99; chmn. Malmgren O'Donnell, 1998-2001; vice-chmn. Cordell Hull Inst., Washington. Adv. coun. Ctr. Strategic and Internat. Studies, Washington, 1987-97; adv. Senate Fin. Com., Washington, 1970-71, 75-76, Interaction Coun., 1985—; chmn. exec. com. Cordell Hull Inst., Washington. Author: International Economic Peace Keeping, 1972; co-author: Assisting Developing Countries, 1972; editor: Pacific Basin Development, 1972; bd. editors: The International Economy, 1987—, The Washington Quarterly, 1987-95, The World Economy, 1980-90; contbr. articles to profl. jours. Mem. Am. Econ. Assn. Met. Club, Reform Club. Home: Summerfield Farm 7620 Cannonball Gate Rd Warrenton VA 20186-7304 E-mail: hm@malmgrenglobal.com.

MALMINIEMI, KIMMO HEIKKI, pharmaceutical company executive, researcher; b. Tampere, Finland, July 2, 1957; s. Matti Henrik and Kaija Hillevi Nieminen; m. Outi Irmeli, Jan. 23, 1988; children: Sini, Satu. MD, Tampere U., 1983; MSc, U. Tampere, 1985, Specialist in Clin. Pharmacology,

1998; PhD, Tampere U., 1999. Lic. physician. Lectr. U. Tampere, 1982-85; internist U. Hosp. Tampere, 1983-85; vis. scientist NIH Inst. Aging, Bethesda, Md., 1985-86; scientist Alko Inc., Helsinki, 1986-87; clin. coord. Leiras Pharms. Inc., Tampere, 1987-96; cons. physician Star Pharms. Inc., 1996—, Santen Inc., Tampere, Finland, 1997-2000; resident physician Tampere U. Hosp., 1997—. Lectr. U. Tampere, 1987—; sr. med. officer Nat. Agy. Medicine, Finland, 2000—. 2d lt. Finnish mil., 1976-77. Mem. Finnish Med. Assn., European Assn. of Study on Diabetes, Nordic Pharmacology Soc., Soc. for Rsch. in Vision and Ophthalmology. Avocation: amateur radio. Office: Lankiniitynkatu 6 FIN33580 Tampere Finland

MALMSTAD, JOHN EARL, Slavic languages and literatures educator; b. Bismarck, N.D., June 25, 1941; s. Manley Ellsworth and Joyce Evelyn (David) M. BA summa cum laude with distinction and departmental honors in Russian Lang. and Lit., Northwestern U., 1963; MA in Slavic Langs. and Lits., Princeton U., 1965, PhD in Slavic Langs. and Lits., 1969; AM (hon.), Harvard U., 1985. Instr. Columbia U., N.Y.C., 1968-69, asst. prof. Russian Lit., 1969-73, assoc. prof., 1973-79, prof. dept. slavic langs. and lits., 1979-85; Samuel Hazzard Cross prof. Slavic langs. and lits. Harvard U., Cambridge, Mass., 1985—, assoc. dean, 1993-94. Vis. assoc. prof. Stanford U., 1971-72, U. Calif. Berkeley, 1977-78; vis. prof. Harvard U., fall 1982; cons., referee NEH translation awards; lectr. in field; attendee internat. symposia. Editor: (with others) The Poetry of Mikhail Kuzmin (3 vols.), 1977, The Poetry of Andrei Bely (3 vols.), 1982-85, Gibel Senatora, 1986, Vladislav Khodasevich Sobranie sochinenii, 1983, Andrei Bely, Spirit of Symbolism, 1987, Readings in Russian Modernism to Honor Vladimir Markov, 1993, Mikhail Kuzmin: Zhizn' Tvorchestvo, Epokha, 1996, Andrey Bely-Ivanov-Razumnik Perepiska, 1998, Mikhail Kuzmin: A Life in Art, 1999, K.N. Bugaeva Vospominaniia o Belom, 2001; Russian book rev. editor Slavic Rev., 1975-86; assoc. editor Russian Rev., 1986-88; mem. editl. bd. Diaspora, Feniks, Opyty, Novoe Literaturnoe obozrenie, Experiment, Philologica, Diaspora; manuscript rev. profl. jours., univ. presses; contbr. articles to profl. jours. Woodrow Wilson fellow, 1963, NDFL fellow Columbia U., 1963-66, Princeton U., 1967-68, Fulbright-Hays fellow, 1966-67, spring 1981, spring 1987, Woodrow Wilson Dissertation fellow, 1966, ACLS rsch. fellow, 1972, Rsch. fellow Russian Inst. Columbia U., summer 1977, 79, 83, 84, IREX fellow, 1975, John Simon Guggenheim fellow, 1980-81; ACLS grant-in-aid, summer, 1980, IREX/ACLS grantee exch. Acad. Scis. USSR, fall 1981, spring 1987, 91, IREX travel grantee Moscow, 1992. Mem. MLA, Am. Assn. Advancement of Slavic Studies, Assn. Tchrs. of Slavic and East European Langs., Inst. d'Etudes Slaves (Paris), Phi Beta Kappa. Avocations: fine arts, ballet, reading. Home: 8A Cogswell Ave Cambridge MA 02140-2001 Office: Harvard U Dept Slavic Langs/Lit Barker Ctr, 12 Quincy St Cambridge MA 02138 E-mail: malmstad@fas.harvard.edu.

MALMUD, LEON SAMUEL, nuclear medicine physician, health facility administrator; b. Phila., Aug. 12, 1939; m. Elsa C. Kravitz; children: Susan Nancy, Anne Cara. BSEE, U. Pa., 1961, MD, 1965. Diplomate Am. Bd. Nuclear Medicine. Intern Albert Einstein Med. Ctr., Phila., 1965-66; resident dept. psychiatry U. Pa., 1966-67; resident dept. medicine Temple U. Hosp., 1969-71; fellow dept. radiology sect. nuc. medicine Johns Hopkins Med. Instns., Balt., 1971-73; asst. prof. medicine Temple U. Sch. Medicine, Phila., 1973-78, assoc. prof. medicine, 1978-83, prof. medicine, 1983—, asst. prof. radiology in nuc. medicine, 1973-76, assoc. prof. radiology in nuc. medicine, 1976-80, prof. radiology in nuc. medicine, 1980-81, prof. diagnostic imaging, 1981—, chmn. dept. diagnostic imaging, 1983-88, Herbert M. Stauffer prof. diagnostic imaging, 1987—, sr. v.p., 1988—, acting chmn. dept. diagnostic imaging, 1989-93, dean, 1997—; CEO Temple U. Hosp., 1991—; pres. and CEO Temple U. Health Sys., 1995—. Staff mem. Temple U. Hosp., Phila., 1973—, assoc. dir. dept. nuc. medicine, 1973-80, acting chmn. dept. nuc. medicine, 1980-81, chmn. dept. nuc. medicine, 1981-83, chmn. dept. diagnostic imaging, 1983-88, CEO, 1990—, chmn. med. staff exec. com., 1982-88, chmn. med. staff steering com., 1982-88, bd. govs., 1982—; staff mem. St. Christopher's Hosp. for Children, 1976-93, Episcopal Hosp., 1978-86, Rolling Hill Hosp., 1978-93. Editor Am. Bd. Nuc. Medicine, Am. Jour. Physiologic Imaging; reviewer Digestive Diseases and Scis., Gastroenterology, Jour. Nuc. Medicine, Pediat., Radiology; contbr. chpts. to books and articles to profl. jours. Capt. USAF, 1967-69. Grantee NIH, 1976-81, 84-87, 84-86. Fellow Am. Coll. Nuc. Physicians; mem. AMA, Radiol. Soc. N.Am., Soc. Chmn. Acad. Radiology Depts., Soc. Nuc. Medicine (self assessment examination subcom. 1978-79, med. student edn. subcom. 1982-83, manpower com. 1982-83, trustee 1986-90, v.p. elect 1987-88, v.p. 1988-89, pres.-elect 1990-91, pres. 1991-92, gov. Greater N.Y. chpt. 1975-77, pres. Greater N.Y. chpt. 1979-81, trustee Greater N.Y. chpt. 1986-90), Am. Coll. Nuc. Medicine, Am. Coll. Radiology, Am. Roentgen Ray Soc., Assn. Univ. Radiologists, Pa. Coll. Nuc. Medicine, Pa. State Med. Soc., Phila. Coll. Physicians, Phila. County Med. Soc. (ins. com. 1986—, com. on acad. 1986—), Phila. Nuc. Medicine Club, Phila. Roentgen Ray Soc., Johns Hopkins Med. and Surg. Soc., Phi Mu Epsilon, Eta Kappa Nu, Sigma Tau. Office: Broad and Ontario Sts Philadelphia PA 19140

MALMUTH, NORMAN DAVID, research scientist, program manager; b. Brooklyn, N.Y., Jan. 22, 1931; s. Jacob and Selma Malmuth; m. Constance Nelson, 1970; children: Kenneth, Jill. AE, U. Cin., 1953; MA in Aero. Engring., Polytech. Inst. of N.Y., 1956; PhD in Aeronautics, Calif. Inst. Tech., 1962. Rsch. engr. Grumman Aircraft Engring. Corp., 1953-56; preliminary design engr. N.A. Aviation Div., L.A., 1956-68; teaching asst. Calif. Inst. Tech., 1961; mem. maths. sci. group Rockwell Internat. Sci. Ctr., 1968-75, project mgr. fluid dynamics rsch., 1975-80, mgr. fluid dynamics group, 1980-82, sr. scientist, project mgr., 1982—. Cons. Aerojet Gen., 1986—89; lectr. UCLA, 1971—72; mem. adv. group for aerospace R&D Fluid Dynamics Panel, 1995; vis. scientist Rensselaer Poly. Inst. Referee AIAA Jour.; bd. editors Jour. Aircraft; contbr. articles to Jour. of Heat Transfer, Internat. Jour. Heat Mass Transfer, and others. Named Calif. Inst. Tech. fellow; recipient Outstanding Alumnus award Univ. Cin., 1990. Fellow AIAA (Aerodynamics award 1991), Am. Phys. Soc.; mem. Am. Acad. Mechanics, Am. Inst. Physics (fluid dynamics divsn.), Soc. Indsl. and Applied Math. Achievements include patent in Methods and Apparatus for Controlling Laser Welding, hypersonic transition delay; pioneering development of high aerodynamic efficiency of hypersonic delta wing body combinations, hypersonic boundary layer stability, transonic wind tunnel interference, plasma aerodynamics, flow control web dynamics, combined asymptotic and numerical methods in fluid dynamics and aerodynamics. Home: 182 Maple Rd Newbury Park CA 91320-4718 Office: Rockwell Sci Co PO Box 1085 1049 Camino Dos Rios Thousand Oaks CA 91360-2362 E-mail: nmalmuth@rwsc.com.

MALONE, ALAN LEE, engineer; b. Lincoln, Nebr., Mar. 8, 1953; s. William Franklin and Iona Belle (Norwood) M.; m. Elaine Rose Walters, July 24, 1957; children: Andrew Nathan, Sean William. BS in Arch., U. Nebr., 1977, postgrad., 1979. Electrician Malone Electric, Waverly, Nebr., 1971-77; solar engr. Solar, Inc., Mead, 1977; commd. 2nd lt. USAF/Air Nat. Guard, 1974, advanced through grades to maj., 1987; weapon systems operator Nebr. Air Nat. Guard, Lincoln, 1974-77, pilot, 1977-84; architect Cons. Engring. Group, Omaha, 1980-81, Hoskins-Western-Sondregger, Lincoln, 1981-82; environ. and design engr. Nebr. Air Nat. Guard, 1982-84; base civil engr. Oreg. Air Nat. Guard, Portland, 1984—. Referee Orchards Soccer Club, Vancouver, Wash., 1987-88. Mem. Soc. Mil. Engrs., Air Nat. Guard Civil Engr. Assn., Internat. Coun. Bldg. Ofcls. Avocations: cooking, gardening, camping, photography. Home: 12401 Finigan Rd Lincoln NE 68517-9619 Office: Oreg Air Nat Guard 6801 NE Cornfoot Dr Portland OR 97218-2743

MALONE, DAVID ROY, state legislator, university administrator; b. Beebe, Ark., Nov. 4, 1943; s. James Roy and Ila Mae (Griffin) M.; m. Judith Kaye Huff, June 20, 1965 (div. Feb. 1990); 1 child, Michael David. BSBA, U. Ark., 1965, JD, 1969, MBA, 1982. Bar: Ark. 1969, U.S. Dist. Ct. (we. dist.) Ark. 1969, U.S. Tax Ct. 1972, U.S. Ct. Appeals (8th cir.) 1972, U.S. Supreme Ct. 1972. Pvt. practice, Fayetteville, Ark., 1969-72; atty. City of Fayetteville, 1969-72; asst. prof. bus. U. Ark., Fayetteville, 1972-76, asst. dean law, 1976-91; mem. Ark. Ho. of Reps., 1980-84, Ark. Senate, 1984—; exec. dir. U. Ark. Found., 1991—. Chair Senate edn. com., co-chair legis. coun., 1999-2000; bd. dirs. Bank of Elkins, 1976-98, S.W. Edn. Devel. Lab., Austin, Tex., 1988-94; legal adv. coun. So. Regional Edn. Bd., Atlanta, 1991—. Contbr. articles to profl. jours.; bd. dirs. Ark. Law Rev., 1978-92; contbg. author U. Ark. Press, 1989. Mayor City of Fayetteville, 1979-80; mem. Jud. Article Task Force, Little Rock, 1989-91; chair Motor Voter task force, 1994-95; bd. dirs. Music Festival Ark., 1989-91, Washington County Hist. Soc., 1993-96; bd. dirs. Walton Arts Ctr. Found., 1994-2000, chmn., 1994-98; chmn. bd. dirs. Washington County Law Libr., 1970-84; chmn. Ark. Tuition Trust Authority, 1997-99. Recipient Svc. award Ark. Mcpl. League, 1980, Disting. Service award U. Ark., 1988, Lucas Svc. award, Ark. Alumni Assn., 1998. Mem. Ark. Bar Assn. (ho. of dels. 1977-81, award of merit 1980, exec. 1981-82, Outstanding Lawyer-Citizen award 1990), Washington County Bar Assn., Ark. Inst. Continuing Legal Edn. (bd. dirs. 1979-88), Fayetteville C. of C. (bd. dirs. 1984-99), Ark. Genealogy Soc. (bd. dirs. 1990-99). Democrat. Methodist. Avocations: genealogy, stamp collecting. Home: 2848 Club Oak Dr Fayetteville AR 72701-9168 Office: PO Box 1048 Fayetteville AR 72702-1048

MALONE, EDWARD ALLEN, English educator; b. Redbank, N.J., June 3, 1962; s. Richard George Malone and Helen Marie Tasto; m. Havva Malone, Jan. 10, 1995; children: Aysen, Adem. BA in English, S.W. Mo. State U., 1984, MA in English, 1987; PhD in English, So. Ill. U., Carbondale, 1993. Lectr. in English U. Mo., Rolla, 1994-96; asst. prof. English Mo. Western State Coll., Saint Joseph, 1996-2000, assoc. prof. English, 2000—. Computer lab coord. Mo. Western State Coll., 1996—. Editor: British Rhetoricians and Logicians, 1500-1660, First Series, 2001; author biographies in: Late Victorian and Edwardian Novelists, 1995, author biographies in: British Travel Writers, 1837-1875, Victorian Period, 1996, author biographies in: British Travel Writers, 1940-97, 1999; contbr. articles to profl. jours. Recipient Dr. James V. Mehl Outstanding Scholarship award, 2001, Governor's award for Excellence in Tchg., 2001. Mem. MLA, Renaissance Soc. of Am., Edmund Spenser Soc., Vladimir Nabokov Soc. Office: Mo Western State Coll 4525 Downs Dr Saint Joseph MO 64507-2294

MALONE, HENRY CHARLES, writer, rare book dealer; b. Detroit, May 5, 1939; s. Charles Joseph and Helen Malone; m. Anita Simone Rodman, June 10, 1962 (div. 1973); 1 child Alex Scott ; m. Edith Sharon Kissane, Apr. 14, 1982. BA, Wayne State U., 1961, MSW, 1967. Diplomate clin. psychotherapy Acad. Cert. Social Workers, lic. marriage and family therapy Mich. Dir. pub. housing social svcs. City of Detroit, 1968-71; broadcaster, prodr. Am. Broadcasting Co., Southfield, 1970-75; adminstrv. dir. Highland Park (Mich.) Mental Health Ctr., 1975-80; clin. dir. Calvin Welles Treatment Ctr., Detroit, 1981-83; clin. psychotherapist Metrotag Clinic, Livonia, 1983-93; free-lance writer, 1990—; contract rsch. writer Gale Rsch., Farmington Hills, Mich., 1990—. Author: (book) Survival, Evasion and Escape, 1986, Footstrikes and Spondees, 1992, New Mexico Haiku, 1996, The Folklore of American Holidays, 3d edit., 1998, Experiencing New Mexico, 1998, James Dickey--ON the Eve of the Millennium, 2000; contbg. author: Gale Encyclopedia of U.S. Economic History, 2 vols., 2000. Bd. dirs. Wayne County (Mich.) Mental Health Bd., Detroit, 1975—80; treas. Greenbriar Co-op. Townhouses, Albuquerque, 1997—99. With USAR, 1957—60. Grantee, NEA, 1966, Am. Acad. Poets, 1967. Mem.: Poetry Soc. Am., Am. Mensa, Poetry Club New Eng. (hon.). Avocations: travel, archaeology, photography, amateur astronomy, antiquarian book collecting. Home and Office: 1220-J Nakomis Dr NE Albuquerque NM 87112-6051 E-mail: Hanksharon@aol.com.

MALONE, JAMES HIRAM, graphic artist, painter, writer; b. Winterville, Ga., Mar. 24, 1930; s. Ralph and Sarah Lena (Echols) M.; m. Mary Louise Liebaert, 1972 (div. 1982); children: Andrew Ralph, Matthew Martin. Student, Morehouse Coll., 1949-50, Coll. Art and Design, 1959-62. Art dir., prodn. mgr. Better Brochures, Inc., Detroit, 1963-65; graphics mgr. Fed. Dept. Stores, 1965-69; sr. art cons. Northgate Ad Agy., 1969-75; sr. graphics designer Montgomery Ward Regional Hdqs., Southfield, Mich., 1975-80; layout/prodn. designer K-Mart Internat. Hdqs., Troy, 1980-83; ad/promotions creative dir. Atlanta Jour./Constitution, 1983-90; fine art prodr., painter Bianco Art Collections of Atlanta, Marietta, Ga., 1990-92; cartoonist, newspaper columnist/reporter Atlanta News Leader, Union City, 1992—. Author, artist: Ralph, 1998, Here and There Poetry, Blues Poetry, 1954, Grandma Sarah's Closet, 1960, Brother, 1970, Malone's Atlanta, 1986, No-Job Dad, 1992, The Cart, 1994, April Mae Jones Coloring Book, 1999; contbr. The Total Cartoonist, 1983, Lure of the Local, 1997, Landscape Narratives, 1998, If I Lives an' Nuthin' Happin'...!, 2000; co-authored songs, Talk to Your Child, Willie Lives in the Streets, 1986, Homeless Hope, 1987, The TAP Song, 1995, artist: (literacy drawings) Say (Simply Apply Yourself), 1988, contr. Word-Up Anthology, 1990, (paintings) BIG (Black Inventors Gifts), 1991; one-man shows include AAA Art Gallery, Detroit, 1963-67, Richard Russell Hall Gallery, Atlanta, 1985, C.W. Hill Gallery, Atlanta, 1990, Walker St. Gallery, Atlanta, 1992, Alma Simmons Gallery, 1986-94, The Atlanta Project Collaboration Ctr., 1994, Atlanta's Auburn Ave. Rsch. Libr., African Am. Culture and History Gallery, 1999, Tchg. Mus. South, 1999-2001, Decatur Bapt. Ch., 2000; exhibited in group shows at Red Cross European Exchange Touring Art Exhbn., 1949, Atlanta U., 1949, 53-55, Contemporary Art Studio Gallery, Detroit, 1962, 64-67, 75, Detroit Mus. Art, 1968, Wayne State Coll. Cmty. Gallery, Detroit, 1969, Kumarsi Mart Art Gallery, Detroit, 1970, Scarab Club Mus., Detroit, 1974, United Auto Workers, Detroit, 1977, Salon Internat. De La Caricature, Montreal, Can., 1980-83, 85-86, 88, Artistic Directions Gallery, Atlanta, 1983, Nexus Gallery, Atlanta, 1984, 89, Ctr. Creative Studies Coll. Art and Design Alumni Exhibits, Detroit, 1986-92, Spelman Coll., Atlanta, 1987, Mattress Factory, 1987, 89, Nat. Black Arts Festival, Atlanta, 1988-92, Ga. State U., 1989, Ruth Hall Hodges Gallery, Atlanta, 1990-93, TULA Galleries, Atlanta, 1990, Seven Stages, 1990, 96, EarthFactory, Atlanta, 1991, Art Station, Atlanta, 1991, Atlanta Life, 1992, Trinity Art Gallery, 1992, Samari Art Gallery, 1993, Mobile (Ala.) Coll., 1993-94, Albany Mus. Art, 1994, Alma Simmons Gallery, Atlanta, 1994, Atlanta Project Hdqs., 1994, Avery Gallery, 1995; Buttermilk Bottom Art Proj., 1995-96, Atlanta's Civic Ctr., 1995-96, Alma Simmons Gallery, 1995-96, Atlanta's Auburn Ave Rsch. Libr., African Am. Culture and History Gallery, 1996, City Hall East Gallery, 1996-97, Atlanta Olympic Park, 1997, Eddies' Alley, 1997, Miles Gallery, 1997, House of Colors, 1998, Annie McPheeters Art Gallery, 1999, Tchg. Mus. South, 1999-2001, Atlanta Hartsfield Airport, 2000, New Orleans Art Galleries, 2000, Kennesaw State U. Gallery, 2000, Walt Disney's movie scenery, 2001-, Motion Through Art, 2001, Pilgrimage to Paradise, 2002, Senior Citizen's Project, 2002; represented in permanent collections including Atlanta U., Hatch-Billups, N.Y., Ga. Artists Register, Atlanta, Bianco Collections, Ga. Rsch. libr. African-Am. culture and history, 1995, RepoHistory Assn., 1996, neighborhood schs. mentor Fed. Dept. Stores, Detroit, 1964-69; motivator, sch. lectr. Atlanta Jour./Constitution, 1983-90, minority job fairs guide, 1985; bd. dirs. Neighborhood Planning Unit J, Atlanta, 1984—, Bankhead Hwy. Revitalization Project, Atlanta, 1990—; arts cons. Fulton County Arts Task Force, Atlanta, 1990—; com. chmn. Jimmie Carter's West Fulton and Douglass Atlanta Cluster Project, 1992—; active Feed The Homeless, Inc., Atlanta Olympics Com., Atlanta Mayor's Bicycle Paths Commn., 1995; com. chmn. Atlanta-Fulton County Action Authority Assn., 1994, North Ave Civic League Assn., 2002. Recipient George H. Clapp Meml. Found. award Art Inst. Pitts., 1949, Nat. Art award, Scholastic Art Awards Contest, Atlanta U. Nat. Art award, 1949, Nat. Cartoonist Soc. scholar, 1958, Editorial Cartoon award Nat. Newspapers Pub. Assn., 1973, Bronze Jubilee Cmty. award WPBA TV, Atlanta, 1986, Alumni Art award Ctr. Creative Studies, Coll. Art and Design, Detroit, 1986, Atlanta Symphony Art award, 1986, Youth Motivation award Merit Employment Assn., 1987-89, So. Drawl Art Exhbn. award, 1993, Atlanta'a Centennial Olympic Park Art award, 1997, Annie L. McPheeters Cmty. Medallion award, 1998, Million Man March Srs. award, 1998, Cmty. award Together Atlanta, 1999; grantee Atlanta Jour./Constitution, 1986, Nexus Family History Artbook Project, 1994, Avant Gardening Tour 2000, Daimler/Chrysler Art award, 2001. Mem. Assn. Am. Cultures, 1980, High Mus. Art, 1st World Writers (v.p. 1993-94), Internat. Black Writers (cons., pres. 1996), Atlanta Writing Resource Ctr., Nat. Conf. Artists, Friends of Atlanta/Fulton County Libr., Buttermilk Bottom Cmty. Assn. (cons., v.p. 1996, pres. 1998), Individual Visual Artists' Coalition, Laughing Trees Assn. (pres. 2000). Democrat. Baptist. Avocations: poetry, photography, tennis, rummage sales, reading. Home: 1796 North Ave NW Atlanta GA 30318-6441 Office: 1796 North Ave NW Atlanta GA 30318-6441 E-mail: j.l.t.malone@att.net.

MALONE, JOHN I. pediatrics educator, biomedical researcher; b. Altoona, Pa., Oct. 10, 1941; s. W. Paul and Olive (Romine) M.; m. Gloria Joyce Cromer, Sept. 5, 1964; children: John Irvin Jr., Michael A., Jennifer A., W. Andrew. BS, Pa. State U., 1963; MD, U. Pa., 1967. Diplomate Am. Bd. Pediatrics, Am. Bd. Pediatric Endocrinology; cert. diabetes educator. Straight pediatric intern Children's Hosp. Phila., 1967-68, resident, 1968-69, research fellow div. biochem. devel. and molecular diseases, 1969-71; instr. pediatrics U. Pa. Sch. Medicine, Phila., 1971-72; chief resident Hosp. of U. Pa., 1971-72; asst. prof. U. South Fla. Coll. Medicine, Tampa, 1972-76, assoc. prof., 1976-80, chief divsn. pediatric diabetes & metalbolic diseases, 1976—, prof., 1980—, co-dir. Diabetes Ctr., 1979—. Co-dir. Fla. Camp for Children and Youth with Diabetes, Tampa, 1973—, pres., 1990; mem. clin. and sci. adv. bd. Children's Diabetes Found. at Denver, 1976-86; dir. Suncoast Regional PKU Program, 1976—, Suncoast Regional Diabetes Program, 1976—, chief pediat. endocrinology, diabetes and metabolism, 1995—; mem. Fla. Gov.'s Diabetes Adv. Coun., 1979—; mem. Internat. Study Group Diabetes in Children and Adolescents, Paris, 1982—; vis. prof., cons. in pediatric endocrinology Uniformed Svcs. U. Health Scis., Bethesda, Md., 1990-98; mem. staff various hosps. Contbr. over 110 articles Sci., New Eng. Jour. Medicine, Jour. Pediatrics, Am. Jour. Human Genetics, Am. Jour. Diseases of Children, Diabetes, Jour. Fla. Med. Assn., Diabetes Care, Jour. Clin. Investigation, Jour. Clin. Psychiatry, European Jour. Pediatrics, Proc. NAS, Pediatrics Rsch., Pediatrician, Diabetes Care, Pediatrics, Am. Jour. Med. Scis., Am. Jour. Med. Genetics, Clin. Pediatrics, also chpts. to books. Mem. AAAS, Am. Acad. Pediatrics, Am. Diabetes Assn. (program chmn. youth coun. 1987-88), Lawson Wilkins Pediatric Endocrine Soc., So. Soc. for Pediatric Rsch. (pres. 1986-87), Am. Fedn. for Clin. Rsch., Soc. for Pediatric Rsch., N.Y. Acad. Sci., Am. Inst. Nutrition, Am. Pediatric Soc., Am. Soc. for Clin. Nutrition, Soc. for Inherited Metabolic Disorders. Achievements include research on the metabolic causes of diabetes associated complications and research on the development and prevention of diabetes in relatives of patients with insulin-dependent diabetes. Office: U South Fla Coll Medicine 12901 Bruce B Downs Blvd Tampa FL 33612-4742 E-mail: jmalone@hsc.usf.edu.

MALONE, JOSEPH JAMES, mathematics educator, researcher; b. St. Louis, Sept. 9, 1932; s. Joseph James and Aurelia Theresa (Schomaker) M.; m. Dorothy Sue Cleary, Nov. 24, 1960; children: Michael, Barbara, Philip, Patrick. BS, St. Louis U., 1954, MS, 1958, PhD, 1962. Instr. math. Rockhurst Coll., Kansas City, Mo., 1960-62; asst. prof. U. Houston, 1962-67; assoc. prof. Tex. A&M U., College Station, 1967-70, prof., 1970-71, Worcester (Mass.) Poly. Inst., 1971-2000, prof. emeritus, 2000—, chmn. dept. math., 1971-78. Contbr. articles to profl. jours. Mem. pub. schs. bd. Town of Westborough (Mass.), 1974-83, 84-87, fin. com., 1992-98, selectman, 1998-2001, fin. com., 2001—. With U.S. Army, 1954-56. Mem. AAUP, Am. Math. Soc., Math. Assn. Am. Democrat. Roman Catholic. Achievements include research in near-ring theory and group theory. Home: 45 Adams St Westborough MA 01581-3610 Office: Worcester Poly Inst 100 Institute Rd Worcester MA 01609-2280 E-mail: jjmalone@wpi.edu.

MALONE, KARL, professional basketball player; b. Summerfield, La., July 24, 1963; Student, La. Tech. U., 1981-85. Basketball player Utah Jazz, 1985—. Mem. U.S. Olympic Basketball Team (received Gold medal), 1992. Mem. NBA All-Star team, 1988-94; recipient NBA All-Star Game MVP award, 1989, co-recipient, 1993; mem. All-NBA first team, 1989-94; mem. All-NBA second team, 1988; mem. NBA All-Defensive second team, 1988; mem. NBA All-Rookie Team, 1986; co-leader most seasons (8) with 2000 points, 1987-95; NBA Most Valuable Player, 1997. Office: Utah Jazz Delta Ctr 301 W South Temple Salt Lake City UT 84101-1216*

MALONE, LAURENCE ADAMS, economist, consultant; b. Cleve., Dec. 4, 1911; s. Cornelius Fitzgerald and Grace Adams (True) M.; m. Ethel Whatley, Jan. 2, 1962 (dec. 1987); m. Nettie Allen, July 24, 1987. LLB, Chgo. U., 1962; PhD, Columbia Pacific U., 1967. Contracting officer USN Sea Systems Command, Washington, 1941-79; economist Direct Answer Publishing Inc, Chagrin Falls, Ohio. Author: An Evolving World, 1972, Restoration, 1972, Our Debt Money Systems, 1985, How to Stop Foreclosure, 1982; patentee in field. Decorated Order of St. John, Knights of Malta. Roman Catholic. Avocations: research, writing, poetry. Home: PO Box 23279 Chagrin Falls OH 44023-0279

MALONE, LAURENCE JOSEPH, economics educator, writer; b. Troy, N.Y., Apr. 4, 1957; s. Laurence Bernard and Barbara Ethel (McCormack) M.; m. Eva Trelease Davidson, June 25, 1983; children: Luke, Theo. BA in Econs., SUNY, 1979; PhD in Econs., New Sch. for Social Rsch., 1991. Sr. rsch. assoc. N.Y. State Assembly, Albany, N.Y., 1980-83; assoc. prof. econs. Hartwick Coll., Oneonta, 1986—. Faculty senate, Hartwick Coll., Oneonta, 1993—, dept. chmn., 1996—. Author: Opening the West, 1998; co-editor: The Essential Adam Smith, 1986. Advisor Hartwick Coll. Student Senate, 1988-92, chmn. off campus programs com., 1990-92. Mem. Econ. and Bus. Hist. Soc. (pres. 2000—), Econ. History Assn., Am. Econs. Assn., Order of the Omega. Democrat. Unitarian Universalist. Avocations: tennis, basketball, debate society. Office: Hartwick Coll Yager Hall Oneonta NY 13820

MALONE, LISA R. accountant, scheduler; b. Baytown, Tex., Aug. 14, 1964; d. Bob R. Allen and H. Ruth (Reeder) Allen; 1 child, Valerie Ann Watkins; m. Don Alan Watkins, Oct. 14, 2000. AA in Bus. Adminstrn., Lee Coll., 1985; BBA in Gen. Bus., U. Houston, Clear Lake, 1987, BS in Finance, 1994, MS in Fin., 1998. Accounts receivable supr. D.E. Harvey Builders, Inc., Houston, 1988-89; document contr. Halliburton, 1989-90, cost engr., 1990-94, internal auditor, 1994-95, acct., 1995-96, scheduler, 1996-2000; earned value analyst Lockheed Martin Corp., 2000—. Methodist. Avocation: cross stitch. Office: Lockheed Martin Corp PO Box 58980 Mail Code L1C Houston TX 77258 E-mail: bugsbunny@ev1.net.

MALONE, MARY FRANCES ALICIÁ, university official; b. N.Y.C., Sept. 24, 1946; d. James Patrick and Mary Theresa (McGarry) Hoban; m. Kieran Malone, Oct. 5, 1985. BA in History, Molloy Coll., 1967; MA in History, Fordham U., 1969; PhD in Higher Edn. Adminstrn., NYU, 1977. Placement dir. Molloy Coll., Rockville Centre, N.Y., 1969-71; doctoral rsch. fellow NYU, N.Y.C., 1971-74, exec. asst. to dean of librs., div. of librs., 1974-77; mgr. profl. devel. Spl. Librs. Assn., 1977-83; asst. dean Grad. Sch. Comm., Fairfield (Conn.) U., 1983-89, asst. acad. v.p., 1989—, assoc. acad. v.p. Task force facilitator Fairfield 2000 Regional Plan Assn., Greenwich, Conn., 1987, dir. coll. access program, dir. vis. black scholar program; facilitator mgmt. survival kit Assn. for Mgmt., Greenwich, 1987; facilitator White House Conf. on Libr. and Info. Sci.; contract reviewer U.S. Dept. Edn., Washington, 1982; bd. dirs. Collegium Faith and Intellect in Cath. Higher Edn., 1991-95, 97-2002. Editor Profl. Devel. Series; contbr. articles to profl. jours. Challange grantee NEH, 1977, Lilly Endowment grantee, 1991, 95, 2001, Humanitas grantee, 1997, Hewlett Found. grantee, 1999; named to 1st worldwide conf. on spl. librs., H.W. Wilson Fedn., Exxon Edn. Found., Honolulu, 1979; recipient citation Spl. Librs. Assn., 1983. Mem. Advt Women N.Y. (com. chmn. 981—), Women in Comm. (bd. dirs. 1984-86, 88-89, 92-93), White House Conf. on Libr. and Info. Sci. (facilitator), Continuing Libr. Edn. Network and Exch. (bd. dirs. 1980-82), Pi Lambda Theta, Phi Delta Kappa. Roman Catholic.

MALONE, MICHAEL GLEN, lawyer; b. L.A., Apr. 12, 1943; s. Thomas Daniel and Virginia (Shupe) M.; m. Susan Cornelia Pierson, May 9, 1970 (div. Nov. 1987); m. Linda Kay Thomson, Dec. 26, 1987. Student, U. So. Calif., 1960-61; BS, U.S. Naval Acad., 1965; JD, U. Calif., San Francisco, 1974. Bar: Calif. 1974, U.S. Dist. Ct. (no. dist.) Calif. 1974, U.S. Ct. Mil. Appeals 1979, U.S. Supreme Ct. 1979. Commd. 2d lt. U.S. Marine Corps, 1965, advanced through grades to lt. col., 1980, served in Republic of Vietnam, USS Coral Sea; appellate mil. judge U.S. Navy-Marine Corps Ct. of Mil. Rev., Washington, 1981-83; ret. U.S. Marine Corps, 1986; assoc. Littler, Mendelson, Fastiff & Tichy, San Francisco, 1986-88; staff atty. for SAFECO Ins. Co. Law Offices of James D. Biernat, Foster City, Calif., 1988-97, Law Offices of Donald J. Deshaw, Foster City, 1998-99; mng. atty. Law Offices of Carol L. Ventura, 1999—. Regional trainer Internat. Rugby Bd. Mem. ABA, Assn. Trial Lawyers Am., Bar Assn. San Francisco, Marin County Bar Assn., Sonoma County Bar Assn., Napa County Bar Assn. Republican. Avocation: rugby. Office: Law Offices Carol L Ventura Mng Atty 1300 Oliver Rd Ste 240 Fairfield CA 94533

MALONE, MICHAEL WILLIAM, electronics executive, software engineer; b. Belmore L.I., N.Y., Mar. 31, 1956; s. Daniel Joseph Malone and Frances Ann (Reilly) Coppersmith; m. Jane Pauline Raese, Aug. 20, 1988. BS in Elec. Engring. and Computer Sci., U. Colo., 1986. Test engr. Catalina Controls, Longmont, Colo., 1984-86; design engr. Inlab, Inc., Broomfield, 1986-87, mgr. engring., 1987-89; software engr. UMG, Inc., Golden, 1989-90, sr. software engr., 1990-91, v.p., 1991-94; sr. software engr. RELA, Boulder,

1994-98, Aztek-Engring., Inc., Boulder, 1998—. Developer software. With USN, 1975-79. Avocations: rock climbing, sailing, aikido, skiing. Office: Aztek Engring Inc Ste 202 2477 55th St Boulder CO 80301-2835

MALONE, NICHOLAS SHERLON, systems analyst, consultant; b. Huntington, W.Va., Aug. 6, 1958; s. Clarence Edward Malone and Ernestine (Queen) Vaughn; m. Julie Stratton, Mar. 4, 1985 (div. Dec. 3, 1990); m. Tracy Lynne Prunty, Dec. 21, 1991; 1 child, Nicolle Morgynne Malone. BA in Political Science, Marshall U., Huntington, W.Va., 1981. Owner Mgmt. Resources, Mount Claire, W.Va., 1977-. Dir. W.Va. Science Fiction Assn., Charleston, 1980-86; mem. bd. dirs. UN Ednl. Orgn., N.Y., 1979-82, MARCON, 1983-90. Author: (book) Social Alternatives in Rsch., 1982, Comp. Security Program, 1990; contbr. articles to profl. jours. Rsch. analyst W.Va. Code Reform Orgn., Charleston, 1979, W.Va. GOP, Huntington, 1980; NORML, Huntington, 1985-86; project mgr. U.N. Edn. Org./NGO Soc., N.Y., 1981-82. Served With USMC, 1979-92. Recipient Gold Star award Michelien du France, 1981, award Rikido-USA, 1981, Nat. Top 10 award RPGA, 1978, 79, 80, 81, Nat. Top 100 Rating UFFA, 1975, 76, 77, 78; inducted into Naidh Nasc, 1999. Mem. NRA, Am. Soc. Tran. & Devel., Assn. Computing Machines, Am. Soc. Industry Security, Millennium Soc., Boy Scouts of Am., Soc. Noble Celts. Republican. Mem. Daoist Ch. Avocations: martial arts, gourmet coking, SCA, chess, hunting. Office: Mgmt Resources Int 9450 Tuxford Rd Richmond VA 23236

MALONE, PATRICK MICHAEL, pharmacist, educator; b. Waterloo, N.Y., June 24, 1954; s. Clarence Leslie and Vernice Irene (Reader) M.; m. Mary Jane Kuncel, June 28, 1980; 1 child, Meghan Jean. BS in Pharmacy, Union U., 1977; PharmD, U. Mich., 1979. Clin. pharmacy resident Buffalo (N.Y.) Gen. Hosp., 1978-79; drug info. specialty fellow U. Nebr. Med. Ctr., Omaha, 1979-80; asst. prof. Ohio No. U., Ada, 1980-83, U. Wash., Seattle, 1983-87; clin. pharmacy specialist Ingalls Meml. Hosp., Harvey, Ill., 1987-90; assoc. prof. Creighton U., Omaha, 1990—. Pres. Drug Info. Evaluation Tech., Inc., Ada, 1994-2000; mem. exec. com. Consortium for Advancement Medication Info., Policy, and Rsch., 1996-97. Author, editor: Drug Information—A Guide for Pharmacists, 1996, 2d edit., 2001; asst. editor DRUGDEX Info. Sys., 1984—. U.S. West fellow Creighton U., 1995-96. Fellow Am. Soc. Health Sys. Pharmacists; mem. Am. Med. Informatics Assn., Am. Assn. Colls. Pharmacy, Drug Info. Assn., Nebr. Pharmacists Assn., Phi Delta Chi (worthy corr. 1975-76, faculty advisor 1991—). Avocations: computers, radio control aircraft, reading. Office: Creighton Univ Sch Pharmacy 2500 California Plz Omaha NE 68178-0001 E-mail: pmalone@creighton.edu.

MALONE, PAUL SCOTT, writer, artist; b. Houston, June 15, 1952; s. Robert Walter and Lillian Ann (Hagewood) M.; m. Cheryl Ann Knott, May 20, 1978. BA in Journalism, U. Houston, 1978; MFA in Creative Writing, U. Ariz., 1986. Tchg. asst. English dept. U. Ariz., 1983-86; lectr., part-time instr. English dept. Wayne State U., Detroit, 1986-87; instr. The Authors Resource Ctr., Tucson, 1986. Part-time instr. English dept. Washtenaw C.C., Ann Arbor, Mich., 1986-87, Austin C.C., 1988-94; adj. prof. Oklahoma City C.C., summer 1982. Author: In An Arid Land: 13 Stories, 1995 (Netlibrary initial sales offering 1999), Memorial Day and Other Stories, 2000, This House of Women, 2001; featured author Tex. Book Festival, State Capitol Tex., 2000; contbr. numerous fiction works to popular mags. and publs. including Writers' Forum, So. Humanities Rev., Prairie Schooner; contbr. poetry to anthologies including Am. Poetry Monthly, Poetry Motel, Tex. Poetry Rev.; contbr. book revs. and essays to newspapers and writing publs.; regular contbr. books sect. The Dallas Morning News, 1992-96; corr. editor Writers' Forum, 1993-2002; state editor The Daily Oklahoman, 1982-83; one-man shows include Sandwich Boy Restaurant and Gallery, Urbana, Ill., 1998, 99, 2000, The Southlynn Studio, Champaign, Ill., 1999, Border's Book Store, Champaign, 1999, El Taller Galleries, Austin, Tex., 2000, Pages for All Ages Book Shop, Champaign, 2000; group shows include Champaign Downtown Assn., 1997, Parkland Coll., Champaign, 1998, Sandwich Boy Restaurant and Gallery, 1999, The Southlynn Studio, Champaign, 1998, 99, Nickelodeon Art Gallery, Burbank, Calif., 2001; represented in numerous pvt. collections; represented by galleryNow, 199-2002; One of 28 regional artists listed on the Tuscon-Pima Arts Coun. Public Art Roster, 2001-02. With U.S. Army, 1972-74. Recipient awards for investigative reporting/news writing Corpus Christi Press Club, 1979, Best Reporting award Tex. Com. on Natural Resources, 1979, 1st pl. for interpretive reporting Soc. Profl. Journalists, 1982, 1st pl. for feature writing AP Mng. Editors of Okla., 1983, 1st prize Tucson Weekly Ann. Fiction Contest, 1985, 2d prize Am. Fiction short story contest, 1988, Black Warrior Rev. Literary award in fiction, 1992, Frank O'Connor Meml. award in fiction Descant, 1994, Jesse Jones award for best book of fiction Tex. Inst. Letters, 1996; featured poet Am. Poetry Monthly, 1997; selected for inclusion in Contemporary Authors, 1996; John Huck Meml. scholar U. Ariz., 1985, 86, anonymous scholarship for fiction writing, 1985; grantee Soc. Southwestern Authors, 1986; NEA fellow in creative writing, 1990; award in Contemporary Litery Fiction, women Writing the West, 2001. Avocation: fly fishing, backpacking. Home: 409 E Belmar PO Box 311 Pearce AZ 85625 E-mail: Psmalone@aol.com.

MALONE, RICHARD P. psychiatrist; b. Mount Pleasant, Pa. BA, U. Pitts., 1974; MD, Hahnemann U., 1983. Psychiatry intern Med. Coll. Pa., 1983, resident in psychiatry, 1983-87, fellow in child and adolescent psychiatry, 1986-88, fellow in child psychopharmacology rsch., 1988-90; dir. child and adolescent psychiatry rsch. MCP Hahnemann U., Phila., 1990—.

MALONE, ROBERT ROY, artist, art educator; b. McColl, S.C., Aug. 8, 1933; s. Robert Roy and Anne (Matthews) M.; m. Cynthia Enid Taylor, Feb. 26, 1956; 1 child, Brendan Trevor. BA, U. N.C., 1955; MFA, U. Chgo., 1958; postgrad., U. Iowa, 1959. Instr. art Union U., Jackson, Tenn., 1959-60, Lambuth Coll., 1959-61; asst. prof. art Wesleyan Coll., Macon, Ga., 1961-67, assoc. prof., 1967-68, W.Va. U., 1968-70, So. Ill. U., Edwardsville, 1970-75, prof., 1975—. One-man shows at Gallery Illien, Atlanta, 1969, De Cinque Gallery, Miami, 1968, 71, Ill. State Mus., Springfield, 1974, U. Del., Newark, 1978, Elliot Smith Gallery, St. Louis, 1985, Merida Galleries, Louisville, 1985, Yvonne Rapp Gallery, Louisville, 1990, 92, 93, 96, 98, 2000, St. John's Coll., Santa Fe, 1991, Uzelac Gallery, Pontiac, Mich., 1997, others; group shows include Bklyn. Mus., 1966, Assoc. Am. Artists Gallery, N.Y.C., 1968, Musée d'Art Modern, Paris, 1970, DeCordova Mus., 1973, 74, St. Louis Art Mus., 1985, Wake Forest U., 1985, New Orleans Mus. Art, 1990, Dakota Internat., Vermillion, 1994; represented in numerous permanent collections including Smithsonian Instn., Washington, USIA, Washington, Library of Congress, Calif. Palace of Legion of Honor, San Francisco, N.Y. Pub. Library, N.Y.C., Victoria and Albert Mus., London, Chgo. Art Inst., Indpls. Mus. Art, Humana Inc., Louisville, State of Ill. Ctr., Chgo., Speed Mus., Louisville, N. Ill. Univ., Capital Devel. Bd., Ill.; co-editor: Contemporary American Printmakers, 1999 (English and Chinese edits.). Recipient numerous regional, nat. awards in competitive exhbns.; Ford fellow, 1977; So. Ill. U. at Edwardsville sr. research scholar, 1976, 84 Home: 600 Chapman St Edwardsville IL 62025-1260 Office: So Ill U Dept Art and Design Edwardsville IL 62025 E-mail: rmalone@sive.edu.

MALONE, ROXANNE ENYEART, artist, educator; b. Topeka; d. Clarence J. and Audrey (Wiss) Malone; m. James L. Enyeart, Sept. 7., 1964; children: Mara, Sascha, Megan. BFA, Kans. City Art Inst., 1965; MFA, U. Ariz., 1984. Prof. Pima Coll., Tucson, 1987-89, Rochester (N.Y.) Inst. Tech., 1991-92, Cornell U., Ithaca, N.Y., 1994, Coll. of Santa Fe, N. Mex., 1995-00. Mem. advisory com. MIT, Boston, 1993. Art: Kirlian Photograms, Androgyne Series, 1986 (award 1986), video art, Zen Trilogy, 1987 (award 1987), Plant and Geometric Series, Cibachromes, 1991, Mixed Media, 1997 (award 1997), (photo montage) Power Grid/Off Grid, 2000, (photo jet prints) Ironic Feminity, 2001, (video/photo/montage) Survival Series, 2002. Mem. art com. Rochester, N.Y. Diocese, 1993-94, arts advocate Women, Montage, Rochester, 1994. Art award Woman's Gallery, Tucson, 1992. Mem. Soc. for Photographic Edn., George Eastman House, Ctr. for Creative Photography Avocation: horticulture. Office: Coll of Santa Fe 1600 Saint Michaels Dr Santa Fe NM 87508-7615

MALONE, THOMAS FRANCIS, academic administrator, meteorologist; b. Sioux City, Iowa, May 3, 1917; s. John and Mary (Hourigan) M.; m. Rosalie Doran, Dec. 30, 1942; children: John H., Thomas Francis, Mary E., James K., Richard K., Dennis P. BS, S.D. Sch. Mines, 1940, D.Eng., 1962; Sc.D., MIT, 1946; L.H.D., St. Joseph Coll., West Hartford, Conn., 1965; Sc.D. (hon.), Bates Coll., 1988. Instr. MIT, 1942-43, asst. prof., 1943-51, assoc. prof., 1951-56; dir. Travelers Rsch. Ctr., Travelers Ins. Co., Hartford, Conn., 1955-56, dir. rsch., 1956-69, sr. v.p., 1968-70, chmn. bd., 1961-70; dean Grad. Sch., U. Conn., Storrs, 1970-73; chmn. bd. Ctr. for Environment and Men, 1970-71; dir. emeritus Holcomb Rsch. Inst., Butler U., Indpls., 1983—; scholar in residence St. Joseph Coll., 1983-91; Nat. Scis. fellow Resources for Future, 1983-84; Univ. Disting. scholar N.C. State U., 1991—98. Chmn. bd. Univ. Corp. for Atmospheric Rsch., 1973—76; mem. Conn. Weather Control Bd., 1959—73; mem. panel on sci. and tech. com. on sci. and astronautics U.S. Ho. of Reps., 1960—70; nat. adv. com. cmty. air pollution HEW, 1962—66; mem. sci. info. coun. NSF, 1962—66; rep. Am. Geophys. Union to U.S. Nat. Commn. for UNESCO, 1963—73, chmn. U.S. Nat. Commn., 1965—67; mem. nat. adv. com. on oceans and atmosphere, 1972—75; mem. Conn. Rsch. Commn., 1965—71; mem. com. application sci. and tech. New Eng. Coun.; chmn. Nat. Motor Vehicle Safety Adv. Coun., 1967—70; mem. sci. adv. com. climate impact assessment and response program UN Environ. Program, 1992—; mem. adv. com. on accreditation Conn. Dept. Higher Edn., 2000—; mem. acad. adv. bd. S.D. Sch. Mines and Tech., 1991—; bd. dirs. Conn. Acad. for Edn., 2001—. Editor: Compendium of Meteorology, 1951; contbg. editor: Environment, 1992-99; bd. editors: Jour. of the Marine Tech. Soc., 1995-99. Bd. dirs. Engrs. Joint Coun., 1968-70; bd. govs. Ins. Inst. Hwy. Safety, 1968-70; mem. oversight rev. bd. Nat. Acid Precipitation Assessment Program, 1990-96. Recipient Robert M. Losey award Inst. Aero. Sci., 1960, Charter Oak Leadership medal Greater Hartford C. of C., 1962, Charles Franklin Brooks award, 1964, Cleveland Abbe award Am. Meteorol. Soc., 1968, Conn. Conservationist of Yr. award, 1966, Guy E. March Silver medal S.D. Sch. Mines, 1976, Internat. Meteorol. Orgn. prize, 1984, Internat. St. Francis Assissi prize for environment, 1991, AAAS Internat. prize, 1994, Irving award Distance Edn. Consortium, 1997, Disting. Alumni award S.D. Sch. Mines, 1998; N.C. State U. disting. scholar, 1990-99, emeritus, 1999—. Fellow AAAS (internat. sci. coop., 1994), N.Y. Acad. Scis., Am. Meteorol. Soc. (pres. 1960-62), Am. Geophys. Union (past pres., sec. internat. participation 1964, Waldo E. Smith award 1986); mem. NAS (chmn. geophysics research bd. 1969-76, chmn. bd. on internat. orgns. and programs, dep. fgn. sec. 1969-73, fgn. sec. 1978-82), NRC (space application bd. 1973-77), Am. Acad. Arts and Scis., Internat. Council Sci. Unions (v.p., sec.-gen. sci. com. problems environ. 1970-76, treas. 1978-82) Am. Geog. Soc. (council 1971-77), Royal Irish Acad. (hon.), Conn. Acad. Sci. and Engring. (exec. scientist 1987-91, 97-2000), Acad. Polit. Scis., Sigma Xi (bd. dirs. 1983-96, pres. 1988-89, dir. Sigma Xi Ctr. 1992-95, chief scientist 1996-98). Home: 5 Bishop Rd Apt 203 West Hartford CT 06119-1536 E-mail: tfmalone@aol.com.

MALONE, THOMAS W. management educator, researcher; b. Roswell, N.Mex., June 2, 1952; s. Ernest P. Jr. and Virginia Malone; m. Joan L. Goldberg, Aug. 28, 1988; children: Robert, Laura. BA in Math. Scis. magna cum laude, Rice U., 1974; MA in Psychology, Stanford U., 1977, MS in Engring.-Econ. Sys., 1979, PhD in Psychology, 1980. Cons. for computer-based instrn. Region IV Edn. Svc. Ctr., Houston, 1974-75; rsch. intern Xerox Corp., Palo Alto (Calif.) Rsch. Ctr., 1979-80, mem. rsch. staff, 1980-83; from asst. prof. to assoc. prof. MIT, Sloan Sch. Mgmt., Cambridge, 1983-89, Patrick McGovern prof. info. sys., 1989, dir. Ctr. for Coord. Sci., 1989—, head info. tech. group, 2000—. Vis. prof. Harvard Bus. Sch., Boston, 1992; co-dir. Initiative on Inventing the Orgns. of 21st Century, MIT, Sloan Sch. Mgmt., 1994-99, Douglas Drane Career Devel. assoc. prof. info. tech. and mgmt., 1985; co-founder, cons. Palladian Software, Cambridge, 1984-88, Agility Sys., Waltham, Mass., 1989-91; mem. adv. bd. Perot Sys. Corp., Dallas, 1992-98; co-founder, chmn. Phios Corp., Cambridge, 1996—, CEO, 1998-99; mem. adv. bd. ELance, Inc., Sunnyvale, Calif., 2000—, Oco Corp., Wayland, Mass., 2000—; spkr. and presenter in field. Author books; contbr. articles to profl. jours.; patentee in field. U.S. Presdl. scholar U.S. Presdl. Scholars Commn., 1970; grad. fellow NSF, 1976. Mem. Assn. for Computing Machinery (program chair conf. on computer supported coop. work 1993-94), Phi Beta Kappa. Office: MIT Sloan Sch Mgmt E53-333 Cambridge MA 02142 E-mail: malone@mit.edu.

MALONE, THOMAS WILLIAM, lawyer; b. Seattle, Sept. 16, 1946; s. James Edward and Marie Cecilia (Anderson) M.; m. Drexel Cox, June 19, 1978; children: Jason, Cary, Jane Marie. BA, U. Wash., 1968, JD, 1972; MBA, Golden Gate U., 1982. Bar: Wash. 1972, U.S. Ct. Appeals (9th cir.) 1972, U.S. Tax Ct. 1980, U.S. Ct. Claims 1981, U.S. Supreme Ct. 1980. Prin. Treece Richale Malone PS, Seattle, 1973-2000, Malone, Galvin & Spicer PS, Seattle, 2001—. Pres. Seattle Marine Bus. Coalition, 1983-86; bd. dirs. Ballard Cmty. Hosp., 1982-91, North Seattle C.C. Found., 1989-97, chmn. 1992-93; bd. dirs. Swedish Med. Ctr.-Ballard Found., 1991-95; chmn. bd. dirs. Ballard Cmty. Hosp., 1986-88; bd. dirs. Swedish Health Systems, 1992—; vice-chmn. Swedish Health Systems, 1995, chair 1996-99; chmn. City of Seattle Fair Campaign Practices Commn., 1986-92; bd. ethics City of Seattle, 1986-92; chmn. City of Seattle Ethics and Elections Com., 1992; trustee Seattle C.C. Dist., 1997—, chmn. 1998-2000. Mem. ABA, Wash. Bar Assn., Seattle-King County Bar Assn., Ballard C. of C. (pres. 1981-84). Office: Malone Galvin Spicer PS 10202 5th NE #201 Seattle WA 98125

MALONE, WILLIAM GRADY, retired lawyer; b. Minden, La., Feb. 19, 1915; s. William Gordon and Minnie Lucie (Hortman) M.; m. Marion Rowe Whitfield, Sept. 26, 1943; children: William Grady, Gordon Whitfield, Marion Elizabeth, Helen Ann, Margaret Catherine. BS, La. State U., 1941; JD, George Washington U., 1952. Bar: Va. 1952, U.S. Supreme Ct 1971. Statis. analyst Dept. Agr., Baton Rouge, 1941; investigator VA, Washington, 1946-59, legal officer, dep., gen. counsel, asst. gen. counsel, 1959-79; pvt. practice law Arlington, Va., 1979-97. Editor: Fed. Bar News, 1972-73. Pres. Aurora Hills Civic Assn., 1948-49; spl. asst. to treas. Com. of 100, 1979-81, chmn., 1982-83; pres. Children's Theater, 1968-69; trustee St. George's Episc. Ch., 1979— ; chmn. Arlington County Fair Assn., 1979-83. Lt. col. AUS, 1941-46, ETO. Decorated Legion of Merit; recipient Disting. Svc. award, 1979, 3 Superior Performance awards, 1952-72, Outstanding Alumni award George Washington Law Sch., 1978 Mem. Fed. Bar Assn. (pres. D.C. chpt. 1970-71, nat. pres. 1978-79), Va. Bar Assn., Arlington County Bar Assn., Nat. Lawyers Club (dir.), Arlington Host Lions, Ft. Myer Officers Club. Home: 224 N Jackson St Arlington VA 22201-1253 E-mail: wgmalone@juno.com. *Success is not measured by dollars accumulated but by service to others.*

MALONE, WINFRED FRANCIS, health scientist; b. Revere, Mass., Feb. 10, 1935; s. Winfred and Margurite (Meehan) M.; m. Eleanor Malone, Aug. 1974. BS, U. Mass., 1957, MS, 1961, Rutgers U., 1963; PhD, U. Mich., 1970. Health scientist Nat. Cancer Inst., Bethesda, Md., 1970-81, chief chemoprevention br., 1981-95, acting assoc. dir., 1991-93, program dir., 1995—. Contbr. articles on drug devel. scis. to profl. jours. Mem. AAAS, Am. Coll. Toxicology, N.Y. Acad. Scis., Drug Info. Assn. Home: 3209 Wake Dr Kensington MD 20895-3216 Office: Nat Cancer Inst EpN # 2122 Bethesda MD 20892-0001

MALONEY, CAROLYN BOSHER, congresswoman; b. Feb. 19, 1948; d. R.G. and Christine (Clegg) Bosher; m. C.H.W. Maloney, 1976; children: Christina, Virginia. Student, Greensboro Coll. Various sr. staff positions N.Y. State Assembly and Senate, 1977-82; mem. N.Y.C Council dist. 8, 1983-93, U.S. Congress from 14th N.Y. dist., Washington, 1993—; mem. fin. svcs. com., ranking mem. subcom. domestic monetary policy, tech. and econ. growth; mem. fin. instns. and consumer credit subcom., internat. monetary policy and trade subcom.; mem. govt. reform and oversight com.; mem. joint economic com. Past chmn. Common Cause; active Assn. for a Better N.Y., Manahattan Women's Polit. Caucus. Mem. NAACP, Nat. Orgn. Women, Hadassah. Home: 49 E 92nd St Apt 1A New York NY 10128-1326 Office: US Ho of Reps 2430 Rayburn HOB Washington DC 20515-0001*

MALONEY, CHARLES WAYNE, gunsmith; b. Washington, June 5, 1945; s. Nicholas and Madeline Atkins Maloney; m. Lee J. Mullikin; m. Sue Vleck; m. Patricia Ann Mostad Maloney, Sept. 9, 1988 (dec. Feb. 1996); 1 child, Nicholas George. BFA, Va. Commonwealth U., 1973, MFA, 1976; cert., U.S. Nat. Match Firearms Sch. Owner, mgr. Firing Pin Gunshop, Catonsville, Md., 1976-80; armorer D.I.O. Weapons Br., Ft. Meade, 1980-82; nat. match gunsmith U.S. Army Marksmanship Unit, 1982-89; chief gunsmith Fulton Armory, Savage, Md., 1989-96; owner, gunsmith Gunning Arts, Inc., Balt., 1986—. Author screenplay: House Divided, 1997. Artistic dir. Pasadena Theatre Co., Millersville, Md., 1994—; active profl. and comty. theater; dir./actor numerous theatrical prodns. and films. With USNR, 1964-70, Vietnam, 1965-67. Mem. NRA (life). Avocations: guitar, photography, collecting coins and books. Home: 1920 Edmondson Ave Catonsville MD 21228-4232 Office: Gunning Arts Inc 5305 East Dr Arbutus MD 21227-2687 E-mail: charliesarts@comcast.net.

MALONEY, CHERYL ANN, foundation, consultant, business executive; b. Mpls., Aug. 30, 1949; d. Arlie Chester and Mary Dawn (Holm) M. AA, U. Minn., 1969, BA in Speech and Theatre, 1972; MA in Theology/Spirituality, Coll. St. Catherine, St. Paul, 1989, MA cert. in Pastoral Ministry, 1990; postgrad., Calif. Inst. Integral Studies, 1994—95; DMin, U. Creation Spirituality, 2001. Cert. grantsmanship, Calif., financial mgmt. Assn. Gov. Accts. Bus. adminstr. Al's Auto Crushing, Inc., Mpls., 1980-81; rsch. assoc. St. Paul Ramsey Med. Ctr., 1981-83; cons. Autowoman Consulting, Mpls., 1982—; adjustor Dependable Auto Appraisal, Inc., Bloomington, 1983; dir. mktg. and devel. Health Recovery Center, Mpls., 1983-85; dir. sales and mktg. Dashe and Thomson, 1987-89, Fredrickson Comm., Mpls., 1989-91; chaplain U. St. Thomas, St. Paul, 1989-90; ind. cons. Mpls., 1991-94; dir. devel. Sisters of Holy Family, Fremont, Calif., 1994-98; co-owner, founder Bras for Body and Soul, 1995—; dir. Fremont Festival Arts, 1998; co-founder & exec. dir. HERS Found., Fremont, 1999—. Dir. Women's Network, Mpls., 1974—77; dir. cultural arts City of Bloomington, Minn., 1977—78; spkr. U. Bethlehem, Israel, 1993; tchr. Holy Childhood High Sch., Jamaica, 1992; presenter M.R.A. Internat. 50th Anniversary Conf., Caux, Switzerland, 1996; prodr. Keep Abreast-Walking Together for HER 5K Run/Walk, 2000, 01, 02; dir. devel. Sisters Holy Family, editor Family of Friends Newsletter, co-coord. Women's Spirituality Workshop series, 1996—97; participant World Media Forum, 1996—; cons. Sisters of St. Joseph of Carondelet, St. Paul, 1992—94; assoc. exec. dir. San Mateo Cmty. Colls. Found., 2000; ofcl. photographer Internat. Women's Ecumenical Decade Chs. Solidarity Women, 1993; quality cons. Author: Housing Resource Book for Minneapolis, 1974, ; contbr. . Presenter Internat. Youth Leadership Conf., Brazil, 1993, Uruguay, 1993, Argentina, 1993, coord. Switzerland, 1996; presenter Reaching Beyond Borders, San Diego, 1996; cmty. organizer Mpls. Crime Prevention Program, 1979—80; dir. Gov.'s Com. Women in Econ. Concern, St. Paul, 1972—77; co-founder HERS Found., Calif., 1999; state Dem. del. St. Paul, 1976; U.S. rep. Gov.Gen's Conf., Jamaica, 1992; coach, youth leader Unity South Ch., Bloomington, 1967—93; coach Ind. Ch., Mpls., 1984—92; chaplain U. St. Thomas, St. Paul, 1989—92, chair women and religion com.; outreach min. Unity of Valley, 1990—93; lay consociate Sisters St. Joseph, 1992, apptd. peace and justice commn. and comm. adv. bd., 1993—95; chair 125th Anniversary Celebration Sisters of the Holy Family, 1997. Recipient Celtic Studies award Coll. St. Catherine, St. Paul, 1988; honoree Hamnline U., St. Paul, 1993; Great Lakes Region scholar, 1986. Mem.: NAFE, AAUW, Nat. Fedn. Ind. Bus., M.R.A. Internat. (nat. team planners for M.R.A. N.Am. and S.Am. activities, conf. presenter), Sales and Mktg. Execs. Am., Mission San Jose C. of C. (pres. 1999—2000, sec. 2000—01, co-founder olive festival 2001—), Minn. Coun. Quality (editor newsletter 1993—94), Le Group (founder), Self-Employed Women Rotary (co-dir. 1992—94), Mpls. Women's Rotary (parliamentarian 1980—, bd. dirs. 1990—94), Commonwealth Club Calif. Independent. Avocations: integrating spirituality and work, cultural arts, sports, international relations. Home: PO Box 3273 Fremont CA 94539-0327 Office: HERS Breast Cancer Found Inc 38775 Stivers St Ste C Fremont CA 94536 E-mail: cmaloney@dnai.com.

MALONEY, GERALD P. retired utility executive; b. Lawrence, Mass., Mar. 9, 1933; s. Thomas P. and Concetta M.; m. Dorothea Ames. BSEE, BSBA, MIT, 1955; MBA, Rutgers U., 1962. With Am. Electric Power Co., Inc., Columbus, Ohio, 1955-98, controller, 1965-70, v.p. fin., 1970-75, sr. v.p. fin., 1975-90, exec. v.p., CFO, 1990-98, vice chmn., 1998; ret. Mem. Beta Gamma Sigma. Home: 275 S Parkview Ave Bexley OH 43209-1649

MALONEY, J. PATRICK, minister, educator, seminary administrator; b. Pitts., Feb. 19, 1929; s. James Deasy and Helen (Crouse) M.; m. Bettie Jean Silvus, Dec. 1, 1953; children: Sharon Shakespeare, Lori Spencer, Mitzi Kelley, Patricia Hawkins, Kathleen Brown (dec.), James D. Maloney. BA, Jacksonville U., 1961; BD, New Orleans Bapt. Theol. Sem., 1964; PhD, St. Marys Sem. and U., Balt., 1973. Ordained to ministry So. Bapt. Conv., 1960. Pastor Fairfield Bapt. Chapel, Jacksonville, Fla., 1958-61, 1st Bapt. Ch., Thomas, La., 1963-64, Hayne Boulevard Bapt. Ch., New Orleans, 1964-67, Kent Bapt. Ch., Landover, Md., 1969-77, Fisher Rd. Bapt. Ch., 1977-83, Mission Oaks Bapt. Ch., East Ridge, Tenn., 1983—. Prof. Sem. Extension So. Bapt. Conv., Nashville, 1973—; acad. v.p. Oxford Grad. Sch., Dayton, Tenn., 1982-86. Mem. Cath. Theol. Soc. Am., Evang. Theol. Soc., Oxford Soc. Scholars. Home: 1210 John Ross Rd Chattanooga TN 37412-1466 E-mail: patrickmlny@juno.com, bro_pat@bellsouth.net. *The "real" change of direction for my life came when in 1957 (Dec.) I became a Christian.*

MALONEY, JAMES HENRY, congressman; b. Quincy, Mass., Sept. 17, 1948; s. James Henry Jr. and Katherine Smith (Murphy) M.; m. Mary Angela Draper, Aug. 16, 1980; children: Adele, Anna, Ellen. BA cum laude, Harvard U., 1972; JD, Boston U., 1980. Vol. VISTA, Gary, Ind., 1969-70; exec. dir. Community Action Com. Danbury, Conn., 1974-78; atty. Pinney, Payne, VanLenten, Burrell, Wolfe & Dillman, P.C., Danbury, 1980-86; ptnr. Dice, Maloney & Lenz, P.C., 1986-93, Maloney, Leaphart & Assocs., PC, Danbury, 1995-97; mem. Conn. Senate, Hartford, 1987-95, 105-106th Congress from 5th Conn. dist., 1997—. Asst. majority leader and senate chair fin., revenue and bonding com., 1993-95. Chmn. Danbury Cmty. Endowment, 1984-94, dem. candidate for U.S. Congress, 1994, 96, 98. Recipient Disting. Svc. award Jaycees North Fairfield County, 1984, Community Svc. award Midwestern Conn. Coun. on Alcoholism, 1990, Spl. Recognition award Jewish Home for the Elderly, Fairfield County, 1993; named Legislator of Yr., Caucus Conn. Dems., 1990, Conn. Assn. Ind. Ins. Agts., 1992. Roman Catholic. Avocation: sailing. Office: 1427 Longworth Ho Office Bl Washington DC 20515-0001*

MALONEY, JAMES JOHN, librarian; b. Chgo., July 20, 1949; s. James Frederick and Raphael Ann (Stachowiak) M. BA in History, Bradley U., 1971; MA in History, No. Ill. U., 1976; MSLS, U. Ill., 1979. Head info. retrieval svcs. dept. Biblio. Ctr. for Rsch., Denver, 1981-83; sr. mktg. rep., project mgr. Dialog Info. Svcs., Palo Alto, Calif., 1983-87; automation cons. Kepler's Books and Mags., Menlo Park, 1987-88; mktg. cons. Computer Advanced Software Products, Cupertino, 1988-89, dir. sales Sunnyvale, 1992—; libr. automated systems mgr. Contra Costa County Libr., Pleasant Hill, 1989-92. Libr. automation cons. Mission San Antonio Libr. and Archives, Jolon, Calif., 1988—; registered rschr. Hoover Instn. Libr. and Archives, 1990—; mem. Bibliographic Retrieval Svcs. User Adv. Bd., 1981-83. Editor: Online Searching Technique and Management, 1983; contbr. articles to profl. jours. Mem. Peninsula Open Space Trust, 1986. Mem. ALA (mem. and chair machine-assisted ref. sect. 1980-85). Home: 172 Del Vale Ave San Francisco CA 94127-1835

MALONEY, JAMES MICHAEL, lawyer, writer; b. Jersey City, 1958; BS, SUNY, Bronx, 1980; JD, Fordham U., 1995; postgrad., LLM, NYU, 1997—. Bar: N.Y. 1996. Pvt. practice, Port Washington, N.Y. Contbr. articles to law jours. Port Washington leader Independence Party Nassau County, 2000—. Mem. Maritime Law Assn. U.S. (proctor 2000—), Assn. Bar City N.Y. (admiralty com. 1997-99), Marine Soc. City N.Y., NRA (life), Mensa. Libertarian. Office: PO Box 551 Port Washington NY 11050

MALONEY, JAMES MICHAEL, retired writer, editor; b. Trenton, N.J., Apr. 4, 1935; s. Matthew Joseph and Margaret Mary Maloney; m. Helen Claire Roche, Apr. 12, 1958; children: Mark, Paul, Brian, Matthew, Brendan. BS Edn., Trenton State Coll., 1957; MA English Lit., Rutgers U., 1963. Cert. Secondary English Tchr. N.J., 1957, Secondary Supr. of English N.J., 1973. English tchr., libr. Jr. HS No. One, Trenton, NJ, 1957—61; English tchr., dept. chairperson Ewing HS, 1961—91; copy editor, proofreader Caliper Mgmt., Inc., Princeton, 1991—2001. English curriculum evaluator Atlantic Middle States Assn., Jersey City, Bergen, Middletown, NJ, 1973—90; state writing assessment participator N.J. Dept. Edn., Trenton, 1984—90; writer of Advanced Placement practice tests Rsch. and Edn. Assn., Piscataway, NJ, 1989—90. Author: (novels) Dark Motions, 1997, The Stump Man, 2000, (2 opinion editorials) New York Times, 1984, (short stories) Kelsey Rev., 1987, BlueMurder.com, 2002; co-author: (novels) AP English Literature and Composition, 1990; editor: (ednl. jour.) Viewpoints, 1977. Block capt. Pine Ridge

South Residents Assn., Whiting, NJ, 2001. Cpl. N.J. Nat. Guard, 1958—60. Recipient "A+ For Kids" award, WWOR TV Channel 9 Newark, New Jersey, 1988; fellow Independent Study fellow, Nat. Endowment for the Humanities, Summar 1986, Summer Seminar fellow at Princeton U., 1987. Mem.: N.J. Edn. Assn., Nat. Edn. Assn. Democrat. Roman Catholic. Avocations: freelance writing, travel, gardening, reading. Home: 906 Oak Ridge Terr Whiting NJ 08759-3515 Personal E-mail: james.m.maloney@att.net.

MALONEY, JOHN JOSEPH, writer; b. N.Y.C., Jan. 15, 1929; s. John J. and Breda T. (O'Leary) M.; m. Helen Martin; children: Peter, Elizabeth, Mary Ellen. BA, Fordham Coll., 1951. City editor Patent Trader, Mt. Kisco, N.Y., 1953-59; news bureau mgr. N.Y. Stock Exchange, N.Y.C., 1959-63; dir. pub. rels. Lehman Bros., 1963-71, Warnaco, Inc., Bridgeport, Conn., 1971-77; v.p. charge of media rels. Citigroup (formerly Citicorp/Citibank), N.Y.C., 1977-91; writer Easton, Conn., 1991—. Cons. capital formation markets Kenyan govt., 1991, Bulgarian govt., 1999. With U.S. Army, 1951-53. Avocation: sailing. Home: 65 Sport Hill Pkwy Easton CT 06612-2239 E-mail: johnhelenmaloney@cs.com.

MALONEY, KEVIN JOHN, investment company executive; b. Waterbury, Conn., Oct. 31, 1957; s. John Stephen and Jane Phyllis (Christolini) M.; m. Leslie Cay Warner, July 25, 1980; children: Shannon Kaye, Laura Jane, Erik John. BA in Econs., Trinity Coll., 1979; MA in Econs., Washington U., St. Louis, 1981, PhD in Econs./Fin., 1983. Asst. prof. Dartmouth Coll., Hanover, N.H., 1983-88, assoc. prof., 1988-95; dir. quantitative rsch., fixed income Putnam Investments, Boston, 1995—99, dir. fin. engring., 1999—2001, dir. product design team, 2001—. Contbr. articles to profl. jours. Mem. Am. Fin. Assn., Fin. Mgmt. Assn. (dir. 1998—). Home: 91 Hemlock Dr Westwood MA 02090-2150 Office: Putnam Investments 1 Post Office Sq Boston MA 02109-2106

MALONEY, MARYNELL, lawyer; b. Hutchinson, Kans., Jan. 14, 1955; d. Robert Edgar and Marian Ellen (Benson) Baker; m. Michael D. Maloney, Nov. 30, 1977; children: Michelle M., Erica O., Dennis Jr. BA, Oberlin Coll., 1975; MA, Trinity U., San Antonio, 1978; JD, St. Mary's U., San Antonio, 1980. Cert. by Tex. bd. of legal specialization. Assoc. Law Offices Pat Maloney, P.C., San Antonio, 1981-82; ptnr., owner Maloney & Maloney, 1982—. Bd. dirs. San Antonio Internat. Keyboard Competition, 1988-90; bd. govs. St. Peters/St. Joseph's Children's Home, San Antonio, 1989-92. Mem. ACLU of Tex. (bd. dirs. 1990—, v.p. 1995-96, SACLU 1990—), Am. Trial Lawyers Assn., State Bar Tex., Tex. Trial Lawyers Assn. (assoc. bd. dirs. 1989-90, bd. dirs. 1991—, chair coun. local leadership 1990-92, cert. personal injury trial law), San Antonio Bar Assn., San Antonio Trial Lawyers Assn. (pres. 1991-92). Democrat. Avocations: reading, writing, film. Office: Maloney & Maloney PC 2000 Milam 115 E Travis San Antonio TX 78205

MALONEY, MICHAEL PATRICK, lawyer, mediator, arbitrator; b. Syracuse, N.Y., June 1, 1944; s. Randolph Bartholomew and Alice Mary (Loban) M.; m. Jane McBurney, May 21, 1977; children: Christopher, Kara. AB, Georgetown U., 1966; MBA, Cornell U., 1968, JD, 1971. Bar: N.Y. 1972. Assoc. Donovan Leisure Newton and Irvine, N.Y.C., 1971-78; asst. dir. div. market regulation SEC, Washington, 1978-79; sr. v.p., gen. counsel, sec. Orion Capital Corp., N.Y.C., 1979-98; pres. OSOWA Enterprises, LLC, 1998—. Mem.: Am. Corp. Counsel Counsel Assn., Am. Soc. Corp. Secs., The Kapalua Club. Home: 891 Holopuni Rd Kula HI 96790

MALONEY, MILFORD CHARLES, retired internal medicine educator; b. Buffalo, Mar. 15, 1927; s. John Angelus Maloney and Winifred Hill; m. Dione Ethyl Sheppard. BS, Canisius Coll., 1947, postgrad., 1947-49; MD, U. Buffalo, 1953. Diplomate Am. Bd. Internal Medicine. Rsch. chemist Buffalo Electrochem. Co., 1947-49; intership Mercy Hosp./Georgetown U., 1953-54; med. residency Buffalo VA Hosp., 1954-56; cardiology fellow Buffalo Gen. Hosp., 1956-57; chmn. dept. medicine Mercy Hosp., 1969-94, program dir., internal medicine residency, 1972-89; with steering com. Assn. Program Dirs. in Internal Medicine, 1976, coun. mem., 1977-80; clin. prof. medicine SUNY, Buffalo, 1981-94; trustee Am. Soc. Internal Medicine, 1984-90, edn. leader med. seminar Austria, Switzerland, France, 1987, Argentina, Brazil, Paraguay, 1988; faculty instr. Christopher Wren Assn. Coll. William and Mary, Williamsburg, Va., 1997—. Bd. dirs. Internal Medicine Ctr. for Advancement and Rsch. Edn.; pres. Heart Assn. Western N.Y., Buffalo, 1969; sr. cancer rsch. physician Roswell Park Meml. Cancer Inst., 1959-62; mem. internal medicine liaison com. N.Y. State, 1980-90; faculty instr., mem. curriculum com. Christopher Wren Assn. Coll. William & Mary, Williamsburg, Va., 1997-99. Editor (newsletter) N.Y. State Soc. Internal Medicine, 1972-78. Bd. dirs. Health Sys. Agy. Western N.Y., Buffalo, 1981; mem. exec. com., bd. dirs. Blue Cross Western N.Y., Buffalo, 1987; mem. bd. regents Canisius Coll., Buffalo, 1987—; mem. pres. assocs. SUNY, Buffalo; founding mem. Greater Williamsburg Va. Symphony Soc., 1998; bd. dirs. Va. Symphony, Norfolk, 2001. Capt. M.C., U.S. Army, 1957-59. Recipient award of merit N.Y. State Soc. Internal Medicine, 1980, Man of Yr. award Heart Assn. Western N.Y., 1982, ann. honoree award Trocaire Coll., 1986, Disting. Alumni award Canisius Coll., 1991, Berkson Excellence award in tchg. and art of medicine, SUNY at Buffalo, 1992, Outstanding Med. Tchg. Attending award Mercy Hosp./SUNY Med. Residents, 1994, Lifetime Career Achievement award Med. Alumni Assn. SUNY, Buffalo, 1998; named to Sports Hall of Fame, Canisius Coll., 1978. Fellow ACP (Upstate Physician Recognition award 1989), Am. Coll. Cardiology; mem. AMA (SUNY rep. 1986-94, rep. to sect. med. schs. at ann. meetings 1984-94, chmn. sect. on internal medicine 1990-91), Am. Soc. Internal Medicine (bd. dirs. Internal Medicine Ctr. for Advancement of Rsch. Edn. 1988-91, trustee 1984-90, pres. 1990-91, chmn. long range planning com., rep. to Federated Coun. on Internal Medicine 1990-91, rep. to AMA nat. practice parameters and guidelines com. 1989-91), N.Y. State Soc. Internal Medicine (pres. 1974-75), Alumni Assn. SUNY (pres. 1975), Med. Soc. County Erie (pres. 1991-82), Va. Soc. Internal Medicine (hon.), Greater Williamsburg Va. Symphony Soc. (founding mem. 1998). Home: 116 Cove Point Ln Williamsburg VA 23185-8613 E-mail: mcmaloney@widomaker.com.

MALONEY, PATRICIA DIANA, artist, educator; b. Louisville, Oct. 15, 1948; d. Bernard Joseph and Dorothy (Schoo) M. BFA, Louisville Sch. Art, 1972; MA, Murray State U., 1974; MFA, Okla. U., 1976. Cert. tchr. K-12, Ky., 1974. Artist-in-residence Allied Arts & Humanities Council, Bartlesville, Okla., 1976-77; prof. art Washington and Jefferson Coll., Washington, 1977—. Vis. researcher Smithsonian Instn. Dept. of Anthropology, Nat. Mus. Natural. History, Washington, summer 1987; instr. studio arts program, resident assoc. program, Smithsonian Instn., summer 1987; research assoc. in ceramics Harvard Semitic Mus., 1988-89. Contbr. to Ceramics Monthly. Merit badge counselor The Boy Scouts of Am., Washington, Pa., 1978—; lectr. Am. Assn. Univ. Women, washington, Pa., 1982. Recipient 1st place visual arts award Wm. Penn Meml. Mus., Harrisburg, Pa., 1981, ceramic cons. grant NEH. 1985, vis. fellow grant The Smithsonian Instn., Nat. Mus. Natural History, 1987, presdl. discretionary fund grant Washington and Jefferson Coll., 1987; named one of outstanding and prominent women of Washington County, Jay Stock, Photographer, 1988; Fulbright scholar, Ghana, Africa, 1993-95. Mem. West Africa Rsch. Assn., Fulbright Assn., Carnegie Instn.-Mus. of Art & Natural History Mus., Pitts. Ctr. for the Arts, Washington County Hist. Soc. Roman Catholic. Avocations: ice skating, walking, herb gardening. Office: Washington and Jefferson Coll S Lincoln St Washington PA 15301

MALONEY, PATSY LORETTA, university official, nursing educator; b. Murfreesboro, Tenn., Feb. 19, 1952; d. Buford Leon Browning and Ina (Bush) DuBose; m. Richard J. Maloney, July 26, 1975; children: Katherine Nalani, Nathaniel Allen, Elizabeth Maureen. BS in Nursing, U. Md., 1974; MA, MS in Nursing, Cath. U., 1984; EdD, U. So. Calif., 1994. Commd. 1st lt. U.S. Army, 1974, advanced through grades to lt. col., 1989; asst. chief nurse evenings and nights DeWitt Army Hosp., Ft. Belvoir, Va.; chief nurse, tng. officer 85th EVAC Hosp., Ft. Lee; clin. head nurse emergency rm./PCU Tripler Army Med. Ctr., Honolulu, chief nursing edn.; chief surg. nursing sect. and acute care nursing sect. Madigan Army Med. Ctr., Tacoma, 1991-94; ret., 1994; dir. Ctr. for Continued Nursing Learning Pacific Luth. U., Tacoma, 1994—. Asst. prof., dir. continuing nursing edn. Pacific Luth. U., Tacoma, 1994—2000, assoc. prof., 2000—. Mem. Emergency Nurses Assn., Nat. Nursing Staff Devel. Orgn., Acad. Med. Surg. Nurses, Sigma Theta Tau, Phi Kappa Phi. Home: 7002 53rd St W Tacoma WA 98467-2214 Office: Pacific Luth U Continuing Nursing Edn Tacoma WA 98467 E-mail: malonepl@plu.edu.

MALONEY, ROBERT E., JR. lawyer; b. San Francisco, Sept. 17, 1942; s. Robert E. and Mara A. (Murphy) M.; children: Michael, Sarah, Paul. BA magna cum laude, U. Portland, 1964; JD summa cum laude, Willamette U., Salem, Oreg., 1967. Bar: Oreg., Wash., U.S. Dist. Ct. Oreg., U.S. Dist. Ct. (we. dist.) Wash., U.S. Dist. Ct. (ea. dist.) Wash., U.S. Ct. Appeals (9th cir.). Ptnr. Lane Powell Spears Lubersky, LLP, Portland, 1967—. Bd. dirs., sec. Norm Thompson Outfitters, Inc., Portland; chmn. bd. visitors Willamette U. Law Sch., 1993-95, bd. dirs. emeritus, 1998—; past chair, mem. exec. com. Portland Trial Dept.; lawyers del. 9th Cir. Jud. Conf., 1995-97; pres. adv. coun. U. Portland, 2001—. Bd. dirs., Oreg. chpt. Multiple Sclerosis Soc., 1990-2002, Children's Cancer Assn., Oreg. Independent Coll. Found., Oreg. Lawyers Against Hunger, 1997-99; judge pro tem Multnomah County Cir. Ct., 1994-99. Mem. ABA (co-chair products liability com., trial practice com. 1990-94), Nat. Assn. R.R. Trial Counsel, Fedn. Ins. Corp. Counsel, Oreg. Assn. Def. Counsel (bd. dirs. 1987-94, sec. 1991-92, v.p. 1993-94, pres. 1994), Fed. Bar Assn. (exec. com. Oreg. divsn. 1988-96, pres. 1994-95), Multnomah Athletic Club. Republican. Roman Catholic. Office: Lane Powell Spears Lubersky LLP 601 SW Second Ave Ste 2100 Portland OR 97204-3158 Fax: 503-778-2200.

MALONEY, ROBERT KELLER, ophthalmologist, medical educator; b. May 1, 1958; AB in Mathematics summa cum laude, Harvard U., 1979; MA in Philosophy, Politics and Econs., Oxford (Eng.) U., 1981; MD, U. Calif., San Francisco, 1985. Diplomate Am. Bd. Ophthalmology. Rsch fellow dept. physiology Cambridge (Eng.) U., 1985; intern U. Calif., L.A., 1985-86; resident Wilmer Ophthalmol. Inst. Johns Hopkins Hosp., Balt., 1986-89; Heed fellow cornea and refractive surgery Emory U., Dept. Ophthalmology, Atlanta, 1989-91; assoc. prof. ophthalmology UCLA Sch. Medicine, Jules Stein Eye Inst., 1991-98. Bd. dirs. Lasik Inst., Clear Ctrs of Am., Calhoun Vision. Contbr. numerous articles to profl. jours.; presenter and spkr. in field; assoc. editor (N.Am.) Jour. Refractive and Corneal Surgery, 1991-95; internat. editl. bd. European Jour. Implant and Refractive Surgery, 1995; reviewer Am. Jour. Ophthalmology, Ophthalmology, Archives of Ophthalmology, Jour. Cataract and Refractive Surgery, Ophthalmic Surgery and Lasers; editl. bd. Ophthalmology Times. Rhodes scholar, 1979, Heed Found. fellow, 1989-90, Heed/Knapp fellow, 1990-91, John Harvard scholar, 1978; recipient Detur and Edward Whitaker prizes, Harvard U., Rsch. to Prevent Blindness Career Devel. award, 1992, Mericos Whittier award, 1997, VISX Star Surgeon award, 1999, 2000. Mem. Am. Acad. Ophthalmology (long-range planning com. 1989-92, quality of care com. 1987-91, retina preferred practice pattern subcom., refractive errors preferred practice pattern subcom.; chmn. ann. meeting program com. for young ophthalmologists, 1990-92; adv. group to ad hoc com. on orgnl. design 1991, young ophthalmologists' com. 1992-94; Honor award 1993, 97), Assn. Rsch. in Vision and Ophthalmology, Internat. Soc. Refractive Surgery (Disting. Lans award 2001), Calif. Assn. Ophthalmology, Max Fine Corneal Soc., Phi Beta Kappa. Office: Maloney Vision Inst 10921 Wilshire Blve Ste 900 Los Angeles CA 90024

MALONEY, THERESE ADELE, insurance company executive; b. Sept. 15, 1929; d. James Henry and F. Adele (Powers) M. BA in Econs., Coll. St. Elizabeth, Convent Station, N.J., 1951; AMP, Harvard U., 1981. CPCU. With Liberty Mut. Ins. Co., Boston, 1951-94, asst. v.p., asst. mgr. nat risks, 1974-77, v.p., asst. mgr. nat. risks, 1977-79, v.p., mgr. nat. risks, 1979-86, sr. v.p. underwriting mktg. and adminstrn., 1986-87, exec. v.p. underwriting, policy decision, 1987-94, also bd. dirs.; pres. and bd. dirs. subs. Liberty Mus. (Bermuda) Ltd., 1981-94, LEXCO Ltd.; cons. Exec. Svc. Corp., 1994—. Bd. dirs., dep. chmn. Liberty Mut. (U.K.) Ltd., London; bd. dirs. Liberty Mut. Ins. Co., Liberty Mut. Fire Ins. Co., Liberty Mut. Life Assurance Co., Liberty Fin. Cos.; mem. faculty Inst. Northeastern U., Boston, 1969—74; mem. adv. bd., risk mgmt. studies Ins. Inst. Am., 1977—83; mem. adv. coun. Suffolk U. Sch. Mgmt., 1984—96; mem. adv. coun. to program in internat. bus. rels. Fletcher Sch. Law and Diplomacy, 1985—94; cons. Exec. Svc. Corp., Boston, 1994—2002. Trustee Coll. St. Elizabeth, N.J., 1993—. Mem. Soc. CPCUs (past pres. Boston chpt.), Univ. Club, Boston Club, Neighborhood Club of Quincy.

MALONEY, WILLIAM JAMES, dentist, educator; b. White Plains, N.Y., Feb. 16, 1967; BS, Siena Coll., Loudonville, N.Y., 1989; DDS, 1992. Dentist. Contbr. articles to profl. jours. Mem.: ADA. Home: 12 Ellis Pl Ossining NY 10562 Office: 12 Ellis Pl Ossining NY 10562

MALOOF, FARAHE PAUL, lawyer; b. Boston, Feb. 10, 1950; s. Farahe and Emily Suzanna (Puchy) M.; divorced; children: Alexandre F., Melissa F. BS, Georgetown U., 1975, JD, 1978. Bar: D.C. 1978, Va. 1981, Md. 1990. Assoc. Corcoran & Rowe, Washington, 1978-82; ptnr. Berliner & Maloney, 1982-84; internat. legal counsel Advocacia Oliveira Ribeiro, Sao Paulo, Brazil, 1984-85; sole practice Washington, 1985-86; prin. Maloof & Assocs., 1986-97; of counsel Haas & Anderson, P.C., McLean, Va., 1997-99; mem. Brincefield Hartnett Maloof & Paleos, P.C., Alexandria, 2000—. Lectr. Am. U., Washington, 1984-85, Internat. Law Inst., Washington, 1986-87. Active Reagan-Bush campaign, Washington, 1984, Frank Wolf re-election campaign, Arlington, Va., 1986, Bush-Quayle campaign, Washington, 1988. Served to cpl. USMC, 1968-70, Vietnam. Mem. ABA, Va. Bar Assn., D.C. Bar Assn. (litigation and corps. sects.), Fed. Bar Assn. (immigration law sect.), Georgetown U. Alumni Assn. (co-chmn. 1983-84). Republican. Roman Catholic. Avocations: tennis, water skiing. Home: 1506 Dewberry Ct Mc Lean VA 22101-5629 Office: Brinafield Hartnett Et Al 526 King St Ste 423 Alexandria VA 22314-3143 E-mail: FPMaloof@aol.com.

MALOOF, GILES WILSON, academic administrator, educator, author; b. San Bernardino, Calif., Jan. 4, 1932; s. Joseph Peters and Georgia (Wilson) M.; m. Mary Anne Ziniker, Sept. 5, 1958 (dec. Oct. 1976); children: Mary Jane, Margery Jo. BA, U. Calif., Berkeley, 1953; MA, U. Oreg., 1958; PhD, Oreg. State U., 1962. Petroleum reservoir engr. Creole Petroleum Corp., Venezuela, 1953-54; mathematician electronics divsn. rsch. dept. U.S. Naval Ordnance Rsch. Lab., Corona, Calif., 1958-59; asst. prof. math. Oreg. State U., Corvallis, 1962-68, rsch. assoc. dept. oceanography, 1963-68, vis. prof. math., 1977-78; prof. math. Boise (Idaho) State U., 1968—, head dept., 1968-75, dean grad. sch., 1970-75. Author, reviewer of coll. textbooks; contbr. to profl. jours. Served with Ordnance Corps, AUS, 1950, 54-56. Recipient Carter award, 1963, Mosser prize, 1966, Oreg. State U., Alumni Found. scholar Teaching award Boise State U., 2000. Mem. Math. Assn. Am., Am. Math. Soc., Soc. Indsl. and Applied Math., N.W. Coll. and Univ. Assn. for Sci. (dir. 1973—, pres. 1990-92), N.W. Sci. Assn. (trustee 1977-80), Assn. Western Univs. (mem. edn. and rsch. com. 1993—), Sigma Xi, Pi Mu Epsilon, Phi Kappa Phi. Home: 1400 Longmont Ave Boise ID 83706-3730 E-mail: giles@diamond.idbsu.edu.

MALOOF, GLORIA DIANA, photographer, actress; b. Paris, Mar. 20, 1933; d. Charles Manuel Idrau and Rachel Gabrielle Pachoud; m. Maurice Nassir Maloof, July 11, 1959; 1 child, Julin Nassir. BA in Visual Arts, Ga. State U., Atlanta, 1978, MA in Visual Arts, 1982. Co-dir. Atlanta Theatre Lab, 1988—. Exhbns. include High Mus., 1972, 99, Piedmont Arts Festival, 1982, Dancer's Collective Theatre, 1982, 84, A Woman's Place, 1982, Acad. Theatre, 1984, 87, Dorothy McRae Gallery, 1993, Atlanta Photography Gallery, 1995, 99, 2000, 02, State Bar of Ga. Arts Exhbn., 1995, Photography Ctr. Atlanta, 1995, 96, 97, Jackson (Ga.) Fine Arts Festival (merit award), 1996, 97, 98, Chateau Elan Art Gallery, 1997, Art Sta. at Stone Mt., 1999, Allen Ashton Gallery, 2000, Brenau U., 2000; represented in permanent collections Heery & Heery, Lefkoff, Duncan, Grimes & Dermer, Kaufmann Diagnostic Clinic, Coopers & Lybrand, Northside Hosp. Bd. dirs. Actors in Renaissance, Atlanta, 1984-88, Seven Stages Theatre, Atlanta, 1990-96; adv. bd. Atlanta Photography Group, 1996—. Avocations: sewing, metal work, travel. Home: 2066 N Ponce de Leon Ave Atlanta GA 30307-1340

MALOOLEY, DAVID JOSEPH, electronics and computer technology educator; b. Terre Haute, Ind., Aug. 20, 1951; s. Edward Joseph and Vula (Starn) M. B.S., Ind. State U., 1975: M.S., Ind. U., 1981, doctoral candidate. Supr., Zenith Radio Corp., Paris, Ill., 1978-79; assoc. prof. electronics and computer tech. Ind. State U., Terre Haute, 1979—; cons. in field. Served to 1st lt. U.S. Army, 1975-78. Mem. Soc. Mfg. Engrs., Nat. Assn. Indsl. Tech., Nat. Fire Protection Assn., Instrument Soc. Am. (sr.), Phi Delta Kappa, Pi Lambda Theta, Epsilon Pi Tau. Democrat. Christian. Home: 11420 Spring Creek Rd Terre Haute IN 47805-9679 Office: Ind State U Dept Electronics and Computer Tech Terre Haute IN 47809-0001

MALOON, JEFFREY LEE, lawyer; b. Columbus, Ohio, May 14, 1958; s. Jerry Lee Maloon and Patricia Ann (Wright) Maloon Spradling: m. Lesa Lynn Hodson, June 14, 1980; children: Ashley Nicole, Adam Jeffrey. BS, Ball State U., 1980; JD, Capital U., 1983. Bar: Ohio 1983, U.S. Dist. Ct. (so. dist.) Ohio 1984, U.S. Supreme Ct. 1987, U.S. Ct. Appeals (6th cir.) 1989. Law clk. to assoc. justice Ohio Supreme Ct., Columbus, 1983-85; pvt. practice, 1985—. Mem. bd. commrs. on unauthorized practice law Ohio Supreme Ct., Columbus, 1988-94; prof. nurse-paralegal program Capital U. Sch. Law, 2001—. Mem. editorial bd. Ohio Trial Mag., 1991-94, editor, 1993-94. Mem. Survivors of Crime Adv. Com., Columbus, 1987-91. Fellow Roscoe Pound Inst.; mem. ABA, ATLA, Ohio State Bar Assn., Columbus Bar Assn., Ohio Acad. Trial Lawyers (vice-chmn. med. negligence sect. 1991-96, trustee 1992—, mem. exec. com. 1993-94, chmn. med. negligence sect. 1996-98, Pres. award 1994), Franklin County (Ohio) Trial Lawyers Assn. Methodist. Avocations: golf, other sports. Home: 8068 Holyrood Ct Dublin OH 43017-9700 Office: Jeffrey L Maloon LLC Ste 350 175 S 3rd St Columbus OH 43215-5188 *Notable cases include: Hardy vs. VerMeulen, 1987 32 Ohio St 3d 45, in which med. negligence statute of repose was held unconstitutional; Griffith vs. ARC, 1988, 678 F Supp. 18Z, which determined the ARC is not allowed to remove a state action to fed. ct.; Estates of Morgan vs. Fairfield Family Counseling Center (Ohio 1997), 673 N.E. 2d 1311, Ohio State Supreme Court places legal duty on mental health care providers to reasonably protect third parties.*

MALOON, JERRY L. trial lawyer, physician, medicolegal consultant; b. Union City, Ind., June 23, 1938; s. Charles Elias and Bertha Lucille (Creviston) M.; children: Jeffrey Lee, Jerry Lee II. BS, Ohio State U., 1960, MD, 1964; JD, Capital U. Law Sch., 1974. Intern Santa Monica (Calif.) Hosp., 1964-65; tng. psychiatry Ctrl. Ohio Psychiat. HOsp., 1969, Menninger Clinic, Topeka, 1970; clin. dir. Orient (Ohio) Devel. Ctr., 1967-69, med. dir., 1971-83; assoc. med. dir. Western Electric, Inc., Columbus, 1969-71; cons. State Med. Bd. Ohio, 1974-80; pvt. practice law Columbus, 1978—; pres. Jerry L. Maloon Co., L.P.A., 1981—. Medicolegal cons., 1972—; pres. Maloon, Maloon & Barclay Co., L.P.A., 1990-95; guest lectr. law and medicine Orient Devel. Ctr. and Columbus Devel. Ctr., 1969-71; dep. coroner Franklin County (Ohio), 1978-84. Dean's coun. Capital U. Law Sch. Capt. M.C., AUS, 1965-67. Fellow: Columbus Bar Found., Am. Coll. Legal Medicine; mem.: ATLA, AMA, ABA, Am. Profl. Practice Assn., Columbus Trial Lawyers Assn., Ohio Trial Lawyers Assn., Columbus Bar Assn., Ohio Bar Assn., Ohio State U. Alumni Assn., U.S. Trotting Assn., The Country Club at Muirfield Village, Ohio State U. Pres.'s Buckeye Club. Home: 2140 Cambridge Blvd Upper Arlington OH 43221-4104 Office: 9155 Moors Pl North Dublin OH 43017 Office Fax: 614-798-8747.

MALOTT, ADELE RENEE, editor; b. St. Paul, July 19, 1935; d. Clarence R. and Julia Anne (Christensen) Lindgren; m. Gene E. Malott, Oct. 24, 1957 BS, Northwestern U., 1957. Coordinator news KGB Radio, San Diego, 1958-60; asst. pub. relations dir. St. Paul C. of C., 1961-63; night editor Daily Local News, West Chester, Pa., 1963-65; editor, co-pub. Boutique and Villager, Burlingame, Calif., 1966-76; sr. editor mag. The Webb Co., St. Paul, 1978-84; editor GEM Pub. Group, Reno, 1985-2001. Faculty Reader's Digest Writers' Workshops. Co-author: Get Up and Go: A Guide for the Mature Traveler, 1989, The Mature Traveler's Book of Deals, 1997; columnist The Mature Traveler, 1989—. Recipient numerous awards Soc. Am. Travel Writers, Nat. Fedn. Press Women, Calif. Newspaper Pubs. Assn., San Francisco Press Club, Calif. Taxpayers Assn., White House Citations. Mem. Internat. Assn. Bus. Communicators (Merit award 1984), Press Women Minn. (numerous awards), Press Women Nev., Soc. Am. Travel Writers (v.p. 1999, chair Western chpt. 1996-98, pres. 2002-). Avocations: historical research, golf, travel, photography, reading. E-mail: maturetrav@aol.com.

MALOTT, JOHN RAYMOND, writer, consultant; b. Kankakee, Ill., Nov. 5, 1946; s. Raymond Roderick and Ruth Pearl (Jacobs) M.; m. Hiroko Iwami, Nov. 23, 1971; children: David Iwami, Rumi Justine. BA, Northwestern U., 1967; grad., Nat. War Coll., 1983. Civilian advisor U.S. Dept. State, Vietnam, 1969-70, China desk officer, 1970-71, Am. consul Kobe, Japan, 1971-73, 1st sec. Am. Embassy Tokyo, 1974-77, Sri Lanka desk officer Washington, 1977-78, India desk officer, 1978-80; Am. consul &, Bombay, 1980-82, with Nat. War Coll. Washington, 1982-83, dep. dir. Japan Affairs, 1983-85, spl. asst. to Under Sec. State Econ. Affairs, 1985-86, Am. consul gen. Osaka, Japan, 1986-89, dir. Japan Affairs Washington, 1989-91, sr. seminar, 1991-92, dep. asst. sec. state South Asian Affairs, 1992-93; sr. advisor to Undersec. State for Econ. Affairs, 1993-95; U.S. amb. to Malaysia Dept. State, 1995-98; exec. chmn. Malott & Assocs., 1999—; pres. World Affairs/Coun. of Orange County, 2000—02. Author: Partners, 1992. Recipient Vietnam Svc. award, 1970, Meritorious Honor award Dept. State, 1982, Superior honor award, 1991. Presbyterian. Home: 25211 Via Piedra Roja Laguna Niguel CA 92677-1822

MALOUF-CUNDY, PAMELA BONNIE, visual arts editor; b. Reseda, Calif., July 9, 1956; d. Jubert George and Marguerite I. (Llido) Malouf. AA in Cinema with honors, Valley Community Coll., 1976. Asst. film editor various film studios including Paramount, 20th Fox, CBS/MTM, and others, 1976-80; post prodn. coordinator, supr. David Gerber Co., Culver City, Calif., 1981-82; post prodn. coordinator Paramount TV, Los Angeles, 1982-84; sole proprietor Trailers, Etc., North Hollywood, Calif., 1984-85; film and video editor Paramount Pictures, L.A., 1985-86; film editor Universal Studios, Universal City, Calif., 1987-89; film, video editor New World TV, L.A., 1991-92; associate dir. Tri-Star TV, Studio City, Calif., 1992-93; film and video editor various studios, 1993—. Owner, mgr. Choice Editing Systems, Northridge, Calif., 1993—. (film and video editor): (TV series) Rude Awakening; Anna Says; Magnificent 7; A Year in the Life; MacGyver; Call to Glory; The Making of Shogun; Nightingales; Mission Impossible, Muder C.O.D., I'll Take Romance; Get a Life; A Fire in the Dark; The Fifth Corner; (movies) Search for Grace; Eyes of Terror; Then There Was One; Sweet Bird of Youth; Without You I'm Nothing; All in the Family; Rockford Files; Is There Life Out There?; Thrill, Breaking Free; Something Borrowed...Something Blue; A Time to Stay Goodbye?; An Unexpected Life; A Father For Brittany; Love Song, Custody of the Heart, 2000; Snap Decision, The Familiar Stranger, Taking Back Our Town, 2001; (asst. film editor) (moveies) King of Gypsies, Star Wars, others; : (films) Stong Medicine. Mem. Internat. Alliance of Theatrical Stage Employees and Moving Picture Machine Operators of U.S. and Can., Tri-Network (pres. 1979-80), Acad. Magical Arts, Inc., Am. Cinema Editors, Acad. TV Arts and Scis., Dir.'s Guild of Am. Democrat. Roman Catholic. Avocations: water skiing, snow skiing, sand castle building, script writing.

MALOUIN, JEAN-LOUIS, university educator; b. Three-Rivers, Que., Can., Oct. 5, 1943; m. Hélène Pépin; children: Pascale, Philippe. B in Commerce, Université Laval, Que., 1965, MSc, 1966; PhD, UCLA, 1970. Prof. Bus. Sch., U. Laval, 1966-89, dir. OSD dept., 1971-75, 78-79, assoc. dean acad. affairs, 1979-84, dean, 1984-89; dean faculty of bus. U. Alta., Edmonton, Alta., Can., 1989-92; dean faculty of adminstrn. U. Ottawa, Ottawa, Ont., Can., 1992-2000. Coord. Can. Consortium for the Support of the Sea PhD program; bd. dirs. Corel Corp., Acerra Corp. Editor: The Generation of Scientific Administrative Knowledge, 1986; co-author: L'Innovation Technologique dans les PME Manufacturières: études de cas enquête, 1992. Bd. dirs. Centre québécois de Productivité, du Vêtement, Montréal, 1983-86, Nat. Rsch. Ctr., London, 1986-87, Banff Sch. Advancement Mgmt., 1989-92. Mem. Can. Fedn. Deans (v.p. 1987), Edmonton C. of C. (bd. dirs. 1989-92). Home: 1410 Clay Ct Gloucester ON Canada K1C 4T2 E-mail: malouin@uottawa.ca.

MALPHURS, ROGER EDWARD, biomedical marketing executive; b. Lake Worth, Fla., Dec. 15, 1933; s. Cecil Edward and Muriel Thelma (Ward) M.; m. Carolyn Sue Calapp, Feb. 2, 1963(div. 1993); children: Steven, Brian, Darren, Regina, Victoria. BS, U. Utah, 1961; D of Chiropractic, Palmer Coll. Chiropractic West, 1990. Cert. med. technologist; lic. chiropractor, Calif., Ariz. Supr. spl. chemistry Cen. Pathology Lab., Santa Rosa, Calif., 1968-73; mgr. lab. Cmty. Hosp., 1973-76; supr. chem., staff asst. Meml. Hosp., 1976-85; pres., CEO R.E. Malphurs Co., Sunnyvale, Calif., 1972—. Owner, developer

REMCO Mktg. Assocs., Santa Rosa, 1970-71; pvt. commodity trader, 1974—; owner Better Bus. Forms and Typeset, Santa Rosa, 1977-81, commodity pool operator, 1979-80; dept. mgr. immunochemistry Spectra Labs., Fremont, Calif., 1990-95; clin. trials cons. hematology, tech. writer Abbott Diagnostics, Santa Clara, Calif., 1995-2000; tech. writer Healtheon/WebMD, Santa Clara, Calif., 2000—, Hewlett-Packard, Roseville, Calif., 2000-. Author: A New, Simple Way to Win at Blackjack, 1972. Served as squadron commdr. CAP USAF Aux., 1982-84. Mem. APHA, Am. Chiropractic Assn., Calif. Chiropractic Assn., Optimists Internat. (youth awards chmn. 1969-74), Toastmasters (sec./treas. 1988-89), Rep. Senatorial Inner Circle. Republican. Avocations: flying, computers, pistol shooting, oil painting, writing.

MALSACK, JAMES THOMAS, retired manufacturing company executive; b. Milw., Apr. 4, 1921; s. Leonard Henry and Florence Alice (Webb) M.; widowed; children: Thomas James, Claudia Irene, Robert Richard, Thomas John, Pamela Joyce. BSBA, Marquette U., 1946; D Pub. Svc. (hon.), No. Mich. U., 1990. Acct. Price Waterhouse & Co., Milw., 1946-51; with Lake Shore, Inc., Iron Mountain, Mich., 1951-88, exec. v.p., 1959-72, pres., chief exec. officer, 1972-84, chmn., 1984-88. Bd. control No. Mich. U., trustee emeritus. With USN, 1942-45. Mem. Masons, Shriners. Republican. Episcopalian.

MALSON, VERNA LEE, special education educator; b. Buffalo, Mar. 29, 1937; d. Guy James and Vera Pearl (Curtis) Mayer; m. Jack Lee Malson, Apr. 20, 1955; children: Daniel Lee, Thomas James, Mark David, Scott Allen. BA in Elem. Edn. and Spl. Edn. magna cum laude, Met. State Coll., Denver, 1975; MA in Learning Disabilities, U. No. Colo., 1977. Cert. tchr., Colo. Tchr.-aide Wyo. State Tng. Sch., Lander, 1967-69; spl. edn. tchr. Bennett Sch. 29J, Colo., 1975-79, chmn. health, sci. social studies depts., 1977-79; spl. edn. tchr. Deer Trail Sch., Colo., 1979-98, chmn. careers, gifted and talented, 1979-87, spl. edn./presch. tchr., 1992-98, ret., 1998. Course cons. Regis Coll., Denver, 1990; mem. spl. edn. parent adv. com. East Central Bd. Coop. Ednl. Services, Limon, Colo. Colo. scholar Met. State Coll., 1974; grantee Colo. Dept. Edn., 1979, 81; recipient Cert. of Achievement, Met. State Coll., 1993. Mem. Coun. Exceptional Children, Bennett Tchrs. Club (treas. 1977-79), Kappa Delta Pi. Republican. Presbyterian. Avocations: coin collecting, reading, sports. Home: PO Box 208 Edgerton WY 82635-0208

MALT, RONALD BRADFORD, lawyer; b. Boston, Aug. 1, 1954; s. Ronald A. and Geraldine (Sutton) M.; m. Sharon Lynn Harford, Feb. 14, 1981; 2 children. AB, Harvard U., 1976, JD, 1979. Bar: Mass. 1979. Assoc. Ropes & Gray, Boston, 1979-86, ptnr., 1987—, mem. policy com., 1993—; dir. Fenway Ptnrs., Inc., N.Y.C., 1999—. Asst. treas. Butler Capital Corp., N.Y.C., 1983—; sec. to adv. bd. Mezzanine Lending Assocs., N.Y.C., 1983—; mem. policy com. Ropes & Gray, Boston, 1993—. Mem. corp. Mass. Gen. Hosp., Boston, 1989—; trustee Butler Found., 1989—, Black River Environ. Improvement Assn., Inc., 1991—. Mem. Republican. Episcopalian. Office: Ropes & Gray One International Pl Boston MA 02110 E-mail: bmalt@ropesgray.com.

MALTBY, FLORENCE HELEN, library science educator; b. Sumner, Iowa, Mar. 2, 1933; d. Harold George and Blanche Theresa (Gritzner) Garland; m. George Robert Maltby, June 3, 1964 (dec. Oct. 1985); 1 child, Patricia Garland Martby Clark. BA, U. No. Iowa, Cedar Falls, 1954; MS in Libr. Sci., U. Ill., 1960, cert. advanced study librarianship, 1967. Elem. sch. libr. Barrington (Ill.) Pub. Sch., 1954-57, USAF Dependent Sch. Europe, Sculthorpe, Eng., 1957-58, Ramstein, Fed. Republic of Germany, 1958-59, Wiesbaden, Fed. Republic of Germany, 1960-61; grad. asst. U. Ill., Champaign, 1959-60; reference asst., instr. Libr. Cen. Mich. U., Mt. Pleasant, 1961-63; asst. prof. libr. sci. Southwest Mo. State U., Springfield, 1963-66, 67-80, assoc. prof. libr. sci., 1980-97; instr. libr. sci. U. Ill., Champaign, 1966-67; archivist Diocese of Springfield-Cape Girardeau, 2001—. Evaluator North Cen. Assn., Springfield, 1989, Dept. Elem. and Secondary Edn., Mo. Sch. Improvement, 1989; com. mem. Children's Lit. Festival, Springfield, 1990, treas., 1991. Contbr. to Masterplots II: Juvenile and Young Adult Fiction, 1991, 97. Mem. AAUP, ALA, Assn. Libr. and Info. Sci. Edn., Mo. Assn. Sch. Librs. (mem. standards rev. com. for state sch. libr. media standards 1994), Assn. Cath. Diocesan Archivists, Beta Phi Mu, Alpha Beta Alpha, Kappa Delta Pi. Roman Catholic. Avocations: reading, playing organ and piano, cert. literary braille transcriber.

MALTBY, RICHARD ALLEN, urban planner; b. Midland, Mich., May 21, 1937; s. Roy Alvan and Florence Isabella M.; m. George-Ann Maltby, June 17, 1961; children: Michael R., Holly Ann. AA in Architecture, Bay City Jr. Coll., Bay City, Mich., 1957; BS in Urban Planning, Mich. State U., 1960, M in Urban Planning, 1965. Urban planner Mich. Dept. State Hwys., Lansing, 1960-62; chief planner Washtenaw County Met. Planning Commn., Ann Arbor, Mich., 1962-67; exec. dir. Champaign County Regional Planning Commn., Urbana, Ill., 1967-70; dep. dir. Erie & Niagara Counties Regional Planning Bd., Amherst, N.Y., 1970-82; dir. Midland County Planning Dept., Midland, Mich., 1983-98. Mem. Am. Planning Assn. (Dist. Chpt. Improvement award 1992), Mich. Chpt. Am. Planning Assn. (pres. 1991-93, disting. svc. award 1995), Beta Alpha Sigma. Avocations: reading, classical music, secular humanism. Home: 5312 Swede Ave Midland MI 48642-7135

MALTESE, JOHN ANTHONY, political scientist, educator; b. Point Pleasant, N.J., Aug. 19, 1960; s. John and Eva May (Campbell) Maltese. BA, Duke U., 1982; MA, PhD, Johns Hopkins U., 1988. Asst. prof. U. Ga., Athens, 1989—95, assoc. prof., 1996—. Author: Spin Control: The White House Office of Communications and the Management of Presidential News, 1992 (Frank Luther Mott-Kappa Tau Alpha Rsch. award, 1992), The Selling of Supreme Court Nominees, 1995 (C. Herman Pritchett award, 1996), The Politics of the Presidency, 5th edit., 2002; co-author: The Heifetz Collection, 1994 (Grammy award, 1996); editor: The Accompanist: The Autobiography of Andre Benoist, 1978. Participant Renaissance Weekend, Kiawah Island, SC, 2000. Mem.: Authors Guild, So. Polit. Sci. Assn., Midwest Polit. Sci. Assn., Assn. for Recorded Sound Collections, Am. Polit. Sci. Assn. Presbyterian. Avocations: collecting historical sound recordings and autograph manuscripts, writing. Home: 226 Westview Dr Athens GA 30606 Office: Polit Sci Dept Univ Ga Athens GA 30602-1615

MALTESE, SERPHIN RALPH, state legislator, lawyer; b. N.Y.C., Dec. 7, 1932; s. Paul and Frances (Scafidi) M.; m. Constance Mary Del Vecchio, Aug. 27, 1955; children— Andrea Constance, Leslie Serphine, Serphin Ralph (dec.). BA, Manhattan Coll., 1958; LL.B., JD (War Service scholar 1958-62), Fordham U., 1962. Bar: N.Y. bar 1963. Trial atty. for ins. cos., 1963-66; asst. dist. atty., dep. chief homicide bur. Queens County, N.Y., 1966-69; asso. counsel N.Y. State Com. Campus Disorders, 1969-70; counsel N.Y. State Com. Deaf and Multiple Impaired, 1970; chmn. law com. Buckley for U.S. Senator, 1970; counsel N.Y. State Assembly, 1972-76, N.Y. State Senate, Albany, 1976-88, state senator, 1988—, chmn. senate standing com. on elections, mem. com. on aging, cities, civil svc. and pensions, mem. codes higher edn., investigations and govt. ops. com. Past pres. N.Y. Conf. of Italian Am. Legislators; exec. dir. N.Y. State Conservative Party, 1971-86, exec. vice chmn., 1978-86, state chmn., 1986-88. Chmn. trustees Christ the King Regional H.S., 1976—; N.Y. State chmn. Conservatives for Ronald Reagan, 1980; chmn. Queens (N.Y.) Rep. Party; mem. Stuyvesant High Sch. Alumni Exec. Bd. With AUS, 1952-54, Korea. Recipient Charles Edison Meml. award N.Y. State Conservative Party, 1977, St. John's U. Pres.'s medal, 1994, Pres.'s award LaGuardia C.C., 1998; named Man of Yr. Commn. for Social Justice, 1998. Mem. Italian Am. Profl. Bus. Assn. (hon. chmn.), N.Y. State Bar Assn., Queens Asst. Dist. Attys. Assn., Christopher Columbus Assn. (chmn. 1970—), Young Ams. for Freedom (nat. sr. adv. bd.), Am. Conservative Union (nat. bd. dirs.), Internat. Assn. Space Philatelists, Queens C. of C., Catholic War Vets., Harold Gray Collectors Soc. (pres.), Am. Legion, VFW, Alpha Phi Delta. Roman Catholic. Office: 71-04 Myrtle Ave Glendale NY 11385-7254 also: 409 Legislative Office Bldg Albany NY 12247

MALTIN, FREDA, retired university administrator; b. Calgary, Alta., Can., June 4, 1923; came to the U.S., 1958; d. Meyers Wolfe and Ida (Kohn) Rosen; m. Manny Maltin, Aug. 25, 1950; 1 child, Richard Allan. Diploma Garbutt's Bus. Coll., Calgary, 1942. Various secretarial and bookkeeping positions, 1951; mem. adminstrv. staff U. So. Calif., 1960-92, asst. to exec. dir. Davidson Conf. Ctr., 1987-92, Grad. Sch. Bus. Adminstrn., 1981-92. Recipient staff achievement award U. So. Calif., 1991. Mem. U. So. Calif. Staff Club (charter), U. So. Calif. Skull and Dagger (hon.), U. So. Calif. Town and Gown.

MALTIN, LEONARD, television commentator, writer; b. N.Y.C., Dec. 18, 1950; s. Aaron Isaac and Jacqueline (Gould) M.; m. Alice Tlusty, Mar. 15, 1975; 1 child, Jessica Bennett. BA, NYU, 1972. Mem. faculty New Sch. for Social Rsch., N.Y.C., 1973-81; curator Am. Acad. Humor, 1975-76; guest curator dept. film Mus. Modern Art, 1976; film critic and corr. Entertainment Tonight, Hollywood, Calif., 1982—; columnist Modern Maturity, 1996-99; film critic Playboy mag., 1998—. Adj. prof. Sch. Cinema & TV, U. So. Calif., 1998—. Author: Movie Comedy Teams, 1970, rev. edit., 1985, Behind the Camera (reprinted as The Art of the Cinematographer), 1971, The Great Movie Shorts (reprinted as Selected Short Subjects), 1971, The Disney Films, 1973, rev. edit., 2000, The Great Movie Comedians, 1978, Of Mice and Magic: A History of American Animated Cartoons, 1980, rev. edit., 1987, The Great American Broadcast, 1997; co-author: Our Gang: The Life and Times of the Little Rascals, 1977, reprinted as The Little Rascals: The Life and Times of Our Gang, 1992; editor: Leonard Maltin's Movie & Video Guide, 1969, rev. annually, Leonard Maltin's Movie Encyclopedia, 1994, Leonard Maltin's Family Film Guide, 1999; producer, writer, host (video) Cartoons for Big Kids, 1989; writer (TV spl.) Fantasia: The Making of a Disney Classic, 1990; writer, host (video) The Making of The Quiet Man, 1992, The Making of High Noon, 1992, Cartoon Madness: The Fantastic Max Fleischer Cartoons, 1993, Cliffhanger!, 1993. Mem. steering com. Hollywood Entertainment Mus., 1989—. Mem. Authors Guild, Soc. for Cinephiles (pres. 1990-91, Man of Yr. 1973), L.A. Film Critics Assn. (pres. 1995-96). Office: c/o Entertainment Tonight Paramount TV 5555 Melrose Ave Los Angeles CA 90038-3112

MALTZ, ROBERT, surgeon; b. Cin., July 21, 1935; s. William and Sarah (Goldberg) M.; m. Sylvia Moskowitz, Aug. 24, 1958; children: Mark Edward, Deborah Lynn, Steven Alan, David Stuart. BS in Zoology, U. Cin., 1958, MD, 1962. Diplomate Am. Bd. Otolaryngology, 1970. Intern Cin. Gen. Hosp., 1962-63; resident Barnes Hosp., St. Louis, 1965-69; asst. prof. surgery Stanford U. Med. Ctr., Palo Alto, Calif., 1969-71; asst. prof. otolaryngology U. Cin. Med. Ctr., 1971-75, assoc. prof. otolaryngology, 1975—; dir. dept. otolaryngology Jewish Hosp., Cin., 1992—. Chief, divsn. head and neck surgery, dept. otolaryngology and maxillofacial surgery U. Cin. Med. Ctr., 1972-76; bd. dirs. Cancer Control Council, U. Cin. Med. Cntr.; cons. Bur. Crippled Children's Svcs., State of Ohio; on staff Univ. Hosp., Cin., Jewish Hosp., Cin., Children's Hosp. Med. Ctr., Bethesda Hosp., Cin., Christ Hosp., Our Lady of Mercy Hosp.; del. to numerous profl. confs.; mem. health affairs adv. com. Cmty. Mut. Ins. Co.; mem. mng. bd. PIE Mut. Ins. Co.; bd. dirs. UCATS, 1995-98; trustee Health Found. Greater Cin., 1997—, vice-chmn., 2000-01, chmn. 2001—, chmn. program com., 2000-01; instr. short term courses in field; pres.-elect alulmni exec. coun. U. Cin. Coll. Medicine, 1998-2000, pres., 2000-2002. Contbr. articles to profl. jours. Bd. dirs. Jewish Cmty. Rels. Coun.; bd. trustees Cin. Art Acad., 1998—; faculty adv. com. U. Cinn. Capt. USAF, 1963-65, PTO. USPHS fellow, 1968-69; grantee Eli Lilly Co. grantee, 1971-76, Burroughs Wellcome Co., 1972. Fellow ACS, Am. Acad. Facial and Reconstructive Surgery (edn. com. 1972, future plans com. 1973-75, sci. program com., budget and fin. com. 1975, chmn. credentials com., no. sect. 1980-85), Royal Soc. Health, Internat. Cosmetic Surgeons, Am. Acad. Cosmetic Surgeons, Am. Assn. Cosmetic Surgeons (sec.-treas. 1976-81); mem. Am. Acad. Otolaryngology and Head and Neck Surgery, Am. Coun. Otolaryngology, Soc. Univ. Otolaryngologists, Pan-Am. Assn. Oto-Rhino-Laryngology and Broncho-Esophagology, Ohio State Med. Assn., Cin. Acad. Medicine (trustee 1992-95, treas. 1993-95, pres. 1996-97, chmn. pub. rels. com. 1980, chmn. comm. com. 1994-96, chmn. sply. soc. com. 1995, legis. com. 1985, editl. bd. 1994-96, jud. com. 1995—, chmn. managed care med. dirs. com. 1997—), U. Cin. Alumni Assn. (bd. govs., sec. 1994, fin. v.p. 1995, 1st v.p. 1996, pres. 1997-98), Acad. Medicine Found. (bd. dirs., v.p., pres. 2002--), Cin. Ear, Nose and Throat Soc., Losantiville Country Club (bd. govs. 1996—, pres. 1999-2001), Omicron Delta Kappa, Sigma Sigma, Sigma Alpha Mu. Avocations: tennis, golf, traveling. Home: 2601 Willowbrook Dr Cincinnati OH 45237-3725 Office: 10496 Montgomery Rd Cincinnati OH 45242-5223

MALTZMAN, IRVING MYRON, psychology educator; b. Bklyn., May 9, 1924; s. Israel and Lillian (Mass) M.; m. Diane Seiden, Aug. 21, 1949; children— Sara, Kenneth, Ilaine. BA, NYU, 1946; PhD, State U. Iowa, 1949. Mem. faculty UCLA, 1949—, assoc. prof., 1957-60, prof. psychology, 1961—, chmn. dept., 1970-77. Co-author: Handbook of Contemporary Soviet Psychology, 1969, Alcoholism: A Review of it Characteristics, Etiology, Treatments, and Controversies, 2000. Fellow: APA, AAAS; mem.: Psychonomic Soc., APS, Phi Beta Kappa, Sigma Xi. Home: 11260-22B Overland Ave Culver City CA 90230-5559

MALTZMAN, STANLEY, artist; b. N.Y.C., July 4, 1921; s. Aberaham and Sarah (Kirsner) M.; m. Rachel Marie Petruzelli, Aug. 17, 1946; children: Carole Kavanagh, Susan Story. Student, N.Y. Phoenix Sch. Design, 1946-49. Staff artist Transparetn Products, N.Y.C., 1949-50; asst. product supr. Lever Bros., 1950-53; ptnr. Art Studio, 1953-55; from studio mgr. to art dir. Morse Internat. Advt., 1955-64; freelance artist, 1964-66; sr. designer Donald Desky Assoc., 1966-69; account exec. Charles Heston Assoc., 1969-73; freelance artist and printmaker Freehold, N.Y., 1974—. Instr. Hudson Valley Workshops, Greenville, N.Y., 1986—. Author: Drawing-Nature, 1995, 2d edit., 1998, Drawing Trees, 1999. Curator Greenville Libr. Gallery. With USCG, 1942-46, PTO. Greene County Coun. on the Arts grant, 1983, Schoharie Coun. on the Art grant, 1984. Mem. Pastel Soc. Am., Greene County Coun. on the Arts (visual arts com. Catskill, N.Y. chpt. 1983—). Jewish. Avocations: swimming, bird study. Home: PO Box 333 Freehold NY 12431-0333

MALVEAUX, FLOYD JOSEPH, academic dean; BS, Creighton U., 1961; MS, Loyola U.; PhD in Microbiology and Pub. Health, Mich. State U., 1968; MD, Howard U., 1974; postgrad., Washington Hosp. Ctr., 1974-76, Johns Hopkins U., 1976-78. Asst. prof. microbiology Howard U. Med. Sch., Washington, 1968-70, chmn. microbiology, assoc. prof. microbiology and medicine, 1989-94, dean, v.p. health affairs, prof. microbiology and medicine, 1995—; mem. faculty Johns Hopkins U., Balt., 1984-89. Founder, pres. Urban Asthma and Allergy Ctr., Balt., 1986-89; mem. numerous med. panels; lectr. in field. Contbr. articles to profl. jours. Recipient Nat. Rsch. Svc. award NIH, Clemens von Pirquet Rsch. award Georgetown U. Sch. Medicine, 1991; Vivian B. Allen Found. fellow; Grantee Nat. Inst. Allergy and Infectious Diseases, Nat. Heart, Lung and Blood Inst. of NIH, Hasbro Children's Found., Robert Wood Johnson Found. Mem. NAACP (life), Alpha Omega Alpha, Sigma Xi, Sigma Pi Phi, Kappa Alpha Psi. Office: Howard U Med Sch 520 W St NW Washington DC 20059-0001*

MALVERN, DONALD, retired aircraft manufacturing company executive; b. Sterling, Okla., Apr. 22, 1921; s. George Michael and Anna Francesca (Elsass) M.; m. Ruth Marie Vogler, June 4, 1949; 1 son, Michael John. BSME, U. Okla., 1946. Engr. Victory Architects and Engrs., Clinton, Okla., 1943, Douglas Aircraft Co., Santa Monica, Calif., 1943; with McDonnell Aircraft Co., St. Louis, 1946-88, exec. v.p., 1973-82, pres., 1982-86; v.p. McDonnell Douglas Corp., 1973-88; aerospace cons. St. Louis, 1988—; pres. McDonnell Douglas Services, Inc., 1978-82. Trustee Falcon Found., 1983—; bd. visitors Def. Sys. Mgmt. Coll., 1983-86, U. Okla. Coll. Engring., 1988-91; pres. Wings of Hope, 1989-92, chmn., 1992—. 1st lt. USAAF, 1943-46; capt. Mo. Air NG, 1946-51. Inducted into Okla. Aviation and Space Mus.'s Hall of Fame, 1987; recipient Disting. Alumni award U. Okla., 1999, Unsung Hero award United Way of St. Louis, 2000. Fellow AIAA (Tech. Mgmt. award 1968, Reed Aeros. medal 1980); mem. Am. Def. Preparedness Assn. (pres. St. Louis chpt. 1979-80), Navy League U.S. (life), Nat. Aeros. Assn., Air Force Assn., Armed Forces Mgmt. Assn., Pi Tau Sigma, Tau Beta Pi, Tau Omega, Sigma Tau Beta. Clubs: Bellerive Country, St. Louis. Home: 213 Grand Banks Ct Chesterfield MO 63017-9507

MALVEY, DONNA M. health sciences educator; MHSA, George Washington U., 1985; PhD, U. Ala., Birmingham, 1996. Asst. prof. U. Ark. at Little Rock, 1996-97, U. South Fla., Tampa, 1997—. Contbr. chpts. to book, articles to profl. jours. Mem. Fla. Cancer Control and Rsch. Adv. Coun., 1997—. Office: U South Fla MDC56 13201 Bruce B Downs Blvd Tampa FL 33612-3805

MALVIYA, VINAY KUMAR, obstetrician-gynecologist; b. Nagpur, India, Sept. 28, 1953; s. Bhagchandra and Chandra Ran Jain; m. Shobha Goel Malviya, Nov. 20, 1985; children: Samir, Sanjana. Interscience degree, SIES Coll., 1970; MBBS, Grant Med. Coll., 1976. Cert. Am. Bd. Ob-Gyn. Rotating intern Sir. J.J. Group Hosps., Bombay, 1975-76; resident St. George Hosp., 1976-77; resident in ob-gyn. Long Island Jewish Hillside Med. Ctr., N.Y.C., 1977-80; fellow in ob-gyn. Mt. Sinai Med. Ctr., 1980-82; asst. prof. in ob-gyn. Case Western Res. U., Cleve., 1982-83; from asst. prof. to assoc. prof., vice chief ob-gyn. Wayne State U., Detroit, 1983-97; dir. divsn. gynecol. oncology Prondence Hosp., Southfield, Mich., 1997—. Lectr. in field; staff Mt. Sinai Med. Ctr., N.Y.C, 1980-82, McDonald House Case Western Res. U., 1982-83, Harper-Grace Hosps., Detroit, 1983—, Detroit Med. Ctr., 1983—, St. John Hosp., Detroit, 1983—, St. John Hosp., Detroit, 1984—, Providence Hosp., Southfield, Mich., 1984—; mem. staff, various coms. Hutzel Hosp., Detroit, 1983—. Contbr. articles to med. jours. Fellow Am. Coll. Ob-Gyns; mem. AMA, Cen. Assn. Ob-Gyns., Southwest Oncology Group, Soc. Gyn. Oncologists, Am. Assn. Gyn. Laparoscopists, Am. Soc. for Colposcopy and Cervical Pathology. Office: Providence Care Ctr 22301 Foster Winter Dr Fl 3 Southfield MI 48075-3707 Fax: 248-483-8108. E-mail: vmalviya@med.wayne.edu.

MALY, KURT JOHN, computer science educator; b. Modling, Austria, Aug. 20, 1944; came to U.S., 1969; s. Anton and Editha (Gneist) M.; m. Christiana Peterlik, Mar. 18, 1972; 1 child, Angela Claudia Diplom Ingenieur summa cum laude, U. Tech., Austria, 1968; MS, Courant Inst. NYU, 1970, PhD, 1973. Asst. prof. U. Minn., Mpls., 1972-78, assoc. prof., 1978-85, acting head, 1980-82, head, 1982-85; eminent prof., chmn. computer sci. Old Dominion U., Norfolk, Va., 1985—, Kaufman prof., 1991—. Hon. prof. Chengdu U. of Sci. and Tech., People's Republic of China, 1986—, Hefei U., People's Republic of China, 1991—, Guangxi Computer Inst., People's Republic of China, 1993—; bd. dirs. Inst. of Info. Tech., Ctr. for Innovative Tech., Blacksburg, Va., 1988-92; bd. dirs., exec. co-dir. Microelectronic and Info. Scis. Ctr., Mpls., 1980-85. Author: Fundamentals of the Computing Sciences, 1978; assoc. editor: Jour. for Microcomputer Application Tech., PRC; contbr. articles to profl. jours. Served with Austrian Air Force, 1963-64 Fellow Sorbonne U., Paris, 1966, Courant Inst., N.Y.C., 1968-72 Mem. Assn. Computing Machinery, IEEE, Sigma Xi Roman Catholic. Office: Old Dominion U Norfolk VA 23529 E-mail: maly@cs.oolu.edu.

MALY, WOJCIECH P. engineering educator, researcher; b. Inowroclaw, Poland, Jan. 5, 1946; came to U.S., 1979; s. Feliks and Maria (Gordzialkowska) M.; m. Halina Zarembowska, Apr. 11, 1970; 1 child, Katarzyna. MSc, Tech. U. Warsaw, 1970; PhD, Polish Acad. Sci., Warsaw, 1975. Asst. prof. Tech. U. Warsaw, 1975-86; assoc. prof. dept. elec. and computer engring. Carnegie Mellon U., Pitts., 1986-90, prof., 1990-96, Whitaker prof., 1996—. Author: Atlas of IC Technologies, 1986; contbr. chpts. to books, numerous articles to profl. jours. Recipient Teare Tchg. award Carnegie Mellon U., 1989; SRC Tech. Excellence award Semicondr. Rsch. Corp., 1993. Fellow IEEE. Roman Catholic. Achievements include development of methodologies of design for manufacturability of integrated circuits; patents in field. Office: Carnegie Mellon U ECE Dept 5000 Forbes Ave Pittsburgh PA 15213-3890

MAMALAKIS, MARKOS JOHN, economics educator; b. Salonica, Greece, Oct. 30, 1932; came to U.S., 1957; s. John Paul and Renate (Rocha) M.; m. Angelica Mamalakis, Jan. 30, 1960; children: Anna, Catherine, Marina, John, Andreas, Philip, Irene, Peter, Joanna, Alexandra, Emmanuel, Thomas. BA in Law., U. Salonica, 1955; postgrad., U. Munich, 1955-57; MA in Econs., U. Calif., Berkeley, 1959, PhD in Econs., 1962. Teaching asst. U. Calif., Berkeley, 1959-61; instr. U. Western Ontario, London, Canada, 1961-62, asst. prof. Canada, 1962-63, Yale U., New Haven, 1963-67; assoc. prof. U. Wis.-Milw., 1967-69, prof., 1969—. Vis. prof. U. Chile, Santiago, 1964-66, U. Gottingen, Germany, 1975-76; cons. Yale U., 1971-72; dir. Ctr. for L.Am. U. Wis., 1967-72; guest scholar Woodrow Wilson Internat. Ctr. Scholars, Washington, 1990, 91; vis. scholar Inter-Am. Devel. Bank, Washington, 19941 guest prof., Giessen (Germany) U., summer 1999, 2000. Author: Growth and Structure of Chilean Economy, 1976, Historical Statistics of Chile, 1978-89, Theory of Sectoral Clashes and Coalitions, 1976. German Exch. program grantee, 1955-57, Can. Coun. grantee, 1961, 62, Social Sci. Rsch. Coun. grantee, 1969-70, Fulbright grantee, 1971-89, 1999, Tinker Found. grantee, 1977-79, NEH grantee, 1981-87, Fromkin grantee, 2001. Mem. Am. Econ. Assn., Latin Am. Studies Assn., Nat. Acad. Econs. Uruguay (corr. acad.). Greek Orthodox. Avocations: climbing, walking, swimming, collecting stamps. Home: 2977 N Shepard Ave Milwaukee WI 53211-3435

MAMALI, CATALIN, psychology educator, researcher; b. Bucharest, Romania, Nov. 10, 1945; came to U.S., 1990; s. Stamate I. and Natalia M. Mamali; m. Ioana V. Mamali. MS in Psychology, U. Bucharest, Romania, 1968, PhD in Social Psychology, 1976. Psychologist Centre for Youth Problems and Rsch., Bucharest, 1968-85; asst. prof. Polytech. Inst., 1976-80, psychology Inst. Typified Bldgs., 1985-90; sr. rschr. Inst. Psychology Romanian Acad., 1990. Instr. Kirkwood C.C., Cedar Rapids, 1992-94, Mt. Mercy Coll., Cedar Rapids, 1996-97, St. Francis U., 1996-97, Clarke Coll., 1997-98, N.E. Iowa C.C., Peosta, 1996—, Loras Coll., 1996—; rsch. team U. UN, 1979-86. Mem. editl. bd. Jour. Personal and Interpersonal Relationships and Loss, 1996; author: The Gandhian Mode of Becoming, 1998; contbr. articles to profl. jours. including Internat. Conf. Reversal Psychology, Revista de Filozofie, among others. Fulbright fellow, 1990-91. Mem. Am. Psychol. Soc., Internat. Network for Personal Relationships, European Assn. for Exptl. Social Psychology. Avocations: mountain hiking, chess, skiing, tennis. Home: PO Box 1221 Dubuque IA 52004-1221 Office: 1450 Alta Vista St Dubuque IA 52001-4327

MAMAN, ARIE, endocrinologist; b. Petah Tikva, Israel, Dec. 18, 1944; came to U.S., 1974; s. Raphael and Mazal (Pariente) M.; m. Jenny Mendel, Oct. 23, 1976; children: Daniel, Michele. MD, Faculty of Medicine of Paris, 1974. Intern, then resident Jewish Hosp. and Med. Ctr., Bklyn., 1974-77; fellow in endocrinology U. Colo. Med. Ctr., Denver, 1977-79; chief clin. endocrinology Naval Regional Med. Ctr., Oakland, 1979-82; endocrinologist Rutgers Cmty. Health Plan, New Brunswick, N.J., 1982-90, physician in chief, 1991—; endocrinologist in pvt. practice East Brunswick, 1991—. Clin. assoc. prof. medicine Robert Wood Johnson Med. Sch. U. N.J., 1986. Fellow ACP, Am. Coll. Clin. Endocrinologists; mem. Endocrine Soc., Am. Diabetes Assn. Jewish. Avocations: skiing, swimming, reading, traveling. Office: D3 Brier Hill Ct East Brunswick NJ 08816-3335

MAMAT, FRANK TRUSTICK, lawyer; b. Syracuse, N.Y., Sept. 4, 1949; s. Harvey Sanford and Annette (Trustick) M.; m. Kathy Lou Winters, June 23, 1975; children: Jonathan Adam, Steven Kenneth. BA, U. Rochester, 1971; JD, Syracuse U., 1974. Bar: D.C. 1976, U.S. Ct. Appeals (D.C. cir.) 1976, Fla. 1977, U.S. Supreme Ct. 1979, US. Dist. Ct. (ea. dist.) 1983, U.S. Ct. Appeals (6th cir.) 1983, Mich. 1984, U.S. Dist. Ct. (no. dist.) Ind. 1984. Atty. NLRB, Washington, 1975—79; assoc. Proskauer, Rose, Goetz & Mendelsohn, Washington, N.Y.C. and L.A., 1979—83, Fishman Group, Bloomfield Hills, Mich., 1983—85, ptnr., 0985—1987; sr. ptnr. Honigman, Miller, Schwartz and Cohn, 1987—94; pres., CEO Morgan Daniels Co., Inc., West Bloomfield, Mich., 1994—; ptnr. Clark Klein & Beaumont, P.L.C., Detroit, 1995—96, Clark Hill, P.L.C., Detroit, 1996—, mem. exec. com., 1999—2001. Bd. dirs. Mich. Food and Beverage Assn., Air Conditioning Contractors of Am., Air Conditioning Contractors of Mich., Am. Subcontractors Assn., Mich. Mfrs. Assn. Labor Counsel, Jewish Vocat. Svcs., Constrn. Fin. Mgmt. Assn., Mich. Assn. Home Bldg. Gen. counsel Rep. Com. of Oakland County, 1986—; chmn. Constrn. Code Commn. Mich., 1993—; bd. dirs. 300 Club, Mich., 1984-90; pres. 400 Club, 1990-93, chmn., 1993—; mem. Associated Gen. Contractors Labor Lawyers Coun.; mem. Rep. Nat. Com. Nat. Rep. Senatorial Com., Presdl. Task Force, Rep. Labor Coun., Washington; city dir. West Bloomfield, 1985-87; pres. West Bloomfield Rep. CLub, 1985-87; fin. com. Rep. Com. of Oakland County, 1984-93; pres. Oakland County Lincoln Rep. Club, 1989-90; bd. dirs. camping svcs. and human resources com. YMCA, 1989-93, Anti-Defamation League, 1989—; vice chmn. Lawyers for Reagan-Bush, 1984; v.p. Fruehauf Farms, West Bloomfield, Mich., 1985-88; mem. staff Exec. Office of Pres. of U.S. Inquiries/Comments, Washington, 1981-83. Fellow Coll. Labor and Employment Attys.; mem. ABA, FBA, Mich. Bar Assn., Fla. Bar Assn. (labor com. 1977—), Rep. Nat. Lawyers Assn., Mich. Bus. and Profl. Assn., Am. Acad. Constrn. and Labor Attys. (exec. dir. 1998—), Am. Subcontractors Assn. (Southeastern Mich., bd. dirs.), Founders Soc. Detroit Bar Assn., Oakland County Bar Assn., B'nai B'rith (v.p. 1982-83, trustee 1987-88, bd. dirs. Detroit Barristers unit 1983-91, pres. 1985-87), Am. Soc. Employers (vice chmn. 2002-), Oakpointe Country Club, Detroit Soc. Clubs, Skyline

Club, Fairlane Club, Detroit Athletic Club, Renaissance Club, Econ. Club Detroit. Office: Clark Hill PLC 500 Woodward Ave Ste 3500 Detroit MI 48226-3435 also: Morgan Daniels Co Inc 5484 Crispin Way Rd West Bloomfield MI 48323-3402 E-mail: fmamat@aol.com., fmamat@clarkhill.com.

MAMATEY, VICTOR SAMUEL, history educator; b. North Braddock, Pa., Feb. 19, 1917; s. Albert Paul and Olga (Darmek) M.; m. Denise M. Perrone, Nov. 20, 1945; children: Albert R., Peter V. Student, Wittenberg Coll., 1938-39, U. Chgo., 1939-40; AM, Harvard U., 1941; PhD, U. Paris, 1949. Asst. prof. history Fla. State U., Tallahassee, 1949-55, assoc. prof., 1955-58, prof., 1958-67, chmn. dept. history, 1964-67; rsch. prof. hist. U. Ga., Athens, 1967-82, acting dean Coll. Arts and Scis., 1972-73. Vis. prof. Columbia U., 1961, Tulane U., 1963. Author: The United States and East Central Europe, 1914-18, 1957, Soviet RussianImperialism, 1964, (with Geoffrey Brunn) The World in the Twentieth Century, 1967, The Rise of the Hapsburg Empire, 1526-1815, 1971, (with Radomir Luza) History of the Czechoslovak Republic, 1918-1948, 1973. With U.S. Army, 1942-46. Guggenheim fellow, 1959. Mem. Am. Hist. Assn. (George Louis Beer prize for best book on internat. history 1958), Am. Assn. For Advancement Slavic Studies. Home: 142 Spruce Valley Rd Athens GA 30605-3332

MAMEDOV, EDOUARD AKHMED, chemist, researcher; b. Gyandja, Azerbaijan, Nov. 1, 1941; s. Akhmed and Vera (Belokoz) M.; m. Irada Akhoundova, Mar. 3, 1979; 1 child, Narmina Mamedova. BSc, State U., Baku, Azerbaijan, 1964; PhD, Inst. Catalysis, Novosibirsk, Russia, 1971; DSc, Inst. Petrochemistry, Baku, 1986. Jr. staff scientist Inst. Catalysis, Novosibirsk, Russia, 1970-71; sr. staff scientist Inst. Petrochemistry, Baku, 1971-86; head of lab. Inst. Phys. Chemistry, 1986-93; sabbatical leave Inst. Catalysis, Madrid, 1993-95; catalyst advisor Saudi Basic Industries Corp., Riyadh, 1995-97; sr. rschr. Sabic Tech. Ctr., Houston, 1997—. Internat. expert UN Indsl. Devel. Orgn., Vienna, Austria, 1982-91; lectr. State U., Baku, 1986-93; expert Cert. Commn., Baku, 1991-93. Co-author: Oxidative Coupling of Hydrocarbons, 1992, Ammoxidation of Alkylaromatics, 1992; contbr. over 100 articles to profl. jours.; patentee in field. Mem. N.Y. Acad. Scis. Moslem. Office: Sabic Tech Ctr 1600 Industrial Blvd Sugar Land TX 77478-2589 E-mail: edouard.mamedov@sabiscusa.com.

MAMER, JAMES MICHAEL, secondary education educator; b. L.A., Oct. 8, 1948; s. James Robert and Annette (Babue) M.; m. Jessica Puma, Aug. 31, 1963. BA in Polit. Sci., Calif. Poly. U., Pomona, 1970; MA in Internat. Studies, Immaculate Heart Coll., 1990. Tchr. Irvine (Calif.) Unified Sch. Dist., 1978—. Mentor tchr. Irvine Sch. Dist., 1988-95. Mem. editl. bd. Global Pages, L.A., 1991-96. Recipient Global Teaching award Western Internat. Studies Consortium, L.A., 1991, Am. Coun. Internat. Edn. award, 1998; Fulbright-Hays grantee, India, 1977; Coe fellow, 1984. Mem. Nat. Coun. Social Studies (Nat. Social Studies Tchr. of Yr. 1992), Irvine Tchrs. Assn. Democrat. Avocation: reading. Home: 29102 Kommers Ln Silverado CA 92676-9726

MAMER, STUART MIES, lawyer; b. East Hardin, Ill., Feb. 23, 1921; s. Louis H. and Anna (Mies) M.; m. Donna E. Jordan, Sept. 10, 1944; children: Richard A., John S., Bruce J. AB, U. Ill., 1942, JD, 1947. Bar: Ill. bar 1947. Assoc. Thomas & Mulliken, Champaign, 1947-55; partner firm Thomas, Mamer & Haughey, 1955—. Lectr. U. Ill. Coll. Law, Urbana, 1965-85; Mem. Atty. Registration and Disciplinary Commn. Ill., 1976-82 Chmn. fund drive Champaign County Community Chest, 1955; 1st pres. Champaign County United Fund, 1957; Pres., dir. U. Ill. McKinley Found., Champaign, 1957-69; trustee Children's Home and Aid Soc. of Ill., v.p., 1977-96. Served as pilot USAAF, 1943-45. Mem. Am. Coll. Trust and Estate Counsel (bd. regents 1984-90), Phi Beta Kappa, Phi Gamma Delta. Republican. Presbyterian. Home: 101 W Windsor Rd # 3105 Urbana IL 61802-6663 Office: Thomas Mamer & Haughey 30 E Main St Fl 5 Champaign IL 61820-3629 E-mail: smamer@tmh-law.com.

MAMET, DAVID ALAN, playwright, director, essayist; b. Chgo., Nov. 30, 1947; s. Bernard Morris and Lenore June (Silver) M.; m. Lindsay Crouse, Dec. 1977 (div.), m. Rebecca Pidgeon, Sept. 22, 1991. BA, Goddard Coll., Plainfield, Vt., 1969; DLitt (hon.), Dartmouth Coll., 1996. Artist-in-residence Goddard Coll., 1971-73; artistic dir. St. Nicholas Theatre Co., Chgo., 1973-75; guest lectr. U. Chgo., 1975, 79, NYU, 1981; assoc. artistic dir. Goodman Theater, Chgo., 1978; assoc. prof. film Columbia U., 1988. Chmn. bd. Atlantic Theater Co. Author: (plays) The Duck Variations, 1971, Secual Pervisity in Chicago, 1973 (Village Voice Obie award, N.Y. Drama Critics Cir. award), Reunion, 1973, Squirrels, 1974, American Buffalo, 1976, A Life in the Theatre, 1976, The Water Engine, 1976, The Woods, 1977, Lone Canoe, 1978, Prairie du Chien, 1978, Lakeboat, 1980, Donny March, 1981, Edmond, 1982 (Village Voice Obie award, 1983), the Disappearance of the Jews, 1983, The Shawl, 1985, Glengarry Glen Ross, 1984 (Pulitzer prize for drama, N.Y. Drama Critics Cir. award), Speed-the-Plow, 1987, Bobby Gould in Hell, 1989, The Old Neighborhood, 1991, Oleanna, 1992, The Cryptogram, 1994, Ricky Jay and His 52 Assistants, 1994; author: (one act) Death Defying Acts, 1995; author: Boston Marriage, 1999, (screenplays) The Postman Always Rings Twice, 1979, The Verdict, 1980, The Untouchables, 1986, House of Games, 1986; author: (with Shel Silverstein) Things Change, 1987; author: We're No Angels, 1987, Homicide, 1991, Hoffa, 1991, Oleanna, 1994, The Edge, 1996, The Spanish Prisoner, 1996, Wag the Dog, 1997, Ronin, 1998, The Winslow Boy, 1999; dir.: (films) State and Main, 2000, Heist, 2001; author: (children's books) Warm and Cold with drawings by Donald Sultan, 1985, The Duck and the Goat, Jafsie & John Henry, 1999, Bar Mitzvah, 1999, (essays) Writing In Restaurants, 1986, SomeFreaks, 1989, on Directing Film, 1990, The Cabin, 1992; actor: (essays) Make-Believe-Town, 1996; author: (novels) The Village, 1994, The Old Religion, 1996, True and False, 1996, 3 Uses of the Knife, 1996, Wilson, 2001, (screenplays) State & Main, 2000, Heist, 2001, Passover, The Duck and the Goat, 1996, Henrietta, 1999, the Hero Pony, 1990, (poetry) The China Man, 1999, Wilson, 2000; dir.: (films) House of Games, 1986, Oleanna, 1994, The Spanish Prisoner, 1996, The Winslow Boy, 1988; (plays) Dangerous Corner, 1995. Recipient Outer Critics Circle award for contbn. to Am. theater, 1978; Acad. award nominee for best screenplay adaptation, 1983, 98; Rockefeller grantee, 1977; CBS Creative Writing fellow Yale U. Drama Sch., 1976-77

MAMLOK, URSULA, composer, educator; b. Berlin, Feb. 1, 1928; d. John and Dorothy Lewis; m. Dwight G. Mamlok, Nov. 27, 1947. Student, Mannes Coll. Music, 1942-45; MusB, Manhattan Sch. Music, 1955, MusM, 1958. Mem. faculty dept. music NYU, 1967-74, CUNY, 1971-74; prof. composition Manhattan Sch. Music, N.Y.C., 1974—. Composer numerous works including Variations and Interludes for 4 percussionists, 1973, Sextet, 1977, Festive Sounds, 1978, When Summer Sang, 1980, piano trio Panta rhei, 1981, 5 recital pieces for young pianists, 1983, From My Garden for solo viola or solo violin, 1983, Concertino for wind quintet, strings and percussion, 1984, Der Andreas Garten for voice, flute and harp, 1986, Alariana for recorder, clarinet, bassoon, violin and cello, 1986, 3 Bagatelles for harpsichord, 1987, 5 Bagatelles for clarinet, violin, cello, 1988, Rhapsody for clarinet, viola, piano Inward Journey for Piano, 1989, Sonata for violin and piano, 1989, Music for flute, violin, cello, 1990, Girasol, a sextet for flute, violin, viola, cello and piano, 1991, Constellations for orch., 1993, Polarities for flute, violin, cello, piano, 1995, Festive Sounds for Organ, String Quartet II, 1996-97, Two Thousan Notes for Piano, 2000-01, Confluencies for Clarinet, Violin, Cello, Piano, 2002. Recipient Opus One Rec. award Am. Composers Alliance, 1987, Serge Koussevitzky Found. commn., 1988, Walter Hinrichsen award Acad. Inst. Arts and Letters, 1989, commn. San Francisco Symphony, 1990; Nat. Endowment Arts grantee, 1974, Am. Inst. Acad. Arts and Letters grantee, 1981, 89, Martha Baird Rockefeller grantee, 1982; John Simon Gugenheim fellow, 1995. Mem. Am. Soc. Univ. Composers, Am. Women Composers, N.Y. Women Composers, Internat. League Women Composers, Am. Music Ctr., Internat. Soc Contemporary Music (bd. dirs.), Fromm Found. Commn., Am. Guild Organists Continuum Commn. Address: 315 E 86th St New York NY 10028-4714 *In my music, I have never striven for novelty nor originality for its own sake. Rather, my primary concern as a composer has been the consolidation of older and newer techniques, as they best serve the work at hand.*

MAMMEL, RUSSELL NORMAN, retired food distribution company executive; b. Hutchinson, Kans., Apr. 28, 1926; s. Vyvian E. and Mabel Edwina (Hursh) M.; m. Betty Crawford, Oct. 29, 1949 (dec. Oct. 1994); children: Mark, Christopher, Elizabeth, Nancy. BS, U. Kans., 1949. With Mammel's Inc., Hutchinson, 1949-57, pres., 1957-59; retail gen. mgr. Kans. divsn. Nash Finch Co., 1959-61, retail gen. mgr. Iowa divsn. Cedar Rapids, 1961-66, dir. store devel. Mpls., 1966-75, v.p., 1975-83, exec. v.p., 1983-85, pres., COO, 1985-91, also bd. dirs., 1991-97; pvt. investments, 1991—. With AUS, 1944-46. Home: 6808 Cornelia Dr Minneapolis MN 55435-1608 Office: Nash Finch Co 7600 France Ave S Ste 200 Minneapolis MN 55435-5920

MAMMOLA, GEORGE CHARLES, business executive; b. Garfield, N.J., Dec. 20, 1940; s. Charles and Anna (Cascino) M.; m. Virginia A. Pasquariello, Mar. 12, 1941. BBA, U. Notre Dame, 1962; postgrad. Bus. Sch., Harvard U., 1975. Fin. mgmt. trainee GE, N.Y., 1962-64; v.p., contr. Interpace, Parsippany, N.J., 1964-74, v.p. sales and mktg., 1974-80; exec. v.p. PPS, Cranford, 1980-89; exec. v.p., gen. mgr. REECO, Morris Plains, 1989-92; exec. v.p. svc. and maintenance Rsch.-Cottrell, Somerville, 1993, sr. v.p., gen. mgr., 1994, pres. indsl. group, 1994, pres., CEO, 1994-99; pres. Boyden Cons. Corp., Morristown, 1999, MT Consulting Corp., Wayne, 2000—. Mem. State of N.J. Sm. Bus. Compliance Adv. Panel. Mem. Inst. Mgmt. Accts., N.J. Country Club (pres. 1987-88). Office: MT Consulting Corp 48 Darlington Dr Wayne NJ 07470-2806

MAMMONE, RICHARD JAMES, engineering educator; b. N.Y.C., Sept. 3, 1953; s. Americo Anth and Helen (Kowalski) M.; m. Christine Podilchuk, Aug. 19, 1989; children: Robert, Jason, Richard, James Jr. BE, CCNY, 1975, ME, 1977; PhD, CUNY, 1981. Computer systems analyst Picatinny Arsenal, Dover, N.J., 1975-77; rsch. fellow CCNY, 1977-81; asst. prof. Manhattan Coll., Riverdale, N.Y., 1981-82; assoc. prof. engring. Rutgers U., Piscataway, N.J., 1981-93, prof., 1993—. Co-founder Computed Anatonomy Inc., N.Y.C., 1982; founder SpeakEZ, Inc., N.J., 1992, chmn. of bd., 1995—; chief tech. advisor, bd. dirs T-NETIX, Inc., Colo., 1995—; founder, CEO Visionary Systems Inc. (VSI), 1999; cons. in field. Co-author: Image Recovery: Theory and Applications, Acad. Press Pubs., 1987, Computational Methods of Signal Recovery and Recognition, 1992; co-editor: Neural Networks: Theory and Applications, 1991; editor: Artificial Neural Networks for Speech and Vision, 1993; editor Pattern Recognition Jour., 1989—; series editor Chapman-Hall on Neural Networks, 1991—; editor artificial neural networks speech and vision Chapman-Hall Pubs., 1993—; asst. editor IEEE Transactions on Speech and Audio Processing, IEEE Transactions on Neural Networks; contbr. articles to profl. jours.; patentee in filed. Assoc. Whitaker Found. grant, 1982, NSF grant, 1992; Internat. Tel. & Tel. grant, 1984; CAIP Rsch. Ctr. grant, 1985; Henry Rutgers fellow, 1985-87; U.S. Nat. Security Agy. grant, 1986—, USAF grant, 1986—, Temeplex grant, 1986—. Mem. IEEE (sr., editor Comms. Jour. 1983-89), N.Y. Acad. Scis. Office: Rutgers U Dept Elec Engring Piscataway NJ 08854

MAMON, DORIS ELAINE, laboratory administrator; b. Chgo., Jan. 31, 1943; d. Julius S. and Helen M. Bonk; children: Deborah, Vincent. BS, Mundelein Coll., 1976; MBA, Marquette U., 1981; MT, St. Mary of Nazareth Sch. Med. Tech., 1964; Diplomate lab. mgmt., 1989. Sect. head immunohematology Alexian Bros. Med. Center, Elk Grove Village, Ill., 1969-78; supr. implementation Medistat, Milw., 1978-80; supr. product analyst Tymshare Med. Systems, Brookfield, Wis., 1980-81; sr. mgmt. cons. The Kennedy Group, Menlo Park, Calif., 1981-83; lab. mgr. Sherman Hosp., Elgin, Ill., 1984-93; mgr. Healthcare Devel. Svcs., Northbrook, Ill., 1993-94; sr. cons. HBO & Co., Atlanta, 1994—. Mem. Am. Soc. Clin. Pathologists, Clin. Lab. Mgmt. Assn.

MAMUT, MARY CATHERINE, retired entrepreneur; b. Calabria, Italy, Oct. 17, 1923; came to U.S., 1928; d. Carmelo Charles and Caterina (Tripodi) Cogliandro; m. Michael Matthew Mamut, May 15, 1954; children: Anthony Carl, Charles Terrance. Student, Stenotype Comml. Coll., 1946-50. Sec. to pres. Thomas Goodfellow, Inc., Detroit, 1942-50; asst. to v.p. R.G. Moeller Co., 1951-52; sec. to pres. United Steel Supply Co., 1952-54; sec. to libr. Farmington (Mich.) Schs., 1962-68; real estate agt., 1969; owner, mgr. Crystal Fair, Birmingham, Mich., 1969-88, ret. Tchr. Stenotype Comml. Coll., Detroit, 1952-54. Vol. Henry Ford Mus., Dearborn, Mich., 1989-90, Greenfield Village, 1989-90, West Bloomfield Libr., 1993-95. Recipient World Lifetime Achievement award Am. Biog. Inst. U.S.A., 1993. Mem. Am. Bus. Women's Assn., Birmingham-Bloomfield C. of C., Profl. Secs. Internat, NAFE. Roman Catholic. Avocations: reading, music, art, theater. Home: 7423 Coach Ln West Bloomfield MI 48322-4022

MAN, LAWRENCE KONG, architect, entrepreneur, graphics, furniture and fashion designer; b. Kowloon, Hong Kong, July 4, 1953; s. Hon-Kwong Man and Sau-Ching Luk. Student, U. Redlands, 1971-72; BArch, U. Oreg., 1977; MArch, Harvard U., 1978. Registered architect, Mass., Calif. Designer, project architect Shepley Bulfinch Richardson & Abbott, Boston, 1978-86; project designer, project architect E. Verner Johnson & Assoc., 1987-91; owner Lawrence Man Architect, Cambridge, Mass., 1992-95, L.A., 1994—. Bd. dirs. Fashion Bus. Incubator. Prin. works include MAN studio, Fong House, San Marino, Calif., Tighe Summer House, Sagamore Beach, Mass, Frozen Fusion Juice Bar, L.A. schs., Fed. Credit Union, L.A., Pub. Mus. Grand Rapids, Mich. (AIA Grand Valley Disting. Bldg. award 1997), LCP Studio, Somerville, Mass., New Asia Restaurants, Danvers and Arlington, Mass., Tai Pan Restaurant, Cambridge, Mass. (Honor award AIA 1993, New Eng. award Excellence in Architecture 1993, Design Excellence award Nat. Orgn. Minority Architects 1993), Ti-Sales Office, Sudbury, Mass. (Design Excellence award Nat. Orgn. Minority Architects 1993), Dental Clinic, Reading, Mass. (AIA Interior Architecture award 1992, Interior Design Project award Am. Soc. Interior Designers 1991, Boston Exports citation AIA 1990, Boston Soc. of Architects/New Eng. Healthcare Assembly honor award, 1994), Mus. Ctr. Union Terminal, Cin. (Reconstrn. award 1991), Ramesses Pavilion Boston Mus. Sci. (Double Vision award/Double Silver Soc. Environ. Graphics 1990), Smithsonian South Quadrangle Mus., Washington (Boston Exports award/citation AIA 1990, Honor award AIA 1989), U. Vt. Student Ctr., Burlington, Campus Ctr. Study and Libr. addition Franklin & Marshall Coll., Andover (Mass.) Co. Corp. Hdqs., Emerson Hosp., Concord, Mass., pvt. residences, others. Mem. AIA, Am. Assn. Mus., Fashion Bus. Incubator (bd. dirs.). Avocations: dancing, traveling, music. E-mail: lawrencemanarchitects@hotmail.com. *There are ups and downs in life. It is more rewarding to experience them all, no matter how hard it may get sometimes. It allows you to become a more complete person. That is, in my view, a true achievement.*

MAN, MARY ANN, medical technologist; b. Durham, N.C., Apr. 14, 1945; d. Robert Martin and Edna Lee (Henley) M. BS, Ctrl. Mich. U., 1968. Med. technologist Branch County Community Health Ctr., Coldwater, Mich., 1967-68, Good Samaritan Hosp., Cin., 1968-77, Lykes Meml. Hosp., Brooksville, Fla., 1977, South Fla. Bapt. Hosp., Plant City, 1977-78, James A. Haley Vets. Hosp., Tampa, Fla., 1978—, social chmn. lab. svc., 1990. Mem. disability com. Vets. Hosp., 1990-92; mem. abilities guild Abilities of Fla., 1993, Ams. with Disabilities Act Ctr., 1993—. Named Outstanding Handicapped Fed. Employee of Yr., Vets. Adminstrn., 1981. Democrat. Episcopalian. Avocations: tennis, swimming, biking, collecting hummingbirds and shells. Office: James A Haley Vets Hosp 13000 Bruce B Downs Blvd Tampa FL 33612-4745

MANABE, SYUKURO, climatologist; b. Shingu-Mura, Uma-Gun, Ehime-ken, Japan, Sept. 21, 1931; came to U.S., 1958; s. Seiichi and Sueko (Akashi) M.; m. Nobuko Nakamura, Jan. 21, 1962; children: Nagisa M., Yukari C. BS, Tokyo U., 1953, MS, 1955, DS, 1958. Rsch. meteorologist U.S. Weather Bur., Washington, 1958-63; sr. rsch. meteorologist Geophys. Fluid Dynamics Lab. NOAA, 1963-68, sr. rsch. meterologist geophys. fluid dynamics lab. Princeton, N.J., 1968-95, mem. sr. exec. svc. of U.S., 1979-95, sr. scientist, 1995-97; dir. global warming rsch. program Frontier Rsch. Sys. for Global Change , Yokohama, Japan, 1997—2001; vis. rsch. collaborator Program in Atmospheric and Oceanic Scis. Princeton U., 2002—. Lectr. with rank of prof. Princeton U., 1968-98; joint sci. com. World Climate Rsch. Program, 1981-87; bd. atmospheric sci. and climate NRC, 1988-91; com. on Geoscis., Environ. and Resources, NRC, 1990-93, climate rsch. com., 2001--; panel on climate and global change NOAA, 1988-97. Recipient Gold medal U.S. Dept. Commerce, 1970, Presdl. Rank Meritorious Exec. award Pres. of U.S., 1989, Acad. award of Blue Planet prize Asahi Glass Found., 1992, Asahi prize Asahi Daily Found., 1996, Volvo Environ. prize Volvo Found., 1997, Milankovitch medal European Geophys. Soc., 1998. Fellow AAAS, Am. Geophys. Union (Revelle medal 1993), Am. Meteorol. Soc. (hon. mem., Meisinger award 1967, 2d half century award 1977, Rossby medal 1992); mem. NAS, Acad. Europaea (fgn.), Royal Soc. Can. (fgn.), Japan Meteorol Soc. (hon., Fujiwara award 1966). Achievements include the first numerical modeling study of global warming. Home: 6 Governors Ln Princeton NJ 08540-3666 Office: Princeton U Sayre Hall Forrestal Campus PO Box CN710 Princeton NJ 08544-0710

MANAHAN, JAMES HINCHON, lawyer; b. Madelia, Minn., Aug. 27, 1936; s. Cecil James and Ruth Pearl (Hinchon) M.; m. Suzanne Colette Laurendeau, June 14, 1958 (div. 1975); children: Theodore, Corinne, Matthew, Anne; m. Vanda Botts Hedges, Jan. 30, 1989. AB, Harvard U., 1958, JD, 1961; BA in Spanish, Minn. State U., Mankato, 2001. Bar: Minn. 1961, U.S. Dist. Ct. Minn. 1961, U.S. Ct. Appeals (8th cir.) 1962, U.S. Supreme Ct. 1971, Hawaii 1989, Colo. 1990. Ptnr. Farrish, Zimmerman, Johnson & Manahan, Mankato, Minn., 1962-72, Manahan, Bluth and Kohlmeyer, Mankato, 1972—. Asst. prof. mass comm. law and law enforcement Mankato State U., 1970-82; pub. defender Blue Earth County, 1980-2000; apptd. by Minn. Supreme Ct. to Lawyers Trust Account Bd., 1983-91, Bd. Legal Certification, 1996-99, Jud. Selection Commn., 2001—; Fulbright Scholar, U. Austral, Chile, tchg. US criminal law and procedure, 2002. Chair Common Cause in Minn., 1974-75; sec. Mankato Police CSC, 1971-76; pres. Mankato LWV, 2000-2001; sec.-treas. Mankato Area NOW, 1977-79; precinct chair Democratic Farm Labor Party, Mankato, 1976-78, conv. del., 1976, 78, 82, 84, 88, 98. Fellow Am. Bar Found. (life); mem. Minn. Bar Assn. (CLE lectr., 1966, 78, 82, 89, 90, 91, 92, 93, 2000, pres. 6th dist. Bar Assn. 1974-75, chair Criminal Law Sect. 1977-78, chair com. human rights 1981-83), ABA (exec. coun. Sect. Individual Rights and Responsibilities 1978-84, chair com. freedom of speech and press 1980-82, news editor Human Rights mag. 1976-92), Minn. Trial Lawyers Assn. (bd. dirs. 1990-99), Acad. Cert. Trial Lawyers of Minn. (dean 1987-88), ACLU (nat. bd. dirs. 2000—), Minn. Civil Liberties Union (pres. 1998-2000), Nat. Bd. Trial Advocacy (cert. civil and criminal trial specialists 1982—), Am. Acad. Matrimonial Lawyers (pres. Minn. chpt. 1991-92, nat. bd. 1990-96). Home: 1200 W River Dr Mankato MN 56001-1735 Office: Manahan Bluth and Kohlmeyer PO Box 287 Mankato MN 56002-0287 E-mail: vandajim@mnic.net.

MANAHAN, JOAN ELSIE, health and physical education educator; b. Haskell, N.J., Jan. 18, 1940; d. Edward A. and Elsie G. (Beckmann) M. BA, Trenton State Coll., 1962; MA, Columbia U., 1966, EdD, 1975. Tchr., coach Bloomfield (N.J.) Bd. Edn., 1962-97. Cons. Nat. Dairy Coun., 1970s. Cons. (book): Basic Stuff: Motor Learning and Performance; contbr. articles to profl. jours. Grantee A+ For Kids Tchr. Network, Inc., 1992-93; recipient Proclamation, N.J. State Legislature, 1997. Mem. NEA, AAHPER (cons. 1980s, 1990s), Am. Archery Assn., N.J. AHPER, N.J. Athletic Assn. (treas. 1966-67, co-editor newsletter 1967-68, archery tournament chairperson 1965-75), N.J. Edn. Assn., Essex County Coaches Assn., Kappa Delta Pi, Pi Lambda Theta. Roman Catholic. Avocations: collecting playing cards and swizzle sticks, life master bridge.

MANAKER, ARNOLD MARTIN, mechanical engineer, consultant; b. N.Y.C., Feb. 11, 1947; s. Paul Bernard and Rose Norma (Malakoff) M.; m. Ellen Conant, Nov. 21, 1970; children: Ryan Scott, Heidi Cora, Jana Ashley. BSME, Newark Coll. of Eng., 1968; MS in Mech. Engring., U. Mass., 1970, PhD in Mech. Engring., 1973. Asst. to plant engr. J. Wiss & Sons Co., Newark, 1965-68; rsch. asst. Dept. Mech. and Aerospace Engring., U. Mass., Amherst, 1968-73, teaching asst., 1970-72; pvt. practice cons., 1972—; staff engr., Clinch River Breeder Reaction Project TVA, Oak Ridge, 1976-77, mech. engr. Chattanooga, 1977-79, project mgr. adv. energy, 1979, project mgr. AFBC R & D, 1979-81, project mgr. AFBC Demonstration Plant, 1984-88, AFBC devel. project engr., 1988-91, mgr. NOx/CEMS projects, 1991-95, mgr. program svcs., 1995-97; project mgr. Strategic Sourcing, 1997-99, Paradise SCR, 1999—. Adminstrv. asst. NASA, 1968-69; rsch. asst. NSF, 1971-73. Contbr. numerous articles to profl. jours. Vol. United Way Leadership Club, 1987-92, Friends Always Indian Guide Program/YMCA, 1988-92. Named Engr. of Yr., TVA, 1989; recipient Product Champion award Electric Power Rsch. Inst., 1992. Fellow ASME (officer coms.). Jewish. Avocations: racquetball, tennis, baseball, sports car racing. Home: 9420 Mountain Shadows Dr Chattanooga TN 37421-3444

MANAKOS, FROSO P. real estate executive; b. Bethlehem, Pa., Feb. 27, 1931; d. Dimitrios N. and Voula (Coumides) Perdikis; m. Peter George Manakos, Sept. 1, 1957; 1 child, George Peter. Dep. sec. adminstrn. Dept. of State Commonwealth of Pa., 1950; treasury fin. dept. Bethlehem Steel Corp., 1950-85; pres. Manakos Co., Bethlehem, 1963—. Heritage affairs commr. Commonwealth of Pa., Harrisburg, 1980-88; mem. leadership com. Rep. State Com. Pa., 1984—; chmn. Pa. Rep. Heritage, 1994; vice chmn. Rep. City Com., Bethlehem, 1994; events chmn. Lehigh County Rep., Allentown, Pa.,1982-94; treas., past pres. Lehigh County Coun. Rep. Women, Allentown, 1994; chmn. Lehigh County Rep. Com., 1994—; sec. parish coun. St. Nicholas Greek Orthodox Ch., 1994-96. Mem. Pa. Soc., Order of Ea. Star (matron 1984-85), Daus. Penelope (dist. gov. 1961-62, pres. 1960-61). Avocations: political activities, travel to Europe, stock market. Fax: 610-434-8034.

MANARY, RICHARD DEANE, manufacturing executive; b. Des Moines, Nov. 11, 1944; s. Robert Claude and Veronica (Cornwell) M.; m. Eileen Cecile, Aug. 16, 1986; children: Erica (dec.), Matthew, Stephen, Lauren. AA in Indsl. Engring., Southwestern Coll., 1976; BA in History, Calif. State U., San Diego, 1967, BS in Edn., 1973; grad., Stanford U. Bus. Ext., 1991; MBA, Nat. U., 1993. Registered profl. engr., Calif.; cert. elem. tchr., Calif. Mfg. engr. Rohr Industries, San Diego, 1967-78, chief R&D divsn. Riverside, 1978-80, project mfg. mgr., 1980-84, dep. program mgr. Wichita, Kans., 1984-87, mgr. Titan 3d, Titan IV missile programs Riverside, 1987-89, program mgr. MD-11, 1989-91, gen. program mgr. Boing mil. programs Calif., 1991-95, gen. mgr. space products divsn., 1995-97; program mgr. tactical mil. fighters Goodrich, 1997-99; dir. ops. B.F. Goodrich, 1999-2000; plant mgr. Goodrich Co., Dallas, 2000—01, ops. dir. Riverside, Calif., 2001—02, dir. plant facilities and indsl. engring., 2002—. Contbr. articles to profl. jours. Chmn. employee and community assistance program Rohr Industries, Riverside, 1981-85; adv. Riverside chpt. Jr. Achievement, 1978-79. Mem. Soc. Mfg. Engrs. (sr., assoc., chmn. 1978-79), Soc. Automotive Engrs., Soc. Material and Process Engrs., Am. Soc. Metals, Nat. Mgmt. Assn. (chmn. 1980-81), Aerospace Industries Assn. (space com.), Air Force Assn., San Diego Port Tenants Assn., KC. Democrat. Roman Catholic. Avocations: backpacking, skiing, stamp collecting, travel, Little League baseball. Home: 4098 Martin Canyon Ct Bonita CA 91902-2562 Office: 850 Lagoon Dr Chula Vista CA 91910-2001

MANAS, GERALD BENNETT, systems consultant, project manager; b. Phila., Mar. 15, 1960; s. Sidney Ralph and Barbara M.; m. Sharon Erica Olson, Sept. 10, 1989; 1 child: Elizabeth Rose. Student, Temple U., 1978-79. Cert. project mgmt. Am. Mgmt. Assn., project mgmt. profl. Project Mgmt. Inst., Microsoft Project Users Group. Programmer Alfred Angelo, Inc., Willow Grove, Pa., 1978-81, Pepper, Hamilton & Scheetz, Phila., 1981-82; programmer, analyst Hurst Performance, Warminster, 1982-85; systems analyst C&D Power Systems, Plymouth Meeting, 1985-87; mgr. product devel. Centennial Systems, Wayne, 1987-89; mgr. edn. Responsive Software Solutions, 1989-90; client mgr. Lever 8 Solutions, a Safeguard Co., 1990—. Pres. Manas Comm., Inc., Phila., 1994-96; chmn. round table Del. Valley Computer Users Group, Phila., 1987-88. Songwriter September Forever, 1996; author: Project Management According to Napoleon, 2002. Mem. Nat. Acad. Songwriters, Alliance Francaise Phila., Del. Valley Entrepreneur's Club (pres., founder 1994-96). Democrat. Jewish. Avocations: music, art, photography, writing, French studies. Office: Lever 8 Solutions 950 W Valley Rd Ste 2301 Wayne PA 19087-6890

MANAS, MIROSLAV, economics educator, researcher; b. Prague, Czech Republic, July 10, 1935; s. Jan and Bozena (Berankova) M.; m. Vera Hlucha, Dec. 20, 1960; children: Jan, Petr. CSc, Charles U., Prague, 1965, RNDr, 1966; DSc in Quantitative Econs., U. Econs., Prague, 1988. Lectr. quantitative econs. U. Econs., Prague, 1961-62, sr. lectr., 1962-78, asst. prof., 1978-84, prof., 1984—, dir. Ctrl. and East European Studies Program, 1993—, vice rector sci. and rsch., 1998-2000. Author: Theory of Games and Optimal Decisions, 1974, Theory of Games and Its Applications, 1991; co-author:

Mathematical Models in Economics, 1989. Mem. Czech Soc. for Ops. Rsch., Czech Econometrical Soc. Avocation: gardening. Office: U Econs Nam W Churchilla 4 13067 Prague 3 Czech Republic

MANASC, VIVIAN, architect, consultant; b. Bucharest, Romania, May 19, 1956; d. Bercu and Bianca (Smetterling) M.; m. William A. Dushenski, Feb. 25, 1984; children: Peter Gabriel, Lawrence Alexander. BS in Architecture, McGill U., Montreal, Que., Can., 1977, BArch, 1979; MBA, U. Alta., Edmonton, 1982. Architectural insp. Transport Can., Edmonton, 1977-79; project architect Bell Spotowski Architects, 1980-82; asst. dir. design constrn. Edmonton Pub. Schs., 1982-84; mgr., prin. Ferguson, Simek, Clark Architects Ltd., Edmonton, 1985-88; mng. dir. FSC Groves Hodgson Manasc Architects Ltd., 1988-97; pres. Manasc Isaac Archs., 1997—. Adj. asst. prof. of architecture, U. Calgary; bd. dirs. Can. Archtl. Accreditation Bd. Contbr. articles to profl. jours. Co-chair innovative practice group in arch. United Way Edmonton, sect. chair, cabinet mem., Edmonton, 1980-82; mentor RAIC Syllabus Program, Edmonton, 1982-88; bd. dirs. Econ. Devel. Edmonton. Scholar McGill U., 1974. Fellow Royal Archtl. Inst. Can. (bd. dirs.); mem. Alta. Assn. Archs., Manitoba Assn. Archs., B.C. Assn. Archs., Saskatchewan Assn. Archs., Coun. Edn. Facility Planners, Nat. Coun. Jewish Women (past pres. Edmonton sect.), Jewish Fedn. Edmonton (v.p. planning). Avocations: extensive internat. travel, photography, writing. Fax: (780) 426-3 70. E-mail: vivian@miarch.com.

MANASSAH, EDWARD E. publisher; b. Sharon, Pa., Mar. 8, 1947; BS, BA, Youngstown State Univ. Pres., publ. The Courier-Journal, Louisville, 1993—. Office: The Courier Journal 525 W Broadway Louisville KY 40202-2137*

MANASSAH, JAMAL TEWFEK, electrical engineering educator, research and technology management consultant; b. Haifa, Palestine, Feb. 23, 1945; s. Tewfek George and Alia Nasrallah (Kardoush) M.; m. Azza Tarek H.I. Mikdadi, Mar. 16, 1979; children: Tala, Nigh. BSc, Am. U., Beirut, Lebanon, 1966; MA, Columbia U., 1968, PhD, 1970. Mem. Inst. Advanced Study, Princeton, N.J., 1970-72, 74-79; asst. prof. Am. U. Beirut, 1972-75; chief sci. adviser Kuwait Inst. Sci. Rsch., 1976-81; COO Kuwait Found., 1979-81; prof. dept. elec. engring. CUNY, N.Y.C., 1981—. Cons. Columbia Radiation Labs., N.Y.C., 1970-73, Ford Found., N.Y.C., 1973-79, NSF, Washington, 1978-83; chmn. Internat. Symposium Series, Kuwait, 1979-81; bd. dirs. Technopro, N.Y.C., 1982-86; mng. dir. Khayatt and Co., Inc., N.Y.C., 1982; mem. organizing com. Chem. Rsch. Applied to World Needs II, 1980-83; mem. Welfare Assn., Geneva, 1984-92; mem. steering com. Internat. Workshop on Laser Physics, 1993-2000; editl. bd. Internat. Jour. Laser Physics, 1994—. Editor: Alternate Energy Sources (2 vols.) 1981; (with others) Advances in Food Producing Systems for Arid and Semiarid Lands (2 vols.), 1981, Innovations in Telecommunication (2 vols.), 1982, (with others) Transient Coherent Phenomena, 1995, Elementary Mathematical and Computational Tools for Electrical and Computer Engineering Using MATLAB, 2001; contbr. more than 150 monographs, reports and rsch. papers in statis. field theory, nonlinear and quantum optics, photonics, ultrafast phenomena and new techs. assessment. Commr. Lebanese Boy Scouts Assn., Beirut, 1972-75; adviser internat. program NSF, 1979-83. Columbia U. faculty fellow, 1966-68, Pfister fellow, 1968-70; grantee NSF, 1982-87; recipient ABI Key award, 1987, Commemorative medal of honor, 1988; named Man of Yr., 1990. Mem. Assn. Inst. for Advanced Study. Internat. Platform Assn., Princeton Club. Christian Orthodox. Achievements include the theoretical discovery or co-discovery of resonant absorption coefficient frequency shift, collective Lamb shift, pion minus condensation in nuclear matter, blackbody frequency shift, dynamical Lorenz shift, reflectivity frequency shift, induced coherent pulse compression, induced spectral broadening, induced frequency shift, three-photons frequency shift, twin peaks in second harmonics generation, induced waveguiding and focusing, time-space superspike, non-linear compression of noise correlation time, soliton phases, coherently inhibited amplification, induced channeling, delayed reflectivity, two-color photon echos, superradiance without inversion, pressure induced cavities. Home: 55 E 87th St Apt 15G New York NY 10128-1051 Office: CUNY Dept Elec Engring Convent Ave New York NY 10031 E-mail: manassah@ccny.cuny.edu.

MANASSE, ARLYNN H. pediatric nurse practitioner; b. Aurora, Ill., Apr. 10, 1947; d. Oliver J. and Arlene M. (Lehman) Hem; m. Henri R. Manasse Jr., Aug. 9, 1969; children: Bryan, Sheralynn. BSN, U. Ill., Chgo., 1969, MPH, 1989; pediatric nurse practitioner cert., Rush-Presbyn.-St. Luke's Ctr., 1971. Pub. health nurse, pediatric nurse practitioner, acting dir. Infant Welfare Soc., Chgo., 1969-72; pediatric nurse practitioner Mpls. Health Dept., 1972-74; pub. health nurse, pediatric nurse practitioner LaGrange (Ill.) Cmty. Nurse and Svc. Assn., 1978-88; pediatric nurse practitioner Bethel Wholistic Health Ctr., Chgo., 1991-93, Circle Family Care, Chgo., 1994—; adj. nursing faculty U. Ill., 1994—. Regional health adv. bd. Cmty. and Econ. Devel. Assn., Head Start, Chgo., 1978-88. Active, mem. of choir Western Springs (Ill.) Bapt. Ch., 1976—; bd. dirs., officer Westside Holistic Family Svcs., Chgo., 1990—. Fellow Nat. Assn. Pediatric Nurse Assocs. and Practitioners; mem. ANA, Ill. Nurses Assn., Am. Pub. Health Assn., Ill. Pub. Health Assn. Avocations: professional sports, travel.

MANASSE, HENRI RICHARD, JR. association executive; b. Amsterdam, The Netherlands, Nov. 27, 1945; came to U.S., 1954, naturalized, 1963; s. Henri David and Janny Lynn (Borst) M.; m. Arlynn Hem, Aug. 9, 1969; children: Bryan, Sheralynn. BS in Pharmacy, U. Ill., Chgo., 1968; MA, Loyola U., Chgo., 1972; PhD, U. Minn., 1974; DSc (hon.), Campbell U., 1997, Union U., 1997, Mercer U., 1998. Lic. pharmacist, Ill. Rsch. pharmacist Xttrium Labs., Chgo., 1968-69; asst. to dean Coll. Pharmacy U. Ill., 1969-72, asst. prof. pharmacy adminstrn., 1974-77, assoc. dean, 1977-80, acting dean, 1980-81, dean, prof., 1981-93, interim vice chancellor for health svcs., 1992-93; prof. coll. pharmacy and medicine U. Iowa, v.p. for health scis., 1993-96; exec. v.p.-designate Am. Soc. Health-Sys. Pharmacists, 1996—, CEO, exec. v.p., 1997—. Sr. policy fellow Ctr. on Drugs and Pub. Policy, U. Md., 1988—; mem. Ill. Bd. Pharmacy, Springfield, 1982-94; pub. mem. Am. Soc. Hosp. Pharmacists Commn. on Credentialling, Bethesda, Md., 1984-86; chair bd. dirs. Nat. Patient Safety Found. AMA, 1999-2001; mem. adv. bd. PEW Found. Health Professions Edn. Reform Commn.; bd. dirs. Am. Soc. Cons. Pharmacists Rsch. and Edn. Found. Mem. editl. bd. Am. Jour. Hosp. Pharmacy, 1990-92; contbr. chpts. to books and articles to profl. jours. Pres. Downers Grove Sch. Bd. Caucus, Ill., 1984-85; bd. dirs. med. svc. Westside Holistic Ctr., Chgo., 1979—. Recipient Lederle Faculty award Lederle Pharm. Co., 1975, Outstanding Achievement award U. Minn., 1998; named Alumnus of Yr., U. Ill. Alumni Assn., 1983. Fellow Inst. Medicine Chgo.; mem. Am. Assn. Colls. Pharmacy (pres., adminstrv. bd. 1982-86, bd. dirs. 1984-86, pres. 1988-89), Am. Soc. Health Sys. Pharmacists, Nat. Acad. Scis., Inst. Medicine-NAS, Am. Pharm. Assn., Am. Soc. Assn. Execs. Baptist. Avocations: computers, international travel. Home: 10118 Vanderbilt Cir Rockville MD 20850-4674 E-mail: hrmjr@ashp.org.

MANASSON, VLADIMIR ALEXANDROVICH, physicist; b. Chernovtsy, Ukraine, Mar. 4, 1952; came to U.S., 1991; s. Alexander and Chaya (Finkelsteyn) M.; m. Katrine Kokhanovskaya, Aug. 2, 1975; children: Alexander, Julia. BSEE, Moscow Inst. Electronic Mfg., 1973, MSEE, 1974; PhD in Physics, Chernovtsy U., 1984. Entr. Acad. Scis. Ukraine Material Sci. Inst., 1975-78, sr. engr., 1978-80, jr. rsch. assoc., 1980-85, sr. rsch. assoc., 1985-90; rsch. scientist Phys. Optics Corp., Torrance, Calif., 1991-94, sr. scientist, 1994-95; leader antenna devel. WaveBand Corp., 1996-98, dir. rsch., 1999-2000, v.p. R&D, 2000—. Patentee several photosensitive devices and antennae. Grantee, NSF, 1993—94, 1997, 1998, Dept. Def., 1994, 1995, 1996, 1997, 1998, 1999, 2001, U.S. Dept. Commerce, 1997, Nat. Rsch. Coun./Nat. Acad. of Sci., 1995, 1998, L.A. Regional Tech. Alliance, 1999, NASA, 2001, 2002, DOE, 2002. Mem. IEEE, Optical Soc. Am., Assn. of Old Crows. Avocations: piano improvising, reading, children, cooking. Office: 375 Van Ness Ave Torrance CA 90501-1497 E-mail: vmanasson@earthlink.net.

MANATOS, ANDREW E. public relations executive; b. Washington, July 7, 1944; m. Tina G. Weber, June 25, 1967; children: Mike A., Nick A., Tom A., George A. BA, Am. U., 1968, MA, 1969. Staff post office and civil service com. U.S. Senate, Washington, 1969-73; assoc. staff dir. of Senate Senator Thomas Eagleton, 1973-77; asst. sec. congl. affairs Dept. Commerce, Washington, 1977-81; owner Manatos & Manatos Inc., 1981—. Creator White House Conf. on Productivity, U.S. Senate Productivity Award, Greek Independence Day Resolution, (videotapes) U.S. Congress and You, Your Court System and You, The Executive Branch and You, Where We Stand; bd. dirs. Washington Coord. Coun. Productivity, 1981-88, Com. for Citizen Awareness, 1985—. Contbr. articles to N.Y. Times, Washington Post, Indianapolis Star. Bd. dirs., mem. nat. fin. com., co-chmn. Dukakis for Pres., 1987-88; mem. Archdiocesan Coun. & Leadership 100 Greek Orthodox Ch. Recipient Cross of Holy Sepulcher, Medal of St. Andrew, Ellis Island Medal of Honor Nat. Ethnic Coalition of Orgns.; named Archon, Greek Orthodox Ch. Office: Manatos & Manatos 601 13th St NW Ste 1150S Washington DC 20005-3883

MANATT, CHARLES TAYLOR, lawyer; b. Chgo., June 9, 1936; BS, Iowa State U., 1958; JD, George Washington U., 1962. Bar: Calif. 1962, U.S. Supreme Ct. 1967, D.C. 1985. Ptnr. Manatt, Phelps & Phillips, Washington, now chmn.; U.S. ambassador Dominican Republic, 1999—2001. Bd. editors George Washington Law Rev., 1960-62. Pres. Calif. Bankers Assn.; chmn. Nat. Democratic Inst., Calif. Democratic Com., Nat. Democratic Com., Internat. Found. for Election Sys. Mem. ABA, Calif. State Bar, L.A. County Bar Assn., San Fernando Valley Bar Assn. (pres. 1971-72), Century City Bar Assn., Phi Delta Phi, Delta Sigma Rho. Office: Manatt Phelps & Phillips 1501 M St NW Ste 700 Washington DC 20005-1737 also: Manatt Phelps & Phillips Trident Ctr E Tower 11355 W Olympic Blvd Los Angeles CA 90064-1614

MANATT, RICHARD, education educator; b. Odebolt, Iowa, Dec. 13, 1931; s. William Price and Lucille (Taylor) M.; m. Sally Jo Johnson, Aug. 20, 1952; children— Tamra Jo, Ann Lea, Joel Price; m. Jacquelyn M. Nesset, Feb. 25, 1970; 1 child, Megan Sue. BSc, Iowa State U., 1953, MS, 1956; PhD, U. Iowa, 1964. Prin. Oskloosa (Iowa) Schs., 1959-62; rsch. assoc. U. Iowa, Iowa City, 1962-64; mem. faculty Iowa State U., Ames, 1964—, prof., 1972—, chmn. dept. ednl. adminstrn., 1970-80, 93-98, dir. Sch. Improvement Model Projects, 1980—, univ. prof., 1998. Cons. performance evaluation for public and independent schs.; disting. vis. prof. Calif. State U., L.A. Author: Educator's Guide to the New Design, When Right is Wrong, Fundamentalists and the Public Schools, Clinical Manual for Teacher Performance Evaluation Compendias of Professional Growth Plans, (computer software program) Computer Assisted Teach Evaluation/Supervision. Served with AUS, 1953-55. Named Disting. Prof., Nat. Acad. Sch. Execs., 1979, Regents' Prof. Edn., 1994; recipient faculty citation Iowa State U. Alumni Assn., 1998, Margaret White Grad. Faculty award, 2001, Pres.'s award NAACP, 2002. Mem. NEA, NASSP, ASCD (Outstanding Cons. 1981), Am. Assn. Sch. Adminstrs., Phi Kappa Phi, Phi Delta Kappa, Delta Chi. Democrat. Methodist. Home: 2926 Monroe Dr Ames IA 50010-4362 E-mail: manatt@ames.net.

MANCALL, ELLIOTT LEE, neurologist, educator; b. Hartford, Conn., July 31, 1927; s. Nicholas and Bess Tuch M.; m. Jacqueline Sue Cooper, Dec. 27, 1953; children: Andrew Cooper, Peter Cooper. BS, Trinity Coll., Hartford, 1948; MD, U. Pa., 1952. Diplomate Am. Bd. Psychiatry and Neurology (dir. 1983-91, dir. emeritus, 1991—). Intern Hartford Hosp., 1952-54; clk. in neurology Nat. Hosp. Nervous Disease, London, 1954-55; asst. resident neurology Neurol. Inst. N.Y., 1955-56; resident neuropathology Mass. Gen. Hosp., 1956-57, clin. and research fellow, 1957-58; teaching fellow neuropathology Harvard Med. Sch., 1956-57; from asst. prof. neurology to assoc. prof. Jefferson Med. Coll., 1958-65; prof. medicine Hahnemann Med. Coll. and Hosp., 1965-76; prof. neurology Med. Coll. Pa.-Hahnemann U., 1993-95; prof. neurology, chmn. dept. Hahnemann Med. Coll. and Hosp., 1976-93; prof. neurology Jefferson Med. Coll., Phila., 1995—, interim chmn. dept. neurology, 1997—. Dir. Hahnemann U. ALS Clinic, 1985-95; chmn. bd. dirs. Phila. Profl. Standards Rev. Orgn., 1981-84. Author: (with others) The Human Cerebellum: A Topographical Atlas, 1961; (with B.J. Alpers) Clinical Neurology, 1971, Essentials of the Neurological Examination, 1971, 81; contbr. articles to profl. jours. With USN, 1945-47. Recipient Christian R. and Mary F. Lindback award, 1969, Oliver Meml. prize ophthalmology U. Pa., 1952 Fellow Am. Acad. Neurology (alt. del. to AMA 1982-86, gen. editor CONTINUUM 1991—, A.B. Baker award for excellence in neurol. edn. 1997); mem. Am. Neurol. Assn., Am. Assn. Neuropathology, Assn. Rsch. in Nervous and Mental Diseases, Soc. Neurosci., AAUP, Pa. Med. Peer Rev. Orgn. (dir. 1979-84), Phila. Neurol. Soc., Alpers Soc. Clin. Neurology, Coll. Physicians Phila., Sydenham Coterie, Phila. County Med. Soc., Pa. State Med. Soc., AMA (sec.-treas. sect. coun. neurology 1983-86), Am. Med. Soc. on Alcoholism, Neurology Intersoc. Liaison Group, Intersoc. Com. Neurol. Resources, Assn. Univ. Prof. Neurology (pres. 1988-90), Soc. for Exptl. Neuropathology, Am. Bd. Med. Specialties (exec. bd., chmn. com. study of evaluation procedures, 1992-99, rep. accreditation com. continuing med. edn. 1998—), Am. Bd. Psychiatry and Neurology (v.p. 1990, del. to Am. Bd. Med. Specialties, emeritus dir. 1991—), Pa. Blue Shield (profl. adv. coun. 1991-98). Home: PO Box 498 Lafayette Hill PA 19444-0498 Office: 1025 Walnut St Philadelphia PA 19107-5001 E-mail: elliott@mancall@mail.tju.edu.

MANCHESTER, ARTHUR HERSCHELL, English and foreign language educator; b. Aberdeen, Wash., July 25, 1933; s. Forrest E. and Annie (Nuttall) M.; m. Barbara Jane Sanford, Aug. 10, 1962; children: Vance Arthur, Eric Andrew. AB, N.W. Nazarene Coll., Nampa, Idaho, 1955; MA, U. Colo., 1958. Cert. in secondary edn., Oreg. Teaching asst. U. Colo., Boulder, 1957-58; prof. N.W. Nazarene Coll., 1958-60; tchr. R.E. Bennett Jr. H.S., Chehalis, Wash., 1960-62, Gresham (Oreg.) Union H.S., 1962-91; home instr. Multnomah County (Oreg.) Pub. Schs., 1996; home and hosp. tchr. Portland (Oreg.) Pub. Schs., 1991—; tchr. Gresham (Oreg.) Sam Barlow H.S., 1996-97. Analytical writing scorer Multnomah County and State of Oreg. Schs., 1987—. Author: Math Puzzles and Games, 1977, 2d edit., 1994. Recipient Dankstipendium, Deutscher Akademischer Austauschdienst, 1956-57, summer stipend NDEA, 1963, Honorarium, NEH, 1978. Mem. NEA, Oreg. Edn. Assn., Confedn. Oreg. Fgn. Lang. Tchrs. (pres. 1981-82, bd. dirs. 1978-80, 82-83). Republican. Nazarene. Avocations: walking, reading, word puzzles. Home: Apt 617 2545 SW Terwilliger Blvd Portland OR 97201-6307

MANCHESTER, KENNETH EDWARD, electronics executive, consultant; b. Winona, Minn., Mar. 22, 1925; s. Laurence Edwin and Daisy Idel (Finley) M.; m. Bonnie Lee Hardgrave, June 24, 1946; children: Cynthia Lee, David Scott. AB, San Jose State Coll., 1949; MS, Stanford U., 1950, PhD, 1955. Sr. chemist Shell Devel. Co., Emeryville, Calif., 1955-62; head chemistry sect. Sprague Electric Co., North Adams, Mass., 1962-63, head chemistry dept., 1963-69, dir. semiconductor rsch., devel. and engring., 1969-79, dir. quality assurance and reliability Worcester, 1979-85, v.p. corp. R & D North Adams, 1985-89, Sprague fellow, 1985; cons. semiconductor industry, 1989—. Lectr. Rensselaer Poly. Inst., Troy, N.Y., 1967. Contbr. articles to profl. jours.; patentee in field. Chmn. com. Troop 70 Boy Scouts Am. Sgt. U.S. Army Ground Forces, 1943-46, ETO. Mem. Am. Chem. Soc., AIME, Optimist Club, Sigma Xi. Republican. Avocations: woodworking, golf. E-mail: kmbucko@netzero.com.

MANCHESTER, PAUL BRUNSON, economist; b. Winsted, Conn., Oct. 7, 1942; s. Elbert Grant and Eleanor Elizabeth (Jones) M.; m. Ruth Elaine Garbisch, Oct. 25, 1969; children: Sarah H., Daniel P. BA, Yale U., 1964; PhD, U. Minn., 1973. Vol. Peace Corps, Colombia, 1964-66; teaching assoc. U. Minn., Mpls., 1966-69; asst. prof. Mary Washington Coll., Fredericksburg, Va., 1971-74; cons. U.S. Dept. Treasury, Washington, 1974-75; asst. prof. Cath. U. Am., 1974-78; cons. Robert R. Nathan Assocs., 1975-78; economist joint econ. com. U.S. Congress, 1978-89; econ. adviser to Tenn. senator U.S. Senate, 1988; sr. economist U.S. League Savs. Insts., 1989-90; economist Office Thrift Supervision, 1990-91; fin. economist U.S. Dept. HUD, 1991—. Contbr. articles to profl. jours. Pres. Woodmoor-Pinecrest Citizens' Assn., Silver Spring, Md.; del. Allied Civic Group, Silver Spring. Mem. Am. Econ. Assn., Soc. Govt. Economists, Nat. Economists Club (v.p. 1985, 87, bd. dirs. 1989-92). Lutheran. Avocations: tennis, skiing, bowling. Home: 105 Lexington Dr Silver Spring MD 20901-2546 Office: US Dept HUD 451 7th St SW Rm 8234 Washington DC 20410-0001

MANCHESTER, WILLIAM, writer; b. Attleboro, Mass., Apr. 1, 1922; s. William Raymond and Sallie Elizabeth (Thompson) M.; m. Julia Brown Marshall, Mar. 27, 1948 (dec. May 1998); children: John Kennerly, Julie Thompson, Laurie. BA, U. Mass., 1946; AM, U. Mo., 1947; LHD (hon.), U. Mass., 1965, U. New Haven, 1979, Russell Sage Coll., 1990; LittD (hon.), Skidmore Coll., 1987, U. Richmond, 1988. Reporter Daily Oklahoman, 1945-46; reporter, fgn. corr., war corr. Balt. Sun, 1947-55; mng. editor Wesleyan U. Publs., 1955-64; fellow Ctr. for Advanced Studies Wesleyan U., Middletown, Conn., 1959-60, writer-in-residence, 1975—, adj. prof. history, 1979-92; fellow Pierson Coll. Yale U., 1991—; prof. of history emeritus Wesleyan U., 1992—. Author: Disturber of the Peace, 1951, The City of Anger, 1953, Shadow of the Monsoon, 1956, Beard the Lion, 1958, A Rockefeller Family Portrait, 1959, The Long Gainer, 1961, Portrait of a President, 1962, The Death of a President, 1967 (Book-of-the-Month Club selection), The Arms of Krupp, 1968 (Lit. Guild selection), The Glory and the Dream, 1974 (Lit. Guild selection), Controversy and Other Essays in Journalism, 1976, American Caesar: Douglas MacArthur, 1880-1964, 1978 (Book-of-Month Club selection), Goodbye, Darkness, 1980 (Book-of-the-Month Club selection), The Last Lion: Winston Spencer Churchill Visions of Glory 1874-1932, 1983 (Book-of-the-Month Club selection), One Brief Shining Moment: Remembering Kennedy, 1983 (Book-of-the-Month Club selection), The Last Lion: Winston Spencer Churchill Alone 1932-1940, 1988 (Book-of-the-Month Club selection), In Our Time, 1989, A World Lit Only by Fire: The Medieval Mind and the Renaissance, Portrait of an Age, 1992; contbr. to Ency. Brit., various publs. Pres. bd. trustees Friends of U. Mass. Libr., 1970-71, trustee, 1970-74; bd. dirs. Winston Churchill Travelling Fellowships, 1990-99. Sgt. USMC, 1942-45, PTO. Decorated Purple Heart; recipient Dag Hammarskjöld prize Assn. Internationale Correspondents Diplomatiques, Rome, 1967, citation for best book on fgn. affairs Overseas Press Club, 1968, U. Mo. Honor award for disting. svc. in journalism, 1969, Conn. Book award, 1975, Pres.'s Cabinet award U. Detroit, 1981, Frederick S. Troy medal U. Mass., 1981, McConnaughy award Wesleyan U., 1981, N.Y. Pub. Libr. Lit. Lion award, 1983, Disting. Pub. Svc. award Conn. Bar Assn., 1985, Lincoln Lit. award Union League Club N.Y., 1983, Blenheim award Internat. Churchill Soc., 1986, Washington Irving award, 1988, Sarah Josepha Hale award, 1993, Helmerich Disting. Author award, 2000, Nat. Humanities medal, 2002; Guggenheim fellow, 1959-60. Mem. PEN, Soc. Am. Historians, Am. Hist. Assn., Authors Guild, Century Club. Democrat. Avocation: photography.

MANCINELLI, JUDITH, piano teacher, recitalist, chamber music performer; b. Johnstown, Pa., Sept. 23, 1948; m. Aldo L. Mancinelli, June 1, 1971; children: Michelle, Brian. BA, Maryville (Tenn.) Coll., 1970; MMusic, U. Tulsa, 1971. Piano tchr. U. Tulsa, 1971-80, staff accompanist, 1978-80; piano tchr. Millikin U., Decatur, Ill., 1980—, supr. student accompanying, 1998—. Pianist with Kirkland Trio, Decatur, 1988—; violinist Millikin-Decatur Symphony, 1980—, Lee Pondel Quartet, Decatur, 1985—. Mem. Music Tchrs. Nat. Assn., Nat. Guild Piano Tchrs. (judge), Ill. Music Tchrs. Assn. (chair dist. competition 1994-99), Pi Kappa Lambda, Tau Kappa Chi. Avocations: stained glass, fish keeping, gardening. E-mail: JMancinelli-!mail.millikin.edu. Office: Millikin U Dept Music 1184 W Main St Decatur IL 62522-2084

MANCINI, ELAINE CAROL, public relations executive, marketing consultant; b. Chgo., Sept. 21, 1953; d. Edward A. and Adeline (Renella) M.; m. Alan G. Morrice, Aug. 14, 1974; children: Zachary, Fiona. BA, U. Ill., 1975; MA, NYU, 1977, PhD, 1981. Dir. Film Archive and Film Libr. Svcs., N.Y.C., 1980-86; asst. prof. Sch. Visual Arts St. John's U., CUNY, S.I., N.Y., 1980-86; account exec. Ruder Finn & Rotman, N.Y.C., 1985-86; sr. v.p. GCI Group subs. Grey Advt., 1986-92; assoc. ptnr. Strategy XXI Group, 1993-95; sr. v.p., dir. econ. devel. Makovsky & Co., 1996-97; -pres. Mancini Comm., White Plains, NY, 1997—2002. Bd. dirs. Internat. Bus. Network of Greater N.Y., 1996-2002; mem. 20th congl. dist. Internat. Trade Adv. Coun. Author: The Free Years of the Italian Film Industry, 1985, Luchino Visconti: A Guide to References and Resources, 1986, D.W. Griffith and The Biograph Company, 1986. Recipient Golden World award Internat. Pub. Rels. Assn., 1992; Fulbright teaching grantee U. Bologna, Italy, 1983. Mem. Internat. Bus. Network Greater N.Y. (bd. dirs. 1996-2002). E-mail: mancini@toast.net.

MANCINI, ERNEST ANTHONY, geologist, educator, researcher; b. Reading, Pa., Feb. 27, 1947; s. Ernest and Marian K. (Filbert) M.; m. Marilyn E. Lee, Dec. 27, 1969; children: Lisa L., Lauren N. BS, Albright Coll., 1969; MS, So. Ill. U., 1972; PhD, Tex. A&M U., 1974. Petroleum exploration geologist Cities Svc. Oil Co., Denver, 1974-76; asst. prof. geology U. Ala., Tuscaloosa, 1976-79, assoc. prof., 1979-84, prof., 1984—. State geologist, oil and gas supr. State Ala., Tuscaloosa, 1982-96; dir. Ea. Gulf Region of the Petroleum Tech. Transfer Coun., 1995—, Ctr. for Sedimentary Basin Studies, U. Ala., 1998—. Contbr. articles to profl. jours. Cushman Found. fellow, Geol. Soc. Am. fellow; recipient Nat. Coun. Citation Albright Coll., 1983, Pratt-Haas Disting. Lectr. Am. Assn. Petroleum Geologists, 1987-88, Outstanding Educator award Gulf Coast Assn. Geol. Socs., 1998. Mem. Geol. Soc. Am. (past chmn. S.E. sect.), Am. Assn. Petroleum Geologists (A.I. Levorsen petroleum geology Meml. award Gulf Coast assn., geol. socs. sect. 1980, chair rsch. com. 2001—, Disting. Educator award 2000), Assn. Am. State Geologists (hon., past pres.), Nat. Assn. State Univs. and Land-Grant Colls. (past chair, mineral and energy resources sect. mem. bd. natural resources), Soc. Econ. Paleontologists and Mineralogists Gulf Coast sect. (hon., past pres.), Paleontol. Soc. (past pres. southeast sect.), N.Am. Micropaleontology Soc., Ala. Geol. Soc. (past pres.), Sigma Xi (past chpt. pres.), Phi Kappa Phi (past chpt. pres.), Phi Sigma. Presbyterian. Home: 15271 Four Winds Loop Northport AL 35475-3325 Office: U Ala Dept Geology PO Box 870338 Tuscaloosa AL 35487-0338 E-mail: emancini@wgs.geo.ua.edu.

MANCINI, FRANK ANTHONY, software developer; b. Dubois, Pa., Oct. 21, 1965; s. Frank and Mary Frances (Battaglino) M. BS in Applied Math., U. Pitts., 1988. Programmer Computing & Info. Systems Inc., Pitts., 1987-88; programmer/analyst Peak Tech. Svcs. Inc., 1988; software engr. Specialized Office Systems Inc., Wilmerding, Pa., 1988-89, Infocap Systems Inc., Pitts., 1989-90; project leader, developer, systems programmer DXI Inc., 1990—. Author: (software) Multiplexor, Municor Systems Inc., 1989. Avocations: automobile and house restoration. Home: 1421 Great Oak Dr Pittsburgh PA 15220-2015 Office: DXI Inc 200 Hightown Blvd Ste 202 Pittsburgh PA 15205

MANCINI, GILDA MARIANN, musician, music educator; b. Detroit, Apr. 15, 1933; d. Peter and Rose Mancini. AA, L.A. City Coll., 1971. Tchr. Cath. Schs., L.A., Detroit, Unified Sch. Sys., L.A. Mem.: Third Order St. Dominic. Jewish. Avocations: painting, drawing. Home: Apt 212 3882 Dobie Rd Okemos MI 48864-3791

MANCINI, MARY CATHERINE, cardiothoracic surgeon, researcher; b. Scranton, Pa., Dec. 15, 1953; d. Peter Louis and Ferminia Teresa (Massi) M. BS in Chemistry, U. Pitts., 1974, MD, 1978; PhD in Anatomy and Cellular Biology, La. State U. Med. Ctr., 2000; M in Med. Mgmt., U. Tex. Southwestern, 2002. Diplomate Am. Bd. Surgery (speciality cert. critical care medicine), Am. Bd. Thoracic Surgery. Intern in surgery U. Pitts., 1978-79, resident in surgery, 1979-87; fellow pediatric cardiac surgery Mayo Clinic, 1987-88; asst. prof. surgery, dir. cardiothoracic transplantation Med. Coll. Ohio, Toledo, 1988-91; assoc. prof. surgery, dir. cardiothoracic transplantation La. State U. Health Scis. Ctr., Shreveport, 1991-98, prof. surgery, chief cardiothoracic surgery, 1999—2002; dir. cardiovascular rsch. Willis Knighton Med. Ctr. Med. advisor Total Artificial Heart Devel., ABIOMED Corp. Author: Operative Techniques for Medical Students, 1983; editor-in-chief: Cardiothoracic Surgery and Transplantation EMedicine Textbooks; contbr. articles to profl. jours. Mem. physicians adv. bd. Rep. Com. Recipient Pres. award, Internat. Soc. Heart Transplantation, 1983, Charles C. Moore Tchg. award, U. Pitts., 1985, Internat. Order of Merit award, 1995, Nina S. Braunwald Career Devel. award, Thoracic Surgery Found., 1996—98, Nat. Leadership award, Rep. Com., 2000, Disting. Alumni award, U. Pitts. Dept. Chemistry, 2002; grantee Am. Heart Assn., 1988, Whittaker, 1998, NIH, 2000. Fellow ACS, Am. Coll. Chest Physicians, Internat. Coll. Surgeons (councillor 1991—); mem. Assn. Women Surgeons, Am. Assn. Thoracic Surgery, Am. Physiol. Soc., So. Surg. Assn., Rotary (gift of life program 1991). Roman Catholic. Achievements include first multiple organ transplant in La., first pediatric heart transplant in La., 1993. Office: La State U Med Ctr 1501 Kings Hwy Shreveport LA 71103-4228

MANCINI, MARY ELIZABETH, nursing executive; b. Providence, Nov. 7, 1953; d. Thomas Anthony and Letitia (Gentile) Rando; m. David Lee Mancini, Feb. 10, 1974; children: Laura Letitia, Carla Elizabeth. Student, Providence Coll., 1971-73; ADN, R.I. Jr. Coll., 1975; BSN, R.I. Coll., 1976; MS in Nursing in Adminstrn., U. R.I., 1982. RN, Tex., FAAN, 1994; cert. ACLS instr. Staff nurse Roger Williams Gen. Hosp., Providence, 1976-77; charge nurse Good Samaritan Hosp., Cin., 1977-78; staff nurse ICU and CCU, Miriam Hosp., Providence, 1978-79, asst. head nurse, 1979-81, head nurse,

1981-83; asst. dir. nursing R.I. Hosp., 1983-84; dir. emergency svcs. Parkland Meml. Hosp., Dallas, 1984-86, v.p. nursing adminstrn., 1986-93, sr. v.p. nursing adminstr., 1993-2000, sr. v.p. nursing and profl. svcs., 2000—. Mem. affiliate nursing staff U. R.I., Kingston, 1981-83; mem. clin. faculty U. Tex. Southwestern Med. Ctr., Dallas, 1986—; adj. clin. prof. U. Tex., Arlington, 1986—, mem. adv. bd. for grad. edn. in nursing adminstrn. Sch. Nursing, 1990—; adj. assoc. prof. U. N.D., Grand Forks, 1987—; mem. select com. on doctoral nursing programs U. Tex. System, 1989; asst. clin. prof. Tex. Woman's U. Coll. of Nursing, 1993; adj. prof. Sch. Law Baylor U., 1993—; mem. healthcare manpower shortage com. Dallas-Ft. Worth Hosp. Coun., 1989—; mem. assoc. degree nursing adv. com. El Centro Coll., 1991—; mem., chairperson mem. com. Am. Hosp. Assn. Inst. for Clin. Nursing Edn., 1992—. Contbr. articles to profl. jours. Founder, chairperson Dallas, Ft. Worth Great 100 Nurses Celebration, 1991-93. Grantee Laerdal Found. for Acute Medicine, 1984-87; Wharton nurse fellow Johnson & Johnson, 1987. Fellow Am. Acad. Nursing; mem. AACN, ANA (cert. nursing adminstrn.), Nat. Assn. Pub. Hosp. (Mgmt. Fellowship 1993), Tex. Nurses Assn. (Nurse of Yr. award dist. 4, 1991), Am. Heart Assn. (nat. working group for ACLS 1983-85, 94-96), NLN (nominations com. 1993, bd. rev. 1996—), Emergency Dept. Nurses Assn. (profl. practice com. Greater Dallas chpt., sec. 1985-86, editor Tex. newsletter 1986-87), Dallas-Ft. Worth Hosp. Coun. Nurse Adminstrs. Forum (pres. 1991), Tex. Soc. for Nursing Svc. Adminstrs., Am. Orgn. Nurse Execs., Soc. Trauma Nurses (editl. bd. 1991—), Phi Theta Kappa, Sigma Theta Tau. Office: Parkland Health & Hosp System 5201 Harry Hines Blvd Dallas TX 75235-7708

MANCINI, ROSE C. lawyer; b. Chgo. m. James G. Alviti. JD, Ill. Inst. Tech., 1980; BS in Psychology, U. Ill., 1997. Bar: Ill. 1980. Asst. regional counsel Prudential Ins. Co. of Am., Chgo., 1981—85; atty. Household Fin. Corp. and subsidiaries, Prospect Hts., 1985—. Mem. Am. Fin. Svcs. Assn. Office: Household Auto Fin Corp 2700 Sanders Rd Prospect Heights IL 60070-2701

MANCINI, WILLIAM LAWRENCE, chemistry educator; b. Paterson, N.J., July 5, 1945; m. Elizabeth Papageorge, July 27, 1967; children: Elisa Henson, Denise. PhD in Organic Chemistry, U. N.H., 1972. Prof. organic chemistry Paradise Valley C.C., Phoenix, 1994—. Cons. in field. Mem. Am. Chem. Soc. Avocation: football. Office: Paradise Valley CC 18401 N 32d St Phoenix AZ 85032 Fax: 602-787-6675. E-mail: hank.mancini@pvmail.maricopa.edu.

MANCINO, DOUGLAS MICHAEL, lawyer; b. May 8, 1949; s. Paul and Adele (Brazaitis) M.; m. Carol Keith, June 16, 1973. BA, Kent State U., 1971; JD, Ohio State U., 1974. Bar: Ohio 1974, U.S. Tax Ct. 1977, Calif. 1981, D.C. 1981. Assoc. Baker & Hostetler, Cleve., 1974-80; ptnr. Memel & Ellsworth, L.A., 1980-87, McDermott, Will & Emery, L.A., 1987—. Bd. dirs. Health Net of Calif. Inc. Author: Taxation of Hospitals and Health Care Organizations, 2000, (with others) Hospital Survival Guide, 1984, Navigating the Federal Physician Self-Referral Law, 1998; (with F. Hill) Taxation of Exempt Organizations, 2002; co-author quar. tax column Am. Hosp. Assn. publ. Health Law Vigil, (with L. Burns) Joint Ventures Between Hosps. and Physicians, 1987; contbr. articles to profl. jours. Chmn. bd. dirs. The Children's Burn Found. Mem. ABA (tax, bus., real property, probate and trust sects., chair exempt orgns. com. 1995-97, coun. dir. 1999—), Calif. State Bar Assn. (tax, bus. law sects.), Ohio Bar Assn., Calif. State Bar, D.C. Bar Assn., Am. Health Lawyers Assn. (bd. dirs. 1986-95, pres. 1993-94), Calif. Soc. for Healthcare Attys., Bel Air Country Club, The Regency Club, Calif. Yacht Club. Office: McDermott Will & Emery 2049 Century Park E Fl 34 Los Angeles CA 90067-3101 E-mail: dmancino@mwe.com.

MANCINO, JOHN GREGORY, software company executive; b. N.Y.C., Nov. 14, 1946; s. John D. and Carmela A. Mancino. BA, Colgate U., 1968. Chief appraiser Rusciano Appraisers & Cons., N.Y.C., 1968-70; v.p. Pisces Prodns., Boulder, Colo., 1971-73; v.p. ops. Celestial Seasonings, Inc., 1973-84, also dir.; dir. Strategic Info. Group, 1994—. Bd. dirs. Computer Connection, Inc., Mr. Software, Inc., Spruce St. Mktg., Inc., Fortune 44 Co., Inc.; pres., bd. dirs. Decision Makers Software, 1984—; chmn. Generation 5 Tech., 1985-89. Preferred Bus. Investments, Ltd., 1986-90. Author: (software) Tattletale, 1991. Office: 214 Mountain Meadows Rd Boulder CO 80302-9256 E-mail: mancino@decismkr.com.

MANCINO, LAWRENCE A. physician; b. Bklyn., May 13, 1961; s. Lawrence and Concetta Mancino; m. Stacy A. Mancino, Apr. 24, 1993. BS in Biology, Wagner Coll., 1984; DO, N.Y. Coll. Osteo. Medicine, 1988. Diplomate Am. Bd. Internal Medicine, Am. Bd. Gastroenterology. Intern Union (N.J.) Hosp., 1988-89; resident in medicine S.I. U. Hosp., 1989-92, chief med. resident, 1992-93; fellow in gastroenterology L.I. Coll. Hosp., Bklyn., 1993-95; attending physician Sottile, Megna, MD, PC, S.I., N.Y., 1995—. Fellow ACP; mem. AMA, Am. Gastroent. Assn., Richmond County Med. Soc., Bklyn. Gastroent. Assn., Am. Coll. Gastroenterology. Office: Sottile Megna MD PC 360 Edison St Staten Island NY 10306-3041

MANCKE, RICHARD BELL, economist, educator, investor; b. Bethlehem, Pa., Jan. 11, 1943; s. Donald Bell and Elizabeth (Schlottman) M.; m. Barbara Hobbie, Sept. 4, 1970; 1 child, Max. BA, Colgate U., 1965; PhD, MIT, 1969. Instr. MIT, Cambridge, Mass., 1968-69; staff economist U.S. President's Oil Imports Task Force, Washington, 1969-70; asst. prof. Grad. Sch. Bus., U. Chgo., 1969-7l; asst. prof. econs. and law U. Mich. Law Sch., Ann Arbor, l97l-74; assoc. prof. Fletcher Sch. Tufts U., Medford, Mass., 1974-8l, prof., l98l-86; mng. ptnr. Wolfeboro (N.H.) Ventures, 1985-92, 96-98; vis. prof. Fgn. Affairs Coll., Beijing, 1987, Colgate U., Hamilton, N.Y., 1990; prof. Fletcher Sch. Tufts U., 1990-96; acad. dean Fletcher Sch., Tufts U., 1991-94; interim dean Fletcher Sch. Tufts U., Medford, Mass., 1994-95; dean bus. sch., SAP prof. entrepreneurial leadership Internat. U. in Germany, Bruchsal, 1999-2000; prof., dir. MBA program Leipzig Grad. Sch. Mgmt., 2000—. Expert witness Cravath, Swaine & Moore, N.Y.C., 1974-82; dir. Intellitech Corp., Key Largo, Fla., 1985-90; rsch. dir. Twentieth Century Fund Energy Policy Task Force, N.Y.C., 1976-77. Author: The Failure of U.S. Energy Policy, 1974, Squeaking By, 1976, Mexican Oil and Natural Gas, 1979; co-author: IBM and the U.S. Data Processing Industry, 1983 (outstanding acad. book award Choice) 1984. Testified before various coms. U.S. Senate, 1972-76; mem. various town bds., Wolfeboro, N.H., 1981-94. Fellow NSF, 1967, Earhart Found., 1981, Goethe Inst., 1995. Mem. Am. Econs. Assn., Appalachian Mountain Club, Mt. Washington Obs. Avocations: reading, cycling, hiking. Office: Leipzig Grad Sch of Mgmt Jahnallee 59 D-04109 Leipzig Germany E-mail: mancke@mba.hhl.de.

MANCUSO, DONNA MARIENE, psychiatrist; MD, La. State U., New Orleans, 1983. Diplomate Am. Bd. Psychiatry and Neurology in gen. psychiatry and forensic psychiatry. Intern Ochsner, New Orleans, 1983-84; resident La. State U., 1984-87; now assoc. prof. clin. psychiatry La. State U. Med. Ctr., 1987—. Mem. La. Psychiat. Med. Assn. (pres. 2000), New Orleans Area Psychiat. Assn. (pres. 1999-2000). Office: La State U MC 1542 Tulane Ave New Orleans LA 70112-2825

MANCUSO, JAMES CARMIN, psychologist, educator; b. Hazleton, Pa., Jan. 17, 1928; s. Vincent and Dolores (Carrato) M.; m. Susan Rose Kuca, Sept. 4, 1954; children: Renée Clare, Michele Ann, Martin Vincent. AB, Dickinson Coll., Carlisle, Pa., 1951; PhD, U. Rochester, N.Y., 1958. Lic. psychologist, N.Y.; cert. secondary sch. tchr., Pa. Psychologist Wyoming County Bd. Coop. Ednl. Svcs., Attica, N.Y., 1956-58; psychol. counselor Counseling and Testing Svcs. Lehigh U., Bethlehem, Pa., 1958-61; asst. prof. dept. psychology U. Albany, N.Y., 1961-62, assoc. prof., 1962-70, prof., 1970—, assoc. dean Coll. Social and Behavioral Scis., 1985-91, prof. emeritus, 1993—; interim dean Sch. Math. and Scis. Coll. St. Rose, Albany, 1991-92. Psychol. cons. Sch. Dist., Coxasakie-Athens, N.Y., Learning Disabilities Ctr., Albany, N.Y., State Dept. Correction, Albany, Child Guidance Ctr., Albany, Dept. Phys. Medicine, Albany Med. Ctr., St. Catherine's Ctr. for Children, Albany. Editor: Readings for a Cognitive Theory of Personality, 1970; (with J.R. Adams-Webber) The Construing Person, 1982, Applications of Personal Construct Theory, 1983; (with M.L. Shaw) Cognition and Personal Structure, 1988; author: (with T.R. Sarbin) Schizophrenia: Medical Diagnosis or Moral Verdict, 1980; contbr. articles to profl. jours., chpts. to books; mem. editl. bd. Internat. Jour. Personal Construct Psychology. Bd. dirs., v.p. cultural affairs Italian-Am. Cultural Found., Capital Dist. N.Y., Albany; bd. dirs., mem. urban affairs com. Coun. Cmty. Svcs. Northeastern N.Y., Albany, 1984-90; mem. budget rev. panel United Way of Northeastern N.Y., Albany, 1986-88. Recipient Lifetime Career Achievement award N.Am. Personal Construct Psychology Network, 1999; named Alumnus of Yr. Milton Hershey Sch., Hershey, Pa., 1986. Mem. APA, Eastern Psychol. Assn., Sons of Italy (immediate past pres. 1996-98—, Golden Lion award 1985), Sigma Xi. Home: 15 Oakwood Pl Delmar NY 12054-2006 E-mail: mancusoj@capital.net.

MANCUSO, JOHN H. lawyer, bank executive; b. Utica, N.Y., June 5, 1944; s. Sam A. and Frances H. (Nelson) M.; m. Etel Tumma, July 18, 1970; children: Christa E., John A. BA in English magna cum laude, Boston Coll., 1968; MA in English, Lehigh U., 1970; MS in Higher Edn. Adminstrn., Syracuse U., 1973, PhD in Higher Edn. Adminstrn., 1978, JD, 1975. Bar: N.Y. 1976, Ohio 1976, U.S. Dist. Ct. (no. dist.) N.Y. 1976, U.S. Dist. Ct. (no. dist.) Ohio 1994. Assoc. Hiscock & Barclay, Syracuse, 1976-80, ptnr., 1981-90; gen. counsel Key Bank of N.Y., Albany, 1992-94; sr. v.p., dep. gen. counsel KeyCorp, Cleve. and Albany, NY, 1990—2001, exec. v.p., gen. coun., 2001—; dir., gen. counsel, sec. Key Bank Nat. Assn., Cleve., 1994—, vice chmn., 2001—. Mem. U.S.Seante Banking Com. Task Force on Fin. Modernization Bill, 1998; adj. prof. law Syracuse U., 1976-87, tchr. higher edn. adminstrn. grad. sch.; English tchr. at various colls., secondary schs., 1968-73; spkr. in field; bd. dirs. Key Bank Nat. Assn., Key Corporate Capital Inc., KeyCorp Ins. Co. Ltd. Author: Home Equity Update: A Manual for Lenders and Lawyers, 1989; co-author: Compliance Examinations Update for Financial Institutions, 1985-2001, The Law of Truth in Lending: 1989, Supplement, Reporting to Bank Regulators: Requirements and Forms Manual, 1990, Bank Regulatory Update: Beyond Consumer Issues, 1995-97; contbr. numerous articles to profl. publs. Chmn. planning bd. Village of Manlius, N.Y., 1983-86; bd. trustees Cleve. Hearing and Speech Ctr., 2000—. Mem. ABA (chair housing fin. subcom., consumer fin. svcs. com., bus. law sect. 1990-92), Am. Bankers Assn. (bank counsel com. 1996-98), Am. Coll. Consumer Fin. Svcs. Lawyers (founding mem.), N.Y. State Bar Assn. (chair bus. law sect. 1994-95, chmn. cinsumer fin. svcs. com. bus. law sect. 1988-91, chmn. subcom. on equal credit opportunity/truth-in-lending 1985-86, chmn. subcom. on credit cards/fair credit billing 1982-83), N.Y. State Bankers Assn. (mem. lawyers retail legis. com. 1992-94, ops. and payments sys. com. 1988-90, legal advisor to residential mortgage com. of consumer banking divsn. 1986-87, mem. lawyers adv. com. 1994—), Consumer Bankers Assn. (mem. ad hoc com. on bank investment products 1993-97, mem. lawyers com. 1987-97), Justinian Soc., Order of Coif. Republican. Avocations: skiing, golf, tennis, reading, chess. Office: KeyCorp 127 Public Sq Cleveland OH 44114-1306 E-mail: john_mancuso@keybank.com.

MANCUSO, J(OHN) JAMES, librarian; b. Olean, N.Y., Apr. 19, 1958; s. Frank A. and Josephine (Romano) M. m. Kathleen M. Petrie, June 29, 1985; children: Nicholas, Victoria, Benjamin. BA, Syracuse U., 1979, MLS, 1983. Bibliographic asst. Ctrl. Libr. Coun., Syracuse, N.Y., 1980-83; quality control specialist BRS, Latham, 1983-86; asst. dir. libr. Capital Dist. Libr. Coun., Albany, 1986-2000; libr. Mid-Am. Bapt. Theol. Sem., Schenectady, 2000—. Reference libr. Schenectady County Pub. Libr., Schenectady, N.Y., part-time 1993—; book reviewer Pub. Rsch. Quar., 1995-97. Editor, compiler: Directory of Repositories, 2000; contbr. articles to profl. jours.; inventor Orderly Arrangement of Knowledge (OAK)libr. classification sys.; designer Internet web-sites. Ch. libr. 1st Presbyn. Ch., Schenectady, 1993— Mem. N.Y. Libr. Assn. (legis. com. 1992-97, sect. on mgmt. of resources and tech. smart Dewey fellow 1992)., Hudson-Mohawk Libr. Assn. (pres. 1993-97), Capital Area Archivists N.Y. (v.p. 1992-94). Republican. Avocations: Victorian architecture, genealogy, seashells, calligraphy. Office: Mid-Am Bapt Theol Sem 2810 Curry Rd Schenectady NY 12303 E-mail: jmancuso@mabtsne.edu.

MANCUSO, JOSEPH EDWARD, medical psychotherapist; b. Rockford, Ill., Dec. 1, 1955; s. Robert Fredrick and Anne Mancuso. Student, Bradley U., Peoria, Ill., 1974-76; BA in Psychology, Marquette U., 1984, MEd in Ednl. Psychology, 1987. Cert. alcohol and drug abuse counselor III, WCB, ICR; cert. clin. assoc. med. psychotherapist, nat.; diplomate, fellow med. psychotherapist ABMP; cert. ind. clin. social worker, Wis.; cert. profl. counselor, Wis.; cert. trauma responder and trauma specialist ATSS. Child care worker Community Care Svcs. Inc., Milw., 1984; day care dir. Mich. Street Day Care; adminstrv. unit clk. Milw. Jewish Nursing Home; day care tchr. St. Mary's Children's Sch., Milw.; psychotherapist Wis. Correctional Svcs.; coord. alcohol and other drug abuse St. Mary's Psychiat. Hosp., 1990-92; cons. social worker St. Mary's Med. Hosp., 1990-91; pvt. practice, 1993-99; emergency rm. social worker Sinai Samaritan Med. Ctr., Milw., 1994-99; intake psychotherapist psychiat. svcs. Behav. Health Intake Ctr.-Sinai Samaritan Med. Ctr., 1999-2000; childrens psychotherapist Sinai Samaritan Med. Ctr., 2000—. Presenter in field. Cartoonist, published and shown in galleries throughout Milw. Mem. Am. Psychol. Assn., Wis. Psychol. Assn. (assoc.), Am. Ednl. Rsch. Assn. Avocations: hiking, drawing, painting, birding. Home: 1612 E Hartford Ave Milwaukee WI 53211-3036 Office: Sinai Samaritan Med Ctr Dept Psychiatry 1020 N 12th St Milwaukee WI 53233-1305

MANCUSO, LENI, artist, poet, educator; b. Bklyn., Aug. 24, 1926; d. John and Christina (Tanzillo) M.; m. Thomas Rawson Barrett, June 14, 1952; 1 child, Kedron Ryon. Student, Pratt Inst., 1944, The New Sch., 1945-50, Bklyn. Mus. Art Sch., 1946-52. Art dir. Columbia Broadcasting Sys., N.Y.C., 1944-46, William Weintraub Agy., N.Y.C., 1946-51; art instr. Currier Gallery Art, Manchester, N.H., 1962-70, St. Paul's Sch., Concord, 1965-75. Art cons. Hargate Art Gallery, Concord, N.H., 1970-89. Solo exhibits include New Eng. Coll., Hennicker, N.H., 1974, Maine Art Gallery, Wiscasset, 1975, Arnold Klein Gallery, Royal Oak, Mich., 1976, Lamont Gallery, Exeter, N.H., 1976, U. Maine, Orono, 1977, Currier Gallery of Art, Manchester, N.H., 1980, Colby Sawyer Coll., New London, N.H., 1983, St. Anselm Coll., Goffstown, N.H., 1985, Manchester Inst. Arts and Scis., N.H., 1987, Blackthorne Gallery, Portsmouth, N.H., 1989, Leighton Gallery, Blue Hill, Maine, 1991, Maine Arts Commn., Augusta, 1995, Maine Coast Artists, Rockport, 1996, Trinity Gallery, Castine, Maine, 2002; represented in pub. and corp. collections include Portland Mus. Art, N.H. State Art Bank, Newberry collection, Detroit, U. Mich., Mich. Bell Telephone, First Nat. Bank Boston, Hargate Art Ctr., N.H., U.S. Dept. State; poems published in Beloit Poetry Jour., Christian Sci. Monitor, Puckerbrush Rev. Portfolio, Maine Times, Off the Coast; contbr. poems to profl. publs. Mem. Maine Writers and Pubs. Alliance, Maine Coast Artists, Acad. Am. Poets, Poets & Writers. Home: PO Box 303 Castine ME 04421-0303

MAND, MARTIN G. financial executive; b. Norfolk, Va., Sept. 26, 1936; s. Meyer J. and Lena (Sutton) M.; m. Shelly Cohen, Aug. 29, 1965; children: Gregory S., Michael E., Brian C. BS in Commerce, U. Va., 1958; MBA, U. Del., 1964. Various fin. staff and mgmt. positions E.I. du Pont de Nemours & Co., Wilmington, Del., 1961-81, v.p. taxes and fin. svcs., 1981-84, v.p., comptr., 1984-88, v.p., treas., 1989-90; sr. v.p., CFO, Nortel Networks, Mississauga, Canada, 1990—93, exec. v.p., CFO, 1993—94; chmn. pres., CEO Mand Assocs., Ltd., Wilmington, 1995—; mng. ptnr. PFP Seminars, 2001—. Bd. dirs. Fuji Bank & Trust Co, N.Y.C., Townsends, Inc., Wilmington, Del., Imagyn Med. Techs., Inc., Irvine, Calif., Factory Card and Party Outlet, Naperville, Ill.; pres. Fin. Execs. Rsch. Found., 1988-90; adv. dir. Global IP Sound, Stockholm, 2001—. Co-author: Partnering for Performance: Unleashing the Power of Finance in the 21st Century Organization, 2000. Lt. USN, 1958-61. Mem. Fin. Execs. Inst., Am. Mgmt. Assn. (chmn. fin. coun.). Office: 618 Berwick Rd Ste 100 Wilmington DE 19803-2204 E-mail: mandassociates@comcast.net.

MANDAL, ANIL KUMAR, nephrologist, medical educator; b. West Bengal, India, Nov. 12, 1935; came to U.S., 1967; s. Nirmal Chandra and Kamala Bala (Sarkar) M.; m. Pranati Ganguly, June 18, 1964 (dec.); children: Aditi, Atashi. MB, BS, Calcutta Nat. Med. Coll., 1959. Diplomate Am. Bd. Internal Medicine, Am. Bd. Nephrology, Am. Bd. Forensic Medicine. Instr. U. Ill., Chgo., 1971-72; asst. prof. U. Okla., Oklahoma City, 1972-75, assoc. prof., 1975-82; VA career investigator VA Med. Ctr., 1975-77; prof. medicine Med. Coll. Ga., 1982-87, Wright State U., Dayton, Ohio, 1987-96; chief nephrology VA Med. Ctr., 1987-99. Cons. Vets. Affairs Med. Ctr., Chillicothe, Ohio, 1995-99; chmn. med. adv. bd. Nat. Kidney Found., 1996-98. Author: Nephrology Asian Pacific Physicians, 1995, Diagnosis and Management Renal Disease and Hypertension, 1994, Kidney Disease in Primary Care, 1998; editl. bd. Jour. Clin. Pharmacology, 1994-96, Kidney, 1994—. Recipient Disting. Svc. award Nat. Kidney Found. USA, 1998; Fulbright scholar, 1992, 96. Avocation: rose gardening. Home: 571 Pine Needles Dr Centerville OH 45458-3323 Office: Med Specialists of St Augustine 240 Southpark Cir E Saint Augustine FL 32086-5137 E-mail: tinaf@med-spec.com.

MANDAL, ASHIS K. cardiothoracic surgeon; b. Burdwan Town, India, Sept. 1, 1931; came to U.S., 1959; s. Mrigendra N. and Sarala Bala Mandal; m. Bina Bhatacharjee, July 14, 1957 (dec. June 1978); 1 child, Aloke; m. Mina R. Mandal, Apr. 24, 1987. MB BChir, Calcutta Nat. Med. Coll., 1957. Civil asst. surgeon Govt. India, Nefa, 1957-59; resident in gen. surgery Howard U., Washington, 1960—65; fellow in cardiovasc. surgery U. Minn., Mpls., 1965-66; resident in cardiothoracic U. Alta., Edmonton, Can., 1966-67, in-charge cardiovasc. rsch. lab. Can., 1967-69; cons. surgeon Ft. St. John (B.C., Can.) Med. Clinic, 1969-73; from asst. prof. surgery to assoc. prof. surgery Drew-UCLA Med. Ctr., L.A., 1973-84, prof. surgery, 1984-98, prof. surgery emeritus, 1999—. Author: Anatomical Basis of Infectious Disease, 1985 (Assam Govt. award 1956), Antimicrobial Therapy in Abdominal Surgery, 1991. Fellow ACS, Royal Coll. Surgeons, Am. Coll. Chest Physicians; mem. Am. Assn. Thoracic Surgeons, Soc. Thoracic Surgeons. Office: King-Drew Med Ctr 12021 Wilmington Ave Los Angeles CA 90059-3019

MANDAL, PURNENDU, information management educator, researcher; b. Lalugeria, W Bengal, India, June 20, 1958; came to U.S., 2000; s. Dhirendranath and Sukhadabala M.; m. Ratna Karak, Aug. 24, 1986; children: Partha, Prasun. B in Tech. with honors, Indian Inst. Tech., Kharagpur, 1979, M in Tech., 1981; PhD, Bradford, Eng., 1986. Chartered profl. engr., Australia. Engr. Indian Oil Corp., Calcutta, 1981-82; lectr. Indian Inst. Tech., Kharagpur, 1986-90, asst. prof., 1990-92; lectr. Monash U., Melbourne, Australia, 1992-93, Deakin U., Geelong, Australia, 1993-2000; prof. Marshall U., Huntington, W.Va., 2000—. Cons. Indian Army, New Delhi, 1989-91, Ford Australia, Geelong, 1994-95. Co-author: Introduction to System Dynamics Modelling, 1994; pub. Sys. Dynamics: An Internat. Jour. of Policy Modelling, 1986-92; contbr. articles to profl. jours. Pres. Moyne Rabindra Club, India, 1990-92. Recipient Nat. Overseas scholarship Govt. of India, 1982-86, Overseas Rsch. Students scholarship Com. of Vice Chancellors and Prins. of Univs., Eng., 1984-86, fellowship German Acad. Exch. Mem. Internat. System Dynamics Soc., Systems Dynamics Soc. of India (founder, publ. sec. 1986-92), Instn. of Engrs. Australia (sr.). Avocations: photography, travel, fishing. Office: Marshall U Lewis Coll Bus 400 Hal Greer Blvd Huntington WV 25705

MANDANIS, GEORGE PETER, electrical engineer, consultant; b. Spartanburg, S.C., Sept. 29, 1927; s. Paraskevajohn and Haido Mandanis; m. Christel Suzanne Utsch, July 17, 1961; children: Michael, Stefan; m. Marjorie Garette Salonites, Aug. 10, 1952 (div. July 1961); 1 child Gregory. BSEE, Clemson Coll., 1949; student, U. Calif., Berkeley, U. Calif., L.A., 1963. Founder Inst. for the Future, Santa Monica, Calif., 1967—; chmn. exec. tng. McLarran Sch. Mgmt., San Francisco, 1985—95; bd. dir. Compaxion Tech., Inc., L.A., 1984—. Co-author: Technological Forecasting, 1969. Grantee, NSF, 1973—75. Democrat. Achievements include invention of of telemail (electronic mail); of SMR mobile telephone. Avocations: painting, singing. Home: 31 Montecito Rd San Rafael CA 94901-2361 Fax: 415-457-4842. E-mail: georgemandanis@msn.com.

MANDEL, CAROLA PANERAI (MRS. LEON MANDEL), foundation trustee; b. Havana, Cuba, 1920; d. Camilo and Elvira (Bertini) Panerai; m. Leon Mandel, Apr. 9, 1938. Mem. women's bd. Northwestern Meml. Hosp., Chgo.; trustee Carola and Leon Mandel Fund Loyola U. Foundation trustee; b. Havana, Cuba; d. Camilo and Elvira (Bertini) Panerai; ed. pvt. schs., Havana and Europe; m. Leon Mandel, Apr. 9, 1938. Mem. women's bd. Northwestern Meml. Hosp., Chgo. Trustee Carola and Leon Mandel Fund Loyola U., Chgo. Life mem. Chgo. Hist. Soc., Guild of Chgo. Hist. Soc., Smithsonian Assos., Nat. Skeet Shooting Assn. Frequently named among Ten Best Dressed Women in U.S.; chevalier Confrerie des Chevaliers du Tastevin. Capt. All-Am. Women's Skeet Team, 1952, 53, 54, 55, 56; only woman to win a men's nat. championship, 20 gauge, 1954, also high average in world over men, 1956, in 12 gauge with 99.4 per cent; European women's live bird shooting championship, Venice, Italy, 1957, Porto, Portugal, 1961; European woman's target championship, Torino, Italy, 1958; woman's world champion live-bird shooting, Sevilla, Spain, 1959, Am. Contract Bridge League Life Master, 1987. Named to Nat. Skeet Shooting Assn. Hall of Fame, 1970; inducted in U.S. Pigeon shooting Fedn. Hall of Fame, 1992. Mem. Soc. Four Arts. Club: Everglades (Palm Beach, Fla.), The Beach. Capt. All-Am. Women's Skeet Team, 1952, 53, 54, 55, 56. Frequently named among Ten Best Dressed Women in U.S.; chevalier Confrerie des Chevaliers du Tastevein; only woman to win a men's nat. championship, 20 gauge, 1954; high average in world over men, 1956, in 12 gauge with 99.4 per cent; European woman's world champion live-bird shooting, Sevilla, Spain, 1595, Am. Contract Bridge League Life Master, 1987; inducted to U.S. Pigeon Shooting Fedn. Hall of Fame, 1992. Mem. Chgo. Hist. Soc., Guild Chgo. Hist. Soc., Smithsonian Assn., Nat. Skeet Shooting Assn. (named to Hall of Fame 1970), Soc. Four Arts, Everglades Club, Beach Club. Home: 324 Barton Ave Palm Beach FL 33480-6116

MANDEL, H(AROLD) GEORGE, pharmacologist, educator; b. Berlin, June 6, 1924; came to U.S., 1937, naturalized, 1944; s. Ernest A. and Else (Crail) M.; m. Marianne Klein, July 25, 1953; children: Marcia Mandel Halgren, Audrey Lynn Todd. BS, Yale U., 1944, PhD, 1949. Lab. instr. in chemistry Yale U., 1942-44, 47-49; research asso. dept. pharmacology George Washington U., 1949-50, asst. research prof., 1950-52, assoc. prof. pharmacology, 1952-58, prof., 1958—, chmn. dept. pharmacology, 1960-96. Advanced Commonwealth Fund fellow Molteno Inst. Cambridge (Eng.) U., 1956; Commonwealth Fund fellow U. Auckland (N.Z.) and U. Med. Scis., Bangkok, Thailand, 1964; Am. Cancer Soc. Eleanor Roosevelt Internat. fellow Chester Beatty Research Inst. London, 1970-71; Am. Cancer Soc. scholar U. Calif., San Francisco, 1978-79; fellow Med. Research Council toxicology unit, Carshalton, Eng., 1986; Burroughs Wellcome Rsch. travel grant, Carshalton, 1988; hon. rsch. fellow dept. biochemistry and molecular biology U. Coll., London, 1993, 96, 97; mem. com. problems drug safety NRC-NAS, 1965-76, mem. com. on toxicology, 1978-82, mem. various panels, 1981-86; mem. cancer chemotherapy com. Internat. Union Against Cancer, 1966-73, fellow, Lyon, France, 1989; mem. external rev. com. Howard U. Cancer Research Center, 1972-74 ; cons. Bur. Drugs, FDA, 1975-79, EPA, 1978-82; mem. toxicology adv. com. FDA, 1975-78; mem. med. research service merit rev. bd. in alcoholism and drug dependence VA, 1975-78; mem. cancer spl. program adv. com. Nat. Cancer Inst., 1974-78, chmn., 1976-78; mem. Nat. Large Bowel Cancer Project Working Cadre, 1980-84; mem. Kettering award selection com. GM Cancer Rsch. Found., 1979-81; bd. advisors Roswell Park Cancer Inst., Buffalo, 1972-74. Editorial bd.: Jour. Pharmacology and Exptl. Therapeutics, 1960-65, field editor, 1978-94; editorial bd.: Molecular Pharmacology, 1965-69, Rsch. Comm. in Chem. Pathology, Pharmacology, 1972-98, Cancer Drug Delivery, Selective Cancer Therapeutics, 1983-92, Cancer Research, 1974-76, assoc. editor, 1977-81. Served with AUS, 1944-46. Recipient John J. Abel award in pharmacology Eli Lilly and Co., 1958, Disting. Achievement award Washington Acad. Scis., 1958, Golden Apple Teaching award AMA, 1969, 85, 97, Sci. Emeritus award Soc. Biology & Medicine, 1999. Mem. AAAS, Am. Chem. Soc., Am. Soc. Biochemistry and Molecular Biology, Am. Soc. Pharmacology and Exptl. Therapeutics (pres. 1973-74), Am. Assn. Cancer rsch., Assn. Med. Sch. Pharmacology (pres. 1976-78), Nat. Caucus of Basic Biomed. Sci. Chairs (chmn. 1991—), Citizens Pub. Rsch. and Edn. Funding (sec. 1996-99), Cosmos Club (Washington), Sigma Xi, Alpha Omega Alpha. Democrat. Achievements include research, numerous publs. on cancer chemotherapy, mechanism of growth inhibition, antimetabolites, drug disposition, chemical carcinogenesis. Home: Apt 302 4956 Sentinel Dr Bethesda MD 20816-3594 Office: George Washington U Dept Pharmacology 2300 I St NW Washington DC 20037-2336 E-mail: hgmandel@aol.com., phmhgm@gwumc.edu.

MANDEL, HERBERT MAURICE, civil engineer; b. Port Chester, N.Y., May 11, 1924; s. Arthur William and Rose (Schmeiser) M.; m. Charlotte Feldman, Aug. 22, 1954; children: Rosanne Mandel Levine, Elliott D., Arthur M. BSCE, Va. Poly. Inst., 1948; M Engring., Yale U., 1949. Registered profl. engr., N.Y., Conn., Fla., Md., Mich., Minn., Ohio, Pa., Va., W.Va.. Structural engr. Madigan Hyland Co., L.I., N.Y., 1949-50; with firm Parsons, Brinckerhoff, Quade & Douglas, Inc., 1950-86; v.p. GAI Cons., Inc., Monroeville, Pa., 1986—, prin. staff cons., 1993—. Resident engr., Chgo., 1961, Atlanta, 1962, project. mgr., N.Y.C., 1963-70, Honolulu, 1970-74, v.p., 1974, sr. v.p., Pitts., 1977-86; mem. faculty Yale U., 1948-49; adj. faculty Bklyn. Poly. Inst., 1956-64, U. Pitts., 1986; gen. chmn. 6th Internat. Bridge Conf., Pitts., 1989. Prin. works include (prin.-in-charge) Williamstown-Marietta Bridge, W.Va.-Ohio, Dunbar Bridge, W.Va., I-64 Bridge over Big Sandy River, W.Va.-Ky., Davis Creek Bridge, Charleston, W.Va., Tygart R. Bridge, W.Va., Easley Bridge, Bluefield, W.Va., Fayette Sta. Bridge, Fayetteville, W.Va., Mon Valley Expwy., W.Va., King Coal Hwy, W.Va., Romney Bridge, W.Va., (project mgr.) Newport Bridge, Narragansett Bay, R.I., (designer/project engr.) Hackensack River Bridge, N.J., Housatanic River Bridge, Conn., Arthur Kill Vertical Lift R.R. Bridge, S.I., N.Y., 62d St. Bridge, Pitts., Savannah River Cantilever Bridge, Ga., I-84 Bridges, Danbury, Conn., (structural rehab. designer) Avondale Bridge, N.J, Lincoln Bridge, N.J., B&O R.R. Bridge, Vincennes, Ind., Hawk St. Viaduct, Albany, N.Y., Congress Ave. Bridge, Austin, Tex., Ohio St. Bridge, Buffalo, Panhandle Bridge, Pitts.; project dir. design and constrn. Pitts. Light Rail Transit Sys., 1977-84; designer Elizabeth R. Tunnel, Norfolk, Va., 1950. Served to 1st lt. U.S. Army, 1943-46, 50-52, ETO. Fellow ASCE, Soc. Am. Mil. Engrs., Engrs. Soc. Western Pa. (exec. com. Internat. Bridge Conf. 1986—, gen. chmn. 1988-89); mem. NSPE, Am. Rwy. Engring. and Maintenance of Way Assn. (steel structures specifications com. 1974—), Profl. Engrs. in Pvt. Practice (bd. govs. 1994-96, profl. devel. coun. 1995-97), Pa. Profl. Engrs. in Pvt. Practice (state vice-chmn. 1992-94, chmn. 1994-96), Pa. Soc. Profl. Engrs. (dir. Pitts. chpt. 1995-98), Internat. Assn. Bridge and Structural Engring., Assn. for Bridge Constrn. and Design, Engrs. Club Pitts., Tau Beta Pi, Chi Epsilon, Omicron Delta Kappa, Phi Kappa Phi, Pi Delta Epsilon, Scabbard and Blade. Jewish. Home: 920 Parkview Dr Pittsburgh PA 15243-1116 Office: GAI Cons Inc 570 Beatty Rd Monroeville PA 15146-1334 E-mail: hmandel@gaiconsultants.com.

MANDEL, IRWIN DANIEL, dentist; b. Bklyn., Apr. 9, 1922; s. Samuel A. and Shirley (Blankstein) M.; m. Charlotte Lifschutz, Apr. 1, 1944; children: Carol, Nora, Richard. BS, CCNY, 1942; DDS, Columbia U., 1945; DSc (hon.), U. Medicine and Dentistry N.J., 1981, U. Göteborg, 1984, Columbia U., 1996. Rsch. asst. Dental Sch. Columbia U., 1946-48, mem. faculty Dental Sch., 1946—, prof. dentistry, dir. div. preventive dentistry Dental Sch., 1969-84, dir. Ctr. Clin. Rsch. in Dentistry Dental Sch., 1984-91, assoc. dean rsch., 1991-92; prof. emeritus Dental Sch., 1992—; pvt. practice dentistry, 1946-68; vis. prof. various dental schs.; chmn. oral biology and medicine study sect. Nat. Inst. Dental Rsch., 1974-76. Co-author: The Plaque Diseases, 1972; contbr. over 250 articles to profl. jours., chpts. to books. Active local chpt. Peace Action, Physicians for Social Responsibility. Lt. Dental Corps USNR, 1945-46, 52-54. Recipient Career Scientist award, N.Y.C. Health Rsch. Coun., 1969—72, Leadership award in periodontology, Tufts U. Dental Sch., 1971, Internat. award, U. Conn. Sch. Dental Medicine, 1979, Seymour J. Kreshover NIDR Lectr. award, 1986, Townsend Harris medal, CCNY, 2000. Fellow AAAS, Am. Coll. Dentists; mem. ADA (chmn. coun. dental rsch. 1978-80, Gold medal for excellence in rsch. 1985), Dental Soc. (Henry Spenadel award 1973, Jarvie-Burkhart Internat. award 1990), Am. Assn. Dental Rsch. (pres. 1980), Am. Assn. Pub. Health Dentists (Disting. Svc. award 1991), Fed. Dentair Internat. (W. D. Miller prize 1992), Internat. Assn. Dental Rsch. (Salivary Rsch. award 1994, Disting. Svc. award 2001), N.Y. Acad. Scis., Sigma Xi, Omicron Kappa Upsilon. Home: 60 Pine Dr Cedar Grove NJ 07009-1036 Office: 630 W 168th St New York NY 10032-3702

MANDEL, JACK KENT, marketing and advertising educator, publishing consultant; b. Bklyn., Dec. 31, 1947; s. Phillip and Molly (Strum) M.; m. Ronni Linda Goldpin, July 12, 1970; children: Jason Garet, Joshua Jared, Jordan Scott, Jaron Paul. BBA, Baruch Coll., 1969; MBA, 1975. Career edn. specialist N.Y.C. Bd. Edn., 1975-77; prof. mktg. and advt. Nassau Community Coll., Garden City, N.Y., 1978—. Prin. Island Craft & Bus. Cons., Oyster Bay Cove, N.Y., 1980—; pub. L.I. Arts, Fine Crafts, and Collectibles Directory, 10 edits., 1980—. Pres. Baldwin Harbor (N.Y.) Homeowners Assn. 1981-83; arbitrator, L.I. Better Bus. Bur. (pres. 1983); bd. dirs. Master Crafters (pres. 1984). Mem. Nat. Mail Order Assn., Am. Entrepreneurs Assn., Massapequa C. of C. (bd. dirs. 1988-92). Republican. Jewish. Avocations: magic, numismatics, jogging, basketball, Doo-wop rock 'n' roll.

MANDEL, JACK N. manufacturing company executive; b. Austria, July 16, 1911; s. Sam and Rose M.; m. Lilyan, Aug. 14, 1938 (dec.) Student, Fenn Coll., 1930-33. Founder, former pres., chmn. Premier Indsl. Corp., Cleve.; chmn., pres. Manbro Corp.; exec. dir. Parkwood Corp.; gen. ptnr. Courtland Assocs. Former mem. exec. com. NCCJ; former life trustee Wood Hosp.; trustee Fla. Soc. for Blind; life trustee South Broward Jewish Fedn., Cleve. Jewish Welfare Fedn.; former pres., life trustee Montefiore Home for Aged; pres. adv. bd. Barry U.; hon. trustee Hebrew U.; trustee Tel Aviv U. Mus. of the Diaspora; life trustee The Temple, Woodruff Found.; trustee Cleve. Play House. Mem. Beachmont Country Club, Commede Club, Union Club, Club at Williams Island. Office: Parkwood Corp 2829 Euclid Ave Cleveland OH 44115-2413

MANDEL, JACK SHELDON, epidemiologist, educator; b. Nov. 24, 1944; MPH, U. Minn., 1973, PhD, 1981. Assoc. prof. U. Minn., Mpls., 1981-88, prof., 1988-99, head divns. environ. and occupl. health, 1995-99, Mayo chair pub. health, 1996-99; group v.p. Exponent, Menlo Park, Calif., 1999—. Home: 201 Los Robles Dr Burlingame CA 94010-5927 Office: Exponent 149 Commonwealth Dr Menlo Park CA 94025-1133 E-mail: jmandel@exponent.com.

MANDEL, JAMES A. civil engineer, educator; b. Pittsburgh, Pa., Dec. 25, 1934; s. Isadore and Jennie Mandel; m. Carolyn D. Lisi, June 24, 1998; m. Rita J. Sommer, May 10, 1959 (dec. Sept. 11, 1991); children: Belinda E. Anderson, Robert K. BS, Carnegie Inst. of Tech., Pittsburg, PA, 1956; MS, Carnegie Inst. of Tech., Pittsburgh, PA, 1962; PhD, Syracuse U., Syracuse, NY, 1967. Design engr. Richardson Gordon & Associates, Pittsburgh, Pa., 1956—61; sr. stress engr. Goodyear Aerospace Corp., Akron, Ohio, 1962—64; asst. prof. Syracuse U., Syracuse, NY, 1967—70, assoc. prof., 1970—78, prof., 1978—95, prof. emeritus, 1995—. Contbr. articles to profl. jours. Pvt. US Army, 1957—57, United States. Achievements include development of Developed CBRIDGE, software for analysis of horizontally curved bridges. Home: 7262 Leaforest Lane East Syracuse NY 13057 Office: Syracuse University Department of Civil & Enviornmental Engi Syracuse NY 13244

MANDEL, JOEL EMANUEL, orthopedist; b. Brooklyn, Mar. 1, 1930; s. Morris and Minnie Mandel. BA, N.Y. U., 1951; MS, Ga. Inst. Tech., 1952; MD, Chgo. Med. Sch., 1956. Diplomate Am. Bd. Med. Examiners, Am. Bd. Orthopedic Surgery. Intern D.C. Gen. Hosp., 1956—57; resident in gen. surgery VA Hosp., 1957—58; resident in orthopedic surgery D.C. Gen. Hosp., 1958—60, N.Y. U., Bellevue, 1960—61; pres., founding ptnr. The New City (N.Y.) Orthopedic Group, P.C., 1961—85; med. dir. Post-Trauma Med. Svcs., New Windsor, 1985—. Host weekly radio program Medicine Today, 1973—76. Assoc. eidtor Jour. Disability, 1990—93, editl. adv. bd. Disability, 1995—96. Bd. govs. Rockland County (N.Y.) Health Complex, 1977—88; mem. coord. coun. Rockland County Emergency Med. Svc., 1977—81. Recipient Rockland County Dist. Svc. award, 1973. Fellow: N.Y. State Soc. Surgeons, Am. Acad. Orthopedic Surgeons, Internat. Coll. Surgeons, Am. Acad. Disability Evaluating Physicians (bd. dirs. 1988—93, sec. 1990—93); mem.: Rockland County (N.Y.) Med. Soc. (mem. peer rev. com. 1973—85, pres. 1974—75, exec. coun. 1967—76, dir. pub. rels. 1967—73, chmn. bd. censors 1975—76), Orange County (N.Y.) Med. Soc. (mem. peer rev. com. 1987—, exec. com. 1994—), Ea. Orthopedic Assn., N.Y. State Soc. Orthopedic Surgeons (bd. dirs. 1976—82). Avocations: sailing, windsurfing. Office: Post-Trauma Med Svc PC 833 Blooming Grove Tpk New Windsor NY 12553 Fax: 845-561-1570. E-mail: bonedoc@frontiernet.net.

MANDEL, JOSEPH DAVID, academic administrator, lawyer; b. N.Y.C., Mar. 26, 1940; s. Max and Charlotte Lee (Goodman) M.; m. Jean Carol Westerman, Aug. 18, 1963; children: Jonathan Scott, Eric David. AB, Dartmouth Coll., 1960, MBA with distinction, 1961; JD, Yale U., 1964. Bar: Calif. 1965. Law clk. U.S. Ct. Appeals, 9th cir., L.A., 1964-65; lectr. law U. So. Calif. Law Ctr., 1965-68; assoc. atty. Tuttle & Taylor, 1965-69, mem., 1970-82, 90-91, of counsel, 1984-90; vice chancellor UCLA, 1991—, lectr. in law, 1993; v.p., gen. counsel, sec. Natomas Co., San Francisco, 1983; lectr. in law UCLA, 2001—02. Mem. Calif. Legal Corps, 1993—; bd. dirs. LRN, The Legal Knowledge Co., 1994—. Mem. bd. editors Yale Law Jour., 1962-64. Pres. Legal Aid Found., L.A., 1978-79; trustee Southwestern U. Sch. Law, 1982, UCLA Pub. Interest Law Found., 1981-82, L.A. County Bar Found., 1974-79, 82, Coro Found., 1989-92, UCLA Armand Hammer Mus. Art and Cultural Ctr., 1995—, Geffen Playhouse, Inc., 1995-98, Coro So. Calif. Ctr., 1985-92; bd. dirs. pub. coun., 1989-94, cmty. v.p., 1992-94; mem. L.A. Bd. Zoning Appeals, 1984-90, vice-chmn., 1985-86, 89-90, chmn., 1986-87; mem. L.A. City Charter Reform Commn., 1996-99; bd. dirs. Western Justice Ctr. Found., 1989—, v.p., 1992-95, 1st v.p., 1995-97, sr. v.p., 1997-99, pres., 1999—; bd. dirs. Harvard Water Polo Found., 1990-96; bd. advisors Pub. Svc. Challenge Nat. Assn. for Pub. Interest Law, 1990—; bd. govs. Inner City Law Ctr., 1991—; mem. Blue Ribbon Screening Com. to Select Insp. Gen., L.A. Police Commn., 1999; mem. bd. overseers Inst. for Civil Justice, RAND, 1999—. Recipient Maynard Toll award Legal Aid Found. of L.A., 1991, Shattuck-Price award L.A. County Bar Assn., 1993, West Coast Liberty award Lambda Legal Def. and Edn. Fund, 1994, Cmty. Achievement award Pub. Coun., 1996; named One of Calif.'s 100 Most Influential Attys. by Calif. Bus. Jour., 2000. Mem. State Bar Calif. (legal svcs. trust fund commn. 1985-87, chmn. 1985-86), Yale U. Law Sch. Assn. (exec. com. 1983-88, 90-96, v.p. 1986-88, chmn. planning com. 1990-92, pres. 1992-94, chmn. exec. com. 1994-96), mem. alumni Coun. Dartmouth Coll., 1992-95, Dartmouth Coll. Assn. Alumni (exec. com. 1997—v.p. 2001), L.A. Co. Bar Assn. (trustee 1974-74, 1975-81, pres. 1980-81, sr. v.p. 1978-79, chair pro bono council 1986-87), Order of Coif. Democrat. Jewish. Home: 15478 Longbow Dr Sherman Oaks CA 91403-4910 Office: UCLA Office Chancellor 2135 Murphy Hl Los Angeles CA 90095-1405 E-mail: jmandel@conet.ucla.edu.

MANDEL, KARYL LYNN, accountant; b. Chgo., Dec. 14, 1935; d. Isador J. and Eve (Gellar) Karzen; m. Fredric H. Mandel, Sept. 29, 1956; children: David Scott, Douglas Jay, Jennifer Ann. Student, U. Mich., 1954-56, Roosevelt U., 1956-57; AA summa cum laude, Oakton Community Coll., 1979. CPA, Ill; registered investment advisor; lic. life ins. provider. Pres. Excel Transp. Service Co., Elk Grove, Ill., 1958-78; tax mgr. Chunowitz, Teitelbaum & Baerson, CPA's, Northbrook, 1981-83, tax ptnr., 1984—. Sec-treas. Lednam, Inc., Coffee Break, Inc.; mem. acctg. curriculum adv. bd. Oakton C.C., Des Plaines, Ill., 1987—; pres. Lednam Enterprises, LLC, 2001—. Contbg. author: Ill. CPA's News Jour., Acctg. Today. Recipient State of Israel Solidarity award, 1976. Mem. AICPA, Am. Soc. Women CPA, Women's Am. ORT (pres. Chgo. region 1972-74, v.p. midwest dist. 1975-76, nat. endowment com., nat investment adv. com.), Ill. CPA Soc. (chmn. estate and gift tax com. 1987-89, legis. contact com. 1981-82, pres. North Shore chpt., award for Excellence in Acctg. Edn., Bd. dirs. 1989-91), Chgo. Soc. Women CPA, Chgo. Estate Planning Coun., Nat. Assn. Women Bus. Owners, Lake County Estate Planning, Coun., Greater North Shore Estate Planning Coun. Office: 401 Huehl Rd Northbrook IL 60062-2300 E-mail: KLM@CTBLTD.COM.

MANDEL, LESLIE ANN, investment advisor, business owner, author; b. Washington, July 29, 1945; d. Seymour and Marjorie (Syble) Mandel; m. Arthur Herzog III. BA in Art History, U. Minn., 1967; cert., N.Y. Sch. Interior Design, 1969. Cert. Brailled Libr. Congress. Pres. Leslie Mandel Enterprises, Inc., N.Y.C., 1968—; sr. v.p. Maximum Entertainment Network, L.A. and N.Y.C., 1988-90; pres. Rich List Co., 1968—; pres., CEO Mandel Airplane Funding and Leasing Corp., N.Y.C., Hong Kong, China and Mongolia, 1990—; CEO Mandel-Khan Inc., Ulaanbaatar, Mongolia, 1994—, keep hers, keep his, 2002—. Fin. advisor Osmed, Inc., Mpls., 1986—, Devine Comm./Allen & Co., N.Y., Del., Utah, N.Mex., N.Y. WUWV, Utah KBER, WKTC-AM-FM, 1984-89, Am. Kefir Corp., N.Y.C., 1983-89, Shore Group (Internat., Guyana), Flight Internat., 1991—; owner The Rich List Co., 150 internat. catalogs, mags. and fundraising lists; joint venture Mongolian Ind. Broadcasting Channel, Ulaanbaatar, 1995; pres., owner Mandel Airplane Funding and Leasing Corp.; rep. Israeli govt. IAI Satellite, China, Romania, Costa Rica, Mongolia, Amos Satellite Network, China, 1992—; advisor rep. Gt. Wall Corp., Long March Corp., China, 1992—, Chinese Silk, 1993—, Am. Oil Refinery, 1993—; bd. dirs. Coastal Equipment Co., Bristol Airlines; cons. Exclusive Miat Airlines, Mongolia; purchasing agt. Peoples Republic of China-Aircraft; advisor Aeropostalis, Mex., 1994-95; photographer; lectr. UN Internat. Direct Mail; advisor Aruba Airlines, Mexicana Airlines; aircraft agt. Lazorlines Landing Equipment, 1997—; lease Estafada Airlines 737-200-C, 2000—; advisor Guyana 2000 Arilines. Photographer: Vogue, 1978, New Earth Times, 1995, Fortune mag.; Braille transcriber: The Prophet (Kalil Gibran), 1967, Getting Ready for Battle (R. Prawe Jhabuala), 1967; exec. prodr. film: Hospital Audiences, 1975 (Cannes award 1976); author: Hungry at the Watering Hole, Gardiners Island, 1636-1990, 1989, Expedition: In the Steps of Ghengis Kahn, 1994; advisor Port Libertè Ptnrs., 1988-94; contbr. articles to profl. jours. Fin. advisor Correctional Assn., Osborn Soc., 1977—; founder, treas. Prisoners Family Transportation and Assistance Fund, N.Y., 1972-77; judge Emmy awards of Acad. TV Arts and Scis., N.Y.C., 1970; bd. dirs. Prisoners Assn., 1990; chmn. U.S.A. com. Violeta B. de Chamarro for Pres. of Nicaragua Campaign. Recipient Inst. for the Creative and Performing Arts fellowship, N.Y.C., 1966, Appreciation cert. Presdl. Inaugural Com., Washington, 1981. Fellow N.Y. Women in Real Estate, Explorers Club (lectr. on Mongolia, fin. com.); mem. Com. on Am. and Internat. Fgn. Affairs, Lawyers Com. on Internat. Human Rels., Bus. Exec. Nat. Security, Venture Capital Breakfast Club, The Coffee Club House, Sigma Delta Tau, Sigma Epsilon Sigma. Democrat. Avocations: painting, writing, fishing, canoeing, horseback riding, breeding cockatiels. Home: 4 E 81st St New York NY 10028-0235 Office: Mandel-Khan Inc PO Box 97 care Boldbaatar Mandel Kahn Ulaanbaatar 210648 Mongolia also: Leslie Mandel Enterprises PO Box 294 Wainscott NY 11975-0294 also: PO Box 29A Wainscott NY 11975-0029

MANDEL, LEWIS RICHARD, pharmaceutical company executive; b. Bklyn., Nov. 13, 1936; s. Murray and Belle (Teller) M.; m. Rochelle Holtzman, Mar. 27, 1960; children: Beth, Susan, Stefanie. BS, Columbia U., 1958, PhD, 1962. Registered pharmacist, N.Y., N.J., Pa. Lectr. biochemistry, then asst. prof. pharmacology Columbia U., N.Y.C., 1961-64; rsch. biochemist Merck & Co., Inc., Rahway, N.J., 1964-76, dir. biochemistry, 1976-79, sr. dir. univ. and indsl. rels., 1979-89, exec. dir. indsl. and acad. rels., 1989—, exec. dir. external sci. affairs worldwide, 1993-99, v.p. external sci. affairs worldwide NJ, 1999—2002, emeritus, external rsch. and acad. affairs, 2002—. Patentee in field; contbr. articles to profl. publs. Grantee NIH, 1963-64; recipient Wellcome travel award Burroughs Wellcome, 1963. Mem. Am. Soc. Pharmacology and Exptl. Therapeutics, Am. Soc. Biochemistry and Molecular Biology. Office: Merck and Co Inc PO Box 2000 Rahway NJ 07065-0900

MANDEL, MARTIN LOUIS, lawyer; b. L.A., May 17, 1944; s. Maurice S. and Florence (Byer) M.; m. Duree Dunn, Oct. 16, 1982; 1 child, Max Andrew. BA, U. So. Calif., 1965, JD, 1968; LLM, George Washington U., 1971. Bar: Calif. 1969, U.S. Dist. Ct. (cen. dist.) Calif. 1972, U.S. Ct. Claims 1971, U.S. Tax Ct. 1971, U.S. Supreme Ct. 1972. With office of gen. csl. IRS, Washington, 1968-72; ptnr. Stephens, Jones, LaFever & Smith, L.A., 1972-77, Stephens, Martin & Mandel, 1977-79, Fields, Fehn, Feinstein & Mandel, 1979-83; sr. v.p., gen. counsel Investment Mortgage Internat., Inc., 1983-84; ptnr. Feinstein, Gourley & Mandel, 1984-85, Mandel & Handin, San Francisco, 1985—; gen. counsel L.A. Express Football Club, 1983-85. Instr. corps. U. West L.A., 19873-83. Mem. ABA, L.A. County Bar Assn., L.A. Athletic Club, Phi Delta Phi. Office: 652 Bair Island Rd #210 Redwood City CA 94063 E-mail: martin@tmgtalent.com.

MANDEL, MAURICE, II, lawyer, educator, mediator; b. Hollywood, Calif. s. Maurice and Wynne Mandel. BSBA, U. So. Calif., 1971, MEd, 1972; JD, Western State U., 1979. Bar: Calif. 1980, U.S. Dist. Ct. (ctrl. dist.) Calif. 1982, U.S. Ct. Appeals (fed. and 9th cirs.) 1983, U.S. Dist. Ct. (we. dist.) Tenn. 1987, U.S. Dist. Ct. Ariz. 1990, U.S. Dist. Ct. (so. dist.) Calif. 1991, U.S. Supreme Ct. 1991, U.S. Ct. Appeals (5th cir.) 1995; cert. level I ski instr. PSIA Nat. Acad. 1998, child specialist 1999, settlement officer, USDC-CDCa. Tchr. Orange County (Calif.) Sch. Dist., 1972-82; pvt. practice law Newport Beach, Calif., 1982—; fed. settlement officer CDCA, 1998—. Instr. Coastline C.C., 1987-95, prof., 1995—, Coastline C.C. Acad. Senate, Coastline C.C. Parlimentarian 1996-99; prof. law Irvine (Calif.) U. Coll. of Law, 1994-98; instr. Orange County Bar Assn. Coll. of Trial Advocacy, 1994—; instr. Orange County Bar Assn. Mandatory Continuing Legal Edn., 1992—, Bear Mountain Calif. Ski Sch., 1996—, Ziet Maros, 1998—; FBA/OCC Mandatory Continuing Legal Edn. provider, 1994—, COURSE Vail Co. Alpine World Cup Finals, 1997, Alpine World Championships, 1999, World Cup, 1999, COURSE St. Anton am Arlberg, Alpine World Championships, 2001, COURSE Ladie's' Norams, Snowbasin, Utah, 2001, COURSE XIX Olympic Games, Salt Lakae City, 2002, Alpine Ski. Counselor Troy Camp, 1969-72; chmn. Legal Edn. for Youth, 1984-86; active Ctr. Dance Alliance, Orange County, 1986-97; JOC racing dir. So. Cal, 1998-2000; mem. Friends Am. Ballet Theatre, Opera Pacific Guild, Opera Pacific Bohemians, Calypso Soc., World Wildlife Found., L.A. County Mus. Art, Newport Beach Art Mus., Met. Mus. Art, Laguna Beach Mus. Art, Smithsonian Instn., Friend of Ballet Pacifica, Friends of Joffrey Ballet; assoc. U.S. Ski Team, 1975—; com. assoc. U.S. Olympics, 1988—; 100th Olympics vols., 1996, XIX Olympics, 2002; F.I.S. vol., 1997—, COURSE Alpine World Cup Finals, Vail, Colo., 1997, Alpine World Championships, 1999, 2001, XIX Olympics, 2002; mem. alumni and scholarship com. Beverly Hills H.S.; Opera Pacific Bohemians, Friends of Ballet Pacifica. Recipient cert. of appreciation U.S. Dist. Ct., L.A., 1985, U.S. Dist. Ct. Mediation award O.C., 2000, Thwarted Thwart award Newport Harbor C. of C., 1989, Tovarich award Kirov Ballet, 1989, 92, Perostroika award Moscow Classical Ballet, 1988-89, 94, Skrisivi Nogi award Bolshoi Ballet, 1990, Marinskii Dance award St. Petersburg, 1993; ABT Romeo & Juliet, 1996, Thwarted Thwart award Newport Harbor, 1996; Ziet Maros award Moscow Classical Ballet, 1998, 99, 2000, 2nd Place award JOC Slalom, 1998, 1st place award JOC Slalom, 2000, 2d place award Big Bear Instrs. Giant Slalom, 2000, 1st place award JOC Concourse, 2000, 14th pl. nat. standing JCNA Slalom, 1999. Mem. ABA, ATLA, Assn. Bus. Trial Lawyers, Federal Bar Assn., (founding pres. Orange Country chpt. 1986, nat. del. 1988-90, founder criminal indigent def. panel 1986, mem. numerous other coms., nat. chpt. activity award 1987, nat. membership award 1987, chpt. svc. award 1989, nat. regional membership chmn. 1990, spl. appointee nat. membership com. 1991), Calif. Bar Assn. (Pro Bono awards 1985-89), Pres.'s Coun. (founder 1996—), Orange County Bar Assn. (legal edn. for youth com. 1982-90, chmn, 1985, fed. practice com., sports com., mandatory fee arbitration com. 1985—, lawyer's referral svc. com. 1984-98, Merit award 1986), Orange County Bar Found. (trustee 1984-87), Women Lawyers of Orange County, U.S. Supreme Ct. Hist. Soc., 9th Jud. Cir. Hist. Soc., Am. Inns of Ct., Calif. Trial Lawyers Assn., Calif. Employee Lawyers Assn., Plaintiff Employee Lawyers Assn., Employees Rights Coun., Bar Leaders Coun. Dist. 8, Amicus Publico, U. So. Calif. Alumni Assn., Mensa, Cougar Club of Am., So. Calif. Cougar Club, San Diego Cougar Club, So. Calif. Jaguar Owners Assn. Clubs: Balboa Yacht. Avocations: skiing, yachting, tennis. Home: PO Box 411 Newport Beach CA 92662 Office: Ste 360 881 Dover Dr Newport Beach CA 92663-6929

MANDEL, MORTON, molecular biologist; b. Bklyn., July 6, 1924; s. Barnet and Rose (Kliner) M.; m. Florence H. Goodman, Apr. 1, 1952; children: Robert, Leslie. BCE, CUNY, 1944; MS, Columbia U., 1949, PhD in Physics, 1957. Scientist Bell Telephone Labs., Murray Hill, N.J., 1956-57; asst. prof. physics dept. Stanford (Calif.) U., 1957-61; scientist Gen. Telephone & Telegraph, Mountain View, Calif., 1961-63; rsch. assoc. dept. genetics Stanford U., 1963-64; rsch. fellow Karolinska Inst., Stockholm, Sweden, 1964-66; assoc. prof. sch. of medicine U. Hawaii, Honolulu, 1966-68, prof., 1968—; founder, dir. Hawaii Biotechnology Group, Inc., 1982-95. Cons. Fairchild Semiconductor, Hewlett Packard, Lockheed, Rheem, Palo Alto, Calif., 1957-61. Contbr. articles to profl. jours. Lt. (j.g.) USN, 1944-46. Recipient Am. Cancer Soc. Scholar award Am. Cancer Soc., 1979-80, Eleanor Roosevelt Internat. Cancer fellowship, 1979; named NIH Spl. fellow Karolinska Inst., 1964-66. Fellow Am. Phys. Soc.; mem. Sigma Xi. Achievements include citation classics; optimal conditions for mutagenesis by N-methyl-N-nitro-N-nitrosoguanidine in E. coli K12; calcium dependent bacteriophage DNA infection. Office: Dept Biochemistry 1960 E West Rd Honolulu HI 96822-2319

MANDEL, OSCAR, literature educator, writer; b. Antwerp, Belgium, Aug. 24, 1926; came to U.S., 1940; m. Adrienne Schizzano. BA, NYU, 1947; MA, Columbia U., 1948; PhD, Ohio State U., 1951. Asst. prof. English U. Nebr., 1955-60; Fulbright lectr. U. Amsterdam, 1960-61; vis. assoc. prof. English Calif. Inst. Tech., 1961-62, assoc. prof. English, 1962-68, prof. Lit., 1968—. Author: A Definition of Tragedy, 1961, The Theater of Don Juan, 1963, Chi Po and the Sorcerer, 1964, The Gobble-Up Stories, 1967, Seven Comedies by Marivaux, 1968, Five Comedies of Medieval France, 1970, The Collected Plays, 1970—72, Amphitryon, 1976, The Land of Upside Down by Tieck, 1978, The Ariadne of Thomas Corneille, 1982, Collected Lyrics and Epigrams, 1981, Three Classic Don Juan Plays, 1981, Philoctetes and the Fall of Troy, 1981, Annotations to Vanity Fair, 1981, The Book of Elaborations, 1985, The Kukkurrik Fables, 1987, Sigismund, Prince of Poland, 1989, August von Kotzebue: The Comedy, The Man, 1990, The Virgin and the Unicorn: Four Plays, 1993, The Art of Alessandro Magnasco: An Essay on the Recovery of Meaning, 1994, The Cheerfulness of Dutch Art: A Rescue Operation, 1996, Two Romantic Plays: The Spaniards in Denmark and The Rebels of Nantucket, 1996, Fundamentals of the Art of Poetry, 1998, L'Arc de Philoctete, 2002, Prosper Merimee: Plays on Hispanic Themes, 2002; contbr. articles to profl. jours. Office: Calif Inst Tech Humanities Divsn Pasadena CA 91125-0001 E-mail: om@hss.caltech.edu.

MANDEL, PETER BEVAN, writer, columnist; b. N.Y.C., June 7, 1957; s. Paul William and Sheila (Emslie) M.; m. Kathryn Evelyn Byrd, June 13, 1981. BA, Middlebury Coll., 1979; MA, Brown U., 1981. Editl. assoc. Brown Alumni Monthly, Providence, 1983-85; editor, staff writer Antioch Pub. Co., Yellow Springs, Ohio, 1985-87; asst. to pres. Bryant Coll., Smithfield, R.I., 1987-90; freelance writer, Paris and Providence, 1990-96; columnist Providence Jour.-Bull., 1996—. Author: The Official Cat IQ Test, 1991 (Japanese, Chinese, German, Italian, Dutch, Swedish, Danish edits.), (poetry) If One Lived on the Equator, 1993, The Cat Dictionary, 1994, (juvenile) Red Cat White Cat, 1994 (Am. Bookseller Pick of Lists award), The Official Dog IQ Test, 1995 (Chinese edit.), (juvenile) Say Hey! A Song of Willie Mays, 2000, (juvenile) My Ocean Liner: Across the North Atlantic on the Great Ship Normandie, 2001; contbr. articles and poetry to various publs., including Harper's, Reader's Digest, Washington Post, Cosmopolitan, Yankee. Bd. dirs. Vol. Svcs. for Animals, Providence, 1996—. Me. Soc. Children's Book Writers and Illustrators, Cat Writers' Assn. Am. (Best Humorous Book medal 1996, Best Newspaper Article medal 1997). Home: 239 Transit St Providence RI 02906-3040 E-mail: pmandel@worldnet.att.net.

MANDEL, REID ALAN, lawyer; b. Mpls., Mar. 31, 1954; s. Irwin A. and Sandra Harriet (Fink) M.; m. Jeanne Claire Smith, Aug. 29, 1981. BA, Yale U., 1977; JD, NYU, 1980. Bar: Minn. 1981, Ill. 1981, U.S. Dist. Ct. (no. dist.) Ill. 1981, U. S. Tax Ct. 1981. Law clk. to justice Supreme Ct. Minn., St. Paul, 1980-81; assoc. Katten, Muchin & Zavis, Chgo., 1981-87, ptnr., 1987--. Adj. prof. LLM program John Marshall Sch. Law. Contbr. articles to profl. jours. Mem. Chgo. Vol. Legal Svcs.; bd. dirs., past chmn. Chgo. Lawyers Com. for Civil Rights Under Law, 1985—. Mem. ABA, Chgo. Bar Assn. Jewish. Office: Katten Muchin Zavis 525 W Monroe St Ste 1600 Chicago IL 60661-3693 E-mail: reid.mandel@kmz.com.

MANDELBAUM, DAVID EZRA, pediatric neurologist; b. N.Y.C., Oct. 24, 1952; s. Bernard Mandelbaum and Judith Louise Werber; m. Elana Katz, June 24, 1975 (div. Aug. 1992); 1 child, Danya Judith. BA, Columbia U., 1974, MD, PhD, Columbia U., 1980. Diplomate Am. Bd. Psychology and Neurology; cert. child neurology, clin. neurophysiology, neurodevel. disabilities. Intern Yale-New Haven Hosp., 1980-81, resident in pediat., 1981-82; resident in neurology Neurol. Inst. Columbia-Presbyn. Med. Ctr., N.Y.C., 1982-83, fellow pediat. neurology, 1983-85; dir. divsn. child neurology U. Med. & Dentistry N.J., New Brunswick, 1985—, asst. prof. pediat. and neurology, 1985-91, assoc. prof., 1991-2001, prof., 2001—. Chief child neurology svc. Robert Wood Johnson U. Hosp., New Brunswick, 1985—, St. Peters U. Hosp., New Brunswick, 1985—; chmn. profl. adv. bd. Epilepsy Found. N.J.; cons., lectr. and presenter in field. Contbr. articles to profl. jours. Bd. dirs. YM/YWHA Raritan Valley, Highland Park, N.J., 1997-2001, Princeton (N.J.) Pro Musica, 1998. Grantee NIH, 1974-80, U. Med. & Dentistry N.J. Found., 1986-88, Ortho-McNeil Pharm. Corp./Johnson & Johnson, 1997-98, Parke-Davis Corp., 1998. Mem. Profs. Child Neurology, Child Neurology Soc., Am. Acad. Neurology, Am. Acad. Pediat., Am. Epilepsy Soc. Jewish. Avocations: music, swimming. Office: U Med & Dentistry NJ 97 Paterson St New Brunswick NJ 08901-2160 Fax: (732) 235-7346. E-mail: mandelde@umdnj.edu.

MANDELBAUM, DAVID MICHAEL, electrical engineer; b. Tel Aviv, Israel, Dec. 28, 1933; arrived in U.S., 1941; s. Isaac Mandelbaum, Jean Mandelbaum; m. Stefanie Singer, June 8, 1965; children: Andrew, Richard. AB, Princeton U., 1956; MSEE, Columbia U., 1960. Contbr. Achievements include development of first frequency domain decoder for cyclic codes; invention of Mandelbaum-Barrows Codes. Home: 118 Tunicflower Ln Princeton Junction NJ 08550 Office: CECOM R&D Command & Control Myer Center Fort Monmouth NJ 07703

MANDELBAUM, HAROLD NEIL, accountant; b. Englewood, N.J., Sept. 13, 1967; s. Diane M. (Kaufman) Kubik; m. Shari Patt, Sept. 9, 1995. BA in Econs. , Syracuse U., 1990; BS in Acctg., William Paterson Coll., 1993. CPA; CFP; cert. personal fin. specialist; lic. ins. N.Y.; lic. securities. Brokerage Lehman Brothers, N.Y.C., 1990-91; accountant NSCSA Am. Inc., Staten Island, N.Y., 1992; accountant, fin. cons. Joseph A. Salamo, CPA, N.Y.C., 1992-96, Harold N. Mandelbaum CPA, PFS, CFP, N.Y.C., 1996—. Mem. AICPA, N.Y. State Soc. CPAs. Office: 555 5th Ave Fl 9 New York NY 10017-2416 E-mail: hnmandelbaum@msn.com.

MANDELBAUM, SAMUEL ROBERT, lawyer; b. N.Y.C., June 9, 1951; s. Alvin J. and Florence (Geller) M.; m. Erica Gottfried Mandelbaum, Sept. 27, 1980; children: Lia, Ben. BA, SUNY, 1973; student, Columbia U., 1974-75; JD, Vermont Law Sch., 1977; LLM, Georgetown U., 1995. Bar: Fla. 1979, N.Y. 1985, U.S. Dist. Ct. (mid. dist.) 1979, U.S. Dist. Ct. (so. dist.) 1983, U.S. Ct. Appeals (11th cir.) 1981, U.S. Ct. Appeals (4th cir.) 1984, U.S. Supreme Ct. 1982. Sr. asst. atty. gen. Atty. Gen's. Office, Tampa, Fla., 1981-82; ptnr. Smith, Williams & Bowles, 1986-95, Becker & Poliakoff, P.A. (formerly Anderson & Orcutt, P.A.), Tampa, 1996-2001, Mandelbaum & Fitzsimmons PA, Tampa, 2001—; adj. prof. law Stetson U. Coll. of Law, De Land, Fla., 1995—. Editor, trial section Fla. Bar Jour., Tallahassee, 1988—. Fund distbr. com. mem. United Way, Tampa, Fla., 1991—. Recipient Outstanding Svc. to Ct. Arbitration Program award U.S. Dist. Ct. Fla., Tampa, 1991. Mem. Fla. Bar Assn. (exec. coun. internat. sect.), Hillsborough County Bar Assn. (chmn. internat. sect.), Davis Island Yacht Club, Rotary Club. Avocations: sailing, golf, jogging, photography. Office: Mandelbaum & Fitzsimmons PA PO Box 3373 Tampa FL 33601-3373

MANDELBROT, BENOIT B. mathematician, scientist, educator; b. Warsaw, Poland, Nov. 20, 1924; came to U.S., 1958; s. Charles and Belle (Lurie) M.; m. Aliette Kagan, Nov. 5, 1955; children: Laurent, Didier. Diploma, Ecole Polytechnique, Paris, 1947; MS in Aeronautics, Calif. Inst. Tech., 1948; PhD in Math., U. Paris, 1952; DS (hon.) , Syracuse U., 1985, Laurentian U., 1986, Boston U., 1987, SUNY, 1988, U. Bremen, 1988, U. Guelph, Ont., Can., 1989, U. Dallas, 1992, Union Coll., 1993, U. Buenos Aires, 1993, U. Tel Aviv, 1995, Open U., U.K., 1998; DHL (hon.) , Pace U., 1989, Athens U. Bus. and Fin., 1998; AM (hon.) , Pace U., 1989; DHL (hon.) , U. St. Andrews, Scotland, 1999; AM (hon.) , Yale U., 2000. Jr. mem. and Rockefeller scholar Inst. for Advanced Study, Princeton, N.J., 1953-54; jr. prof. math. U. Geneva, 1955-57, U. Lille and Ecole Polytechnique, Paris, 1957-58; rsch. staff mem. IBM Watson Rsch. Ctr., Yorktown Heights, N.Y., 1958-74, IBM fellow, 1974-93, IBM fellow emeritus, 1993—; prof. math. scis. Yale U., New Haven, 1987-99; prof. Acad. des Scis., Paris, 1995; Sterling prof. Yale U., New Haven, 1999—. Vis. prof. econs. Harvard U., 1962-63, vis. prof. applied math., 1963-64, vis. prof. math., 1979-80, prof. practice math., 1984-87; vis. prof. engring. Yale U., 1970; vis. prof. physiology Einstein Coll. Medicine, 1970; Hitchcock prof. U. Calif., Berkeley, 1992; visitor MIT, 1953, also Inst. lectr.; visitor U. Paris, 1966, Coll. de France, Paris, 1973, Inst. des Hautes Etudes Scientifiques, Bures, 1980, Mittag-Leffler Inst., Sweden, 1984, 2001, Max Planck Inst. Math., Bonn, Germany, 1988, Gonville and Caius Coll., Newton Inst.; lectr. Yale U., 1970, Cambridge (Eng.) U., 1990, 99, Oxford U., 1990, Imperial Coll., London, 1991, Accademia di Lincei, Rome, Math. Centrum, Amsterdam, The Netherlands, U. Barcelona, Spain, U. Uppsala, Sweden, London Sch. Econs., Oslo U., Coimbra U., Portugal, Stockholm Tech. U.; spkr. and organizer profl. confs. *Science would be ruined if (like the Olympics) it were to put competition above everything else, and if it were to clarify the rules of competition by withdrawing entirely into narrowly defined specialties. The rare scholars who are wanderers-by-choice are essential to the intellectual welfare of the settled disciplines. He is a recipient of the Barnard medal which read "In the great tradition of natural philosophers past, looked at the world around you on a broader canvas". The American Journal of Physics has said, concerning his work, "It is possible to believe that no one will be considered scientifically literate tomorrow who is not familiar with fractals". Science has said that Mandelbrot "Points out that nature has played a joke on mathematicians". The Interdisciplinary Science Review called one of his books "The most extraordinarily beautiful book in thought and in form that I have read for many years."* Author: Logique, Langage et Théorie de l'Information, 1957, Les objets fractals: forme, hasard et dimension, 1975, 4th edit., 1995, Fractals: Form, Chance and Dimension, 1977, The Fractal Geometry of Nature, 1982, La Geometria della Natura, 1987, Fractals and Scaling in Finance: Discontinuity, Concentration, Risk, 1997, Fractales, hasard et finance, 1997, Multifractals and 1/f Noise: Wild Self-Affinity in Physics, 1999, Gaussian Self-Affinity and Fractals, 2002, Nel mondo dei frattali, 2001, (with M.L. Frame) Fractals, Graphics and Mathematics Education, 2002, Fractals in Chaos and Statistical Physics, 2002; contbr. articles to profl. jours. Recipient Franklin medal Franklin Inst., 1986, Alexander von Humboldt Preis, 1987, Caltech disting. svc. award, 1988, Moet-Hennessy prize, 1988, Harvey prize, 1989, Nev. prize U. Nev. Sys., 1991, Wolf prize for physics, 1993, Honda prize, 1994, Medal of City of Paris, 1996, John Scott award City of Phila., 1999, L.F. Richardson medal European Geophys. Soc., 2000; nat. lectr. Sigma Xi, 1980-82; Guggenheim fellow, 1968. Fellow AAAS, IEEE (Charles Proteus Steinmetz medal 1988), Am. Acad. Arts and Scis., European Acad. Arts, Scis. and Humanities, Am. Phys. Soc., French Physics Soc. (hon.), Inst. Math. Stats., Econometric Soc., Am. Geophys. Union, Am. Statistic Assn.; mem. NAS U.S.A. (Barnard medal 1985), Internat. Statis. Inst. (elected.), Am. Math. Soc., Norwegian Acad. Sci. and Letters (fgn. mem.), Sigma Xi (Procter prize 2002). Achievements include origination of theory of fractals, an interdisciplinary theory of roughness it is concerned with financial data, mountains, clouds, dynamic attractors, and all other shapes and phenomena that are equally irregular or broken-up at all scales; the best known fractal is called Mandelbrot set. Office: Yale Univ Math Dept New Haven CT 06520-8283 E-mail: Fractal@watson.ibm.com.

MANDELKER, DANIEL ROBERT, law educator; b. Milw., July 18, 1926; s. Adolph Irwin and Marie (Manner) M.; divorced; children: Amy Jo, John David. BA, U. Wis., 1947, LLB, 1949; JSD, Yale U., 1956. Bar: Wis. 1949. Asst. prof. law Drake U., 1949-51; atty. HHFA, Washington, 1952-53; asst. prof., then assoc. prof. law Ind. U., 1953-62; mem. faculty Washington U., St. Louis, 1962—, prof. law, 1963-74, Howard A. Stamper prof. law, 1974—. Walter E. Meyer rsch. prof. law Columbia U., 1971-72; Ford Found. law faculty fellow, London, 1959-60; cons. State of Hawaii Dept. Planning and Econ. Devel., 1972-78, State of Hawaii Office of State Planning, 1993-94; legal resources adv. group Transp. Rsch. Bd., 1991-94; mem. local govt. adv. bd. intergovtl. rels. U.S. Adv. Commn., 1985-88; mem. devel. regulations coun. Urban Land Inst., 1980-96; cons. housing subcom., banking and currency com. U.S. Ho. of Reps., 1970-71, cons. policy studies, ins. subcom., banking, fin., urban affairs coms., 1989-91; mem. commn. on environ. law World Conservation Union, 1997—; cons. state and local govts. on land use regulation; Nat. Disting. lectr. Fla. State Jour. Land Use and Environ. Law, 1992; 15th Denman lectr. U. Cambridge, Eng., 1992, Inaugural Robert E. Boden lectr. Marquette U. Sch. Law, 1997; cons. Master Plan Coalition, New Orleans, 2001--; frequ.nt spkr. at nat. confs. on land use law. Author: Green Belts and Urban Growth: English Town and Country Planning in Action, 1962, Controlling Planned Residential Developments, 1966, Managing Our Urban Environment-Cases, Text and Problems, 1966, 2d edit., 1971, Case Studies in Land Planning and Development, 1968, The Zoning Dilemma, 1971, (with W.R. Ewald) Street Graphics and the Law, 1971, 2d edit., 1988, (with R. Montgomery) Housing in America: Problems and Perspectives, 1973, 2d edit., 1979, Housing Subsidies in the United States and England, 1973, New Developments in Land and Environmental Controls, 1974, Environmental and Land Controls Legislation, 1976, supplement, 1982, (with D. Netsch) State and Local Government in a Federal System, 1977, (with D. Netsch and P. Salsich) 2d edit., 1983, (with Netsch, Salsich and Wegner) 3rd edit., 1990, 5th edit., 2002, (with R. Cunningham) Planning and Control of Land Development, 1979, 3d edit., 1990, (with R. Cunningham and J. Payne) 4th edit., 1995, (with J. Payne) 5th edit., 2001, Environment and Equity, 1981, (with others) Cases and Materials on Housing and Urban Development, 1981, 2d edit., 1989, 3rd edit., 1999, Land Use Law, 1982, 4th edit., 1997, supplement 2001 (with F. Anderson, D. Tarlock and R. Glicksman) Environmental Protection Law and Policy, 2d edit., 1990, 3d edit., 1999, NEPA Law and Litigation, 2d edit., 1992, supplement, 2001, (with J. Gerard and T. Sullivan) Federal Land Use Law, 1986, supplement, 2000, (with others) Property Law and the Public Interest, 1998; mem. editl. adv. bd. various land use jours. Mem. nat. adv. com. on outdoor advt. and motorist info. Dept. Transp., 1980-81; mem. adv. com. on housing Dem. Caucus, U.S. Ho. of Reps., 1981-82; pres. Nat. Coalition for Scenic Beauty, 1987-88; sr. fellow Urban Land Inst., 1989-95; mem. law sch. editl. bd. Lexis Law Pub., 1989-97. Mem. NAS (com. social and behavioral urban rsch. 1967-68), Am. Planning Assn. (bd. dirs. 1981-84, Housing Policy Task Force 1990-93, property rights task force 1994-95, amicus curiae com. 1995—, prin. cons. growing smart model legislation project 1996-2001), Nat. Assn. Environ. Profls. (chair legal issues com. NEPA working group 1999-01), Order of Coif, Phi Beta Kappa, Phi Kappa Phi. Office: PO Box 1120 Saint Louis MO 63188-1120 E-mail: mandelker@wulaw.wustl.edu.

MANDELKER, LAWRENCE ARTHUR, lawyer; b. N.Y.C., Dec. 2, 1943; s. Murray and Sally (Levine) M.; m. Carolyn Anne Bareish, Oct. 4, 1970; children: Daniel H., Benjamin E. BA, Queens Coll., CUNY, 1964; JD, NYU, 1968. Bar: N.Y. 1968, Pa. 1981, U.S. Dist. Ct. (so. and ea. dists.) N.Y. 1973, U.S. Dist. Ct. (ea. dist.) Wis. 1980, (no. dist.) N.Y., 1995, U.S. Ct. Appeals (2d cir.) 1979, U.S. Ct. Appeals (9th cir.) 1989. Law sec. N.Y.C. Civil Ct., 1970-71, N.Y. State Supreme Ct., 1972; mem. Kantor, Davidoff, Wolfe, Mandelker & Kass, P.C.; mem. com. character and fitness 9th Jud. Dist., Coun., N.Y. State Athletic Commn., 1995—2001. Bd. dirs. NYU Law Alumni Assocs. Mem. Lewisboro Bd. Assessment Rev., N.Y., 1979—, chmn., 1984—; chmn. Lewisboro Bd. Ethics. Former mem. bd. editors: NY Law Jour.; contbr. articles. Served as staff sgt. USAR, 1968-74. Mem. Assn. Bar City N.Y. (mem. coun. on jud. adminstrn., past mem. com. on state cts. superior jurisdiction civil ct. com., former chmn. spl. com. on election law). Home: 206 Todd Rd Katonah NY 10536-2410 Office: Kantor Davidoff Wolfe Mandelker & Kass PC 51 E 42nd St New York NY 10017-5404

MANDELKERN, LEO, biophysics and chemistry educator; b. N.Y.C., Feb. 23, 1922; s. Israel and Gussie (Krostich) M.; m. Berdie Medvedoff, May, 1946; children: I. Paul, Marshal, David. BA, Cornell U., 1942, PhD, 1949. Postdoctoral rsch. assoc. Cornell U., Ithaca, N.Y., 1949-52; phys. chemist Nat. Bur. Standards, Washington, 1952-62; prof. chemistry and biophysics Fla. State U., Tallahassee, 1962—, R.O. Lawton Disting. prof., 1984—. Vis. prof. U. Miami (Fla.) Med. Sch., 1963, U. Calif. Med. Sch., San Francisco, 1964, Cornell U., 1967; mem. biophysics fellowship com. NIH, 1967-70; mem. study panel crystal growth and morphology NRC, 1960; cons. in field. Author: Crystallization of Polymers, 1964, An Introduction to Macromolecules, 1972, 1983; contbr. numerous articles to profl. jours. 1st lt. USAAF, 1942-46, PTO. Recipient Meritorious Svc. award U.S. Dept. Commerce, 1957, Arthur S. Fleming award Washington Jaycees, 1958, Mettler award N.Am. Thermal Analysis Soc., Phila., 1984, Disting. Svc. in Advancement of Polymer Sci. award Soc. Polymer Sci., Japan, 1993. Fellow AAAS, Am. Chem. Soc. (Polymer Chemistry award 1975, Fla. award 1984, Rubber divsn. Whitby award 1988, Charles Goodyear medal 1993, Applied Polymer Sci. award 1989, Disting. Svc. in Advancement of Polymer Sci. 1993, Polymer Divsn. P.J. Flory award 1994, Polymer Materials Sci. & Engring. Divsn. Coop. Rsch. award 1995, Herman F. Mark award 2000), Polymer Soc. Japan, Biophys. Soc., Am. Phys. Soc. (Outstanding Educator of Am. 1973, 75), Cosmos Club Washington, Alpha Epsilon Pi. Home: 1503 Old Ft Dr Tallahassee FL 32301-5637 Office: Fla State U Dept Chemistry Tallahassee FL 32306

MANDELL, ARLENE LINDA, communications educator; b. Bklyn., Feb. 19, 1941; d. George and Esther Kostick; m. Lawrence M. Mandell, May 23, 1982; children from previous marriage: Bruce R. Rosenblum, Tracey B. Brimaldi. BA magna cum laude, William Paterson U., 1973; MA, Columbia U., 1989. Newspaper reporter Suburban Trends, Riverdale, NJ, 1972-73; writer Good Housekeeping mag., N.Y.C., 1976-78; account exec. Carl Byoir & Assocs., 1978-86; v.p. Porter/Novelli, 1986-88; adj. prof. composition, lit., poetry, women's studies William Paterson U., Wayne, NJ, 1989-99; writer, collage artist Sonoma County, Calif., 1999—. Author: Variations on a Theme, a poetry chapbook, 2001; co-author: 7 anthologies; contbr. articles to profl. jours. and newspapers, poetry to N.Y. Times and poetry jours. Recipient 1st pl. women's interest writing, N.J. Press Assn., 1973.

MANDELL, BARBARA D. clinical social worker, educator; b. Boston, Aug. 9, 1950; d. Leo and Helen (Steloff) M.; m. Edward Samuel Steinberg, June 12, 1983; children: Daniel, Jonathan. BA in Psychology, Carnegie-Mellon U., 1972; MSW, Smith Coll., 1975. Lic. ind. clin. social worker, Mass.; diplomate Am. Bd. Examiners in Clin. Social Work. Adminstrv. asst. Psychol. Testing Lab., Peter Bent Brigham Hosp., Boston, 1972-73; psychiat. social worker Mass. Mental Health Ctr., 1977-80, Bath (Maine)-Brunswick Mental Health Ctr., 1975-77, Boston VA Med. Ctr., 1980-87; adj. asst. prof. Boston U. Sch. Social Work, 1987-89; pvt. practice, Sudbury and Brookline, Mass., 1980-89, Portland, Oreg., 1990—. Instr. Portland State U., 1990—; mem. NW Women's Therapy Project, 1990—. Mem. NASW, Acad. Cert. Social Workers, Portland Acad. Hypnosis. Avocations: aerobic exercise, reading, travel. Office: 5330 Amberwood Ct Lake Oswego OR 97035-8792

MANDELL, GERALD LEE, physician, medicine educator; b. N.Y.C., Aug. 20, 1936; s. Herman and Sylvia (Keller) M.; m. Judith Rensin Mandell, Dec. 22, 1960; children: James, Pamela, Scott. BA, Cornell U., 1958; MD, Cornell U., N.Y.C., 1962. Diplomate Am. Bd. Internal Medicine. Intern, resident N.Y. Hosp. Cornell Med. Ctr., N.Y.C., 1965-67; instr. Med. Coll., Cornell U., 1968-69; asst. prof. U. Va., Charlottesville, 1969-71, assoc. prof., 1972-75, prof., 1976—, Owen R. Cheatham prof. sci., 1981—, head infectious diseases, 1970—. Editor: Principles and Practice of Infectious Diseases, 1979, 5th edit., 2000. Lt. comdr. USPHS, 1963-65. Recipient MERIT award NIH, 1986. Master ACP; fellow AAAS, Infectious Diseases Soc. Am. (Bristol award 2000); mem. Assn. Am. Physicians, Am. Soc. Clin. Investigation, Inst. of Medicine, Nat. Inst. Allergy and Infectious Diseases (mem. adv. coun.), Phi Beta Kappa, Alpha Omega Alpha. Jewish. Avocations: photography, tropical fish, sculling. Office: U Va Med Ctr PO Box 385 Charlottesville VA 22902-0385 E-mail: gm@virginia.edu.

MANDELL, GORDON KEITH, aerospace engineer; b. N.Y.C., Mar. 6, 1947; s. Bertram Herman and Maria Catherine (O'Hagan) M. BS, MIT, 1969, MS, 1970. Research aerospace engr. MIT, Cambridge, Mass., 1970-72; aero. cons. Eagle River, Alaska, 1972-76; designated engring. rep., 1976-82; aerospace engr. FAA, Anchorage, 1982—. Author/editor: Topics in Advanced Model Rocketry, 1973; mng. editor Model Rocketry mag., Cambridge, 1968-72; contbr. articles to profl. jours. NSF fellow, MIT, 1969; scholar Grumman Aerospace Corp., MIT, 1965. Mem. Nat. Assn. Rocketry, Planetary Soc., Nat. Space Soc., Sigma Xi, Sigma Gamma Tau, Tau Beta Pi. Buddhist. Avocations: rural living, model building, home computing. Home: PO Box 671388 Chugiak AK 99567-1388 Office: FAA Aircraft Cert Office ACE-115N 222 W 7th Ave Unit 14 Anchorage AK 99513-7587 E-mail: gordon.mandell@faa.gov.

MANDELL, JOEL, lawyer; b. Hartford, Conn., July 1, 1939; s. Max Edward and Harriet (Shafer) M.; m. Ellen Solomon, Aug. 23, 1964; children: Peter, Ross, Jason. BA, U. Conn., 1961, JD, 1966. Bar: Conn. 1966, U.S. Dist. Ct. Conn. 1967, U.S. Supreme Ct. 1971. Ptnr. Rosenthal, Clayman & Mandell, Hartford, 1966-72; prin. Levy & Droney, Farmington & West Hartford, Conn., 1972—. Mem. adv. bd. First Am. Title Ins. Co., Hartford, 1984—. Bd. dirs. Farmington Valley Jewish Congregation, Simsbury, Conn., 1980-83; mem. State of Conn. Title Ins. Task Force, 1989-90; selectman Town of Simsbury, 1993—, dept. first selectman, 1999—; mem. Town of Simsbury Charter Revision Commn., 1990-92, Simsbury Housing Authority, 1992-93. Mem.: Real Estate Exch., Conn. Assn. Real Estate Profls. (panel mem. 1991, real estate exch. panel moderator 1996, 2000), New Eng. Land Title Assn. (panel mem. 1991, 2000, bd dirs. 1996—, panel me. 2000—01), Conn. Bar Assn. (ho. of dels. 1983—86, real estate exec. com. 1978—2001, emeritus 2001—, chmn. 1995—97), Am. Legion Simsbury, KP (chancellor comdr. 1981—82). Office: Levy & Droney PC 74 Batterson Park Rd Farmington CT 06032-2565 E-mail: joelmandell@attbi.com., jmandell@ldlaw.com.

MANDELL, LEONARD CHARLES, engineer, company executive; b. Providence, July 6, 1919; s. Charles Lawrence and Florence (Greenleaf) M.; m. Sylvia Evelyn Schwartz; children: Howard A., Lynda R., Mark S. BSME, U. Ala., Tuscaloosa, 1941; MSME, MIT, 1946; MS in Indsl. Hygiene, Harvard U., 1953. Cert. environ. engr.; diplomate Am. Bd. Indsl. Hygiene. Chief engr. Enginaire, Inc., Providence, 1947-53; prin., pres. L.C. Mandell Assocs., Providence/E. Providence, R.I., 1953-83, Safety Svcs., Inc., Providence/E. Providence, 1973—. Mem. faculty U. R.I. Ext. Mem. AIChE, ASME, Human Factors Soc., Am. Soc. Gas Engrs., Am. Indsl. Hygiene Assn., Am. Soc. Safety Engrs., Air Pollin Control Assn. (pres. N.E.), Am. Acad. Forensic Scis. (diplomate). Jewish. Avocations: golf, sailing. Office: Safety Svcs Inc PO Box 16150 Rumford RI 02916-0697 Home: Apt 553 355 Blackstone Blvd Providence RI 02906-4953

MANDELL, MARSHALL, physician, allergist, consultant; b. N.Y.C., Feb. 4, 1922; s. Albert and Beatrice (Roth) M.; m. Thelma Sylvia Cantor, Aug. 1, 1944 (div. 1974); children: Joan Arlene, Steven Marshall, Nori Lyn; m. Blanca Aurora Abrego, June 22, 2001. BA in Zoology, U. Conn., 1943; MD, L.I. Coll. Medicine, 1946. Diplomate Am. Bd. Pediats., Pediat. Allergy, Am. Bd. Allergy and Immunology, Am. Bd. Environ. Medicine. Intern in pediats. Yale U. Med. Sch./New Haven Hosp., 1946—47; jr. resident in pediats. St. Louis Children's Hosp./Washington U. Med. Sch., 1949-50; resident in pediats. Gen. Hosps. #1 and #2, Kansas City, Mo., 1950-51; instr., clin. asst. N.Y. Med. Coll., 1955-58, asst. prof. allergy, 1958-80. Adj. prof. nutrition and allergy U. Bridgeport, Conn., 1976—90; cons. in allergy and bio-ecologic disorders in mental illness Fuller Meml. Sanitarium, South Attleboro, Mass., 1972—76; cons. in cerebral allergy Ctr. Neurol. Rehab. , Morton, Pa., 1980—; guest lectr Antwerp U., Belgium, 1998, European Congress Allergology, Stockholm, 1968, First World Congress Biologic Psychiatry, Buenos Aires, 1971, Nat. Multiple Sclerosis Soc. Ann. Tri-state Meeting, N.Y.C., 1987. Author: 5-Day Allergy Relief System, 1979, Lifetime Arthritis Relief System, 1983, It's Not Your Fault You're Fat Diet, 1983; editor: Let's Have Healthy Children, 1981; contbr. more than 35 articles to profl. jours. Capt. U.S. Army, 1947-49. Recipient Founders medal demonstrating the role of brain allergy in schizophrenia, Huxley Soc., 2 awards Citizens Commn. Human Rights showing the role of nervous sys. sensitivity to dietary and environ. factors in mental and behavioral disorders. Fellow: Internat. Acad. Nutrition and Preventive Medicine, Acad. Orthomolecular Medicine and Psychiatry (Spl. Commendation for Contbns. to Mental Illness), Am. Acad. Environ. Medicine (Recipient Jonathan Forman Gold medal), Am. Coll. Allergy, Asthma and Immunology (Jonathan Forman gold medal); mem.: Am. Acad. Allergy, Lions (pres. Norwalk club 1956—58), Phi Sigma Delta (pres. 1941—43). Avocations: medical writing, computers, wood carving, gardening, swimming. Home and Office: 112 Canterbury Ln Laredo TX 78041

MANDELSTAM, CHARLES LAWRENCE, lawyer; b. Brookline, Mass., July 6, 1927; s. Felix and Sarah (Odence) M.; m. Gloria Messinger, June 2, 1957; children: Emily F., Peter D. BA, Harvard Coll., 1949; LLB, Yale U., 1952. Bar: Conn. 1952, N.Y. 1953, D.C. 1953. Mem. staff office of gen. counsel Internat. Ladies' Garment Workers Union, N.Y.C., 1952-56; assoc. Kaye, Scholer, Fierman, Hays & Handler, 1956-60; ptnr. Dornbush Mensch Mandelstam & Schaeffer, LLP, 1968—. Bd. dirs. Société d' Exploitation Agricole Rhodanienne, Ampuis, France; counsel North Salem (N.Y.) Open Land Found., 1975—. Comment editor Yale Law Jour., 1951-52; contbr. articles to Yale Law Jour., 1951, 52 Bd. dirs. Samuel Rubin Found., 1975—; trustee Rubin Mus. of Art, N.Y.C., 2001—. Mem. Assn. of the Bar City of N.Y., Phi Beta Kappa. Home: 27 W 86th St New York NY 10024-3615 Office: 747 3d Ave New York NY 10017-2803

MANDELSTAMM, ALLAN BERYLE, economics educator, consultant; b. Saginaw, Mich., Oct. 18, 1928; s. Jonas and Helen G. (Weinburg) M.; m. Maria T. Buhlmeyer, Sept. 1, 1967. B.A., U. Mich., 1950, M.A., 1951, Ph.D., 1962. Instr. Northwestern U., Evanston, Ill., 1957-59; asst. prof. Vanderbilt U., Nashville, 1959-63; assoc. prof. Mich. State U., East Lansing, 1963-67, prof., 1967-74; prof. econs. Va. Poly. Inst. and State U., Blacksburg, 1974-90, prof. emertus, econ. cons., 1990—; vis. prof. Dartmouth Coll., 1970, U. Fla., 1972; cons. Dept. State, AID, U.S. Dept. Labor, others. Contbr. articles to profl. jours. and encys. Recipient Disting. Teaching award Mich. State U., 1968, Best Prof. award U. Fla., 1972, Va. Poly. Inst., 1976, 77, Sporn award, 1987; Rockefeller Found. grantee, 1958-62. Mem. AAUP, Am. Econ. Assn., Indsl. Rels. Rsch. Assn., Acad. Polit. Sci., Va. Assn. Scholars (treas.). Home: 600 Landsdowne Dr Blacksburg VA 24060-5926

MANDELSTAMM, JEROME ROBERT, lawyer; b. St. Louis, Apr. 3, 1932; s. Henry and Estelle (London) M.; m. Carolyn A. White; stepchildren: John M. Gagliardi, Maria A. Amundson, Amy E. Gagliardi. AB, U. Pa., 1954; LL.B., Harvard U., 1957. Bar: Mo. 1957. Since practiced in, St. Louis; partner Greenfield, Davidson, Mandelstamm & Voorhees, 1969-81, Schmitz, Mandelstamm, Hawker & Fischer, 1981-82; sole practice, 1982—. Bd. dirs. Legal Aid Soc. City and County St. Louis, 1967-75, pres., 1969-70; bd. dirs. Lawyers Reference Service Met. St. Louis, 1976-83, chmn., 1978-83; bd. dirs. Mo. Legal Aid Soc., 1977-82; mem. 22d Jud. Cir. Bar Com., 1983-85, gen. chmn., 1984-85 Mem. St. Louis County Bd. Election Commrs., 1973-77. Served with AUS, 1957. Mem. ABA, Mo. Bar Assn., Am. Arbitration Assn. (panel of arbitrators 1984—), Bar Assn. Met. St. Louis (v.p. 1974-75, treas. 1975-76). Home: 7217 Princeton Saint Louis MO 63130-3000 Office: 1010 Market St Ste 1600 Saint Louis MO 63101-2032

MANDERS, CONSTANCE ELENA, community agency executive, environmental analyst; b. Weisbaden, Germany, Oct. 7, 1954; came to U.S., 1955, naturalized, 1956; d. William George and Gloria Nikki (Caporal) M. A.A., Am. River Coll., 1976; B.S., U. Calif.-Davis, 1979; B.A., Calif. State U.-Sacramento, 1982, postgrad. in bus. adminstrn. Pres., chmn. bd. Head Trauma Support Project Inc., Sacramento, 1979-82, dir. project devel., 1982—; adminstrv. asst. Calif. Farm Bur. Fedn., Sacramento, 1980-82; environ. analyst Aerojet Gen. Corp., Sacramento, 1982— ; chmn. internat. med. confs. Producer dir. brain injury video tng. tapes. Recipient Vol. Activist award Vol. Bur. Sacramento, 1982. Mem. Nat. Head Injury Found., Am. Hellenic Profl. Soc. (bd. dirs. Sacramento chpt. 1980-84), Met. Mus. Art, U. Calif. Aggie Alumni Assn., Daus. of Penelope (Artemis chpt.). Greek Orthodox. Office: Aerojet Gen Corp Box 15699C Dept 9020/43 Sacramento CA 95813

MANDERS, KARL LEE, neurosurgeon; b. Rochester, N.Y., Jan. 21, 1927; s. David Bert and Frances Edna (Cohan) Mendelson; m. Ann Laprell, July 28, 1969; children: Karlanna, Maidena; children by previous marriage: Karl, Kerry, Kristine. Student, Cornell U., 1946; MD, U. Buffalo, 1950. Diplomate Am. Bd. Neurol. Surgery, Am. Bd. Clin. Biofeedback, Am. Bd. Hyperbaric Medicine, Am. Bd. Pain Medicine, Nat. Bd. Med. Examiners. Intern U. Va. Hosp., Charlottesville, 1950-51, resident in neurol. surgery, 1951-52, Henry Ford Hosp., Detroit, 1954-56; pvt. practice Indpls., 1956—. Med. dir. Cmty. Hosp. Rehab. Ctr. for Pain, 1973—; chief hosp. med. and surg. neurology Cmty. Hosp., 1983, 93; coroner Marion County, Ind., 1977-85, 92-96. *Over 45 years in practice of Neurological Surgery and the development of one of the first multidisciplinary pain centers in the country over a quarter of a century ago. Dr. Manders also established the first hyper-baric centers in Indiana. He has also served as Marion County coroner in Indianapolis for twelve years and his continued interest in forensic medicine have developed into further development of medical-legal consultation services.* With USN, 1952-54, Korea. Recipient Cert. achievement Dept. Army, 1969, Disting. Physician award Comm. Hosp., 1997. Fellow ACS, Internat. Coll Surgeons, Am. Acad. Neurology; mem. Congress Neurol. Surgery, Internat. Assn. Study of Pain, Am. Assn. Study of Headache, N.Y. Acad. Sci., Am. Coll. Angiology, Am. Soc. Contemporary Medicine and Surgery, Am. Holistic Med. Assn. (co-founder), Undersea Med. Soc., Am. Acad. Forensic Sci., Am. Asssn. Biofeedback Clinicians, Soc. Cryosurgery, Pan Pacific Surg. Assn., Biofeedback Soc. Am., Acad. Psychosomatic Medicine, Pan Am. Med. Assn., Internat. Back Pain Soc., North Am. Spine Soc., Am. Soc. Stereotaxic and Functional Neurosurgery, Soc. for Computerized Tomography and Neuroimaging, Ind. Coroners Assn. (pres. 1979), Royal Soc. Medicine, Nat. Assn. Med. Examiners, Am. Pain Soc., Midwest Pain Soc. (pres. 1988), Am. Acad. Pain Medicine,

Cen. Neurol. Soc., Interurban Neurosurg. Soc., Internat. Soc. Aquatic Medicine, James A. Gibson Anat. Soc., Am. Bd. Med. Psychotherapists (mem. profl. adv. council), James McClure Surg. Soc., Brendonwood Country Club, Highland Country Club. Home: 5845 High Fall Rd Indianapolis IN 46226-1017 Office: 7369 Shadeland Sta Ste 100 Indianapolis IN 46256-3958

MANDERS, SUSAN KAY, artist; b. Burbank, Calif., Dec. 29, 1948; d. Gus H. and Erika (Stadelbauer) M.; m. Allan D. Yasnyi, Dec. 18, 1992; children: Brian Mallut. Attended, U. Guadalajara, 1969; BA, Calif. State U., 1971; postgrad., Otis Parsons, L.A., 1985, Royal Coll. of the Arts, London, 1987; grad., Silicon Digital Arts. Owner, dir., tchr. The Art Experience Sch. and Gallery, Studio City, Calif., 1978—. Cons. in field. One-woman shows include La Logia, Studio City, Calif., 1991, Il Mito, Studio City, 1991, Bamboo, Sherman Oaks, Calif., 1991—, L.A. Art Installations, 1990, 92, Fed. Bldg., L.A., 1993, Art Experience, Studio City, 1993, Emerson's Gallery, Sherman Oaks, 1994, Raphael's, Beverly Hills, Calif., 1994, KL Fine Arts, Chgo., 1999, L.A.C.M.A., 1999; group shows include Beverly Hills Affair in the Gardens, 1984, 94, Otis Parsons, L.A., 1987, Hilderbrand Galleries, New Orleans, 1993, Studio City Art Festival, 1994, Parents Found., New Haven, Conn., 1994, Project Studio 8, San Francisco, 1994, Bistango Studio-Gallery, Irvine, Calif., 1994—, Montserrat Gallery, N.Y.C., 1995, Annenberg Ctr., U. So. Calif., 1997—, U. So. Calif. Entertainment Tech. Ctr., 1997—, K.L. Fine Arts Chgo., 1999, LACMA, 1999, Angel Project, L.A., 2001, Anti Reformation League Exhbn., 2001; creator, publ. prints Iron Jane Collections, 1994, Children's Hosp., ASI Entertainment, 1998, ASPCALA, 1998; producer (film) Fifi Good and the Bad Ass. Docent UCLA; active Tuesday's Child, Pillars of Hope Project San Fernando Valley County Fair, 1995. Mem. AAUW, L.A. Art Assn., Beverley Hills Art Assn., Nat. Mus. Women in the Arts, Nat. Assn. Univ. Women, L.A. County Mus. of Art, Dada, L.A., Mus. Contemporary Art Coun., Women in Animation, Nat. Assn. Univ. Women, Vidamation Assn. (bd. dirs.). Office: The Art Experience 11830 Ventura Blvd Studio City CA 91604-2617 E-mail: skmanders@aol.com.

MANDERSCHEID, LESTER VINCENT, agricultural economics educator; b. Andrew, Iowa, Oct. 9, 1930; s. Vincent John and Alma (Sprank) M.; m. Dorothy Helen Varnum, Aug. 29, 1953; children: David, Paul, Laura, Jane. BS, Iowa State U., 1951, MS, 1952; PhD, Stanford U., 1961. Grad. asst. Iowa State U., Ames, 1951-52, Stanford (Calif.) U., 1952-56; asst. prof. Mich. State U., East Lansing, 1956-65, assoc. prof., 1965-70, prof., 1970-73, prof., assoc. chmn., 1973-87, prof., chmn., 1987-92, prof., 1992-95, prof. emeritus, 1996—, coord. Grad. Sch., 1993—. Reviewer Tex. A&M Agrl. Econ. Program, College Station, 1989; cons. Consortium Internat. Earth Sci. Info. Network, Ann Arbor, 1990. Co-author: Improving Undergraduate Education, 1967; contbr. articles to jours. in field. Pres. parish coun. St. Thomas, East Lansing, 1984-87; coll. coord. United Way, East Lansing, 1983-84; pres. bd. dirs. Cristo Rey Cmty. Ctr., 1998-2001. Recipient Disting. Faculty award Mich. State U., 1977. Mem. Am. Agrl. Econ. Assn. (pres. 1988-89, bd. dirs. 1982-85, excellence in teaching award 1974), Am. Statis. Assn., Am. Evaluation Assn., Am. Econ. Assn., University Club, Sigma Xi (pres. 1986-87), Phi Kappa Phi (pres. 1979-80). Roman Catholic. Home: 2372 Burcham Dr East Lansing MI 48823-3885 Office: Mich State U Dept of Agrl Econs Circle Dr East Lansing MI 48824-1039 E-mail: mandersc@msu.edu.

MANDERSCHEID, RONALD WILLIAM, federal program administrator; b. LaCrosse, Wis., Sept. 28, 1943; s. William Joseph and Norene Elsine (Batteen) M.; m. Frances Elizabeth Fedkiw, Sept. 1, 1973; children: William Derrick, Kristen Elizabeth, Erika Marie. BA maxima cum laude, Loras Coll., 1965; MA, Marquette U., 1967; PhD, U. Md., 1975; Cert., Fed. Exec. Inst., 1986. Research asst. U. Md., College Park, 1970-72; research assoc. NIMH, Adelphi, Md., 1972-75, sr. research sociologist, 1975-80, chief evaluation research sect. Rockville, Md., 1980-81, chief stats. rsch. br., 1981-92; acting dir. div. state and community systems devel. Ctr. for Mental Health Svcs., 1992-93, chief survey & analysis, 1992—. Cons. George Washington U., Washington, 1978-83, World Health Orgn., 1993—, Pan Am. Health Orgn., 1995—, Columbia U., 1998-2001; mem. Internat. Consortium Mental Health Policy & Rsch., 2000—. Author, editor: Mental Health in the United States, 1987, 90, 92, 94, 96, 98, 2000, 02; editor: System Science and the Future of Health, 1976; producer: Making the Numbers Work for You, 1987; contbr. articles to profl. jours. Active West Montgomery Citizens Assn., Potomac, Md., 1983—. With U.S. Army, 1967-69. Decorated Army Commendation medal; recipient Disting. Alumni award, Loras Coll., 1998, Sec. Disting. Svc. award, 2999, Mental Health Stats. Improvement Program Leadership award, 2001. Fellow Washington Acad. Scis. (life; pres. 1987-88), World Acad. Art and Sci.; mem. N.Y. Acad. Scis., Am. Pub. Health Assn. (chair mental health 1997-98, Mental Hlth. Sect. award 2000, Mental Health Chairperson's Disting. Svc. award 2001), Am. Sociol. Assn. (chmn. various coms. 1983-91, chmn. com. on fed. standards for sociologists 1983-88), Soc. for Gen. Systems Rsch. (chmn. Washington chpt. 1976—), Ea. Sociol. Soc. (exec. com. 1979-84, chmn. various coms., Peter Gellman award 1984), D.C. Sociol. Soc. (pres. 1992-93), Fed. Exec. Inst. Alumni Assn. (exec. bd. 1997—, chair policy issues com. 1995-2000, Meritorious Svc. award 1999), Soc. Applied Sociol. (Nat. Sociol. Practice award 1995), Cosmos Club, Alpha Kappa Delta (pres. 1972-73), Delta Epsilon Sigma, Phi Kappa Phi. Avocations: coin collecting, historical reading. Office: CMHS 5600 Fishers Ln Rm 15C-04 Rockville MD 20852-1750 E-mail: rmanders@samhsa.gov.

MANDEVILLE, HUBERT TURNER, JR. oil company executive; b. N.Y.C., Apr. 24, 1974; s. Hubert Turner Mandeville and Judith Knudsen. BBA, So. Meth. U., 1994, JD, 1998. Fin. analyst Amerada Hess Corp., Houston, 1994-95; sr. fin. analyst Santa Fe Energy, 1995-96; v.p. Mandeville Oil Co., 1996—; pres. Mandeville Corp., 1997—, EncrypTech Corp., Miami, 1999—. Cons. Oracle Software, Houston, 1996-97. Mem. Dallas Symphony, Houston Symphony. Mem. Dallas Hall Soc., Houstonian Club, Houston Livestock Show and Rodeo, One Hundred Club, River Oaks Country Club, Petroleum Club, Met. Racquet Club. Republican. Presbyterian. Avocations: financial markets, golf, tennis, snow skiing, fundraising. Home: 111 N Post Oak Ln Houston TX 77024-7703 Office: Mandeville Oil Corp 2323 N Field St Apt 2500 Dallas TX 75201-1761 also: EncrypTech Corp 1101 Brickell Ave Fl 5 Miami FL 33131-3105 Address: 1111 Brickell Bay Dr Ph 2 Miami FL 33131-2950

MANDIA, STEPHEN ERNEST, urologist; b. Engelwood, N.J., Dec. 30, 1958; s. Ernest James and Anita Joan (Turrisi) M. BS, Georgetown U., Washington, 1980; MSA in Health Svcs. Adminstrn., Cen. Mich. U., Mt. Pleasant, 1996; MD, Georgetown U., 1984. Diplomate Am. Bd. Urology, Am. Coll. Healthcare Execs. Resident in surgery St. Vincent's Med. Ctr., Bridgeport, Conn., 1984-85; commd. ensign USN, 1980, advanced through grades to comdr., 1995, flight surgeon, 1985-88, resident in urology, 1988-92, head urology dept. Rota, Spain, 1992-94, chief surg. svcs. Spain, 1994, head urology dept. Jacksonville, Fla., 1994—. Assoc. clin. prof. Uniformed Svcs. U. of Health Scis., Bethesda, Md., 1994—. Fellow ACS; mem. AMA, Am. Urol. Assn., Fla. Med. Assn. (bd. govs. 1995—). Republican. Roman Catholic. Avocations: private pilot, motorcycling, golf. Office: US Naval Hosp 2080 Child St Jacksonville FL 32214-5005

MANDIBERG, DAVID MICHAEL, sculptor; b. Detroit, June 30, 1942; s. Jack Norman and Helen (Jaffe) M. Student, Art Students League, N.Y.C., 1965-68, San Francisco Art Inst., 1970-71, Ctr. for Creative Studies, Detroit, 1991-93; BA, Wayne State U., 1981. Tchr. sculpture Cunniff Studio Gallery, Lake Orion, 1995-96. One-man shows include Cunniff Studio Gallery, Lake Orion, Mich., 1989, 91, 93-95, 97, Swann Gallery, Detroit, 1997, 99; exhibited in group shows at Detroit Artists Market, 1970, Helen Cunniff Studio Gallery, Lake Orion, 1987, 88, 90, Detroit Focus Gallery, 1988, Ariel Gallery, N.Y.C., 1988, 89, Sculptors Guild Mich., Detroit, 1993, Gallery One Twenty Eight, N.Y.C., 1994, 96, Scarab Club, Detroit, 1998, Mus. Contemporary Art, Pontiac, Mich., 1999, State of the Art Gallery, Ithaca, N.Y., 2002; represented in permanent collections Rosemary McNaughton, Toronto, Can., Helen Cunniff, Lake Orion, Mich., Swords into Plowshares Peace Ctr., Detroit, Dr. Jack Levine, N.Y.C., Sol Lewitt, N.Y.C., Takao Nagai, Chgo., Irving Berg, Detroit, Joan Brace, Lake Orion, Mich., Mus. New Art, Detroit; sculptures include life-size David, Life, Psalm, Reality, Peace at Swords into Ploughshares Peace Ctr., Detroit, bust of William Clinton, bust of Andy Warhol, Progress-3 part woodcarving, Stardom, Andy Worhol Bust; TV appearances include Metro Art and Book Talk, Channel11, Media One, 1999. Recipient 12 award ribbons Metro Carvers Mich., 1994-97, 2d place award for sculpture Sister Kenny Inst., Mpls., 1991; scholar Art Students League, 1966-67. Mem. Sculptors Guild Mich. (treas. 1992-97), Metro Carvers Mich., Detroit Blues Soc. (bd. dirs. 1994-96), Met. Detroit Recorder Soc., Nat. Sculpture Soc. Avocations: playing piano, guitar and recorder, Italian, tennis. Home: Apt 101 2688 Patrick Henry St Auburn Hills MI 48326-2241 Studio: Ste 318 40 W Howard St Pontiac MI 48342-1293 E-mail: dmandiberg@aol.com.

MANDIL, I. HARRY, nuclear engineer; b. Istanbul, Turkey, Dec. 11, 1919; s. Harry Robert and Bertha (Presente) M. (parents Am. citizens); m. Beverly Ericson, June 22, 1946; children: Jean Dale, Eric Robert. BS, U. London, 1939; MS, MIT, 1941; grad., Oak Ridge Sch. Reactor Tech., 1950; DSc (hon.), Thiel Coll., Greenville, Pa., 1960. Devel., design process controls for textile mills and chem. plants Norcross Corp., 1941-42, asst. to pres. charge field engrng., 1946-49; asst. to tech. dir. naval reactors br. reactor devel. div. AEC, 1950-54, dir. reactor engrng. div. Bur. Ships, Navy Dept. and chief reactor engrng. br. Naval Reactors, 1954-64; prin. officer, dir. MPR Assos., Inc. (engrs.), Washington, 1964-85, cons., dir. Alexandria, Va., 1985—. Developer nuclear power for propulsion naval vessels, also for Shippingport Atomic Power Ctrl. Sta.; mem., sec. Energy Adv. Bd., Washington, 1990-93; mem. corp. vis. com. for nuclear engring. dept. MIT, 1984-93; mem. sr. tech. rev. group for plutonium, Amarillo, Tex., 1995-99. Author numerous papers in field. Served with USNR, 1942-46. Recipient Naval Letter of Commendation, 1946, Meritorious Civilian Svc. award Navy Dept., 1952, ASME Prime Movers award, 1956, Disting. Civilian Svc. award, 1959. Mem. Nat. Acad. Engrng. Home: 701 Heathery Ln Pelican Bay Naples FL 34108 Office: 320 King St Alexandria VA 22314-3238 Fax: (703) 519-0224.

MANDL, HERBERT JAY, rabbi; b. Balt., Jan. 9, 1945; s. Sigmund and Ruth (Lefkowitz) M.; m. Barbara Sue Toltzis, Aug. 18, 1968; children: Aron M., Seth S., Debra A., Miriam D. AB, Johns Hopkins U., 1965; MHL, Jewish Theol. Sem., 1967, DDiv, 1994; PhD, U. Montreal, 1981. Ordained rabbi, 1969. Lectr. U. Alta., Edmonton, 1969-71; sr. rabbi Beth Shalom Synagoge, Alta., Can., 1969-71; asst. rabbi Congregation Shaar Hashomayim, Montreal, Que., Can., 1971-77; sr. rabbi Kehilath Israel Synagogue, Kansas City, Mo., 1977—; chaplain Overland Park Police Dept., Kans., 2000—. Vis. lectr. U. Mo., Kansas City, 1978-80, Rockhurst Coll., adj. prof., 1989—; chaplain Kansas City Police Dept., 1988—. Bd. dirs. Shalom Geriatric Group, Kansas City, 1985—, Jewish Fedn., Kansas City, 1977—; chmn. State Mo. Health Facilities Rev. Commn., Jefferson City, 1980-86; chmn. Kansas State Holocaust Commn., Topeka, 1987—; mem. Kansas City Sister City Commn., 1980—, Kans. Pub. Disclosure Commn., 1991-97. Mem. Rabbinical Assembly (com. Jewish law and standards 1989-94), Internat. Order Police Chaplains, Rabbinical Assn. Kansas City (pres. 1980-81, 94-96), Union for Traditional Judaism (panelist on Jewish law 1985—), B'nai Brith. Office: Kebilath Israel Synagogue 10501 Conser St Shawnee Mission KS 66212-2600

MANDLER, GEORGE, psychologist, educator; b. Vienna, Austria, June 11, 1924; came to U.S., 1940, naturalized, 1943; s. Richard and Hede (Goldschmied) M.; m. Jean Matter, Jan. 19, 1957; children: Peter Clark, Michael Allen. BA, NYU, 1949; MS, Yale U., 1950, PhD, 1953; postgrad., U. Basel, Switzerland, 1947-48. Asst. prof. Harvard U., 1953-57, lectr., 1957-60; prof. U. Toronto, Ont., Can., 1960-65; prof. psychology U. Calif., San Diego, 1965-94, chmn. dept. psychology, 1965-70, prof. emeritus, 1994—; dir. Ctr. Human Info. Processing, U. Calif., 1965-90. Hon. rsch. fellow Univ. Coll. London., 1977-78, 82-90, vis. prof., 1990—. Author: Mind and Emotion, 1975, (German edit.), 1980, Mind and Body, 1984, (Japanese edit.), 1987, Cognitive Psychology, 1985, Japanese edit., 1991, Human Nature Explored, 1997, Interesting Times, 2001; co-author: (with W. Kessen) The Language of Psychology, (Italian edit.), 1959, (with J.M. Mandler) Thinking: From Association to Gestalt, 1964; contbr. articles and revs. to profl. jours.; editor: Psychol. Rev., 1970-76. Served with U.S. Army, 1943-46. Fellow Ctr. for Advanced Study in Behavioral Scis., 1959-60; vis. fellow Oxford U., Eng., 1971-72, 78; Guggenheim fellow, 1971-72. Fellow AAAS, Am. Acad. Arts and Scis.; mem. AAUP, Am. Assn. Advancement Psychology (1974-82); Psychonomic Soc. (governing bd., chmn. 1983), Am. Psychol. Soc., Am. Psychol. Assn. (pres. div. exptl. psychology 1978-79, pres. div. gen psychology 1982-83, mem. coun. reps. 1978-82, William James prize 1986), Internat. Union Psychol. Scis. (U.S. com. 1985-90), Soc. Exptl. Psychologists, Fedn. Behavioral Psychol. and Cognitive Scis. (pres. 1981). Home: 1406 La Jolla Knoll La Jolla CA 92037-5236 Office: U Calif San Diego Dept Psychology La Jolla CA 92093-0109 also: 3 Perrins Lane London NW3 1QY England E-mail: gmandler@ucsd.edu.

MANDLER, JEAN MATTER, psychologist, educator; b. Oak Park, Ill., Nov. 6, 1929; d. Joseph Allen and May Roberts (Finch) Matter; m. George Mandler, Jan. 19, 1957; children: Peter Clark, Michael Allen. Student, Carleton Coll., 1947-49; BA with highest honors, Swarthmore Coll., 1951; PhD, Harvard U., 1956. Rsch. assoc. lab. social rels. Harvard U., 1957-60; rsch. assoc. dept. psychology U. Toronto, Ont., Can., 1961-65; assoc. rsch. psychologist, lectr. U. Calif. at San Diego, La Jolla, 1965-73, assoc. prof., 1973-77, prof. psychology, 1977-88, prof. cognitive sci., 1988-2000, rsch. prof., 2000—; mem. adv. com. memory and cognitive processes NSF, 1978-81. Hon. rsch. fellow U. Coll., London, 1978-89, vis. prof., 1990—; hon. mem. Med. Rsch. Coun. Cognitive Devel. Unit, 1982-98. Author: (G. Mandler) Thinking: From Association to Gestalt, 1964, Stories, Scripts and Scenes, 1984; assoc. editor Psychol. rev., 1970-76; mem. editl. bd. Child Devel., 1976-89, Discourse Processes, 1977-94, Jour. Exptl. Psychology, 1977-85, Text, 1979-97, Jour. Verbal Learning and Verbal Behavior, 1980-88, Lang. and Cognitive Processes, 1985—, Cognitive Devel., 1990-99, Jour. Cognition and Devel., 1999—; contbr. articles to profl. jours. Pres. San Diego Assn. Gifted Children, 1968-71; v.p. Calif. Parents for Gifted, 1970-71; mem. alumni council Swarthmore Coll., 1975-78. NIMH research grantee, 1968-81; NSF research grantee, 1981-99. Fellow: APA (mem. exec. com. divsn. 3 1983—85), Am. Acad. Arts and Scis.; mem.: Soc. Exptl. Psychologists, Cognitive Devel. Soc., Cognitive Sci. Soc., Psychonomic Soc. (mem. governing bd. 1982—87, chmn. 1985—86), Phi Beta Kappa. Office: U Calif San Diego Dept Cognitive Sci La Jolla CA 92093-0515

MANDLER, THOMAS YALE, lawyer; b. Chgo., Oct. 26, 1946; s. Martin and Florence (Hurovitz) M.; m. Cathy Jane Buchbinder, June 29, 1969; children: Lisa Beth, Amy Lyn, Jason Scott. BA, U. Wis., 1968; JD, U. Ill., 1971. Bar: Ill. 1972, U.S. Dist. Ct. (no. dist.) Ill. 1972, U.S. Ct. Appeals (7th cir.) 1972, U.S. Supreme Ct. 1976. Assoc. Goldberg, Weigle Mallin & Gitles, Chgo., 1971-74; ptnr., assoc. Jenner & Block, 1974-85; ptnr. Arvey, Hodes, Costello, 1985-88, Schwartz & Freeman, Chgo., 1988—2001, Quarles & Brady, Chgo., 2001—. Author: Analysis of a Typical Employment Handbook, 1988, How Employers Can Minimize Employment Discrimination, 1998, Understanding the Negotiaion Process, 1987, How to Hire, Manage and Terminate Employees, 1999; mem. U. Ill. Law Rev., 1969-71; assoc. and chpt. editor Discipline and Discharge in Arbitration, 1998—. Pres. H.S. Dist. 113, Highland Park, Ill., 1996-97, 2000—; chmn. Highland Park Human Rels. Commn., 1987-88; bd. dirs. Ill. Inst. CLE, mem. exec. com., 1988-95. Recipient Iron Cross award U Wis., 1968. Mem. ABA, Chgo. Bar Assn. Office: Quarles & Brady 500 W Madison St Ste 3700 Chicago IL 60661 E-mail: tmandler@quarles.com.

MANDLY, CHARLES ROBERT, JR. lawyer; b. Greenwood, Miss., Dec. 31, 1957; s. Charles Robert and Carole Burney (Williams) M.; m. Sara Anne Biro, Sept. 29, 1996. BA, U. Ala., 1980; JD, Vanderbilt U., 1983. Assoc. Pattishall, McAuliffe & Hofstetter, Chgo., 1983-89, ptnr., 1989-93, Wildman, Harrold, Allen & Dixon, Chgo., 1993-2001, London, 2001—. Guest lectr. John Marshall Law Sch., Chgo., 1984-88. Contbr. INTA State Trademark and Unfair Competition Law, 1986; contbr. articles to profl. jours. Mem. Internat. Bar Assn., Inst. for Advanced Legal Studies, Lawyers Club of Chgo., The Caxton Club, Selden Soc., Nat. Eagle Scout Assn. Avocation: bibliophile. Office: Tower 3 11th Fl Clements Inn London WC2A 2AZ England Home: 4 Redfield Mews London SW5 0RH England

MANDRA, YORK T. geology educator; b. N.Y.C. s. Raymond and Irene (Farruggio) M.; m. Highoohi Kechijian, Jan. 26, 1946. BA, U. Calif., Berkeley, 1947, MA in Paleontology, 1949; PhD in Geology, Stanford U., 1958. From instr. to assoc. prof. geology San Francisco State U., 1950-63, prof., 1964—, head geology sect., chmn. dept., 1960-67. Vis. prof. U. Aix-Marseille, France, 1959, Syracuse U., summer 1963, U. Maine, summer 1969, U. Calif., Santa Barbara, summers 1972—; research assoc. U. Glasgow, 1959, Calif. Acad. Scis., 1966-88; vis. scientist New Zealand Geol. Survey, fall 1970. Contbr. numerous articles to profl. jours. Pres. David S. Sohigian Found., 1975—. Served with USAAF, 1942-46. Recipient Neil A. Miner Disting. Coll. Teaching award, 1984; Danforth Found. teaching fellow, 1958, NSF fellow, 1959; NSF rsch. grantee, 1967-77. Fellow Geol. Soc. Am. (Sr.), Calif. Acad. Scis., AAAS; mem. Nat. Assn. Geology Tchrs. (pres. Far Western sect. 1953-54, 73-74, Robert Wallace Webb award 1977), Paleontol. Soc., Soc. Econ. Mineralogists and Paleontologists, Soc. for Environ. Geochemistry and Health. Avocations: walking, reading, music. Office: San Francisco State U Dept Geoscis 1600 Holloway Ave Dept Geoscis San Francisco CA 94132-1722 E-mail: ytjmandra@sfsu.edu.

MANDRACCHIA, VIOLET ANN PALERMO, psychotherapist, educator; b. N.Y.C. d. Anthony and Anna (Yetto) Palermo; m. John J. Mandracchia (dec. 1979); children: Dona Williams, Anne Marino, Marisa, John, Matthew, Lisa Williams. Student, Coll. Mt. St. Vincent; BA, St. John's U.; MA, Bklyn. Coll.; cert. in ednl. adminstrn. & supervision, Hofstra U.; MSW, SUNY, Stony Brook, 1990; advanced study in psychotherapy, L.I. Gestalt Ctr., 1988-92. Cert. social worker, secondary sch. adminstr., supr., English and social studies, practitioner Eye Movement Desensitization and Restructuring. Tchr. English Bay Ridge H.S., Bklyn., Ctrl. Islip (N.Y.) H.S., Smithtown (N.Y.) H.S.; asst. prin. Shoreham-Wading River (N.Y.) H.S., 1977-81; prin. West Islip (N.Y.) H.S., 1981-83; pvt. practice as psychotherapist Stony Brook and Manhattan, 1990—. Satellite psychotherapist Health House, Islandia, N.Y., 1988-97, supr., 1990-97. Active Suffolk County (N.Y.) Human Rights Commn., 1979-84, 88-92; chair adv. bd. Office for Women, Suffolk County, 1986-89; treas. bd. dirs. Women's Ctr., SUNY, Farmingdale, N.Y., 1985-87; chair Women's Equal Rights Coalition, Suffolk County, 1979-84, 88-92; chair North Fork Task Force in Arts, Suffolk County, 1977-79. Recipient Woman of Yr. award Suffolk County Exec. Office for Women, 1989; named Citizen of Yr., Smithtown LWV, 1984, Educator of Yr., Suffolk County Exec. & Women's Equal Rights Coalition, 1982; practitioner writing grantee Harvard U. Grad. Sch. Edn., 1981. Mem. NASW, NOW, Nat. Assn. Secondary Sch. Prins. Avocations: writing, film, theater, travel, painting. Home: 15 Shore Oaks Dr Stony Brook NY 11790-1417 Office: 211 Thompson St New York NY 10012-1365 E-mail: vmandr6889@aol.com.

MANDRELL, GENE DOUGLAS, retired management consultant; b. Clinton, Okla., Jan. 7, 1944; s. Glen Douglas and Mary Emma (Spears) M. BA, U. Okla., 1966; MS, Ctrl. Mich. U., 1995; diploma, Indsl. Coll. Armed Forces, 1976, Armed Forces Staff Coll., 1977. Logistics officer Hdqrs. AF Logistics Command, Wright-Patterson AFB, Ohio, 1971-79; asst. for supply policy Office Sec. AF, Washington, 1979-81; congl. fellow U.S. Ho. of Reps., 1981; dep. dir. command policy and current issues Hdqrs. AF Logistics Command, Wright-Patterson AFB, Ohio, 1982-87, dep. dir. concept devel. and integration, 1987; spl. asst. strategic planning DCS/Communication Computer Systems, Hdqrs. AF Logistics Command, 1988-89, dir. strategic planning & policy, 1989-93; dep. dir. corp. info. HQ AF Materiel Command, 1993-95; dir. sys. engrng. Hdqrs. Material Sys. Group, Wright-Patterson AFB, Ohio, 1995, tech. dir., 1996-97; sr. cons. Battelle Meml. Inst., 1997-99. Vis. lectr. Air War Coll., Maxwell AFB, Ala., 1977-85. Co-author: Public Policy for the 1980's, 1981. Chmn. City Planning Commn., Huber Heights, Ohio, 1983-93, 2000—; chmn. citizens adv. group Miami Valley Regional Planning Commn., 2001—. Served to sgt. U.S. Army, 1967-70. Named one of Outstanding Young Men of Am., U.S. Jaycees, 1982. Mem. Internat. Inst. Forecasters, Soc. Logistics Engrs. (life, Dayton chpt. vice-chmn. 1977-78), Am. Def. Preparedness Assn. (life, v.p.), Air Force Assn. (life), World Future Soc. (Dayton chpt. bd. dirs. 1984-93, pres. 1987-88), Am. Planning Assn., Am. Acad. Polit. and Social Scis., Am. Acad. Polit. Sci., Logistics Edn. Found., Ohio Soc. SAR, Huber Heights C. of C., Engrs. Club. Republican. Avocations: music, photography, travel. Home: 5261 Coco Dr Dayton OH 45424-5701 E-mail: gmandrell@ameritech.net.

MANDRI, DANIEL FRANCISCO, psychiatrist; b. Camaguey, Cuba, Apr. 22, 1950; came to U.S., 1962; s. Adalberto Froilan and Estrella (Pereiro) M.; m. Monica A. Ruffing, May 21, 1983; children: Nicholas, Natalie. MD, U. Cen. Del Este, Dominican Republic, 1977. Diplomate Am. Bd. Psychiatry and Neurology. With internal medicine PGY-1 Christ Hosp., Oak Lawn, Ill., 1979-80; with psychiatry PGY 2 plus 3 U. Miami/Jackson Meml. Hosp., Miami, Fla., 1980-82, chief resident psychiatry, 1982-83; pvt. practice psychiatry Coral Gables, 1983-86; dir. acute care unit Broward County Mental Health Div., Hollywood, 1986-87; dir. psychiat. svcs. Douglas Gardens Community Mental Health Ctr., Miami, 1987—, Douglas Gardens Home and Hosp. for the Aged, Miami, 1989-92. Asst. instr. psychiatry dept. of psychiatry U. Miami, 1982-83. Mem. N.Y. Acad. Scis., Am. Psychiatry Assn., World Psychiat. Assn., World Fedn. for Mental Health, Am. Assn. Community Psychiatrists. Office: Douglas Gardens Cmty Mental Health Ctr 701 Lincoln Rd Miami Beach FL 33139-2879

MANDRY, CHRISTINE M. public adminstator; b. Waukegan, Ill., June 16, 1964; d. James and Linda LaPonsie; m. Dennis Robert Mandry; children: Sherri Ann, Casey Lynn, Nicole, Rebekah. Records tech. Adminstrv. Office of Cts., Montgomery, Ala.; restitution officer Dist. Attorney's Office, 2000—. Softball coach Millbrook Girls Softball League. Mem.: Am. Soc. for Pub. Adminstrators, Toastmasters Internat. Home: 40 Green Ct Deatsville AL 36022 Office: Dist Atty's Office 100 South Lawrence St Montgomery AL 36102 Personal E-mail: cmandry@justice.com. Business E-mail: christinemandry@mc-ala.org.

MANDULA, JEFFREY ELLIS, physicist; b. N.Y.C., July 23, 1941; s. Andrew and Gertrude Phyllis (Entenberg) M.; m. Barbara Blumenstein, June 2, 1963. BA, Columbia U., 1962; MA, Harvard U., 1964, PhD, 1966. Fellow Harvard U., Cambridge, Mass., 1966-67; rsch. fellow Calif. Inst. Tech., Pasadena, 1967-69, asst. prof. theoretical physics, 1970-73; mem. Inst. for Advanced Study, Princeton, N.J., 1969-70; assoc. prof. applied math. MIT, Cambridge, 1973-79; prof. physics Washington U., St. Louis, 1979-87; sr. scientist theoretical physics Dept. Energy, Washington, 1987—. Program dir. for theoretical physics NSF, Washington, 1980-81; sec. Signition Corp., Los Alamos, N.Mex., 1986—; vis. prof. U. Minn., Mpls., 1979, U. Southampton, Eng., 1979; invited prof. U. Louvain, Belgium, 1980; adj. prof. physics Washington U., St. Louis, 1987—. Contbr. over 90 articles to profl. jours. NSF fellow, 1966, Alfred P. Sloan Found. fellow 1973; recipient Cottrel Rsch. award Rsch. Corp., 1984. Mem. AAAS, Am. Phys. Soc., Fedn. Am. Scientists. Home: 500 23d St NW Washington DC 20037-2828 Office: US Dept Energy Divsn High Energy Physics Washington DC 20585-0001 E-mail: jeffrey.mandula@science.doe.gov.

MANEA, NORMAN, writer, educator; b. Suceava, Bukovina, Romania, July 19, 1936; came to U.S., 1988; s. Marcu and Janeta (Braunstein) M.; m. Josette-Cella Boiangiu, June 28, 1969. MS in Engring., Inst. Constrn., Bucharest, Romania, 1954. Engr., Romania, 1959-74; writer Romania, 1969-86; fellow Deutscher Akademischer Austauschdienst, West Berlin, Germany, 1987; fellow Internat. Acad. Scholarship and the Arts Bard Coll., Annandale On Hudson, N.Y., 1989-92, writer in residence, 1992-96, Francis Flournoy prof. in European studies and culture, 1997—. Author: October, eight o'clock, 1992, On Clowns: The Dictator & the Artist, 1992, Compulsory Happiness, 1993, The Black Envelope, 1995; contbr. articles, stories to profl. jours. Recipient MacArthur Found. award, 1992, Nat. Jewish Book award Jewish Book Coun., 1993, Literary Lion award Nat. Pub. Libr., 1993, Nonino Internat. Lit. prize, Italy, 2002; Guggenheim grantee, 1992; Fulbright fellow, 1988. Mem. Am. Pen. Office: Bard Coll Dept Lang and Lit Annandale On Hudson NY 12504

MANEKER, MORTON M. lawyer; b. N.Y.C., Nov. 14, 1932; s. Arthur and Estelle (Hochberg) M.; m. Roberta S. Wexler, 1985; children: Meryl Colle, Amy Jill, Marion Kenneth. AB, Harvard U., 1954, LL.B., 1957. Bar: N.Y. State 1957. Assoc. Shearman & Sterling, N.Y.C., 1957-62; trial atty. antitrust div. Dept. Justice, 1962-63; ptnr. Proskauer Rose LLP, N.Y.C., 1963-94; ret., 1994. Trustee Beth Israel Hosp., N.Y.C., 1977—2001. Mem. Am. Law Inst., N.Y. State Bar Assn., Harmonie Club. Jewish. Home: 30 E 65th St New York NY 10021-7013 E-mail: maneker@aol.com.

MANEKER, ROBERTA S(UE), public relations executive; b. N.Y.C., July 9, 1937; d. Maxwell Roy and Esther (Gerson) Scheff; m. Hannan Wexler, June 4, 1961 (div. 1983); children: Daniel, Joanna; m. Morton M. Maneker, June 1, 1985. BA, Oberlin Coll., 1957. Mng. editor True Love mag., N.Y.C., 1960-62; publicity dir. Capt. Kangaroo, CBS, N.Y.C., 1962-66; syndicated columnist Oleg Cassini, N.Y.C., 1967-69; freelance writer, N.Y.C., 1967-70; dir. pub. rels. Direct Mktg. Assn., N.Y.C., 1983-85, v.p. pub. rels., 1985-87; v.p. pub. rels. Christie's, N.Y.C., 1987-91, sr. v.p. corp. comm./mktg., 1991—. dir. Lechters, Inc. Ford Found. scholar, 1953-57. Mem. Oberlin Coll. Alumni Assn. (pres. 1989-91), Phi Beta Kappa. Home: 30 E 65th St New York NY 10021-7013 Office: Christie's 20 Rockefeller Plz New York NY 10020-1902

MANELLI, DONALD DEAN, screenwriter, film producer; b. Burlington, Iowa, Oct. 20, 1936; s. Daniel Anthony and Mignon Marie (Dean) M.; m. Susan Linda Allen, June 16, 1964 (div. Aug. 1973); children: Daniel, Lisa. BA, U. Notre Dame, 1959. Communications specialist Jewel Cos., Melrose Park, Ill., 1959; script writer Coronet Films, Chgo., 1960-62; freelance writer, 1962-63; creative dir. Fred A. Niles Communications Ctrs., 1963-67; sr. writer Wild Kingdom NBC-TV, 1967-70; freelance film writer, producer, 1970-76; pres. Donald Manelli & Assocs., Inc., Chgo. and Paris, 1976—. Screenwriter, prodr. more than 225 documentary films, 1970—, numerous episodes Wild Kingdom, 1967-82 (Emmy award 1969, 70). Recipient numerous awards various orgns. including N.Y. Internat. Film Festival, Houston Internat. Film Festival, Berlin, Paris, Venice Internat. Film Festivals, CINE, 1976—. Mem. Writers Guild Am. Roman Catholic. Avocations: photography, traveling, tennis. Office: 1 E Delaware Pl Chicago IL 60611-1449 also: 1 Rue Goethe 75116 Paris France E-mail: dmanelli@earthlink.net. *A simple truth is played out in most lives: what we believe ourselves to be, we are. We may be tested with adversity, our own failed efforts, and plain bad luck, but our personal vision gives us strength and persistence. Success brings the satisfaction of fulfilled dreams, and the responsibility to help others form and follow their own visions.*

MANERI, NORMAN EDWARD, music educator; b. Cleve., Oct. 18, 1951; s. Onorio P. and Mildred Maneri; m. Kathleen Lois Watson; children: Christopher, Matthew, Andrew. MusB , Baldwin-Wallace Coll., 1973; MA , Case-Western Res. U., 1981. Music educator Cleve. Pub. Schools, 1973—78; asst. dir. All-Ohio State Fair Band, Columbus, 1995—; music educator Richmond Heights local schs., 1978—. Pres. South-Euclid/Lyndurst Kiwanis Club, Lyndhurst, 1983—84. Named Tchr. of the Yr., Richmond Heights Local Schools, 1989; grantee Summer Creativity Project, Martha Holden Jennings Found., 1975. Mem.: Music Educators Nat. Conf., Ohio Music Edn. Assn., Ohio Edn. Assn., Richmond Heights Edn. Assn. (pres. 1988—91). Roman Catholic. Avocation: reading, all types of sports. Home: 23 Church St Hudson OH 44236 Office: Richmond Heights Local Schs 447 Richmond Rd Cleveland OH 44143

MANERI, REMO R. management consultant; b. Cleve., Aug. 16, 1928; s. Quinto Peter and Lucia (Massenzi) M.; m. Camille Ann Caranna, Aug. 26, 1950; children: Peter, Alisa, Leonard, Celia. BS in Chem. Engring., Case Inst. Tech., 1950; grad., Advanced Mgmt. Program, Harvard U., 1969. Devel. engr. Dow Corning, 1950-53, market researcher, 1956, comml. devel. mgr., 1957-63, chief engr., 1964-66, unit mfg. mgr., 1967-69, dir. tech. service and devel., 1970-72, bus. mgr., v.p., 1973-74, mgr. bus., group v.p., 1975-76; pres. Dow Corning U.S.A., 1977-80; exec. v.p. Dow Corning Corp., 1981-82, also bd. dirs.; chmn. bd. Quantum Composites, 1982-85, pres., chmn. bd., 1985-87, chmn. bd., 1987-89, also bd. dirs.; mgmt. cons., 1989—. Bd. dirs. Comerica Bank-Midland, Duro-Last Roofing, Inc., Quantum Composites, Inc.; cons. in field. Contbr. articles to profl. jours.; patentee in field. Bd. dirs. Midland Hosp. Assn. Served with Signal Corps, U.S. Army, 1954-56. Named Man of Year Adhesives and Sealants Coun., 1988. Mem. AAAS, Chem. Spltys. Mfg. Assn. (dir.), Am. Chem. Soc., Sigma Xi, Tau Beta Pi, Alpha Chi Sigma. Clubs: Midland Country. Roman Catholic. Home and Office: 5808 Siebert St Midland MI 48640-2753

MANESS, EDWIN CLINTON, III, highway patrol officer, video coordinator; b. Charlotte, N.C., Feb. 5, 1955; s. Ed Clinton Jr. and Blanche (Jones) M.; m. Diane Mease, July 15, 1981; 1 child, Brooke. Grad. in radio/TV comm., Carolina Sch. Broadcasting, Charlotte, 1974. Sgt., video sect. N.C. Hwy. Patrol, Raleigh, 1981—. Mem. adv. bd. Boy Scouts Am., Morganton, N.C., 1979, Charlotte, 1991. Named Trooper of Yr., Mecklenburg County Rotary Club, Charlotte, 1991, Man of Yr. Morganton Jaycees, 1979; recipient Gov.'s Heroism award, 2000. Mem. Law Enforcement Video Assn. Baptist. Avocation: golf. Home: 7121 Westworth Dr Willow Spring NC 27592-9607 Office: NC State Hwy Patrol 3318 Garner Rd Raleigh NC 27610-5618

MANETH, DAVID SCOTT, secondary school educator; b. Great Bend, Kans., Aug. 29, 1964; s. William Francis and Kay Maneth; m. Angie Marie Detmer; 1 child Mary Helen. Assoc. degree, Barton County C.C., 1985; BA, Marymount Coll., 1987; BS, Newman U., 1998. Cert. secondary tchr. Kans., picture framer. Math. and sci. tchr. Christ the King Cath. Sch., Wichita, Kans., 1999—2002. Freelance photographer, Wichita, 1982—99; apprentice photographer Scenic Documentary, 1981. Vol. photographer Sedwick County Zoo, Wichita, 1990—95; Officer- Chancellor, Warden Knights of Columbus #4118, KS, 1993—2002. Recipient 1st Place-News Divsn., Kans. Associated Collegiate Press, 1998, finalist, Photographer's Forum Mag., 1986. Mem.: KC (4th degree) (Honor Guard 1997—2002). Roman Catholic. Home: 2043 Sunridge St Wichita KS 67235-1522 Office: Christ the King Cath Sch 4501 Maple St Wichita KS 67209 Personal E-mail: maneth@onemain.com.

MANEVAL, DAVID RICHARD, mineral engineering consultant; b. Williamsport, Pa., Dec. 18, 1928; s. Paul David and Julia May (Heisler) M.; m. Lyne Page Heisley, Feb. 25, 1951 (dec.); children: David R. Jr., Michael W. (dec.), Holly M. McDonough, Laurie M. Zellers. BS, Pa. State U., 1950, MS, 1957, PhD, 1961. Asst. prof. Pa. State U., State College, 1961-63, dir. rsch. Pa. dept. of mines, 1963-69, dep. sec. Pa. dept. environment, 1969-70; sci. advisor Appalachian Regional Com., Washington, 1971-78; asst. dir. Office of Surface Mining, 1979-81; prof. U. Alaska, Fairbanks, 1981-89; mineral engring. cons., State College, 1989—. Cons. in field, 1961—; extramural reviewer Alaska Sci. and Engring. Found., Anchorage, Alaska, 1989—; lectr. Pa. State U., 1992—. Author: (book chpts.) Mining Engineering Handbook, 1973, Coal Preparation, 1979; contbr. articles to profl. jours. Mem. College Area Sch. Bd., State College, 1957-63; mem. adv. com. Bur. Land Mgmt., Fairbanks, 1983-89; exec. bd. dirs. Juniata Valley Boy Scout Coun., 1993—. With U.S. Army, 1950-52. Recipient Superior Svc. award U.S. Dept. of Interior, 1979, Silver Beaver award Juniata Valley Boy Scout Coun., 1962. Mem. Am. Inst. Mining, Metallurg. and Petroleum Engrs. (disting. mem. 1990, Distin. Svc. award for environ. conservation 1980), Pa. State Ret. Faculty Club (treas. 1995-98), Rotary (sr. active State College, bd. dirs. 1995-97, 2001-02, Paul Harris fellow 1988). Republican. Presbyterian. Avocations: gardening, travel, photography. Home: 126 W Lytle Ave State College PA 16801-5925

MANEY, MICHAEL MASON, lawyer; b. Taihoku, Japan, Aug. 13, 1936; s. Edward Strait and Helen M. M.; m. Suzanne Cochran, Oct. 22, 1960; 1 child, Michele. BA, Yale U., 1956; MA, Fletcher Sch. Law and Diplomacy, Tufts U., 1957; LL.B., U. Pa., 1964. Bar: N.Y. 1966, D.C. 1977. Case officer CIA, 1957-61; law clk. Justice John Harlan, Supreme Ct. U.S., Washington, 1964-65; asso. Sullivan & Cromwell, N.Y.C., 1965-70, ptnr., 1971-77, 81—, mng. ptnr. Washington, 1977-81. Law fellow Salzburg Seminar in Am. Studies, 1967; mem. bd. overseers Fletcher Sch. Law and Diplomacy. Mem. bd. overseers U. Pa. Law Sch. 1st lt. USAF, 1957-61. Mem. ABA, Am. Law Inst., Am. Coll. Trial Lawyers, N.Y. State Bar Assn., Union Club, Down Town Assn., Madison Beach Club, Madison Country Club, Met. Opera Club, New Haven Country Club. Home: 1220 Park Ave New York NY 10128-1733 also: 48 Neptune Ave Madison CT 06443-3210 Office: Sullivan & Cromwell 125 Broad St New York NY 10004-2498 E-mail: maneym@sullcrom.com.

MANFREDI, DEANNA ANN, psychologist; b. Wilmington, Del., Mar. 12, 1968; d. Richard Lewis and Anna Gloria (Vallorani) M. BA, Franklin & Marshall Coll., Lancaster, Pa., 1990; MA, Princeton U., 1992, PhD, 1994; MBA, Widener U., 1999. PA Psych. Lic., 1999. Asst. instr. Princeton (N.J.) U., 1990-93; project mgr. Nat. Analysts, Inc., Phila., 1994-96; resident N.E. Treatment Ctrs., 1996-97; psychology intern Allegheny Health, Edn. and Rsch. Found., 1997-98, Integra, Inc., 1998-99. Contbr. chpt. to book and articles to profl. jours. Mem. APA, Am. Coll. Healthcare Execs., Sigma Xi. Republican. Roman Catholic. Home: 301 Race St Apt 205 Philadelphia PA 19106-1843 Office: TVG Inc 520 Virginia Dr Fort Washington PA 19034-2707 E-mail: deannaman@aol.com.

MANG, DOUGLAS ARTHUR, lawyer; b. Little Falls, N.Y., Mar. 25, 1942; s. Willard D. and Mary L. (Murray) M.; m. Nora Ladeane Geren; 1 child, Brittany Nandeana. BS, Cornell U., 1964; LLB, Syracuse U., 1967. Bar: N.Y. 1971, Fla. 1971, U.S. Dist. Ct. (no. dist.) Fla. 1977, U.S. Ct. Appeals (5th and llth cirs.) 1981, U.S. Dist. Ct. (mid. dist.) Fla. 1982, U.S. Supreme Ct. 1988. Atty. Mut. Life Ins. Co., N.Y.C., 1971-73; asst. gen. counsel Am. Gen. Capital Mgmt., 1973-77; gen. counsel Fla. Dept. of Ins., Tallahassee, 1977-79; ptnr. Mang & Stowell PA, 1979-86, Mang Law Firm PA, Tallahassee, 1986—. Served to 1st lt. U.S. Army, 1968-70, Vietnam. Mem. Fla. Def. Lawyers Assn., Tiger Bay Club, Fla. Econs. Club, Rotary, Fedn. Regulatory Counsel (regional dir.). Methodist. Avocations: sailing, golf. Office: Mang Law Firm PA 660 E Jefferson St Tallahassee FL 32301-2582 E-mail: dmang@manglaw.com.

MANGA, MICHAEL, science educator; b. Hamilton, Ont., Can., July 22, 1968; s. Pran and Louise Manga; m. Susan Storch. BSc, McGill U., Montreal, Que., Can., 1990; SM, Harvard U., 1992, PhD, 1994. Miller rsch. fellow Miller Inst. for Basic Rsch. Sci., Berkeley, Calif., 1994—96; asst. prof. U. Oreg., Eugene, 1996—2001; assoc. prof. U. Calif., Berkeley, 2001—. Recipient Career award, NSF, 1997—2001; fellow, Sloan Found., 2001. Fellow: Am. Geophys. Union (James B. Macelwane medal 2002). Office: Univ Calif Berkeley 307 McCone Hall Berkeley CA 94720-4767 Office Fax: 510-643-9980. Business E-Mail: manga@seismo.berkeley.edu.

MANGALARAMANAN, SATHYA PRASAD, mechanical engineer, researcher; b. Madurai, India, Mar. 19, 1969; arrived in Can., 1992,arrived in U.S.A., 2000; s. Narayanan and Lakshmi Mangalaramanan; m. Bama Srinivasan Sathyaprasad, Oct. 11, 1999; 1 child Narayanan Sathyaprasad Aiyer. BE, Anna U., India, 1990; MS, U. Regina, Can., 1993; PhD, Meml. U., 1997. Mktg. engr. Larsen & Toubro Ltd., Chennai, India, 1990—92; rsch. assoc. U. Regina, Saskatchewan, Canada, 1992—93; rsch. & tchg. assoc. Meml. U., St. Johns, Canada, 1993—97; design engr. Babcock & Wilcox Can., Cambridge, Canada, 1997—2000; prin. engr. Dana Corp., Kalamazoo, 2000—. Adj. prof. Meml. U., Newfoundland, Canada, 1998—2001. Author: Simplified Inelastic Analysis and Code Perspectives, 2001; contbr. articles to profl. jours. Recipient Gov. Gen. Gold Medal award, Gov. Gen. of Can., 1997, Alien of Extraordinary Ability award, U.S. Immigration & Naturalization Svcs., 2001. Mem.: ASME (tech. reviewer 1997—, Jour. Editor's Choice award 2002), Soc. Automotive Engrs. Hindu. Avocations: So. Indian cooking, handy man. Office: Dana Corp 6938 Elm Valley Drive Kalamazoo MI 49009

MANGAN, JOAN MARY, medical educator; b. Bronx, N.Y., Oct. 7, 1966; AA, Edison C.C., 1986; BS in Med. Tech., Fla. Atlantic U., 1989, MS in Tchg., 1994. Sr. med. technologist Broward Gen. Med. Ctr., Ft. Lauderdale, Fla., 1989-96; regional mgr. lab. Imperial Point Med. Ctr., 1996-97; acad. coord. surg. physician asst. program U. Ala., Birmingham, 1999—2001, dir. admissions surg. physician asst. program, 2001—. Chairperson Sheridan, Ft. Lauderdale. Mem. Am. Soc. of Clin. Pathologists, Am. Pub. Health Assn. Home: 1104 Gables Dr Birmingham AL 35244 E-mail: manganj@shrp.uab.edu.

MANGAN, JOHN LEO, retired electrical manufacturing company executive, international trade and trade policy specialist; b. Lakewood, Ohio, May 24, 1920; s. Mark A. and Celia M. Mangan; m. Mildred J. Livingston, June 21, 1946; children: John, Scott. BSME, Carnegie Inst. Tech., 1942. Registered profl. engr., Mass., N.Y. Turbine design engr. Gen. Electric Co., Lynn, Mass., 1946-48, turbine application and sales engr. Fitchburg and Lynn, Mass., Schenectady, St. Louis, 1948-55, mgr. gas turbine indsl. sales Schenectady, 1955-60, mgr. gas turbine product planning, 1960-64, mgr. turbine bus. strategy devel., 1966-86; mgr. turbine indsl. customer requirements Boeing Co., Seattle, 1964-66. Contbr. articles profl. jours., chpts. in books; inventor in field. Mem. com. Boy Scouts Am., 1955-59, 64-66; bd. dirs. United Way Schenectady County, Inc., 1991-96, chmn., 1992-93. 1st lt. U.S. Army, 1942-46. Recipient Profl. and Social Activities award GE, 1977, cert. of merit N.Y. State Assembly, 1995. Fellow ASME (v.p. 1975-79, bd. govs. 1983-87, Gas Turbine citation, Centennial medal 1980, Dedicated Svc. award 1988); mem. Internat. Combustion Engine Coun. (permanent com. 1974-81, v.p. 1977-81), Mohawk Golf Club (Schenectady). Home: 1345 Ruffner Rd Niskayuna NY 12309-2505

MANGAN, MONA, association executive, lawyer; b. Pittston, Pa., Dec. 29, 1945; d. Joseph H. and Mona C. Mangan; m. Roy N. Watanabe, Oct. 24, 1987 (div. 2000); 1 child, Julia. BA, Lock Haven U., 1966; AM, Duke U., 1969; JD, Columbia U., 1975. Bar: N.Y. 1976, U.S. Dist. Ct. (ea. and so. dists.) N.Y. 1979. Mem. congrl. staff Sen. Wayne Morse of Oreg., 1967-68; staff atty. U.S. Dept. Labor, N.Y.C., 1975-79; trial atty. EEOC, 1979; asst. exec. dir. Writers Guild Am. East Inc., 1979-84, assoc. exec. dir., 1984, exec. dir., 1984—. Recipient Gross award for contbn. to journalism Lock Haven U., 1984. Mem.: AFL-CIO (v.p., v.p. dept. for profl. employees), ABA, N.Y. NATAS (treas. 2000—), NATAS (bd. govs. 2001—), Internat. Affiliation Writers Guilds (treas.), Unions for Performing Arts (treas.), Pan Am. Fedn. Arts, Mass Media and Entertainment Unions (v.p. 1993—), Coalition on Motion Picture and TV Unions (v.p.), Assn. Bar City of N.Y., Nat. Policy Assn., Columbia U. Law Sch. Alumni Assn. Office: Writers Guild Am East Inc 555 W 57th St New York NY 10019-2925

MANGAN, PATRICIA ANN PRITCHETT, statistician; b. Hammond, Ind., Feb. 4, 1953; d. Edward Clayton and Helen Josephine (Mills) Pritchett; m. William Paul Mangan, Aug. 30, 1980; 1 child, Ryan Christopher. BS in Maths. and Stats., Purdue U., 1975, MS in Applied Stats., 1977. Tobacco devel. statistician R.J. Reynolds Tobacco Co., Winston-Salem, N.C., 1978-82, R&D statistician, 1982-86, sr. R&D statistician, 1986-90, sr. staff R&D statistician, 1990-93; dir. software devel. ARJAY Equipment Corp., 1993-96; sr. staff scientist R.J. Reynolds Tobacco Co., 1996-99; statis. analyst N.C. Bapt. Hosp., 1999-2000; staff specialist N.C. Baptist Hosp., 2000—. Cons. Lab. for Application of Remote Sensing, West Lafayette, Ind., 1976-77; statis. engr. Corning Glass Works, Harrodsburg, Ky., 1977. Editor Jour. of Sensory Studies, 1992-95; contbr. articles to sci. jours. Rep. United Way, Winston-Salem, 1985. Recipient G.R. DiMarco award, 1990, 96, Excaliber award for Outstanding Performance, 1991, 93. Mem. Am. Statis. Assn., Wash. Statis. Assn., Purdue Alumni Assn. E-mail: pmangan@wfubmc.edu.

MANGAN, TERENCE JOSEPH, federal agency professional, retired protective services official; b. Utica, N.Y., Feb. 17, 1938; BA, St. Mary's Coll., 1961; MA, St. Albert's Coll., 1965; postgrad. in pub. adminstrn., U. So. Calif., 1972-76; Grad., FBI Nat. Acad., N.W. Law Enforcement Exec., 1986. Cert. Wash. State Criminal Justice Tng. Commn., Calif.; cert. Gov.'s Rev. Team Child Abuse Svscs., 1986. With Seaside (Calif.) Police Dept., 1967-72, Lakewood (Calif.) Police Dept., 1972-76, chief, dir. cmty. safety, 1976; chief Bellingham (Wash.) Police Dept., 1976-87, Spokane (Wash.) Police Dept., 1987-98; ret., 1998; mem. FBI leadership and mgmt. sci. unit FBI Acad., Quantico, Va., 1998—; program mgmt. FBI Nat. Exec. Inst. and Major City Chiefs Program. Past chair Wash. Stae Criminal Justice Tng. Commn.; mem.Mgmt. Adv. Group Organized Crime and Narcotics Enforcement; apptd. to death investigations coun. Spl. Task Force on Child Abuse, Gov.'s Criminal Justice Adv. Bd.; master mentor Waspc's Exec. Leadership Inst., coord. N.W. Law Enforcement Command Coll. Program; mem. Wash. Law Enforcement Exec. Forum, past chair; mem. Wash. State Inst. Cmty. Oriented Policing. Mem. archdiocesan steering com. Ann. Catholic Appeal, 1982; chair fund-raising drives Am. Cancer Soc., Am. Heart Assn., Salvation Army, Easter Seal Soc., Assn. Retarded Citizens; bd. advs. Holy Names Ctr.; exec. bd. Inland Empire coun. Boy Scouts Am.; bd. dirs. Spokane Goodwill Industries, United Way, Whatcom County, Calif. Paul Harris fellow Rotary Internat., 1986; recipient citation U.S. Secret Svc., 1969, Congl. Com. Internal Security, 1971, Svc. award City of Seaside, 1972, Disting. Svc. award City of Lakewood, Wash. Assn. Sheriffs and Police Chiefs, 1978-81, Cmty. Svc. award Wash. Toastmasters Internat., 1980, Pres. award Pacific Luth. U., 1981; named Police Officer of Yr. Nat. Exch. Club, 1979, Lawman of Yr. VFW, 1980, Law Enforcement Officer of Yr. VFW, 1980. Secret Svc. Honor award, 1998, Defender of Freedom award, 1998. Mem. Internat. Assn. Chiefs of Police (com. terrorism), Nat. Coun. Crime and Delinquency, Wash. Assn. Sheriffs and Police Chiefs (life mem.; past pres.), Internat. Peace Artch Law Enforcement Coun., VFW (life). Roman Catholic. Office: FBI Acad L Msu Rm 112 Quantico VA 22135-0001

MANGAN, THOMAS P. band director; b. Braddock, Pa., Oct. 24, 1966; s. Robert A. and Frances A. Mangan; m. Kimberly T. Turner, Sept. 26, 1998. Student, Armed Forces Sch. Music, 1994; BS in Bus. Mgmt., U. Phoenix, 2000. Trombonist 3rd Marine Aircraft Wing Band, El Toro, Calif., 1985—93, III Marine Expeditionary Force Band, Okinawa, Japan, 1993—94; asst. dir. Marine Corps Band, San Diego, 1995—2001, dir. & officer in charge Twentynine Palms, 2001—. Guest condr. various U.S. & Can. mil. and h.s. bands, 1995—. With USMC, 2001—. Recipient Navy & Marine Corps Commendation medal, USMC, 2001. Mem.: Marine Corps Musicians Assn., Calif. Music Educators Assn., Music Educators Nat. Conf., Audi TT Owners' Club, BonesWest, San Diego Bay Bones, Tubists' Universal Brotherhood Assn., Internat. Trombone Assn. Roman Catholic. Avocations: music, trombone choir, racquetball, dogs. Home Fax: 760-830-6647. Personal E-mail: TomMangan@aol.com.

MANGANARO, FRANCIS FERDINAND, naval officer; b. Providence, Feb. 27, 1925; s. Ralph and Ada Susanna (Hobden) M.; m. Carol Anne Slater, Sept. 8, 1948; children: Carol Sue, William Francis, John Thomas, Linda Anne, Mary Kathryn. Student, U. R.I., 1943-44; BS in Elec. Engring, U.S. Naval Acad., 1944-47; Post MD, Naval Engr., MIT, 1956; cert., Advanced Mgmt. Program, Harvard U. Sch. Bus., 1971; cert. pub. utilities exec. program, U. Mich., 1984. Registered profl. engr., Conn. Commd. ensign U.S. Navy, 1947, advanced through grades to rear adm., 1975; served in destroyers Atlantic Fleet, 1947-49; served in submarines Pacific Fleet, 1949-53; repair officer, submarines Pearl Harbor Naval Shipyard, 1956-59; design project officer, submarines Bur Ships, 1959-63; inspection and planning officer Office Supr. of Shipbldg. Groton, Conn., 1963-68; prodn. officer Portsmouth Naval Shipyard, 1968-72; comdg. officer Puget Sound Naval Shipyard, 1972-76; chmn. navy claims settlement bd. Naval Material Command, 1976-78; vice comdr. Naval Sea Systems Command Washington, 1978-80; ret. (Naval Sea Systems Command), 1980. V.p., dir. GPU Nuclear Corp., 1980-90; cons. Burns & Roe Utility Mgmt. Cons., 1990-94; cons. Raytheon Engrs. & Constructors, Inc., 1994-96. Decorated DSM, Legion of Merit. Mem. Soc. Naval Architects and Marine Engrs., Am. Soc. Naval Engrs., Sigma Xi, Tau Beta Pi, Beta Psi Alpha.

MANGANELLO, JAMES ANGELO, psychologist; b. Cambridge, Mass., Nov. 30, 1944; s. Almando and Carmella (Spera) M.; m. Rosemarie Bombara, Dec. 26, 1965; children: Jason, Jennifer. BA, Eastern Nazarene Coll., 1966; MA, Boston U., 1970; EdM, Suffolk U., 1969; EdD, Boston U., 1977; M in Pub. Health, Harvard U., 1980. Instr. biology N.Y. Christian Acad., Bklyn., 1966-67; minister youth, edn. St. Paul Ch., Somerville, Mass., 1967-69; dir., founder Community Nursery Sch., 1967-69; resident dir., instr. Malone Coll., Canton, Ohio, 1969-70; clin., research fellow dept. psychiatry Mass. Gen. Hosp., Boston, 1973-75; psychologist North Shore Counseling Ctr., Beverly, Mass., 1975-79; instr. North Shore Community Coll., 1975-78; pres. Health Integration Services, Peabody, Mass., 1978-83; clin. fellow dept. psychiatry Harvard U. Med. Sch., Boston, 1983-84; pres. Dr. Manganello & Assocs., Danvers, Mass., 1983—, The Charis Inst., Lexington, 1994—. Cons. psychologist Erich Lindemann Mental Health Ctr., Boston, 1971-75, Westwood Lodge, 1973-74. Contbr. articles to profl. jours. Chpt. mem. Rep. Presdl. Task Force, Washington, 1983—; mem. guidance adv. bd., bd. trustees Lexington Christian Acad., Mass., 1977—; mem. pres.'s council Gordon-Conwell Theol. Sem., Hamilton, Mass., 1983—. Mem. AAAS, Am. Orthopsychiat. Assn., Am. Pub. Health Assn., Am. Coll. Health Care Execs., Am. Sci. Affiliation, Soc. for Sci. Study of Religion, MIT Enterprise Forum, Pi Lambda Theta. Avocations: tennis, basketball, music. Home: 2 Crest Cir Lexington MA 02421-7144 Office: 3 Militia Dr Lexington MA 02421-4739

MANGANELLO, JOSEPH JAMES, communication and management consultant, writer; b. N.Y.C., Jan. 30, 1949; s. Joseph Anthony and Aida Angelina (Capone) M.; married June 27, 1970 (div. Apr. 1985); children: Aida Michelle, Jacqueline Marie. BBA in mktg. and econs., Iona Coll., 1970. Retail environment designer Patrick's Things Ltd., Mt. Vernon, N.Y., 1970-72; retail environment designer and fabricator Tiffany II Designs, Tuckahoe, 1972-73; tng. mgr. Friendly Ice Cream Family Restaurants, Wilbraham, Mass., 1973-75; dir. human resources and devel. Pier I Imports, Ft. Worth, 1975-81; exec. dir. mgmt. devel. Club Corp. Am., Dallas, 1981-83; ptnr. Hadden Manganello & Assocs., 1983—. Author: (monthly feature) Dallas Bus. Jour., 1989—. Recipient Excellence award Cable Access TV, 1988, Silver medal Internat. Film and TV Festival N.Y., 1984, 89, Internat. Matrix award Women in Comm., 1989, Best of Tex. award U.S.A. Film Festival, 1984; named Most Outstanding Exhibitor, Nat. Assn. for Display Industry, 1971. Mem. Internat. Assn. Bus. Communicators, Internat. TV Assn. (Silver Reel award 1985), Am. Soc. Tng. and Devel. (v.p. mktg. and pub. relations 1985-86, Outstanding Contribution by Cons. 1984), Am. Mgmt. Assn., Nat. Club Assn. (assoc.), Tex. Restaurant Assn., Dallas Restaurant Assn. (bd. dirs. 1987-89), Dallas C. of C., Century II Club, Elks. Roman Catholic. Avocations: writing, cooking, music composition. Address: Manganello Communicat 6110 E Mockingbird Ln # 102-606 Dallas TX 75214-2628

MANGANIELLO, JANICE MARIE, peri-operative nurse; b. Pittston, Pa., July 29, 1966; d. Ludwig Sr. and Dorothy Manganiello; m. Michael LaBella, 1995; children: Christina LaBella, Gianna LaBella. AAS, Luzerne County C.C., Nanticoke, Pa., 1989; student, Coll. Misericordia, Dallas, Pa., 1989—; cert., Luzerne County C.C., 1992. RN; cert. first asst. CNOR, nat. cert. peri-operative nurse. Emergency svcs. nurse Pittston Med. Emergency Ctr., 1989; obstetrics nurse Wilkes Barre (Pa.) Gen. Hosp., 1989, surg. svcs. nurse, 1989-91; RN first asst. Office of Sam C. DePasquale, 1992-93; perioperative nurse, charge nurse urology/renal transplant Temple U. Hosp., Phila., 1993—, clin. specialist laser surgery, 1993—, clin. coord. for students, 1993—. Instr. continuing edn. planning Luzerne County C.C., 1993. Vol. Big Bros./Big Sisters, Am. Cancer Soc., Valley Santa; religious edn. tchr. St. Rocco's Ch., Pittston; mem. long range planning com. Pittston Area Sch. Dist., 1992. Recipient St. John Neumann award, St. Pius X award religious edn. Mem. ANA, NAFE, Am. Heart Assn., Assn. Operating Rm. Nurses (chair project Alpha 1990-91, chair rsch. 1993-94, RN 1st asst. interest group), Soc. for Urology Nurses Assn., Orgn. for Advancement Assoc. Degree Nurses, Nat. League for Nursing, Soc. Peripheral Vascular Nursing, Nat. Assn. Orthopaedic Nurses, Couns. Cardiovascular Nursing and Circulation.

MANGANIELLO, LOUIS OTTO JOSEPH, retired neurosurgeon; b. Waterbury, Conn., June 6, 1915; s. Angelo M. and Raimonda (Membrino) M.; m. Carol Graham Pryor, June 11, 1950; children: Carol Helen, Victoria R. AB, Harvard U., 1937; MD, U. Md., 1942; JD, Augusta Law Sch., 1967. Diplomate Am. Bd. Neurol. Surgery. Intern Uuniv. Hosp., Balt., 1942-43, resident in neurol. surgery, 1946-50; pvt. practice medicine specializing in neurosurgery Augusta, Ga., 1951-96; ret., 1996. Mem. staff Univ. Hosp., Doctors Hosp., St. Joseph Hosp., Augusta; mem., past pres. composite state bd. Med. Examiners Ga.; cons. VA Hosp., Augusta; dir. Blue Cross/Blue Shield; assoc. prof. neurosurgery Med. Coll. Ga., 1951-96, ret., 1996. Contbr. articles to profl. jours. Bd. dirs. ARC. Served with USN, 1942-46. Fellow ACS; mem. AMA, Richmond County Med. Soc., Med. Assn. Ga., Am. Assn. Neurol. Surgery, Congress Neurosurgeons, So. Neurosurg. Soc., Southeastern Surg. Congress, Am. Assn. Cancer Rsch., Am. Assn. Med. Colls., Internat. Assn. Lex and Sci., Ga. Neurosurg. Soc. (past pres.), Country Club of Augusta, Pinnacal Club, Rotary. Home: 656 Milledge Rd Augusta GA 30904-4388

MANGANO, LOUIS, lawyer; b. Passaic, N.J., Sept. 19, 1939; s. Salvatore and Mary Mangano; m. Arlene M. Triolo, Sept. 20, 1964; children: Kenneth L., Eileen M., Louis M., Michael S. BS in Bus. Adminstrn., Seton Hall U., 1970; MA in Criminal Justice, John Jay Coll., 1973; JD, Seton Hall U., 1979. Bar: N.J. 1981, U.S. Dist. Ct. N.J. 1981, U.S. Supreme Ct. 1985. With Elmwood Park (N.J.) Police Dept., 1966-83; pvt. practice atty. Elmwood Park, 1981—. Adj. prof. Fairleigh Dickinson U., Rutherford, N.J., 1973-75, Jersey City (N.J.) State Coll., 1973-75; asst. prof. William Paterson Coll., Wayne, N.J., 1983-84; adv. bd. mem. Berkeley Coll., West Paterson, N.J., 1983, 93-99.

Trustee, pres. Elmwood Park (N.J.) Bd. Edn., 1980-83, 89-93. With U.S. Army, 1959-61. Mem. Bergen County Bar Assn. Office: PO Box 305 395 River Dr Elmwood Park NJ 07407-1622

MANGANO, SALVATORE NICHOLAS, surgeon; b. Cambridge, Mass., 1922; s. Santo and Rose (Costa) M.; m. Anna Barney Stevenson, Apr. 28, 1956; children: Paul Stephen, John Joseph. AB, Harvard U., 1944; MD, Tufts U., 1947. Diplomate Am. Bd. Surgery. Intern Cambridge City Hosp., 1947-48, resident in surgery, 1949-51; resident Carney Hosp., Boston, 1948-49; pvt. practice gen. and colon-rectal surgery, 1953-90; cons. Mass. Dept. Correction, 1990—. Surgeon Lemuel Shattuck, Boston; asst. clin. prof. surgery Tufts U. Sch. Medicine, 1994—. Capt. USAF, 1951-53. Fellow ACS; mem. Am. Soc. Colorectal Surgery, Nat. Bd. Med. Examiners, Mass. Bd. Registration in Medicine (sec. 1984-87), Fedn. State Med. Bds. (cert. of appreciation 1987), Middlesex Dist. Med. Soc. (exec. sec. 1970—). Roman Catholic. Home: 145 Black Bear Dr Unit 2011 Waltham MA 02451-0229 Office: 145 Black Bear Dr #2011 Waltham MA 02451 Fax: 781-209-1938.

MANGAPIT, CONRADO, JR. manufacturing company executive; b. Cavite, Philippines, Oct. 17, 1946; s. Conrado Lebang Sr. and Amparo Ajuste (Odion) M.; m. Rosalinda Martinez Travis, Dec. 19, 1970; 1 child, Regina. BEE, U. So. Calif., Los Angeles, 1969; MA in Human Resource Mgmt., Pepperdine U., 1978. Commd. ensign USN, 1969, advanced through grades to lt. comdr., resigned, 1979; project engr. Continental Can Co., Houston, 1979-80; applications engr. Toshiba Houston Internat. Corp., 1980-83, asst. mktg. mgr., asst. product mgr., 1983, mgr. mktg., products, 1983-89, mgr. power apparatus div., 1989-96, mktg. mgr. packaging group, 1995-96, dir. ops.-contract, 1995-96, mktg. mgr. switchgear products group, 1996-97, sr. sales exec., 1997-98; sales mgr. Power Conversion Divsn., Liteon, Houston, 1998-99; dir. engring. Factory Automation Sys., College Park, Ga., 1999-2000; product mgr. IMC, Tucson, 2000—01; sales mgr. Magtrol/A.E.A., 2001—02; regional mgr. Rosens Power Sys., 2002—. Advisor Filipino-U.S. Mil. Assn., Guam, 1977-78; co. rep. Japan-Am. Soc., Houston, 1985—, Houston Minority Bus. Coun., 1997—. Recipient Humanitarian Service medal U.S. Dept. Def., 1978; named Outstanding Young Man of Am. U.S. Jaycees, 1980. Mem. IEEE, Am. Mgmt. Assn. Clubs: Mission Bend Homeowners Assn. (Houston). Republican. Roman Catholic. Avocations: reading, guitar, electronics, camping, college recruiting for the University of Southern California. E-mail: conradmangapit@myexcal.com., conradm@rosenelec.com.

MANGELSDORF, THOMAS KELLY, psychiatrist, consultant; b. St. Louis; s. Albert Henry and Hazel (Kelly) M.; m. Helen Louise Kareth, Apr. 12, 1958 (div. Jan. 1986); children: Ellen S., Steven T., Thomas K. Jr., Laura E. BS, U. Notre Dame, 1952; MD, St. Louis U., 1956. Diplomate Am. Bd. Psychiatry and Neurology (examiner 1968, 95), Am. Bd. Forensic Examiners; cert. Am. Bd. Profl. Disability Cons. Cons. in mental health various municipalities and pvt. practice, 1972—. Author and editor computerized system to interpret Minn. Multiphasic Personality Inventory profiles of patients to predict optimal psychiat. and pharmacologic interventions. Served to capt. U.S. Army, 1960-62. Fellow Am. Psychiat. Assn.; mem. Eastern Mo. Psychiat. Assn. (sec. 1983-85). Avocation: sailing. Office: 621 S New Ballas Rd Saint Louis MO 63141-8232

MANGER, GERALD H. real estate broker; b. Jersey City, Feb. 10, 1948; s. Henry C. and Irene M. Manger; children: Christopher, Paul. BFA, Pratt Inst., 1970; postgrad., Rutgers U., 1970-73. Real estate salesperson Max E. Spann Realtors, Bernardsville, N.J., 1976-82; adminstrv. broker Weichert Referrals, Morris Plains, 1982-95; pres. Wyndemere Real Estate Co., Inc., Blairstown, 1996—. Co-chmn. Main St. & Village Assn., Blairstown, 1997-99. Mem. Nat. Assn. Realtors, N.J. Assn. Realtors, Warren County Bd. Realtors (sec. 1998—), Blairstown Bus. Assn. (pres. 2000). Office: Wyndemere Real Estate Co Inc PO Box 669 3 Main St Blairstown NJ 07825-2601 E-mail: wyndemere@goes.com.

MANGER, WILLIAM MUIR, internist, educator; b. Greenwich, Conn., Aug. 13, 1920; s. Julius and Lilian (Weissinger) M.; m. Lynn Seymour Sheppard, May 30, 1964; children: William Muir, Jr., Lilian Wade (Mrs. Porter Fleming), Stewart Sheppard, Charles Seymour. BS, Yale U., 1944; MD, Columbia U., 1946; PhD, Mayo Found., U. Minn., 1958. Diplomate Nat. Bd. Med. Examiners, Am. Bd. Internal Medicine. Intern Presbyn. Hosp., N.Y.C., 1946-47, resident, 1949-50; fellow internal medicine Mayo Found., 1950-55; asst. physician Presbyn. Hosp., 1957—; dir. Manger Rsch. Found., 1961-77; clin. asst. attending physician Columbia divsn. Bellevue Hosp., 1964-68; asst. attending physician NYU Bellevue Hosp., 1969-77, assoc. attending physician, 1977-83, attending physician, 1983—; instr. medicine Columbia U. Coll. Phys. and Surg., 1957-66, assoc. medicine, 1966-70, lectr., 1981—. Asst. attending physician Presbyn. Hosp., 1966—68; asst. clin. prof. medicine NYU Med. Ctr., 1968—75, assoc. clin. prof. medicine, 1975—83, clin. prof. medicine, 1983—; mem. devel. com. Mayo Clinic, 1981—87; vice chmn. bd. Manger Hotels, Inc., , 1957—73. Co-author: Chemical Quantitation of Epinephrine and Norepinephrine in Plasma, 1959, Pheochromocytoma, 1977, Clinical and Experimental Pheochromocytoma, 1996; author: Catecholamines in Normal and Abnormal Cardiac Function, 1982; editor, co-author: Hormones and Hypertension, 1966, 100 Questions and Answers About Hypertension, 2000; editor: Am. Lecture Series in Endocrinology, 1962-75; guest editor First Irvine H. Page Internat. Hypertension Rsch. Symposium, 1990; contbr. articles to profl. and lay jours. Mem. bd. govs. St. Albans Sch., Washington, 1958-64, 67-73, 83-89, chmn., 1967-69; trustee Found. Rsch. in Medicine and Biology, 1971-77, Buckley Sch., 1975-85, Lycee Francais, N.Y., 1996-98, Found. for Advancement Internat. Rsch. in Microbiology, 1977-82, Thyroid Found., 1980-85; mem. bd. visitors Boston U. Med. Sch., 1992—; trustee Found. for Depression and Manic Depression, 1978-89, pres., 1980-89; elder Presbyn. Ch., 1968-70, 92-93, trustee, 1962-67, 80-84, deacon, 1959-61. Lt. (j.g.) M.C., USNR, 1947-49. Recipient Mayo Found. Alumni award for Meritorious Rsch., 1955, Disting. Alumnus award, 1992. Fellow ACP, Acad. Psychosomatic Medicine, Am. Geriatric Soc., Coun. on Geriatric Cardiology, N.Y. Acad. Medicine (admission com. 1976-78, edn. com. 1979-92) Am. Coll. Cardiology, Am. Coll. Clin. Pharmacology, Royal Soc. Health, Am. Inst. Chemists; trustee Nat. Hypertension Assn. (chmn. 1977—), AMA, Am. Soc. Internal Medicine, N.Y. State Med. Soc., N.Y. County med. Soc., Am. Heart Assn. (fellow coun. on circulation and coun. for high blood pressure rsch.), Nat. High Blood Pressure Edn. Program (mem. Coord. Com.), Inter-Am. Soc. Hypertension, Internat. Soc. Hypertension, Am. Soc. Hypertension (designated hypertension specialist), Am. Thoracic Soc., N.Y. Acad. Sci., AAAS, Am. Physiol. Soc., Am. Chem. Soc., Am. Soc. Pharmacology and Exptl. Therapeutics, Am. Soc. for Clin. Pharmacology and Therapeutics, Clin. Autonomic Rsch. Soc., Am. Autonomic Soc., Med. Strollers, N.Y.C., Endocrine Soc., Pan Am. Med. Assn., Harvey Soc., Soc. Exptl. Biology and Medicine, Rsch. Discussion Group (founding mem., sec.-treas. 1958-80), Am. Fedn. Clin. Rsch. Am. Soc. Nephrology, Royal Soc. Medicine (affiliate), Fellows Assn. Mayo Found. (v.p., pres. 1953), Mayo Alumni Assn. (v.p. 1981-82, exec. com. 1981-89, pres. elect 1982-85, pres. 1985-87), Chatecholamine Club (founder, sec.-treas. 1967-80, pres. 1981-82), Doctors Mayo Soc., Albert Gallatin Assocs., New Eng. Soc., S.R. (chmn. admissions com. 1959-67, bd. mgrs. 1959-67, 69-70), Soc. Colonial Wars, Soc. of the Cin., Sigma Xi, Nu Sigma Nu, Phi Delta Theta, Explorers, Meadow (L.I., N.Y.), Univ. Club, Yale Club, N.Y. Athletic Club (N.Y.C.), Southampton Bathing Club, Jupiter Island Club. Achievements include research on the mechanism of salt-induced hypertension, the mechanism whereby potassium lowers blood pressure and prevents stroke, and on pheochromocytoma. Home: 8 E 81st St New York NY 10028-0201 Fax: (212) 447-7032.

MANGES, JAMES HORACE, investment banker; b. N.Y.C., Oct. 8, 1927; s. Horace S. and Natalie (Bloch) M.; m. Joan Brownell, Oct., 1969 (div.); m. Mary Seymour, 1974 (div. Oct. 2000); children: Alison, James H. Jr. Grad., Phillips Exeter Acad., 1945; BA, Yale U., 1950; MBA, Harvard U., 1953. With Kuhn, Loeb & Co., N.Y.C., 1954-77, ptnr., 1967-77; mng. dir. Lehman Bros., Kuhn Loeb Inc., 1977-84, Shearson Lehman, Inc., N.Y.C., 1984-90; adv. dir. Lehman Bros., 1990-96. Dir. Baker Industries, 1967—77, Proudfoot PLC, 1996—98; dir., exec. com. Metromedia, Inc., 1970—86. Trustee The Episcopal Sch., 1978-92, St. Bernard's Sch., 1985-2000, Phillips Exeter Acad., 1985-89, mem. trustee coun., 1989-95. Mem. Bond Club, Yale Club (N.Y.C.), Century Country Club (Purchase, N.Y.). Home: 888 Park Ave Apt 7A New York NY 10021-0235 Office: 45 Rockefeller Plz New York NY 10111-0100

MANGHAM, MACK ROBERT, writer; b. Macon, Ga., Nov. 24, 1928; s. William Gill Mangham, Allene (none) Jones. AB, Fla. State U., 1950, MS, 1954; postgrad., U. Ark., 1966, Fla. A&M U., 1966, U. Nebr., 1967, U. Okla., 1967, U. Fla., 1968, U. Tenn., 1968; MA, Goddard Coll., 1978. Cert. tchr. Fla., 1966. Instr. Fla. State U., Tallahassee, 1950—51; attache to pres. Florida State Senate, 1951—52; attache to gov. State of Fla., 1952—53; psychologist Jenkins Psychiat. Clinic, Daytona Beach, 1955—65; instr. Carrabelle High Sch., Carrabelle, Panama City, 1966—92, Gulf Coast C.C., Panama City, 1978—92; author, lectr. Maxbooks.net, Balsam, NC, 1992—. Author: The Accidental Agent, 2000 (Frankfurt International e-Book award Nomination, 2000), The Shadow of the Hawk, 2001 (Pulitzer prize nomination, 2002), Crazy Dog Song, 2001, Things Left Undone, 2002, Who Will Tie Your Shoes?, 2002, A Pause in the Sound of Killing, 2002, (plays) Hello, Willow Tree, 1955 (Hallmark Hall of Fame, 1955), (screenplays) PT 109, 1963 (Acad. award nomination, 1964); editor: Fla. Wildlife mag., 1953—55. Mem.: Am. Mensa Soc., Omicron Delta Kappa. Episcopalian. Avocations: movies, concerts, plays, running, piano, reading, fishing, baseball, travel, sailing, swimming. Home: Box 28/ 225 Cabin Flats Rd Balsam NC 28707 Office: MaxBooks.net PO Box 28 Balsam NC 28707-0028 Home Fax: (828) 452-1388; Office Fax: (828) 452-1388.

MANGIA, ANGELO JAMES, lawyer; b. Bklyn., Mar. 12, 1954; AB in Govt. cum laude, Georgetown U., 1975; JD, St. John's U., 1978. Bar: N.Y. 1979, U.S. Dist. Ct. (so. and ea. dists.) N.Y. 1979, U.S. Ct. Appeals (2d cir.) 1985. Asst. atty. Town of North Hempstead, N.Y., 1979-81; assoc. Ain, Libert & Weinstein, Garden City, 1981; atty. Town of North Hempstead, 1982; counsel senate com. on crime State of N.Y., 1983-85, counsel senate com. on banks, 1985-88; chief counsel to majority N.Y. State Senate, 1989-94; mng. dir. Sandler, O'Neill & Ptnrs., L.P., N.Y.C., 1995-2001; pres. Std. Funding Corp., Woodbury, NY, 2001—. Mem. bd. editors N.Y. Law Jour., 1994-96. Recipient Outstanding Work in Field of Criminal Justice Legis. award N.Y. State Bar Assn., 1985, Disting. Svc. award Civil Trial Inst./St. John's Law Sch., 1987, Luther Gulick award for Outstanding Achievement in Pub. Svc. Long Island U., 1992; Toll fellow, 1991. Mem. ABA, Nassau County Bar Assn., Coun. of State Govts. (exec. com., intergovernmental affairs com., internat. task force, legal affairs task force, legis./exec. staff task force 1989-94), Nat. Conf. of State Legislatures. Office: 335 Crossways Park Dr Woodbury NY 11797

MANGIAPANE, JOSEPH ARTHUR, consulting company executive, applied mechanics consultant; b. N.Y.C., Aug. 1, 1926; s. Michael and Rose D'Amico M.; m. Marcia Balut, Oct. 30, 1954 (div. Apr. 1974); children: Rosemarie, Michael, Diana, Joseph J., Susan. BS, Fordham U., 1950. Stress analyst Republic Aviation, Farmingdale, N.Y., 1951-55; pvt. practice tech. cons., 1955-58; sect. mgr. Aerojet-Gen., Sacramento, 1958-61; project engr. Pratt & Whitney Aircraft, East Hartford, Conn., 1961-71; pvt. practice tech. cons., 1971-79; pres. Joseph A. Mangiapane & Assocs., Inc., Tampa, Fla., 1979-92. Author numerous tech. reports. Served as cpl. USAAF, 1945-47, ETO. Assoc. fellow AIAA; mem. Pine Acres Club (Wethersfield, Conn.) (pres. 1968-69). Republican. Roman Catholic. Avocations: reading, photography, genealogical research. Home: 5410 Aragon Ct Tampa FL 33624-4884 E-mail: Jam50ram@aol.com.

MANGIARDI, JOHN RAGUE, neurosurgeon; b. N.Y.C., Mar. 10, 1950; s. Joseph L. and Patricia E. (Pearson) M.; m. Tina Mangiardi; children: Ian R., Tess M. BA in Philosophy, Holy Cross Coll., Worcester, Mass., 1972; degree in biochemistry, U. Mass., 1973; MD, Wayne State U., 1977. Diplomate Am. Bd. Neurol. Surgery. Intern in surgery U. Calif., San Francisco, 1978-79; asst. resident in neurosurgery NYU Med. Ctr., 1979-82, chief resident, 1982-83, attending physician, 1996—, Westchester County Med. Ctr., N.Y.C., 1989-92; from asst. to assoc. prof. neurosurgery N.Y. Med. Coll., 1984-92; chief neurosurgery Lincoln Hosp., 1984-91, Lenox Hill (N.Y.) Hosp., 1991—; clin. prof. neurosurgery NYU, 1994—. Cons. Western Queens Cmty. Hosp., 1992—; chmn. Found. Neurosurg. Rsch., 1991—; med. staff Clin. Rsch. Ctr., Brookhaven Nat. Lab., 1996—. Bd. dirs. Jour. Radiosurgery; presenter in field; contbr. articles to profl. jours. Fellow ACS; mem. Am. Assn. Neurol. Surgeons, Congress Neurol. Surgeons, Soc. Surg. Oncology, N.Y. State Med. Soc., N.Y. Acad. Medicine, N.Am. Soc. Neuro-Oncology. Office: 50 E 72nd St New York NY 10021-4246

MANGIN, CHARLES-HENRI, electronics company executive; b. Riom, France, Apr. 16, 1942; s. Louis Eugene and Monique (Mathivon) M.; m. Marguerite Stern, Nov. 27, 1974; children: Charlotte, Louis-David, Maxence. MBA, Ecole Superieure de Commerce, Reims, France, 1965. Computer salesman IBM, Paris, 1967-68; asst. to pres. EDC, Rome, 1969-71; gen. mgr. CEGI, Paris, 1971-77; pres. CEERIS, 1977-81, CEERIS Internat., Inc., Old Lyme, Conn., 1982—. Cons. The Mitre Corp., Washington, 1973-78, Coyne & Bellier, Paris, 1973-76, IITRI, Chgo., 1979-81, PRC, London, 1980-81. Author: Lebanon, 1965, The Atlantic Facade, 1973, Flights Over Europe, 1974, Surface Mount Technology, 1986, Managing the SMT Challenge, 1990; contbg. editor Electronic Packaging and Prodn., 1988-91; contbr. articles to profl. jours. Mem. Surface Mount Tech. Assn., N.Y. Yacht Club, Ocean Cruising Club, Cruising Club Am., Ski Club (Les Arcs, France). Roman Catholic. Avocations: sailing, skiing, opera. Office: Ceeris Internat Inc PO Box 939 Old Lyme CT 06371-0939 E-mail: ceeris@aol.com.

MANGINO, MATTHEW THOMAS, lawyer; b. New Castle, Pa., Oct. 3, 1962; s. Thomas Michael and Connie (Frigone) M.; m. Juliann Galmarini, Aug. 6, 1988. BA, Westminster Coll., 1985; JD, Duquesne U., 1988. Bar: Pa. U.S. Dist. Ct. (we. dist.) Pa., U.S. Ct. Appeals (3d cir.), U.S. Supreme Ct. Jud. clk. Hon. Francis X. Caiazza, New Castle, 1988-89; asst. pub. defender County of Lawrence, 1989; pvt. practice, 1990—; dist. atty. Lawrence County, 1998—. Chmn. New Castle Airport Authority, 1990-92; solicitor County of Lawrence, New Castle, 1992-96; instr. Pa. State U., 1992—; legal cons. O.J. Simpson Trial, Sta. WBZY-AM, New Castle, 1995; bd. dirs. Allied Human Svcs.; seminar plan mem. on gang violence Pa. Bar Inst., 1996; guest lectr. Westminster Coll., Slippery Rock U.; participant White House Conf. on Sch. Safety, 1998. Prodr. TV program Gang Violence Curbing the Epidemic, 1996; columnist, New Castle News, 1989-90; prodr. (cable TV) Task Force Program; host TV program Lawrence County's Most Wanted; contbr. chpt. to book, article to profl. jours.; guest numerous TV news programs. Mem. campaign staff Dukakis for Pres., Pitts., 1988; del. Dem. Nat. Conv., Atlanta, 1988; com. mem. Lawrence County Econ. Devel. Corp.; sec. Lawrence County Bd. Assistance, New Castle; bd. dirs. Family Ctr. of Lawrence County, Lawrence County chpt. ARC, Workforce Investment Bd., Youth Coun.; mem. Leadership Lawrence County, 1997, Lawrence County Pride; trustee Western Pa. Youth Devel. Ctrs.; Dem. candidate for Congress, 2000; bd. dirs. Lawrence County Social Svcs.; adv. bd. Lawrence County Learning Ctr.; active Pa. Atty. Gen.'s Task Force on Elder Abuse. Mem. ABA (vice chmn. law and media com. 1996-97), Pa. Bar Assn. (state exec. bd. young lawyers divsn. 1994-97, jud. selection and reform com., co-chair spl. project on gang violence 1996-97), Pa. Dist. Atty.'s Assn., Lawrence County Bar Assn., Lawrence County C. of C. (bd. dirs. 1990), Wolves (bd. dirs., pres. 1996-97), Kiwanis. Roman Catholic. Avocations: golf, writing, reading. Office: 2nd Fl 315 N Mercer St New Castle PA 16101-2222 E-mail: matthewmangino@aol.com.

MANGION, RICHARD MICHAEL, health care executive; b. Haverhill, Mass., Apr. 26, 1941; s. Michael Anthony and Evelyn (Cote) M.; m. Gail Elizabeth Donne, Apr. 27, 1968; children: Catherine Jean, James Richard, Ian Kyle. BBA, Suffolk U., 1963; MBA, Syracuse U., 1965; MPH, U. Calif., Berkeley, 1972. Asst. adminstr. Nashua (N.H.) Meml. Hosp., 1972-75, assoc. adminstr., 1975-77; pres. and chief exec. officer Harrington Meml. Hosp., Southbridge, Mass., 1977—. Lectr. U. N.H., Durham, 1972-74. Pres. Tri-Community Devel. Corp., Southbridge, 1983-88. Capt. USAF, 1966-70. Fellow Am. Coll. Health Care Execs. (regent Mass. area B 1995-99); mem. Am. Hosp. Assn., Mass. Hosp. Assn., Ctrl. Mass. Hosp. Coun. (pres. 1982-84), Ctrl. Mass. Health Care Found., Tri-Cmty. C. of C. (pres. 1983-84). Clubs: Hosp. Supts. Lodges: Rotary. Democrat. Roman Catholic. Avocations: tennis, swimming, hiking. Home: 50 Old Village Rd Sturbridge MA 01566-1069 Office: Harrington Meml Hosp 100 South St Ste 1 Southbridge MA 01550-4047 E-mail: rmangion@harringtonhospital.org.

MANGIONE, GORDON, information technology executive; Degree in engring., U. Waterloo, Ont., Can. Developer, PC/telephony integration Bell No. Rsch.; product unit mgr., Internet svcs. bus., devel. mgr. SNA Server Microsoft, Redmond, Wash., 1991, v.p. Exch. team, corp. v.p., SQL server team. Office: One Microsoft Way Redmond WA 98052-6399*

MANGLER, ROBERT JAMES, lawyer, judge; b. Chgo., Aug. 15, 1930; s. Robert H. and Agnes E. (Sugrue) M.; m. Geraldine M. Delich, May 2, 1959; children: Robert Jr., Paul, John, Barbara. BS, Loyola U., Chgo., 1952, MA, 1983; JD, Northwestern U., 1955. Bar: Ill. 1958, U.S. Dist. Ct. (no. dist.) Ill. 1959, U.S. Supreme Ct. 1976, U.S. Ct. Appeals (7th cir.) 1980. Author: (with others) Illinois Land Use Law, Illinois Municipal Law. Village atty., prosecutor Village of Wilmette, 1965-93; mcpl. prosecutor City of Evanston, 1963-65, adminstrv. law judge, 2000—; chmn. Ill. Traffic Ct. Conf., 1977—; pres. Ill. Inst. Local Govt. Law; mem. home rule attys. com. Ill. Mcpl. League. Mem. ABA (chmn. adv. com. traffic ct. program), Nat. Inst. Mcpl. Law Officers (past pres.), Ill. Bar Assn. (former chmn. traffic laws and ct. com.), Chgo. Bar Assn. (former chmn. traffic ct. seminar, former chmn. traffic laws com.), Caxton Club, Phi Alpha Delta.

MANGLITZ, MARJORIE JOAN, religious education director; b. Milford, Nebr., June 11, 1930; d. Harry George and Irma Mildred (Belka) Welsch; m. George Rudolph Manglitz, Oct. 20, 1953; children: Ruth Ann, Harry George, Paul Adolph, Mary Margaret, Joel David. Student, Doane Coll., 1947-49; BS in Religious Edn., Schauffler Coll., 1951; postgrad., George Washington U., 1951-52. Cert. ch. educator for United Ch. of Christ. Parish worker Bd. Nat. Missions, Takoma Park, Md., 1951-52; dir. religious edn. Bd. Nat. First Reformed, Cin., 1952-53; vol. dir. religious edn. 1st Congl. Ch., Minot, N.D., 1953-54, 1st Presbyn. Ch., Tifton, Ga., 1954-56, Trinity United Ch., Takoma Park, Md., 1956-58, Trinity UCC, Lincoln, Nebr., 1958-70; dir. resource libr. Nebr. Conf. UCC, 1969-91; supt. ch. sch. N.E. UCC, 1970-74, visual arts min., 1974—. Preview com. Ecumenical Media Ctr., Lincoln. Commr., chair Area Agy. on Aging, Lincoln; cons. emm. Family Preservation Team, Lincoln, 1994—; bd. dirs. Prairie Peace Park, Pleasant Dale, Nebr., 1986-95; charter on-line vol. Personal Crisis Svc., Lincoln, 1970-2000; hearings monitor State Parole Bd., Lincoln, 1970's; vice-chair Lancaster County Dem. Ctrl. Com., Lincoln, 1985-88; active Nebraskans for Peace, 1970—; vol. Hospice of Tabitha, 1998—. Named Vol. of Yr. Personal Crisis Svc., 1981; recipient Disting. Svc. award UNA-USA, 1985-87, Honored Woman award 17th Gen. Synod UCC, 1989, Quality of Life award LWV, 1991, Paul Kersenbrock Humanities award Doane Coll. Alumni Assn., 1994, YWCA Tribute to Women award 1998, Outstanding Citizen award Rotary, 2001, Arnold Goodman Leadership award, 2000. Mem. Assn. United Ch. Educators, Ch. Women United (exec. bd., pres. legis. act 1985-87, Valiant Woman award 1992), UN Assn. (leadership corps regional coord. 1995-96), Alliance for Mentally Ill (treas. governing bd. Nebr. chpt. 1995-98—), Bread for the World (shared leadership treas. 1989—), Justice and Peace Ministry (sec. Nebr. conf. 1976—), Older Womans League. Avocations: reading, gardening, activities with grandchildren. Home: 955 N 67th St Lincoln NE 68505-2218 E-mail: unalincoln@hotmail.com.

MANGO, CHRISTINA ROSE, psychiatric art therapist; b. Garden City, N.Y., May 13, 1962; d. Camillo Andrew and Dorothy Mae (Harrison) Mango; m. Keith Hurdman, Sept. 11, 1993 (div. 2001); children: Clarissa Rose Hurdman, Andrew James Hurdman. BFA summa cum laude, Coll. of New Rochelle, 1984; MA, NYU, 1987. Registered art therapist; bd. cert. structural family therapy tng.; cert. psycho-edn. multi family therapy tng. Art therapist Bronx Mcpl. Hosp. Ctr., 1984-88; clin. supr. Fordham-Tremont Cmty. Mental Health Ctr., Bronx, 1988-98, unit dir., 1998—. Art therapy fieldworker Bronx State Hosp., 1984, art therapy intern Bronx Children's Hosp., 1985, Saint Lukes Hosp., N.Y.C., 1986. Contbr. articles to profl. jours. Mem. N.Y. Art Therapy Assn., No. N.J. Art Therapists Assn., Am. Art Therapy Assn. Home: 234 Garfield St Haworth NJ 07641-1420 E-mail: crm07641@aol.com.

MANGO, WILFRED GILBERT, JR. real estate and construction company executive; b. Weehawkin, N.J., July 11, 1940; s. Wilfred Gilbert and Mildred B.M.; children from previous marriage; Christian P., Peter H.; m. Charlene Holt, Feb. 14, 1985; children: Alison L., David H. BS, Lehigh U., 1963; MBA, NYU, 1969. Auditor Hurdman & Cranstown, N.Y.C., 1963-69; dir. fin. Thomas Crimmins Contracting Co., 1969-77; v.p. fin., mgr. fin. controls ITT Teleplant, Inc., 1977-78; v.p. fin. George A. Fuller Co. div. Northrop Corp., 1978-81, now pres., CEO, dir., 1981—; chmn., CEO Fuller Internat. Devel., Ltd. Past chmn. bd. trustees Marymount Manhattan Coll.; adv. bd. N.Y. Real Estate Inst.; bus. adv. coun. emeritus Lehigh U.; bus. coun. Lighthouse for the Blind; mem. Urban Land Inst.; chmn. The Stanwich Sch., Greenwich, Conn. Mem.: Univ. Club (N.Y.C.), Lehigh U. of N.Y. Club. Home: 14 Buckingham Ln Greenwich CT 06830

MANGOLD, ARCHIE WAYNE II, insurance agent; b. Pekin, Ill., Dec. 8, 1973; s. Archie Wayne Sr. and Rebecca Ann Mangold. BA in English, The U. of No. Iowa, 1996. Bean walker Arthur Milikins Farm, Hedrick, Iowa, 1991; telephone sales rep. APAC Customer Svcs., 1995, telephone sales rep., ins. agt. Iowa, 1996—. Editor: Literary: The Magazine of Writing, 1990—2000. Mem. Reform Party of Am. Lutheran. Home: PO Box 116 117 1/2 1st Ave W #12 Oskaloosa IA 52577 Office: APAC Customer Svcs 200 High Ave E Oskaloosa IA 52577

MANGOLD, JOHN FREDERIC, manufacturing company executive, former naval officer; b. La Grange, Ill., Jan. 24, 1927; s. John Frederic and Helvig Victoria (Anderson) M.; m. Margaret Ellen Gore, Oct. 25, 1947; children: John, Andrew, Jennifer. BS, U.S. Naval Acad., 1947; MSEE, U.S. Naval Postgrad. Sch., Monterey, Calif., 1958. Registered profl. engr., Conn. Commd. ensign USN, 1947, advanced through grades to comdr., 1962, comdg. officer nuclear submarine U.S.S. Halibut, 1962—63, comdg. officer nuclear tng. unit, 1963—67, ret., 1967; v.p. mfg. Combustion Engring., Inc., Windsor, Conn., 1972—78, group pres., 1982—86, v.p. utility boilers, 1990—91; pres. Vetco, Inc., Ventura, Calif., 1978—82; cons., 1992; pres. Detrex Corp., Southfield, Mich., 1992—93. Bd. dirs. Detrex Corp. Mem. IEEE, U.S. C. of C. (energy com. 1984-87). Republican.

MANGOLD, SYLVIA PLIMACK, artist; b. N.Y.C., Sept. 18, 1938; d. Maurice and Ethel (Rein) Plimack; m. Robert Mangold. Student, Cooper Union, 1956-59; BFA, Yale U., 1961. Exhibited one-person shows Daniel Weinberg Gallery, San Francisco, 1974, 75, Fischbach Gallery, N.Y.C., 1974, 76, Fischbuch, 1974, 76, Annemarie Verna Gallery, Zurich, 1978, 91, 97, Droll-Kolbert Gallery, N.Y.C., 1978, 80, Young Hoffman Gallery, Chgo., 1980, Ohio State U., Columbus, 1980, Pa. Acad., 1981, Contemporary Arts Mus., Houston, 1981, Madison Art Ctr., (Wis.), 1982, Brooke Alexander, Inc., 1982, 83, 84, 85, 86, 89, 92, 95, Duke Art Mus., N.C., 1982, Rhona Hoffman Gallery, Chgo., 1982, 85, Tex. Gallery, 1986, Fuller Goldeen Gallery, San Francisco, 1987, U. Mich, Ann Arbor, 1992, Minn. Inst. Arts, 1992, Grunwald Ctr. for Graphic Arts, UCLA, 1992, Neuberger Mus. Art, SUNY, Purchase, 1993, Davison Art Ctr., Wesleyan U., Middletown, Conn., 1993, Albright-Knox Art Gallery, Buffalo, 1994, Wadsworth Atheneum, Hartford, Conn., 1994, Blaffer Gallery U. Houston, 1994, Mus. Fine Arts, Boston, 1994, Herbert F. Johnson Museum, 1998, Cornell U., Ithaca, N.Y., 1998, Alexander and Bonin, N.Y., 2000; group shows at Young Hoffman Gallery, Chgo., 1979, Walker Art Ctr., Mpls., 1979, Droll-Kolbert Gallery, 1979, Denver Art Mus., 1979, U. So. Calif., 1979, Honolulu Acad. Art, 1979, Oakland Mus., (Calif.), 1979, Univ. Art Mus. of U. Tex.-Austin, 1979, Cornell U., Ithaca, N.Y., 1979, The New Museum of Contemporary Art, N.Y.C., 1979, Nat. Museum, Belgrade, Yugoslavia, 1979, Internat. Biennial Ljibljana, Yugoslavia, Phoenix Art Mus., 1979, Art Latitute Gallery, N.Y.C., 1980, Thorpe Intermedia Gallery, Sparkhill, N.Y., 1980, U. Colo. Art Galleries, Boulder, 1980, Nina Freudenheim Gallery, Buffalo, 1980, U.S. Pavillion of Venice Biennial, 1980-81, Indianapolis Museum of Art, 1980, Civici Musei e Gallerie di Storia e Arte, Sala Ajace, Udine, Italy, 1980, Young Hoffman, Chicago, 1980-81, Delahurty, Dallas, 1980, Museum of Modern Art, 1981, Wesleyan U. Art Gallery, 1981, Davison Art Ctr., Middleton, Conn., 1981, Virginia Museum of Fine Arts, Richmond, 1981, Oakland Museum, Calif., 1981, Inst. Contemporary Art of U. Pa., Phila, 1980-81, Yale U. Art Gallery, 1981, San Antonio Mus. Art, 1981, Indpls. Mus. Art, 1981, Tucson Mus. Art, 1981, Pa. Acad., 1981, Mus. Art of Carnegie Inst., Pitts., 1981, Brooke Alexander, Inc., N.Y.C., 1982, Ben Shahn Ctr. Visual Arts, 1982, Castle Gallery, Coll. of New Rochelle, N.Y., 1983,

Thomas Segal Gallery, Boston, 1982-83, Siegel Contemporary Art, N.Y., 1983, Freedman Gallery, Albright Coll., Reading, Pa., 1983, Fuller Goldeen, San Francisco, 1983, Yale U. Art Gallery, New Haven, 1983-84, 86, Wilcox Gallery, Swarthmore, Pa., 1984, The Hudson River Mus., Yonkers, N.Y., 1984, Sardonia Art Gallery, Wilkes Coll., Wilkes-Barre, Pa., 1985, Kent State U. Gallery, Ohio, 1985, Brooke Alexander, N.Y., 1985, John C. Stoller Co., Minn., 1985, Knight Gallery, Spirit Sq. Arts Ctr., Charlotte, N.C., 1986, Mus. Art, R.I. Sch. Design, Providence, 1986, Yale U. Gallery, 1986, CUNY, 1986-87, Lorence Monk Gallery, N.Y.C., Vanquard Gallery, Phila., 1986-87, Aldrich Mus., Ridgefield, 1986-87. Flander's Contemporary Art, Mpls., 1987, Annemarie Verna Galerie, Zurich, 1988, U. N.C., 1988, R.I. Sch. Design, 1988, Grace Borgenicht Gallery, N.Y.C., 1988, Fay Gold Gallery, Atlanta, 1988, U. N.C., Greensboro, Three Rivers Arts Festival, Pitts., 1989, Cin. Art Mus., New Orleans Mus. Art, Denver Art Mus., Pa. Acad. Fine Arts, 1989, U. Mich., 1992, Mpls. Inst. Arts, 1992, Grunwald Ctr. Graphic Arts, UCLA, L.A., Neuberger Mus. Art, SUNY Purchase, 1993, Davison Art Ctr., 1993, Montgomery Glasoe Fine Art, Mpls., 1993, Yale U. Art Gallery, New Haven, 1993, Daniel Weinberg Gallery, Santa Monica, Calif., 1993, Museum of Fine Arts, Boston, 1993, Barbara Mathes Gallery, N.Y.C., 1993, Nina Freudenheim Gallery, Buffalo, 1993, Kansas City Gallery of Art, U. Mo., 1994, Midtown Payson, N.Y.C., 1994, Katonah Museum of Art, N.Y., 1994, Rhona Hoffman Gallery, Chgo., 1994, Feigen Inc., Chgo., 1994, Brooke Alexander, N.Y.C., 1994, Elga Wimmer Gallery, N.Y.C., 1995, Aargauer Kunsthaus Aarau, Austria, 1995, The Am. Acad. of Arts and Letters, N.Y.C., 1995, Andre Zarre Gallery, N.Y.C., 1996, Aspen Art Museum, Colo., 1996, The Am. Acad. of Arts and Letters, N.Y.C., 1996, Anne Marie Verna Gallery, Zurich, Switzerland, 1997, Queens Museum of Art, 1997, Aspen Art Museum, 1997, U. Gallery, Fine Arts Ctr., U. Mass., Amherst James Graham & Sons, N.Y.C., 1997, The Museum of Modern Art, 1997, Seattle Art Museum, 1997, State U. N.Y., 1998, N.Y.C. Dowd Fine Arts Gallery, 1998, The Am. Acad. of Fine Arts and Letters, 1998, Karen McCready Fine Art, 1999, Alexander and Bonin, N.Y.C., 1999, Henry Art Gallery, Seattle, 2000; exhibited in permanent collections, Albright-Knox Art Gallery, Buffalo, Allen Meml. Art Mus., Oberlin, Ohio, Bklyn. Mus., Dallas Mus. Fine Arts, Detroit Inst. Art, Mus. Fine Arts, Houston, Indpls. Mus. Art, Madison (Wis.) Art Ctr., Milw. Art Mus., Yale U. Art Gallery, Mus. Modern Art, N.Y.C., Mus. Fine Arts, U. Utah, Tampa (Fla.) Mus., Walker Art Mus., Mpls., Whitney Mus. Am. Art, N.Y., Weatherspoon Art Gallery, Greensboro, N.C., Wadsworth Athenaeum, Hartford, U. Mich., Utah Mus. Fine Art, Museum of Fine Arts, Boston, N.Y.C. Public Library, Smith Coll. Museum, Northampton, Mass., Achenbach Found. for Graphic Arts, San Francisco, St. Louis Art Museum, The Tampa Museum. Achievements include work reviewed in newspapers and mags.

MANGONE, GERARD J. international and maritime law educator; b. N.Y.C., Oct. 10, 1918; s. Gerard Francis and Viola (Schumm) M.; m. Emma Haddad, Apr. 13, 1958; children— Cleopatra, Regina, Flaminia. AB, CCNY, 1938; MA, Harvard, 1947, PhD (Charles Summer prize), 1949. Asst. prof. polit. sci. Wesleyan U., Middletown, Conn., 1948-51; assoc. prof. Swarthmore Coll., 1951-56; prof. polit. sci. and internat. relations Syracuse U., 1956-67; dir. grad. overseas tng. program, exec. officer Maxwell Center Study Overseas Operations, 1958-60; exec. asst. to dean Maxwell Grad. Sch., 1961-64, asso. dean dir. internat. relations program, 1961-67; dean Coll. Liberal Arts, v.p., provost Temple U., Phila., 1967-69; sr. fellow Woodrow Wilson Internat. Ctr., 1970-72; prof. internat. law U. Del., Newark, 1972-74, dir. Ctr. for Study of Marine Policy, 1973-89, H. Rodney Sharp prof. internat. law and orgn., 1975-89, univ. rsch. prof. internat. and maritime law, 1989—, prof. legal studies, 2001—, coord. grad. studies, 1976-79; adj. prof. Maine Maritime Acad., 1992—94. Vis. prof. Trinity Coll., Mt. Holyoke Coll., Yale, Princeton, Johns Hopkins; Tagore law prof. U. Calcutta, 1979; disting. lectr. U. Ind., 1980; vis. scholar U. Western Australia, 1983, 87, Peking U., 1984, Capetown U., 1986, 89, U. Natal, 1989, Hanyand U., 1994, Hong Kong U., 1997; mem. Presdl. Commn. Trust Territory Pacific, 1963; cons. AID, 1965-67, Nat. Commn. Marine Resources and Engring. and State Dept., 1967-73, UN, 1965, U.S. Corps Engrs., 1975; vice chmn. exec. com. Commn. Study Orgn. Peace; exec. dir. Pres.' Commn. on UN, 1970-71; dir. diploma program, shipping and pt. mgmt. Pt. of Singapore, 1990-97. Author: The Idea and Practice of World Government, 1951, A Short History of International Organization, 1954, The Elements of International Law, 2d edit, 1967, Marine Policy for America, 1977, 2d edit., 1989, Law for the World Ocean, 1981, Mangone's Concise Marine Almanac, 2d edit., 1991, United States Admiralty Law, 1997; co-author, editor: The Art of Overseasmanship, 1958, The Overseas Americans, 1960, European Political Systems, 1960, UN Administration of Economic and Social Programs, 1966, Energy Policies of the World, 3 vols, 1976-79, Internat. Straits of the World, 13 vols., 1978-3003; editor: Future of Gas and Oil from Sea, American Strategic Minerals, 1984; editor in chief: Marine Policy Reports, 1981-91, Internat. Jour. Marine and Coastal Law, 1991— . Capt. AUS, 1942-46, maj. res., 1946-54. Mem. Am. Soc. Internat. Law, Internat. Law Assn., Maritime Law Assn., Port of Wilmington Maritime Soc. (bd. dirs. 1980—, chmn. 1989), Francis Alison Soc. (sec. 1990—, award 1983), Del. Acad. Sci. (pres. 1993), Cosmos Club (Washington), Harvard Club (N.Y.C.). Home: 201 Unami Trl Newark DE 19711-7508 Office: Univ Del Grad Coll Marine Studi Newark DE 19716

MANGOUNI, NORMAN, publisher; b. Detroit, Oct. 19, 1932; s. Nazareth Lazarus and Isabelle (Garabedian) M.; m. Anahid Apelian, May 10, 1964; 1 child, Marie-Isabelle. AB, U. Mich., 1954; MS, Columbia U., 1955; postgrad., U. Mich., 1957-58. Reporter Ann Arbor (Mich.) News, 1957-59; editor Mich. Alumnus, U. Mich., Ann Arbor, 1959-62; sr. editor Coll. Entrance Exam. Bd., N.Y.C., 1962-64; dir. fin. aid U. Miami, Coral Gables, Fla., 1965-66; dir. State U. N.Y. Press, Albany, 1966-78; pres., gen. editor Scholars' Facsimiles & Reprints, Ann Arbor, Mich., 1972—; pres. Caravan Books, 1972—, Acad. Resources Corp., Las Vegas, Nev., 1988—; corr. DuPont-Columbia Survey and Awards, 1976-78; rep. to com. on standards in field of library work, documentation and related pub. practices Am. Nat. Standards Inst., 1974-78. Exec. asst. to majority caucus Mich. State Senate, 1964 Co-translator: The Gaucho Martin Fierro, 1974; contbr. articles to profl. jours.; mem. editorial bd. Ararat mag, 1962-66, 77-78. Served to lt. USAF, 1955-57. Mem. Modern Lang. Assn. Am., Middle East Studies Assn. N.Am., Mensa, Phi Sigma Kappa, Sigma Delta Chi, Phi Alpha Delta. Clubs: Rotary Internat. Home: 410 Lenawee Dr Ann Arbor MI 48104-1866 E-mail: nm320@columbia.edu.

MANGRU, BASDEO, secondary education educator; b. Guyana; came to U.S., 1987; m. Doreen Nadia Permaul, Aug. 4, 1965; children: Rajendra, Tricia Nadini (Mangru) Dhanraj. Tchr. cert., Tchrs. Coll., Guyana, 1964; BA, U. Guyana, 1970, MA in Guyanese, West Indian History, 1976; PhD in South Asian Studies, U. London, 1981. Cert. social studies tchr., NYC bd. edn.; grade I, class I, trained tchrs. cert., Guyana. Tchr. Guyana High Sch., 1959-74; lectr. U. Guyana, 1974-76, asst. prof., 1976-80, assoc. prof., 1980-84, also coord. Caribbean studies course for non-history majors; student evaluator, interviewer freshmen history majors; tchr., rschr., London, Eng., 1984-87; tchr. social studies N.Y.C. Bd. Edn., 1987—. Participant in seminars, symposiums, lectr. on East Indian Diaspora to ednl. and cultural groups; adj. assoc. prof. York Coll. Author: Benevolent Neutrality, Indian Government Policy and Labour Migration to British Guiana, 1854-1884, 1987, Indenture and Abolition, Sacrifice and Survival on the Guyanese Sugar Plantations, 1993; editor: (with others) The East Indian Diaspora: 150 Years of Survival, Contributions and Achievements, 1993, A History of East Indian Resistance on the Guyana Sugar Estates, 1996, Indians in Guyana: A Concise History From Their Arrival to the Present, 1999; asst. editor The East Indian Diaspora Newsletter; resident historian The East Indian Diaspora Com.; contbr. articles to profl. jours. Vol. civilian asst. to Richmond Hill police dept. working with youth and teenage problems; organizer remedial reading and citizenship classes for local residents. Recipient Bookers' Sugar Estates scholarship, Guyana, 1966-70, Commonwealth Acad. Staff fellowship, Commonwealth Scholarship Commn., UK, 1978-81, Ednl. Achievement award, Corentyne Comprehensive High Sch. Student-Tchr. Reunion Orgn., 1989, Rockefeller Residency fellowship in Humanities, Queens Coll. Asian-Am. Ctr., CUNY, 1990-91. Mem. Am. Hist. Assn. (Albert J. Beveridge Rsch. award 1990), Assn. Caribbean Historians, Assn. Caribbean Studies, Assn. Third World Studies, E. Indian Diaspora Com. (asst. sec., history cons., conf. coord.). Avocations: reading, writing, music, cricket, lawn tennis. Home: 10941 115th St Jamaica NY 11420-1112

MANGRUM, DEBRA KIRKSEY, elementary school educator; b. Jonesboro, Ark., May 17, 1955; d. Hayward Leon and Marguerite (Bailey) Kirksey; children: Wayne, Marissa, Martina. BS in Mktg., Ark. State U., Jonesboro, 1979, BSE in Edn., 1990, MSE in Counselor Edn., 1992; postgrad., Edn. Specialist in psychology and Counseling. Cert. elem. edn. tchr. Ark. Adminstrv. sec. to pres. Planters Prodn. Credit Assn., Jonesboro, 1983-85; owner, mgr. Goodship Lollipop Children's Shop, 1985-88; grad. and rsch. asst. Ark. State U., 1990-92. Mem. MSE in Counselor Edn. curriculum com. Ark. State U., 1990-91, mem. tchr. edn. program com., 1991-92; presenter papers ann. conf. Mid.-South Ednl. Rsch. Assn., ann. spring conf. Ark. Assn. Colls. of Tchr. Edn./Assn. Tchr. Educators, 1992. Mem. Valley View PTA, Jonesboro, 1979—, Valley View Athletic Booster Club, Jonesboro, 1979—; cert. judge Miss Ark. Pageant Sys., Hot Springs, 1989—; dir. Miss Mistletoe Pageant, Jonesboro, 1989-93. Mem. ASCD, Am. Sch. Counselor Assn., Ark. Edn. Assn., Phi Delta Kappa, Kappa Delta Pi. Avocation: reading. Home: 4507 Southwest Dr Jonesboro AR 72404-8929

MANGUM, GARTH LEROY, economist, educator; b. Delta, Utah, July 23, 1926; s. James L. and Golda (Elder) M.; m. Marion Poll, Nov. 20, 1953; children: Stephen, David, Mary, Elizabeth. BS, Brigham Young U., 1956; MPA, Harvard U., 1958, PhD, 1960; JD, U. Utah, 1989. Instr. econs. Harvard U., 1960; asso. prof. econs. Brigham Young U., 1960-63; sr. staff analyst Presdl. R.R. Commn., 1961; research dir., subcom. employment and manpower U.S. Senate, 1963-64; exec. dir. President's Com. Manpower, 1964-65; exec. sec. Nat. Com. Tech., Automation and Econ. Progress, 1965-66; research prof. econs. George Washington U., 1967-71; co-dir. George Washington U. (Center Manpower Policy Studies), 1967-69; Max McGraw prof. econs. and mgmt. U. Utah, Salt Lake City, 1969-97, prof. emeritus, 1997—, dir. Inst. Human Resource Mgmt., 1969-90. Lectr. U. Tel Aviv, Israel, 1969, 84, Am. Seminar at Salzburg, 1975, U. South Africa, 1977, Monash U., Australia, 1984; Spl. mediator Fed. Mediation and Conciliation Service, 1962-63; mem. Adv. Council Vocational Edn., 1966-67; vice chmn. Nat. Manpower Policy Task Force, 1966-69, chmn., 1969-71, mem., 1966-76; mem. Nat. Council on Employment Policy, 1976—, chmn., 1979-81, sec.- treas., 1990—; chmn. Nat. Inst. Career Edn., 1976-81; cons. fed., state and local govts., bus. firms, govts. of, Saudi Arabia, Kuwait, Jordan, Yemen, Bahrain, United Arab Emirates, Indonesia, Yugoslavia, Romania, Uganda, Nigeria, Israel, South Africa, Russia, Korea, China, other countries; cons. AID, ILO, World Bank; also arbitrator. Author: The Operating Engineers: Economic History of a Trade Union, 1964, MDTA, Foundation of Federal Manpower Policy, 1968, The Emergence of Manpower Policy, 1969, Federal Work and Training Program in the 1960's, 1969, Economic Opportunity in the Ghetto, 1970, Human Resources and Labor Markets, 1971, Career Education: What It Is and How To Do It, 1972, A Decade of Manpower Development and Training, 1973, Career Education and the Elementary School Teacher, 1973, Career Education in the Middle/Junior High School, 1973, Manpower Planning for Local Labor Markets, 1974, Career Education for the Academic Classroom, 1975, Employability, Employment and Income, 1976, Career Education in the High School, 1976, Your Child's Career, 1977, The Lingering Crisis of Youth Unemployment, 1978, Coming of Age in the Ghetto, 1978, Job Market Futurity, 1979, The Coal Industry and its Industrial Relations, 1985, Capital and Labor in American Copper, 1992, Labor Struggle in The Post Office, 1992, The Mormons War on Poverty, 1993, Union Resilience in Troubled Times, 1994, Portable Pension Plans for Casual Labor Markets, 1995, Transnational Industrial Marriages, 1996, The Rise, Fall and Replacement of Industry-Wide Bargaining in the Basic Steel Industry, 1996, Programs in Aid of the Poor, 1997, 2d edit., 2002, On Being Poor in Utah, 1997, The Public Employment Svc. In a One Stop World, 1998, Poverty Ain't What It Used To Be, 1999, Confronting The Youth Demographic Challenge, 2000, The Persistance of Poverty in the United States, 2002; also articles, monographs.; editor: The Manpower Revolution: Its Policy Consequences, 1965, Automation and Economic Progress, 1966, Metropolitan Impact of Manpower Programs, 1973, The T in CETA, 1981, Of Heart and Mind: Social Policy Essays in Honor of Sar A. Levitan, 1996. With USAAF, 1944-45. Mem. Ch. of Jesus Christ of Latter-day Saints (missionary 1950-53, bishop 1971-78). Home: 2130 Ridgewood Way Bountiful UT 84010-1632

MANGUM, RONALD SCOTT, army officer; b. Chgo., Nov. 14, 1944; s. Roy Oliver and Marjorie Wilma (Etchason) M.; m. Kay Lynn Booton, July 14, 1973 (div. July 1983); children: Scott Arthur, Katherine Marie; m. Anna Maria Moser, Feb. 14, 1999. BA, Northwestern U., 1965, JD, 1968. Bar: Ill. 1968, Wis. 1986; lic. nursing home adminstr., Ill. Asst. atty. Northwestern U., 1968-73; assoc. Lord, Bissell & Brook, Chgo., 1974-76; ptnr. Liss, Mangum & Beeler, 1976-80, Mangum, Beeler, Schad & Diamond, Chgo., 1980-82, Azar, Mangum & Jacobs, Chgo., 1982-84, Mangum, Smietanka & Johnson, Chgo., 1984-2000. Instr. U. St. Francis Grad. Sch., Joliet, Ill.; adj. instr. Mallinkroft Coll. North Shore, Wilmette, Ill.; lectr. Northwestern U., 1972-74, NYU Inst. Fed. Taxation, 1980, Loyola U. Med. Sch., Chgo., 1994-96; lectr. health care topics; faculty Healthcare Fin. Mgmt. Assn. Ann. Nat. Inst., Boulder; pres. Creative-Health Mgmt., Inc., 1978—, 1426 Chgo. Ave. Bldg. Corp., 1975-76, Parkinson Rsch. Corp., 1970-74. Author: (with R.M. Hendrickson) Governing Board and Administrator Liability, 1977, Tax Aspects of Charitable Giving, 1976, Designing Your Compliance Plan, 1997; contbr. articles to profl. jours. Commr. Evanston Preservation Commn., 1981-83; chmn. Am. Hearing Rsch. Found., 1977-79, v.p., 1972-77; bd. dirs. Episcopal Charities, 1978-80, U. Hosp. Chgo., 1989-97, sec. 1991-97; trustee Evanston Art Ctr., 1977-78; healthcare subcom. Nat. Fire Protection Assn., 1980-82; bd. dirs. Am. Schs. Profl. Psychology, Chgo., 1991-97; bd. trustees U. Sarasota, Fla., 1992-97. Brig. gen. U.S. Army. Decorated knight Order of Jerusalem, comdr. Order of St. Lazarus of Jerusalem; recipient Appreciation cert. Ill. Inst. Continuing Legal Edn., 1972. Mem. ABA, NRA (life) Chgo. Bar Assn., Ill. Bar Assn., Art Inst. Chgo. (life), Civil Affairs Assn. (life), Res. Officers Assn. (life), Assn. U.S. Army, Army Res. Assn. (sec., gen. counsel, bd. dirs. 1993—), Alumni Assn. U.S. Army War Coll. (life), John Evans Club (bd. dirs.), Order Temple Jerusalem (grand croix, internat. grand magistral chancellor 1996—), Order St. Lazarus Jerusalem (comdr.), Order of Constantine the Great (knight), Order of the Red Branch (Ireland, Champion), Psi Upsilon. Home: 15106 Pleasant Valley Rd Woodstock IL 60098-8942 Office: Spl Ops Command Korea Unit 15622 APO AP 96205-0328 E-mail: rmangum410@aol.com.

MANGUM, WILLIAM GOODSON, artist; b. Kinston, N.C., Jan. 31, 1924; s. Charles Preston and Margaret Edwards Mangum; m. Ariana Holliday Mangum; children: Ariana, William, Alice, Laura, Grace. BA in Art, U. N.C., 1956, MA in Art History, 1959; postgrad., Notre Dame U.; student, U. Florence, Italy, Art Students League N.Y., 1948-50, Corcoran Sch. Art, Washington, 1946-48. Prof. art emeritus Salem Coll. One-man shows include U. N.C., Chapel Hill, 1957, Western Carolina U., U. Tenn., Winthrop Coll., 1957, N.C. Mus. Art, Va. Mus. Art, 1959, Salem Coll., 1960, Southeastern Ctr. for Creative Art, 1958, Lynn Kottler Galleries, N.Y., 1960, Philip Morris Corp. Hdqs., Richmond, Va., 1962; exhibited in group shows Art Students League of N.Y., Bodley Gallery, N.Y.C., 1963, Springfield (Mass.) Mus. Art, N.C. Mus. Art, Va. Mus. Art, 1959, Isaac Delgado Mus., New Orleans, 1964, High Mus., Atlanta, 1964, Mint Mus., Charlotte, N.C., 1964, Southeastern Ctr. for Creative Art, 1968; ; represented in permanent collections N.C. Mus. Art, U. N.C., Chapel Hill, Greensboro, Salem Coll., R.J. Reynolds Industries, Wachovia Bank, various pvt. collections; executed Prometheus monument The Lamp of Learning, Greensboro, 1962, portrait bust of Carl Sandburg, Sandburg Mus., Flat Rock, N.C., 1962; trombonist in concert band and jazz groups. Served with 8th Air Force USAF, Eng., WW II. Recipient awards N.C. Mus. Art, Va. Mus. Art, SECCA, Isaac Delgado Mus., High Mus. Address: 106 Ascot Dr Chapel Hill NC 27517-7991

MANGUN, CLARKE WILSON , JR. public health physician, consultant; b. Iowa Falls, Iowa, Feb. 12, 1919; s. Clarke Wilson and Vallie Hazel (Hoffman) M.; m. Edith Lauretta DuBois, May 13, 1945; children: Edith Ann, Nancy June, Laura Jane. BS, U. Iowa, 1940, MD, 1943; MPH, Columbia U., 1947. Diplomate Am. Bd. Preventive Medicine. Commd. officer USPHS, 1945-66; med. adminstr. Am. Hosp. Assn., Chgo., 1966-67, Chgo. Heart Assn., 1967-68, AMA, Chgo., 1969-80; long-term cons. Abbott Labs., North Chicago, Ill., 1980—. Recipient award Nat. Bd. Med. Examiners, 1944. Fellow APHA, Am. Coll. Preventive Medicine; mem. AMA (Physician's Recognition award, 1970—), Ill. State Med. Soc., Chgo. Med. Soc. Avocations: photography, travel, gardening. Home and Office: 733 S Greenwood Ave Park Ridge IL 60068-4539

MANGUS, CARL WILLIAM, technical safety and standards consultant, engineer; b. Broken Bow, Okla., Aug. 20, 1930; s. Nathaniel M. and Eva Tennessee (Johnson) M.; m. Dorotha Marie Wood; children: Steven Neal, Roy Gene, Carla Anne. BSME, Okla. State U., 1958. Registered profl. engr., La. Various positions, 1948-63; project mgr. Chalkley Gas Processing Plant, 1964; project devel. Seven Natural Gas Plants, 1965; project mgr. N. Terrebonne Plant Expansion & Dual 36 Pipeline Loop, 1966-67; with Project Devel.-Two Natural Gas Plants, 1967-68; project mgr. Calumet Gas Processing Plant, 1968, offshore engring. sect. leader facilities, 1969; offshore prodn. supt. Maintenance and Operating Standards, 1970; with tech. safety rev. & approval engring. procedures Plus Regulations and Industry Standards, 1971; mgr. regulatory affairs Shell Offshore Inc., 1982, sr. staff tech. safety specialist, 1985; pvt. practice tech. safety and standards Lacombe, La., 1986—. Com. mem. Am. Bur. Shipping, N.Y.C., 1974-88; Dept. State cons. Internat. Maritime Orgn., London, 1975-79; Am. Petroleum Inst. rep. to Exploration/Prodn. Forum, London, 1979-83; com. mem. NAS, Washington, 1979-84; mem. spl. adv. ad hoc com. Internat. Assn. Drilling Contractors, Houston, 1978, human resources com., 1978-80; past mem. offshore operators com. Am. Petroleum Inst., New Orleans; past U.S. industry rep. safety code for constrn. offshore structures, ILO, Geneva. Staff sgt. USAF, 1951-55. Recipient Am. Petroleum citation for svc. Am. Petroleum Inst., 1987. Mem. La. Engring. Soc., Am. Soc. Safety Engrs., Gulf Coast Safety and Tng. Group, Soc. Petroleum Engrs. Republican. Avocations: hunting, fishing, woodworking, swimming, boating, traveling. Home and Office: 59131 Cypress Bayou Ln Lacombe LA 70445-3603

MANGUS, THOMAS EUGENE, band director; b. Oklahoma City, Mar. 28, 1953; s. Richard (Stepfather) and Carol Ann Wood; m. Jennifer Erin Bell; children: Greg, Andrew. M in Music Edn., U. Ctrl. Okla., 1979. Cert. tchr. Okla. Band dir. Big Cabin (Okla.) Pub. Schs., 1975—76, Maud (Okla.) Pub. Schs., 1976—79, Crescent (Okla.) Pub. Schs., 1979—82, Northeastern Okla. A&M Coll., Miami, 1982—86, Miami Pub. Schs., 1986—97, Mustang (Okla.) Pub. Schs., 1997—. Pres. Northeastern Okla. B and Dirs. Assn., Miami, 1995—97. Mem.: NEA, Ctrl. Okla. Band Dirs. Assn. (pres. 2001—02), Okla. Music Adjudicators Assn., Okla. Edn. Assn., Mustang Assn. Tchrs., Okla. Bandmasters Assn., Okla. Music Educators Assn. (band chmn. 1997—98, All-Okla. Music Educators Assn. band chmn. 1997—98), U. Ctrl. Okla. Alumni Assn. (life), Phi Beta Mu. Office: Mustang Pub Schs 906 S Heights Dr Mustang OK 73064 Office Fax: 405-376-7852. Business E-Mail: mangust@mustang.k12.ok.us.

MANHART, MARCIA Y(OCKEY), art museum director; b. Wichita, Kans., Jan. 14, 1943; d. Everett W. and Ruth C. (Correll) Yockey; children: Caroline Manhart Sanderson, Emily Alexandrea Morrison. BA in Art, U. Tulsa, 1965, MA in Ceramics, 1971. Dir. edn. Philbrook Art Ctr., Tulsa, 1972-77, exec. v.p., asst. dir., 1977-83, acting dir., 1983-84; exec. dir. Philbrook Mus. Art (formerly Philbrook Art Ctr.), 1984—. Instr. Philbrook Art Ctr. Mus. Sch., Tulsa, 1963-72; gallery dir. Alexandre Hogue Gallery, Tulsa U., 1967-69; NEH Challenge Grant panelist, 1991, presenter to AAM Conv., 1991; MAAA Craft Fellowship panelist, 1988, 93, NEA Craft Fellowship panelist, 1990; NEA spl. exhbn. panelist, 1996; curator nat. touring exhibit Nature's Forms/Nature's Forces: The Art of Alexandre Hogue, 1984-85; co-curator internat. exhbn.: The Eloquent Object, 1987-90; curator Sanford and Diane Besser Collection exhbn., 1992. Author essays in field. Vis. com. Smithsonian Instn./Renwick Gallery, Washington, 1986; cultural negotiator Gov. George Nigh's World Trade Mission (Okla.), China., 1985; com. mem. State Art Coll. of Okla., 1985—; mem. Assocs. of Hillcrest Med. Ctr., 1983-88, exec. com., 1985-88; com. mem. Neighborhood Housing Services, 1985-87; mem. City of Tulsa Arts Commn., 1996—; steering com. Harwelden Isnt. for Aesthetic Edn., 1983; com. mem. River Parks Authority, 1976; mem. Jr. League of Tulsa Inc., 1974-78; adv. panel mem. Nat. Craft Planning Project, NEA, Washington, 1978-81; craft adv. panel mem. Okla. Arts and Humanities Council, 1974-76; juror numerous art festivals, competitions, programs; reviewer Inst. Mus. Services, Washington, 1985, 88, 92, 95, 98; auditor Symposium on Language & Scholarship of Modern Crafts, NEA and NEH, Washington, 1981; nominator MacArthur Fellows Program, 1988; panelist Lila Wallace Reader's Digest Internat. Artists Fellowship, 1992, panelist Pew Charitable Trust, 1996. Recipient Harwelden award for Individual Contbrn. in the Arts, 1989, Gov.'s award State of Okla., 1992. Mem. Assn. Am. Mus., Assn. Art Mus. Dirs., Art Mus. Assn. Am., Mountain Plains Assn. Mus., Am. Craft Coun., Okla. Mus. Assn., Tulsa Met. C. of C. (bd. dirs. 1997-99), Rotary, Phi Beta Kappa. Office: Philbrook Mus Art PO Box 52510 Tulsa OK 74152-0510 E-mail: mmanhart@philbrook.org.

MANHART, PAUL IGNATIUS, writer, priest; b. Omaha, Jan. 2, 1927; s. Paul Ignatius Sr. Manhart and Eleanor Catherine Steinauer. BA, St. Louis U., 1952, BTh, 1959. Ordained priest Roman Cath. Ch., 1964. H.S. tchr. Red Cloud Indian Sch., Pine Ridge, SD, 1952—64; pastor Rapid City (SD) Diocese, 1964—. H.S. counselor Red Cloud Sch., 1960—64. Editor: (books in Lakota) Lakota-English Dictionary, 1970, Lakota Hymnal, 1993, Lakota Tales and Text in Translation, 1998. Bd. dirs. Rosebud Edn. Soc., St. Francis, SD, 1998. Mem.: Soc. of Jesus. Democrat. Roman Catholic. Avocations: hiking, athletics, writing, carpentry, metalwork. Home and Office: Holy Rosary Mission 100 Mission Dr Pine Ridge SD 57770-2100 Fax: 605-867-1291. E-mail: pimsj@redcloudschool.org.

MANHEIM, CAMRYN, television and film actress; b. N.J., 1961; MFA, NYU. Star TV series The Practice, 1997—; appeared in TV movies Jackie's Back!, 1999, The Loretta Claiborne Story, 2000, TV miniseries The 10th Kingdom, 2000; Appeared in films What Planet are You From?, Joe the King, Happiness (Nat. Bd. Rev. award 1998), Romy and Michele's High School Reunion, Eraser, Jeffrey, The Road to Wellville, Bonfires of the Vanities, David Searching, Wide Awake, Mercury Rising, Fool's Gold; prodr., performer Kiss My Act, 2000; appeared on TV shows Law and Order, Touched By an Angel, New York Undercover, Ally McBeal, Oh Baby, Chicago Hope, Will and Grace; star one-woman show Wake Up, I'm Fat, 1995; theater appearances include N.Y. Shakespeare Festival, Lincoln Ctr., Yale Repertory, N.Y. Theatre Workshop, Classic Stage Co., Home for Contemporary Theater. Recipient Obie award, 1995, Emmy award as best supporting actress, 1998, Golden Globe award, 1999, Quality TV for Viewers Award, 1999. Address: David E Kelly Prodns c/o 20th Century Fox 9057 Nemo St Ste C West Hollywood CA 90069-

MANHEIM, JAROL B. political communication researcher, educator; b. Cleve., Apr. 17, 1946; s. Harvey and Norma Manheim; m. Amy Lowen. BA, Rice U., 1968; MA, Northwestern U., 1969, PhD, 1971. Asst. prof. polit. sci. CCNY, N.Y.C., 1971-74; from asst. to assoc. prof. polit. sci. Va. Poly. Inst. and State U., Blacksburg, 1975-87; founding dir. Sch. Media and Pub. Affairs George Washington U., Washington, 1987, prof. media and pub. affairs, 1987—. Cons. Market/Media Scis., Bethesda, Md. Author: (books) The Politics Within: A Primer in Political Attitudes and Behavior, 2d edit., 1982, All of the People, All the Time: Strategic Communication and American Politics, 1991, Strategic Public Diplomacy and American Foreign Policy: The Evolution of Influence, 1994, Empirical Political Analysis, 1995, The Death of a Thousand Cuts: Corporate Campaigns and the Attack on the Corporation, 2001, others; contbr. numerous articles to scholarly jours. Named D.C. Prof. of Yr., Carnegie Found. for Advancement of Tchg., 1995, McGannon award for Social and Ethical Relevance in Comm. Policy, Donald McGannon Ctr., Fordham U., 1994, Outstanding Reference Source of 1984, ALA, 1985; grantee AT&T Found., 1992-95, rsch. grantee Mainichi Newspapers, 1991, travel grantee Office of Press Sec. to Pres. of Korea, 1988, rsch. grantee U.S. EPA, 1988-90. Mem. Internat. Comm. Assn., Am. Polit. Sci. Assn. Home: 8506 Beech Tree Ct Bethesda MD 20817-2901 Office: George Washington U Sch Media and Pub Affairs Washington DC 20052 E-mail: jarolb@gwu.edu.

MANHEIM, MICHAEL PHILIP, photographer; b. Canton, Ohio, June 20, 1940; s. Robert B. and Clara B. Manheim; m. Carolyn B. Olson, Oct. 30, 1965 (div. Jan. 1995); children: Jonathan, Allison. BSE, U. Pa., 1962. Mgr. Clothing Retailer, Alliance, Ohio, 1962-69; profl. photographer Marblehead and Beverly, Mass., 1969-94, 94—. Artist-in-residence Bates Coll., Lewiston, 2001, Phillips Exeter (NH) Acad., 2002. Solo shows include (fine art photography) Fitchburg (Mass.) Art Mus., 1993, Arthur Griffin Ctr. for Photographic Art, Winchester, Mass., 1994, Mythos Gallery, Burbank, Calif., 1995, Terrakotta Gallery, Thessaloniki, Greece, 1996, Spazio Pellegrin, Riva del Garda, Italy, 1996, Panopticon Gallery, Boston, 1996, Nat. Mus. Dance, Saratoga Springs, N.Y., 1999, 2000, Bates Coll. Mus. Art, 2002; exhibited in group shows at Danforth Mus. Art, Framingham, Mass., 1994, Chgo. Photog. Print Fair, 1996, Photographic Resource Ctr., Boston, 1996, Alinder Gallery, Gualala, Calif., 1997, Santa Monica (Calif.) Mus. Art, 1997, EverColor Fine Art, Worcester, Mass., 1997, Lamont Gallery, Phillips Exeter Acad., N.H., 1998, Long Beach Arts, Calif., 1998, Edward Carter Gallery, Gualala, Calif., 1999, Rice/Polak Gallery, Provincetown, Mass., 2000, Radiant Light Gallery, Portland, Maine, 2000, Jacob's Pillow Dance Festival, Becket, Mass., 2001, DeCordova Mus. and Sculpture Park, Lincoln, Mass., 2001; represented in permanent collections at Bates Coll. Mus. Art, Lewiston, Maine, Danforth Mus. Art, Framingham, Jacob's Pillow Dance Festival, Becket, Mass. Mem. Am. Soc. Media Photographers. Office: 39 Dodge St # 333 Beverly MA 01915-1705

MANI, RAMASWAMY, chemist, researcher; b. Namakkal, India, May 19, 1964; came to U.S., 1996; s. Vellaiya Gounder and Ramaswamy (Ramayee) R.; m. Gandhi Kavitha, June 9, 1997. PhD in Chemistry, Nat. Chem. Lab., Pune, India, 1995. Rsch. assoc. Nat. Chem. Lab., Pune, 1995-96, U. Minn., St. Paul, 1996—. Rsch. assoc. Coun. Sci. and Indsl Rsch., Govt. India, 1995. Reviewer Macromolecules, Jour. Am. Chem. Soc., Washington, 1998—, European Polymer Jour, Leis, Eng., 1999—; contbr. articles to profl. jours., chpts. to books. Mem. AAAS, Am. Chem. Soc., Bio/Environmentallly Degradable Polymer Soc., Soc. Plastics Engrs. Avocations: reading, music. Office: U Minn 1390 Eckles Ave Saint Paul MN 55108-1038 E-mail: manix002@tc.umn.edu.

MANIERI-HARVEY, MICHELE DAWN, musician, educator; b. Melbourne, Fla., Apr. 25, 1955; d. Ettore Don and June Laclaire (Spaur) Manieri; m. Joseph Howard Harvey, May 27, 1989. AA, U. Fla., 1976, B in Music Edn., 1978; M in Early Childhood and Elem. Edn., Nova U., 1983; M in Guidance and Counseling, U. South Fla., 1993. Cert. tchr., Fla. Profl. vocalist, Fla., 1973—; pvt. practice vocal tchr. Gainesville, 1978-80; substitute tchr. Alachua Sch. Bd., 1978-79; music specialist Levy County Sch. Bd., Williston, Fla., 1979-82, kindergarten tchr., 1982-83; tchr. 2d grade Hernando County/Moton Elem., Brooksville, 1983-84, tchr. 1st grade, 1984—86, music specialist with integrated counseling concepts and basic skills, 1986—. Chair calendar plus com. Moton, 1994-99; adj. prof. St. Leo U., 1984—; adj. prof. Pasco-Hernando C.C.; Fla. cert. observer and peer tchr., 1986—, master scheduling com., 1983-99; mem. Hernando County Fine Arts Curriculum Writing Team, 1994-96, accreditation steering com., chair music SAC com., Tchr. of Yr. selection com., 1994-2000; staff devel. trainer integrating music and counseling with academics Connections, Classroom Managed Assessment, Responsibility Tng., Coop. Learning. Featured vocalist Hernando Symphony Orch., Spring Hill, Fla., 1992, 95, 96, Hillsborough Edn. Gala, Tampa, Fla., 2002, Hillsborough County Music Specialists ann. banquet, 2002; featured soloist with Nature Coast Festival Singers, 1994, 96, Brooksville Music Club Christmas Ho., 1985, 94; dir., prodr. 26 sacred cantata-dramas, 52 children's musicals. Music dir. 1st Bapt. Ch., Brooksville, 1989-98; mem., actress Playhouse 19, Crystal River, Fla., Stage West Cmty. Theater, Spring Hill, Richey Suncoast Theatre, New Port Richey, Fla.; min. of music 1st Bapt. Ch., Spring Hill, 1999-2001; pvt. concerts. Named 1994 Hernando County Tchr. of Yr., 1994, Best Musical Actress, Stage West, 1995, Best Musical Supporting Actress, Favorite Female Performer, 2000; named to Outstanding Young Women of Am., 1981. Mem. Am. Fedn. of Tchrs., Hillsborough County Elem. Music Tchrs. Assn. (entertainment com.), Hillsborough Edn. Found., Hillsborough Classroom Tchrs. Assn., FTP-NEA, Nat. Music Educators Assn., Fla. Music Educators Assn., Fla. League Tchrs., Fla. Mental Health Counseling Assn., Fla. Counseling Assn., Fla. Assn. Staff Devel., Hernando Counseling Assn. (Counseling Advocate of Yr. 1994), Hernando County Bd. Fine Arts Coun., Hernando Edn. Found. (sec. 1995-96), Hernando Classroom Tchrs. Assn. (exec. bd. 1985-86), Hernando Acad. Tchrs. (vice-chair 1994-95, chair 95-96), Alpha Delta Kappa. Office: Hillsborough County 9855 Harney Rd Thonotosassa FL 33592-3301 Fax: 813-987-6755. E-mail: michele.manieri-Harvey@newideas.sdhc.k12.fl.us.

MANIFOLD, GREGORY LEE, sportswriter; b. Vallejo, Calif., Mar. 15, 1976; s. Jerry Lee Manifold, Carole Lee Murio. BS in Journalism, Calif. Poly Tech. at San Luis Obispo, 1999. Sports editor, design editor, writer Mustang Daily, San Luis Obispo, 1995—98; sports designer, reporter The Tribune, 1997—2001; sr. sports designer San Diego Union-Tribune, San Diego, 2001—. Mem.: Soc. News Design, Soc. Profl. Journalists. Avocations: soccer, golf, tennis, writing. Home: 6293 Caminito Del Oeste San Diego CA 92111 Office: San Diego Union-Tribune PO Box 120191 San Diego CA 92111

MANIKA, JOHN FRANCIS, computer systems educator, computer information systems analyst; b. Phila., Jan. 22, 1922; s. John F. and Mary T. (Johnston) M.; m. Marie Susan Valeo, Feb. 20, 1944; 1 child, Suzanne Manika Frauenhoffer. A in Bus. Adminstrn., U. Pa., 1967, BBA, 1979, postgrad., 1979-85; grad., U.S. Army Mgmt. Sch., 1968. Mgmt. analyst, internal mgmt. cons. VA, 1946-49; mgr. mgmt. engring. dept. Aviation Supply Office, USN, 1949-51, mgr. mgmt. engring. dept. Shipbldg. Activity, 1951-53; dir. mgmt. planning dept. U.S. Army Ordnance Dist., Phila., 1953-59; computer sys. mgr., sys. analyst Def. Logistics Agy., 1959-79; faculty Peirce Coll., Phila., 1967-98, prof. computer info. sys., 1979-98, chmn. computer info. system dept., 1982-89. Adj. instr. Temple U., 1951-56; cons. in field, 2000—. Capt. U.S. Army, 1942-46; lt. col. USAR ret. Fellow Assn. Data Comm. Users (chmn. ednl. com. 1986-86); mem. AAUP, Am. Soc. Profl. Cons., Toastmasters (past pres., founder Mil. Clothiers chpt.), Wharton Club, U. Pa. Faculty Club.

MANIMTIM, WINSTON MENDOZA, pediatrician, neonatologist; b. The Philippines, July 11, 1961; arrived in U.S., 1994; s. Florencio and Suprema (Mendoza) Manimtim. BS in Zoology, U. St. Tomas, The Philippines, 1981, MD, 1985. Diplomate Am. Bd. Pediatrics. Pediatric resident Philippine Children's Med. Ctr., 1987-90; registrar neonatology Mercy Hosp. Women, Melbourne, Australia, 1992-94; pediatric resident Albert Einsten Coll. Medicine, Bronx, N.Y., 1995-97; fellow in neonatology U. Md., Balt., 1997—2000, clin. instr. Instr. Neonatal Resucitation Program, Balt.; attending neonatologist Rsch. med. Ctr., 2000-. Capt. Philippine Med. Corps., 1986. Resident scholar Philippine Pediatric Soc., 1987; Internat. fellow Am. Respiratory Care Found., 1991; recipient Alien of Extraordinary Ability in field of medicine. Fellow Am. Acad. Pediat.; mem. AMA, Ea. Soc. Pediatric Rsch. Avocations: reading, Russian art. Home: 4949 Wornall Rd #409 Kansas City MO 64112 Office: Rsch Med Ctr 2316 E Myer Blvd Rm 526 Kansas City MO 64132

MANION, DANIEL ANTHONY, federal judge; b. South Bend, Ind., Feb. 1, 1942; s. Clarence E. and Virginia (O'Brien) Manion; m. Ann Murphy Manion, June 29, 1984. BA, U. Notre Dame, 1964; JD, Ind. U., 1973. Bar: Ind., U.S. Dist. Ct. (no. dist.) Ind., U.S. Dist. Ct. (so. dist.) Ind. Dep. atty. gen. State of Ind., 1973—74; from assoc. to ptnr. Doran, Manion, Boynton, Kamm & Esmont, South Bend, 1974—86; judge U.S. Ct. Appeals (7th cir.), 1986—. Mem. Ind. State Senate, Indpls., 1978—82. With U.S. Army, 1965—66. Office: US Ct Appeals US Courthouse & Federal Bldg 204 S Main St Rm 301 South Bend IN 46601-2122 Home: 20725 Riverlan Rd South Bend IN 46637-1029*

MANION, PAUL THOMAS, lawyer; b. Decatur, Ill., Apr. 7, 1940; s. Charles F. and Jeannette (Kaufman) M.; m. Bonnie J. Rivard, Aug. 12, 1961; children: Christine, Sheila, Tessy, Michael, Brian, Daniel. BBA in Fin., Notre Dame U., 1961; JD, DePaul U., 1964. Bar: Ill 1964, U.S. Ct. Appeals (7th cir.) 1975. Ins. investigator Hooper Holmes Bur., South Bend, Ind., 1958-61; supr. U.S. Dist. Ct., Chgo., 1961-64; asst. states atty. Iroquois County, Watseka, Ill., 1964-67; sr. ptnr. Manion, Devens & McFetridge, Ltd., Hoopeston, 1967—. Author: With Friends Like These, 1985. Mem. exec. com. Vermilion County Dem. Party, Danville, Ill., 1974—, county chmn. 1983-87; pres. Vermilion Mental Health Ctr., Danville, 1975-78. Mem. ATLA, Ill. Bar Assn., Ill. Trial Lawyers Assn. (bd. mgrs. 1997—). Democrat. Roman Catholic. Home: RR 2 Box 80 Hoopeston IL 60942-9706 Office: Manion Devens & McFetridge 216 S Market St Hoopeston IL 60942-1508

MANION, SHARON GREEN, curriculum director; b. Dallas, Dec. 14, 1947; d. Frank Wilfred and Loreda (Dunfield) Green; m. Kenneth J. Manion, Jr., Mar. 29, 1969; children: Jennifer, Christopher. BA, So. Meth. U., 1969; MEd, Coll. William & Mary, 1975. Cert. tchr., Ala., Washington. Tchr. hearing impaired Guam Pub. Schs., Agana, 1969-70, Tacoma (Wash.) Pub. Schs., 1975-80; resource tchr. Montgomery (Ala.) Pub. Schs., 1980-81; resource tchr., job coord., dept. chair, computer tchr. Anchorage Sch. Dist., 1981-92; spl. educator, dept. chair Auburn (Wash.) Sch. Dist., 1992-94, coord. curriculum, instrn., staff devel., 1994—. Mem. ASCD, Coun. Exceptional Children (pres.-elect 1990-91, v.p. 1991-92), Learning Disabilities Assn., Phi Delta Kappa, Delta Kappa Gamma. Home: 4143 SW 322nd St Federal Way WA 98023-2417 Office: Tukwila Sch Dist 4640 S 144th St Tukwila WA 98168

MANIRE, JAMES MCDONNELL, lawyer; b. Memphis, Feb. 22, 1918; s. Clarence Herbert and Elizabeth (McDonnell) M.; m. Nathalie Davant Latham, Nov. 21, 1951 (div. 1979); children: James McDonnell, Michael Latham, Nathalie Manire Willard; m. Nancy Whitman Colbert, Dec. 30, 1995. LL.B., U. Va., 1948. Bar: Tenn. 1948, U.S. Supreme Ct. 1957. Pvt. practice, Memphis, 1948—; city atty., 1968-71; of counsel Williams, McDaniel, Wolfe & Womack, 1986—. Editor in chief Va. Law Rev., 1947-48. Served to lt. comdr. USNR, 1941-46. Fellow Am. Coll. Trial Lawyers, Am. Bar Found. (life); mem. Tenn. Bar Assn. (pres. 1966-67), Memphis and Shelby County Bar Assn. (pres. 1963-64, Lawyer's Lawyer award 1995), Tenn. Bar Found. (charter), 6th Circuit Jud. Conf. (life), Raven Soc. Clubs: Memphis Country, Memphis Hunt and Polo. Home: 2927 Frances Pl Memphis TN 38111-2401 Office: 5521 Murray Rd Memphis TN 38119-3717

MANIS, MELVIN, psychologist, educator; b. N.Y.C., Feb. 18, 1931; s. Alex and Hanna (Oyle) M.; m. Jean Denby, May 28, 1954; children: Peter Eugene, David Denby. AB in Psychology, Franklin and Marshall Coll., 1951; PhD, U. Ill., 1954. Instr. psychology U. Pitts., 1956-58; rsch. psychologist Ann Arbor VA Med. Ctr., Mich., 1958-89; prof. psychology U. Mich., Ann Arbor, 1966-98, assoc. chmn. dept., 1990-91; ret., 1998. Author: Cognitive Processes, 1966, An Introduction to Cognitive Psychology, 1971; editor Jour. Personality and Social Psychology, 1980-84. Served with USPHS, 1954-56 Mem. APA, Soc. Exptl. Social Psychology, Phi Beta Kappa. Clubs: Racquet (Ann Arbor). Democrat. Jewish. Home: 20 Harvard Pl Ann Arbor MI 48104-1726 E-mail: Melmanis@umich.edu.

MANISCALCO, JOSEPH, artist, educator; b. Tampa, Fla., Feb. 24, 1921; s. Michaelangelo and Rosa (Belluccia) M.; m. Ann Lynn Laurence Cadman, Sept. 24, 1954 (div. June 1962); children: Michael, James, Elizabeth, Robert; m. Barbara Ann Fisher Insley, Jan. 3, 1976. Student, Art Students League of N.Y., 1939-41, 46-49. Portrait artist, 1941—. Lectr. in field; judge exhbns. Represented in permanent collections including Mich. Supreme Ct., U.S. House of Reps., Nat. Archives, Washington. With U.S. Army, 1942-46, ETO and PTO. Recipient Fitch award Mich. Acad. Letters, Arts and Sci., Artistic Excellence and Cmty. Commitment award Wayne County Coun. of the Arts, 1992. Mem. Scarab Club (bd. dirs. 1967—, pres. 1972-73, 80-81, 4 gold medals, 1st prize Silver Medal Show), Prismatic Club of Detroit (pres. 2000), Grosse Point Theatre (scenic artist), Fine Art Soc. of Detroit (chmn. art com. 1975), Adcraft Club of Detroit. Avocations: acting and singing in community theater productions, church choral singing. Home: 5232 Mirror Lake Ct Orchard Lake MI 48323-1536 Studio: 217 Farnsworth St Detroit MI 48202-4018

MANJURA, BONNIE DOREEN, marketing and advertising executive, educator; b. Duluth, Minn., Mar. 2, 1956; d. Maximilian Karl and Charlotte Erna (Jaeschke) M.; divorced; 1 child, Robert Maximilian Bonafide Manjura-Boody. BA, Rollins Coll., 1977, MA, 1979. Internat. promotion specialist dept. commerce State of Fla., Tallahassee, 1979-80, motion picture liaison dept. econ. devel. Orlando, 1981-85; dir. tourism devel. Greater Orlando C. of C., 1980-85; exec. dir. Centerra Group, Heathrow, Fla., 1985-91; pres. small bus. Longwood, 1989-91; exec. dir. spl. project Heathrow Land & Devel. Corp., 1985-90; vice chmn. JFP & Assocs. Fla., Inc., Heathrow, 1988-90; CFO, pres. Gilbert & Manjura Mktg. and Advt., Longwood, Fla., 1992—; pres. Gilbert & Manjura Merchandise, 1998—. Mem. Christopher Columbus Quincentennial Core Commn., 1992; prof. MBA program Webster U., 1994—, mentor mktg. dept., 1994—. Contbg. editor Lake Mary Progress, 1988-90. Mem. golf tournament com. Internat. Embassy House, 1992-93; ACS 125 Com., 1991-93, Seminole C.C. Bus. and Industry Coun., 1988-93; bd. dirs. Hospice of the Comforter, 1994-95, Hist. Preservation Bd., Longwood, 1998—; pub. rels. com. Orlando Day Nursery, 1995-96; cmty. trustee Seminole County Visions, 1996-98; founder, chmn., co-chmn. Lake Mary Heathrow Festival Arts, 1987-90; bd. dirs. Am. Diabetes Assn., 1987-89, Internat. Visitors Coun., 1987-90; bd. dirs. Ctrl. Fla. chpt. Leukemia Soc., 1986-88; mem. adv. bd. Vis. Nurses Assn., 1988-90. Nominee William T. Kenper award Excellence in Teaching, 2002; named One of Movers and Shakers, Ctrl. Fla. mag., 1987, Grant Patron, Tunon Internat. Sch., 1986; recipient scholarship award, Notre Dame Ctrl. Fla. Soc. Assn. Execs., 1984, Silver Addy for Creative Excellence, 1994, William Duggan award, Webster U., Orlando, 1997, Outstanding Vol. award, HRS Dept. Children and Families, 1998, Bus. Woman of Month award, Longwood, 1998. Mem. Fla. Motion Picture and TV Assn., Greater Orlando C. of C. (steering com. on suburban mobility 1991), Seminole County C. of C. (CEO's roundtable 1988), Variety Club Internat. (bd. dirs. 1988-90), Seminole Ornament Soc. (pres. 1988—). Republican. Lutheran. Avocations: tennis, gardening, children and senior charities. Office: 346 Freeman St Longwood FL 32750-4171 Also: 101 W Palmetto Ave Longwood FL 32750-4144

MANK, EDWARD WARREN, marketing professional; b. Boothbay Harbor, Maine, Oct. 2, 1962; s. Edward Raymond Jr. and Sandra Gail (Strahan) M. Assoc. in Liberal Arts, C.C. Vt., 1985; cert. ophthalmic technician, Nat. Edn. Ctr., San Francisco, 1992; cert. real estate broker, Am. Sch. Mortgage Banking, Walnut Creek, Calif., 1994. Lic. real estate salesman, Calif.; cert. Am. Bd. Optometry Dispensing. Tng. coord. Burger King Corp., South Burlington, Vt., 1985-87, San Francisco, 1988-89; asst. mgr. Bonanza Family Restaurant, South Burlington, 1987-88; supr. U.S. Census Bur., San Francisco, 1990; sales rep. Viacom Cablevision, 1991; programming researcher NBC, 1992; mktg. cons. Calyx & Corolla, 1993; mktg. rep. Alliance Bancorp, Millbrae, Calif., 1993—. Sustaining mem. Rep. Nat. Com., Washington, 1989—; sponsor Heritage Found., Washington, Cato Inst., Washington. Mem. Acad. Polit. Sci., Coun. Fgn. Rels., World Affairs Coun., Nat. Rifle Assn. (life), Reason Found. Republican. Episcopalian. Home: 3401 E 18th St Apt 3 Oakland CA 94601-3003 Office: Alliance Bancorp 800 El Camino Real Millbrae CA 94030-2010 E-mail: edmank@canada.com.

MANKA, RONALD EUGENE, lawyer; b. Wichita, Kans., Dec. 12, 1944; s. James Ashford and Jane Bunn (Meeks) M.; m. Frances Ann Patterson, Aug. 7, 1965 (dec. Dec. 1985); children: Kimberly Ann, Lora Christine; m. Linda I. Bailey, Mar. 11, 1995. BBA cum laude, U. Kans., 1967; JD cum laude, U. Mich., 1970. Bar: Conn. 1970, Mo. 1974, Kans. 1985, Colo. 2001. Assoc. Day, Barry & Howard, Hartford, Conn., 1970-73, Lathrop & Gage L.C., Kansas City, Mo., 1973-78, mem., 1979-82, 85—; group counsel Butler Mfg. Co., 1982-83, div. gen. mgr., 1983-84. Legal com. Boulder County Cmty. Found., Colo., 2002—. Trustee, clk., elder Village Presbyn. Ch., Prairie Village, Kans.; dir., treas. Lyric Opera of Kansas City, 1995—; pres. Genesis Sch., Kansas City, 1987-89; devel. chmn. Kansas City Friends of Alvin Ailey, 1987-89; chmn. Kansas City Mus., 1988-92, gen. counsel, 1994—; gen. counsel Spirit Festival, Kansas City, 1985-87, Kansas City C. of C., 1989-96; pres. Ctr. for Mgmt. Assistance, Kansas City, 1991-93; dir. Colo. Music Festival, 2002-. Mem. ABA, Mo. Bar Assn. (alt. dispute resolution com. 1986—), Lawyers Assn. Kansas City, Silicon Prairie Tech. Assn. (bd. dirs. 1990-92), Homestead Country Club (pres. 1984-85). Democrat. Avocations: bicycling, swimming. Home: 812 Walnut Apt F Boulder CO 80302 Office: 4845 Pearl East Cir Ste 300 Boulder CO 80301 Fax: 720-931-3001. E-mail: RManka@LathropGage.com.

MANKEL, FRANCIS XAVIER, former principal, priest; b. Knoxville, Tenn., Nov. 8, 1935; s. George Whitehead Sr. and Willia Frances (Duncan) M. BA, St. Ambrose U., 1957; STB, St. Mary's Sem. and U., Balt., 1959, STL, 1961; MEd, Loyola Coll., Balt., 1965. Ordained priest, Roman Cath. Ch., 1961. Assoc. pastor Holy Ghost Ch., Knoxville, 1962-67; prin. Knoxville Cath. High Sch., 1967-79; pastor Sacred Heart Ch., Lawrenceburg, Tenn., 1979-84, St. John Neumann Ch., Knoxville, 1984-87, Sacred Heart Cathedral, Knoxville, 1987-97, Holy Ghost Ch., Knoxville, 1997—. Chancellor Cath. Diocese Knoxville, 1988-96, vicar gen., 1988-98, 99—; supt. Cath. Schs., Diocese of Knoxville, 1989-92. Bd. dirs. Knoxville area chpt. ARC, 1986—. Mem. Knoxville Ministerial Assn. Home and Office: 111 Hinton Ave Knoxville TN 37917-6418

MANKIEWICZ, THOMAS FRANK, screenwriter, director, producer; b. L.A., June 1, 1942; s. Joseph Leo and Rosa M. Student, Yale U., 1959-63. Author: (book, Broadway musical) Georgy!, 1970; screenwriter: (teleplay, musical spl.) Movin' with Nancy, 1967, The Sweet Ride, 1968, (teleplay, musical spl.) The Beat of the Brass, 1968, Diamonds Are Forever, 1971, Live and Let Die, 1973, The Man With with the Golden Gun, 1974, The Eagle Has Landed, 1976, The Cassandra Crossing, 1977, Ladyhawke, 1985; screenwriter, co-prodr.: Mother, Juggs and Speed, 1976; creative cons.: Superman, 1978, Superman II, 1980; dir. (teleplay, tv pilot) Hart to Hart, 1979-80, (screenplay) Dragnet, 1987, Delirious, 1991, (cable tv series) Tales from the Crypt, 1992, (cable tv movie) Taking the Heat, 1993; exec. prodr. Hot Pursuit, 1985. Bd. dirs. William Holden Wildlife Found., L.A., 1995—. Mem. Greater L.A. Zoo Assn. (bd. trustees 1997—, chmn. 2002--), Motion Picture Acad. Arts and Scis. (bd. govs. 1979-81). Avocations: wildlife conservation, thoroughbred horse racing and breeding.

MANKIN, CHARLES JOHN, geology educator; b. Dallas , Jan. 15, 1932; s. Green and Myla Carolyn (Bohmert) M.; m. Mildred Helen Hahn, Sept. 6, 1953 (dec. Oct. 26, 1995); children: Sally Carol, Helen Francis, Laura Kay. Student, U. N.Mex., 1949-50; BS, U. Tex., Austin, 1954, MA, 1955, PhD, 1958. Asst. prof. geology Calif. Inst. Tech., 1958-59; asst. prof. geology U. Okla., 1959-63, asso. prof., 1963-64, prof., 1964—; dir. Sch. Geology and Geophysics, 1963-77, Energy Resources Inst., 1978-87. Mem. U.S. Nat. Commn. on Geology, 1977-80; dir. Okla. Geol. Survey, 1967—, Sarkeys Energy Ctr., U. Okla., 2000—; former chmn. bd. mineral and energy resources, former mem. commn. on phys. sci., math. and resources NAS; former commr. Commn. Fiscal Accountability of Nation's Energy Resources; mem. royalty policy com. Dept. Interior, past chmn. royalty mgmt. adv. com.; past bd. dirs. Environ. Inst. for Waste Mgmt. Studies, U. Ala.; trustee Nat. Inst. Global Environ. Change; mem. adv. bd. geoscis. Sandia Nat. Labs.; mem. adv. com. Idaho Nat. Labs.; trustee Drake Well Found.; vice chair royalty policy adv. com. Dept. of Interior. Contbr. articles profl. jours. Recipient Conservation Service award Dept. Interior, 1983, Energy Adv. od Yr., Internat. Assn. of Energy Advs., 2000. Fellow Geol. Soc. Am. (co-project leader Decade N.Am. Geology, former councillor, former chmn. found., Disting. Svc. award 1998), Mineral. Soc. Am.; mem. Am. Assn. Petroleum Geologists (com. on resource evaluation, govt. affairs com., chair govt. liaison subcom., pub. svc. award 1988, hon. life), Am. Inst. Profl. Geologists (v.p., past pres., Martin Van Couvering Meml. award 1988, Ben H. Parker medal, mem. found., hon. life), Clay Minerals Soc., Geochem. Soc., AAAS, Assn. Am. State Geologists (past pres.), Am. Geol. Inst. (past pres., Ian Campbell medal 1987), Soc. Econ. Paleontologists and Mineralogists (past pres. Mid-Continent sect.), Internat. Soc. Energy Advocates (Energy Advocate of Yr. 2000), Oklahoma City Geol. Soc. (hon., life), Sigma Gamma Epsilon (hon. life, nat. sec.-treas.). Home: 2220 Forister Ct Norman OK 73069-5120 Office: Okla Geol Survey 100 E Boyd St Rm N131 Norman OK 73019-1028 E-mail: cjmankin@ou.edu.

MANKIN, HENRY JAY, physician, educator; b. Pitts., Oct. 9, 1928; s. Hyman Isaac and Mary (Simons) M.; m. Carole Jane Pinkney, Aug. 20, 1952; children: Allison Joan, David Philip, Keith Pinkney. BS magna cum laude, U. Pitts., 1952, MD, 1953; MA (hon.), Harvard U., 1973. Diplomate Am. Bd. Orthopaedic Surgery (mem. bd. 1976-82, pres. bd. 1980-81). Intern U. Chgo. Clinics, 1953-54; resident orthopaedics Hosp. for Joint Diseases, N.Y.C., 1957-60; instr. orthopaedics U. Pitts. Sch. Medicine, 1960-62, asst. prof., 1962-64, assoc. prof., 1964-66; dir., prof. orthopaedics Hosp. for Joint Diseases and Mt. Sinai Sch. Medicine, 1966-72; chief orthopaedics Mass. Gen. Hosp., Boston, 1972-96, chief orthopaedic oncology, 1972—. Edith M. Ashley prof. orthopaedics Harvard Med. Sch., 1972—; mem. surgery B study sect. NIH, 1969-73; mem. adv. com. on surg. treatment FDA, 1973-75; corporator Boston Five Cent Savs. Bank, 1982-83; mem. exec. com. Am. Bd. Med. Spltys., 1982-85; adv. council on grad. med. edn., 1986-96; mem. Nat. Arthritis Avd. Bd., 1986-89; mem. human resources and research rev. group A Nat. Inst. Arthritis, Metabolism and Digestive Diseases, 1981-85, chmn., 1983-85. Assoc. editor Arthritis and Rheumatism, 1967-77, Jour. Bone and Joint Surgery, 1967-82; mem. editorial bd. Jour. Orthopedic Research, 1982-85; trustee Jour. Bone and Joint Surgery, 1985-91, chmn. bd., 1988-91; contbr. more than 530 articles to profl., med. jours. Served to lt. comdr. USNR, 1955-57. Fellow ACS, Royal Coll. Surgeons (hon.); mem. Am. Acad. Orthopaedic Surgeons, Acad. Orthopaedic Soc. (pres. 1991-92), Am. Orthopaedic Assn. (pres. 1982-83), Orthopaedic Research Soc. (pres. 1969-70), Musculoskeletal Tumor Soc. (pres. 1991-92), Brit. Orthopaedic Research Soc., Argentine Orthopaedic Assn. (hon.), N.Y. Acad. Medicine (chmn. orthopaedic sect. 1971-72), Am. Rheumatism Assn., Soc. Internat. Chirurgerie Orthopaedice et Traumatologia, Hip Soc., Interurban, Forum Orthopaedic clubs, Brit. Orthopaedic Assn. (hon.), Can. Orthopaedic Assn. (hon.), Australian Orthopaedic Assn. (hon.), N.Z. Orthopaedic Assn. (hon.), Japanese Orthopaedic Assn. (hon.), Israel Orthopaedic Assn. (hon.), Thai Orthopaedic Assn (hon.). Office: Mass Gen Hosp 55 Fruit St Boston MA 02114-2696 E-mail: hmankin@partners.org.

MANKINS, KENT WAYNE, minister, consultant; b. Floydada, Tex., Sept. 14, 1965; s. Bruce Edward Mankins and Lynda Nell Thomas; m. Tonya Lynn Lee, Dec. 20, 1987; children: Logan, Ethan. MEd in Counseling and Human Svcs., U. Idaho, 2000. Ordained to ministry Assembly of God, 1994. Pre., cons. Lead to Succeed, A Mgmt. Cons. Firm, Post Falls, Idaho; pastor Southridge Cmty. Ch., Spokane, Wash., 2000—. Counselor Union Gospel Mission, Spokane, Wash. Beulah Martin scholarship U. Idaho, 1998. Mem. ACA, Am. Assn. of Marriage and Family Therapists, Am. Assn. of Chrisitan Counselors. Avocations: horsemanship, hiking, music, travel. Home: 24123 E Garland Otis Orchard WA 90027 Office: Southridge Cmty Ch 2607 S Ray Spokane WA 99223 E-mail: kentmankins@psychgrowth.com.

MANKO, JOSEPH MARTIN, SR. lawyer; b. Phila., Oct. 7, 1939; s. Horace David and Vivian (Greenberg) M.; m. Lynn Kimmelman, June 17, 1962; children: Joseph Jr., Glenn, Wendy. BA magna cum laude, Yale U., 1961; JD cum laude, Harvard U., 1964. Bar: Pa. 1964. Regional counsel EPA, Phila., 1973-75; assoc. Wolf, Block, Schorr & Solis-Cohen, 1964-72, ptnr., 1972-73, 75-89, chmn. environ. law, 1978-89; founding ptnr. Manko, Gold & Katcher, LLP, Bala Cynwyd, Pa., 1989—. Adj. prof. U. Pa. Law Sch., 1988—, Grant Irey lectr., 1989-90, Thomas A. O'Boyle lectr., 2000-01; lectr. in law Vt. Law Sch., 1988—; dir. Pa. Environ. Council, Phila., 1978-85, 99—2000, treas., 1986-87, pres., 1987-89, chmn. 1989-98, 10,000 Friends of Pa.; chair or co-chair numerous environ. bar assn. coms. Commr. Lower Merion Twp., Ardmore, Pa., 1979-91, 94—, v.p., 1992, pres. 1993; mem. Com. of 70, Phila., 1978-88; pres. Beth David Reform Congregation, Gladwyne, Pa., 1983-86, trustee, 1978-83, 86—; trustee Fedn. Jewish Agys., Phila., 1982-86; bd. dirs. Golden Slipper Camp, 1981-84, 88—, Jewish Cmty. Rels. Coun., 1983-88, Lower Merion Conservancy, 1976-2002, Phila. Geriatric Ctr., 1990-98, 99—, Delaware River Basin Water Resources Assn., 1993-96; mem. Dem. State Com., 1986-90; bd. dirs. 21st Century Environ. Commn., 1997-98. Recipient Outstanding Conservation Profl. award Pa. Wildlife Fedn., 2000; named Disting. Environ. Neutral, CPR Inst. for Dispute Resolution, 2000, Dem. of Yr., Montgomery County Dem. Com., 2000, Montgomery County (Pa.) Dem. of Yr., 2000. Mem.: ABA, Pa. Bar Inst. (bd. dirs. 1997—2000, 2001—), Phila. Bar Assn., Pa. Bar Assn. (Environ. Atty. of Yr. 2001, Outstanding Environ. Atty. 2001), Vesper Club, Bala Golf Club (Phila.), Germantown Cricket Club, Hamilton Bridge Club, Lambda Alpha, Phi Beta Kappa. Avocations: tennis, golf, jogging, bridge, classical music. Home: 96 E Levering Mill Rd Bala Cynwyd PA 19004-2611 Office: Manko Gold Katcher & Fox LLP 401 E City Ave Ste 500 Bala Cynwyd PA 19004-1167 E-mail: Jmanko@mgkflaw.com.

MANKOFF, ALBERT WILLIAM, cultural organization administrator, consultant, writer; b. Newark, Aug. 24, 1926; s. Albert and Dorothy M.; m. Audrey Emery, Mar. 18, 1972; 1 child, Robert Morgan. BLS, U. Okla., 1967. With Am. Airlines, Inc., 1947-69; mgr. mgmt. tng. and devel. Am. Airlines Inc., 1957-67; mgr. orgn. devel. Am. Airlines, Inc., Tulsa, 1968-69; dir. personnel Peat, Marwick, Mitchell & Co., Chgo., 1969-72; ptnr. Lexicon, Inc.

Cons., Raleigh, N.C., 1972-77; Pacific area mgr. safety and tng. Trailways, Inc., L.A., 1978-80; tng. cons. State of Calif., Sacramento, 1980-91; pres. Inst. Am. Hist. Tech., Hendersonville, N.C., 1987—. Author: Trolley Treasures, 4 vols., 1986-87, The Glory Days, 1989, Tracks of Triumph, 1993, Tarnished Triumph, The Edison Paradigm, 1994, Sacramento's Shining Rails, 1995, Trolleys in America: The Long Road Back, 1995; contbr. articles to profl. jours. Bd. dirs., v.p. OASIS; Midwest Centre for Human Potential, Chgo., 1970-72, Tulsa Urban League, 1962-69; v.p., bd. dirs. Meditation Groups Inc., Ojai, Calif., Psychosynthesis Internat., Psychosynthesis, Ctr. World Servers, Henersonville, N.C. Avocations: street car and light rail technology, historical trolley photographs, cat humor. Home and Office: 1300 Brevard Rd #18 Hendersonville NC 28791-2503 E-mail: awmank@bellsouth.net. *Personal philosophy: I believe that the love principle is the most powerful force in the universe, and fear is the most destructive; that we create our own heaven or hell as a consequence of our thought; that we die and are reborn countless times until we master life in the human framework.*

MANKOFF, DAVID ABRAHAM, nuclear medicine physician; b. July 10, 1959; BS in Physics summa cum laude, Yale U., 1981; MD, PhD in Bioengring., U. Pa., 1988. Diplomate Am. Bd. Internal Medicine, Am. Bd. Nuclear Medicine. Rsch. scientist UGM Med. Systems, Phila., 1988-89, dir. engring., 1989-90; rsch. assoc. nuclear medicine sect. U. Pa., 1988-90; resident in internal medicine U. Wash., Seattle, 1990-92, resident in nuclear medicine, 1992-96, asst. prof. radiology, 1996—2001, assoc. prof. radiology, 2001; 0. Office: Divsn Nuc Medicine U Wash Med Ctr Box 356113 1959 NE Pacific St Seattle WA 98195-0001 E-mail: dam@u.washington.edu.

MANKOFF, RONALD MORTON, lawyer; b. Gettysburg, S.D., Oct. 13, 1931; s. Harry B. and Sarah (Frank) M.; m. Joy Faith Shechtman, Nov. 3, 1959; children: Jeffrey Walker, Douglas Frank. BSL, U. Minn., JD, 1954; LLM in Taxation, NYU, 1959. Bar: Minn. 1954, Tex. 1959. With Leonard, Street & Deinard, Mpls., 1957-58; research analyst Inst. Jud. Adminstrn., N.Y.C., 1958-59; assoc. Lyne, Blanchette, Smith & Shelton, Dallas, 1959-60; ptnr. Durant and Mankoff, 1960-85; pres. Brice & Mankoff P.C., 1985-89, Mankoff, Hill, Held & Metzger, L.L.P., Dallas, 1989-95; chmn./gen. counsel RAC Fin. Group, Inc. (now 1st Plus Fin Group, Inc.), 1994-96. Lectr. law So. Meth. U., 1974-77; speaker in field. Contbr. articles to profl. jours. Chmn. bd. Dallas chpt. Am. Cancer Soc., 1976-77, bd. dirs. Tex. divsn., 1981-94; chmn. Dallas Crusade, 1974-75, bd. dirs., mem. exec. com., 1963-88; mem. Dallas Mcpl. Libr., 1973-75; exec. com. Dallas Citizens Charter Assn., 1971-75; pres. Dallas Arts Found., Inc., 1973-75; mem. exec. com. Nat. Pooled Income Fund, Coun. Jewish Welfare Fedns. and Funds, 1975-77; adv. dir. Dallas Cmty. Chest Trust Fund, 1976-78; chmn. Found. Dallas Jewish Fedn., 1976-77; pres. Temple Emanu-el, Dallas, 1977-79; bd. dirs. Jewish Fedn. Greater Dallas, 1977-79, 99—, Dallas Civic Opera, 1981-83, World Union Progressive Judaism, 1981-90; mem. S.W. regional liaison com. IRS, 1980-83; exec. com. Union Am. Hebrew Congregations, 1979-89, trustee, 1979-97, chmn. nat. coll. com., 1983-87, vice chmn. bd. dirs., 1984-88, vice chmn. devel. commn., 1997-99; sec. Dallas Assembly, 1979-84; exec. com. Jewish Cmty. Rels. Coun., 1982-83, Com. for Qualified Judiciary, 1982—; sec. Child Care Partnership, 1984-86, bd. dirs., 1986-88; bd. dirs. Dallas Women's Found., 1985-89, adv. coun., 1989—, chair adv. coun., 1997-99; bd. dirs. Am. Jewish Com., 1982-88, pres. Dallas chpt. 1986-90; bd. dirs. Tex. coun. Girl Scouts U.S., 1982-85, Goodwill Industries of Greater Dallas, 1979-83, Title One Home Improvement Lender's Assn., 1994-96; mem. Mayor's Task Force on Child Care, 1984; bd. govs. Dallas Symphony Assn., 1988-92, 98—; chmn. Temple Emanu El Found., 1988-95; bd. dirs. Dallas Inst. Humanities and Culture, 1998—, Ctr. for Interreligious Understanding, 2001--, Cardio-Pulmonary Rsch. Inst., 2002--, Jane's Due Process, Inc., 2002--. Lt. (j.g.) USN, 1954-57. Mem. ABA, State Bar Tex., Dallas Bar Assn., Columbian Country Club (bd. dirs. 1967-73), LaJolla Country Club, Crescent Club, Zeta Beta Tau, Delta Sigma Rho. Democrat. Jewish. Home: 22 Lakeside Park Dallas TX 75225 Office: 5950 Berkshire Ln Ste 550 Dallas TX 75225-5833

MANKOWITZ, BARRY JOEL, surgeon; b. Newark, Jan. 2, 1942; AB, Kenyon Coll., 1963; MD, Tufts U., 1967. Diplomate Am. Bd. Surgery; cert. gen. surgery, 1973, vascular surgery, 1983, 93. Intern Newark-Beth Israel Med. Ctr., 1967-68, resident in surgery, 1968-72; staff Fishermen's Hosp., Marathon, Fla., 1973—2001, ret., 2001. Fellow Am. Coll. Surgeons, Internat. Soc. Cardiovasc. Surgery; mem. Soc. Clin. Vasc. Surgery, Soc. Laparoscopic Surgery, Fla. Vasc. Soc., SSC. Home: 58477 Morton St Grassy Key FL 33050

MANLEY, AUDREY FORBES, academic administrator, pediatrician, military officer; b. Jackson, Miss., Mar. 25, 1934; d. Jesse Lee and Ora Lee (Buckhalter) Forbes; m. Albert Edward Manley, Apr. 3, 1970. AB with honors (tuition scholar), Spelman Coll., Atlanta, 1955; MD (Jesse Smith Noyes Found. scholar), Meharry Med. Coll., 1959; MPH, Johns Hopkins U.-USPHS traineeship, 1987; LHD (hon.), Tougaloo (Miss.) Coll., 1990, Meharry Med. Coll., Nashville, 1991; LLD (hon.), Spelman Coll., 1991, Tskegee U., 1998; DSc (hon.), Coll. New Rochelle, 1998. Diplomate: Am. Bd. Pediatrics. Intern St. Mary Mercy Hosp., Gary, Ind., 1960; from jr. to chief resident in pediatrics Cook County Children's Hosp., Chgo., 1960—62; NIH fellow neonatology U. Ill. Rsch. and Ednl. Hosp., 1963—65; staff pediatrician Chgo. Bd. Health, 1963—66; practice medicine specializing in pediatrics Chgo., 1963—66; assoc. Lawndale Neighborhood Health Ctr. North, 1966—67; asst. med. dir., 1967—69; asst. prof. Chgo. Med. Coll., 1966—67; instr. Pritzker Sch. Medicine, U. Chgo., 1967—69; asst. dir. ambulatory pediatrics, asst. dir. pediatrics Mt. Zion Hosp. and Med. Center, San Francisco, 1969—70; med. cons. Spelman Coll., 1970—71, med. dir. family planning program, chmn. health careers adv. com., 1972—76; med. dir. Grady Meml. Hosp. Family Planning Clinic, 1972—76; with Health Services Adminstrs., Dept. Health and Human Services, 1976—97; commd. officer USPHS, 1976—97; chief genetic diseases services br. Office Maternal and Child Health, Bur. Community Health Services, Rockville, Md., 1976—81; acting assoc. adminstr. clin. affairs Office of Adminstr. Health Resources and Services Adminstrn., 1981—83, chief med. officer, dep. assoc. adminstr. planning, evaluation and legis., 1983—85; sabbatical leave USPHS Johns Hopkins Sch. Hygiene and Pub. Health, 1986—87; dir. Nat. Health Service Corps.; asst. surgeon gen., 1988; dep. asst. Sec. for Health USPHS/HHS, 1989—93, acting asst. Sec. Health, 1993, dep. asst. Sec. Health/intergovtl. affairs, 1993—94; dep. surgeon gen., acting dep. asst. sec. for minority health USPHS, 1994—95, acting surgeon gen., 1995—97; pres. Spelman Coll., 1997—. Mem. U.S. del. UNICEF, 1990-94, Am. Acad. Family Physicians (pub. adv. bd.), Am. Coun. Learned Socs., Am. Med. Assn. Minority Affairs Consortium (sr. advisor), Ctrs. for Disease Control Found. (bd. visitors), Moorehouse Sch. Medicine (clin. Prof. Pediats., Pub. Health Lectr.), Rollins Sch. Pub. Health Emory U (Commrs., Adv. Coun., Ga. Leadership Commn. Organ, Tissue, Blood Marrow donation amont African Ams. Author numerous articles, reports in field. Trustee Spelman Coll., 1966-70; bd. dirs. March of Dimes, 1998; The Coll. Fund(UNCF (com. Archives, Hist. Govtl. Affairs Com.), Coun. Fgn. Rels., bd. dirs. coun. Ind. Colls., bd. dirs. Nat. Merit Scholarship, Nat. bd. dirs. March of Dimes, Nat. Minority Mil. Mus. Found. Edl. Adv. Coun., Downtown Atlanta Chpt. Rotary, Atlanta 2000 Adv. Com., adv. bd. Atlanta Regional Health Summit, Commerce Club, Ga. Found. Ind.. Recipient Meritorious Svc. award USPHS, 1981, Mary McLeod Bethune award Nat Coun. Negro Women, 1979, Dr. John P. McGovern Ann. Lectureship award Am. Sch. Health Assn., Disting. Alumni award Meharry Med. Coll., 1989, Spelman Coll. 108 Founder's Day Convocation, 1989, Disting. Svc. medal USPHS, 1992, Hildrus A. Poindexter award OSG/PHS, 1993, numerous other svc. and achievement awards. Fellow Am. Acad. Pediatrics; mem. Nat. Inst. Medicine of Nat. Acad. Sci., Nat. Med. Assn., APHA, AAUW, AAAS, Spelman Coll. Alumnae Assn., Meharry Alumni Assn., Operation Crossroads Africa Alumni Assn., Atlanta C. of C., Rotary, Delta Sigma Theta (hon.), Phi Beta Kappa. Address: 2807 18th St NW Washington DC 20009

MANLEY, DAVID BOTT, III, lawyer; b. Jacksonville, Fla., June 19, 1953; s. David Bott and Bernadette Claire Manley; m. Gayle Aileen Whitney, Nov. 1, 1978; children: David Jeremiah, Alexandra Ina Claire. BA with honors magna cum laude, U. Ga., 1975, JD, 1982. Bar: Ga. 1983, U.S. Dist. Ct. (no. dist.) Ga. 1983, U.S. Ct. Appeals (11th cir.) 1986. Auditor So. Hostess Sys., Inc., Augusta, Ga., 1975-76; prosecutorial asst. fraud investigator State Ga., Atlanta, 1976-79; assoc. Gadrix & Green, P.C., 1982-83, Lowe, Barham, Eubanks & Lowe, Atlanta, 1983-85; mem. Barham & Manley, 1985-89; dir., ptnr. Campbell Martin & Manley, LLP, 1989—. Corp. counsel Highland Homes, Inc., Dallas and Atlanta, 1990—, Mast Advt. and Pub. Inc., Houston and Nashville, 1991—; corp. sec., counsel Agrisel USA, Inc., Atlanta and Hong Kong, 1998—; mem. Ga. Law Related Edn. Constorium of Carl Vinson Inst. Govt., U. Ga., 2000—. Pres. U.S. Jaycees, Mt. Park/Lilburn, 1985; cert. coach Lucky Shoals Youth Athletic Assn., Norcross, Ga., 1992-98; bd. dirs Fulton County, Ga. Dept. Family and Children's Svcs. (commendation, bd. resolution for bravery, 1978); svc. provider Parent to Parent of Ga.; mem. Dekalb Vol. Lawyers Found., Lawyers Found. Ga. Named Jaycee of Yr., U.S. Jaycees-Mt. Park/Lilburn, Ga., 1984. Mem. ABA, State Bar Ga. (legis. com. corp. and banking law sect. 1987-88, mem. corp. and banking law sect. 1987—, adv. mem. law revision com. 1989-90, mem. trial sect. 1984—, mem. real property sect. 1996—, advocate for spl. needs children 1996—), Nat. Youth Sports Coaches Assn. (continuing mem. 1996—), Sandy Springs Bar Assn. (treas. 1987-88, pres. 1988-89, dir. 1989-90), Omicron Delta Kappa. Avocations: coaching youth sports, model railroading, photography, collecting, travel. Home: 4390 Flippen Trl Norcross GA 30092-3902 Office: Campbell Martin & Manley LLP 990 Hammond Dr NE Ste 800 Atlanta GA 30328-5510 E-mail: dbmanley@chb-cmm.com.

MANLEY, DAVID THOMAS, employee benefits plan administration executive; b. Youngstown, Ohio, Apr. 13, 1938; s. Harry T. and Margaret M. (Stein) M.; m. Virginia Borcik, Sept., 1961 (div. 1975); children: Kelly A., Scott D., Lynne M., Brian D., Leslie; m. Ruth Ann Osterhage, Dec. 31, 1975; children: David Louis, Mollie O. Student, Youngstown U., 1956-60. Dist. sales mgr. Res. Life, Dallas, 1960-63, Guarantee Res. Life, Hammond, Ind., 1963-64; mgr. brokerage CNA Ins. Group, Chgo., 1964-68; pres. Greater Del. Corp., Dover, 1981-85, Variable Protection Adminstrn., Cleve., 1968—, also bd. dirs.; pres. VPA Ins., Ltd., 1985—, also bd. dirs.; with VPI, Inc. Rep. precinct committeeman, 1966-72, ward leader, 1970-72; mem. Cuyahoga County Rep. Com., 1970-72; mem. Bd. Zoning Appeals, Hinckley, Ohio Twp.; pres. Our Lady of Grace Bd. Fin., 1980-89; bd. trustees Cath. Charities. Mem. Soc. Profl. Benefit Adminstrs., Mass Market Ins. Inst., Internat. Found. Employee Benefits, Am. Mgmt. Assn., KC. Roman Catholic. Home: 2485 Bethany Ln Hinckley OH 44233-9741 Office: Variable Protection Adminstrs Inc 6902 Pearl Rd Ste 500 Cleveland OH 44130-3625

MANLEY, EDWARD HARRY, JR. association executive, former navy officer; b. S.I., N.Y., Sept. 12, 1941; s. Edward H. and Dorothy I.; m. Judith Manley; children: Deborah Szymchack, Michael E. BS, Cornell U., 1975; MS, Rollins Coll., 1978. Cert. food svc. exec. Joined USN, 1959, commd. ensign, 1970, advanced through grades to lt. comdr., 1979; food svc. dir. Naval Hosp., Annapolis, Md., 1972-73; asst. food svc. dir. Nat. Naval Med. Ctr., Bethesda, 1971-72; food svc. dir. Naval Regional Med. Ctr., Orlando, Fla., 1975-80, ret., 1980; food svc. dir. North Broward Hosp., Pompano Beach, Fla., 1981-89; pres. Creative Food Concepts, Inc.; founder Workaholics Internat. Network, 1999—. Mem. adv. bd. Mid-Fla. Tech. Food Svc. Program, 1978-80, Atlantic Vo-Tech Dietetic Program, 1981-89; chmn. Skills Std. Bd., Hospitality and Tourism. Mem. evaluation team Hennessey award U.S. Air Force, 1982; mem. adv. bd. Broward Community Coll., 1985—. Ed Manley Scholarship Fund established, 1984; named Accomplished Health Care Food Svc. Adminstr., 1985; recipient Peter Gust Economou award, 1987. Mem. Internat. Food Svc. Execs. Assn. (pres. Orlando br. 1979-80, pres. South Fla. br. 1983-84, internat. sec., treas. 1986-87, internat. pres. 1988—, named mem. of yr. Orlando br. 1978, mem. of yr. South Fla. br. 1984, Disting. Svc. award 1984, chmn. bd. 1988-89, pres. 1989—, Dignified Order of the Dinner Gong 2001), Cornell Soc. Hotelmen (pres. Ctrl. Fla. chpt. 1976-80), Cornell Hotel Soc. (Las Vegas, treas. 2001—), Fla. Restaurant Assn. (bd. dirs. 1980), Am. Soc. Hosp. Food Svc. Adminstrs. (sec. South Fla. chpt.), Chaine des Rotisseurs, Cornell of Ctrl. Fla. Club, Naval Tng. Ctr. Officers Club (pres. 1978-80), Pompano Sq. Mall Walkers Club (founder). Home and Office: 2609 Surfwood Dr Las Vegas NV 89128-1282

MANLEY, FRANK, retired English language educator, writer; b. Scranton, Pa., Nov. 13, 1930; s. Aloysius F. and Kathryn L. (Needham) M.; m. Carolyn Mary Holliday, Mar. 14, 1952; children: Evelyn, Mary. BA, Emory U., 1952, MA, 1953; PhD, Johns Hopkins U., 1959. Instr., then asst. prof. Yale U., New Haven, 1959-64; assoc. prof., then prof. dept. English Emory U., Atlanta, 1964-2000, chmn. dept., 1968-70, Candler prof. English, 1982-2000, dir. creative writing program, 1990-2000, retired, 2000. Editor: The Anniversaries (John Donne), 1963, A Dialogue of Comfort (St. Thomas More), vol. 12, 1977 and Epistola ad Pomeranum, vol. 7, 1990, Yale edit. More's complete works; author: Resultances, 1980 (Devins award for poetry 1980), Two Masters (co-winner Gt. Am. New Play Contest 9th Ann. Humana Festival New Am. Plays 1985), (with F. Watkins) Some Poems and Some Talk About Poetry, 1985, Within the Ribbons: 9 Stories, 1989, (play) The Trap, 1993, The Cockfighter: a Novel, 1998, Among Prisoners: Stories, 2000, (poems) The Emperors, 2001, Truc Hope: A Novel, 2002. With U.S. Army, 1952-55. Guggenheim Found. fellow, 1966-67, 78-79; recipient NEH transl. program fellowship, 1981-83, Nat. Endowment Arts Creative Writing Fellowship in Fiction, 1995-97, Disting. Teaching award, 1984, Univ. scholar/Tchr. of yr. award, 1989, Disting. Alumnus award The Marist Sch., 1993. Mem. MLA, AAUP. Roman Catholic. Home: 401 Adams St Decatur GA 30030-5207 also: Doublehead Gap Rd Ellijay GA 30540 Office: Emory U Dept Theater Studies 212 Rich Bldg Atlanta GA 30322-0001 E-mail: fmanley@emory.edu.

MANLEY, GERTRUDE ELLA, librarian, media specialist; b. Phila., Dec. 29, 1930; d. William Eugene and Anna G. (Price) Lomas; m. Harley E. Manley, Jr., July 20, 1957; children: Marc Alan, Karen Sue Manley Thornton, Gail Ann Manley Rivera. BRE, Shelton Coll., 1955; MSEd, MS in Libr. Edn., Queens Coll., 1958; postgrad., various. Libr. tchr. Plainedge (N.Y.) Sch. Dist., 1955-60; libr. dir. Huntington (N.Y.) Christian Sch., 1968-70; libr./media specialist Connetquot Ctrl. Sch. Dist. of Islip, Bohemia, N.Y., 1970—. Editor: Manley Family Newsletter, 1983—, LomasLines Newsletter, 1996—. Mem. nursery sch. bd. New Life Cmty. Ch., Sayville, N.Y., 1985-89, mem. missions com., 1996—, missionary corresponder, 1997—; adminstr. pre-sch. story time program, E.J. Bosti Sch., Bohemia, 1972—, sign lang. instr., 1988—, Huffine award chairperson, 1985—, spell bee judge, 1984—, arranger spkrs. program, 1988—, kindergarten screening participant, 1988—, numerous in-house site-base planning and mgmt. coms., 1990-93. Mem. N.Y. State Ret. Tchrs. Assn. (life), N.Y. State United Tchrs., Western Suffolk Ret. Tchrs. Assn. (life), Connetquot Tchrs. Assn. (chmn. scholarship com. 1978-93), Connetquot Ret. Tchrs. Assn. (rec. and corr. sec. 1993—), Descendants and Friends of 51st Pa. Vol. Infantry (charter). Baptist/Reformed Ch. of Am. Avocations: family history rsch., genealogy, authoring history articles, reading. Home: 171 Nathan Dr Bohemia NY 11716-1319 Office: Connetquot Ctrl Sch Dist Islip 780 Ocean Ave Bohemia NY 11716-3631 E-mail: trugem@optonline.net.

MANLEY, JOAN A(DELE) DANIELS, retired publisher; b. San Luis Obispo, Calif., Sept. 23, 1932; d. Carl and Della (Weinmann) Daniels; m. Jeremy C. Lanning, Mar. 17, 1956 (div. Sept. 1963); m. Donald H. Manley, Sept. 12, 1964 (div. 1985); m. William G. Houlton, May 31, 1991. BA, U. Calif., Berkeley, 1954; DBA (hon.), U. New Haven, 1974; LLD (hon.), Babson Coll., 1978. Sec. Doubleday & Co., Inc., N.Y.C., 1954-60; sales exec. Time Inc., 1960-66, v.p., 1971-75, group v.p., 1975-84, also bd. dir.; circulation dir. Time-Life Books, 1966-68, dir. sales, 1968-70, pub., 1970-76; chmn. bd. Time-Life Books Inc., 1976-80. Vice chmn. bd. Book-of-the-Month Club, Inc., N.Y.C., until 1984; supervising dir. Time-Life Internat. (Nederland) B.V., Amsterdam, until 1984; bd. dirs. Dreyfus Founders Funds, Sara Lee Corp., Moore Corp., Ltd. Past trustee Mayo Found., Rochester, Minn., Nat. Repertory Orch., William Benton Found.; former mem. adv. coun. Stanford U. Bus. Sch., Haas Sch. Bus. U. Calif. Named to Direct Mktg. Hall of Fame, 1993; U. Calif.-Berkeley fellow, 1989. Mem. Assn. Am. Pubs. (past chmn.).

MANLEY, JOHN, Canadian government official; b. Ottawa, Ontario, Canada, Jan. 5, 1950; s. John Joseph and Mildred Charlotte (Scharf) Manley; m. Judith Mary Rae, Apr. 21, 1973; children: Rebecca Jane, David John, Sarah Kathleen. Attended, Carleton U.; Doctorate (hon.), U. Ottawa. Law clerk for Rt. Hon. Bora Laskin Chief Justice Can., 1976-77; chair Ottawa-Carleton Bd. Trade, 1985-86; min. Industry Govt. of Can., 1993-2000, min. Western Econ. Diversification, min. Atlantic Can. Opportunities Agy., 1996; min. for Can. Econ. Devel. for Que. Regions, 1996-2000; min. fgn. affairs, 2000—02; dep. prime minister of Can. and minister infrastructure and crown corps., 2002—; chair cabinet com. on pub. security and anti-terrorism, 2001—. Chmn. cabinet com. on pub. security and anti-terrorism Ho. of Commons, Ottawa, Canada, 2001—, min. infrastructure and crown corps., 2002—, polit. min. for Ontario and chmn. cabinet com. on econ. union and social union, 2002—. Elected to H. of C. g.e., 1988. Named Time Can. Mag. Newsmaker of the Yr., 2001. Avocation: marathon running. Office: House of Commons Rm 209S Centre Block Ottawa ON K1A 0A6 Canada Mailing: Office of Dep Prime Minister Canada 55 Metcalfe St 15th Floor Ottawa ON K1A 0A3 Canada Office Fax: 613-995-1534. E-mail: manlej@parl.gc.ca.

MANLEY, JOHN HUGO, computing technology executive, educator; b. Highland Park, Mich., July 9, 1932; s. Hugo Edward and Linda Amelia (Kuure) M.; m. Josephine Theresa Catanzaro, Sept. 3, 1958; children: Lisa Linn, Michele Ann, John David, Marc Darrin. B. Metall. Engring., Cornell U., 1955; MS Indsl. Engring., U. Pitts., 1965, PhD, 1971. Metall. engr. GE, Schenectady, N.Y., 1955-56; commd. 2d lt. USAF, 1956, advanced through grades to lt. col., 1973, ret., 1976; asst. to dir. Johns Hopkins Applied Physics Lab., Laurel, Md., 1976-80; exec. ITT Corp., Stratford, Conn., 1980-83; v.p. Nastec Corp., Southfield, Mich., 1983-85; dir. Software Engring. Inst. Software Engring. Inst. Carnegie Mellon U., Pitts., 1985-87; pres., chmn. Computing Tech. Transition, Inc., Wilmington, Del., 1983—; prof. manufacturing and info. tech. systems engring., dir. mfg. sys. engring. prog. U. Pitts., 1987—2002. Mem. tech. adv. bd. Tartan Inc., Pitts.; dir. Concurrent Techs. Corp., Johnstown, Pa.; mem. com. on nat. weather svc. modernization NRC, 1991-94. Editor-in-chief Jour. Systems and Software, 1978-82; contbr. articles to profl. jours. Pres. Point Field Community Assn., Millersville, Md., 1979-80; v.p. Greater Severna Park Coun., Severna Park, Md., 1980. Lt. col. USAF, 1955-76, Vietnam. Decorated Legion of Merit, Bronze Star. Mem. IEEE Computer Soc. (TC exec. bd.), Soc. Mfg. Engrs., Assn. Computing Machinery, Am. Soc. Engring. Edn., Pitts. Athletic Assn. Republican. Episcopalian.

MANLEY, JUDITH L. director; b. Columbus, Ohio; B in Bus., Ohio State U., 1970; MEd, Xavier U., 1986. Copy writer advt. agy., Columbus, 1970—74; program asst. Ohio State U., 1974—. Advisor, counselor dept. Spanish and Portuguese Ohio State U., Columbus, 1991—. Author poems. Area commr. Greater Hilltop Area Commn., Columbus, 1989—; bd. mem. Greater Hilltop Cmty. Devel. Corp., 1989—; alumnae Leadership Columbus, 1993. Named Vol. of the Month, Children's Hosp., Columbus, 2002. Mem.: ACA. Avocations: writing, photography, music, theater .

MANLEY, LANCE FILSON, data processing consultant; b. Atlanta, Dec. 8, 1945; s. Vern Paul and Beth (Filson) M.; m. Sandra Faye Parris, Oct. 31, 1964 (div. 1967); 1 child, Lance Filson Jr.; m. Elizabeth Jane Wallace, Oct. 31, 1968; children: Jeffrey Lance, Heather Leigh. Student, John Marshall Law Sch., 1964-66, Shorter Coll., Rome, Ga., 1967-68, Brevard Coll., Cocoa, Fla., 1968-69, U. Mid Fla., 1972-74; tech. cert., Programming Systems Inst., Atlanta, 1967, RCA Edn. Ctr., L.A., 1968, Burroughs Edn. Ctr., Detroit, 1973, Honeywell Edn. Ctr., Atlanta, 1976, Info. Sci., San Antonio, 1977, IBM Edn. Ctr., Atlanta, 1978, Emory U., 1988, Platinum Tech., Atlanta, 1993, 96. Cert. in systems analysis and design Am. Mgmt. Assn., 1979; cert. brainbench. Sr. computer operator Fed. Elec. Corp., Cape Kennedy, Fla., 1966-68, Universal Studios, Universal City, Calif., 1968-70; program analyst State of Fla., Jacksonville, 1970-73, Fla. Nat. Bank, Jacksonville, 1973-76; sr. program analyst Fulton Nat. Bank, Atlanta, 1977-78, 1st Nat. Bank Atlanta, 1978-80; cons. Ins. Systems Am., Atlanta, 1980, Cotton States Ins., Atlanta, 1981, State of Ga., Atlanta, 1981-83, Decatur Fed., Atlanta, 1981, C&S Bank, Atlanta, 1982, Cox Communication, Atlanta, 1983, Emory U., Atlanta, 1984-88; staff cons. So. Co. Svcs., 1988-93; sr. info. sys. software engr. Ga. Bapt. Med. Ctr., 1993-96; database adminstr. State of Ga. Dept. Adminstrv. Svcs., Tucker, 1996-97; sr. cons. GEAC, 1997, Federated Syss. Group, 1997—. Avocations: skiing, camping, fishing, music. Home: 2856 Langley Rd Loganville GA 30052-2227 Office: Federated Systems Group 5985 State Bridge Rd Duluth GA 30097 E-mail: lancemanley@hotmail.com.

MANLEY, NANCY JANE, environmental engineer; b. Ft. Smith, Ark., Sept. 13, 1951; d. Eugene Hailey and Mary Adele (Chave) M. BSE, Purdue U., 1974; MSE, U. Wash., 1976; postgrad., U. Minn., 1976-77; grad., Air Command and Staff Coll., 1984, Exec. Leadership Devel. Program Dept. Def., 1988. Lic. profl. engr., Ga.; registered environ. mgr. Sanitary engr. Minn. Dept. Health, Mpls., 1976-77; sanitary engr. water supply EPA, Chgo., 1977, leader primacy unit water supply Atlanta, 1977-79, leader tech. assistance team, 1979-82; chief environ. and contract planning, project mgr. Grand Bay Range design USAF, Moody AFB, Ga., 1982-84, dep. base civil engr. Carswell AFB, Tex., 1984-86, Scott AFB, Ill., 1986-89, mem. tech. adv. com. Scott AFB master plan study Belleville, 1986-89, dep. base civil engr. Robins AFB, Ga., 1989-91, acting chief engr., 1990-91, chief pollution prevention divsn., dir. environ. mgmt., 1991-93; chief engr. divsn. 78 Civil Engr. Group, 1993—. Mem. Fla. Tech. Adv. Com. for Injection Wells, Tallahassee, 1980-82, Nat. Implementation Team for Underground Injection Control Program, Washington, 1979-82, tech. panel Nat. Groundwater Protection Strategy Hearings, 1981; judge Internat. Sci. and Engring. Fair, 1986. Active various ch. support activities, 1969-74; sec. Perry Area Hist. Soc., 1991-93; vol. Meals-on-Wheels, Girl Scouts U.S., Ga. Voluntary Tech. Assistance Group, others, various locations, 1982—; founder, crisis intervention counselor Midwest Alliance, West Lafayette, Ind., 1970-74; active St. Louis Math. and Sci. Network Day, 1989, Adopt-a-Sch. Program, Lebanon, Ill., 1987-89; scientist by mail Boston Mus. Sci., 1989-99, Mathcounts, 1991—; mentor Purdue U., U. Washington, others, 1986—. Recipient Presdl. Point of Light award USAF, 1991, Disting. Govt. Svc. award Dallas/Ft. Worth Fed. Exec. Bd., 1986, Lady of the Black Knights award 19th Air Refueling Wing, 1991, Celebration of Women in Engring. award Nat. Acad. Engring., 2000; named Engr. of Yr., Air Force Material Command, 1998, 2000, Robins AFB, 1997, 99, Ga. Engr. of Yr., Ga. Soc. Profl. Engrs., 2001, others. Fellow ASCE (vol. Ga. sect.); mem. NSPE (bd. dirs. 1991-94, 97—, v.p. local chpt. 1994-95, pres.-elect local chpt. 1995-96, pres. 1996-97, 2001, nat. govt. and legis. affairs com. 1999—, state dir. 2000—), Soc. Women Engrs. (regional mem.-at-large rep. 1990-93, sr. mem. local officers 1979-82, 84-86), Am. Women in Sci., Soc. Am. Mil. Engrs. (local membership and contingency coms., local bd. dirs., profl. soc. liaison 1998, sec. 1999-2001). Achievements include assignment as 1st woman dep. base civil engr. USAF, Carswell AFB. Office: 778 CES/CEC Robins AFB GA 31098 E-mail: nancy.manley@robins.af.mil., nanjmanley@ccs.com.

MANLEY, RICHARD WALTER, insurance executive; b. Malone, N.Y., Dec. 26, 1934; s. Walter E. and Ruth (St. Mary) M.; m. Linda Kimberlin, Dec. 18, 1965; children: Stephanie, Christopher. BS in Bus., U. So. Miss., 1960. Cert. real estate broker. Account exec. Colonial Life and Accident, Hattiesburg, Miss., 1960-63, dist. mgr. Oklahoma City, 1963-66, regional dir. Denver, 1966-76, zone dir., 1976-82; pres. Commonwealth Gen. Group, 1982-98, Manley Properties Inc., Denver, 1982-90, Richard W. Manley Commonwealth Gen. Grps., Inc., Denver, 1982—. Cons. Capitol Am. Life Ins. Co., Cleve., 1987-96; bd. dirs. (merco) Mercy Hosp., Denver, 1982-87. With USAF, 1956-59. Mem. Cherry Hills C. of C., Rotary, Alpha Tau Omega. Roman Catholic. Avocations: golfing, racquetball, running. Home: 6510 E Lake Pl Englewood CO 80111-4421 E-mail: manleydick@aol.com.

MANLEY, ROBERT EDWARD, lawyer, economist; b. Cin., Nov. 24, 1935; s. John M. and Helen Catherine (McCarthy) M.; m. Roberta L. Anzinger, Oct. 21, 1971 (div. 1980); 1 child, Robert Edward. ScB in Econs, Xavier U., 1956; AM in Econ. Theory, U. Cin., 1957; JD, Harvard U., 1960; postgrad., London Sch. Econs. and Polit. Sci., 1960, MIT, 1972. Bar: Ohio 1960, U.S. Supreme Ct. 1970. Pvt. practice law, Cin., 1960—; chmn. Manley Burke, 1977. Taft teaching fellow econs. U. Cin., 1956-57, vis. lectr. community planning law Coll. Design, Architecture and Art, 1967-73, adj. assoc. prof. urban planning Coll. Design, Architecture, Art and Planning, 1972-81, adj. prof., 1981—, adj. prof. law, 1980—. Author: Metropolitan School Desegregation, 1978, (with Robert N. Cook) Management of Land and Environment, 1981, others; chmn. editl. adv. bd. Urban Lawyer, 1986-95. Mem. Hamilton County Pub. Defender Commn., 1976-79; trustee HOPE, Cin., Albert J. Ryan Found.; counsel, co-founder Action Housing for Greater Cin.; mem. Spl. Commn. on Formation U. Cin. Health Maintenance Orgn., Mayor Cin. Spl. Com. on Housing; chmn. Cin. Environ. Adv. Coun., 1975-76; trustee The Americas Fund for Ind. Univs., 1987-2000; trustee Ohio Planning Conf., 1982-91, pres., 1987-89, trustee, 1987-90; sec. Cin. Mounted Patrol Com., 1993—; active Bd. Cin. Downtown Coun., 1991-98. Mem. ABA (coun. sect. local govt. law 1976-80, 81-85, 88-92), Ohio Bar Assn., Cin. Bar Assn., Am. Judicature Soc., Law and Soc. Assn., Nat. Coun. Crime and Delinquency, Harvard U. Law Sch. Assn.

Cin. (pres. 1970-71), Am. Econ. Assn., Am. Acad. Polit. and Social Sci., Queen City Club, Explorers Club (N.Y.C.) (trustee, sec. Clark chpt. 1992—), Athenaeum Club (Phila.), S.Am. Explorers Club (Lima, Peru). Republican. Roman Catholic. Office: Manley Burke 225 W Court St Cincinnati OH 45202-1052 E-mail: info@manleyburke.com.

MANLEY, ROBERT JOSEPH, school administrator; b. N.Y.C., Apr. 27, 1942; s. Joseph Anthony and Edith Ruth (Hopkins) M.; m. Kathryn Ann McCormick, Aug. 28, 1965' children: Michael, Patrick. BA in Spanish, Iona Coll., 1963; MA in Humanities, Hofstra U., 1970; Profl. Diploma in Adminstrn., St. John's U., 1975, PhD in Adminstrn., 1979. Tchr. W. Babylon (N.Y.) Union Free Sch. Dist., 1965-79, asst. supt., 1984-87, dep. supt., 1987-90, supt., 1990—; asst. prin. Babylon (N.Y.) Union Free Sch. Dist., 1979-82; prin. Plainedge High Sch. Union Free Sch. Dist., N. Massapequa, N.Y., 1982-84. Adj. prof. St. John's U., Jamaica, N.Y., 1980—; pres. con. Nat. Edn. Leadership Services, W. Islip, N.Y., 1979—; pres. Suffolk coop. library system bd., Bellport, N.Y., 1985—. Author: (poems) The Bark, 1969. Mem. N.Y. State Commrs. Council on Gifted, Albany, N.Y., 1983—. Recipient Community Service proclamation Town of Islip, 1980. Mem. Nat. Assn. for Supervision and Curriculum, N.Y. Assn. for Supervision and Curriculum, N.Y. Acad. Scis., ALA, N.Y. Library Assn., W. Islip C. of C. (pres. 1979-80), Phi Delta Kappa. Democrat. Roman Catholic. Avocations: racquetball, swimming, golf. Office: West Babylon Union Free Schs 10 Farmingham Rd West Babylon NY 11704

MANLEY, WALTER WILSON, II, lawyer, business educator; b. Gainesville, Fla., Mar. 16, 1947; s. Walter Wilson and Marjorie Iley (Watkins) M.; children: Marjorie, Benjamin. BA, Fla. So. Coll., 1969; JD, Duke U., 1972; MBA, Harvard U., 1975. Assoc. Blackwell, Walker & Gray, Miami, Fla., 1972-75; pvt. practice, Lakeland, 1975-84; prof. bus. adminstrn. Fla. State U., Tallahassee, 1985—; ptnr. MacFarlane, Ferguson, Allison & Kelly, 1991-94. Vis. prof. bus. adminstrn. Ridley Hall Coll. and Cambridge Fedn. Theol. Colls., Eng., 1988-90, Cambridge U. Faculties of Mgmt. Studies, Philosophy, Law, Social and Polit. Scis. and Divinity, 1989-90; pres. Exeter Leadership Cos. Inst., Inc., Tallahassee, 1989-94, Fla. North Shore Tech. Ctrs., Inc., 1995-97. Author: Critical Issues in Business Conduct, 1990, Executive's Handbook of Model Business Conduct Codes, 1991, Handbook of Good Business Practice, 1992, What Florida Thinks, 1997, The History of the Supreme Court of Florida and Its Predecessor Courts, 1821-1917, 1997 (nominated Littleton Griswold prize in Am. Law & Soc. 1998) Chmn. Fla. Endowment Found. for Vocat. Rehab., 1991-93; bd. dirs. Fla. Real Property and Casualty Joint Underwriters Assn., 1987-91, Consumer Coun. Fla., 1992-99; bd. visitors Duke U. Sch. Law, 1991-98; trustee The Webb Sch., BellBuckle, Tenn., 1983-92, nat. fund chmn., 1982; trustee Ctr. for Fla. History; pres. Polk County Legal Aid Soc.; legal editor Harbus, ofcl. Class of 1975 rep. 350th anniversary Harvard U. Recipient Outstanding Alumnus award Fla. So. Coll., 1999. Fellow Fla. Supreme Ct. Hist. Soc. (disting. historian); mem. ABA, Fla. Bar Assn. (Pres.' Pro Bono Svc. award 1985), Lakeland Bar Assn. (pres.), Capital Duke Club (founder, past pres.), Tallahassee Quarterback Club Found. (past chmn., Biletnikoff award), Psi Chi, Omicron Delta Kappa, Sigma Alpha Epsilon (Nation's Outstanding Educator award 1998), Phi Delta Phi. Episcopalian. Avocations: hot air balloons, gliders, fly fishing, wing shooting. Home: 2804 Rabbit Hills Rd Tallahassee FL 32308-0837

MANLY, BRYAN FREDERICK JOHN, statistics educator; b. London, May 27, 1944; s. Ronald Eric George Manly and Joan Amelia (Rose) Edwards; m. Liliana Gonzalez, May 30, 1991. BSc, City Univ., London, 1966, DSc, 1993. Chartered statistician, Eng. Statistician Fisons Ltd., Felixstowe, Eng., 1967-68; lectr. U. Salford, Eng., 1969-71, U. Papua & New Guinea, 1971-73; sr. lectr. U. Otago, New Zealand, 1973-81, assoc. prof. New Zealand, 1982-86, prof. New Zealand, 1987—. Author: The Statistics of Natural Selection, 1983, Multivariate Statistical Methods, 1986, 94, Stage Structural Populations, 1990, Randomization and Monte Carlo Methods in Biology, 1991. Fellow Royal Soc. of New Zealand (treas. Otago br. 1992—), Royal Stats. Soc. Avocation: wining and dining. Office: U Otago PO Box 56 Dunedin New Zealand

MANLY, SAMUEL, lawyer; b. Louisville, Aug. 8, 1945; s. Samuel III and Nell Thornton (Montgomery) M.; m. Tacie Jarrett Bond, Aug. 8, 1970 (div. 1978); children: Julie Elder, Elizabeth Meriwether. BA cum laude, Yale U., 1967; JD, U. Va., 1970. Bar: Ky. 1971, U.S. Dist. Ct. (we. and ea. dists.) Ky. 1972, U.S. Dist. Ct. (so. dist.) Ind. 1972, U.S. Dist. Ct. (we. dist.) Mich. 1995, U.S. Ct. Appeals (6th cir.) 1972, U.S. Ct. Appeals (10th cir.) 1997, U.S. Supreme Ct. 1997. Pres. Madison House, U. Va., Charlottesville, 1968-70; assoc. Greenebaum Doll & McDonald, Louisville, 1970-76; ptnr. Reisz Blackburn Manly & Treitz, 1976-78; sr. ptnr. Manly & Sears, 1978-81, Manly & Heleringer, Louisville, 1981-84; pvt. practice Law Offices of Samuel Manly, 1984—. Sec., gen. counsel Gibbs-Inman Co., Louisville, 1972-78; contract atty. FDIC, Washington, 1976-84; counsel Winston Products Co., 1988—; dir. defender svcs. U.S. Dist. Ct. (we. dist.) Ky., 1992-94; mem. drug policy com. Ky. Criminal Justice Coun., 1998-2000. Contract atty. Jefferson County, 1977-78, City of Louisville, 1978-83. Capt. USAR, 1967-86. Fellow: Ky. Bar Found. (life); mem.: ATLA, ABA (com. on products liability, subcom uninsured mfrs. sect. ligitation, com. on self-insurers and risk mgrs. sect. tort and ins. law practice), Am. Bankruptcy Inst., Assn. Fed. Def. Attys., Am. Judicature Soc., Comml. Law League of Am., Fed. Bar Assn., Ky. Acad. Trial Lawyers, Nat. Assn. Criminal Def. Lawyers, Ky. Assn. Criminal Def. Lawyers (pres. 2001—, bd. dirs., exec. com. 1986—), Louisville Bar Assn., Ky. Bar Assn. (com. on legal ethics 1978—84, 1996—98), Louisville Boat Club. Republican. Avocations: classical music, fishing, golf. Home: 407 S Sherrin Ave Louisville KY 40207-3817 Office: Law Offices of Samuel Manly 239 S 5th St Ste 1606 Louisville KY 40202-3208

MANLY, SARAH LETITIA, retired state legislator, ophthalmic photographer, angiographer; b. Greenville, S.C., Feb. 1, 1927; d. Victor Harris and Elsie Clippard (Burnett) Gillespie; m. Basil Manly IV, Sept. 11, 1947; children: Sarah Manly Cornish, Basil V, Jean Manly McDowell, Mary Manly Mounce. BS cum laude, Furman U., 1947; postgrad., MIT, 1972; MEd, Clemson U., 1974; postgrad., Cambridge (Eng.) U., 1981. Cert. physics tchr., Pa., S.C.; cert. retinal angiographer. Ward sec. Roper Hosp., Charleston, S.C., 1947; analytical chemist Parker Labs., 1948; tchr. sci. Upper Darby (Pa.) Sch. Dist., 1961-63; tchr. physics Sch. Dist. Greenville (S.C.) County, 1963-64, 70-76; ophthalmic photographer Basil Manly IV, MD, Greenville, 1976-96; lectr. physics Clemson (S.C.) U., 1979-81. Cons. MIT, Cambridge, 1972-75, Georgetown U., Washington, 1974-76, NASA, Houston, 1974-76. Editor, cons. physics study guides MIT, 1972-75; editor lab. materials NASA, 1974-76; contbr. articles to profl. jours. Trustee Sch. Dist. Greenville County, 1976-88. Named S.C. Legislator of Yr., S.C. Sch. Bds. Assn., 1991, Hon. Alumnus of Phi Beta Kappa, 1994. Mem. Greenville County Med. Aux. (sec. 1953-54), Delta Kappa Gamma. Democrat. Baptist. Avocations: travel, reading, volunteering. Home: 2 Chanticleer Dr Greenville SC 29605-3106

MANLY, WILLIAM DONALD, metallurgist; b. Malta, Ohio, Jan. 13, 1923; s. Edward James and Thelma (Campbell) M.; m. Jane Wilden, Feb. 9, 1949; children: Hugh, Ann, Marc, David. Student, Antioch Coll., 1941-42; BS, U. Notre Dame, 1947, MS, 1949; postgrad., U. Tenn., 1950-55; PhD in Engring. (hon.), U. N.D., 2000. Metallurgist Oak Ridge Nat. Lab., 1949-60, mgr. gas cooled reactor program, 1960-64; mgr. materials research Union Carbide Corp., N.Y.C., 1964-65; gen. mgr. Union Carbide Corp. (Stellite div.), 1967-69, v.p. Kokomo, Ind., 1969-70; sr. v.p. Cabot Corp., Boston, 1970-83, exec. v.p., 1983-86; ret., 1986; also dir. chmn. adv. com. for reactor safety AEC, 1964-65. Served with USMC, 1943-46. Recipient Honor award U. Notre Dame, 1974, Nat. Medal of Tech., Nat. Sci. Found., 1993. Fellow Am. Soc. Metals (hon. mem., pres. 1972-73, medal for advanced rsch. 1987), AIME, Am. Nuclear Soc. (Merit award 1966); mem. Nat. Acad. Engring., Nat. Assn. Corrosion Engrs., Metall. Soc., Masons. Presbyterian. Home: 103 Cypress Ln Oak Ridge TN 37830-8772

MANN, ALFRED, pharmaceutical executive; b. Portland, Oreg., 1925; MS in Physics, UCLA; DHL (hon.) , U. So. Calif., 2001, Johns Hopkins U., 2001. Chmn., CEO MannKind Corp., Sylmar, Calif.; chmn., co-CEO Advanced Bionics Corp.; chmn. emeritus MiniMed Inc.; founder, chmn. Med. Rsch. Group, Inc.; chmn., CEO Siemens-Pacesetter, Inc. and predecessor Pacesetter Sys., Inc.; pres. Spectrolab, Heliotek. Chmn. bd. trustees Alfred Mann Found., Alfred Mann Inst., U. So. Calif.; U. So. Calif. trustee mem. bd. overseers Keck U. So. Calif. Sch. Medicine; chmn. So. Calif. Biomed. Coun., Second Sight, LLC, Allecure Corp., Quallion, LLC, CTL Immunotherapy, Inc., Pharm. Discovery Co., Inc. Named Man of Yr., WISE Sr. Svcs., 1999, Humanitarian of Yr., House Ear Inst., 1999; named one of 10 Most Influential People on Tch Coast, L.a. Times, 1999; recipient Spirit of Edison award for cmty. svc., Thomas Edison State Coll., 1999, Vision of the Future award, RP Internat., 1999, Reynolds Soc. Achievement award, Harvard Med. Sch., 1999. Fellow: Am. Inst. Med. and Biol. Engring.; mem.: NAE. Office: MannKind Corp 12744 San Fernando Rd Lake View Terrace CA 91342-3728

MANN, ALFRED N. chemical engineer; b. Cin., July 27, 1929; s. Jacob Mann and Margit Klein; m. Genevieve Elaine Wilkinson, Sept. 28, 1951; children: Carolyn, Martha. BS in Chem. Engring., Cornell U., 1951; MS in Chem. Engring., U. Pitts., 1961. Cert. profl. engr. Pa. Engr. Shell Chem. Co., Wilmington, Calif., 1951-57, Gulf R&D Co., Pitts., 1957-83; cons. United Energy Group, 1984-90; prin. engr. Burns & Roe Svcs., 1991-99, Parsons Corp., Pitts., 1999—. Co-author: Economics of Present and Future Fossil-Based Electricity Generation, 1985. With U.S. Army, 1953-55. Mem. Air and Waste Mgmt. Assn., Assn. Energy Engrs. Episcopalian. Avocations: nutrition, fitness, gardening. Home: 1251 N Sheridan Ave Pittsburgh PA 15206-1757 Office: Parsons Corp PO Box 10940 Pittsburgh PA 15236-0940 Fax: 412-661-4732. E-mail: al.mann@pp.netl.doe.gov., mann@netl.doe.gov.

MANN, ANTHONY, minister, dean; b. N.Y.C., Jan. 3, 1959; s. William Benjamin and Patricia Claudette Mann; m. Tanya Yvonne Duncan, Dec. 26, 1980; children: William Anthony, Tiffany Kimberly. BA, Coll. New Rochelle, 2000; cert. in theology, Princeton Theol. Sem., 1998. V.p. C & L Badger Inc., N.Y.C., 1982; optical technician SUNY, 1982—85; corrections officer NY State Correctional Svcs., Bedford Hills, 1985—93; dean of students N.Y.C. Bd. Edn., Bronx, 2000—02; pastor Bapt. Temple Ch., N.Y.C., 2001—. Bd. dirs., clergy Harlem Hosp., N.Y.C., 1994—97; bd. dirs. Partnership for Homeless, 1994—98, Salvation Army, N.Y.C., 1997—2000. Specialist 4 U.S. Army, 1976—82. Recipient proclamation, Gov. George Pataki, NY. Mem.: Bapt. Min. Conf. Greater N.Y. Baptist. Avocations: horseback riding, tennis, researching ancient icons and artifacts, analyzing Hebrew scripture. Office: Bapt Temple Ch 18 W 116th St New York NY 10026 Office Fax: 212-996-0334. E-mail: anthonyshalom@aol.com.

MANN, BARLOW TREADWELL, financial consultant, lawyer; b. Mobile, Ala., Sept. 5, 1953; s. Cameron Mann and Jane Snowden (Treadwell) Mann Martin; m. Roma Joyce Crockett, Apr. 23, 1981; children: Arthur Barlow Treadwell, Jr., Lawson Henderson. B.A. with honors, Tulane U., 1975; J.D., Memphis State U., 1978. Bar: Tenn. 1978, U.S. Dist. Ct. (we. dist.) Tenn. 1979. Assoc. Memphis Area Legal Clinic, Memphis State U. Clinic, 1977-78; asst. dir. devel. Memphis State U., 1978-82; dir. devel. U. Tenn., Memphis, 1982-84; COO, v.p., legal counsel Robert F. Sharpe and Co., Memphis, 1984— . Contbr. articles to profl. jours. Mem. ABA, Tenn. Bar Assn., Memphis Bar Assn., Shelby County Bar Assn., Council for Advancement and Support of Edn., Nat. Soc. Fundraising Execs., Phi Alpha Delta (pres. 1977-78), Delta Kappa Epsilon (pres. 1974-75). Clubs: Memphis Country, University (Memphis). Home: 4581 Normandy Ave Memphis TN 38117-2421

MANN, BILLIE ARNELL, neuroscience nurse, radiologic technologist; b. Oceanside, Calif., Jan. 20, 1952; d. William Amos and Peggy Joyce (Steele) Mann. Radiology Technologist, Norfolk Gen. Sch. Radiology, Va., 1975; ASN, Tidewater C.C., Portsmouth, Va., 1983; BS in Health Care Adminstrn., St. Joseph's Coll., 1989; MS in Health Care Adminstrn., Ctrl. Mich. U., 1990; BSN, Graceland Coll., 1999; postgrad., Touro U. Internat., 2000—. Registered radiologic technologist; RN, Va., N.C.; cert. rehab. nurse; cert. neurosci. nurse. Radiology technologist Norfolk Gen. Hosp., 1976-83; shift head nurse Brain Injury unit Med. Coll. of Va., Richmond, 1984-89; staff nurse Southea. Regional Rehab., Fayetteville, N.C., 1989-90; staff primary nurse stroke acute care unit Duke Med. Ctr., Durham, 1990-91; clin. charge nurse II Cysto Ste. U. N.C., Chapel Hill, 1991-92, nurse edn. clinician divsn. neurosurgery, 1992-95; clin. evaluator for rehab. svcs. U. N.C. Hosps., 1995-97, nurse edn. clinician divsn. neurosurgery, 1997—. Recipient Nursing Process award Med. Coll. Va., 1987, Excellence in Adminstrv. Practice award, 1988. Mem. Assn. for Rehab. Nursing, Am. Registry of Radiologic Technologists, Am. Congress of Rehab. Medicine, Nat. Head Injury Found., N.C. Assn. Rehab. Nursing, N.C. Head Injury Found., Neurosurgery Nursing Assn., Nat. Soc. Neurosurg. Nursing, Sigma Iota Epsilon. Roman Catholic. Avocations: Russian, needlepoint, stained glass. E-mila. Home: Apt 303 5122 Copper Ridge Dr Durham NC 27707-5592 Office: U NC Hosps at Chapel Hll Divsn Neurosurgery C B7060 Chapel Hill NC 27599-7060 E-mail: Bmann7742@aol.com.

MANN, BOB BAKER, urologist; b. Newnan, Ga., June 6, 1953; s. Frances (King) M.; m. Linda Jean Hibbs, Nov. 28, 1986; children: Spencer, Staci, Baker, Shrader. BS, Emory U., 1975; MD, Emory U. Sch. Medicine, 1979. Diplomate Am. Bd. Urology. Intern Emory U. Affiliated Hosps., Atlanta, 1979-80; urologist PAPP Clinic, Newnan, 1984—; resident in urology Emory U. Affiliated Hosps., Atlanta, 1980-84. Bd. dirs. OutMed, Inc., Newnan. Bd. dirs. Ctrl. Bapt. Ch., Newnan, 1994—. Fellow Am. Coll. Surgeons; mem. Am. Urol. Assn., Ga. Urol. Assn., Atlanta Urol. Assn. Avocations: golf, reading, travel. Office: PAPP Clinic 15 Cavender St Newnan GA 30263-1931

MANN, BRUCE ALAN, lawyer, investment banker; b. Chgo., Nov. 28, 1934; s. David I. and Lillian (Segal) M.; m. Naomi Cooks, Aug. 31, 1980; children: Sally Mann Stull, Jonathan Hugh, Andrew Ross. BBA, U. Wis., 1955, SJD, 1957. Bar: Wis. 1957, N.Y. 1958, Calif. 1961. Assoc. Davis, Polk & Wardwell, N.Y.C., 1957-60, Pillsbury, Madison & Sutro, San Francisco, 1960-66, ptnr., 1967-83; adminstrv. mng. dir. L.F. Rothschild Unterberg Towbin, 1983-87; ptnr. Morrison & Foerster, 1987—; sr. mng. dir. W.R. Hambrecht & Co., 1999—. Cons. SEC, 1978; vis. prof. law Georgetown U., 1978; lectr. in field. Author: (with Mattson) California Corporate Practice and Forms, 1999; contbr. articles to profl. jours. Served with USAR, 1957. Mem.: NASD (gov.-at-large 1981—83), ABA (chmn. fed. regulation of securities com. 1981—83, mem. bus. law sect. coun. 1996—99, standing com. on ethics and profl. responsibility 1997—, standing com. on venture capital 2000—), Bar Assn. San Francisco (bd. dirs. 1974—75), State Bar Calif., Am. Law Inst., The Family Club. Office: Morrison & Foerster 425 Market St Ste 3100 San Francisco CA 94105-2482 E-mail: bmann@mofo.com.

MANN, CEDRIC ROBERT, retired institute administrator, oceanographer; b. Auckland, N.Z., Feb. 14, 1926; came to Can., 1949; s. Duncan and Winifred Mary (Hood) M.; m. Muriel Frances May, Dec. 19, 1950; 1 child, Robin Carl B.Sc., U. N.Z., Auckland, 1948, M.Sc., 1950; PhD, U. B.C., Vancouver, Can., 1953; D.Eng., N.S. Tech. Coll., Halifax, Can., 1972. Physicist Naval Research Establishment, Halifax, N.S., Can., 1953-61; oceanographer Atlantic Oceanographic Lab., Can., 1961-75, dir. Can., 1975-78; dir. gen. Bedford Inst. Oceanography, Can., 1978-79, Inst. Ocean Scis., Sidney, B.C., Can., 1979-87. Assoc. prof. Dalhousie U., Halifax, 1961-75; chmn. sci. adv. bd. Intergovtl. Oceanographic Commn., Paris, 1978-81; mem. Can. Climate Planning Bd., Ottawa, 1983-86; chmn. Sea Use Council, Seattle, 1981-86. Contbr. articles to profl. jours. Fellow Royal Soc. Can.; mem. Can. Meteorol. and Oceanographic Soc. (life, recipient J.P. Tully medal in Oceanography, 1994). Anglican. Avocations: golf; gardening. Home: 301-2373 Henry Ave Sidney BC Canada V8L 2B4

MANN, CHARLES FREDERICK, language educator, translator, author; b. Gloucester, Mass., July 27, 1946; s. John Jacob Mann and Evelyn Ann Salah. BA cum laude, U. Ottawa, Ont., Can., 1969; MA, Boston Theol. Inst., 1973; license-es-lettres, La Sorbonne, Paris, 1974; PhD, l'Inst. Catholique de Paris, 1978. Ordained to ministry Cath. Ch., 1973. Admissions officer U. Ottawa, 1964-66; H.S. tchr. Ottawa schs., 1966-69; head religious edn. St. Mary's Parish, Marlborough, Mass., 1973-75; French interpreter Claude Davie Media, Paris, 1975-78; French translator, linguistic cons. Univers Pubs., 1978-80; French tchr. Boston Sch. Modern Langs., 1980-82; dir. students Tutoring Svc. of San Francisco, 1982-90; fgn. lang. tutor U. Calif., Berkeley, 1991—. ESL coord. Fgn. Lang. Inst., San Francisco, 1991—2001. Author: Madeleine Delbrêl: A Life Beyond Boundaries, 1996; translator: Jeanne Jugan, 1997, God Behind Bars, 1999, We, the Ordinary People of the Streets, 2000. Elections inspector San Francisco City Hall, 1982—; reading tutor San Francisco Pub. Libr., 1982—; vol. Project Head Start, San Francisco, 1995—; vol. literacy program Ctrl. YMCA of San Francisco, 1995—. Named Vol. of Yr., San Francisco Elections Office, 1995; recipient Favorite Book of Yr. award Nat. Cath. Reporter, 1999, Excellence in Translation award Paulist Press, 1999, Univers Media, 2000. Fellow Book Coun. San Francisco; mem. Amnesty Internat., Small Pubs. Assn. No. Calif., Fgn. Lang Tchrs. Assn. Am. Democrat. Roman Catholic. Avocations: writing, language research, weightlifting, global affairs, contemporary spirituality. Home: 954 Geary St Apt 55 San Francisco CA 94109

MANN, CHARLES ROY, statistician; b. N.Y.C., Mar. 27, 1941; s. Gerard and Gertrude (Krieger) M. BS in Applied Math., Poly. U. N.Y., 1961; MS in Math. Stats., Mich. State U., 1963; PhD in Stats., U. Mo., 1969. Asst. prof. stats. George Washington U., Washington, 1969-73; head stats. divsn. Group Ops., Inc., 1973-77; pres. Charles R. Mann Assocs., Inc., 1977—. Cons. in field. Contbr. articles to profl. jours. Mem. No. Va. C.C. Bd., 1978-82. Fellow Am. Statis. Assn.; mem. Inst. Math. Stats., Washington Statis. Soc., Profl. Testing Coun. of Met. Washington. Home: 2920 Hickory St Alexandria VA 22305-2513 Office: 1730 K St NW Washington DC 20006-3833

MANN, CLARENCE CHARLES, real estate company official; b. Oradell, N.J., Oct. 15, 1929; s. Clarence Theodore and Martha Barbara (Koster) M.; m. Joan Elizabeth Schnoor, Nov. 25, 1951 (div. Jan. 1985); 1 child, Gary John. BA, NYU, 1951; MA, U. Pa., 1958, Am. U., Beirut, Lebanon, 1963. Grad. Realtors Inst.; accredited buyers rep. grad. Commd. 2d. lt. U.S. Army, 1951, advanced through grades to col., ret., 1977; def. attache to Jordan, 1973-77; mktg. mgr. Litton Industries, Jordan, Saudi Arabia, 1977-81; mktg. mgr. Mid-East Hughes Aircraft Co., Fullerton, Calif., 1981-91; dir. relocation ERA Gem Realty, Tucson, 1992-97; realtor Realty Execs., 1997—. Author: Abu Dhabi: Birth of an Oil Shaikhdom, 1964. Decorated Legion of Merit. Mem. Met. Tucson Conv. and Visitors Bureau, Tucson C. of C. Avocations: music, gardening, travel.

MANN, CLAUD PRENTISS, JR. retired television journalist; b. Galveston, Tex., June 30, 1925; s. Claud Prentiss and Henrietta Anno (Cline) M.; m. Loris Lea Padgett, Sept. 18, 1948; children: Beatrice Anno, Claudea Padgett, Claud Prentiss III. BS, U. Houston, 1949. Cert. tchr., Calif.; lic. real estate agt., Wash. Fellow Fund for Adult Edn. Mass Media U. Calif., Berkeley, 1958-59; anchor, reporter, writer, prodr., commentator Sta. KTVU-TV, San Francisco, Oakland, Calif., 1962-87; news dir., anchor, prodr. Sta. KTIE-TV, Oxnard, Santa Barbara, 1987-88; freelance writer, producer, pub. info. specialist, 1988—; journalism instr. Highline and South Seattle Community Colls., 1990-92. Past v.p. bd. dirs. Vashon-Maury Sr. Ctr. Recipient No. Calif. Emmy awards for reporting and anchor work, 1975, 76, 77, 79, 81, John Swett award for Edn. Reporting; commendations U.S. State Dept., City of Oakland, City of San Francisco, Calif. State Legis. Mem. AFTRA, NATAS (Silver Circle), Vashon Allied Arts (bd. dirs. 1989-91), Soc. Profl. Journalists. Home: 25115 122nd Ave SW Vashon WA 98070-7820 E-mail: cmanX2@aol.com.

MANN, DANIEL, religious organization worker; b. Cin., Feb. 14, 1932; s. Jacob and Margit (Klein) M.; m. Elaine Scherr, Dec. 23, 1956; 1 child, David J. Student, Spertus Coll. of Judaica, Chgo., 1949-53, Berl Katznelson Inst., Israel, 1950-51; BA, U. Chgo., 1952; MA, Columbia U., N.Y.C., 1959; postgrad., Georgetown U., 1985-94. Nat. sec. Habonim Labor Zionist Youth, N.Y.C., 1955-58; dir. youth and young adult activities Fedn. Jewish Agys., Phila., 1959-61; exec. dir. Labor Zionist Movement, N.Y.C., 1961-68; nat. coord. Am. Zionist Fedn., 1969-73; exec. dir. Jewish Cmty. Coun. Greater Washington, 1973-79; dir. Israel commn. B'nai B'rith, Washington, 1979-91. Adj. prof. Jewish communal studies Balt. Hebrew U., 1977-95. Mem. editorial bd. Jewish Frontier. Founding chmn. Habonim Dror Found.; bd. dirs. Jewish Hist. Soc. of Greater Washington; chmn. libr. com. Bd. Jewish Edn. of Greater Washington; mem. Israel and overseas com. Jewish Fedn. Greater Wash.; nat. pres. Labor Zionist Alliance, 1994-2000; bd. gov.'s coms. Jewish Agy. for Israel; mem. gov. bodies Am. Zionist Movement, Am. Israel Pub. Affairs Com., Jewish Labor Com.; mem. congregation Beth El Montgomery County, Md. Mem. ACLU, Nat. Symphony Orch. Assn., Jewish Communal Svc. Assn. N.Am. (pres. 1982-84), Consumers Union. Democrat.

MANN, DAVID, energy and services company executive; b. Drummondville, Que., 1939; m. Lois Dyer Mann; children: Geoffrey, Peter, Gillian. B.Commerce, Dalhousie U., Halifax, N.S., 1961, B.Laws, 1965; M.Laws, U. London, 1966. With Cox Hanson O'Reilly Matheson, Halifax, 1967-96, mng. ptnr., 1974-91; pres., CEO Emera Inc. and Nova Scotia Power Inc., 1996—; also bd. dirs. Chmn. Emera Fuels, Maritimes & N.E. Pipeline L.P., L.L.C., Bangor Hydro-Electric Co.; bd. dirs. Logistec Corp., Can. Coun. Chief Exec. Gov. Olympic Trust of Can.; mem. adv. bd. Dalhousie Sch. Bus.; chmn. Atlantic Salmon Fedn.; bd. dirs. Found. for Ednl. Exch. between Can. and U.S. (The Can.-U.S. Fulbright Program), Atlantic Inst. for Mkt. Studies, Greater Halifax Econ. Devel. Partnership. Queen's Counsel, 1982. Fellow: Coll. Law Practice Mgmt.; mem.: Can. Electricity Assn. (bd. dirs., vice chmn.). Avocations: golf, sailing, skiing, fly fishing, cooking. Office: Emera Inc PO Box 910 Halifax NS Canada B3J 2W5 Fax: (902) 428-6112. E-mail: david.mann@emera.com.

MANN, DAVID O'BRIEN, venture capitalist, military officer; b. Clarksville, Ind., Aug. 15, 1969; s. David O. and Mary S. Mann; m. Julia M. Young, May 11, 1996. BS, U.S. Naval Acad., Annapolis, 1991; MBA, Harvard U., 1999. Lt. comdr. USNR, 1991—; supply corps officer Naval Info. Sys. Mgmt. Ctr., Arlington, Va., 1991; supply corps officer U.S.S. Mississippi USN, Norfolk, 1992-95, White House liaison officer Washington, 1995—97; co-founder WeServeHomes, Inc., Downers Grove, Ill., 1999—2001; ptnr. ServiceMaster Venture Fund LLC, 1999—2000, Spring Mill Venture Ptnrs., Bloomington, Ind., 2001—. Dir. Alumni Leaders in Nat. Comm., Chgo., 1999-2001; scoutmaster Boy Scouts Am., Bethesda, Md., 1996-97; exec. advisor Jr. Achievement, Washington, 1994-96. Recipient numerous pub. svc. awards, including Pub. Speaking award Toastmasters, 1995-97. Mem. IEEE, U.S. Naval Acad. Alumni Assn. (life, dir. Greater Washington chpt. 1996-97), Am. Entrepreneurs for Econ. Growth, Harvard Bus. Sch. Alumni Assn., World Future Soc., Navy League of U.S., Navy Supply Corps Assn., The Hudson Inst., Am. Legion, Crimson Investment Fund. Roman Catholic. Avocations: physical fitness, economic development. Office: Spring Mill Venture Ptnrs Historic Hirons Bldg 555 N Morton St Bloomington IN 47404 Home: 1317 Fenbrook Ln Bloomington IN 47401-4265 E-mail: dmann@mba1999.hbs.edu.

MANN, DAVID DOUGLAS, English educator, retired; b. Oklahoma City, Sept. 13, 1934; s. Loftin Harry and Jeannette (Kneer) M.; m. Susan Garland, Aug. 15, 1983. BS, Okla. State U., 1956, MA, 1963; PhD, Ind. U., 1969. Instr. English Wabash Coll., Crawfordsville, Ind., 1965-67; from instr. to prof. Miami U., Oxford, Ohio, 1968-2000; ret., 2000. Author: A Bibliography to the Works of Sir George Etherege, 1982; co-author: Women Playwrights in England, Ireland, and Scotland, 1660-1823, 1996; editor: Concordance to the Dramas of William Congreve. 1973, Concordance to the Works of Sir George Etherege, 1985, The Dramatic Works of Theophilus and Susanna Cibber, 1982; co-editor: The Enchantress by Robert Louis Stevenson, 1989; contbr. articles to profl. jours. With USN, 1956-59, res., 1959-68. Fellow Folger Shakespeare Libr., 1970, Am. Soc. Bibliog. Studies, 1988, Beinecke Libr. at Yale, 1989, Lily Libr. at Ind. U., 1992. Mem. Modern Lang. Assn., Samuel Johnson Soc. of Midwest. Avocations: children's literature, cooking, gardening. Home: 2101 Twin Hill Rd Louisville KY 40207 E-mail: ddmann@iglou.com.

MANN, DAVID SCOTT, lawyer; b. Cin., Sept. 25, 1939; s. Henry M. and Helen Faye M.; m. Elizabeth Taliaferro, Oct. 5, 1963; children: Michael, Deborah, Marshall. AB cum laude, Harvard Coll., 1961, LLB magna cum laude, 1968. Bar: Ohio 1968. Assoc. Dinsmore & Shohl, Cin., 1968-74, ptnr., 1974-83, Taliaferro and Mann, Cin., 1983-92; councilman City of Cin., 1974-92, mayor, 1980-82, 91; mem. 103d Congress 1st Ohio dist., Washington, 1993-94; mem. armed svcs. com., mem. jud. com.; of counsel Thompson, Hine and Flory, Cin., 1995-96; pvt. practice Mann & Mann, LLC, 1997—. Adj. prof. Coll. of Law, U. Cin., 1995—. Editor Harvard Law Rev., 1966-68, notes editor, 1967-68; contbr. articles to profl. jours. Mem., chmn. Cin. Bd. Health, 1972-74. With USN, 1961-65. Mem. Cin. Bar Assn. Democrat. Methodist. Home: 568 Evanswood Pl Cincinnati OH 45220-1527

MANN, DELBERT, film, theater, television director and producer; b. Lawrence, Kans., Jan. 30, 1920; s. Delbert Martin and Ora (Patton) M.; m. Ann Caroline Gillespie, Jan. 13, 1942; children: David Martin, Frederick G.,

Barbara Susan, Steven P. BA, Vanderbilt U., 1941; MFA, Yale U.; LLD (hon.), Northland Coll. Dir. Town Theatre, Columbia, S.C., 1947-49; stage mgr. Wellesley Summer Theater, 1947-48; floor mgr., asst. dir. NBC-TV, N.Y.C., 1949, dir., 1949-55; freelance film and TV dir., 1954—. Pres. Dirs. Guild Benevolent Found.; former bd. govs. Acad. TV Arts and Scis.; former co-chmn. Tenn. Film, Tape and Music Commn.; former pres. Cinema Circulus; former lectr. Claremont (Calif.) McKenna Coll., U. N.C., Chapel Hill. Dir., Philco-Goodyear TV Playhouse, 1949-55, also Omnibus, Ford Star Jubilee, Playwrights 56, Producers Showcase, DuPont Show of the Month, Playhouse 90; films Marty, 1954 (Palme d'Or, Cannes Internat. Film Festival, Acad. Award), The Bachelor Party, 1956, Desire Under the Elms, 1957, Separate Tables, 1958, Middle of the Night, 1959, The Dark at the Top of the Stairs, 1960, The Outsider, 1960, Lover Come Back, 1961, That Touch of Mink, 1962, A Gathering of Eagles, 1962, Dear Heart, 1963, Mister Buddwing, 1965, Fitzwilly, 1967, Kidnapped, 1972, Birch Interval, 1976, Night Crossing, 1982; TV spl. Heidi, 1968, David Copperfield, 1970, Jane Eyre, 1971, The Man Without a Country, 1973, A Girl Named Sooner, 1975, Breaking Up, 1977, Tell Me My Name, 1977, Home To Stay, 1978, All Quiet on the Western Front, 1979, To Find My Son, 1980, All the Way Home, 1981, Bronte, 1982, The Member of the Wedding, 1982, The Gift of Love, 1983, Love Leads the Way, 1984, A Death in California, 1985, The Last Days of Patton, 1986, The Ted Kennedy Jr. Story, 1986, April Morning, 1987, Ironclads, 1991, Against Her Will: An Incident in Baltimore, 1992, Incident in a Small Town, 1993, Lily in Winter, 1994, The Memoirs of Abraham Lincoln, 1996; plays include A Quiet Place, 1956, Speaking of Murder, 1957, Zelda, 1969, The Memoirs of Abraham Lincoln, 1996,; opera Wuthering Heights, N.Y.C. Ctr., 1959; author: Looking Back...At Live Television and Other Matters, 1998. Bd. trustees Vanderbilt U., 1962—. 1st lt. USAAF, WWII; B-24 pilot and squadron intelligence officer, 1944-45. Recipient Acad. Award for dir. Marty, 1955. Mem. Dirs. Guild Am. (past pres. 1967-71) (Dirs. Guild award, 1955), Kappa Alpha. Democrat. Presbyterian. Avocation: reading history. Home and Office: Caroline Prodns Inc 556 S Ogden Dr Los Angeles CA 90036-5376

MANN, DONALD CAMERON, marketing company executive; b. Memphis, Jan. 31, 1949; s. Cameron Mann and Jane Snowden (Treadwell) Martin; m. Natacha Luba Plotnikoff, June 1, 1972 (div. Nov. 1998); 1 child, Cameron Alexander; m. Donna Marie Reed, April 17, 1999. BA, Brown U., 1971; MBA, Columbia U., 1978. Assoc. pub. Portfolio Mag., N.Y.C., 1978-80; mktg. dir. Bloom & Gelb, 1980-82; gen. mgr. Malmo Dir. Advt., Memphis, 1982-88; pres. Fusion Mktg. Group unit Axiom Corps., 1988—2002; pres., founder Memphis Records, 2002—. Spkr. Fin. Inst. Mktg. Assn., Chgo., 1988-90, Bank Mktg. Assn., Database Mktg. Conf., 1995, OKRA Mktg. User Conf., Tampa, Fla., 1989-94, Customer Insights Corp. Conf., 1989, Bank Mktg. Assn. Argentina, Buenos Aires, 1994, Strategic Rsch. Inst., N.Y., 1994-95; founder, dir. Advanced Fin. Database Mktg. Sch. Northwestern U., Chgo., 1990-2000. Editor, author: (book) The New Age of Financial Marketing, 1991. Bd. dirs. Concerts Internat., Memphis, 1989, Memphis Arts Festival, 2001--; mem. Leadership Memphis, 1993; mem. adv. bd. Case-in-Point, Axciom Corp., 1995-99. Recipient Cert. Merit Direct Mktg. Assn., 1983, Fin. Inst. Mktg. Assn., 1987, ADDY, Am. Assn. Advt. Agys., 1988. Mem. The Univ. Club, The Porsche Club Am., The Dixon Gallery and Gardens, Memphis Brooks Mus. of Art, The Gullwing Owners Group, The Ferrari Club Am., Shelby Am. Automobile Club, Mercedes Benz Club Am. Avocation: automobile restoration. Office: Memphis Records 2258 Young Ave Memphis TN 38104 E-mail: don@memphisrecordsonline.com.

MANN, DONEGAN, lawyer; b. Birmingham, Ala., Mar. 6, 1922; s. Ephriam DeValse and Edna Atkins (Donegan) M.; m. Frances Virginia Hindman, Apr. 6, 1957 (dec. May 1993); m. Frances M. Jenkins, Jan. 7, 1995 (dec. Dec. 1997). Student, Birmingham-So., 1940-41; AB, George Washington U., 1947, JD, 1950. Bar: U.S. Dist. Ct. D.C. 1950, U.S. Ct. Appeals (D.C. cir.) 1950, U.S. Ct. Claims 1957, U.S. Supreme Ct. 1961, U.S. Ct. Appeals (fed. cir.) 1982. Acting bur. counsel Civil Aeronautics Bd., Washington, 1953-55; gen. rates atty. GAO, 1955-57; spl. rate counsel Gen. Svcs. Administrn., 1957-60; assoc. Wolf & Case, 1960-66; sr. atty., office gen. counsel. U.S. Dept. Treasury, 1966-79; of counsel Shands & Stupar, 1979-82; pvt. practice, 1984—. Pres. Friends of Historic Great Falls Tavern, Inc., Potomac, Md., 1977-80, bd. dirs., 1980-83. With USN, 1943-46, PTO. Mem. ABA (treas. pub. contracts sect. 1965-66, chmn. awards com. 1975-76, svc. award sr. lawyers' divsn. 1991, counsel sr. lawyers divsn., 1995-97, chmn. guardianship and conservatorship com. 1989-95, sr. lawyers' divsn. task force to reform guardianship laws 1992-94, vice chmn., wills probate and trust com., 1995—, chmn. citizenship com. 1996-97, vice chmn. Law Day and citizenship com. 1997—), FBA, Fed. Energy Bar Assn., D.C. Bar Assn., Montgomery County Hist. Soc. (exec. v.p. 1980-83, bd. dirs. 1984-86). Democrat. Episcopalian. Avocations: fishing, hunting, golf, tennis, gardening. Office: 1000 Connecticut Ave NW Ste 204 Washington DC 20036-5337

MANN, ELAINE RENEE, marketing manager; b. Witchita, Kansas, Nov. 25, 1969; d. Delbert E. Mann and Carol Ann Shockey. BA, West Chester Univ., 1991. Comm. asst. Ecogen, Inc., Langhorne, Pa., 1992-94; sales admnstr. Medx, Inc., Trevose, 1994-95; dist. dir. Muscular Dystrophy Asn., Southampton, 1995-97; mktg. comm. mgr. NovaCare, Inc., King of Prussia, 1997-99; global conventions dir. Pharmacia & Upjohn, Peapack, N.J., 1999-2000; dir. nat. conventions Merck, West Point, Pa., 2000—. Mem. Health Care Exhibitors Assn., Trade Show Exhibitors Assn. Home: 1292 Harrow Cres Yardley PA 19067-6006 Office: Merck WP39-139 West Point PA 19486 E-mail: elaine_mann@merck.com.

MANN, EMILY BETSY, writer, artistic director, theater director; b. Boston, Apr. 12, 1952; d. Arthur and Sylvia (Blut) M.; m. Gary Mailman; 1 child, Nicholas Isaac Bamman. BA, Harvard U., 1974; MFA, U. Minn., 1976; D of Fine Arts (hon.) , Princeton U., 2002. Resident dir. Guthrie Theater, Mpls., 1976-79; dir. BAM Theater Co., Bklyn., 1980-81; freelance writer, dir. N.Y.C., 1981-90; artistic dir. McCarter Theater Ctr. for the Performing Arts, Princeton, N.J., 1990—. Author: (plays) Annulla, An Autobiography, Still Life (6 Obie awards 1981, Fringe First award 1985), Execution of Justice (Helen Hayes award, Bay Area Theatre Critics Circle award, HBO/USA award, Playwriting award Women's Com. Dramtists Guild for Dramatizing Issues of Conscience 1986), Greensboro: A Requiem, Having Our Say (L.A. NAACP award for Best Play), Meshugah; co-author: (with Ntozake Shange) (musical) Betsey Brown; (screenplays) Fanny Kelly, The Winnie Mandela Story, Having Our Say (Christopher award, Peabody award), Having Our Say (Peabody award); dir. Hedda Gabbler, A Doll House, Annulla, Still Life (Obie award), Execution of Justice (Guthrie and Broadway), Betsey Brown, The Glass Menagerie, Three Sisters, Cat on a Hot Tin Roof, Twilight: L.A., 1992 (L.A. NAACP award for best dir.), The Perfectionist, The Matchmaker, Safe as Houses, The Mai, Betrayal, Fool for Love, The Cherry Orchard, Because He Can, Romeo and Juliet, All Over; adaptor, dir. Miss Julie, Having Our Say (Tony nomination-direction of a play 1995, Dramatist Guild's Hull Warriner award, L.A. NAACP award), Greensboro, A Requiem, The House of Bernarda Alba, Meshugah, The Cherry Orchard, Because He Can, Romeo and Juliet All Over (McCarter and the Roundabout Theatres); translator: Nights and Days (Pierre Laville), 1985; pub. in New Plays U.S.A. 1, New Plays 3, American Plays and the Vietnam War, The Ten Best Plays of 1986, Out Front, Testimony: 4 Plays by Emily Mann, 1997; co-editor: Political Stages, 2002. Recipient BUSH fellowship, 1975-76, Rosamond Gilder award New Drama Forum Assn., 1983, NEA Assocs. grant, 1984, Guggenheim fellowship, 1985, McKnight fellowship, 1985, CAPS award, 1985, NEA Playwrights fellowship, 1986. Mem. Soc. Stage Dirs. and Choreographers, Theatre Comms. Group (v.p.), New Dramatists, PEN, Writers' Guild, Dramatists' Guild (exec. bd. mem.), Phi Beta Kappa.

MANN, FRANK BERT, visual artist, painter; b. Washington, Apr. 22, 1950; s. Frank Bert and Wilda Vendetta Kaufman. BS, High Point Univ., 1972; BA, George Washington Univ., 1979; MFA, Pratt Inst., 1981. Guest lectr. Corcoran Sch. of Art, Washington, 1979, Pennsylvania State U., Reading, 1986-87, Pratt Inst., Bklyn., 1987-88, Parsons Sch. Art & Design, N.Y.C., 1996-97. Exec. dir. Colaborative Projects, Inc., N.Y., 1987-88, Basicarts Network, N.Y., 1989-90; vis. artist Coalition for the Homeless Camp, 1997, Children's Friends for Life, N.Y., 1997, Project for St. Cyrils Ch., N.Y., 1992. Author: Eye of the Painter, 1997; book, exhibitions include Biennale Internazionale, Florence, Italy, 2001 (Lorenzo Il Magnifico medal in painting, 2001), Represented in permanent collections Guggenheim Mus., N.Y.C. U.S. rep. Biennale Internazionale, Florence, Italy, 1999, 2001. Recipient Mable Sanger Webb award, Ford Found., 1980; grantee, N.Y. State Coun. Arts, 1988, N.Y. City Dept.Cultural Affairs, 1989, 2000—02. Mem.: Contemporary Artists' Guild, Am. Soc. Contempoarary Artists, Drawing Soc., Artists Equity (bd. dirs. 2000—01), Am. for the Arts. Lutheran. Home and Office: 212 E 34th St Apt 3E New York NY 10016-4846 E-mail: fmann100@hotmail.com.

MANN, GEORGE STANLEY, real estate and financial services corporation executive; b. Toronto, Ont., Can., Dec. 23, 1932; s. David Philip and Elizabeth (Green) M.; m. Saundra Sair, Jan. 2, 1955; children: Michael, Tracy. Attended, North Toronto Collegiate Sch.; LLD (hon.), U. Windsor. Ptnr. Mann & Martel Co. Ltd., 1959-68, CEO, 1968-70, United Trust Co., 1970-76; pres. Unicorp Canada Corp., Toronto, 1972-76, chmn. bd., 1976-90; dir. Nat. Bank Canada, 1978-91; chmn. bd. Union Gas Ltd., 1986-93; owner co., Toronto. Pres. chmn. bd. Lincorp Holdings, Inc., N.Y.C. Bd. govs. Mt. Sinai Hosp., Toronto. Mem. Oakdale Golf & Country Club (Toronto), High Ridge Country Club (Palm Beach, Fla.), Mar-a-Lago Club (Palm Beach, Fla.), Trump Internat. Golf Club (Palm Beach, Fla.). Avocation: golf. Home: 18 Old Forest Hill Rd Toronto ON Canada M5P 2P7 also: 930 S Ocean Blvd Palm Beach FL 33480-4909 Office: 2 St Clair Ave W Ste 1004 Toronto ON Canada

MANN, HAROLD EARLE, physician; b. Phila., Mar. 8, 1920; s. Louis and Jeanette Ruth M.; m. Muriel Mann, July 25, 1948; children: Deborah Hoffman, Carol Mann, Lisa Ricketts Mann, Jennifer Mann. BA, U. Pa., 1940, MD, 1944. Cert. psychiatry, child psychiatry, psychoanalysis. Intern Michael Reese Hosp., Chgo., 1944-45; resident-psychiatry Worcester (Mass.) State Hosp., 1945-46, Boston State Hosp., 1946-47; resident in child psychiatry Judge Baker Ctr., Boston, 1947-51; capt. U.S.P.H.S., Washington, 1951-53; pvt. practice San Francisco, 1953-58, Berkeley, Calif., 1958—. Mem. East Bay Psychiat. Assn. (pres. 1971), No. Calif. Psychiat. Soc. (pres. 1973), Am. Coll. Psychiatrists, Am. Coll. Psychoanalysts, others. Home: 2634 Saklan Indian Dr Apt 6 Walnut Creek CA 94595-3031 Office: 2006 Dwight Way Berkeley CA 94704

MANN, HENRY DEAN, accountant; b. El Dorado, Ark., Feb. 8, 1943; s. Paul L. and Mary Louise (Capps) M.; m. Rebecca Balch, Aug. 14, 1965; children: Julie Elizabeth, Betsey Sawyer Mann. BSBA, U. Ark., 1965. CPA, Mo., Tex. Staff acct., mgr. Ernst & Whinney, Houston, 1967-76, ptnr., 1976-77; regional personnel ptnr. Ernst & Whinney (now Ernst & Young), St. Louis, 1977-78, mng. ptnr., 1978-88; pres. Mann Industries, Inc., 1988-89; pres., dir. 1st Capital Corp., Ft. Scott, Kans., 1989—, chmn., CEO, dir., 1989—. Citizens Bank, N.A., Fort Scott, 1989—. CEO, chmn. bd. dirs. Humble (Tex.) Nat. Bank, 1992-98; adv. bd. U. Mo. Sch. Accountancy, Columbia, 1979-82; bd. dirs. Cupples Co. Mfrs., St. Louis. Treas. Jr. Achievement, St. Louis, 1984-98, bd. dirs., 1986-98; treas., bd. dirs. United Way, St. Louis, 1986-92, Art and Edn. Coun., St. Louis, 1986-91; bd. dirs. St. Louis Symphony, 1988-89, Mercy Hosp. Found., Ft. Scott, Kans., 2000—, Bankers Bank of Kans., Wichita, 2000—; bd. dirs. Kammergild Chamber Orch., St. Louis, 1986, pres., 1983-85. Mem. AICPA, Mo. Soc. CPAs, Ft. Scott C. of C. (bd. dirs., pres.2001—), Bellerive Country Club (treas. 1986-87, v.p. 1988-89), Beta Gamma Sigma, Beta Alpha Psi. Presbyterian. Office: Citizens Bank NA 200 S Main St Fort Scott KS 66701-2045

MANN, J. KEITH, arbitrator, law educator, lawyer; b. May 28, 1924; s. William Young and Lillian Myrle (Bailey) M.; m. Virginia McKinnon, July 7, 1950; children: William Christopher, Marilyn Keith, John Kevin, Susan Bailey, Andrew Curry. BS, Ind. U., 1948, LLB, 1949; LLD, Monmouth Coll., 1989. Bar: Ind. 1949, D.C. 1951. Law clk. Justice Wiley Rutledge and Justice Sherman Minton, 1949-50; pvt. practice Washington, 1950; with Wage Stblzn. Bd., 1951; asst. prof. U. Wis., 1952, Stanford U. Law Sch., 1952-54, assoc. prof., 1954-58, prof., 1958-88, prof. emeritus, 1988—, assoc. dean, 1961-85, acting dean, 1976, 81-82, cons. to provost, 1986-87. Vis. prof. U. Chgo., 1953; mem. Sec. of Labor's Adv. Com., 1955-57; mem. Pres.'s Commn. Airlines Controversy, 1961; mem. COLC Aerospace Spl. Panel, 1973-74; chmn., mem. Presdl. Emergency Bds. or Bds. of Inquiry, 1962-63, 67, 71-72; spl. master U.S. vs. Alaska, U.S. Supreme Ct., 1980-97. Editor book rev. and articles Ind. U. Law Jour., 1948-49. Ensign USNR, 1944-46. Sunderland fellow U. Mich., 1959-60; scholar in residence Duke U., 1972. Mem. ABA, AAUP, Nat. Acad. Arbitrators, Indsl. Rels. Rsch. Assn., Acad. Law Alumni Fellows Ind. U., Order of Coif, Tau Kappa Epsilon, Phi Delta Phi. Democrat. Presbyterian. Home: 872 Lathrop Dr Stanford CA 94305-1053 Office: Stanford U Sch Law Stanford CA 94305-8610 E-mail: jkmann@leland.stanford.edu.

MANN, JACK MATTHEWSON, bottling company executive; b. Marshall, Tex., Apr. 14, 1932; s. Jack Slater and Mary (Matthewson) M.; m. True Sandlin, Sept. 4, 1954 (div. 1989); children: Jack, Robert, Daniel, Nathaniel. Student, N.Mex. Mil. Inst., 1952; BBA, U. Tex., 1954; MBA, Harvard U., 1960. Credit analyst Republic Nat. Bank, Dallas, 1959; chem. coord. Humble Oil and Refining Co., Baytown, Tex., 1960-61; asst. sales mgr. The Made-Rite Co., Marshall, 1957-58; asst. gen. mgr. The Made Rite Co., 1961-63, gen. mgr. Longview, 1963-92, pres., 1972—, owner, chmn., 1982—; v.p. Longview Econ. Devel. Corp., 1994-2000, treas., 1995-96, pres., 1996-97. Bd. dirs. Longview Nat. Bank, Region's Bank; mem. pres.'s adv. coun. Le Tourneau U., 1994-97, mem. devel. coun. U. Tex.-Tyler Longview U. Ctr., 2000—; chancellor's coun. U. Tex., 2001—. Exec. com. Rep. Party Tex., 1962-65; mem. Trinity Episcopal Ch., Longview, 1963-, sr. warden, jr. warden, treas.; mem. exec. bd. Episcopal Diocese Tex., Houston, 1974-76; mem. small bus. adv. com. Tex. Dept. Commerce, 1988-91. Mem. Tex. Soft Drink Assn. (pres. 1972), Nat. Dr. Pepper Bottlers Assn. (pres. 1983-85), Longview C. of C. (dir. 1965-68, 84-86). Clubs: Summit (Longview) (gov. 1982-94). Avocation: University of Texas athletics. Home: 45 Stonegate Dr Longview TX 75601-3600 Office: The Made Rite Co PO Box 3283 Longview TX 75606-3283

MANN, JAMES DARWIN, mathematics educator; b. Lambric, Ky., Feb. 27, 1936; s. Glinn W. and Wanda (Collins) M.; 1 child, Terry Brian. BS, Morehead State U., 1962; M in Math., U. S.C., 1965; postgrad., Ind. U., 1968-69, Obelin Coll., 1968. High sch. tchr. math., 1962-64; instr. math. Presbyn. Coll., Clinton, S.C., 1965-66; assoc. prof. math. Morehead (Ky.) State U., 1966-95, assoc. prof. emeritus, 1995—. Fundraiser United Way, 1977-78; vol. coach Little League Baseball, 1973-76; coach Babe Ruth Baseball, 1977; chmn. N.E. Ky. Sci. Fair Rules, 1969-76; judge N.E. Ky. Sci. Fair, 1967, 68, 77, 79, 80, 81. NSF grantee U. S.C., 1964-65, Vanderbilt U., 1967, Oberlin Coll., 1968, N.C. State U., 1972; recipient Outstanding Alumni award Ky. Zeta chpt. Sigma Phi Epsilon, 1977. Mem. Math. Assn. Am., Nat. Coun. Tchrs. Math. Baptist. Home: 4200 Christy Crk Morehead KY 40351-9075

MANN, JAMES ROBERT, former congressman; b. Greenville, S.C., Apr. 27, 1920; s. Alfred Cleo and Nina (Griffin) M.; m. Virginia Thomason Brunson, Jan. 15, 1945; children— James Robert, David Brunson, William Walker, Virginia Brunson. BA, The Citadel, 1941, LL.D. (hon.), 1978; JD, U. S.C., 1947. Bar: S.C. 1947, U.S. Ct. Appeals (4th cir.) 1948, U.S. Supreme Ct. 1970. Practice in, Greenville, 1947—; del. S.C. Ho. of Reps. from, Greenville County, 1949-52; solicitor 13th Jud. Circuit, 1953-63; mem. 91st-95th Congresses 4th Dist. SC. Sec. Greenville County Planning Commn., 1963-67; Trustee Greenville Hosp. System, 1965-68; bd. govs. Greenville Shriners Hosp., 1983-90. Served to lt. col. AUS, 1941-46; col. USAR ret. Mem. Am., S.C., Greenville County bar assns., Am. Judicature Soc., Greater Greenville C. of C. (pres. 1965), V.F.W. (dep. comdr. 1951-52), Am. Legion. Lodges: Mason; Shriners; Kiwanis; Elks; Woodmen of World. Democrat. Baptist. Office: 414 Univ Park Greenville SC 29601

MANN, JEAN ADAH, artist; b. Schenectady, N.Y., June 27, 1927; d. Allan B. and Esther Copeland Mann. Student, Mannes Coll., N.Y.C., Hunter Coll., Mavros Studio, Irma Rothstein Studio. Pvt. art tchr. The Kick Wheel, New Fairfield, Conn. Tchr. Adult Edn. Program, Newtown, Conn., 1966-77, Heritage Village, Southbury, Conn., 1967-75, 89-91, RESCUE Vis. Artists Program, Conn., 1969, Adult Edn. Program, New Fairfield, 1976-81, 94—, Brookfield (Conn.) Craft Ctr., 1981, 82, 86, George Walker Vincent Smith Art Mus., Springfield, Mass., 1984, Heritage House Sr. Ctr., Redding, Conn., 1987, Old Church Art Sch., Demarest, N.J., 1994. One-woman shows include Hammond Mus., North Salem, N.Y., 1975, 77, 82, 85, 88, 89, 93, 94, 95, 99, 2001, GWS Gallery, Southport, Conn., 1987, Atelier Gallery, New Milford, Conn., 1989, Weslayan Potters, Middletown, Conn., 1989, The Silo Gallery, New Milford, 1996, Ferguson Libr., Stamford, Conn., 1997, Dirs. Choice, Silvermine Guild of Artists, New Canaan, Conn., 2000; exhibited in group shows including Farmington Valley Ctr., Fisher Gallery, 1989, Variations, Riverton, Conn., 1992; represented in permanent collections Met. Mus. Art, N.Y.C., Smithsonian Inst., Washington, Mus. Art and Archaeology, U. Mo. Columbia, Everson Mus. Art, Syracuse, others. Grantee Conn. Commn. on the Arts, 1981. Mem. Silvermine Guild, Am. Crafts Coun., Brookfield Craft Ctr., Soc. for Conn. Crafts (Master Craftsman/Educator award 1995), Oriental Brush Artist's Guild, Internat. Netsuke Soc., New Haven Paint and Clay Club. Home and Office: c/o The Kick Wheel 154 Route 39 New Fairfield CT 06812-4203

MANN, JOHN MARTIN, minister; b. McKeesport, Pa., Nov. 18, 1946; s. Glenn Grant and Mary Dorothy (Flaherty) M. BA, Clarion State Coll., 1967; MDiv, Duke U., 1970, ThM, 1972; D Ministry, Wittenberg U., 1976. Ordained to ministry Luth. Ch. in Am., 1972. Pastor 1st Luth. Ch., Edinboro, Pa., 1971-82; sr. pastor St. John's Luth. Ch., Erie, 1982-91. Instr. Edinboro State Coll., 1971-82; adj. prof. religion Thiel Coll. Greenville, Pa., 1980-82, baccalaureate preacher, 1980-84, trustee, 1974-80, 82—; chmn. synod vocations examining com. N.W. Pa.-W.Va. Synod, 1984-88; chmn. intersynodical candidacy com. N.W. Pa.-Allegheny Synods, 1988-90; chmn. ch. vocations examining com. N.W. Pa. Synod, 1990—; chmn. Luth. Coalition of Erie, 1990-91; dean Cond. I, Northwestern Pa. Synod, 1991—. Contbr. articles to profl. jours. Bd. dirs. Luth. Home, Erie, 1976-79, 82—, Inter-Ch. Ministries N.W. Pa., 1979-84, South Erie Hillside Cmty. Orgn., 1982—, Holy Trinity Cmty. Ctr., Erie, 1984-88, Nesting Inn, 1988—, Hospice Met. Erie, 1988—; chmn. Erie City Strategy for Luths., 1989—; pastor Trinity Luth. Ch., Canton, Ohio, 1992—; pres. UrbanArk Urban Ministry Coalition; active ELCA N.E. Ohio Synod, ecumenical com., synod outreach com., 1998—, dean conf., Canton; founding chmn. Interfaith Roundtable of Canton and N.W. Neighborhood Assn., Canton Downtown Pastors Assn. Recipient Outstanding Young Man of Am. award Jaycees, 1982. Mem. Luth. Assn. Larger Chs., Am. Assn. Pastoral Counselors, Luth. Campus Ministry Assn., Interdenominational Ministerial Assn. (sec.). Home: 6671 Firestone Ave NE Canton OH 44721-2514 Office: Trinity Luth Ch 415 Tuscarawas St W Canton OH 44702-2017 *In a word where materialism, hedonism and the selfish concerns of humanity have threatened the survival of nations and the planet, on the eve of the third millenium, we need now as never before to be convinced of the Gospel and to proclaim it in life.*

MANN, KAREN, consultant, educator; b. Kansas City, Mo., Oct. 9, 1942; d. Charles and Letha (Anderson) M. BA, U. Calif., Santa Barbara, 1964; MPA, Golden Gate U., 1975, PhD, 1994. Cert. lay min. Order of Buddhist Contemplatives. Mem., tchr. Sisters of Immaculate Heart, L.A., 1964-68; group counselor San Francisco and Marin County Probation Depts.; parole agt. Calif. Dept. Corrections, Sacramento, San Francisco, 1970-86; rschr. and cons. Non-profit Orgnl. Devel., 1986—, Computer Applications for Persons with Disabilities, 1986—. Adj. faculty Grad. Theol. Uion, Berkeley, 1984—; Compuserve Disabilities Forum, 1985-2000; forum adminstr., 1988-2000; mem. faculty Golden Gate U., 1990. Co-author: Prison Overcrowding, 1979, Community Corrections: A Plan for California, 1980. Sec., bd. dirs. Spirit Rock Mediation Ctr., 1989-93; co-founder Network Ctr. for Study of Ministry, San Francisco, 1982; pres. San Francisco Network Ministries, 1980-82; mem. Disabled Children's Computer Resource Group, 1988-90, Spingwater Ctr. for Mediative Inquiry and Retreats, 1986-88; emotional support counselor Marin AIDS Project, 1992-97. Fellowship of Reconciliation, N.Y., 1970—. Office: 400 Shasta Ave Mount Shasta CA 96067 E-mail: blueroof@surfree.com.

MANN, KENNETH HENRY, marine ecologist; b. Dovercourt, Essex, Eng., Aug. 15, 1923; emigrated to arrived Canada, 1967, naturalized, 1973; s. Harry and Mabel (Ashby) M.; m. Isabella Gilmour Ness, Apr. 18, 1946; children: Ian Malcolm, Sheila Helen, Colin Gilmour. B.Sc., U. London, 1949; PhD, U. Reading, 1953; D.Sc., U. London, 1965. Lectr. zoology, then reader U. Reading, Eng., 1949-64; 64-67; sr. biologist marine ecology lab. Bedford Inst. Oceanography, Dartmouth, Can., 1967-72, dir. marine ecology lab. Can., 1980-87, sr. rsch. scientist Can., 1987-93, emeritus rsch. scientist Can., 1993—. Prof., chmn. biology Dalhousie U., Halifax, N.S., Can., 1972-80, adj. prof. biology, 1980— Author: Leeches: Their Structure, Physiology, Ecology and Embryology, 1961, Ecology of Coastal Waters: A Systems Approach, 1982, Ecology of Coastal Waters: Implications for Management, 2000; co-author: (with J. Lazier) Dynamics of Marine Ecosystems: Biological-Physical Interactions in the Sea, 1991; 2d edit., 1996; (with R.S. Barnes) Fundamentals of Aquatic Ecology, 1991; editor, contbr.: Network Analysis in Marine Ecology, 1989; editor Jour. Animal Ecology, 1966-67. Served with Royal Air Force, 1942-46. Fellow Royal Soc. Can.; mem. Brit. Ecol. Soc., Am. Assn. Limnology and Oceanography. Home: 23 Woodward Cres Halifax NS Canada B3M 1J6 Office: Bedford Inst Oceanography Box 1006 Dartmouth NS Canada B2Y 4A2 E-mail: ken.mann@ns.sympatico.ca.

MANN, KENNETH WALKER, retired minister, psychologist; b. Nyack, N.Y., Aug. 22, 1914; s. Arthur Hungerford and Ethel Livingston (Walker) M. AB, Princeton U., 1937; STB, Gen. Theol. Sem., N.Y.C., 1942; MS, U. Mich., 1950, PhD, 1956. Ordained priest Episcopal Ch., 1942; diplomate Am. Assn. Pastoral Counselors; lic. clin. psychologist, Calif., Conn.; lic. marriage, family and child counselor, Calif. Vicar in Valley Cottage, Pearl River, N.Y., 1941-43; priest in charge Yonkers, 1943-45. Dir. youth work and Christian edn. Diocese L.A., 1945-47; curate in Beverly Hills, Calif., 1947-49; counselor Bur. Psychol. Svcs., U. Mich., 1951-52; chaplain, clin. psychologist dept. psychiatry St. Luke's Hosp., N.Y.C., also priest-psychotherapist Cathedral St. John Divine, N.Y.C., psychol. examiner ministerial candidates Diocese N.Y., 1952-58; assoc. chaplain Hosp. Good Samaritan, L.A., 1958-65; exec. pastoral svcs., exec. coun. Episc. Ch. N.Y.C., 1965-70; program officer Acad. Religion and Mental Health, N.Y.C., 1970-72; sr. adviser profl. affairs Inst. Religion and Health, 1972-74; sr. psychol. staff Silver Hill Found., New Canaan, Conn., 1974-84; pres. Rockland County (N.Y.) Mins. Assn., 1942-43; exec. sec. social svc. commn. Diocese N.Y., 1943-45; chmn. div. pastoral svcs. Diocese L.A., 1958-65; field dir. Western region Acad. Religion and Mental Health, 1958-61; assoc. nat. chaplain U.S. Power Squadrons, 1956-57. Author: On Pills and Needles, 1969, Deadline for Survival—A Survey of Moral Issues in Science and Medicine, 1970; contbr. articles to profl. jours. Pres. Adoption Inst. L.A., 1964; mem. edn. com. Calif. Heart Assn., 1962-64; trustee, treas. Acad. Religion and Mental Health, 1954-59, mem. profl. bd., 1960-70; trustee Vis. Nurse Assn. L.A., 1963-65, Children's Home Soc. Calif. in L.A., 1964-65, North Conway Inst., 1966-80. USPHS grantee, 1950-51. Fellow AAAS; mem. APA (chmn. com. rels. between psychology and religion 1956-58), Western Psychol. Assn., Calif. Psychol. Assn., L.A. County Psychol. Assn., N.Y. Acad. Scis., Planetary Soc., Assembly Episc. Hosps. and Chaplains, Upper Nyack Tennis Club, Princeton Club N.Y., Exch. Club Beverly Hills (pres.). Republican. Home: 32 Tallman Ave Nyack NY 10960-1606 *I have strongly held to the principle that the total "health" of mankind cannot be considered apart from the values and aspirations by which people live, and by which they may even be prepared to die. Amidst the confusions that exist today over loyalties, traditions, and ideals, many are asking: What is the right way to behave? How should I think? What kind of person am I supposed to be? To help such people in quandary to live responsibly, and still be true to their individuality, is a large task, but it is one that is central to a religious ministry. It has always been my chief concern.*

MANN, LAWRENCE MOSES, lawyer; b. Wilmington, N.C., Jan. 30, 1940; s. Irving Murray and Ada (Frohm) M.; m. Susan Beth Bernstein, Dec. 1, 1961 (div. Nov. 1994); children: Rachel (dec.), Michael, Debra; m. Pat Rosenthal, Mar. 3, 1996. BA, U. N.C., 1962; LLB, Georgetown U., 1966. Bar: D.C. 1967, U.S. Dist. Ct. D.C. 1967, U.S. Ct. Appeals (D.C. and 7th cirs.), 1967, U.S. Ct. Claims, 1970, U.S. Tax Ct. 1970, U.S. Supreme Ct. 1972, U.S. Ct. Appeals (9th, 8th and 4th cirs.) 1975, U.S. Ct. Appeals (10th cir.) 1978, U.S. Ct. Appeals (11th and 5th cirs.) 1981, U.S. Dist. Ct. (ea. dist.) Ky. 1983, U.S. Ct. Appeals (3d cir.) 1987, U.S. Ct. Appeals (2d cir.) 1988, U.S. Ct. Appeals (6th cir.) 1990. Spl. asst. to Sen. Vance Hartke, U.S. Senate, Washington, 1964-65; legal asst. post office and civil svc. com. U.S. Ho. of Reps., 1965-66; counsel Commn. on Polit. Activity of Govt. Pers., 1967; ptnr. Alper & Mann , 1968—. Author: What Every Railroad Worker Should Know About Federal Railroad Safety Laws, 1988. Former mem. bd. dirs. Washington Hebrew Congregation. Mem. ABA, ATLA, Acad. Rail Labor Attys., D.C. Bar Assn. Avocations: art, collecting shells. Office: Alper & Mann 1730 K St NW Ste 1107 Washington DC 20006-3808

MANN, LESTER PERRY, mathematics educator; b. Milford, Mass., May 30, 1921; s. Lester P. and Viola E. (Tracy) M.; m. Dorothy M. Davis, Oct. 11, 1947; children: Kelly P., Leslie P. BS with high honors, U. Md., 1964; MEd, U. Alaska, Anchorage, 1974; EdD, Boston U., 1983. Cert. elem. tchr., reading specialist and supr., Mass.; cert. elem. tchr., reading specialist, Alaska. Commd. 2nd lt. USAAF, 1941; advanced through grades to maj. USAF, 1954, navigator, weather officer, 1941-64; ret., 1964; resident counselor OEO-Job Corps, 1965-66; flight navigator Südflug, Braniff, Capitol and Japan Air Lines, 1966-73; instr. math., adminstr., curriculum developer U. Alaska, 1974-86, adj. instr., 1987-99; instrnl. assoc. Mann Assocs., Applied Lifelong Learning, Anchorage, 1983-99. Instr. Anchorage Community Coll., 1974-86; asst. prof. Embry-Riddle Aero. U., Anchorage, 1987-98, acad. advisor, 1987-90; mem. for remedial reading Alaska Talent Bank; vis. adult educator German Adult Edn. Assn., 1984. Mem. Math. Assn. Am., Nat. Coun. Tchrs. Math., Internat. Reading Assn., Am. Assn. Adult and Continuing Edn. (profl., past mem. nomination and election com.), Am. Meteorol. Soc. (emeritus), Phi Alpha Theta, Phi Kappa Phi. Avocations: fishing, sport flying, classical guitar. MANN. Home and Office: 2304 Turnagain Pky Anchorage AK 99517-1124 Fax: 907-243-. E-mail: lesmann@alaska.net.

MANN, LOUIS EUGENE, financial planner; b. Balt., Jan. 24, 1947; s. Manfred and Ruth Eleanor (Kates) M.; m. Marjorie Ruth Friedman, Mar. 23, 1971; children: Lisa Renee, Brian Michael. Student, Balt. Poly. Inst., 1964, Towson State Coll., 1964-67; postgrad., U. Pa., 1969-70; CFP, Coll. for Fin. Planning, 1993. CFP; securities licenses; lic. ins. broker, N.J., Pa., N.Y. Clk. Food Fair Stores, Inc., Balt., 1964-68; v.p. Friendly Grocer, Inc., Cherry Hill, N.J., 1968-79; sales mgr. Frito-Lay Inc., Cinnaminson, 1979-82; salesman N.Y. Life Ins. Co., Cherry Hill, 1982-89; ptnr. Custom Fin. Svcs., Marlton, N.J., 1988-93; pres. Louis E. Mann Fin. Svcs., Inc., Mt. Laurel, 1993—; comptroller Shusterman & Davis, LLC, Phila., 1996-2000; exec. v.p. Orion Fin. Svcs. LLC, 2001. Developer: (math. formula) Law of Squares of Consecutive Numbers, 1963. Mgr., coach Greentree Athletic Assn., Mount Laurel, N.J., 1985-94; pres. Congregation Beth Tikvah Men's Club, Marlton, 1988-89, 90-91, 94-95, bd. dirs., exec. bd. mem., 1994-95. Recipient Coll. scholarships State of Md.-Senatorial and Ednl., 1964. Mem. Delaware Valley Inst. CFPs, Fin. Planning Assn., Million Dollar Round Table (membership com. 1984), Rotary Club of Moorestown (com. chmn., bd. dirs. 1984-94, 1st v.p. 1996-97, pres. 1997-98), Rotary Internat. (dist. planned giving chmn. Dist. 7500, 1994-95, asst. dist. annual giving chair dist. 7500 2001—), Fedn. Jewish Men's Clubs (trustee Mid-Atlantic region 1995-96). Democrat. Jewish. Avocations: sports, hist. readings, fin. readings, music, gardening. Home: 121 Colony Pl Mount Laurel NJ 08054-2404 E-mail: manncfp@aol.com.

MANN, LYNNE MARIE, executive secretary; b. Columbus, Ohio, Dec. 22, 1964; d. Robert James Greenlee and Lois Etta Mann. Assocs. Degree, Hocking Coll.; Bachelors Degree, DeVry Inst. Tech. Med. lab. asst. Progenitor, Athens, Ohio; crew mgr. Marlboro Van Promotions, Columbus; massage therapist San Francisco, Columbus; part-time makeup artist Glamour Shorts; adminstrv. asst.; exec. adminstrv. asst. various cos., San Francisco. Founder, pres., CEO Madame Diva/LM Mann, Columbus, 2001. Author, editor: Poems & Story Stories of a Fat Woman, 2001. Leader, founder Large and Lovely Club-NFAA, Columbus, 2001; voting poll officer Athens County Dem. Party, Nelsonville, 1988. Recipient 2nd prize cake design, Athens County Fair, 1978, 2nd prize future clothing design, 1982. Avocations: tai-chi, sewing, cooking, swimming, hiking.

MANN, MARCIA L. state agency administrator; b. Pitts., May 20, 1944; d. Walter W. and Helen Mann. BA, Thiel Coll., 1965; MEd, U. Pitts., 1966; PhD, U. Nebr., 1970. Elem. tchr. Montgomery County Schs., Rockville, Md., 1966, Lincoln (Nebr.) City Schs., 1966-69; grad. asst. U. Nebr., Lincoln, 1969-70; asst. prof. edn. U. South Fla., Tampa, 1970-75, assoc. prof. edn., 1976-85, prof. edn., 1986—, assoc. dean clin. edn. and spl. projects, 1984-91; sec. Fla. Lottery, Tallahassee, 1991—. Evaluator dept. edn. Pinellas County Inservice Evaluation, 1978, Fla. Tech. U., 1978; vice chairperson Nat. Forum of Field Dirs., 1977, chairperson, 1978; del. dept. edn. State Conv., 1979; mem. Fla. State program Am. Coun. on Edn., 1978; coord. Hillsborough County for Gov. Graham, 1979-83; chair State Adv. Com. on Tchr. Edn., 1987; vis. scholar N.C. Disting. Vis. Scholars Program, Chapel Hill, 1989; mem. edn. stds. commn. State of Fla., 1990-93; active Nat. Coun. for Accreditation Tchr. Edn. Rev. Team Banks, 1977—, Thirteenth Cir. Jud. Nominating Commn., 1979-83, Gov. Commn. on Status of Women, 1981-85, Gov. Adv. Com. on Edn. Block Grants, 1981-85, Joint Exec. and Legis. Task Force for Tchr. Edn. Quality Improvement, 1982-84, Human Resource Devel. Adv. Com., 1987, Gov.-Elect Lawton Chiles' Edn. Core Task Force, 1990-91; cons., presenter in field. Contbr. articles to profl. jours. Vol. dir. comm. network for Graham Campaign, Tampa, 1976-78; vol. coord. rsch. and adminstrv. transition staff Gov. Graham, Tallahassee, 1978-79; vol. mgr. Hillsborough Campaign for Graham, 1978, Hillsborough County Campaign for Commr. Edn. Ralph Turlington, Tampa, 1982, Hillsborough Campaign for U.S. Senate Bob Graham, Tampa, 1986; bd. dirs. March of Dimes, 1986; active Pres. Adv. Com. for Women, 1980, Mil. Acad. Nominating Bd., 1987—. Recipient Gov. award for outstanding Fla. woman, 1981, Profl. Accomplishment award Thiel Coll., 1989. Mem. ASCD, Am. Assn. Colls. for Tchr. Edn. (Showcase of Excellence award for outstanding accomplishments with talented students 1985), Am. Ednl. Rsch. Assn., Assn. Tchr. Educators (del. 1978-82, mem. exec. bd. 1978-82, chairperson nat. ad hoc com. to establish coun. state pres. 1979-80, mem. '90 com. 1984-86), Fla. Assn. Tchr. Educators (chairperson pub. rels. and publicity com. 1975-76, v.p. 1977, chairperson com. for pub. rels. 1977, program chmn. 1977-78, pres. 1978-79, legis. liaison 1979-80), Greater Tampa C. of C. (mem. edn. coun. 1982—, chair state task force on govt. 1984-85), Phi Delta Kappa (chair scholarship fund 1988-89, 90-91). Democrat. Lutheran. Avocations: reading, gardening, flower arranging. Office: Fla Lottery Capitol Complex Tallahassee FL 32399-4002

MANN, MARION, physician, educator; b. Atlanta, Mar. 29, 1920; s. Levi James and Cora (Casey) Mann; m. Ruth Maurine Reagin, Jan. 16, 1943; children: Marion Jr., Judith Walk. BS in Edn., Tuskegee Inst., Ala., 1940; MD, Howard U., 1954; PhD, Georgetown U., 1961; grad., 1965, U.S. Army War Coll., 1970; DSc (hon.) , Georgetown U., 1979, U. Mass., 1984, Tuskegee U., 1998; grad., U.S. Army War Coll., 1970. Diplomate Nat. Bd. Med. Examiners, Am. Bd. Pathology. Intern USPHS Hosp., Staten Island, NY, 1954—55; resident Georgetown U. Hosp., 1956—60; practice medicine, specializing in pathology Washington, 1961—; instr. pathology Georgetown U., 1960—61; professorial lectr. Georgetown U. Sch. Medicine, 1970—73; asst. prof. pathology Howard U. Coll. Medicine, 1961—67, assoc. prof., 1967—70, prof., 1970, dean, 1970—79; v.p. rsch. Howard U., 1988—91. Capt. U.S. Army, 1942—50, brig. gen. Res. U.S. Army. Mem.: Nat. Acad. Scis., Inst. Medicine, Sigma Pi Phi, Alpha Omega Alpha. Mem. United Ch. Of Christ. Home: 1453 Whittier Pl NW Washington DC 20012-2845 Office: 520 W St NW Washington DC 20059-0001

MANN, MICHAEL MARTIN, electronics company executive; b. N.Y.C., Nov. 28, 1939; s. Herbert and Rosalind (Kaplan) M.; m. Mariel Joy Steinberg, Apr. 25, 1965. BSEE, Calif. Inst. Tech., 1960, MSEE, 1961; PhD in Elec. Engring. and Physics, U. So. Calif., 1969; MBA, UCLA, 1984. Cert. bus. appraiser, profl. cons., mgmt. cons., lic. real estate broker, Calif. Mgr. high power laser programs office Northrop Corp., Hawthorne, Calif., 1969-76; mgr. high energy laser systems lab. Hughes Aircraft Co., El Segundo, 1976-78, mgr. E-0 control systems labs., 1978-83, asst. to v.p., space & strategic, 1983-84; exec. v.p. Helionetics Inc., Irvine, Calif., 1984-85, pres., chief exec. officer, 1985-86, also bd. dirs.; ptnr. Mann Kavanaugh Chernove, 1986-87; sr. cons. Arthur D. Little, Inc., 1987-88; chmn. bd., pres., CEO, Blue Marble Devel. Group, Inc., 1988—; exec. assoc. Ctr. Internat. Cooperation and Trade, 1989—; sr. assoc. Corp. Fin. Assocs., 1990—; exec. assoc. Reece and Assocs., 1991—; dir. Reece & Assocs., 1991—; mng. dir. Blue Marble Ptnrs. Ltd, 1991—; chmn. bd. dirs., CEO Blue Marble Ptnrs., 1992—; chmn., CEO, En Compass Techs., Inc., Torrance, Calif., 1994-98; chmn. En Compass Knowledge Systems, Inc., 2000—. Mem. Army Sci. Bd., Dept. Army, Washington, 1986-91; chmn. Ballistic Missile Def. Panel, Directed Energy Weapon Panel, Rsch. and New Initiatives Panel; cons. Office of Sec. of Army, Washington, 1986—. Inst. of Def. Analysis, Washington, 1978—, Dept. Energy, 1988—, Nat. Riverside Rsch. Inst., 1990—; bd. dirs. Datum, Inc.,1988—, Fail-Safe Tech., Corp., 1989-90, Safeguard Health Enterprises, Inc., 1988—, Am. Video Communications, Inc., Meck Industries, Inc., 1987-88, Decade Optical Systems, Inc., 1990—, Forum Mil. Application Directed Energy, 1992—, Am. Bus. Consultants, Inc., 1993—; chmn. bd. Mgmt. Tech., Inc. 1991—, Encompass Tech., Inc., 1994-98; bd. dirs., mem. adv. bd. Micro-Frame, Inc., 1988-91; chmn. bd. HLX Laser, Inc., 1984-86; bd. dirs. Cons's. Roundtable, 1992—, Am. Bus. Cons., Inc., 1993—, Country Home Bakers, Inc., 1999—, C.L.E.A.R., Inc., 1999—; chmn. TEC, 1999—; rsch. assoc., mem. extension teaching staff U. So. Calif., L.A., 1964-70; chmn. Ballistic Missile Def. Subgroup, 1989-90, Tactical Directed Energy Weapons Subgroup, 1988-90; chmn., chief exec. officer Mgmt. Tech., Inc., 1991—; dir. Am. Bus. Cons., Inc., 1993—; faculty mem. Asia Pacific Inst., 1998—; faculty Nat. Technol. U., 1997—. Contbg. editor, mem. adv. bd. Calif. High-Tech Funding Jour., 1989-90; contbr. over 50 tech. articles to profl. jours.; patentee in field. Mem. adv. com. to Engring. Sch., Calif. State U., Long Beach, 1985—; chmn. polit. affairs Am. Electronics Assn., Orange County Coun., 1986-87, mem. exec. com., 1986-88; adv. com. several Calif. congressmen, 1985—; mem. dean's coun. UCLA Grad. Sch. Mgmt., 1984-85; bd. dirs. Archimedes Circle U. Soc. Calif., 1983-85, Ctr. for Innovation and Entrepreneurship, 1986-90, Caltech/MIT Venture Forum, 1987-91; chmn. adv. coun. and adj. prof., indsl. and sys. engring. U. So. Calif., 1996—; mem. bd. examiners Nat. Quality Award, 1998—. Hicks fellow in Indsl. Rels. Calif. Inst. Tech., 1961, Hewlett Packard fellow. Mem. IEEE (sr.), So. Calif. Tech. Execs. Network, Orange County CEO's Network, Orange County CEO's Roundtable, Pres. Roundtable, Nat. Assn. Corp. Dirs., Aerospace-Def. CEO's Roundtable, Am. Def. Preparedness Assn., Security Affairs Support Assn., Acad. Profl. Cons. and Advisors, Internat. Platform Assn., Inst. Mgmt. Cons. (bd. dirs. So. Calif. chpt.), Pres. Assn., Cons. Roundtable, King Harbor Yacht Club. Republican. Avocations: sailing, photography, writing. Home: 4248 Via Alondra Palos Verdes Peninsula CA 90274-1545 Office: Blue Marble Partners 406 Amapola Ave Ste 125 Torrance CA 90501-7238 E-mail: drmmmann@bluemarblecorp.com.

MANN, NANCY LOUISE (NANCY LOUISE ROBBINS), entrepreneur; b. Chillicothe, Ohio, May 6, 1925; d. Everett Chaney and Pauline Elizabeth R.; m. Kenneth Douglas Mann, June 19, 1949 (div. June 1979); children: Bryan Wilkinson, Laura Elizabeth. BA in Math., UCLA, 1948, MA in Math., 1949, PhD in Biostatistics, 1965. Sr. scientist Rocketdyne Divsn. Rockwell Internat., Canoga Park, Calif., 1962-75; tech. staff Rockwell Sci. Ctr., Thousand Oaks, 1975-78; rsch. prof. UCLA Biomath., L.A., 1978-87; pres., CEO, owner Quality Enhancement Seminars, Inc., 1982—; pres., CEO Quality and Productivity, Inc., 1987—. Curriculum adv. UCLA Ext. Dept. of Bus. and Mgmt., L.A., 1991—; mem. com. on Nat. Statistics, Nat. Acad. Scis., Washington, 1978-82; mem adv. bd. to supt. U.S. Naval Posgrad. Sch., Monterey, Calif., 1979-82. Co-author: Methods for Analysis of Reliability and Life Data, 1974; author: Keys to Excellence, 1985, The Story of the Deming Philosophy, 2d edit., 1987, 3d edit., 1989; contbr. articles to profl. jours. Recipient award IEEE Reliability Soc., 1982, ASQC Reliability Divsn., 1986. Fellow Am. Stats. Assn. (v.p. 1982-84); mem. Internat. Statis. Inst. Office: Quality Productivity Inc 10724 Wilshire Blvd # 711 Los Angeles CA 90024-4463

MANN, NICK ROBERT, research scientist; b. Moscow, Dec. 29, 1970; s. Danny L. Mann, Susan Mann; m. Toni Lynn Jarolimek; children: Logan, Caleb. BA in Geology, Idaho State U., 1996. Geologist Eratham-Vanir Geol. Consulting, Pocatello, Idaho, 1996—96; scientist Lockheed Martin Idaho Techs. Co., Idaho Falls, 1996—2000, Bechtel BBWI, Idaho Falls, 2000—. Contbr. articles to profl. jours. Recipient Idaho Innovation in Industry award in the Agr. and Food Industry Category, Dept. Energy Office Indsl. Tech., 2001. Achievements include research in crossflow filtration testing on INEEL radioactive and nonradioactive waste slurries; INEEL EM chemical separations program; cesium sorption from concentrated acidic tank waste using ammonium molybdophosphate-polyacrylonitrile composite sorbents; evaluation and testing of inorganic ion exchange sorbent for the removal of cesium-137 from Idaho Chemical Processing Plant acidic tank waste; patents pending in field. Office: INEEL PO Box 1625 Idaho Falls ID 83415 Business E-Mail: mannnr@inel.gov.

MANN, NIRMAL SINGH, internist, educator; b. India, Aug. 10, 1936; came to U.S., 1964, U.S. citizen, 1978; s. Harinder Singh nd Udar Kaur (Punia) M.; m. Surinder Kaur Nijjar, Jan. 14, 1970; children: Neel K., Sheel K. BSc in Chemistry and Biology, Delhi (India) U., 1956; MD, Panjab (India) U., 1962; MS in Gastroenterology, Northwestern U., 1969; DSc in Gastroenterology, San Juan (P.R.) Bautista U., 1987; PhD in Nutrition, Pan Am. U., Mex., 1998. Chief of gastroenterology dept. VA Med. Ctr., Louisville, 1973-83, Temple, Tex., 1984-2000; asst. prof. medicine U. Louisville, 1973-78, assoc. prof. medicine, 1978-83, Tex. A&M U., College Station, 1983-84, prof. medicine, 1985-2000; dir. gastroenterology VA Med. Ctr., Martinez, Calif., 2000—; prof. medicine U. Calif., Davis, 2000—. Author: Selected Annotated Bibliographies, 1995, 20 Golden Hits in Gastroenterology, 1996; editor, assoc. editor Am. Jour. Gastroenterology, Proctology; contbr. numerous articles to profl. jours. Mem. Poetical Symposium, Dallas, 1988—. Fellow ACP, Royal Coll. Physicians Can., Am. Coll. Nutrition, Am. Coll. Gastroenterology (gov. 1986-92), Am. Coll. Med. Quality; mem. Am. Gastroenterology Assn., Am. Soc. G.I. Endoscopy. Avocation: writing poetry. Home: 2705 Rockwell Dr Davis CA 95616-7665 Office: VA Med Ctr 111G 150 Muir Rd Martinez CA 94553-4695

MANN, OSCAR, retired physician, internist, educator; b. Paris, Oct. 13, 1934; arrived in U.S., 1953; s. Aron and Helen (Biegun) Mann; m. Amy S. Mann, July 19, 1964; children: Adriana, Karen. AA with distinction, George Washington U., 1958; MD cum laude, Georgetown U., 1962. Diplomate Am. Bd. Med. Examiners, Am. Bd. Internal Medicine, Am. Bd. Cardiovasc. Disease, cert. advanced achievement in internal medicine. Intern Georgetown U. Med. Ctr., Washington, 1962-63, jr. asst. med. resident, 1963-64, clin. fellow in cardiology with Proctor Harvey program, 1965-66; sr. asst. resident in medicine Georgetown svc. D.C. Gen. Hosp., 1964-65; clin. prof. medicine Georgetown U. Sch. Medicine, 1985—; nat. chmn. med. alumi fund Georgetown U. Med. Sch., Washington, 1993-95; pvt. practice internal medicine and cardiology, 1966-99. Mem. med. nursing com. Georgetown U. Med. Ctr., mem. adv. com. CME, mem. tchg. adv. com., opthalmology dept. rev. com., surgery dept. rev. com., faculty com., search com. for a new dean for acad. affairs; appointed coun. to the dean Georgetown U. Sch. Medicine, 1977—; mem. Instnl. Self Study Task Force. Contbr. articles to profl. jours. Nat. chmn. med. alumni fund Georgetown U., 1997—99. Served with U.S. Army, 1953—55, with U.S. Army, 1953—55. Recipient Mead Johnson Postgrad. Scholar ACP, 1964—65, Physicians Recognition award, AMA, 1987—96, Advanced Achievement in Internal Medicine, 1987, John Carroll award, Georgetown U., 1999. Fellow: ACP, Am. Coll. Chest Physicians, Am. Coll. Cardiology; mem.: AMA, Med. Soc. D.C., Am. Heart Assn. (coun. clin. cardiology), Am. Soc. Internal Medicine, Georgetown U. Alumni Assn. (bd. govs. 1993—, chair med. alumni bd. 1995—, nat. chmn. med. alumni fund 1997—99), Cosmos Club, Phi Delta Epsilon, Alpha Omega Alpha. Home: 5137 Yuma St NW Washington DC 20016 E-mail: oscarmann@peoplepc.com.

MANN, PAMELA A. lawyer; b. Chgo., Sept. 30, 1948; d. Fred and Sada Lea (Rudin) Mann; m. Walter M. Meginniss, Jr., July 25, 1982; 1 child, Emma E. Mann-Meginniss. BA in History, Oberlin Coll., 1970; JD, U. Pitts., 1973. Bar: Pa. 1974, N.Y. 1977, U.S. Supreme Ct. 1987. Jud. law clk. Judge Marion K. Finkelhor, Pitts., 1973-74; staff atty. Susquehanna Legal Svcs., Sunburg, 1974-76; sr. staff atty. Nat. Employment Law Project, N.Y.C., 1976-82; clin. prof. Law Sch. Constnl. Litigation Clinic Rutgers U., Newark, 1982-84; dep. chief charities bur. N.Y. State Atty. Gen., NYC, 1984—85, chief charities bur., 1985—95; prin. pvt. practice, 1995—. Lectr. in field. Co-author: Advising Non-Profits, 1988, 2d edit. 1995; contbr. articles to profl. jours. Mem. govt. rels. com. Non-Profit Coording Com., 1996. Mem. Nat. Assn. State Charities Ofcls. (pres. 1994-95), N.Y. State Bar Assn. (charitable orgns. com. 1996—), Assn. Bar City N.Y. (com. on non-profit orgns. 1984-94, chmn. 1998-2001). Office: 225 Broadway Rm 2501 New York NY 10007-3088 E-mail: pmann@pamelamann.com.

MANN, PHILLIP LYNN, data processing company executive; b. Charleston, W.Va., July 26, 1944; s. Clarence Edward and Virginia Charlotte (Rupe) M.; m. Edith Jane Dewell, Dec. 28, 1966 (div. 1977); 1 child, Cynthia Lynn; m. Phyllis Anita Berg, May 18, 1979; children: Stacia Lynn, Brandon Granville. BSEE, Purdue U., 1970; MBA, U. Chgo., 1975. Devel. engr. Western Electric Co., Inc., Lisle, Ill., 1970-77; v.p. Uniq Digital Techs., Inc., Batavia, 1977-88; pres. ProTech Computer Group, Inc., 1988—. Served with USN, 1962-66. Avocations: radio control helicopters, fishing. Home: 428 Meadowrue Ln Batavia IL 60510-2815 Office: ProTech Computer Group Inc 428 Meadowrue Ln Batavia IL 60510-2815

MANN, PREM SINGH, economics educator; b. Punjab, India, Nov. 20, 1947; came to U.S., 1980; s. Malkiat Singh and Darshan Kaur (Gill) M.; m. Sarabjeet K. Bains, May 9, 1975; children: Harpreet K., Kulwinder S., Sukhwinder S. BA, Panjab U., Chandigarh, India, 1968, MA in Econs., 1970, U. Manchester (Eng.), 1977; PhD in Econs., UCLA, 1988. Tchr. D.S.N. High Sch., Nawanshahr, India, 1970-71; lectr. Panjab U., 1971-75, Calif. State U., L.A., 1981-82, asst. prof. Fullerton, 1982-86, Ea. Conn. State U., Willimantic, 1986-89, assoc. prof., 1989-94, prof., 1994—, chair dept. econs., 1994—. Author: Introductory Statistics, 1992, 4th edit., 2001, Statistics for Business and Economics, 1995; contbr. articles to profl. publs. Mem. Am. Econ. Assn. Sikh. Avocations: sports, reading. Office: Ea Conn State U Willimantic CT 06226

MANN, RICHARD EVANS, lawyer, arbitrator; b. Jacksonville, Ill., Jan. 9, 1922; s. Roberts John and Lecie Evans M.; m. Theodosia Ross, June 17, 1943; children: Theodosia Evans, Kristin, Richard R., Kathryn Herring, William P. AB, U. Ill., 1946, JD, 1947. Bar: Ill. 1948. State's atty. Scott County, Winchester, Ill., 1948-60; ptnr. Hutchens & Mann, 1948-80; cir. judge 7th Jud. Cir., 1980-88; ptnr. Bell & Mann, 1988—. 1st lt. U.S. Army AC, 1942-45. Republican. Episcopalian. Home: RR 2 Box 108 Winchester IL 62694-9534 Office: Bell & Mann PO Box 109 Winchester IL 62694-0109

MANN, RICHARD LYNN, lawyer; b. Columbus, Ohio, June 22, 1946; s. Clyde Earl and Kathryn Ann (Mock) M.; children: Richard Sean, Shannon Michele. BA, Ohio State U., 1968, JD, 1971. Bar: Ohio 1972, U.S. Dist. Ct. (so. dist.) Ohio 1979. Ptnr. Bolla, Mann & Caulfield, Columbus, 1973-76, Caulfield & Mann, Columbus, 1976-78, Mann & Stuhr, Columbus, 1978-81, White, Rankin, Co., LPA, Columbus, 1981-88, Shrim and Henry, 1988-89; pvt. practice Columbus, 1989—; state counsel Ohio Assn. Secondary Adminstrs., 1976—. Author article series Legal Notes, 1976—; co-author pamphlet Due Process in Schools, 1977, Ohio Title Insurance PSI, 1990, Ohio Title Insurance Ipdate PSI, 1994. 1st lt. U.S. Army, 1971-73. Decorated Army Commendation medal. Mem. Edn. & Law Assn. Clubs: Little Turtle Country (Westerville, Ohio). Republican. E-mail: mannr@titlemrst.com.

MANN, RICHARD O. public relations consulting company executive; b. N.Y.C., July 1, 1933; s. Otto and Ruth (Buchwald) M.; m. Anne Marie Seidenschwang, Apr. 28, 1956; children: Melinda, Susan, Carolyn. BA in History and Polit. Sci., Hofstra U., 1955. Reporter Newsday, Garden City, N.Y., 1951-56; pub. relations v.p., cons. Carl Byoir & Assoc., N.Y.C., 1957-76; v.p. corp. affairs Mack Trucks, Inc., Allentown, Pa., 1976-79; v.p. pub. relations Transway Internat., N.Y.C., 1979-85; pres. Mann Assoc., Mt. Kisco, N.Y., 1985—. Track and field official, U.S. Internat. meets, including 1984 Olympics, 1970— Bd. dirs. Vol. Ctr. United Way, Westchester County, Internat. Waldenstrom's Macroglobulinemia Found. 1st lt. U.S. Army, 1956-57. Mem. Pub. Relations Soc. Am., Met. Golf Writers Assn., N.Y. Sales Execs. Club, Mt. Kisco Country Club. Republican. Presbyterian. Avocations: golf, sports. Home and Office: 37 Indian Hill Rd Mount Kisco NY 10549-3826

MANN, ROBERT, academic administrator; Chair dept. physics U. Waterloo, Canada. Contbr. articles to profl. jours. Achievements include research in gravitation and particle physics; tests of gravitational theory; black holes; quantum gravity and string theory. Office: U Waterloo Dept Physics Waterloo ON N2L 3G1 Canada

MANN, ROBERT DAVID, lawyer; b. Chgo., May 27, 1941; s. Robert Lewis and Leona M. (Merillat) M. BA, DePauw U., 1963; JD, Ind. U., 1966. Bar: Ind. 1966, U.S. Dist. Ct. (so. dist.) Ind. 1966. Ptnr. Baker, Andrews Barnhart, et al., Bloomington, Ind., 1966-74, Andrews, Harrell, Mann, et al., P.C., Bloomington, 1974—. Bd. dirs. Citizens Bank Ctrl. Ind., Bloomington Community Found. Chmn., mem. Bd. Pub. Safety City of Bloomington, 1969-72; chmn., bd. dirs. South Cen. Community Mental Health Ctrs., Inc., Bloomington, 1968-74; pres., bd. dirs. Mental Health Assn. of Monroe County, Bloomington, 1972; bd. dirs. WonderLab Mus., 1997—, Bloomington Area Arts Coun., 1997-99. Fellow Ind. Bar Found.; mem. ABA (constrn. forum), Am. Assn. Arbitrators (former constrn. arbitrator), Ind. State Bar Assn., Monroe County Bar Assn. (pres. 1988-89), Assn. Trial Lawyers Am., Ind. Trial Lawyers Assn., Ind. Assn. Mediators (cert. mediator), Greater Bloomington C. of C. (bd. dirs., sec. 1969). Office: Andrews Harrell Mann et al PC PO Box 2639 400 W 7th St Ste 104 Bloomington IN 47402 Fax: 812-331-4511. E-mail: bobmann@ahmcp.com.

MANN, ROBERT WELLESLEY, biomedical engineer, educator; b. Bklyn., Oct. 6, 1924; s. Arthur Wellesley and Helen (Rieger) M.; m. Margaret Ida Florencourt, Sept. 4, 1950; children: Robert Wellesley, Catherine Louise. SB, MIT, 1950, SM, 1951, ScD, 1957. With Bell Telephone Labs., N.Y.C., 1942-43, 46-47; with U.S. Army Signal Corps, 1943-46; research engr. MIT, 1951-52, rsch. supr., 1952, mem. faculty, 1953—, prof. mech. engring., 1963-70, Germeshausen prof., 1970-72, prof. engring., 1972-74, Whitaker prof. biomed. engring., 1974-92, Whitaker prof. emeritus, sr. lectr., 1992—, head systems and design div., mech. engring. dept., 1957-68, 82-83, founder, dir. engring. projects lab., 1959-62; founder, chmn. steering com. Center Sensory Aids Evaluation and Devel., 1964-86, chmn. div. health scis., tech., planning and mgmt., 1972-74, founder, dir. Newman biomechanics and human rehab. lab., 1975-92; dir. bioengring. programs Whitaker Coll. MIT, 1986-89; dir. Harvard-MIT Rehab. Engring. Ctr., 1988-93. Mem. exec. com. Divsn. Health Scis. and Tech. Harvard U. MIT, 1972-85; prof., 1979—, mem. Com. on Use of Humans as Exptl. Subjects MIT, 1984-93, co-chair Pub. Svc. Ctr., 1988-92; lectr. engring. Faculty of Medicine, Harvard U., 1973-79; rsch. assoc. in orthopedic surgery Children's Hosp. Med. Ctr., 1973—; cons. in engring. sci. Mass. Gen. Hosp., 1969—; cons. in field, 1953—; mem. Nat. Commn. Engring. Edn., 1962-69; com. prosthetics rsch. and devel. NRC, 1963-69; chmn. sensory aids subcom., 1965-68, com. skeletal sys., 1969; mem. com. interplay engring. with biology and medicine Nat. Acad. Engring., 1969-73; mem. bd. health scis. policy Inst. Medicine, 1973-74, 82-86; mem. com. on nat. needs for rehab. physically handicapped Nat. Acad. Scis., 1975-76; mem.-at-large confs. com. Engring. Found., 1975-81; chair sensory aids panel scis. merit rev. bd. Rehab., R & D Svc., Dept. Vets. Affairs, 1983-95, 99—, mem. Visual/Hearing Impairment Rehab. Panel, 1999—; mem. Commn. on Life Scis. NRC, 1984-88, Com. on Strategic Tech. for U.S. Army, NRC, 1989-93; NRC Com. on Space Biology and Medicine, 1992-95. Consulting editor: Ency. Sci. and Tech., 1962-67; assoc. editor: IEEE Trans. in Biomed. Engring., 1969-78, ASME Jour. Biomech. Engring., 1976-82; mem. editl. bd. Jour. Visual Impairment and Blindness, 1976-80, SOMA, 1986-92; mem. editl. adv. bd. new liberal arts program Alfred P. Sloan Found., 1986-92; contbr. over 400 articles to profl. jours. Pres., trustee Amanda Caroline Payson Scholarship Fund, 1965-86; bd. dirs. Carroll Ctr. for Blind, 1967-74, pres., 1968-74; mem. corp. Perkins Sch. for Blind, 1970-2000, Mt. Auburn Hosp., 1972-2000; trustee Nat. Braille Press, 1982—, pres., 1990-94; mem. Cardinal's adv. com. on social justice Archdiocese of Boston, 1993-96; bd. overseers St. Marguerite D'Youville Found., Youville Lifecare Inc., 1994-98. With U.S. Army Signal Corps, 1943-46. Recipient Sloan award for Outstanding Performance, 1957, Talbert Abrams Photogrammetry award, 1962, Assn. Blind of Mass. award, 1969, IR-100 award for Braillemboss, 1972, Bronze Beaver award MIT, 1975, UCP Goldenson Rsch. for Handicapped award, 1976, New Eng. award, 1979, J.R. Killian Faculty Achievement award MIT, 1983, Martin Luther King Leadership award MIT, 1995, Distng. Alumnus lectr. dept. mech. engring. MIT, 1997. Fellow Am. Acad. Arts and Scis., Am. Inst. Med. and Biol. Engring., IEEE (mem. editl. bd. Spectrum 1984-86), AAAS, ASME (gold medal 1977, H.R. Lissner award for biomed. engring. 1977); mem. NAS, Inst. Medicine NAS, NAE, Biomed. Engring. Soc. (bd. dirs. 1981-84), Orthopedic Rsch. Soc., Rehab. Soc. N.Am., MIT Alumni Asssn. (pres. 1983-84, Alumni Fund Bd. 1978-80, bd. dirs. 1980-86, 93-95, corp. joint adv. com. 1983-84, chair nat. selector com. 1985-88, awards com. 1992-94, chmn. 1994, bd. Tech. Rev. 1986-95, chmn. 1993-95), Sigma Xi (nat. lectr. 1979-81), Tau Beta Pi, Pi Tau Sigma, Sigma Xi. Roman Catholic. Achievements include patents on missile power units, founding of computer aided design in 1963, earliest braille translation software and hardware in

1962, cybernetic amputation prosthesis, 1966, in vivo measurements of human cartilage pressures, 1984. Home: 5 Pelham Rd Lexington MA 02421-5707 Office: MIT 77 Massachusetts Ave Rm 3-137 Cambridge MA 02139-4307 E-mail: rwmann@mit.edu.

MANN, ROBERT CHRISTOPHER, communications educator, television host, producer; b. Bklyn., Mar. 18, 1953; s. Alvin Charles and Marion Theresa (Hensch) M.; m. Virginia Rohan, Apr. 29, 1979 (div. Feb. 1995); 1 child, Christopher Robert. BA, Fordham U., 1975; MA, Montclair State U., 1993. Radio newscaster, sportscaster Sta. WOBM-AM-FM, Toms River, N.J., 1976-77; TV host, prodr. United Artists Cable (now Cablevision), Oakland, 1977-84; on air host Sta. WNET-TV, N.Y.C., 1983-85; feature reporter Sta. WOR-AM, 1985; prof. comm., chair dept. Caldwell (N.J.) Coll., 1988—; TV host, prodr. Mann Media Inc., Bergenfield, N.J., 1989—. Mem. faculty coun. Caldwell Coll., 1990—. Host, prodr. (TV show) Healthview From Hackensack U. Med. Ctr., 1989— (Percy award 1990), Healthtalk, 1996—; host (radio program) Healthbeat, 1991— (Percy award 1996). Class father Roy Brown Mid. Sch., Bergenfield, 1994; vol. TV host Am. Cancer Soc., Bergen County, N.J., 1996. Recipient Cable Programming award Cable TV Network N.J., 1996. Mem. AFTRA, Nat. Acad. Cable Programming (CableACE award (3), 1984-85), Soc. Profl. Journalists, AAUP. Avocations: tennis, travel, N.Y. Yankees baseball, comedy, movies. Home: 163 Phelps Ave Bergenfield NJ 07621-1422 Office: Caldwell Coll 9 Ryerson Ave Caldwell NJ 07006-6109 E-mail: profmann@aoo.com.

MANN, ROBERT PAUL, retired lawyer; b. Pitts., July 24, 1929; s. O. Paul and Floy Melinda (Foster) M.; m. Dorothy Neeld, Sept. 4, 1953; children: Robin Duvall Francik, Stewart Neeld Mann. BS, U. Md., College Park, 1951; JD, U. Md., Balt., 1953. Bar: Md. 1954, U.S. Dist. Md. 1965, U.S. Tax Ct. 1976. Pvt. practice, Ruxton, Md., 1956-96; ret., 1996. Trial magistrate, 1957-59. Past pres. Artists Equity, Timonium Rotary, Towson Libr.; active wildlife orgns.; art donor to numerous major mus. Mem. Omicron Delta Kappa, Delta Theta Phi, Sigma Chi. Episcopalian.

MANN, ROGER, economist; b. Lake Forest, Illinois, Oct. 18, 1955; s. Richard E. and Mary Louise Mann; m. Kimberly Wheatley, June 14, 1986; children: Cory Lee, Eric Tyler. BS, U. N.H., 1976; MS, U. Nev. Reno, 1979; PhD, Colo. State U., 1988. Economist Hydrosphere Resources Inc., Boulder, Colo., 1986—91, Biosys. Analysis Inc., Tiberon, Calif., 1991—94, CHZM HILL, Sacramento, 1995—99; prin., founder RMecon, Davis, 1999—. Author: Water Resources Research, 1986, Antimarket Economics, 1996. Soccer coach AYSD, Davis, 1996—2001; treas. Davis United 2001. Achievements include noted for contributions to application of economics and water resource economics. Office: RMecon 1677 Colusa Ave Davis CA 95616-3140

MANN, ROGER ELLIS, business development, food service and real estate executive; b. N.Y.C., Jan. 12, 1948; BA, Wesleyan U., Middletown, Conn., 1971, MA in Tchg., 1972; MBA, Yale U., 1986. Africa mgmt. cons. and journalist, Tanzania, Kenya, Zambia, 1973-84; sr. dir. devel. Marriott Corp. and Host Marriott Corp., Washington, 1986-94; mng. dir., CEO Lifesource Internat. Ltd., 1994-95; pres. Rainbow Ventures, Inc., Naples, Fla., 1995—. Mng. dir. Bagel Internat., Washington, 1996-99, Bagel Internat. UK Ltd., London, 1996-99; founder, pres. Picnic, Inc., Washington, 1997-2000; pres. Care-Free Corp., Naples, Fla., 2001-2002. Contbr. articles on Africa to profl. jours. Pres. Friends of Tanzania. Nat. Resource fellow Yale U., 1985-86.

MANN, SAM HENRY, JR. lawyer; b. St. Petersburg, Fla., Aug. 2, 1925; s. Sam Henry and Vivian (Moore) M.; m. Mary Joan Bishop, Sept. 7, 1948; children: Vivian Louise, Sam Henry III, Wallace Bishop. BA, Yale U., 1948; LLB, Fla. U., 1951, JD, 1967. Bar: Fla. 1951, U.S. Dist. Ct. (mid. and so. dists.) Fla. 1951, U.S. Ct. Appeals (5th cir.) 1955, U.S. Ct. Appeals (11th cir.) 1996, U.S. Supreme Ct. 1971. Ptnr. Greene, Mann, Rowe, Stanton, Mastry & Burton, St. Petersburg, 1951-84, Harris, Barrett, Mann & Dew, St. Petersburg, 1984—. Trustee, v.p. Mus. Fine Arts, St. Petersburg, 1980-94, Eckerd Coll., St. Petersburg, 1976-79, Webb Sch., Bell Buckle, Tenn., 1966-75; bd. dirs. Regional Cmty. Blood Ctr., St. Petersburg, 1966-93, Fla. Blood Svcs., 1993-94, mem. emeritus 1996—; mem. Disting. Alumni Soc. Webb Sch.; mem., chmn. H. Milton Rogers Heart Found.; bd. dirs., pres. Family and Children's Svc., Inc., 1956-61. Lt. (j.g.) USNR, 1943-48. Fellow Am. Coll. Trial Lawyers, Am. Bar Found., Fla. Bar Found.; mem. ABA, Fla. Bar Assn., Fla. Supreme Ct. Hist. Soc., Am. Counsel Assn., Def. Rsch. Inst., Internat. Assn. Def. Counsel, Pinellas County Trial Lawyers Assn., Nat. Assn. Railroad Trial Counsel, Fla. Def. Lawyers Assn., Assn. Hostp. Attys., Bay Area Vanderbilt, St. Petersburg Bar Assn., Yale and U. Fla. Alumni Assns., Phi Alpha Delta, Delta Kappa Epsilon. Republican. Presbyterian. Avocations: RV travel, boating, gardening, workshop. Home: 531 Brightwaters Blvd NE Saint Petersburg FL 33704-3713 Office: Harris Barrett Mann & Dew Southtrust Bank Bldg 150 Second Ave N Saint Petersburg FL 33731-1441

MANN, SEYMOUR ZALMON, political science and public administration educator emeritus, union official; b. Chgo., Mar. 29, 1921; s. Morris and Sarah (Julius) M.; m. Irene Eincig, Aug. 30, 1942; children: Martin R., Sheldon H., Jeanette P. Student, Wright Coll., 1938-40; BE, No. Ill. U. (formerly No. Ill. State Tchr.'s Coll.), 1942; MA, U. Chgo., 1948, PhD, 1951. Instr. polit. sci. Triple Cities Coll., Syracuse U., 1948-51; asst. prof. Harpur Coll., State U. N.Y., 1951-55, asso. prof. polit. sci., 1955-60, chmn. dept., 1953-58; dir. pub. adminstrn. and met. affairs program, prof. govt. So. Ill. U., Edwardsville, 1960-67; chmn., prof. urban affairs dept. urban affairs Hunter Coll./CUNY, 1967-77; dir. Urban Research Center, 1967-68, chmn. dept. urban affairs, 1968-73; dep. to execs. dist. council 37, Am. Fedn. State, County and Mcpl. Employees, AFL-CIO, 1977-79; prof. govt. and public adminstrn., assoc. dir. Nat. Center Public Productivity, John Jay Coll. Criminal Justice, CUNY, 1980-86. Vis. expert Office Pub. Affairs, High Commr.'s Office, Germany, 1954; cons. Southwestern Ill. Govtl. Study Commn., 1961-62; vis. prof. U. So. Calif. Sch. Pub. Adminstrn., 1967; co-chmn. Ill. U.-State Agy. Coun., 1965-67; chmn. nat. commn. on urban affairs Am. Jewish Congress, 1977-81, mem. nat. governing coun., 1991-97; cons., coord. spl. projects dist. coun. 37 Am. Fedn. State, County and Mcpl. Employees, N.Y.C., 1972-77, dep. to dir., DC 37, 1977-82. Author: (with others) From the Wagner Act to the Taft-Hartley Act, 1950, (with Charlotte B. Smart) Land Use and Planning in the Cleveland Metropolitan Area, 1959, (with R.R. Boyce) Urbanism in Illinois: Its Nature Importance and Problems, 1965, Chicago's War on poverty, 1966; contbr. to: Cases in State and Local Government, 1961, Cases in American National Government and Politics, 1978, The Politics of Productivity: State and Local Focus, 1980, Labor Management Cooperation and Worker Participation: A Public Sector Focus, 1989, play Summing Up in Public Voices, 1993; contbr. poetry to anthologies, vols. of poetry; mem. editl. bd. Pub. Voices. Served with AUS, 1943-45, ETO. Fellow Social Sci. Research Council, 1949-50; Fulbright prof. W. Germany, 1953-54; Fulbright prof. Tel Aviv (Israel) U., 1974-75 Mem. Am. Soc. for Pub. Adminstrn. (pres. St. Louis met. chpt. 1964-65), Am. Arbitration Assn. (nat. labor panel), Soc. of Children's Book Writers and Illustrators, Poetry Soc. Va., Live Poets Soc. (Alexandria, Va.). Home and Office: 203 S Yoakum Pky Apt 1111 Alexandria VA 22304-3731 E-mail: szmann@home.com. *It will have to be left to others to judge what success I may have obtained. There have, however, been some guiding principles which seemed to have given direction to my life's course and undoubtedly impacted on whatever professional recognition has come my way. These include: a profound respect for democratic ideology— particularly the notion that each person should have the opportunity to achieve his/her fullest potential; a clear recognition that wisdom and knowledge are not the same; and that listening is harder than talking, though it is the most important element in human communication.*

MANN, STEPHEN ASHBY, financial counselor; b. Richmond, Va., Feb. 20, 1947; s. Milton Ashby and Rebecca (George) Mann; m. Patricia Ann Kofron, Aug. 25, 1982; 1 child Michael Joseph Ashby stepchildren: Christine Ferguson, Tracy Kofron. BS in Gen. Bus., Va. Poly. Inst. and State U., 1970. CLU, cert. sr advisor 2001. Supr. mfg. Brown & Williamson Tobacco Corp., Petersburg, Va., 1970-72; pres. Cumberland (Va.)) Woodyard, 1972-79; mgr. Ragland Woodyards, Goochland, Va., 1980-81; advt. mgr., rep. Gazette Newspapers, 1982-85; fin. counselor, ins. and fin. planner Peoples Security Ins. Co., Mechanicsville, Va., 1986-98, Monumental Life Ins. Co., Mechanicsville, 1999—. Pres Millquarter Property Owners Asn, Powhatan, Va., 1987. Named to All-Star Honor Roll, Ins Sales Mag, 1989, 1990. Mem.: SCV (lt comdr Powhatan 1980—82, inspector gen state div 1981, nat adc 1982—83, comdr), All Harley Drag Racing Asn (nat ranked # 4 street eliminator 1996—97, Racer of the Yr Award 1996, nat ranked #2 super sport 1999), Richmond Asn Ins and Financial Advisors (bd dirs 1989—92), Asn Health Inst Agts, Soc Financial Serv Profls, Nat Asn Ins and Financial Advisors (Nat Quality Award 1986, Nat Sales Achievement Award 1986, Nat Health Inst Award 1986), Sons of the South Motorcycle Club, Masons (master 1990, 1994, chaplain Powhatan Lodge # 295 1995—, 16th dist blood coord 1995—96, Samis Grotto treas 1991—93, Scottish Rite, life mem Royal Arch), Golden Key Soc (mem comt 1991—96). Republican. Baptist. Avocations: church pianist/organist, history, motorcycling. Home: 1433 E Overlook Dr Powhatan VA 23139 Office: Monumental Life Ins Co 5980 Chamberlayne Rd Mechanicsville VA 23116-2511

MANN, SUSAN, history educator; b. Ottawa, Ont., Can., Feb. 10, 1941; d. Walter and Marjorie Mann; m. Nicholas Trofimenkoff; 1 child, Britt. BA in Modern History, U. Toronto, 1963; MA in History, U. Western Ont., 1965; PhD, U. Laval, Que., Can., 1970; LLD (hon.), Concordia U., Montreal, Que., 1989, U. Ottawa, 1994, U. Montreal, 1997. Lectr. English Toyo Eiwa Jogakuin, Tokyo, 1963-64; lectr. in history U. Montreal, 1966-70; asst. prof. history U. Calgary, Alta., Can., 1970-72; from asst. to assoc. prof. U. Ottawa, 1972-83, prof. history, 1983-92, chmn. dept. history, 1977-80, vice rector acad., 1984-90; pres. York U., Toronto, Ont., 1992-97. Mem. stamp adv. com. Can. Post Corp., Ottawa, 1988-92; chmn. adv. bd. Nat. Archives Can., 1989-91. Author: (as Susan Mann Trofimenkoff) Action Française: French Canadian Nationalism in the 1920s, 1975, Stanley Knowles: The Man From Winnipeg North Centre, 1982, Dream of Nation: A Social and Intellectual History of Quebec, 1983, 2002 (Sec. of State Canadian Studies prize 1984), Visions nationales: Une histoire du Québec, 1986; editor: The Twenties in Western Canada, 1972, Abbé Groulx: Variations on a Nationalist Theme, 1973, (with Alison Prentice) The Neglected Majority: Essays in Canadian Women's History, vol. I, 1977, vol II, 1985; editor: (as Susan Mann) The War Diary of Clare Gass 1915-1918, 2000; acad. editor Social Scis. in Can., 1974-76; assoc. editor Social History, 1982-84; contbr. articles to profl. jours. Assessor of projects Social Scis. and Humanities Rsch. Coun. Can., 1972—; chmn., aid to scholarly publs. com. Social Sci. Fedn. Can., 1976-79; mem. appraisals com. Ont. Coun. Grad. Studies, 1983-84; pres. Can. Hist. Assn., 1984-85; chair status of women com. Coun. Ont. Univs., 1985-88; mem. Summer Inst. Women in Higher Edn. Adminstrn. Bryn Mawr (Pa.) Coll., 1986; co-founder Sr. Women Acad. Adminstrs. Can. Publ. grantee Social Scis. and Humanities Rsch. Coun. Can., 1975, Leave fellow, 1980-81, Doctoral fellow Can. Coun., 1968-70; U. Toronto scholar, 1959-61, U. Western Ont. scholar, 1964. Fellow Royal Soc. Can., Order Can., Canadian Rsch. Inst. Advancement Women (hon., life, founder, bd. dirs. 1976-78). Office: York Univ Dept History 4700 Keele St Toronto ON Canada M3J 1P3

MANN, TED RUSSELL, retired music educator; b. Tallassee, Ala., July 16, 1952; s. Fred Wright and Julia Atkins Mann; m. Amy Ellis Plott, Aug. 23, 1975; children: Russell. MusB in Edn., Troy State U., 1970. Cert. Elem. Educator Ala., 1989. Band dir. Pvt. Sch., Union Springs, Ala., 1975—76, Pickens County H.S., Reform, 1976—82, Childersburg H.S., Childersburg, 1982—84, Brookwood H.S., Brookwood, 1984—87; band dir., music tchr. Marbury Sch., Marbury, 1987—. Musician Montgomery Recreators Jazz Band, Montgomery, Ala., 1990—, Prattville, Ala., 1990—; music judge, Prattville, 1990—; pvt. music tchr., Prattville, 1990—. Mem.: Ala. Edn. Assn., Music Educators Nat. Conf., Phi Mu Alpha (warden 1973—74). Methodist. Home: 112 Croydon Dr Prattville AL 36066 Personal E-mail: tmslidz@aol.

MANN, THEODORE R. lawyer; b. Czechoslovakia, Jan. 31, 1928; came to U.S., 1929, naturalized, 1930; s. Aaron and Bertha (Schreiber) M.; m. Rowena Joan Weiss, 1954; children: Julie Ellen, Rachel Beth, Marcus Eliyahu. Pvt. practice, Phila., 1953—; ptnr. Wolf, Block, Schorra, Solis & Cohen; advocate in civil liberties, anti-trust and securities fraud cases. Chmn., pres. Nat. Jewish Community Rels. Adv. Coun., 1976-80; Conf. Pres. Major Am. Jewish Orgns., 1978-80; Nat. Conf. Soviet Jewry, 1981-83; Am. Jewish Congress, 1984-88; Mazon-A Jewish Response to Hunger, 1985-90; Project Nishma, 1988-97; exec. com. chair Israel Policy Forum, 1997-2001. Fellow Temple U. Alumni. Office: 1650 Arch St Fl 22 Philadelphia PA 19103-2097

MANN, THOMAS EDWARD, political scientist; b. Milw., Sept. 10, 1944; s. Edward Emil and Eleanor (Hoffman) M.; m. Sheilah Rosenhack, June 4, 1976; children: Edward Matthew, Stephanie Rachael. BA, U. Fla., 1966; MA, U. Mich., 1968, PhD, 1977. Staff assoc. Am. Polit. Sci. Assn., Washington, 1970-76, asst. dir., 1977-81, exec. dir., 1981-87; co-dir. congress project Am. Enterprise Inst., 1979-81; dir. govtl. studies Brookings Instn., 1987-99, W. Averell Harrimann sr. fellow in Am. governance, 1991—. Mem. bd. overseers Nat. Election Study, 1987-94, chmn., 1990-94. Author: Unsafe At Any Margin, 1978; co-author: Vital Statistics on Congress, 1980, 82, 84-85, 87-2002, Campaign Finance Reform: A Sourcebook, 1997; Renewing Congress, 1992, 93; co-editor: The New Congress, 1981, The American Elections of 1982, 1983, Media Polls in American Politics, 1992, Values and Public Policy, 1994, Elections at Home and Abroad, 1994, Congress, the Press, and the Public, 1994, Intensive Care: How Congress Shapes Health Policy, 1995, The Permanent Campaign and Its Future, 2000, The New Campaign Finance Sourcebook, 2002, Governance for a new Century: Japanese Challenges, American Experience, 2002; editor: A Question of Balance: The President, The Congress and Foreign Policy, 1990. Mem. Democratic Nat. Com.'s Commn. on Presdl. Nomination and Party Structure, 1975-78; mem. tech. com. Dem. Nat. Com. Commn. on Presdl. Nominations, 1981-82, The Fairness Commn., 1985. U. Mich. NDEA grad. fellow, 1966-69; Am. Polit. Sci. Assn. Congl. fellow, 1969-70 Fellow Am. Acad. Arts and Scis., Nat. Acad. Pub. Adminstrn.; mem. Coun. on Fgn. Rels., Phi Beta Kappa. Home: 6508 Goldleaf Dr Bethesda MD 20817-5837 Office: Brookings Instn 1775 Massachusetts Ave NW Washington DC 20036-2103 E-mail: tmann@brook.edu.

MANN, TRUE SANDLIN, psychologist, consultant; b. Longview, Tex., Aug. 4, 1934; d. Bob Murphy and Stella True (Williams) Sandlin; m. Jack Matthewson Mann, Sept. 4, 1954 (div. Dec. 1989); children: Jack Matthewson Jr., Bob Sandlin, Daniel Williams, Nathaniel Currier. BS, Stephen F. Austin State U., Nacogdoches, Tex., 1973, MA, 1977; PhD, East Tex. State U., 1982. Lic. psychologist, Tex., Ark. Instr. Stephen F. Austin State U., 1975-76, vis. asst. prof. psychology, 1986-87; instr. East Tex. State U., Commerce, 1980-81; postdoctoral fellow Southwestern Med. Sch., Dallas, 1982-83; pvt. practice, Longview, Tex., 1983-92; psychologist dept. family practice U. Tex. Health Sci. Ctr., Tyler, 1990-92; dir. psychol. svcs. St. Michael's Hosp., Texarkana, Tex., 1992-93; cons. psychologist, Longview, 1993—. Weekly newspaper columnist HARBUS, Cambridge Mass., 1959-60; cons. Made-Rite Co., Longview, 1989—. Mem. candidate com. Assoc. Reps. Tex., Austin, 1990—; bd. dirs. Mental Health Assn. Tex., 1977-82, 84-92, Longview Symphony, 1995-99, Dallas Opera Guild, 1999—, Longview Mus. of Art, 1995; mem. Leadership Tex., 1988—. Mem. APA, Tex. Psychol. Assn., N.E. Tex. Field Ornithologists. Episcopalian. Avocations: photography, travel, history of civilizations. Home: 1906 N 4th St Longview TX 75601-3202 Office: 1203 Montclair St Longview TX 75601-3565

MANN, WILLIAM CRAIG, lawyer; b. Norwalk, Ohio, Nov. 17, 1953; s. Abraham and Shirley (Smith) M. BA, Case Western Res. U., 1976; JD, U. Dayton, 1979. Bar: Ohio 1979, U.S. Dist. Ct. (no. dist.) Ohio 1979, U.S. Supreme Ct. 1986, U.S. Dist. Ct. (so. dist.) Ohio 1988. Law clk. Ohio Supreme Ct., 1985-86; pvt. practice Cleve., 1986-87; assoc. Wolske & Blue, Columbus, Ohio, 1987-97; ptnr. Sunbury, Mann & Young, 1997-99; of counsel Mitchell, Allen, Catalano & Boda, 1997—. Spkr. various orgns. in field, including Ohio Legal Ctr. Inst., Ohio Acad. of Trial Lawyers; mem. Ohio Supreme Ct. commn. on professionalism, 1997—. Contbr. articles to profl. jours. Bd. dirs. United Way, Huron County, Ohio, 1983; mem. exec. and cen. coms. Huron County Dem. Com., 1976-79. Mem. Ohio State Bar Assn. (ethics com. 1987—), Columbus Bar Assn., Ohio Acad. Trial Lawyers (pres. 2001—), Franklin County Trial Lawyers Assn. (pres. 2001—). Avocations: football, jogging. Home: 2041 Ramblewood Ave Columbus OH 43235-7340 Office: Mitchell Allen Catalano & Boda 490 S High St Columbus OH 43215-5603 E-mail: Mannlaw99@aol.com.

MANN, WILLIAM JOSEPH, JR. gynecologic oncologist; b. Wilkes Barre, Pa., Apr. 13, 1947; s. William Joseph and Irene Bertha M.; m. Katie Gallagher, Aug. 8, 1980; children: William Joseph Mann III, Kelly Catherine Rena. BA cum laude, Amherst Coll., 1969; MD, Pa. State U., 1973; MBA, Coll. of William and Mary, 1997. Diplomate Am. Bd. Ob-Gyn. Intern, resident M.S. Hershey Med. Ctr., Hershey, Pa., 1973-78, ACOG-Ortho fellow, 1976-77; fellow in gynecol. oncology U. Ala., Birmingham, 1978-80; assoc. prof., dir. gynecol. oncology SUNY, Stony Brook, 1980-91; dir. ob-gyn. residency Riverside Regional Med. Ctr., Newport News, Va., 1991-2001; prof. ob-gyn. Med. Coll. of Va., Richmond, 1993-2001; chmn., dept. ob-gyn., residency dir. Jersey Shore Med. Ctr., Neptune, NJ, 2001—. Prof. clin. ob-gyn. Ea. Va. Med. Sch., Norfolk; cons. Mary Immaculate Hosp., Newport News, Williamsburg Community Hosp., Sentara Hampton Gen. Hosp. Contbr. numerous articles to profl. jours., chpts. in books, revs. in various publs. Coach Smithtown Kickers soccer league, 1988-89, Rugby Club, SUNY at Stony Brook, 1988-91; vol. fireman Nissequogue Fire Dept., St. James, N.Y., 1988-91, Setauket (N.Y.) Vol. Fire Dept., 1983-88 Recipient Silver Sword award Am. Cancer Soc., 1991. Fellow ACS, Am. Coll. Ob-Gyn.; mem. Soc. Gynecol. Oncologists, Assn. Profs. Ob-Gyn., So. Med. Soc., So. Oncology Assn. (founding), Gyn. Urology Soc., Am. Soc. for Colposcopy and Cervical Pathology, Suffolk County Soc. Ob-Gyns., Internat. Gyn. Cancer Soc., Am. Soc. for Laser Medicine and Surgery, Inc., Newport News Med. Soc., Va. Ob-Gyn. Soc., Am. Soc. for Parenatal and Enteral Nutrition, Mid-Atlantic Gyn. Oncologic Soc. Avocations: rugby, karate. Office: 1945 State Route 33 Neptune NJ 07753-4859

MANN, ZANE BOYD, editor, publisher; b. St. Paul, Jan. 28, 1924; s. Michael M. and Rose Lee (Reuben) M.; m. Esther Zeesman, Mar. 25, 1945; children: Michael L., Eric F. Personal Fin. Planning, U. Calif., Riverside, 1986. Registered investment advisor Securities and Exch. Commn. Mcpl. fin. cons. Ehlers Mann & Assoc., Mpls., 1956-64; v.p. mcpl. bond underwriter Ebin Robertson, 1964-70; v.p. mcpl. dept. Piper Jaffrey & Co., 1970-72; ret., 1972; editor, pub. monthly investment newsletter Calif. Mcpl. Bond Advisor, Palm Springs, Calif., 1984—. Author: Fair Winds and Far Places, 1978; contbr. articles to profl. jours. Mem. Twin City Met. Planning Commn., St. Paul, 1958-70; bd. dirs. CORAL, Riverside County, Calif., 1984-91. Staff sgt. U.S. Army, 1942-45. Decorated DFC with cluster, Air medal with cluster, Soldier's medal, Purple Heart U.S. Army Air Corp. Mem. Nat. Fedn. Mcpl. Analysts, Calif. Soc. Mcpl. Analysts, Internat. Combat Camera Assn., Writers Guild Am. (ret.), Com. for the Sci. Investigation of Claims of the Paranormal (assoc.), Royal Corinthian Yacht Club (life, Cowles, Eng.), Mensa., Sports Car Club Am. Avocations: sailing, racing and cruising, scuba, SCCA competition driver, pilot. Home: 1300 E Verbena Dr Palm Springs CA 92262-5873 Office: Calif Mcpl Bond Advisor 1037 S Palm Canyon Dr Palm Springs CA 92264-8378

MANNAN, M. SAM, chemical engineer, educator, consultant; b. Comilla, Bangladesh, Nov. 10, 1954; came to U.S., 1981; s. Abdul and Nargis Ara Mannan; m. Afroza Mannan, Dec. 26, 1982; children: Joya, Rumki. BSChemE, Engring. U., Dhaka, Bangladesh, 1978; MSChemE, U. Okla., 1983, PhDChemE, 1986. Registered profl. engr., Tex., La. Engr. Devel. Bank, Dhaka, 1978; chem. engr. Ministry Mcpls., Agedabia, Libya, 1978-81; grad. rsch. asst. U. Okla., Norman, 1981-86, vis. asst. prof., 1986-89; program dir. RMT, Inc., Austin, Tex., 1990-94, v.p. Ausitn, 1994-97; assoc. prof., dir. chem. engring. Tex. A&M U., College Station, 1997—. Presenter papers at numerous confs., meetings, and symposia. Author: Guidelines for Safe Process Operations and Maintenance, 1995; contbr. articles to profl. jours. including Oil and Gas Jour., Chem. Engring. Process, and Internat. Jour. Physics. Recipient Quality Recognition award PPG Industries, 1998. Mem. AIChE (IIA com. 1998—, dir. safety and health divsn. 1999—), Am. Soc. Safety Engrs., Sys. Safety Soc. Mem. AIChE (IIA com. 1998—, safety and health divsn. 1999—), Am. Soc. Safety Engrs., Sys. Safety Soc. Avocations: travel, fishing, hunting. Office: Tex A&M U Dept Chem Engring College Station TX 77843-0001

MANNE, DEBORAH SUE, oncology nurse, consultant, dental hygienist; b. Vincennes, Ind., Nov. 20, 1954; d. Charles Kenneth and Susan Jane (Fox) Thornberry; m. Marshall Stanley Manne, Dec. 21, 1985. AA, Maplewoods C.C., Kansas City, Mo., 1973; BS in Dental Hygiene, U. Mo., 1975; BSN, St. Louis U., 1991, MSN in Oncology Nursing, 1998. RN, reg. dental hygienist, Mo. Dental hygienist Dr. Marshall S. Manne, St. Louis, 1978—, office nurse, 1991—; oncology nurse CIRCLE Barnes-Jewish Hosp., 1993-98; staff nurse Radiation Oncology Ctr. Barnes-Jewish Hosp. North, 1997; nurse educator Cancer Family Care, St. Louis, 1998; clin. asst. prof. divsn. dental hygiene Sch. Dentistry U. Mo., Kansas City, 1999—. Instr. dental hygiene dept. St. Louis C.C., Forest Park, 1999—; clin. instr. So. Ill. U., Carbondale, 2000—; coord., cons. Oncology Dental Support Svcs., St. Louis, 1992—; mem. curriculum rev. com. dental hygiene program St. Louis C.C., 1993; mem. adv. bd. ACCESS Dental Hygiene Jour., 1994—. Contbr. articles to profl. jours. Bd. dirs., v.p. Am. Cancer Soc., St. Louis, 1992-93, chair Gt. Am. Smokeout, 1992, mem. Breast Cancer task force, 1994-98; mem. profl. adv. com. Wellness Cmty., St. Louis, 1994—; chmn. Tobacco-Free Mo. Super Coalition, St. Louis, 2000—. Recipient Vol. Recognition award Am. Cancer Soc., 1992, Mo. Dental Hygienist of Yr. award, 1995, Irene Newman award, 1997, Susan Brockman-Bell Humanitarian award U. Mo. Kansas City Dental Hygiene Alumni Assn., 2000. Mem. Am. Dental Hygienists Assn. (council on pub. rels., coun. on edn.), Oncology Nursing Soc. (chair oral care focus group, pres.-elect St. Louis chpt. 1998, pres. 1999, editor patient edn. sig newsletter 1999-2000), Mo. Dental Hygienists' Assn. (pres.), Greater St. Louis Hygienists' Assn. (pres.), Sigma Phi Alpha, Sigma Theta Tau. Avocations: walking, raising golden retrievers and cats. Home: 11617 Larkmont Dr Creve Coeur MO 63141-6907 Office: Oncology Dental Support Svc 3009 N Ballas Rd Ste 211 Saint Louis MO 63131-2323

MANNE, HENRY GIRARD, lawyer, educator; b. New Orleans, May 10, 1928; s. Geoffrey and Eva (Shainberg) M.; m. Bobbette Lee Taxer, Aug. 19, 1968; children: Emily Kay, Geoffrey Adam. BA, Vanderbilt U., 1950; JD, U. Chgo., 1952; LL.M., Yale U., 1953, J.S.D., 1966; LLD, U. Seattle, 1987, U. Francisco Marroquin, Guatemala, 1987, George Mason U., 2000. Bar: Ill. 1952, N.Y. 1969. Practice in, Chgo., 1953-54; assoc. prof. St. Louis U. Law Sch., 1956-57, 59-62; vis. prof. law U. Wis., Madison, 1957-59; prof. George Washington U. Law Sch., 1962-68; Kenan prof. law and polit. sci. U. Rochester, 1968-74; vis. prof. law Stanford (Calif.) Law Sch., 1971-72; disting. prof. law, dir. Law and Econs. Center, U. Miami Law Sch., 1974-80; prof. law Emory U. Law and Econs. Ctr., Atlanta, 1980-86; dean Law Sch., chmn. Law and Econs. Ctr. George Mason U., 1986-96, univ. prof., 1986-99, dean emeritus, 2000—. Vis. prof. law U. Wis., Madison, 1957-59, Stanford (Calif.) Law Sch., 1971-72, U. Chgo. Law Sch., 2000—; dir. Econs. Insts. Fed. Judges, 1976-89. Author: Insider Trading and the Stock Market, 1966, (with H. Wallich) The Modern Corporation and Social Responsibility, 1973, (with E. Solomon) Wall Street in Transition, 1974, Med. Malpractice Guidebook: Law and Economics, 1985; editor: (with Roger LeRoy Miller) Gold, Money and the Law, 1975, Auto Safety Regulation: The Cure or the Problem, 1976; editor: Economic Policy and the Regulation of Corporate Securities, 1968, The Economics of Legal Relationships, 1975; editor: (with James Dorn) Econ. Liberties and the Judiciary, 1987. Served to 1st lt. USAF, 1954-56. Recipient Salvatori award Excellence in Acad. Leadership, 1994; named Cultural Laureate of Va., 1992. Adj. scholar CATO Inst.; fellow Am. Law and Econs. Assn. (hon. life), Mont Pelerin Soc., Order of Coif, Phi Beta Kappa. E-mail: hmanne@mediaone.net.

MANNEPALLI, YELLAMANDESWARA RAO, software engineer, consultant; b. Mannepalli, India; s. Subbaramaiah and Tulasamma Mannepalli; m. Usha Khadarbad, May 9, 1982; children: Bharadwaj, Aswin Bhargava. BS in Computer Engring., Inst. Electron/Telecomm Engrs., New Delhi, 1982; MS in Computer Sci. with Gold medal, U. Hyderabad, India, 1986. Scientist/engr.-SC Indian Space Rsch. Orgn., Sriharikota, 1982-86, scientist/engr.-SD, 1987-90, scientist/engr.-SE, 1991-95, scientist/engr.-SF, 1995; software cons. Bell Labs, Lucent Techs., Middletown, N.J., 1996—. Author more than 125 tech. reports in field; contbr. 30 papers to nat. and internat. confs. and jours. Fellow Instn. Engrs., Inst. Electronics and Telecomm. Engrs.; mem. IEEE (sr.), AIAA (sr.), Astronautical Soc. India (life), Non-Destructive Soc. India (life). Achievements include: discovery of a mistake in a method followed all over the world for over 50 years for the computation of burning time of solid rocket motors; development of new automatic method for computation of burning time of solid rocket motors, with the potential of becoming an international standard; development of simpler method for source location without using intersecting hyperbolas and which can be extended to any number of dimensions; development of new algorithm for generating the guaranteed shortest path for radars and telescopes, which can avoid sun and moon, using hill-climbing technique; discovery of a mistake in the highest sound level produced in the world; development of star calibration software for Precision Coherent Monopulse C-Band Radar; development of random vibration control system, shock control system, programmable logic control system for High Altitude Test Facility for Indian Space Research Organization; and others; increasing the capacity of the Network Management system for Integrated Transport Management, from 500 Nodes to 25,000 Nodes; development of a new method to find the route in large networks which reduces the time required to find the route by an order of magnitude; development of a new method to find the route in large networks to have 100% success rate. Home: 94 Winding Wood Dr Apt 8A Sayreville NJ 08872-2717 Office: Bell Labs Lucent Technologies Rm IL-118 480 Red Hill Rd Middletown NJ 07748-2406

MANNER, JENNIFER FOUSE, social worker; b. Balt., June 15, 1964; d. Richard Erb and Patricia Ann (Matthews) Fouse; m. David Bruce Manner, Aug. 16, 1986; 1 child, Jessica Lynn. BA in Psychology, Hop Coll., 1986; MS in Social Adminstrn., Case Western Reserve U., 1988. Lic. ind. social worker, Ohio; cert. chem. dependency counselor. Adolescent continuing care coord. Lakeland Inst. Lorain (Ohio) Cmty. Hosp., 1988-90; dir. Laurelwood Counseling Ctr., Mayfield Heights, Ohio, 1990-93; field instr. Mandel Sch. Applied Social Scis. Case Western Res. U., Cleve., 1991-95; ind. social worker, chem. dependency counselor Elyria, Ohio, 1993—. Lectr. in field; adj. instr. Lorain County C.C., 1998—. Mem. NASW, Psi Chi. Democrat. Presbyterian. Avocations: canoing, writing children's books, skiing. Home: 6641 Myrtle Hill Rd Valley City OH 44280-9300 Office: Psychiat & Psychol Svcs 412 E River St Elyria OH 44035-5231

MANNERING, JERRY VINCENT, agronomist, educator; b. Custer, Okla., June 14, 1929; s. James Bryan and Verta (Bates) M.; m. Marjorye McVicker, June 20, 1953; children: Debra Lynn Mannering Zerman, Stephen Scott, Lisa Gaye Mannering Schwingendorf. BS, Okla. State U., 1951; MS, Purdue U., 1956, PhD, 1967. Cert. profl. soil scientist, profl. soil erosion and sediment control specialist. Grad. asst. Purdue U., West Lafayette, Ind., 1954-56, extension agronomist, prof. agronomy, 1967-89; prof. emeritus, 1990—; research agronomist U. Idaho, Aberdeen, 1956-58; research soil scientist Agrl. Research Sta., USDA, West Lafayette, 1958-67; cons. FAO, Bulgaria, 1972, Govt. of Brazil, 1975. Contbr. numerous articles on agronomy to profl. jours. Served to 1st lt. U.S. Army, 1951-54 Decorated Purple Heart; recipient Hovde award Purdue U. and Ind. Farm Bur., 1982 Fellow Soil Conservation Soc. Am., Soil Sci. Soc. Am., Am. Soc. Agronomy; mem. Internat. Soil Sci. Soc., Internat. Soil Tillage Research Orgn., Lions Club.

MANNERS, NANCY, retired mayor; b. Catania, Sicily, Italy; d. Gioacchino Jack and Maria Providenza (Virzi) Marasa; m. George Manners, Dec. 20, 1941; children: Gene David, Nancy Ellen Manners Sieh, Joan Alice. BA in Pub. Adminstrn., U. La Verne, 1979. Asst. city mgr. City of Covina, 1963-74; mcpl. mgmt. cons., 1975-85; mem. city coun. City of West Covina, Calif., 1984-97; pres. Ind. Cities Risk Mgmt. Authority, West Covina, 1988; mayor City of West Covina, 1988-89, 92-93; pres. Ind. Cities Assn., 1989-90. Pres. Covina Coord. Coun., 1970-71, Altrusa Club of Covina-West, 1971-72, Ea. San Gabriel Valley Regional Occupation Program, 1974-76, San Gabriel Valley Planning Com., 1986-87, Mid-Valley Mental Health Coun., 1988-89; regional chmn. San Gabriel Valley Lung Assn., 1971-73; trustee Covina-Valley Unified Sch. Dist., 1973-77; foreman pro tem L.A. County Grand Jury, 1980-81; chmn. L.A. County Solid Waste Mgmt. Com., 1986-89; treas., bd. dirs. San Gabriel Valley Commerce and Cities Consortium, 1991, policy and steering com. Nat. League Cities, 1991-96; chmn. employee rels. policy com. League Calif. Cities; bd. dirs. L.A. County Sanitation Dist., 1992-94, San Gabriel Valley Coun. of Govts., San Gabriel Valley Mosquito Abatement Dist., 1994-97; hon. chair, grand marshall July 4th Parade, City of West Covina, 1997. Named Covina Citizen Yr., 1977, West Covina Citizen Yr., 1983, Woman Yr., Calif. State Legislature, 1990; recipient Woman of Distinction award Today's Woman Forum, 1988, Woman of Achievement award YWCA, 1987, 88, Community Svc. award West Covina C. of C., 1989, Meritorious Pub. Svc. award Rsch. Inst. Claremont McKenna Coll., 1990, Disting. Leader award San Gabriel Valley Boy Scouts of Am., 1997, others. Mem. LWV (pres. San Gabriel Valley 1978-79), Am. Heart Assn. (mem. bd. dirs.), Mcpl. Mgmt. Assocs. of So. Calif. (v.p. 1972-73), Queen of the Valley Hosp. 2100 (pres. 1996-97), Ind. Cities Assn. (v.p. 1988, pres. 1989), West Covina C. of C. (bd. dirs. 2001-), West Covina Hist. Soc. (v.p. 1995-99, pres. 1999-2000), West Covina Rotary (bd. dirs.). Home: 734 N Eileen Ave West Covina CA 91791-1042

MANNERS, PAMELA JEANNE, middle school educator; b. Holyoke, Mass., Mar. 20, 1951; d. Francis Edward and Helen Mary (Kurtyka) Herbert; div. 1985; children: Tracy, Kristen. BA, U. So. Miss., 1986, MEd, 1993. Cert. elem. edn. K-3, 4-8, secondary Eng., Social Studies; cert. elem. prin., secondary prin., elem. and secondary adminstrn. Registrar Michel Mid. Sch., Biloxi, Miss., 1987-88, tchr. Eng. and Social Studies, 1988-90, tchr. reading/law related edn., 1990-95; curriculum coord. Biloxi Pub. Schs., 1995-98; administrator Fernwood Jr. High Sch., Biloxi Pub. Schs., 1998-2000; dir. ABA Reading Curriculum Program, 1989-95; prin. Michel Jr. H.S., Biloxi Pub. Schs., 2000—. Law-related edn. trainer Miss. Law-Related Edn. Ctr., Jackson, 1990—; law-related trainer Ctr. Civic Edn., Calabasas, Calif., 1993; law-related trainer Constitutional Right Found., 1994—. Participant program Lawyer in Every Class Miss. Bar Assn., Jackson, 1990-93 On-site target grantee Miss. Bar/Dept. Justice, 1992; A+ Site recognition U.S. Dept. Edn. Mem. Leadership Gulf Coast C. of C. (edn. com. 1996—). Roman Catholic. Office: Biloxi Pub Schs 1400 Father Ryan Ave Biloxi MS 39530 E-mail: PamonCoast@aol.com.

MANNES, ELENA SABIN, film and television producer, director; b. N.Y.C., Dec. 3, 1943; d. Leopold Damrosch and Evelyn (Sabin) M. BA, Smith Coll., 1965; MA, Johns Hopkins U., 1967. Researcher Pub. Broadcast Lab. Nat. Ednl. TV, N.Y.C., 1968-70; writer Sta. WPIX-TV, 1970-73; assignment editor Sta. ABC-TV, 1973-76; producer, writer Sta. WCBS-TV, 1976-80; producer CBS News, 1980-87, Pub. Affairs TV/Bill Moyers PBS Documentaries, N.Y.C., 1987-90. Ind. documentary dir. and producer, 1987— Recipient Emmy award NATAS, 1984, 85, 87, 90, 94, 96, Peabody award, 1985, Cine Golden Eagle award, 1988, 90, 93, 94, 95, 99, Robert F. Kennedy journalism award, 1989, DGA awards, 1987, 90. Mem. Writers Guild Am., Dirs. Guild Am., Am. Film Inst. (dir. Workshop for Women). Avocations: tennis, still photography.

MANNEY, SHERRITA GLYNN, women's health nurse; b. El Paso, Tex., Aug. 28, 1954; d. Robert DeWitt Jr. and Margaret (Durrill) Garland; m. Michael Wayne Manney, Aug. 5, 1978 (div. Aug. 1986). BA, U. Tex., 1975; BSN, U. Tex., El Paso, 1992. Cert. in patient ostetric nurse, fetal monitoring instr. Mgr. Swenson's, El Paso, 1977-81; pers. trainer Iron Tender, 1981-83; mgr., bookkeeper Gasoline Alley, 1984-91; nurse tech., grad. nurse Thomason Gen. Hosp., 1992—, nurse preceptor, 1994. Dir. tel med health bd. Tel Med Teen Health Bd., El Paso, 1979-85; instr. English S.W. Inst., El Paso, 1985; rsch. asst. human papalliomavius study Tex. Tech.-The U. Tex., El Paso, 1992. Cost accounts YWCA Day Care Ctrs., El Paso, 1978-79; chmn. El Paso St. Festival, 1983-86; vol. El Paso Pub. Schs., 1986-87; health speaker Girl Scouts-Rio Grande Troop 348, El Paso, 1991; mem. Goodtime Singers: Music Therapy for the Elderly, 1993-95, People to People Ambassador Program, 2001. Recipient scholarship Thomason Gen. Hosp., El Paso, 1991-92. Mem. Assn. Women's Health Obstet. and Neonatal Nurses, Tex. Nursing Student Assn. (project chmn. 1990-91), The Jr. League El Paso (vol.), Sigma Theta Tau. Avocations: swimming, painting, music, arts and crafts. Home: 6632 Fiesta Dr El Paso TX 79912-5032 Office: Thomason Gen Hosp 4815 Alameda Ave El Paso TX 79905-2794 E-mail: sherritagarland@aol.com.

MANNHEIMER, MICHAEL JAY, lawyer; b. Bklyn., Jan. 12, 1969; s. Ralph and Roberta Helene (Shulman) M. BA, SUNY, Binghamton, 1991; JD, Columbia U., 1994. Bar: N.Y. 1995, U.S. Dist. Ct. (so. dist.) N.Y. 1996, U.S. Dist. Ct. (ea. dist.) N.Y. 1997, U.S. Ct. Appeals (3d cir.) 1997. Staff atty. Legal Aid Soc., N.Y.C., 1994-95; law clk. to Hon. Sidney H. Stein U.S. Dist. Ct. (so. dist.) N.Y., 1995-96; law clk. to Hon. Robert E. Cowen U.S. Ct. Appeals (3d cir.) N.J., Trenton, 1996-97; assoc. Paul, Weiss, Rifkind, Wharton & Garrison, N.Y.C., 1997-99; appellate counsel Ctr. for Appellate Litigation, 1999—. Contbr. articles to profl. jours. Recipient Pro Bono award Legal Aid Soc., 1998. Mem.: N.Y. County Lawyers Assn. Avocations: writing, golf, travel, film, bicycling. Office: Ctr Appellate Litigation 11th Fl 74 Trinity Pl New York NY 10006

MANNICK, JOHN ANTHONY, surgeon; b. Deadwood, S.D., Mar. 24, 1928; s. Alfred and Catherine Elizabeth (Schuster) M.; m. Alice Virginia Gossard, June 9, 1952; children— Catherine Virginia, Elizabeth Eleanor, Joan Barbara. BA, Harvard U., 1949, MD, 1953. Diplomate: Am. Bd. Surgery (dir. 1971-77). Intern Mass. Gen. Hosp., 1953-54, resident in surgery, 1956-60; instr. in surgery to asst. prof. Med. Coll. Va., 1960-64; asso. prof. to prof. surgery Boston U., 1964-76, chmn. div. surgery, 1973-76; Moseley prof. surgery Harvard U., 1976-94, Moseley Disting. prof. surgery, 1994—; dir. ednl. programs Harvard Med. Internat., 1994-96; chmn. dept. surgery Peter Bent Brigham Hosp. and Brigham and Women's Hosp., Boston, 1976-94. Mem. surgery, anesthesiology and trauma study sect. NIH, 1978-82, mem. medicine study sect., 1967-70; rsch. com. Med. Found., Inc., 1970-76. Author: (with others) Modern Surgery, 1970, Core Textbook of Surgery, 1972, Surgery of Ischemic Limbs, 1972, The Cause and Management of Aneurysms, 1990; mem. editorial bd. AMA Archives of Surgery, 1973-84, Clin. Immunology and Immunopathology, 1972-84, Surgery, 1982-97, Brit. Jour. Surgery, 1982-92, European Jour. Vascular Surgery, 1988-96, Shock, 1997—; mem. editl. bd. Advances in Surgery, 1979—, editor, 1984-86; mem. editl. bd. Jour. Vascular Surgery, 1984-97, assoc. editor, 1990-97; also articles. Served to capt. M.C. USAF, 1954-56. Markle scholar in acad. medicine, 1961-66 Fellow ACS (gov.), Royal Coll. Surgeons (hon., Eng.), Royal Coll. Surgeons (hon., Edinburgh), Vascular Soc. Gt. Britain and Ireland; mem. Am. Fedn. Clin. Rsch., Am. Assn. Immunologists, Am. Soc. Exptl. Pathology, Soc. Clin. Investigation, Soc. Clin. Surgery, Soc. Univ. Surgeons, Soc. Surg. Chmn. (sec. 1985-87, pres. 1987-88), Am. Surg. Assn. (pres. 1989-90), Internat. Cardiovascular Soc. (recorder N.Am. chpt., 1973-76, pres. N.Am. chpt. 1991-92, internat. v.p. 1993), Soc. Vascular Surgery (pres. 1981), N.E. Surg. Soc., New Eng. Soc. Vascular Surgery (pres. 1994-95), So. Soc. Assn., So. Soc. Vascular Surgery, Surg. Infection Soc., Halstead Soc., Lifeline Found. (pres. 1997—), Shock Soc. (Sci. Achievement award 2000), Phi Beta Kappa. Home: 81 Bogle St Weston MA 02493-1056 Office: 75 Francis St Boston MA 02115-6110 Fax: 617-582-6169.

MANNINA, GEORGE JOHN, JR. lawyer; b. Washington, Oct. 14, 1949; s. George J. Sr. and Mary Lee (Shupe) M.; m. Susan Marie Mannina, Mar. 15, 1975; 1 child, Christopher. BS, Cornell U., 1971; JD, Am. U., 1979. Bar: U.S. Dist. Ct. D.C. 1985, U.S. Ct. Appeals (D.C. cir.) 1985, U.S. Claims Ct. 1987, U.S. Ct. Appeals (7th cir.) 1995, U.S. Ct. Appeals (fed. cir.) 1988, Ct. of Internat. Trade 2000, U.S. Supreme Ct. 1996. Adminstrv. aide Congressman Gude, Washington, 1971-73; legis. dir. Congressman Forsythe, 1973-75; consel subcom. Fisheries, Wildlife Conservation and Environment, 1975-82; chief minority counsel, staff dir. House Merchant Marine and Fisheries Com., 1982-85; partner O'Connor & Hannan, LLP, 1985—. Recipient Emily Dworkin award Montgomery County (Md.) Commn. Children and Youth, 1996. Mem. ABA, D.C. Bar Assn., Lutheran Ch. St. Andrew (chairman youth bd., 1980—). Republican. Avocations: gardening, photography. Office: O'Connor & Hannan LLP 1666 K St NW Ste 500 Washington DC 20006

MANNING, ARLENE M. healthcare administrator; b. Liberty, N.Y., Aug. 14, 1943; d. Mark A. Schmouth and Catherine Sedlacek Schmouth Watson; m. Thomas J. Manning, Sept. 12, 1964; children: Kathleen Marie, Sean Mark. Diploma, Binghampton Gen. Hosp., 1964; BSN, U. Phoenix, 1993. RN, Pa., Ariz.; cCert. oncology. nurse ANCC. Staff nurse, charge nurse, asst. head nurse Binghamton (N.Y.) Gen. Hosp., 1964-69; staff nurse, head nurse, rehab. coord. supr. River Mede Manor, Binghamton, N.Y., 1969-74; staff nurse, rehab. Read Meml. Hosp., Hancock, 1974-76; resident care dir. Susquehanna Nursing Home, Binghamton, 1977-78; nurse coord. Read Meml. Hosp., Hancock, 1978-79; staff nurse ICU Phoenixville (Pa.) Hosp., 1980-81; asst. dir. nursing Phoenixville Manor, 1981-83; case mgr. No. Chester County Nursing Svc., Phoenixville, 1983-86; staff nurse, intake coord. John C. Lincoln Home Health, Phoenix, 1987-88, quality assurance coord., 1988-94; assoc. dir., area dir. Home Care So. Ariz., Green Valley, 1994-96; home health coord. Integra Home Health and Hospice, Tucson, 1996-97; care mgr. MatureWell, 1997-2000; resident svc. dir. Silver Springs, Green Valley, 2000-01, Atria Campana Del Rio, Tucson, 2001—. Home: 124 E El Viento Green Valley AZ 85614-2222 Office: Atria Campana Del Rio 1550 E River Rd Tucson AZ 85718

MANNING, BARTON HARLEY, neuroscientist; b. St. John's, Nfld., Can., Apr. 28, 1968; s. Barton Harley and Audrey Yvonne (Hatcher) M. BSc, McGill U., 1991; PhD, Va. Commonwealth U., 1996. Postdoctoral fellow U. Calif., San Francisco, 1996-2000; asst. prof. Ohio State U., 2000; sr. rsch. biologist Merck Rsch. Labs., Merck & Co., Inc., West Point, Pa., 2001—. Contbr. chpt. to book, articles to profl. jours. Centennial fellow Med. Rsch. Coun. Can., 1999; Life Scis. Rsch. Found. fellow, 1999; U.S. NIH fellow, 1999. Mem. AAAS, Soc. for Neurosci., Internat. Assn. Study of Pain, Am. Pain Soc. Avocations: piano, guitar. Office: Merck and Co Inc Merck Rsch Labs WP46-300 770 Sumneytown Pike West Point PA 19486-0004 E-mail: barton_manning@merck.com.

MANNING, BRENT V. lawyer; b. Preston, Idaho, Jan. 18, 1950; s. Leon W. and Gwen (Briscoe) M.; m. J. Christine Coffin, Oct. 25, 1969; children: Justin, Britten, John. BA, Idaho State U., 1972; JD, Harvard U., 1975. Bar: Colo. 1975, Utah 1981, U.S. Ct. Appeals (10th cir.) 1978. Assoc. Holme Roberts & Owen, Denver, 1975-80, ptnr., 1980-97, Salt Lake City, 1981-97; founding ptnr. Manning Curtis Bradshaw & Bednar, LLC, 1997—. Mem. panel mediators and arbitrators U.S. Dist. Ct. Utah, 1993—; mediation & settlement judge pro tempore 3rd Jud. Dist. State of Utah, 1996—; mem. jud. nominating commn., 2d Jud. Dist. Ct. Utah. Trustee Bountiful (Utah) Davis Art Found., 1985-91, Utah Tibetan Resettlement Project; chair ...and Justice for All Campaign, 2001—. Mem. ABA, Utah Bar Assn. (chmn. continuing legal edn. com. 1988, mem. disciplinary com. 1991-93, cts. and judges com. 1993—, chmn. 1996-97, chmn. And Justice for All campaign, 2001—), Am. Inns of Ct. (pres. 1997-98, master of bench 1988—), Am. Alpine Club (N.Y.C.) Democrat. Avocations: climbing, bicycling, running. Home: 2079 Maple Grove Way Bountiful UT 84010-1005 Office: Manning Curtis 3d Fl Newhouse Bldg 10 Exchange Pl Salt Lake City UT 84111-2714 E-mail: BManning@mc2b.com.

MANNING, CHRISTOPHER ASHLEY, finance educator, consultant; b. L.A., June 26, 1945; s. Ashley and Vivian LaVerne (Wagner) M.; m. Cathy Ann Nichols, July 30, 1977 (div. Sept. 1993). BS, San Diego State U., 1967; MBA, Northwestern U., 1971; PhD, UCLA, 1983. Corp. loan officer Security Pacific Nat. Bank, L.A., 1971-75; v.p. fin. Solitude Ski Resort, Bravo Ski Corp., Salt Lake City, 1975-78; pres. Sequoia Spa Co., L.A., 1976-79, Manning and Co., L.A., 1971-86, Manning's Little Red Piano Shop, L.A., 1971-86; instr. corp. fin. Pepperdine U., 1979-83; instr. corp. fin. and real estate Long Beach (Calif.) State U., 1983-86; assoc. prof. fin. Loyola Marymount U., L.A., 1986-92, prof. fin., 1992—. Mng. prin. Denver office Houlihan Valuation Advisors, 1993-94; founder, mng. prin. Manning Advisors. Mem. editl. bd. Jour. of Real Estate Rsch., 1988-90, 91-93, 94-96, 97-99; contbr. articles to profl. jours. 1st lt. U.S. Army, 1967—70. Decorated Bronze Star. Mem.: Am. Real Estate Soc. (bd. dirs. 1994—96, 1997—99, 2000—, v.p./program chair 2001—02, pres.-elect 2002—, pres. 2002—), Phi Eta Sigma, Beta Gamma Sigma. Republican. Episcopalian. Home: 29438 Quailwood Dr Palos Verdes Peninsula CA 90275-4929 Office: Manning Advisors 29438 Quailwood Dr Palos Verdes Peninsula CA 90275-4929

MANNING, DAVID LEE, financial executive; b. Birmingham, Ala., Jan. 30, 1950; s. William L. and Lula L. (Lively) M.; m. Donna H. Holley, Dec. 29, 1972; children: Emily Anne, Laura Elizabeth. BA, U. Ala., Tuscaloosa, 1973, MPA, 1974. Budget analyst State of Tenn., Nashville, 1974-79, asst. state treas., 1979-87, commr. fin. and adminstrn., 1987-95; v.p. Columbia/HCA Healthcare Corp., 1995-97, sr. v.p., 1997-98, healthcare cons., 1998-99; dir. fin. Met. Govt. Nashville and Davidson County, 1999—. So. Regional Tng. Program in Pub. Adminstrn. fellow, 1973. Democrat. Baptist. Office: 106 Metropolitan Courthouse Nashville TN 37201

MANNING, DIANA MARIE, artist, educator; b. Decatur, Ill., Nov. 27, 1949; d. Chester Allen and Marjorie Marie (Matthews) Locke; m. David Lynn Manning, Aug. 25, 1973; children: Joshua David, Jacob Allen. BS in Art Edn., Ea. Ill. U., 1971; postgrad., Richland C.C., 1982, Ill. State U., 1987. Art tchr. Eisenhower H.S., Decatur, Ill., 1972-73; art tchr., dept. head St. Teresa H.S., 1974-95; owner Diana Manning Studio, Inc. Pvt. art tchr. for numerous orgns. Sculptor numerous pvt. collections; designer notecards and clothing with original drawings; sculptures mass-produced by Christhomas Corp., Irvine, Calif.; licensed sculptures produced for Family of Friends collection Chris Thomas Corp. Home: 470 E Park St Argenta IL 62501

MANNING, ELLIOTT, lawyer, educator; b. Atlanta, June 7, 1935; s. Edwin Morris and Pauline (Spielberger) M.; m. Gail Helene Washor, July 16, 1959; children: Evan Marshall, Thomas Mark, Shari Lisa. AB with honors, Columbia Coll., N.Y.C., 1955; JD magna cum laude, Harvard U., 1958. Bar: Ga. 1957, N.Y. 1959, Fla. 1983, U.S. Tax Ct. 1961, U.S. Claims Ct. 1969. Assoc. Cleary Gottlieb Steen and Hamilton, N.Y.C., 1958-67, ptnr., 1968-80; acting prof. law Stanford (Calif.) U., 1978; prof. law U. Miami, Coral Gables, Fla., 1980—. Vis. prof. McGeorge Law Sch., Sacramento, 1984, U. So. Calif., L.A., 1994; cons., Miami, 1983—; mem. Tax Adv. Bd., Chgo., 1984-94, Boston, 1994-95. Author: Choosing the Business Entity, 1989, revised edit., 1995, Corporate Buy-Sell Agreements, 1990, revised edit., 1995; contbr. articles to profl. jours. Treas., bd. dirs. The Fla. Appleseed Ctr. for Law and Justice Inc., 1996—. Staff sgt. USAR, 1958-64. Fellow Am. Coll. Tax Counsel; mem. Am. Law Inst., N.Y. County Lawyers Assn., N.Y. State Bar Assn. Democrat. Jewish. Home: 7605 SW 126th St Miami FL 33156-6013 Office: Sch Law U Miami PO Box 248087 Coral Gables FL 33124-8087

MANNING, ERIC, computer science and engineering educator, university dean, researcher; b. Windsor, Ont., Can., Aug. 4, 1940; g. George Gorman and Eleanor Katherine (Koehler) M.; m. Betty Goldring, Sept. 16, 1961; children: David, Paula. BSc, U. Waterloo, Ont., 1961, MSc, 1962; PhD, U. Ill., 1965. Registered profl. engr., B.C. With MIT and Bell Telephone Labs., 1965-68; prof. computer sci. U. Waterloo, 1968-86, founding dir. computer comms. networks group, 1973-82; founding dir. Inst. for Computer Rsch., 1982-86; prof., dean engring. U. Victoria, B.C., Can., 1986-92, prof. computer sci., elec. engring. Can., 1993-2000, New Media Ctr./Nortel Networks Prof. Network Performance Can., 2000—. NewMIC Chief Scientist, Networks Cluster, 2000—; dir. Natural Sci. and Engring. Rsch. Coun. Can., mem. exec. com., chair strategic grants com., 1982-87; dir. Comms. Rsch. Centre, Govt. of Can., 1995-97, Consortium for Software Engring. Rsch., Ottawa, 1997-99; trustee B.C. Advanced Sys. Found., 1986-93; dir. Sci. Coun. B.C., 1988-91; bd. dirs. Can. Microelectric Corp.; adv. com. on artificial intelligence NRC, 1987-91; IBM chair computer sci. Keio U., Yokohama, 1992-93; hon. prof. South East U., Nanjing, People's Republic of China. Author: Fault Diagnosis of Digital Systems, 1970; also numerous articles. V.p. Greater Victoria Concert Band, 1995-96; trumpet sect., Sooke Philharmonic & 5th Field Artillery Band, Royal Canadian Artillery. Fellow IEEE, Engring. Inst. Can.; mem. Assn. Computing Machinery (mem. snowbird com. 1999—), Assn. Profl. Engrs. B.C., Soc. for Computer Simulation, Can. Inst. for Advanced Rsch. (adv. com. on artificial intelligence and robotics 1986-90), Can. Assn. for Computer Sci. (pres. 1994-2000), Can. Soc. for Fifth Generation Rsch. (trustee 1987-88), B.C. Microelectronics Soc. (bd. dirs. 1986-87). Avocations: squash, scuba diving, sailing, flying, musical performance. Home: 2909 Phyllis St Victoria BC Canada V8N 1Y8 Office: U Victoria Faculty Engring PO Box 3055 Victoria BC Canada V8W 3P6 E-mail: Eric.Manning@engr.UVic.ca.

MANNING, JAMES MATTHEW, biochemistry educator; b. Boston, Jan. 3, 1939; s. Matthew Francis and Mary (Nee) M.; m. Lois Radin, May 9, 1964; children: Robert, Laura. BS in Chemistry, Boston Coll., 1960; PhD in Biochemistry, Tufts U., 1966. USPHS postdoctoral fellow Tufts U., Medford, Mass., 1960-66; NSF postdoctoral fellow U. Rome, Italy, 1966-67; rsch. assoc. Rockefeller U., N.Y.C., 1967-69, asst. prof., 1967-72, assoc. prof., 1972-95; prof. Northeastern U., Boston, 1995—. Cons. Am. Heart Assn., 1976-78, Am. Soc. Biol. Chemists, 1979, NSF, 1979. Contbr. articles to Jour. Biol. Chemistry, Ann. N.Y. Acad. Sci.; contbr. articles to profl. jours. Grantee NIH, 1987. Mem. Am. Soc. Biol. Chemists, Am. Chem. Soc., Am. Soc. Hematology, The Harvey Soc., Soc. Am. Protein Chemists. Achievements include research in demonstration of covalent anti-sickling agents, mechanism of enzymatic transamination, protein biosynthesis and processing. E-mail: jmanning@lynx.neu.edu.

MANNING, JEROME ALAN, retired lawyer; b. Bklyn., Dec. 31, 1929; s. Emanuel J. and Dorothy (Levine) M.; m. Naomi Jacobs, Oct. 31, 1954; children: Joy, Stephen, Susan. BA, NYU, 1950, LLB, 1952; LLM, Yale U., 1953. Bar: N.Y. 1953, Fla. 1977. Assoc. Joseph Trachtman, N.Y.C., 1956-61; ptnr. Stroock & Stroock & Lavan, 1961-96; prof. NYU Sch. Law, 1956-96. Editor: NYU Law Rev.; author: Estate Planning, 1980, rev. edit., 1995, Estate Planning for Laymen, 1992. Trustee N.Y.U. Sch. Law. Capt. USAF, 1953-56. Mem. ABA. Home: 1835 Franklin St San Francisco CA 94109-3483 E-mail: jmanning@stroock.com.

MANNING, JOHN WARREN, III, retired surgeon, medical educator; b. Phila., Nov. 24, 1919; s. John Warren Jr. and Edith Margaret (Reagan) M.; m. Muriel Elizabeth Johnson, Oct. 11, 1944; children: John, Melissa, Susan. BS in Chemistry with honors, Ursinus Coll., 1940; MD, U. Pa., 1943; postgrad., 1978. Diplomate Am. Bd. Surgery. Naval intern Pa. Naval Hosp., 1946; resident Saginaw (Mich.) Gen. Hosp., 1947-50; preceptor Dr. H.M. Bishop, 1950-52; pvt. practice Saginaw, 1950—. Sr. staff mem. Saginaw Gen. Hosp., St. Luke's Hosp., Saginaw; past chief of surgery, chmn. tissue com. St. Mary's Hosp., Saginaw; cons. VA Hosp., Saginaw; assoc. clin. prof. surgery Mich. State U., assoc. prof. surgery, 1976-92, prof. emeritus, 1992—; mem. search com. Saginaw Coop. Hosp. Contbr. articles to profl. publs. Lt. USN, 1942-46, PTO. Fellow ACS; mem. AMA, Mich. State Med. Soc., Saginaw Surg. Soc., Soc. Abdominal Surgeons, Am. Coll. Angiology, Soc. Am. Gastrointestinal Endoscopic Surgeons. Office: 4515 Gratiot Rd Saginaw MI 48603-6261

MANNING, KENNETH ALAN, lawyer; b. Buffalo, July 22, 1951; Jack Edwin and Dorothea Ann (Ruhland) M.; m. Diane Louise Garrold, Aug. 11, 1973; children: Michael John, Kathryn Ann. BS in Engring. Sci., SUNY, Buffalo, 1974, JD, 1977. Bar: N.Y. 1978, U.S. Dist. Ct. (we. dist.) N.Y. 1978, U.S. Dist. Ct. (no. dist.) N.Y. 1980, U.S. Ct. Appeals (2d cir.) 1983, U.S. Ct. Appeals (3d cir.) 1988. Confidential law asst. to assoc. justice Appellate Div. 4th Dept., Buffalo, 1977-79; assoc. Phillips, Lytle, Hitchcock, Blaine & Huber, 1979-84, ptnr., 1985—. Vol. Lawyers Project, Erie County, 1985—, Criminal Appeals Program, Erie County, 1988-89; mem. coun. Western N.Y. region NCCJ. Woodburn fellow SUNY, Buffalo, 1973-76. Mem. ABA (TIP sect.), N.Y. State Bar Assn. (ins. negligence sect.), Erie County Bar Assn., Gyro Club (pres. 1988), Park Club, One Hundred Club Buffalo. Avocations: sports, hunting. Office: Phillips Lytle Hitchcock Blaine & Huber 3400 HSBC Ctr Buffalo NY 14203-2887

MANNING, KENNETH PAUL, technologies company executive; b. N.Y.C., Jan. 18, 1942; s. John Joseph and Edith Helen (Hoffmann) M.; m. Maureen Lambert, Sept. 12, 1964; children: Kenneth J., John J., Elise, Paul, Carolyn, Jacqueline. BME, Rensselaer Poly. Inst., 1963; postgrad., George Washington U., 1965-66; MBA in Ops. Rsch., Am. U., 1968. With W.R. Grace & Co., N.Y.C., 1973-87, v.p. European consumer divsn., 1975-76, pres. ednl. products divsn., 1976-79, pres. real estate divsn., 1979-81, v.p. corp. tech. group, 1981-83, pres., CEO, Ambrosia Chocolate Co. divsn. Milw., 1983-87; group v.p. Sensient Techs. Corp., 1987-89, exec. v.p., dir., 1989-92, pres., COO, dir., 1992-96; pres., CEO, dir. Universal Foods Corp., 1996—, chmn., CEO, 1997—. Bd. dirs. Firstar Corp., Milw., Badger Meter, Inc., Milw. Vice chmn. Greater Milw. Com.; bd. dirs. Milw. Harbor Commn. Served as lt. USN, 1963-67; rear adm. USNR, ret. Decorated Legion of Merit, Nat. Def. medal, others. Mem. Am. Chem. Soc., Navy League, U.S. Naval Inst., Naval Res. Assn., Milw. Metro Assn. Commerce (bd. dirs.), Union League (N.Y.C.), Milw. Club, Knights of Malta. Republican. Roman Catholic. Home: 5240 N Lake Dr Milwaukee WI 53217-5369 Office: Sensient Techs Corp 777 E Wisconsin Ave Milwaukee WI 53202-5304

MANNING, KEVIN JAMES, academic administrator; b. N.Y.C., Nov. 8, 1944; s. James and Helen (Gurry) M.; m. Sara Garrity; children: Elizabeth Ann, Meagan Garrity, Kevin James. BA in Theatre, Webster U., St. Louis, 1967; MS in Pers., Shippensburg (Pa.) U., 1976; PhD in Ednl. Adminstrn., Ohio State U., 1982; attended, Inst. Ednl. Mgmt., Harvard U., 1989. Adminstr., intr. Webster U., St. Louis, 1967-68; mgmt recruiter L.S. Brady, Inc., 1969; adminstr. Washington U., 1969-71; admissions counselor Elizabethtown (Pa.) Coll., 1972-76, dir. admissions, 1976-80, spl. asst. to pres., 1982-83; rsch. asst. Ohio State U., Columbus, 1980-82; chief staff Gov.'s Commn. Higher Edn., Harrisburg, Pa., 1983-84; v.p. devel. Immaculata (Pa.) Coll., 1984-2000; pres. Villa Julie Coll., Md., 2000—. Workforce adv. panel Commonwealth of Pa. Mem. attractions com. Phila. Econ. Devel. Coalition, 1988—; bd. trustees Peirce Coll., 1998—2001; bd. dirs. Chester County Export Ctr., Exton, Pa., 1990. Mem. Sr. Devel. Officers Phila. (chmn. 1995-96), Great Valley C. of C. (bd. dirs.). Avocations: reading, arts, film, golf. Home: 1907 Billy Barton Cir Reisterstown MD 21136 Office: Villa Julie Coll 1525 Greenspring Valley Rd Stevenson MD 21153-0641

MANNING, LAUREN FORSHAY, financial service company executive; b. Belleville, N.J., Feb. 15, 1961; d. Thomas Owen Pritchard; m. Kenneth DeMille Butler, Dec. 12, 1991 (div. Mar. 1998); m. Gregory Peter Manning, March, 2000; 1 child, Tyler. BA, Fordham U., N.Y.C., 1981-84; postgrad. in bus., N.Y.U., 1985—. Cert. Series 7, 63 NASD, SEC. Asst. v.p. Lehman Bros., Inc., N.Y.C., 1985-86; asst. v.p., v.p. Dean Witter Reynolds, Wayne, N.J., 1986-88; sales mgr. Reuters Am., N.Y.C., 1988-91; regional sales mgr. Fusion Sys. Corp., 1991-93; v.p. bus. devel. Cantor Fitzgerald Securities, 1993-96, ptnr., 1994—, v.p. sales Market Data Corp., 1996-97, sr. v.p., dir. global information svcs., 1997—. Pres., chmn. Perry St. Assn., N.Y.C., 1999—; jr. com. mem. N.Y.C. Ballet, 1997. Mem.: Fin. Womens Assn., Women's Bond Club. Avocations: golf, horseback riding, real-estate.

MANNING, MONICA ANN, nurse practitioner; b. Plymouth, N.C., Aug. 29, 1965; d. Carlos Ervin and Jacquelyn (Respess) M. BSN, East Carolina U., 1987; MSN, Duke U., 1999. RN, N.C.; cert. adult nurse practitioner; cert. cardiovasc./geriatric nurse practitioner; cert. BLS, ACLS Am. Heart Assn. Staff nurse in cardiology Pitt County Meml. Hosp., Greenville, N.C., 1987-94, charge nurse cardiology, 1988-94; RN III/charge nurse cardiovasc. surgery Univ. Med. Ctr. Pitt County, 1994-97; nurse practitioner Eastern Nephrology Assocs., NC, 2000—01; nurse practitioner endocrinology East Carolina U. Sch. Medicine, 2001—. Counselor, camp nurse Carolina Bible Camp, 1986-91. Mem. Am. Heart Assn. (coun. cardiovasc. nursing 1996—), Am. Coll. Nurse Practitioners, Am. Acad. Nurse Practitioners, Am. Geriatrics Soc., N.C. Nurses Assn., East Carolina Sch. Nursing Profl. Soc., Grad. Nursing Student Assn. Duke U. (founding mem., student rep. 1999), Nat. Kidney Found., Am. Diabetes Assn., Sigma Theta Tau, Phi Kappa Phi. Avocations: reading, swimming, Internet use in medicine and healthcare.

MANNING, PETER KIRBY, sociology educator; b. Salem, Oreg., Sept. 27, 1940; s. Kenneth Gilbert and Esther Amelia (Gibbard) M.; m. Victoria Francis Shaughnessy, Sept. 1, 1961 (div. 1981); children— Kerry Patricia, Sean Peter, Merry Kathleen; m. Betsy Cullum-Swan, Aug. 4, 1991 (div. 1997). BA, Willamette U., 1961; MA, Duke U., 1963, PhD, 1966; MA (hon.), Oxford U., Eng., 1983. Instr. sociology Duke U., 1964-65; asst. prof. sociology U. Mo., 1965-66, Mich. State U., East Lansing, 1966-70, assoc. prof. sociology and psychiatry, 1970-74, prof., 1974—; prof. criminal justice, 1993—. Beto chair lectr. Sam Houston State U., 1990; Ameritech lectr. E. Ky. U., 1983; vis. prof. U. Victoria, 1968, MIT, 1982, SUNY, Albany, 1982, U. Mich., 1990—91, York U., Toronto, 1999; vis. sr. scholar Northeastern U. Coll. Criminal Justice, 2001, E.V. and E.M. Brooks chair; cons. Nat. Inst. Law Enforcement and Criminal Justice, U.S. Dept. Justice, Rsch. Triangle Inst., NSF, Nat. Health and Med. Rsch. Coun., Australia, 1980—, Social Sci. Rsch. Coun. Eng., AID, Jamaica, 1991, Sheehy com. Police Pay and Performance, England, 1993. Author: Sociology of Mental Health and Illness, 1975, Police Work, 1977, 2d edit., 1997, The Narcs' Game, 1980, 2d edit., 2002, Semiotics and Fieldwork, 1987, Symbolic Communication, 1988, Organizational Communication, 1992, Private Policing, 1999, other books; also book chpts., articles in profl. jours.; cons. editor series: Principal Themes in Sociology; co-editor Sage Series in Qualitative Methods; mem. editorial bd. numerous jours. in social scis. Recipient Bruce Smith Sr. award Acad. Criminal Justice Scis., 1993, O.W. Wilson award, 1997, Charles H. Cooley award Mich. Sociol. Assn., 1994; NDEA fellow, 1962-64, NSF fellow, 1965, fellow Balliol Coll., Oxford U., 1982-83, vis. fellow Wolfson Coll., Oxford U., 1981, 82-83, fellow, 1984-86; Am. Bar Found. rsch. fellow, 1998; Rockefeller resident, Bellagio, Italy, 2000. Mem. Am. Soc. Criminology, Am. Sociol. Assn., Brit. Soc. Criminology, Internat. Sociol. Assn., Midwest Sociol. Soc., Soc. Study of Social Problems, Soc. for the Study of Symbolic Interaction (spl. recognition award 1990, v.p. 1992-93, program chair 1993), Internat. Soc. for Semiotics and Law. Office: Northeastern U Coll Criminal Justice Boston MA 02115 E-mail: manningpk@hotmail.com.

MANNING, PEYTON, professional football player; b. Mar. 24, 1976; Grad., U. Tenn. Quarterback Indpls. Colts, 1998—. Office: Indianapolis Colts PO Box 535000 Indianapolis IN 46253-5000 also: Indianapolis Colts 7001 West 56th Streeet Indianapolis IN 46254*

MANNING, RANDOLPH H. academic administrator; b. Bronx, Dec. 18, 1947; s. Ruthfoy M. and Gertrude (Webber) M.; m. Monica S. McEvilley, May 15, 1972; children: Randolph, Craig, Corey. AA, Suffolk Community Coll., 1969; BA, SUNY, Stony Brook, 1971, MALS, 1975, PhD, 1998. Owner, operator R.H. Manning Enterprises, Coram, N.Y., 1973—; counselor Suffolk County Community Coll., Riverhead, 1971-80, prof. psychology and sociology, 1980-85, dean instrn., 1985—. Pres. emeritus Spl. Program Personnel Assn., SUNY, 1978-82; ednl. cons. Bds. Coop. Ednl. Svcs., Westhampton, N.Y., 1980; adv. bd. Re-Route Dept. Labor, Suffolk County Sheriff's Dept., 1980—; assoc. commr. N.Y. State Task Force on Race Rels. N.Y.; co-dir. Counsel Internat. Programs, 1990—; Mid. States evaluator, 1990—; cons. to N.J. Dept. Higher Edn., 1990—; curriculum and program evaluator. Pres. N.Y. State Program Personnel Assn., 1978-82; bd. dirs. Gordon Heights FCU, L.I., 1975-82, treas, bd. dirs. L.I. Sickle Cell Inc., Hempstead, 1981—, adv. bd. Suffolk County Farm Coop. Extension, USN. Named one of Outstanding Young Men Am., 1981; recipient Proclamation for Service, County of Suffolk, 1986. Mem. Am. Sociol. Assn., Black Faculty and Staff Assn., N.Y. State Bd. Profl. Med. Conduct, Cmty. Coll. Gen. Edn. Assn. (pres.). Home: 3 Indian Valley Rd East Setauket NY 11733-4037 Office: Suffolk County CC Crooked Hill Rd Brentwood NY 11717

MANNING, ROBERT HENDRICK, media consultant; b. Soerabaja, Java, Indonesia, Aug. 23, 1941; s. William and Gertrude (Unk) M. BS, No. Mich. U., 1974. Instr. sailing USCG Acad., New London, Conn., 1959-63; dir. audio visual/media svcs. No. Mich. U., Marquette, 1965-93, capt. univ. rsch. vessel, 1977-79, dir. audio visual svcs. emeritus, 1997—; dir. devel. Bresnan Comm. Co., 1993-97. Ind. media cons., Marquette, 1969—, comm. cons., 1996—. Pub. TV host "Ask the Doctors", PBS Sta. WNMU-TV, 1977-98. Hon. mem. Marquette-Alger County Med. Soc., 1970-2000; pub. rels. dir. Charter Comm., 2000—. Mem. Marquette-Alger County Med. Soc. (hon. mem., employed as exec. dir. 1975-2000). Avocations: astronomy, navigation, med. history, sailing, amateur radio. Home and Office: PO Box 309 Marquette MI 49855-0309 E-mail: sailor@chartermi.net.

MANNING, ROBERT JOSEPH, editor; b. Binghamton, N.Y., Dec. 25, 1919; s. Joseph James and Agnes Pauline (Brown) M.; m. Margaret Marinda Raymond, Dec. 28, 1944 (dec. 1984); children: Richard Raymond, Brian Gould, Robert Brown; m. Theresa M. Slomkowski, July 11, 1987. Nieman fellow, Harvard, 1945-46; LittD (hon.), Tufts U., 1966; LHD, St. Lawrence U., 1971. Reporter Binghamton (N.Y.) Press, 1936-41, AP, 1942; State Dept. and White House corr. UPI, 1944-46; chief UN corr. United Press, 1946-49; writer Time mag., 1949-55, sr. editor, 1955-58; chief London bur. Time, Life, Fortune, Sports Illus. mags., 1958-61; Sunday editor N.Y. Herald Tribune, 1961-62; asst. sec. state for pub. affairs Washington, 1962-64; exec. editor Atlantic Monthly, 1964-66, editor-in-chief, 1966-80; v.p. Atlantic Monthly Co., 1966-80; editor-in-chief Boston Pub. Co., 1981-87; pres., editor-in-chief Bobcat Books Inc., Boston, 1987—. Served with AUS, 1942-43. Fellow Kennedy Inst. Politics, Harvard U., 1980. Mem. AAAS, Century Assn. (N.Y.C.), Tavern Club, St. Botolph Club. Home and Office: 1200 Washington St #507 Boston MA 02118 E-mail: bobcat1225@rcn.com.

MANNING, ROBERT THOMAS, physician, educator; b. Wichita, Kans., Oct. 16, 1927; s. Thomas Earl and Mary Francis (Schlegel) M.; m. Jane Bell, July 29, 1949; children: Mary Kay Travers, Phillip Trenton, Susan Ann Shiba. AB, Wichita U., 1950; MD, Kans. U., 1954; DHL, Med. Coll. Hampton Rds., 1991. Diplomate Am. Bd. Internal Medicine. Intern Kansas City (Mo.) Gen. Hosp., 1954-55; resident Kans. U., Kansas City, 1955-58; from assoc. prof. to prof. Kans. U. Med. Ctr. Sch. of Medicine, 1958-71, assoc. dean students, 1969-71; dean Eastern Va. Med. Sch., Norfolk, Va., 1971-74, chmn., prof. internal medicine, 1974-77; prof. internal medicine U. Kans. Sch. of Medicine, Wichita, 1977-93; prof. emeritus U. Kans. Sch. Medicine, 1993—; assoc. dean, clin. affairs U. Kans. Sch. of Medicine, 1985-89; chmn. internal medicine U. Kans. Sch. Medicine, 1987—89; pres. Wesley Med. Rsch. Inst., 1986-88. Nat. cons. surgeon gen. USAF, 1973-78. Author: Major's Physical Diagnosis, 9th edit., 1982; contbr. articles to profl. jours. Pres. Kans. Health Ethics, Inc., 1994-96. Served with USAF, 1945-47. Recipient Advanced Achievement award Am. Bd. Internal Medicine, 1987. Fellow ACP (laureate Kans. chpt., bd. govs. Kans. 1984-88); mem. Am. Fedn. Clin. Rsch., Cen. Soc. Clin. Rsch., Am. Assn. Study Liver Disease, Sigma Xi, Alpha Omega Alpha. Presbyterian. Avocations: woodworking, golf. Home: 126 Trail Of The Flowers Georgetown TX 78628-4814

MANNING, ROBERTA THOMPSON, historian, educator; b. Austin, Tex., Jan. 24, 1940; d. Robert Bennet and Lucille Luby Thompson; m. Gerald Stuart Manning, Mar. 24, 1964; children: Innessa Anne, Rebecca Emily. BA, Rice U., 1962; MA, Columbia U., 1967, PhD, 1975. Acting asst. prof. U. Calif., San Diego, 1975; asst. prof. Boston Coll., Chestnut Hill, Mass., 1975-81, assoc. prof., 1981—2002, prof., 2002—. Pres. The Tragedy of the Soviet Village Inc., Newton, Mass., 1998—. Author: The Crisis of the Old Order in Russia: Gentry and Government, 1982 (Herbert Baxter Adams prize Am. Hist. Assn. 1983), Bel'skii Raion 1937g, 1998; editor: Stalinist Terror, 1993, Tragediia Sovietskoi Derevni: Kollektivization, 1927-1939, Vols. 1-4, 1999-2002; mng. editor Russian History, 1975-88; editor Sci. and Soc., 1981-96. Guggenheim fellow, N.Y.C., 1989; Collaborative Projects fellow NEH, Washington, 1997, 99, 2002. Fellow Davis Ctr. for Russian Studies; mem. Am. Hist. Assn., Am. Assn. for the Advancement Slavic Studies. Democrat. Office: Boston Coll Dept History Commonwealth Ave Chestnut Hill MA 02467 E-mail: manning@bc.edu.

MANNING, RONALD LEE, banker; b. Hillsboro, Ohio, Jan. 15, 1951; s. George Charles and Margaret Alice (Hail) M. BSBA, Bowling Green State U., 1973; Cert., U. Okla., 1984. Teller, collection coordinator Bank of Wood County, Bowling Green, Ohio, 1972-73; mgr. Park Nat. Bank, Newark, 1973-76; mgr., asst. v.p. BancOhio Nat. Bank, Cin., 1976-78, br. adminstr., 1978-81, mgr. comsumer credit, 1981-83, v.p., dist. lending mgr. Newark, 1983-88, pres. Bellefontaine and Kenton, 1988-92, Nat. City Bank, Newark-Licking, Perry, 1993-96, regional mgr. Newark/Lancaster region, 1996-99, area exec. Toledo/N.W. area, 1999-2000; regional sales mgr., head pvt. banking Unizan Bank, N.A., Columbus, Ohio, 2000—. Mem. adv. com. Ctrl. Ohio Tech. Coll., Newark, 1983-90; lectr. U. Cin., 1978-85, Camp Enterprise, Newark, 1993-99; chmn. Manningstead Farms, Howard, Ohio, 1986—. Mem. adv. com. Am. Cancer Soc., Newark, 1976—, lay trustee Ohio div., 1990; mem. United Way of Licking County, 1993-99, United Way of Lucas County, 1999-2000; pres. Mann, Inc., 1990—; bd. dirs. Par Excellence Sch., 1995-99; bd. dirs. Licking County Indsl. Growth Corp., 1994-99; mem. fin. com. Inst. Indsl. Tech., 1995-99; mem. governing com. Licking County Found., 1993-2000; mem. bus. and industry coun. Licking Meml. Hosp., 1993-99. Named to Hon. Order of Ky. Col., 1972. Mem. Mental Health Assn., Newark Area C. of C. (dir. 1993-99), Am. Inst. Banking, Ohio Oil & Gas Assn., Rotary, Valley of Cin., Masons. Avocations: sports, hunting. Home: 1440 Sedgefield Dr New Albany OH 43054 Office: Unizan Bank 66 S 3rd St Columbus OH 43215-4201

MANNING, SHERRY FISCHER, college president emeritus, business executive; b. Washington, Apr. 28, 1943; d. Fred W. and Eleanor A. (Mertz) Fischer; m. Charles W. Manning, Dec. 23, 1966; children: Shannon Marie, Charles Fischer, Kelly Eleanor. BA in Math., Western Md. Coll., 1965, LHD, 1979; MS in Math., William and Mary Coll., 1967; PhD in Mgmt. Sci., U. Colo., 1973. Mktg. rep., systems engr. IBM, 1967-71; staff assoc. Nat. Ctr. for Higher Edn. Mgmt. Sys., 1971-72; exec. asst. to exec. dir. Nat. Commn. of the Financing of Postsecondary Edn., 1972-73; adj. prof. U. Colo., 1973-74; asst. prof. U. Kans., 1975-77; cons. to pres. for acad. planning Universidade Fed. de Ceara, 1976-77; exec. v.p. Colo. Women's Coll., 1977-78, pres., 1978-81, 1981—; CEO John Madden Co., Englewood, Colo., 1982-87, bd. dirs., 1984—; founder, chmn., and CEO ECCI, 1988—. Bd. dirs. Solar Energy Rsch. Inst., 1987-90, Regis Coll., 1987-91, Univ. So. Colo. Found., 1987-91, United Bank Svcs. Co., 1978-81, Imperial Am. Energy Inc., Adopt-A-School, 1979-82, Denver Symphony, 1979-82, Colo. Council on Econ. Edn., 1984-87, Colo. Assn. Commerce and Industry, 1985-89. Host community affairs program KHOW Radio, 1979-80; contbr. articles in field. Trustee Fountain Valley Sch., Colorado Springs; co-chmn. Armstrong Campaign for U.S. Senate, 1986, Kramer Campaign for U.S. Senate, 1988. Recipient DAR Outstanding Citizen award, 1961, Faculty Devel. award U. Kans., 1976, Soroptimists Women Helping Women award, 1980. Mem. Nat. Assn. Christians & Jews, Nat. Women's Coalition, Women's Forum, Zonta, Altrusa., Com. of 200 Club, Newcomen Soc. of U.S., Sports Hall of Fame Western Md. Coll., Phi Beta Kappa, Denver Met. Club. Republican. Presbyterian. Office: The Tech Bldg 511 Central Ave Charleston WV 25302-1909 E-mail: sherry@campusecci.com.

MANNING, SYLVIA, English studies educator; b. Montreal, Que., Can., Dec. 2, 1943; came to U.S., 1967; d. Bruno and Lea Bank; m. Peter J. Manning, Aug. 20, 1967; children— Bruce David, Jason Maurice BA, McGill U., 1963; MA, Yale U., 1964, PhD in English, 1967. Asst. prof. English Calif. State U.-Hayward, 1967-71, assoc. prof., 1971-75, assoc. dean, 1972-75; assoc. prof. U. So. Calif., 1975-94, prof., assoc. dir. Ctr. for Humanities, 1975-77, assoc. dir. Ctr. for Humanities, 1975-77, chmn. freshman writing, 1977-80, chmn. dept. English, 1980-83, vice provost, exec. v.p., 1984-94; prof. English U. Ill., Champaign, 1994—, v.p. for acad. affairs, prof. English, 1994—, interim chancellor Chgo., 1999-2000, chancellor, 2000—. Author: Dickens as Satirist, 1971; Hard Times: An Annotated Bibliography, 1984. Contbr. essays to mags. Woodrow Wilson fellow, 1963-64, 66-67 Mem. MLA, Dickens Soc. Office: U of Ill Office of Chancellor 2833 University Hall 601 S Morgan St Chicago IL 60607-7100

MANNING, WALTER SCOTT, JR. veterinarian; b. Bryan, Tex., Mar. 3, 1945; s. Walter Scott and Eleanor Mary (Jones) M.; m. Mary Ann Hurliman, Mar. 11, 1972; children: Adrienne Emily, Walter Scott III. BS, Tex. A&M U., 1967, 76; MS, East Tex. State Univ., 1972; DVM, Tex. A&M U., 1977, PhD, 1986. Mixed practitioner Benton (Ark) Veterinary Hosp., 1977-81; vet. clin. assoc. Coll. Vet. Medicine, Tex. A&M U., College Station, Tex., 1981-84; regional animal care specialist USDA Animal and Plant Health Inspec. Svc., Regulatory Enforcement Animal Care, Ft. Worth, 1986-89; clin. veterinarian Alcon labs., Inc., 1989-90, mgr., 1990-94, asst. dir., 1995-98, prin. scientist III, 1998—. Charter orgn. rep. troop 431 Santa Fe Dist., Longhorn Coun., Boy Scouts Am. Mem. AVMA, Am. Assn. Indsl. Veterinarians, Tex. Vet. Med. Assn., Tarrant County Vet. Med. Assn., Dallas County Vet. Med. Assn., Am. Soc. Lab. Animal Practitioners, Am. Assn. Lab. Animal Sci., Tex. Br. Lab. Animal Sci., Assn. Primate Veterinarians, Nat. Eagle Scout Assn., SAR, Beta Beta Beta, Phi Eta Sigma. Presbyterian. Avocations: genealogy, numismatics, photography. Home: 2055 Mary Ann Ln Burleson TX 76028-2229 Office: Alcon Labs Inc 6201 South Fwy R3-12 Fort Worth TX 76134-2099 E-mail: scott.manning2@alconlabs.com.

MANNING, WILLIAM DUDLEY, JR. retired specialty chemical company executive; b. Tampa, Fla., Mar. 7, 1934; s. William Dudley and Rebecca (Reid) M.; m. Carol Randolph Gillis, June 30, 1962; children: Carol Randolph, Rebecca Barrett, Anne Gillis. BA in Chemistry, Fla. State U., 1957. Sales rep. Amoco Chem. Co., St. Louis and Cleve., 1959-63; sales engr. The Lubrizol Corp., Tulsa, 1963-64, southwestern regional sales mgr., 1964-66, mgr. chem. product sales Wickliffe, Ohio, 1966-72, sales mgr., western U.S., 1972, gen. sales mgr., asst. div. head-sales, 1972-79, mktg. mgr., asst. div. head-sales, 1979-80, v.p. mktg., 1980-81, v.p., bus. devel. div., 1981-85, sr. v.p. sales and mktg., 1985-87; pres. Lubrizol Petroleum Chems. Co., 1987-94; sr. v.p., asst. to pres. The Lubrizol Corp., 1994; cons., investor, 1994—. Bd. dirs. NYCO Am. LLC, Spartanburg, SC, Robbins and Myers, Dayton, Ohio, UNIFRAX Corp., Niagara Falls, N.Y. Trustee Vocat. Guidance Svcs., Cleve., 1991-2000, Borromeo Sem., 2000—. With USAR, 1957-63. Mem. Soc. Automotive Engrs. (assoc.), Kirtland Country Club (v.p. 1986-88, pres. 1988-89), Tavern Club (trustee 1986-91), Chagrin Valley Hunt Club, Sand Ridge Golf Club. Republican. Roman Catholic. Office: 2550 SOM Center Rd Ste 120 Willoughby OH 44094 E-mail: wdmann@compuserve.com.

MANNING, WILLIAM FREDERICK, wire service photographer; b. Gardner, Mass., Aug. 18, 1920; s. Seth Newton and Jennie May (Bennett) M.; m. Yvonne J.C. Winslow, Feb. 29, 1964; children: Pamela Ann, Jeffrey Newton. AA, Boston U., 1950, BS in Communications, 1952. With AP, Boston, 1951-53; photographer UPI, 1953-88; ret. Contbr. photos to books, mags., newspapers throughout the world. Served with USN, 1940-46, PTO. Recipient Look 1st Prize All Sports award, 1958; Pictures of the Yr. award U. Mo., 1964, 74; Nat. Headliners Club award for outstanding syndicate photography, 1974 Mem. Boston Press Photographers Assn., Delta Kappa Alpha. Clubs: Nat. Headliners. Congregationalist. Home: 23 Sunset Dr Beverly MA 01915-2319 Office: One Herald Sq 300 Harrison Ave Boston MA 02118-2237

MANNING, WINTON HOWARD, psychologist, educational administrator; b. St. Louis, Feb. 9, 1930; s. Winton Harry and Jane (Swanson) M.; m. Nancy Mercedes Groves, Aug. 1, 1959; children: Cecelia Groves Tazelaar, Winton H. III. AB with honors, William Jewell Coll., 1951; PhD in Psychology, Washington U., St. Louis, 1959. Instr. psychology William Jewell Coll., Liberty, Mo., 1954-55, asst. prof., acting head dept. psychology, 1955-56; rsch. psychologist Washington U., St. Louis, 1956-58, rsch. assoc., 1958-59; from asst. prof. to prof. psychology Tex. Christian U., Ft. Worth, 1959-65, assoc. dir. univ. honors program, 1962-65; from assoc. dir. rsch. to exec. dir. R & D Coll. Entrance Examination Bd., N.Y.C., 1965-69; from dir. devel. rsch. divsn. to sr. v.p. R & D Ednl. Testing Svc., Princeton, N.J., 1969-83, v.p., 1970-77, sr. v.p. devel. and rsch., 1977-83, sr. scholar, 1983-93; pres. Ednl. Devel. Svc., 1993—. Vis. fellow Princeton U., 1982-83; cons. Gallup Internat. Inst., 1990—, Applied Ednl. Rsch., 1993-95; cons. Grad. Mgmt. Admissions Coun., 1992-95, Carnegie Found. for the Advancement of Tchg. 1993-95; vis. lectr. Washington U., St. Louis, summer, 1961. Author: The Pursuit of Fairness in Admissions to Higher Education, 1977; Student Manual for Essentials of Psychology, 1960. Contbr. articles on ednl. measurement and psychology of learning to profl. publs. Patentee in field U.S. and Europe. Trustee Assn. for Advancement of Mentally Handicapped, 1975-78, Nat. Chicano Coun. on Higher Edn., 1977-85, N.J. Arts Festival, 1980-85; vice-chmn. Found. for Books to China, 1980-98; chmn. bd. trustees Princeton Day Sch., 1981-93; trustee Princeton Area Found., 1991-94, Our House Found., 1991-92; bd. dirs. The Princeton Singers, 1992-99, Christian Renewal Effort in Emerging Democracies, 1992-94, George H. Gallup Internat. Inst., 1992-98; chmn., trustee Trinity-All Saints' Cemetery, 1993-98; chmn. Affordable Housing Bd. of Princeton Borough, 1987-89; chmn., commr. Princeton Pub. Housing Authority, 1995-99, 2001—; sr. warden All Saints Episc. Ch., 1987-89; chmn. ins. com. Diocese N.J., 1993-95; coun. mem. Diocese of N.J., 1996-99, audit com., 1997-98, mem. standing com., 1998—; adv. coun. U. Okla. Ctr. for Rsch. on Minority Edn., 1987-92, Ind. Sch. Chmn. Assn., 1987-92; trustee Friends of Princeton Open Space, 1995-98; trustee Russian Ministry Network, 1995-98; cons. Carnegie Found. for Advancement of Teaching, 1987-95; cons. The Coll. Bd., 1988-91; spl. cons. Commn. on Admission to Grad. Mgmt. Edn., 1987-89; chair Princeton Residents Traffic Safety Com., 1994—. Recipient Alumni Achievement citation William Jewell Coll., 1970; named Gallup Scholar in Edn., 1995. Fellow Am. Psychol. Soc. (charter), Eastern Psychol. Assn., Psychometric Soc., Nat. Assn. Scholars, Am. Ednl. Rsch. Assn., Nat. Coun. on Measurement in Edn. (mem. com. on legal issues in measurement 1977-79), N.Y. Acad. Scis., Nassau Club, Pendragon Club, Old Guard of Princeton, Oratory of Good Shepherd, Phi Beta Kappa, Sigma Xi, Order of St. John of Jerusalem. Home: 12 Morven Pl Princeton NJ 08540-3024 Office Fax: 609-924-9528. E-mail: win.manning@verizon.net.

MANNING-WEBER, CLAUDIA JOY, medical radiography administrator, consultant, author, writer; b. Oak Park, Ill., Mar. 17, 1950; d. Charles Lawrence and Carrie Joy (Lund) Manning. AAS, Coll. of DuPage, 1980; BA with honors, Nat. Coll. of Edn., 1986, MS, 1989. Registered med. radiography technologist, Am. Registry of Radiologic Technologists; cert. med. radiography technologist, Ariz.; cert. adult and continuing edn. tchr., Ariz. State Cmty. Coll. Bd. Faculty Coll. of DuPage, Glen Ellyn, Ill., 1987-90, South Suburban Coll., South Holland, 1989-91; mentor tchr. Prescott (Ariz.) Coll., 1992—; dir. Ariz. Continuing Edn. Svcs., Avondale, 1992—; clin. instr. Phoenix Bapt. Hosp., 1992-93; program dir. PTR Bryman Sch., 1993-95; program dir. med. radiography Apollo Coll., 1995-96; now writer, edn. cons. Avondale, Ariz. Contbr., cons. EDUMED Co., Minnetonka, Minn., 1995—; treas. ASSRT, Mesa, Ariz., 1993-94; cons. Coll. of DuPage, 1988-91. Author: Distance Delivered Education in Nuclear Medicine Technology, 1989, Multiskilling: Radiography for Health Care Providers. Mem. ASCD, AAUW, Internat. Soc. Radiographers and Radiologic Technicians, Assn. for Educators in Radiologic Sci., Am. Soc. Radiologic Technologists, Ariz. State Soc. Radiologic Technologists (ednl. dir. 1992-93, treas. 1993-94, seminar presenter 1991, 92), Delta Kappa Gamma. Avocations: reading, writing, hiking, horseback riding. Home: 10938 W Bermuda Dr Avondale AZ 85323-4304

MANNINO, EDWARD FRANCIS, lawyer, educator; b. Abington, Pa., Dec. 5, 1941; s. Sante Francis and Martha Anne (Hines) M.; m. Mary Ann Vigilante, July 17, 1965 (div. 1990); m. Antoinette K. O'Connell, June 25, 1993; children: Robert John, Jennifer Elaine. BA with distinction, U. Pa., 1963, LLB magna cum laude, 1966. Bar: Pa. 1967. Law clk. 3d cir. U.S. Ct. Appeals, 1966-67; assoc. Dilworth, Paxson, Kalish & Kauffman, Phila., 1967-71, ptnr., 1972-86, co-chmn. litigation dept., 1980-86, sr. ptnr., 1982-86; sr. prin. Elliott, Mannino & Flaherty, PC, 1986-90; chmn. Mannino Griffith PC, 1990-95; sr. ptnr. Wolf, Block, Schorr & Solis-Cohen, 1995-98; ptnr. Akin, Gump, Strauss, Hauer & Feld LLP, 1998—. Hearing examiner disciplinary bd. Supreme Ct. Pa., 1986—89, mem. adv. com. on appellate ct. rules, 1989—95; lectr. Temple U. Law Sch., 1968—69, 1971—72; mem. Phila. Mayor's Sci. and Tech. Adv. Com., 1976—79; project mgr. Pa. Environ. Master Plan, 1973; chmn. Pa. Land Use Policy Study Adv. Com., 1973—75; chmn. adv. com., hon. faculty history dept. U. Pa., 1980—85, lectr. Am. history, 2001—. Author: Lender Liability and Banking Litigation, 1989, Business and Commercial Litigation: A Trial Lawyer's Handbook, 1995, The Civil RICO Primer, 1996; mem. editl. bd. Litigation mag., 1985-87, Comm. Lending Litigation News, 1988-2001, Bank Bailout Litigation News, 1989-93, Bus. Torts Reporter, 1988-99, Practical Litigator, 1989—, Civil RICO Report, 1991-2001; contbr. articles to profl. jours. Pres. parish coun. Our Mother of Consolation Ch., 1977-79; bd. overseers U. Pa. Sch. Arts and Scis., 1985-89, chmn. recruitment and retention of faculty com.; commonwealth trustee Temple U., 1987-90, audit, bus. and fin. coms. Named one of Nation's Top Litigators Nat. Law Jour., 1990, Pa.'s Top Ten Trial Lawyers, 1999. Fellow Am. Bar Found., ABA (chmn. various coms.), Am. Law Inst., Hist. Soc. U.S. Dist. Ct. Ea. Dist. Pa. (bd. dirs.), Pa. Bar Assn., Phila. Bar Assn. (gov. 1975), Pa. Soc., Order of Coif, Phi Beta Kappa, Phi Beta Kappa Assocs. Democrat. Office: Akin Gump Strauss Hauer & Feld LLP One Commerce Sq 2005 Market St Ste 2200 Philadelphia PA 19103-7014 E-mail: emannino@akingump.com.

MANNINO, J(OSEPH) ROBERT, medical educator; b. Altoona, Pa., May 6, 1941; s. Joseph Robert and Helen La Rue (Menza) M.; m. Rosemary Kathleen McGrath, Apr. 8, 1978; 1 child, Angela Christine. BS, Juniata Coll., 1963; MA, East Carolina U., 1965; PhD, Colo. State U., 1974; DO, Kansas City Coll. Osteo. Med., 1971. Diplomate Am. Osteo. Bd. Family Practice. Intern Rocky Mountain Hosp., Denver, 1971-72; physician pvt. practice, 1972-77; dir. med. edn.nt Kansas City Coll. Osteo. Medicine, 1977-80; prof. family medicine Ohio U. Coll. Osteo. Medicine, Athens, 1981-94, Nova Southeastern U., Coll. Osteo. Medicine, North Miami Beach, Fla., 1994—. Teaching asst. physiology East Carolina U., 1965; coord. rsch. Phila. Coll. Osteo. Medicine, 1966-67; asst. dir. med. edn. Rocky Mountain Hosp., Denver, 1972-73, dir. med. edn., 1975-77, bd. trustees, 1975-77; dir. gen. practice residency Drs. Hosp., Columbus, 1980-94; dir. med. edn. & program dir. family practice residency North Broward Hosp. Dist., Ft. Lauderdale, Fla., 1994-96; clin.

assoc. Cleveland Clinic, Ft. Lauderdale, 1996-2000; cons. in field. Contbr. articles to profl. jours. Rsch. fellow Colo. State U., 1968-69. Fellow Am. Coll. Osteo. Family Practice, Am. Soc. Colposcopy & Cervical Pathology, Am. Soc. Laser Medicine & Surgery; mem. Am. Osteo. Assn., Am. Coll. Cyrosurgery, N.Y. Acad. Scis., Fla. Soc. Osteo. Medicine, Fla. State Soc. Am. Coll. Osteo. Family Physicians, Broward County Acad. Fla. Soc. Osteo. Medicine, Endocrine Soc., Chi Beta Phi. Republican. Roman Catholic. Avocation: restoring antique cars.

MANNION, BARBARA L. secondary school educator; b. Adelsberg, Germany, May 2, 1945; d. Gerhard and Lieselotte (Koch) Voet; divorced; children: Liselotte A., Donna P. BS in Biology cum laude, U. Mary Hardin-Baylor, 1980; MA in Adminstrn. and Supr. Curriculum, Wash. State U., 1992. Cert. tchr., adminstr., Wash., N.C. Sci. and math. tchr. Western Harnett (N.C.) Sch. Dist.; head sci. dept., trainer outcome driven edn. and 4-MAT Pasco (Wash.) Sch. Dist.; now prin. Columbia H.S., Columbia Sch. Dist. 400, Burbank, Wash. NSF grantee, 1979; Woodrow Wilson fellow in biology. Mem. ASCD, Nat. Assn. Biology Tchrs., N.Y. Acad. Sci., Wash. State Sci. Tchrs. Assn., Phi Delta Kappa. Home: 4815 Desert Plateau Dr Pasco WA 99301-9420

MANNIS, VALERIE SKLAR, lawyer; b. Green Bay, Wis., May 26, 1939; d. Phillip and Rose (Aaron) Sklar; m. Kent Simon Mannis, Dec. 28, 1958; children: Andrea, Marci. BS, U. Wis., 1970, JD, 1975, PhD, 1997. Bar: Wis. 1974. Staff atty. Legis. Coun., Madison, Wis., 1974-75; sole practice, 1975-84; asst. to pres. Bank of Shorewood Hills, Wis., 1984-86; trust officer, sr. account exec. First Wis. Nat. Bank, Madison, 1986-90; devel. dir. YWCA-Madison, 1990-92. Assoc. lectr. U. Wis., Madison, 1997—. Pres. Nat. Women's Polit. Caucus Dane County, Madison, 1984; bd. dirs. Madison Estate Planning Coun., 1980-84, Madison Jewish Cmty. Coun., 1975-79, 82-84. Mem. State Bar Wis. (gov. 1980-86), Dane County Bar Assn. (chmn. property com. 1978-84), Legal Assn. for Women (founding), Bus. Forum Bd. (bd. dirs. 1988-91, 98—), Rotary (pres. 1992-93).

MANNIX, CHARLES RAYMOND, law educator; b. Elizabeth, N.J., Aug. 2, 1950; s. Charles Raymond and Helen Joan (French) M. BA, Duquesne U., 1972, MA, JD, Duquesne U., 1976; MPA, Harvard U., 1998. Bar: Iowa 1976, N.Y. 1996, Va. 1980, D.C. 1980, U.S. Ct. Claims 1976, U.S. Tax Ct. 1976, U.S. Ct. Mil. Appeals 1976, U.S. Ct. Internat. Trade 1976, U.S. Ct. Appeals (4th and 5th cirs.) 1977, U.S. Ct. Appeals (D.C. cir.) 1977, U.S. Dist. Ct. Va. 1980, U.S. Supreme Ct. 1980, U.S. Ct. Appeals (D.C. cir.) 1980, U.S. Ct. Appeals (fed. cir.) 1982, N.Y. 1996. Commd. 2d lt. USAF, 1973, advanced through grade to lt. col., 1982; intern UN Office of Legal Affairs, N.Y.C., 1975; various legal assignments; lectr. USAF Med. Law Cons. Program, 1981-99. Adj. faculty Georgetown U., Washington, 1984-99; assoc. prof. and chmn. dept. med. jurisprudence, asst. prof. mil. medicine, v.p. and gen. counsel Uniformed Svcs. U. Health Scis. Decorated Meritorious Svc. medal with Oak Leaf Cluster, Air Force Commendation medal with Oak Leaf Clusters. Mem. ABA, FBA, ATLA, D.C. Bar Assn., Va. State Bar Assn., Am. Soc. Internat. Law, Am. Soc. Law and Medicine, Am. Arbitration Assn. (arbitrator), Am. Acad. Hosp. Attys., Nat. Assn. Coll. and Univ. Attys., N.Y. State Bar Assn., Bar Assn. of the City of N.Y., Assn. Mil. Surgeons U.S., Harvard Club of N.Y. Home: 10205 Walker Lake Dr Great Falls VA 22066-3558 Office: Uniformed Svcs U Health Scis Gen Coun Jones Bridge Rd Bethesda MD 20815-5737 E-mail: charlesmannix@msn.com.

MANNIX, KEVIN LEESE, lawyer; b. Queens, N.Y., Nov. 26, 1949; s. John Warren Sr. and Editta Gorrell M.; m. Susanna Bernadette Chiocca, June 1, 1974; children: Nicholas Chiocca, Gabriel Leese, Emily Kemper. BA, U. Va., 1971, JD, 1974. Bar: Oreg. 1974, U.S. Ct. Appeals (9th cir.) 1976, U.S. Supreme Ct. 1978, Guam 1979. Law clk. to judge Oreg. Ct. Appeals, Salem, 1974-75; asst. atty. gen. Oreg. Dept. Justice, 1975-77, Govt. of Guam, Agana, 1977-79; judge adminstrv. law Oreg. Workers' Compensation Bd., Salem, 1980-83; assoc. Lindsay, Hart, Neil & Weigler, Portland, Oreg., 1983-86; pres. Kevin L. Mannix Profl. Corp., Salem, 1986—. Chmn. St. Joseph Sch. Bd., Salem, 1981-86; pres. Salem Cath. Schs. Corp., 1985; v.p. Salem Cath. Schs. Found., 1985-88, pres., 1988-90, 91-94, 2000—, state rep., 1989-97, 99-2001; pres. bd. dirs. Blanchet Sch.; v. chair Oregon Rep. Party, 1998—; State Senator, 1998-99. Mem. Marion Bar Assn., Rotary (bd. dirs. East Salem 1985-89, pres. 1987-88), KC. Republican. Avocations: photography, scuba diving, travel. Home: 375 18th St NE Salem OR 97301-4307 Office: 2003 State St Salem OR 97301-4349

MANNO, BRUNO VICTOR, foundation administrator; BA, U. Dayton, 1970, MA, 1972; PhD, Boston Coll., 1975. Mem. faculty U. Dayton, 1975-78; dir. rsch. Data Bank and In-svc. programs Nat. Cath. Edn. Assn., Washington, 1979-86; dir. planning Office of Ednl. Rsch. and Improvement Dept. Edn., 1986, chief staff, acting asst. sec., 1986-91, asst. sec. edn., 1991-93; sr. fellow edn. policy studies program Hudson Inst., 1993-98; sr. fellow edn. The Annie E. Casey Found., Balt., 1998-99; sr. program assoc. The Annie E. Carey Found., 1999—. Vis. sr. lectr. Cath. Tchrs. Coll., Sydney, Australia; vis. rsch. assoc. Nat. Opinion Rsch. Ctr., U. Chgo.; vis. lectr. Inst. for Cath. Ednl. Leadership, U. San Farncisco. Co-author: Charter Schools in Action: Renewing Public Education, 2000; co-editor book; author 150 articles and 30 book revs. Office: The Annie E Casey Found 701 Saint Paul St Baltimore MD 21202-2311

MANNO, RITA, state agency administrator; b. Buffalo, Sept. 11, 1946; d. Anthony Joseph and Irene Pawlowski; m. Donald F. Manno, July 11, 1970; children: Kimberly, Rebecca. Student, Exetr (Eng.) U., 1965-66; BA, Canisius Coll., Buffalo, 1967; MA, U. Wis., 1968. State polit. editor Courier-Post, Cherry Hill, N.J., 1980-93; press sec. Gov. Christine Whitman, 1994-95; dir. comms. N.J. Dept. Health and Sr. Svcs., 1996—. Mem. exec. bd. Nat. Pub. Health Info. Coalition, 1996—. Recipient Best of Gannett award Gannett Corp., 1990-93; Knight scholar, 1993. Mem. N.J. C. of C. (N.J. 300 Women 1998-99). Avocations: hiking, weight training, movies, motorcycles. Office: NJ Dept Health and Sr Svcs PO Box 360 Trenton NJ 08625-0360

MANNS, LINDA GREENE, community health nurse coordinator; b. Bklyn., May 21, 1951; d. Gaston A. and Cleopatra (Frier) Greene; m. Nov. 25, 1978 (div. 1984); 1 child, Temeca E. AAS, Bronx Community Coll., 1971; BSN, Hunter Coll., 1973; MSN, U. Va., 1988. Staff nurse Kings County Hosp., Bklyn., 1971-73; charge nurse St. John's Episcopal Hosp., 1974-78; pub. health nurse Dept. Health, 1973-78; staff nurse Roanoke (Va.) Meml. Hosp., 1979, VA Med. Ctr., Salem, Va., 1979-83, primary nurse oncology clinic, 1983-84, weekend nurse supr., 1986-87, community health nurse, 1984-90, community health nurse coord., 1990—. Coord. Community Awareness Health Fair, High St. Bapt. Ch., 1987; vol. coord. Roanoke City Health Dept. Cardiovascular Risk Reduction Program. Mem. Va. Pub. Health Assn., Roanoke Valley Black Nurses' Assn. (treas.), Sigma Theta Tau. E-mail: LGManns@hotmail.com.

MANNWEILER, MARY-ELIZABETH, painter; b. Norwood, Ohio, June 23, 1916; d. Wilbur Lawrence Young and Augusta Minnis (Newman) Davis; m. Robert Mays Lang, Sr., May 25, 1940 (dec. July 1981); children: Robert Mays Lang, Jr., Gary Davis Lang, Julianna Elizabeth Lang Crawford; m. Gordon Bannatyne Mannweiler, Apr. 17, 1982(dec. Aug. 2001). Student, Miami U., Oxford, Ohio, 1935-37. Portrait painter; permanent collections; donated (with husband) stained glass window to Congl. Ch., Naugatuck, Conn. Past pres. Athena Club, Freeport, N.Y., Woodbury (Conn.) Women's Club, 1977-78, Watertown (Conn.) Art League; past dir. Waterbury (Conn.) Symphony Orch.; pres. Mannweiler Found., Naugatuck, Conn. Recipient blue ribbons for artwork; Paul Harris fellow Rotary, 2001; music room named in honor of Mr. and Mrs. Mannweiler Conn. Jr. Republic, Litchfield, 1997. Mem. DAR (regent Ruth Floyd Woodhull chpt. 1966-67, pres.). Home: 435 Hillside Ave Naugatuck CT 06770-2727

MANNY, CARTER HUGH, JR. architect, foundation administrator; b. Michigan City, Ind., Nov. 16, 1918; s. Carter Hugh and Ada Gage (Barnes) M.; m. Mary Alice Kellett, Dec. 6, 1942 (dec. Jan. 1994); children: Elizabeth, Carter Hugh III; m. Maya Moran, Dec. 27, 1995. AB magna cum laude, Harvard U., 1941, Indsl. Adminstr., 1942; Taliesin fellow, Scottsdale, Ariz., 1946; BS in Architecture, Ill. Inst. Tech., 1948. With Murphy/Jahn (name formerly Naess & Murphy and C.F. Murphy Assocs.), Chgo., 1948-83, partner, 1957-61; dir. 1st Citizens Bank, Michigan City, Ind., 1970-86; sr. v.p. Murphy/Jahn (name formerly Naess & Murphy and C.F. Murphy Assocs.), 1978-83. Mem. adv. com. on architecture Art Inst. of Chgo., 1982—, oversight com. Ill. Inst. Tech. Sch. of Architecture, Chgo., 1989-94; trustee Graham Found. Advanced Studies in Fine Arts 1956-74, exec. dir., 1972-93, hon. trustee, 1994—. Projects include O'Hare Internat. Airport, Chgo., FBI Hdqrs, Washington, First Nat. Bank Chgo. Civic Center, Chgo. Bd. Trade. Fellow SAH, AIA (pres. Chgo. chpt. 1973, dir. Ill. council 1972-73), Soc. Archtl. Historians (dir. 1982-85), Chgo. Bldg. Congress (dir. 1978-83), Soc. Archtl. Historians; mem. Phi Beta Kappa, Pottawattomie Country Club, Mich. City Yacht Club, Tavern Club, Arts Club, Cliff Dwellers Club (Chgo., hon.). Home: 200 Lake Ave Michigan City IN 46360 also: 1448 N Lake Shore Dr Chicago IL 60610-6655

MANOFF, RICHARD KALMAN, advertising executive, public health consultant, author; b. Bklyn., June 24, 1916; s. Kalman and Sarah (Glatman) M.; m. Lucy B. Deutscher, Nov. 27, 1942; children: Robert K., Gregory P. BS, CCNY, 1937, MS, 1940. Asst. regional dir. War Manpower Commn., 1942-45; marketing dir. Welch Grape Juice Co., 1949-53; v.p. Kenyon & Eckhardt Advt., N.Y.C., 1953-56; pres., chmn. bd. Richard K. Manoff Inc. Advt., from 1956; now pres. Manoff Internat. Inc.; spl. adv. mktg. and communications to exec. dir. UNICEF, 1980—. Dir. Thomas J. Lipton, Inc.; adj. prof. dept. health Scis. Sargent Coll. Allied Health Professions, Boston U., 1978— ; lectr. pub. health Columbia U. Sch. Medicine, 1982-83; Mem. U.S. del. FAO World Conf., Rome, Italy, 1966; spl. advisor UNICEF and WHO, 1968-78; cons. spl. mission to Food and Agr. Ministry, Govt. India, AID, 1969; Ford Found. offices Pub. Edn. Pub. Broadcasting for children's TV; participant 1st World Conf. on Social Communication for Devel. Mass Communications, Mexico, 1970, 7th Asian Advt. Congress, Delhi, 1970, 3d Western Hemisphere Nutrition Congress, Fla., 1971, Internat. Conf. Nutrition, Nat. Devel. and Planning, Mass. Inst. Tech., 1971, Symposium Eating Patterns and Their Influence on Purchasing Behavior and Nutrition, Nev., 1971, Nutrition Workshop, AID, 1971, 9th Annual Summer Workshop Family Planning, 1971, 4th & 5th Seminar Workshop on Mgmt. and Planning of Population Family Planning Programs, 1971, New Products Symposium, 1971, Communication Seminar series Cornell U., 1971, Exploration The Frontiers of Nutritional Edn. Seminar, 1972, 9th Internat. Congress of Nutrition, Mexico, 1972, East-West Center Comml. Resources Conf. on Family Planning, Hawaii, 1972; Protein adv. group UN Systems Annual Mtg., 1973; mem. panel White House Conf. Food, Nutrition and Health, 1969; mem. Sec.'s Adv. Com. on Population Affairs, Dept. HEW, 1971-76; mem. adv. com. Population Reference Bur., Washington, 1977— , Population Inst., 1980—; mem. Nelson A. Rockefeller's Commn. on Critical Choices for Ams.; cons. HRSA Healthy Start Campaign to reduce infant mortality, 1991; bd. dirs. Population Comm. Internat.; Martin J. Forman Meml. lectr., Washington, 1993. Author: Social Marketing: New Imperative for Public Health, 1985. Bd. dirs. Planned Parenthood World Population, Pathfinder Fund, Boston, 1977-80, United Nutrition Edn. Found., Alexandria, Va., 1978—; mem. com. on internat. nutrition programs NAS-NRC, 1973; founder, mem. Com. for Shakespeare Festival, N.Y.C.; bd. visitors Grad. Sch. and Univ. Ctr., CUNY; mem. adv. bd., cons. to the pres. Henry J. Kaiser Family Found., 1987-91; dir. City Coll. Fund, 1990—. Recipient 5th Ann. Global award for media excellence Population Inst., China, 1985, Townsend Harris medal Alumni Assn. CCNY, 1986. Mem. Am. Assn. Advt. Agys. (gov. 1967—, sec.-treas. 1975—), Population Comms. Internat. (dir. 1992—), Friars Club, Harmonie Club (N.Y.C.), Century Assn. Home: 322 E 57th St New York NY 10022-2949 also: PO Box 1276 14 Donahue Rd Litchfield CT 06759

MANON-ESPAILLAT, RAMON, physician, educator; b. Feb. 2, 1956; MD, U. P.R., 1980. Diplomate Am Bd. Psychiatry and Neurology. Asst. prof. Case Western Res. U., Cleve., 1985-90; assoc. prof. Temple U., Phila., 1990-94; clin. prof. Jefferson Med. Coll., 1994—. Office: Neurology and Neurophysiology 125 S 9th St Philadelphia PA 19107-5125

MANOOGIAN, RICHARD ALEXANDER, manufacturing company executive; b. Long Branch, N.J., July 30, 1936; s. Alex and Marie (Tatian) M.; children: James, Richard, Bridget. BA in Econs, Yale U., 1958. Asst. to pres. Masco Corp., Taylor, Mich., 1958-62, exec. v.p., 1962-68, pres., 1968-85, chmn. bd., CEO, 1985—. Chmn., dir. Mascotech, Inc., Trimas Corp.; dir. First Chgo. NBD Corp., Detroit Renaissance, Am. Bus. Conf. Trustee U. Liggett Sch., State Dept. Fine Arts Comsn., Founder's Soc., Detroit Inst. Arts, Center for Creative Studies; trustee coun. Nat. Gallery Art. Mem. Yale Alumni Assn. Clubs: Grosse Pointe Yacht, Grosse Pointe Hunt, Country Club Detroit, Detroit Athletic. Office: Masco Corp 21001 Van Born Rd Taylor MI 48180-1300*

MANOOGIAN, WILLIAM, lawyer; b. Fresno, Calif., Mar. 29, 1946; s. Morris Anthony and Doris Eunice (Parigian) M.; m. Margaret Ann Solt, Oct. 18, 1975; children: Nicole-Helene, Claire-Louise. BA, Stanford U., 1968; postgrad., U. Paris, 1968-70; JD, Am. U., Washington, 1973. Legis. atty. Rep. Nat. Com., Washington, 1973-75; minority counsel Civil Svc. com. Civic Svc. com. Ho. of Reps., 1975-83; spl. counsel Dept. of Edn., 1983-84; counsel to Amb. John Gavin Dept. of State, Mexico City, 1984-86; cons. to Dr. Armand Hammer Occidental Petroleum, L.A., 1986; gen. atty. Criminal divsn., Dept. of Justice, Washington, 1987-89, Immigration and Naturalization Svc., San Diego, 1989—. Advisor to William Saroyan, Paris, 1969-70. Contbr. articles to profl. jours. Legal advisor to Rep. campaigns, Washington, 1974. Mem. D.C. Bar Assn., Chi Psi. Armenian Orthodox. Avocations: swimming, foreign languages. Home: 12992 Carmel Creek Rd San Diego CA 92130-2132 Office: Justice Dept 880 Front St Ste 1234 San Diego CA 92101-8834

MANOS, JOHN M. federal judge; b. Cleve., Dec. 8, 1922; m. Viola Manos; 4 children. BS, Case Inst. Tech., 1944; JD, Cleve.-Marshall Coll. Law, 1950. Bar: Ohio 1950. Asst. plant mgr. Lake City Malleable Iron Co., Cleve., 1946-50; atty. Manos & Manos, 1950-63; law dir. City of Bay Village, 1954-56; industries rep. Cleve. Regional Bd. of Rev., 1957-59; judge Ohio Ct. Common Pleas, Cuyahoga County, 1963-69, Ohio Ct. Appeals, Cuyahoga County, 1969-76; sr. judge U.S. Dist. Ct. (no. dist.) Ohio, Cleve., 1976-91, 1991—. With USN, 1942-45. Named Phi Alpha Delta Man of Yr., 1972, Outstanding Alumnus Cleve.- Marshall Law Alumni Assn., 1976. Mem. ABA, Fed. Bar Assn., Ohio State Bar Assn., Nat. Lawyers Club (hon.), Bar Assn. Greater Cleve., Cuyahoga County Bar Assn., Delta Theta Phi (Man of Yr. 1970). Office: US Dist Ct 201 Superior Ave E Cleveland OH 44114-1201

MANOS, SARANTOS JOHN, physics educator; b. Bronx, N.Y., Dec. 7, 1941; s. Peter Sarantos and Carol Manos; m. Anna A. Manos; 1 child, Erika. AAS, Williamsville C.C., Buffalo, 1961; BS, U. So. Miss., 1968; MED in Biology, Boston State Coll.; postgrad., Pa. State U., U. Mass. Tchr. sci. Boston Tech. H.S., 1969—; prof. Massasoit C.C., Brock, Mass., 1983—. Coord. Simmons Math. Sci. Minority Enrichment Program, Boston Tech. H.S., 1998—; coord. after-sch. programs in elec. and mech. engring., biology and chemistry, Tufts U., 1978-84; instr. pre-engring. program North Shore C.C.; participant Hubble Space Telescope Workshop. Mem. Am. Assn. Physics Tchrs., Nat. Sci. Tchrs. Assn., Am. Inst. Physics Soc., New Eng. Sci. Tchrs. Assn., Mass. Assn. Sci. Tchrs., Greater Boston Physics Tchrs. Assn., N.Y. Acad. Scis. Home: 26 Kimberly Pl Randolph MA 02368-5524

MANOSEVITZ, MARTIN, psychologist; b. Mpls., June 22, 1938; s. Julius and Ethel (Cohen) M.; m. Carolyn Heather Margulius, Sept. 17, 1959; children— Bradley, Jason. BA, U. Minn., Mpls., 1960, PhD, 1964. Diplomate in clin. psychology, psychoanalysis Am. Bd. Profl. Psychology. Asst. prof. psychology Rutgers U., 1964-67; asst. prof. psychology U. Tex., Austin, 1967-69, assoc. prof., 1969-75, prof., 1975-87; pvt. practice clin. psychology Austin, 1975-99, Aspen, Colo., 1999—. Adj. prof. psychology U. Tex., 1987-93; dir. psychol. svcs. CPC Capital Hosp., Austin, 1987-93, Shoal Creek Hosp., Austin, 1994-99; allied profl. staff Aspen Valley Hosp., 2000—; founding ptnr. Aspen Dispute Resolution, 2001--. Trustee Austin-Travis County Mental Health-Mental Retardation Center, 1978-80. Fellow APA (bd. dirs. divsn. psychoanalysis, 1999-2000, membership chmn. 1997-2000, bd. mem. at large 1999-2000, treas. 2002—), Acad. Clin. Psychology, Acad. Psychoanalytic Psychology; mem. Colo. Psychol. Assn., Austin Soc. for Psychoanalytic Psychology (pres. 1994-95), Denver Psychoanalytic Soc. Office: Ste 200 106 S Mill St Aspen CO 81611 Mailing: PO Box 7976 Aspen CO 81612 E-mail: mmanosev@earthlink.net.

MANOUS, PETER J. lawyer; m. Susan Severtson Manous. BS in pub. adminstrn. & mgmt., Ind. Univ., 1984; law degree, Valparaiso U., 1987. Bar: Ind. State Bar Assn. Pvt. atty., 1994—; coord. Frank O'Bannon's Campaign , 1996—2000; adv. Governor Residence Commn. Bd. dirs. Lake Area United Way; past pres. Millennium Housing Found.; Lake County Welfare to Work Coun.; mem. N.W. Ind. Quality Life Coun.; bd. dirs. Tradewinds; mem. Ind. Dem. Party Deputy Chairmen; regional coord. Evan Bayh U.S. Senate; vol. Kennedy for Pres. Campaign, 1980; mem. St. George Greek Orthodox Ch. Mem.: Am. Bar Assn., Lake County Bar Assn. Democrat. Office: 9111 Broadway Ste GG Merrillville IN 46410*

MANOUSAKIS, EFSTRATIOS, physicist, educator; b. Ithaca, Kefalinias, Greece, July 11, 1957; s. Stavros and Persephone (Lyviaki) Manousakis; children: Jacob. Diploma, U. Athens, Greece, 1980; M.S, U Ill., Urbana-Champaign, 1983; PhD, U, Ill., Urbana-Champaign, 1985. Rsch. asst. Nuclear Rsch. Ctr. Democritos, Athens, Greece, 1980—81; tchg. asst. U. of Ill., Urbana-Champaign, 1981—82, rsch. asst. Ill., 1982—85; rsch. assoc. MIT, Cambridge, Mass., 1985—87; assoc. prof. Fla. State U., Tallahassee, 1988—92, prof. of physics, 1992—. Adv. bd. mem. Jpl, Nasa, Pasadena, Calif., 2000—02; adv. bd. Dept. of Energy, Washington, 1989—89. Contbr. articles including original rsch. ons; editor: (Conf. Proceedings) Physical Phenomena at Higj Magnetic Speeds, 1991. Recipient Second Panhellenic Math. Soc. Award, Greek Math. Soc., 1975, Ross J. Martin, U. of Ill., 1985. Mem.: Am. Phys. Soc., Sigma Xi. Achievements include research in On antiferromagnet on the square lattice and its application to cuprous articles. Office: Florida State Univ 612 Dept Physics Tallahassee FL 32306 Office Fax: 850-644-8630. E-mail: stratos@martech.fsu.edu.

MANOWITZ, PAUL, biochemist, researcher, educator; b. Monticello, N.Y., Dec. 13, 1940; s. Jacob M. and Rose (Levine) M.; m. Joyce L. Swartz, June 16, 1968; children: Neal J., Lauren H. BA in Chemistry with honors, Cornell U., 1962; PhD in Biochemistry, Brandeis U., 1967. Fellow NYU Sch. Medicine, 1967-70, instr., 1970-72; asst. prof. psychiatry U. Medicine and Dentistry N.J. Robert Wood Johnson Med. Sch., Piscataway, 1972-78, assoc. prof. psychiatry, 1978-96, prof. psychiatry, 1996—. Rsch. cons. VA Med. Ctr., Lyons, N.J., 1987—. Mem. edit. bd. Jour. of Studies on Alcohol, 1993—; contbr. articles to profl. jours. Grantee Nat. Inst. on Alcohol Abuse and Alcoholism. Mem. AAAS, World Fedn. of Socs. Biol. Psychiatry, Internat. Soc. for Biomed. Rsch. on Alcoholism, Am. Soc. Human Genetics, Soc. Biol. Psychiatry, Rsch. Soc. on Alcoholism. Home: 7 Guernsey Ln East Brunswick NJ 08816-3506 Office: U Medicine and Dentistry NJ Robert Wood Johnson Med Sch 671 Hoes Ln Piscataway NJ 08854-5627

MANROSS, MARY, mayor; m. Larry; 4 children. BS in Polit. Sci. Mayor City of Scottsdale, Ariz., 2000—. Mem. Scottsdale (Ariz.) City Coun., 1992-2000. Chmn. Scottsdale (Ariz.) Parks and Recreation Commn., Maricopa Assn. Govts. Youth Policy Adv. Com.; bd. dirs. Ariz. Women in Mcpl. Govt.; mem. Planning Commn.; vice chmn. Scottsdale Bond Com.; mem. Sub-com. TPC-Westworld, City Ct., C. of C./Econ. Devel.; mem. Govs. Task Force on Urban Planning, Ariz. Town Hall, Nat. League of Cities Energy, Environment and Nat. Resource Policy Com.; mem. steering com. NLC Transp., Infrastructure and Svcs. Address: 3939 N Drinkwater Blvd Scottsdale AZ 85251-4433 Office: City Hall 3939 N Drinkwater Blvd Scottsdale AZ 85251-4433*

MANS, WALTER A. engineer; b. Inglewood, Calif., July 11, 1942; s. Walter Adolf and Grace M.; m. Martha Laverne Voiner, Aug. 10, 1968; children: Wade Walter, Shane Michael. BS, Mont. State U., 1964; MS, U. So. Calif., 1971. Enlisted USAF, 1964, advanced through grades to maj.; mathematician, astroengineer Nat. Security Agy., Ft. Meade, Md., 1964-68, U.S. Dept. Def., El Segundo, Calif., 1968-72; prof. ROTC USAF, Waterville, Maine, 1972-74, chief engr. El Segundo, 1974-76; regional area comdr. CAP, Great Falls, Mont., 1976-80; chief plans divsn. USAF, Sunnyvale, Calif., 1981-85, chief planner Albuquerque, 1985-89; plans and resources Lockheed Martin, 1989-94; project engr. mgmt. Hughes Aircraft Co. Registered rep. Dain, Boswell, Great Falls, 1976-80. Author: NASA/Department of Defense: Ten Years of the Future, 1971, Economic Balance 1983, 1983; contbr. articles to profl. jours. Mem. IEEE, IAAA. Lodges: Optimists, Rotary. Methodist. Avocations: reading, hiking, fishing, tennis, computers.

MANSBERGER, ARLIE ROLAND, JR. surgeon; b. Pitts., Oct. 13, 1922; s. Arlie Rol and Mayme (Smith) M.; m. Anna Ellen Piel, July 27, 1946; children— Ellen Lynn, John Arlie, Leigh Ann. BA, Western Md. Coll., 1943, D.Sc. (hon.), 1974; MD, U. Md., 1947, D.Sc. (hon.), 1978. Diplomate: Am. Bd. Surgery (dir., vice chmn.). Intern U. Md. Hosp., 1947-49, resident in surgery, 1947-54; chief wound shock br. biophysics div. Army Chem. Center, 1954-56; instr. surgery U. Md., 1956-59, asst. prof., 1959-61, asso. prof., 1961-69, prof. surgery, 1969-73; clin. dir. shock-trauma unit, 1962-73; prof. surgery, chmn. dept. Med. Coll. Ga., Augusta, 1973-91; prof. surgery emeritus, chmn., 1991—. Cons. surgeon Dwight David Eisenhower Army Med. Center, VA Hosp. Editor: Essence of General Surgery, 1975; chmn. editorial bd.: Bull. U. Md, 1971-73; editor-in-chief: The Am. Surgeon, 1973-89; surg. editor: Resident and Staff Physician, 1979-91; contbr. articles to profl. jours., chpts. to books. Trustee Western Md. Coll., 1971— , Med. Research Found. Ga., 1973-91; bd. dirs. Nicholas J. Pisican Found., 1993—. Served to col. U.S. Army, 1943-46, 54-56. Recipient Man of Yr. award U. Md., 1970, 72, Golden Apple teaching award U. Md., 1968, 72, Disting. Faculty award Med. Coll. Ga., 1979, Gold Medal Alumni award U. Md., 1989, Disting. Svc. award (medal) Southeastern Surg. Congress, 1990. Fellow A.C.S. (gov.); mem. Am. Surg. Assn., Soc. Univ. Surgeons, So. Surg. Assn., Soc. Internationale de Chirurgie, Am. Assn. Surgery of Trauma, Southeastern Surg. Congress, Soc. Surgery of Alimentary Tract, AMA, Soc. Consultants to Armed Forces, Med. Assn. Ga. (editorial bd. 1987-92), Am. Bd. Family Practice (bd. dirs. 1987-92), 29th Div. Assn., Alpha Omega Alpha (Tchg. award 2001). Episcopalian. Home: One 7th St Unit 1502 Augusta GA 30901-1343 Office: Dept Surgery Med Coll Ga Augusta GA 30912

MANSBRIDGE, JANE JEBB, political scientist, educator; b. N.Y.C., Nov. 19, 1939; d. Ronald and Georgia St. Claire (Mullen) M.; m. Christopher Jencks; 1 child, Nathaniel Mansbridge Jencks. BA, Wellesley Coll., 1961; MA, Harvard U., 1966, PhD, 1971. Asst. prof. polit. sci. U. Chgo., 1973-80; assoc. prof. Northwestern U., Evanston, Ill., 1980-86, prof. polit. sci., 1986-91, Jane W. Long prof. arts and scis., 1991-96; prof. J.F. Kennedy Sch. Govt. Harvard U., 1996-98, Adams prof. polit. leadership and democratic values, 1998—. Author: Beyond Adversary Democracy, 1980, Why We Lost the ERA, 1986; editor: Beyond Self-Interest, 1990; editor: (with Susan M. Okin) Feminism 2 vols., 1994; editor: (with Aidon Morris) Oppositional Consciousness, 2001; mem. editorial bd. Signs, Jour. Polit. Philosophy. Russell Sage Found. scholar , 1991-92; fellow Inst. for Advanced Study, 1985-86, Rockefeller Humanities, 1982-83, NSF, 1971-72, Ctr. Advanced Study in the Behavioral Scis., 1997-98, 2001-02. Mem. Am. Acad. Arts and Scis., Am. Polit. Sci. Assn. (v.p. 1992-93, program chair 1990, exec. com. 1987-89, coun. 1987-89, pres. Women's Caucus 1996), Soc. Advancement of Socio-Econs. (pres. 1992-93), Internat. Polit. Psychology Assn. (governing coun. 1993-94). Office: JF Kennedy Sch Govt 79 JFK St Cambridge MA 02138-5801

MANSELL, DARREL LEE, JR. English educator; b. Canton, Ohio, Apr. 9, 1934; s. Darrel Lee and Virginia (Shepherd) M.; m. Elizabeth Meihack, Jan. 1957 (div. July 1970); 1 child, Benjamin Lloyd; m. Adriana Saviane, July 16, 1983. BA, Oberlin Coll., 1956; student, Oxford U., 1961-62; PhD, Yale U., 1963; MA (hon.), Dartmouth Coll., 1975. Instr. Dartmouth Coll., Hanover, N.H., 1962-64, asst. prof., 1964-68, assoc. prof., 1968-74, prof., 1974-99, prof. emeritus, 1999—. Author: The Novels of Jane Austen, 1973; contbr. articles to scholarly jours. Mem. Victorian Lit. Assn., Internat. Assn. for Phenomenology and Lit., Soc. for Literature and Sci., Jane Austen Soc. N.Am. (founding patron), Phi Beta Kappa. Home: 2 Dana Rd Hanover NH 03755-2227 Office: Dartmouth Coll Dept English Hanover NH 03755 E-mail: darrel.mansell@dartmouth.edu.

MANSELL, JOYCE MARILYN, special education educator; b. Minot, N.D., Dec. 17, 1934; d. Einar Axel and Gladys Ellen (Wall) Alm; m. Dudley J. Mansell, Oct. 31, 1954; children: Michael, Debra Mansell Richards. BS, U. Houston, 1968; MEd, Sam Houston State U., 1980. Cert. provisional elem. tchr. 1-8, provisional mentally retarded tchr., provisional lang. and/or learning disabilities tchr., profl. elem. tchr. gen. 1-8, profl. reading specialist. From 1st grade tchr. to 3rd grade tchr. Johnson Elem. Sch., 1968-77; spl. edn. tchr. mentally retarded/learning disabled Meml. Parkway Jr. H.S., 1982-86, Waller Mid. Sch., 1986-90; spl. edn. tchr. mentally retarded Royal Mid. Sch., Tex., 1990-95, Royal H.S., 1995-96; ret., 1996. Tchr. Am. sign lang. for retarded students in pub. schs. Active Holy Three and One Luth. Ch. of Deaf. Lutheran. Avocations: reading, fishing, grandchildren and family, signing choir, watercolor painting. Home: 2155 Paso Rello Dr Houston TX 77077-5622

MANSELL, L. ALMA, state legislator; b. Midvale, Utah, Jan. 23, 1944; m. Margurite Mansell. Student, U. Utah. Lic. real estate broker. Real estate broker; mem. Utah Senate, Dist. 10, Salt Lake City, 1994—; asst. majority whip Utah Senate, 1999—2000; mem. legis. mgmt. com., state and local affairs com.; co-chair econ. devel. and human resources appropriations. Mem. Salt Lake Bd. Realtors (pres. 1983, Realtor of Yr. 1986), Utah Assn. Realtors (pres. 1990, Realtor of Yr. 1988, Pres.'s award 1992), Nat. Assn. Realtors (v.p. 1992), Sandy Rotary Club (past pres.). Republican. Office: 6995 Union Park Ctr Ste 100 Midvale UT 84047-4135*

MANSEN, STEVEN ROBERT, manufacturing company executive; b. Chgo., Nov. 26, 1955; s. Robert Lee and Dorothy Nora (Nichols) M.; m. Leesa mansen, May 7, 1988; children: Ambur, Christopher. B in Indsl. Adminstrn., Gen. Motors Inst., 1978. Data processing sys. analyst in traffic Gen. Motors Corp., Oklahoma City, 1979-81, premium freight sys. coord., rate analyst in traffic, 1981-83; sr. mfg. sys. analyst Tech. Oil Tool Co. divsn. Baker Internat., Norman, Okla., 1983-86; v.p. mgmt. infosys. W. Pat Crow Forgings, Inc., 1986-88; material mgr. Aerospace Techs. Inc. divsn. Alco Standard Group, Ft. Worth, 1988-89; mgr. infosys. Wynn-Kiki divsn. Diesel-Kiki (now Zexel Tex., Inc. divsn. Zexel Corp.), Grand Prairie, 1989-98; MIS/material mgr. Spray Booth Sys., Inc., Ft. Worth, 1999—. Ind. systems implementation cons., 1998. Pres. Emerald Park Neighborhood Assn., 1997—, treas. 2000. Mem. S.W. States ASK Users Group (v.p. 1984-86, pres. 1986, Hewlett Packard liaison 1992), Camus. Home: 2214 Diamond Point Dr Arlington TX 76017-4517 Office: Spray Booth Sys Inc 4720 Esco Dr Fort Worth TX 76140-2208

MANSFIELD, CARL MAJOR, radiation oncology educator; b. Phila., Dec. 24, 1928; m. Sarah Lynn Flower; children: Joel, Kara. AB in Chemistry, Lincoln U., 1951; postgrad., Temple U., 1952; MD, Howard U., 1956; ScD (hon.), Lincoln U., 1991. Diplomate Am. Bd. Radiology, Am. Bd. Nuclear Medicine. Rotating intern Episcopal Hosp., Phila., 1956-57, resident in radiology, 1957-58, 60, 61-62; resident in radiation therapy and nuclear medicine Thomas Jefferson Med. Coll. Hosp., 1960-61, NIH fellow in radiation therapy and nuclear medicine, 1962-63, instr. radiology, chief div. nuclear medicine, 1964-65, Chernicoff fellow in pediatric radiation therapy, 1964-66, assoc. in radiology, chief div. nuclear medicine, 1966-67, asst. prof. radiology, chief div. nuclear medicine, 1967-69, assoc. prof. dept. radiation therapy and nuclear medicine, chief sect. of ultrasound, 1970-74, prof., chief div. nuclear medicine and sect. of ultrasound, 1974-76, prof., chmn. dept. radiation therapy and nuclear medicine, 1983-95; assoc. dir. divsn. cancer treatment Nat. Cancer Inst. NIH, Bethesda, Md., 1995-97; prof., chmn. dept. radiation oncology U. Md., Balt., 1997—. NIH postdoctoral fellow in radiation therapy Middlesex Hosp. and Med. Sch., London, 1963-64; lectr. in radiology U. Pa. Sch. Medicine, Phila., 1967-73; vis. prof. radiation therapy and nuclear medicine Hahnemann Med. Coll. Hosp., 1971; sabbatical leave Myerestein Inst. Radiotherapy, Middlesex Hosp. and Med. Sch., London, 1972-73; mem. grad. faculty in radiation biophysics U. Kans. Med. Ctr., Kansas City, 1977-83, prof. , chmn. dept. radiation therapy, 1976-83; chmn. dept. radiation therapy Menorah Med. Ctr., Kansas City, Mo., 1977-83. Author 2 books, also author or co-author over 129 articles in med. jours. Served with USAF, 1958-60. Fellow Am. Coll. Radiology, Coll. Physicians of Phila., Am. Coll. Nuclear Medicine; mem. AMA, Am. Coll. Radiology, Am. Cancer Soc. (dir.-at-large, nat. bd. dirs. 1981-85, med. and sci. com. 1981-88, profl. edn. com. 1981-88, pres. Phila. divsn. 1989), Am. Radium Soc. (pres. 1988), Radiation Rsch. Program Nat. Cancer Inst. (dir.), Sigma Xi. Office: U Md Med Sys 22 S Greene St Baltimore MD 21201-1544 E-mail: cmansfiel@QIS.net.

MANSFIELD, CHRISTOPHER CHARLES, insurance company legal executive; b. 1950; married. BA, Boston Coll., 1972, JD, 1975. With Liberty Mut. Ins. Co., Boston, 1975—, v.p., 1983, sr. v.p., gen. counsel, 1983—; underwriter Liberty Lloyds of Tex. Ins. Co., 1984-94; v.p., dir. Liberty Ins. Corp., 1985—; v.p. Liberty Mut. Fire Ins. Co., 1985—; v.p., gen. counsel LEXCO Ltd., 1986—; sr. v.p., gen. counsel Liberty Mut. Capital Corp., 1986—. Bd. dirs. Liberty Mut. Ins. Co., Liberty Fin. Cos., Liberty Mut. Bermuda, Liberty Internat., Employers Ins. Wausau, Golden Eagle Ins. Corp., Wausau Gen. Ins. Co., Pine Street Inn; bd. overseers Rand Inst. Civil Justice, 2002--. Office: Liberty Mut Ins Co PO Box 140 175 Berkeley St Boston MA 02117-5066

MANSFIELD, DIANNE LYNN, minister; b. Kokomo, Ind., July 31, 1945; d. George Armour and Ardys Jane (Tinkler) Duncan; m. Jarold Birson Mansfield, Apr. 20, 1968; children: Gregory Birson, Kristine Lynn, Kimberly Jane. BS in Elem. Edn., Ind. State U., 1967, MS in Elem. Edn., 1969; MA in Christian Edn., Christian Theol. Sem., 1990, MDiv, 1993. Interim min. 1st Christian Ch., Casey, Ill., 1990-91; min. edn. Ctrl. Christian Ch., Terre Haute, Ind., 1993-97, interim min., 1996-97, Hillsboro (Ind.) Christian Ch., 1997-98; edn. min. First Christian, Greencastle, Ind., 1998—. Mem. NAACP, Terre Haute, 1997; participant Stand By Me Ministry, Terre Haute, 1994—. Mem. Religious Edn. Assn., Assn. Christian Ch. Educators. Democrat. Avocations: gardening, cross-stitch. Home: 6010 E Devonald Ave Terre Haute IN 47805-9607 E-mail: revmansfield@aol.com.

MANSFIELD, DONALD H. biologist, educator; b. Salem, Oreg., Oct. 30, 1951; s. Oliver T. and Helen R. Mansfield; children: Ethan, Anna. BA, Colo. Coll., Colorado Springs, 1973; MS, U. B.C., Vancouver, 1977; DA, Idaho State U., 1979. Postdoctoral plant physiologist U. Calif., Davis, 1979-81; asst. prof. biology Colo. Coll., Colorado Springs, 1981-84; assoc. prof. biology and environ. studies Rollins Coll., Winter Park, Fla., 1984-89; prof. biology Albertson Coll. of Idaho, Caldwell, 1989—. Author: Flora of Steens Mountain, 2000. Mem. Idaho Acad. Sci. (pres. 2000-2001). Democrat. Christian Ch. Avocations: mountaineering, ice hockey, travel. Office: Albertson Coll of Idaho 2112 Cleveland Blvd Caldwell ID 83605 E-mail: dmansfield@albertson.edu.

MANSFIELD, EDWARD PATRICK, JR. advertising executive; b. Warren, Pa., Oct. 29, 1947; s. Edward Patrick and Frieda (Dahler) M.; m. Norma L. Johnson, Apr. 17, 1971. AS in Acctg., Jamestown Bus. Coll., 1967; BS in Mktg. Advt., Myers U., 1970. Promotion mgr., ad dir. The News-Herald, Lake County, Ohio, 1973-77; dir. advt. The Eagle, Butler, Pa., 1977-78; dir. mktg. Baltimore Mag., 1978-79; dir. advt. The Washingtonian, Washington, 1979—. Founder, chmn. Warm-A-Heart Fund, 1988—; bd. dirs. Columbia Lighthouse for the Blind, 1988—, chmn., 1988-93; bd. dirs. The Lighthouse; mem. adv. bd. Ann Arundel County Mental Health. Avocations: amateur radio operator gen. class, sailing. Home: 347 Cottswold Pl Riva MD 21140-1528 Office: Washingtonian Mag 1828 L St NW Ste 200 Washington DC 20036-5169 Business E-Mail: emansfield@washingtonian.com.

MANSFIELD, GORDON H. federal agency administrator; Degree, Villanova U.; law degree, U. Miami. Commd. U.S. Army, 1964, co. comdr. 101st Airborne Divsn. Vietnam; lawyer Ocala, Fla.; various positions including assoc. exec. dir. govt. rels. Paralyzed Vets. Am., 1981—89, exec. dir., 1993—2001; asst. sec. fair housing and equal opportunity Dept. Housing and Urban Devel., 1989—93; asst. sec. congl. and legis. affiars Dept. Vets. Affairs, Washington, 2001—. Decorated Bronze Star, Purple Heart (2), Combat Infantryman's badge, Presdl. Unit Citation. Office: US Dept Vets Affairs Congl and Legis Affairs 810 Vermont Ave Washington DC 20420*

MANSFIELD, JAMES NORMAN, III, lawyer; b. Chattanooga, Feb. 15, 1951; s. James Norman and Doris June (Hilliard) M.; m. Terry Ann Thomas, Dec. 28, 1975; children: Seth Thomas, James Norman, Scott Michael. BA, U. Tenn., Chattanooga, 1973; MA, La. State U., 1976, JD, 1979. Bar: La. 1979, U.S. Dist. Ct. (we. dist.), La. 1979. Shareholder Liskow and Lewis, Lafayette and New Orleans, La., 1979—. Pres. Raven Soc., Chattanooga, 1973; mem. sch. bd. St. Thomas More H.S. Mem. ABA, La. Bar Assn., La. Min. Law Inst. (adv. coun. mem.), Am. Assn. Profl. Landmen, Lafayette Assn. Petroleum Landmen, Order of Coif. Roman Catholic. Avocations: photography, jogging, fishing. Home: 103 Asbury Cir Lafayette LA 70503-3632 Office: Liskow & Lewis PO Box 52008 Lafayette LA 70505-2008

MANSFIELD, JERRY WAYNE, librarian; b. Garrett, Ind., Jan. 26, 1952; s. William Wayne Mansfield and Beverley June Ridgway; m. Melberne Anne Crellin, June 2, 1984; 1 child, Melberne Elizabeth. BA, Hanover (Ind.) Coll., 1974; MS in Libr. Sci., U. Ky., 1975. Reference libr. Ga. State U., Atlanta, 1975-78; asst. engring. libr., asst. prof. Purdue U., West Lafayette, Ind., 1978-83; dir. med. librs. King Faisal Specialist Hosp. and Rsch. Ctr., Riyadh, Saudi Arabia, 1983-87; chief advisor for libr. affairs Nat. Ctr. for Financial and Econ. Info., Saudi Arabia, 1987-90; head pub. svcs. U.S. Postal Svc. Corp. Libr., Washington, 1990-2000; mgr. Info. Resource Ctrs., Congrl. Rsch. Svc., 2000—. Author: The Nuclear Power Debate: A Guide to the Literature, 1984; contbr. articles to profl. jours. Pres. Friends of the Bowie (Md.) Libr., 1994, 96, 98. Recipient Excellence in Librarianship award Ga. State U. Found., 1977. Mem. Spl. Librs. Assn., Am. Libr. Assn. (life, D.C. chpt.), Internat. Fedn. Libr. Assns. Avocations: travel, gardening, miniature books, volunteerism. Office: Congrl Rsch Svc/Libr Congress 101 Independence Ave SE Rm 324 Washington DC 20540-0002

MANSFIELD, KAREN LEE, lawyer; b. Chgo., Mar. 17, 1942; d. Ralph and Hilda (Blum) Mansfield; children: Nicole Rafaela, Lori Michele. BA in Polit. Sci., Roosevelt U., 1963; JD, DePaul U., 1971; student U. Chgo., 1959-60. Bar: Ill. 1972, U.S. Dist. Ct. (no. dist.) Ill. 1972. Legis. intern Ill. State Senate, Springfield, 1966-67; tchr. Chgo. Pub. Schs., 1967-70; atty. CNA Ins., Chgo., 1971-73; law clk. Ill. Apellate Ct., Chgo., 1973-75; sr. trial atty. U.S. Dept. Labor, Chgo., 1975—, mentor Adopt-a-Sch. Program, 1992-95. Contbr. articles to profl. jours. Vol. Big Sister, 1975-81; bd. dirs. Altgeld Nursery Sch., 1963-66, Ill. div. UN Assn., 1966-72, Hull House Jane Addams Ctr., 1977-82, Broadway Children's Ctr., 1986-90, Acorn Family Entertainment, 1993-95; mem. Oak Park Farmers' Market Commn., 1996—; rsch. asst. Citizens for Gov. Otto Kerner, Chgo., 1964; com. mem. Ill. Commn. on Status of Women, Chgo., 1964-70; del. Nat. Conf. on Status of Women, 1968; candidate for del. Ill. Constl. Conv., 1969. Mem. Chgo. Council Lawyers, Women's Bar Assn. Ill., Lawyer Pilots Bar Assn., Fed. Bar Assn. Unitarian. Clubs: Friends of Gamelan (performer), 99's Internat. Orgn. Women Pilots (legis. chmn. Chgo. area chpt. 1983-86, legis. chmn. North Cen. sect. 1986-88, legis. award 1983, 85). Home: 204 S Taylor Ave Oak Park IL 60302-3307 Office: US Dept Labor Office Solicitor 230 S Dearborn St Fl 8 Chicago IL 60604-1505

MANSFIELD, NORMAN CONNIE, bookkeeper; b. Rayle, Ga., Apr. 27, 1916; s. Boykin Carswell and Cleo (Norman) M.; m. Ila Ruth Poss, Jan. 3, 1943; children: Jonathan Norman, Jerry Carswell. Cert., U. Ga. Notary Pub., Ga. Mgr. Railway Express Agy., Washington, 1943-78; semi-retired bookkeeper Russell Transfer Co. Inc., 1979—. Mgr. Rwy. Express. Exec. bd. mem. Ga. Carolina Coun.; deacon First Baptist Ch., Washington; cubscout master, Washington, Ga., 1962. With USNG. Recipient Baseball and Little League award Coca Cola Co., Washington, Ga., 1951, 68, Woodmen of World award Life Ins. Soc., Augusta, Ga., 1978; named Boy Scout of Yr., Ga. Carolina Coun., Thomson, 1956. Mem. Masons (Shriner, worship master 1984), Order of Eastern Star (worthy patron), Woodman of the World (pres.), Lions (pres.), Washington (Ga.) Country Club, Ida Cason Callaway Found., Ga. Sheriffs Assn. Home: 209 Hudson Dr Washington GA 30673-1527 Office: The News-Reporter 116 W Robert Toombs Ave Washington GA 30673-1664

MANSFIELD, ROGER LEO, astronomy and space publisher; b. Boston, Feb. 18, 1944; s. Roy D. Sr. and Nellie E. Mansfield; m. Alice Lee Waring, Nov. 1, 1969 div. Mar. 1983); 1 child, Jason Benjamin; m. Karen June Sprout, June 27, 1987. BS in Chemistry with high honors., U. Cin., 1965; MA in Math., U. Nebr., 1972. Chemist Lockheed Missiles & Space Co., Palo Alto, Calif., 1967; orbital analyst USAF, Offutt AFB, Nebr., 1967-73; instr. Dept. of Math. USAF Acad., Colorado Springs, Colo., 1973-74; aerospace engr. Philco-Ford Corp., Palo Alto, 1974-75, Data Dynamics Inc., Mountain View, Calif., 1975-76, Ford Aerospace & Communications Corp., Colorado Springs, 1976-90; prin. engr. Loral Aerospace Corp., 1990-95; owner Astron. Data Svc., 1976—; asst. prof. adjoint U. Colo., Colorado Springs, 1996—99. Pub. Skywatcher's Almanac, Local Planet Visibility Report, Photographer's Almanac, Comparative Ephemeris, Space Birds, WeatherBirds Utilities, Skywatcher; contbr. articles to profl. jours. Mem. Am. Astron. Soc., Math. Assn. Am., Internat. Planetarium Soc., Rocky Mountain Planetarium Assn., Phi Beta Kappa, Phi Eta Sigma. Avocations: satellite tracking and orbital mechanics. Home and Office: 3922 Leisure Ln Colorado Springs CO 80917-3502

MANSI, JOSEPH ANNEILLO, public relations company executive; b. Oct. 8, 1935; s. Joseph C. and Vinnie (Chirico) M.; m. Mary P. Fusco, Aug. 1, 1959; children: Karen M. D'Attore, Jeanine V. Dimenna. BS, NYU, 1957. Newsman Internat. News Service, UPI, 1953-58; mem. pub. relations staff Lawrence Orgn., N.Y.C., 1960-63; acct. supr. Philip Lesly Co., 1963-67; dir. corp. communications Ward Foods, Inc., 1967-72; dir. pub. relations Metromedia Inc., 1973-75; pres. Corp. Relations Network, Inc., 1975-80; mng. ptnr. KCSA Pub. Rels. Worldwide, 1980—. Served with AUS, 1958-60. Mem. Pub. Rels. Soc. Am. (accredited). Home: 10 Beatrice Ln Glen Cove NY 11542-1202 Office: KCSA Pub Rels Worldwide 800 2nd Ave New York NY 10017-4709 E-mail: jmansi@kcsa.com.

MANSKE, CONNIE LYNN, physician; b. Mpls., Nov. 3, 1951; m. J. Bruce Redmon; children: Katie, Kevin, Joe. AB Biology, Brown U., 1973; MA Learning Disabilities, Northwestern U., 1975; MD, U. Conn., Hartford, 1979. Diplomate Am. Bd. Internal Medicine, Am. Bd. Nephrology. Nephrology fellow Vanderbilt U., Nashville, 1983-85, chief resident in medicine, 1982-83, instr. medicine, 1985-86; assoc. prof. medicine U. Minn., 1986—. Ad hoc adv. panel mem. renal rsch., NIH, 1997; task force on vascular disease in end stage Renal Disease Nat. Kidney Found., 1997-98. Contbr. articles to profl. jours. Named among Best Doctors in America Ctrl. Region, 1996-97, National, 1999-2000, 2001-02. Mem. Am. Soc. Nephrology, Internat. Soc. Nephrology, Am. Heart Assn., Am. Soc. Transplantation, Nat. Kidney Found. Office: U Minn Sch of Medicine Box 736 516 Delaware St SE Minneapolis MN 55455-0356 E-mail: mansk002@tc.umn.edu.

MANSKE, LYNN DARLENE, surgical nurse; b. Milw., Feb. 10, 1955; d. Warren Clayton and Lois Joan (England) M. BSN, No. Mich. U., 1978. RN, Wis. Staff nurse St. Vincent Hosp., Green Bay, Wis., 1988, team leader plastic, maxillofacial and podiatry, 1991—2002, resource RN plastics and maxillofacial/dental, 2002—. Mem. Assn. Operating Room Nurses (cert.). Home: 2516 Finger Rd Green Bay WI 54302-4864

MANSKI, CHARLES FREDERICK, economist, educator; b. Boston, Nov. 27, 1948; s. Samuil and Estelle Jean (Zonn) M.; m. Catherine Fowler Moss, Feb. 20, 1972; children: Benjamin Robert, Rebecca. BS in Econs., MIT, 1970, PhD, 1973. Asst. prof. econs. Carnegie-Mellon U., Pitts., 1973-77, assoc. prof., 1977-80, Hebrew U. of Jerusalem, Israel, 1979-83; prof. econs. U. Wis., Madison, 1983-98, Wolfowitz prof., 1989, Hilldale prof., 1993; bd. trustees prof. Northwestern U., Evanston, Ill., 1997—. Dir. Inst. for Rsch. on Poverty, Madison, 1988-91. Author: Analog Estimation Methods in Econometrics, 1988, Identification Problems in the Social Sciences, 1995; co-author: College Choice in America, 1983; co-editor: Structural Analysis of Discrete Data, 1981, Econometric Soc. Monograph Series, 1983-88, Evaluating Welfare and Training Programs, 1992; editor Jour. Human Resources, 1991-94; assoc. editor Jour. Econ. Perspectives, 1986-89, Econometrica, 1980-88, Jour. Am. Statis. Assn., 1983-85, Transp. Sci., 1978-84; contbr. articles to profl. jours. Mem. adv. panel HHS, 1990-94, NSF, 1985-87, 1999-2000; mem. com. NAS, 1984-87, 91, 92—. Grantee NSF, 1984, 86, 88, 93, 97, 2000, NIH, 1989, HHS, 1989. Fellow AAAS, Econometric Soc., Am. Acad. Arts and Scis.; mem. Am. Econ. Assn., Am. Statis. Assn., Inst. Math. Stats. Office: 2003 Sheridan Rd Evanston IL 60208-0826 E-mail: cfmanski@northwestern.edu.

MANSKI, WLADYSLAW JULIAN, microbiology educator, medical scientist; b. Lwow, Poland, May 15, 1915; came to U.S., 1958, naturalized, 1964; s. Julian and Helena (Lewicka) M.; m. Anna Z. Artymowicz, June 20, 1941; children: Chris, Louis. M.Phil., U. Warsaw, Poland, 1939, D.Sc., 1951. Instr. U. Warsaw, 1936-39; rsch. asst. Inst. Lwow, 1940-41, Inst. Lwow (Inst. Agr.), Pulawy, Poland, 1942-44; instr. U. Lublin, Poland, 1944-45; instr. dept. microbiology Med. Sch., Wroclaw, Poland, 1945-49; Rockefeller fellow Columbia U., N.Y.C., 1949-50; head immunochemistry lab. Inst. Immunology and Exptl. Therapy, Polish Acad. Sci., Wroclaw, 1951-55, head Macromolecular Biochemistry Lab. Warsaw, 1955-57; head dept. virology Biochemistry Lab., State Inst. Hygiene, 1955-57; research worker Coll. Physicians and Surgeons, Columbia U., 1958-62, rsch. assoc., 1962-64, asst. prof., 1964-67, assoc. prof. microbiology, 1967-74, prof. microbiology, 1974-85, prof. emeritus, 1986; dir. rsch. Harkness Eye Inst., Columbia U., N.Y.C., 1985-90. Contbr. articles to profl. jours. NIH grantee, 1960-86. Mem. AAAS, Am. Assn. Immunologists, AAUP, Research in Vision and Ophthalmology Assn., Am. Chem. Soc., Brit. Biochemical Soc., N.Y. Acad. Scis., Soc. Exptl. Biology and Medicine, Soc. Study of Evolution, Internat. Soc. Eye Research, Harvey Soc., Transplantation Soc. Home: 10 Downing St New York NY 10014-4734 E-mail: wm6@columbia.edu.

MANSMANN, PARIS TAYLOR, medical educator; b. Pitts., Feb. 19, 1957; s. Herbert Charles Jr. and Margaret Marshal (Miller) M.; m. Leslie Ann Windstein, July 8, 1978; children: Erin Hart, Paris Corey, Maureen Ellyse. Student, Lafayette Coll., 1975-76; BS in Math., St. Joseph's U., Phila., 1980; MD, Jefferson Med. Coll., 1984. Diplomate Am. Bd. Medicine, Am. Bd. Internal Medicine, Am. Bd. Pediatrics, Am. Bd. Allergy and Immunology. Resident in medicine, pediatrics Geisinger Med. Ctr., Danville, Pa., 1984-88, chief resident, 1987-88; fellow in allergy, immunology Duke U. Med. Ctr., Durham, N.C., 1988-90; asst. prof. medicine and pediat. W.Va. U., Morgantown, 1990-93, asst. prof. medicine, 1990-95, assoc. prof. medicine, 1995-2000. Program coord. medicine, pediat., W.Va. U., Morgantown, 1990-93. Author: (with others) Current Pediatric Therapy, 1994; contbr. articles to profl. jours. Recipient Outstanding Commitment award Vis. Clinicians, 1990. Fellow Am. Acad. Pediatrics, Am. Coll. Allergy and Immunology, ACP, Am. Acad. Allergy and Immunology, European Acad. Allergy and Clin. Immunology, W.Va. Allergy Soc. (pres. 1992—). Republican. Roman Catholic. Avocations: fishing, farming, cross country skiing, soccer. Office: Shearwater Allergy Sch Medicine PO Box 1298 Yarmouth ME 04096 E-mail: pmansba@aol.com.

MANSO, LEIRA A. Latin American literature educator, poet; BA cum laude, U. Puerto Rico, 1986; MA, NYU, 1989; PhD in Comparative Lit., SUNY, Binghamton, 1996. Asst. prof. Hartwick Coll., Oneonta, N.Y., 1999-2000, Broome C.C., Binghamton, 2000—. E-mail: manso_l@sunybroome.edu.

MANSON, ANNE, music director; Grad., Harvard U.; postgrad., King's Coll., London, Royal Coll. Music, Royal Northern Coll. Music; studied with Norman Del Mar, James Lockhart. Music dir. Kansas City (Mo.) Symphony, 1998—. Condr. Mecklenburgh Opera, 1991, Endymion Ensemble, 1992-93, London Mozart Players, 1993-94, BBC Scottish Symphony and Iceland Symphony Orch., 1994-95, Northern Sinfonia, Resedentie Orch. in The Hague, Ensemble Inter Contemporain, Paris, 1996-97, Bournemouth Symphony Orch., Royal Scottish Nat. Orch., 1997-98. Dir. operas The Emperor of Atlantis, Die Weisse Rose, Manekiny, Hansel and Gretel, Marriage of Figaro, Cosi fan Tutte, The Magic Flute, Il Combattimento, Echoes, Royal Opera House, Don Pasquale, Don Giovanni, English Touring Opera, House of the Dead, Salzburg Festival, Lohengrin, Blood Wedding, 1992-93, Petrified, The Place Theatre, London, 1992, Brundibar, Queen Elizabeth Hall, London, 1993, Craig's Progress, 1994, Boris Godunov, Vienna State Opera, 1994, Vanessa, 1994-95, Rise and Fall of the City of Mahagonny, Netherlands Touring Opera, 1996, Dangerous Liaisons, Washington Opera, 1997, Voices, Berlin Biennale, 1997-98. Marshall scholar Royal Coll. Music; Conducting fellow Royal Northern Coll. Music. Office: Kansas City Symphony 1020 Central St Ste 300 Kansas City MO 64105-1663*

MANSON, DAVID JOSEPH, producer, director; b. N.Y.C., Jan. 6, 1952; s. Eddy Lawrence and Margery May (Abramson) M.; m. Arla Mae Nudelman, Apr. 4, 1982; 1 stepchild, Elena Jo Sorkin. BA magna cum laude, U. Calif., Irvine, 1974. Dir. devel. Stonehenge Prodns., Los Angeles, 1975-76, v.p. creative affairs, 1977-80; pres. Sarabande Prodns., 1980—. Producer: Sessions, 1983, (feature films) Bring on the Night, 1985 (Grammy award 1986), Birdy, 1985 (Cannes Spl. Jury prize 1985), Eye on the Sparrow, 1987 (Christopher award 1988), Cemetery Club, 1993, Mad Love, 1995, others, (TV films) Nightjohn, 1996 (Nat. Soc. Film Critics Special Citation), Baby, 2000 (Writers Guild award nomination, Christopher award), Rising Son, 1990, The Wedding Dress, 2001, others, (TV miniseries) A Rumor of War, 1980 (Writers Guild award 1980); dir., exec. producer TV series Those Secrets; co-creator, exec. producer; Against the Law, 1990, Nothing Sacred (Peabody WGA Humanitas award 1998).

MANSON, GARY LYLE, lawyer; b. Reno, Dec. 28, 1951; s. Gerald Lee and Betty Helen (Ferrari) M.; m. Carla Lynette Coleman, Mar. 23, 1985; children: Morgan Leigh, Coleman Jordan. BA magna cum laude, U. Nev., 1974; JD, U. San Francisco, 1977. Bar: Nev. 1977. Law clk. to Hon. William N. Forman Washoe County Dist. Ct. 2nd Judicial Dist., Reno, 1977-78; assoc. Bissett & Logar, 1978-83; assoc., ptnr. Law Offices of Ronald J. Logar, 1983-92; pvt. practice Law Offices of Gary L. Manson, 1992—. Lectr. Bar Review, Reno, 1986-91; lectr. in field. Contbr. articles to profl. jours. Coach Pop Warner Football, Reno; legis. intern State Senator Thomas "Spike" Wilson, 1973; pro tem judge Reno Mcpl. Ct., 1988—. Mem. Washoe County Bar Assn., Nev. State Bar Assn. (family law section 1985—), ABA, Phi Kappa Phi, Phi Alpha Theta, Sigma Nu, Blue Key Svc. Club, Phi Delta Phi. Republican. Avocation: sports. Home: 3075 W Plumb Ln Reno NV 89509-3032 Office: 575 Forest St Ste 205 Reno NV 89509-1689 E-mail: gmanson@yellowsub.net.

MANSON, HAROLD CRAIG, federal agency administrator; b. Mo. Grad., USAF ACad.; JD, U. of the Pacific. Asst. sec. Fish, Wildlife and Parks U.S. Dept. Interior, Washington, 2002—. Faculty McGeorge Sch. Law, 1992—. With USAF, with Air Nat. Guard. Office: US Dept Interior Fish Wildlife and Parks 1849 C St NW Washington DC 20240*

MANSON, JOANN ELISABETH, endocrinologist; b. Cleve., Apr. 14, 1953; d. S. Stanford and Therese (Palay) M.; m. Christopher N. Ames, June 12, 1979; children: Jennifer, Jeffrey. AB magna cum laude, Harvard U., 1975; MD, Case Western Res. U., 1979; MPH, Harvard Sch. Pub. Health, 1984, DPH, 1987. Bd. cert. internal medicine; bd. cert. in subspecialty of endocrinology and metabolism. Intern and resident internal medicine NEDH, Harvard Med. Sch., Boston, 1979-82; fellowship in endocrinology U. Hosp. Boston, 1982-84; rsch fellow in medicine Brigham and Women's Hosp., Boston, 1984-87, Andrew W. Mellon Found. fellow, 1987-89; dir. endocrinology, co-dir. women's health Brigham and Women's Hosp., Divsn. Preventive Medicine, 1993—; chief Divsn. Preventive Medicine Brigham and Women's Hosp., 1999—; staff physician, consulting endocrinologist Harvard Vanguard Med. Assocs., Peabody, 1986—; prof. medicine Harvard Med. Sch., Boston, 1999—. Mem. editl. bd. Am. Jour. Preventive Medicine, 1992—, Jour. Women's Health, 1996—; author textbooks and monographs; contb. more than 400 articles to profl. jours. Vol. physician Lynn (Mass.) Shelter for the Homeless, 1989-93; med. adv. bd. Harvard Health Letter, Boston, 1992—, Greater Boston (Mass.) Diabetes Soc., 1993—, Harvard Women's Health Watch, Boston, 1993—; vol. Am. Heart Assn., 1992—. Named Hero in Women's Health, Am. Health for Women Mag., 1997, one of Top 10 Champions of Women's Health, Ladies Home Jour., 2000, one of Top Docs for Women. Boston mag., 2001; recipient Connors award for outstanding leadership in women's health, 1999—. Fellow ACP, ACE; mem. AMA, Am. Med. Women's Assn., Am. Heart Assn., Women's Health Initiative (mem. steering com.), Alpha Omega Alpha. Avocations: playing with my children, reading, hiking, music, travel. Home: 14 Washington St Beverly MA 01915-5820 Office: Brigham and Women's Hosp 900 Commonwealth Ave E Fl 3 Boston MA 02215-1204 E-mail: jmanson@rics.bwh.harvard.edu.

MANSON, JOSEPH LLOYD, III, lawyer; b. Richmond, Va., May 5, 1949; s. Joseph Lloyd Jr. and Nan Smith (Copley) M.; m. Martha Forman Foltz, Sept. 8, 1973; children: Martha Stuart, Joseph Scott, Rachel Smith. BS, U. Va., 1970; JD, Emory U., 1974. Assoc. Verner, Liipfert, Bernhard & McPherson, Washington, 1974—80; ptnr. Verner, Liipfert, Bernhard, McPherson & Hand, 1981—, co-chmn. exec. com., 1998—2001; bd. dirs. Pres., CEO, bd. dirs. Barrow Grocery Co., DBM Group. Founder Alexandria Youth Sports Found., 1993; bd. govs. St. Stephens and St. Agnes Sch., Emory U. Law Sch. Coun., Mesa Air Group; vice chmn., bd. dirs., bt. trustees St. Stephens and St. Agnes Sch. 2d lt. U.S. Army, 1973. Mem. ABA (ry. and airline labor law com., co-chmn. mgmt. 1993-94), D.C. Bar Assn. Republican. Episcopalian. Avocations: music, tennis, theatre, movies. Office: Verner Liipfert Bernhard McPherson & Hand 901 15th St NW Ste 700 Washington DC 20005-2327

MANSON, KEITH ALAN MICHAEL, lawyer; b. Warwick, RI, Oct. 26, 1962; s. Ronald Frederick and Joan Patricia (Reardon) M.; m. Jennifer Annette Stearns; children: Kristin Elizabeth, Michelle Nicole. BA, R.I. Coll., 1985; cert. computer info. systems, Bryant Coll., 1988; cert. law, U. Notre Dame, London, 1990; JD, Thomas M. Cooley Law Sch., 1991. Bar: Ind. 1991, U.S. Dist. Ct. (no. dist.) Ind. 1991, U.S. Dist. Ct. (so. dist.) Ind. 1991, U.S. Dist. Ct. (so. dist.) Ga. 1992, U.S. Dist. Ct. Mil. Appeals 1991. Spl. asst. U.S. atty. U.S. Dist. Ct. Ga., Brunswick, 1992-93; pvt. practice Fernandina Beach, Fla., 1994—; atty., securities compliance divsn. Prudential Ins. Co., 1997-98; counsel Stonier Transportation Group, Jacksonville Beach, Fla., 1998—99; prof., law area chmn. U. Phoenix, Jacksonville, 1999—. Cons. The Law Store Ltd. Paralegal Svcs., Fernandina Beach., 1994—, Barnett Bank, Nations Bank, 1998. Contbr. articles to profl. jours. Dist. fin. and mem. chmn. North Fla. coun. Boy Scouts Am., , Jacksonville, 1993—; com. mem. sea scout ship 660 St. Peter's Ch., Fernandina Beach, 1994—96; chmn. Scouting for Food Drive, Nassau County, Fla., 1994—; teen ct. judge Duval County, 2001—. Lt. USN, 1985—86, lt. USN, 1990—96. Recipient Nassau Dist. award of merit Boy Scouts Am., 1999, God and Svc. award, 2000, Silver Beaver award, 2002; F.C. Tanner Trust, Fed. Products Inc. scholar, Providence, 1981-85, Esterline Corp. scholar, Providence, 1986. Mem.: ABA, Jacksonville Bar Assn. (professionalism com.), Judge Advocate Assn., Ind. Bar Assn., Rotary (project mgr. Webster-Dudley Mass. chpt. 1986—88), Am. Legion, Navy League U.S., Phi Alpha Delta. Avocations: gardening, rugby, sports history, military history, collecting historical items. Home and Office: 1908 Reatta Ln Fernandina Beach FL 32034-8937 E-mail: mansonjk@netscape.net.

MANSON, LEWIS AUMAN, energy research executive; b. Cleve., July 12, 1918; s. Lewis Frederick and Ina Josephine (Auman) M.; m. Alva Anne London, Sept. 3, 1960 (div. 1982); children: Anita, Howard; m. Shirley Anne Traeger, Jan. 27, 1982; children: Lewis, Jean, Phillip, Edward. Student, Gen. Motors Tech. U., 1943-44, Purdue U., 1942-43, Rice U., 1950-54. Cons. numerous oil, gas, and mining cos., 1951-57; cons. The Space Agy., Washington, 1958-59, Douglas Aircraft, El Segundo, Calif., 1964; dir. Copper Range Mines, Wyo., 1965; dir. explorations, cons. Nico Internat., S.A. de C.V., Mex., 1968-71; builder Spring, Tex., 1971-74; dir., conductor explorations Minerals of the Sun, S.A. de C.V., Honduras, 1975; dir. Asheville Petroleum Corp., Ill., 1976; conductor explorations Neozoic Minerals & Petroleum, Ltd., Colo., N.Mex., Tex., 1976-77; conductor explorations, dir. Primal Energy Rsch. Found., Houston, 1982—. Pres. Transzoic Orebody Locators, Ltd., Vancouver, B.C., Pleiades Petroleum Corp., Lexington, Tenn. and Houston; pres., dir. Neozoic Geophys. Survey, Ltd., 1999; lectr. grade schs., high schs., Kiwanis, and Rotary, 1962—. Author: The Primal Energy Transverter, 1966, Birth of the Moon, 1978, Origins of Solar Flares and Keys to Predicting Them, 1978, Automatic Recording of Deep Space (interplanetary) Gravity, 1978, Arriving Ionospheric High Energy (Solar Generated), 1978, Out of the Grey Mist, 1992, Life's Continuum, 1992, The Real Origin of Stellar Energy, 1993, The Great Mystery, 1994; patentee in field. Scoutmaster Boy Scouts Am., Houston, 1956-63; cubmaster Cub Scouts, Pasadena, Calif., 1962. With Ind. NG, 1942-43. Republican. Achievements include developed and placed in service new equipment, The Affinity System, that indicates petroleum or gas from the surface to any depth and defines if commercial quality. Avocations: mineral and fossil collecting, mountaineering, boating, archeology, metal and wood working. Office: Primal Energy Rsch Found 31 Rush Haven Dr The Woodlands TX 77381-3227

MANSOUR, GEORGE P. Spanish language and literature educator; b. Huntington, W.Va., Sept. 4, 1939; s. Elia and Marie (Yazbek) M.; m. Mary Ann Rogers, Dec. 27, 1961; children: Alicia, Philip. AB, Marshall U., 1961; MA, Mich. State U., 1963, PhD, 1965. Assoc. prof. Mich. State U., East Lansing, 1968-77, prof., 1977—, chmn. dept. Romance and Classical langs., 1982—. Cons. Mich. Dept. Edn., Lansing, 1984-85. Contbr. articles to profl. jours., including Hispania, Revista de estudias, hispanicos, also chpts. to books. Mem. Am. Assn. Tchrs. Spanish and Portuguese (v.p. 1969-71), Mich. Fgn. Lang. Assn. (pres. 1982-84). Democrat. Mem. Eastern Orthodox Ch. Avocations: Pysanky, golf. Home: 1303 Lucerne Dr Dewitt MI 48820-9528 Office: Mich State U Dept Romance & Classical Langs East Lansing MI 48824

MANSOUR, STEPHEN MALIK, software developer, mathematician; b. Washington, Oct. 3, 1952; s. Farris and Annie Laurie (Riley) M.; m. Heide Nanette Hartley, Apr. 14, 1984 (div. Jan. 1997); children: George, Lisa. BA in Math., U. Calif., Berkeley, 1981; MS in Statistics, Union Coll., 1992. Printer Tyler Bus. Svcs., Washington, 1971-72; yeoman 1st class USCG, San Francisco, 1972-80; programmer/statistician IBM Corp., East Fishkill, N.Y., 1982-94; computer programmer CheckFree Corp., Jersey City, 1994-96; cons. The Carlisle Group, Scranton, Pa., 1996—. Contbr. articles to profl. jour. Mem. Am. Contract Bridge League, Assn. Computing Machinery (APL 99 conf. chmn.), Soc. Preservation and Encouragement of Barbershop Quartet Singing in Am., Phi Beta Kappa. Republican. Avocations: barbershop quartet singing, bridge. E-mail: steve@carlislegroup.com.

MANSOUR, TAG ELDIN, pharmacologist, educator; b. Belkas, Egypt, Nov. 6, 1924; came to U.S., 1951, naturalized, 1956; s. Elsayed and Rokaya (Elzayat) M.; m. Joan Adela MacKinnon, Aug. 6, 1955; children— Suzanne, Jeanne, Dean. DVM, Cairo U., 1946; PhD, U. Birmingham, Eng., 1949, DSc, 1974. Lectr. U. Cairo, 1950-51; Fulbright instr. physiology Howard U., Washington, 1951-52; sr. instr. pharmacology Case Western Res. U., 1952-54; asst. prof., assoc. prof. pharmacology La. State U. Med. Sch., New Orleans, 1954-61; assoc. prof., prof. molecular pharmacology Stanford U. Sch. Medicine, 1961—, chmn. dept. pharmacology, 1977-91, Donald E. Baxter prof., 1977-98, prof. emeritus, 1999—. Cons. USPHS, WHO, Nat. Acad. Scis.; Mem. adv. bd. Med. Sch., Kuwait U.; Heath Clarke lectr. London Sch. Hygiene and Tropical Medicine, 1981 Contrbr. sci. articles to profl. jours. Commonwealth Fund fellow, 1965; Macy Found. scholar NIMR, London, 1982. Fellow AAAS; mem. Am. Soc. Pharmacology and Exptl. Therapeutics, Am. Soc. Biol. Chemists, Am. Heart Assn., Sierra Club, Stanford Faculty Club. Office: Stanford Sch Medicine Dept Molecular Pharm CCSR 269 Campus Dr Rm 3155 Stanford CA 94305-5174

MANSOURI, LOTFOLLAH (LOTFI MANSOURI), retired general director of opera company; b. Tehran, June 15, 1929; arrived in Can., 1976; s. Hassan and Mehri (Jalili) M.; m. Marjorie Anne Thompson, Sept. 18, 1954; 1 child, Shireen Melinda. AB, UCLA, 1953. Asst. prof. UCLA, 1957-60; resident stage dir. Zurich Opera, 1960-65; chief stage dir. Geneva Opera, 1965-75; gen. dir. Can. Opera Co., Toronto, Ont., 1976-88, San Francisco Opera, 1988—2001; dramatic coach Music Acad. West, Santa Barbara, Calif., 1959; dir. dramatics Zurich Internat. Opera Studio, 1961-65, Centre Lyrique, Geneva, 1967-72; artistic adviser Tehran Opera, 1973-75; opera adviser Nat. Arts Centre, Ottawa, Ont., 1977; v.p. Opera America, 1979—. Operatic cons. dir. Yes, Giorgio, MGM, 1981; dir. opera sequence for film Moonstruck (Norman Jewison), 1987. Guest dir. opera cos. including Met. Opera, San Francisco Opera (70 prodns.), N.Y.C. Opera, Lyric Opera of Chgo., L.A. Opera, Teatro Colon, Buenos Aires, Utah Opera, Canadian Opera Co. (30 new prodns.), Houston Grand Opera, La Scala, Covent Garden, Verona Opera, Kirov Opera, Australian Opera, Vienna Staatsoper, Vienna Volksoper, Salzburg Festival, Amsterdam Opera, Holland Festival, Nice (France) Opera, Festival D'Orange, France, Verona Arena Festival; co-author: An Operatic Life, 1982. Decorated chevalier Order Arts and Letters (France), 1992. Mem. Am. Guild Mus. Artists, Can. Actors Equity Assn. Achievements include initiating above-stage projection of subtitles as a simultaneous translation of opera, 1983. Address: Columbia Artists Mngmt Crittenden Divsn 165 W 57th St New York NY 10019-2201 E-mail: lotfimansouri@hotmail.com.

MANSSON, JOAN, librarian, consultant; b. Sacramento, June 9, 1950; d. Gunnar Emanuel Månsson and Signe Evy Jönsson. BA in Fine Arts, N.J. City U., 1982, MA in Studio Art, 1983, postgrad., 1983-84; MLS, Rutgers U., 1985. Grad. asst. art dept. N.J. City U., Jersey City, 1982-84; tchg. asst. Rutgers Art Libr., 1984-85; pub. svcs. libr. Maitland (Fla.) Pub. Libr., 1986—; rsch. cons. Tradingwise, Casselberry, Fla., 1989—; ind. rsch. cons., 1995—. One-woman shows include Maitland Pub. Libr., 1999, W.T. Bland Pub. Libr., 2000, Maitland Pub. Libr., 2001. Mem. steering com. One Cmty, One Book: Ctrl. Fla. Reads, 2002. Mem. ALA, Fla. Libr. Assn. (chair young adult network 1988-92, steering com. 1994-96, chair YA caucus 1996-97, Transformers Honor Roll 1996), Fla. Pub. Libr. Assn. (spkr. conf. 1988), Ctrl. Fla. Libr. Consortium (continuing edn. com. 1994-96). Lutheran. Avocations: pastel artist, weaver, painter. Office: Maitland Pub Libr 501 S Maitland Ave Maitland FL 32751-5672 E-mail: jmansson@cflc.net.

MANSUETTA, CHERI COLAGROSS, optometrist, public health educator; b. Sheffield, Ala., May 15, 1961; d. Charles Clement and JoNell (Vann) Colagross; m. Nicholas Thomas Mansuetta, May 26, 1995. BS, U. Ala., 1984; OD, Nova S.E. U., 1993, MPH with honors, 1997, DO, 2002. Cert. optometrist, Fla., Ala. Pvt. practice, Hialeah and Cooper City, Fla., 1993-98; asst. prof. pub. health Nova Southea. U., Ft. Lauderdale, 1996-98; pvt. practice Cullman, Ala., 1998-2000; rsch. fellow Callahan Eye Found. Hosp., Birmingham , 2002—. Mem. Jr. League Boca Raton, Fla., 1995-96, Jr. League Ft. Lauderdale, 1996-98, Jr. League of Birmingham, Ala., 1998—. Mem. AMA, APHA, Am. Optometric Assn., Ala. Optometric Assn. Avocations: antiques, art, hiking.

MANSUKHANI, SUNDER HASHMATRAI, pathology educator; b. Hyderabad, Sindh, Pakistan, Jan. 14, 1931; came to U.S., 1969; s. Hahmatrai C. and Putli H. (Shahani) M.; m. Devika B. Kripalani, Sept. 2, 1961; children: Kiron, Ashwin, Sharad. B in Medicine and Surgery, B.J. Med. Coll., Ahmedabad, India, 1954; DPH, Bombay U., 1958; MD, Grant Med. Coll., Bombay, 1959. Diplomate Am. Bd. Pathology. Resident Sir J.J. Hosps./U. Bombay, 1956-59; intern Presbyn. Hosp.-U. Pitts., 1961-62; sr. lectr. Grant Med. Coll., Bombay U., 1959-67; prof. pathology Mahatma Gandhi Med. Coll., Jamshedpur, India, 1967-69; rsch. assoc. U. Pitt. Med. Sch., 1969-71; assoc. prof. pathology Med. Coll. Pa., Phila., 1971-76, prof. pathology, 1976—; chmn. pathology and lab. medicine Bucks County Campus, Med. Coll. Hosp., Warminster, Pa., 1991-94; pres. S.J. Pathology Assocs., 1989—; prof. pathology Hahnemann U., Phila., 1994—. Dir. med. edn. in pathology Med. Coll. Pa., Phila., 1971-79; dir. continuing med. edn. Zurbrugg Meml. Hosps., Riverside, N.J., 1979-91. Contbr. abstracts, articles to profl. jours. Recipient Gold medal, Bombay U., 1959, Lindbach Excellence in Tchg. award, Med. Coll. Pa., 1976. Fellow Royal Coll. Pathologists (Eng.), Am. Soc. Clin. Pathologists; mem. AMA, Internat. Acad. Pathology, Am. Assn. Physicians from India (bd. trustees 1990, chmn. health sys. reform 1995, Spl. Achievement award 1987, 88), Asian Indian Profls. Inc. (founder, pres.). Avocations: reading, music, traveling. Home: 64 Regan Ln Kirkwood Voorhees NJ 08043-4146

MANSY, HANSEN A. biomedical researcher, educator; b. Egypt, Jan. 15, 1959; s. Amonem B. and Wagha H. Mansy. PhD, Ill. Inst. Tech., 1990. Rsch. assoc. prof. Ill. Inst. Tech., Chgo., 1999—; v.p. Biomed. Acoustic Rsch. Co., Evanston, 1997—. Cons. Aurea Industries, Chgo., 1993—95. Mem.: Acoustic Soc. Am. Achievements include patents for trapped vortex pair fluidic oscillator; invention of method and apparatus for characterizing gastrointestinal sounds.

MANTEGAZZA, SERGIO, executive; b. Mendrisio, Switzerland, Oct. 31, 1927; s. Antonio and Angela (Ribolzi) M.; m. Sebastiana Hernandez, Feb. 25, 1955; children: Fabio, Dolores, Paolo. D of Bus. Adminstrn., Gademann Handelschule, 1945. With Globus Gateway Tours, Lugano, Switzerland, 1945-48, mgr. Switzerland, 1948-52, gen. mgr. Switzerland, 1952-56, dir. Switzerland, 1956-60; mng. dir. Globus and Cosmos Groups, Switzerland, 1960—, pres. Switzerland; main shareholder Monarch Airlines Ltd., 1967. Named Knight of the Order of St. Gregorio Magno and Hon. Consul of Mexico. Mem. Lyford Cay, Maxims Bus. Club, Mark's Club. Avocations: tennis, yachting, golf. Office: Globus Travel Svcs Via alla Roggia CH-6916 Grancia Switzerland

MANTEL, ALLAN DAVID, lawyer; b. N.Y.C., June 27, 1951; s. Bernard and Ruth (Weichman) M.; m. Janet Mantel, June 17, 1985; children: Bernard, Elizabeth. BA, NYU, 1973; JD, SUNY, Buffalo, 1976. Bar: N.Y. 1977, U.S. Dist. Ct. (so. and ea. dists.) N.Y. 1977. Assoc. Rosenthal & Herman P.C., N.Y.C., 1977-82; ptnr. Rosenthal, Herman & Mantel, 1983-94, Hofheimer, Gartlir & Gross, LLP, N.Y.C., 1995-98, Stein Riso & Mantel LLP, N.Y.C., 1999—. Fellow Am. Acad. Matrimonial Lawyers (bd. mgrs. 1998-2000, N.Y. chpt. treas. 2001—); mem. ABA (family law sect.), N.Y. State Bar Assn. (equitable distbn. com.), Assn. Bar City N.Y. (matrimonial law com. 1985-88), N.Y. County Lawyers Assn. (matrimonial law and bus. and comml. law com.). Jewish. Office: Stein Riso & Mantel LLP 405 Lexington Ave New York NY 10174-0002 E-mail: allan.mantel@steinrisomantel.com.

MANTEL, SAMUEL JOSEPH, JR. management educator, consultant; b. Indpls., Nov. 17, 1921; s. Samuel Joseph and Beatrice Smith (Talmas) M.; m. Dorothy Jean Friedland, June 28, 1950; children— Michael Lee, Samuel Joseph, III, Margaret Irene, Elizabeth Baer. AB, Harvard U., 1948, M.P.A., 1950, PhD, 1952. Asst. prof. social sci. Ga. Inst. Tech., 1953-56; asst. prof., then assoc. prof. econs., dir. Econs.-in-Action program, Case Western Res. U., 1956-69; prof. mgmt. and quantitative analysis U. Cin., 1969-89, prof. emeritus quantitative analysis and ops. mgmt., 1989—, Joseph S. Stern prof. mgmt., 1973-89, emeritus, 1989, exec. dir. Grad. Ctr. for Mgmt. of Advanced Tech. and Innovation, 1987-89, emeritus, 1989. Mgmt. cons., condr. mgmt. seminars. Author: Cases in Managerial Decisions, 1964, Project Management: A Managerial Perspective, 1985, Operations Management for Pharmacists: Strategy and Tactics, 1992, Project Management: A Managerial Perspective, 4th edit., 2000, Project Management in Practice, 2001; contbr. to several books, editl. bd. Technovation; contbr. articles to profl. jours. Vice pres. Jewish Fedn. Cin., 1978-80; past pres., life mem. Cin. Hillel Found., Cleve. Hillel Found.; historian Rockdale Temple, 1969-77; mem. mgmt. and adminstrn. com. Anti-Defamation League, B'nai B'rith, 1976; trustee Jewish Hosp., Cin., 1975-84, Sarah Marvin Found. for Performing Arts, 1990—; mem. mgmt. adv. com. Cin. Police Dept., 1991-92. Maj. USMCR, 1942-46, 51-53. Decorated D.F.C. with 3 oak leaf clusters, Air medal with 11 oak leaf clusters; Econs.-in-Action fellow, 1955; fellow Inst. Policy Research, 1980; named Prof. of Year, Delta Sigma Pi, 1974 Mem. IEEE, Project Mgmt. Inst., Iota Epsilon, Beta Gamma Sigma. Home: 608 Flagstaff Dr Cincinnati OH 45215-2525 E-mail: mantelsj@email.uc.edu.

MANTELL, KEITH C. chemical engineer; b. N.Y.C., May 3, 1939; s. Charles L. and Adelaide Marie Mantell; m. Leticia Carriedo, June 20, 1970 (dec. 1991); children: Kevin Phillip, Charles Edward, Christopher Arthur. BSChemE, Polytechnic Inst. Bklyn., 1967. Registered profl. engr., N.J., Pa. Jr. process engr. Air Reduction, Piscataway, N.J., 1967-70; project/process engr. Cornell Design, 1978-85; cons. engr. Lark Labs., SBA Francis, Negromex, IDSFYA, Unitas Corp., El Reyo Farms; dir. Nurex Industiers, Montvale, N.J., 1990—, The Isogenics Inst., San Francisco, 1985-90; pres., dir. Isogenics, Inc., Montvale, N.J., 1975—. Purchasing mgr. Gentry Internat., Fairlawn, N.J., 1971-73; project engr. Chlorox Co., Jersey City. Patents pending for Power Blast device on motor cars and Mantellcyllin and Manetllmycin antibiotics. Mem. AAAS, N.Y. Acad. Scis. Avocations: sport car racing, pool, golf, cross-country skiing. Office: Isogenics Inc 96 Powder Hill Montvale NJ 07645

MANTELL, SUZANNE RUTH, editor; b. West Orange, N.J., Nov. 26, 1944; d. Milton A. and Florence B. M.; m. Peter Gray Friedman, 1985; 1 child, Erica Mantell Friedman Student, U. Chgo., 1962; B.F.A., Pratt Inst., 1967. Formerly assoc. editor Harper's mag., N.Y.C., exec. editor, 1977-80; editor Harper's Bookletter, 1974-77, Learning Mag., 1980-81, Family Learning Mag., 1983-84; reader Book of the Month Club, 1985-87, 91-99; editor Travel Bookstore Catalogue, Banana Republic, 1985-87; assoc. editor The N.Y. Observer, N.Y.C., 1987-91; acting Book News editor Pubs. Weekly, 1992-93, contbg. editor, 1993—. Also lectr. mag. writing Stanford U., U. Calif. at Santa Cruz. Consulting editor Spelman Coll. Messenger, 1994-98; columnist L.A. Times Book Review, 1998-99; arts editor New Times L.A., 1999-2001; author Art of the State: Vermont, 1998. Mem. PEN, PEN West USA, Nat. Book Critics Circle. Home: 101 Warwick Pl South Pasadena CA 91030-4062

MANTELLA, TINO J. medical association administrator; m. Deb Mantella; children: Cara, Dana, Brock. MS, Temple U.; postgrad., Columbia U. Inst. Non-Profit Mgmt. Pres. and CEO Arthritis Found., 2001—. Office: Arthritis Found PO Box 7669 Atlanta GA 30357-0669*

MANTEY, ELMER MARTIN, food company executive; b. Malone, Tex., July 20, 1926; s. Edward G. and Margaret H. Mantey; m. Donna May Scritsmier, Dec. 27, 1948; children: Patricia Mantey Rooks, Carol Mantey Callis, Cynthia Mantey Stockdale. BS in Chemistry with honors, Bradley U., 1949. Chemist, plant mgr. Am. Petrochem. Co., Mpls., 1949-63, v.p. ops., 1963-66; v.p. Polychem. Group Whittaker Corp., L.A., 1966-69, pres. textile divsn., 1969-71; CEO, pres., chmn. bd. dirs. Flavorite Labs. Inc., Memphis, 1971-89; chmn. emeritus. Bd. dirs. A.M. Todd Co., dir. emeritus; bd. dirs. The Dupps Co.; chmn. bd. trustees Chrichton Coll. Trustee John Brown U., 1991-2000. Served with USN, 1944-46. Mem. Rotary (Memphis), Summit Club. Home: 6925 Sugar Maple Cv Memphis TN 38119-5619 Office: PO Box 1315 Memphis TN 38101-1315

MANTHE, CORA DE MUNCK, real estate company executive; b. Alton, Iowa, Oct. 10, 1928; d. Cornelius John and Bessie Bell (Miller) De Munck; m. Carl Robert Manthe, Apr. 5, 1952 (dec. Dec. 1987); children: Barry Paul, David Glenn. BA in Econs., U. Iowa, 1950; postgrad., U. Wis., Madison and Oshkosh, 1972-75; grad., Realtors Inst., 1983. Cert. residential appraiser. Rsch. analyst Dept. Def., Washington, 1951-52; social work investigator Dane County, Madison, 1960-62; civic hostess Welcome Wagon, Beaver Dam, Wis., 1963-70; real estate broker "C" Manthe Realty, Ltd., 1979—, property mgr., investment mgr., pres., treas., 1982—. Deacon Grace Presbyn. Ch., 1974-77, elder, 1979-82, ruling elder, 1989-92; staff worker Kohl Senate Campaign, 1994. Mem. AAUW (life), Internat. Platform Assn., Beaver Dam C. of C., U. Iowa Alumni Assn. (life), Optimist Internat. (life). Avocations: bridge, golf, travel, reading. Home and Office: 404 Declark St Beaver Dam WI 53916-1714 *Attendance at meetings, classes, family reunions throughout the world has consumed time. The Crystal Cathedral California Hour of Power Television Ministry has been a participating meeting place since the early 70s. The International Platform Association in wAshington, D.C., featuring classes in Speech, Journalism, Art, Acting, etc. has been attended. Charitable work includes Optimist International and the American Association of University Women with their emphasis on Women's issues has taken time and endeavors.*

MANTHEI, RICHARD DALE, retired lawyer, health care company executive; b. Olivia, Minn., Dec. 23, 1935; s. Alvin R. and Sidonia (Klatt) M.; m. Karen J. Peterson, Sept. 6, 1959 (dec. Mar. 1985); children: Steven, Jana, Kari, John, Rebecca; m. Lynn E. Graham, Aug. 9, 1986. BS in Pharmacy (Rexall award 1960), S.D. State U., 1960; JD, U. Minn., 1967. Bar: Ind. 1967, Ill. 1970, D.C. 1987, U.S. Supreme Ct. 1987. Sales rep. Eli Lilly & Co., Indpls., 1962-64, atty., 1967-70; atty., then asst. corp. sec., dir. regulatory affairs Am. Hosp. Supply Corp., Evanston, Ill., 1970-79, corp. sec., dep. gen. counsel, 1979-85; assoc. gen. counsel Baxter Travenol Labs., Deerfield, 1986-87; ptnr. Burditt, Bowles & Radzius, Washington, 1987-90, McKenna & Cuneo, Washington, 1990-96; sr. v.p. regulatory scis. C.R. Bard, Inc., Murray Hill, N.J., 1996-2000. Author articles in field.; Editorial adv. staff: Med. Devices and Diagnostic Industry, 1979. Mem. bd. edn. Libertyville H.S., 1984-87; mem. governing bd. Spl. Edn. Dist. of Lake County, Ill., 1985-87; trustee N.J. Ctr. for Visual Arts. With AUS, 1954-56. Mem. ABA, Health Industry Mfrs. Assn. (chmn. law sect. 1976), Health Industry Assn. (chmn. legal com. 1973), Am. Soc. Corp. Secs. (corp. practices com. 1983-88, group pres. 1985-86, Chgo. regional group 1986-87), Ill. Bar Assn., Ind. Bar Assn., D.C. Bar Assn., Univ. Club (Evanston, Ill., bd. dirs. 1984-86). Home: 11608 Stonewall Jackson Dr Spotsylvania VA 22553

MANTHEI, ROBIN DICKEY, project coordinator; b. Tucson, May 16, 1956; d. Wilbur Dunbar French and Barbara Dickey; m. Joel Robert Manthei, Sept. 4, 1976; children: Nicholas Robert, Charles Dickey. AS, Augsburg Coll., 1976; cert. med. lab. technician, Med. Inst. Minn., 1978; BS, U. Minn., 1994. Med. lab. technician Lufkin Med. Lab., Mpls., 1978-82; jr. scientist U. Minn., 1982-86; rsch. tech. Mayo Found., Rochester, Minn., 1986-89; chpt. leader Young Astronaut Program, 1987-94; jr. scientist Inst. Human Genetics U. Minn., 1989-90; rsch. asst. Mpls. Med. Rsch. Found., 1990-93; lab. instr. North Hennepin C.C., Brooklyn Park, Minn., 1994-98, tech. coord., 1999—. Contbr. articles in field. Mem. Maple Grove Rotary Club. Episcopalian. Avocation: family genealogy. Home: 7630 Lanewood Ln N Maple Grove MN 55311-2670 E-mail: robin.manthei@nhcc.mnscu.edu.

MANTHEY, FRANK ANTHONY, physician, director; b. N.Y.C., Dec. 2, 1933; s. Frank A.J. and Josephine (Roth) M.; m. Douglas Susan Falvey, Sept. 14 1958 (div. 1979, dec. 1989); children: Michael P., Susan M., Peter J.; m. Doris Jean Pulley, Oct. 11, 1979. BS, Fordham U., 1954; MD, SUNY, Syracuse, 1958. Diplomate Am. Bd. Anesthesiology, Am. Bd. Med. Examiners. Intern Upstate Med. Ctr., Syracuse, 1958-59; resident in anesthesiology Yale-New Haven Med. Ctr., 1962-64; physician Yale-New Haven Hosp., 1964-75; pvt. practice medicine Illmo, Mo., 1975-79; dir. Manthey Med. Clinic, Elkton, Ky., 1979—. Clin. instr. anesthesiology Yale U. Med. Sch., New Haven, 1964-69, asst. clin. prof. anesthesiology, 1969-75; cons. Conn. Dept. Aeros., Hartford, 1969-70; sr. med. examiner Fed. Aviation Adminstrn., Illmo, 1975-79. Contbr. articles to profl. jours. Chmn. gen. works Little Folks Fair, Guilford, Conn., 1967-71; mem. Rep. Town Com., Guilford, 1969-75; chmn. Guilford Sch. Bldg. Com., 1973-75. Capt. USAF (M.C.), 1956-62. Mem.: Flying Physicians Assn. (v.p. NE chpt. 1973—75, v.p. nat. 1974—75, 1979—80, bd. dirs. 1970—73, 1975—78, bd. dirs. nat. 1975—78), Aerospace Med. Assn. (assoc. fellow 1973—75), Ky. Med. Assn., Mercedes Benz ClubAm., Alpha Kappa Kappa. Avocations: philately, numismatics, aviation, auto restoration, skiing. Home: 105 Sunset Dr Elkton KY 42220-9257 Office: Manthey Family Practice Clinic 203 Allensville St PO Box 368 Elkton KY 42220-0368

MANTHEY, MERRILY RUTH, psychotherapist, educator, consultant, artist, photographer; b. Mar. 25, 1943; Office: 317 W Meeker St # E Kent WA 98032-6005 Home: PO Box 279 Kent WA 98035-0279

MANTLE, PETER JOHN, aerospace executive, consultant; b. London, Apr. 29, 1935; came to U.S., 1960; s. George Henry and Winifred Mantle; m. Lisa Margaret Taylor, June 26, 1965 (div. July 1979); children: Tracy Lynn Gage, Christopher James; m. Kathleen Anne Kinney, Dec. 27, 1987. MSc in Aero, Cranfield Tech., Bedford, Eng., 1958; MSc in Math. magna cum laude, Laval U., 1960; AeE, CalTech, 1964. Program mgr. Bell Aerospace, New Orleans, 1965-73; pres. Mantle Engring., Rosslyn, Va., 1976-78; dir. tech. assessment U.S. Navy, Pentagon, Washington, 1978-84; dir. surveillance programs Lockheed Martin, Sunnyvale, Calif., 1984-87, dir. European bus., 1987-97; cons. Mantle & Assocs., Vashon Island, Wash., 2000—. Chmn. NATO indsl. adv. group on missile def., Brussels, 1990-2000. Author: Tech Summary of Air Cushion Craft, 1975, Air Cushion Craft Development, 1980; designer fastest U.S. Navy ship, 1972; patentee advanced marine vehicles. Recipient Nat. Cert. prize Insn. Mech. Engrs., London, 1955, Superior Civilian Svc. award Sec. of Navy, 1984. Mem. Masons, Scottish and York Rites. Avocations: sculpture, art, photography, skiing. Home: 7703 SW 259th St Vashon WA 98070-8540 E-mail: mantlep@ix.netcom.com.

MANTLE, RAYMOND ALLAN, lawyer; b. Painesville, Ohio, Oct. 15, 1937; s. Junius Dow and Ada Louise (Stinchcomb) M.; m. Judith Ann LaGrange, Nov. 26, 1967; children: Amanda Lee, Rachel Ann, Leah Amy. BSBA summa cum laude, BA summa cum laude, Kent State U., 1961; LLB cum laude, NYU, 1964. Bar: N.Y. 1964, N.J. 1976, U.S. Supreme Ct. Asst. counsel Gov. Nelson A. Rockefeller, N.Y., 1964-65; assoc. Paul Weiss Rifkind Wharton & Garrison, 1967-69; mem. Varet & Fink P.C. (formerly Milgrim Thomajan & Lee, P.C.), N.Y.C., 1969-95; ptnr. Piper & Marbury L.L.P., 1995-98; mem. Reitler Brown LLC (formerly Brock Silverstein, LLC), 1998—. Lectr. in computer law field. Contbr. author: Doing Business in China and Intellectual Property China, 1990—. Capt. U.S. Army, 1965-67. Mem.: N.J. Bar Assn., N.Y. State Bar Assn. (co-chmn. seminar on intellectual property and internet 2000, 2001, 2002, co-chair internet com., mem. exec. com. intellectual property sect.). Republican. Methodist. Office: Reitler Brown LLC 800 3rd Ave Fl 21 New York NY 10022-7604 E-mail: rmantle@reitlerbrown.com.

MANTON, EDWIN ALFRED GRENVILLE, insurance company executive; b. Earls Colne, Essex, Eng., Jan. 22, 1909; came to U.S., 1933; s. John Horace and Emily Clara (Denton) M.; m. Florence V. Brewer, Feb. 1, 1936; 1 child, Diana H. Manton Morton. Student, London (Eng.) U., 1925-27, N.Y. Ins. Soc., 1933-35; DHL (hon.), Coll. of Ins., 1994. With B.W. Noble Ltd., Paris, 1927-33; casualty underwriter Am. Internat. Underwriters Corp.,

N.Y.C., 1933-37, sec., 1937-38, v.p., 1938-42, pres., 1942-69, chmn., 1969-75. Sr. advisor Am. Internat. Group, Inc.; hon. dir. C.V. Starr & Co., Inc. Trustee St. Luke's-Roosevelt Hosp., N.Y.C. Mem. Salmagundi Club, Mendelssohn Glee Club, Williams Club, St. George's Soc., Downtown Assn. Episcopalian. Office: Am Internat Group Inc 70 Pine St New York NY 10270-0002

MANTON, PAUL K, retired music educator; b. Niagara Falls, Ny, Jan. 2, 1948; s. Richard Moore and Lillian Martha, Theiss Manton; m. Sharon A. Donato, Feb. 17, 1999; children: Christopher M., Stephanie A., Cheryl M.; m. Margaret E. Brown, June 7, 1970 (div.); children: Amy L., Timothy P. MusB in Music Edn., Suny Fredonia, Fredonia, NY, 1970, MusM in Music Edn., 1975. Cert. EMT NY, 1998. Music educator Akron Ctrl. Schools, Akron, NY, 1970—2002. Condr., chmn., adjudicator NY State Music Assn., NY, 1970—2002, Erle County Music Educator Assn., Erle County, NY, 1970—2002; condr., chmn. Niayona County Music Educaton Assn., Niayona County, NY, 1990—2002; del. NY State Teachrs Retirement Sys., Albany, NY, 1992—2002. Fireman, emt, sec. Alden Hook & Ladder Fire Co., Alden, NY, 1980—94; cpr educator ARC, Buffalo, 1983—90; dir. Habitat for Humanity of Genesee, County Hill, 1999—2002; ruling elder First Presbyn. Ch., 1996—2001. Recipient membership, Phi Mi Alpha Sinfonia, 1969-2002. Mem.: Akron Faculty Assn. (pres. 1975—75), NY State Sch. Music Assn. (adjucator 1978—), Erie Country Music Edn. Assn. Presbyterian. Avocations: gold, gold, gold. Home: 170 Ross St Batavia NY 14020-2321

MANTON, WILLIAM JEFFREY, operating engineer, fleet consultant; b. Oak Park, Ill., Sept. 29, 1959; s. Herman Charles Manton and June Gertrude Kasman; m. Joanne Marie Maciejewski ((div. Oct. 1987); children: Jessica Lynn, Jeffrey William; m. Kimberly Ann May, Sept. 3, 1988; children: Charles James (dec.), Amanda Nicole and Courtney Elizabeth (twins). Grad. high sch., Hillside, Ill., 1977. Svc. mgr. Warnimont's Farm Supply, Bloomingdale, Ill., 1983-88; fleet mgr. Crane & Steel Inc., Addison, 1988—. Trustee, Village of Hanover Park, Ill., 1996—, vice chmn. Devel. Commn., 1994-96. Mem. Internat. Union Operating Engrs., Knights of Columbus. Republican. Roman Catholic. Avocations: sporting clays, trap shooting. Home: 1819 Seneca Dr Hanover Park IL 60133-6751 Office: 2121 W Lake St Hanover Park IL 60133-4301 E-mail: williammanton@msn.com., w.manton@hanoverparkillinois.org.

MANTONYA, JOHN BUTCHER, lawyer; b. Columbus, Ohio, May 26, 1922; s. Elroy Letts and Blanche (Butcher) M.; m. Mary E. Reynolds, June 14, 1947 (dec. 1987); children: Elizabeth Claire, Mary Kay, Lee Ann; m. Carole L. Lugar, Sept. 28, 1989. AB cum laude, Washington and Jefferson Coll., 1943; postgrad., U. Mich. Law Sch., 1946-47; JD, Ohio State U., 1949. Bar: Ohio 1949. Assoc. A.S. Mitchell (Atty.), Newark, 1949-50, C.D. Lindrooth, Newark, 1950-57; partner firm Lindrooth & Mantonya, 1957-74; firm John B. Mantonya, 1974-81, John B. Mantonya, L.P.A., 1981—. Mem. North Fork Local Bd. Edn., 1962-69; adv. com. Salvation Army, Licking County, 1965—, Mayor of, Utica, Ohio, 1953-59. Served with AUS, 1943-45. Mem. Am. Bar Assn., Ohio Bar Assn., Licking County Bar Assn. (pres. 1967), Phi Delta Phi, Beta Theta Pi. Home: 11055 Reynolds Rd Utica OH 43080-9549 Office: 3 N 3rd St Newark OH 43055-5506

MANTOOTH, JOHN ALBERT, judge; b. Oklahoma City, June 13, 1947; s. Albert and Thelma (Kerr) M.; m. Robin M. McColley, Jan. 17, 1993; children from previous marriage: Susan, Jan, Meredith. BA, Okla. U., 1969, JD, 1972. Bar: Okla. 1973, U.S. Dist. Ct. (we. dist.) Okla. 1973, U.S. Ct. Appeals (10th cir.) 1975, U.S. Supreme Ct. 1976, U.S. Army Ct. Mil. Rev. 1987, U.S. Ct. Mil. Appeals 1987, U.S. Ct. Appeals (fed. cir.) 1999. Sole practice, Purcell, Okla., 1973-79; ptnr. Elder, Mantooth & Haxel, 1979-85, Mantooth & Haxel, Purcell, 1985-91; sole practice law, 1992—. Judge City of Purcell, 1974-88, City of Lexington, Okla., 1976—; owner, bd. dirs. M-Quad Land Devel., Purcell, 1979-82, Cartier Jewelry, Dallas, 1982-87; mem. com. on uniform jury instructions civil Okla. Supreme Ct. Mem. Gov.'s Task Force on Vocat.-Tech. Edn., 1975; chmn. Purcell Mcpl. Hosp., Purcell, 1974-76; co-founder Cleve. County Crisis Pregnancy Ctr., 1996—; mem. Purcell Pub. Sch. Found., 1993—. Served to Col. JAGC U.S. Army, 1976—; 95th Divsn. staff judge advocate, 1996-2000, staff judge advocate 5045 Garrison support unit, 2000-02, comdr. 174th legal support orgn., 2002—. Mem. Okla. Trial Lawyers Assn. (editor mag. 1976-80), Rotary (pres. Purcell Club 1978-79), Beta Theta Pi, Phi Alpha Delta. Republican. Presbyterian. Avocations: tennis, skiing, hunting, fishing, traveling. Office: 111 N 3d St Purcell OK 73080-0667

MANTOVANI, JOHN F. pediatric neurologist; b. St. Louis, Jan. 17, 1949; s. John F. and Marinelle Mantovani; children: John R. and Ann Marie. BA cum laude, U. Evansville, 1971; MD, U. Mo., 1974. Diplomate Am. Bd. Pediat., Am. Bd. Psychiatry and Neurology in child neurology and in neurodevel. disabilities. Resident pediatrics, neurology, fellow child neurology Washington U.-St. Louis Childrens Hosp., 1974-79; practitioner adult and child neurology Dean Clinic, Madison, Wis., 1979-84; dir. child neurology, vice chmn. dept. pediatrics St. John's Mercy Med. Ctr., St. Louis, 1984—. Clin. asst. prof. neurology U. Wis., Madison, 1980-84; instr. clin. pediatrics and neurology Washington U., 1985-95, asst. prof., 1995-99, assoc. prof., 1999—. Contbr. articles to profl. jours. Fellow Am. Acad. Pediatrics; mem. AMA, Am. Acad. Cerebral Palsy and Devel. Medicine (bd. dirs. 1994-2001, v.p. 1997-98, pres.-elect 1999, pres. 2000), Am. Acad. Neurology, Child Neurology Soc., Alpha Omega Alpha. Office: 621 S New Ballas Rd Ste 5009 Saint Louis MO 63141-8232

MANTSCH, HENRY HORST, chemistry educator; b. Mediasch, Transylvania, Romania, July 30, 1935; emigrated to Can., 1968; s. Heinrich Johann and Olga Augusta (Gondosch) M.; m. Amy Emilia Kory, Nov. 2, 1959; children: Monica, Marietta. BSc, U. Cluj, Transylvania, 1958, PhD, 1964. Rsch. scientist Romanian Acad. Sci., Cluj, 1958-65, Tech. U. Munich, Germany, 1966-68; with NRC, Ottawa, Can., 1968-72; prof. biochemistry U. Cluj, 1973-74, Liebig U., Giessen, Germany, 1975-76; head molecular spectroscopy NRC, Ottawa, 1977—; mem. Can. Rsch. Coun., 1977-91, Winnipeg, Can., 1992—. Adj. prof. Carleton U., Ottawa, 1978-90, U. Ottawa, 1990-92, U. Manitoba, Winnipeg, 1992—. Contbr. articles to profl. jours.; patentee in field. Recipient medal Ministry of Edn., Bucharest, 1972, Humboldt Found. medal Bonn, 1980, Herzberg award, 1984, Marcus Marci medal, 1998; Chem. Inst. Can. fellow, 1979, Royal Soc. Can. fellow, 1982. Mem. Am. Biophys. Soc., Soc. Applied Spectroscopy, Chem. Inst. Can. (chmn. biol. chem. divsn. 1980-81), Can. Spectroscopy Soc. (nat. exec. com. 1981-90), Can. Biophys. Soc. (sec. 1999—). Home: 2222 W Taylor Blvd R3P 2J5 Winnipeg MB Canada R3P 2J5 Office: NRC Can 435 Ellice Ave Winnipeg MB Canada R3B 1Y6 E-mail: henry.mantsch@nrc.ca.

MANTY, BRIAN ALAN, high technology company executive; b. Quincy, Mass., Aug. 2, 1944; s. Allan E. and Ellen Manty; m. Barbara Adamson, Mar. 13, 1965; children: George, Mark. BS in Chemistry, Fla. State U., 1966; MS in Electrochemistry, Fla. Atlantic U., 1969; MBA, Nova U., 1989. Chemist Pratt & Whitney Aircraft Co., West Palm Beach, Fla., 1966-71, group leader, surface finishing, 1971-77, supr. chemistry and machining, 1976-93, program mgr. govt. contracts, 1975-93; tech. dir. Concurrent Techs. Corp., Johnstown, Pa., 1993-97, gen. mgr. so. divsn. Largo, Fla., 1997—. Adj. instr. Palm Beach C.C., 1989-93; cons. in field. Patentee in field. Mem. Am. Chem. Soc., Am. Electroplaters and Surface Finishers Soc. (dir. 1991-95, pres. 1995-96, elected fellow 1997), Soc. Mfg. Engrs., Robotics Internat. (cert. mfg. engr.), Nat. Assn. Corrosion Engrs. (cert. corrosion specialist), Am. Metals Soc., Air Force Assn. Home: 1811 Weatherstone Dr Safety Harbor FL 34695-5515 Office: Concurrent Techs Corp 7990 114th Ave Largo FL 33773-5026

MANTYLA, KAREN, distance learning consultant; b. Bronx, N.Y., Dec. 31, 1944; d. Milton and Sylvia (Diamond) Fischer; m. John A Mantyla, May 30, 1970 (div. 1980); 1 child, Michael Alan. Student, Rockland Community Coll., Suffern, N.Y., 1962, NYU, 1967, Mercer U., 1981. Mktg. coordinator Credit Bur., Inc., Miami, Fla., 1973-79; dist. mgr. The Research Inst. Am., N.Y.C., 1979-80, regional dir., 1980-85, field sales mgr., 1985-86, nat. sales mgr., 1986-87; nat. accounts mgr. The Rsch. Inst. Am., 1989; v.p. sales Bur. Bus. Practice/Paramount Comm., Inc., Waterford, Conn., 1989-93; pres. Quiet Power, Inc., Washington, 1993—. Author: Consultative Sales Power, 1995, Interactive Distance Learning Exercises That Really Work, 1999, The 2000/2001 ASTD Distance Learning Yearbook, 2000, Blending e-Learning: The Power is in the Mix, 2001; co-editor The 2001/2002 ASTD Distance Learning Yearbook; co-author: Distance Learning: A Step-By-Step Guide for Trainers, 1997, Blending E-Learning: The Power is in the Mix, 2001. Bd. dirs. Federal Govt. Distance Learning Assn. Mem. ASTD, Sales and Mktg. Execs. (past bd. dirs. N.Y. chpt., v.p. Ft. Lauderdale chpt. 1979), U.S. Distance Learning Assn. (editor Distance Learning News, mem. tech. and comm. com. Fla. chpt.), Nat. Assn. Women Bus. Owners, U.S. C. of C., Women Entrepreneurs. Avocations: antiques, tennis, writing, swimming. Home: 6500 Majestic Prince Loop Gainesville VA 20155 Office: Quiet Power Inc 1201 Pennsylvania Ave NW Washington DC 20004-2401 E-mail: quietpower@aol.com.

MANTZ, ARLAN W. physics educator; b. Slatington, Pa., July 25, 1940; s. Harold H. and Irene A. (Herber) M.; m. Barbara Dae Mantz, Dec. 28, 1963; 1 child, Yves Andre. BA, Catawba Coll., 1962; MSc, Ohio State U., 1966, PhD, 1969. Sr. scientist Air Force Avionics Lab., Ohio, 1966-73; postdoctoral fellow Labo Aime Cotton, Orsay, France, 1973-74; sr. scientist Digilab, Inc., Cambridge, Mass., 1974-76; engrng. mgr. Laser Analytics Inc., Bedford, 1976-79, pres., gen. mgr., 1979-89; assoc. prof. Franklin and Marshall Coll., Lancaster, Pa., 1990-95; Oakes Ames prof. physics Conn. Coll., New London, 1995—. Editl. adv. bd. Spectrochemica Acta, 1990, revs. editor, 1995. Mem. AAAS, Optical Soc. of Am., Am. Chem. Soc., Am. Phys. Soc., N.Y. Acad. Sci. Avocation: sailing. Home: 145 Wamphassuc Rd Stonington CT 06378-2816

MANTZELL, BETTY LOU, school health administrator; b. Brookville, Pa., Oct. 16, 1938; d. Elmer William and Wilda Mae (Enterline) M. Diploma, Ind. (Pa.) Hosp. Sch. Nursing, 1959; BSN, Case Western Res. U., 1969, MA, 1978; cert. supr. ednl. adminstrn., Cleve. State U., 1983; cert. supr., John Carroll U., 1989. RN, Ohio, Pa. Oper. room nurse Univ. Hosps. of Cleve., 1963-69; sch. nurse various locations Cleve. Pub. Schs., 1969-85, coord. sch. nurses, 1976-85, acting asst. supr. health svcs., 1985-86, supr. health svcs., 1986—. Mem. adv. com. to baccalaureate nursing program Cleve. State U.; prevention of blindness adv. com. Cleve. Sight Ctr.; active All Kids Count Consortium Cleve. Dept. Pub. Health; mem. sch. health com. Acad. Medicine Cleve.; Frances Payne Bolton Sch. Nursing, mem. alumni assn.; clin. instr. cmty. health nursing Case We. Res. U., Cleve., 1988-90, women's connection; mem. coun. econ. opportunities Greater Cleve.; mem. adv. com. Headstart Health Svcs. Mem. Am. Sch. Health Assn., Nat. Assn. Sch. Nurses, Ohio Assn. Sch. Nurses, Northeastern Ohio Assn. Sch. Nurses, Ohio Assn. Secondary Sch. Adminstrs., Cleve. Coun. Adminstrs. and Suprs., Cleve. Med. Libr. Assn. Office: Buhrer Elem Sch 1600 Buhrer Ave Cleveland OH 44109

MANUEL, BERNARD M. investment banker; b. Paris, June 9, 1947; s. Andre Alexis and Jeanine (Steel) M.; m. Isabelle L. Lowengard; came to U.S., 1971; M.S. cum laude in Mathematics, U. Paris, 1968, cum laude in Econs., 1970; M.B.A. with high distinction (Baker scholar), Harvard U., 1973; children— Gregory, Vladimir, Severine, Olivier, Laurent. Lectr. econs. U. Paris, 1968-70; investment analyst Louis-Dreyfus S.A., Paris, 1970-71, asst. to pres. Louis-Dreyfus Corp., N.Y.C., 1973-77; pres. Portescap U.S. Inc., N.Y.C., 1977-83; pres. Amvent Inc., N.Y.C., 1983— . French Govt. scholar, 1971-73, Loeb Rhodes fin. fellow, 1971-72; Melvin T. Copeland awardee, 1971-72. Clubs: Meadow Brook, Hasty Pudding (Boston); Travellers, St. Germain des Pres, Morfontaine (Paris). Home: 25 E 86th St New York NY 10028-0553 Office: Cygne Designs Inc 1410 Broadway Rm 1002 New York NY 10018-5010

MANUEL, CHARLIE FUQUA, JR. professional baseball manager; children: Charles Jr., Julie. Outfielder Minn. Twins, 1963-74; with Bklyn. Dodgers, 1974-75, Yakult Swallows and Kintetsu Buffaloes, Japan, 1976-81; scout Minn. Twins, 1982; mgr. class A Wisconsin Rapids, 1983; various coaching and mgr. positions, 1983-99; mgr. Cleve. Indians, 1999—. Inducted Salem-Roanoke Baseball Hall of Fame, 1995. Office: Cleve Indians 2401 Ontario St Cleveland OH 44115-4003*

MANUEL, JERRY, professional sports team manager; b. Hahira, Ga., Dec. 23, 1953; m. Renette Caldwell; children: Angela, Jerry, Anthony, Natalie. Switch-hitting infielder Detroit Tigers, 1972, Class A Lakeland, Class AAA Toledo, 1973, Class AAA Evansville, 1974-75, Detroit Tigers, 1975-76, Montreal, Can., 1980-81, San Diego, 1982, Class AAA Iowa, 1983, Class AAA Denver, 1984; scout White Sox, 1985; player, coach Indpls. orgn., 1986, infield instr., 1987; minor-league fielding coord. Expos orgn., 1988-89; mgr. Class AAA Indpls. Montreal Expos Sys., 1991; coach maj. league baseball Montreal Expos, 1991-96; mgr. Chgo. White Sox, 1997—. Bench coach Fla. Marlins, 1997. Named So. League Mgr. of Yr., 1992. Office: Chgo White Sox 333 W 35th St Chicago IL 60616-3651*

MANUEL, RALPH NIXON, former private school executive; b. Frederick, Md., Apr. 21, 1936; s. Ralph Walter and Frances Rebecca (Nixon) M.; m. Sarah Jane Warner, July 22, 1960; children: Mark, David, Stephen, Bradley. AB, Dartmouth Coll., 1958; M.Ed., Boston U., 1967; PhD, U. Ill., 1971. Assoc. dean Dartmouth Coll., Hanover, N.H., 1971-72, dean of freshmen, 1972-75, dean, 1975-82; pres. Culver (Ind.) Acad. and Culver Edn. Found., 1982-99. Bd. dirs. Ind. Sch. Cen. States, 1986-99, chair, 1993-95. Mem. Assn. Mil. Colls. and Schs. of U.S. (pres., bd. dirs.), Nat. Assn. Ind. Schs. (bd. dirs. 1995-99). E-mail: ralph.n.manuel@valley.net.

MANUEL, SANDRA LORRAINE, minister; b. Lakewood, NJ, July 29, 1951; d. Samuel Blackstone and Curtis Burnett; m. Alexander Manuel, July 12, 1967 (dec. Feb. 27, 1995); children: Darnell, Tasha, Alexia;. Diploma in nursing, Charles Gregory Sch. Nursing, 1985; B in Religious Edn., United Bible Coll., 1991. RN NJ; cert. student group adviser Kean U., 00. HIV and AIDS instr. NJ Dept. Criminal Justice, Police Tng. Commn., NJ; med. supr. NJ Tng. Sch. for Boys, Jamesburg; head nurse, group advisor Kean U., Union; pastor Mission of Faith Ministry, Neptune. Pres. Euphrates Project, Neptune, NJ; developer workshop on non-violence Tchg. Non-Violence: Begin in Infancy, 1996. Organizer: first gospel program for cable TV in Monmouth County. Active Neighborhood Leadership Initiative Cmty. Found. of NJ, Morristown, 2002. Recipient plaque, Harde Hank Cable, 1984, Letter of Accomodation, NJ Tng. Sch., 1990. Mem.: Nat. Coun. Netro Women. Avocation: bird watching. Home: PO Box 653 Neptune NJ 07753

MANUEL, VIVIAN, public relations executive; b. Queens County, N.Y., May 6, 1941; d. George Thomas and Vivian (Anderson) M. BA, Wells Coll., 1963; MA, U. Wyo., Laramie, 1965. Mgmt. analyst Dept. Navy, 1966-68; account supr. GE Co., N.Y.C., 1968-72, corp. rep. bus. and fin., 1972-76; dir. corp. comm. Std. Brands Co., 1976-78; pvt. cons., 1978-80; pres. V M Comm. Inc., 1980-97; pub. info. officer Mont. Dept. Commerce, Helena, 1997—. Mem. com. Girls Club N.Y., 1983—84; mem. adv. bd. Glenholme Sch., 1991—92; mem. audit com.-disaster relief agys. and youth orgns. United Way Mont., 1998—; bd. dirs. Am. Lung Assn. of No. Rockies, 1999—2002; trustee Wells Coll., 1983—90. Mem. AAUW, N.Y. Women in Comms. (bd. v.p. 1983-85, chair Matrix awards 1985), Women Execs. in Pub. Rels. (bd. dirs. 1985-88), Women's Econ. Roundtable. Address: 1400 Flowerree St Helena MT 59601-6024 Office: 301 S Park Ave Helena MT 59601-4503 E-mail: vmanuel@state.mt.us.

MANUELL, LYNN MARIE, booking agent, singer, actress; b. Grand Rapids, Mich., Apr. 17, 1961; d. Richard James and Barbara Ann (Reeves) M. AA, Prairie State Coll., Chicago Heights, Ill., 1983; BA with honors, Columbia Coll., Chgo., 1985; postgrad., Am. Acad. Dramatic Arts, N.Y.C., 1985-86, Wavendon Allmusic Plan, U.K., 1987-89. Singer, actress Ill. Theatre Ctr., Park Forest, 1975-83; pub. rels. photographer Columbia Coll., Chgo., 1983-84, Connie Zonka and Assocs., Chgo., 1984; promotional sales agt. Cliff Steward & Assocs., N.Y.C., 1985; mgr. Raymond Annlisa Promotional, 1985; office coord., agt. Nat. Shakespeare Co., 1985-86; singer Whaler/Madison Towers, 1986; spl. events coord. Cultural Coun. Found., 1986-89; exec. asst./booking NAMCO Booking, 1990-91; assoc. in booking devel. Shofer/Gold/Lamero Ltd., 1991—. Coord. Minority Arts Mgmt., N.Y.C., 1987; events coord. Soho Booking, N.Y.C., 1987; assoc. Gatchell & Neufeld Ltd., N.Y.C., 1990; exec. dir. Tour de Force Internat., Inc., 1992, AIS Prodns. assoc. and co. mgr., 1994; internat. sales assoc. Bresner Mgmt., Inc., 1996; co. mgr. Donald Byrd Dance Found., 1999, (broadway show) Grease!, 2000—, Smokey Joe's Cafe, 2001; founder Internat. Prodn. Mgmt. Author: (poetry) Unicorns and Golden Traces, 1981, Standing Tall--the journals, emails, and creative writings since 9/11; contbr. articles to profl. jours.; performer in Remember Me from Holy Redeemer High at Don't Tell Mama's, N.Y.C.; recorded CD: Return to Love, 1999; in over 150 theatrical prodns.; performs for Am. Theatre Wing is lyricist on music recorded and performed by singers of note. Friend, Community Literacy Rsch. Project, N.Y.C., 1986-87; polit. worker NOW, Chgo., 1978-80. Mem. Nat. Orgn. Female Execs., Theatre Devel. Fund, Am. Friends of Royal Shakespeare Co., Dickens Fellowship of N.Y. Avocations: photography, writing poetry, antiques, cabaret theatre. Home and Office: 12 Dongan Pl Apt 201 New York NY 10040-1592 E-mail: lynn.manuell@gte.net.

MANUS, NANCY MANNING, writer, former social services administrator, medical social services director; b. Jesup, Ga., Jan. 13, 1945; d. Charlie Dalton and Zellie Adell (Flowers) Manning; children: Andrew Ceaphus, Kevin Charles, Thomas Lindsey. BA in Journalism, U. Ga., 1967. Ga. state merit sys. cert. caseworker, 1968, level II, 1969, eligibility supr., 1970. Case worker I Wayne County Dept. Family and Children Svcs., Jesup, 1968-69; case worker II Coffee County Dept. Family and Children Svcs., Douglas, Ga., 1969-70, eligibility supr., 1970-73; freelance writer Odum, Ga., 1975-80; dir. med. social svcs. Wayne Meml. Hosp., Jesup, 1981-98. Com. mem. Edn./Cons. Social Work Found. of Ga. Hosp. Assn., 1989-98. Vol. hosp. blood drive coord. Red Cross Low Country Chpt., Hinesville, Ga., 1982-87; mem. Adv. Coun. Health and Edn., Wayne County, Ga., 1985-98; assisted living cons. in cmty., 1992—. Recipient Recognition for Svc. award Red Cross Low Country Chpt., Hinesville, 1985. Mem. NOW, Ga. Soc. Social Workers in Health Care of Ga. Hosp. Assn. (dist. chmn. S.E. dist. 1996-97, sec. 1996-97, Com. Achievement award 1996, cert. appreciation service, 1997-98). Democrat. Avocations: Do-It-Yourself building projects, gardening, exploring nature, dancing, reading. Home: 3790 Beards Bluff Rd Odum GA 31555-8117

MANUTA, DAVID MARK, research chemist, consultant; b. Bklyn., June 10, 1957; s. Gerald and Vivian Bernice (Chartoff) M.; m. Ruth Pauline Krog, Mar. 27, 1988 (dec. Dec. 1993). BS in Chemistry, SUNY, Oneonta, 1979; PhD in Chemistry, SUNY, Binghamton, 1985. Lab. tech. Sci. Process & Rsch., Somerset, N.J., 1980-81; from tchg. asst. to postdoctoral fellow SUNY, Binghamton, 1981-86; asst. prof. Upper Iowa U., Fayette, 1986-88; asst. prof. II Shawnee State U., Portsmouth, Ohio, 1989-90; rsch. staff U.S. Enrichment Corp., Piketon, 1990-2000; founder Manuta Chem. Consulting Inc., 1998. Tchr. Christ the King Regional H.S., N.Y.C., 1986; instr. Stanley Kaplan Exam. Prep. Svcs., Garden City, N.Y., 1986; cons. City of Portsmouth, 1989; mem. strategic planning com. Ohio Acad. Sci., 1996. Sec. Big Bros./Big Sisters of South Ctrl. Ohio, 1996; pres. Waverly Heights Crime Watch, 1995; treas. Pike County Humane Soc., Ohio, 1997; fin. chair Portsmouth employees chpt. Nat. Mgmt. Assn., 1997. With USN, 1978-79. IBM Corp. grad. fellow, 1984-85. Fellow: Am. Inst. Chemistry; mem.: ASTM, AAAS, Internat. Assn. Arson Investigators, Nat. Fire Protection Assn., Nat. Forensic Ctr., Assn. Consulting Chemists Chem. Engrs., Am. Chem. Soc. Avocations: chess, reading, running, bicycling, traveling. Home: 431 Gordon Ave Waverly OH 45690-1208 Fax: 740-947-1565. E-mail: dmanuta@dmanuta.com., dmanuta@zoomnet.net., mc2@dmanuta.com.

MANVILLE, STEWART ROEBLING, archivist; b. White Plains, N.Y., Jan. 15, 1927; s. Leo and Margaret (Roebling) Manville; m. Ella V. Grainger, Jan. 19, 1972 (dec.). *Late wife had previously been spouse to composer-pianist Percy Grainger, and pursued a career of her own as an artist, working with paintings and tiles.* Student, U. Wyo., 1944-46; BS, Columbia U., 1962. Various office positions, N.Y.C., 1947-51, 56-58; asst. stage dir. several European opera houses, 1951-55; editor Jas. T. White & Co., N.Y.C., 1959-63; archivist, curator Percy Grainger Library, White Plains, 1963—. Author: (book) The Manville/Manvel Families in America; contbr. artlcs and revs. on music to mags. and newspapers. Mem.: SAR, St. Nicholas Soc. N.Y., Westchester Trails Assn. (pres. 2001—), Brit. Music Soc., Société des Antiquaires de Picardie, Victorian Soc. Am. (past. dir. N.Y. chpt.), Nat. Trust Hist. Preservation. Mem. Soc. Of Friends. Office: 7 Cromwell Pl White Plains NY 10601-5005

MANY, ROBERT TODD, telecommunications executive; b. Oneonta, N.Y., Dec. 3, 1958; s. Wesley Allen and Margaret Louise (Ames) M.; m. Marina Ann Teglia, June 20, 1982; children: Michael Wesley, Julie Ann, Kristine Marie. BS, No. Ill. U., 1980, MBA, 1990. Tchr. Riverside-Brookfield High Sch., Riverside, Ill., 1980-84; sr. account mgr. sales NCR Corp., Dayton, Ohio, 1984-86; sales mgmt. MCI, Chgo., 1986-90; dir. sales Teradyne, 1990-93, nat. sales mgr., 1994-95, dir. N.Am. sales, 1995-96; bus. devel. dir. Accenture, 1996-2000, alliance dir., 2000—. Mem. Am. Mgmt. Assn., Beta Gamma Sigma. Avocations: sports, books, travel, wine, cooking. Home: 483 Quail Dr Naperville IL 60565-4159

MANYAM, BALA VENKATESHA, healthcare administrator, neurology educator; b. Bangalore, India, Oct. 15, 1942; came to U.S., 1972; d. Kolar Venktesha and Swarnam (Venktesha) Iyer; m. Rani Manyam; 1 child, Shaila. MB, BS, Bangalore Med. Coll., 1967. Diplomate Am. Bd. of Psychiatry and Neurology. With Thomas Jefferson U., Phila., 1975-83, 83-84, asst. prof. pharmacology, 1981-83, assoc. prof. pharmacology, 1983-84; staff neurologist VA Med. Ctr., Wilmington, Del., 1975-80, asst. chief neurology, 1982-84; assoc. prof. neurology Sch. of Medicine So. Ill. U., Springfield, 1984-92, prof., 1992—, dir. neurology residency program, 1993—. Founding dir. Movement Disorders Clinic, Wilmington, 1977-84, Parkinson's Disease & Movement Disorders Clinic, Springfield, 1984—. Contbr. numerous articles to profl. jours. Adviser organizing com. Parkinson's Disease Support Group of Ctrl. Ill., Springfield, 1987—. Grantee VA, 1978-83, Merck, Sharp & Dohme Rsch. Labs., 1988-89, NIH, 1993-94, DuPont, 1993-95, PACT/Zander, 1993-96, Allergan, 1993-94. Fellow Am. Acad. Neurology; mem. World Fedn. Neurology (rsch. com.), Am. Neurologic Assn., Am. Soc. Pharmacology and Exptl. Therapeutics. Hindu. Avocations: creative writing, history of medicine, collecting old coins and stamps, photography. Office: So Ill U Sch Medicine PO Box 19230 Springfield IL 62794-9230

MANZ, AUGUST FREDERICK, welding technology and safety consultant; b. Newark, Mar. 7, 1929; BSEE, N.J. Inst. Tech., 1957, MSEE, 1959. Devel. engr. Linde div. Union Carbide, Newark, 1957-64, project engr., 1964-69, spl. project engr., 1969-73, project scientist Tarrytown, N.Y., 1973-76, assoc. mgr. regulations tech. Danbury, Conn., 1976-82, mgr. regulations tech., 1982-85, sr. engr. Somerset, N.J., 1985-86; pres. A.F. Manz Assocs., Union, 1986—. Chmn. Z49.1 safety in welding and cutting, ANSI, N.Y.C.; adj. prof. Kean Coll., Union, N.J. Author: Power Supply Handbook, 1973, Welding Processes and Practices, 1988; co-author/contbr. 18 books on welding; patentee in field of welding. With USAF, 1947-54. Named Inventors of Yr., N.J. Inventors Hall of Fame, 1992. Fellow Am. Welding Soc. (chmn. labeling and safe practices, Safety & Health award, 1996, Airco Welding award 1991, William Irrgang award 1990, Nat. Meritorious award 1988, Plummer Meml. Ednl. Lectr. 1974); mem. Nat. Welding Supply Assn., The Authors Guild, Edison Soc. of N.J. Avocations: welding history, stamps. Office: 470 Whitewood Rd Union NJ 07083-8218

MANZ, CALVIN KIM, technology sector entrepreneur; b. Regina, Can., May 31, 1953; married, July 5, 1980. CEO, pres. Horizon, Inc., Calgary, Alta., Can., 1978-82, Interalia, Inc., Calgary, 1982-87, Manz Devels. Inc., Calgary, 1985—; dir. Telebackup Sys. Inc., 1997-99; CEO, pres. Odyssey Fin. Inc., 1997—; dir. Internat. Properties Group Ltd., 1997—; chmn. J-Commerce, 1999—; dir., founder LAUNCHworks Inc., 1999—. Founder, dir. MCK Comm., Inc., Boston; bd. dirs. Scyther Corp., Investorplus.com. Avocation: golf. Office: Manz Devels Inc Ste 30 Box 1 RR # 12 Calgary AB Canada T3E 6W3 Fax: 403-242-3670.

MANZ, CHARLES C. management educator; Nirenberg prof. bus. leadership U. Mass., Amherst, 1997—. Author: The Art of Self-Leadership: Strategies for Personal Effectiveness in Your Life and Work, 1983, Mastering Self-Leadership: Empowering Yourself for Personal Excellence, 1992, 2d edit., 1999; co-author: Superleadership, 1990, Business Without Bosses: How Self-Managing Teams are Building High-Performance Companies, 1993, Company of Heroes: Unleashing the Power of Self-Leadership, 1996, For Team Members Only, 1997, The Leadership Wisdom of Jesus: Practical Lessons for Today, 1998, Teamwork and Group Dynamics, 1999, The Wisdom of Solomon at Work: Ancient Virtues for Living and Leading Today, 2001, The New Super Leadership: Leading Others to Lead Themselves, 2001, The Power of Failure: 27 Ways to Turn Life's Setbacks Into Success, 2002. Office: U Mass Sch of Mgmt Amherst MA 01003

MANZ, JOHANNES JAKOB, Swiss diplomat; b. Zurich, Switzerland, Dec. 15, 1938; s. Jakob J. and Margaret (Ruegg) M.; m. Marie-Antoinette Kunz, May 26, 1966; children: Alexander Cyril, Isabel Carmela. Student, Oreg. State U., 1958-59; LLD, U. Zurich, 1969. Sec. Mission of Switzerland, N.Y.C., 1971-75; counselor Swiss Embassy, Vienna, Austria, 1975-81; min., dep. head mission Mission of Switzerland, Geneva, 1981-84; amb., chief protocol Swiss Confedn., Bern, 1984-88; amb., dir. adminstrn. and pers. Swiss Dept. for Fgn. Affairs, 1988-91; under sec. gen., spl. rep. to sec. gen. for Western Sahara, UN, N.Y.C., 1990-91; amb., head of mission, permanent observer to UN, Mission of Switzerland, 1992-97; amb. to Japan, Swiss Embassy, Tokyo, 1997—. Contbg. author: Manual of Swiss Foreign Policy, 1991. Pres. Platform for Young Citizens, Zollikon, Switzerland, 1967-68. Mem. Delta Upsilon (hon. Oreg. State U. chpt.). Avocations: cross-country skiing, golf, swimming, classical music. Address: Embassy of Switzerland 5-9-12 Minami Azabu Minato-ku Tokyo 106-8589 Japan

MANZELLA, JOHN P. infectious disease physician; b. Buffalo, Dec. 23, 1948; BA in Biology, Canisius Coll., 1970; MD, SUNY, Buffalo, 1974. Diplomate Am. Bd. Internal Medicine, Am. Bd. Infectious Diseases, Nat. Bd. Med. Examiners. Intern U. N.C., Chapel Hill, 1974-75, resident, 1975-77; fellow in infectious disease U. Rochester Sch. Medicine and Dentistry, 1977-79; mem. staff York (Pa.) Hosp., 1979—; cons. Meml. Hosp. York, 1979—, Healthsouth of York, 1983—, VA Hosp. Balt., 1980-89; clin. assoc. prof. medicine Pa. State U. Coll. Medicine, 1996—; clin. assoc. medicine U. Md. Sch. Medicine, 1979—. Reviewer Am. Jour. Diseases of Children, 1979-82, Annals Internal Medicine, 1996—; mem. editl. bd. Family Practice Survey, 1983-84; chmn. infectiou control. com. Healthsouth of York, 1983—; mem. steering com. on AIDS Hosp. Adminstrn. Pa., 1985-89; bd. dirs. York Apothecary; presenter, lectr. in field. Contbr. numerous articles to profl. jours., chpts. to books. Fellow ACP, Infectious Diseases Soc. Am.; mem. AAAS, AMA, Am. Soc. Microbiology, Am. Fedn. Clin. Rsch., Pa. Med. Assn. (interspecialty rep. 1995-96), Pa. Soc. Infectious Diseases (counsellor 1992—, York Med. Soc., Alpha Omega Alpha. Office: York Hosp Divsn Infectious Diseases Kettlerman Bldg 4th Fl 1001 S George St York PA 17403-3676 E-mail: jmanzella@wellspan.org.

MANZITTO, ARTHUR SEBASTIAN, nursing and hospital administrator; b. Omaha, Jan. 30, 1943; s. Sebastian John and Lela Mae (Hike) M.; m. Sara Esther Rovetto, Dec. 31, 1962 (div. July 1969); 1 child, Kevin Dale. BSN, U. N.Mex., 1973; M of Healthcare Adminstrn., Chapman U., 1989. Cert. profl. in healthcare quality., C.P.H.Q. Commd. ensign USN, 1962, advanced through grades to lt. comdr., 1983; nurse educator St. Joseph Hosp., Albuquerque, 1983-85; asst. adminstr. West Mesa Healthcare Ctr., 1985-86; night nursing supr. Carrie Tingley Hosp., 1986-89; adminstr. Ft. Bayard (N.Mex.) Healthcare Ctr., 1989-91; owner, CEO Ivory Healthcare Mgmt. Sys., Albuquerque, 1991-93; coord. quality programs U. N.Mex./Carrie Tingley Hosp., 1993-2000; dir. nursing Turquoise Lodge, 2000—02; ret., 2002. Creator edn. programs physician orientation to navy medicine, 1983. Mem. N.Mex. Healthcare Quality Assn. (pres. 1998-00). Democrat. Roman Catholic. Avocations: model railroading, pianist, rose enthusiast, arts and crafts. Home: Apt 315 1111 Cardenas Dr SE Albuquerque NM 87108-1544 E-mail: amanzito1@juno.com.

MANZO, EDWARD DAVID, patent lawyer; b. N.Y.C., Nov. 23, 1950; s. Edward Joseph and Elvira Helen (Melone) M.; m. Fern Rita Siegel, Oct. 30, 1978 (div. 1984); 1 child, Justin Edward; m. Margaret Ruth Johnson, Oct. 11, 1985; children: Hunter Roy, Kira Nicole. BS in Physics, Poly. Inst. Bklyn., 1972; JD cum laude, SUNY, Buffalo, 1975. Bar: N.Y. 1976, Ill. 1979, U.S. Patent and Trademark Office 1976, U.S. Ct. Appeals (fed. cir.) 1982, U.S. Supreme Ct. 1982. Assoc. Darby & Darby, P.C., N.Y.C., 1975-77; group patent counsel Schlumberger Ltd., 1977-79; ptnr. Cook, Wetzel & Egan, Chgo., 1979-85, 88-90, Jenner & Block, 1985-88; sr. ptnr. Cook McFarron & Manzo, Ltd., Chgo., 1990-99; sr. ptnr., exec. v.p., treas., CFO Cook, Alex, McFarron, Manzo, Cummings & Mehler, Ltd., 1999—. Instr. DePaul U., Chgo., 1989-91. Author (with others): Intellectual Property Law in Illinois, 1988; contbr. articles to profl. jours. Bd. dirs. Concertante di Chgo., 1997—; grantor Edward Manzo Patent Law scholarship DePaul Law Sch., 2001—. Jaeckle Fleishman grantee, 1973. Mem. Am. Intellectual Property Law Assn., Intellectual Property Law Assn. Chgo., Stradivari Soc., Sicilian Am. Cultural Assn. (treas. 1996-98, v.p. 1998-99, pres. 2000—). Avocations: classical piano and guitar, tennis, bridge. Office: Cook Alex McFarron Manzo Cummings & Mehler Ltd 200 W Adams St Ste 2850 Chicago IL 60606-5206 E-mail: emanzo@cammcm.com.

MANZULLO, DONALD A, congressman, lawyer; b. Rockford, Ill., 1944; s. Frank A. Sr. and Catherine M.; m. Freda Teslik; children: Neil, Noel, Katie. BA in Polit. Sci./Internat. Rels., American U., 1967; JD, Marquette U. Law Sch. Atty., 1970—; mem. U.S. Congress from 16th Ill. Dist., 1993—. Mem. House Com. on Internat. Rels., subcom. internat. econ. policy and trade, subcom. on Asia and the Pacific, House Com. on small bus., chmn. on subcom. on tax, fin. and exports, Banking Com. and its capital markets, securities and govt.-sponsored enterprises subcom. Mem. No. Ill. Alliance for Arts, Friends of Severson Dells, Citizens Against Govt. Waste, Rep. Nat. Com. Recipient George Washington honor medal for excellence in pub. comm. Freedoms Found., Valley Forge, Pa., 1991. Mem. ABA, Ill. Bar Assn., Ogle County Bar Assn. (pres. 1971, 73), Nat. Legal Found., Acad. Polit. Sci., Ill. Press Assn., Ill. C. of C., Oregon City C. of C., Nat. Land Inst., Nat. Fedn. Ind. Bus., Ogle County Hist. Soc., Aircraft Owners and Pilots Assn., Ogle County Pilots Assn., Ill. Farm Bur., Ogle County Farm Bur. Office: US Ho of Reps 409 Cannon Bldg Ofcbld Washington DC 20515-1316*

MAPEL, WILLIAM MARLEN RAINES, retired banking executive; b. Maryville, Mo., Sept. 17, 1931; s. William and Evelyn (Raines) M.; m. Gail Manchee, June 21, 1958; children: Daniel B., Susan L., Stephen W. BA, Yale U., 1953. Indsl. relations asst. Union Carbide Corp., N.Y.C., 1953-57; with Citibank (N.A.), 1957-88, asst. cashier, 1959-62, asst. v.p., 1962-64, v.p., 1964-69, sr. v.p., 1969-88. Bd. dirs. Brundage, Story & Rose Investment Trust, Churchill Capital Ptnrs., Galey & Lord, Atlantic Salmon Fedn., Que.-Labrador Found. Mem. U.S. Srs. Golf Assn., Woodway Country Club, Anglers Club, Pine Valley Golf Club, Wolf's Head, Delta Kappa Epsilon. Home: 18 Stephanie Ln Darien CT 06820-2723

MAPES, GLYNN DEMPSEY, newspaper editor; b. N.Y.C., July 15, 1939; s. John George and Dorothy (Glynn) M.; m. Elizabeth Adlum, Apr. 13, 1963; children— Timothy Glynn, Susannah Glynn. BA, Williams Coll., 1961. Reporter Wall St. Jour., San Francisco, 1965-67, bur. chief Phila., 1967-70, fgn. editor N.Y.C., 1970-71, bur. chief, 1971-75, Page One editor, 1975-88, Reports editor, 1988-89, bur. chief London, 1989-93, money and investing editor N.Y.C., 1993-99, asst. mgn. editor, 1999—. Served to lt. (j.g.) USN, 1961-65. Mem.: Bronx Opera Chorus, London Concert Choir Club, Collegiate Chorale Club. Democrat. Home: 37 W 12th St Apt 2H New York NY 10011-8503 Office: Wall St Jour 200 Liberty St New York NY 10281-1003 E-mail: gmapes@pipeline.com.

MAPES, JEFFREY ROBERT, journalist; b. San Francisco, Nov. 21, 1954; s. James Robert and Phyllis June (Bloemker) M.; m. Karen Jane Minkel, Aug. 20, 1978; children: Katharine, James. BA, San Jose State U., 1976. Reporter Napa (Calif.) Register, 1976-79; Washington corr. Scripps League Newspapers, 1979-83; reporter The Oregonian, Portland, 1984-87, chief polit. reporter, 1987—. Office: The Oregonian 1320 SW Broadway Portland OR 97201-3499

MAPLE, JAMES ALAN, consulting engineer, civil engineer; b. Rushville, Ind., Apr. 22, 1937; s. William Kenneth and Nellie Marie (Cameron) M.; m. Betty Jean Allman, Feb. 16, 1963; children: Melissa Alayn Maple Eitel, Maura Marie. . BSCE, Purdue U., 1960, MSCE, 1965, PhD, 1969. Registered profl. engr. Alaska, Texas, Indiana. Maintenance engineering officer U.S. Navy, Crane, Ind., 1960-63; constrn. engr. Ind. Dept. Transp., Crawfordsville, 1964; refining engring. advisor Humble Oil Co. (Exxon), Baytown, Tex., 1969-73, 78-81, 83-89, 1992; pipeline engring. advisor Ayeska Pipeline, Anchorage, 1973-78, 81-82, 89-92; engring. cons. J.A. Maple and Assocs., Baytown, Tex., 1992—. Adv. coun. Sch. of Civil Engring., Purdue U., 1995-2001. Bd. dirs. Chinquapin Prep Sch., Highlands, Tex., 1995—, Baytown Family YMCA, 1989-2000; mem. sch. bd. Goose Creek Sch. Dist., Baytown, 1989. Lt. jg. U.S. Navy, 1960-63. Mem. AAAS, ASCE, ASME, Am. Concrete Inst., Ind. Acad. of Sci., Internat. Soc. Offshore and Polar Engrs., Sigma Xi, Tau Beta Pi, Chi Epsilon (chpt. hon. mem. 1996). Achievements include 3 Canadian and 2 U.S. patents for pipeline supports: U.S. patent for pipeline failure analysis. Retired U.S. Naval Reserve with rank of Comdr., 1988. Office: JA Maple Assocs 3405 Winter Ln Baytown TX 77521-2616

MAPLE, MARILYN JEAN, educational media coordinator; b. Turtle Creek, Pa., Jan. 16, 1931; d. Harry Chester and Agnes (Dobbie) Kelley; 1 child, Sandra Maple. BA, U. Fla., 1972, MA, 1975, PhD, 1985. Journalist various newspaper including Mountain Eagle, Jasper, Ala., Boise (Idaho) Statesman, Daytona Beach (Fla.) Jour., Lorain (Ohio) Jour.; account exec. Frederides & Co., N.Y.C.; prodr. hist. films Fla. State Mus., Gainesville, 1967-69; writer, dir., prodr. med. and sci. films and TV prodns. for 6 medically related colls. U. Fla., 1969—. Pres. Media Modes, Inc., Gainesville. Author: On the Wings of a Butterfly; columnist Health Care Edn. mag.; contbr. Fla. Hist. Quar. Recipient Blakslee award, 1969, spl. award, 1979; Monsour lectr., 1979. Mem. Health Edn. Media Assn. (bd. dirs., awards 1977, 79), Phi Delta Kappa, Kappa Tau Alpha. Home: 1927 NW 7th Ln Gainesville FL 32603-1103 Office: U Fla PO Box 16J Gainesville FL 32602-0016 E-mail: mmaple@atlantic.net.

MAPLE, OPAL LUCILLE, school psychologist; b. Canton, Ill., Nov. 15, 1935; d. Dwight Willard and Eileen Beatrice (Cadwalader) Beaty; m. Gilbert Roy Maple, June 30, 1967 (dec. 1985). BA, Wheaton (Ill.) Coll., 1958; MS, We. Ill. U., 1962. Cert. sch. psychologist, Ill. Tchr. Community Dist. #5, Cuba, Ill., 1958-60, Community Dist. #66, Canton, 1960-61; asst. dean women Moody Bible Inst., Chgo., 1961-64; sch. psychologist intern Chgo. Pub. Schs., 1964-65; sch. psychologist Peoria (Ill.) pub. schs., 1965-69, Waukegan (Ill.) pub. schs., 1969-81, Knox-Warren Spl. Edn., Galesburg, Ill., 1986-96, ret., 1996. Co-author pre-sch. test, 1975. Deaconess, treas. Antioch Evang. Free Ch., 1971-81; deaconess, fin. sec. Bethel Bapt. Ch., Galesburg, 1982-94. Mem. Cen. Ill. Sch. Psychologists Assn. (pres. 1967-68), Ill. Psychol. Assn. (sec. 1977-79), DAR, Knox County Genealogical Soc., Ill. Sch. Psychologists Assn. Republican. Baptist. Avocations: genealogical research, travel.

MAPLES, JIMMIE KAY, mechanical engineer; b. Berryville, Ark., Jan. 11, 1940; s. William Floyd and Edith (Bowman) M.; m. Beverly Florence Hadden, June 12, 1965 (div. Dec. 1968); children: Myrtle Venita, Beverly Sue; m. Sharon Gay Jennings Stewart (div. June 1974). BSME, U. Ark., 1962; MSRP, S.W. Mo. State U., 1991. Registered profl. engr., Mo., Ala., Ga., W.Va., Ark. Assoc. engr. Lockheed Aircraft Service Co., Ontario, Calif., 1962-63; design engr. McDonnell Aircraft Co., St. Louis, 1965-68; bookkeeper, salesman, co-owner Glen Isle Shoes, Springfield, Mo., 1969-72; mech. engr. Warren and Goodin, Inc., 1972-77; engr. systems and equipment Piper Aircraft Corp., Lakeland, Fla., 1977-81; sr. facility engr. Zenith Electronics Corp., Springfield, 1981-88; with Boone Internat. Corrugated Svcs., Inc., Waco, Tex., 1988-89; cons., author Maples Enterprizes, Springfield, 1989—; v.p. Corrugated Mech. Svcs. Inc., Nixa, Mo., 1990-95, Heartland Electronics Corp., 1995-97; engr. Godwin & Assocs., 1997—; treas. Mohawk Quality Remodeling Inc., 2000—. Mem. Boone County Hist., Harrison, Ark., Carroll County Hist. and Geol., Berryville, Ozark Geol., Springfield, The Air Force Hist. Found., White River Valley Hist. Soc. Served with U.S. Army, 1963-65. Mem. Air Force Assn., Am. Aviation Hist. Soc., Nat. Rifle Assn., Nat. Geog. Soc., The Rich Family Assn., The Maples Family News, U. Ark. Alumni Assn., Frontiersmen Camping Fraternity (Royal Rangers Daniel Boone chpt.), Am. Soc. Programmetric and remote Sensing. Democrat. Mem. Assembly of God. Avocations: stamp collecting, genealogy, computers. Home: 2545 W Swallow St Springfield MO 65810-3623 Office: Maples Enterprizes 2545 W Swallow St Springfield MO 65810-3623 also: Godwin & Assocs 1200 E Woodhurst Bldg P Springfield MO 65804 E-mail: godwinae@aol.com., jkmtree@aol.com.

MAPLES, KAREN LORRAINE, personnel official; b. Norfolk, Va., July 21, 1954; d. James Wilson and Helen (Stevens) M.; B.B.A., Coll. of William and Mary, 1976, M.B.A., 1978. Staff assoc. C&P Telephone Co., Arlington, Va., 1978, staff supr., Washington, 1979-81, supr., 1981-83, staff mgr., 1983— , cons. community action team, Arlington, 1985—, com. mem. Greater Washington Bd. Trade: Regulatory Adv. Com., 1983—, com. mem. Arlington C. of C. (legi. com. 1986—), com. mem. Teenage Pregnancy Prevention Panel, Washington, D.C., 1986—; contbr. newletter column 1985-86. Mem. Human Resource Planning Soc., 1987. Avocations: travel, music, tennis.

MAPLESDEN, CAROL HARPER, marital and family therapist, music educator; b. Phila., Aug. 27, 1947; d. Emmitt Dewain and Helen Esther (Davison) Harper; m. James Paul Maplesden, May 27, 1967; children: Andrew James, Elizabeth Elvira. BA, Holy Family Coll., Phila., 1979; MA, La Salle U., Phila., 1984. Cert. counselor Nat. Bd. Cert. Counselors, lic. profl. counselor of mental health Del., Pa. Child, youth and family therapist People Acting To Help (PATH), Phila., 1983-86, Benjamin Rush Cmty. Mental Health, Phila., 1987-88; clin. dir. N.E. Treatment, 1988-89; outpatient supr. Interact Com. Mental Health, 1989; program supr. Cath. Charities Christopher House, Trenton, N.J., 1989-90; dir. Carden Family Inst., Phila., 1984—, instr. keyboard, organist, vocal performer Carden music div., 1993—; clinician Family Svc. Assn. Bucks County, 2000—. Seminar lectr. in Phila. area. Author: (piano course and audio tape) Young Beginnings Piano Course, Part I, 1993. Mem.: ACA, Internat. Assn. Marriage and Family Counselors, Daus. Union Vets. Civil War (Pa. state pres. 2001—). Republican. Methodist. Avocations: history studies, genealogy, crafts. Home: PO Box 16096 Philadelphia PA 19114-0096

MAPOTHER, DILLON EDWARD, physicist, university official; b. Louisville, Aug. 22, 1921; s. Dillon Edward and Edith (Rubel) M.; m. Elizabeth Beck, June 29, 1946; children: Ellen, Susan, Anne. BS in Mech. Engring, U. Louisville, 1943; D.Sc. in Physics, Carnegie-Mellon U., 1949. Engr. Westinghouse Research Labs., East Pittsburgh, Pa., 1943-46; instr. Carnegie Inst. Tech., Pitts., 1946; mem. faculty U. Ill., Urbana, 1949-94, prof. physics, 1959-94, dir. acad. computing services, 1971-76, assoc. vice chancellor for research, 1976-94, acting dean grad. coll., vice chancellor research, 1977-78, assoc. dean grad. coll., 1979-94, assoc. vice chancellor rsch. emeritus, 1995—, assoc. dean emertus grad. coll., prof. emeritus physics, 1995—. Cons. in field. DuPont fellow, 1947-49; Alfred P. Sloan fellow, 1958-61; Guggenheim fellow, 1960-61 Fellow Am. Phys. Soc.; mem. AAAS, Assn. Univ. Tech. Mgrs., Am. Assn. Physics Tchrs., Sigma Xi. Achievements include research on ionic mobility in alkali halides, thermodynamic properties of superconductors, calorimetric study of critical points, administration of university research, commercialization of academic research technology. Home: 1013 Ross Dr Champaign IL 61821-6631 Office: U Ill Physics Dept Loomis Lab 1110 W Green St Urbana IL 61801-9013 E-mail: mapother@staff.uiuc.edu.

MAPOTHER, TOM CRUISE See CRUISE, TOM

MAPP, ALF JOHNSON, JR. writer, historian; b. Portsmouth, Va., Feb. 17; s. Alf Johnson and Lorraine (Carney) M.; m. Hartley Lockhart, Mar. 28, 1953; 1 son, Alf Johnson III; m. Ramona Hartley Hamby, Aug. 1, 1971. *A 13-th generation Virginian in paternal descent and 12th in maternal, Mapp is the son of Alf Johnson Mapp, Sr., internationally honored public educator. He is a direct descendant of Alfred the Great and Charlemagne. Ancestors include more than 60 persons with separate sketches in the Encyclopedia Britannica.* AA, Coll. William and Mary, 1945, AB summa cum laude, 1961. Editorial writer Portsmouth Star, 1945-46, assoc. editor, 1946-48, editorial chief, 1948-54; news editor, editorial writer Virginian-Pilot, Norfolk, 1954-58; free-lance writer, 1958—; lectr. Old Dominion U., 1961-62, instr., 1962-67, asst. prof. English and history, 1967-73, asso prof. English, journalism, creative writing, history, 1973-79, prof., 1979-82, eminent prof., 1982-89, eminent scholar, 1989-92, eminent scholar emeritus, 1992—, Louis I. Jaffe prof. English, 1990-92; Louis I. Jaffe prof. emeritus, 1992—. Radio commentator WSAP, Portsmouth, Va., 1947-48; profl. lectr., 1984—; frequent analyst or guest on radio and TV including individual stas. and Universal Studio and BBC radio networks, CBS-TV, 1985—, C-SPAN, 1998—, PBS, 2001, NPR, 2001, CNN, 2001—; mem. Nat. Jefferson-Hemings Scholars commn., 2001-2002. *Mapp's writings have circulated around the world in nine languages. The Worldmark Encyclopedia of the States lists him as one of the two most important historians, and one of the seven most important writers in any category, born in 20th century Virginia. One of America's leading biographers, he is one of the world's three principal living authorities on Thomas Jefferson. He is the author of internationally acclaimed works on American and British history, and is an outstanding scholar in cultural history and interdisciplinary studies. He is in demand nationally and internationally as an informative and lively speaker and interviewee. "Reared in an intellectual family with high ethical standards, enthusiasm for the arts, and a firm belief in hard work, I also had impressed on me that advantages conferred obligations. In an historic environment, I became aware of my generation's responsibility to those that had preceded it (to preserve the good that they had created) and to those who would follow (to create things that would enrich their lives). This concept, with personal ambition, imbues my professional life"* Host TV series Jamestown to Yorktown, 1975-77; author: The Virginia Experiment, 1975, 3d edit., 1987, Frock Coats and Epaulets, 1963, 5th edit., 1996, America Creates Its Own Literature, 1965, Just One Man, 1968, The Golden Dragon: Alfred the Great and His Times, 1974, 4th edit., 1990, Thomas Jefferson: A Strange Case of Mistaken Identity, 1987, 3d edit., 1989 (Book-of-Month Club feature selection 1987), Thomas Jefferson: Passionate Pilgrim, 1991, 3d edit., 1993 (Book-of-Month Club feature selection 1991), (novel) Bed of Honor, 1995, 2d edit., 2000, Three Golden Ages: Discovering the Creative Secrets of Renaissance Florence, Elizabethan England, and America's Founding, 1998; co-author: Chesapeake Bay in the Revolution, 1981, Portsmouth: A Pictorial History, 1989, Constitutionalism: Founding and Future, 1989, Constitutionalism and Human Rights, 1991, Great American Presidents, 1995; mem. editl. bd. Jamestown Found., 1967—; author lyrics for symphonic composition, world debut with Va. Symphony, 1998; author nationally distributed AP editl., 1998; contbr. to N.Y. Times, Wall St. Jour., other newspapers and mags. Mem. Portsmouth-Norfolk County Savs. Bond Com, 1948-51, Va. Com. on Libr. Devel., 1949-50; mem. publs. com. 350th Anniversary of Rep. Govt. in the Western World, 1966-69, War of Independence Commn., 1967-83; chmn. Portsmouth Revolutionary Bicentennial Com., 1968-81; chmn. awards jury Baruch award United Daus. Confederacy-Columbia U., 1976, mem., 1980; chmn. Portsmouth Mus. and Fine Arts Commn., 1983-85, Southeastern Va. Anglo-Am. Friendship Day, 1976, Bicentennial Commemoration of Cornwallis' Embarkation for Yorktown, 1981, World Premiere of Mary Rose Marine Archeol. Exhibit, 1985; mem. grant rev. com. Va. Commn. for the Arts, 1986-87; bd. dirs. Portsmouth Pub. Libr., 1948-58, v.p., 1954-56; bd. dirs. Va. Symphony, 1986-87, trustee, 1987—; mem. taxes and mandates com. City of Portsmouth, 1982-86; mem. adv. com. City Mgr. of Norfolk, 1988-94; bd. dirs. Portsmouth Area Cmty. Chest, 1948-52, Va. YMCA Youth and Govt. Found., 1950-52; mem. All-Am. cities com. for award-winning city Nat. League Municipalities, 1976; bd. advisors Ctr. Study Interactive Learning, Pasadena, Calif., 1993—; mem. steering com. Old Dominion U. Friends of the Libr., 1994-95, dir., 1995—; trustee Coun. for Am.'s First Freedom, 1994-98; chair ad hoc com. Joint Portmouth-Suffolk Libr., 1999—; dir. Va. R.R. Mus., 2000–. Named Portsmouth Young Man of Year, 1951; recipient honor medal Freedoms Found., 1951, Disting. Rsch. award Old Dominion U., 1987, Great Citizen award Hampton Roads 8 Cities, 1987, Notable Citizen award Portsmouth, Va., 1987; English award Old Dominion Coll., 1961; Troubadour, Great Tchrs. award, 1969; Outstanding Am. Educator award, 1972, 74; Nat. Bicentennial medal Am. Revolution Bicentennial Adminstrsn., 1976; medal Comité Francais du Bicentenaire de l'Independence des Etats-Unis, France, 1976; (with Ramona Mapp) Nat. Family Svc. award Family Found. Am., 1980; Laureate award Commonwealth of Va., 1981; Disting. Alumnus award Old Dominion U., 1982; Liberty Bell award Portsmouth Bar Assn., 1985; Old Dominion U. Triennial Phi Kappa Phi Scholar award, 1986, 91; History medal Nat. Soc. Daus. Am. Revolution; Portsmouth Downtown Merchants award, 1984, 85, Nat. Founders and Patriots award, 1995; Old Dominion U. Outstanding Achievement award, 1995; Gladstone Hill Friend of the Arts award (with Ramona H. Mapp), 1995, Richard Hakluyt award for Am. history, 1996; named to Order of the Crown of Charlemagne, 1993. Mem. Am. Hist. Assn., Va. Hist. Soc., Portsmouth Hist. Soc. (historiographer 1975-82, v.p. 1982-84, pres. 1985), Norfolk Hist. Soc. (dir. 1965-72), No. Neck Hist. Soc., Hist. Socs. Eastern Va. (dir. 1971—), SAR, Am. Assn. U. Profs., Authors Guild, Va. Library Assn. (legislative com. 1950-51), Poetry Soc. Va. (pres. 1974-75, adv. com. 1976—), Va. Writers Club, Assn. Preservation of Va. Antiquities, Order of Cape Henry (dir. 1970—, nat. pres. 1975-76), Jamestowne Soc. (chief historian 1975-77, internat. sec. state 1978-79), English Speaking Union (dir. 1976-77), Modern Lang. Assn., Order of First Families Va. 1607-1624 (councillor 1996-99), Nat. Historians Circle, Phi Theta Kappa, Delta Phi Omega (chpt. pres. 1961), Phi Kappa Phi. Baptist. Home: Willow Oaks 2901 Tanbark Ln Portsmouth VA 23703-4828

MAPP, EDWARD CHARLES, speech educator; b. N.Y.C., Aug. 17, 1929; s. Edward Cameron and Estelle Viola (Sampson) M.; children: Andrew, Elmer, Everett. BA, CCNY, 1953; MS, Columbia U., 1956; PhD, NYU, 1970. Tchr. Bd. Edn., N.Y.C., 1957-64; dir. libr. N.Y.C. Tech. Coll., CUNY, Bklyn., 1964-77; dean of faculty Borough of Manhattan Community Coll., CUNY, N.Y.C., 1977-81, prof. speech and communication, 1983-92; prof. emeritus, 1994—; vice chancellor City Colls. of Chgo., 1982-83. Commr. N.Y.C. Commn. on Human Rights, N.Y.C., 1987-94, vice chair, 1992-94; treas. U. Faculty Senate of CUNY, 1974-77; model, 1994—. Author: Blacks in American Films: Today and Yesterday, 1972; co-author: A Separate Cinema, 1992; editor: Puerto Rican Perspectives, 1974; compiler Books for Occupational Edn. Programs, 1971, Directory of Blacks in the Performing Arts, 1978, 2d edit., 1990; columnist Movie/TV Mktg., Tokyo, 1979-91. Bd. dirs UN Assn. of N.Y., 1975-78; mem. Bklyn. Borough Pres. Adv. Panel, 1981-84; trustee N.Y. Met. Ref. and Rsch. Agy., N.Y., 1980-82; exec. com. The Com. for Pub. Higher Edn., N.Y.C., 1978-81. Recipient Founders Day award NYU, 1970, Acad. Motion Picture Arts and Scis. award, 1996; inducted into Black Collectors Hall of Fame, 1992. Mem. Archons of Colophon (convenor 1985-86), Black Filmmakers Found., Audelco, Theatre Libr. Assn., Friends of Thirteen (bd. dirs. 2000—). Democrat. Avocations: collector, black cast film posters and other black memorabilia.

MAQUET, JACQUES JEROME PIERRE, anthropologist, writer; b. Brussels, Belgium, Aug. 4, 1919; came to U.S., 1967, naturalized, 1974; s. Jerome and Jeanne (Lemoine) M.; m. Emma de Longrée, June 17, 1946; children: Bernard, Denis; m. Gisèle Cambresier, Nov. 13, 1970. JD, U. Louvain, Belgium, 1946, D.Phil., 1948; student, Harvard, 1946-48; PhD, U. London, Eng., 1952; Dr. ès-lettres, Sorbonne, France, 1973. Field anthropologist Inst. Sci. Research in Central Africa, 1949-51; head Inst. Sci. Research in Central Africa (Social Scis. Center), 1951-57; prof. State U. of Congo, Elisabethville, 1957-60; research dir. Ecole pratique des Hautes Etudes, U. Paris, 1961-68; prof. anthropology Case Western Res. U., 1968-71; prof. UCLA, 1971-91, chmn. dept. anthropology, 1978-83, prof. emeritus anthropology, 1991—. Vis. prof. Northwestern U., 1956, Harvard, 1964, U. Montreal, 1965, U. Pitts., 1967; extraordinary prof. U. Brussels, 1963-68 Author: The Sociology of Knowledge, 1951, Aide-mémoire d'ethnologie africaine, 1954, Ruanda, 1957, (with others) Elections en Société féodale, 1957, The Premise of Inequality in Ruanda, 1961, Power and Society in Africa, 1971, Civilizations of Black Africa, 1972, Africanity, The Cultural Unity of Black Africa, 1972, Introduction to Aesthetic Anthropology, 1979, The Aesthetic Experience, 1986, L'Anthropologue et l'esthétique, 1993, La Experiencia Estética, 1999; co-editor: (with others) Dictionary of Black African Civilization, 1974. Recipient Waxweiler award Royal Acad. Belgium, 1961; First World Festival of Negro Arts award Dakar, 1966 Mem. Am. Anthrop. Assn., Internat. Assn. Buddhist Studies, Pali Text Soc., AAUP, Fedn. Am. Scientists. Address: UCLA Dept Anthropology Los Angeles CA 90095-0001 E-mail: jmaquet@ucla.edu.

MARA, JOHN LAWRENCE, retired veterinarian, consultant; b. Whitesboro, N.Y., May 17, 1924; s. William Edward and Olive Pearl (Brakefield) M.; m. Kathleen Keefe, 1946 (div. 1958); children: William, Michael, Daniel, Patrick; m. Patricia Louise Paulk, 1970 (div. 1994); children: Jennifer Lee, Kennon. DVM, Cornell U., 1951. Diplomate Am. Coll. Vet. Nutrition. Intern N.Y. State Coll. Vet. Medicine, Cornell U., Ithaca, 1951-52; assoc. veterinarian L.W. Goodman Animal Hosp., Manhasset, N.Y., 1952-55; owner, pres. Mara Animal Hosp., Huntington, 1955-79; profl. rep. Hills Pet Products, Topeka, 1979-80, mgr. profl. rels., 1980-81, dir. profl. affairs, 1981-88, dir. vet. affairs, 1988-94, sr. fellow profl. and acad. affairs, 1994-97, sr. fellow global vet. bus. devel., 1997-2000; ret., 2000. V.p. Huntington United Fund; chmn. Huntington Taxpayers Party, 1968-78, Ch. in the Garden, Garden City, N.Y., 1975-77, trustee, 1975-77; trustee, v.p. vet. divsn. Morris Animal Found. Sgt. U.S. Army, 1943-45, ETO. Recipient Disting. Svc. award We. Vet. Conf., 1988; named hon. alumnus Coll. Vet. Medicine, Wash. State U.; Jack L. Deans scholarship named in his honor Sch. Vet. Medicine U. Pa. Mem. AVMA (Pres.'s award, Jack L. Mara vet. technician program), L.I. Vet. Medicine Assn., N.Y. State Vet. Medicine Assn. (Outstanding Svc. award 2001), Am. Animal Hosp. Assn. (disting. life, Outstanding Svc. award 1996-97), Kans. Vet. Medicine Assn., Am. Coll. Vet. Nutrition (hon. diplomate). Republican. Baptist. Avocations: gardening, swimming, reading. Home: 6439 SW Castle Ln Topeka KS 66614-4392 E-mail: jmara@kscable.com

MARA, TIMOTHY GERALD, lawyer; b. Cin., July 30, 1949; s. Thomas James and Rose Marie (Sansone) M. B in Community Planning, U. Cin., 1972; JD, No. Ky. U., 1978. Bar: Ohio 1978, U.S. Dist. Ct. Cin. 1979, U.S. Ct. Appeals (6th cir.) 1983. Regional planner Ohio-Ky.-Ind. Regional Coun. of Govts., Cin., 1972-77; spl. asst. U.S. Rep. Thomas A. Luken, 1977-78; pvt. practice, 1979—. Trustee Green Twp., Hamilton County, Ohio, 1982-86. Mem. Ohio State Bar Assn., Cin. Bar Assn., Hamilton County Dem. Steering Com. Roman Catholic. Avocations: nature walks, biking. Office: 1500 Chiquita Ctr 250 E 5th St Cincinnati OH 45202-4119

MARA, VINCENT JOSEPH, college president; b. Worcester, Mass., Sept. 19, 1930; s. Edward Stephan and Mary Stephanie (Kavanaugh) M.; m. Clare Owens, Feb. 15, 1958; children: John, Kevin, Maryellen, Thomas, Clare. BS in Edn., Worcester State Coll.; EdM, U. Conn.; PhD; LLD (hon.), Framingham State Coll., 1995; LHD, Fitchburg State Coll., 1995. From asst. prof. to assoc. prof. Framingham (Mass.) State Coll., 1960-63, dir. admissions, 1963-69, acad. dean, 1969-76; acting pres. Salem (Mass.) State Coll., 1974-75; pres. Fitchburg (Mass.) State Coll., 1976-95, prof. emeritus, 1995—, pres. emeritus, 1995—. Corporator Fitchburg Savs. Bank, 1976-85; mem. Montachusett Region Pvt. Industry Coun., 1983—; dir. Safety Fund Nat. Bank. Contbr. articles to profl. jours. Trustee Notre Dame Prep. Sch., Fitchburg, 1985-86, Worcester Pub. Libr., 1967-70, pres. bd. trustees, 1970; bd. dirs Fitchburg Civic Ctr., 1977-80, Cushing Acad., 1978-80, North Ctrl. Mass. Mental Health Assn., 1979-81, United Way, 1981-87, Montachusett Region Pvt. Industry Coun., 1983-93, Thayer Symphony Orch., 1987-90, pres., 1994-95; active Mass. Commn. Edn. Telecomm., 1983-90, Fitchburg Bd. Health, 1982-93, Fitchburg Sch. Com., 1998-2002. With U.S. Army, 1953-55. Named Outstanding Young Man of Yr. Worcester C. of C., 1960; recipient Disting. Citizen award City of Fitchburg, 1989. Mem. NEA, Am. Conf. Acad. Deans, Am. Assn. State Colls. and Univs., N.Am. C. of C. (bd. dirs. 1984-91), Fitchburg C. of C. (bd. dirs. 1977-83), Fay Club, Phi Delta Kappa, Kappa Delta Pi. Democrat. Roman Catholic. Home: 242 Pearl Hill Rd Fitchburg MA 01420-2019 Office: Fitchburg State Coll 160 Pearl St Fitchburg MA 01420-2631 E-mail: vmara@fsc.edu.

MARA, WELLINGTON T. professional football team executive; b. Aug. 8, 1916; Pres. N.Y. Giants, East Rutherford, N.J., also co-chief exec. officer. Elected to Pro Football Hall of Fame, 1997. Office: NY Giants Giants Stadium East Rutherford NJ 07073 also: Nat Football League 410 Park Ave New York NY 10022-4407*

MARABELLA, DAWN MARIE, ESL educator; b. Chicago, Ill., June 9, 1969; d. Paul Joseph and Mary-Ann Marabella; m. Victor C. Chang, May 24, 2002. MA Linguistics, U. of Ill. at Chgo., Chicago, Illinois, 1994; BS Comm., Ill. State U., Normal, Illinois, 1991. English as a second lang. educator Song-A Lang. Inst., Pupyung, Korea, 1994—95, Nat. Taiwan Normal U., Taipei, Taiwan, 1995—96, Ching-Mae Girl's Sr. H.S., Taipei, Taiwan, 1995—96, Columbia Coll., Chicago, Ill., 1996—. Recipient Alpha Lamda Delta Honors Soc., 1988, Onnecion Deta Kappa Honor's Soc., 1990. Mem.: TESOL, Pub. Action to Deliver Shelter, Quill and Scroll Soc. Avocations: writing poetry, writing poetry.

MARABLE, SIDNEY THOMAS, lawyer; b. Henderson, N.C., Dec. 4, 1954; s. Nathaniel and Julia M. (Vann) M.; m. Frances J. Marable; 1 child, Marcus Latham. BA in Polit. Sci., N.C. Agrl. & Tech. State U., 1976; JD, U. N.C., 1979. Bar: N.C. 1979, Ariz. 1983, U.S. Supreme Ct. 1979. Assoc. Castro, Zipf & Rogers, Phoenix, 1983-87, ptnr., 1987-92; pvt. practice, 1992—. Mem. Civil Practice Procedure Com., Phoenix, 1994-97, Maricopa County Bench/Bar Com., Phoenix, 1994-96, Fed. Dist. Ct. Local Rules Com., Phoenix, 1995—. Bd. dirs. Ctrl. Ariz. Arthritis Found., Phoenix, 1987-88; mem. Mayor's Profl. Sports Adv. Com., Phoenix, 1988-91, Bus. Ptnrs. of Phoenix Symphony, 1993-95. Capt. JAG, USAF, 1979-83. Master Sandra Day O'Connor Inn of Ct.; mem. ABA, ATLA, Nat. Bar Assn., Ariz. Trial Lawyers Assn., Ariz. State Bar Assn., N.C. State Bar Assn., Fed. Bar Assn., Maricopa County Bar Assn. (mem. pub. rels. com. 1993-95, chair 1995-96), Continuing Legal Edn. Committee, Cmty. Legal Svcs. (chair bd. dirs. 1997-98), Alpha Edn. Found. of Phoenix, Inc. (chair, bd. dirs. 1996-98). Avocations: flying, camping, skiing, sailing, hiking. Office: Ste 250 3707 N 7th St Phoenix AZ 85014-5057

MARABLE, SIMEON-DAVID, artist; b. Phila., May 10, 1948; s. Daniel Berry and Marsima (Maddela) M.; m. Pamela Joyce Sorenson, June 1, 1969; children: Simeon-David dePaul, Daniel-Dale Christopher (dec.), Jason-Andrew Bartley, Jo Anna Lee, Benjamin Arthur Kurtis. BA in Art and English, Lea Coll., Minn., 1970; postgrad., Tyler Sch. Art, Phila. Art tchr. 7-8th grade Pennsbury (Pa.) Sch. Sys., 1970—88; Art tchr. 9-10th grade Charles H. Boehm H.S., Pennsbury, 1988—, Medill Bair H.S., Pennsbury, 1990—; Art tchr. 9-12th grade Pennsbury H.S. West , 2002—. Tchr. Neshaminy Adult Edn., 1972-82; resident artist Middletown Hist. Assn., 1976, Three Arches Corp., 1975, also treas.; founder, creator Rivulet Art 2000. Permanent collections include Albert Lea (Minn.) Libr., chapel Ft. Dix, N.J.; portraits of Mr. Mike Schmidt, Mr. Lee Elia; creator Phila. City of Champs logo, 50th anniversary logo Fairless Hills, Pa. 1951-2001 Celebration; creator children's ednl. programs Falls Twp. 300th Pa. statehood; artwork represented in Middletown Twp. calendar, 1992, Falls Twp. calendar, 1992; creator Olde Phila. Ednl. Program and Pa. Statehood Program, Nat. Rep. Conv., Phila., 2000; creator scale model homes exhibit Pa. Historic Mus., 2002; author, creator Levittown Pennsylvania, 1952-2002 A Garden Community, 2002; sketch presented to Gov. of Pa. 2002. Vol. Rep. Nat. Convention, Phila., 2000; mgr. Boys Soccer League, Boys Little League, Middletown Twp.; sr. Babe Ruth coach, mgr. Langhorne Athletic Assn., 1988-89; sr. coach Babe Ruth League, 1989; J.V. baseball coach, 1989; mem. Presdl. Task Force; elected to Nat. Trust for Historic Preservation, 1995; involved with ednl. program Honoring the 200th Anniversary U.S. Constn. Commemorative Olde Phila. Constn. Atty. Served with USAR, 1970. Named Artist of Yr., Albert Lea Lions Club, 1970. Mem. Buck County Art Educators (pres. 1973-74), Levittown Artists Assn., Nat. Soc. Arts and Lit., Internat. Platform Assn. Roman Catholic. Home: 18 Spindletree Rd Levittown PA 19056-2215 Office: 600 S Olds Blvd Fairless Hills PA 19030-2441 E-mail: amx_12345@hotmail.com.

MARADUDIN, ALEXEI A. physics educator; b. San Francisco, Dec. 14, 1931; BS, Stanford U., 1953, MS, 1954; PhD in Physics, Bristol U., 1957. Rsch. assoc. physics U. Md., College Park, 1956-57, rsch. asst. prof., 1957-58; asst. rsch. prof. Inst. Fluid Dynamics & Applied Math., 1958-60; physicist Westinghouse Rsch. Labs., Churchill Borough, Pa., 1960-65; cons. semicondr. br. U.S. Naval Rsch. Lab., Washington, 1958-60, Los Alamos Sci. Lab., 1965-67, 83-89; cons. semiconductor br. Gen. Atomic Divsn. Gen. Dynamics Corp., 1965-71; chmn. dept. U. Calif., Irvine, 1968-71, prof. physics, 1965—. Recipient Alexander von Humboldt U.S. sr. scientist award, 1980-81. Fellow Am. Phys. Soc., Optical Soc. Am., Am. Assn. Advancement of Sci., Inst. Physics, U.K.; mem. Phi Beta Kappa, Tau Beta Pi, Sigma Xi. Office: U Calif Irvine Dept Physics & Astronomy Frederick Reines Hl # 2180 Irvine CA 92697-0001 E-mail: aamaradu@uci.edu.

MARAK, LOUIS BERNARD, JR. artist, educator; b. Shawnee, Okla., Sept. 9, 1942; s. Louis Bernard and Ann Elizabeth (Sakach) M.; m. Noelle Stephanie Cusumano, Dec. 10, 1966; children: Jason Matthew, Ethan Andrew. Assoc. in Bus. Adminstrn., St. Gregory's Jr. Coll., 1962; BFA in Crafts, U. Ill., Champaign, 1965; MFA in Ceramics, Alfred U., 1967. Instr. of art Keuka Coll., Keuka Park, N.Y., 1967-69; prof. art Humboldt State U., Arcata, Calif., 1969—. Nat. Endowment for the Arts Craftsmen's fellowship grantee, 1975; Calif. Arts Coun. artist fellowship grantee, 1994. Home: 1110 Freshwater Rd Eureka CA 95503-9558

MARAKAS, GEORGE MICHAEL, real estate executive; b. Harvey, Ill., Mar. 23, 1953; s. George Constantine and Martilla Ruth (Holcombe) M.; m. Susan Lynn Witte, June 28, 1983; 1 child, Stephanie Lynn. BA, Gov.'s State U., 1986. Cert. in Data Processing. Dir. learning Valcom Computers, Bourbonnais, Inc., 1983-84; dir. data processing Crest Savings & Loan, Kankakee, Ill., 1984-85, v.p., 1985, Exec. Affiliates, Big Rock, Ill., 1986-87, Continental Ill. Nat. Bank, Chgo., 1987-88; pres. CMC Mgmt. Group, Inc., Miami, 1988—. Dir. Imperial Condo Assn., Miami, 1986—. Mem. Community Assn. Inst., Dade County Apt. Assn., Lions. Avocations: scuba diving, golf, karate. Office: CMC Mgmt Group Inc 800 Brickell Ave # 2ph Miami FL 33131-2911

MARALDO, ANGELA MARIE, civil engineer; b. Grosse Pointe, Mich., Sept. 26, 1966; d. Mario Victor and Judith Ann (Raether) M. BSCE, Mich. Tech. U., 1989. Registered profl. engr. Mich. Project engr. City of Monroe (Mich.), Mich., 1989-97; constrn. project engr. Genesee County Rd. Commn., Flint, 1997-98; civil engr. II City of Port Huron, 1998—. Mem. ASCE, Mich. Soc. Profl. Engrs. Avocations: travel, four wheeling. Office: City of Port Huron 100 Mcmorran Blvd Rm City Port Huron MI 48060-4007

MARAMOROSCH, KARL, virologist, educator; b. Vienna, Austria, Jan. 16, 1915; came to U.S., 1947, naturalized, 1952; s. Jacob and Stefanie Olga (Schlesinger) M.; m. Irene Ludwinowska, Nov. 15, 1938; 1 dau., Lydia Ann. MS magna cum laude in Entomology, Agrl. U., Warsaw, Poland, 1938; student, Poly. U. Bucharest, Rumania, 1944-46; fellow, Bklyn. Bot. Garden, 1947-48; PhD (predoctoral fellow Am. Cancer Soc. 1948-49), Columbia, 1949. Civilian internee in, Rumania, 1939-46; asst., then assoc. Rockefeller U., N.Y.C., 1949-61; sr. entomologist Boyce Thompson Inst., Yonkers, N.Y., 1961-74, program dir. virology and insect physiology, 1962-74; prof. microbiology Waksman Inst., Rutgers U., New Brunswick, N.J., 1974-85; prof. entomology Cook Coll., Rutgers U., 1985—, Robert L. Starkey prof., 1983—; vis. prof. agr. U. Wageningen, Netherlands, 1953, Cornell U., 1957, Rutgers U., 1967-68, Fordham U., 1973, Hokkaido U., Sapporo, Japan, 1980, Justus Liebig U., Giessen, Ger., 1983. Mendel lectr. St. Peters Coll., Jersey City, 1963; virologist FAO to Philippines, 1960; Disting. Vis. prof. Fudan U., Shanghai, 1982; cons. FAO-UN, World-wide survey, 1963; chmn. U.S.-Japan Coop. Seminar, 1965, 74, 85; mem. panel food and fiber Nat. Acad. Scis., 1966; cons. rice virus diseases AID-IRRI, Hyderabad, India, 1971; cons. UNDP, Bangalore, India, 1978-79; virologist FAO/UNDP, Sri Lanka, 1981, 82, 83, Mauritius, 1985; AIBS lectr., 1970-72, Found. Microbiology Nat. lectr., 1972-73, Fulbright Disting. prof., Yugoslavia, 1972, 78; mem. tropical medicine and parasitology study sect. NIH, 1972-76; chmn. 1st-3d Internat. Confs. Comparative Virology, 1969, 73, 76. Author: Comparative Symptomatology of Coconut Diseases of Unknown Etiology, 1964; editor: Biological Transmission of Disease Agents, 1962, Insect Viruses, 1968, Viruses, Vectors and Vegetation, 1969, Comparative Virology, 1971, Mycoplasma Diseases, 1973, Viruses, Evolution and Cancer, 1974, Invertebrate Immunity, 1975, Legume Diseases in the Tropics, 1975, Invertebrate Tissue Culture: Research Applications, 1976, Invertebrate Tissue Culture: Applications in Medicine, Biology and Agriculture, 1976, Aphids as Virus Vectors, 1977, Insect and Plant Viruses: An Atlas, 1977, Viruses and Environment, 1978, Practical Tissue Culture Applications, 1979, Leafhopper Vectors and Plant Disease Agents, 1979, Vectors of Plant Pathogens, 1980, Invertebrate Systems in Vitro, 1980, Vectors of Disease Agents, 1981, Mycoplasma Diseases of Trees and Shrubs, 1981, Mycoplasma and Allied Pathogens of Plants, Animals and Human Beings, 1981, Plant Diseases and Vectors: Ecology and Epidemiology, 1981, Invertebrate Cell Culture Applications, 1982, Pathogens, Vectors and Plant Diseases: Approaches to Control, 1982, Subviral Pathogens of Plants and Animals, 1985, Viral Insecticides for Biological Control, 1985, Biotechnology Advances in Insect Pathology and Cell Culture, 1987, Mycoplasma Diseases of Crops, 1988, Invertebrate and Fish Tissue Culture, 1988, Biotechnology for Biological Control of Pests and Vectors, 1991, Viroids and Satellites: Molecular Parasites at the Frontier of Life, 1991, Plant Diseases of Uncertain Etiology, 1992, Insect Cell Biotechnology, 1994, Arthropod Cell Culture Systems, 1994, Forest Trees and Palms: Diseases and Control, 1996, Invertebrate Cell Culture: Novel Directions and Biotechnology Applications, 1997, Invertebrate Cell Culture: Looking Toward the XXI Century, 1997, Biotechnology and Plant Protection in Forestry Sci., 1998, Maintenance of Human, Animal, and Plant Pathogen Vectors, 1999; Methods in Virology, 1964—, Advances in Virus Research, 1972—, Archives of Virology, 1973-78, Intervirology, 1973-77, Advances in Cell Culture, 1979—; editor in chief Jour. N.Y. Entomol. Soc. 1972-84; assoc. editor: Virology, 1964-68, 75-79. Recipient Sr. Rsch., Lalor Found., 1957, Nat. Ciba-Geigy awad in agr., 1976, Wolf prize in agr., 1980, Jurzykowski prize in biology, 1980, Disting. Svc. award, Am. Inst. Biol. Scis., 1983, Lifetime Achievement award, Soc. In Vitro Biology, 2001. Fellow AAAS (hon., Campbell award 1958), Entomol. Soc. Am., Am. Phytopath. Soc., N.Y. Acad. Scis. (A. Cressy Morrison prize natural sci. 1951, chmn. div. microbiology 1956-60, rec. sec. 1960-61, v.p. 1962-63), Nat. Acad. Scis. India (hon.); mem. Harvey Soc., Growth Soc., Phytopath. Soc., Indian, Japan, Can. phytopath. socs., Leopoldina Acad., Internat. Com. Virus Nomenclature, Electron Microscopy Soc., Am. Soc. Microbiology (Waksman award 1978), Soc. In Vitro Biology (Tissue Culture Assn., pres. N.E. br. 1978-81, pres. history br. 1988-90, Disting. Lifetime Achievement award 2001), Soc. Invertebrate Pathology (founder's lectr., Adelaide 1990, Founder's honoree Sapporo 1998), Internat. Assn. Medicinal Forest Plants (pres. 1989—), Sigma Xi (pres. Rugers chpt. 1978, Khailshanker Durlabhji award Jaipur 1993). Home: 17 Black Birch Ln Scarsdale NY 10583-7456 Office: Rutgers U Dept Entomology New Brunswick NJ 08901 E-mail: maramors@rci.rutgers.edu.

MARAN, MICHAEL JOSEPH, publisher, writer, lawyer; b. Mt. Pleasant, Mich., Nov. 19, 1952; s. Anthony John and Lucile Mildred (Newton) M. BA, Mich. State U., 1973; JD, U. Wis., 1977. Bar: Mich. 1977, Wis. 1977. Pvt. practice law, Mt. Pleasant, 1977-79; asst. prof. bus. law and regulation Ctrl. Mich. U., 1979-80; campaign coord. Ferency for Gov., Lansing, Mich., 1981-82; staff atty. UAW-GM Legal Svcs., 1983-84; pub. Grand River Press, 1985—. Author: Michigan Divorce Book, 1986, 4th edit., 1998, After the Divorce, 1999, Make Your Own Will, 1990, Michigan Power of Attorney Book, 1991. Bd. dirs. Mt. Pleasant Zoning Bd., 1978-81, East Lansing (Mich.) Zoning Bd., 1991-95. Mem. Mich. State Bar Assn., Wis. State Bar Assn., Phi Beta Kappa. Avocations: reading, skiing. Home: 1517 Erica Ln East Lansing MI 48823-2256 Office: Grand River Press 411 W Lake Lansing Rd Ste B-110 East Lansing MI 48823-8468

MARAN, STEPHEN PAUL, astronomer; b. Bklyn., Dec. 25, 1938; s. Alexander P. and Clara F. (Schoenfeld) M.; m. Sally Ann Scott, Feb. 14, 1971; children: Michael Scott, Enid Rebecca, Elissa Jean. BS, Bklyn. Coll., 1959; MA, U. Mich., 1961, PhD, 1964. Astronomer Kitt Peak Nat. Obs., Tucson, 1964-69; project scientist for orbiting solar observatories NASA-Goddard Space Flight Center, Greenbelt, Md., 1969-75; head advanced systems and ground observations br. NASA-Goddard Space Flight Ctr., 1970-77, mgr. Operation Kohoutek, 1973-74, sr. staff scientist Lab. for Astronomy and Solar Physics, 1977-95; asst. dir. Space Scis. for Info. and Outreach, 1995—. Cons. Westinghouse Rsch. Labs., 1966; vis. lectr. U. Md., College Park, 1969-70; sr. lectr. UCLA, 1976; press officer Am. Astron. Soc., 1985—; A. Dixon Johnson lectr. in sci. comm., Pa. State U., 1990; vis. scholar Univ. Ctr. Ga., 1997; lectr. on astronomy cruises and eclipse tours. Author: (with John C. Brandt) New Horizons in Astronomy, 1972, 2d edit., 1979, Arabic edit., 1979, (with Jacqueline Mitton) Gems of Hubble-Superb Images from the Hubble Telescope, 1996, Astronomy for Dummies, 1999, German edit. 2000; editor: Physics of Nonthermal Radio Sources, 1964, The Gum Nebula and Related Problems, 1971, Possible Relations Between Solar Activity and Meteorological Phenomena, 1975, New Astronomy and Space Science Reader, 1977, A Meeting with the Universe, 1981, Astrophysics of Brown Dwarfs, 1986, The Astronomy and Astrophysics Encyclopedia, 1991; assoc. editor: Earth, Extraterrestrial Scis, 1969-79; editor: Astrophys. Letters, 1974-77, assoc. editor, 1977-85; contbg. editor Air & Space/Smithsonian, 1990—; mem. editl. adv. bd. Astronomy Mag., 1997—, Astronomy and Geophysics, 1997—; contbr. articles on astronomy, space to popular mags. Named Disting. Visitor Boston U., 1970; recipient Group Achievement awards NASA, 1969, 74, Exceptional Achievement medal, 1991, Klumpke-Roberts award Astron. Soc. of Pacific, 1999. Fellow AAAS; mem. Internat. Astron. Union (editor daily newspaper 1988, Minor Planet 9768 named Stephenmaran in honor 2000), Am. Astron. Soc. (Harlow Shapley vis. lectr. 1981—), press. officer 1985—), Royal Astron. Soc., Am. Phys. Soc., Am. Geophys. Union. Office: Code 600 Nasa Goddard Space Flight Ctr Greenbelt MD 20771-0001

MARANDA, GUY, oral maxillofacial surgeon, Canadian health facility executive, educator; b. Paris, Sept. 9, 1936; arrived in Canada, 1937; s. Emilien and Lucille (Fortin) M.; married; children: Lucille, Jean, Isabelle. BA, U. Ottawa, Ont., Can., 1957; DDs, U. Montreal, Can., 1962; cert. oral surgeon, U. Pa., 1965. Pvt. practice, Quebec, 1965-70; mem. faculty U. Laval, Ste. Foy, Que., Can., 1970—, asst. prof. Can., 1987-94, prof. Can., 1995—; ret., 2001. Bd. dirs. Ordre Dentistes du Québec; pres. Quebec Assn. Oral Surgeons, 1979-80; cons. Quebec Health Bd., Assurance Auto Quebec, various law firms. Mem. Royal coll. Dentists Can. (diplomate, pres. 1991), Internat. Assn. Oral Surgeons, Can. Assn. Oral Surgeons, Can. Dental Assn. Ordre Dentistes Que. Roman Catholic. Home: 6031 Route De Fossambaunt Fossambaunt Sur Le Lac QC Canada G0A-3M0 Office: U Laval Faculte Medecine Dentaire Sainte Foy QC Canada G1K 7P4

MARANGI, VITO ANTHONY, SR. claim administrator; b. Utica, N.Y., Jan. 1, 1932; s. Gregorio and Carmella (Consoli) Marangi; m. Mary Margaret Lokey, Apr. 10, 1960 (div. July 1973); children: Vito Anthony Jr., Vanetta Gayle, Gregory Alan; m. Diann Louise Bunch, Apr. 11, 1987. BS, SUNY, Potsdam, 1958. Cert. mentor/tng. asst., 2000. Asst. regional claims mgr. Hartford Ins. Group, Fresno, Calif., 1958-67; supervising adjuster Underwriters Adjusting Co., 1967-70; home office claim supr. Meritplan Ins. Co., Newport Beach, Calif., 1970-71; appeals referee State of Nev., Reno and Carson City, 1971-73, 76-79; br. mgr. Brown Bros. Adjusters, Reno, 1974-87; ind. ins. adjuster Tony Marangi, Adjuster, Carson City, 1987—; vice chmn., bd. trustees Carson-Tahoe Hosp., 1991-96. Scout master Boy Scouts Am., Utica, N.Y., Fresno, Calif., Carson City, 1953-85; vol. tng. asst., mentor Mentor Ctr. of Western Nev., 2000—; mem. Carson City Storm Drainage Adv. Com., 2000—. With USN, 1949-53. Mem. Nev. State Claims Assn. (pres., v.p., treas., sec.), No. Nev. Claims Assn. (pres., v.p., treas., sec.), Nat. Assn. of Adminstrv. Law Judges, Internat. Assn. of Arson Investigators (Nev. chpt.), Carson City Elks Lodge, VFW, Carson City C. of C. (bus. edn. com. 1987—, transp. com. 1987—). Avocations: photographer, bowling, dancing, classic car owner, musician. Home and Office: PO Box 843 Carson City NV 89702-0843

MARANO, ANTHONY JOSEPH, cardiologist; b. White Plains, N.Y., Apr. 14, 1934; s. Anthony Joseph and Mary Antoinette (Perrotta) M.; m. Mary Regina Marbach, Aug. 23, 1958; children— Thomas, Kathryn, Michele. B.A., Williams Coll., 1956; M.D., Cornell Med. Coll., 1960. Diplomate Am. Bd. Internal Medicine, Am. Bd. Cardiovascular Disease. Intern Bellevue Hosp., N.Y.C., 1960-61; resident St. Luke's Hosp., N.Y.C., 1961-63; NIH fellow in cardiology Mt. Sinai Hosp., N.Y.C., 1963-64, research assoc., 1964-75; clin. assoc. in medicine Coll. Physicians and Surgeons, N.Y.C., 1970-86; pres. med. staff White Plains Hosp., 1984-86, chief cardiology, 1985-91, chief cardiology emeritus, 1991—, bd. dirs., 1983-88; cons. in cardiology Burke Rehab. Ctr.; med. dir., founder Paramedic Ambulance, White Plains, 1976-82. Contbr. articles to med. jours. Trustee Pace U., N.Y.C., 1975— , Home Savs. Bank, White Plains, 1973-90; bd. dirs. YMCA, White Plains, 1978-82 ; team physician White Plains High Sch., 1967— ; cons. physician Dept. Pub. Safety, White Plains, 1968—; cons. physician City of White Plains Sch. System, 1994—; bd. dirs. Westchester County Sports Hall of Fame, 1993—; alumni trustee Tyng Found., Williams Coll., 1994—. Tyng scholar Williams Coll., 1952-59; recipient Outstanding Achievement award Emergency Med. Services Council, 1982; named to White Plains High Sch. Hall of Fame, 1998. Fellow ACP, Am. Coll. Cardiology; mem. AMA, Am. Coll. Sports Medicine, Am. Heart Assn., N.Y. State Heart Assn. (bd. dirs. 1982-85), Westchester Heart Assn. (v.p. 1983-86, pres. 1987-90), Phi Beta Kappa. Clubs: University (White Plains) (pres. 1970-71); Westchester Country (Harrison, N.Y.). Avocations: tennis, skiing, gardening. Home: 46 Eagle Ct White Plains NY 10605-5116 Office: 20 Old Mamaroneck Rd White Plains NY 10605-2060

MARANO, RICHARD MICHAEL, lawyer; b. Waterbury, Conn., June 22, 1960; s. Albert Nicholas and Angeline Domenica (Viotti) M.; m. Eileen N. Barry. BA, Fairfield U., 1982; JD, Seton Hall U., 1985. Bar: Conn. 1985, U.S. Dist. Ct. Conn. 1985, U.S. Tax Ct. 1986, U.S. Supreme Ct. 1990, U.S. Ct. Appeals (2d cir.) 1991; cert. criminal trial advocate. Assoc. Moynahan, Ruskin, Mascolo & Mariani, Waterbury, 1985-87; ptnr. Marano & Diamond, 1987—2001. Bd. of examiners Nat. Bd. Trial Advocacy, 1999—. Author: History of the Order Sons of Italy of Waterbury, Connecticut, 1995, Connecticut Criminal Legal Forms, 1999; co-author: Growing Up Italian and American in Waterbury, 1997; co-editor: Counsel for the Defense, 1991-93, editor, 1993-98; contbr. law articles to Conn. Bar Jour. Bd. dirs. Italian-Am. Dem. Club, Waterbury, 1988—, Ctrl. Naugatuck Valley HELP, 1992—, Anderson Boys Club, 1989—, pres. 1996-98, Waterbury Housing Police Fund, 1992-94, Waterbury Crime Stoppers Inc., 1994-97; pres. Conn. Young Dems., 1981-82; state coord. McGovern for U.S. Presdl. campaign, 1983-84; campaign mgr. Orman for Congress, 1984; active Oxford Dem. Town Com., 2002-; commr. Waterbury Pub. Assistance, 1986-88, Waterbury Fire Bd., 1996-98; justice of the peace, Waterbury, 1989-99; gen. counsel Waterbury Dem. Town Com., 1990-96; trustee Our Lady of Lourdes Ch., 1993—; alderman City of Waterbury, 1988-90. Mem. ABA, ATLA, KC, Conn. Bar Assn., Nat. Assn. Criminal Def. Lawyers (life), Conn. Criminal Def. Lawyers Assn. (pres.-elect 1997-98, pres. 1998-99), Conn. Italian-Am. Bar Assn. (pres. 1993-95), Conn. Trial Lawyers Assn., Waterbury Bar Assn. (bd. dirs. 1993-2002, pres. 1996-98), New Haven County Bar Assn., Nat. Italian-Am. Bar Assn. (Conn. delegate 1993—), Sons of Italy (pres. lodge #66 1994-96), Unico Club (pres. Waterbury chpt. 1997-99), Cath. Lawyers Guild, Conn. Acad. Cert. Trial Lawyers, Nat. Eagle Scout Assn. (life), Elks, Alpha Mu Gamma, Pi Sigma Alpha. Roman Catholic. Home: 24 Lake Dr Oxford CT 06478-1172 Office: Marano Law Offices 61 Field St Waterbury CT 06702-1907 E-mail: RichardMarano@aol.com.

MARANS, J. EUGENE, lawyer; b. Butte, Mont., May 26, 1940; s. Edward and Florence M.; m. Anne Marie Borger, Sept. 3, 1978; children: Julia C., John E. AB, Harvard U., 1962, LLB, 1965. Bar: N.Y. 1966, D.C. 1971. Law clk. to Judge John M. Wisdom U.S. Ct. Appeals (5th cir.), New Orleans, 1965-66; assoc. Cleary, Gottlieb, Steen & Hamilton, N.Y.C., 1966-70, Paris, 1970-71, Washington, 1971-74, ptnr., 1975-90, 93-00, of counsel, 2001—, ptnr. Hong Kong, 1990-93. Mem. N.Y. State adv. com. U.S. Commn. Civil Rights, 1969-70; mem. nat. eval. com. on simplified method of determining eligibility in pub. assistance HEW, 1969-70; sec., counsel Bipartisan Com. on Absentee Voting, 1973— Contbr. articles to legal jours. Bd. dirs. New Leadership Fund, chmn. 1977-79; mem. Sabre Found., pres. 1990; trustee Internat. Inst. Rural Reconstrn., vice chair, 2001—. Mem. Assn. Ams. Resident Overseas, Ripon Soc. (nat. governing bd. 1962-2001, chmn. 1969-70), Coun. on Fgn. Rels., ABA, D.C. Bar (chmn. internat. sect. 1978-79), Assn. of Bar of City of N.Y., Am. Soc. Internat. Law, Union Internat. des Avocats, Washington Fgn. Law Soc. (pres. 1985-86), Am. Law Inst. Office: 2000 Pennsylvania Ave NW Washington DC 20006-1812 E-mail: emarans@cgsh.com.

MARASHIO, PAUL WILLIAM, humanities educator; b. Woburn, Mass., May 30, 1941; s. Peter and Catherine (Danizio) M.; m. Nancy Feeney, June 24, 1967. BEd, Keene State Coll., 1963; MA, U. N.H., 1968; cert. advanced studies, Wesleyan U., 1977. Tchr., Somersworth, N.H., 1963-66; history dept. head Salem, 1966-69; supr. instrn. and curriculum, 1969-71; prin. Woodbury Sch., 1971-77; curriculum coord. Salem Sch. Dist., 1977-83, educator, 1983-86; prof. humanities N.H. Cmty. Tech Coll., Claremont, 1986—. Mem. N.H. Excellence in Edn. Commn., 1983-84. Editor: Myth in U.S. Culture; editor Pedagogy Jour.; contbr. articles to profl. jours. Pres. Salem Hist. Soc., 1977-80; mem. Salem Com. on Environ. Issues, 1977, Old Town Hall Restoration Com., Salem Mus. Com.; rschr. N.H. Bicentenial Celebration U.S. Constn., 1985. Recipient award N.H. Coun. Better Schs., 1974, Tchrs. Who Inspire award Lawrence Eagle Tribune, 1983; Ariz. State U. fellow, 1968; scholar U.S. Constn. Bicentenial, 1986—. Mem. Am. Hist. Assn., Orgn. Am. Historians, Coll. Humanities Assn., Nat. Assn. for Humanities Edn., Sunapee Yacht Club, Phi Delta Kappa. Roman Catholic. Address: PO Box 2211 Mount Sunapee NH 03255-2211

MARATHE, BHASKAR, development engineer; b. Mumbai, India, Dec. 31, 1964; s. Vishnu R. and Neela V. Marathe; m. Ashwini S. Dandekar, June 9, 1991. B in Tech., Banaras Hindu U., Varanasi, India, 1986; M in Tech., Indian Inst. Tech., Mumbai, 1989; PhD, Pa. State U., 1998. Exec. engr. Bharat Electronics Ltd., Taloja, India, 1986-87; sr. engr. Bombardier Motor Corp. Am., Grant, Fla., 1995-98; devel. engr. Luk Inc., Wooster, Ohio, 1999—. Reviewer Jour. Fluid Engring, 1998—; contbr. articles to profl. jours.

Organizer, vol. India-Fest India Assn., Melbourne, Fla., 1996-98. Mem. ASME, Soc. Automotive Engrs. Home: 2750 Winchester Woods Apt K Wooster OH 44691-2594 Office: Luk Inc 3401 Old Airport Rd Wooster OH 44691-9544 Fax: 330-202-6299.

MARATTA SNYDER, GRACE ELVIRA, volunteer; b. Jackson, Ohio, July 22, 1922; d. John William and Mary Ann (Lewis) Matthews; m. James Edward Maratta, Oct. 14, 1957 (div. May 1971); m. Price Knapp Snyder, Sept. 19, 1998. Student, Rio Grande Coll., 1940-41, Columbus Bus. U., 1941-42. Clk.-typist Ohio State Dept. Trans., Columbus, 1942-44; adminstrv. office mgr. Div of Police City of Columbus, 1944-77, ret., 1977; legis. agt. Police and Fire Retirees of Ohio, Reynoldsburg, 1978—. Trustee Columbus Police Sub-Relief Fund, 1967—, Adult Life Care Ctr., Reynoldsburg, Ohio, 1990—; lobbyist Police and Fire Retirees of Ohio, Columbus, 1978—. Past pres. Reynoldsburg Womens Civic Club, 1979-81, Reynoldsburg Womens Rep. Club, 1982-84; pres. Reynoldsburg Sr. Citizens Ctr., 1988—; trustee Wesley Ridge Retirement and Health Complex, 1996—. Recipient Disting. Svc. award Ohio Gen. Assembly, 1970, Cmty. Builders award Masonic Lodge 340, 1996; named Outstanding Svc. Sr. Citizen Reynoldsburg Jaycees, 1987, Outstanding Eldercare Work, Ohio State Dept. Aging, 1989; inducted into Ohio Sr. Citizens Hall of Fame, 1994. Mem. Columbus Police Retirees Assn. (Outstanding Svc. 1981). Republican. Methodist. Avocations: musical theatre, reading, TV watching, shopping, eating out. Office: Police & Fire Retirees 7335 E Livingston Ave Reynoldsburg OH 43068 E-mail: pfro@iwaynet.net.

MARAYNES, ALLAN LAWRENCE, filmmaker, television producer; b. N.Y.C., Apr. 26, 1950; s. Harry and Dorothy (Kaufman) M.; m. Bitsy Healy, Oct. 14, 1978; children: Sean, Megan, Matthew. BA, Queens Coll., 1972; MA, Loyola U., L.A., 1974. Assoc. prodr. CBS News, N.Y.C., 1976-77, prodr. 60 Minutes, 1974-88, writer, dir. 60 Minutes, 1976-88; pres. No. Films, 1988-90; exec. prodr. "SST" program ABC, 1989; prodr. 20/20 ABC News, N.Y.C., 1990-93, sr. investigative prodr. 20/20, 1994-96; sr. investigative prodr. Dateline NBC, 1996—. Lectr. New Sch., N.Y.C., 1979, Columbia U., N.Y.C. Author: (play) A Straight Line to the Market Place, 1975, (screenplay) Smithereens, 1999. Recipient Emmy award NATAS, 1981, 85, 89, 91, 93, 95, 97, 98, George Foster Peabody award, 1989, 2000, Edward R. Murrow award, 1997, 98, 2000, DuPont Columbia Journalism award, 2000, George Polk award, 2000, Investigative Reporters and Editors award, 1997, 2000. Mem. NATAS, Writers Guild Am. Avocations: N.Y. Yankees. Office: NBC 30 Rockefeller Plz Fl 2 New York NY 10112-0036 E-mail: ALLAN.MARAYNES@NBC.COM.

MARAZITA, ELEANOR MARIE HARMON, retired secondary education educator; b. Madison County, Ind., Oct. 25, 1933; d. William Houston Harmon and Martha Belle (Savage) Hinds; m. Philip Marazita; children: Mary Louise, Frank, Dominic, Vincent, Elizabeth Faye, Candice Marie, Daniel William. BS in Home Econs., Ctrl. Mich. U., 1955; MA in Human Ecology, Mich. State U., 1971. Cert. vocat. home econs. tchr., K-Jr. Coll., cert. speech correction tchr. Tchr. adult edn., Mt. Pleasant, Mich., 1956; substitute tchr. North Branch (Mich.) Schs., 1961-64; tchr. Pied Piper Coop. Nursery Sch., Lansing, Mich., 1964-69, Lansing C.C., 1971-81, Grand Ledge (Mich.) H.S., 1969-98. Mich. tchr. del. World Conf. Tchg. Profls., 1985, 98; adv. mem. Mich. Tchr. Competency Testing Program, 1992. Bd. dirs. Greater Lansing chpt. U.N., 1995-98; vol. St. Lawrence Mental Health Hosp., 1972-73, Listening Ear Crisis Intervention Ctr., 1973-77, Capital City Convalescent Home, 1969-73; chmn. study com. Delta Twp. Libr., 1969-73, Jr. League, 1969—; interviewer Youth for Understanding, 1978-83; active exch. student orientation program Mich. State U., 1977, exch. trips, 1979-82; mem. adv. bd. Mich. League Human Svcs., 1988-91, Eaton County Extension Svcs., 1988-91, Mich. Women's Assembly, 1986-91; mem. Friends of Waverly Libr., 1963—; participant 3rd Congress Educators Caucus, 1986-92; 4-H leader, 1950-65. Recipient State Tchr. Multicultural award, 1989, UN Global Educator award, 1991, State Tchr. Maureen Wyatt feminist award, 1996. Mem. AAUW, LWV, NEA (del. 1998, observer 2nd annual Ednl. Internat. Congress 1998), DAR (co-chair State Good Citizen 1999—), PEO, Mich. Edn. Assn. (mem. polit. action exec. bd. 1986-98, v.p. women's caucus 1986-93, Liz Siddell State Internat. Cultures award 1992), Circumnavigators Club (travel around world in one trip 1993), Century Club (travel in 100 countries outside U.S. 1994), Delta Kappa Gamma (co-chair State World Fellowship 1993-95, chair state legislation com. 1997-99, chpt. Women of Distinction award 1993), Phi Delta Kappa (Tchr. of Yr. Mich. State U. 1992). Avocation: travel in U.S. and foreign countries. Home: 214 Farmstead Ln Lansing MI 48917-3015

MARAZITA, MARY LOUISE, genetics researcher; b. Cheboygan, Mich., June 13, 1954; m. Richard T. McCoy, 1984; 5 children. BS, Mich. State U., 1976; PhD in Genetics, U. N.C., 1980. Fellow U. So. Calif., 1980-82; statistician, instr. UCLA, 1982-86; asst. prof. human genetics Med. Coll. Va., 1986-93; dir. Cleft Palate-craniofacial Ctr. U. Pitts., 1993-00, head divsn. oral biology, 1999—, asst. dean for rsch. Sch. Dental Medicine, 2000-2001, assoc. dean rsch., 2001—. Instr. biomath. U. Calif., 1984-86; asst. prof. dentistry Med. Coll. Va., 1992-93; assoc. prof. human genetics and oral maxillofacial surgery U. Pitts., 1993-97, prof. human genetics and oral and maxillofacial surgery, 1997—. Fellow Am. Coll. Med. Genetics, Am. Cleft Palate Assn., Am. Soc. Human Genetics, Internat. Genetic Epidemiol. Soc., Internat. Assn. Dental Rsch. Achievements include research in genetics of cleft lip, cleft palate and other craniofacial anomalies, including statistical genetic analysis and gene mapping studies. Office: U Pitts Divsn Oral Biology/Genetics 693A Salk Hall Pittsburgh PA 15261-1903

MARBACH, JOSEPH R. political science educator, consultant; b. Phila. s. Joseph John and Florence Marbach; m. Paula Ann Marbach, June 24, 1989; children: Joseph, Jillian. BA, LaSalle Coll., Phila., 1983; MA, Temple U., 1986, PhD, 1993. Asst. dir. Ctr. for Study of Federalism, Phila., 1990-94; assoc. prof. Seton Hall U., South Orange, N.J., 1994—; co-dir. Inst. for Svc. Learning, 1998—; chair dept. polit. sci. Seton Hall U., 2000—. Cons. USIA, Novosibirsk, 1993-94, Seoul, Korea, 1999, mem. faculty Fulbright Summer Insts., 1995-. Contbr. articles to profl. jours. Advisor Coll. Reps., 1995—, Seton Hall UN Assn., 1995-99. Fellow Earhart Found., 1985-87. Mem. Am. Polit. Sci. Assn., Acad. Polit. Sci., Northea. Polit. Sci. Assn., Turners Orgn. Roman Catholic. Office: Seton Hall U 400 S Orange Ave South Orange NJ 07079-2697

MARBER, PAUL ANDREW, lawyer; b. Glen Cove, N.Y., Jan. 19, 1960; s. Philip Marber and Ruth Brown; m. Randy Sue Kornfeld, Aug. 18, 1985; children: Elana Susan, Matthew William. BA, U. Rochester, 1982; JD, Boston U., 1985. Bar: N.Y. 1986, N.J. 1986, U.S. Dist. Ct. (ea. and so. dists.) N.Y. 1986, U.S. Dist. Ct. N.J. 1986. Asst. corp. counsel N.Y.C. Law Dept., Office of Corp. Counsel, 1985-88; assoc. Budd Larner Gross et al, N.Y.C., 1988-97, The Cochran Firm/Schneider Kleinick Weitz Damashek & Shoot, N.Y.C., 1997—. Active West Birchwood Civic Assn., Jericho, 1990—; committeeman Nassau County (N.Y.) Dem. Com., 1994—; dist. ct. judge candidate 4th Dist. Ct. Nassau County, Oyster Bay, 1995, 96. Mem. N.Y. State Bar Assn., N.Y. State Trial Lawyers Assn., Nassau County Bar Assn. Office: The Cochran Firm/Schneider Kleinick Weitz Damashek & Shoot 233 Broadway Fl 5 New York NY 10279-0599

MARBLE, DUANE FRANCIS, geography educator, researcher; b. Seattle, Dec. 10, 1931; s. Francis Augustus and Beulah Belle (Simmons) M.; m. Jacquelynne Hardester, Aug. 18, 1957; children: Kimberley Eileen Beauclair, Douglas Craig. BA, U. Wash., 1953, MA, 1956, PhD, 1959. Asst. prof. real estate U. Oreg., Eugene, 1959; asst. prof. regional sci. U. Pa., Phila., 1960-63; from assoc. prof. geography to prof. geography Northwestern U., Evanston, Ill., 1963-73, assoc. dir. Transp. Ctr., 1966-73; prof. geography and computer sci. SUNY at Buffalo, Amherst, N.Y., 1973-87; prof. geography and natural resources Ohio State U., Columbus, 1987-98, prof. emeritus, 1998—. Chmn. com. on geog. data sensing and processing Internat. Geog. Union, 1980-88; bd. dirs. Castlereagh Enterprises, Phoenix; founder Internat. Symposium Spatial Data Handling; cons. on geog. info. systems to U.S. Bur. Census, UN, also pvt. orgns. Editor: Intro Readings in GIS, 1990, Taylor & Francis, 1990-95; author computer program (best software award Assn. Am. Geogs. 1990); mem. editl. bd. Annals of Assn. Am. Geography, 2000—. Recipient Legend in Leadership award Environ. Sys. Rsch. Inst., 1997. Mem.: IEEE Computer Soc., AAAS, Assn. Am. Geographers (honors 1993). Home: 1310 Langston Dr Upper Arlington OH 43220-3900 Office: Ohio State U Ctr for Mapping Columbus OH 43212

MARBLE, GORDON ERIC, administrator; b. Cin., Dec. 14, 1952; Assoc. degree, Compton Coll., 1984. Contbr. poetry to anthologies. With USN, 1973—75. Personal E-mail: gmarble@hotmail.com.

MARBLE, MELINDA SMITH, writer, editor; b. Ponca City, Okla., June 17, 1960; d. Monte Gene and Dorothy Worthington Smith; m. Sanford Marble. BA with high hons., spl. hons. English, U. Tex., 1984. Mktg. Data Base Publs., Austin, Tex., 1986-87; assoc. editor Austin Area Bus. Women Directory, 1987-88; asst. pub. Travelers' Times, Austin, 1988-89; assoc. editor Tex. Bar Jour., 1989-95. Freelance editor, Austin, 1989-95, novelist, freelance journalist, Morristown, N.J., 1995—. Contbr. articles to newspapers and profl. jours. Recipient Gold Quill award of merit Internat. Assn. Bus. Communicators, 1993, Gold Quill Excellence award for First Person Articles, 1995; Best of Austin 4 Color Mag. award, 1993, 2 awards of merit, 1995, Presdl. Citation, State Bar of Tex., 1993, Nat. Assn. Govt. Communicators award of Honor 4 Color Mag., 1994, Best of Austin Feature Writing award, 1995, Best of Austin Advocacy Writing award, 1995. Avocations: reading, travel, skiing.

MARBURGER, JOHN HARMEN, III, federal agency administrator; b. S.I., N.Y., Feb. 8, 1941; s. John H., Jr. and Virginia A. (Smith) M.; m. Carol Preston Godfrey, June 12, 1965; children: John Harmen, Alexander Godfrey. BA in Physics magna cum laude, Princeton U., 1962; PhD in Applied Physics (NASA trainee), Stanford U., 1967; LHD (hon.) , Hofstra U., 2000; DS (hon.) , Stony Brook U., 2002, Moscow State U., 2002. Physicist Goddard Space Flight Center, NASA, 1962—63; asst. prof. physics and elec. engring. U. So. Calif., Los Angeles, 1966—69, assoc. prof., 1969—75, prof., 1975—80, chmn. physics dept., 1972—75, interim dean Coll. Letters, Arts and Scis., 1976—77, dean Coll. Letters, Arts and Scis., 1977—80; pres. SUNY, Stony Brook, 1980—94, prof. physics and elec. engring., 1994—98; pres. Brookhaven Sci. Assoc., 1998—2001; dir. Brookhaven Nat. Labs, 1998—2001, Off. Sci. & Tech. Policy, Washington, 2001—. Cons. laser fusion program Lawrence Livermore Labs., 1972-76; chmn. N.Y. State fact finding panel on Shoreham Nuclear Power Facility, 1983; chmn. bd. trustees Universities Rsch. Assn., 1988-94; co-chair NASULGC Bd. on Oceans and Atmosphere, 1992-93; bd. dirs. N.Y. State Edn. and Rsch. Network, Inc., 1986-98; bd. dirs., chair L.I. Rsch. Inst., 1989-95; bd. dirs. L.I. High Tech. Incubator Corp., 1992-98, chair 1994-98. Contbr. articles to tech. publs. Bd. dirs. Mus. at Stony Brook, 1980-92, 94-98, L.I. Assn., Inc., 1983-93, 98—, Action Com. for L.I., 1980-83, L.I. Forum for Tech., Inc., 1980—, Rsch. Found. SUNY, 1990—; bd. trustees Princeton U., 1985-89; chmn. N.Y. State Energy Office Rev. Commn., 1980-81, Suffolk County (N.Y.) Task Force on Priorities in Fin., 1980-81; campaign chmn. United Way of L.I., 1991-92. Recipient Shuichi Kusaka Meml. Prize Princeton U., 1962 Fellow AAAS, APS; mem. Assn. of Colls. and Univs. State of N.Y. (pres. 1988-90), Coleman Chamber Music Assn. (bd. dirs. 1969-80). Office: OSTP Eisenhower Exec Office Bldg 17th and Pennsylvania Ave NW Washington DC 20502 Office Fax: 202-456-6021.*

MARBURG-GOODMAN, JEFFREY EMIL, lawyer; b. Taipei, Taiwan, Feb. 20, 1957; s. Samuel and Lisl (Marburg) G. BA, Amherst Coll., 1979; JD, Harvard U., 1983; postgrad., U. Aix-Marseille, France, 1983-84. Bar: N.Y. 1986, U.S. Dist. Ct. (so. and ea. dists.) N.Y. 1988. Assoc. Shearman & Sterling, Paris, 1984, N.Y.C., 1985-89, Patton & Boggs, Washington, 1989-91; legal counsel U.S. AID, U.S. Dept. State, 1991-2000, asst. gen. counsel, 2000—. Mem. nat. steering com. Clinton-Gore '96, Gore 2000, Washington; cons. Gore 2000, Washington. Rotary fellow, 1984. Mem. Harvard Club, Phi Beta Kappa. Avocations: running, weight training, music, theatre, travel. Home: 1401 17th St NW Ph Apt1008 Washington DC 20036-6400 Office: US AID Office Gen Counsel Ronald Reagan Bldg & Interna C Washington DC 20523-0001 E-mail: jmarburg-goodman@usaid.gov.

MARBURY, RITCHEY MCGUIRE, III, engineering executive, surveyor; b. Albany, Ga., May 18, 1938; s. Ritchey McGuire and Shirley Kathryn (VanHouten) M.; m. Fonda Gayle Starnes, June 16, 1962; children: Mary Kathryn, Ritchey McGuire IV. BCE, Ga. Tech. Inst., 1960, M in City Planning, 1966. Registered profl. engr., Ga., Fla., Idaho, Ala.; land surveyor, Ga. V.p. Marbury Engring. Co., Albany, Ga., 1965-78, pres., chmn. bd., 1981—; pres. Marbury, Ritter, Scott & Turner, Inc., 1970-78, 81-92, Marbury Assocs., Inc., 1991—, Idaho Boise Mission of Latter-day Saints Ch., 1978-81. Presenter seminars on total quality mgmt. to nat. convs. of Am. Cons. Engrs. Coun., Design Constrn. Quality Inst., Sml. Firm Coalition of Cons. Engrs., Assn. for Project Mgrs. Exec. bd. Boy Scouts Am., Southwest Ga., 1982—. Served to 1st lt. U.S. Army, 1963-65. Mem. NSPE (South Ga. chpt. pres. 1993-95), Am. Cons. Engrs. Coun., Surveying and Mapping Soc. of Ga. (bd. dirs. 1966-78), Ga. Planning Assn., Home Builders Assn. (bd. dirs. 1985-86), Rotary. Mem. Lds Ch. Avocations: fishing, writing, music, computer, golf. Home: 1824 Green Valley Dr Albany GA 31707-3116 Office: 2334 Lake Park Dr Albany GA 31707-3132 E-mail: rmm3@marbury.com. *Always be a role model of Christlike behavior and do those things that make a significant differenc for good. Do what's right simply because it's the right thing to do. The greatest results come through kindness.*

MARBURY, STEPHON, professional basketball player; b. Feb. 20, 1977; Student, Ga. Tech., 1996. Guard Minn. Timberwolves, 1996-98; guard, forward N.J. Nets, 1998—2001; player Phoenix Suns, Phoenix, 2002—. Named to 1996-97 NBA All-Rookie First Team, NBA Rookie of the Mo. for Jan., 1997 Achievements include becoming only 5th player in NBA history to top 40 points and 10 assists in game without a turnover; led the Timberwolves in 1997-98, ranked 4th in the NBA in assists; has appeared in 8 NBA playoff games, averaging 16.6 points per game; hit a Timberwolves franchise record 8 three-pointers in 11 attempts, totaling a game-high 35 points, 7 assists and 4 rebounds, many others. Office: Phoenix Suns America West Arena 201 E. Jefferson St Phoenix AZ 85042*

MARBURY, VIRGINIA LOMAX, insurance and investment executive; b. Ruston, La., June 25, 1918; d. Dallas Daniel and Della (Southern) Lomax; m. William A. Marbury Jr., Sept. 5, 1943; children: Rebekah, Caroline. BA, La. Tech. U., 1936, LLD (hon.), 1987; MusB, La. State U., 1938. Exec. v.p. Marbury Corp., Ruston, La., 1944—; sec.-treas. Bankers Life La., 1959—. 1st v.p., membership chmn. Lincoln Parish Mus. and Hist. Soc., Ruston, La., 1992—. Recipient Tower Medallion award La. Tech. U., 1991. Mem. Shreveport Symphony Soc. Republican. Episcopalian. Office: Marbury Corp 601 N Trenton St Ruston LA 71270-3840

MARBURY, WILLIAM ARDIS, banker; b. Ruston, La., July 22, 1917; s. William Ardis Sr. and Leola (Ridgdill) M.; m. Virginia Lomax, Sept. 5, 1943; children: Rebekah, Caroline. BA, La. Tech. U., 1936, LLD (hon.), 1987. Pres., chmn. Bankers Life of La., Ruston, 1959—; pres. Ruston State Bank & Trust Co., 1972-81; also bd. dirs. Bankers Life of La., Ruston, 1959—. Bd. dirs., chmn. Ruston State Bank & Trust Co., La. Tech Univ. Found. Bd. dirs., pres. Lincoln Gen. Hosp., Ruston, 1962-82. Recipient Silver Beaver award Boy Scouts Am., Washington, 1979, Alumnus of Yr. award La. Tech. U., Ruston, 1976, Disting. Svc. award Kiwanis, Ruston, 1990. Mem. Ruston C. of C. (pres. 1955, Robert E. Russ award 1990). Republican. Episcopalian. Home: 601 N Trenton St Ruston LA 71270-3840 Office: The Marbury Corp 601 N Trenton St Ruston LA 71270-3840

MARBUT, ROBERT GORDON, communications and broadcast executive, investor; b. Athens, Ga., Apr. 11, 1935; s. Robert Smith and Laura Gordon (Powers) M.; m. Margo Susan Spitz, Sept. 24, 1989; children: Robert Gordon, Laura Dodd, Michael Powers, Marcy Lizbeth. B Indsl. Engring., Ga. Inst. Tech., 1957; MBA with distinction, Harvard U., 1963. Registered profl. engr., Calif. Engr. Esso Standard Oil Co., Baton Rouge, 1957; corp. dir. engring. and plans Copley Press, La Jolla, Calif., 1963-70; v.p. Harte-Hanks Newspapers, Inc., San Antonio, 1970-71; pres., CEO Harte-Hanks Comm., Inc., 1971-91, also dir., 1971-91, vice chmn. bd. dirs., 1991; founder, chmn., CEO Argyle Comm., Inc., 1992—; founder, CEO, dir. Argyle TV Holding, Inc., 1993-95; co-founder, chmn., CEO Argyle TV, Inc., 1994-97; chmn., co-CEO Hearst-Argyle TV, Inc., N.Y.C., 1997-2000, chmn., 2001—; co-mng. ptnr. Argyle Global, LP, 2001—. Dir. AP, 1979-88, vice chmn. 1987-88; chmn. Newspaper Advt. Bur., 1988-90, exec. com. dir. 1974-80, 82-90; bd. dirs Valero Energy Corp., Tupperware, Inc., Proact Techs., IKnowledge, Inc., Bus. Execs. Nat. Security; mem. adv. bd. U Ga. Henry W. Grady Sch. Journalism, 1975-83; mem. adv. bd. Ga. Tech., 1978-81, 98—; founding mem. Am. Bus. Conf., 1981-89; mem. U. Tex. Centennial commn., 1981-83; pres. adv. coun. U. Tex. Coll. Comm., 1982-83; bd. dirs. Up With People, 1983-2001, exec. com., 1984-2001; instr. Armstrong Coll., 1951, Calif. State U., L.A., 1964, Woodbury Coll., 1964. Author: (with Healy, Henderson and others) Creative Collective Bargaining, 1965. Coordinating chmn. San Antonio Target 90 commn., 1983-84; campaign chmn. United Way, San Antonio, 1985, chmn. bd. trustees 1988-89; vice chmn. Tex. select com. on Tax Equity, 1987-89; mem select com. Tex. Revenues, 1991-92; mem. Tex. World Trade Coun., 1986-87. Capt. USAF, 1958-61. Salzburg Inst. Am. Studies sr. fellow, 1997—; recipient Isaiah Thomas award Rochester Inst. Tech., 1980, EXCEL award in comm., 1987, People of Vision award, 1991; selected to Acad. Disting. Engring. Alumni Ga. Tech., 1995. Mem. Am. Newspaper Publs. Assn. (chmn. task group on future, chmn. telecomm. com. 1974-81, bd. dirs. 1976-84, chmn. future task group), So. Newspaper Pubs. Assn. (pres. 1979-80, dir. 1975-81, treas. 1977), Am. Newspaper Pubs. Assn. Found. (trustee 1976-79), Tex. Daily Newspaper Assn. (pres. 1979, Tex. Newspaper Leader of Yr., 1981), N.Y. Met. Club, Doubles, San Antonio Country Club, Argyle Club, Greater San Antonio C. of C., Delta Tau Delta (Alumni Achievement award 2000), Omicron Delta Kappa, Phi Eta Sigma. Office: Hearst-Argyle Television Inc 200 Concord Plaza Dr Ste 700 San Antonio TX 78216-6941

MARCALI, JEAN GREGORY, chemist, retired; b. Jermyn, Pa., May 29, 1926; d. John Robert and Anna Marie Gregory; m. Kalman Marcali, Oct. 6, 1956; children: Coleman, Frederick. Student, U. Pa., 1948-52, U. Del., 1971-72. Microanalyst E.I. du Pont de Nemours & Co., Deepwater, N.J., 1943-60, tech. info. analyst, organic chems. dept., 1960-64, tech. info. analyst info. systems dept. Wilmington, Del., 1964-67, sr. adviser tech. info., 1967-70, supr. tech. info., 1970-82, 85-89, supr. adminstrv. svcs. Ctrl. Rsch. Dept., 1982-85, cons., 1989-92, retired, 1992. Sec. Alfred I. Dupont Elem. PTA, 1971, pres. 1972; pres. PTA Brandywine Sch. Dist., 1973; mem. Wilmington Dist. Rep. Com., 1976—. Mem. Am. Chem. Soc. (treas. div. chem. info. 1976-81, chmn.-elect 1981, chmn. 1982, 83, div. councilor 1983-90), Am. Chem. Soc. (com. on chem. abstracts svc. 1983-85, 87-93, mem. joint bd. coun. com. on chem. abstracts svc. 1994-96, 98, 99, 2000, Del. sec. chem. lit. topical group, chmn. 1979-80, chem. vets. chmn.-elect 1999), Order Ea. Star, Du Pont Country. Lutheran. Home: 312 Waycross Rd Wilmington DE 19803-2950

MARCANO, SORAYA, visual artist; b. Cidra, P.R., July 5, 1965; d. Mariano Marcano and Luz Velazquez. BFA, U. P.R., 1988; MFA, Pratt Inst., Bklyn., 1995. One-woman shows include U. P.R., 1991, Colegio de Abogados, P.R., 1991, Charas Art Ctr., N.Y.C., 1991, Higgins Gallery, 1994, P.R. Workshop, 1997, Ctrl. Conn. State U., New Britain, 1997, El Museo Francisco Oller, Inc., Buffalo, 1998, Jamaica (N.Y.) Ctr. for Arts and Learning, 1999, Mixta Gallery, NY, 2002, exhibited in group shows at Mus. City of N.Y., 1991, Art in Gen., N.Y.C., 1994, San Juan (P.R.) Conservation Studio, 1994, U. Panama, 1994, 1995, Longwood Gallery, Bronx, N.Y., 1995, Mexic-Arte Mus., Tex., 1996, John Jay Gallery, N.Y.C., 1996, Museo de las Americas, P.R., 1996, Bronx Mus. Arts, 1996—97, Dalton Gallery, Ga., 1997, Jamaica (N.Y.) Art Ctr., 1997, Musee d'Art Contemporain de Chamaleires, France, 1997, Mus. Contemporary Art, San Juan, 1998, Found. Ctr. Cultural Altos de Chavon, La Romana, Dominican Republic, 1998, U.S. Dept. State/Art in Embassies Program, U.S. Embassy, San Salvador, 2000—, Off-Centre Gallery, Bristol, Eng., 2001, Town Hall, Queens, NY, 2001, Ctr. for Book Arts, NY, 2001. Home: 8005 6th Ave Apt 2B Brooklyn NY 11209-4038

MARCATANTE, JOHN JOSEPH, educational administrator; b. N.Y.C., Mar. 3, 1930; s. Joseph and Matilda Clara (Grasso) M. Student, NYU, 1948-50; AB, Bklyn. Coll., 1955; MS in Edn., Hunter Coll., 1958. English tchr. secondary schs., N.Y.C., 1955-72; asst. prin. Astoria Intermediate Sch., 1967—. Instr. Hunter Coll., 1963; lectr. in edn. Grad. Sch., Queens Coll., N.Y.C., 1965-67. Cons., Anglo-Am. Seminar on Teaching English, Dartmouth Coll., 1966, Anglo-Am. Seminar on Teaching the Disadvantaged, West Midlands Coll., Great Britain, 1968. Author: Identification and Image Stories, 1964, American Folklore and Legends, 1967, (with others) Macmillan Gateway English Series, 1969, Tales from World Epics, 1990; also numerous articles in profl. jours., poetry; editor: Fourteenth Yearbook N.Y. Society for Experimental Study for Education, 1970. Mem. Nat. Coun. Tchrs. English, N.Y.C. Tchrs. English, Coun. Supervisory Assns., Cath. Tchrs. Assn., Columbia Assn. N.Y.C., Poetry Soc. Am. Home: 52 Daffodil Ln Wantagh NY 11793-1802

MARCEAU, JUDITH MARIE, elementary education educator; b. Gardner, Mass., Aug. 10, 1946; d. George Joseph and Bernice Victoria (Johnson) Babineau; m. James Victor Krymowski, Aug. 20, 1976 (div. Mar. 1985); children: Kathryn Victoria, Kenneth James; m. Glenn Francis Marceau, Aug. 30, 1989. Grad., Sch. Worcester Art Mus., 1967; BFA, Clark U., 1971. Tchr. elem. art Quabbin Regional Pub. Schs., Barre, Mass., 1967-70, Gardner (Mass.) Pub. Schs., 1970-81, tchr. elem., 1981—. Author, editor: Fascinating Facts of Gardner, 1977, 2d edit., 1999, Hubbardston as Seen Through the Eyes of its Children, 1987; author numerous poems. Active Hubbarston Hist. Commn.; vol. Hubbarston Recycling Initiative; bd. dirs. Gardner Edn. Assn., 1975-86; bd. dirs. Youth Advocacy and Counseling Ctr., Gardner, 1979-82. Recipient Citation of Outstanding Edn. City of Gardner, 1994,2000, Nat. Libr. Poetry, 1998, editor's choice award Nat. Libr. Poetry, 1999, Cert. of Commendation for outstanding achievement Mayor of City of Garner. Mem. Mass. Tchrs. Assn., Nat. Tchrs. Assn. Avocations: writing history, poetry, antiques, watercolor painting, sketching. Home: 221 Gardner Rd Hubbardston MA 01452-1655 Office: Prospect Sch 75 E Broadway Gardner MA 01440-3339

MARCEAU, LISA LYNN See **MOORE, LISA LYNN**

MARCELLA, JOSEPH, information system administrator; BS in Biochemistry, Temple U., 1970. Computer operator/sys. programmer, asst. mgr. King Kullen Grocery Co./Gen. Fire & Casualty, L.I., 1971-72; asst. v.p., electronic banking Bank of Am., Las Vegas, 1972-83; sr. v.p., dir. info. svcs. Primerit Bank of Nev., 1983-96; dir. info. technologies City of Las Vegas, 1997—. Bd. dirs., past pres. Bank Adminstrn. Inst.; past pres., v.p. Nev. Clearing House Assn.; bd. dirs. Western Payments Alliance; mem. Rules Com. Nat. Automated Clearning House, Task Force to Build Acad. Advanced Tech., Focus Sch. Partnership program. Mem. South Nev. Entities Tech. Alliance (bd. dirs.). Office: City Las Vegas Dept Info Techs City Hall 5th Fl 400 Stewart Ave Las Vegas NV 89101-2927

MARCELLO, FRANK F. lawyer, educator; b. Chgo., Aug. 11, 1961; s. Fred Anthony and Antoinette Marie (Colombo) M. BS, DePaul U., 1983; MBA, Dominican U., 1996; JD, The John Marshall Law Sch., 1986. Exec. legal coord. Office of Cook County Pub. Defender, Chgo., 1985-87, asst. dep. chief, 1987-89; v.p. exec. counsel Connaught Corp., 1989-93; v.p. sr. counsel Internat. Cons. Group, 1993-96; prof. law Northwestern Bus. Coll., 1996—, Dominican U., River Forest, 1996—. Active Joint Civic Com. Italian Ams., Chgo. Mem. ABA, AAUP, Justiniam Soc., Nat. Italian Am. Bar Assn., Sons of Italy Found., Assn. Cath. Colls. and Univs. Office: Dominican U 7900 W Division St River Forest IL 60305 E-mail: ffm@abanet.org.

MARCELLUS, JOHN ROBERT, III, trombonist, educator; b. Overton, Tex., Sept. 17, 1939; s. John Robert and Grace (Stockman) M.; children: Robert Gray, John Frederick. BS, U. Md., 1964; Mus.M., Catholic U. Am., 1970, D.Mus. Arts, 1972. Adj. prof. trombone Cath. U. Am., dir. trombone choir and brass ensembles, 1966-78; prof. N.C. Sch. Arts, 1965-68; mem. rotating faculty Inst. Advanced Mus. Studies, Montreux, Switzerland, 1974, Am. U., 1970-78; prof. trombone Eastman Sch. Music, Rochester, N.Y., 1978—, acting chmn. woodwind, brass and percussion, 1981-98, chmn. woodwind, brass and percussion, 1998—, dir. internat. trombone workshop, 1991. Co-dir. Ea. Trombone Workshop, Towson, Md., 1974-80, Internat. Trombone Workshop, 1991; guest condr. Chautauqua Symphony Orch., Penfield Symphony Orch., Chautauqua Wind Ensemble, U.S. Naval Acad. Band, Nat. Music Camp, Interlochen. Trombonist USN Band, Washington, 1960-64, Balt. Symphony, 1964-65; trombonist Nat. Symphony, Washington, 1965-78, prin. trombone, 1970-78; prin. trombone Chautauqua Symphony Orch., 1978; mem. Eastman Brass Quintet; clinician, soloist King Benge Mus. Instruments; solo tours to Scandinavia, Japan, Germany, Greece, Austria,

Poland, Australia, England, France, Switzerland; performer with Art Mooney, Ray Eberle, Charlie Spivak, Vaughn Monroe, Henry Mancini Orchs.; music dir. Brighton Symphony Orch., 1980—; contbr. articles to Music Educators Jour., Instrumentalist, Accent, Internat. Trombone Assn. Jour. Named Musician of Yr. Mu Phi Epsilon. Mem. Internat. Trombone Assn. (founder, bd. dirs., pres. 1988-90, award 1999), Am. Fedn. Musicians, Nat. Assn. Wind and Percussion Instruments, Music Educators Nat. Conf., Phi Mu Alpha. Office: Eastman Sch Music 26 Gibbs St Rochester NY 14604-2599 *Dedication, drive and determination to the art of music has been center front on my career in music.*

MARCELYNAS, RICHARD CHADWICK, management consultant; b. New London, Conn., Aug. 21, 1937; s. Anthony F. and Elizabeth A. (Chadwick) M.; m. Betty A. Forray, July 1, 1961; children: Michael R., Thomas R. BA in Bus. Adminstrn., U. Wash., 1961; postgrad. Seattle U., 1971-72. Mgmt. trainee, installation foreman Pacific Bell, Fullerton, Calif., 1964-65; cost acct. Scott Paper Co., Everett, Wash., 1965-68; asst. v.p. pers. and adminstrn. Nat. Pub. Svc. Ins. Co., Seattle, 1968-77; pers. ops. mgr. Olympia Brewing Co., 1977-78; mgr. indsl. rels. Heath Tecna Precision Structures Inc., Kent, Wash., 1978-85; mgmt. cons., recruiter Pilon Mgmt. Co., Seattle, 1985-90; pers. adminstr. Peninsula Group Olympia, Wash., 1990-94; pres. Chadwick & Assocs., Olympia, 1994-2000; info. tech. recruiter Red Rover Solutions, Bellevue, Wash., 2000—. Served to maj. USMCR, 1961-77. Decorated commendations for bravery and tech. expertise, 1962-64; recipient Seattle chpt. Pacific N.W. Personnel Mgrs. Assn. Bd. Dirs. award, 1975. Mem. Pacific N.W. Personnel Mgrs. Assn. (past pres. Tacoma chpt.), Oreg. Lodging Assn., Human Resources Consultants Network. Office: 623 Sherman St SW Olympia WA 98502-5454

MARCH, CATHLEEN CASE, education educator; b. Port Jervis, N.Y., Dec. 8, 1942; d. Fred Baker Case and Elizabeth (Mayes) Allen; children: Elizabeth, Brian, Matthew, Melinda. BS, U. Pa., 1963; MS, SUNY, Buffalo, 1979, PhD, 1998. Cert. K-12 tchr., N.Y. 1st grade tchr. Anna Merritt Sch., Lockport, N.Y., 1964-65; kindergarten tchr. Dewitt Clinton Sch., 1966-69; asst. librarian Lockport Pub. Libr., 1970-72; reading tchr. Starpoint Ctrl. Sch., Lockport, 1975-78, Medina (N.Y.) Ctrl. Schs., 1979-98; prof. D'Youville Coll., 1998—. Adj. prof. Canisius Coll., Buffalo, 1992-98. Editor: Niagara Frontier Reading Coun., 1991-96. Named Educator of Excellence N.Y. State English Coun., 1994. Mem. Internat. Reading Assn., Internat. Whole Lang. Umbrella, N.Y. State Reading Assn. (Svc. to Reading award 1996), Niagara Frontier Reading Coun. (pres. 1997-98). Avocations: reading, writing. Home: 6801 Lilac Dr Apt A Lockport NY 14094-6824 E-mail: Cathread@aol.com.

MARCH, DARLENE J. secondary school educator, news correspondent; b. Odell, Nebr., Apr. 24, 1936; d. Albert Lawrence and Anna S. (Kostal) Hubka; m. Ronald D. March, Dec. 20, 1958; children: Teresa Ann Hunzeker, Ronald S., Rhonda Jean Heier. BS in Vocat. Home Econs., U. Nebr., 1956. Cert. tchr. Nebr., substitute tchr. Tchr., volleyball coach, FHA advisor Randolph (Nebr.) H.S., 1956—58, Barneston (Nebr.) H.S., 1958—61; substitute tchr. various schs., 1983—; news corr. Beatrice (Nebr.) Daily Sun Newspaper, 1987—. Sch. bd. mem. Barneston Consol. Sch. Dist., 1982—86; leader 4-H; clk., organist, session mem. Barneston Presbyn. Ch. Named Leader of Day, 4-H, 1983. Mem.: Order of the Ea. Star (worthy matron 1976, asst. warder Nebr. Grand chpt., Grand rep. Vt. in Nebr. 1979, 1993—95). Presbyterian. Home: 103 W Grand Ave Barneston NE 68309

MARCH, JAMES GARDNER, social scientist, educator; b. Cleve., Jan. 15, 1928; s. James Herbert and Mildred (MacCorkle) M.; m. Jayne Mary Dohr, Sept. 23, 1947; children: Kathryn Sue, Gary Clifton, James Christopher, Roderic Gunn. BA, U. Wis., 1949; MA, Yale U., 1950, PhD, 1953; PhD (hon.), Copenhagen Sch. Econs., 1978, Swedish Sch. Econs., 1979, U. Wis., Milw., 1980, U. Bergen, 1980, Uppsala U., 1987, Helsinki Sch. Econs., 1991, Göteborg U., 1998, U. Poitiers, 2001. From asst. prof. to prof. Carnegie Inst. Tech., 1953-64; prof., dean Sch. Social Scis. U. Calif., Irvine, 1964-70; prof. mgmt., higher edn., polit. sci. and sociology Stanford (Calif.) U., 1970-95, prof. emeritus, 1995—. Cons. in field; mem. Nat. Council Ednl. Research, 1975-78, Nat. Sci. Bd., 1968-74; mem. sociol.-social psychology panel NSF, 1964-66; social sci. tng. com. NIMH, 1967-68; mem. math. social sci. com. Social Sci. Research Council, 1958-60; mem. Assembly Behavioral and Social Sci., NRC, 1973-79, chmn. com. on aging, 1977-82, chmn. com. on math., sci., tech. edn., 1984-86 Author: (with H.A. Simon) Organizations, 1958, 2nd edit., 1993, (with R.M. Cyert) A Behavioral Theory of the Firm, 1963, 2nd edit., 1992, Handbook of Organizations, 1965; (with B.R. Gelbaum) Mathematics for the Social and Behavioral Sciences, 1969; (with M.D. Cohen) Leadership and Ambiguity, 1974, 2nd edit., 1986, Academic Notes, 1974; (with C.E. Lave) An Introduction to Models in the Social Sciences, 1975; (with J.P. Olsen) Ambiguity and Choice in Organizations, 1976, Aged Wisconsin, 1977, Autonomy as a Factor in Group Organization, 1980, Pleasures of the Process, 1980, Slow Learner, 1985; (with R. Weissinger-Baylon) Ambiguity and Command, 1986, Decisions and Organizations, 1988; (with J.P. Olsen) Rediscovering Institutions, 1989, Minor Memos, 1990, A Primer on Decision Making, 1994, Fornuft og Forandring, 1995; (with J.P. Olsen) Democratic Governance, 1995; The Pursuit of Organizational Intelligence, 1999, (with M. Schulz and X. Zhou) The Dynamics of Rules, 2000, Late Harvest, 2000; contbr. articles to profl. jour. Fellow Ctr. Advanced Study in Behavioral Scis., 1955-56, 73-74; recipient Wilbur Lucius Cross medal Yale U., 1968; named knight 1st class Royal Norwegian Order of Merit, 1995, Comdr. of Order of Lion of Finland, 1999. Mem. NAS, Nat. Acad. Edn., Accademia Italiana di Economia Aziendale, Royal Swedish Acad. Scis., Norwegian Acad. of Sci. and Letters, Am. Acad. Arts and Scis., Am. Econ. Assn., Am. Polit. Sci. Assn. (v.p. 1983-84, John Gaus award 1997), Am. Psychol. Assn., Am. Sociol. Assn., Acad. Mgmt. (Disting. Scholar award 1999), Russell Sage Found. (trustee 1985-94, chmn. 1990-93), Finnish Soc. Scis. and Letters, Citigroup Behavioral Scis. Rsch. Coun. (chmn. 1994-2000), Am. Philos. Soc., Phi Beta Kappa, Sigma Xi. Home: 501 Portola Rd Box 8136 Portola Valley CA 94028 Office: Stanford U 71 Cubberley Stanford CA 94305-3096 E-mail: march@stanford.edu.

MARCH, KATHLEEN PATRICIA, judge; b. May 18, 1949; married; 2 children. BA, Colo. Coll., 1971; JD, Yale U., 1974. Bar: N.Y. 1975, Calif. 1978. Law clk. to hon. judge Thomas J. Griesa U.S. Dist. Ct. (so. dist.) N.Y., 1974-75; assoc. Cahill, Gordon & Reindel, N.Y.C., 1975-77; asst. U.S. atty. criminal div. Office of U.S. Atty. Cen. Dist. Calif., L.A., 1978-82; assoc. Adams, Duque & Hazeltine, 1982-85; ptnr. Demetriou, Del Guercio & Lovejoy, 1985-88; judge U.S. Bankruptcy Ct. Cen. Dist. Calif., Calif., 1988—. Bd. editors Yale U. Law Jour. Mem.: ABA, Fin. Lawyers Assn., L.A. Bankruptcy Forum (bd. dirs.), Nat. Assn. Women Judges, Women Lawyers Assn., L.A. County Bar Assn., Fed. Bar Assn., Phi Beta Kappa. Avocations: horseback riding, scuba diving, photography. Office: Roybal Fed Ct Bldg 255 E Temple St Ste 1460 Los Angeles CA 90012-3332

MARCH, LIONEL JOHN, architecture educator, researcher; b. Hove, Sussex, Eng., Jan. 26, 1934; came to U.S., 1984; s. Leonard James and Rosina Amelia March; m. Maureen Mary Francis; children: Candida, Ben Oliver, Ben, Talitha, Anna, Sarah. BA with honours, Cambridge (Eng.) U., 1959, Dip Arch, 1961, MA, 1962, ScD, 1978. Lectr. Cambridge U. Sch. Architecture, 1968-76; prof. U. Waterloo (Ont., Can.) Faculty Engring., 1974-76, Open U. Faculty Tech., Milton Keynes, Eng., 1976-81; rector, v.p. Royal Coll. Art, London, 1981-84; prof. Grad. Sch. Architecture and Urban and Design, UCLA, 1984-94, prof. Sch. Architecture and Arts, 1994—. Dir. Ctr. for Land Use and Built Form Studies, Cambridge, 1969-73; chmn. Applied Rsch. Lbd., Cambridge, 1969-73; gov. Imperial Coll. Sci. and Tech., London, 1981-84. Author: The Geometry of Environment, 1971, Architectonics of Humanism, 1998, Schindler and How Houses, 1999; editor, author: Urban Space and Structures, 1972, The Architecture of Form, 1976, R.M. Schindler, 1995; gen. editor: Cambridge Architectural and Urban Studies, 12 vols., 1970-89; founding editor Planning and Design, 1974—. Sub-lt. Royal Navy, 1953-55. Commonwealth Fund Harkness fellow Joint Ctr. for Urban Studies, Harvard U. and MIT, 1962-64. Fellow Inst. Math. and Its Applications, Royal Soc. Arts, Royal Coll. Art. Avocations: restoration, gardening, family. Home: How House 2422 Silver Ridge Ave Los Angeles CA 90039-3322 E-mail: lmarch@ucla.edu.

MARCH, MICHAEL FRANCIS, propulsion systems analyst, consultant; b. Detroit, Mar. 3, 1962; s. Stanley and Dorothy M. AAS in Archtl. Design, Macomb C.C., Warren, Mich., 1983; BS in Mech. Engring., Lawrence Technol. U., 1986; ME, U. Fla., 1994. Sr. analytical engr. United Techs. Corp.-Pratt & Whitney, West Palm Beach, Fla., 1986-93; pvt. practice propulsion analysis cons. Tullahoma, Tenn., 1994—. Mem. ASME.

MARCH, XAVIER, systems analyst; b. Guayaquil, Ecuador, Mar. 13, 1932; came to U.S., 1953; s. Francscio and Nieves (Hernández) M.; m. Carol ann Heiser, Sept. 29, 1962; children: Gregory Fancis, Christopher John. BA, Dartmouth Coll., 1957; MS in Computer Sci., Iona Coll., 1985. Applied scientist IBM Corp., Caracas, Venezuela, 1957-61, data ctr. rep. N.Y.C., 1961-63, scientific developer White Plains, N.Y., 1963-70, advisory programmer, 1972-80, project leader Croydon, U.K., 1970-72, systems assurance rep. Sterling Forest, N.Y., 1980-86, sr. programmer Norwalk, Conn., 1986-88, application devel. auditor Southbury, 1988-93, ad effectiveness cons., 1993—. Author/editor: Application Development Guide, 1986 (IBM award 1987), Application Development Process, 1991, Testing of Boject-Oriented Methods, Calsses and Systems, 1994; author: (software tools) Risk Assessment Expert System, 1987 (IBM award 1989), Ad Maturity Audit Expert System, 1989 (IBM award 1990). Mem. Assn. Computing Machinery, IEEE Computer Soc. Home: 216 Saint Andrews Blvd Campobello SC 29322-9516 Office: IBM Consulting Group 150 Kettletown Rd Southbury CT 06488-2685

MARCHAK, MAUREEN PATRICIA, anthropology and sociology educator; b. Lethbridge, Alta., Can., June 22, 1936; d. Adrian Ebenezer and Wilhelmina Rankin (Hamilton) Russell; m. William Marchak, Dec. 31, 1956; children: Geordon Eric, Lauren Craig. BA, U. B.C., Vancouver, Can., 1958, PhD, 1970. Asst. prof. U. B.C., Vancouver, 1972-75, assoc. prof., 1975-80, prof., 1980—, head dept. anthropology and sociology, 1987-90, dean faculty arts, 1990-96, disting. scholar in residence Peter Wall Inst., 2000-01, fellow Lio Centre for Study of Global Issues, prof., dean emerita of arts, 2002—. Author: Ideological Perspectives on Canada, 1975, 2d edit., 1981, 3d edit., 1988, In Whose Interests, 1979, Green Gold, 1983 (John Porter award 1985), The Integrated Circus, The New Right and The Restructuring of Global Markets, 1991, Logging the Globe, 1995, Falldown, Forest Policy in British Columbia, 1999, Racism, Sexism and the University, the Political Science Affair at UBC, 1996, God's Assassins. State Terrorism in Argentina in the 1970's, 1999 (Wallace J. Ferguson prize, Hon. Mention); author, co-editor: Uncommon Property, 1987; mem. editl. bd. Can. Rev. Sociology and Anthropology, Montreal, Que., 1971-74, Studies in Polit. Economy, Ottawa, Ont., Can., 1980-87, Current Sociology, 1980-86, Can. Jour. Sociology, 1986-90, B.C. Studies, 1988-90, 2000—. Bd. dirs., chair ethics com. Univ. Hosp., 1992-93, Cedar Lodge Trust Soc., 1989-92; mem. adv. coun. Ecotrust, 1991-93, bd. dirs., 1993-97, Eco-trust Can., 1995-99; chmn. bd. dirs. B.C. Bldgs. Corp., 1992-95; mem. B.C. Forest Appeals Commn., 1992-2002; bd. govs. U. B.C., 1999-2001; bd. dirs. Pub. Svc. Employees for Environ. Ethics, 2002--. Fellow Royal Soc. Can. (v.p. Acad. II 1994-98, pres. Acad. II 1998-2000); mem. Can. Sociology and Anthropology Assn. (pres. 1979-80, other offices), Internat. Sociol. Assn., Can. Polit. Sci. Assn., Assn. for Can. Studies, Forest History Soc. (mem. exec. com. 1991-92). Avocations: hiking, swimming, traveling. Home: 4455 W 1st Ave Vancouver BC Canada V6R 4H9 Office: U BC Dept Anthrop & Sociology 6303 NW Marine Dr Vancouver BC Canada V6T 1Z1 also: Lio Centre for Study of Global Issues 6476 NW Marine Dr Vancouver BC Canada V6T 1Z2 E-mail: pmarchak@interchange.ubc.ca.

MARCHALONIS, JOHN JACOB, immunologist, educator; b. Scranton, Pa., July 22, 1940; s. John Louis and Anna Irene (Stadner) M.; m. Anne B. Caldwell, 1969 (div. 1976); 1 child, Lee; m. Sally Ann Sevy, May 5, 1978; children: Elizabeth, Emily. AB summa cum Laude, Lafayette Coll., 1962; PhD, Rockefeller U., 1967. Grad. fellow Rockefeller U., 1962-67; fellow Am. Cancer Soc. Walter and Eliza Hall Inst. Med. Research, 1967-68; asst. prof. biomed. scis. Brown U., 1969-70; head molecular immunology lab. Walter and Eliza Hall Inst. Med. Research, Melbourne, Australia, 1970-76; head cell biology and biochemistry sect. Frederick Cancer Research Ctr., 1977-80; adj. prof. dept. pathology U. Pa., 1977-83; prof., chmn. dept. biochemistry and molecular biology Med. U. S.C., Charleston, 1980-88; prof., chmn. dept. microbiology and immunology U. Ariz., Tucson, 1988—, prof. pathology, 1991—, prof. medicine, 1992—. Bd. dirs. Type Tissue Culture Collection; vis. prof. human immunology Pierre et Marie Curie U., Paris, 2001. Author: Immunity in Evolution, 1977; editor: Comparative Immunology, 1976, the Lymphocyte: Structure and Function, 1977; (with N. Cohen) Self/Non-Self Discrimination, 1980; (with G.W. Warr) Antibody as a Tool, 1982, The Immunobiology and Molecular Biology of Parasitic Infections, 1983, Antigen-Specific T Cell Receptors and Factors, 1987, The Lymphocyte: Structure and Function, 2d edit., 1987; (with Carol Reinisch) Defense Molecules, 1989; (with Gregory Beck, Edwin L. Cooper and Gail S. Habicht) Primordial Immunity, 1994; editl. bd. jours. in field. Active Nat. Commn. Damon Runyon-Walter Winchel Cancer Fund. Named among 1,000 most highly cited sci. authors Inst. for Sci. Info.; Frank R. Lillie fellow, 1974; grantee in field. Fellow Am. Inst. Chemists, Am. Acad. Microbiology; mem. AAAS, Am. Assn. Immunology, Am. Soc. Biol. Chemists, Henry Kunkel Soc., Sigma Xi, Phi Beta Kappa. Episcopalian. Achievements include development of microchemical (radioimmunochemical) approaches for proteins and surface receptors of living cells; characterization of immunoglobulin-like antigen receptors of thymus-derived lymphocytes; application of synthetic peptide technology to antibodies, T cell receptors and autoimmunity; pioneered investigation of the molecular evolution of immunity, peptides therapies for acquired immunodeficiency and autoimmunity. Home: 5661 N Camino Arturo Tucson AZ 85718-3933 Office: U Ariz Health Sci Ctr Tucson AZ 85724-0001

MARCHAM, TIMOTHY VICTOR, pharmacist; b. New Britain, Conn., June 15, 1943; s. John Nelson and Eileen Agnes (Mannings) M. BS in Pharmacy, U. Conn., 1966. Diplomate Am. Bd. Forensic Examiners. Staff pharmacist Kensington (Conn.) Pharmacy, Inc., 1968-72, New Britain Meml. Hosp., 1972-75; cons. pharmacist Health Care Cons. Corp., West Hartford, Conn., 1976-85; staff pharmacist Conn. Dept. Mental Health/Cedarcrest Regional Hosp., Newington, 1978-85, dir. pharmacy, 1985-91, N.C. Dept. Corrections/McCain Correctional Hosp., 1992-2000; corporator New Britain (Conn.) Gen. Hosp., 1974—. Radiol. officer Civil Preparedness/Emergency Mgmt. Div., Town of Plainville, Conn., 1965-91; life mem. New Britain Gen. Hosp. Aux.; pres. New Britain Meml. Hosp. Credit Union, 1974-75; provider, SAC officer Health Systems Agy. of North Cen. Conn., 1976-82. Capt. CAP, 1974—. Fellow Am. Soc. Cons. Pharmacists, Am. Coll. Forensic Examiners; mem. Am. Pharm. Assn., Am. Soc. Hosp. Pharmacists, Conn. Pharm. Assn. (awards and scholarship), Conn. Soc. Hosp. Pharmacists, Pharmacy Alumni Assn. U. Conn. (life), N.C. Pharm. Assn., N.C. Soc. Hosp. Pharmacists, Moore County Pharm. Assn., Am. Meteorol. Soc. (assoc. 1974-2001), Am. Numismatic Assn. (life.). Republican. Episcopalian. Avocations: coins, stamps, electronics, computers. Home: 612 Sun Rd Aberdeen NC 28315-2128

MARCHAND, JACQUELYN, foundation administrator; b. Rochester, N.Y., Oct. 17, 1961; d. Leo R. and Frances Mary (Popp) M. BA magna cum laude, SUNY, Albany, 1983; postgrad., U. Rochester, 1990—. Devel. asst. Internat. Ctr. Integrative Studies, N.Y.C., 1984-85; nat. mgr. spl. events Nat. Multiple Sclerosis Soc., 1985-88; devel. officer Christie Sch., Portland, Oreg., 1988-89; assoc. dir. devel. Monroe Community Coll., Rochester, 1989-90; dir. devel. SUNY Coll. at Brockport Found., 1990—. Bd. dirs. Genesee Valley, Inc. coun. Girl Scouts U.S.A., Rochester, 1991—. Mem. Nat. Soc. Fund Raising Execs., Planned Giving Coun. Upstate N.Y., Rochester Women's Network. Avocation: cycling. Office: SUNY Coll at Brockport Found 350 New Campus Dr Brockport NY 14420-2997

MARCHAND, JEFFREY BURKE, financial advisor; b. Cleve., July 6, 1943; s. Robert Walter and Gladys Geraldine (Burke) M.; m. Freya Corinne Liechty, Sept. 24, 1966; children: Meredith Elizabeth Marchand Feeney, Hilary Corinne, John Liechty. BS in Bus., Miami U., 1966; Ms, Coll. Fin. Planning, 1995. CFP; cert. investment mgmt. cons.; cert. investment mgmt. analyst. Lic. stockbroker Ball Burge & Kraus, Cleve., 1967-69; 1st v.p. investments Prudential Securities Inc., Akron, Ohio, 1969—. Advisor Coll. Fin. Planning, Denver, 1989—; Akron Tax and Estate Planning. Creator, author (computer programs) IRA Rollover Distbn., 1984, The Alpha Report, 1998. Vol. of the yr. YMCA, Akron, Ohio, 1986; vol. Haven of Rest, Akron, 1991. Mem. Akron Chess Club (pres. 1972-74), Kiwanis Club (treas. 1968), Akron Pension Coun. (pres. 1987), Masons, Torch Club (pres. 1997). Republican. Avocations: fishing, chess, scuba diving. Home: 214 Grayling Dr Akron OH 44333-2846 Office: Prudential Fin Inc 50 S Main St Ste 500 Akron OH 44308-1830 E-mail: jeffrey_marchand@prusec.com.

MARCHAND, MICHAEL J. military officer; b. Rice, Minn. BA, St. John's U., Collegeville, Minn., 1970. Commd. Judge Advocate Gen.'s Corps, U.S. Army, 1974, asst. staff judge advocate Tex., 1974—77, US Army Forces Command, Ft. McPherson, Ga., 1977—79; instr., sr. instr. contract law Judge Advocate Gen.'s Sch., Charlottesville, Va., 1980—83; dep. staff judge advocate U.S. Army Transp. Ctr. and Ft. Eustis, Ft. Eustis, 1983—85; plans officer Office of the Judge Advocate Gen., Washington, 1986—88; staff judge advocate 6th Inf. Divsn. (Light) Alaska, 1988—91, U.S. Army Garrison, Ft. Polk, La., 1991—93; chief adminstrv. law divsn. Office of Judge Advocate Gen., Washington, 1994—95, exec. to Judge Advocate Gen., 1995—97, asst. judge advocate gen. for civil law and litigation, 1997—98; comdr. U.S. Army Svcs. Agy., 1998—2001; chief judge U.S. Army Ct. Criminal Appeals, 1998—2001; asst. judge advocate gen. Judge Advocate Gen. Corps, 2001—. Decorated Legion of Merit, Meritorious Svc. medal with 3 oak leaf clusters, Army Commendation medal with one oak leaf cluster, Army Achievement medal with one oak leaf cluster, Nat. Def. Svc. medal with one svc. star. Office: Office of Judge Advocate General US Army Pentagon Washington DC 20310-1500*

MARCHANT, FRANK RICHARD, database administrator, state official; b. Waukesha, Wis., Apr. 4, 1952; s. Frank Lockyer and Marcella Virginia (Loescher) M. Grad., Springfield (Ill.) High Sch., 1971. Various position main computer facility State of Ill., Springfield, 1977-80, tape media supr., 1980-89, database mgr., 1989-00. Lectr. Frank Lloyd Wright's life and work. Performer in one man shows as Mark Twain. Docent Dana-Thomas House Frank Lloyd Wright Historic Site, 1991-00; mem. Dana House Found. Avocations: designing and constructing art glass windows and lamps in Prairie and Usonian styles. Home: 2325 Grinnell Springfield IL 62704-5442

MARCHANT, JOANN REVICZKY, English language educator, actress; b. Putnam, Conn., May 22, 1964; d. James and Joan Alicia (Gronus) Reviczky; m. Jonathan Edward Marchant, June 24, 1995; 1 child, Zoltán. BFA, U. Conn., 1985, MA, 1991; MEd, Plymouth (N.H.) State Coll., 1995; grad., Creative Sch. Cosmetology, Manchester, Conn., 1989. Cert. tchr., English, N.H. Rsch. asst. U. Conn., Storrs, 1990-91, lectr., 1990-91; educator N.H. Coll., Laconia, 1992-95; educator English and drama Coe-Brown Northwood (N.H.) Acad., 1995-97; actress Players' Ring, Portsmouth and Alton, N.H., 1997—; educator Hesser Coll., Portsmouth, 1997—, Franklin Pierce Coll., Concord, N.H., 1997—. Owner Theatre for Life, Sanborton, 1996—; tchr. spl. edn., English, and drama Brentwood Sch., Merrimack, 1999-2002; model East Coast Focus, Concord, N.H., 1997—; stage mgr. premier Tom Dulack's Ah! Bright Wings, Storrs, Conn., extra in film Meet Joe Black; lectr. Plymouth State Coll., 1997-99; bd. dirs. Plymouth Writer's Group. Vol.l campaign worker Nancy Wyman, Conn., Christopher Dodd, Conn., Michael Helfgott, Conn.; vol. Habitat for Humanity, N.H., 1995. Mem. Nat. Coun. Tchrs. English, New Eng. Theatre Conf., N.H. Coun. English Tchrs., Friends of the Bard, Phi Delta Kappa. Democrat.

MARCHASE, RICHARD BANFIELD, cell biologist, educator; b. Sayre, Pa., Mar. 12, 1948; s. Nicholas and Vivian H. (Banfield) M.; m. Susan Elizabeth Darrow, Apr. 14, 1979; children: Nicolas Darrow, Allison Elizabeth. BS in Engring., Cornell U., 1970; PhD in Biophysics, Johns Hopkins U., 1976; postgrad., Duke U., 1978. Muscular Dystrophy Assn. postdoctoral fellow div. neurology Duke U. Med. Ctr., 1976-77, USPHS postdoctoral fellow dept. anatomy, 1977-78, asst. prof. anatomy, 1978-86; assoc. prof. cell biology U. Ala.-Birmingham, 1986—90, prof., 1990—, chmn., 1992—2000, sr. assoc. dean biomed. rsch., 2000—. Contbr. chpts. to books, articles to profl. jours. Recipient Hamilton Watch award Cornell U., 1970, award Juvenile Diabetes Found., 1995; Grad. fellow NSF, 1970-73, Danforth Found. grad. fellow, 1973-76; Nanaline H. Duke scholar, 1982-85; grantee USPHS, NSF, Presdl. Young Investigator grant, 1982-87. Mem. AAAS, Am. Soc. Cell Biology, Am. Soc. Zoology, Assn. of Anatomy, Cell Biology, and Neurobiology Chairpersons (pres. 1995-96), Am. Assn. Anatomists, Nat. Caucus of Basic Biomed. Sci. Chairs, Coun. Acad. Socs. (rep.), Am. Assn. Med. Colls. (rep.), Fed. Am. Soc. Exptl. Biology (bd. dirs. 2000—), Sigma Xi. Home: 2117 Magnolia Way Birmingham AL 35243-2024 Office: U Ala Dept Cell Biology Birmingham AL 35294-0001 E-mail: marchase@uab.edu.

MARCHE, GARY ELDON, economics educator; b. Ft. Riley, Kans., Nov. 17, 1953; s. Don Clair Marche and Clara Marie (Keim) Davidson; m. Mary Kasten, June 13, 1987. BS in Econs., Kans. State U., 1975, MA in Econs., 1978, PhD in Econs., 1989. Grad. teaching asst. Kans. State U., Manhattan, 1976-78; landlord, 1975-79; grad. teaching asst. U. Nebr., Lincoln, 1984-87; asst. prof. Francis Marion Coll., Florence, S.C., 1988-89; asst. prof. econs. Ark. State U., Jonesboro, 1989—. Author: Economics of Law Enforcement, 1989, Aggregation Biases and Economies of Scale in the Metropolitan Police Unit Production Function, 1992, The Production of Homicide Solutions: An Empirical Analysis, 1994. Rep. United Way, Jonesboro, 1989. Lt. USNR, 1980-83. Mem. Am. Econ. Assn., Southwestern Econs. Assn., Decision Sci. Inst., Omicron Delta Epsilon. Republican. Avocations: sports, basketball, running, football, baseball, tennis. Office: Ark State U PO Box 239 State University AR 72467-0239

MARCHESE, MICHAEL JAMES, JR. radiation oncologist; b. N.Y.C., Mar. 9, 1955; s. Michael James Sr. and Mabel Gladys (Rosero) M.; m. Kathryn Allen, Aug. 7, 1982 (div. May 1993); 1 child, Michael James III; m. Kathleen Spahr, Oct. 18, 1997; 1 child, Melissa June. BA magna cum laude, NYU, 1976; MD, Baylor Coll. Medicine, 1979. Diplomate Am. Bd. Radiology. Intern Monmouth Med. Ctr., Hahnemann Med. Coll., Long Branch, N.J., Phila., 1979-80; resident and chief resident radiation therapy Presbyn. Hosp., Columbia U. Coll. Physicians and Surgeons, N.Y.C., 1980-83, asst. attending physician radiation oncology, 1983-87; resident brachytherapy svc. Meml. Sloan Kettering Cancer Ctr., Cornell U. Med. Coll., 1982; asst. clin. prof. radiation oncology Columbia U. Coll. Physicians & Surgeons, 1983-84, asst. prof. radiation oncology, 1984-87; attending staff radiology/radiation oncology Cmty. Med. Ctr., Toms River, N.J., 1987-96, Kimball Med. Ctr., Lakewood, 1994—, Med. Ctr. Ocean County, Brick, 1996—; dir. Ocean Radiation Therapy Ctr., Toms River, 1997—. Investigator Nat. Cancer Inst., 1983-87, investigator radiation therapy oncology group, 1983-87, 95—, physician surveyor, 1983-85, investigator cancer and leukemia group B, 1986-87, investigator Ea. Coop. Oncology Group, 1995—; physician surveyor practice accreditation program Am. Coll. Radiology, 1986-87; Cancer liason Am. Coll. Surgeons, Kimball Med. Ctr., 2001—. Author: (with others) Radiation Therapy of Gynecological Cancers, 1987, Frontiers of Radiation Therapy and Oncology, vol. 22, 1988; contbr. articles to profl. jours. Bd. dirs. Am. Cancer Soc., Ocean County, N.J., 1993—, v.p., 1993-94, pres., 1994-98, chief med. officer, 2000-01. Recipient Resident/Fellow award Am. Radium Soc., Travel award European Soc. Therapeutic Radiology and Oncology, Clin. Oncology Career Devel. award Am. Cancer Soc., Physician of the Year, Amer. Canc. Soc., 1998. Mem. Am. Coll. Radiology, Am. Soc. Therapeutic Radiology and Oncology, Am. Soc. Clin. Oncology, Acad. Medicine N.J., Radiation Rsch. Soc., N.Y. Acad. Sci., Ocean County Med. Soc. (bd. trustees 1997—), Med. Soc. N.J. (del. 2000—). Roman Catholic. Home: 44 Lake Shore Dr Red Bank NJ 07701-5840 Office: Ocean Radiation Therapy Ctr 19 Mule Rd Toms River NJ 08755-5029

MARCHESE, RONALD THOMAS, ancient history and archaeology educator; b. Fresno, Calif., Mar. 17, 1947; s. John Anthony and Julie Rita (Ferrarese) M.; m. Marcia Lynn Schneider, Apr. 6, 1974 (div. Apr. 1980); 1 child, Stephanie Jo; m. K. Werdin, 1988; children: Alexander Joseph, Kayla Marie. BA summa cum laude, Calif. State U., Fresno, 1970; MA, N.Y.U., 1972, PhD with distinction, 1976; postgrad., Columbia U., 1972-73. Asst. prof. Va. Poly. Inst., Blacksburg, 1976-77; asst. to assoc. prof. ancient history and archaeology U. Minn., Duluth, 1977-87, prof., 1987—. Rsch. assoc. dept. classics NYU, 1972-74; evaluator grant proposals NEH, HSF; excavator numerous sites in Israel, Turkey, and Greece; lectr. in field. Author, editor 7 books; author articles on nomadic material culture and religious textiles. Recipient Fulbright-Hays Sr. Research fellowship, Turkey, 1984-85, 91-92, The Am. Council Learned Socs. fellowship, 1977-78, NDEA Title VI Fgn.

Languages fellowship, 1972-75, Spl. Commendation for Excellence award Phi Alpha Theta, 1979; grantee NEH, 1978, 80, nat. Geographic Soc., 1974, Andrew Mellon Found., NSF, Ford Found., 1971-72, U. Minn., others. Mem. NEH, Nat. Assn. Scholars, Coun. for Internat. Exchange, Am. Coun. Learned Socs., Fulbright Alumni Assn., Phi Alpha Theta, Sigma Xi, Alpha Phi Omega. Roman Catholic. Avocations: tennis, golf, dressage. Home: 5789 220th St N Forest Lake MN 55025-9677 E-mail: ronmarchese@hotmail.com.

MARCHESSAULT, THOMAS EDWARD, economist; b. Cambridge, Mass., July 25, 1948; s. Edward George and Ann Regina (Sieverts) M.; m. Sally Sheedy Jackson, July 14, 1979; 1 stepchild, Sean DeGuerre Jackson BA in Econs., U. Mass., Boston, 1970; postgrad., U. Md., 1970-75. Economist rsch. & coord. divsn. DOT, Washington, 1974-78, economist energy policy divsn., 1978-82, economist office econs., 1982-97, spl. asst. office asst. sec. for transp. policy, 1997-99, economist mobility and infrastructure leom, 1999—. Recipient Sec.'s Award for Meritorious Achievement, Sec. Transp., 1985, Way-to-Go Cert., 1995, Asst. Sec.'s Award for Superior Achievement, 1991, Intelligent Vehicle-Hwy. Soc. Am. Cert. of Appreciation, 1991, Sec.'s Partnership for Excellence award, 2000. Mem. Am. Econs. Assn., Soc. Govt. Economists, Intergovtl. Transp. Soc. Am., Mobility 2000, Intelligent Transp. Soc. Am. Home: 432 Inspiration Ln Gaithersburg MD 20878-5664 Office: US Dept Transp 400 7th St SW Washington DC 20590-0001 E-mail: Tom.Merchessault@ost.dot.gov.

MARCHETTI, DONNA, writer; b. Cin., June 25, 1953; d. Francis Niles Estes and Victorine Murphy; m. Anthony Marchetti, Aug. 26, 1984; 1 child Justin. BA, Coll. Mount St. Joseph, Cin., 1975; MA, Case We. Res. U., 1984. Freelance writer, 1990—; editor The Orff Echo (profl. jour. for music tchrs.), Cleve., 1994—2001; book critic Cleve. Plain Dealer, 1996—. Lectr. We. Res. Writers Conf., Cleve., 1997—; pub. spkr. on Great Lakes and their history librs., civic clubs, Cleve., 1998—. Author: Lake Michigan, 2000, Around the Shores of Lake Erie, 1998; contbr. chapters to books. Vol. ESL tutor Project: LEARN, Cleve., 1987—. Mem.: Poets and Writers League of Gtr. Cleve., Am. Orff-Schulwerk Assn. (hon.). Avocations: bicycling, reading, scuba diving, travel. Home and Office: 3105 Lincoln Blvd Cleveland Heights OH 44118

MARCHETTI, MARILYN H. lawyer; b. Whiting, Ind., Mar. 10, 1947; d. Stephen D. and Helen F. (Ajdinovich) Hrpka; m. George Arthur Marchetti, Aug. 21, 1976; 1 child, Christine Stephanie. BA in English, Ind. U., 1969; JD, IIT, 1979. Bar: Ill. 1980. Tchr. jr. high school North Easton (Mass.) schs., 1969-70; social worker Ind. Dept. Pub. Welfare, Gary, 1970-74; medicaid specialist U.S. Dept. Health, Edn., Welfare, Chgo., 1974-78; law clk. to Justice Thomas Moran Ill. Supreme Ct., Waukegan, 1979-81; assoc. Mayer, Brown & Platt, Chgo., 1982-84; ptnr. Keck, Mahin & Cate, 1984-94, Oppenheimer, Wolff & Donnelly, Chgo., 1994-97, Seyfarth, Shaw, Fairweather & Geraldson, Chgo., 1997-99, Great Banc Trust Co., Oak Brook, Ill., 1999—. Guest lectr. Harvard U.; cons. USSR marine industry privatization, 1990-91; speaker The Employee Stock Ownership Plan Assn. Paris Internat., London, 1991, 92; mem. U.S. del. promoting concept of employee ownership, to China, 1994, to Zimbabwe, 1995. Contbr. articles to profl. jours., chpts. to books. Asst. troop leader Girl Scouts U.S., Western Springs, Ill., 1990—; mem. parish coun. St. John of the Cross Ch., Western Springs, 1991-92; fundraiser Carol Mosely Braun Campaign, Chgo., 1992; founder Girls' Cir., 1994—; mem. bd. edn. Lyons Twp. H.S. Dist. 204, 1997—; bd. dirs., sec. Dist. 106 Ednl. found., 1995-97. Mem. Employee Stock Ownership Plan Assn. (bd. dirs., administrv. com. 1989—, legis. com. 1990—, founder, sec., treas. Ill. chpt.), Nat. Assn. of Women Bus. Owners, Nat. Ctr. Employee Ownership, Women in Employee Benefits (steering com. 1987). Avocations: golf, bridge, writing. Office: Great Banc Trust Co 1301 W 22nd St Oak Brook IL 60523-2006

MARCHETTI, REESA, web manager, editor; b. Philadelphia, PA, Dec. 29, 1948; married. High School, Cherry Hill High School West, Cherry Hill, N.J., 1962—66. Editor and Web Manager Association of Educational Publishers, Swedesboro, NJ, 1999—2002; Editor and Writer South Jersey News Group, Salem, 1993—98. Public relations consultant Reesa Marchetti Publishing, Glassboro, NJ, 1980—2002; Web designer, developer, manager SpideRee Web Design, Glassboro, NJ, 1996—2002. Author: (Newspaper) Today's Sunbeam, three articles, 1998 (NJ Press Association first place column writing, 1999). Recipient 1st place column writing, N.J. Press Assn., 1999. Mem.: BMI, PR Network, International Webmasters Association, Society of Professional Journalists. Avocation: Musician (vocals, guitar, keyboard). Personal E-mail: reesa@usa.net.

MARCHI, JON, former investment brokerage executive, cattle rancher, exporter; b. Aug. 6, 1946; s. John Robert and Joan Trimble (Toole) M.; m. Mary Stewart Sale, Aug. 12, 1972 (div. 1999); children: Aphia Jessica, Jon Jacob. Student, Claremont Men's Coll., 1964-65; BS, U. Mont., 1968, MS, 1972. Sec., treas. Marchi, Marchi & Marchi, Inc., Morris, Ill., 1968-69; account exec. D. A. Davidson & Co., Billings, Mont., 1972-75, asst. v.p., office mgr., 1976-77, v.p. mktg. and adminstrn. Great Falls, 1977—. Sec., dir., v.p. fin. svcs. and exec. devel. D. A. Davidson Realty Corp., Great Falls, 1978-85, chmn. rsch. com., 1980; bd. dirs. Ligocyte Corp., Bozeman, Mont., Big Sky Airlines, Billings, chmn. bd. dirs., 1995; bd. dirs. Implemax Equipment Co., Inc., Bozeman, Energy Overthrust Found., Mansfield Found., Mont. Beverages, Mont. Venture Capital Network, Direct Advantage, Inc., Hamilton, Mont., Mont. Naturals Internat., Inc., Eclipse Techs., Inc., Mont. Small Bus. Investment Corp., Phillips Environ. Corp., Bozeman, Mont.; chmn., dir. Devel. Corp. Mont., Helena, 1995; cattle rancher, Polson, Mont., 1986—; dir. Mont. Econ. Devel. Action Group, 2001-. Chmn. Mont. Gov.'s Subcom. for Venture Capital Devel., Mont. Cmty. Fin. Corp., Helena; chmn. investment com. State of Mont. Sci. and Tech. Alliance, 1985—; chmn. seed capital com. State of Mont., bd. dirs. job svc. com.; mem. Mont. Peoples Action; sec.-treas. Valley View Assn., 1987—; trustee sch. dist. # 35, Polson, Mont., 1990—, chmn., 1991—; bd. dirs. Mont. Entrepreneurship Ctr., Missoula, Mont., 1990—; pres., dir. sec.-treas. Mont. Pvt. Capital Network, Bozeman, Mont., 1990—, pres., 1992—; chmn., dir. Mont. Naturals Internat., Inc., 1991; dir. Mont. State Rural Devel. Coun., 1992, Mont. SBA Adv. Coun., 1992; dir. Ctr. Econ. Renewal and Tech. Transfer Mont. State U., Bozeman, 1994—; del. to White House Conf. on Small Bus., Washington, 1994-95; chmn. Glacier Venture Fund, Helena, Mont., 1996—; mem. investment adv. com. DCC Growth Fund, Washington, 1998—. With U.S. Army, 1969-71; dir. Mont. State U., Billings, Coll. of Bus. Bd., 1995-, Mont. Econ. Devel. Action Group, 2001-; mem. Gov.'s Com. Tax Restructuring, 2002-, Gov.'s Task Force on Access to Capital, 2002-. Mem. Nat. Cattlemen's Assn. (fgn. trade com.), Am. Wagyu Assn. (dir. 2000—, treas.), Can. Wagyu Assn., Polson C. of C. (bd. dirs.), Valley View Assn. (bd. dirs.), Mont. Cattle Feeders Assn., Mont. Angus Assn., Western Mont. Angus Assn., Am. Angus Assn., Western Mont. Stockgrowers Assn., Securities Industry Assn., Mont. Stock Growers Assn., Mont. Ambassadors (dir. 1995, pres. 2001—), Polson C. of C. (dir.), Leadership Great Falls Club, Ski Club, Mont. Club, Helena Wilderness Riders Club, Rotary. Episcopalian. Office: Marchi Angus Ranches 7783 Valley View Rd Polson MT 59860-9302

MARCHI, LORRAINE JUNE, social services executive; b. June 5, 1923; d. Leopold and Josephine Lillian (Trieber) Heiman; m. Gene Marchi, Apr. 10, 1943 (div. 1973); children: Gene, Jeffrey, Debra, Beth; m. Robert L. Fastie, Oct. 21, 1973. Student, Stanford U., 1941-42, U. Calif., Berkeley, 1942-43; LHD (hon.) , SUNY, 2002. Founder Com. to Aid Visually Handicapped Children, San Francisco, 1954-57; pres. Aid to Visually Handicapped, 1957-59; founder, CEO Nat. Assn. for Visually Handicapped, N.Y.C. and San Francisco, 1972—. Sec. Calif. Conf. for Exceptional and Rehab. Needs, San Francisco, 1955-66; chmn. bd. Langley Porter Neuropsychiat. Inst., San Francisco, 1966-73. Recipient spl. svc. award Los Angeles County Soc. Ophthalmology, 1971, award for visual awareness N.Y. Acad. Optometry, 1997, honor award Am. Acad. Ophthalmology and Otolaryngology, 1971, Lifetime Achievement award Nat. Assn. for Visually Handicapped, 1989, cert. of appreciation Am. Acad. Ophthalmology, 1978, cert. of appreciation Lions Club Internat., 1998; named woman of Yr. San Francisco sect. Nat. Coun. Jewish Women, 1957, one of Ten Disting. Women San Francisco Examiner Bay Area, 1959. Home: 305 E 24th St New York NY 10010-4011 E-mail: staff@navh.org.

MARCHI, SERGIO SISTO, Canadian government official; b. Buenos Aires, May 12, 1956; s. Ottavio and Luisa (D'Agostinis) M.; m. Laureen Storozuk, Oct. 1, 1983. BA with honors, York U., Toronto, 1979. Alderman City of North York, 1982-84; M.P. for York West dist. Ho. of Commons, Ottawa, 1984-99, min. citizenship and immigration, 1993-96; min. of environment, 1996-97; min. internat. trade Govt. Canada, 1997-99; Canadian amb. of UN and WTO Permanent Missions of Can. to Office of UN, Geneva, 2000—; chmn. WTO Coun. for Trade in Svcs., 2000—01; chair working party on accession of Ukraine WTO, 2000—; mem. policy adv. commn. WIPO, 2000—; chair gen. coun. WTO, 2002—. Mem. cabinet coms. on treasury bd., social policy and program review. Mem. Cabinet Com. on Treas. bd., Social Policy and Program Review; vice chmn. North York Planning Bd., Toronto, 1982-84, Standing Com. on Transport, Ottawa, 1990-93; chmn. Nat. Liberal Caucus, Ottawa, 1990-93. Office: Perm Mission Amb of Can #5 Ave de L'Ariana Geneva 1202 Switzerland E-mail: sergio.marchi@dfait-maeci.gc.ca.

MARCHINI, CLAUDIA CILLONIZ, artist; b. Lima, Peru, Feb. 3, 1959; came to U.S., 1983; d. Alberto Peschiera and Matilde Spiers (Toledo) Cilloniz; m. Carlos Edwards, Nov. 14, 1983; 1 child, Renzo. BFA in Painting, Memphis Coll. Art, 1987; MFA in Painting, U. Tex., San Antonio, 1989. Part-time mgr. Lung Clinic, Grants Pass, Oreg. Executed mural Oreg. State Capitol bldg., Salem, 1994 (2d place Ea. N.Mex. U. 1997), Southern Oregon Art Exhibit, 1998 (2d place, third place and hon. mention, 1999, Individual artist fellow grant award Oreg. Arts Commn., 2000), mural for Asante/Three Rivers Cmty. Hosp., Grants Pass, Oreg., 2001; one woman shows at Foyer Auditorium and Gallery, U. Tex., San Antonio, 1990, GPHS Libr. Gallery, Oreg., 1991, Instituto Cultural Peruano Norteamericano, Lima, 1992, 93, Rogue Gallery, Medford, Oreg., 1992, Portland (Oreg.) State U., 1994, Firehouse Gallery, Grants Pass, Oreg., 1995, D.O.T. N.W., Portland, 1995, Galeria Cecilia Gonzalez, Lima, 1996, Gallery at Stevenson Union, So. Oreg. State Coll., Ashland, 1996, Lisa Harris Gallery, Seattle, 1997, Galeria Cecilia Gonzalez, Lima, Peru, 1998, Grants Pass (Oreg.) Frameworks Gallery, 1999, Wiseman Gallery, Grants Pass, 1999, Josephine County Libr. Grants Pass (Oreg.), 2000, Frameworks Gallery, Grants Pass, 2001; group exhbns. include Instituto Cultural Peruano Norteamericano, 1988, 110 Broadway, San Antonio, 1988, Mexico-Arte, Austin, Tex., 1988, Bank One, San Antonio, 1989, Rolling Oaks Mall, San Antonio, 1989, Art League Gallery, Beaumont, Tex., 1990, U. Toronto, Can., 1990, Art Gallery at Lower Columbia Coll., 1991, Newport (Oreg.) Visual Arts Ctr., 1991, 92, Grants Pass Mus., 1991, 92, 93, Rogue Gallery, 1991, 92, 95, Stonington Gallery, Seattle, 1992, 93, Wiseman Gallery, Grants Pass, 1993, Paris Gibson Sq. Mus. of Art, Great Falls, Mont., 1993, Ctr. Contemporary Art, Seattle, 1993, Pulliam Deffengaugh Gallery, Portland, 1994, Ctr. for Visual Arts, Oakland, Calif., 1994, Washington State Convention and Trade Ctr., 1995, D.O.T. Northwest, 1995, Graven Images Gallery, Ashland, Oreg., 1995, Portland Mus. of Art, 1995, 99, So. Oreg. Art Exhbn., Grants Pass, 1996, Coleman Gallery, Albuquerque, 1996, Museo de Osma, Lima, 1996, Ea. N.Mex. U., 1997, Ctr. Visual Arts, Oakland, Calif., 1997, Grants Pass Mus., 1998, Ea. N. Mex. Univ., 1998, Museo de Osma, Lima, 1998, Jega Gallery, Ashland, 1998, Lisa Harris Gallery, Seattle, 1998, Grants Pass Mus. Art, Oreg., 1998, Ga. N.Mex. U., 1998, East N.Mex. U., 1999, Tacoma Art Museum, Wash., 1999, El Haras, Lima, Peru, 1999, Runnels Gallery, East N.Mex. U., 1999, Whatcom Mus., Bellingham, Wash., 2000, Country Club, Medford, Oreg., 2000, Grants Pass Mus. Art, Oreg., 2000, Josephine County Libr., Oreg., 2000, Touchstone Gallery, Washington, 2001, Muroff-Kotler Visual Arts Gallery, 2001, Rogue Gallery and Art Ctr., 2001, 02, Grants Pass Mus. Art, 2001, 02, Scarlet Palette Gallery, Jacksonville, Oreg., 2001, Womanmade Gallery, Chgo., 2002, others; represented in various pvt. collections. Recipient 2d place award Ea. N.Mex. U., 1997, Recipient of Yr. Individual Artist fellowship award Oregon Arts Commn., 2000, 1st pl. Pacific N.W. Exhbn. Rogue Gallery, Medford, Oreg., 2002. Mem. Seattle's Ctr. Contemporary Art, Grants Pass Mus. of Art, Greenpeace, Wofld Wildlife Fund, Jame Goodall Inst., Arts Coun. So. Oreg., U.S. Squash Racquet Assn. Avocations: squash, hiking, travel, animals. Office: Lung Clinic 874 NE 7th St Grants Pass OR 97526-1635

MARCHISHIN, DANIEL, construction executive; b. Paterson, N.J., May 16, 1934; s. William and Mary (Hepak) Marchisen; m. Marie Gruber, Oct. 31, 1965; children: Rita, Geoffrey, Rachel, Michael. BSCE, Newark Coll. Engring. Hwy. engr. U.S. Forest Svc., Placerville, Calif., 1961-67; environ. engr. U.S. EPA, N.Y.C. and Edison, N.J., 1967-72; gen. engr. U.S. Dept. HUD, Newark, 1972-80; modernization coord., constrn. mgr. Newark Housing Authority, 1980-89; self-employed constrn. mgr. cons. Bound Brook, N.J., 1990—. Commr. U.S. Commn. on Ukrainian Famine, Washington, 1985-90, N.J. Commn. on Eastern European History, 1985—, chmn., 1991—; fin. officer N.J. Divsn. Ukrainian Am. Vets., 1991—; pres. Plainfield Area Coalition for Environment, 1970, St. Andrew's Fed. Credit Union, 1992-94, Masthope Property Owners Assn., 1995—; chmn. Captive Nations Com., N.J., 1967-72; treas. Ascension of Our Lord Serbian Orthodox Ch., 1974-75, N.J. Coalition for Dem. Majority, 1975; coord. Henry Jackson for Pres., N.J. Citizens, 1976, Com. for Def. Valentin Moroz, 1978-80; shop steward, Nat. Fedn. Fed. Employyees profl. staff, HUD Newark office, 1975-81; v.p. Ams. for Human Rights in Ukraine, 1980-87; chmn. N.J. Ethnic Cmtys. Congress, 1974-81; active Orgn. for Def. Lemkivshchina; pres. U.S. EPA Employees Sunshine Club, 1969-72; coord. Pan-Orthodox Youth Group, 1963-67; chmn. Captive Nations Com., San Francisco, 1963-67; treas. St. John Serbian Orthodox Ch. Choir, 1963-67. With U.S. Army, 1954-55. Mem. NAACP, League of Ukranian Voters (bd. dirs., coord. 1985-96), Serbian Am. Voters Alliance (bd. dirs.), Ukrainian Congress Com. Am., Serb Nat. Def. Coun. Democrat. Ukrainian Orthodox. Avocations: reading, chess, football, golf, singing. Home and Office: 518 Church St Bound Brook NJ 08805-1729

MARCHMAN, FREDERICK ALAN, artist; b. Apr. 12, 1941; BFA, U. Ala., 1963; MFA, Tulane U., 1965. Mem. artist Contemporary Art Ctr. Mobile (Ala.), 1979-83, Seven Artists (co-op.), Mobile, 1986; prof. visual art, art history Ala. Sch. Math. and Sci., 1992-95; mem. artist Cathedral Square Art Gallery (co-op.), Mobile, 1995-2000, Ala. Printmaker's Portfolio, 1986, Ala. Artists on Billboards Project, 1996; artist Hawthorne Gallery, Mountain Brook, Ala., 2001—. White House easter egg artist, Washington, 1987, 88. Article in Mobile Bay Monthly, May 1993; poetry presented on The Romantic Hour, Nat. Pub. Radio, 1999; featured in Moments with Eugene, 2000; The Harbinger cartoon strip Dr. Jo-Mo; art rev. writer, critic, 1986, 96—; author: Portals of Paradise, 2002.

MARCIALIS, ROBERT LOUIS, planetary astronomer; b. N.Y.C., Sept. 14, 1956; s. Louis Angelo and Joan Regina (Dippolito) M. SB in Aero. and Astronautical Engring., MIT, 1978, SB in Earth and Planetary Scis., 1980; MS in Physics and Astronomy, Vanderbilt U., 1983; PhD in Planetary Scis., U. Ariz., 1990. Teaching asst. dept. earth and planetary scis. MIT, Cambridge, 1976-80; lab. instr. dept. physics and astronomy Vanderbilt U., Nashville, 1981, 82-83, rsch. asst. Arthur J. Dyer Obs., 1981-82; rsch. asst. Lunar and Planetary Lab. U. Ariz., Tucson, 1983-86, rsch. assoc., 1986-90; JPL postdoctoral fellow Jet Propulsion Lab., Pasadena, Calif., 1990-92; adj. faculty Pima C.C., Tucson, 1992—; sr. rsch. specialist U. Ariz., 1996—. Founding mem. Pluto/Charon Mut. Eclipse Season Campaign. Contbr. articles to Nature, Bull. Am. Astron. Soc., Astron. Jour., Minor Planet Circular, Lunar and Planetary Sci., Sci., Jour. Brit. Astron. Assn., Astrophys. Jour., Icarus, also others. Instr. water safety ARC, 1981-82; ednl. counselor MIT, 1983—; fastpitch softball umpire, 1975—. Rsch. fellow NASA, 1986-89. Mem. AAAS, Am. Astron. Soc., Am. Geophys. Union, Astron. Soc. Pacific, Internat. Occultation Timing Assn., Sigma Pi Sigma. Roman Catholic. Achievements include discovery of water ice on surface of Pluto's moon Charon; construction of an albedo map for surface of Pluto; research on Pluto, Charon and Triton, icy satellites, outer solar system formation and evolution, solar system photometry, occultation astronomy, construction and calibration of Imager for Mars Pathfinder, cameras for the Mars Polar Lander missions and Mars Odyssey gamma ray spectrometer. Office: U Ariz Lunar Planetary Lab Tucson AZ 85721-0001 E-mail: umpire@lpl.arizona.edu.

MARCILLA, MARY H. writer; b. Rocky Ford, Colo., Jan. 31, 1935; d. Elmer Hamby and Agnes Stark; children: Janna Laree, James Jauier. BA, U. New Maxico, Albuquerque, 2002—02. Author: (book) Below the Gallows-Tree; contbr. articles to profl. jours. Home: 2114 Oxford SE Albuquerque NM 87106

MARCI-MARIANI, ANITA, designer, illustrator, fine artist; b. Carbondale, Pa., Feb. 11, 1960; d. William Frank and Anita Mae (Sachele) Marci; m. Robert Joseph Mariani, Dec. 31, 1988. BFA summa cum laude, Kutztown (Pa.) U., 1982. Designer, illustrator Lukasiewicz Design, N.Y.C., 1982-84, Art and Design Assocs., N.Y.C., 1984-85; prin., designer, illustrator Anita Marci Studios, 1985-91, White Plains, N.Y., 1992-97, Hartsdale, 1997—. Lect. ednl. orgns., Pa., 1989—. One person shows S.I. shows, 1992, 94, Mamaroneck Artist's Guild, Larchmont, N.Y., 1996; group shows include Soc. of Illustrators, N.Y.C. (student scholarship award 1982—), Gallery 2000, Carmel, Calif., 1997, Articoli Fine Arts Gallery, White Plains, N.Y., 1998-2000, Scarsdale Art Assn, 1999— (watercolor award 2000, 01), Women's Club of White Plains (watercolor award 2000). Mem. Soc. Illustrators (student scholarship award 1982), Graphic Artists Guild, Mamoroneck Artist's Guild, Scarsdale Art Assn.

MARCINEK, MARGARET ANN, nursing educator; b. Uniontown, Pa., Sept. 29, 1948; d. Joseph Hugh and Evelyn (Bailey) Boyle; m. Bernard Francis Marcinek, Aug. 11, 1973; 1 child, Cara Ann. RN, Uniontown Hosp., 1969; BSN, Pa. State U., 1970; MSN, U. Md., 1973; EdD, W.Va. U., 1983. Staff nurse Presbyn. U., Pitts., 1970-71; instr. nursing W.Va. U., Morgantown, 1973-77, asst. prof., 1977-80, assoc. prof., 1980-83, Calif. U. Pa., 1983-87, prof., 1987—, dept. chmn., 1985—. Program evaluator Commn. on Collegiate Nursing Edn., Nat. League for Nursing Accrediting Commn.; mem. adv. coun. In Home Health, Inc.; mem. adv. coun. Albert Gallatin VNA. Contbg. author: Critical Care Nursing; contbr. articles to profl. jours. Mem.: ANA, Commn. on Collegiate Nursing Edn. (site evaluator), Oncology Nursing Soc., Sigma Theta Tau.

MARCINIAK, CHRISTINA MARIA, physician; b. Chgo., Sept. 28, 1955; d. Edward Allen and Viginia Cecelia Marciniak; m. Michael D. Brown. BA, U. Notre Dame, 1977; MD, U. Ill., Chgo., 1981. Diplomate Am. Bd. Phys. Medicine and Rehab., Am. Bd. Spinal Cord Injury, Am. Bd. Electrodiagnosis. Internal medicine intern Michael Reese Hosp., Chgo., 1981-82; resident in phys. medicine and rehab. Northwestern U., 1982-85; attending physician Rehab. Inst. Chgo., 1985—; med. dir. rehab. svcs. Northwestern Meml. Hosp., Chgo., 1986—; exec. dir. inpatient svcs. Rehab. Inst. Chgo. Co-author: (chpts.) Electrodiagnosis in Muskuloskeletal Medicine, 1990, Medical Management of Long Term Disability, 1996, Palliative Care, 1999; contbr. articles to profl. jours. Fellow Am. Assn. Electrodiagnostic Medicine, Am. Acad. Phys. Medicine and Rehab. Office: Rehab Inst Chgo 345 E Superior St Chicago IL 60611-4805 E-mail: cmarciniak@rehabchicago.org.

MARCIS, DAVE, professional sports team executive; b. Wausau, Wis., Mar. 1, 1941; m. Helen Marcis; children: Shawn Marie, Richard. Team owner Marcis Racing, Arden, NC. Recipient 5 Winston Cup victories, 2d pl., Winston Cup Points, 1975, record for most consecutive starts in Daytona 500, Buddy Schuman award, 2001. Mem.: Darlington Record Club. Avocations: fishing, hunting. Office: Marcis Racing 71 Beale Rd Arden NC 28704-9797

MARCOCCIA, LOUIS GARY, accountant, university administrator; b. Syracuse, N.Y., Nov. 6, 1946; s. George A. and Rose J. (Misita) M.; m. Susan Evelyn Miller, June 21, 1974; 1 child: Rachel Kathryn. BS, Syracuse U., 1968, MS, 1969. CPA, N.Y. Acct. Price Waterhouse & Co., Syracuse, N.Y., 1969-75; dir. internal audit Syracuse U., 1975-76, comptroller, 1976-82, v.p., comptroller, 1982-95, sr. v.p. bus., and fin., 1985-95, sr. v.p. bus., fin. and adminstrv. svcs., 1995—. Bd. dirs. Syracuse Bd. Chase Manhattan Bank, Syracuse Divsn., 1985-2001, Lincoln Life and Annuity Co. N.Y., Univ. Hill Corp., Upstate Med. Univ. Found.; pres. Syracuse U. Hotel and Conf. Ctr., LLC; spkr. Harvard U. Inst. Ednl. Mgmt., 1984-88, 90-91. Pres. parish coun. St. Michael's Ch., Syracuse, 1985-88; pres. Syracuse U. Theatre Corp., 1987—; bd. dirs. Friends of Burnet Park Zoo, 1987-93, Syracuse U. Press., 1982—, Syracuse Sports Corp., 1990-91. Mem. AICPA, N.Y. Soc. CPA, Nat. Assn. Accts., Fin. Execs. Inst., Inst. Internal Auditors. Clubs: Drumlins (pres. 1976—); Century. Republican. Roman Catholic. Avocations: swimming, tennis. Home: Hedge Ln Cazenovia NY 13035 Office: Syracuse U Off of VP Bus Fin Adminstrv Svc Skytop Rd Syracuse NY 13244-0001 E-mail: lmarcocc@syr.edu.

MARCOLINA, KATHRYN WATKINS, personal and professional success coach; b. West Chester, Pa., Jan. 17, 1959; d. Dwain Joseph and Kathryn Gertrude (Wood) W.; m. Peter Jerome Marcolina, Feb. 11, 1984. BS in Edn., U. Del., Newark, 1981; MSW, Bryn Mawr (Pa.) Coll., 1985. Cert clin. social worker, N.C. Family therapist Family Svc. Burlington County, Mt. Holly, N.J., 1985-89, Family Svc. Lower Cape Fear, Wilmington, N.C., 1989-90, The Parkside Clinic, Wilmington, 1990-96, Cape Fear Pschol. and Psychiat. Svcs., Wilmington, 1996-97; student counselor U. N.C., 1997-98; personal and profl. success coach Wrightsville Beach, NC, 2000—. Mem. NASW (chairperson local chpt. 1992), Acad. Cert. Social Workers, N.C. Cert. Bd. Social Work. Avocations: protection of sea turtles and wetlands, environmental awareness, study of nutrition, health and healing. Home: 2301-F Cordgrass Bay Wrightsville Beach NC 28480

MARCONI, DOMINIC ANTHONY, clergyman; b. Newark, Mar. 13, 1927; s. Sabato Joseph and Antoinette (Ricciardi) M. BA, Seton Hall U., 1949; postgrad., Immaculat Conception Sem., Mahwah, N.J., 1952; S.T.L., Catholic U., Washington, 1953. Ordained priest Roman Cath. Ch., 1953; asso. pastor St. Anthony's Ch., Union City, N.J., 1953-66; asso. dir. family life apostolate Archdiocese of Newark, 1966-70, dir., 1970-75; co-dir. div. for services to elderly Associated Cath. Charities, 1975-76; aux. and regional bishop Union County, Newark, 1976—. Mem.: K.C. Address: 238 E Blancke St Linden NJ 07036-3004

MARCONI, PETER PAUL, JR. financial analyst; b. Worcester, Mass., Aug. 26, 1963; s. Peter Paul and Sally Ann Marconi; m. Gail Ann Marconi, Apr. 30, 1994; children: Nicholas Peter, Evan Charles. BS, Worcester State Coll., 1985; MBA, Nichols Coll., 1999. Bus. analyst Gulf Oil Co., Canton, Mass., 1986-91; internal auditor Fallon Cmty. Health Plan, Worcester, 1991-97; fin. analyst U. Mass. Med. Ctr., 1997-98; sr. fin. analyst Southboro (Mass.) Med. Group, 1998—2001; sr. bus. analyst Fallon Cmty. Health Plan, Worcester, Mass., 2001—. Mem. Delta Mu Delta. Avocations: sports, music, travel. Office: 10 Chestnut St Worcester MA 01608 E-mail: SkipSMG@aol.com, skip11mass@yahoo.com.

MARCOPOULOS, GEORGE JOHN, history educator; b. Salem, Mass., June 30, 1931; s. John George and Urania Christou (Moustakis) M. BA, Bowdoin Coll., 1953; MA, Harvard U., 1955, PhD, 1966. Instr. Tufts U., Medford, Mass., 1961-66, asst. prof., 1966-71, assoc. prof., 1971-92, prof., 1992—. Contbr. articles to profl. jours. and Am. Ann. yearbooks. Bd. dirs. Gerondelis Found., Inc., Lynn, Mass., 1987—, treas., 1994—. Recipient Mellon Faculty Devel. grant Tufts U., 1983. Mem. AAUP, Am. Assn. Advancement Slavic Studies, Am. Hist. Assn., New Eng. Hist. Assn., Danforth Assocs. New Eng., Modern Greek Studies Assn., Phi Beta Kappa. Greek Orthodox. Avocations: music, films, reading, performing arts, excursions. Office: Tufts U Dept History East Hall Medford MA 02155

MARCOSSON, THOMAS I. service company executive; b. N.Y.C., Jan. 31, 1936; s. Mark and Mollie (Schreiber) M.; m. Carla F. Hunt, May 15, 1988; children: Mark, Susan, Samuel, Jill. Student, Union Coll., Schenectady, 1953-55; BS, NYU, 1959. CPA, N.Y. Mgr. Touche Ross & Co., N.Y.C., 1959-63; v.p. fin., dir. Superior Surg. Mfg. Co., Inc., Huntington, N.Y., 1964-66; div. pres., gen. mgr. OEI div., Vernitron Corp., Great Neck, 1967-71; controller Allied Maintenance Corp., N.Y.C., 1972-75, v.p. fin., 1975-82; chief fin. officer Remco Maintenance Corp., N.Y.C., 1982-84, exec. v.p., chief operating officer, 1984-88; pres. MBW Advt. Network Inc., N.Y.C., 1988-89; founder, pres. Dunmarc Assocs., Inc., 1989—; pres., dir. Square Arch Realty Corporation, 1986—. Exec. v.p. Greater Talent Network, Inc., 1991—; co-founder, dir. Village Alliance Bus. Improvement Dist., 1993—. Office: 437 5th Ave 7th Fl New York NY 10016 E-mail: t.marcosson@verizon.net.

MARCOTTE, BRIAN, transportation executive; BAS in Civil Engring., U. Toronto, Ont., 1971; Diploma in Local Govt. Adminstrn., U. Alta., 1985; Cert., U. Va., 1994. With Ont. Ministry of Transp., North Bay, Toronto, 1971-74, Regional Municipality of York, Newmarket, Ont., 1974-81; asst. dep. min. Alta. Transp., Edmonton, 1981—. Office: Alberta Transp Policy & Planning Divsn 4999 98 Ave 3rd Flr Edmonton AB Canada T6B 2X3 Fax: 780-427-1066. E-mail: brian.marcotte@gov.ab.ca.

MARCOTTE, MICHAEL STEVEN, municipal administrator; b. New Orleans, Jan. 17, 1951; s. Steven Stephen and Gloria Catherine (DeValcourt) Marcotte; m. Mary Jane Kilgore, May 28, 1972; children: Matthew David, Margaret Katherine. BA, M of Environ. Engring., Rice U., 1973. Cert. profl engr, DC, Tex, Colo. Engr., sr. engr., mgr. Turner, Collie & Braden, Inc., Houston, 1973-82; chief maintenance engr. water div. City of Houston, 1982-83, mng. engr. water div., 1984-85, asst. to the dir. pub. works dept., 1985-87, exec. asst. to the dir. pub. works dept., 1987-88, acting dir. dept. planning and devel., 1988-89; dir. Dallas Water Utilities, 1989-95; dir. econ. devel. City of Dallas, 1995-97; chief engr. D.C. Water & Sewer Authority, 1997—. Fellow: ASCE; mem.: Am Acad Environ Engrs (trustee), Tex Water Conservation Asn (bd dirs), Metropolitan Washington Coun Govts, Water Environ Fedn, Am Water Works Asn (trustee Research Found), Water Resources Coun. Presbyterian. Avocation: high school and college sports official. Home: 900 N Stafford St Apt 2522 Arlington VA 22203-4138 Office: DC Water Sewer Authority 5000 Overlook Ave SW Washington DC 20032-5212 E-mail: mmarcotte@asa.com.

MARCOTTE, PAUL JOHN, neurosurgeon, educator; b. Ottawa, Ont., Can., Oct. 15, 1958; (parents Can. and Am. citizens); s. Paul John and Elinor Ann (Simeone) M. BSc, U. Ottawa, 1980, MD, 1984. Intern Ottawa Civic Hosp., 1984-85; resident U. Ottawa, 1985-90, asst. prof., 1990-92; fellow in spinal surgery Barrow Neurol. Inst., Phoenix, 1991-92; asst. prof. U. Pa., Phila., 1993—. Contbr. articles to profl. jours., chpts. to books. Fellow: ACS, Royal Coll. Physicians and Surgeons (Can.); mem.: Can. Congress Neurol. Surgeons, Am. Assn. Neurol. Surgeons, Congress Neurol. Surgeons. Roman Catholic. Avocations: hockey, model railroading, automobiles. Office: Hosp U Pa 3400 Spruce St Philadelphia PA 19104-4206

MARCOUX, CARL HENRY, former insurance executive, writer, historian; b. San Francisco, Jan. 6, 1927; s. Henry Roderick and Margaret (Carlin) M.; m. Ana Virginia Penate-Melara, Nov. 11, 1967; children: Eric Henry, Grant Reynold. BA, Stanford U., 1950; MBA, Golden Gate U., San Francisco, 1958; MA in Latin Am. History, U. Calif., Irvine, 1988; PhD in Latin Am. History, U. Calif., Riverside, 1994. Gen. mgr. Nat. Union Ins. Co., Pitts., 1953-68; exec. v.p. Transam. Ins. Co., 1968-85. Author: (novels) Sailing West, 2001. Served with U.S. Mcht. Marine, 1944-46; USAF, 1951-53. Mem. Stanford Alumni Assn. Republican. Home: 1967 Port Cardigan Pl Newport Beach CA 92660-5347

MARCOUX, JULIA A. midwife; b. St. Helens, England, Aug. 7, 1928; d. Robert Patrick and Margaret Mary Theresa (White) Ashall; m. Albert Marcoux, Apr. 23, 1955; children: Stephen, Ann Marie, Richard, Michael, Maureen, Patrick, Margaret, Julie. Diploma, Withington Hosp., Manchester, England, 1950; grad., Cowley Hill Hosp., St. Helens, England, 1952; BS in Pub. Adminstrn., St. Joseph's Coll. RN, Conn.; lic. midwife, Conn. Nurse, labor, delivery rm. and nursery Day Kimbal Hosp., Putnam, Conn.; sch. nurse Marianapolis Prep. Sch., Thompson; occupational nurse U.S. Post Office, Hartford; pvt. duty and gerontology nurse. Nurse cons. to day care babies, toddlers and pre-schoolers. Contbr. articles to profl. jours. Named Internat. Cath. Family of Yr., 1982.

MARCOUX, WILLIAM JOSEPH, lawyer; b. Detroit, Jan. 20, 1927; s. Lona J. and Anna (Ransom) C.; m. Kae Marie Sanborn, Aug. 23, 1952; children: Ann K., William C. BA, U. Mich., 1949, JD, 1952. Bar: Mich. 1953. Pvt. practice, Pontiac, Mich., 1953; assoc. McKone, Badgley, Domke and Kline, Jackson, 1953-65, ptnr., 1965-75; dir. Marcoux, Allen, Abbott, Schomer & Bower, P.C., 1975—. Mem. exec. bd. Great Sauk Trail council Boy Scouts Am., pres., 1965-66; bd. dirs. Jackson County United Way, pres., 1983-84. Served with USNR, 1945-46. Recipient Silver Beaver award Boy Scouts Am., 1969, Disting. Citizen award Land O'Lakes coun. Boy Scouts Am., 1991. Fellow Am. Coll. Trial Lawyers, Mich. State Bar Found.; mem. Mich. State Bar Assn., Jackson County Bar Assn. (pres. 1979-80), Jackson Rotary Club (pres. 1963-64), Country Club of Jackson, Clark Lake Yacht Club (hon., commodore 1959). Methodist. Home: 1745 Malvern Dr Jackson MI 49203-5378 Office: Marcoux Allen Abbott Schomer & Bower PC PO Box 787 Jackson MI 49204-0787 E-mail: wmarcoux@marcouxallen.com.

MARCOVICI, SEBASTIAN, ballet dancer; b. Paris; Student, Sch. of Paris Opera Ballet; studied with, Chautauqua Sch. Dance. Mem. corps de ballet N.Y.C. Ballet, 1993—98, soloist, 1998—. Dancer (ballets) Liebeslieder Walzer, Appalachia Waltz, Dances at a Gathering, Glass Pieces, The Goldberg Variations, Ancient Airs and Dances, Polyphonia, Quartet for Strings, La Stravaganza, Brandenburg, West Side Story Suite, The Beethoven Seventh, numerous others. Office: NYC Ballet NY State Theatre 20 Lincoln Ctr Plz New York NY 10023-6913*

MARCOVITZ, LEONARD EDWARD, retail executive; b. Bismarck, N.D., Sept. 6, 1934; s. Jacob and Frieda Marcovitz. Asst. mgr. Greengard's Clothing, Mandan, N.D., 1955-58; mgr. K-G Men's Stores, Inc., Bismarck, 1958-61, Billings, Mont., 1961-69, v.p. store ops., 1969-73; pres. Leonard's Men's Stores, Yakima, Wash. and Billings, Mont., 1973-77; chief exec. officer K-G Retail div. Chromalloy Am. Corp., Englewood, Colo., 1977-81; pres. DeMarcos Men's Clothing, Casper, Wyo., 1982—, Idaho Falls, Idaho, 1984—, Billings, Mont., 1986-96, Twin Falls, Idaho, 1996—, Ft. Collins, Colo., 1999—, Boise, Idaho, 2000—. Mem. Menswear Retailers Am. (past dir.), Order of Demolay (Degree of Chevalier 1952, Internat. Master Councilor 1953, Demolay Dad 1959), Elks. Home: PO Box 95124 Las Vegas NV 89193-5124

MARCUCCIO, PHYLLIS ROSE, retired association executive, editor; b. Hackensack, N.J., Aug. 25, 1933; d. Filippo and Rose (Henry) Marcuccio. AB, Bucknell U., 1955; MA, George Washington U., 1976. Trainee Time, Inc., 1956—57; art prodn. for mags. of Med. Econs., Inc., 1958—60; mem. staff Nat. Sci. Tchrs. Assn., Washington, 1961—99; assoc. editor Sci. and Children, 1963, editor, 1964—93, dir. divsn. elem. edn., 1974—78, dir. divsn. program devel. and continuing edn., 1978—83, pub., 1993—99; dir. publs. Nat. Sci. Tchrs. Assn., 1983—99, assoc. exec. dir., 1990—99; pub. Dragonfly, 1996—99. Lectr., cons. in field. Author (photographer, illustrator numerous articles) ; co-author: Investigation in Ecology, 1972; editor: Science Fun, 1977, Science Fun, 2d edit., 1994; ; compiler: Opportunities for Summer Studies in Elementary Science, 1968, compiler: Opportunities for Summer Studies in Elementary Science, 2d edit., 1969, pub.: Sci. and Children, 1993—99, pub.: Dragonfly Mag., 1997—99. Apptd. commr. Rockville (Md.) Housing Authority, 1981—91, chairperson, 1984—86; bd. dirs. Nat. Sci. Resource Ctr., NAS, 1986—96, Hands on Sci. Outreach, Inc., 1991—2001; pres. East Rockville Civic Assn. , 2000—. Recipient Citizenship medal, DAR, 1951, Golden Lamp award, Edpress, 1998. Mem.: AAAS, NSTA (life), Pocono Environ. Edn. Ctr. (bd. dirs. 1989—98), Sci. Tchg. Assn. N.Y. (Outstanding Svc. to Sci. Edn. award 1987), Press Assn. Am. (regional dir. 1969—71, sec. 1979—, Disting. Achievement award 1969, 1971—74, 1976, 1977, 1980, 1988, 1993, 1995, Eleanor Fishburn award 1978), The Washington Forum, Washington edn. Press Assn. (treas. 1966—67, pres. 1975—76), Ohio Coun. Elem. Sch. Sci. (life), Nat. Assn. Industry Edn. Coop. (bd. dirs. 1980—86), Nat. Press Club, Am. Nature Study Soc., Coun. Elem. Sci. Internat. (Internat. award for outstanding contbns. sci. edn. 1971, 1972, 1986, 1994), Sigma Delta Chi, Phi Delta Kappa, Phi Delta gamma, Theta Alpha Phi. Home: 406 S Horners Ln Rockville MD 20850-1556 E-mail: marcu@erols.com.

MARCUM, DEANNA BOWLING, library administrator; b. Salem, Ind., Aug. 5, 1946; d. Anderson and Ruby (Mobley) Bowling; m. Thomas P. Marcum, June 13, 1974; 1 child, Ursula. BA, U. Ill., 1967; MA, So. Ill. U., 1969; MLS, U. Ky., 1971; PhD, U. Md., 1991. Tchr. Deland-Weldon (Ill.) High Sch., 1967-68; instr. English U. Ky., Lexington, 1969-70, cataloging librarian, 1970-73, asst. to dir., 1973-74; asst. dir. pub. svcs. Joint U. Librs., Nashville, 1974-77; mgmt. tng. specialist Assn. Rsch. Librs., Washington, 1977-80; sr. cons. Info. Systems Cons., Inc., 1980-81; v.p. Coun. on Libr. Resources, 1981-89; dean Sch. Libr. and Info. Sch. Cath. U., 1989-92; dir. pub. svcs. and collections mgmt. Libr. of Congress, 1993-95; pres. Coun. on Libr. Resources and Info., 1995—. Adv. bd. So. Edn. Found., Atlanta, 1986-91; chmn. grants com. Coun. on Libr. resources, Washington, 1990-94. Author: Good Books in a Country Home, 1993, Development of Digital Libaries, An American Perspective, 2001; co-author: (with Richard Boss) The Library Catalog, 1980, On-Line Acquisitions Systems, 1981; contbr. articles to profl. jours. Pres., Commn. on Preservation and Access, 1995—. Mem. ALA, Am. Studies Assn., Orgn. Am. Historians, Am. Antiquarian Soc. (adv. bd. 1989—), Beta Phi Mu, Phi Kappa Phi. Home: 3315 Wake Dr Kensington MD 20895-3218 Office: Coun on Libr and Info Resources Ste 500 1755 Massachusetts Ave NW Washington DC 20036-2124 E-mail: dmarcum@clir.org.

MARCUM, WALTER PHILLIP, manufacturing executive; b. Bemidji, Minn., Mar. 1, 1944; s. John Phillip and Johnnye Evelyn (Edmiston) M.; m. Barbara Lynn Maloof, Apr. 17, 1976. BBA, Tex. Tech. U., 1967. Rschr. Collins Securities, Denver, 1968-70, Hanifin Imhoff, Denver, 1970-71; cons. Marcum-Spillane, 1971-76; with MGF Oil Corp., Midland, Tex., 1976-87, sr. v.p., 1978, exec. v.p., 1979-83, pres., CEO, 1983-87; sr. v.p. corp. fin. Boettcher & Co., Denver, 1987-90; pres., CEO Marcum Natural Gas Svcs., Inc., 1991-99, Metretek Techs., Denver, 2000—. Dir. TestAmerica Inc., Asheville, N.C., Key Energy Group, East Brunswick, N.J. Republican. Presbyterian. Home: 342 Monroe St Denver CO 80206-4445 Office: 303 East 17th Ave Ste 660 Denver CO 80203

MARCUS, ALFRED ALLEN, finance educator, consultant; b. Pitts., Jan. 21, 1950; s. James Marcus and Alice Freed; m. Judith Esther Davis, July 1, 1973; children: David, Isaac, Ariel Jonathan. BA in History, U. Chgo., 1971, MA in Polit. Sci., 1973; PhD in Govt., Harvard U., 1977. Asst. prof. U. Pitts. Bus. Sch., 1977—79; rsch. scientist Buttelle Human Affairs Ctrs., Seattle, 1979—84; asst. prof. U. Minn. Carlson Sch. Mgmt., Mpls., 1984—88, assoc. prof., 1988—92, prof., 1992—. Author: The Adversary Economy, 1984, Business and Society, 1995; editor (with Ken Sexton): Better Environmental Decisions, 2000.

MARCUS, BERNARD, lawyer, consultant; b. Wilkes-Barre, Pa., Mar. 10, 1924; m. Frances Frank; children: Kate, Aaron, Charles, Mary. Student, U. Pa., 1941-43, Carnegie-Mellon U., 1943-44; LL.B., Harvard U., 1948; postgrad., Loyola U. of South, New Orleans, 1958. Bar: D.C. 1949, La. 1958. Atty. legis. reference service Library of Congress, 1949-50; acting counsel small bus. com. Ho. of Reps., 1950; atty. NLRB, Washington, Cin., Buffalo and New Orleans, 1950-57; assoc. Deutsch, Kerrigan & Stiles, New Orleans, 1957-58, ptnr., 1958-95, mng. ptnr., 1985-89, emeritus ptnr., 1995—. Cons. Dept. State, 1965-69; labor arbitrator Am. Arbitration Assn., Fed. Mediation and Conciliation Svc., NASD, Arbitration Forum, USDA, U.S. Dept. Def., U.S. Dept. Transp., City of Houston, Houston Lighting & Power Co., Houston Met. Transit Authority, Sanyo Mfg. Co., TU Elec., Internat. Paper Co., Inland Paper, Gaylord Container, ADM Corp., GTE, SW Bell, Ingalls Shipbldg., PPG Industries, Ga. Pacific Corp., Westvaco, Hertz, Schering Plough, Chevron, Bryan Foods, Savannah Elec. & Power, Citgo, SBC Corp., Verizon, GTE, GAF, Citgo, Conoco, Phillips Petroleum Co., others. Author: Congress and the Monopoly Problem, 1950; contbr. to casebooks. Pres. New Orleans Jewish Community Center, 1973-75; mem. Nat. Jewish Welfare Bd., 1974-83; bd. dirs. New Orleans Jewish Welfare Bd., Jewish Family and Children's Service, New Orleans, Communal Hebrew Sch.; v.p. New Orleans Home for Jewish Aged, 1978-80, Florence Heller Rsch. Found. Served U.S Army, 1943-46. Mem. ABA, Fed. Bar Assn., La. Bar Assn., New Orleans Bar Assn. (exec. com. 1971-74), D.C. Bar Assn. Home: 630 Burdette St New Orleans LA 70118-3937 Office: 755 Magazine St New Orleans LA 70130-3698 E-mail: bmarcus@dks.com.

MARCUS, BERNARD, retired retail executive; b. 1929; married. BS, Rutgers U., 1954. V.p. Vornado Inc., 1952-68; pres. Odell Inc., 1968-70; v.p. Daylin Inc., 1970-73; with Handy Dan Home Improvement, Los Angeles, 1972-78; co-founder Home Depot Inc., Atlanta, 1978—2002, ret., 2002. Office: Home Depot Inc 2455 Paces Ferry Rd SE Atlanta GA 30339-4024

MARCUS, CLAUDE, advertising executive; b. Paris, Aug. 28, 1924; s. Jacques and Louise (Bleustein) M.; m. Claudine Pohl, May 27, 1948; children: Michele, Pierre, Anne-Marie, Isabelle. Diploma in Econs., U. Paris, 1947; Lic., Paris Law Sch., 1947. Sec. gen. Publicis, Paris, 1948-55, dir. comml. to dir. gen. adjoint, 1961, dir. gen., 1962-68; mng. dir. Publicis Conseil, 1968-83; pres. Publicis Internat., 1984-88; vice-chmn. Publicis Communication, 1988—. Decorated chevalier de la Legion d'Honneur. Mem. Bur. Verification de la Publicite (vice-chmn.), Racing Club (France). Home: 12 Rue Felicien David 75016 Paris France Office: Publicis 133 Champs Elysees 75008 Paris France E-mail: claudius6@wanadoo.fr.

MARCUS, DEVRA JOY COHEN, internist; b. Bronx, N.Y., Sept. 5, 1940; d. Benjamin and Gertrude (Siegel) Cohen; m. Robert A. Marcus, Apr. 1963 (div. 1974); children: Rachel, Adam; m. Michael J. Horowitz, Mar. 2, 1975; 1 child, Naomi. BA, Brandeis U., 1961; MD, Stanford U., 1966. Diplomate Am. Bd. Internal Medicine. Intern Stanford U., 1966-67, resident in internal medicine, 1967-68; gen. internist D.C. Dept. Pub. Health, 1968-69, Cardozo Neighborhood Health Ctr., Washington, 1969-73; med. dir. East of the River Health Assn., 1973-75; fellow in infectious disease Washington Hosp. Ctr., 1975-77; gen. internist Police and Fire Clinic, Washington, 1977-78; pvt. practice, 1977—; assoc. clin. prof. medicine George Washington U. Med Ctr., 1978—; gen. internist World Bank, 1978-81; ptnr. Traveller's Med. Svc. D.C., 1980-82; gen. internist Community of Good Hope Med. Clinic, Washington, 1984-85; assoc. clin. prof. medicine Georgetown U. Med. Ctr., 1987—. Preceptor Georgetown U. Hosp., 1986—. Contbr. articles to profl. jours. Exec. com. Woodley Park Citizen's Assn., 1979-80; chair mayor's adv. com. on prevention, 1982-83; bd. dirs. Exodus Youth Svcs., 1987-89. Named Best Physicians of Washington, Washingtonian Mag., 1999. Fellow ACP; mem. AMA (Physicians Recognition award, 1981, 84, 87, 90, 93, 96, 99), Med. Soc. D.C. (credentials com., communicable disease com., founder com. on women 1983, pres. 1985-87, med. ethics and judiciary com. 1987-91, judiciary coun. 1992-96), Physicians for Human Rights Med. Mission. Home: 1205 Crest Ln Mc Lean VA 22101-1837 Office: 1145 19th St NW Ste 510 Washington DC 20036-

MARCUS, DONALD HOWARD, advertising executive; b. Cleve., May 16, 1916; s. Joseph and Sarah (Schmitman) Marcus; m. Helen Olen Weiss, Feb. 12, 1959; children: Laurel Kathy Heifetz, Carol Susan, James Randall(dec.) , Jonathan Anthony. BA, Cleve. State U., 1996. Mem. publicity dept. Warner Bros. Pictures, Cleve., 1935-37; mem. advt. dept. RKO Pictures, 1937-40; mem. sales dept. Monogram Pictures, 1940-42; pres. Marcus Advt. Inc., 1946-85, chmn., 1986-2000; chmn. emeritus Marcus Thomas, 2001—. Vice-chmn. comm. divsn. Jewish Welfare Fund Appeal Cleve., 1964—70, chmn., 1971—72; trustee Cleve. Jewish News, 1974—96, v.p., 1983—85; mem. Ohio Dem. Exec. Com., 1969—70, del. nat. conv., 1968; trustee Jewish Cmty. Fedn., 1973—74, No. Ohio regional office Anti-Defamation League of B'nai B'rith, 1986—, Jewish Cmty. Ctr., 1988—90; bd. dirs. Cuyahoga County unit Am. Cancer Soc., 1979—, Cleve. State U. Devel. Found., 1987—. Recipient Disting. Alumnus award, Cleve. State U., 2001. Mem.: NATAS (Silver Cir. award 1994), Cleve. Advt. Club (elected to Hall of Fame), Mensa, Clee. Growth Assn., Beechmont Country Club (past pres.), Union Club Cleve., Ohio Commodores. Jewish. Home: 22449 Shelburne Rd Cleveland OH 44122-2053 Office: Marcus Thomas 25700 Science Park Dr Cleveland OH 44122-7319

MARCUS, DOROTHY MANN, social worker, speech pathologist; b. Chgo., Sept. 3, 1926; d. Sigmund Mann and Sarah (Newman) Maslansky; m. Irwin M. Marcus, Jun 29, 1948; children: Randall, Sherry Marcus Wise, Melinda Marcus Jacobson. BS, Northwestern U., 1947; MSW, Tulane U., 1977. Lic. social worker, La. Social worker Irwin M. Marcus MD & Assocs., New Orleans, 1978-80; pvt. practice, 1981—. Contbr. articles to profl. jours. Pres., bd. dirs. women's aux. Touro Inf. Bd. of Mgrs., New Orleans, 1973-75. Fellow Internat. Conf. for Advancement of Clin. Social Work (bd. dirs. 1980—, pres.-elect 1991); mem. NASW, Am. Bd. Examiners in Clin. Social Work, La. Soc. Clin. Social Work. Avocations: golf, travel, gardening. Home and Office: 5 Muirfield Pl New Orleans LA 70131-3309

MARCUS, EDWARD, economist, educator; b. Bklyn., Apr. 29, 1918; s. Herman and Rose (Marayna) M.; m. Mildred Rendl, Aug. 10, 1956. BS, Harvard, 1939, MBA, 1941; student, King's Coll., Cambridge (Eng.) U., 1946-47; PhD, Princeton, 1950. Economist Fed. Res. Bd., 1950-52; prof. econs. Bklyn. Coll., 1952-81, chmn. dept., 1966-79. Cons. Nat. Acad. Scis., 1959, UN Conf. Trade and Devel., 1966; dir. Syracuse U. Maxwell Sch. Nigerian Project, 1961; participant Internat. Econometrics Assn., Amsterdam, Holland, 1968 Author: Canada and the International Business Cycle, 1927-1938, 1954, (with Mildred Rendl Marcus) Investment and Development Possibilities in Tropical Africa, 1960, International Trade and Finance, 1965, Monetary and Banking Theory, 1965, Economic Progress and the Developing World, 1971, Economics, 1978. Served with AUS, 1941-42; Served with USCGR, 1942-46. Grantee Merrill Found., 1953 Mem. Am. Econ. Assn., Canadian Econ. Assn., N.Y. Met. Econ. Assn. (pres. 1966-67), Am. Finance Assn., Royal Econ. Soc., Econ. Soc. S. Africa, Am. Assn. U. Profs., New Canaan Hist. Soc. Treas. 1983—), Phi Beta Kappa. Home: PO Box 814 New Canaan CT 06840-0814

MARCUS, EDWARD LEONARD, lawyer, political organization administrator, former chairman; b. Bklyn., June 14, 1927; s. Isaac Horatio and Dorothy (Kirchsten) M.; m. Phyllis Betzes, Sept. 19, 1948 (div. 1984); children: Shelley A., Susan E., Nicole Marie; m. Lisa E. Munson, 1984 (div. 1989); m. Lorraine Jill Surprenant, Aug. 9, 1989. BA, Yale Coll., 1948, LLB, LLD, 1950. Bar: Conn. 1950, U.S. Dist. Ct. Conn. 1952, U.S. Ct. Appeals (2d dist.) 1954, U.S. Supreme Ct. 1955. Sr. ptnr. Marcus Law Firm, New Haven, 1950—. Mem. Overseas Pvt. Invest Corp, Washington, 1978-81; bd. dirs. exec. com. Branford (Conn.) Savs. Bank, Boca Raton (Fla.) First Nat. Bank. Alderman City of New Haven, 1951-56; majority leader State Senate, Conn., 1958-70; chmn. Commn. Inter Govt. Rels., 1962-70, senate majority leader, 1966-70; chmn. Coun. State Govts., 1968-69; del. Dem. Nat. Conf., 1976, 92, 96; mem. Conn. Tourism Task Force, 1991—; mem. Dem. State Ctrl. Com., Conn., 1986—, chmn. fin. com., 1991-92; chmn. Conn. del. Dem. Nat. Conv., 1992, 96, 2000. Mem. ABA, Conn. Bar Assn., New Haven Bar Assn. Democrat. Avocations: tennis, swimming. Home: 100 Stony Creek Rd Branford CT 06405-3236 Office: Marcus Law Firm 111 Whitney Ave Ste 2 New Haven CT 06510-1261 E-mail: emarcus@marcuslawfirm.com.*

MARCUS, ERIC PETER, lawyer; b. Newark, Aug. 31, 1950; s. John J. and Alice M. (Zeldin) M.; m. Terry R. Toll, Oct. 9, 1983. BA, Brown U., 1972; JD, Stanford U., 1976. Bar: N.Y. 1977, N.J. 1977. Assoc. Kaye, Scholer, Fierman, Hays & Handler LLP, N.Y.C., 1976-84, ptnr., 1985—. Contbr. articles to profl. jours. Mem. Phi Beta Kappa. Office: Kaye Scholer LLP 425 Park Ave New York NY 10022-3506

MARCUS, ERIC ROBERT, psychiatrist; b. N.Y.C., Feb. 16, 1944; s. Victor and Pearl (Maddow) M.; m. Eslee Samberg, Nov. 24, 1985; children: Max, Pia. AB, Columbia U., 1965; MD, U. Wis., 1969. Diplomate Am. Bd. Psychiatry and Neurology. Intern NYU Med. Ctr. Bellevue Hosp., 1969-70; resident Columbia Presbyn. Med. Ctr.-N.Y. State Psychiatric Inst., 1972-75; dir. St. Marks Free Clinic, N.Y.C., 1971-75; from co-dir. to dir. neuropsychiatric/diagnostic treatment unit Columbia-Presbyn. Med. Ctr., 1975-84; dir. med. student edn. in psychiatry Columbia U. Coll. Physicians and Surgeons, 1981—; supervising-tng. analyst Columbia U. Ctr. for Psychoanalytic Tng.-Rsch., 1994—; clin. prof. psychiatry and social medicine Columbia U. Coll. Physicians and Surgeons, 1995—. Bd. govs. student health Columbia U., 1986—. Author: Psychosis and Near Psychosis, 1992, revised 2d edit., 2002; mem. editl. bd.: The Psychoanalytic Study of Society, 1989—94, mem. editl. bd.: Jour. Clin. Psychoanalysis, 1998—; co-editor: Psychiatry1, 1998; contbr. articles to profl. jours. Recipient Weber Rsch. award Columbia U. Psychoanalytic Ctr., 1991, O'Connor Tchg. award, 1995, Columbia Univ. Presdl. Awd. for Outstanding Tchg., 1999. Fellow: Am. Psychiat. Assn. (pres. NY County Dist. 2001—02, Roeske award 1991); mem.: NY Acad. Medicine, Assn. Psychoanalytic Medicine (pres. 1999—2001), Am. Coll. Psychoanalysts, Am. Psychoanalytic Assn. (chmn. coun. on univ. and med. edn. 1999—, mem. editl. bd. Jour. 2000—). Avocations: classical music, photography, swimming, reading. Office: Columbia U Dept Psychiatry 1051 Riverside Dr New York NY 10032-1013

MARCUS, FRANK ISADORE, cardiologist, educator; b. Haverstraw, N.Y., Mar. 23, 1928; s. Samuel and Edith (Sattler) M.; m. Janet Geller, June 30, 1957; children: Ann, Steve, Lynn. BA, Columbia U., 1948; MS, Tufts U., 1951; MD cum laude, Boston U., 1953. Diplomate Am. Bd. Internal Medicine, subspecialty cardiovascular diseases. Intern Peter Bent Brigham Hosp., Boston, 1953-54, asst. resident, 1956-57, research fellow in cardiology, 1957-58; clin. fellow in cardiology Georgetown U. Hosp., 1958-59, chief med. resident, 1959-60; chief of cardiology Georgetown U. Med. Service, D.C. Gen. Hosp., Washington, 1960-68; instr. medicine Georgetown U. Sch. Medicine, 1960-63, asst. prof., 1963-68, assoc. prof., 1968; prof. medicine, chief cardiology sect. U. Ariz. Coll. Medicine, Tucson, 1969-82, disting. prof. internal medicine (cardiology), 1982-99, emeritus prof., 1999—, dir. electrophysiology, 1982—2001. Cons. cardiology VA Hosp., Tucson, 1969, USAF Regional Hosp., Davis-Monthan AFB, Tucson, 1969; mem. panel drug efficacy study, panel on cardiovascular drugs Nat. Acad. Scis.-NRC, 1967-68; chmn. undergrad. cardiovascular tng. grant com. HEW-NIH, 1970; dir. Arrhythmia Svcs., 1996—. Editor: Modern Concepts of Cardiovascular Disease, 1982—84; : mem. editl. bd. Circulation, 1976—81, : mem. editl. bd. Current Problems in Cardiology, 1976—80, : mem. editl. bd. Cardiovascular Drugs and Therapy, 1986—, : mem. editl. bd. New Trends in Arrythmias, 1984—, : mem. editl. bd. Jour. Am. Coll. Cardiology, 1984—87, : mem. editl. bd., 1996—2000, : mem. editl. bd. Am. Jour. Cardiology, 1984, : mem. editl. bd. Jour. Cardiovasc. Drugs and Therapy, 1994—, : mem. editl. bd. Jour. Cardiovasc. Pharmacology and Therapeutics, 1994—, : mem. editl. bd. Pacing and Clin. Electrophysiology, 1995—, : mem. editl. bd. Annals of Noninvasive Electrocardiology, 1996—, : mem. editl. bd. Cardiology, 2000—; contbr. articles to med. jours. Chmn. Washington Heart Assn. High Sch. Heart Program, 1966-68. Served to capt. USAF, 1954-56. Recipient Career Devel. award NIH, 1965, Student AMA Golden Apple award Georgetown U. Sch. Medicine, 1968; Mass. Heart Assn. fellow, 1957-58; John and Mary Markle scholar, 1960-65 Fellow Coun. on Clin. Cardiology Am. Heart Assn., ACP (Ariz. laureate award 1987), Am. Coll. Cardiology (bd. govs. Ariz. 1984-87, asst. sec. 1987-89, trustee); mem. Assn. Univ. Cardiologists, Inc. (v.p. 1989-90, pres. 1990-91), Ariz. Heart Assn. (dir. 1970, v.p. 1972-73, chmn. rsch. com. 1970-72), So. Ariz. Heart Assn. (dir. 1969), N.Am. Soc. for Pacing and Electrophysiology, Alpha Omega Alpha. Home: 4949 E Glenn St Tucson AZ 85712-1212 Office: U Ariz Univ Med Ctr 1501 N Campbell Ave Tucson AZ 85724-0001

MARCUS, GREIL GERSTLEY, critic; b. San Francisco, June 19, 1945; s. Gerald Dodd and Eleanore (Hyman) M.; m. Jenelle Bernstein, June 26, 1966; children: Emily Rose, Cecily Helen. BA, U. Calif., Berkeley, 1967, MA, 1968. Record editor Rolling Stone mag., San Francisco and N.Y.C., 1969-70, book columnist, 1975-80, Calif. Mag., L.A., 1982-83, 88-90; pop music columnist Music Mag., Tokyo, 1978-94, New West mag., L.A., 1978-82, Artforum mag., N.Y.C., 1983-87, 90-98, Village Voice newspaper, N.Y.C., 1986-90, Interview Mag., N.Y.C., 1992—; dir. Falter newspaper, Vienna, 1997-98; cultural columnist N.Y. Times, 1998, Esquire mag., 1998-99; music columnist Salon-.com, 1999—. Seminar presenter U. Calif., Berkeley, Princeton U., 2000. Author: Mystery Train: Images of America in Rock 'n Roll Music, 1975, U.S. rev. , 1982, 90, 97 (Brit., German, Greek, Dutch, Japanese and French edits.), Real Life Rock (Japanese), 1984, Lipstick Traces: A Secret History of the 20th Century, 1989 (Brit., Italian, Spanish, German, French and Turkish edits.), Dead Elvis: A Chronicle of a Cultural Obsession, 1991 (Brit., Japanese and German edits., rev. 1999), Ranters and Crowd Pleasers: Punk in Pop Music, 1977-92, 93, In The Fascist Bathroom: Writings on Punk, 1999 (Brit. and German edits.), The Dustbin of History (Brit. and German edits.), 1995, Invisible Republic: Bob Dylan's Basement Tapes, 1997 (Brit., Italian, German, Dutch and French edits.), Double Trouble: Bill Clinton and Elvis Presley in a Land of No Alternatives, 2000 (Brit. edit.), The Old, Weird America: The World of Bob Dylan's Basement Tapes, 2001; editor: Stranded, 1979, rev. 1996, Psychotic Reactions and Carburetor Dung (Lester Bangs), 1987; contbr. criticism to publs. including Creem, Express-Times, New Mus. Express, Another Room, RAW, Rock and Roll Confidential, Threepenny Rev., Representations, Salon, Interview, Common Knowledge; curator Whitney Mus. Am. Art, N.Y., 1998.

MARCUS, GWEN ELLEN, sculptor; b. N.Y.C. d. David Oscar and Doris (Sherman) M. BS, NYU, 1977. One-woman shows include Galeries Lafayette Trump Tower, N.Y.C., 1994, exhibited in group shows at Silvermine Guild Art, New Canaan, Conn., 1967, Nat. Acad. Galleries, Audubon Artists, N.Y., 1968, Grannymede Gallery, 1992, Sher Galleries, Miami, Fla., 1994—99, Bal Harbour Gallery, Fla., 2000, Sundance Gallery, Bridgehampton, N.Y., 1994—98, Allied Artists Am. Inc., N.Y., 1995, CFM Gallery, 1993—95, Catharine Lorillard Wolfe Art Club Inc., 1996, 1999, 2000, 2001, 2002,

Broome St. Gallery, N.Y., Musee d'Art et d'istoire of Neuchatel, Switzerland, 1996, Newark Mus., Am. Nimismatic Soc., 1996, Rotunda Cannon House, Washington, 1996, Bonatirer Fine Art Gallery, Piermont, N.Y., 1997—2000, Nat. Sculpture Soc., N.Y.C., 1997—2002, Cavalier Gallery, Greenwich, Conn., 1998—2002, Kaleidoscope Gallery, Mission Viejo, Calif., 1998—2002, DeVorzon Gallery, Beverly Hill, Calif., 1999, 2000, The Sculpture Showcase Ltd., New Hope, Pa., 1998—2002, Kerygma Gallery, Ridgewood, N.J., 1999—2002, New Cannan for the Arts Soc., 1999, Crysalis Gallery, South Hampton, N.Y., 2000—02, Bal Harbour Gallery, Fla., 2000, Fleischer Mus. Am. Masters Then and Now: Two Centuries of Sculpture from the Nat. Sculpture Soc., Scottsdale, Ariz., 2000, 2001, Hilligoss Gallery, Chgo., 2000, 2001, Studio Long Grove Galleries Find Art, Grove, Ill., 2000, 2001, Champs Hill, Coldwaltham, Pulborough, West Sussex, England, 2001—02, Frank T. Sabin Gallery, London, 2001—02, Wobun Abbey, Bedfordshire, Eng., 2002, Sudeley Castle, Gloucestershire, Eng., 2002, Stoneleigh Abbey, Warwickshire, Eng., 2002, Castle Howard, Yorkshire, Eng., 2002. Recipient Elliot Liskin Meml. awawrd, Salmagundo Photography & Sculpture Exhbn., N.Y., 1993, Excellence award, 1994, BBI award, 1995, Excellence award, Knickerbocker Artists, Washington, 1993, cert. Merit, Nat. Acad. Design Mus., N.Y., 1996, Agop Agopoff award, Hudson Valley Art Assn., Inc., 1998, Gold medal honor, 2000, Elliot Liskin award, 2001, Coun. Am. Artists Soc. award, 1998, Michael Gressel Meml. award, 2001. Fellow Nat. Sculpture Soc.; mem. Allied Artists Am. (Philip Eisenberg award 1990, Lindsey Morris Meml. award 1994, Gold Medal 1996, Josephine Beardsley Sander Meml. award 1999, 2001), Catharine Lorillard Wofe Art Club (Medal of Honor 1993, Harriet W. Frishmuth Meml. award 1994, Anna Hyatt Huntington Bronze Medal 1995, CLWAC Centennial award 1996), Pen and Brush Club (sculpture soc., Solo Show award 1995, Leonard J. Meiselman Meml. award 1997, Charlotte Dunwiddie Meml. award 2001), Am. Medallic Sculpture Assn., Nat. Assn. Women Artists Inc., Am. Artist Profl. League Inc. (Medal of Honor 1994, 96, President's award 1995, Granville Carter Meml. award 1998, Frank C. Wright Meml. award 1999, Am. Artists Fund award), Nat. Sculpture Soc. (Gloria Medal 1990), Medallic Sculpture Assn. (bd. dirs.), Audubon Artists (Gold medal 1998). Avocations: travel, theater, music, dance, vol. work. Home and Office: 401 E 80th St Apt 19E New York NY 10021-0651 E-mail: marcustudio@aol.com.

MARCUS, HAROLD, retired physician, health facility administrator; b. N.Y.C., May 28, 1915; s. Abraham and Yetta (Salb) M.; m. Beatrice Falk, Apr. 27, 1943; children: Robert Michael, Alan David. BS, Columbia U., 1935; BS in Medicine, W.Va. U., 1936; MD cum laude, Boston U., 1939. Diplomate Nat. Bd. Med. Examiners, Am. Bd. Internal Medicine. Intern Maimonides Med. Ctr., Bklyn., 1939-41; resident in pathology Nassau County Med. Ctr., Hempstead, 1941, 46, resident in internal medicine, 1947-48; resident in neurology Kingsbrook Med. Ctr., Bklyn., 1948-49; pvt. practice, 1949-88; chief medicine Internat. Ladies Garment Workers Union Health Ctr., N.Y.C., 1953-96; ret., 1997. Contbr. articles to profl. jours. Lt. col. U.S. Army, 1941-46. Decorated Bronze Star; recipient Merit Citation Gen. Chiang Kai Shek, China, 1945. Mem. ACP, Phi Delta Epsilon. Avocations: golf, tennis, leather work. Home: Apt 4026 6815 Willowwood Dr Boca Raton FL 33434-3520

MARCUS, HARRIS LEON, materials science educator; b. Ellenville, N.Y., July 5, 1931; s. David and Bertha (Messite) M.; m. Leona Gorker, Aug. 29, 1962; children: Leland, M'Risa. BS, Purdue U., 1963; PhD, Northwestern U., 1966. Registered profl. engr., Tex. Tech. staff Tex. Instruments, Dallas, 1966-68, Rockwell Sci. Ctr., 1968-70, group leader, 1971-75; prof. mech. engring. U. Tex., Austin, 1975-79, Harry L. Kent Jr. prof. mech. engring., 1979-90, Cullen Found. prof., 1980-95, dir. ctr. for Materials Sci. and Engring., dir. program, 1979-95; prof. metallurgy and materials engring., dir. Inst. for Material Sci., U. Conn., 1995—. Cons. numerous orgns. Contbr. numerous articles to profl. publs. Recipient U. Tex. faculty U. Tex. Engring. Found., 1983; Krengel lectr. Technion, Israel, 1983; Alumni Merit medal Northwestern U., 1988, Disting. Purdue Univ. Engring. Alumnus award, 1994. Fellow Am. Soc. Metals; mem. ASTM, ACS, AIME (bd. dirs. Metall. Soc. 1976-78, 84-86), Materials Rsch. Soc. Achievements include 18 patents. Home: 78 Ellise Rd Storrs Mansfield CT 06268-1424 Office: Inst Materials Scis 97 N Eagleville Rd Unit U-3136 Storrs Mansfield CT 06269-3136 E-mail: hmarcus@mail.ims.uconn.edu.

MARCUS, JAMES ELBERT, manufacturing company executive; b. Helena, Ala., July 3, 1949; s. James Edward and Ora Dee (Shanks) M.; m. Willie Mae Murry, June 30, 1980; children: Charsie Latrice, Chareka Lenita, Carlisle Lamar. BS in Biology, Chemistry, Tuskegee U., 1971. Soft drink technician Custom Canners, Inc., Norcross, Ga., 1972-73; comml. inventory supr. Washington Inventory Svc., Inc., Atlanta, 1973-76; shipping and receiving specialist Norrell Temporary Svc., 1977-78; enology lab. technician Monarch Wine Co., 1978-80; R & D technician Pave-Mark Corp., 1980-82; mfg. tech. support specialist Dynatron Bondo Corp., 1982-85; equipment operator Circuit City, Inc., 1985-86; air filter technician Comml. Air Filter Co., 1987-88; owner, pres. Marcus Industries, 1989—, Group 38 Transp. Svcs., Inc., Atlanta, Group 38, Inc. Bus. Concerns, Atlanta. Sub-contractor, advt. distbr., investment profl., 1998. Prin. developer pavement marking material, 1981. Cub scout master Southeastern dist. Traveler's Rest Bapt. Ch. Boy Scouts Am., 1988, 89, 90. Mem.: Nat. Hon. Soc. Pershing Rifles. Democrat. Baptist. Avocations: basketball, bowling, writing, electronics, billiards. Home: 2009 Rocking Ter Conley GA 30288-2109 Personal E-mail: clean38sweep@yahoo.com. E-mail: mae7673@aol.com.

MARCUS, JOEL DAVID, pediatrician; b. Bklyn., June 16, 1932; BA, Columbia Coll., 1954; MD, George Washington U., 1958. Diplomate Am. Bd. Pediats. Rotating intern/pediat. resident The Jewish Hosp. of Bklyn., 1958-61; pvt. practice Rye, N.Y., 1963—; attending pediatrician United Hosp., Port Chester, 1963—; assoc. pediatrician Sound Shore Med. Ctr., New Rochelle, 1997—; assoc. phys., pediatrician St. Agnes Hosp., White Plains, NY. Sch. pediatrician Rye Sch. Sys., 1963—. Capt. USAF, 1961-63. Fellow Am. Acad. Pediats. Avocations: sculpture, barbershop quartet. Office: Unitd Hosp 406 Boston Post Rd Port Chester NY 10573-

MARCUS, JOHN, wholesale distribution executive; b. N.Y.C., Oct. 18, 1941; s. Sam and Margaret (McCoy) M.; m. Helen S. Bondurant, Aug. 14, 1965; children: Lisa Marie, Lynn Michelle. AA, Wentworth Mil. Acad., Lexington, Mo., 1961. Buyer Foley Bros. Dept. Stores, Houston, 1963-65; owner JOMARC, 1965-66; sales mgr. Firestone Tire & Rubber Co., 1966-67; distbn. mgr. Matthews Book Co., St. Louis, 1967-69, office mgr., 1969, gen. mgr., 1970, v.p. ops., 1971, pres., 1972, chmn., CEO, 1974—. Pres., CEO McCoy Collegiate Svcs., St. Louis, 1969—, NACSCORP Inc., Oberlin, Ohio, 1983, Coll. Stores Rsch. and Edn. Found., 1984-85, chmn., CEO Founders Bookstore Svcs.; CEO Coll. Bookstores of Am., St. Louis, 1986—. Contbr. articles to publs. Bd. dirs. YMCA, Wentworth Mil. Acad. Mem. Nat. Assn. Coll. Stores (pres. 1981-82), The Employee Stock Ownership Plans Assn. Office: Matthews Book Co 11559 Rock Island Ct Maryland Heights MO 63043-3596

MARCUS, JOSEPH, child psychiatrist; b. Cleve., Feb. 27, 1928; s. William and Sarah (Marcus) Schwartz; m. Cilla Furmanovitz, Oct. 3, 1951; children: Oren, Alon. B.Sc., Western Res. U., 1963; MD, Hebrew U., 1958. Intern Tel Hashomer Govt. Hosp., Israel, 1956-57; resident in psychiatry and child psychiatry Ministry of Health, Govt. of Israel, 1958-61; acting head dept. child psychiatry Ness Ziona Rehab. Ctr., 1961-62; sr. psychiatrist Lasker dept. child psychiatry Hadassah U. Hosp., 1962-64; research asso. Israel Inst. Applied Social Research, 1966-69; practice medicine specializing in psychiatry Jerusalem, 1966-72; assoc. dir. devel. neuropsychiatry Jerusalem Infant and Child Devel. Ctr., 1969-70; dept. head Eytanim Hosp., 1970-72; cons. child psychiatrist for Jerusalem Ministry of Health, 1970-72; dir. dept. child psychiatry and devel. Jerusalem Mental Health Ctr., 1972-75; prof. child psychiatry, dir. unit for research in child psychiatry and devel. U. Chgo., 1975-85, prof. emeritus, co-dir. unit for research in child psychiatry and devel., 1986—; vis. research psychiatrist UCLA Dept. Psychiatry, 1987—. Chief editor: Early Child Devel. and Care, 1972-76; mem. editorial bd.: Israel Annals of Psychiatry and Related Disciplines, 1965-70, Internat. Yearbook of Child Psychiatry and Allied Professions, 1968-74; contbr. articles to med. jours. Mem. Am. Acad. Child Psychiatry (com. on research, com. on psychiat. aspects of infancy), Soc. Research in Child Devel., Internat. Assn. Child Psychiatry and Allied Professions (asst. gen. sec. 1966-74), European Union Paedopsychiatry (hon.), World, Israel psychiat. assns., Internat. Coll. Psychosomatic Medicine, Israel Center Psychobiology. Home: 910 Chelham Way Santa Barbara CA 93108-1049 Office: # MC 3077 5841 S Maryland Ave Chicago IL 60637-1463 E-mail: jmarcusmd@cox.net.

MARCUS, KAREN MELISSA, foreign language educator; b. Vancouver, B.C., Can., Feb. 28, 1956; came to the U.S., 1962; d. Marvin Marcus and Arlen Ingrid (Sahlman) Bishop; m. Jorge Esteban Mezei, Jan. 7, 1984 (div. Mar. 1987). BA in French, BA in Polit. Sci., U. Calif., Santa Barbara, 1978, MA in Polit. Sci., 1981; MA in French, Stanford U., 1984, PhD in French, 1990. Lectr. in French Stanford (Calif.) U., 1989-90; asst. prof. French No. Ariz. U., Flagstaff, 1990-96, assoc. prof. French, 1996—. Cons. Houghton Mifflin, 1993, Grand Canyon (Ariz.) Natural History Soc., 1994. Vol., letter writer Amnesty Internat. Urgent Action Network, 1991-95; vol. No. Ariz. Aids Outreach Orgn., Flagstaff, 1994-95. Recipient medal for outstanding achievement in French, Alliance Française, Santa Barbara, 1978; named Scholarship Exch. Student, U. Geneva, Switzerland, 1979-80; doctoral fellow Stanford (Calif.) U., 1981-85. Mem. MLA, Am. Assn. Tchrs. French, Am. Coun. on the Tchg. Fgn. Langs., Am. Literary Translators Assn., Women in French, Coordination Internat. des Chercheurs Sur Les Litteratures Maghrebines, Phi Beta Kappa, Pi Delta Phi, Alpha Lambda Delta. Democrat. Jewish. Avocations: walking, yoga, reading, writing short stories. Office: No Ariz Univ Modern Lang Dept PO Box 6004 Flagstaff AZ 86011-6004 E-mail: melissa.marcus@nau.edu.

MARCUS, KENNETH HEARNE, historian, educator; b. N.Y.C., Jan. 21, 1961; s. Rudolph Arthur and Laura Hearne M.; m. Christine Ersig-Marcus, Dec. 23, 1997. BA, U. Calif., Berkeley, 1984; MBA, Ecole Superieure de Commerce, Paris, 1987; PhD, Cambridge U., Eng., 1992. Lectr. Boston Coll., 1992; tutor Harvard U., Cambridge, Mass., 1992-93, rsch. asst., 1992-93; lectr. Calif. State Polytech. U., Pomona, 1994-2001, Woodbury U., Burbank, Calif., 1995-99; vis. asst. prof. U. La Verne (Calif.), 2001—02, asst. prof., 2002—. Author: The Politics of Power: Elites of an Early Modern State in Germany, 2000; composer, musician: (CD) Some American Music, 1999, Colorado Boulevard, 2000. Scholar Am. Friends of Cambridge U., 1989, fellowship Inst. for European History, Mainz, Germany, 1995, Huntington Libr., 2001, 2002. Mem. Clare Coll. Assn., Am. Hist. Assn., Am. Musicol. Soc. Avocations: music, skiing, tennis, gardening. Home: 1111 Blanche St Apt 110 Pasadena CA 91106-3018 Office: U La Verne Dept History and Polit Sci 1950 Third St La Verne CA 91750 E-mail: marcusk@ulv.edu.

MARCUS, LEE EVAN, small business owner, consultant, accountant; b. Cleve., 1953; s. Morton and Bluma Marcus. BA in English, Amherst Coll., 1975. CPA, Fla. Audit staff acct. Arthur Andersen, Tampa, 1976-78; tax mgr. Price Waterhouse, Miami, Fla., 1978-83; controller Williams Island Assocs., Ltd., North Miami Beach, 1983-84; corp. contr. Suncoast Land Devel. Co., Inc., and Affiliates, Stuart, 1984-85; fin. officer, contr. Haydn Cutler Cos., Ft. Worth, 1985-89; pres. Global Solutions Co., Plantation, Fla., 1989-2000, Positive Changes Broward, Inc., Coral Springs, 2000—. Office: Positive Changes Broward Inc 2236 N University Dr Coral Springs FL 33071-6184 E-mail: LeeMcpa@aol.com.

MARCUS, LINDA SUSAN, dermatologist; b. Brooklyn; d. Nathaniel and Eugenia (Portnay) Marcus; m. Ronald Carlin, July 5, 1976; children: Robert Adam, Neal Marc. BS, Adelphi U., Garden City, N.J., 1970; MD, Downstate Med. Sch., Brooklyn, 1975. Diplomate Am. Bd. Dermatology. Intern Long Island (N.Y.) Jewish Med. Ctr., 1975-76; resident in dermatology Columbia-St. Luke's, N.Y.C., 1976-77, Boston U.-Tuft's, 1977-79; pvt. practice Wyckoff, N.J., 1980—. Dir. dermatology Valley Hosp. Ridgewood. Contbr. articles to profl. jours. Mem. Am. Acad. Dermatology, Am. Soc. Dermatology Surgeons, Internat. Soc. Dermatology Surgeons. Avocations: swimming, ice skating. Office: 271 Godwin Ave Wyckoff NJ 07481-2057 E-mail: marcusmd@pubtek.net.

MARCUS, MARIA LENHOFF, lawyer, law educator; b. Vienna, Austria, June 23, 1933; came to U.S., 1938, naturalized, 1944; d. Arthur and Clara (Gruber) Lenhoff; m. Norman Marcus, Dec. 23, 1956; children: Valerie, Nicole, Eric. BA, Oberlin Coll., 1954; JD, Yale Law Sch., 1957. Bar: N.Y. 1961, U.S. Dist. Ct. (so. and ea. dists.) N.Y. 1962, U.S. Ct. Appeals (2d cir.) 1962, U.S. Supreme Ct. 1964. Assoc. counsel NAACP, N.Y.C., 1961-67; asst. atty. gen. N.Y. State, 1967-78; chief litigation bur. Atty. Gen. N.Y. State, 1976-78; adj. assoc. prof. NYU Law Sch., 1976-78; assoc. prof. Fordham U. Law Sch., N.Y.C., 1978-86, prof., 1986—, Joseph M. McLaughlin prof., 1997—. Arbitrator Nat. Assn. Securities Dealers; chair subcom. interrogatories U.S. Dist. Ct. (so. dist.) N.Y., 1983-85. Contbr. articles to profl. jours. Recipient Teacher of Year award, Fordham Law School Students, 2001. Fellow N.Y. Bar Found.; mem. Assn. Bar City of N.Y. (v.p. 1995-96, long range planning com. 1996-2000, exec. com. 1976-80, com. audit 1988-95, labor com. 1981-84, judiciary com. 1975-76, chmn. civil rights com. 1972-75), N.Y. State Bar Assn. (exec. com. 1979-81, ho. dels. 1978-81, com. constitution and by-laws 1984-93), N.Y. Women's Bar Assn. (Pres.'s award 1999). Office: Fordham U Law Sch 140 W 62nd St New York NY 10023-7485

MARCUS, MARVIN, mathematician, educator; b. Albuquerque, July 31, 1927; s. David Clarence and Esther (Rosenthal) M.; m. Arlen Ingrid Sahlman, Sept. 14, 1951; children: Jeffrey Thomas, Karen Melissa; m. Rebecca Elizabeth Michael, Oct. 12, 1965. BA, U. Calif. at Berkeley, 1950, PhD, 1953. Instr., then asst. prof. U. B.C., 1954-56, asso. prof., 1957-62; postdoctoral research fellow Nat. Bur. Standards, Washington, 1956-57; prof. U. Calif. at Santa Barbara, 1962—; dir. Inst. for Interdisciplinary Applications of Algebra and Combinatorics, 1973-79, chmn. dept. math., 1963-68, dean research devel., 1978, assoc. vice-chancellor research and acad. devel., 1979-86. Vis. distinguished prof. U. Islamabad, West Pakistan, 1970; Cons. Bur. Naval Ordnance, Pasadena, Calif. Author books and articles in field.; Editor: Linear and Multilinear Algebra. Served with USN, 1945-46. Mem. Am. Math. Soc., Math. Assn. Am., Soc. Indsl. and Applied Math., Assn. for Computing Machinery, Sigma Xi, Pi Mu Epsilon. Home: 2937 Kenmore Pl Santa Barbara CA 93105-2223

MARCUS, PAUL, law educator; b. N.Y.C., Dec. 8, 1946; s. Edward and Lillian (Rubin) M.; m. Rebecca Nimmer, Dec. 22, 1968; children: Emily, Beth, Daniel. AB, UCLA, 1968, JD, 1971. Bar: Calif. 1971, U.S. Dist. Ct. (cen. dist.) Calif. 1972, U.S. Ct. Appeals (D.C. cir.) 1972, U.S. Ct. Appeals (7th cir.) 1976. Law clk. U.S. Ct. Appeals (D.C. cir.), 1971-72; assoc. Loeb & Loeb, L.A., 1972-74; prof. law U. Ill., Urbana, 1974-83; dean Coll. Law U. Ariz., Tucson, 1983-88, prof., 1988-92; Haynes prof. law Coll. William and Mary, Williamsburg, Va., 1992—, interim dean, 1993-94, 97-98. Reporter, cons. Fed. Jud. Ctr. Commn. Author: The Entrapment Defense, 1989, 3d edit., 2003, The Prosecution and Defense of Criminal Conspiracy, 1978, 5th edit., 2002, Gilbert Law Summary, 1982, 7th edit., 2001, Criminal Law: Cases and Materials, 1982, 5th edit., 2003, Criminal Procedure in Practice, 2001; nat. reporter on criminal law Internat. of Comparative Law, 1978—. Nat. reporter on criminal law Internat. of Comparative Law, 1978—. Office: Coll William & Mary Sch Law Williamsburg VA 23185 E-mail: pxmarc@wm.edu.

MARCUS, PHILIP IRVING, virology educator, researcher; b. Springfield, Mass., June 3, 1927; s. Julius and Marley Amelia (Speir) M.; m. Angela Joan Francis, Dec. 4, 1953; children: Craig F., Wendy L., Valerie L. BS, U. So. Calif., 1950; MS, U. Chgo., 1953; PhD, U. Colo., 1957. Asst. prof. biophysics U. Colo. Sch. Medicine, Denver, 1957-60; asso. prof. microbiology Albert Einstein Coll. Medicine, Bronx, N.Y., 1961-66, prof., 1967-69; prof. microbiology U. Conn., Storrs, 1969-75, head dept., 1969-75, prof. virology, 1969—, dir. Biotech. Ctr., 1990-95. Dir. Nat. Cancer Inst. Program Project, 1973-83; cons. NIH, NSF; mem. sci. adv. coun. Damon Runyon-Walter Winchell Cancer Fund, 1970-74, Am. Cancer Soc., 1986-88, Am. Found. for AIDS Rsch., 1990—. Editor Jour. Cellular Physiology, 1969-96; editor in chief Jour. Interferon Rsch., 1984-95, Jour. Interferon & Cytokine Rsch., 1995—; contbr. numerous articles to profl. jours.; patentee in field. Served with USAAC, 1945-47. Recipient USPHS rsch. career devel. award, 1960-70, excellence in rsch. award U. Conn. Alumni Assn., 1987; NIH grantee, 1960-94, NSF, USDA grantee. Mem. AAAS, Am. Soc. Microbiology, Am. Soc. Cell Biology, Am. Soc. Virology, Brit. Soc. Microbiology, Internat. Soc. Interferon and Cytokine Research, Soc. In Vitro Biology, Harvey Soc., Conn. Acad. Sci. and Engring. Home: 24 Thompson Rd Storrs Mansfield CT 06268-1806 Office: U Conn Dept Molec & Cell Biol U-3044 Storrs Mansfield CT 06269

MARCUS, RICHARD ANDREW, accountant, mayor; b. N.Y.C., Apr. 14, 1954; s. Richard Andrew and Joan Rose Mary Marcus; m. Janet Marcus, May 6, 1978; children: Richard A. III, John Patrick. BBA in Acctg., Iona Coll., 1976. Pub. acct. Alexander Grant & Co., N.Y.C., 1975-79; audit supr. Polygram Corp., 1979-82; mgr. internal audit MGM/UA Entertainment, Culver City, Calif., 1982-84, dir. internal audit, 1984-86, Turner Entertainment, Culver City, 1986-88; contr. Consolidated Film Industries, Hollywood, 1989-97; pres. Marcus Acctg. Svcs., Culver City, 1997—; city councilman Culver City, 1996-99, mayor, 1999-2000. Bd. dirs. Am. Heart Assn., Culver City, 1997—, Culver City Pks. and Svc. Found., 1995—; civil svc. commr. City of Culver City, 1994-96; patron Culver City Edn. Found., 1994—; asst. den leader Pack 18 Boy Scouts Am., Culver City, 1994—, asst. scoutmaster Boy Scouts Am. Troop 113, 1998—; mem. Culver City PTA, 1993—, Culver City Sister Cities Com., 1994—. Mem. Culver City C. of C., Culver City Homeowners Assn., Elks, YMCA Century Plus Club. Democrat. Avocations: music, gardening, camping, military history, writing. Home: 5426 Diller Ave Culver City CA 90230-5331

MARCUS, RICHARD GREENWALD, manufacturing company executive; b. N.Y.C., Sept. 24, 1947; s. Robert Greenwald and Natalie (Snider) M.; m. Beth Applebaum; children: Teri Applebaum, Todd Snider. SB, MIT, 1969, SM, 1971. Sales and mktg. assoc. Am. Biltrite Inc., Wellesley Hills, Mass., 1971-83, v.p., 1981-83, pres., 1983—. Office: Am Biltrite Inc 57 River St Wellesley MA 02481-2013

MARCUS, RICHARD LEON, lawyer, educator; b. San Francisco, Jan. 28, 1948; s. Irving Harry and Elizabeth (McEvoy) M.; m. Andrea June Saltzman, Apr. 26, 1981; 1 child, Ruth. BA, Pomona Coll., 1969; JD, U. Calif., Berkeley, 1972. Bar: Calif. 1973, U.S. Dist. Ct. (no. dist.) Calif. 1976, U.S. Dist. Ct. (cen. dist.) Calif. 1978, U.S. Ct. Appeals (9th cir.) 1981. Law clk. to judge Calif. Supreme Ct., San Francisco, 1972; assoc. Boalt Hall U. Calif., 1973-74; law clk. to judge U.S. Dist. Ct. Calif., San Francisco, 1974-75; from assoc. to ptnr. Dinkelspiel, Pelavin, Steefel & Levitt, 1976-81; assoc. prof. law U. Ill., Champaign, 1981-84, prof. law, 1984-89, U. Calif. Hastings Sch. Law, San Francisco, 1989-97, disting. prof. law, 1997-99, Horace O. Coil '57 prof. litigation, 1999—. Vis. prof. law U. Mich., 1986-87, U. Calif., Hastings, 1988; assoc. reporter Fed. Cts. Study Com., 1989-90; reporter com. civil motions Ill. Jud. Conf., Chgo., 1984, com. on evidence, 1985; cons. Nat. Commn. on Judicial Discipline and Removal, 1992-93; reporter Civil Justice Ref. Act Adv. Group No. Dist. of Calif., 1992—, chair local rules adv. com. No. Dist. Calif., 1994-99; spl. reporter advisory commn. on the civil rules, jud. conf. of the U.S., 1996—; mem. 9th Cir. local rules and internal operating procedures com., 1996—. Author: Complex Litigation, 1985, 3rd edit., 1998, Civil Procedure: A Modern Approach, 1989, 3rd edit., 2000, Federal Practice and Procedure, vols. 8, 8A, and 12 , 2d edit., 1994, 1997; rsch. editor U. Calif. Law Rev., 1971-72; contbr. articles to profl. jorus. Named Order of Coif. Mem. ABA, Am. Law Inst., Am. Assn. Law Schs. (chmn. sect. civil procedure 1988,chmn. complex litigation com. 1991). Democrat. Home: 70 Domingo Ave Berkeley CA 94705-2436 Office: U Calif Coll Law 200 Mcallister St San Francisco CA 94102-4707

MARCUS, RICHARD SARGON, research scientist; AB, U. Pa., 1954, BSEE, 1955; MSEE, MIT, 1957, EE, 1958. Rsch. fellow MIT Rsch. Lab. for Electronics, 1955-58; prin. rsch. scientist MIT Lab. for Info. and Decision Systems, 1958-62, 67—; sr. systems engr. Itek Corp., 1962-67. Editl. bd. Info. Processing and Mgmt., Jour. of Intelligent Info. Systems; reviewer other jours. Mem. Am. Soc. for Info. Sci. (Best article of Yr. to Jour.), Assn. for Computing Machinery, Assn. for Computational Linguistics. Achievements include research on modeling of indexing and retrieval processes for bibliographic and textual databases and the application of those models in the development of expert search assistance systems. E-mial. Office: MIT LIDS 77 Mass Ave Rm 35-421 Cambridge MA 02139-4307 E-mail: rmarcus@mit.edu.

MARCUS, ROBERT, aluminum company executive; b. Arlington, Mass., Feb. 24, 1925; s. Hymen David and Etta (Arbetter) M.; m. Emily Patricia Ulrich, 1988; children: Lawrence Brian, Janie Sue, Clifford Scott, Emily. AB, Harvard U., 1947; MBA, U. Mich., 1949; MEd, Tufts U., 1950. Market analyst Govt. Commodity Exch., N.Y.C., 1952-54; market rsch. analyst Gen. Electric Co., 1954-55; corp. market analyst Amax Inc., N.Y.C., 1955-62, staff market mgr. aluminum group, 1962-65, pres. internat. aluminum div., 1965-70, v.p., 1970-71; exec. v.p. Amax Pacific Corp., San Mateo, Calif., 1971-72; exec. v.p., dir. Alumax Inc., 1973-82, pres., chief exec. officer, dir., 1982-86; ptnr. Am. Indsl. Ptnrs., San Francisco, 1987-92; dir. Saybrook Inst., 1992-99. Dir. Domtar, Montreal, 1984-90, Kaiser Aluminum Corp., 1990-99. Trustee Mex. Mus., 1988-93, 97-98, World Affairs Coun., 1975-90. Ensign USN, 1943-46. Mem. Japan Soc. (bd. dirs.), Harvard Club (N.Y.C.). Home: 2700 Scott St San Francisco CA 94123-4637

MARCUS, ROBERT BRUCE, lawyer; b. N.Y.C., June 19, 1942; s. Henry Edward and Fannie S. (Siegler) M.; children: Peter J., Gabrielle Beth; m. Jeanie Elizabeth Neyer, Dec. 14, 1984. Bar: N.Y. 1967, N.Y. Dist. Ct. (so., ea. and no. dists.) N.Y. 1968, U.S. Supreme Ct. 1980. Assoc. Shatzkin & Cooper, P.C., N.Y.C., 1967-69, Jay Wallman, P.C., N.Y.C., 1969-72, Klotz & Gould, P.C., N.Y.C., 1972-75; sr. assoc. Weiss, Molod, Berkowitz & Godosky, P.C., 1975-79, Richard Frank, P.C., N.Y.C., 1979-82; ptnr. Wallman & Wechsler, P.C., 1982-84, Metnick & Bernstein, P.C., N.Y.C., 1984-88, Metnick, Marcus & Schuchman, P.C., N.Y.C., 1988-89; pres. Robert B. Marcus, P.C., 1989—; counsel to Kelner and Kelner Esq., 1989-97; ptnr. Marcus and Yodowitz, LLP, New City, N.Y., 1998—. Bd. advisors Art Hazzards Inst., N.Y.C., 1981—; chmn., founder Willow Tree Civic Assn., Ramapo, N.Y., 1977-81; bd. dirs. Rockland Family Shelter. Mem. ABA, Assn. Trial Lawyers Am., N.Y. State Trial Lawyers Assn., Assn. Trial Lawyers of City of N.Y. Home: 203 Strawtown Rd New City NY 10956-6815 Fax: (845) 638-6303. E-mail: boblawpc@tco.com.

MARCUS, RUDOLPH ARTHUR, chemist; b. Montreal, July 21, 1923; arrived in U.S., 1949, naturalized, 1958; s. Myer and Esther (Cohen) Marcus; m. Laura Hearne, Aug. 27, 1949; children: Alan Rudolph, Kenneth Hearne, Raymond Arthur. BS in Chemistry, McGill U., 1943, PhD in Chemistry, 1946, DSc (hon.) , 1988, U. Chgo., 1983, Poly. U., 1986, U. Göteborg, Sweden, 1987, U. N.B., Can., 1993, Queens U., 1993, U. Oxford, Eng., 1995, Yokohama Nat. U., 1996, U. N.C., 1996, U. Ill., 1997, Technion-Israel Inst. Tech., 1998, Polytechnic U. Valencia, 1999, Northwestern U., 2000. Rsch. staff mem. RDX Project, Montreal, 1944—46; postdoctoral rsch. assoc. NRC of Can., Ottawa, 1946—49, U. N.C., 1949—51; asst. prof. Poly. Inst. Bklyn., 1951—54, assoc. prof., 1954—58, prof., 1958—64, acting head, div. phys. chem., 1961—62; prof. U. Ill., Urbana, 1964—78, head, div. phys. chem., 1967—68; Arthur Amos Noyes prof. chem. Calif. Inst. Tech., Pasadena, 1978—; vis. prof. theoretical chem. U. Oxford, 1975—76; Baker lectr. Cornell U., Ithaca, NY, 1991; Linnett vis. prof. chemistry Cambridge (Eng.) U., 1996; hon. prof. Fudan U., Shanghai, 1994—; hon prof. Inst. Chem. Chinese Acad. Scis., Beijing, 1995—; hon. fellow Univ. Coll., Oxford, 1995—. Professorial fellow Univ. Coll., Oxford, 1975—76; mem. Courant Inst. Math. Scis., NYU, 1960—61; trustee Gordon Rsch. confs., 1966—69; assoc. mem. Ctr. Advanced Studies, U. Ill., Urbana, 1968—69; chmn. bd. dirs. Gordon Rsch. confs., 1968—69, mem. coun., 1965—68; mem. rev. panel Argonne Nat. Lab., 1966—72, chmn., 1967—68; mem. rev. panel Brookhaven Nat. Lab., 1971—74; mem. rev. com.Radiation Lab., U. Notre Dame Radiation Lab., U. Notre Dame, 1975—80; mem. panel on atmospheric chemistry climatic impact com. NAS-NRC, 1975—78, mem. com. kinetics of chem. reactions, 1973—77, chmn., 1975—77, mem. com. chem. scis., 1977—79; lectr. in field, 1982; mem. com. to survey opportunities in chem. scis., 1982—86; mem. math. panel Internat. Benchmarking of U.S. Rsch. Fields, 1996—97; mem. panel on accountability of federally funded rsch. Com. on Sci., Engring. and Pub. Policy, 2000—01; adv. com. for chemistry NSF, 1977—80; external adv. bd. NAS Ctr. Photoinduced Charge Transfer, 1990—; mem. presdl. chairs com., Chile, 1994—96; advisor, Ctr. for Molecular Scis. Chinese Acad. Scis. and State Key Lab. for Structural Chemistry of Unstable and Stable Species, Beijing, 1995—; co-hon. pres. 29th Internat. Chemistry Olympiad, 1997; hon.

visitor Nat. Sci. Coun., China, 1999. Former mem. editl. bd. Jour. Chem. Physics, Ann. Rev. Phys. Chemistry, Jour. Phys. Chemistry, Accounts Chem. Rsch., Internat. Jour. Chem. Kinetics Molecular Physics, Theoretica Chimica Acta, Chem. Physics Letters, Faraday Trans., Jour. Chem. Soc., editl. bd. Laser Chemistry, 1982—, Advances in Chem. Physics, 1984—, World Sci. Pub., 1987—, Internat. Revs. in Phys. Chemistry, 1988—, Progress in Physics, Chemistry and Mechanics (China), 1989—, Perkins Transactions 2, Jour. Chem. Soc., 1992—, Chem. Physics Rsch. (India), 1992—, Trends in Chem. Physics Rsch. (India), 1992—, hon. editor Internat. Jour. Quantum Chemistry, 1996—. Named Hon. Citizen, City of Winnipeg, 1994, Treasure of L.A., Ctrl. City Assn., 1995; recipient Anne Molson prize in chem., McGill U., 1943, Sr. U.S. Scientist award, Alexander von Humboldt-Stiftung, 1976, Electrochem. Soc. Lecture award, 1979, 1996, Robinson medal, Faraday divsn. Royal Soc. Chemistry, 1982, Centenary medal, 1988, Chandler medal, Columbia U., 1983, Wolf prize in Chem., 1985, Nat. medal of Sci., 1989, Evans award, Ohio State U., 1990, Nobel prize in Chem., 1992, Hirshfelder prize in Theoretical Chemistry, U. Wis., 1993, Golden Plate award, Am. Acad. Achievement, 1993, Lavoisier medal, French Chem. Soc., 1994, Oesper award, U. Cin., 1997, Key to City of Taipei, Taiwan, 1999, William Jost lectr. and medal, Deutsche Bunsenges and Acad. Sci., Göttingen, 1999; fellow Alfred P. Sloan, 1960—61, NSF sr. postdoctoral, 1960—61; scholar sr. Fulbright-Hays, 1972. Fellow: AAAS, Royal Soc. Can. (hon.), Internat. Acad. Quantum Molecular Sci. (hon.), Royal Soc. (London) (hon.), Royal Soc. Chemistry (hon.), Chinese Acad. Scis. (hon.), Internat. Soc. for Theoretical Chem. Physics (hon.), Am. Acad. Arts and Scis. (hon.; exec. com. western sect., co-chmn. 1981—84, rsch. and planning com. 1989—91), Internat. Soc. Electrochemistry (hon.); mem.: NAS (hon.), Am. Chem. Soc. (past divsn. chmn., mem. exec. com., mem. adv. bd. petroleum rsch. fund, Irving Langmuir award in chem. physics 1978, Peter Debye award in physic. chemistry 1988, Willard Gibbs medal Chgo. sect. 1988, S.C. Lind Lecture, East Tenn. sect. 1988, Theodore William Richards medal Northwestern sect. 1990, Edgar Fahs Smith award Phila. sect. 1991, Ira Remsen Meml. award Md. sect. 1991, Pauling medal Portland, Oreg., and Puget Sound sect. 1991, Auburn-Kosolapoff award 1996, Theoretical Chemistry award 1997, Top 75 Chem. & Engring. News award 1998), Am. Phys. Soc., Korean Chem. Soc. (hon.), Am. Philos. Soc. (hon.), Alpha Chi Sigma. Achievements include development of the Marcus Theory of electron transfer reactions in chemical systems and RRKM theory of unimolecular reactions. Home: 331 S Hill Ave Pasadena CA 91106-3405 E-mail: ram@caltech.edu.

MARCUS, RUTH BARCAN, philosopher, educator, writer, lecturer; b. N.Y.C. d. Samuel and Rose (Post) Barcan; divorced; children: James Spencer, Peter Webb, Katherine Hollister, Elizabeth Post. BA, NYU, 1941; MA, Yale U., 1942, PhD, 1946; DLH (hon.), U. Ill., 1995. Rsch. assoc. in anthropology Inst. for Human Relations, Yale U., New Haven, 1945-47; AAUW fellow U. Chgo., 1947-48; vis. prof. (intermittently) Northwestern U., 1950-57, Guggenheim fellow, 1953-54; asst. prof., assoc. prof. Roosevelt U., Chgo., 1957-63; NSF fellow, 1963-64; prof. philosophy U. Ill. at Chgo., 1963-70, head philosophy dept., 1963-69; fellow U. Ill. Center for Advanced Study, 1968-69; prof. philosophy Northwestern U., 1970-73; Reuben Post Halleck prof. philosophy Yale U., 1973-93; sr. rsch. scholar, 1994—. Fellow Ctr. Advanced Study in Behavioral Sci., Stanford, Calif., 1979; vis. fellow Inst. Advanced Study, U. Edinburgh, 1983, Wolfson Coll., Oxford U., 1985, 86; vis. fellow Clare Hall, Cambridge U., 1988, lifetime mem. coll. room, 1989—; past or present mem. adv. coms. Princeton U., MIT, Calif. Inst. Tech., Cornell U. Humanities Ctr., Columbia U., UCLA, Ohio State U., U. Calif. Santa Barbara, Carnegie Mellon, Brown U., U. Va., U. Tex., others; vis. prof. U. Calif., Irvine, 1995—. Author: Modalities, 1993; editor: The Logical Enterprise, 1975, Logic Methodology and Philosophy of Science VII, 1986; mem. editorial bd. Past or Present Metaphilosophy, Monist, Philos. Studies, Signs, Jour. Symbolic Logic, The Philosophers Annual; editor, contbr. to profl. jours. and books. Recipient Machette prize for contbn. to profession; Medal, College de France, 1986, Wilbur Cross medal Yale U., 2000; Mellon sr. fellow Nat. Humanities Ctr., 1992-93; vis. disting. prof. U. Calif., Irvine, 1994, 96, 97, 98, 99; fellow Conn. Acad. Arts & Scis. Fellow Am. Acad. Arts and Scis.; mem. Coun. on Philos. Studies (pres. 1988-90), Assn. for Symbolic Logic (past exec. coun., exec. com. 1973-83, v.p. 1980-82, coun. 1980-85, pres. 1982-84), Am. Philos. Assn. (past sec., treas., nat. bd. dirs. 1977-83, pres. ctrl. divsn. 1975-78, chmn. nat. bd. officers 1977-85), Philosophy of Sci. Assn., Inst. Internat. Philosophie (past exec. com., v.p. 1983-86, pres. 1990-93, hon. pres. 1994—), Fedn. Internat. Philosophy (exec. com., steering com. 1985-99), Elizabethan Club (v.p. 1989, pres. 1989-90), Phi Beta Kappa. Office: Yale U Dept Philosophy PO Box 208306 New Haven CT 06520-8306 E-mail: ruth.marcus@yale.edu.

MARCUS, SHELDON, social sciences educator; b. N.Y.C., Aug. 4, 1937; s. Manny and Sarah (Lande) M.; m. Phyllis Knight; children: Beth, Jonathan, Evan. BA, CCNY, 1959, MS, 1960; Ed.D., Yeshiva U., 1970. Tchr. N.Y.C. Pub. Schs., 1959-68; lectr. social sci. CUNY, 1965-68; mem. faculty Fordham U., N.Y.C., 1968-70, chmn. div. urban edn., 1970-76, assoc. dean grad. edn. Tarrytown campus, 1976-93, prof., 1993—. Mem. exec. bd. tchr. corps program U.S. Office Edn., 1974-82; trustee Doctoral Assn. N.Y., 1973-82; co-dir. Fordham Inst. for Rsch. on Supervision and Tchg., 1992-94, Fordham U./N.Y.C. Supts. Network, 1995—. Author or co-author: Conflicts in Urban Education, 1970; Urban Education: Crisis or Opportunity?, 1972; Father Coughlin: The Tumultuous Life of the Priest of the Little Flower, 1973, (nominated for Pulitzer Prize); The Urban In-Service Education Experience, 1977; Administrative Decision Making in Schools: A Case Study Approach to Strategic Planning, 1986, Strategic Planning: A Case Study Approach to Administrative Decision Making. Case Teaching Notes, 1987; contbr. articles to profl. jours. Recipient Scanlon award for contbns. to edn., 1992, Adminstr. of Yr. award Phi Delta Kappa, 1993. Mem. Am. Ednl. Rsch. Assn. (proposal reviewer 1992-97). Home: 36 Pocantico River Rd Pleasantville NY 10570-3510 Office: Fordham U Sch Educ Tarrytown NY 10591 E-mail: marcus@fordham.edu.

MARCUS, STANLEY, federal judge; b. New York, NY, 1946; BA, CUNY, 1967; JD, Harvard U., 1971. Assoc. Botein, Hays, Sklar & Herzberg, N.Y.C., 1974-75; asst. atty. U.S. Dist. Ct. (ea. dist.) N.Y., 1975-78; spl. atty., dep. chief U.S. organized crime sect. Detroit Strike Force, 1978-79, chief U.S. organized crime sect., 1980-82; U.S. atty. So. Dist. of Fla., Miami, 1982-85; judge U.S. Dist. Ct. (so. dist.) Fla., 1985-97, U.S. Ct. Appeals (11th cir.), 1997—. Office: US Ct of Appeals 11th Cir 99 NE 4th St Rm 1262 Miami FL 33132-2185*

MARCUS, STEPHEN CECIL, printing company executive; b. Phila., Mar. 8, 1932; s. Jerome Milton and Helen Gertrude (Jacobs) M.; m. Seena Hymowitz, Nov. 2, 1958; children: Nancy Joy, Julie Bea; m. Lois Simon, Oct. 7, 1984. BS, Drexel U., 1957. Jr. ptnr. Liess-Marcus Co., Inc., Phila., 1957-59; v.p. sales Mid-City Press, Inc., 1959-70; pres., CEO, founder Mars Graphic Svcs., Inc., Westville, N.J., 1970-86, chmn., 1986-97; prin., chmn. Emerging Growth Equities, King of Prussia, Pa., 1999—. Mem. Phila. Mgmt. Negotiating Com.; mem. Phila. br. Jr. Execs./Graphic Arts; bd. dirs. Covenant Ptnrs., Phila., Rodale Press Inst., 1990—, First Pa. Bancorp , Phila., First Pann Bank, IZ Co., San Diego, Harte Hanks, Inc.; mem. adv. bd. First Virtual Co. Holding Co., San Diego. Active Am. Cancer Soc., Phila. Big Bros.; trustee Friends Ctrl. Sch., 1977—80; trustee, co-founder Beth Tovin Synagogue, Phila.19, 1972—; bd. dirs. Eastern Penitentiary Prison, 1999—, Philly Pops Orch., Phila., Maritime Mus., 2002. With U.S. Army, 1953—55. Recipient Ann. award Exch. Club N.J., 1981, Big Bros. Am. award, Am. Cancer Soc. award. Mem. Am. Arbitration Assn. (various awards), Nat. Direct Mail Mktg. Assn., Graphic Arts Tech. Found., South Jersey Graphic Arts Assn., Graphic Arts Assn. Del. Valley (bd. dirs. 1988), Poor Richard Club (Phila.), Tau Kappa Epsilon. Republican. Jewish. Home: 915 Exeter Crst Villanova PA 19085-2001 Office: Emerging Growth Ewuities 1150 1st Ave King Of Prussia PA 19406 Fax: 610 783 4761. E-mail: stephenmarcus@egequities.com.

MARCUS, STEPHEN HOWARD, lawyer; b. N.Y.C., June 30, 1945; s. Jacob and Mildren (Cohen) M.; m. Carol Sylvia Beatrice, June 11, 1967; children: Joshua David, Rebecca Lynn, Daniel Benjamin. BME, MIT, 1967; JD, Harvard U., 1970. Bar: Calif. 1971, U.S. Dist. Ct. (cen. dist.) Calif. 1971, U.S. Dist. Ct. (so. dist.) Calif. 1974, U.S. Dist. Ct. (so. dist.) Calif. 1975, U.S. Ct. Appeals (9th cir.) 1980. Assoc. Mitchell, Silberberg & Knupp, L.A., 1971-72, Greenberg, Bernhard, Weiss & Karma, L.A., 1972-76; ptnr. Greenberg, Bernhard, Weiss & Rosin, 1976-85; assoc. Frandzel & Share, 1985-87, ptnr., 1987-97, Gittler & Bradford, L.A., 1997—; dir. Cerriton Valley Bancorp., 2001—02. Bd. dirs. Cerritos Valley Bancorp; judge pro tem L.A. Mcpl. Ct., 1976-83. Editor Harvard Law Rev., 1970. Dir. legal com. Temple B'Nai Huyim, 1999—; bd. dirs. Temple B'nai Hayim, 1999—. Mem. Los Angeles County Bar Assn. (client rels. com. arbitrator 1982—, vice chair, 1996—), Century City Bar Assn. (bd. govs. 1984-90), MIT Club So. Calif. (pres. 1978-79, bd. govs. 1979—), Sigma Xi, Tau Beta Pi. Democrat. Jewish. Avocations: senior soccer, skiing, square dancing. Office: Gittler & Bradford 11620 Wilshire Blvd Ste 800 Los Angeles CA 90025-1793 E-mail: csmarcus@aol.com., smarcus@gblaw.net.

MARCUS, STEVEN IRL, electrical engineering educator; b. St. Louis, Apr. 2, 1949; s. Herbert A. and Peggy L. (Polishuk) M.; m. Jeanne M. Wilde, June 4, 1978; children: Jeremy A., Tobin L. BA, Rice U., 1971; SM, MIT, 1972, PhD, 1975. Research engr. The Analytic Scis. Corp., Reading, Mass., 1973; asst. prof. U. Tex., Austin, 1975-80, assoc. prof., 1980-84, prof., 1984-91, assoc. chmn., dept. elec. and computer engring., 1984-89, L.B. Meaders prof. engring., 1987-91; prof. elec. and computer engring. U. Md., College Park, 1991—, acting chair dept., 2000-01, chair, 2001—, dir. Inst. for Sys. Rsch., 1991-96, acting chair, 2000-01. Cons. Tracor Inc., Austin, 1977, 90, ALPHATECH Inc., Arlington, 1999—. Assoc. editor Math. of Control Signals and Systems, 1987—, Jour. on Discrete Event Dynamic Systems, 1990, Acta Applicandae Mathematicae, 1983—. NSF fellow, 1971-74; Werner W. Dornberger Centennial Teaching fellowship in engring., U. Tex., Austin, 1982-84. Fellow IEEE (prize paper awards com. 1985-88, field awards com. 1989-90, assoc. editor Transactions Info. Theory 1990-92), IEEE Control Systems Soc. (bd. govs. 1985-90, chmn. conf. on decision and control program com. 1983, chmn. working group on stochastic control and estimation 1984-87, assoc. editor Transactions Automatic Control 1980-81); mem. Am. Math. Soc., Soc. Indsl. and Applied Math. (corr. editor Jour. Control and Optimization 1990—, editor-in-chief, 2000—), Acta Applicandae Math., 1983—, Eta Kappa Nu, Tau Beta Pi. Home: 9516 Thornhill Rd Silver Spring MD 20901-4836 Office: U Md Inst for Systems Rsch 2227 Ave Williams Bldg 115 College Park MD 20742-0001

MARCUS, WALTER F., JR. retired state supreme court justice; b. New Orleans, July 26, 1927; married; children: Walter III, Adam, Barbara Ann. BA, Yale U.; JD, Tulane U. Bar: La. 1955. Mem. New Orleans City Council, 1962-66; judge Civil Dist. Ct., 1966-73; justice Supreme Ct. La., 1973—2000. Mem. ABA*

MARCUS, WILLIAM MICHAEL, rubber and vinyl products manufacturing company executive; b. Boston, Jan. 31, 1938; s. Richard and Diana (Litch) M.; m. Cynthia Steinman, Dec. 9, 1962; children: Melanie, Daniel, Richard. BS in Bus. Adminstrn., Babson Inst., 1959. With Am. Biltrite Inc., Wellesley Hills, Mass., 1960—, exec. v.p., treas., 1983—, also dir. Bd. dirs. Congoleum Corp. Served with U.S. Army, 1960-61. Office: Am Biltrite Inc 57 River St Wellesley MA 02481-2013

MARCUSA, FRED HAYE, lawyer; b. Paterson, N.J., Jan. 31, 1946; s. Harry and Alice Marcusa; m. Andrea Disario, June 28, 1986; children: Michael, Daniel. AB, Dartmouth Coll., 1967; JD, U. Pa., 1970. Bar: N.Y. 1971. Assoc. Davis, Polk & Wardwell, N.Y.C., 1970-79; v.p., gen. counsel The Coca-Cola Bottling Co. of N.Y., Inc., 1979-81; ptnr. Kaye Scholer LLP, 1981—. Office: Kaye Scholer LLP 425 Park Ave New York NY 10022-3506 E-mail: fmarcusa@kayescholer.com.

MARCUSE, ADRIAN GREGORY, academic administrator; b. N.Y.C., Mar. 25, 1922; s. Maxwell Frederick and Mildred Ann (Hitter) M.; m. Janet Constance Radlo, Oct. 28, 1945 (dec. Mar. 22, 1980); children: Nancy Ruth Marcuse Marshall, Sally Ann Marcuse Crawford, Elizabeth Susan; m. Betty Jane Lieberman Rossman, Jan. 11, 1985; 1 stepchild, Amy Beth Rossman Schurtz. BS, MIT, 1942, MS, 1946; LLD (hon.), Lab Inst. Merchandising, 1992. Registered profl. engr. N.Y., Fla. Rsch. assoc. MIT, Cambridge, Mass., 1945-46; rsch. scientist United Aircraft Co., E. Hartford, Conn., 1946-47; application engr. Westinghouse Electric Corp., Boston, N.Y.C., 1947-60; consulting engr. pvt. practice, N.Y.C., 1955-62; v.p. mktg. and sales Corrosion Control Corp., 1960-62; sales & merchandising mgr. B. Altman & Co., 1962; v.p., COO Lab. Inst. of Merchandising, 1962-72, pres., CEO, 1972—2002, prof. emeritus, counsel to pres., 2002—. Pres. LIM Fashion Edn. Found., 1978—; chmn. Assn. Regionally Accredited Prvt. Colls. and Univs., Washington, 1990-93. Charter commr. City of Glen Cove, N.Y., 1964, chmn. bd. engrs., 1964-68, mem. planning bd., 1980-87; past treas. Community Concert Assn., Glen Cove; past trustee and budget chmn. North Country Reform Temple, Glen Cove; past mem. YMCA Fund-Raising Coun., Glen Cove. 1st lt. USAAF, 1942-45, PTO. Mem. Am. Assn. Higher Edn., Nat. Assn. Coll. Admissions Counselors, Am. Coun. on Edn., Assn. Proprietary Colls. (former pres., chmn.), N.Y. State Assn. Two-Yr. Colls., N.Y. State Counselors Assn., Soc. Sigma Xi, Sigma Beta Delta. Republican. Avocations: sailing, bicycling, travel, theater. Office: Lab Inst of Merchandising 12 E 53rd St Fl 2 New York NY 10022-5268 Address: 356 Golfview Rd #306 North Palm Beach FL

MARCUSE, DIETRICH, retired physicist; b. Koenigsberg, East Prussia, Germany, Feb. 27, 1929; came to U.S., 1957; s. Richard and Gertrud (Solty) M.; m. Haide Schwarz, Jan. 13, 1959; children: Christina, Mikel. Diplom Physiker, Freie Universität, Berlin, 1954; Doktor Ingenieur, Karlsruhe Universität, 1962. Mem. tech. staff Siemens and Halske, Berlin, 1954-57, AT&T Bell Labs., Holmdel, N.J., 1957-94, dist. mem. tech. staff, 1982-94; ret., 1994. Vis. rsch. prof. U. Md., Balt. County, 1995-99. Author: Principles of Quantum-Electronics, 2d edit., 1980, Light Transmission Optics, 2d edit., 1982, Theory of Dielectric Optical Wave-guides, 1972, 2nd edit.,1991, Principles of Optical Fiber Measurements, 1981; also over 200 articles. Fellow IEEE (Quantum Electronics award 1981), Optical Soc. Am. (Max Born award 1989). E-mail: dietermarcuse@aol.com.

MARCUSS, ROSEMARY DALY, economist; b. Stamford, Conn., Aug. 27, 1945; d. Eugene Lawrence and Margaret Mary (Murphy) Daly; B.A. in Econs. cum laude, Newton (Mass.) Coll., 1967; M.S., U. Md., 1973, Ph.D., 1979; m. Stanley J. Marcuss, July 6, 1968; children— Elena Daly, Aidan Stanley. Jr. staff economist President's Council of Econ. Advisers, 1968-70; economist, asst. to pres. Am. Fedn. State, County and Mcpl. Employees, Washington, 1973; economist, mgmt. cons. Data Resources, Inc., Washington, 1974-78; dep. asst. dir. tax analysis Congressional Budget Office, Washington, 1980-83, asst. dir. tax analysis, 1983-98; dep. dir. Bur. Econ. Analysis, Washington, 1998—. NSF fellow, 1970-73. Mem. Am. Econ. Assn., Nat. Tax Assn., Tax Inst. Am., So. Econ. Assn., Soc. Govt. Economists, Nat. Economists Club, Washington Women Economists. Home: 4616 29th Pl NW Washington DC 20008-2105 Office: Congressional Budget Office 2nd & D Sts SW Washington DC 20515-0001

MARCUSS, STANLEY JOSEPH, lawyer; b. Hartford, Conn., Jan. 24, 1942; s. Stanley Joseph and Anne Sutton (Leone) M.; m. Rosemary Daly, July 6, 1968; children: Elena Daly, Aidan Stanley. BA, Trinity Coll., 1963, Cambridge U., 1965, MA, 1968; JD, Harvard U., 1968. Bar: D.C., N.Y., Conn., U.S. Supreme Ct. Staff atty. office of gen. counsel HUD, Washington, 1968; atty. firm Hogan and Hartson, 1968-73; counsel to internat. fin. subcom. U.S. Senate Com. on Banking, Housing and Urban Affairs, 1973-77; dep. asst. sec. for trade regulation Dept. Commerce, Washington, 1977-78, sr. dep. asst. sec. for industry and trade, 1978-79, acting asst. sec. for industry and trade, 1979-80, acting asst. sec. for trade regulation, 1980; mem. firm Milbank, Tweed, Hadley & McCloy, Washington, 1980-93, Bryan Cave, 1993—. Former adj. prof. Am. U. Law Sch. Author: Effective Washington Representation, 1983; mem. bd. overseers U. Calif. Berkeley Law Jour.; contbr. articles to profl. jours. Former trustee Trinity Coll., Hartford. Marshall scholar. Mem. ABA, D.C. Bar (former chmn., steering com. internat. law div.), Phi Beta Kappa. Home: 4616 29th Pl NW Washington DC 20008-2105

MARCUVITZ, NATHAN, electrophysics educator; b. Bklyn., Dec. 29, 1913; s. Samuel and Rebecca (Feiner) M.; m. Muriel Spanier, June 30, 1946; children— Andrew, Karen. B.E.E., Poly. Inst. Bklyn., 1935, M.E.E., 1941, D.E.E., 1947; Laurea Honoris Causa, Politecnico Di Torino, 1993; D in Engring. (hon.), Polytechnic U., 2000. Engr. RCA Labs., 1936-40; research asso. Radiation Lab., Mass. Inst. Tech., 1941-46; asst. prof. elec. engring. Poly. Inst. Bklyn., 1946-49, asso. prof., 1949-51, prof., 1951-65; dir. Poly. Inst. Bklyn. (Microwave Research Inst.), 1957-61; v.p. research, acting dean Poly. Inst. Bklyn. (Grad. Center), 1961-63, prof. electrophysics, 1961-66, dean research, dean, 1964-65; asst. dir. def. research and engring. Dept. Def., Washington, 1963-64; prof. applied physics N.Y.U., 1966-73; prof. electrophysics Poly. Inst. N.Y., 1973—, prof. emeritus, 1978—. Vis. prof. Harvard U., spring 1971 Author: Waveguide Handbook, Vol. 10, 1951, (with L. Felsen) Radiation and Scattering of Waves, 1973; also numerous articles. Recipient Microwave Career award IEEE Microwave Theory and Techniques Soc., 1985. Fellow IEEE (Heinrich Hertz medal 1989); mem. Nat. Acad. Engring., Am. Phys. Soc., Sigma Xi, Tau Beta Pi, Eta Kappa Nu. Home: Apt 1403 7225 Pelican Bay Blvd Naples FL 34108-5524 E-mail: marc@rama.poly.edu.

MARCY, ALVIN NEWELL, contractor; b. Southbridge, Mass., Sept. 28, 1935; s. Herman Alvin and Pauline Grace Marcy; m. Laura Erma Ripley, June 14, 1958; children: Laura Lee, Steve, Grace, James. BA, Wheaton Coll., 1958; BD, Gordon Divinity Sch., Wenham, Mass., 1961. Active Fairfax County Taxpayers Assn.; active govtl. orgns. Mem. John Birch Soc. Avocations: long distance running, reading, writing, grandchildren.

MARCY-GEYSTON, STEPHANIE VIVIAN, interior designer; b. Springfield, Ill., Aug. 15, 1966; d. Louis Allen and Judith Ann Marcy; m. John Jeffery Geyston; 1 child Sydney Vivian Geyston. BS, U. Ill., Champaign, 1988. Interior designer Jim Wilson Interiors, Springfield, 1984-92; interior designer, owner Stephanie V. Marcy Interior Design, 1992—. Tchr. interior design Lincoln Land C.C., Springfield, 1992—. Contbr. articles to Builder mag. Recipient Show Case People's Choice award, Springfield Home Builders Assn., 1992, Festival of Trees People's Choice award, Meml. Med. Ctr., 1994, 1996, 1999, 2001. Mem. Am. Soc. Interior Designers, Civic Garden Club, Phi Upsilon Omicron. Home and Office: 3431 Tuxhorn Rd Springfield IL 62707-8361

MARDEN, BRICE, artist; b. Bronxville, N.Y., Oct. 15, 1938; s. Nicholas Brice and Kathryn (Fox) M.; m. Pauline Thalia Baez, 1960 (div. 1964); 1 son, Nicholas Brice; m. Helen Regina Harrington, Nov. 7, 1968; 2 daus., Maya Mirabelle Zahara, Melia Io Bricia. Student, Fla. So. Coll., 1957-58; BFA, Boston U., 1961; MFA, Yale U., 1963. Pres. Plane Image, Inc. Exhibited in one man shows including Wilcox Gallery, Swarthmore, Pa., 1964, Bykert Gallery, N.Y.C., 1966, 68-70, 72-74, Galerie Yvon Lambert, Paris, 1969, 73, Galleria Francoise Lambert, Milan, Italy, 1970, 73, Konrad Fischer, Dusseldorf, Fed. Republic of Germany, 1971-73, 75, 80, Gian Enzo Sperone, Turin, Italy, 1971, 77, Locksley-Shea Gallery, Mpls., 1972, 74, Jack Glenn Gallery, Corona del Mar, Calif., 1973, Cirrus Gallery, Los Angeles, 1974, Sable-Castelli Gallery, Toronto, Can., 1974, Contemporary Arts Mus., Houston, 1974, Loretto Hilton Gallery, St. Louis, 1974, Ft. Worth (Tex.) Art Mus., 1974, Mpls. Inst. Arts, 1975, D'Allesandro/Ferranti, Rome, 1975, Solomon R. Guggenheim Mus., N.Y.C., 1975, Sperone Westwater Fischer, N.Y.C., 1976, Max Protech Gallery, Washington, 1977, Bell Gallery, Providence, 1977, Jean and Karen Bernier, Athens, 1977, Pace Gallery, N.Y.C., 1978, 80, 82, 84, Kunstraum, Munich, 1979, Inst. für Moderne Kunst, Nurnberg, Fed. Republic of Germany, 1979, Ink, Zurich, 1980, Stedelijk Mus., Amsterdam, 1981, Daniel Weinberg Gallery, Los Angeles, 1984, Mary Boone Gallery, N.Y.C., 1987, Mary Boone/Michael Werner Gallery, N.Y.C., 1988, 89, Gallery Montenay, Paris, 1988, Anthony d'Offay Gallery, London, 1988, Van Straaten Gallery, Chgo., 1989, Galerie Michael Werner, Cologne, 1990, Kunsthalle im Kulturhaus Palazzo, Baselland, Switzerland, 1991, Gagosian Gallery, N.Y., 1993, Mus. Fine Arts, Boston, 1993, Matthew Marks Gallery, N.Y., 1993, 95, 96, 98, Dia Ctr. for the Arts, N.Y., 1993, Walker Art Ctr., Mpls., 1993, Menil Collection, Houston, 1993, Mus. Nat. Ctr. de Arte, Madrid, 1993, Kunstmus., Bonn, Germany, 1993, Tate Gallery, London, 1993, Mus. d'Art Moderne de la Ville de Paris, 1993, Balt. Mus. Art, 1993, Curwen Gallery, London, 1993, Kunstmus. Basel, 1995, Mus. fur Gegenwartskunst, 1995, Mus. Fridericianum, Kassel, 1995, Kunsthalle, Bern, 1995, Vienna Secession, 1995, Stedelijk, Amsterdam, 1995, St. Louis Art Mus., 1995, Pace Gallery, N.Y., 1996, Thomas Ammann Fine Art AG, Zurich, Switzerland, 1997, Staatliche Graphisch Sammlung, Munchen, 1998, Kunstmus., Winterthur, Switzerland, 1998, Wexner Art Ctr., Ohio, 1999, Fogg Art Mus., Cambridge, Mass., 1999, Dallas Mus. Art, 1999; represented in group shows including Lyman Allen Mus., New London, Conn., 1960, Leo Castelli Gallery, N.Y.C., 1966, Park Place Gallery, N.Y.C., 1966, Ithaca (N.Y.) Coll. Mus. Art, 1967, Krannert Art Mus., Champaign, Ill., 1967, Bykert Gallery, 1967-68, 70-71, 74, Inst. Contemporary Art, Phila., 1967, U. Omaha, 1967, Mus. Fine Arts, Houston, 1967, Clemson U. Sch. Architecture, 1968, Vassar Coll. Art Gallery, Poughkeepsie, N.Y., 1969, Stadtische Kunsthalle, Dusseldorf, 1969, Ft. Worth Art Mus., 1969, 74, Carmen Lamanna Gallery, Toronto, 1969, Whitney Mus. Am. Art, N.Y.C., 1969, 71, 73, 77, 83, Locksley-Shea Gallery, 1970, Albright-Knox Gallery, Buffalo, 1970, Found. Maeght, St. Paul-de-Vence, France, 1970, Utah Mus. Fine Arts, Salt Lake City, 1970, Minn. Mus. Art, St. Paul, 1971, Henry Gallery, Seattle, 1972-73, Ariz. State U., Tempe, 1972, Ga. Mus. Art, Athens, 1972, Mus. Contemporary Art, Chgo., 1972, 86, Indpls. Mus. Art, 1972, Walker Art Ctr., Mpls., 1972, Univ. Art Mus., Berkeley, Calif., 1972, Art Inst. Chgo., 1972, Mus. Friderichianum and Neue Galerie, Kassel, Fed. Republic of Germany, 1972, Galerie Yvon Lambert, 1972, Yale U. Art Gallery, New Haven, 1973, Genthofte Kunstvenner and Genthofte Kommune, Denmark, 1973, Stadtisches Mus., Monchengladbach, Fed. Republic of Germany, 1973, I.C.C., Antwerp, Belgium, 1973, Centro Communitario di Brera, Milan, 1973, Royal Coll. Art, London, 1973, Parcheggio di Villa Borghese, Rome, 1974, Kathonah (N.Y.) Gallery, 1974, Nat. Gallery of Victoria, Australia, 1974, Art Gallery of New South Wales, Australia, 1974, Art Gallery of South Australia, Akelaide, 1974, West Australian Art Gallery, Perth, 1974, City of Auckland (Australia) Art Gallery, 1974, Westfalischer Kunstverein, Munster, Fed. Republicof Germany, 1974, Scottish Arts Council, Edinburgh, 1974, Mus. Modern Art, N.Y.C., 1974, 76, Rice Mus. and Sewall Gallery, 1975, Rijksmuseum Kroller-Muller, Otterlo, Holland, 1975, Basel (Switzerland) Kunstmuseum, 1975, Kunstahlle, Zurich, 1976, Staatliche Kunsthalle, Baden-Baden, Fed. Republic of Germany, 1976, Graphische Sammlung Albertina, Vienna, 1976, Sidney Janis Gallery, N.Y.C., 1977, Wildenstein and Co., London, 1980, Bklyn. Mus., 1980, Mus. Contemporary Art, Los Angeles, 1983, Hayden Gallery, Cambridge, Mass., 1983, Pratt Inst. Gallery, N.Y.C., 1983, Gallery Maeght Lelong, N.Y.C., 1983, The Renaissance Soc., Chgo., 1984, Blum Helman Warehouse, N.Y.C., 1984, Daniel Weinberg Gallery, Los Angeles, 1985, Guggenheim Mus., N.Y.C., 1985, Condeso Lawler Gallery, N.Y.C., 1985, Mary Boone Gallery, 1985, Carnegie Inst., Pitts., 1985, Ft. Lauderdale (Fla.) Mus. Art, 1986, P.S. 1, L.I. City, 1986, Charles Cowles Gallery, N.Y.C., 1986, Musee d'Art Moderne, Paris, 1986, Los Angeles County Mus., 1986, Gemeentemuseum, The Hague, The Netherlands, 1986, Ludwig Mus., Kolm, Fed. Republic of Germany, 1986, Galerie Nachst St. Stephan, Vienna, 1986, CAPC Musee d'Art Contemporain de Bordeaux, France, 1986, Anthony d'Offay Gallery, London, 1987, The SAra Hilden Art Mus., Tampere, Finland, 1988, Carnegie Mus. Art, Pitts., 1988, Musee d'art contemporain, Lyon, 1988, Hirschl and Adler Modern, New York, 1989, Whitney Mus. Am. Art, N.Y., 1989, Albright Knox Art Gallery, Buffalo, Ctr. for the Fine Arts, Miami, Fla., Milwaukee Art Mus., Wis., Yale U. Art Gallery, New Haven, Conn., 1989, The Albertina, Vienna, 1990, Musee du Louvre, Paris, 1990, The Mus. of Modern Art, New York, 1992, Margo Leavin Gallery, L.A., 1992, The Balt. Mus. Art, 1992, Kassel, Germany, 1992, The Aldrich Mus., Ridgefield, Conn., 1993, Luhring Augusting, N.Y., 1994, Nat. Gallery, Washington, 1994, The Art Inst. Chgo., 1995, Nat. Mus. Modern Art, Tokyo, 1995, Whitney Mus. Am. Art, N.Y., 1995, Musee national d'art modern, Centre Georges Pompidou, 1995, Mus. Contemporary Art, Chgo., 1996, La Biennale di Venizia, Venice, Italy, 1997, Mitchell-innes & Nash, N.Y., 1998, Hirshhorn Mus. and Sculpture Garden, Washington, Miami (Fla.) Art Mus., 1999-2000, Carnegie Mus. Art, Pitts., 2000, Serpentine Gallery, London, 2000, Kunst Mus., Luzern, Switzerland, 2000, Boston U. Gallery, 2002, Matthew Marks Gallery, N.Y.C., 2002. Office: 170 Varick St New York NY 10013-1221

MARDEN, KENNETH ALLEN, advertising executive; b. Dec. 12, 1928; s. Allen H. and Doris (Littlefield) M.; m. Julia Lee Black, June 11, 1949; children: Priscilla Anne, Emily Gage. BA, U. Maine, 1950. Hosp. salesman Johnson & Johnson, New Brunswick, N.J., 1959-61, product dir. hosp divsn., 1962-68, advt. and pub. rels. mgr. hosp. divsn., 1969-71, group product dir., patient care divsn., 1972-74, advt. dir. patient care divsn., 1974-78; v.p. E.J. Axelrod, Inc., N.Y.C., 1978-80; v.p. account mgmt. Vicom/FCB, Phila., 1980-87; pres. Am. Kennel Club, N.Y., 1987-90. Cons. on dog legislation, 1990—, also bd. dirs.; pres. Crossing Creek Comm., 1991—; bd. dirs. The

Dog Mus., 1995—. 1st lt. U.S. Army, 1951-53; capt. Md. N.G., 1956-59. Mem. Dog Writers Assn. Am., German Shorthaired Pointer Am. Club (del. 1976—, v.p. 1985-96), Eastern German Shorthaired Pointer Club (pres. 19072-74, 94-98), Jersey Rag Racers (pres. 1994-96), Kennel Club Phila. (bd. dirs.), Hunterdon Hills Kennel Club, Nat. Animal Interest Alliance (bd. dirs. 1994—), Nat. Breed Clubs Alliance (v.p. 1996—). Republican. Episcopalian. Home: 183 E River Rd Whitefield ME 04353 Office: Crossing Creek Communications 183 E River Rd Whitefield ME 04353

MARDER, CAROL, advertising specialist and premium firm executive; b. Bklyn., Sept. 20, 1941; d. Simon and Sylvia (Rothstein) Cohen; m. Edwin Marder, Apr. 15, 1961; children: Elisa, Steven Alan, Susan. Prin. owner Boys Ego Retail Clothing, Englishtown, N.J., 1974-76; pres. Motivators, Inc., Old Bridge, 1976-83, Inkwell Promotions Corp., Morganville, 1983—. Cons. Specialty Advt. of N.Y., 1988—. Recipient citation Monmouth County Bd. Recreation Commrs., Lincroft, N.J., 1987. Mem. East Flatbush League Retarded Children (bd. dirs. 1965-69), Marlboro Chpt. Retarded Children (founder, pres. 1969-71, 73-74, bd. dirs. 1971-76), Marlboro Jewish Ctr. Sisterhood (bd. dirs. 1971-73), N.J. Women in Bus., Middlesex County C. of C., Western Monmouth C. of C. Democrat. Jewish. Avocations: golf, cooking, travel. Office: Inkwell Promotions 1020 Campus Dr W Morganville NJ 07751-1260

MARDER, JOHN G. real estate investor, marketing consultant, corporate director, bison rancher; b. N.Y.C., Dec. 27, 1926; s. Joseph T. and Rhea Marder; m. Barbara Sand, 1956 (div. 1971); children; Jonathan A., Susan Zelouf, Jane Martin; m. Joan Kron, 1971. Student, Cornell U., 1944-45; BS in Bus., Columbia U., 1950. Merchandising exec. Macy's, N.Y.C., 1951-56; exec. v.p. Grey Advt. Inc., 1956-86; real estate investor-developer Miami Beach, Anguilla B.W.I., 1986—; ptnr. buffalo ranch and mktg. enterprise Belle-Air Farms, Thompson, Pa., 1999—. Bd. dirs. several profit, not-for-profit and ednl. corps. Served as radio officer U.S. Maritime Service, U.S. Army Transport Service, 1945-46; 2d Lt. Q.M.C. U.S. Army, 1951-53. Home: 205 E 63rd St New York NY 10021-7425 also: 18 Hedges Banks Dr East Hampton NY 11937-3505 E-mail: jgm@buffalobelle.com.

MARDER, MICHAEL ZACHARY, dentist, researcher, educator; b. N.Y.C., Aug. 30, 1938; s. Jospeh Theodore and Rhea (Greenspun) M.; (widowed); children: Sherri Ellen, Robert Whitney. Student, Tufts U., 1959; D.D.S., Columbia U., 1963. Diplomate: Am. Bd. Oral Medicine. Practice dentistry, N.Y.C., 1963-66, 68—; asst. Sch. Dental and Oral Surgery, Columbia U., 1963-66, instr., 1968, asst. clin. prof., 1968-72, assoc. clin. prof., 1972-76, clin. prof. dentistry, 1976—, researcher, 1963—; dir. oral medicine, 1972-84; dir. clin. cancer tng., 1993—; asst. attending dental surgeon Presbyn. Hosp., 1972-76; assoc. attending dentist, 1976-82; attending dentist, 1982—; cons. Good Samaritan Hosp., Suffern, N.Y. Lectr. in field. Author 2 textbooks in dental medicine; contbr. chpts. to med. and dental textbooks, articles to profl. jours. Served to capt. U.S. Army, 1966-68. Recipient Cert. of Achievement U.S. Army, 1968. Fellow N.Y. Acad. Dentistry; mem. ADA, Internat. Assn. Dental Rsch., Am. Acad. Oral Medicine, Frist Dist. Dental Soc. N.Y., Omicron Kappa Upsilon, Sigma Xi. Office: 119 W 57th St New York NY 10019-2303

MARDER, STEPHEN R. psychiatrist, educator; b. N.Y.C., May 19, 1945; s. Fred and Ida M.; m. Paula Smith, Aug. 19, 1976; 1 child, Jennifer R. AB, U. Pa., 1967; MD, SUNY, Buffalo, 1971. Intern Denver Gen. Hosp., 1971-72; resident in psychiatry U. So. Calif., 1972=75; staff psychiatrist Brentwood VA Med. Ctr., L.A., 1977—; chief psychiatry West L.A. VA Med. Ctr., 1994—; prof., vice chair dept. psychiatry UCLA, 1994—. Office: VA Med Ctr MIRECC 210A 11301 Wilshire Blvd Los Angeles CA 90073-1003

MARDER, TOD A. art historian, educator; PhD, Columbia U. Prof. Rutgers U., New Brunswick, N.J., chmn. dept. art history, 1999—. Author: Bernini's Scala Regia at the Vatican Palace, 1997, Bernini and the Art of Architecture, 1998; editor-in-chief Jour. Soc. Archtl. Historians, 1987-90; contbr. articles to profl. jours. Fellow Am. Acad. in Rome. Office: Dept Art History Rutgers U Vorhees Hall 71 Hamilton St New Brunswick NJ 08903

MARDER, WILLIAM DAVID, health economist; b. Phila., Apr. 5, 1947; s. Nathan and Sylvia (Roseman) M.; m. Donna Rhae, Jan. 22, 1975; children: Jessica E., Andrew N., Julia A. AB, U. Chgo., 1968, AM, 1972, PhD, 1990. Tchr. jr. high sch. Phila. Pub. Schs., 1970-71; asst. prof. Roosevelt U., Chgo., 1975-80; economist AMA, 1980-82, sr. economist, 1982-84, dept. dir., 1985-89; dir. health labor mkt. rsch. Abt Assocs. Inc., Cambridge, Mass., 1990-92, area mgr., 1993-94, mng. v.p., 1994-95; v.p., gen. mgr. The MEDSTAT Group, 1995—. Author: Organizational Medical Practice, 1985, Physician Supply and Utilization by Specialty, 1988; contbr. articles to profl. jours. Traineeship NIMH, 1971-75. Mem. APHA (chmn. economists com. 1990-91), Internat. Health Econs. Assn., Am. Econ. Assn., Ill. Econ. Assn. (pres. 1986-87). Office: The MEDSTAT Group 125 Cambridgepark Dr Cambridge MA 02140-2329 E-mail: bill.marder@medstat.com.

MARDIAN, ROBERT CHARLES, JR. restaurateur; b. Orange, Calif., Feb. 1, 1947; s. Robert Charles Sr. and Dorothy Driscilla (Denniss) M.; m. Jayne Marie Garvin, June 21, 1970 (div. 1977); 1 child, Robert Charles III; m. Kathleen Frances Dixon, Oct. 13, 1984 (div. 1991); children: Alexandra Quinn, Ashley Michele. BA, Stanford U., 1969; MBA, Pepperdine U., 1986. Gen. mgr. Loft Restaurant, San Jose, Calif., 1969-71; chief exec. officer/chmn. bd. Wind & Sea Restaurants, Inc., Dana Point, 1971—. Bd. dirs. Dana Niguel Bank, cons. U.S. Olympic Com., Colorado Springs, 1984-88. Commr. Dana Point Econ. Devel. Mem. Young Pres. Orgn. Republican. Avocations: skiing, surfing, beach volleyball, running, snowboarding. Office: Wind & Sea Restaurants Inc 34699 Golden Lantern St Dana Point CA 92629-2908

MARDINKHA, KHNANIA, IV, church administrator; Catholic patriarch Apostolic Catholic Assyrian Ch. of the E. Office: Apostolic/Cath Assyrian Ch 3d Ave # 32 Tehran 14 Iran also: Apostolic & Cath Assyrian Ch East 7201 N Ashland Blvd Chicago IL 60626-2503

MARDIROSS, EDWARD, civil, soil and earthquake engineer; b. Tehran, Iran, Nov. 5, 1947; came to U.S., 1982; s. Yerwand Mardiross and Eliz Abramian; m. 1946; children: Edward, Seda, Medick, Shahick. BSc, Imperial Coll. Sci and Tech., 1972, PhD, 1978. Dir. Soils & Founds. Ltd., London, 1978-83; dir. real estate devel. Contbr. articles on engring. to profl. jours.

MARDIROSSIAN, JONATHAN, surgeon; b. Waterbury, Conn., 1946; BA, Williams Coll., Williamstown, Mass., 1968; MD, Cornell U., 1972. Diplomate Am. Bd. Ophthalmology. Asst. prof. ophthalmology U. Louisville Sch. Medicine, 1978-79; staff retinologist U. Tuebingen, Germany, 1980; chief ophthalmology St. Agnes Hosp., White Plains, N.Y., 1988-92. Adv. bd. The Lighthouse, Inc., White Plains, 1984-90, programs com., 1990-2000; com. on stds. and costs in med. care Westchester County Med. Soc., Purchase, N.Y., 1984-90. Contbg. author: Anesthesia for Ophthalmic Surgery, 1992, Ambulatory Anesthesia, 1995, Anesthesia & Transplantation, 1999. N.Y. State regents scholar, 1964. Fellow ACS, Am. Acad. Ophthalmology, Pan Am. Assn. Ophthalmology; mem. Vitreous Soc., N.Y. Soc. for Clin. Ophthalmology, N.Y. Retinal Study Club. Office: 33 Davis Ave White Plains NY 10605-1015

MARDIS, ELIZABETH WILLIAMS, occupational health nurse; b. Colbert County, Ala., July 31, 1953; d. Bobby Joe and Nell Elizabeth (Cochran) Williams; m. Danny Richard Mardis, Dec. 18, 1976; children: Paige, Patrick. Diploma nursing, Sanford U., 1973; student, U. North Ala. Cert. occupl. health nurse; cert. occupl. hearing conservationist. Occupl. health mgr. Goodyear Dunlop Tire Corp., Huntsville, Ala.; occupl. health nurse Delphi Automotive Systems, Athens; dir. case mgmt. Parkway Med. Ctr., Decatur, emergency rm. supr.; asst. dir. nursing svcs. Lawrence County Hosp., Moulton; patient edn. and infection control nurse Humana Hosp., Russelville. Instr. prepared childbirth. Mem. Am. Assn. Occupl. Health Nurses. Home: 2006 Cotaco Valley Trl SE Decatur AL 35603-5145

MARDIS, HAL KENNEDY, urological surgeon, educator, researcher; b. Lincoln, Nebr., Apr. 4, 1934; s. Harold Corson and Marie (Swaim) M.; m. Janet Reimers Schenken, June 22, 1956; children: Michael Corson, Anne Lucille, Jeanne Marie. BS, U. Nebr., Lincoln, 1955; MD, U. Nebr., Omaha, 1958. Diplomate Am. Bd. Urology. Intern Nebr. Meth. Hosp., Omaha, 1958-59, med. dir. The Stone Ctr., 1966—; resident in urology Charity Hosp. La., New Orleans, 1959-62, chief resident in urology, 1962-63; pvt. practice Omaha, 1965—; instr., asst. prof. La. State U. Sch. Medicine, New Orleans, 1963-65; asst. prof., assoc. prof. surgery U. Nebr. Med. Ctr., 1965-85, prof., 1985—. Investigator North Cen. Cancer Treatment Group, Rochester, Minn., 1988—, Technomed Internat., Inc., Danvers, Mass., 1988—; cons. Boston Sci. Corp., Watertown, Mass., 1988—. Assoc. editor Jour. Stone Disease; contbr. articles to Jour. AMA, So. Med. Jour., Jour. Urology, Urology, Urol. Clinics N.Am., Seminars in Interventional Radiology. Sec., pres. Omaha Symphony Assn., 1973-76; advisor United Arts Omaha, 1983-88. Recipient Outstanding Contbn. award dept. surgery U. Nebr. Med. Ctr., 1990. Fellow ACS; mem. AMa (del. med. staff sect. 1983-86), Am. Urol. Assn. (pres. South Cen. chpt. 1990-91, 1st prize 1976, best clin. exhibit award 1977, Gold Cane achievement award 2001), Am. Lithotripsy Soc. (pres. 1989-90), Alpha Omega Alpha (pres. 1991-92). Republican. Achievements include development of guidewire techniques for angiography and endourology, thermoplastic internal ureteral stent; description of benefits of hydrophilic polymers for endourologic devices. Office: The Urology Ctr 111 S 90th St Omaha NE 68114-3907 E-mail: hkmardis@urologycenterpc.net.

MARDIS, RICHARD LYLE, television producer and director, production manager; b. Ponca City, Okla., Dec. 30, 1963; s. Richard Leon and Geneva Louise (Peterson) M.; widowed; 2 foster children. BA, Cen. State U., 1986; AA, No. Okla. Coll., 1984. Prodr. Sta. KCSC-TV, Edmond, Okla., 1985-86; prodr., dir., prodn. mgr. Sta. KAUT-TV, Oklahoma City, 1986-91; sr. prodr., dir., prodn.mgr. Sta. KOKH-TV, 1991—; freelance dir., slo-mo dir. Sooner Vision, 1996—. Freelance photographer John Crowe Prodns., 1988-89, 91, Home Sports Entertainment, 1988-90, Challenger Prodns., 1989, ESPN, 1988-89, Cox Cable, 1989, Sports Comm. Inc., 1985; prodr.-dir. (TV comml.) All Asian Auto Parts, 1989 (Telly award 1990), Cimarron Pottery, 1992-96, Alzheimer's Couch Potato Gala, 1992-99, Muscular Dystrophy Assn., 1992—, OKC Blazers, 1996-98, OKC Cavalry, 1996-97, Tulsa Ice Oilers, 1996-98, IGA Tennis Classic, 1997-99, Salvation Army, 1998-99 (Telly award 1999), Sprint PCS It's Clearly Christmas, 1997-99, (TV shows) Colorado Dreamer, 1985, Snake Charmer, 1986; dir. (TV show series) Around Campus, 1985-86, Camp Kids Club, 1987-98 (Telly award 1997, 98), Spotlight on Oklahoma, 1990-92, Oklahoma Football, 1991-98, The Gary Gibbs Show, 1991-94, OU Sooners Football, 1991—, The Billy Tubbs Show, 1991-94, Discover Oklahoma, 1992-2000, Dance Magic, 1989-99, Carpenters Children, 1994-97, The Magic Forest, 1994-98, Revival for Christ, 1994-98, The Howard Schnellenberger Show, 1995, The John Blake Show, 1996-98, The Kelvin Sampson Show, 1995—, Oklahoma Medical News, 1996, Easter Comedy Show, 1998, (made-for-TV play) Weird Ducks, 1986; launched Fox 25 News, 1996. Democrat. Avocations: music, playing drums, aviculture. Office: Sta KOKH-TV 2301 Gladstone Terr Oklahoma City OK 73120-3616

MARDON, AUSTIN ALBERT, geographer, writer, researcher; b. Edmonton, Alta., Can., June 25, 1962; came to U.S. 1985; s. Ernest George and May Gertrude (Knowler). BA in Geography, U. Lethbridge, Alta., 1985; MSc in Geography, S.D. State U., 1988; MEd Edn. Curriculum and Instruction, Tex. A&M U., 1990; grad. work in space sci., U. N.D., 1990; PhD in Geography, Greenwich U., Australia, 2000; postgrad., U. Alberta; student, U. Calgary, U. Grenoble; postgrad., Newman Coll., 2001. Research scientist NASA/NSF, Antarctica, 1986-87; freelance writer, 1991—; dir. pres. Antarctic Inst. Canada, Edmonton, 1985—. Mem. meteorite recovery expedition, Antarctic, 1986-87; mem. Com. Space Rsch. Internat. Com. Sci. Unions; geoophys. con. Stargate Rsch. Lab., Calif., 1999—; self-help network coord., 1999—; adj. faculty mem. Greenwhich U., 2000—. Author/co-author 21 books in areas of space sci., meteorite sci., astronomy, Alberta history, space exploration tech., polar sci., Medieval English history, and geography; contbr. more than 108 articles to profl. jours. Vol. Schizophrenia Soc. Alberta Edmonton Bd., 1999—, Schizophrenia Soc. Alberta Provincal Bd., 2000—; bd. dirs. Regional Mental Health Adv. Com., 1999—, chair, 2000—01, mem. chairs com. for Alberta, 2000—01; bd. dir. Nation Network for Mental Health, 1999—2000. Recipient Antarctic Svc. medal, U.S. Navy, 1987; Duke of Edinburgh award, Can., 1987; Tex. State Proclamation, 1989; Polar Continental Shelf Proj. Arctic Research grantee, 1988, personal audience with Pope in Rome, 1996, Gov. Generals Caring Canadian Award, 1998, Nadine Stirling award Can. Mental Health Assn., 1999, Flag of Hope award Schizophrenia Soc. Can., 2001.. Fellow: Internat. Explorers Club; mem.: Russian Acad. Arts and Sci. (fgn. mem.), Am. Polar Soc. (life), Antarctic Inst. Can., Sigma Pi Sigma (Physics Honor Soc.), Gamma Theta Upsilon (Geography Honor Soc.). Progressive Conservative. Roman Catholic. Office: Main Post Office PO Box 1223 Edmonton AB Canada T5J 2M4 E-mail: mardon@freenet.edmonton.ab.ca.

MARE, OLINDO FRANCO, football player; b. Hollywood, Fla., June 6, 1973; m. Sandy. Student, MacMurray Coll., Valencia C.C., Orlando, Fla., Syracuse U. Kicker Miami Dolphins, 1996—. Active Cystic Fibrosis Found., Habitat for Humanity. Named to Pro Bowl, 1999; named first-team All-Pro, AP, USA Today, The Sporting News, Football Digest, Pro Football Weekly, Coll. and Pro Football Newsweekly, 1999, NFL Alumni Assn. Spl. Teams Player of Yr., 1999. Office: Miami Dolphins Tng Facility 7500 SW 30th St Davie FL 33314*

MAREADY, WILLIAM FRANK, lawyer; b. Mullins, S.C., Sept. 13, 1932; s. Jesse Frank and Vera (Sellers) M.; m. Brenda McCanless, Nov. 3, 1979. AB, U. N.C., 1955, JD with honors, 1958. Bar: N.C. 1958, U.S. Dist. Ct. N.C. 1960, U.S. Ct. Appeals (4th cir.) 1962, U.S. Supreme Ct. 1968. Assoc. Mudge, Stern, Baldwin & Todd, N.Y.C., 1958-60, Hudson, Ferrell, Carter, Petree & Stockton, Winston-Salem, N.C., 1960-65; ptnr. Petree, Stockton & Robinson, 1965-92, Robinson, Maready, Lawing & Comerford, 1992-97, Maready, Comerford & Britt, 1997-99; prin. Law Offices of William F. Maready, 1999—. N.C. chmn. Winston-Salem/Forsyth County Bd. Edn., 1968-70, chmn., bd. dirs. and mem. exec. com., N.C. State Port Authority, 1984-97. With Green Berets, U.S. Army, 1952-54. Recipient Disting. Svc. award N.C. Sch. Bds. Assn., Freedom award John Locke Soc., 2000. Fellow Am. Coll. Trial Lawyers, Am. Bar Found.; mem. ABA (chmn. standing com. on aero. law 1979-82, chmn. forum com. on air and space law 1982-86), N.C. Bar Assn. (chmn. litigation sect. 1981-82, adminstrn. of justice com. 1981-82), Nat. Parent Tchr. Assn. (life), Forsyth Country Club, Rotary (Winston-Salem), Order of Coif, Phi Delta Phi, Phi Beta Kappa. Republican. Methodist. Office: 1076 W 4th St Ste 100 Winston Salem NC 27101-2411 E-mail: bmaready@mareadylaw.com.

MARECAUX, MARIE-LAURE, consultant, writer; b. Dec. 23, 1956; , permanent resident, U.S., 2001; Diploma, Inst. Etudes Politiques, Paris, 1978; MA in German, U. Sorbonne, Paris and Munich, 1980; PhD with distinction, U. Minn., 1998. Internat. auditor Dannon Group, Paris, 1980-83; audit supr. Price Waterhouse, 1983-87; tchg. asst. Colo. State U., Ft. Collins, 1987-89; instr. U. Minn., Mpls., 1990-97; owner Creative Solutions Internat., Paris, 1998—. Faculty mem. U. No. Colo., Greeley, 2000—. Mem. MLA, Club Price Waterhouse, Assn. Anciens Sc.-Po, Assn. Anciennes Ste. Marie, Rotary Club, Phi Kappa Phi, Phi Sigma Iota. Address: 45 rue Boileau 75016 Paris France Office: PO Box 5203 Greeley CO 80634 E-mail: xaerem@hotmail.edu.

MAREE, JENNIFER, lawyer; Postgrad., Gertzen U., St. Petersburg, Russia, 1994—95; BA in Polit. Sci., BA in Russian Lang. and Lit., U. Utah, 1995; postgrad., Moscow State U., 1998; JD cum laude, Am. U., 2001. Bar: N.Y. 2002. Adjudicator State of Utah, Dept. of Workforce Svcs., Salt Lake City, 1997—98; law clk. Barnes Richardson & Colburn, Washington, 1999—2000, ABA, Cen. and East European Law Initiative, Washington, 2000; atty. LaPlaca McKenzie, P.Z., Rockville, Md., 2001—. Contbr. articles to law revs. (Dean's Award in Banking Law, 2001); editor: (newsletter) The Network Newsletter, ABA Business Law Section, Women's Interest Network, 2002; contbg. author: report Bosnia and Herzegovina: Study of Administrative Barriers to FDI, 2001, contbg. author: report Macedonia: Removing Impediments to the Business Registration Process, 2001. Organizer, fundraiser and participant hurricane relief mission to Belize Am. U., Wash. Coll. of Law, Washington, 2000—01, organizer, fundraiser and participant hurricane relief mission to Honduras, 1998—99; vol. Stradania, St. Petersburg, Russia, 1994—95. Fellow, Am. Coun. Tchrs. of Russian, 1994, Fulbright Commn., 1997; scholar, U.S. Dept. of Edn., 1994, anonymous scholarship, Am. U., 2000, Melrod scholar, 1999. Mem.: ABA (bus. law sect., banking law sect., fin. svcs. sect. 2001—02), Women's Bar Assn. D.C. (co-chair ann. awards dinner, hon. com. and fundraising com. 2001—02). Personal E-mail: jasjen@sprynet.com.

MAREK, JAMES DENNIS, lawyer; b. Chgo., Feb. 19, 1943; s. James John and Ardis McBroom Marek; m. Shelley R. Forbess (div. May 1993); children: James J., Elizabeth A., Jordan A., Lacey A.; m. Cathleen Marcotte, 1999. Student, Durham (Eng.) U., 1962-63; BA, DePauw U., 1964; JD, Northwestern U., Chgo., 1967. Bar: Ill. 1967, U.S. Dist. Ct. (ctrl. dist.) Ill. 1974, U.S. Tax Ct. 1977. With CIA, Washington, 1967-70; ptnr. Ackman, Marek & Boyd Ltd., Kankakee, Ill., 1970—. Trustee Kankakee C.C., 1992—. 1st lt. USAF, 1967-70. Fellow Am. Coll. Trial Attys., Am. Bd. Trial Advs.; mem. Ill. Def. Trial Counsel (bd. dirs. 1991-2001). Avocations: skiing, golf, raising llamas. Office: Ackman Marek & Boyd Ltd One Dearborn Sq Kankakee IL 60901 E-mail: llamalaw@aol.com.

MAREK, KIERSTEN L. social worker; b. Windham, Conn., Oct. 7, 1968; d. Leland J. and Ann Marie Stoppleworth; m. Kevin Michael Krcmarik; 1 child Katrina. BA, Hunter Coll., 1990; MSW, Smith Coll., Northampton, Mass., 1996. LCSW, lic. ind. clin. social worker. Assoc. editor Merlyn's Pen, East Greenwich, RI, 1995—2001; clin. social worker Child and Family Svcs. Newport County, Newport, 1996—98, R.I. Hosp., Lifespan, Providence, 1998—; assoc. editor Pif Mag., Seattle, 2001—; asst. editor The Hudson Rev., N.Y.C. Workshop tchr. Kmareka.com, Cranston, RI, 2002—; editor-in-chief Kmareka.com and Saga City, Cranston, RI, 2002—. Contbr. short stories to mags. and anthologies. Campaign vol. Kate Coyne-McCoy for Congress, Providence, 2001. Home: 109 Waterman Ave Providence RI 02910 Office: Kmareka.com and Saga City 109 Waterman Ave Providence RI 02910 Personal E-mail: kmarek@kmareka.com. Business E-Mail: kmarek@kmareka.com.

MARELLA, PHILIP DANIEL, broadcasting company executive; b. Italy, Sept. 9, 1929; came to U.S., 1930; s. T. Joseph and Julia (Santolina) M.; m. Lucinda Minor, Dec. 30, 1955; children: Philip Daniel, Laura Ann, William Scott. BS, Calif. State U., 1955; MS, Syracuse U., 1956. Account exec. WGR-TV, Buffalo, 1956-57; account exec., sales mgr. WIIC-TV, Pitts., 1957-66; gen. mgr. WCHS-TV, Charleston, W.Va., 1966-68; v.p. radio and television Rollins, Inc., Atlanta, 1968-70; pres. WAVY-TV, Inc., Tidewater, Va., 1970—; v.p. ops. Lin Broadcasting, Inc., N.Y.C.; also dir.; pres., owner WMGC-TV, Binghamton, N.Y., 1978-86; CEO, pres. Pinnacle Comm., Inc., 1987—. CEO Pinnacle Broadcasting Co., 1987; owner radio stas. WFXC-FM, WDUR, WFXK, Raleigh, N.C., WRNS-AM-FM, WANG-FM, WMSQ-AM, WERO-FM, WCPQ, WDLX-AM, Coastal, N.C., WKOO-FM, WKJA-FM, Jacksonville, N.C., WYAV-FM, WRNN-FM, WMYB-FM, WYAK-FM, Myrtle Beach, S.C., KLLL-AM-FM, KONE-FM, KMMX-FM, Lubbock, Tex., WYNG-FM, Evansville, Ind., WSOY-AM-FM, WDZQ-FM, WDZ-AM, WCZQ-FM, Decatur, Ill., WPXX-FM, Danville, Va.; bd. dirs. Radio Advt. Bur., N.C. Assn. Broadcasters. Bd. dirs. Salvation Army, 1966-68; bd. dirs., v.p. United Fund; bd. dirs. Portsmouth chpt. ARC, Tidewater Regional Health and Planning Commn.; bd. dirs., v.p. Binghamton Symphony. Served with USMC, 1948-49, 50-52. Mem. Nat. Assn. Broadcasters (v.p., radio advt. bd. dirs.), Va. Assn. Broadcasters, N.C. Assn. Broadcasters (bd. dirs.), Nat. Adv. Bur. (bd. dirs.), Variety Club Pitts., Radio and TV Club, Portsmouth C. of C. (pres.-elect), Norfolk C. of C., Newport News C. of C., Cavalier Golf and Yacht Club (Virginia Beach, Va.), N.Y. Athletic Club, Binghamton Country Club. Home: 2073 Cheshire Rd Binghamton NY 13903-3199 also: Central Pk Pl 301 W 57th St Apt 43C New York NY 10019-3180

MARES, MICHAEL ALLEN, ecologist, educator; b. Albuquerque, Mar. 11, 1945; s. Ernesto Gustavo and Rebecca Gabriela (Devine) M.; m. Lynn Ann Brusin, Aug. 27, 1966; children: Gabriel Andres, Daniel Alejandro. BS in Biology, U. N.Mex., 1967; MD, Ft. Hays Kans. State U., 1969; PhD, U. Tex.-Austin, 1973. From asst. to assoc. prof. U. Pitts., 1973-81; assoc. prof., curator mammals U. Okla., Norman, 1981-83; dir. Okla. Mus. Nat. Hist., 1983—; assoc. prof. zoology U. Okla., 1983-85, prof., 1985—. Adj. prof. U. Nacional de Cordoba, Argentina, 1971-72, U. Nacional de Tucuman, Argentin, 1972, vis. prof., 1974; vis. scientist U. Ariz., Tucson, 1980-81; cons. Argentine Nat. Sci. Found., Inst. Arid Zone Rsch., Mendoza, 1983, World Wildlife Fund, Brazil, 1986; mem. Coun. Internat. Exch. Scholars, Am. Republics Bd., Fulbright Commn., 1983-86, 88-91; bd. dirs. Coun. Internat. Exch. of Scholars, 1988-91; NUS cons., Venezuela, 1980-81; sci. cons. interim working group White House Biodiversity, Ecology, and Ecosystems, 1992-94; apptd. adv. bd. Ctr. Biol. Diversity, Dept. Interior; mem. Commn. on Future of Smithsonian Instns., 1993-96, Smithsonian Coun., 2000—. Contbr. articles to profl. jours. NSF grantee, 1974-79, 82-93, 99-2000; Nat. Fulbright Rsch. fellow, 1976; Nat. Geo. Soc. grantee, 1992-95, 99; rsch. fellow Chicago Coun. on Higher Edn., 1978, Ford Found. Minority Rsch., 1980-81; recipient Brazilian Nat. Acad. Sci. Rsch. award, 1975-78. Mem. AAAS (Western Hemispheric coop. com. 1989-93), Am. Soc. Mammalogists (1st. v.p. 1990-94, C. Hart Merriam award 2000), Am. Ecol. Soc., Interam. Assn. Advancement Sci., Am. Inst. Biol. Sci., Am. Soc. Naturalists, Soc. Study of Evolution, Southwestern Assn. Naturalists (Donald W. Tinkle rsch. excellence award), Paleontol. Soc., Sigma Xi, Phi Kappa Phi, Beta Beta Beta. Home: 3930 Charing Cross Ct Norman OK 73072-3201 Office: U Okla Okla Mus Natural History 2401 Chautauqua Ave Norman OK 73072

MARESCO, PETER ANTHONY, education educator; b. Bridgeport, Conn., Jan. 26, 1948; s. Peter and Victoria Maresco; m. Margaret Kelly Maresco, June 15, 1985; 1 child Juli Anne. BA in History, U. Charleston, W.Va., 1969; MA in Comm., Fairfield U., Conn., 1984; PhD in Edn., Walden U., Mpls., 1998. Cert. tchr. K-8 Conn., adminstr. Conn. V.p. mktg. Mechanics & Farmers Bank, Bridgeport, Conn., 1972—91; tchr. Bridgeport Pub. Schs., 1992—99; asst. prof. edn. Sacred Heart U., Fairfield, 2000—. Cons. Subway Corp., Milford, Conn., 1999. Bd. dirs. Vis. Nurse Assn., Bridgeport, 1986—88; pres. Barnum Festival, 1993. Mem.: Elks, Sigma Phi Epsilon. Republican. Baptist. Avocations: music, art. Mailing: Sacred Heart Univ 5151 Park Ave Fairfield CT 06432-1000

MARES-GUIA, MARCOS LUIZ, biochemist, consultant; b. Santa Barbara, Brazil, June 3, 1935; came to U.S., 1994; s. Jose Maria and Judith (Coelho) M-G.; m. Henriqueta Martins, May 22, 1959; children: Frederico, Christiana, Juliana, Luciana, Tatiana, Fabiana. MD, Fed. U. Minas Gerais, Belo Horizonte, Brazil, 1958; PhD, Tulane U., 1964. Prof. Biochemistry Fed. U. Minas Gerais, Belo Horizonte, 1958-93; emeritus prof., 2000—; v.p. rsch. Biobras S.A., Belo Horizonte, 1971-93; pres. Biomm, Inc., Miami, Fla., 1993—. Cons. Diabetes Rsch. Inst., U. Miami, 1994—; bd. dirs. Biobras S.A., 1994—. Patentee in field. Recipient Order of Scientific Merit Ministry of Sci., Brasilia, 1992. Mem. Am. Chem. Soc., N.Y. Acad. Scis., Brazilian Acad. Scis. Achievements: founder of Biobras S.A., 1971; co-founder Pythagoras Ednl. Sys. in Brazil, 1966; founder of Biomm, Inc., 1993; work on active ctr. chemistry of proteolytic enzymes. Office: Biomm Inc 14775 SW 132nd Pl Miami FL 33186-7685 E-mail: maresguia@aol.com.

MARESH, ALICE MARCELLA, retired educational administrator; b. Chgo., Sept. 17, 1922; d. Joseph Anton and Barbara Magdalene (Slad) M. BEd, Chgo. Tchrs. Coll., 1944; MEd, Loyola U., Chgo., 1962. Chemist Best Foods, Inc., Chgo., 1944-54; tchr. Chgo. Bd. Edn., 1954-65, counselor, 1965-67, asst. prin., 1967-69, prin., 1969-93; retired, 1993. Recipient Outstanding and Dedicated Svc. award Puerto Rican Congress, 1975, Those Who Excel award Ill. Bd. Edn., 1978, Whitman award for excellence in ednl. mgmt. Whitman Acad., Chgo., 1990, Outstanding Svc. to Edn. in Chgo. award Nat. Coun. Negro Women, 1992. Mem. Chgo. Prins. Assn., Aquin Guild (Dedicated Svc. award 1976), Delta Kappa Gamma (pres. 1976-78), Phi Delta Kappa, Pi Lambda Theta (sec. 1995—). Democrat. Roman Catholic. Avocations: music, travel, calligraphy, theater. Home: 3850 W Bryn Mawr Ave Apt 308 Chicago IL 60659-3141

MARET, ELIZABETH GARDNER, sociology educator; b. Phila., Nov. 9, 1943; d. Raymond and Elizabeth (Clark) M.; m. Sam House, Jan. 1, 1977; 1 child, David Stanley. BA, U. Tex., 1967, MA, 1971, PhD, 1973. Asst. prof. Huston-Tillotson Coll., 1972-73, Tex. Tech. U., 1973-76; assoc. prof. sociology Tex. A&M U., College Station, 1976—; ptnr. Grassburr Cattle Ptnrs. Coord. Women in Devel., 1984-86. Author: Women and the American Occupational Structure, 1978, Women's Career Patterns, 1983, Women of the Range, 1993; contbr. articles to profl. jours. Mem.: Nat. Women's Polit. Caucus, Tex. Coun. Family Rels., N.Y. Acad. Scis., Sociologists for Women in

Society, S.W. Sociol. Assn., Am. Sociol. Assn., Emily's List, Am. Simmental Assn., Internat. Platform Assn., U.S. Canoe and Kayak Team. Democrat. Office: Tex A&M U Dept Sociology College Station TX 77843-0001

MARETH, PAUL DAVID, multimedia producer; b. N.Y.C., Nov. 16, 1945; s. Josef Gleicher and Elisabeth Gay; m. Evelyn Heineman, Dec. 26, 1968 (div. 1980); children: Leda J., Joanna R. BA, Brandeis U., 1967; MFA, UCLA, 1969. Lectr. U. Pitts., 1976-77; asst. prof. communications Temple U., Phila., 1977-81; vis. faculty fellow in history of sci. Princeton (N.J.) U., 1981-82; founder, owner Projections Co., Asheville, NC, 1983—. Cons. IBM, RCA, Bell Labs., Ednl. Testing Svc., Children's TV Workshop, Prodigy. Author: Fidel & Leo, 2001; co-author multimedia sect. Peter Norton's Outside IBM PC, 1992; contbr. to Acad. Am. Ency., 1985—, Channels of Communications, 1983-85; editorial advisor IEEE Jour., IEEE Spectrum, 1983-84; contbr. numerous articles to profl. jours. Bd. dirs. Westchester Choral Soc., 1991-95. Grantee WGBH Pub. TV, Boston, 1974, Swedish Film Inst./Swedish Broadcasting Corp., 1973, Pa. Coun. on the Arts, 1976, 79. Mem. Soc. Motion Picture and TV Engrs., Internat. Interactive Communications Soc. (chmn. program com. 1987-90), Univ. Film/Video Assn. Avocation: choral singing. Office: Projections Co 39 Patton Ave Asheville NC 28801-3314 E-mail: pdm@projco.com.

MARGALIT, SHLOMO, educator; b. Tiberias, Israel, Apr. 30, 1914; s. Nehemiah and Bath-Sheva (Kuperman) M.; m. Dina Rivlin, Feb. 8, 1938; children: Nehemiah, Yael Margalit Moses. DHL (hon.), Gratz Coll., 1985. Ordained rabbi, 1933. Rabbi Kefar Vitkin, Israel, 1934; religion instr. Haifa, Israel, 1937; assoc. rabbi Congregation Rodeph Shalom, Atlantic City, 1955; prof. Hebrew, Bible and rabbinics Gratz Coll., Phila., 1959-85. Author: Agartal, 1996; contbr. articles to profl. jours. With Israel Def. Forces. Mem. Am. Assn. of Jewish Edn., Nat. Coun. of Jewish Edn., Hebrew Tchrs. and Prins. of Am. (chtp. past pres.), Histadruth Ivrith of Am., Master Har-Zion Lodge-Jerusalem. Avocations: poetry, singing. Home: 2903 Fallstaff Rd Unit 407 Baltimore MD 21209-3561

MARGALITH, HELEN MARGARET, retired librarian; b. N.Y.C., Nov. 19, 1914; d. Louis and Caroline (Stern) Fleischer; m. Aaron Margalith, Jan. 26, 1947 (dec.); children: Carol Lenore, Joan Louise. BA, Hunter Coll., 1936, MA, 1944; MLS, Columbia U., 1958. Editl. corr. Book of the Month Club, 1936-47; rschr. libr. N.Y.C. Bd. Edn., 1955-80; prof. pibr. Touro Coll., N.Y.C., 1980-90; mentor in libr. Empire State Coll., SUNY, 1991—. Cons. in field. Fellow Royal Soc. Medicine (libr. com., gerontology com., history of medicine com.); mem. Ch. and Synagogue Libr. Assn. (book reviewer), Internat. Honor Soc. Women in Edn., Delta Kappa Gamma. Democrat. Avocations: reading, baking, travel, research. Home: 205 W End Ave New York NY 10023-4804

MARGARYAN, ALFRED, physical chemistry engineer, material science researcher; b. Tehran, Iran, Apr. 19, 1936; came to U.S., 1988; s. Ashot and Almast (Babakhanian) M.; m. Anahit Kouradjian, Mar. 1, 1968; children: Ashot, Ara. BS, Poly. Inst., Yerevan, Armenia, 1959; MS, Tech. Inst., St. Petersburg, Russia, 1966, DS, 1985. Rsch. engr. Inst. Inorganic Chemistry, Yerevan, 1959-63; asst. prof. Tech. Inst., St. Petersburg, 1963-66; chief scientist Inst. Inorganic Chemistry, 1966-76; sr. rsch. scientist Vavilov State Optical Inst., St. Petersburg, 1976-88; sr. scientist Control Optics Corp., Baldwin Park, Calif., 1988-93; sr. rsch. scientist Material Sci. Co., Glendale, 1990-93; prof. U. La Verne, 1991-94; chief scientist U&M Sci. Co., Glendale, 1994—. Author: Germanate Glasses, 1993, Ligands and Modifiers in Vitreous Materials: Spectroscopy of Condensed Systems, 1999; contbr. over 120 articles to profl. jours. Mem. Am. Armenian Soc. Archs. and Scientists, Internat. Soc. Optical Instrumentation Engring. Roman Catholic. Avocations: classical music, sports, arts. Home: 1139 E Maple St Apt 5 Glendale CA 91205-4420 Office: U&M Sci Co 1139 E Maple St Apt 5 Glendale CA 91205-4420

MARGED, JUDITH MICHELE, information technology educator; b. Phila., Nov. 27, 1954; d. Bernard A. and Norma Marged. Student, Drexel U., 1972-73; AA in Biology, Broward Community Coll., Ft. Lauderdale, Fla., 1975; BA in Biology, Fla. Atlantic U., 1977, BA in Exceptional Edn., 1980, MEd in Counseling, 1984; EdD in Early and Middle Childhood, Nova U., 1991. Cert. tchr., Fla.; cert. tech. trainer; Microsoft cert. sys. engr.; Microsoft cert. profl., trainer. Tchr. Coral Springs (Fla.) Mid. Sch., 1979-80, Am. Acad., Wilton Manors, Fla., 1980-83, Ramblewood Mid. Sch., Coral Springs, 1984-96; info. tech. prof. Am. InterContinental U., Plantation, Fla., 1999—. Creator programs for mid. sch. students. Author: A Program to Increase the Knowledge of Middle School Students in Sexual Education and Substance Abuse Prevention, An Alternative Education Program to Create Successful Learning for the Middle School Child At-Risk. Mem.: Assn. for Career and Tech. Edn., Phi Delta Kappa. Home: 9107 NW 83d St Tamarac FL 33321-1509 Office: Am InterContinental U 8151 Peters Rd Ste 1000 Plantation FL 33324-4005

MARGEN, SHELDON, public health educator; b. Chgo., May 19, 1919; s. Paul and Sarah M.; m. Jeanne Carmel Sholtz, Mar. 16, 1943; children: Claude, Paul, Peter, David. BA, UCLA, 1938, MA, 1939; MD, U. Calif., San Francisco, 1943. Diplomate Am. Bd. Internal Medicine. Assoc prof. U. Calif., Berkeley, 1963-68, prof. pub. health and nutrition, 1968-89, prof. emeritus, 1989—. Cons., mem. adv. coms. NIH, WHO,; bd. dirs. Omnicare. Cin., 1980—. Editor-in-chief U. Calif. Wellness Letter; author and editor 10 books on Nutrition and/or Pub. Health. Bd. dirs. Calif. Wellness Found., Woodland Hills, 1991-96. Capt. M.C., U.S. Army, 1943-48, ETO. Grantee NIH, State of Calif., Ford Found., numerous others. Fellow Am. Inst. Nutrition and many other profl. orgns. in fields of ntutrition and pub. health. Office: U Calif Sch Pub Health Berkeley CA 94720-0001

MARGER, EDWIN, lawyer; b. N.Y.C., Mar. 18, 1928; s. William and Fannie (Cohen) M.; m. Kaye Sanderson, Oct. 1, 1951; children: Shari Ann, Diane Elaine, Sandy Ben; m. L. Suzanne Smyth, July 5, 1968; 1 child, George Phinney; m. Mary Susan Hamel, May 6, 1987; 1 child, Charleton Faye. BA, U. Miami, 1951, JD, 1953. Bar: Fla. 1953, Ga. 1971, D.C. 1978. Pvt. practice, Miami Beach, Fla., 1953-67, Atlanta, 1971—. Gen. counsel Physicians Nat. Risk Retention Group, 1988-91, Physicians Reliance Assn., 1988-91, Physicians Nat. Legal Def. Corp., 1988-91; spl. asst. atty. gen. Fla., 1960-61; atty., agt. Republic of Haiti, 1962-67, City of Port-au-Prince for Transp. and Housing, 1962, Dominican Republic for Trade and Industry, 1964-65; of counsel Richard Burns, Miami, 1967—. Contbr. articles to profl. jours. Tchr. Nat. Inst. Trial Advocacy; mem. Miami Beach Social Svc. Commn., 1957; chmn. Fulton County Aviation Adv. Com., 1980—; trustee Forensic Scis. Found., 1984-88; v.p., 1986-88; lt. col., a.d.c. Gov. Ga., 1971-74, 80-84; col., a.d.c. Gov. La., 1977-87; Khan Bahador and mem. exiled King of Afghanistan Privy Council, 1980—. With USAAF, 1946-47. Fellow Am. Acad. Forensic Scis. (chmn. jurisprudence sect. 1977-78, sec. 1976-77, bd. dirs. 1978-79, exec. com. 1983-86); mem. ATLA, ABA, Fla. Bar Assn. (aerospace com. 1971-83, bd. govs. 1983-87, 90-94, exec. com. 1993-94), State Bar Ga. (chmn. sect. environ. law 1974-75, aviation law sect. 1978, bd. govs. 1999—, stds. of the profession com.), Ga. Trial Lawyers Assn., Nat. Assn. Criminal Def. Lawyers, Ga. Assn. Criminal Def. Lawyers, Am. Judicature Soc., Am. Arbitration Assn. (commn. panel 1978), Inter-Am. Bar Assn. (sr.), World Assn. Lawyers (founding), Lawyer-Pilots Bar Assn. (founding, v.p. 1959-62), VFW, Rotary, Advocates Club. Office: 44 N Main St Jasper GA 30143-1501

MARGERISON, RICHARD WAYNE, diversified industrial company executive; b. Phila., Nov. 5, 1948; s. Kenneth Hilton and Edythe Margerison; m. Leah Blythe Margerison, July 18, 1970; children: Andrew Kenneth, Ashley Creed. BA in Econs., U. N.C., 1970; MBA with distinction, Harvard U., 1977. Mgr. So. Bell Telephone Co., Greensboro, N.C., 1972-75; mgr. sub. liaison Atlas Powder Co. subs. Tyler Corp., Dallas, 1978-79, dir. mktg. svcs., 1979-80; exec. v.p. Micro-Term, Inc., St. Louis, 1980-83, pres., chief exec. officer, 1983-85; mgr. acquisitions Tyler Corp., Dallas, 1977-78, v.p., 1985-88, sr. v.p., 1988-89, exec. v.p., 1989-94, pres., COO, 1994-97, also bd. dirs.; CEO Sammons Distbn., Inc., 1997—2001, Legacy Assocs. Investments, 2001—. Mem. Northway Christian Ch., Dallas, 1985--; coach Youth Soccer, Dallas, 1987—; advisor YMCA Indian Princess and Indian Guides, 1987-89; adult leader Boy Scouts Am., 1988-93; active Dallas United Way, 1990. Love fellow Harvard Grad. Sch. Bus., 1975-77. Mem. Harvard Bus. Sch. Club of Dallas, Lakewood Country Club, Order of Old Well, Phi Beta Kappa. Avocations: golf, youth soccer, running. Home: 3115 Stanford Ave Dallas TX 75225-7702

MARGERUM, DALE WILLIAM, chemistry educator; b. St. Louis, Oct. 20, 1929; s. Donald C. and Ida Lee (Nunley) M.; m. Sonya Lora Pedersen, May 16, 1953; children: Lawrence Donald, Eric William, Richard Dale. BA, S.E. Mo. State U., 1950; PhD, Iowa State U., 1955. Research chemist Ames Lab., AEC, Iowa, 1952-53; instr. Purdue U., West Lafayette, Ind., 1954-57, asst. prof., 1957-61, assoc. prof., 1961-65, prof., 1965-97, disting. prof. chemistry, 1997—, head dept. chemistry, 1978-83. Inorganic-analytical chemist, vis. scientist Max Planck Inst., 1963, 70; vis. prof. U. Kent, Canterbury, Eng., 1970; mem. med. chem. study sect. NIH, 1965-69; mem. adv. com. Research Corp., 1973-78; mem. chemistry evaluation panel Air Force Office Sci. Research, 1978-82 Cons. editor McGraw Hill, 1962-72; mem. editorial bd. Jour. Coordination Chemistry, 1971-81, Analytical Chemistry, 1967-69, Inorganic Chemistry, 1985-88. Recipient Grad. Rsch. award Phi Lambda Upsilon, 1954, Alumni Merit award S.E. Mo. State U., 1991, Sagamore of the Wabash, State of Ind., 1994; NSF sr. postdoctoral fellow, 1963-64. Fellow AAAS; mem. AAUP, Am. Chem. Soc. (chmn. Purdue sect. 1965-66, com. on profl. tng. 1993—, Disting. Svc. award in advancement of inorganic chemistry 1996), Sigma Xi (Monie A. Ferst award 2000), Phi Lambda Upsilon. Office: Dept Chemistry Purdue U West Lafayette IN 47907

MARGERUM-LEYS, JON, education educator, researcher; s. Ron and Marilyn Leys; m. Julie Margerum; children: Meagan, Emma. PhD, U. Mich., Ann Arbor, 2001. Asst. prof. Ea. Mich. U., Ypsilanti, Mich., 2000—. Participating investigator The Ctr. for Learning Techs. in Urban Schs., Ann Arbor, Mich., 2001—. Author: (dissertation) Teacher knowledge of educational technology: A case study of student teacher/mentor teacher pairs, 2001 (Am. Assn. of Colleges for Tchr. Edn. Outstanding Dissertation Award, 2002). Grantee Spencer Found. Rsch. Tng. Award, The U. of Mich., 1995-2000. Home: 3564 Inverness Dexter MI 48130 Office: Eastern Michigan Univ 315 M Porter Bldg Ypsilanti MI 48197

MARGESON, THEODORE EARL, judge; b. New Glasgow, N.S., Can., Aug. 15, 1938; children: Theodore Jason, Mark Andrew Earl. BA, Mt. Allison U., Sackville, N.B., Can., 1959, BEd, 1960; LLB, Dalhousie U., Halifax, N.S., 1965. Barrister, solicitor, notary pub. Tchr. Shelburne (N.S.) H.S., 1960-61, New Glasgow H.S., 1961-62; barrister, solicitor New Glasgow and Toronto, Ont., 1965-90; judge Tax Ct. of Can., Ottawa, 1990—. Bd. dirs. N.S. Legal Aid. Recipient Confedn. medal Govt. of Can., 1992. Mem. Can. Judges Conf., N.S. Barrister's Soc. (mem. of coun.), Continuing Legal Edn. Soc. (dir.). Avocations: golf, hockey, squash. Office: Tax Ct of Can 200 Kent St 3d Fl Ottawa ON Canada K1A OM1

MARGETON, STEPHEN GEORGE, law librarian; b. Elizabeth, N.J., Mar. 22, 1945; s. Louis George and Josephine A. (Bednarik) M.; m. Margaret Mary Salter, May 14, 1977; children: Catherine Ann, Elizabeth Ann. AB, Mt. St. Mary's Coll., 1967; JD, George Washington U., 1970; MSLS, Cath. U., 1973. Reference librarian Am.-Brit. law div. Library of Congress, Washington, 1968-72; law libr. Steptoe & Johnson, 1972-85; librarian Supreme Ct. of U.S., 1985-88; dir. Judge Kathryn J. DuFour Law Libr. The Cath. Univ. Am., 1988—. Instr. George Mason Law Sch., Arlington, Va., 1977-80. Mem. Am. Assn. Law Libraries, Internat. Assn. Law Libraries. Office: Cath U Am Judge Kathryn J DuFour Law Libr 3600 John Mccormack Rd NE Washington DC 20064-0001

MARGID, LEONARD, lawyer; b. N.Y.C., May 13, 1927; s. Irving Bert and Jean (Davis) M.; m. Loretta B. Berman, Aug. 23, 1958; 1 child, Elizabeth S. BA, U. Iowa, 1949; JD, NYU, 1951. Bar: N.Y. 1952, U.S. Dist. Ct. (ea. and so. dists.) N.Y. 1954. Assoc. Proskauer, Rose, Goetz & Mendelson, N.Y.C., 1951-58; ptnr. Otterbourg, Steindler, Houston & Rosen, 1958-90; pvt. practice, 1991—. Sgt. U.S. Army, 1945-46, ETO. Mem. Assn. of Bar of City of N.Y. Avocations: travel, tennis, hiking, theater, investments. Home and Office: 4455 Douglas Ave Bronx NY 10471-3519

MARGILETH, ANDREW MENGES, physician, former naval officer; b. Cin., July 17, 1920; s. Elmer C. and Bertha (Menges) M.; m. Catherine Lanier, Oct. 31, 1994; children: R. Lynn, Andrew C., Elle C., David Lanier. BA, Washington and Jefferson Coll., 1943; BS, MIT, 1944; MD, U. Cin., 1947. Diplomate Am. Bd. Pediat. Commd. ensign USN, 1943, advanced through grades to capt., 1963; intern, then residen in pediat. Nat. Naval Med. Ctr., 1947-49; resident in pediat. Johns Hopkins Hosp., 1949-50; chief pediat. U.S. Naval Hosps., Corona, Calif., 1953-57, Chelsea, Mass., 1957-63, Bethesda, Md., 1963-67; prof. Uniformed Svcs. U. Health Scis., 1979-90; clin. prof. U. Va. Health Scis. Ctr., 1990-95, Mercer U. Sch. Medicine, 1995—, U. Fla., Jacksonville, 2001—. Mem. coun. Nat. Inst. Child Health and Human Devel., 1963-67; sr. attending physician Childrens Hosp., Washington; assoc. clin. prof. pediat. Med. Sch., Howard U.; adj. prof. pediat. Med. Sch., George Washington U. Contbr. chpt. to Current Pediatric Therapy, 1970, 72, 74, 76, 80, 83, 85, 90, 93, 95; contbr.: (textbooks) Neonatology, 1975, 81, 86, 94, 99, Pediatrics, 1977, 81, 86, 91, 95, 96, 2001, Medicine, 1978, 82, 86, 88, 91, Current Therapy Medicine, 1996, 99, Current Therapy of Infectious Disease, 1996, 2000, Pediatric Dermatology, 1978, 86, 88, also 160 articles to profl. jours.; co-editor Clin. Procs. of Children's Hosp. Nat. Med. Ctr., 1970-79; co-editor: An Atlas of Pediatric Infectious Diseases, 1998. Fellow ACP, Am. Acad. Pediat.; mem. Assn. Mil. Surgeons, Am. Pediat. Soc., Soc. Pediat. Dermatologists, Soc. Pediat. Infectious Diseases, Alpha Omega Alpha. Address: 655 W 8th St 5th Fl Jacksonville FL 32209

MARGIOTTA, MARY-LOU ANN, software engineer; b. Waterbury, Conn., June 14, 1956; d. Rocco Donato and Louise Antoinette (Carosella) M. AS Gen. Edn., Mattatuck C.C., Waterbury, 1982; BSBA, Teikyo Post U., 1983; MS Computer Sci., Rensselaer Polytech. Inst., 1989. Programmer analyst Travelers Ins. Co., Hartford, Conn., 1985-87; sr. programmer analyst Conn. Bank and Trust Co., East Hartford, 1987-88; programmer analyst Ingersoll-Rand Corp., Torrington, 1990-91; sr. programmer analyst Orion Capital Cos. Inc., Farmington, 1991-92; pres., prin., software engr. A.M. Consultants, New Britain, 1992—. Pres. C++ Spl. Interest Group, 1995-96; bd. dirs. Conn. Object Oriented Users Group, 1995-96; tech. team leader Computer Scis. Corp., East Hartford, Conn., 1998—. Mem. social action com. St. Helena's Parish, West Hartford, Conn., 1988-95; advisor Jr. Achievement, Waterbury, 1981-83; tutor Traveler's Ins. Co. Tutorial Program, West Hartford, 1986-87; trainer CPR, ARC, Hartford, 1986-87; mem. Lang. and Cultural Adoptation Programs, Conn. and Mass., 1998— Clayborn Pell grantee Post Coll., 1982-83, State of Conn. grantee, 1982-83; recipient Citation, Jr. Achievement, 1982; Bd. Trustees scholar Post Coll., 1982-83. Mem. IEEE, Am. Acculturation Assocs. (bd. dirs.), Toastmasters Internat., Tau Alpha, Beta Gamma. Roman Catholic. Avocations: European travel, gourmet cooking, reading, tennis, golf. Home: 210 Brittany Farms Rd Ste E New Britain CT 06053-1282

MARGO, KATHERINE LANE, family physician, educator; b. Buffalo, June 3, 1952; d. Warren Wilson and Virginia (Penney) Lane; m. Geoffrey Myles Margo, Apr. 20, 1980; 1 child Benjamin stepchildren: Jenny, Judy. BA, Swarthmore Coll., 1974; MD, SUNY Health Sci. Ctr., Syracuse, 1978. Resident physician St. Joseph's Hosp., Syracuse, 1979-82; attending physician Health Svcs. Assn., 1982-90, asst. med. dir. for quality assurance, 1985-90; asst. prof. family medicine SUNY-HSC at Syracuse, 1990-94; mem. residency faculty Harrisburg (Pa.) Hosp., 1994-2000; med. dir. Harrisburg Kline Family Practice Ctr., 1996-2000; assoc. residency dir. Harrisburg Family Practice Residency, 1997-2000; predoctoral dir. dept. family practice cmty. medicine U. Pa., 2000—, assoc. residency dir. family practice residence, 2000—. Clin. assoc. prof. Allegheny Med. Sch., 1997—2000. Contbr. Bd. trustees Pt. Choice, Syracuse, 1993—94; chair med. com. Planned Parenthood, 1984—94; bd. dirs. Planned Parenthood Susquehanna Valley, 1996—2000; active Friends of Chamber Music, Syracuse, 1985—94; keyboard player Old World folk Band. Mem.: Am. Acad. Family Practitioners (v.p. Syracuse chpt.), Soc. Tchrs. of Family Medicine. Home: 426 Carpenter Ln Philadelphia PA 19119-3040 E-mail: margok@uphs.upenn.edu.

MARGO, ROBERT CRAVENS, lawyer; b. Indpls., Mar. 1, 1949; s. Marvin Kenneth and Bobbie (Cravens) M.; m. Martha L. Johnson, June 12, 1971; children: Amy E., Bradley J. BA, So. Meth. U., 1971; JD, Oklahoma City U., 1974. Bar: Okla. 1974, U.S. Dist. Ct. (ea. dist.) Okla. 1974, U.S. Ct. Appeals (10th cir.) 1974, U.S. Supreme Ct. 1989. Assoc. Pierce Couch et al, Oklahoma City, 1974-77; ptnr. Short Wiggins Margo & Butts, 1977—. Bd. dirs. Okla. Attys. Mut. Ins. Co., Oklahoma City. Fellow Am. Coll. Trial Lawyers; mem. Okla. Bar Assn., Oklahoma County Bar Assn. (bd. dirs. 1993-95), Fedn. Defendants and Corp. Counsel, Am. Bd. Trial Advocates (pres. Okla. chpt. 1994-95). Home: 1615 Dorchester Dr Oklahoma City OK 73120-1204 Office: Short Wiggins Margo & Butts 3100 Oklahoma Tower 210 Park Ave Oklahoma City OK 73102-5605

MARGOL, IRVING, personnel consultant; b. St. Louis, May 28, 1930; s. William and Dora (Karsh) M.; m. Myrna Levy, Dec., 1960; children—Bradley, Lisa, Cynthia. BA, Washington U., St. Louis, 1951, MA, 1952. Employment mgr. Am. Car & Foundry div. ACF, St. Louis, 1955-59; asst. personnel dir. Vickers Inc. div. Sperry-Rand, 1959-60; instr. personnel mgmt. Washington U. (St. Louis), 1960-62; personnel dir. Energy Controls div. Bendix Corp., South Bend, Ind., 1962-69; exec. v.p. community/employee affairs group, community rels. dept., employee assistance program Security Pacific Nat. Bank, L.A., 1969-92; mng. dir. Southern Calif. Jannotta, Bray & Assocs., Inc., 1992—; pres. Security Pacific Found., L.A., 1989-94; mng. dir. Jannotta Bray & Assocs., 1992-94, Right and Assocs., L.A., 1995-99; prin. Eddy Assocs., Inc., 2000—. Instr. UCLA Extension Div., Los Angeles; Grad. Sch. Banking, Rutgers U., Notre Dame U.; bd. dirs. Gateway Hosp. Bd. dirs. L.A. chpt. ARC, Am. Heart Assn., Am. Cancer Soc., Nat. Conf. Christians & Jews, Braille Inst.; bd. overseers Southwestern U. Law. Mem. Am. Bankers Assn. (exec. com. 1979—), Am. Soc. Tng. and Devel., Am. Soc. Personnel Adminstrs., Am. Inst. Banking, Washington U. Alumni Assn. Democrat. Jewish. Office: Eddy Assocs Inc 3500 W Olive Ave Ste 300 Burbank CA 91505-4647

MARGOLIN, ABRAHAM EUGENE, lawyer, director; b. St. Joseph, Mo., Oct. 16, 1907; s. Jacob and Rebecca (Cohn) M.; m. Florence Solow, Feb. 1, 1931 (dec. Feb. 1998); children: Robert J., Judith (Mrs. Goodman), James S. BA, Dartmouth Coll.; LLB, Mich. U., Ann Arbor, JD, 1929. Pvt. practice, Kans. City. Bd. mem. Tension Envelope Corp., UMB Mortgage Co.; pres. ctrl. governing bd. Children's Mercy Hosp., 1972-76, life mem.; dir. life Truman Med. Ctr., Menorah Med. Ctr.; mem. bd. govs. City Trust Kansas City, Rsch. Mental Health Found.; dir., v.p. Jewish Fedn. Greater Kansas City. Bd. govs. Hebrew Acad. Kans. City; gov. Am. Royal Assn.; pres. coun., fellow Brandeis U.; trustee B'nai B'rith Found.; mem. adv. bd. Anti-Defamation League; mem. nat. exec. coun. Am. Jewish Com., Am. Joint Distbn. Com. Named Disting. Law Alumnus, Washington U.; recipient Man of Yr. award Congregations Beth Shalom. Mem. ABA, ATLA, Am. Judicature Soc., Fed. Bar Assn., Mo. Bar Assn., Met. Kans. City Bar Assn., U.S. Supreme Ct. Hist. Soc., Heritage Found., Cato Inst., World Jewish Congress, Am. Jewish Congress, Kans. City Club, Oakwood Golf and Country Club, Nat. Lawyers Club, Order of Coif, Delta Sigma Rho. Office: 2345 Grand Blvd Ste 2500 Kansas City MO 64108-2603 Home: # E206 5500 W 123rd St Shawnee Msn KS 66209-3193

MARGOLIN, CARL M. psychotherapist; b. N.Y.C., Jan. 23, 1939; s. Samuel and Henrietta (Kressel) M.; B.A., CUNY, 1961; M.S.W., Columbia U., 1965; postgrad. Nat. Psychol. Assn. for Psychoanalysis, 1968-70; m. Susie Echols Watts, Feb. 10, 1964; children— Christopher, Andrew; m. Paula Jean Beatty, March 26, 1993. Sr. psychiat. social worker W.J.C.S., White Plains, N.Y., 1964-76; psychotherapist Whitehill Counseling Service, Yorktown Hights, N.Y., 1973-76; pvt. practice psychotherapy, 1976— ; tng. supr. Yeshiva U., 1972-76. Mem. exec. com. No. Westchester Mental Health Council, 1973-79, chmn. planning com., 1975-79. Cert. social worker, N.Y. State. Mem. Nat. Assn. Social Workers (diplomate), Acad. Cert. Social Workers, Soc. Clin. Social Work Psychotherapists (bd. cert. diplomate in clin. social work). Office: 19 Long Ridge Rd Bedford NY 10506-1529

MARGOLIN, FREDERICK A. lawyer; b. Bklyn., June 5, 1945; s. Leo H. and Ann Margolin. BA, Am. U., Washington, 1966; JD, NYU, 1969. Bar: N.Y. 1971, U.S. Dist. Ct. (ea. and so. dists. 1975) N.Y. Asst. counsel, pub. adminstr. Kings County, Bklyn., 1971-81. Mem. Bklyn. Bar Assn. Office: Marriott Renaissance Plz 335 Adams St Ste 2720 Brooklyn NY 11201

MARGOLIN, HAROLD, metallurgical educator; b. Hartford, Conn., July 12, 1922; s. Aaron David and Sonia (Krupnikoff) M.; m. Elaine Marjorie Rose, July 4, 1946; children: Shelley, Deborah, Amy. B in Engring., Yale U., 1943; M in Engring., Yale Univ., 1947, DEng, 1950. Rsch. assoc./scientist divsn. rsch. NYU, N.Y.C., 1949-56, assoc. prof. metall. engring., 1956-62, prof., 1962-73; prof. phys. metallurgy Poly. U., N.Y., Bklyn., 1973-93, disting. rsch. prof., 1993—. Theodore W. Krengel vis. prof. Technion, Haifa, Israel, 1983; cons. in field. Contbg. author books; contbr. articles to profl. publs.; patentee in field. With USNR, 1944-46. Fellow Am. Soc. Metals (edn. award N.Y. chpt. 1967); mem. Metall. Soc. (honoree symposium in his name San Francisco 1994), ASM Internat., TMS. Democrat. Jewish. Home: 81 Stony Run New Rochelle NY 10804-3415 E-mail: hmemxox@aol.com. *Achievement, work, and refusal to accept defeat are intimately intertwined.*

MARGOLIN, JEAN SPIELBERG, artist; b. N.Y.C., Oct. 12, 1926; d. Jack and Ida (Grossman) Spielberg and Bess Liebowitz Spielberg (stepmother); m. Paul Margolin, May 19, 1946 (dec. Mar. 1989). Student, Ind. U., 1951-55, Skowhegan Sch. Painting/Sculp., 1954. Tchr. painting and drawing Ind. U., Bloomington, 1954-55; curator group show Pace U. Gallery, N.Y.C., 1984. Paintings exhibited John Herron Art Mus., Indpls., 1952-55, J.B. Speed Art Mus., Louisville, 1953, Cin. Mus. Art, 1955, L.A. County Mus. Art, 1956, A.C.A. Gallery, N.Y.C., 1959-60, Pa. Acad. Fine Arts, Phila., 1962, Heckscher Mus., Huntington, N.Y., 1964, Skowhegan Benefit Exbhn., Nat. Arts Club, N.Y.C., 1974, Arthouse, Storrs, Conn., 1979, Landmark Gallery, N.Y.C., 1980-82, Pace U. Gallery, N.Y.C., 1980, 84, The Artists Choice Mus., Alex Rosenberg Gallery, N.Y.C., 1983; paintings exhibited by appointment only, N.Y.C., 1985—. Recipient 1st prize purchase award for painting Skowhegan Sch. Painting and Sculpture, 1954, scholar, 1954. Home: 4 Washington Square Vlg Apt 12S New York NY 10012-1908

MARGOLIN, ROBERT JEREMY, lawyer; b. Kansas City, Mo., Mar. 21, 1935; s. Abraham Eugene and Florence Margolin; m. Dorothy Ann Macy, Sept. 20, 1959; children: Kathryn R. Margolin Richter, Charles D. AB, Dartmouth Coll., 1957; JD, LLB, U. Mich., 1960. Bar: Mo., U.S. Ct. Appeals (8th cir.). Ptnr. Margolin and Kirwan, Kansas City, 1960—. Bd. dirs. Kansas City Kings, Feld Leasing. Asst. editor Mich. Law Rev. Bd. dirs. Menorah Med. Ctr., Kansas City, Kansas City Philharm. Assn.; mem. exec. com. Jewish Vocat. Svc., Kansas City. Mem. ABA, Nat. Basketball Assn. (bd. govs.), Mo. Bar Assn., Kansas City Bar Assn. Avocations: golf, skiing. Home: 1628 River Ridge Williamsburg VA 23185-7546 E-mail: bobj757@aol.com.

MARGOLIN, SOLOMON BEGELFOR, pharmacologist, consultant; b. Phila., May 16, 1920; s. Nathan and Fannie (Begelfor) M.; m. Gerda Levy, Jan. 17, 1947 (div. Feb. 1985); children: David, Bernard, Daniel; m. Nancy A. Cox, Apr. 30, 1987. BSc, Rutgers U., 1941, MSc, 1943, PhD, 1945. Asst. Rutgers U., New Brunswick, N.J., 1943-45; rsch. biologist Silmo Chem. Co., Vineland, 1947-48; rsch. pharmacologist Schering Corp., Bloomfield, 1948-52, dir. pharmacology dept., 1952-54; chief pharmacologist Maltbie Labs., Belleville, 1954-56, Wallace Labs, Carter-Wallace, Inc., Cranbury, 1956-60, dir. pharmacology dept., 1960-64, v.p. biol. rsch., 1964-68; pres. AMR Biol. Rsch., Inc., Princeton, 1968-78; from prof., chmn. pharmacology dept. to emeritus prof. St. George's (Grenada) U. Sch. Medicine, 1978—; pres. MARNAC, Inc., Dallas, 1990—. Author: Harper's Handbook Therapeutic Pharmacology, 1981; author: (with others) Physiological Pharmacology, 1963, World Review, Nutrition and Dietetics, 1980; contbr. more than 100 articles to profl. jours. Mem. AAAS, Endocrino Soc., Am. Chem. Soc., Soc. Exptl. Biology and Medicine, Am. Soc. Pharmacology and Exptl. Therapeutics, N.Y. Acad. Scis., Drug Information Assn. Achievements include over 40 U.S., European, and Japanese patents for prevention and treatment of fibrotic lesions, multiple sclerosis and other neurodegenerative disorders; research in anti-histamines anti-cholinergics, endorphins, sedative-hypnotics, tranquilizers, muscle relaxants, glucocorticoids, cardiovascular agents, anti-inflammatory drugs, anti-fibrotic agents, multiple sclerosis agents. Home: 6723 Desco Dr Dallas TX 75225-2704 E-mail: marnacinc@aol.com.

MARGOLIS, ANITA JOY, lawyer; b. Mpls., May 29, 1959; d. Herbert A. and Ursula (Ries) M. BA, U. Wis., 1981; JD, Calif. Western Sch. of Law, 1985. Bar: Calif. 1985, U.S. Dist. Ct. (so. dist.) Calif. 1985, U.S. Dist. Ct. (ctrl.

dist.) Calif. 1993. Assoc. Phillips, Campbell, Haskett, Noone & Ingwalson, San Diego, 1986-93; pvt. practice The Law Offices of Anita J. Margolis, 1993—; judge pro tem San Diego Superior Court, 2001—, arbitrator, 2001—; G. Mem. task force Women's Resource Fair, 1989—; vol. lawyer San Diego Vol. Lawyers Program, 1993-97; mem. gender equity adv. bd. San Diego C.C. Dist., 1990—, chair, 1994—; mem. single parent/displaced homemakers adv. bd. San Diego C.C. Dist., 1990—; judge mock trial Calif. Sch. Law, 1991-95; mem. Citizens Adv. Coun. to Bd. Trustees S.D. City Sch. Dist., 1997-2001; mem. alumni bd. Calif. Western Sch. Law, 1996-98. Mem. San Diego County Bar Assn. (bd. dirs. 2000—, sec. 2001, v.p. 2002—), Consumer Attys. San Diego, Lawyers Club of San Diego (bd. dirs. 1989-93, sec. 1991-92, asst. sec. 1992-93, chmn. cmty. rels. com. 1989-91, chmn. continuing edn. com. 1992-93). Avocations: soccer, golf, skiing. Office: 600 B St Ste 2400 San Diego CA 92101-4520 E-mail: anitau2@pacbell.net.

MARGOLIS, BENJAMIN ROBERT, lawyer, pharmacist; b. Phila., Jan. 15, 1945; s. Daniel and Sylvia (Rubin) M.; m. Lia Ordaz, Dec. 27, 1971; 1 child, Jonathan Daniel. BSc, U. of the Scis. in Phila., 1967; PharmD, U. So. Calif., 1969; JD, Southwestern U. Sch. Law, 1984. Bar: Calif. 1986, D.C. 1987, U.S. Dist. Ct. (cen. dist.) Calif. 1986, U.S. Tax Ct. 1986, U.S. Ct. Appeals (9th cir.) 1987, U.S. Supreme Ct. 1989. Dir. pharmacy Rancho Los Amigos Nat. Rehabilitation Ctr., Downey, Calif., 1993-2000; pvt. practice Pacific Palisades, 1986—. Expert witness pharmacy and med. malpractice. Mem. ABA, ATLA, Los Angeles County Bar Assn., L.A. Trial Lawyers Assn. E-mail: benmar12001@yahoo.com.

MARGOLIS, BERNARD ALLEN, library administrator; b. Greenwich, Conn., Oct. 2, 1948; s. Sidney S. and Rose (Birkenfeld) M.; m. Amanda Batey, Nov. 2, 1973. BA in Polit. Sci., U. Denver, 1970, MLS, 1973; Doctorate (hon.), Wentworth Inst. Tech., 1999. Cert. libr., Mich. Libr. asst. Denver Pub. Libr., 1970-72; br. head Virginia Village Libr., Denver Pub. Libr., 1972-73; dep. dir. Monroe County Libr. Sys., Mich., 1973-75; dir. Raisin Valley Libr. Sys., Monroe, 1976-88, Pikes Peak Libr. Dist., Colorado Springs, Colo., 1988-97; pres. Colo. Ctr. for Books, 1989-92, Colo. Ctr. for the Book, 1993-97, Boston Pub. Libr., 1997—. Cons. in libr. pub. rels., 1976—; founding trustee United Colo. Investment Trust, 1993-95; chmn. Colo. Gov.'s Conf. on Libr. and Info. Svcs., 1990; lectr. Western Mich. U., Kalamazoo, 1978-81; appraiser rare books, Monroe, Colorado Springs, 1970—. Contbr. articles to profl. jours.; mem. editl. bd. Bottom Line Mag. Fin. Mgmt. for Librs., 1986—. Bd. dirs. Monroe Sen. Citizens Ctr., 1976-80, Monroe Fine Arts Coun., 1978-81, Am. the Beautiful Centennial Celebration, Inc., 1993, The Libr. Consortium, 1993-97, Downtown Colorado Springs, Inc., 1994-97, Friends of Copley Sq., 1998—, Care & Share, Inc., sec., 1994-95, vice chmn., 1995, chmn., 1995-97; chmn. Blue Cross-Blue Shield Consumer Coun., Detroit, 1984-88; mem. adv. bd. Access Colo. Libr. and Info. Network (ACLIN), 1991-97, Mercy Meml. Hosp., Monroe, 1984-86, 5th Congl. Art Competition Com., 1992-97; Dem. candidate for Mich. Senate, 1986; mem. allocations com. Pikes Peak United Way, 1988-91, chmn., 1990-91, bd. dirs., 1990-91, 94-97; chmn. Great Pikes Peak Cowboy Poetry Gathering, 1990, 91, 92, 94, 95, 96; del. White House Conf. on Libr. and Info. Scis.; mem. El Paso County Colo. Retirement Bd., 1995-97, sec., 1996-97; fellow Boston Found., 1998—; overseer Hancock Shaker Village, Pittsfield, Mass., 1999—. Recipient Mayoral Cert. Commendation award Denver, 1972, 73; named Mich. Libr. of Yr., 1985, Colo. Libr. of Yr., 1990, commendation John F. Kennedy Ctr. for Performing Arts, 1993, Frank Waters award Pikes Peak Writer's Conf., 1996. Mem.: ALA (governing coun. 1986—, endowment trustee 1989—93, sr. endowment trustee 1993—2001, chmn. resolutions com. 1991—92, cons. ann. swap and shop 1979—84, John Cotton Dana award 1977, 1991, Libr. Awareness Idea Search award Washington 1982), Pub. Libr. Assn., Libr. Adminstrv. Mgmt. Assn., Colo. Libr. Assn. (mem. legis.com., Intellectual Freedom award 1993), Internat. Fedn. Libr. Assns. and Instns., New Eng. Libr. Assn., Mass. Libr. Assn. Democrat. Jewish. Office: Boston Pub Libr Copley Sq 700 Boylston St Boston MA 02116 E-mail: bmargolis@bpl.org.

MARGOLIS, DANIEL HERBERT, lawyer; b. Feb. 11, 1926; s. Morris Abraham and Miriam M.; m. Anabel Tendler, Dec. 23, 1951 (dec.); children: Peter, Beth, Laura, James; m. Sidney Millman Moore, Feb. 5, 1983. BA, Johns Hopkins U., 1948; LLB, Harvard U., 1951. Bar: D.C. 1951, U.S. Supreme Ct. 1959. Atty. adv. Office Price Stablzn., Washington, 1951-52; trial atty. Antitrust divsn. Dept. Justice, 1952-56; sr. ptnr. Bergson, Borkland, Margolis & Adler, 1962—86, McGuire, Woods, Battle & Boothe, Washington, 1986-89, Patton, Boggs LLP, Washington, 1989—2001; sr. counsel DC Office of Corp. Counsel, 2001—. Mem. adv. bd. Internat. Human Rights Law Group, 1989—. With USN, 1945—46. Fellow ABA (chmn. spl. com. on jury comprehension, litig. sect.), Washington Lawyers for Civil Rights. Democrat. Avocations: sailing, skiing, cooking. Office: OCC 1350 Pennsylvania Ave NW Washington DC 20001

MARGOLIS, DAVID I(SRAEL), industrial manufacturing executive; b. N.Y.C., Jan. 24, 1930; s. Benjamin and Celia (Kosofsky) M.; m. Barbara Schneider, Sept. 7, 1958; children: Brian, Robert, Peter, Nancy. BA, CCNY, 1950, MBA, 1952; postgrad., NYU, 1952-55. Asst. treas. Raytheon Co., 1956-59; treas. IT&T, N.Y.C., 1959-62; with Coltec Industries Inc., 1962-95, pres., 1968-91, CEO, 1984-95, chmn. bd. dirs., 1985-95; chmn. exec. com., 1995-99. Mem. bd. trustees Presbyn. Hosp. City N.Y.; bd. overseers NYU Stern Sch. Bus. Mem. Coun. Fgn. Rels. Office: 147 E 48th St New York NY 10017-1223

MARGOLIS, DORIS MAY ROSENBERG, editor, writer; b. Washington, May 10, 1936; d. Samuel Jacob and Eva (Mendelsohn) Rosenberg; m. Lawrence S. Margolis, Jan. 30, 1960; children: Mary Aleta, Paul Oliver. BA, George Wash. U., 1958. Founder, v.p., CEO Editorial Assocs., Washington, 1963-82, founder, pres., CEO, 1982—. Founder, pub., exec. editor Margolis Health Report, 1999—; bd. govs. Nat. Press Club, 1991-94; mem. adv. bd. Washington Journalism Conf., 1991-96; judge Biomed. Writing awards Am. Med. Writers Assn.-Mid-Atlantic, 1987-91, Blue Pencil Writing awards Nat. Assn. Govt. Contractors, 1992, 94, Rose Kushner Breast Cancer Writing award Am. Med. Writers Assn., 1992, Nat. Essay competition Pres.'s Com. on Employment of the Handicapped, Nat. Worker of Yr. competition Goodwill Industries of Am., Nat. Essay Competition Hospitalized Vets. Assn., others. Author: This Is Goodwill, 1968; editor-in-chief Jour. Rehab., 1960-67, (newsletters) Nat. Assn. Sheltered Workshops and Homebound Programs News, 1964-68, Jewish Occupational Coun. News, 1968-70, Aspen Update, 1976-80; contbg. editor (newspapers) Pediatric News, 1968-69, Ob-Gyn News, 1968-69, Internal Medicine News, 1968-69; columnist Jour. Rehab., 1960-67, Washington Jewish Week, 1968-73, Sports Medicine Monthly, 1984-85, Gazette Newspapers, 1999-2000; radio news corr. Physicians Radio News Network, 1969, 1976; contbr. articles to profl. jours.; editor: Rehabilitation of the Mentally Ill, 1961, Rehabilitation International, 1962, Rehabilitation of the Mentally Retarded, 1962, To Aid the Disabled, 1963, The Stroke Spectrum: Prevention, Treatment, and Rehabilitation, 1963, Workshops at the Crossroads, 1964, Sheltered Workshops: The Road Ahead, 1965, Sheltered Workshops, 1965, The Coronary Spectrum: Prevention, Treatment, and Rehabilitation, 1966, Medical Rehabilitation Model Delivery Systems, 1978; asst. editor NEA News, 1958-59. Singer, dancer Montgomery Light Opera Co., 1970's, Washington Civic Opera, 1978-84; singer, dancer, actress Hexagon Players, 1970-72; bd. dirs. Jewish Social Svcs. Agy., 1970-72; bd. govs. Am. Newspaper Women's Club, 1982-84, Woman's Nat. Dem. Club, 1983-88; exec. com. bd. dirs. People-to-People Com. on Disability, 1992-2000, vice-chmn., 1995-2000; pres. Inner Wheel Club of Washington, 1993-94. Recipient Ellen Woodhull scholastic scholarship George Washington U., 1957, Disting. Alumni Achievement award George Washington U., 1978, Nat. Press Club Vivian award, 1997, 99; personal commendations Pres. John F. Kennedy, 1963, Pres. Lyndon B. Johnson, 1966; Paul Harris fellow Rotary Internat., 1996. Fellow Am. Med. Writers Assn. (bd. dirs. 1989-94, nominating com. 1990-91, chair pub. rels., advt. and mktg. sect. 1989-90, pres. Mid-Atlantic chpt. 1990-91, exec. com. bd. dirs. 1993-94); mem. Nat. Assn. Sci. Writers, Rotary (bd. dirs. 1999-2001, 2002—), Cosmos Club, Alpha Epsilon Phi Alumni Assn. (pres. 1959-60), Mortar Bd. (treas. 1957-58), Pi Delta Epsilon (v.p. 1957-58), Psi Chi, Alpha Theta Nu. Office: Editorial Assocs Nat Press Bldg Washington DC 20045

MARGOLIS, EMANUEL, lawyer, educator; b. Bklyn., Mar. 18, 1926; s. Abraham and Esther (Levin) M.; m. Edith Cushing; m. Estelle Thompson, Mar. 1, 1959; children: Elizabeth Margolis-Pineo, Catherine, Abby Margolis Newman, Joshua, Sarah. BA, U. N.C., 1947; MA, Harvard U., 1948, PhD, 1951; JD, Yale U., 1956. Bar: Conn. 1957, U.S. Dist. Ct. Conn. 1958, U.S. Supreme Ct. 1969. Instr. dept. govt. U. Conn., 1951-53; assoc. Silberberg & Silverstein, Ansonia, Conn., 1956-60, Wofsey Rosen Kweskin & Kuriansky, Stamford, 1960-66, ptnr., 1966-96, of counsel, 1996—. Arbitrator State of Conn., 1984-85; adj. prof. Quinnipiac U. Sch. Law, 1986—. Sr. editor Conn. Bar Jour., 1971-80, 83—, editor-in-chief, 1980-83; contbr. to profl. jours. Mem. nat. bd. ACLU, 1975-79; mem. Westport (Conn.) Planning and Zoning Commn., 1971-75; chmn. Conn. CLU, 1988-95, legal advisor, 1995—; exec. com. Yale Law Sch., 2000—. With U.S. Army, 1944-46. Decorated Purple Heart; recipient First Award for Disting. Svc. to Conn. Bar, Conn. Law Tribune, 1987. Fellow Conn. Bar Found. (James W. Cooper fellow 1996); mem. ABA, Conn. Bar Assn. (chmn. human rights sect. 1970-73), Nat. Assn. Criminal Def. Lawyers, Am. Arbitration Assn. (arbitrator 1998—, trial referee 1985—). Office: 600 Summer St Stamford CT 06901-1990 Home: 72 Myrtle Ave Westport CT 06880-3512 E-mail: veecha@optonline.net.

MARGOLIS, GERALD JOSEPH, psychiatrist, psychoanalyst; b. Bronx, N.Y., May 7, 1935; s. Max and Sophie (Siegel) M.; m. June Edelman Greenspan, July 13, 1976; children: David J., Peter S., Steven J. AB, U. Rochester, 1957; MD, U. Chgo., 1960; postgrad., Inst. Phila. Assn. Psychoa., 1972. Diplomate Am. Bd. Psychiatry and Neurology. Intern, resident in psychiatry Upstate Med. Ctr./SUNY, Syracuse, 1960-64, instr. psychiatry, 1966-67; from instr. to clin. prof. psychiatry Med. Sch., U. Pa., Phila., 1967—. Practice medicine specializing in psychiatry and psychoanalysis, Cherry Hill, NJ; tng. and supervising analyst Inst. of the Psychoanalytic Ctr. Phila. Contbr. articles to profl. jours. Served with M.C., USAF, 1964-66. Mem.: AMA, Psychoanalytic Ctr. Phila. (tng. and supervising analyst), Am. Psychiat. Assn., Am. Psychoanalytic Assn. (cert.), B'nai B'rith, Phi Beta Kappa. Home: 408 Park Ln Moorestown NJ 08057-2000

MARGOLIS, HOWARD, public policy studies educator; b. Boston, Mar. 20, 1932; s. Abraham and Ann Margolis; m. Joan Olva Thuma, Jan. 17, 1962; children: Peter, Jenny, Sarah. BA, Harvard U., 1953; PhD, MIT, 1979. Speechwriter Sec. of Def., Washington, 1962-64; journalist Sci. Mag., Washington Post, 1960-62, 64-65; rsch. staff Inst. Def. Analyses, Arlington, Va., 1965-72; rsch. fellow MIT, Cambridge, 1972-81; vis. scholar Inst. Advanced Study & Russell Sage Found., N.Y.C. and Princeton, 1981-83; lectr. U. Calif., Irvine, 1983-85; prof. U. Chgo., 1985—. Author: Selfishness, Altruism and Rationality, 1982, Patterns, Thinking and Cognition, 1987, Paradigms and Barriers, 1993, Dealing With Risk, 1996, It Started with Copernicus, 2002. Avocations: skiing, hiking, windsurfing. Office: U Chgo Harris Sch Chicago IL 60637 E-mail: hmarg@uchicago.edu.

MARGOLIS, JEFFREY ALLEN, program specialist; b. Phila., July 13, 1948; s. Alex Harry and Sara Blanche (Schwartz) M.; m. Ida Rose Moskowitz, June 14, 1970; 1 child, Jamibeth. BS in Edn., Temple U., 1970; MA, Rowan U., 1975. Cert. student personnel svcs. specialist, social studies tchr., N.J. Tchr./counselor Ventnor (N.J.) Pub. Schs., 1971-84; pres./CEO Jami Trading Co. Inc., Ocean City, 1978-87; investor rels. mgr. Wilmington (Del.) Savs. Fund Soc., 1986-87; counselor Lower Cape May (N.J.) Regional Sch. Dist., 1987—2002; program specialist Rowan U., Glassboro, NJ, 2002—. Adj. instr. Richard Stockton Coll. N.J., 1999—. Author: On Your Own, 1991, Teen Crime Wave, 1997, Violence in Sports: Victory at What Price, 1999, Kids Who Kill, 1999; contbr. Ency. of N.J., 2001. With USAR, 1970-76. Recipient Citation, N.J. Gen. Assembly, 1990. Mem. NEA, N.J. Edn. Assn., N.J. Counseling Assn., Nat. Acad. Advising Assn., Bethel Investment Club (v.p.), Masons (officer 1993-98), Shriners, Phi Delta Kappa (past pres., Svc. Key award 1996). Avocations: scripophily, fishing, travel, biking, investing. Home: 304 N Lafayette Ave Ventnor City NJ 08406-1625 Office: Rowan U . Glassboro NJ 08028

MARGOLIS, JEFFREY ROBERT, financial services executive; b. Englewood, N.J., July 2, 1957; s. Frederick Paul and Florence (Goldner) M.; m. Nancy Dee Epstein, Oct. 28, 1984; 1 child, Lisa. BA, Cornell U., 1979, MBA, 1980. CPA, N.Y.; chartered fin. analyst. Acct. Arthur Young & Co., N.Y.C., 1980-83; COO Continental Asset Mgmt., 1983-94; mng. dir. Morgan Stanley Dean Witter Investment Mgmt., 1994—. Media contbr., interviewee and critic for fin. community; speaker in field. Editor, contbr. various publs. Mem. AICPA, Assn. for Investment Mgmt. and Rsch., N.Y. Soc. CPAs, Ins. Investment Strategy Group (founder, chmn.). Home: 85 Barberry Ln Roslyn Heights NY 11577-1501 Office: Morgan Stanley Dean Witter Investment Mgmt 5th Fl 1221 Avenue Of The Americas Fl 5 New York NY 10020-1001

MARGOLIS, JULIUS, economist, educator; b. N.Y.C., Sept. 26, 1920; s. Sam and Fannie (Weiner) M.; m. Doris Lubetsky, Oct. 30, 1942; children—Jane S., Carl W. BSS., City Coll. N.Y., 1941; Ph.M. in Econs, U. Wis., 1943; M.P.A. in Econs, Harvard, 1947, PhD, 1949. Instr. econs. Tufts Coll., 1947-48; asst. prof. econs. and planning U. Chgo., 1948-51; asst. prof. econs. Stanford, 1951-54; prof. bus adminstrn. U. Calif. at Berkeley, 1954-64; prof. econs. and engrng. econ. systems Stanford, 1964-69; prof., dir. Fels Center of Govt., U. Pa., 1969-76; prof. econs. U. Calif. at Irvine, 1976—. Dir. Ctr. on Global Peace and Conflict Studies, 1985—; cons. to govt. and industry, 1958— Author: (with others) The Public Economy of Urban Communities, 1965, The Northern California's Water Industry, 1966, Public Economics, 1969, Public Expenditure and Policy Analysis, 1984; also articles. Served with AUS, 1943-46. Mem. Am. Econ. Assn., Royal Econ. Soc. Home: 45 Whitman Ct Irvine CA 92612-4059 Office: U Calif Dept Econ Irvine CA 92697-0001 E-mail: jmargoli@uci.edu.

MARGOLIS, LAWRENCE STANLEY, federal judge; b. Phila., Mar. 13, 1935; m. Doris May Rosenberg, Jan. 30, 1960; children: Mary Aleta, Paul Oliver. BSME, Drexel U., 1957; JD, George Washington U., 1961. Bar: D.C. 1963. Patent examiner U. S. Patent Office, Washington, 1957-62; patent counsel Naval Ordnance Lab., White Oak, Md., 1962-63; asst. corp. counsel D.C., 1963-66; atty. criminal div., spl. asst. U.S. atty. Dept. of Justice, Washington, 1966-68; asst. U.S. atty. for D.C., 1968-71; U.S. magistrate judge U.S. Dist. Ct., Washington, 1971-82; judge U.S. Ct. Fed. Claims, 1982—; chmn. task force on discovery reform U.S. Claims Ct., chmn. alt. dispute resolution. Chmn. Space and Bldg. com., mem. faculty Fed. Jud. Ctr. Editor-in-chief The Young Lawyer, 1965-66, D.C. Bar Jour., 1967-73; bd. editors The Dist. Lawyer, 1978-82. Trustee Drexel U., 1983-89; bd. govs. George Washington U. Alumni Assn., 1978-85, 93-96 Recipient Contbn. award D.C. Jaycees, 1966, Svc. award Boy Scouts Am., 1970, Alumni Svc. award George Washington U., 1976, Disting. Alumni Achievement award George Washington U., 1985, Disting. Alumni Achievement award Drexel U., 1988, Drexel 100 award, 1992, Alternative Dispute Resolution award Ctr. for Pub. Resources, 1988, Alternative Dispute Resolution Svc. award Ct. of Fed. Claims, 1996, Alumni Recognition award George Washington U., 1996. Fellow Inst. Jud. Adminstrn., Am. Bar Found.; mem. ABA (chmn. jud. adminstrn. divsn., Disting. Svc. award 1981), ABA Nat. Conf. Spl. Ct. Judges (chmn., Disting. Svc. award 1978), D.C. Jud. Conf., Bar Assn. D.C. (bd. dirs. 1970-72, jour. editor-in-chief, Contbn. award young lawyers sect. 1983), Fed. Bar Assn., George Washington U. Nat. Law Assn. (pres. D.C. chpt. 1974-76, pres. 1983-84), Univ. Club., Rotary (bd. dirs. Washington 1984-90, pres. 1988-89, dist. gov. 1991-92, Rotarian of Yr. 1984, Rotary Internat. Rep. to the World Bank and Orgn. of Am. States, 1998-99, pres. Rotary Found. 1999-2000), Charles Fahy Am. Inn of Ct. (Nat. Program award, 1997), Phila. Cen. High Sch. Alumni (bd. mgrs. 2001—). Office: US Ct Fed Claims 717 Madison Pl NW Ste 703 Washington DC 20439-0002 E-mail: lawrence_margolis@ao.uscourts.gov.

MARGOLIS, MARK NEAL, actor; b. Phila., Nov. 26, 1939; s. Isidore and Fanya (Fried) M.; m. Jacqueline Petcove, June 3, 1962; 1 child, Morgan. Studied with, Stella Adler, Lee Strasberg, Bill Hickey, Barbara Loden. Actor: (films) Short Eyes, The Cotton Club, Delta Force II, Tales from the Darkside, Scarface, 1492-Conquest of Paradise, Ace Ventura Pet Detective, The Pallbearer, I Shot Andy Warhol, Where The Rivers Flow North, Jacob the Liar, Mickey Blue Eyes, PI, The Thomas Crown Affair, End of Days, Tailor of Panama, others; (TV) Crime Story, Jake and the Fatman, Star Trek The Next Generation, Santa Barbara, Quantum Leap, Columbo, Law and Order, N.Y. Undercover, Oz, others; (Broadway prodns.) The World of Sholom Aleichem, Infidel Caesar; (off-Broadway prodns.) Three Americanisms, My Uncle Sam, Balm in Gilead, Hospitality, Child of the Clay Country, The Big Knife, others; (regional theatre) The Substance of Fire, Ghosts, Love Me or Leave Me, Once in a Lifetime, The Boys Next Door, A Shayna Maidel, Hunting Cockroaches, The Seagull, Split Decision, The Front Page, Broken Glass, Quills. Office: HWA Talent Reps 220 E 23d St Ste 400 New York NY 10010

MARGOLIS, MARVIN ALLEN, lawyer; b. Milw., Sept. 30, 1934; s. Ben William and Jen (Dekelboum) M.; m. Ann Lubell, Dec. 3, 1961; children: David, Michael, Jeffrey. BS, U. Wis., 1956, JJD, 1958. Bar: Wis. 1958, U.S. Dist. Ct. (ea. dist.) Wis. 1960. Ptnr. Margolis & Cassidy, Milw. Ct. Commr. City of Milw., 1975—; lectr. in field. Contbr. numerous articles to profl. jours. Fellow Am. Acad. Matrimonial Lawyers (Wis. chpt. treas. 1978, v.p. 1979, pres. 1980-81), Wis. Acad. Trial Lawyers; mem. ABA, ATLA, Wis. Bar Assn. (bd. attys. profl. responsibility 1975—, dir. family law sect. 1982—), Milw. Bar Assn. (jud. selection com. 1999), Jr. Milw. Bar Assn., Am. Inns of Ct. (Leander J. Foley, Jr. matrimonial chpt.). Avocation: golf. Office: Margolis & Cassidy 324 E Wisconsin Ave Ste 700 Milwaukee WI 53202-4308

MARGOLIS, MICHAEL STEPHEN, political science educator, consultant; b. Chgo., Mar. 27, 1940; s. Ralph Victor and Annette (Krassner) M.; m. Ellen Louise Freedman, Dec. 26, 1964; children: Karen, Jennifer, Abby, Max, Nicola; m. Elaine Cajano Camerota, June 23, 1990. AB, Oberlin Coll., 1961; MA, U. Mich., 1962, PhD, 1968. Lectr. Politics U. Strathclyde, Glasgow, Scotland, 1965-67; instr. polit. sci. U. Pitts., 1967-68, asst. prof., 1968-73, assoc. prof., 1973-85, prof., 1985-90; prof. U. Cin., 1990—, dept. head, 1990-95; lectr. politics U. Glasgow, 1973-74; Fulbright lectr./rschr. Hankuk U. Fgn. Studies, Seoul, Korea, 1997; cons. in field. Author: (with others) Political Stratification and Democracy, 1972, Viable Democracy, 1979; editor: (with G. Mauser) Manipulating Public Opinion, 1989, (with John Green) Machine Politics, Soundbites & Nostalgia, 1993, Free Expression, Public Support & Censorship, 1994; mem. Allegheny County Democratic Com., Pa., 1971-73. Mem. Am. Polit. Sci. Assn., Am. Assn. Pub. Opinion Rsch., Midwest Polit. Sci. Assn. (exec. coun. 1997—) Home: 658 Pointe Benton Ln Covington KY 41014-1100 Office: U Cin Dept Polit Sci 375 Mill St Cincinnati OH 45215-4616

MARGOLIS, PHILIP MARCUS, psychiatrist, educator; b. Lima, Ohio, July 7, 1925; s. Harry Sterling and Clara (Brunner) M.; m. Nancy Nupuf, July 26, 1959; children: Cynthia, Marc, David, Laurence. BA magna cum laude, U. Minn., 1945, MD, 1948. Diplomate Am. Bd. Psychiatry and Neurology (examiner 1973—). Intern Milw. County Hosp., 1948-49; resident VA Hosp. and U. Minn., 1949-52, Mass. Gen. Hosp. and Harvard U., Boston, 1952-54; instr. U. Minn., Milw., 1953-55; asst. prof. dept. psychiatry Med. Sch., U. Chgo., 1955-60, assoc. prof., 1960-66; prof. psychiatry Med. Sch. U. Mich., 1966—, prof. cmty. mental health, 1968—; prof. psychiatry emeritus L.S.A., 1997—, instr., 1977-97; mem. civil liberties bd. U. Mich., 1995—, chair civil liberties bd., 1996—; chief psychiat. inpatient service U. Chgo. Hosps. and Clinics, 1956-66; dir. Civil Forensic Tng. Program, 1997—. Cons. Forensic Psychiat. Ctr., State of Mich., 1972—, coord. med. student edn. program, 1975-78, dir., 1978-82; cons. Turner Geriatric Clin., 1978-86, cons. Breast Cancer Clinic, 1988, Powertrain subs. Gen. Motors, 1984—, Dept. Mental Health, U.S. Dept. Justice; assoc. chief clin. affairs U. Mich. Hosps., 1981-85, chair legis. govt. com., 1996—, chmn. ethics com.; bd. dirs., mem. profl. rev. com. PSRO Area VII, 1982-86; mem. Mich. State Bd. Medicine, 1986-94, chmn. 1992-94, senate adv. com. Univ. Affairs., 1986-89; bd. dirs. Fedn. of State Med. Bds., 1994-98, spl. com. on profl. conduct and ethics, 1998—, Mich. del., 1988-96, FLEX Com. Nat. Bd. Med. Examiners, 1988-98. Author: Guide for Mental Health Workers, 1970, Patient Power: The Development of a Therapeutic Community in a General Hospital, 1974; also articles.; cons. editor: Community Mental Health jour, 1967— . Recipient Commonwealth Fund fellow award, 1964, Career Svc. award, 1992, Resident Appreciation award, 1991. Fellow: Am. Coll. Psychiatrists (chmn. bylaws com. 1997—), Am. Psychiat. Assn. (life; chmn. membership com. 1979—83, cons. ethics com. 1983—86, trustee 1985—88, sec. 1989—91, chmn. ethics appeals bd. 1989—, cons. steering com. on practical guidelines 1991—, budget com. 1991—, mem. assembly 1992, coun. med. edn. and career devel. 1993—, pres. Lifers 1994—, recertification com. 1998—, annual Lifers award 1999); mem.: Am. Acad. Psychiatry and Law (com. on psychoanalytic edn. 1995—, edn. com. 1998, treas. midwest chpt. 1998—2000, pres. 2001—02), Am. Acad. Psychoanalysis, Mich. State Med. Soc. (bioethics com. 1989—, com. on med. licensure and discipline 1995—, mental health liaison com. 1995—, legis. and regulations com. 1995—, liaison com. Gen. Motors 1998—, chair 2000—), Mich. Psychiat. Soc. (pres. 1980—81, chmn. ethics com. 1983—86, resolutions officer student rights responsibilities 1996—, chmn. legislation and govt. com. 1996—, v.p. 2000—, Career Achievement award 2000), Washtenaw County Med. Soc. (exec. coun. 1982—, chmn. ethics com. 1983—87, pres. 1987—88, editl. bd. 1995—, chair legis. commn. 1999—). Home: 228 Riverview Dr Ann Arbor MI 48104-1846 Office: 900 Wall St Ann Arbor MI 48105-1910

MARGOLIS, SUSAN ELLEN, psychiatric clinical nurse specialist, artist; b. Cleve., May 11, 1955; d. William Nathan and Sarah Aranow Zuckerman; m. Larry S. Margolis; children: William Zuckerman, Jacob Nathan. BSN, U. Tex., 1981, MSN, 1989; PhD, Tex. Woman's U., 2000. RN, Tex.; cert. clin. nurse specialist-psychiat./mental health. Charge/staff nurse NurseFinders, Arlington, Tex., 1984-88; clin. asst. Post Oak Psychiatry Assocs., Waxahachie, 1988-89; team leader Ft. Worth (Tex.) Vet.'s Ctr., 1989-90; nursing instr. Tarleton State U., Stephenville, Tex., 1990; pvt. practice cons., educator, lectr., therapist Benbrook, 1991-92; geri-psychiat. nurse therapist Ft. Worth Family Inst., 1992-93; dir. geriatric svcs. Psychiat. Ctr. of North Tex., DeSoto, 1993—. Spkr. Alzheimer's Assn., Tarrant Area Gerontol. Soc., Dallas/Ft. Worth County, Dallas and Ft. Worth, 1989—. Vol. Arlington (Tex.) Night Shelter, 1988-96, Presbyn. Night Shelter, Ft. Worth, 1997—; del. to China, Am. Del. Psychol. Nurses, 1990; foster parent; active local Orthodox synagogue. With U.S. Army, 1973-75; lt. USAF, 1982-83. Full chemistry scholar Stephen F. Austin State U., 1972; selected for individual study Royal Acad. Nursing, Edinburgh, Scotland, 1973. Mem. ANA, Tex. Nurse's Assn., Disabled Vet.'s Assn., U. Tex. at Arlington Alumni Assn., Tex. Woman's U. Alumni Assn., Sigma Theta Tau. Jewish. Avocation: stained glass art. Home: 10166 Trail Ridge Dr Benbrook TX 76126-9516 E-mail: margolis7@hotmail.com.

MARGOLIS, VIVIENNE O. psychotherapist, educator; b. Dayton, Ohio, Jan. 11, 1922; d. Sol and Cecelia (Salowitz) M.; m. Leonard Eisner (div. 1976); children: Charna, Andrew, Jonathan. BS, George Washington U., 1944; MS with honors, So. Conn. U., 1966; PhD with honors, Calif. Coast, 1980. Tchr. Fairfield (Conn.) U., 1970-72, Norwalk (Conn.) Community Coll., 1970-75, Bicultural Day Sch., Stamford, Conn., 1960-70; therapist Hackensack (N.J.) Hosp., 1976-81; tchr. Towson (Md.) State U., 1987-89, Towson State U., Columbia, 1988-90; pvt. practice Washington, 1985-87, Columbia, 1989—. Professorial connection with Riverhill Wellness Ctr., Clarksville, Md., 2001—. Author: Newspaper Everything Book, 1975, 77, Boat, Bat and Beanie, 1977, Quick and Easy Holiday Costumes, 1977, Fanfare for a Feather, 1991; art exhibit of newspaper craft work U. City Arts League, Phila., 1999. Avocations: collage, small-box constructions, clay sculpture. Home and Office: 6037 Majors Ln Columbia MD 21045-4133

MARGOLIUS, HARRY STEPHEN, pharmacologist, physician; b. Albany, N.Y., Jan. 29, 1938; s. Irving Robert and Betty (Zweig) M.; m. Francine Rockwood, May 22, 1964; children: Elizabeth Anne, Craig Matthew. BS, Union U., 1959, PhD, 1963; MD, U. Cin., 1968. Diplomate Nat. Bd. Med. Examiners, 1969, pharmacology test com., 1990-94. Intern, resident Harvard Med. Svc. Boston City Hosp., 1968-70, pharmcology rsch. assoc., 1970-72; sr. clin. investigator NHLBI NIH, Bethesda, 1972-74; assoc. prof. pharmacology, asst. prof. medicine Med. U. S.C., Charleston, 1974-77, prof. pharmacology, assoc. prof. medicine, 1977-80, prof. pharmacology, prof. medicine, 1980—, chmn. pharmacology, 1989—. Cons. NIH, FDA, VA, NSF, Washington, Bethesda, 1975—; mem. editorial bd. Am. Heart Assn., Dallas, 1980—. Editor: Kinins IV, 1986, Renal Function, Hypertension and Kallikrein-Kinin System, 1988; contbr. numerous articles to profl. jours. Commdr. USPHS, 1967-74. Recipient S.C. Gov.'s award for sci. S.C. Acad. Scis., 1988, Frey-Werle Commemorative medal for biomed. rsch., 1997; Burroughs-Wellcome scholar, 1976; vis. scholar U. Cambridge, Eng., 1980-

81; sr. fellow Fitzwilliam Coll., 1996; NIH grantee, 1975—; named Theodore Cooper Meml. Lectr., 1995. Fellow Coun. for High Blood Pressure Rsch., Am. Heart Assn.; mem. Am. Soc. for Pharmacology and Exptl. Therapeutics, Am. Soc. for Clin. Investigation and 10 additional med., sci. socs. Jewish. Achievements include studies of the role of kallikreins and kinins in human and animal forms of hypertension; discovery of abnormalities which signify roles in causing high blood pressure. Office: Medical Univ of SC College of Medicine 171 Ashley Ave Charleston SC 29425-0001

MARGON, BRUCE HENRY, astrophysicist, educator; b. N.Y.C., Jan. 7, 1948; s. Leon and Maxine E. (Margon) Siegelbaum; 1 dau., Pamela. AB, Columbia U., 1968; MA, U. Calif.-Berkeley, 1971, Ph.d., 1973. Asst. rsch. astronomer U. Calif.-Berkeley, 1973-76; assoc. prof. astronomy UCLA, 1976-80; prof. astronomy U. Wash., Seattle, 1980—, chmn., 1981-87, 90-95, sci. dir. Sloan Digital Sky Survey, 1998-99; assoc. dir. Space Telescope Sci. Inst., Balt., 2001—. Bd. govs. Astrophys. Rsch. Consortium, Inc., Seattle; chmn. bd. dirs. AURA, Inc., Washington; co-investigator Hubble space telescope NASA, Washington, 1977—. NATO postdoctoral fellow, 1973-74; Sloan Found. research fellow, 1979-83 Fellow AAAS, Am. Phys. Soc.; mem. Internat. Astron. Union, Am. Astron. Soc. (Pierce Prize 1981), Royal Astron. Soc. Office: Space Telescope Sci Inst 3700 San Martin Dr Baltimore MD 21218 E-mail: margon@stsci.edu.

MARGOSHES, MIRIAM KAGAN, information specialist; b. Cambridge, Mass., Feb. 10, 1932; d. Baruch and Raizl (Rozinko) Kagan; m. Marvin Margoshes, Aug. 7, 1955; children: Bethia Anne, Sara Amy, Jessa Abi, Dan Raphael. BS, Simmons Coll., 1953; MS, CUNY, 1976. Cert. libr. media specialist, N.Y. Libr. aide Harvard U. Librs., Cambridge, 1947-53; asst. libr. Wheelock Coll., Boston, 1954-57; libr., cons. Combined Book Exhibit, Briarcliff Manor, N.Y., 1971-73; instrnl. svcs. libr. Westchester C.C., Valhalla, 1974-77; libr. dir., editor Pergamon Press, Inc., Elmsford, 1978-83; libr. supr. Joseph E. Seagram & Sons, N.Y.C., 1984-87; sr. rsch. assoc. House of Seagram, 1987-92; database specialist Towers Perrin, Valhalla, 1992—. Cons. D.C. Welfare Dept., Washington, 1965-70; libr. cons. Pocantico Hills (N.Y.) Sch., 1973-74. Contbr. articles to profl. jours. Trustee Bethesda-Chevy Chase (Md.) Libr. Bd., 1968-71; dist. leader Tarrytown Dem. Com., 1972-74; trustee Temple Beth Abraham, Tarrytown, N.Y., 1980-89; chmn., sec. Warner Libr. Bd., Tarrytown, 1982, 84-94; trustee, sec. Westchester Libr. Sys. Bd., Elmsford, 1984-89; publicity com. Temple Beth Abraham 100th Anniversary, 1999-2000. Recipient Westchester Libr. System Luminary award, 1999. Mem. Spl. Librs. Assn., Westchester Libr. Adv. Com.(v.p.), Hadassah. Avocations: travel, cultural anthropology, aerobics. Office: Towers Perrin 100 Summit Lake Dr Valhalla NY 10595-1347 E-mail: margosm@towers.com., mirkamar@telocity.com.

MARGOTTA, MAURICE HOWARD, JR. management consultant; b. Tarrytown, N.Y. s. Maurice Howard Sr. and Mary (Hritz) M.; children: Maureen Rancourt, Gregory. BA, U. Hartford, 1974, MS, 1976; postgrad., U. Conn., 1979-80; MA, Columbia U., 1989, EdD, 1990. Cert. credit exec. Asst. mgr., br. mgr. Sperry Rand Corp., 1968—70; credit svcs., corp. credit mgr. RBM div. Litton Industries, Hartford, Conn., 1970-78; adj. prof. mgmt.continuing edn. div. U. Hartford, 1975-84, coord. div., 1978-84; credit mgr., trainer Mercantile Acceptance Corp., Hartford, 1978-84; dir. edn. Nat. Assn. of Credit Mgmt., N.Y.C., 1985-87, v.p., dir. edn. Columbia, Md., 1987-94, Credit Rsch. Found., Columbia, 1988-94; exec. officer Corp. Rsch. Assocs., 1994-97; corp. credit mgr. Heath Cons., Inc., Houston, 1998—. Chmn. curriculum group Grad. Sch. Credit and Fin. Mgmt., Columbia, 1987-94, chief acad. officer, 1987, exec. officer, Corp. Rsch. Assoc., Inc., 1994. Author: Credit Management Review, 1987, rev. 2d edit., 1992; contbr. numerous articles on mgmt. topics to profl. jours. and mags.; presenter speeches on mgmt. and fin. at pub. forums. Town chmn. United Cerebral Palsy Assn., East Windsor, Conn., 1970—. With USMC, then res., Korea, Vietnam. Recipient merit award U. Hartford, 1979, Teaching Excellence award, 1985. Fellow Nat. Inst. Credit (assoc.); mem. ASTD, Internat. Platform Assn., Am. Assn. Adult Continuing Edn., Am. Soc. Assn. Execs., Nat. Econs. Club, Nat. Assn. Credit Mgmt. (cert. credit exec., bd. dirs. Conn. chpt. 1978-80, chmn. edn. com. 1978-84, nat. edn. com. 1985—; nat. accreditation bd. 1987—), Fin. Mgmt. Assn., Phi Delta Kappa. Roman Catholic. Avocations: hiking, fishing, tennis, walking, reading. Office: Heath Cons Inc 9030 Monroe Rd Houston TX 77061-5229 E-mail: credit@heathus.com., mauredn@cs.com.

MARGRAVE, JOHN LEE, chemist, educator, university administrator; b. Kansas City, Kans., Apr. 13, 1924; s. Orville Frank and Bernice J. (Hamilton) M.; m. Mary Lou Davis, June 11, 1950; children: David Russell, Karen Sue. BS in Engring. Physics, U. Kans., 1948, PhD in Chemistry, 1950. AEC postdoctoral fellow U. Calif. at Berkeley, 1951-52; from instr. to prof. chemistry U. Wis., Madison, 1952-63; prof. chemistry Rice U., 1963—, E.D. Butcher chair, 1986—, chmn. dept., 1967-72, dean advanced studies and rsch., 1972-80, v.p., 1980-86. V.p. rsch. Houston Advanced Rsch. Ctr., chief sci. officer, 1989—; vis. prof. chemistry Tex. So. U., 1993; vis. disting. prof. U. Wis., 1968; vis. disting. prof. U. Iowa, 1969, Ga. Inst. Tech., 1970, U. Colo., 1975; dir. Materials Sci. Ctr., 1986—93; dir. Coun. Chem. Rsch. , 1985—88; dir. Woodlands Sci. and Art Ctr., 1999—; chmn. tech. rev. coun. Environ. Tech. Develop. and Commercialization Ctr. (ETDCC), Texas City, 1998—; various nat. and internat. confs. on chem. vapor deposition of thin diamond films , 1989—98; advisor NROTC Assn., 1984—; mem. Wilhelm und Else Heraeus Stiffung Found. Symposium on Alkali Metal Reactions, Germany, 1988; chmn. tech. rev. coun. Environ. Tech. Devel. and Commercialization Ctr., Texas City, Tex., 1998—; mem. com. on stockpile of chem. weapons NRC, 2001—; Reilly lectr. Notre Dame, 1968; Patrick lectr. Kans. State U., 2002; Dupont lectr. U. S.C., 1971; Abbott lectr. U. N.D., 1972; Cyanamid lectr. U. Conn., 1973; Sandia lectr. U. N.Mex., 1981; Phi Lambda Upsilon lectr. Kans. State U., 1995; Seydel-Wooley lectr. Ga. Inst. Tech., 1970; lectr. NSF-Japan Joint Thermophys. Properties Symposium, 1983, Ohio Aerospace Inst., 1999; orgnl. com. NATO Conf. on Supercooled Metals, Il Ciocio, Italy, 1993, Internat. Symposia Fluorine Chemistry, Santa Cruz, 1988, Vancouver, B.C., 96, Durham, England, 2000, First, Second, Third and Fourth World Superconductivity Congresses, 1989, 90, 92, 94; chmn. com. chem. processes in severe nuc. accidents NRC, 1987—88, chmn. molten salt reactor armarments panel , 1996—99, mem. com. alt. techs. demilitarization assembled chem. weapons, 1997—2000; cons. to govt. and industry, 1954—; dir. Rice Design Ctr., Houston Area Rsch. Ctr., U. Kans. Rsch. Found., Gulf Univs. Rsch. Consortium, Energy Rsch. and Edn. Found., Spectroscopic Assocs., World Congress on Superconductivity; mem. adv. coms. chem., materials sci., rsch. U. Tenn., Knoxville, Ohio State U., Tex. So. U., La. Bd. Regents; sci. adv. bd. SI Diamond Tech., 1992—96, BioNumerik, 1993—, Intrepid Tech., 1994—96; pres. Mar Chem., Inc., 1970—, High Temperature Sci., Inc., 1976—99. Editor: Modern High Temperature Sci., 1984; contbg. editor Characterization of High Temperature Vapors, 1967, Mass. Spectrometry in Inorganic Chemistry, 1968; editor High Temperature Sci., 1969-99, Procs. XXIII and XXIV Confs. on Mass Spectrometry, 1975, 76; author: (with others) Bibliography of Matrix Isolation Spectroscopy, 1950-85, 87; contbr. articles to profl. jours.; patentee in field. Served with AUS, 1943-46; capt. Res. ret. Sloan research fellow, 1957-58; Guggenheim fellow, 1960; recipient Kiekhofer Teaching award U. Wis., 1957; IR-100 award for CFX lubricant powder, 1970, IR-100 award for Cryolink, 1986; Tex. Honor Scroll award, 1978; Disting. Alumni citation U. Kans., 1981, Sci. and Tech. award North Harris Montgomery Cmty. Coll., 1994., Chemical Pioneer award, Am. Inst. Chemists, 2002. Fellow AAAS, Am. Inst. Chemists, Am. Phys. Soc., Tex. Acad. Sci.; mem. AAUP, NAS, Am. Chem. Soc. (Inorganic Chemistry award 1967, S.W. Regional award 1978, Fluorine Chemistry award 1980, S.E. Tex. Sect. award 1993, chem. edn. com. 1968-70, publs. com. 1973-74, patents and related matters com. 1994-96), Am. Ceramic Soc., Am. Soc. Mass Spectrometry (dir.), Am. Soc. Metals, Electrochem. Soc., Chem. Soc. London, Tex. Philos. Soc., Materials Rsch. Soc., Sigma Xi (Disting. Svc. award 1994), Omicron Delta Kappa, Sigma Tau, Tau Beta Pi, Alpha Chi Sigma. Methodist. Home: 4511 Verone St Bellaire TX 77401-5513 Office: Rice University Dept of Chemistry MS-60 6100 Main St Houston TX 77005-1892 Fax: 713-523-8236. E-mail: margrav@rice.edu.

MARGRAVE, KATHY CHRISTINE, nurse anesthetist; b. Pittsburg, Kans., Oct. 23, 1957; d. James Raymond and Nancy Jeanne (Evans) M.; 1 child, Erica. BSN, Marymount Coll., Salina, Kans., 1980; MS, U. Kans., 1996. With St. Mary's Hosp., Manhattan, Kans., 1980; med./surg. staff nurse S.W. Jefferson Community Hosp., Louisville, 1980-81; commd. U.S. Army, 1981-93, advanced through grades to maj., 1991; operating rm. staff nurse Frankfurt Army Reg. Med. Ctr., W. Ger., 1981-85, Brooke Army Med. Ctr., San Antonio, 1985-88; sr. clin. staff nurse Dwight D. Eisenhower Army Med. Ctr., Fort Gordon, Ga., 1989-90, 91-94; 86th Evacuation Hosp., Saudi Arabia, 1990-91; neuro ICU staff nurse U. Hosp., Augusta, Ga., 1993-94. Faculty Acad. Health Scis., U.S. Army, Ft. Sam Houston, Tex. Decorated Army Commendation medal, Expert Field Medical Badge. Mem.: Am. Assn. Nurse Anesthetists. Office: Anesthesia Assocs of Savannah 8 Stephenson Ave Savannah GA 31405-5802

MARGULIES, ANDREW MICHAEL, chiropractor; b. Bklyn. s. Irving R. and Marion (Steiner) Margulies; m. Lorraine Raffa, Dec. 23, 1990; children: Samantha Cara, Maxwell Scott. D. Chiropractic, Palmer Coll. Chiropractic, Davenport, Iowa, 1981; MSc in Spinal Biomechanics, Intercontinental U., 1995. Diplomate Nat. Bd. Chiropractic, Am. Acad. Pain Mgmt., Am. Bd. Disability Analyst (sr. disability analyst), Am. Bd. Disability Analysis, cert. chiropractic sports physician. Dir., chiropractic physician Margulies Chiropractic and Sports Injuries Ctr., Massapequa, N.Y., 1981—; adminstrv. dir. Physician Multicare, 1998-2001; practice adminstr. Allied Med. and Rehab., P.C., 2001—. Chiropractor, mem. med. team N.Y. LI Marathon, 1986—, USA/Mobil Track and Field Nat. Championships, 1991—; cons. Massapequa Rd. Runners, LI, 1985—; bd. dirs. Bay Ridge Fed. Credit Union. Recipient Silver Star award, Markson/Svc. to Cmty., Flushing, N.Y., 1984, Markson Mgmt. Ann. award, 1984, Cmty. Svc. and Profl. award, Success Sys., 1993. Fellow: Am. Acad. Applied Spinal Biochem. Engring.; mem.: AAAS, APHA, N.Y. State Chiropractic Assn., Found. Chiropractic Edn. and Rsch., Am. Chiropractic Assn. (coun. sports injuries and phys. fitness, coun. diagnostic imaging), N.Y. Acad. Scis. Office: Allied Med & Rehab PC 1350 Hicksville Rd Massapequa NY 11758-1219

MARGULIES, BETH ZELDES, assistant attorney general; b. Hartford, Conn., Apr. 24, 1954; d. Benjamin and Edith Rose (Herrmann) Zeldes; m. Martin B. Margulies, July 26, 1981; children: Max, Adam. BA in Anthropology, McGill U., Montreal, 1976; JD summa cum laude, U. Bridgeport, 1983; LLM, Yale U., 1985. Bar: Conn. 1983, U.S. Dist. Ct. Conn. 1983, U.S. Ct. Appeals (D.C. cir.) 1988, U.S. Supreme Ct., 1989, U.S. Ct. Appeals (2d cir.) 1992. Asst. atty. gen. Atty. Gen.'s Office State of Conn., Hartford, 1985—. Contbr. articles to profl. jours. Home: 79 High Rock Rd Sandy Hook CT 06482-1623 Office: Atty Gen Office State of Conn 55 Elm St Hartford CT 06106-1746 E-mail: beth.margulies@po.state.ct.us.

MARGULIES, JAMES HOWARD, editorial cartoonist; b. Bklyn., Oct. 8, 1951; s. Henry Norman and Miriam Margulies; m. Martha Anne Golub, May 21, 1978; children: Elana, David. BFA, Carnegie-Mellon U., 1973. Editorial cartoonist Jour. Newspapers, Springfield, Va., 1980-84, Houston Post, 1984-90, The Record, Hackensack, N.J., 1990—. Syndicated cartoonist various newspapers, 1985—. Author: My Husband Is Not a Wimp, 1988, Hitting Below the Beltway, 1998; contbr. columns to profl. jours.; cartoons featured on TV programs. Mem. leadership com. Jewish Community Ctr., Houston, 1987, 88. Recipient Best Cartoon award Population Inst., 1985, Global Media award, 1985, 2d Place Editl. award Pavillion of Humor, 1985, Judges award World Hunger Media awards, 1986, Katie award Press Club of Dallas, 1989, Best Black and White Illustration in Advt. and Graphic Arts Addy award Houston Advt. Fedn., 1990, John Peter Zenger award N.Y. State Bar Assn., 1992, Nat. Headliner award for editl. cartoons Press Club of Atlantic City, 1996, 1st prize Fischetti Editl. Cartoon Competition, Columbia Coll., Chgo., 1996, Deadline Club award for editl. cartoons N.Y. chpt. Soc. Profl. Journalists, 1998, 1st pl. for editl. cartoons Garden State Assn. of Black Journalists, 1999, 2000; named One of Texans Who Made the Eighties Winter, Ultra mag., 1990. Mem. Assn. Am. Editl. Cartoonists. Avocation: running. Office: The Record 150 River St Hackensack NJ 07601-7155 E-mail: jimmarg@aol.com.

MARGULIES, JULIANNA, actress; b. Spring Valley, NY, June 8, 1966; BA, Sarah Lawrence Coll., 1989. Actress (film) Out for Justice, 1991, Traveller, 1997, Paradise Road, 1997, A Price Above Rubies, 1997, The Newton Boys, 1998, What's Cooking, 2000, Ten Unknowns, 2001 (Lucille Lortel Award for outstanding featured actress, 2001), The Man From Elysian Fields, 2001, Ghost Ship, 2002, (voice) Dinosaur, 1998, (TV) Murder, She Wrote, Law and Order, Homicide, Philly Heat, ER, 1994-2000 (Emmy award for supporting actress Drama, 1995, Golden Globe award nominee, SAG award nominee), The Mists of Avalon, 2001 (theater) The Substance of Fire, At Home, Fefu and Her Friends, Living Expenses, Dan Drift, and Book of Names, The Vagina Monologues, 2000. Office: c/o William Morris Agency 151 S El Camino Dr Beverly Hills CA 90212*

MARGULIES, MARTIN B. lawyer, educator; b. N.Y.C., Oct. 6, 1940; s. Max N. and Mae (Cohen) M.; m. Beth Ellen Zeldes, July 26, 1981; children: Max Zeldes, Adam Zeldes. AB, Columbia Coll., 1961; LLB, Harvard U., 1964; LLM, NYU, 1966. Bar: N.D. 1968, N.Y. 1974, Mass. 1977, Conn. 1988, U.S. Dist. Ct. Mass. 1977, U.S. Ct. Appeals (2d cir.) 1984, U.S. Supreme Ct. 1995. Asst. prof. law U. N.D., Grand Forks, 1966-69; editor-in-chief Columbia Coll. Today, Columbia U., N.Y.C., 1969-71; assoc. editor Parade Mag., 1971-72; assoc. prof. law Western New Eng. Law Sch., Springfield, Mass., 1973-76; Bernard Hersher prof. law U. Bridgeport, Conn., 1977-92; prof. law Quinnipiac U., 1992—, Neil H. Cogan Pub. Svc. prof. law, 1997-99. Author: The Early Life of Sean O'Casey, 1970; contbr. articles to profl. jours. Cooperating atty. Conn. Civil Liberties Union, Hartford, 1979—, bd. dirs., 1982-94; bd. dirs. Conn. Attys. for Progressive Legislature, New Haven, 1982; bd. dirs. ACLU, 1987-94, mem. free speech-assn. and poverty constl. rights com., 1988-94; chmn. bd. dirs. Fairfield County Civil Liberties Union, 1982-87, Hampden County Civil Liberties Union, 1976-78; bd. dirs. Civil Liberties Union Mass., Boston, 1975-78, Greater Springfield Urban League, 1976-78, Conn. Civil Liberties Union, 1982-94, ACLU, 1987-94, Ctr. for First Amendment Rights, Inc., 1993—. Recipient Media award N.Y. State Bar Assn., 1972, Gavel award ABA, 1973, Outstanding Tchr. award U. Bridgeport Law Sch., 1986, 87. Mem. Mass. Bar Assn., N.Y. State Bar Assn. Jewish. Home: 79 High Rock Rd Sandy Hook CT 06482-1623 Office: Quinnipiac Univ Sch Law 275 Mt Carmel Ave Hamden CT 06518-1947

MARGULIES, PAUL, internist, endocrinologist, educator; b. N.Y.C., Nov. 28, 1944; s. Ralph and Tillie (Sher) M.; m. Leslie Hoffer, June 18, 1967; children: Elizabeth, Suzanne. BS in Biochemistry, U. Chgo., 1966, MD, 1970. Diplomate Am. Bd. Internal Medicine with subspecialty in endocrinology and metabolism. Med. intern N.Y. Hosp., N.Y.C., 1970-71, resident in medicine, 1973-75; fellow in endocrinology Cornell U. Med. Coll., 1975-76; physician-in-chg. endocrinology dept. North Shore Univ. Hosp., Manhasset, N.Y., 1979-85, in chg. Endocrinology Clinic, 1979—, attending physician, 1989—. Clin. assoc. prof. medicine Cornell U. Med. Coll., 1991-96, NYU, N.Y.C., 1996—; med. dir. Nat. Adrenal Diseases Found., Gt. Neck, N.Y., 1985. Contbr. articles to profl. jours. Capt. U.S. Army, 1971-73. Fellow ACP, Am. Coll. Endocrinology; mem. Am. Thyroid Assn. Avocations: theater, music. Office: 444 Community Dr Manhasset NY 11030-3820

MARGULIS, ALEXANDER RAFAILO, physician, educator; b. Belgrade, Yugoslavia, Mar. 21, 1921; arrived in U.S., 1946; s. Rafailo and Olga (Weiss-Belic) Margulis; m. Hedvig Hricak, Feb. 26, 1983; 1 child Peter Hricak. Student, U. Belgrade, 1939—41; MD, Harvard U., 1950; hon. doctorates, Aix-Marseille U. Sch. Medicine, 1980, Med. Coll. Wis., 1986, Cath. U. Louvain, 1986, Karolinska Inst., Stockholm, 1986, U. Munich, 1987, U. Toulouse, 1987, U. Montpellier, 1993; student, U. Belgrade, 1945—46. Diplomate Am. Bd. Radiology. Intern Henry Ford Hosp., Detroit, 1950—51; resident in radiology U. Mich. Hosps., 1951—53; jr. clin. instr. U. Mich., 1953—54; instr., then asst. prof. U. Minn., 1954—59; asst. prof. sch. medicine Washington U., St. Louis, 1959—60, assoc. prof. to prof., 1960—63; prof. radiology, chmn. dept. U. Calif., San Francisco, 1963—89, dir. magnetic resonance Sci. Ctr., assoc. chancellor spl. projects, 1989—93, spl. cons. to vice chancellor, 1993—2000; clin. prof. radiology Cornell U. Weill Med. Coll., N.Y.C., 2000—; radiologist N.Y.-Presbyn. Med. Ctr., 2000—. Radiologist in chief U. Calif. Hosps., 1963—89; cons. VA Hosp., Letterman Gen. Hosp., San Francisco, U.S. Naval Hosp., Oakland, Calif.; cons. in radiology Office Surgeon Gen., 1967—71. Author (with others): Roentgen Diagnosis of Abdominal Tumors in Childhood, 1957; editor: Modern Alimentary Tract Radiology; co-editor: Alimentary Tract Roentgenology; editl. bd. Calif. Medicine, 1964—74, Radiology, 1975—93, assoc. editor Investigative Radiology, 1980—89; editor: Opinion in Radiology, 1988—91. Capt. U.S. Army, 1957—59. Recipient J.P. Allyn medal, P. Roberts Rsch. Inst., 1989, UCSF medal, 2000. Master: NAS-Inst. Medicine; fellow: Royal Coll. Surgeons (hon.), Royal Coll. Radiologists (hon.); mem.: Japan Radiol. Soc., Royal Coll. Surgeons Ireland, French Radiol. Soc., Swiss Radiol. Soc., Italian Radiol. Soc., Russian Acad. Scis. (fgn.), Serbian Acad. Scis. (fgn.), Soc. Magnetic Resonance in Medicine (pres. 1983), Calif. Acad. Medicine (pres. 1978), Rocky Mountain Radiol. Soc. (hon.), German Radiol. Soc. (hon.), San Francisco Radiol. Soc. (pres. 1973—74), Radiol. Soc. N.Am., Soc. Chmn. Acad. Radiology Depts. (pres. 1968—69), Am. Gastroenterology Assn., Assn. Univ. Radiologists (pres. 1966—67, chmn. adv. com. acad. radiology 1971), Roentgen Ray Soc., AMA (cons. drugs 1961—). Office: NY Presbyn Hosp Rm N-09 Box 141 525 E 68th St New York NY 10021-4870 E-mail: arm2001@med.cornell.edu.

MARGULIS, GREGORY A. mathematics educator, researcher; b. Moscow, Feb. 24, 1946; came to U.S., 1991; s. Alexander Y. Margulis and Tsilya M. Osherenko; m. Raisa T. Kristal, Aug. 30, 1972; 1 child, Boris. Diploma, Moscow U., 1967, PhD, 1970; DSc, Belorrussian Acad. Scis., Minsk, 1983. Rschr. Inst. Problems in Info. Transmission, Soviet Acad. Scis., Moscow, 1970-91; prof. math. Yale U., New Haven, 1991—. Mem. scientific adv. coun. Math. Scis. Rsch. Inst., Berkeley, Calif., 1993-97. Author: Discrete Subgroups of Semisimple Lie Groups, 1991; mem. editl. bds. several math. jours. Recipient prize for young mathematicians Moscow Math. Soc., 1968, Fields medal Internat. Math. Union, 1978, Humboldt Found. prize, 1995, Lobachevski prize Russian Acad. Scis., 1996. Mem. AAAS (fgn. hon. mem.), N.Y. Acad. Scis. Avocations: chess, jogging, swimming. Home: 20 Vista Ter New Haven CT 06515-2402 Office: Yale U Dept Math 10 Hillhouse Ave Dept Math New Haven CT 06511-6814

MARGULIS, HOWARD LEE, lawyer; b. St. Louis, Oct. 7, 1961; s. Lawrence and Rosalyn Rae (Chait) M.; m. Sharlene R. Harris, Aug. 12, 1984; children: Jennifer Lynne, Michelle Lisa, David Jonathan. BA in History, Northwestern U., 1984; JD summa cum laude, IIT, 1987. Bar: Ill. 1987, N.J. 1990, N.Y., 1999, U.S. Dist. Ct. (no. dist.) Ill. 1987, U.S. Dist. Ct. N.J. 1990, U.S. Ct. Appeals (7th and D.C. cirs.) 1989, U.S. Ct. Appeals (9th and 3d cirs.) 1989, U.S. Dist. Ct. (ea. and so. dists.) N.Y. 1998, U.S. Dist. Ct. (ea. dist.) Mich. 1998, U.S. Ct. Appeals (2d cir.) 1998; registered lobbyist, N.J. Assoc. Seyfarth, Shaw, Fairweather & Geraldson, Chgo., 1987-89, Saiber Schlesinger Satz & Goldstein, Newark, 1989-90; spl. counsel Guardian Life Ins. Co., Iselin, N.J., 1990-91; gen. counsel Energy Consortium, Inc., NJ, 1991—94, Skadden Arps Slate Meagher & Flom, Newark, 1994—99; ptnr. Baker & McKenzie, N.Y.C., 1999—2000, Squire, Sanders & Dempsey, LLP, NYC, 2001—. Active Middlesex County Human Rels. Commn., 1997—. IIT Acad. scholar, 1984-87. Mem. N.Y. State Bar Assn., NYC Bar Assn. (energy law steering com.), N.J. Assn. Energy Engrs. (sr. dir.). Democrat. Jewish. Avocation: golf. Office: 350 Park Ave New York NY 10022

MARGULIS, LYNN (LYNN ALEXANDER), biologist, educator; b. Chgo., Mar. 5, 1938; d. Morris and Leone (Wise) Alexander; m. Carl Sagan, June 16, 1957; children: Dorion Sagan, Jeremy Sagan; m. Thomas N. Margulis, Jan. 18, 1967; children: Zachary, Jennifer Margulis diProperzio. AB, U. Chgo., 1957; A.M., U. Wis., 1960; PhD, U. Calif., Berkeley, 1965. Mem. faculty Boston U., 1966—68, asst. prof. biology, 1967—71, assoc. prof., 1971—77, prof., 1977—88, Univ. prof., 1986—88; Disting. Univ. prof. U. Mass., Amherst, 1988—. Sherman Fairchild Disting. scholar Calif. Inst. Tech., 1976—77; vis. prof. dept. microbiology U. Autónoma de Barcelona, Spain, 1986, Spain, 88; Disting. univ. prof. U. Mass. Author: Origin of Eukaryotic Cells, 1970, Symbiosis in Cell Evolution, 1981, Symbiosis in Cell Evolution, 2d edit., 1993, Early Life, 1982; author: (with K.V. Schwartz) Five Kingdoms, 1982; author: (with K.V. Schwartz) Five Kingdoms, 3d edit., 1998; author: (with Dorion Sagan) Microcosmos, 1986, Origins of Sex, 1986, Garden of Microbial Delights, 1988, Garden of Microbial Delights, 2d edit. , 1993, Garden of Microbial Delights, paperback edit., 1997, Garden of Microbial Delights, 3d edit., 1998; author: (with Dorion Sagan) Biospheres From Earth To Space, 1988, Mystery Dance: On the Evolution of Human Sexuality, 1991; author: (with René Fester) Symbiosis as a Source of Evolutionary Innovation: Speciation and Morphogenesis, 1991; author: (with Lorraine Olendzenski) Environmental Evolution: The effect of the origin and evolution of life on planet Earth, 1992; author: (with L. Olendezski and H. McKhann) Glossary of Protoctista, 1993; editor (with René Fester): Global Ecology, 1989; editor: (with others) Handbook of Protoctista, 1990; editor: What Happens to Trash and Garbage: An Introduction to the Carbon Cycle, 1993; editor: (with Dorion Sagan) What is Life?, 1995; editor: (with Dorion Sagan) Slanted Truths: Essays on Gaia, Evolution and Symbiosis, 1977, What Is Sex?, 1998; editor: Looking at Microbes, An Introduction to the Microbiology Laboratory for Students, Symbiotic Planet. A New Look at Evolution, 1998; editor: (with K. V. Schwartz and M. Dolan) Diversity of Life: The Illustrated Guide to the Five Kingdoms, 2d edit., 1999; (prodr. videos of live microorganisms): ; contbr. ; author (with Michael Dolan): Early Life, 2nd edit., 2001; author: (with Dorian Sagan) Acquiring Genomes: A Theory of the Origins of Species, 2002. Recipient Nat. Medal Sci., 1999, Humboldt Prize, 2002; fellow Guggenheim fellow, 1979. Fellow: AAAS; mem.: NAS, Soc. Evolutionary Protistology (co-founder). Office: U Mass Geosci Dept 611 No Pleasant St Amherst MA 01003-2820 *We must, as E. M. Forster admonished, "only connect" and lower our population's growth rate. The sciences, the quest for knowledge about the universe, life and man, are intrinsically united. Like all other species ever to have lived on Earth, ours too will be replaced. The quality of that demise depends directly on our attitudes towards our planetmates, our growth, death and their control.*

MARGULIS, MICHAEL HENRY, lawyer; b. N.Y.C., Oct. 30, 1959; s. David H. and Eleanor Weinberg Margulis; m. Amy M. Sturmer, Mar. 19, 1989; children: Rebekah Geri, Daniel Aaron. AB, Princeton (N.J.) U., 1981; JD, Stanford U., 1984. Bar: N.Y. 1985. Assoc. Shea & Gould, N.Y.C., 1984-93, ptnr., 1993-94, Duane Morris LLP, N.Y.C., 1994—. Office: Duane Morris LLP 380 Lexington Ave New York NY 10168-0002

MARIAM, THOMAS FRED, public relations executive, radio producer; b. N.Y.C., Feb. 26, 1957; s. Rudolph Karl and Lisa Gertrude (Silbermann) Mariam; m. Alyce Beth Appleman, Aug. 20, 2000; 1 child Michael Reese. BA in Polit. Sci., Columbia U., 1978; MS in Broadcast Journalism, Boston U., 1980. News dir. Sta. WNBP, Newburyport, Mass., 1979-80; sports dir. Sta. WKCR-FM, N.Y.C., 1976-78; editor, writer The Wall St. Jour. Report, 1980-84; nat. copy editor Dow Jones News Svc., 1984; dir. news svcs. Am. Stock Exch., 1984-95; sr. v.p. Rubenstein Assocs. Pub. Rels., 1995-96; sr. mgr. pub. rels. Booz-Allen & Hamilton, 1996-99; dir. mktg. and comm. Cadwalader, Wickersham & Taft, 1999-2000; dir. global comm. Clifford Chance Rogers & Wells LLP, 2000—02; pres. Mariam Comms. LLC, 2002—. Radio sports reporter Sports Final Radio Network, Boston, 1987—; N.Y. corr. The Sports File, 1989-93. Producer, host (radio program) Amex Business Talk, 1985-94; producer, anchor (radio feature) Sports Folks, 1987-89. Voting mem. Self-Help, Inc., N.Y.C., 1985-92; trustee Congregation Habonim. Mem. ABA, Legal Mktg. Assn., N.Y. Fin. Writers Assn. (bd. dirs. 1992—), Radio-TV News Dirs. Assn., Pub. Rels. Soc. Am., Deadline Club N.Y., Nat. Assn. Broadcasters, Nat. Assn. Sportscasters and Sportswriters, Columbia Club N.Y. (dir.-at-large 1984-96, activities chmn. 1986-94, 1st v.p. 1988-96). Democrat. Jewish. Home: 6 Bonnit Rd Port Chester NY 10573-1937 E-mail: tfm0226@aol.com.

MARIANI, DAVID FRANK, artist; b. Buffalo, Jan. 19, 1942; s. Guido James and Mable Lucretiam (Pantano) M.; children: Mack David, Todd James. Asst. art dir. Gelia and Wells Advt., Snyder, N.Y., 1967-72; art dir. Rich Advt., Buffalo, 1972-74, Mainspring Advt., Buffalo, 1974-76; freelance illustrator N.Y., 1976-86; sr. artist rsch. and devel. Fisher-Price, East Aurora, 1986-88, sr. project artist, 1988-93, illustrator, art dir., product stylist, 1993—. Instr. visual communications SUNY, Buffalo, 1974-78, lectr. casual comms., 1999; with editorial dept. Courier-Express, Buffalo, 1982. Com. chmn. Elma (N.Y.) Wheat and Barley Festival, 1991. With USAF, 1960-64. Recipient 1st place Addy award Am. Advt. Fedn., 1973. Mem. Graphic Artist Guild Western N.Y.

(pres., co-founder 1981-82), Art Dirs. Club Buffalo (best of show, 1978). Republican. Roman Catholic. Avocations: bagpipe music, rodeo clowning. Home and Office: 14 Portsmouth Terr Ste 4 Rochester NY 14607 E-mail: sylvia4159@aol.com.

MARIANO, ANA VIRGINIA, pathologist; b. Baguio City, The Philippines, Nov. 20, 1938; came to U.S., 1963; d. Celestino Chuongco and Ana (Tanseco) Juan; m. Gregorio Torres Mariano, June 4, 1966; children: Joel, Eric, Greg, Anita. AA, U. St. Tomas, Manila, 1957, MD, 1962. Bd. cert. in anatomic pathology and clin. pathology Am. Bd. Pathology; lic. physician, N.Y., Pa. Med. intern Youngstown (Ohio) Hosp., 1963; pathology resident I R.I. Hosp., Providence, 1964; pathology resident II-IV Wayne State U. Med. Sch., Detroit, 1965-68; assoc. pathologist Newark-Wayne Comty. Hosp., Newark, 1979-83; interim pathologist Clifton Springs (N.Y.) Hosp., 1983; lab. dir. VA Med. Ctr., Altoona, Pa., 1996-97, staff pathologist, 1997-99. Locum tenens Altoona (Pa.) Hosp., 1999-2001; mem. courtesy med. staff Newark-Wayne Cmty. Hosp., 1983-92, Clifton Springs (N.Y.) Hosp., 1983-89; mem. adv. bd. Cath. Physicians Guild, Rochester, N.Y., 1991-92; cons. in pathology VA Med. Ctr., Altoona, 1993-96. Tchr. religious edn. St. Michael's Ch., Newark, 1978-80, 82-84. Fellow Am. Soc. Clin. Pathologists, Coll. Am. Pathologists. Roman Catholic. Avocations: swimming, aerobics, gardening. Home and Office: 320 Bristol Ln Hollidaysburg PA 16648-2901

MARIANO, RAYMOND V. former mayor; b. Worcester, Mass., Sept. 23, 1950; m. Antonia Kouvaros; children: Gina Marie, Raymond, Anthony. BA in Sociology, Worcester State Coll., 1974; MPA, Clark U., 1982. Former cons. various polit. campaigns; co-founder Mariano & Wright, 1984—; mayor City of Worcester, 1993—2001. Mem. Worcester Sch. Com., 1975-81; mem City Coun., 1981—, vice chmn., 1985-87; chmn. Pub. Works and Rules Com.*

MARICK, MICHAEL MIRON, lawyer; b. Chgo., Nov. 20, 1957; s. Miron Michael and Geraldyne Marilyn (Lid) M.; m. LIsa Amy Gelman, May 17, 1986. BA, Denison U., 1979; JD, Ill. Inst. Tech., 1982. Bar: Ill. 1982, U.S. Dist. Ct. (no. dist.) Ill. 1982, Fla. 1983, U.S. Ct. Appeals (3rd cir.) 1988, U.S. Ct. Appeals (6th cir.) 1992, U.S. Supreme Ct. 1992. Assoc. Hinshaw, Culbertson, Moelmann, Hoban & Fuller, Chgo., 1982-85, Phelan, Pope & John, Chgo., 1985-90; ptnr. Pope & John, 1990-94, Meckler Bulger & Tilson, Chgo., 1994—. Adj. prof. Ill. Inst. Tech./Chgo.-Kent Coll. Law, 1983-84, 87-99; comml. arbitrator Am. Arbitration Assn., Chgo., 1983—. Mem. Ill. Inst. Tech./Chgo.-Kent Law Rev., 1980-82; contbr. articles on ins. law and litigation to profl. jours. Treas., mem. exec. com. 42d Ward Rep. Orgn., 1984-87. Denison U. Econs. fellow, 1978, State of Ill. Gov.'s fellow, 1978; recipient Disting. Svc. award Ill. Inst. Tech./Chgo. Kent Coll. Law, 1996. Mem. ABA (mem. exec. com., com. on legis. action young lawyers divsn. 1983-84, vice chmn. TIPS excess surplus lines and reins. com. 1990-92), Ill. Bar Assn. (ins. law sect. coun. 1991-96, chair 1994-95, assembly rep. 1993-96), Fla. Bar Assn., Chgo. Bar Assn., Def. Rsch. Inst., Internat. Assn. Def. Counsel, Ill. Inst. Tech./Chgo.-Kent Coll. Law Alumni Assn. (v.p. 1990-94, pres. 1994-95), Trial Lawyers Club, Omicron Delta Upsilon, Pi Sigma Alpha, Alpha Tau Omega. Presbyterian. Home: 3605 Pebble Beach Rd Northbrook IL 60062-3109 Office: Meckler Bulger & Tilson 123 North Wacker Dr Ste 1800 Chicago IL 60606-6339 E-mail: michael.marick@mbtlaw.com.

MARICLE, ROBYN LUANN (FORD), band director, choir director; b. Waco, Tex., Dec. 29, 1959; d. Robert Charles and Peggy Lou (Brown) Ford; m. Dale Louis Maricle; children: Alan Louis, Aaron Lee. AA, McLennan C.C., 1981; MusB Edn., Baylor U., 1984. Cert. all-level music. Asst. dir. of music First United Meth. Ch., Waco, Tex., 1977—95, music sec., 1982—84; music tchr. Waco I.S.D. (Mountainview Elem.) , 1984—85; music tchr. Waco I.S.D. (Parkdale Elem.), 1990—99; dir. music Florence United Meth. Ch., Florence, 1995—98; choral dir. middle sch. and hs Lorena I.S.D., Lorena, 1999—2002. Cub scout/boy scout leader Pack 308/Troop 308, Waco, 1991—2001; chmn. worship com. Mooreville United Meth. Ch., Mooreville, 2000—02, leader children's time, 1999—2002; asst. leader for youth Mooreville United Methodist Ch., 2000—02; youth Sunday sch. tchr. Mooreville United Meth. Ch., 2001—02. Recipient Harry Hosier award, Ctrl. Tex. Conf. of the United Meth. Ch., 2000. Mem.: Ctrl. Tex. Conf. Music Edn., Music Educators Nat. Conf., Tex. Music Educator Assn. Methodist. Avocations: outdoors, crafts. Home: 1029 Fm 1239 Eddy TX 76524-2442 Office: Lorena ISD PO Box 97 Lorena TX 76655 Office Fax: 254-857-3419. Business E-Mail: RobynMaricle@lorena-isd.net.*

MARICQ, HILDEGARD RAND, physician, researcher; b. Rakvere, Estonia, Apr. 23, 1925; came to U.S., 1954; d. August and Elvine Rosalie (Vunderlich) Rand; m. John George Maricq, Oct. 9, 1948; children: Michel Matti, Andres Villu, Peter Toivo. Candidate in natural and med. sci., Free U., Brussels, 1946-49, MD, 1953; post-doctoral fellow, Columbia U., 1965-67. Clin. investigator VA Hosp., Lyons, N.J., 1963-65, dir. Schizophrenic Research Sect., 1970-73; post-doctoral fellow in psychology Columbia U., N.Y.C., 1965-67, research assoc., 1973-75; assoc. profl. research medicine Med. U. S.C., Charleston, 1975-81, prof. research medicine, 1981—. Contbr. articles to sci. jours. Mem. Am. Physiol. Soc., Am. Rheumatism Assn., Microcirculatory Soc., Soc. Psychophysiol. Research, Soc. Biol. Psychiatry. Office: Med U SC Div Rheumatology 171 Ashley Ave Charleston SC 29425-0001

MARIE, LINDA, artist, photographer; b. Cheverly, Md., Nov. 8, 1960; d. Thomas Grason Jr. and Rosalinda (Wepf) McWilliams; 1 child, Ann Marie. AA with honors, Cecil C.C., North East, Md., 1991. One-woman shows include Franklin Hall Arts Ctr., Chesapeake City, Md., 1993, Humanities and Arts Gallery-Essex (Md.) C.C., 1993, Widener Art Mus., Chester, Pa., 1996, Gallery B.A.I., N.Y.C., 1997, Environ. Elements Corp., Balt., 1999-2000; group exhbns. include Del. Ctr. Contemporary Art, Wilmington, 1991, Md. Fedn. Art, Annapolis, 1991-93, Acad. of Arts, Easton, Md., 1992, Elkton (Md.) Arts Ctr., 1990-92, Md. Gallery East, Havre de Grace, 1992, Chautaqua (N.Y.) Inst., 1992, Washington Project for Arts, 1992, Ward-Nasse Gallery, N.Y.C., 1994, Sinclair C.C., Dayton, Ohio, 1994, AAAS, Washington, 1994-95, ACP, College Park, Md., 1994, Gallery B.A.I., Barcelona, Spain, 1996, Sullivan County Mus., N.Y., 1997, Gallery Art Addiction, Stockholm, 1997, Sharon Art Ctr., Peterborough, N.H., 1998; represented in permanent collections at AAAS, Cecil C.C. Mem. Del. Ctr. Contemporary Arts, Md. Fedn. Art, Cecil County Arts Coun., Alpha Alpha Theta. Address: 6 W Walnut St North East MD 21901-4132 E-mail: witsendbengals@sprynet.com., wghadyk@sprynet.com.

MARIEN, ROBERT, producer, director, naturalist, photographer, designer; b. San Juan, P.R., Oct. 3, 1952; came to U.S., 1980; s. Jorge Marién and Conchita Hernáiz. BS, U. Sacred Heart, Santurce, P.R., 1976; MS, U. P.R., 1978; MFA, Calif. Inst. Arts, 1982. Producer Dept. Natural Resources, San Juan, 1976-77; film editor Guastella Film Producers, Inc., 1977-78; dir. photography Publi Co-Op, 1978-79; photographer Expo-Foto 80, 1980; prodn. photographer M3 Effects, Inc., North Hollywood, Calif., 1982-83; film research Dennis Film Services, Inc., Hollywood, 1983-84; cinema coordinator XXIII Olympic Games, Los Angeles, 1984; host spl. shows Universal Studios Tour, Inc., Universal City, Calif., 1984-86; prodn. asst. Columbia Picture Industries, Inc., Burbank, 1984-86; cameraman Jerry Kramer Prodns., Inc., Hollywood, 1986; prof. basics of filmmaking Art Ctr. Coll. Design, Pasadena, 1986-87; producer promotions, copywriter Sta. KVEA-TV, Glendale, 1986-88; contractor, producer Spanish TV/radio spots The Disney Co., 1989—. Owner, photographer Stock Photo Agy., Rom-Ma Stock Images, Pasadena, Calif., 1989—; prof. cinema and scis., documentary prodr. Columbia Coll., Hollywood, 1989-95; interior/exterior designer; watergardens designer. Producer, dir., editor: (documentaries) Marine Environments, 1977, The Forests of Puerto Rico, 1978 (Environmental award 1979), (visual essay) Sojourn Earth, 1982 (Gold medal 1982, Filmex 1983, Golden Halo 1984, Gold Lone Star award Houston Internat. Film & Video Festival, 1988); producer, cameraman The VIII PanAmerican Games in Puerto Rico, 1979; producer, cameraman Through the World of Nutrition, 1979; dir. photography, cameraman Chef's Delight, 1983; dir. photography The Puerto Rican Cuatro, 1978, Celebrity On Course, 1985; camera asst. The Computer Question, 1983. Prodr., dir., editor: (documentaries) Marine Environments, 1977, The Forests of Puerto Rico, 1978 (Environmental award 1979), (visual essay) Sojourn Earth, 1982(Gold medal 1982, Filmex 1983, Golden Halo 1984, Gold Lone Star award Houston Internat. Film & Video Festival 1988); prodr., dir. Documentary for Frank Capra Jr., 1997; prodr., cameraman The VIII Pan-American Games in Puerto Rico, 1979, Through the World of Nutrition, 1979; dir. photography, cameraman Chef's Delight, 1983; dir. photography The Puerto Rican Cuatro, 1978, Celebrity on Course, 1985; camera asst. The Computer Question, 1983. E-mial. Office: Ro-Ma Stock Images PO Box 50983 Pasadena CA 91115-0983 E-mail: romastock@aol.com.

MARIENCHILD, EVA, consultant, editor, writer; b. N.Y.C., Mar. 24, 1957; d. Benjamin Beauchamp de Jesus Rodriquez and Marien (Engracia) Martinez-Ceberio. Student, Dominican Comml. Sch., 1976. Acct. mgmt. exec. sec. Warwick, Welsh & Miller, N.Y.C., 1978-80; chem. patent trademark paralegal Davis, Hoxie, Faithfull & Hapgood, 1980-82; dir. publicity, exec. sec. Waring & LaRosa Advt., 1981-82; assoc. acct. exec. Stiefel/Raymond Advt., 1982-83; copy editor personal fin. E.F. Hutton, 1983-84; acct. exec. Anderson Stone & Jason, 1984-85; v.p. sales Computer Rsch. Tabs, 1985-86; pres., CEO Collection Resource Team, 1986—, Eva Marienchild Cons., N.Y.C., 1988—; copywriter Del Labs., N.Y., 1999—. Dir. promotion Motion Picture & TV Media Registry, N.Y.C., 1983; copywriter, translator Del Labs., 1999—. Editor, pub. Sidelines mag., 1984, various newsletters; contbr. to Seventeen mag., others. Graphic artist fin. div. UNICEF, N.Y.C., 1983; collaborator sci. and tech. entry program Manhattan Coll.; co-creator, overseer Pub. Assistance Group Recertification Coordination, County of Nassau, Dept. Spl. Svcs., 1993-99. Mem. NAFE, Am. Women's Econ. Devel. Avocations: voice, sketching, handwriting analysis, classic lit., classical music. Home and Office: 1444 Park Ave Merrick NY 11566

MARIENTHAL, GEORGE, telecommunications company executive; b. Kansas City, Mo., Nov. 15, 1938; s. George and Sadie (James) M.; children: Shawn Ann Capon, Patrick James, Shannon Lee Van Winter. BS, U.S. Naval Acad., 1962; MS, Stanford U., 1963; MBA, Am. U., 1974. Sr. rsch. assoc. Logistics Mgmt. Inst., Washington, 1967-71; dir. regional ops. EPA, 1971-75, dir. water policy, 1984-85; dep. asst. sec. def. Dept. Def., Washington, 1975-81; v.p. Survival Tech., Inc., Bethesda, Md., 1981-84; dep. asst. sec. agr. Dept. Agr., Washington, 1985-86; dep. adv. programs Titan Systems, Inc., 1986-87; mgr. mktg. Computer Scis. Corp., Falls Church, Va., 1987-89; dir. WorldCom, Inc., McLean, 1989—. Bd. dirs. Home Security Title Ins. Co. Served with USAF, 1962-67. Mem.: Internat. Telephone Pioneers Assn., Armed Forces Comms. and Electronics Assn., Masons. Republican. Episcopalian. Home: 2157 Sandcastle Ct Annapolis MD 21403-5505 E-mail: george.marienthal@wcom.com.

MARIER, ROBERT L. dean, hospital administrator; b. Mar. 29, 1943; m. Joanne Marier; 2 children. AB, Boston Coll., 1965; MD, Yale U., 1969; MHA, Tulane U., 1990. Diplomate Am. Bd. Internal Medicine. Intern in internal medicine Mass. Gen. Hosp., Boston, 1969-70, asst. resident in medicine, 1970-71; epidemic intelligence svc. officer Nat. Ctr. Disease Control USPHS, Atlanta, 1971-73; clin. rsch. fellow in inflammatory disease Yale U., New Haven, 1973-75, asst. prof. medicine, 1975-78; assoc. prof. medicine La. State U., New Orleans, 1978-83, acting head sect. infectious disease, 1982-83, dir. intro. to clin. medicine, 1982-85, dir. residency program, 1982-86, prof. medicine, 1983—; dir. adult closed care Charity Hosp., 1982-83, dir. office infection control, 1982—89, asst. dean, 1986—89, assoc. med. dir., 1986-88; Dean LSU School of Med, 1989—. Vis. physician Yale-New Haven Hosp., 1975-78; mem. La. State AIDS Task Force, 1985—; mem. Met. Hosp. Coun. New Orleans, 1988—; physician advisor La. Health Care Review, New Orleans, 1991—. Mem. editorial bd. Infections in Surgery, 1983-88, Jour. Orthopedics, 1983—, AHPS Drug Info. Monographs, 1986—. Remsey Meml. scholar Yale U., 1968—; rsch. fellow in infectious disease NIH, 1975-77. Fellow ACP, Infectious Disease Soc. Am.; mem. AMA, Am. Soc. Microbiology, Am. Fedn. Clin. Rsch., So. Soc. Clin. Investigation, La. State Med. Soc., Orleans Parish Med. Soc., Alpha Omega Alpha. Office: La State U Med Ctr 1542 Tulane Ave New Orleans LA 70112-2825*

MARIL, DAVID C. editor; b. Balt., Apr. 2, 1950; s. Herman and Esta Cook Maril. BA in English, Clark U., 1972. Sports editor News Recorder, Worcester, Mass., 1972-75, Milford (Mass.) Daily News, 1975-2000; news copy editor Brockton (Mass.) Enterprise, 2000—. V.p. Herman Maril Paintings, Balt., 1995—; sports editor AP Assn. Editor, writer Baseball Odyssey supplements, 1977-98 (award UPI 1988); columnist Off the Field, 1999. Bd. dirs. Highwood Condo Assn., Franklin, Mass., 1995—; mem. cable adv. com. Town of Franklin, 1988-91; mem. art adv. bd. Univ. Coll. of Univ. Md., 2001—. Recipient sports column awards UPI, 1986, 87, New Eng. Newspaper Assn., Boston, 1999, Cmty. Newspapers, Needham, Mass., 1999. Mem. Baseball Writers Assn. (Hall of Fame voter), Soc. Baseball Rsch., Boston Baseball Writers (bd. dirs.). Avocations: reading, cinema history, baseball history. Home: 37 Highwood Dr Franklin MA 02038

MARIMOW, WILLIAM KALMON, journalist; b. Phila., Aug. 4, 1947; s. Jay and Helen Alma (Gitnig) M.; m. Diane K. Macomb, Oct. 18, 1969; children: Ann Esther, Scott Macomb. BA, Trinity Coll., Conn., 1969. Asst. editor Comml. Car Jour., Chilton Co., Bala Cynwyd, Pa., 1969-70; asst. to econ. columnist Phila. Bull., 1970-72; staff writer Phila. Inquirer, 1972—, city hall bur. chief, 1979-81, editor Main Line Neighbors, 1986-87, N.J. editor, 1987-89, city editor, 1989-91; city editor, asst. to pub. Phila. Inquirer and Daily News, 1991-93; met. editor Balt. Sun, 1993, assoc. mng. editor, 1993-95, mng. editor, 1995-2000, editor, sr. v.p., 2000—. Instr. urban studies U. Pa., 1979; instr. English Rutgers U., Camden, NJ, 1981; nominating jury Pulitzer Prize, 1991—92, 1996—97, 2002; bd. fellows Trinity Coll., 1998—2000; mem. adv. bd. Knight Ctr. for Specialized Journalism at U. Md., 1999—2000; bd. visitors U. Md. Sch. Journalism, 2000—. Recipient 1st pl. award for team reporting Phila. Press Assn., 1977, 1st pl. award for deadline reporting AP Mng. Editors of Pa., 1977, Pub. Svc. awards, 1978, 85, Nat. Pub. Svc. award Sigma Delta Chi, 1978, 1st pl. award for best news story Sigma Delta Chi Phila., 1977, 2nd pl. award for deadline reporting, 1980, Pub. Svc. awards, 1978, 85, Pub. Svc. awards Sigma Delta Chi N.J., 1978, Pulitzer prize for disting. pub. svc., 1978, Pulitzer prize for investigative reporting, 1985, Silver Gavel award ABA, 1978, 82, Roy W. Howard Pub. Svc. award Scripps-Howard Found., 1978, Robert F. Kennedy Journalism award, 1978, 2nd pl. award for investigative reporting Keystone Press Assn., 1978, 85, 1st pl. award for best news story, 1982, Media Achievement award Phila. Bar Assn., 1982, William Schnader award Pa. Bar Assn., 1982, Nat. Headliners award, 1985, Trinity Coll. Alumni Achievement award, 1984; Nieman fellow Harvard U., 1982-83. Mem. Am. Soc. Newspaper Editors, Pen and Pencil Club, Investigative Reporters and Editors, Inc. Home: 1025 Winding Way Baltimore MD 21210-1232 Office: The Baltimore Sun PO Box 1377 501 N Calvert St Baltimore MD 21278-0001

MARIN, CYNTHIA MYERS (CHERYL MARIN), systems engineer; b. Rocky Mount, Va., July 17, 1958; d. Edward Douglas and Ethel Beatrice (Cassidy) Myers. AAS in Avionics Tech., C.C. Air Force, 1982, AAS in Electronics Engring., 1987; BSEE, Ariz. State U., 1987; MS in Indsl. Engring., U. Ctrl. Fla., 1998. Cert. program mgr., acquisition mgr., electronics engr., space comm. engr., network contr. Avionics specialist USAF, Luke AFB, Ariz., 1976-78, avionics technician, analyst Eglin AFB, Fla., 1978-81, instr. leadership, mgmt. Zaragoza AFB, Spain, 1981-84, office tng. program Tempe, Lackland AFB, Ariz., Tex, 1984-88, engr. space comms. Vandenberg AFB, Calif., 1988-90, sys. engr., network contr. Cape Canaveral, Fla., 1990-92; mgr. ITTFSC, Cocoa Beach, 1992-93; mgr. integrated product LORAL, Rockledge, 1993-95; mgr. engring. Lockheed Martin, 1996-99, program mgr., sys. engr. Gaithersburg, Md., 1999—. Mem. AFCEA (past dir., pres., life), Air Force Assn. (life), Tau Beta Pi, Eta Kappa Nu. Avocations: space sci., education. Home: 45639 Paddington Sta Ter Sterling VA 20166 Office: Lockheed Martin 182 700 N Frederick Ave Gaithersburg MD 20879 E-mail: cynthia.c.marin@lmco.com.

MARIN, DEBORAH B. psychiatrist, educator; b. Cleve., Oct. 9, 1957; d. Emanuel and Klara Blumenthal; m. Michael Marin; children: Lea, Max. BA, Wellesley Coll., 1979; MD, Mt. Sinai Med. Sch., 1984. Vice chair, prof. psychiatry Mt. Sinai Med. Ctr., N.Y.C., 1992—. Office: Mt Sinai Med Ctr PO Box 1230 New York NY 10029-0313

MARIN, ROSARIO, federal agency administrator; m. Alex Marin; children: Eric, Carmen, Alex. Grad., Calif. State U., L.A., Harvard U. Chief legis. affairs Calif. Dept. Devel. Svcs.; chair Calif. State Coun. Developmental Disabilities; asst. dep. dir. Calif. State Dept. Social Svcs.; dep. dir. Gov.'s Office Cmty. Rels., L.A.; mayor, councilwoman City of Huntington Park; 41st U.S. treas. U. S. Dept. Treasury, Washington, 2001—. Office: US Dept Treasury Treas US 1500 Pennsylvania Ave NW Washington DC 20220

MARINACCIO, CHARLES LINDBERGH, lawyer, consultant; b. Stratford, Conn., Dec. 10, 1933; BA, U. Conn., 1957; JD with honors, George Washington U., 1962. Bar: Conn. 1962, D.C. 1982. Trial lawyer U.S. Dept. Justice, Washington, 1963-69; advisor supervisory and regulation div. Fed. Res. Bd., 1969-73; dir., exec. sec. law enforcement asstistance adminstrn. U.S. Dept. Justice, 1973-75; gen. counsel banking housing and urban affairs com. U.S. Senate, 1975-84; commr. SEC, 1984-85; ptnr. Kelley, Drye & Warren, 1985-94; ind. cons., 1995—. Apptd. by Pres. Clinton to bd. dirs. Securities Investor Protection Corp.; bd. dirs. AmeriTrade Holding Corp., Omaha. Home and Office: 4911 Massachusetts Ave NW Washington DC 20016-4310

MARINACE, KENNETH ANTHONY, financial advisor; b. N.Y.C., May 2, 1944; s. Anthony and Hilda Marinace; children: Steven Joseph, Douglas Anthony. Student, Am. Inst. Fin., 1962-63, Am. Coll., 1975; CLU, Coll. Fin. Planning, 1981. CFP, CFP Bd. Owner, CEO Comprehensive Fin. Svcs., Burbank, Calif., 1967—. Bd. dirs. Life Underwriters Assn. L.A., 1980-82. Host radio series You and Your Money, 1988-90, TV series You and Your Money, 1990—. Bd. dirs. San Gabriel coun. Girl Scouts U.S., Arcadia, Calfi., 1987, Burbank Family YMCA, 1989, Econ. Coun., Mus. Sci. and Industry, L.A., 1990-93, Providence, St. Joseph Med. Ctr. Found., 1997—, Burbank corps Salvation Army, 1996-99; mem. adv. panel Royal Alliance Assocs., Inc., N.Y.C., 1989-91; pres. Burbank Cmty. Healthcare Found., 1989. Recipient Bus. Person of Yr. award Profl. Econs. Svcs., 1974, Outstanding Citizen Commendations, City of Burbank, 1988, 98, City of L.A., 1988, 98, County of L.A., 1993, 98, Calif. State Senate, 1998, Calif. State Assembly, 1998. Mem. Fin. Planning Assn., Inst. CFP, Kiwanis (bd. dirs. Burbank Found. 1989—), Oakmont Country Club, Jonathan Club. Avocations: golf, music, travel. Office: Comprehensive Fin Svcs 3811 W Burbank Blvd Burbank CA 91505-2116

MARINCHEK, SCOTT MICHAEL, entrepreneur; b. Park Ridge, Ill., Nov. 6, 1966; s. John Andrew and Connie (Ruttin) M. BS in Econs., U. Pa., Phila., 1988. Trader Phibro Energy-Salomon Bros., Westport, Conn., 1987-91; v.p. Credit Suisse Fin. Products, London, 1991-94; dir. Merrill Lynch, 1994-96, The Conquistador Group, London, 1995—. Committeman Rep. Party, Phila., 1987. Named Derivatives Superstar Global Fin. mag., 1995. Office: 287 Regent St Ste 10 London W1R 7PB England Home: 2529 New Haven Cir Sun City Center FL 33573-7136

MARINCOLA, ELIZABETH MARK, scientific society executive; b. New Haven, Aug. 31, 1959; d. James B.D. and Jean M. (Rambar) Mark; m. Francesco M. Marincola, Jan. 1, 1982; children: James Paul, Paula Rambar, Rachel Angela. AB, Stanford U., 1981, MBA, 1986. Dir. devel. Stanford (Calif.) U. Hosp., 1987-90; dep. dir. policy rsch. analysis NIMH, Rockville, Md., 1990-91; exec. dir. The Am. Soc. Cell Biology, Bethesda, 1991—. Mem. cell biology com. of visitors NSF, 2001; com. for divsn. on earth and life studies Nat. Acad. Sci., 2001—; mem. PubMed Ctrl. Nat. adv. com. Nat. Libr. of Medicine Nat. Inst. Health, 2000—; 20th Annual Fae Golden Kass lectr. Harvard Med. Sch., 1999. Home: 10110 Chapel Rd Potomac MD 20854-4143 Address: Amer Society for Cell Biology 8120 Woodmont Ave Suite 750 Bethesda MD 20814-2755 E-mail: emarincola@ascb.org.

MARINCOLA, JOHN, classics educator; b. Phila., Dec. 14, 1954; Student, Swarthmore Coll., 1972-74; BA magna cum laude, U. Pa., 1979; PhD, Brown U., 1985. Instr. Coll. Holy Cross, Worcester, Mass., 1984-85, asst. prof., 1985-86; vis. asst. prof. Union Coll., Schenectady, N.Y., 1986-88, asst. prof., 1989-93, assoc. prof., 1994-97; exec. dir. Am. Philol. Assn., 1997-99; assoc. prof. of classics NYU, N.Y.C., 1999—. Vis. rschr. Inst. Alte Geschichte U. Munich , Germany, 1989—90; Astor vis. lectr. Oxford U., 2002—. Author: Authority and Tradition in Ancient Historiography, 1997, (introductory matters and notes) Herodotus: The Histories, 1996, Greek Historians, 2001; corr. Histos. A New Jour. of Ancient Historiography, 1996—; reviewer, contbr. numerous articles to profl. jours. William A. Michaelides fellow in Greek studies, 1983, jr. fellow Ctr. Hellenic Studies-Harvard U., Washington, 1999-2000; faculty scholar Brown U., 1983-84; recipient Deutscher Akademischer Austauschdienst stipendium, 1990. Mem. Interna. Plutarch Soc., New Eng. Ancient History Colloquium, Cambridge Philol. Soc., Classical Assn. (Eng.), Classical Assn. Atlantic States, Classical Assn. Empire State, Columbia U. Classical Civilization Sem., Women's Classical Caucus, Assn. Ancient Historians. Home: Apt 9-I 2 Washington Sq Village New York NY 10012 Office: Dept of Classics NYU New York NY 10003 Fax: (212) 995-4209. E-mail: john.marincola@nyu.edu.

MARINE, ANDREW CRAIG, lawyer; b. Norman, Okla., Nov. 3, 1960; s. I. Wendell and Helen R. (Landsman) M. BA in Polit. Sci., BS in Gen. Bus., Va. Poly. Inst. and State U., 1982; JD, U. S.C., 1985. Bar: S.C. 1986, U.S. Dist. Ct. S.C. 1988. Assoc. Huguenin, Trueblood & Floyd, Martinez, Ga., 1986-87; ptnr. Floyd & Marine, Aiken, S.C., 1987-93; pvt. practice, 1993—. Chmn. Aiken County Young Republican Com., 1986-89; treas. Aiken County Rep. Party, 1989-95, chmn., 1995-97; mem. City of Aiken Election Commmn., 1988-98, S.C. State Ethics Commn., 1998—, vice chmn., 2000-01, chmn., 2001—; bd. dirs. Golden Harvest Food Bank, 1995—; dist. chmn. Boy Scouts Am., 1997-2000. Mem. ABA, S.C. Bar Assn., Aiken C. of C., Sunrise Rotary (pres. 2000-01), Phi Alpha Delta. Republican. Home: 1010 Williams Dr Aiken SC 29803-5372 Office: 106 Trafalgar St Aiken SC 29801

MARINE, CLYDE LOCKWOOD, agricultural business consultant; b. Knoxville, Tenn., Dec. 25, 1936; s. Harry H. and Idelle (Laue) M.; m. Eleanor Harb, Aug. 9, 1958; children: Cathleen, Sharon. BS in Agr., U. Tenn., 1958; MS in Agrl. Econs., U. Ill., 1959; PhD in Agrl. Econs., Mich. State U., 1963. Sr. market analyst Pet Milk Co., St. Louis, 1963-64; mgr. market planning agr. chems. div. Mobile Chem. Co., Richmond, Va., 1964-67; mgr. ingredient purchasing Central Soya Co., Ft. Wayne, Ind., 1970-73, corp. economist, 1967-70, v.p. ingredient purchasing, 1973-75, sr. v.p., 1975-90; pres. Marine Assocs., 1991—; bd. dirs. SCAN, 1992—. Mem. agrl. policy adv. com. U.S.D.A. Bd. dirs. Ft. Wayne Fine Arts Found., 1976-79, Ft. Wayne Pub. Transp. Corp., 1975-83, Libr. Found.; commr. Metro Human Rels. Commn.; v.p. Ft. Wayne Philharm., 1974-76. Served with U.S. Army, 1959-60. Mem. Nat. Soybean Processors Assn. (chmn.), U.S. C. of C., Am. Agrl. Econs. Assn., Am. Feed Mfrs. Assn. (chmn. purchasing coun.). Clubs: Ft. Wayne Country. Episcopalian. Office: Marine Assocs 4646 W Jefferson Blvd Fort Wayne IN 46804-6842 E-mail: lmarine@attglobal.net.

MARINE, MICHAEL R. healthcare company executive; b. Mar. 12, 1954; BS in Econs. and Pub. Policy, Cornell U., 1976; MPH in Hosp. Adminstrn., Tulane U., 1979. CPA, Md. Asst. dir. reimbursement Georgetown U., Washington, 1988-90; divsn. mgr. Columbia/HCA, Ft. Lauderdale, Fla., 1995-97; CFO Pharmacy Svcs. Group, 1999—. Seminar leader Bus. Network, Nashville, 1995—; nat. seminar instr. Optimizing Medicare Reimbursement, 1995—. Home: 16792 Royal Poinciana Dr Fort Lauderdale FL 33326-1541 E-mail: mmarine@rxmail.com.

MARINE, SUSAN SONCHIK, analytical chemist, educator; b. Maple Heights, Ohio, Mar. 10, 1954; d. Stephen Robert and Gloria Ann (Hach) Sonchik; m. Michael David Marine; 1 child, Matthew Robert Marine. BS in Chemistry magna cum laude, John Carroll U., 1975; MS in Analytical Chemistry, Case Western Res. U., 1978, PhD in Phys. Chemistry, 1980. Asst. chemist Horizons Research Inc., Beachwood, Ohio, 1974-75; chemist specialist Standard Oil of Ohio, Warrensville Heights, 1975-79; organic chemistry br. mgr. Versar, Inc., Springfield, Va., 1980-83; mgr. gas chromatography program IBM Instruments Inc., Danbury, Conn., 1983-87, radiation safety officer, 1985-87; expert witness, cons. Martin, Craig, Chester & Sonnenschein, Chgo., 1981-83; adv. engr. in advanced lithography IBM Corp., Essex Junction, Vt., 1987-95; vis. assoc. prof. chemistry Centre Coll., Danville, Ky., 1995-98; asst. prof. chemistry and biochemistry, coord. tech. program Miami U., Middletown, Ohio, 1998—. Vis. asst. prof. chemistry and math. Heritage Coll., 1991-92; spkr. in field. Author: African Walking Safari, 1985; editorial adv. bd. Jour. Chromatographic Sci., 1977-93, guest editor, 1987. Mem. Danbury Conservation Commn., 1986-87, tchr. and tutor chemistry, 1985-89, 91-92, 94; troop leader Lake Erie coun. Girl Scouts U.S.A., 1971-80, Southwestern

Conn., 1983-87; leader explorer post Cleve. coun. Boy Scouts Am., 1977-78; managerial advisor Jr. Achievement, Warrensville Heights, Ohio, 1977-78; judge State or Regional Sci. Fair, 1977, 80, 89-91, 99, 2000, Odyssey of the Mind, 1994; asst. leader Internat. Folk Dancers, Newtown, Conn., 1985-87; tchr. religion, 1981-84, 87-90, 93-94. Recipient Overall Best Paper award Eastern Analytical Symposium, 1984, First Gas Chromatograph award IBM Instruments Inc., 1985, contbn. award (tech. paper) 10th Internat. Congress of Essential Oils, Flavors, Fragrances, Washington, 1986. Mem. ASTM (exec. com. E-19 1985-2000, chmn. subcom. 1986-2000, vice chmn. arrangements 1994-98), Am. Chem. Soc. (chmn. membership com. Green Mountain sect. 1988-89, chair elect 1989-90, chmn. 1990-91, local coord. Nat. Chemistry Week 1991, 93-98, 2002, Phoenix award 1994, 97), Iota Sigma Pi (pres. N.E. Ohio chpt. 1978-79, mem.-at-large fin. mgr. 1993-97, nat. v.p. 1996-99, nat. pres. 1999-2002, immediate past pres. 2002-), No. Vt. Canoe Cruisers (treas. 1990-92), Green Mountain Steppers (sec. 1993-95), Centre Coll. Outdoors Club (faculty liaison 1996-98). Roman Catholic. Avocations: camping, dancing, travel. Home: 4667 Sebald Dr Franklin OH 45005-5328 Office: Miami U Middletown 4200 E University Blvd Middletown OH 45042-3458 E-mail: mariness@muohio.edu.

MARINELLI, JOSEPH MARCELLO, aerospace advisor; b. Phila., Aug. 15, 1948; s. William Marinelli and Lillian (Nicolena) Navarro. Grad. high sch., Phila. Aerospace advisor Rissler Sci. Orgn., Phila., 1982—. Mem. Air Force Assn. (life), U.S. Naval Inst. (life), Navy League (life), Am. Def. Preparedness Orgn. (life), World Future Soc. (life), Tailhook Assn. (life), Assn. Am. Politics (life), Assn. Naval Aviation (life), Cruiser Olympia Assn. Inc. (life), F-4 Phantom 2 Soc. (life), Am. Aviation Hist. Soc. (life), Nat. Space Soc., Planetary Soc., Nat. Air and Space Soc. Democrat. Roman Catholic. Home: 2141 S 21st St Philadelphia PA 19145-3502

MARINER, WILLIAM MARTIN, chiropractor; b. Balt., Jan. 2, 1949; s. William Joseph and Ellen (Dexter) M. AA, Phoenix Coll., 1976; BS in Biology, D Chiropractic summa cum laude, L.A. Coll. of Chiropractic, 1980; DD (hon.), Universal Life Ch., Modesto, Calif., 1986. Health food restaurant mgr. Golden Temple of Conscious Cookery, Tempe, Ariz., 1974-75; health food store mgr. Guru's Grainery, Phoenix, 1975; physical therapist A.R.E. Clinic, 1975-76; research dir., founder G.R.D. Healing Arts Ctr., 1974-77; aminstrv. asst., acad. dean L.A. Coll. Chiropractic, Whittier, Calif., 1977-80; faculty Calif. Acupuncture Coll., L.A., 1978-80; ednl. cons. Avanti Inst., San Francisco, 1985-91; found, dir., head clinician Pacific Healing Arts Ctr., Del Mar, Calif., 1980-93, Mt. Shasta, 1993—. Ednl. cons. John Panama Cons., San Francisco, 1991-99. Patentee in field. Co-dir. "We Care We Share" Charitable Orgn., San Diego, 1985-86. Named Outstanding Sr., L.A. Coll. Chiropractic, 1980. Mem. Calif. Chiropractic Assn., Am. Chiropractic Assn., Internat. Coll. Applied Kinesiology, Holistic Dental Assn., Brit. Homopathic Assn. Avocations: Yoga, meditation, personal growth, natural healing methods, cooking. Office: Pacific Healing Arts Ctr PO Box 192 Mount Shasta CA 96067-0192 E-mail: wmariner@jps.net.

MARINESCU, DAN CRISTIAN, computer sciences educator, consultant; b. Craiova, Dolj, Romania, Mar. 4, 1942; s. Nicolae and Aurelia Marinescu; m. Gabriela Magdalena Sezon; children: Andrei. PhD in EECS, Polytechnic Inst., Bucharest, Romania, 1972—75. Prof. computer sci. Purdue U., West Lafayette, Ind., 1984—2001, U. Ctrl. Florida, Orlando, 2001—02; sr. rschr. GSI, Darmstadt, Germany, 1980—84, Inst. Atomic Physics, Bucharest, Romania, 1965—79; assoc. prof. Polytechnic Inst., Romania, 1970—79. Vis. prof. INRIA Rocquencourt, Paris, 2000—00, Paris, 1999—99, IBM Rsch., Yorktown Heights, NY, 1985—85, Intel Supercomputer Sys., Portland, 1992—92. Author: Internet-Based Workflow Management, 2002; contbr. articles to profl. jours. Recipient Grand Challenge, National Science Foundation, 1995-2002, Virtual Lab for Computational Biology, Nat. Sci. Found., 2001—, Workflow Management, 2001—, 3D Reconstruction of Viruses, 2000—. Greek Orthodox. Avocations: skiing, photography, travel. Home: 14449 Dover Forest Dr Orlando FL 32828 Office: Computer Sci Dept UCF 4000 Central Florida Blvd Orlando FL 32816

MARINETTI, GUIDO V. biochemistry educator; b. Rochester, N.Y., June 26, 1918; s. Michael and Nancy (Lippa) M.; m. Antoinette Francione, Sept. 19, 1942; children: Timothy D., Hope L. BS, U. Rochester, 1950, PhD, 1953. Research biochemist Western Regional Lab., Albany, Calif., 1953-54; instr. U. Rochester, N.Y., 1954-57, asst. prof., 1957-60, assoc. prof., 1960-66, prof. sch. medicine and dentistry, 1966—97; prof. emeritus dept biochemistry and biophysics, 1997—. Cons. Eastman Kodak, 1978, Rochester Gas & Electric, 1979 Author: Disorders of Lipid Metabolism, 1990; editor: Lipid Chromatographic Analysis, 3 vols., 1969, 2nd edit., 1976; contbr. 160 pub. articles in sci. jours. Served with USAAF, 1942-46. Recipient Nat. Infantile Paralysis award, 1952; recipient Glycerine Research award, 1957; NSF grantee, 1953; recipient Lederle Med. Faculty award, 1955, 56 Mem. Am. Soc. Biol. Chemists, Am. Chem. Soc., AAAS, Sigma Xi, Phi Beta Kappa Achievements include research in membrane structure and function, biochemistry of phospholipids, phosphatidylinositiol metabolism in isolated synaptomsomes.

MARING, NORMA ANN, military academy administrator; b. Humboldt, Kans., Oct. 1, 1933; d. Edward Simon and Anna Agnes (Friederich) Breiner; m. L. Keith Maring, Dec. 27, 1951 (dec. July 1988); children: Stan, Steve, Scot, Ron. Grad. high sch., Chanute, Kans. Cert. swimming pool operator. Instr. dance, water safety courses Wentworth Mil. Acad., Lexington, Mo., 1968-91, alumni dir., 1979—. Operator Chanute Mcpl. Swimming Pool, 1956—; water safety trainer ARC, Kans., Mo., 1969-1996. Bd. dirs., chmn. water safety Neosho County unit ARC, Chanute, 1965—85; pres. Lexington PTA, 1960—64, Lafayette County PTA, 1965—70; active Wentworth-Lexington Cmty. Coun., 1991—2000. Recipient Disting. Svc. award Nat. ARC, 1982, Employee of the Month, Outstanding Pub. Rels., City of Chanute, 1993, Pub. Cmty. Svc. award, 1993; named 1st hon. alumnus Wentworth Mil. Acad. Alumni Assn., 1992; coll. scholarship in her name given by PTA Coun., Chanute, 1982. Mem.: Kans. Swimming Pool Assn., Kans. PTA (hon.), Kans. PTA (life), Am. Contract Bridge League, Gen. Fed. Women's Club (pres. Lexington 1970—72), Lexington Garden Club (v.p. 1969—70), Wentworth Mil. Acad. Alumni Assn. (sec. coun. 1986—, named 1st hon. mem. 1992, dedication Norma Maring Alumni Hall 2000). Roman Catholic. Avocations: bridge, swimming. Home: 1622 South St Lexington MO 64067-1432 Office: Wentworth Mil Acad 18th and Washington Sts Lexington MO 64067

MARIN-GARCIA, JOSE, researcher, cardiologist; b. Lorqui, Spain; s. Jose and Facunda Marin; m. Daniele M. Marin, July 1, 1967; 1 child, Melanie. MD, Granada, Spain, 1960. Dir. The Molecular Cardiology and Neuromuscular Inst., Highland Park, NJ, 1993—. Office: The Molecular & Neuromuscular Cardiology Inst 75 Raritan Ave Highland Park NJ 08904-2442 E-mail: tmci@att.net.

MARINI, ANN MARIE, medical researcher, educator; b. Stamford, Conn., May 27, 1949; d. Alfred Francis Marini and Theresa Marchitto; m. Robert Henry Lipsky, Sept. 6, 1990; 1 child, Sarah. BA, Erskine Coll., 1971; PhD, Georgetown U., 1978, MD, 1980. Diplomate Am. Bd. Internal Medicine, Am. Bd. Psychiatry and Neurology. Med. resident U. Mass., Worcester, 1980-83; neurology resident Albert Einstein Coll. Medicine, Bronx, N.Y., 1983-86; post-doctoral fellow NIH, Bethesda, Md., 1986-93; staff neurologist Dept. Vet. Affairs, Washington, 1993-94; asst. prof. Uniformed Svcs. U. Health Scis., Bethesda, 1994-2001, assoc. prof., 2001—. Mem. Am. Acad. Neurology (tech. and therapeutics subcom. 1994-99), Soc. for Neurosci., Sigma Xi. Office: Uniformed Svcs U Health Scis 4301 Jones Bridge Rd Bethesda MD 20814-4712 E-mail: ann.marini@na.amedd.army.mil.

MARINI, DOMINIC , JR. elementary and secondary education educator; b. Niagara Falls, N.Y., Nov. 18, 1950; s. Dominic and Maria M.; m. Patricia S. Plunkett, Mar. 23, 1974; children: Dawn Davina, Dominic III. BA, Roberts Wesleyan Coll., 1972; M in Tchg., Niagara U., 1976; postgrad., Rochester Inst. Tech., 1990. Tchr. Niagara Wheatfield Sch., Sanborn, N.Y., 1974-80, Fairport (N.Y.) Ctrl. Sch., 1982—. Mem. Am. Fedn. Tchrs., N.Y. State Tchrs. Assn. Roman Catholic. Avocations: little league baseball, pony league baseball, club volleyball.

MARINI, JOHN JOSEPH, medical scientist, educator, physician; b. Syracuse, N.Y., Oct. 6, 1946; s. Warren John and Theresa Josephine (Palermo) M.; m. Margaret Elizabeth Mooney, June 13, 1970. B in Engring. Sci., Johns Hopkins U., 1969, MD, 1973. Intern internal med. U. Wash., Seattle, 1973-74, resident internal med., 1974-76, fellow respiratory diseases, 1976-78, asst. prof., assoc. prof. medicine, 1978-83; assoc. prof. medicine Vanderbilt U., Nashville, 1983-89; prof. medicine U. Minn., Mpls., St. Paul, 1989—; dir. pulmonary and critical care medicine St. Paul-Ramsey Med. Ctr./Regions Hosp., 1989—; chief academic medicine Regions Hosp., 1997—. Chmn. critical care section Am. Thoracic Soc., 1989-90; mem. policy and exam writing com. Am. Bd. Internal Medicine, 1991-96; disting. Simmons lectr. UCLA, 1991; Eagan Sci. lectr. Am. Assn. for Respiratory Care, 1992. Author 7 books on pulmonary and intensive care; mem. editl. bds. 5 profl. jours.; contbr. numerous articles to profl. jours. Named one of Outstanding Pulmonologists/Critical Care Physicians in U.S., Town & Country, 1989, 95, One of Best Doctors in Am. Woodward Whyte, 1992, 95, 97, 99; recipient Lifetime Achievement award Am. Assn. Respiratory Care, 1998. Fellow Am. Coll. Chest Physicians (Cecil Lehman Mayer award 1980, 86), Am. Bd. Internal Medicine; mem. ACP, European Soc. Intensive Care, European Respiratory Soc., Am. Thoracic Soc., Soc. Critical Care Medicine. Avocations: skiing, tennis, foreign languages, computer science. Office: Regions Hosp 640 Jackson St Saint Paul MN 55101-2502

MARINI, ROBERT CHARLES, environmental engineering executive; b. Quincy, Mass., Sept. 29, 1931; s. Larry and Millie (Cirillo) M.; m. Myrna Lydia Pellegrini, June 26, 1955 (dec. June 1994); children: Debra, Robert Charles, Larry; m. B. Anne Jones, May 27, 1995. BSCE with honors, Northeastern U., 1954, hon. dr., 1997; SMSE, Harvard U., 1955, postgrad. Advanced Mgmt. Program, 1985. Registered profl. engr., Mass., N.Y., Calif., Mich., Fla., Va. Jr. engr. Camp Dresser & McKee Inc., Boston, 1955-56, project engr., 1958-64, assoc., 1964-67, ptnr., sr. v.p., 1967-77, pres. environ. engring. div., 1977-82, exec. v.p., 1982-84, pres., 1984-90, CEO, 1989-98, chmn. bd. dirs., 1998—99, vice chmn. bd. dirs., 1999-2001, chmn. emeritus, 2001—. Mem. civil engring. adv. com. Worcester (Mass.) Poly. Inst., 1985-90, U. Mass., 1986-90, U. Tex., Austin, 1989-91, chmn., 1991-92, mem. engring. found. adv. coun., 1991-98; active South Shore Savs. Bank, 1990—. Contbr. articles to profl. jours. Dir. nat. coun. Northeastern U., Boston, 1983—, mem. corp. bd., 1983—, bd. overseers, 1985-89, trustee, 1989—; chmn. Leadership Phase Century II Fund, 1989-91, chmn. devel. com., 1991-98, vice chmn. bd. trustees, 1997—; bd. dirs. Mass. Bus. Round Table, 1991-99, vice chmn., 1995-97, chmn., 1997-99. Recipient Disting. Eagle Scout award Boy Scouts Am., 1986, Mass. Patriots award Old Colony Coun., 1998, W. Erwin Story award, 1991, Outstanding Civil Engring. Alumni award Northeastern U., 1992, Outstanding Alumni award, 1993; named Man of Yr., Don Orione, 1999. Fellow ASCE (hon.), NAE, Boston Soc. Civil Engrs. (hon.); mem. Am. Pub. Works Assn. (Man of Yr. award New Eng. chpt. 1981), Am. Water Works Assn., Mass. Soc. Profl. Engrs. (Young Engr. of Yr. award 1966), Am. Acad. Environ. Engrs. (diplomate, trustee at large 1989-92, v.p. 1992-93, pres.-elect 1993-94, pres. 1994-95, Stanley E. Kappe award 1992), Water Environment Fedn. (hon., N.E. chpt., Founders award 1999), Internat. Assn. Water Pollution Rsch. and Control, Engring. Soc. New Eng. (New Eng. award 1994), Greater Boston C. of C. (bd. dirs. 1997-99), Water Environ. Rsch. Found. (bd. dirs. 1998-2001), Tau Beta Pi, Phi Kappa Phi. Roman Catholic. Home: 1 Nevin Rd Weymouth MA 02190-1610 Office: Camp Dresser & McKee Inc 50 Hampshire St Cambridge MA 02139

MARINIS, THOMAS PAUL, JR. lawyer; b. Jacksonville, Tex., May 31, 1943; s. Thomas Paul and Betty Sue (Garner) M.; m. Lucinda Cruse, June 25, 1969; children: Courtney, Kathryn, Megan. BA, Yale U., 1965; LLB, U. Tex., 1968. Bar: Tex. 1968. Assoc. Vinson & Elkins, Houston, 1969-76, ptnr., 1977—. Bd. dirs. Phoenix House of Tex., Inc., Covenant House Tex. Fellow Tex. Bar Found.; mem. ABA (sec. taxation sect. 1986-87), Houston Country Club, Houston Ctr. Club, Coronado Club. E-mail: tmarinis@velaw.com.

MARINO, EUGENE LOUIS, publishing company executive; b. N.Y.C., Jan. 7, 1929; s. Salvatore A. and Florence M. (Casabona) M.; m. Patricia Ryan, Mar. 11, 1948; children: Jeanette, Anthony, John, Eugene III. Student, Columbia U., 1945-48. Credit mgr. Sears, Roebuck Inc., L.I., N.Y., 1951-60; gen. credit mgr. Davison-Paxon div. R.H. Macy, Inc., Atlanta, 1960-63, Grand-Way div. Grand Union Co., N.Y.C., 1963-66; v.p., gen. credit mgr. Consumer Products div. Singer Co., 1966-75, Grolier, Inc., Danbury, Conn., 1975-90; ret. Officer, v.p., gen. credit mgr., dir. numerous subsidiaries. Recipient Quarter Century cert. Internat. Consumer Credit Assn., 1981. Mem. Mchts. Research Council, Internat. Consumer Credit Assn., Nat. Assn. Credit Mgmt., Alpha Sigma Phi. Home: 4858 Tivoli Ct Sarasota FL 34235-3653 E-mail: elmarino@comcast.net.

MARINO, IGNAZIO ROBERTO, transplant surgeon, educator, researcher; b. Genoa, Italy, Mar. 10, 1955; s. Pietro Rosario and Valeria (Mazzanti) M.; m. Rossana Parisen-Toldin, Sept. 15, 1990; 1 child, Stefania Valeria. Maturità-Classica, Coll. of Merode, Rome, 1973; MD, Cath. U., Rome, 1979. Diplomate Nat. Bd. Gen. Surgery, Nat. Bd. Vascular Surgery. Intern, then resident Gemelli U. Hosp., Rome, 1979-84; temp. asst. dept. surgery Cath. U., 1981, asst. prof. surgery, 1983-92; asst. prof. surgery Transplantation Inst. U. Pitts., 1991-95, assoc. prof. surgery Transplantation Inst./, 1995-99, prof. surgery, 1999—; prof. surgery postgrad. Sch. Microsurgery, Exptl. Surgery U. Milan, 1994—; prof.surgery Sch. Medicine U. Perugia, 1994—; attending surgeon U. Pitts. Med. Ctr., Pitts., 1991—; assoc. dir. transplant divsn. VA Med. Ctr., 1992—; attending surgeon Children's Hosp. Pitts., 1993—; prof. surgery Transplantation Inst., U. Pitts., 1999—. Mem. surg. team 1st and 2d baboon to human liver transplants U. Pitts. Med. Ctr., 1992, 93, dir. European med. divsn., 1995—; sci. journalist Agenzia Nazionale Stampa Associata, 1992—; mem. nat. ad hoc donations com. United Network for Organ Sharing, 1995—; dir. Ist. Mediterraneo per i Trapianti e Terapie ad Alta Specializzazione, 1997—; cons. Nat. Transplant Com. Italy, 1999—; mem. regional com. Organ Procurement Orgn. for Sicily, 1999—; mem. Nat. Tech. Commn. for Informative Campaign on Organ Donation of Italy, 1999—, Nat. Ctr. for Transplantation of Italy, 2000—. Author: New Technique to Avoid the Revascularization Syndrome in Liver Transplantation, 1985 (Ann. prize Italian Soc. Surgery, 86), New Technique in Liver Transplantation, 1996 (De Angelis award, 86); mem. editl. bd.: Clin. Transplantation, mem. editl. bd.: Leadership Medica, mem. editl. bd.: Transplantation, mem. editl. bd.: Jour. Investigative Surgery; contbr. over 500 articles to profl. jours. Grantee Italian Nat. Coun. Rsch., 1979, 86, 87, 88, 89-93, Gastroenterology Soc., 1988; recipient award Instituto Nazionale Previdenza Dirigenti Aziende Industriali, 1982. Mem. ACS, Am. Soc. Transplantation Surgeons, Am. Soc. Transplant Physicians, Italian Soc. Surgery, Transplantation Soc. (grant 1988), European Soc. for Organ Transplantation, Soc. Surgeons Under 40 (ann. prize 1986), Cell Transplant Soc. (founding mem.), Acad. Surg. Rsch., Soc. Critical Care Medicine, Internat. Liver Transplantation Soc., Italian Order Journalists, Assn. Italian Corrs. in N.Am. (assoc.), Xenotransplantation Club (founding mem.), Internat. Coll. Surgeons, Assn. for Acad. Surgery, Nat. Assn. VA Physicians, Univ. Physician Practice Assn., Xenotransplantation Assn., Am. Assn. for the Study of Liver Diseases. Avocations: reading (history books), sailing, yoga, Annibale (pet cat). Home: Corso Italia 29 Rome 00198 Italy Office: U Pitts Transplantation Inst European Med Divsn 200 Lothrop St Ste 10097 Pittsburgh PA 15213-2546 E-mail: marinoir@msx.upmc.edu.

MARINO, JOSEPH THOMAS, physician; b. Bklyn., Apr. 25, 1947; s. Joseph Thomas and Jeannette Theresa (Pontolillo) M.; m MAry Alice Dubuisson, Sept. 18, 1976; children: Joseph, Katherine. BS, Boston Coll., 1968; BMS, Dartmouth U., 1970; MD, Harvard U., 1972. Diplomate Am. Bd. Pediats., Am. Bd. Allergy and Immunology, Am. Bd. Pediat. Pulmonology. Intern Johns Hopkins Hosp., Balt., 1972-73; resident USPHS/NIH, 1973-75, Children's Hosp., Boston, 1975-77, fellow, 1977-79; pvt. practice Carmichael, Calif., 1982—; assoc. med. dir. Children's Hosp., Fresno, 1980-82; dir. pediat. ICU Valley Med. Ctr., 1979-80. Fellow Am. Acad. Pediats., Am. Coll. Chest Physicians, Am. Acad. Allergy, Asthma and Immunology; mem. Am. Thoracic Soc., Calif. Thoracic Soc., Calif. Med. Assn., Sacramento Med. Assn. Avocations: jogging, travel, wine, foods, biostatistics. Office: 6555 Coyle Ave Ste 215 Carmichael CA 95608-0303

MARINO, MICHAEL FRANK, III, lawyer; b. Little Falls, N.Y., Feb. 19, 1948; s. Michael Frank and Betty (Roberts) M.; m. Catherine Viladesau, Aug. 31, 1970 (div. Nov. 1996); m. Ann Buttfield Feb. 15, 1997; children: Michael John, Lisa Kathryn, Matthew Christopher. BS, Cornell U., 1971; JD, Syracuse U., 1974; LLM, Georgetown U., 1982. Bar: D.C. 1975, U.S. Dist. Ct. D.C. 1975, U.S. Ct. Mil. Appeals 1975, N.Y. 1976, U.S. Dist. Ct. (ea. and we. dists.) Va. 1977, U.S. Dist. Ct. Md. 1980, U.S. Ct. Appeals (4th cir.) 1982, Va. 1982, U.S. Ct. Appeals (9th cir.) 1994. Civilian employee head rels. br. Office of the Judge Adv. of the Navy, Washington, 1975-76; spl. asst. to the gen. counsel Office of Sec. of Navy, 1977; asst. gen. counsel labor and employment Office of the Gen. Counsel of the Navy, 1978; assoc. Pierson, Ball & Dowd, 1978-81; ptnr. Boothe, Prichard & Dudley, Fairfax and Mc Lean, Va., 1981-87, McGuire, Woods, Battle & Boothe, Mc Lean, 1987-89, Reed, Smith, Shaw & McClay, N.Y.C., 1989-2000, Hunton & Williams, McLean, Va., 2000—. Labor group head, Washington, Va.; mng. ptnr. McLean Office. Author: Virginia Employer's Guide to Labor Law, 1982; co-author: New York Employer's Guide, 1989, 1992—2001, Florida Labor and Emloyment Law, 2001, Labor Employment Law in Pennsylvania, 1994. Mem. planning com. SMU Multi State labor Law Conf., Dallas; chmn. Arlington (Va.) Chamber Employee Rels. Com.; bd. dirs. Arlington Chamber; mem. Va. Chamber Mgmt. Rels. Com. Richmond, 1980—; bd. dirs. Dan Marino Found. Capt. USMC, 1971-78. Mem.: ABA (labor law com. 1974—), Fairfax Bar Assn. (Pro Bono award 2000), N.Y. Bar Assn. (labor law com. 1974—), Va. Bar Assn. (labor law com. 1974—, sec.-treas. labor law sect. 1995, vice chair 1996—97), D.C. Bar Assn. (labor law com. 1974—). Roman Catholic. Avocations: fitness, boating. Office: Hunton & Williams 1751 Pinnacle Dr Ste 1700 Mc Lean VA 22102-3836 E-mail: mmarino@hunton.com.

MARINO, MIGUEL ANGEL, engineering educator; b. Cienfuegos, Cuba, Nov. 10, 1940; s. Ramon and Julia Marino; m. Irma Padovani, July 27, 1968; 1 child, Raquel Christina. AA, Andrew Coll., 1959; BS, N.Mex. Inst. of Mining and, Tech., Socorro, 1962, MS, 1965; PhD, UCLA, 1972. Cert. profl. hydrologist, Am. Inst. Hydrology. Asst. geohydrologist N.Mex. State Engrs. Office, Santa Fe, 1964; asst. hydrologist Ill. State Water Survey, Champaign, 1965-69; asst. prof. U. Calif., Davis, 1972-76, assoc. prof., 1976-80, prof., 1980-99, dir. hydrology program, 1996-98, prof. above-scale, 1999—. Author: (book) Groundwater and Seepage, 1982; editor: (monograph) Subsurface Flow and Contamination, 1987, (book) Integrated Water Resource Management, 2001, Regional Management of Water Resources, 2001, Integrated Water Resources Management, 2001, Regional Management of Water Resources, 2001, (jour.) Jour. of Water Resources Planning and Mgmt., 1984-88; contbr. articles to profl. jours. Bd. dirs. Univs. Coun. on Water Resources; v.p. Internat. Commn. Water Resource Sys. Recipient Richard R. Torrens award Am. Soc. Civil Engrs., 1986. Fellow Am. Water Resources Assn.(hon. mem.), Am. Geophys. Union; mem. ASCE (hon. mem. 1999, Outstanding Jour. Paper awards 1986, 90, Julian Hinds award 1996), N.Y. Acad. Scis., Am. Water Resources Assn., Am. Inst. Hydrology, Internat. Assn. Hydrol. Scis. (Best Paper award), Tau Beta Pi, Sigma Xi. Home: 813 Harrier Pl Davis CA 95616-0173 Office: Univ Calif 139 Veihmeyer Hall Davis CA 95616

MARINO, NANCY A. marketing professional; b. N.Y.C., Aug. 11; d. Thomas and Ruth Firriolo; m. J. Richard Marino. BA in Mktg., Hunter Coll., 1971. Exec. v.p. AMC, N.Y.C., 1990—97; pres., CEO Frederick Atkins, 1997—99; pres. Linmark, 1999—. Bd. dirs. USA-ITA, N.Y.C., Cotton Inc., N.Y.C.; mem. steering com. Fashion Group Internat., N.Y.C., 1999—. Mem. found. bd. Fashion Inst. Tech., N.Y.C., 1999—. Mem.: Retail Mktg. Soc. (bd. dirs. 1998—). Office: Linmark 485 Seventh Ave Ste 611 New York NY 10018 Business E-Mail: nmarino@gxmart.com.

MARINO, NATALIE MARIE, artist; b. Elizabeth, N.J., July 4, 1951; d. John T. and Stefana (Sarullo) Marino; m. Anthony Paul D'Alessio, Aug. 28, 1968 (div. 1998); 1 child, Stephanie Elsbeth; m. Brian James Blackmore, Mar. 27, 1998; children: Jonathan Brian, Ronnie Marin, Stefana. BA, NYU, 1969; postgrad., New Sch., N.Y.C., 1969-72; cert., N.J. Ctr. Visual Arts, 1977. One-woman shows include Exxon Corp., Linden, N.J., 1985, Florence Gallery, Dallas, 1985, Rosalyn Sailors, Phila., 1993, ART Insights, N.Y., Marino Galleries, Millburn, N.J., 1994, 96; exhibited in group shows at N.J. State Mus., 1979, Bergen Cmty. Mus., Paramus, N.J., 1980, Nat. Art Club, N.Y.C., 1981, Lincoln Ctr., N.Y.C., 1983, Cork Art Gallery, N.Y.C., 1983, Phila. Port of History Mus., 1984, numerous others; represented in permanent collections, including Rosalyn Sailor Gallery and Mus. Fine Art, Margate, N.J., Phila., Tom Weiner's Art Insights, N.Y.C., Marino Galleries, Inc., Millburn; contbr. illustrations to books; author: (screenplay) The Successor, 1989; illustrator: Art Lovers Cookbook, 1975; host cablecast series Art Forum; prodr., dir. video and TV programs. Vol. cons. N.J. Ctr. for Visual Arts, Summit, 1989; trustee TV 36, Communities on Cable, Summit, 1989; judge for sr. citizen art shows, Newark, 1989. Recipient Bee Co. award Pastel Soc. Am., 1981, European Banner of Arts, Accademia d'Europa, 1984, award-artists grant Union County Divsn. of Art and Cultural Affairs; N.J. state Coun. for Arts grantee Union County Cultural Commn., 1985-86, Ludwig Vogelstein Found. grantee, 1989. Fellow Artists Equity, Women's Caucus for Art, Riker Hill Art Park (exec. com.); mem. N.J. Ctr. Visual Art (award 1979). E-mail: fine-art-gallery.com. Home: PO Box 225 Springfield NJ 07081-0225

MARINO, PAMELA ANNE, health sciences administrator; b. Milford, Conn., Feb. 28, 1951; d. Angelo and Christine M. BA in Biology with honors, U. Conn., 1973; PhD in Biomed. Scis., U. Conn., Farmington, 1986. Rsch. assoc. to lab. supr. Yale Med. Sch., New Haven, 1973-80; from postdoctoral fellow to sr. staff fellow Nat. Cancer Inst., Bethesda, Md., 1986-93; sr. staff fellow FDA, 1993-94; program dir. Nat. Inst. Gen. Med. Scis., 1994—. Contbr. articles to profl. jours. Tchr. NIH Sci. Alliance with Pub. Schs., Rockville, Md., 1994-96. Conn. State scholar, 1969-73; U. Conn. fellow, 1980-86, Nat. Cancer Soc. fellow, 1986-90; recipient Performance award NIGMS, 1994, 98, 99, 2000, 01, 02. Mem. Fedn. Am. Socs. Exptl. Biology, Am. Soc. Biol. Chemists and Molecular Biologists, Women in Cancer Rsch. (co-chair mentoring com. 1995-96, chair database com., chair commns. com. 1995—, selection com. 1998—), Am. Assn. for Cancer Rsch. (edn. com.). Home: 17128 King James Way Apt 201 Gaithersburg MD 20877-2219 Office: Nat Inst Gen Med Scis 45 Center Dr Bethesda MD 20892-0001

MARINO, PAUL MICHAEL, science education educator; b. Hazleton, Pa., Nov. 1, 1945; m. Joan M. Marino, June 12, 1976; children: Kristen, Jeffrey, Jonathan. MEd in Biology, Pa. State U., 1971, MEd in Earth Sci., 1973, PhD, 1976. Lic. tchr., Pa., N.J., N.Y., Mass. Assoc. prof. Del. Valley Coll., Doylestown, Pa., 1992—. Mem. ASCD, Phi Delta Kappa. Office: Del Valley Coll 700 E Butler Ave Doylestown PA 18901-2607

MARINO, RONALD VINCENT, pediatrician, educator; b. Dec. 11, 1950; BS, SUNY, Brockport, 1972; MPH, U. Okla., 1973; DO, Mich. State U., 1978. Bd. cert. Am. Osteo. Bd. Pediatrics; cert. pediatric advanced life support instr. Am. Heart Assn., 1988—. USPH traineeship U. Okla., 1972-73; grad. asst. dept. cmty. medicine Mich. State U. Sch. Medicine, Coll. Osteo. Medicine, 1974-75, rsch. fellow dept. biomechanics, 1975-78; intern Doctor's Hosp., Columbus, Ohio, 1978-79, resident, chief resident, 1979-81; attending physician Kennedy Meml. Hosp.-Univ. Med. Ctr., Stratford, N.J., 1981-86; chief Ctr. for Ambulatory Pediatrics Interfaith Med. Ctr., Bklyn. (N.Y.) Jewish Hosp., 1986-87; chmn. quality assurance com. dept. pediatrics Winthrop U. Hosp., Mineola, N.Y., 1987—, dir. ambulatory and behavioral pediatrics, dept. pediatrics, 1987-93, dir. gen. pediatrics, dept. pediatrics, 1993—, assoc. dir. faculty devel., 1997—. Instr. health edn. SUNY, Coll. Brockport, N.Y., summer 1974; clin. faculty Ohio U. Coll. Osteo. Medicine, Athens, 1979-81; biomechanics cons. Doctors Hosp. Divsn. Osteo. Svcs., Columbus, 1980-81; pediatric cons. State of Ohio, Dept. Mental Health, Ctrl. Ohio Adolescent Ctr., Columbus, 1981; attending pediatrician Cooper Med. Ctr., Camden, N.J., 1982-85; chief sch. physician Mineola (N.Y.) Union Free Sch. Dist., 1991—, Westbury (N.Y.) Union Free Sch. Dist., 1992—; lectr. in field; clin. assoc. prof. pediatrics SUNY, Stony Brook, 1987-96, clin. prof., 1996—; adj. asst. prof. pediatrics N.Y. Coll. Osteo. Medicine, 1986-89, adj. prof., 1989-98, prof., 1998—; clin. asst. prof. pediatrics SUNY, Bklyn., 1986-87; asst. prof. pediatrics U. Medicine and Dentistry N.J., 1982-86, clin. asst. prof., 1981-82; cons. Nat. Bd. Osteo. Med. Examiners, 1987-90, exec. com. Nassau County Regional Planning Group for Early Intervention Svcs., 1988-91, HHS, 1990, Mich. State U., 1991, assoc. chair Community Affairs dept Pediatrics, Winthrop U. Hosp., 1999—. Editorial cons.: Jour. Devel. and Behavioral Pediatrics Patient Care, Jour. Am. Osteo. Assn., Clin. Pediatrics; contbr. articles to profl. jours. Recipient award of excellence Mich. Assn. Osteo. Physicians and Surgeons, 1978, Cmty. Advocacy award Am. Cancer Soc., 1998. Fellow Am. Acad. Pediatrics (catch facilitator 1997), Am. Coll. Osteo. Pediatricians (Pediatrician of Yr. award 1998); mem. APHA, Am. Coll.

Osteopathic Physicians (mem. residency tng. com., evaluation com., chmn. cont. med. edn. com.), Am. Osteo. Assn., Soc. for Behavioral Pediatrics, Ambulatory Pediatric Assn. (nat. faculty devel. scholar 1997-99, chmn. faculty devel. spl. interest group 1998—), Am. Acad. for Cerebral Palsy and Devel. Medicine, Nassau Pediatric Soc. (exec. coun. 1996—, v.p. 1998-99, pres. 2000-2001). Office: Winthrop Univ Hosp 259 1st St Mineola NY 11501-3987 E-mail: RMarino@winthrop.org.

MARINO, WILLIAM FRANCIS, telecommunications industry executive, consultant; b. Phila., Dec. 28, 1948; s. William F. and Edith Ellen (Dougherty) M.; m. Mary Ellen Klems, Sept. 29, 1979; children: Kiersten Leigh, Meghan Lyn. Student, Ohio State U., 1967; BS in Fin. and Acctg., Widener U., 1970. Sr. acctg., fin. positions U.S. Steel Corp., Pitts., 1970-83; v.p. U.S. Steel Credit Corp., 1983-85; dir. fin. programs CIS Corp., Syracuse, N.Y., 1985, v.p. instl. sales, 1986; pres. CIS Credit Corp., 1987, v.p. fin., 1988; v.p., chmn. reorganization com. Continental Info. Systems Corp., 1989; v.p. fin., CFO ITEC Corp., Lake Bluff, Ill., 1990-91, pres., CEO, 1991—, Global Telecom Svcs. Corp., 2000—. Advisor, cons. Chong & Assocs., N.Y.C., 1989. Advisor Hiawatha coun. Boy Scouts Am., Syracuse, 1987; dir. Cystic Fibrosis Found., Syracuse, 1987-88. Recipient Century award Boy Scouts Am., Syracuse, 1988. Mem. Am. Assn. Equipment Lessors, Am. Mgmt. Assn., Fin. Execs. Inst., Aircraft, Owners & Pilots Assn. Republican. Avocations: pvt. pilot, cross country skiing. Home: 8763 Muirfield Dr Naples FL 34109-4352 Office: Global Telecom Svcs Corp 8763 Muirfield Dr Naples FL 34109-4352

MARINO, WILLIAM J. insurance executive; Various positions Prudential Ins. Co. Am., 1968-91, Horizon Blue Cross & Blue Shield of N.J., Inc., Newark, 1991-94; pres., CEO Horizon Blue Cross & Blue Shield of NJ Inc, 1994—. Mem. exec. com. Blue Cross/Blue Shield Assn. (BCBSA), chair Inter-Plan Operating Com. and Emerging Issues of BCBSA, bd. dirs. of Health Insurance Assn. of America, Nat. Inst. for Health Care Mgmt. Trustee, chmn. United Way of Essex and West Hudson, N.J., campaign chmn., 1993-94; chmn., bd. dirs., mem. exec. com. Regional Bus. Partnership; trustee N.J. Network Found., St. Peter's Coll., Newark Mus.; bd. pres. advisors Fairleigh Dickinson U.; mem. chief justice com. on efficiency N.J. Jud. Sys.; past trustee Kessler Inst. for Rehab., Inc. Mem. N.J. State C. of C., past chmn. bd. dirs., exec. com. Blue Cross/Blue Shield Assn. (BCBSA), Inter-Plan Operating Com., mem. Emerging Issues Com. of BCBSA, bd. dirs. Health Insurance Assn. of Amer., Nat. Inst. for Health Care Mgmt. Office: Horizon Blue Cross/Blue Shield of NJ Inc 3 Penn Plz E Newark NJ 07105-2245*

MARINOFF, ELAINE, artist; b. L.A., Sept. 24, 1934; d. George Lawrence and Lena (Brown) M.; m. Robert Glen Good, June 9, 1957 (div. 1980); children: Cynthia Ellen Good Reiman, Glendon Robert, Bradley Lawrence Good. Student, Chinouard Art Inst., 1950, U. Calif., Berkley, 1953-55, Ecole Guerre Lavigene, Paris, 1955-56; BA, UCLA, 1957; postgrad., Sch. Visual Arts, N.Y.C., 1989. Pres. Elaine Good Interiors, L.A., 1960-72; instr. The Serigraphic Process UCLA, 1986-88. Author, illustrator: (books) Windows, 1988, Power Sources, 1989; exhibited in group shows and one-woman shows at Laguna (Calif.) Mus. Art, 1974, Brand Mcpl. Mus. Gallery, Glendale, Calif., 1979, L.A. County Mus. Art, L.A., 1979, 80, 81, Calif. Mus. Sci. and Industry, 1980, Sateria Galeria fur Erotisch Kusnt, Kronberg, Germany, 1981, Downey (Calif.) Mus. Art, 1981, Heritage Gallery, L.A., 1982, Galerie Das Bilderhaus, Frankfurt, Germany, 1983, Cabrillo Marine Mus., San Pedro, Calif., 1984, Galerie Woeller Paquet, Frankfurt, 1984, Criteria Gallery, Denver, 1985, Artworks Gallery, L.A., 1988, Eva Cohon Gallery, Chgo., 1992, Kouros Gallery, N.Y.C., 1993, Claudia Chapline Gallery Stinson Beach, Calif., 1993, 95, Andre Zarre Gallery, N.Y.C., 1994, NYU, 1995, Noyes Mus., Oceanville, N.J., 1995, Bedford (N.Y.) Hist. Soc., 1996, Korean Cultural Ctr., L.A., 1998, U. Judaism, L.A., 1999. Mem. Cmty. Bd. # 1, N.Y.C., 1998—. Mem. Fine Arts Fedn., Artists Talk on Art, Artists Equity (bd. dirs. L.A. chpt. 1980), Women's Caucus for the Arts, Bus. and Profl. Women, Artists for Econ. Action. Democrat. Jewish. Avocations: writing, researching, lecturing. Studio: 110 Franklin St New York NY 10013-2910

MARINSKY, HARRY, artist; b. London, May 8, 1909; s. Isaac and Debora (Divorkin) M. Student, R.I. Sch. of Design, Providence, 1927; grad., Pratt Inst. Art, Bklyn., 1928-29. Art editor Am. Home Country Life, N.Y.C., 1935-39. One-man shows include One War One Peace Grand Central Palace, N.Y.C., 1946, Adelphia U., Garden City, N.Y., 1965, Interiors Anna-Maria, Stephen Kellen Archives of Parsons Sch. Design, 1972, Hammer Galleries, N.Y.C., 1981, 84, 94, La Galerie Shayne, Montreal, 1984, Montclair (N.J.) Art Mus., 1988; group exhbns. include Whitney Mus. Annual Sculpture Exhibit, N.Y.C., 1956, Internat. Sculpture Exhbn., Pietrasanta, Italy, 1993, Naples, Italy, 1990; represented in permanent collections Vets. Meml. Pk., Norwalk, Conn., 1960, The Great Bird Smell & Touch Garden, Stamford (Conn.) Mus., 1960, York U., Ont., Can., Commedia Dell Arte Group, Englewood, Colo., Rivotorto Assisi, Italy, Mus. of Outdoor Art, Englewood, Hunt Botanical Libr., Pa., Westmoreland Mus., Greenburg, Pa., Alice in Wonderland Park, Englewood, One War One Peace Hist. Mus. The Resistance, St. Anna, Stazzema, Toscany, Italy, 1996, (sculpture) St. Francis Commn. Inaugurated Pietrasanta, Italy, 2000; illustrator Mexico in Your Pocket, 1937, Isabelle Elizabeth, 1946, Puffy Goes to Sea, 1946, Woman's Day Book of Houseplants, 1963. Recipient Award of Distinctive Merit, Art Dirs. Club, N.Y.C., 1945, Henry Hering Meml. Medal award Nat. Sculpture Soc., N.Y.C., 1988. Fellow Nat. Sculpture Soc. 1988. Home: Via Pozzodonico 35 Pietrasanta Lucca Italy 55045

MARINSTEIN, ELLIOTT FRED, lawyer; b. N.Y.C., June 15, 1928; s. Joseph and Rose (Zessman) M.; m. Leita A. Adeson, Dec. 1, 1957; children: Edward Ross, Jay Drew. BA, Bklyn. Coll., 1950; JD, NYU, 1953. Bar: N.Y. 1955, U.S. Dist. Ct. (no. dist.) N.Y. 1956, U.S. Supreme Ct. 1970, U.S. Dist. Ct. (so. and ea. dists.) N.Y. 1986. Sole practice, Troy, N.Y., 1956-86; asst. dist. atty. County of Rensselaer, 1965-67; ptnr. Marinstein & Marinstein, 1986-2000, Marinstein & Marinstein, Esqs., PLLC, Troy, 2000—. Counsel charter rev. com. City of Troy, 1972-73; mem. com. on profl. standards Third Jud. Dept., 1988-94. Committeeman Rensselaer County Dem. Com., Troy, 1960-65; del. jud. convention Dem. State Com., Troy, 1978-88; chmn. housing bd. rev. City of Troy, 1979-90. Served to cpl. U.S. Army, 1953-55. Mem. ABA (corp., banking and bus. law sect.,), N.Y. State Bar Assn. (count county courts com., lectr. 1978-83), Rensselaer County Bar Assn. (chmn. grievance com. 1972-75, pres. 1979-80), N.Y. State Dist. Attys. Assn., Comml. Law League Am. (practice com.). Lodges: Knights of Pythias (past chancellor), Masons. Avocation: tennis. Home: 2354 Burdett Ave Troy NY 12180-2409 Office: Marinstein & Marinstein 200 Broadway Troy NY 12180-3289 Fax: (518) 274-5039. E-mail: mmlaw@capital.net.

MARION, ANN, school psychologist, educator; b. Mobile, Ala., Apr. 30, 1936; d. Edmund Charles and Lela Marie (Franklin) Guidroz; m. Donald Orrin Marion, June 25, 1965; children: Janet Marie, Kathryn Elizabeth. BA, Millsaps Coll., Jackson, Miss., 1963; MEd, U. So. Miss., Hattiesburg, 1972. Cert. tchr., cert. sch. psychologist, Miss. Classrm. tchr. Natchez-Adams Sch. Dist., Natchez, Miss., 1963-72, tchr. Title III ESEA, 1967-69, psychometrist, 1969-72, sch. psychologist, 1977-94. Past pres. Mental Health Assn., Adams County Assn. for Child Protection; mem. Gov.'s Criminal Justice Task Force, 1991; bd. dirs. Natchez Child Protection Assn.; mem. craft com. Natchez Career and Tech. Ctr. Mem. Pilgrimage Garden Club, Nat. Rep. Assn., Phi Delta Kappa. Avocations: reading, study broups, bridge, collecting antiques, dollhouses. Home: 105 Mansfield Dr Natchez MS 39120-4930 E-mail: agmarion@netscape.net.

MARION, DONALD WILLIAM, neurosurgeon; b. Hettinger, N.D., July 18, 1953; s. Claude and Geraldine (White) M.; m. Helene Sharon Wolkowitz, May 6, 1988; 1 child, John Patrick. BS, U. N.D., 1970; MD, U. Calif., San Francisco, 1982; MSc, U. Pitts., 1989. Diplomate Am. Bd. Neurol. Surgery. Intern, resident U. Pitts., 1982-89; fellow Med. Coll. Va., Richmond, 1989-90; from asst. prof. to prof., attending neurosurgeon U. Pitts., 1990—; dir. Brain Trauma Rsch. Ctr., Ctr. Injury Rsch. and Control UPMC Presby. Fellow Am. Coll. Surgeons; mem. AMA, Am. Assn. Surgery Trauma, Am. Assn. Neurol. Surgeons, Congress Neurol. Surgeons. Office: U Pitts Med Ctr 200 Lothrop St Ste B400 Pittsburgh PA 15213-2546 E-mail: dmarion@neuronet.pitt.edu.

MARION, GAIL ELAINE, reference librarian; b. Bloomington, Ill., May 31, 1952; d. Ralph Herbert and Norma Mae (Crump) Nyberg; m. David Louis Marion, May 13, 1972 (div. Apr. 1983). AA in Liberal Arts, Fla. Jr. Coll., 1976; BA in U.S. History, U. North Fla., 1978; MS in Libr. and Info. Sci., Fla. State U., 1985. Law libr., legal rschr. Mathews Osborne et al, Jacksonville, Fla., 1979-82; reference libr. City of Jacksonville-Pub. Librs., 1982—. With U.S. Army, 1970-72, maj. U.S. Army Res., 1978—, with Fla. Army N.G., 1974-78. Named to Outstanding Young Women of Am., 1985; N.G. Officers Assn. scholar, 1980. Mem. ALA, WAC Vets. Assn., Adj. Gen. Regimental Corps, Res. Officers Assn., Fla. Libr. Assn., Fla. Paleontol. Soc. Republican. Methodist. Avocations: art, photography, reading, rock hounding, Nascar auto racing. Home: 3200 Hartley Rd Apt 70 Jacksonville FL 32257-6719 Office: Jacksonville Pub Librs 122 N Ocean St Jacksonville FL 32202-3314

MARION, JOHN MARTIN, academic administrator; b. Fitchburg, Mass., Jan. 11, 1947; s. Don Louis and Violet Pearl Marion; m. Joann Elizabeth Trzcinski, Aug. 8, 1970; children: Benjamin Andrew, Jessica Noelle. BS in Edn., Fitchburg State Coll., 1969, MEd, 1971; postgrad., Pepperdine U. Tchr. Groton (Mass.) Dunstable Regional Schs., 1969-84; computer tchr. Littleton (Mass.) Pub. Schs., 1985-86; computer coord. K-12th grades Newburyport (Mass.) Pub. Schs., 1986-90; chair Acad. Computing Endicott Coll., Beverly, Mass., 1990-98; dir. tech. Reading (Mass.) Pub. Schs., 1998-00; media tech. specialist Dracut Pub. Schs., Mass., 2000—. Instr. Merrimack Edn. Ctr., Chelmsford, Mass., 1980-90; trainer, cons. Logo Computer Sys., Inc., N.Y.C., 1984-90; tchr. trainer Lego-Decta, Lego Sys., Inc., Enfield, Conn., 1987-90; mem. adv. bd. Claris Software Co.; bd. dirs. Mass. Computer Using Educator, 1989-90. Bd. dirs. Reading Cmty. TV, Inc., 1998-99. Fulbright scholar tchr. exch., Southampton, Eng., 1973-74. Mem. Internat. Soc. Tech. in Edn., Mass. Computer Using Educators, Phi Delta Kappa. Home: 123 Chestnut St Pepperell MA 01463-1019 Office: Dracut Pub Schs 2063 Lakeview Ave Dracut MA 01826 E-mail: jmarion@aol.com.

MARION, MARJORIE ANNE, English language educator, education consultant; b. Winterset, Iowa, May 6, 1935; d. Virgil Arthur and Marilyn Ruth (Sandy) Hammon; m. Robert H. Marion, Dec. 20, 1964; 1 child, Kathryn Ruth. BA, Colo. Coll., 1958; MA, Purdue U., 1969; postgrad., Inst. Mgmt. Lifelong Edn. Harvard U., 1981. Chairperson English dept. Lincoln-Way H.S., New Lenox, Ill., 1964-68; dir. pub. rels. U. St. Francis, Joliet, 1968-70, chairperson English dept., 1971-75, chairperson divsn. humanities and fine arts, 1975-79, coord. instrnl. devel., 1979-80, dir. continuing edn., 1980-84, acting v.p. acad. affairs, 1984-85, dean of faculty, 1985-89, assoc. prof. English, 1989-97, dir. Freshman Core Program, 1993-95; dir. Writing Ctr., 1996; prof. emeritus U. St. Francis, 1997—. Cons. to presdl. search U. St. Francis, 2001—02; mem. vis. team North Ctrl. Assn., Joliet and Lockport, Ill., 1975—79; lectr. at ednl. workshops and instns.; condr. writing workshops for adults returning to coll., 1995—; TV and radio appearances regarding lifelong edn., Chgo., St. Louis, Albuquerque, Phoenix, 1982—85; lectr. writing workshops. Author: A Guide to Writing for the Faint at Heart, 1996; author monograph; drama critic Joliet Herald News, 1970-82. Recipient Pres.'s award Coll. St. Francis, 1975. Mem. Am. Assn. Higher Edn., Nat. Coun. Tchrs. of English, Nat. Acad. Advising Assn. Roman Catholic. E-mail: rhmarion@msn.com.

MARION, SUZANNE MARGARET, music educator; b. Hutchinson, Kans., May 6, 1938; d. Charles Myers and Margaret Lansden (Foster) Davis; m. Stuart Eli Marion, June 2, 1962; children: John Stuart, David Evan, Matthew Charles. BA in Psychology, U. Ariz., 1960; BA in Music, U. Houston, 1982. Psychiat. social worker Ariz. State Hosp., Phoenix, 1960-62; tchr. voice, theory, piano Houston Music Inst., 1978-81; pvt. practice Houston, 1970—. Performer Class Act, Houston, 1994—. Soloist Emerson Unitarian Ch. choir, Houston, 1983—. Voice scholarship Madrigal Club, 1964. Mem. Music Tchrs. Natl. Assn., Houston Music Tchrs. Assn. (theory chmn. 1987-89), Houston Music Tchrs. Assn. (chamber music and ensemble chmn. 1990-95, bd. dirs., Tchr. Svc. award 1995), Houston Tuesday Musical Club (pres. 1996-98), Treble Clef Club, Sigma Alpha Iota. Republican. Unitarian Universalist. Avocations: creative writing, study of Spanish, computer, reading, working with dogs. Home: 910 Briarbrook Dr Houston TX 77042-2006

MARIOTTE, MICHAEL LEE, environmental activist, environmental publication director; b. Indpls., Dec. 9, 1952; s. Richard H. and Rozetta Mae (Dorton) M.; m. Lynn W. Thorp, Mar. 3, 1984; children: Nicole Lynn, Richard Matthew. BA, Antioch Coll., 1978. Editorial asst. ABA, Washington, 1979-81; mng. editor, gen. mgr. City Paper, 1981-84; editor Nuclear Info. & Resource Svc., 1985-86, exec. dir., 1986—, dir. Ea. European/Newly Ind. States project, 1997—. Dir. Safe Energy Comm. Coun., Washington, 1990—; dir. Rainforest Internat., 1995; mem. adv. bd. GE Stockholder Alliance, 1991—; advisor Coun. on Econ. Priorities, 1990-95; webmaster NIRS Website. Editor (newsletter) Nuclear Monitor, 1985—. E-mal. Office: Nuclear Info & Resource Svc 1424 16th St NW Ste 404 Washington DC 20036-2237 E-mail: nirsnet@nirs.org.

MARIOTTI, MARGARET, executive secretary; b. Derby, Conn., Nov. 1, 1956; d. Peter J. and Matrona (Iannotti) M. Student, Stone Sch. Bus., New Haven, 1975-76. Sec. Sikorsky Aircraft, Stratford, Conn., 1977—. Mem. Alpha Iota. Home: 411 Coram Ave Shelton CT 06484-3134 E-mail: mmmariotti@aol.com.

MARIOTTI, STEVE J. entrepreneur, financial educator, president and founder NFTE; b. Ann Arbor, Mich., Aug. 14, 1953; s. John and Nancy Gilbert (Mason) M. BBA, U. Mich., 1975, MBA, 1977; PhD in Bus. and Entrepreneurship (hon.), Johnson & Wales U., 1990. Fin. analyst Ford Motor Co., Dearborn, Mich., 1977-79; pres., founder Mason Import/Export, N.Y.C., 1979-82; spl. edn. tchr. N.Y.C. Pub. Schs., 1982-88; pres. Nat. Found. for Tchg. Entrepreneurship, 1988—. Author: Homeboys: Diary of an Inner-City Teacher, 1990; co-author: (with Tony Towle) Entrepreneurship How to Start and Operate a Small Business, 1995, (with Debra DeSalvo and Tony Towle) The Young Entrepreneurs Guide to Starting and Running a Business, 1996; contbr. articles to profl. jours. Recipient Leavey award for Outstanding Achievement in the Field of Free Enterprise Edn., 1985, Best Bus. Tchr. of Year. Nat. Fedn. Ind. Bus., 1988, Entrepreneur of Yr. award N.Y. State in Supporter of Enterpreneurship Inc. mag., 1992, Appel award Price Inst. for Entrepreneurial Studies, 1994. Home: 125 W 12th St New York NY 10011-8269 Office: 120 Wall St Fl 29 New York NY 10005-4001 E-mail: stevem@nfte.com.

MARIS, CHARLES ROBERT, surgeon, otolaryngologist; b. Champaign, Ill., Nov. 24, 1948; s. Harold Franklin and Marjorie Ellen (Beermann) M.; m. Karen Lynne Richardson, Dec. 27, 1970; children: Katherine, Emily, Charles Jr. BS, Eastern Ill. U., 1971; MD, U. Ill., 1975. Diplomate Am. Bd. Surgery, Am. Bd. Otolaryngology. Resident in otolaryngology U. Nebr. Med. Ctr., Omaha, 1982; chief of surgery Sarah Bush Lincoln Health Ctr., Mattoon, Ill., 1984-85, chmn. exec. com., 1985, 89, 94, chief of staff, 1986, 90, 95; bd. dirs. Carle Found., Urbana, 1998—. Bd. dirs. 1st Mid-Ill. Bank & Trust. Mem. Charleston Cmty. Unit Dist. #1 Sch. Bd., 1984-88; v.p. fin., pres.-elect, pres. Lincoln Trails coun. Boy Scouts Am. Col. USAR, 1990-91, Desert Storm. Named one of Outstanding Young Men in Am., 1985. Fellow ACS, Am. Acad. Otolaryngology-Head and Neck Surgery. Republican. Methodist. Office: 200 Lerna Rd S Mattoon IL 61938-9388

MARIS, STEPHEN S. lawyer, educator; b. Dallas, Dec. 19, 1949; children: Shane, Kara. BS, Stephen F. Austin State, 1971; JD, So. Meth. U., 1975. Bar: U.S. Dist. Ct. (no. dist.) Tex. 1975, U.S. Dist. Ct. (ea. dist.) Tex. 1986, U.S. Dist. Ct. (so. dist.) Tex. 1992, U.S. Ct. Appeals (5th cir.) 1980, U.S. Ct. Appeals (11th cir.) 1981, U.S. Supreme Ct. Tex. 1975. Assoc. Passman & Jones, Dallas, 1975-80, ptnr., 1980-87, Fulbright & Jaworski, Dallas, 1987-97, Jenkens & Gilchrist, Dallas, 1997—. Prof. So. Ill. U., 1979-80, So. Meth. U., Dallas, 1980—; mem. faculty Nat. Inst. Trial Advocacy, 1980—. Editor: Southwest Law Journal, 1973-75. Mem. ABA, State Bar Tex., Dallas Bar Assn., Barristers, Order Coif, Phi Delta Phi. Office: Jenkens & Gilchrist 1445 Ross Ave Ste 3200 Dallas TX 75202-2785

MARISCALO, ROSEMARY JEAN, real estate broker; b. Oyster Bay, N.Y., Dec. 1, 1939; Grad. high sch., Oyster Bay. Translator Baroid Internat., Rome, Italy, 1963-65, U.S. Govt., Rome, 1965-68; ct. reporter Barrister Reporting Svc. Ct., N.Y.C., 1975-83; owner, broker Oyster Bay Real Estate Co. Mem. Oyster Bay C. of C., L.I. Bd. Realtors, Friends of Raynham Hall, St. Bartholomew City Club (N.Y.C.). Office: Oyster Bay Real Estate Co 32 E Main St Oyster Bay NY 11771-2406

MARITIME, GEORGE, writer, photographer; b. Yonkers, N.Y., Feb. 19, 1942; s. Archie Fetchko and Ann Bernadine Macko; m. Dorothy Eiss, Sept. 16, 1968 (div. 1978). BA, Syracuse U.; postgrad., Sarah Lawrence Coll. Dir. Folk Music Hall Fame, Yonkers, 1991. Author: Columbus, 1991, The Cricket's Song, 1992, The Story of John Keats, 1992, The Ballad of Christopher Marley, 1994, The Communists in Shanghai, 2000, Steel Rocks, 2000. Schubert fellow, 1978-79. Mem. Marlowe Assn. Am., N.Y. Shelley Soc., Melville Soc., Marlowe Lives Assn. Home: 44 Cherwing Rd Yonkers NY 10701-5325

MARIUCCI, STEVE, professional football coach, former college coach; b. Iron Mountain, Mich., Nov. 4, 1955; m. Gayle Mariucci; 4 children. Football coach No. Mich. U., 1978-79, Calif. State U., Fullerton, 1980-82; asst. head coach U. Louisville, 1983-84; receivers coach Orlando Renegades U.S. Football League, 1985; quality control coach L.A. Rams, 1985; receivers/spl. teams coach U. So. Calif., L.A., 1986, wide receivers/spl. teams coach, 1987-89, quarterbacks coach, offensive coord., 1990-91; quarterbacks coach Green Bay (Wis.) Packers, 1992-95; head coach Golden Bears U. Calif., 1996-98; head coach San Francisco 49ers, 1996—. Office: San Francisco 49ers 4949 Centennial Blvd Santa Clara CA 95054-1229*

MARJANCZYK, JOSEPH ANICETUS, priest; b. Elizabeth, N.J., Apr. 17, 1921; s. Joseph John and Catherine Frances (Cwik) M. BA, Seton Hall U., 1941; MDiv, Darlington Sem., 1975. Ordained priest Roman Cath. Ch., 1945; named monsignor, 1979. Asst. pastor St. Valentine's Ch., Bloomfield, N.J., 1945-72; pastor St. Adalbert's Ch., Elizabeth, 1972-83, Our Lady of Mt. Carmel Ch., Bayonne, N.J., 1983-96; named protonotary apostolic, 1988; vicar episcopal South Hudson Vicariate, 1991—96; prof. Polish Master Sch. Fgn. Langs., Seton Hall U., 1948-60; pastor emeritus Our Lady of Mt. Carmel Ch., Bayonne, 1996—. Chmn. pers. bd. Archdiocese of Newark, 1972-74, mem. pastoral coun., 1972-83, archdiocesan trustee 1975-86; chmn. adminstrv. com., mem. exec. bd. Archdiocesan Pastoral Coun., 1972-84; dean Union County East Deanery, 1975-83; Polish Apostolate rep. Nat. Conf. Cath. Bishops Com. on Migration, 1989-96, chmn. Polish adv. bd. to conf. office for pastoral care of migrants and refugees, 1989-96. Chmn. bd. dirs. Polish Cultural Found., 1974-90, 92-97, 98-2000; trustee Seton Hall U., 1978-96, Immaculate Conception Sem., South Orange, N.J., 1979-86; commr. bd. edn. City of Elizabeth, 1979-83; nat. chaplain Polish Army Vets. Assn. Am., 1980-98; founder, pres. emeritus N.J. chpt. John Paul II Found., 1986-2000; chmn. exec. bd. Polish chapel renovation and rededication Nat. Shrine of Immaculate Conception, Washington, 1986-89. Decorated Gold Order of Merit (Republic of Poland), 1988; recipient Polish Apostolate Pride of Polonia award, 1996; named Canon of Cathedral chpt. Archdiocese Warsaw, Poland, 1995. Mem. Archdiocesan Polish Clergy Soc. (hon. pres. 1979—), Polish Am. Priests Assn. (exec. com. 1991-99), Polish Am. Congress, Polish Am. Hist. Assn., N.J. Hist. Soc., Polish Am. Numis. Assn., Polonians Club, KC. Home: PO Box 456 Point Pleasant NJ 08742-0456

MARK, DANIEL BENJAMIN, cardiologist; b. Boston, Aug. 1, 1953; s. Vernon H. and Alexandra M.; m. M. Lee Cheney. BA, Hampshire Coll., 1974; MD, Tufts U., 1978; MPH, Harvard Sch. of Pub. Health, 1979. Intern U. Va. Hosp., Charlottesville, 1979-80, resident, 1980-82; fellow Duke U. Med. Ctr., Durham, N.C., 1982-85, assoc. in medicine, 1985-86, asst. prof. of medicine, 1987-92, assoc. prof. of medicine, 1993-98, prof. of medicine, 1998—, dir. Outcomes Rsch. and Assessment Group, 1994—. Editor: Am. Heart Jour., 1996—; author: (book) Acute Coronary Care; contbr. articles to numerous profl. jours. and publs. Recipient Rsch. Excellence award Assn. of Pharmacoecons. and Outcomes Rsch., 1997. Fellow: AHA (rsch. and evaluation com. 1999—), Am. Soc. Clin. Investigation, Am. Coll. Physicians, Am. Coll. Cardiology (guideline com. AHCPR-NIH Unstable Angina Guideline 1994, database R&D com. 1998—2001, Coronary Stent Consensus Guidelines 2001—02, Exercise Testing Guidelines 2002); mem.: Assn. Am. Physicians, Assn. Health Svcs. Rsch., Soc. for Med. Decision Making. Office: Duke Clin Rsch Inst 2400 Pratt Ave Rm 311 Durham NC 27705-3976 E-mail: daniel.mark@duke.edu.

MARK, HANS MICHAEL, physicist, government official; b. Mannheim, Germany, June 17, 1929; arrived in U.S., 1940, naturalized, 1945; s. Herman Francis and Maria (Schramek) M.; m. Marion G. Thorpe, Jan. 28, 1951; children: Jane H., Rufus J. AB in Physics, U. Calif. at Berkeley, 1951; PhD, MIT, 1954; Sc.D. (hon.), Fla. Inst. Tech., 1978; D. Eng. (hon.), Poly. U. N.Y., 1982; DEng (hon.), Milw. Sch. Engring., 1991; LHD (hon.), St. Edward's U., 1993. Rsch. assoc. MIT, Cambridge, 1954-55, asst. prof., 1958-60; rsch. physicist Lawrence Radiation Lab., U. Calif., Livermore, 1955-58, 60-69, exptl. physics div. leader, 1960-64, assoc. prof. nuclear engring. Berkeley, 1960-66, prof., 1966-69, chmn. dept. nuclear engring., 1964-69, lectr. dept. applied sci. Davis, 1969-73; cons. prof. engring. Stanford U., 1973-84; dir. NASA-Ames Rsch. Ctr., 1969-77; undersec., dir. Nat. Reconnaissance Office USAF, Washington, 1977-79, sec., 1979-81; dep. adminstr. NASA, 1981-84; chancellor U. Tex. System, Austin, 1984-92; prof. aerospace engring. and engring. mechanics U. Tex., 1988—; dir. defense rsch. and engring. Dept. Defense., Washington, 1998-2001. Mem. Pres.'s Adv. Group Sci. and Tech., 1975-76; bd. dirs. Astronautics Corp. Am.; trustee Poly. U., 1984—. Author: (with N.T. Olson) Experiments in Modern Physics, 1966 (with E. Teller and J.S. Foster, Jr.) Power and Security, 1976, (with A. Levine) The Management of Research Institutions, 1983, The Space Station-A Personal Journey, 1987, (with Victor G. Szebehely) Adventures in Celestial Mechanics, 1998; also numerous articles.; Editor: (with S. Fernbach) Properties of Matter Under Unusual Conditions, 1969, (with Lowell Wood) Energy in Physics, War and Peace, 1988. Recipient Disting. Svc. medal NASA, 1972, 77, medal for exceptional engring. achievement, 1984, Exceptional Civilian Svc. award USAF, 1979, Disting. Pub. Svc, medal, Dept. Def., 1981, 2001, Sec.'s Gold medal Dept. Energy, 2001. Fellow AIAA (hon., Von Karman lectr. astronautics 1992), Am. Phys. Soc.; mem. Nat. Acad. Engring., Am. Nuclear Soc., Am. Geophys. Union, Coun. Fgn. Rels., Cosmos Club. Achievements include research on nuclear energy levels, nuclear reactions, applications, nuclear energy for practical purposes, atomic flourescence yields, measurement X-rays above atmosphere, spacecraft and experimental aircraft design. Office: U Tex Dept Aerospace Engring/Engr Austin TX 78712

MARK, HARRY HORST, ophthalmologist, researcher; b. Breslau, Germany, Jan. 21, 1931; came to U.S., 1957; s. Lothar and Ruth Mark. MD, U. Vienna, Austria, 1957. Diplomate Am. Bd. Ophthalmology. Intern George Washington U., Washington, 1957; resident Boston U., 1958-60, SUNY, Bklyn., 1960-62; pvt. practice New Haven, 1963—; attending ophthalmologist Yale-New Haven Hosp., 1963—, St. Raphael Hosp., New Haven, 1963—. Author: Optokinetics, 1982; contbr. articles to profl. jours. Avocations: optics, history, sailing. Home: 16 Broadway North Haven CT 06473-2301 Office: 2 Church St S New Haven CT 06519-1717

MARK, JAMES B. D. surgeon, educator; b. Nashville, June 26, 1929; s. Julius and Margaret (Baer) M.; m. Jean Rambar, Feb. 5, 1957; children: Jonathan, Michael, Margaret, Elizabeth, Katherine. BA, Vanderbilt U., 1950, MD, 1953. Intern, resident in gen. and thoracic surgery Yale-New Haven Hosp., 1953-60; instr. to asst. prof. surgery Yale U., 1960-65; assoc. prof. surgery Stanford U., 1965-69, prof., 1969-97, prof. emeritus, 1997—, Johnson and Johnson prof. surgery, 1972-97, head div. thoracic surgery, 1972-97, assoc. dean clin. affairs, 1988-92; chief staff Stanford U. Hosp., 1988-92. Governing bd. Health Systems Agy., Santa Clara County, 1978-80; sr. Fulbright-Hays fellow, vis. prof. surgery U. Dar es Salaam, Tanzania, 1972-73 Mem. editl. bd.: Jour. Thoracic and Cardiovasc. Surgery, 1986-94, World Jour. Surgery, 1995—, The Pharos, 2002-; contbr. numerous articles to sci. jours. Bd. dirs. Stanford U. Hosp., 1992-94. With USPHS, 1955-57. Fellow ACS (pres. No. Calif. chpt. 1980-81), Am. Coll. Chest Physicians (pres. 1994-95); mem. Am. Assn. Thoracic Surgery, Am. Surg. Assn., Western Surg. Assn., Pacific Coast Surg. Assn., Halsted Soc. (pres. 1984), Western Thoracic Surg. Assn. (pres. 1992-93), Calif. Acad. Medicine (pres. 1978), Santa Clara County Med. Soc. (pres. 1976-77), Internat. Surg. Soc. Home: 921 Casanueva Pl Stanford CA 94305-1001 Office: Stanford U Med Ctr CVRB Stanford CA 94305 E-mail: jbdm@stanford.edu.

MARK, JONATHAN GREENFIELD, political science educator, writer, air force officer; b. N.Y.C., Dec. 22, 1948; s. Sidney Carl and Patricia (Greenfield) M. BA, U. Tex., Austin, 1971; MA, U. Pa., 1976; PhD, U. Okla., 1981; grad., Indsl. Coll. Armed Forces, 1987. Vice-pres. Stas. KAKC-KBEZ, Tulsa,

1976-80; instr. polit. sci. Tulsa Jr. Coll., 1981-84; admissions liaison officer USAF Acad., 1981—. Vis. lectr. mass communications, 977; detachment commdr. USAFR, 1985-86; mem. .C. Congressional adv. com. svc. acad. appointments, 1989—; res. asst. to dep. asst. res. affairs Sec. of USAF, Washington, 1989-91; res. asst. Office of Asst. Sec. of Def. for Res. Affairs, Washington, 1991-2001; adj. faculty Nat. Def. U., Washington, 1986-2001; vis. lectr. polit sci. U. Tulsa, 1977, Air Command and Staff Coll., Montgomery, Ala., 1988. Contbr. articles and photography on travel to L.A. Herald-Examiner, Dallas Morning News, Kans. City Star, Balt. Sun, others. Served to capt. USAF, 1971-75; col. USAFR, 1975-2001. Decorated Def. Superior Svc. medal, 2 Meritorious Svc. medals, Air Force Commendation medal, Vietnam Svc. medal; recipient grad. rsch. prize U. Okla., 1981. Mem. Res. Officers Assn. U.S., Air Force Assn., Washington Ind. Writers.

MARK, LAURENCE MAURICE, film producer; b. N.Y.C., Nov. 22; s. James Mark and Marion Lorraine (Huebner) Green. BA, Wesleyan U., 1971; MA, NYU, 1973. Exec. dir., publicity Paramount Pictures, N.Y.C., 1978-80, v.p., West Coast mktg. L.A., 1980-82, v.p., prodn., 1982-84; exec. v.p., prodn. Twentieth Century Fox, 1984-86; pres. Laurence Mark Prodns., 1986—. Exec. prodr.: (films) Black Widow, 1987, My Stepmother is an Alien, 1988, Working Girl, 1988, Mr. Destiny, 1990, Sister Act 2: Back in the Habit, 1993, As Good As It Gets, 1997, (TV) Sweet Bird of Youth, 1989, Oliver Twist, 1997, The Last Laugh, 2000, These Old Broads, 2001; prodr.: (films) Cookie, 1989, True Colors, 1991, One Good Cop, 1991, The Adventures of Huck Finn, 1993, Cutthroat Island, 1995, Tom and Huck, 1995, Jerry Maguire, 1996, Romy and Michele's High School Reunion, 1997, Deep Rising, 1998, The Object of My Affection, 1998, Simon Birch, 1998, Anywhere But Here, 1999, Bicentennial Man, 1999, Hanging Up, 2000, Center Stage, 2000, Finding Forrester, 2000, Glitter, 2001, Riding In Cars With Boys, 2001; prodr. (theatre) Brooklyn Laundry, 1991, (Broadway) Big, 1996. Mem. Acad. Motion Pictures Arts and Scis. Office: Columbia Pictures Sony Studios 10202 Washington Blvd Culver City CA 90232-3119 Home: 12437 Mulholland Dr Beverly Hills CA 90210-1336

MARK, LAURENCE PETER, anesthesiology educator; b. N.Y.C., Jan. 30, 1953; s. Lester Charles and Muriel Harriet (Widman) M.; m. Elizabeth Sue Collier, Aug. 29, 1982; children: Torin and Ryan (twins). BS in Physics, Harvey Mudd Coll., 1975; MD, Columbia U., 1979. Diplomate Am. Bd. Anesthesiology, Nat. Bd. Med. Examiners. Intern surgery St. Vincent's Hosp., N.Y.C., 1979-80; resident anesthesia Mass. Gen. Hosp., Boston, 1980-82, anesthesia fellow, 1982-83; asst. prof. anesthesiology Columbia-Presbyn. Med. Ctr., N.Y.C., 1983—, head divsn. anesthesia for ophtalmol. procedures, 2000—. Expert witness Kopff, Nardelli & Dopf, N.Y.C., 1988—; article reviewer Anesthesia and Analgesia; bd. dirs. Columbia-Presbyn. Phsycians Network. Mem. Am. Soc. Anesthesiologists, N.Y. State Soc. Anesthesiologists (speaker closed cir. anesthesiology postgrad. assembly 1988). Democrat. Jewish. Avocations: computers, flying, sailing, electronics. Home: 210 W 90th St Apt 9B New York NY 10024-1243 Office: Columbia U 622 W 168th St New York NY 10032-3720

MARK, MARION THORPE, writing educator; b. Hayward, Calif., Sept. 28, 1930; d. Milton William and Johanna Altgelt (Schwab) Thorpe; m. Hans Michael Mark, Jan. 28, 1951; children: Jane, Rufus. BS in Edn., Boston U., 1952, MS in Edn., 1953; EdD, George Washington U., 1982. Diagnostician, tchr. Boston U. Reading Clinic, 1951-53; tchr. remedial reading, dir. ednl. testing and diagnosis Natick (Mass.) Pub. Schs., 1953-55; pvt. tutor of adults and children in reading Livermore, Calif., 1955-61; pvt. turor, home tchr. Berkeley, Calif, 1961-68; instr. reading McKinley Continuation H.S., 1968-69; chmn. dept. English Ravenswood H.S., Redwood City, Calif., 1969-71; honors English tchr. San Mateo Sch. Dist., 1971-76; instr. George Washington U., Washington, 1981-82; reading specialist Prince Georges County, Camp Springs, Md., 1971-76; curriculum specialist Austin (Tex.) Ind. Sch. Dist., 1984-91; tchr. advanced placement English St. Michael's Acad., Austin, 1993-97; instr. writing St. Edward's U., 1995—. Mentor handicapped students St. Edward's U., 1997—, mentor migrant students, 1995—. Author: (lession series) Teaching Literary Appreciation, 1953, The Pious Tiger, 1964, The Scientific Grammarian, 1985, The Mathematical Historian, 1986; author diagnostic test: Mathematics Skills, 1975. Bd. dirs. ARC, Austin, 1989, Camp Fire Boys and Girls, Austin, 1984-92, U. Tex. Migrant Edn., Austin, 1984-92, Ballet Austin; leader Camp Fire Boys and Girls, Berkeley, Calif., 1961-69; adv. coun. U. tex. Migrant Edn.; vol. adv. com. Austin Ind. Sch. Dist. Named Tchr. of the Yr., Menlo-Atherton Student Coun., 1975; recipient Leadership award Camp Fire Boys and Girls, 1991. Mem. The English Speaking Union, PEO, Pan Am. Round Table, Austin Women's Club, Am. History Club, Univ. Ladies Club, Tuesday Club, Tex. Phios. Soc. Democrat. Episcopalian. Avocations: piano, reading, needlepoint, antique dolls, family history. Home: 1710-III Rockmoor Pl Austin TX 78703 Office: 1715 Scenic Dr Austin TX 78703-2000

MARK, MELVIN, consulting mechanical engineer, educator; b. St. Paul, Nov. 15, 1922; s. Isadore William and Fannye (Abrahamson) M.; m. Elizabeth J. Wyner, Sept. 9, 1951; children: Jonathan S., David W., Peter B. B.M.E., U. Minn., 1943, MS, 1946; Sc.D. (Teaching, Research fellow), Harvard, 1950. Registered profl. engr., Mass., Minn. Instr. N.D. State U., 1943-44, U. Minn., 1945-47; project mgr. Gen. Electric Co., Lynn., Mass., 1950-52; mgr. Raytheon Co., Wayland, 1952-56; cons. engr., 1956—; prof. Lowell Technol. Inst., 1957-59, dean faculty, 1959-62; prof. mech. engring. Northeastern U., Boston, 1963-84, dean engring., 1968-79, provost, sr. v.p. for acad. affairs, 1979-84. Vis. lectr. Mass. Inst. Tech., 1955, Brandeis U., 1958; vis. prof. U. Mass., 1984-86; mem. Mass. Bd. Registration of Profl. Engrs. and Land Surveyors, 1990-2001. Author: Thermodynamics: An Auto-Instructional Text, 1967, Concepts of Thermodynamics, 1975, Thermodynamics: Principles and Applications, 1979, Engineering Thermodynamics, 1985; contbr. articles to profl. jours.; patentee in field. Served with USAAF, 1944-45. Recipient prize Lincoln Arc Welding Found., 1947 Hon. fellow ASME (fellow 1948-50); mem. Am. Soc. Engring. Edn., Sigma Xi, Tau Beta Pi, Pi Tau Sigma, Phi Kappa Phi Home: 17 Larch Rd Waban MA 02468-1413 Office: 93 Union St Ste 400 Newton Center MA 02459-2241 E-mail: mel@cartesianinc.com

MARK, MICHAEL DAVID, lawyer; b. Bklyn., Sept. 16, 1944; s. Irving and Mildred Mark; children: Dana Lynne, Stephanie Lauren. BA, Rutgers U., 1966; JD, U. Tenn., 1969. Bar: Tenn. 1969, N.J. 1970, U.S. Dist. Ct. N.J. 1970, U.S. Supreme Ct. 1973; cert. civil trial atty., N.J. Supreme Ct. 1992. House counsel Liberty Mut. Ins. Co., East Orange, N.J., 1969-71; assoc. Skoloff & Wolfe, Newark, 1971-73; pvt. practice, Union, N.J., 1973—. Past assoc. bd. dirs. United Jersey Bank, Union; Police Benevolent Assn. lawyer City of Linden, N.J., 1980—, Clark Twp., Clark, N.J., 1986; mem. Union-Essex County Early Settlement Panels, Elizabeth and Newark. Mem. Am. Acad. Matrimonial Lawyers (bd. mgrs. 1982—), N.J. Bar Assn., Union County Bar Assn., Union Lawyers Club (past pub. defender). Republican. Avocation: private pilot. Office: 2444 Morris Ave Union NJ 07083-5711

MARK, MICHAEL LAURENCE, retired music educator; b. Schenectady, N.Y., Dec. 1, 1936; s. David and Ruth (Garbowitz) M.; m. Lois Nitekman, Jan. 28, 1942; children: Michelle, Diana. BM, The Cath. U. of Am., 1958, DMA, 1969; MA, George Washington U., 1960; M in Music Edn., U. Mich., 1962. Tchr. Prince George's County, Md. Pub. Schs., 1958-60, 61-66; assoc. prof. music Morgan State U., Balt., 1966-70; supr. music Auburn (N.Y.) Enlarged Sch. Dist., 1970-72; dir. music Elmira (N.Y.) Enlarged Sch. Dist., 1972-73; assoc. prof., sch. music Cath. U. Am., Washington, 1973-81; dean grad. sch., prof. music Towson (Md.) U., 1981-95, prof. music, 1995-98; prof. emeritus, 1998. Edtl. com. five jours. in field. Author: Contemporary Music Education, 1978, 3rd rev. edit., 1996, Source Readings in Music Education History, 1982, 2nd edit., 2002; co-author: A History of American Music Education, 1992. Mem. Music Educators Nat. Conf. (numerous coms.), Coll. Music Soc., Md. Music Educators Assn. (pres. 1999—). Avocations: travel, woodworking. E-mail: mmark@towson.edu.

MARK, PETER, director, conductor; b. N.Y.C., Oct. 31, 1940; s. Irving and Edna M.; m. Thea Musgrave, Oct. 2, 1971. BA (Woodrow Wilson fellow), Columbia U., 1961; MS, Juilliard Sch. Music, 1963. Prof. music and dramatic art U. Calif., Santa Barbara, 1965-94. Fellow Creative Arts Inst., U. Calif., 1968-69, 71-72; guest condr. Wolf Trap Orch., 1979, N.Y.C. Opera, 1981, L.A. Opera Theater, 1981, Royal Opera House, London, 1982, Hong Kong Philharm. Orch., 1984, Jerusalem Symphony Orch., 1988, Tulsa Opera, 1988, Compania Nacional de Opera, Mexico City, 1989, 92, N.Y. Pops, Carnegie Hall, 1991. Concert violist U.S., S.Am., Europe, 1961-67; artistic dir., condr. Va. Opera, Norfolk, 1975—, art dir., 1978—; condr.: Am. premier of Mary, Queen of Scots (Musgrave), 1978; World premier of A Christmas Carol (Musgrave), 1979, of Harriet, the Woman Called Moses (Musgrave), 1985, of Simon Bolivar (Musgrave), 1984, Porgy and Bess, Buenos Aires, Mexico City and São Paulo, 1992, Orlando Opera co., 1993, Richmond Symphony, 1993, Krakow Opera, 1995, Pacific Opera Victoria (Can.), 1996, Cleve. Opera, 1996, Festival Pucciniano-Torre del Lago, Italy, 1996. Recipient Elias Lifchey viola award Juilliard Sch. Music, 1963; named hon. citizen of Norfolk (Va.) Mem. Musicians Union, Phi Beta Kappa. Office: Va Opera PO Box 2580 Norfolk VA 23501-2580 E-mail: pmark@vaopera.com.

MARK, REUBEN, consumer products company executive; b. Jersey City, Jan. 21, 1939; s. Edward and Libbie (Berman) M.; m. Arlene Slobzian, Jan. 10, 1964; children: Lisa, Peter, Stephen. AB, Middlebury Coll., 1960; MBA, Harvard U., 1963. With Colgate-Palmolive Co., N.Y.C., 1963—, pres., gen. mgr. Venezuela, 1972-73, Can., 1973-74, v.p., gen. mgr. Far East div., 1974-75, v.p., gen. mgr. household products div., 1975-79, group v.p. domestic ops., 1979-81, exec. v.p., 1981-83, chief operating officer, 1983-84, pres., 1983-86, CEO, 1984—, chmn. bd., 1986—. Lectr. Sch. Bus. Adminstrn., U. Conn., 1977 Served with U.S. Army, 1961. Mem. Soap and Detergent Assn. (bd. dirs.), Grocery Mfrs. Am. (dir.), Nat. Exec. Service Corp. Office: Colgate-Palmolive Co 300 Park Ave Fl 8 New York NY 10022-7499*

MARK, RICHARD KUSHAKOW, internist; b. N.Y.C., Feb. 11, 1951; s. Eugene and Gertrude (Kushakow) M.; m. Harriet Bass, Sept. 17, 1989; children: Sabrina, Ari, Etan. BS, Hofstra U., 1972; MD, U. Autonomous Guadalajara, 1976, SUNY, Bklyn., 1977. Diplomate Am. Bd. Internal Medicine. Resident in medicine Maimonides Med. Ctr., Bklyn., 1977-82; clin. instr. medicine Downstate Med. Ctr., 1982-90, asst. prof. medicine, 1990-93; prof. clin. medicine CUNY, 1993—; pvt. practice internal medicine Bklyn., 1982—. Dept. attending emergency Cabrini Med. Ctr., N.Y.C., 1982-84; med. cons. The Lighthouse. Author: Consumer's Guide to Preventive Medicine, 1996. Mem. N.Y.C. Coalition for the Homeless, 1986—, The Children's Fund., N.Y.C., 1990—. Recipient Cmty. Svc. award Borough of Bklyn., 1986, Physicians Recognition award AMA, 1993-97, Preceptorship award ACP, 1996, Tchr. of Yr. Maimonides Clin. Tchg. award CUNY, 1995, 96, 97, 98, 99, 2001; recipient Tchr. of the Yr. 1982, 83. Fellow ACP; mem. Acad. Medicine, Inter-Am. Coll. Medicine, King's County Med. Soc. Democrat. Jewish. Avocations: sailing, photography, skiing. Office: 8023 19th Ave Brooklyn NY 11214-1753

MARK, ROBERT ALAN, federal judge; b. 1951; BA, Brandeis U.; JD, U. Calif., Berkeley. Law clk. to Hon. Sidney Aronovitz, U.S. Dist. Ct. for So. Dist. Fla., Miami, 1978-79; assoc. Stearns, Weaver, Miller et al, 1979-90; bankruptcy judge U.S. Bankruptcy Ct. for so. Dist. Fla., 1990-99, chief bankruptcy judge, 1999—. Office: 1404 Federal Bldg 51 SW 1st Ave Miami FL 33130-1608

MARK, SARALYN, endocrinologist; b. Denver, May 14, 1961; d. Andre and Idella Betty (Kauvar) M. BA in Biology magna cum laude, Columbia U., 1983; MD, NYU, 1988. Intern and resident in internal medicine U. Calif., San Francisco, 1988-91, fellow in gen. and reproductive endocrinology and geriatrics, 1992—; ambulatory care clin. staff physician Kaiser Permanente Hosp., South San Francisco, Calif., 1991-92. Tchr. nurse practitioner students U. Calif., San Francisco, 1990-91, tchr. med. students, 1991—; sr. med. advisor USPHS Office on Women's Health, Dept. HHS, also NASA; asst. clin. prof. Yale U. Sch. Medicine. Contbr. articles to profl. publs. Nat. Honor Soc. scholar; recipient Gallery of Fame award for pub. svc. Denver Post, Dr. Abe Ravin Spl. Meml. award Colo. Heart Assn.; summer rsch. honors fellow NYU Sch. Medicine; grantee Sterling-Winthrop, 1993—, Merck Rsch. Labs., 1994—, Procter & Gamble Pharms., 1994—, NIH, 1994—. Mem. ACP, AMA, Am. Assn. Clin. Endocrinologists, Endocrine Soc., Bay Area Women in Endocrinology, Phi Beta Kappa. Democrat. Avocations: mountain biking, skiing, hiking, horseback riding, tennis.

MARK, SHELLEY MUIN, economist, educator, government official; b. China, Sept. 9, 1922; came to U.S., 1923, naturalized, 1944; s. Hing D. and S. (Wong) M.; m. Janet Chong, Sept. 14, 1946 (dec. Mar. 1977); children—Philip, Diane, Paul, Peter, Steven; m. Tung Chow, July 8, 1978. BA, U. Wash., 1943, PhD, 1956; MS, Columbia, 1944; postgrad. (Ford Found. fellow), Harvard, 1959-60. Fgn. news reporter CBS, N.Y., 1945-46; instr. U. Wash., 1946-48; asst. prof. Ariz. State Coll., 1948-51; territorial economist OPS, Honolulu, 1951-53; prof. econs. U. Hawaii, 1953-62, dir. econ. rsch. ctr., 1959-62; dir. planning and econ. devel. State of Hawaii, 1962-74, state land use commr., 1962-74, state energy coord., 1973-74; dir. Office Land Use Coordination EPA, Washington, 1975-77; prof. econs. U. Hawaii, 1978—. Rsch. fellow East-West Ctr., Inst. Econ. Devel. and Policy, 1984-94; Asian advisor Internat. Ctr. Econ. Growth, 1992—; sr. advisor Dept. Bus., Econ. Devel. and Tourism, Hawaii, 1995—; vis. scholar Harvard U., 1986; vis. faculty Grad. Sch. People's Bank of China, 1988; also econ. cons. Philippines Inst. Devel. Studies, Devel. Rsch. Ctr. State Coun., China, also other orgns.; mem. Gov.'s Adv. Com. Sci. and Tech., 1963-74, Oahu Transp. Policy Com., 1964-74, Regional Export Expansion Coun., 1964-74 Author: Economics in Action, 4th edit., 1969, Macroeconomic Performance of Asia-Pacific Region, 1985, Development Economics and Developing Economies, 1990, Aspects of Chinese Economic Development, 1991; editor: Economic Interdependence and Cooperation in Asia-Pacific, 1993, Asian Transitional Economies, 1996; contbr. articles to profl. jours. Bd. dirs. U. Hawaii Rsch. Corp.; bd. dirs. Coun. State Planning Agys., pres., 1973-74, hon. mem., 1975—; governing bd. Coun. State Govts., 1972-74. Recipient Sackett Meml. award Columbia, 1944 Mem. Hawaii Govt. Employees Assn. (pres. univ. chpt., dir. 1958-59), Am. Econ. Assn., Royal Econ. Soc., Western Regional Sci. Assn. (pres. 1974-75, dir.), Phi Beta Kappa, Sigma Delta Chi. Mem. United Ch. of Christ. Home: 2036 Keeaumoku St Honolulu HI 96822-2526

MARK, WAYNE MICHAEL, technical education marketing professional; b. Rochester, N.Y., June 26, 1952; s. Henry S. and Mary (Bucci) M.; m. Peggy Halling, Apr. 1, 1971 (div. Apr. 1987); children: Crystal, Jonathan; m. Janet Louise Richards, Dec. 18, 1987 (div. Aug. 1996); children: Michael, Christopher, Joshua; m. Candace F. Crosnoe, Apr. 18, 1998. Grad. high sch., Rochester. Cert. automotive technician. Mgr. NAPA Auto Parts, Hollywood, Fla., 1970-73, Canandaigua, N.Y., 1973-78, gen. mgr., 1978-80; sales rep. Echlin, Inc., Branford, Conn., 1980-83, tech. tng. specialist, 1983-88, dir. advanced tech. edn., 1988-93, mgr. spl. tng. svcs., 1994-96; mgr. Tech. Tng. Mktg. Svcs., 1996-99; auto group sales mgr. Sierra Internat., Inc., 1999—. Cons. Genuine Parts Co., Atlanta, 1991—, T.H. Pickens Tech. Ctr., Aurora, Colo., 1992-96, Automotive Svc. Excellence, Hampton, Va., 1992—, Internat. Platform Assn., 1994—. Editor, dir, advisor: (video prodn.) Automotive Servicing, 1990, 92, Soc. of Automotive Engineers, 1995—; contbr. editorials to profl. publ. Roman Catholic. Avocations: model railroading, camping, auto restoration, gardening. Office: Sierra Internat Inc 1 Sierra Pl Litchfield IL 62056-3029

MARK, WENDY, artist; b. N.Y.C., 1950; d. Lawrence and Annette Mark. BA, Brandeis U., 1972; MFA, Columbia U., 1974. Represented by ACA Gallery, N.Y.C. Workshop presenter The Mus. Sch., Provincetown, Mass., 1989, Sweet Briar (Va.) Coll., 1991, Castle Hill Monotype Workshop, Truro, Mass., 1993; vis. artist Dartmouth Coll., Hanover, N.J., 1993. One-woman shows include Hell's Kitchen Gallery, N.Y.C., 1989, 1990, 1991, U. Maine Mus. Art, Orono, 1990, Forum Gallery, N.Y.C., 1991, 1992, Louise Newman Gallery, Beverly Hills, Calif., 1992, Phillipe Staib Gallery, Kent, Conn., 1992, The Arsenal Gallery, Pks. and Recreation, N.Y.C., 1995, Glenn Horowitz Bookseller, East Hampton, N.Y., 1996, exhibited in group shows at Louise Newman Gallery, Beverly Hills, 1992, 1993, NYU, 1993, The League at the Cape, Provincetown, Mass., 1993, Riverside Art Mus., L.A., 1993, Hiroshima (Japan) Mus. Fine Art, 1993, The Drawing Ctr., N.Y.C., Berta Walker Gallery, Provincetown, 1993, Brooke Alexander Gallery, N.Y.C., 1994, Sotheby's, 1995, The Sharon Arts Ctr., N.H., 1996, Nat. Mus. Am. Art, Washington, 1997, ACA Gallery, N.Y.C., 1998, Lyman Allyn Mus. Art, New London, Conn., 1998, Represented in permanent collections Met. Mus. Art, N.Y.C., The Ringling Mus. Art, Sarasota, Fla., U. Maine Mus. Art, Orono, The Berg Collection, N.Y. Pub. Libr., N.Y.C., Morgan Libr., Readers Digest, Pleasantville, N.Y., and pvt. collections; contbr. lit. edit. books Wendy's Pinball, The Figure You, 89 Clouds. Recipient Alice Melrose prize for watercolor painting Nat. Acad. Design, Sch. Fine Arts, N.Y., 1985, Purchase prize The Art Students League, N.Y.C., 1986, Dr. Ralph Weller prize for painting Nat. Acad. Design, Sch. Fine Arts, N.Y.C., 1986; scholar The Mus. Sch., Provincetown, 1985; residency grantee The Vt. Studio, 1987; MacDowell Colony fellow, 1990, Yaddo fellow, 1990, 1993, Va. Ctr. for the Creative Arts fellow, Sweet Briar, 1992; Garner Tullis Monotype Workshop residency, N.Y.C., 1990, 92. Home: 2 W 67th St New York NY 10023-6241

MARKANDA, RAJ KUMAR, mathematics educator; b. Amritsar, Panjab, India, Nov. 15, 1940; came to U.S. 1983; s. Gurunditta Mall and Maya Devi (Sharma) Markanda; m. Manjula Shukla, Oct. 16, 1974; children: Neha, Sonal. BA with honors, Panjab U., 1959, MA, 1961; PhD, U. Colo., 1973. Sr. rsch. asst. Irrigation & Power Rsch. Inst., Amritsar, 1961-63; lectr. Govt. Coll., Kapurthala, Panjab, India, 1963-64; jr. rsch. fellow Panjab U., 1964-68; teaching asst. U. Colo., Boulder, 1968-69, 70-71, fellow, 1969-70, 71-72, Universite' de Paris X, Paris, 1972-73; vis. mem. Tata Inst., Bombay, India, 1973-74; lectr. Panjab U., Chandigarh, India, 1974-75; assoc. prof. Nat. U. Colombia, Bogota, 1975-77; assoc. prof. math. No. State U., Aberdeen, S.D., 1986-91, prof., 1991—. Assoc. prof. Universidad de Los Andes, Merida, Venezuela, 1977-83; vis. assoc. prof. U. Iowa, 1983-86. Co-author: College Algebra Exam File, 1990; contbr. articles to profl. jours. S.D. Bd. Regents grantee, 1990, 92, 93, S.D. Gov.'s Tech. grantee, 1999. Mem. Am. Math. Soc., Indian Math. Soc. (life mem.), S.D. Acad. Sci. Achievements include discovery of a new infinite class of arithmetic Euclidean rings whose existence had not been suspected. Office: No State Univ Dept Math Aberdeen SD 57401

MARKE, JULIUS JAY, law librarian, educator; b. N.Y.C., Jan. 12, 1913; s. Isidore and Anna (Taylor) M.; m. Sylvia Bolotin, Dec. 15, 1946; 1 child, Elisa Hope. BS, CCNY, 1934; LLB, NYU, 1937; BS in Lib. Sci., Columbia U., 1942. Bar: N.Y. 1938. Reference asst. N.Y. Pub. Libr., 1937-42; pvt. practice law N.Y.C., 1939-41; prof. law, law libr. NYU, 1949-83, prof. law emeritus, 1983—, interim dean of librs., 1975-77; Disting. Prof., dir. Law Libr. St. John's U. Sch. Law, 1983-95, disting. rsch. prof. law N.Y., 1995—. Lectr. Columbia Sch. Library Service, 1962-78, adj. prof., 1978-85; cons. Orientation Program Am. Law, 1965-68, Found. Overseas Law Libraries Am. Law, 1968-79, copyright Ford Found., law libraries, Coun. Fgn. Rels., 1990—, Shubert Archives, 1991, others. Author: Vignettes of Legal History, 1965, 2d series, 1977, rev. edit., 2000, Copyright and Intellectual Property, 1967 (with R. Sloane) Legal Research and Law Library Management, rev. edit., 1990, 2002; editor: Modern Legal Forms, 1953, The Holmes Reader, 1955, The Docket Series, 1955—, Bender's Legal Business Forms, 4 vols., 1962; compiler, editor: A Catalogue of the Law Collection at NYU with Selected Annotations, 1953, Dean's List of Recommended Reading for Pre-Law and Law Students, 1958, 84, and others; chmn. editl. bd. Oceana Group, 1977—, Index to Legal Periodicals and Books, 1978—; columnist N.Y. Law Jour., 1970—; contbr. articles to profl. jours. Mem. publs. coun. N.Y.U., 1964-80. Sgt. AUS, 1943-45. Decorated Bronze Star. Mem. ABA, Am. Assn. Law Librs. (pres. 1962-63, Disting. Svc. award 1986), Assn. Am. Law Schs., Coun. of Nat. Libr. Assns. (exec. bd., v.p 1959, 60), Law Libr. Assn. Greater N.Y. (pres. 1949, 50, chmn. joint com. on libr. edn. 1950-52, 60-61), NYU Law Alumni Assn. (Judge Edward Weinfeld award 1987, mem. exec. bd. 1988—), Columbia Sch. Libr. Svc. Alumni Assn. (pres. 1973-75), Order of Coif (pres. NYU Law Sch. br. 1970-83), NYU Faculty Club (pres. 1966-68), Field Inn, Phi Delta Phi. Home: 4 Peter Cooper Rd Apt 8F New York NY 10010-6746

MARKEE, KATHERINE MADIGAN, librarian, educator; b. Cleve., Feb. 24, 1931; d. Arthur Alexis and Margaret Elizabeth (Madigan) M. AB, Trinity Coll., Washington, 1953; MA, Columbia U., 1962; MLS, Case Western Res. U., 1968. Employment mgr., br. store tng. supr. The May Co., Cleve., 1965-67; assoc. prof. libr. sci., data bases libr. Purdue U. Libr., West Lafayette, Ind., 1968—, interim head spl. collections, 1996—. Contbr. articles to profl. jours. Mem. ALA, AAUP, Spl. Librs. Assn., Ind. Online Users Group, Sigma Xi (Rsch. Support award 1986). Avocations: photography, sailing, gardening. Office: Purdue U Libr West Lafayette IN 47907-1530 E-mail: kmarkee@purdue.edu.

MARKEL, PAUL DENNIS, psychologist, geneticist; b. Bismarck, N.D., Apr. 12, 1968; s. Gordon Francis and Phyllis Rose M.; m. Milissa Ann Vetter, June 1, 1990; children: Zane, Jacob, Evan, David. BA, U. Mary, Bismarck, 1990; MA, U. Colo., 1993, PhD, 1995. Faculty rsch. assoc. Sch. Pharmacy U. Colo. Health Scis. Ctr., Denver, 1995; statis. geneticist Millennium Pharms., Cambridge, Mass., 1995-96; assoc. prof. psychology Minot (N.D.) State U., 1996—. Vis. prof. Limburgs U. Centrum, Diepnboek, Belgium, 1999—; lectr. medicine Harvard Med. Sch., Boston, 1998-2002; dir. Alcohol Genomics Consortium, 1998-99; cons. Millennium Pharms., Cambridge, 1996-99; prin. cons. GenoPlex, Denver, 1998-99; bd. dirs. Med. Arts Ednl. and Sci. Found., Minot, 1998-2002. Pres.-elect faculty senate Minot State U. NIMH Tng. Grant fellow for alcoholism rsch., 1990-93; Nat. Alliance Rsch. Schizophrenia and Affective Disorders fellow for genetic rsch., 1994. Mem. Am. Psychol. Soc., Math. Soc. Am., Sigma Xi (treas. 1998—). Avocations: writing, music, drawing, hunting. Home: 1113 23rd St NW Minot ND 58703-1760 Office: Dept Psychology Minot State U 500 University Ave W Minot ND 58707-0001 Fax: 701-839-6933. E-mail: markel@minotstateu.edu.

MARKELLO, JEFFREY PHILIP, lawyer; b. Buffalo, Dec. 14, 1964; s. Anthony Philip and Nancy Hammond M. BA, U. Rochester, 1987; JD, SUNY, Buffalo, 1990. Bar: N.Y. 1991, Mass. 1991. Atty. pvt. practice, Elma, N.Y., 1991-97; ptnr. Sakowski & Markello, 1998—. Trustee East Aurora (N.Y.) Bd. Edn., 1993—, dep. and prosecuter Town of Aurora, 2002—. Office: Sakowski & Markello PO Box 200 6890 Seneca St Elma NY 14059-0200

MARKEN, WILLIAM RILEY, magazine editor; b. San Jose, Calif., Sept. 2, 1942; s. Harry L. and Emma Catherine (Kraus) M.; m. Marilyn Tonascia, Aug. 30, 1964; children— Catherine, Elizabeth, Michael, Paul Student, Occidental Coll., 1960-62; BA, U. Calif., Berkeley, 1964. Editor-in-chief Sunset Mag., Menlo Park, Calif., 1981-96, eHow.com, 1999-2001, Garden Design Mag., 2001—. Bd. dirs. Calif. Tomorrow, 1979-83; pres. League to Save Lake Tahoe, 1994-97. Avocations: tennis, skiing, basketball.

MARKER, MARC LINTHACUM, lawyer, investor; b. Los Angeles, July 19, 1941; s. Clifford Harry and Voris (Linthacum) M.; m. Sandra Vocom. Aug. 29, 1965; children: Victor, Gwendolyn. BA in Econs. and Geography, U. Calif.-Riverside, 1964; JD, U. So. Calif., 1967. Asst. v.p., asst. sec. Security Pacific Nat. Bank, L.A., 1970-73; sr. v.p., chief counsel, sec. Security Pacific Leasing Corp., San Francisco, 1973-92; pres. Security Pacific Leasing Svcs. Corp., 1977-85, dir., 1977-92. Bd. dirs., sec. Voris, Inc., 1973-86; bd. dirs. Refiners Petroleum Corp., 1977-81, Security Pacific Leasing Singapore Ltd., 1983-85, Security Pacific Leasing Can. Ltd., 1989-92; lectr. in field. Served to comdr., USCGR. Mem. ABA, Calif. Bar Assn., D.C. Bar Assn; Club: Army and Navy. Republican. Lutheran.

MARKERT, MARY LOUISE, pediatrics educator; MD, Duke U., 1982. Resident Duke U., Durham, N.C., 1982-84, assoc. prof. pediatrics, 1984—; chmn. American Board of Allergy & Immunology, 1998—. Office: Duke U Med Ctr PO Box 3068 Durham NC 27715-3068*

MARKESBERY, MARIA SABA, lawyer; b. Cin., June 2, 1961; d. Khamis Alexander and Judith Diehl Saba; m. Glenn Alan Markesbery, Aug. 26, 1987; children: Michael, Katherine, Emily. BS, Xavier U., 1983; JD, U. Cin., 1986. Bar: Ohio. Dir. risk mgmt., legal svcs. Franciscan Health System, Cin., 1988-98, gen. counsel, 1998-99; assoc. counsel Mercy Health Ptnrs. S.W. Ohio, 1999—. Mem. Cin. Bar Assn. Office: Mercy Health Ptnrs 2446 Kipling Ave Cincinnati OH 45239-6621

MARKEVICIUS, NIKOLAS VYTAS, bank officer, writer; b. LaGrange, Ill., May 13, 1978; s. Mindaugas and Patricia Markevicius. Grad., Columbia Coll., Chgo., 2002. Mgr. Mary's Corner Market, Westmont, Ill., 1994—2001; tutor writing skills Columbia Coll., Chgo., 2000—02; teller Mid Am. Bank, Clarendon Hills, 2001—02; trainer retail ops. Mid Am. Bank, Westchester, 2002—. Author: The Posse, 2000, Today Was Friday, 2001, The Pilgrim, 2002.

Founder Columbia Cir., 2000—02; pres. United Meth. Ch. Youth Group, 1994—96. Named Ill. State scholar, 1996; recipient 1st pl., Suburban Prairie Writer's Festival, Ill., 1996. Avocations: reading, hockey, advocate for cinema etiquette, comedy.

MARKEY, BRIAN MICHAEL, lawyer; b. Teaneck, N.J., Feb. 10, 1956; s. Raymond Joseph and Sheila (Barry) M.; m. Virginia M. Lincoln, Oct. 26, 1986. BA cum laude, Rider Coll., 1978; JD, Suffolk U., 1985. Bar: N.J. 1985, U.S. Dist. Ct. N.J. 1985, N.Y. 1988. Assoc. Kohler & Clinch, Hackensack, NJ, 1985—90, Law Office J. Dennis Kohler, Hackensack, 1990—91; pvt. practice law Glen Rock, 1991—94; ptnr. Lincoln & Markey, 1995—. Dir. Glen Rock Savs. Bank. Chmn. Glen Rock Planning Bd. Mem. ABA, N.J. Bar Assn., Glen Rock Independence Day Assn. Office: 126 Valley Rd Glen Rock NJ 07452-1796

MARKEY, EDWARD JOHN, congressman; b. Malden, Mass., July 11, 1946; s. John E. and Christine M. (Courtney) M. BA, Boston Coll., 1968, JD, 1972. Bar: Mass. Mem. Mass. Ho. of Reps., 1973-76, U.S. Congress from 7th Mass. dist., 1975—, New Eng. Congl. Caucus, N.E.-Midwest Econ. Advancement Coalition, Dem. Study Group; mem. energy and commerce com. Mem. editorial staff: Boston Coll. Law Rev. Served with USAR, 1968-73. Mem. Mass. Bar Assn. (Mass. Legislator of Year 1975) Clubs: K.C. Home: 7 Townsend St Malden MA 02148-6322 Office: US Ho of Reps 2108 Rayburn House Office Bldg Washington DC 20515-0001*

MARKEY, PAUL VICTOR, videographer, videotape editor, production manager; b. Washington, Feb. 26, 1959; s. Hugh Victor and Patricia Ann (Collins) M.; m. Kathleen Marie Wirts, Feb. 14, 1981; children: Robert William, Julie Faye. AA, Ga. State U., 1979. Film cinematographer U.S. Army, Berlin, 1974-76; on-line editor, videographer Video One, Inc., Owings Mills, Md., 1987-88; live sound engr. various touring bands, 1976-87; pres. East Coast Pictures, Balt., 1988-89; on-line editor, videographer Flite Three Recordings, Ltd., 1989-91; on-line editor KLM Video, Inc., Bethesda, Md., 1992-96; sr. on-line editor, post-prodn. mgr. Big Shot Prodns., Inc., Balt., 1996-99; mgr. post prodn. svcs. Discovery Comm., Inc., Bethesda, 1999—. Editor, videographer Ga. State CCTV, Atlanta, 1977-79; lighting designer Berlin Am. Theater, 1974-76. Lighting designer (plays) Fantastiks, 1974, Love on the Rooftop, 1975; video editor (film) He Said, She Said, 1991; on-line editor various TV programs, indsl. films and documentaries, including The World Wrestling Fedn. (a.k.a. Titan Sports), America's Most Wanted, Beyond 2000, Arthur C. Clarke's Mysterious Universe, History's Turning Points, Histories Mysteries, Scandinavia, The Learning Channel's Mind Twisters, Century of Flight, TLC Legends, The Clintons: A Marriage of Power, Extremists, (with Mark Hammil) Forbidden Places, (with Cheryl Tiegs) Next to Nothing, Wild India, UFO's Explained, Behind the Terror; World's Mightiest Bank; videographer: (TV program) Inside the NFL, 1990; chief video editor: U.S. Holocaust Meml. Mus., Washington. Mem. NATAS, Internat. TV Assn. Avocations: sailing, movies, books, family activities. Office: Discovery Comm Inc 7700 Wisconsin Ave Fl 5 Bethesda MD 20814-3557 Home: 2902 Tweed Dr Finksburg MD 21048-2006 E-mail: paulvmarkey@hotmail.com., paul_markey@dicovery.com.

MARKEY, ROBERT GUY, lawyer; b. Cleveland, Ohio, Feb. 25, 1939; s. Nate and Rhoda (Gross) Markey; m. Nanci Louise Brooks, Aug. 25, 1990; children: Robert Guy, Randolph. AB, Brown U., 1961; JD, Case Western Res., 1964. Bar: Ohio 1964. Ptnr. Baker & Hostetler, Cleve., 1983—. Office: Baker & Hostetler 3200 National City Ctr 1900 E 9th St Ste 3200 Cleveland OH 44114-3475

MARKEY, WILLIAM ALAN, health care administrator; b. Cleve., Dec. 29, 1927; s. Oscar Bennett and Claire (Feldman) M.; m. Irene Nelson, Oct. 31, 1954; children— Janet Ellen Markey-Hisakawa, Suzanne Katherine Markey-Johnson. Student, Case Inst. Tech., 1945-48; BA, U. Mich., 1950; MS, Yale U., 1954. Resident hosp. adminstrn. Beth Israel Hosp., Boston, 1953-54; asst. dir. Montefiore Hosp., Pitts., 1954-56; asst. adminstr. City of Hope Med. Ctr., Duarte, Calif., 1956-57, adminstrv. dir., 1957-66; assoc. dir. cancer hosp. project, instr. pub. health U. So. Calif. Sch. Medicine, 1966-67, asst. clin. prof. pub. health and community medicine, 1968-70, asst. prof., 1970-75, dep. dir. regional med. programs, 1967-71; adminstr. Health Care Agy., County of San Diego, 1971-74, health services cons., 1974-75; dir. Maricopa County Dept. Health Services, Phoenix, 1975-79, cons., 1979-80; adminstr. Sonoma Valley Hosp., Calif., 1980-83. Lectr. pub. health Sch. Pub. Health, UCLA, 1969-74; lectr. comty. medicine Sch. Medicine, U. Calif.-San Diego, 1973-75; cons. L.A. County Dept. Hosps., 1966-71, cons. Hosp./Health Svcs., 1983—; CEO Chinese Hosp., San Francisco, 1985-86, 90-91; adj. instr. Golden Gate U., 1992-96. Mem. bd. edn. Duarte Unified Sch. Dist., 1967-72, pres., 1970-72; bd. dirs. Hosp. Coun. So. Calif., 1963-67, sec., 1966-67, Duarte Pub. Libr. Assn., 1965-72, Duarte-Bradbury chpt. Am. Field Svc., 1965-72, Duarte-Bradbury Comty. Chest, 1961-68, Cen. Ariz. Health Svcs. Agy., 1975-80, Vis. Nurse Assn. The Redwoods, Santa Rosa, Calif., 1985-86, Sonoma Greens Homeowners Assn., 1990-95, Sonoma City Opera, 1987, 93, United Way, Sonoma, 1996—; com. chmn. Sonoma County Bd. Realtors, 1990-92; active Sonoma County Multiple Listing Svc., 1987—. With AUS, 1950-52. Fellow Am. Coll. Health Care Execs. (life); mem. Am. Hosp. Assn. (life), Am. Pub. Health Assn., Royal Soc. Health, Calif. Hosp. Assn. (trustee 1966-69, dir. 1966-69), Internat. Fedn. Hosps., Hosp. Coun. No. Calif. (dir. 1981-83), Kiwanis, Rotary (past pres. Duarte). Home: 866 Princeton Dr Sonoma CA 95476-4186 Office: PO Box F Sonoma CA 95476-0370

MARKEY, WINSTON ROSCOE, aeronautical engineering educator; b. Buffalo, Sept. 20, 1929; s. Roscoe Irvin and Catherine L. (Higgins) M.; m. Phoebe Anne Sproule, Sept. 10, 1955; children: Karl Richard, Katherine Ilse, Kristina Anne. BS, MIT, 1951, Sc.D., 1956. Engr. MIT, 1951-57, asst. prof., 1957-62, assoc. prof., 1962-66, prof., 1966—, undergrad. officer, 1988-2000, dir. Measurement Systems Lab., 1961-89. Chief scientist USAF, 1964-65, mem. sci. adv. bd., 1966-69 Author: (with J. Hovorka) The Mechanics of Inertial Position and Heading Indication, 1961; Assoc. editor: AIAA Jour, 1963-66. Recipient Exceptional Civilian Service award USAF, 1965 Mem. Sigma Xi, Tau Beta Pi, Gamma Alpha Rho. Home: 11 Edgewood Rd Lexington MA 02420-3501 Office: MIT Bldg 33-208 Cambridge MA 02139 E-mail: wrmarkey@mit.edu.

MARKGRAF, J(OHN) HODGE, chemist, educator; b. Cin., Mar. 16, 1930; s. Carl A. and Elizabeth (Hodge) M.; m. Nancy Hart, Apr. 4, 1957; children: Carrie G., Sarah T. AB, Williams Coll., 1952; M.Sc., Yale U., 1954, PhD, 1957; postgrad., U. Munich, W. Ger., 1956-57. Research chemist Procter & Gamble Co., Cin., 1958-59; asst. prof. chemistry Williams Coll., Williamstown, Mass., 1959-65, assoc. prof., 1965-69, prof., 1969-98, Ebenezer Fitch prof. chemistry, 1977-85, 94-98, prof. emeritus, 1998—, provost, 1980-83, v.p. for alumni relations and devel., 1985-94, coll. marshal, 1995-98. Vis. prof. U. Calif., Berkeley, 1964-65, 68-69, 76-77, Duke U., 1983-84, 2001, U. Houston, 1999. Contbr. articles to profl. jours.; patentee in field. NSF sci. faculty fellow, 1964-65; NSF grantee, 1961-63, Am. Chem. Soc.-Petroleum Rsch. Fund grantee, 1965-68, 70-72, 93-95, Merck & Co. grantee, 1967, Rsch. Corp. grantee, 1963, 75, 90-92, Pfizer Inc. grantee, 1996, 97, 98, Camille and Henry Dreyfus Found. grantee, 2000-2001. Mem. Am. Chem. Soc., Phi Beta Kappa, Sigma Xi. Home: 104 Forest Rd Williamstown MA 01267-2029 Office: Williams College Dept Chemistry Williamstown MA 01267-2692 E-mail: j.hodge.markgraf@williams.edu.

MARKGRAF, ROSEMARIE, real estate broker; b. Grantsburg, Wis., Oct. 31, 1934; d. Helen Elizabeth Pribil. BS, U. Wis., 1957, MS, 1958. Cert. tchr. Tchr. H.S., Wis., Conn, 1958-61; office mgr. Robert S. Palmer, Middletown, Conn., 1962-64; edn. adv. Girl Scouts U.S.A., N.Y.C., 1964-66; cmty. rels. assoc. Motion Picture Assn. Am., N.Y., 1967-69; mgr. The Chateau Inn, Stamford, N.Y., 1970-78; real estate salesman Atkins Realty, Ltd., Bklyn., 1979-80; real estate broker, prin. The Markgraf Group, Ltd., 1980—. Cons. Real Estate Counseling Group Conn., Storrs, 1963-91; pres. Tuff Transport, Inc., 1977-2000; adj. prof. Real Estate Inst., 1995—. Pres. Brownstone Rep. Club; candidate 12th Congl. Dist., Bklyn., 1998, 2000; exec. com. Kings County Rep. Com.; conservative candidate 52d State Assembly Dist., 2002. Mem. Real Estate Bd. N.Y., Steuben Soc. (pres.), Yeats Soc. N.Y. Roman Catholic. Avocations: water aerobics, crossword puzzles, oenology. Home and Office: The Markgraf Group Ltd 60 Remsen St Brooklyn NY 11201-3453 E-mail: rmarkgraf@worldnet.att.net.

MARKHAM, CHARLES BUCHANAN, retired lawyer; b. Durham, N.C., Sept. 15, 1926; s. Charles Blackwell and Sadie Helen (Hackney) M. AB, Duke U., Durham, N.C., 1945; postgrad., U. N.C. Law Sch., Chapel Hill, 1945-46; LL.B., George Washington U., Washington, 1951. Bar: D.C. 1951, N.Y. 1961, N.C. 1980, U.S. Ct. Appeals (2d cir.) 1962, U.S. Ct. Appeals (D.C. cir.) 1955, U.S. Supreme Ct. 1964. Reporter Durham Sun, N.C., 1945; asst. state editor, editorial writer Charlotte News, 1947-48; dir. publicity and research Young Democratic Clubs Am., Washington, 1948-49, exec. sec., 1949-50; polit. analyst Dem. Senatorial Campaign Com., 1950-51; spl. atty. IRS, Washington and N.Y.C., 1952-60; assoc. Battle, Fowler, Stokes and Kheel, N.Y.C., 1960-65; dir. research U.S. Equal Employment Opportunity Commn., Washington, 1965-68; dep. asst. sec. U.S. Dept. Housing and Urban Devel., 1969-72; asst. dean Rutgers U. Law Sch., Newark, 1974-76; assoc. prof. law N.C. Central U., Durham, 1976-81, prof. law, 1981-83; mayor City of Durham, N.C., 1981-85; ptnr. Markham and Wickham, Durham, 1984-86. Trustee Hist. Preservation Soc. Durham, 1982-86; bd. dirs. Stagville Ctr., 1984-86; mem. Gov.'s Crime Commn., Raleigh, 1985; dep. commr. N.C. Indsl. Commn., Raleigh, 1986-93. Editor: Jobs, Men and Machines: The Problems of Automation, 1964 Mem. Carolina Club, Phi Beta Kappa, Omicron Delta Kappa, Phi Delta Phi, Phi Delta Theta. Republican. Episcopalian. Home: 204 N Dillard St Durham NC 27701-3404

MARKHAM, CHARLES HENRY, neurologist; b. Pasadena, Calif., Dec. 24, 1923; s. Fred Smith and Maziebelle Valeta (Glover) M.; m. Kathleen Tiernan, Sept. 29, 1945 (div. 1971); children: Charles H., Arthur Tiernan, Daphne, James Daniel; m. Lisa Wells Overly, July 10, 1971; children: John Wells, Sara Brennan. Student, Colo. Sch. Mines, 1941-43; AB, Stanford U., 1947, MD, 1951. Intern, med. asst. resident Lane Hosp., San Francisco, 1950-52; fellow in neurology Children's Med. Ctr., Boston, 1952-53; asst. resident Boston City Hosp., 1953-54, chief resident, 1954-55; asst. prof. neurology UCLA Sch. Medicine, 1958-65, assoc. prof., 1965-70, assoc. prof. neurology, 1970-71, prof. neurology, 1971-94, prof. emeritus, 1994—; rsch. prof. dept. psychology U. Calif., Santa Barbara, 1995—. Sci. dir. Dystonia Med. Rsch. Found., Chgo., 1985-94, mem. bd. trustees, 1994—; sci. dir. Hereditary Disease Found., L.A., 1979-81; mem. adv. bd. Am. Parkinson Disease Assn., N.Y.C., 1976-83; attending physician UCLA Sch. Medicine, 1957—, cons. in neurology St. John's Hosp., Santa Monica, Calif., 1960-94. Contbr. articles to profl. jours.; author numerous books and abstracts. Trustee Westlake Sch. for Girls, L.A., 1965-74, St. Matthews Parish Sch., L.A., 1985-87; bd. dirs. Jubilee Christian Acad., 1996-99, Wildling Mus., 1997—, Las Positas Park Found., 1998-2000. With U.S. Army, 1943-45, ETO. Grantee NIH, NASA. Mem. Am. Acad. Neurology, AAAS, Am. Bd. Psychiatry and Neurology, Am. Epilepsy Soc., Am. Neurol. Assn., Am. Pain Soc., Am. Soc. for Gravitational and Space Biology, Bárány Soc. (Hallpike-Nylen prize 1990), Internat. Brain Rsch. Orgn., Internat. League Against Epilepsy, L.A. Soc. Neurology and Psychiatry, N.Y. Acad. Scis., Soc. for Neurosci., Western Inst. on Epilepsy, Rsch. Soc. for Parkinson Disease and Movement Disorders (pres. 1984-2000). Republican. Achievements include research in L-dopa and medical and surgical therapy for Parkinson's disease, dystonia, brain stem mechanisms for vestibular and quick and slow eye movements, long-term exposure to microgravity, space motion sickness. Office: UCLA Sch Medicine Dept Neurology Los Angeles CA 90095-0001

MARKHAM, CHARLES RINKLIN, financial executive, tax accountant; b. Travis AFB, Calif., May 13, 1959; s. Charles Whitlow Markham and Helen (Roberson) Williams. BS, MIT, 1984; MS, Bentley Coll., 1995. Assoc. cons. Bain and Co., Boston, 1984-87; cons., 1987-89; investment analyst Hancock Venture Capital, Boston, 1989-91; pvt. practice acct., 1990—; CFO Bus. Matters, Inc., Waltham, Mass., 1993-95, Clin. Networx, Waltham, 1995-97. Dir. Harvard Coop. Soc., 1980-81, 83-84; mem. subcom. United Way Citizens Allocation 1982-87; alt. del. Rep. Nat. Conv., 1984; nat. gov. bd. Common Cause, 1984-85; state gov. bd. Common Cause, Mass., 1987-91; mem. fin. com. Town of Norwell, 1994-98; mem. Bd. Assessors, Town of Norwell, Mass., 1998—. Mem. Sigma Chi. Home: 45 Woods Rd Norwell MA 02061-1238 Office: 454 Washington St Norwell MA 02061

MARKHAM, CLAIRE AGNES (M. CLARE MARKHAM), retired chemistry educator, consultant; b. New Haven, Aug. 12, 1919; d. James J. and Agnes V. (Manning) M. BA, St. Joseph Coll., West Hartford, Conn., 1940; PhD, Cath. U. Am., 1952; DHL (hon.) , St. Joseph Coll., 1989. Joined Sisters of Mercy, Roman Cath. Ch., 1940. Tchr. chemistry and math. Sacred Heart H.S., Waterbury, Conn., 1945-49; mem. faculty chemistry St. Joseph Coll., West Hartford, 1952-97, cons. instl. advancement, 1996—. Dept. chair St. Joseph Coll., 1959-70, dean grad. sch., 1979-87, asst. to pres. acad. affairs, 1987-95; dir. numerous tchr. insts., 1959-89; mem. vis. faculty Calvin's Lab., NSF, U. Calif., Berkeley, 1967-68. Contbr. articles to profl. jours.; editor sci. series McGraw Hill, 1956-60. Undersec. for Energy, Office of Policy and Mgmt., State of Conn., Hartford, 1977—79; mem. adv. com. Permanent Commn. Status of Women, 1995—; mem. adv. coun. Dept. Higher Edn., State of Conn., 1970—80; energy advisor Nat. Gov.'s Assn., 1977—79; bd. dirs. Conn. Energy Co-op., 2000—. Faculty fellow NSF, Trondheim, Norway, 1967, travel grantee, cons., Madras, India, 1974-77; recipient Equity award AAUW, 1992. Fellow Conn. Acad. for Edn.; mem. AAAS, Am. Chem. Soc. (councilor 1968-88, chair Conn. Valley sect. 1955-67, 20 Yr. award 1988), Conn. Acad. Sci. and Engring. (founding mem., chair tech. bd. 1994-98), Sigma Xi (sect. chair 1993-95). Democrat. Avocations: photography, music, literature. Home: 1678 Asylum Ave West Hartford CT 06117-2791 Office: St Joseph Coll West Hartford CT 06117

MARKHAM, J. DAVID, educator, writer, historical consultant; b. Austin, Tex., Dec. 26, 1945; s. James Walter and Myrtle (Sturges) M.; m. Barbara Ann Munson, May 14, 1983. BS, U. Iowa, 1971; MA, U. No. Iowa, 1972; postgrad., So. Ill. U., 1972-74, U. Wis., 1981-82; MEd, Ariz. State U., 1991; postgrad., Fla. State U., 1996—97, Oxford (Eng.) U., 1996. Instr. sociology U. Wis., Fond du Lac/Stevens Point, 1974-76; dir. Vietnam edn. grants Wis. Dept. Vet. Affairs, Madison, 1979-83; coordinator internat. edn. AFSCME, Phoenix, 1983-84; vets. svc. officer Ariz. Vets. Service Commn., 1984-86; asst. to dir. Commn. on Ariz. Environ., 1986-88; div. supr. Ariz. Dept. Liquor Lics. and Control, 1988-89; world history and English tchr. Tolleson Union H.S. Dist., 1990-92; world history tchr. Lake Worth H.S., Palm Beach, Fla., 1992-2000; history tchr. Tumwater H.S., 2000—01, Centralia H.S., 2001—02. Instr. sociology and polit. sci., Maricopa C.C. Dist., Phoenix, 1985-91; instr. Palm Beach C.C., 1993-95. Co-author: Napoleon: The Final Verdict, 1996; contbr. articles in 20 jours. Bd. dirs. World Affairs Coun. Ariz., 1987-90; v.p. Ariz. Com. for Bicentennial of the French Revolution, 1988-89; exec. v.p. Napoleonic Alliance, 1996—. With U.S. Army, 1968-69, Vietnam. Decorated Bronze Star; recipient medal of Landtag of Badden-Württemberg, Germany, 1987, Spl. Svc. award Alliance Francaise of Phoenix, 1992, Marengo medal Province of Alessandria, Italy, 1997, medal City of Ajaccio, Corsica, France, 1997. Mem. Internat. Napoleonic Soc. (exec. v.p. and editor-in-chief 1995—, Legion of Merit 1996), Napoleonic Alliance (bd. dirs. 1992—, editor conf. procs., editor bull., Pres. medal 1998), Inst. on Napoleon and the French Revolution, Western Soc. for French History, Am. Byron Soc., Sierra Club, Zero Population Growth, Alpha Kappa Delta, Phi Kappa Phi, Phi Alpha Theta. Democrat. Avocations: collecting Napoleonic items, writing history, outdoor activities, travel, music. Home: 1841 52nd Way SE Olympia WA 98501-8000 E-mail: imperialglory@attbi.com.

MARKHAM, JESSE WILLIAM, economist, educator; b. Richmond, Va., Apr. 21, 1916; s. John James and Edith (Luttrell) M.; m. Penelope Jane Anton, Oct. 15, 1944; children: Elizabeth Anton Markham McLean, John James, Jesse William. AB, U. Richmond, 1941; postgrad., Johns Hopkins U., 1941-42, U.S. Fgn. Svc. Sch., 1945; MA, Harvard U., 1947, PhD, 1949. Acct. E.I. duPont de Nemours Co., Richmond, 1935-38; tchg. fellow Harvard U., 1946-48; asst. prof. Vanderbilt U., 1948-52, assoc. prof., 1952-53; chief economist FTC, Washington, 1953-55; assoc. prof. Princeton U., 1955-57, prof. econs., 1957-68; prof. Harvard Grad. Sch. Bus. Adminstrn., 1968-72, Charles Edward Wilson prof., 1972-82, prof. emeritus, 1982—; prof. Harvard U. Ext. Svcs., 1984—. Vis. prof. Columbia U., 1958; Ford Found. vis. prof. Harvard Grad. Sch. Bus. ADminstrn., 1965-66; rsch. prof. Law and Econs. Ctr., Emory U., 1982-84; rsch. staff, mem. bd. editors Patent Trademark Copyright Rsch. Inst., George Washington U., 1955-70; econs. editor Houghton Mifflin Co., 1961-71; U.S. del. comm. experts on bus. practices European Productivity Agy., OEEC, 1956, 57, 58, 59, 61; vis. prof. Harvard U., 1961-62; dir. Ford Found. Seminar Region II, 1961; adv. com. mktg. to sec. commerce, 1967-71; mem. Am. Bar Assn. Commn. to study FTC, 1969. Author: Competition in the Rayon Industry, 1952, The Fertilizer Industry: Study of an Imperfect Market, 1958, The American Economy, 1963, (with Charles Fiero and Howard Piquet) The European Common Market: Friend or Competitor, 1964, (with Gustav Papnek) Industrial Organization and Economic Development, 1970, Conglomerate Enterprise and Public Policy, 1973, (with Paul Teplitz) Baseball Economics and Public Policy, 1982; sect. on oligopoly Internat. Ency. Social Scis.; contbr. articles to econ. jours. Del. People to People Diplomacy Mission to USSR, 1989; active Boy Scouts Am.; chmn. Harvard Parents Com., 1969-72. Served as lt. USNR, World War II. Ford Found. rsch. prof., 1958-59. Mem. Am. Econ. Assn., U.S. C. of C. (econ. policy com.), Harvard Club (N.Y.C., Sarasota, Fla.), The Cedars Club, Phi Beta Kappa. Episcopalian. Home: 4425 Gulf Of Mexico Dr Longboat Key FL 34228-2403 Office: Harvard U Grad Sch Bus Adminstrn 300 Cumnock Boston MA 02163

MARKHAM, REED B. education educator, consultant; b. Alhambra, Calif., Feb. 14, 1957; s. John F. and Reeda (Bjarason) M. BA, MA, Brigham Young U., 1982; BS, Regents Coll., 1981, MA, 1982; MPA, U. So. Calif., 1983; MA, UCLA, 1989; PhD, Columbia Pacific U., 1991. Mem. faculty Brigham Young U., Provo, Utah, 1984, Calif. State U., Fullerton and Long Beach, 1984, Northridge, 1985, El Camino Coll., Torrance, Calif., 1986, Orange Coast Coll., Costa Mesa, 1986, Pasadena (Calif.) Coll., 1986, Fullerton (Calif.) Community Coll., 1986; instr., mem. pub. rels. com. Chaffey (Calif.) Coll., 1986-87; prof., CARES dir. Calif. State Poly. U., Pomona, 1987-98; adj. prof. Calif. State U., L.A., 1992-93, dir. Ctr. for Student Retention, 1995—; prof. East L.A. Coll., 1996-98, Salt Lake C.C., 1998—. Rsch. asst. to pres. Ctr. for the Study of Cmty. Coll., 1985; mem. faculty Riverside (Calif.) Coll., 1989-90, Rio Hondo (Calif.) Coll., 1989-90, English Lang. Inst., 1994, Calif. Poly Summer Bridge, 1989-95, East L.A. Coll.; adj. prof. Citrus Coll., 1998—; speechwriter U.S. Supreme Ct., Washington, 1980; cons. gifted children program Johns Hopkins U./Scripps Coll., Claremont, Calif., 1987-88; mem. faculty PACE Program East L.A., 1995-96; faculty East L.A. Coll., 1996-97; adj. prof. U. So. Calif., 1998—; prof. Salt Lake C.C., 1998-99; mem. Pres.'s Coalition for Am. Reads Challenge, 1999; mem. Olympic News Svc. 2002, 2001-. Author: Power Speechwriting, 1983, Power Speaking, 1990, Public Opinion, 1990, Advances in Public Speaking, 1991, Leadership 2000: Success Skills for University Students, 1995, Excellence in Public Speaking, 1997; co-author: Student Retention: Success Models in Higher Education, 1996, Upward Bound Program Grant Proposal, 1996, Making Marriage Magnificent, 1998; editor Trojan in Govt., U. So. Calif., 1983; editl. bd. mem. Edn. Digest, Speaker and Gavel, Innovative Higher End., Pub. Rels. Rev., Nat. Forensic Jour., The Forensic Educator, Clearinghouse for the Contemporary Educator, Hispanic Am. Family Mag.; writer N.Y. times, Christian Sci. Monitor; ednl. columnist San Bernardino (Calif.) Sun., 1992-98. VOICE, 2000-01. Pres. bd. trustees Regents Coll., 1986; appointed to Pres.'s Coalition for Am. Reads Challenge; mem. Olympic News Svc., 2001—; mem. Coun. Study of Cmty. Colls., 2002—; torchrearer Olympic Winter Games, 2002; unit commr. Boy Scouts of Am., 2002— Mem. Am. Comm. Assn., Doctorate Assn. N.Y. Scholars, Nat. Assn. Pvt. Nontraditional Colls. (accrediting com. 1989—), Pub. Rels. Soc. Am. (dir.-at-large inland empire 1992-93, faculty advisor). Mem. Lds Ch. Office: Salt Lake CC Comm Dept PO Box 30808 Salt Lake City UT 84130-0808 E-mail: markhare@slcc.edu.

MARKHAM, RICHARD GLOVER, research executive; b. Pasadena, Calif., June 18, 1925; s. Fred Smith and Maziebelle (Glover) M.; m. Jonne Louise Pearson, Apr. 29, 1950; children: Janet B., Fred S., Charles R., Richard G., Marilyn A. Student, Stanford U., 1943; BS, Calif. Inst. Tech., Pasadena, 1945; MS, Stanford U., 1947. Pres., owner Aquarium Pump Supply, Prescott, Ariz., 1957-78; 1st v.p., dir. Bank of Prescott, 1981-87; also v.p., bd. dirs. Oxycal Labs., Prescott, 1981-97, ret., 1997. Patentee in field. Mem. Ariz. Dept. Econ. Planning and Devel., 1967-72; treas. Ariz. State Rep. Com., 1970-72; active Ariz. Acad., 1974—; trustee Orme Sch., Mayer, Ariz., 1970-83, Prescott Coll., 1979-83. Home: Prescott, Ariz. Died Mar. 31, 2002.

MARKHAM, RICHARD LAWRENCE, chemist; b. Texarkana, Ark., July 31, 1940; s. Andre Lawrence and Elizabeth Ella (Beck) M.; m. Judith Lynn Roberts, Aug. 5, 1972. BS, Okla. State U., 1962; MS, U. Ariz., 1969. Rsch. scientist Celanese Plastics Co., Summit, N.J., 1969-72; narcotics analyst U.S. Army Crime Lab., Frankfurt, Germany, 1973-74; from plant chemist to mfg. mgr. Amerace Corp., Kehlen, Luxembourg, Butler, NJ, Johnson City, Tenn., 1974-79; from project mgr. to product mgr. Battelle Meml. Inst., Columbus, Ohio, 1979-90, bus. devel. mgr., 1991-98; rsch. mgr. Nextec Applications Inc., Vista, Calif., 1998—2001; ind. cons., 2000—; cons. Poway, Calif., 2001—. Adv. bd. Plastics Cons. Dir., Tucson, 1990-95. Author, editor: Identification of Major Developments in Polymer Blends, 1987, Reactive Processing of Polymeric Materials, 1988, Compatibilization of Polymer Blends, 1994; contbr. articles to profl. jours.; patentee in field. Founder, pres. East. Tenn. chpt. St. Jude Rsch. Hosp., Johnson City, 1977, 78, 79; pres., trustee Lakeside Forest Homeowners Assn., Westerville, Ohio, 1993-94. Mem. Am. Chem. Soc. (polymer chem. div., polymeric materials sci. & engring. div.), Sigma Xi. Avocations: fastpitch softball, racquetball, photography. Home: 13108 Decant Dr Poway CA 92064-1116 E-mail: markhamr@san.rr.com.

MARKHAM, SANFORD MAX, obstetrician-gynecologist, educator; b. Pittsburg, Kans., 1934; BS, U. Kans., 1956, MD, 1960. Intern Ind. Med. Ctr., Indpls., 1960-61; resident ob-gyn. Cornell Med. Ctr., N.Y.C., 1963-67; fellow reproductive endocrinology Johns Hopkins Hosp., Balt., 1986-88; assoc. prof. ob-gyn. U. Iowa. Hosps. and Clinics, Iowa City. Mem. ACS, AMA, Am. Coll. Ob-Gyn., Am. Soc. for Reproductive Medicine. E-mial. Office: U Iowa Hosps and Clinics Dept Ob-Gyn 200 Hawkins Dr Iowa City IA 52242-1009 E-mail: sanford-markham@uiowa.edu.

MARKIDES, KYRIAKOS SOCRATES, gerontology educator; b. Nicosia, Cyprus, Mar. 21, 1948, came to U.S., 1968; s. Socrates and Persoulla Markides; m. Evelyn A. Stanton, Dec. 18, 1971; 1 son, Michael. BA, Bowling Green State U., 1972; MA, La. State U., 1973, PhD, 1976. Asst. prof. U. Tex. Health Sci. Ctr., San Antonio, 1976-82; assoc. prof. , 1982-87, U. Tex Med. Br., Galveston, prof., 1987—. Author: (with others) Older Mexican Americans, 1983; Ethnicity and Aging: A Bibliography, 1984, Aging and Ethnicity, 1987, Retirement in Industrialized Societies, 1987, Aging and Health, 1989, Aging, Stress and Health, 1989; editorial bd. The Gerontologist Jour., 1980—, Jour. Gerontology, 1984—; founding editor Jour. of Aging and Health. Nat. Inst. Aging research grantee, 1980—; Hogg Found. research grantee, 1984—, Rockefeller Found. rsch. grantee. Fellow Gerontol. Soc. Am.; mem. Am. Sociol. Assn., Population Assn. Am., Am. Pub. Health Assn. Office: Univ Tex Medical Branch Galveston TX 77550

MARKIN, KARL EDWARD, obstetrician/gynecologist; b. Rochester, N.Y., 1929; MD, SUNY Syracuse, 1955. Diplomate Am. Bd. Ob-Gyn. Intern, resident pathology Ea. Maine Gen. Hosp., Bangor, 1955-56; resident ob-gyn St. Mary's Hosp., Rochester, N.Y., 1958-61; ob-gyn Selah, Wash., 1961—. Fellow Am. Coll. Ob-Gyn, Am. Fertility Soc.; mem. YCMS, Ducks Unltd., Pheasants Forever, Mule Deer Found., Safari Club Internat. (pres. ctrl. Wash. chpt., chmn. Amazon Project). Home: 181 Reitmeier Ln Selah WA 98942-8713

MARKING, T(HEODORE) JOSEPH, JR. transportation and urban planner; b. June 28, 1945; s. Theodore Joseph and Alvena Cecilia (Thieman) M.; m. Kathy K. Hagerman, Nov. 25, 1969. BA, So. Ill. U., 1967, M City and Regional Planning, 1972. Intelligence rsch. specialist Def. Intelligence Agy., Washington, 1967-68; planner 1 St. Louis City Plan Commn., 1970; transp. planner Alan M. Voorhees & Assocs., St. Louis, 1970-74, sr. transp. planner, 1974-78, assoc., 1978; sr. transp. planner Booker Assocs Inc., 1978-80, chief traffic and transp. sect., 1980-85; mgr. transit planning East-West Gateway Coord. Coun., 1985-88; mgr. planning dept. Harland Bartholomew & Assocs., 1988-91; sr. transp. planner Burns & Mcdonnell Engring. Co., 1992-95, PB Booker Assoc. Inc., St. Louis, 1996-98, Parsons Brinckerhoff, St. Louis, 1998—. Planner-in-charge, Mo.; guest lectr. St. Louis C.C. Dist., Webster U., St. Louis U. Mem. am. Inst. Cert. Planners (charter), Am. Planning Assn. (charter, treas. transp. planning divsn., past pres., pres., sec., bd. dirs. St. Louis sect.), Inst. Transp. Engrs., Traffic Engrs. Assn. Met. St. Louis (past pres.), Transp. Rsch. Bd. Office: 1831 Chestnut St Ste 700 Saint Louis MO 63103-2225 E-mail: marking@pbworld.com.

MARKKULA, A.C., JR. entrepreneur, computer company executive; Co-founder, former pres., chief exec. officer Apple Computer Inc., now chmn. bd. dirs.; founder, vice chmn. Echelon, Los Gatos, Calif.; with ACM Investments, Woodside. Office: ACM Investments PO Box 620170 Woodside CA 94062-0170

MARKLAND, BARBARA CAROLYN, sales and leasing professional; b. Winter Park, Fla., Nov. 11, 1972; d. Roger Vaughn and Virginia Marie (Hudson) M. BA, U. Ctrl. Fla., 1995, MPA, 1997. Notary pub., Fla. Prodn. leader Daugar, Casselberry, Fla., 1992-96; intern Orange County Corrections Divsn., Orlando, 1996; asst. grad. coord. U. Ctrl. Fla., 1995-97; adminstrv. asst. Glatting Jackson Kercher Anglin Lopez Rinehart Inc., 1998; sales and leasing coord. Club Car Inc./Ingersoll Rand, 1998—. Caseworker Prosecution Alternatives Youth, Sanford, Fla., 1994. Vol. Seminole County Humane Soc., Sanford, 1990—, Habitat for Humanity, Orlando, 1993, Coalition for the Homeless, Orlando, 1998-99; mem. Dean's Adv. Coun., Orlan do, 1995-97; citizen on patrol Seminole County, 2001—. Disney scholar Walt Disney World, 1991. Mem. ASPA, Golden Key, Beta Sigma Phi, Phi Theta Kappa, Phi Kappa Phi, Pi Alpha Alpha, Alpha Phi Sigma. Republican. Lutheran. Avocations: reading, sewing, collectables, walking, cooking. Home: 1939 Carrigan Ave Winter Park FL 32792-1010

MARKLAND, FRANCIS SWABY, JR. biochemist, educator; b. Phila., Jan. 15, 1936; s. Francis Swaby Sr. and Willie Lawrence (Averritt) M.; m. Barbara Blake, Jun. 27, 1959 - April 5, 1996; children: Cathleen Blake, Francis Swaby IV. BS, Pa. State U., 1957; PhD, Johns Hopkins U., 1964. Postdoctoral fellow UCLA, 1964-66, asst. prof. biochemistry, 1966-73; vis. asst. prof. U. So. Calif., Los Angeles, 1973-74, assoc. prof., 1974-83, prof., 1983—, acting chmn. dept. biochemistry, 1986-88, vice-chmn., 1988-92. Cons. Clin. Lab. Med. Group, L.A., 1977-88, Cortech, Inc., Denver, 1983-88, Maret Corp., Wayne, Pa., 1996-2000; mem. biochem., endocrinology study sect. NIH, 1986-90. Contbg. editor: Toxicon, Internat. Jour. Toxinology, Jour. Natural Toxins; contbr. articles to profl. jours.: Mem. Angeles Choral, L.A. Capt. USNR, 1957-59 Recipient NIH rsch. career devel. award USPHS, NIH, 1968-73; rsch. grantee Nat. Cancer Inst., 1979-86, 91-93, Nat. Heart Lung and Blood Inst., 1984-88, 95-99, State of Calif. Breast Cancer Rsch. Program, 1995—, State Calif. Cancer Rsch. Program, 2000—. Mem. AAAS, Am. Soc. Biochem. and Molecular Biology, Am. Chem. Soc., Internat. Soc. on Toxinology, Soc. Fibronolysis & Proteolysis, Internat. Soc. on Thrombosis and Haemostasis (subcom. exogenous hemostatic factors, chair 1994-96, 99-2001), Am. Assn. Cancer Rsch., Am. Soc. Hematology, Sigma Xi, Alpha Zeta. Avocations: singing, skiing, aerobics, golf. Office: U So Calif Keck Sch Medicine Cancer Rsch Lab Rm 106 1303 N Mission Rd Los Angeles CA 90033-1020 E-mail: markland@usc.edu.

MARKLE, CHERI VIRGINIA CUMMINS, nurse; b. N.Y.C., Nov. 22, 1936; d. Brainard Lyle and Mildred (Schwab) Cummins; m. John Markle, Aug. 26, 1961 (dec. 1962); 1 child, Kellianne. RN, Ind. State U. and Union Hosp., 1959; BS in Rehab. Edn., Wright State U., 1975; BSN, Capital U., 1987; postgrad. in nursing adminstrn., Wright State U., 1987-89; MS, Calif. Coll. Health Sci. Administration, 1994; postgrad., Columbia Pacific U., 1996-2000. Cert. clin. hypnotherapist Nat. Guild Hypnotherapists. Coordinator Dayton (Ohio) Children's Psychiat. Hosp., 1962-75; dir. nursing Stillwater Health Ctr., Dayton, 1975-76; rehab. cons. Fairborn, Ohio, 1976-91, N.Y.C.; sr. supr. VA, Dayton, 1977-85, nurse coord. alcohol rehab., 1985-86; DON Odd Fellows, Springfield, Ohio, 1987-88, Miami Christel Manor, Miamisburg, 1988-99; DON, rehab. cons. NMS Tng. Sys., Dayton, 1989-91. Psychiat. nurse VA Med. Ctr., N.Y. Rehab., 1991, mem. com. women vets., 1991-93; advisor Calif. Coll. Health Sci. Newspaper columnist Golden Times, Clark County. Bd. dirs. Temple Universal Judaism, 1992, 97; mem. Town and Village Synagogue, 1999—. 1st lt. USAF, 1959-61. Mem. ANA (cert. adminstrn. 1983, cert. gerontology 1984), AAUW, Nurse Mgrs. Assembly, Gerontol. Nurse Assembly, Rehab. Soc., Nat. Guild Hypnotherapists, Internat. Assn. Counselors and Therapists, Nat. Coun. Jewish Women, Jewish War Vets. (sr. vice comdr. Post 1), Wright State U. Alumni Assn., Am. Legion (life), Hadassah, Women's City Club N.Y., Gilbert and Sullivan Soc., Internat. Consortium Parse Scholars, Alpha Sigma Alpha, Sigma Theta Tau. Democrat. Jewish. Avocations: cats, reading, music, needlework, swimming, grandchildren. E-mail: cherimarklern@yahoo.com.

MARKLE, JOHN, JR. lawyer; b. Allentown, Pa., July 20, 1931; s. John Markle II and Pauline (Powers) Mulligan; m. Mary B. McLean, Apr. 19, 1952 (div. Apr. 1990); children: Ellen, John III, Patricia, Stephen, Mary; m. Kathryn E. Wheeler, July 14, 1990. Grad., The Hill Sch., Pottstown, Pa., 1949; BA, Yale U., 1953; LLB, Harvard Law Sch., 1958. Bar: Pa. 1959, U.S. Dist. Ct. (ea. dist.) Pa. 1959, U.S. Supreme Ct. 1980, U.S. Ct. Appeals (3d cir.) 1973. Assoc. Drinker Biddle & Reath, Phila., 1958-64, ptnr., 1964-97, counsel, 1997-2000. Chmn. Pa. Labor Rels. Bd., 1996—; bd. dirs. Main Line Health. Contbg. editor: The Developing Labor Law, 1976—. Bd. dirs. Paoli (Pa.) Meml. Hosp. Found., 1982—, chmn., 1995—2000; bd. dirs. The Hill Sch., Pottstown, Pa., 1970—, chmn., 1985—93. Lt. col. USMC, 1950—73. Named Most Outstanding Young Rep. (Pa.), 1966. Mem. ABA, Pa. Bar Assn., Am. Arbitration Assn., Coll. Labor and Employment Lawyers, Yale Club (Phila.), Merion Golf Club, Ekwanok Country Club. Republican. Avocations: golf, photography. Home: 205 Cambridge Chase Exton PA 19341-3137 Office: Drinker Biddle & Reath 1000 Westlakes Dr Ste 300 Berwyn PA 19312-2409 E-mail: jackmarkle@prodigy.net., marklej@dbr.com.

MARKLE, ROGER A(LLAN), retired oil company executive; b. Sidney, Mont., Dec. 12, 1933; m. Mary Elizabeth Thompson, Jan. 13, 1967. BS in Mining Engring, U. Alaska, 1959; MS, Stanford U., 1965; MBA, U. Chgo., 1972. Mgr. mine devel. Amoco Minerals, Inc., Chgo., 1973-74; pres. western div. Valley Camp Coal Co., Salt Lake City, 1974-78, pres., chief exec. officer Cleve., 1979-82; pres. Quaker State Corp., Oil City, Pa., 1982-86, chief operating officer, 1986-88, also bd. dirs., vice chmn., 1988-89; pres. Nerco Oil & Gas, Vancouver, Wash., 1990-92. Dir. U.S. Bur. Mines, Washington, 1978-79 Served with USN, 1951-54. Mem. AIME.

MARKLE, WILLIAM HOWARD, family physician, educator; b. Pitts., Apr. 11, 1947; s. Howard Elmer and Doris (Bland) M.; m. Mary Margaret Pollock, Aug. 23, 1969; children: Alex William, Elizabeth Irene, Mary Ruth, Dorothy Joy. BA, Washington Jefferson Coll., 1969; MD, Pa. State U., 1973. Diplomate Am. Bd. Family Practice; cert. of knowledge in clin. tropical medicine. Resident Med. Coll., Blackstone, Va., 1973-76; pvt. practice Mannboro (Va.) Med. Ctr., 1976-86; physician Nat. Health Svcs. Corp., Mannboro, 1976-78; med. dir. Ind. br. Wycliffe Bible Translators, Irian Jaya, Indonesia, 1987-94; asst. prof. family physician U. Pitts., 1994—; program dir. family practice residency UPMC Mckeesport, 2002—. Fellow: Am. Acad. Family Physicians; mem.: World Orgn. Family Doctors, Internat. Health Med. Edn. Consortium (governing coun. 1995—2001), Am. Soc. Tropical Medicine and Hygiene, Christian Med. Dental Soc. Mem. Assembly of God. Avocations: running exercise, gardening, reading. tropical fish. Office: U Pitts Dept Family Med 3518 5th Ave Pittsburgh PA 15261-0001 E-mail: whm@pitt.edu.

MARKMAN, PAIGE BEAVERS, communications executive; b. Ft. Walton Beach, Fla., June 3, 1965; d. Charles Willis B. and Kaye (McKnight) Beavers; m. Eric Jon Markman, Apr. 6, 1991 (div. 1994). BA in Media Arts, Rhodes Coll., 1987. Classified mgr. Ark. Bus. Mag., Little Rock, 1987-88; publs. mgr. Ark. Children's Hosp., 1988-89; dir. communications Ark. Bar Assn., 1989-94; owner Builders' Showcase Mag., 1994-96; pub. rels. specialist Wills Thompson Paschall, 1996-97; dir. comm. and devel. Ark. Advs. for Children and Families, 1997—. Bd. dir. pub. rels. Ark. Leadership, Inc., Little Rock, 1989-90; mem. editors adv. bd. West Pub. Co., St. Paul, speaker editors exch., 1992; mem. bus. devel. bd. Cornerstone Project, Little Rock. Editor AR Lawyer mag., 1989-94, (newsletter) Newsbulletin, 1989-94. Spl. events chair Riverfest, Inc., Little Rock, 1991-92; mem. Jr. League of Little Rock, 1991, sec.-treas. pub. rels.-mktg. com., 1991-92; bd. dirs. Little Rock C. of C., 1987-89. Named New Mem. of Quarter, Little Rock Jr. C. of C., 1987, New Mem. of Yr., 1988. Mem. Internat. Assn. Bus. Communicators (editor Inside IABC Ark. 1990-91), Nat. Assn. Bar Execs (speaker pub. rels. sect. workshop 1990). Democrat. Roman Catholic. Avocations: snow skiing, jogging, reading. Home: 7 Cedar Branch Dr Little Rock AR 72223-2362 Office: Ark Advs Children and Family Donaghel Bldg 7th and Main Sts Ste 913 Little Rock AR 72201

MARKMAN, RONALD, artist, educator; b. Bronx, N.Y., May 29, 1931; s. Julius and Mildred (Berkowitz) M.; m. Barbara Miller, Sept. 12, 1959; 1 dau., Ericka Elizabeth. B.F.A., Yale U., 1957, M.F.A., 1959. Instr. Art Inst. Chgo., 1960-64; prof. fine arts Ind. U., 1964—. Color cons. Hallmark Card Co., 1959-60 One-man shows Kanegis Gallery, 1959, Reed Coll., 1966, Terry Dintenfass Gallery, 1965, 66, 68, 70, 76, 79, 82, 85, The Gallery, Bloomington, Ind., 1972, 79, Indpls. Mus., 1974, Tyler Sch. Art, Phila., 1976, Franklin Coll., 1980, Dart Gallery, Chgo., 1981, Patrick King Gallery, Indpls., 1983, 86, John Heron Gallery, Indpls., 1985, New Harmony Gallery, 1985; two-man show Dintenfass Gallery, 1984; group shows include Kanegis Gallery, Boston, 1958, 60, 61, Boston Arts Festival, 1959, 60, Mus. Modern Art, 1959, 66, Whitney Mus., N.Y.C., 1960, Art Inst. Chgo., 1964, Gallery 99, Miami, Fla., 1966, Ball State Coll., 1966, Butler Inst., 1967, Indpls. Mus., 1968, 69, 72, 74, Phoenix Gallery, N.Y.C., 1970, Harvard U., 1974, Skidmore Coll., 1975, Am. Acad. Arts and Letters, 1977, 89, Tuthill-Gimprich Gallery, N.Y.C., 1980, Patrick King Gallery, 1988, numerous others; represented in permanent collections Met. Mus. Art, Mus. Modern Art, Art Inst. Chgo., Library of Congress, Cin. Art Mus., Bklyn. Mus., Ark. Art Center, others; commns. include 5 murals Riley Children's Hosp., Indpls., 1986; installation Evanston (Ill.) Art Ctr., 1989, 2-part installation Ortho Child Care Ctr., Raritan, N.J., 1991; illustrator Acid and Basics-A Guide to Acid-Base Physiology, 1992. Served with U.S. Army, 1952-54. Recipient Ind. Arts Commn. award, 1990, 93; Fulbright grantee, Italy, 1962, grantee Ctr. for New TV, Chgo., 1992; Lilly Endowment fellow, 1989, honorable mention, Ohio Film Festival, 1995. Home and Office: 1623 Saint Margarets Rd Annapolis MD 21401-5540 Office: Ind U Dept Fine Arts Bloomington IN 47401

MARKMAN, SHERMAN, investment banker, venture capitalist, corporate financier; b. Denver, Aug. 21, 1920; s. Abe and Julia (Rosen) M.; m. Paula Elaine Henderson; children: S. Michael, Joan, Lori. Student, So. Meth. U., 1962-64. V.p. Lester's Inc., Oklahoma City, 1940-59; exec. v.p. Besco Enterprises, San Francisco, 1960-61; sr. v.p. Zale Corp., Dallas, 1962-69; pres., CEO Leased Jewelry divsn., 1965-69, Designcraft Industries, N.Y.C., 1969-75, Tex. Internat. Export Co., Dallas, 1975—; pres. CAC Fin. Group, 1975—. Fin. advisor Vocational Video, Huntington, N.Y., Consolidated Transplant Network, Metairie, La., Thera-Test Diagnostic Labs., Chgo., Kemper Mil. Acad., Boonville, Mo., Soft-Trac Info. Systems, Jasper, Ala., client referal arrangement The Dai-Ichi Kangyo Bank, Ltd.; former cons. Homecare Mgmt., Ronkonkoma, N.Y., Credicorp, Chgo., The Windy City Group, Chgo.; charter mem. N.Y. Ins. Exch.; guest lectr. fin. risk confs., 1982—, spkr. Am. Real Estate Investment Conf., London, 1986; pres., CEO The Markman Fin. Orgn., Dallas, 1975—. Contbr. articles to profl. jours. Vol. social worker Presbyn. Hosp., Dallas; mem. Dallas Coun. World Affairs, 1962—; active NCCJ. With USMCR, 1942-45, PTO. Mem. Press Club, City Club (Dallas), India Temple Club (Oklahoma City), L.A. Athletic Club, Columbian Golf and Country Club, Young Men's Philanthropic League (N.Y.C.). Address: 3013 W Country Hill Dr Tucson AZ 85742 E-mail: shermanmarkman@aol.com.

MARKO, ANDREW PAUL, school system administrator; b. Kingston, Pa., Aug. 16, 1936; s. Andrew Paul and Anna (Stragis) M.; m. Janet Thimm, Aug. 10, 1988; 1 child, Danielle. BA, Kings Coll., Wilkes-Barre, Pa., 1962; MA, Scranton U., 1968, prin.'s cert., 1971; postgrad., Oxford (Eng.) U., 1988, Lehigh U., 1991, Widener U., 1991—. Cert. tchr., secondary prin., supt.'s letter of eligibility, Pa. Elem. tchr. Dundalk Elem. Sch., Balt., 1963-64; English tchr. Kingston (Pa.) High Sch., 1964-66, Wyoming Valley West High Sch., Plymouth, Pa., 1966-90, vice prin., 1980, 89; secondary curriculum adminstr. Wyoming Valley West Sch. Dist., Kingston, 1990, dir. instrnl. svcs. and pupil svcs., 1991-95, apptd. supt., 1995—. Wrestling coach Kingston High Sch., 1964-69; jr.-sr. class advisor Wyoming Valley West High Sch., Plymouth, 1968-88, newspaper advisor, 1970-90, literary mag. advisor, 1970-90, publs. bus. mgr., 1988-90. Councilman Kingston Borough Coun., 1969-77; pres. Holy Name Soc.; ward capt. Heart Fund and March of Dimes; bd. dirs. Childrens Svc. Ctr. United Way, Diversity Bd. Coll. Misricordia, Dallas, Pa.; exec. dir. Northeastern Health Trust Pa.; mem. adv. bd. Blue Cross/Blue Shield; chmn. Sch. to Work; bd. dirs. libr. bd. Leham campus Pa. State U. With USN, 1954-57. Fellow Ednl. Policy and Leadership Pa.; mem. ASCD, Pa. Assn. Student Assistance Profls., Pa. Assn. for Supervision and Curriculum Devel., Pa. Assn. Pupil Svcs. Adminstrs., Nat. Assn. Pupil Svcs. Adminstrs., Pa. Staff Devel. Coun., Nat. Mid. Sch. Assn., Ptnrs. for Quality Learning, VFW, Am. Legion, KC. Democrat. Roman Catholic. Avocations: sports, gardening, building, reading. Home: 6 Halowich Rd Harveys Lake PA 18618-9629 Office: Wyoming Valley West Sch Dist 450 N Maple Ave Kingston PA 18704-3683

MARKOE, ARNOLD MICHAEL, radiation oncologist; b. N.Y.C., Apr. 15, 1942; s. Joseph Markoe and Claire (Hershkowitz) Markoe Berger; m. Tana Kates, Sept. 3, 1967; 1 child, Zaharah. BA, Adelphi U., 1963; MS, U. Rochester, 1966; ScD, U. Pitts., 1972; MD, Hahnemann U., 1977. Diplomate, Am. Bd. Radiology (Therapeutic Radiology). Rsch. assoc. Albert Einstein Coll. Medicine, Bronx, N.Y., 1966-69; USPHS postdoctoral fellow Allegheny Gen. Hosp., Pitts., 1972-73; Am. Cancer Soc. spl. postdoctoral fellow Hahnemann Med. Coll., Phila., 1975-77; from sr. instr. to assoc. prof. radiation oncology Hahnemann U., 1977-89; staff physician Jackson Meml. Hosp., Miami, Fla., 1990—; mem. Sylvester Comprehensive Cancer Ctr., 1990—; assoc. prof. radiation oncology U. Miami, 1989-92, prof., 1992—, interim chmn. radiation oncology Sch. Medicine, 1994-96; chmn., 1996—; staff physician U. Miami Hosp. & Clinics, 1990—, VA Hosp., Miami, 1996—, JFK Med. Ctr., Atlantis, Fla., 1997—. Cons. Anna Bates Leach Hosp. of Bascom-Palmer Eye Inst., 1990—, Cancergrams Info. Ventures, Inc., Phila., 1989-92; spl. site vis. radiation oncology Accreditation Coun. for Grad. Med. Edn., 1986—; adv. bd. radiation therapy tech. tng. program Gwynedd-Mercy Coll., Gwynedd Valley, Pa., 1988-89, Miami Dade C.C./Jackson Meml. Hosp. Consortium, 1989—, med. advisor, 1995—; adv. panel Radiation Oncology Self-Assessment Program, 1992-97, Pro Bono Expert Witness Program, State of Fla., Dept. Health and Human Svcs., 1997—. Mem. editl. bd. Am. Jour. Clin. Oncology, 1991—, Radiation Oncology Investigations, 1992-97; reviewer Cancer, 1994—, Jour. Neuro-Oncology, 1994—; ad hoc reviewer Internat. Jour. Radiation Oncology Biol. Physics, 1996—; contbr. articles to profl. jours. Bd. dirs. Jewish Leadership Inst.; exec. bd. Young Israel of Miami Beach. Grantee, Soc. Nuclear Medicine, 1976; named One of Best Drs. in Am., 1996-. Mem Am. Radium Soc., Am. Soc. Clin. Oncology, Am. Coll. Radiology, Am. Coll. Radiation Oncology, Am. Soc. Therapeutic Radiation Oncology, So. Med. Soc., Fla. Med. Soc., Dade County Med. Soc., Fla. Soc. Clin. Oncology, Alpha Omega Alpha, Beta Beta Beta. Avocations: reading, music, fishing.

MARKOE, FRANK, JR. lawyer, business and hospital executive; b. Balt., Sept. 5, 1923; s. Frank and Margaret (Smith) M.; m. Margaret McCormack (div.); children: Andrée Markoe Caldwell, Ritchie Harrison Markoe Scribner. AB, Washington and Lee U., 1947; LLB, U. Md., 1950. Bar: Md. 1950. Pntr. Karl F. Steinmann, Balt., 1948-50, 50-53, Cable & McDaniel, Balt., 1954-55; gen. counsel, dir. Emerson Drug Co., 1955-56, adminstrv. v.p., 1957-58; v.p., sec., dir., gen. counsel Warner-Lambert Pharm. Co., 1958-67, exec. com., sr. v.p., dir., gen. counsel, sec., 1967-69, exec. asst. chmn. bd., 1970-71, sr. v.p., 1971-73; exec. v.p. Warner-Lambert Co., Morris Plains, N.J., 1973-77, vice chmn. bd., 1977-81; vice chmn. adv. bd. N.Y. Hosp.-Cornell Med. Ctr., 1987—, also chmn. major gifts com. Capital Campaign; hon. holder Alfred E. Driscoll chair Fairleigh Dickinson U. Bd. dirs. N.J. Coll. Medicine and Dentistry, Bd. Internat. Broadcasting, Radio Free Europe/Radio Liberty, Kips Bay Boys; bd. dirs., exec. com., pres. N.J. Ballet. With USAAF, 1942-45, PTO. Mem. U.S. C. of C., Proprietary Assn. (chmn., bd. dir., exec. com.), Pharm. Mfrs. Assn. (bd. dir., exec. com.), N.J. State C. of C. (bd. dir.), Phi Beta Kappa. Home and Office: 201 Grenville Rd Hobe Sound FL 33455-2414 also: Cleft Rd Mill Neck NY 11765

MARKOFF, BRAD STEVEN, lawyer; b. N.Y.C., July 29, 1957; s. Daniel and Geri (Skitol) M.; m. Danna Kay Schmidt, May 17, 1980; children: Andrew David, Paul Steven, Samuel Joseph. AB, Duke U., 1979; JD, Washington U., St. Louis, 1982. Bar: Mo. 1982, U.S. Tax Ct. 1984, N.C. 1985. Assoc. Stolar Partnership, St. Louis, 1982-84; assoc., ptnr. Moore & Van Allen, Raleigh, N.C., 1984-92; ptnr. Smith Helms Mulliss & Moore, 1992-97, Alston & Bird LLP, Raleigh, 1997—; ptnr. in charge Research Triangle Park, 1997—. Bd. dirs. Coun. for Entreprenurial Devel., Research Triangle Park, N.C.; spl. coun. apptd. by N.C. Gov. N.C. R.R. Study Group, 1992-93; practice group head Alston & Bird's N.C. Bus. Practice, 1997—. Contbr. articles to profl. jours. Mem. ABA, Nat. Assn. Bond Lawyers, Nat. Assn. Real Estate Investment Trusts, Mo. Bar Assn., N.C. Bar Assn. Avocations: golf, astronomy. Office: Alston and Bird LLP 3605 Glenwood Ave Ste 310 Raleigh NC 27612-4957

MARKOFF, GARY DAVID, investment executive; b. Brookline, Mass., July 29, 1956; s. Leon Fred and Marylyn Sue (Goldstein) M.; m. Cicely Beston Butler, Sept. 23, 2000. BA in Econs., Trinity Coll., Hartford, Conn., 1978. From acct. exec. to v.p. E.F. Hutton & Co., Inc., Chestnut Hill, Mass., 1978-88; first v.p. investments Salomon Smith Barney, Boston, 1988-99, corp. client group dir., 1999-2000, sr. v.p., 2001—. Founding mem. Intuition Network Bus. Cons. Group, 1994. Co-author: Intuition at Work: An Anthology, 1996. Fundraiser Hunger Project, 1985—; active Spl. Olympics, 1988; founding mem. fin. profls. unit B'nai B'rith, 1988; class agent class of 1978 Trinity Coll., 1993—. Named one of Best Stockbrokers in Am., Money mag., 1987. Mem. Boston Jaycees, World Runners Club. Clubs: World Runners (San Francisco). Avocations: marathons (Goodwill Games, Moscow, 1986), triathlons, tennis, skiing, windsurfing. Home: Jamaica Pond Estates 100 Pond St Apt 7 Boston MA 02130-2759 Office: Salomon Smith Barney 28 State St Fl 26 Boston MA 02109-1775

MARKOFF, JOHN, reporter; b. Oakland, Calif., Oct. 24, 1949; married. Bachelors, Whitman Coll., 1971; Masters, U. Oreg., 1976. Reporter, editor Infoworld, 1981—83; w. coast editor Byte Mag., 1984—85; reporter San Francisco Examiner, 1985—88, NY Times, 1988—. Columnist San Jose (Calif.) Mercury, 1981—83. Co-author (with Lennie Siegel): The High Cost of High Tech, 1985; co-author: (with Katie Hafner) Cyberpunk: Outlaws and Hackers on the Computer Frontier, 1991. Recipient award for best new reporting, Software Pub. Assn., 1988. Office: NY Times 229 W 43d St New York NY 10036*

MARKOPOLOS, HARRY M. investment professional; b. Erie, Pa., Oct. 22, 1956; s. Louis Harry and Georgia Ann (Pappas) M. BABA, Loyola Coll., Balt., 1981; MS in Fin., Boston Coll., 1997. Chartered Fin. Analyst. Dist. mgr. ATFC Fin. Corp., Towson, Md., 1981—87; trader Makefield Securities Corp., Washington Crossing, Pa., 1987—88; asst. portfolio mgr. Darien Capital Mgmt., Greenwich, Conn., 1988—91; portfolio mgr. Rampart Investment Mgmt., Boston, 1991, chief investment officer, 2002—; v.p. edn. Boston Security Analysts Soc., 2000—02, pres., 2002—. Bd. dirs. Boston Security Analysts, QWAFAFEW, Boston, Boston GARP; derivatives instr. Boston Security Analysts. Maj. U.S. Army Res., 1978-95. Decorated U.S. Army Achievement medal, 1990, Nat. Def. Svc. medal, 1990. Mem. Internat. Assn. Fin. Engrs., Am. Fin. Assn., Fin. Mgmt. Assn., Assn. for Investment Mgmt. and Rsch., Boston Security Analysts Soc. (v.p. edn. 2000-02, pres. 2002--), U.S. Army Command and Gen. Staff Coll. Alumni (life mem.). Avocations: trout fishing, hunting. Office: Rampart Investment Mgmt 1 International Pl Boston MA 02110-2602

MARKOS, CHRIS, retired real estate company executive; b. Cleve., Nov. 25, 1926; s. George and Bessie (Papathatou) Markos; m. Alice Zaharopoulos, Dec. 11, 1949 (dec.); children: Marilyn Martin, Irene Matthews, Betsy Feierabend. BA, Case Western Reserve, Cleve., 1960; LLB, LaSalle U., Chgo., 1964. Cert. gen. real estate appraiser, Ohio. Vice-pres. Herbert Laronge Inc., Cleve., 1963-76; v.p. Calabrese, Racek and Markos Inc., 1976-83, Herbert Laronge Inc., Cleve., 1983-87, pres., 1987-88; v.p. Cragin Lang, Inc., 1989-91; sr. cons. Grubb & Ellis, 1991-93; sr. v.p. Realty One Appraisal Divsn., Independence, Ohio, 1993-98. Pres. Alcrimar Inc., 1989-98. Co-author: Ohio Supplement to Modern Real Estate Practice, 5th-7th edits.; cons. editor, co-author: Modern Real Estate Practice in Ohio, 1st-3rd edits. Bd. dirs. David N. Meyers Coll., Cleve., 1984-97. With U.S. Army, 1945-46. Mem. Am. Soc. Appraisers (sr., pres. 1973, state dir. 1976), Cleve. Bd. Realtors (hon. life mem., pres. 1974, Realtor of Yr. award 1976). Republican. Greek Orthodox. Home: Corinthian Condominium 936 Intracoastal Dr Apt 6-H Fort Lauderdale FL 33304 E-mail: alcrimar@webtv.net. *Everyone's life has a beginning and an ending. It is what happens between these two points that makes up the essence of a person.*

MARKOVCHICK, VINCENT J. surgeon; b. Hazleton, Pa., 1944; MD, Temple U., 1970. Intern Presbyn. Med. Ctr., Denver, 1970-71; resident emergency medicine U. Chgo. Hosps.-Clinics, 1974-76; mem. staff Denver Gen. Hosp.; assoc. prof. U.Colo. Health Sci. Ctr.; pres. Am. Bd. Emer. Med., East Lansing; dir. emergency med. Denver Health Med. Center, Denver, 2000—. Mem. Am. Coll. Emergency Physicians, Colo. Med. Soc., STEM. Office: Denver Gen Hosp Emergency Medicine Dept 777 Bannock St Denver CO 80204-4507 also: Amer Bd Emerg Med 3000 Coolidge Rd East Lansing MI 48823-6319*

MARKOVIC, NENAD S. internist, hematologist, oncologist, educator; b. Skopje, Macedonia, Jan. 24, 1938; came to the U.S., 1993; s. Svetomir K. and Olga R. Markovic; m. Olivera T. Markovic, 1961; 2 children. MD, Med. Faculty, Skopje, 1962, specialist internist, 1968, primarius, 1981; DSc, Med. Faculty, Belgrade, Yugoslavia, 1975. Prof. internal medicine Med. Faculty, Skopje, 1978-85; sci. dir. Clinic of Hematology, 1981-85; vis. prof. dept. pathology U. Pa., Phila., 1985-88; prof. oncology Inst. Oncology, Novi Sad, Yugoslavia, 1988-93; med. officer FDA Ctr. for Drug Evaluation and Rsch., Rockville, Md., 1994-98. Vis. prof. pharmacology Med. Coll. Pa., Phila., 1988-94; chmn. oncology Med. Faculty, Novi Sad, 1991-94, dir. English speaking med. program, 1991-94; expert cons. BioSciCon., Rockville, Marcons Cons., Rockville, 1999—; adj. prof. Am. U., Washington, 2000. Author: Quantitative Cytochemistry of Enzymes, 1986, Manual on Bone Marrow Morphology Screening, 1989; editor: UICC Manual of Cancer Chemotherapy, 1982; contbr. articles to profl. jours. Mem. Fed. Physicians Assn., Am. Assn. for Clin. Rsch., Am. Soc. Hematology, Yugoslav Cancer Soc. (pres. 1979-83). Avocation: chess.

MARKOVICH, PATRICIA, economist; b. Oakland, Calif. children: Michael S. Treece, Bryan Treece, Tiffany Treece. MS in Econs., U. Calif., Berkeley; postgrad., Stanford U. Cert. emergency mgmt. planner. Pub. rels. Pettler Advt., Inc.; pvt. practice polit. and econs. cons.; aide to majority whip Oreg. Ho. of Reps.; lectr., instr. various Calif. instns., Chemeketa (Oreg.) Coll., Portland (Oreg.) State U.; commr. City of Oakland (Calif.), 1970-74. Chairperson, bd. dirs. Cable Sta. KCOM; econ. and emergency mgmt. cons. Mem. Piedmont (Calif.) Gen. Plan Commn.; mem. Econ. Devel. City of Berkeley, Calif. NSF grant Oreg. Grad. Rsch. Ctr., Lilly Found. grant. Mem.: NAFE, Am. Econ. Assn., Nat. Coording Coun. Emergency Mgmt., No. Calif. Pub. Ednl. and Govt. Access Cable TV Com., Mensa.

MARKOVITS, ANDREI STEVEN, political science educator; b. Timisoara, Romania, Oct. 6, 1948; came to U.S., 1960, naturalized, 1971; s. Ludwig and Ida (Ritter) M. BA, Columbia U., 1969, MBA, 1971, MA, 1973, MPhil, 1974, PhD, 1976. Mem. faculty NYU, 1974, John Jay Coll. Criminal Justice, CUNY, 1974, Columbia U., 1975; rsch. assoc. Inst. Advanced Studies, Vienna, Austria, 1973-74, Wirtschafts und Sozialwissenschaftliches Inst., German Trade U. Fedn., Düsseldorf, Germany, 1979, Internat. Inst. Comparative Social Rsch., Sci. Ctr. Berlin, 1980; asst. prof. govt. Wesleyan U., Middletown, Conn., 1977-83; assoc. prof. polit. sci. Boston U., 1983-92; prof., chair dept. politics U. Calif., Santa Cruz, 1992-99; prof. dept. Germanic langs. and lit. U. Mich., Ann Arbor, Mich., 1999—; Fulbright prof. U. Innsbruck, Austria, 1996. Vis. prof. Tel Aviv U., 1986, Osnabruck U., 1987, Bochum U., 1991; sr. rsch. assoc. Ctr. for European Studies, Harvard U., 1975-99, vis. prof. social studies, 2002--. Author, editor books and papers in field; TV and radio commentator. Univ. Pres.'s fellow Columbia U., 1969, B'nai B'rith Found. fellow, 1976-77, Kalmus Found. fellow, 1976-77, Ford Found. fellow, 1979, Hans Boeckler Found. fellow, 1982 Inst. for Advanced Study Berlin fellow, 1998-99; N.Y. State scholar Columbia U., 1969. Mem. N.Y. Acad. Scis., Am. Polit. Sci. Assn., Internat. Polit. Sci. Assn., AAUP. Home: 718 Onondaga St Ann Arbor MI 48104-2611 Office: Univ Mich 3110 Modern Lang Bldg 812 E Washington St Ann Arbor MI 48109-1275 also: Harvard U Ctr European Studies 27 Kirkland St Cambridge MA 02138-2043 E-mail: andymark@umich.edu., andreimarkovits@cs.com.

MARKOVSKY, BARRY NEIL, sociology educator; b. Framingham, Mass., Apr. 3, 1956; s. Louis Joseph and Freida Judith Markovsky; m. Rose Marcia Garfinkle, July 15, 1987; 1 child, Tess. BA, U. Mass., 1978; PhD, Stanford U., 1983. NIMH postdoctoral fellow Stanford (Calif.) U., 1983; asst. prof.

sociology U. Iowa, Iowa City, 1983-88, assoc. prof. sociology, 1988-94, prof. sociology, 1994-2001; prof., chair sociology U. S.C., Columbia, 2001—. Dir. Ctr. Study of Group Processes, U. Iowa, 1992-2001; grant rev. panelist, NSF, 1988—, sociology program dir., NSF, Arlington, Va., 1997-99. Editor (ann. vol.) Advances in Group Processes, 1987-97; contbr. over 60 articles to profl. jours., including Am. Sociol. Rev. NSF fellow, 1990. Mem. Am. Sociol. Assn., Internat. Network Social Network Analysis, Skeptics Soc., ACLU (bd. mem. Iowa chpt. 1997-2001), Phi Beta Kappa. Democrat. Avocations: guitar, softball. Office: Univ SC Sloan Hall Columbia SC 29208 E-mail: barry@sc.edu.

MARKOWICZ, ELAINE C. writer; b. Phila., Apr. 10, 1951; d. Benjamin Joseph and Marie Castellano; m. James Michael Markowicz, Nov. 16, 1974; children: David, Jimmy, Andrew, Eric. Student, Art Inst., Phila., 1996-97. Sec. Colonial Pann, Phila., 1972-78. Author: Tender Temptation, 1978, Secret of Evergreen, 2000. Avocations: drawing children's series, painting, karate, violin.

MARKOWITZ, DEBORAH LYNN, state government official; b. Tarrytown, N.Y., Sept. 14, 1961; d. Gerald Harvey and Sandra Lee (Schulner) M.; m. Paul William Markowitz, June 19, 1988; children: Aviva Lee, Sandra Rose, Ari David. BA with honors, U. Vt., 1982; JD magna cum laude, Georgetown U., 1987. Bar: Vt. 1988, U.S. Dist. Ct. Vt. 1989. Assoc. Covington & Burling, Washington, summer 1986; jud. law clk. Justice Peck-Vt. Supreme Ct., Montpelier, 1987-88; assoc. Langrack, Sperry & Wool, Burlington, Vt., 1988-90; dir. Law Ctr. Vt. League of Cities and Towns, Montpelier, 1990—97; devel. cons. Vt. Law Sch., South Royalton, 1997—; sec. of state State of Vt., 2000—. Adj. faculty Vt. Law Sch., South Royalton, 1992; examiner Vt. Bd. Bar Examiners, Montpelier, 1994-98. Contbr. articles to profl. jours. Bd. dirs. Ctrl. Vt. Cmty. Action Agy., Vt. Hist. Soc.; trustee Woodbury Coll. Mem. ABA (state and local govt. sect.), Vt. Bar Assn. (mcpl. com.), Internat. Mcpl. Lawyers Assn. (chair pers. sect. 1993—), Nat. Assn. Secs. of State, Nat. Mus. of Women in the Arts (bd. dirs. Vt. chpt.), Order of Coif. Avocations: cross-country skiing, singing, sketching, gardening. Office: Sec of State Redstone Bldg 26 Terrace Street, PO Box 9 Montpelier VT 05609-0001

MARKOWITZ, HARRY M. finance and economics educator; b. Chicago, Ill., Aug. 24, 1927; s. Morris and Mildred (Gruber) M.; m. Barbara Gay. PhB, U. Chgo., 1947, MA, 1950, PhD, 1954. With research staff Rand Corp., Santa Monica, Calif., 1952-60, 61-63; tech. dir. Consol. Analysis Ctrs., Inc., 1963-68; prof. UCLA, Westwood, 1968-69; pres. Arbitrage Mgmt. Co., N.Y.C., 1969-72; pvt. practice cons., 1972-74; with research staff T.J. Watson Research Ctr. IBM, Yorktown Hills, N.Y., 1974-83; Speiser prof. fin. Baruch Coll. CUNY, N.Y.C., 1982-93; dir. rsch. Daiwa Securities Trust Co, Jersey City, 1990-2000. V.p. Inst. Mgmt. Sci., 1960-62. Author: Portfolio Selection: Efficient Diversification of Investments, 1959, Mean-Variance Analysis in Portfolio Choice, 1987; co-author: SIMSCRIPT Simulation Programming Language, 1963; co-editor: Process Analysis of Economic Capabilities, 1963. Recipient John von Neumann Theory prize Ops. Rsch. Soc. Am. and Inst. Mgmt. Sci., 1989, Nobel Prize in Econs., 1990. Fellow Econometric Soc., Am. Acad. Arts and Scis.; mem. Am. Fin. Assn. (pres. 1982—). Office: Ste 245 1010 Turquoise St San Diego CA 92109

MARKOWSKI, JOHN JOSEPH, human resources executive; b. N.Y.C., Jan. 12, 1947; s. Stanley J. and Helen (Krawiecki) M.; m. Christine Cipriano, Sept. 15, 1974; children: Alexis Marie, Laura Jane. BSEE, Poly. U., Bklyn., 1968, MS in Mgmt., 1973. Engr. Gen. Dynamics Corp., Pomona, Calif., 1968-69; mgr. employee rels. Unisys Corp., Great Neck, N.Y., 1969-82; dir. compensation Merck & Co. Inc., Rahway, N.J., 1982-91; dir. human resources Astra Merck, Wayne, Pa., 1991-95; asst. v.p. human resources Wyeth, Madison, NJ, 1995—. Mem. coun. on compensation The Conf. Bd., N.Y.C., 1988-91; sponsor Ctr. for Advanced Human Resources Studies, Ithaca, N.Y., 1991-95. Named Exec. Human Resources Champion, Cornell U., 1993; recipient Lifetime Achievement award Am. Compensation Assn., 2000. Mem. Soc. for Human Resources Mgmt., Human Resources Planning Soc. Avocation: Dept. 56 Dickens Village collecting. Office: Wyeth 5 Giralda Farms Madison NJ 07940-1027 E-mail: markowj@wyeth.com.

MARKS, BERNARD BAILIN, lawyer, director; b. Sioux City, Iowa, Sept. 6, 1917; s. Meyer A. and Beulah (Bailin) M.;m. Betty L. Marks; 1 child, Susan E. BA, Harvard U., 1939, JD, 1942. Bar: Iowa 1942. With firm Shull, Marshall & Marks, Sioux City, 1946-85, ptnr., 1949-85, Marks & Madsen, Sioux City, 1985-97, of counsel, 1998-99, ret., 2000, sec., asst. treas., dir., 1962-81; sec., dir. KTIV-TV Co., 1965-74; bd. dirs. First Nat. Bank, Firstar Bank, 1963-91; with Flavorland Industries, Inc. Bd. dirs. Iowa Heart Assn., 1960, Woodbury County chpt., 1958-64, pres., 1962-64; bd. dirs. Sioux City Art Center, 1952-54, Sioux City United Fund, 1965-71, Sioux City Community Appeals Bd., 1965-68; trustee Briar Cliff Coll., Sioux City, 1968-74. Served with USAAF, 1942-46. Fellow Iowa Bar Assn. Found.; mem. ABA, Iowa Bar Assn., Woodbury County Bar Assn. (pres. 1958), Am. Coll. Trust and Estate Counsel, Sioux City C. of C. (bd. dirs. 1964-67, treas. 1965-66), Sioux City Lawyers Club (pres. 1951), Sioux City Country Club (bd. dirs. 1963-64).

MARKS, BRUCE, artistic director, choreographer; b. N.Y.C., Jan. 23, 1937; s. Albert and Helen (Kosersky) M.; m. Toni Pihl Petersen, Jan. 27, 1966 (dec. May 1985); children: Erik Antony, Adam Christopher, Kenneth Rikard. Student, Brandeis U., 1954-55, Juilliard Sch., 1955-56; DFA (hon.), D (hon.), Northeastern U., 1997. Prof. U. Utah, 1981, 84-86; artistic dir. Boston Ballet Co., 1985-97, artistic dir. emeritus, 1998—. Mem. dance adv. panel Nat. Endowment for Arts, 1979, chmn. internat. selection com., 1979, chmn. dance adv. panel, 1981, mem. nat. adv. bd. on arts and edn., 1989; bd. dirs., mem. exec. com., Dance/USA 1989, 92—, chmn., 1990-92, chmn. govt. affairs, 1992—; mem. U.S.-USSR Commn. on Dance and Theatre Studies, Am. Coun. Learned Socs./IREX; mem. jury Internat. Moscow Internat. Ballet Competition, 1989; mem. arts in edn. adv. coun. Harvard U., 1997; chmn. 3d Japan Internat. Ballet and Modern Dance competition, 1999; jury mem. Prague Internat. Ballet Competition, 2001; artistic advisor Ft. Worth/Dallas Ballet, 2000-01. Prin. dancer Met. Opera, 1956-61, Am. Ballet Theatre, 1961-72, Royal Swedish Ballet, 1963, Festival Ballet, London, 1965, Royal Danish Ballet, 1971-76; artistic dir. Ballet West, Salt Lake City, 1976-85; choreographer Eliot Feld Ballet Co., 1970, Royal Danish Ballet, 1972-73, Netherlands Dance Theatre, 1974, Ballet West, 1976-85; artistic fellow Aspen Inst. for Humanistic Studies, 1979—. Bd. dirs. Am. Arts Alliance, 1983-85, Am. Coun. for Arts, 1985—; bd. dirs. Dance U.S.A., 1988-94, chmn., 1990-92; chmn. U.S.A. Internat. Ballet Competition, Jackson, Micc., 1990—, vice chair jury Helsinki, Finland, 1991, judge Helsinki Ballet Competition 1995; mem. nat. adv. bd. on arts and edn. NEA, 1989-91; mem. internat. jury 1st and 2d Japan Internat. Ballet Competition, Nagoya, Japan, 1993, 96, Am. jury for Prix de Lausanne, 1994, 98; mem. Brandeis Creative Arts Awards Commn., 1993, chmn. Brandeis Creative Arts Awards Dance, 1994; chair Grants to Dance Cos. panel NEA, 1993, overview panel, 1994; chmn. 3d Japan Internat. Ballet Competition, Nagoya, 1999; artistic advisor Ft. Worth/Dallas Ballet, 2000-2001. Recipient Disting. Svc. award for artistic prodn. Nat. Govs. Assn., 1994, Capezio award Balletmakers, Inc., 1995, Dance Mag. award, 1997, Honors award Dance/USA, 1998, Proscenium award, Boston, 2001.

MARKS, CHARLES, architect; b. Bklyn., May 19, 1938; s. Louis and Nettie Marks; m. Margery Green; children: Melissa Gabrielle, Joshua Wolf. BFA, Carnegie Mellon U., 1960; BArch, Columbia U., 1967, MArch, 1968. Registered N.Y., Conn., NCARB. Architect Harrison & Abramovitz, N.Y.C., 1964-68, Fischer/Jackson, N.Y.C., 1968-69; architect, long-range planner Am. Airlines, 1969-79; prin. Graves Marks Assocs., 1979-86, Charles Marks Assocs., Greenwich, Conn., 1986—. Advisor, cons. Republic of Haiti, 1976-84; chmn. airlines planning com. San Francisco Airport, 1976-80; mem. planning com. Cin. Airport, 1972-78, Pan Am. Flight Ctr., JFK Airport, Engrng. Ctr., JFK Airport; mem. U.S. Dept. Commerce, U.S.-Haiti Bus. Devel. Coun., 1998—. Projects include Republic of Haiti New Passenger Terminal and Office, Port-au-Prince, numerous banks and office bldgs., residences in the N.E. and in the Caribbean. With U.S. Army, 1961-63. Mem. AIA, Nat Coun. Archtl. Registration Bds. Avocation: triathlons. Address: 111 Mason St Greenwich CT 06830-6605 Fax: 203-661-7920.

MARKS, CHARLES, surgeon, educator; b. Kiev, Ukraine, Jan. 28, 1922; came to U.S., 1968; s. Abe and Sonia (Beck) M.; m. Joyce Wernick, Dec. 11, 1949; children: Malcolm, Peter, Ian, Anthony. MD, U. Cape Town, South Africa, 1945; MS, Marquette U., 1966; PhD, Tulane U., 1973. Intern and surg. resident Groote Schuur Hosp., Cape Town, 1946-49; surg. resident Royal Coll. Surgeons Affiliated Hosps., London, 1950-53; cons. surgeon Salisbury (Rhodesia) Gen. Hosp., 1953-63; assoc. prof. surgery Marquette U. Med. Sch., Milw., 1963-67; dir. dept. surgery Mt. Sinai Hosp., Cleve., 1967-71; assoc. clin. prof. surgery Case Western Res. U. Sch. Medicine, 1967-71; prof. surgery La. State U. Sch. Medicine, New Orleans, 1971-88; sr. attending surgeon Charity VA, Touro and Hotel Dieu Hosps., 1971—88; med. exec. dir. Fla. Dept. Corrections, Charlotte, Fla., 1994-97. Cons. cardiothoracic surgeon Ministry of Health, Govt. Zimbabwe, Harare, 1989-94; Hunterian prof. Royal Coll. Surgeons, 1956. Mem. bd. govs. Drs. Hosp. Sarasota, 1997-2000, chmn. bd. govs., 2001—; mem. inner senatorial com. Rep. Party, Washington, 1997—. Recipient Schlieder Rsch. award, 1975. Fellow ACS, Royal Coll. Physicians Edinburgh, Am. Coll. Cardiology; mem. Internat. Cardiovasc. Soc., Am. Transplantation Soc., New Orleans Surg. Soc. (pres.). Republican. Avocations: tennis, golf, travel. Home: # 1517 988 Blvd of the Arts Sarasota FL 34236

MARKS, CHARLES DENNERY, insurance consultant; b. New Orleans, Nov. 22, 1935; s. Sidney Leroy Marks and Melanie Dennery; m. Gillian E. Otter, Sept. 1, 1963; children: Elizabeth Dennery, Richard Dennery. BA, Yale U., 1957. CLU; ChFC; accredited estate planner; cert. long term care. With Charles Dennery, Inc., 1959-63; sales rep. Prudential Ins. Co., New Orleans, 1964-97. Past bd. dirs. Boys Club Greater New Orleans, Big Bros. Greater New Orleans, United Way; past pres. Goodwill Rehab. Ctr.; vice chmn. Jr. Achievement; active Temple Sinai Synagogue; bd. dirs. Am. Coll., 2000—, mem. exec. com., 2001—. 1st lt. U.S. Army, 1957-59. Recipient award Volunteer Activist, 1983. Mem.: Nat. Assn. Ins. and Fin. Advisors (vice chmn. fin. com. 1993—99), Million Dollar Round Table (exec. com. 1990—94, pres. 1993, Top of the Table 1986—89), New Orleans Estate Planning Coun., La. Assn. Ins. and Fin. Advisors (pres. 1986—87, Life Underwriter of Yr. 1985, 1987), Soc. Fin. Svc. Profls. (pres. New Orleans chpt. 1984—85), Nat. Assn. Ins. and Fin. Advisors (New Orleans, polit. action com.), Life and Health Found. for Edn. (life; chmn. 1996—98). Republican. Home: 1525 Eleonore St New Orleans LA 70115-4242 E-mail: cdmdrt@msn.com.

MARKS, CHARLES CALDWELL, retired investment banker, retired industrial distribution company executive; b. Birmingham, Ala., June 1, 1921; s. Charles Pollard and Isabel (Caldwell) M.; m. Jeanne Vigeant, Jan. 12, 1945 (dec.); children: Randolph C., Margaret Marks Porter, Charles P.; m. Alice V. Scott, Sept. 18, 1999. Student, Birmingham U., 1930-38; BS in Physics, U. of South, 1942; grad. mgmt. seminar, Harvard U., 1957; DCL (hon.), U. of the South, 1989; LLD (hon.), U. Ala., Birmingham, 1990. With Owen-Richards Co. (name changed to Motion Industries, Inc. 1970), Birmingham, 1946—, chmn. bd., 1952-73, pres., 1973-83; vice chmn. bd. Porter White & Yardley Cos., Inc., 1984-92, ret., 1992. Bd. dirs. emeritus Genuine Parts Co., BE & K Inc., emeritus; bd. dirs., chmn. Birmingham br. Fed. Res. Bank of Atlanta. Bd. dirs. So. Rsch. Inst., exec. com., 1987-95, dir. emeritus, 1995—; bd. govs. Indian Springs Sch., dir. emeritus, 1995—; pres., bd. dirs. Workshop for Blind, Birmingham, 1958-61, Children's Aid Soc. Birmingham, 1962; chmn. Com. of 100, Birmingham, 1963; co-chmn. United Appeals of Jefferson County, 1963; trustee, regent U. of South; pres. St. Vincent's Found., 1987; bd. dirs. U. Ala.-Birmingham Rsch. Found., Exec. Svcs. Corps. of Birmingham, 1984-96. Lt. USNR, WWII, ATO, MTO. Mem. The Club, Redstone Club, John's Island Club, Mountain Brook Club, Ala. Newcomen Soc., Blue Key, Phi Beta Kappa, Sigma Alpha Epsilon. Episcopalian. Home: 500 Olde English Ln Apt 516 Birmingham AL 35223-1078 Office: Ste 104 402 Office Park Dr Birmingham AL 35223

MARKS, DAVID HUNTER, civil engineering educator; b. White Plains, N.Y., Feb. 22, 1939; s. Sidney M. and Jean (Berger) M.; div.; 1 child, Joanna; m. Lilian Kemp, Dec. 17, 1998. BCE, Cornell U., 1962, MS in Environ. Engrng., 1964; PhD, Johns Hopkins U., 1969. Registered profl. engr., N.Y., Mass.; registered hydrologist, Am. Inst. Hydrology. Sr. sanitary engr. USPHS, Phila., 1964-66; asst. prof. civil engrng. MIT, Cambridge, Mass., 1969-72, assoc. prof., 1972-75, prof., 1975—. head dept., 1985-92, dir. program in environ. edn. and rsch., 1991-2000, James Mason Crafts prof., 1992-2000, Goulder Family prof., 2001—; coord. Alliance for Global Sustainability, 1996—; dir. Ctr. Environ. Initiatives, 1997-2001, Lab. for Energy and the Environment, 2001—. Office: Mit 1 Amherst St Rm E40-455 Cambridge MA 02142-1309

MARKS, EDWARD B. retired international relief administrator; b. N.Y.C., Apr. 22, 1911; s. Edward B. and Miriam (Chuck) M.; m. Margaret Levi (dec. 1980); 2 children; m. Vera J. Barad, 1987. BA cum laude, Dartmouth Coll., 1932; MA in Sociology, Columbia U., 1938. Assoc. editor Am. Wine and Liquor Jour., N.Y.C., 1933-36; mng. editor Better Times mag. Welfare Coun. N.Y.C., 1937-38; dir. div. for social and cultural adjustment Nat. Refugee Svc., N.Y.C., 1938-42; refugee program officer War Relocation Authority, Dept. Interior, Washington, 1942-46; chief of mission for Greece UN Internat. Refugee Orgn., Geneva and Athens, 1947-50; chief of mission successively for Greece, N.Y., and Yugoslavia Internat. Migration Orgn., 1951-58; exec. dir. U.S. Com. for Refugees, N.Y.C., 1958-62; dep. chief office cen. African affairs AID, Washington, 1962-65, asst. dir. for relief and rehab., Vietnam, 1965-66, aid coordination officer, Am. Embassy, U.K., 1966-68, asst. dir. for relief and rehab., Nigeria, 1969-71, voluntary agy. liaison officer for Asia, 1973-75; various emergency and liaison assignments UNICEF, N.Y.C., Paris, Geneva, 1971-73, dep. dir. secretariat Internat. Yr. of Child N.Y.C., 1976-80, liaison rep. for UN Yr. for Disabled, 1981-82, internat. cons., 1983-85; interim pres. U.S. Com. for UNICEF, 1985, bd. dirs., mem. exec. com., chmn. nominating com., 1986-92. Pres. then chmn. Immigration and Refugee Svcs. Am., 1985-98; instr. Boston U. Sch. Social Work, 1988, 89. Author: A World of Art--The United Nations Collection, 1996, For A Better World - Posters from the United Nations, 2000; contbr. articles to The New Yorker, N.Y. Times Mag., other jours. Bd. dirs. Nat. Com. for an Effective Congress, 2001. Recipient 1st Disting. Career award AID, 1976; Nat. Endowment for Arts grantee, 1994. Address: 333 E 46th St New York NY 10017-7401 : 102 Sycamore Ave Mill Valley CA 94941 E-mail: eb1marks@aol.com.

MARKS, EDWIN S. investment company executive; b. N.Y.C., June 3, 1926; s. Carl and Edith R. (Smith) M.; m. Nancy Lucille Abeles, June 21, 1949; children: Carolyn Gail, Linda Beth, Constance Ann. Student, Princeton U., 1944-45; BS, U.S. Mil. Acad., 1949. V.p. Carl Marks & Co., Inc., N.Y.C., 1958-61, pres., 1961-2000, also bd. dirs., chmn., 2000; dir., exec. v.p. CMNY Capital Co. Inc., 1962—. Chmn. emeritus North Shore Hosp.'s Rsch. Inst. Author: What I Know about Foreign Securities, 1958. Trustee Lincoln Ctr. Fund, 1966-77, Hofstra U., 1974-79, Sarah Lawrence Coll., 1979-81, North Shore Univ. Hosp., Manhasset, N.Y.; chmn. bd. overseers Rsch. Lab., North Shore Univ. Hosp.; bd. dirs. Chief Execs. Orgn. Cold Spring Harbor Labs., 1992, vice chmn.; bd. dirs. Smith New Court PLC, London, 1988-94; bd. dirs., exec. com. Lincoln Ctr. for the Performing Arts, vice chmn., 1998—. Mem. West Point Soc., N.Y. Bd. Trade, Harmonie Club. Office: Carl Marks & Co Inc 135 E 57th St New York NY 10022-2050 E-mail: emarks@carlmarks.com.

MARKS, FRANCES, obstetrician-gynecologist, educator; b. N.Y.C., Oct. 1, 1956; d. Arthur and Ruth (Flamberg) Marks; divorced; children: Jeffrey Harrison, Adam Daniel. BS summa cum laude, Fairleigh Dickinson U., 1978; MD, Columbia U., 1982. Diplomate Am. Bd. Ob-gyn., Am. Bd. Maternal-Fetal Medicine. Resident in ob-gyn Presbyn. Hosp., N.Y.C., 1982-85, chief resident, 1985-86, asst. attending, 1988—; fellow maternal-fetal medicine NYU, 1986-88; clin. instr. ob-gyn NYU Med. Ctr., N.Y.C., 1986-88; asst. prof. clin. ob-gyn Columbia-Presbyn. Med. Ctr., 1988—; asst. dir. residency Columbia-Presbytn. Med. Ctr., 1988-89; co-dir. residency Columbia-Presbyn. Med. Ctr., 1989-92, dir. residency, 1992-94; pvt. practice Riverdale and Manhattan, N.Y., 1988-93. Presenter in field. Contbr. articles to med. jours.; reviewer for med. jours. Mennen scholar, 1977; Sebrell fellow, 1979. Fellow Am. Coll. Obstetricians and Gynecologists; mem. AMA, Assn. Profs. of Gynecology and Obstetrics, Soc. Perinatal Obstetricians, Am. Med. Women's Assn., N.Y. Perinatal Soc., Sigma Xi. Democrat. Jewish. Avocations: swimming, tennis, racquetball, reading, whitewater rafting. Office: Columbia Presbyn Med Ctr Ob/Gyn New York NY 10032 E-mail: francym@aol.com.

MARKS, HERBERT EDWARD, lawyer; b. Dayton, Ohio, Nov. 3, 1935; s. I.M. and Sarah S. M.; m. Marcia Frager; children: Jennifer L., Susan E. AB with high distinction, U. Mich., 1957; JD, Yale U., 1960; postgrad., George Washington U. Law Sch., 1965-67. Bar: Ohio 1960, D.C. 1964, U.S. Supreme Ct. 1965. Law clk. to chief judge U.S. Ct. Claims, 1964-65; assoc. Wilkinson, Cragun & Barker, Washington, 1965-69, ptnr., 1969-82, Squire, Sanders & Dempsey, Washington, 1982—. Assoc. gen. counsel Presdl. Inaugural Coms., 1969, 73, 81; chmn. U.S. State Dept. Adv. Panel on Internat. Telecom. Law, 1987—91; mem. adv. com. on internat. comm. and info. policy U.S. State Dept., 1988—91; mem. U.S. del. ITU European Telecom. Devel. Conf., 1991, ITU Plenipotentiary Conf., 1998, ITU Coun., 2000; mem. ITU Sec. Gen.'s Expert Group, 1999—2002. Contbr. articles to legal jours. Served to capt. JAG USAF, 1960-64. Mem. ABA (chair sci. and tech. sect. 1990-91, chmn. communications div. 1986-88), D.C. Bar Assn., Computer Law Assn. (pres. 1975-77, bd. dirs. 1972-85, adv. bd. 1985—), Fed. Communications Bar Assn., Cosmos Club, Kenwood Golf & Country Club, Phi Beta Kappa. Office: Squire Sanders & Dempsey 1201 Pennsylvania Ave NW PO Box 407 Washington DC 20044-0407 also: 5317 Cardinal Ct Bethesda MD 20816-2908

MARKS, JAMES GARFIELD, JR. dermatologist; b. Trenton, N.J., May 19, 1945; s. James Garfield and Lavinia May (Ellis) M.; m. Joyce Lynne Turner, Aug. 9, 1969; 1 child, Shannon. BA, Wilkes Coll., 1967; MD, Temple U., 1971. Intern Geisinger Med. Ctr., Danville, Pa., 1971-72; resident Wilford Hall USAF Med. Ctr., San Antonio, 1975-78; clin. instr. dermatology U. Tex. Health Sci. Ctr., 1978-80; staff dermatologist Pa. State U. Coll. Medicine, Hershey, 1980—, asst. prof., 1980-85, assoc. prof., 1985-91, prof. dermatology, 1991—; chair dept. dermatology Hershey Med. Ctr. Author: Atlas of Differential Diagnosis in Dermatology, 1998, Principles of Dermatology, 2000, Handbook of Contact Dermatitis , 2000, Contact and Occupational Dermatology, 2002; author: (with others) Principles of Clinical Diagnosis , 1992; author: Principles and Practice of Dermatology , 1990, 2d edit., 1996, Occupational Skin Diseases , 1999, Conn's Current Therapy, 1988, 2d edit., 1989; contbr. articles. Bd. dirs. Braun Sta. East Cmty., 1976. Lt. col. USAF, 1972-80. Decorated Meritorious Svc. Commendation meadl; Am. Acad. Dermatology Exch. fellow, 1984; recipient Roerig Pharms. Challenges in Dermatology Ednl. award, 1982. Mem. Am. Acad. Dermatology, Am. Contact Dermatitis Soc. (v.p. 1993, pres. 2001), N.Am. Contact Dermatitis Group, Pa. Acad. Dermatology, Phila. Dermatology Soc., European Soc. Contact Dermatitis, World Fragrance Rsch. Team, Soc. Investigative Dermatology, Assn. Mil. Dermatologists, Dermatology Found., Agromedicine Consortium, Lions (v.p. 1982, pres. 1983). Office: Hershey Med Ctr 500 University Dr # 850 Hershey PA 17033-2360 E-mail: jmarks@psu.edu.

MARKS, JAMES FREDERIC, pediatric endocrinologist, educator; b. Pitts., Dec. 18, 1928; s. Alfred Mozelle and Cecil (Cuff) M.; m. Susan Grace Benson, Nov. 18, 2001; 1 child, Roland Phillip. BA, Princeton U., 1950; MD, Harvard U., 1954; MPH, U. Pitts., 1984. Intern Montefiore Hosp., Pitts., 1954-55; resident in pediatrics Children's Hosp. of Pitts., 1955-57; rsch. fellow in pediatric endocrinology U. Pitts., 1959-61; asst. prof. dept. pediatrics U. Tex. Southwestern Med., Dallas, 1961-68, assoc. prof. pediatrics, 1968-98, clin. prof. internal medicine, 2001—. Bd. dirs. State Newborn Screening Program, Tex., 1980-98. Contbr. articles to profl. publs., chpts. to med. textbooks. Capt. U.S. Army, 1957-59. Sr. rsch. fellow USPHS, 1983-84. Mem. Am. Diabetes Assn. (bd. dirs. Tex. affiliate 1992-97), Am. Acad. Pediatrics, Endocrine Soc., Soc. for Pediatric Rsch. Achievements include research in thyroid function in infancy, delineation of early clinical course in Lesch-Nyhan disease, observations on the possible genetic factors in diabetic microvascular disease. Office: U Tex Southwestern Med 5323 Harry Hines Blvd Dallas TX 75390-7208

MARKS, JAMES S. public health service administrator; b. May 13, 1948; AB cum laude, Williams Coll., 1969; MD, SUNY, Buffalo, 1973; MPH, Yale U., 1980. Diplomate Am. Bd. Pediatrics. Intern in pediat. U. Calif., San Francisco, 1973-74, resident in pediat., 1974-75, chief resident pediatric outpatient dept., 1975-76; resident in preventive medicine Ctrs. for Disease Control, Atlanta, 1977-78; fellow Robert Wood Johnson Clin. Scholars Program Yale U., New Haven, 1978-80; resident in preventive medicine Ctrs. for Disease Control, Atlanta, 1981-82, chief epidemiology and rsch. br., nutrition divsn., 1982-84, asst. dir. preventive medicine residency program, 1985-87, dir. divsn. reproductive health, 1987, coord. for chronic disease control activities, 1987-88, acting dir. divsn. diabetes transl., 1988-89, acting dir. divsn. chronic disease control, 1990-91, dir. divsn. reproductive health, 1992-95, dir. Nat. Ctr. Chronic Disease Prevention/Health Promotion, 1995—; adj. assoc. prof. Emory U. Sch. Pub. Health, 1990—. Asst. surgeon general, 1996—; editor Chronic Disease Notes and Reports, 1989-92; clinic physician Planned Parenthood of San Francisco Teen Clinic, San Francisco, 1975-76; cons. physician Ohio Dept. Health Bur. Preventive Medicine, 1978-79; cons. PAHO Consultative Group on Perinatal Care, Washington, 1982, WHO Malaysia Ministry of Health, 1982, 83, WHO Maternal and Child Health Unit Geneva, 1983, World Bank China Program Third Health Project, 1988, 1991, World Bank Poland, Health Promotion/Chronic Disease Prevention, 1992, World Bank China, Seventh Health Project, 1993. Contbr. articles to profl. jours, chpts. to books. Exec. sec. Diabetes Tech. Adv. com., 1989-92; liaison mem. Nat. Diabetes Adv. Bd., 1988-89; mem. Diabetes Mellitus Interagy. Coording. com., 1988-89; mem. subcom. adult edn., Am. Cancer Soc., 1987-92; staff White House Task Force on Infant Mortality, 1989; presenter in field. Epidemic Intelligence Svc. Officer USPHS Field Svcs. Divsn., 1976-78. Recipient Alexander D. Langmuir award, 1978, CDC Group award, 1984, Commendation Medal USPHS, 1984, and many other awards and citations. Fellow Am. Coll. Epidemiology; mem. APHA (active in com. work), Am. Epidemiol. Soc., Soc. Epidemiol. Rsch., Am. Acad. Pediat. (com. pediatric rsch. 1994-95), Internat. Epidemiol. Assn., Physicians for Social Responsibility, Soc. on Med. Decision Making, Epidemic Intelligence Svc. Alumni Assn., Sigma Xi. Home: 3158 Kings Arms Ct NE Atlanta GA 30345-2153 Office: Ctrs for Disease Control 4770 Buford Hwy NE Mail Stop K40 Atlanta GA 30341-3717*

MARKS, JANET GOLDBERG, poet, writer; b. Oct. 30, 1918; children: Leonard Stephen, Dianne Marks Bettag, Lisa Marian. BA in English cum laude, U. Houston, 1972; MA in Creative Writing and English, San Francisco State U., 1975. Instr. English, Paine Coll., Augusta, Ga., 1975-76; lectr. English, U. Houston, 1976-78; instr. English Houston C.C., 1978; writer, editor Rice Comms., Ltd., Kentfield, Calif., 1979; lectr. English U. San Francisco, 1980; instr. ESL, San Francisco C.C. Dist., 1980-82. Freelance writer, 1983-2000; proctor John Adams Coll. Ctr., San Francisco, 1991-92. Contbr. works to Cardinal, Border, Bitterroot, South and West, Latitudes, New Eng. Rev., Forum, Miss. Rev., Transfer, Travois, An Anthology of Contemporary Texas Poetry, Songs of Our Voices, Poets on Parnassus Anthology, others. Recipient 1st prize essay award Harvest, U. Houston, 1966, Sr. award Rosenberg Award for Poems on the Jewish Experience, 1992, Rosenberg Commendation award, 1993, Runner-up award Frances Shaw Fellowship for Older Women Writers, 1994.

MARKS, JEFFREY ALAN, freelance/self-employed writer; b. Georgetown, Ohio, Oct. 8, 1960; s. Gerald Ronald and Barbara Ann (Cummins) M. BS in Applied Sci., Miami U., Oxford, Ohio, 1983; MBA, Xavier U., Cin., 1986. Client support mgr. GE, Cin., 1983-99; staff writer Tech Decisions, 1999-2001; pub. rels. mktg. Intrieve, Cin., 2001—. Freelance writer, Cin., 1989-99. Auditor: Intent to Sell: Marketing the Genre Novel, 2002; editor: Canine Crimes, 1998, A Canine Christmas, 1999, Magnolias & Mayhem, 2000, Who Was That Lady?, 2001, The Ambush of My Name, 2001, Murder, Mystery and Malone, 2002. Recipient Barnes & Noble prize, Green River Writers, 1996; grantee Malice Domestic, 1994. Mem. Mystery Writers Am., Sisters in Crime. Office: 312 Plum St Cincinnati OH 45202 E-mail: jeff@jeffreymarks.com.

MARKS, JOHN HENRY, Near Eastern studies educator; b. Denver, Aug. 6, 1923; s. Ira and Clara E. (Dralle) M.; m. E. Aminta Willis, July 21, 1951; children: Peter A., Fleur A., John B. BA, U. Denver, 1946; BD (O.T. fellow), Princeton Theol. Sem., 1949; ThD, U. Basel, (Switzerland), 1953. Instr. Princeton Theol. Sem., 1953-54, Princeton U., 1954-55, asst. prof. to assoc. prof. Near Eastern studies, 1955-61, prof., 1979-93. Dir. Am. Schs. Oriental Research, Jerusalem, 1966-67; pres. Am. Ctr. Oriental Research, Amman, Jordan, 1969-79; trustee Am. Schs. Oriental Research, Phila, 1971-86 ; Acting dean Princeton U. Chapel, 1980 Author: Der Textkritische Wert des Psalterium Hieronymi iuxta Hebraeos, 1956, Visions of One World, Legacy of Alexander,

1985; also translator. Pres. Sch. Bd. Princeton, 1969-71; mem. Planning-Zoning Bds. Princeton, 1964-66. Served with U.S. Army, 1943-45. Democrat. Presbyterian. Home: 107 Moore St Princeton NJ 08540-3308 Office: Princeton U 110 Jones Hl Princeton NJ 08544-0001

MARKS, JON OWEN, physician; b. Bklyn., Dec. 28, 1946; s. Peter J. and Lily I. (Fagelson) M.; m. Ellen A. Zimmerman, June 10, 1967 (div.); m. Eileen M. Rich; children: Ian, Lana, Laura. BS in Aerospace Engring., NYU, 1967, MS in Aerospace Engring., 1969; MD, N.Y. Med. Coll., 1976. Diplomate Am. Bd. Urology. Rsch. engr. Grumman Aerospace, Bethpage, N.Y., 1969-72; resident Lenox Hill Hosp., N.Y.C., 1976-78, 78-81; staff urologist Beth Israel Med. Ctr., 1981-84; physician pvt. practice, 1984—; med. dir. Met. Lithotriptor Assocs., 1987—, Repro Lab, N.Y.C., 1994—. Mem. AMA, Am. Urologic Assn., Am. Soc. Reproductive Medicine, Am. Lithotripsy Soc., Endourology Soc., Soc. Urology and Engring., Tau Beta Pi, Sigma Gamma Tau. Avocation: piano. Office: Advanced Urology PC 55 E 9th St New York NY 10003-6311

MARKS, JONATHAN BOWLES, lawyer, mediator, arbitrator; b. Dec. 17, 1943; s. Herbert Simon Marks and Rebecca (Bowles) Marks Hawkins; m. Nandita Wagle, Dec. 18, 1971; children: Joshua Benegal, Natasha Bowles. BA cum laude, Harvard U., 1966, JD cum laude, 1972. Asst. U.S. Atty., Washington, 1973-76; assoc. Munger, Tolles & Rickershauser, L.A., 1976-78, ptnr., 1979; counsel, assoc. dir. planning and evaluation Peace Corps, Washington, 1979-80; gen. counsel Internat. Devel. Coop. Agy., 1980-81; dispute resolution cons., 1981-82; pres. EnDispute, Inc., 1982-94; vice chmn. Jams-EnDispute, 1994-99; prin. MarksADR, LLC, 1999—. Home: 4410 Chalfont Pl Bethesda MD 20816-1804 Office: 1120 G Street NW Suite 410 Washington DC 20005

MARKS, KAREN ANNETTE SPEECE (KAREN A. SPEECE), management consultant, school administrator; b. Novato, Calif., Nov. 17, 1956; d. Robert G. and Irene B. (Erickson) Speece; m. John (Pixley) Marks, Nov. 23, 1985; children: Allison, Jordan. BA, U. No. Iowa, 1978; MS, San Francisco State U., 1984. Editor Americas Beh. Rsch. Corp., San Francisco, 1979-81; orgn. devel. cons. Levi Strauss & Co., 1981-84; sr. orgn. devel. cons. Mervyns, Hayward, Calif., 1985-87, dist. pers. mgr., 1987-89; mgmt. cons., prin. self-employed Novato, 1989-97. Sch. adminstr. Good Shepherd Luth. Sch., Novato, Calif., 1996—. Editor: (book) Handbook for Women Scholars, 1980. Pres. sch. bd. Good Shepherd Sch., Novato, 1992-95. Mem. Bay Area Orgn. Devel. Democrat. Lutheran. Avocations: skiing, running, reading. Home and Office: 200 Adams St Novato CA 94947-4436

MARKS, LAWRENCE EDWARD, psychologist, educator; b. N.Y.C., Dec. 28, 1941; s. Milton and Anne (Parnes) M.; m. Joya Ellen Cazes, Dec. 24, 1963; children: Liza, Laura. AB, Hunter Coll., N.Y.C., 1962; PhD, Harvard U., Cambridge, Mass., 1965; PhD honoris causa, Stockholm U., 1994. Rsch.-assoc. prof. Yale U., New Haven, 1966-84; asst.-assoc. fellow John B. Pierce Lab., 1966-84; prof. epidemiology and psychology Yale U., 1984—; fellow John B. Pierce Lab., 1984—, dir., 1999—. Author: Sensory Processes: The New Psychophysics, 1974, The Unity of the Senses, 1978. Named to Hall of Fame, Hunter Coll., N.Y.C., 1985; recipient Jacob Javits award NIH, Washington, 1987. Fellow AAAS, Am. Psychol. Assn., Am. Psychol. Soc., N.Y. Acad. Sci. Democrat. Jewish. Achievements include elucidation of common principles underlying sensory processes in various sense modalities; development of validational scheme for quantifying magnitudes of sensory experience; indication of role of cross-modal (synesthetic) perception in relation to language and literature. Home: 48 Maplevale Dr Woodbridge CT 06525-1118 Office: John B Pierce Lab 290 Congress Ave New Haven CT 06519-1403 E-mail: marks@jbpierce.org.

MARKS, LEE ROBERT, lawyer, director; b. N.Y.C., Oct. 22, 1935; s. George L. and Shirley (Chassy) M.; m. Lisl Zach; children: Jan Philip, Benjamin Eli. BA with honors, U. MIch., 1957; LLB cum laude, Harvard U., 1960. Bar: N.Y. 1960, D.C. 1964, U.S. Supreme Ct. 1980, Va 1999. Lectr. law George Washington U., Washington, 1961-68; atty. Office Legal Adviser, Dept. State, 1961-65, sr. dep. legal advisor, 1977-79, mem. adv. com. on internat. investment, tech. and devel., 1983; ptnr. Ginsburg, Feldman & Bress, 1965-77, 79-98, Greenberg, Traurig, McLean, Va., 1998—. Past mem. bd. dirs. Washington Opera. Mem. ABA (chmn. com. on fgn. claims 1983). Office: Greenberg Traurig 1750 Tysons Blvd Ste 1200 Mc Lean VA 22102-4211 E-mail: marksl@gtlaw.com.

MARKS, LEONARD, JR. retired corporate executive; b. N.Y.C., May 22, 1921; s. Leonard M. and Laura (Colegrove) Rose; m. Antonia Saldaña Riley, July 19, 1986; children from previous marriage: Linda, Patricia Anne, Peter K. AB in Econs., Drew U., 1942; MBA, Harvard U., 1948, D.BA, 1961. Asst. prof. bus. adminstrn. Harvard U., 1949-55; prof. fin. Stanford U., 1955-64; asst. sec. USAF, Washington, 1964-68; v.p. corp. devel. Times Mirror Co., Los Angeles, 1968-69; sr. v.p. Wells Fargo Bank, San Francisco, 1969-72; exec. v.p. Castle & Cooke Inc., 1972-85; gen. ptnr. Marks-Hoffman Assocs., Venture Capital, 1985-92; corp. dir., 1992-2000, Airlease Mgmt. Svcs., San Francisco, 2000—, also bd. dirs. Co-author: Case Problems in Commercial Bank Management, 1962; contbg.: Credit Management Handbook, 1958. Capt. AUS, 1942-46, ret. brig. gen. USAFR. E-mail: proftmarks@aol.com.

MARKS, LEONARD HAROLD, lawyer; b. Pitts., Mar. 5, 1916; s. Samuel and Ida (Levine) M.; m. Dorothy Ames, June 3, 1948; children: Stephen Ames, Robert Evan. BA, U. Pitts., 1935, LL.B., 1938. Bar: Pa. 1938, D.C. 1946. Asst. prof. law U. Pitts. Law Sch., 1938-42; prof. law Nat. U., 1943-55; asst. to gen. counsel FCC, 1942-46, ops. counsel, 1986—; ptnr. Cohn & Marks, Washington, 1946-65, 69-86. Chmn. exec. com. Nat. Savs. and Trust Co., 1977-85; chmn. Internat. Conf. on Comm. Satellites, 1968-69; Am. del. Internat. Broadcasting Confs., 1948-69; pres. Internat. Rescue Com., 1973-79, Honor Am. Com., 1977-86; chmn. U.S. Adv. Commn. on Internat. Ednl. and Cultural Affairs, 1973-78; chmn. Fgn. Policy Assn., 1981-87, exec. com., 1987-96; head U.S. del. Internat. Telecom. Union, 1983, 87; chmn. U.S. del. to London Info. Forum, Commn. on Security and Cooperation in Europe, 1989. Mem. ABA (ho. of dels. 1962-64), Fed. Comm. Bar Assn. (pres. 1959-60), Bar Assn. D.C., Acad. Diplmacy (chmn. exec. com. 2000—), World Affairs Council Washington (chmn.), Cosmos Club, Metropolitan Club (v.p., gov.), Federal City Club, Broadcasters Club (pres. 1957-59), Alfalfa Club (Washington), Order of Coif, Phi Beta Kappa, Omicron Delta Kappa, Sigma Delta Chi. Clubs: Cosmos, Metropolitan, Federal City, Broadcasters, (pres. 1957-59), Alfalfa (Washington). Home: 2700 Calvert St NW Washington DC 20008-2621 Office: 1920 N St NW Washington DC 20036-1601

MARKS, LILLIAN SHAPIRO, secretarial studies educator, author; b. Bklyn., Mar. 16, 1907; d. Hayman and Celia (Merowitz) Shapiro; m. Joseph Marks, Feb. 21, 1932; children: Daniel, Sheila Blake, Jonathan. BS, NYU, 1928. High sch. tchr., N.Y.C., 1929-30; tchr. Evalina de Rothschild Sch., Jerusalem, 1930-31; social worker United Jewish Aid Bklyn., 1931-32; tchr. Richmond Hill High Sch., 1932-40, Andrew Jackson High Sch., Cambria Heights, N.Y., 1940-71; mem. faculty New Sch. Social Rsch., N.Y.C., 1977-87; staff Vassar Summer Inst., 1946. Vol. tchr. English Israel schs., 1987—. Am. editor: Teeline, A System of Fast Writing, 1970; author: College Teeline, 1977, College Teeline Self Taught, 1988, Touch Typing Made Simple, 1985; contbr. articles to profl. jours. Mem. Am. Fedn. Tchrs. Democrat. Home and Office: 300 E46 St 17J New York NY 10017

MARKS, LOUIS DENTON, JR. economist, educator, researcher; b. Memphis, Sept. 10, 1949; s. Louis Denton and Frances (Fraser) M.; m. Tessa Kristine Hoeter, June 12, 1982. BA, Yale U., 1971; M in Pub. Affairs, Princeton U., 1973, MA in Econs., 1977, PhD in Econs., 1981. Economist HEW, Washington, 1974-75; asst. prof. policy analysis U. B.C., Vancouver, 1980-86; asst. prof. econs. Simon Fraser U., 1986-90; assoc. prof. econs. U. Wis., Whitewater, 1990—. Cons. Health and Welfare Can., Ottawa, Ont., 1973, Ont. Commn. of Inquiry Into Residential Tenancies, Toronto, 1983-84, Employment and Immigration Can., Ottawa, 1990-91. Contbr. articles to profl. jours. U.S. Dept. Labor grantee, 1978-80. Mem. Am. Econs. Assn., Midwest Econs. Assn., Yale Club Wis. Office: U Wis Whitewater Dept Econs 800 W Main St Whitewater WI 53190-1745

MARKS, MARTHA ALFORD, writer; b. Oxford, Miss., July 27, 1946; d. Truman and Margaret Alford; m. Bernard L. Marks, Jan. 27, 1968. BA, Centenary Coll., 1968; MA, Northwestern U., 1972, PhD, 1978. Tchr. Notre Dame High Sch. for Boys, Niles, Ill., 1969-74; teaching asst. Northwestern U., Evanston, 1974-78, lectr., lang. coord., 1978-83; asst. prof. Kalamazoo (Mich.) Coll., 1983-85; writer Riverwoods, Ill., 1985—. Cons. WGBH Edn. Found., Boston, 1988-91, Am. Coun. on the Tchg. of Fgn. Langs., 1981-92, Ednl. Testing Svcs., 1988-90, Peace Corps., 1993. Co-author: Destinos: An Introduction to Spanish, 1991, 96, Al corriente, 1989, 93, 97, Que tal?, 1986, 90; author: (workbook) Al corriente, 1989, 93; contbr. articles to profl. jours. Mem. Lake County (Ill.) Bd., Forest Preserve Commn., 1992—, Lake County Conservation Alliance; vice chmn. Friends of Ryerson Conservation Area Bd.; co-founder, pres. Rep Am., Reps. for Environ. Protection. Home: 2940 Cherokee Ln Deerfield IL 60015-1609 Office: County Bd Office 18 N County St Waukegan IL 60085-4351

MARKS, MAURICE J. chemist; b. Tampa, Fla., Nov. 1, 1954; AA, Polk C.C., Winter Haven, Fla., 1973; BA in Chemistry, Vanderbilt U., 1976; PhD in Chemistry, Fla. State U., 1981. Rsch. chemist PPG Industries, Inc., Corpus Christi, Tex., 1981-83, The Dow Chem. Co., Freeport, 1983-96, Terneuzen, The Netherlands, 1996-98, Freeport, Tex., 1998—. Contbr. articles to profl. jours.; patentee in field. Mem. Am. Chem. Soc. (local sect. program chair 1986, nat. chemistry day chair 1987, awards chair 1988), Sigma Xi, Phi Beta Theta. Office: Dow Chemical Co Bldg B-1603 Freeport TX 77541 E-mail: mjmarks@dow.com.

MARKS, MELVIN I. physician, educator, health services consultant; b. Montreal, July 30, 1940; came to U.S., 1979; s. Irving and Kate Marks; div. March 1999; children: Suzanne, Jennifer, Daniel. BSc, McGill U., 1961, MD CM, 1965; Cert. in Exec. Mgmt., UCLA, 1990. Diplomate Am. Bd. Pediat., Am. Bd. Pediat. Infectious Disease. Intern Montreal Gen. Hosp., 1965-66; resident in pediat. Montreal Children's Hosp., 1966-68; fellow in pediat. infectious diseases U. Colo. Med. Ctr., 1968-70; asst. prof. McGill U., Montreal, 1970-75, assoc. prof., 1975-79; prof. U. Okla., Oklahoma City, 1979-86; prof., vice-chmn. dept. U. Calif., Irvine, 1986—; clin. prof. U. So. Calif., 1997-99. Author: Pediatric Infectious Disease for the Practitioner, 1985; editor: Cystic Fibrosis, 1996. Bd. dirs. StarBright Found., L.A., 1995—. Office: Miller Childrens Hosp 2801 Atlantic Ave Long Beach CA 90806-1737 E-mail: mmarks@memorialcare.org.

MARKS, MERTON ELEAZER, lawyer, arbitrator, mediator; b. Chgo., Oct. 16, 1932; s. Alfred Tobias and Helene Fannie (Rosner) M.; m. Radee Maiden Feiler, May 20, 1966; children: Sheldon, Elise Marks Vazelakis, Alan, Elaine Marks Ianchiou. BS, Northwestern U., 1954, JD, 1956. Bar: Ill. 1956, U.S. Ct. Mil. Appeals 1957, Ariz. 1958, U.S. Dist. Ct. Ariz. 1960, U.S. Ct. Appeals (9th cir.) 1962, U.S. Supreme Ct. 1970; cert. arbitrator U.S. Dist. Ct. Ariz. Assoc. Moser, Compere & Emerson, Chgo., 1956-57; ptnr. Morgan, Marks & Rogers, Tucson, 1960-62; asst. atty. gen. State of Ariz., Phoenix, 1962-64, counsel indsl. commn., 1964-65; from assoc. to ptnr. Shimmel, Hill, Bishop & Greunder, 1965-74; ptnr. Lewis & Roca, 1974—2001. Lectr. on arbitration and mediation, product liability and ins. subjects; Judge Pro Tempore Ariz. Ct. Appeals, 1994; legal columnist Exec. Golfer mag.; comml. panelist Am. Arbitration Assn.; spl. master Ariz. Superior Ct., 2001—. Contbr. articles to profl. jours. Bd. trustees Ariz. Opera Co., past chmn. endowment commn.; past mem. U.S. Olympic Com. for Ariz. Capt. JAGC, USAR, 1957-64. Fellow Chartered Inst. Arbitrators (London); mem. ABA (tort and ins. practice sect., chmn. spl. com. on fed. asbestos legis. 1987-89, chmn. workers compensation and employers liability law com. 1983-84, dispute resolution sect., internat. law and practice sect.), Am. Bd. Trial Advocates, Am. Coll. Legal Medicine, Internat. Bar Assn. (sect. on bus. law, product liability, advt., unfair competition and consumer affairs com., internat. litigation com., ins. com., arbitration and alt. dispute resolution com.), State Bar Ariz. (chmn. workers compensation sect. 1969-73), Fedn. Ins. and Corp. Counsel (chmn. pharm. litig. sect. 1989-91, chmn. workers compensation sect. 1977-79, v.p. 1978-79, 81, bd. dirs. 1981-89, mem. products liability sect., mem. reinsurance sect.), Internat. Assn. Def. Counsel, Ariz. Assn. Def. Counsel (pres. 1976-77), Maricopa County Bar Assn., Pima County Bar Assn., Def. Rsch. Inst. (drug and device com., chmn. workers compensation com. 1977-78), Assn. Internat. de Droit des Assurances (cert. arbitrator), Reinsurance and Ins. Arbitration Soc., Union Internat. des Avocats, London Ct. of Internat. Arbitration.. Office: Scottsdale Exec Office Pk Ste G-223 8655 E Via De Ventura Scottsdale AZ 85258-3363

MARKS, MICHAEL E. electronics company executive; BA, MA, Oberlin Coll.; MBA, Harvard U. Formerly pres., CEO Metcal Inc.; chmn. bd. dirs. Flextronics, 1993—, CEO, 1994—. Office: Flextronics 2090 Fortune Dr San Jose CA 95131-1823*

MARKS, MICHAEL PAUL, medical administrator; b. N.Y.C. BA, Brandeis U., 1975; MD, Boston U., 1980. Bd. cert. Am. Bd. Radiology, spl. qualification in neuroradiology, diagnostic radiology; lic. Nat. Bd. Med. Examiners. Dir. neuroradiology Stanford (Calif.) Stroke Ctr. Stanford U. Med. Ctr., 1991—, chief interventional neuroradiology, 1992—; assoc. prof. radiology and neurosurgery Stanford U. Sch. Medicine, 1998—. Mem. Radiologic Soc. N.Am., Am. Soc. Neuroradiology, Am. Soc. Interventional and Therapeutic Neuroradiology, World Fedn. Interventional Neuroradiology, Am. Assn. Neurol. Surgeons (joint sect. cerebrovascular surgery). Office: Stanford U Med Ctr 300 Pasteur Dr Stanford CA 94305-5105 Office Fax: 650-498-5374.

MARKS, MURRY AARON, lawyer; b. Carbondale, Ill., July 14, 1933; Student, Northwestern U., 1951-52; BA, Washington U., 1954; attended, U. So. Calif., 1956; JD, Washington U., 1963. Bar: Mo. 1963, U.S. Dist. Ct. (ea. and we. dists.) Mo. 1969, U.S. Ct. Appeals (8th cir.) 1969, U.S. Supreme Ct. 1972, U.S. Tax Ct. 1984. Asst. county counsellor County of St. Louis, 1963-67; ptnr. Elliott, Marks & Freeman, St. Louis, 1967-1971; pvt. practice, 1971—. With U.S. Army, 1954-56. Fellow St. Louis Bar Found.; mem. ABA, ATLA, Nat. Assn. Criminal Def. Lawyers (life), St. Louis County Bar Assn., Mo. Bar Assn., Am. Coll. Legal Medicine, Mo. Assn. Trial Attys., Mo. Assn. Criminal Def. Attys. (bd. dirs. 1986-90), First Amendment Lawyers Assn., Met. Bar Assn. St. Louis, Lawyers Assn. St. Louis, Trial Lawyers for Pub. Justice, The Roscoe Pound Found. Office: 7700 Clayton Rd Ste 307 Saint Louis MO 63117-1347

MARKS, PAUL ALAN, oncologist, cell biologist, educator; b. N.Y.C., Aug. 16, 1926; s. Robert R. and Sarah (Bohorad) Marks; m. Joan Harriet Rosen, Nov. 28, 1953; children: Andrew Robert, Elizabeth Susan Marks Ostrer, Matthew Stuart. AB with gen. honors, Columbia U., 1945, MD, 1949; D in Biol. Sci. (hon.) , U. Urbino, Italy, 1982; PhD (hon.) , Hebrew U., Jerusalem, Israel, 1987, U. Tel Aviv, 1992; DSc, Columbia U., 2000. Fellow Columbia U. Coll. Physicians and Surgeons, 1952—53, assoc., 1955—56, mem. faculty, 1956—82, dir. hematology tng., 1961—74, prof. medicine, 1967—82, prof. human genetics and devel., 1969—82, dean faculty of medicine, v.p. med. affairs, 1970—73, dir. Comprehensive Cancer Ctr., 1972—80, v.p. health scis., 1973—80, Frode Jensen prof. medicine, 1974—80; prof. medicine and genetics Cornell U. Coll. Medicine, N.Y.C., 1982—, prof. medicine Grad. Sch. Med. Scis., 1983—; pres. emeritus Meml. Sloan-Kettering Cancer Ctr., 2000—. Instr. Sch. Medicine George Washington U., 1954—55; cons. VA Hosp., N.Y.C., 1962—66; attending physician Presbyn. Hosp., N.Y.C., 1967—82, Meml. Hosp. for Cancer and Allied Diseases, 1980—; mem. Sloan-Kettering Inst. for Cancer Rsch., 1980—; adj. prof. Rockefeller U., 1980—; vis. physician Rockefeller U. Hosp. , 1980—; hon. staff N.Y. Hosp., 1981—; bd. sci. counselors divsn. cancer treatment Nat. Cancer Inst., 1980—83; mem. steering com. Nat. Cancer Inst. Frederick Cancer Rsch. Facility, 1982—86; chmn. program adv. com. Robert Wood Johnson Found., 1983—89; mem. Gov.'s Commn. on Shoreham Nuc. Plant, 1983, Mayor's Commn. Sci. and Tech. City of N.Y., 1984—87; mem. adv. com. on NIH to Sec. HHS, 1989—90, 1993—; external adv. com. Intramural Rsch. Program Rev. NIH; mem. gov. com. NYPRHA, 1996; mem. Mayor's Task Force Biomed. Rsch. and Tech., N.Y.C., 1999; mem. tech. adv. group UN Assn. U.S.; mem. coun. biol. scis. Pritzker Sch. Medicine U. Chgo., 1977—88; first lectr. Nakasone Program for Cancer Control U. Tokyo, 1984; Ayrey fellow, vis. prof. Royal Postgrad. Med. Sch. U. London, 1985; William Dameshek vis. prof. hematology Mt. Sinai Med. Ctr., 1985; nat. vis. com. CUNY Med. Sch., 1986—89; trustee Feinberg Grad. Sch. Weizmann Inst. Sci., Rehovot, Israel, 1986—; William H. Resnick lectr. in medicine Stamford Hosp., 1986; disting. faculty lectr. M.D. Anderson Hosp. U. Tex., 1986; Maurice C. Pincoffs lectr. U. Md., Balt., 1987; vis. prof. Coll. de France, 1988; Alpha Omega Alpha vis. prof. N.Y. Med. Coll., 1990; Mario A. Baldini vis. prof. Harvard Med. Sch., 1991; mem. sci. adv. bd. City of Hope Nat. Med. Ctr., Duarte, Calif., 1987—92, Raymond and Beverly Sackler Found., Inc., 1989, Jefferson Cancer Inst., Phila., 1989; mem. Found. Biomed. Rsch., 1989—; mem. sci. adv. com. Imperial Cancer Rsch. Fund, 1994. Editor: Monographs in Human Biology, 1963; author: 11 books; contbr. over 375 articles to profl. jours.; mem. editl. bd.: Blood, 1964—71, assoc. editor: , 1976—77, editor-in-chief: , 1978—82, assoc. editor: Jour. Clin Investigation, 1967—71, mem. editl. bd.: Cancer Treatment Revs., 1981—, mem. editl. bd.: Cancer Preventions, 1989, mem. editl. bd.: Sci., 1990, mem. editl. bd.: Current Opinion Oncologic Endocrine and Metabolic Drugs, 1998, guest editl. bd. : Japanese Jour. Cancer Rsch., 1985—, assoc. editor: Molecular Reprodn. and Devel., 1988—, expert analyst: Chemistry and Molecular Biology edit. of Chemtracts, 1990—92, mem. adv. bd.: Internat. Jour. Hematology, 1992, mem. adv. bd.: Stem Cells, bd. contbg. editors: Blood Cells, Molecules and Diseases, 1994, bd. contbg. editors: Comité des Sages, 1994. Trustee St. Luke's Hosp., 1970—80, Roosevelt Hosp., 1970—80, Presbyn. Hosp., 1972—80, Metpath Inst. Med. Edn., 1977—79, Hadassah Med. Ctr., Jerusalem, 1996; mem. jury Albert Lasker Awards, 1974—82; bd. dirs. Revson Found., 1976—91, Am. Found. for Basic Rsch. Israel, Israel Acad. Scis., 1991; mem. tech. bd. Milbank Meml. Fund, 1978—85; bd. govs. Friends of Sheba Med. Ctr., Tel Hashomer. Recipient Charles Janeway prize, Columbia U., 1949, Joseph Mather Smith prize, 1959, 1995, Stevens Triennial prize, 1960, Swiss-Am. Found. award in Med. Rsch., 1965, Columbia U. Coll. Physicians and Surgeons Disting. Achievement medal, 1980, Centenary medal, Inst. Pasteur, 1987, Disting. Oncologist award, Hipple Cancer Ctr. and Kettering Ctr., 1987, Found. for Promotion of Cancer Rsch. medal (Japan), 1984, Disting. Svc. medal, Robert Wood Johnson Found., 1989, Outstanding Achievement award in hematopoiesis, U. Innsbruck, 1991, Pres.'s Nat. Medal Sci., 1991, Gold medal for Disting. Acad. Accomplishments, Coll. Physicians and Surgeons, 1994, japan Found. for Cancer Rsch. award, 1995, John Jay award for disting. profl. achievement, Columbia Coll., N.Y., 1996, Lifetime Achievement award, Greater N.Y. Hosp. Assn., 1997, Katherine Berken Judd award, Meml. Sloan-Kettering Cancer Ctr., 1999, Lifetime Achievement award, Am. Italian Cancer Found., 1999, Humanitarian award, Breast Cancer Rsch. Found., 2000; fellow Commonwealth Fund fellow, Pasteur Inst., 1961—62. Master: ACP, Coll. Phys. Surgeons; fellow: AAAS, Pasteur Inst. Paris (Commonwealth Fund fellow 1961—62), Am. Acad. Arts and Scis., Royal Soc. Medicine; mem.: UN Assn. U.S.A. (tech. adv. group), Health Scis. Adv. Coun. Columbia U., Weizmann Inst. Sci. (bd. govs. 1976—, gov. emeritus, Israel), Chinese U. Hong Kong, Sci. Adv. Bd. Hong Kong Cancer Inst., Third World Acad. Scis. (advisor), Soc. for Study Devel. and Growth, Internat. Leadership Ctr. on Longevity and Soc. Interurban Clin. Club, Japan Soc. Hematology (Disting. lectr. 1989, Disting. lectr. 1989), Soc. for Devel. Biology, Internat. Soc. Devel. Biologists, Harvey Soc. (pres. 1973—74), Assn. Am. Physicians, Am. Soc. Hematology (pres.-elect 1983, pres. 1984, chmn. adv. bd. 1985), Soc. Cell Biology, Assn. Am. Cancer Insts. (bd. dirs. 1983—88), Am. Assn. Cancer Rsch., Italian Assn. Cell Biology and Differentiation (hon.), Chinese Anti-Cancer Assn. (hon.), Japanese Cancer Assn. (hon.), Am. Soc. Human Genetics (past mem. program com.), Am. Soc. Biol. Chemists, Am. Soc. Clin. Investigation (pres. 1972—73), Am. Fedn. Clin. Rsch. (past councillor Ea. dist.), Red Cell Club (past chmn.), Inst. Medicine (coun. 1973—76, chmn. com. study resources clin. investigation with NAS 1988), NAS (chmn. sect. med. genetics, hematology and oncology 1980—83, chmn. Acad. Forum Adv. Com. 1980—81, coun. 1984—87, del. biol. warfare com. Internat. Security and Arms Control 1986—89), Univ. Club (N.Y.C.), Century Assn., Econ. Club (N.Y.C.), Alpha Omega Alpha. Office: Meml Sloan-Kettering Cancer Ctr 1275 York Ave New York NY 10021-6094

MARKS, PETER WAYNE, hematologist, oncologist, educator; b. Bklyn., Nov. 5, 1963; s. Philip and Shirley Ann (Mueller) M.; m. Erika Cleveland, June 21, 1987. BA, Columbia Col., 1985; MS, NYU, 1988, PhD, 1990, MD, 1991. Med. lic. Mass. Resident in internal medicine Brigham and Women's Hosp., Boston, 1991-93, fellow in hematology and oncology, 1993-96, assoc. physician, 1996—; instr. medicine Harvard Med. Sch., 1996—; med. dir. Genzyme Corp., Framingham, 1999-2000; clin. dir. hematology Brigham and Women's Hosp., Boston, 2000—; med. dir. Boston hemophilia Ctr., 2002—. Contbr. articles to profl. jours. Mem. AAAS, Am. Soc. Cell Biology, Am. Soc. Hematol., Am. Soc. Clin Oncology. Office: Brigham Women's Hosp 75 Francis St Boston MA 02115 E-mail: pmarks@partners.org.

MARKS, RICHARD DANIEL, lawyer; b. N.Y.C., June 21, 1944; s. Morris Andrew and Dorothy (Schill) M.; m. Cheryl L. Hoffman, Nov. 13, 1971. BA, U. Va., 1966; JD, Yale U., 1969. Bar: D.C., U.S. Ct. Appeals (3rd, 4th, 8th, 11th and D.C. cir.), U.S. Supreme Ct. Assoc. Dow, Lohnes & Albertson, Washington, 1972-78, ptnr., 1978-97, Vinson & Elkins, Washington, 1997-2000, Davis Wright Tremaine, Washington, 2000—. Co-author: Legal Problems in Broadcasting, 1974. Trustee U. Va. Coll. Found., 2001—. Capt. U.S. Army, 1970-72. Mem. ABA (chmn. contracting for computer com., sect. for sci. and tech., computer law div., chmn. computer law div. 1994-2002), Fed. Comms. Bar Assn., Am. Law Inst., Computer Law Assn. (dir. 1999-02), Capital Area Assn. Flight Instrs. (pres. 1989-90), UVA Club of Washington (pres. 1991-92). Avocations: aviation, skiing. Office: Davis Wright Tremaine LLP 1500 K St NW Ste 450 Washington DC 20005-1272 Business E-Mail: richardmarks@dwt.com.

MARKS, ROBERT, music director, composer, educator; b. N.Y.C., May 10, 1955; s. Peter R. and Eve (Hoffenreich) Sonnenmark; m. Elayne K. Bloom; children: Erica Allyn, Arielle Nichole. BA, Montclair State Coll., 1984. Pvt. vocal coach, N.Y.C., 1971—; assoc. condr. St. Louis Mcpl. Opera, 1976-77; pianist Broadway prodn. of Annie, N.Y.C., 1977-79; pres. Mus. Theater Cons., Inc., 1979—; mus. dir. The Rocky Horror Show Westbury Music Fair, L.I., N.Y., 1979; instr., condr. seminars Weist-Barron Sch., N.Y.C., 1981—96. Mus. dir. various N.J. dinner theaters, 1976—; guest speaker Speech and Theater Assn. of N.J., 1985-87; guest instr. St. Johns Univ., N.Y.C., 1986; mus. dir. over 200 prodns. including stock, regional and dinner theaters. Composer (mus. revue) The Safety Kids, 1981; mus. dir., arranger: Madison Avenue at Palsson's N.Y.C., 1988, (off-Broadway prodn.) Oh Johnny, 1982. Recipient Lyric award Am. Song Festival, 1980. Mem. ASCAP (ASCAP award 1982, Popular Music award 1983-86), Nat. Assn. Tchrs. Singing, N.Y. Singing Tchrs. Assn., Am. Soc. Music Copyists, Nat. Acad. Rec. Arts and Scis. Office: MTC Inc 850 7th Ave Ste 804 New York NY 10019-5230

MARKS, ROBERT BOSLER, television producer, consultant; b. Atlantic City, Apr. 9, 1953; s. Albert Aubrey Jr. and Elizabeth (Cramer) M.; m. Gloria Maria Berglund, Oct. 30, 1976. Communications dir. Miss Am. Pageant, Atlantic City, 1972-76; mgr., TV facility FAA Tech. Ctr., 1976-87, mgr. imaging tech. br., 1987—. Pres. Shore Prodns., Inc., Mays Landing, N.J., 1978—. Mem. Internat. TV Assn. Episcopalian. Avocations: electronics, flying, computers. Home: 146 Asbury Rd Egg Harbor Township NJ 08234 Office: William J Hughes FAA Tech Ctr ACX-60 Advanced Imaging Internat Airport Atlantic City NJ 08405-0001 E-mail: marksr@erols.com.

MARKS, SCOTT CHARLES, lawyer; b. Gloucester, MA, Nov. 19, 1956; s. Wilfred Elliot and Marjorie (Bloom) M.; m. Rhonda Ann Levine, Aug. 22, 1982; children: Eric Ian, Jesse Robert. BS, Boston U., 1978; JD, New Eng. Sch. Law, 1982. Bar: Mass. 1982, U.S. Dist. Ct. Mass. 1983. Assoc. Kline & Gardner, PC, Gloucester, Mass., 1982-87; ptnr. Channell & Marks, Beverly, 1987-90; assoc. Peter C. DiGangi, Salem, 1990-97, DiGangi & Legasey P.C., Salem, 1997—2002; pres. Law Office of Scott C. Marks, 2002—. Mem. ABA, Mass. Bar Assn., Salem Bar Assn., Essex County Bar Assn. Democrat. Jewish. Office: Law Office of Scott C Marks 70 Washington St Ste 405 Salem MA 01970-3733

MARKS, SHARON LEA, primary school educator, nurse; b. Arroyo Grande, Calif., June 12, 1942; d. Donald Elmore and Gertrude (Grieb) Shaffer; m. George Conrad Schmidt, June 23, 1963 (div. 1975); children: Kerrilynn, Robert, Marianne; m. Keith Dalton Marks, June 4, 1978 (div. 1999); children: Joseph, Erik, Alice. Diploma, Sch. Nursing Samuel Merritt Hosp., 1963; BSN, Lewis and Clark State Coll., 1984, BS in Mgmt., 1986; MA in Environ. Edn., Calif. State U., San Bernardino, 2001. RN, Calif.; cert. tchr., Calif. Staff nurse Vesper Meml. Hosp., San Leandro, Calif., 1968-74; night nurse supr. Tuolumne Gen. Hosp., Sonora, 1975; nurse Orleans (Calif.) Search and Rescue Team, 1975-78; instr. nursing Pasadena (Calif.) City Coll., 1978-79; resource coord. learning ctr. div. health sci. Spokane (Wash.) Community Coll.,

1979-84; staff nurse Kootenai Med. Ctr., 1979-85; instr. North Idaho Coll., Coeur d'Alene, 1984-85; staff nurse North Idaho Home Health, 1985-86; coord. br. office Family Home Care, Spokane, 1986-87; devel., dir. Good Samaritan Home Health Plummer, Idaho and Fairfield, Washington, 1987-88; mgr. patient svcs. VNS Seattle-King County, Tukwila, Wash., 1988-89; co-owner, v.p. The Wooden Boat Shop, Seattle, 1989-97; primary sch. tchr. Marisposa Sch., 1994-95, Corona Sch., 1995-96, West Randall Sch., Fontana, Calif., 1996—. Owner Marks and Assocs., 1994—; instr. in emergency med. tech. Orleans campus Coll. Redwoods, Eureka, Calif., 1977-78; book reviewer Brady Co., Besterfield and Assocs., 1994; film reviewer Olympia Media Info., 1999. Author: The Chumash Indians: San Luis Obispo County's First Environmentalists, 2001. Network Environ. Sci. Tchg. liaison West Randall Sch., 1996—. Recipient Leader in Edn. award Calif. State. U.-San Bernardino, 2001; grantee NORCAL. Avocations: travel, gardening, hiking, train watching. Office: 35621 Wildwood Canyon Rd Yucaipa CA 92399-5130 E-mail: markss2@cybertime.net.

MARKS, STEPHEN PAUL, law, international affairs and public health educator, international official; b. San Francisco, June 13, 1943; s. Marion Harris and Ruth Wise (Rosenblum) M.; m. Kathleen A. Modrowski, Feb. 28, 1978; children: Joshua, Emmanuel. BA, Stanford U., 1964; diploma, Inst. Advanced Internat. Studies, Paris, 1972; D in Law, U. Nice, 1979; advanced degree, U. Strasbourg, France, U. Besançon, U. Damascus, Syria. Sr. staff Internat. Inst. Human Rights, Strasbourg, 1969-73; sr. program specialist UNESCO, Paris, 1973-83; program officer Ford Found., N.Y.C., 1983-88; lectr. Law Sch. Columbia U., 1985-99, adj. prof. polit. sci., 1989, adj. prof. Sch. of Internat. and Pub. Affairs, 1989-95, sr. lectr., 1995-99, dir. UN studies program, 1996-99; vis. prof. law Cardozo Sch. Law, Yeshiva U., N.Y.C., 1989-92, dir. program in internat. law and human rights, 1989-92; asst. to ind. jurst UN Mission for Referendum in Western Sahara, 1991-92; chief sect. UN Transitional Authority, Phnom Penh, Cambodia, 1992-93; François-Xavier Bagnoud prof. health and human rights Sch. Pub. Health, Harvard U., 1999—, dir. Françis-Xavier Bagnoud Ctr. Health & Human Rights. Univ. fellow New Sch. for Social Rsch., N.Y.C., 1989-92; mem. consultative coun. Lawyers Com. for Nuclear Policy, N.Y.C., 1985—; rep. to UN Internat. Svc. for Human Rights, Geneva, 1989—; cons. MacArthur Found., 1992, UN Devel. Program, 1998, Parliamentarians for Global Action, 1999; human rights advisor Asia Found., Cambodia, 1998; vis. fellow Ctr. Internat. Studies, Woodrow Wilson Sch., Princeton U., 1993-95, lectr., 1995; pres., chmn. of bd. U.S. Com. for Internat. Svc. for Human Rights, 1995—. Mem. adv. com. Human Rights Watch/Mid. East, 1991—; bd. dirs. Cambodian Inst. Human Rights, 1993—, Albert Einstein Inst., 1994—, People's Decade of Human Rights Edn., 1990—; mem. editl. bd. Health and Human Rights, Boston; mem. nat. adv. com. human rights, UN Assn. of the U.S., 1996; mem. rev. panel U.S. Inst. of Peace, Washington, 1998; mem. human rights adv. bd. Carnegie Coun. on Ethics and Internat. Affairs, 1999—; adv. panelist Human Devel. Report, UN Devel. Program, 2000; adv. com. Carr Ctr. Kennedy Sch. Govt., Harvard U. Hague Acad. Internat. Law fellow, 1967, 73, Peaslee fellow Columbia U., 1985, MacArthur Found. fellow, 1994-95. Mem. Acad. Coun. on UN Sys., Am. Soc. Internat. Law, Am. Polit. Sci. Assn., Internat. Law Assn., Assn. of Bar of City of N.Y., Ind. Commn. on Human Rights Edn., Société Française pour le Droit Internat., Acad. Polit. Sci., Internat. Studies Assn., Am. Pub. Health Assn. Home: 65 Mount Auburn St Apt 72 Cambridge MA 02138-4914 Office: Harvard Sch Pub Health 651 Huntington Ave # Rom705 Boston MA 02115-6009 Fax: (617) 432-4310. E-mail: smarks@hsph.harvard.edu.

MARKS, THEODORE LEE, lawyer; b. N.Y.C., Oct. 18, 1935; s. Irving Edward and Isabel (Goodman) M.; m. Benita Cooper, July 13, 1958; children: Eric, Robert, Jennifer BS, NYU, 1956, LL.B., 1958. Bar: N.Y. 1959, U.S. Dist. Ct. (so. dist.) N.Y. 1963, U.S. Supreme Ct. 1964, U.S. Ct. Appeals (2d cir.) 1975, U.S. Dist. Ct. (ea. dist.) N.Y. 1978. Assoc. Silver, Bernstein, Seawell & Kaplan, N.Y.C., 1959-65; sole practice, 1965-70; ptnr. Lee, Cash & Marks, 1970-76, Vogel, Marks & Rosenberg, N.Y.C., 1976-79, Bromberg, Gloger, Lifschultz & Marks, N.Y.C., 1979-85, Epstein Becker Borsody & Green, P.C., N.Y.C., 1985-86, Gelberg & Abrams, 1986-87, Morrison Cohen Singer & Weinstein, 1987—. Speaker at meetings of profl. assns. Contbr. articles to profl. jours. Served with Army N.G., 1958-61. Mem. N.Y. State Bar Assn. (mem. real property, banking, corp. and bus. law sects.), N.Y. County Lawyers Assn., Fed. Bar Coun., T&M. Office: Morrison Cohen Singer & Weinstein LLP 750 Lexington Ave New York NY 10022-1200

MARKSON, DANIEL BEN, real estate developer, consultant, syndicator; b. Boston, Dec. 19, 1959; s. Morris Eliot and Gertrude (Hurvitt) M. BA, Clark U., 1981; MBA, Babson Coll., 1983. Projects mgr. Hist. Mill Properties, Milton Village, Mass., 1983-84; freelancer Markson Devel., Boston, 1984-85; asst. v.p. New England Communities Inc., Wellesley, Mass., 1985-88; sr. v.p. Boston Capital Ptnrs. Inc., 1988-96; exec. v.p. Nat. Housing Corp., Virginia Beach, Va., 1996-97; prin. Royal Castle Develop. Corp., N. Miami, Fla., 1998—. Exec. v.p. Affordable Landmarks Inc., Miami Beach, Fla., 1989-91; pres. Charlesview Inc., Allston, Mass., 1988-91, dir., 1981—; dir. North Harvard, Allston, 1981-91. Participant Boston City Housing Task Force, 1990—; v.p. Miami Supportive Housing Corp., 1994-98. Mem. Nat. Home Builders (trustee, multi-family coun. 1996-2001, past chair housing credit group 2000), Tex. Assn. Affordable Housing Providers (v.p. 1999-2000, dir.) Republican. Avocations: historic property restoration, antique Cadillacs, swimming, weight training. Home: 2421 Lake Pancoast Dr Miami FL 33140-4804 Office: Royal Castle Dev Corp 12550 Biscayne Blvd Ste 215 North Miami FL 33181-2536

MARKSON, DAVID M. writer; b. Albany, N.Y., Dec. 20, 1927; s. Samuel Albert and Florence (Stone) M.; m. Elaine Kretchmar, Sept. 30, 1966 (div. May 26, 1994); children: Johanna, Jed. BA, Union Coll., 1950; MA, Columbia U., 1952. Reporter Albany (N.Y.) Times-Union, 1944-45, 48-49; editor Dell Books, N.Y.C., 1953-54, Lion Books, N.Y.C., 1955-57; instr. L.I. U., Bklyn., 1964-66; lectr. Columbia U., N.Y.C., 1979-84, 86-87, New Sch. for Social Rsch., N.Y.C., 1994, 97-99. Author: (novels) The Ballad of Dingus Magee, 1966, Going Down, 1970, Springer's Progress, 1977, Wittgenstein's Mistress, 1988, Reader's Block, 1996 (Salon Book award 1997), This Is Not a Novel, 2001, (entertainments) Epitaph for a Tramp, 1959, Epitaph for a Dead Beat, 1961, Miss Doll, Go Home, 1965, (lit. criticism) Malcolm Lowry's Volcano, 1978, (poetry) Collected Poems, 1993. Staff sgt. U.S. Army, 1946-48. Recipient fellowship Centro Mexicano De Escritores, 1960-61, Nat. Endowment for Arts, 1990, N.Y. Found. for Arts, 2000. Mem. PEN, Louis Norman Newsom Soc. (commr. 1973-91). Democrat. Jewish. Avocations: opera, baseball. Home and Office: 215 W 10th St Apt 3E New York NY 10014-2913

MARKULIS, HENRYK JOHN, career military officer; b. Columbia, S.C., July 10, 1945; s. Henryk F. Markulis and Judith E. (Taylor) Kassman; children: Mark C., Melinda L. BA, U. Buffalo, 1968; MA, Ctrl. Mich. U., 1977. Commd. USAF, 1969; advanced through ranks to col.; aircraft cmdr. 53d Weather Recon Squadron Ramey AFB, P.R., 1970-74; gunship aircraft cmdr. 16th Spl. Ops. Squadron Korat RTAB, Thailand, 1974-75; cmdr. 437th Field Maintenance Squadron Sect. Charleston AFB, S.C., 1975-78; exercise and contingency support 1701st Mobility Support Shaw AFB, 1978-82; air staff action officer Joint Chiefs of Staff Pentagon, 1982-84; chief internat. programs Singapore, Malaysia & Brunei, 1984-93; dep. cmdr., chief staff Iceland Def. Force NATO, 1993-95, ret., 1995; pres., CEO Internat. Security and Mktg. Cons., 1996—. Cons. Nissan Motor Acceptance Corp., 1996—, Infiniti Fin. Svcs., 1996—. Mem. Am. Legion, VFW, Ret. Officers Assn., Aircraft Owners & Pilots Assn., Army Navy Country Club, Order of Daedalians, Kiwanis. Avocation: golf. Office: 52 Union St Hamburg NY 14075 Home: 56 Union St Hamburg NY 14075-4910

MARKUS, KENT RICHARD, lawyer; b. Cleve., Feb. 1, 1959; s. Richard and Carol (Slater) M.; m. Susan Mary Gilles, Apr. 15, 1987. BS, Northwestern U., 1981; JD with honors, Harvard U., 1984. Bar: Ohio 1984, U.S. Dist. Ct. (no. dist.) Ohio 1984, U.S. Dist. Ct. (so. dist.) Ohio 1996, U.S. Ct. Appeals (6th cir.) 1986. Jud. clk. to Hon. Alvin I. Krenzler U.S. Dist. Ct. (no. dist.) Ohio, Cleve., 1984-86; litigation assoc. Gold, Rotatori, Schwartz & Gibbons, 1986-89; transition dir. Ohio Atty. Gen. Office, Columbus, 1990-91, first asst. atty. gen., chief of staff, 1991-93; counsel to dep. atty. gen. U.S. Dept. Justice, Washington, 1994, dep. assoc. atty. gen., 1994-95, acting asst. atty. gen. legis affairs, 1995, counselor to atty. gen., 1996-98, dep. chief of staff, 1997-98; prof., dir. Dave Thomas Ctr. for Adoption Law, Capitol U. Law Sch., 1998—; nominated to U.S. Ct. Appeals (6th cir.), 2000. Adj. prof. law Cleveland-Marshall Coll. Law, 1987-88. Co-editor: Trial Handbook for Ohio Lawyers, 2nd edit., 1988; contbn. editor for law Webster's New World Dictionary, 4th edit., 1999. Former bd. dirs., former legis. chair Handgun Control Fedn. of Ohio, 1984-93; mem. adv. coun. Northwestern U. Sch. Speech, 1985—; spl. projects dir. Celeste for Gov. Com., Cleve., 1986; campaign mgr. Lee Fisher for Atty. Gen., Cleve. and Columbus, 1989-90; bd. dirs., former trustee, life mem. Cleve. NAACP, 1986-87; chief of staff Dem. Nat. Com., Washington, 1993-94; at-large mem. bd. dirs. Search, Inc., 2000--. Named Rising Star of Dem. Party, Campaigns and Elections mag., 1991. Mem. ABA, Ohio State Bar Assn. (former chair young lawyers divsn.), Columbus Bar Assn. Home: 5636 Indian Hill Rd Dublin OH 43017-8209 Office: Capital Univ Law Sch 303 E Broad St Columbus OH 43215-3201 E-mail: kmarkus@law.capital.edu.

MARKUS, LAWRENCE, retired mathematics educator; b. Hibbing, Minn., Oct. 13, 1922; s. Benjamin and Ruby (Friedman) M.; m. Lois Shoemaker, Dec. 9, 1950; children: Sylvia, Andrew. *Son Andrew Markus (1954-1995) was a phenomenal linguist and a brilliant scholar. His early talents (spelling champion of Minnesota, top pupil at Ecole Nouvelle, Lausanne) anticipated his BA, summa cum laude at Harvard, 1975, fellowship with Keio University, Tokyo, and PhD from Yale, 1985. The publication of his book, "The Willow in Autumn: Ryutei Tanehiko, 1783-1842" (Harvard University Press 1992), brought acclaim as an authority on the cultural history of Edo and an appointment as an Associate Professor of Japanese at the University of Washington, where his scholarship is now commemorated through an endowed lectureship.* BS, U. Chgo., 1942, MS, 1946; PhD, Harvard U., 1951. Instr. meteorology U. Chgo., 1942-44; rsch. meteorologist Atomic Project, Hanford, 1944; instr. math. Harvard U., 1951-52; instr. Yale U., 1952-55; lectr. Princeton U., 1955-57; asst. prof. U. Minn., Mpls., 1957-58, assoc. prof., 1958-60, prof. math., 1960-93, assoc. chmn. dept. math., 1961-63, dir. control scis., 1964-73, Regents' prof. math., 1980-93, Regents' prof. emeritus, 1993—, dir. Control Sci. and Dynamical Sys. Ctr., 1980-89. Leverhulme prof. control theory, dir. control theory ctr. U. Warwick, Eng., 1970-73, Nuffield prof. math., 1970-85, hon. prof., 1985—; regional conf. lectr. NSF, 1969; vis. prof. Yale U., Columbia U., U. Calif., U. Warsaw, 1980, Tech. Inst. Zurich, 1983, Peking U. (China), 1983; dir. conf. Internat. Ctr. Math., Trieste, 1974; lectr. Internat. Math. Congress, 1974, Iranian Math. Soc., 1975, Brit. Math. Soc., 1976, Japan Soc. for Promotion Sci., 1976, Royal Instn., London, 1982, U. Beer Sheva, Israel, 1983; vis. prof. U. Tokyo, 1976, Tech. U., Denmark, 1979; mem. panel Internat. Congress Mathematicians, Helsinki, 1978; sr. vis. fellow Sci. Rsch. Coun., Imperial Coll., London, 1978; mem. UNESCO sci. adv. com. Control Symposium, U. Strasbourg, France, 1980; IEEE Plenary lectr., Orlando, Fla., 1982; Sci. and Engring. Rsch. Coun. vis. prof. U. Warwick, Eng., 1982-90; Neustadt Meml. lectr. U. So. Calif., 1985, prin. lectr. symposium U. Minn., 1988, dir. NSF workshop, 1989, prin. lectr. symposium in honor of his 75th birthday, 1997; Tate lectr. U. Cin., 1998; mem. adv. bd. Office Naval Rsch., Air Force Office Sci. Rsch. Author: Flat Lorentz Manifolds, 1959, Flows on Homogeneous Spaces, 1963, Foundations of Optimal Control Theory, 1967, rev. edit., 1985, Lectures on Differentiable Dynamics, 1971, rev. edit., 1980, Generic Hamiltonian Dynamical Systems, 1974, Distributed Parameter Control Systems, 1991, Boundary Value Problems and Symplectic Algebra, 1998, Multi-Interval Linear Ordinary Boundary Value Problems and Complex Symplectic Algebra, 2001; editor Internat. Jour. Nonlinear Mechanics, 1965-73, Jour. Control, 1963-67; mem. editl. bd. Proc. Georgian Acad. Sci. Math., 1993—; contbr. articles to profl. jours. Lt. (j.g.) USNR, 1944-46. Recipient Rsch. prize Internat. Conf. Nonlinear Oscillations, Ukrainian Acad. Sci., Kiev, 1969, Festschrift volume, 1993; Fulbright fellow Paris, 1950; Guggenheim fellow Lausanne, Switzerland, 1963. Fellow Royal Soc. of Edinburgh (hon.); mem. Am. Math. Soc. (past mem. nat. coun.), Am. Geophys. Soc., Soc. Indsl. and Applied Math. (past nat. lectr.), Phi Beta Kappa, Sigma Xi. Office: U Minn Math Dept 127 Vincent Hall Minneapolis MN 55455 E-mail: markus@math.umn.edu.

MARKUS, RICHARD M. judge, mediator; b. Evanston, Ill., Apr. 16, 1930; s. Benjamin and Ruby M.; m. Carol Joanne Slater, July 26, 1952; children: Linda, Scott, Kent. BS magna cum laude, Northwestern U., 1951; JD cum laude, Harvard U., 1954. Bar: D.C. 1954, Ohio 1956, Fla. 1994. Appellate atty., civil div. Dept. Justice, Washington, 1954-56; ptnr. civil litigation law firms Cleve., 1956-76, 89-98; judge Cuyahoga County (Ohio) Common Pleas Ct., 1976-80, Ohio Ct. Appeals, 1981-88. Instr. M.I.T., 1952-54; adj. prof. Case Western Res. U. Law Sch., 1972-78, 84-87, Cleve. State U. Law Sch., 1960-80, prof. 1999-2000; prof. Harvard Law Sch., 1980-81; mem. Nat. Commn. on Med. Malpractice, 1971-73; chmn. Nat. Inst. Trial Advocacy, 1978-81, trustee 1971—. Author: Trial Handbook for Ohio Lawyers, 5th edit., 2002, Ohio Evidence Rules with Commentary, 1999; contbr. articles to profl. jours.; editor Harvard U. Law Rev, 1952-54. Republican nominee Justice of Ohio Supreme Ct., 1978; bd. dirs. Luth. Metro Ministry, 1988—, Fairview Luth. Hosp., 1985—. Mem. Ohio State Bar Assn. (pres. 1991-92), Cuyahoga County Bar Assn., Greater Cleve. Bar Assn. (trustee 1967-70, 85-90), Assn. Trial Lawyers Am. (nat. pres. 1970-71), Ohio Acad. Trial Lawyers (pres. 1965-66), Phi Beta Kappa, Pi Mu Epsilon, Delta Sigma Rho, Phi Alpha Delta. Home and Office: Pvt Judicial Svcs Inc 3903 N Valley Dr Cleveland OH 44126-1716

MARKUS, ROBERT MICHAEL, journalist, retired; b. Chgo., Jan. 30, 1934; s. David White and Anna (Tonkonogy) M.; m. Leslie Winnifred Ator, Aug. 25, 1962; children— Catherine Mary, Patricia Anne, Michael Hughes. B.J., U. Mo., 1955. Gen. assignment reporter Moline (Ill.) Dispatch, 1955-59; successively copy editor, sports columnist, feature writer, baseball writer, coll. sports writer, hockey writer Chgo. Tribune, 1959-96, ret., 1996. Mem. Northbrook (Ill.) Caucus, 1967. Served with U.S. Army, 1956-58. Recipient Nat. Headliner award as best columnist, 1973; named Ill. Sports Writer of Year, 1970, 71, 72 Mem. Football Writers Assn. Am., Baseball Writers Assn. Am., Am. Auto Racing Writers and Broadcasters Assn. Home: 3000 Holiday Dr #1102 Fort Lauderdale FL 33316

MARKUS, STEPHEN ALLAN, lawyer; b. Harvey, Ill., Mar. 14, 1954; s. Fred Herman and Ruth (Kahn) M.; m. Nancy Lynn Adams, July 29, 1978; children: Andrew, Peter. BA, Case Western Res. U., 1976, JD, 1979. Bar: Ohio 1979, U.S. Dist. Ct. (no. and so. dist.) Ohio 1979, U.S. Ct. Appeals (6th cir.) 1984, U.S. Supreme Ct. 1990. Ptnr. dept. labor and employment Ulmer & Berne, Cleve., 1979—. Trustee Cleve. Internat. Film Festival, 1977—. Jewish. Home: 2611 Ashton Rd Cleveland Heights OH 44118-4225 Office: Ulmer & Berne 1300 E 9th St Ste 900 Cleveland OH 44114-1583 E-mail: smarkus@ulmer.com.

MARKUSON, RICHARD K. pharmaceutical association executive; Mem. adv. com. on pharmacy practice Nat. Assn. Bds. Pharmacy, pres.; exec. dir. Idaho State Bd. Pharmacy; adj. prof. pharmacy law Idaho State U.; chmn. Nat. Assn. Bds. Pharmacy. Mem.: Idaho State Pharm. Assn., Idaho Soc. Health Sys. Profls. (life). Office: 700 Busse Hwy Park Ridge IL 60068*

MARKWELL, DICK R(OBERT), retired chemist; b. Muskogee, Okla., Feb. 20, 1925; s. Alex J. and May (Albright) M.; m. Virginia Ann Gass, Aug. 28, 1949; children: Steven R., Scot L., Eric R., Cheryl F. BS, Wichita State U., 1948, MS, 1950; PhD, U. Wis., 1956. Commd. 2d lt. U.S. Army, 1951, ret. lt. col., 1967; with Office Chief Rsch. and Devel.; assoc. prof. chemistry San Antonio Coll., 1967-74; chemist Corpus Christi Dept. Health, 1975-77; supr. chemistry sect. lab. div. San Antonio Met. Health Dist., 1977-87. With USMC, 1942-45. Mem. Am. Chem. Soc. Home: 7887 Broadway St Apt 501 San Antonio TX 78209-2537

MARLAIS, HELEN MARA, music educator, pianist; b. Gorizia, Italy, July 14, 1965; came to U.S., 1965; BA, U. Toledo, 1987; MFA, Carnegie Mellon U., 1989; MusD, Northwestern U., 1995. Cert. master tchr., Iowa. Instr. piano Gustavus Adolphus Coll., St. Peter, Minn., 1995, Iowa State U., 1995-97; coord. piano pedagogy Crane Sch. Music SUNY, Potsdam, 1997-98; psalmist coord. piano pedagogy Grand Valley (Mich.) State U., 1998—. Clinician Frederick Harris Music Pub.; adjudicator, master class clinician state and nat. levels, piano soloist, collaborative artist, Ill., Minn., Iowa, N.Y., Mich., 1992—. Dorothy L. Pound scholar Northwestern U., 1993; mini grantee Iowa Arts Coun., 1996, travel grantee Iowa State U., 1996. Mem. Nat. Assn. Music Tchrs. (state and nat. cert.). Avocations: travel, Italian cooking.

MARLAND, ALKIS JOSEPH, leasing company executive, computer science educator, financial planner; b. Athens, Greece, Mar. 8, 1943; came to U.S., 1961, naturalized, 1974; s. Basil and Maria (Pervanides) Mouradoglou; m. Anita Louise Malone, Dec. 19, 1970; children: Andrea Weber, Alyssa. BS, Southwestern U., 1963; MA, U. Tex., Austin, 1967; MS in Engring. Adminstrn., So. Meth. U., 1971. Cert. in data processing, enrolled agt., fund specialist, ChFC, CLU, CFP, RFC, CTP, ATA, ATP. With Sun Co., Richardson, Tex., 1968-71, Phila., 1971-76; mgr. planning and acquisitions Sun Info. Svcs. subs. Sun Co., Dallas, 1976-78; v.p. Helios Capital Corp. subs. Sun Co., Radnor, Pa., 1978-83; pres. ALKAN Leasing Corp., Wayne, 1983—, bd. dirs., 1983—. Prof. dept. computer scis. and bus. adminstrn. Eastern Coll., St. Davids, Pa., 1985-87; prof. math. Villanova (Pa.) U., 1987-89. Bd. dirs. Radnor Twp. Sch. Dist., 1987-91, Delaware County Intermediate Unit, 1988-91. Mem. IEEE, Assn. Computing Machinery, Data Processing Mgmt. Assn., Fin. Planners Assn. Phila. (mem. Tri-State area chpt., bd. dirs. 2000—, treas. 2000-01, pres.-elect 2002), Soc. Fin. Svc. Profls., Am. Assn. Equipment Lessors, Inst. Cert. Fin. Planners (bd. dirs. Phila. Tri-State Area 1993-99, v.p. mem. 1994-95, treas. 1995-99), Nat. Assn. Enrolled Agts., Nat. Assn. Tax Practitioners, Nat. Assn. Pub. Accts., Fin. Analysts Phila., Fin. Planning Assn. (bd. dirs. Delaware Valley Soc. 2000—, treas. 2000—), Phila. Fin. Assn. (sec. 1989-92, mem. award 1988, bd. dirs. 1989-92), Fgn. Policy Rsch. Inst., World Affairs Coun. Phila., Phila. Union League, Main Line C. of C., Assn. Investment Mgmt. and Rsch., Rotary (pres. Wayne club 1989-90, gov.'s rep. dist. 7450, 1990-91, 93-94), Masons (32 degree). Republican. Home: 736 Brooke Rd Wayne PA 19087-4709 Office: PO Box 8301 Radnor PA 19087-8301 E-mail: almarland@aol.com., marlandatalkan@aol.com.

MARLAND, MELISSA KAYE, judge; b. Beckley, W.Va., Feb. 16, 1955; d. James Robert and Fannie Evelyn (Cook) M. BA in Polit. Sci., W.Va U., 1976, JD, 1979. Bar: W.Va. 1979, U.S. Dist. Ct. (so. dist.) W.Va. 1979, U.S. Supreme Ct. 1983. Law clk. Pub. Svc. Commn. W.Va., Charleston, 1979-82, hearing examiner, 1982-87, dep. chief adminstrv. law judge, 1987-89, chief adminstrv. law judge, 1989—. Faculty mem. ann. regulatory studies program Nat. Assn. Regulatory Commrs./Inst. Pub. Utilities, Mich. State U., 1994—. Assoc. editor: West Virginia Digest of Public Utility Decisions, vols. 1-7, 1986-91; contbr. articles to profl. jours. Mem. ABA, NAFE, W.Va. State Bar (com. on corp., banking and bus. law 1987—, adminstrv. law com. 1995—), Nat. Assn. Regulatory Commrs. (chmn. subcom. on adminstrv. law judges 1991-95), Phi Beta Kappa, Phi Alpha Delta, Pi Sigma Alpha. Democrat. Avocations: music, reading. Office: Pub Svc Commn WVa 201 Brooks St Charleston WV 25301-1803 E-mail: mmarland@worldnet.att.net.

MARLAR, DONALD FLOYD, lawyer; b. Little Rock, Jan. 15, 1944; s. Floyd Howard and Ruth May (Lawson) M.; m. Janet Jeanne Clark, Mar. 29, 1963; children: Jennifer Clark, Christopher Decker. BA, Ark. State U., 1966; JD, U. Tulsa, 1969; Masters in Taxation, George Washington U., 1972. Bar: Okla. 1969. Ptnr. Pray, Walker, Jackman, Williamson & Marlar, Tulsa, Okla., 1973-96, pres., 1996—. Chmn. Okla. Bar Tax Section, 1979-80. Dir. Tulsa Ballet Theatre, 1987—, pres., 1991-92; gen. coun., v.p. Gilcrease Mus., Tulsa, 1989—, pres., 2000-01, chmn. bd. dirs., 2001—; trustee Grace and Franklin Bernsen Found., Tulsa, 1992—. Capt. U.S. Army, 1969-73. Mem. Am. Bar Assn., Tulsa Bar Assn., The Summit Club (bd. govs. 1986-92, pres. 1992). Home: 3517 E 70th Pl Tulsa OK 74136-2647 Office: Pray Walker Jackman Williamson & Marlar 900 Oneok Plz 100 W 5th St Tulsa OK 74103 E-mail: DFM@praywalker.com.

MARLAR, JANET CUMMINGS, retired public relations officer; b. Burnsville, Miss., Dec. 22, 1942; d. James E. and Juanita (Hale) Cummings; m. David C. Linton, May 21, 1961 (div. 1984); 1 child, Jeffory Mark; m. Thomas Gilbert Cupples, Mar. 5, 1984 (div. 1990); m. Frederick Marlar, Nov. 19, 1994. Student, NE Miss. Jr. Coll., 1960-61, Memphis State U., 1975-76, Sheffield Tech. Ctr., Memphis, 1984-85. Property owner, Burnsville, 1974—, Glen, Miss., 1993—. Mem. bus. adv. com. Sheffield Tech. Ctr., 1997—; docent Curlee House, Corinth, Miss., 1989—; exec. bd. Internat. Heritage Commn., Memphis, 1987-92; ret.; pub. rels. officer Internat. Heritage Ethnic Festival, Memphis; mem. pub. rels. com. BHS Club of 1960 com., 1994-2000. Co-editor: Internat. Heritage Bull./Newsletter; contbr. articles. Vol. Memphis Brooks Mus. Art, 1980—; mem. exec. co., pub. info. officer Bldg. Bridges for A Better Memphis, 1985—; pres. Eagle Watch Assn.; founder Janet C. Cupples Citizenship awards, Memphis City Inter-City Sch., 1975, Founded Citizenship award, 1975, Memphis City Schs.; founder, chair women's com. on crime City of Memphis, 1985—, chair Heritage-City of Memphis, chair internat. heritage program, 1987, 88—, Ethnic Outreach Neighborfest, 1988—; hon. mem. city coun., 1987; donor, exec. com. Women of Achievement, Inc., Memphis, 1986; mem. spkrs. bus. United Way of Greater Memphis, Friends of Shelby County Libr., 1986—, YMCA; chair ethnic outreach com. Neighborfest, Memphis, 1987, chairperson exec. com., 1988; amb. Memphis Internat. Heritage Commn., 1988; youth mentor Memphis Youth Leadership Devel. Inst.; internat. coord. Neighborfest '88; chairperson Internat. Heritage City of Memphis, 1987; mem. cmty. coun. Memphis City Schs., Memphis Cablevision Edn. Task Force; apptd. col. aide de camp to staff of Gov. Ned McWherter of Tenn., 1988; apptd. hon. mem. Tenn. State Senator Steve Cohen's staff, 1989; sec. safety com. St. Francis Hosp., 1992, sec. BHS com., 1960; participant Vol. Miss. Food Network Distbn. for Disabled Persons, 1996; active Dem. Nat. Com., 1994—; founder Inter City Sch. Citizenship award, 1986; founder Burnsville Elem. Sch. Accelerated Reader Awards, Libr. award, Citizenship Essay award, 2001—. Recipient 11 certs. of recognition Memphis City Coun., 1986-89, Outstanding Svc. to Pub. Edn. award 1986, merit award City of Memphis, 1987, Royal award HRH Prince Kevin, 1996; named Outstanding Female Participant, Neighborhood, Inc., 1987; named Woman of Achievement 1988; honored by Pres. George Bush as Outstanding Vol., 1989; featured as one of top 1000 Vols. in Mid-South, 1989; Svc. award Cummings Sch., 1993; apptd. Hon. Memphis City Councilwoman, 1995-96; recognized by Gen. Colin Powell, 1997. Mem. NAFE, NOW (2d v.p. Memphis chpt. 1987, del. nat. conf. 1987, 2d v.p.), Network Profl. Women's Orgn., NCCJ, Rep. Career Women, Memphis Peace and Justice Ctr., Women's Polit. Caucus Tenn., Nat. Children's Cancer Soc. (friend 1995-96). Methodist. Avocations: community service, writing, teaching.

MARLAR, JOHN THOMAS, environmental engineer; b. Jackson, Ala., Sept. 24, 1939; s. John Thomas and Ada Jean (Hamilton) M.; m. Maryjo Borges, June 22, 1963 (div. 1979); children: John Thomas III, Jeannine Marie, Jennifer Joanne; m. Joyce A. Moon, Aug. 12, 1988 (dec. June 1997); children: Regina Etheridge, Preston E. Moon. Student, Miss. So. Coll., 1957-58; BCE, Auburn U., 1963; MS, Ga. Inst. Tech., 1968. Coop. student U.S. Amry C.E., Mobile, Ala., 1958-63; staff engr. Fed. Water Pollution Control Adminstrn., Atlanta, 1967-68, Alameda, Calif., 1968-69; superfisory san. engr. Fed. Water Quality Adminstrn., San Francisco, 1969-71; chief tech. assessment unit U.S. EPA, Atlanta, 1971-73, chief tech. support br., 1973-76, chief water quality planning br., 1976-81, chief facilities performance br., 1981-91, chief environ. compliance br., 1991-97, ret., 1997, sr. tech. authority internat program-Ukraine, 1996-97; prin. J.T. Marlar, Inc., 1997—. With USPHS, 1963-66. Recipient Bronze medal EPA, 1973, 86, 94, 97, Silver medal, 1985, Gold medal, 1988; Alcoa scholar, 1962-63. Mem. Water Pollution Control Fedn., Sigma Xi, Chi Epsilon, Phi Kappa Phi. Home: 85 Sims Rd Winder GA 30680-3594 Office: EPA Sci and Ecol Support Divsn 980 College Station Rd Athens GA 30605-2720 E-mail: JTMarlar@aol.com.

MARLAS, JAMES CONSTANTINE, holding company executive; b. Chgo., Aug. 22, 1937; s. Constantine J. and Helen (Cotsirilos) M.; m. Kendra S. Graham, 1968 (div. 1971); m. Glenn Close, 1984 (div. 1987); m. Marie Nugent-Head, 1993. AB cum laude, Harvard U., 1959; MA in Jurisprudence, Oxford (Eng.) U., 1961; JD, U. Chgo., 1963. Bar: Ill. 1963, N.Y. 1966. Assoc. firm Baker & McKenzie, London and N.Y.C., 1963-66; exec. v.p. South East Commodity Corp., N.Y.C., 1967-68; chmn. bd. Union Capital Corp., 1968—; vice chmn. bd. Mickelberry's Food Products Co., 1970-71; pres., dir. Mickelberry Comm. Corp., 1972—, chief exec. officer, 1973—; chmn. bd. Mickleberry Commn. Corp., 1984—; chmn. bd., CEO Newcourt Industries, Inc., 1976—. Chmn. bd. dirs. Bowmar Instrument Corp., chmn. exec. com., 1983-92. Co-editor: Univ. Chgo. Law Rev, 1962-63; Contbr. articles to profl. jours. Bd. dirs. N.Y.C. Opera, Commanderie de Bordeaux, Brasenose Coll. Charitable Found. Mem. Am. Fgn. Law Assn., Young Pres.'s Orgn. Clubs: Boodle's (London); Racquet and Tennis (N.Y.C.). Office: Mickelberry Comm Corp 405 Park Ave New York NY 10022-4405

MARLATT, DOROTHY BARBARA, university dean, education consultant; b. Tarrytown, N.Y., Dec. 01; d. Joseph S. and Evelyn M. (McGinnis) Porcano; m. Gene R. Marlatt, Aug. 20, 1960; children: David D., Julia Jeanne Marlatt Kelley. BA, Wheaton (Ill.) Coll., 1960; MA, U. Colo., 1966; EdD, Internat. Grad. Sch., St. Louis, 1987. Tchr. Alexandria (Va.) Pub. Schs., 1961-62, Westminster (Colo.) Pub. Schs., 1962-66, Jeffco Pub. Schs., Lakewood, Colo., 1966-69; elem. prin. Denver Pub. Schs., 1970-94; assoc. prof. edn. Rockmont Coll., Lakewood, 1976-93; prof. edn. Colo. Christian U., 1993-98, dean edn., 1994-97; adj. prof. Union Grad. Sch., Cin., 1995—; prin. Twin Peaks Charter Acad., Longmont, Colo., 1997-99; v.p. New Century Assocs., Denver, 1999—. Author: Leadership to a Higher Power, 1998. Recipient Svc. to Youth award YMCA, 1960, Svc. award Big Bros., 1970, Pub. Rels. Recognition award Denver Pub. Schs., 1972. Fellow Acad. Nat. Staff Devel., Inst. for Devel. of Edn1. Activities, Nat. Elem. Sch. Prins. Assn.; mem. Optimists, Kappa Delta Pi. Republican. Presbyterian. Avocation: music.

MARLATT, MICHAEL JAMES, lawyer; b. L.A., Jan. 15, 1957; s. James Raymond and Norma Jean (Greenfield) M.; m. Donna Marie Healey, Apr. 13, 1985. BA, U. So. Calif., Calif. Poly., Pomona, 1981; JD, Pepperdine U., 1984. Bar: Calif. 1984, U.S. Dist. Ct. (ctrl. dist.) Calif. 1985, U.S. Supreme Ct. 1990. Project liaison U. So. Calif., Sch. Medicine, L.A., 1975-78; documentation rschr. NASA-Jet Propulsion Lab., Pasadena, Calif., 1978-81; ptnr. Thompson & Colegate, Riverside, 1984—. Bd. dirs. Assn. So. Calif. Def. Counsel, L.A., U. Calif., Riverside; lectr. Calif. Trial Lawyers Assn., 1991-94, Princeton U., 1993, U. Amsterdam Law Sch., 1994, Loma Linda (Calif.) U. Sch. Medicine, 1991-94, 99, Boston Coll. Law Sch., 1997, U. London, 1998; chair Am. Legal Sys. Internat. Law Program Civil Litigation U. of Calif., 1997; lectr., spkr. to ins. cos. on health care, 1988—; radio commentator Stas. KCKC, KCAL, KMEN and KPRO. Pres. U. Calif., Riverside, 1996—99; v.p. Mission Inn Found., 1996—98, pres., 1999—2001; mem. bioethics com. Riverside Cmty. Hosp., 1999—2002; Mem. ctr. com. Calif. Rep. Party, Sacramento, 1990—93; bd. dirs. U. Calif., Riverside, Mission Inn Found., Riverside County Regional Med. Ctr., ARC. Mem. Am. Bd. Trial Advocates, So. Calif. Assn. Hosp. Risk Mgrs. (bylaws com. 1996-99), Victoria Country Club, Lincoln Club Riverside County, Phi Alpha Delta. Roman Catholic. Avocations: rare book collecting, collegiate athletics, traveling. Office: Thompson & Colegate PO Box 1299 3610 14th St Riverside CA 92501-3843 E-mail: mmarlatt@thompson-Colegate.com.

MARLEAU, DIANE, Canadian government official; b. Kirkland Lake, Ont., Can., June 21, 1943; d. Jean-Paul and Yvonne (Desjardins) LeBel; m. Paul C. Marleau, Aug. 3, 1963; children: Brigitte, Donald, Stéphane. Student, U. Ottawa, Ont., 1960-63; BA in Econs., Laurentian U., Sudbury, Ont., 1976. With Donald Jean Acctg. Svcs., Sudbury, 1971-75; receiver mgr. Thorne Riddell, 1975-76; treas. No. Regional Residential Treatment Program for Women, 1976-80, Com. for the Industry and Labour Adjustment Program, Sudbury, 1983; mem. transition team Ont. Premier's Office, Toronto, 1985; firm adminstr. Collins Barrow-Maheu Noiseux, Sudbury, 1985-88; M.P. from Sudbury House of Commons, Ottawa, 1988—; min. of health for Can., 1993-96; min. of public works Canada, 1996-97; min. for internat. cooperation, min. responsible for La Francophonie, 1997-99. Councilor Regional Municipality of Sudbury, 1980-85, chair fin. com., 1981; alderman City of Sudbury, 1980-85; mem. No. Devel. Coun., Sudbury, 1986-88; vice chair Nat. Liberal Standing Com. on Policy, 1989; chair Ont. Liberal Caucus, 1990; apptd. nat. exec. Liberal Party Can., 1990, assoc. critic Govt. Ops., 1990, Dep. Opposition Whip, 1991, assoc. critic Fin., 1992; vice chair standing com. fin., 1992. Chmn. fund-raising Canadian Cancer Soc., Sudbury, 1987-88; co-chmn. Laurentian Hosp. Cancer Care Svcs. fund-raising campaign, Sudbury, 1988; chair bd. govs. Cambrian Coll., 1987-88, bd. govs., 1983-88; mem. Sudbury and Dist. Health Unit Bd., 1981-82; mem. fin. com., bd. dirs. Laurentian Hosp., 1981-85; chair Can. Games for the Physically Disabled, 1983; apptd. Ont. Adv. Coun. Women's Issues, 1984. Recipient Paul Harris award, 1996. Mem. Sudbury Bus. and Profl. Women Club. Avocations: playing piano, gardening, cooking. Office: House of Commons Parliament Bldgs Ottawa ON Canada K1A 0A6 also: 36 Elgin St Sudbury ON Canada P3C 5B4

MARLEN, JAMES S. chemical, plastics and building materials manufacturing company executive; b. Santiago, Chile, Mar. 14, 1941; came to U.S., 1961; m. Carolyn S. Shields, Jan. 23, 1965; children: James, Andrew, John. Grad., U. Ala., 1965; MBA, U. Akron, 1971. With GenCorp., Akron, Ohio, 1965-93, engrng., mktg. and gen. mgmt. positions domestic and internat. ops., 1965-76; pres. GTR Coated Fabrics Co., 1977-80, group pres. fabricated plastics, 1980-87; pres. consumer and indsl. sects. GenCorp Polymer Products, Akron, Ohio, 1988—; v.p. and officer GenCorp, 1988-93; pres., CEO Ameron Internat. Corp., Pasadena, Calif., 1993—. Bd. dirs., Ameron, Inc., chmn. bd. dirs., pres. and CEO, 1995—; dir. A. Schulman, Inc., Tamco Steel, Parsons Corp.; gen. and hon. chmn. Nat. Inventors Hall of Fame Induction, 1993. Bd. dirs. YMCA Met. L.A., The Employers Group of Calif., Town Hall of L.A., gov.; mem. the Beavers; dir. L.A. Sports Coun. Mem. Chem. Mfrs. Assn. (past pres.), Assocs. Caltech, Calif. C. of C., L.A. C. of C. (dir.), Portage Country Club (Akron, Ohio), Calif. Club (L.A.), Annandale Golf Club (Pasadena), L.A. Country Club, Valley Hunt Club (Pasadena), Soc. Fellows of Huntington Libr. (L.A.). Office: Ameron Internat Corp 245 S Los Robles Ave Pasadena CA 91101-2820

MARLER, CHARLES HERBERT, journalism educator, historian, consultant; b. Garfield, Ark., Apr. 13, 1933; s. William Owen and Velma Valentine (Poe) M.; m. Peggy Lucille Gambill, Dec. 30, 1954; children: David Owen, Todd Alan, Scott Ladd. BA, Abilene Christian U., 1955, MA, 1968; PhD, U. Mo., 1974. Publicity asst. Abilene (Tex.) Christian U., 1955-56, sports info. dir., 1958-63, assoc. dir. devel., 1963-64, dir. info. and pubs., 1964-71, prof. journalism, 1974—, chmn. dept. journalism and mass comm., 1987-98; rsch. asst. U. Mo., Columbia, 1973-74. Editor: Horizons, 1963-71, Lone Star Christmas, 1989, No Ordinary University, 1998; cons. Parenting Today, Christian Woman, Gospel Advocate, IdeaShop, Christian Chronicle; mem. editl. bd. Am. Journalism, Southwestern Mass Comm. Jour.; contbr. articles to profl. jours. Elder Univ. Ch. Christ, Abilene, 1977—; trustee Christian Village of Abilene, 1981-2000, Members of Chs. of Christ for Scouting, Abilene, 1985—, nat. chmn., 1989-91; mem. coun. bd. Boy Scouts Am., Abilene, 1981-2001. With U.S. Army, 1956-57, Germany. Frank Luther Mott Hist. Rsch. fellow U. Mo., Columbia, 1972-74, Cullen Fund grantee, 1982-84, 85-87; recipient Improvement award Time/Life Alumni Mag., 1966, Journalism Excellence award 20th Century Christian Mag., 1968, Clinton H. Denman Freedom of Info. Writing award U. Mo., 1974, Scoutmaster's key Boy Scouts Am., 1981, Dist. Merit award, 1982, Keith Ware award U.S. Army Journalism Competition, 1985, Tchr. of Yr. Trustees award, 1987, Silver Beaver award Boy Scouts Am., 1988, Christian Journalism award The Christian Chronicle, 1993; named Advisor of Yr., Tex. Intercollegiate Press Assn., 1982, Faithful Servant, Chs. Christ for Scouting, 1990, Faculty Senate award, 2000, Coll. Arts and Scis. Career Achievement award, 2000, Charlie Marler scholarship, Southwestern Journalism Congress, 2001. Mem. Am. Journalism Historian Assn. (bd. dirs. 1985-88, chmn. pub. com. 1983-87, 95-96, chmn. election and site com. 1987-90), Nat. Conf. Editorial Writers, S.W. Edn. Coun. for Edn. in Journalism and Mass Comm. (pres. 1988-89), SW Journalism Congress (pres 1987-88, 1997-98, 1998-99, 99-2000), Texas Intercollegiate Press Assn. Advs. (pres. 1987-89), Soc. Newspaper Design, Soc. Profl. Journalists (dep. dir. journalism edn. 1988-90, mem. nat. journalism edn. com. 1988-90), Assn. for Edn. in Journalism and Mass Comm. and Religion and Media Interest Group (chair 1999-2000). Avocations: geneaology, newspaper coffee mug collecting, travel, research, camping. Home: 818 Radford Dr Abilene TX 79601-4613 Office: Dept Journalism and Mass Comm ACU Box 27892 Abilene Christian U Abilene TX 79699-7892 E-mail: charlie.marler@jmc.acu.edu.

MARLER, LARRY JOHN, private investor, leadership consultant; b. Chgo., Sept. 22, 1940; s. Walter William and Lena Inez (Killen) M.; m. Katy Jo Hibbits, Oct. 17, 1962 (div. Apr. 1971); 1 child, Preston Scott; m. Linda Lee Sorg, Sept. 2, 1982. BA, Christian Coll. Am., 1987; MA, Houston Grad. Sch. Theology, 1988; PhD, U.S. Internat. U., San Diego, 1992. Acct. Shell Oil Co., New Orleans, Houston, 1964-73; acctg. supr. We. Geophys. Co. Am., Houston, 1974; payroll supr. Olsen Inc., 1975-77; corp. credit mgr. Grant Corps., 1977-82; rschr., student contractor Navy Pers. R&D Ctr., San Diego, 1990-92; entrepreneur Denver, 1992-97; ESL coord., acct. Galilee Bapt. Ch., 1998—. With USCG, 1959-62. Mem. Am. Psychol. Soc., Am. Soc. Quality Control, Toastmasters Internat. Republican. Protestant. Avocations: reading, jogging, swimming, hiking, downhill skiing.

MARLETTA, MICHAEL A. biochemistry educator, researcher, protein chemist; b. Rochester, N.Y., Feb. 12, 1951; m. Margaret Gutowski, 1991. BA, SUNY, 1973; PhD in Pharm. Chemistry, U. Calif., 1978. Fellow MIT, Cambridge, 1978-80, from asst. prof. to assoc. prof. toxicology, 1980-87; assoc. prof. med. chemistry U. Mich., Ann Arbor, 1987-91, assoc. prof. biol. chemistry, 1989-91, John G. Searle prof. med. chemistry, prof. biol. chemistry, 1991—2001; prof., dept. of chem. and biology U. Calif. at Berkeley, 2001—; prof., dept. of cellular and molecular pharmacology U. Calif. at San Franciso, 2001—. Investigator Howard Hughes Med. Inst., 1997. John D. and Catherine T. MacArthur fellow, 1995. Mem. AAAS, Am. Soc. Biochem. and Molecular Biology, Am. Chem. Soc. Achievements include research in protein/structure function with a particular interest in enzyme reaction mechanisms and molecular mechanisms of signal transduction, study of nitric oxide synthase, guanylate cyclase and related enzymes in this signaling system. Office: U of Calif at Berkeley Dept of Chemistry 211 Lewis Hall 1460 Berkeley CA 94720-1460*

MARLIN, ARTHUR EDWARD, pediatric neurosurgeon, educator; b. Boston, Jan. 28, 1947; s. Herman and Eva Marlin; m. Bebby Marlin; children: Sarah Jane, Tamara Eve, Evan Seth. BSc with distinction, McGill U., 1968, MD, 1972; MHA, Trinity Sch. Health Care Admn., 1999. Diplomate Am. Bd. Neurol. Surgery; lic. surgeon, N.Y., Tex. Surg. intern U. Minn. Hosps., 1972-73; resident NYU Med. Ctr., 1973-78; clin. instr. neurosurgery NYU Sch. Medicine, 1978; asst. prof. surgery/neurosurgery, asst. prof. pediatrics U. Tex. Health Sci. Ctr., San Antonio, 1978-80, clin. asst. prof. surgery/neurosurgery, 1980-84, clin. asst. prof. pediatrics, 1980-82, clin. assoc. prof. pediatrics, 1982-91, clin. assoc. prof. orthopedics, 1985-91, clin. prof. pediatrics, 1991—2001; CEO, Meth. Womens and Childrens Hosp., 1998, Meth. Childrens Hosp. of So. Tex., 1998—. Chief sect. pediatric neurosurgery Santa Rosa Childrens Hosp., San Antonio, 1984-97; mem. adv. bd. South Tex. Organ Bank, 1987-90; mem. tech. adv. com. to gen. program Crippled Children's Svcs., Tex. Dept. Health, Austin, 1983-84; mem. Childrens Hosps. and Related Instns. Tex. Author: Handbook of Pediatric Neurology and Neurosurgery, 1993; editor: Concepts in Pediatric Neurosurgery, Vol. VII, 1987, Vol. VIII, 1988, Vol. IX, 1989, Vol. X, 1990, Vol. XI, 1991, Shortcuts, 1989-91; mem. editl. bd. Clin. Neurosurgery, 1981, 82, 83; ann. meeting editor Jour. Pediatric Neurosurgery, 1992—, mem. editl. bd., 1992—; prodr. movies Brain Retraction Pressure Monitoring, 1983, The Use of Surgical Isolation Bubble, 1986; contbr. articles to profl. jours. Fellow ACS, Am. Acad. Pediatrics; mem. AMA, Bexar County Med. Soc., Tex. Med. Assn., Internat. Soc. Pediatric Neurosurgery, San Antonio Pediatric Soc., Am. Soc. Pediatric Neurosurgery (chmn. edn. com. 1986-91), Tex. Pediatric Soc., Am. Assn. Neurol. Surgeons (chmn. pediatric sect. 1993-95, chmn. surg. policy com. 1990-91), Am. Acad. Pediatrics (neurology sect.). Office: 4499 Medical Dr Ste 397 San Antonio TX 78229-3713 E-mail: aem@pediatric-neurosurgery.com.

MARLIN, DANIEL, finance educator; b. Miami, July 25, 1966; s. Richard and Dorotha Marlin; m. Stacie Marlin; children: Brittany, Brendan. PhD, Fla. State U., 1995. Asst. prof. U. Tex., San Antonio, 1995—99, Coll. Charleston, SC, 1999—. Mem.: Southern Mgmt. Assn., Acad. Mgmt. Republican. Avocations: golf, fishing. Office: Coll Charleston Dept Mgmt and Mktg Charleston SC 29424 Business E-Mail: marlind@cofc.edu.

MARLIN, JOHN TEPPER, economist, writer, consultant; b. Washington, Mar. 1, 1942; s. Ervin Ross and Hilda (van Stockum) M.; m. Alice Rose Tepper, Sept. 25, 1971; children: John Joseph Tepper (Jay), Caroline Alice Tepper. AB cum laude, Harvard U., 1962; MA, Oxford U., 1969; PhD in Econs., George Washington U., 1968. Fin. economist Fed. Res. Bd., 1964-66, SBA, Washington, 1966-67, FDIC, Washington, 1967-69; asst. prof. Baruch Coll., CUNY, 1969-73; founder, pres. Coun. Mcpl. Performance, N.Y.C., 1973-88; pres. JTM Reports, Inc., 1989-92; first social auditor Ben and Jerry's Homemade, 1989; dir. Conversion Info. Ctr., Coun. Econ. Priorities, 1991-92; chmn., bd. advisors CIC, CEP, 1992-95, advisor internat. security program, 1995—2001. Cons. J.M. Kaplan Fund, 1991-92; chief economist Office Comptr., City of N.Y., 1992-94, 97—, sr. policy advisor, 1994-97; adj. prof. Pace U. Lubin Sch. Bus., N.Y.C., 2000—; adj. prof. ethics, markets and law NYU Stern Sch. Bus., N.Y.C., 2002--. Author: The Wealth of Cities, 1974, Cities of Opportunity, 1988, Catalogue of Healthy Food, 1990, The Livable Cities Almanac, 1992, Take up the Song, 1998 (prod. in Rochester's Geva Theatre, 1988, video produced, 2000); co-author: Let's Go Guide to Europe, 1961, Book of American City Rankings, 1983, Contracting Municipal Services, 1984, Book of World City Rankings, 1986, Soviet Conversion, 1991, Building a Peace Economy, 1992, NYC's Sports Economy, 1996, N.Y.C.'s Software/Information Technology Industry, 1999, The Impact of the September 11 WTC Attack on NYC's Economy and City Revenues, 2001; founding editor: Jour. Fin. Edn., 1972—73; editor: Nat. Civic Rev., 1987—88, Privatization Report, 1986—88, Econ. Notes, 1992—94, 1997—. Donor-advisor E.R. Marlin Fund, N.Y. Cmty. Trust, 1994--; chmn. budget and fin. com. Springs Cmty. Presbyn. Ch., 2000—. Mem. Am. Econ. Assn. (life), Fin. Mgmt. Assn. (life), Economists Allied Arms Reduction (treas., mem. exec. com. 1994-2002, bd. dirs. 1994--), Harvard Club (N.Y.C.), Devon Yacht Club, Trinity (Oxford) Soc. U.S.A. (pres. 1969-94), Oxford U. Soc. (trustee, exec. com. 1999-2002), Brit. Schs. and Univs. Found. (treas. 2002—), Oxford U. Alumni Assn. N.Y. (sec. 1994-99, mem. exec. com., archivist 1999—), Oxford-Cambridge Dinner Com. (N.Y.C., pres. 1992—), Money Marketeers NYU, N.Y. Assoc. Bus. Economists (v.p. 2000-02, pres. 2002—). Home: 360 W 22nd St New York NY 10011-2600 Office: City of New York Office Comptr 1 Centre St Rm 621 New York NY 10007-1602 E-mail: jmarlin@comptroller.nyc.gov., jtmarlin@post.harvard.edu., TepperMarlin@aol.com.

MARLIN, RICHARD, lawyer; b. N.Y.C., June 1, 1933; s. Edward and Lillian (Milstein) M.; m. Merrel Pincus, June 12, 1955 (div. 1972); children: John F., Elizabeth; m. Jenesta Rutherford, July 29, 1974 (div. 1981); m. Caroline Mary Hirsch Magnus, Nov. 1, 1981. BA magna cum laude, Yale U., 1955, LLB, 1958; LLM, NYU, 1964. Bar: N.Y. 1959, Fla. 1978. Law clk. to presiding justice U.S. Dist. Ct. Conn., New Haven, 1958-59; assoc. Cleary, Gottlieb, Steen & Hamilton, N.Y.C., 1959-62, Wien Lane & Klein, N.Y.C., 1962-64; ptnr. Mnuchin Moss & Marlin, 1964-66, Marshall, Bratter, Greene, Allison & Tucker, N.Y.C., 1966-79; sr. ptnr. Kramer, Levin, Naftalis & Frankel LLP, 1979—. Bd. dirs. FAB Industries, Inc., N.Y.C. Bd. editors Yale Law Jour. Mem. ABA, Assn. Bar City N.Y., N.Y. County Lawyers' Assn. (corp. law com., chmn. subcom.), Glen Oaks Club (Old Westbury, N.Y.) (bd. govs. 1979-85, 92-94), Phi Beta Kappa. Office e-mail: kramerlevin.com. Office: Kramer Levin Naftalis & Frankel LLP 919 3rd Ave New York NY 10022-3902

MARLIN, ROBERT MATTHEW, secondary school educator; b. Buffalo, June 11, 1940; s. Clarence Lewis and LaVerna (Haentgus) M.; m. Margaret Mary Steve, July, 1962 (div. July 1970); 1 child, Wendy. BEd, U. Alaska, 1967; postgrad., Alaska Pacific U., 1967-71, U. Ga., 1970, U. Salamanca, Spain, 1987, Calif State U., 1984-87. Cert. tchr., Calif. Radio traffic analyst USAF Security Svc., Anchorage, 1958-63; copywriter Anchorage Daily Times, 1963-67; tchr. Anchorage Sch. Dist., 1967-72; mgr. Transamerica Corp., L.A., 1972-84; tchr. L.A. Unified Sch. Dist., 1984—. Participant sci. seminar on quality of edn., Pinar de Rio, Cuba, 1995, Matanzas, Cuba, 1996, Manzanillo, Cuba, 1997, Cienfuegos, Cuba, 1998. Bd. dirs. Upward Bound, Alaska Meth. Univ., Anchorage, 1969; vol. counselor Gay and Lesbian Cmty. Svcs. Ctr., L.A., 1975-76; cons. Constl. Rights Found., L.A., 1994—; gay and lesbian edn. comm. site liason L.A. Bd. Edn., 1996—. With USAF, 1958-63. Grantee Dept. Commerce, 1969, NSF, 1970, 71, L.A. Unified Sch. Dist., 1988. Mem. NEA, Gay, Lesbian, Straight Edn. Network, Calif. Tchrs. Assn., United Tchrs. L.A. (gay lesbian issues com.), Calif. Coun. for Social Studies. Democrat. Home: 531 W Avenue 46 Los Angeles CA 90065-5007 Office: Berendo Middle Sch 1157 S Berendo St Los Angeles CA 90006-3301

MARLING, KARAL ANN, art history and social sciences educator, curator; b. Rochester, N.Y., Nov. 5, 1943; d. Raymond J. and Marjorie (Karal) M. PhD, Bryn Mawr Coll., 1971. Prof. art history and Am. studies U. Minn., Mpls., 1977—. Author: Federal Art in Cleveland, 1933-1943: An Exhibition, 1974, Wall-to-Wall America: A Cultural History of Post-Office Murals in the Great Depression, 1982, 2d edit., 2000, The Colossus of the Roads: Myth and Symbol along the American Highway, 1984, 2d edit., 2000, Tom Benton and His Drawings: A Biographical Essay and a Collection of His Sketches, Studies, and Mural Cartoons, 1985, Frederick C. Knight (1898-1979), 1987, George Washington Slept Here: Colonial Revivals and American Culture, 1876-1986, 1988, Looking Back: A Perspective on the 1913 Inaugural Exhibition, 1988, Blue Ribbon: A Social and Pictorial History of the Minnesota State Fair, 1990; (with John Wetenhall) Iwo Jima: Monuments, Memories, and the American Hero, 1991, Edward Hopper, 1992, As Seen on T.V.: The Visual Culture of Everyday Life in the 1950's, 1994, Graceland: Going Home with Elvis, 1995; editor (with Jessica H. Foy) The Arts and the American Home, 1890-1930, 1994, Norman Rockwell, 1997, Designing the Disney Theme Parks: The Architecture of Reassurance, 1997, Merry Christmas! Celebrating America's Greatest Holiday, 2000, Looking North: Canadian Mounted Police Paintings, 2002; contbr. essays to catalogs. Recipient Minn. Humanities Commn. award 1986, Minn. Book award History, 1994, Robert C. Smith award Decorative Arts Soc., 1994, Internat. Assn. of Art Critics award, 1998. Office: 1920 S 1st St Ste 1301 Minneapolis MN 55454-1190

MARLING-BUSSARD, ROSE MARIE, geriatrics nurse; b. Lowell, Mass., July 18, 1934; d. Edward Mark and Alice (Godsell) Culleton; m. James F. Marling, Aug. 3, 1952 (div. Sept. 1982); m. William J. Bussard, June 4, 1988 (dec. Sept. 1991); children: Kathleen Marling Persinger, James M. Marling, Dianne Marling Good, David P. Marling. LPN, B.M. Spurr Sch. Practical Nursing, 1980; ADN, Hocking Tech. Coll., 1987; postgrad. RN-MSN, Wesley Coll., 1999—2002. RN, Del. Soc. editor The Times Leader, Martins Ferry, Ohio; staff reporter Wheeling (W.Va.) News Register, 1978—99; nurse Ohio Valley Med. Ctr., Wheeling, W.Va.; staff nurse telemetry, med.-surg. Beebe Med. Ctr., Lewes, Del.; charge nurse, dir. nursing Lewes Convalescent Ctr.; dir. nursing Milford Manor Nursing and Rehab. Ctr., Milford, Del.; skilled unit mgr. IHS of Del. at Kent, Smyrna; staff float pool RN Naples Cmty. Hosp. Camp nurse 4-H; RNC investigative Nurse Longterm Care Residents Protection Del. Divsn. Health and Social Svcs. Parish Coun. pres. St. Mary's Cath. Ch., Shadyside, Ohio; mem. Salt and Light com., advocacy and social justice St. Edmond's Ch., Rehoboth, Del.; mem. Upper Ohio Valley Girl Scout coun. Recipient Writing award Writer's Digest, Journalism award Shadyside Woman's Club; Bus. and Profl. Women Nursing grantee. Mem. ANA (cert. gen. nurse), Nat. League Nursing, Del. Nurses Assn., Del. Dir. Nursing Assn., Nat. Writers Club, Bus. and Profl. Women. Home: 28 Gunpowder Ln Rehoboth Beach DE 19971-9758

MARLOW, AUDREY SWANSON, artist, designer; b. N.Y.C.; d. Sven and Rita (Porter) Swanson; student (scholarships) Art Students League, 1950-55; spl. courses SUNY (Stony Brook), L'Alliance Française m. Roy Marlow, Nov. 30, 1968. With Cohn-Hall-Marx Textile Studio, 1961-65, R.S. Assocs. Textile Studio, 1965-73; freelance designer, illustrator Prince Matchabelli, Lester Harrison Agy., J. Walter Thompson Agy., 1957-78; portrait and fine artist, Wading River, N.Y., 1973—; instr. Phoenix Sch. Design (N.Y.C.); illustrator children's books: Breads of Many Lands and 4H Club Bakes Bread, 1966, Anna Smith Strong and the Setauket Spy Ring, 1991, Timothy and the Acrobat, 1992; exhibits include: Nat. Arts Club, NAD, Parish Art Mus., South Hampton, N.Y., Guild Hall, East Hampton, N.Y., Portraits Inc., Lincoln Ctr., Chung-Cheng Art Gallery, St. John's U., Mystic (Conn.) Art Assn., Harbour Gallery, St. Thomas, V.I., Palais Rameau, Lisle, France, 1988, Sumner Mus., Washington, 1992, East End Arts & Humanities Coun., L.I., N.Y., 1996; one-person shows: Salmagundi Club, 1982, Rockefeller Gallery, N.Y.C., 1992; portrait commns. include: Millicent Fenwick, Harrison J. Goldin, Thomas R. Bayles, Mons. John Fagan, others. Trustee, Middle Island Public Library, 1972-76. Recipient John W. Alexander medal, 1976, award Council on Arts, 1978, award of excellence Cork Gallery, Lincoln Center, 1982; Grumbacher Bronze medal, 1983; Grumbacher Silver medal 1986; Best in Show award N.Y. Arts Council, 1986, Suburban Art League, 1993, Excellence award Town of Oyster Bay, 1995, Brookhaven Arts & Humanities Coun., 1996. Mem. Pastel Soc. Am. (award 1977, 80, 90), Am. Artists Profl. League (2 1st prize awards), Hudson Valley Art Assn. (award), Knickerbocker Artists (2 awards), Catharine Lorillard Wolfe Art Club (award 1982), Salmagundi Club (5 awards), Nat. League Am. Pen Women (Gold award, Gold medal of Honor, Best in Show 1990). Works represented at NYU, Longwood Pub. Libr., Sr. Citizen's Complex, Newark, St. Theresa of the Child Jesus Convent, Wading River Congl. Ch., L.I., pvt. collections. Home: 147 N Side Rd Wading River NY 11792-1112

MARLOW, EDWARD A. former army officer; b. Cleve., Nov. 22, 1946; m. Gari Ann Dill, Sept. 20, 1975. AA, Long Beach City Coll., 1971; cert., Officer Candidate Sch., Ft. Benning, 1974, Basic Infantry Officer Course, 1976; student, Am. Law Inst., N.Y., 1979-80; cert., Advance Armor Officer Course, Ft. Knox, 1982, U.S. Army Command and Gen. Staff Coll., 1986; BS in Bus. Mgmt. and Polit. Sci., SUNY, 1987; MPA, U. So. Calif., 1990; cert., Advance Intelligence Officer Course, Ft. Huachuca, 1991. Registered investment adv. with SEC, 1978-90. Commd. 2d lt. inf. U.S. Army, 1974, advanced through grades to maj., 1988; chief real property br. Mil. Dept., Sacramento, 1968—; pres. and dir. TEAM Mgmt. Corp., 1978—; pres. Western Res. Corp., Goldfield, Nev., 2000—, also bd. dirs. Mng. sr. ptnr. Caribbean Basin Latin Am. Devel. Orgn., Sacramento, 1988-98; trustee Hosp. Relief Fund Caribbean, Inc., Washington, 1989-92; mem. Caribbean Pvt. Sector Disaster Coord. subcom. White House Internat. Disaster Adv. Com., 1991-92; sr. ptnr. Caribbean Basin Latin Am. Devel. Orgn. Endowment Group, Sacramento, 1992—; chair bd. trustees CABALADO Relief Fund, Inc., 1993-99; provided disaster assistance and med. equipment to Glendon Hosp., Plymouth, Montserrat, West Indies, 1994-95. Mem. DAV (life), Am. Assn. Retired Persons. Avocations: sailing, fishing.

MARLOW, IAN MICHAEL, real estate company executive; b. Bklyn., Jan. 18, 1975; s. David Zachary and Ann Marlow. BSChemE, Rensselaer Poly. Inst., 1996. Environ. engr. Dept. Def., N.Y., 1993-96; nuc. engr. Dept. Energy, 1996-97; v.p., dir. info. scis. Homestead Ins. Co., Florham Park, NJ, 1997-99; v.p.,chief engring. and mktg. officer Signet Star Re, 1999—2002; chief info. and bus. ops. officer The Gale Co. LLC, 2002—. Mem. Datawarehousing Inst., Phi Lambda Phi (Nat. Engring. award). Avocations: sailing, automobiles, travel. Home: 11 Champion Blvd Livingston NJ 07039-8240

MARLOW, JAMES ALLEN, lawyer; b. Crossville, Tenn., May 23, 1955; s. Dewey Harold and Anna Marie (Hinch) M.; m. Sabine Klein, June 9, 1987; children: Lucas Allen, Eric Justin. BA, U. Tenn., 1976, JD, 1979; postgrad., Air War Coll., Maxwell AFB, Ala., 1990-91, Internat. Studienzentrum, Heidelberg, Germany, 1985-86. Bar: Ga. 1979, D.C. 1980, Tenn. 1980, U.S. Dist. Ct. (mid. dist.) Tenn. 1984, U.S. Ct. Fed. Claims 1987, U.S. Ct. Internat. Trade 1988, U.S. Tax Ct. 1987, U.S. Ct. Mil. Appeals 1980, U.S. Ct. Appeals (fed. cir.) 1987, U.S. Supreme Ct. 1987. Assoc. Carter & Assocs., Frankfurt, Fed. Republic Germany, 1984-85; chief internat. law USAF, Sembach AFB, Germany, 1986-96; pvt. practice Crossville, 1997—. Instr. Ctrl. Tex. Coll., 1997—; asst. prof. Embry-Riddle Aero. U., Kaiserslauten, Fed. Republic Germany, 1985—. Capt. USAF, 1980-84, Lt. Col. USAFR. Mem. Phi Beta Kappa. Avocations: genealogy, basketball, chess, German and Spanish languages. Home and Office: 5746 Highway 127 S Crossville TN 38572

MARLOW, JAMES ELLIOTT, English language educator; b. Feb. 14, 1938; s. Charles Henry and Louise Roberta (Frisby) M.; m. Sondra Kane, Apr. 1, 1966 (div. Mar. 1988); m. Corinne Thomas, Oct. 8, 1988; children: Jennifer Figueroa, Benjamin. AB, Dartmouth Coll., 1960; MA, U. Calif., Davis, 1968, PhD, 1972. Asst. prof. Coll. William and Mary, Williamsburg, Va., 1969-73; prof. English, U. Mass., Dartmouth, 1973—. Author: (lit. criticism) Uses of Time, 1995; contbr. articles to profl. jours. With U.S. Army, 1960-62. Home: 1 Timberledge Mattapoisett MA 02739 Office: U Mass Dept English Old Westport Rd Dartmouth MA 02747

MARLOW, JEANNETTE, retired pediatrician; b. N.Y.C., Oct. 30, 1922; d. Charles William and Dorothy Edna (Clarke) M.; m. John Shami, June 14, 1947 (div. 1978); children: Susan Evans, Dorothy Shami, John Shami, Wendy Shami. BA, Denison U., 1943; MD, Womans Med. Coll. of Pa., 1947. Diplomat Am. Bd. Pediatrics. Pvt. practice, Bedford Hills, N.Y., 1953-60; sch. physician Chappaqua (N.Y.) Pub. Schs., 1960-67; pediatric unit chief Letchworth Devel. Ctr., Thiells, N.Y., 1967-74; dir. med. svcs. Wassaic (N.Y.)

Devel. Ctr., 1974-90. Vol. clin. physician pediatrician Collier County Pub. Health, Naples, Fla., 1993-97. Recipient Alumnae Citation Alumnae Assn. Denison U., 1993. Fellow Am. Acad. Pediatrics; mem. AMA, AAUW (pres. 1964-65), Am. Med. Women's Assn., Women's Emergency Svcs. (bd. dirs. 1980-82), Ret. Physicians Assn. of AMA, Ret. Physicians Assn. of Collier County. Congregationalist. Avocations: painting, golf, walking. Home: 320 Seaview Ct Marco Island FL 34145-2914 E-mail: jmarlow18@aol.com., jmarlow@comcast.net.

MARLOW, LYDIA LOU, elementary education educator; b. Aledo, Ill., Aug. 21, 1954; d. Dwayne Elwood Irwin and Phyllis Jean (McKeown) Graff; m. Sidney G. Marlow Jr.; children: Erika Lynn, John Andrew. BA in Edn. with honors, Stephens Coll., 1976; MA in Reading, U. Mo., Kansas City, 1983. Cert. elem. tchr., Mo. Tchr. 2d grade Atlanta (Mo.) C-3 Sch. Dist., 1976-81; from tchr. headstart to tchr. 2d grade Independence (Mo.) Sch. Dist., 1982-92; reading clinician Santa Fe Trail & Procter Elem. Sch., Independence, 1993-99; Title 1 reading tchr. George Caleb Bingham 7th Grade Ctr., 1999-2000; gifted and talented tchr., 2001—. Adj. prof. children's lit. Webster U., Kansas City, Mo., 1994; developer program Focus on Reading, Independence, Mo., 1996; dept. chair, contbr. Missouri Reader, 1998—; presenter in field. Author: (novels) The Master Teacher: Memorable Moments, 2001; contbr. articles. Facilitator attention deficit hyperactivity disorder support group Caring Cmty. Santa Fe Trail Sch., Independence, 1996—97; rschr., author Truman Whistlestop Project, 1996—97; reading clinician Literacy Learning Ctr., 1997—2001. Recipient True Friend award Friends United Ednl. Support, Independence, 1994, Excellence in Tchg. award Govt. Employees Hosp. Assn., 1997, 2002. Mem.: Cmty. Assn. for the Arts, Children and Adults with Attention Deficit Disorder, Internat. Reading Assn. (local pres., publicity com. 1989—90, publicity co-chmn., editor Indep. IRA local 1991—93, editor Mo. state IRA 1992—95, Pres. award 1989), AAUW (publicity chair 1982—83), NEA (MNEA/Reliant grantee 1997), ASCD, Writers Club (coord. 1993—99, Editor's Choice 2001). Avocations: writing, gardening, reading, collecting antiques and elephant figurines. Home: 14609 E 44th St S Independence MO 64055-4810 Office: Christian Ott Elem School 1525 N Noland Rd Independence MO 64050 E-mail: Lydz14609@yahoo.com.

MARLOW, ORVAL LEE, II, lawyer; b. Denver, May 1, 1956; s. Jack Conger and Barbara A. (Stolzenburg) M.; m. Paige Wood, June 8, 1985; children: Lorri Wood, Orval Lee III. BA, U. Nebr., 1978, JD, 1981. Bar: Tex. 1981, U.S. Dist. Ct. (so. dist.) Tex. 1984, U.S. Ct. Appeals (5th cir.) 1984. Assoc. Krist & Scott, Houston, 1981-82; prin. Marlow & Assocs., 1982-83; ptnr. Lendais & Assocs., 1983-91; dir. Morris, Lendais, Hollrah & Snowden, 1992—. Mem. ABA, Internat. Bar Assn., Tex. Bar Assn., Houston Bar Assn., Phi Delta Phi. Lutheran. Avocations: golf, snow skiing, chess. Office: Morris Lendais Hollrah & Snowden 1980 Post Oak Blvd Ste 700 Houston TX 77056-3881 E-mail: omarlow@mlhs.net.

MARLOWE, CHRIS SEAN, safety engineer; b. Newark, Dec. 2, 1950; s. Thomas John and Elaine Marie (Kall) M.; m. Mary Haddad, July 1, 1972; children: Charles, Danelle, Jon, Fred, Karen, Leila. BA in Chemistry, Rutgers U., 1976; M Environ. Engring., N.J. Inst. Tech., 1984. Cert. indsl. hygienist, hazardous materials mgr., qualified environ. profl. Indsl. hygienist OSHA, U.S. Labor Dept., Newark, 1977-82; chemist Jacobs Engring., Edison, N.J., 1984-85; mgr. safety and health Envireponse, Inc., Livingston, 1985-87; health and safety mgr. Camp Dresser & McKee, Edison, 1987—. Author: Safety Now Action Levels for Hazardous Waste Operations. Exxon NJDEP fellow in environ. engring., 1982-84. Mem. Am. Chem. Soc. (past chair divsn. chem. health and safety), Am. Indsl. Hygiene Assn. (past chair hazardous waste com., Drum Buster award 1996). Democrat. Unitarian Universalist. Avocations: contra dancing, computers, peace activism. Home: 42 Highlander Dr Scotch Plains NJ 07076-2424 Office: Camp Dresser & McKee Inc Raritan Plz I 42 Highlander Dr Scotch Plains NJ 07076 E-mail: chrismarlowe@comcast.net., Marlowecs@cdm.com.

MARLOWE, EDWARD, pharmaceutical company executive; b. N.Y.C., May 5, 1935; children: Shari Marlowe Kasten, Steven Richard. BS, Columbia U., 1956, MS, 1958; PhD, U. Md.-Balt., 1962. Rsch. assoc. Merck, Sharp & Dohme Rsch. Lab., West Point, Pa., 1962-64; sr. scientist Ortho Pharm. Corp. div. Johnson & Johnson, Raritan, N.J., 1964-67; dir. R&D Whitehall Labs. div. Am. Home Products Corp., Hammonton, 1967-72; v.p. R&D Plough Products div. Schering-Plough Corp., Memphis, 1972-81; v.p. R&D, consumer products group Warner-Lambert Co., Morris Plains, N.J., 1981-83, pres. consumer products div. R&D, 1983-91, v.p., 1984-91, v.p. parent Co.; v.p. R&D Clairol Inc., Stamford, Conn., 1992-97; sr. v.p. Bristol-Myers Squibb World Wide Beauty Care, 1997-2000. Contbr. articles to profl. publs. Chmn. bd. Papermill Playhours, Millburn, NJ, 2000—; bd. dirs. Lowenstein Found., Overlook Hosp., 1985—94. Recipient award Skin Cancer Found., 1979; Pfizer fellow, 1958; Robert Lincoln McNeil fellow, 1961 Mem. Am. Pharm. Assn., Acad. Pharm. Scis., Soc. Cosmetic Chemists, Indsl. Rsch. Inst., Cosmetic Toiletry & Fragrance Assn. (sci. adv. exec. com. 1998-2000), Non-Prescription Drug Mfrs. Assn. (sci. affairs com. 1976-91, policy planning subcom. 1977-91, bd. dirs. 1981-83), N.Y. Acad. Sci., Sigma Xi, Rho Chi. Home: 56 Kean Rd Short Hills NJ 07078-1430

MARLOWE, MARY LOUISE, lawyer; b. Pasadena, Calif., Sept. 3, 1957; d. Robert Emmet and Mary Louise (Gelera) Coughlan); m. Daniel Robert Marlowe, Aug. 16, 1986; children: Benjamin, Marisa. BS, James Madison U., 1979; JD, George Mason U., 1983. Bar: N.Mex. 1984. Law clerk tax div. Dept. Justice, Washington, 1979-81, Nat. Assn. Mfrs., Washington, 1982-83; assoc. producer The McLaughlin Group, 1983-84; asst. atty. gen. N.Mex. Atty. Gen's Office, Santa Fe, 1984-87; ptnr. Marlowe & Marlowe, Taos, N.Mex., 1987-90; gen. counsel Securities Div. State of N.Mex., Santa Fe, 1990; ptnr. The Marlowe Law Firm, 1990—. Mem. ABA, N.Mex. State Bar Assn. Democrat. Roman Catholic. Office: Marlowe Law Firm 200 W Marcy St Ste 216 Santa Fe NM 87501-2036

MARLOWE, WILLIE, artist, fine arts educator; b. Whiteville, N.C., Jan. 17, 1943; d. John David and Tessie Ernestine (McLawhorn) M.; m. Thomas Blakeslee Speight, July 11, 1980. Student, Pa. Acad. Fine Arts, Phila., 1964; BS, East Carolina U., 1965; MFA, U. Idaho, 1969; postgrad., Peace Coll., 1993. Instr. dept. art Skidmore Coll., Saratoga Springs, N.Y., 1970-74, mentor univ. without walls, 1972-74; instr. dept. art Columbia-Greene C.C., Hudson, 1973-74; instr. Empire State Coll. SUNY, Albany, 1974; prof. divsn. fine arts The Sage Colls., 1977—, chmn., 1979-81. Co-founder, tchr. Saratoga Arts Workshop, Saratoga Springs, N.Y., 1970-74; watercolor tchr. abroad Sage Colls., Scotland, Ireland, 2001; tchr. Somerville Coll., Oxford U., Eng., 1992; vis. artist U. Ga. studies abroad program, Cortona, Italy, 1989; vis. artist, Wexford Arts Ctr., Ireland, artist-in-residence for Ptnrs. of the Americas, Barbados, W.I., 1986, The Millay Colony for the Arts, Austerlitz, N.Y., 1999; artist selection com. Albany Ctr. Gallery, 1998; lectr. in field. One-woman shows include The Mint Mus. Art, Charlotte, N.C., 1971, Schenectady Mus., N.Y., 1975, Marist Coll., Poughkeepsie, N.Y., 1976, Stockton State Coll., Pomono, N.J., 1977, The Greenville Mus. Art, N.C., 1982, 97, Ann Grey Gallery The Casino, Saratoga Springs, N.Y., 1985, The Barrett Art Gallery Utica Coll. Syracuse U., N.Y., 1986, The Atrium Gen. Electric Corp. R&D Ctr., Schenectady, 1988, The Forum Gallery, Gütersloh, Germany, 1992, Albany Ctr. Gallery, 1992, 97, McHenry County Coll., Crystal Lake, Ill., The Main St. Gallery, Dobbs Ferry, 1995, The Wexford Arts Ctr., Ireland, 1998, The Saratoga Arts Ctr., Saratoga Springs, N.Y., 2000, Rathbone Gallery, Albany, 2001, Fondo del Sol Gallery and Visual Arts Ctr., Washington, 2002, Martinez Gallery, Troy, N.Y., 2002, Arts Ctr. of Capital Region, Troy, 2002, others; exhibited in group shows at Martinez Gallery, Troy, NY, 2002, Artemisia Gallery, Chgo., 2000, Nexus Gallery, N.Y.C., 1997-99, The Gang Gallery, N.Y.C., Eng. & Co., London, 1993, Steinbaum-Krauss Gallery, N.Y.C., 1990, Stux Gallery, Boston, 1987, Nat. Mus. Women Arts, Washington, 1987, Westbeth Gallery, N.Y.C., 1994, Clocktower, N.Y.C., 1986, The Rice Gallery The Albany Inst. History & Art, 1986, others; represented in pvt. collections; represented in permanent collections Legis. Offices Empire State Plz., Albany, First Albany Corp., The Md. Dept. Econ. & Cmty. Devel., Balt., Quad Graphics, Boston, SUNY Albany, N.C. Nat. Bank, Charlotte, The Greenville Mus. Art, East Carolina U., Greenville, N.C., Boston Pub. Libr., The Budapest Gallery, Russell Sage Coll., Troy, N.Y., The Mint Mus. Art, Charlotte, N.C., Four Winds Ctr., Saratoga Springs, The Univ. Mus. SUNY Albany, Bullard and McLeoud Atty., N.Y.C.; co-curator and curator for mail art shows. Recipient Purchase award in painting Hudson Mohawk Regional Ann., SUNY Albany, 1977, 95, 97, honorable mention in watercolor The Oswego Art Guild, N.Y., 1986, medal Internat. Art Competition Metro Arts, Inc., Scarsdale, N.Y., 1986, honorable mention in painting Third Ann. Nat. C.C. Miniature Painting Show, Lexington, 1987, Sywer award, 1995, and numerous others; N.Y. State Coun. on the Arts grantee Barrett Art Gallery Syracuse U., 1986, grantee Artists' Space, 1988, Y.Y. found. for the Arts. Mem. Nat. Assn. Women Artists, Albany Inst. History and Art, Fulton St. Gallery, Albany Ctr. Gallery, Woman's Caucus For Art. Avocations: painting, visual poetry, mail art.

MARMADUKE, JOHN H. retail executive; b. Amarillo, Tex., May 6, 1947; m. Martha Ann Harter, July 29, 1975; children: Margaret, Owen, Samuel. Student, Amarillo Coll., 1965-67; BBA in Fin., U. Tex., Austin, 1969. Advt. mgr., salesman Western Merchandisers, Inc., Amarillo, 1969-73, pres., dir., chief exec. officer, 1982-94; v.p. Hastings Books & Records, Inc., Amarillo, 1973-76, pres., dir., chief exec. officer, 1976—. Pres., Gift of Music Found., 1982-84. Past bd. dirs. Amarillo Art Ctr.; bd. dirs. Ctr. for Non-Profit Mgmt., Amarillo, 1988—, Amarillo Area Found., 1989; chmn. Don & Sybil Harrington Cancer Ctr., Amarillo, 1988-91. Recipient spl. merit award, Internat. Music Industry Conf., Berlin, 1982, Golden Nail award, Amarillo, 1987; named Vol. of Yr., Panhandle chpt. Tex. Multiple Sclerosis assn., 1988. Mem. Nat. Assn. Recording Merchandisers (pres. 1981-82), Video Software Dealers Assn. (bd. dirs.). Republican. Roman Catholic. Avocations: skiing, fly fishing, cooking, travel, racquetball. Office: Hastings Entertainment Inc 3601 Plains Blvd Amarillo TX 79102

MARMANN, SIGRID, software development company executive; b. Voelklingen, Saarland, Germany, Feb. 8, 1938; s. Leo and Karoline Anna (Weidenhof) M. Postgrad., Norwood Coll., London, 1962; BS in Acctg., Ind. & Handelskammer, Saarbruecken, Fed. Republic Germany, 1956; postgrad., Golden Gate U., 1970-85; BA in Mgmt., St. Mary's Coll., Moraga, Calif., 1984. Controller M.O.M., Paris, 1965-69; bookkeeper Chrissa Imports, Brisbane, Calif., 1970-78; acctg. mgr. Highcity Internat., San Anselmo, 1978-80; acctg. mgr., system analyst Kukje Korean Trading Co., Rutherford, N.J., 1980-81; asst. treas. Am. Mercantile Co., Brisbane, 1981-84; controller Provident Credit Union, Burlingame, Calif., 1984; owner Datatech EDI Systems, San Rafael, 1984—, pres., chief owner, 1989—; pres. Telepay Express, Inc., 1989. Founder No. Calif. Electronic Data Interchange Users Group, San Francisco, 1990. Mem. ANSI ASC X12 Electronic Data Interchange (fin. subcom. Alexandria, Va. chpt., nominee Membership award 1990) Great Plains Software (qualified installer), Computer Assocs. Internat. (installer). Avocations: travelling, skiing, swimming, sailing, fishing, baking. Home: 30 Newport Way San Rafael CA 94901-4411

MARMARELIS, VASILIS ZISSIS, engineering educator, writer, consultant; b. Mytilini, Greece, Nov. 16, 1949; came to U.S., 1972; s. Zissis P. and Elpis V. (Galinos) M.; m. Melissa Emily Orme, Mar. 12, 1989; children: Zissis Eugene and Myrl Galinos. Diploma in elec. and mech. engring., Nat. Tech. U. of Athens, Greece, 1972; MS in Info. Sci., Calif. Inst. Tech., 1973, PhD in Engring. Sci., 1976. Rsch. fellow Calif. Inst. Tech., Pasadena, 1976-78; asst. prof. U. So. Calif., L.A., 1978-83, assoc. prof., 1983-88, prof., 1988—, also dir. biomed. simulations resource, 1985—, chmn. dept. biomed. engring., 1990-96; pres. Multispec Corp., 1986-2000. Author: Analysis of Physiological Systems, 1978, translated in Russian 1981, translated in Chinese 1990; Advanced Methods of Physiological Systems Modeling, vol. I, 1987, vol. II, 1989, vol. III, 1994; contbr. numerous articles to profl. jours. Fellow IEEE, Am. Inst. for Med. and Biol. Engring.; mem. N.Y. Acad. Scis., Biomed. Engring. Soc., Neural Networks Soc. Office: U So Calif Ohe 500 Los Angeles CA 90089-0001

MARMAS, JAMES GUST, retired business educator, retired college dean; b. Virginia, Minn., July 11, 1929; s. Gust George and Angela (Fatili) M.; m. Ruth Phyllis Leinonen, May 23, 1952; children— James Matthew, Lynn Marie, Brenda Kay. BS, St. Cloud (Minn.) State Coll., 1951; MA, U. Minn., 1956; Ed.D., Stanford, 1961. Tchr. bus. Littlefork (Minn.) High Sch., 1951-53, Lake City (Minn.) High Sch., 1953-55, Austin (Minn.) High Sch., 1955-59; asst. prof. bus. edn. Los Angeles State Coll., 1961-62; chmn. dept. bus. edn., dir. Ctr. Econ. Edn. St. Cloud State U., 1962-66, dean Coll. of Bus., 1966-87. Bd. dirs. Ins. and Savs. and Loan Author articles in field. Bd. dirs., mem. exec. com. Minn. Council Econ. Edn.; bd. dirs. St. Cloud (Minn.) Econ. Devel. Ptnrship., chmn. research and planning com. (sec., bd. dirs.). Mem. Nat. Bus. Edn. Assn., Minn. Bus. Edn. Assn., N. Central Bus. Edn. Assn. (2d v.p.), Midwest Bus. Adminstrn. Assn., St. Cloud C. of C., Phi Delta Kappa, Delta Pi Epsilon (nat. research com.), Beta Gamma Sigma. Clubs: Rotary (pres. St. Cloud). Home: 26194 County Road 4 Nisswa MN 56468-2185

MARMER, NANCY, editor; b. N.Y.C., Nov. 19, 1932; d. Carl and Frances Marmer; m. Gerald Jay Goldberg, Jan. 23, 1954; 1 child, Robert. BA magna cum laude, Queens Coll., 1954; postgrad., U. Minn., 1954-57, UCLA, 1968-71. L.A. corr. Art Internat., 1965-67; West Coast editor Artforum, 1976-77; sr. editor Art in America, N.Y.C., 1979-81, exec. editor, 1981-83, book rev. editor, 1983-97, mng. editor, 1983-97, editor-at-large, 1997-98, contbg. editor, 1998—. Lectr. Mellon seminar R.I. Sch. Design, 1983; lectr. art criticism Visual Arts dept. U. Calif., San Diego, 1978; faculty expository writing Dept. English, U. Minn., 1954-57. Author: The Modern Critical Spectrum, 1962; contbr. numerous articles to profl. jours.; art critic/reviewer for Art in America, Art Internat., Artforum, L.A. Times. Recipient Samuel Kress Found. Award in Art History; Nat. endowment for the Arts fellow in art criticism. Mem. Phi Beta Kappa. E-mail: 102424.711@compuserve.com.

MARMET, GOTTLIEB JOHN, lawyer; b. Chgo., Mar. 24, 1946; s. Gottlieb John and Margaret Ann (Saylor) M.; m. Jane Marie Borkowski, Sept. 12, 1970; children: Gottlieb John, Philip Stanley, Thomas Jacob. BS with distinction in Acctg., San Diego State U., 1967; JD, Northwestern U., 1970. Bar: Ill. 1970, U.S. Dist. Ct. (no. dist.) Ill. 1970, U.S. Tax Ct. 1981; CPA, Calif., Ill., Minn. Tax acct. Touche Ross & Co., Chgo., 1970-75; assoc. atty. Howington, Elworth, Osswald & Hough, 1975-79; tax mgr. Peat, Marwick, Mitchell & Co., Mpls., 1979-81; assoc. Shefsky, Saitlin & Froelich, Ltd., Chgo., 1981-83; prin. G. John Marmet, Glenview, Ill., 1983—. Lectr. corp. law William Rainey Harper Coll., Arlington Heights, Ill., 1984; instr. Ill. Soc. CPAs, 1976, 77, Minn. Soc. CPAs, 1980. Author: Farm Corporations and Their Income Tax Treatment, 1970, 74; contbr. articles to jours., pubs. Active Northeast Ill. Coun. Boy Scouts Am., 1984—, dist. chmn. Skokie Valley, 1988, mem. exec. bd., 1989-91, 99—; bd. dirs. North Shore Sr. Ctr., 1995-99. Recipient Hon. Mention Chgo. Bar Assn. Art Show, 1972, Boy Scouts Am. Dist. award of merit, 1990, Silver Beaver award, 1997. Mem. AICPA, ABA, Ill. Bar Assn., Chgo. Bar Assn., Rotary (Service Above Self award 1986, 96, bd. dirs. 1988-90, v.p. 1990-91, pres. 1991-92), Beta Gamma Sigma, Beta Alpha Psi, Phi Alpha Delta. Office: 950 Milwaukee Ave Ste 318 Glenview IL 60025-3779 E-mail: gmarmet@aol.com.

MARMON, LOUIS MICHAEL, pediatric surgeon; b. Pitts., Oct. 7, 1956; s. Harold and Beverly (Goss) M.; m. Andrea Caren Felzer, May 29, 1983; children: Eric, Allison, Katelyn. MD, Temple U., 1981, PhD, 1994. Diplomate Am. Bd. Surgery; cert. gen. surgery, pediat. surgery, surg. crit. care. Dir. pediat. surgery Shady Grove Adventist Hosp., Rockville, Md. Avocations: baseball history, medical history. Office: 9707 Med Ctr Dr Ste 200 Rockville MD 20850-3323

MARMOR, JUDD, psychiatrist, educator; b. London, May 1, 1910; came to U.S., 1911, naturalized, 1916; s. Clement K. and Sarah (Levene) M.; m. Katherine Stern, May 1, 1938; 1 son, Michael Franklin. AB, Columbia U., 1930, MD, 1933; DHL, Hebrew Union Coll., 1972. Diplomate: Am. Bd. Psychiatry and Neurology, Nat. Bd. Med. Examiners. Intern St. Elizabeth Hosp., Washington, 1933-35; resident neurologist Montefiore Hosp., N.Y.C., 1935-37; psychiatrist Bklyn. State Hosp., 1937; psychoanalytic tng. N.Y. Psychoanalytic Inst., N.Y.C., 1937-41; pvt. practice psychiatry, psychoanalysis and neurology, 1937-46, L.A., 1946—; adj. neurologist, neurologist-in-charge clinic Mt. Sinai Hosp., N.Y.C., 1939-46; lectr. New Sch. Social Rsch., 1942-43; vis. prof. social welfare UCLA, 1949-64, clin. prof. psychiatry sch. medicine, 1953-80, adj. prof. psychiatry, 1980-85, emeritus prof., 1985—. Tng. analyst, also pres. So. Calif. Psychoanalytic Inst., 1955-57; sr. attending psychiatrist L.A. County Gen. Hosp., 1954-80; dir. divs. psychiatry Cedars-Sinai Med. Ctr., L.A., 1965-72; Franz Alexander prof. psychiatry U. So. Calif. Sch. Medicine, 1972-80, emeritus, 1980— ; sr. cons. regional office social svc. VA, L.A., 1946-50; cons. psychiatry Brentwood VA Hosp., Calif., 1955-65; mem. Coun. Mental Health of Western Interstate Commn. Higher Edn., 1966-72. Editor: Sexual Inversion-The Multiple Roots of Homosexuality, Modern Psychoanalysis: New Directions and Perspectives, Psychiatry in Transition: Selected Papers of Judd Marmor, Homosexual Behavior: A Modern Reappraisal; (with S. Woods) The Interface Between the Psychodynamic and Behavioral Therapies, Psychiatrists & Their Patients: A National Study of Private Office Practice; (with S. Elsenstein and N.A. Levy) The Dyadic Transaction: An Investigation into the Nature of the Psychotherapeutic Process; (with P. Nardi and D. Sanders) Growing Up Before Stonewall; mem. editl. bd. Am. Jour. Psychoanalysis, Contemporary Psychoanalysis, Archives Sexual Behavior; contbr. articles in field to profl. jours. Served as sr. attending surgeon USPHS USNR, 1944-45. Fellow Am. Psychiat. Assn. (life mem., pres. 1975-76), N.Y. Acad. Medicine (life mem.), Am. Acad. Psychoanalysis (pres. 1965-66), Am. Orthopsychiat. Assn. (dir. 1968-71), AAAS, Am. Coll. Psychiatrists; mem. AMA, Calif. Med. Assn., Group for Advancement Psychiatry (dir. 1968-70, pres. 1973-75), Am. Fund for Psychiatry (dir. 1955-57), So. Calif. Psychiat. Soc., So. Calif. Psychoanalytic Soc. (pres. 1960-61), Am. Psychoanalytic Assn., Los Angeles County Med. Soc., Phi Beta Kappa, Alpha Omega Alpha. Home and Office: 10660 Wilshire Blvd # 1007 Los Angeles CA 90024-4526 Fax: (310) 446-4186.

MARMOR, MICHAEL FRANKLIN, ophthalmologist, educator; b. N.Y.C., Aug. 10, 1941; s. Judd and Katherine (Stern) M.; m. C. Jane Breeden, Dec. 20, 1968; children: Andrea K., David J. AB, Harvard U., 1962, MD, 1966. Diplomate Am. Bd. Ophthalmology. Med. intern UCLA Med. Ctr., 1967; fellow neurophysiology NIMH, 1967-70; resident in ophthalmology Mass. Eye and Ear Infirmary, Boston, 1970-73; asst. prof. ophthalmology U. Calif. Sch. Medicine, San Francisco, 1973-74; asst. prof. surgery (ophthalmology) Stanford (Calif.) U. Sch. Medicine, 1974-80, assoc. prof., 1980-86, prof., 1986—, head. div. ophthalmology, 1984-88, chmn. dept., 1988-92, dir. Basic Sci. Course Ophthalmology, 1993—. Faculty mem. program in human biology Stanford U., 1982—; chief ophthalmology sect. VA Med. Ctr., Palo Alto, Calif., 1974-84; mem. sci. adv. bd. No. Calif. Soc. to Prevent Blindness, 1984-92, Calif. Med. Assn., 1984-92, Nat. Retinitis Pigmentosa Found., 1985-95. Author: The Eye of the Artist, 1997, Degas Through his own Eyes, 2002; editor: The Retinal Pigment Epithelium, 1975, The Effects of Aging and Environment on Vision, 1991, The Retinal Pigment Epithelium: Function and Disease, 1998; editor-in-chief Doc. Ophthalmologica, 1995-99; history editor: Survey of Ophthalmology; editl. bd. Healthline; contbr. more than 200 articles to sci. jours., 50 chpts. to books. Mem. affirmative action com. Stanford U. Sch. Medicine, 1984-92. Sr. asst. surgeon USPHS, 1967-70. Recipient Svc. award Nat. Retinitis Pigmentosa Found., Balt., 1981, Rsch. award Alcon Rsch. Found., Houston, 1989; rsch. grantee Nat. Eye. Inst., Bethesda, Md., 1974-94. Fellow Am. Acad. Ophthalmology (bd. councillors 1982-85, pub. health com. 1990-93, rep. to NAS com. on vision 1991-93, Honor award 1984, Sr. Honor award 1996), Internat. Acad. Sports Vision (rsch. com.); mem. Internat. Soc. Clin. Electrophysiology of Vision (v.p. 1990-98), Assn. Rsch. in Vision and Ophthalmology, Internat. Soc. for Eye Rsch., Macula Soc., Retina Soc. Democrat. Avocations: tennis, race-walking, chamber music (clarinet), art, medical history. Office: Stanford U Sch Medcine Dept Ophthalmology Stanford CA 94305-5308

MARNEY, MILTON CARNELL, research scientist; b. Harriman, Tenn., Oct. 3, 1922; s. John Leonard and Sarah Victoria (Mays) M.; m. Jane Helen Nelson, Oct. 19, 1950 (div. Mar. 1967); children: Matthew Ley, Nathan Leonard, Stephen Carlyle, David Charles, Angela. EE Cert., U. Tenn., 1943; BS in Math. and Physics, Wake Forest U., Winston-Salem, 1946. Process operator Tenn. Eastman Corp., Oak Ridge, 1943-45; faculty math. Wake Forest (N.C.) U., 1949-50; jr. physicist Oak Ridge Nat. Lab., 1946-48, 50-52; instrumentation engr. Airesearch Inc., L.A., 1952-55; naval rsch. in sonar U. Tex. Def. Rsch. Lab., Austin, 1955-59; ops. rschr. Johns Hopkins U., Bethesda, Md., 1959-61; basic rsch. in philosophy of sci. Rsch. Analysis Corp., McLean, Va., 1961-71; ind. rschr. George Washington U., Washington, 1972-82. Sci. advisor NIH, Washington, 1967, Institut de la Vie, Paris, 1973-74, Institut Nat. de la Recherche, Massy, France, 1973; spl. lectr. Indsl. Coll. U.S. Armed Forces, Washington, 1965, Johns Hopkins U., Balt., 1964, U. Md., 1965, George Washington U., 1969. Contbr. numerous articles to profl. jours., chpts. to books.; author books in systems theory, philosophy of science and behavior and evolution of adaptive systems. Oldright fellow U. Tex., 1956-58, NIMH Rsch. fellow, 1972-74. Achievements include research in wave-particle duality for thermal neutrons; taxonomy of adaptive systems; foundations of the prescriptive sciences; intellectual basis for an "exploration ethic." Avocations: poetry composition, big-band jazz, a capalla choral performance. Home: 4016 Wexford Dr Kensington MD 20895-1523

MARNEY, SAMUEL ROWE, JR. physician, educator; b. Bristol, Va., Feb. 15, 1934; m. Elizabeth Ann Bingham, Oct. 1, 1966; children: Samuel Rowe III, Annis Morison. BA in Chemistry, U. Va., 1955, MD, 1960. Diplomate Am. Bd. Internal Medicine, Am. Bd. Allergy and Immunology; cert. in Diagnostic Lab. Immunology, 1988. Staff physician VA Hosp., Nashville, 1968-69, clin. assoc., 1969-71, clin. investigator, 1971-74, staff physician, infectious disease and allergy cons., 1974—; asst. prof. medicine Med. Ctr. Vanderbilt U., 1971-76, assoc. prof., 1976—, dir. allergy and immunology, 1974—. Vis. investigator Scripps Clinic and Rsch. Found., La Jolla, Calif., 1973-74. Capt. USAF, 1962-64, Korea. Fellow ACP, Am. Acad. Allergy and Immunology, Am. Coll. Allergy and Immunology; mem. Southeastern Allergy Assn. (pres. 1986-87, Hal M. Davison Meml. award, 1981, 99), Tenn. Soc. Allergy and Immunology. Home: 4340 Sneed Rd Nashville TN 37215-3242 Office: Vanderbilt U Med Ctr Allergy & Immunology 2611 W End Ave Nashville TN 37203-6013 E-mail: samuel.marney@mcmail.vanderbilt.edu.

MAROHN, ANN ELIZABETH, health information management professional; b. Grand Rapids, Mich., Feb. 26, 1946; d. Luther Alfonse and Mary Inez (Pinkstaff) M. BS, Ind. U., 1968; MS, SUNY, Buffalo, 1978. Asst. med. record dir. Highland Park (Mich.) Gen. Hosp., 1968-70; asst. dir. med. record svcs. Meml. Hosp., Elmhurst, Ill., 1970-73; dir. med. record tech. program Alfred (N.Y.) State Coll., 1974-76; mem. faculty med. record adminstrn. dept. Lincoln Coll., Melbourne, Australia, 1977-78, Kean Coll., Union, N.J., 1984-85, Med. U. S.C., Charleston, 1985-87; mem. faculty health record dept. Ferris State Coll., Big Rapids, Mich., 1979-80; dir. health info. mgmt. Armstrong State Coll., Savannah, Ga., 1980-84; dir. med. record dept. Tucson Gen. Hosp., 1988-89, N.D. State Hosp., Jamestown, 1990-92; cons. Prospective Payment Specialists, Tucson, 1992-93; health info. mgr. Sierra Med. Ctr., El Paso, Tex., 1993-94; dir. health info. mgmt. program Southern U., Shreveport, La., 1994-97; dir. health info. mgmt. N. VA Mental Health Inst., Falls Church, Va., 1997; dir. health info. tech. program Molloy Coll., Rockville Centre, N.Y., 1997-99; coord. health info. mgmt. program Santa Fe C.C., Gainesville, Fla., 1999—2001. Cons. Oglethorpe Ctr., Savannah, 1983-84. Columnist Australian Med. Record Jour., 1981-87, Communique, 1981-84, Palmetto Breeze, 1985-87, Progress Notes, 1984-85, 2000. Recipient disting. mem. award Ga. Med. Record Assn., 1984; fellow Aspen Inst., 1988. Mem. Assembly on Edn., Am. Health Info. Mgmt. Assn., Ariz. Health Info. Mgmt. Assn. (program chmn. 1988-89, sec. 1989—), Tex. Health Info. Mgmt. Assn. (dist. III v.p.), L.I. Health Info. Mgmt. Assn., Fla. Health Info. Mgmt. Assn., N.E. Fla. Health Info. Mgmt. Assn. (del. 2000 state house dels.; incoming pres.-elect, 2000—), Alachua County Vocat. Edn. Assn., Internat. Fedn. Health Record Orgns. Episcopalian. Avocations: swimming, reading, travel, photography, cooking. Home: Apt 26 800 NW 18th Ave Gainesville FL 32609-3583 E-mail: annmarohn@netscape.net.

MAROLDA, ANTHONY JOSEPH, management consulting company executive; b. Winthrop, Mass., Sept. 7, 1939; s. Daniel Arthur and Rose Marie (Pagliarulo) M.; m. Maria Theresa Rizzo, Oct. 10, 1970; children: Matthew, Ria. BS in Physics, Northeastern U., 1962; MS in Physics, Northeaster U., 1968; MBA, Harvard U., 1970. Rsch. physicist High Voltage Engring. Corp., Burlington, Mass., 1962-65; sr. scientist E.G. & G. Inc., Wellsley, 1965-68; v.p. Arthur D. Little, Inc., Cambridge, 1970-85; pres. The Winbridge Group, Inc., 1985—. Bd. advs. Daetwyler N.Am., Burlington, N.J., Altdorf, Switzerland, 1995-96; bd. dirs. Stratbridge, Inc., Cambridge, Mass. Inventor Apparatus High Density Plasma, 1965; co-author: Business Problem Solving, 1980, Modern Marketing, 1986, Regional Resiliance and Defense Conversion, 1997. Adv. Waterbury-Leningrad. Intersport, Waterbury, Conn., 1988-92; mem.

comty. action program Harvard Bus. Sch. Alumni Orgn., 1997--. Recipient Hayden Meml. Scholarship, Northeastern U., 1957. Mem. Harvard Club, Harvard Bus. Sch. Alumni Assn. Republican. Roman Catholic. Avocations: hiking, sailing, tennis. Office: The Winbridge Group Inc Blanchard House 249 Ayer Rd Ste 203 Harvard MA 01451 E-mail: amarolda@winbridgegroup.com.

MARONDE, ROBERT FRANCIS, internist, clinical pharmacologist, educator; b. Monterey Park, Calif., Jan. 13, 1920; s. John August and Emma Florence (Palmer) M.; m. Yolanda Cerda, Apr. 15, 1970; children: Robert George, Donna F. Maronde Varnau, James Augustus, Craig DeWald. BA, U. So. Calif., 1941, MD, 1944. Diplomate: Am. Bd. Internal Medicine. Intern L.A. County-U. So. Calif. Med. Ctr., 1943-44, resident, 1944-45, 47-48; asst. prof. physiology U. So. Calif., L.A., 1948-49, asst. clin. prof. medicine, 1949-60, assoc. clin. prof. medicine, 1960-65, assoc. prof. medicine and pharmacology, 1965-67, prof. medicine and pharmacology, 1968-90, emeritus, 1990—, prof. emeritus, 1990—; spl. asst. v.p. for health affairs, 1990—. Cons. FDA, 1973, Medco Containment Co. Inc., 1991-97, State of Calif. Dept. Health Svcs., 1993; mem. adv. panel State of Calif., 1997—. Served to lt. (j.g.) USNR, 1945-47. Fellow ACP; mem. Am. Soc. Clin. Pharmacology and Therapeutics, Alpha Omega Alpha. Home: 785 Ridgecrest St Monterey Park CA 91754-3759 Office: 2025 Zonal Ave Los Angeles CA 90089-0110 *Scientific integrity, objectivity, concern for the quality of life and adherence to the ethics of Nuremberg are ingredients for the evaluation of therapy for human illness. This is the ultimate objective of the practice of medicine.*

MARONEY, JAMES F. music educator; b. Hartford, Conn., Oct. 28, 1955; m. Marina L. Ghio, Sept. 14, 1985. Diploma in Art, U. of Hartford; MusM, Ithaca Coll.; EdD , Columbia U. Asst. dir. of choral activities Western Carolina U., Cullowhee, NC, 1997—2001; dir. of choral activities East Stroudsburg U., East Stroudsburg, Pa., 2001—. Founder, music dir. Harmonia Choral Ensemble, Cheshire, Conn., 1993—97. Author: Music for Voice and Classical Guitar, 1997; contbr. music reviews for choral jour. Mem.: Nat. Assn. of Teachers of Singing, Coll. Music Soc., Music Educators Nat. Conf., Am. Choral Directors Assn. Office: Dept of Music East Stroudsburg University East Stroudsburg PA 18301 Business E-Mail: jmaroney@po-box.esu.edu.

MARONEY, JANE P. former state legislator, consultant; b. Boston, July 29, 1923; d. John Henry and Mary (Boland) Perkins; m. John Walker Maroney, July 7, 1956; children: Jane Maroney El Dahr, John Walker Jr. Student, Radcliffe Coll., 1940-41, Katharine Gibbs Sch., 1941-42; LHD (hon.), Golden Beacom Coll., 1995. Elected official Del. Gen. Assembly, Dover, 1978-98; former project mgr. Milbank Meml. Fund, N.Y.C. Del. Family Law Commn., 1990—99, Health and Human Devel. Com., 1984—99; moderator, panelist Pub. Policy Conf., annually; past mem. Jr. League Wilmington; vice chair Creative Grandparenting, Inc., 1999—; bd. dirs. YWCA, New Castle County, Family and Workplace Connection, Coord. Coun. Children with Disabilities, chmn., 1990—91; mem. adv. bd. Rockwood Mus., Del. Hospice, Girl Scouts Del., Del. Internat. Yr. of Family, March of Dimes, Coalition for Literacy, Inst. Human Behavior. Named 1 of 10 Best Rep. Legislators of Yr., Pres. Reagan, 1985; named to, Women's Hall of Fame, Del., 1996, Outstanding Legislator of Yr., Easters Seals of Del., 1998; recipient Outstanding Svc. to Children award, Acad. Pediat., Disting. Svc. award, Del. Bar Assn., Alfred R. Shands Disting. Svc. award, 1992, Order of Merit award, U. Del., 1993, J. Donaldson Brown Disting. Svcs. award, Children and Family Svcs. Del. to Dr. & Rep. Maroney, 1992, Nathan Davis award, AMA, 1996, Order of the First State award, Gov. of Del., 1998, Advocacy and Leadership in Children's Issues award, Epilepsy Found. Del., 2000, Outstanding Lifetime Contbn. award, Health Edn. Network Del., 2001, Cmty. Builder award, Nat. Conf. for Cmty. and Justice, 2001, Woman Pioneer award, Boy Scouts Am., 2001. Roman Catholic. Avocations: travel, pub. policy, human svcs., domestic and international affairs. Fax: (302) 478-2677.

MARONEY, THOMAS JOSEPH, lawyer; b. Nassau County, N.Y., Sept. 27, 1955; s. George Edward and Elaine (Murphy) M.; m. Michelle Carol Entin, Nov. 15, 1997; 1 child, Susan Isabella. BA, Siena Coll., 1977; JD, St. John's U., 1980. Bar: N.Y. 1982, U.S. Ct. Appeals (fed. dist.) 1981. Shareholder, founding ptnr. Hawkins, Feretic, Daly, Maroney & Hayes, P.C., N.Y.C., 1990—. Mem. com. on character and fitness Appellate Divsn., N.Y. State, 1998. Mem. N.Y. State Bar Assn., N.Y. County Lawyers Assn., N.Y. Trial Lawyers, Def. Assn. N.Y. Office: Hawkins Feretic Daly Maroney & Hayes PC 60 John St New York NY 10038-3714

MARONEY, THOMAS P. lawyer, political party executive; AB, Marshall U.; JD, Am. U. Pvt. practice, Charleston, WV. Chmn. W.Va. State Dem. Party, 1996—. Office: West Virginia Democratic Party 405 Capitol St Ste 501 Charleston WV 25301-2157*

MARONI, YVES, retired economist; b. Paris, Aug. 31, 1920; came to U.S., 1940; s. Robert and Valentine M.; m. Frances Tower, June 24, 1950; children: Stephen T., Alice C., Roger S. Diploma, Ecole Libre des Scis. Polits., Paris, 1940; MA, U. Va., 1941, Harvard U., 1943, PhD, 1946. Instr. in econs. Brown U., Providence, 1946-48, asst. prof. econs., 1948-50, U. Buffalo, N.Y., 1950-51; economist FTC, Washington, 1951-52, Bd. of Govs. Fed. Reserve System, Washington, 1952-63, sr. economist, 1963-94, ret., 1994. Contbr. articles to profl. jours., chpts. to books. Mem. exec. com. Fairfax County Fedn. Citizens' Assns., 1958-64, 1st v.p., 1961-62, pres. 1962-63. Home: 3440 S Jefferson St Apt 437 Falls Church VA 22041

MAROON, MICKEY, clinical social worker; b. Flint, Mich., July 20, 1948; d. Harold Clifford and Dorothy Ruth (Fuller) McDaniel; m. Michael Martin Maroon, Aug. 22, 1970. BA, Bradley U., 1970; MSW, Denver U., 1975. Lic. clin. social worker, Colo.; bd. cert. diplomate. Social worker Ill. Dept. Children and Family Svcs., Peoria, Ill., 1970-73; clin. social worker Adams County Social Svcs., Westminster, Colo., 1975-77, Bethesda Hosp., Denver, 1977-84; pvt. practice, 1979—. Clin. cons. Human Svcs., Inc., Denver, 1988-91; vol. faculty Health Sci. Ctr. U. Colo., Denver, 1987—; chair attending social work staff West Pines Hosp., Wheat Ridge, Colo., 1988-89. Recipient Clin. Faculty award U. Colo. Health Scis. Ctr. Dept. Psychiatry, 199, Pacesetter award Nat. Assn. Soc. Workers, 1998. Mem. NASW (pres. Colo. chpt. 1994-96, chair clin. social work com. 1996, Social Worker of Yr. Colo. chpt. 1997, interim exec. dir. 1997—), Colo. Soc. Clin. Social Work (Denver chpt. pres. 1992, state pres. 1993, Cmty. Svc. award 1996).

MAROPIS, NICHOLAS, engineering executive; b. Slovan, Pa., May 14, 1923; s. Speros N. and Argero (Skinakis) M.; widowed; children: Samuel, Colin, Janice, Michelle. BA, Washington and Jefferson U., 1949; MS, Pa. State U., 1967. Physicist Naval Ordinance Lab., White Oak, Md., 1950-53; sr. project engr., physicist RM Parsons Inc., Frederick, 1953-55; v.p. engring. Aeroprojects Inc., Westchester, Pa., 1955-71; v.p UTI Corp., Collegville, 1972-91; prin. Maropis Tech. Enterprises, Inc. (M-TEI), Baden, 1991—. Mem. allocations Com. United Way Chester County, Exton, Pa., 1989-90; pres. St. Sophia Greek Orthodox Ch., 1985-87. Sgt. USAAF, 1942-45. Recipient Commendation AEC, 1964, NASA, 1970. Mem. Hellenic Ednl. Progressive Assn. (officer 1979-91). Republican. Achievements include patents for high powered ultrasonic systems and their applications to metal deformations. E-mail: mtei@stargate.net.

MAROT, LOLA, retired accountant; b. Providence, Oct. 6, 1939; d. Frank and Iola (Lombardi) Ansuini; m. Joseph Marot (div. 1973); 1 child, David Joseph BA with distinction, U. R.I., 1973; postgrad., Bryant Coll. Bookkeeper Diamond Paper Box Co., Providence, 1958-69; export sales adminstr. Brite Industries, 1973-77; property svcs. asst. Met. Property and Liability Ins. Co., Warwick, R.I., 1977-79, buyer, 1979-83, sr. buyer, 1983-86, supr. printing adminstrn., 1986-87, expense control adminstr., 1987-88; acct. Dept. Adminstrn. State of R.I., Divsn. Ctrl. Svcs., 1992-99; ret., 1999. Mem. Univ. Soc. Providence (pres. 1978)

MAROTO-VALER, MARIA MERCEDES, chemical engineer, researcher, educator; b. Vitoria, Spain, Nov. 30, 1971; d. Avelino Maroto and Consuelo Valer. BSc in Applied Chemistry with honours, U. Strathclyde, Glasgow, Scotland, 1993, PhD in Applied Chemistry, 1997; BSc in Indsl. Chemistry, U. Basque Country, Bilbao, Spain, 1994, DChE, 1998. Tchg. asst. U. Strathclyde, 1993-96, rsch. scientist, 1997; rsch. scholar U. Ky., Lexington, 1997-99; rsch. assoc. Pa. State U., University Park, 1997-99, asst. prof. energy and geo-environ. engring., 2000—; program coord. for sustainable energy The Energy Inst., 2000—. Cons. in industry; conf. chair and conf. symposium organizer. Contbg. author: Encuclopedia of Separation Science, 2000; contbr. articles to profl. jours.; author conf. procs. Recipient Bellahouston award, Glasgow, 1996, Ritchie prize U. Strathclyde, 1997, prize Coal Rsch. Forum, U.K., 1995, 97, NMR Discussion Group award, U.K., 1997. Mem. Am. Chem. Soc. (R.A. Glenn award, fuel divsn. 1996). Avocations: hill-walking, cinema, travel, sports, foreign cultures. Office: Pa State U 405 Acad Activities Bldg University Park PA 16802 E-mail: mmm23@psu.edu.

MAROTTA, JOSEPH THOMAS, medical educator; b. Niagara Falls, N.Y., May 28, 1926; emigrated to Can., 1930; s. Alfred and Mary (Montemuro) M.; m. Margaret Hughes, Aug. 31, 1953; children: Maureen, Patricia, Margaret, Fred, Thomas, Jo Anne, Michael, Martha, John, Virginia. MD, U. Toronto, 1949. Trainee in internal medicine U. Toronto, 1949-52; trainee in neurology Presbyn. Hosp., N.Y.C., 1952-55, U. London, Eng., 1955-56; mem. faculty U. Toronto, 1956—, prof. medicine, 1969—; former assoc. dean clin. affairs U. Toronto (Faculty of Medicine), 1981-89; hon. prof. of neurology U. Western Ontario, 1990—. Fellow Royal Coll. Physicians (Can.); mem. Alpha Omega Alpha, Phi Chi. Home and Office: 46 Carnforth Rd London ON Canada N6G 4P6

MAROTTI, ARTHUR FRANCIS, language educator; b. N.Y.C., Apr. 3, 1940; s. Arthur Vincent and Adeline Dorothy Marotti; m. Alice Neale Moger; children: William, Stephen. PhD, The Johns Hopkins U., 1965. Asst. prof. English Wash. U., St. Louis, 1965—70; prof. English Wayne State U., Detroit, 1970—2002. Vis. assoc. prof. English The Johns Hopkins Univ., Balt., 1983—83. Author: (book) John Donne, Coterie Poet, 1986, Manuscript, Print, and the English Renaissance Lyric, 1995; editor: Critical Essays on John Donne, 1994, Catholicism and Anti-Catholicism in Early Modern English Texts, 1999. Fellow John Simon Guggenheim Meml. Fellowship, Guggenheim Found., 1975—76, Am. Coun. of Learned Societies, 1988—89, NEH, 2000. Mem.: Renaissance English Text Soc. (exec. coun. 1991—2003). Office: Wayne State U 51 W Warren Detroit MI 48202 Home Fax: 313-577-8618; Office Fax: 313-577-8618. Business E-Mail: a.marotti@wayne.edu.

MAROY, MICHEL, European affairs consultant; b. Uccle, Belgium, Dec. 18, 1952; s. Pierre Maroy and Nicole Janssen; m. Jacqueline de Dorlodot; 1 child, Gabriel. Law candidate, Facultes U. St. Louis, Brussels, 1973; grad. in law, Cath. U. Louvain, Belgium, 1976. Bar: Brussels 1977. Attaché Cabinet Min. Edn., Brussels, 1977-80; dir. Bie Press Agy., 1981-83; attaché Cabinet Min. Pres., 1985-86; v.p. Imterel, S.A., 1987-88; sr. cons. G.J.W., Ltd., London, 1988-89; dir. 2M Pub. Affairs, Brussels, 1990—. Spkr., Team Europe, Brussels, 1992—; dir. Telex Africa, 1981-87, Telex Mediterranean, European Movement. Roman Catholic. Home: Manypré B-1325 Corroy LeGrand Belgium Office: 2M Public Affairs Square Vergote 39 B-1030 Brussels Belgium E-mail: michel.maroy@skynet.be.

MAROYKA, ERIC MARTIN, pharmacist; b. Jan. 2, 1970; BS, Rutgers U., 1992, postgrad., 2001—. Asst. chief inpatient pharmacy, chief outpatient pharmacy Landstuhl (Germany) Army Regional Med. Ctr., 1992-95; chief inpatient/support pharmacy Martin Army Cmty. Hosp., Ft. Benning, Ga., 1995-98; resident pharmacy practice Walter Reed Army Med. Ctr., Washington, 1998-99; chief pharmacy svc. Ft. Meade, Md., 1999—2001. E-mail: emaroyka@eden.rutgers.edu.

MARPLE, DOROTHY JANE, retired church executive; b. Abington, Pa., Nov. 24, 1926; d. John Stanley and Jennie (Stetler) M. AB, Ursinus Coll., 1948; MA, Syracuse U., 1950; Ed.D., Columbia U. Tchrs. Coll., 1969; L.H.D., Thiel Coll., 1965, Gettysburg Coll., 1979, Ursinus Coll., 1981; D. Humanitarian Services, Newberry Coll., 1977; DD, Trinity Luth. Sem., 1987. Counselor, asst., office dean undergrad. women Women's Coll., Duke, 1950-53; dean women, fgn. student adv. Thiel Coll., 1953-61; asst. social dir. Whittier Hall, Columbia Tchrs. Coll., 1961-62; exec. dir. Luth. Ch. Women, Luth. Ch. Am., Phila., 1962-75; asst. to bishop Luth. Ch. Am., 1975-85; coord. Transition Office Evang. Luth. Ch. Am., 1986-87; asst. gen. sec. ops. Nat. Coun. Chs. of Christ in U.S., N.Y.C., 1987-89. Coordinator Luth. Ch. in Am. commn. on function and structure, 1970-72 Home: 8018 Anderson St Philadelphia PA 19118-2936

MARPLE, GARY ANDRE, management consultant; b. Mt. Pleasant, Iowa, Feb. 22, 1937; s. Kenneth Lowry and Truma Janice (Cook) M.; m. Ellen I. Metcalf, May 29, 1971 (div. 1981); m. Meredith Ann Rutter, July 23, 1988; children: Brian Edward, Stephen Lowry. BS, Drake U., 1959; MBA, Mich. State U., 1962, DBA, 1963. Postdoctoral fellow mgmt. MIT, 1963; cons. Arthur D. Little Inc., Cambridge, Mass., 1963-82; pres. Commonwealth Strategies, Inc., Acton, 1982—, Oceanus Holding, Ltd., S.W., Harbor, Maine, 1985—, Answer Pharm. Corp., Norwood, Mass., 1997-99, Lessac Techs., Inc., White Plains, NY, 1999—. Exec.-in-residence Ctr. for Entrepreneurial Leadership, Ewing Marion Kauffman Found., Kansas City, Mo., 1996-99; pres. Lessac Techs., Inc., White Plains, N.Y., 2002 Editor, author: Grocery Manufacturing in the U.S., 1968; contbr. to Conquering Government Regulation, 1982. Trustee Nat. Arts & Learning Collaborative, Natick, Mass., Linden Hill Sch., Northfield, Mass. Mem. Arthur D. Little Alumni Assn. (bd. dirs., past pres. Lexington, Mass. 1992—), Am. Bonanza Soc., Minuteman Bearded Collie Club (bd. dirs., past pres. 1996—), Bearded Collie Club Am. (treas. 2000-02). E-mail: gary@cwstrategies.com.

MARPLE, THOMAS FRANKLIN, columnist, reporter; b. Winchester, Va., June 24, 1956; s. Thomas Franklin Marple Jr. and Mary Ellen Marple. BS in Mgmt., Shenandoah U., 1980. Reporter The Journal, Martinsburg, W.Va., 1997—2001; writer Mid-Atlantic Thoroughbred, Timonium, Md., 2001—, Horsemen's Jour., Austin, Tex., 2000—. With U.S. Army, 1980—82. Named Best Sports Columnist, W.Va. Press Assn., 2001. Mem.: W.Va. Sports Writers Assn., W.Va. Breeders Assn. (publicity dir. 2001—). Avocations: fishing, bicycling, weightlifting, basketball, gardening. Home: 1801 Sam Mason Rd Bunker Hill WV 25413

MARQUAND, JEAN MACMURTRY, educational administrator; b. Schenectady, N.Y., Feb. 1, 1947; d. Louis Frederick Jr. and Eleanore Jean (Noyes) McM. BA in Edn. with honors, Simmons Coll., 1969; MEd, U. Vt., 1975; grad. cert. advanced studies in mgmt., Radcliffe Coll., 1993. Elem. tchr., Pittsford, N.Y., 1969-70; reading specialist Lincoln, Vt., 1971-73, Pembroke, Mass., 1976; grad. teaching asst U. Vt., 1975; elem tchr. Chatham, Mass., 1977-80; with Arthur D. Little, Cambridge, 1981-82; exec. sec. Meredith & Grew, Inc., Boston, 1982—. V.p. alumnae fund Simmons Coll., Boston, 1994-96. Bd. mgrs. Jr. League Boston, 1990-92, v.p. pres., 1993-94, sustainer com., 1997—; Boston chpt. Philanthropic Ednl. Orgn., 1993—, chair Mass. state bylaws com., 1998; mem. Greater Boston Real Estate Bd., 2001—. Recipient Vol. Recognition award Jr. League Boston, 1989. Mem. The Coll. Club (pres. 1994-98, chair bylaws com. 1998—, parliamentarian 2001-), PEO, The Internat. Alliance, Chowder Soc.

MARQUARD, STEVEN SANDEL, economist, financial consultant; b. Yakima, Wash., Sept. 6, 1947; s. Martin William and Yvonne L. (Jacobs) M. BSChemE, U. Wash., 1969; MBA in Applied Econs., U. Calif., 1975. CPA, Mont. Metallurgist US Steel, Pitts., 1969-72, Spectra Flux, Watsonville, Calif., 1972-73; chief economist So. Pacific, San Francisco, 1975-82; asst. treas. Bio Rod, Richmond, 1982-84; treasury staff mgr. Pacific Telesis, San Francisco, 1985—; fin. cons. Smilodon Fin. Consulting, Berkeley, 1985—. Author: Distortion Theory of Macro-economic Forecasting, 1994. 1st lt. USAR, 1977-83. Republican. Episcopalian. Home and Office: Smilodon Fin Consulting Ste 32 2732 Haste St Apt 32 Berkeley CA 94704-2437

MARQUARDT, ANN MARIE, small business administrator; b. Plainview, N.Y., Oct. 28, 1964; d. Steven Peter Paul and Virginia Ann (Gallo) Marquardt; m. Paul W. Minerva, Dec. 24, 1996; children: Paul Steven Minerva, Anthony Joseph Minerva. Grad., Harry B. Ward Occupational Ctr, Riverhead, N.Y., 1982; student, Dowling Coll., 1982-84; Assoc. Acctg., Suffolk Community Coll., 1990; BS in Bus. Mgmt., St. John's U., 1993. Sec. Dowling Coll., Oakdale, N.Y., 1982-84; sec., office mgr. Pudge, Peteco & Peanuts Corp., Southold, 1984-86, Era Albo Agy., Mattituck, 1986-87; legal asst. manage estate dept. Wickham, Wickham & Bressler, P.C., 1987-89, 93—; bus., gen. mgr. Mattituck Laundromat, 1987-89, Gaslight Cafe, Ltd., Mattituck, 1989; office/bus. mgr., bookkeeper accounts payable/receivable Minerva's Tree Svcs. Ltd., Cutchogue, N.Y., 1990-96; owner, operator Cranky Yankee Bus. Svcs. (now Estate Trust Adminstrn. Svcs.), 1998-99, AMMinerva, Legal Asst., Estate, Trust Adminstrn. Svcs., 1999—. Office/bookkeeping cons. Dickerson's Marine, Mattituck, 1990, Hobby's Plus, Southold. Author poetry and short stories. Mem. NOW, NAFE, AAUW, Am. Mgmt. Assn., Nat. Arborist Assn., Nat. Assn. for Self-Employed, Legal Secs. Ea. L.I., Am. Soc. Notaries. Avocations: modeling, dance, creative writing, boating, fishing. Office: Wickham Wickham & Bressler 10315 Main Rd Mattituck NY 11952-1529 E-mail: ammestates@worldnet.att.net.

MARQUARDT, CHRISTEL ELISABETH, judge; b. Chgo., Aug. 26, 1935; d. Herman Albert and Christine Marie (Geringer) Trolenberg; children: Eric, Philip, Andrew, Joel. BS in Edn., Mo. Western Coll., 1970; JD with honors, Washburn U., 1974. Bar: Kans. 1974, Mo. 1992, U.S. Dist. Ct. Kans. 1974, U.S. Dist. Ct. (we. dist.) Mo. 1992. Tchr. St. John's Ch., Tigerton, Wis., 1955-56; pers. asst. Columbia Records, L.A., 1958-59; ptnr. Cosgrove, Webb & Oman, Topeka, 1974-86, Palmer & Marquardt, Topeka, 1986-91, Levy and Craig P.C., Overland Park, Kans., 1991-94; sr. ptnr. Marquardt and Assocs., L.L.C., Fairway, 1994-95; judge Kans. Ct. Appeals, 1995—. Mem. atty. bd. discipline Kans. Supreme Ct., 1984—86. Mem. editorial adv. bd. Kans. Lawyers Weekly, 1992-96; contbr. articles to legal jours. Bd. dirs. Topeka Symphony, 1983-92, 95-2002, Arts and Humanities Assn. Johnson County, 1992-95, Brown Found., 1988-90; hearing examiner Human Rels. Com., Topeka, 1974-76; local advisor Boy Scouts Am., 1973-74; bd. dirs., mem. nominating com. YWCA, Topeka, 1979-81; bd. govs. Washburn U. Law Sch., 1987-2002, v.p., 1996-98, pres., 1998-2000; mem. dist. bd. adjudication Mo. Synod Luth. Ch., Kans., 1982-88. Named Woman of Yr., Mayor, City of Topeka, 1982; Obee scholar Washburn U., 1972-74; recipient Jennie Mitchell Kellogg Atty. of Achievement award, 1999, Phil Leives medal of Distinction, 2000, Atty. of Achievement award Kans. Women Attys. Assn., Disting. Svc. award Washburn U. Law Sch., 2002. Fellow: Kans. Bar Found. (trustee 1987—89), Am. Bar Found.; mem.: ABA (specialization com. 1987—93, mem. ho. dels. 1988—, chmn. 1989—93, lawyer referral com. 1993—95, state del. 1995—99, bar svcs. and activities 1995—99, bd. govs., program and planning com. 1999—2002, bd. govs. 1999—, ctrl. and ea. European law initiative 2001—, del-at-large ho. of dels. 2002—), Law and Organizational Econ. Ctr. (bd. dirs. 2000—02), Am. Bus. Women's Assn. (lectr., corr. sec. 1983—84, pres. career chpt. 1986—87, named one of Top 10 Bus. Women of Yr. 1985), Topeka Bar Assn., Kans. Trial Lawyers Assn. (bd. govs. 1982—86, lectr.), Kans. Bar Assn. (sec., treas. 1981—85, bd. dirs. 1983—, v.p. 1985—86, pres. 1987—88). Home: 3408 SW Alameda Dr Topeka KS 66614-5108 Office: 301 SW 10th Ave Topeka KS 66612-1502 E-mail: marquardt@kscourts.org.

MARQUARDT, SANDRA MARY, activist, lobbyist, researcher; b. Dhahran, Saudi Arabia, Mar. 5, 1959; parents Am. citizens; d. Donald Edward and Mary Eleanor (Lindsay-Rea) M.; m. Hans Kristensen. BA, U. Wis., 1982. Editor, organizer Nat. Coalition Against the Misuse of Pesticides, Washington, 1983-87; rschr., author Environ. Policy Inst., 1987-88; rschr., lobbyist Greenpeace, 1988-95; rschr. Consumer's Union, 1995-96; program dir. Mothers and Others for a Livable Planet, San Francisco, 1996-97; coord. organic fiber coun. Organic Trade Assn., Richmond, 1997—. Authored reports on domestic and internat. pesticide use, bottled water, organic cotton, golf courses, sanitary products. Avocation: Hiking, swimming, photography.

MARQUARDT, STEVE ROBERT, library director; b. St. Paul, Sept. 7, 1943; s. Robert Thomas and Dorothy Jean (Kane) M.; m. Judy G. Brown, Aug. 4, 1968; 1 child, Sarah. BA in History, Macalester Coll., 1966; MA in History, U. Minn., 1970, MLS, 1973, PhD in History, 1978. History instr. Macalester Coll., St. Paul, 1968-69; cataloger N.Mex. State U. Libr., Las Cruces, 1973-75; acting univ. archivist, acting dir. Rio Grande Hist. Collections N. Mex. State U. Libr., 1973-74; acquisitions librarian Western Ill. U. Libr., Macomb, 1976-77, head cataloger, Online Computer Libr. Ctr. coord., 1977-79; asst. dir. resources & tech. svcs. Ohio U. Libr., Athens, 1979-81; dir. librs. U. Wis., Eau Claire, 1981-89; dir. univ. librs. No. Ill. U., DeKalb, 1989-90; dir. librs. U. Wis., Eau Claire, 1990-96; dean of librs. S.D. State U., Brookings, 1996—. Editor Jour. Rio Grande History, 1974; contbg. editor: Library Issues, 1994-99; contbr. articles to profl. jours. Coord. Amnesty Internat. Adoption Group 275, Eau Claire, 1985-88; pres. Chippewa Valley Free-net, 1994-96. Mem. ALA, Assn. Coll. and Rsch. Librs. (chmn. performance measures in acad. librs. com. 1985-89). Lutheran. Avocations: tennis, bicycling. Office: SD State U Briggs Libr PO Box 2115 Brookings SD 57007-0001 E-mail: steve_marquardt@sdstate.edu.

MARQUES, PAUL JOSEPH, secondary school educator, consultant; b. Revere, Mass., Mar. 27, 1969; s. James John and Marie Teresa Marques. BS in Computer Sci., U. Mass., 1993, MEd, 2002. Computer sci. dir. Malden H.S., Malden, Mass., 1998—. Web cons. Youth Tech Entrepreneurs, Malden, 1998—. Mem.: Nat. Math. Tchr. Assn. Home: 32 Fairfax Street Somerville MA 02144 Office: Malden High School 77 Salem Street Malden MA 02148

MARQUESS, LAWRENCE WADE, lawyer; b. Bloomington, Ind., Mar. 2, 1950; s. Earl Lawrence and Mary Louise (Coberly) M.; m. Barbara Ann Bailey, June 17, 1978; children: Alexander Lawrence, Michael Wade. BSEE, Purdue U., 1973; JD, W.Va. U., 1977. Bar: W.Va. 1977, Tex. 1977, U.S. Dist. Ct. (so. dist.) W.Va. 1977, U.S. Dist. Ct. (no. dist.) Tex. 1977, Colo. 1980, U.S. Dist. Ct. Colo. 1980, U.S. Ct. Appeals (10th cir.) 1980, U.S. Supreme Ct. 1984, U.S. Dist. Ct. (no. dist.) Ohio 1988, U.S. Ct. Appeals (DC cir.) 1997, U.S. Dist. Ct. Nebr. 1999. Assoc. Johnson, Bromberg, Leeds & Riggs, Dallas, 1977-79, Bradley, Campbell & Carney, Golden, Colo., 1979-82, ptnr., 1983-84, Stettner, Miller & Cohn P.C., 1984-87, Nelson & Harding, Denver, 1987-88, Heron, Burchette, Ruckert & Rothwell, 1989-90, Harding & Ogborn, 1990-94, Otten, Johnson, Robinson, Neff & Ragonetti, Denver, 1994-2001, Littler Mendelson, P.C., Denver, 2001—. Mem. faculty Am. Law Inst. - ABA Advanced Labor and Employment Law Course, 1986, 87. Mem. ABA (labor, antitrust and litigation sects.), ACLU, Colo. Bar Assn. (co-chmn. labor law com. 1989-92), Denver Bar Assn., 1st Jud. Dist. Bar Assn., Sierra Club, Nat. Ry. Hist. Soc. Democrat. Methodist. Home: 11883 W 27th Dr Lakewood CO 80215-7000 Office: Littler Mendelson PC 1200 17th St Ste 2850 Denver CO 80202 E-mail: lmarquess@littler.com.

MARQUEZ, JOAQUIN ALFREDO, lawyer; b. Humacao, P.R., Aug. 1, 1942; s. Joaquin and Emelina (Tudela) M.; m. Jocelyn Christiansen, Mar. 27, 1967; children: Joaquin A. Jr., Julian A. BS in Econs., U. Pa., 1964; LLB, U. P.R., 1967; LLM in Taxation, Georgetown U., 1974. Bar: P.R. 1967, U.S. Dist. Ct. P.R. 1968, U.S. Ct. Appeals (1st cir.) 1968, D.C. 1972, U.S. Dist. Ct. D.C. 1972. Assoc. Goldman, Antonetti & Subira, San Juan, P.R., 1967-68; adminstrv. asst. to resident commr. from P.R. Washington, 1971-72, 77-78; sr. atty.-advisor AID U.S. Dept. State, 1973-76; dir. P.R. Fed. Affairs Adminstrn., 1978-81; ptnr. Hopkins & Sutter, 1981-94, Drinker, Biddle & Reath, Washington, 1994—. Mem. P.R. Export Promotions Coun., San Juan, 1979-81; staff dir. So. Govs.' Assn., Washington, 1980-81. Capt. U.S. Army, 1968-70, Vietnam. Decorated Bronze Star. Mem. ABA, P.R. Bar Assn., D.C. Bar Assn. Republican. Roman Catholic. Avocations: sailing, reading. Office: Drinker Biddle & Reath 1500 K St NW # 1100 Washington DC 20005-1209

MARQUEZ, MARK LYNN, education educator; b. Farmington, N.Mex., May 11, 1958; s. Frank O. Marquez and Elsie E. Giron-Marquez, Jose Giron (Stepfather); m. Cynthia Ann Colvin, Oct. 21, 1999; children: Danial Ruiz, Jessica Ruiz, Jennifer Romero. AA, San Juan Coll., 1988; BS, Regents Coll., 1989; DSc (hon.) , Nova Coll. Europe, Can., 1995; MA, U. Berkley, Southfield, Mich., 1996. Cert. tchr. Colo. Radio comm./ intelligence USMC, 1976—82; with Farmington Pub. Schs., 1986—94; youth dir. Youth Svcs., Jicarilla Apache Tribe, Dulce, 1995—99; dep. program dir. Boys and Girls Club of Farmington, 2000—01, Youth Opportunity Program, Towaoc, Colo., 2001; instr. edn. and social sci. Pueblo C.C., 2002—; sales assoc. Wal*Mart Supercenter, Cortez, 2002—; career counselor Lockheed Martin IMS GAIN, Panorama City, Calif., 2002; radio operator N.Mex. Army N.G., Farmington. Devel. dir. AMEN Ministries, Glendora, Calif., 1999—2000; instr. history/polit. sci. Pueblo C.C., Cortez. Editor: (evangelical news) Political, 2001. Youth monitor N.Mex First, Albuquerque, 1997—98; youth steering com. Denver Olympic Com., Colorado Springs, Colo., 1972—73; del. N.Mex. Boys States Am. Legion, Roswell, 1976—77; campaign worker, youth for carter Dem., Farmington, 1975—76; v.p. Farmington H.S., 1975—76. Cpl. USMC, 1976—82. Mem.: Am. Legion (mem. youth svcs. 1999—2002).

Conservative. Mem. Assembly Of God. Avocations: fishing, music, book collecting. Home: PO Box 413 Farmington NM 87401 Office: Youth Development 2707 E 30th St Farmington NM 87401 Personal E-mail: mmarquez19582002@yahoo.com. E-mail: mmarquez2@excite.com.

MÁRQUEZ-MAGAÑA, LETICIA MARIA, biology educator; b. Sacramento, Aug. 15, 1963; d. Jesús José and Guadalupe María Márquez; married; children: Joaquin, Elias. BS,MS in Biol. Scis., Stanford U., 1986; PhD in Biochemistry, U. Calif., Berkeley, 1991. Postdoctoral fellow Stanford (Calif.) U., 1991-94; assoc. prof. biology San Francisco State U., 1994—, microbial geneticist, 1994—. Contbr. articles to profl. jours., including Jour. Bacteriology and Jour. Biol. Chemistry. Motivational spkr. to minority students, No. Calif., 1994—. Named One of 100 Most Influential Hispanics, Hispanic Bus. Mag., 1998. Mem. AAAS (Mentor award 2001), Am. Soc. Microbiology, Soc. Advancement of Chicanos and Native Americans in Sci. (bd. dirs. 1989-91). Office: San Francisco State U Dept Biology 1600 Holloway Ave San Francisco CA 94132

MARQUIS, HARRIET HILL, social worker; b. Rocky Mount, N.C., Sept. 4, 1938; d. Robert Foster and Anne Ruth (Daughtry) Hill; m. James Ralph Marquis, Apr. 23, 1967; children: Margaret Anne, Karen Lee. BA in English, Meredith Coll., 1960; MA in English, Seton Hall U., 1971; PhD in English, Drew U., 1984; MSW, NYU, 1987; cert., N.Y. Sch. Psychoanalytic Psychotherapy, 1991, Inst. Study Psychotherapy & Psychoanalysis N.J., 1998. Tchr. English S.C. Pub. Schs., 1960-62, Peace Corps, Sierra Leone, West Africa, 1963-65; adj. prof. English Farleigh Dickinson U., Madison, 1983-85; psychotherapist Child Guidance & Family Svc. Ctr., Orange, N.J., 1987; staff clinician Esther Dutton Counseling Ctr., Morristown, 1987-90; psychotherapist Ctr. Evaluation & Psychotherapy, 1990-93; pvt. practice Madison, 1990-98, Brevard, N.C., 1998—. Mem. Internat. Conf. Advancement of Pvt. Practice Clin. Social Work; speaker in field. Fellow N.C. Soc. Clin. Social Workers; mem. NASW (bd. cert. diplomate in social work), Nat. Fedn. of Socs. for Clin. Social Work (nat. membership com. psychoanalysis in clin. social work). Democrat. Methodist. Avocations: reading, walking, writing, travel. E-mail: harrieth@brinet.com.

MARR, CARMEL CARRINGTON, retired lawyer, retired state official; b. Bklyn., June 23, 1921; d. William Preston and Gertrude Clementine (Lewis) Carrington; m. Warren Marr II, Apr. 11, 1948; children: Charles Carrington, Warren Quincy III. BA, Hunter Coll., 1945; JD, Columbia U., 1948. Bar: N.Y. 1948, U.S. Dist. Ct. (ea. dist.) N.Y. 1950, U.S. Dist. Ct. (so. dist.) N.Y. 1951. Clk. Dyer & Stevens, N.Y.C., 1948-49; pvt. practice, 1949-53; adviser legal affairs U.S. mission to UN, 1953-67; sr. legal officer Office Legal Affairs UN Secretariat, 1967-68; mem. N.Y. State Human Rights Appeal Bd., 1968-71, N.Y. State Pub. Svc. Commn., 1971-86; cons. Gas. Rsch. Inst., 1987-91. Lectr. N.Y. Police Acad., 1963-67. Contbr. articles to profl. jours. Mem. N.Y. Gov.'s Com. Edn. and Employment of Women, 1963-64; mem. Nat. Gen. Svcs. Pub. Adv. Council, 1969-71; mem., former chmn. adv. coun. Gas. Rsch. Inst.; mem. chmn. tech. pipeline safety standards com. Dept. Transp., 1979-85; former mem. task force Fed. Energy Regulatory Commn. and EPA to examine PCBs in gas supply system; past chmn. gas com. Nat. Assn. Regulatory Utility Commrs.; past pres. Great Lakes Conf. Pub. Utilities Commrs., mem. exec. com.; mem. UN Devel. Corp., 1969-72; bd. dirs. Amistad Rsch. Ctr., New Orleans, 1970—, chmn. bd. dirs., 1981-94; bd. dirs. Bklyn. Soc. Prevention Cruelty to Children, Nat. Arts Stblzn. Fund, 1984-93, hon. bd. mem., 1998, Prospect Park Alliance, 1987-98; bd. visitors N.Y. State Sch. Girls, Hudson, 1964-71; mem. exec. bd. Plays for Living, N.Y.C., 1968-75; pres. bd. dirs. Billie Holiday Theatre, 1972-80; mem. nat. adv. coun. Hampshire Coll.; pres.'s coun. Tulane U., 1988-95. Mem. Phi Beta Kappa, Alpha Chi Alpha, Alpha Kappa Alpha. Republican. Episcopalian.

MARR, J(AMES) JOSEPH, biotechnology company executive; b. Hamilton, Ohio, Oct. 21, 1938; s. J. Joseph and Mildred Adele Marr; m. Martha Eleanor Marr, June 29, 1963; children: Kathleen, Joseph, John, Kerry, James. BS, Xavier U., 1959; MD, Johns Hopkins U., 1964; MS, St. Louis U., 1968. Diplomate Am. Bd. Internal Medicine, Am. Bd. Infectious Diseases. Intern Johns Hopkins Hosp., Balt., 1964-65; resident Barnes Hosp., Washington U., St. Louis, 1969-70; postdoctoral fellow in microbiology St. Louis U., 1967-69; asst. prof. medicine and microbiology Wash. U., St. Louis, 1970-75, assoc. prof., 1975-76; prof. medicine and microbiology St. Louis U., 1976-82; prof. medicine and biochemistry U. Colo., Denver, 1982-89; sr. v.p. drug discovery Monsanto/Searle, Skokie, Ill., 1989-93; v.p. R&D Ribozyme Pharms., Boulder, Colo., 1993-96; CEO Immunologic Pharm. Corp., Waltham, Mass., 1996-99. Bd. dirs. Sequitur, Inc., Immunologic Pharms. Contbr. articles to profl. jours.; patentee in field. Bd. trustees Estes Park (Colo.) Med. Ctr., 1994-96; advisor Cub Scouts/Boy Scouts Am., St. Louis, 1975-82; adv., lectr. schs., St. Louis, Denver, 1976-89; physician Free Med. Clinic, St. Louis, 1970-80; advisor Jefferson County Sch. Dist., 1986-89. Capt. U.S. Army Spl. Forces, 1966-68. Fellow ACP, Am. Acad. Microbiology, Infectious Diseases Soc. of Am., Am. Assn. of Physicians; mem. Am. Soc. Clin. Investigation, Am. Coll. Physician Execs., Phi Beta Kappa, Alpha Omega Alpha, Sigma Xi. Avocations: scuba diving, climbing, skiing, martial arts (2 black belts), writing poetry. Home and Office: 180 Centennial Dr Estes Park CO 80517-6901

MARR, PHEBE ANN, historian, educator; b. Mt. Vernon, N.Y., Sept. 21, 1931; d. John Joseph and Lillian Victoria (Henningsen) Marr. BA, Barnard Coll., 1953; PhD, Harvard U., 1967. Rsch. assoc. ARAMCO, Dhahran, Saudi Arabia, 1960-62; dir. mid. east program Fgn. Svc. Inst., 1963-66; asst. prof. Stanislaus State Coll., Turlock, Calif., 1970-71, assoc. prof., 1971-74; assoc. prof. history U. Tenn., Knoxville, 1974-85, chmn. Asian studies program, 1977-79. Cons. ARAMCO, 1979-83. Author: The Modern History of Iraq, 1985; co-editor: Riding the Tiger: Middle East Challenge After the Cold War, 1993; contbr. articles to profl. jours. Rsch. fellow Mid. East Ctr., Harvard U., Cambridge, Mass., 1968-70, sr. fellow Nat. Def. U., Washington, 1985-97, Woodrow Wilson Ctr. fellow, 1998-99, Coun. on Fgn. Relations. Mem. Mid. East Inst., Mid. East Studies Assn. Home: 2902 18th St NW Washington DC 20009-2954 E-mail: marrphebe@aol.com.

MARR, ROBERT BRUCE, physicist, educator; b. Quincy, Mass., Mar. 25, 1932; s. Ralph George and Ethel (Beals) M.; m. Nancy Rosa Parkes, June 12, 1954; children: Richard, Jonathan, Rebecca. BS, MIT, 1953; MA, Harvard U., 1955, PhD, 1959. Research asso. Brookhaven Nat. Lab., Upton, N.Y., 1959-61, asso. physicist, 1961-64, physicist, 1964-68, sr. physicist, 1968-95, assoc. chmn. applied math. dept., 1974-75, 83-88, chmn., 1975-78; ret., 1995. Adj. assoc. prof. Columbia U., 1969; lectr. SUNY at Stony Brook, 1969-70, vis. prof. dept. computer sci., 1979; guest mathematician U. Colo., 1970; vis. mathematician Lawrence Berkeley Lab., 1978; cons. NSF, NIH, 1969— Contbr. articles to profl. jours. Served with U.S. Army, 1958-59. NSF grantee, 1974 Mem. Soc. for Magnetic Resonance in Medicine (trustee 1982-87, sec.-treas. 1984-86, treas. 1986-87). Home: 368 Private Rd Patchogue NY 11772-5827

MARR, STEVE, foundation executive; b. Detroit, Oct. 24, 1949; s. Robert B. and Dorthery Erlyne Marr; m. Mary L. Marr, Apr. 24, 1994; 1 child, Michael. BA, Northwood U., 1972. Pres., CEO J.V. Carr-Son, IUC, Detroit, 1972-96; pres. Widows Mite Found., Tucson, 1996—. Dir. Ctr. for Ariz. Policy, Phoenix, 1997—. Author: (books) How to Manage a Million Dollars, 2000, Business Proverbs, 2001; radio host: Business Proverbs. Mem. Detroit Athletic Club. Republican. Home: Widows Mite Found # 144 4729 E Sunrise Dr Tucson AZ 85718 E-mail: stevemarr@businessproverbs.org.

MARRA, ANTHONY TULLIO, audio visual specialist; b. Newark, June 26, 1947; s. John and Christine (Sapparito) M.; m. Erica Jane Curci, Nov. 25, 1987; children: Becky Michelle George, Antonio Tullio, Becky Lynn George, Crystal Marra, Heather Leigh Marra, Megan Marra. Advisor Govt. Liason for Ednl. Insts., Washington, 1978-91; media specialist, advisor Washington & Lee U., Lexington, Va., 1978-91; media specialist Longwood Coll., Farmville, 1978-91, Hollins Coll., Salem, 1978-91, Lynchburg (Va.) Coll., 1978-91, Randolph Macon Women's Coll., Lynchburg, Va., 1978-91; dir. audio-visual Sweet Briar (Va.) Coll., 1978-91; media cons. Africa Global Perspectives, 1994—; pres., owner Audio/Visual Advisors, 1997—; agt. bus. comms. sys. divsn. Lucent Techs./Bell Labs, 1997—. Acoustic expert rsch. and devel. NASA Langley Field, Hampton, Va., 1971-78. Author: (books) Poetry in LIfe To Be in Death I Am, 1972, The Holy Quran-The Hereafter, 1989; inventor: overhead copy stand for ch.-sch. system, 1991, marking device for NASA Test Flights, 1972; designer TV studio and control room, 1994. Bd. dirs. S.W. Va. Free Clinic. With USMC, 1964-68, Vietnam. Recipient cert. appreciation NASA for rsch. 1976, 78. Avocations: photgraphy, videography, working with bldg. computers, cmty. work. Home: PO Box 575 Madison Heights VA 24572-0575 Office: 3421 Plymouth Pl Lynchburg VA 24503-1300

MARRA, KACEY G. research scientist, educator; b. Washington, Sept. 24, 1970; d. John W. (.) and Kathleen A. Gribbin; m. William M. Marra, Nov. 26, 1994; children: Ethan, LeeAnna. BS, U. Pitts., 1992, PhD, 1996. Postdoctoral fellow Emory U. Sch. Medicine, Atlanta, 1996—97; rsch. scientist Carnegie Mellon U., Pitts., 1998—. Mem. study sect. NIH, 2000—01; mem. panel rev. NSF, 2002. Contbr. Organizer charity event Genesis, Washington, 2000—01. Named Rschr. of the Month, Pitts. Tissue Engring. Initiative, Inc., 1998; named one of PUMP's "40 under 40" Most Influential Pittsburghers, Pitts. Urban Magnet Project, 2001. Mem.: Carnegie Mellon Women's Assn., Materials Rsch. Soc., Am. Chem. Soc. (Sherwin Williams Student Award Competition finalist 1994), Tissue Engring. Soc. Roman Catholic. Avocations: reading, golf. Office: Carnegie Mellon U 5000 Forbes Ave Pittsburgh PA 15213 Office Fax: 412-268-5229. Personal E-mail: kmarra@cs.cmu.edu. Business E-Mail: kmarra@cs.cmu.edu.

MARRA, RALPH PETER, lawyer; b. S.I., N.Y., Jan. 1957; BA, St. John's U., 1979; JD, Nova Southeastern Law Sch., 1982. Assoc. ct. atty. N.Y. State Unified Ct. System, S.I., 1983-95, prin. law clk., 1996—. Mem. SMA II Claims Arbitrator, S.I., 1988—. Mem. Meals on Wheels, S.I., 1996—; dist. capt. Dem. Party of Richmond, S.I., 1996—. With USMCR, 1976-78. Mem. NAACP, Cath. Ct. Attaché Assn., Amicus Curine Columbia Assn., Assn. of Arbitrators, Nova Southeastern U. Law Alumni Assn., Phi Delta Phi. Office: NY State Supreme Ct 18 Richmond Ter Staten Island NY 10301-1935

MARRA, SAMUEL PATRICK, retired pharmacist, small business owner; b. Sault Ste Marie, Mich., Apr. 15, 1927; s. Leonard and Nancy (Clement); m. Jeanette L. Rohr, Sept. 2, 1949; children: Rebecca, Nancy, David, Dana, Janet. BS in Pharmacy, Ferris State Coll., 1949. Ret. Bd. dirs. Chem. Bank, No. States Bancshares, Chem. Bank North. Bd. dirs. Houghton Lake Edn. Found.; pres. Houghton Lake Grenadier Band; co-chmn. Scheutte for Congress, Roscommon County, 1984, 86. Mem. Nat. Assn. Retail Druggists. Republican. Avocations: music, photography. Home: 10672 Westshore Dr Houghton Lake MI 48629-8636

MARRACCI, THOMAS KENNETH, software executive, consultant; b. Oakland, Calif., Apr. 29, 1965; s. Louis Thomas and Susan Joan (Storment) M. Student, Grinnell (Iowa) Coll., 1983-84; BA in Math., UCLA, 1989. Programmer Synergy, Inc., Torrance, Calif., 1984-85, chief programmer, 1985-86, v.p., 1986, Computers for Industry & Fin., Inc., Torrance, 1986-88, pres., 1988—; v.p. Internat. Software Techs., Inc., Glendale, Calif., 1987-88; pres. Nimbus Computers, Palos Verdes, 1989—. Cons. Continental Airlines, Houston, 1985-88, Banco Do Brasil, Internat., L.A., 1987-88; bd. dirs. C.I.F., Inc., Torrance. Developer L.A. software, banking, gen. bus. and trucking software. Grinnell Coll. athletic scholar, 1983. Mem. UCLA Bus. Soc., So. Calif. Assn. Pick Profls., Am. Trucking Assn. Republican. Roman Catholic. Avocations: cricket, golf, classical guitar, model building.

MARRACK, DAVID, pathologist; b. Sawbridgeworth, Herts., England, Dec. 25, 1922; came to U.S., 1961; s. John Richardson and Alice May (Milward) M.; m. Patricia Franklin, June 1949; children: Jane, Paul, Mary. BS, MB, U. London, England, 1947, MD, 1952. Rsch. fellow Royal Postgrad. Med. Sch., London, 1951-53; travelling fellow Washington U., St. Louis, 1953-54; assoc. prof. pathology U. Tex. M.D. Anderson Hosp., Houston, 1961-68; pathologist Harris County Hosp., 1965-75; with Fort Bend Med. Clinic. Contbr. articles to profl. jours. With RAF, 1949-51. Mem. Air Waste Mgmt. Assn., Am. Soc. Clin. Pathology, Audubon Soc. Office: Fort Bend Med Clinic PO Box 271907 Houston TX 77277-1907 Fax: 713 666-1397.

MARREN, JUDY ANN, paramedic; b. N.Y.C., May 5, 1962; d. Martin Frances and Dolores Teresa M. AS, Laguardia C.C., 2000. EMT-paramedic N.Y.C. Emergency Med. Svcs., 1988-91; officer mgr. PRP, L.I., N.Y., 1992-96; physicians asst. CUNY, N.Y.C., 2000—. Photographer N.Y.C. Emergency Med. Svcs., N.Y.C., 1988-91. Instr. ARC, N.Y.C., 1985—; mem. paramedic Corona Vol. Ambulance Corps., Corona, 1988-92; EMT Astoria Vol. Ambulance Corps., 1985-88. Mem. N.Y. Acad. of Scis., Nat. Assn. of EMT's and Paramedics. Avocations: guitar, environmental protection, animal rights, skiing, cycling.

MARRERO, VICTOR, lawyer, judge; b. Santurce, P.R., Sept. 1, 1941; s. Ezequiel Marrero and Josefina (Sanabria) Santos M.; m. Veronica M. White, Dec. 1987. BA, NYU, 1964; LLB, Yale U., 1968; postgrad. (Fulbright scholar), U. Sheffield, Eng., 1966-67. Bar: N.Y. 1982. Exec. dir. N.Y.C. Dept. City Planning, 1973-74; spl. counsel to comptroller City of N.Y., 1974-75; 1st asst. counsel to gov. State of N.Y., Albany, 1975-76; chmn. N.Y.C. City Planning Commn., 1976-77; commr. N.Y. State Divsn. Housing and Cmty. Renewal, N.Y.C., 1977-79; under-sec. HUD, Washington, 1979-81; ptnr. Tufo & Zuccotti, N.Y.C., 1982-85, Brown & Wood, N.Y.C., 1986-93; amb., U.S. rep. UN Econ. and Social Coun., 1993-97; amb., permanent U.S. rep. OAS, Dept. State, Washington, 1998-99; judge U.S. Dist. Ct., N.Y.C., 1999—. Vis. lectr. Yale U. Law Sch., New Haven, 1986, Columbia U. Law Sch., 1991-93. Trustee N.Y. Pub. Libr., 1989—, SUNY, Albany, 1985-93, Cooper Union, 1989-93, Consolidated Edison Co., 1988-93; bd. dirs. P.R. Legal Def. and Edn. Fund., N.Y.C., 1972-86, N.Y. Telephone Co., 1987-93; chmn. N.Y. State Chief Judge's Com. to Improve Availability of Legal Svcs., 1988-90. Mem. ABA (Pro Bono Publico award 1993), N.Y. State Bar Assn. (Root/Stimson Pub. Svc. .award 1992), Assn. Bar City N.Y. (mem. com. modern cts. 1980-93, exec. com. 1986-89, judiciary com. 1991-92, v.p. 1992-93). Office: US Dist Court of NY 40 Centre St New York NY 10007-1502

MARRESE, BARBARA ANN, nurse, educator, program planner; b. Dover, N.J., Mar. 24, 1936; d. Andrew A. and Eleanor C. (Connelly) Brown; m. Thomas G. Marrese, Nov. 27, 1959; children: Guy A., Holly A. Karker. BA, Jersey City State Coll., 1973; MS, East Stroudsburg (Pa.) U., 1989. Scrub nurse Orange (N.J.) Meml. Hosp., 1956-58; head scrub nurse Columbus Hosp., Newark, 1959-60; sch. nurse/tchr. Mt. Olive Twp. Bd. of Edn., Budd Lake, N.J., 1964-90; asst. supr. Childrens Med. Svcs., Ft. Lauderdale, Fla., 1990-92; program planner Sch. Dist. Palm Beach County, 1992-2000; ret., 2000. Mem.: Morris County Ret. Tchrs. Assn., Fla. Nurses Assn., Fla. Sch. Health Assn. (pres. 2001—02), Am. Sch. Health Assn. Republican. Roman Catholic. Avocations: crewel, reading, golf, walking. Home: 2142 NW 60th Cir Boca Raton FL 33496-2647 E-mail: tmarrese@aol.com.

MARRETT, CORA B. b. Richmond, Va., June 15, 1942; d. Horace Sterling and Clora Ann (Boswell) Bagley; m. Louis Everard Marrett, Dec. 24, 1968. BA, Va. Union U., 1963; MS, U. Wis., 1965, PhD, 1968. Asst. prof. U. N.C., Chapel Hill, 1968-69; from asst. to assoc. prof. Western Mich. U., Kalamazoo, 1969-73; from assoc. prof. to full prof. U. Wis., Madison, 1973-97; asst. dir. NSF, Arlington , Va., 1992-96; provost, vice chancellor for acad. affairs U. Mass., Amherst, 1997—2001; sr. v.p.. for acad. affairs U. Wis. System, 2001—. Mem. sci. adv. panel U.S. Army, Washington, 1976-77; mem. Naval Rsch. Adv. Com., Washington, 1978-81, Pres. Commn. on the Accident at Three Mile Island, 1979; bd. govs. Argonne (Ill.) Nat. Lab., 1983-90, 96-99. Editor: Research in Race and Ethnic Relations, 1988, Gender and Classroom Interaction, 1990. Resident fellow NAS, 1973-74; fellow Ctr. for Advanced Study in Behavioral Scis., 1976-77. Mem. AAAS, ASA, Phi Kappa Phi. Avocations: reading, travel, film appreciation. Home: 7517 Farmington Way Madison WI 53717 Office: Office of Acad Affairs U of Wisconsin Syatem 1620 Van Hise Hall Madison WI 53706 E-mail: cmarrett@uwsa.edu.

MARRIÉ, WILLIAM, dancer; b. Montreal, Quebec, Can. Student, L'École Supérieur de Danse du Quebec. Mem. Nat. Ballet Can., Toronto, Canada, 1990—97, first soloist Canada, 1997—. Guest artist Metropolitan Opera House, Am. Ballet Theatre, New York, 2000. Dancer (ballets) The Taming of the Shrew, Onegin, Swan Lake, Romeo and Juliet, Giselle, Rite of Spring, Soldiers' Mass, Cruel World, Herman Schmerman pas de deux, Petruchio The Taming of the Shrew, Am. Ballet Theatre, N.Y., 2000. Office: Walter Carsen Ctr Nat Ballet Can 470 Queens Quay West Toronto ON Canada M5V 3K4*

MARRIN, CHARLES AINSWORTH STAVELEY, cardiovascular and thoracic surgeon, educator; b. Santa Monica, Calif., Dec. 19, 1947; s. Charles Ainsworth and Cecilia Margaret (Staveley) M.; m. Marian Anthon Bruen, Apr. 19, 1976; 1 child, Minet A. B. MB, BS, U. London, Royal Free Hosp. Sch. Medicine, London, 1971. Ho. physician Willesden Gen. Hosp., London, 1971, Royal Free Hosp., London, 1972; resident in gen. surgery St. Luke's Hosp. Ctr., N.Y.C., 1973-76, chief resident, 1976-77, fellow in cardiovasc. surgery, asst. physician, 1977; fellow in cardiovasc. surg. rsch. Coll. Physicians and Surgeons, Columbia U., 1978; resident in cardiovasc. and thoracic surgery Columbia-Presbyn. Med. Ctr., 1979-80, chief resident, 1980; staff surgeon Hitchcock Clinic and Dartmouth-Hitchcock Med. Ctr., Lebanon, N.H., 1981—; prof. surgery Dartmouth (N.H.) U. Med. Sch., 2000—. Author chpts. to books; contbr. articles to profl. jours. Co-prin. investigator Am. Heart Assn., 1993—; co-investigator U.S. Agy. for Health Care Policy and Rsch., 1993—. Fellow ACS, Am. Coll. Cardiology, Am. Coll. Chest Physicians; mem. AMA, Am. Assn. Thoracic Surgery, Soc. Thoracic Surgeons. Office: Dartmouth-Hitchcock Med Ctr 1 Medical Center Dr Lebanon NH 03756-0002

MARRINGA, JACQUES LOUIS, manufacturing company executive; b. Rotterdam, The Netherlands, Aug. 8, 1928; arrived in U.S., 1965; s. Jakob and Christine Antoinette (Vandervalk) Marringa; m. Joan Kathryn Potter, Oct. 23, 1965; children: Jack, Bob, Katy. Student, Erasmus U., Rotterdam, 1946—49, D in Econ., 1954; grad., Advanced Mgmt. Program Harvard U., 1984. Rsch. asst. Chem. Projects, N.Y.C., 1955; product mgr. Philips, N.V., Eindhoven, The Netherlands, 1956—61; product line mgr. ITT, Brussels and N.Y.C., 1961—70; v.p. Elco Corp., Willow Grove, Pa., 1970—72, Crouse-Hinds, Syracuse, NY, 1972—77; group v.p. Sta-Rite Industries, Milw., 1977—94; pres. Marringa Internat. Corp., 1994—. Bd. dirs. Marlo Inc., Racine, Wis. Mem.: Rotary (Milw.), Milw. Country Club. Home: 2520 W Dean Rd Milwaukee WI 53217-2019

MARRINGTON, BERNARD HARVEY, retired automotive company executive; b. Vancouver, B.C., Can., Nov. 9, 1928; s. Fredrick George and Constance Marie (Hall) M.; m. Patricia Grace Hall, Sept. 3, 1953 (dec. 1999); children: Jodie Lynn, Stacey Lee. Student, U. Pitts., 1982, Bethany Coll., W.Va., 1983; BS in Mktg. Mgmt., Pacific Western U., 1955. V.p., sales mgr. W & L of La Mesa, Calif., 1960-66, pres., gen. mgr., 1966-68, terr. mgr., 1968-77; regional mgr. PPG Industries, Inc., L.A., 1977-88, regional mgr. profit ctr., 1988-91. Cons. L.A. Unified Sch. Dist., 1972, South Coast Air Quality Mgmt. Dist., El Monte, Calif., 1987-91; adv. com. So. Calif. Regional Occupational Ctr., Torrance, 1978-91; mem. Ford Arbitration bd. U. Wis., 1997-99. Contbr. articles to profl. jours. Sustaining sponsor Ronald Reagan Presdl. Found., Simi, 1987—; sustaining mem. Rep. Nat. Com., L.A., 1985-92, Rep. Presdl. Legion of Merit, 1986-99; del. Rep. Platform Planning com., L.A., 1992; charter mem. Nat. Tax Limitation Com., Washington, 1988, Jarvis Gann Taxpayers Assn., L.A., 1978-2002; sponsor Reagan Presdl. Libr., 1986; mem. Ford Arbitration Bd., U. Wis., 1997-99; mem. Daimler Chrysler Arbitration bd. U. Wis., 1999-2000. Recipient Award for Outstanding Community Support, So. Calif. Regional Occupational Ctr., 1986. Episcopalian. Avocations: rose gardening, citrus culture, golf, sailing, classical music.

MARRIOTT, MARCIA ANN, internet business owner, educator, consultant; b. Rochester, N.Y., Mar. 21, 1947; d. Coyne and Alice (Schleper) M.; children: Brian, Jonathan. AA, Monroe C.C., Rochester, 1967; BS, SUNY, Brockport, 1970, MA, 1975; PhD, S.W. U. La., 1985. Program adminstr. N.Y. Dept. of Labor, N.Y.C., 1970-75; employment mgr. Rochester Gen. Hosp., 1975-77, salary adminstr., 1982-98, compensation mgr., 1996—; corp. dir. wage and salary dept. Gannett Newspapers, Rochester, 1977-80; compensation and benefits adminstr. Sybron Corp., 1980-82; compensation mgr. Rochester Gen. Hosp., 1996—; dir. compensation Via Health, Rochester, 1995-98; pres. Compensation Link, 1997—; prof. Grad. Sch. Bus. Rochester Inst. Tech., 1998—, SUNY, Brockport, 1998—. Instr. N.Y. State Sch. Indsl. Rels., Cornell U., N.Y.C., 1976-79; assoc. prof. Rochester Inst. Tech., 1978—, Monroe C.C., 1981—, dir. career adv. coun., 1989—; assoc. prof. SUNY, Brockport; assoc. prof. Nazareth Coll., 1998; dir. Rochester Presbyn. Home, 1987-91, 96—, v.p. bd. dirs., 1997-98, pres. bd. dirs., 1998—; dir. area hosp. coun. Kidney Svc. Ctrs., Rochester, 1988-91; cons. in field. Author: (pamphlets) Guideline for Writing Job Descriptions, 1983, (manual) Career Planning Manual, 1985, (booklet) Guideline for Writing Criteria-Based Job Descriptions, 1988, Skill-based Job Descriptions: A Quality Approach, 1994, Redesigning the Performance Appraisal Process, 1996. Campaign mgr. Carter Campaign Commn., Rochester, 1975; mem. coun. Messiah Luth. Ch., Rochester, 1991-94. Davenport-Hatch Found. grantee, 1973, Wegman Found. grantee, 1975. Mem. Am. Compensation Assn., Single Adopted Parents Group (pres. 1988-93). Avocations: tennis, hiking, reading, swimming, skiing. Office: Rochester Gen Hosp 1425 Portland Ave Rochester NY 14621-3095

MARRIOTT, SALIMA SILER, state legislator, social work educator; b. Batl., Dec. 5, 1940; d. Jesse James and Cordie Susie (Ayers) Siler; m. David Small Marriott, Sept. 24, 1964 (div. 1972); children: Terrez Siler, Patrice Kenyatta. BS, Morgan State Coll., 1964; M in Social Work, U. Md., 1972; D in Social Work, Howard U., 1988. Tchr. Balt. City Pub. Sch., 1964-65; social worker N.Y.C. Social Svcs., 1965-67, Balt. City Social Svcs., 1968-72; instr., asst. prof. Morgan State U., Balt., 1972-96; mem. Md. Gen. Assembly, 1990—. Chair Park Heights Devel. Corp., Balt., 1976-92, Nat. Black Women's Health Project, 1993-94; chair Balt. City Del. to Md. Gen. Assembly. Co-editor: U.S. Policy Toward Southern Africa, 1984. Cons. Balt. City Head Start, 1985-94; sec. Nat. Rainbow Coalition; exec. bd. Nat. Black Caucus of State Legislators; vice chmn. Md. Legis. Black Caucus, 1995-96, chair law and justice com.; trustee Bethel A.M.E. Ch., Balt.; bd. dirs. Balt. Substance Abuse Sys. Flemming fellow, 1995. Mem. Delta Sigma Theta. Office: Md House of Dels 2901 Druid Park Dr Ste 200E Baltimore MD 21215-8177

MARRO, ANTHONY JAMES, newspaper editor; b. Middlebury, Vt., Feb. 10, 1942; s. Francis James and Esther Martha (Butterfield) M.; m. Jacqueline Helen Cleary, June 5, 1965; 1 child, Alexandria. BA in History, U. Vt., 1965; MS in Journalism, Columbia U., 1968. Reporter Rutland (Vt.) Herald, 1964-67, Newsday, L.I., N.Y., 1968-74, chief Washington bur., 1979-81, mng. editor, 1981-86, exec. editor, 1986-87, editor, 1987—; reporter Newsweek, Washington, 1974-76, N.Y. Times, Washington, 1976-79. Co-recipient Pulitzer prizes for Pub. Service Reporting, 1970, 74. Office: Newsday 235 Pinelawn Rd Melville NY 11747-4250

MARRO, MATTHEW SHAWN, chemist; BS in Biology, Fitchburg State Coll., 1986. Lab. analyst Wheelabrator EOS, Leominster, Mass., 1986-88; environ. inspector City of Leominster, 1988—; pvt. consulting practice, 1999—. Mem. Am. Chem. Soc., Am. Water Works, Water Environment Fedn. Office: City of Leominster 109 Graham St Leominster MA 01453-4234

MARRON, DARLENE LORRAINE, real estate development executive, financial and marketing consultant; b. Auburn, N.Y., July 20, 1946; d. William Chester and Elizabeth Barbara (Gervaise) Kulakowski; m. Edward W. Marron Jr., Apr. 28, 1973. BS cum laude, Rider U., 1968; MBA, NYU, 1970. Lic. securities broker. Dir. mktg. Am. Airlines, N.Y.C., 1970-79; asst. v.p. Merrill Lynch, 1979-83; v.p. Kidder, Peabody & Co., 1983-86; prin. Marron Bros. Realty Corp., Upper Saddle River, N.J., 1990—; prin. real estate fin. svcs. firm Hendrickson Advisors, LLC, 2000—. Avocations: pianist, flutist, skiing, fly fishing. Home: 9 Normandy Ct Ho Ho Kus NJ 07423-1217 Office: Marron Cos 118 State Rt 17 Upper Saddle River NJ 07458

MARRONE, DANIEL SCOTT, business, production and quality management educator; b. Bklyn., July 23, 1950; s. Daniel and Esther (Goodman) M.; m. Portia Terrone, Sept. 1, 1979; children: Jamie Ann. BA, Queens Coll., 1972, MLS, 1973; MBA, N.Y. Inst. Tech., 1975; PhD, NYU, 1988; diploma in Quality Engring., Seifer Quality Inst. L.I., 1992, diploma in Mfg. Engring., 1993; cert. in reliability engring., 1995; cert. in quality tech., Total Bus. Svc. Ctr., 1997. Cert. integrated resource mgmt., mech. inspector, quality auditor, quality engr., quality mgr., quality technician, software quality engr., prodn. and inventory mgmt. Auditor/investigator N.Y. State Spl. Pros., N.Y.C., 1977-78; asst. prof. Delehanty Inst., 1978-79, Ladycliff Coll., Highland Falls, N.Y., 1979-80, Am. Bus. Inst., Bklyn., 1980-82; asst. dir. Adelphi Inst., 1982-85; asst. prof. Coll. St. Elizabeth, Convent Station, N.J., 1986-88; prof. SUNY Coll. of Tech., Farmingdale, 1987—. Editor: Research Techniques in Business Education, NYU Business Education Doctoral Abstracts, 1981—,

Agnew lecture by P.M. Sapre, 1989, NYU Symposium, 1989. Recipient Paul S. Lomax award, NYU, 1989, Bus. Edn. Leadership award, 1993. Mem. Inst. Mgmt. Accts., Am. Prodn. and Inventory Control Soc. (cert. prodn. and inventory mgmt.), Prodn. and Ops. Mgmt. Soc., Nat. Assn. Purchasing Mgmt. (cert. purchasing mgr.), Delta Pi Epsilon (Cert. of Merit 1988). Republican. Home: 493 Lariat Ln Bethpage NY 11714-4017

MARRONE, STEPHEN RICHARD, critical care nurse, educator; b. Bklyn., May 17, 1957; s. Anthony Leonard and Patricia Marie (Mercatante) M. BSN cum laude, L.I. U., 1979; MSN, U. Del., 1985. RN. Staff nurse critical care, edn. specialist critical care Mt. Sinai Med. Ctr., N.Y.C., 1979-93, 99—; edn. coord. critical care nursing King Faisal Hosp. & Rsch. Ctr., Riyadh, Saudi Arabia, 1993-98. Author, editor: Basic Dysrhythmia, 1994, Advanced Dysrhythmia, 1995, Intra-aortic Balloon Pump, 1997; contbr. articles to profl. jours. Mem.: Coun. on Anthropology and Nursing, Global Nursing and Health, N.Y. State Nurses Assn., Nat. Nursing Staff Devel. Orgn., Assn. Perioperative Registered Nurses, Am. Assn. Critical Care Nurses (leadership fellow Ctr. for Leadership Excellence), Sigma Theta Tau. Democrat. Roman Catholic. Avocations: travel, reading. Office: Mt Sinai Med Ctr Nursing Edn Box 1144 1 Gustave L Levy Pl New York NY 10029-6500 E-mail: stephenmarrone@smtplink.mssm.edu., stephenmarrone@hotmail.com.

MARROQUIN-MERINO, VICTOR MIGUEL, lawyer; b. Lima, Peru, Feb. 10, 1962; s. Victor S. and Maria Isabel (Merino) M.; m. Marisa Jenny Torres, May 2, 1987; 1 child, Victor Andres. AB, Univ. Miami, 1989, JD, 1992; LLM, Harvard Law Sch., 1993. Staff mem. legal dept. Internat. Monetary Fund, Washington, 1993-94; sr. assoc. Baker & McKenzie, Chgo., 1994—. Contbr. articles to profl. jours. Recipient Disting. Svc. award Chgo. Vol. Legal Svcs. Found., 1994, Merit award Legal Clinic for the Disabled, 1996; named Internat. Lawyer of Yr. Univ. Miami, 1994. Avocations: writing, reading, foreign travel, tennis. Office: Baker & McKenzie One Prudential Plaza Chicago IL 60601

MARROU, CHRIS RENÉ, television newscaster; b. San Antonio, Nov. 12, 1947; s. André Noel and Annette (Deason) M.; m. Kathleen Mary O'Connor, Aug. 17, 1974; children: Mirage Marie and Molly O'Connor (twins). Student, Princeton U., 1964-67. News editor, anchor KRLD Radio, Dallas, 197-73; news anchor KENS-TV, San Antonio, 1973-80, news anchor, mng. editor, 1981—; news anchor WBZ-TV, Boston, 1980-81. Bd. dirs. Alliance Media Group; co-owner Ties.com. Contbr. weekly column San Antonio Light, 1986-93. Recipient award Tex. AP Broadcasters, 1976, 77, 87, Most Respected Local TV News Anchor award TV-Radio Age Mag., 1985, My Turn, Newsweek mag., 1996. Office: KENS-TV 5400 Fredericksburg Rd San Antonio TX 78229-3597

MARROW, DEBORAH, foundation executive, art historian; b. N.Y.C., Oct. 18, 1948; d. Seymour Arthur and Adele (Wolin) M.; m. Michael J. McGuire, June 19, 1971; children: David Marrow McGuire, Anna Marrow McGuire. BA cum laude, U. Pa., 1970, PhD, 1978; MA, Johns Hopkins U., 1972. Resch. asst. Phila. Mus. of Art, 1974-75; mng. editor Chrysalis Mag., L.A., 1978-80; asst. prof. Occidental Coll., 1979, 81-82; publs. coord. The J. Paul Getty Trust, 1983-84; program officer The Getty Grant Program, 1984-86, asst. dir., 1987-89, dir., 1989—; interim dir. The Getty Res. Inst., 1999—. Mem. internat. com. Coun. on Founds., Washington, 1992-96; mem. internat. adv. Group Nat. Endowment for the Arts, 1992; mem. adv. com. Calif. Cmty. Found., L.A., 1991—; mem. Excellence and Equity task force Am. Assn. of Mus., Washington, 1989-91. Author: The Art Patronage of Maria de Medici, 1982; contbr. articles to profl. jours. Chair cultural diversity com. The J. Paul Getty Trust, L.A., 1995-98; mem. Save Am.'s Treas. com., Nat. Trust for Historic Preservation in partnership with White Ho. Millenium Com., 1998—; mem. trustees coun. on Penn Women, U. Pa., 1997—; bd. govs. U. Calif. Humanities Rsch. Inst., 2000—. Samuel H. Kress Found. fellow, N.Y.C., 1975-77. Mem. Coll. Art Assn. of Am., So. Calif. Assn. for Philanthropy (program com., 1988-89, 97), Grantmakers in the Arts, Art Table, Internat. Coun. of Mus. Office: The Getty Rsch Inst 1200 Getty Center Dr Ste 800 Los Angeles CA 90049-1600

MARRS, BARRY LEE, executive director; b. Newark, Sept. 23, 1942; s. Donald Lee and Goldie (Mack) M.; m. Barbara Abbe Griswold, Aug. 20, 1966; children: Abbe Lea, Gwendolyn. BA, Williams Coll., 1963; PhD, Case Western Res. U., 1968. NSF postdoctoral fellow U. Ill., Urbana, 1967-69; Am. Cancer Soc. postdoctoral fellow Stanford (Calif.) U., 1969-71; rsch. assoc. Ind. U., Bloomington, 1971-72; asst. prof. Sch. Medicine St. Louis U., 1972-75, assoc. prof., 1975-78, prof., 1978-83; sr. rsch. assoc. Exxon Rsch. and Engring. Co., Clinton, N.J., 1983-85; rsch. mgr. E. I. duPont de Nemours & Co., Wilmington, Del., 1985-90, sci. dir., 1990-94; CEO, pres. Recombinant BioCatalysis, Inc., Sharon Hill, Pa., 1994-96, Photosynthetic Harvest, Inc., Willingboro, N.J., 1996-98; dir. corp. rsch. Hercules Inc., Wilmington, 1998-2001; exec. dir. Fraunhofer Ctr. for Molecular Biotech., Newark, 2001—. Sci. editor PBS video series Intimate Strangers: Unseen Life on Earth, 1999; contbr. over 50 articles to profl. publs. Trustee U. Del. Rsch. Found., Newark, 1994-99. Recipient Career Devel. award NIH, 1973-78. Office: Fraunhofer Ctr for Molecular Biotech Rsch Ctr 15 Innovation Way Newark DE 19711 E-mail: bmarrs@fraunhofer.org.

MARRS, JAMES F., JR. (JIM MARRS), author, journalist, educator; b. Ft. Worth, Dec. 5, 1943; s. James Marrs; m. Carol Ann Worcester, May 25, 1968; children: Cathryn Nova Ayn, Jayme Alistar. BA in Journalism, U. North Tex., 1966; postgrad., Tex. Tech. Coll., 1967-68. Editor/owner Magpie Mag., 1963-64; sports/news writer, cartoonist Denton (Tex.) Record Chronicle, 1965-66; reporter, copy editor, cartoonist and photographer Lubbock (Tex.) Avalanche-Jour., 1967-68; news and feature writer, cartoonist, photographer Lubbock Sentinel, 1968; reporter, feature writer, photographer, cartoonist Ft. Worth Star-Telegram, 1968-80; prodr. "Texas Roundup" Sammons Cable TV, Ft. Worth, 1982-83; scriptwriter Spindletop Prodns., Dallas, 1982-83; pub. rels. cons. The Mktg. Group, 1982-83; pubr., co-owner The Springtown (Tex.) Current, 1983-84; comm. dir. Continental State Bank, Springtown, 1985-95. Editl. page editor Campus Chat, North Tex. State U., 1965-66; part-time copywriter, pub. rels. dir., cartoonist Jerre R. Todd & Assocs., 1972-74, dir. spl. projects, account exec., pub. rels. dir., 1980-81; editor/pub. and co-owner Cowtown Trails, Ft. Worth, 1983-84; faculty Office Continuing Edn. U. Tex., Arlington, 1976—; comm. dir. N.E. HealthCare Ctr., Hurst, Tex., 1985-86. Author: Crossfire: The Plot That Killed Kennedy, 1989, Alien Agenda, 1997, Rule by Secrecy, 2000, Psi Spies, 2001; scriptwriter, dir. video: Fake, 1991, The Many Faces of Lee Harvey Oswald, 1992; contbr. articles to profl. jours. Prodr. Tex. Gridiron Show, Ft. Worth, 1978-79, dir., 1980; chmn. pub. info. subcom. Ft. Worth Mayor's Com. on Employment of Handicapped, 1979-82; co-chmn. Springtown Centennial Com., 1984; workshop tchr. Operation CLASP, Neighborhood Adv. Coun., Community Devel. Block Grant, City of Ft. Worth, 1984; community rels. cons. All Church Home for Children, Ft. Worth, 1984-95. With USAR, 1969-70. Recipient White Helmet award Ft. Worth Fire dept., 1969, 71, Assoc. Press writing awards, 1969-76, Nat. Writing award Aviation/Aerospace Writers Assn., 1972, Human Rights Leadership award Freedom Mag., 1993; named Arts and Entertainment Newsmaker of the Yr., Tex. Gridiron Club, Soc. Profl. Journalists, 1991. Mem. Tex. Mil. Hist. Soc., Springtown Optimist Club, Delta Sigma Phi, Sigma Delta Chi. Libertarian. Methodist. Avocation: civil war reenactor. Home and Office: Wise Comms PO Box 189 Springtown TX 76082-0189 E-mail: jmarrs@ntws.net.

MARS, JACQUELINE BADGER, food products executive; V.p., co-owner Mars, Inc., McLean, Va. Office: Mars Inc 6885 Elm St Mc Lean VA 22101

MARSALA-CERVASIO, KATHLEEN ANN, medical/surgical nurse, administrator; b. Mar. 22, 1955; d. James Patrick and Kathleen (McLoughlin) Waters. AAS with honors, S.I. Coll., 1974, BS in Nursing with honors, 1984; MSN with honors, CUNY, 1986; PhD in Pub. Adminstrn., Kensington U., 1997. RN, N.Y.; cert. CS, CCRN, CNAA. Staff nurse USPHS Hosp., S.I., 1974-80; head nurse MICU-critical care unit-surg. ICU Bayley Seton Hosp., N.Y., 1980-82; staff nurse surg. ICU, MICU, critical care unit East Orange (N.J.) VA Med. Ctr., 1982-86, critical care nurse specialist; clin. specialist, cons. Med. Ctr. Bklyn. VA Med. Ctr., 1989-95; dir. nursing svcs., asst. prof. nursing U. Hosp./SUNY Health Sci. Ctr., Bklyn., 1990-2000. Asst. clin. prof. SUNY Health Sci. Ctr.; adj. prof. L.I. U., 2001—. Mem. ANA (coun. clin. nurse specialists), AACN (no. N.J. chpt., N.J. chpt.), Am. Coll. Healthcare Execs. (assoc.), N.Y. Orgn. Nurse Execs., Nat. League for Nursing, Sigma Theta Tau. Home: 8898 16th Ave Brooklyn NY 11214-5804

MARSCHER, WILLIAM DONNELLY, engineering company executive; b. Utica, N.Y., Feb. 18, 1948; s. William Ransford and Margaret Elizabeth (Donnelly) M.; m. Deborah Lynn Schmidt, May 27, 1972; children: Michael, Colleen, Megan. BS, Cornell U., 1970, MS in Engring., 1972; MS in Applied Mechanics, Rensselaer Poly. Inst., 1976. Sr. engr. Bendix EFI Divsn., Troy, Mich., 1970-73, Pratt & Whitney Aircraft, East Hartford, Conn., 1973-78; project supr. Creare Inc., Hanover, N.H., 1978-82; engring. mgr. Dresser Pump Divsn., Liberty Corner, N.J., 1982-92; v.p. Concepts ETI, Inc., Norwich, Vt., 1992-96; pres. Mech. Solutions, Inc., Parsippany, N.J., 1996—. Short course lectr. U. Va., Tex. A&M U., Concepts ETI, Brit. Pump Mfrs. Assn. Author: Predictive Maintenance, 1993; co-author: Centrifugal Pumps, 1997; editor: Tribology Transaction Mag., 1988—; contbr. chpts. to books, articles to profl. jours. Edn. dir. St. Denis Ch., Hanover, 1980-82; tchr. St. Margaret's Ch., Morristown, N.J., 1982—; head coach Morris County 12/14 yr. old Soccer, Morristown, 1985-90. NASA fellow, 1971-72; recipient Creativity Gold medal Dresser Industries, 1986, ASLE, Hodson Best Paper award, 1983. Mem. ASME (chmn. tribol. conf. chair 1995, co-chmn. rotating machinery conf. 1993, chair predicative maintenance tech. com. 1999—), ASTM (fatigue stds. com., wear stds. com. 1980—), Soc. Tribologists and Lubrication Engrs. (fellow, chmn. wear com. 1988-90, bd. dirs. 1989—, chmn. awards com. 1992, chmn. ann. mtg. 1989, chmn. seals tech. com. 1998—, treas. 1995, sec. 1996, v.p. 1997, pres. 1998). Republican. Roman Catholic. Achievements include patents in field. Office: Mechanical Solutions Inc 1719 Route 10 Ste 205 Parsippany NJ 07054-4507

MARSDEN, BRIAN GEOFFREY, astronomer; b. Cambridge, Eng., Aug. 5, 1937; came to U.S., 1959; s. Thomas and Eileen (West) M.; m. Nancy Lou Zissell, Dec. 26, 1964; children: Cynthia Louise, Jonathan Brian. BA, Oxford U., U.K., 1959, MA, 1963; PhD, Yale U., 1965. Rsch. asst. Yale U., New Haven, 1959-65; lectr. astronomy Harvard U., Cambridge, Mass., 1966-83; astronomer Smithsonian Astrophys. Obs., 1965-86; assoc. dir. planetary scis. Harvard-Smithsonian Ctr. for Astrophysics, 1987—2002. Dir. Ctrl. Bur. Astron. Telegrams, 1968-2000, Minor Planet Ctr. Internat. Astron. Union, 1978—. Editor: The Earth-Moon System, 1966, The Motion, Evolution of Orbits and Origin of Comets, 1972, Catalogue of Orbits of Unnumbered Minor Planets, 1996, Catalogue of Cometary Orbits, 2001. Recipient Merlin medal Brit. Astron. Assn., 1965, Goodacre medal, 1979; Van Biesbroeck award U. Ariz., 1989, Camus-Waitz prize Societé astronomique de France, 1993, Dirk Brouwer award Am. Astron. Soc., 1995, Lacchini prize Unione Astrofili Italiani, 2001. Fellow Royal Astron. Soc.; mem. Am. Astron. Soc. (chmn. div. on dynamical astronomy 1976-78), Internat. Astron. Union (pres. commn. 1976-79), Astron. Soc. Pacific, Sigma Xi. Office: Harvard-Smithsonian Ctr Astrophysics 60 Garden St Cambridge MA 02138-1516 E-mail: bmarsden@cfa.harvard.edu.

MARSDEN, LAWRENCE ALBERT, retired textile company executive; b. Mpls., May 28, 1919; s. Lawrence N. and Carrie Elizabeth (Ross) M.; m. Millicent Irene Snyder, Mar. 24, 1941; children: Millicent Carrie, Andrea Leigh, Lawrence Stewart, John Daniel. BS in Law, U. Minn., 1941; LL.B., George Washington U., 1946. Bar: D.C. 1946. Ptnr. Onion, Marsden & New, Washington, 1947-48; pres. Marsden-Slate, Inc., High Point, N.C., 1949-68; v.p. Guilford Mills, Inc., Greensboro, 1968-72, sr. v.p., 1973-84. Chmn. Marcor, Inc., High Point, 1980—; ptnr. SPM Investments; pres. Fabrilux Products, Inc., High Point, 1995-96. Author: Attack Transport, 1946, Gemini Ship, 2002. Served to lt. comdr. USN, 1941-46, PTO. Mem. Am. Assn. Textile Chemists and Colorists, Sportsman Pilots Assn. (past pres.), Aircraft Owners and Pilots Assn., Rolls Royce Owner's Club, Quiet Birdmen, High Point Country Club, Willow Creek Golf Club (High Point), Isla Del Sol Yacht and Country Club (St. Petersburg, Fla.), Phi Delta Phi, Phi Delta Theta. Republican. Home: 1706 Maryfield Ct High Point NC 27260-2684

MARSE, LINDA MOODY, music educator; b. Kansas City, Kans., Jan. 6, 1946; d. Jay K. and Nell Arville (Hayes) Moody; m. John Pat Marse, Aug. 31, 1968; 1 child, Melissa Janel. MusB, U. Colo., 1967, MusM, 1970. Piano tchr. U. Colo., Boulder, 1967-68, Cordova Music Ctr., Sacramento, 1968-71; office mgr. Weinstein & Spira, CPAs, Houston, 1972-73; legal sec. Thompson, Ogletree & Deakins, Atlanta, 1974-75; piano tchr. Houston, 1975-82, Linda Marse Piano Studio, Austin, Tex., 1982—. Judge Jr. Miss, Tex. Performer: (recording) Linda Moody Marse Plays the Memorial Organ, 1976. Mem. Tex. Music Tchrs. Assn., Nat. Guild Piano Tchrs., Music Tchrs. Nat. Assn., Austin Dist. Music Tchrs. Assn. (pres. 1995-97, Tchr. of Yr. 1997). Home and Office: 11012 Centennial Trl Austin TX 78726-1409

MARSEE, SUSANNE IRENE, mezzo-soprano; b. San Diego, Nov. 26, 1941; d. Warren Jefferson and Irene Rose (Wills) Dowell; m. Mark J. Weinstein, May, 1987; 1 child, Zachary. Student, Santa Monica City Coll., 1961; BA in History, UCLA, 1964. Mem. voice faculty Am. Mus. and Dramatic Acad., N.Y.C., 1994-97, Pitts. Civic Light Opera Acad., 1997—, Duquesne U., 1998-2000; artist's lectr. Carnegie Mellon U., 2000—. Assoc. prof. La State U. Appeared with numerous U.S. opera cos., 1970—, including N.Y.C. Opera, San Francisco Opera, Boston Opera, Houston Grand Opera; appeared with fgn. cos., festivals, Mexico City Bellas Artes, 1973, 78, Canary Islands Co., 1976, Opera Metropolitana, Caracas, Venezuela, 1977, Spoleto (Italy) Festival, 1977, Aix en Provence Festival, France, 1977, Calgary, Alta., Can., 1986; recorded Tales of Hoffmann, ABC/Dunhill Records; TV appearances include Live from Lincoln Center, Turk in Italy, Cenerentola, 1989, Live from Wolftrap Roberto Devereux, 1975, Rigoletto, 1988, A Little Night Music, 1990, Marriage of Figaro, 1991, (PBS TV) Rachel, La Cubana; recs. and CDs Anna Bolena with Ramey, Scotto, Roberto Devereux with Beverly Sills, Roberto Devereux with Monserat Caballé Carreras, Tales of Hoffmann with Beverly Sills, Rigoletto with Quilico and Carreras; videotape Roberto Devereux with Beverly Sills. Recipient 2d place award Met. Opera Regional Auditions, 1968, San Francisco Opera Regional Auditions 1968; named winner Liederkranz Club Contest, 1970; Gladys Turk Found. grantee, 1968-69; Corbett Found. grantee, 1969-73; Martha Baird Rockefeller grantee, 1969-70, 71-72 Mem. AFTRA, Am. Guild Mus. Artists (past bd. dirs.), Nat. Assn. Tchrs. of Singing (past bd. dirs. for N.Y.). Democrat.

MARSEL, ROBERT STEVEN, law educator, mediator, arbitrator; b. N.Y.C., July 23, 1947; s. Bernard and Vivian (Gilbert) M. JD, U. Calif., 1971. Bar: N.Y., D.C., U.S. Supreme Ct. Mem. Worcester Coll., Oxford, Eng.; vis. lectr. Faculty Law, U. Auckland N.Z.; spl. asst. U.S. atty., San Francisco; legal counsel U.S. Supreme Ct., Washington; vis. asst. prof. law U. Miami, 1983-84; prof. South Tex. Coll. Law, Houston, 1984-97, prof., dean Inst. for Advanced Studies, 1995—, v.p., gen. counsel Houston Mediation Project, 1995—; chmn. com. on privacy and confidentiality U.S. Dept. Commerce; trainer, lectr. on mediation and arbitration; mediator pro bono Houston Dispute Resolution Ctr.; faculty mem. Ctr. for Legal Responsibility. U. Calif. hon. traveling fellow. Fellow Houston Bar Found.; mem. Am. Arbitration Assn., Tex. Assn. Mediators, Accts. and Lawyers for the Arts (bd. dirs. mediation com.), Soc. Profls. in Dispute Resolution. Office: 425 Courtleigh St Wichita KS 67218-1715

MARSELIS-MOORE, JADEH, emergency room nurse, alcohol/drug abuse nurse; b. La., Aug. 13, 1960; s. Willie and Mildred (Marselis) M. Diploma lic. practical nurse, Hinds Jr. Coll., Vicksburg, Miss., 1980; AAS, Utica (Miss.) Jr. Coll., Utica, Miss., 1982; ADN, N.Mex. State U., 1984; BSN, City U., L.A., 1993; MS, Am. Inst. of Holistic Theology, 1999; grad., Brodsky Sch. Real Estate, 2001; PhD, Madison U., 2001. Lic. realtor. Charge nurse, relief adminstrv. supr. Miss. State Hosp., Whitfield, 1980-81; RN, relief charge nurse Med. Unit Meml. Gen. Hosp., Las Cruces, N.Mex., 1982-88; dir. med./surg. unit Physicians & Surgeons Hosp., Atlanta, 1988-89; asst. head nurse drug addictions/behavior South Fulton Med. Ctr., East Point, Ga., 1989-93, charge nurse Emergency dept., 1993-2000; adminstr. supr. Desert Gardens Clin. Care Campus, Tucson, 1999—; RN in emergency dept. Eldorado Hosp., Tuscon, 1999—. Recipient The Samaritan award, Libr. Svc. award. Mem. Emergency Nurses Assn., Tucson Assn. Realtors, Multiple Listing Svc. E-mail: Jadehmmoore@hotmail.com.

MARSH, BENJAMIN FRANKLIN, lawyer; b. Toledo, Apr. 30, 1927; s. Lester Randall and Alice (Smith) M.; m. Martha Kirkpatrick, July 12, 1952; children: Samuel, Elizabeth. BA, Ohio Wesleyan U., 1950; JD, George Washington U., 1954. Bar: Ohio 1955. Pvt. practice law, Toledo, 1955-88, Maumee, 1988—; assoc., ptnr. Doyle, Lewis & Warner, Toledo, 1955-71; ptnr. Ritter, Boesel, Robinson & Marsh, 1971-88, Marsh & McAdams, Maumee, 1988-98; personnel officer AEC, 1950-54; asst. atty. gen. State of Ohio, 1969-71; asst. solicitor City of Maumee, 1959-63, solicitor, 1963-92; ptnr. Marsh McAdams Scharty Brogan & Schaefer, Ltd., 1999—. Mem. U.S. Fgn. Claims Settlement Commn., Washington, 1990-94; counsel N.W. Ohio Mayors and Mgrs. Assn., 1990-2000; mem. regional bd. rev. Indsl. Commn. Ohio, Toledo, 1993-94; mem. Ohio Dental Bd., 1995-2000; trustee Corp. for Effective Govt., 1998—; mem. Ohio Elections Commn., 2001—. U.S. rep. with rank spl. amb. to 10th Anniversary Independence of Botswana, 1976; past pres. Toledo and Lucas County Tb Soc., citizens for metro pks.; past mem. Judges Com. Notaries Pub.; formerly mem. Lucas County Bd. Elections; former chmn. bldg. commn. Riverside Hosp., Toledo; past trustee Com. on Rels. with Toledo, Spain; past chmn. bd. trustee Med. Coll., Ohio; past treas. Coglin Meml. Inst.; chmn. Lucas County Rep. Exec. Com., 1973-74; precinct commiteeman, Maumee, 1959-73; legal counsel, bd. dirs. Nat. Coun. Rep. Workshops, 1960-65; pres. Rep. Workshops, Ohio, 1960-64; alt. del. Rep. Nat. Conv., 1964; candidate 9th dist. U.S. Ho. of Reps., 1968; adminstrv. asst. to Rep. state chmn. Ray C. Bliss, 1954; chmn. Lucas County Bush for Pres., 1980; co-chmn. Reagan-Bush Com. for Northwestern Ohio, 1980, vice chmn. fin. com. Bush-Quayle, 1992; co-chmn. Ohio steering com. Bush for Pres., mem. nat. steering com., 1988; del. Rep. Nat. Conv., 1988; past bd. dirs. Ohio Tb and Respiratory Disease Assn.; apptd. Ohio chmn. UN Day, 1980, 81, 82; adminstrv. asst. Legis. Svc. Commn., Columbus, 1954-55; mem. Lucas County Charter Commn., Toledo, 1959-60; vice-chmn. U.S. Nat. Commn. for UNESCO, mem. legal com., del. 17th gen. conf., Paris, 1972, U.S. observer meeting of nat. commns., Africa, 1974, Addis Ababa, Ethiopia; past mem. industry functional adv. com. on standards trade policy matters; mem. nat. def. exec. res. Dept. Commerce; active Am. Bicentennial Presdl. Inauguration, Diplomatic Adv. Com. With USNR, 1945-46. Named Outstanding Young Man of Toledo, 1962. Mem. ABA, Maumee C. of C. (past pres.), Ohio State Bar Assn., Toledo Bar Assn., Ohio Mpcl. League (past pres.), Am. Legion, Lucas County Maumee Valley Hist. Soc. (trustee, past pres.) George Washington Law Assn., Internat. Inst. Toledo, Ohio Mcpl. Attys. Assn. (past pres.), Orgn. Security and Cooperation in Europe (registration supr., adjudicator, elections supr. in Bosnia), Ohio Hist. Soc., Canal Soc. Ohio, Toledo Mus. Art, Ohio Wesleyan U. Alumni Assn. (past pres.), Toledo C. of C., Ohio State Bar Found., Toledo Bar Found., Rotary, Faculty Club Med. Coll., Toledo Country Club, Omicron Delta Kappa, Delta Sigma Rho, Theta Alpha Phi, Phi Delta Phi. Presbyterian. Home: 124 W Harrison St Maumee OH 43537-2119 Office: 204 W Wayne St Maumee OH 43537-2125 E-mail: bmarsh124@aol.com.

MARSH, BRIAN RICHARD, management executive, playwright, educator, clergyman; b. Montague, Mass., Nov. 7, 1948; s. Walter Raymond and Elizabeth Hazel (McClary) M.; m. Ljuba Greene, July 25, 1977; children: Alexandra Whitney, Colin Webster. BA, U. Mass., 1970, MA, Bowling Green U., 1971; MDiv, The Gen. Theol. Sem., 1996; DMin, Laud Hall. Pres. Profl. Tng. Inc., Springfield, Mass., 1982—, Almadan Inc., Belchertown, 1984-95; prodr. The Hampshire Shakespeare Co., 1989-94; pres. Marsh Co., 1997—; dir. theatre Pioneer Valley Performance Arts, 1997—; rector St. George Anglican Ch., 1998—2000, Ch. of Good Shepherd, 2000—. Clergy del. Nat. Synod, 1999. Playwright: This Particular Place, 1988, Play for 21 Voices, 1988, The Church-250 Years, 1987, The Search for Emily, 1988, The Letter from Hope, 1989, The Passenger Pigeon, 1991, Home to Hawley, 1991, Julian (The Moment is a Mask), 1993, Lear Solo, 1993, Fellowship of the Mystery, 1994, The Christmas Copier, 1995, Mala's Story, 1999. Pres. Carriage Towne Players, 1980—84. Mem. Founders of Hartford (Councillor 1988-90), Colonial Wars. Anglican. Home: 21 Sherwood Dr Belchertown MA 01007-9541

MARSH, BRUCE DAVID, geologist, educator; b. Munising, Mich., Jan. 4, 1947; s. William Roland and Audrey Jane (Steinhoff) M.; m. Judith Anne Congdon, Jan. 24, 1970; children: Hannah Eyre, William Noah. BS, Mich. State U., 1969; MS, U. Ariz., 1971; PhD, U. Calif.-Berkeley, 1974. Geologist, geophysicist Anaconda Co., Tucson, 1969-71; asst. prof. dept. earth/planet sci. Johns Hopkins U., Balt., 1974-78, assoc. prof., 1978-81, prof., 1981—. Chmn., 1989-93; vis. prof. Calif. Inst. Tech., Pasadena, 1985, U. Maine, 1992-93; co-chmn. Gordon Rsch. Conf. on Inorganic Geochemistry, Holderness, N.H., 1983-84; advisor NASA, Washington, 1975-84, NSF, Washington, 1978-90, NRC, 1985-91; Hallimond lectr. Mineral. Soc. Great Britain and Ireland, 1995. Assoc. editor Geology, 1981-83, Jour. Volcanology and Geothermal Rsch., 1978—, Jour. Petrology, 1986—; editor Jour. Volcanology and Geothermal Rsch., 1990—. Fellow Geol. Soc. Am. (assoc. editor Bulletin 1986-92), Royal Astron. Soc., Mineral. Soc. Am., Am. Geophys. Union (sec. sect. on volcanology, geochemistry and petrology 1984-86, pres. elect 1988-90, pres. 1990-92, Bowen award 1993, Daly lecture 2000); mem. Model A Ford Club Am. Office: Johns Hopkins U Dept Earth-Planetary Scis 322 Olin Hall Baltimore MD 21218 E-mail: bmarsh@jhu.edu.

MARSH, CAROL K. adult community administrator; b. Elloree, S.C., Sept. 15, 1933; d. William Conrad and Allie (Ulmer) Kemmerlin; m. Edward A. Peeples, Sept. 20, 1963 (div. Dec. 1988); 1 child, William E. Kemmerlin Peeples; m. Charles Marsh, March 15, 1953 (div. Sept. 1961), remarried May. 27, 1989; children: Shera Marsh Chupa, Mickee Brown. Operator So. Bell Telephone, Allendale, SC, 1951-54; bookkeeper Colonial Stores, Chamblis, Ga., 1955-57, Florence, SC, 1957-58; retail acct. Piggly Wiggly Carolina, Charleston, 1958-65; ptnr. Southern Inventory Svc., SD, 1976-85; substitute tchr./trainer Charleston County Schs., 1979-88; gen. mgr. Beachwood at the Heritage, Myrtle Beach, SC, 1988—. Ptnr. Marsh Contractors Ltd., 1990—. Contbr. poetry to Internat. Libr. Poetry. Bd. dirs. Mfrd. Housing Inst. S.C., Columbia, 1996—; life mem. Luth. Sem. Aux./So. Sem., Columbia; pres. Women of Evang. Luth. Ch. Am. St. Matthews Luth. Ch., 1984-86. Named Vol. of the Yr., Charleston County Schs., 1984. Mem. NAFE, Myrtle Beach C. of C., Am. Bus. Women's Assn. (pres. 1996-98, Woman of Yr. 1998), PTA (life, hon.), S.C. PTA (hon. life), Am. Soc. Notaries. Lutheran. Home: PO Box 3111 Myrtle Beach SC 29578-3111 Office: Beachwood at the Heritage 1712 Club House Dr Myrtle Beach SC 29577-5090 E-mail: ccc2x1@cs.com.

MARSH, CAROLE, author, photographer, publisher; b. Marietta, Ga., Mar. 22, 1946; CEO, Gallopade Internat., Peachtree City, Ga. Author more than 10,000 books and software including: (children's ednl. series) CArole Marsh State Books, Our Black Heritage Series, Smart Sex Stuff for Kids 7-17, Quantum Leap Books, The Naked Gourmet, Lifewrite and Propub Books, History Mystery Books, Lost Colony Collection; author curriculum materials based on state standards for all 50 state and Can. Recipient Top Honors, Nat. C. of C.; named Communicator of Yr., Assn. Bus. Communicators. Office: Gallopade Publishing Group 665 Hwy 74 S Peachtree City GA 30269

MARSH, CARYL AMSTERDAM, museum exhibitions curator, psychologist, advisor; b. N.Y.C., Mar. 9, 1923; d. Louis and Kitty (Weitz) Amsterdam; m. Michael Marsh, Sept 3, 1942 (dec. 1993); children: Susan E., Anna L. BA, Bklyn. Coll., 1942; MA, Columbia U., 1946; PhD, George Washington U., 1978. Lic. psychologist, D.C. Asst. cultural attache Am. Embassy, Paris, 1946-48; psychologist D.C. Recreation Dept., 1957-69; spl. asst. Smithsonian Instn., Washington, 1966-73; curator exhbns. Nat. Archives, 1978-85, sr. exhbns. specialist, 1985-86; dir. traveling psychology exhbn. Am. Psychol. Assn., 1986-93, sr. advisor, 1993-95; chair humanities seminars in sci. mus. Assn. Sci. Tech. Ctrs., 1994—. Rsch. fellow exptl. gallery Smithsonian Instn., 1992; rsch. cons. Nat. Zoo, 1981-92, Smithsonian Folk Life Festival, Nat. Mus. Am. History, 1977-78; organizer Discovery Room Nat. Mus. Natural History, 1969-73; cons. Meyer Found., 1964-66; advisor Lemelson Ctr. for Study of Invention and Innovation, Nat. Mus. Am. History, 1999-2000. Editor: Exhibition: The American Image, 1979. Organizer Anacostia Neighborhood Mus., Washington, 1967, bd. dirs., 1974—, v.p. 1993—; sec. D.C. Commn. on Arts and Humanities, 1969-72; pres. Pre-Sch. Parents Coun., Washington, 1956-57; adv. bd. Youth Alive, 1997-99. Fellow Nat. Mus. Am. Art, 1975-77; vis. scholar Nat. Mus. Am. Art, 1978—; grad. fellow CUNY, 1945-46; scholar George Washington U.; noted for Design. Contbn. to Pub. Understanding of Psychology, APA, 1993. Mem. AAAS, APA (Outstanding Svc. award 1992,

Disting. Contbn. to Pub. Understanding of Psychology award 1993), D.C. Psychol. Assn., Am. Assn. Mus., Mus. Edn. Roundtable (bd. dirs. 1983-87). Home and Office: 10450 Lottsford Rd # 3011 Mitchellville MD 20721-2734

MARSH, CLARE TEITGEN, retired school psychologist; b. Manitowoc, Wis., July 7, 1934; d. Clarence Emil and Dorothy (Napiezinski) Teitgen; m. Robert Irving Marsh, Jan. 30, 1955; children: David, Wendy Marsh Tootle, Julie Marsh Domino, Laura Marsh Beltrame. MS in Ednl. Psychology, U. Wis., Milw., 1968. Sch. psychologist Milw. Pub. Schs., 1975-76; lead psychologist West Allis (Wis.)-West Milw. Pub. Schs., 1968-95; sch. psychologist Wauwatosa (Wis.) Pub. Schs., 1987; instr. Milw. Sch. Engring., 1989-90, Alverno Coll., 1990-91. NDEA fellow, 1966-68. Mem. Internat. Sch. Psychologists Assn., Nat. Assn. Sch. Psychologists (del.), Suburban Assn. Sch. Psychologists (pres. 1976-77, 86-87), Wis. Assn. Sch. Psychologists (pres. 1990-91, chmn. membership com. 1980-84, sec. 1985-89, chmn. conv. 1987), Wis. Fedn. Pupil Svcs., Phi Kappa Phi, Pi Lambda Theta (pres.), Kappa Delta Pi, Phi Delta Kappa, Sigma Tau Delta, Alpha Chi Omega. Home: 14140 W Honey Ln New Berlin WI 53151-2442 E-mail: cclare@marsh@cs.com.

MARSH, DONALD JAY, medical school dean, medical educator; b. N.Y.C., Aug. 5, 1934; m. Wendy G. Clough; 2 children. AB, U. Calif., Berkeley, 1955; MD, U. Calif., San Francisco, 1958. Intern in medicine UCLA Hosp., 1958-59; postdoctoral fellow dept. physiology NYU, 1959-60, instr. dept. physiology, 1960-61, asst. prof. physiology and biophysics, 1963-67, assoc. prof. physiology and biophysics, 1967-71; prof. biomed. engring. U. So. Calif., 1971-92, prof., chmn. dept. physiology and biophysics, 1978-92, prof. medicine, 1982-92, rsch. prof. physiology and biophysics, 1992—; prof. physiology Brown U., Providence, 1992—, dean medicine and biol. scis., 1992—, Frank L. Day prof. biology, 1995—. Mem. engring. in medicine and biology tng. com. NIH, 1973, cardiovascular renal study sect., 1983-86, ad hoc mem. med. lab. scis. rev. com., 1976, inst. gen. med. scis. adv. com., 1982; ad hoc reviewer NSF; mem. rsch. com. Am. Heart Assn., 1979-82, rev. coms. for grants-in-aid, pub. affairs com., 1986-88; cons. com. interdisciplinary rsch. Nat. Rsch. Coun.- Inst. of Medicine, 1989; mem. med. schs. sect. task force AMA, 1994—; lectr. in field. Mem. editorial bd. Annals of Biomed. Engring., 1972-74, mng. editor, 1974-78; mem. editorial bd. Am. Jour. Physiology and Jour. of Applied Physiology, 1972-76, Am. Jour. Physiology: Regulatory, Integrative and Comparative Physiology, 1977-79, Am. Jour. Physiology: Renal, Fluid and Electrolyte Physiology, 1977-82, 88-94, Am. Jour. Physiology: Modelling Methodology Forum, 1984-91; guest reviewer Biophys. Jour., Circulation Rsch., Jour. Clin. Investigation, Jour Theoretical Biology, Kidney Internat., Sci., Pfluegers Archiv European Jour. Physiology; contbr. articles to profl. jours., chpts. to books. Named Career Scientist, Health Rsch. Coun. N.Y., 1964-71; Spl. fellow NIH, 1970-71; NIH grantee, 1963—. Fellow AAAS; mem. Assn. Am. Med. Colls. (coun. of deans), Am. Soc. Nephrology, Am. Physiol. Soc. (com. on coms. 1980-83, chmn. renal sect. 1982-83, long range planning com. 1990-93), Biophys. Soc., Microvascular Soc., Soc. Gen. Physiologists, Soc. Math. Biology (nominating com. 1983, publs. com. 1984-85, bd. dirs. 1986-88), Alpha Omega Alpha. Home: 148 Pratt St Providence RI 02906-1411 Office: Brown U Sch of Medicine PO Box G-a1 Providence RI 02912-0001

MARSH, DONALD REPPERT, holding company executive; b. Beaver Falls, Pa., Apr. 7, 1930; s. Donald Excell and Ruth Isabelle (Reppert) M.; m. Josephine Newell Roberts (div. Dec. 1980); children: Duncan Roberts, Tobin Clark, Kevin Reppert; m. Takako Satoh, Feb. 13, 1981. BA in Econs., U. Mich., 1955. V.p. Morgan Guaranty Trust Co., N.Y.C., 1957-76, New Eng. Mchts. Nat. Bank, Boston, 1976-77; sr. v.p. Rainier Nat. Bank, Seattle, 1977-84; v.p. internat. Burlington No., Inc., 1984-89; pres. Burlington No. Internat. Services, Inc., 1985-89; sr. adv. Pacific N.W. Advisors, 1992—; adj. prof. Seattle U., 1993—. Mem. Wash. Export Council, Seattle, 1979-86, Keizai Doyukai, Japan, 1987-91; bd. dirs., treas. Wash. Council Internat. Trade, Seattle, 1978-86; chair bd. dirs. Wash. Coun. Econ. Edn. Contbr. articles on internat. fin. and trade to profl. jours. D. dirs. YMCA, Seattle, 1978-80; trustee Blakemore Found.; bd. dirs. World Affairs Coun., 1990-94, Am.-Japan Soc. Served as cpl. U.S. Army, 1951-53. Mem. Bankers' Assn. Fgn. Trade (bd. dirs., exec. com. 1979-83), Japan Am. Soc. (bd. dirs.), Seattle C. of C. (chmn. internat. trade com. 1982-85), Olympic Club(Seattle); Internat. House (Tokyo). Avocations: skiing, backpacking, sailing, travelling. Home and Office: 8170 Grand Ave Bainbridge Island WA 98110-2947 E-mail: DonaldMarshNova@aol.com.

MARSH, ELLA JEAN, pediatrician; b. Chgo., Dec. 16, 1941; d. Charles and Eleanor (Canfield) M. BA, St. Mary of Woods (Ind.) Coll., 1963; DO, Chgo. Coll. Osteo. Medicine, 1971. Diplomate Am. Coll. Osteo. Pediatricians (chmn. evaluating com. 1981-89), Nat. Osteo. Bds. Intern Doctor's Hosp., Columbus, Ohio, 1971-72; resident in pediatrics Chgo. Coll. Osteo. Medicine, 1972-74, asst. prof., 1974-78, assoc. prof. pediatrics, 1978-82; assoc. prof. W.Va. Coll. Osteo. Medicine, 1975-86; clin. assoc. prof. pediatrics South Eastern Osteo. Sch. Medicine, 1984-96, chmn. pediatric and newborn nursery, 1982-94; assoc. dir. med. edn. Orlando (Fla.) Gen. Hosp., 1985-88. Mem. staff Arnold Palmer Children's Hosp., Fla. Hosp., Health Ctr.; pediatric cons. Nat. Bd. Osteo. Examiners; lectr., cons. in field. Alumni bd. dirs. St. Mary of Woods Coll., 1992-95, Ctrl. Fla. Primary Care, 1994-97. Donald Bucknar Moore scholar, 1963. Fellow Am. Coll. Osteo. Pediatricians (v.p. 1986, pres. 1988), Am. Acad. Pediat.; mem. AMA, Am. Osteo. Assn., Fla. Osteo. Assn., Fla. Med. Soc., Orange County Med. Soc., Cen. Fla. Pediatric Soc., Chgo. Coll. Osteo. Medicine Alumni Assn., Am. Coll. Osteo. Pediatricians, Am. Acad. Pediatricians, Irish Am. Pediatric Soc., Am. Acad. of Osteopathy. Roman Catholic. Home: 8210 Imber St Orlando FL 32825-8233 E-mail: emarsh16@aol.com.

MARSH, GARY W. interior designer; b. Independence, Mo., Jan. 5, 1948; s. James Albert and Dorothy Jean (Adams) M. BS, Cen. Mo. State U., 1970. Designer/apprentice Sermon-Anderson Inc., Independence, 1967-70; designer Savage Furniture Co., 1970-71, J.C. Penney Corp., Kansas City, Mo., 1971-76; owner, designer Marsh-LeFevbre & Assocs., 1980—2002; pres., CEO Sermon-Anderson Inc., 2002—. Mem. Am. Soc. Interior Designers (bd. dirs. 1982-90, chmn. home yr. com. 1986-90, presdl. citation 1987, chair hist. preservation 1983—, pres.-elect Mo./West Kans. chpt. 1993), Nat. Trust Conf., Design Excellence Awards (bd. dirs. 1986, dir. 1982), Nat. Trust Hist. Preservation, Hist. Kansas City Found. Episcopalian. Avocations: theatre, opera, travel, reading, woodworking. Office: Sermon-Anderson Inc 10815 Winner Rd Independence MO 64052 E-mail: Mgwmarsh@aol.com.

MARSH, HAROLD MICHAEL, anesthesiologist; b. Sydney, Australia, Mar. 7, 1939; came to U.S., 1974; m. Elizabeth Eleanor. BSc in Medicine, U. Sydney, 1956, MBBS, 1963. Intern Royal Prince Alfred Hosp., Sydney, Australia, 1964, resident Australia, 1965-68, Mayo Grad. Sch. Medicine, Rochester, Minn., 1969-71; clin. assoc. dept. anesthesiology Toronto Western Hosp., 1971; dir. dept. intensive care Royal Prince Alfred Hosp., 1972-74; instr. anesthesiology Mayo Med. Sch., Rochester, 1975-76, asst. prof. anesthesiology, 1976-83; assoc. prof. anesthesiology Mayo Grad. Sch., Minn., 1981-89, prof. anesthesiology, 1989; chmn. dept. anesthesiology Henry Ford Hosp., Detroit, 1989-98; prof. chmn. dept. anesthesiology Wayne State U., 1998—; spec.-in-chief anesthesiology Detroit Med. Ctr., 1998—. Part-time lectr., tutor faculty medicine U. Sydney, 1972-74; cons. anesthesiology Mayo Clinic, 1974-89, med. dir. surg. and respiratory intensive care units, 1977-81, dir. critical care svcs., 1981-83, 87-89, assoc. dir. critical care svcs., 1984-87, chmn. divsn. intensive care & respiratory therapy, 1985-89; vis. prof. dept. anesthesia U. Pa., 1976, Nat. Naval Med. Sch., 1981, Northwestern U., 1982, 89, Royal Prince Alfred Hosp., 1983, Sir Charles Gairdner Hosp., 1984, U. Md., 1987, Sloan-Kettering Inst., 1990, Rush-Presbyn.-St. Luke's Med. Ctr., Chgo., 1991, U. Hosp., London, Ont., 1993; invited lectr. dept. anesthetics IV Pan Am. Congress of Diseases of Chest, Caracas, Venezuela, 1987, Uniformes Svcs. U. Health Scis. Med. Sch., Bethesda, Md., 1987, Walter Reed Amry Med. Ctr., 1987, Naval Hosp., 1987, Bethesda, World Congress Intensive Care, Kyoto, Japan, 1989, Uddevalla (Sweden) Hosp., 1993, Karolinska Hosp., Stockholm, Sweden, 1993, Nat. Inst. Cardiology, Mexico City, Mexico, 1993; presenter in field. Contbr. chpts. to books and articles to profl. jours. With Australian Mil., 1958-61. Faculty of Anaesthetists, Royal Australasian Coll. Surgeons fellow, 1968. Fellow Am. Coll. Chest Physicians; mem. AAAS, Am. Bd. Anesthesiology, Am. Coll. Anesthesiologists. Achievements include research on general anesthesia and the lung, acute lung injury, metabolism, epidemiology in critical care. Office: Detroit Med Ctr DHR/UHC Dept Anesthesiolog 4201 Saint Antoine St Detroit MI 48201-2153

MARSH, JANET ZIMMERMAN, humanities educator; d. William Robert and Mary Paterson Thomson Zimmerman; m. Alan Bartky Marsh, Oct. 12, 1980; children: Alexander, Natalie. AA, Ill. Valley C.C., Oglesby, Ill., 1978; BA in English, North Ctrl. Coll., Naperville, Ill., 1983; MA in English, No. Ill. U., DeKalb, 1996, doctoral student, 1997—. Acad. team coach Rutland Grade Sch., Ottawa, 1996—; substitute tchr. LaSalle County Schs., 1996—; instr. English Ill. Valley C.C., Oglesby, 2001—02. Mem. sch. bd., v.p. Rutland Grade Sch., Ottawa, 1993—2002; sec. bd. dirs. Rutland Grade Sch. Found., 1997—2002. Mem.: MLA, Ill. Assn. Tchrs. English, Nat. Coun. Tchrs. English, Assn. Study Am. Indian Lits., Sigma Tau Delta. Avocations: Okinawan Shuri-ryu Karatedo (3rd degree black belt), Shorei-Goju Karatedo (3rd degree brown belt). Home: 2275 N 3559th Rd Ottawa IL 61350 Office: Dept English No Ill U Dekalb IL 60115 Personal E-mail: marsh@theramp.net. E-mail: jmarsh1@niu.edu.

MARSH, JOAN KNIGHT, educational film, video and computer software company executive, publisher children's books; b. Apr. 8, 1934; d. E. Lyle and Ruth (Hopkins) Knight; m. Alan Reid Marsh, Sept. 27, 1958; children: Alan Reid, Clayton Knight. BA, Tex. Tech U., 1956. Owner, pres. MarshMedia, Kansas City, Mo., 1969—. Mem. ctrl. governing bd. Children's Mercy Hosp., 1996—; mem. coun. Family Study Ctr., U. Mo., Kansas City, 1983-89, Children's Relief Assn. Mercy Hosp., Kansas City, 1984—, pres., 1989-91; pres. Friends of Children's Mercy Hosp., 1996-98; chmn. The Jewel Ball, 1997, Great Ball of China II, 1999. Mem. Jr. League (sustaining chmn. 1982-84, Cmty. Svc. award 1999), Gamma Phi Beta. Republican. Presbyterian. Avocations: Egyptology, filmology.

MARSH, JOSEPH VIRGIL, commercial real estate and investment broker; b. Winston-Salem, N.C., Apr. 28, 1952; s. Gilliam Hughes and Dovie Elizabeth (Watson) M. Student, Surry C.C., 1970-72; student coop. engring. program, U.S. Govt. Schs., Md., S.C., Washington, 1972-74; BSEE, U. Md., 1976; grad., N.Y. Inst. Fin., 1978, NYU, 1978, MBA, 1980. Comml. real estate broker, N.C. With Joint Armed Svcs. Tech. Liaison, Washington, 1974-75; cons. U.S. Govt., 1975-76; corr., cons. individuals, bus. on tech. matters Ararat, N.C., 1977—. Registered adviser SEC, 1981-2000, ret. Active U.S. Presdl. Task Force, 1981-2000; tech. liaison NASA, 1992; founder The Marsh Found., 1989. Recipient Presdl. Medal of Merit Pres. of U.S., 1988, 90. Mem. Internat. Entrepreneurs Assn., VFW (hon.), Armed Forces Assn., Ind. Cons. Assn., Internat. Assn. Sci. Devel., Coun. Civilian Tech. Advisers. Republican. Office: Hwy 2019/2026 Ararat NC 27007-0120 Fax: 336-374-4405.

MARSH, JOSEPH FRANKLIN, JR. emeritus college president, educational consultant; b. Charleston, W.Va., Feb. 24, 1925; s. Joseph Franklin and Florence (Keller) M. Student, Concord Coll., 1941-42, W.Va. U., 1942-43; AB, Dartmouth Coll., 1947; student, Nat. Inst. Pub. Affairs, Washington, 1947-48; M.P.A., Harvard U., 1949; LL.D., Davis and Elkins Coll., 1968; L.H.D., Alderson-Broaddus Coll., 1982. Cons. Hoover Commn., Washington, 1948; instr. in gt. issues Dartmouth, 1952—54, instr. econs., 1953—55, asst. prof., 1955—59; pres. Concord Coll., Athens, W.Va., 1959—73, pres. emeritus, 1985—; ednl. cons., 1973—74; pres. Waynesburg (Pa.) Coll., 1974—83, pres. emeritus, 1983—; v.p. The Armand Hammer United World Coll. of the Am. West, Montezuma, N.Mex., 1984—85; pres. Marsh Edn Cons., Athens, W.Va., 1985—. Dir. One Valley Bank of Mercer County, 1987-98, hon. dir., 1998-2000. Author articles. Mem. State Dept. Ednl. Mission to U.A.R., 1964, Mercer County (W.Va.) Planning Commn., 1964-74, 83-94, hon., 1994—; vice chmn. W.Va. Com. for Constnl. Amendments, 1966; mem. regional coun. Internat. Edn. Study Mission to Europe, 1970; bd. dirs. Am. Assn. State Colls. and Univs., 1972-73, Regional Coun. for Internat. Edn., 1973, Hospice Care Mercer County, W.Va., 1987-91, Faculty Merit Found. W.Va., 1990—, Greater Mercer County Charitable Found., Inc., W.Va., 1998--, exec. com. 2001-, chmn., pres., 1998-2001; bd. dirs. Pa. Assn. Colls. and Univs., 1974-83, exec. com., 1980-82; bd. dirs. Pa. Commn. for Ind. Colls. and Univs., 1974-83, sec.-treas., 1976-77, vice chmn., 1977-80, chmn., 1980-82; trustee Found. Ind. Colls. Pa., 1974-83, mem. exec. com., 1979-82; bd. visitors Midway Coll., Ky., 1979-93; adv. com. Pa. State Coun. Higher Edn., 1980-82; trustee Concord Coll. Found., 1986, bd. dirs., 1987—; active Town of Athens Planning Commn., 1986-94, pres. commn. 1987-94; bd. trustees, Princeton (W.Va.) Cmty. Hosp. Found., 1989-98, vice chmn., 1989-97; Gov's. appointee to bd. dirs. State Coll. System W.Va., 1989-96, chmn. adminstrv. com., 1990-91, vice chmn. of bd., 1991-95, chmn., 1995-96; gov.'s appointee to the W.Va. Parkways, Econ. Devel. and Tourism Authority, 1998—, Edn. Commn. of the states, 1998-2002. Served as gunnery officer USNR, 1943-46. Named Outstanding Young Man, W.Va. Jr. C. of C., 1960; recipient Alumnus of Yr. award Concord Coll., 1973, Golden Alumnus award, 1992, Outstanding Alumnus award for Career Achievement, 1996; Outstanding Citizen award Athens Woman's Club, 1992, Total Community Involvement Award, Town of Athens, WV, 2001; Rotary fellow Oxford (Eng.) U., 1950-52. Mem. AAUP, Am. Assn. Univ. Adminstrs., Am. Econ. Assn., Royal Inst. Pub. Adminstrn., Oxford Union Debating Soc. (life), Oxford Soc. (life), Pa. Soc., Duquesne Club (Pitts.), Univ. Club (Bluefield), Masons, Rotary (dist. gov. 1992-93), The Guild of Carillonneurs N.Am. (hon.), Phi Beta Kappa, Phi Tau, Phi Delta Pi, Phi Sigma Kappa, Alpha Kappa Psi (hon.). Methodist. Home: 106 First Ave Athens WV 24712 Office: PO Box 734 Athens WV 24712-0734

MARSH, LEONARD ROY, lawyer; b. Watertown, N.Y., May 21, 1928; s. Roy Leonard and Ruby May Marsh; married; children: Jeffrey, Peter, Melissa. BS in Bus., U. Buffalo, 1953; JD, Syracuse U., 1956. Bar: N.Y. 1957. Lectr., instr. numerous magistrate and police schs. and orgns.; former asst. dist. atty. Jefferson County, N.Y.; former adminstr. Indigent Defendant Program, Jefferson County. Former dir. March of Dimes, Watertown, Family Counseling Svc., Watertown, United Fund, Watertown. Sgt. USAF, 1946-49. Mem.: ABA, Jefferson County Bar Assn., NY State Bar Assn. Nazarene. Home: 1325 Holcomb St Watertown NY 13601-4419 Office: Renee Renzi Law Office 1201 Washington St Watertown NY 13601-4339 E-mail: lenm@capital.net.

MARSH, MALCOLM F. federal judge; b. Portland, Oreg., Sept. 24, 1928; m. Shari Marsh. BS, U. Oreg., 1952, LLB, 1954, JD, 1971. Bar: Oreg. 1954, U.S. Dist. Ct. Oreg. 1955, U.S. Ct. Appeals (9th cir.) 1968. Ptnr. Clark & Marsh, Lindauer & McClinton (and predecessors), Salem, Oreg., 1954-87; judge U.S. Dist. Ct. Oreg., Portland, 1987—98, sr. judge, 1998—. With U.S. Army, 1946-47. Fellow Am. Coll. Trial Lawyers; mem. ABA, Oreg. Bar Assn. Office: US Dist Ct 1507 US Courthouse 1000 SW 3d Ave Portland OR 97204

MARSH, MALCOLM ROY, JR. electronics engineer; b. Bedford, Va., Oct. 12, 1932; s. Malcolm Roy and Mildred (Overstreet) M.; BEE, U. Va., 1956; children: Lauranne Ashton, James Overstreet. Elec. engr. Sperry Piedmont, Inc., Charlottesville, Va., 1957-58, Martin Orlando Co., Orlando, Fla., 1958-60; electronic engring. cons., Orlando, 1960—. Served with U.S. Army, 1958. Mem. IEEE. Methodist. Home and Office: 2609 Tradewinds Trail Orlando FL 32805-5840

MARSH, MARTHA, hospital administrator; BS, U. Rochester; MPH, MBA, Columbia U. Pres. and CEO Matthew Thornton Health Plan, Dartmouth-Hitchcock Med. Ctr., 1986—94; sr. v.p., profl. svcs. and managed care and v.p, managed care U. Pa. Health Sys., 1994—98; dir. U. Calif.-Davis Health Care Sys., 1998—2001; pres. and CEO Stanford (Conn.) Hosp. and Clinics, 2002—. Office: Stanford Hosp 300 Pasteur Dr Ste H3200 Stanford CA 94305*

MARSH, MARY ELIZABETH TAYLOR, recreation administrator, dietician, nutritionist; b. Medina, N.Y., Dec. 10, 1933; d. Glenn Aaron and Viola Hazel (Lansill) Grimes; m. Wilbur Alvin Fredlund, Apr. 12, 1952 (div. Jan. 1980); 1 child, Wilbur Jr.; m. Frederick Herbert Taylor, Mar. 15, 1981 (dec. Dec. 1996); children: Martha Dayton, Jean Grout, Beth Stern, Cindy Hey, Carol McLellan, Cheryl Dearborn, Robert, Marilyn Ridens, Janice Emory, Gordon Marsh, Margaret Hana; m. Earl R. Marsh, Apr. 4, 1998. BS in Food and Nutrition, SUCB, Buffalo, 1973; MEd in Health Sci. Edn. and Evaluation, SUNY, 1978. Registered dietitian, 1977. Diet cook Niagara Sanitorium, Lockport, N.Y., 1953-56; cook Mount View Hosp., 1956-60, asst. dietician, 1960-73, dietician, food svc. dir., 1973-79, cons. dietician, 1979-81; instr. Erie Community Coll., Williamsville, 1979-81; sch. lunch coord. Nye County Sch. Dist., Tonopah, Nev., 1982-93, retired, 1993; food svc. mgmt. cons., fin. mgmt. advisor pvt. practice, 1994—; activity dir. Preferred Equity Corp. Recreation Vehicle Resort, Pahrump, Nev., 1993-95; tchr. maturing body and nutrition Nev. Cmty. Coll., Fall 1997; nutritionist Equal Opportunity Bd. Clark County, Las Vegas, 1997-2000; ind. travel agt. Hello World Travel, 2001—; activity dir. Preferred R.V. Resort, 2001—. Cons. dietitian Nye Gen. Hosp., Tonopah, 1983-88; adj. instr. Erie C.C., Williamsville, 1978-79, So. Nev. C.C., 1997; nutrition instr. for coop. extension Clark County C.C., 1990—; cons. Group Purchasing Western N.Y. Hosp. Adminstr., Buffalo, 1975-79, vice-chmn. adv. com., 1976-78; cons. BOCES, Lockport, 1979-81. Nutrition counselor Migrant Workers Clinic, Lockports, 1974-80; mem. Western N.Y. Soc. for Hosp. Food Svc. Adminstrn., 1974-81; nutritionist Niagara County Nutrition Adv. Com., 1977-81; mem. Helping Hands, Pahrump, 1997—; nutritionist Equal Opportunity Bd. Clark Conty, 1997-2000; activity dir. Perfered Equities RV Resort, 2001-. Recipient Outstanding Woman of the Yr., YWCA-UAW Lockport, 1981, Disting. Health Care Food Adminstrn. Recognition award Am. Soc. for Hosp. Food Svc. Adminstrs., 1979, USDA award Outstanding Lunch Program in Nev. and Western Region, 1986, 91. Mem. Am. Assn. Ret. Persons, Am. Sch. Food Svc. Assn. (bd. dirs. 1987, 92-93, cert. dir. II 1987, 5-yr. planning com. 1990, mem. ann. confs. 1988-93), Am. Dietetic Assn. (nat. referral system for registered dietitians 1992-93), So. Nev. Dietetic Assn. (pres. 1985-86), Nev. Food Svc. Assn. (participant ann. meetings 1990-93), Nutrition Today Soc., Nev. Sch. Food Svcs. Assn. (dietary guidelines com. 1991-93), Pahrump Kawians. Republican. Lutheran. Avocations: travel, knitting, crocheting, sewing. Home: 481 N Murphy St Pahrump NV 89060-3851 E-mail: mrshtrvl@usintouch.com.

MARSH, MERRILYN DELANO, sculptor, painter; b. Larchmont, N.Y., Dec. 26, 1923; d. Merrill Potter and Hazel (Holmes) Delano; m. George Estabrook Marsh, Sept. 18, 1954; children: Merrill Delano, George Estabrook Jr., Robert Houston. Diploma, Sch. of Mus. of Fine Arts, Boston, 1947; postgrad., Acad. Grande Chaumière, Paris, 1947-48. Art tchr. Choate Sch., Brookline, Mass., 1948, 49, Brookline Cmty. Ctr., 1948, 49; pvt. art tchr. Newton, Mass., 1948-49; comml. sculptor for display and mfg. cos., 1948-55; sculpture tchr. De Cordova Mus., Lincoln, Mass., 1950-54. Juror for numerous art exhbns., New Eng. area, 1954-55, 72-74. One-woman show at Copley Soc. of Boston, 1996; commd. 7 reliefs for Sch. for Environ., Levine Sci. Ctr., Duke U., Durham, N.C., 1994, bronze statue for cloister garden St. Andrew's Episcopal Ch., Wellesley, Mass., 1995, bronze portrait reliefs for Houston and Sargent Athletic awards Tufts U., Medford, Mass., 1997, 2 bronze reliefs, Ellis Oval Athletic Field Tufts U., 2001, bronze portrait relief of Clarence P. "Pop" Houston, Houston Hall, Tufts U., 1965, others. Mrs. David Hunt Sculpture scholar Mus. Fine Arts, 1947; recipient Katherine Thayer Hobson award Pen and Brush Soc., 1991, Best in Show award Juliani Gallery, 1991, Pres.'s Cup award for golf Wellesley (Mass.) Country Club, 1998. Mem. Copley Soc. Boston (Copley master, Maria Maravigna award 1988, 1st prize in sculpture and large works 1994, other awards, 1983, 89), New Eng. Sculptors Assn. (bd. dirs. 1986, award 1988), Wellesley Soc. Artists (awards 1985, 87, 89, 91-92, 95, 2001-02, bd. dirs. 1970, 88—), Cambridge Art Assn. (Jack Schultz award, 2000, other awards 1993-94). Republican. Episcopalian.

MARSH, MICHAEL LAWRENCE, track and field athlete; b. Hawthorne, Calif., Aug. 4, 1967; Grad., UCLA, 1989. Olympic runner, Barcelona, Spain, 1992. Recipient 200m Track and Field Gold medal, Olympics, Barcelona, 1992, 1st USA outdoor 200m, 1993, 1st USA outdoor 100m, 1995. Office: US Track and Field 1 Rca Dome Ste 140 Indianapolis IN 46225-1023

MARSH, NELSON LEROY, military officer; b. Ft. Worth, Sept. 27, 1937; s. Edward Donald and Joyce Estelle (Taif) M.; m. Janice Ferguson, Nov. 20, 1960 (div. 1965); m. Anne Schreiweis, Sept. 6, 1966; children: Michele Maria, Sharon Catherine, Glenn Edward. BA, Tex. Christian U., 1959; LLB, LaSalle U., Chgo., 1973; cert., Nat. War Coll., 1980, Army Command & Gen. Staff Coll, 1973. Commd. 2nd lt. U.S. Army, 1959, advanced through grades to col., 1979, office dep. dir. office of chief of pers., 1965-68, div. personnel officer 101st Airborne Div. Bien Hoa, Vietnam, 1968-69, adjutant gen. 3rd infantry div. Wuerzburg, Fed. Republic of Germany, 1969-72, comdr. 3d infantry div. Rear, editor in chief Soldiers Mag. Alexandria, Va., 1973-75, commdr. various battalions Chgo., Frankfurt, 1975-79, dir. various offices Washington, San Antonio, 1980-86, dir. Army/Air Force News Service San Antonio, 1986-89. Owner NLM Income Tax Svc., San Antonio, 1987-95; bd. dirs. Bright Eyes Vision, Starbuck Svc., Inc.; pres., CEO NLM Tax Svc. Inc., 1995—. Author, editor: Army Enlisted Management, 1965; contbr. articles to mags. and newspapers. Pres. Armed Forces Pub. Affairs Coun., San Antonio, 1987-88. Decorated Bronze Star (3 awards), Legion of Merit (5 awards), Meritorious Svc. medal (3 awards), Army Commendation medal (5 awards). Mem. Order of Mil. Med. Merit, Tex. Christian U. Alumni Assn., VFW, Phi Alpha Theta. Democrat. Presbyterian. Avocations: computers, war games, baseball, chess. Home: 18003 Green Knls San Antonio TX 78258-3418 E-mail: NMarsh5339@aol.com.

MARSH, ROBERT BUFORD, chemical engineer, consultant; b. Chgo., Nov. 16, 1946; s. Ivar Buford and Blanche Julien (Morrisette) M.; m. Claudia Ann Werner, Feb. 14, 1970; children: Julie Ann, Kristy Louise. BSChemE, Mich. Tech. U., 1968. Registered profl. engr., Mass. Engr. 1 design engr. Chevron Rsch., Richmond, Calif., 1968-70, tech. svc. engr., 1970-73; lustrex supr. Monsanto, Long Beach, 1973-78, mfg. supr. Everett, Mass., 1978-83, environ. engr., 1984-85, mfg. tech. specialist, 1986-91, worldwide plasticizer tech. expert engring. specialist Everett, Indian Orchard, 1992-93; pres. Marsh Engr., Inc., Andover, 1992—. Environ. instr., U. Mass., 1994; cons. Mass. Dept. Environ. Protection, Lowell, 1993-94; cons. EPA Rsch. grant, 1994; speaker in field. Adv., co. leady Jr. Achievement, Long Beach, 1975-77; vol. Andover Sch. System, 1983-84, Chicopee River Watershed Assn., Springfield, Mass., 1993, Shawsheen River Watershed Assn., Tewksbury, Mass., 1994, 98; election com. State Senator O'Brien com., 1994-97, State Senator Tucker, 1998; mem. Andover Citizen Environ. Com. Independent. Methodist. Achievements include rsch. in ammonia-Hydrogen Sulfide Equilibrium in the 10-50% range. Avocations: reading, camping, tennis, swimming, stock market. Home: 8 Mulberry Cir Andover MA 01810-3231 Office: Marsh Engring Inc 8 Mulberry St Andover MA 01810-0804

MARSH, ROBERT HARRY, chemical company executive; b. Camden, N.J., Sept. 6, 1946; s. Harry Louis and Margaret Charlotte (Starke) M.; m. Margaret Sammartino, Mar. 21, 1970. BA, BS in Mech. Engring., Rutgers U., 1969; MBA in Mgmt. and Fin., Temple U., 1980. Registered profl. engr., N.J., Pa., Del. From mech. engr. to mech. specialist and project engr. Rohm & Haas Engring., Bristol, Pa., 1969-76; from staff engr. to sr. engring. specialist Hercules, Inc., Wilmington, Del., 1976-80, sr. fin. analyst for corp. strategic planning, 1980-81, sr. bus. analyst bus. group, 1982-83; mgr. bus. analysis Himont, Inc., 1983-86, dir. strategy and planning, 1986-88, dir. bus. mgmt., 1988-91, mng. dir. China, 1991-95, dir. strategy, 1991-95; prin. Marsh & Assocs., 1995. Founder, bd. dirs. various news cos. Contbr. articles to profl. jours. Active Haddonfield (N.J.) Civic Affairs. Mem.: NSPE, ASME (nat. power com. 1977—84, vice chmn. awards com. 1980, membership chmn. 1982), Engrs. Club Phila., Pyramid Club Phila., Beta Gamma Sigma. Home: 225 Flagstone Dr Bethlehem PA 18017

MARSH, ROBERT MORTIMER, sociologist, educator; b. Everett, Mass., Jan. 22, 1931; s. Henry Warren and Ruth (Dunbar) M.; children: Eleanor L., Christopher S.H., Diana E. Student, Boston U., 1948-50; AB, U. Chgo., 1952; MA, Columbia, 1953, PhD, 1959. Fellow Ford Found., Japan, Taiwan, Hong Kong, 1956-58; instr. sociology U. Mich., 1958-61; asst. prof. sociology Cornell U., 1961-65; asso. prof. Duke, 1965-67; mem. faculty Brown U., 1967—, prof. sociology, 1968—, chmn. dept., 1971-75. Manpower personnel and tng. rsch. prof. U.S. Naval Acad., Annapolis, 1987-88; vis. prof. Nat. Tsing Hua U., Taiwan, 1991. Author: The Mandarins: The Circulation of Elites in China, 1961, Comparative Sociology: A Codification of Cross-Societal Analysis, 1967; (with H. Mannari) Modernization and the Japanese Factory, 1976, Organizational Change in Japanese Factories, 1988, The Great Transformation: Social Change in Taipei, Taiwan Since the 1960s, 1996; also articles; assoc. editor Adminstrv. Sci. Quar., 1963-67, Jour. Comparative Family Studies, 1970-74; co-editor: (with J. Michael Armer) Comparative Sociological Research in the 1960s and 1970s. East Asian Inst. summer fellow Chinese Columbia, 1955; Ford Found. and Guggenheim Found. fellow Japan, 1969-70; Japan Soc. Promotion Sci. fellow, 1976, 83; Chiang Ching Kuo Found. and Nat. Sci. Coun. fellow (Taiwan, Republic of China). 1991-93. Mem. Am.

Sociol. Assn., Ea. Sociol. Assn., Assn. Asian Studies, Internat. Studies Assn. (exec. com. comparative interdisciplinary studies sect. 1971-76), Japan Human Rels. Assn. (councilor 1970—). Office: Dept Sociology Brown Univ Providence RI 02912-0001 E-mail: robert_marsh@brown.edu.

MARSH, SUE ANN, special education educator; b. Marshall, Tex., Dec. 5, 1949; d. Orman and Della Florence (Floyd) M. BS in Edn., Stephen F. Austin State U., Nacogdoches, Tex., 1971, MEd, 1975. Cert. elem. tchr., reading tchr., spl. edn. in mental retardation, Tex. Tchr. Title 45 Dickinson (Tex.) Ind. Sch. Dist., 1971, tchr. Title I, 1971-72; tchr. trainable mentally retarded Conroe (Tex.) Ind. Sch. Dist., 1972-85, tchr. Option III, 1985—. Coach, asst. coach Vol. Spl. Olympics, Conroe, 1973—, advt. chmn for golf tournament, 1989-90. Editor: Almost Reader Series. Leader for mentally retarded boys and girls Boy Scouts Am., Conroe, 1990—; chmn. Crockett Cougars Year Book Advertisement 50th Anniversary Edit. Named Crockett Intermediate Tchr. of Yr., 1992; recipient Sam Houston Disting. Scouting award of merit, 1993, Sam Houston Disting. Scouting award of Merit, 1996; co-recipient State Centennial Farm award, Career Ladder, 1984-93. Mem. Assn. Tex. Profl. Educators (bldg. rep. 1983—), Classroom Tchrs. Assn. (bldg. rep. 1975-78), Floyd Family Assn. (sec.-treas. Plantersville, Tex.), River Plantation Lions (camp chmn. 1990-94, chmn. attendance 1990-91, bd. dirs. 1990-96, 3rd v.p. 1992-93, 2nd v.p. 1993-94, v.p. 1994-95, pres. 1995-96, treas. 1996). Democrat. Baptist. Avocations: travel, needlecrafts, plays, concerts. Office: Wash Intermediate Sch 507 Avenue K Conroe TX 77301-3881

MARSHAK, ALAN HOWARD, electrical engineer, educator; b. Miami Beach, Fla., Mar. 21, 1938; s. Jerome and Yetta (Feiner) M.; children: Jerry Brian; m. Joan Grode Milner, May 25, 1997. BScEE, U. Miami, 1960; MS, La. State U., 1962; PhD, U. Ariz., 1969. Asst. prof. elec. engring. La. State U., Baton Rouge, 1969-73, assoc. prof., 1973-78, prof., 1978—2002, chmn. dept. elec. and computer engring., 1983—2002, prof. emeritus, 2002—. Vis. prof. Electron Device Rsch. Ctr., U. Fla., Gainesville, 1979-80; tech. reviewer NSF, 1976—, panelist, 1993-96; panelist NRC, 1993, 2001; mem. Southeastern Ctr. Elec. Engring. Edn., 1984—, chmn., CEO, 1992-2001, trustee, 1994--; spkr. profl. confs. Tech. referee various jours. including Solid-State Electronics, Jour. Applied Physics; editor: Device and Process Modeling, IEEE Trans. Electron Devices, 1991-2001; author: (with D. J. Hamilton and F. A. Lindholm) Principles and Applications of Semiconductor Device Modeling, 1971, Basic Experiments in Electronics: A Laboratory Manual, 1978, also tech. papers. NSF grad. trainee, 1967-69; grantee, 1970, 73, 75, 78; named F.H. Coughlin/CLECO prof. of elec. engring., 1993. Fellow IEEE; mem. Electron Devices Soc., Sigma Xi, Eta Kappa Nu. Home: 113 Clipper Cove Lafayette LA 70508-7023

MARSHAK, HILARY WALLACH, psychotherapist, owner, small business owner; b. N.Y.C., May 27, 1950; d. Irving Isaac and Suni (Fox) Wallach; m. Harvey Marshak, Jan. 1, 1981; children: Emily Fox, Jacob Randall. BA, U. Conn., Storrs, 1973; MSW, N.Y.U., 1992; cert., Inst. for Study of Culture, and Ethnicity, N.Y.C., 1994. Cert. social worker, N.Y.; Qualified Clin. Social Worker, 1999. Tchr. English. Glastonbury (Conn.) H.S., 1973; instr. English, U. Autonoma de Guerrero, Acapulco, Mexico, 1974; administrv. asst. 4M Pub. Svcs. Corp., N.Y.C., 1975, bus. mgr.; exec. v.p. Vitalmedia Enterprises Inc., 1977-87, pres., CEO, 1987-2001; psychotherapist Fifth Avenue Ctr. Counseling and Psychotherapy, 1992-95; pvt. practice, 1992—; co-dir. Inst. for Advanced Thinking, 2000—. Mktg. cons. Frana Ltd., London, 1988-89; infertility counselor; v.p. Think Impossible, 2000—. Editor: Before the Bar, 1978-80, Guide to Higher Edn., 1980; reviewer vol 32, The Jour. of Sex Rsch. Founder Women's Radical Caucus, U. Conn., 1970; broadcaster Sta. WHUS; bd. dirs. N.Y. Theater Ballet, 1990—, Am. AIDS Assn., 1992-97; mem. writers coun. Writers in Performance series Manhattan Theater Club. Recipient 2nd Place Flowers Ulster County Agrl. Fair, New Paltz, N.Y., 1987, 1st Place Herbs, 1988. Mem. NASW (qualified clin. social worker), Soc. for Sci. Study of Sex, Sex Edn. and Info. Coun. of U.S., Nat. Coun. Family Rels., Am. Infertility Assn., Am. Soc. for Reproductive Medicine, Resolve. Jewish. Avocations: gardening, birdwatching, cooking, reading. Home and Office: 41 River Terrace #1706 New York NY 10282

MARSHAK, MARVIN LLOYD, physicist, educator; b. Mar. 11, 1946; s. Kalman and Goldie (Hait) M.; m. Anita Sue Kolman, Sept. 24, 1972; children: Rachel Kolman, Adam Kolman. AB in Physics, Cornell U., 1967; MS in Physics, U. Mich., PhD in Physics, 1970. Rsch. assoc. U. Minn., Mpls., 1970-74, from asst. prof. to assoc. prof., 1974-83, prof. physics, 1983-96, dir. grad. studies in physics, 1983-86, prin. investigator high energy physics, 1982-86, head Sch. Physics and Astronomy, 1986-96, sr. v.p. for acad. affairs, 1996-97, Morse-Alumni disting. tchg. prof. physics, 1996—, dir. residential coll., 1997—, faculty legis. liason, 1997—2001. Contbr. articles to profl. jours. Trustee Children's Theater Co., 1989-94. Mem. Am. Phys. Soc. Home: 2855 Ottawa Ave S Minneapolis MN 55416-1946 E-mail: marshak@umn.edu.

MARSHAK, ROBERT REUBEN, former university dean, medical educator, veterinarian; b. N.Y.C., Feb. 23, 1923; s. David and Edith (Youselovsky) Marshak; m. Ruth Emilie Lyons, Dec. 4, 1948; children: William Lyons, John Ball, Richard Best; m. Margo Post Marshall, June 25, 1983. Student, U. Wis., 1940—41; DVM, Cornell U., 1945, U. Bern, 1968; MA (hon.) , U. Pa., 1971. Diplomate Am. Coll. Vet. Internal Medicine (charter). Practice vet. medicine, Springfield, Vt., 1945—56; prof., chmn. dept medicine Sch. Vet. Medicine, U. Pa., Phila., 1956—58; prof. medicine Grad. Sch. Medicine, 1957—64; chmn. dept. clin. studies Sch. Vet. Medicine, 1958—73; dir. Bovine Leukemia Research Center, 1965—73; dean Sch. Vet. Medicine, 1973—87; co-dir. Center on Interactions Animals and Soc., 1975—79, also mem. grad. group com. in comparative med. scis.; prof. medicine, chief sect. epidemiology and pub. health Sch. Vet. Medicine U. Pa., 1990—93, prof. medicine emeritus, 1993—. Mem. adv. bd. Pa. Dept. Agr., 1973—87; chmn. Gov.'s STudy Group on Horse Racing Industry in Pa., 1979; mem. del. to evaluate vet. med. and rsch. Chinese Ministry Agr.; mem. adv. com. Stround Water Rsch. Ctr., 1992—; mem. adv. coun. Coll. Vet. Medicine, Cornell U., 1993—. Sr. co-editor: Advances in Veterinary Science and Comparative Medicine; contbr. numerous articles to sci. jours. Mem. sci. adv. bd. Sch. Vet. Medicine The Hebrew U., Jerusalem, 1984—, mem. rev. com., 1997—; chmn. external com. Sch. Vet. Medicine Tuskegee U.; trustee Upland Country Day Sch., 1988—91; mem. animal adv. com. City of Phila., 1989—93; mem. Pres.'s Rev. Com. Korest Sch. Vet. Medicine Hebrew U. Jerusalem, 1997—98; bd. dirs. Humane Soc. U.S., 1978—82, Bide-a-wee Home Assn., 1980—85. With U.S. Army, 1943—44. Recipient Disting. Vet. award, Pa. Vet. Med. Assn., 1984, Barn-raiser award, Pa. Farmers Assn., 1987. Fellow: Phila. Coll. Physicians; mem.: AAAS, NAS Inst. Medicine (sr.), Pa. Livestock Assn. (dir.), Pa. Vet. Med. Assn., Am. Vet. Med. Assn., Am. Assn. Cancer Rsch., John Morgan Soc. (pres. 1967—68), Phila. Zool. Soc. (bd. dirs. 1986—87), Phila. Soc. for Promoting, James A. Baker Inst. for Animal Health (mem. adv. coun. 1977—), Pa. Friends Agr. Found., Westminster Kennel Club, Phi Zeta, Sigma Xi. E-mail: rmarshak@uchicago.edu.

MARSHALL, ALAN GEORGE, chemistry and biochemistry educator; b. Bluffton, Ohio, May 26, 1944; s. Herbert Boyer Marshall Jr. and Cecile (Mogil) Rosser; m. Marilyn Gard, June 13, 1965; children: Gwendolyn Scott, Brian George. BA in Chemistry with honors, Northwestern U., 1965; PhD in Phys. Chemistry, Stanford U., 1970. Instr. II U. B.C., Vancouver, Can., 1969-71, asst. prof. Can., 1971-76, assoc. prof. Can., 1976-80; prof. chemistry and biochemistry Ohio State U., Columbus, 1980-93; prof. chemistry Fla. State U., Tallahassee, 1993-2000, Kasha prof., 2000—. Cons. Extrel FTMS, Madison, Wis., 1989-92, Oak Ridge (Tenn.) Nat. Lab., 1990—; dir. ion Cyclotron Resonance Program Nat. High Magnetic Field Lab. Author: Biophysical Chemistry, 1978, Fourier Transforms in Spectroscopy, 1990; editor: ICR/ION Trap newsletter, 1986—, Rapid Comm. on Mass Spectrometry, 1988—; mem. editl. bd.: Analytical Chemistry, 1990—92, mem. editl. bd.: Internat. Jour. Mass Ion Procs., 1987—, mem. editl. bd.: Jour. Am. Soc. Mass Spectrometry, 1989—97; mem. editl. bd. (jour.) Jour. Am. Soc. Mass Spectrometry, 2001—; mem. editl. bd.: Mass Spectrometry Rev., 1994—, mem. editl. bd.: Jour. Magnetic Resonance, 1995—98; contbr. more than 335 articles to profl. jours. Recipient Disting. Scholar award Ohio State U., 1988, Maurice F. Hasler award Spectroscopy Soc. Pitts., 1997, gold medal N.Y. Soc. Applied Spectroscopy, 1998, Pitts. Spectroscopy award Spectroscopy Soc. Pitts., 2002. Fellow: AAAS, Am. Phys. Soc.; mem.: Am. Soc. Mass Spectroscopy (bd. dirs. 1991—92, 2002—, Disting. Contbn. award 1999), Soc. Applied Spectroscopy (chmn. local sect. 1990—91), Am. Chem. Soc. (award in analytical chemistry 2002, award in chem. instrumentation, Akron sect. award, Frank H. Field and Joe L. Franklin award 1995), Internat. Mass Spectrum Soc. (Thomson medal 2002). Office: Fla State Univ Nat High Magnetic Field Lab 1800 E Paul Dirac Dr Tallahassee FL 32310-3748

MARSHALL, ALLEN WRIGHT, III, communications executive, financial consultant; b. Griffin, Ga., Dec. 4, 1941; s. Allen Wright Jr. and Evelyn Louise (Halliburton) M.; m. Carole Anne Moore, Dec. 24, 1964; 1 child, Allen Wright IV. BA in Journalism, U. Ga., 1964; diploma, Elkins Inst. Radio, Atlanta, 1964; postgrad., Ga. State U., 1968, MBA, 1988; cert., Coll. Fin. Planning, Denver, 1991. 1st class radio telephone lic. FCC; cert. fin. planner. Pres. Sta. WKEU-AM-FM, Griffin, 1954-86; co-founder, v.p. Griffin Cable TV, 1971-74; co-founder, pres. Custom Svcs. Inc. (now Marshall Plans Inc.), Griffin, 1974—; co-founder, v.p. Cobbwells Marshall Inc., 1982-87, Page One, Griffin, 1983-87; co-founder, pres. Toolware Inc., 1993-97; co-founder, sec./treas. Magnolia Broadcasting Inc., laGrange, Ga., 1993-95; founder, mng. mem. Spalding Speculators LLC, Griffin, 1995—. Bd. dirs. First Union Nat. Bank, Griffin, Face Internat. Corp., Norfolk, Va.; spkr. in field. Author radio progrms, editorials (Ga. AP award 1969-84); also articles. Bd. dirs. Goals for Griffin and Spalding Counties INc., 1981-92, pres. 1991; mem. adv. com. Griffin Vocat.-Tech. Sch., 1982-87; bd. dirs. Jr. Achievement, Griffin, 1977-87; chmn. Griffin-Spalding Indsl. Authority, 1984; mem. Gov.'s Adv. Com. on Area Planning and Devel. Commns., 1971-72; bd. dirs. McIntosh Trail Area Planning and Devel. Commn., Ga., 1971-73; founding trustee, vice chair, dir. St. George's Episc. Sch., 1995-2001; treas., trustee Nat. Episc. Radio/TV Found., 1986-93. Sgt. U.S. Army, 1966-68. Named Man of Yr., Exch. Club of Griffin, 1984. Mem. Ga. Assn. Broadcasters 9bd. dirs. 1970-74, Radio Sta. of Yr. 1977), Griffin Area C. of C. (bd. dirs. 1980, chmn. indsl. com. 1980, 81), C.C. (charter mem. 1966), Rotary (pres. 1976-77). Avocations: photography, landscape design, archtl. renovation. Home and Office: 1800 Maple Dr Griffin GA 30224-7405

MARSHALL, ALTON GARWOOD, real estate counselor; b. Flint, Mich., Sept. 19, 1921; s. William Robert and Lela Christine (Brabon) M.; m. Mary Lee Golden, June 22, 1945 (div. July 1971); children: William A., Stephen B., Bruce S., Mary Ann Marshall Trebian, John L.; m. Sarah Elizabeth DeLand, Sept. 4, 1971; 1 child, Sarah Graham. BA, Hillsdale Coll., 1942; MS, Syracuse U., 1948, LLD (hon.), 1974; D Pub. Service & Bus. Adminstrn. (hon.), Hillsdale Coll., 1980. Sec. utility regulations pub. svc. commn. N.Y. State, Albany, 1953-61, dep. dir. div. budget, 1961-65, exec. officer, then sec. to gov., Office of Gov., 1965-70; pres., bd. dirs. Rockefeller Ctr., N.Y.C., 1971-81; pres. A.G. Marshall Assocs., 1981—; chmn., pres., chief exec. officer Lincoln Savs. Bank, 1984-88, chmn., chief exec. officer, 1988-91, also bd. dirs. Mem. exec. com. Nat. Realty Com., Washington, 1970-99; bd. dirs. N.Y. State Electric & Gas Corp., 1971-98; ind. gen. ptnr. Equitable Capital Ptnrs. and Equitable Capital Ptnrs. Retirement Fund, 1989-99; trustee Hudson River Trust, 1991-97. Mem. exec. com., steering com. Assn. for a Better N.Y., 1971—; mem. exec., landmarks and polit. action coms. Real Estate Bd. N.Y.; chmn. Nat. Assn. on Drug Abuse Problems, 1990-92. Sr. fellow The Nelson A. Rockefeller Inst. Govt., 1991-94. Mem. Am. Soc. Real Estate Counselors. Office: Alton G Marshall Assocs Inc 136 E 79th St New York NY 10021-0328

MARSHALL, ANN LOUISE, pastoral counselor; b. Hazleton, Pa., Feb. 19, 1954; d. David Harold and Mary Louise (Rohrbach) M.; m. David Wilcox Main, Aug. 14, 1976; children: Eric David, Jeremy Scott. BA in French, Susquehana U., Selinsgrove, Pa., 1976; MLS, U. Md., 1979; MS in Pastoral Counseling, Loyola Coll., Columbia, Md., 1996. Nat. cert. counselor.; lic. profl. counselor, Washington. Libr. Intelsat, Washington, 1979-94; pastoral counselor Brookland Pastoral Ctr., 1997—. Fellow Assn. Music and Imagery; mem. ACA, Am. Assn. Pastoral Counselors. Mem. United Ch. of Christ. Avocations: choral music, swimming, reading. Office: Brookland Pastoral Ctr 1325 Quincy St NE Washington DC 20017-2615

MARSHALL, BRIAN LAURENCE, trade association executive; b. Kingston-on-Thames, England, Apr. 6, 1941; arrived in US, 1949; s. John and Marguerite Elizabeth (Sandele) Marshall. BA in European History, U. N.C., 1963; MS in Internat. Mgmt., Am. Grad. Sch. Internat. Mgmt., Glendale, Ariz., 1973. Commd. 2d lt. USAF, 1964, advanced through grades to capt., 1972; instr. Armed Forces Air Intelligence Tng. Ctr., Denver, 1965-68; intelligence analyst Task Force Alpha, Nakhon Phanom, Thailand, 1968-69; intelligence systems analyst Headquarters Tactical Air Command, Langley AFB, Va., 1969-72, resigned, 1972; sr. analyst Computer Scis. Corp., Falls Ch., 1974-87; dir. U.S. membership and pubs. U.S.-Mexico C. of C., Washington, 1987-91; v.p. pub. affairs, bd. dirs. N.Am. Free Trade Assn., 1991-96; v.p. N.Am. Trade and Investment Group, 1991-97, also bd. dirs. Contract team leader strategic planning studies and analyses US Dept Def, Joint Chiefs Staff, Washington, 1976—82; regional opers supr elections in Bosnia Orgn Security and Coop in Europe (OSCE), 1997, election supr, Bosnia and Kosovo, 1997—98, Bosnia and Kosovo, 2000; int trade consult, 1998—. Contbr. articles to booklets and newsletters. Bd dirs Columbia Plaza Tenants Asn, Washington, 1981—84; vol Pres Ford Comt, 1976. Mem.: VFW, Washington Mgt and Bus Asn (vice chmn 1981—83, treas 1987—91), Thunderbird Alumni Asn (pres Washington chpt 1980—87), Foreign Policy Asn (group leader discussion program), World Affairs Coun, Asn Former Intelligence Officers, Has House Harriers. Republican. Avocations: jogging, tennis, travel, discussion groups, reading. Home: 5304 Albemarle St Bethesda MD 20816-1827 Office: US Mex C of C 1300 Pennsylvania Ave NW Washington DC 20004 E-mail: brnmarsh@hotmail.com.

MARSHALL, CAK (CATHERINE ELAINE MARSHALL), music educator, composer; b. Nashville, Nov. 24, 1943; d. Dean Byron and Petula Iris (Bodie) M. BS in Music Edn., Ind. U. Pa., 1965; cert., Hamline U., 1981, 82, 83, Memphis State U., 1985; MME, Duquesne U., 1992. Nat. registered music educator, 1993; vocal music tchr., Pa. Tchr. music Mars (Pa.) Area Sch. Dist., 1965-66; music specialist Fox Chapel (Pa.) Area Sch. Dist., 1966—, Duquesne U. City Music Ctr., Pitts., 1994-98. Orff specialist Chatham Coll. Fine Arts Camp, Pitts., 1977-91; instrn. rep. elem. curriculum Dist. I, Pitts., 1986-92; arts curriculum project Pa. Dept. Edn., 1988. Author: (plays) The Rainbow Recorder, 1988, The Gift Disk Dilemma, 1989; composer, author: (play) Pittsburgh-The City with a Smile on Her Face, 1986, (holiday musical) The Dove That Could Not Fly, 1986, (book) Seasons in Song, 1987, (play) The Search for Happiness, 1990; composer: What Color Was the Baby, 1990, Kaia, 1990, Sing Praises To His Name, 1990, Go In Peace, 1990, Sing Unto The Lord, 1990, Simple Gift, 1991, I Love America, 1992, The Cost Is Correct Caper, 1993, The Adventures of Arffie, 1997, The Greatest Snow on Earth, 1997, A Second Grade "Informance", 1998, Stopping by Woods, 1999, A Play-Party Play-in, 1999, Give Thanks, 1999. Actor North Star Players, Pitts., 1975-80; soloist Landmark Bapt. Ch., Penn Hills, Pa., 1981-86, Bible Bapt. Ch., 1987; performer Pitts. Camerata, 1977-89; group leader Pitts Recorder Soc., 1985-86; soloist Grace Bapt. Ch., Monroeville, 1991—. Recipient Citation of Excellence award Pa. Dept. Edn., 1996. Mem. NEA, Am. ORFF-Schulwerk Assn., Pitts. Golden Triangle Chpt. (pres. 1985—), Music Educators Nat. Confl., Pa. Music Educators Assn. (elem. jour. 1986—), Am. Recorder Assn., Pi Kappa Lambda. Baptist. Avocations: cake decorating, bargello, needlework, swimming, folk dancing. Office: O'Hara Elem Sch 115 Cabin Ln Pittsburgh PA 15238-2500 Home: 2494 Percheron Ct SE Salem OR 97301-6273

MARSHALL, CAROL SYDNEY, labor market analyst, employment counselor; b. N.Y.C., Nov. 21, 1930; d. Charles Herbert and Tillie (Muriel) Helman; m. Bogdan Branislav Denitch, 1952 (div. 1954); m. Charles Marshall, Oct. 9, 1954 (div. Aug. 1973); children: Katrina, Peter Morgan Helman, Bonnie Sophia Brija, Athena. Student, Antioch Coll., 1948-50, Hunter Coll., 1953-61, U. Mo., 1967-68; AB in Geography & Urban Planning with honors & distinction, San Diego State U., 1971, postgrad., 1972-73. Copy person, cub reporter Chgo. Sun-Times, 1949-50; adminstrv. asst. Hudson Guild Child Care Ctr., N.Y.C., 1951-54; rsch. asst. City of Antioch Planning Dept., Calif., 1971-72; planning aide San Diego County Planning Dept., 1972-73; labor market analyst Labor Market Info. Divsn. Calif. Employment Devel. Dept., San Francisco, 1973-94; employment rep. Job Svc. Calif. Employment Devel. Dept., 1994—. Speaker, panelist on labor mkt. issues, 1985-94; labor mkt. rsch. cons. San Francisco Pvt. Industry Coun., 1986-94, San Mateo Pvt. Industry Coun., 1986-91, Alameda County Econ. Devel. Adv. Bd., 1991-94; mem. profl. working group Health Occupations Study Nat. Ctr. for Rsch. in Vocat. Edn., Berkeley, Calif., 1989-91; mem. adv. bd. Dept. Health Info. Tech. City Coll. San Francisco, 1992-94. Contbr. articles to profl. jours. Mem. Young Peoples Socialist League, N.Y.C., 1947-54, nat. sec., 1952-53; mem. Young Socialist League, N.Y.C., 1954-62; organizer, co-founder San Diego State U.Child Care Ctr., 1971. Mem. Dem. Socialists of Am. (East Bay exec. com.), Ctr. for Sci. in the Pub. Interest, Pub. Citizens Health Rsch. Group, East Bay Bicycle Coalition, San Francisco Bicycle Coalition, League of Am. Bicyclists. Jewish. Avocations: bicycling, classic rock & roll, photography, theatre. Office: Calif Employment Devel Dept Job Svc 363 Civic Dr Pleasant Hill CA 94523-1920

MARSHALL, CAROLYN ANN M. church official, executive; b. Springfield, Ill., July 18, 1935; d. Hayward Thomas and Isabelle Bernice (Hayer) McMurray; m. John Alan Marshall, July 14, 1956 (dec. Sept. 1990); children: Margaret Marshall Bushman, Cynthia Marshall Kyrouac, Clinton, Carol Bentler. Student, De Pauw U., 1952-54; BSBA, Drake U., 1956; D of Pub. Svc. (hon.), De Pauw U., 1983; LHD (hon.), U. Indpls., 1990. Corp. sec. Marshall Studios, Inc., Veedersburg, Ind., 1956-89, exec. cons., 1989-93; sec. Gen. Conf., lay leader South Ind. conf. United Meth. Ch., 1988-96; exec. dir. Lucille Raines Residence, Inc., Indianapolis, 1996—. Carolyn M. Marshall chair in women studies Bennett Coll., Greensboro, N.C., 1988; fin. cons. Lucille Raines Residence, Inpls., 1977-95. Pres. Fountain Ctrl. Band Boosters, Veedersburg, 1975-77; del. Gen. Conf., United Meth. Ch., 1980, 84, 88, 92, 96, 2000, pres. women's divsn. gen. bd. global ministries, 1984-88; bd. dirs. Franklin (Ind.) United Meth. Ch. Home: 204 N Newlin St Veedersburg IN 47987-1358 Office: Lucille Raines Residence Inc 947 N Pennsylvania St Indianapolis IN 46204-1070 E-mail: cmarshall@sprintmail.com.

MARSHALL, CHARLES, communications company executive; b. Vandalia, Ill., Apr. 21, 1929; s. William Forman and Ruth (Corson) M.; m. Millicent Bruner, Jan. 2, 1953; children: Ruth Ann, Marcia Marshall Rinek, William Forman, Charles Tedrick. BS in Agr, U. Ill., 1951. With Ill. Bell Telephone Co., 1953-59, 61-64, 65-70, 71-72, 77-81, pres., chief exec. officer, 1977-81; with AT&T, 1959-61, 64-65, 70-71, 76-77, 81-89; chmn., chief exec. officer Am. Bell, Morristown, N.J., 1983-84, AT&T Info. Systems, 1984-85; vice chmn. AT&T, N.Y.C., 1985-89. Bd. dirs. Hartmarx. Bd. dirs. Moorings Park, Naples; trustee U. Ill. Found.; vice-chmn. Naples Philharm. Soc. for the Arts. Served to 1st lt. USAF, 1951-53. Mem. Econ. Club Chgo., Comml. Club Chgo., Club of Pelican Bay, Chgo. Club. Avocations: fishing, golfing, reading. Home: 6001 Pelican Bay Blvd Ph B Naples FL 34108-8168

MARSHALL, CHARLES NOBLE, railroad executive; b. Phila., Feb. 18, 1942; s. Donnell and Cornelia Lansdale (Brooke) M.; m. Ann Shaw Donovan, Jan. 12, 1971; children— Elizabeth, Caroline, Cornelia, Edward BS in Engring., Princeton U., 1963; JD, U. Mich., 1967. Bar: Md. 1967, D.C. 1975, Pa. 1978. Atty. Balt. & Ohio R.R., Balt. and Cleve., 1967-73; gen. atty. So. Ry., Washington, 1973-78; gen. counsel commerce Conrail, Phila., 1978-83, v.p. mktg., 1983-85, sr. v.p. mktg. and sales, 1985-89, sr. v.p. devel., 1989-95; pres., COO Genesee & Wyoming Inc., 1997—. Bd. dirs. Phila. Reg. Port Authority, Rails to Trails Conservancy, Pa. Hort. Soc.

MARSHALL, CODY, bishop; Bishop No. Ill. Ch. of God in Christ, Chgo. Office: Freedom Temple Church of God in Christ 6028 S Champlain Ave Chicago IL 60637-2512

MARSHALL, LORD COLIN (LORD MARSHALL OF KNIGHTSBRIDGE), airline executive; b. Edgware, Middlesex, Eng., Nov. 16, 1933; s. Edward Leslie and Florence Mary Marshall; m. Janet Winifred Cracknell, May 10, 1958; 1 child. Student, U. Coll. Sch., Hampstead, Eng., 1946-51. From cadet purser to dep. purser Orient Steam Navigation Co., 1951-58; mgmt. trainee Hertz Corp., Chgo. and Toronto, Ont., Can., 1958-59; gen. mgr. Hertz Corp., Mexico City, 1959-60, asst. to pres. N.Y.C., 1960, gen. mgr. U.K. divsn. London, 1961-62, gen. mgr. U.K. The Netherlands and Belgium divsn., 1962-64; regional mgr., v.p. Avis Co., London, 1964-66, gen. mgr. Europe and Middle East divsn., 1966-69, v.p. gen. mgr. Internat. divsn., 1969-71, exec. v.p., chief operating officer, 1971-75, pres., chief operating officer, 1975-76, pres., chief exec. officer, 1976-79; exec. v.p., sector exec. Norton Simon Inc., N.Y.C., 1979-81; dir. dep. chief exec. Sears Holdings Plc, London, 1981-83; CEO Brit. Airways, 1983-95, apptd. dep. chmn. bd. dirs., 1989-93, exec. chmn. bd. dirs., 1993-95, chmn. bd. dirs., 1996—, Invensys Plc, London, 1999—. Bd. dirs. Brit. Airways, HSBC Holdings, Brit. Telecomm.; chair internat. adv. bd. Brit. Am. Bus. Coun., 1994—. Awarded Knight Bachelor, Her Majesty the Queen, 1987. Mem. Queens Club, All Eng. LTC. Clubs: Queens. Avocations: tennis, cross country skiing. Office: British Airways Plc Waterside PO Box 365 Harmondsworth UB7 OGB England Fax: 020 7495 4845.

MARSHALL, CONRAD JOSEPH, entrepreneur; b. Detroit, Dec. 23, 1934; s. Edward Louis Fedak and Maria Magdalena Berzsenyi; m. Dorothy Genieve Karnafil, Dec. 1, 1956 (div. 1963); children: Conrad Joseph Jr., Kevin Conrad, Lisa Marie; m. Beryle Elizabeth Callahan, June 15, 1965 (div. 1972); children: Brent Jasmer, Farah Elizabeth. Diploma, Naval Air Tech. Tng. Ctr., Norman, Okla., 1952; student, Wayne State U., 1956-59; Diploma, L.A. Police Acad., 1961. Dir. mktg. Gulf Devel., Torrance, Calif., 1980-83; sales mgr. Baldwin Piano Co., Santa Monica, 1977-80; dir. mktg., v.p. Western Hose, Inc., L.A., 1971-76; city letter carrier U.S. Post Office, 1969-71; writer freelance, 1966—; police officer L.A. Police Dept., 1961-66; asst. sales mgr. Wesson Oil Co., Detroit, 1958-60; agt. Life Ins. Co. of Va., Wayne, Mich., 1956-58; pres. Am. Vision Mktg., L.A., 1990—, Con-Mar Prodns., L.A., 1983—; sr. v.p. Pacific Acquisition Group, 1992—, Invest. Admin. HealthCom., Int., 1993—; pres. Midway TV Co., 1994—. Tech. advisor Lion's Gate Films, Westwood, Calif., 1970-74, Medicine Wheel Prodns., Hollywood, Calif., 1965-75; mng. gen. ptnr. Encino Wireless #1, 1994—; CEO Midway TV Inc., 1995; v.p. nat. bus. affairs MMA Internat., 1997; v.p. mktg. Kidkritter, Inc., 1998; sr. prodn. exec. Alpine Pictures Inc., 1999. Author: (series) "Dial Hot Line", 1967, (screenplay) "Heads Across the Border", 1968, "The Fool Card", 1970, "Probable Cause", 1972; co-author: The Fedak File, 1995; albums include Song Shark, 1992, Conrad Marshall Quintet, 1991. Campaign vol. Dem. Ctrl. Com., L.A., 1976, Rep. Ctrl. Com., 1994. Mem. Screen Actors Guild, Internat. Platform Assn. Avocations: poetry, song writing, club singing, philosophy, theology. Home: 11853 Kling St Valley Village CA 91607-4073 Office: Con Mar Prodns 2026 Holly Hill Ter Hollywood CA 90068-3812

MARSHALL, DALE ROGERS, college president, political scientist, educator; b. Mar. 22, 1937; m. Donald J. Marshall; children: Jessica, Cynthia, Clayton. BA in Govt., Cornell U., 1959; MA in Polit. Sci., U. Calif., Berkeley, 1960; PhD in Polit. Sci. with distinction, UCLA, 1969. Lectr. in polit. sci. UCLA, 1969-70, U. Calif., Berkeley, 1970-72, from asst. prof. to prof. Davis, 1972-86, faculty asst. to vice chancellor acad. affairs, 1980-82, assoc. dean Coll. Letters and Scis., 1983-86; acting pres. Wellesley (Mass.) Coll., 1987-88, dean of coll., prof. polit. sci., 1986-92; pres. Wheaton (Mass.) Coll., 1992—. Mem. exec. bd. Calif. Assembly Fellowship Program, 1980-86; bd. trustees, bd. overseers Newton-Wellesley Hosp., 1989-93; bd. trustees Cornell U., Ithaca, N.Y., 1983-93, chair Cornell Fund, co-chair Coll. Arts and Scis. Capital Campaign, 1990-93; bd. trustees New Eng. Zenith Fund, New Eng. Mut. Life Ins. Co., 1995—; bd. dirs. Am. Student Assistance Guarantor, Am. Student Assistance Corp, 1994-2001. Author: (with John C. Bollens) Guide to Participation: Field Work, Role Playing Cases and Other Forms, 1973, (with Roger Montgomery) Housing Policy for the 80's, 1980, (with Rufus P. Browning and David H. Tabb) Protest is Not Enough: The Struggle of Blacks and Hispanics for Equality in Urban Politics, 1984 (APSA Ralph J. Bunche award for best book on ethnic rels. 1985, Gladys Kammerer award for best book in Am. policy 1985); editor: Urban Policy Making, 1979, (with David K. Leonard) Institutions of Rural Development for the Poor: Decentralization and Organizatonal Linkages, 1982, (with Rufus P. Browning and David H. Tabb, co-editor), Racial Politics in American Cities, 1990, 2d edit., 1997; mem. editl. bd. Am. Polit. Sci. Rev., 1972-76, Pub. Adminstrn. Rev., 1985-86; contbr. articles to profl. jours. Woodrow Wilson fellow, 1959-60, Calif. Regents fellow, 1966-67, 67-68; NSF grantee, 1976-78, 79-80; recipient Disting. Teaching award Significant Contbn. to Status of Women citation Chancellor's Com. on Status of Women at U. Calif. at Davis, 1978. Mem. Am. Polit. Sci. Assn. (mem. exec. coun. 1974-76, v.p. 1985-86, mem. nominating com. 1988-90), Western Polit. Sci. Assn. (mem. exec. coun. 1973-75, pres.

1984-85), Nat. Acad. Pub. Adminstrn., Nat. Assn. Ind. Colls. and Univs. (bd. dirs.), Assn. Ind. Colls. and Univs. Mass. (exec. com.), Mortar Bd., Phi Beta Kappa, Phi Kappa Phi. Office: Wheaton Coll Office of Pres Norton MA 02766 E-mail: dmarshal@wheatonma.edu.

MARSHALL, DAVID STANLEY, lawyer; b. Seneca Falls, N.Y., Aug. 23, 1950; s. James Stanley and Ruth Catherine (Cratty) M.; m. Jo Ann Breuninger, Mar. 20, 1993; children: Matthew Stanley, Peter David. BA, Cornell U., 1970; JD, U. Calif., Berkeley, 1974. Bar: Wash. 1981, Calif. 1975. Dep. pros. atty. Pierce County, Tacoma, 1981-84; assoc. atty. Williams Kastner & Gibbs, Seattle, 1984-85; shareholder Prince, Kelley, Marshall & Coombs, 1985-96; pvt. practice, 1997—. Chmn. fellowship bd. Univ. Congl. Ch., 1985-85; chmn. citizens' adv. com. Metro Transit, Seattle, 1988-90; vol. Big Brothers King County, Seattle, 1992-2000; bd. dirs. Transit Discussion Group, 1995-96. Democrat. United Church of Christ. Avocations: squash, cycle touring, alpine skiing, Romance languages. Home: 1703 Warren Ave N Seattle WA 98109-2823 Office: 900 4th Ave Ste 3250 Seattle WA 98164-1005 E-mail: dmarshall@davidsmarshall.com.

MARSHALL, DONALD GLENN, English language and literature educator; b. Long Beach, Calif., Sept. 9, 1943; s. Albert Louis and Margaret Corinne (Morrison) M.; m. Kathleen Bonann, June 21, 1975; children: Stephanie Deborah, Zachary Louis AB summa cum laude, Harvard U., 1965; MPhil, Yale U., 1969, PhD, 1971. Asst. prof. English UCLA, 1969-75; from assoc. prof. to prof. English U. Iowa, Iowa City, 1975-90; honors dir. U. Iowa Coll Liberal Arts, 1981-85; prof., head English dept. U. Ill., Chgo., 1990—2000. Editor: Philosophy as Literature/Literature as Philosophy, 1986; compiler: Contemporary Critical Theory: A Selective Bibliography, 1993; translator: (with Joel Weinsheimer) Truth and Method by Hans-Georg Gadamer, 1989; contbr. articles and revs. to profl. jours. Recipient Bell prize Harvard U., 1965, Webster prize Yale U., 1967; NEH Younger Humanist fellow, 1973-74; grantee UCLA, U. Iowa Mem.: MLA, Ill. Humanities Coun. (bd. dirs. 1994—2000, Chgo. Humanities Festival 1997—), Modern Poetry Assn. (pres. 1998—2000), Conf. Christianity and Lit. (bd. dirs. 2000—). Democrat. Roman Catholic. Office: U Ill Dept English Univ Hall 601 S Morgan St Chicago IL 60607-7120 E-mail: marshall@uic.edu.

MARSHALL, DONALD THOMAS, medical technology consultant, retired; b. Omaha, June 9, 1955; s. William A. and Alma J. Marshall; m. Beverly Ann Everett, Sept. 22, 1990. Med. tech., Pikes Peak Inst. Med. Tech., 1977; EMT, Pikes Peak C.C., Colorado Springs, 1979; PhD of Religion, D of Metaphysics (hon.), Universal Life Ch., 1995. Registered med. technologist; cert. clin. lab. technologist. X-ray and med. lab. technician St. Joseph Hosp. of Plains, Cheyenne Wells, Colo., 1977-79; med. lab. technician Conejos County Hosp., La Jara, 1979-84; med. technologist Nat. Health Lab., Englewood, 1984-91; med. technologist, tech. cons., quality assurance officer Cmty. Health Svcs. Denver Health, Denver, 1996-2001, med. technologist, 1996-2001. Cons. in field. EMT, fireman La Jara Vol. Fire Dept., 1979-84, Meritorious Svc. Citation, 1983; drum major Colo. Irish Pipeband, 2002-. Mem.: Am. Med. Technologists, Am. Assn. Bio-Analysts, Shriners (pipeband 1999—, drummer 1999—, drum maj. 2000—01, drum maj. Colo. Irish pipeband 2002—), Scottish Rite, York Rite, Mason (worshipful master 1994). Republican.

MARSHALL, DOUGLAS WILLIAM, medical administrator, educator; b. Indpls., July 1, 1943; s. William Pryor and Virginia (Guthrie) M.; m. Heidi Christina Amenda, May 30, 1985; 1 child, W. Parker. BA, Denison U., 1965; AB, U. Mich., 1967, PhD, 1975. Western field mgr. U. Mich. Alumni Assn., San Francisco, 1967-69; assoc. curator W.L. Clements Libr. Am. History U. Mich., Ann Arbor, 1970-82; project dir. Campbell-Ewald Co., Warren, Mich., 1982-83; sr. account exec. N.W. Ayer, Inc., Detroit, 1984; mgr. strategic planning GM, 1985-91; program mgr. GM Internat., 1991-96; CEO Onkoservices, 1996-97; v.p. new bus. devel. Innovative Solution in Healthcare, 1997-99; prin. Blitz and Assoc. LLC, 2000—. Adj. assoc. prof. radiation oncology Sch. Medicine, Wayne State U., Detroit, 1996-2000; coord. program in history of discovery U. Mich., Ann Arbor, 1973-81. Co-author: (with H.H. Peckham) Campaigns of the American Revolution: An Atlas Manuscript Maps, 1976; exec. editor Terrae Incognitae: Annals of the Soc. for the History of Discoveries, 1975-82; editor: Research Catalog of Maps of America to 1860, 4 vols., 1972; writer, narrator: (ednl. TV series) Maps: Horizons to Knowledge, 1981. Dir. Gt. Lakes region Am. Cancer Soc. Found., 1996—; mem. S.E. Mich. strategic planning bd. United Found., Detroit, 1982-83. Rsch. fellow Nat. Geog. Soc., 1977; recipient Bicentennial award Bicentennial Commn., State of Mich., 1974; Fulbright lectr. U.S. Fulbright Commn., Helsinki U., 1980-81; William Andrews Clark postdoctoral fellow UCLA, 1979. Mem. Mich. Map Soc. (pres. 1984-85), Soc. for the History of Discoveries (coun. 1979--81), Bohemian Club Calif. Episcopalian. Home: 545 University Pl Grosse Pointe MI 48230-1639 also: 7090 Windemere Harbor Springs MI 49740 Office: 21 Kercheval Ave Ste 270 Grosse Pointe MI 48236 E-mail: marshall@karmanos.org.

MARSHALL, DOYLE, real estate executive; b. Frederick, Okla., July 22, 1932; s. Dallas H. and Sally Vada (Hicks) M.; m. Glenda Ruth Pawley, May 7, 1955; children: William Donald, Sheryl Ruth, David Weston. AS, U. Tex., Arlington, 1957. Realty specialist Corps Engrs., Ft. Worth, 1955-70; realty officer Gen. Svcs. Adminstrn., 1971—, dep. dir. real estate sales, 1981—. Pub. Annetta Valley Farm Press, Aledo, Tex., 1987—. Author: Aledo Country Sketchbook, 1987, A Cry Unheard, 1990, The Liveoak Tree School, 1994; contbr. articles to mags. and newspapers. Scoutmaster Boy Scouts Am., Ft. Worth, 1969-72. Mem. Tex. State Hist. Assn., West Tex. Hist. Assn., various county hist. assns. Baptist. Avocations: Texas history, collecting Texana books, raising cattle, collecting for private farm and ranch museum, writing.

MARSHALL, ELAINE FOLK, state official; b. Lineboro, Md., Nov. 18, 1945; d. Donald and Pauline Folk; m. Sol Marshall; 3 stepchildren. BS in Textiles and Clothing, U. Md., 1968; JD, Campbell U., 1981. Bar: N.C., U.S. Dist. Ct. (ea. and mid. dists.), U.S. Ct. Appeals (4th cir.), U.S. Supreme Ct. Owner retail bus., 1968-79; assoc. Bain Law Firm, Lillington, N.C., 1981-84; ptnr. Bain & Marshall, 1985-92, Marshall & Marshall, Lillington, 1993-96; sec.of state State of N.C., 1997-. Legal advisor Bus. and Profl. Women, N.C., 1982-90; mem. 15th dist. N.C. Senate, 1993-94, N.C. Planning Commn., 1993-94, N.C. Cts. Commn., 1993-94. Bd. dirs. Harnett County United Way, 1987-97, N.C. 4-H Devel. Fund, Inc., 1990—, N.C. Rural Econ. Devel. Fund, 1993-95, N.C. Bd. Econ. Devel., 1993-94, 97—, N.C. Ctr. Pub. Policy Rsch., 1994—, N.C. Justice Acad. Found., 1994—; mem. Divine St. United Meth. Ch.; founding chmn., hon. chmn. Harnett HelpNet Children, 1992—; trustee Meredith Coll., 1997—. Recipient N.C. Friends Ext. award, 1992. Fellow N.C. Inst. Polit. Leadership (bd. dirs. 1996—); mem. Women's Forum N.C. Office: Office Sec State 300 N Salisbury St Raleigh NC 27603-5925*

MARSHALL, FRANCIS JOSEPH, aerospace engineer; b. N.Y.C., Sept. 5, 1923; s. Francis Joseph and Mary Gertrude (Leary) M.; m. Joan Eager, June 14, 1952; children— Peter, Colin, Stephen, Dana. BS in Mech. Engring, CCNY, 1948; MS, Rensselaer Poly. Inst., 1950; Dr. Eng. Sci., N.Y. U., 1955. Engr. Western Union Co., N.Y.C., 1948, Gen. Electric Co., Schenectady, 1948-50; engr. Wright-Aero Corp., Woodridge, N.J., 1950-52; group leader Lab. for Applied Scis., U. Chgo., 1955-60; instr. Ill. Inst. Tech., 1957-59; prof. Sch. Aeros. and Astronautics, Purdue U., West Lafayette, Ind., 1960—. Engr. U.S. Naval Underseas Warfare Center, Pasadena, Calif., 1966-68; faculty fellow NASA-Langley, 1969-70; vis. prof. Inst. Tech. Mara-Midwest Univs. Consortium for Internat. Activities, Malaysia, 1989. Contbr. articles to profl. jours. Served with U.S. Army, 1943-46. Decorated Combat Inf. badge.; NASA research grantee, 1970-76; Fulbright scholar, Turkey, 1988-89. Asso. fellow AIAA; mem. Am. Soc. Engring. Edn., AAUP. Home: 120 Leslie Ave West Lafayette IN 47906-2410 Office: Sch Aeros and Astronautics Purdue U West Lafayette IN 47907

MARSHALL, GARLAND ROSS, biochemist, biophysicist, medical educator; b. San Angelo, Tex., Apr. 16, 1940; s. Garland Ross and Jewel Wayne (Gray) M.; m. Suzanne Russell, Dec. 26, 1959; children: Chris, Keith, Melissa, Lee. BS, Calif. Inst. Tech., 1962; PhD, Rockefeller U., 1966; DSc (hon.), Politechnika, Lodz, Poland, 1993. Instr. Washington U., St. Louis, 1966-67, asst. prof., 1967-72, assoc. prof., 1972-76, prof. biochemistry, 1976—, prof. pharmacology, 1985-2000, dir. Ctr. for Molecular Design, 1988-2000; pres. MetaPhore Pharm. Inc., 1995—. Vis. prof. Massey U., Palmerston North, New Zealand, 1975; vis. prof. chemistry U. Florence, Italy, 1991; pres. Tripos Assocs., Inc., St. Louis, 1979-87; chmn. 10th Am. Peptide Symposium, St. Louis, 1986-88; councilor Am. Peptide Soc., 1990-93; established investigator Am. Heart Assn., Washington, 1970-75. Editor: Peptides: Chemistry and Biology, 1988, Peptides: Chemistry, Structure and Biology, 1990; editor-in-chief Jour. Computer-Aided Molecular Design, 1986-98. Recipient medal L-Lecia Tech. U., Lodz, Poland, 1987, Vincent de Vigneaud award Am. Peptide Soc., 1994, Sci. and Tech. award St. Louis Regl. Commerce and Growth Assn., 1996. Mem. Am. Chem. Soc. (Medicinal Chemistry award 1988, Midwest award 1996), Am. Soc. for Biochemistry and Molecular Biology, Am. Soc. for Pharmacology and Exptl. Therapeutics, Biophys. Soc., Am. Peptide Soc. (Vincent du Vigneaud award 1994, Merrifield award 2001), Chinese Peptide Soc. (Cathay award 2000). Office: Washington U Ctr for Computational Biol 700 S Euclid Ave Saint Louis MO 63110-1012 E-mail: garland@pcg.wustl.edu.

MARSHALL, GEORGE DWIRE, retired supermarket chain executive; b. Washington, Feb. 7, 1940; s. Joseph Paull and Jane Schouler (Dwire) M.; m. Sharon Ruth Carter, Nov. 17, 1968; children: Sarah Dwire, Benjamin Carter. BA, Amherst Coll., 1962; JD, U. Calif., Berkeley, 1965. Bar: Calif. 1966. Atty., then sr. atty. legal div. Safeway Inc., Pleasanton, Calif., 1970-79, v.p., mgr. labor rels. divsn., 1979-97. Employer trustee UFCW Internat. Union-Industry Pension Fund, 1980—. Served to lt. USNR, 1966-70, Korea, Vietnam. Mem. State Bar Calif., Psi Upsilon, Phi Delta Phi. Republican. Presbyterian.

MARSHALL, GERALD FRANCIS, physicist; b. Seven Kings, Eng., Feb. 26, 1929; BSc in Physics, London U., 1952. Physicist Morganite Internat., London, 1954—59; sr. rsch. devel. engr. Ferranti Ltd., Edinburgh, Scotland, 1959—67; project mgr. Diffraction Limited Inc., Bedford, Mass., 1967—69; dir. engring. Medical Lasers, Inc., Burlington, 1969—71; staff cons. Speedring Systems, Troy, Mich., 1971—76; dir. optical engring. Energy Conversion Devices, Inc., 1976—87; sr. tech. staff specialist Kaiser Electronics, San Jose, Calif., 1987—89; cons. in optics design and engring., 1989—. Editor(contbg. author): Laser Beam Scanning, 1985, Optical Scanning, 1991. Fellow: Optical Soc. Am. (program chair 1979—80, pres. Detroit sect. 1980—81, bd. dirs. No. Calif. sect. 1990—92), Internat. Soc. Optical Engring. (symposia chair 1990, bd. dirs. 1991—93, exec. chair Internat. Symposium on Electronic Imaging Device Engring., 1993), Inst. Physics. Achievements include patents in field. E-mail: marshallgf@aol.com.

MARSHALL, GRAYSON WILLIAM, JR. biomaterials scientist, health sciences educator; b. Balt., Feb. 12, 1943; s. Grayson William and Muriel Marie Marshall; m. Sally Jean Rimkus, July 4, 1970; children: Grayson W. III, Jonathan Charles. BS in Metall. Engring., Va. Poly. Inst., 1965; PhD in Materials Sci., Northwestern U., 1972, DDS, 1986; MPH, U. Calif., Berkeley, 1992. Rsch. assoc., design and devel. ctr. Northwestern U., Evanston, Ill., 1972-73, NIH fellow, 1973, instr. Dental and Med. Schs. Chgo., 1973-74, asst. prof. Dental Sch., 1974-78, assoc. prof. Dental Sch. and Grad. Sch., 1978-87; prof. preventive and restorative dental scis. U. Calif., San Francisco, 1987—, chief biomaterials sect., 1988-92, chmn. biomaterials and bioengring. divsn., 1992—. With bioengring. program U. Calif., San Francisco and Berkeley, 1988—; with oral biology program U. Calif., San Francisco, 1991—; guest scientist Lawrence Livermore Nat. Lab., 1989—, Lawrence Berkeley Nat. Lab., 1989—; cons. oral biology and medicine study sect. NIH, 1988-92; dir. Clin. Rsch. Unit, 1992-96, Dentist-Sci. Award Program, 1996—, Integrated DDS-PhD Program, 1996—, Comprehensive Oral Health Rsch. Tng. Program, 2001—. Contbr. articles to profl. jours. Recipient Spl. Dental Rsch. award Nat. Inst. Dental Rsch., 1975; vis. fellow U. Melbourne, Australia, 1981. Fellow: AAAS, Acad. Dental Materials (exec. sec. 1983—85, chmn. credentials 1984—91, bd. dirs. 1985—93, mem. editl. bd. Scanning Microscopy 1987—93, sec. 1988—91, pres. 1991—93, Cells and Materials 1992—2000, sect. editor 1993—2000, Jour. Oral Rehab. 1994—, Dent Mater 1998—), Am. Coll. Dentists, Internat. Coll. Dentists; mem.: Am. Assn. Pub. Health Dentistry, AIME, Am. Assn. Pub. Health Dentistry, APHA, ADA (assoc. editor Jour. ADA 2002—), U.S. Power Squadrons, U.S. Naval Inst., Calif. Pub. Health Assn.-North, Calif. Acad. Scis., N.Y. Acad. Scis., Am. Assn. Dental Rsch. (bd. dirs. 1996—98, San Francisco coun. 1997—), Microscopy Soc. Am., Am. Soc. Metals, Am. Coll. Sports Medicine, Internat. Assn. Dental Rsch. (Chgo. sect. officer 1978—80, dental materials coun. 1990—96, pres. 1998—99), Soc. Biomaterials, Am. Assn. Dental Schs. (sect. officer 1981—83), Omicron Kappa Upsilon, Sigma Gamma Epsilon, Sigma Xi, Alpha Sigma Mu. Office: U Calif Dept Preventive and Restorative Dental Scis San Francisco CA 94143-0001 E-mail: graymar@itsa.ucsf.edu., grayson_marshall@cal.berkeley.edu.

MARSHALL, GROVER EDWIN, retired French and Italian language educator; b. Portland, Maine, Mar. 28, 1930; s. Carroll Oakes and Marguerite Velma (Hoffman) M.; m. Linda Kay Curtis, July 2, 1966; 1 child, Sarah Elizabeth. BA, Bowdoin Coll., 1951; MA, Princeton U., 1954, PhD, 1971. Instr. Romance langs. Princeton (N.J.) U., 1954-58; asst. prof. Williams Coll., Williamstown, Mass., 1958-65; assoc. prof. French and Italian, U. N.H., Durham, 1965-2000, retired, 2000. Fulbright fellow, Besançon, France, 1951-52. Mem. Am. Assn. Tchrs. French, N.E. MLA, Phi Beta Kappa. Democrat. Episcopalian. Avocations: reading, writing, music, hiking. Office: U New Hampshire 15 Library Way Durham NH 03824-3596 E-mail: thegems@earthlink.net.

MARSHALL, IRL HOUSTON, JR. franchise company executive; b. Evanston, Ill., Feb. 28, 1929; s. Irl H. and Marjorie (Greenleaf) M.; m. Barbara Favill, Nov. 5, 1949; children: Alice Marshall Vogler, Irl Houston III, Carol Marshall Allen. AB, Dartmouth Coll., 1949; MBA, U. Chgo., 1968; cert. franchise exec., La. State U., 1991. Gen. mgr. Duraclean Internat., Deerfield, Ill., 1949-61; mgr. Montgomery Ward, Chgo., 1961-77; pres., chief exec. officer Duraclean Internat., 1977-98; pres. Franchise Cons. Svcs., 1998—. Cons. Exec. Svc. Corps., 1999—. Inventor/patentee in field. Pres. Cliff Dwellers, Chgo., 1977; exec. com., treas., dir. Highland Park Hosp., 1971-80; bd. dirs. Better Bus. Bur. Chgo. & No. Ill., Chgo., 1988—. Mem. Internat. Franchise Assn. (bd. dirs. 1981-90, pres. 1985, chmn. 1985-86, bd. dirs. Ednl. Found. 1984—), Inst. Cert. Franchise Execs. (bd. govs. 1995—), Econ. Club Chgo., Exmoor Country Club, Univ. Club Chgo. Presbyterian. Home: 1248 Ridgewood Dr Northbrook IL 60062-3725

MARSHALL, JAMES ANDREW, civil engineer, real estate developer; b. Chgo., May 27, 1932; s. William Emmet and Margaret (Fitzgerald) M. BSCE, Ill. Inst. Tech., 1955, MS in City and Regional Planning, 1960. Registered profl. engr., Ill. Civil engr. Hoyer-Schlesinger-Turner, Chgo., 1973-76, Harza Engrs., Chgo., 1990-91. Mem. Ill. and Mich. Canal Nat. Historic Corridor, Lockport, Ill., 1993—. Served with U.S. Army, 1955-57. Mem. Adventurers Club Chgo., Caxton Club Chgo., Chgo. Lit. Club, Cliff Dwellers Chgo. Democrat. Achievements include discovery of mathematical knowledge of prehistoric Native Americans. Avocations: surveying and mapping Indian mounds and earthworks. Home and Office: 1828 S Roselle Rd Roselle IL 60172-5016

MARSHALL, JAMES HILTON, retired secondary education educator; b. Ft. Erie, Ont., Can., Oct. 10, 1938; came to U.S., 1957; s. Thomas Robert and Doris Marshall; m. Virginia Lee Lewis, Jan. 20, 1962; children: Thomas Walter, Debra Lee Marshall Fenton. BS, Springfield (Mass.) Coll., 1961; MA, U. Conn., 1963, PhD, 1970. 2000tchr. Glastonbury (Conn.) H.S., 1964; ret., 2000. Past mem. adj. faculty Mattatuck C.C., Waterbury, Conn., Middlesex C.C., Middletown, Conn., Manchester (Conn.) C.C., U. Hartford, West Hartford, Conn., 1984, Quinabaug C.C., Danielson, Conn., 2000, U. Conn., 2001, Ea. Conn. State U., 2001; adj. faculty U. Conn., 2001, Capital CC. Chmn. Bolton (Conn.) Bd. Edn., 1976-2001. Recipient cert. of outstanding svc. Conn. Bd. Edn.; named Tchr. of Yr., Trinity Coll., Hartford. Mem. Masons, Shriners. Republican. Avocations: jogging, skating, swimming. Home: 14 Fernwood Dr Bolton CT 06043

MARSHALL, JAMES PETER, accountant, educator; b. Bklyn., Feb. 19, 1942; s. Henry Marshall and Evelyn Berg; m. Esther Marshall, Dec. 28, 1971; children: Dan Yonah, Gad Asher, Yael Evelyn. BA, Yale U., 1966; MA, Hebrew U., Jerusalem, 1975. Copy editor, assoc. editor Keter Pub., Jerusalem, 1968—71; English tchr., fac. head Beit Hinukh H.S., 1971—89; acctg. coord. Four Seasons Hotel, Boston, 1989—. Avocation: reading. Home: 327 St Paul St Apt 2 Brookline MA 02446-3504 Office: Four Seasons Hotel 200 Boylston St Boston MA 02116

MARSHALL, JAMES THOMAS, physician assistant; b. Great Falls, Mont., Nov. 7, 1947; s. James and Joye (Cunningham) M.; m. Jonnie Reese Owens, Jan. 6, 1973; children: Dustin, Jamie. BSBA, Mont. State U., 1989; M in Health Scis., Duke U., 1994. Cert. physician asst. Physician asst. Duke U. Med. Ctr., Durham, N.C., 1994-96, Park Clinic, Livingston, Mont., 1996-97, Bridger Orthopedic & Sports Medicine, Bozeman, 1997—. Adj. faculty Rocky Mtn. Coll., Billings, Mont., 1996—. Fellow Am. Acad. Physician Assts., Mont. Acad. Physician Assts. Avocations: photography, fishing, skiing. Home: 308 Teton Ave Bozeman MT 59718-6241

MARSHALL, JEAN MCELROY, physiologist; b. Chambersburg, Pa., Dec. 31, 1922; d. Frank Lester and Florence (McElroy) M. AB, Wilson Coll., 1944; MA, Mt. Holyoke Coll., 1946; PhD, U. Rochester, 1951. Instr. Johns Hopkins U. Med. Sch., Balt., 1951-56, asst. prof., 1956-60; research postdoctoral fellow Oxford (Eng.) U., 1954-55; asst. prof. Harvard U. Med. Sch., Boston, 1960-66; asso. prof. physiology Brown U., Providence, 1966-69, prof., 1969-88, prof. emerita, 1988, E. Brintzenhof Prof. Med. Sci., 1987—. Mem. physiology study sect. NIH, 1967-71, mem. tng. com. engring. in biology and medicine, 1971-74, mem. tng. com. lab. medicine, 1976-77; physiol. test com. Nat. Bd. Med. Examiners, 1972-76, neurobiology adv. com., 1977-80 Editor: The Initiation of Labor, 1964; mem. editorial bd. Jour. Pharmacology and Exptl. Therapeutics, 1963-69, Am. Jour. Physiology, 1969-73, Circulation Research, 1973-81; contbr. articles to profl. jours. Mem. Am. Physiol. Soc., Am. Pharmacol. Soc., N.Y. Acad. Scis., Soc. Reproductive Biology, Soc. Gen. Physiologists, Phi Beta Kappa, Sigma Xi. Home: 14 Aberdeen Rd Weston MA 02493-1733

MARSHALL, JEFFREY SCOTT, mechanical engineer, educator; b. Cin., Feb. 10, 1961; s. James C. and Norma E. (Everett) M.; m. Marilyn Jane Patterson, July 16, 1983; children: Judith K., Eric G., Emily J., Paul E. BS summa cum laude, UCLA, 1983, MS, 1984; PhD, U. Calif., Berkeley, 1987. Asst. rsch. engr. U. Calif., Berkeley, 1988; engr. Creare, Inc., Hanover, N.H., 1988-89; from asst. to assoc. prof. dept. ocean engring. Fla. Atlantic U., 1989-93; from assoc. prof. to prof. dept. mech. engring. U. Iowa, Iowa City, 1993—2001, prof., chair dept. mech. and indsl. engring., 2001—. Assoc. editor Jour. Fluids Engring.; contbr. articles to profl. jours.; textbook author. Recipient Young Investigator award, 1992-95. Mem. ASME (assoc. editor jour. Fluids Engring. 2001-03, Henry Hess award 1992), Am. Phys. Soc., Tau Beta Pi. Achievements include research in fluid mechanics, three-dimensional vortex dynamics and vortex-structure interaction and thin film flows. Office: U Iowa Dept Mech & Indsl Engring Iowa City IA 52242 E-mail: jeffrey-marshall@uiowa.edu.

MARSHALL, JENNIFER CIZIK, language educator; b. Norwalk, Conn., June 25, 1969; d. Donald Cizik and Sharon Hastings Johnson; m. Raymond Marshall (div.); m. Patrick Edmond. BA, Boston U., 1991; MA, Yale U., 1992, MPhil, 1995, PhD, 1998. Lectr., tchg. fellow Yale U., New Haven, 1993—98; asst. prof. of German Centre Coll., Danville, Ky., 1998—. Author: (novels) Violence, Betrothal and the Beloved Sacrifice, 2001; contbr. articles. Grantee Tech. Initiative grant, Assn. Colls. of the South, 2002. Mem.: MLA, AATA, Phi Beta Kappa. Democrat. Avocation: Irish traditional music, travel, food, wine. Office: Centre Coll 600 W Walnut St Danville KY 40422

MARSHALL, JO TAYLOR, social worker; b. N.Y.C. d. Ralph Taylor. *Jo Marshall's father, Ralph Taylor, was the former owner of Caswell-Massey Company Ltd., est. 1752 (The oldest chemist and perfumers in America). Her mother, Sydney Taylor, was the award-winning children's author of the "All-of-a-Kind Family" series, which is currently being made into a motion picture.* BA, Sarah Lawrence Coll., 1957; MSW, Columbia U., 1959. Cert. social worker, N.Y.; clin. diplomate. Caseworker Youth Cons. Svcs., 1960-62; program cons. Social Work Recruiting Ctr., 1962-63; casework supr. Louise Wise Svcs., 1963-68; faculty field instr. sch. social work Columbia U., N.Y.C., 1968-70; coord. social work vol. and student tng. programs St. Lukes/Roosevelt Hosp. Ctr., 1970-75; asst. dir. fieldwork, faculty lectr. in health care Columbia U., N.Y.C., 1975-78; dir. social work and psychiat. emergency svcs. Morristown Meml. Hosp., 1978—95; social worker pvt. practice, 1995—2002; ret., 2002. Adj. prof. Columbia U.; adv. bd., faculty Nat. Discharge Planning Inst. SUNY, Buffalo; prin. speaker, cons. Hosp. Assn. Pa., 1983, Mid-Atlantic Health Congress, 1985, VA, East Orange, N.J., 1986, Hosp. Assn. Tenn., 1987; adv. com. Rutgers GGrad. Sch. Social Work; mem. multidisciplinary state rev. com. for discharge planning standards in N.J. Contbr. articles to profl. jours.; produced and cons. on numerous film and TV prodns. Mem. NASW, Soc. Hosp. Social Wk. Dirs. (exec. bd., pres. N.J. chpt. 1988-89, chmn. nat. media task force). Address: PO Box 40 Far Hills NJ 07931-0040 also: 1230 Hillsboro Mile Hillsboro Beach FL 33062

MARSHALL, JOHN, federal agency administrator; b. Omaha; B, M, U. Va. Apptd. Gov. Va.'s Commn. Govt. Reform; fin. mgmt. analyst Pres.'s Office Mgmt. and Budget; deputy adminstr. mgmt. Agrl. Stabilizatin and Conservation; CEO Fed. Crop. Ins. Corp.; sr. advisor to chmn. Senate Com. Govt. Affairs, 1995—97; prin. IBM Bus. Innovations Svcs., Bethesda, Md., 1997—2001; asst. adminstr. USAID, Washington, 2001—. Contbr. articles to profl. jours. Office: USAID RRB 1300 Pennsylvanis Ave NW Washington DC 20523*

MARSHALL, JOHN PAUL, broadcast engineer; came to U.S., 1967. Degree, U. Grenoble, France, 1963; student, U. Munich, 1964-65, San Francisco State, 1969-71, John O'Connell Tech. Inst., 1973-74. Cert. Novell adminstr., cert. broadcast technologist, A+ computer svc. technician Microsoft Cert. Profl.; cert. Networkplus Tech., Microsoft Cert. Profl., Microsoft Cert. Sys. Engr. Mem. faculty law and econ. scis. U. Grenoble, 1963-64; mem. Expo '67 staff City of Montreal, Que., Can., 1967; filmmaker Cinemalab, San Francisco, 1970; engr. film and TV Able Studios, 1971-73; radio and TV engr. Sta. KALW-FM (Nat. Pub. Radio), 1973-74; broadcast engr. Sta. KRON-TV (NBC), 1974-91; intern Centre d'Informatique et de Maintenance Automatisme, 1993; founder Marshall U.S.A., San Francisco, 1994; freelance broadcast engr. KPIX-TV (CBS), KGO-Radio (ABC), KSFO-Radio (ABC), KPST-TV, 1995—, also Sta. KPST-TV (Home Shopping Network), San Francisco. Freelance audio visual tech. advisor, San Francisco area, 1975—, lectr. radio, TV, motion pictures, 1975—, cons. customized electronic effects; tech. advisor, assoc. Broadkast Skills Bank. Translator tech. pubs. and manuals, 1975—. Mus. dir., participant in theater prodns., 1950-59; active Boy Scouts Am. Govt. of France scholar, 1960-63. Mem. Rolls Royce Owners Club Found. (life), Internet Soc., Soc. Broadcast Engrs. (cert. broadcast networking technologist), Elec. Tech. Assn. Avocations: classical pianist, polyglot, world traveler. E-mail: johnpaul@ispwest.com. *Personal philosophy: (French proverb) Aide toi, le ciel t'aidera--Use your own resources and you will always receive a helping hand from heaven.*

MARSHALL, JOHN CROOK, internal medicine educator, researcher; b. Blackburn, Lancashire, Eng., Feb. 28, 1941; came to U.S., 1976; s. Albert Acey and Marion Miller (Crook) M.; m. Marilyn Dallas Parry, Sept. 20, 1969; children: Samantha Jane, Susannah Crook. BS, Victoria U., Manchester, Eng., 1962, MB, ChB, 1965, MD, 1973. Diplomate Am. Bd. Internal Medicine, Am. Bd. Endocrinology and Metabolism. Intern Manchester Royal Infirmary, 1965-66; resident Brompton Hosp., Nat. Heart Hosp., London, 1966-69, Hammersmith Hosp., London, 1966-69, rsch. fellow, 1969-72; lectr. U. Birmingham, Eng., 1972-76; assoc. prof. internal medicine U. Mich., Ann Arbor, 1976-79, prof., 1979-91, chief endocrinology and metabolism, 1987-91; prof. U. Va., Charlottesville, 1991—, dir. Ctr. for Rsch. in Reprodn., 1996—. Sci. counselor NIH, Bethesda, Md., 1983-84. Editor Endocrinology Text, 1990—; contbr. articles to profl. jours. Grantee NIH, 1977-2005. Fellow ACP, Royal Coll. Physicians, Royal Soc. Medicine; mem. Ctrl. Soc. for Clin. Rsch. (coun. 1983—), Assn. Am. Physicians, Am. Soc. for Clin. Investigation, Am. Clin. and Climatological Soc. Anglican. Avocations: vintage racing cars, golf. Office: U Va Sch Medicine Dept Internal Medicine Charlottesville VA 22908-0001

MARSHALL, JOHN DAVID, lawyer; b. Chgo., May 19, 1940; s. John Howard and Sophie (Brezenk) M.; m. Marcia A. Podlasinski, Aug. 26, 1961; children: Jacquelyn, David, Jason, Patricia, Brian, Denise, Michael, Catherine. BS in Acctg., U. Ill., 1961; JD, Ill. Inst. Tech., 1965. Bar: Ill. 1965, U.S. Tax Ct. 1968, U.S. Dist. Ct. (no. dist.) Ill. 1971; CPA, Ill. Ptnr. Mayer, Brown & Platt, Chgo., 1961—. Bd. dirs. Levinson Ctr. for Handicapped Children, Chgo., 1970-75. Fellow Am. Coll. Probate Counsel; mem. Ill. Bar Assn., Chgo. Bar Assn. (agribus. com. 1978—, trust law com. 1969—, probate practice com. 1969—, com. on coms. 1983—, vice chmn. 1988-89, chmn. 1989-90, legis. com. of probate practice com. 1983—, chmn. and vice chmn. legis. com. of probate practice com. 1983-84, chmn. exec. com. probate practice com. 1982-83, vice chmn. exec. com. 1981-82, sec. exec. com. 1980-81, div. chmn. 78-79, div. vice chmn. 1977-78, div. sec. 1976-77, Appreciation award 1982-83), Chgo. Estate Planning Council. Clubs: Union League (Chgo.). Roman Catholic. Office: Mayer Brown & Platt 190 S La Salle St Ste 3100 Chicago IL 60603-3441 Home: 429 N Willow Wood Dr Palatine IL 60074-3831

MARSHALL, JOHN DAVID, retired librarian, author; b. McKenzie, Tenn., Sept. 7, 1928; s. Max Cole and Emma (Walpole) M. BA, Bethel Coll., McKenzie, 1950; MA in Libr. Sci., Fla. State U., 1951, postgrad., 1951-52, Oxford (Eng.) U., summer 1989. Grad. asst. Sch. Libr. Sci. Fla. State U., 1951-52; ref. libr. Clemson (S.C.) U. Libr., 1952-55; head ref. dept. Auburn (Ala.) U. Libr., 1955-57; head acquisitions divsn. U. Ga. Libr., Athens, 1957-67; libr., assoc. prof. Mid. Tenn. State U., Murfreesboro, 1967-76, univ. bibliographer, assoc. prof., 1976-80, prof., 1980-93, prof. emeritus, 1994—; Mary Ball Holmes lectr. Bethel Coll., 1999. Book rev. staff Libr. Jour., 1953-64. Contbg. editor So. Observer, 1953-66; gen. editor Contributions to Library Literature series, 1963-78; book rev. editor Jour. Libr. History, 1966-76, Southeastern Librarian, 1979-82; author: Books in Your Life, 1959, Louis Shores: A Bibliography, 1964, A Fable of Tomorrow's Library, 1965, Louis Shores, Author-Librarian: A Bibliography, 1979, One Librarian's Credo, 1986, Lizzie Borden and the Library Connection, 1990, Churchill's Fulton Speech, 1994, Books are STILL Basic, 1994, And Now Buzz Off: Wit and Wisdom of Sir Winston S. Churchill, 2000; co-editor: Books-Libraries-Librarians, 1955; editor: Of, By, and For Librarians (1st series), 1960, An American Library History Reader, 1961, In Pursuit of Library History, 1961, Mark Hopkins' Log and Other Essays by Louis Shores, 1965, Approaches to Library History, 1966, The Library in the University, 1967, Of, By, and For Librarians: Second Series, 1974, Southern Books Competition at Twenty-Five: A Silver Anniversary Tribute, 1980, Books are Basic: The Essential Lawrence Clark Powell, 1985. Bd. govs. Friends of Linebaugh Pub. Libr., Murfreesboro, Tenn., 1994—, pres., 1984, treas., 1996; mem. Murfreesboro City Libr. Bd., 1985-93, treas., 1990-93; mem. Highland Rim Reg. Libr. Bd., 1989-95, treas., 1993-95, Rutherford County Libr. Br., 1989-95; bd. govs. Winston Churchill Meml. Libr., 1989—. Recipient Disting. Alumni award Sch. Libr. and Info. Sci., Fla. State U., 1989, Alumni Achievement award Bethel Coll., 1989, Disting. Alumni Svc. award, 1992; Churchill fellow Westminster Coll., 1982. Mem. ALA (membership com. 1953-55, libr. history round table 1956—, sec. 1969-72), Assn. Coll. and Rsch. Librs. (pubs. com. 1957-62), Southeastern Libr. Assn. (hon. life, chmn. awards com. 1986-88, Outstanding Author Award com. 1990-92, 96—, Mary Utopia Rothrock award 1994), Tenn. Libr. Assn. (chmn. intellectual freedom com. 1968-70, 84-85, mem. Tenn. History Book Award com. 1985—, chmn. 1985-86, Frances Neel Cheney award 1984, Honor award 1992), Internat. Churchill Soc., Phi Kappa Phi, Beta Phi Mu. Avocations: reading, writing/editing, collecting Churchilliana. Home: PO Box 2506 Murfreesboro TN 37133-2506

MARSHALL, JOHN ELBERT, III, foundation executive; b. Providence, July 2, 1942; s. John Elbert Jr. and Millicent Edna (Paige) M.; m. Diana M. Healy, Aug. 16, 1968; children: Nelson John, Priscilla Anne. BA, Brown U., 1964. Advt. mgr. U.N. Alloy Steel Corp., Boston, 1968-70; assoc. dir. devel. Brown U., 1970-74; exec. dir. R.I. Found., Providence, 1974-79; v.p. Kresge Found., Troy, Mich., 1979-82, exec. v.p., 1982-87, pres., 1987—, trustee, 1991—; CEO, 1993—. Bd. dirs. Ind. Sector; former chmn. Mich. Cmty. Found. Youth Project. Bd. dirs. United Way Cmty. Svcs., Detroit Symphony Orch. Hall, Greater Downtown Partnership, Schs. for 21st Century; former bd. dirs. Mich. Campus Compact; former bd. dirs., vice chmn. Family Svc. Detroit and Wayne County; past pres. Bloomfield Village Assn.; former trustee Coun. on Founds., Washington. Office: Kresge Found PO Box 3151 Troy MI 48007-3151

MARSHALL, JOHN HARRIS, JR. geologist, oil company executive; b. Dallas, Mar. 12, 1924; s. John Harris and Jessie Elizabeth (Mosley) M.; m. Betty Eugenia Zarecor, Aug. 9, 1947; children: John Harris III, George Z., Jacqueline Anne. BA in Geology, U. Mo., 1949, MA in Geology, 1950; LHD, Garrett Evangelical Theolgical, 1996. Registered geologist, Calif., Wyo., Ky. Geologist Magnolia Oil Co., Jackson, Miss., 1950-59; assoc. geologist Magnolia/Mobil Oil, Okla. City, Okla., 1959-63; from dist. and divsn. geologist to chief geologist worldwide Mobil Oil Corp., various, 1963-81, gen. mgr. exploration for Western Hemisphere N.Y.C., 1981-82; chief geologist Amberx, 1982—84; prin., owner Marshall Energetics, Inc., Dallas, 1982—. Dir. exploration Anschutz, 1985-91; pres. Summit Oil and Gas Worldwide, 1993-99, Madera Prodn. Co., 1992—; adv. bd. Salvation Army, Manhattan, 1980-82; trustee The Sci. Place, Dallas, 1995—. Active geology devel. bd. U. Mo., past pres., 1982—, pres. Coll. Arts and Sci. devel. program, 1996—, mem. devel. coun., 1996-2000, arts and scis. strategic devel. bd., 2000—; councilman, City of Warr Acres (Okla.), 1962-63; active United Meth. Ch., 1951—, Boy Scouts Am., 1960-68; chair Found. of Evangelism, United Meth. Ch., 1988-96. With U.S. Army, 1943—46. Decorated 3 Battle Stars U.S. Army; recipient Curator's medal, U. Mo., 1949, Disting. Alumni Svc. award, 1996, Arts and Sci. award, The Mosaic Soc., U. Mo., 2000, Faculty-Alumni award, U. Mo., 2001. Mem. Am. Assn. Petroleum Geologists (Pub. Svc. award 2000), Am. Geol. Inst., Am. Geol. Soc. (Dallas, Alaska, Oklahoma City; L.A. Basin pres. 1969-70), Rocky Mountain Assn. Geologists, N.Y. Acad. Sci., Pacific Petroleum Geologists, Am. Sci. Affiliation, Assn. Christian Geologists, Meth. Men Club, Denver Petroleum Club, Sigma Xi. Democrat. Office: 9526 Moss Haven Dr Dallas TX 75231-2608 Fax: 214-348-0543.

MARSHALL, JOHN PATRICK, lawyer; b. Bklyn., July 3, 1950; s. Harry W. and Mary Margaret (Kelly) M.; m. Cheryl J. Garvey, Aug. 10, 1975; children: Kelly Blake, Logan Brooke. BA, Rutgers U., 1972; JD cum laude, N.Y. Law Sch., 1976. Bar: N.Y. 1977, N.J. 1977, U.S. Dist. Ct. N.J. 1977, U.S. Dist. Ct. (so. and ea. dists.) N.Y. 1978, U.S. Ct. Appeals (3rd cir.) 1982, U.S. Dist Ct. (no. dist.) N.Y. 1991. Assoc. Kelley Drye & Warren, N.Y.C., 1976-84, ptnr., 1985-98. Mem. editl. bd. N.Y. Law Sch. Law Rev., 1975-76, staff mem., 1974-75; contbr. articles to profl. jours. Mem. jud. screening com. N.Y. Dem. Com., N.Y. New Dem. Coalition, 1988; exec. v.p. Humanitarian Found. for Nicaragua, 1991; mem., sec. Respect for Law Found., 1996; mem. Southern Dist. N.Y. Mediation Panel, 1994—; mem. Coun. on Jud. Adminstrn., 1996-98. Fellow Am. Bar Found.; mem. ABA, N.Y. County Lawyers' Assn. (sec. 1984-87, mem. com. on Supreme Ct. 1984-94, mem. legal edn., admission to bar and lawyer placement com. 1983-93), Am. Arbitration Assn. (mem. nat. panel arbitrators N.Y. and N.J. regions 1991—, mem. corp. counsel com. 1993-98), Assn. of Bar of City of N.Y. (sec. judiciary com. 1989-92, mem. com. on arbitration 1994-96, sec. coun. on judical adminstrn. 1996-98). Home and Office: 50 Highland Ave Short Hills NJ 07078-2812 E-mail: marshall.highland@prodigy.net.

MARSHALL, JOHN RICHARD, opera director; b. Schenectady, N.Y., July 28, 1929; s. Abraham Lincoln and Edith (Lambert) M.; m. Jean Deresienski, May 23, 1953 (div. Oct. 1982); m. Maria Tomasz, June 11, 1988. BA, U. Rochester, 1951; MMus, Ind. U., 1953, DMus, 1964. Head of opera and choral music U. Buffalo, N.Y., 1959-62; head of opera Boston Conservatory, 1969-72; dir. New Eng. Regional Opera, Boston, 1971-76; gen. dir. Charlotte (N.C.) Opera, 1976-82; founder, gen. dir., artistic dir. Ctr. for Contemporary Opera, N.Y.C., 1982—. With U.S. Army, 1954-55. Recipient Svc. to Opera award Performing Arts Assn., 1975. Mem. Opera Am., Nat. Opera Assn., Arts and Bus. Coun., Am. Music Ctr., Am. Composers Forum. Democrat. Unitarian Universalist. Avocation: photography. Office: Ctr for Contemporary Opera PO Box 258 Island Station New York NY 10044-0205 E-mail: conopera@mindspring.com.

MARSHALL, JOHN ROMNEY, obstetrician; b. L.A., Apr. 27, 1933; s. Harold and Olive (Romney) M.; m. Rose Anne Evans, Aug. 16, 1956 (div. Aug. 1995); children: Karen, Alecia, Kirk, Robin, Rebekah; m. Elaine Sorenson, July 2, 1996. Student, Pomona Coll., 1954; MD, U. Pa., 1958. Diplomate Am. Bd. Ob-Gyn. Resident in ob-gyn. George Washington U., Washington, 1960-63, asst. prof., 1963-70; prof. ob-gyn., vice chair dept. UCLA Med. Sch., 1970-86; v.p., med. dir. Fertility and Genetics Rsch., Inc., Chgo., 1986-88, Life Blood Trust, Torrance, Calif., 1988-91; clin. prof. ob-gyn. UCLA Med. Sch., 1991—. Sr. investigator Nat. Cancer Inst., Bethesda, 1963-70; chmn. ob-gyn. dept. Harbor/UCLA Med. Ctr., Torrance, Calif., 1970-86. Fellow Am. Coll. Ob-Gyn., Am. Gynecol. and Obstet. Soc.; mem. Soc. Gynecol. Investigation, L.A. Ob-Gyn. Soc. Office: 875 B 29th St San Pedro CA 90731 E-mail: jrmarshl@concentric.net.

MARSHALL, JOHN TREUTLEN, lawyer, educator; b. Macon, Ga., Nov. 1, 1934; s. Hubert and Gladys (Lucas) M.; m. Katrine White, May 1, 1959; children: Allison, Rebecca, Paul, Mary Anne. BA, Vanderbilt U., 1956; LLB, Yale U., 1962. Bar: Ga. 1962, U.S. Dist. Ct. (no., mid. and so. dists.) Ga. 1962, U.S. Ct. Appeals (5th cir.) 1962, U.S. Supreme Ct. 1978, U.S. Ct. Appeals (11th cir.) 1982. Ptnr. Powell, Goldstein, Frazer & Murphy, Atlanta, 1962—. Adj. prof. law Emory U. Sch. Law, 1968-86, mem. coun.; chmn. No. Dist. Ga. Bar Coun., 1989; chmn. Ga. State Commn. on Continuing Lawyer Competency, 1991-93, Ga. State Commn. on Standards of Profession, 1996--. Bd. editors: Yale Law Jour. Bd dirs. Atlanta Legal Aid, 1972-73; trustee Ga. Inst. Continuing Legal Edn., 1983-90; chmn. adv. bd. Atlanta Vol. Lawyers Found. Recipient S. Phillip Heiner award Atlanta Vol. Lawyers Assn., 1992, A. Gus cleveland award Ga. Commn. on Continuing Edn., Tradition of Excellence award State Bar Ga., 1995. Fellow Am. Coll. Trial Lawyers (state chmn. 1985-86), Am. Acad. Appellate Lawyers, Am. Bar Found., Ga. Bar Found.; mem. ABA (ho. of dels. 1976-86, Harrison Tweed award 1986), Am. Arbitration Assn., State Bar Ga. (chair stds. of profession com.), Atlanta Bar Assn. (pres. 1974-75, Charles E. Watkins Jr. award 1988, Leadership award 1996), Ga. Inst. Trial Advocacy (chmn. 1982-830, Cherokee Town and Country Club, 191 Club, Lawyers Club. Office: Powell Goldstein Frazer & Murphy 191 Peachtree St NE Fl 16 Atlanta GA 30303-1740

MARSHALL, JONATHAN, charitable foundation administrator, journalist; b. N.Y.C., Jan. 20, 1924; s. James and Lenore (Guinzburg) M.; m. Maxine Besser, Apr. 6, 1955; children: Lucinda, Laura, Robert Louis, Jonathan Herbert. BA in Econs., U. Colo., 1946; postgrad., U. N.C., 1947—49; MS in Journalism, U. Oreg., 1962; LHD (hon.) , Ariz. State U., 1994. Program assoc. Planning Dept., West Chester County, NY, 1949—52; editor, pub. Arts mag., N.Y.C., 1953-58, Scottsdale (Ariz.) Daily Progress, 1963-87; program assoc. Ford Found., N.Y.C., 1958-59; pres. New Hope Found., 1985-98, Marshall Fund Ariz., Scottsdale, 1987—. Pulitzer prize juror, 1983, 84; Ruhl fellow lectr. U. Oreg., 1986, Allen lectr., 91. Former mem. editl. bd. Amicus Jour.; contbr. articles to various publs., including Masthead, ASNE Bull., Quill, Amicus Jour. Chmn. Oreg. Vols. for Stevenson, 1960, Ariz. Grandparents Day, 1972, 73; bd. dirs. Ariz. Theatre Co., Phoenix Art Mus., Nat. Com. for Effective Congress; former mem. bd. dirs. Am. Jewish Com., Camelback Hosp., Phoenix Urban League, Phoenix Symphony Assn. Recipient Nat. Phys. Fitness Leadership award U.S. Jaycees, 1973, Ariz. Newspapers' Master Editor-Pub. award, 1978, Disting. Svc. award Ariz. Press Club, 1988, Ariz. Philanthropist award Nat. Soc. Fundraising Execs., 1997, Ariz. State U. Coll. Liberal Arts, 1988, Pub. Interest award Ariz. Ctr. for Law in Pub. Interest, 1998, John W. Creasman award for excellence Ariz. State U., 1999, Martin Luther King, Jr. Diversity Champion award, 2001; named Ariz. Civil Libertarian of Yr., 1996; inducted into Ariz. Newspapers Hall of Fame, 1996; named to U. Oreg. Journalism Sch. Hall of Achievement, 2001. Mem. Nat. Conf. Editl. Writers, Am. Soc. Newspapers Editors (past mem. editl. bd. Bull.), Soc. Profl. Journalists (1st Amendment award 1979). Democrat. Jewish. Office: Marshall Fund Ariz 3295 N Drinkwater Blvd Scottsdale AZ 85251

MARSHALL, JULIE W. GREGOVICH, investor relations executive; b. Pasadena, Calif., Mar. 3, 1953; d. Gibson Marr and Anna Grace (Peterson) Wolfe; m. Michael Roy Gregovich Dec. 18, 1976 (div. June 1994); children: Christianna, Kerry Leigh; m. Robert Brandon Marshall, Aug. 6, 1994. BA magna cum laude, Randolph-Macon Woman's Coll., 1975; MBA, Pepperdine U., 1983. cert. tchr. K-12, Calif. Test engr. Westinghouse Hanford, Richland, Wash., 1975-76; startup engr. Bechtel Power Corp., Norwalk, Calif., 1976-77; test engr. Wash. Pub. Power, Richland, 1978-80; from mgr. to v.p. Sun Tech. Svcs., Mission Viejo, Calif., 1983-93; cons. Mission Energy Co., Irvine, 1993-94; owner, CEO, pres. Key Employee Svcs., Inc., Key Largo, Fla., 1994-97; from assoc. to pres. Hawk Assocs., Inc. Investor Rels., Tavernier, 1996—. Contbr. article to jour. Named Young Career Woman of the Yr. Wash. Pub. Power Supply System, 1979. Mem. Phi Beta Kappa. E-mail: jmarsh@hawkassociates.com.

MARSHALL, KATHRYN SUE, lawyer; b. Decatur, Ill., Sept. 12, 1942; d. Edward Elda and Frances M. (Minor) Lahniers; m. Robert S. Marshall, Sept. 5, 1964 (div. Apr. 1984); m. Robert J. Arndt, June 25, 1988; children: Stephen Edward, Christine Elizabeth. BA, Lake Forest Coll., 1964; JD, John Marshall Law Sch., Chgo., 1976. Intern U.S. Atty.'s Office, Chgo., 1974-76; mng. ptnr. Marshall and Marshall Ltd., Waukegan, Ill., 1976-84; pvt. practice, 1984-93, Preemptive Solutions, Wash., Calif. Contbr. articles to profl. jours. Cert. jud. candidate Dem. party, Lake County, Ill.; bd. mem. Camerata Soc., Lake Forest; bd. mem., v.p. Lake Forest (Ill.) Fine Arts Ensemble; bd. dirs. Island Hosp. Health Found.; mem. steering com. Equal Justice Coalition. Fellow: ABA (gov. 1993—96), Coll. Law Practice Mgmt., Ill. Bar Assn.; mem.: Navy League (life). Avocations: boating, reading, travel.

MARSHALL, LAURENCE PAUL, social services administrator; b. Portland, Maine, Aug. 12, 1951; s. James Edward and Jane Wynne (Horslin) M.; 1 child, Luke Paul. BA in Social Work, U. So. Maine, 1973; MSW, U. Louisville, 1976. Cert. social worker. Rsch. technician Human Svcs. Devel. Inst., Portland, 1973-75; dir. discharge planning and aftercare Elan One, Poland Spring, Maine, 1976-80; regional planner Maine Dept. Mental Health, Augusta, 1980-82; program dir. Four County Mental Health Svcs., St. Charles, Mo., 1982-85; dir. Friendship House, Dover, N.H., 1985-89, Pioneer House, Salem, Mass., 1989—. Mem. faculty Internat. Ctr. Clubhouse Devel., N.Y.C., 1988—. Mem. Nat. Assn. Social Workers. Avocations: sports, stamps. Home: 151 Indigo Hill Rd Somersworth NH 03878-3040 Office: Pioneer House 2 Washington St Peabody MA 01960-5521

MARSHALL, LAWRENCE FRANCIS, neurological surgeon; b. N.Y.C., July 29, 1943; s. Frederic Mac and Margaret (Linde) M.; m. Sharon Bowers; children: Derek, Kathryn, Samantha. BA, U. Rochester, 1965; MD, U. Mich., 1969. Diplomate Am. Bd. Neurol. Surgery. Intern U. Pa. Children's Hosp., 1969-70, neurosurgery resident, 1970-74, fellow, 1974-75; chief neurosurg. svcs. U. Calif., San Diego, 1980—, chair practice plan, 1983-88, prof. surgery divsn. neurol. surgery, 1984—, assoc. dean faculty practice affairs Sch. Medicine, 1986-88, dir. managed care, 1989-92, exec. dir. managed care, 1992-95, dir. residency tng. program neurol. surgery, 1994—, chmn. divsn. neurol. surgery, 1995—. Author: Neuroscience Critical Care: Pathophysiology and Patient Management, 1990; reviewer AMA residency review com. Neurol. Surgery, 1999—; mem. editl. bd. Jour. Neurosurgery, 1997—; contbr. articles to profl. jours. Chmn. Hispanic-Jewish Rels. of Antidefamation League, San Diego, 1981-84. Recipient William F. Caveness award Nat. Head Injury Found., Inc., 1986, Jamieson medal Neurosurg. Soc. Australasia, 1990, Wakeman award Duke U., 1990, Brain Trauma Found. Lectureship award, 1993. Mem. Soc. Neurotrauma, Congress Neurol. Surgeons, Am. Assn. Neurol. Surgeons, Soc. Neurol. Surgeons. Jewish. Avocations: sports, reading, travel. Home: PO Box 1242 Rancho Santa Fe CA 92067-1242 Office: Univ Calif Divsn Neurol Surgery 200 W Arbor Dr San Diego CA 92103-9000 Fax: 619-543-2769.

MARSHALL, LINDA LANTOW, pediatrics nurse; b. Tulsa, Dec. 13, 1949; d. Lawrence Lee and Lena Mae (Ross) Lantow; m. David Panke Hartson, Aug. 25, 1970 (div. 1982); children: Michael David, Jonathan Lee; m. Roger Nathan Marshall, Dec. 11, 1985; 1 child, Sarabeth Megan. A, U. Okla., 1970; BSN, U. Tulsa, 1983. Cert. pediatric nurse, 1995. Pediats. nurse Youthcare, Claremore, Okla., 1983-85, 87-98; staff nurse ICU Doctors Hosp.; Tulsa, 1985-87; sch. nurse Wilson Tulsa Pub. Schs., 1998—. Bd. dirs. PTA Barnard, Tulsa, 1993-95; leader Brownie troop Girl Scouts U.S., Tulsa, 1994-95, leader jr. scouts, 1995—. Mem. Sigma Theta Tau. Avocation: gardening. Home: 2628 E 22nd St Tulsa OK 74114-3123 Office: Wilson Middle Sch 1127 S Columbia Ave Tulsa OK 74104-3928

MARSHALL, LINDA MURPHY, linguist, government official; b. St. Louis, Aug. 6, 1950; d. Samuel Baldwin and Barbara Anne (Chivvis) Murphy; m. Joseph A. Kelley, Aug. 31, 1974 (div. Sept. 1987); children: Alex, Mia; m. William Peyton Marshall, July 8, 1989. BA, U. Denver, 1972; MA, St. Louis U., 1974, PhD, 1978; postgrad., Washington U., 1981-85, Georgetown U., 1997-98. Translator Aerospace Ctr., Def. Mapping Agy., St. Louis, 1978-81; multi-linguist U.S. Fed. Govt., Washington, 1985—. Cons.: Sotho Newspaper Reader, Reference Grammar and Lexicon, 1998; contbr. articles to profl. jour. Mem. Phi Beta Kappa. Episcopalian. Avocations: classical piano, poetry, travel, foreign languages. Home: 10391 Green Mountain Cir Columbia MD 21044-2455

MARSHALL, MARGARET HILARY, state supreme court chief justice; b. Newcastle, Natal, South Africa, Sept. 1, 1944; came to U.S., 1968; d. Bernard Charles and Hilary A.D. (Anderton) M; m. Samuel Shapiro, Dec. 14, 1968 (div. Apr. 1982); m. Anthony Lewis, Sept. 23, 1984. BA, Witwatersrand U., Johannesburg, 1966; MEd, Harvard U., 1969; JD, Yale U., 1976; LHD (hon.), Regis Coll., 1993. Bar: Mass. 1977, U.S. Dist. Ct. Mass., U.S. Dist. Ct. N.H., U.S. Dist. Ct. D.C., U.S. Dist. Ct. (ea. dist.) Mich., U.S. Tax Ct., U.S. Ct. Appeals (1st, 11th and D.C. cirs.), U.S. Supreme Ct. Assoc. Csaplar & Bok, Boston, 1976-83, ptnr., 1983-89, Choate, Hall & Stewart, Boston, 1989-92; v.p., gen. counsel Harvard U., Cambridge, Mass., 1992-96; justice Supreme Jud. Ct. Commonwealth Mass., 1996-99, chief justice, 1999—. Mem. jud. nominating coun., 1987-90, 92; chairperson ct. rules subcom. Alternative Dispute Resolution Working Group, 1985-87; mem. fed. appts. commn., 1993; mem. adv. com. Supreme Judicial Ct., 1989-92, mem. gender equality com., 1989-94; mem. civil justice adv. group U.S. Dist. Ct. Mass., 1991-93; spl. counsel Jud. Conduct Commn., 1988-92; trustee Mass. Continuing Legal Edn., Inc., 1990-92. Trustee Regis Coll., 1993-95; bd. dirs. Internat. Design Conf., Aspen, 1986-92, Boston Mcpl. Res. Bur., 1990-94, Supreme Judicial Ct. Hist. Soc., 1990-94, sec., 1990-94. Fellow Am. Bar Found. (Mass. state chair); mem. Boston Bar Assn. (treas. 1988-89, v.p. 1989-90, pres.-elect 1990-91, pres. 1991-92), Internat. Women's Forum, Mass. Women's Forum, Boston Club, Phi Beta Kappa (hon.). Office: Supreme Jud Ct Pemberton Sq 1300 New Courthouse Boston MA 02108-1701*

MARSHALL, MARILYN JOSEPHINE, lawyer; b. Dayton, Ohio, May 31, 1945; d. Foy Wylie and Inez Virginia (Smith) Gard; m. Alan George Marshall, June 13, 1965; children: Gwendolyn Scott, Brian George. Student, Northwestern U., 1963-65; BA, Stanford U., 1967; cert. in teaching, U. B.C., Vancouver, 1977; JD, Capital Law Sch., Columbus, Ohio, 1985. Bar: Ohio 1985, Fla. 1993, U.S Dist. Ct. (so. dist.) Ohio 1986, U.S. Dist. Ct. (no. dist., mid. dist. and so. dist.) Fla. 1994, U.S. Ct. Appeals (6th cir.) 1986, U.S. Ct. Appeals (11th cir.) 1994. Tchr. Sutherland Secondary Sch., North Vancouver, B.C., 1977-79; instr. Brit. Coll. Inst. Tech., Burnaby, 1979-80; assoc. Crabbe, Brown, Jones, Potts & Schmidt, Columbus, Ohio, 1985-86; clk. to judge U.S. Dist. Ct. (so. dist.) Ohio, 1986-88; clk. to justice Ohio Supreme Ct., 1988-89; assoc. Squire, Sanders & Dempsey, 1989-92; with Columbus City Atty.'s Office, Columbus, Ohio, 1992-93; asst. atty. gen. civil divsn. State of Fla., Tallahassee, 1994-96; pvt. practice, 1996—. Bd. dirs. Tallahassee Symphony. Mem. ABA, Ohio Bar Assn., Fla. Bar Assn., Tallahassee Bar Assn., Tallahassee Women Lawyers Assn., Capital U. Law Sch. Alumni Assn. Republican. Avocations: tennis, gardening, music. Office: 254 E 6th Ave Tallahassee FL 32303-6208 E-mail: mjmarshall@aol.com.

MARSHALL, MARK F. lawyer; b. 1954; BS, U. S.D., 1977, JD, 1981. Bar: S.D. 1981, U.S. Dist. Ct. S.D. 1981, U.S. Ct. Appeals (8th cir.) 1981, U.S. Supreme Ct. 1984. Law clk. hon. Fred J. Nichol, 1981-83; assoc. Bangs, McCullen, Butler, Foye & Simmons, Rapid City, SD, 1983-96; of counsel Johnson, Heidepriem, Miner, Marlow & Janklow, Sioux Falls, 1996—2000; magistrate judge U.S. Dist. Ct. S.D., 1996-2000; ptnr. Davenport Law Firm, 2000—. Office: 513 S Main Ave # 1030 Sioux Falls SD 57104-6813

MARSHALL, MARTIN VIVAN, business administration educator, business consultant; b. Kansas City, July 22, 1922; s. Vivan Dean and Marie (Church) M.; m. Rosanne Borden, Sept. 5, 1951 (dec. Feb. 8, 1986); children: Martin Dean, Michael Borden, Neil McNair; m. Hildegard Meyer, June 24, 1988. AB, U. Mo., 1943; MBA, Harvard U., 1947, D.C.S., 1953. Instr. mktg. and advt. U. Kans., 1947-48; mem. faculty Harvard U., 1948—, Henry R. Byers prof. bus. adminstrn., 1960—, chmn. mktg. area faculty, 1962-66, chmn. Smaller Co. Mgmt. Program, 1981-84, chmn. Owner/Pres. Mgmt. Program, 1985-94, mem. faculty Inst. Ednl. Mgmt., 1981-90, endowed chair, Martin Marshall prof. bus. adminstrn., 1999. Cons. U.S. and internat. bus., 1950—; dir. ann. seminar mktg. and advt. Am. Advt. Fedn., 1958-78; vis. prof. mktg. IMEDE Mgmt. Inst., Lausanne, 1965-66; sr. prof., ednl. dir. Internat. Mktg. Inst., 1967-71; vis. prof. Indian Inst. Mgmt., Agra, 1968, IPADE, Mexico City, 1969, U. Melbourne, Australia, 1977, 79; bd. dirs. Western Stone & Metal.; lectr. Templeton Coll., Oxford, summer 1998. Author: Automatic Merchandising, 1954, (with N.H. Borden) Advertising Management, 1960, Notes on Marketing, 1983, 88, 90, 92, 93. Bd. dirs. Youth Svcs. Internat., Inc., 1994-97, Moclean Co., 1998-99. Served to lt. (s.g.) USNR, 1943-46. Home: 130 Mount Auburn St Apt 309 Cambridge MA 02138-5779 Office: Harvard U Cumnock Hall Boston MA 02163

MARSHALL, MARY JONES, civic worker; b. Billings, Mont.; d. Leroy Nathaniel and Janet (Currie) Dailey; m. Harvey Bradley Jones, Nov. 15, 1952 (dec. 1989); children: Dailey, Janet Currie, Ellis Bradley; m. Boyd T. Marshall, June 27, 1990. Student, Carleton Coll., 1943-44, U. Mont., 1944-46, UCLA, 1959. Owner Mary Jones Interiors. Founder, treas. Jr. Art Council, L.A. County Mus., 1953-55, v.p., 1955-56; mem. costume council Pasadena (Calif.) Philharm.; co-founder Art Rental Gallery, 1953, chmn. art and architecture tour, 1955; founding mem., sec. Art Alliance, Pasadena Art Mus., 1955-56; benefit chmn. Pasadena Girls Club, 1959, bd. dirs., 1958-60; chmn. L.A. Tennis Patron's Assn. Benefit, 1965; sustaining Jr. League Pasadena; mem. docent council L.A. County Mus.; mem. costume council L.A. County Mus. Art., program chmn. 20th Century Greatest Designers; mem. blue ribbon com. L.A. Music Ctr.; benefit chmn. Venice com. Internat. Fund for Monuments, 1971; bd. dirs. Art Ctr. 100, Pasadena, 1988—; pres. The Pres.'s L.A. Children's Bur., 1989; co-chmn. benefit Harvard Coll. Scholarship Fund, 1974, steering com. benefit, 1987, Otis Art Inst., 1975, 90th Anniversary of Children's Bureau of L.A., 1994; mem. Harvard-Radcliffe scholarship dinner com., 1985; mem. adv. bd. Estelle Doheny Eye Found., 1976, chmn. benefit, 1980; adv. bd. Loyola U. Sch. Fine Arts, L.A., Art Ctr. Sch. Design, Pasadena, Calif., 1987—; patron chmn. Benefit Achievement Rewards for Coll. Scientists, 1988; chmn. com. Sch. Am. Ballet Benefit, 1988, N.Y.C.; bd. dirs. Founders Music Ctr., L.A., 1977-81; mem. nat. adv. council Sch. Am. Ballet, N.Y.C., nat. co-chmn. gala, 1980; adv. council on fine arts Loyola-Marymount U.; mem. L.A. Olympic Com., 1984, The Colleagues; founding mem. Mus. Contemporary Art, 1986; chmn. The Pres.'s Benefit L.A. Children's Bur., 1990; exec. com. L.A. Alive for L.A. Music Ctr., 1992; mem. exec. com. Children's Bur. of L.A. Found., 1992; chmn. award dinner Phoenix House, 1994, 96; bd. dirs. Andrews Sch. Gerontology, U. So. Calif., 1996—, Leakey Found., 1996—; bd. regents Children's Hosp. L.A., 1996—. Mem. Am. Parkinson Disease Assn. (steering com. 1991), Valley Hunt Club (Pasadena), Calif. Club (L.A.), Kappa Alpha Theta. Home: 10375 Wilshire Blvd Ste 8B Los Angeles CA 90024-4712

MARSHALL, MARYANN CHORBA, office administrator; b. Scranton, Pa., Apr. 18, 1952; d. Edward M. and Mildred (Polc) Chorba; m. Daniel V. Marshall III. BA, Emmanuel Coll., 1974. Personal, social sec. Jordan Embassy Mil. Office, Washington, 1974-76; exec. asst, office mgr. Jordan Embassy Info. Bur., 1976-81; asst. to pres. Nat. Press Club, 1982-91; adminstr. Harvard Bus. Sch. Club, 1995-96; co-coord. frontiers in clin. genetics lecture series George Washington U. Med. Ctr., 1999-2000; exec. sec. The Gridiron Club, 2001—. Mem. League Rep. Women. Republican. Roman Catholic. Office: The Gridiron Club Capital Hilton Hotel 1001 16th St NW Washington DC 20036 Home: Watergate South # 805 700 New Hampshire Ave NW Washington DC 20037

MARSHALL, MERIAM DORIS, federal agency administrator; b. N.Y.C., Aug. 26, 1930; d. Nathan and Ethel Blaustein; m. Lawrence I. Marshall, Nov. 12, 1960; 1 child, Nanette D. Grad., Allderice Sch., Pitts., 1950. Postmistress substa. post office U.S. Postal Svc. Mem. NOW. Home: 5551 Centre Ave # 804 Pittsburgh PA 15232-1213

MARSHALL, MICHAEL BORDEN, marketing executive; b. Boston, Mar. 16, 1957; s. Martin Vivan and Rosanne (Borden) M.; m. Susan Diane Parks, June 15, 1991; children: Samantha Rosanne, Brenton Alexander. BA, Oberlin Coll., 1979; MBA, Harvard U., 1983. Analyst Benton & Bowles, Inc., N.Y.C., 1979-80; mktg. mgr. Thor Metal Works, Ltd., Syracuse, N.Y., 1980-81; asst. mgr. Am. Express Co., N.Y.C., 1982; sr. analyst Bank of Boston Corp., 1983-85; cons. John Hancock Mut. Life Ins. Co., Boston, 1985-89; corp. v.p. N.Y. Life Ins. Co., N.Y.C., 1989—. Cons. assoc. Bank Mktg. Assn., Boston, 1983-89, N.Y., 1991—; advisor bus. analysis Arthur D. Little, Inc., Cambridge, Mass., 1985-93. Contbr. articles to profl. jours. Adv. bd. Youth Enrichment Svcs. of Boston, 1984-90; treas. St. James Episcopal Ch., North Salem, N.Y., 1996-99. Recipient Jerome Davis award Oberlin Coll., 1979, Copeland Sect. award Harvard Bus. Sch., 1982, Corp. Spl. award John Hancock Exec. Com., 1986. Mem. Am. Mktg. Assn. (sr. v.p. 1984-93), Mktg. Sci. Inst. (bd. dirs. 1985-89), Life Ins. Mktg. and Rsch. Assn. (devel. bd. 1991-98, market rsch. com. 1995—, chmn. 2002—), Coun. on Fin. Competition (adv. bd. 1991—), Soc. Ins. Strategists (founding mem. 1992), Fin. Industry Rsch. Study Team (founding mem. 1993), Am. Coun. on Life Ins. (rsch. advisor 1994—), N.Y. Mktg. Coun., Harvard Club. Office: NY Life Ins Co 51 Madison Ave New York NY 10010-1603 E-mail: mmarshall@newyorklife.com.

MARSHALL, MONTY GLENN, political research scientist, consultant; b. Anamosa, Iowa, Feb. 5, 1952; s. Glenn Nelson and Jacqueline Anne M.; m. Beth Julia Rose Elzinga, Aug. 15, 1987 (div. May 1994); 1 child, Gabrielle Elzinga-Marshall; m. Donna Faye Ramsey, Mar. 20, 1999; 1 child, Nathan. BA, U. Colo., 1983-87; MA, U. Md., 1990; PhD, U. Iowa, 1996. Vis. asst. prof. U. S.Fla., Tampa, 1994-97; integrated network societal conflict rsch. program mgr. U. Md. Ctr. Internat. Devel. and Conflict Mgmt., College Park, 1998—. Dir. Ctr. Systemic Peace, Severn, Md., 1997—; sr. cons. State Failure Task Force, Washington, 1998—; mem. adv. bd. Minorities at Risk Project, College Park, 1998—; dir., mem. adv. bd. Polity IV Project, College Park, 1999—. Author: Third World War: System, Process, and Conflict Dynamics, 1999, Peace and Conflict 2001: A Global Survey of Armed Conflicts, Self-Determination Movements, and Democracy, 2001; contbg. author: Minorities at Risk, 1993, Federalism Against Ethnicity?, 1997, Wars in the Midst of Peace, 1997, Peoples versus States, 2000, From Reaction to Conflict Prevention: Opportunities for the UN System, 2001. Fellow, U. Iowa, 1990-93. Mem. Internat. Studies Assn., Am. Polit. Sci. Assn., Peace Sci. Soc. Avocations: biking, hiking, squash, stained glass, traveling. Home: 7939 Heather Mist Dr Severn MD 21144 Office: CIDCM U Md Tydings Hall College Park MD 20742 Fax: 301-314-9256. E-mail: CSPmgm@aol.com., mmarshall@cidcm.umd.edu.

MARSHALL, NATALIE JUNEMANN, economics educator; b. Milw., June 13, 1929; d. Harold E. and Myrtle (Findlay) Junemann; m. Howard D. Marshall, Aug. 7, 1954 (dec. 1972); children: Frederick S., Alison B.; m. Phillip Shatz, May 27, 1988. AB, Vassar Coll., 1951; MA, Columbia U., 1952, PhD, 1963, JD, 1994. Instr. Vassar Coll., Poughkeepsie, N.Y., 1952-54, 59, 59-60, 63, dean studies, prof. econs., 1973-75, v.p. for student affairs, 1975-80, v.p. for adminstrn. and student services and prof. econs., 1980-91, prof. econs., 1991-94; teaching fellow Wesleyan U., Middletown, Conn., 1955-56; from asst. prof. to prof. SUNY, New Paltz, 1964-73; prof. econs. Vassar Coll., Poughkeepsie, N.Y., 1973-94; of counsel Donoghue, Thomas, Auslander & Drohan, Hopewell Junction, 1997—. Editor: (with Howard Marshall) The History of Economic Thought, 1968; Keynes, Updated or Outdated, 1970; author: (with Howard Marshall) Collective Bargaining, 1971. Trustee St. Francis Hosp., 1979-88, Area Fund Dutchess County, 1981-87, Coll. New Rochelle, 1994-2000, Hudson Valley Philharm., 1985-92, pres., 1989-91. Mem. AAUP, Am. Assn. Higher Edn., Am. Econ. Assn., AAUW (v.p. N.Y. State div. 1964-66), Poughkeepsie Vassar Club (pres. 1965-67). Home: 157 Skidmore Rd Pleasant Valley NY 12569-5001

MARSHALL, PETER, actor, singer, game show host; b. Clarksburg, W.Va., Mar. 30, 1930; s. Ralph and Jeanne (Frampton) Lacock; m. Laurie L. Stewart, Aug. 19, 1989; children: Suzanne, Peter, David, Jaime. Grad. high sch., Huntington, W.Va. Big band singer; night club entertainer; part of comedy team Noonan and Marshall; appeared in motion pictures, musicals, comedies, Broadway and tv; host Hollywood Squares (5 Emmys: Best Game Show Host, 1973-74, 74-75, 79-80, 80-81, Best Day Time Entertainer, 1973-74). Master sgt. U.S. Army, 1944—46. Avocations: golf, tennis. E-mail: gloent@al.com.

MARSHALL, PHYLLIS ELLINWOOD, mental health system executive, consultant; b. Kansas City, Mo., Dec. 20, 1929; d. Herbert Dwight and Mildred (Gillham) Ellinwood; m. John D. Reich, July 1, 1950 (div. 1964); children: Martha Reich Millican, Michael David, Donald Martin; m. C. Randolph Marshall, Nov. 27, 1969. BA, Washington U., St. Louis, 1951, MSW, 1969. Adult program dir. St. Louis YWCA, 1964-67; alcoholism caseworker Malcolm Bliss Mental Health Ctr., St. Louis, 1968; exec. dir. Cobb County YWCA, Ga., 1969-72; dir. Coastal Area Cmty. Mental Health Crt., Brunswick, 1973-77; dir. mental health svcs. Ga. Dept. Human Resources, Atlanta, 1977-84; exec. dir. Integrated Mental Health, Inc., Rochester, N.Y., 1984-92, No. Va. Mental Health Inst., Falls Church, Va., 1992-95; mgr. MHMRSA Reorgn., Alexandria, 1995-96; state health reform dir. Nat. Mental Health Assn., 1997; project mgr. nat. women's health info. ctr. Soza & Co., Ltd., Fairfax, 1998-99; ret. Bd. dirs. Anne Arundel Co. Md. Mental Health Agy.; cons. NIMH, Washington, 1979-84, So. Regional Ednl. Bd., Atlanta, 1979-84, N.Y. State Office Mental Health, Albany, 1980-84, State of Ill. Dept. Mental Health, 1988, WHO, 1989, Ont., Can., 1990-91, The Netherlands, 1991-91, 93, 97, Sch. Medicine U. Md., 1997-98, ind. behavioral health cons., P.E.M. cons., 1996—; with mental health programs in Ohio, Mich., Ariz., Md., S.C., N.Y.; co-chair Metro Atlanta Deinstitutionalization Task Force, 1983-85; bd. dirs. Children Have All Rights, Legal, Ednl. and Emotional, Menninger Found. project, Atlanta, 1983-84; bd. dirs. Fingerlakes Health Sys. Agy., Rochester, 1985-92, bd. dirs., 1991-92; chair Monroe County Adv. Com. on Women's Issues, 1992, chmn., 1991-92; mem. steering com. Mental Health Liaison Group, Com. on Health Care Reform, Washington, 1994-99. Contbg. author: Perspectives in Mental Health Svcs., 1998, New Frontiers in Mental Health, 1989; contbr. articles to profl. pubs. Bd. dirs., pres. Ga. Human Resources Credit Union, Atlanta, 1982-84; bd. dirs. Annapolis Chorale, 2001-02. Recipient Boss of Yr. award Brunswick Jaycees, 1977, Good Friend award Brunswick Mental Health Assn., 1977, Cmty. Mental Health award Atlanta U., 1980, Outstanding Achievement award Am. Soc. for Pub. Adminstrn., 1990. Mem. AAUW (chpt. pres. 1978), Assn. Mental Health Adminstrs. (chair health policy com. 1995-96), Assn. Behavioral Healthcare Mgmt. (newsletter columnist 1996-99), Ga. Assn. Cmty. Mental Health Ctrs. (pres. 1975-77), Rochester Women's Network (bd. dirs., treas. 1990-92), New Annapolitans (pres. 2000-01, bd. dir. Annapolis Chorale, 2001-). Avocations: program development in women's sailing, music, tennis. E-mail: pemcon@att.net.

MARSHALL, RICHARD TREEGER, lawyer; b. N.Y.C., May 17, 1925; s. Edward and Sydney (Treeger) M.; m. Dorothy M. Goodman, June 4, 1950; children: Abigail Ruth Marshall Bergerson, Daniel Brooks; m. 2d Sylvia J. Kelley, June 10, 1979. BS, Cornell U., 1948; JD, Yale U., 1951. Bar: Tex. 1952, U.S. Ct.. Appeals (5th cir.) 1966, U.S. Ct. Appeals (10th cir.) 1980, U.S. Supreme Ct. 1959; lic. Tex. Dept. Ins. Pvt. practice, El Paso, Tex., 1952-59, 61-79; assoc. Fryer & Milstead, 1952; sr. ptnr. Marshall & Wendorf, 1959-61, Marshall & Volk, El Paso, 1979-81; sr. atty. Richard T. Marshall & Assocs., PC, 1981-85; sr. ptnr. Marshall, Thomas & Winters, 1985-87; sr. atty. Marshall & Winters, 1987-88, Marshall, Sherrod & Winters, 1988-90; pvt. practice El Paso, 1990—. Instr. polit. sci. U. Tex., El Paso, 1961-62; instr. ins. law C.L.U. tng. course Am. Coll.; officer, dir. Advance Funding, Inc., El Paso. Editor El Paso Trial Lawyers Rev., 1973-80; contbr. articles to profl. jours. Mem. ATLA (sec. personal injury law sect. 1967-68, nat. sec. 1969-70, sec.-treas. environ. law sect. 1970-71, vice chmn. family law litigation sec. 1971-72), El Paso Bar Assn., El Paso Trial Lawyers Assn. (pres. 1965-66), Tex. Trial Lawyers Assn., Roscoe Pound-Am. Trial Lawyers Found. (commn. on profl. responsibility 1979-82), Nat. Acad. Elder Law Attys., Soc. Cert. Sr. Advisors, Nat. Assn. Charitable Estate Counselors. Office: 5959 Gateway Blvd W El Paso TX 79925-3331 E-mail: marshall@texseniorlaw.com.

MARSHALL, ROBERT CHARLES, computer company executive; b. Berwyn, Ill., June 19, 1931; s. Joseph H. and Rose M.; m. Sarane Virruso, Aug. 1, 1954; children— Joseph, Lisa, Jim. BSE.E., Heald Engring. Coll., 1956; MBA, Pepperdine U., 1976. Engr. Lawrence Radiation Lab., Livermore, Calif., 1956-64; systems engr. Electronics Assos., Palo Alto, 1964-69; v.p. mfg. Diablo Systems, Hayward, 1969-75; with Tandem Computers, Inc., Cupertino, 1975—, sr. v.p., chief operating officer, dir., 1979-96; pres., CEO Info Gear, 1996-97; gen. ptnr. Selby Venture Ptnrs., 1998—. Served with U.S. Army, 1952-54. E-mail: Bob@selbyventures.com.

MARSHALL, ROBERT HERMAN, economics educator; b. Harrisburg, Pa., Dec. 6, 1929; s. Mathias and Mary (Bubich) M.; m. Billie Marie Sullivan, May 31, 1958; children: Mellisa Frances, Howard Hylton, Robert Charles. AB magna cum laude, Franklin and Marshall Coll., 1951; MA, Ohio State U., 1952, PhD, 1957. Teaching asst. Ohio State U., 1952-57; mem. faculty, then prof. econs. U. Ariz., Tucson, 1957-95, prof. emeritus, 1995; dir. Internat. Bus. Studies Project, 1969-71. Research observer Sci.-Industry Program, Hughes Aircraft Co., Tucson, summer 1959 Author: Commercial Banking in Arizona: Structure and Performance Since World War II, 1966, (with others) The Monetary Process, 2d edit. 1980. Bd. dirs. Com. for Econ. Opportunity, Tucson, 1968-69. Faculty fellow Pacific Coast Banking Sch., summer 1974 Mem. Am. Econ. Assn., Phi Beta Kappa, Beta Gamma Sigma, Pi Gamma Mu, Phi Kappa Phi, Delta Sigma Pi. Democrat. Roman Catholic. Home: 6700 N Abington Rd Tucson AZ 85743-9795

MARSHALL, ROBERT LEWIS, musicologist, educator; b. N.Y.C., Oct. 12, 1939; s. Saul and Pearl (Shapiro) M.; m. Traute Maass, Sept. 9, 1966; children— Eric, Brenda. AB, Columbia U., 1960; M.F.A., Princeton U., 1962, PhD, 1968; postgrad., U. Hamburg, W. Ger., 1965. Instr. dept. music U. Chgo., 1966-68, asst. prof., 1968-71, assoc. prof., chmn. dept., 1972-78, prof., 1978-83, Brandeis U., 1983-2000, chmn. dept., 1985-93, incumbent endowed chair Louis, Frances and Jeffrey Sachar prof. music, 1986-2000; emeritus, 2000—. Vis. assoc. prof. Princeton U., 1971-72; endowed prof. Univ. Ala., 1994; mem. rev. bd. rsch. materials program NEH, 1982, rev. bd. edits., 1991. Author: The Compositional Process of J.S. Bach, 2 vols., 1972, The Music of Johann Sebastian Bach: The Sources; The Style; The Significance, 1989, Mozart Speaks: Views on Music, Musicians and the World, 1991, Dennis Brain on Record: A Comprehensive Discography of His Solo, Chamber, and Orchestral Recordings, 1996; editor New Bach Edit., Eighteenth Century Keyboard Music, 1994; contbr. articles to musical jours. in U.S., Gt. Brit., Germany. Mem. music adv. bd. Ill. Arts Council, 1977-79. Recipient Deems Taylor award ASCAP, 1990; NEH fellow, 1978-79; Hon. Harold Spivacke consultantship Library of Congress. Mem. Am. Musicol. Soc. (bd. dirs. 1974-75, v.p. 1985-86, editl. bd. jour. 1975-80, rev. editor 1986-89, chmn. publs. com. 1991-94, Otto Kinkeldey prize 1974), New Bach Soc. (chmn. Am. chpt. 1977-80), Phi Beta Kappa. Home: 100 Chestnut St Newton MA 02465-2538 E-mail: rmarshall@brandeis.edu.

MARSHALL, RUSSELL FRANK, consulting company executive; b. Fort Madison, Iowa, Sept. 10, 1941; s. William Frank and Dorothy Eleanor (Mikels) M.; m. Mary Jean Bailey, June 19, 1966; children: William Russell, Robert Scott (dec.), Gregory Howard. AB, Monmouth Coll., 1963; MS, U. Ill., 1965, PhD, 1971. Rsch. engr. Materials Rsch. Lab, Urbana, Ill., 1970-75; mgr. acad. computing Drake U., Des Moines, 1975-80; v.p. GMI Ltd., 1980-83; sr. v.p., treas. Communication Devel. Co., West Des Moines, 1983-96; pres. Marshall Assocs., Iowa, 1996—; dir. info. svcs. Grand View Coll., Des Moines, 1996—. Contbr. articles to profl. jours. Active Boy Scouts Am., 1982—; mem. Des Moines Cmty. Theatre. Grantee AEC, 1964-71. Mem. Assn. Computing Machinery, Am. Phys. Soc., Assn. Info. Tech. Mgrs., Des Moines Symphony Assn. Presbyterian. Avocations: music, reading. Home: 1625 19th St West Des Moines IA 50265-1622 E-mail: RMarshall@gvc.edu.

MARSHALL, SHEILA HERMES, lawyer; b. N.Y.C., Jan. 17, 1934; d. Paul Milton and Julia Angela (Meagher) Hermes; m. James Josiah Marshall, Sept. 30, 1967; 1 child, James J.H. BA, St. John's U., N.Y.C., 1959; JD, NYU, 1963. Bar: N.Y. 1964, U.S. Ct. Appeals (2d, 3d, 5th and D.C. cirs.), U.S. Supreme Ct. 1970. Assoc. LeBoeuf, Lamb, Greene & MacRae, N.Y.C., 1963-72, ptnr., 1973—. Specialist in field. Mem. ABA, N.Y. State Bar Assn., Assn. of Bar of City of N.Y. Republican. Home: 325 E 72nd St New York NY 10021 Office: LeBoeuf Lamb Greene & MacRae 125 W 55th St New York NY 10019-5369

MARSHALL, SIRI SWENSON, corporate lawyer; BA, Harvard U., 1970; JD, Yale U., 1974. Bar: N.Y. 1975. Assoc. Debevoise & Plimpton, 1974-79; atty., sr. atty., asst. gen. counsel Avon Products, Inc., N.Y.C., 1979-85, v.p. legal affairs, 1985-89, sr. v.p., gen. counsel, 1990-94, Gen. Mills, Inc., Mpls., 1994-99, sr. v.p. corp. affairs, gen. counsel, sec., 1999—. Bd. dirs. Jafra Cosmetics, Am. Arbitration Assn.; mem. exec. com. Ctr. Pub. Resources. Trustee Mpls. Inst. Arts. Office: Gen Mills Inc Number One Gen Mills Blvd Minneapolis MN 55426

MARSHALL, SUSAN, lawyer; b. Ellsworth, Kans., July 8, 1950; d. Daniel Benjamin and Elizabeth Jean (Bailey) M. BA, U. Kans., 1972; JD with honors, Washburn U., 1976. Bar: Kans. 1976. Summer legal intern Campbell, Erickson, Cottingham, Morgan & Gibson, Kansas City, Mo., 1975; rsch. asst., lobbyist Kans. County and Dist. Attys. Assn., Topeka, 1975-76; assoc. Metz & Metz, Lincoln, Kans., 1977-83; county atty. Lincoln County, 1980-85, 89-97; pvt practice Lincoln, 1983—. Atty. position Kans. Commn. on Civil Rights, Topeka, 1978-86. Pres. Lincoln Carnegie Libr., 1982-88; bd. dirs. Lincoln Housing Authority, 1998—. Mem. ABA, Kans. Bar Assn., Kans. County and Dist. Attys. Assn., Nat. Dist. Attys. Assn., Kans. Assn. County Commrs. (bd. dirs. 1995-97), Nat. History Soc. Republican. Office: PO Box 389 117 S 4th St Lincoln KS 67455-2325

MARSHALL, SUSAN LOCKWOOD, civic worker; b. Orange, N.J., Dec. 2, 1939; d. Richard Rouglas and Helen Lockwood (Stratford) Nelson; m. William Pendleton Marshall, Aug. 20, 1960; children: Jill, James. BE, Wheelock Coll., 1961. Vol. Newton-Wellesley (Mass.) Hosp., 1962—63, New Eyes for Needy, Inc., 1963—64; vol. amblyopia screening program Short Hills, NJ, 1969—71; fund raising vol. Children's Aid and Adoption Soc. NJ, 1969—73, dir., 1970—73, asst. sec., 1970—72, 1st v.p., 1972—73; vol. Voluntary Action Ctr., 1975—76; coun. parent bd. Darien Sch., 1978—83, rec. sec., 1981—83; bd. dirs. Middlesex Jr. H.S. Parents Assn., 1979—83, treas., 1982—83; active Vol. Ctr., 1984—2001; vol. mgmt. assistance program adv. com. Darien chpt. Am. Field Svc., 1984—87; chmn. Darien H.S. Parents Assn., 1984—85; bd. dirs. Episcopal Churchwomen St. Luke's Parish, 1974—81, 2d v.p., 1976—77, asst. treas., 1977—78, treas., 1978—80, pres., 1980—81; vol. St. James by the Sea, 2002—; bd. dirs. Jr. League Oranges and Short Hills, Inc., 1967—72, corr. sect., 1970—72; bd. dirs. Jr. League Stamford-Norwalk (Conn.), 1974—78, asst. treas., 1976—77, treas., 1977—78; bd. dirs. Program One to One, Inc., 1975—76, treas.; bd. dirs., treas. Lockwood Mathews Mansion Mus., 1979—95, vol., 1979—2000, v.p., 1983—88; bd. dirs. Darien United Way, 1984—2001, asst. treas., 1988—95, treas., 1995—98, 1st v.p., 1998—99, pres., 1999—2001. Address: 2915 Woodford Dr La Jolla CA 92037-3545

MARSHALL, THOMAS CARLISLE, applied physics educator; b. Cleveland, Ohio, Jan. 29, 1935; s. Stephen Irby and Bertha Marie (Bieger) M.; children— Julian, John B.Sc., Case Inst. Tech., 1957; M.Sc., U. Ill., 1958, PhD, 1960. Asst. prof. elec. engring. U. Ill., 1961-62; mem. faculty Columbia U., 1962—, assoc. prof. elec. engring., 1962-65, assoc. prof., 1965-70, prof. engring. sci., 1970-78, prof. applied physics, 1978—. Author: Free Electron Lasers, 1985, Book of the Toade, 1992; contbr. articles to profl. jours. Research grantee Dept. Energy, Office Naval Research, NSF. Fellow: Am. Phys. Soc. (study group on directed energy weapons 1985—87); mem.: Free Election Lasers and Advanced Concepts in Accelerator Physics. Office: Columbia U 213 Mudd Bldg New York NY 10027 E-mail: tcm2@columbia.edu.

MARSHALL, THOMAS OLIVER, JR. lawyer; b. Americus, Ga., June 24, 1920; s. Thomas Oliver and Mattie Louise (Hunter) M.; m. Angie Ellen Fitts, Dec. 20, 1946; children: Ellen Irwin Marshall Beard, Anne Hunter Marshall Peagler, Mary Olivia Marshall Hodges. BS in Engring., U.S. Naval Acad., 1941; JD, U. Ga., 1948. Bar: Ga. 1947. Pvt. practice law, Americus, Ga., 1948-60; judge S.W. Judicial Circuit, 1960-74, Ga. Ct. Appeals, Atlanta, 1974-77; justice Ga. Supreme Ct., 1977-86, chief justice, 1986-89; pvt. practice, 1989—. Chmn. bd. visitors U. Ga. Law Sch., 1970. Trustee Andrew Coll., So. Ga. Meth. Home for Aged; active ARC, 1948-60, United Givers Fund, 1948-54. Served with USN, World War II, Korean War. Decorated Bronze Star; named Young Man of Yr. Americus, 1953. Mem. ABA, Ga. Bar Assn. (bd. govs. 1958-60), Atlanta Bar Assn., State Bar Ga., Am. Judicature Soc., Nat. Jud. Coll., Jud. Coll. Ga., VFW, Am. Legion. Lodges: Kiwanis, Masons, Shriners. Methodist. Home: 238 15th St NE Apt 3 Atlanta GA 30309-3594 Office: 1 Atlantic Ctr 1201 W Peachtree St NW Atlanta GA 30309-3449

MARSHALL, TIM I. entertainment company executive; b. LaCrosse, Wis., Dec. 27, 1961; s. Donald Charles and Mary Ann (Hein) M. Student, Winona State U., 1986-88. Prodr. Brandon Marsh Entertainment, Milw., 1993-95, exec. prodr., 1994—; pres. Brandon Marsh Entertainment, Inc., 1996—. Prodn. cons. State Bar Wis., Madison, 1996-97; CEO Future Pride Found., Milw., 1997—. Prodr., author (TV) TRUE to Desire, 1995-96, Dark of the Night, 1998, Reverse World, 1999; author: End of the Wind, 1996; dir. (TV) Law Talk, 1996-99; prodr., host. (TV) In A Fishbowl, 1997-98. Mem. leadership circle United Way, Milw., 1996, gov.'s circle, 1997-99. Sgt. U.S. Army, 1982-86. Recipient Philo award Milw. Access Telecom., 1993, 95, 97, Exceptional Support for Cmty. TV awards Milw. Access Telecom., 1994, 96. Mem. NATAS, Alliance for Cmty. Media. Avocations: weightlifting, backpacking, writing, photography. Office: Brandon Marsh Entertainment Inc 316 N Milwaukee St Milwaukee WI 53202-5885

MARSHALL, VINCENT DE PAUL, industrial microbiologist, researcher; b. Washington, Apr. 5, 1943; s. Vincent de Paul Sr. and Mary Frances (Bach) M.; m. Sylvia Ann Kieffer, Nov. 15, 1986; children from previous marriage: Vincent de Paul III, Amy. BS, Northeastern State Coll., Tahlequah, Okla., 1965; MS, U. Okla. Health Sci. Ctr., Oklahoma City, 1967, PhD, 1970. Rsch. assoc. U. Ill., Urbana, 1970, postdoctoral fellow, 1971-73; rsch. scientist The Upjohn Co., Kalamazoo, 1973-74, rsch. head, 1975, sr. rsch. scientist, 1976-91, sr. scientist, 1991-2000; cons., 2000—. Mem. editl. bd. Jour. of Antibiotics, 1990-2001, Jour. Indsl. Microbiology, 1989-2001, Devels. in Indsl. Microbiology, 1990; contbr. numerous articles to profl. jours., chpts. to books; patentee in field. Served with U.S. Army Nat. Guard, 1960-65. NIH predoctoral fellow, 1967-70; NIH postdoctoral fellow, 1971-73. Fellow Am. Acad. Microbiology; mem. Soc. for Indsl. Microbiology (membership com. 1988-90, co-chair edn. com. 1989-93, local sects. com. 1991-96, chair nominating com. 1993-94, mem. nominating com. 1999-2000, co-chair program com. 1993-94, dir. 1994-96, pres. So. Great Lakes sect. 1992-95), Am. Soc. Microbiology, Am. Soc. Biochemistry and Molecular Biology, Internat. Soc. for Antimicrobial Activity of Non-Antibiotics (sci. adv. bd.), Sigma Xi. Republican. Lutheran. Home and Office: 203 Paisley Ct Kalamazoo MI 49006-4359 E-mail: vince3795@aol.com.

MARSHALL, WAYNE KEITH, anesthesiology educator; b. Richmond, Va., Feb. 9, 1948; s. Chester Truman and Lois Ann (Tiller) M.; m. Dale Claire Reynolds, June 18, 1977; children: Meredith Reynolds, Catherine Truman, Whitney Wood. BS in Biology, Va. Poly. Inst. and State U., 1970; MD, Va. Commonwealth U., 1974. Diplomate Am. Bd. Anesthesiology, Nat. Bd. Med. Examiners; bd. cert. in pain mgmt. Surg. intern U. Cin., 1974-75, resident in surgery, 1975-77; resident in anesthesiology U. Va. Coll. Medicine, Charlottesville, 1977-79, rsch. fellow, 1979-80; asst. prof. anesthesia Pa. State U. Coll. Medicine, Hershey, 1980-86, assoc. prof., 1986-95, assoc. clin. dir. oper. rm., 1982-95, dir. pain mgmt. svc., 1984-95, chief divsn. pain mgmt., 1992-95; prof., chmn. dept. anesthesiology Med. Coll. Va., Richmond, 1995-99; med. dir. operating rms. MCV Hosp., 1995-99; prof. anesthesiology Coll. Medicine Pa. State U., Hershey, 1999—. Moderator nat. meetings. Mem. editorial bd. Am. Jour. Anesthesiology, 1987-99, Jour. Neurosurg. Anesthesiology, 1988—; contbr. articles and abstracts to med. jours. Recipient Antarctic Svc. medal NSF, 1980. Mem. AMA, Soc. Neurosurg. Anesthesia and Critical Care (sec.-treas. 1985-87, v.p. 1987-88, pres. 1989-90, bd. dirs. 1985-91), Assn. Univ. Anesthetists, Am. Soc. Anesthesiologists (del. ASA ho. of dels. 1990-92), Internat. Anesthesia Rsch. Soc., Pa. Soc. Anesthesiology. Republican. Baptist. Office: Dept Anesthesiology Penn St Univ Coll of Med PO Box H-187 Hershey PA 17033-2360 E-mail: wkmarshall@psu.edu.

MARSHALL, WENDE ELIZABETH, anthropologist, educator; b. New Haven, Oct. 12, 1961; d. Carter Lee, Jr. and Julie Adelaide Marshall. PhD, Princeton U., 1999. Co-author: (book) Criminality and Citizenship: Implicating the White Nation, 1999. Mem. adv. bd. Action Cmty. Empowerment, N.Y.C., 1992—2002; bd. dirs. Prevention Point Phila., 1993—95; mem. adv. bd. Carter G. Woodson Inst., Charlottesville, Va., 2001—02. Fellow Postdoctoral, Yale U./NIMH, 1999-2001. Mem.: Am. Anthrop. Assn. Home: 128 Shamrock Rd Charlottesville VA 22903 Office: U Va PO Box 400120 Charlottesville VA 22904 Office Fax: 434-924-1350. E-mail: wm3f@virginia.edu.

MARSHALL, WILLIAM EDWARD, historical association executive; b. St. Paul, Apr. 19, 1925; s. William Edward and Louise (White) M.; m. Ruth Marie Winner, Sept. 3, 1947 (div.); children: Michael Scott, Terry Lee, Sharon; m. Loretta E. Slota, Nov. 6, 1976; children: Marc William, Matthew Ryan. BA, U. Mont., 1950; BFA, Wittenberg U., 1951; postgrad., Ohio State U., 1951-52. Owner, operator Public Library Public Relations Service, 1952-55, Specialized Press, 1952-60; graphic and exhibits designer Ohio Hist. Soc., 1952-60, State Historic Soc. Colo., Denver, 1960-61, dep. exec. dir., 1961-63, exec. dir., 1963-79; cons. to hist. agys., author, 1979—. Founding mem. Little Kingdom Hist. Found.; condr. historic interpretation seminars and workshops. Author historic TV and film prodns., books, fiction and non-fiction in nat. publs.; editor: Humboldt Historian, 1990-91, CEO MediFacts, 1992—; illustrator, photographer books and periodicals; contbr. articles to profl. jours. Bd. dirs. Rocky Mountain Center on Environment, 1967-72, Trinidad Mus. Soc., 1986-89; chmn. Colo. Humanities Program Com., 1971, 75. With USMCR, 1943-45. Mem. Am. Assn. Museums (exec. com. 1973-74, mus. accreditation evaluator), Am. Assn. State and Local History (mem. council 1966-72, awards com. 1966-80, com. on fed. programs in history), Orgn. Am. Historians (hist. sites com. 1974-75) Presbyterian. Home: Moonstone Heights 719 Driver Rd Trinidad CA 95570-9722 E-mail: marshall@marshallgallery.com.

MARSHALL, WILLIAM JEFFREY, journalist, author; b. N.Y.C., Mar. 17, 1949; s. Albert Edward Jr. and Barbara (Stevenson) M.; m. Judith Marie Smith, July 2, 1983. AB, Princeton U., 1971; MSJ, Northwestern U., 1974. Reporter Bergen Record, Hackensack, N.J., 1974-80, AP, Newark, 1982; editor Northwest News, Midland Park, N.J., 1980-82; writer, editor American Banker, N.Y.C., 1983-90; mng. editor U.S. Banker, 1991-97, exec. editor, 1997-98, editor-in-chief, 1998-00; dir. publs., editor-in-chief Fin. Execs. Internat., Morristown, N.J., 2000—. Author: Staying Ahead of CRA, 1991; freelance contbr. to nat. and regional publs.; contbr. poetry to nat. anthologies. Co-recipient Neal award, Am. Bus. Press, 1993; finalist, 1996; recipient cert., Am. Soc. Assn. Execs. Gold Circle Awards, 2001. Mem. Am. Soc. Mag. Editors, Princeton Alumni Schs. Com., Chatham Fish and Game Club, Trout Unltd. Avocations: tennis, fly fishing, golf, gardening. Home: 49 Canfield Rd Morristown NJ 07960-6936 Office: 10 Madison Ave Morristown NJ 07960-7303 E-mail: jeffmall@aol.com.

MARSHALL, WILLIAM TAYLOR, lawyer; b. Dallas; s. Willis A. and Jane T. Marshall; m. Peggy Taylor, May 18, 1973; 1 child, Taylor. BSPA with honors, U. Ark., 1973, MBA with honors, 1975; JD with honors, U. Ark., Little Rock, 1981. Bar: Ark. 1981, U.S. Dist. Ct. (fed. dist.) 1982, U.S. Ct. Appeals (8th cir.) 1982, U.S. Supreme Ct. 1984; CPA, Ark. Fin. analyst Hosp. Affiliates Internat., Nashville, 1975-76, sr. fin. analyst, 1976-78; CFO Hosp. Affiliates Internat./Doctor's Hosp., Little Rock, 1978-81; assoc. House Holmes & Jewell, 1981-83, ptnr., 1983-85, Robinson, Staley, Marshall & Duke, Little Rock, 1985—. Lectr. in field. Contbr. articles to profl. jours. Mem. ABA, AICPAs, Ark. Bar Assn. (cert. tax specialist, health law sect. 1985—), Am. Health Lawyers Assn. Home: 1900 Beechwood St Little Rock AR 72207-2004 Office: Robinson Staley Marshall & Duke PA 400 W Capitol Ave Ste 2891 Little Rock AR 72201-3463 E-mail: bmarshall@rsmd.com.

MARSHALL-DANIELS, MERYL, telecommunications executive, lawyer; b. L.A., Oct. 16, 1949; d. Jack and Nita Corinblit; m. Raymond Daniels, Aug. 19, 2000. BA, UCLA, 1971; JD, Loyola Marymount U., L.A., 1974. Bar: Calif. 1974. Dep. pub. defender County of L.A., 1975-77; sole practice L.A., 1977-78; ptnr. Markman and Marshall, 1978-79; sr. atty. NBC, Burbank, Calif., 1979-80, dir. programs, talent contracts bus. affairs, 1980, asst. gen. atty. N.Y.C., 1980-82, v.p., compliance and practices Burbank, 1982; v.p. program affairs Group W Prodns., 1987-89, sr. v.p. future images, 1989-91, TV producer, Meryl Marshall Prodns., 1991-93; pres. Two Oceans Entertainment Group, 1991—. Chmn., Nat. Women's Polit. Caucus, Westside, Calif., 1978-80; mem. Calif. Dem. Ctrl. Com., 1978-79; mem. Hollywood Women's Polit. Com., 1988. Mem.: Women in Film, Acad. TV Arts and Scis. (treas. 1985, treas. 1993—97, bd. govs. 1989—2001, pres. 1997—99, chmn. bd., CEO 1999—2001). Democrat. Jewish. Office: Two Oceans Entertainment Group 2017 Lemoyne St Los Angeles CA 90026 E-mail: twooceans@aol.com.

MARSHELLA, THOMAS JOSEPH, financial analyst; b. Bridgeport, Conn., Mar. 13, 1957; s. Thomas Albert and Dorothy Corrine (D'Elia) M.; m. Linda Elizabeth Humphrey, July 9, 1988; children: Julia Dorothy, Casey May. BS in Acctg., U. Conn., 1979; MBA in Fin., Tulane U., 1983. CPA, Conn. Staff intern Zolan, Bernstein, Dworken and Klein, CPAs, Bridgeport, 1978; auditor Ernst & Young, New Haven, 1979-81; fin. intern, then investment analyst Met. Life Ins. Co., N.Y.C., 1982-85; sr. fin. analyst Moody's Investors Svc., Inc., 1985-87, asst. v.p. fin. planning and devel., 1987-88; assoc. dir. energy, tech. and communications dept. Pub. Utility Group, 1988-93; mng. dir. Moodys Australia, Sydney, 1993-97, Global Project Fin., N.Y.C., 1996—, Speculative Grade Ratings, N.Y.C., 1996—. Speaker at profl. meetings. Pub. rels. vol. Conn. State Spl. Olympics, New Haven, 1980. Mem. AICPA, Wall St. Utility Group. Avocations: golf, running. Office: 99 Church St New York NY 10007-2707

MARSICO, THOMAS, investment company executive; married; 3 children. Mgr. Janus Funds; founder Marsico Capital Mgmt., Denver, 1999, CEO. Office: Marsico CapitalMgmt 1200 17th St Ste 1300 Denver CO 80202-9813*

MARSOCCI, VELIO ARTHUR, engineering educator, researcher; b. N.Y.C., June 7, 1928; s. Frank and Jennie (Cioffi) M.; m. Frances Siracusa, Sept. 3, 1955; children: Christopher (dec.), Francesca. BEE, NYU, 1953, MEE, 1955, D of Engring. Sci., 1964. Registered profl. engr., N.Y., N.J. Instr. in elec. engring. NYU, Bronx, 1954-56; asst. prof. elec. engring. Stevens Inst. Tech., Hoboken, N.J., 1956-63, assoc. prof. elec. engring., 1964-65, SUNY, Stony Brook, 1965-67, prof., 1967-94, Disting. Svc. prof., 1994—2000, Disting. Svc. prof. emeritus, 2000—. Pvt. practice electronics cons. Contbr. articles to profl. jours. With USN, 1946-49. Grantee NSF, 1985. Mem. IEEE, NSPE, Am. Soc. Engring. Edn., Eta Kappa Nu, Tau Beta Pi, Sigma Xi, Golden Key. Achievements include first to achieve experimental measurements and theorectical model for spin-orbit interaction in single-crystal ferromagnetic thin films, experimental and theoretical models of superconducting linear amplifiers.

MARSTON, EDGAR JEAN, III, lawyer; b. Houston, July 5, 1939; s. Edgar Jr. and Jean (White) M.; m. Graeme Meyers, June 21, 1961; children: Christopher Graham, Jonathan Andrew. BA, Brown U., 1961; JD, U. Tex., 1964. Bar: Tex. 1964. Law clk. to presiding justice Supreme Ct. Tex., Austin, 1964-65; assoc. Baker & Botts, Houston, 1965-71; ptnr. Bracewell & Patterson, 1971-89, 96—, of counsel, 1990-96; exec. v.p., gen. counsel Southdown, Inc., 1987-95, also bd. dirs. Mem. ABA, Tex. Bar Assn., Tex. Bar Found., Houston Bar Assn., Houston Country Club, Coronado Club. Episcopalian. Avocations: hunting, fishing, philately, reading. Office: Bracewell & Patterson 711 Louisiana St Ste 2900 Houston TX 77002-2781 E-mail: emarston@bracepatt.com.

MARSTON, MICHAEL, urban economist, asset management executive; b. Oakland, Calif., Dec. 4, 1936; s. Lester Woodbury and Josephine (Janovic) M.; m. Alexandra Lynn Geyer, Apr. 30, 1966; children: John, Elizabeth. BA, U. Calif., Berkeley, 1959; postgrad. London Sch. Econs., 1961-63. V.p. Larry Smith & Co., San Francisco, 1969-72, exec. v.p. urban econ. divsn., 1969-72; chmn. bd. Keyser Marston Assocs., Inc., San Francisco, 1973-87; gen. ptnr. The Sequoia Partnership, 1979-91; pres. Marston Vineyard and Winery, 1982—, Marston Assocs., Inc., 1982—, The Ctr. for Individual and Instnl. Renewal, 1996—. Cert. rev. appraiser Nat. Assn. Rev. Appraisers and Mortgage Underwriters, 1984—. Chmn., San Francisco Waterfront Com., 1969-86; chmn. fin. com., bd. dirs., mem. exec. com., treas. San Francisco Planning and Urban Rsch. Assn., 1976-87, Napa Valley Vintners, 1986—, mem. gov. affairs com.; trustee Cathedral Sch. for Boys, 1981-82, Marin Country Day Sch., 1984-90; v.p. St. Luke's Sch., 1986-91; pres. Presidio Heights Assn. of Neighbors, 1983-84; chmn. Presidio Com. 1991—; v.p., bd. dirs., mem. exec. com. People for Open Space, 1972-87; mem. Gov.'s Issue Analysis Com. and Speakers Bur., 1966; mem. speakers bur. Am. Embassy, London, 1961-63; v.p., bd. dirs. Dem. Forum, 1968-72; v.p., trustee Youth for Service. Served to lt. USNR. Mem. Napa Valley Vintners, Urban Land Inst., World Congress Land Policy (paper in field), Order of Golden Bear, Chevalier du Tastevin, Bohemian Club, Pacific Union Club, Lambda Alpha. Contbr. articles to profl. jours. Home: 3375 Jackson St San Francisco CA 94118-2018 *Personal philosophy: Success is what you do with what you have not what others think or what is in vogue.*

MARSTON, ROBERT ANDREW, public relations executive; b. Astoria, N.Y., Aug. 6, 1937; s. Frank and Lena (DiDomenico) M.; m. Maryann Doherty, Sept. 23, 1990; children: Robert Brendan, Bradford Scott. BA, Hofstra U., 1959. Sr. v.p. Rowland Co., N.Y.C., 1959-68, Rogers & Cowen, Inc., N.Y.C., 1968-70; founder, chmn., CEO Robert Marston And Assocs., Inc., 1970—. Contbr. articles and photographs to profl. jours. and popular mags. Mem. Pub. Rels. Soc. Am. (counselors sect.), Doubles Club, Southampton Bath & Tennis Club, Sky Club. Roman Catholic. Home: 570 Park Ave New York NY 10021-7370 also: 130 Captains Neck Ln Southampton NY 11968-4561 Office: 485 Madison Ave New York NY 10022-5803

MARSZALEK, JOHN EDWARD, lawyer; b. Chgo., Oct. 24, 1951; s. Edward J. and Virginia F. (Yaks) M.; m. Therese E. Finn, Jan. 26, 1985. BA, Rollins Coll., Winter Park, Fla., 1972; JD, John Marshall Law Sch., Chgo., 1976. Bar: Ill. 1976, U.S. Dist. Ct. (no. dist.) Ill. 1977, Fla. 1979, U.S. Supreme Ct. 1986, U.S. Ct. Appeals (7th cir.) 1986. Assoc. Goldstein, Goldberg & Fishman, Chgo., 1976-79, John G. Phillips & Assocs., Chgo., 1979-83; proprietor Law Office of John E. Marszalek, 1983-84; owner Marszalek & Marszalek, 1984—. E-mail. Home: 910 N Lake Shore Dr Apt 517 Chicago IL 60611-1585 Office: Marszalek & Marszalek 29 S La Salle St Ste 830 Chicago IL 60603-1561 E-mail: jmarszalek@aol.com.

MARTAN, JOSEPH RUDOLF, lawyer; b. Mar. 28, 1949; s. Joseph John and Margarete Paula (Rothenbock) M. BA with honors, U. Ill., 1971; JD with honors, Ill. Inst. Tech., 1977; cert., Masaryk U., Brno Czech Republic, 1993, 94, 95. Bar: Ill. 1977, U.S. Dist. Ct. (no. dist.) Ill. 1977. Assoc. V.C. Lopez, Chgo., 1978-80; corp. counsel Goldblatt Bros., Inc., 1980-81; br. counsel Ill. br. Am. Family Ins. Group, Schaumburg, Ill., 1981-87; atty. Judge & Knight Ltd., Park Ridge, 1987-91, Judge & James, Ltd., Park Ridge, 1991-92; staff counsel Alliance of Am. Insurers Liability Ins. Rsch. Bur., Downers Grove, 1992—. Mem. Czech Republic program adv. bd. John Marshall law Sch., 1996—; mem. West Suburban Concert Band, Inc., Western Springs, Ill., 1975—, pres., 1979-81, v.p. 1989-90. with U.S. Army, 1972-74; capt. USAR, 1974-85. Mem. Ill. State Bar Assn., West Suburban Bar Assn., DuPage County Bar Assn., Bohemian Lawyer's Assn. Chgo. (pres. 1990), Windjammers Unltd. Inc., Chgo. Coun. Fgn. Rels., Czech-Am. C. of C., Res. Officer's Assn., Assn. U.S. Army, Met. Opera Guild, Pi Sigma Alpha. Home: 4056 Gilbert Ave Western Springs IL 60558-1235 Office: Alliance Am Insurers Liability Ins Rsch Bureau 3025 Highland Pkwy Ste 800 Downers Grove IL 60515-5506 E-mail: hundd44@hotmail.com.

MARTARELLA, FRANC DAVID, television executive, not-for-profit fundraiser; b. Bklyn., Jan. 23; s. Frank James and Ann (Barbarito) M. BFA, NYU, 1972, MBA, 1974. Producer/writer/dir. WNYC-TV, 1971-72; unit mgr. ABC News, N.Y.C., 1972-74; prodn. mgr. Feature Films, 1974-76; prodn. controller WNET/Fin., 1976-80; prodn. supr. CBS Cable, 1980; mgr. arts programming for fin. Sta. WNET, 1981, assoc. dir. bus. affairs, 1982-84, bus. mgr. Prodn. Ctr., 1984-86; dir. co-prodn. financing and prog. adminstrn. Sta. WNET-TV, 1986-89, dir. bus. affairs, 1989-92; supr. spl. projects Sta. WNYC Radio and TV, N.Y.C., 1992-98; budget and grant dir. CASES, 1999-2000; budget mgr. GMHC, 2000—. Cons. ABC News, 20/20, Raintree Prodns., Martin Carr Prodns., Office for Telecommunications, U.S. Cath. Conf., Smithsonian Instn., WETA-TV, Cen. TV, London. Contbr. articles to profl. jours. Recipient Emmy Award Certificates, Nat. Acad. TV Arts and Scis., 1982, 86. Mem. NATAS, Am. Coun. Exercise, Idea Found. Avocations: piano, voice, photography, marathon aerobic competitions (cert. aerobics instr.).

MARTAS, JULIA ANN, special education administrator; b. Bronx, N.Y., July 30, 1949; d. Julio and Emilia (Guerra) M. BS, CCNY, 1972, MS, 1975; postgrad., NYU. Cert. spl. edn. tchr., N.Y., sch. adminstrn. and supr. Tchr bilingual spl. edn. N.Y.C. Bd. Edn., 1972-82, regional coord. bilingual-spl. edn. div. spl. edn. Manhattan, 1982-86, profl. assocs., div. personnel, 1986-87, chancellor's monitor spl. edn. office of monitoring, 1987-88, dist. adminstr. spl. edn., 1988-95; dir. spl. edn. Instrl. Svcs., Rockford, Ill., 1995-99; asst. dir. spl. edn. tech. support svcs. D.C. Pub. Schs., Washington, 1999—. Instr. grad. spl. edn. dept. Coll. of New Rochelle, L.I. U., Adelphi U., CCNY, 1984-95, U. Ill., Chgo., 1999; cons. sch. div. McGraw Hill Pub. Co., Globe Pub. Co., Bowmar Noble, Economy Pub. Co. Recipient Congl. Recognition USA, 1992, Cert. of Merit N.Y. State Senate, 1992. Mem. ASCD, Coun. for Exceptional Children, Ill. Coun. for Exceptional Children (regional dir., exec. bd. dirs. 1996-99), P.R. Educators Assn., N.Y.C. Assn. Dist. Adminstrs. Spl. Edn., Odd Fellows, House of Ruth. Office: DC Pub Schs 825 N Capitol St NE Washington DC 20002-4210

MARTEL, EVA LEONA, accountant; b. Bristol, Conn., Feb. 14, 1945; d. Samuel L. and Irene A. (Beaulieu) Martel. BS in Acctg., N.H. Coll., 1986; MBA, Plymouth State Coll., 1990. Cert. mgmt. acct.; cert. continuing edn. educator. Accts. payable Elliot Hosp., Manchester, N.H., 1971-79, bookkeeper, 1979-84, dir. acctg., 1984-94; portfolio mgr. Optima Health Inc., N.H., 1994-97, mgr. managed care contracting, 1997-98, dir. managed care, 1998-2000; exec. dir. managed care Elliot Hosp., 2000—. Adj. faculty N.H. Coll., 1991—; speaker Daniel Webster coun. Boy Scouts Am., Manchester, 1988, Med. Assts. Workshop, 1997; panel mem. ednl. seminar, 1993. Treas. N.H. Indian Cun., 1980-84; vol. United Way, Manchester, 1988—, accountexec., 1990, 91; mem. adv. coun. health care adminstrn. N.H. Coll., 1990, faculty advisor weekend program, 1990-91; vol. N.H. Heart Assn., 1990-92; bd. dirs. N.H. chpt. Am. Cancer Soc., 1991—; road race com. Elliot Hosp.; mem. scholarship com. Jewett Sch. Recipient Excellence in Tchg. award N.H. Coll., 2000. Mem. NAFE, Hosp. Fin. Mgmt. Assn., Speaker's Bur. (smoke free com., recycling com. 1991), IMA, Healthcare Fin. Mgmt. Assn. Roman Catholic. Avocations: physical fitness, reading, music, writing, teaching. Home: 129 Riverledge Dr Goffstown NH 03045-6203 E-mail: emartel@optima.org.

MARTEL, JOHN SHELDON, lawyer, writer; b. Stockton, Calif., Jan. 1, 1931; s. Henry T. and Alice L. M.; m. Bonnie Martel; children: John Sheldon, Melissa Ann. BS, U. Calif.-Berkeley, 1956, JD, 1959. Bar: Calif. 1959. Dep. dist. atty., Alameda County, 1960-61; assoc. trial atty. firm Bronson, Bronson & McKinnon, San Francisco, 1961-64; ptnr. firm Farella, Braun & Martel, 1964—. Lectr., mem. adv. bd. Hastings Ctr. for Trial and Appelate Adv., 1983—. Author: (novels) Partners, 1988, Conflicts of Interest, 1994, The Alternate, 1999, Billy Strobe, 2001; author, editor legal publs.; composer-writer popular songs; profl. musician. Pilot USAF, 1951-54. Winner Am. Song Festival awards, 1978-80, 82, 85, 87. Fellow Am. Coll. Trial Lawyers (state chmn. 1985-87, bd. regents 1993-98); mem. ABA (litigation, antitrust, tort and ins. sects.), Calif. Bar Assn., San Francisco Bar Assn. (former chair litigation sect.), Am. Bd. Trial Advocates (bd. dirs. 1991-93), Am. Fedn. Musicians, Phi Delta Phi, Kappa Sigma. Office: Farella Braun & Martel 235 Montgomery St Ste 3100 San Francisco CA 94104-2902

MARTEL, WILLIAM, radiologist, educator; b. N.Y.C., Oct. 1, 1927; s. Hyman and Fanny M.; m. Rhoda Kaplan, Oct. 9, 1956; children: Lisa, Pamela, Caryn, Jonathan, David. MD, NYU, 1953. Intern, Kings County Hosp., N.Y., 1953-54; resident in radiology Mt. Sinai Hosp., N.Y.C., 1954-57; instr. radiology U. Mich., Ann Arbor, 1957-60, asst. prof., 1960-63, asso. prof., 1963-67, prof., 1967—, Fred Jenner Hodges prof., 1984—, chmn. dept. radiology, 1981-92, dir. skeletal radiology, 1970-81, Fred Jenner Hodges prof. emeritus radiology, 1997—. Contbr. articles to Radiol. Diagnoses of Arthritic Diseases. Served with USAAF, 1945-46. Recipient Amoco U. Mich. Outstanding Teaching award, 1980; established William Martel professorship in radiology U. Mich., 1997. Mem. Radiol. Soc. N.Am., Am. Roentgen Ray Soc., Assn. Univ. Radiologists. Home: 2972 Parkridge Dr Ann Arbor MI 48103-1737 Office: Univ Mich Hosps Dept Radiology 1500 E Med Ctr Dr Ann Arbor MI 48109 E-mail: wmartel@umich.edu.

MARTELL, DANIEL ALLEN, forensic neuropsychologist, researcher, educator; b. Elkhart, Ind., Oct. 22, 1957; m. Christine Purzycki. BA, Washington & Jefferson Coll., 1980; MA, U. Va., 1985, PhD, 1991. Lic. clin. psychologist, N.Y. Fellow in forensic psychology Bellevue Hosp./NYU, N.Y.C., 1987-88; clin. asst. prof. NYU Sch. Medicine, 1989-94; rsch. scientist Nathan Kline Inst., Orangeburg, N.Y., 1989-94; dir. forensic neuropsychology lab. Kirby Forensic, N.Y.C., 1989-94; asst. clin. prof. UCLA Neuropsychiat. Iinst., 1994—; pvt. practice Park Dietz & Assocs., Newport Beach, Calif., 1994—. Contbr. articles to profl. jours. Recipient Disting. Lectr. award N.Y. State Dist. Attys. Assn., 1996. Mem. APA, AAAS, Nat. Assn. Neuropsychology (profl.), Am. Acad. Forensic Scis. (sec. 1997—), Am. Psychology Law Soc., Am. Soc. Criminology. Avocations: gardening, cooking, music. Office: 537 Newport Ctr Dr # 200 Newport Beach CA 92660-6937

MARTELL, KEITH, bank executive; Chmn. First Nations Bank Can., Saskatoon. Avocation: scuba diving. Office: First Nations Bank Can 224 4th Ave S Saskatoon SK S7K 5M5 Canada*

MARTEN, GORDON CORNELIUS, research agronomist, educator, federal agency administrator; b. Wittenberg, Wis., Sept. 14, 1935; s. Clarence George and Cora Levina (Verpoorten) M.; m. Lynette Joy Hanson, Sept. 9, 1961; 1 dau., Kimberly Joy. BS, U. Wis., 1957; MS, U. Minn., 1959, PhD, 1961; postgrad., Purdue U., 1962. Rsch. agronomist U.S. Dept. Agr., U. Minn., St. Paul, 1961-72, supervisory rsch. agronomist, rsch. leader, 1972-89; adj. prof. agronomy U. Minn., 1971-96; assoc. dir. USDA-Agr. Rsch. Svc., Beltsville, Md., 1989-96; prof. emeritus U. Minn., St. Paul, 1996—. Mem. governing body and U.S. rep. to OECD Biol. Resource Mgmt. Program, Paris, 1990-96; adminstrv. coun. USDA Sustainable Agrl. Rsch. and Edn. Program, 1993-95. Assoc. editor: Crop Sci., 1972-74; sr. editor USDA Handbook Near Infrared Reflectance Spectroscopy: Analysis of Forage Quality, 1985, rev. edit., 1989; mem. edit. bd. Sci. of Food and Agriculture, 1985-90; contbr. numerous articles to profl. jours. NSF grad. fellow, 1959-61; recipient Merit award Am. Forage and Grassland Coun., 1976, Outstanding Svc. award, 1981, Civil Servant of Yr. award Twin Cities, Minn., 1976, Cert. of Merits, USDA Agrl. Rsch. Svc., Northrup King Faculty Outstanding Performance award U. Minn., 1986, Superior Svc. award USDA, 1987; named to Hall of Fame, Wausau Wis. Sch. Dist., 1998. Fellow: Crop Sci. Soc. Am. (bd. dirs. 1975—77), Am. Soc. Agronomy; mem.: Agronomic Sci. Found. (trustee 1984—89), Coun. Agr. Sci. and Tech. (bd. dirs. 1985—90), Am. Forage and Grassland Coun. (bd. dirs. 1977—80), North Suburban St. Paul Golden K Kiwanis (bd. dirs. 1998—2001), Biol. Club, Sigma Xi, Phi Kappa Phi, Delta theta Sigma, Alpha Zeta, Gamma Sigma Delta (Adminstrn. award of merit Nat. Capital Area 1994). Lutheran. Home: 1312 Willow Cir Roseville MN 55113-3235

MARTEN, ROBERT DANIEL, obstetrician/gynecologist, retired; b. Milw., 1929; MD, Marquette U., 1954. Diplomate Am. Bd. Ob-Gyn. Intern St. Mary's Hosp., Milw., 1954-55; resident ob-gyn Kaiser Found. Hosp., Oakland, Calif., 1958-61; ret., 1996. Ob-gyn Kaiser Found. Hosp., Walnut Creek, Calif.; clin. instr. U. Calif. San Francisco. Fellow ACS, Am. Coll. Ob-Gyn; mem. AMA. E-mail: marten@jps.net.

MARTENS, DAN E. lawyer; b. Oklahoma City, Mar. 27, 1945; s. Frank M. and Estele Alice Martens; m. Susan Jo Farmer, Apr. 3, 1976; children: Kathryn T., Daniel C. BA in Social Sci., So. Meth. U., 1967, JD, 1974. Bar: Tex. 1974, U.S. Dist. Ct. (no. dist.) Tex. 1974, U.S. Dist. Ct. (ea. dist.) Tex. 1991, U.S. Dist. Ct. (we. dist.) Okla. 1983, U.S. Ct. Appeals (5th cir.) 1984, U.S. Ct. Appeals (10th cir.) 1995, U.S. Tax Ct. 1988, U.S. Supreme Ct. 1993. Assoc. atty. Golden Potts Boeckman & Wilson, Dallas, 1974-77; ptnr. Hiersche Martens Hayward Drakeley & Urbach, 1977-2000, Moseley & Martens LLP, Plano, 2001—. Bd. dirs., pres. Ronald McDonald House of Dallas, 1996-98, Journey of Hope Grief Support Ctr., Plano, 1998-2000. Lt. USNR, 1967-70, Viet Nam. Methodist. Avocations: flying, hunting, golf. Home: 5810 Knightsbridge Dr Dallas TX 75252-5011 Office: Moseley & Martens LLP Ste 270 Hedgcoxe Plz 4949 Hedgcoxe Rd Plano TX 75024 E-mail: dmartens@moseleymartens.com.

MARTENS, DONALD MATHIAS, orthodontist; b. Coleman, Wis., June 25, 1925; s. Harry Alfred and Emma Genevive (Laurent) M.; m. Fern Ann Krejcarek, June 24, 1950; children: Daniel, Nance, Dean, Cathy, Cynthia, Linda, James, Jeffrey, Michele. DDS, Marquette U., 1952. Diplomate Internat. Bd. Orthodontics. Practice dentistry specializing in orthodontics, Green Bay, Wis., 1952-91. Pres. San Luis Manor, Inc., Green Bay, 1973-86. Pres. Martens Found., Green Bay, 1982—. Served with USAAF, 1943-46. Fellow Am. Acad. Orthodontics (pres. 1971-72); mem. Brown Door Kewaunee Dental Soc. (pres. 1964), Fedn. Orthodontics Assn. (pres. 1979-81). Lodges: Optimist (pres. Green Bay club 1964). Republican. Roman Catholic. Avocations: golfing, skiing, hunting, fishing.

MARTENS, HELEN EILEEN, elementary school educator; b. Atkinson, Nebr., Jan. 13, 1926; d. Robert McKinley and Minnie Viola (Alfs) M. BS, Dana Coll., 1971; postgrad., U. Nebr., 1971-94, Wayne (Nebr.) U., 1971-94. Cert. tchr., Nebr. Rural sch. tchr. Dist. 231, Atkinson, Nebr., 1943-44, Dist. 77, Atkinson, 1944-45, Dist. 119, Atkinson, 1945-47; tchr. Emmet (Nebr.) Pub. Sch., 1947-59, O'Neill (Nebr.) Pub. Sch., 1959-99. Mgr. Saddle Horn Ranch for Youth. Mem. Holt County 4-H Coun., 1986-90, leader, 1946—; mem. youth edn. com. Holt County Cancer Soc., 1976-94; activity sec. Dr. Boots and Saddle Club, Holt County, 1969-95; demonstration tchr. Nebr. Tchrs. Help Mobile. Recipient Good Neighbor citation Knights of Aksarben, 1986, Amb. award O'Neill C. of C., 1986, Tchr. of Yr. World Herald Newspaper, 1986, Outstanding Elem. Tchr. Nebr. Rural Cmty. Schs., 1994; named Grand Marshall O'Neill St. Patrick's Parade, 1986. Mem. NEA, Nebr. Edn. Assn., O'Neill Edn. (sec., v.p., pres. 1960-94), Order Eastern Star, Alpha Delta Kappa, Delta Kappa Gamma (sec., v.p. 1959-94). Republican. Methodist. Avocation: ranching. Home: HC 69 Box 41 Atkinson NE 68713-9615

MARTENS, LESLIE VERNON, dentistry educator, consultant; b. Peoria, Ill., Oct. 15, 1938; s. Vernon Christ and Lydia Rachel (Weisenburger) M.; m. Judith A., June 15, 1961 (div. Nov. 1988); children: Michael J., Philip S., Eric W., Pamela A. Student, Bradley U., Peoria, Ill., 1956-59; DDS, Loyola U. Chgo., 1963; MPH, U. Minn., Mpls., 1969. Dental officer, maj. U.S. Army Dental Corps., Tex., 1963-68, Germany, 1963-68, Ky., 1963-68; asst. prof., assoc. dir. Grad. Program in Dental Pub. Health, U. Minn., 1969-72; assoc. prof. Sch. of Dentistry and Pub. Health, Mpls., 1972-82; prof. Sch. Pub. Health U. Minn., 1982—; prof., chair dept. preventive scis. Sch. Dentistry U. Minn., 1982—. Cons. to 13 dental schs. and 31 other health related agys. and orgns., 1972-99. Author of 74 manuscripts and rsch. abstracts in numerous jours.; patentee in field. Chmn. Red Cross Vol. Program, U.S. Army, 1963-67; merit badge counselor Boy Scouts Am., Anoka, Minn., 1972-89. Maj. U.S. Army, 1963-68, Germany. Grantee, U. Minn., 1970—; recipient commanding gen. citation U.S. Army, Fort Campbell, Ky., 1968, 84. Mem. ADA, Am. and Internat. Assns. for Dental Rsch., Am. ssn. of Dental Schs., Omicron Kappa Upsilon, Delta Omega. Avocations: thoroughbred racing. Office: Sch Dentistry U Minn 515 Delaware SE Minneapolis MN 55455 E-mail: marte001@tc.mn.edu.

MARTENS, LYLE CHARLES, state education administrator; b. Wausau, Wis., June 22, 1935; s. Norman Theodore and Eloise Loretta (Kreger) M.; m. Darlene Carrol Pyatt, Dec. 22, 1956; children: William Lyle, Robert Michael. BS in Indsl. Edn., Stout State U., 1957, MS in Indsl. Tech., 1962. Tchr. indsl. arts Mercer (Wis.) Pub. Schs., 1957-62; high sch. prin. Seymour (Wis.) Community Schs., 1962-65, supt. schs., 1965-87, Green Bay (Wis.) Area Pub. Schs., 1987-89; asst. state supt. State Dept. Edn., Madison, Wis., 1989-90, dep. state supt., 1990-93; coord. sch.-to-work Cesa 7, Green Bay, 1993-98; ret., 1998; dir. Ctr. for Edn. and Workforce Competitiveness, U. Wis., Green Bay, 1996-98. Chair United Way Edn. Fund Dr., Brown County, Wis., 1989; mem. bd.dirs. Green Bay C. of C., Good Shepherd Nursing Home, Seymour, Wis., 1975-87; mem. Econ. Devel. Corp., Outagamie County, Wis., 1985-86; founder Fallen Timber's Environment Ctr., 1972. Recipient Martens Praire Honor, 1995, Disting. Alumni award U. Wis., Stout, 1997. Mem. ASCD, Am. Assn. Sch. Dist. Adminstrs., Wis. Assn. Sch. Dist. Adminstrs. (pres. 1978-79, Disting. Educator award 2000), North Cen. Regional Ednl. Lab., Fox Valley Tech. Inst., Masons, Phi Delta Kappa. Lutheran. Avocations: fishing, hunting, flying, woodworking, raising and showing dogs. Home: 6504 County Road R Denmark WI 54208-9729

MARTENS, PATRICIA FRANCES, adult education educator; b. St. Louis, Nov. 27, 1943; d. John William and Mary Ruth (Bolds) Martens; m. George Joseph Miller, Aug. 7, 1965 (div.); children: Nicolette, George Jr., Jeffrey; m. Garrett Balke, Apr. 5, 2002. BS in Psychology, So. Ill. U., 1975; MA in Counseling, St. Louis U., 1990, PhD in Psychol. Founds., 1996. Cert. sexuality educator, hypnotherapist; lic. profl. counselor Nat. Bd. Cert. Counselors; cert. therapist and cons. Eye Movement Desensitization and Reprocessing. Primary, intermediate tchr. St. Hedwig Sch., St. Louis, 1961-66; tchr. jr. h.s. Assumption Sch., 1976-81; tchr. trainer grad. students Paul VI Cathechetical Inst., 1986-88; nat. tchr. trainer, 1989—; pvt. practice psychotherapy, 1997—. Cons. Archdiocese L.A., Archdiocese St. Louis, Nat. Coun. Cath. Bishops, 1991; del. Nat. Cath. Ednl. Del. to Russia and Lithuania, 1993; frequent spkr. and presenter at schs., parishes ednl. confs., nat. and internat. religious edn. mtgs.; TV appearances on ABC and CTNA; nat. ednl. cons. Tabor Pub. Author: (videos) In God's Image: Male and Female, 1989, God Doesn't Make Junk, 1989 (Cath. Audio Visual Educators award 1991), (books) Parent to Parent, 1989, Sex Is Not A Four-Letter Word!, 1994. Recipient Award Cath. Press Assn., 1995. Mem. AACD, Nat. Cath. Educators Assn., Am. Assn. Sex Educators, Counselors, Therapists, Assn. for Religious Values in Counseling, Am. Sch. Counselor Assn., Am. Coll. Personnel Assn., Soc. for Sci. Study of Sex, Pi Lambda Theta. Avocations: travel, swimming, biking, movies, sharing youth activities. Office: 10411 Clayton Rd Ste 2 Saint Louis MO 63131

MARTH, FRITZ LUDWIG, sports association executive; b. Essen, Germany, Feb. 23, 1935; s. Fritz and Elizabeth (Dietrich) M.; came to U.S., 1952, naturalized, 1959; student pub. schs. Essen; m. Sonja Wiehl, June 17, 1964; children: Fritz Thomas, William Robert. Stock clk. Hamilton Art Metal Co., N.Y.C., 1952-55; with Keystone Metal Finishers, Inc., Secaucus, N.J., 1955—, asst. plant mgr., 1962-66, plant mgr., 1966-83; adminstr. amateur div. U.S. Soccer Fedn., N.J. 1983—. Pres. N.J. State Soccer Assn., 1965-70; sec. So. N.Y. State Soccer Assn., 1972-83; gen. sec. Cosmopolitan Soccer League, 1961—; mem. div. soccer U.S. Olympic Com. With U.S. Army, 1958-59, Korea. Lutheran. Mem. Hoboken (N.J.) Soccer Football. Home: 121 W Passaic Ave Bloomfield NJ 07003-4528 Office: 7800 River Rd North Bergen NJ 07047-6245

MARTH, MARY ELLEN (KIM MARTIN), entertainer; b. Atkinson, Minn., July 15, 1936; d. Sigvard B. Kanikkeberg and Beatrice M. (Lundberg) Wangen; m. T.A. Martinez (div.); m. Luther H. Marth (div.); children: Mitzie, Leslie, Tina, Allen. Entertainer The Kim Martin Show, 1960—. Band leader Kim Martin Show, 1960—; real estate owner Marth Properties, Mpls., 1972—. Author of poems, songs, articles, short stories, childrens books, historian, humanitarian. Sec. Hennepin County Adult Foster Care, Mpls, 1983—; mem. Summit Ministries, Colo, 1995, Columbia Heights Owners Assn., 1990—, Multi-Housing Assn., Mpls, 1993—, Vesterheim Geneal. Mus., 1990, Norwegian Am. Mus., 1988—. Named Queen of Country Music, Country Entertainers Assn., Mpls., 1977, Entertainer of Yr. 1978, Female Vocalist of Yr., 1978, Best Band of Yr., 1979, Songwriter of Yr., 1980. Mem. Winnesheik Geneal. Soc., Fillmore County Hist. Soc., Vesterheim Geneal. Soc., Minn. Historical Soc. Lutheran. E-mail: kimtonem@aol.com.

MARTICH, DAWNA, nurse; b. McKeesport, Pa., June 14, 1958; d. Daniel and Julia (Medich) Martich; widow. BSN, U. Pitts., 1980, MSN, 1984. RN, Pa. Staff nurse Presbyn. Univ. Hosp., Pitts., 1980-84; tchr. sch. of nursing Shadyside Hosp., 1984-86; nursing edn. specialist Mercy Hosp., 1986-90, patient care delivery specialist, 1990-92, mgr. adminstrv. svcs., 1992-94; freelance health care cons., 1994—; dir. Medi-Home Health, 1995-96; clin. mgr. Univ. Family Practice, Moon Township, 1997-98; clin. trainer Am.

Healthways Liberty Tech. Ctr., 1998—. Author various nursing textbooks and manuals. Mem. Sigma Theta Tau. Serbian Orthodox. Avocations: writing, reading, oil painting, walking. Home: 4001 Greenridge Rd Apt 201 Pittsburgh PA 15234-1346 Office: Liberty Tech Ctr 2200 Liberty Ave Ste 200 Pittsburgh PA 15222-4500 E-mail: dawna.martich@worldnet.att.net.

MARTIG, JOHN FREDERICK, anesthesiologist; b. Salem, Oreg., Mar. 19, 1947; s. Kenneth W. and Virginia P. (Young) M.; m. Susan J. Chinworth; children: Daniel R., Thomas. A of Tech. Arts, Olympic Coll., 1968, AS, 1972; BSEE, U. Wash., 1974; DO, COMP, 1987. Registered profl. engr., Wash. Cons. Rockwell Internat., Anaheim, Calif., 1984, Honeywell, Silverdale, Wash., 1985; resident Ball Meml. Hosp., Muncie, Ind., 1987-89; physician Drs. Imediate Med. Ctr., 1988—; resident Met. Hosp., Grand Rapids, Mich., 1990-93; chief anesthesia, v.p. med. staff Jay County Hosp., Portland, Ind., 1993-2000; chief anesthesia Wells Cmty. Hosp., Blufton, 2000—. Mem. bd. dirs. United Way Jay County, 1996—. With USN, 1969-83. Mem. AMA, Am. Osteo. Assn., Am. Soc. Anesthesiologists, Am. Osteo. Coll. Anesthesiologists, Am. Coll. Osteo. Family Physicians, Am. Soc. Regional Anesthesia, Ind. State Med. Assn. Avocations: flying, tennis, hiking, photography, gardening. Home: 703 W 7th St Portland IN 47371-2314 Office: Jay County Hosp 500 W Votaw St Portland IN 47371-1399 E-mail: johnmartig@aol.com.

MARTIKAINEN, A(UNE) HELEN, retired health education specialist; b. Harrison, Maine, May 11, 1916; d. Sylvester and Emma (Heikkinen) M. AB, Bates Coll., 1939, DSc (hon.), 1957; MPH, Yale U., 1941; DSc, Harvard U., 1964; DSc (hon.), Smith Coll., 1969. Health edn. sec. Hartford Tb and Pub. Health Assn., 1941-42; cons. USPHS, 1942—49; chief health edn. WHO, Geneva, 1949—74; chair internat. affairs AAUW-NC, 1986—94, rep. to N.C. Coalition on Aging, 2001—, bd. dirs., 2001—; mem. N.C. Health Adv. Bd. for Aging, 2001—. Hon. trustee Bridgton Acad., North Bridgton, Maine; mem. N.C. Women's Forum, 1984—; bd. dirs. N.C. Ctr. of Laws Affecting Women, Inc.; bd. dirs. West Triangle chpt. UNA-USA; chair residents health and social svcs. com., mem. residents coun., mem. residents com. for cmty. rels. Carol Woods. Recipient Delta Omega award Yale U., Nat. Adminstrv. award Am. Acad. Phys. Edn., Key award Bates Coll., Internat. Svc. award, France, 1953, Prentiss medal, 1956, Spl. medal, cert. for internat. health edn. svc. Nat. Acad. Medicine for France, 1959, Profl. award Soc. Pub. Health Educators, 1963, Benjamin Elijah Mays award Bates Coll. Alumni Assn., 1989, Legacy of Leadership honoree Pines of Carolina coun. Girl Scouts U.S., 2002. Fellow APHA (chmn. health edn. sect., Excellence award 1969); mem. AAUW, LWV, Women's Internat. League for Peace and Freedom, U.S. Soc. Pub. Health Educators, Internat. Union Health Edn. (Parisot medal, tech. adviser), Acad. Phys. Edn. (assoc.), N.C. Coun. Women's Orgns. (mem. coun. assembly 1988-92, Women of Distinction award 1989), Phi Beta Kappa. Home: 3113 Carol Woods 750 Weaver Dairy Rd Chapel Hill NC 27514-1443

MARTIN, AGNES, artist; b. Maklin, Sask., Can., 1912; came to U.S., 1932, naturalized, 1950; Student, Western Wash. State Coll., 1935-38; BS, Columbia U., 1942, MFA, 1952. One-woman shows include Betty Parsons Gallery, N.Y.C., 1958, 59, 61, Robert Elkon Gallery, N.Y.C., 1961, 63, 72, 76, Nicolas Wilder Gallery, Los Angeles, 1963-66, 67, Visual Arts Ctr., N.Y.C., 1971, Kunstraum, Munich, 1973, Inst. Contemporary Art U. Pa., Phila., 1973, Pace Gallery, N.Y.C., 1975, 76, 77, 78, 79, 80-81, 81, 83, 84, 85, 86, 89, 91, 92, 94, 95, Mayor Gallery, London, 1978, 84, Galerie Rudolf Zwirner, Cologne, Fed. Republic Germany, 1978, Harcus/Krakow Gallery, Boston, 1978, Margo Leavin Gallery, Los Angeles, 1979, 85, Mus. N.Mex., Santa Fe, 1979, 98, Richard Gray Gallery, Chgo., 1981, Garry Anderson Gallery, Sydney, Australia, 1986, Waddington Galleries Ltd., London, 1986, Stedelijk Mus., Amsterdam, 1991, Whitney Mus. Am. Art, N.Y.C., 1992, 2000, Wildenstein Gallery, Tokyo, 1993, Serpentine Gallery, London, 1993, Galerie Michael Werner, Cologne, 1994, Pace Wildenstein, N.Y.C., 1995, 96, 97, 98, 2000, 2001, Santa Fe Mus. Fine Arts, 1994, Galerie Daniel Blau, Munich, 1996, Harwood Mus., Taos, N.Mex., 1997, 2002, Galeria 56, Budapest, 1998, Royal Botanic Garden, Edinburgh, Scotland, 1999, Anthony d'Offay Gallery, London, 2001, Menil Collection, Houston, 2002; exhibited in group shows at Carnegie Inst., Pitts., 1961, Whitney Mus. Am. Art, N.Y.C., 1962, 66, 67, 74, 77, 92, Tooth Gallery, London, 1962, Gallery Modern Art, Washington, 1963, Wadsworth Atheneum, Hartford, Conn., 1963, Solomon R. Guggenheim Mus., N.Y.C., 1965, 66, 76, Mead Corp., 1965-67, Mus. Modern Art, N.Y.C., 1967, 76, 85, Inst. Contemporary Art, Phila., 1967, Detroit Inst. Art, 1967, Corcoran Gallery Art, Washington, 1967, 81, Finch Mus., N.Y., 1968, Phila. Mus., 1968, Zurich Art Mus., Switzerland, 1969, Ill. Bell Telephone Co., Chgo., 1970, Mus. Contemporary Art, Chgo., 1971, Inst. Contemporary Art U. Pa., Phila., 1972, Randolph-Macon Coll., N.C., 1972, Kassel, Fed. Republic Germany, 1972, Stedelijk Mus., Amsterdam, 1975, U. Mass., Amherst, 1976, Venice Biennale, Italy, 1976, 80, Cleve. Mus. Art, 1978, Albright-Knox Gallery, Buffalo, 1978, Inst. Contemporary Art, Boston, 1979, Art Inst. Chgo., 1979, San Francisco Mus. Modern Art, 1980, ROSC Internat. Art Exhbn., Dublin, Ireland, 1980, Marilyn Pearl Gallery, N.Y.C., 1983, Kemper Gallery, Kansas City Art Inst., 1985, Am. Acad. and Inst. Arts and Letters, N.Y.C., 1985, Charles Cowles Gallery, N.Y.C., 1986, Moody Gallery Art U. Ala., Birmingham, 1986, Butler Inst. Am. Art, 1986, Art Gallery Western Australia, Perth, 1986, Mus. Contemporary Art, Los Angeles, 1986, Boston Fine Arts Mus., 1989; represented in permanent collections Mus. of Modern Art, N.Y.C., Albright-Knox Gallery, Aldrich Mus., Ridgefield, Conn., Art Gallery Ont., Can., Australian Nat. Gallery, Canberra, Grey Art Gallery and Study Ctr., N.Y.C., Solomon R. Guggenheim Mus., High Mus. Art, Atlanta, Hirshhorn Mus. and Sculpture Garden, Washington, Israel Mus., Jerusalem, La Jolla (Calif.) Mus. Contemporary Art, Los Angeles County Mus. Art, Mus. Art R.I. Sch. Design, Providence, Mus. Modern Art, Neuegalerie der Stadt, Aachen, Fed. Republic Germany, Norton Simon Mus. Art at Pasadena, Calif., Stedelijk Mus., Amsterdam, The Netherlands, 1992, Mus. Modern Art, paris, 1992, Tate Gallery, London, Wadsworth Atheneum, Walker Art Ctr., Mpls., Whitney Mus. Am. Art, 1993, Sofia, Madrid, 1993, Huosten, 1993, Worcester (Mass.) Art Mus., Yale U. Art Gallery, New Haven; subject of various articles. Office: 414 Placitas Rd # 37 Taos NM 87571-2513

MARTIN, ALAN JOSEPH, lawyer; b. Berwyn, Ill., Dec. 9, 1959; s. Daniel George and Lillie (Chalupa) M.; m. Dawne Michelle Martin, June 24, 1989; children: Rebecca Marie, Melissa Nicole, Sarah Anne, reid Anthony. BA summa cum laude, U. Ill., 1982; JD, U. Va., 1985. Bar: Ill. 1985, U.S. Dist. Ct. (no. dist.) Ill., 1985, U.S. Ct. Appeals (7th cir.) 1997, U.S. Ct. Appeals (3d cir.) 1999. Analyst office politico-mil. analysis, bur. intelligence and rsch. Dept. State, Washington, 1981; assoc. Isham, Lincoln & Beale, Chgo., 1985-87, Mayer, Brown & Platt, Chgo., 1987—, ptnr., 1993. Mng. and exec. editor Jour. Law and Politics, 1984-85. Counselor terminally ill Mercy Hosp. Hospice, Urbana, Ill., 1980-82; pro bono lawyer, 1985—. Merriam scholar, 1980-82, James, 1982. Mem. ABA, Phi Beta Kappa, Phi Delta Phi. Avocations: racquetball, running, chess. Home: 1500 White Eagle Dr Naperville IL 60564-9761 Office: Mayer Brown & Platt 190 S La Salle St Ste 3100 Chicago IL 60603-3441

MARTIN, ALBERT CHARLES, manufacturing executive, lawyer; b. San Lucido, Italy, Sept. 20, 1928; s. Joseph and Carmela M.; m. Jean Perrin, Aug. 22, 1953 (dec.); children: Lynne, Ken; m. Frances Doughty, June, 1996. BS, Mich. State U., 1952; MS, U. Mich., 1953; JD, Detroit Coll. Law, 1962. Bar: Mich. 1962. Corp. counsel, sec. Udylite Corp., Detroit, 1963-68; corp. counsel Hooker Chem. Corp., N.Y.C., 1968-70, Grow Chem. Co., N.Y.C., 1970-71; group v.p. Leeds & Northrup Internat., North Wales, Pa., 1971-79, pres., 1979—. Served with U.S. Army, 1946-48. Mem. Mich. Bar Assn.

MARTIN, ALDEN JEFFREY, petrophysicist, geologist; b. Houston, Oct. 13, 1948; s. A.J. and Jessie Mae (Whittaker) M.; m. Marie Patricia Martin, Mar. 17, 1979. BS in Geology, Lamar U., 1970. Geologist Texaco, Inc., New Orleans, 1970-76; sr. staff petrophysicist Conoco, Inc., Houston, 1976—. With U.S. Army, 1970-72. Mem. Soc. Profl. Well Log Analysts, Soc. Petroleum Engrs., Am. Assn. Petroleum Geologists. Methodist. Avocations: unpublished sci-fi author, golf, sailing, antique autos. Home: PO Box 480 Fulshear TX 77441-0480 E-mail: a-j-jeff.martin@conoco.com., martimj@fbns.net.

MARTIN, ALISON CADY, interior designer; b. N.Y.C., May 12, 1949; d. Everett Ware Jr. and Ruth Anne (Payan) Cady; m. Robin Bradley Martin, Jan. 29, 1972 (div. 1979); m. Frederic Bradley Underwood, Oct. 8, 1988 (div. 1999). BA, Middlebury (Vt.) Coll., 1971. Pres. Alison Martin Interiors, Ltd., Washington, 1976—. Sec. Great Falls (Va.) Concert Series, 1983-88, treas., 1988-96. Mem. Colony Club (N.Y.C.). Republican. Episcopalian. Avocation: classical singing. Office: PO Box 949 Berryville VA 22611 E-mail: amiltd@shentel.net.

MARTIN, ALLEN, lawyer; b. Manchester, Conn., Aug. 12, 1937; s. Richard and Ruth Palmer (Smith) M.; m. Bonnie Reid, Sept. 8, 1979; children: Elizabeth Palmer, Samuel Bates. BA, Williams Coll., 1960, Oxford U., 1962; LLB, Harvard U., 1965. Ptnr. Downs, Rachlin and Martin, Burlington, Vt., 1971—. Chmn. bd. dirs. Wicor Ams., 1991—; bd. dirs. IDX Systems Corp.; bd. dirs., chmn. fin. com. Union Mut. Ins. Co., New Eng. Guaranty Ins. Co.; mem. Vt. Jud. Responsibility Bd., vice-chmn., 1978-80. Chmn. Vt. Bd. Edn., 1978-83; chmn. Vt. Rep. Party, 1991-95; mem. Rep. Nat. Com., 1991-95, 97-99; trustee Vt. Law Sch., 2000—. Mem. ABA, Am. Law Inst. (life), Vt. Bar Assn. Republican. Home: 283 S Union St Burlington VT 05401-5507 also: Six Chimneys Orford NH 03777 Office: PO Box 190 199 Main St Burlington VT 05401-8309 E-mail: amartin@drm.com.

MARTIN, ANDREW AYERS, lawyer, physician, educator; b. Toccoa, Ga., Aug. 18, 1958; s. Wallace Ford and Dorothy LaTranquil (Ayers) M.; children: William Ayers, Malorie Ayers. BA, Emory U., Atlanta, 1980, MD, 1984; JD, Duke U., 1988. Bar: Calif. 1989, La. 1990, D.C. 1991; diplomate Am. Bd. Pathology, Nat. Bd. Med. Examiners; lic. physician, La., Miss., Ark. Intern in pediatrics Emory U./Grady Meml. Hosp., Atlanta, 1984; intern Tulane U./Charity Hosp., New Orleans, 1989-90, resident in anatomic and clin. pathology, 1990-94; surg. pathology fellow Baylor Coll. Medicine, Houston, 1994-95; law clk. Ogletree, Deakins, Smoak, Stewart, Greenville, S.C., summer 1986, Thelen Marrin Johnson Bridges, L.A., summer 1987, Duke Hosp. Risk Mgmt., 1987-88; assoc. Haight Brown Bonesteel, Santa Monica, Calif., 1988; pvt. practice L.A., 1989; physician/atty. Tulane Med. Ctr./Charity Hosp., New Orleans, 1989-94, Baylor Coll. Medicine/Tex. Med. Ctr., Houston, 1994-95; lab. dir. King's Daus. Hosp., Greenville, Miss., 1995—; asst. clin. prof. pathology Tulane U.; lab. dir., owner Vicksburg Pathology Lab., Bolivar Med. Ctr., Cleveland, Miss.; staff pathologist Delta Regional Ctr., Greenville, N.W. Miss. Regional Medical Ctr., Clarksdale, No. Sunflower County Hosp., Ruteville, Tallahatchie County Hosp., Charleston. Sr. ptnr. Mid-South Pathology Assocs.; med. dir. of labs. Vicksburg Pathology Lab., N.W. Miss. Regional Med. Ctr., Bolivar Med. Ctr., Delta Regional Med. Ctr., North Sunflower County Hosp., 1997—, Tallahatchie (Miss.) County Hosp., N.W. Miss. Regional Med. Ctr., Clarksdale, Lab Corp., Southaven, Miss., Tallahatchie County Hosp.; adj. faculty Moorhead U.; bd. dirs. Martin Bldrs., Inc., Toccoa; mem. AIDS Legis. Task Force for La.; case cons. Office of Tech. Assessment, Washington; tech. cons. and autopsy extra Oliver Stone's "JFK"; adj. clin. faculty Moorhead Coll. Contbr. articles to profl. jours.; author: Reflections on Rusted Chrome (book of poetry). Fellow Coll. Am. Pathologists, Coll. Legal Medicine, La. State Med. Soc. (del. meeting 1992-93). Home: 935 Lakehall Rd Lake Village AR 71653-6096 also: 4104 Alabama Ave Kenner LA 70065-5603 also: 3850 Old Highway 27 Vicksburg MS 39180-8829 Office: Mid-South Pathology Assocs PO Box 5880 Greenville MS 38704-5880

MARTIN, ANGELA CARTER, nursing educator; b. Reidsville, N.C., June 24, 1957; d. R. Philip and Carol (Walker) Carter; m. Dale Martin, Apr. 3, 1976; children: Melissa, Christopher. BSN, U. N.C., Greensboro, 1979; MS in Nursing, U. N.C., Chapel Hill, 1983. Cert. family nurse practitioner, N.C. Dir. Children's Med. Clinic Person-Chatman-Caswell County Health Dept., Yanceyville, N.C., 1983; family nurse practitioner Nat. Health Svc. Corps, Atlanta, 1983-86; asst. prof. dept. family and community medicine Med. Coll. Hampton Rds., Norfolk, Va., 1986—; asst. prof., coord. family nurse practitioner program Sch. Nursing, Old Dominion U., 1987-92, 94-98; asst. prof., assoc. program dir. Uniformed Svcs. U. of Health Scis. and dept. Vet. Affairs, Bethesda, Md., 1998—. Cons. in field. Mem. editl. bd.: Jour. Nursing Risk Mgmt.; contbr. articles to profl. publs. Mem. ANA, Va. Nurses Assn., Nat. Orgn. Nurse Practitioners Faculties (bd. dirs. 1992-93), Am. Acad. Nurse Practitioners (state award for excellence 1992), Sigma Theta Tau (Rsch. award 1988, award for excellence Epsilon Chi chpt.). Home: 3228 Pineridge Dr Chesapeake VA 23321-5404 E-mail: amartin@usuhs.mil.

MARTIN, ARTHUR LEE, JR. lawyer; b. Montgomery, Ala., Jan. 13, 1949; s. Arthur Lee and Blanche (Bush) M.; children by previous marriage: Elizabeth Leah, Rachel Blanche; m. Diane S. Lamon, Mar. 23, 1993. BA cum laude, Vanderbilt U., 1971; JD, U. Chgo., 1974. Bar: U.S. Dist. Ct. (no. dist.) Ill. 1972, U.S. Ct. Appeals (7th cir.) 1972, Ill. 1975, Ala. 1979, U.S. Dist. Ct. (no. dist.) Ala. 1979, U.S. Ct. Appeals (5th cir.) 1979. Law clk. to sr. judge U.S. Ct. Appeals (5th cir.), Montgomery, 1974-75; assoc. D'Ancona & Pflaum, Chgo., 1975-78; ptnr. Haskell, Slaughter & Young, Birmingham, Ala., 1978-89, Dominicik, Fletcher & Yeilding, Birmingham, 1989-95, Berkowitz, Lefkovitz, Isom & Kushner, Birmingham, 1995-98, Johnston & Conwell, Birmingham, 1998—2001, Miller Hamilton Sailer & Odom, Birmingham, 2001—. Gov. Ala. ctrl. dist. Civitan Internat., internat. judge adv. Mem. ABA, Nat. Assn. Bond Lawyers, Ala. State Bar, Birmingham Bar Assn., Am. Acad. Hosp. Lawyers, Downtown Dem. Club, Phi Delta Phi. Democrat. Methodist. Home: 2463 Chuchura Rd Birmingham AL 35244-3254 Office: Miller Hamilton Sailer & Odom 2501 20th Place S Birmingham AL 35223 E-mail: alm@johnstonconwell.com.

MARTIN, ARTHUR MEAD, lawyer; b. Cleveland Heights, Ohio, Mar. 29, 1942; s. Bernard P. and Winifred (Mead) M. AB, Princeton U., 1963; LLB, Harvard U., 1966. Bar: Ill. 1966, U.S. Dist. Ct. (no. dist.) Ill. 1969, U.S. Ct. Appeals (7th cir.) 1970, U.S. Supreme Ct. 1980, U.S. Ct. Appeals (fed. cir.) 2000. Instr. law U. Wis., Madison, 1966-68; assoc. Jenner & Block, Chgo., 1968-74, ptnr., 1975—. Co-trustee Dille Family Trust, 1982—; bd. dirs. Sleepeck Printing Co. Author: Historical and Practice Notes to the Illinois Civil Practice Act and Illinois Supreme Court Rules, 1968-88. Trustee 4th Presbyn. Ch., Chgo., sec. 1997-99, exec. com. 1997-99; bd. dirs. Stop Colon/Rectal Cancer Found., 1998—. Mem. ABA, Am. Law Inst., Ill. Bar Assn., Chgo. Bar Assn. (bd. editors 1972-86), Ill. State Hist. Soc. (adv. bd. 1998-99, bd. dirs. 1999—, exec. com. 1999—, fin. com. 1999—, treas. 2002--), Ill. Centennial Bus. Com., Lake Mich. Fedn. (bd. dirs. 1993—, exec. com. 1994—, treas. 1994-99, 2001--, sec. 1999-2001), Law Club Chgo., Legal Club Chgo. Office: Jenner & Block 1 IBM Plz Fl 4400 Chicago IL 60611-7603 E-mail: amartin@jenner.com.

MARTIN, BARBARA LEE, computer programmer, analyst; b. Warsaw, Feb. 11, 1941; d. Eldon Merritt Glor and Ora Elizabeth (Putney) Newton; m. Brent Robert Martin, July 7, 1962 (div. Jan. 1979); children: Dane Robert, Dale Eldon. BS, Otterbein Coll., 1962; postgrad., Marion (Ohio) Tech. Coll., 1977-78. Tchr. math. Avon (Ohio) High Sch., 1962, Taft Jr. High Sch., Marion, 1962-66; computer programmer Nationwide Ins. Co., Columbus, Ohio, 1978-80; lead programmer/analyst The Scotts Co. (formerly O.M. Scott & Sons Co.), Marysville, 1980—. Sec. bd. zoning appeals Delaware (Ohio) Twp., 1989-92, chair, 1993, 94, 95, 96; chair outreach com. Olentangy River Valley Assn., Del., 1988-90, chair assn. 1990, 91. Mem. AAUW (membership v.p. Del. br. 1993, 94, 95). Unity. Avocations: bird watching, bridge, theater, travel, crafts. Office: The Scotts Co 14111 Scottslawn Rd Marysville OH 43040-9506

MARTIN, BENJAMIN GAUFMAN, ophthalmologist; b. Louisville, Aug. 18, 1937; s. Benjamin and Catherine L. Martin; m. Caroline Sue Martin, May 25, 1975; children: Benjamin, Lori, Tamara, Farrell, Steven, David. BME, U. Louisville, 1954, M. Engring., 1973; MD, U. So. Calif., 1964. Design engr. Philco/Ford, Palo Alto, Calif., 1957-60; rsch. engr. N.Am./Rockwell, Inglewood, 1961-63; intern Wright-Patterson Med. Ctr., Dayton, Ohio, 1964-65; ophthalmology resident Wilford Hall Med. Ctr., San Antonio, 1968-71; commd. USAF, 1963, advanced through grades to col., ret., 1980; CEO Cape Coral (Fla.) Eye Ctr., 1980—. With USN, 1954-57. Decorated Legion of Merit, DFC, Bronze Star, Air medal. Mem.: DFC Soc., Daedalions, Elks, Shriners, Masons. Republican. Lutheran. Office: Cape Coral Eye Ctr 4120 Del Prado Blvd S Cape Coral FL 33904-7165

MARTIN, BERNARD LEE, former college dean; b. Dayton, Ohio, May 29, 1923; s. Harley L. and Clare (Murphy) M.; m. Mary Patricia McDonald, Nov. 23, 1950; children: Joseph, Mary, David, Patrick, Paul, Timothy, Michael, Christopher. BA, Athenaeum of Ohio, 1941-45; MA in History, Xavier U., 1950, MBA, 1955; PhD in Econs, U. Cin., 1963; PhD honoris causa, Canisius Coll., 1978. Mem. faculty Xavier U., Cin., 1948-65, asst. prof. bus. adminstrn., 1955-62, assoc. prof. mktg., 1962-65, chmn. mktg. dept., 1961; chmn., prof. mktg. Eastern Mich. U., Ypsilanti, 1965-66; dean Sch. Bus. Adminstrn. Canisius Coll., Buffalo, 1968-72, acting acad. v.p. of coll., 1972-74, dean Sch. Bus., 1974-78; dean McLaren Coll. Bus. Adminstrn., U. San Francisco, 1978-86, prof. mktg., 1986-91; prof. emeritus U. San Francisco, 1992. Author: (with others) Contemporary Economic Problems and Issues, 3d edit, 1973. Ford Found. grantee Harvard, 1964 Mem. Am. Mktg. Assn., Am. Econ. Assn. Home: 1062 Cherry Ave San Jose CA 95125-4311

MARTIN, BOE WILLIS, lawyer; b. Texarkana, Ark., Oct. 6, 1940; s. E.H. and Dorothy Annette (Willis) M.; m. Carol J. Edwards, June 12, 1965; children: Stephanie Diane, Scott Andrew. BA, Tex. A&M U., 1962; LLB, U. Tex., 1964; LLM, George Washington U., 1970. Bar: Tex. 1964. Law clk. Tex. Supreme Ct., 1966-67; assoc. Snakard, Brown & Gambill, Ft. Worth, 1967-69, assoc., ptnr., 1971-72; asst. counsel U.S. Senate Labor and Pub. Welfare Com., 1969; legal asst. U.S. Senator Ralph W. Yarborough, 1969-71; assoc., ptnr. Stalcup & Johnson, Dallas, 1972-77; assoc. ptnr. Coke & Coke, 1977-80; ptnr., shareholder Johnson & Gibbs, 1981-96, Bell, Nunnally & Martin, Dallas, 1996—. Vis. prof. law So. Meth. U. Sch. Law, 1972-73, 75, 88-89, 95, 99-2000, 02, U. Tex. Sch. Law, 1977, 79. Contbr. articles to profl. jours. Staff Carter-Mondale Campaign, 1976, 80; cons. to v.p. of U.S., 1977-80; cons. Mondale for Pres. Campaign, 1983-84, Dukakis for Pres. Campaign, 1988; dep. coord. of visit of Pres. Mikhail Gorbachev to State of Minn., 1990. Capt. U.S. Army, 1964-69. Mem. ABA, Tex. Bar Assn., Dallas Bar Assn. Democrat. Methodist. Home: 4435 Arcady Ave Dallas TX 75205-3604 Office: Bell & Nunnally & Martin 3232 Mckinney Ave Ste 1400 Dallas TX 75204-2426

MARTIN, BOYCE FICKLEN, JR. federal judge; b. Boston, Oct. 23, 1935; s. Boyce Ficklen and Helen Artt Martin; m. Mavin Hamilton Brown, July 8, 1961; children: Mary V.H., Julia H.C., Boyce Ficklen III, Robert C.G. II. AB, Davidson Coll., 1957; JD, U. Va., 1963. Bar: Ky. 1963. Law clk. to Hon. Shackelford Miller, Jr. U.S. Ct. Appeals 6th Cir., Cin., 1963—64; asst. U.S. atty. Western Dist. Ky., Louisville, 1964; U.S. atty. Western Dist. Ky., 1965; pvt. practice Louisville, 1966—74; judge Jefferson Circuit Ct., 1974—76; chief judge Ct. Appeals Ky., 1976—79; judge U.S. Ct. Appeals 6th Cir., Cin. and Louisville, 1979—96, chief judge, 1996—. Jud. coun. U.S. Ct. Appeals (6th cir.), 1979—96, chmn., 1996—; mem. Jud. Conf. of U.S., 1996—, exec. com., 1998—. Trustee Isaac W. Bernheim Found., Louisville, 1981—97, chmn., 1982—95; trustee Blackacre Found., Inc., Louiville, 1983—94, chmn., 1986—94; trustee Hanover (Ind.) Coll., 1982—, vice-chmn., 1992—97, chmn., 1998—; exec. bd. Old Ky. Home coun. Boy Scouts of Am., 1968—72; pres. Louisville Zool. Commn., 1971—74; vestry mem. St. Francis in the Fields Episcopal Ch., Harrods Creek, 1979—83; bd. vis. Davidson (N.C.) Coll., 1980—86, trustee, 1994—98. Capt. JAGC U.S. Army, 1958—66. Fellow: Am. Bar Found.; mem.: ABA (com. effective appellate advocacy Conf. Appellate Judges), Louisville Bar Assn., Ky. Bar Assn., Fed Bar Assn., Am. Judicature Soc., Inst. Jud. Adminstrn. Office: US Ct Appeals 209 US Courthouse 601 W Broadway Louisville KY 40202-2227*

MARTIN, BRADLEY L, legal consultant, composer; b. Grand Forks, Nd, Jan. 29, 1949; s. William Joseph Martin and Darlyne Ione Montgomery; m. Rose Marie Austin, Aug. 9, 1974 (div. Apr. 0, 1988); children: Nichole, Jeremy. BA, U. ND, Grand Forks, ND, 1974—77, MA, 1977—79. Fed. employee US Govt., Grand Forks and Fargo, ND, 1976—90; songwriter Broadcast Music Inc, Nashville, 1974—; legal cons. Self Employed, Fargo, ND, 1992—. Grad. tchg. asst. U. ND, Grand Forks, ND, 1997—98; union local pres. Am. Fedn. of Govt. Employees, Fargo, ND, 1989—90. Leader Campfire, ND, 1992—94, Boy Scouts of Am., 1994—96; chmn. state fin. com. Dem. Party, 1976—77. E-4 (rm3) USN, 1969—72, San Diego, CA & Vietnam. Recipient Vol. in Svc. to Children, ND Pub. Schools, 1982, Superior Performance Award, Social Security Adminstrn., 1989. Mem.: DAV (life; chpt. comdr. 1976), North Am. Hunting Club (life). Democrat-Npl. Roman Catholic. Achievements include 30 Songs Copywrited. Avocations: hunting, fishing, camping, community service. Home: 2100 E Main Ave West Fargo ND 58078

MARTIN, BURCHARD SAMUEL, lawyer; b. Vineland, N.J., Sept. 3, 1961; s. Burchard Viliger and Elizabeth Marie (DelRossi) M.; m. Paula Ann Miutovicz, June 13, 1987; children: Caroline Mary Elizabeth, Burchard W.J. BA in Polit. Sci., Villanova U., 1983, JD, 1986. Bar: N.J. 1986, Pa. 1986, U.S. Dist. Ct. (ea. dist.) Pa. 1986, U.S. Dist. Ct. N.J. 1986, U.S. Ct. Appeals (3d cir.) 1986, U.S. Supreme Ct. 1990. Assoc. Tomar, Seliger, Simonoff, Adourian & O'Brien, P.C., Haddonfield, N.J., 1986-87, Martin, Crawshaw & Mayfield, P.A., Westmont, 1987-91; ptnr. Martin, Gunn & Martin, P.A., 1991—. Instr. bus. law Burlington County Coll. Mem. Camden County Environ. Law Com., 1989—. Mem. Internat. Assn. Def. (counsel 1997-), Am. Arbitration Assn. (arbitrator), N.J. Bar Assn. (product liability and toxic/tort com. 1990), Camden County Bar Assn., Justinian Soc. Roman Catholic. Avocations: golf, travel, coaching basketball and baseball. Home: 5 Winston Ct Medford NJ 08055-8200 Office: Martin Gunn Martin PA PO Box 358 216 Haddon Ave Ste 420 Westmont NJ 08108-2812

MARTIN, BURCHARD V. lawyer; b. Millville, N.J., May 9, 1933; s. William J. and Helen (Mullane) M.; m. Elizabeth Del Rossi, June 11, 1955; children: Doris, Burchard S., William J., Thomas O. BS in Econs., Villanova (Pa.) U., 1954, LLB, 1958. Bar: N.J. 1960, U.S. Dist. Ct. N.J. 1960, U.S. Ct. Appeals (3d cir.), U.S. Supreme Ct. 1976. Assoc. Carroll, Taylor & Bischoff, Camden, N.J., 1960-63; ptnr. Taylor, Bischoff, Neutze & Williams, 1963-70, Taylor, Bischoff, Williams & Martin, Camden, 1970-72, Martin, Crawshaw & Mayfield, Haddonfield-Westmont, N.J., 1972-91, Martin, Gunn & Martin, Westmont, 1991—. Bd. cons. Villanova Law Sch., 1983—. Recipient Trial Bar award, Trial Attys. of N.J., 1987. Fellow Am. Coll. Trial Lawyers (state chmn. 1982-83); mem. ABA, N.J. Bar Assn., Camden County Bar Assn. (bd. dirs., Peter J. Devine award 1981). Avocation: golf. Office: Martin Gunn & Martin PA 216 Haddon Ave Apt 420 Collingswood NJ 08108-2812

MARTIN, CAROL JACQUELYN, educator, artist; b. Ft. Worth, Oct. 6, 1943; d. John Warren and Dorothy Lorene (Coffman) Edwards; m. Boe Willis Martin, Oct. 6, 1940; children: Stephanie Diane, Scott Andrew. BA summa cum laude, U. N. Tex., 1965; MA, U. Tex., El Paso, 1967. Tchr. Edgemere Elem. Sch., El Paso, Tex., 1965-66, Fulmore Jr. H.S., Austin, 1966-67, Monnig Jr. H.S., Ft. Worth, 1967-68, Paschal H.S., Ft. Worth, 1968-69; instr. Tarrant County Jr. Coll., 1968-69, 71-72; press sec. U.S. Sen. Gaylord Nelson, Washington, 1969-71; instr. Eastfield C.C., Dallas, 1981, Richland C.C. Dist., 1982. Artist Vt. Studio Ctr., 1998. Editor The Avesta Mag., 1964-65; exhibited in group shows at City of Richardson's Cottonwood Park, 1970-86, Students of Ann Cushing Gantz, 1973-85, Art About Town, 1979, 80, shows by Tarrant County and Dallas County art assns. Active Dallas Symphony Orch. League, Easter Seal Soc., Women's Auxiliary of Nexus, Dallas Hist. Soc., Women's Bd. of the Dallas Opera, Dallas Arboretum and Garden Club, Dallas County Heritage Soc., Nat. Mus. Women in Arts. Mem. Internat. Platform Assn., Mortar Bd., Alpha Chi, Sigma Tau Delta, Kappa Delta Pi, Delta Gamma. Democrat. Methodist. Avocations: travel, photography, snow skiing, oil painting. Address: 4435 Arcady Ave Dallas TX 75205-3604

MARTIN, CATHERINE ELIZABETH, anthropology educator; b. N.Y.C., Feb. 14, 1943; d. Walter Charles and Ruth (Crucet) Strodt; children: Kai Stuart, Armin Wade. BA, Reed Coll., 1965; MA, UCLA, 1967, PhD, 1971. Cert. C.C. tchr., Ariz., Calif. From asst. to full prof. anthropology Calif. State U., L.A., 1970-96, prof. emeritus, 1996, coord. women's studies, 1979-88, acting dir. acad. advisement, 1992-93, dir. Can. studies, 1991, advisement coord., 1996, prof. emeritus, 1996; assoc. faculty Mohave C.C., Kingman, Ariz., 1996-99; adj. prof. No. Ariz. U., 1997-99, affiliate Women's Studies, 1998-99; adj. faculty anthropology Shasta Coll., 2001—. Contbr. chpts. to books and poetry to profl. publs. Cubmaster, den mother Boy Scouts Am., L.A. and Pasadena, 1982-85; leader Tiger Cubs, Boy Scouts Am., 1983. Recipient Outstanding Tiger Cub Leader award Boy Scouts Am., L.A., 1983, Cub Scout Growth award Boy Scouts Am., L.A., 1984. Fellow Soc. Applied Anthropology; mem. Am. Anthropol. Assn., Southwestern Anthropol. Assn. Avocations: reading, traveling, exploring cultural diversity.

MARTIN, CATHIE JO, political scientist, educator; b. Panama Canal Zone, U.S., Nov. 22, 1951; d. Robert M. Martin and Mary Jo Mackenzie; m. James R. Milkey, July 7, 1990; 2 children. BA, Carleton Coll., 1974; MSW, U. Wash., 1979; PhD, MIT, 1986. Asst. prof. Northwestern U., Evanston, Ill.,

1988—90; prof. Boston U., 1990—. Vis. prof. Copenhagen U., Denmark, 2000—01; vis. scholar Russell Sage Found., N.Y.C., 1994—95. Author: (novels) Shifting the Burden, 1991, Stuck in Neutral, 2000. Grantee grant, NSF, 1986, Robert Wood Johnson Found., 1992—93, German Marshall Fund, 2001. Mem.: Am. Polit. Sci. Assn. Home: 24 Woodcliff Rd Newton MA 02461 Office: Boston Univ Dept Polit Sci 232 Bay State Rd Boston MA 02461

MARTIN, CATHLEEN A. lawyer; b. St. Charles, Mo., Apr. 26, 1971; d. David and Bonnie Arnold; m. Jeffrey S. Martin, June 4, 1994. BA in Bus. Adminstrn., BA in Journalism, Truman State U., 1993; JD, U. Mo., 1996. Bar: Mo. 1996, U.S. Dist. Ct. (we. dist.) Mo. 1996, U.S. Ct. Appeals (8th cir.) 1996. Asst. atty. gen. Mo. Atty. Gen.'s Office, Jefferson City, 1996—97; shareholder Newman, Comley & Ruth P.C., 1997—. Mem., children's leader Grace Evang. Free Ch., Jefferson City, 1996—; bd. dirs. Jefferson City Rape and Abuse Crisis Svc., 1999—, vice chair, 2000, chair, 2001; com. mem. Jefferson City Young Life, 1996—. Mem.: ABA, Jefferson City C. of C., Cole County Bar Assn., Soc. for Human Resource Mgrs., Mo. Bar Assn. (chair labor and employment law com. 2001—02), Jefferson City Breakfast Rotary (club svc. chair 1997—98, cmty. svc. chair 1998—2001, sgt.-at-arms 2001—02), Order of Barristers. Avocations: gardening, running, church activities. Office: Newman Comley & Ruth PC PO Box 537 Jefferson City MO 65102-0537

MARTIN, CHARLES SEYMOUR, middle school educator; b. Lewiston, Maine, Dec. 26, 1961; s. Robert Charles and Annette Marion (Card) Martin; m. Margaret Ilene Davis, Aug. 20, 1988; 1 child, Danielle Elizabeth. BS in Health Edn., U. Maine, Farmington, 1984; MEd, Plymouth State Coll., 1988; cert. advanced studies, U. Maine, Orono, 1991. Cert. coach, health edn. tchr. K-12, life sci. tchr. 7-12. Health educator Stephens Meml. Hosp., Norway, Maine, 1984; health sci. tchr./coach Oxford Hills Jr. H.S., South Paris, 1984—. Contbr. articles to profl. jours. Dir. Paris Conservation Commission, 1990; asst. leader Boy Scouts Am. troop #130, South Paris, 1985. Named Blaines House Scholar State of Maine Dept. Edn., 1988; recipient metropolitan Life grant, 1988. Mem. Phi Delta Kappa, Phi Kappa Phi, Eta Sigma Gamma, Kappa Delta Pi. Republican. Avocations: fishing, camping, hiking, studying nature, athletics. Home: 67 E Oxford Rd South Paris ME 04281-6018 Office: Oxford Hills Mid Sch 100 Pine St South Paris ME 04281-1518

MARTIN, CHARLES WADE, pastor; b. Athens, Ga., June 7, 1952; s. William Edward and Winifred (Maxwell) M.; m. Rebecca Hankins, May 26, 1973; children: John Wade, Elizabeth Lynn. BA, Asbury Coll., 1974; MDiv, MA in Religion, Asbury Theol. Sem., 1977; postgrad. in hist. geography of Palestine, Inst. Holy Land Studies, 1977; postgrad. in audience psychology and behavior, Wheaton Coll., 1981, postgrad. in principles of rsch., 1982-83; DMin in Preaching and Worship, Fuller Theol. Sem., 1982; postgrad. in missiology and cultural anthropology, Trinity Evangelical Div. Sch., 1986-87, D in Missiology, 1989; postgrad. in missiology and cultural anthropology, Ft. Wayne Bible Coll., 1987. Lic. to preach by United Meth. Ch., 1972; ordained deacon United Meth. Ch., 1975; ordained elder United Meth. Ch., 1978; ordained to ministry First Bapt. Ch., 1983; ordained elder First Christian Ch., 2001. Pulpit supply preacher Statesboro Dist. United Meth. Ch., 1970-72, pulpit supply preacher Ky. Annual Conf., 1972-77; pastor Mt. Moriah United Meth. Ch., Matthews, Ga., 1977-80; staff min. in youth work and leadership devel. First United Meth. Ch., Sylvania, 1981-83; co-pastor Black Creek United Meth. Ch., Newington, 1982-87; interim pastor Little Horse Creek Bapt. Ch., Woodcliff, 1986-87, pastor, 1987-96. Exec. dir. Evan. Ministries of Sylvania, Inc., 1978—; tour escort to Israel, 1979, Israel and Egypt, 1981, Greece, 1982; interim Bible tchr., First Bapt. Ch., Sylvania, 1983-84. Contbr. articles to profl. jours. Avocations: archaeology, linguistics, social psychology, human development, educational psychology. Home: 206 Pinecrest Dr Sylvania GA 30467-2144 Office: Evang Ministries Sylvania PO Box 1664 Sylvania GA 30467-1664

MARTIN, CHESTER Y. sculptor, painter; b. Chattanooga, Nov. 2, 1934; s. Woodfin Ballenger and Mabel Willett (Young) M.; m. Patricia Ann Parnell, Aug. 15, 1963; 1 child, Sharon Elizabeth (Mrs. Christopher Pruitt). Student, U. Chattanooga, 1952-55, 60-61, Internat. Medallic Workshop-Pa. State U., 1984. Freelance artist, Chattanooga, 1967-86; sculptor, engraver U.S. Mint, Phila., 1986-92. One-man shows include Hunter Mus. Art, Chattanooga, 1979; group shows: Kottler Galleries, N.Y.C., 1966; Internat. Exposition Contemporary Medals, Italy, 1983, Sweden, 1985, Finland, 1990; U.S. Dept. State, 1984, Nat. Sculpture Soc., N.Y.C., 1984, 85, 99, Cast Iron Gallery, N.Y.C., 1992, Internat. Exhbn. of Contemporary Medals, Brit. Mus., London, 1992, Hungarian Nat. Gallery, Budapest, 1994, Neuchatel, 1996, Nat. Sculpture Soc., N.Y.C., 1999, Weimar, 2000, Paris Mint, 2002, numerous others; permanent collections: British Mus., London; Smithsonian Instn.; Food and Agrl. Orgn., Rome; Am. Numismatic Soc., N.Y.C.; Julius Wile Sons and Co., N.Y.C.; Brookgreen Gardens, S.C., U.S. Mint, Phila.; major comms.: World Food Day Medal, UN, 1984, others; other major works: History of Chattanooga Mural, 1974; theme painting of Br. Colonial Ft. Loudon, 1975; Centennial Mural for Chattem Inc., Chattanooga, 1980; sculptured Congl. Bicentennial Silver Dollar, 1989, Eisenhower Centennial Dollar reverse, Mt. Rushmore Dollar obverse, 1991; designer Andrew Wyeth Congl. medal, 1989, George Bush Presdl. medal reverse; designer Yosemite Nat. Park Centennial Congressional Medal, 1991, Gen. Colin L. Powell Congressional Medal, 1992, White House Bicentennial Dollar reverse, 1992; designer mural Chattanooga Met. Airport, 1999. Served with USAF, 1956-60. Recipient numerous art awards, most recent being Purchase award Benedictine Art Competition, 1975, Medallic Sculpture award Am. Numismatic Assn., 1993. Mem. Fedn. Internationale de la Medaille (Am. del.), Am. Medallic Sculpture Assn. (v.p. 1987). Methodist. Avocations: modern languages. Mailing: 4110 Sunbury Ave Chattanooga TN 37411-5232

MARTIN, CHRISTOPHER EDWARD, accountant, personal finance consultant; b. Bayport, N.Y., Dec. 18, 1969; s. Thomas Charles and Lorraine (Van Eyk) M.; m. Debra Spangler, Aug. 1, 1998. BS in Accountancy, Bentley Coll., 1992. CPA, N.Y. Staff acct., auditor Tonneson & Co., CPA's, P.C., Wakefield, Mass., 1992-93; fin. and tax cons., owner Christopher E. Martin, CPA, Bayport, 1994—; grant coord. Devel. Disabilities Inst., Inc., Smithtown, N.Y., 1996—. Vol. Okeanos Ocean Rsch. Found., Riverhead, N.Y., 1995. Mem. AICPA, N.Y. State Soc. CPA's (Leadership Acad. 1997—). Republican. Avocations: scuba diving, ocean lifeguard, boating, skiing. Home: 314 Greenbelt Pkwy Holtsville NY 11742-2226

MARTIN, CLARA RITA, elementary education educator; b. Steubenville, Ohio, Oct. 14, 1953; d. Robert Emmett and Mary Agnes (Flynn) Joyce; m. Gary Dean Martin, July 8, 1978; children: Bradley A., Douglas A. BS in Elem. Edn., Coll. Steubenville, 1975; MS in Interdisciplinary Skillls, U. Dayton, 1984. Cert. tchr., Ohio. Reading specialist Steubenville City Sch. Dist., 1975; tchr. elem. schs. Harrison Hills City Sch. Dist., Jewett and Hopedale, Ohio, 1975—. Coord. spelling bee Harrison News Herald Spelling Bee, Cadiz, Ohio, 1984-2001. Jump Rope for Heart coord., asst. coord. Meml. Day Program, 1992. Mem. Harrison Hills Tchrs.' Assn. (grievance chair, chief negotiator 1980—, bldg. rep. 1985—, del. Ohio Edn. Assn. Conv., 1981—, co-pres. 1999-), Ladies Ancient Order Hibernians (sec. 1991-92). Roman Catholic. Avocations: reading, travel. Home: 4059 State Hwy 43 Richmond OH 43944-7912

MARTIN, CLARENCE EUGENE, III, lawyer; b. Martinsburg, W.Va., Mar. 24, 1946; s. Clarence Eugene Jr. and Catherine Dubois (Silver) M.; m. Judith Anne Gray; 2 children: McKenna Gray Martin, Morgan Elizabeth Martin. AB in English, U. Ariz., 1968; JD, Cath. U., Washington, 1974. Bar: W. Va. 1974, D.C. 1974, Md. 1987, Pa., 1992, U.S. Dist. Ct. D.C. 1975, U.S. Ct. Appeals (D.C. cir.) 1975, U.S. Dist. Ct. (no. dist.) W.Va. 1976, U.S. Dist. Ct. (so. dist.) W.Va., U.S. Dist. Ct. Md. 1986, U.S. Ct. Appeals (4th cir.) 1976, U.S. Supreme Ct. 1979, U.S. Dist. Ct. (no. and ea. dists.) Pa. 1984, U.S. Ct. Appeals (3d cir.) 1984. Asst. couonsel U.S. Ho. Reps., Washington, 1974-75; trial atty. U.S. Dept. Justice, 1975-76; assoc. Martin & Seibert, L.C., Martinsburg, 1976-79, ptnr., 1979—. Bd. dirs. Mchts. & Farmers Bank, Martinsburg, W.Va. Legal Svcs. Plan. Author: (seminar) Impeachment of Witnesses, 1984; co-author ABA publ. Emerging Problems Under the Federal Rules of Evidence, 2d edit., Bad Faith Litigation, The Ethics of Surveillance. Mem. W.Va. Ho. Dels., Charleston, 1976-82; trustee Nat. Parks and Conservation Assn., Washington, 1980-85; bd. govs. Def. Trial Counsel W.Va., 1984-92; commr. Interstate Commn. Potomac River Basin, 1980-86, U.S. Commn. on Agrl. Workers, 1988-94; bd. advs. Shepherd Coll., 1989-93, 95-99, chmn. 1990-93, 95-97; mem. W.Va. Coun. Cmty. and Econ. Devel.; chmn. W.Va. Devel. Found., W.Va. Devel. Corp.; pres. Discover the Real W.Va. Found.; mem. Greater Ea. Panhandle Ch. Com., 1988—, chmn. 1988—; chmn. St. Joseph's Parish Coun., 1997-99. Recipient Am. Jurisprudence Scholastic Achievement award, 1972, Assn. Govt. Employees award, 1980. Mem. ABA, W.Va. Bar Assn. (pres. 1990-91), W.Va. State Bar, D.C. Bar Assn., Berkeley County Bar Assn. (pres. 1984), Nat. Assn. R.R. Trial Counsel, Am. Legis. Exch. Coun., Am. Judicature Soc., Def. Rsch. Inst., D.C. Bar Assn., Md. Bar Assn., Pa. Bar Assn., Am. Bd. Trial Advocates (bd. dirs. 1986-94), Internat. Assn. Def. Counsel, Def. Trial Counsel of W.Va. (founding mem., bd. dirs. 1984-92), Md. Def. Trial Counsel, W.Va. Law Inst., Berkeley County Roundhouse Authority (chmn. 1999—), City Tavern Club, Rotary, KC, Elks, Univ. Club, Order of Malta. Home: Pendleton House 6393 Arden Nollville Rd Martinsburg WV 25401-8866 Office: Martin & Seibert LC PO Box 1286 Martinsburg WV 25402-1286 E-mail: cemartin@martinandseibert.com.

MARTIN, CLAUDE RAYMOND, JR. marketing consultant, educator; b. Harrisburg, Pa., May 11, 1932; s. Claude R. and Marie Teresa (Stapf) M.; m. Marie Frances Culkin, Nov. 16, 1957; children: Elizabeth Ann, David Jude, Nancy Marie, William Jude, Patrick Jude, Cecelia Marie. BS, U. Scranton, 1954, M.B.A, 1963; PhD, Columbia U., 1969. Newsman Sta. WILK-TV, Wilkes-Barre, Pa., 1953-55; news dir. Sta. WNEP-TV, Scranton, 1955-60; dir. systems Blue Cross & Blue Shield Ins., Wilkes-Barre, 1960-63; lectr. mktg. St. Francis Coll., Bklyn., 1964, U. Mich., Ann Arbor, 1965-68, asst. prof., 1968-73, asso. prof., 1973-77, prof., 1977-80, Isadore and Leon Winkelman prof. retail mktg., 1980—, chmn. mktg. dept., 1986-90. Bd. dirs. Perry Drug Stores, cons. mktg., 1983-89; spl. cons. on rsch. changes in U.S. currency Fed. Res. Sys., 1978—; pub. mem. Nat. Advt. Rev. Bd., 1989-94. Contbr. articles on mktg. analysis, consumer research to profl. publs. Trustee U. Scranton, 1996—. Served with USNR, 1955-57. Mem. Acad. Mktg. Sci., Am. Mktg. Assn., S.W. Mktg. Assn., Bank Mktg. Assn., Assn. Consumer Rsch., Am. Collegiate Retailing Assn., Am. Acad. Advt. (Disting. Fellow). Roman Catholic. Home: 1116 Aberdeen Dr Ann Arbor MI 48104-2812

MARTIN, CLYDE VERNE, psychiatrist; b. Coffeyville, Kans., Apr. 7, 1933; s. Howard Verne and Elfrieda Louise (Moehn) Martin; m. Barbara Jean McNeilly, June 24, 1956; children: Kent Clyde, Kristin Claire, Kerry Constance, Kyle Curtis. Student, Coffeyville Coll., 1951—52; AB, U. Kans., 1955, MD, 1958; MA, Webster Coll., St. Louis, 1977; JD, Thomas Jefferson Coll. Law, L.A., 1985. Diplomate Am. Bd. Psychiatry and Neurology. Intern Lewis Gale Hosp., Roanoke, Va., 1958—59; resident in psychiatry U. Kans. Med. Ctr., Kansas City, 1959—62, Fresno br. U. Calif.-San Francisco, 1978; staff psychiatrist Neurol. Hosp., Kansas City, 1962; practice medicine specializing in psychiatry Mo., 1964—84; founder, med. dir., pres. bd. dirs. Mid-Continent Psychiat. Hosp., Olathe, Kans., 1972—84; adj. prof. psychology Baker U., Baldwin City, 1969—84; staff psychiatrist Atascadero State Hosp., Calif., 1984—85; clin. prof. psychiatry U. Calif., San Francisco, 1985—; chief psychiatrist Calif. Med. Facility, Vacaville, 1985—87. Pres., editor Corrective and Social Psychiatry, Olathe, 1970—84, Atascadero, 1984—85, Fairfield, Calif., 1985—97; cons. psychiatrist Brit. Health Svc. Plymouth (Eng.) Trust, 1999—2001. Contbr. articles to profl. jours. Bd. dirs. Meth. Youthville, Newton, Kans., 1965—75, Spofford Home, Kansas City , 1974—78; del. Kans. East Conf. Meth. Ch., 1972—80, bd. global ministries, 1974—80. Served to capt. USAF, 1962—64, ret. col. USAF. Scholar Oxford Law and Soc., 1993. Fellow: Am. Orthopsychiat. Assn., World Assn. Social Psychiatry, Royal Soc. Health (London), Am. Assn. Mental Health Profls. in Corrections, Am. Psychiat. Assn. (life); mem.: AMA, Assn. Mental Health Adminstrs. (cert.), Am. Assn. Sex Educators, Counselors and Therapists (cert.), Assn. for Advancement Psychotherapy, St. James Club (London), Capitol Hill Club (Washington), Marines Meml. Club (San Francisco), Pi Kappa Alpha, Phi Beta Pi. Office: PO Box 3365 Fairfield CA 94533-0587

MARTIN, CONNIE RUTH, retired lawyer; b. Clovis, N.Mex., Sept. 9, 1955; d. Lynn Latimer and Marian Ruth (Pierce) M.; m. Daniel A. Patterson, Nov. 21, 1987; step-children: David Patterson, Dana Patterson. B in Univ. Studies, Ea. N.Mex. U., 1976, MEd, 1977; JD, U. Mo., Kansas City, 1981. Bar: N.Mex. 1981, U.S. Dist. Ct. N.Mex. 1981, Colo. 2002. Asst. dist. atty. State of N.Mex., Farmington, 1981-84; ptnr. Tansey, Rosebrough, Gerding & Strother, PC, 1984-93; pvt. practice Connie R. Martin, P.C., 1993-94; domestic violence commr. 11th Judicial Dist. Ct., State of N.Mex., 1993-94; with Jeffrey B. Diamond Law Firm, Carlsbad, N. Mex., 1994-96; assoc. Sager, Curran, Sturges and Tepper PC, Las Cruces, 1996-97, Holt & Babington PC, Las Cruces, 1997-2000; ret., 2000. Dep. med. investigator State of N.Mex., Farmington, 1981-84; instr. San Juan Coll., 1987, N.Mex. State U., 1995; spkr. N.Mex. Jud. Edn. Ctr., 1993-94; chair paralegal program adv. com., 1988, Adv Com., St Francis Clin., Presbyn. Med. Svs., 1994-96; bd. Bar Examiners State of N.Mex., 1989—, vice-chair, 1995-97, chair, 1997-99; asst. bar counsel Disciplinary Bd.; mem. profl. adv. com. Meml. Med. Ctr. Found., 1997-2000, trustee, 1997-2000; mem. So. N.Mex. Estate Planning Coun., 1997-2000; mem. character and fitness com. Nat. Conf. Bar Examiners, 2002. Bd. dirs., exec. com. San Juan County Econ. Opportunity Coun., Farmington, 1982-83; bd. dirs. Four Corners Substance Abuse Coun., Farmington, 1984, N.Mex. Newspapers, Inc.; chmn. Cmty. Corrections-Intensive Supervision Panel, Farmington, 1987-88; jud. selection com. mem. San Juan County, 1991, Chavez County, 1995; nominating com. Supreme Ct./Ct of Appeals, 1991-96; treas. Ft. Morgan United Meth. Ch., 2001—. Recipient Distinguished Svcs. award for Outstanding Young Woman San Juan County Jaycees, 1984. Mem. N.Mex. Bar. Assn. (bd. dirs. elder law sect. 1993-96, peer rev. task force 1994-95, asst. to new lawyers com. 1986-87, local bar com. 1988, bd. dirs. young lawyers divsn. 1989-91, bd. dirs. real property probate and trust sect. 1994-97), San Juan County Bar Assn. (treas. 1985-87, v.p. 1987, pres. 1988), Farmington C. of C. (bd. dirs. 1991-93). Methodist. Avocations: health, fitness, reading.

MARTIN, CURTIS, professional football player; b. Pitts., May 1, 1973; Student, U. Pitts. Running back New Eng. Patriots, Foxboro, Mass., 1995-98, N.Y. Jets, 1998—. Selected to Pro Bowl, 1995, 96. Office: care NY Jets 1000 Fulton Ave Hempstead NY 11550-1030*

MARTIN, CURTIS HARMON, political scientist; b. Plainfield, N.J., July 21, 1945; s. Harmon C. and Audrey (Smith) Martin; m. Janet May Morahan, June 2, 1979; 1 child Gwendolyn May. AB, Harvard U., 1967; PhD, Tufts U., 1974. Rsch. assoc. Nat. Bur. Econ. Rsch., Cambridge, Mass., 1974; prof. Merrimack Coll., North Andover, 1974—, chair, 1979—94. Co-author: (book) Politics East and West, 1992, Local Economic Development, 1978; author: (book chpt.) Sanctions as Economic Statecraft, 2000; contbr. articles to profl. jours. Grantee grantee for pub. policy curriculum devel., Sloan/Ford Found., 1979. Avocations: landscape painting, swimming. Office: Merrimack Coll Polit Sci Dept 315 Turnpike St North Andover MA 01845 E-mail: curtis.martin@merrimack.edu.

MARTIN, D. JOE, accountant; b. Greenville, Ohio, May 19, 1947; s. Stanley E. and Mildred E. (Ford) M.; m. Kathleen Brosmer, Dec. 22, 1991. BS in Acctg., Capital U., 1969. CPA, Ohio. Staff acct. Peat Marwick & Mitchell & Co., Columbus, Ohio, 1969-71; audit supr. First Banc Group of Ohio, 1971-74; asst. treas. First Trust Co. of Ohio, 1974-76; v.p. fin. Buckeye Fin. Corp., 1976-80; prin., ptnr., owner D. Joe Martin Co., CPAs, 1979—; treas., dir. So. Fin. Holding Corp., West Palm Beach, Fla., 1984-85; vice chair, corp. sec., dir. Ravenna Savs. Bank, Columbus, 1987—; pres., CEO Sterling Fin. Holdings, Inc., West Palm Beach, fla., 1995—. Mem. AICPA, Ohio Soc. CPAs. Republican. Lutheran. Avocations: tennis, skiing. Home: 663 Overbrook Dr Columbus OH 43214-3130 Office: D Joe Martin Co CPAs 3404 Riverside Dr Upper Arlington OH 43221-1743

MARTIN, DALLAS REA, lawyer; b. Kansas City, Kans., Aug. 3, 1954; s. H. Thayne and Frances Colleen (Hay) M.; m. Lianne Marie Taylor, June 2, 1979; 1 child, Elise Taylor. BA in Philosophy with honors and distinction, U. Kans., Lawrence, 1976, JD, 1979. Bar: Kans. 1979, U.S. Dist. Ct. Kans., 1979, U.S. Ct. Appeals (10th cir.) 1979, Colo. 1985, U.S. Dist. Ct. Colo. 1985. Pvt. practice, Olathe, Kans., 1979-81; contracts counsel Midwest Rsch. Inst., Kansas City, Mo., 1981-84; counsel and contracts mgr. Precision Visuals, Inc., Boulder, Colo., 1984-90; mgr. tech. transfer Nat. Renewable Energy Lab., Golden, 1990-94; dir. intellectual property, tech. transfer office U.S. West Advt. Tech., Inc., Boulder, 1994-97; sr. counsel intellectual property First Data Corp., Englewood, Colo., 1997-2000; v.p., gen. counsel, sec. SwitchPoint Networks, Inc., 2001—. Contbr. articles to profl. jours. Bd. dirs. Blue Knights, Inc., Denver, 1997—. Mem. ABA (intellectual property sect. 1991—), Tech. Transfer Soc. (bd. dirs. 1996-98), Licensing Execs. Soc. (co-chair Denver chpt. 2001—). Office: SwitchPoint Networks Inc 4582 S Ulster St Denver CO 80237 E-mail: drmartin@switchpointnetworks.com.

MARTIN, DANIEL C. surgeon, gynecologist, educator; b. St. Louis, Apr. 7, 1946; s. Dan Allen and Ruth Keel (Fields) M.; m. Glenn Ann Blakemore, July 7, 1970; children: Josh, Adam. BS in Physics, Emory U., 1968, MD, 1972. Diplomate Am. Bd. Ob-Gyn. Rsch. asst. physics and radiology Emory U., Atlanta, 1968-69; intern, resident, fellow, instr. The Johns Hopkins Med. Instns., Balt., 1972-77; from asst. prof. to clin. asst. prof. U. Tenn., Memphis, 1977-90, clin. assoc. prof., 1990—; surgeon Reproductive Surgery, P.C., 1977—. Gynecologist, reproductive surgeon Bapt. Meml. Hosp., 1977—; Axel Munthe presenter, Naples, Italy, 1992; guest spkr. 15th Annual Japanese Endometriosis Symposium, Osaka, 1994; dir. gynecologic laser and endoscopy workshops, 1982-93. Editor: (textbooks) Lasers in Endoscopy, 1990, Laparoscopic Appearance of Endometriosis, 1990, Manual of Endoscopy, 1990, Atlas of Endometriosis, 1993, Endoscopic Management of Gynecologic Disease, 1996. Basketball coach Grace St. Luke's Ch., Memphis, 1992-95. Picker Found. fellow Emory U., 1969; Tex. Assn. Ob-Gyn. hon. fellow, 1989; recipient Bridges trophy for athletics Emory U., 1968, Codman surg. award, 1982, 83, Video award Am. Fertility Soc., 1992, Physician Recognition awrd Endometriosis Assn., 1995; named one of Best Drs. Am. Woodward and White Inc., 1992, 94, 96, 98, Hon. mem. Australian Gynecol. Endoscopy Soc., 1993. Mem. ACOG (sect. chair jr. fellows Md.), Tenn. Med. Assn., Memphis and Shelby County Med. Soc. (comm. com.), Am. Nat. Std. Inst. (subcom. on laser safety in med. facility), Am. Assn. Gynecol. Laparoscopists (pres. 1990-91, Videoendoscopy award 1993), Gynecologic Surgery Soc. (pres. 1994-96, chmn. bd. 1996-98), Australian Gynecol. Endoscopy Soc. (hon.), Argentinian Ob-Gyn. Soc. (hon.). Office: Reproductive Surgery PC 1717 Kirby Pkwy Ste 100 Memphis TN 38120-4331 E-mail: dnmartin46@aol.com.

MARTIN, DANIEL RICHARD, pharmaceutical company executive; b. Lima, Peru, June 9, 1937; s. James Marion and Clemmy Caroline (Valencia) M.; m. Barbara Artemis Cyrus, June 23, 1962; children: Daniel Richard Jr., John Alexander, Christopher Andrew. BA, Cornell U., 1958; MS, Columbia U., N.Y.C., 1959. Area sales supr. Schering Corp., Bloomfield, N.J., 1960-64; assoc. McKinsey & Co., N.Y.C., 1964-69; treas. Harper & Row, Pubs., 1969-72; mng. dir. Merck & Co., Rahway, N.J., 1972-77; group v.p. Bell & Howell Co., Chgo., 1977-80; pres. Howland Martin Corp., N.Y.C., 1980-85; pres. Sterling Europe, Middle East, Africa Sterling Drug, Inc., 1986-89; pres., CEO, also bd. dirs. E-Z-EM, Inc., Westbury, N.Y., 1990-97; pres., also bd. dirs. Milestone Scientific, Inc., Livingston, N.J., 1998-99. Adj. prof. mgmt. Pace U., N.Y.C., 1996—. Co-chmn. Accion Internat., Cambridge, Mass., 1988-98; trustee Bangor (Maine) Theol. Sem., 1991-2000; dir. Americas Found.; bd. dirs., fin. com. White Plains (N.Y.) Hosp. Decorated Order of Merit (Ecuador). Mem. Coun. on Fgn. Rels., Americas Soc., Cornell Club (N.Y.C.). Republican. Congregationalist. Home: 31 Rochambeau Dr Hartsdale NY 10530-3017 E-mail: drm1937@aol.com.

MARTIN, DARRYL JAMES, audio-visual specialist; b. St. Albans, N.Y., Sept. 4, 1950; s. Sydney and Helen Martin; m. Theresa McCarthy, July 29, 1978 (div. 1986); children: Jamielynn, Kristina Marie. Student in bus. adminstrn., Nassau C.C., 1971-73; assoc. in fire sci., Fire Svc. Acad., 1971-78; paramedic tng. in advanced cardiac care, St. Francis Hosp., Roslyn, N.Y., 1973-77; BA in Audio Visual Tech., N.Y. Inst. Tech., 1975; M in Computer Sci. and Tech., U. Berkeley, 1999. Audio-visual coord. Farmingdale (N.Y.) Pub. Schs., 1971-79; dir. audio-visual svcs. Bethpage (N.Y.) Pub. Schs., 1979—. Audio-visual coord. evening classes C.W. Post Coll., L.I.U., Green Vale, N.Y., 1982-85, lead call ctr. ops. Cablevision L.I., 1996—. Author: Security Procedures for An Educational Institution, 19981, Poems of the Heart, 1990, Class of 68, 1991, Suffer In Silence, 1999. Engine capt. Bethpage Fire Dept., 1972-82. With U.S. Army, 1968-71. Mem. Nat. Assn. Ednl. Radio, N.Y. State Ednl. Comm. Assn., Nat. Audio Visual Assn. Home: 36 Acme Ave Bethpage NY 11714-4610 Office: Bethpage Pub Schs Adminstrn Bldg Cherry Ave Bethpage NY 11714

MARTIN, DAVID ALAN, law educator; b. Indpls., July 23, 1948; s. C. Wendell and Elizabeth Bowman (Meeker) M.; m. Cynthia Jo Lorman, June 13, 1970; children: Amy Lynn, Jeffrey David. BA, DePauw U., 1970; JD, Yale U., 1975. Bar: D.C. Law clk. to Hon. J. Skelly Wright U.S. Ct. Appeals (D.C. cir.), 1975-76; law clk. to Hon. Lewis F. Powell U.S. Supreme Ct., Washington, 1976-77; assoc. Rogovin, Stern & Huge, 1977-78; spl. asst. bur. human rights and humanitarian affairs U.S. State Dept., 1978-80; from asst. prof. to assoc. prof. U. Va. Sch. Law, Charlottesville, 1980-86, prof., 1986-91, Henry L. & Grace Doherty prof. law, 1991—, F. Palmer Weber Rsch. prof. civil liberties and human rights, 1992-95, 2000—. Cons. Adminstrv. Conf. U.S., Washington, 1988-89, 91-92, U.S. Dept. Justice, 1993-95; gen. counsel U.S. Immigration and Naturalization Svc., 1995-98. Author: Immigration: Process and Policy, 1985, 4th edit., 1998, Asylum Case Law Sourcebook, 1994, 3rd edit., 2001, The Endless Quest: Helping America's Farm Workers, 1994; editor: The New Asylum Seekers, 1988, Immigration Admissions, 1998, Immigration Controls, 1998; contbr. articles to profl. jours. Nat. governing bd. Common Cause, Washington, 1972-75; elder Westminster Presbyn. Ch., Charlottesville, 1982-84, 89-92; bd. dirs. Internat. Rescue Com., 2000—. German Marshall Fund Rsch. fellow, Geneva, 1984-85. Mem. Am. Soc. Internat. Law (Book award 1986), Internat. Law Assn. Democrat. Office: U Va Sch Law 580 Massie Rd Charlottesville VA 22903-1738 E-mail: dam3r@virginia.edu.

MARTIN, DAVID EDWARD, health sciences educator; b. Green Bay, Wis., Oct. 1, 1939; s. Edward Henry and Lillie (Luckman) M. BS, U. Wis., 1961, MS, 1963, PhD, 1970. Ford Found. research trainee Wis. Regional Primate Ctr., Madison, 1967-70; asst. prof. health scis. Ga. State U., Atlanta, 1970-74, assoc. prof., 1974-80, prof., 1980-91, regents prof., 1992-00, regents prof. emeritus, 2000—. Affiliate scientist Yerkes Primate Rsch. Ctr., Emory U., Atlanta, 1970-98; U.S. rep. to Internat. Olympic Acad., 1978; sports medicine rsch. assoc. U.S. Olympic Com., 1981-84; chmn. sports scis. U.S.A. Track and Field; mem. coaching staff U.S. teams to world championships in distance running, Rome, 1982, Gateshead, Eng., 1983, Budapest, Hungary, 1994, Vilamoura, Portugal, 2000, head coach, Paris, 1980, Madrid, 1984, Hiroshima, Japan, 1985, Warsaw, Poland, 1987, Antwerp, Belgium, 1991; mem. Olympic med. support group Atlanta Olympic Games. Author: Laboratory Experiments in Human Physiology, 4th edit., 1980, The Marathon Footrace, 1979, La Corsa Di Maratona, 1982, The High Jump Book, 1982, The High Jump Book, 2d edit., 1987, Respiratory Anatomy and Physiology, 1987, Training Distance Runners, 1991, Training Distance Runners, 2d edit., 1997, Training Distance Runners, German edit., 1992, Training Distance Runners, Spanish edit., 1995, Training Distance Runners, Japanese edit., 2001. Trustee Ga. Found. for Athletic Excellence. Recipient fed. and univ. grants for physiol. research; named Disting. prof. Ga. State U., 1975, 81, 85 Fellow Am. Coll. Sports Medicine; mem. Internat. Soc. Olympic Historians, Am. Physiol. Soc., Atlanta Track Club. Home: 510 Coventry Rd Apt 13A Decatur GA 30030-5038 Office: Ga State U Dept Cardiopul Care Atlanta GA 30303

MARTIN, DAVID GEORGE, historian, Latin educator, author; b. Midland, Mich., Feb. 8, 1949; s. Robert A. Martin and Viola B. Weaver; 1 child, Peter Joseph Martin. BA, U. Mich., 1971; MA, Princeton (N.J.) U., 1973, PhD, 1975. Latin instr. The Peddie Sch., Hightstown, N.J., 1975—. Editor Longstreet House, Hightstown, N.J., Combined Publs., Conshohocken, Pa. Author: Gettysburg, July 1, 1995 (award 1997), Jackson's Valley Campaign, 1988; co-author: Regimental Strengths at Gettysburg, 1982; author, editor 20 books on civil war. Recipient Good Citizenship award N.J. Dept. Sons of Union Vets. of the Civil War, 1984, 96. Fellow Company of Mil. Historians; mem. SAR, N.J. Civil War Heritage Assn. (2d v.p. 1998—), Friends of Monmouth Battlefield (bd. trustees 1996—), Sons of the Unions Vets. of the Civil War (comdr. N.J. dept. 1993-95), Sons of Vets. Res. (capt. 1990-92). Office: The Peddie Sch South Main St Hightstown NJ 08520

MARTIN, DAVID HUBERT, physician, educator; b. Detroit, Mar. 24, 1943; s. Hubert Cillis and Mable Anita (Stewart) M.; m. Jane Ellen Schlichtemeier, Nov. 22, 1970; children: Jennifer, Jason. BA with distinction, U. Kans., 1965; MD cum laude, Harvard Coll., 1969. Diplomate Nat. Bd. Med. Examiners,

Am. Bd. Internal Medicine, Infectious Disease Subspecialty Bd. Am. Bd. Internal Medicine. Intern Bronx (N.Y.) Mcpl. Hosp. Ctr., 1969-70; staff assoc. Nat. Inst. Allergy and Infectious Diseases, Mid. Am. Rsch. Unit, NIH, Panama Canal Zone, 1970-73; med. resident U. Wash. Affiliated Hosps., 1973-75; sr. fellow in infectious diseases U. Wash., 1976-78; chief resident in medicine USPHS Hosp., Seattle, 1975-76, staff internal medicine clinic, 1975, attending physician internal medicine, 1976-78, staff dept. internal medicine New Orleans, 1979-81; staff Hotel Dieu Hosp., 1982-94; clin. asst. prof. medicine La. State U. Med. Sch., 1979-81, asst. prof. medicine divsn. infectious diseases, 1981-82, assoc. prof. medicine divsn. infectious diseases, 1982-88, assoc. prof. microbiology, 1986-88, prof. internal medicine and microbiology, 1988, asst. chief sect. infectious diseases, 1988-89, chief sect. infectious diseases, 1990—, Harry E. Dascomb M.D. prof. of medicine, 1990—. Instr. dept. medicine U. Wash. Sch. Medicine, Seattle, 1975-78, acting asst. prof. medicine, 1978-79; chmn. infection control com., chmn. instnl. rev. bd. human rsch. com., chmn. antibiotic utilization com., sec. rsch. and editl. com., sec. animal welfare com. USPHS Hosp., New Orleans, 1979-81, dep. chief clin. rsch. dept., 1979-81, chmn. credentials com., 1980-81; mem. infection control com. Hotel Dieu Hosp., New Orleans, 1983-84, chmn. pharmacy and therapeutics com., 1988-94, mem. infection control com., 1990-94; vis. physician Charity Hosp. (now Med. Ctr. of La. at New Orleans), New Orleans, 1982—, chmn. antibiotics com., 1982—, dir. infection control program, 1993—, chmn. infection control com., 1993—, vice chmn. pharmacy and therapeutics com., 1995—; cons. sexually transmitted diseases control program Dept. Health and Human Resources, State of La., 1985—; staff physician Jefferson Parish Venereal Disease Clinic, 1986-90, New Orleans (La.) Sexually Transmitted Disease Clinic, 1992—; cons. pharmacy and therapeutics com. Mercy Hosp., New Orleans, 1989-91; cons. La. AIDS Cmty. Rsch. Project, 1989-92; chmn. comprehensive medicine head search com. La. State U. Med. Sch., 1989-90, dept. medicine faculty promotion com., 1988—, AIDS policy com., 1992; mem. La. State Labs. Adv. Bd., 1993—, State La. Pub. Health Lab. Adv. Com., 1994—, U.S. Pub. Health Region 6 Infertility Prevention Adv. Com., 1995—; mem. nat. STD treatment guidelines com. Ctrs. Disease Control, 1993, 98, nat. Chlamydia and gonorrheadiagnosis guidelines com., 1997—. Peer reviewer various jours. including Sexually Transmitted Diseases, The Jour. of Infectious Diseases, The Am. Jour. of the Med. Scis., Archives of Internal Medicine, Clin. Infectious Diseases, New Eng. Jour. Medicine, Annals Internal Medicine, Jour. AMA; contbr. chpts. to books and articles to profl. jours. Dir. La. STD/HIV Rsch. Ctr., 2002—. With USPHS, 1970-82. Achievements include established the first chlamydia laboratory in the Gulf South. Fellow ACP (La. chpt. program chmn. 1994-95), Infectious Diseases Soc. Am.; mem. Internat. Soc. for Sexually Transmitted Disease Rsch. (bd. dirs. 1991-99, chmn. 1995 meeting organizing com., pres. 1993-95, sec.-treas. 1999—), Am. Fedn. for Clin. Rsch., Am. Sexually Transmitted Diseases Assn. (v.p. 1992-94, pres. 1994-96), Am. Soc. for Microbiology, European Soc. for Clin. Microbiology and Infectious Diseases, So. Soc. for Clin. Investigation, La./Miss. Infectious Diseases Soc. (bd. dirs., sci. program chmn. 1993, pres. 1997-99), Phi Beta Kappa. Achievements include research in the effect of sexually transmitted microorganisms on pregnancy outcome, antibiotic treatment of sexually transmitted diseases and in particular C. trachomatis, epidemiology of C. trachomatis in normal populations, chancroid and other genital ulcer diseases; being the director of La. STD/HIV rsch. ctr., 2001-. Office: La State U Med Sch 1542 Tulane Ave New Orleans LA 70112-2825

MARTIN, DAVID O'BRIEN, congressman; b. St. Lawrence County, N.Y., Apr. 26, 1944; s. Edson Albert and Anne (O'Brien) M.; children: Victoria, Kelly, Julia. BBA, U. Notre Dame, 1966; JD, Albany Law Sch., 1973. Mem. N.Y. State Assembly from 112th Dist., 1977-80; mem. 97th-102nd Congresses from 26th N.Y. dist., 1981—. Served to capt. USMC, 1966-70, Vietnam. Mem. ABA, N.Y. State Bar Assn., Am. Legion. Clubs: Elks. Republican. Roman Catholic. Office: US Ho of Reps Cannon House Office Bldg Rm 442 Washington DC 20515-0001*

MARTIN, DAVID S. retired educator, administrator; b. N.Y.C., May 14, 1941; s. Perry Johnson and Polly Edith (Shedlov) M.; m. Florence E. Martin, Jan. 14, 1989; children: Drew Michael, Amy Davida. BA, Adelphi Coll., 1962, MA, 1966; profl. cert., Hofstra U., 1969. Cert. secondary tchr., sch. dist. adminstr., N.Y. Adj. assoc. prof. Pace U., White Plains, N.Y., 1978-92; tchr., computer coord. Jericho (N.Y.) Pub. Schs., 1962-99. Author: Teachers Manual for Introduction to Pascal; co-author: How To Prepare for SAT II: Physics, 6th edit.; also author other books; contbr. articles to profl. jours. Fulbright-Hays grantee, 1967-68; recipient Grand award L.I. Sci. Congress, 1958, Disting Achievement award Electronic Learning, 1983, Outstanding Accomplishment award RITEC, 1984. Mem. IEEE (sr.), Am. Assn. Physics Tchrs., Assn. Computing Machinery, Authors Guild, Jericho Tchrs. Assn., N.Y. State United Tchrs., Flambeau, Phi Delta Kappa, Sigma Pi Sigma. Home: 16 Elm Pl Sea Cliff NY 11579-1634

MARTIN, DAVID STANDISH, education educator; b. New Bedford, Mass., Aug. 24, 1937; s. Theodore Tripp and Elinor Louise (Raymond) M.; m. Susan Katherine Orowan, June 30, 1962. BA, Yale U., 1959; MEd, Harvard U., 1961, CAS, 1968; PhD, Boston Coll., 1971. Cert. tchr., prin. Tchr. Newton (Mass.) Pub. Schs., 1961-68, asst. prin., 1969-70; teaching asst. Boston Coll., Chestnut Hill, Mass., 1968-69; curriculum dir. Beverly (Mass.) Pub. Schs., 1970-73; prin. Mill Valley (Calif.) Pub. Schs., 1973-75, curriculum dir., 1975-80; chmn. dept. edn. Dominican Coll., San Rafael, Calif., 1978-80; coordinator undergrad. tchr. edn. Gallaudet U., Washington, 1980-85, dean sch. edn. and human svcs., 1985-95, prof. edn., 1995—2001, prof., dean emeritus, 2002—. Cons. Curriculum Devel. Assocs., Washington, 1975-2001; mem. bd. examiners Nat. Coun. Accreditation Tchr. Education; bd. dirs. USA-SINO Tchr. Education Consortium, Western Pa. Sch. for the Deaf. Author: Case Studies in Curriculum, 1989; editor: Cognition, Education and Deafness, 1985, Advances in Cognition Education and Deafness, 1991; contbr. articles to profl. jours. Grantee Dept. Edn., 1970, 85, Knight Found., 1995-2001, Ford Found., 1998-2001. Mem. D.C. Assn. Colls. Tchr. Edn. (pres. 1989-92), Assn. for Supervision and Curricum Devel., Nat. Coun. for Social Studies, Am. Ednl. Rsch. Assn., Am. Assn. Colls. for Tchr. Edn. (bd. dirs.), Coun. for Exceptional Children, Phi Delta Kappa, Kappa Delta Pi (chair publ.), Ednl. Consulting Schs. and Univs. Democrat. Unitarian Universalist. Avocations: genealogy, sailing, classical organ, astronomy. Home and Office: 10 Colonial Farm Cir Marstons Mills MA 02648

MARTIN, DAVID WARREN, management consultant; b. West Grove, Pa., Apr. 21, 1941; s. Raymond Conard and Katharine (McLimans) M.; m. Hope Wingate, Aug. 17, 1963; children: Jennifer W., Jonathan W. BA, Lincoln U., 1964; MSA, G. Washington U., 1974; grad., USAF Air War Coll., 1974; postgrad., U. Va., 1984. Tchr. of English Mt. Pleasant H.S., Wilmington, Del., 1963-66; commd. 2d lt. USAF, 1966, advanced through grades to col., 1988; ret. USAFR, 1993; pers. mgr. S.E. Nat. Bank of Pa., Malvern, 1976-81; regional pers. officer U.S. Nuclear Regulatory Commn., King of Prussia, Pa., 1981-83; sr. dir. human resources Amtrak, Washington, 1985-97; CEO, pres. HRA Svcs., Inc., Chadds Ford, Pa., 1998—. Bd. trustees Upland Sch., Kennett Sq., Pa., 1987-93, chmn. strategic planning, fin., pers. coms. Home: 582 Coatesville Rd West Grove PA 19390-9232 Office: HRA Svcs PO Box 818 Chadds Ford PA 19317-0628 E-mail: dave@hraservices.com.

MARTIN, DEBORAH ANN, intensive care nurse, educator; b. Chester, Pa., June 4, 1957; d. Clarence Hayden and Freida Florence (Hubacher) Williams; m. Gary Gene Martin, Aug. 14, 1982; children: Sean, Jeremy, Kyle. BSN, U. Del., 1979; MSN, U. Ctrl. Ark., 1994. RN, Ark.; cert. ACLS. Staff RN renal transplant and surg. ICU Hosp. U. Pa., Phila., 1979-81; staff RN burn treatment ctr., charge nurse ICU relief Crozer-Chester Med. Ctr., Upland, Pa., 1981-83; staff RN ICU, ICU clin. educator Bapt. Med. Ctr., Jacksonville, Fla., 1983-85; staff nurse ICU Med. Pers. Pool and Staff Builders, Tampa, 1985-88; staff RN ICU Berwick (Pa.) Hosp., 1988-89; staff RN ICU, spl. recovery, relief cardiac/diabetes educator, instr. dysrhythmia and pacemaker instr. St. Edward's Mercy Med. Ctr., Ft. Smith, Ark., 1990—. Part-time faculty Westark C.C., Ft. Smith, 1996-99, full-time instr., 1999—. Mem. AACN, Sigma Theta Tau. Home and Office: 7515 Bear Hollow Rd Fort Smith AR 72916-7408 E-mail: dmartin@westark.edu.

MARTIN, DENNIS DALE, religious studies educator; b. Elkhart, Ind., Mar. 5, 1952; s. Dale Ernest Martin and Sylvia Ethel Schrock; m. Carol Ann Nearpass, May 3, 1980. BA, Wheaton Coll., Ill., 1974; MA, U. Waterloo, Ont., Can., 1975, PhD, 1982. Asst. editor Brethren Ency., Inc., Oak Brook, Ill., 1979-83; assoc. editor Inst. Mennonite Studies, Mennonite Ency. Project, Elkhart, 1983-89; asst. prof. ch. history Associated Mennonite Bibl. Sems., 1983-89; asst. prof. hist. theology Loyola U., Chgo., 1991-97, assoc. prof. hist. theology, 1997—. Charter governing bd. mem. Lumen Christi Inst., Chgo., 1997—; collaborateur Ctr. de Rsch. et D'Etudes de Spiritualite Cartusienne, Inst. Cath. de Paris, 1998—. Author, editor: Brethren Encyclopedia, 1983, Mennonite Encyclopedia, 1990; author: Fifteenth-Century Carthusian Reform, 1992; author, translator: Carthusian Spirituality, 1997; adv. editor Christian History mag., 1994—. Fulbright scholar Fulbright Commn., Tuebingen, Germany, 1976-77; summer fellow NEH, 1989, resident fellow Inst. for Rsch. in the Humanities, U. Wis., Madison, 1990-91. Mem. The Historical Soc., Am. Cath. Hist. Assn., Medieval Acad. Am. Roman Catholic. Office: Loyola Univ Chgo 6525 N Sheridan Rd Chicago IL 60626-5344 E-mail: dmarti1@wpo.it.luc.edu.

MARTIN, DONALD JAMES, marketing professional; b. Brantford, Ont., Can., May 2, 1928; s. Norman Wilfred and Leeta Maude (Woodley) M.; m. Annette Roselyn Mills, Aug. 25, 1952; children: Paul Stuart, Cheryl Anne. PhB, Northwestern U., 1964; postgrad., U. Chgo., 1965-66. Account rep. J. Walter Thompson, Toronto, Can., 1951-56, supr. mgmt. Sao Paulo, Brazil, 1956-60, v.p. Chgo., 1960-66; dir. corp. rels. Kraft, Inc., N.Y.C., Chgo., 1966-73; v.p. external affairs Scott Paper, Phila., 1973-76; v.p. com.. Conrail, 1976-79; pres. Rennoc Corp., Vineland, N.J., 1979-84, Martin Broadcasting Inc., Vineland, 1979-84; v.p. internat. paper real estate Hilton Head Island, S.C., 1979-84; pres. Marcom Inc., 1989—; talk show host Sta. WHHI-TV, 1992—. Instr. internat. mktg. Northwestern U., Evanston, Ill., 1964-66; prof. broadcast mgmt. Mercer (N.J.) Coll., 1980-83; dir. Broadcast Pioneers Am.. Mgr. Hilton Head Concert Orch., 1985-89; exec. prodr. summer festival Hilton Head Eastman Sch. Music, 1986-89; bd. dirs. Hilton Head Dance Theater, 1986, 87, Cultural Coun. Hilton Head Island, 1987-90; mem. cmty. adv. bd. Hilton Head Med. Ctr. Clinics, 1995—; actor Hilton Head Playhouse. Recipient Svc. Appreciation award Sunshine Found., 1979, Outstanding Media award United Way, 1998. Mem. Rotary (Svc. Above Self award 1992-93), S. C. Yacht Club. Avocations: tennis, sailing, acting. Office: WHHI-TV Courtyard Building Ste 103 Hilton Head Island SC 29928-4637

MARTIN, DONNA ATKINS, textile designer; b. Ft. Ord, Calif., July 25, 1956; d. James Edward and Mary Ward (Shearin) Atkins; m. Glen Alan Downs, Jan. 2, 1982 (div. Nov. 1990); m. Robert Blair Martin, June 29, 1991 (div. 1998); 1 child, Parker James Blair Martin. AAS in Fashion Design, SUNY, 1977; BS in Textile Tech., N.C. State U., 1978. Head designer Chatham Mills, Pittsboro, N.C., 1978-81; dept. mgr. JC Penney, Wilson, 1982-85; house mem.'s asst. N.C. Legislature, Raleigh, 1985-86; dir. product devel. Doblin Fabrics, Morganton, 1989-94; pres., CEO Martin Textiles, Ltd., Hickory, 1994—. Freelance designer, stylist Carolina Mills, Hickory, 1995-97; automotive textile designer, CMI Industries, Elkin, N.C., 1998-2000; design ops. mgr. Chatham-Borgstena Automotive Textiles, Mt. Airy, N.C., 2001—. Southern Baptist. Avocations: traveling, choral singing. E-mail: donna.martin@us.borgstena.com.

MARTIN, DONNA LEE, publishing company executive, retired; b. Detroit, Aug. 7, 1935; d. David M. Paul and Lillian (Paul); m. Rex Martin, June 5, 1956; children: Justin, Andrew. BA, Rice U., 1957. Mng. editor trade dept. Appleton-Century-Crofts Co., N.Y.C., 1961-62; dir. publs. Lycoming Coll., Williamsport, Pa., 1966-68; editor Univ. Press of Kans., Lawrence, 1971-74; mng. editor Andrews McMeel Publ., Kansas City, Mo., 1974-80, v.p., editorial dir., 1980-95, v.p., editor-at-large, 1995-98; v.p. Universal Press Syndicate, 1980-98. Lectr. U. Mo., Kansas City, Johnson County Cmty. Coll., Kans.; free-lance writer, editor; cons. Kansas City Star Books. Author: (adaptation) Charles Dickens' A Christmas Carol: Adapted for Theatre; contbr. articles to profl. jours. Named Disting. Alumna Rice U., 1990. Mem. Ctrl. Exchange (Kansas City), The Groucho Club (London), Phi Beta Kappa. Home: 6810 W 66th Ter Shawnee Mission KS 66202-4147 E-mail: donnaMartin@compuserve.com.

MARTIN, EARIN MILLER, grant administrator, program director, educator, trainer; b. Austin, Tex., July 6, 1952; d. Alse Edward Jr. and Wilma Nell (Maufrais) Ethridge; m. Paul Chapman Goggan, Jan. 11, 1975 (div. Nov. 1982); m. Bobby Lee Martin, May 24, 1986. BA, S.W. Tex. State U., 1974; MA, U. Tex., 1987, EdD, 1996. Cert. English and sociology tchr., Tex. Tchr. aide, tchr. English Irving (Tex.) Ind. Sch. Dist., 1976-78; tchr. English Frenship Ind. Sch. Dist., Wolforth, Tex., 1978-79; staff asst. Farm Credit Banks Tex., Austin, 1982-85, tng. specialist, 1985-87; fiscal program specialist II Tex. Edn. Agy., 1987-90, ednl. program dir., 1990, dir. programs II, 1990-98, assoc. sr. dir., 1998-99, sr. dir., 1999—. Strategic planning com. Tex. Edn. Agy., 1994—, bus. reingineering task force, 1995—, coord. funding adv. com., 1997—; chairperson Title VI Nat. Steering Com., 1996-98, 2000—; mem. state electronic grant tech. assistance workgroup, 2001—; legis. com. chair Title VI Nat. Steering Com. Recipient fellowship Alexander Caswell Ellis, 1986-87. Mem. ASCD, Phi Kappa Phi, Kappa Delta Pi, Phi Delta Kappa. Methodist. Avocations: water sports, gardening, reading, writing. Home: 5301 Waterbrook Dr Austin TX 78723-4042

MARTIN, EARL RICHARD, theology educator; b. Milton, Pa., Nov. 13, 1927; s. Luther Hause and Maude Ellen (Arner) M.; m. Mary Jane Winchester, July 30, 1948; children: Judith C. Smalling, Susan L. Sakaguchi, Charlene J. Gray, Wayne E. BA, Maryville Coll., 1949; BDiv, Southwestern Bapt. Theol. Sem., 1953; M in Theology, Southeastern Bapt. Theol. Sem., 1966; PhD, U. Nairobi, Kenya, 1974. Ordained to Gospel Ministry, Fountain Meml. Bapt. Ch., 1950. Minister Temple Hills Bapt. Ch., Md., 1953-57; missionary Fgn. Mission Bd., Kenya, Tanzania, Rwanda, 1957-82; prof. Southwestern Bapt. Theol. Sem., Ft. Worth, 1982-87, Internat. Bapt. Sem., Ruschlikon, Switzerland, 1987-92; dir. Inst. Mission Evangelism, European Bapt. Fedn., 1987-94; sr. prof. Carson-Newman Coll., Tenn., 1994—. Vis. prof. Golden Gate Bapt. Theol. Sem., Mill Valley, Calif., 1969-70, Kenyatta U. Coll., Kenya, 1976-77. Author: MuKoma of Lion Country, 1964, PAssport to Servanthood, 1988. Avocations: reading, hiking, dog. Home: 285 Battlefield Dr Dandridge TN 37725

MARTIN, EDWARD BRIAN, electrical engineer; b. Lawrence, Kans., Feb. 9, 1936; s. Edward Brian and Dorothy Irene (Dowers) M.; m. Sharon Anne Zimmerman, Dec. 21, 1955; children: Terry Brian, Ricky Lynn, Mindy Anne, Timothy Alan. BSEE, U. Kans., 1958; MSEE, St. Louis U., 1969. Registered profl. engr., Mo. Program mgr. McDonnell Douglas, St. Louis, 1980-85, mgr. avionics, 1985-86, dir. engring., 1986-88, dir. electronics, 1988-89, sr. dir. tech. processes, 1989-91, sr. dir. avionics tech., 1991-92, dir. advanced missile systems, 1992-95, dir. advanced weapon systems, 1995-97; dir. advanced tactical missiles The Boeing Co., 1997—2000. Chmn. bd. dirs. Martin Internat., Ltd. Contbr. numerous articles to profl. jours. Pres. PTA, St. Louis, 1972; founder Martin Family Found. Mem. AIAA. Avocations: running, mountain climbing, writing. Home: 5335 Lancelot Dr Saint Charles MO 63304-5742

MARTIN, EDWARD CURTIS, JR. landscape architect, educator; b. Albany, Ga., Aug. 21, 1928; s. Edward Curtis and Mildred Lee (Tyler) M.; m. Roberta Inman Parker, Mar. 18, 1967; children: Edward Curtis III, Andrew Parker. BFA, U. Ga., 1950, M of Landscape Architecture, 1969. Landscape architect Norman C. Butts Landscape Contractor, Atlanta, 1950; M.T. Brooks Office of Landscape Architecture, Birmingham, Ala., 1950-56; univ. landscape architect, horticulturalist Miss. State U., Mississippi State, 1956-70, prof. landscape architecture, 1970-92, Disting. prof., 1988, prof. emeritus, 1993—, part-time prof., 1992—93; originator, chmn., lectr. Miss. Landscape Design Symposium, 1957—. Guest lectr. U. San Luis Potosi, Mex., 1990, U. Mexico, Mex. City, 1991, La. State U., 1990, 91, 92, 94, 96, Biendenharn Found., Monroe, La., 1991, Longue Vue Found., New Orleans, 1991, So. Garden Symposium. 1993, 2001, St. Francisville, La., 1993, 2001, Southern Regional Meeting Garden Writers Assn. Am., Memphis, 1993, Rotary Internat. Dist. Conf., Memphis, 1993, Deep S. Regional Conf. Nat. Coun. State Garden Clubs, Lafayette, La., 1993, Nat. Capital Area Garden Coun., U. Md., 1996; guest instr. Nat. Landscape Design Study Courses Nat. Coun. State Garden Clubs, Inc., U.S., Mex., 1960—, Guatemala first study course, 1995, 96; originator, lectr. Garden Design Workshops, Miss. State U., 1988—; host Flower and Garden Tour of British Isles, Southland Travel Svcs., 1985, Flower and Garden Tour of Europe, 1981, 82; host, lectr. Hampton Ct. Palace Flower Show and English Gardens Tour, 1996, 98, Ireland and Scotland Gardens Tour, 1997, 99, 2001, Italian Gardens Tour, 1998, 2000, French Gardens Tour, 1999, 2000, 2001, So. Germany Tour, 2000, Austria Gardens Tour, 2000; host, lectr. Gardens of Spain and Portugal Tour, 2001; So. hist. gardens lectr., tour host Elderhostel Conf., Miss. U. for Women, 1997, 98, 99, 2000; photographic landscape arch. rsch. study: Europe, 1958, 66, 74, 85, S.Am., 1960, Israel, 1993, 95, Greece, Turkey, 1998; vis. prof. La. State U., 1990-93, vis. landscape architecture prof., 1994, 97; instr. landscape design Botanical Gardens, Huntsville, Ala., 1996; host, lectr. historic southern gardens on Miss. River, New Orleans to Vicksburg, Delta Queen Steamboat, 1994, Am. Queen Steamboat, 1999, 2000, New Orleans to St. Francisville, La., The Garden Clubs of Miss., Inc., Miss. Queen Steamboat, 1996, Memphis to New Orleans, 1997, 98; host Chelsea Flower Show and English Gardens Tour, 1994, Nat. Coun. State Garden Clubs, 1994, Fla. Wild Flower Conf. Fla. Fedn. Garden Clubs, Inc., 1994; instr. ecology tour Copper Canyon, Mex., 1994; spkr. Miss. Urban Foresters, Miss. Arboriculturist Ann. Conv., Vicksburg, 1999, Ga. Nursery Men's Ann. Winter Landscaping Seminar, Athens, 1999, Crosby Arboretum, Picayunne, Miss., 1999, Hist. Preservation Regional Conf. Am. Soc. Landscape Archs., Natchez, Miss., 1999, Urban Landscape Design Pascagula, Miss., 1999, Hist. Preservation City Starkville, Miss., 2000, 44th Ann. Conv. Constrn. Specifications Inst., Atlanta, 2000; lectr. 65th Colonial Williamsburg Garden Symposium, 2001; lectr. in field. Author: Landscape Plants in Design, A Photographic Guide, 1983; co-author: Home Landscapes, Planting Design and Management, 1994; invited to participate in Attingham Summer Program in Historic Preservation (English country houses and gardens) Eng., 1985; author/photographer of 80-captioned slide series, one on Home Landscapes, another on Urban Landscape Design for use by Nat. Coun. State Garden Clubs, Inc., 1994. Mem. Miss. State Bd. Landscape Architects for Profl. Registration, 1973-74; mem. Starkville (Miss.) Park and Recreation Bd., 1973-79. Recipient Silver Seal award Nat. Coun. State Garden Clubs 1969, honoree 1995; recipient Landscape Heritage award Fraser Found. Calif. 1986, Helent S. Hull Lit. award, 1996. Fellow Am. Soc. Landscape Architects (chmn. edn. com. 1960-61, pres. Miss. sect. S.W. chpt. 1975, chmn. S.W. chpt. ann. awards com. 1976, trustee Miss. chpt. 1977-81); mem. Nat. Trust for Historic Preservation, So. Garden History Soc., Nat. Coun. State Garden Clubs (chmn. landscape design 1993-97), Garden Clubs Miss. (bd. dirs. 1958—, Silver Trophy 1961, Spl. Silver award 1980, Gold trophy 1993). Presbyterian. Home: 464 Chapel Rd Black Mountain NC 28711-2640 Office: Dept Landscape Architecture Box 9725 Mississippi State MS 39762-9725

MARTIN, EDWARD THOMAS, cardiologist, researcher; b. Cleve., Feb. 4, 1961; s. Edward James and Mary Ellen Agnes Martin; m. Barbara Jean Davis, June 8, 1991; children: Edward IV, Ryan. BS in Physics, Xavier U., 1984; MSME, U. Cin., 1987; MD, Med. Coll. Ohio, 1991. Diplomate Am. Bd. Internal Medicine, Am. Bd. Cardiovascular Disease. Project engr. TTEEMD, Inc., Derwood, Md., 1985-88; intern Temple U. Hosp., Phila., 1991-92, resident in internal medicine, 1993-94; emergency rm. physician Cooper Green Hosp., Birmingham, Ala., 1994-95; fellow in cardiology U. Ala., 1994-98; internist Lloyd Nolan Hosp., Ala., 1995-96; cardiologist Regional Med. Ctr., Anniston, 1996-98, Okla. Heart Inst., Tulsa, 1998—, dir. cardiovascular MRI. Clin. assoc. prof. medicine U. Okla. Coll. Medicine, Tulsa, 1999—; dir. cardiovasc. MRI Ctr. Okla. Heart Inst.; dir. nuclear cardiology Southcrest Hosp.; dir. cardiac MRI Hillcrest Med. Ctr. Author: Technologies for Small Water and Wastewater Systems, 1991; mem. editl. bd. Jour. Cardiovascular Magnetic Resonance. Bd. dirs. Tulsa region Am. Heart Assn. Grad. scholar U. Cin., 1985-87. Fellow ACP, Am. Coll. Cardiology; mem. AMA, Internat. Soc. Magnetic Resonance in Medicine, Am. Soc. Nuclear Cardiology, Soc. for Cardiovascular Magnetic Resonance (founding mem.), So. Med. Assn. Roman Catholic. Avocations: golf, sports, crossword puzzles, travel. Office: Okla Heart Inst 9228 S Mingo Rd Tulsa OK 74133 E-mail: martin@oklahomaheart.com.

MARTIN, ELLIOT EDWARDS, theatrical producer; b. Denver, Feb. 25, 1924; m. Marjorie Cuesta, Oct. 7, 1949; children: Richard, Linda Lisa. Student, U. Denver, 1943-46. Actor, singer, stage mgr., assoc. producer Theatre Guild, N.Y.C. and London, 1947-53; prodn. stage mgr. 20 Broadway plays and musicals, 1953-61; theatrical producer Never Too Late, Nobody Loves an Albatross, N.Y.C., 1962-66; theatre producer London, 1963; mng. dir. Center Theatre Group, Music Ctr., Los Angeles, 1966-71; producer Elliot Martin Prodns., N.Y.C., 1972—. Mem. exec. bd. Nat. Theatre of the Deaf, Chester, Conn., 1981— , Westport-Weston Arts Council, 1976— Prodns. on Broadway include: Dinner at Eight, 1966, More Stately Mansions, 1967, Abelard and Heloise, 1971, Emperor Henry IV, 1973, A Moon for the Misbegotten, 1973 (spl. Tony award), When You Comin' Back, Red Rider, 1974 (Outer Critics award), Of Mice and Men, 1975, Touch of the Poet, 1976, Dirty Linen and New Found Land, 1977, Caesar and Cleopatra, 1977, Kingfisher, 1979, Clothes for a Summer Hotel, 1980, Kingdoms, 1981, American Buffalo, 1981, Angels Fall, 1983, Glengarry Glen Ross, 1984 (Pulitzer prize), Woza Albert, 1984, American Buffalo, 1984, Harrigan 'n' Hart, 1985, Arsenic and Old Lace (Broadway and nat. tour), 1986-87, Joe Turner's Come and Gone (7 Tony nominations, N.Y. Drama Critic's award best play), 1988, Steel Magnolias (nat. tour), 1989, The Circle, 1989-90, Shadowlands, 1990-91, Breaking Legs, 1991-92, She Loves Me (9 Tony noms.), 1993-94, Death of a Salesman, 1995-96, A Moon For the Misbegotten, 2000, Down the Gaden Paths, 2001, I'm Not Rappaprot, 2002. Mem. bd. assocs. U. Bridgeport, 1978-83. Recipient Tony award for most innovative revival, 1977-78, Larry Tajiri award for outstanding contbn. to arts Denver Post, 1970, Congl. commendation, 1970, Profl. Achievement award U. Denver, 1987. Mem. Platform Speakers Am., League N.Y. Theatres and Prodrs. (gov.), Am. Friends Royal Shakespeare Co. (pres.), Players Club. Clubs: N.Y. Athletic (N.Y.C.). Republican. Office: Elliot Martin Prodns 152 W 58th St New York NY 10019-2139

MARTIN, FRED, artist, college administrator; b. San Francisco, June 13, 1927; s. Ernest Thomas and Leona (Richey) M.; m. Genevieve Catherine Fisette, Jan. 29, 1950 (dec.); children: T. Demian, Frederica C., Anthony J.; m. Stephanie Zuperko Dudek, 1992. BA, U. Calif., Berkeley, 1949, MA, 1954; postgrad., Calif. Sch. Fine Arts, 1949-50. Registrar Oakland (Calif.) Art Mus., 1955-58; dir. exhbns. San Francisco Art Inst., 1958-65, dir. coll., 1965-75, dean acad. affairs, 1983-92; dean acad. affairs emeritus; represented by Frederick Spratt Gallery, San Jose, Calif., Ebert Gallery, San Francisco. Exhibited one man shows, Zoe Dusanne Gallery, Seattle, 1952, M.H. deYoung Meml. Mus., San Francisco, 1954, 64, Oakland Art Mus., 1958, San Francisco Mus. Modern Art, 1958, 73, Dilexi Gallery, San Francisco, 1961, Minami Gallery, Tokyo, 1963, Royal Marks Gallery, N.Y.C., 1965-70, Hansen Fuller Gallery, San Francisco, 1974, 75, 76, Quay Gallery, San Francisco, 1979, 81, 84, Natsoulas Gallery, Davis, Calif., 1991, Belcher Studios Gallery, San Francisco, 1994, Frederick Spratt Gallery, San Jose, 1996, Ebert Gallery, San Francisco, 1997, 98, 99, 2000, Art and Consciousness Gallery/John F. Kennedy U., Berkeley, 1997, Shasta Coll., 1998, Han Art Contemporaire, Montreal, 1999; represented in permanent collections, Mus. Modern Art, N.Y.C., San Francisco Mus. Modern Art, Oakland Art Mus., Whitney Mus., Fogg Mus.; author: Beulah Land, 1966, Log of the Sun Ship, 1969, Liber Studiorum, 1973, A Travel Book, 1976, From an Antique Land, 1979; Bay area corr.: Art Internat., 1967-69, 75-76; contbg. editor Art Week, 1976-93. Recipient prizes Oakland Art Mus., 1951, 58, prizes San Francisco Mus. Art, 1957, 58, prizes Richmond (Calif.) Art Center, 1962, prizes Nat. Found. for Arts, 1970 E-mail: Fred T. Home: 232 Monte Vista Ave Oakland CA 94611-4922 Office: San Francisco Art Inst 800 Chestnut St San Francisco CA 94133-2206 E-mail: Martin@IBM.net.

MARTIN, FREDERICK KANE, portfolio manager, investor; b. Elkhart, Ind., Oct. 29, 1946; s. William Frederick and Mary Amalia (Kohlhaas) M.; m. Margery Hickey, Dec. 20, 1969; children: Peter, Thomas, William. BA, Dartmouth Coll., 1968, MBA, 1969. CFA. Analyst, portfolio mgr. Northwestern Nat. Bank, 1973-78; sr. portfolio mgr., mng. dir. Mitchell Hutchins Asset Mgmt., Mpls., 1978-97; founder, sr. portfolio mgr. Disciplined Growth

Investors, 1997—. Lt. USN, 1969-73, Vietnam. Mem. Two Cities Soc. Security Analysis, Mpls. Club. Avocations: flight instructor, soccer coaching. Office: Disciplined Growth Investor 900 2d Ave S Minneapolis MN 55402

MARTIN, FREDERICK NOEL, audiology educator; b. N.Y.C., July 24, 1931; s. Philip and Mildred Ruth (Austin) M.; m. Mary Catherine Robinson, Apr. 4, 1954; children: David C., Leslie Anne. BA, Bklyn. Coll., 1957, MA, 1958; PhD, CUNY, 1968. Audiologist, Lenox Hill Hosp., N.Y.C., 1957-58; Audiologist Ark. Sch. for the Deaf, Little Rock, 1958-60; dir. audiology Bailey Ear Clinic, 1960-66; mem. faculty Bklyn. Coll., 1966-68, U. Tex., Austin, 1968—, endowed prof. audiology, 1982—. Author: Introduction to Audiology, 1975, 7th edit., 2000, Pediatric Audiology, 1978, Medical Audiology, 1981, Basic Audiometry, 1986; editor: Remediation of Communication Disorders, Vol. 10, 1978, Hearing Disorders in Children, 1986, Effective Counseling in Audiology, 1994, Hearing Care for Children, 1996, Exercises in Audiometry, 1998; contbr. numerous articles to profl. jours. Served with USAF, 1951-55. Fellow Am. Speech-Language Hearing Assn., Am. Acad. Audiology; mem. Tex. Speech-Lang.-Hearing Assn., Am. Auditory Soc., Tex. Acad. Audiology. Home: 8613 Silver Ridge Dr Austin TX 78759-8144 Office: U Tex Austin TX 78712

MARTIN, G. STEVEN, biochemist, educator; b. Oxford, Eng., July 19, 1943; came to U.S., 1968; s. Kurt and Hanna M.; m. Gail R., June 30, 1969; 1 child, Nicholas. BA, Queens' Coll., Cambridge, Eng., 1964; MA, PhD, U. Cambridge, 1968. Staff Imperial Cancer Rsch. Fund, London, 1971-75; from asst. prof. zoology to prof. molecular & cell biology U. Calif., Berkeley, 1975—. NIH grantee, 1975—. Fellow Royal Soc. Avocations: hiking, bicycling, reading. Home: 818 Spruce St Berkeley CA 94707-2043 E-mail: smartin@socrates.berkeley.edu.

MARTIN, GARY J. retired business executive, mayor; b. Des Moines, Feb. 8, 1937; s. William Carl Martin and Mary Louise Sweeney; m. Carolyn J. Karau, July 28, 1956; children: Victoria, Cheryl, Dennis. BBA, Marquette U., 1972. CPA Wis., 1973. Mfr. GM, Milw., 1957-68, engring. mgr., 1968-73; CFO Miller Brewing Co., 1974-76, dir. corp. planning, 1977-78; pres. Better Brands of N.Y., N.Y.C., 1978-79; exec. v.p. Seven Up Co., St. Louis, 1979-85; v.p. mktg. Schenley Industries, Dallas, 1985-86; cons. Martin & Assocs., 1986-89; mayor Osage Beach, Mo., 1992-95. Bd. dirs. Family Hosp., Milw., 1976-78; mem. lay bd. St. Mary Health Ctr., St. Louis, 1980-85. With USN, 1954-57. Avocations: computers, boating, golf, travel. Home: 2349 Fairskies Dr Spring Hill FL 34606-7257 E-mail: gama@tampabay.rr.com.

MARTIN, GARY JOSEPH, medical educator; b. Chgo., Mar. 12, 1952; m. Helen Gartner; children: Daniel T., David G. BA in Psychology, U. Ill., 1974, MD, 1978. Diplomate Am. Bd. Internal Medicine, Am. Bd. Cardiovascular Disease, Nat. Bd. Med. Examiners; lic. physician, Ill. Intern, resident internal medicine Northwestern U. Med. Sch., Chgo., 1978-81, instr. medicine, 1981-82, asst. prof. medicine, 1984-90, assoc. prof., 1990-96, prof., 1996—, divsn. chief, divsn. gen. internal medicine, 1988-2001, assoc. chmn. dept. medicine, 1998-2000, vice chmn. dept. medicine, 2001—; cardiology fellow Loyola U. Med. Ctr., 1982-84; attending physician Northwestern Meml. Hosp./Northwestern Med. Faculty Found., Chgo., 1984—; chief med. resident, attending physician Northwestern Meml. Hosp., 1981-82; dir. primary care clerkship Nat. Ctr. for Advanced Med. Edn., 1984—. Chmn. outpatient utilization rev. and quality assurance com., 1985-93; chmn. Northwestern Meml. Hosp./Lakeside VA Rsch. Com., 1988-91; dir. tng. gen. internal medicine residency program, 1985-95; bd. dirs. com. Northwestern Med. Faculty Found., 1993—; cons. health care divsn. Ernst & Young, 1991—; peer reviewer Faculty Devel. Rev. Com. Panel 1, 1994. Contbr. articles to profl. jours. Fellow Buehler Ctr. on Aging. Fellow Am. Coll. Cardiology; mem. ACP, Soc. Gen. Internal Medicine, Am. Heart Assn. Office: Northwestern U Med Sch Divsn Gen Internal Medicine 675 N Saint Clair St Ste 18-200 Chicago IL 60611-5929

MARTIN, GARY LACY, aerospace engineer; b. Richmond, Va., June 6, 1955; s. Thomas Leon and Nancy Ella M.; m. Ellen Doran, Aug. 17, 1985; children: Zach Austin, Doran Thomas. BA in Anthropology, Colo. State U., 1979; BS in Applied Math. & Physics, Va. Commonwealth U., 1986; MS in Astronautical Engring., George Washington U., 1988. Chief advanced programs and tech. NASA, Washington, 1991-94, dep. dir. microgravity sci. divsn., 1994-96; program integration mgr. NASA Goddard Space Ctr., Greenbelt, Md., 1996-97, chief tech., planning and integration, 1997-2001; dir. advance programs Office of Space Flight, NASA Hq., Washington, 2000—. Contbr. articles to profl. jours. Mem. Am. Inst. Aeronautics and Astronautics, Phi Kappa Phi. Home: 2603 Arden Forest Ln Bowie MD 20716-3810 E-mail: gmartin@hq.nasa.gov.

MARTIN, GARY WAYNE, lawyer; b. Cin., Feb. 14, 1946; s. Elmer DeForrest and Nellie May (Hughes) M.; m. Debra Lynn Goldsmith, June 25, 1982; children: Christopher, Jeremy, Joie, Casey. BA, Wilmington Coll., 1967; JD, U. Cin., 1974. Bar: Fla. 1974. Casualty practice leader Fowler White Gillen Boggs Villareal & Banker, Tampa, Fla., 1974—, also bd. dirs. Lt. USNR, 1967-71. Mem. Harbour Island Athletic Club. Republican. Presbyterian. Avocation: tennis. Office: Fowler White Gillen Boggs Villareal & Banker 501 E Kennedy Blvd Ste 1600 Tampa FL 33602-5240 E-mail: gmartin@fowlerwhite.com.

MARTIN, GEORGE (GEORGE WHITNEY MARTIN), writer; b. N.Y.C., Jan. 25, 1926; s. George Whitney and Agnes Wharton (Hutchinson) M. BA, Harvard U., 1948; student, Trinity Coll., Cambridge (Eng.) U., 1950; LL.B., U. Va., 1953. Bar: N.Y. 1955. With firm Emmet, Marvin & Martin, N.Y.C., 1955-59; engaged in writing, 1959—. Author: The Opera Companion, A Guide for the Casual Operagoer, 1961, 5th edit., 1997, The Battle of the Frogs and Mice, An Homeric Fable, 1962, 2d edit., 1987, Verdi, His Music, Life and Times, 1963, 4th edit., 2001, The Red Shirt and The Cross of Savoy, The Story of Italy's Risorgimento, 1748-1871, 1969, Causes and Conflicts, The Centennial History of the Association of the Bar of the City of New York, 1870-1970, 1970, 2d edit., 1997, Madam Secretary: Frances Perkins, 1976, The Damrosch Dynasty, America's First Family of Music, 1983, Aspects of Verdi, 1988, 2nd edit., 1993, Verdi at the Golden Gate, San Francisco in the Golden Years, 1993, Twentieth Century Opera, A Guide, 1999; contbr. articles to profl. jours., mags. Home: 53 Crosslands Dr Kennett Square PA 19348-2010

MARTIN, GEORGE FRANCIS, lawyer; b. Yuba City, Calif., July 7, 1944; s. John Severd and Albina Marie M.; m. Linda Louise D'Aoust, Mar. 17, 1968; children: Brandon, Bry. BA in Govt., Calif. State U., Sacramento, 1968; JD, U. Calif., Davis, 1971. Bar: Calif. Adminstr. asst. Assemblyman E. Richard Barnes, Sacramento, 1967-68; with Borton, Petrini & Conron, Bakersfield, Calif., 1971—, mng. gen. ptnr., 1977—; dean Calif. Pacific Sch. Law, 1993-95. Holdings numerous ventures, partnerships; lectr. in field; founder, owner theatrical bus. Mgmt. by Martin, Inc., Shower of Stars, Frantic Records, 1962-67. Editor-in-chief Verdict Jour. of Law, 1984-85, Calif. Def. Mag.; newspaper reporter Appeal Democrat, Marysville, Calif., 1959-62. Former vice chmn. Kern County Rep. Ctrl. Com.; past pres. So. Calif. Def. Counsel; past chmn. Ctrl. Calif. Heart Inst.; bd. dirs. Calif. State U. at Bakersfield Found., chair, 1998; bd. dirs. Calif. Coun. Partnerships, Kern Econ. Devel. Corp; mem. adv. bd. Automobile Club So. Calif.; chmn. adv. bd. Witkin Legal Inst. Mem. Greater Bakersfield C. of C. (bd. dirs., past pres.). Office: Borton Petrini & Conron 1600 Truxtun Ave Bakersfield CA 93301-5111

MARTIN, GEORGE J., JR. lawyer; b. Port Chester, N.Y., June 7, 1942; s. George J. and Eileen Ann (Buckley) M.; m. Joanne L. Frost, Aug. 21, 1965 (div. May 1986); children: Amy Anne, Ryan Frost; m. Anna Marie Cipriati, June 21, 1986; children: Marissa McCreay, Jill McCreay. BA, Georgetown U., 1964, JD, 1967. Bar: N.Y. 1969; conseil juridique, France, 1977-82. From assoc. to ptnr. Mudge Rose Guthrie Alexander & Ferdon, N.Y.C., 1967-95; ptnr. Coudert Bros., 1995—. Mem. French Heritage Soc. (gen. counsel, dir.). Roman Catholic. Home: 163 Congress St Brooklyn NY 11201-6103 Office: Coudert Bros 1114 Ave of The Americas New York NY 10036-7710 E-mail: geojmartin@aol.com., marting@coudert.com.

MARTIN, GEORGE J. investment banker, financial consultant; b. N.Y.C., Apr. 20, 1932; m. Katherine Cecelia Whitt, Apr. 10, 1986. BA, Columbia Coll., N.Y.C., 1954; BSME, Columbia Coll., 1955, postgrad., 1958. Commd. ensign USN, 1954; advanced through grades to comdr. USNR, ret., 1982; design engr. IBM, Poughkeepsie, N.Y., 1958-60; mktg. mgr. Electronic Assocs. Inc., West Long Branch, N.J., 1960-67; gen. ptnr. Coleman & Co., N.Y.C., 1968-75, C.E. Unterberg Towbin, N.Y.C., 1975-77; mng. dir., gen. ptnr. L.F. Rothschild, Unterberg Towbin, 1977-87; mng. dir. Fort Point Fin. Group, N.J. and San Francisco, 1988-93; dir. tech. corp. fin. group Foley, Mufson, Howe, Phila., 1993, Fort Point Fin. Group, 1994-96; mng. dir. Silver Strand Venture Mgmt., Melbourne, Fla., 1997—. E-mail: mayflower1075@worldnet.att.net.

MARTIN, GEORGE M. pathologist, gerontologist, educator; b. N.Y.C., June 30, 1927; s. Barnett J. and Estelle (Weiss) M.; m. Julaine Ruth Miller, Dec. 2, 1952; children: Peter C., Kelsey C., Thomas M., Andrew C. BS, U. Wash., 1949, MD, 1953. Diplomate Am. Bd. Pathology, Am. Bd. Med. Genetics. Intern Montreal Gen. Hosp., Quebec, Can., 1953-54; resident-instr. U. Chgo., 1954-57; instr.-prof. U. Wash., Seattle, 1957—. Vis. scientist Dept. Genetics Albert Einstein Coll., N.Y.C., 1964, Rockefeller U., 1998-99; chmn. Gordon Confs. Molecular Pathology, Biology of Aging, 1974-79; chmn., nat. res. Plan on Aging Nat. Inst. on Aging, Bethesda, Md., 1985-89; dir. Alzheimer's Disease Rsch. Ctr. U. Wash., 1985—, assoc. dir., 1999—. Editor Werner's Syndrome and Human Aging, 1985, Molecular Aspects of Aging, 1995; contbr. articles in field to profl jours. Active Fedn. Am. Scientists. With USN, 1945-46. Recipient Allied Signal award in Aging, 1991, Rsch. medal Am. Agy. Assn., 1992, Kleemeier award, 1994, Paul Glenn award for aging rsch., 1998; named Disting. Alumnus, U. Wash. Sch. Medicine, 1987; USPHS rsch. fellow dept. genetics, Glasgow U., 1961-62; Eleanor Roosevelt Inst. Cancer Rsch. fellow Inst. de Biologie, PHysiologie, Chimie, Paris, 1968-69; Josiah Macy faculty scholar Sir William Din Sch. Pathology, Oxford (Eng.) U., 1978-79, Humboldt Disting. scientist dept. genetics U. Wurzburg, Germany, 1991. Fellow: AAAS, Tissue Culture Assn. (pres. 1986—88), Gerontol. Soc. Am. (chmn. Biol. Sci. 1979, pres.-elect 2001, Brookdale award 1981, Lifetime Acheivement award for rsch. in alzheimer's disease World Alzheimer's Congress 2000); mem.: Am. Fedn. Aging Rsch. (pres. 1999—2001), Am. Soc. Investigative Pathology, Am. Soc. Human Genetics, Am. Assn. Univ. Pathologists (emeritus), Inst. Medicine. Democrat. Avocations: internat. travel, jazz music, biography. Home: 2223 E Howe St Seattle WA 98112-2931 Office: U Wash Sch Medicine Dept Pathology Rm K543 Seattle WA 98195 E-mail: gmmartin@u.washington.edu.

MARTIN, GEORGE WILLIAM, priest; b. Chatham, N.B., Can., Sept. 21, 1924; s. John Stephen and Mary Florence (Cassidy) M. BA, St. Thomas Coll., N.B., 1945; B.Th., Holy Heart Sem., Halifax, N.S., 1949; LL.D., St. Francis Xavier U., N.S., 1980. Ordained priest Roman Cath. Ch., 1949. Tchr. St. Thomas High Sch., Chatham, N.B., Can., 1949-58; registrar St. Thomas U., Can., 1958-71, v.p. Fredericton, Can., 1971-75, pres. Can., 1975-90. Vicar gen. Diocese of St. John, N.B., 1975-95; exec. mem. Assn. Atlantic Univs., Halifax, 1979-81. Mem. Assn. Univs. and Colls. Can., Assn. Atlantic Univs. Roman Catholic (prelate of honor) Address: Diocese of Saint John 1 Bayard Dr Saint John NB Canada E2L 3L5

MARTIN, GLADYS CHRISTINE, housing executive; b. Arlington, Tex., Aug. 24, 1948; d. Grady Taylor and Bessie Marie (Parker) Pointer; m. Arthur Ray Martin, Nov. 18, 1968; children: Kriste, Arthur II, Kandace, Maribeth. Student, Tarrant County Jr. Coll. Exec. dir. Housing Authority/City of Cooper, Tex., 1991—. Recipient award Girl Scouts Am. Recipient award Girl Scouts U.S., 1991. Mem. NAACP, Nat. Assn. Housing Ofcls., Pub. Housing Dirs. Assn., Tex. Housing Assn. (bd. dirs.), S.W. Nat. Orgn. Housing Ofcls. (vice chair commn., S.W. Media award 1994), N.E. Tex. Housing Assn., Lamar County Housing Assn. (v.p. 1994-95), Delta County Ext. Agy. (bd. dirs. 1995-96). Home: 3935 Holbrook St Paris TX 75462-6643

MARTIN, GLENN MICHAEL, military officer; b. Pittsfield, Mass., Sept. 13, 1950; s. Thomas Claude and DeLima Rose Marie (Gelinas) Martin; m. Dawn Star Schile, Mar. 26, 1983. BS in Biology, Norwich U., 1973; BSBA in Acctg., Mass. Coll. Liberal Arts, 1981; postgrad., Air U., Maxwell AFB, Ala., 1983. Cert. tchr. Mass., real estate broker. Sci. tchr. North Adams (Mass.) Mid. Sch., 1977-78; sales mgr. Doverbrook Estates, Chicopee, 1982-83; mortgage officer ComFed Savs. Bank, Leominster, 1983-85, Bank of Boston, Fitchburg, 1985-86; v.p. br. mgr. Northeastern Mortgage Co., Inc., Worcester, 1986-87; br. mgr. First NH Mortgage Corp., Marlboro, 1988-89; bus. broker VR Bus. Brokers, Leominster, 1989-90; mktg. dir. Equity Group, Inc., Fitchburg, 1989-90; USAF liaison officer to joint forces command J337 Sect., Norfolk Naval Base, Va., 2001—. Dep. sheriff Berkshire County Sheriff's Dept., Pittsfield, 1981; mem. Ashburnham (Mass.) Planning Bd., 1990—2001. Scholar Alumni, Norwich U., 1969—73. Mem.: Res. Officer Assn. (treas. 1983—84), Norwich Rugby Club, Rotary Internat. Roman Catholic. Avocations: tennis, skiing, sailing, bicycling, hiking. Home: 1303 Plantation Lakes Cir Chesapeake VA 23320-8111 E-mail: glenn.martin@afnsep.af.mil.

MARTIN, GREGORY KEITH, lawyer, mayor; b. Conway, S.C., Nov. 7, 1956; s. George Henry Martin and Julia Ann (Johnson) M. Land. BS in Fin. Mgmt., Clemson U., 1979; JD, U. S.C., 1983. Bar: S.C. 1983. Intern U.S. Senate, 1980; law clk. to presiding judge 15th Jud. Cir. Ct., Conway, 1983; assoc. Johnson & Martin, 1983-88, ptnr., 1988-93, Martin & Smith, Conway, 1993-98; mayor City of Conway, 1995—; pvt. practice, Conway, 1998—. Mem. Conway Planning Commn., 1986-89, chmn., 1989; bd. dirs. Conway-Main St. U.S.A., 1986-90, chmn., 1988; mem. Conway Bd. Appeals, 1987-89, Horry County Bd. Archtl. Rev., 1987-90; mem. Conway City Coun., 1991-94; pres., Horry County Hist. Soc., 1988, 90, mayor pro tem, 1994; mem. adv. bd. Pee Dee Heritage Ctr., 1988—. Mem. ABA, S.C. Bar Assn., Horry County Bar Assn., Sigma Nu, Phi Delta Phi. Methodist. Avocations: tennis, coin collecting. Home: 706 Elm St Conway SC 29526-4373 Office: PO Box 736 Conway SC 29528-0736

MARTIN, GUY, lawyer; b. Los Angeles, Jan. 22, 1911; s. I.G. and Mary Pearl (Howe) M.; m. Edith Kingdon Gould, Oct. 12, 1946; children— Guy III, Jason Gould, Christopher Kingdon, Edith Maria Theodosia Burr. AB, Occidental Coll., 1931; BA (1st class hons.), Oxford U., 1934, MA, 1944; LL.B., Yale, 1937. Bar: N.Y. 1938, D.C. 1947. Practiced with Donovan, Leisure, Newton & Lumbard, N.Y.C., 1938-41; gen. counsel All Am. Aviation, Inc., 1942, Am. Mexican Claims Commn., U.S. Dept. State, 1945-47; ptnr. Martin, Whitfield, Smith & Bebchick (and predecessors), Washington, 1952-80; counsel Martin and Smith (and predecessors), 1981-86; pres., vice chmn. bd., dep. chief exec. officer Internat. Bank, 1981-86; with Law Office of Saltzstein & Martin, 1988-99. Served with USN; sea duty 1942-45. Mem. ABA, Assn. of Bar of City of N.Y., Bar Assn. D.C, Phi Beta Kappa, Sigma Alpha Epsilon. Clubs: Yale, Brook, Knickerbocker (N.Y.C.); Metropolitan, City Tavern (Washington). Episcopalian. Home: 3300 O St NW Washington DC 20007-2813

MARTIN, HAROLD CLARK, humanities educator; b. Raymond, Pa., Jan. 12, 1917; s. Henry Floyd and Anna May (Clark) M.; m. Elma Hicks, Dec. 21, 1939; children— Thomas, Joel, Ann, Rebecca. AB, Hartwick Coll., Oneonta, N.Y., 1937, LL.D. (hon.), 1965; AM, U. Mich., 1941; PhD, Harvard, 1954; student, U. Wis., 1936, Columbia, 1941; LHD (hon.), Elmira Coll., 1967, Siena Coll., 1968, Concord Coll., 1968; DHL (hon.), Trinity Coll., Conn., 1970; Litt.D. (hon.), Skidmore Coll., 1974; LHD (hon.), Coll. St. Rose, 1974, Union Coll., 1975. High sch. tchr. English and French langs., Adams, N.Y., 1937-39; high sch. tchr. English Goshen, 1939-44; prin. high sch., 1944-49; mem. faculty Harvard U., 1951-65, dir. gen. edn., 1951-63, lectr. comparative lit., 1954-65; chancellor Union U.; also pres. Union Coll., Schenectady, 1965-74; pres. Am. Acad., Rome, Italy, 1974-76; Margaret Bundy Scott prof. Williams Coll., 1977; Charles A. Dana prof. humanities Trinity Coll., Conn., 1977-82, prof. emeritus, 1982—, sr. lectr. humanities, 1982—. Author: Logic and Rhetoric of Exposition, 1958, Spanning Three Centuries, 1984, Outlasting Marble and Brass, 1986; editor: Inquiry and Expression (with Richard Ohmann), 1958, Style in Prose Fiction, 1959, Pearson Diary, 2 vols., 2001. Chmn. Mass. Com. Fulbright Awards, 1955-65, Coll. Bd. Com. English, 1959-64; Trustee Hartwick Coll., Siena Coll., Franklin Coll., Switzerland, Wenner-Gren Found. With USNR, 1945-46. Home: 70 Matthew Dr Brunswick ME 04011-3275

MARTIN, HAROLD G. engineering consultant; b. Scotland, Pa. s. Abram Earl and Eula Mae Martin; m. Christina Shipley Martin, June 5, 1948; children: Susan (dec.), Judith Krieger, Bruce. BSCE, Pa. State U., 1944. Stress analyst, chief structures Fairchild Republic Co., Hagerstown, Md., 1967-70, mgr. tech. engring., 1970-71, chief problem analysis and corrective action, 1977-81, chief quality engring., 1981, project engr. F14, FAA airworthiness coord., 1981-84; engring. cons., FAA designated engring. rep. Waynesboro, Pa., 1984—. Mem. sch. bd. Waynesboro Area Sch. Bd., 1978-84. Staff sgt. U.S. Army, 1944-46. Mem.: Mid Atlantic Air Mus., Am. Aviation Hist. Soc., Engring. Soc. for Advancing Mobility Land Sea Air and Space. Avocations: auto restoration, travel, writing, boating, fishing. Home and Office: 833 Anthony Ave Waynesboro PA 17268

MARTIN, HAROLD SHEAFFER, minister, educator; b. Ephrata, Pa., Aug. 7, 1930; s. Noah Weaver Martin and Helen White Schaeffer; m. Priscilla Ann Miller, Aug. 31, 1950; children: Stephen A., H. Stanley, Sherwood J., Christine F., Delphine K., Berdene M. BS, Millersville State Tchrs. Coll., 1952; MEd, Western Md. Coll., 1956; BA, Messiah Coll., 1962; D.Min., Covington Theol. Sem., 1981. Cert. secondary sch. prin. Pa., 58, ordained min. Ch. of the Brethren, 52. Math. tchr. Gettysburg (Pa.) H.S., 1952, Spring Grove (Pa.) Jr. H.S., 1952—77; min. Pleasant Hill Ch. of the Brethren, 1952—. Writer Bible Helps Bible Helps, Inc., Hanover, Pa.; editor BRF Witness, Brethren Revival Fellowship, Ephrata, 1966—; adj. prof. Bethany Theol. Sem., Oak Brook, Ill., 1992; lesson tchr., radio Sunday Sch. Meditations, Lancaster, Pa., 1999—; Bible tchr. Brethren Revival Fellowship, 1955—; mem. conf. study com. Ch. of the Brethren, Elgin, Ill., 1966—90, mem. conf. study coms., Ill., 1966—79. Contbr. over 370 articles to profl. publs.; author: Sermons on Eternal Themes, 1971, Glimpses from the Book of Revelation, 1981, What Every New Christian Should Know, 1974, Simple Messages on Romans, 1974, New Testament Beliefs, 1989, Simple Messages on Matthew, 2000, A Study in Brethren Heritage, 2001. Recipient Svc. award, Ch. of the Brethren Gen. Bd., 1983—85. Republican. Mem. Brethren Ch. Avocations: travel, study. Home: 20 United Zion Cir Lititz PA 17543-7956

MARTIN, HARRY CORPENING, lawyer, retired state supreme court justice; b. Lenoir, N.C., Jan. 13, 1920; s. Hal C. and Johnsie Harshaw (Nelson) M.; m. Nancy Robiou Dallam, Apr. 16, 1955; children: John, Matthew, Mary. AB, U. N.C., 1942; LLB, Harvard U., 1948; LLM, U. Va., 1982. Bar: N.C. 1948. Pvt. practice, Asheville, N.C., 1948-62; judge N.C. Superior Ct., 1962-78, N.C. Ct. Appeals, Raleigh, 1978-82; justice N.C. Supreme Ct., 1982-92; ptnr. Martin & Martin, Attys., Hilllsborough, N.C., 1992—. Adj. prof. U. N.C. Law Sch., 1983-92, Duke U., 1990-91, Dan K. Moore disting. vis. prof., 1992-94; sr. conf. atty. U.S. Ct. Appeals for 4th Cir., 1994-99; chief justice Supreme Ct. ea. bd. of Cherokee Indians, 2000—. With U.S. Army, 1942-45, South Pacific. Mem. U.S. Supreme Ct. Hist. Soc., N.C. Supreme Ct. Hist. Soc. (pres.). Democrat. Episcopalian. Home: 1 Hilltop Rd Asheville NC 28803-3017 Office: Cherokee Supreme Ct PO Box 455 Cherokee NC 28719 Fax: 828-497-5705. E-mail: judgemartin@home.com.

MARTIN, HELEN ELIZABETH, educational consultant; b. West Chester, Pa., Feb. 19, 1945; d. Thomas Edwin and Elizabeth Temple (Walker) M. BA, The King's Coll., N.Y.C., 1967; MEd, West Chester U., 1970; postgrad., Goethe Inst., Freiberg, Fed. Republic Germany, 1979, Oxford (Eng.) U., 1979. Nat. bd. cert. tchr. adolescent/young adult sci., 2000. Tchr. math. and sci. Unionville (Pa.) H.S., 1967-99; ret., 1999; ednl. cons. Adj. prof. West Chester U., 1989—; mem. Carnegie Forum on Edn. and the Economy. Mem. Pa. Rep. State Com., 1982-90, Rep. Com. of Chester County, 1984-94. Named Alumna of Yr., The King's Coll., 1987; recipient State Presdl. award, 1989, Frank G. Brewer Civil Air Patrol Meml. Aerospace award, 1989, Outstanding Achievement award U.S. Dept. Commerce, 1993; Bus. Week/Challenger Seven fellow, 1991. Fellow Am. Sci. Affiliation; mem. AAAS, Nat. Bd. Profl. Tchg. Stds. (founding dir.), Satellite Educators Assn. (pres. 1990-2000), Nat. Sci. Tchrs. Assn., Nat. Coun. Tchrs. Math., Nat. Sci. Tchrs. Assn. (internat. lectr. 1987), Assn. for Sci. Edn. in U.K. (internat. lectr. 1987). Home: PO Box 605 Unionville PA 19375-0605 E-mail: SatTeacher@aol.com.

MARTIN, HENRY ANTHONY, security officer; b. Aruba, Netherlands Antilles, Dec. 5, 1953; s. Joseph Martin, Rachel Agatha Martin; m. Julie Ann Oneal; children: Henry Jr, Andrew, Shanika. Associates, College of Lake County, GrayLake, IL, 1977—80, University of Louisville, Louisville, Kentucky, 1995—97, Eastern Kentucky University, Richmond, Kentucky, 1992—92, North Eastern Illinois University, Chicago, Illinois, 1987—87. Security Officer Jewish Hospital, Louisville, 1993—2002; Police Officer Veterns Administration, North Chicago, IL, 1984—92, Great Lakes Navy Base, Great Lakes, 1980—84. Art Teacher Emma L. Minnis Junior Academy, Louisville, 1998—2001; Probation Officer Adult Division of Court Services, Waukegan, IL, 1985—92; Young Democrat Leader St. Thomas Legislature, St. Thomas, Virgin Islands. SFC, E-7 United States Army Reserve, 1974—2002, Louisville, Kentucky. : Magazine Street Development Corporation (Fundraising Chair 1999—2002). Seventh Day Adventist. Avocation: swimming, bike riding, camping, and cooke.

MARTIN, HERBERT WOODWARD, English educator, poet; b. Birmingham, Ala., Oct. 4, 1933; s. David Nathaniel and Willie Mae (Woodward) M.; m. Elizabeth Susan McAfee Altman, Dec. 13, 1952; children: Sarah Elizabeth Altman, Julia Johanna Martin. BA in English, U. Toledo, 1964; MLitt in Drama, Middlebury (Vt.) Coll., 1972; DA in Poetry, Carnegie Mellon U., 1979; LHD (hon.), Urbana (Ohio) U., 1998; LHD (hon.) , U. Dayton, 2002. From instr. to asst. prof. English Aquinas Coll., Grand Rapids, Mich., 1967-70; from asst. prof. to assoc. prof. U. Dayton, Ohio, 1970-98. Disting. vis. prof. Ctrl. Mich. U., Mt. Pleasant, 1972; advisor Ohio Arts Coun., Columbus, 1980; cons. Ohio Humanities Coun., Columbus, 1996. Author: (poems) N.Y. The Nine Million, 1968, The Shit-Storm Poems, 1972, The Persistence of the Flesh, 1976, The Forms of Silence, 1980, Galileo's Suns, 1999, In His Own Voice: The Uncollected Works of Paul Laurence Dunbar, 2002, The Log of the Vigilante, 2000; librettest (with Joseph Fennimore) Six Songs, 1989, (with Philip Magnuson) Seven Songs, 1992, (with Adolphus Hailstork) Common Ground, 1995, (with Philip Magnuson) It Pays to Advertise, 1996, Magnificat, 2000, Voices: A Requiem, 1998. Paul Laurence Dunbar laureate City of Dayton, 1996; Paul Laurence Dunbar writer-in-residence Dunbar Ho., Dayton, 1996. Recipient Opus award Culture Works, 1996, Richard Bjornson Humanities award Ohio Humanities Coun., 1996, Paul Laurence Dunbar Humanities award Inner-W. Priority Bd., 1996, Gov.'s award Ohio Arts Coun., 2002, Mark Twain award Soc. for Study of Midwestern Lit., 2002; named 10 Top African Males City of Dayton, 1996; Fullbright scholar Janus Pannonius U., 1990-91. Avocations: singing, acting, giving public readings of poetry. Home: 5193 Chapin St Dayton OH 45429-1905 Office: U Dayton Dept English 300 College Park Ave Dayton OH 45469-0001 E-mail: Herbert.Martin@notes.udayton.edu.

MARTIN, HORACE FELECIANO, pathologist, law educator; b. St. Miquel, Azores, Portugal, Jan. 11, 1931; came to U.S., 1941; s. Manuel Feleciano and Maria (Rapozo) M.; m. Florence Jadach, Nov. 25, 1954; children: Michael, Paul, Kathleen, Peter, Susan, John, Mary. BS in Biology, Providence Coll., 1953; MS, U. R.I., 1955; PhD, Boston U., 1961; MS (hon.), Brown U., 1965, MD, 1975; JD, So. New England Sch. Law, 1991. Diplomate Am. Bd. Med. Examiners, Am. Bd. Clin. Chemistry. Rsch. group leader Monsanto Rsch., Boston, 1957-59; dir. clin. chemistry R.I. Hosp., Providence, 1963-93; prof. pathology Brown U., 1963-93; adj. prof. law Providence Coll., 1991—. Mem. device panel FDA, Washington, 1989—; commr. Gulf War Info. and Relief Commn., R.I., 1999—. Author: Determination of Normal Values, 1975. Named Man of Yr., Commn. of Volunteerism. Master Am. Coll. Occupational Environ. Medicine; fellow Coll. Legal Medicine; mem. Maine Toxicological Inst. (bd. dirs. 1992) Brown U. Med. Alumni (pres. 1991), Sigma Xi. Home: 57 Spring St Pawtucket RI 02860-3018

MARTIN, HOSEA L. public relations and marketing professional; b. Montezuma, Ga., Aug. 10, 1937; s. Hozie L. and Marion Turner Martin. BA, U. Chgo., 1960. Jr. exec. Sears, Chgo., 1963-65; publs. editor Prudential Ins. Co., 1966-67; promotins mgr. Coca Cola Co., Atlanta, 1967-75; programs mgr. Safeway Inc., Oakland, Calif., 1975-84; assoc. v.p. United Way, San Francisco, 1989-2000; media rels. dir. IABC, 2000—. Pres., founder Paragraphs Unltd., Oakland, 1984-89. Contbr. articles to newspapers and mags. including Wall St. Jour., Boston Globe, Essence mag., others. With U.S. Army, 1960-63. Avocations: writing, long distance running. Home: 6 Greenbank Ave Piedmont CA 94611 E-mail: HMartin191@aol.com.

MARTIN, HOWARD FRANKLIN, otolaryngologist; b. San Francisco, Mar. 10, 1928; MD, Washington U., St. Louis, 1954. Diplomate Am. Bd. Otolaryngology. Intern San Francisco County Hosp., 1954-55; resident in otolaryngology Ill. Hosps. and Ill. EE Infirmary, Chgo., 1955-58; with El Camino Hosp., Mountain View, Calif., El Camino Surg. Ctr., Mountain View. Clin. assoc. prof. surgery Stanford Sch. Medicine. Fellow AAAS, ACS, AAO, Am. Acad. Facial Plastic and Reconstructive Surgery. Office: 2500 Hospital Dr Bldg 4B Mountain View CA 94040-4167

MARTIN, HUGH, asset manager, securities dealer, educational materials developer; b. Chgo., Aug. 31, 1939; s. Charles Francis and Elizabeth Louise (Wyant) M.; m. Susan Preston Martin, June, 1962 (div. Aug. 1966); 1 child, Jennifer; m. Bonita Jean Felgenhauer, June, 1967 (div. Aug., 1972); 1 child, Naomi; m. Amalia Kaye Contino, Aug. 17, 1974; children: Amalia, Rebecca, Joshua, Samuel, Olivia. BA, Swarthmore Coll., 1961; MA, U. Pa., 1962. Registered investment advisor; CFP. Acct. exec. Reynolds Securities, Oakland, Calif., 1974-76, Blyth Eastman Dillon, San Francisco, 1976-78; pres., CEO Hugh Martin & Co., Sebastopol, Calif., 1978—. Registered investment advisor Securities and Exch. Commn., 1980; spkr. nat. profl. confs. Guest various TV and radio talk shows. Mem. Nat. Assn. Securities Dealers (broker, dealer 1978), Internat. Assn. Fin. Planning. Republican. Avocations: home exchanging, backpacking, biking, travel. Office: PO Box 1736 Sebastopol CA 95473-1736 E-mail: MartinHugh@aol.com.

MARTIN, IONE EDWARDS, social worker; b. Davenport, Okla., Sept. 11, 1912; d. Rila Dewitt and Mae Eliza (Brown) Edwards; m. Lawrence Joseph Martin, Aug. 9, 1946 (dec.); 1 child, David L. BA, Southwestern Coll., 1934; MSW, St. Louis U., 1945. Caseworker Wichita (Kans.) Welfare, 1934-35; state child welfare worker Kans. Child Welfare, Topeka, 1937-38; social worker VA, Denver, 1949-51; psychiat. social worker Patton, Calif., 1953-55; med. social worker County Gen. Hosp., Denver; sch. social worker Denver Pub. Schs., 1958-70. Lectr. local questers and retirement homes; lectr. on bead heritage local Questers orgn., retirement facilities. Mem. AAUW (mem. book rev. group), NEA, Colo. Edn. Assn., Questers Internat. (pres. Aurora chpt. 1986-88, 92-93, lectr. 1996-97). Avocations: collecting and studying antiques, bridge.

MARTIN, IONIS B, artist, educator; b. Chicago, Ill., 1936; d. Francis Wright and Hattie R Bracy; m. Allyn Aubrey Martin; children: Allyn Bracey Fletcher. MFA, pRATT I NSTITUTE, Brooklyn ,Ny, 1987; MED, U. Of Hartford, West Hartford,Ct, 1996; BS, Fisk U., Nashville,Tn, 1957. Lectr./and adj. prof. Ctrl. Ct State U., New Britain, Conn., 1985; art tchr. h.s. Bloomfield Bd. of Educatiion, Hartford, 1971—2001; art instr. co pounder Artists Collective, 1972—74; art tchr. weaver h.s. Hartford Bd. of Edn., 1961—67, art tchr. arsenals elem sch., 1961—61; ct child wearfare assn CT Child Welfare Assn, New Haven, 1959—61; y-teen associated dir. YWCA of Greater Hartford, Hartford, 1957—59. Co founder v.p. Artist collective bd. of Dir, Hartfoed, Conn., 1972; corporatur U. of Hartford bd. of Dir., West Hartford, Conn., 2001; trustee Wadsworth Atheneam Mus. of art, Hartford, Conn., 1978—97. Author: (book) A Curriculum Sampler, (almanac entry) Gale Researchers'African American. Co-trustee of abaurr mall Ella Burr Monies Trust, Hartaford, Conn., 1985; am. boaard of ground dir. Ancient Buriol Grand, Hartford, 1998; dir. Huntington Ho. Mus., Windsor, 2001. Recipient Felloeship, Dubois Inst., Harvard ,CT, 1994, Grant Through Young Black, Ct Commn. on the Arts, Hartford,CT. Mem.: Greater Hartford Chpt. (assoc.; pres. 1954), Greater Hartford Chpt. (assoc.; pres. 1985—2002), Art Works Gallery (assoc.; pres. 1981—86). Home: 1234 Prospect Avenue Hartford CT 06105 Home Fax: 860-523-5000. Personal E-mail: dr.a.martin@sner.net.

MARTIN, J. PETER, utility company executive; b. New Bethlehem, Pa., Dec. 14, 1939; s. W. Clement and Agnes (Shilling) M.; m. Jacqueline Diane Gleason, Dec. 29, 1984; children: Andrew, Sarah, Angelica. BSME, U. Notre Dame (Ind.), 1962; MBA, Harvard U., 1964. Mkt. analyst Roots-Connersville div. Dresser Ind., Inc., Connersville, Ind., 1964-66, reg. sales mgr. Toronto, Ont., 1966-67; staff cons. Donald R. Booz & Assocs., Chgo., 1967-68; gen. mgr. Ready Power Co., Detroit, 1968-69, So. Gulf Utilities, Inc., Miami, Fla., 1969-73, pres., 1973-80, Atlantic Utilities Corp., Miami, 1980—. Mem. Fla. Waterworks Assn. (dir. 1973—), Assoc. Gas Distbrs. of Fla. (del. 1985—), Fla. Natural Gas Assn. (del.), Gas Inst. S. Fla. (sec.-treas.), Coral Gables Country Club, Notre Dame Club of S Fla., Harvard Bus. Sch. Club. S. Fla., Ferrari Club of Am. Republican. Roman Catholic. Home: 11100 Snapper Creek Rd Coral Gables FL 33156-4216

MARTIN, JACK, physician; b. Northport, Ala., Aug. 11, 1927; s. Marvin Oscar and Glenavis (Rice) M.; m. Ann Inman, Apr. 7, 1957; children: Sarah, Richard, Charles Randall, Robert. BS, U. Ala., 1949; MD, Vanderbilt U., 1953. Intern Charity Hosp., New Orleans, 1953-54; resident in adult and child psychiatry Cin. Gen. Hosp., Cincinnati, Ohio, 1954-58; dir. child psychiatry U. Tex. Health Scis. Ctr., Dallas, 1958-67; med. dir. Shady Brook Res. Ctr., Richardson, Tex., 1963-81; physician pvt. practice, Dallas, 1981—. With USNR, 1945-47. Independent. Episcopalian. Avocations: bridge, golf. Office: 3636 Dickason Ave Dallas TX 75219-4911 E-mail: jam4757@aol.com.

MARTIN, JACK, federal agency administrator; m. Bettye Martin; children: Randy, Ingrid. BS, MBA, Wayne State U.; postgrad., U. Minn. CPA. With Gen. Motors Corp., Det.; various mgmt. positions Control Data; cons. acct. Touche Ross & Co. (now Deloitte and Touche); mng. dir., CEO, founder Jack Martin and Co. P.C., CPAs; chmn., acting CEO Home Fed. Savings Bank, Det.; chmn. provider reimbursement rev. bd. U.S. Dept. Health and Human Svcs., 1991—94; CFO Dept. Edn., Washington, 2001—. Chmn. of bd. Health Alliance Plan; mem. investment com. Mercy Health Sys. (now Trinity Health); chair Mich. adv. com. U.S. Civil Rights Commn.; v.p. Merrill Palmer Inst. Wayne State U. Treas. Alzheimer's Assn. Mem.: AICPA (mem. practice stds. subcom.), Det. Athletic Club (bd. dirs.). Office: Dept Edn Office CFO 400 Maryland Ave SW Washington DC 20202-4110*

MARTIN, JAMES ALFRED, JR. religious studies educator; b. Lumberton, N.C., Mar. 18, 1917; s. James Alfred and Mary (Jones) M.; m. Ann Bradsher, June 1, 1936 (dec. 1982); m. Nell Gifford, Jan. 6, 1984. AB, Wake Forest Coll., 1937, LittD, 1965; MA, Duke U., 1938; PhD, Columbia U., 1944; student, Union Theol. Sem., 1940-43; MA (hon.), Amherst Coll., 1950. Ordained to ministry Bapt. Ch., 1944; asst. pastor Roxboro (N.C.) Ch., 1937-38; instr. philosophy and psychology Wake Forest Coll., 1938-40; asst. philosophy religion Union Theol. Sem., N.Y.C., 1941-44, Danforth prof. religion in higher edn., 1960-67, adj. prof. philosophy religion, 1967-82; prof. religion Columbia U., 1967-82, prof. emeritus, 1982—, chmn. dept., 1968-77; asst. prof. religion Amherst Coll., 1946-47, asso. prof., 1947-50, prof., 1950-54, Marquand and Stone prof., 1954-57, Crosby prof. religion, 1957-60. Ordained deacon P.E. Ch., 1953; vis. prof. Cornell U., summer 1948, Mt. Holyoke Coll., 1949-50, 52-53, 59-60, State U. Iowa, summer 1959, U. N.C., summer 1964; Univ. prof. Wake Forest U., 1984— ; vis. prof. religious studies U. Va., 1984; asso. mem. East-West Philosophers Conf., U. Hawaii, 1949 Author: Empirical Philosophies of Religion, 1944, (with J.A. Hutchison) Ways of Faith, 1953, rev., 1960, Fact, Fiction, and Faith, 1960, The New Dialogue between Philosophy and Theology, 1966, Beauty and Holiness, 1990; contbr. articles to profl. jours. and encys., chpts. to books. Chmn. bd. visitors Wake Forest Coll., 1981-83. Served as lt. chaplain USNR, 1944-46, PTO. Recipient Disting. Alumnus award Wake Forest U., 1971, Nat. Faculty award Assn. of Grad. Liberal Studies Programs, 1995. Mem. Soc. Values in Higher Edn. (Kent fellow, pres. 1964-69), Am. Theol. Soc. (v.p. 1981-82, pres. 1982), Soc. Theol. Discussion, Soc. Philosophy of Religion, Phi Beta Kappa, Omicron Delta Kappa, Pi Kappa Alpha. Home: PO Box 6746 Winston Salem NC 27109-6746 E-mail: martinja@wfu.edu. *My experience of life has increasingly underscored the central importance of honesty-in understanding of oneself, and in perceptions of and relations to others. The quest for honesty entails a relentless and often painful search for truth. Acceptance of truth, and of others as they truly are, requires grace. The goal is to speak the truth in love.*

MARTIN, JAMES CHANDLER, lawyer; b. Newport News, Va., Mar. 14, 1956; s. Francis Chandler and Glenna Faye (Dunkum) M. MusB, U. Md., 1978; JD, George Mason U., 1987. Bar: Va. 1987, D.C. 1989, N.C. 1991. Asst. commonwealth's atty. City of Danville, Va., 1987-90, 92—; pvt. practice law Danville, 1990-92. Prin. trombonist Philharm. Greensboro, N.C. 1988—, bd. dirs., 1991-93; prin. trombonist Danville Symphony Orch., 1992—, bd. dirs., 1992-94, 97-98. Mem. Nat. Dist. Attys. Assn., K.C. (4th degree navigator 1997-98). Roman Catholic. Avocations: musician (trombonist, vocalist, composer), writer. Home: 258 Manor Pl Danville VA 24541-2633 Office: Commonwealths Attys Office 115 S Union St Danville VA 24541-1105

MARTIN, JAMES DOUGLAS, neurologist; b. Cullman, Ala., Dec. 10, 1926; s. Charles L. and Sylvia J. (Johnson) M.; m. Elizabeth Mason, June 22, 1956; children: James, Julia, Ann. BA, Vanderbilt U., 1949, MD, 1959. Diplomate Am. Bd. Psychiatry and Neurology. Med. intern U. Va., Charlottesville, Va., 1959-60, neurology resident, 1960-63; fellow in neuropathology Harvard Med. Sch., Boston, 1963-65; asst. prof. neurology W. Va. U., Morgantown, 1965-70, assoc. prof., 1970-72, prof., 1972—. Fellow Am. Acad. Neurology. Office: W Va Univ Dept Neurology PO Box 9180 Morgantown WV 26506-9180

MARTIN, JAMES FRANKLIN, physician, lawyer; b. Chattanooga, Feb. 22, 1929; s. Delbert Chester and Doshia (Locke) M.; m. Mary Edna Connelly, June 5, 1950; children: Samuel Franklin, Mary Karen, John Delbert, Molly Frances. MD, U. Tenn., Memphis, 1960; LLB, U. Tenn., Knoxville, 1952. Bar: Tenn. 1952, U.S. Ct. Mil. Appeals 1953. Engring. draftsman Combustion Engring. Co., Chattanooga, 1947-48; engr. mech. Combustion Engring. Co., 1952; lawyer Harold Stone Law Firm, Knoxville, 1955-60; atty. Tenn. Valley Authority, 1955-56; intern James Walker Meml. Hosp., Wilmington, N.C., 1960-61, attending staff mem., 1962-66; pvt. practice in family practice, 1961-66, Yuma, Ariz., 1968—; med. dir. Provident Life Accident Ins. Co., Chattanooga, 1966-68. Instr. medicine James Walker Meml. Hosp., 1962-64; bd. dirs. Yuma Regional Med. Ctr., Mutual Ins. Co. of Ariz., Phoenix. Editor Tenn. Law Rev., 1951-52; author: Principal Security Devices in Tennessee, 1952. Capt. U.S. Army, 1952-55. Fellow Am. Acad. Family Practice, Am. Coll. Legal Medicine; mem. AMA, Ariz. Med. Assn., Am. Coll. Legal Medicine. Democrat. Avocations: reading, Southwest border history, Spanish language, quail hunting, tennis. Home: 1733 W Arcadia Ln Yuma AZ 85364-5064 Office: 2053 S Avenue A Yuma AZ 85364-8305

MARTIN, JAMES FREDERICK, broadcasting executive; b. Sebring, Fla., June 29, 1944; s. George William and Elizabeth (Knudson) M.; m. Hope Hamilton McCulloch, May 31, 1969; children: Faith Hamilton, Aimee Leavenworth. BFA in Visual Communications, Syracuse U., 1967; MA in Non-Verbal Communication, Mich. State U., 1968. Film producer Foote, Cone & Belding, Chgo., 1968-73, sr. producer, v.p., 1973-77, exec. producer, 1977-80, dir. broadcast prodn., 1980-97, dir. advt. services, 1983-84, sr. v.p. broadcast prodn., 1984—. Home: 1115 Normandy Ln Glenview IL 60025-3211 Office: Foote Cone & Belding 101 E Erie St Fl 14 Chicago IL 60611-2850

MARTIN, JAMES GRUBBS, medical executive, former governor; b. Savannah, Ga., Dec. 11, 1935; s. Arthur Morrison and Mary Julia (Grubbs) M.; m. Dorothy Ann McAulay, June 1, 1957; children: James Grubbs, Emily Wood, Arthur Benson. BS, Davidson Coll., 1957; PhD, Princeton U., 1960. Assoc. prof. chemistry Davidson (N.C.) Coll., 1960-72; mem. 93d to 98th Congresses from N.C., 1973-85; gov. State of N.C., 1985-92; v.p. Carolinas HealthCare System, Charlotte, N.C., 1993—. Mem. Mecklenburg (N.C.) Bd. County Commrs., 1966-72, chmn., 1967-68, 70-71; pres. N.C. Assn. County Commrs., 1970-71; mem., tuba player Charlotte Symphony, 1961-66; dir. J.A. Jones Constrn., Family Dollar Stores, Inc., Duke Energy Co., Applied Analytical Industries, Inc., Palomar Med. Technologies, Inc. Chmn. Global TransPark Found., 1993—; trustee Davidson Coll., 1998—; trustee Union Theol. Sem., Va., 2002-. Danforth fellow, 1957-60. Mem. Beta Theta Pi (v.p., trustee 1966-69, pres. 1975-78), Masons (33 deg.), Shriners. Presbyterian. Office: Carolinas Med Ctr PO Box 32861 Charlotte NC 28232-2861 E-mail: jgmartin@carolinas.org.

MARTIN, JAMES HANLEY, deputy state attorney general; b. N.Y.C., Dec. 22, 1960; s. James Patrick and Josephine Anne (Hanley) M. AB, Georgetown U., 1983; JD, Fordham U., 1986. Bar: N.J. 1986, U.S. Dist. Ct. N.J. 1986, N.Y. 1987, D.C. 1988, U.S. Dist. Ct. (so. and ea. dists.) N.Y. 1991, U.S. Ct. Appeals (D.C. and 3d cirs.) 1991, U.S. Supreme Ct. 1991. Dep. atty. gen. State of N.J., Newark, 1987—. Mem. ABA, Am. Judicature Soc., Bergen County Bar Assn., N.J. State Bar Assn., D.C. Bar, Assn. Bar of City of N.Y. Roman Catholic. Office: State of NJ Divsn Law PO Box 45029 124 Halsey St Newark NJ 07101

MARTIN, JAMES JOHN, JR. retired consulting research firm executive, systems analyst; b. Paterson, N.J., Feb. 3, 1936; s. James John and Lillian (Lea) M.; m. Lydia Elizabeth Bent, June 11, 1954; children: David, Peter, Laura, Daniel, Lucas BA, U. Wis.-Madison, 1955; postgrad., Div. Sch., Harvard U., 1955-57; MS, Navy Postgrad. Sch., 1963; PhD, MIT, 1965. Commd. ensign USN, 1957, advanced through grades to comdr., 1971, ret., 1977; sector v.p. Sci. Applications Internat. Corp., La Jolla, Calif., 1977-95. Author: Bayesian Decision Problems and Markov Chains, 1967; editor: On Not Confusing Ourselves, 1991; author articles on nat. security. Bd. dirs. Mil. Conflict Inst., 1986-92. Decorated Legion of Merit; recipient Superior Svc. medal Dept. Def. Mem. Internat. Inst. Strategic Studies, Ops. Research Soc. Am., Mil. Ops. Research Soc. (bd. dirs. 1974-77) Democrat. Avocation: cooking. Home: 6603 Aranda Ave La Jolla CA 92037-6216

MARTIN, JAMES KAY, government official; b. Montreal, Que., Sept. 20, 1948; s. Douglas Kay and Margaret (Sherren) M.; m. Emma Lim Abrenica, Sept. 12, 1986. B of Math., U. Waterloo, Ont., 1970; PhD, U. Toronto, 1974. Sr. analyst Health & Welfare, Ottawa, 1974-79; asst. dir. transfer payments Social Devel. Ministry, 1980-84; exec. dir. planning Dept. Agr., 1984-90; exec dir. regulatory affairs Treasury bd. Can., 1990-96; dir. gen. Internal Audit and Risk Mgmt. Human Resources Can., 1997—. Chmn. regulatory mgmt. group OECD, Paris, 1995-97. Contbr. articles to profl. jours. Chmn. grad. students union U. Toronto, 1973, mem. bd. govs., 1974. Fellow Nat. Rsch. Coun., 1970, Ont. Inst. for Edn., 1971, Can. Coun., 1972, 73. Mem. Ottawa Humane Soc. Roman Catholic. Avocations: running, canoeing, skiing, swimming. E-mail: james.martin@hrdc-drhc.gc.ca.

MARTIN, JAMES KIRBY, historian, educator; b. Akron, Ohio, May 26, 1943; s. Paul Elmo and Dorothy Marie (Garrett) M.; m. Karen Wierwille, Aug. 7, 1965; children: Darcy Elizabeth, Sarah Marie, Joelle Kathryn Garrett. BA summa cum laude, Hiram Coll., 1965; MA, U. Wis., 1967, PhD, 1969. Asst. prof. history Rutgers U., New Brunswick, N.J., 1969-73, assoc. prof., 1973-79, prof., 1979-80, asst. provost, 1972-74, v.p. acad. affairs, 1977-79; vis. prof. Rutgers Ctr. of Alcohol Studies, 1978-88; prof. history U. Houston, 1980-97, disting. univ. prof., 1997—, chmn. dept., 1980-83; vis. prof. history Rice U., Houston, 1992. Chmn. bd. sponsors Papers of Thomas Edison Project, 1977-80; mem. editl. adv. bd. Papers of William Livingston Project, 1973-80; founding ptnr. PastQuest Rsch. Svcs., 1999. Author: Men in Rebellion, 1973, In the Course of Human Events, 1979, (with M.E. Lender) A Respectable Army: The Military Origins of the Republic, 1982 (contemporary mil. reading list), Drinking in America: A History, 1982, rev. edit. 1987, (with others) America and Its Peoples, 1989, 4th edit., 2001, concise edit. 1995, Benedict Arnold: Revolutionary Hero, 1997 (Homer D. Babbidge, Jr. award), audio edit., 2001; editor: Interpreting Colonial America, 1973, 2d edit. 1978, The Human Dimensions of Nation Making, 1976, (with K. Stubaus) The American Revolution, Whose Revolution?, 1977, 81, (with M.E. Lender) Citizen-Soldier: The Revolutionary War Journal of Joseph Bloomfield, 1982 (R.P. McCormick prize), Ordinary Courage: The Revolutionary War Adventures of Joseph Plumb Martin, 1993, 2d edit., 1999; mem. bd. editors Houston Rev., 1981—, N.J. History, 1986—, Conversations with the Past Series, 1993-95; gen. editor Am. Social Experience Series, 1983-2002. Recipient N.J. Soc. of the Cin. prize for Disting. Achievement in Am. History, 1995, Hiram Coll. Alumni Achievement award, 1996. Mem. Tex. Assn. for Advancement History (bd. dirs. 1981-93, v.p. 1986-90), Inst. for Internat. Bus. Analysis (adv. coun. 1982-86), Am. Hist. Assn. (Beveridge-Dunning prize com. 1990-93), Orgn. Am. Historians, So. Hist. Assn., Soc. Historians Early Am. Republic (adv. coun. 1985-88), Soc. for Mil. History, Phi Beta Kappa, Phi Kappa Phi, Pi Gamma Mu, Omicron Delta Kappa, Phi Alpha Theta. Office: U Houston Dept History 4800 Calhoun Rd Houston TX 77204-0001

MARTIN, JAMES LARENCE, dentist, educator; b. Dubuque, Iowa, Sept. 3, 1940; s. James Larence and Ada Virginia (Boone) M.; m. Willie Mae Walker, Jan. 23, 1941; children: Linda Gail, James Larence III, John Lance. BS, Loras Coll., Dubuque, 1959, LittD, 1982; MS, Tenn. State U., 1960; DDS, Meharry Med. Coll., 1966; MPH, U. Mich., 1975. Dental dir. children and youth Meharry Med. Coll., Nashville, 1967-72, acting dir. children and youth program, 1972-73, dir. primary dental svcs., 1973-75, coord. dental component Ctr. for Health Care Rsch., 1975-77, prof., 1981—; owner Martin Dental, 1980—. Dental cons. Medically Dedicated, Washington, 1992—; pres. faculty senate Meharry Med. Coll., 1989-93, mem. pres.'s exec. mgmt. team, 1989-93, dir. divsn. dental public health 1999—, chair dept. dental pub. health, 1999—. Contbr. articles to profl. jours., chpts. to books. Bd. regents Loras Coll., 1997—. Recipient Meritorious Svc. award Acad. Oral Medicine, 1977. Mem. ADA, Am. Pub. Health Assn. (med. com.), Am. Assn. Pub. Health Dentistry, Nat. Assn. Cmty. Health Ctrs., Am. Acad. Goil Foil Operators, Soc. of the Upper 10th, Nashville Area C. of C., Beta Kappa Chi, Phi Sigma. Avocations: reading, swimming, photography. Home: 3515 Geneva Cir Nashville TN 37209-2524 Office: 908 34th Ave N Nashville TN 37209-2502 E-mail: jmartin@mmc.edu.

MARTIN, JAMES NEAL, lawyer; b. Glasgow, Ky., Jan. 11, 1950; s. J. Jack and Olive Katherine (Conover) M.; 1 child, Amelia Anne. BA, U. Louisville, 1972, JD, 1980. Bar: Ky. 1980, U.S. Dist. Ct. (ea. dist.) Ky. 1987. Pvt. practice, Tompkinsville, Ky., 1980-82; spl. commr. Cumberland Cir. Ct. for 29th Jud. Cir. Ky., Burkesville, 1982-84; ptnr. Martin & Martin, Richmond, Ky., 1984-89; pvt. practice, 1989—; Asst. Ccommonwealth Atty., prosecutor 25th Judicial Cir., Ky., 2000—. Asst. county atty., prosecutor, criminal div. Office Madison County Atty., Richmond, 1986; adj. instr. Bur. Criminal Justice Tng., Ky. Law Enforcement Coun., 1988--. Bd. dirs. Richmond Little League, Inc., 1987—, chmn. exec. bd., 1988-89. Mem.: Madison County Bar Assn., Ky. Bar Assn., Rotary (bd. dir. Richmond 1986, v.p., pres. 1991—92), Richmond C. of C. (legis. affairs com. 1986—88). Avocations: water sports, landscape gardening. Office: 619 West Main St PO Box 828 Richmond KY 40476-0828 Fax: 859-623-9096.

MARTIN, JAMES RICHARD, music educator; MusB in Edn., Fla. State U., 1977. Choral dir. Harllee Mid. Sch., Bradenton, Fla., 1977—91, Braden River Mid. Sch., Bradenton, 1991—. Mem.: Fla. Vocal Assn. (chmn. dist. 11 1989—90).

MARTIN, JAMES ROBERT, identification company executive; b. Indpls., Mar. 31, 1943; s. Walter and Helen (Snider) M.; m. Jan. 24, 1970 (div. Dec. 1990); children: Julia, Justin; m. Tamara Hicks, Dec. 21, 1991; stepchildren: Hunter Hoskins, Laura Hoskins. BA, DePauw U., 1965; MBA, Ind. U., 1967. Bus. analyst TRW, Inc., Redondo Beach, Calif., 1967-70; fin. analyst Internat. Industries, Beverly Hills, 1970; v.p. fin., treas. A & E Plastik Pak Co., Inc., Industry, 1970-75; pres. Plasti-Line, Inc., Knoxville, Tenn., 1975-92, chmn., CEO, 1992—. Bd. dirs. 1st Am. Corp., Nashville, Signal Thread Co., Chattanooga, Tenn. Bd. dirs. Knoxville Symphony Soc., 1976, Knoxville United Way, 1986, Knoxville Mus. Art; bd. dirs., chmn. fin. com. Thompson Cancer Survival Ctr., Knoxville, 1985. Mem. Chief Execs. Orgn., Club LeConte (bd. dirs.), East Tenn. Automobile Club (bd. dirs.), St. Francis Yacht Club, Cherokee Country Club. Aspen Mountain Club. Republican. Episcopalian. Home: 1029 Scenic Dr Knoxville TN 37919 Office: Plasti-Line Inc PO Box 59043 Knoxville TN 37950-9043

MARTIN, JAMES VICTOR, JR. foreign service officer, writer; b. Tokyo, Nov. 15, 1916; (parents Am. citizens); s. James Victor Sr. and Esther Belle (Ludwig) M.; m. Elizabeth Shaler Smith, June 28, 1941; children: Sarah Martin Brown, Susan P. Martin, David Ludwig Martin. BA, DePauw U., 1938; MA, Tufts U., 1939, PhD, 1948; postgrad. in Japanese lang., Harvard U., 1941-42, Yale U., 1948-49. Vice consul U.S. Consulate Gen., Bombay, 1946-48; polit. officer, head transl. sect. Office of Polit. Adviser, Tokyo, 1949-50; econ. officer U.S. Consulate Gen., Kobe-Osaka, Japan, 1951-53; prin. officer U.S. Consulate, Fukuoka, Japan, 1953-56; officer-in-charge Japanese Affairs U.S. Dept. State, Washington, 1956-58, personnel planning staff, 1958-61; chief polit. sect. U.S. Embassy, Rangoon, Burma, 1962-64; U.S. polit. adviser Office of U.S. High Commn. to the Ryukyu Islands, Okinawa, 1964-67; polit. counselor U.S. Embassy, Canberra, Australia, 1968-70; country dir. for Australia, N.Z. and Pacific Islands, U.S. Dept. State, Washington, 1970-73. Lectr. Far East internat. rels. Am. U., Washington, summer 1961; occasional lectr. U.S. Asian policy U. Md. Extension, Okinawa, 1965-67; cons. Pacific Islands, U.S. Dept. of Interior, Washington, 1973-74. Contbr. articles to profl. jours. Trustee Japan-Am. Soc. Washington, Inc., 1982-89; bd. dirs. Com. for Community Democracies-U.S.A., Washington, 1983-92, v.p., 1986-87; sec., treas. Com. for Community of Democracies (D.C.), Washington, 1985-88. Lt. USN, 1941-46, PTO. Mem. Assn. for Asian Studies, Mid-Atlantic Region Chpt. Assn. for Asian Studies (treas. 1972-76), Diplomatic and Consular Officers Ret. Methodist. Avocations: painting, woodblock printing, photography.

MARTIN, JAMES WILLIAM, lawyer; b. Turlock, Calif., Dec. 20, 1949; Student, Ga. Inst. Tech., 1967-69; BS, Stetson U., 1971, JD, 1974. Bar: Fla. 1974, U.S. Dist. Ct. (mid. dist.) Fla. 1974, U.S. Ct. Appeals (5th cir.) 1974, U.S. Ct. Appeals (11th cir.) 1987, U.S. Supreme Ct. 1978. Ptnr. Brickley & Martin, St. Petersburg, Fla., 1974-79; pres. James W. Martin, P.A., 1979—. Presenter in field. Author: West's Florida Corporation System, 1984, West's Legal Forms, 3d edit., Non-Profit Corporations, 1991, 92, 93, 94, 96, 97, 98, 99, 2000, 2001, West's Florida Legal Forms, Business Organizations, Real Estate, Specialized Forms, 1990, 91, 92, 93, 94, 95; supplement editor Fla. Jur. Forms, Legal and Bus., 1998, 99; contbr. articles to profl. jours. including Word Perfect mag., ALI-ABA Practical Lawyer, Fla. Bar News, Fla. Bar Jour. City councilman, St. Petersburg, 1982-83; active Leadership St. Petersburg; active charter class Leadership Tampa Bay; founding trustee, sec., counsel Salvador Dali Mus., 1980—; founding dir., sec., counsel Fla. Internat. Mus., 1992-94. Recipient Outstanding Young Man award Jaycees, 1982, Outstanding Contbn. to City award St. Petersburg C. of C., 1980. Mem.: St. Petersburg C. of C. (gen. counsel 1991—92, arts task force 1987, chmn. parking com., chmn. urban solutions com. 1992—93, chmn. downtown com. 1993—94), St. Petersburg Bar Assn. (chair probate sect. 1999—2000), Fla. Bar (chmn. coordinating com. tech. 1992—93, probate rules com. 1994—2000), Pinellas County Arts Coun. (councilman 1997—2001), Pres. Club (founder, hon. bd. dirs. 1985—91). Fax: 727-823-3479. E-mail: jamesmartinpa@msn.com.

MARTIN, JANICE LYNN, special education educator; b. Louisville, Feb. 24, 1952; d. Thomas Joseph and Agnes Marie (Singhiser) Duddy; m. Reed Ammerman Martin Jr., Aug. 14, 1976; children: Susan, John. BS magna cum laude, U. Ga., 1974; MEd, U. Louisville, 1976, grad. dean's citation, 1984; cert., Western Ky. U., 1984. Tchr. Jefferson County Pub. Schs., Louisville, 1974—. Mem. curriculum coun. Jefferson County Pub. Schs., 1979-82. Mem. St. Joseph Cath. Orphan Soc., Louisville, 1981—; mem., adult asst. Troop 513 Girl Scouts U.S., Louisville, 1988—. Recipient Grad. Dean's citation U. Louisville, 1976, Achievement in Edn. award Middletown Optimist Club, 1999, finalist Stella Edwards award for outstanding spl. edn. tchr. yr. Ky. Dept. Edn., 1998, 2000 Spirit award Middletown C. of C.; grantee Eisenhower Title II math. and sci., 1992, 93, Appalachian Ednl. Lab. Eisenhower Math. Grant Project, 1994. Mem. NEA, ASCD, Ky. Edn. Assn., Coun. for Exceptional Children (Outstanding Spl. Edn. Tchr. of Yr. 1990), Louisville Coun. Tchrs., Ky. Coun. Tchrs. of Math., Nat. Coun. Tchrs. Math., Jefferson County Tchrs. Assn., AAUW, Alpha Delta Kappa, Phi Kappa Phi, Phi Delta Kappa, Sigma Kappa. Democrat. Home: 9005 Cardiff Rd Louisville KY 40242-3362 Office: Jefferson County Pub Schs Middletown Elem 218 N Madison Ave Louisville KY 40243-1018

MARTIN, JASON EUGENE, music educator; b. Jefferson City, Mo., Dec. 15, 1972; s. Jesse Eugene and Carol Beth Martin; m. Tammy Jean Burrus, Apr. 8, 1998; children: Lucas Kyle. BME, Ctrl. Mo. State, Warrensburg, MO, 1995; MA, U. Mo., Columbia, MO, 2002. Band dir. Eldon Pub. Schools, Eldon, Mo., 1995—. Mem.: Mo. State Teachers Assn., Music Educators Nat. Conf., Mo. Band Masters Assn., Mo. Music Educators Assn. R-Consevative. Baptist. Avocations: softball, movies, reading. Office: Eldon High School 101 S Pine Eldon MO 65026 Office Fax: 573-392-5057. E-mail: j-martin@mail.eldon.k12.mo.us..

MARTIN, JASON ULYATTA, management consultant, entrepreneur; b. Georgetown, Guyana, May 17, 1960; came to U.S., 1981; s. Harold Wilfred and Elaine Martin; m. Moronke Oshin, Sept. 3, 1990; children: Alexander, Jason II. Cert. in internat. bus., Sannd Coll., Nagoya, Japan, 1983; BSc, NYU, 1984. Cert. mgmt. cons. Rschr., ops. specialist Merrill Lynch, N.Y.C., 1985-86; ind. cons. N.Y. and Caribean, 1986-91; prin. MCCG LLC, White Plains, N.Y., 1999; pres., mng. dir. Mgmt. Cons. Controls Group Inc., N.Y.C., 1991—. Bd. dirs. Flatbush Cmty. Devel. Corp., Bklyn., 1998-99, Caribbean C. of C. and Industry; mem. fin. com. Urban Health Plan Inc., Bronx, 1997-99; adv. bd. Harlem Jazz Found., 1997-98. Mem. Inst. of Mgmt. Cons. (cert.), Am.

Mgmt. Assn., Cmty. Healthcare Assn. of N.Y. State. Avocations: tennis, basketball, reading, history, travel, writing. Office: MCCG LLC Wall Street Sta PO Box 227 New York NY 10268-0227

MARTIN, JAY GRIFFITH, lawyer; b. Washington, Oct. 13, 1951; s. Drexel Reese and Joyce (Towne) M.; 1 child, Trevor. BBA, So. Meth. U., 1973, MPA, JD, So. Meth. U., 1976. Bar: Tex., D.C., U.S. Ct. Appeals (5th cir.), U.S. Dist. Ct. (so. dist.) Tex., U.S. Dist. Ct. D.C., U.S. Supreme Ct. Counsel Pennzoil Co., Houston, 1976-78, sr. counsel, 1978-81; divsn. counsel The Superior Oil Co., 1981-85; sr. counsel Mobil Natural Gas, 1985-87, gen. counsel, 1987-91; asst. gen. counsel Mobil Oil Corp., Fairfax, Va., 1991-96; ptnr. Andrews & Kurth LLP, Washington, 1996-2000, Phelps Dunbar LLP, Houston, 2000—01, Winstead Sechrest & Minick, Houston, 2001—. Mem. sr. adv. bd. Bus. Laws Inc., Chesterland, Ohio, 1997—; mem. adv. bd. Inst. Transnat. Arbitration, Southwestern Legal Found., 1996—. Author: (books) Environmental Management Systems, 1998, Dispute Resolution for Oil and Gas Practitioners, 2000; contbr. articles; mem. adv. bd.: jour. Natural Gas Contracts, 1991—. Chmn. fundraising com. So. Meth. U., Washington, 1996—97, mem. dean's adv. coun. Sch. Law, 1995—; bd. trustees Rocky Mountain Mineral Law Found. Named one of World's Outstanding Energy Lawyers, Euromoney, 2001. Fellow: Tex. Bar Found., State Bar Tex. (life; adv. bd. 1985—, chmn. corp. counsel sect. 1990—91); mem.: Fed. Bar Assn. (chmn. 1986—87, bd. dirs. 1990—92, antitrust sect. 1991—98, chmn. internat. energy com. 1997—), Delta Theta Phi, Rocky Mountain Law Inst. (trustee 1991—), Am. Soc. Internat. Law, Assn. Internat. Petroleum Negotiators, Houston Bar Assn., ABA (litig. sect. rep. on ABA coord. com. on energy law 1991—97, sect. pub. utility law 1991—, chmn. natural resources, energy and environ law internat. energy com. 1996—98, exec. coun., budget chmn. sect. on environment, energy and law 1996—, liaison to Fed. Energy Bar Assn. 1997—, ad hoc mem. of com. 1997—, sr. liaison oversight responsibility for all energy and resource coms. 1998—, vice chmn. sect. on environment, energy and resources' natural gas and oil 1998—), Energy Bar Assn. (chmn. antitrust sect. 1986—87, chmn. internat. energy com. 1998—99, chmn. internat. com.), Internat. Bar Assn. (sect. energy and natural resources 1994—), D.C. Bar Assn. (internat.sect.), State Bar Coll. of Tex., Tex. Bar Assn. Avocations: history, current events and politics, tennis, golf, jogging. Home: 3133 Buffalo Speedway Apt 7207 Houston TX 77098-1828 Office: Winstead Sechrest & Minick 910 Travis St Ste 2400 Houston TX 77002 E-mail: jmartin@winstead.com.

MARTIN, JAY HERBERT, psychoanalysist, English educator; b. Newark, Oct. 30, 1935; s. Sylvester K. and Ada M. (Smith) M.; m. Helen Bernadette Saldini, June 9, 1956; children: Helen E., Laura A., Jay Herbert. AB with honors, Columbia U., 1956; MA, Ohio State U., 1957, PhD, 1960; PhD in Psychoanalysis, So. Calif. Psychoanalytic Inst., 1983. Instr. English Pa. State U., 1957-58; instr., then asst. to assoc. prof. English and Am. Studies Yale U., New Haven, 1960-68; prof. English and comparative culture U. Calif., Irvine, 1968-79; asst. prof. psychiatry and human behavior, clin. supr. residency program Calif. Coll. Medicine Calif. Coll. Medicine U. Calif.-Irvine, 1978—96; Leo S. Bing prof. English and Am. lit. U. So. Calif., L.A., 1979-96, dir. undergrad. program in Am. studies, 1968-69, dir. program in comparative culture, 1969-71, dir. edn. abroad program, 1971-75; prof. govt., Edward S. Gould prof. humanities Claremont McKenna Coll., 1996—; dir. civilization program Claremont (Calif.) McKenna Coll., 1996—2000, acting dir. Gould Ctr. for Humanistic Studies, 1998-2000. Instr. psychoanalysis So. Calif. Psychoanalytic Inst., 1984-96; Bicentennial prof. Am. lit. and culture Moscow State U., USSR, 1976, Dai Ho Chun (Wisdom) chair Prof. U. Hawaii, 2000-01; vis. Parmenter lectr. Children's Hosp., San Francisco, 1989, Ann. William Faulkner Lecture, 1991, Herman Serota Found. lecture, 1992; cons. to pub. houses; lectr. USSR, Poland, Norway, France, Costa Rica, Germany, Brazil, Can., U. London, Hebrew U., Jerusalem, Seoul, Rep. Korea, China, Peru, Durham, Eng., Helsinki; dir. NEH summer sems., 1976, 77; mem. evaluation com. dept. pvt. post-secondary edn. State of Calif., 1986; cons. numerous univs., pubs., NEA, NEA, J.S. Guggenheim Found., Calif. Coun. for Humanities and Pub. Policy, U.S. Congress Com. on Edn. and Labor; faculty assoc. Coun. Internat. Exch. of Scholars; frequent speaker profl. orgns. and sems., univs., confs., hosps. Author: (criticism and biography) Conrad Aiken: A Life of His Art, 1962, Harvests of Change: American Literature 1865-1914, 1967, Nathanael West: The Art of His Life, 1970 (U. Calif. Friends Libr. award), Robert Lowell, 1970, Always Merry and Bright. The Life of Henry Miller, 1978, (U. Calif. Friends of Libr. award, Phi Kappa Phi Best Faculty Publ. prize U. So. Calif., transl. in French, Japanese and German), (fiction) Winter Dreams: An American in Moscow, 1979, Who Am I This Time, Uncovering the Fictive Personality, 1988 (trans. Portuguese, Burlington No. Found. award 1989); Swallowing Tigers Whole, 1996, A Corresponding Leap of Love: Henry Miller, 1996, Henry Miller's Dream Song, 1996, Journey to heavenly Mountain, 2002, Biography and Humanity, 2000; author one hour radio drama, William Faulkner. Sound Portraits of Twentieth-Century Humanists, starring Tennessee Williams, Glenn Close, Colleen Dewhurst, Nat. Pub. Radio, 1980; author one-act docudrama Trial Days in Coyocoan, Antioch Rev., 2001; author sects. 24 books including most recently American Writing Today, vol. I, 1982, The Haunted Dusk: American Supernatural Fiction, 1820-1902, 1983, Frontiers of Infant Psychiatry, vol.II, 1986, Centenary Essays on Huckleberry Finn, 1985, Robert Lowell: Essays on the Poetry, 1987, William Faulkner: The Best from American Literature, 1989, The Homosexualities: Reality, Fantasy and the Arts, 1991, Life Guidance Through Literature, 1992, Biography and Source Studies, 1995, William Faulkner and Psychology, 1995, Psychotherapy East and West, 1996, Readings on Huckleberry Finn, 1999, John Fante: A Critical Gathering, 2000, Uncollected Works By...Paul Laurence Dunbar, 2000 ; contbr. numerous articles and revs. to profl. jours., bulls., L.A. Times Book Rev., Partisan Rev., N.Y. Times Book Rev., Internat. Rev. Psycho-Analysis, Am. Lit., London Times Lit. Supplement, Psychoanalytic Quarterly, Jour. Applied Psychoanalysis; editor: Winfield Townley Scott (Yale series recorded poets), 1962, Twentieth Century Interpretations of the Waste Land: A Collection of Critical Essays, 1968, Twentieth Century Views of Nathanael West, 1972, A Singer in the Dawn: Reinterpretations of Paul Laurence Dunbar (with intro.), 1975, Economic Depression and American Humor (with intro.), 1986; mem. editl. bd. Am. Lit., 1978-81, Humanities in Society, 1979-1983; editor-in-chief Psychoanalytic Edn., 1984-89; editor Humanitas/Communitas, 1998-2000; appearances on TV and radio including Connie Martinson Talks Books, Barbara Brunner Nightline, Sonya Live in L.A., Oprah Winfrey Show, 1988-89 Pres. Friends of Irvine Pub. Libr., 1974-75; mem. Com. for Freud Mus. Recipient Fritz Schmidl Meml. prize for rsch. applied psychoanalysis Seattle Assn. Psychoanalysis, 1982, Marie H. Briehl prize for child psychoanalysis, 1982, Franz Alexander prize in psychoanalysis, 1984; Morse rsch. fellow, 1963-64, Am. Philos. Soc. fellow, 1966, J.S. Guggenheim fellow, 1966-67, Rockefeller Found.humanities sr. fellow, 1975-76, Rsch. Clin. fellow So. Calif. Psychoanalytic Soc. 1977-81, Rockefeller fellow, Bellagio, Italy, 1983, NEH sr. fellow, 1983-84. Mem. So. Calif. Am. Studies Assn. (pres. 1969-71), Am. Studies Assn. (exec. bd. 1969-71, del. to MLA Assembly 1974, chmn. Ralph Gabriel prize com. 1975-77), MLA (chmn. prize com. Jay B. Hubbell Silver medal in Am. lit. 1978-84), Nat. Assn. Arts and Letters (prize com. 1987-88), Nat. Humanities Faculty (advisor to Valhalla High Sch., El Cajon, Calif. 1979-81), Nat. Am. Studies Faculty, Internat. Psychoanalytic Assn., Internat. Assn. Empirical Aesthetics, Internat. Assn. U. Profs. English, Internat. Karen Horney Soc., Phi Beta Kappa. Home: 748 Via Santo Tomas Claremont CA 91711-1569 E-mail: jay_martin@claremontmckenna.edu.

MARTIN, JEAN ANN, school administrator, educational diagnostician; b. Omaha, June 27, 1942; d. Clarid Fee and Frances Catherine (Dugan) McNeil; m. Robert William Martin, Dec. 28, 1968. BS, Pa. State U., 1963; MEd, U. Del., 1968; EdD, Wilmington Coll., 1997. Cert. English tchr., Pa., N.Y., Del., reading specialist, Va., N.Y., Del., secondary prin., reading supr., dir. of instrn., Del. Tchr. English Neshaminy Sch. Dist., Langhorn, Pa., 1963-65; tchr. English and reading Unionville (Pa.) Sch. Dist., 1965-68; tchr. reading Jamesville-DeWitt (N.Y.) Sch. Dist., 1968-69, South Colonie Sch. Dist., Albany, N.Y., 1969-70; tchr. English Bethlehem Ctrl. Sch. Dist., Delmar, 1970-71, Smyrna (Del.) Sch. Dist., 1971-73; reading specialist, tchr. English Delmar (Del.) Sch. Dist., 1973-88; reading specialist Accomack (Va.) County Schs., 1988-93; sch. adminstr., diagnostician Del. Dept. Svcs. for Children, Youth and Their Families, Middletown, Del., 1994—. Adj. prof. Del. State U., 1997—99, Wilmington Coll., 2000—; chairperson H.S. Reading Task Force, Del. Commn. on Reading Success, 1999. Mem.: ASCD, CEC, Cedar Shores Condominium Assn. (sec.), Internat. Reading Assn. (ea. regional conf. gen. conf. chair 1997—99, regional conf. com. 1999—), Del. Assn. Sch. Adminstrs., Diamond State Reading Assn. (pres. 1985—86, editor DSRA Reader), Nat. Assn. Secondary Sch. Prins., Lions Club (New Castle, Del., pres. 2001), Alpha Delta Kappa (past pres. Theta chpt. and Del.). Home: 33 E 6th St New Castle DE 19720-5087 Office: Silver Lake Treatment Ctr 493 E Main St Middletown DE 19709-1463 E-mail: jmartin@state.de.us., jmart000@aol.com.

MARTIN, JEANETTE ST. CLAIR, adult education educator; b. Jackson, Mich., Sept. 25, 1947; d. George Washington and Doris Janette (Robins) St. Clair; m. Stevens John Martin Jr., July 17, 1976; 1 child, Andrea Lynne. BA in Bus. Edn., Mich. State U., 1970; MBA in Mktg., U. Chgo., 1974; EdD in Curriculum and Instrn., U. Memphis, 1991. Product availability coord. Quaker Oats Co., Chgo., 1971-74; market analyst and inventory mgr. Robert Bosch Corp., Broadview, Ill., 1974-76; materials sys. analyst Zenith Corp., Chgo., 1976-77; purchasing rsch. analyst Baxter, Deerfield, Ill., 1977-78; owner Carriage Gallery, Memphis, 1981-85; instr. Shelby State Coll., 1986-90; instr., tchg. asst. U. Memphis, 1986-91; asst. prof. U. Miss., University, 1991-98, assoc. prof., 1999—. Cons. Sharp Corp., Memphis, 1989-90, Benchcraft, Blue Mountain, Miss., 1995, IPR, 1997—. Author: (with L. Chaney) Intercultural Business Communication, 1995, 2d edit., 2000. Mem. Intercultural Comm. Assn., Assn. Bus. Comm. (assoc. editor 1990—), Internat. Assn. Intercultural Rels. Republican. Episcopalian. Avocations: golf, swimming. Office: U Miss Sch Bus Adminstrn University MS 38677

MARTIN, JERRY HAROLD, bank examiner; b. Richwood, W.Va., Apr. 28, 1945; s. Weaver Eugene and Hazel Lee (Adkins) M.; m. Phyllis Lowe, Apr. 26, 1967 (div. 1980); m. Deborah Ann Perry, June 6, 1983 (div. 1994); children: Marlene, Renee; m. Mamie E. Scott, Mar. 1, 1994. BA in Econs., U. Charleston (W.Va.), 1967; Cert. Banking, La. State U., Baton Rouge, 1980. Asst. examiner Comptroller of the Currency, Charleston, 1969-74, bank examiner, 1974-77, examiner-in-charge, 1977-84, field mgr., 1984-97; banker Wesbanco Bank, 1998—; sr. fin. instn. examiner W.Va. Banking Divsn., 1998—. With U.S. Army, 1967-69. Recipient Cert. of Appreciation, Comptroller of Currency, 1986. Methodist. Avocations: jogging, coin collecting. Home: PO Box 3934 Charleston WV 25339-3934

MARTIN, JERRY LEE, organization executive, educator; b. Turkey, Tex., Oct. 16, 1941; m. Abigail L. Rosenthal, 1998. Student, San Diego State Coll., 1961; BA in Polit. Sci., U. Calif., Riverside, 1963; MA in Philosophy and Polit. Sci., U. Chgo., 1966; PhD in Philosophy, Northwestern U., 1970. Asst. prof. U. Colo., Boulder, 1967-74, chmn. dept. philosophy, 1979-81, assoc. prof., 1974-84, adjunct prof., 1984—; rsch. analyst House Rep. Rsch. Com., 1982-87; legis. asst. Congressman Hank Brown, 1982-87; dir. divsn. edn. programs NEH, Washington, 1987-88, asst. chmn. studies and evaluation, 1988-89, asst. chmn. programs and policy, 1989-95, acting chmn., 1993. Adj. prof. Georgetown U., 1993-95; adj. scholar Am. Enterprise Inst., 1993—; dir. Ctr. Study Values and Social Policy, U. Colo., Boulder, 1981-82; founding mem. organized rsch. program State of Colo., 1981-82; mem. exec. com. faculty adv. coun. Colo. Commn. Higher Edn., 1980-82; pres. Am. Coun. Trustees and Alumni, 1995—; spkr. in field, frequent guest on radio and TV. Contbr. articles to profl. jours. Mem. Gov.'s Blue Ribbon Commn. on Higher Edn., 1998—2000. Andrew W. Mellon Found. Congl. fellow, 1992-93. Mem. AAUP (state pres. 1977-79), Am. Philos. Assn., Soc. Historians Early Am. Republic, Am. Polit. Sci. Assn., Soc. Social, Polit. and Legal Philosophy. Avocations: tennis, baseball, hist. tours. Home: 145 C Selner Ln Doylestown PA 18901 Office: Am Coun Trustees and Alumni 1726 M Street NW # 800 Washington DC 20036

MARTIN, JOAN ELLEN, secondary education educator; b. Oak Park, Ill., Sept. 1, 1937; d. Emil and Jessie R. (Kotva) M. BS, North Cen. Coll., 1959; MA, Northwestern U., 1962; EdD, Okla. State U., 1983. Cert. tchr., phys. edn., adminstrn., driver edn. tchr., Ill. Tchr. Naperville (Ill.) Cen. High Sch., 1959-94, dept. chair, 1966-77. Instr. phys. edn. Triton Jr. Coll., Leyden, Ill., Naperville Pk. Dist., Girls Scouts, 1965-78; instr. Aurora U., 1997, Chgo. State U., 1999-2000. Contbr. articles to profl. jours. Established tchr. stress/burnout Cons. Svc. Naperville Ctrl. H.S., 1983; chmn. health edn. com. North Ctrl. Evaluatioin team Thornton Twp. H.S., Harvey, Ill., 1984; rep. Naperville Tchrs. Assn. Bldg., 1985-94. Recipient NASPE Pres. Citation, 1990, YWCA Outstanding Woman Leader in DuPage County (Atletics) award, 1988, Ill. Assn. Health Phys. Edn. Recreation and Dance Honor award, 1981, Naperville Sch. Dist. (twenty five yeard award, 1984), Am. Red Cross (ten year svc.) award, 1980, Ill. Presdl. citation, 1999, Midwest Dist. Presdl. citation, 2000; Humble Oil scholar, 1965. Mem. ASCD, NEA, AAHPERD (meritorious svc. award 1987, honor award 1995), Midwest Assn. Health Phys. Edn. Recreation and Dance (v.p. phys. edn. divsn. 1980, 81, v.p. gen. divsn. 1994-96, bd. dirs., v.p. health divsn. 1999-02, honor award 1998), Ill. Assn. Health, Phys. Edn. Recreation and Dance (ad hoc com., long range planning com., exec. bd. and rep. assembly, rsch. com. chmn., jour. mng. editor, conv. program chmn., Pepi, honor fellow, quarter century award), Secondary Sch. Phys. Edn. Soc. (v.p., pres.), Ill. Edn. Assn., U.S. Orienteering Assn., Chgo. Area Orienteering Assn., Naperville Tchrs. Assn., Ill. H.S. Coll. Driver Edn. Assn., Women's Sports Found., Phi Epsilon Kappa. Home: 317 Elmwood Dr Naperville IL 60540-7206

MARTIN, JOANNE, educator; b. Salem, Mass., Sept. 25, 1946; d. Richard Drake and Nathalie (Ashton) M.; m. Beaumont A. Sheil, July 9, 1977; 1 child, Beaumont Martin Sheil. BA, Smith Coll., 1968; PhD in Social Psychology, Harvard U., 1977; PhD in Econs. and Bus. Adminstrn. (hon.) , Copenhagen Bus. Sch., 2001. Assoc. cons. McBer & Co. (formerly Behavior Sci. Ctr. of Sterling Inst.), 1968-70, dir. govt. mktg., 1970-72; asst. prof. orgnl. behavior and sociology Grad. Sch. Bus., Stanford (Calif.) U., 1977-80; assoc. prof. grad. sch. bus. Stanford (Calif.) U., 1980-91, prof. grad. sch. bus., 1991—, dir. doctoral programs, grad. sch. bus., 1991-95, Fred H. Merrill prof. orgn. behavior and sociology, 1996—, vice-chair adv. bd., 1995—97. Vis. scholar Australian Grad. Sch. Mgmt. U. N.S.W., Copenhagen Bus. Sch., 1998; vis. scholar dept. psychology Sidney (Australia) U., 1989—90; Ruffin fellow bus. ethics Darden Grad. Sch. Bus. Adminstrn. U. Va., 1990; bd. dirs. Cons. Psychologists Press, Inc., iMahal, Internat. Ctr. for Rsch. in Orgnl. Discourse, Strategy and Change; guest lectr. dept. psychology MIT, 1976—77; cons. in field. Mem. editl. bd. Adminstrv. Sci. Qtrly., 1984—88, Jour. Social Issues, 1981—83, Acad. Mgmt. Jour., 1984—85, Social Justice Rsch., 1985—90, Jour. Mgmt. Inquiry, 1991—; co-author: five books; mem. editl. bd. Orgn., 1994—; contbr. articles to profl. jours. Lena Lake Forrest Rsch. fellowship Bus. and Profl. Women's Found., 1978, James and Doris McNamara Faculty fellowship Grad. Sch. of Bus., Stanford U., 1990-91. Fellow: APA, Grad. Sch. of Bus. Trust Faculty, Am. Psychol. Soc. (bd. dirs.), Acad. Mgmt. (rep.-at-large 1983—85, divsn. program chair 1985—87, divsn. chair 1987—89, bd. govs. 1992—95, we. divsn. Promising Young Scholar award 1982, Disting. Educator award 2000); mem.: Internat. Ctr. for Rsch. in Orgnl. Discourse, Strategy and Change (adv. bd. 2000—), Silicon Valley Chpt. of Nat. Assn. of Corp. Dir. (adv. bd. 2000—), Cons. Psychologists Press. Office: Stanford U Grad Sch Bus Littlefield Ctr 353 Stanford CA 94305

MARTIN, JOHN BRUCE, chemical engineer; b. Auburn, Ala., Feb. 2, 1922; s. Herbert Marshall and Lannie (Steadham) M.; m. Mildred Jane Foster, Aug. 7, 1943 (dec. Nov. 1960); children— Shirlie Martin Briggs, John Bruce; m. 2d, Phyllis Barbara Rodgers, June 25, 1963; 1 child, Richard Kipp BS, Ala. Poly. Inst., 1943; M.Sc., Ohio State U., 1947, PhD, 1949. Registered profl. engr., Ohio. With Procter & Gamble Co., Cin., 1949-82, coordinator orgn. devel., research and devel., 1967-77, mgr. indsl. chem. market research, 1977-82; sr. assoc. Indumar Inc., 1982-86, sr. v.p., 1986-87. Lectr. U. Cin., 1982-88; adj. assoc. prof. Auburn U., 1983-88. Author: Martin's Mini Mysteries, 1998; contbr. articles to profl. jours.; patentee in field Served with AUS, 1943-46 Decorated Air Medal, Bronze Star with oak leaf cluster; recipient Disting. Alumnus award Coll. Engring., Ohio State U., 1970, Disting. Engr. award Tech. Socs. Council Cin., 1982 Fellow AIChE (bd. dirs. 1968-70, chmn. mktg. divsn. 1985, Mktg. Hall of Fame 1988, Chem. Engr. of Yr. award Ohio Valley 1971); mem. Am. Chem. Soc., Am. Soc. Engring. Edn., Engring. Soc. Cin. (pres. 1972-73), Tech. and Sci. Socs. Cin. (pres. 1972-73), Comml. Devel. and Mktg. Assn., Soc. for Preservation and Encouragement of Barber Shop Quartet Singing in Am., Mystery Writers Am., Sisters in Crime, Sigma Xi, Tau Beta Pi, Phi Kappa Phi, Phi Lambda Upsilon. Republican. Presbyterian. Home: 644 Doepke Ln Cincinnati OH 45231-5045 E-mail: jbrucem@aol.com.

MARTIN, JOHN DRISCOLL, school administrator; b. Chgo., July 28, 1954; s. Walter Roy and Constance Kathleen (Driscoll) M.; children: Patrick, Kelsey; m. Caroline J. Martin, Mar. 28, 1996. BA, Augustana Coll., 1976; MA, Northwestern U., 1982. Cert. tchr., Ill. Tchr. J.D. Darnall High Sch., Geneseo, Ill., 1976-77, St. Viator High Sch., Arlington Heights, 1977-79, Hoffman Estates (Ill.) High Sch., 1979-88, athletic dir., 1988-90, Adlai E. Stevenson High Sch., Lincolnshire, Ill., 1990—. Adv. com. Ill. High Sch. Assn., Bloomington, 1989-92; master tchr. Gov.'s Master Tchr. Program, 1984—. Mem. AAHPERD, Ill. Assn. Health, Phys. Edn., Recreation and Dance, Nat. Athletic Adminstrs. Assn., Ill. Athletic Dirs. Assn. (conf. chair 1995, cert. athletic adminstr.). Avocations: golf, reading. Office: 1 Stevenson Dr Lincolnshire IL 60069-2824 E-mail: jmartin@district125.k12.il.us.

MARTIN, J(OHN) EDWARD, architectural engineer; b. L.A., Oct. 23, 1916; s. Albert C. and Carolyn Elizabeth (Borchard) M.; m. Elizabeth Jane Hines, May 27, 1944; children: Nicolas Edward, Peter Hines, Sara Jane McKinley Reynolds, Christopher Carey, Elizabeth Margaret Ferguson. Student, U. So. Calif., 1934-36; BS in Archtl. Engring., U. Ill., 1939. Registered profl. engr., Calif., Ill. Structural engr. Albert C. Martin & Assocs., L.A., 1939-42, ptnr., 1945-75, mng. ptnr., 1975-86. Founding mem. bd. trustees Thomas Aquinas Coll., Santa Paula, Calif., 1971-98, emeritus, 1998. Lt. USNR, 1942-45. Fellow ASCE; mem. Structural Engrs. Assn. Calif., Cons. Engrs. Assn. Calif., Jonathan Club (bd. dirs. 1978-81), Calif. Club, Ranchero Visitadores, Valley Hunt Club, Flintridge Riding Club, West Hills Hunt Club (Master of Fox Hounds 1975-88), Saddle & Sirloin Club, Heritage Found., Traditional Mass Soc. (founder), Pacific Legal Found. (charter). Republican. Roman Catholic. Avocation: horsemanship. E-mail: bzmartin@pacbellnet. Office: AC Martin Ptnrs 444 S Flower St Los Angeles CA 90017-3475 Fax: 626-440-0889.

MARTIN, JOHN JOSEPH, journalist; b. N.Y.C., Dec. 3, 1938; s. John and Marie Agnes (Jacobsen) M.; children from previous marriage: Sophie Suzanne, Claire Catherine; m. Katherine Fitzhugh, Feb. 14, 1987. BA in Journalism, San Diego State U., 1995. Copy editor, reporter San Diego Union, 1958-62; copy editor Augusta (Ga.) Chronicle, 1963, N.Y. Times Internat. Edit., Paris, 1964-65; editorial asst. Temple Fielding Publs., Mallorca, Spain, 1965-66; reporter, producer Sta. KCRA-TV News, Sacramento, 1966-75; corr. ABC-TV News, 1975—2002; Adjunct Prof., Journalism Columbia U., 2002—. Adj. prof. journalism Columbia U., 2002—. Editor, pub. Aztec Tennis Reporter, 1999—; contbg. writer Tennisone.com, 2000— Served with U.S. Army, 1962-64. Recipient Nat. Headliner awards, 1980, 89, NSPE award, 1982, Nat. Assn. Home Care award, 1992, Emmy award, 1993, George Polk award, 1994, DuPont-Columbia U. Gold baton, 1994, Nat. Assn. Black Journalists award, 2002. Mem. AFTRA, U.S. Tennis Assn., Coffee House Club N.Y.C., Nat. Press Club, Overseas Press Club, U.S. Tennis Writers Assn. Office: 1528 Corcoran St NW Washington DC 20009

MARTIN, JOHN L. airport executive; Dir. San Francisco Airport Commn. Office: San Francisco Airport Commn PO Box 8097 San Francisco CA 94128-8097*

MARTIN, JOHN LEWIS, state legislator; b. Eagle Lake, Maine, June 5, 1941; s. Frank and Edwidge (Raymond) M. BA in History and Govt., U. Maine, 1963, postgrad., 1963-64. Tchr. Am. govt. and history Ft. Kent (Maine) Community High Sch., 1966-72; instr. U. Maine, Ft. Kent, 1972-89, asst. prof., 1989—; mem. from Eagle Lake and St. Francis dist. Maine Ho. of Reps., 1964-94, minority fl. leader, 1970-74, speaker of ho., 1975-94, chmn. com. on energy & natural resources, 1994-95, mem. from dist. 151, 1998-2000. Mem. Maine Senate, Dist. 1, 2000—; chmn. Com. Natural Resources, 1999-2000; adj. lectr.; mem. intergovtl. rels. com. Nat. Legis. Conf., 1970-74; chmn. Maine Land Use Regulation Commn., 1972-73, Maine Bur. Human Rels., 1972, State Legis. Leaders Found., 1979-83; mem. exec. bd. Nat. Conf. State Legislatures, chmn. state-fed. assembly, 1985-86, chair task force on reapportionment, 1987-88, vice chmn. budget, fiscal and rules com., 1986-87, v.p., 1988-89, pres.-elect, 1989-90, pres., 1990-91, immediate past pres., 1991-92; mem. exec. com. New Eng. Caucus of State Legislatures, 1978-95, chmn., 1982; mem. regional exec. com. Nat. Dem. State Legis. Leaders Assn., 1991-95, chmn., 1987-89; bd. dirs. Found. for State Legislatures, 1988-94; mem. exec. com. Dem. Nat. Com., 1991-94. Trustee Eagle Lake Water and Sewer Dist., 1966—, No. Maine Gen. Hosp., Ft. Kent, Ea. Maine Health Care, 1991-92; mem. rural health steering com. Nat. Acad. for State Health Policy; advisor White House Task Force on Health Care Reform; dir. intergovtl. affairs Nat. Health Care Campaign, 1994. Mem. New Eng. Polit. Sci. Assn. Home: PO Box 250 Eagle Lake ME 04739-0250 Office: Maine Senate State House Augusta ME 04333-0003

MARTIN, JOHN STEWART, software engineer; b. Tacoma, June 20, 1965; s. Richard and Catherine Jesse (Stewart) M.; m. Tami Renee Ewing, Feb. 25, 1992 (div. 1999); 1 child, Devon Irene. Adrd. high sch., Portland, Oreg. Rsch. asst. Inst. Neurosci. U. Oreg., Eugene, 1990-93; asst. dir. software devel. Covox, Inc., 1993-95; pres. EIJA, Inc., 1995-2000; software engr. Maxim. Group, Portland, Oreg., 2000—. Creator: (Internet virtual world) Singlenesia, 1991. Mem. Eugene Area C. of C. Avocations: radio controlled model aircraft, collecting music, robotics. E-mail: jmartin@mindless.com.

MARTIN, JOHN SWANSON, retired educator; b. Sulligent, Ala., May 7, 1939; s. Judson Roby and Frances Susan (Rutland) M.; m. Linda Ferrell Isaacs, June 3, 1978; 1 child, Belinda Frances. AA, Marion (Ala.) Mil. Inst., 1959; BA, Livingston U., 1961; MEd, Auburn U., 1965; EdS, U. Ala., 1975. Tchr., chmn. social studies dept. W.P. Davidson H.S., Mobile, Ala., 1961-92, dept. chmn., 1962-92; ret., 1992; instr. U. Ala., summers 1973-75; tchr. Internat. Lang. Sch./Mobile Bapt. Assn., Mobile, 1992—, Jesus Film Project, Russia, 1993, Bulgaria, 1994, Nicaragua, 1995, Republic of Macedonia, 1996, Tanzania, 1997, Uganda, 1998, Republic of Georgia, 1999, M-Fuge Project, London, 2000, Mongolia, 2001, India, 2002. Contbg. author publs. in field. Adv. com. sch. bd. race, Mobile County Pub. Schs.; sponsor, mem. adv. bd. Fellowship of Christian Athletes Davidson H.S., Mobile; deacon, vice-chmn. deacon fellowship Dauphin Way Bapt. Ch., Mobile; mem. steering com. Cottage Hill Christian Acad. H.S.; So. Baptist projects, Mongolia 2001, India 2002. Recipient award for work with driver edn. Chrysler Corp., Outstanding Tchr. award Davidson Key Club, 1990, others; spl. recognition support Davidson NJROTC 1978-79 and 1980-81. Mem. NEA, Ala. Edn. Assn., Mobile County Edn. Assn. (past treas., exec. bd.), Retired Tchrs. of Ala., Retired Tchrs. of Mobile County, Nat. Coun. for Social Studies, Ala. Coun. for Social Studies, Mobile County Coun. for Social Studies (v.p. 1977-78), Ala. Hist. Assn., Capstone Coll. of Edn. Soc., Livingston Alumni Assn. (v.p. local chpt.), Phi Delta Kappa.

MARTIN, JOHN THOMAS, physician, author, educator; b. Cleve., June 8, 1924; s. Clarence Henry and Clara May (Feeney) M.; m. Marion Elizabeth George, Feb. 18, 1946; children: Thomas R., David B., Richard G., Janet E., Patricia L., Robert W. MD, U. Cin., 1948. Commd. 1st lt. USAF, 1949, advanced through grades to maj., 1953; resident in anesthesiology Lackland AFB Hosp., San Antonio, 1953-55; asst. chief USAF Sch. Anesthesiology, Lackland AFB, 1955-57; attending anesthesiologist Baylor U. Hosp., Dallas, 1957-58; cons. dept. anesthesiology Mayo Clinic, Rochester, Minn., 1958-72, head Meth sect. anesthesiology, 1966-72; assoc. clin. prof. anesthesiology, 1968-72; chmn. dept. anesthesiology Ochsner Med. Ctr., New Orleans, 1972-74; clin. assoc. prof. anesthesiology Tulane U. Sch. Medicine, 1972-74; prof. anesthesiology Med. Coll. Ohio, Toledo, 1974-90, chmn. dept. anesthesiology, 1980-89, emeritus prof. anesthesiology, 1990—. Editor, author: Positioning Patients Anesthesia/Surgery, 1978, 2d edit., 1987, 3d edit., 1997; editor ASA Handbook of Hosp. Facilities for Anesthesia, 1972, 2d edit., 1974; contbr. articles to profl. jours. Chmn. conductor selection com. Rochester Symphony Orch., 1963-66; pres. Rochester Civic Music, 1965. Mem. Internat. Anesthesia Rsch. Soc. (chmn. 1979-81, trustee 1965-90), Minn. Soc. Anesthesiologists (pres. 1966-67), Ohio Soc. Anesthesiologists (pres. 1988-89), Am. Med. Writers Assn. (pres. Minn. chpt. 1970-71), Assoc. Physicians Med. Coll. Ohio (bd. dirs. 1974-89), Am. Soc. Anesthesiology, Sigma Xi, Alpha Omega Alpha, Sigma Chi, Phi Chi. Republican. Avocations: medical writing, computers, music, fishing. Home: 4605 Woodland Ln Sylvania OH 43560-3221 Office: Med Coll of Ohio PO Box 10008 Toledo OH 43699-0008

MARTIN, JOHN WILLIAM, JR. retired lawyer, automotive industry executive; b. Evergreen Park, Ill., Sept. 1, 1936; s. John William and Frances (Hayes) M.; m. Joanne Cross, July 2, 1966; children: Amanda Hayes, Bartholomew McGuire. AB in History, DePaul U., 1958, JD, 1961. Bar: Ill. 1961, D.C. 1962, N.Y. 1964, Mich. 1970. Antitrust trial atty. Dept. Justice, Washington, 1961-62; assoc. Donovan, Leisure, Newton & Irvine, N.Y.C., 1962-70; sr. atty. Ford Motor Co., Dearborn, Mich., 1970-72, assoc. counsel, 1972-74, counsel, 1974-76, asst. gen. counsel, 1976-77, assoc. gen. counsel, 1977-89, v.p., gen. counsel, 1989-99; ret., 1999. Trustee DePaul U., 1998—; bd. dirs. Ctr. Social Gerontology, Inc., Nat. Women's Law Ctr. Contbr. articles to profl. jours. Mem. Assn. Gen. Counsel, Am. Law Inst. Coun., Little Traverse Yacht Club. Republican. Roman Catholic. E-mail: jwmartinjrsail@netscape.net.

MARTIN, JOHNNY BENJAMIN, accountant; b. Gainesville, Ga., June 9, 1947; s. John Daniel and Helen Amanda (Meeks) M.; m. Mary Sue West, June 8, 1969; 1 child, Tammy Michelle. BBA, U. Ga., Athens, 1969, MA, 1971. CPA, Ga. Tchr. high sch. Hall County Sch. Systems, Gainesville, 1969-70; instr. acctg. Austin Peay State U., Clarksville, Tenn., 1972-76; instr. bus. Gainesville Jr. Coll., 1976-77; contr. Home Fed. Savs. and Loan, Gainesville, 1977-83; ptnr. Kendrick & Jessup, CPA's, 1983-92; pvt. practice, 1992—. Mem. AICPA, Ga. Soc. CPAs, Civitan (bd. dirs., treas. 1981-82, treas. 1986-87), Phi Kappa Phi, Beta Gamma Sigma. Democrat. Baptist. Home: 3751 Robinson Dr Oakwood GA 30566-3408 E-mail: Jmartin512@aol.com.

MARTIN, JOSÉ GINORIS, education administrator; b. Feb. 4, 1941; married; two children. BS in Nuclear Engring. with honors, Miss. State U., 1964; MS in Nuclear Engring., U. Wis., 1966, PhD in Engring., 1970; MDP, Harvard U., 1997. Asst. prof. U. Mass., Lowell, 1975-77, assoc. prof., 1977-79, prof. energy engring., 1979—, grad. coord. for energy engring., 1984-90; chmn. chem. and nuclear engring. dept. Coll. of Engring., U. Mass., 1990-96; dean Coll. Sci., Math and Tech. U. Tex., Brownsville, 1996—2000, provost and v.p. acad. affairs, 2000—. Bd. dirs. Enersol, Inc., Tech Prep of the Rio Grande Valley, Inc., Valley Regiona Hosp.; Fulbright prof. Curso de Postgraduacão em Ecologia, U. Federale do Rio Crande do Sul, Porto Alegre, Brazil, 1995; vis. prof. Ariz. State U. Coll. of Architecture, 1983, U. Mex., 1976-77, I.M.E., Rio de Janeiro, 1973; dir. Mass. Photovoltaic Ctr., 1987-96; cons. Corp. for Energy Devel. of Andalucia, 1992-96, Corp. for the 1992 Universal Exposion in Seville, Spain, 1982-88; prin. gov.'s task force on energy Commonwealth of Mass., 1994. Contbr. numerous articles to profl. jours. Mem.: Sigma Xi. Home: RR 3 Box 12 Los Fresnos TX 78566-9710 E-mail: jmartin@utbl.utb.edu.

MARTIN, J(OSEPH) PATRICK, lawyer; b. Detroit, Apr. 19, 1938; s. Joseph A. and Kathleen G. (Rich) M.; m. Denise Taylor, June 27, 1964; children: Timothy J., Julie D. AB magna cum laude, U. Notre Dame, 1960; JD with distinction, U. Mich., 1963; postgrad., London Sch. Econs., 1964. Bar: Mich. 1963, U.S. Dist. Ct. (ea. dist.) Mich. 1963, U.S. Ct. Appeals (6th cir.) 1967, U.S. Supreme Ct. 1979, U.S. Dist. Ct. (we. dist.) Mich. 1981, U.S. Ct. Fed. Claims 1999. Spl. asst. to gen. counsel Ford Motor Co., Dearborn, Mich., 1962; assoc. Dykema, Wheat, Spencer et al, Detroit, 1963-66; assoc., then ptnr. Poole Littell Sutherland, 1966-76; sr. atty., ptnr., shareholder Butzel Long, Detroit and Birmingham, Mich., 1976-94; sr. atty., shareholder Vlcko, Lane, Payne & Broder PC, Bingham Farms, 1994-96; sr. atty. Gourwitz and Barr PC, Southfield, 1996-99; pvt. practice, 2000—. Adj. prof. remedies and alternative dispute resolution U. Detroit Law Sch., 1989—, Wayne State U. Law Sch., 1996—, Cooley Law Sch., 2001--; arbitrator Am. Arbitration Assn., Southfield, Mich., 1968—, Nat. Assn. Security Dealers, 1988—, N.Y. Stock Exch., 1991—; state court adminstrv. office approved mediator all Mich. Cts. under new ADR rules; case evaluator, discovery master Oak County Cir. Ct., Pontiac, Mich., 1985—; mediator Lex Mundi, Coll. of Mediators, 1992—; case evaluator, mediator Mediation Tribunal Assn. for Wayne County Cir. Ct., 1992—; moderator Mich. State Ct. Appeals, 1995—; case evaluator Oakland County Dist. Cts., 1998—. Author, editor: Laches-Oak County Bar Assn. Legal Jour., 1984, 92, 96, Real Property Rev., 1989-90, Mich. Law Weekly, 1990; ADR Newsletter, 2000. Scholar Cook Found., Ford Found., London, 1963-64. Mem. ABA, State Bar Mich. (chair alternative dispute sect.), Oakland County Bar Assn. (chair fed. ct. com., chair Mich. dist. ct com., ADR com.), Mich. State Bar Found. Roman Catholic. Avocations: gardening, golf, walking. Home and Office: 1663 Hoit Tower Dr Bloomfield Hills MI 48302-2630 Fax: 248-932-0368. E-mail: jpatrickmartin@aol.com.

MARTIN, JOSEPH ROBERT, financial executive; b. Phila., Dec. 9, 1947; s. Robert and Elva Ruth (Griffen) M.; m. Catherine Marie Kelly, Sept. 5, 1970; children: Joseph Robert Jr., Jennifer H., Patrick F., Kathleen K., Mariah E. BS, Embry Riddle U., 1974; MBA, U. Maine, 1976. Sr. corp. fin. analyst Keyes Fibre Co., Waterville, Maine, 1976-80; mgr. fin. analysis and planning Schlumberger, Fairchild, South Portland, 1980-83; div. contr. Schlumberger, Factron, Clifton Park, N.Y., 1983-84; corp. contr. VTC, Inc., Bloomington, Minn., 1984-87, v.p. fin., chief fin. officer, 1987-88, sr. v.p., chief fin. officer, 1989-90; dir. fin. Nat. Semiconductor, South Portland, Maine, 1990-91; v.p. fin. std. products group Nat. Semicondr., Santa Clara, Calif., 1991-95; v.p. fin. worldwide ops. Nat. Semiconductor, 1995-96; exec. v.p., CFO, bd. dirs. Fairchild Semiconductor, South Portland, Maine, 1996—. Bd. dirs. Brooks Automation, Inc., Synqor, Inc.; bd. visitors U. So. Maine, 1998-2001. Served to capt. U.S. Army, 1967-72, Vietnam. Decorated D.F.C., Purple Heart, Bronze Star medal, Air medal. Home: 17 Stornoway Rd Cumberland Foreside ME 04110 Office: Fairchild Semicondr Corp 82 Running Hill Rd South Portland ME 04106 E-mail: joseph.martin@fairchildsemi.com.

MARTIN, JOSEPH BOYD, neurologist, educator; b. Bassano, Alta., Can., Oct. 20, 1938; s. Joseph Bruce and Ruth Elizabeth (Ramer) Martin; m. Rachel Ann Wenger, June 18, 1960; children: Bradley, Melanie, Douglas, Neil. BSc, Eastern Mennonite Coll., Harrisonburg, Va., 1959; MD, U. Alta., 1962; PhD, U. Rochester, N.Y., 1971; MA (hon.), Harvard U., 1978; ScD (hon.), McGill U., 1994, U. Rochester, 1996, U. Wis., 1997, U. Alta., 1998. Resident in internal medicine Univ. Hosp., Edmonton, 1962—64; resident in neurology Case-Western Res. U. Hosps., 1964—67; rsch. fellow U. Rochester, NY, 1967—70; mem. faculty McGill U. Faculty Medicine, Montreal, Canada, 1970—78; prof. medicine and neurology, neurologist-in-chief Montreal Neurol. Inst., 1976—78; chmn. dept. neurology Mass. Gen. Hosp., Boston, also Dorn prof. neurology Harvard U. Med. Sch., 1978—89; dean Sch. Medicine U. Calif., San Francisco, 1989—93; chancellor U. Calif., 1993—97; dean faculty medicine Harvard U., Boston, 1997—. Mem. med. adv. bd. Gairdner Found., Toronto, 1978—83, Toronto, 1997—; adv. coun. neurol. disorders program Nat. Inst. Neurol., Communicative Disorders and Stroke, 1979—82. Co-author: Clinical Neuroendocrinology, 1977, The Hypothalamus, 1978, Clinical Neuroendocrinology: A Pathophysiological Approach, 1979, Neurosecretion and Brain Peptides: Implications for Brain Functions and Neurological Disease, 1981, Brain Peptides, 1983; editor: Harrison's Principles of Internal Medicine, 1980—99, Molecular Neurology, 1998—. Recipient Moshier Meml. gold medal, U. Alta. Faculty Medicine, 1962, John W. Scott gold med. award, 1962, Abraham Flexner award, AAMC, 1999; scholar, Med. Rsch. Coun. Can., 1970—75. Mem.: NAS, Inst. of Medicine, Am. Acad. Arts and Scis., Assn. Am. Physicians, Soc. Neurosci., Royal Coll. Phys. and Surg. Can., Am. Physiol. Soc. (Bowditch lectr. 1978), Am. Neurol. Assn. (pres. 1990). Office: Dean of the Faculty of Medicine Harvard U 25 Shattuck St Boston MA 02115-6027

MARTIN, JOSEPH VINSON, neurobiologist, educator; b. Boston, Sept. 17, 1952; s. James Cullen and Mary Louise (Echols) M.; m. Jean Ann Rusteberg, Apr. 27, 1989; 1 child, Lara Jean. BA, Northwestern U., 1973; PhD, U. So. Calif., 1987. Rsch. asst. L.A. Harbor Commn., 1978-79; chemist NIMH, Bethesda, Md., 1982-87; postdoctoral rsch. assoc. dept. psychiatry & behavioral sci. SUNY, Stony Brook, 1987-88, rsch. instr. dept. psychiatry and behavioral sci., 1988-89; asst. prof. zoology dept. biology Rutgers U., Camden, N.J., 1989-95, assoc. prof. zoology dept. biology, 1995—. Proposal reviewer NSF; manuscript reviewer European Jour. Pharmacology, Pharmacology Biochemistry and Behavior, Sleep; lectr. in field. Contbr. articles to profl. jours. Recipient Nat. Merit Letter of Commendation, 1969, NSF Undergrad. Summer Rsch. fellowship, 1972, NIMH Predoctoral Rsch. fellowship, 1977-78, Rutgers U. Acad. Svc. Increment award, 1991, 93, 98, NSF Rsch. grantee, 1994-97, 98—. Mem. AAAS, Assn. Profl. Sleep Socs., Internat. Brain Rsch. Orgn., N.J. Acad. Sci., N.Y. Acad. Scis., Sleep Rsch. Soc., Soc. for Neuroscience. Office: Dept Biology Rutgers Univ Camden NJ 08102 E-mail: jomartin@camden.rutgers.edu.

MARTIN, JUDITH SYLVIA, journalist, author; b. Washington, Sept. 13, 1938; d. Jacob and Helen (Aronson) Perlman; m. Robert Martin, Jan. 30, 1960; children: Nicholas Ivor, Jacobina Helen. BA, Wellesley Coll., 1959; DHL (hon.), York Coll., 1985, Adelphi U., 1991. Reporter-critic, columnist Washington Post, 1960—83; syndicated columnist United Feature Syndicate, N.Y.C., 1978—; columnist Microsoft, 1996—. Critic-at-large Vanity Fair, 1983-84. Author: The Name on the White House Floor, 1972, Miss Manners' Guide to Excruciatingly Correct Behavior, 1982, Gilbert, 1982, Miss Manners' Guide to Rearing Perfect Children, 1984, Common Courtesy, 1985, Style and Substance, 1986, Miss Manners' Guide for the Turn-of-the-Millennium, 1989, Miss Manners on (Painfully Proper) Weddings, 1996, Miss Manners Rescues Civilization, 1996, Miss Manners' Basic Training: Communications, 1997, Miss Manners' Basic Training: Eating, 1997, Miss Manners' Basic Training: The Right Thing to Say, 1998, Miss Manners' Guide to Domestic Tranquility, 1999. Bd. dirs. Washington Concert Opera, Friends of Scuola San Rocco. Mem. Cosmos Club, Literary Soc. Office: United Feature Syndicate 200 Madison Ave Fl 4 New York NY 10016-3911

MARTIN, JUNE JOHNSON CALDWELL, journalist; b. Toledo, Oct. 06; d. John Franklin and Eunice Imogene (Fish) Johnson; m. Erskine Caldwell, Dec. 21, 1942 (div. Dec. 1955); 1 child, Jay Erskine; m. Keith Martin, May 5, 1966. AA, Phoenix Jr. Coll., 1941; BA, U. Ariz., 1943, 59; postgrad., Ariz. State U., 1939, 40. Freelance writer, 1944—; columnist Ariz. Daily Star, Tucson, 1956-59, 70-94, book reviewer, 1970-94, co-founder Ann. Book and Author Event; editor Ariz. Alumnus mag., 1959-70; ind. book reviewer, audio tape columnist, 1994—; coord. S.W. Books of Yr. Tucson Pima Pub. Libr., 2000—. Panelist, co-producer TV news show Tucson Press Club, 1954-55, pres., 1958. Contbg. author: Rocky Mountain Cities, 1949; contbr. articles to World Book Ency., and various mags. Mem. Tucson CD Com., 1961; vol. campaigns of Samuel Goddard, U.S. Rep. Morris Udall, U.S. amb. and Ariz. gov. Raul. Castro. Recipient award Nat. Headliners Club, 1959, Ariz. Press Club award, 1957-59, 96, Am. Alumni Coun., 1966, 70. Mem. Nat. Book Critics Circle, Ariz. Press Women, Jr. League of Tucson, Tucson Urban League, PEN U.S.A. West, Planned Parenthood So. Ariz., Tucson Press, Pi Beta Phi. Democrat. Methodist. Home: Desert Foothills Sta PO Box 65388 Tucson AZ 85728-5388

MARTIN, KAREN SIEBENTHAL, community health nurse; b. Bloomington, Ill., Sept. 15, 1942; d. Arthur A. and Evelyn R. (Ehresman) Siebenthal; m. Stanley A. Martin, Mar. 31, 1963; children: Steven, Kathleen, Kelly. Diploma, Meth. Hosp. Sch. Nursing, 1963; BSN, U. Iowa Coll. Nursing, 1969; MS in Nursing, U. Nebr. Coll. Nursing, 1977. Staff nurse, dir. nursing Champaign (Ill.)-Urbana Pub. Health, 1966-67, 69-73; dir. rsch. Vis. Nurse Assn. Omaha, 1978-93. Prin. investigator Nat. Ctr. for Nursing Rsch., 1989—93; health care cons., 1993—; adj. prof. Midland Luth. Coll. Divsn. Nursing, Fremont, Nebr., 1994—; vis. prof. Japan and Taiwan, 1998, U.K., 2000—01, Ireland, 2001; workshops and cons. Europe, 1992—93, Canada, 1997, New Zealand, 2000; spkr. in field. Author: 4 books, 1 translated into Japanese; editor: Home Health Focus, 1994—2000; mem. editl. adv. bd.: Pub. Health Nursing, 1990—, mem. editl. bd.: Outcomes Mgmt. for Nursing, 1997—, mem. editl. bd.: Home Care Provider, 1996—, bd. of review: Nursing Outlook, 1990—; contbr. Recipient Alumnus of Yr. award Meth. Med. Ctr. of Cen. Ill. Sch. Nursing, Peoria, Ill., 1995. Mem.: Am. Acad. Nursing (expert panel on electronic networks 1995—97), APHA, ANA (Congress of Nursing Practice 1994—98, dist. bd. dirs. 1999—2001), Am. Med. Informatics Assn., Internat. Coun. Nurses (internat. classification of nursing practice adv. com. 1994—), Midwest Nursing Rsch. Soc., N.Am. Nursing Diagnosis Assn., Sigma Theta Tau.

MARTIN, KATHLEEN L. military officer, hospital administrator; BSN, Boston U., 1973; MS in Nursing Adminstrn., U. San Diego, 1992. Commd. ensign USN, 1973; advanced through grades to rear admiral Nat. Naval Med. Ctr.; staff nurse, then charge nurse in pediats. Naval Hosp., Camp Lejeune, NC, 1973—76, charge nurse pediat. ward Jacksonville, Fla., 1979—82; med. programs officer Navy Recruiting Dist., Phila., 1976—79; divsn. officer mil. medicine, credentials coord., risk mgr., quality assurance coord. Naval Med. Clinic, Pearl Harbor, Hawaii, 1982—86; head amb. med. nursing dept. Naval Hosp., San Diego, 1986—90; dir. nursing svcs. Naval Med. Clinic, Port Hueneme, 1992—93, commdg. officer, 1993—95, Naval Hosp., Charleston, SC, 1995—98, med. inspector gen., 1998—99; 19th dir. Navy Nurse Corps, 1998—99; comdr. Nat. Naval Med. Ctr., Bethesda, Md., 1999—. Decorated Legion of Merit (3), Def. Meritorious Svc. medal, Meritorious Svc. medal, Navy Commendation medal. Mem.: Assn. Mil. Surgeons of the U.S., Am. Acad. Amb. Care Nursing, Am. Coll. Healthcare Execs., Sigma Theta Tau. Office: National Naval Med Ctr 8901 Wisconsin Ave Bethesda MD 20889-5600*

MARTIN, KELLIE (NOELLE), actress; b. Riverside, Calif., Oct. 16, 1975; Movie and motion picture actress. Actress T.V. series Life Goes On, 1989, (voice) Taz-Mania, 1992, Christy, 1994-1995, Crisis Ctr., 1997, ER, 1998-2000, others; movies and TV movies include Jumpin' Jack Flash, 1986, Secret Witness, 1988, Troop Beverly Hills, 1989, Matinee, 1993, If Someone Had Known, 1995, Her Last Chance, 1996, On The Edge of Innocence, 1997, About Sarah, 1999, All You Need, 2001; voice characterization A Goofy Movie, 1995, also T.V. guest appearances. Office: c/o The Gersh Agy 232 N Canon Dr Beverly Hills CA 90210-5302*

MARTIN, KENNETH FRANK, insurance company executive; b. Milw., Feb. 27, 1948; s. John Fred Martin and Paula Christine (Lochstampfer) Rodgers; m. Patricia Ann Liggett, Dec. 23, 1970; children: Theodore Dieter, Oliver Derek. Student, U. Wis., Oshkosh, 1966-69, Career Acad. Broadcasting, Milw., 1969. Lic. Tex. ins. group I, HMO; registered health underwriter. Radio announcer Sta. KRGI, Grand Island, Nebr., 1970, Sta. WLVA, Lynchburg, Va., 1970-71; freelance writer Milw., 1971-73; radio journalist Stas. WRIT, WBCS, 1973-74, Sta. KTRH, Houston, 1974-75; with ins. sales staff Combined Am. Ins. Co., 1975-77; with office equipment sales staff Pitney Bowes, 1977-80; owner Bayou Benefits Group (formerly The Ken Martin Co.), 1980-96, Sr. Security of Tex., Houston, 1995-96; pres. Bayou Benefits Group, Inc., from 1996. Corr. Moscow Bus. Jour. Report, Open Radio AM 918, 1993. Nation chief, pres. Indian Guides Westside Family YMCA, Houston, 1987-89, trail guide, pres. Trailblazers, 1990-96; judge Westside Swim League, Houston, 1990; umpire, coach, mgr. Meml. Ashford Little League, 1993—; bd. dirs. Greater Houston YMCA Camping Svcs., 1991-95. Named Vol. of Yr. YMCA of Greater Houston Area, 1989. Mem. Nat. Assn. Health Underwriters (comm. com. 1999-2001, named to Pres.'s Coun. Leading Prodrs. Round Table 1991-99, Nat. Conv. master of ceremonies Atlanta 1996, Disting. Svc. award 1998), Houston Assn. Health Underwriters (bd. dirs. 1991-92, 2d v.p. 1992-93, pres.-elect 1993-94, pres. 1994-95, immediate past pres. 1995-96, trustee 1996—, Kowalski Meml. award for Excellence 1997), Tex. Assn. Health Underwriters (bd. dirs. 1996—, sec. 2000-01, Outstanding Texan award 1997, Ken Martin and Hollis Roberson awards 2001). Avocations: youth leadership, auto racing. Home: Houston, Tex. Died Oct. 10, 2001.

MARTIN, KEVIN DOUGLAS, surgeon; b. Kansas City, Mo., Oct. 26, 1955; BA, MS, Northwestern U., 1978; MD, Vanderbilt U., 1982. Diplomate Am. Bd. Surgery. Resident in surgery Vanderbilt Med. Ctr., Nashville, 1982-84, Baystate Med. Ctr., Springfield, 1984-87; fellow in vascular surgery U. Cin., 1987—; mem. staff Good Samaritan Hosp., Cin., St. Elizabeth, Edgewood, Ky., St. Luke's Hosp., Ft. Thomas. Mem. Internat. Soc. for Endovascular Surgery, Peripheral Vascular Surgery Soc., Midwest Vascular Surgery Soc., Ky. Med. Soc., Ohio State Med. Assn., Cranley Surg. Assocs., Am. Assn. for Vascular Surgery, Am. Coll. Surgeons. Office: Ste 355 20 Medical Village Dr Covington KY 41017

MARTIN, KEVIN J. federal agency administrator; m. J. Catherine Martin. BA, U. N.C., Chapel Hill; M Pub. Policy, Duke U.; JD, Harvard U. Bar: Fla., D.C. Ud. clk. Judge William M. Hoeveler U.S. Dist. Ct., Miami; assoc. Wileu, Rein & Fielding, Washington; with Office Ind. Counsel; advisor commr. Harold Furchtgott-Roth FCC; deputy gen. counsel Bush Campaign; with transition team Bush-Cheney; commr. FCC, 2001. Mem.: D.C. Bar Assn., Fla. Bar Assn., Fed. Comm. Bar Assn. Office: FCC 445 12th St SW Washington DC 20554*

MARTIN, KEVIN JOHN, nephrologist, educator; b. Dublin, Ireland, Jan. 18, 1948; came to U.S., 1973; s. John Martin and Maura Martin; m. Grania E. O'Connor, Nov. 16, 1972; children: Alan, John, Ciara, Audrey. MB BCh, Univ. Coll. Dublin, 1971. Diplomate Am. Bd. Internal Medicine, Am. Bd. Nephrology. Intern St. Vincent's Hosp., Dublin, 1971-72, resident, 1972-73, Barnes Hosp., St. Louis, 1973-74, fellow, 1974-77; asst. prof. Washington U., 1977-84, assoc. prof., 1984-89; prof., dir. div. nephrology St. Louis U., 1989—. Contbr. numerous articles to med. jours. Office: Saint Louis Univ Med Ctr 3635 Vista Ave Saint Louis MO 63110-2539

MARTIN, KIM See MARTH, MARY

MARTIN, KIMBERLY SUE, critical care nurse, educator; b. Pitts., Aug. 24, 1966; d. Raymond R. and Helen G. (Tawney) Coughanour; m. Curtis L. Martin, June 4, 1989; 1 child, Carolyn Nicole. BSN, Carlow Coll., Pitts., 1988; MSN, U. Phoenix, 2000. CCRN, Fla.; BLS, Fla.; ACLS, Fla.; ACLS instr., Fla. Nurse technologist Montefiore Hosp., Pitts., 1987-88, staff nurse II, 1988-89; staff nurse Halifax Hosp. Med. Ctr., Daytona Beach, Fla., 1989-92, Humana Hosp., Daytona Beach, 1991-92, Meml. Hosp.-Ormond Beach, Fla., 1992-94, asst. dir. nursing, 1994-96, adminstrv. coord., 1996—2001; staff nurse ICU Meml. Hosp. Peninsula, Ormond Beach, 2001—. Asst. prof. Daytona Beach C.C., 1991-2000, skills lab. coord., 2001—. Mem.: AACN (sec. Volusia Flagler chpt. 1993—95, bd. dirs. 1997—98, 2000—01, pres. elect 2001—02). Home: 49 Wicksfield Ct Ormond Beach FL 32174-4849 Office: Daytona Beach CC Dept Nursing 2811 Internat Spdwy Blvd Daytona Beach FL 32120-2811 E-mail: martink@dbcc.cc.fl.us., kimberlymartin@bellsouth.net.

MARTIN, KIMBRA, editor, writer; d. Francis Foster Farnworth and Mary Belle Nelson; m. David Joseph Martin, Apr. 18, 1998; m. Daniel Dennis Phillips, July 2, 1983 (div. May 30, 1989); 1 child Daniel Bracken Phillips. AA, Mesa Coll., San Diego, 1978. Assoc. editor Amateur Chief Mag., Newark, 1999—2001; poetry editor Small Spiral Notebook, 2001—. Author: (book) Snapshots, A Rare Look at Childhood Trauma and Abuse, 1999. Dir. Planned Parenthood So. Oreg., Grants Pass, 1987—89. Liberal. Avocation: cooking.

MARTIN, KIRK L. writer; b. Balt., Mar. 1, 1966; s. James Hamilton and Nancy Lee Martin; m. Anita J. Perkins, Dec. 30, 1989; children: Casey. BS in Internat. Bus. and Mktg., Towson U., 1988. Mktg. cons. Cantwell-Hamilton, Greensboro, NC, 1992—2002. Author: (novels) Shade of the Maple, 2002. Spokesperson Friends You Can Count On, Greensboro, 2001—02; vol. Big Bros., Chattanooga, 1996—98. Business E-Mail: kirkmartin@shadeofthemaple.com.

MARTIN, LARRY D. technical manager; b. Saginaw, Mich., June 10, 1955; s. Orville J. and Louise J. Martin; m. Annette M. Jedlowski; children: Jenna, Shane. AAS in Machine Tool Tech., Ferris State U., Big Rapids, Mich., 1976, BS in Mfg. Engring., 1980. Project engr. United Def., San Jose, 1980—93, Mpls., 1993—96; bus. unit mgr. FMC, Material Handling Divsn., Homer City, Pa., 1996—2000; tech. mgr. Allen Systems, FMC Technologies Inc., Newberg, Oreg., 2000—. Mem.: Internat. Mgmt. Counsel, Soc. of Mfg. Engrs. (treas. 1975—76). Home: 16966 Summer Pl Lake Oswego OR 97035 Office: Allen Systems, FMC Technologies Inc. 500 E Illinois St Newberg OR 97132 Business E-Mail: larry.martin@fmcti.com.

MARTIN, LAURA BELLE, real estate and farm land owner and manager; b. Jackson County, Minn., Nov. 3, 1915; d. Eugene Wellington and Mary Christina (Hanson) M. BS, Mankato State U., 1968. Tchr. rural schs., Renville County, Minn., 1936-41, 45-50, Wabasso (Minn.) Pub. Sch., 1963-81; pres. Renville Farms and Feed Lots, 1982-86. Author: Historical Biography of Joseph Renville, 1996; published poet Nat. Libr. Poetry. Pres. Wabasso (Minn.) Edn. Assn., 1974-75, publicity chmn., 1968-74; sec. and publicity agt. Hist. Renville Preservation Com., 1978-86; publicity chmn., sec. Town and Country Boosters, Renville, 1982-83. Mem. Genealogy Soc. Renville County, Am. Legion Aux. Democrat. Lutheran. Avocations: antique furniture, travel, sewing, writing poetry. Home and Office: 334 NW 1201st Rd Holden MO 64040-9378

MARTIN, LELAND MORRIS (PAPPY MARTIN), history educator; b. Patrick Springs, Va., Aug. 8, 1930; s. Rufus Wesley and Mary Hilda (Biggs) M.; m. Mildred Greer, May 12, 1956; children: Lee Ann Martin Powell, Mitzi Jo. AB, Berea Coll., 1953; MS, U. Tenn., 1954; grad., Air War Coll., Maxwell AFB, Ala., 1978; MA in History, U Tex. Pan-Am., 1993; cert. machinist, Tex. State Tech. Coll., 1997, AAS in Machining Technology-Tool and Die Making, 1999. Enlisted USAF, 1954, advanced through grades to col., 1977; comdr. RAF, Greenham Common, Welford, 1974-76; comdt., comdr. Mil. Airlift Command Noncommisioned Officers Acad., McGuire AFB, N.J., 1976-79; vice comdr., comdr. RAF Mildenhall and RAF Chicksands, Eng., 1979-83; chief of staff 21st Air Force, McGuire AFB, 1983-84; pres. Air Force Phys. Evaluation Bd., Randolph AFB, N.J., 1984-86; ret., 1986; dep. exec. dir. Confederate Air Force, Harlingen, Tex., 1986-88; exec. dir. Am. Airpower Heritage Found., 1986-88; tchg. asst., lectr. in history U. Tex. Pan Am., Edinburg, 1989-93; adj. prof. history Tex. State Tech. Coll., Harlingen, 1994—2001. Co-chair (with Sir Douglas Bader) 1976 Internat. Air Tatoo at RAF Greenham Common; chair Air Fete 80 and 81, RAF Mildenhall, Eng. Co-editor: History of Military Assistance Command, Vietnam, 1970. Decorated Legion of Merit with two oak leaf clusters, Bronze Star; Cross of Gallantry (Vietnam); recipient Amb.'s award Ct. St. James, London, 1974, 83. Mem. Air Force Assn., Am. Watchmakers Inst., Nat. Assn. Watch and Clock Collectors, Brit. Officers Club Phila. (hon.), Rotary (gov. internat. dist. 5930 1995-96), Order of Daedalians, Phi Alpha Theta, Phi Kappa Phi Republican. Presbyterian. Avocations: clock repairs, photography, golf, fishing. Home: 3001 Emerald Lake Dr Harlingen TX 78550-8621 Office: Tex State Tech Coll Dept History Harlingen TX 78550-3697

MARTIN, LEONARD AUSTIN, II, music educator; b. McCook, Nebr., July 18, 1949; s. Austin Berwell and Marie Elizabeth (Kimbro) M. BA summa cum laude, Metro State Coll. Denver, 1971; MA, Denver U., 1972, PhD, 1984. Cert. tchr., adminstr., Colo. Music instr. Cross Exec. Sch. Music, Aurora, Colo., 1965—, Peetz (Colo.) elem. and secondary schs., 1972, 5 area sch. dists., Denver, 1973, Adams County Sch. Dist. 12, Denver, 1974-94. Prof. U. Colo., Denver, 1990—, U. No. Colo., 1996—, Adams State Coll., 1996—, U. Phoenix, 1997—; mem. faculty tchr. edn. program U. Denver, 1994—, prof. Educator's Inst., 1994—; presenter in field. Author: High School Music Theory, 1978, Basic Music Theory, 1989, A Curriculum for Educational Licensure, 1994; contbr. articles to profl. jours. Youth choir dir. Faith Presbyn. Ch., Aurora, 1973-75, substitute dir. adult choir, 1987-90; mem. worship team, mem. choir Cornerstone Cmty. Ch., Glendale, Colo., 1991-93; substitute dir., Presbyn. Ch. Aurora, 1995-97 (choir dir. 1998—); cornetist Aurora Summer Cmty. Band, 1965-71; mem. Colo. All-State Band, 1967; choir dir. Aurora First Presbyn. Ch., 1998—; lay preacher Presbyn. Ch. and Care Ctr., 2000—. Mem. NEA, ASCD, Colo. Edn. Assn., Music Educators Nat. Conf., Colo. Music Educators Assn., Denver Musicians Soc. (pres.), Nat. Geog. Soc. Republican. Presbyterian. Avocations: collecting chime/strike clocks, elephants, silent 8 mm movies, swimming, bowling. E-mail: leomarti@du.edu.

MARTIN, LEONARDO S.J. urologist, surgeon; b. Macati, Rizal, The Philippines, Nov. 26, 1926; came to U.S., 1953; s. Nemesio Martin and Felicidad San Juan; m. Helen Mary Dougherty, May 24, 1958; children: Leonard, John and David (twins), Mark, Regina Mary Martin Dawson, Daniel. AA, U. The Philippines, 1947; MD, U. Santo Tomas, Manila, The Philippines, 1952. Diplomate Am. Bd. Urology; cert. physician and surgeon, Calif. Resident in urology Phila. Gen. Hosp., 1954-57; fellow in urology Mass. Gen. Hosp., Boston, 1957-59; urologist Manila Specialists Med. Ctr., 1959-63; instr. urology U. Santo Tomas, 1959-63; assoc. cancer urologist Roswell Pk. Meml. Hosp., Buffalo, 1963-65; urologist Sunnyvale (Calif.) Med. Ctr., 1965-94; mem. clin. tchg. staff Stanford (Calif.) Med. Ctr., 1965-94; cons. urology Los Altos, 1994—. Commr., med. expert Calif. Med. Bd. Licensure, Sacramento, 1987-2000. Contbr. some 40 articles to profl. jours. Bd. dirs. Flint Cultural Ctr., Cupertino, Calif., 1970-80; mem adv. bd. Santa Clara County unit Boys and Girls Club Am. Named one of 10 Outstanding Young Men, Jaycees, The Philippines, 1960, Disting. Men of Medicine, U. The Philippines Coll. Medicine, 1960. Fellow ACS (cert. merit 1964); mem. AMA (cert. Inc. merit 1964), Am. Urol. Assn. (AUA, Inc. cert. merit 1964), Am. Assn. Clin. Urologists, Philippine-Am. Urol. Soc. (founding pres. 1972), U. Santo Tomas Med. Alumni Assn. in Am. (pres. 1996-97, Most Outstanding Alumnus of Yr. 2000). Republican. Roman Catholic. Avocations: oil painting, piano and organ, stained glass, tennis, golf. Home and Office: 1931 Deodara Dr Los Altos CA 94024-7055

MARTIN, LESLIE, performing arts association administrator; 3d v.p. Am. Dance Guild, N.Y.C. Office: American Dance Guild Inc PO Box 2006 Lenox Hill Station New York NY 10021*

MARTIN, L(ESLIE) JOHN, retired journalism educator and dean; b. Budapest, Hungary, Jan. 5, 1921; came to U.S., 1948; s. Joseph and Elizabeth Caroline Martin; m. Lois Ann Henze, Mar. 22, 1951; children: Keith Douglas, Brian John. BA, Am. U., Cairo, 1947; postgrad., U. Oreg., 1948-49; MA, U. Minn., 1951, PhD, 1955. Corr., reporter, editor various newspapers, London, Paris, others, 1941-47; asst. prof. comm. U. Nebr., Lincoln, 1954-57; copy editor, night editor Detroit Free Press, 1957-58; prof. comm. U. Fla., Gainesville, 1958-61; divsn. chief, overseas rsch. dir. USIA, Washington, 1961-69; prof. internat. and cross-cultural comm., rsch. methods in mass communication, public opinion and propaganda U. Md., College Park, 1969-89, prof. emeritus, 1989—, dir. grad. studies, 1974-79, 82-89, dean Coll. Journalism, 1975, 79-80, assoc. dean, 1988-89, dir. PhD program in pub. comm., 1983-85, faculty ombuds officer, 1999—. Author: International Propaganda: Its Legal and Diplomatic Control, 1958, rev. edits., 1969, 94, (Sigma Delta Chi nat. award 1959); editor: (with A. Chaudhury) Comparative Mass Media Systems, 1983, (in Arabic) 1991, (in Malaysian) 1997, (with R. Hiebert) Current Issues in International Communication, 1990, 3 other books; contbr. 20 chpts. to books; contbr. 3 encys.; contbr. numerous articles to profl. jours. and conf. procs. Recipient Disting. Svc. to Internat. Comm. award, Assn. Edn. in Journalism and Mass Comm., Washington, 1989. Mem. Kappa Tau Alpha. Avocations: reading, writing, travel, walking, computers. Home: 5313 Iroquois Rd Bethesda MD 20816-3104 Office: U Md Office Of Pres College Park MD 20742-0001 E-mail: ljmartin@wam.umd.edu.

MARTIN, LINDA GAYE, demographer, economist; b. Paris, Dec. 17, 1947; d. Leslie Paul and Margie La Verne (Thomas) Martin. BA in Math., Harvard U., 1970; MPA, Princeton U., 1972, PhD in Econs., 1978. Dir. mgmt. info. sr. ctrs. bur. purchased social svcs. for adults City of N.Y., 1972—74; rsch. assoc., rsch. dir. U.S. Ho. of Reps. Select Com. on Population, Washington, 1977—79; rsch. assoc. East-West Population Inst., Honolulu, 1979—89, asst. dir., 1982—84; asst. prof. econs. U. Hawaii, 1979—81, assoc. prof., 1981—89, prof., 1989; dir. com. on population Nat. Acad. Scis., Washington, 1989—93; dir. domestic rsch. divsn., v.p. RAND, Santa Monica, Calif., 1993—95, v.p. for rsch. devel., 1995—99; pres. Population Coun., N.Y.C., 1999—. Mem. neurosci. behavior and sociology of aging rev. com. Nat. Inst. on Aging, Bethesda, 1991—95; chair panel on aging in developing countries NAS, Washington, 1987, mem. com. on population, 1993—99, mem. panel on internat. aging data, 1999—2001; mem. peer rev. oversight group NIH, 1998—. Editor: The ASEAN Success Story, 1987; co-editor: Demographic Change in Sub-Saharan Africa, 1993, The Demography of Aging, 1994, Racial and Ethnic Differences in the Health of Older Americans, 1997; author: (monograph) The Graying of Japan, 1989; contbr. articles to profl. jours. Mem. adv. coun. Woodrow Wilson Sch. Pub. and Internat. Affairs, Princeton U., NJ, 2000—; mem. faculty scholars selection com. William T. Grant Found., 2000—. Recipient Fulbright Faculty Rsch. award, Coun. for Internat. Exch. of Scholars, 1988. Mem.: Population Assn. Am. (bd. dirs. 1991—93), Internat. Union for Sci. Study Population, Gerontol. Soc. Am. Democrat. Office: Population Council 1 Dag Hammarskjold Plz New York NY 10017-2220

MARTIN, LINDA ANN, geriatrics nurse, educator; b. Elizabeth, N.J., Aug. 15, 1958; d. Julian Edward and Carolyn H. (Hudak) Szurley; m. James Richard Martin, June 4, 1989 (dec. 1998); 1 child Christopher John. BSN, Trenton State Coll., 1980; MSN, Rutgers U., Newark, 1989. Cert. clin. specialist in gerontol. nursing. Staff nurse, gen. med. unit Robert Wood Johnson Univ. Hosp., New Brunswick, N.J., 1980-83, asst. head nurse, oncology, patient care coord., 1983-91; coord. insvc. edn. Roosevelt Hosp., Edison, 1991—. Faculty coord. St. Francis Med. Ctr. Sch. Nursing, Trenton, N.J. Fellow N.Am. Acad. Arts and Scis.; mem. Nat. League for Nursing, ADSPN, Sigma Theta Tau. Office: St Francis Med Ctr Sch Nursing 601 Hamilton Ave Trenton NJ 08629-1915 E-mail: RNFaculty@worldnet.att.net.

MARTIN, LINDE BENISON, artist, interior designer; b. Erlangen, Germany, Jan. 2, 1930; came to U.S., 1953; d. Michael and Thea (Jetzelsberger) Kuchenreuther; m. James Bruce Martin, Nov. 16, 1966 (div.); 1 child, Cornelia Johnson. Student, Sorbonne, Paris, 1947-50, Cabrillo Coll., Aptos, Calif., 1961-65, San Jose (Calif.) State U., 1965. Tchr. Creativity Workshop, Zurich, 1988-90. Exhibited works in solo shows at Redding Gallery, Carmel, Calif., 1963, Jungain Ctr., San Francisco, 1973, Stanford U., 1975, Carmel Gallery Fine Arts, 1985, Kunsthalle, Nuremberg, Germany, 1991, U. Calif. Santa Cruz Women's Ctr., 1993, Christ Luth. Ch., Tiberon, Calif., U. Phoenix, Santa Cruz, 1994, others; group shows include Vorpal Gallery, San Francisco, Open Studios Art Tour, Santa Cruz, O Gallery, Westport, Conn., Syntex Corp., San Jose, Met. Art Care, Los Altos, Calif., Mus. Modern Art, Miami, Fla., Montreal Internat. Competition, San Jose, Wax Lander Galleries, Santa Fe, 1997; represented in collections at U. Phoenix,, U. Calif. at Santa Cruz, First Congl. Ch., Santa Cruz, Malton Gall., Cinn., COvner's Gall., Arcadia, Mich., also pvt. collections including that of Itzac Perlman, N.Y.C.; commns. include watercolor illustration for children's books, art glass windows and paintings. Named Best Artist of 1996 Spectra Art Mag., Grand Prize Crabby Award Art Calendar Mag., 1998. Avocations: gardening, reading, theater, classical music. Home: 213 Juniper PO Box 1482 Carmel CA 93921 Gallery: Linde Fine Art PO Box 1482 Carmel CA 93921 E-mail: infoLinde@LindebMartin.com.

MARTIN, LIPMAN F, statistician, management consultant; b. Long Branch, NJ, Dec. 23, 1959; s. Stanley and Florence Lipman; m. Marla A Sherman, Nov. 1, 1981; children: Sora, Avraham, Aharon. BS, Case Western Res. U., Cleve., 1982, MS, 1986. User svcs. statistician NASA Glenn Rsch. Ctr., Cleve., 1987—89; sr. statis. assoc. Booz Allen Hamilton, Cleveland, 1989—. Works statistician LTV Steel, Cleve., 1982—87. Mem.: Am. Statis. Assn. Home: 4379 Baintree Rd University Heights OH 44118 Office: Booz Allen Hamilton 127 Public Square Ste 5300 Cleveland OH 44114 Office Fax: 216-696-0359. E-mail: lipman_martin@bah.com.

MARTIN, LORI YVONNE, secondary education educator; b. Dayton, Ohio, Jan. 30, 1965; d. Jesse Willard Moore Jr. and Susan Diane Martin Berry; 1 child, Sara. Nursing cert., Ohio Hi-Point Sch. Nursing, Bellefontaine, 1991; BA, Wright State U., 1996, MEd, 2000. Nurse Mercy Meml. Hosp., Urbana, Ohio, 1991-94; tchr. Hillsboro (Ohio) City Schs., 1997-98, Calvary Christian Sch., Bellefontaine, 1999-2000, Ohio Hi Point Joint Vocat. Sch., Bellefontaine, 2000—01; with Logan County Sheriffs Office, 2002—. Author: An Angel for Sara, 1993. Mem. Am. Cancer Soc., Va. Hist. Soc., Smithsonian Instn., U.S. Holocaust Meml. Mus., Kappa Delta Phi. Republican. Avocations: cooking, travel, reading, puzzles, history. E-mail: snlmartin@hotmail.com.

MARTIN, LORRAINE B. humanities educator; b. Utica, N.Y., Aug. 18, 1940; d. Walter G. and Laura (Bochenek) Bolanowski; m. Charles A. Martin; children: Denise M. Stringer, Tracy M. Weinrich. Student, SUNY, Albany, 1958-60, postgrad., 1992—; BA in English and Edn. magna cum laude, Utica Coll. of Syracuse U., 1977; MS in Edn. and Reading, SUNY, Cortland, 1979, CAS in Edn. Adminstrn., 1984; postgrad., Syracuse U., 1990—. Cert. nursery, elem. tchr., secondary tchr., sch. adminstr. and supr., sch. dist. adminstr., reading specialist, N.Y. From tchr. to reading specialist, adminstrv. intern Poland (N.Y.) Cen. Sch., 1972-84; instr. reading Utica Coll. of Syracuse U., summer 1982-84; adminstr. spl. edn. and chpt. 1 remedial program Little Falls (N.Y.) City Sch. Dist., 1984-85; adminstr. adult and continuing edn. Madison-Oneida Bd. Coop. Ednl. Svcs., Verona, N.Y., 1985-86; dir. gen. programs Herkimer (N.Y.) Bd. Coop. Ednl. Svcs., 1986-88. Prof. English, SUNY SLN Internet English 1, children's lit., intro. edn., and honors program Herkimer County C.C. of SUNY, 1988—, participant brainstorming session on underprepared students SUNY, 1993, trainer tchr. performance evaluation program N.Y. State Dept. Edn., Herkimer, 1984, facilitator effective schs. program, 1986-88; cons. Two-Yr. Coll. Devel. Ctr. SUNY, 1985-89, tchr. trainer for the Writing Process; developed summer reading, writing and study skills course for Bridge program; tchr. asst. cert. program; cons. in field. Author: The Bridge Program-Easing the Transition from High School to College, 1990; editorial bd. Research and Teaching in Developmental Education; contbr. to Teaching Writing to Adults Tips for Teachers: An Idea Swap, 1989; textbook reviewer for pubs., 1993—. Vol. arts and crafts fair HCCC Found.; active Myasthenia Gravis Found., 1988—, Muscular Dystrophy Assn., 1989—, Thyroid Found. of Am., 1988—; past advisor Network for Coll. Re-Entry Adults; mem. Coun. of Profs., Parents Weekend Com. Recipient Leader Silver award for volunteerism 4-H Coop. Extension, Utica, 1980; HCCC Found. grantee, Writing grantee Reader's Digest. Mem. Internat. Reading Assn., Assn. Supervision and Curriculum Devel., Nat. Coun. Tchrs. English, Conf. on Coll. Composition and Communication, Phi Kappa Phi, Alpha Lambda Sigma. Avocations: English, current events, travel, public and satellite television, computers. Home: 7099 Crooked Brook Rd Utica NY 13502-7203 Office: Herkimer County Comm Coll SUNY Reservoir Rd Herkimer NY 13350-1545

MARTIN, LOUIS FRANK, surgery and healthcare outcomes analyst; b. Troy, N.Y., Nov. 7, 1951; s. Eugene Lavern and Lois Jane (Perkins) Martin; m. Deborah Lynn Tjarnberg, Mar. 12, 1977; children: Jesse Tjarnberg, James Casey, Tyler Gene. BA, Brown U., 1973, MD, 1976; MS in Health Adminstrn., U. Louisville, 1993. Diplomate Am. Bd. Surgery, Am. Bd. Med. Mgmt. Resident in gen. surgery U. Wash. Affiliated Hosps., Seattle, 1977-78, U. Louisville, 1978-83, rsch. fellow trauma rsch. and health care edn. adminstrn., 1980-82; asst. prof. surgery Pa. State U., Hershey, 1983-88, asst. prof. physiology, 1986-88, assoc. prof. surgery and cellular and molecular physiology, 1988-92; prof. surgery La. State U., New Orleans, 1992—, prof. preventative medicine and pub. health, 1994—; prof. neurosci., 1995—; med. dir. St. Charles Weight Mgmt. Ctr. La. State U., New Orleans, 1995—. Vis. scientist INSERM, Poste Orange, France, 1990-91; cons. TENET Health Care Corp. Med. Affairs Dept., 1995—, Ethicon Endo-Surgery, Inc., 2000—. Mem. editl. bd., Shock, 1994-97, Obesity Surgery, 1997—, Jour. Surgical Outcomes, 1997-99; author med. books; contbr. articles to newspapers and profl. jours. Recipient Loyal Davis Traveling Surg. scholar ACS, 1990, Clin. Investigator award NIH, 1985-90. Mem.: ACS, Shape Up Am., New Orleans Surg. Soc. (pres. 1999), Soc. Univ. Surgeons, Soc. Internat. Chirurgie, Collegium Internat. Chirurgiae Digestivae, Assn. for Acad. Surgery (councilman 1988—90), Am. Physiol. Soc., Am. Coll. Critical Care Medicine, Am. Soc. Bariatric Surgery (program chmn. 1997, 1998, mem. exec. coun. 1997—2000). Home: 3005 Palm Vista Dr Kenner LA 70065-1560 Office: La State U Dept Surgery 1542 Tulane Ave New Orleans LA 70112-2825

MARTIN, LUAN, accountant, payroll and timekeeping supervisor; b. Dimmitt, Tex., Dec. 9, 1952; d. Walter Johnnie and Nellie Beth (Connell) Martin; 1 child, Dani D'Ann; m. Richard Cordi, Feb. 2000. Grad., Amarillo Jr. Coll., 1986; BS Occupational Edn., Wayland Bapt. U., 1997. Credit mgr. Castro County Credit Bur., Dimmitt, 1978-79; parts mgr. Case Power and Equipment, 1979-82; bookkeeper Dimmitt Agri Industries, Inc., 1982; personnel dir. Deaf Smith Gen. Hosp., Hereford, Tex., 1983-84; payroll acct. Mason & Hanger-Silas Mason Co., Inc. (now named BWXT Pantex), Amarillo, 1984—; owner, pres. Dugan Mgmt., 1987-94, Martin Enterprises, Amarillo, 1997—; v.p. CorMar Enterprises, 2001—. Vol. local sch.; spkr. in behalf of blood, bone marrow and organ donations. Mem. Toastmasters Internat. (Pantex Lunch Bunch chpt.). Methodist. Avocations: reading, computers, sports, helping teenagers, bowling. Home: 7505 Countryside Dr Amarillo TX 79119-6488 Office: BWXT-Pantex PO Box 30020 Amarillo TX 79120-0020

MARTIN, M. GERTRUDE, artist; b. Pitts., July 31, 1931; d. George Urquhart and Gertrude (Wilson) M.; m. Roger Sanger Barnes, Aug. 19, 1956 (div.); children: Matthew Martin Barnes, Anna Martin Barnes. BS in art edn., Ohio State U., 1953; student, Ohio State U. Grad Sch., 1953-54, Art Student's League N.Y.C., 1954-56, Pratt Graphic Ctr., 1961, Creative Graphic Workshop, 1961, Brookfield Craft Ctr., 1963-76, Sch. Am. Craftsmen, 1965. Cert. art tchr., Conn. Art instr. Manhattanville Coll., Purchase, N.Y., 1960-63, Hartford (Conn.) Art Sch., 1972-74; head of arts Westover Sch., Middlebury, Conn., 1962—94, dir. summer Creative Arts Program, 1973-75. Del. World Crafts Coun. Meeting, Oaxtepec, Mex., 1976; evaluation com. mem. New Eng. Assn. Schs. Colls., 1976; historian Soc. Conn. Crafts, 1982—; archivist Women's Caucus Art, Conn., 1990—. One-woman shows include Washington Art Assn., Conn., 1967, 78, Mattatuck Mus., Waterbury, Conn., 1972, The Silo Gallery, 1975, 95, Peters Vally Gallery, Lawton, N.J. Bd. mem. Planned Parenthood, Waterbury, 1973-75. Named Disting. Advocate for Arts 2000, Conn. Commn. on Arts, Vol. of Yr., Flanders Nature Ctr. and Land Trust, 2002; recipient Silver Gavel award Artwell Gallery, Torrington, Conn., 2001, Jushua Point Studio pfize for coll. New Haven Paint and Clay Club, 2002, Amelia Peabody Meml. award Nat. Assn. Women Artists, 2002; Out -of-Town scholar Art Students' League, N.Y.C., 1954; McDowell Travelling grantee Art Students' League, N.Y.C., 1956, Fullbright grantee, U.S. Info. Svc. Florence, Italy, 1958-59, Artist's grantee Vt. Studio Ctr., Johnson, 1997; Art fellow Skidmore Coll., Saratoga Springs, N.Y., 1985. Mem. Soc. Conn. Crafts (v.p. 1981-91), Arcosanti Ariz. Alumni. Democrat. Unitarian Universalist. Office: M G Martin Studios 580 Upper Grassy Hill Rd Woodbury CT 06798-3107 E-mail: mgmartin@snet.net.

MARTIN, MALCOLM ELLIOT, lawyer; b. Buffalo, Dec. 11, 1935; s. Carl Edward and Pearl Maude (Elliot) M.; m. Judith Hill Harley, June 27, 1964; children; Jennifer, Elizabeth, Christina, Katherine. AB, U. Mich., Ann Arbor, 1958, JD, 1962. Bar: N.Y. 1963, U.S. Ct. Appeals (2d cir.) 1966, U.S. Supreme Ct. 1967. Assoc. Chadbourne Parke Whiteside & Wolff (now Chadbourne & Parke LLP), N.Y.C., 1962-73, ptnr., 1974—. Dir., sec. Carl and Dorothy Bennett Found., Inc.; sec., counsel Copper Devel. Assn., Inc. With U.S. Army, 1958-60. Mem. ABA, N.Y. State Bar Assn., Assn. Bar City of N.Y., St. Andrew's Soc. of N.Y., Met. Opera Guild, Oratamin Club (Blauvelt, N.Y.), Nyack Boat Club, Rockefeller Ctr. Club, Copper Club (N.Y.C.). Home: 74 S Highland Ave Nyack NY 10960-3609 Office: Chadbourne & Parke LLP 30 Rockefeller Plz Fl 31 New York NY 10112-0129 E-mail: mmartin@chadbourne.com.

MARTIN, MARCELLA EDRIC, retired community health nurse; b. Rosedale, Miss., Jan. 25, 1930; d. Amos and Alma Allen; m. Reuben Clifton Martin, Jan. 25, 1969; children: Brunetta, Jacqueline, Cornnel, Constance. Student, Marygrove Coll., Detroit, 1971; ADN, Highland Park Sch. Nursing, Mich., 1979; ThB, Cmty. Bible Coll., Detroit, 1968. Lic. LPN. LPN VA Hosp., Ann Arbor, Mich., Crittendon Hosp., Detroit, Vis. Nurses Assn., Detroit. Instr. Charles H. Mason Bible Sch., Detroit, 1991—95. Author: (book) Women Who Struggle, 2001. Founder Prime of Life Adult Foster Care Home, 1979; missionary over women Chs. of God in Christ, 1986—2002; vol. Redford Geriatric Home, Mich., 1999—. Recipient Spirit of Detroit award, City of Detroit, 1978, 2000, 2002, Disting. Citizen of Detroit award, 1980, Testimonial Resolution award, 1985. Mem.: Detroit Writers Guild. Democrat. Pentecostal Ch. Avocations: reading, writing. Home: 25332 Shiawassee Cir Apt 106 Southfield MI 48034

MARTIN, MARCI, writer, advertising executive; b. Corsicana, Tex., Oct. 20; d. Roy Rhoston McNutt and Maggie Mae Price; m. Howard Durward Martin, May 31, 1947 (dec. Dec. 15, 1998); children: Jennifer Ann Martin Svihus, Gary Durward. Student, North Tex. State U., 1945—46, So. Meth. U., 1946, Miracosta Coll., 1990—91. Bus. rep. Southwestern Bell, Dallas, 1946—55; advt. rep. Christian Sci. Monitor, San Diego, 1982—89. Author: Go To Hell and Make a U-Turn, 1996, rev. edit., 2000, Secrets and Lies, 2000, License To Steal, 2001, (short stories, essays, articles) The Muse on My Shoulder, 2001. Vol. prison chaplain, San Diego. Recipient 1st place for poetry, Nat. U., 1991, 3d place for essay, Writer's Jour., 2d place and hon. mention, Ann. Showcase Writers Club, 1994. Mem.: Sisters in Crime, Ariz. Mystery Writers (coord./pres. 1998—), Soc. Southwestern Authors (mentor 1998—), Mystery Writers Am. Avocation: golf. Home: 3011 W Sawmill Spring Trail Tucson AZ 85742

MARTIN, MARGARET GATELY, elementary education educator; b. Teaneck, N.J., July 24, 1928; d. Martin F. and Grace (Hammell) Gately; m. Phillips H. Martin, June 27, 1953 (div. 1977); children: Paul H., Patrick W., Thomas P. BA, Hunter Coll., 1950, MA, 1953. Cert. elem. tchr., N.Y. Tchr. Pub. Sch. # 5, Queens, N.Y., 1950-53, Wappingers Cen. Sch., Wappingers Falls, 1953-55, Jamestown (N.Y.) Pub. Schs., 1977-95; ret., 1996; tchr. Wenzler Day Care and Learning Ctr., Kettering, Ohio, 2000—02; tchr. religious edn. St. Francis of Assissi, Centerville, 2001. Tchr. Sunday sch. Sts. Peter and Paul Ch., Jamestown, 1977-95; citizen amb. to Prague and Russia, People to People Program, 1995. Mem. NEA, AAUW (pres. 1980-82, 92-94, Edn. Found. Program award 1985), Jamestown Tchrs. Assn. (membership chair 1976-78, sec. 1982-84), Jamestown Inter Club Coun. (pres. 1984-86, v.p. 1995-96, Woman of Yr. 1991), Green Thumb Garden Club (pres. 1986-88, 96—, v.p. 1991-93, 95-96), Delta Kappa Gamma (membership chair 1991-94, corr. sec. 1988-90, v.p. 1994-96, pres. 1998-2000). Republican. Roman Catholic. Avocations: gardening, needle work, travel, theater, geneology. Home: 3708 Wenzler Dr Kettering OH 45429-3366 E-mail: peg3708@aol.com.

MARTIN, MARGARET MCNEILL, home economist, educator; b. Laurens, S.C., Feb. 22, 1955; d. William S. and Mary Ann (Wharton) McNeill; children: Keri Lee, Travis McNeill. BS, Lander U., 1977; MEd, Converse Coll., 1991. Cert. tchr., S.C. Social worker Laurens County DSS, 1978; tchr. Laurens Dist. 55 H.S., 1978—. Mem. NEA, S.C. Edn. Assn., Laurens County Edn. Assn. Methodist. Avocations: cooking, painting, staining, sewing, bookkeeping/management consulting. Home: 40 Sesame St Laurens SC 29360-8936 Office: Laurens Dist 55 HS 5058 Hwy 76 W Laurens SC 29360-9378 E-mail: mknmartin@prtcnet.com.

MARTIN, MARILYN MANN, library media specialist; b. Greencastle, Ind., July 14, 1939; d. Emil Albert and Edith Costa Mann; m. Max Lee Martin; children: Michael Lee, Melanie Sue Martin Boesen. BS, Ind. State U., 1960, MS, 1970, 88. Tchr. Latin, sch. libr. Danville (Ind.) H.S., 1960; libr., media specialist Greencastle (Ind.) H.S., 1971—. Mem. tech. connections com. Greencastle H.S., 1997-98; mem. exec. bd. Stone Hills Libr. Svcs., Bloomington, Ind., 1990-96. Mem.: Greencastle Classroom Tchrs. (scholarship chmn. 1985—), Assn. Ind. Media Educatoris (dist. advocacy chmn. 1998), Ind. Coop. Libr. Svcs., Ind. Libr. Found., Ind. Tchrs. Assn., NEA, ASCD, Phi Kappa Phi. Avocations: gardening, reading, volunteering. Office: Greencastle High Sch 910 E Washington St Greencastle IN 46135-1898

MARTIN, MARK D. state supreme court justice; b. Apr. 29, 1963; s. M. Dean and Ann M. BSBA summa cum laude, Western Carolina U., 1985; JD with honors, U. N.C., 1988; grad., Nat. Jud. Coll., 1993; LLM, U. Va., 1998. Bar: N.C., U.S. Dist. Ct. (ea. and mid. dists.) N.C., U.S. Ct. Appeals (4th crct.). Law clk. to Hon. Clyde H. Hamilton U.S. Dist. Ct., Columbia, S.C., 1988-90; pvt. practice McNair Law Firm, Raleigh, N.C., 1990-91; legal counsel to gov. Office of Gov., 1991-92; superior ct. judge Jud. Dist. 3A, Greenville, N.C., 1992-94; judge N.C. Ct. Appeals, 1994-99; assoc. justice N.C. Supreme Ct., 1999—. Mem. N.C. Dept. Correction Master Plan Adv. Com., 1992; designated hearing officer Commutation Revocation Hearing of Zedie T. Smith, 1992; mem. N.C. Coun. for Women, 1992; legis. and law reform com. Conf. Superior Ct. Judges, 1993-94; co-chair legis liason com. N.C. Jud. Conf., 1995-97; mem. computer com. N.C. Appellate Cts., 1995—; sec. N.C. Jud. Conf., 1997-99; adj. faculty Univ. N.C., Chapel Hill, N.C. Ctrl. Univ. Sch. Law. Office coord. United Way Ann. Combined Campaign, 1991, 92. Recipient Book award, 1987, Order of Long Leaf Pine, 1992, Disting. Alumnus award We. Carolina U., 1995; Lloyd C. Balfour fellow, 1987, N.C. Inst. Polit. Leadership, 1992. Mem. ABA (jud. adminstrv. divsn.), N.C. Bar Assn. (minorities in profession com. 1995—, multidisciplinary practice task force 1999—, v.p. 2000-01), N.C. Assn. Black Lawyers, Wake County Bar Assn., Mortar Bd. Sr. Hon. Soc., Carolina Law Alumni Assn. (bd. dirs.), Internat. Hon. Soc., Alpha Lambda Delta, Phi Kappa Phi, Pi Gamma Mu, Omicron Delta Epsilon, Phi Alpha Delta, Delta Sigma Phi (scholar 1986), Beta Gamma Sigma (hon.). Office: North Carolina Supreme Court PO Box 2170 Raleigh NC 27602*

MARTIN, MARSHALL ALLEN, agricultural economist; b. Kewanee, Ill., Dec. 16, 1943; s. Marion R. and Lucille (Myers) M.; m. Berdine R. Kipp, June 5, 1966; children: Melanie A., Matthew A. BS, Iowa State U., 1966; MS, Purdue U., 1972, PhD, 1976. Dir. tchr. Instituto Rural de Montero, Santa Cruz, Bolivia, 1966-71; grad. rsch. asst. Purdue U., West Lafayette, Ind., 1971-73, from asst. prof. to prof., 1976-90, prof. agrl. econs., 1990—, assoc. head dept. agrl. econ., 1995—2002, assoc. dir. agrirsch. programs, 2002—; vis. scholar U. Sao Paulo, Brazil, 1974-75. Cons. Ford Found., Brazil, 1978, World Bank, Brazil, 1979, U.S. C. of C., Mexico, 1990; mem. adv. bd. Fed. Res. Bank of Chgo., 1989-90; dir. Ctr. for Agrl. Policy and Tech. Assessment, Purdue U., 1988-2002; mem. biotech. com. Nat. Assn. State Univs. and Land Grant Colls., 1988-97; mem. oper. com. Nat. Agrl. Biotech. Coun., 1991—; mem. adv. com. agri biotech. USDA, 2000-02; bd. dirs. Agrl. Alumni Seed Improvement Assn., 1999—; sci. adv. bd. Revista Argentina de Economia Agraria, 1998—. Author: Commercial International Agricultural Policies, 1991; author/editor: Agricultural Biotechnology, 1991; contbr. articles to profl. jours. Sch. supt. search com., West Lafayette Community Sch. Corp., 1989; pres., bd. dirs. Global Ministries of the North Ind. Conf., United Meth. Ch., 1980-85; pres. bonds adv. bd. Purdue U., 1996-. Recipient Rsch. Grant German Marshall Fund, 1987, rsch. awards Am. Agrl. Econs. Assn., 1981, 82, 83, 92. Mem. AAAS, Nat. Acad. Sci. (Russia), Atlantic Econ. Soc. (exec. com. 1995-97), Sigma Xi (chpt. pres. 1987). Achievements include research on U.S. agricultural policy, economic impacts of pesticide use and the adoption of agricultural biotechnology. Home: 108 Crimson Ct West Lafayette IN 47906-1602 Office: Purdue U Dept Agrl Econs Krannert Rm 655 West Lafayette IN 47907-1145 E-mail: marshallmartin@purdue.edu.

MARTIN, MARTA, learning disability specialist, educator; b. Miami, Fla., Apr. 30, 1952; d. Martin Nemerof and Rita Auletta. BA in Psychology, Fla. Atlantic U., 1975; MAT, Nova U., Ft. Lauderdale, 1985; student, U. Tenn., 1970-73. Specific learning disability instr. Univ. Sch. of Nova U., 1980-85; dir. edn. Sylvan Learning Ctr., Palm Beach Gardens, Fla., 1987-89; specific learning disabilities tchr. Palm Beach Gardens Elem. Sch., 1989-92; owner, dir. Marta Martin Tutoring, Lake Park, Fla., 1990—; coord. learning resource labs. Progressive Sch., West Palm Beach, 1997-98; learning resource specialist Rosarian Acad., 1999—2001.

MARTIN, MARY, secondary education educator; b. Detroit, May 17, 1954; d. Enos and Sara (Evans) M. AS, Highland Park C.C., 1975; BA, Wayne State U., 1975, MA in Teaching, 1981; postgrad., So. Calif. Sch. Ministry, Detroit, 1992—. Dietary aide Allan Dee Nursing Home, Detroit, 1972, Harper Hosp., Detroit, 1973, 74, nurse aide, 1974-75, respiratory technician, 1975-80, Dr.'s Hosp., Detroit, 1980; head cook, supr. Focus Hope, 1981; substitute tchr. Detroit Bd. Edn., 1984-90, tchr. adult edn., 1990-93, tchr., 1993—. Interim advisor student coun. Wayne State U., Detroit, 1985. Sunday sch. teaching trainer People's Missionary Bapt. Ch., Detroit, 1986, del., 1984-87, mem. All Aid, 1984-87, mem. choir, 1984, usher, 1984; precinct del. 13th Congl. Dist., 1986-88, 90-92, model, 1985. Recipient Spirit of Detroit award Detroit City Coun., 1993, Spl. Congl. cert. Hon. Barbara Rose Collins, 1994, Proclamation, Wayne County Commr. George Cushingberry, 1994. Mem. Nat. Sociol. Honor Soc. Democrat. Avocations: reading, shopping, movies, golf, driving.

MARTIN, MARY-ANNE, art gallery owner; b. Hoboken, N.J., Apr. 26, 1943; d. Thomas Philipp and Ruth (Kelley) M.; m. Henry S. Berman, June 9, 1963 (div. 1976); 1 child, Julia Coyote. Student, Smith Coll., 1961-63; BA, Barnard Coll., 1965. Head dept. painting Sotheby Parke Bernet, N.Y.C., 1971-78; founder Latin Am. dept. Sotheby's, 1977, sr. v.p., 1978-82; pres. Mary-Anne Martin, Fine Art, 1982—. Mem. Art Dealers Assn. Am. (bd. dirs.). Avocations: art collecting, scuba diving. Office: Mary-Anne Martin Fine Art 23 E 73rd St New York NY 10021-3522 E-mail: mamartin@mamfa.com.

MARTIN, MARYANNE, computer professional, juvenile literature author; b. Salem, Mass., May 22, 1964; d. Ralph Cornelius Jr. and Norma Joan (Rossi) M. BA in English Lit., St. Anselm Coll., Manchester, N.H., 1986; BFA in Graphic Design, Montserrat Coll. Art, Beverly, Mass., 1995; student, Northea. U., Boston. Graphic design profl. GTE Elec. Products Corp., Danvers, Mass., 1990-92, Tufts-New England Med. Ctr., Boston, 1992-93; pvt. practice Peabody, Mass., 1993—; graphic, web designer Lahey Hitchcock Clinic, Burlington, 1995-98; web mgr. Authoria, Inc., Waltham, 1999—. Design cons. Paint for Pets Mass. Soc. Prevention Cruelty to Animals, Boston, 1993, Osborn Communications Corp., Greenwich, Conn., 1994—, Snow Harbor Graphics, Danvers, 1994—, Montserrat Coll. Art, 1995. Vol. J.B. Thomas Hosp., Peabody, 1979-81, Big Brother/Big Sister Assn., Manchester, N.H.,

1983-84; mem., Mass. Soc. Prevention Cruelty to Animals, 1988—, lobbyist, 1993—. Mem. Am. Inst. Graphic Artists, Mass. Audubon Soc. Roman Catholic. Avocations: yoga, walking, reading. Home: 32 Woodbriar Rd Wakefield MA 01880-1154

MARTIN, MELISSA CAROL, radiological physicist; b. Muskogee, Okla., Feb. 7, 1951; d. Carl Leroy and Helen Shirley (Hicks) Paden; m. Donald Ray Martin, Feb. 14, 1970; 1 child, Christina Gail. BS, Okla. State U., 1971; MS, UCLA, 1975. Cert. radiol. physicist, Am. Bd. Radiology, radiation oncology, Am. Bd. Med. Physics. Asst. radiation physicist Hosp. of the Good Samaritan, L.A., 1975-80; radiol. physicist Meml. Med. Ctr., Long Beach, Calif., 1980-83, St. Joseph Hosp., Orange, 1983-92, Therapy Physics, Inc., Bellflower, 1993—. Cons. in field. Editor: (book) Current Regulatory Issues in Medical Physics, 1992. Fund raising campaign div. mgr. YMCA, Torrance, Calif., 1988-92; dir. AWANA Youth Club-Guards Group, Manhattan Beach, Calif., 1984—. Named Dir. of Symposium, Am. Coll. Med. Physics, 1992. Fellow Am. Coll. Med. Physics (chancellor western region 1992-95), Am. Assn. Physicists in Medicine (profl. coun. 1990-95, treas. 1998—, bd. dirs. 1994—), Am. Coll. Radiology (econs. com. 1992-95, govt. rels. com. 1998—); mem. Calif. Med. Physics Soc. (treas. 1991-98), Am. Soc. for Therapeutic Radiology and Oncology, Health Physics Soc. (pres. So. Calif. chpt. 1992-93), Am. Brachytherapy Soc. Baptist. Avocations: Christian youth group dir. Home: 507 Susana Ave Redondo Beach CA 90277-3953 Office: Therapy Physics Inc 9156 Rose St Bellflower CA 90706-6420 E-mail: melissamartin@compuserve.com.

MARTIN, MICHAEL ALBERT, surveillance agent; b. Akron, Ohio, Feb. 29, 1940; s. Albert Leo and Beatrice Marie (Flasck) M.; m. Jeanine E. Johnson, June 10, 1972 (div. Dec. 1976). Hotel Sch. diploma, Universal Schs., Miami, Fla., 1969. Security officer Boyd Group, California Hotel, Las Vegas, Nev., 1991-97, surveillance agt., 1998—. Author: Atlantis Secrets Revealed, 1994, Hilltop Country Songbook, 1997, (poetry) Noet You Poet, 1995; author (songs) To Eva My Love, Western Song, Your Song of Love, Reaching Out; contbr. to The Best Poems of 1995, The Best Poems of 1997, The Best Poems of the 90s. Staff sgt. USAF, 1964-68. Recipient Ednl. awards USAF, 1964-65, others; named to the Internat. Poetry Hall of Fame, 1996. Mem. Internat. Soc. Poets (hon., 13 Editors Choice award for poetry), Am. Legion, Masons (Scottish Rite pres. 1973—), Shriners. Democrat. Roman Catholic. Avocations: travel, photography, book writing, poetry writing, song writing. Home: Duck Creek Village 5330 Duralite St # 103 Las Vegas NV 89122-7364 Office: Calif Hotel and Casino PO Box 630 Las Vegas NV 89125-0630

MARTIN, MICHAEL LAWRENCE, informaiton assurance educator; b. Wallace, Idaho, Oct. 6, 1946; s. Howard E. and Bette Lee (Williams) M.; m. Susan Mary Forbes, Nov. 27, 1987. BA, U. Mont., 1968; MBA, St. Louis U., 1972; MS, Johns Hopkins U., 1985; PhD, George Mason U., 1995. From gen. supply asst. to computer programmer U.S. Army, 1968-73; computer specialist Social Security Adminstrn., Balt., 1973-78; computer sys. analyst Health Care Financing Adminstrn., 1978-86; sr. computer scientist Def. Info. Sys. Agy., Falls Church, Va., 1986-94, tech. dir., 1994-95; prof. info. assurance info. resources Mgmt. Coll. Nat. Def. U., Washington, 1995—. Mem. I*EEE, Assn. Computing Machinery, Armed Forces Comm. and Electronics Assn. Democrat. Episcopalian. Avocations: bridge, tennis, skiing, racquetball, chess. Home: 912 Maryland Ave NE Washington DC 20002-5308 Office: Nat Def U/Info Resources Mgmt Coll/Rm 132 Marshall Hl Bldg 62 Washington DC 20319-0001 E-mail: martinml@ieee.org.

MARTIN, MICHAEL LEE, orthotist; b. Long Beach, Calif., May 30, 1947; s. Troy Lee and Ruth Elizabeth (Hummer) M.; m. Sharon Lee Johnson, Aug. 23, 1969; 1 child, Tanya Lee. Student, Northwestern U., 1973; AA, Cerritos (Calif.) Coll., 1976; student, UCLA, 1976. Diplomate Am. Bd. Orthotists and Prosthetist. Cable splicer Gen. Telephone, Dairy Valley, Calif., 1965-66; orthotic technician Johnson's Orthopedic, Santa Ana, 1969-73, orthotist, 1974-96; pres. Johnson's Orthopedic Designs, Corona, 1989-97; rsch. orthotist Rancho Los Amigos Hosp., Downey, 1973; clin. dir. ops. Rehab Designs of Am., Orange, Calif., 1996. Mem. rsch. adv. bd. Rancho Los Amigos Hosp. Mem. rsch. adv. com. on tech. for children Rancho Los Amigos Hosp., Downey. With U.S. Army, 1966-68, Vietnam. Mem. Am. Acad. Orthotists and Prosthetists (sec., pres. So. Calif. chpt. 1976-79, sec., pres. Region IX 1979-87, bd. dirs. 1994—, Practitioner of Yr. award 1992), Orthotic and Prosthetic Provider Network (pres. Calif. chpt. 1988—), Internat. Soc. for Prosthetics and Orthotics. Democrat. Avocations: fishing, golf, surfing. Home: 22453 Bear Creek Dr S Murrieta CA 92562-3010 Office: Rehab Designs ofAm 1920 E Katella Ave Ste G Orange CA 92867-5146

MARTIN, MICHAEL REX, lawyer; b. Lawton, Okla., Feb. 16, 1952; s. Rex R. and Mary L. (Smith) M.; m. Janet E. Becker, Aug. 25, 1979; children: Katy, Donnie, Melissa. BS in Bus. Adminstrn., Tulsa U., 1974, JD, 1979. Bar: Okla. 1979, U.S. Dist Ct. (we. dist.) Okla. 1984. Ptnr. Musser, Musser & Martin, Enid, Okla., 1981-85, Crowley, Martin & Lovell, Enid, 1985—. Republican. Methodist. Office: Crowley Martin & Lovell PO Box 3487 Enid OK 73702-3487

MARTIN, MICHAEL TOWNSEND, racing horse stable executive, sports marketing executive; b. N.Y.C., Nov. 21, 1941; s. Townsend Bradley and Irene (Redmond) M.; m. Jennifer Johnston, Nov. 7, 1964 (div. Jan. 1977); children: Ryan Bradley, Christopher Townsend; m. Jean Kathleen Meyer, Mar. 1, 1980 Grad., The Choate Sch., 1960; student, Rutgers U., 1961-62. Asst. gen. mgr. N.Y. Jets Football Club, N.Y.C., 1968-74; v.p. NAMANCO Prodns., 1975-76; v.p., gen. mgr. Cosmos Soccer Club, 1976-77; exec. asst. Warner Communications, 1978-84; owner, operator Martin Racing Stable, 1983—; pres. Sports Mark, Inc., 1990—. Bd. dirs. Mote Marine Lab., Sarasota, Fla., Phipps Houses, VZV Rsch. Found., Inc., Morris Animal Found., Coun. of Visitors, Woods Hole Marine Biol. Lab., Nat. Lighthouse Ctr. and Mus.; bd. advisors The Pennington Sch., Dir.'s Cir., Scripps Instn. Oceanography. Mem. Athletics Congress (life, cert. official 1984—), U.S. Tennis Assn. (life), Internat. Oceanographic Found. (Miami life mem.), Fla. Thoroughbred Breeders Assn., Quogue Field Club, The Union Club. Republican. Episcopalian. Avocation: collecting Inuit (Eskimo) art. Home: 131 E 69th St Apt 11A New York NY 10021-5158 Office: 575 Madison Ave Ste 1006 New York NY 10022-2511 E-mail: mmarti1237@aol.com.

MARTIN, MIKE W. philosophy educator; b. Salt Lake City, Nov. 6, 1946; s. Theodore R. and Ruth Martin; m. Shannon Snow, Aug. 1, 1968; children: Sonia Renée, Nicole Marie. BS, U. Utah, 1969, MA, 1972; PhD, U. Calif., Irvine, 1977. Instr. dept. philosophy Chapman U., Orange, Calif., 1976-78, asst. prof., 1978-82, assoc. prof., 1982-86, prof., 1986—. NEH sponsor Nat. Project Philosophy and Engring. Ethics, 1978-80. Co-author: Ethics in Engineering, 1996, Introduction to Engineering Ethics, 2000; author: Self-Deception and Morality, 1986, Virtuous Giving, 1994, Love's Virtues, 1996; ; editor: Self-Deception and Self-Understanding, 1985; contbr. articles to profl. jours. Recipient Graves award Pomona (Calif.) Coll., 1983, Matchette Found. award U. Calif., Irvine, 1976; Coll. Tchrs. fellow NEH, 1981-82. Mem. Am. Philos. Assn., Soc. Bus. Ethics, Soc. Study Profl. Ethics, Phi Beta Kappa, Phi Kappa Phi. Democrat. Office: Dept Philosophy Chapman U 1 University Dr Orange CA 92866-1005

MARTIN, MYRON GREGORY, foundation administrator; b. Houston, Jan. 14, 1958; s. Monty Gene and Vera Mae (Saurage) M. MusB, U. North Tex., 1980; MBA, Golden Gate U., 1989. Various sales and mktg. positions Baldwin Piano Co., N.Y.C., 1980-1990, dir. concert and artists, 1990-95; exec. dir. Liberace Found., Las Vegas, Nev., 1995-98; dir. U. Las Vegas, 1998—. Mem. adv. bd. Thelonious Monk Inst., Washington, D.C., 1994-95; bd. dirs. Cystic Fibrosis Found., Chgo., 1990, Liberace Found., 1993-95, Museums and Attractions, Las Vegas, 1996—. Recipient Special award Cystic Fibrosis Found., 1990. Mem. Nev. Mus. Assn. (bd. dirs. 1997—). Avocations: tennis, judging scholarship pageants for Miss America organization. Home: 3996 Placita Del Rico Las Vegas NV 89120-2629 Office: U Las Vegas Performing Art Ctr 4505 S Maryland Pkwy Las Vegas NV 89154-9900

MARTIN, NATHANIEL FRIZZEL GRAFTON, mathematician, educator; b. Wichita Falls, Tex., Oct. 10, 1928; s. James Thelbert and Ethel Elizabeth (Nycum) M.; m. Joan Bowman, Apr. 10, 1954; children: Nathaniel Grafton, Jonathan Bowman. BS, North Tex. State U., 1949, MS, 1950; PhD, Iowa State U., 1959. Instr. Midwestern U., Wichita Falls, 1950-52; teaching asst. Iowa State U., Ames, 1955-59; from instr. to prof. math. U. Va., Charlottesville, 1959-96, prof. emeritus math., 1996, assoc. dean Grad. Sch. Arts and Scis., 1976-82; rsch. assoc. U. Calif., Berkeley, 1965-66. Guest lectr. U. Copenhagen, 1969-70; rsch. assoc. U. Warwick, Coventry, Eng., 1982; vis. mem. MSRI, Berkeley, 1992; vis. faculty Univ. Coll., London, 1992. Author: Mathematical Theory of Entropy, 1981; editor: McGraw-Hill Dictionary of Physics & Math, 1978, Sci. & Tech. Terms, 1974. Lt. USNR, 1952-55. Mem. Am. Math. Soc., Math. Assn. Am., Sigma Xi, Pi Mu Epsilon. Office: U Va Dept Math PO Box 400137 Kerchof Hall Charlottesville VA 22904-4137 E-mail: nfm@virginia.edu.

MARTIN, NOEL, graphic design consultant, educator; b. Syracuse, Ohio, Apr. 19, 1922; s. Harry Ross and Lula (Van Meter) M.; m. Coletta Ruchty, Aug. 29, 1942; children— Dana, Reid Cert. in Fine Arts, Art Acad. Cin., Doctorate (hon.), 1994. Designer Cin. Art Mus., 1947-93, asst. to dir., 1947-55; freelance designer for various ednl., cultural and indsl. orgns., 1947—; instr. Art Acad. Cin., 1951-57, artist-in-residence, 1993—. Design cons. Champion Internat., 1959-82, Xomox Corp., 1961—, Federated Dept. Stores, 1962-83, Hebrew Union Coll., 1969—; designer-in-residence U. Cin., 1968-71, adj. prof., 1968-73; mem. adv. bd. Carnegie-Mellon U., R.I. Sch. Design, Cin. Symphony Orch., Am. Inst. Graphic Arts; lectr. Smithsonian Instn., Libr. of Congress, Am. Inst. Graphic Arts, Aspen Design Conf., various additional schs. and orgns. nationally. One man shows include Contemporary Arts Ctr., Cin., 1954, 71, Addison Gallery Am. Art, 1955, R.I. Sch. Design, 1955, Soc. Typographic Arts, Chgo., 1956, White Mus. of Cornell U., 1956, Cooper & Beatty, Toronto, Ont., Can., 1958, Am. Inst. Graphic Arts, 1958, Ind. U., 1958, Ohio State U., 1971; exhibited in group shows at Mus. Modern Art, N.Y.C., Library of Congress, Musee d'Art Moderne, Paris, Grafiska Inst., Stockholm, Carpenter Ctr., Cambridge, Gutenberg Mus., Mainz, U.S. info. exhbns. In Europe, South America and USSR; represented in permanent collections Mus. Modern Art, Stedelijk Mus., Amsterdam, Cin. Art Mus., Boston Mus. Fine Arts, Cin. Hist. Soc., Library of Congress; contbr. to various publs. Served to sgt. U.S. Air Force, 1942-45 Recipient Art Directors medal, Phila., 1957, Sachs award, Cin., 1973, Lifetime Achievement award Cin. Art Dirs., 1989.

MARTIN, PAIGE ARLENE, lawyer; b. Pitts., Nov. 27, 1951; d. James William and Mildred Jean (Toplis) M.; m. Barry Rosenbaum, June 15, 1974 (div. 1977); m. David Kern, Feb. 21, 1988 (div. July 1996). AB, Wellesley (Mass.) Coll., 1973; JD, Case Western Res. U., Cleve., 1978. Bar: Ohio 1978, U.S. Dist. Ct. (no. dist.) Ohio 1978. Assoc. Sindell, Sindell & Rubenstein, Cleve., 1978-83, Spangenberg, Shibley, Traci & Lancione, Cleve., 1983-89; pvt. practice, 1989—. Instr. Cuyahoga Community Coll., Cleve., 1979-80; adj. faculty Case Western Res. U., Cleve., 1984-85; lectr. Assn. Trial Lawyers Assn., Dallas, 1986, Ohio Acad. Trial Attys., Cin., Columbus, 1984, Ohio Legal Ctr. Inst., Sandusky, Ohio, 1985, Cleve. Acad. Trial Attys., 1987. Contbr. chpt. to book. Child advocate CASA program Franklin County. Recipient award of merit Ohio Legal Ctr. Inst., 1985; named to Outstanding Young Women of Am., 1987. Mem. Cleve. Bar Assn. (chair hospice com. 1982-83, Merit Svc. award), Greater Cleve. Bar Assn. (joint med.-legal com. 1983-90, chair 1986-87), Cleve. Acad. Trial Lawyers (dir. 1984-87), Assn. Trial Attys. Am. (diptheria, pertussis, tetnus litigation sect. 1985-87), Ohio State Bar Assn., Ohio Acad. Trial Attys. (constnl. law com. 1989-90). Office: 77 Outerbelt St Columbus OH 43213-1548

MARTIN, PARKER, accountant, financial consultant; b. Barbourville, Ky., Dec. 6, 1947; s. Stanley Chester Martin and Georgia Thelma (Bullock) Lofgren. BS in Acctg., Calif. State U., Los Angeles, 1976. CPA, Calif. Acctg. mgr. Coca Cola, Los Angeles, 1970-76; staff acct. Tilles and Gest, CPA's, Beverly Hills, Calif., 1977-86; owner Parker Martin, CPA, Burbank, 1986—. Co-author: The Mansions of Beverly Hills, 1967. Mem. Am. Inst. CPA's, Calif. Soc. CPA's. Clubs: Valley Bus. Alliance (Burbank). Republican. Avocations: reading, swimming. Home: PO Box 58067 Los Angeles CA 90058-0067 Office: 1178 Hartford St Cambria CA 93428-2908

MARTIN, PATRICK A. federal agency administrator; BS, Ind. U. Pa. Engring. support NASA GSFC, 1983—88; sr. engr. Vitro Corp., 1988—98; aerospace engr. Fed. Aviation Adminstrn.'s Office of Comml. Space Trans., 1998—99; SMA lead for sci. missions NASA Office of Safety and Mission Assurance, 1999—. OSMA liaison to Space Sci. Enterprise, NASA Jet Propulsion Lab. NASA. Office: NASA Hdqrs Mail Code Q 300 E St SW Washington DC 20546*

MARTIN, PATRICK ALBERT, investment adviser; b. Green Bay, Wis., Apr. 25, 1950; s. Patrick Henry and Mary Ellen (Neufeld) M.; m. Sandra Marie Staskon, May 31, 1980; children: Sarah, Patrick William, Philip A. AB, Dartmouth Coll., 1972, MBA, 1974. CFA. Assoc. Northern Trust Co., Chgo., 1974-77; v.p. The Abacus Group, 1977-84, Heller Fin., Chgo., 1984-87, GMAC Mortgage Corp., Chgo., 1987-88, Nat. Bank Canada, Chgo., 1988-89; mng. ptnr. Martin & Co., Winnetka, Ill., 1989—. Mng. ptnr. Martin Investments, Green Bay, 1982—, Cherry St. Investments, Green Bay, 1990—. Mng. trustee Martin Charitable Trust, Green Bay, 1982—, E.A. Neufeld Charitable Trust, Green Bay, 1992—, Village of Kenilworth Pub. Libr. Br., 1999—; dist. enrollment dir. Dartmouth Coll., Chgo., 1977-83; governing mem. Chgo. Symphony Orch., 1995—. Mem. AICPA, Ill. CPA Soc., Assn. for Investment Mgmt. and Rsch., Dartmouth Club Chgo. (bd. dirs. 1979-82), Univ. Club, Michigan Shores Club, Sheridan Shores Yacht Club, Oneida Golf and Riding Club. Office: Martin & Co PO Box 618 Winnetka IL 60093-0618

MARTIN, PAUL, Canadian government official; b. Windsor, Ont., Can., Aug. 28, 1938; s. Paul Joseph and Eleanor (Adams) M.; m. Sheila Ann Cowan, Sept. 11, 1965; children: Paul William James, Robert James Edward, David Patrick Anthony. BA in Philosophy and History, U. Toronto, Can., 1962, LLB, LLB, U. Toronto, Can., 1965. Bar: Ont. 1966. Exec. asst. to pres. Power Corp. Can. Ltd., 1966-69, v.p., 1969-71; v.p. spl. projects Consol.-Bathurst Ltd., 1971-73; v.p. planning and devel. Power Corp., Can., 1973-74; pres. Can. S.S. Lines Ltd., Montreal, 1974-80, chief exec. officer, 1976-80; pres., chief exec. officer CSL Group Inc., 1980-88; M.P. Ho. of Commons, 1988—; min. of fin. Dept. of Fin. Can., 1993—2002; former min. for fed. office of regional devel. Can. Govt., 1993-95. Co-chair Nat. Platform Com. of Liberal Party of Can. Co-author (with Chaviva Hosek): Creating Opportunity: The Liberal Plan for Canada. Former mem. C.D. Howe Inst. Policy Analysis Com., Birt, N.Am. Com., Ctr. Rsch. Action on Race Rels.; former bd. dirs. Can. Coun. Christians and Jews; founding dir. emeritus North-South Inst., Can., Coun. Native Bus.; bd. govs. Concordia U., coun., v.p., past mem. bd. advisors; inaugural chair G-20, 1999. Liberal. Avocations: sports, reading. Office: Rm 458 Conf Bldg House of Commons Ottawa ON Canada K1A 0A6

MARTIN, PAUL CECIL, physicist, educator; b. Bklyn., Jan. 31, 1931; s. Harry and Helen (Salzberger) M.; m. Ann Wallace Bradley, Aug. 7, 1957; children: Peter, Stephanie Glennon, Daniel. AB, Harvard U., 1952, PhD, 1954. Mem. faculty Harvard U., Cambridge, Mass., 1957—, prof. physics, 1964-82, J. H. VanVleck prof. pure and applied physics, 1982—, chmn. dept. physics, 1972-75, dean divsn. engring. and applied scis., 1977-98, assoc. dean Faculty Arts and Scis., 1981-98, dean rsch. and info. tech., 1998—. Vis. prof. Ecole Normale Superieure, Paris, 1963, 66, U. Paris, Orsay, 1971; mem. materials rsch. adv. coun. NSF, 1986-89; bd. dirs. Mass. Tech. Pk. Corp., 1990—, exec. com., 1992—. Bd. editors: Jour. Math Physics, 1965-68, Annals of Physics, 1968-82, Jour. Statis. Physics, 1975-80, Proc. Nat. Acad. Scis., 2000—. Bd. dirs. Assoc. Univs. for Rsch. in Astronomy, 1979-85; bd. dirs. Assoc. Univs ., Inc., 1981—, exec. com., 1986-90, 92-94, chmn. bd. dirs., 1996-2000. NSF postdoctoral fellow, 1955; Sloan Found. fellow, 1959-62; Guggenheim fellow, 1966, 71 Fellow: AAAS (chair physics sect. 1986), Am. Phys. Soc. (councillor-at-large 1982—84, panel on pub. affairs 1983—86, chmn. nominating com. 1994), Am. Acad. Arts and Scis., NAS. Office: Harvard U Dept Physics Cambridge MA 02138 E-mail: martin@harvard.edu.

MARTIN, PAUL EDWARD, retired insurance company executive; b. Santa Claus, Ind., Sept. 10, 1914; s. James F. and Anna (Singer) M.; m. Pauline Peva, Dec. 22, 1939 (dec. Feb. 1982); 1 child, Peter McDowell; m. Ann Parker, Oct. 14, 1983. BA, Hanover Coll., 1936. With actuarial dept. State Life Ins. Co., Indpls., 1936-42; asst. actuary Ohio Nat. Life Ins. Co., Cin., 1946-48, asso. actuary, 1948-49, actuary, 1949-55, actuarial v.p., 1955-56, adminstrv. v.p., 1956-67, sr. v.p. ins. adminstrn., 1967-71, pres., 1971-72, chmn. bd., chief exec. officer, 1972-79, also dir. Trustee Hanover (Ind.) Coll. Served to maj. F.A. AUS, 1942-46, PTO. Fellow Soc. Actuaries, Acad. Actuaries; mem. Comml. Club, Skyline Club, Masons, Shriners, Gamma Sigma Pi, Beta Theta Pi. Presbyterian. Home: 7146 N Finger Rock Pl Tucson AZ 85718-1406

MARTIN, PAUL EDWARD, lawyer; b. Atchison, Kans., Feb. 5, 1928; s. Harres Crawford and Thelma Fay (Wilson) M.; m. Betty Lou Crawford, Aug. 28, 1954; children: Cherry Gayle Martin Luna, Paul Alexander, Mary Lou Martin Brieger. BBA, Baylor U., 1955, LLB, JD, 1956; LLM, Harvard U., 1957. Bar: Tex. 1956, Pa. 1958; cert. in estate planning and probate law Tex. Bd. Legal Specialization. Assoc. Ballard, Spahr, Andrews & Ingersoll, Phila., 1957-59; ptnr. Fulbright & Jaworski, Houston, 1959-77, Chamberlain, Hardlicka, White, Williams & Martin, Houston, 1977—2002, shareholder. Former instr. estate planning U. Houston. Co-author: How To Live and Die with Texas Probate, 1968, 7th edit., 1995. Pres. devel. coun. Baylor U., Waco, Tex., 1973-74; past chmn. bd. deacons West Meml. Bapt. Ch., Houston; past trustee fgn. missions bd. So. Bapt. Conv.; past trustee Baylor U., Meml. Hosp. Sys., Houston. Lt. comdr. USN, 1947-53, Korea. Fellow Am. Coll. Trust and Estate Counsel; mem. State Bar Tex., Houston Bar Assn., Houston Estate and Fin. Forum (pres. 1965-66), Houston Bus. and Estate Planning Coun. Republican. Home: 126 Lakeside Dr Montgomery TX 77356 Office: Chamberlin Hrdlicka Et Al 1200 Smith St Ste 1400 Houston TX 77002-4401 Fax: (713) 658-2553. E-mail: paul.martin@chamberlainlaw.com.

MARTIN, PAUL ROSS, editor; b. Lancaster, Pa., May 14, 1932; s. Paul Rupp and Amanda (Minnich) M.; m. Julia Ibbotson, June 5, 1954 (div. Apr. 1979); children: Monica Martin Goble, Julia, Paul Jr., Barbara, Drew, Eric. BA, Dartmouth Coll., 1954. Reporter, wire editor Lancaster New Era, Lancaster Newspapers Inc., 1954-60; copyreader, makeup man Wall St. Jour. divsn. Dow Jones & Co., N.Y.C., 1960-63, copy editor nat. news, 1963-69, editor bus. and fin. column, 1969-72, nat. copydesk chief, 1972-75, page one sr. spl. writer, 1975-90, asst. to mng. editor, 1990-93, asst. mng. editor, 1993—2002. Editor: The Possible Dream, 1978, Retirement Without Fear, 1981, Wall Street Journal Style Book, 1981, 4th edit., 1995, The Wall Street Journal Guide to Business Style and Usage, 2002; co-author, editor: American Dynasties Today, 1983. Bd. dirs. Community Bd. 1, S.I., N.Y., 1976-84. Mem. N.Y. Fin. Writers Assn. (past officer). Avocations: basketball, tennis, travel. Office: Wall St Jour 200 Liberty St New York NY 10281-1003 E-mail: paul.martin-sr@wsj.com.

MARTIN, PETER ROBERT, psychiatrist, pharmacologist; b. Budapest, Hungary, Sept. 6, 1949; came to U.S.,1980; s. Nicholas M. and Eva (Horvat) M.; m. Barbara Bradford, Dec. 23, 1985; 1 child, Alexander Bradford. BSc with honors, McGill U., Montreal, Que., Can., 197l, MD, CM, 1975; MSc, U. Toronto, Ont., Can., 1978. Diplomate Am. Bd. Psychiatry and Neurology, Psychiatry, Addiction Psychiatry. Resident in internal medicine U. Toronto, Can., 1975-76, resident in psychiatry, 1978-80; fellow clin. pharmacology Addiction Rsch. Found., Toronto, 1976-78; chief sect. clin. sci. Nat. Inst. on Alcohol Abuse & Alcoholism, Bethesda, 1983-86; assoc. prof. Vanderbilt U. Sch. Medicine, Nashville, 1986-92, prof., 1992—, dir. divsn. addiction medicine, 1986—, dir. addiction ctr., 1994—; dir. Vanderbilt Inst. for Coffee Studies, 1999—. Vis. scientist Lab. of Clin. Sci., NIMH, Bethesda, Md., 1980-83; investigator John F. Kennedy Ctr. for Rsch. on Human Devel., Nashville, 1993—. Fellow Royal Coll. Physicians (Can.), Am. Psychiatric Assn.; mem. AAAS, Am. Soc. Clin. Pharmacology and Therapeutics, Am. Acad. Addiction Psychiatry, Am. Coll. Psychiatrists, Rsch. Soc. on Alcoholism, Internat. Soc. Biomed. Rsch. in Alcoholism. Office: Vanderbilt U Sch Medicine Dept Psychiatry MCN AA2206 Nashville TN 37232-0001 E-mail: peter.martin@uvanderbilt.edu.

MARTIN, PETER WILLIAM, lawyer, educator; b. Cin., Apr. 11, 1939; s. Wilfred Samuel and Elizabeth (Myers) M.; m. Ann Wadsworth, Nov. 28, 1964; children: Leah, Elliot, Isaac. BA, Cornell U., 1961; JD, Harvard U., 1964. Bar: Ohio 1964. Atty. AF Gen. Counsel's Office, 1964-67; asso. prof. law U. Minn., 1967-71; vis. asso. prof. law Cornell U., 1971-72, prof. law, 1972—, dean, 1980-88, Edward Cornell prof. law, 1989-92, Jane Foster prof. law, 1992—; co-dir. Legal Info. Inst., 1992—; pres. Ctr. for Computer Assisted Legal Instrn., 1986-88. Cons. Adminstrv. Conf. U.S., 1977-79; reporter Am. Bar Assn. Task Force on Lawyer Competency and the Role of the Law Schs. Author: The Ill-Housed, 1971, (with others) Social Welfare and the Individual, 1971, Cases and Materials on Property, 1974, 3d edit., 1992, Social Security Law, 1990, Basic Legal Citation, 1992, Social Security Plus, 1994, Introduction to Copyright, 2000; editor Jour. Legal Edn., 1985. Chmn. Ithaca Bd. Zoning Appeals, 1974-79. Served to capt. USAF, 1964-67. Mem. ABA (task force on law schs. and legal profession 1990-92), Am. Bar Found. (vis. com.), Am. Assn. Law Schs. (chmn. law and computers sect. 1987-88, 93-94). Office: Cornell U Law Sch Myron Taylor Hall Ithaca NY 14853 E-mail: martin@lii.law.cornell.edu.

MARTIN, PHILLIP DWIGHT, bank consulting company executive, mayor; b. Nevada, Mo., Jan. 4, 1943; s. E. Dwight and Berniece E. (Leedy) M. BS, U. Mo., 1964, MBA, 1965, cert. math. and bus. edn., 1966. Tchr. Warson (Mo.) Pub. Schs., 1966-68; investment analyst Bus. Men's Assurance Co. Am., Kansas City, Mo., 1968-70; exec. v.p. Farmer's Bank Walker, 1970-71; banking cons. Howard J. Blender Co., Dallas, 1971-84; chmn. Profit Motivators Internat., Inc., Boulder, Colo., 1984—; mayor City of Walker, 1986-2000. Mem. Walker R-4 Alumni Assn. (co-founder, life mem. scholarship com., pres. 1994-96). Home: 214 E Marvin Ave Walker MO 64790-0069 E-mail: pdm19@centurytel.net.

MARTIN, PHILLIP HAMMOND, lawyer; b. Tucson, Jan. 4, 1940; s. William P. and Harriet (Hammond) M.; m. Sandra S. Chandler, June 17, 1961 (div. Mar. 1989); children: Lisa, Craig, Wade, Ryan; m. Erika Zetty, May 9, 1990. BA, U. Minn., 1961, JD, 1964. Bar: Minn. 1964, U.S. Tax Ct. 1967, U.S. Dist. Ct. Minn. 1968, U.S. Ct. Appeals (8th cir.) 1973, U.S. Supreme Ct. 1981, U.S. Claims Ct. 1983, U.S. Ct. Appeals (fed. cir.) 1988, U.S. Ct. Appeals (7th cir.) 1989. Assoc. Dorsey & Whitney, Mpls., 1964-69, ptnr., 1970—. Home: 487 Portland Ave Saint Paul MN 55102-2216 Office: Dorsey & Whitney Ste 1500 50 S 6th St Minneapolis MN 55402-1498 E-mail: martin.phil@dorseylaw.com.

MARTIN, QUINN WILLIAM, lawyer; b. Fond du Lac, Wis., Mar. 12, 1948; s. Quinn W. and Marcia E. Martin; m. Jane E. Nehmer; children: Quinn W., William J. BSME, Purdue U., 1969; postgrad., U. Santa Clara, 1969-70; JD, U. Mich., 1973. Bar: Wis. 1973, U.S. Dist. Ct. (ea. dist.) Wis. 1973, U.S. Ct. Appeals (7th cir.) 1973. Sales support mgr. Hewlett-Packard, Palo Alto, Calif., 1969-70; assoc. Quarles & Brady, Milw., 1973-80, ptnr., 1980—. Bd. dirs. Associated Bank Milw., U-Line Corp., Gen. Timber and Land, Inc., Fond du Lac. Chmn. gov. McCallum Trans Com., Wis., U. Mich. Law Sch. Fund; bd. dirs. Milw. Zool. Soc., Found. for Wildlife Conservation. Mem. ABA, Wis. Bar Assn., Milw. Club, Ozaukee Country Club, Chaine des Rottiseurs, Delta Upsilon (sec.), Milw. Alumni Club, Rotary. Office: Quarles & Brady 411 E Wisconsin Ave Ste 2550 Milwaukee WI 53202-4497

MARTIN, R. BRAD, retail executive; Chmn., ceo Proffitts, Inc. (now Saks Inc.), Memphis. Office: Saks Inc 750 Lakeshore Pkwy Birmingham AL 35211-4400*

MARTIN, R. KEITH, business and information systems educator, consultant; b. Seattle, Sept. 5, 1933; s. Jerome Milton and Winifred (Gifford) M.; m. Carolyn Joanne Carosella, June 15, 1957; children: Jefferson, Sean, Jennifer, Katherine. AB, Whitman Coll., 1955; MBA with high honors, CCNY, 1965; PhD, U. Wash., 1973. Registered, lic. profl. engr.; cert. data processing, cert. systems profl., cert. computer profl. Div. mgr. Campus Merchandising Bur., Inc., N.Y.C., 1955-56; sales rep. IBM, Seattle, 1956, Service Bur. Corp. subs. IBM, N.Y.C., 1957-58; specialist mgmt. adv. services Price Waterhouse & Co., 1959-65, Seattle, 1965-66, mgr., 1966-67; dir. mgmt. systems dept. U. Wash., 1967-71, lectr. dept. acctg. Sch. Bus. Adminstrn., 1971-73; asst. prof. dept. accountancy Baruch Coll., CUNY, 1973-76, assoc. prof., 1977-79; prof. acctg. Fairfield U., 1979-84, prof. acctg. and info. systems, 1984-94, assoc. dean Sch. Bus., 1980-82, dean, 1982-93, acting dean grad. Sch. of Communications, 1988-90, prof. info. systems, 1994-2001, prof. info. systems and ops. mgmt., 2001—, dept. chmn., 2001—, holder Stephen and Camille Schramm chair in bus., 2000—. V.p. Eastalco Systems, 1971-72; faculty fin. div. Am. Mgmt. Assn., 1963-64; part-time lectr. Bellevue Community Coll., 1967-69, Shoreline Community Coll., 1968-72, Seattle U., 1971-72 Co-author: Management

Control of Electronic Data Processing, 1965; author: Management Information Systems in Higher Education: Case Studies at Three Universities, 1973, Effective Business Communications, 1976, 79, 91, Systems Development and Computer Concepts, 1977; assoc. editor: Industry Guides for Accountants and Auditors, 2 vols., 1980; mem. editorial rev. bd. Dickenson Pub. Co., 1974-75, Prentice-Hall, Inc., 1977-78, 87-88, 90-91, Reston Pub. Co., 1977-78, Jour. Acctg. Edn., 1981-83; featured roles (Amateur Comedy Club prodns.) Guys and Dolls, Our Town, The Fantastics, stage mgr. Some Assembly Required, Arcadia, house mgr. The Real Thing, The Tempest; author numerous monographs; contbr. numerous articles to profl. jours. Mem. Mendelssohn Choir of Conn. Recipient cert. of appreciation Am. Mgmt. Assn., 1966, cert. of merit for disting. service to Mgmt. Scis., 1969, for disting. service to info. systems profession, 1973; Merit award Assn. Systems Mgmt., 1971, Achievement award, 1972, Internat. award World Assn. for Case Method Rsch. and Application, 1996; cert. for service City of Seattle, 1973; named Outstanding Young Man Am., 1970, One of 300 Outstanding Alumni, Whitman Coll., 1979; Kellogg fellow, 1971-72, Price Waterhouse faculty fellow, 1976 Mem. Am. Inst. Indsl. Engrs. (dir. Seattle chpt. 1967-70, chmn. regional conf. 1969), World Assn. for Case Method Rsch. and Application (adv. bd. 1996-99, exec. bd. dirs. 1999—), Acad. for Creative Tchg. (exec. bd. 1998—), Inst. Mgmt. Accts. (assoc. dir. N.Y. chpt. 1963-64, 75-85 Seattle chpt. 1967-70), Assn. Systems Mgmt. (sec. 1968-69, v.p. 1969-70, pres. Pacific N.W. chpt. 1970-71), Data Processing Mgmt. Assn., Assn. Computing Machinery, Soc. Cert. Data Processors, NSPE, N.Y. Soc. Profl. Engrs., Soc. Mgmt. Info. Systems, AAUP, Am. Acctg. Assn., Phi Delta Theta (province pres. 1986-87), Beta Gamma Sigma, Mu Gamma Tau, Phi Delta Kappa, Beta Alpha Psi Clubs: Bronxville Field. Home: 338 Collins Ave Mount Vernon NY 10552-1602 E-mail: rkmartin@mail.fairfield.edu.

MARTIN, RALPH DRURY, lawyer, columnist; b. Pittsburg, Kans., Mar. 4, 1947; s. Kent Wills and Kathleen (Drury) M.; m. Ruchirawan Meemeskul, Oct. 28, 1982; 1 child, Chanida Kathleen. BA, Tulane U., 1969; JD, Washington U., 1972. Bar: La. 1972, D.C. 1981, Calif. 1992, U.S. Dist. Ct. (mid. dist.) La. 1985, U.S. Dist. Ct. D.C. 1991, U.S. Ct. Appeals (9th cir.) 1979, U.S. Ct. Appeals (D.C. cir.) 1991, U.S. Supreme Ct. 1976. Law clk. to Hon. Frederick J.R. Heebe U.S. Dist. Ct., Ea. Dist. La., New Orleans, 1972-74; spl. asst. to U.S. atty. U.S. Dept. Justice, Washington, 1974-75, trial atty. civil rights div., 1975-80; dep. asst. legal advisor U.S. Dept. State, 1980-82; sr. prosecutor pub. integrity sect. U.S. Dept. Justice, 1982-90; spl. counsel U.S. Dept. State, 1990-91; ptnr. Storch & Brenner, 1991-2000, Dilworth Paxson PLLC, Washington, 2001—02; sr. counsel Nat. Assn. Securities Dealers, 2002—. Adj. prof. Washington Coll. Law, The Am. Univ., 1991-92; chmn. Lawyers Com. Effective Assistance of Counsel, 1995—. Comments editor Washington U. Law Quarterly, 1971-72 (honors scholar award 1971). Bd. dirs. Thomas and Bertie T. Smith Arts Found., 1996—, James Madison Project, 1999—. Mem. ABA, Am. Soc. Internat. Law, Nat. Assn. Criminal Def. Lawyers, Univ. Club, D.C. Assn. Criminal Def. Lawyers (v.p. 1995-97), Order of Coif, Stan Musial Soc., E.B. Williams Inn of Ct. (master). Office: Dilworth Paxson PLLC 1200 19th St NW Washington DC 20036 E-mail: khaki@verizon.net.

MARTIN, RANDI CHRISTINE, psychology educator; b. Salem, Oreg., May 24, 1949; d. Harold Raymond and Maxine Constance (Torgeson) M.; m. Lawrence P. Chan, Aug. 30, 1974. BA, U. Oreg., 1971; MA, Johns Hopkins U., 1977, PhD, 1979. Lectr. U. Calif., Santa Cruz, 1979-80; assoc. rsch. scientist Johns Hopkins U., Balt., 1980-82; asst. prof. Rice U., Houston, 1982-87, assoc. prof., 1987-93, prof., 1993—, chair psychology dept., 2002—. Assoc. editor Psychonomic Bulletin & Rev., Austin, Tex., 1995—; editl. bd. mem. Cognitive Neuropsychology, London, 1994—, Jour. Neurolinguistics, Cambridge, Eng., 1994—; contbr. articles to profl. jours. Recipient Claude Pepper award NIH Deafness and Comm. Disorders Inst., 1995—. Fellow APA; mem. Psychonomic Soc. (sec./treas. 1993-95, bd. dirs. 1997—), Acad. Aphasia (program com. 1990-93). Achievements include research in short term memory deficits in brain damaged patients. Office: Rice U Dept Psychology 6100 Main St Houston TX 77005-1892

MARTIN, RAYMOND ANTHONY, neurologist, educator; b. Far Rockaway, N.Y., July 11, 1942; s. John R. and Sara Martin; m. Josephine M. Artino, June 26, 1965; children: Sandra, David R. BA, SUNY, Buffalo, 1964, MD, 1968. Diplomate Am. Bd. Psychiatry and Neurology. Resident in neurology Mayo Clinic, Rochester, Minn., 1971-73, 74-75, fellow in immunology, 1975; exch. fellow in clin. neurology Royal Victoria Infirmary and U. Newcastle upon Tyne, Eng., 1973-74; cons. Mayo Clinic and Mayo Grad. Sch. Medicine, Rochester, 1976-77; pvt. practice, Houston, 1977—. Instr. neurology U. Minn. Sch. Medicine, Mpls., 1976-77; clin. asst. prof. dept. neurology and dept. family practice and cmty. medicine U. Tex. Health Sci. Ctr., Houston; bd. dirs. health net bd. Meml. Hermann Health Care Sys., Houston, 1993—; cons. in neurology Tex. Bd. Med. Examiners, 1991—. Capt. M.C., U.S. Army, 1969-70, Vietnam. Recipient outstanding edn. award U. Tex. Family Practice Residents-Meml. S.W. Hosp., 1984; John S. Dunn Sr. Outstanding Tchr. award Meml. family practice residency program U. Tex. Health Sci. Ctr., 1992, 99, Dean's Tchg. Excellence award in family medicine, 1994, 95; Robert E. Elliott scholar SUNY, 1965, Avalon Found. scholar, 1965, Orton Heyer scholar, 1966; postdoctoral fellow NIH, 1975-78. Fellow Am. Acad. Neurology (liaison legis. affairs com. 1990-93, mem. subcom. on edn. for non-neurologists, 1994—, chmn. consortium neurology tchrs. family practice, honor roll of neurology tchrs. 2002), Am. Acad. Disability Evaluating Physicians; mem. AMA, Am. EEG Soc., Am. Assn. Electrodiagnostic Medicine, Soc. Tchrs. Family Medicine, Am. Heart Assn. (fellow stroke coun., bd. dirs. Houston divsn. 1997-99), Nat. Multiple Sclerosis Soc. (med. adv. com. Lone Star chpt. 1981—, chmn. 1989-95, bd. dirs. 1999-2001; vice chmn. 1998-00, mem. chpt. svcs. com. 1989-93, exec. com. 1991—, vice chmn. exec. com. 1998-20, chmn. bd. 1999—), Tex. Med. Assn., Tex. Neurol. Soc. (v.p. 1985-86, pres. 1987-88, peer rev. com. 1986—, membership com. 1986—), Houston Neurol. Soc., Harris County Med. Soc. (liaison to Houston Bar Assn. com. 1992-94, alt. del. to Tex. Med. Assn. 1994—), Mayo Alumni Assn., SUNY Buffalo Med. Alumni Assn., James A Gibson Anat. Soc., Alpha Omega Alpha. Avocation: running. Office: Houston Neurology Assocs 8200 Wednesbury Ln Ste 111 Houston TX 77074-2998 E-mail: ramart@houston.rr.com.

MARTIN, RAYMOND BRUCE, plumbing equipment manufacturing company executive; b. N.Y.C., Oct. 23, 1934; s. Raymond M. and Margaret (Lennon) M.; m. Suzanne Ruth Longpre, Sept. 3, 1960; 1 son, Christopher Haines. AB, Villanova U., 1956. With Corning Glass Works (N.Y.), 1956-68, nat. plumbing sales mgr., 1966-68; v.p. mktg. Briggs Mfg. Co., Warren, Mich., 1968-69, v.p., gen. mgr. plumbing fixture div., 1969-72; pres., chief exec. officer Water Control Internat. Inc., Troy, 1972-91; dir. Internat. Tech. Corp.; pres., chief exec. officer W/C Technology Corp., 1991; mem. plumbing harmonization Fed. North Am. Free Trade Delegation, 1992. Served with AUS, 1957-58. Mem. Am. Soc. Plumbing Engrs., Plumbing Mfrs. Inst. (chmn. HUD Task Group 1981-82, chmn. communications com. 1983-86, chmn. fed. water conservation com. 1988-90, chmn. flushing devices com. 1999—, chmn. info. tech. com. 2002—), Am. Soc. Sanitary Engrs., ASME (panel 19, chmn. definitions task group 1993-94, chmn. water closet hydraulic performance task group 1993-94, chmn. flushing devices com. 2000—). Republican. Roman Catholic. Office: 37685 Interchange Dr Farmington Hills MI 48335

MARTIN, RAYMOND S. international health consultant; b. Jan. 29, 1940; BA, Goshen (Ind.) Coll., 1966; MPH, Johns Hopkins U., 1985. Health devel. officer U.S. AID, Rabat, Morocco, 1968-70, Washington, 1970-78, Accra, Ghana, 1978-80, Yaounde, Cameroon, 1980-84, Islamabad, Pakistan, 1985-89, Kinshasa, Zaire, 1989-92; pub. health specialist World Bank, Washington, 1992—. Cotnabr. articles to profl. jours. Exec. dir. Christian Connections for Internat. Health, McLean, Va., 1997—. Mem. APHA (chair-elect. internat. health sect.). Office: 1817 Rupert St Mc Lean VA 22101-5434 E-mail: martinrs@aol.com.

MARTIN, RICHARD H. principal; b. Washington, Feb. 25, 1956; s. Henderson E. and Margaret Roxena Martin; m. Lori Confer Martin, Nov. 6, 1982. BS in Edn., Calif. State Coll., 1978, MA in Comms., 1980; EdD in Edn. Adminstrn., W.Va. U., 1991. Cert. tchr., supr., prin., supt. schs. Asst. to dean Calif. State Coll., 1978-80; tchr. Turkeyfoot Sch. Dist., Confluence, Pa., 1980-81, Somerset (Pa.) Sch. Dist., 1981-82, Frazier Sch. Dist., Perryopolis, Pa., 1982-85, dept. chair, 1985-90, prin., 1990-96, Mt. Lebanon Sch. Dist., Pitts., 1996-99, Bethlehem Ctr. High Sch., 1999—. Cons. W.Va. Dept. of Edn., Charleston, 1990—, Intermediate Unit #1, Calif., 1982-90; mem. safety coun. Mt. Lebanon Sch. Dist., Pitts., 1997—; trainer in IDEA Allegheny Intermediate Unit, Pitts., 1998—; adj. asst. prof. W.Va. U., 1991—. Contbr. articles to profl. jours. Recipient Cmty. Svc. award Perrypolis Heritage Soc., 1991. Mem. NASSP/PASSP, AASA, ASCD, CEFPI, Mt. Lebanon Found., Masons (floor officer 1985—), Monessen Commandary Knights Templar (floor officer 1985—), Shriners, Uniontown Masons, Phi Delta Kappa. Avocations: fly fishing, hunting, good cigars. Home: 225 Nobles Rd Brownsville PA 15417-9283 E-mail: lmartin@mail.mlynk.com.

MARTIN, RICHARD JAY, medical educator; b. Detroit, May 16, 1946; s. Peter Aaron and Tillie Jean (Munch) M.; m. Helene Iris Horowitz, Dec. 23, 1967; children: Elizabeth Hope, David Evan. BS, U. Mich., 1967, MD, 1971. Diplomate Am. Bd. Internal Medicine and Pulmonary Disease. Intern, Ariz., 1971-72; resident Tulane U., New Orleans, 1974-76; pulmonary fellow, 1976-78; asst. prof. medicine U. Okla., Okla. City, 1978-80, U. Colo., Denver, 1980-85, assoc. prof., 1985-92, prof., 1992—. Dir. Cardiorespiratory Sleep Rsch., Nat. Jewish Med. and Rsch. Ctr., Denver, 1980-89, staff physician, 1980—, head divsn. pulmonary medicine, 1993—, vice chair dept. of medicine, 1997—. Author: Cardiorespiratory Disorders During Sleep, 1984, 2d edit., 1990, (with others) Current Therapy in Internal Medicine, 1984, Clinical Pharmacology and Therapeutics in Nursing, 1985, Interdisciplinary Rehabilitation of Multiple Sclerosis and Neuromuscular Disorders, 1984, Drugs for the Respiratory System, 1985, Current Therapy in Pulmonary Medicine, 1985, Abnormalities of Respiration During Sleep, 1986, Mitchell's Synopsis of Pulmonary Medicine, 1987, Pulmonary Grand Rounds, 1990, Asthma and Rhinitis, 1994, The High Risk Patient: Management of the Critically Ill, 1995, Manual of Asthma Management, 1995, 2000, Severe Asthma: Pathogenesis and Clinical Management, 1995, Curret Pulmonology, 1995, Pulmonary and Respiratory Therapy Secrets, 1996, (book chpts.) Lung Biology in Health and Disease, 1995, 97, 2000, Allergy, 1997, Asthma, 1997, Emergency Asthma, 1999, Difficult Asthma, 1999, Asthma and Rhinitis, 1999, Imaging of Diffuse Lung Disease, 2000; editor: Nocturnal Asthma: Mechanisms and Interventions, 1993, Cardiothoracic Interrelationships in Clinical Practice, 1997; author, editor: Nocturnal Asthma: Mechanisms and Treatment, 1993, Combination Therapy for Asthma and Chronic Obstructive Pulmonary Disease, 2000; mem. editl. bd.: (jour.) Chronobiology Internat., 1997—, Am. Jour. of Respiratory and Critical Care Medicine, 1994-98, Bronchial Asthma: Index and Review, 1996-97; assoc. editor: Clinical Care for Asthma, 1995-97; contbr. articles, reviews, reports on respiratory and neuromuscular diseases to profl. jours. Pres. Congregation Rodef Shalom, Denver, 1984-85; regional v.p. United Synagogues of Am., Denver, 1988-89. Pulmonary fellow Am. Lung Assn., 1977-79; James F. Hammarsten Outstanding fellow U. Okla. Health Scis. Ctr., 1978; grantee Am. Lung Assn., VA, U. Okla. Lung Assn., NIH, Parker B. Francis Found.; recipient Best Paper in Internal Medicine award Okla. Soc. Interna. Medicine, 1977, 78, U. Okla. Gastroenterology sect, 1977. Mem. Am. Thoracic Soc., Am. Fedn. for Clin. Rsch., Am. Coll. Chest Physicians (rep. to Young Pulmonary Physician Conf., St. Charles, Ill. 1979), ACP, Colo. Trudeau Soc., Western Soc. Clin. Investigation. Avocations: biking, golf, karate. Office: Nat Jewish Med Rsch Ctr 1400 Jackson St Denver CO 80206-2761 E-mail: martinr@njc.org.

MARTIN, RICHARD KELLEY, lawyer; b. Tulsa, June 30, 1952; s. Richard Loye and Maxine (Kelley) M.; m. Reba Lawson, June 12, 1993; children from previous marriage: R. Kyle, Andrew J. BA, Westminster Coll., 1974; JD, So. Meth. U., 1977. Bar: Tex. 1977, U.S. Tax Ct. 1979. Ptnr. Akin, Gump, Strauss, Hauer & Feld, LLP, Dallas, 1977-95, Haynes and Boone LLP, Dallas, 1995—. Bd. dirs. Goodwill Industries, Dallas, 1986-2000, v.p., 1986-91; bd. dirs. Greater Dallas Youth Orchs., 1987-90; bd. dirs., v.p., pres. Big Bros. and Sisters Met. Dallas, 1988-91; bd. dirs. Tejas coun. Girl Scouts U.S., 1997-2001. Mem. Tex. Bar Assn., Salesmanship Club Dallas. Republican. Methodist. Office: Haynes and Boone LLP 1505 N Plano Rd Ste 4000 Richardson TX 75082-4101 E-mail: rick.martin@haynesboone.com.

MARTIN, RICHARD L. retired insurance executive; b. Franklin, N.J., Feb. 2, 1932; s. Richard Lewis and Elizabeth (Roe) M.; m. Susan Mazuy, June 20, 1970; children: David Cory, Scott Mazuy; m. Victoria Lee Morton, May 30, 1998; 1 stepchild, Robert M. Ferguson. BEd, U. Miami, 1958; MA, Columbia U., 1963. Chartered Property Casualty Underwriter. Educator Franklin (N.J.) Sch. Dist., 1958-60; mng. dir. Sparta (N.J.) Sch. Dist., 1960-66; adminstr. Orange (N.J.) Sch. System, 1966-71; chief exec. officer Montague (N.J.) Sch. Dist., 1971-72, Stanhope (N.J.) Sch. System, 1972-73; v.p. Selective Ins. Group, Branchville, N.J., 1973-87; pres., chief exec. officer Med. Malpractice Ins. Assn., N.Y.C., 1987-98; ret., 1998. Chmn. N.J. Anti-Car Theft Com., Trenton, 1980-87; treas. N.J. Ins. News Svc., Newark, 1982-87; chmn. AIA-N.J. State Conf., Trenton, 1983-87. Contbr. several articles to mags. With USMC, 1952-54. Mem. CPCU, Am. Mgmt. Assn., Soc. Ins. Research, Soc. for Corp. Planning, City Midday, Newton Country, Branchville Rotary, Sons of Am. Revolution, Mayflower Soc. Presbyterian. Avocations: golf, hunting. Home: Two Plains Rd Augusta NJ 07822

MARTIN, ROBERT, CEO; m. Theresa Martin. PhD in econ. & fin., Southern Mehodist U.; MA in econ. & fin., Southern Methodist U.; graduate, U. North Tex. CEO U. Pa. Health Sys., 2001—, COO; exec. dir. Clinical Care Assoc., 1997—99; chief adminstrv. officer, treas. Bd. Gov. Meml. Health Sys., Ariz. Office: U Penn Hosp Sys 21 Penn Tower Philadelphia PA 19104*

MARTIN, ROBERT BRUCE, chemistry educator; b. Chgo., Apr. 29, 1929; s. Robert Frank and Helen (Woelffer) M.; m. Frances May Young, June 7, 1953. BS, Northwestern U., 1950; PhD, U. Rochester, 1953. Asst. prof. chemistry Am. U., Beirut, Lebanon, 1953-56; research fellow Calif. Inst. Tech., 1956-57, Harvard U., 1957-59; asst. prof. chemistry U. Va., Charlottesville, 1959-61, assoc. prof., 1961-65, prof., 1965—, chmn. dept., 1968-71. Spl. fellow Oxford U., 1961-62; Program dir. Molecular Biology Sect., NSF, 1965-66 Author: Introduction to Biophysical Chemistry, 1964. Fellow AAAS; mem. Am. Chem. Soc. Office: Univ Va Dept Chemistry Charlottesville VA 22901

MARTIN, ROBERT BURTON, management and marketing consultant; b. Takoma Park, Md., Mar. 17, 1935; s. Herbert Lester and Lenora Marie (Sponseller) M.; m. Mary Lou Rushworth, Sept. 7, 1959 (div. Dec. 1982); children: Laurajean, Kenneth, Donna Beth. BEE, Cornell U., 1958; MS, Northwestern U., 1966, PhD, 1967. Dir. mgmt. systems Denver and Rio Grande Western R.R., 1967-71; v.p. Mgmt. Design Assoc., Denver, 1971-79; owner Martin & Assoc., 1979—; founder Martin Aquatics, LLC, 1993—. Treas. Rocky Mountain chpt. Inst. of Mgmt. Sci., Denver, 1968-70; opening speaker AICPAs, Las Vegas, Nev., 1988. Author, pub.: (newsletter) Martin Reports, 1981-90, Bob Martin-Chris Frederiksen Marketing and Management Report for CPAs, 1990-94. Served to lt. USN, 1958-63. Mem. Inst. Mgmt. Cons., Alpha Pi Mu, Sigma Xi. Avocations: hiking, camping, ultralight aviation, watersports. Home and Office: PO Box 6886 Denver CO 80206-0886

MARTIN, ROBERT DALE, lawyer; b. Canton, Ohio, Oct. 1, 1937; s. Charles Leroy and Edith Ruby (Turnbull) M.; m. Carla Jean Kibler, Dec. 27, 1966; 1 child, Kendall Dalene. BA, Ohio U., 1960; JD, U. Akron, 1969, M in Taxation, 1989; MBA, Ashland U., 1995; postgrad., Kent State U., 1998. Bar: Ohio 1969, U.S. Dist. Ct. (no. dist.) 1984, U.S. Ct. Appeals (6th cir.) 1984. Pers. adminstr. Hoover Co., North Canton, Ohio, 1966-67; atty. Allmon and Benson, Carrollton, 1967-69; legal staff asst. Republic Steel Corp., Canton, 1969-71, indsl. rels. counsel, 1971-73, supt. labor rels., 1973-78, asst. supt. indsl. rels., 1978-85; mgr. human resources Republic Engineered Steel Corp., 1985-91; gen. counsel, dir. adminstrn. Office of Summit County Engr., Akron, 1991-95; adminstr. bus. and human svcs. Ohio Dept. Transp., New Philadelphia, 1995—. Adj. prof. bus. law Ashland (Ohio) U., 1988; gen. counsel mgmt. consulting Labor Rels. Assocs., Dayton, Ohio, 1991-93; gen. counsel human resource consulting Human Resources Assocs., Dayton, 1993-95. Sgt. U.S. Army, 1960. Sgt. U.S. Army, 1960. Mem. Ohio State Bar Assn. (gen. sect. 1970-97, labor/employment law sect. 1995-99, probate/trust sect. 1996-99, corp. law 1996-99), Nat. Assn. Cert. Govt. Fin. Mgmt. Avocations: walking, fishing, reading, fitness. Home and Office: 850 Mcdaniel Ave Minerva OH 44657-1240 Fax: (330) 868-6161.

MARTIN, ROBERT DAVID, judge, educator; b. Iowa City, Oct. 7, 1944; s. Murray and G'Ann (Holmgren) M.; m. Ruth A. Haberman, Aug. 21, 1966; children: Jacob, Matthew, David. AB, Cornell Coll., Mt. Vernon, Iowa, 1966; JD, U. Chgo., 1969. Bar: Wis. 1969, U.S. Dist. Ct. (we. dist.) Wis. 1969, U.S. Dist. Ct. (ea. dist.) Wis. 1974, U.S. Supreme Ct. 1973. Assoc. Ross & Stevens, S.C., Madison, Wis., 1969-72, ptnr., 1973-78; chief judge U.S. Bankruptcy Ct. We. Dist. Wis., 1978—. Instr. gen. practice course U. Wis. Law Sch., 1974, 76, 77, 80, lectr. debtor/creditor course, 1981-82, 83, 85, 87, 2001, farm credit seminar, 1985, advanced bankruptcy problems, 1989, 91, 96; co-chmn. faculty Am. Law Inst.-ABA Fin. and Bus. Planning for Agr., Stanford U., 1979; faculty mem. Fed. Jud. Ctr. Schs. for New Bankruptcy Judges, 1985-96; chmn. Ann. Continuing Legal Edn. Wis. Debtor Creditor Conf., 1981—. Author: Bankruptcy: Annotated Forms, 1989; co-author: Secured Transactions Handbook for Wisconsin Lawyers and Lenders, Bankruptcy-Text Statutes Rules and Forms, 1992, Ginsberg and Martin on Bankruptcy, 4th edit., 1996. Chmn., bd. dirs., mem. exec. com. Luth. Social Svc. Wis. and Upper Mich.; bd. dirs., mem. exec. com. Turnaround Mgmt. Assn., 1997—. Mem. Wis. State Bar, Am. Coll. Bankruptcy, Am. Judicature Soc., Nat. Conf. Bankruptcy Judges (bd. govs. 1989-91, sec. 1993-94, v.p. 1994-95, pres. 1995-96), Nat. Bankruptcy Conf. Office: 120 N Henry Rm 340 PO Box 548 Madison WI 53701-0548

MARTIN, ROBERT EDWARD, architect; b. Dodge City, Kans., Mar. 17, 1928; s. Emry and Alice Jane (Boyce) M.; m. Billie Jo Lange, Aug. 16, 1952 (div. Feb. 1970); m. Kathryn M. Arvanitis, June 26, 1971; children: Lynn, Amy, Blaine. Student, McPherson Coll., 1946-48; BArch, U. Cin., 1954. Registered architect, Ohio. Architect Samborn, Steketee, Otis & Evans, Inc., Toledo, 1956-58; prin. Schauder & Martin, 1958-72, The Collaborative, Inc., Toledo, 1972-93. Mem. Bd. Examiners Archs., Ohio, 1985-95, pres., 1989-94; bd. examiners Nat. Coun. Archtl. Registration Bds., 1986-95, edn. com., 1992; chmn. site design divsn. Archtl. Registration Exam., 1989, 90, 91; mem. Nat. Coun. Archtl. Registration Bds. Grading, 1987-94; chmn. study of Toledo Fire & Rescue Dept., Corp. for Effective Govt., 1994. Artist numerous paintings. Mem. Toledo Planning Commn., 1971-74, Toledo Zoning Appeals Bd., 1973, Toledo Bd. Bldg. Stds., 1967-84, Citizens Fire Adv. Commn., 1974-80, Citizens Urban Area Adv. Commn., 1962, Toledo Area Coun. Govts., 1977-80, Com. of 100, Toledo, 1987-89, Spectrum Friends Fine Arts, Inc., Toledo; chmn. bd. Toledo Area Govtl. Rsch. Assn., 1981-90; chmn. Corp. for Effective Govt., Study of Toledo Fire and Rescue Dept., 1994; chmn. Cystic Fibrosis, Toledo. 1985. Served to capt. USAF, 1954-56. Recipient numerous watercolor awards. Fellow AIA (pres. Toledo chpt. 1966, Arch. of Yr. 1993), Archs. Soc. Ohio (pres. 1975), Ohio Watercolor Soc. (trustee 1999—), N.W. Ohio Watercolor Soc., Toledo Fedn. Art Socs. (pres. 1989, 90), Spectrum, Tile Club (v.p.), Toledo Artists Club, Sylvania Country Club, Rotary, Masons, Shriners, Jesters. Mem. Ch. of Brethren. Avocation: painting. Home: 5119 Regency Dr Toledo OH 43615-2946 Office: 1700 N Reynolds Rd Toledo OH 43615-3628

MARTIN, ROBERT FRANCIS, roof maintenance systems company executive; b. Bronx, N.Y., Sept. 16, 1942; s. James Edward and Loretta Rita (Martin); children: Craig, Keith, Dana. Student, St. Mary's Coll., Ky., 1960-64; BS in Mktg. Econs., Fordham U., 1967. Registered roof cons. Mgr. Owens Corning Fiberglass, N.Y.C., 1965-70; gen. sales mgr. Bradco Supply, Avenel, N.J., 1970-73; pres. Roof Maintenance Systems, Farmingdale, 1973—. Mem. teaching staff Ctr. for Profl. Advancement, 1989—. Coach referee Jackson Vics Soccer Club, N.J., 1973-91; coach Holbrook Little League, N.J., 1976-86, Pop Warner Football, N.J., 1979-85; founder Drug Prevention Program for Children, N.Y.C., 1965-69. Fellow Am. Inst. Plant Engrs. (pres. 1987-89, Engr. of Yr. 1981), Roof Cons. Inst. (past officer, region I bd. dirs., registered roof cons., past officer); mem. Constrn. Specification Inst., Bldg. Owners and Mgrs., Nat. Roofing Contractors, N.E. Roofing Contractors Assn., Bldg. Trades Assn., Single Ply Roofing Inst. Republican. Office: Roof Maintenance Systems PO Box 67 Farmingdale NJ 07727-0067

MARTIN, ROBERT LESLIE, physician; b. Abilene, Tex., Oct. 28, 1934; s. Leslie Resa and Garnet Iva (Brown) M.; m. Henrietta Montgomery, 1956; children: Randal, Christopher. BA, U. Kans., 1956, MD, 1960. Diplomate in clin. pathology Am. Bd. Pathology; diplomate Nat. Bd. Med. Examiners; lic. physician, Calif., Fla. Intern U. Kans., 1960-61, resident and fellow in pathology, 1964-67; asst. prof. pathology Case We. Res. U., Cleve., 1967-78; dir. clin. labs. Univ. Hosps. of Cleve., 1972-76; assoc. prof. pathology U. South Fla., Tampa, 1978-82; chief clin. pathology James A. Haley Vets. Hosp., 1978-82; project mgr. Scott Sci. & Tech., Albequerque, N.Mex., 1982-83; physician advisor Profl. Found. for Health Care Inc., Tampa, 1984-89; primary care physician Fla., 1986-98; med. rev. officer MBA Meditest, Bartow, 1995—. Contbr. articles to profl. jours. Fellow Coll. Am. Pathologists; Alpha Omega Alpha, Phi Gamma Delta. Republican. Episcopalian. Home: 15840 Sanctuary Dr Tampa FL 33647-1075 E-mail: rlmartinmd@aol.com.

MARTIN, ROBERT SIDNEY, federal agency administrator; b. Houston, Aug. 13, 1949; s. Sidney A. and Elizabeth Ann Martin. BA, Rice U., 1971; MLS, U. N. Tex., 1979; PhD, U. N.C., 1988. Libr. assoc. U. Tex., Austin, 1972-76; debt claims adjustor U.S. Gen. Accounting Office, Washington, 1977; libr. U. Tex., Arlington, 1977-80; instr. Sch. Libr. and Info. Sci. U. Wis., Madison, 1984; assoc. dean Librs. La. State U., Baton Rouge, 1985-95; dir., libr. Tex. State Libr. and Archives Commn., Austin, 1995—99; dir. Inst. of Museum and Library Serv., Washington, 2001—. Co-author: Countours of Discovery, 1982, Maps of Texas and the Southwest, 1513-1900, 1984 (Kate Broock Bates award 1985); editor: Scholarly Communication in an Electronic Environment: Issues for Research, 1993, Carnegie Denied: Communities Rejecting Carnegie Library Construction Grants, 1993; mem. editl. bd. Am. Archivist, 1994—, Libr. Quar., 1995—. Mem. ALA (councilor 1998—), Nat. Assn. Govt. Archivists and Records Adminstrs. (mem. exec. bd. 1996—), Tex. Map Soc. (v.p. 1996—), Book Club Tex. (v.p. 1996—). Avocations: hiking, photography, music. Office: Inst of Museum and Library Serv 1100 Pennsylvania Ave NW Washington DC 20506 Office Fax: 202-606-8591. E-mail: martin@tsl.state.tx.us.*

MARTIN, ROBERT WILLIAM, corporate director; b. Toronto, Ont., Can., June 7, 1936; s. William George and Evelyn Irene (Phillips) M.; m. Patricia Lorraine Norris, June 27, 1959; children: Stephen Gregory, Robert Scott, Adrienne Christine Teron. BASc., U. Toronto, 1958. Pres., CEO Consumers Gas, Toronto, 1973-92. Bd. dirs. Enbridge Inc., Cara Ops. Ltd., Aon Reed Stenhouse, HSBC Bank Can.; chmn. Acres Inc. Gov. York U.; campaign chmn. United Way Toronto; past chmn. Toronto Symphony Orch. Recipient Meritorious Svc. award U. Toronto, 1983, Arbor award. Mem. Assn. Profl. Engrs. Ont., Can. Gas Assn. (past chmn.), Ont. Natural Gas Assn. (past pres.), Mad River Golf Club, Toronto Club. Home: 118 Farnham Ave Toronto ON Canada M4V 1H4

MARTIN, ROBERT WILLIAM, econometrician; b. Elizabeth, N.J., Nov. 14, 1961; s. Edward Robert Martin and Vivienne Angela Schaul. BA in English, U. N.C., 1984, BA in Econs., 1985; MA in Econs., Clemson U., 1989. Rsch. asst. dept. econs. Clemson (S.C.) U., 1988-89, lectr., policy analyst Ctr. Policy Studies, 1989-90; econometrician, exec. mgr. Bd. Econ. Advisors, Columbia, S.C., 1990—. Cons. Clemson U., 1990; adj. instr. Midlands Tech. Coll., Columbia. Contbr. articles to profl. jours. Mem. Am. Econ. Assn., Nat. Assn. Bus. Economists (Carolinas chpt. regional v.p. and sec.), Omicron Delta Epsilon, Sigma Tau Delta. Avocations: golf, running. Home: 933 Paces Run Ct Columbia SC 29223-7951 Office: Bd Econ Advisors Rembert Dennis Buildin Ste 446 Columbia SC 29201

MARTIN, ROBLEE BOETTCHER, retired cement manufacturing executive; b. St. Louis, Apr. 21, 1922; s. Henry W. and Esther (Boettcher) M.; m. Lillian Seegraves, July 15, 1940; children: Mary Katherine, Bruce Daniel, Amy Lee. BS in Chem. Engring., Columbia U., 1943, MS in Chem. Engring., 1947; D.Sc. in Bus. Adminstrn. (hon.), Cleary Coll., 1962. Prodn. supr. Monsanto Chem. Co., St. Louis, 1946-49; dir. research and devel. Miss. Lime Co., Ste. Genevieve, Mo., 1949-59; pres. Dundee Cement Co., Mich., 1959-69; v.p. Fruehauf Corp.; gen. mgr. (Fruehauf Bldgs. div.), Detroit, 1969-72; pres. Presidents Assn. div. Am. Mgmt. Assn., N.Y.C., 1972-74; pres. insulation div. Keene Corp., Princeton, N.J., 1974-76; chmn., chief exec. officer Keystone Cement Co., Bath, Pa., 1976-89, Giant Cement Co., Harleyville, S.C., 1985-89; sr. v.p., dir. Giant Group Ltd., Beverly Hills, Calif., 1985-89. Served to lt. (j.g.) USNR, 1944-46, PTO. Mem. Sigma Xi, Tau Beta Pi, Phi Lambda Upsilon. Baptist. Home: 2151 Palermo Pl Charleston SC 29406-9231

MARTIN, ROGER BOND, landscape architect, educator; b. Virginia, Minn., Nov. 23, 1936; s. Thomas George and Audrey (Bond) M.; m. Janis Ann Kloss, Aug. 11, 1962; children: Thomas, Stephen, Jonathan. BS with high distinction, U. Minn., 1958; M. Landscape Arch., Harvard U., 1961. Asst. prof. U. Calif.-Berkeley, 1964-66; from assoc. prof. to prof. emeritus U. Minn., Mpls., 1966—99, prof. emeritus, 1999—; owner Roger Martin & Assoc., site planners and landscape architects, 1966-68, 99—; prin. InterDesign, Inc., 1968-84, Martin & Pitz Assocs., Inc., 1984-98; vis. prof. U. Melbourne, 1979-80. Vis. prof. coll. architecture, 2000—02. Prin. works include Minn. Zool. Gardens, 1978 (merit award Am. Soc. Landscape Archs., 1978), Mpls. Pkwy. Restorations, 1972—87 (merit award, 1978, Minn. Classic award Am. Soc. Landscape Archs., 1994), South St. Paul Ctrl. Sq., 1978 (merit award, 1978), Festival Park, Chisholm, Minn., 1986 (merit award, 1986), Miss. Wildlife Refuge Visual Image assessment (merit award, 1989), Nicollet Island Park, Hennepin Avenue Master Plan, 1995 (merit award, 1995). Recipient Fredrick Mann award for svc. to edn. U. Minn., 1990, Disting. Educator award Sigma Lambda Alpha, 1990, Bradford Williams medals for outstanding articles in landscape Architecture mag., 1968, 69, Minn. chpt. Lob Pine award for outstanding svc. to landscape architecture, 1988, Mpls. Com. on Urban Environ. award for design of Whittier Park, 1997; fellow Am. Acad. in Rome, 1962-64. Fellow Am. Soc. Landscape Archs. (pres. Minn. chpt. 1970-72, trustee 1980-84, nat. pres. 1987, chmn.-elect coun. fellows 1991, chmn. 1992-94, past chmn. 1994-96, Pub. Svc. award 1985, Minn. chpt. Classic award 1994); mem. Nat. Coun. Instrs. Landscape Architecture (pres. 1973-74), Can. Soc. Landscape Archs. (hon.). Home and Office: 2912 45th Ave S Minneapolis MN 55406-1829 E-mail: marti009@tc.umn.edu.

MARTIN, ROGER HARRY, college president; b. N.Y.C., June 26, 1943; s. Edwin Diller and Emma (Neuenburg) M.; m. Susan Bradford, Aug. 29, 1970; children: Katherine R., Emily G. BA, Drew U., 1965; BD, Yale U., 1968, STM, 1969; DPhil, Oxford (Eng.) U., 1974. Program officer Edn. Incentive Program, N.Y.C., 1969-70; devel. officer NYU, 1970-71, 75-76; asst. dir. devel. Rensselaer Polytech Inst., Troy, N.Y., 1974-75; asst. prof. history, exec. asst. to pres. Middlebury (Vt.) Coll., 1976-80; assoc. dean Harvard Div. Sch., Cambridge, Mass., 1980-86; prof. history, pres. Moravian Coll., Bethlehem, Pa., 1986-97; pres. Randolph-Macon Coll., 1997—. Author: Evangelicals United: Ecumenical Stirrings in Pre-Victorian Britain, 1795-1830, 1983. Mem. Harvard Club (N.Y.C.), Commonwealth Club (Richmond). Mem. Soc. Of Friends. Avocations: skiing, running. Home: 305 Caroline St Ashland VA 23005-1602 Office: Randolph-Macon Coll Office of Pres PO Box 5005 Ashland VA 23005-5505

MARTIN, ROGER JOHN, computer scientist; b. Ft. Atkinson, Iowa, Sept. 11, 1947; s. Raymond Charles and Linda R. (Kuennen) M.; m. Jane Degnan, Nov. 21, 1970; children: John, Kathryn, Susan, Jacquelyn. BS in Computer Sci., Iowa State U., 1969, MS in Computer Sci., 1971. Computer specialist Naval Ship R & D Ctr., Bethesda, Md., 1971-76; supervisory sys. analyst Exec. Office of Pres., Washington, 1976-82; computer scientist, mgr. software engrng. group Inst. Computer Scis. and Tech., Nat. Inst. Stds. and Tech., 1982-92, chief sys. and software tech. divsn., 1993-95, mgr. software methods, 1995-96; mgr. stds. strategy. Sun Microsys., Palo Alto, Calif., 1996—2002; dir. stds. AOL-TW, Dulles, Va., 2002—. Program co-chmn. Conf. on Software Maintenance, 1985, gen. mgr., 1987; gen. chmn. Computer Stds. Comf., 1988. Soccer coach Montgomery County Recreation Dept., Rockville, Md., 1979-83; treas., del. Mill Creek Towne Elem. Sch. PTA, Rockville, 1981-84, pres., 1986-87; Magruder clustr PTA coord., 1984-856; leader Cub Scouts Am., Rockville, 1983-84, asst. troop scoutmaster, 1984-92. Recipient award for tech. excellence Interagy. Com. on Info. Resources Mgmt., 1989, Fed. Computer Week 100 award, 1992, cert. of recognition Nat. Bur. Stds., 1983, bronze medal Dept. Commerce, 1984, silver medal, 1989, Hans Karlsson award IEEE, 1995, Standards Medallion, 1992. Mem. Assn. for Computing Machinery, IEEE Computer Soc. (chmn. working group on test methods for POSIX 1986-93, tech. com. on conformance testing 1989-94, mem. tech. com. on operating sys. project mgmt. com. 1991-93, cert. of recognition 1987, Meritorious Svc. award 1991, Stds. medal 1992). Home: 1418 Rosalia Ave San Jose CA 95130-1249 Office: Sun Microsystems 901 San Antonio Rd Palo Alto CA 94303-4900 E-mail: rjmartin99@aol.com.

MARTIN, ROGER LLOYD, educator, management consultant; b. Kitchener, Ont., Can., Aug. 4, 1956; s. Lloyd Milton and Delphine Elvera (Horst) M.; m. Nancy Lorraine Lang, Sept. 24, 1983; children: Robert Lloyd, Jennifer Frances, Daniel Roger. BA in Econs., Harvard U., 1979, MBA, 1981. Prin. Can. Cons. Group, Toronto, Ont., Can., 1981-85; chmn. Monitor Co. Can. Ltd., 1986-98; dir. Monitor Co. Inc., Boston, 1988—2000, co-head, 1995-96; chmn., CEO Monitor U., 1993-98; dean, prof. strategy Rotman Sch. Mgmt. U. Toronto, 1998—. Bd. dirs. Celestica Inc., Thomson Corp., Superbuild Corp., XDL Intervest, Hosp. Sick Children, Co. DNA, Workbrain Inc., Butterfield & Robinson, Can. Film Ctr. Contbr. antitrust and internat. trade articles to profl. jours. Mem. Osler Bluffs Ski Club Collingwood, York Club (Toronto). Home: 57 Highland Ave Toronto ON Canada M4W 2A2 Office: U of T Rotman Sch Mgmt 105 St George St Toronto ON Canada M55 3E6 also: Monitor Co Two Canal Pk Cambridge MA 02141 E-mail: martin@rotman.utoronto.ca.

MARTIN, RON, editor, superintendent of schools, consultant, minister; b. Rock Island, Tenn., Aug. 5, 1942; s. Houston and Bernie (Gribble) M.; m. Carolyn J. Odineal, Oct. 5, 1969. AA, Freed-Hardeman Coll., Henderson, Tenn., 1963; BA with honor, David Lipscomb Coll., 1973; MEd with highest honors, Mid. Tenn. State U., 1983; student, Leadership Inst., Harvard U. Grad. Sch. Edn., Oxford (England) U. Entered ministry Ch. of Christ, 1963. Cons. Tenn. Dept. Edn., Nashville, 1977-82; tchr. remedial reading Warren County Schs., McMinnville, Tenn., 1972-74, elem. prin., 1974-77, tchr. Viola, 1981-82, asst. prin. sr. high sch. McMinnville, 1982-85, supt. schs., 1987-92, editor newsletter, 1987—. Min., Bible tchr. Warren County Chs. of Christ, McMinnville, 1963—; announcer, news reporter Cumberland Valley Broadcasting, McMinnville, 1963-90. Vice chmn. Warren County Dem. Com., 1984-86; mem. bd. rev. Eagle Scouts, Boy Scouts Am., McMinnville, 1986—, chmn. 1999—; pres. Warren County Drug Task Force, 1987, 92; chmn. Leadership McMinnville, 1997; pres. Leadership Warren, 1998; chmn. cmty. svcs. K-T Dist. Com.; chmn. Boy Scouts Am. Dist. Named Young Educator of Yr., Warren County Jaycees, 1976, Leader of Yr., 4-H Club, Warren County, 1974-76; recipient Leadership award Tenn. Acad. Sch. Leaders, 1983, Long Rifle award Disting. Dist. Boy Scouts Am. Svc., 2000, Vol. of Yr. award McMinnville-Warren County C. of C., 2001; named Hometown Hero, So. Std., 2002. Mem. NEA, ASCD, Am. Adult Edn. Coun., Nat. Assn. Secondary Sch. Prins., Nat. Staff Devel. Coun., Am. Assn. Sch. Adminstrs., Coun. Adult Basic Edn., Tenn. Edn. Assn., Tenn. Adult Edn. Coun., Tenn. Literary Coun., Warren County Edn. Assn. (rep. assembly 1976, 83, Leadership award), Warren County Aviators and navigators (sec.), Commn. on Adult Basic Edn. (southeast regional rep. 1003-95), Commn. on Adult Basic Edn. (nat. sec. 1995, pres.-elect 1997, pres. 1998), Kiwanis (Warren County pres., disting. pres. 1995, disting. lt. gov. 1997—, cmty. svc. Ky.-Tenn. dist. chmn. 1999, dist. trainer 1997, new club builder 2000, edn. com. 2001, chmn. leadership edn. 2002-), Tenn. Assn. Adult and Cont. Edn. (pres. 2000, co-chair nat. conf. 2001). Avocations: reading, working on community projects, visiting outstanding school systems, teaching young people, developing educational ideas. Home: 4200 Crisp Springs Rd Mc Minnville TN 37110-5239 Office: Warren County Schs 2548 Morrison St Mc Minnville TN 37110-3617

MARTIN, ROY BUTLER, JR. museum director, retired broker; b. Norfolk, Va., May 13, 1921; s. Roy Butler and Anne (Holman) M.; m. Louise Eggleston, Apr. 17, 1948; children: Roy Butler III, Anne Beverly Martin Sessoms. Student, William and Mary Coll., Norfolk, 1939-40; BS in Commerce, U. Va., 1943. Chmn. bd. Commonwealth Brokers Inc., 1955-88; mayor City of Norfolk, 1962-74; pres. Chrysler Mus., Norfolk, 1989-961989—. Pres. U.S. Conf. Mayors, Washington, 1973-74; trustee Sentara Health System, 1985-96. Chmn. Douglas MacArthur Found., 1963-2000, Civic Facilities Commn., Norfolk, 1986—; bd. dirs. Norfolk Forum; exec. com., pres. Va. Mcpl. League, 1968-69; past mem. Va. State Water Control Bd.; past mem. exec. com., adv. bd. Nat. League of Cities, com. on community devel., U.S. Conf. Mayors, Southeastern Va. Planning Dist. Commn; chmn. Southeastern Tidewater Area Manpower Planning System, Mayor's Youth Commn.; Gov.'s Com. on Youth; past bd. dirs. Norfolk Urban Coalition; past mem. VALC Zoning Procedures Com.; past bd. dirs. Norfolk Symphony Orch., Boys Club Norfolk, Old Dominion U. Edns. Found.; past mem. Norfolk Cerebral Palsy Tng. Ctr., vestry Ch. of Good Shepherd, Norfolk. Lt. USNR, 1943-46, USNR, 1948-52. Decorated officer in Order of the Crown (Belgium); recipient Outstanding Alumni award Old Dominion U., 1964, Sales of Yr. award Sales and Mktg. Club Tidewater, 1971, Meritorious Pub. Svc. Citation Dept. Navy, 1974, Cmty. Svc. award Jewish Cmty. Ctr., 1974, Cert. Appreciation Va. Food Dealers Assn., 1974, Fall Guy award Saints and Sinners, 1974, Brotherhood award NCCJ, 1976, First Citizen award City of Norfolk, 1974. Mem. Norfolk Yacht and Country Club (pres. 1990-92), Va. Club (bd. dirs. 1991-93), Chi Phi, Alpha Kappa Psi. Episcopalian. Home: 1519 Commonwealth Ave Norfolk VA 23505-1719

MARTIN, ROY CLAYTON, clinical neuropsychologist; b. St. Petersburg, Fla., Mar. 1, 1961; s. Jim Orlopp and Barbara Martin; m. Cindy Lawrence, June 20, 1986; 1 child, James D. BS, Augusta State U., 1984, MS, 1987; PhD, La. State U., 1995. Lic. psychologist, Ala. Asst. prof. U. Ala., Birmingham, 1995—. Contbr. articles to profl. jours. Chair adv. bd. Epilepsy Found. North Ctrl. Ala., Birmingham, 1999—. Recipient Young Investigator award Epilepsy Found. Am., 1999—. Mem. APA, Am. Psychol. Soc., Internat. Neuropsychol. Soc., Nat. Acad. Neuropsychology, Am. Epilepsy Soc. Office: Dept Neurology U Ala 312 Cir 1719 6th Ave S Birmingham AL 35294-0001

MARTIN, SHANE PATRICK, education educator, consultant; b. L.A., Aug. 7, 1958; s. Robert Curtis and Lucille Catherine (Koch) M. BA in History, Loyola Marymount U., 1980; MDiv, Jesuit Sch. Theology, Berkeley, Calif., 1991, ThM, 1992; PhD, U. So. Calif., 1995. Clear secondary tchg. credential, Calif. Mem. faculty Bellarmine Coll. Prep. Sch., San Jose, Calif., 1984, 85-88, dir. campus ministry, 1987-88; grad. tchg. asst. Jesuit Sch. Theology, 1990-92; lectr. Loyola Marymount U., L.A., 1994-95, assoc. prof. edn., 1995—, coord. secondary edn., 2000—02, acting coord. bilingual and multicultural edn. programs, 1999-2000, assoc. dean of edn., 2002—. Adj. prof. U. San Francisco, 1996—; cons., sr. assoc. Karadenes & Assocs., L.A., 1998—; sr. rsch. cons. Imoyase Group, Inc., 2001—. Author: Cultural Diversity in Catholic Schools, 1996. Trustee Loyola H.S., L.A., 1997—98; bd. mem. Greendot Pub. Charter Schs., 2000—; bd. dirs., chmn. com. Coun. on Anthropology and Edn. Grantee Loyola Marymount U., 1996, 1998, 1999, 2001, 2002. Mem. Am. Anthrop. Assn., Am. Ednl. Rsch. Assn., Am. Assn. for Colls. Tchr. Edn., Assn. Tchr. Educators, Nat. Assn. for Multicultural Edn., Nat. Cath. Edn. Assn. (McGivney Meml. Fund grantee 1993). Avocations: travel, cultural events, music, technology, mentoring. Office: Loyola Marymount U Sch Edn 1 LMU Dr UH Ste 2612 Los Angeles CA 90045-2659 E-mail: smartin@lmu.edu.

MARTIN, SIDNEY A. ophthalmologist; b. New Haven, May 28, 1929; s. Frank and Isabelle Martin; m. Susan Patricia Martin, Feb. 16, 1962; children: Steven, John, Jeff, Elizabeth. BA, Princeton U., 1951; MD, SUNY, Bklyn., 1955. Diplomate Am. Bd. Ophthalmology. Intern Beth Israel Hosp., N.Y.C., 1955-56; resident Balt. Eye and Ear Hosp., 1958—61; ophthalmologist North Shore Eye Care, Smithtown, N.Y., 1962—; attending St. Catherine's Hosp. Office: North Shore Eye Care 260 Middle Country Rd Smithtown NY 11787-3501

MARTIN, STACEY, accountant; b. Dallas, Dec. 5, 1951; d. Orval Calvin and Adella Aloise (Morgan) M.; m. Bryan Keith Ellis, Jan. 31, 1987; children: Martin Harrison, Morgan Houston Ellis. BA in Bus. Adminstrn., Austin Coll., 1973; MBA in Acctg., So. Meth. U., 1974. CPA, 1982. Jr. acct. MacIver & Bell, CPA's, Dallas, 1974-76; staff acct. Steak & Ale Restaurants, Inc., 1975-76; internal auditor Columbia Gen. Corp., 1976-80; tax specialist MARC, Inc., 1981—. Owner Sallie's Baby, Infant & Toddler Knitwear, 1988—. Mem. Greenland Hills Neighborhood Assn., Dallas, 1983-94, Dallas Heritage Soc., 1987, Dallas Arboretum Soc., 1987. Mem. AICPA, Tex. Soc. CPA's, DAR (treas. White Oak chpt. 1990—), United Daus. of the Confederacy, Daus. Republic of Tex. (treas. Peter James Bailey chpt. 1993—). Presbyterian. Office: MARC Inc 7850 N Belt Line Rd Irving TX 75063-6098

MARTIN, STANLEY A. lawyer; b. Logansport, Ind., Apr. 9, 1955; s. Richard James and Helen Elizabeth (Newburn) M.; m. Kellie Lea McCabe, Aug. 14, 1988. BS, MIT, 1977; JD, Boston Coll., 1984. Bar: Mass. 1985, U.S. Dist. Ct. Mass. 1985, U.S. Ct. Appeals (1st cir.) 1985, N.H. 1986, U.S. Dist. Ct. N.H. 1987. Prin. Stan Martin, Designer/Builder, Andover, Mass., 1977-84; assoc. Gadsby & Hannah LLP, Boston, 1984-91, ptnr., 1992—2001, Holland & Knight LLP, Boston, 2001—. Lectr. Northeastern U., Boston, 1989—95, MIT, 2000—01. Author: Mechanic's Liens, Performance and Payment Bonds under Massachusetts Law, 1989, 7th rev. edit., 1996; co-author: Architect-Engineer Liability Under Massachusetts Law, 1985, 5th rev. edit., 1990, Aspen Construction Law Update Annual; contbr. articles to profl. jours. Bd. dirs. Andover Com./A Better Chance-ABC, 1981—84, Associated Gen. Contractors of Mass., 1999—2001, Boston Archtl. Ctr., 2000—, Edgewood Retirement Cmty., 2001—. Mem. ABA (pub. contract sect., chair region I 1990-96), Am. Arbitration Assn. Constrn. Industry Panel, Mass. Bar Assn. (chair pub. law sect. 1993-94), Internat. Bar Assn., N.H. Bar Assn. Home: 13 Brown St Andover MA 01810-5302 Office: Holland & Knight LLP 10 St James Ave Boston MA 02116 Fax: 617-523-6850. E-mail: smartin@hklaw.com.

MARTIN, SUSAN KATHERINE, librarian; b. Cambridge, Eng., Nov. 14, 1942; came to U.S., 1950, naturalized, 1961; d. Egon and Jolan (Schonfeld) Orowan; m. David S. Martin, June 30, 1962. BA with honors, Tufts U., 1963; MS, Simmons Coll., 1965; PhD, U. Calif., Berkeley, 1983. Intern libr. Harvard U., Cambridge, Mass., 1963-65, systems libr., 1965-73; head systems office gen. libr. U. Calif., Berkeley, 1973-79; dir. Milton S. Eisenhower Libr. Johns Hopkins U., Balt., 1979-88, exec. dir. Nat. Commn. on Libraries and Info. Sci., 1988-90; univ. libr. Georgetown U., Washington, 1990-2001, tchr., cons., 2001—; pres. SKM Assocs., 2001—. Mem. libr. com. Princeton (N.J.) U., 1987—95; mem. vis. com. Harvard U. Libr., 1987—93, 1994—2000; bd. overseers for univ. libr. Tufts U., 1986—2001, Tufts U. Sch. Arts and Scis., 2001—; cons. various librs. and info. cos., 1975—; mem. libr. adv. com. Hong Kong U. Sci. Tech., 1988—95; mem. acad. libr. adv. group U. Md. Sch. Librs. and Info. Scis., 1994—96; mem. adv. bd. ERIC, 1990—92; mem. Chadwyck-Healey N.Am. Adv. Com. on Lit. Online, 1997—99; vice chair, chair Chesapeake Info. and Rsch. Libr. Alliance, 1996—98; cons. libr. devel. & fundraising, 1998—; spkr. in field; mem. bd. trustees Marstons Mills Pub. Libr., 2002—; mem. adv. coun. Georgetown U. Libr., 2001—. Author: Libary Networks: Libraries in Partnership, 1986—87; editor: Jour. Libr. Automation, 1972—77; co-editor: Portal: Libraries and the Academy, 2000—; mem. editl. bd.: Advanced Tech./Librs., 1973—93, mem. editl. bd.: Jour. Libr. Adminstrn., 1986—2000, mem. editl. bd.: Libr. Hi-Tech., 1989—93, mem. editl. bd.: Jour. Acad. Librarianship, 1994—99; contbr. articles to profl. jours. Trustee Phila. Area Libr. Network, 1980—81; bd. dirs. Universal Serials and Book Exch., 1981—82, v.p., 1983, pres., 1984; trustee Capital Consortium, 1992—95; mem. bd. Potomac Internet, 1995—96; pres., trustee Marstons Mills Pub. Libr., 2002—. Named Samuel Lazerow disting. lectr., Drexel U., 1984, L.I. U., 2002; recipient Simmons Coll. Disting. Alumni award, 1977; fellow Coun. on Libr. Resources fellow, 1973. Mem.: ALA (coun. 1988—92, structure revision TF 1995—97, chair task force on external accrediting body 1999—2002, web adv. com. 2001—02), Assn. Coll. and Rsch. Librs. (pres. 1994—95, program officer for scholarly comms. 2002—), Coalition for Networked Info. (leader working group 1990—92), Assn. Jesuit Colls. and Univ. Librs. (chair 1997—98), Libr. of Congress (optical disk pilot project adv. com. 1985—89), Assn. Rsch. Librs. (info. policy com. 1995—97, stats. com. 1998—2000), Libr. and Info. Tech. Assn. (pres. 1978—79), Rsch. Librs. Group (exec. com. 1985—87, gov.), Internat. Fedn. Libr. Assns. Commn. on Access to Info. and Freedom of Expression, Sweet Adelines Internat., Georgetown Club, Cosmos Club (libr. com. 1986—96), Phi Beta Kappa (chair Georgetown U. chpt. 2000—01). Home and Office: 10 Colonial Farm Cir Marstons Mills MA 02648 E-mail: martin@skmassociates.net.

MARTIN, SUSAN WORK, educator; b. Croswell, Mich., Oct. 24, 1950; d. Samuel McCreery and Ruth (Laramie) Work; m. James L. Winckler, May 22, 1971 (div. Dec. 1983); 1 child, Diana; m. Lawrence Wesley Martin, Jan 3, 1985; 1 son, Samuel; 1 stepson, Brian. BS in Pub. Speaking, Cen. Mich. U., 1971; MBA in Acctg., Mich. State U., 1976, postgrad. in Acctg., 1980—. CPA, Mich.; cert. mgt. acct.; CIA. Tax intern Ernst & Whinney, Lansing, Mich., 1976; asst. auditor gen. Mich. Dept. Auditing Gen., 1976-80; grad. asst. Mich. State U. Acctng., East Lansing, 1980-81, 83-84; dep. state treas. Mich. Dept. Treasury, Lansing, 1981-84, commr. revenue, 1985-88; assoc. prof. Grand Valley State U., 1988—. Chmn. Mich. com. on Govtl. Acctg. and Auditing, 1983-85. Editor Municipal Forum, The Michigan CPA. Mem. Nat. Tax Assn. (com. 1984—), Am. Inst. CPA's (doctoral fellow 1984-85), Am. Acctg. Assn., Inst. Internal Auditors (bd. govs. Lansing chpt. 1979), Govt. Fin. Officers Assn. (com. on acctg., auditing and fin. reporting), Assn. Govt. Accts. (Disting. Leadership award), Midwestern Assn. of State Tax Adminstrs. (sec. 1986, v.p. 1987), Mich. Assn. of CPA's Acctg. and Auditing (vice chmn. 1986), Multistate Tax Commn. (exec. com. 1986), Cen. Mich. U. Alumni Assn. (nat. bd. Dirs. 1976-77, Lansing State Jour.) Clubs: Porsche of Am. (pres. Motorstadt region 1979). Avocation: golf. Office: Mich Dept Treasury Bur of Revenue Allegan St Lansing MI 48922-0001

MARTIN, TERRELL OWEN, university administrator; b. Florence, Ala., Mar. 25, 1937; s. Terrell Owen and Ruth Alice (Nowell) M. BS in Bus. Adminstrn., Erskine Coll., 1959; MS in Student Pers., Ind. U., 1964, D in Recreation, 1972. Dir. student activities Franklin Coll., Ind., 1964-66; acad. adv. U. Akron, Ohio, 1966-68; counselor, 1972-74; resident counselor Ind. U., Bloomington, 1968-72; dir. spl. programs and orgns. Indiana U. Pa., 1974-82; dean student devel. Tex. A&M U., Kingsville, 1982-87; dir. acad. counseling and advising So. Ill. U., Edwardsville, 1987—. 2d lt. U.S. Army, 1960. Mem. ACD, Am. Coll. Pers. Assn., Nat. Assn. Campus Activities, Nat. Assn. Student Pers. Adminstrs., Nat. Recreation and Park Assn., Phi Delta Kappa, Order of Omega. Democrat. Methodist. Avocations: traveling, swimming, reading. Office: So Ill U PO Box 1640 Edwardsville IL 62026-1640

MARTIN, TERRENCE KEECH, lawyer, city councilor; b. Lynchburg, Va., Apr. 21, 1939; s. Walter Worth and Frances Louise (Keech) M.; m. Cecilia Rudy, Nov. 5, 1983 (div. 1999); children: Theodore Worth, Timothy Francis. BA, U. Notre Dame, 1961; JD, U. Va., 1964. Bar: Va. 1964. Asst. city atty. City of Newport News, Va., 1967-69; assoc. Bert A. Nachman, Atty., Newport News, 1969-70; pvt. practice, 1970-72; ptnr. Martin & Rilee, 1972-74, Martin & Bensten, Newport News, 1974-78; atty. Terrence K. Martin & Assocs., 1978-83; ptnr. Mason, Gibson, Cowardin & Martin, 1983-88, Overman, Cowardin & Martin, PLC, Newport News, 1988-98; pvt. practice pvt. practice, 1998—. Mem. coun. City of Newport News, 1990—2002; bd. dirs. Va. Peninsula Econ. Devel. Coun., 1996-99, Youth Svcs. Commn., 1993-2000, Transp. Safety Commn., 1990—2002; mem. edn. com. Va. Mcpl. League, 1994-95; mem. task force City's Role in Edn., Nat. League of Cities, mem. comty. and econ. devel. steering com., 1999—2002; pres. Newport News Sister Commn.; bd. dirs. Va. Living Mus., 2001-02; pres. Sister Cities of Newport News, Inc., 2002—. Capt., Mil. Police Corps, U.S. Army, 1965-67, France. Republican. Roman Catholic. Home: 17349 Warwick Blvd Newport News VA 23603-1331 Office: 714 J Clyde Morris Blvd Newport News VA 23601-1500 Fax: 757-599-9824. E-mail: terry@visi.net.

MARTIN, THEODORE KRINN, former university administrator (deceased); b. Blue Mountain, Miss., Jan. 2, 1915; s. Thomas Theodore and Ivy (Manning) M.; m. Lorene Garrison, Sept. 6, 1947; children: Glenn Krinn, Mary Ann, Janet Kay. AB, Georgetown (Ky.) Coll., 1935; MA, La. State U., 1941; PhD, George Peabody Coll., 1949. Tchr. Consol. Sch., Dumas, Miss., 1935-36; prin. Mississippi Heights Acad., 1936-39; tchr. Murphy High Sch., Mobile, Ala., 1940-41; registrar Miss. State U., 1949-53, registrar, adminstrv. asst. to pres., 1953-56, dean Sch. Edn., 1956-61, exec. asst. to pres., 1961-66, v.p., 1966-85, dir. Summer Sch., 1956-70, ret., 1985. Served as capt. AUS, 1941-46. T.K. Martin Ctr. for Tech. and Disability on Miss. State U. Campus named in his honor. Mem. Masons, Kappa Alpha, Phi Kappa Phi, Omicron Delta Kappa, Kappa Delta Pi, Phi Delta Kappa. Home: 1151 East Dr Starkville MS 39759-9491

MARTIN, THOMAS HENRY, JR. water resource engineer, software writer; b. Plainfield, N.J., Aug. 3, 1957; s. Thomas Henry Sr. and Audrey May (Goldhammer) M.; m. Lisa Marie Burley, July 1, 1995. BS in Civil Engring., U. Vt., 1981; cert. advanced studies in applied electronics, Harvard U., 1988. Registered profl. engr., Maine, Wash.; cert. water distbn. mgr., Wash. Hydropower engr. ind. cons., Fanwood, N.J., 1981; geotech. engr. Geotech Assocs., 1981; water resource engr. Camp Dresser & McKee Inc., Boston, 1982-86, systems engr., 1986-88; software engr. WSI Corp., Billerica, Mass., 1988-90; civil engr. EA Engring., Redmond, Wash., 1991-92; water resource engr. Foster Wheeler Environ. Corp. (formerly Ebasco), Bellevue, 1992—. Coauthor: Vermont Hydro-Logic: Small-Scale Licensing and Governing Issues, 1981, (computer automated weather info. system) WxWindows: Touchscreen System, 1989; engr. removal of dam from East Fork Salmon River, Idaho, 1991; engr. water quality computer model Columbia River System Operation Rev. EIS, 1994; mem. ecology water reuse adv. com. Washington Dept. Health, 1996. Andrew Mellon Environ. and Natural Resources grantee, Burlington, Vt., 1979. Mem. ASCE, IEEE, Am. Water Works Assn. Avocations: playing harmonica, basketball, telemark and downhill skiing, beachcombing. Home: 7550 Roosevelt Way NE Seattle WA 98115-4221

MARTIN, THOMAS LYLE, JR. university president; b. Memphis, Sept. 26, 1921; s. Thomas Lyle and Malvina (Rucks) M.; m. Helene Hartley, June 12, 1943 (dec. Sept. 1983); children: Michele Marie, Thomas Lyle; m. Mildred L. Moore, June 5, 1984. B.E.E., Rensselaer Poly. Inst., 1942, M.E.E., 1948, D.Eng., 1967; PhD, Stanford U., 1951. Prof. elec. engring. U. N.Mex., 1948-53; prof. engring. U. Ariz., 1953-63, dean engring., 1958-63, U. Fla., Gainesville, 1963-66, So. Meth. U., Dallas, 1966-74; pres. Ill. Inst. Tech., Chgo., 1974-87, pres. emeritus. Bd. dirs. Cherry Corp. Capt. Signal Corps AUS, 1943-46. Mem. ASEE Hall of Fame. Fellow IEEE; mem. Nat. Acad. Engring. Achievements include being one of the founders of Dallas-Ft. Worth Internat. Airport. Home and Office: PO Box 167845 Irving TX 75016-7845

MARTIN, THOMAS MACDONALD, lawyer; b. Huntington, N.Y., Dec. 17, 1947; s. Raleigh Lloyd and Elizebeth Battle (Gutwein) M.; m. Sheila Lynn Wilkens, July 13, 1968. AAS in Bus. Adminstrn., SUNY, Selden, 1967; BS in Criminal Justice, SUNY, Westbury, 1976; JD, Touro Coll., 1986. Bar: Va. 1988, U.S. Ct. Appeals (4th cir.) 1988, U.S. Supreme Ct. 1993, U.S. Ct. Fed. Claims 1993, U.S. Ct. Appeals (fed. cir.) 1993, U.S. Ct. Mil. Appeals 1993; cert. fraud examiner. Customs officer, sky marshall U.S. Customs Agy. Svc., N.Y.C., 1971-75; spl. agt. U.S. Dept. Agr., 1975-78; supervisory spl. agt. Office of Insp. Gen., 1978-81, asst. regional insp. gen. then regional insp. gen., 1981-86, dep. div. dir. Washington, 1986-88, chief internal affairs, 1988-91, sr. spl. agt. gen. investigations divsn., 1991-93, sr. spl. agt. program investigation divsn., 1993-98; ret. Fairfax, Va., 1998; pvt. practice law, 1998—; magistrate 19th Jud. Dist., Fairfax County, Va., 1999—2001. With USN, 1967-71. Mem. ABA (litigation sect. 1989—), Fairfax Bar Assn., Va. Trial Lawyers Assn., Assn. Trial Lawyers Am., Va. Magistrates Assn., Nat. Geog. Soc., Fed. Law Enforcement Officers Assn., Nat. Assn. Fraud Examiners. Methodist. Avocations: karate, marksmanship, golf, fishing, reading. E-mail: MARTINLAW1@excite.com.

MARTIN, THOMAS R. medical educator, medical association administrator; b. Cincinnati, Ohio, Oct. 27, 1947; MD, U. Pa., 1973; BA in Chemistry, Macalester Coll., St. Paul, 1969. Asst. prof. medicine U. Wash., Seattle, 1982-85, assoc. prof. medicine, 1985—, v. chair dept. medicine, dir., Pulmonary Rsch. Training Prog., 1990—; chief medicine svc. VA Pugent Sound Health Care Sys. Pres. Am. Thoracic Soc., 2002—. Office: Seattle VA Medical Ctr 1660 S Columbian Way Seattle WA 98108-1532*

MARTIN, THOMAS RHODES, communications executive, writer; b. Memphis, July 10, 1953; s. Otis Knox and Joe Anne (Coggin) M.; m. Wanda C. Benderman, Dec. 1, 1984; children: Seth Knox, Cyrus Rhodes. BA, Vanderbilt U., 1975. Sales communication writer Schering-Plough Corp., Memphis, 1976-78; media devel. specialist Fed. Express Corp., 1978-81, sr. media devel. specialist, 1981-82, mgr. of mgmt. communication, 1982-84, mng. dir. employee communication, 1984-92, mng. dir. pub. rels., 1992-95, v.p. corp. comm., 1995-96; v.p. corp. rels. ITT Industries, White Plains, N.Y., 1996-99, sr. v.p. corp. rels., 1999—. Contbg. editor Memphis mag., 1984-94; contbr. numerous articles to mags. Bd. dirs. Big Bros./Big Sisters, Memphis, 1983-87, Memphis Oral Sch. for the Deaf, 1985-91, Leadership Memphis, 1986-87, 92-96, Pub. Rels. Soc. Am. Found., 1999—, Inst. for Pub. Rels., 1999—. Recipient Journalism award Sigma Delta Chi, 1983, Mobius Advt.

award, 1998. Mem. Pub. Rels. Soc. Am., Internat. Assn. Bus. Communicators, Internat. TV Assn., Pub. Rels. Soc. Am. (Silver anvil award 1995, Bronze Anvil award 1996), Arthur W. Page Soc., The Wisemen, Pub. Rels. Seminar. Avocations: writing, backpacking, sailing, skiing. Office: ITT Industries 4 W Red Oak Ln Fl 2 White Plains NY 10604-3617 E-mail: tom.martin@itt.com.

MARTIN, THOMAS RUSSELL, music educator, musician; b. Bay City, Mich., Mar. 5, 1950; s. Irvin Joseph and Margaret Catherine (Carmell) Martin; m. Elizabeth Anne Richardson, Aug. 28, 1982 (div. Sept. 0, 1998); children: Eleanor, Riley, Lucia; m. Jo-Anne Regan, Jan. 1, 2000; stepchildren: Sarah Sandri, John Sandri, Benjamin Sandri. B of Theater Arts, Boston Coll., 1972; MusB in Composition, Berklee Coll. Music, 1976; MEd, Keene State Coll., 1989. Voice dept. faculty Berklee Coll. Music, Boston, 1976—83, asst. chair voice dept., 1979—83; choral dir. Winchendon (Mass.) Pub. Schs., 1985—88, Quabbin Regional Sch. Dist., Barre, 1988—94, Keene (N.H.) H.S., 1994—. Mus. dir., pianist, arranger, N.Y.C., 1983—85; staff pianist New Eng. Theatre Conf., Boston, 1975—2001; mus. dir., pianist, arranger, Monadnock Region, NH, 1985—; mus. dir., condr. Boston Coll. Dramatics Soc., Chestnut Hill, Mass., 1972—83; adj. faculty voice Franklin Pierce Coll., Rindge, NH, 1986—89; mus. dir., condr., music prodr. Am. Dance Heritage, Wellesley, Mass., 1980—83; clinician N.H. Music Educators Assn., Concord, NH, 1995, New Eng. Theatre Conf., New Haven, 1990; guest condr. S.W. dist. N.H. Music Educators, New Ipswich, NH, 1990; guest condr. Vt. Music Educators Assn., Townsend, 1989, Monadnock Valley Music Festival, Amherst, NH, 2000; guest vocalist Keene Pops Choir, 2001. Composer: (children's mus.) Androcles And The Lion, 2001. Mem.: NEA, N.H. Music Educators Assn. (choral com. 2000—02, 2000), Am. Choral Dirs. Assn. (pres. N.H. chpt. 1998—2001), Monadnock Valley Music Festival Assn. (choral mgr. 2001—), New Eng. Music Festival Assn. (accompanist 2002—), Music Educator Nat. Conf. Office: Keene H S 43 Arch St Keene NH 03431 Office Fax: 603-357-1512. E-mail: tmartin@sau29.k12.nh.us.

MARTIN, TONY, humanities educator; b. Port of Spain, Trinidad, Feb. 21, 1942; came to U.S 1969. s. Claude G. and Vida Beryl M. BSc in econ. with honors, U. Hull, England, 1968; MA, Mich. State U., 1970, PhD, 1973. Barrister-at-law Honorable Soc. Gray's Inn, London, 1965; asst. prof. of history, African-Afro Am. studies U. Mich., Flint, 1971-73; assoc. prof. in Africana studies Wellesley Coll., Wellesley, Mass., 1973-79, prof. Africana studies, 1979—. Vis. prof. of history U. Minn., 1975, The Colo. Coll., Colo. springs, 1985-86, vis. prof. of Afro-Am studies Brown U., Providence, R.I., 1991, Brandeis U., Waltham, Mass., 1974, 81; hon. rsch. fellow U. of the West Indies, Trinidad, 1986-87; lectr. DuBois-Padmore-Ukramah, Ghana, 1990; cons. founds.; expert witness Congl. Hearings, 1987. Author: Race First, 1976, Literary Garveyism, 1983, The Pan-African Connection, 1983, The Jewish Onslaught, 1993; reviewer articles for profl. jours.; contbr. articles to profl. jours., encys., and other ref. books; contbr. editor profl. jours. Recipient Rsch. award Am. Philosophical Soc., Phila., 1990, Cmty. award Emancipation Support Com. Mem. Assn. of Caribbean Historians, African Heritage Studies Assn., Assn. for the Study of Classical African Civilizations (John Henrik Clarke Living Legacy award), Nat. Coun. for Black Studies. Office: Wellesley Coll Africana Studies Dept Wellesley MA 02481 E-mail: amartin@wellesley.edu.

MARTIN, TONY DERRICK, professional football player; b. Miami, Fla., Sept. 5, 1965; Student, Bishop Coll., Mesa State U. Wide receiver Miami Dolphins, 1990-93, San Diego Chargers, 1994-98; wide reciever Miami Dolphins, 1999—2000. Named to Pro Bowl, 1996. Office: Miami Dolphins 7500 SW 30th St Davie FL 33314-1020*

MARTIN, VERNON EMIL, librarian; b. Guthrie, Okla., Dec. 15, 1929; s. Vernon E. Sr. and Marian (Brandon) M.; m. Arlan Stone, June 30, 1956 (div. 1977); children: Vernon Martin III, Jeffrey Martin; m. Elizabeth Jean Chapin, June 16, 1979; 1 child, Amy Chapin Hathaway. MA in Music, Columbia U., 1959, MS in Libr., 1965. Libr. Lincoln Ctr. Libr. Mus., N.Y.C., 1964-66; music libr. North Tex. State U., Denton, 1966-70; libr. dir. Morningside Coll., Sioux City, Iowa, 1970-74; head art dept. Hartford (Conn.) Pub. Libr., 1974-93, ret., 1993. Composer operas including Ladies Voices, 1956, Waiting For the Barbarians, 1956, Fables By Thurber, 1986, (ballet) Dancing Back The Buffalo, 1996, What Happened*An Opera, 1999; singer Raylynmor Opera Co. Chmn. Cultural Affairs Commn., Hartford, 1984-86. Mem. ASCAP (Standard award 1969-99). Home: 110 Arch St Keene NH 03431-2169 E-mail: Vermart@monad.net.

MARTIN, VINCENT GEORGE, management consultant; b. N.Y.C., Feb. 9, 1922; s. Joseph R. and Mae B. (Mulligan) M.; m. Alice Ann McGovern, June 8, 1946; children— Kathleen (Mrs. Michael Greiner), Joseph F. Student, Pace Coll., 1948-49, Am. Internat. Coll., 1950. Salesman Lavigna Jewels, N.Y.C., 1945-47; indsl. engr. Barton Watchcase Mfg., 1948-49; office procedures Local Loan Co., 1950-51; sr. time study engr. Perkins Machine & Gear Co., West Springfield, Mass., 1951-52; with Milton Bradley Co., East Longmeadow, 1952-79, mgr. mfg., 1962-64, v.p. mfg., 1964-69, exec. v.p., 1969—, dir., 1971—, gen. mgr., 1972-79. With Vincent G. Martin Assos. (Mgmt. Consultants), 1979— ; trustee Springfield Inst. for Savs., 1978-81; dir. Armoury Corp., Stockbridge Corp., 1978-80 Past pres. Springfield Speech and Hearing Center; mem. East Longmeadow Indsl. Park Steering Com.; gen. campaign chmn. United Fund Pioneer Valley, 1976; bd. dirs. Springfield Symphony Orch.; corporate Springfield Coll., 1976-79, Wesson Meml. Hosp., 1976-80. Served with AUS, 1942-45. Decorated Bronze Star. Mem. Soc. Advancement Mgmt. (pres. Western Mass. chpt. 1954-56), Am. Mgmt. Assn., Toy Mfrs. Am. (dir. 1973-75), Springfield C. of C. (dir. 1974-78), Newcomen Soc. N.Am., East Longmeadow C. of C. (pres., dir. 1965-68) Clubs: Rotarian (dir. 1970-72). Home and Office: 8 Flume Ave PO Box 505 Marstons Mills MA 02648-0505 E-mail: vgmarzy@msn.com.

MARTIN, VINCENT LIONEL, manufacturing company executive; b. Los Angles, June 29, 1939; s. Arthur Seymon and Alice Maria (Miller) M.; m. Janet Ann Dowler, Mar. 25, 1961; children: Jennifer Lynn, Karen Arlene, Timothy Paul. BS, Stanford U., 1960; MBA, Harvard U., 1963. Various staff positions FMC Corp, Chgo, 1966-74, gen. mgr. Crane and Excavator div. Cedar Rapids, Iowa, 1974-79; pres. Equipment Systems div. AMCA Internat. Corp., Houston, 1979-81, group v.p. Brookfield, Wis., 1981-85; CEO, pres. Jason Inc., Milw., 1986-96, chmn. CEO, 1996-99, chmn., 1999—. Mem. Phi Beta Kappa, Tau Beta Pi Republican. Presbyterian. Home: 2601 W Cedar Ln Milwaukee WI 53217-1138 Office: Jason Inc 411 E Wisconsin Ave Milwaukee WI 53202-4461 E-mail: Vmartin@jasoninc.com.

MARTIN, VIVIAN, soprano; b. Detroit, May 09; d. George W. and Lillie (Champion) M.; m. Clement A. McDowell. Student, Detroit Conservatory Music; BS in Edn., Wayne State U.; studied with, Nadia Boulanger, Germaine Martinelli, France, Samuel Margolis, N.Y.C., Paul Daubner, Munich, Elsa Verena, Berlin, Celeste Cole, Detroit. Educator Bd. of Edn., Detroit, N.Y.C. Soloist with Robert DeCormier Singers, Munich Philharm., Neurnberg Symphony and Philharm. Chorus, 1970, Gävleborgs Symfoniorkester, Gavle, Sweden, 1978, Symphony Radio Concert, Paris, 1978, Warsaw Symphony Orch.; operatic debut as Leonora in La Forza del Destino, 1971; appeared in Antigone and Carmina Burana with Munich Philharm. Orch. and Chorus, Das ewige Evangelium with Nürnberg Symphony Orch. and Philharm. Chorus, L'Africaine in Ghent, Belgium, Oberon in Wexford (Ireland) Opera Festival, 1972, Bess from Porgy and Bess, Bratislava, 1979, Il Travatore, Constantza, 1980; performed with Royal Opera Ghent, Stadt Opera Essen, Badische Opera Karlsruhe, Stadt Opera Bonn, Mainz Opera, Royal Opera Lisbon, Portugal, Stadtheatre Bremen; TV broadcasts include BBC, BRT Belgium, Bratislava (Czechoslovakia) Philharm. Orch. and Opera, Bavarian Radio; rec. artist RCA, Command Records, Concord Records, Halo Records; tour India, Iran, Afghanistan, U.S. State Dept., 1976; toured with Gävleborgo Symphony Orch., Sweden, 1981-84; appeared in opera concert on radio and TV, Bucharest, 1979; sang Leonora in Il Travatore in opera festival, Constantza, Rumania, 1979; concerts in Belgrade, Tivoli Gardens, Copenhagen, Zagreb, Yugoslavia, 1979; opera concert tour of Sweden with Gävle Symphony Orch., 1979; soloist Belgium TV Flanders Expo, Gent, Belgium, 1990, concert tour Czechoslovakia, 1991, performed New Opera House, Maastricht, Holland with Limburgs Symphony Orchestra, 1992, Concert Koor, 1992, Olavshallen, Trondheim, Norway with Trondheim Symfoniorkester and Trondheim Kammerkor, 1993, concert tours U.S.A., 1994-96, soprano soloist Gershwin Gala Porgy and Bess, 1989-96, (with Philharm. Orch.) World of Gershwin, 1998; concert tours Belgium, Germany, (with St. Petersburg (Russia) Phil. Orch.) Shostakovich, 1998, (with Russian Nat. Symphony Orch.), Moscow, 1998; solo recitals festival St. Petersburg, 1998, Moscow, 1998. Recipient Jean Paul Alaux award Conservatoire de Fontianbleau, 18 singing scholarships and awards. Mem. AFTRA, Am. Guild Mus. Artists, Actors Equity Assn., New Initiatives for the Arts, Wayne State U. Alumni Assn., Alpha Kappa Alpha. Office: Dr Gosta Schwarck Intl Ltd 18 Groennegade 1st Fl DK-1007 Copenhagen K Denmark

MARTIN, WADE HAMPTON, III, physician, scientist; b. Dallas, Mar. 23, 1951; s. Wade Jr. and Martha Jane (Emerson) M.; m. Mary Havelka, Apr. 14, 1999. BA, U. Kans., 1973, MD, 1977. Diplomate in internal medicine and cardiovasc. diseases Am. Bd. Internal Medicine, Cert. Bd. Nuc. Cardiology, Nat. Bd. Echocardiography. Intern and resident in internal medicine St. Louis U., 1977-80; fellow preventive medicine Washington U., St. Louis, 1980—82; fellow cardiovasc. diseases U. Tex. Southwestern, Dallas, 1982—85; asst. prof. medicine Washington U., St. Louis, 1985-99, assoc. prof. medicine, 1999—; staff physician Barnes Hosp., 1985—, John Cochran VA Hosp., St. Louis, 1989—. Manuscript reviewer Am. Jour. Physiology, Am. Jour. Cardiology, Jour. Am. Coll. Cardiology, Circulation, Annals of Internal Medicine, Medicine & Sci. in Sports and Exercise; ad hoc mem. applied physiology study sect. NIH, 1986, heart failure study sect., 1989; VA merit grant reviewer, 2001, 02. Contbr. more than 40 articles to profl. jours. Grantee NIH, 1989-94, VA, 1995-2000. Fellow ACP, Am. Coll. Sports Medicine, Am. Coll. Cardiology; mem. Am. Physiol. Soc., Am. Fedn. Clin. Rsch. Avocations: competitive running, tennis, travel. Home: 6626 Waterman Ave University City MO 63130-4659 Office: John Cochran VA Hosp Divsn Cardiology 111A/JC 915 N Grand Blvd Saint Louis MO 63106-1621 E-mail: martinw@medicine.wustl.edu., Wade.Martin@med.va.gov.

MARTIN, WALTER, retired lawyer; b. Crookston, Minn., Nov. 7, 1912; s. Frederick and Rosalie (Mertz) M.; m. Catherine Mary Severin, May 1, 1942 (dec. May 1979); children: Frederick H., Jacqueline K., Patricia, Priscilla, Walter Jr., John E. BA, Albion Coll., 1937; JD, U. Mich., 1939. Bar: Mich. 1939, U.S. Dist. Ct. (fed. dist.) 1939, U.S. Ct. Appeals (6th cir.) 1947, U.S. Supreme Ct. 1958. Ptnr. Martin & Martin, Saginaw, Mich., 1939-94; ret., 1994. Fellow Mich. Bar Assn., Saginaw County Bar Assn. (pres. 1958). Lutheran. Avocations: hunting, fishing. Office: 803 Court St Saginaw MI 48602-4223

MARTIN, WALTER FRANCIS, 3RD, librarian; b. Salem, Mass., July 10, 1943; s. Walter Francis Martin, Jr. and Cynthia Winslow Northey. BA, Yale U., 1968; MLS, Pratt Inst., 1972. Ref. libr. Tabor Libr., Marion, Mass., Lewiston Libr., Maine, Milford Pub. Libr., Conn., East Haven Libr., Hewitt Meml. Libr., New Haven. Mem. ALA, Am. Studies. Democrat. Home: 55 Whalley Ave Apt C New Haven CT 06511-3230

MARTIN, WAYNE A. clinical social worker; b. N.Y.C., Jan. 26, 1945; s. Bernard and Juliet (Aurbach) M.; m. Barbara Jo Goodman, Aug. 16, 1970; 1 child, Jason David. BA in Social Sci., Fla. State U., 1966; MS, Columbia U., 1968; postgrad., Old Dominion U., 1978—. Lic. clin. social worker, Va., cert. diplomate. Day camp dir. Jewish Cmty. Ctr., Norfolk, Va., 1968-71, children's dept. dir., 1968-69, youth dept. dir., 1969-71; psychiat. social worker Psychiat. Assocs., Ltd., Portsmouth, 1971-77; clin. social worker Human Resource Inst., Norfolk, 1977-79; part-time caseworker Cath. Home Bur., Hampton, Va., 1977-78; primary therapist Charter Colonial Inst., Newport News, 1980-91; pvt. practice clin. social work Virginia Beach, Norfolk and Newport News, 1980—. Program coord. for adolescent psychiat. unit Peninsula Psychiat. Hosp., Hampton, Va., 1979-80; field supr. Va. Commonwealth U. Sch. Social Work, 1978-84, Norfolk State U. Sch. Social Work, 1982-90, chmn. adv. com. Upjohn Health-care Svcs., 1979-80; dir. social svcs. Colonial Hosp., Newport News, 1995-99; oral examiner/adviser Va. Bd. Social Work. Chmn. Crisis Ctr., 1977-78; pres. Arnold Gamsey Lodge of B'Nai B'rith, 1975-77; 1st v.p. B'nai B'rith, Va. State Assn., 1977-78, pres. 1979-80, mem. B'Nai B'rith dist. 5 bd. govs., 1978—, 3d v.p./treas. dist. 5, 1983-84, 1st v.p. 1985-86, pres.-elect 1986-87, pres. 1987-88, chmn. dist. 5 personnel com., bd. govs. B'nai B'rith Internat., 1986-88, 94-2000; v.p. Chesapeake Bay region, 1997-2000; chmn. Hillel Found. for State of Va., 1978-79, 90—; bd. dirs. Jewish Cmty. Ctr., Norfolk, 1973-79, Anti-Defamation League; exec. bd. Temple Israel Synagogue, 1981-84, pres. Men's Club, 1981-82, temple sec. 1982-84. Recipient Charles Olshansky Lodge Svc. award B'nai B'rith, 1991, Outstanding Svc. Presdl. citation, 1991; named Outstanding Lodge Pres. B'nai B'rith, 1977, Outstanding State Pres. 1980, Man of Yr., Va. State Assn. B'nai B'rith, 1980. Mem. NASW (v.p. Hampton Roads unit 1974-76, dist. chmn. 1982-83, state dir. 1977-83), Va. Soc. Clin. Social Work (bd. dirs. Ea. Va. chpt. 1989-96, 99-02, state dir. at large 1999-02, 02--, pres. 1991-95, legis. v.p. 1999—), Nat. Fed. Socs. Clin. Social Work (pres. clin. social work guild opeiu #49 Va., bd. dirs. 1991-95), Acad. Cert. Social Workers (bd. cert. diplomate), ACLU, Family Therapy Practice Acad. (charter mem., mem-at-large 1995-2000), Mogul Ski Club (v.p. 1970-71), Kappa Delta Pi, Phi Alpha Theta, Pi Sigma Alpha. Democrat. Jewish. Home: 1827 Longdale Dr Norfolk VA 23518-4943

MARTIN, WESLEY GEORGE, electrical engineer; b. Chgo., Apr. 15, 1946; s. Chester W. and Marie L. (Seifarth) M.; m. Margaret Rose Kowach, Aug. 17, 1968; children: Patrick, Christopher. BS, Milw. Sch. Enging., 1969; Cert., Alexander Hamilton Inst., N.Y.C., 1976. Registered profl. engr., Ill., Ind., Wis. Elec. engr., estimator The Austin Co., Des Plaines, Ill., 1969-78; elec. estimator Skidmore, Owings & Merrill, Chgo., 1978-83; elec. engr. Holabird & Root, 1983-95, assoc. ptnr., 1986-95, dir. elec. engring., 1988-89, project engr., 1989-95; owner W.G. Martin & Assocs., Cons., Palatine, 1978—; sr. elec. engr. Consoer Townsend Envirodyne Engrs., Chgo., 1995—, assoc., 1996—2002, sr. assoc., 2002—, project mgr., 1996—. Contbr. articles to profl. jours. Dem. precinct capt., Palatine, 1979-82; cubmaster pack # 91 Boy Scouts Am., 1986-88. Recipient Award of Merit, Chgo. Lighting Inst., 1981-83, 90-92, 97-98. Mem. NSPE, Illuminating Engring. Soc. N.Am. (Internat. Illumination Design award 1992), Ill. Soc. Profl. Engrs., Nat. Eagle Scout Assn., Loyal Order of the Moose. Roman Catholic. Home: 918 W Colfax St Palatine IL 60067-2316 Office: 303 W Wacker Dr Chicago IL 60606-1204 E-mail: wes.martin@cte-eng.com.

MARTIN, WILFRED WESLEY FINNY, psychologist, property owner and manager; b. Rock Lake, N.D., Dec. 3, 1917; s. William Isaac and Anna Liisa (Hendrickson-Juntunen) M.; m. Stella Helland, Sept. 25, 1943; children: Sydney Wayne, William Allan. BA, Jamestown Coll., 1940; army specialized tng. program, Hamilton Coll., 1944; MS, EdD, U. So. Calif., 1956. Highsch. prin., coach pub. sch., Nekoma, N.D., 1940-42; contact rep., psychologist VA, L.A., 1946-49, psychologist, chief rehab., 1972-77; guidance dir. Moorhead (Minn.) Pub. Schs., 1951-53; instr. Concordia Coll., Moorhead, 1951-53; from intern to resident Fargo (N.D.) VA Hosp., 1953-58; psychologist VA, Fargo, 1953-58; assoc. Sci. Rsch. Assoc./IBM, Boulder, Colo., 1958-65, regional dir. L.A., 1966-72; owner, mgr. Martin Investments, Huntington Beach, Calif., 1977—. Adjutant U. Miss., Oxford, 1942; trustee Wilfred W. and Stella Martin Trust, Huntington Beach, 1991. Author: Veterans Administration Work Simplification, 1948, 57. Charter mem. Rep. Presdl. Task Force, 1980; adv. sr. ptnrs. bd. dirs. U. Calif. Med. Sch., Irvine, 1990; donor Dr. and Mrs. W.W. Martin Endowment, Jamestown Coll., N.D., 1985; mem. Assocs. of James Ford Bell Libr., U. Minn. With U.S. Army, 1942-45. Mem. Am. Psychol. Assn., Cardinal & Gold U. So. Calif., Jamestown Coll. Heritage Circle (charter), Suomi Coll. Second Century Soc., Elks. Republican. Lutheran. Avocations: reading, Finnish heritage, swimming, sports, card playing. Home: PO Box 5445 Huntington Beach CA 92615-5445 *The dominant force in my life is described by the Finnish word SISU, which means perseverence, determination, competitiveness, and tenacity toward goal-oriented achievements. Due to SISU, faith, and hard work I enjoy an active successful life.*

MARTIN, WILLIAM ALLEN, sociology educator; b. Galveston, Tex. s. James F. and Myra F. (Lide) M.; m. Debra J. Taylor; children: Zachary, Michelle. BA, So. Meth. U., 1970; MA, Tex. Christian U., 1971; PhD, U. Tex., 1976. Rsch. assoc. II U. Tex., Austin, 1970-74, part-time instr., 1974-75; instr. Ark. State U., State University, 1975-77; asst., assoc. prof. U. Tex. at Tyler, 1977-89, prof., 1989—. Faculty adv. coun. U. Tex. Sys., 1994-99; pres. faculty senate U. Tex. at Tyler, 1994-98; rsch. cons. Nat. Pk. Svc., 1984; mem. spl. com. AAUP, 1998-99. Author: (book) Race & Ethnic Relations, 1999; contbr. articles to profl. jours. Mem. Phys. Environment Com. Tex. Coun. of Govts., 1995—. Recipient Tex. Higher Edn. Coordinating Bd. fellowship, 1992. Mem. Am. Sociol. Assn., Population Assn. Am., Assn. Am. Geographers, Southwestern Sociol. Assn. (v.p.), Tex. Assn. Coll. Tchrs. (pres. 1999-2001). Office: U Tex 3900 University Blvd Tyler TX 75799-0001 E-mail: Amartin@mail.uttyl.edu.

MARTIN, WILLIAM C. sociology educator, writer; b. San Antonio, Dec. 31, 1937; s. Lowell Curtis and Joe Bailey (Brite) M.; m. Patricia Dale Summerlin, Dec. 31, 1957; children: Rex Martin, Jeff Martin, Elisabeth Dale Martin Thomas. BA, Abilene Christian U., 1958, MA, 1960; BD, Harvard Divinity Sch., 1963; PhD, Harvard U., 1969. Instr. history Dana Hall Sch., Wellesley, Mass., 1965-68; instr. sociology Rice U., Houston, 1968-69, asst. prof. sociology, 1969-73, assoc. prof. sociology, 1973-79, prof. sociology, 1979—, Chavanne prof. religion and pub. policy, 1996—, master Sid W. Richardson Coll., 1976-81, chair dept. sociology, 1983-86, 89-94. Cons. films and TV documentaries; speaker in field. Author: These Were God's People, 1966, Christians in Conflict, 1972, A Prophet With Honor: Billy Graham Story, 1991 (Christianity Today's Critic's Choice award 1992), My Prostate and Me: Dealing With Prostate Cancer, 1994, With God on our Side: The Rise of the Religious Right in America, 1996; contbg. editor Tex. Monthly (Nat. Headliner award 1982); contbr. numerous articles to profl. jours. and pop mags.; numerous radio and TV appearances. Dir. House of the Carpenter, Inc., inner-city youth program, Boston, 1963-66, pres. and bd. dirs. non-profit housing corp.; bd. dirs. Fellowship Racial and Econ. Equality, 1970-71; mem. exec. com. Houston Coun. Human Rels. Recipient Nicholas Salgo Outstanding Tchr. award Rice U., 1971, 93, Brown Coll. award for Teaching in the Humanities Rice U., 1974, 76, George R. Brown Award for Superior Teaching, alumni Rice U., 1974, 76, 77, 84, for Excellence in Teaching, 1975, 82, Life Honor award, 1985, Sr. scholar James A. Baker III Inst. Pub. Policy; grantee Am. Coun. Learned Socs. and Am. Philos. Soc., 1974. Mem. Am. Sociol. Assn., Soc. Scientific Study Religion, Religious Rsch. Assn., Tex. Inst. Letters (J. Frank Dobie/Paisano fellowship 1980). Democrat. Protestant. Avocation: bicycling. Home: 2148 Addison Rd Houston TX 77030-1222 Office: Rice U Dept Sociology 6100 Main St Dept Houston TX 77005-1892 E-mail: wcm@rice.edu.

MARTIN, WILLIAM CLIFFORD, III, judge; b. Longview, Tex., July 15, 1938; s. William Clifford Jr. and Frankie Judith (Farmer) M.; m. Janet Marie Geist, June 3, 1961; children Melissa Marie, Charles William. AB cum laude with honors, Davidson Coll., 1961; JD, U. Tex. Sch. Law, 1963. Bar: Tex. 1966. Pvt. practice, Longview, Tex., 1966; ptnr. DeWitt & Martin, 1966-67, Adams, Sheppard & Martin, Longview, 1968-70; judge, ct. domestic rels. Gregg County, 1971-77; judge, 307th jud. dist. Family Dist. Ct., 1977-90; sr. dist. judge, family law 1st Admin. Jud. Region of Tex., Dallas, 1991—. Formerly mem. Juvenile Probation Commn. Tex., Govs. Juvenile Justice and Delinquency Prevention Adv. Com. Contbr. articles to profl. jours. Lt. U.S. Army, 1964-66. Mem. ABA, Tex. Bar Assn. (coun. family law sec.). Republican. Presbyterian. Avocations: history, genealogy, bladesmithing. Office: PO Box 8 Longview TX 75606-0008

MARTIN, WILLIAM COLLIER, hospital administrator; b. Atlanta, Aug. 16, 1926; s. William Henry and Lillian (Collier) M.; m. Alice Elizabeth Nickle, Jan. 12, 1952 (dec.); children: Mary Anne, Patricia Jean, William Collier, Nancy Lee; m. Carol J. Sullivan, July 25, 1998. BS, U. Ga., 1950; diploma, Charlotte Meml. Hosp., 1952; postgrad., U. Okla., 1969. Operating room technician Athens (Ga.) Gen. Hosp., 1949-50; hosp. adminstrn. intern/resident Charlotte (N.C.) Meml. Hosp., 1950-52; hosp. adminstr. Rockmart-Aragon Hosp., Rockmart, Ga., 1952-54; asst. hosp. adminstr. St. Agnes Hosp., Raleigh, N.C., 1954-56; hosp. adminstr. Florence-Darlington Tb. Sanitorium, Florence, S.C., 1956-58; commd. 1st lt., MSC U.S. Army, 1959; advanced through grades to lt. col.; adj. U.S. Army Hosp. Ft. Campbell, Ky., 1959; comdg. officer med. co. U.S. Army Hosp., 1959-61; comdg. officer U.S. Army Med. Svc. Detachment Ft. Gulick, G.Z., 1961-64; exec. officer 5th Evacuation Hosp. Ft. Bragg, N.C., 1964; comdg. officer, 1964-65; adj. personnel officer 55th Med. Group Ft. Bragg, 1965-66, Qui Nhon, Rep. of Vietnam, 1966-67; comdg. officer 47th Gen. Hosp., Fitzsimons Gen. Hosp. Denver, 1967-68; exec. officer Evans Health Care Facility Ft. Buckner, Okinawa, Japan, 1968-69; dir. security plans and ops. U.S. Army Med. Ctr., Camp Kue, Okinawa, 1969-71; med. ops. officer VII Corps Moehringen, Germany, 1971-73; chief tng., exercise and readiness U.S. Army Med. Command Heidelberg, W. Germany, 1973-74; dir. security plans and tng. Fitzsimons Army Med. Ctr., 1974-77; retired, 1977. Guest lectr. healthcare adminstr. U.S. Army Med. Command in Europe, 1973-74; exec. dir. Thoms Rehab. Hosp., Asheville, N.C., 1977-78; pres./chair Escambia County Pub. Health Trust, 1978-86; founder Hospice of Northwest Fla. and Exec. Dir., 1979-86. Mem. Pres.'s Com. on Employment of the Handicapped, 1978; sec. United Meth. Bd. Pastoral Care and Counseling, 1988-90; mem., v.p., bd. ministries Pensacola Dist. United Meth. Ch., Inc., 1988-98; dir. lay speaking, bd. laity, coun. on ministries Pensacola Dist. United Meth. Ch., Inc., 1988-98; dir. lay speaking, bd. laity Ala.-West Fla. Conf. United Meth. Ch., 1988-97; mem. Health and Human Svcs. task force citizens goals for Pensacoloa, 1981-86; vice chmn. adminstrv. bd. Pine Forest United Meth. Ch., Pensacola, 1979-86; mem. fin. com., 1979-86; dir. lay speaking Pensacola Dist. United Meth. Ch., 1985-88; bd. dirs. Hispanic Ministries, Inc., 1986-93, Meth. Homes for the Aging, Inc., 1990—. Served with USN, 1944-46. Decorated Legion of Merit, Bronze Star, Meritorious Svc. medal (3); Vietnam Royal Cross of Gallantry with bronze palm; cert. lay speaker United Meth. Ch. Fellow Am. Acad. Med. Adminstrs.; mem. Am. soc. Tng. and Devel. (dir. 1977-78), Ret. Officers Assn., Assn. U.S. Army (dir. Denver-Centennial chpt. 1974-77, Greater Gulf Coast chpt. 1979-86), U.S. Power Squadrons, Ret. Officers Assn. (bd. dirs. Bob Sikes chpt. 1996-2000, bd. dirs. Escarosa chpt. 1985-99, pres. ESCAROSA chpt. 1989-90), V.F.W., Masons, Phi Delta Theta. Democrat.

MARTIN, WILLIAM EDWIN, business executive, lawyer, government official; b. Bowling Green, Ky., Oct. 16, 1943; s. John Edwin and Bess Carolyn (Matherly) M.; children: Anne Whitson, William Whitson; m. Jean Clinton Nelson, Aug. 1, 1981. BA, Vanderbilt U., 1965, JD, 1968. Bar: Tenn. 1968. Ptnr. Waller Lansden Dortch & Davis, Nashville, 1968-75; sr. ptnr. Harwell Martin & Stegall, 1975-93; dep. asst. sec. for internat. affairs U.S. Dept. Commerce-NOAA, Washington, 1993-98; chmn. Will Martin Co., 1998—; sr. v.p. Pvt. Bus. Inc., Brentwood, Tenn., 1999; vice chmn. Tecniflex, Inc., Nashville, 2000—01; chmn. Imagic Corp., 2000—01. Sr. fellow World Wildlife Fund, 1999—; bd. dirs. Marine Stewardship Coun., London, Board Mem. Inc., Brentwood. Contbr. articles to newspapers and law revs. Dir. polar programs Wilderness Soc., Washington, 1990—92. Democrat. Episcopalian. Avocations: mountain climbing, photography, running, tennis, biking. Office: 9020 Overlook Blvd Brentwood TN 37027

MARTIN, WILLIAM FRANCIS, JR. lawyer; b. Lowell, Mass., Sept. 13, 1961; s. William F. and Patricia A. Martin; m. Martha Doherty, Oct. 23, 1988; children: William F. III, Daniel J., Jacqueline E. BA in English, Coll. of Holy Cross, Worcester, Mass., 1983; JD, Boston Coll., 1986. Bar: Mass. 1986, N.H. 1991. Law clk. to Hon. Joseph R. Nolan Mass. Supreme Jud. Ct., Boston, 1986-87; assoc. Hale and Dorr, Boston and Manchester, 1987-93; ptnr. Eno, Boulay, Martin Donahue, LLP (and predecessor firm), Lowell, 1994—. Bd. dirs. Lowell Parks and Conservation Trust, Lowell, 1991—; mem. Lowell Conservation Commn., 1993-94, chmn., 1994-99. Articles editor Boston Coll. Law Review, 1985-86. Mem. Lowell City Coun., 2000—. Mem. Omicron Delta Epsilon, Order of the Coif. Home: 115 Moore St Lowell MA 01852-5046 Office: Eno Boulay Martin & Donahue LLP 21 George St Lowell MA 01852

MARTIN, WILLIAM J. economist; b. Brisbane, Australia, Oct. 19, 1953; came to U.S., 1990; s. William Bernard and Joan May (White); m. Kristine Lynette Riding, Sept. 2, 1978; 1 child: Samuel David. B in agrl. sci., U. Queensland, Brisbane, Australia, 1975; B in econ., Australian Nat. U., Canberra, Australia, 1979; PhD, Iowa State U., 1982. Rsch. officer Bureau of Agrl. Econ., Canberra, Australia, 1975-79, rsch. mgr. Australia, 1983-86; vis. rsch. fellow Australian Nat. U., Australia, 1987, sr. rsch. fellow Australia, 1988-90; economist to sr. economist, Internat. Trade Divn. World Bank, Washington, 1991-97, prin. economist, Rsch. Group, 1998—, lead economist, 2000—. Mem. Econ. Rsch. Advisory, Canberra, Australia, 1986-88, adv. bd. Global Trade Analysis Project, Lafayette, Ind., 1993—. Editor: Uruguay

Round and the Developing Economics, 1986; contbr. articles to profl. jours. Sec. Econ. Grad. Students Assn., Ames, Iowa, 1980-81, pres. 1981-82. Recipient Outstanding Svc. award Purdue U., 1997; rsch. fellow Australian Govt., Canberra, Australia, 1987. Mem. Am. Econ. Assn., Am. Agrl. Econ. Assn., Econ. Soc. Australia, Australian Agrl. Econ. Soc. (br. pres. 1985). Avocations: travel, golf, skiing, tennis, reading. Home: 8619 Coral Gables Ln Vienna VA 22182-2308 Office: World Bank Rsch Group 1818 H St NW Washington DC 20433-0001 E-mail: wmartin1@worldbank.org.

MARTIN, WILLIAM J., II, academic administrator; MD, U. Minn. Resident in internal medicine Mayo Grad. Sch. Medicine, Rochester, Minn., fellow in pulmonary medicine; faculty and med. staff Mayo Clinic, 1981—88; Floyd and Reba Smith prof. respiratory disease Ind. U. Sch. Medicine, 1988—2002, exec. assoc. dean clin. affairs, dir. divsn. pulmonary, allergy, critical care and occupl. medicine, 1988—2000; Christian R. Holmes prof. and acting sr. v.p. U. Cin. Coll. Medicine, 2002—, dean, 2002—. Pres. and CEO Ind. U. Med. Group; health policy fellow U.S. Sen. for Sen. Labor and Human Resources Com., 1995—96; funded prin. investigator Nat. Heart, Lung and Blood Inst. Mem.: Am. Thoracic Soc. (pres. 2000—01), Assn. Pulmonary and Critical Care Medicine Program Dirs. (past pres.), Am. Lung Assn. Ind. (past pres.). Office: Coll of Medicine 231 Albert Sabin Way Cincinnati OH 45267*

MARTIN, WILLIAM JOSEPH, III, lawyer; b. New Brunswick, N.J., Nov. 30, 1953; s. William Joseph, Jr. and Martha Jane Martin; m. Ann Blom, Aug. 21, 1977; children: William Clay, David John. BA with high honors, U. Del., 1975; JD with honors, Rutgers U., 1978; ML in Taxation, Georgetown U., 1987. Bar: Del. 1978, U.S. Tax Ct. 1979, Pa. 1996. Assoc. David Nicol Williams, PA, Wilmington, Del., 1978-81; ptnr. Williams, Gordon & Martin, PA, 1981-94, William J. Martin, P.A., Wilmington, 1994-96; ptnr., exec. com. mem. Prickett, Jones & Elliott, P.A., Wilmington and Dover, Del., 1996—; ptnr. Prickett, Jones & Elliott P.A., Kennett Square, Pa., 1996—, mng. ptnr., 2001—. Spkr. Del. Tax Inst., Wilmington, 1987, 89, 91, 94. Trustee, pres. Concord Presbyn. Ch., Wilmington, 1987-90; mem. staff Del. section Am. Radio Relay League, Wilmington, 1987-88. Mem. ABA (health law sect.), Del. State Bar Assn. (tax sect. and estates and trusts sect.). Avocation: amateur radio. Home: 719 Burnley Rd Wilmington DE 19803-1730 Office: Prickett Jones Elliott P A 1310 King St Wilmington DE 19801-3220 E-mail: wjmartin@prickett.com.

MARTIN, WILLIAM RAYMOND, retired financial manager; b. Phila., Oct. 16, 1939; s. Clyde Davis and Mary Anna (Coates) M.; m. Michaela Roberta Smink, Sept. 8, 1962 (div. 1969); 1 child, James; m. Margaret Scouten, Oct. 16, 1970 (div. 1983); children: Mary Frances, Susanna; m. Joan Friedman Kennedy, Jan. 29, 1988 (div. 1999). BSME, Lehigh U., 1960; MBA, U. Pa., 1973. Mem. engring. staff Pa. R.R., 1960-65; asst. gen. mgr. Excelsior Truck Leasing, Phila., 1965-71; sr. analyst Assn. Am. R.R.s, Washington, 1973-76, mgr. engring. econ., 1976-78; mgr. fin. analysis So. Ry., 1978-83; dir. fin. planning Norfolk (Va.) So. Corp., 1984-92, asst. v.p. fin., 1992-95. Contbr. articles to profl. jours. Bd. dirs. Williams Sch., Norfolk, 1988—96, pres., 1992—96; bd. dirs. Va. Stage Co., 1995—2001, Feldman Chamber Music Soc., 2001—, Norfolk Chamber Consort, 1998—, treas., 2001—. Mem. ASME, Soc. Automotive Engrs. Home: 2725 River Rd Virginia Beach VA 23454-1210

MARTIN, WILLIAM ROBERT, accountant; b. Cocoa, Fla., Nov. 26, 1927; s. Roy Nmi and Ella (Barton) M.; m. Lurline Lillian Powell, Apr. 30, 1954; children: Lurline Lillian, Nancy Louise, William Robert, Jr. BA in Acctg., Stetson U., 1949. CPA, Fla. Staff acct. Potter, Loucks & Bower, CPAs, Orlando, 1949-51; in-svc. auditor Army Audit Agy., Atlanta, 1951-53; sr. acct. Potter, Bower & Co., CPAs, Orlando, 1954-55; ptnr. Kurtz and Martin, CPAs, 1956-68, Osburn, Henning & Co., CPA, Orlando, 1968-92. Mem. Bd. of Accountancy Dept. Profl. Regulation, 1987-92, vice chmn. 1989, chmn. 1990; adj. faculty Valencia Community Coll. Acctg. Founding treas., past bd. dirs. Orlando Opera Co., Inc.; bd. dirs., fin. advisor Open Door Mission, Inc.; treas. Bill McCollum for Congress, 1982—; v.p., bd. dirs. Cen. Fla. Crew Boosters Assn., Inc., 1979-81; charter dir. Cen. Fla. Crime Watch Program, Inc., 1977-79; mem. Fla. Symphony Orch., Inc., Assoc. Bd., 1959-72; active Indsl. Devel. Commn. Mid-Fla., 1977-89; past treas., bd. dirs. United Cerebral Palsy Orange County, 1960-64, We Care, Inc., 1971; bd. dirs. Orlando Day Nursery, 1995—, treas., 1998—. Mem. AICPA (hon. life, mem. legis. key contact program), Fla. Inst. CPAs (founding chmn., local practitioners com., chmn. pub. rels. com., 1984-85), Nat. Assn. Bds. Accountancy administrv. and fin. com. 1991—), Greater Orlando C. of C. (bd. dirs. 1985, asst. v.p. fin. 1986, v.p. fin. 1987). Republican. Presbyterian. Avocations: fishing, water sports. Office: Osburn Henning & Co CPAs 617 E Colonial Dr Orlando FL 32803-4691

MARTIN, WILLIAM ROYALL, JR. retired association executive; b. Raleigh, N.C., Sept. 3, 1926; s. William Royall and Edith Ruth (Crocker) M.; m. Betty Anne Rader, June 14, 1952; children: Sallie Rader Martin Busby, Amy Kemp Martin Lewis. AB, U. N.C., 1948, MBA, 1964; BS, N.C. State U., 1952. Chemist Stamford (Conn.) rsch. labs. Am. Cyanamid Co., 1952—54; chemist Dan River Mills, Danville, Va., 1954—56, Union Carbide Corp., South Charleston, W.Va., 1956—59; rsch. assoc. Sch. Textiles N.C. State U., 1959—63; tech. dir. Am. Assn. Textile Chemists and Colorists, Research Triangle Park, NC, 1963—73, exec. dir., 1974—96. Adj. asst. prof. Coll. Textiles, N.C. State U., 1966-88, adj. assoc. prof., 1989-97; del. Internat. Orgn. Standardization, Pan Am. Standards Commn. With USNR, 1944-46. Fellow Am. Inst. Chemists, Soc. Dyers and Colourists, Textile Inst.; mem. Am. Chem. Soc., Coun. Engring. and Sci. Soc. Execs. (past pres. 1992-93), Fiber Soc., Am. Assn. Textile Chemists and Colorists, Masons, Rotary, Phi Kappa Phi, Phi Gamma Delta. Methodist. Home and Office: 224 Briarcliff Ln Cary NC 27511-3901 E-mail: wrbrm@aol.com.

MARTIN, WILLIAM RUSSELL, nuclear engineering educator; b. Flint, Mich., June 2, 1945; s. Carl Marcus and Audrey Winifred (Rosene) M.; m. Patricia Ann Williams, Aug. 13, 1967; children: Amy Leigh, Jonathn William. BSE. in Engring. Physics, U. Mich., 1967; MS in Physics, U. Wis., 1968; MSE. in Nuclear Engring., U. Mich., 1975, PhD in Nuclear Engring., 1976. Prin. physicist Combustion Engring., Inc., Windsor, Conn., 1976-77; asst. prof. nuclear engring. U. Mich., Ann Arbor, 1977-81, assoc. prof. nuclear engring., 1981-88, prof. nuclear engring., 1988—, dir. lab. for sci. computation, 1986—2001, chmn. nuclear engring., 1990-94, assoc. dean for acad. affairs Coll. Engring., 1994-99, dir. Ctr. for Advanced Computing, 2002—. Cons. Lawrence Livermore Nat. Lab., Livermore, Calif., 1982—, Los Alamos (N.Mex.) Nat. Lab., 1980-89, 2001—, IBM, Inc., Kingston, N.Y., 1984, Rockwell Internat., Pitts., 1985. Author: Transport Theory, 1979; author tech. and conf. papers. Recipient Glenn Murphy award Am. Soc. for Engring. Edn., 1993; Disting. scholar U. Mich. Coll. Engring., 1967; vis. fellow Royal Soc., London, 1989. Fellow Am. Nuclear Soc.; mem. Am. Phys. Soc., Soc. for Indsl. and Applied Math., IEEE. Avocations: running, reading, skiing, sailing. Home: 1701 Crestland St Ann Arbor MI 48104-6329 Office: U Mich Dept Nuclear Engring Ann Arbor MI 48109 E-mail: wrm@umich.edu.

MARTIN, YVONNE CONNOLLY, pharmaceutical company executive; b. St. Paul, Sept. 13, 1936; d. Elvert Farrell and Irene Mildred (Aitken) C.; m. William Brady Martin, Dec. 14, 1963; children: Margaret Anne, Catherine Irene. BA, Carleton Coll., 1958; PhD, Northwestern U., Evanston, Ill., 1964. Pharmacology asst. Abbott Labs, North Chgo., Ill., 1958-60, sr. pharmacologist, 1964-67, Abbott Park, 1968-70, assoc. rsch. fellow, 1970-74, rsch. fellow, 1974-85, sr. project leader, 1983—, sr. rsch. fellow, 1985—; instr. in chemistry Northwestern U., 1963-64. Vis. instr. Pomona Coll., Claremont, Calif., 1967-68. Author: Quantitative Drug Design, 1978; editor: Paths to Better and Safer Drugs, 1989, Perspectives in Drug Discovery and Design, 1999—; contbr. articles to profl. jours. Recipient predoctoral fellowship NSF, Northwestern U., 1960-63. Fellow, AAAS; mem. Am. Chem. Soc., Am. Crystall. Assn., Molecular Graphics Soc., Protein Soc., Phi Beta Kappa, Sigma Xi. Office: Abbott Labs D47E AP10 100 Abbott Park Rd Abbott Park IL 60064-3502

MARTIN-BOWEN, LINDSEY, freelance writer; b. Kansas City, Kans., Aug. 4, 1959; d. Lawrence Richard and V. Marie (Schaffer) Pickett; m. Frederick E. Nicholson (div.); 1 child, Aaron Frederick; m. Edwin L. Martin, June 18, 1980 (div. 1987); 1 child, Ki Elise; m. Michael L. Bowen, Dec. 23, 1988 (div. 1997). BA in English Lit., U. Mo., Kansas City, 1972, MA in English and Creative Writing, 1988, postgrad., 1991-94; JD, U. Mo. Kansas City Sch. Law, Kansas City, 2000. Bar: Mo. 2001. Tech. editor Office Hearings and Appeals, U.S. Dept. Interior, Washington, 1976-77; reporter, photographer Louisville Times, 1982-83; reporter, features editor Sun Newspapers, Overland Park, Kans., 1983-84; assoc. editor Modern Jeweler, Overland Park and N.Y.C., 1984-85; writer Coll. Blvd. News, Overland Park, 1985-89, KC View, Kansas City, Mo., 1988-89; editor Number One, 1986-88, cons., 1988-89; copywriter Sta KXEO/KWWR Radio, Mexico, 1989; editorial asst. New Letters, 1985—; features writer, columnist The Squire, Prairie Village, Kans., 1990-95. Instr. lit., fiction writing, intro. to journalism, reporting, English, cultural studies, tech. writing, acad. writing and lit. U. Mo., Kansas City, 1986-88, 97—, Johnson County C.C., 1988-95; instr. writing Rockhurst U., 2002--; tchr. English and fiction Longview C.C., 1988-95, 97-98; instr. writing and mass comm. Webster U., 1990-98; instr. world lit., Am. lit., women in lit., creative writing Penn Valley C.C., 1993-97, faculty sponsor The Penn; owner, writer Paladin Freelance Writing Svc., Kansas City, 1988—; prodn. editor Nat. Paralegal Reporter, 1992-95, editor 1994-97; staff writer, columnist, Nat. Fedn. Paralegal Assns., Inc. books and pubs., NPR, 1992-; writing contest judge New Letters, 1987—; judge poetry contest BkMk Press, U. Mo., Kansas City, 1998—. Author: (novel) The Dark Horse Waits in Boulder, 1985, (poetry) Waiting for the Wake-Up Call, 1990, Second Touch, 1990, (fiction) Cicada Grove and Other Stories, 1992; contbr. poems, book revs., features, cartoon artwork, and photographs to numerous publs. including New Letters, Lip Service Contemporary Lit. Criticism, UMKC Law Rev., River King Poetry Supplement, Black Bear Review, The Kans. City Star; lead actress prodns. Coach House Players, 1969-70; extra HBO film Truman, 1995; staff mem., contbr. U. Mo.-Kansas City Law Rev., 1998-99. Campaigner McGovern for Pres. Campaign, Kansas City, 1971-72. Regents scholar, 1967; GAF fellow, 1986. Mem. U. Mo.-Kansas City Alumni Assn. (media com. 1983-84), Phi Kappa Phi. Roman Catholic. Avocations: acrylic and oil painting, downhill skiing, music, Greek cooking, paralegal work. Home: 7109 Pennsylvania Ave Kansas City MO 64114-1316 Office: U Mo Kansas City English Dept Cockefair Hall Rm 16B 5100 Rockhill Rd Kansas City MO 64110-2481

MARTINCIC, JOHN EDWARD, engineering executive; b. Hampton, Va., Oct. 5, 1967; s. John Joseph and Karen Elain (Black) M.; m. Lorraine Beck, June 15, 1996; children: John Paul, Kara Elizabeth. BSEE, Bob Jones U., 1989. Broadcast engr. WBJU, Greenville, S.C., 1985-87; dir. field engring. Magnum Tech., Warren, Pa., 1989-95; pres. Forest Scientific, Tionesta, 1983—; dist. mgr. Paxton/Patterson, Chgo., 1995-98; regional mgr. Allegheny Ednl. Sys., Pitts., 1998-99. Mem. IEEE, Tech. Edn. Assn. Pa. Avocations: fishing, hunting, amateur radio, computers, electronics. Home and Office: HC 2 Box 213 Tionesta PA 16353-9219 E-mail: jem@forestscientific.com.

MARTINDALE, CARLA JOY, librarian; b. Ladysmith, Wis., Sept. 9, 1947; d. Howard Walter and Audrey Elizabeth (Stanton) M. BA, Mt. Senario Coll., 1970; MLIS, U. South Fla., 1990. Libr. Blackhawk Schs., South Wayne, Ind., 1975-79, Osceola County Libr., Kissimee, Fla., 1989-90, Fla. Tech. Coll., Orlando, 1991-92, Orlando Coll. South, 1993-98; ret., 1998; vis. prof. distance learning libr. St. Leo (Fla.) U., 1999—. Chair for libr. 21st curriculum Phillips Coll., Orlando, 1995, acad. com., 1993-98, accreditation steering com., 1996. Library named in her honor Orlando Coll. South, 1995. Mem.: ALA, Fla. Libr. Assn. Avocations: reading, pets, stock investing. Home: 39637 Otis Allen Rd Zephyrhills FL 33540-6801 E-mail: carla.martindale@saintleo.edu.

MARTINDALE, COLIN EUGENE, psychology educator, author; b. Ft. Morgan, Colo., Mar. 21, 1943; s. Roy Woodrow and Martha Martindale; m. Mee Lee Goh, May 15, 1993. BA summa cum laude, U. Colo., 1964; PhD, Harvard U., 1970. From asst. prof. to prof. dept. psychology U. Maine, Orono 1970—. Author: Romantic Progression: The Psychology of Literary History, 1975, Cognition and Consciousness, 1981, The Clockwork Muse: The Predictability of Artistic Change, 1990, Cognitive Psychology: A Neural-Network Approach, 1991; editor sci. jours., 1982—. Recipient 1st prize 9th Ann. Creative Talent Awards program Am. Insts. for Rsch., 1970, Sociopsychol. prize AAAS, 1984. Fellow APA; mem. Assn. for Computers and the Humanities, Internat. Assn. Empirical Aesthetics, Assn. for Lit. and Linguistic Computers, Phi Beta Kappa. Republican. Home: 89 3rd St Bangor ME 04401-6104 Office: Dept Psychology Univ Maine Orono ME 04469-0001 E-mail: rpy393@maine.edu.

MARTINEAU, JULIE PEPERONE, social worker; b. Kilgore, Tex., Oct. 31, 1956; d. Angelo Gerad and Jane Margaret (Reppel) Peperone; m. Russell Joseph Martineau, Dec. 30, 1950; children: Adria Helen, Brittany Jane. AA, Marymount Palos Verdes Coll., Calif., 1976; BA, Calif. State U., Long Beach, 1979. Staff cons. United Way of L.A., 1979-83; group mgr. United Way of the Tex. Gulf Coast, Houston, 1983; dir. cmty. devel. Tri-County Mental Health and Mental Retardation Svcs., Conroe, Tex., 1984-87; exec. dir. Montgomery County Com. on Aging, 1987-97; pres. Montgomery County United Way, The Woodlands, 1997—. Chmn. Project CARE Monitoring Coun., Conroe, 1989-97; mem. long term care task force Tex. Health and Human Svcs. Commn., Austin, 1993-95; mem. aging programs adv. coun. Houston-Galveston Area Coun., 1987-97; mem. aging and disabled adv. coun. Dept. Human Svcs., Houston, 1993-98. Bd. dirs. Conroe Regional Med. Ctr., 1993—, United Way of Montgomery County, Conroe, 1984-87, Montgomery County Cmty. Found., 1998—; mem. United Way of Tex., United Way of Am.; congl. del. 1995 White House Conf. on Aging; chmn. Leadership Montgomery County, 1995-96, South Montgomery County Healthier Cmty. Forum, Conroe, 1996-98; v.p. Bluebonnet chpt. Nat. Charity League; mem. Consortium of Cmty. Assistance Programs, 1998—. Named Outstanding Woman of Yr., YWCA of Montgomery County, 1990; recipient Hometown Hero award, The Woodlands, 1999, Paul Harris fellow, 2001. Mem.: Area Agy. on Aging Execs. Network, Leadership Conroe (pres. 1990—92, v.p. 1995—97, pres. 1997—99), John Ben Sheperd Leadership Forum, Leadership Montgomery County Alumni Assn., South Montgomery C. of C. (chmn. bd. 1992—93), LWV of Montgomery County, Greater Conroe C. of C. (bd. dirs. 1999—2001), Rotary (Woodlands). Roman Catholic. Avocations: singing, cooking, volleyball, riding. Office: Montgomery County United Way 1600 Lake Front Cir The Woodlands TX 77380-3613

MARTINEN, JOHN A. travel company executive; b. Sault Ste Marie, Mich., Mar. 26, 1938; s. John Albert and Ina Helia (Jarvi) M. BS with highest honors, Mich. State U., 1960; LLB, NYU, 1963. With Grace Line, N.Y.C., 1963-69; cons. Empresa Turistica Internat., Galapagos Cruises, Quito, Ecuador, 1969-70; regional mgr. Globus & Cosmos (Group Voyagers Inc.), N.Y.C., 1970-73, v.p., 1974-76, exec. v.p., 1977-78, pres., CEO, 1979-92, Littleton, Colo., 1993-98, chmn., 1998; pres., CEO Vista Travel Ventures, Inc., Denver, 1999—2001; pres. Trofolger Tours, Long Island City, NY, 2002—. Pres., bd. dirs. Edbrooke Condominium Assn. Mem. U.S. Tour Operators Assn., Am. Soc. Travel Agts., Tour Operator Plan, Denver Acad. Travel and Tourism (bd. dirs.) Lotus, Sky and Wings Club (N.Y.), Columbine Country Club, Denver Athletic Club. Democrat. Office: Trofolger Tours 29-76 Northern Blvd Long Island City NY 11101 Home: 915 W End Ave New York NY 10025 E-mail: JohnMartinen@TrofolgerTours.com.

MARTINES, EUGENIA BELLE, elementary school educator; b. Marion, Va., Feb. 28, 1939; d. Howard Kelly Gullion and Mary Enias Edwards-Gullion; m. Frank Fuentes Martines, May 23, 1959 (dec. Oct. 25, 1991). Student, Marion Jr. Coll., 1958; AA, Coll. of Sequoias, 1960; BEd, Calif. State U., Fresno, 1966; cert. in bilingual edn., Calif., 1996. Kindergarten tchr. Five Points (Calif.) Sch., 1962—63; 3d grade spl. edn. tchr., 6th grade and 1st grade tchr. Corcoran (Calif.) Joint Unified Schs., 1963—97. Mem. Kings County Citizens Adv. Bd. on Alcohol and Other Drugs, Hanford, Calif., 1986—2001, chmn., 1992; mem. Red Ribbon Com. on Kings County and Corcoran, 1989—2001, Kings County Health Adv. Bd., Hanford, 1997—2001, Kings County Master Plan on Alcohol and Other Drugs, Hanford, 1991—2001; credentials person region 6 Reform Party of Calif., 1997—. Mem.: NEA, Corcoran Faculty Assn., Calif. Tchrs. Assn., Internat. Soc. Poets, Soc. Children's WRiters, Romance Writers of Am., Valley Writer's Network (pres. 1991—92), Fiction Writers' Connection, Photographers Assn., Kings County Critiquing (cofounder), PTA (life), Nat. Writers' Club. Reform. Roman Catholic. Avocations: reading, writing, breeding chihuahuas, political activism. Address: PO Box 458 Corcoran CA 93212-0458 E-mail: eugenia@savy2k.net.

MARTINETTI, RONALD ANTHONY, lawyer; b. N.Y.C., Aug. 13, 1945; s. Alfred Nathan and Frances Ann (Battipaglia) M. Student, U. Chgo., 1981-82; JD, U. So. Calif., 1982. Bar: Calif. 1982; U.S. Dist. Ct. (cen. and no. dists.) Calif. 1982, U.S. Dist. Ct. Ariz., 1992; U.S. Ct. Appeals (9th cir.) 1982. Ptnr. Kazanjian & Martinetti, Glendale, Calif., 1986—. Co-founder Am. Legends Website, 1995, Am. Legends Pub., 1996. Author: James Dean Story, 1995; co-author: Rights of Owners of Lost, Stolen or Destroyed Instruments Under UCC Section3-804: Can They Be Holders in Due Course, 1993; contbr. to Wall St. Jour., Washington Post, Newsday, Balt. Sun, The New Leader, Columbia U. Forum, 1968-76; pub. James Dean Scrapbook, 1996. Vol. trial lawyer Bet Tzedek Legal Svcs., 1987—; vol. arbitrator L.A. Sup. Ct., 1987—; judge pro tem L.A. Superior Ct., 1994—. Mem. Calif. Bar Assn. Roman Catholic. Office: Kazanjian & Martinetti 520 E Wilson Ave Glendale CA 91206-4374 Fax: 818-241-2193. E-mail: amlegends@aol.com.

MARTINEZ, ALEX J. state supreme court justice; b. Denver, Apr. 1, 1951; m. Kathy Carter; children: Julia, Maggie. Diploma, Phillips Exeter Acad., N.H., 1969; student, Reed Coll., 1969-72; BA, U. Colo., 1973, JD, 1976. Bar: Colo. 1976. Dep. state pub. defender, Pueblo and Denver, 1976-83; county ct. judge Pueblo, 1983-88; dist. ct. judge, 1988-97; justice Colo. Supreme Ct., Denver, 1997—. Supreme Ct. liaison Colo. Criminal Rules Com., Colo. Criminal Jury Instrns.; chmn. Child Welfare Appeals Workgroup, 1997; mem. standing com. Integrated Info. Svcs. Chmn. Pueblo adv. bd. Packard Found., 1993-96; chmn. site-based governing coun. Pueblo Sch. Arts and Scis., 1994-95; mem. site-based governing coun. Roncalli Mid. Sch., 1993-94; bd. dirs. Colo. U. Law Alumni. Mem. Colo. Bar Assn. (regional v.p. 1995-96), Colo. Hispanic Bar Assn., Pueblo Bar Assn. (mem. exec. coun. 1994-96), Pueblo Hispanic Bar Assn. Office: Colo Supreme Ct 2 E 14th Ave Denver CO 80203-2115 E-mail: AJMarti@aol.com.*

MARTINEZ, ALMA R. actor, director, educator; b. Monclova, Coahuila, Mex. Student, U. Guadalajara-Artes Plasticas, Mex., 1972-73, Ibero-Am. U., 1976, UNAM, Mexico City, 1976-77; BA in Theatre, Whittier Coll., 1984; MFA in Acting, U. So. Calif., 1995; postgrad., Stanford U., 1994—; student, Jerzy Grotowski Para Theatre, Berkeley, Calif., 1977, Lee Strasberg Theatre Inst., Hollywood, Calif., 1982, Royal Acad. Dramatic Arts, London, Eng., 1987, Mnouchkine/Theatre du Soleil, Paris, 1993. Asst. prof. theatre arts U. Calif., Santa Cruz. Appeared in plays including In the Summer House, Lincoln Ctr., N.Y.C., Greencard, Joyce Theatre, N.Y.C., Zoot Suit, Mark Taper Forum, L.A., Bocon, Mark Taper Forum, L.A., Macbeth, Oreg. Shakespeare Festival, The Skin of Our Teeth, Oreg. Shakespeare Festival, Hello Dolly, Long Beach Civic Light Opera, A Christmas Carol, South Coast Repertory, House of Blue Leaves, Pasadena Playhouse, Sundance Inst., Sundance, Utah, Fuente Ovejuna, Berkeley Repertory Theatre, Burning Patience, San Diego Repertory Theatre, Marriage of Figaro, Ariz. Theatre Co., Sons of Don Juan, Asolo Theatre, Fla., Wait Until Dark, Pa. Stage Co., La Carpa de los Rasquachis, Teatro Campesino; TV appearances include Gen. Hosp., Twilight Zone, Sequin, Corridos (Peabody award), Tough Love, Dress Gray, The Boys, In a Child's Name, The Gambler Returns, Quiet Killer, The New Adam 12 (series regular), 500 Nations, Nash Bridges (guest star); film appearances include Ballad of a Soldier, Jacaranda, The Novice, Trial by Terror, Dollie Dearest, Maria's Story, For A Loves One, Soldado Razo, Shattered Image, Zoot Suit, Barbarosa, Born in East L.A., Under Fire, among others; dir. (plays) Bed of Stone, 1996, La Gran Carpa de los Rasquachis, 1997, Heroes & Saints, 2001. Active Assistance with Alcohol and Sobriety Uniting Latinas, United L.Am. Youth, Med. Aid for El Salvador, Save the Children, the Christian Children's Fund; vol. and charity work in refugee camps in Ethiopia, India, Thailand, Sri Lanka, and The Philippines; bd. dirs. Mexican Mus., El Teatro Compresing. Recipient Cert. of Appreciation El Teatro Campesino, 1978, Recognition award Barrio Sta., 1980, Alumni Hall of Fame, El Rancho H.S., 1982, Outstanding Hispanic Alumni award Whittier Coll., 1984; co-recipient with Anthony Quinn and Edward James Olmos Hispanic Entertainer of Yr., The Equitable Co., 1987; Escobedo fellow Stanford U., 1996, Dorothy Danforth Compton Rsch. fellow, 1996. Mem. MLA, Nat. Acad. of Television Arts & Scis., AFTRA, SAG (John Dales scholar 1995-96, 98), TCG, Assn. for Theatre in Higher Edn., Nat. Theatre Conf., Nat. Assn. Chicas and Chicano Studies, Actors Equity Assn. Office: U Calif JW-14Theatre Arts Ctr Santa Cruz CA 95064 Agent: STARS Agency 23 Grant Ave 4th Fl San Francisco CA 94108 E-mail: bneducda@leland.stanford.edu.

MARTINEZ, ANTHONY JOSEPH, real estate appraiser; b. San Pedro, Calif., Nov. 2, 1947; s. Antonio Jose and Frances (Gonzales) M.; m. Judith Lyn Miller, July 24, 1971; children: Ronda Adrienne, Amanda Elizabeth, Melanie Melissa. AA, Cerritos Coll., 1968; BA, U. Americas, Mexico City, 1970. Cert. secondary tchr., Calif.; cert. gen. real estate appraiser, Ariz. Corp. officer Canyon Savs. & Loan, Prescott, Ariz., 1976-80; Ariz. dir. Nat. Assn. Ind. Fee Appraisers, Phoenix, 1989-91; with bd. dirs. Ariz. State Bd. Appraisal, 1990-96, chmn., 1990-94; owner RAM Enterprises, Prescott, 1980-86, A.J. Martinez & Assocs., Prescott, 1986—2001. Instr. Yavapai Coll., Prescott, 1973—; chmn. Bus. Adv. Coun. Yavapai Coll., 1988-89; with accredited residential sq. footage stds. com. Am. Nat. Stds. Instn., 1995-96. Tech. editor: Principios De La De Bienes Raicdes Residenciales, 1983. Elected Yavapai County Assessor, 2001—; charter mem. Prescott Town Hall. Mem. Nat. Assn. Ind. Fee Appraisers (sr., cert. instr. 1984—), Assn. Regulatory Ofcls. (nat. pres. 1994-95), Outward Bound-Prescott (bd. dirs. 1976-80), West Yavapai Guidance Clinic (bd. dirs. 1978-84), Prescott Sister Cities Assn. (pres. 1975-78), Lions (pres. Prescott Sunrise club 1979-80, Melvin Jones Fellow award, 2001). Republican. Lutheran. Avocations: reading, camping, hunting. Office: Yavapai County Assessor 1015 Fair St Prescott AZ 86305 Fax: 928-771-3181. E-mail: tony.martinez@co.yavapai.az.us.

MARTINEZ, BONNIE YVONNE, retired social services worker; b. Billings, Mont., Apr. 16, 1925; d. John Aaron and Dorothy Vernon (Best) Lewis; m. Antonio Avalos Martinez, Jan. 6, 1950 (div. Nov. 1974); children: Karla Dababneh, Yvette A., Anthony K., Robin M., Dana M., Lance M., Maria B. Van Haren. Grad. in Cosmetology, Edison Tech., 1950; student, Rocky Mountain Coll., 1970. Clk. Prudential Ins., L.A., 1967-68; crime/traffic auditor L.A. Police Dept., 1968-70; clk. Dept. Motor Vehicles, L.A., 1970-71; comty. action social worker Billings, 1971-74; eligibility technician San Diego County Welfare, 1974-76, Yellowstone County Welfare, Billings, 1976-91. House rep. State of Mont., Helena, 1994—, bd. Liftt, Rape Task Force, Granparents Raising Grandchildren. Mem. Hispanics and Friends Phyllis Wheatley (pres. 1971). Republican. Pentecostal. Avocations: people, betterment of society. Home: 769 Fallow Ln Billings MT 59102-7000

MARTINEZ, DAVID BRIAN, lawyer; b. Albuquerque, Aug. 9, 1956; s. Joe R. and Henrietta A. Martinez; m. Kimberley J. Gilbert, Aug. 17, 1984; children: Kellen, Madelaine. BBA, U. Notre Dame, 1978; JD, U. N.Mex., 1982. Bar: N.Mex. 1982, U.S. Dist. Ct. N.Mex. 1982. Pers. mgr. Springer Corp., 1978-79; assoc. Gilman & Maguire, Albuquerque, 1982-85; ptnr. Gilman, Maguire & Martinez, 1985-90, Maguire & Martinez, Albuquerque, 1990-92; mng. ptnr., v.p. Eaton, Martinez Hart & Valdez PC, 1993—. Bd. dirs. Albuquerque Acad., 1987-95, Manzano Day Sch., Albuquerque, 1996-99; trustee Sandia Prep. Sch., 2000—. Mem. ATLA, N.Mex. Trial Lawyers Assn., Albuquerque Bar Assn., U. N.Mex. Alumni Assn. (bd. dirs. 1986—). Office: Eaton Martinez Hart & Valdez PC 1801 Rio Grande Blvd NW Albuquerque NM 87104-2566 E-mail: david@emhpc.com.

MARTINEZ, DAVID R. electrical engineer, science educator; BSEE, N.Mex. State U., 1976; MS in Elec. Engring., MIT, 1979; EE in Elec. Engring., MIT/Woods Hole Oceanographic Instn., 1979; MBA, So. Meth. U., 1986. Prin. rsch. engr. Atlantic Richfield Co., 1979—88; group leader, assoc. divsn. head MIT Lincoln Lab., Lexington, Mass., 1988—. Mem. Army Sci. Bd. Recipient Spl. Achievement award, ARCO. Mem.: IEEE, Assn. for Computing Machinery. Achievements include patents for in field. Office: Lincoln Lab MIT 244 Wood St Lexington MA 02420-9108*

MARTINEZ, DONNA F. federal judge; BA, U. Conn., 1973, MSW, 1975, JD, 1978. Bar: Conn. 1979. Corp. counsel City of Hartford, Conn., 1979-80; asst. U.S. atty. Office U.S. Atty., Hartford and New Haven, 1980-94; chief organized crime drug enforcement task force Dist. of Conn., New Haven, 1989-94; magistrate judge U.S. Magistrate Ct., Hartford, 1994—. Instr. trial practice Yale U. Law Sch., New Haven, 1996-2001. Mem. Conn. Bar Assn.,

Fed. Bar Assn., Hispanic Bar Assn., Fed. Magistrate Judges Assn., Am. Inns of Ct. (past. v.p., past pres.), Am. Leadership Forum (bd. dirs.). Office: US Magistrate Ct 450 Main St Rm 262 Hartford CT 06103-3002

MARTINEZ, EDUARDO VIDAL, lawyer; b. Travis AFB, Calif., Sept. 27, 1955; s. Vidal and Isidora (Lee) M.; m. Mary Kim Sullivan, Apr. 7, 1984. BA, U. Tex., 1978; MA, Antioch Ctr. for Legal Studies, Washington, 1983; JD, Miss. Coll., 1990. Bar: Miss. 1991, U.S. Dist. Ct. (no. and so. dist.) Miss. 1991, U.S. Ct. Mil. Appeals 1991, U.S. Ct. Appeals (5th cir.) 1991, U.S. Supreme Ct. 1994. Gen. counsel Home-Land Title & Abstract Co. Inc., Jackson, Miss., 1991; pvt. practice, 1991-92; spl. asst. atty. gen. Office of the Atty. Gen., 1992-97; legal counsel, site adminstr. SkyTel Corp., 1997—98, corp. counsel, 1999—; dir. site leasing and acquisition WorldCom Broadband Solutions, Inc., 2001. Editor Legal Eye, 2000-2002. Comdr. USNR, 1994-2001. Scholar Miss. Bar Found., 1988, scholar in environ. law Am. Law Inst., 1990. Mem. ABA, Miss. Bar Assn., Naval Res. Assn. (chpt. pres.), Navy League, Res. Officer Assn. (chpt. pres., nat. naval sect. committeeman 2000-2002), Nat. Jr. Officer (co-chairperson), Sea Svcs. (nat. jr. v.p.). Roman Catholic. Office: 515 E Amite St Jackson MS 39201 E-mail: evmart@juno.com.

MARTINEZ, FERNANDO J. academic physician, medical educator; b. Havana, Cuba, Sept. 23, 1958; s. Fernando José and Bertha Adelfa Martinez; m. Colleen Mary Brennan; children: Margaret, Fernando. MD, U. Fla., 1983; MS, U. Mich., 2001. Cert. internal medicine and pulmonary disease 1983, critical care medicine. Lectr. medicine Harvard Med. Sch., Burlington, Mass.; asst. prof. internal medicine U. Mich., Ann Arbor, 1991—95, assoc. prof. internal medicine, 1995—2002, prof. of medicine, 2002—. Dir. pulmonary diagnostic svcs., lung volume reduction surgery program U. Mich., Ann Arbor; chmn. clin. descriptors writing com., Nat. Emphysema Treatment Trial Nat. Heart and Blood Inst., Bethesda, Md., 1998—2002. Mem. editl. bd.: Am. Jour. Respiratory and Critical Care Medicine. Fellow: Am. Coll. Chest Physicians (Dupont Critical Care/Young Investigator award 1986); mem.: Am. Thoracic Soc., European Respiratory Soc. Home: 4293 Sherwood Forest Ct Ann Arbor MI 48103 Office: U Mich TC 3916 1500 E Med Ctr Dr Ann Arbor MI 48109-0360 Home Fax: 734-936-5048; Office Fax: 734-936-5048. E-mail: fmartine@umich.edu.

MARTINEZ, FERNANDO V. civil engineer; b. Blewett, Tex., July 2, 1927; s. Catarino G. and Refugia V. M.; m. Dora Garza, Sept. 27, 1953; children: Fernando G., Karen Martinez Solano, Edward A. BS in Civil Engring, Tex A&M U., 1951. Registered profl. engr., Tex. Field engr. Farnsworth & Chambers Co, Houston, 1953-54; design engr. Link Belt Co., 1954, Anderson Clayton & Co., Houston, 1954-59; project engr. Olin Mathieson Chem. Corp., Pasadena, Tex., 1959-80; project mgr. Mobil Oil Corp., 1980—. 1st lt. U.S. Army, 1951-53, Korea. Republican. Roman Catholic. Home: 710 Skylark Rd Pasadena TX 77502-4560 Office: Mobil Oil Corp 2001 Jackson Rd Pasadena TX 77501

MARTINEZ, GAYLE FRANCES, protective services official; b. Joplin, Mo., June 25, 1954; d. Jackie Ray Jackson and Shirley Joann (Williams) Jackson Hulett; m. Randy Louis Brown (div. Sept. 1974); 1 child, Randy Louis Brown II; m. Alan John Dwinells, July 15, 1975 (div. Sept. 1977); children: Christopher Ray Dwinells. AA, Longview Coll., 1979; indsl. drafting cert., Marin County Adult Sch., 1984; BA, Sacramento State Coll., 1989. Cert. peace officer. Computer operator JC Penney, Kans., 1977-81; air cargo specialist USAF, 1980-92; ins. agent Prudential, Richmond, Calif., 1983-85; peace officer Calif. State Prison, Vacaville, 1985—. Trainer Calif. Dept. Corrections, Vacaville, 1989—; piano tchr.; dog trainer for hosp. and convalescent home therapy dogs. Author: Whispers in the Wind. Mem. Calif. Correctional Peace Officers Assn. (union rep.). Democrat. Assembly of God. Avocations: sewing, interior decorating, bowling, piano. Home: 1525 Willow Lake Rd Discovery Bay CA 94514-9394

MARTINEZ, GUSTAVE See SOLOMONS, GUS JR.

MARTINEZ, HERMINIA S. economist, banker; b. Havana, Cuba; came to U.S., 1960, naturalized, 1972; d. Carlos and Amelia (Santana) Martinez Sanchez; m. Mario Aguilar, 1982; children: Mario Aguilar, Carlos Aguilar. BA in Econs. cum laude, Am. U., 1965; MS in Fgn. Svc. (Univ. fellow); MS in Econs., Georgetown U., 1967, PhD in Econs., 1969; postgrad., Nat. U. Mex. Instr. econs. George Mason Coll., U. Va., Fairfax, 1967-68; researcher World Bank, 1967-69, indsl. economist, devel. econs. dept., 1969-71; economist World Bank Latin Am. (Ctrl. Am., Mex., Venezuala, Equador, Panama and Dominican Republic, Washington, 1971-79; sr. loan officer for Middle East and North Africa World Bank, 1977-81, sr. loan officer for Western Africa region, 1981-84, sr. economist Africa Region, 1988-91, prin. ops. officer pvt. sector fin. group Africa region, 1992-96, lead specialist, sub-regional mgr., 1996-2000; pres. pvt. practice, 2000—. Contbg. author: The Economic Growth of Colombia: Problems and Prospects, 1973, Central American Financial Integration, 1975. Mid-Career fellow Princeton U., 1988-89. Mem. Am. Econ. Assn., Soc. Internat. Devel., Brookings Inst. Latin Am. Study Group. Roman Catholic. Home: 5145 Yuma St NW Washington DC 20016-4336 Office: World Bank 1818 H St NW Washington DC 20433-0001

MARTINEZ, JACQUELINE MURPHREE, writer, real estate broker; b. Mesa, Ariz., July 10, 1924; d. Eugene Loid Murphree and Orleta Grace Drain; m. Lawrence King Cox, June 8, 1942 (div. Oct. 5, 1955); children: Sherry Ann Cox, Sunny Lynn Cox; m. Joseph B. Martinez Sr., Dec. 30, 1965. Student, Stanford U., 1945—51. Real estate broker, San Diego, 1958—71; freelance writer Idaho Falls, Idaho, 1994—. Author: Journey West. Democrat. Roman Catholic. Avocations: tennis, fishing, travel, cooking, gardening. Home: 1875 Peggy's Ln Idaho Falls ID 83402

MARTINEZ, JOAQUIN OSVALDO, production control professional; b. San Juan, P.R., Oct. 9, 1960; s. Joaquín Martínez and Luz Nery Rios; m. Yvette Divina Molina; children: Jessica, María. BBA, Met. U., San Juan, P.R., 1985. Store mgr. Tiendas Militares Guardia Nacional PR, Inc., Cayey, PR, 1990—91, mktg. mgr. Carolina, 1991—93, area mgr., 1993—95; mgr. Blockbuster Video, San Antonio, 1996—99; prodn. control USAA Fed. Savs. Bank, 1999—. Pub. affairs officer U. S Army Pr N.G., San Juan, 1993—96. Author: (childens book) Bicycle Ride, 2002. Capt. USAR, 1988—96. Mem.: U.S. Army Officer Club. Office: USAA Fed Savs Bank 10750 McDermott Fwy San Antonio TX 78288-0544

MARTINEZ, JOE LOUIS, JR. neurobiologist, educator; b. Albuquerque, Aug. 1, 1944; s. Joe Louis and Maria Elena (Werner) M.; m. Janice Susanna Hepner, Sept. 17, 1967 (div. Oct. 1987); children: Adan, Adria, Aric; m. Kimberly Smith, Dec. 2, 1990; 1 child, Ariel. BA, U. San Diego, 1966; MS, N.Mex. Highlands U., 1968; PhD, U. Del., 1971. From asst. to assoc. prof. Calif. State U., San Bernardino, 1971-75; assoc. researcher U. Calif., Irvine, 1975-82, prof. Berkeley, 1982-94; prof. neurobiology, dir. Cajal Neurosci. Rsch. Ctr. U. Tex., San Antonio, 1994-2001, assoc. vice provost for rsch., 2001—. Mem. AAAS (lifetime mentor award 1994), NIDA (bd. sci. counselors 1999—), Am. Coll. Neuropsychopharmacology. Office: U Tex 6900 N Loop 1604 W San Antonio TX 78249-1130 E-mail: jmartinez@utsa.edu.

MARTINEZ, JOSE RAFAEL, writer, educator, poet; b. Monte Vista, Colo., Aug. 16, 1943; s. Jose Delfino Martinez and Rose Madril Fennell; m. Fredrika Audrey McGraw, Dec. 24, 1975; children: Ashley Rose, Brian Thomas. BS in Journalism, U. Colo., 1972. News reporter KMGH-TV, Denver, 1971-73; freelance journalist La Voz de Colo., Focus, others, 1974-77; info. officer City and County of Denver, 1977-86; instr. U. Colo., Boulder, 1986-99; freelance writer, 1995—. Dir. writing workshop The Frank Waters Found., Arroyo Seco, N.Mex., 1995—; lit. judge The Peter and Madeleine Martin Found., Taos, N.Mex., 1996—; lit. presentations/workshops The Millicent Rogers Mus., Taos, 1996-97; lit. judge for Oreg. Arts Coun., Colo. Coun. on Arts, 1998. Author short fiction, poetry, acad. criticism, lit. journalism. Sgt. USAF, 1964-68. Recipient The Frank Waters Writing award for lit. achievement Peter and Madeleine Martin Found., 1994; Artist fellow in lit. and poetry Colo. Coun. on Arts, 1998-99. Avocations: photography, hiking, birdwatching. Home: 1834 Marine St Boulder CO 80302-6420 E-mail: joseralph@aol.com.

MARTINEZ, JOSEMARIA ESPINO, computer services administrator; b. Manila, Philippines, Nov. 10, 1963; came to U.S., 1974; s. Rogelio Alaras and Rosita (Espino) M.; m. Kamala Lynn Hendricks, July 27, 1991; 1 child, Christian Sinclair Garrison Martinez. Student, U. Ill., Chgo., 1980-81; BA, DePaul U., Chgo., 1993; postgrad., Northwestern U., 1999—. Data processing mgr. Nationwide Credit & Collection, Chgo., 1982-84; project leader/analyst Met. Chgo. Coun., 1984-86; systems dir. Fifield Cos., Ltd., Chgo., 1986-90; dir. MIS Thorek Hosp. and Med. Ctr., 1991-93; MIS dir. Chgo. Zool. Soc. and Brookfield Zoo, 1993-97; prin. Whittman-Hart, Chgo., 1997—. Contbr. articles to mags. and profl. jours. Mem. Assn. for Systems Mgmt., Common Users Group. Republican. Presbyterian. Avocations: tennis, racquetball, golf. Home: 4312 Camelot Cir Naperville IL 60564-3189 Office: Whittman-Hart #3500 311 S Wacker Dr Ste 3500 Chicago IL 60606-6621

MARTINEZ, LUIS FERNANDO, journalist, writer, historian; b. Medellin, Antioquia, Colombia, Apr. 29, 1946; s. Edelberto Antonio Martinez and Myriam Carlota Solis; m. Alicia Ester Posada; children: Isabel Kristina, Ludoviko Ernesto, Enver Kamilo. BA in Journalism, Antioquia U., Medellin, 1987; Tchg. Cert., Nat. Learn Svc., Apartado, Colombia, 1996; Historian and Academic (hon.) , Antioquia History Acad., Medellin, 1998. Speech writer CORVIDE, Medellin, 1992—99; human develoment SENA, Apartado, 1996—99; Spanish composition Cooperativ U., Turbo, Colombia, 1997—98; comm. theory Apya Yala U., Apartado, 1997—98; columnist, editor El Periodiko, St. Louis, 1999—. Journalist Comunal Action, Medellin, 1970—85, Patriot Union, Medellin, 1985—99. Author: (17 books) Geopolitics and Comunications, 1998; editor: (newspaper) EL PERIODIKO, 2001. Recipient Gold Medal, SEDUCA, 1987, Heroic Journalism award, SIP, 1989, Ariza Flower flower, COMFENALCO, 1998. Mem.: Universala Esperanto Asocio (rotterdam 1970—). Avocations: walking, athletics. Office: El Periodiko 2nd Fl 3337 Texas Ave Saint Louis MO 63118 Home Fax: 314-776-3362; Office Fax: 314-776-3362. Personal E-mail: elperiodiko@cs.com. Business E-Mail: elperiodiko@cs.com.

MARTINEZ, LUIS OSVALDO, radiologist, educator; b. Havana, Cuba, Nov. 27, 1927; came to U.S., 1962, naturalized, 1967; s. Osvaldo and Felicita (Farinas) M.; children Maria Elena, Luis Osvaldo, Alberto Luis; m. Nydia M. Ceballos. MD, U. Havana, 1954. Cert. in diagnostic radiology. Intern Calixto Garcia Hosp., Havana, 1954-55; resident in radiology Jackson Meml. Hosp., Miami, Fla., 1963-65, fellow in cardiovascular radiology, 1965-67; instr. radiology U. Miami, 1965-68, asst. prof., 1968, clin. asst. prof., 1968-70, assoc. prof., 1970-76, prof., 1976-91, clin. prof., 1991-94; chief radiol. svcs. VA Med. Ctr., 1991—. Assoc. dir. dept. radiology Mt. Sinai Med. Ctr., Miami Beach, Fla., 1969-91, chief divsn. diagnostic radiology, 1970-91, dir. residency program in diagnostic radiology, emeritus mem. med. staff, 1991; dir. Spanish Radiology Seminar. Reviewer Am. Jour. Radiology, Radium Therapy and Nuclear Medicine, 1978; contbr. articles to profl. jours. Former pres. League Against Cancer. Recipient Gold medal Interam. Coll. Radiology, 1975, Antoine Bèclere medal Internat. Congress Radiology, 1989, Carlos J. Finlay Gold medal Cuban Med. Convb., 1990, Honors Achievement award, Cert. of Merit Mallinckrodt Pharms., 1972-74; Luis O. Martinez M.D. Lecture named in his honor, Interam. Coll. Radiology. Mem. AMA (Physician's Recognition award 1971, 74-83), AAUP, Radiol. Soc. France (hon. 1991), Internat. Soc. Lymphology, Interam. Coll. Radiology (pres.), Internat. Coll. Surgeons, Internat. Coll. Angiology, Internat. Soc. Radiology, Cuban Med. Assn. in Exile, Am. Coll. Chest Physicians (assoc.), Radiol. Soc. N. Am., Am. Coll. Radiology, Am. Roentgen Ray Soc., Am. Assn. Fgn. Med. Grads., Am. Profl. Practice Assn., Am. Thoracic Soc., Pan Am. Med. Assn., Am. Assn. Univ. Radiologists, Brit. Inst. Radiology, Am. Heart Assn. (mem. council cardiovascular radiology), Faculty Radiologists, Soc. Gastrointestinal Radiologists, Am. Geriatrics Soc., Am. Coll. Angiology, Royal Coll. Radiologists, Am. Soic. Therapeutic Radiologists, Assn. Hosp. Med. Edn., Cuban Radiology Soc. in exile (founder, pres.), Cuban chpt. Inter Am. Coll. Radiology (founder, pres.), Am. Coll. Med. Imaging, Interasma, So. Med. Assn., N.Y. Acad. Scis., Fla. Thoracis Soc., Fla. Radiol. Soc., Dade County Med. Assn., Greater Miami Radiol. Soc., cuban Radiol. Soc. (sec.), Can. Assn. Radiologists, Soc. Thoracic Radiologists (founding mem.), Emeritus mem. Am. Coll. Angiology, 1989, Emeritus mem. Am. Heart Assn., 1992; hon. mem. numerous med. socs. of Mex., Cen. and S. Am. Roman Catholic. Office: 1201 NW 16th St Miami FL 33125-1624

MARTINEZ, MARIA DOLORES, pediatrician; b. Cifuentes, Cuba, Mar. 16, 1959; d. Demetrio and Alba Silvia (Perez) M.; m. James David Marple, Apr. 25, 1992. MD, U. Navarra, Pamplona, Spain, 1984. Med. diplomate. Resident in pediatrics Moses Cone Hosp., Greensboro, N.C., 1986-89; pvt. practice Charlotte, 1989-93, Mooresville, 1993-96; pediat. pulmonary fellow Univ. Med. Hosp., Tucson, 1996-99; pediatric pulmonologist, also in sleep medicine/transplants Duke U., Durham, N.C., 1999—, dir. pediat. lung transplant svcs., assoc. dir. sleep medicine lab., 2000—. Mem. AMA, Am. Acad. Pediatrics, N.C. Med. Soc., Mecklenburg County Med. Soc. Republican. Roman Catholic. Avocations: horseback riding, travel. Office: Duke U Med Ctr Dept Pediats PO Box 2994 Durham NC 27710-0001

MARTINEZ, MARIANELA, state agency administrator; b. McAllen, Tex., June 27, 1956; d. Francisco Martínez and Maria Lidia Villarreal. BS, U. Tex. Pan Am., Edinburg, 1979; chem. tech. cert., Tex. State Tech. Inst., 1987; student, Ind. U., 1999. Cert. intoxilyzer 5000 breath alcohol analysis instrument op., maint., repair and instrn. oper. CMI, Inc., 2000, breath test op. Tex. Dept. Pub. Safety, 2000, tech. supr. Tex. Dept. Pub. Safety, 2000. Tchr. Mission (Tex.) H.S., 1981-86, Alamo (Tex.) Mid. Sch., 1998; agent analyst II S.W. Rsch. Inst., 1987-95, 97-99; tech. supr. Breath Test Svcs., McAllen, 1999—. Shift rep. Johnston Island Mgmt. Action Com., Johnston Atoll, 1989—91; lab. rep. Comm. Improvement Team, Johnston Atoll, 1999. Poll judge Dems., McAllen, 1986; sgt. at arms Gathering Christ Ministries, Inc., McAllen, 2000. Mem.: Intoxilyzer 5000 Users' Group, Alcohol Testing Alliance, Am. Chem. Soc. Avocations: swimming, reading, board games, traveling. Office: Breath Test Svcs 4309 N 10th St Ste F4 Mcallen TX 78504 E-mail: nelbo1@aol.com.

MARTINEZ, MATTHEW GILBERT, former congressman; b. Walsenburg, Colo., Feb. 14, 1929; children: Matthew, Diane, Susan, Michael, Carol Ann. Cert of competence, Los Angeles Trade Tech. Sch., 1959. Small businessman and bldg. contractor; mem. 97th-106th Congresses from 31st Calif. dist., 1982-2001; mem. edn. and labor com., fgn. affairs com. Mem. Monterey Park Planning Commn., 1971-74; mayor City of Monterey Park, 1974-75; mem. Monterey Park City Council, 1974-80, Calif. State Assembly, 1980-82; bd. dirs. San Gabriel Valley YMCA. Served with USMC, 1947-50. Mem. Congl. Hispanic Caucus, Hispanic Am. Democrats, Nat. Assn. Latino Elected and Apptd. Ofcls., Communications Workers Am., VFW, Am. Legion, Latin Bus. Assn., Monterey Park C. of C., Navy League (dir.) Lodges: Rotary. Democrat.*

MARTINEZ, MELQUIADES R. (MEL MARTINEZ), federal official; b. Sagua La Grande, Cuba, Oct. 23, 1946; came to U.S., 1962; naturalized, 1971; s. Melquiades C. and Gladys V. (Ruiz) M.; m. Kathryn Tindal, June 13, 1970; children: Lauren Elizabeth, John Melquiades, Andrew Tindal. BA, Fla. State U., 1969, JD, 1973. Bar: Fla. 1973, U.S. Dist. Ct. (mid. dist.) Fla. 1973, U.S. Supreme Ct. 1979, U.S. Dist. Ct. (so. dist.) Fla. 1986; cert. Nat. Bd. Trial Advocacy. Civil trial atty. Fla. Ptnr., Martinez, Dalton, Dellecker and Wilson, Orlando, Fla., 1973-85, Martinez, Dalton, Dellecker, Wilson and King, 1985-98; chmn. Orange County, 1998-2001; sec. HUD, Washington, 2001—. Bd. dirs. Cath. Social Svcs. Orlando, 1978-86; founder, chmn. Mayor's Hispanic Adv. Com., Orlando, 1981-82; chmn. bd. commrs. Olando Housing Authority, 1983-86; commr. Orlando Utilities Commn., 1992-97, pres. 1995-97; chmn. Orange County, 1998. Mem. Fla. Bar (bd. govs. young lawyers sect. 1980-81), Acad. Fla. Trial Lawyers (dir. 1981-85, treas. 1986-87, pres. 1988-89), 9th Jud. Cir. (jud. nomination commn. 1986). Roman Catholic. Office: HUD 451 7th St SW Washington DC 20410*

MARTINEZ, MIGUEL ACEVEDO, urologist, consultant, lecturer; b. Chihuahua, Mex., Aug. 18, 1953; came to U.S., 1956; s. Miguel Nuñez and Velia (Acevedo) M. AB, Stanford U., 1976; MD, Yale U., 1983. Diplomate Am. Bd. Urology. Intern U. S.C. Med. Ctr., 1983-84; resident in urology White Meml. Med. Ctr., L.A., 1984-89, urologist, 1989—. Cons., lectr. physician asst. program U. So. Calif., L.A., 1990—, clin. instr.; patient edn. cons. ICI Pharm., Del., 1991—, Zeneca's Speaker Forum; patient edn. and med. cons., lectr. Abbott Labs., 1991—; mem. edn.cons. several radio/TV stas., 1991—; mem. subcom. for diseases on kidney and transplantation NIH, Washington, 1991; mem. nat. Hispanic adv. bd. Pfizer Pharms., Inc., 1998—. Author: Intercellular Pathways, 1981. Polit. cons. Xavier Becerra, U.S. Congress, 1992, Martin Gallegos, Gil Cedillo, Calif. State Assembly, 1993, others; bd. dirs. Latino Ctr. for Prevention and Action in Health, Orange County, calif.; bd. govs., sec., rep. Zeneca Urology Econ. Summit, Washington, 1993; mem. Pfizer Nat. Hispanic Adv. Bd. Named one of Outstanding Young Men of Am., 1981; Nat. Hispanic Med. Assn. Pub. Policy fellow, 2000-01. Mem. AMA, Nat. Hispanic Med. Assn. (public policy fellow), Am. Urological Assn., Calif. Med. Assn. (polit. action com. bd. dirs. 1997—, del.), L.A. Med. Assn. (polit. action com. 1992—), L.A. County Med. Assn., Yale Alumni Assn., Stanford Alumni Assn., L.A. Athletic Club. Office: White Meml Med Ctr Rm 500 1701 Cesar Chavez Ave Los Angeles CA 90033-2438

MARTINEZ, MIGUEL EDUARDO, development bank executive; b. Nov. 21, 1943; MA in Econs., U. Chgo., 1968, PhD in Econs., 1970. Prof. econs. U. Cuyo, Mendoza, Argentina, 1968-74; mgmt., advisor World Bank, Washington, 1974-94; mgr. InternAm. Devel. Bank, 1994—. Home: 9421 Winterset Dr Potomac MD 20854-2845

MARTINEZ, MILTON M. language educator; b. Camagüey, Cuba, Nov. 15, 1947; arrived in U.S., 1980; s. Juvenal and Catalina B. Martinez; m. Maria C. Madrigal, 1975 (div. 1980); 1 child Milton M. Martinez Madrigal ; m. Erika Arguello Martinez, 1982; children: Erika F., Michelle F. BA in Spanish Grammar and Lit., U. Central, 1968; BA in Pedagogy and Spanish Methodology, Inst. Superior Edn., Camagüey, 1974; M in Spanish Methodology, Inst. Superior Pedagógico, Camagüey, 1979; MA, N.Mex. State U., 1995. Prof. Spanish lang. Ministry Armed Forces, Matanzas, Cuba, 1966—68; prof. methodology Edn. Adults Ministry, Camagüey, 1968—72; provincial tech. adv. Ministry Edn., 1972—77, chmn. Spanish dept., 1977—80; tchg. asst. Spanish N.Mex. State U., Las Cruces, 1993—95; instr. Spanish lang. Internat. Baccalaureate Program, Tampa, Fla., 1996—98, Xavier U., New Orleans, 1998—. Lectr. in field. Author: Sitio de Máscaras, 1987, Espacio y albedrio, 1990, Domingo, el abuelo astral, 2000; contbr. articles to profl. jours. Mem.: La. Fgn. Lang. Tchrs. Assn., La. Assn. Tchrs. Spanish and Portuguese, Am. Assn. Tchrs. Spanish and Portuguese, Circulo de Cultura Panamericana. Avocations: reading, writing. Home: 814 27th St Kenner LA 70062 Office: Xavier Univ 1 Drexel Dr New Orleans LA 70125 Fax: 504-485-7907. E-mail: mmartine@xula.edu.

MARTINEZ, PEDRO JAIME, professional baseball player; b. Manoquayabo, Dominican Republic, July 25, 1971; With L.A. Dodgers, 1992-93; pitcher Montreal Expos, 1994-97, Boston Red Sox, 1998—. Named Minor League Player Sporting News, 1991. Office: Boston Red Sox 4 Yawkey Way Boston MA 02215-3496*

MARTINEZ, RICARDO, research and development company executive; m. Robin Rosser. MD, La. State U. Sch. Medicine, 1980. Intern Lafayette (La.) Charity Hosp., 1980-81; resident Charity Hosp., New Orleans, 1983-85; vis. fellow accident rsch. unit Ctr. Automotive Engring./U. Birmingham, U.K., 1989; adminstr. Nat. Hwy. Traffic Safety Adminstrn, Washington, 1994—99; sr. v.p. health affairs Healtheon Web MD Corp., Atlanta, 1999—2000; pres., CEO Safety Intelligence Sys., 2000—. Clin. prof. emergency medicine Emory U. Sch. Medicine, Atlanta, assoc. dir. Ctr. for Injury Control. Home: 1254 Spring Creek Way Decatur GA 30033-2643 Office: Safety Intelligence Systems 790 Atlantic Drive S 0355 Atlanta GA 30332

MARTINEZ, ROSE MARIE, health facility administrator; PhD, Johns Hopkins Sch. Hygiene and Pub. Health. Former asst. dir. health fin. and policy U.S. Gen. Acctg. Office; sr. health rschr. Mathematica Policy Rsch.; dir. IOM Bd. Health Promotion and Disease Prevention , 2002—. Office: 2101 Contitution Ave NW Washington DC 20418*

MARTINEZ, RUBEN MARTIN, logistics engineer; b. L.A., Mar. 12, 1948; s. Elias and Emma Louise (Jurado) M.; m. Deanna Jean Rein, May 1969 (div. 1976); children: Ruben Jr., Victor; m. Linn Ann Hampton, Apr. 5, 1980; children: Michael, Martin, Linnita, Loretta. AA in Bus., Rio Hondo Coll., 1973; AA in Logistics, BA in Computer System, Nat. U., 1989, Cert. in Exec. Computer Mgmt., 1990, MBA in Mgmt. Info. Systems, 1991; cert. in sys. engring. mgmt., Calif. Inst. Tech., 1995. Registered engr., Calif. Sr. data analyst Continental Data Graphics, Culver City, Calif., 1972-79; provisioning engr. Hughes Aircraft, Ground Systems, Fullerton, 1979-83; sr. logistics engr. Rockwell Internat., Anaheim, 1987—87; sr. logistics engr. divsn. air combat sys. Northrop Grumman Corp., El Segundo, 1987—. Officer Civil Air Patrol, Compton, Calif., 1984. Mem. Soc. Logistics Engr., Am. Defense Preparedness Assn., Nat. Mgmt. Assn., KC, Elks. Republican. Roman Catholic. Avocations: martial arts (registered 3d degree black belt in Tae Kwon Do). Home: 9605 Armley Ave Whittier CA 90604-1006 Office: Aircraft Combat Sys LW61/W3 1 Hornet Way El Segundo CA 90245-2804 E-mail: tpgn1948@cs.com, martiru@mail.northgram.com.

MARTINEZ, STEVEN FRANK, organization executive; b. St. Louis, May 7, 1956; s. Frank and Charline (Stueymeyer) Martinez; m. Kathy M. O'Shaughnessy, July 11, 1996; children: Maria Suzanne, Monica Lee. BS, U. Mo., 1979; MA, Webster U., 1984. With Mo. dept. mental health, 1979-83; dir. activity therapy Creidon Spring Hosp. , 1983—84; with Mo. Baptist Hosp. , 1984—86, St. Joseph Health Care Ctr., St. Charles, 1986—87. Mem. exec. bd. Jaycee Fairground Village, 1986-94, All Saints Parish, 2000-; dir. develop. Childhaven Treatment Ctr., 1989—92; exec. v.p. Am. Floral Endowment, 1999—. Mem.: St. Charles Jaycees (pres. 1988—89, Outstanding Health Care Provider 1988), St. Charles Crime Stoppers (pres. 1989—99). Avocations: racquetball, volunteer, volleyball, fishing, hunting. Office: Am Floral Endowment 11 Glen Ed Profl Park Glen Carbon IL 62034 E-mail: afe@endowment.org.

MARTINEZ, SUSAN BARBARA, human rights advocate; b. N.Y.C., May 31, 1943; d. Irving Ehrman and Rose Yelnick; children: Alexander Isaac, Liliana Rose. BA, Bklyn. Coll., 1965; PhD, Columbia U., 1972. Gemmologist Tropical Gems, West Palm Beach, Fla., 1988-92; Pan-Am. activist Ragged Feather Lodge, 1993-98; editor Oahspe Scriptorium, Tiger, Ga., 1995-99; adv. Children of War, Afghanistan, 2001—. Designer (gems and jewelry) Designers Handbook, 1991; author: The Quickening, Chronicles of Kosmon. Newsletter editor World Peace Tonite, Clayton, Ga., 1995—; foster parent Iluision Freedom Inst., Clayton, 1996—; founder, peace activist, min. Ch. of Tae, 1998—. Recipient Poetry award Poets of Palm Beach, 1994. Avocations: music, vegetarian cooking, prehistory research, new science. Office: Lodge Publs PO Box 194 Clayton GA 30525

MARTINEZ, WALTER BALDOMERO, architect; b. Havana, Cuba, Sept. 21, 1937; came to U.S., 1961; s. BaldomerO and Maria J. Amparo (Rodriguez) M.; m. Olga Justa Sardina, July 23, 1961; children: Teresita Maria, Gabriel Jose. Cert. in civil constrn., Arts and Craft Vocat. Sch., Havana, 1957; student, U. Havana, 1958-60, U. Miami, 1963-64, cert. fallout shelter analyst, 1970. Registered architect, Fla.; cert. gen. contractor, Fla. Job capt. Tony Sherman Architect, Miami, Fla., 1961-63; project mgr. Ken Miller Architect, 1968-69; designer, project mgr. Russell-Melton & Assocs., 1969-70; head archtl. dept. Sanders & Thomas, 1971-72; assoc. Russell-Wooster & Assoc., 1973-77; prin. Russell-Martinez & Holt, 1977-84; prin., pres. The Russell Partnership, 1985—. Uniform bldg. code insp., 1991—; insp. So. Bldg. Code Cong. Internat. Inc., 1997—. Contbr. articles to Constrn. mag. Bd. dirs. Biscayne Nature Ctr., Miami, 1982—97; vice chmn. Latin Quarters Rev. Bd., 1989—2002. Fellow AIA (nat. chmn. minority resources com. 1985, pres. Miami chpt. 1982, Silver medal 1981); mem. Nat. Assn. Cuban Archs. (bd. dirs. Miami chpt. 1986, Gold medal 1984), Fla. Bd. Archs. (chmn. 1991), NCARB, Fla. Home Builders Assn. (Aurora award 1999), Greater Miami C. of C. (Hispanic affairs com. 1988-93, chmn. affordable housing com. 1989), Nat. Arch. Accrediting Bd., Inc. (accreditation team mem. 1992-95). Republican. Roman Catholic. Avocations: boating, photography, travel. Home: 4130 Malaga Ave Coconut Grove FL 33133-6325 Office: Russell Partnership Inc 5815 SW 68th St Miami FL 33143-3620

MARTINEZ, YOLANDA R. social services administrator; b. Feb. 11, 1936; d. Eduardo R. and Consuelo (Rincon) Martinez; m. William Edward Hawkins, Mar. 27, 1963 (dec. May 11, 1996); children: Ricardo, Eduardo, William T. AA, San Bernardino Valley Coll., 1959; BA, U. Wash., 1974. Tchr. pub. schs., Calif., 1958—59; parole adviser, project dir., counselor Active Mexicanos,

Seattle, 1972—76; instr. Everett (Wash.) C.C., 1975—76; rschr., translator Wash. State Coun. Crime and Delinquency, Seattle, 1977; program asst., minority affairs Seattle Ctrl. C.C.; cons. to cmty. offenders programs, 1977—81; sr. cmty. svc. rep. Seattle Dept. Human Resources, 1981—. Cons. Chicago mental health. Author: Usted y La Ley, 1977. Translator ARC Lang. Bank, 1975—; chmn. Region 10 Chicago Task Force on Drug Abuse, 1977—79; mem. Seattle Cable Citizens Adv. Bd., 1988—90; v.p. Concilio for Spanish Speaking; state dir., mem. nat. exec. bd. League United L.Am. Citizens, 1980—82; chmn. Hispanic adv. bd. Seattle Cmty. Coll. Dist. 6, 1981—83; chmn. Seattle/Mazatlan Sister City Assn., 1981—83; v.p. Neighborhoods U.S.A., 1987—92, 1995—, bd. dirs., 1986, United Way of King County; dist. adv. com. group health Northgate Clinic; del. White House Conf. on Families, L.A., 1980; bd. dirs. N.W. Kidney Ctr. Regional Coun., 2002; bd. mem. Northgate Chamber, 2002; Dem. precinct committeeman, 1968, 1970, 1988—2002; vol. worker various local and state polit. campaigns. Named One of 100 Women Role Models for Pub. Schs., State Office Pub. Instrn., Lake City Citizen of Yr., 2000; recipient Gov.'s citation, 1974, award for committment to hither edn., Seattle C.C. Dist., 1983, One of 10 Unsung Heroes in Seattle, Radical Women, 1983, Cmty. Svc. award, Am. G.I. Forum, 1984, Golden Maple Leaf award, Maple Leaf Cmty. Coun., 1991, Commn. award, Seattle Commn. on Children and Youth, 1991, 1993, assoc. mem., Eastern Washington U. Found., Seattle Works award, Cmty. Ambassador, 2001, Seattle Works Award, 2002. Mem.: Northgate C. of C. (founding mem.), Rotary. Home: 12018 17th Ave NE Seattle WA 98125-5116 E-mail: yolanda.martinez@ci.seattle.wa.us., ymart@earthlink.net.

MARTINEZ-BANTA, MARCELLA, language educator; b. Durango, Colo., Sept. 25, 1958; d. Antonio José and Antonia Rosa (Montaño) Martinez; m. Stephen P. Banta, Sept. 24, 2001; children: Jamie, Sean. BA, So. Oreg. State Coll., Ashland, 1990. Migrant bilingual resource tchr. Klamath Falls (Oreg.) City Schs., 1990-2000, Mills Elem., Ponderosa Jr. HS, Klamath Falls, 1990-93, Fairview Elem. Sch., Klamath Falls, 1993-94, Fairview Elem., Mills Elem., Klamath Falls, 1994-95, Mills Elem. Sch., Klamath Falls, 1994-2000; vol. Klamath Basin Sr. Citizen Svcs., 2000—01. Mem. 2d Lang. Com., 1994-2000. Troop leader Girl Scouts U.S., Klamath Falls, Oreg., 1986-91; bilingual translator, 1996-99. Home: 101 S 2d St Gallup NM 87301-6219

MARTINEZ-CARBONELL, KARELIA, not-for-profit fundraiser; b. Havana, Cuba, Jan. 6, 1962; arrived in U.S., 1968, naturalized; d. Francisco and Amada Martinez; m. Marino E. Carbonell, May 29, 1983; children: Brenden Marino Carbonell. BA, Fla. Internat. U., Miami, FL, 1994, MBA, 1997; DPA, Nova Southeastern U., Fort Lauderdale, FL, 2002. Dir. of devel. Carrollton Sch. of the Sacred Heart, Coconut Grove, Fla., 1998—. Bd. mem. St. Philip's Episcopal Sch., Coral Gables, Fla., 1995—, Assn. of Fund Raising Professionals, Miami, Fla., 2000—; editl. bd. mem. Am. Soc. of Pub. Adminstrn., Fla., 2000—. Contbr. articles to profl. jours. Mem. Jr. League of Miami, Coral Gables, Fla., 1995—2002; adv. com. Blue Ribbon Ethics Commn., Miami, 2000—02. Recipient finalist, Chivas Regal Order of Distinction, 2000. Mem.: Ocean Reef Club, Rivera Country Club (arts committeee 1992—2002). Republican. Roman Catholic. Avocations: reading, traveling, researching, researching. Office: Carrollton School of the Sacred Heart 3747 Main Highway Coconut Grove FL 33133 E-mail: kcarbonell@carrollton.org.

MARTINEZ-HERNANDEZ, ANTONIO, pathology educator; b. Calahorra, Rioja, Spain, Apr. 20, 1944; came to U.S., 1968; s. Manuel Martinez and Antonia Hernandez; m. Carla Froitzheim, June 3, 1968; children: Daniel, Michelle. MD, U. Madrid, l968. Diplomate Am. Bd. Pathology. Intern Tucson Med. Edn., 1968-69; resident in pathology U. Colo., Denver, l969-73, instr., l973-74, asst. prof., 1974-77, assoc. prof., 1977-78, Hahnemann U., Phila., 1978-80, prof., 1980-86; prof. pathology Thomas Jefferson U., 1986-90; prof. U. Tenn., Memphis, 1990—. Mem. pathobiochemistry study sect. NIH, Bethesda, Md., 1978-81; cons. Med. Rsch. Coun. Can., 1987—. Mem. editorial bd. Lab. Investigation, 198l—; contbr. over l50 articles to profl. jours., chpts. to books. Recipient Louis M. Katz rsch. prize Am. Coll. Cardiology, l975; NIH grantee, l980, 82; Max-Planck Soc. fellow, Fed. Republic Germany, 1985-86. Mem. Am. Assn. Pathologists, Am. Histochem. Soc., Am. Soc. Cell Biology. Avocations: tennis, air brushing, bonsai. Office: VA Med Ctr Dept Pathology Lab Medicine 1030 Jefferson Ave Memphis TN 38104-2127

MARTINEZ-MALDONADO, MANUEL, medical service administrator, physician; b. Yauco, P.R., Aug. 25, 1937; s. Manuel and Josefa Maldonado (Josefa Maldonado) Martinez; m. Nivia Elena Rivera, Dec. 18, 1959; children: Manuel, David, Ricardo, Pablo. BS, U. P.R., 1957; MD, Temple U., 1961. Diplomate Am. Bd. Internal Medicine, Am. Bd. Nephrology. Intern St. Charles Hosp., Toledo, 1961—62; resident VA Hosp., San Juan, 1962—65, chief resident, 1964—65; instr. U. Tex. Southwestern Med. Sch., Dallas, 1967—68; from asst. prof. to prof. medicine, dir. renal sect. Baylor Coll. Medicine, Houston, 1968—73; prof. medicine U. P.R. Sch. Medicine, 1973—90, prof. physiology, 1974—90; prof. medicine U. Caribbean, Bayamon, PR, 1980—90; chief med. services VA Hosp., San Juan, 1973—90, dir. renal metabolic lab, 1973—90; prof., vice chmn. dept. medicine Emory U. Sch. Medicine, 1990—98; chief med. svcs. and clin. affairs Atlanta VA Med. Ctr., 1990—98; v.p. for rsch., prof. medicine Oreg. Health Scis. U., Portland, 1998—99, v.p. rsch., 1999—2000; pres., dean Ponce (P.R.) Sch. Medicine, 2000—. Assoc. mem. nephrology com. Am. Bd. Internal Medicine , 1982—86; nat. adv. bd. gen. medicine B study sect. Nat. Inst. Arthritis, Metabolism and Digestive Diseases NIH; bd. sci. counselors, sci. advisors com. Nat. Heart, Lung and Blood Inst., NIH. Author: La Voz Sostenida, 1984, Palm Beach Blues, 1986, Por Amor al Arte, 1989, Hotel Maria, 1989, Isla Verde, 1999; film critic: El Reportero, 1983—86, film critic: El Mundo, 1987—90; contbr. articles to profl. jours.; editor/co-editor: in field, mem. editl. bd.: U. P.R. Press; editor: Am. Jour. of Med. Scis., 1994—98, Am. Jour. Kidney Disease, 1997—2001. Com. mem. 500th Anniversary of Discovery Am., PR, 1987—92; health com. Popular Dem. Com., 1982—84. Named one of Outstanding Medicine, P.R. C. of C., 1976; recipient Lederle Internat. award, 1966—67, Faculty Scholar award, Macy Faculty, 1979—80, Grand Mobil prize medicine, Mobil Oil Corp., 1981, Disting. Alumnus award, Temple Med. Sch., 1988, Presdl. award, Nat. Kidney Found., 1988, Donald W. Seldin award, 1994, Disting. Physician award, P.R. Hosps. Assn., 1988, Orden del Cafetal award, Municipality of Yauco, 1989, Abelardo Díaz Sefaro award, Medicine & Humanites, 2002. Fellow: AAAS, ACP, Am. Heart Assn. (hypertension rsch. coun.), Coun. for High Blood Pressure Rsch.; mem.: Nat. Kidney Found. (chmn. pub. policy com. 1992—94), Consortium Southeastern Hypertension Ctrs. (bd. dirs.), Assn. Am. Physicians, Inter-Am. Soc. Hypertension Assn. (bd. govs., chmn. 8th Sci. Congress 1989, U.S. Pharmacopeial Conv. Cardio Renal Drugs com. 1990—96), L.Am. Soc. Nephrology (v.p. 1987—91, pres.-elect 1991—94, pres. 1994—96, Miatello award 1999), Am. Soc. for Clin. Investigation, So. Soc. Clin. Investigation (sec.-treas. 1983—85, pres.'. 1985—86, Founders medal 1990, Pub. Svc. medal, Donald W. Seldin award), Am. Soc. Nephrology (legis. liaison com., chmn. audit com. 1988), Inst. Medicine NAS (com. on human rights 1987—92), Alpha Omega Alpha. Achievements include research in kidney physiology and pathophysiology, treatment of clinical disturbances of blood composition, clinical use of diuretics, mechanisms of the devel. of hypertension. E-mail: mmartinez@psm.edu., martinem_pms@hotmail.com.

MARTINEZ-SAN MIGUEL, YOLANDA MARIA, literature educator, cultural critic; b. Santurce, P.R., May 10, 1966; d. Benjamin Martínez López and Carmen Yolanda San Miguel; m. Eugenio Adolfo Frias-Pardo, Aug. 7, 1988. BA, U. P.R., Rio Piedras, 1989; MA, U. Calif., Berkeley, 1991, PhD, 1996. Instr. U. Calif., Berkeley, 1994-95; asst. prof. U. P.R., Rio Piedras, 1996-97, Princeton (N.J.) U., 1997-2000, Rutgers U., New Brunswick, N.J., 2000—. Vis. prof. U. Calif., Berkeley, 1997; presenter in field. Author: Saberes Americanos: Subalternidad y Epistemología en los Escritos de Sor Juana, 1999; editl. bd.: U. Fla. Press, 2000—, editl. cons.: Revista de Ciencias Sociales, 1997—, editl. cons.: Centro Jour., 1999—; editor: Lucero Jour. of Iberian and Latin Am. Studies, 1992—93; asst. editor: , 1990—92; contbr. Chancellor's Minority fellowship U. Calif., 1992-94. Mem. MLA, Latin Am. Studies Assn., P.R. Studies Assn., Instituto Internacional Literatura Iberoamericana, Caribbean Studies Assn., Am. Assn. of Tchrs. of Spanish and Portuguese. Office: Rutgers U 105 George St New Brunswick NJ 08901 E-mail: yolamsm@rci.rutgers.edu.

MARTING, MICHAEL G. lawyer; b. Cleve., Nov. 5, 1948; BA summa cum laude, Yale U., 1971, JD, 1974. Bar: Ohio 1974. Assoc. Jones, Day, Reavis & Pogue, Cleve., 1974-83, ptnr., 1984—. Mem.: Tavern Club (treas., sec., trustee local chpt. 1985—88), Cleve. Racquet Club, Union Club. Avocations: fly fishing, bird shooting, big game hunting, squash. Office: Jones Day Reavis & Pogue N Point 901 Lakeside Ave E Cleveland OH 44114-1190

MARTIN-GALL, JENNIE MARIE, editor; b. Saint Helena, Calif., Aug. 12, 1958; d. Don L. Martin and Mickie LaDelle; m. Edgar G. Gall, Nov. 22, 1982; children: Jonathan Gall, Jennifer Gall. AA, Mendocino Coll., Ukiah, CA, 1980, AS, 1981. Cert. Medical Transcriptionist Am. Assn. Med. Transcriptionists. Asst. dir. Headstart Preschool, Ukiah, Calif., 1983—85; med. asst. Physician's Clinics, 1977—83; sr. med. transcriptionist Adventist Health Systems, 1980—96; owner, operator Redwood Empire Med. Transcription, Ukiah, 1996—2000, Transpositions, Ukiah, 1989—; editor Lit West Pub. Agy., San Francisco, 1999—. Leadership coord. Am. Assn. Med. Transcriptionists, Sacramento, 1997—99; mentor Redwood Empire Med. Transcription, Ukiah, Calif., 1997—2001, continuing edn. coord., Calif., 1997—2001; organizer local chpt. Am. Assn. Med. Transcriptionists, Ukiah, Calif., 1999—99. Author short story, editor books and articles to journals. Active Am. Cancer Soc., Ukiah, Calif., 2002—02; health educator, chef Ch. programs, health club, Willits, 1990—95. Mem.: Am. Med. Writer's Assn., Am. Assn. Med. Transcriptionists. R-Liberal. Christian. Achievements include research in Two radio segments in Napa Valley, CA, regarding allergies to foods in children and adults. Avocations: reading, vegetarian gourmet cookery, vegetarian gourmet cookery, vegetarian gourmet cookery, quilting. Home: 2151 Arroyo Road Ukiah CA 59482 Office: Transpositions 2151 Arroyo Road Ukiah CA 95482 Home Fax: 707-463-1564; Office Fax: 707-463-1564. Personal E-mail: jenmartingall@pacific.net. E-mail: jenmartingall@pacific.net.

MARTINI, RICHARD K. theatrical producer; b. Bergenfield, N.J., Mar. 11, 1952; s. John F. and June L. (Fenton) M.; m. Susan C. Weaving, Aug. 1, 1981. BA, St. Francis Coll., Loretto, Pa., 1974; MEd, U. S.C., 1975. V.p. Am. Theatre Prodns., N.Y.C., 1975-81; pres. Edgewood Orgn., 1981-86; pres., owner KL Mgmt., 1986—; owner, operator Martini Entertainment, Inc., 1991—. Home: 201 E 37th St New York NY 10016-3159 Office: Martini Entertainment Co 1501 Broadway Ste 1401 New York NY 10036-5601

MARTINI, ROBERT EDWARD, wholesale pharmaceutical and medical supplies company executive; b. Hackensack, N.J., 1932; BS, Ohio State U., 1954. With Bergen Brunswig Corp., Orange, Calif., 1956-92, v.p., 1962-69, exec. v.p., 1969-81, pres., 1981-92, CEO, 1990-97, chmn., 1992—. Chmn. exec. com. Bergen Brunswig Corp. Capt. USAF, 1954.*

MARTINI, WILLIAM J. former congressman, state commissioner; b. Passaic, N.J. m. Gloria Martini; children: William Jr., Marissa. Degree, Villanova U., 1968; JD, Rutgers U., 1972. Elected mem. City Coun. of Clifton, N.J., Passaic County Bd. Chosen Freeholders, U.S. House of Reps., 1994-96; ptnr. Sills Cummis Radin Tischman Epstein & Gross PA, Newark; commr. Port Authority of N.Y. and N.J. Pres. Nicholas Martini Found.; trustee United Way of Passaic County, Ctr. Italian Am. Culture, Passaic Valley Coun. Boys Scouts of Am., Hackensack U. Med. Ctr., Freedom House. Office: Sills Cummis et al One Riverfront Plz Newark NJ 07102

MARTINO, CHERYL DERBY, insurance company secretary; b. Paterson, N.J., Jan. 19, 1946; d. Elles Mayo and Sarah Emma (Steele) D.; m. Leonard D. Martino, Nov. 4, 1995. BA, Elmira Coll., 1967; MBA, NYU, 1982. Tchr. Ramsey (N.J.) High Sch., 1967-70; contbns. analyst Met. Life Ins. Co., N.Y.C., 1970-83, fin. writer investments dept., 1983-93, asst. sec., 1994—. Bd. trustees United Meth. Ch. of Waldwick, N.J., v.p., 1989-91, pres., 1992-93, fin. sec., 2000—. Fellow Life Mgmt. Inst. (bd. dirs. Greater N.Y. chpt. 1984-91, pres. 1986, edn. coun. 1990-93), Life Mgmt. Inst. Edn. Coun. (nat. adminstrv. com. chmn. 1990-92, mktg. subcom. 1985-93), Nat. Orchestral Assn. (bd. dirs. 1990-92); mem. Elmira Coll. Alumni Club N.J. (exec. bd. 1982-87); mem. alumni bd. dirs. Elmira Coll.,1992—. Methodist. Office: Met Life 1 Madison Ave New York NY 10010-3603

MARTINO, DONALD JAMES, composer, musician, educator; b. Plainfield, N.J., May 16, 1931; s. James Edward and Alma Ida (Renz) M.; m. Mari Rice, Sept. 5, 1953 (div. June 1968); 1 child, Anna Maria; m. Lora Harvey, June 5, 1969; 1 child, Christopher James. BMus, Syracuse U., 1952; MFA, Princeton U., 1954; MA (hon.), Harvard U., 1983. Instr. music Princeton U., 1957-59; asst. prof. theory music Yale U., 1959-66, assoc. prof., 1966-69; chmn. dept. composition New Eng. Conservatory Music, Boston, 1969-80; Irving Fine prof. music Brandeis U., 1980-82; prof. music Harvard U., 1983—, Walter Bigelow Rosen prof. music, 1989-93; Walter Bigelow Rosen prof. emeritus, 1993—. Tchr. composition and theory Yale Summer Sch. of Music and Art, 1960-63; tchr. composition Berkshire Music Ctr., summers, 1965-67, 69; composer in residence Berkshire Music Ctr., 1973, Composers' Conf., Johnson, Vt., summer 1979, May in Miami, 1994, Festival Internat. Musica de Morelia, Mex., 1996, Composers' Conf., Wellesley, Mass., 1997, Ernest Block Music Festival Composers Conf., Newport, Oreg., summer 1998; vis. lectr. Harvard U., 1971; Maurice Abravanel vis. disting. composer U. Utah, 1994, Mary Duke Biddle disting. composer Duke U., 1995; master artist-in-residence Atlantic Ctr. for the Arts, 1997; BMI composer in residence Vanderbilt U., 1998. Composer: Separate Songs, 1951; for high voice and piano, Sonata for Clarinet and Piano, 1951, Piano Quartet, 1951, With Little Children In Mind, 1951, String Quartet No. 2, 1951, The Bad Child's Book of Beasts, 1952, Suite of Variations on Medieval Melodies cello sonata, 1952; String Quartet No. 3, 1953, sonata for Violin and Piano, A Set for Clarinet, 1954, Quodlibets for Flute, 1954, Three Dances for Viola and Piano, 1954, String Trio, 1954, Three Songs, 1955, Portraits; a secular cantata for chorus, soloists and orch., 1955, Sette Canoni Enigmatici, 1956, Contemplations for Orch. (commd. by Paderewski Fund), 1956, 24 Tin Pan Alley Tunes, 1956, Quartet for Clarinet and Strings, 1957, After Lennie, Canon Ball, Cathy, Three Way, Late In The Day, Mac Fugal, Lover Come Bach, 1957, Piano Fantasy, 1958, Trio for violin, clarinet and piano, 1959, Cinque Frammenti, 1961, Two Rilke Songs, 1961, Fantasy-Variations for violin, 1962, Concerto for Wind Quintet (commd. by Fromm Found. and Berkshire Music Center), 1964, Parisonatina Al'Dodecafonia; for cello solo, 1964, Concerto for Piano and Orch. (commd. by New Haven Symphony), 1965, B, a, b, b, it, t; for clarinet, 1966, Strata; for bass clarinet, 1966, Mosaic for grand orch. (commd. for Chgo. Symphony by U. Chgo.), 1967, Pianississimo; sonata for piano, 1970, Seven Pious Pieces, 1971, Concerto for Violoncello and Orch., 1972, Augenmusik, 1972, Notturno, 1973 (Naumburg Chamber Music award commn., Pulitzer prize in music 1974), Paradiso Choruses for Chorus, Soloists, Orch. and Tape, 1974 (Paderewski Fund commn., Classical Critics citation Record World mag. 1976), Ritorno for Orch. (Plainfield Symphony Bicentennial commn.), 1975, Triple Concerto for Clarinet, Bass Clarinet and Contrabass Clarinet with Chamber Ensemble (N.Y. State Council on Arts and Andrew W. Mellon Found. commn.), 1977, Impromptu for Roger; piano solo, 1977, Quodlibets II (Am. Music Ctr. commn.); flute solo, 1980, Fantasies and Impromptus, piano solo (Koussevitzky Found. commn.), 1981, Divertissements for Youth Orch. (Groton, Mass. Arts Ctr. Commn.), 1981, Suite in Old Form, piano solo, 1982, String Quartet (Elizabeth Sprague Coolidge Commn., winner 1st prize Kennedy Ctr. Friedheim Awards 1985), 1983, Canzone e Tarantella, clarinet and cello, 1984, The White Island, for chorus and chamber orchestra (Boston Symphony Centennial Commn.), 1985, Concerto for Alto Saxophone and Chamber Orch. (Nat. Endowment Consortium commn.), 1987, From the Other Side, Divertimento for Flute, Cello, Percussion and Piano (commd. by Flederman New Music Ensemble for the Australian Bicentennial, 1988), 12 Preludes (commd. Meet the Composer-Readers Digest), 1990, 15, 5, '92 AB for Carinet solo, 1992, Three Sad Songs, 1993, Viola and Piano (Elizabeth Sprague Coolidge commn.), Concerto for Violin and Orchestra (Nat. Endowment Commn.), 1997, Variazioni sopra un soggetto cavato, cl. solo, 1998, Serenata Concertante (Koussevitzky Found. Com.), 1999, Piccolo Studio, Alto Saxaphone solo, 1999, Romanza, Violin solo, 1999; numerous others; contbr. articles to prof. jours. Recipient BMI Student Composer awards, 1952-53; Bonsall fellow, 1953-54; Kosciuszko scholar, 1953-54; Nat. Fedn. Music Clubs award, 1953; Kate Neal Kinley fellow U. Ill., 1954-55; Fulbright grantee Florence, Italy, 1954-56; Pacifica Found. award, 1961; Creative Arts citation Brandeis U., 1963; Morse Acad. fellow, 1965; Nat. Inst. Arts and Letters grantee, 1967; Guggenheim fellow, 1967-68, 73-74, 82-83; Nat. Endowment on Arts grantee, 1973, 76, 79, 89, Mass. Council on Arts grantee, 1973, 79, 89; recipient Pulitzer prize in music, 1974, Kennedy Ctr. Friedheim Awards 1st prize, 1985, Mark M. Horblit award Boston Symphony Orch., 1987, Paul Revere award for mus. autography Music Publ. Assn., 1990-92. Mem. AAAS, AAAL, Coll. Music Soc., Am. Composers Alliance, Broadcast Music Inc., Am. Music Ctr., Internat. Soc. Contemporary Music (a founder New Haven chpt. 1964, dir. U.S. sect. 1961-64), Am. Soc. U. Composers (founding mem., exec. com. 1965-66, trustee 1965—), Internat. Clarinet Soc. Office: Harvard U Dept Music Cambridge MA 02138 E-mail: dantinfo@dantalian.com.

MARTINO, DONNA FRANCES, newspaper sales administrator; b. N.Y.C., May 8, 1947; d. Samuel Edward and Angelina (Scudieri) M. BA, Coll. Mt. St. Vincent, 1969; MA, Columbia U., 1972. Cert. early childhood tchr., N.Y., N.J. Acct. mgr. Contra Costa Times, Walnut Creek, Calif., 1980-83; nat. acct. mgr. San Francisco Chronicle/Examiner, 1983-85; retail acct. exec. The N.Y. Times, N.Y.C., 1986-94, nat. acct. mgr. pharm. advt., 1994-96; nat. sales mgr. pharms. Newspaper Nat. Network, 1997—. Project leader spl. advertorials to The N.Y. Times, 1994—. Mem. Columbia U. Alumni Club Bergen/Passaic Counties (pres. 1998—), Healthcare Mktg. and Comm. Coun. Avocations: sailing, rock climbing, antiques, art. Office: Newspaper Nat Network 711 3rd Ave New York NY 10017-4014

MARTINO, JOSEPH PAUL, research scientist, researcher; b. Warren, Ohio, July 16, 1931; s. Joseph and Anna Elizabeth (Kubina) M.; m. Mary Lou Bouquot, May 18, 1957 (dec. Jan. 1988); children: Theresa, Anthony, Michael; m. Nancy McCoy, Dec. 28, 2000. AB, Miami U., Ohio, 1953; MS, Purdue U., 1955; PhD, Ohio State U., 1961. Commd. 2d lt. USAF, 1953, advanced through grades to col., 1973, project engr. armament lab. Ohio, 1955-58, mathematician Office Sci. Rsch. Washington, 1961-62, staff scientist Avionics Lab. Wright-Patterson AFB, 1972-73, dir. engring. standardization Def. Electronics Supply Ctr. Dayton, Ohio, 1973-75, ret., 1975; sr. scientist, rsch. inst. U. Dayton, 1975-93. Author: Technological Forecasting for Decision-making, 1972, rev. edit., 1983, 3d edit., 1992, A Fighting Chance-The Moral Use of Nuclear Weapons, 1988, Science Funding: Politics and Porkbarrel, 1992, Research and Development Project Selection, 1995; assoc. editor: Tech. Forecasting and Social Change Jour., 1968—. Fellow IEEE, AAAS, AIAA (assoc.); mem. Inst. for Ops. Rsch. and Mgmt. Sci., Am. Soc. Engring. Mgmt., Engrs. Club of Dayton. Roman Catholic. E-mail: jpmart@bright.net.

MARTINO, MICHAEL CHARLES, entertainer, musician, actor; b. Philadelphia, Pa., Sept. 10, 1950; s. Salvatore Joseph and Marie Angela (Langone) M. Grad. high sch., Upper Darby, Pa. Spokesperson/rep. Petosa Accordion Co., Seattle, 1979—; featured TV entertainer Mike Martino Show, Delaware County, Pa., 1987-89; accordion tchr. Drexel Hill, 1989—. Entertainer/host/producer St. Jude's Children's Hosp. Marathon, King of Prussia, Pa., 1973; opening act comedian Morty Gunty Downingtown, Pa., 1973, opening act comedian Morty Gunty, 1973, Pat Cooper, Phila., 1981; guest artist/entertainer Internat. Platform Assn. Conv., Washington, 1979; nite club performer Glen Mills, Pa., 1989; actor TV commls., Elkton, Md., 1979, Halloween Spl. KYW-TV, Phila., 1986; performed radio contest jingle Sta. KISS 100 radio, Media, Pa., 1992. Author: (movie script) Forever Fiftys, 1990; composer popular songs; directed, produced, starred video Forever Fiftys; composed theme song Forever Fiftys, (movie theme) That First September; creator, performer Suspended Triple Bellows Shake Technique for the Accordion, 1994; composer (ballad) Through the Music, Through the Words I Sing, 1995, Through the Music Through the Words I sing, (sung by Donna Theodore) 1998; actor: (movie) Jesus' Son, 1999. Recipient citation U.S. Ho. Reps., 1989, Proclamation Mike Martino Day Mayor Ward, Del. County, 1988, Danny Thomas Hon. award St. Jude's Hosp., Del. County, 1973, Mayor's Svc. award Upper Darby, Pa., 1994. Roman Catholic. Avocations: antique cars, dogs. Home: 2530 Stoneybrook Ln Drexel Hill PA 19026-1610

MARTINO, PETER DOMINIC, financial software company executive, real estate developer; b. N.Y.C., Sept. 21, 1963; s. Rocco Leonard and Barbara Italia (D'Iorio); 1 child, Elizabeth Marie. BS, U.S. Naval Acad., 1985. Cert. cash mgr., 1992. Commd. ensign USN, 1985, advanced through grades to lt., 1989, resigned, 1990; with USNR, 1990-99; from v.p. mktg. to exec. v.p., COO XRT, Inc., Wayne, Pa., 1990-93, pres., 1993-98, CEO, 1996-98; pres., CEO XRT-CERG Am., Inc., 1998-2000; exec. v.p. XRT-CERG S.A., Paris, 1998-2000; pres., CEO, chmn., founder CharitEx, Inc., N.Y.C., 2000—01; real estate broker Corcoran Group, 2001—; real estate developer, 2002—. Founder, dir. XRT Europe, Ltd., 1994-98; founder, dir., pres Four Star Software, Inc., Wayne, 1994-98; bd. dirs. Nat. Kidney Found. Delaware Valley; founder internet e-commerce bus. for charitable giving. Mem. coun. Phoenixville Borough Coun., 1993, Rep. committeeman, 1994-96; bd. dirs. Nat. Kidney Found. Delaware Valley, 1997-2001; bd. dirs. Martino Found., 1998—, World Affairs Coun. Phila., 1999-2001; adv. bd. Pres.'s Cir., Naval Acad. Found. Mem. Treasury Mgmt. Assn., Naval Acad. Alumni Assn., Naval Acad. Athletic Assn., Naval Submarine League, N.Y. Athletic Club, Pyramid Club (Phila.), Avalon Yacht Club, Met. Rep. Club, N.Y. Young Rep. Club, The Wine Soc. (U.K.). Roman Catholic. Avocations: sailing, boating, real estate, fine wine, art collecting. Office: 660 Madison Ave Fl 11 New York NY 10021-8405 : 168 W Lake Dr Annapolis MD 21403 Fax: 212-230-7242. E-mail: pdm@corcoran.com.

MARTINO, ROBERT SALVATORE, orthopedic surgeon; b. Clarksburg, W.Va., May 31, 1931; s. Leonard L. and Sarafina (Foglia) M.; m. Lenora Cappellanti, May 22, 1954; children: Robert S. Jr., Leslie F. Reckziegal. AB, W.Va. U., 1953, postgrad., 1955-56, BS in Medicine, 1958; MD, Northwestern U., 1960. Diplomate Am. Bd. Orthopaedic Surgery; lic. Ill., Calif., Ind. Intern Chgo. Wesley, 1960-61; resident dept. orthopaedic surgery Northwestern U., 1961-65, Chgo. Wesley Meml., 1961-62, Am. Legion Hosp. for Crippled Children, 1962-63, Cook County Hosp., Chgo., 1964, 64-65; orthopaedic surgeon Gary, Ind., 1965-67; orthopaedic surgeon Merrillville, 1967—. Fellow Nat. Found. Infantile Paralysis, 1956, Office of Vocat. Rehab., Hand Surgery, 1965; chief of staff St. Mary Med. Ctr., 1976, chief of surgery, 1974-85; chief of staff Gary Treatment Ctr./Ind. Crippled Children's Svcs., 1974-84; adj. asst. prof. anatomy Ind. U., 1978, clin. asst. prof. orthopaedic surgery, 1980, others; mem. Zoning Bd., 1989-90. Chmn. Planning Bd. Town of Dune Acres, 1992-96; bd. dirs. United Steel Workers Union Health Plan, 1994—. St. Mary's Med. Ctr., Hobart, Ind.; com. on Health Care Reform. Capt. U.S. Army, 1953-56. Fellow ACS (emeritus)mem. AMA, Ind. Med. Soc., Ill. Med. Soc., Chgo. Med. Soc., Ill. Orthopaedic Soc., Ind. Orthopaedic Soc., Mid-Am. Orthopaedic Assn., Tri-State Orthopedic Soc., Clin. Orthopaedic Soc. Home: Dune Acres 22 Oak Dr Chesterton IN 46304-1016

MARTINO, SILVANA, osteopath, medical oncologist; b. Guardia Piemontese, Italy, Sept. 7, 1948; came to U.S., 1958; d. Antonio and Elena (Iannuzzi) M. BS in Psychology, Wayne State U., 1970; DO, Mich. State U., 1973. Bd. cert. internal medicine and med. oncology, 1984. Intern Detroit Osteo. Hosp., 1973-74; resident in internal medicine Botsford Hosp., Farmington, Mich., 1974-77; fellow in oncology Wayne State U. Sch. Medicine, Detroit, 1977-79, asst. prof. med., 1979-88, assoc. prof., 1988-93; med. dir. Westlake Comprehensive Breast Ctr., Westlake Village, Calif., 1993-97, Breast Ctr., Van Nuys, 1997-99; med. oncologist John Wayne Cancer Inst., Santa Monica, 1999—. Full-time staff Harper-Grace Hosps., Detroit, 1979-93, coord. oncology housestaff 1979-83; univ. affiliate, sect. of oncology, dept. medicine, Hutzel Hosp., Detroit, 1979-93; clin. advisor breast cancer prognostic study Mich. Cancer Found., Detroit, 1981-86; univ. affiliate dept. medicine Detroit Receiving Hosp., 1983-93; adj. faculty dept. medicine Wayne State U. 1989-92. Co-author: Diet & Cancer: Markers, Prevention and Treatment, 1994; contbr. articles to profl. jours., chpt. to book; spkr. in field. Bd. dirs. Wellness Cmty., Conjeo Valley/Ventura, Calif., 1995-99; bd. dirs. ACS Greater Conjeo Valley Unit, Thousand Oaks, Calif., 1994-99. Fellow Am. Coll. Osteo. Internists; mem. AAAS, Am. Osteo. Assn., Am. Soc. Clin. Oncology, Internat. Assn. Breast Cancer Rsch., Am. Soc. of Preventive Oncology, Am. Assn. for Cancer Rsch., Inc., Southwest Oncology Group (chair breast com. 1992-2000, co-chair cancer control rsch. com. 87-92). E-mail: martinos@jwci.org.

MARTIN-O'NEILL, MARY EVELYN, advertising, marketing, business writing, sales training consultant; b. Lexington, Ky. d. George Clarke and Georgann Elizabeth (Bovis) M.; m. John Michael O'Neill, May 24, 1998. BA magna cum laude, Lindenwood Coll.; MA with honors, U. Ky. Asst. to pres. The Hamlets, Ltd/Park Place Country Homes, Louisville, 1984-85; advt. designer, copywriter Park Place Country Homes, Anchorage, 1985-86; creative dir. of advt., mktg., v.p., treas. Park Place Country Homes/Park Place Properties, 1986—; mktg. comm. specialist Mayfield Publ., Mountain View, Calif., 1998; curriculum developer Oracle Corp., Redwood Shores, 1998-2000; sr. info. designer/tech. writer BenefitPoint, Inc., San Francisco, 2000—. Founder, pres. Good Help Cons. Svcs., Louisville and Lexington, Maison Marche Advt. & Promotions, Louisville, 1989; instr. dept. English U. Ky., 1989—91; adj. prof. composition U. Louisville, 1991—97; vis. lectr. lit. Bellarmine Coll., Louisville, 1992; adj. prof. humanities Ind. U. S.E., 1991—95, DeVry U., 2002—; prof. arts and humanities McKendree Coll., Louisville, 1993—97; lectr. Coll. Bus. San Francisco State U., 2000—; writer, historian Home Builders Assn. Louisville, 1996. Editor: (poetry mag.) The Griffin, 1979-80, Bus. Wire, 1997; contbr. series to mag., 1996. Mem. People for the Am. Way, Greenpeace. Recipient Spahmer creative writing award, 1979; Haggin fellow U. Ky., 1987; grantee U. Louisville, 1992-95. Mem. Am. Film Inst., Nat. Assn. Home Builders (affiliate), Ky. Film Artists Coalition, Women in Tech. Internat. Democrat. Avocations: weaving, screenwriting. Office: 915 Cole St # 300 San Francisco CA 94117

MARTINS, HEITOR MIRANDA, foreign language educator; b. Belo Horizonte, Brazil, July 22, 1933; came to U.S., 1960; s. Joaquim Pedro and Emilia (Miranda) M.; m. Teresomja Alves Pereira, Nov. 1, 1958 (div. 1977); children— Luzia Pereira, Emilia Pereira; m. Marlene Andrade, Jan. 11, 1984 AB, U. Federal de Minas Gerais, 1959; PhD, U. Federal de Minas Gerais, 1962. Instr. U. N.M., Albuquerque, 1960-62; asst. prof. Tulane U., New Orleans, 1962-66, assoc. prof., 1966-68; prof. dept. Spanish and Portuguese Ind. U., Bloomington, 1968—, chmn. dept., 1972-76. Vis. prof. U. Tex., Austin, 1963, Stanford U. 1968 Author: poetry Sirgo nos Cabelos, 1961; essay Manuel de Galhegos, 1964; essays Oswald de Andrade e Outros, 1973; critical anthology Neoclassicismo, 1982; Essays Do Barroco a Guimarães Rosa, 1983; editor: essays Luso-Brazilian Literary Studies. Social Sci. Research Council grantee, 1965; Fulbright-Hays Commn. grantee, 1966; Ford Found. grantee, 1970, 71 Mem. MLA, Renaissance Soc. Am., Am. Comparative Lit. Assn., Am. Assn. for 18th Century Studies. Home: 1316 S Nancy St Bloomington IN 47401-6050 Office: Indiana U Dept Spanish and Portuguese Bloomington IN 47405 E-mail: martins@indiana.edu.

MARTINS, NELSON, physics educator; b. Santos, Brazil, Oct. 18, 1930; s. Aniceto and Angelica Martins; m. Maria Lucia, Jan. 8, 1959 (div. Sept. 1983); children: Flavia, Paulo. BS in Physics, Mackenzie U., São Paulo, Brazil, 1958; D in Physics, Pontifica U., Campinas, Brazil, 1977. Cert. physicist. Dir. engring. Mackenzie U., 1971-73, dir. Exact Sci., 1983-90; gen. dir. Ednl. Found., Barretos, Brazil, 1973-76; chief physics dep. Engring. Sch., Araraquara, Brazil, 1991; chief physics dept. U. Santo Amaro, São Paulo, 1990-92; dir. CCET Ctr. Exact Scis. and Tech., 1992-95. Author: (with others) Electriciy and Magnetism, 1973, Dimensional Analysis, 1980, Dynamics, 1982. Mem. Am. Assn. Physics Tcrhs., Brazil Soc. Physics. Office: Sorocaba Engring Sch Rod Sen Jose Ermirio Moraes Sorocaba 18001970 Brazil

MARTINS-GREEN, MANUELA, cell biologist; b. Luso, Moxico, Angola, Dec. 30, 1947; came to U.S., 1973; d. Joaquim P. and Maria Alice (Marques) Martins; m. Harry W. Green, II, May 15, 1975; children: Alice, Harry, Maria Green. BS, U. Lisbon, 1970; MS, U. Calif., Riverside, 1975; PhD, U. Calif., Davis, 1987. Chief scientist EM lab Agronomical Sta., Oeiras, Portugal, 1970-73; electron microscopist, dept. ophthalmology U. Calif., Davis, 1975-82; postdoctoral researcher Lawrence Berkeley Lab., U. Calif., 1987-88, rsch. scientist, 1992-93; adj. asst. prof. Rockefeller U., 1991-92; asst. prof. cell biology U. Calif., Riverside, 1993-2000, assoc. prof. cell biology, 2000—. Vis. lectr. U. Wuhan, China, 1988; vis. scientist Lab. Molecular Immunoreg. Nat. Cancer Inst., Frederick, 2000. Contbr. articles to profl. jours., books. Recipient Nat. Rsch. Svc. award, 1988-91, NIH traineeship, 1986-87; Fulbright Travel grantee Internat. Exch. Scholars, Riverside, 1973, NIH grantee, 1992-98, Am. Heart Assn. grantee, 2000—, Tobacco Related Disease Rsch. Program grantee, 2001—. Mem. Wound Healing Soc., Am. Soc. for Cell Biology, Am. Soc. Devel. Biology, Cytokine Soc., Women for Cell Biology, Wound Healing Soc., Phi Kappa Phi. Avocations: travel, hiking. Office: U Calif Dept Cell Biology Neuros Riverside CA 92521-0001 E-mail: mmgreen@ucrac1.ucr.edu.

MARTINSON, BRADLEY JAMES, lawyer; b. Ortonville, Minn., Oct. 16, 1945; s. Edwin James and Helen Eleanor (Christenson) M.; m. Beth Louise Nelson, June 24, 1967; children: Sara, Timothy. BA, Concordia Coll., Moorhead, Minn., 1967; JD, U. Minn., 1973. Assoc. Robert Hillstrom & Assocs., Mpls., 1973-80; shareholder Hillstrom, Bale & Martinson, 1980-85, Martinson, Schwartz & Corey, Mpls., 1985-87, Salmen, Brinkman & Martinson, St. Paul, 1987-90; shareholder, mng. ptnr. Tews, Squires, Martin & Martinson, Mpls., 1990-97; shareholder Law Offices of Bradley J. Martinson, 1998—. 1st lt. U.S. Army, 1968-71. Mem. Midland Hills Country Club (pres. 1997-98). Home: 1928 29th Ave NW New Brighton MN 55112-1737 Office: 333 S 7th St S5e 1170 Minneapolis MN 55402 E-mail: bmartlaw@aol.com.

MARTINSON, CONSTANCE FRYE, television program hostess, producer; b. Boston, Apr. 11, 1932; d. Edward and Rosalind Helen (Sperber) Frye; m. Leslie Herbert Martinson, Sept. 24, 1955; 1 child, Julianna Martinson Carner. BA in English Lit., Wellesley Coll., 1953. Dir. pub. relations Coro Found., Los Angeles, 1974-79; producer/host KHJ Dimensions, 1979-81, Connie Martinson Talks Books, Los Angeles, 1981—. Instr. dept. humanities UCLA, 1981—; moderator, instr. Univ. Judaism; celebrity advisor Book Fair-Music Ctr., L.A., 1986; advisor, moderator L.A. Times Festival of Books, 1996; bd. dirs. Friends of English UCLA; TV rep. L.A. Pub. Libr. L.A. Cityview, Sta. WNYE, Channel Am. Author Dramatization of Wellesley After Images, 1974; book editor, columnist Calif. Press Bur. Syndicate, 1986—; columnist Beverly Hills Courier, 1997—. Pres. Mayor's adv. council on volunteerism, Los Angeles, 1981-82; chmn. community affairs dept. Town Hall of Calif., Los Angeles, 1981-85; bd. dirs. legal def. fund NAACP, Los Angeles, 1981-84. Mem. Women in Cable, Am. Film Inst., Jewish TV Network (bd. dirs. 1985-87), PEN, Nat. Book Critics Assn., Wellesley Coll. Club (pres. 1979-81), Mulholland Tennis Club. Democrat. Jewish. Avocations: tennis, theater, reading. Home and Office: 2288 Coldwater Canyon Dr Beverly Hills CA 90210-1756 E-mail: talksbooks@lycos.com.

MARTINSON, ELIZABETH ANN, archaeologist; b. Chelan, Wash., Mar. 25, 1970; d. Anthony Ogden and Linda Wall M. BA, U. Wash., 1993; MA, U. N.Mex., 1997; PhD, 2001—. Vol. Initiative 120, Wash., 1990-91. Anthropology fellow U. N.Mex., 1995-98, Lat. Am. and Iberia Inst. fellow, 1999-2001. Mem. Soc. Am. Archaeology, Lake Chelan Hist. Soc. E-mail: eamail@alaska.com.

MARTINSON, IDA MARIE, nursing educator, nurse, physiologist; b. Mentor, Minn., Nov. 8, 1936; d. Oscar and Marvel (Nelson) Sather; m. Paul Varo Martinson, Mar. 31, 1962; children: Anna Marie, Peter. Diploma, St. Luke's Hosp. Sch. Nursing, 1957; BS, U. Minn., 1960, M.N.A., 1962; PhD, U. Ill., Chgo., 1972. Instr. Coll. St. Scholastica and St. Luke's Sch. Nursing, 1957—58, Thornton Jr. Coll., 1967—69; lab. asst. U. Ill. at Med. Ctr., 1970—72; lectr. dept. physiology U. Minn., St. Paul, 1972—82, asst. prof. Sch. Nursing, 1972—74, assoc. prof. rsch., 1974—77, prof., dir. rsch., 1977—82; prof. dept. family health care U. Calif., San Francisco, 1982—, chmn. dept., 1982—90. Vis. rsch. prof. Nat. Taiwan U., Def. Med. Ctr., 1981; vis. prof. nursing Sun Yat-Sen U. Med. Scis., Guang Zhou, China, Ewha Women's U., Seoul, Republic of Korea, Frances Payne Bolton Sch. Nursing, Case Western Res. U., Cleve., 1994—96; chair, prof. dept. health scis. Hong Kong Poly. U., 1996—2000. Author: Mathematics for the Health Science Student, 1977; editor: Home Care for the Dying Child, 1976, Women in Stress, 1979, Women in Health and Illness, 1986, The Child and Family Facing Life Threatening Illness, 1987, Family Nursing, 1989, Home Health Care Nursing, 1989, Home Health Care Nursing, 2d edit., 2002; contbr. chapters to books, articles. Active Am. Cancer Soc. Recipient Book of Yr. award, Am. Jour. Nursing, 1977, 1980, 1987, 1990, Humanitarian award for pediat. nursing, 1993; fellow, Fulbright Found., 1991. Mem.: ANA, Inst. Medicine, Am. Acad. Nursing, Coun. Nurse Rschrs., Sigma Theta Tau, Sigma Xi. Lutheran. Office: U Calif Family Health Care Nursing PO Box 606 San Francisco CA 94143-0606 *The challenge of quality health care to all of society and the critical role nursing has to play in order to achieve this goal has motivated me throughout my professional life. The richness of talent in this country spurs me on.*

MARTINSON, JACOB CHRISTIAN, JR. academic administrator; b. Menomonie, Wis., Apr. 15, 1933; s. Jacob Christian and Matilda Kate (Wisner) M.; m. Elizabeth Smathers, Apr. 29, 1962; children— Elizabeth Anne, Kirsten Kate. BA, Huntingdon Coll., Ala., 1954, LLD (hon.), 1993; MDiv, Duke U., 1957; DDiv, Vanderbilt U., 1972; grad., Inst. Ednl. Mgmt., Harvard U., 1981. Ordained elder United Methodist Ch. Minister Trinity United Meth. Ch., Lighthouse Point, Fla., 1960-67; sr. minister First United Meth. Ch., Winter Park, 1967-71; supervising instr. Vanderbilt U. Div. Sch., Nashville, 1971-72; pres. Andrew Coll., Cuthbert, Ga., 1972-76, Brevard Coll., N.C., 1976-85, High Point (N.C.) U., 1985—. Bd. dirs. First Union Nat. Bank, High Point, chmn. 1989; lectr. St. Mary's Theol. Soc., U. St. Andrews, Scotland; mem. exec. com. N.C. Ind. Colls. and Univs. Bd. advisors Uwharrie coun. Boy Scouts Am.; chmn. N.C. Friends of HIgher Edn., 1986. Recipient Hickman Preaching award Duke U. Div. Sch.; Glen Slough scholar Vanderbilt U., 1971; hon. fellow Westminster Coll., Oxford, Eng., 1994; Rotary Paul Harris fellow. Mem. Nat. Assn. Schs. and Colls. United Meth. Ch. (bd. dirs. 1982-85, 87-90, chmn. fin. com.), So. Assn. Colls. and Schs. (commn. on colls.), Ind. Coll. Fund. N.C. (trustee, exec. com.), Brevard C. of C. (pres. 1979), High Point C. of C. (chmn. 1992), Piedmont Ind. Coll. Assn. (chmn. 1991-93), Carolinas Intercollegiate Athletic Conf. (pres. 1991-93), Phi Theta Kappa. Methodist. Avocation: mountain hiking. Home: 1109 Rockford Rd High Point NC 27262-3607 Office: High Point U Office of Pres High Point NC 27262-3598 E-mail: jmartinson@highpoint.edu.

MARTINUZZI, LEO SERGIO, JR. banker; b. Newton, Mass., Aug. 1, 1928; s. Leo Sergio and Jessica (Stewart) M.; m. Helen Renfrew Gibson, Oct. 26, 1957; children: John James, Georgiana Gibson, Samuel Stewart. BA, Harvard U., 1950; B.Litt., Oxford U., 1952. With Chase Manhattan Bank, N.Y.C., 1956-81, asst. treas., 1960, asst. v.p. Japanese brs., 1961-64, v.p. Japanese brs., 1964-68, marketing exec. internat. staff, 1968-72, sr. v.p., 1971-81; corporate devel. officer Chase Manhattan Corp., 1972-75, group exec. info. services, 1975-81; chmn. Chase Econometric Assocs. Inc., 1975-80; sr. v.p. strategic planning Squibb Corp., 1981-87, cons., 1988-91. Chmn. Strategic Dimensions, Inc., 1990—; adj. prof. econs. Edison C.C., 1993-97. Lt. (j.g.) USNR, 1952-56. Home: 336 Galleon Dr Naples FL 34102-7638

MARTIS, LEO, healthcare researcher; b. Pangala, Karnatka, India, June 3, 1945; s. Gregory and Apolina Martis; m. Jacintha B. Castelino, June 10, 1975; children: Sameeth, Nikhil. MS, U. Wash., 1970, PhD, 1973; MBA, Northwestern U., 1980. Diplomate Am. Bd. Toxicology. Postdoctoral fellow dept. neurosci. U. Wash., Seattle, 1973-74; mgr., dir., v.p. Baxter Healthcare, Deerfield, Ill., 1974—. Guest lectr. U. Ill., Chgo., 1985—. Contbr. over 200 articles and abstracts to sci. jours.; inventor in field. Pres. India Cath. Assn. Am., Chgo., 1992-93. Mem. Am. Soc. Nephrology, Fedn. Am. Socs. Exptl. Biology, Am. Soc. Pharmacology and Exptl. Therapeutics, Am. Soc. Toxicology, Am. Chem. Soc. Avocations: tennis, golf, running. Home: 5524 Old Wood Ln Long Grove IL 60047-8215 Office: Baxter Healthcare 1620 Waukegan Rd Waukegan IL 60085-6730 E-mail: martisl@baxter.com.

MARTLAND, T(HOMAS) R(ODOLPHE), philosophy educator; b. Port Chester, N.Y., May 29, 1926; s. Thomas Rodolphe and Anne Elizabeth (Newbury) M.; m. Agatha Murphy, Apr. 3, 1952; children: David Allen, Luke Thomas. BS magna cum laude, Fordham U., 1951; MA, Columbia U., 1955, PhD, 1959. Asst. prof. Lafayette Coll., Easton, Pa., 1959-65; assoc. prof. So. Ill. U., Carbondale, 1965-66; assoc. prof. philosophy U. Albany, N.Y., 1966-84, prof., 1984-97, rsch. prof., 1997—, dir. religious studies program, 1980-87, dir. philosophy grad studies program, 1988-91. Disting. Jeannette K. Watson vis. prof. of religion, Syracuse U., 1987; dir. Master of Arts in Liberal Studies Program, 1995-97. Author: Religion as Art: An Interpretation, 1982; The Metaphysics of William James and John Dewey, 1969; mem. editl. bd. Jour. Comparative Lit. and Aesthetics, 1982-91; guest editor Annals of Scholarship, 1982. Served to lt. (s.g.) USN, 1944-47, 51-53. Faculty Exch. Guest scholar, 1976-77, rsch. fellow, 1967, 68, 71, 87; Jones Fund award Lafayette Coll., 1962-63, Signum Laudis award for excellence in tchg. and rsch., 1986. Mem. Am. Philos. Assn., Am. Soc. Aesthetics (steering com. 1985-88), Internat. Assn. Philosophy and Lit. (exec. com. 1976-81). Home: 762 McLaren Hill Rd East Ryegate VT 05042-8994 Office: Dept Philosophy Coll Arts and Sci U Albany Albany NY 12222-0001 E-mail: t.martland@albany.edu.

MARTO, PAUL JAMES, retired mechanical engineering educator, consultant, researcher; b. Flushing, N.Y., Aug. 15, 1938; s. Peter Joseph and Natalie Janet (Verrinoldi) M.; m. Mary Virginia Indence, June 10, 1961; children: Terese V. Marto Sanders, Paul J. Jr., Wayne T., Laura C. BS, U. Notre Dame, 1960; SM, MIT, 1962, ScD, 1965. Asst. prof. Naval Postgrad. Sch., Monterey, Calif., 1965-69, assoc. prof., 1969-77, prof., 1977-85, disting. prof., 1985-96, chmn. dept. mech. engring., 1978-86, dean rsch., 1990-96, disting. prof. emeritus, 1996—. Cons. Modine Mfg. Co., Racine, Wis., 1986—. Editor: Power Condenser Heat, 1981; regional editor N.Am. Jour. of Enhanced Heat Transfer, 1993-98; editor-in-chief Internat. Jour. Transport Phenomena, 1997—; contbr. articles to profl. jours. Bd. trustees Naval Postgrad. Sch. Found., Inc., 1997—. Lt. USN, 1965-67. Recipient Rear Adm. John J. Schieffelin award Naval Postgrad. Sch., 1976, Alexander von Humboldt U.S. Sr. Scientist award Humboldt Stiftung, Fed. Republic Germany, 1989-90, Disting. Civilian Svc. award Sec. of Navy, 1996. Fellow ASME (assoc. tech. editor Jour. of Heat Transfer 1984-90); mem. Am. Soc. Naval Engrs., Am. Soc. for Engring. Edn., Sigma Xi. Avocations: walking, tennis, music. Office: Naval Postgrad Sch Dept Mechanical Engring Code ME MX Monterey CA 93943

MARTOF, MARY TAYLOR, retired nursing educator; b. Charlotte County, Va., Feb. 8, 1935; d. James Russell and Ella (Lipscomb) Palmer; m. John Laning Taylor III, Oct. 3, 1959 (div. 1971); children: Tara, Laura; m. Steven Martof, Apr. 7, 1979. BSN, U. Md., Balt., 1973, MS in Nursing, 1976; EdD, N.C. State U., 1984. Clin. nurse Clin. Ctr., NIH, Bethesda, Md., 1969-73, nursing educator, 1973-79; instr. U. N.C., Chapel Hill, 1979-81; asst. prof. Tex. Christian U., Ft. Worth, 1984-88, U. Southwestern La., Lafayette, 1988-92; assoc. prof. nursing La. State U., New Orleans, 1992—2001, chmn. critical thinking Sch. Nursing, 1994-2000; mem. grad. coun. Sch. Nursing La. State U. Health Sci. Ctr., 2000—, ret., 2001. Cons. nephrology nursing NIH, 1974-79; chmn. profl. edn. Am. Cancer Soc., New Orleans, 1990-96; chmn. rsch. com. Sch. Nursing, La. State U., 1995-98; reviewer/rschr. various pubs.; coord. oncology grand rounds La. State U. Med. Ctr., 1995-2001; judge for Rsch. Day, La. State U. Sch. Medicine, 1999-2001. Contbr. articles to profl. jours., rsch. publ., chpts. to books. Mem. faculty Am. Cancer Soc., Cancer Update, Ochsner Hosp., 1996-98. Recipient Merit award NIH, 1977, plaque Am. Cancer Soc., 1991-93. Mem. Sigma Theta Tau (Disting. Writer). Democrat. Episcopalian. Avocations: hiking, writing. Home: 305 Lake Cheohee Rd Tamassee SC 29686-2007

MARTON, EVA, opera singer; b. Budapest, Hungary, June 18, 1943; m. Zoltan Marton; children: Zoltan, Diana. Student, Liszt Acad., Budapest. Debut Budapest State Opera, 1968-72; performed with Frankfurt Opera, 1972-77, Hambrug State Opera, 1977-80, Maggio Musicale Fiorentino, Vienna State Opera, La Scala Milan, Met. Opera, N.Y., Lyric Opera, Chgo., Grand Opera, Houston, San Francisco Opera, Convent Garden, London, Teatro Liceo, Barcelona, Munich State Opera, Berlin, Paris, Sydney, Teatro Colon Buenos Aires, Bayreuth Festival, Salzburg Festival, Area of Verona, others; roles include Manon Lescaut, Tosca, Turandot, Aida Elisabetta in Don Carlo, Leonora in Forza del destino and in II Trovatore, Fedora, Maddalena in A Chenier, Wally, Gioconda, Leonore in Fidelio, Salome, Ariadne, Helene in Agyptische Helene, Chrysothemis and Electra in Electra, Empress/Wife in Die Frau ohne Schatten, Vensu and Elisabeth in Tannhäuser, Elsa and Ortrud in Lohengrin, Sieglinde and Bruünnhilde in the Ring, Isolde, others; rec. include Turandot, Tosca, La Fanciulla del West, A Chenier, Fedora, La Gioconda, Violanta, Tiefland, La Wally, Semirama, Bluebeards Castle, Mefistofele, Electra, Salome, Die Walkuere, Siegfrid, Götterdämmerung, Gurrelider, Forza del destino, Puccini Arias, Wagner arias, Songs by Bartok and Liszt, others. Address: 31 Ave Princesse Grace Monte Carlo 98 Monaco also: Theatrageutur Dr Hilbert Maximilian Str 22 80539 Munchen Germany E-mail: mez_floria1974@compuserve.com.

MARTON, LAURENCE JAY, researcher, educator, clinical pathologist; b. Bklyn., Jan. 14, 1944; s. Bernard Dov and Sylvia (Silberstein) M.; m. Marlene Lesser, June 27, 1967; 1 child, Eric Nolan BA, Yeshiva U., 1965, DSc (hon.), 1993; MD, Albert Einstein Coll. Medicine, 1969. Intern Los Angeles County-Harbor Gen. Hosp., 1969-70; resident in neurosurgery U. Calif.-San Francisco, 1970-71, resident in lab. medicine, 1973-75, asst. research biochemist, 1973-74, asst. clin. prof. depts. lab. medicine and neurosurgery, 1974-75, asst. prof., 1975-78, assoc. prof., 1978-79, prof., 1979-92, asst. dir. div. clin. chemistry, dept. lab. medicine, 1974-75, dir. divsn., 1975-79, acting chmn. dept., 1978-79, chmn. dept., 1979-92; dean med. sch. U. Wis., 1992-95, prof. pathology and lab. medicine and oncology, 1992-2000, prof. dept. human oncology, 1993-95. Interim vice chancellor Ctr. Health Scis., U. Wis., 1993-94; adj. prof. dept. lab medicine U. Calif., San Francisco, 1992—; pres., CEO SLIL Biomed. Corp., 1998-2000, chief sci. and med. officer, 2000—. Co-editor: Polyamines in Biology and Medicine, 1981; Liquid Chromatography in Clinical Analysis, 1981; Clinical Liquid Chromatography, vol. 1, 1984, vol. 2, 1984 Served with USPHS, NIH, 1971-73 Recipient Rsch. Career Devel. award Nat. Cancer Inst., Disting. Alumnus award Albert Einstein Coll. Medicine, 1992. Mem. Am. Assn. Cancer Rsch., AAAS, Acad. Clin. Lab. Physicians and Scientists, Am. Soc. Investigative Pathology, Alpha Omega Alpha. Jewish. Avocations: photography, art, music, travel. Home: 5810 Tree Line Dr Fitchburg WI 53711-5826 Office: SLIL Biomed Corp 37 Kessel Ct Madison WI 53711-6233

MARTON, MICHAEL, cinematographer; b. Berlin, Germany, Dec. 20, 1942; came to U.S., 1970; s. Alfred Freiherr von Schellerer and Käthe Marie (Hampel) Marton; m. Constance E. Kheel, June 24, 1969 (div. 1975); 1 child, Dunja; m. Ketzel Levine, May 22, 1987 (div. 1992); m. Terry Johnson, June 15, 1996. Diploma in photography, Lette Haus, Berlin, 1960. Asst. cameraman Sta. ZDF-TV, Mainz, Fed. Republic Germany, 1962-65, Gerard Vandenberg, throughout Europe, 1965-68; ind. cinematographer Europe and U.S., 1968-72, throughout U.S., 1972—; video prodns. mgr. Loral Cyberstar, 2001—. Cinematographer corp. and indsl. clients. Cinematographer, dir., prodr., editor: (video documentaries) Stonewall Joe, 1974, Arvilla, 1975, Winterlillies, 1976, A Matter of Size, 1976, Mary Lou at Saratoga, 1981, American Trap, 1982, I Don't Matter I Don't Care, 1983 (U.S. Film and Video award 1984), Henry Brant on the Nature of Music, 1983, The Unsettled Ashes, 1984, Watch Me Now, 1985 (Golden Ring award 1986), Expectations, 1987 (Blue Ribbon award N.Y. Film and Video Festival 1987), Noch ist Polen Nicht Verloren, 1992; (with Harald Beckmann) Volga Dreams, 1993, Three in America, 1995, Angel from Moscow, 1996, Trek to the East, The Love Letter Writer, 1999. Bd. Govs. N.Y. Found. for the Arts, N.Y.C., 1987. Recipient Creative Artists Pub. Service Program award, 1976-78, N.Y. Humanities award N.Y. Council for the Humanities, 1978, N.Y. Found. for the Arts award, 1985, Telly award, 1997-99, Communicator Excellence award, 1996; Guggenheim fellow, 1980. Avocations: reading, travel. Home and Office: Michael Marton Prodns 20403 Shadow Oak Ct Montgomery Village MD 20886 E-mail: martoninmaryland@aol.com.

MARTONE, FREDERICK J. judge; b. Fall River, Mass., Nov. 8, 1943; BS, Coll. Holy Cross, 1965; JD, U. Notre Dame, 1972; LLM, Harvard U., 1975. Bar: Mass. 1972, Ariz. 1974, U.S. Dist. Ct. Mass. 1973, U.S. Dist. Ct. Ariz. 1974, U.S. Ct. Appeals (1st cir.) 1973, U.S. Ct. Appeals (9th cir.) 1974, U.S. Supreme Ct. 1977. Law clk. to Hon. Edward F. Hennessey Mass. Supreme Judicial Ct., 1972-73; pvt. practice Phoenix, 1973-85; assoc. presiding judge Superior Ct. Ariz., Maricopa County, judge, 1985-92; justice Supreme Ct. Ariz., 1992—2002; U.S. dist. judge Dist. of Ariz., 2002—. Editor notes and comments Notre Dame Law Rev., 1970-72; contbr. articles to profl. jours. Capt. USAF, 1965-69. Mem. ABA, Ariz. Judges Assn., Maricopa County Bar Assn., Am. Judicature Soc., State Bar Ariz., Horace Rumpole Inn of Ct. Office: US Dist Ct Sandra Day O'Conner US Courthouse 401 W Washington St Spc 62 Ste 526 Phoenix AZ 85003-2158 E-mail: Frederick.martone@azd.uscourts.gov.

MARTONE, JEANETTE RACHELE, artist; b. Mineola, N.Y., June 5, 1956; d. John and Mildred Cecilia (Loehr) M. BFA, SUNY, Purchase, 1978. One woman shows include Ariel Gallery, N.Y.C., 1990, La Mantia Gallery, Northport, N.Y., 1994-96, Inter-Media Arts Ctr., Huntington, N.Y., 1996; exhibited in group shows from 1980 to 2002 including Harbor Gallery, Cold Spring Harbor, 1980, Huntington Coun. Arts, 1986, Pindar Gallery, N.Y.C., 1987, Mills Pond House, Smithtown, N.Y., 1987, Suffolk County Exec. Offices, Hauppage, N.Y., 1988, La Mantia Gallery, Northport, N.Y., 1990, Nassau County Office Cultural Affairs, 1991, Ward-Nasse. Gallery, N.Y.C., 1991, Monsterrat Gallery, N.Y.C., 1991, Priscilla Redfield Roe Gallery, Bellport, N.Y., 1991, L.I. U., Brookville, 1992, Northport B.J. Spoke Gallery, Huntington, N.Y., 1992, Fischetti Gallery, N.Y., 1992, Artists Space, N.Y.C., 1992, N.Y. Botanical Gardens, Bronx, N.Y., 1993, Visions Gallery, Albany, L.I. U., Brookville, N.Y., 1994, Goodman Gallery, Southampton, N.Y., 1994, B.J. Spoke Gallery, Huntington, N.Y., 1994-95, Islip Art Mus., East Islip, N.Y., 1994, L.I. MacArthur Airport, Ronkonkoma, N.Y., 1995, The Stage Gallery, N.Y., 1997, Lightworks Gallery, Glen Cove, N.Y., 1997, Showcase 98, Smithtown Twp. Arts Coun., St. James, N.Y., 1998, Nat. League Am. Pen Women, Inc., 1999, N.Y. Open Ctr., N.Y.C., 1999, Cork Gallery, Lincoln Ctr., N.Y.C., 1999, Omni Gallery, Uniondale, N.Y., 1999, Nat. League of Am. Pen Woman Inc., Bienniel, Belmont, Calif., 2002, Nat. League of Am. Pen Woman, Inc., Smithtown, N.Y., 2001, St. John's Univ. 7th Annual Juried exhb., Jamaica, N.Y., 2001, Huntington Arts Coun., Huntington, N.Y., 2001, Smithtown Township Arts Coun., 2001, others; publs. include The Other Side Mag., 1997, 1999, 2000, 2001, The Artist's Mag., 1999, Art Calendar, 1995, 2000, Portrait Inspirations, 1997, The Best of Oil Painting, 1996; artwork published in profl. publs. Recipient Award of Excellence Gold medal Art League of Nassau County, 1993, Best in Show award Nat. League Am. PEN Women Artists, 1990, 92, Windsor and Newton award for oil Arts Coun. East Islip, N.Y., 1989, award of excellence Art League of Nassau County, 1987, 88, many best in shows including 1st Ann. Juried Art Exhibit, Brookhaven Arts and Humanities Coun., Farmingville, N.Y., 1996, Supervisor's award Babylon Citizens Coun. Arts Juried Exhbn., 1994, Bob Jones Glad Hand Press award Stamford Art Assn., 1995, Faber Biren Nat. Color award Stamford Art Assn., 1995, Nat. League of Am. Pen Woman, Inc. Belmont, Calif. award of Excellence, 2002, Catharine Lorillard Wolfe Art Club Inc. Portrait award, 2002, Ann. Mem. Art Forum award of Excellence, Smithtown, N.Y., 1999, Award of Excellence Smithtown Twp. Arts Coun. Mem. Show, St. James, N.Y., 1997, 1999. Mem. Nat. League of Am. Pen Women, Catherine Lorillard Wolfe Art Club (Frank B. and Mary Anderson Cassidy Meml. award 1992, Award for Oil 1987Margaret Dole Portrait award 2002), Allied Artists of Am. (John Young Hunter Meml. award 1993, Antonio Cerino Meml. award 1990, award of Excellence 1997), Hudson valley Art Assn., Knickerbock Artists of Am., Nat. Art League. Avocations: travel, reading, volunteer work. Home: 47 Summerfield Ct Deer Park NY 11729-5642

MARTONE, MASSIMILIANO MAX, telecommunications consultant; b. Rome, Apr. 20, 1965; s. Giorgio and Gianna (Megone) M. Diploma in science, JFK Lyceum, 1984; D. of elecs., U. Rome, 1990. Design engr. S.P.E. Inc., Rome, 1990; staff engr. TRS X-Cons., 1990-91, Alenia (Space Divsn.), Rome, 1991-94; sr. engr. ATSI, Inc., Waltham, Mass., 1994-95, Watkins-Johnson Co., Gaithersburg, Md., 1995-2000; with W.J. Comms., Inc., San Jose, Calif., 2000—02, Rosum Corp., Redwood City, 2002—. Cons. Alfacons., Inc., Rome, 1991, Staer,Inc., Rome, 1993, Microlab., Inc., Rome, 1993-94; researcher Rensselaer Polytech. Inst. , Troy, N.Y., 1993-94. Authors of tech. books; contbr. articles to profl. jours. Mem. IEEE, N.Y. Acad. Scis., Electrotech. Assn. Italy. Roman Catholic. Home: 2451 Taylor Way Antioch CA 94531-8295 Office: Rosum Corp 1450 Veterans Blvd Redwood City CA 94513 E-mail: mmartone@rosum.com.

MARTONE, MICHAEL, writer; b. Fort Wayne, Ind., Aug. 22, 1955; s. Anthony S. and Patty A. M.; m. Theresa O. Pappas, Apr. 3, 1984; children: Samuel Martone, Nick Pappas. AB, Ind. U., 1977; MA, Johns Hopkins U., 1979. Prof. English dept Iowa State U., Ames, 1980-87, Harvard, Cambridge, Mass., 1987-90, Syracuse (N.Y.) U., 1990-95, U. Ala., Tuscaloosa, 1995—.

Author: Alive and Dead in Indiana, 1984, Safety Patrol, 1987, Fort Wayne is Seventh on Hitler's List, 1989, Pensees The Thoughts of Dan Quayle, 1990, Seeing Eye, 1995, Sex Life of the Fantastic Four, 1998, The Flatness and Other Landscapes, 2000, The Blue Guide to Indiana, 2001; editor: A Place of Sense, 1984, Townships, 1988, The Scribners Anthology of Contemporary Short Fiction, 2000, Trying Fiction, 2001. NEA fellow, Washington, 1984, 88, AWP Creative Nonfiction award, 1998. Home: 29 Country Club Hls Tuscaloosa AL 35401-1300 Office: U Ala Dept English PO Box 870244 Tuscaloosa AL 35487 E-mail: martone@english.as.ua.edu.

MARTONE, PATRICIA ANN, lawyer; b. Bklyn., Apr. 28, 1947; d. David Andrew and Rita Mary (Dullmeyer) M. BA in Chemistry, NYU, 1968, JD, 1973; MA in Phys. Chemistry, Johns Hopkins U., 1969. Bar: N.Y. 1974, U.S. Dist. Ct. (so. and ea. dists.) N.Y. 1975, U.S. Ct. Appeals (2d cir.) 1975, U.S. Ct. Appeals (1st cir.) 1981, U.S. Patent and Trademark Office 1983, U.S. Ct. Appeals (fed. cir.) 1984, U.S. Supreme Ct. 1984, U.S. Dist. Ct. (ea. dist.) Mich. 1985, U.S. Dist. Ct. (no. dist.) Calif. 1995. Tech. rep. computer timesharing On-Line Sys., Inc., N.Y.C., 1969-70; assoc. Kelley Drye & Warren, 1973-77, Fish & Neave, N.Y.C., 1977-82, ptnr., 1983—. Adj. prof. NYU Sch. Law, 1990—; mem. adv. coun. Engelberg Ctr. Innovation Law & Policy, 1996—; participating atty. Cmty. Law Offices, N.Y.C., 1974—78; atty. Pro Bono Panel U.S. Dist. Ct. (so. dist.) N.Y., 1982—84; lectr. Practising Law Inst., N.Y.C., 1995—, mem. conf. bd., 2001; lectr. Aspen Law & Bus., 1990—95, Franklin Pierce Law Sch., 1992—97, Lic. Exec. Soc., 1995; chair, bd. dirs. N.Y. Lawyers for the Pub. Interest, 1996—98, vice chair, 1998—2000, 2002—, Legal Svcs., N.Y.C., 1991—95. Mng. editor NYU Law Sch. Rev. Law and Social Change, 1972-73; contbr. articles to profl. jours. Recipient Founder's Day award NYU Sch. Law, 1973; NSF grad. trainee Johns Hopkins U., 1968-69; NYU scholar, 1964-68. Mem. ABA, Assn. Bar City N.Y. (mem. environ. law com. 1978-83, trademarks, unfair competition com. 1983-86), Fed. Bar Coun., Fed. Cir. Bar Assn., Copyright Soc., Am. Chem. Soc., Licensing Execs. Soc., N.Y. Intellectual Property Law Assn., Univ. Club. Office: Fish & Neave Fl 49 1251 Ave of the Americas New York NY 10020-1105 E-mail: pmartone@fishneave.com.

MARTONE, WILLIAM JAMES, physician; b. Troy, N.Y., May 25, 1947; s. Emilio James and Rose Anna Wassil; 1 child Elizabeth, Virginia. BS, Union Coll., Schenectady, N.Y., 1969; MD, NYU, 1973; MS, U. Va., 1981. Diplomate in internal medicine and infectious diseases Am. Bd. Internal Medicine. Intern, then resident in internal medicine U. Va., 1973-76; sr. exec. dir. Nat. Found. Infectious Diseases, Bethesda, Md., 1995—; dir. hosp. infections program CDC, Atlanta, 1987-95. Mem. Soc. for Healthcare Epidemiology of Am. (sec. 1991-93, v.p. 1994, pres. 1996), Phi Beta Kappa, Alpha Omega Alpha.

MARTONOSI, ANTHONY NICHOLAS, biochemistry educator, researcher; b. Szeged, Hungary, Nov. 7, 1928; came to U.S., 1957; s. Antal and Anna (Zsoter) M.; m. Mary Alice Gouvea, May 2, 1959; children: Mary Anne, Anthony, Margaret, Susan. MD, U. Med. Sch., Szeged, 1953. Asst. prof. dept. physiology Med. Sch., Szeged, 1955-57; rsch. fellow Mass. Gen. Hosp., Boston, 1957-59; rsch. assoc. Retina Found., 1959-62, asst. dir. dept. muscle rsch., 1962-65; assoc. prof. biochemistry St. Louis U. Sch. Medicine, 1965-69, prof., 1969-79; prof. biochemistry SUNY Health Sci. Ctr., Syracuse, 1979-98. Albert Szent-Gyorgyi prof. U. Med. Sch., Szeged, Hungary, 1994; adj. prof. Kwangju Inst. f Sci. and Tech., Korea, 1995—; vis. scientist dept. biochemistry U. Birmingham, Eng., 1963-64. Author: The Development of Sarcoplasmic Reticulum, 2000; editor: The Enzymes of Biological Membranes, Vols. 1-4, 1976, 2d edit., 1985; Membranes and Transport, Vols. 1-2, 1982; contbr. over 180 articles to sci. publs.; mem. editl. bd. Biochimica et Biophysica Acta, 1988-96. Recipient Established Investigator award Am. Heart Assn., 1961-66; rsch. grantee USPHS, NIH, 1959-89, NSF, 1963-96, Muscular Dystrophy Assn., 1975-89. Mem. Am. Soc. Biochemists and Molecular Biologists. Roman Catholic. Home: 110 Stanwood Ln Manlius NY 13104-1412 E-mail: gouveama@aol.com.

MÁRTONYI, CSABA LÁSZLO, ophthalmic photographer, imager; b. Budapest, Hungary, Mar. 23, 1941; came to U.S., 1951; s. Louis Péter and Magda (Gyürky) M.; m. Elnajean Beyst, Sept. 4, 1976; 1 child, Erika Lyn. Cert. retinal angiographer. Chief photographer U. Mich. Photog. Svcs., Ann Arbor, 1967-71; dir. ophthalmic photography, dept. ophthalmology U. Mich., 1971-75, instr. dept. ophthalmic photography, 1975-80, asst. prof., 1980-83, assoc. prof., 1983-2000, assoc. prof. emeritus, 2000—. First author: Clinical Slit-Lamp Biomicroscopy and Photo Slit-Lamp Biomicrography, 1985; author, artist exhibit of eye images Landscapes of the Eye, 1993; author sci. exhibits. With U.S. Naval Air Res., 1965-67. Recipient Disting. Tchg. award Joint Commn. on Allied Health Pers. in Ophthalmology, 1997. Fellow Ophthalmic Photographers Soc. (parliamentarian 1988—, chair hon. life membership com. 1991—, fellowship com., pres. 1978-80, chair bd. certification 1978-84, chmn. editl. com. 1987-89, awards including top award for outstanding contbns. to ophthalmic photography), Am. Acad. Ophthalmology (assoc., Honor award 1984). Avocations: guitar (classical-traditional), woodsculpting, fine arts photography, tennis. Home: 1261 Laurel View Dr Ann Arbor MI 48105-9765

MARTORANA, BARBARA JOAN, secondary education educator; b. N.Y.C., Oct. 18, 1942; d. Samuel and Joan Renee (Costello) M. BA, St. John's U., Jamaica, N.Y., 1970, MS in English Edn., 1972; advanced cert. computers in edn., L.I. U., 1988, profl. diploma in edn. adminstrn., 1990. Cert. sch. dist. adminstr., sch. adminstr. and supr., tchr. English grades 7-12, N.Y. Exec. sec. Am. Petroleum Inst., N.Y.C., 1960-65; exec. asst. to v.p. Goldring, Inc., 1965-67; exec. asst. Rsch. Inst. for Cath. Edn., 1967-69; English tchr. St. Martin of Tours Sch., Amityville, N.Y., 1970-77, Oceanside (N.Y.) Jr. H.S., 1977-78, Freeport (N.Y.) H.S., 1979—. Rec. sec. Freeport (N.Y.) Tchr. Ctr. Policy Bd., 1986-89; co-chair Middle States Steering Com., Freeport, 1988-90; chair Freeport (N.Y.) H.S. Shared Decision Team, 1992-93; adv. bd. L.I. Writing Project, Garden City, N.Y., 1993—, co-leader Summer Insts.; adj. prof. literacy studies dept. Hofstra U., N.Y., 1999—. Co-author: (textbooks) Writing Competency Practice, 1980, Writing Competency Practice-Revised and Expanded, 1989. With Seaford (N.Y.) Rep. Club, 1975—. Mem. ASCD, Nat. Coun. Tchrs. English (conf. on English edn.), N.Y. State English Coun., L.I. Writing Project. Avocations: reading, writing, traveling. Office: Freeport HS 50 S Brookside Ave Freeport NY 11520-3144 E-mail: engteech@aol.com.

MARTORANA, BENEDICT FREDERICK, civil engineer; b. Newark, Sept. 17, 1947; m. Diane Gulla, June 1, 1968; children: Stephen, Wendy. BCE, N.J. Inst. Tech., 1974. Registered profl. engr., N.J., Pa., Calif.; registered profl. planner, N.J. Staff engr. Borough of Glen Ridge, N.J., 1968-71; asst. mcpl. engr. Town of Bloomfield, 1971-73; ptnr. Barbieri, Pluymers Assocs., Totowa, 1973-76; mcpl. engr., adminstr. Twp. of West Caldwell, 1976—. Adj. faculty Essex County Coll., Newark, 1989-90. Active West Caldwell Planning Bd., 1977—; chmn. Passaic River Flood Task Force, Essex County, 1984; exec. bd. N.J. Intergovtl. Ins. Fund, 1991, chmn., 2000—; apptd. to 26th consecutive term as mem. W. Caldwell Planning Bd., 2002. Mem. N.J. Soc. Mcpl. Engrs., ASCE, N.J. Soc. Profl. Planners. Achievements include development of model program for composting leaves for N.J. Office: Twp West Caldwell 30 Clinton Rd West Caldwell NJ 07006-6704

MARTORI, JOSEPH PETER, lawyer; b. N.Y.C., Aug. 19, 1941; s. Joseph and Teresa Susan (Fezza) M. BS summa cum laude, NYU, 1964, MBA, 1968; JD cum laude, U. Notre Dame, 1967. Bar: D.C. 1968, U.S. Dist. Ct. D.C. 1968, U.S. Dist. Ct. Ariz. 1968, U.S. Ct. Appeals (9th cir.) 1969, U.S. Supreme Ct. 1977. Assoc. Sullivan & Cromwell, N.Y.C., 1967-68, Snell & Wilmer, Phoenix, 1968-69; pres. Goldmar Inc., 1969-71; ptnr. Martori, Meyer, Hendricks & Victor, P.A., 1971-85, Brown & Bain, P.A., Phoenix, 1985-94, chmn. corp. banking & real estate dept., 1994—; chmn. bd. ILX Resorts, Inc. Chmn. ILX Inc., Varsity Clubs Am. Inc. Author: Street Fights, 1987; also articles, 1966-70. Trustee Boys' Clubs Met. Phoenix, 1974-99; consul for Govt. of Italy, State of Ariz., 1987-97. Mem. ABA, State Bar Ariz., Maricopa County Bar Assn., Lawyers Com.for Civil Rights Under Law (trustee 1976—), Phoenix Country Club, Plaza Club (founding bd. govs. 1979-90). Republican. Roman Catholic. Office: ILX Resorts Inc 2111 E Highland Ave Ste 210 Phoenix AZ 85016-4786 E-mail: jmartori@ILXresorts.com.

MARTOVETSKY, NICOLAI N. mechanical engineer, researcher; b. St. Petersburg, Russia, July 2, 1955; arrived in U.S., 1992; s. Nicolai M. and Elena V. Martovetsky; m. Irina V. Lebedeva, Apr. 11, 1975; children: Egor, Gleb. MSME, Moscow Power Engring. Inst., 1978; PhD in Mech. Engring., Kurchatov Inst., 1985. Engr., rsch. assoc., head of lab. Kurchatov Inst., Moscow, 1978—92; with Superconducting Super Collider Lab., Dallas, 1992—94; engr., program leader Lawrence Livermore (Calif.) Nat. Lab., 1994—. Cons. Babcock and Wilcox, Lynchburg, Va., 1999; mem. adv. com. U. Irvine, Calif., 2000. Inventor in field; contbr. articles to profl. jours. Mem.: Cryogenic Soc. Am. Avocations: tennis, touring, canoeing, woodworking. Office: Lawrence Livermore Nat Lab 7000 East Ave Livermore CA 94550 Fax: 925-422-2477. E-mail: martovetsky1@llnl.gov.

MARTS, TERRI LOUISE, management executive; b. Wilkinsburg, Pa., June 8, 1958; d. Robert Jackson and Margaret Elaine (Frescura) Gebrosky; m. Norman Vincent Marts, Sept. 27, 1980. BS in Bus. Adminstrn., U. Pitts., 1980; MBA, Robert Morris Coll., 1985. Clk. Westinghouse Electric Corp., Pitts., 1977-79, pers. rep., 1980-81, in quality, mktg. and human resources, 1981-85; quality engr. Westinghouse Energy Systems, 1985-89, mgr. employee svcs., 1989-91, mgr. total quality and nuclear quality assurance, 1991-93; asst. dir. human resources Westinghouse Corp. Hdqs., 1993-95; mng. dir. Westinghouse Source W, 1995-98, pres., 1999—. Faculty mem. Human Resource Planning Soc., N.Y.C., 1992-95; nat. spkr. Am. Soc. Quality Control, 1985-90. Bd. dirs. Jr. Achievement, Pitts., 1995-97. Recipient Am. Legion award, 1970. Mem. Quality Network (sponsorship com. 1992-95), Women in Comm. Avocations: reading, travel, gardening, church activities. Home: 5974 Kremer Hollow Rd Export PA 15632-1544 Office: Westinghouse Electric Corp 11 Stanwix St Pittsburgh PA 15222-1312

MARTSON, WILLIAM FREDERICK, JR. lawyer; b. Carlisle, Pa., May 31, 1947; m. Deborah S. Smith, June 4, 1969; children: Alexander Fenton, Bradford Walter. Student, U. Edinburgh, Scotland, 1967-68; BA in Polit. Sci. magna cum laude, Washington & Jefferson, 1969; JD magna cum laude, U. Mich., 1972. Bar: Oreg. 1972, U.S. Dist. Ct. Oreg. 1972, U.S. Ct. Appeals (9th cir.) 1974, U.S. Ct. Claims 1973, U.S. Supreme Ct. 1979. Assoc. Davies Biggs Strayer Stoel & Boley, Portland, Oreg., 1972-74, Tonkon Torp & Galen, Portland, 1974-78; ptnr. Tonkon Torp LLP (and predecessor firm), 1978—. Chmn. indigent representation com. U.S. Dist. Ct. Oreg. Bd. dirs., treas. Albertina Kerr Ctr., Portland, 1985-90; bd. dirs. Oreg. Hist. Soc., Portland, 1990-2000, treas., 1994-97, pres., 1997-99; bd. dirs., chmn. Molalla (Oreg.) Elem. Sch. Dist. # 35, 1989-93; dir. Oreg. Trail Found., 1994-97. Fellow Internat. Soc. Barristers (bd. mem. 1999—); mem. ABA, FBA, Oreg. State Bar Assn. (chmn. com. on detention correction), Prisoners Legal Svc. of Oreg., Inc. (chmn. of the bd.), Arlington Club, Order of Coif, Phi Beta Kappa. Avocations: skiing, horseback riding. Office: Tonkon Torp LLP 1600 Pioneer Tower 888 SW 5th Ave Portland OR 97204-2012 E-mail: rick@tonkon.com.

MARTUCCI, VINCENT JAMES, composer, pianist; b. Medford, Mass., Oct. 21, 1954; s. Vincent James Sr. and Grace Alice (Giorgio) M.; m. Elizabeth Nicoll Lawrence, Sept. 20, 1981; children: Katharine Amalia, James Lawrence. Student, Berklee Coll. Music, Boston, 1974-75; BA in Music, Colby Coll., 1977; student, Hal Galper, N.Y.C., 1978-80, Dave Holland, Woodstock, N.Y., 1982-84; MM in Music, Purchase Coll., SUNY, 2001. Lectr. music Alfred (N.Y.) U., 1978-80; registrar, instr. Creative Music Studio, Woodstock, 1980-82; owner, composer, performer Vinnie Martucci Prodns., West Hurley, N.Y., 1987—; prof. jazz studies SUNY, New Paltz, 1991—. Performer, composer, 1977—; free-lance composer, producer recordings and TV, 1986—; tchr. SUNY, New Paltz, 1991; cons. synthesis and audio technique, 1985—; mem. U.S. Embassy tour concert series, Bogota, Colombia, 1991; participant conf. Internat. Assn. Jazz Educators, Boston, 1994; instr. music theory and piano Ashokan Fiddle & Dance, 1996—. Composer, performer, corporate spl. events The Dolphins, North Am., South Am., Europe, Canada, including Newport Jazz at Saratoga, North Sea Jazz Festival, JVC Jazz Festival at Nice, France, The Hague in Holland, Jazz Mecca Festival in Holland, Pori Jazz Festival, Finland, Levercusen Jazz Festival Germany, Brubeck Family Project Tours, and many others, 1987—; performed with Hubert Laws, Nick Brignola, Livingston Taylor, Rory Block, Don Mclean; arranger radio concert series Karl Berger Composer, 1985; co-author, arranger Adventures of Comander Crumbcake - TV series, 1987; composer: (rec.) Malayan Breeze, 1991, network theme redesign pkg. lifetime med. TV, 1988; travel channel, 1990, CNN-Daily Menus, 1991; composer, performer, arranger underscore CBS's As the World Turns, 1993—, NBC's Another World, 1993—, Guiding Light; co-composer: (rec.) Old World/New World, 1991, Ain't I a Woman, 1992; author instructional tape series Arranging and Recording Electronic Instruments, 1987—; co-prodr., performer, engr. music for theatrical prodns. McCarter Theatre (1 Tony award), Princeton, Asolo Theatre, Sarasota, Fla.; co-prodr., music for theatre prodn. Having Our Say, 1995—; performer, music dir. numerous live TV and radio performances; music dir. for Eileen Fulton star of As the World Turns, 1990-, music dir. Laurel Massé, 1997-; author: (book series) Introduction to Jazz Keyboards, Introduction to Blues Keyboards, Introduction to Rock Keyboards, 1997. Recipient 2d pl. jazz composition Billboard Mag., 1988. Mem. ASCAP, AFTRA, Am. Fedn. Musicians. Avocations: photography, bicycling, swimming. Home and Office: Vinnie Martucci Prodn 29 Pleasant Ridge Dr West Hurley NY 12491-5441

MARTUZA, ROBERT L. neurosurgeon; b. Wilkes-Barre, Pa., July 1, 1948; BA, Bucknell U., Lewisburg, Pa., 1969; MD, Harvard U., 1973. Diplomate Am. Bd. Neurol. Surgery. Instr. surgery Harvard Med. Sch., Boston, 1980-81, asst. prof., 1981-86, assoc. prof., 1986-91; prof., chmn. dept neurosurgery Georgetown U., Washington, 1991-2000; Higgins prof. neurosurgery Harvard Med. Sch., Boston, 2000—; chief neurosurgery Mass. Gen. Hosp., 2000—. Dir. Georgetown Brain Tumor Ctr., Washington, 1993-2000, Mass. Gen. Hosp. Neurofibromatosis Clinic, Boston, 1990-91; chair Decade of the Brain Task Force, Chgo., 1994—. Contbr. articles to profl. jours. Recipient Von Recklinghauson award Nat. NF Found., N.Y.C., 1989. Mem. Am. Acad. Neurol. Surgeons, Soc. Neurol. Surgery (Grass award), Am. Assn. Neurol. Surgeons, Congress Neurol. Surgeons. Achievements include development of genetically engineered viruses for brain tumor therapy; first development of replication-competent viral vectors for tumor therapy. Office: Mass Gen Hosp White 502 Boston MA 02127-1109

MARTY, ALVIN LEONARD, economist, educator; b. N.Y.C., Jan. 29, 1927; s. Harry and Pearl (Bailin) M. Student, Cambridge (Eng.) U., 1947-50; PhD, U. Calif., Berkeley, 1955; AB, UCLA, 1947. Mem. faculty Northwestern U., Evanston, Ill., 1955-60; prof. econs. CUNY, 1960—, prof. econs. and fin. Ctr. for Study of Bus. and Govt., Baruch Coll., 1960—. Vis. prof. U. Chgo., 1962, U. Hawaii, 1973, Columbia U., 1974, City of London, 1987-88; vis. scholar Fed. Res. Bank of St. Louis, 1993; Simon rsch. prof. Manchester (Eng.) U., 1975-76. Mem. editorial bd. Am. Econ. Assn.; contbr. articles to profl. jours. Ehrman student Cambridge U., 1947-50; Ford Found. fellow, 1956-57. Home: 545 W End Ave New York NY 10024-2713 Office: Baruch Coll Ctr for Study of Bus & Govt 17 Lexington Ave New York NY 10010-5518

MARTY, MARTIN EMIL, religion educator, editor; b. West Point, Nebr., Feb. 5, 1928; s. Emil A. and Anne Louise (Wuerdemann) Marty; m. Elsa Schumacher Marty, 1952 (dec. 1981); children: Frances, Joel, John, Peter, James, Micah, Ursula; m. Harriet Lindemann Marty, 1982. MDiv, Concordia Sem., 1952; STM, Luth. Sch. Theology, Chgo., 1954; PhD in Am. Religious and Intellectual History, U. Chgo., 1956; LittD (hon.) , Thiel Coll., 1964; LHD (hon.) , W.Va. Wesleyan Coll., 1967, Marian Coll., 1967, Providence Coll., 1967; DD (hon.) , Muhlenberg Coll., 1967; LittD (hon.) , Thomas More Coll., 1968; DD (hon.) , Bethany Sem., 1969; LLD (hon.) , Keuka Coll., 1972; LHD (hon.) , Willamette U., 1974; DD (hon.) , Wabash Coll., 1977; LLD (hon.) , U. So. Calif., 1977, Valparaiso U., 1978; LHD (hon.) , St. Olaf Coll., 1978, De Paul U., 1979; DD (hon.) , Christ Sem.-Seminex, 1979, Capital U., 1980; LHD (hon.) , Colo. Coll., 1980; DD (hon.) , Maryville Coll., 1980, North Park Coll. Sem., 1982; LittD (hon.) , Wittenberg U., 1983; LHD, Rosary Coll., 1984, Rockford Coll., 1984; DD (hon.) , Va. Theol. Sem., 1984; LHD (hon.) , Hamilton Coll., 1985, Loyola U., 1986; LLD (hon.) , U. Notre Dame, 1987; LHD (hon.) , Roanoke Coll., 1987, Mercer U., 1987, Ill. Wesleyan Coll., 1987, Roosevelt U., 1988, Aquinas Coll., 1988; LittD (hon.) , Franklin Coll., 1988, U. Nebr., 1993; LHD (hon.) , No. Mich. U., 1989, Muskingum Coll., Coe Coll., Lehigh U., 1989, Hebrew Union Coll. and Governors State U., 1990, Whittier Coll., 1991, Calif. Luth. U., 1993; DD (hon.) , St. Xavier Coll. and Colgate U., 1990, Mt. Union Coll., 1991, Tex. Luth. Coll., 1991, Aurora U., 1991, Baker U., 1992; LHD (hon.) , Luth. U., 1993, Calif. Luth. U., 1993, Midland Luth. Coll., 1995; DD, Hope Coll., 1993, Northwestern Coll., 1993; LHD (hon.) , George Fox Coll., 1994, Drake U., 1994, Centre Coll., 1994, Fontbonne Coll., 1996; DD, Yale U., 1995; LHD (hon.) , Otterbein Coll., 1996; ThD (hon.) , Lycoming Coll., 1997; LHD, Dana Coll., 1998; LittD (hon.) , Alma Coll., 1998, Concordia U. Portland, 1998, Niagara U., 1998; LHD (hon.) , Kalamazoo Coll., 1999, William Jewell Coll., 1999; LittD (hon.) , U. Miami, 1999; DD, DD, Trinity Coll., 2001; DHum, DHum, Westminster Choir Coll., 2001; LHD, LHD, U. Scranton, 2001. Ordained to ministry Luth. Ch., 1952. Pastor, Washington, 1950—51; asst. pastor River Forest, Ill., 1952—56; pastor Elk Grove Village, 1956—63; prof. history of modern Christianity Div. Sch. U. Chgo., 1963—, Fairfax M. Cone Disting. Svc. prof., 1978—98, prof. emeritus, 1998—; assoc. editor Christian Century mag., Chgo., 1956—85, sr. editor, 1985—98; co-editor Ch. History mag., 1963—97. Pres. Park Ridge (Ill.) Ctr., 1989—, sr. scholar, 1989—; pres. Am. Inst. for Study of Health, Faith and Ethics, 1985—89; dir. fundamentalism project Am. Acad. Arts and Scis., 1988—; dir. The Pub. Religion Project, 1996—99; interim pres. St. Olaf Coll., 2000—01; sr. scholar Park Ridge Ctr., 1989—. Author: A Short History of Christianity, 1959, The New Shape of American Religion, 1959, The Improper Opinion, 1961, The Infidel, 1961, Baptism, 1962, The Hidden Discipline, 1963, Second Chance for American Protestants, 1963, Church Unity and Church Mission, 1964, Varieties of Unbelief, 1964, The Search for a Usable Future, 1969, The Modern Schism, 1969, Righteous Empire, 1970, Protestantism, 1972, You Are Promise, 1973, The Fire We Can Light, 1973, The Pro and Con Book of Religious America, 1975, A Nation of Behavers, 1976, Religion, Awakening and Revolution, 1978, Friendship, 1980, By Way of Response, 1981, The Public Church, 1981, A Cry of Absence, 1983, Health and Medicine in the Lutheran Tradition, 1983, Pilgrims in Their Own Land, 1984, Protestantism in the United States, 1985, Modern American Religion, The Irony of it All, Vol. 1, 1986, An Invitation to American Catholic History, 1986, Religion and Republic, 1987, Modern American Religion: The Noise of Conflict, Vol. 2, 1991; author: (with R. Scott Appleby) The Glory and the Power, 1992; editor (with Jerald C. Brauer): The Unrelieved Paradox: Studies in the Theology of Franz Bibfeldt, 1994; editor: (with Micah Marty) Places Along the Way, 1994; editor: Our Hope for Years to Come, 1995, Modern American Religion, Under God, Indivisible, Vol. 3, 1996, The One and the Many, 1997, The Promise of Winter, 1997, When True Simplicity is Gained, 1998, Politics, Religion, and the Common Good, 2000, Education, Religion, and the Common Good, 2001; editor: (jours.) Context, 1969—; editor: Second Opinion; sr. editor: The Christian Century, 1956—98; contbr. articles to religious publs. Chmn. bd. regents St. Olaf Coll., 1996—2001; dir. The Pub. Religion Project, 1996—; sr. regents St. Olaf Coll., 2002—. Recipient Nat. Medal Humanities, 1997, Alumni medal, U. Chgo., 1998; scholar Sr. scholar-in-residence, The Park Ridge Ctr., 1989—. Fellow: Soc. Am. Historians, Am. Acad. Arts and Scis. (dir. fundamentalism project 1988—94); mem.: Am. Antiquarian Soc., Am. Acad. Religion (pres. 1987—88), Am. Cath. Hist. Assn. (pres. 1981), Am. Soc. Ch. History (pres. 1971), Am. Phil. Soc. Office: 239 Scottswood Rd Riverside IL 60546-2223 E-mail: memarty@aol.com.

MARTYL, (MRS. ALEXANDER LANGSDORF JR.), artist; b. St. Louis, Mar. 16, 1917; d. Martin and Aimee (Goldstone) Schweig; m. Alexander Langsdorf, Jr., Dec. 31, 1941; children: Suzanne, Alexandra. AB, Washington U., St. Louis, 1938. Instr. art dept. U. Chgo.; artist in residence Tamarind Inst., U. N.Mex., Albuquerque, 1974 Solo shows include, Calif. Palace of Legion of Honor, 1956, Chgo. Art Inst., 1949, 76, Feingarten Galleries, N.Y.C., Beverly Hills and Chgo., 1961, 62, 63, St. Louis, 1962, Feingarten Gallery, N.Y.C., 1963, L.A., 1964, Kovler Gallery, Chgo., 1967, Washington U., St. Louis, 1967, U. Chgo. Oriental Inst. Mus., 1970, Deson&Zaks Gallery, 1973, Fairweather-Hardin Gallery, 1977, 81, 83, Ill. State Mus., 1978, Fermilab, 1985, 91, Bklyn. Mus., 1986, Oriental Inst. Mus., 1987, Gibbes Art Mus., Charleston, S.C., 1988, Fairweather-Hardin Gallery, 1988, Tokyo Internat. Art Expo, 1990, State of Ill. Art Gallery, Chgo., 1990, Expo Navy Pier, Chgo., 1993, Printworks Gallery Ltd., Chgo., 1995, 97, 99, 2002, Oriental Inst. Mus., Chgo., Martyl: Nature/Artifice Ft. Wayne Mus. Art, 2000; represented in permanent collections, Met. Mus. Art, Chgo. Art Inst., Pa. Acad. Fine Arts, Ill. State Mus., Bklyn. Mus., DuSable Mus., Chgo., Los Angeles County Mus., Whitney Mus. Am. Art, Davenport (Iowa) Municipal Mus., St. Louis Art Mus., Washington U., U. Ariz., Arnot Gallery, Elmira, N.Y., Greenville (S.C.) Mus., Nat. Coll. Fine Arts, Hirshhorn Mus. and Sculpture Gallery, Rockford (Ill.) Mus. Recipient 1st prize City Art Mus., St. Louis, 1943, 44; Armstrong prize Chgo. Art Inst., 1947; William H. Bartels award, 1953; Frank Logan medal and prize, 1950; Walt Disney purchase award Los Angeles Museum; purchase prize Portrait of America competition, Colo. Springs Fine Arts Center, 1961; honor award for mural AIA, 1962, Outstanding Achievement award in the Arts YWCA, 1986; named Artist of Year Am. Fedn. Arts, 1958 Mem. Chgo. Network, Arts Club (Chgo.). Unitarian Universalist. *To be an artist means devoting a lifetime to an intensely difficult activity— one that requires concentration and skill. I've spent my time learning the power of color, line, shape and meaning. I like to think that I have opened out experiences people cannot reveal by themselves.*

MARTZ, CLYDE OLLEN, lawyer, educator; b. Lincoln, Nebr., Aug. 14, 1920; s. Clyde O. and Elizabeth Mary (Anderson) M.; m. Ann Spieker, May 29, 1947; children: Robert Graham, Nancy. AB, U. Nebr., 1941; LLB, Harvard U., 1947. Bar: Colo. 1948, U.S. Ct. Appeals (D.C. cir.) 1968, U.S. Supreme Ct. 1969. Prof. U. Colo., Boulder, 1947-58, 60-62; jud. adminstr. State of Colo., Denver, 1959-60; ptnr. Davis, Graham & Stubbs, 1962-67, 69-80, 81-87, of counsel, 1988—; asst. atty. gen. U.S. Dept. Justice, Washington, 1967-69; solicitor U.S Dept. Interior, 1980-81; exec. dir. dept. natural resources State of Colo., 1987. Adj. prof. U. Denver, 1961-79, U. Colo., Boulder, 1988-96; cons. Pres. Materials Policy Commn., 1951; mem. Colo. Adv. Bd. Bur. Land Mgmt., 1967-69; bd. dirs., adv. bd. Natural Resources Law Ctr., 1982-2002 Author: Cases and Materials on Natural Resources Law, 1951, Water for Mushrooming Populations, 1954; co-author: American Law of Property, 1953, Water and Water Rights, 1963; editor, co-author: American Law of Mining, 1960. Co-chmn. Jud. Reorganization Commn., 1961-63; elder Presbyn. Ch., Boulder; pres. Rocky Mountain Mineral Law Found., 1961-62, others. Comdr. USN, 1942-58, PTO, with Res. Decorated Silver Star, Bronze Star, Letter of Commendation, Disting. Svc. award. Mem. ABA (chmn. natural resources sect. 1985-86), Fed. Bar Assn., Am. Health Lawyers Assn., Colo. Bar Assn. (chmn. water sect. 1957, chmn. mineral sect. 1961, award of merit 1962), Nat. Mining Assn. (Disting. Svc. award 1997), Order of Coif, Phi Beta Kappa. Democrat. Avocations: horticulture, woodworking, mountaineering, skiing. Home: 970 Aurora Ave Apt 205F Boulder CO 80302-7299 Office: Davis Graham & Stubbs PO Box 185 Denver CO 80201-0185

MARTZ, JUDY HELEN, governor; b. Big Timber, Mont., July 28, 1943; m. Harry Martz, June 23, 1965; children: Justin, Stacey. Owner, operator Martz Disposal Svc., 1971—; skater U.S. World Speed Skating Team, Japan, 1963, U.S. Olympic Team, Innsbruck, Austria, 1964; exec. dir. U.S. High Altitude Speed Skating Ctr., Butte, Mont., 1985-89; field rep. Senator Conrad Burns, 1989—95; lt. gov. State of Mont., 1997-2001, gov., 2001—. Coach Mont. Amateur Speed Skating Assn.; bd. dirs. Youth Hockey Assn.; pres. adv. bd. U.S. Internat. Speed Skating Assn. Bd dirs. St. James Cmty. Hosp., Legion Oasis HUD Housing Project. Named Miss Rodeo Mont., 1963; inducted Butte Sports Hall of Fame, 1987.*

MARTZ, LAWRENCE STANNARD, retired periodical editor; b. Bklyn., Apr. 2, 1933; s. Lawrence Stannard Martz and Jean Lee Bailey; m. Anne-Sophie Uldall, May 28, 1955; children: Geoffrey Stannard, Jenny-Anne Horst-Martz. AB, Dartmouth Coll., 1954; postgrad., U. Edinburgh, 1955. Reporter The Pontiac (Mich.) Press, 1955-56, The Detroit News, 1956-59; copy editor The Wall St. Jour., N.Y.C., 1959-60; bus. writer/editor to asst mng. editor, editor internat. editions Newsweek Mag., 1961-93, contbg. editor, 1993-99; editor World Press Rev. Mag., 1993-99. Co-author: Ministry of Greed, 1988; author: Making Schools Better, 1992. Recipient J.C. Penney-Mo. award for bus. writing, U. Mo. Sch. of Journalism, 1969, Silver Gavel award ABA, 1990, Media award N.Y. State Bar Assn., 1986. Mem.: Overseas Press Club of Am. (bd. govs. 1994—, pres. 2000—02). E-mail: larrymartz@aol.com.

MARTZ, MIKE, professional football coach; b. Sioux Falls, S.D., May 13, 1951; BS summa cum laude, Fresno State. Asst. coach Los Angeles Rams, 1992—99, Washington Redskins, 1997-98; offensive coord. St. Louis Rams, 1999—2000, head coach, 2000—. Office: Saint Louis One Rams Way Saint Louis MO 63045

MARTZ, WILLIAM B. management consultant, educator; b. Washington , Apr. 20, 1958; s. William B. and Peggy T. Martz. BBA Mktg., Coll. William and Mary, 1981; MS Mgmt. Info. Scis., U. Ariz., 1985, PhD Mgmt. Info. Scis., 1989. Pres. & coo Ventana Corp., Tucson, 1989—96; assoc. prof. Calif. State U. , Chico, 1996—2000, U. Colo., Colorado Springs, 2000—. Office: U Colo 1420 Austin Bluffs Pkwy Colorado Springs CO

MARTZEN, PHILIP D. physicist, software developer; b. Dinuba, Calif., Oct. 23, 1948; s. Dave and Vivian M.; m. Eloise Thompson, Jan. 29, 1972 (div. May 1988); Children: Natashya, Kinarii; m. Cynthia Stapp Landriz, July 1, 1995 (div. May 1997). BS, U. Calif., Santa Barbara, 1973, PhD, 1979. Staff mem. Geodynamics Corp., Santa Barbara, Calif., 1979-95; cons. Frontier Tech. Inc., 1996; cons. speech tech. lab. Panasonic, 1997; engrng. splst. Aerospace Corp., El Segundo, Calif., 1997—, mem. physics patent com., 1999—. Contbr. to profl. jours. V.p. REACTS, Santa Barbara, 1995-96; mem. Sci. and Engring. Coun. Santa Barbara, 1995—. Republican. Episcopalian. Avocations: golf, rock climbing, sailing, hiking. Home: 4166 San Martin Way Santa Barbara CA 93110-1429

MARUMOTO, WILLIAM HIDEO, management consultant; b. L.A., Dec. 16, 1934; s. Harry Y. and Midori Mary (Koyama) M.; m. Jean Masako Morishige, June 14, 1959; children: Wendy H. Vlahos, Todd M., Lani M. Moore, J. Tamiko Smith. BA, Whittier Coll., 1957; postgrad., U. Oreg., 1957-58. Dir. alumni rels. Whittier (Calif.) Coll., 1958-65; assoc. dir. alumni and devel. UCLA, 1965-68; v.p. planning and devel. Calif. Inst. of the Arts, L.A., 1968-69; sr. cons. Peat, Marwick & Mitchell, 1969; asst. to sec. HEW, Washington, 1969; spl. asst. Pres. of U.S., 1970-73; pres. The Interface Group Ltd., 1973-89; chmn. The Interface Group Ltd./Boyden, 1989-92, mng. dir. ptnr., 1992-2000, chmn., CEO, 2000—. Lectr. on career strategy, planning and diversity, 1973—; mem. White House Pers. Task Force, 1981-88, White House Conf. on Small Bus., 1986. Trustee Whittier Coll., 1978-2002, Japanese Am. Nat. Mus., 1989—, Mex. Am. Legal Def. and Ednl. Fund, 1989-93, Wolf Trap Found. for Performing Arts, 1995-2001, Coun. for Advancement and Support Edn., 1980-84; chmn. Nat. Japanese Am. Meml. Found., 1994-97, chmn., 1995-97; chmn. Leadership Edn. for Asian Pacifics, Inc., 1994-97; bd. dirs. Congl. Asian Am. Caucus Inst., 1997—, chmn. 2001—, Nat. Asian Pacific Ctr. on Aging, 1999—; mem. assocs. coun. George Washington U. Sch. Bus. and Pub. Mgmt., 1997—. Recipient Stanley Suyat Meml. Leadership award Asian Am. Govt. Exec. Network, 2002; named one of Am.'s Top 150 Exec. Recruiters, Harper & Rowe Pubs., 1992, 94, One of 500 Most Influential Asian Americans, Ave. Avenue Mag., 1996, Most Influential Asian Am. in Washington, Asian Week, 1997. Mem. Assn. Exec. Search Cons. (bd. dirs. 1994-97), U.S. Nat. Assn. Corp. and Profl. Recruiters, Congl. Country Club. Republican. Methodist. Home: 8808 Brook Rd Mc Lean VA 22102-1509 Office: The Interface Group Ltd 1054 31st St NW Ste 270 Washington DC 20037 E-mail: intrfacgrp@aol.com.

MARÚN, GIOCONDA, Spanish language educator; b. San Juan, Argentina, Nov. 21, 1942; came to the U.S., 1973; d. Simón and Josefina Victoria Marún. MA in Spanish Am. Lit., St. John's U., 1974; PhD, Nat. U. Buenos Aires, 1979. Chair modern langs. and lits. dept. Fordham U., Bronx, N.Y., 1993-96, prof. Spanish, 1995—. Mem. Ctr. d'Etudes des Lit. et des Civilisations du Rio de la Plata, U. Sorbonne; pres. 6th Internat. Congress, Fordham U., 1998. Author: El modernismo argentino incógnito en La Ondinal del Plata y Revista literaria (1875-1880), 1993; editor: Olimpio Pitango de Monalia, 1994; contbr. articles to profl. jours.; co-author, editor: Selected Procs. Ctr. d'Etudes des Lit. et des Civilisations du Rio de la Plata, 2000. Recipient award, NEH, 1982, OAS, 1992. Mem.: Am. Assn. Tchrs. of Spanish and Portuguese (co-chair biennial N.E. meeting 1986—88, editl. bd. 2001—), Internat. Assn. Iberoam. Lit. (editl. bd. 1992—96), Columbia U. L.Am. Seminar (assoc.). Home: 4-B 470 Halstead Ave Harrison NY 10528 Office: Fordham U Modern Langs Dept 441 E Fordham Rd Bronx NY 10458 Office Fax: 718-817-2655. E-mail: marun@fordham.edu.

MARUOKA, JO ANN ELIZABETH, retired information systems manager; b. Monrovia, Calif., Jan. 1, 1945; d. John Constantine and Pearl (Macovei) Gotsinas; m. Lester Hideo Maruoka, Nov. 8, 1973 (div. Aug. 1992); stepchildren: Les Scott Kaleohano, Lee Stuart Keola. BA with honors, UCLA, 1966; MBA, U. Hawaii, 1971. Office mgr. and asst. R. Wenkam, Photographer, Honolulu, 1966-69; computer mgmt. intern and sys. analyst Army Computer Sys. Command, 1969-78; reservations mgr. Hale Koa Hotel, 1978-79; equal employment opportunity specialist U.S. Army Pacific Hdqs., 1979-80, computer specialist, 1980-87, supervisory info. sys. mgr., chief info. tech. plans and programs, 1987-2001; ret., 2001. Bd. dirs. High Performance Computing and Comm. Coun., Tiverton, R.I.; pacific v.p. Fedn. Govt. Info. Processing Couns., Washington, 1992-95. Mem. Nat. and Hawaii Women's Polit. Caucus, Honolulu, 1987—; pres. Fed. Women's Coun. Hawaii, Honolulu, 1976-77, advisor, 1977—. Recipient Svc. award Fed. Women's Coun. Hawaii, 1986, EEO Excellence award Sec. of Army, 1989, Pacific Fed. Mgr. award Honolulu-Pacific Fed. Exec. Bd., 1990, Info. Resources Mgmt. award Interagy. Com. on Info. Resources Mgmt., 1991, Lead Dog Leadership award Fedn. Govt. Info. Processing Couns., 1993; named One of Fed. 100 (Execs.) of Yr., Fed. Computer Week, 1996. Mem. NAFE, Nat. Women's Polit. Caucus, AAUW, LWV, Armed Forces Comm.-Electronics Assn. (Hawaii chpt., Internat. award for Info. Resources Mgmt. Excellence 1992), Assn. U.S. Army (Pacific Fed. Mgr. award 1990), Federally Employed Women (advisor Aloha and Rainbow chpts. 1977—), Army Signal Corps Regtl. Assn. (Bronze Order of Mercury 1997, Silver Order of Mercury, 2001), Hawaii Intergovt. Info. Processing Coun. (pres. 1988-89, svc. award 1989). Avocations: travel, reading, tai chi, support of performing arts.

MARUPUDI, SAMBASIVA RAO, surgeon, educator; b. Chintalapudi, India, July 1, 1952; came to U.S., 1976; s. Venkateswarlu and Nagendramma (Gaddipati) M.; m. Usha Nandipati, Mar. 25, 1976; children: Neena, Neelima. MB, BS, Guntur (India) Med. Coll., 1974. Diplomate Am. Bd. Surgery, Am. Bd. Colon and Rectal Surgery. Rotation intern St. Clare's Hosp., Schenectady, 1976-77; resident in gen. surgery. St. Agnes Hosp., Balt., 1977-78, Franklin Square Hosp., Balt., 1978-82; fellow in colon and rectal surgery U. Tex. Health Scis. Ctr., Houston, 1982-83; pvt. practice, Amarillo, Tex., 1983—. Clin. asst. prof. dept. surgery Tex. Tech U Health Scis. Ctr., Amarillo, 1984—. Fellow ACS, Am. Soc. Colon and Rectal Surgeons, Internat. Coll. Surgeons; mem. AMA, Tex. Med. Assn., Potter-Randall County Med. Soc. (past pres.), Tex. Soc. Colon and Rectal Surgeons (past pres.). Democrat. Hindu. dr. Office: 800 Quail Creek Dr # 103 Amarillo TX 79124-1609 E-mail: smarupudi@aol.com., drmarupudi@hotmail.com.

MARVEL, L. PAIGE, federal judge; b. Easton, Md., Dec. 6, 1949; d. E. Warner Marvel and Louise Harrington Harrison; m. Robert H. Dyer, Jr., Aug. 9, 1975; children: Alex W. Dyer, Kelly E. Dyer. BA magna cum laude, Notre Dame Coll., 1971; JD with honors, U. Md., 1974. Bar: Md. 1974, U.S. Dist. Ct. Md. 1974, U.S. Tax Ct. 1975, U.S. Ct. Appeals (4th cir.) 1977, U.S. Supreme Ct. 1980, U.S. Ct. Claims 1981, D.C. 1985. Assoc. Garbis & Schwait, P.A., Balt., 1974-76, shareholder, 1976-85, Garbis, Marvel & Junghans, P.A., Balt., 1985-86, Melnicove, Kaufman, Weiner, Smouse & Garbis, P.A., Balt., 1986-88; ptnr. Venable, Baetjer and Howard LLP, 1988-98; judge U.S. Tax Ct., Washington, 1998—. Bd. dirs. Loyola/Notre Dame Libr., Inc.; mem. U. Md. Law Sch. Bd. Vis., 1995—2001; mem. adv. com. U.S. Dist. Ct. Md., 1991—93. Co-editor procedure dept. Jour. Taxation, 1989-98; contbr. chpts. to books, articles to profl. jours. Active Women's Law Ctr., 1974-85, Md. Dept. Econ. and Community Devel. Adv. Comm., 1978-80. Recipient recognition award Balt. Is Best Program, 1981; named One of Md.'s Top 100 Women, The Daily Record, 1998; recipient MSBA Taxation section's Tax Excellence award, 2002. Fellow Am. Bar Found., Am. Coll. Tax Counsel (regent 1995-98); mem. ABA (sect. taxation coun. dir. 1989-92, vice-chair com. ops. 1993-95, Disting. Svc. award), Am. Law Inst. (advisor Ali restatement of law third, law governing lawyers), Md. Bar Assn. (chmn. taxation sect. 1982-83, bd. dirs. 1988-90, 96-98, Disting. Svc. award), Md. Bar Found., Balt. Bar Assn. (at-large exec. coun.), Am. Tax Policy Inst. (trustee 1997-98), Serjeant's Inn, Rule Day Club. Avocations: golf, music, travel. Home: 7109 Sheffield Rd Baltimore MD 21212-1628 Office: US Tax Ct 400 2d St NW Washington DC 20217-0001

MARVEL, M. KIM, psychologist, researcher; b. Manhattan, Kans., Dec. 2, 1952; s. John A. and Frances J. M.; m. Connie McGuinn, May 26, 1976; children: Aron V., Skylar W. BA, U. No. Colo., 1975; MA, San Francisco State U., 1979; PhD, Utah State U., 1987. Asst. prof. Am. Samoa C.C., Pago Pago, 1979-81, U. Wis., Wausau, 1981-89, dir. behavioral medicine dept. family practice, 1989-93; dir. behavioral medicine Ft. Collins (Colo.) Family Practice Ctr., 1993-99, assoc. dir. residency program, 1999—. Chair Colo. Behavioral Sci. Consortium, Denver, 1997-98. Contbr. articles to profl. jours. Fulbright scholar, 1992-93. Mem.: APA, Collaborative Family Health Care Coalition, Soc. Tchrs. Family Medicine. Avocations: running, hiking. Home: 1357 Northern Ct Fort Collins CO 80521 Office: Family Medicine Ctr 1025 S Pennock Pl Fort Collins CO 80524-3257 E-mail: mkm@libra.pvh.org.

MARVEL, THOMAS STAHL, architect; b. Newburgh, N.Y., Mar. 15, 1935; s. Gordon Simis and Madelyn Emigh (Jova) M.; m. Lucilla Wellington Fuller, Apr. 19, 1958; children— Deacon Simis, Jonathan Jova, Thomas Stahl AB, Dartmouth Coll., 1956; MArch, Harvard U., 1962. Registered architect, N.C., P.R., Mass., N.Y. Designer Synergetics, Inc., Raleigh, N.C., 1958; designer IBEC Housing, N.Y.C., 1959; ptnr., architect Torres-Beauchamp-Marvel, San Juan, P.R., 1960-85, Marvel-Flores-Cobian, San Juan, 1985-97; ptnr. Thomas S. Marvel Architects, 1997—. Prof. Sch. Architecture, U. P.R., Rio Piedras, 1967-89. Author: Antonin Nechodoma, Architect, 1994; co-author: Parish Churches of Puerto Rico, 1984. Works include Am. Embassy, Guatemala, 1973, U.S. Courthouse and Fed. Office Bldg., V.I., 1976, City Hall, Bayamon, P.R., 1978, Mcpl. Baseball Stadium, Bayamon, 1975, Am. Embassy, Costa Rica, 1986. Bd. dirs. St. John's Sch., San Juan, 1976-93. Recipient 1st award for regional coll. design U. P.R., Utuado, 1983; Harvard Grad. Sch. Design Julia Amory Appleton travelling fellow, 1962, Henry Klumb prize, 1991. Fellow AIA (bd. dirs. 1993-96, Design award for Fla. Caribbean region 1981, 84-85, 90-91); mem. P.R. Coll. Architects, Acad. Arts and Scis. Clubs: Harvard (N.Y.C.). Roman Catholic. Home: 450 Calle Del Valle San Juan PR 00915-3315 Office: Thomas S Marvel Architects 161 Calle San Jorge Santurce San Juan PR 00911-2018 E-mail: tsmarvel@marvelarch.com.

MARVIN, CATHERINE A. financial consultant; b. Asheville, N.C., Aug. 16, 1966; d. Robert L Morrison and Anne C. Veitch, Thomas H Veitch (Stepfather), Kay Morrison (Stepmother). BBA, S.W. Tex. State U., 1988. Cert. Series 7, 63, 65. Asst. v.p./trust officer Bank of Am., Dallas, 1994—99; fin. cons. Salomon Smith Barney, San Antonio, 1999—2002. Mem. Bexar County Young Republicans, San Antonio, 2001—02. Mem.: Southwest Tex. State U. Alumnae Assn., Humane Soc. U.S., Zeta Tau Alpha Alumnae Assn. (coord. collegiate/alumnae rels. 2000—02). Baptist. Avocations: travel, reading, cooking. Office: Salomon Smith Barney 300 Convent St 28th Fl San Antonio TX 78205 Office Fax: 210-271-6194. Business E-Mail: catherine.a.marvin@rssmb.com.*

MARVIN, CHARLES ARTHUR, law educator; b. July 14, 1942; s. Burton Wright and Margaret Fiske (Medlar) M.; m. Elizabeth Maureen Woodrow, July 4, 1970 (div. July 1987); m. Elizabeth Dale Wilson, Mar. 20, 1999; children: Colin, Kristin. BA, U. Kans., 1964; postgrad., U. Toulouse, France, 1964-65; JD, U. Chgo., 1968, M of Comparative Law, 1970. Bar: Ill. 1969. Legal intern EEC, Brussels, 1970; lectr. law U. Kent, Canterbury, Eng., 1970-71; asst. prof. law Laval U., Quebec City, Que., Can., 1971-73; legal adv. constnl., internat. and adminstrv. law sect. Can. Dept. Justice, Ottawa, Ont., 1973-76; assoc. prof. law U. Man., Winnipeg, Can., 1976-77; dir. adminstrv. law project Law Reform Commn., Ottawa, 1977-80; prof. law Villanova (Pa.) U., 1980-83; dir. Adminstrv. Law Reform Project Can. Dept. Justice, 1983-85; prof. law Ga. State U., 1985—, assoc. dean, 1987-89. Legal advisor on adminstrv. code revision to Govt. of Kazakhstan, 1993; law faculty devel. adviser to Bulgaria, 1993; dir. internat. human rights law summer program Regent U. Sch. Law, 1998; lectr., Ivory Coast, 1998; Fulbright prof. Riga Grad. Sch. Law, Latvia, 2000-2002. Acad. mem. Southwestern Legal Found. Fulbright scholar U. Toulouse, 1964-65, Summerfield scholar U. Kansas, 1961-64, U. Chgo. scholar, 1965-68; Ford Found. Comparative Law fellow, 1968-70. Mem. ABA, Ill. Bar Assn., Chgo. Bar Assn., Am. Soc. Internat. Law, Am. Fgn. Law Assn., Internat. Bar Assn., Internat. Law Assn., Can. Bar Assn., Can. Coun. on Internat. Law, Phi Beta Kappa, Omicron Delta Kappa, Phi Beta Delta, Phi Delta Phi. Office: Ga State U Coll Law PO Box 4037 Atlanta GA 30302-4037 E-mail: cmarvin@gsu.edu.

MARVIN, CHARLES RODNEY, JR. lawyer; b. Elizabeth, N.J., Feb. 26, 1953; s. Charles Rodney and Doris Marie (Richards) Marvin; m. Carol Ann Welterroth, Aug. 30, 1975 (dec.); children: Kathryn, Kristin, Cynthia, Gregory; m. Nancy Agnes Ruggiero, Mar. 24, 2001; 1 stepchild Susanna Myirski. BA in Econs., Mich. State U., 1975; JD, Boston U., 1978; LLM in Mil. Law, Judge Advocate Gen. Sch., 1987; LLM in Govt. Contracts, George Washington U., 1995. Bar: N.J. 1982, U.S. Dist. Ct. N.J. 1982, U.S. Ct. Mil. Appeals 1982, U.S. Ct. Appeals (fed. cir.) 1994, D.C. 1996, U.S. Ct. Fed. Claims 1996. Commd. 2nd lt. U.S. Army, 1975, advanced through grades to major, 1994, nuclear missile officer Germany, 1979-82, mil. prosecutor Fort Sill, Okla., 1983-86; sr. def. counsel U.S. Army Trial Def. Svc., Ft. Polk, La., 1987-89; trial counsel, chief protest br. U.S. Army Contract Appeals Divsn., Arlington, Va., 1990-94; ptnr. Venable, Baetjer, Howard & Civiletti, Washington, 1994—. Mem. ABA (vice-chair, bid protest com., pub. contract law sect. 1992-93), FBA, Bd. Contract Appeals Bar Assn. (bd. govs. 1993-96), Fed. Cir. Bar Assn., John Carroll Soc., Nat. Contract Mgmt. Assn., Bishop McNamara High School (bd. dirs.), Forestville, MD. Roman Catholic. Avocations: musical composing, adult education, golf. Office: Venable Baetjer et al 1201 New York Ave NW Ste 1000 Washington DC 20005-3197

MARVIN, JAMES CONWAY, librarian, consultant; b. Warroad, Minn., Aug. 3, 1927; s. William C. and Isabel (Carlquist) M.; m. Patricia Katharine Moe, Sept. 8, 1947; children: James Conway, Jill C., Jack C. BA, U. Minn., 1950, MA, 1966. City librarian, Kaukauna, Wis., 1952-54; chief librarian Eau Claire, 1954-56; dir. Cedar Rapids (Iowa) Pub. Library, 1956-67, Topeka Pub. Library, 1967-92. ALA-Rockefeller Found. vis. prof. Inst. Libr. Sci., U. Philippines, 1964-65; vis. lectr. dept. librarianship Emporia (Kans.) State U., 1970-80; chmn. Kans. del. to White House Conf. on Librs. and Info. Svcs., Gov.'s Com. on Libr. Resources, 1980-81; mem. Kans. Libr. Adv. Commn., 1992—, chmn., 1998—. Served with USNR, 1945-46. Mem. ALA, Iowa Libr. Assn. (past pres.), Kans. Libr. Assn., Philippine Libr. Assn. (life), Mountain Plains Libr. Assn. Home: 40 SW Pepper Tree Ln Topeka KS 66611-2055

MARVIN, JOHN GEORGE, clergyman, church organization executive; b. Summit, N.J., May 8, 1912; s. George and Caroline (Whitman) M.; m. Elizabeth Anne Wheater, June 30, 1944; children: Caroline Wheater Dorney, Elizabeth Anne West, Martha Jane Hobbs, Frances Alice Heidel. BS, Davidson Coll., 1933; ThB, Princeton Theol. Sem., 1936; DD, Coll. of Emporia, 1964; LLD, Tarkio Coll., 1964. Ordained to ministry Presbyn. Ch., 1936. Pastor, Windsor, N.Y., 1936-37, Montrose, Pa., 1937-44, Lewistown, 1944-52, Denton, Tex., 1952-61; presbytery exec. Greater Kansas City, Mo., 1961-65; pastor 1st Presbyn. Ch., Bartlesville, Okla., 1965-69; sr. min. Chevy Chase Presbyn. Ch., Washington, 1969-77, pastor emeritus, 1978—. Interim sr. min. Catonsville Ch., Balt., 1978, 3d Ch., Rochester, N.Y., 1978-79, 1st Ch., Ft. Worth, 1979-80, Gaithersburg, Md., 1980-81, Westfield, N.J., 1981-82, Ch. of Palms, Sarasota, Fla., 1982-83, Bethel Ch., Balt., 1983-84, Pine Shores Ch., Sarasota, Fla., 1984, Interfaith Chapel, Silver Spring, Md., 1984-87; mem. exec. com. Pa. Coun. Chs., 1949-52, Tex. Coun. Chs., 1953-61; mem. exec. com., long range chmn. Greater Kansas City Coun. Chs., 1962-65; chmn. campus Christian Life Tex. Synod, 1958-61; chmn. nat. mission Pa. Synod, 1949-52; sec. nominations com. Gen. Assemly U.P. Ch., 1955-58, chmn. com. on baptized children, 1969-70, mem. com. of nine on synods bounderies, 1970-72. Contbr. articles to religious publs. Bd. dirs. Midwest Christian Counseling Ctr., Kansas City, Mo., 1963-69, Presbyn. Homes of Okla., Inc., 1966-69; mem. jud. commn. Synod of Okla.-Ark., 1966-69; mem. strategy com. Bd. Nat. Missions, 1968-70, British-Am. Preaching Exch., preaching missions to Alaska and Mex.; leader and lectr. on religious heritage tours in Europe, Middle East, Egypt, Caribbean and Orient, 1972-84; bd. dirs. Tarkio Coll., 1961-67, Westminster Found., Pa. State U., 1945-52, North Tex. State U., 1952-61; mem. ministerial rels. com. Nat. Capital Union Presbytery, 1973-78; bd. visitors Warren Wilson Coll. Mem. Rotary, Beta Theta Pi. Republican. Home: 14500 Elmhan Ct Silver Spring MD 20906-1839 E-mail: Betty4John@aol.com.

MARVIN, MONICA LOUISE WOLF, lawyer; b. San Francisco, Feb. 3, 1947; d. Andrew John and Hazel Louise Wolf; m. Gregory Lewis Marvin, Aug. 17, 1969; children: Brett Lewis, Elizabeth Louise. Student, Pacific U., Forest Grove, Oreg., 1964-66, Sonoma State U., Rohnert Park, Calif., 1966-67; BA in Psychology, Chico (Calif.) State U., 1969; JD, Empire Coll., Santa Rosa, Calif., 1982. Bar: Calif. 1982, U.S. Dist. Ct. Calif. 1982. Assoc. Fitzgerald Fitzgerald and Gowen, Santa Rosa, Calif., 1982-83, Gowen and Marvin, Santa Rosa, 1983-85, Rodeno Robertson & Assocs., Napa, Calif., 1985-86; pvt. practice St Helena, 1986—; of counsel Hardell & Yost, LLP, 2000—. Judge pro tempore Napa County Consol. Cts., Small Claims Divsn., 1991—. Bd. dirs., v.p. Cmty. Resources for Children, Napa, 1991-94; mem. Napa County Commn. on Children, Youth and Family, 1994-97; mem. Napa County Dem. Ctrl. Com., 1994-98; mem. adv. bd. Napa County Vol. Ctr. Ombudsman Program, 1994-95; founder, chair St. Helena C. of C. Jumelage Com., Sister Chamber affiliation with Libourne C. of C. and Industry, France. Mem. State Bar Calif., Napa County Bar Assn. (bd. dirs. 1994), Napa Women Lawyers (past pres., sec. 1987-92). Office: PO Box 271 Saint Helena CA 94574-0271 E-mail: mwmarvin@napanet.net.

MARVIN, ROY MACK, retired foundry executive; b. May 4, 1931; s. Merrill McKinley and Jennie Marie (Larsen) M.; m. Diane Valeri MacKenzie, Nov. 26, 1955. AS, Grays Harbor Coll., 1951; BS, Lewis and Clark Coll., 1954. CPA, Oreg. Acct. Pope, Loback & Co., Portland, Oreg., 1953-54, 56-69; contr. Ranch Homes, Inc., Beaverton, 1959-61, Precision Castparts Corp., Portland, 1961-96, treas., 1967-93, dir., 1967-99, v.p. fin., 1970-80, sec., 1983-96. Dir. Physicians Assn. Clackamas County, Providence, Milwaukie, Oreg.; cons. Precision Castparts Corp., 1996, bd. dirs. Bd. dirs. Dwyer Hosp., 1970-79, 84-86; mem. exec. com. Greater Portland Bus. Group on Health, 1980-90; mem. Clackamas County Econ. Devel. Commn., 1984-91, dep. Oreg. Bus. Coun., 1982-90; bd. dirs. Boys and Girls Aid Soc. Oreg., 1990-2002, non-dir. mem. adminstrn. com., 2002—. With U.S. Army, 1954-56. Mem. AICPA, Nat. Assn. Accts. (past pres. Portland chpt.), Planning Execs. Inst. (past pres. Portland chpt.), Fin. Execs. Inst., Oreg. Soc. CPAs, Associated Oreg. Industries (bd. dirs. 1990-96, vice-chmn. 1992-94), Assoc. Oreg. Indus. Pol. Action Com. (pres. 1991, trustee), North Clackamas C. of C. (pres. 1973), Oreg. Metals Industry Coun. (pres. 1991-94), Multnomah Athletic Club. Republican. Presbyterian.

MARVIN, URSULA BAILEY, retired geologist; b. Bradford, Vt., Aug. 20, 1921; d. Harold Leslie and Alice Miranda (Bartlett) Bailey; m. Lloyd Burton Chaisson, June 28, 1944 (div. 1951); m. Thomas Crockett Marvin, Apr. 1, 1952. BA, Tufts Coll., 1943; MA, Harvard/Radcliffe Coll., 1946; PhD, Harvard U., 1969. Rsch. asst. dept. geology U. Chgo., 1947-50; mineralogist Union Carbide Corp., N.Y.C., 1952-58; instr. dept. geology Tufts U., Medford, Mass., 1958-61; geologist Smithsonian Astrophys. Obs., Cambridge, 1961-98; lectr. geology Harvard U., 1974-92; sr. geologist emeritus Harvard-Smithsonian Ctr. for Astrophysics, 1998. Vis. prof. dept. geology Ariz. State U., Tempe, 1978; trustee Tufts U., 1975-85, trustee emeritus, 1988—; trustee U. Space Rsch. Assn., Columbia Md., 1979-84, chmn., 1982-83; sec.-gen. Internat. Commn. on History Geol. Scis., 1989-96, v.p. for N.Am., 1996—. Author: Continental Drift, 1973; contbr. chpt.: Astronomy from Space, 1983, The Planets, 1985, Les Météorites, 1996, James Hutton-Present and Future, 1999, The Earth Inside and Out: Some Major Contributions to Geology in the Twentieth Century, 2002; assoc. editor Earth in Space, Am. Geophys. Union, 1988-90; contbr. articles to profl. jours. Mem. Lunar and Planetary Sci. Coun., Houston, 1987-91; chair Antarctic Meteorite Working Group NSF-NASA-Smithsonian Instn., 1993-99. Recipient Antarctic Svc. medal NSF, 1983, Sustained Superior Achievement award SAO, 1988, 93, 96, Lifetime Achievement award Women in Sci. and Engring., 1997, Lifetime Achievement award Harvard-Smithsonian Ctr. for Astrophysics, 1997; Asteroid Marvin named in her honor Minor Planet Bur. of Internat. Astron. Union, 1991, Marvin Nunatak (mountain peak rising through the Antarctic ice sheet) named in her honor U.S. Bd. on Geog. Names, 1992. Fellow AAAS, Meteoritical Soc. (pres. 1975-76), Geol. Soc. Am. (chmn. history of geology divsn. 1982-83, History of Geology award 1986); mem. Assn. Women in Sci., Am. Geophys. Union, History of Earth Scis. Soc. (pres. 1991), Sigma Xi (pres. Harvard-Radcliffe chpt. 1971-72). Avocations: worldwide birding. Office: Harvard-Smithsonian Ctr for Astrophysics 60 Garden St Cambridge MA 02138-1516 E-mail: umarvin@cfa.harvard.edu.

MARVIN, WILLIAM GLENN, JR. former foreign service officer; b. Dobbs Ferry, N.Y., Oct. 30, 1920; s. William Glenn and Charlotte (Linden) M.; m. Sheila Wells, June 6, 1945 (dec.); children: Sally Marvin Lockhart, William Glenn III (dec.), Wells.; m. Suzanne Franzon, Oct. 16, 1982. Student, U. Calif., Berkeley, 1938-40; BS, Harvard U., 1942; MA, Stanford U., 1948. European rep. Hoover Instn., 1948-49; polit. scientist Stanford Research Inst., 1949-52; commd. fgn. service officer Dept. State, 1952; vice consul Algiers, 1952-55; consul Berlin, 1955-60; consul, prin. officer Fort de France, Martinique, 1964-66; econ. sec. CENTO, Ankara, Turkey, 1974-76; consul gen. Bordeaux, France, 1977-80; ret., 1980. Served to capt. U.S. Army, 1942-46. Mem. U.S. Fgn. Service Assn., Assn. Bordeaux-L.A. Clubs: Connetablie de Guyenne, Ordre de Tursan.

MARWEDEL, WARREN JOHN, lawyer; b. Chgo., July 3, 1944; s. August Frank and Eleanor (Wolgamot) M.; m. Marilyn Baran, Apr. 12, 1975. BS in Marine Engring., U.S. Merchant Marine Acad., 1966; JD, Loyola U., Chgo., 1972. Bar: Ill. 1972, U.S. Dist. Ct. (no. dist.) Ill. 1972, U.S. Supreme Ct. 1974. With U.S. Merchant Marines, 1966-70. Mem. ABA (Ho. of Dels. 1989-96), Ill. Bar Assn., Chgo. Bar Assn., Maritime Law Assn.(sec.), Propeller Club (Chgo. pres. 1982). Avocations: boating, reading, history. Office: Marwedel Minichello & Reeb PC 10 S Riverside Plz Chicago IL 60606-3708

MARX, ANNE (MRS. FREDERICK E. MARX), poet; b. Germany; came to U.S., 1936, naturalized, 1938; d. Jacob and Susan (Weinberg) Loewenstein; m. Frederick E. Marx, Feb. 12, 1937; children: Thomas J., Stephen L. Student, U. Heidelberg, U. Berlin. Mem. staffs N.Y.C. Writers Conf., 1965, Iona Coll., 1964, 65, 70, Wagner Coll., 1965, Poetry Workshop, Fairleigh Dickinson U., 1962, 63, 64, Poetry Soc. Am. Workshop, 1970-71, 78-79; Bronxville Adult Sch. Lecture Series, 1972; bd. dir. poetry series Donnell Library Ctr. (N.Y. Pub. Library), 1970-74; poetry day chmn. Westchester County, 1959—; Poetry Day Workshop, Ark., 1966, 70, Ark. Writers Conf., 1971, South and West Conf., Okla., 1972; vis. poet So. U., 1979; tchr., poetry readings, Jakarta, Indonesia, summer 1979; poetry workshop leader Scarsdale Cultural Ctr., 1981-82; conv. speaker Nat. Fedn. State Poetry Socs., 1974, 81, 82; condr. symposium Immigrant Voices, Pa. State U., 1986; judge Chapbook Award Nat. Federation of Poetry Socs., 1994, 1996-97; judge various nat. poetry contests; ongoing project: Selected Poems from Half a Century, 1997—. Poet; more than 1500 poems published in nat. mags., anthologies, lit. jours. and newspapers; Author: Ein Buechlein, 1935, Into the Wind of Waking, 1960, The Second Voice, 1963, By Grace of Pain, 1966, By Way of People, 1970, A Time to Mend; selected poems, 1973; A Conversation with Anne Marx; 2 hour talking book for blind, 1974; Hear of Israel and Other Poems, 1975, 40 Love Poems for 40 Years, 1977, Face Lifts for All Seasons, 1980, 45 Love Poems for 45 Years, 1982, Holocaust: Hurts to Healings, 1984, German edit. Wunden und Narben, 1986; A Further Semester, 1985, Love in Late Season (New Poems by Anne Marx), 1993; co-editor: Pegasus in the Seventies, 1973; contbr. to American Women Poets Discuss Their Craft, 1983, The Courage to Grow Old, 1989, A Collection of Essays by Ballantine Books, 1989; nat. editor poetry recs., Lamont Library at Harvard, stas. WFAS, WRNW, WEVD, WRVR, Voice of Am., The Pen Woman, 1986-88, Christian Sci. Monitor Anthology of Poems, 1989, Canadian Anthology, 1991, Irish Anthology, 1991, M. Rukeyser Anthology, 1999. Recipient Am. Weave Chapbook award 1960, Nat. Sonnet 1959, 67, 81, award World Order Narrative Poets, 1981-85 1959, 67, prizes Nat. Fedn. Women's Clubs 1959, 60, Nat. Fedn. State Poetry Socs. 1962, 65, 66, 73, 80-83, South and West Publn. award 1965, Greenwood prize Eng. 1966, 2d Ann. Viola Hayes Parsons award 1977, award Delbrook Center Advanced Studies 1978, 1st prize Nat. Essay Competition, 1990, N.Y. State Outstanding Writer award, 1991; named Poet of the Year N.Y. Poetry Forum, 1981; winner Chapbook competition Crossroads Press, 1984, Ann. Writer's

Digest award, 1983-90; recipient N.Y. State 1st prize for Poetry, 1995. Mem. Poetry Soc. Am. (life, exec. bd. 1965-70, v.p. 1971-72, 2 fellowships, Cecil Hemley Meml. award 1974), Poetry Soc. Gt. Britain, Nat. League Am. Pen Women (pres. Westchester county br. 1962-64, North Atlantic regional chmn. 1964-66, nat. letters bd. 1972-74, biennial poetry workshop leader, nat. poetry editor 1974-78, N.Y. State lit. chmn. 1979-80, N.Y. State pres. 1982-84, 2d nat. v.p. 1984-86, nat. editor Pen Woman mag. 1986-88, contbg. editor 1990—, Biennial Book award 1976, Biennial awards (4), 1982, (2), 1984, Writer of Yr. 1991, N.Y. State Poetry award 1996, 1st prize Biennial Conv. 1998, established Anne Marx Sestina award 1998), Acad. Am. Poets, Poet Soc. Pa., Composers, Authors and Artists Am., Inc. (poetry editor mag. 1973-78), Poets and Writers, Inc., N.Y. Poetry Forum (life). Achievements include being subject of story "An American by Choice, A Poet's Credo" pub. in The PEN Woman mag., Nov. 1988, The Courage to Grow Old, 1989, N.Y. Times interview "Finding Poetry in All of Life's Events," 1993; collected works N.Y. Pub. Libr.: Anne Marx Archives, 1992, early German material added to collection, 1994, Juvenile Diaries, 2000. *To be undeterred is the key to any achievement that is important to our lives. Undeterred by detractors asserting that one's goal is impossible to reach. Undeterred by blame or praise. Undeterred by demands of custom and fashion. Undeterred by all but the most essential bonds of family and friends. Undeterred even by the knowledge that there will be no greatness at the end of the long climb - only the satisfaction that we have tried to bring out the best that is in us, that we have added to our years that special ingredient we needed most to add zest to existence.*

MARX, DONALD LEE, statistician, educator; b. Kansas City, Mo., Feb. 20, 1938; s. George Fred and Elizabeth Barbara Marx; m. Barbara Jo Anderson, June 17, 1961; children: Timothy, Michelle Kuper. BA, St. Benedict Coll., 1959; BSEE, Kans. State U., 1961; MBA, PhD, U. of Houston, 1974. Engr. Boeing Airplane Co., Wichita, Kans., 1961—62; sr. engr. The Bendix Corp., Mishawaka, Ind., 1962—68; sys. engr. TRW, Houston, 1968—69; tchg. asst. and instr. U. of Houston, 1969—74; asst. prof. Mich. Technol. U., Houghton, Mich., 1974—75, La. State U., Baton Rouge, 1975—81; assoc. prof. U. of Alaska Anchorage, Anchorage, 1981—, prof. Cons. D. L. Marx, Anchorage, 1981—; instr. Ctr. for Internat. Mgmt. Devel., Riyadh, Saudi Arabia, 1999—99; vis. scholar Ctr. for Quality and Productivity Improvement, Madison, Wis., 1990—90. Contbr. articles to profl. jours. Referee Anchorge soccer leagues, Anchorage, 1983—88, Baton Rouge youth soccer leagues, Baton Rouge, 1977—81; mem. planning com. Making Statis. More Effective in Sch. and Bus., 1991—2002; mem. of youth ministry team St. Benedict Ch., Anchorage, 1998—2002. Mem.: Decision Sciences Inst., Inst. for Ops. Rsch. and Mgmt. Sci. (faculty rep. 1995—2002), Am. Statis. Assn. (sec. local chpt. 1986—91, v.p. local chpt. 1986—91, pres. local chpt. 1986—91). Roman Catholic. Avocations: softball, camping. Office: University of Alaska 3211 Providence Drive Anchorage AK 99508 Personal E-mail: donmarx@att.net. E-mail: afdlm@uaa.alaska.edu.

MARX, GARY DEAN, international education consultant, association executive; b. Manchester, S.D., Nov. 28, 1938; s. Harvey Fredrick and Lucille (Stemple) M.; m. Judy Rae Marx, June 18, 1961; children: John Fredrick, Daniel Winston. BA, U. S.D., 1960. CAE, ASPR, APR. Newscaster, announcer, dir. Sta. KSOO Radio and TV, Sioux Falls, S.D., 1958-61; newscaster, announcer Sta. WOW Radio and TV, Omaha, 1961-71; dir. comms. Westside Cmty. Schs., 1971-77; exec. dir. comms. Jefferson County Pub. Schs., Denver, 1977-79; sr. assoc. exec. Am. Assn. Sch. Adminstrs., Arlington, Va., 1979-96, exec. dir. Leadership for Learning Found., 1996-98; pres. Ctr. for Pub. Outreach, Inc., Vienna, 1998—. Sr. rsch. fellow Health, Energy and Productivity in Schs. project, Herndon, Va., 2000—; pub. rels. cons. Nat. Sch. Pub. Rels. Assn., RockviPle, Md., 1972—; v.p., owner Sta. KOAK Radio, Red Oak, Iowa, 1977-82; v.p. Comms. Devel. Inc., Denver, 1974-76; chief evaluator CIVITAS Internat. Exch. Program, Calabasas, Calif., 2000—. Author: Radio...Your Publics are Listening, 1976, Radio...Get the Message, 1977, Excellence in Our Schools...Making it Happen, 1984, Public Relations for Administrators, 1984, 88, Working with the News Media, 1993, Preparing Students for the 21st Century, 1996, 99, The Future of Community, 1999, Preparing Schools and School Systems for the 21st Century, 1999, Ten Trends . . . Educating Children for a Profoundly Different Future, 2000; contbr. articles to profl. jours. Founder, chmn. Keystone Cmty. Task Force, Omaha, 1970-77; mem. Omaha Parks and Recreation Bd., City of Omaha, 1975-77, mem. urban growth policy bd., 1976; mem. nat. edn. adv. com. for restoration Statue of Liberty-Ellis Island Found,. N.Y.C., 1984-86; mem. exec. com. edn. Commn. on Bicentennial of the U.S. Constitution, Washington, 1986-92; bd. dirs. Campaign for New Priorities, Washington, 1992-93; bd. dirs., founder Coalition for America's Children, Washington, 1992-98; mem. steering com. Libr. of Congress, Ctr. of the Book, Washington, 1992-99; mem. design arts program steering com. NEA, Washington, 1993-94; mem. grants selection com. Alliance for Arts Edn., John F. Kennedy Ctr. for the Performing Arts, Washington, 1993-96; mem. steering com., judge Disney Salute to the Am. Tchr., Burbank, Calif., 1993-97; mem. steering com., Emmy awards judge NATAS, N.Y.C., 1995-97; mem. adv. bd. NBC The More You Know campaign, N.Y.C., 1992-98; mem. nat. adv. bd. PBS, 1990-98; mem. steering com. Goals 2000 Arts Edn. Partnership NEA, Washington, 1993-98; mem. selection com. Nat. Tchr. of Yr. Program, Washington, 1979-99; judge USA Today All USA Acad. Team, Arlington, Va., 1995—; internat. cons., spkr. Ctr. for Civic Edn., Calabasas, Calif., 1996—, USIA, U.S. Dept. State, Washington, 1996—, internat. steering com. Civitas Internat., Strasbourg, France, 1996—. Mem. Nat. Sch. Pub. Rels. Assn. (numerous offices and bds. 1971—, accredited, Pres.'s award 1999), Pub. Rels. Soc. Am. (accredited), Am. Soc. Assn. Execs. (cert.), Edn. Writers Assn. (bd. dirs. 1979—), Am. Assn. Sch. Adminstrs. (Disting. Svc. award 2000), World Future Soc. (profl. mem.). Avocations: folk art, travel, reading, writing, photography. Office: Ctr for Pub Outreach 1831 Toyon Way Vienna VA 22182-3355 E-mail: gmarxcpo@aol.com.

MARX, GARY T. sociologist, writer; b. Hanford, Calif., Oct. 1, 1938; BA, UCLA, 1960; MA, U. Calif., Berkeley, 1962, PhD, 1966. Rsch. assoc. U. Calif., Berkeley, 1965-67, lectr. dept. sociology, 1966-67; rsch. assoc. Harvard-MIT Joint Ctr. for Urban Studies, 1967-73; asst. prof., lectr. dept. social rels. Harvard U., 1967-73; sr. rsch. assoc. Ctr. for Criminal Justice Harvard Law Sch., 1973-75; assoc. prof. MIT, 1973-79, prof., 1979-94, emeritus prof. dept. urban studies and planning, 1994; prof. U. Colo., Boulder, 1992-98, chair dept. sociology, 1992-96; vis. scholar U. Wash., 1999—. Vis. prof. U. Calif., San Diego, 1977-78, SUNY, Albany, 1980, Cath. U., Louvain, and Louvain La Neuve, Belgium, Tech. U., Vienna, Austria, 1993, Nankai U., China, 1995, U. Calif. Irvine, 2000, Berkeley, 2001—, Northwestern U., 2001; mem. exec. com. Am. Sociol. Assn., 1973-76; mem. adv. bd. Office of Tech. Assessment, 1985-87, NAS, 1989-91, Electronic Privacy Info. Ctr., 1992—; presenter testimony U.S. Congress, 1981, 91, 97. Author: Protest and Prejudice, 1967, rev. edit., 1969, Japanese edit., 1971, Undercover: Police Surveillance in America, 1988, Chinese edit., 1995; co-author: (with others) Inquiries in Sociology, 1972, (with N. Goodman) Society Today, rev. edit., 3d. edit., 1978, 4th edit., 1982, (with Doug McAdam) Collective Behavior and Collective Behavior Process, 1993; contbr. numerous articles to profl. jours.; editor: (book) Muckracking Sociology: Research as Social Criticism, 1972, (jours.) Social Problems, 1969-75, Am. Sociol. Rev., 1972-75, Ann. Rev. Sociology, 1978-84, 97-98, Jour. Conflict Resolution, 1984-91, Qualitative Sociology, Justice Quar., 1990-93, Sociol. Forum, 1991-96, Criminology, 1991-93; co-editor: (books) (with others) Confrontation: Psychology and Problems of Today, 1970, (with N. Goodman) Sociology: Classic and Popular Approaches, 1980, (with C. Fijnaut) Undercover: Police Surveillance in Comparative Perspective, 1995; mem. editl. bd. The Info. Soc., 1995—, The Am. Sociologist, 1997—, Policing and Society, 1997—, Ethics and Info. Tech., 1998—. Recipient Disting. Scholarship award Am. Sociol. Assn., 1990, named Jensen lectr., 1989; Outstanding Book award Acad. Criminal Justice Scis., 1990, Bruce Smith Lifetime Achievement award, 1999; Silver Gavel award ABA, 1991; Guggenheim fellow, 1970-71, rsch. fellow Ctr. for Advanced Study in the Behavioral Scis., 1987-88, 96-97, fellow Woodrow Wilson Internat. Ctr. for Scholars, Washington, 1997-98; rsch. grantee NSF, 1973-75, 85-86, 91-95, 20th Century Fund, 1982-87, Austauschdienst, Whiting Found., Deutscher Akademischer, 1991; resident scholar Rockefeller Study and Conf. Ctr., Belagio, Italy, 1990, Stice Meml. lectr. in social scis. U. Wash., 1992, Appel Disting. lectr. in law and tech., Denver U., 1994; Chancellor's Disting. fellow U. Calif., 2000.

MARX, HERBERT LEWIS, JR. arbitrator; b. Feb. 1, 1922; AB, Dartmouth Coll., 1943; MBA, NYU, 1955. With Office of Strategic Svcs., Washington, London, Paris, 1943-45; assoc. editor Scholastic Mags., N.Y.C., 1945-51; with Gen. Cable Corp., 1951-75, v.p. indsl. rels.; pvt. practice arbitrator, mediator N.Y.C., 1975—. Home and Office: 20 Waterside Plz Apt 23J New York NY 10010-2688 E-mail: waterside20@aol.com.

MARX, MICHAEL WILLIAM, English educator, author; b. Phila., Nov. 1, 1951; s. Elmer Edward Marx and Katharine Scott Marz; m. Il Sun Kang; children: Yong, Tristan, Ashlynn. Student, Loyola U.; BA in Polit. Sci., Hobart Coll., 1973; MFA in Film Making, NYU, 1976; MA in Eng., Ind. State U., 2001. Freelance writer, Calif., 1976-90; owner, head chef Freelandville (Ind.) Novelist Cafe, 1990-95; pub. Marx & Marx Writers & Pubs., 1998—; instr. English lang. and lit. Ind. State U., 1999—; tchr. Lakeland Coll., Danville, Ill., 2000—01, Ivy Tech State Coll., Terra Haute & Greenfield, Ind., 2000—01, Mira Costa Coll., Oceanside, Calif., 2001—, Southwestern Coll., Chula Vista, 2001—, San Diego City Coll., 2001—, Palomar Coll., San Marcos, 2001—, Miramar Coll., San Diego, 2001—, Cuyumaca Coll., El Cajon, 2001—, Inter-Am. Coll., National City, 2001—. Part-time tchr. Vincennes (Ind.) U., 1991-93, Indiana Bus. Coll., 1995. Author: A War Ends, 1977, 2d edit., 1985 (Artisan award Acad. Fine Arts & Friends), Eric Greenfield: Middle American, 1987, Justus: A Utopia, 1999; columnist North Knox Leader, 1997-98, Knox County Daily News, Wabash Weekly News, 1991-92; movie reviewer. Home: PO Box 4180 Carlsbad CA 92018 E-mail: michael@michaelmarx.com.

MARX, NICKI DIANE, sculptor, painter; b. L.A., Oct. 3, 1943; d. Donald F. and Ruth H. (Ungar) M. Undergrad., U. Calif., Riverside, 1965, U. Calif., Santa Cruz, 1973. Represented by Nicki Marx Studio, Taos, N.Mex., Fred Kline Gallery, Santa Fe. One-woman shows include Palm Springs Desert Mus., 1977, Julie Artisans Gallery, N.Y.C., 1975, Phoenix Art Mus., 1975, Weston Gallery, Carmel, Calif, 1981, Kirk de Gooyer Gallery, L.A., 1982, Rocklands Gallery, Monterey, Calif., 1983, Fetish Gallery, Taos, 1988, Fenix Gallery, Taos, 1991, Earthworks, 1993, Lamberts, 1994, Stables Gallery, Taos, 1995, Fred Kline, 1995, Sun Cities Mus. Art, Ariz., 1996, Harwood Mus. Art, Taos, 1999, others; group exhbns. include E.P. Smith Gallery, Santa Cruz, 1994, Lumina Gallery, Taos, 1994, Cafe Gallery, Albuquerque, 1991, Bareiss Gallery, Taos, 1990, Ctr. for Contemporary Art, Santa Fe, 1989, Jordan Gallery, Taos, N.Mex., 1988, 89, Stables Art Gallery, Taos, 1988, 94, Albuquerque State Fair Grounds, 1986, San Francisco Mus. Modern Art, 1977, 78, The Elements Gallery, Greenwich, Conn., 1977, Pacific Design Ctr., L.A., 1976, Lester Gallery, Inverness, Calif., 1976, numerous others; work included in sixteen invitational shows; represented in pub. collections IBM, Milford, Conn., N.Y.C., San Jose, Calif., Bank of Am., San Francisco, The Continental Group, Inc., Stamford, Conn., Cedars-Sinai Hosp., L.A., Farm Bur. Fedn., Sacramento, Calif., Sherman Fairchild Sci. Ctr., Stanford, Calif., Palm Springs (Calif.) Desert Mus., Univ. Mus., Ariz. State U. at Tempe, Mills Coll. Art Gallery, Berkeley, Calif.; exhibited in pvt. collections of Estate of Eugene Klein, Estate of Louise Nevelson, Estate of Georgia O'Keeffe, Fritz Scholder, Ray Graham, Bunny Horowitz, Sue and Otto Meyer, Burt Sugarman, Craig Moody, Paul Pletka, others; subject of numerous articles in jours. and mags. MacDowell Colony fellow, 1975; recipient Adolph and Esther Gottleib Found. grant, 1985. Studio: PO Box 1135 Ranchos De Taos NM 87557-1135

MARX, PETER A. lawyer; b. N.Y.C., June 14, 1942; s. Robert L. and Helen (Sohn) M.; m. Barbara K. Marx, Dec. 21, 1974; children: Laura, Lisa. BA, Cornell U., 1965, MBA, JD, 1968. Bar: N.Y. 1969, D.C. 1970, Mass. 1980. Atty., advisor U.S. Securites & Exch. Commn., Washington, 1968-71; assoc. Shaw, Pittman, Potts & Trowbridge, 1971-74; v.p., gen. counsel Chase Econometrics and Interactive Data Corp., Waltham, Mass., 1975-85; ptnr. Goulston & Storrs, Boston, 1985-87; prin. The Marx Group, Wellesley, Mass., 1987—. Dir. Info. Industry Assn., Washington, 1980-84, hon. counsel to bd., 1993—; chmn. Electronic Bus. Forum, 2002–, N.E. Computer Law Forum, 1982-89; adv. bd. CNC Interactive, 1998, LifetecNet.com, 1999-2001, For-Power.com, 1999-2002, Eye on Interactive, 1999, WebMediate.com, 2000—, Protegent, Inc., 2001—; host Venture Capital Quest, 1998-2000; vice-chmn. bd. dirs. Internet Alliance, 1999-2000; exec.-in-residence Babson Coll., 2002—; chmn. Electronic Bus. Form, 2002—. Editor: Contracts in the Information Industry, 1988, II, 1990, III, 1995; mem. bd. advisors Computer Law Strategist, 1987-99; info. law editor Info. Mgmt. Rev., 1987-90; host program Bus. Insight, Sta. WCAB-TV, 1991—; coord. editor The Info. Industry Deal Making Directory, 1994. Mem. ALI-ABA Computer Law Inst. (chmn. 1980-88), New Eng. Corp. Counsel Assn. (chmn. 1981-82), Cornell Club Boston (dir. 2002—). Office: The Marx Group 60 Valley Rd Wellesley MA 02481-1448 E-mail: peter@marxgroup.com.

MARX, THOMAS GEORGE, economist; b. Trenton, N.J., Oct. 25, 1943; s. George Thomas and Ann (Szymanski) Marx; m. Arlene May Varga, Aug. 23, 1969; children: Melissa Ann, Thomas Jeffrey, Jeffrey Alan. BS summa cum laude, Rider Coll., 1969; PhD, U. Pa., 1973. Fin. analyst Am. Cyanamid Co., Trenton, 1968; economist FTC, Washington, 1973; econ. cons. Foster Assocs. Inc., 1974-77; sr. economist GM, Detroit, 1977-79, mgr. indsl. econs., 1980-81, dir. econs. policy studies, 1981-83, dir. corp. strategic planning group, 1984-86, gen. dir. market analysis and forecasting, 1986-88, gen. dir. econ. analysis, 1988-90, gen. dir. issues mgmt. on industry govt. rels. staff, 1990-96, dir. econ. issues and analysis corp. affairs staff, 1996-97, dir. global climate issue, 1997—. Mem. faculty Temple U., Phila., 1972—73, U. Pa., Phila., 1972—73; adj. prof. Wayne State U., 1981—89, U. Detroit, 1988—. Assoc. editor: Bus. Econs., 1980—98, mem. edit. bd.: Akron Jour. Bus. and Econs., 1981—90; contbr. articles to profl. jours. With USAF, 1961—65. Mem.: Assn. Pub. Policy Analysts, Planning Forum, Western Econ. Assn., So. Econ. Assn., Econ. Soc. Mich., Detroit Area Bus. Economists (v.p.), Nat. Assn. Bus. Economists, Am. Econ. Assn., Nat. Econs. Club, Beta Gamma Sigma, Pi Gamma Mu. Roman Catholic. Home: 3312 Bloomfield Park Dr West Bloomfield MI 48323-3514 Office: GM Corp MC 482-C27-C22 PO Box 300 300 Renaissance Ctr Detroit MI 48265-3000 E-mail: tom.marx@gm.com.

MARY, NOURI Y. pharmacist, educator, dean; b. Baghdad, Iraq, June 25, 1929; arrived in U.S., 1961; s. Yousif Mansoor Mary and Hayat Jajjo Nadhir; m. Nakiya Tominna Mary, May 18, 1958; children: Atheel, Yasmine. Pharm. chemist, Baghdad U., 1951; MSc, Ohio State U., 1953, PhD, 1955. Asst. prof. pharmacognosy Coll. Pharmacy Baghdad U., 1956—61, acting dean, 1960—61; vis. rsch. scientist NAS, Sch. Pharmacy, U. Calif., San Francisco, 1961—63; post-doctoral fellow Pharmacy Rsch. Inst., Sch. Pharmacy, U. Conn., Storrs, 1963—65; assoc. prof. pharmacognosy Bklyn. Coll. Pharmacy, L.I. U., 1965—72; prof. pharmacognosy Arnold and Marie Schwartz Coll. Pharmacy and Health Scis., L.I. U., 1972—, assoc. dean, 1982—. Mem.: Am. Soc. Health Sys. Pharmacists, Am. Assn. Colls. Pharmacy, Am. Soc. Pharmacognosy, Am. Pharm. Assn. Roman Catholic. Avocations: reading, travel, sports. Office: LI Univ Coll Pharmacy 75 DeKalb Ave Brooklyn NY 11201

MARYSCHUK, OLGA YAROSLAVA, artist, executive assistant; b. Greenwich, Conn., July 21, 1928; d. George and Rose Greshchyshyn M. BFA, Cooper Union Sch. Art/Arch., 1979. Exec. asst. I.M. Pei & Ptnrs., N.Y.C., 1966-92. One woman shows include I.M. Pei & Ptnrs., Architects & Planners, N.Y.C., 1984, Fifth Street Gallery, N.Y., 1980, Ukrainian Can. Art Found., Toronto, 1980, Ukrainian Artists Assn. in USA, N.Y.C., 1979, Ukrainian Friendship Soc., 1971, Peter Cooper Gallery, N.Y., 1968; exhibited in group shows at Old New York Gallery, N.Y., 1998, 2000, Tenement Mus., N.Y., 1999, Ukrainian Inst., N.Y., 1999, Richmond (Calif.) Art Ctr., 1997, Chgo. Ctr. for Book and Arts, 1996, The Cooper Union, Houghton Gallery, N.Y.C., 1996, Michael Ingbar Gallery, N.Y.C., 1993, 94, many others; represented in permanent collection AT&T, Atlanta, C&S/Sovran Bank, Atlanta, Carter Wallace, N.Y., Kohn Pedersen Fox, Architects, N.Y.C., Mortgage Bankers Assn., Washington, Ternopil Regional Mus., Ukraine, Ukrainian Mus. of Fine Art, Kiev, United Way, Atlanta, West Allis Meml. Hosp., Milw., Consul Gen. of Ukraine in N.Y. Founding mem. Fulton Art Fair, Bklyn., 1957; vol. Sta. WNYC, N.Y.C., 1992—, UNICEF, N.Y.C., 1999. Scholarship Kiev State Art Inst., 1970-71; fellowship Ragdale Found., 1984, 86, Va. Ctr. for Creative Arts, 1982, 83. Unitarian Universalist. Avocations: Taoist Tai Chi, traveling, writing, curatorial work. Home: 170 Avenue C Apt 2C New York NY 10009

MARZ, LOREN CARL, environmental engineer, chemist, meteorologist; b. Jamestown, N.Y., June 11, 1951; s. Maurice Carl and Dorothy May (Anderson) M.; m. Sharon Lee Mekus, June 2, 1979; children: Brandon, Stephen. BS, Gannon U., Erie, Pa., 1975; MS, SUNY, Fredonia, 1990. Registered environ. profl.; cert. cons. meteorologist. Profl. baseball player Milw. Brewers Class A Team, Newark, 1973; analyst chem. lab. Dunkirk (N.Y.) Ice Cream Co., 1975-80, Ralston-Purina Co., Inc., Dunkirk, 1980-84; environ. engr. CPS, 1985-89; environ. scientist U.S. Army Med. Rsch. Inst. Chem. Def., Aberdeen Proving Ground, Md., 1989-91; environ. engr. U.S. Dept. Energy, Oak Ridge, Tenn., 1991-98; cons. meteorologist pvt. practice, 1997—; meteorologist U.S. Nat. Weather Svc., Brownsville, Tex., 1998-99, Jackson, Ky., 1999—2002, Mortistown, Tenn., 2002—. Site operator Nat. Atmospheric Deposition Program-Nat. Trends Network, Ft. Collins, Co., 1987-89. Mem. Mayville (N.Y.) Emergency Planning Com., 1988-89. Mem. Am. Meteorol. Soc. Baptist. Home: 112 Settlers Ln Talbott TN 37877- 313 Office: Nat Weather Svc 5974 Commerce Blvd Morristown TN 37814 E-mail: lmarz@charter.net., loren.marz@noaa.gov.

MARZINSKI, LYNN ROSE, oncological nurse; b. Milw., Mar. 15, 1951; d. Anthony A. and Delores D. (Moczynski) Miller; m. Ronald M. Marzinski, Aug. 26, 1972; children: Nicholas, Benjamin. BSN, U. Wis., 1973; MSN, U. Wis., 1992. RN, Wis., Mo., Kans.; cert. advanced oncology nurse. Mgr. St. Camillus Health Ctr., Wauwatosa, 1980-87; staff nurse St. Luke's Med. Ctr., Milw., 1972-79, 87-94; oncology rsch. coord. Sinai Samaritan Med. Ctr., 1994-96. Lectr. U. Wis., Milw., 1992-93, Oncology CNS Independence (Mo.) Regional Health Ctr., 1996-2001, Oncology CNS St. Luke's Hosp., Kansas City, Mo., 2001—. Mem. Oncology Nursing Soc., Greater Kansas City Oncology Nursing Soc. (newsletter editor), Am. Assn. Therapeutic Humor, Sigma Theta Tau. E-mail: lmarzinski@saint-lukes.org.

MARZIO, PETER CORT, museum director; b. Governor's Island, N.Y., May 8, 1943; s. Francis and Katherine (Mastroberte) M.; m. Frances Ann Parker, July 2, 1979; children: Sara Lon, Steven Arnold. BA (Neva Miller scholar), Juniata Coll., Huntingdon, Pa., 1965; MA, U. Chgo., 1966, PhD (univ. fellow, Smithsonian Instn. fellow), 1969. Research asst. to dir., then historian Nat. Mus. History and Tech., Smithsonian Instn., 1969-73, assoc. curator prints, 1977-78, chmn. dept. cultural history, 1978; dir., chief exec. officer Corcoran Gallery Art, Washington, 1978-82; dir. Mus. Fine Arts, Houston, 1982—. Instr. Roosevelt U., Chgo., 1966-68; assoc. prof. U. Md., 1976-77u; adv. coun. Anthrop. Film Ctr., Archives Am. Art; mem. adv. bd. Smithsonian Inst. Press; bd. dirs. First Interstate Bank of Tex. Author: Rube Goldberg: His Life and Works, 1973, The Art Crusade, 1976, The Democratic Art: An Introduction to the History of Chromolithography in America, 1979; editor: A Nation of Nations, 1976. Mem. adv. coun. Dumbarton Oaks, 1979-86; trustee, mem. exec. com., pres. Texart 150, Tex. Commn. on the Arts, Tex. Assn. for Promotion of Art, 1990-91; pres. Lila Wallace-Reader's Digest Found. Sr. Fulbright fellow Italy, 1973-74 Mem. Print Council Am., Am. Print Council, Dunlap Soc., Assn. Art Mus. Dirs. (pres. 1988-89), Am. Assn. Mus. (exec. com.), Am. Fedn. of the Arts (trustee), Young Pres. Orgn. Clubs: Cosmos (Washington). Home: 101 Westcott St Houston TX 77007-7044 Office: Mus Fine Arts 1001 Bissonet St PO Box 6826 Houston TX 77265-6826

MARZKE, RONALD OSCAR, physics and astronomy educator; b. Chapel Hill, N.C., Dec. 11, 1966; s. Robert Franklin and Mary (Walpole) M.; m. Heidi May Waterfield, July 20, 1997; 1 child, Cassandra. BS in Physics, Ariz. State U., 1987; AM in Asronomy, Harvard U., 1988, PhD in Astronomy, 1994. Rsch. assoc. Nat. Rsch. Coun. Can., Victoria, B.C., 1994-97; Hubble fellow Obs. Carnegie Instn. Washington, Pasadena, Calif., 1997-2000; asst. prof. physics and astronomy San Francisco State U., 2000—. Contbr. articles to sci. jours., including Astrophys. Jour., Astronom. Jour., Astronomy and Astrophysics, publs. of Astron. Soc. Pacific. Rsch. grantee NSF, 1999, major rsch. instrumentation grantee, 1999. Mem. Am. Astron. Soc., Astron. Soc. Pacific. Avocations: outdoor activities, wilderness preservation. Office: San Francisco Stat U Dept Physics and Astronomy 1600 Holloway Ave San Francisco CA 94132

MARZLUF, GEORGE AUSTIN, biochemistry educator; b. Columbus, Ohio, Sept. 29, 1935; s. Paul Bayhan and Opal Faun (Simmons) M.; m. Zarife Sahenk; children: Bruce, Julie, Philip, Glenn. BS, Ohio State U., 1957, MS, 1960; PhD, Johns Hopkins U., 1964. Postdoctoral fellow U. Wis., Madison, 1964-66; asst. prof. biochemistry Marquette U., Milw., 1966-70; assoc. prof. Ohio State U., Columbus, 1970-75, prof., 1975—, chmn. dept. biochemistry, 1985-2000. Contbr. articles to profl. jours. Mem. Genetics Soc. Am., Am. Soc. Microbiology, AAAS, Am. Soc. Biochemists and Molecular Biologists. E-mail: Marzluf.1@osu.edu. Office: Ohio State U Dept of Biochemistry 484 W 12th Ave Columbus OH 43210-1214

MASA, GEORGE JOHN, retired regional director; b. Chgo., Apr. 29, 1947; s. George John Sr. and Barbara Ann (Kos) M.; m. Judy Ann Martin, Apr. 24, 1971; children: Kimberly Janine, Kristin Marie. BS in Commerce, De Paul U., 1969; cert. in banking, Rutgers U., 1979; cert. in mgmt., Pa. State U., 1987. Field bank examiner FDIC, Chgo., 1969-77, rev. examiner, 1977-82, asst. regional dir. Dallas, 1982-85, asst. dir. policy Washington, 1985-86, asst. dir. ops., 1986-89, regional dir. Chgo., 1989-91, San Francisco, 1991—2002; ret., 2002. With USAF, 1970-76.

MAŚA, RUDOLF, retired chemist, finance executive; b. Zabrzeg, Poland, Nov. 4, 1926; came to U.S., 1956; s. Franciszek and Anna (Puchałka) M.; m. Krystyna Maria Koziarski, June 19, 1954; children: Yvonne, Lydia. BS in Chemistry, Salford (Eng.) U., 1956; MS in Chemistry, Carnegie Mellon U., 1970. Chemist Koppers Co., Pitts., 1956-62; sr. rsch. assoc. PPG Industries, 1962-91; registered rep. Allegheny Investment Ltd., 1992—. Vol. polymer chemist Exec. Svc. Corp., Stamford, Conn., 1992—, cons., Dokki, Egypt, 1995, Port Said, Egypt, 1999. Contbr. chpt. to book: Annual Reviews of Industrial and Engineering Chemistry, 1970; U.S. and fgn. patentee in polymer chemistry. Mem. Am. Chem. soc., Polymer Orgn. Pitts., Internat. Assn. Fin. Planning, Alcoma Golf Club. Republican. Roman Catholic. Avocations: tennis, bee keeping, travel. Home: 117 Hodil Ter Pittsburgh PA 15238-1109

MASCAGNI, MICHAEL, computer scientist, mathematician; b. Bologna, Italy, Nov. 25, 1959; s. Vincent Albert and Marie Teresa Mascagni; m. Becky Jean Fandrei; children: Alexander, Marcus. BS in Math., BS in Biomed. Engring., U. Iowa, 1981; MS in Math., NYU, 1985, PhD in Math., 1987. Staff fellow NIH, Bethesda, Md., 1987—88; National Research Council Postdoctoral Fellow National Institutes of Health, MD, 1988—90; mem. rsch. staff Ctr. for Computing Scis., IDA, Bowie, Md., 1990—96; coord. doctoral program in sci. computing U. So. Miss., Hattiesburg, Miss., 1997—99, assoc. prof. math., 1997—99; dir. PET program Ctr. for Higher Learning, Stennis Space Center, Miss., 1998—99; assoc. prof. computer sci. Fla. State U., Tallahassee, 1999—2002, prof. computer sci., 2002—. Cons. Comdr. Naval Meteorology and Oceanography Command, Stennis Space Center, 1997—99, Arthur D. Little, Cambridge, 1999, Bettis Lab., West Mifflin, 1999—2002, PDH, Internat., Hallandale, 2001. Fellow Nat. Rsch. Coun. postdoctoral fellow, Nat. Acads. Sci./Nat. Rsch. Coun., 1988—2000. Mem.: Assn. of Computing Machinery, Soc. for Applied and Indsl. Math. Roman Catholic. Avocations: violin, bicycling, swimming. Office: Fla State U Dept Computer Sci Tallahassee FL 32306-4530 Home Fax: 775-254-4833; Office Fax: 775-254-4833. Personal E-mail: mascagni@cs.fsu.edu. Business E-Mail: mascagni@cs.fsu.edu.

MASCARA, FRANK, congressman; b. Belle Vernon, Pa., Jan. 19, 1930; married; 4 children. BS, Calif. U. Pa., 1972. Pub. acct., 1956-75; contr. Washington County, 1974-80; chmn. Wash. Bd. County Commrs., 1980-94; mem. U.S. Congress from 20th Pa. dist., 1995—; mem. fin. svcs. com., transp. and infrastructure com. Office: US House Reps 314 Cannon Ho Office Bldg Washington DC 20515-0001 also: Professional Plaza 625 Lincoln Avenue, Ste. 210 North Charleroi PA 15022*

MASCETTA, JOSEPH ANTHONY, principal; b. Canonsburg, Pa., Sept. 2, 1931; s. Joseph Alphonso and Amalia (Ciavarra) M.; m. Jean Verrone, June 18, 1960; children: Lisa Marie, Linda Jo, Lori Jean. BS, U. Pitts., 1954; MS, U. Pa., 1963; cert. advanced study, Harvard U., 1970. Cert. tchr. math., phys. scis., adminstr. secondary sch., Pa. Tchr. chemistry Canonsburg High Sch., 1956-59, Mt. Lebanon High Sch., Pitts., 1959-75, chair sci. dept., 1967-75;

coord. secondary curriculum Mt. Lebanon Sch. Dist., 1975-81; prin. Mt. Lebanon Sr. High Sch., 1981-91; ret., 1991; ednl. cons., 1991—. Vis. team mem. Mid. States Assn. Colls. and Schs., Phila., 1967-78, chair vis. teams, 1981-96, Pa. state adv. com., 1988-91; mem. sch. bd. and edn. commn. St. Patrick Sch., Canonsburg, 1972-85, 95-2002; regional dir. Pa. Jr. Acad. Sci., Pitts., 1976-82; ednl. cons. Pitts. area schs., 1992—; mem. quality edn. com. Pitts. Diocese, 1995-97. Author: Modern Chemistry Review, 1968, Chemistry the Easy Way, 1989, revised, 1995, Barron's SAT II, Chemistry, 1994, rev. edit., 2002; contbg. author: (ency.) Barron's Student Concise Ency., 1988, rev. 1994, Barron's New Student's Concise Ency., 1993, Perry Como Commemorative Booklet, 1998. Recipient Outstanding Tchr. award Spectroscopy Soc., 1973; grantee NSF, 1961, 62-63, 63, 67, 69-70, 73; sci. fellow GE, 1959. Mem. ASCD, Nat. Assn. Secondary Sch. Prins. (cert. recognition 1991), Pa. Assn. Curriculum & Supervision (exec. bd. dirs. 1985-87, regional pres. 1987), Western Pa. Assn. Curriculum & Supervision (v.p. 1983-85, pres. 1985-87, exec. bd. dirs. 1989-2001), Greater Canonsburg Heritage soc., Phi Delta Kappa. Roman Catholic. Avocations: painting, writing. Home: 451 Mcclelland Rd Canonsburg PA 15317-2258 E-mail: jmascetta@bellatlatic.net.

MASCHERONI, ELEANOR EARLE, investment company executive; b. Boston, June 6, 1955; d. Ralph II and Eleanor Forbes (Owens) Earle; m. Mark Mascheroni, May 30, 1981; children: Olivia Forbes, Isabella Starbuck, Rex Owens. AB, Brown U., 1977. Dept. adminstr. Sotheby Parke Bernet, N.Y.C., 1978-79; asst. dir. devel. Inst. Architecture and Urban Studies, 1979-81; assoc. in pub. rels. Prudential Securities Inc., 1981-84, asst. v.p., 1984-86, assoc. v.p., 1986-87, v.p., mgr., 1987-89, lst v.p., dir. corp. commns., 1989-91; v.p. corp. commn.s Zurich Scudder Investments, Inc., 1991-95, prin., sr. v.p., dir. corp. comms., 1996-99, mng. dir., 1999—2001; CMO Ogilvy & Mather, 2001—. N.Y. Alumnae bd. govs. St. Timothy's Sch., Stevenson, Md., 1994—; trustee Hartley House, 2000—. Avocations: running, photography.

MASCI, JOSEPH RICHARD, medical educator, physician; b. New Brunswick, N.J., Nov. 27, 1950; s. Joseph Nicholas and Delfina (Musa) M.; m. Elizabeth Bass, May 21, 1993; 1 child, Jonathan Samuel. BA, Cornell U., 1972; MD, NYU, 1976. Diplomate Am. Bd. Internal Medicine, Am. Bd. Infectious Diseases. Instr. medicine Boston U. Sch. Medicine, 1979—80, Mt. Sinai Sch. Medicine, N.Y.C., 1982—84, asst. prof. clin. medicine, 1984—88, asst. prof. medicine, 1988—90, assoc. prof. medicine, 1990—, chief infectious diseases, 1999—; assoc. dir. medicine Elmhurst Hosp. Ctr., 1987—2002, dir. medicine, 2002—. Peer reviewer NIH, 1994—. Author: Primary and Ambulatory Care of the HIV-Infected Adult, 1992, Outpatient Management of HIV-Infection, 1996, 3d edit., 2001. Fellow Am. Coll. Chest Physicians; mem. ACP, Am. Soc. Microbiology, Assn. Program Dirs. Internal Medicine. Office: Elmhurst Hosp Ctr 79-01 Broadway Elmhurst NY 11373-1329

MASCIA, JOSEPH SERAFINO, banking, economics and finance educator; b. Astoria, N.Y., Mar. 18, 1939; s. Peter and Lucy (Grodio) M.; m. Ritva A. Halinen, Dec. 14, 1966; 1 child, Mark Joseph. BA, CCNY, 1960; MBA, NYU, 1964, MS, 1973, MPA, 1977. Rsch. assoc. 1st Nat. City Bank, N.Y.C., 1962-66; dir. rsch. N.Y. State Bankers Assn., 1966-69, 72-73; asst. v.p. Marine Midland Banks, Inc., N.Y.C. and Buffalo, 1969-71; fin. economist Dept. Treasury, Washington, 1971-72; dir. rsch., economist Irving Bank Corp., N.Y.C., 1973-76; instr. Montclair State Coll., Upper Montclair, N.J., 1977-78; asst. prof. economics Marist Coll., Poughkeepsie, N.Y., 1978-79; assoc. prof. banking, econs. and fin. Adelphi U., Garden City, 1979—, chmn. dept., 1992-95, prof. emeritus NY, 2000—. Arbitrator Mcpl. Securities Rulemaking Bd., Nat. Futures Assn., 1991, N.Y. Stock Exch., N.Y.C., 1990—, Nat. Assn. Securities Dealers, N.Y.C., 1990—. Contbr. articles to profl. jours. 1st lt. USAR, 1961-68. Mem. Am. Econ. Assn., Am. Fin. Assn. Roman Catholic. Avocation: amateur musician. Home: 343 Bronxville Rd Bronxville NY 10708-2111 Office: Adelphi U Garden City NY 11530

MASCOLA, RICHARD F. former medical association administrator; Degree in prosthodontics, N.Y.U. Coll. Dentistry, 1962. Pres. ADA, 2001—02. Recipient Albert L. Borish Award, 2001.*

MASCOLO, RAYMOND ALFRED, dentist, educator; b. Bklyn., Mar. 30, 1955; s. Alfred Raymond and Corinne Ann Mascolo; m. Evelyn Mascolo, May 22, 1976; children: Michele Ann, Thomas Alfred. Dentistry degree, Georgetown U., 1980. Resident Georgetown Hosp., Washington, 1980-81; gen. dentist Alexandria, Va., 1981-83, East Northport, N.Y., 1983—. Adj. prof. Georgetown Dental Sch., Washington, 1981-83, Adelphi U., Garden City, N.Y., 1985—, dental adv. bd., 1985-93 V.p. Leukemia Soc., Melville, N.Y., 1993—. Fellow Suffolk Acad. Medicine; mem. ADA, Acad. Gen. Dentistry, Suffolk County Sheriff's Dept. (spl. dep. 1992—), East Northport C. of C. (pub. safety chmn. 1997—), Father Judge KC (v.p., Knight of the Month 1993, 96), Sons of Italy. Avocations: golf, basketball. Office: 240 Clay Pitts Rd East Northport NY 11731

MASDEU, JOSE CRUZ, neurologist, medical school administrator; b. Madrid, Sept. 15, 1946; arrived in U.S., 1972; s. Jose and Maria Luisa Masdeu. MD, U. Madrid, 1969. Diplomate Am. Bd. Psychiatry and Neurology. Resident in neurology Chgo. Med. Sch., 1972-75; fellow in neuropathology Peter Bent Brigham Hosp., 1976-77; sect. chief neurology Hines (Ill.) VA Hosp., 1978-82; asst. prof. neurology Loyola, 1978-82; head, neurology sect. North Ctrl. Bronx (N.Y.) Hosp., 1982-87; assoc. attending staff Montefiore Med. Ctr., Bronx, 1982-87; assoc. prof. neurology Einstein, 1982-87; dir. neurology St. Vincent's Hosp./Med. Ctr., N.Y.C., 1987—; attending staff, clin. prof. neurology Bellevue Hosp./NYU Med. Ctr., 1987—; prof., chmn. neurology dept. N.Y. Med. Coll./West County Med. Ctr., Valhalla, 1991—. Author (with C. Gonzalez, C.B. Grossman): Head and Spine Imaging, 1985; author: (with P. Brazis, J. Biller) Localization in Neurology, 4 edits., 1985—2001; author: (with L. Sudarsky, L. Wolfson) Gait Disturbances of Aging, 1997; contbr. Named Outstanding New Citizen of Yr., Chgo. Citizenship Coun., 1977, Among Best Neurologists in N.Y., N.Y. Mag., 1991, 1996, Among 22 Best Neurologists in U.S., Am. Health Mag., 1996. Mem.: World Fedn. Neurology (chmn. neuroimaging rsch. group 1997—), Am. Soc. Neuroimaging (pres. 1994—96), Am. Acad. Neurology (chmn. neuroimaging sect. 1996—, chmn. subcom. practice com. 1990—, bd. dirs.). Roman Catholic. Avocation: Avocations: tennis, golf. Address: Neurology CUN Avda Pio XII 31008 Pamplona Spain

MASEK, GEORGE ALLEN, retired rancher; b. St. Louis, Sept. 3, 1926; s. Louis Richard Masek and Stella Cristianna Winkelmeyer; m. Cynthia Jane Hollister, Jan. 13, 1953 (div. May 1967); children: George Allen, Cynthia Hollister; m. Nina Kimberly Carpenter, June 23, 1967. Student, Tulane U., 1944; BS, U. Ariz., 1955. V.p. Stewart Boot Co., Tucson, 1953—54; exec. v.p. Hollister Estate Co., Santa Barbara, Calif., 1955—66; operator Grass Ridge Farm, Sonoita, Ariz., 1967—. Dir. U.S. Combined Tng. Assn., Boston, 1969—70; pres. Ariz. St. Horseman's Assn., Phoenix, 1972—73; dir. Tucson Mus. Art, 1996—2001, Ariz. Hist. Soc., Tucson, 1999—. Mem. Masters Fox Hounds Am., Boston, 1968—79; gov. U.S. Polo Assn., Lexington, Ky., 1993—2000. Col. USN, 1944—47, WWII, 1st lt. U.S. Army, 1950—53, Korea. Recipient Dalmar trophy, U.S. Polo Assn., Lexington, Ky., 2000. Mem.: Mountain Oyster Club (dir. 1999), Woodhill Country Club. Home: PO Box 411 Sonoita AZ 85637

MASEK, JEROME EDWARD, public relations executive; b. Painesville, Ohio, Dec. 6, 1952; s. Perry Edward Jr. and Evelyn Josephine M.; m. Carol Ann Repede, Apr. 9, 1983; children: Tracey, Mathew. BS in Journalism, Bowling Green State U., 1975. City editor The Star-Beacon, Ashtabula, Ohio, 1972-80; energy and environ. reporter The Press, Cleve., 1980-82; city editor The Star, Terre Haute, Ind., 1982-83; editor employee publs. BFGoodrich, Akron, Ohio, 1983-84; press sec., exec. asst. Mayor's Office, Cleve., 1984-89; day city editor The Morning Jour., Lorain, Ohio, 1990-92; supr. publs. Ohio Lottery Commn., Cleve., 1992-2000; media rels. mgr. Greater Cleve. Regional Transit Authority, 2000—. Instr. photojournalism Kent State u., Ashtabula, 1978-79; presenter in field. Mem. comm. com. Cleve. Bicentennial Commn., 1994-96. Mem. Soc. Profl. Journalists (nat. membership chair 1998-2001, pres. Cleve. chpt. 1990-91, 98-99, bd. dirs. 1987-2000, Disting. Svc. award 2000), Press Club Cleve., Toastmasters Internat., Cleve. Hiking Club, Sierra Club. Republican. Roman Catholic. Avocations: photography, hiking. Home: 18914 Fairville Ave Cleveland OH 44135 Office: Greater Cleve Regional Transit Authority 1240 W 6th St Cleveland OH 44113 Fax: 216-566-5240. E-mail: jmasek@gcrta.org.

MASEK, MARK JOSEPH, writer; b. Joliet, Ill., June 13, 1957; s. Glenn James and Helen Margaret (Gleason) Masek; m. Theresa Marie Norton, Oct. 24, 1987. BJ, U. Ill., 1979. Reporter The Daily Illini, Champaign, 1976-79, Joliet Herald-News, 1978-79; columnist, editor Elgin (Ill.) Daily Courier-News, 1979-88; editor The Daily Herald, Arlington Heights, Ill., 1988-90; publs. mgr. Argonne (Ill.) Nat. Lab., 1990-98. Author: Hollywood Remains to Be Seen, 2001. V.p. Recycle Now-Joliet, 1991—; active Environ. Commn. City of Joliet, 1993—96; bd. dirs. Will County Habitat for Humanity, 1994—99, pres., 1997—99. Recipient 1st pl. Pub. Svc. award, Ill. AP Editor's Assn., 3d pl. Pub. Svc. award, 1980, 2d pl. Columns award, No. Ill. Newspaper Assn., 1982, 1st pl. Columns award, Nat. Newspaper Assn., 1982. Mem.: Soc. Profl. Journalists, Mensa. Democrat. Roman Catholic.

MASELLA, ROBERT THOMAS, political science and geography educator, funeral service; b. Bayonne, N.J., Mar. 23, 1948; s. Ralph J. and Ann (Hitchell) M. (dec.). BA, Jersey City U., 1980; MA, Rutgers U., Newark, 1983; cert., Alexander Sch. Real Estate, Bayonne, N.J., 1992. Plant mgr. Hutt Inc., Cliffwood, NJ, 1966-72; funeral svc. Michalski Funeral Home, Jersey City, 1982—, Fryczynski Funeral Home, Bayonne, 1987-92; prof. N.J. City U., 1987—. Real estate referral agt., Bayonne. Author: History of Presidential Elections, The White House--Big Losers. Named one of Outstanding Young Men in Am., 1984, Outstanding Scholar, Intellectual and Genius of the 20th and 21st Centuries, Cambridge U., 2001, Great Minds of the 21st Century. Mem. Pi Sigma Alpha. Democrat. Roman Catholic. Home: 90 W 4th St Bayonne NJ 07002-1151

MASELLI, JOHN ANTHONY, food products company executive; b. N.Y.C., Feb. 18, 1928; s. Anthony and Livia M.; m. Brigitta Degenkolb, Dec. 26, 1948; children: Elisa, John A. Jr. BS in Chemistry, CCNY, 1947; MS in Chemistry, Fordham U., 1949, PhD in Chemistry, 1952. Dir. research and devel. Standard Brands, Stamford, Conn., 1952-64; mgr. product devel. M&M/Mars, Hackettstown, N.J., 1964-67; pres. OZ Food Corp., Chgo., 1967-79; v.p. tech. Nabisco Brands, East Hanover, N.J., 1979-85; v.p. corp. research and devel. RJR Nabisco, Winston-Salem, N.C., 1985-87; sr. v.p. tech. Planters LifeSavers Co., 1987-91, cons., 1991—. Bd. dirs. Cultor Food Scis. (Finland), N.C. Biotech. Ctr., Sci-Works, Winston Salem, Winston Salem Symphony. Patentee in field. Bd. dirs. Chgo. Boy's Club, 1975-79, YMCA, Wilton, Conn, 1980-84. Mem. AAAS, ACS, Inst. Food Tech., Am. Soc. Bakery Engrs., Indsl. Biotechnology Assn., Indsl. Research Inst. Republican. Avocations: sailing, photography, music. Home: 529 Knob View Pl Winston Salem NC 27104-5107

MASER, JACK D. psychology educator; b. Balt., Dec. 15, 1937; s. Louis R. and Naomi S. Maser; m. Irma Visser, Nov. 19, 1962; 1 child, Andrea L. BS, U. Md., 1961; MA, Temple U., 1964, PhD, 1969. From asst. to assoc. prof. Tulane U., New Orleans, 1969-75; health scientist adminstr. NIMH, Rockville, Md., 1975-99; prof. psychiatry dept. U. Calif.-San Diego, La Jolla, 1999—. Cons. dept. psychiatry U. Pisa, Italy, 1995—; bd. dirs. Freedom from Fear, S.I., N.Y. Editor, author: Comorbidity of Mood and Anxiety Disorder, 1990, Handbook of Antisocial Behavior, 1997; also articles. With U.S. Army, 1961-63. Recipient Disting. Friend to Behavior Therapy award Assn. for Advamcement Behavior Therapy, 1995. Fellow Am. Psychopath. Assn.; mem. Assn. for Rsch. in Personality Disorders (bd. dirs.), Soc. for Rsch. in Psychopathology. Home: 2841 Vista Mariana Carlsbad CA 92009-7112 Office: VA Med Ctr Psychiatry Svc 116A 3350 La Jolla Village Dr San Diego CA 92161-0002 Office Fax: 858-642-6442. E-mail: jmaser@VApop.UCSD.edu.

MASEY, JACK, exhibition designer; b. N.Y.C., June 10, 1924; s. Max and Anna Masey; m. Mary Lou Leach, Dec. 27, 1959. Student, Cooper Union, 1941-43; BFA, Yale U., 1950. Pres. MetaForm Inc., N.Y.C., 1979—; co. project mgr. for design of La. Pavilion, World Expo., New Orleans, 1984, Statue of Liberty Exhibit, N.Y.C., 1986; project mgr. for design Johnstown (Pa.) Flood Mus., 1988, Ellis Island Immigration Mus., N.Y.C., 1990; co. project mgr. for design of Nat. D-Day Mus., New Orleans, 1994, designer D-Day Invasion, Pacific Exhbn., 2000; co. project mgr. for design of Harry S. Truman Mus., Independence, 2001. Lectr. Sch. Art and Arch., Yale U., 1968—69; design cons. State Hermitage Mus., St. Petersburg, Russia, 1998; project mgr. for design of Am. air power since WWII exhbn. The Mighty Eighth Air Force Mus., Savannah, Ga., 2001. Cartoonist Esquire mag, 1946; exhibits officer, USIS, New Delhi, 1951-55; designer U.S. Pavilion, Kabul Internat. Fair, 1956; dir. design Am. Nat. Exhbn., Moscow, 1959, chief, East-West exhibits br. USIA, Washington, 1960-67; chief design U.S. Pavilion, Montreal (Que., Can.) World's Fair, 1967, dep. commr. gen. for planning and design Osaka (Japan) World Expn., 1970; dir. design Am. Revolution Bicentennial Commn., Washington, 1971-73; dir. design and exhbns. Am. Revolution Bicentennial Adminstrn., 1974-77, design dir. Internat. Communication Agy., Washington, 1977— ; designer: Medicine-U.S.A. exhbn. for, USSR exchange program, 1962, Tech.-Books exhbns., 1963; co-designer Vis. Complex, UN, UN Found., N.Y.C. Served with AUS, 1943-45, ETO. Recipient Meritorious Service award USIA, 1959, Superior Service award, 1964, Superior Honor award, 1967, 75; award of excellence Fed. Design Council, 1975; Outstanding Achievement award, 1979; award of excellence Soc. Fed. Artists and Designers, 1971; Gold medal Art Dirs. Club, 1965; cert. of excellence Am. Inst. Graphic Arts, 1964; two Fed. Design Achievement awards for Contributions to Excellence in Design, U.S. Govt., 1984, Presdl. awards for Statue of Liberty Exhibit, 1986, for Ellis Island Immigration Mus., 1990. Home: 131 E 66th St Apt 3A New York NY 10021-6129 Office: 15 E 26th St New York NY 10010-1505

MASH, DONALD J. college president; b. Oct. 12, 1942; children: Maria, Christina, Donnie (dec.). BS in Edn., Ind. U. Pa., 1960; MA in Geography, U. Pitts., 1966; PhD, Ohio State U., 1974. Teaching fellow U. Pitts., 1964-65; instr. geography U. Pitts.-Bradford, 1965-68; dean for student svcs. Ohio Dominican Coll., 1968-75; v.p. for student affairs George Mason U., Fairfax, Va., 1975-85, exec. v.p. adminstrn., 1985-88; pres. Wayne (Nebr.) State Coll., 1988-98; chancellor U. Wis.-Eau Claire, 1998—. Office: Univ of Wisconsin-Eau Claire Office of Chancellor PO Box 4004 Eau Claire WI 54702-4004

MASHBERG, ARTHUR, medical educator, medical researcher; b. Nov. 1925; AB in Biology and Chemistry cum laude, Bklyn. Coll., 1945; DDS, NYU, 1949; postgrad., U. Pitts., 1958-59. Diplomate Am. Bd. Oral and Maxillofacial Surgery. Resident in oral surgery VA Hosp., Pitts., 1958-61; chief oral and maxillofacial surgery sect. VA Med. Ctr., East Orange, N.J., 1961-90; clin. prof. to prof. to prof. emeritus of surgery U. Med.-Dentistry N.J. Med. Sch., 1977—, clin. assoc. prof. to clin. prof. to vis. prof. oral and maxillofacial surgery, 1961—90; clin. assoc. prof. to clin. prof. oral and maxillofacial surgery Fairleigh Dickinson U., Hackensack, NJ, 1976—89. Contbr. Capt. U.S. Army, 1951—52. Grantee VA, 1967-72, 71-73, 72-77, NIH, NIDR, 1973-80, NIH, 1980-82, Nat. Cancer Inst., 1981-84, Smokeless Tobacco Rsch. Inst., 1995. Fellow Am. Coll. Dentists; mem. ADA, Acad. Medicine of N.J., Am. Cancer Soc. (profl. edn. com. 1983, med. com. 1993-94, Cancer Achievement award), Am. Soc. Oral and Maxillofacial Surgery, Am. Coll. Oral and Maxillofacial Surgeons, Nat. Assn. V.A. Dentists (pres.), Cancer Inst. N.J. (edn. com. 1976-77), N.J. Soc. Oral Surgeons, Oncology Soc. N.J., Soc. of Head and Neck Surgeons, N.Y. Head and Neck Soc., Soc. of Educators in Oral and Maxillofacial Surgery. Achievements include patents for in field of cancer detection. Home: 13 Kent Dr Roseland NJ 07068 Fax: (973) 403-8029. E-mail: artmash@aol.com.

MASHBURN, DONALD EUGENE, educator; b. Johnson City, Tenn., June 10, 1944; s. Harvey and Martha (McNeese) M.; m. Mary Juanita McKee, May 30, 1970; 1 child, Donna Sue. BS, East Tenn. State U., 1965, MS, 1971. Tchr. Cocke County High Sch., Newport, Tenn., 1965-66, John S. Battle High Sch., Bristol, Va., 1966-94, Wallace Mid. Sch., Bristol, 1994-97; tech. support tchr. Meadowview (Va.) Elem. Sch., 1997-98, Rhea Valley Elem. Sch., Damascus, Va., 1997-98, Valley Inst. Elem. Sch., Bristol, 1997-98, Watanga Elem. Sch., Abingdon, 1997-98; with Info. Sys. and Media Prodn., 1998-99, Washington Coll. Acad., Limestone, Tenn., 2001. Adj. faculty Northeast State Tech. Community Coll., Blountville, Tenn., 1984—. Mem. Ruritan (sec. Conklin club 1986-91, 98, 2001-02, pres. 1985, 92, 99, 2000, Davy Crockett dist. treas. 1993). Republican. Methodist. Avocations: computers, farming. Home and Office: 195 Mashburn Rd Telford TN 37690-3132

MASHECK, JOSEPH DANIEL, art critic, educator; b. N.Y.C., Jan. 19, 1942; s. Joseph Anthony and Dorothy Anna (Cahill) M. AB, Columbia U., 1963, MA, 1965, PhD, 1973; M.Litt., U. Dublin, 2001. Editorial researcher Bollingen Found.-Princeton U. Press, 1967-69; lectr. liberal studies Maidstone Coll. Art, Kent, Eng., 1968-69; preceptor in art history Columbia U., 1970-71; instr. art history Barnard Coll., 1971-73, asst. prof., 1973-82; lectr. visual and environ. studies Harvard U., Cambridge, Mass., 1983-86; assoc. prof. art history Hofstra U., Hempstead, N.Y., 1987-94, prof., 1994—; coord. grad. program in humanities, curatorial cons. Hofstra Mus., 1991—. Author: Historical Present: Essays of the 1970s, 1984, Smart Art (Point 1), 1984, Modernites: Art-Matters in the Present, 1993, Building-Art: Modern Architecture Under Cultural Construction, 1993; editor: Marcel Duchamp in Perspective 1975, reprint, 2002, Van Gogh 100, 1996, A.W. Dow's Composition, 1997; editor-in-chief Artforum mag., 1977-79. Bd. dirs. Crosby St. Project, N.Y., 1995-96; mem. adv. bd. Annals of Scholarship, 1998—. Nat. Endowment Arts fellow, 1972-73, 75-76; Guggenheim fellow, 1977-78, Samuel H. Kress Found. fellow, 1968-69; Hon. Armiger, Coll. Arms, London. Fellow Royal Soc. Arts; mem. AAUP, Coll. Art Assn., Internat. Assn. Art Critics, United Arts Club (Dublin). Roman Catholic. Democrat. Office: Hofstra U Dept Fine Arts and Art History Calkins Hall Hempstead NY 11549

MASHIA, LINDA ROSE, broadcasting company administrator; b. Holyoke, Mass., Oct. 1, 1969; d. Robert Dean and Jacqueline Marguerite Mashia. BA, Smith Coll., 1991; CSS, Harvard U., 2002. Cert. elem. tchr. level 1-6, Mass.; FCC restricted radiotelephone operator permit. Instr. Learning Skills, Inc., Northampton, Mass., 1991-92; traffic asst. Sta. WGBY, Springfield, 1992-93, air/traffic contr., 1993-94, asst. dir. broadcast ops., 1994-95; learning resources coord. Sta. WXEL, West Palm Beach, Fla., 1995-96, ops. mgr., 1996-97, dir. ops., 1997; broadcasting coord. Sta. WGBH, Boston, 1997-2000, traffic supr., 2000—. Mem. PBS Traffic Adv. Com., Alexandria, 1998—2001, vice chmn., 2000—01. Dist. com. mem. Squanto dist. Boy Scouts Am., Brockton, Mass., 1997—99, Knox Trail Coun., 2000—; assoc. advisor Stoughton (Mass.) Police Explorer Post # 57, 1998—2000, Newton (Mass.) Police Explorer Post # 300, 1999—2001, Emergency Svcs. Post # 525, Waltham, Mass., 2001—; dir. Children's Handbell Choir, 1998—. Home: 26 Kensington St Newton MA 02460-1312 Office: Sta WGBH 125 Western Ave Boston MA 02134-1008 Fax: 617-300-1022. E-mail: linda_mashia@wgbh.org.

MASHIN, JACQUELINE ANN COOK, medical sciences administrator, nursing administrator; b. Chgo., May 11, 1941; d. William Hermann and Ann (Smidt) Cook; m. Fredric John Mashin, June 7, 1970; children: Joseph Glenn, Alison Robin. BS, U. Md., 1984; BSN, Cath. U. Am., Washington, 1993. Cert. realtor. Adminstrv. asst. CIA, Washington, 1963-66; asst. to mng. dir. Aerospace Edn. Found., 1966-74; exec. asst. to asst exec. dir. Air Force Assn., 1974-79; v.p., ptnrship. owner Discount Linen Store, Silver Spring, Md., 1979-81; asst. regional polit. dir. Office of Pres.-elect, Washington, 1980-81; confidential asst. to dir. Office of Personnel Mgmt. (US), 1981-83; spl. asst. to dep. dir. Office of Mgmt. and Budget, 1983-86; dir. internat. communications and spl. asst. to commr. Dept. of the Interior, 1986-89, cons., 1989-93; with Washington Hosp. Ctr., 1993—. Chmn., vol. coord. Mo. County Rep. Party, 1999; chmn. Bayclub, Mo. County Fedn. Rep. Women, 1999, 2000, 01. Pres. Layhill Civic Assn., Silver Spring, Md., 1980; state chmn. Md.'s Reagan Youth Delegation, Annapolis, Md., 1980; state treas., office mgr. Reagan-Bush State Hdqrs. of Md., Silver Spring, 1980; mem. Women's Com. Nat. Symphony Orch.; pres. Rock Creek Women's Rep. Club, 1998; chmn. Montgomery County Rep. Party, 1999, Montgomery County Fedn. Rep. Women, 1999—; mem. subcom. Wheaton Redevel. Program, 2001—. Mem.: Air Force Assn. (life), U.S. Capital Hist. Soc., Am. League Lobbyists, Aux. Salvation Army (life), Indian Springs Country Club. Republican. Avocations: golf, horseback riding, collecting wine glasses, Hibel plates, lithos and Lalique crystal. Home and Office: 2429 White Horse Ln Silver Spring MD 20906-2243 E-mail: Jaguar041@aol.com.

MASHKEVICH, STEFAN VLADIMIROVICH, physicist, researcher, computer scientist; b. Kiev, USSR, Aug. 15, 1971; s. Vladimir Stefanovich Mashkevich and Lyudmila Petrovna Godenko; m. Veronica Petrovna Kaninska, Sept. 15, 1995; 1 child, David Stefan. MS, Kiev State U., 1990; PhD in Physics and Math., Joint Inst. for Nuc. Rsch., Dubna, Russia, 1993. Jr. rschr. Inst. Theoretical Physics, Kiev, 1993—95, rschr., 1995—98; systems analyst Optimark Technologies, Jersey City, 1998—2000; sr. specialist Merrill Lynch, N.Y.C., 2000—02; sci. software developer Schrödinger, Inc., 2002—. Vis. scientist Inst. de Physique Nucléaire, Orsay, France, 1995, Ctr. for Advanced Study, Oslo, 1995-96; vis. scholar U. Wash., Seattle, 1996. Contbr. articles to profl. jours. Linkage grantee NATO, 1993-94; fellow Ctr. Nat. Rsch. Sci., Paris, 1995, Norwegian Acad. Sci. and Letters, Oslo, 1995-96. Avocations: poetry, chess, soccer, transit history. Home: 1712 Madison Pl Brooklyn NY 11229-2628 E-mail: mash@mashke.org.

MASHMAN, JAN HOWARD, neurologist, educator, rehabilitation administrator; b. N.Y.C., Oct. 3, 1939; s. Jack and Dorothy (Dimondstein) M.; m. Susan Lee Zuckerman, Aug. 13, 1959; children: Walter, Pamela. BA with honors, U. Vt., 1961, MD cum laude, 1965. Intern in medicine Montefiore Hosp. Med. Ctr., Bronx, 1965-66; resident in neurology Albert Einstein Coll. Medicine, 1966-69, chief resident in neurology, 1968-69; pvt. practice Associated Neurologists, P.C., Danbury, Conn., 1971—; asst. clin. prof. neurology Yale Med. Sch., New Haven, 1980—. Med. dir. Datahr Rehab. Inst., Brookfield, Conn., 1984—; bd. dirs. MedCtr. Home Health Care, Brookfield; chmn., v.p. profession adv. com. Western Conn. M.S. Soc., Norwalk, 1980-92. Contbr. articles to profl. jours. Maj. USAF, 1969-71. Recipient Mosby scholarship award, Med. Sch. faculty, 1965. Fellow Am. Acad. Neurology (cert. neurology, polit. action com. 1990-95); mem. Conn. Neurol. Soc. (pres. 1988—), Fairfield County Neurology Soc. (pres. 1975-85, polit. action com. 1995), Briard Club Am., Alpha Omega Alpha, Sigma Xi. Jewish. Avocations: dogs, computers, antiques, travel, gardening. Office: Associated Neurologists PC 69 Sand Pit Rd Ste 300 Danbury CT 06810-4088 E-mail: janmash@aol.com., assocneuro@aol.com.

MASI, DALE A. research company executive, social work educator; b. N.Y.C. d. Alphonse E. and Vera Avella; children: Eric, Renee, Robin. BS, Coll. Mt. St. Vincent; MSW, U. Ill.; D Social Work, Cath. U. Lectr. Sch. Social Svcs., Ipswitch, Eng., 1970-72; project dir. occupational substance abuse program, asso. prof. Boston Coll. Grad. Sch. Social Work, 1972-79; dir. Office Employee Counseling Svc., Dept. Health/Human Svcs., Washington, 1979-84; pres. Masi Research Cons., Inc., 1984—; prof. U. Md. Grad. Sch. Social Work, 1980—; adj. prof. U. Md. Coll. Bus. and Mgmt., 1980—. Mem. IBM Mental Health Adv. Bd., 1990-95; cons. IBM, Toyota, Mobil Chm., The Washington Post, U.S. Ho. Reps., U.S. Postal Svc., White House, WHO, Bechtel Corp., other orgns. in pub. and pvt. sector; bd. advisors Nat. Security Inst., Wayside Youth and Family Support Network; USIA Ampart lectr. on alcohol, drugs and AIDS in the workplace. Author: Human Services in Industry, Organizing for Women, Designing Employee Assistance Programs, Drug Free Workplace, AIDS Issues in the Workplace: A Response Model for Human Resource Management, The AMA Handbook for Developing Employee Assistance and Counseling Programs, Evaluating Your Employee Assistance and Managed Behavioral Care Program, Internat. Employee Assistance Anthology, Productivity Lost: Alcohol and Drugs in the Workplace; co-author: Shrink to Fit: Answers to Your Questions About Therapy; also over 40 articles. Named Disting. Scholar, Nat. Acad. Practice, 2001—; named to Employee Assistance Program Hall of Fame; recipient award, Employee Assistance Program Digest; fellow Fulbright fellow, 1969—70, 1994, AAUW postdoctoral fellow, NIMH, 1962—64. Mem. AAUW, NASW (Internat. Rhoda G. Sarnat award 1993), Acad. Cert. Social Workers, Employee Assistance Profls. Assn. (nat. individual achievement award 1983), Fulbright Assn. (nat. bd.). Democrat. Roman Catholic. Office: 2549 Virginia Ave NW Washington DC 20037-1903 E-mail: masirsrch@aol.com.

MASI, JOHN ROGER, lawyer; b. Bklyn., Jan. 18, 1954; s. John Roger and Evelyn (Teagno) M.; m. Sherrill Alaine Schlett, June 29, 1985; children: Roger C., Christopher J., Nicholas J. BA, Franklin & Marshall Coll., 1976; JD, Temple U., 1980. Bar: NJ. 1981, Pa. 1981, U.S. Dist. Ct. N.J. 1981. Assoc. Klinger, Nicolette, Mavroudis & Honig, Oradell, N.J., 1982-86, Gern, Dunetz, Roseland, 1986-87; ptnr. J. Roger Masi, Esq., Hackensack, 1987—. Committeeman County Rep., Ridgewood, N.J., 1982-84; mem. Ridgewood Zoning Bd. Adjustment, 1990-94; mem. Ridgewood Edn. Found. Mem. ATLA. Roman Catholic. Office: 55 State St Hackensack NJ 07601-5426

MASI, ROBIN, artist, writer, educator; b. Palo Alto, Calif., July 29, 1960; d. Joseph Louis and Dale (Avella) M.; 1 child, Benjamin Westmont. BFA, Tufts U., 1983; MFA, Acad. of Art Coll., San Francisco, 1994. Adj. faculty fine arts Regis Coll., Weston, Mass., 1994-95, Endicott Coll., Beverly, 1995-96. Vis. faculty Sch. Mus. Fine Arts, 1996—. Author: Shrink-to-Fit: Answers to Your Questions About Therapy, 1998; exhibited in Boston, N.Y., Washington, San Francisco, 1980—; author (screenplay) Searching for Judith, 1997. Dir. The Women's Artist Database Project, 1992; co-founder The Varo Registry of Women Artists, 1995—; moderator Feminist Art History and Women Artist Listserves, 1996—. Democrat. Roman Catholic. E-mail: rmasi@ziplink.net.

MASIE, ELLIOTT, training executive; b. N.Y.C., May 13, 1950; s. Harry H. and Dorothy (Gordon) M. BA, SUNY, 1972. Cons. Irish Ministry Health, Dublin, 1972-73; project evaluator N.Y. State Dept. Edn., 1973-76; dir. Nat. Student Leadership Ctr., Raquette Lake, N.Y., 1977—; pres. Masie Ctr., 1991—. Cons. Disney, CIA, 1990-91, Dow Chem., NASA, Panama C.Z., Bank of Am., Nat. Assn. Secondary Sch. Prins., Washington, 1985; rsch. fellow Picturetel Corp., 1996; mem. Oracle Adv. Edn. Bd., 1996; pres. Ziff Daus Inst., 1992-94; founder On-Line Learning Coun.; mem. White House Commn. on Tng. Opportunities, Nat. Govs. Assn.'s Commn. on Learning. Author: Computers and Student Activities, 1984, The Computer Training Handbook, 1995, Learning in the Digital Age, others; host Microsoft TV. Mem. Assn. Computer Tng. and Support (pres., dir. 1989—, founder 1989—), Nat. Tng. & Computer Projects (bd. dirs., pres. Tools for Tng. 1985—). Jewish. Avocation: technology. Office: Masie Ctr PO Box 397 Saratoga Springs NY 12866-0397

MASIELLO, ROCCO JOSEPH, airlines and aerospace manufacturing executive; b. N.Y.C., Jan. 9, 1922; s. Joseph and Armanda (Mansueti) M.; m. Rita Elizabeth Amoruso, Feb. 19, 1945; children: Richard, Robin, Janet. Student, CCNY, 1946-48, Hofstra U., 1951-54. Registered profl. engr., Maine. With Pan. Am. World Airways, N.Y.C., 1950-59; v.p. maintenance and engring. U.S. Air Group, Pitts., 1959-72, Am. Airlines, Tulsa, 1973-82, sr. v.p. ops. Dallas, 1982-86; founder, exec. v.p. USAfrica Airways, 1990-94, also bd. dirs; founder The Reston Group; aerospace cons., prin. R.J. Masiello and Assoc. Mem. Soc. Aerospace Engr., Royal Aero. Soc. Roman Catholic.

MASIH, TARA LYNN, book editor, writer; b. Syracuse, N.Y., Aug. 22, 1963; d. Lalit Kumar and Sandra Kolyer Masih; m. Robert Edward Padykula, Aug. 29, 1993 (div. May 2000); 1 child, Arun Padykula. BA, C.W. Post Coll., 1985; MA, Emerson Coll., 1986. Pub.'s asst. Pym-Randall Press, Roslindale, Mass., 1987; editl. asst. Little, Brown & Co., Boston, 1987-88; asst. editor STORIES Mag., 1987-88; sr. book editor Bedford Books, 1988-93; freelance book editor, 1993—. Contbr. short stories to anthologies. Recipient 1st pl. for fiction, The Ledge mag., 1995; scholar, Bookbuilders of Boston, 1985. Avocations: gardening, tennis, canoeing, travel, reading. E-mail: masiht@aol.com.

MASILELA, CALVIN ONIAS, land use planner, educator; b. Bulawayo, Zimbabwe, Oct. 27, 1955; s. Stephen Masilela and Martha Ndiweni; m. Sibonisiwe Ntini; children: Zwelihle, Ayanda. Postgrad. diploma, U. Westminster, London, 1981; M in Urban and Regl. Planning, Va. Tech. U., 1983, PhD, 1989. Vis. prof. Indiana U. Pa., 1989—90, asst. prof., 1990—93, assoc. prof., 2001; asst. prof. W.Va. U., 1993—99, assoc. prof., 1999—2001, dir. Ronald E. McNair scholars program, 2000—01. Bd. dirs. Mon Valley Green Space Coalition, Morgantown, 200001. Recipient Outstanding Educator in Conservation Monongahela Soil Conservation Dist., 1999, Cheikh Anta Diop award Ctr. for Black Culture and Rsch., 1995, Urban Indicators award Univ. Consortium for Geographic Info. Sci. U.S. HUD, 2001; named Eberly Coll. Arts and Scis. Outstanding Tchr., 2000. Mem. Am. Planning Assn., W.Va. Planning Assn., Coun. Ednl. Opportunity, Mid-Eastern Assn. Ednl. Opportunity Pers., W.Va. Assn. Ednl. Opportunity Pers. Office: Dept Geography and Regional Planning Indiana U of Pa Indiana PA 15705 Home: 148 Canterbury Commons Indiana PA 15701 E-mail: cmasilel@iup.edu.

MASIN, MICHAEL TERRY, lawyer; b. Montreal, Jan. 28, 1945; came to U.S., 1954; s. Frank J. and Sonia (Ellmann) M.; m. Joanne Elizabeth Combé, June 4, 1966; 1 child, Courtney. BA, Dartmouth U., 1966; JD, UCLA, 1969. Bar: Calif. 1969, D.C. 1970. Assoc. O'Melveny & Myers, Los Angeles, 1969-76, ptnr. Washington, 1976-91, mng. ptnr. N.Y.C., 1991-93; vice chair, pres. GTE, Irving, Tex., 1993—; vice chmn., pres. Verizon Comms., N.Y.C., 2000—. Bd. dirs. Trust Co. the West Citigroup, Puerto Rico Tel. Co. Trustee Carnegie Hall; mem. dean's adv. com. Dartmouth Coll. Mem. Coun. on Fgn. Rels., The Brook, Calif. Club. Republican. Methodist. Office: Verizon Communications 1095 Ave of the Americas 39th Fl Rm 3922 New York NY 10036 E-mail: michael.masin@verizon.com.

MASINELLI, ANTHONY DEAN, journalist, writer; b. Springfield, Ill., Oct. 26, 1964; s. Larry Gene and Carolyn Jean Masinelli; m. Cheryl Lynn Davenport, Oct. 13, 1990; children: Joshua, James, Zachary, Matthew. BS Liberal Arts, Regents Coll., Albany, NY, 2000. Customer svc. Atlanta Legal Copies, Atlanta, 1990—92, First Image Corp., Atlanta, 1992—94; comml. print sales Atlanta Legal Copies, 1994—96, Mac Printing Corp., Atlanta, 1996—98; freelance journalist self-employed, Staunton, Ill., 1998—. Author: (book) Proclaim His Salvation (Concordia Hist. Inst. Award of Commendation, 2002). Vol. Ascension Luth. Ch. Sunday Sch., Atlanta, 1994—95; bd. mem. Stone Mountain Luth. Mission Ch., Stone Mountain, 1996—97, Open Arms Day Care, Atlanta, 1995—96. Recipient President's Award, Concordia Sem., St. Louis, MO, 2001, Blackburn Writer's Prize, Blackburn Coll., Carlinville, IL, 1982, Voice of Democracy, VFW, Staunton, IL, 1981. Mem.: The Acad. Am. Poets. Lutheran. Avocations: reading, writing, running, mountain-biking, mountain-biking. Home: 6A Founders Way Saint Louis MO 63105

MASINTER, PAUL JAMES, lawyer; b. New Orleans, June 28, 1961; s. Milton Paul Masinter and Shirley Mae (Rabé) Bradley; m. Audrey Renee Williams, Oct. 10, 1992. BA in Polit. Sci., La. State U., 1984, JD, 1987. Bar: La. 1987, U.S. Dist. Ct. (ea., mid. and we. dists.) La. 1987, U.S. Ct. Appeals (5th cir.) 1990, U.S. Supreme Ct. 1994. Law clk. to assoc. justice Hon. James L. Dennis La. Supreme Ct., New Orleans, 1987-88; assoc. McGlinchey, Stafford, 1988-90, Stone, Pigman, Walther, Wittmann & Hutchinson, New Orleans, 1990-95; ptnr. Stone, Pigman, Walter, Wittmann & Hutchinson, L.L.P., 1996—. Assoc. editor La. Law Rev., 1986-87. Bd. dirs. Save Our Cemeteries, New Orleans, 1993—, treas., 1998, pres., 1999. Mem. ABA (chair newsletter subcom., bus. and corp. litigation com. bus., law sect.), La. State Bar Assn., New Orleans Bar Assn. Democrat. Roman Catholic. Home: 1820 Octavia St New Orleans LA 70115-5660 Office: Stone Pigman Walther Wittmann & Hutchinson 546 Carondelet St Ste 100 New Orleans LA 70130-3588 E-mail: PMasinter@stonepigman.com.

MASINTER, THOMAS ALAN, composer; b. New Orleans, Dec. 5, 1950; s. Joseph Louis and Dorothy Maderine Masinter; m. Theresa A. Masinter; children: Celeste, Adam. BA in Music Composition, Trinity U., San Antonio, Tex., 1972, MA in Musicology, 1976. Owner Thomas Masinter Piano Studio, San Antonio, 1980—; pres. Star Dreams Prodns., 1998—. Music dir. Josephine Theatre, San Antonio, 2001—02, San Pedro Playhouse, San Antonio, 1998—2000, 1520 AD Theatre, San Antonio, 1975—76. Composer: (mus. compositions) Gone to Texas, 2002, Fire on the Bayou, 1998, Warner Bros. Pub. Co., 1995—. Composer United Way, San Antonio, 1973—74; music dir. Tex. Pub. Radio, 1997—; pianist Opera Guild San Antonio, 1996—2002. Recipient Meritorious Svc. award, USAF Chief of Chaplains, 1983. Mem.: ASCAP, San Antonio Music Tchrs. Assn., Music Tchrs. Nat. Assn. (nat. cert. 1985), Dramatists Guild. Home: 110 Cotillion Dr San Antonio TX 78213 Office: Star Dreams Prodns 110 Cotillion Dr San Antonio TX 78213

MASKALL, MARTHA JOSEPHINE, executive recruiter, publisher, health consultant; b. Kearny, N.J., Mar. 30, 1945; d. Charles Edgar and Mathilda (Comba) M. BA in Biology, Stanford U., 1966; MA, Duke U., 1969. Cert. data processor, 1979. Data base adminstr. Armco Steel, Ashland, Ky., 1972-74; project mgr. Rand Info. Systems, San Francisco, 1974-78; sales rep. Datacom ADR, 1980-81; systems engr. Four-Phase Systems, Sacramento, 1981-83; exec. recruiter, 1983—; owner Attitude Works Pub., Fair Oaks, Calif., 1990—. Health cons., 1994—. Author: The Attitude Treasury: 101 Inspiring Quotations, 1990, The Athena Treasury: 101 Inspiring Quotations by Women, 1993. NDEA fellow, 1966-68. Mem. Data Processing Mgmt. Assn., Sierra Club, Bus. and Profl. Women, Toastmasters (Disting. Toastmaster award 1989). Democrat. Home: 8456 Hidden Valley Cir Fair Oaks CA 95628-6121 Office: Marty Maskall & Assoc PO Box 1765 Fair Oaks CA 95628-1765

MASKET, EDWARD SEYMOUR, television executive; b. N.Y.C., Mar. 3, 1923; s. Isadore and Jennie (Bernstein) M.; m. Frances Ellen Rees, June 11, 1958 (div.); children: Joel Daniel, Johanna Rees Bettaeib, Kate Isobel Smiley. BS, CCNY, 1942; LLB, JD, Harvard U., 1949. Bar: N.Y. 1949. Atty., dir. bus. affairs, v.p. bus. affairs ABC, 1951-68; v.p. to exec. v.p. Columbia Pictures TV, Burbank, Calif., 1968-81; sr. v.p. adminstrn. Universal TV, 1982-86, exec. v.p. adminstrn., 1986-90, MCA TV Group, 1990-93; TV cons., 1994—. Served as 2d lt. AUS, 1942-46, PTO. Mem. Motion Picture Pioneers, Phi Beta Kappa. Avocation: tennis, golf. E-mail: telemogul@aol.com.

MASKET, SAMUEL, medical association administrator; b. N.Y.C., 1943; MD, N.Y. Med. Coll., 1968. Diplomate Am. Bd. Ophthalmology. Intern Bronx Mcpl. Hosp.-Einstein, N.Y.C., 1968—69; resident Metro Hosp. Ctr.-N.Y. Med., 1969—73; fellow Columbia-Presbyn. Med. Ctr., N.Y.C.; asst. clin. prof. ophthalmology UCLA; mem. staff West Hills Hosp., Canoga Park, Calif.; chmn. Am. Bd. Ophthalmology, Bala Cynwyd, Pa.; clinical prof. Jules Stein Eye Inst., Los Angeles, Calif. Fellow: Am. Acad. Ophthalmology; mem.: PAAO, ASCRS, AMA. Office: Am Bd Ophthalmology 111 Presidential Blvd Ste 241 Bala Cynwyd PA 19004-1012 also: 7230 Med Ctr Dr Ste 204 Canoga Park CA 91307 Office: Jules Stein Eye Inst 100 Stein Plaza UCLA Los Angeles CA 90095*

MASKIN, ERIC STARK, economics educator; b. N.Y.C., Dec. 12, 1950; m. Gayle Sawtelle; children: Joseph, Charlotte. AB in Maths., Harvard U., 1972, AM in Applied maths., 1974, PhD in Applied Maths., 1976. Rsch. fellow Jesus Coll. Cambridge (Eng.) U., 1976-77; asst. prof. econs. MIT, Cambridge, Mass., 1977-80, assoc. prof. econs., 1980-81, prof. econs., 1981-84, Harvard U., Cambridge, 1985—. Am. editor: Rev. of Econ. Studies, 1977-82; assoc. editor: Social Choice and Welfare, 1983—, Games and Econ. Behavior, 1988—; editor Quarterly Jour. of Econs., 1984—; adv. editor: Jour. of Risk and Uncertainty, 1987—. Churchill Coll. fellow, 1980-81; Guggenheim fellow, 1980-81, Sloan fellow, 1983-85, St. John's Coll. fellow, 1987-88. Fellow Econometric Soc.; mem. Am. Econ. Assn. Office: Harvard U Dept Econs Cambridge MA 02138

MASKOOKI, KOOROS, educator; s. Askar and Molouk Maskooki; m. Mehrnaz M. Kalani; children: Sam, Kevin. PhD, U. Nebr., 1977. Asst. prof. Shiraz (Iran) U., 1977—78, Earlham Coll., Richmond, Ind., 1979—81; prof. U. Mass., North dartmouth, 1981—. Contbr. articles to profl. jours. (citations for originality and practical application, 1992). Recipient Tchr. of Yr. award, Delta Mu Delta, 1996. Mem.: Emerald Literati Club (citations for excellence in rsch. 2002). Office: U Mass-Dartmouth 285 Old Westport Rd Dartmouth MA 02747 Home Fax: 508-999-8776; Office Fax: 508-999-8776. Personal E-mail: kmaskooki@umassd.edu. E-mail: kmaskooki@umassd.edu.

MASLACH, CHRISTINA, psychology educator; b. San Francisco, Jan. 21, 1946; d. George James and Doris Ann (Cuneo) M.; m. Philip George Zimbardo, Aug. 10, 1972; children: Zara, Tanya. BA, Harvard-Radcliffe Coll., 1967; PhD, Stanford U., 1971. Prof. psychology U. Calif.-Berkeley, 1971—, vice provost for undergrad. edn., 2001—. Author: Burnout: The Cost of Caring, 1982; co-author: Influencing Attitudes and Changing Behavior, 1977, Maslach Burnout Inventory (rsch. scale), 1981, 2d edit., 1986, 3d edit., 1996, Experiencing Social Psychology, 1979, 4th edit., 2001, Professional Burnout, 1993, The Truth About Burnout, 1997, Preventing Burnout and Building Engagement, 2000. Recipient Disting. Teaching award, 1987, Best Paper award Jour. Orgnl. Behavior, 1994, Prof. of Yr. award Carnegie/CASE, 1997. Fellow AAAS, APA, Am. Psychol. Soc., Soc. Clin. and Exptl. Hypnosis (Henry Guze rsch. award 1980), W. Psychol. Assn. (pres. 1989); mem. Soc. Exptl. Social Psychology. Democrat. Office: U Calif Office of Chancellor 200 California Hall # 1500 Berkeley CA 94720-1500 E-mail: maslach@socrates.berkeley.edu.

MASLACH, GEORGE JAMES, former university official; b. San Francisco, May 4, 1920; s. Michael J. and Anna (Pszczolkowska) M.; m. Doris Anne Cuneo, Mar. 12, 1943; children: Christina, James, Steven. AA, San Francisco Jr. Coll., 1939; BS, U. Calif., 1942. Staff mem. radiation lab. Mass. Inst. Tech., 1942-45, Gen. Precision Labs., 1945-49; research engr. Inst. Engring. Research, 1949-52, asst. dir., 1956-58; assoc. prof. U. Calif., Berkeley, 1952-58, prof., 1959-72, dean Coll. Engring., 1963-72, provost profl. schools and colls., 1972-81, vice-chancellor research and acad. services, 1981-83; internat. cons. edn. and econ. devel., 1982—. Adv. aeros. research and devel. NATO, 1960-78, U.S. Naval Acad. Rev. Bd., 1966-75, Dept. Commerce Tech. Adv. Bd., 1964-69, Ford Found. and Am. Soc. Engring. Edn., 1966-78 Mem. ASME, AAAS, Sigma Xi. Home: 265 Panoramic Way Berkeley CA 94704-1831

MASLAND, CHARLES HENRY, IV (CHAD MASLAND), financial services executive; b. Carlisle, Pa., Jan. 26, 1955; s. Charles Henry III and Virignia Lee (Parlin) M.; m. Robin Lynn Jones, Aug. 31, 1985. Student, Dickinson Coll., 1971-72; BA in Psychology, Gordon Coll., 1976; CLU, Am. Coll., 1981, chartered fin. cons., 1983. Cert. NASD Series 7. Dir. youth program Lakeside Youth Svc., Willow Grove, Pa., 1976-77; sales rep. Mut. N.Y., Boston, 1977-79; mktg. cons. advanced sales Paul Revere Co., Worcester, Mass., 1979-82, mktg. cons. life products, 1982-83; dir. competition Nat. Life Vt., Montpelier, 1983-84, dir. competition and proposal svcs., 1984-88, asst. v.p., 1988-89, asst. v.p. mktg., 1989-90, 2d v.p. product mktg., 1990-91, 2nd v.p. product coordination, 1991-93, product exec. non-traditional products, 1992—, v.p. sales, 1993-94, v.p. annuities, 1994-96; sr. v.p. product mgmt./sales/mktg. Citibank/Citicorp Ins. Group, Dover, Del., 1996-2000; pres. Citicorp Internat. Ins. Co., Ltd., 1999-2000, Am. First State Capital Group, Inc., 2000—. Bd. dirs. Citicorp Life Ins. Co., First Citicorp Life Ins. Co., Citicorp Internat. Ins. Co., Citicorp Assurance Co., 1996-2000; cons. Interstate 10 Broadcasting Inc., Lordsburg, N.Mex., 1986-90, bd. dirs.; advisor Gordon Coll., Wenham, Mass., 1978-82; lectr. N.H. Assn. Life Underwriters, Manchester; cons. Nat. Underwriters, Inc., Cin., 1986-90; spkr. in field. Contbr. articles to mags.; photography editor (newspaper) The Tartan, 1974-75. Tchr. 1st Congl. Ch., Hopkinton, Mass., 1978-82; planning com. Bible Fellowship Ch., Fayston, Vt., 1989-92; pres. Psychology Adv. Coun., Wenham, 1974-75; pres. Briarcliff Assn., Warren, Vt., 1988-95; chmn., bd. dirs., actor, singer The Team Inc., Oxford, Mass., 1987-92; co-founder Heartistry Theatre Arts, 1994—. Mem. Nat. Assn. Life Underwriters, Nat. Assn. Securities Dealers, Am. Soc. CLU and ChFC, Am. Coun. Life Ins. (annuity com. 1999-2000), Assn. Advanced Life Underwriters, Small Bus. Coun. Am., Mensa, Assn. Banks in Ins. (chmn. annuity com. 1997-2000), Phi Alpha Chi. Avocations: dramatic arts, soccer, ballroom dance, tennis. Home: 10 Elizabeth Ave Dover DE 19901-5804

MASLANSKY, CAROL JEANNE, toxicologist; b. N.Y.C., Mar. 3, 1949; d. Paul Jeremiah and Jeanne Marie (Filiatrault) Lane; m. Steven Paul Maslansky, May 28, 1973. BA, SUNY, 1971; PhD, N.Y. Med. Coll., 1983. Diplomate Am. Bd. Toxicology; cert. gen. toxicology. Asst. entomologist N.Y. State Dept. Health, White Plains, 1973-74; sr. biologist Am. Health Found., Valhalla, N.Y., 1974-76; rsch. fellow N.Y. Med. Coll., 1977-83, Albert Einstein Coll. Medicine, Bronx, N.Y., 1983; copr. toxicologist Texaco, Inc., Beacon, 1984-85; prin. GeoEnviron. Cons., Inc., White Plains, 1982-97, Maslansky GeoEnviron. Inc., Prescott, Ariz., 1997—. Lectr. in entomology Westchester County Parks and Preserves, 1973-96, lectr. toxicology and hazardous materials, 1985—. Author: Air Monitoring Instrumentation, 1993, Health and Safety at Hazardous Waste Sites, 1997, (with others) Training for Hazardous Materials Team Members, 1991 (manual, video) The Poison Control Response to Chemical Emergencies, 1993. Mem. Harrison (N.Y.) Vol. Ambulance Corps., 1986-91, Westchester County (N.Y.) Hazardous Materials Response Team, 1987-96. Monsanto Fund Fellowship in Toxicology, 1988-90; grad. fellowship N.Y. Med. Coll., 1977-83. Mem. AAAS, Nat. Environ. Health Assn., N.Y. Acad. Sci., Am. Soc. Toxicology, Am. Indsl. Hygiene Assn., Environ. Mutagen Soc. Achievements include participation in development of genetic toxicity assays to identify potential carcinogens; rsch. on air monitoring instrumentation at hazardous materials sites, health and safety for hazardous waste site workers, environmental and chemical toxicology, genetic toxicology.

MASLEN, DAVID KEITH, mathematician; b. Dunedin, Otago, New Zealand, June 17, 1968; s. Keith Ian Desmond and Marjorie (Jones) M. BSc with honors, U. Otago, Dunedin, 1989; PhD, Harvard U., 1993. Rschr. Max-Planck-Inst. for Math., Bonn, Germany, 1993-95, U. Utrecht, The Netherlands, 1995-97, Centrum voor Wiskunde en Informatica, Amsterdam, The Netherlands, 1997—. Vis. asst. prof. dept. math. Dartmouth Coll., 1998—; quantitative rsch. assoc. Susquehanna Investment Group, 1999—. Contbr. articles to profl. jours. Mem. Am. Math. Soc. Office: Susquehanna Investment Group 401 E City Ave Ste 200 Bala Cynwyd PA 19004-1117

MASLEN, DAVID PETER, lawyer; b. Quincy, Mass., Apr. 22, 1948; s. Frederick George and Catherine Elizabeth (Kelly) M.; m. Patricia Ann Ryan, June 17, 1972; children: Pamela Ryan, Julia Kelly. AB, Coll. of Holy Cross, Worcester, Mass., 1972; JD, New Eng. Sch. Law, Boston, 1976; LLM in Taxation, Boston U., 1985. Bar: Mass. 1977, U.S. Dist. Ct. Mass. 1977. Compliance officer U.S. Dept. Labor, Boston, 1975-85; atty. New Eng. Mutual Life Ins. Co., Boston, Burlington, Mass., 1985-87; sr. v.p. Aon Cons., Newburyport, 1987—. Office: Aon Cons PO Box 926 Newburyport MA 01950-5626 E-mail: david_maslen@aoncons.com., dmaslene@attbi.com.

MASLOW, WILL, lawyer, association executive; b. Kiev, Russia, Sept. 27, 1907; came to U.S., 1911, naturalized, 1924; s. Saul and Raeesa (Moonves) M.; m. Beatrice Greenfield, Dec. 21, 1933; children: Laura, Catha. AB, Cornell U., 1929; JD, Columbia U., 1931. Bar: N.Y. 1932, U.S. Supreme Ct. 1932. Reporter N.Y. Times, 1929-31; assoc. Arthur Garfield Hays, 1931-34; assoc. counsel Dept. Investigation, N.Y.C., 1934-36; trial atty., trial examiner NLRB, 1937-43; dir. field operations Pres.'s Com. Fair Employment Practice, 1943-45; gen. counsel Am. Jewish Congress, 1945—60, exec. dir., 1960-72. Faculty N.Y. Sch. Social Research, 1948-60; adj. prof. Coll. City N.Y., 1965-84. Editor: Boycott Report, 1977—94, Radical Islamic Fundamentalism Update, 1995—99. Trustee Meml. Found. for Jewish Culture; bd. dirs. Interracial Council for Bus. Opportunity, A. Philip Randolph Inst. Recipient Nat. award Jewish Coun. Pub. Affairs, 1998. Mem. World Jewish Congress (exec. com.), ACLU (dir. 1963-72), Am. Jewish Congress (Stephen Wise laureate 1972), Phi Beta Kappa. Home: 401 E 86th St New York NY 10028-6403

MASÓ, GEORGE, journalist, press information agency executive; b. Montevideo, Uruguay, Apr. 19, 1929; arrived in U.S., 1953; s. Maximino and Eugenia (Jones) M.; divorced; 1 child, Gonzalo. D of Social Scis., U. Uruguay, Montevideo, 1954; PhD in Polit. Scis., Columbia U., 1958. Founder, dir. Internat. Press Info. Agy., N.Y.C., Madrid, Buenos Aires, 1958—, Boca Raton, Fla., 1991—. Info. adviser of Uruguay to UN, N.Y.C., Geneva, 1972-77. Treas. West Atlantic Redevel. Coalition Inc., Delray Beach, Fla., 1996—; vice chmn. Affordable Housing Adv. Com., Delray Beach, 1996-98; bd. dirs. Pineapple Grove Main Street Inc., Delray Beach, 2000-01, Downtown Devel. Authority, 2000—; mem. Parking Mgmt. Adv. Bd., Delray Beach, 2000—. Mem. Lions (charter pres. UN 1978-80, zone chmn., pres. N.Y. State 1981-83, bd. dirs. UN 1984-2001), Republican. Office: Internat Press Info Agy PO Box 7006 Boca Raton FL 33431 E-mail: georgemaso@webtv.net.

MASON, AIMEE HUNNICUTT ROMBERGER, retired philosophy and humanities educator; b. Atlanta, Nov. 3, 1918; d. Edwin William and Aimee Greenleaf (Hunnicutt) Romberger; m. Samuel Venable Mason, Aug. 16, 1941 (dec. 1988); children: Olivia Elizabeth (Mrs. Mason Butcher), Christopher Leeds. BA, Conn. Coll., 1940; postgrad., Emory U., 1946-48; MA, U. Fla., 1979, PhD, 1980; MA, Stetson U., 1968. Model, coll. shop Saks Fifth Ave., N.Y.C., 1939; jr. exec. merchandising G. Fox & Co., Hartford, Conn., 1940-41; air traffic contr. CAA, Atlanta, 1942; ptnr. Coronado Concrete Products, New Smyrna Beach, Fla., 1953-81; adj. faculty Valencia Jr. Coll., Orlando, 1969; instr. philosophy and Humanities Seminole C.C., Sanford, 1969. Area cons. ARC, 1947-50; del. Nat. Red Cross, Washington, 1949; founding mem. St. Joseph Hosp. Aux., Atlanta, 1950-53; v.p., treas. Nw Smyrna Beach PTA, 1955-60; bd. dirs. Atlanta Symphony Orch., Fla. Symphony Orch., 1954-59; mem Code Enforcement Bd., Edgewater, Fla., 1992-94. Lt. USCGR, 1943-46. Recipient award in graphics Nat. Assn. Women Artists, 1939, 41. Mem. AAUP, AAUW (founding mem. New Smyrna Beach, exec. bd. 1984-85, chmn. scholarship com. 1984-87, coll./univ. liaison 1987-91, citizens code enforcement bd. Edgewater 1992-94), DAV, Am. Philos. Assn., Fla. Philos. Assn. (exec. coun. 1978-79), Collegium Phenomenologicum, Soc. Existencial and Phenomenological Philosophy, Soc. Phenomenology in Human Scis., Merleau-Ponty Circle, Fla. Assn. Cmty. Colls., Univ. Club Winter Park. Home: B216/218 1620 Mayflower Court Winter Park FL 32792

MASON, BARRY JEAN, retired banker; b. Big Spring, Tex., June 3, 1930; s. Vernon E. and Irene E. (Owen) M.; m. Alexana Petroff, Aug. 31, 1958; children: Scott Alexander, Lydia Claire. BS, U. Tex., 1957; B.F.T., Am. Inst. Fgn. Trade, 1958; postgrad., Advanced Mgmt. Program Harvard, Auspices U. Hawaii, 1968. Trainee First Nat. City Bank, N.Y., Hong Kong, 1959-60, asst. accountant Toyko, Japan, 1960-63, asst. mgr. Tokyo, 1963-66, mgr. Hong Kong, 1966-67, resident v.p., 1967-68, Tokyo, 1968-69, v.p. Japan, Korea, Okinawa, 1969, Republic Nat. Bank Dallas, 1969-70, sr. v.p., 1970-72, exec. v.p., 1972-83; chmn., chief exec. officer Republic Bank Las Colinas, 1983-87. Sr. advisor Sumitomo Trust and Banking Co. Ltd., 1989-91; mem. adv. bd. PEFCO. Trustee Am. Sch. Japan; bd. advisers Internat. Sch. Hong Kong. Served with AUS, 1948-49, USNR, 1952-53, USMCR, 1953-55. Mem. Bankers Assn. for Fgn. Trade (past dir.), Am. Bankers Assn. Clubs: Hong Kong, T Bar M Racquet. Home: 7730 Yamini Dr Dallas TX 75230-3231

MASON, BETTY G(WENDOLYN) HOPKINS, school system administrator; b. Tulsa, Mar. 3, 1928; d. Stacy Ervin and Carrie (McGlory) Hopkins; 1 child, Trena Janell Milliner Combs. BA, Bishop Coll., Marshall, Tex., 1949; MEd, Calif. State U., Haywood, 1974; EdD, U. Okla., 1986. Tchr. pub. schs., Kansas City, Mo., 1963-69; asst. Title I schs. Berkeley (Calif.) Unified Schs., 1970-71, asst. prin., 1971-72, dir. elem. edn., 1974-79; prin. Le Conte Elem. Sch., Berkeley, 1972-74; dir. high schs. Oklahoma City Pub. Schs., 1979-82, asst. supt., 1982-88; supt. of schs. Gary (Ind.) Pub. Schs., 1988-90; ednl. cons. Oklahoma City Pub. Schs., 1990-91, asst. supt., 1991-92, supt. of schs., 1992-95, ret., 1995. Mem. exec. bd. supt.'s initiative Nat. Urban League, N.Y.C., 1988-90. Author: Closed Chapter, 1999. Mem. exec. bd. YWCA, Gary, 1988-90, N.W. Ind. chpt. Urban League, Gary, 1988—; vol. supt. St. John Christian Heritage Acad., 1997. Named to, Okla. Educators Hall of Fame, 1999; recipient Citizen of Yr. award, Omega Phi Psi, 1985, Outstanding Woman in Edn. award, Okla. Commn. in Edn., 1987, Youth Svc. award, City and Mayor of Gary, 1988, Outstanding Educator award, Ind. U. Dons, 1989, Disting. Educator's award, 1993, Silver Beaver award, Boy Scouts Am., 1995, Woman of Yr. award, Girl Scouts, 1995, Best in Edn. Leadership award, Kappa Alpha Psi, 1998, Outstanding Sr. Soror award, Alpha Kappa Alpha, 1999. Mem. Am. Assn. Sch. Adminstrs., Nat. Assn. Black Educators, NW Ind. Supts. Coun., Phi Delta Kappa (Soror of yr. 1996), Alpha Kappa Alpha. Home: 2217 NW 119th St Oklahoma City OK 73120-7815

MASON, BOBBIE ANN, novelist, short story writer; b. Mayfield, Ky., May 1, 1940; d. Wilburn A. and Christianna (Lee) M.; m. Roger B. Rawlings, Apr. 12, 1969. BA, U. Ky., 1962; MA, SUNY, Binghamton, 1966; PhD, U. Conn., 1972. Asst. prof. English Mansfield (Pa.) State Coll., 1972-79. Writer-in-residence, U. Ky., Lexington, 2001—. Author: Nabokov's Garden, 1974, The Girl Sleuth: A Feminist Guide to the Bobbsey Twins, Nancy Drew and Their Sisters, 1975, 2d edit., 1995, Shiloh and Other Stories, 1982 (Ernest Hemingway award, Nat. Book Critics Circle award nominee, Am. Book award nominee, PEN Faulkner award nominee), 2d edit., 2001, In Country, 1985, Spence + Lila, 1988, 2d edit., 1998, Love Life, 1989, Feather Crowns, 1993 (Nat. Book Critic's Circle award nominee, So. Book award), Midnight Magic, 1998, Clear Springs, 1999 (Pulitzer prize finalist), Zigzagging Down a Wild Trail, 2001 (So. Book award); contbr. regularly to the New Yorker, 1980—; contbr. fiction to The Atlantic, Redbook, Paris Rev., Mother Jones, Harpers, N.Am. Rev., Va. Quar. Rev., Story, Ploughshares, So. Rev., Crazyhorse, DoubleTake; contbr. works Best American Short Stories, 1981, 83, The Pushcart Prize, Best of the Small Presses, 1983, 86, 97. Recipient O. Henry Anthology awards, 1986, 88, Hillsdale prize, 1999; grantee Pa. Arts Coun.,

1983, 89, Nat. Endowment Arts, 1983, Am. Acad. and Inst. Arts and Letters, 1984; Guggenheim fellow, 1984. Mem.: PEN, Author's Guild, Fellowship of So. Writers. Office: Internat Creative Mgmt care Amanda Urban Agt 40 W 57th St New York NY 10019-4001

MASON, CHARLES ELLIS, III, magazine editor; b. Boston, Oct. 31, 1938; s. Charles Ellis, Jr. and Ada Brooks (Trafford) M. BA, Yale U., 1960. Loan officer State St. Bank, Boston, 1963-68; asso. editor Sail mag., 1968-74, exec. editor, 1974—. Author: (with Buddy Melges) Sailing Smart, 1983; editor: Best of Sail Trim, 1976, Best of SAIL Navigation, 1981. Mem. exec. com. Sierra Club Greater Boston Group, 1992. Served with USNR, 1960-62. Home: 16 Joy St Boston MA 02114-4140 Office: Sail Publs 98 N Washington St Boston MA 02114 E-mail: cmason@primediasi.com.

MASON, CHARLES F. economist; b. Oakland, Calif., Mar. 16, 1955; s. Harold F. and Marian E. C. Mason; m. Glenda L. Earl, Aug. 8, 1981; children: Claire, Anne. BA in Math., BA in Econs., U. Calif., Berkeley, 1977, PhD in Econs., 1982. Asst. prof. U. Wyo., Laramie, 1982—88, assoc. prof., 1988—94, prof. econs., 1994—. Vis. scholar Ctr. for Resource and Environ. Studies, Australian Nat. U., Canberra, ACT, Australia, 1997; vis. prof. dept. econs. U. Waikato, Hamilton, New Zealand, 1997; vis. prof. Grad. Sch. Econs., Oreg. State U., Corvallis, 1996; vis. scholar dept. econs. U. Mich., Ann Arbor, 1990. Co-editor: Jour. Environ. Econs. and Mgmt., 2001—, assoc. editor: , 1999—2000, assoc. editor: Social Sci. Jour., 1988—92; contbr. Mem.: Soc. Econ. Dynamics and Control, Econ. Sci. Assn., Assn. Environ. and Resource Economists, Am. Econs. Assn., Wyo. State Soccer Assn. (state coord. referee assignors 2001—02), Laramie Blizzard Soccer Club (v.p. 2001—02). Avocations: fly fishing, soccer referee. Office: U Wyo Dept Econ and Fin Laramie WY 82071-3985 Office Fax: 307-766-5090. Business E-Mail: bambuzlr@uwyo.edu.

MASON, COLIN MICHAEL, music educator, musician; b. Tamuning, Mar. 22, 1963; s. Jack Meredith and Sarah McMahon Mason; m. Anna Elizabeth Carney, May 13, 1994. MusB in Jazz Studies, San Diego State U., 1993; MusM, No. Ariz. U., 1995; MusD in Edn., The U. of Tex., Austin, Texas, 1996. Coord. of jazz studies The U. N.H., Durham, NH, 1999—2000; asst. dir. of bands, dir. of jazz studies U. of Mary Hardin-Baylor, Belton, Tex., 2000—. Dir.: (jazz performing group) The Southwest Horns , 1999. Mem.: The Internat. Assn. for Jazz Edn. (tex. state chpt. coord. of performing groups 2001—02, artist rels. mgr. 1999—2002). Home: 2911 B Whisper Oaks Ln Georgetown TX 78628 Office: University of Mary Hardin Baylor 900 College Street Belton TX 76513 Home Fax: 254-295-4943; Office Fax: 254-295-4943. Personal E-mail: cmason@umhb.edu. E-mail: cmason@umhb.edu.

MASON, DAVID STEWART, political science educator; b. Washington, Nov. 23, 1947; s. Richard S. and Sheila M. Mason; m. Sharon Ann Wood, June 17, 1970; children: Dana Kathryn, Melanie Elizabeth. BA, Cornell U., 1969; MA, Johns Hopkins U., 1971; PhD, Ind. U., 1978. Asst. prof. Butler U., Indpls., 1975-82, assoc. prof., 1982-90, prof., 1990—, dept. chair, 1991-98. Author: Public Opinion and Political Change in Poland, 1985 (Quincy Wright award 1986), Revolution in East-Central Europe, 1992, rev. edit., 1996, Marketing Democracy, 2000. Rsch. grantee Nat. Coun. for Soviet and East European Rsch., 1990-92, 96-97, Social Sci. Rsch. Coun., 1990, Am. Coun. Learned Socs., 1983. Mem. Am. Polit. Sci. Assn., Am. Assn. for Advancement of Slavic Studies, Internat. Studies Assn.-Midwest (pres. 1986-87). Democrat. Avocations: tennis, guitar. Office: Butler U 4600 Sunset Ave Indianapolis IN 46208-3487

MASON, DEAN TOWLE, cardiologist; b. Berkeley, Calif., Sept. 20, 1932; s. Ira Jenckes and Florence Mabel (Towle) M.; m. Maureen O'Brien, June 22, 1957; children: Kathleen, Alison. BA in Chemistry, Duke U., 1954, MD, 1958. Diplomate Am. Bd. Internal Medicine, Am. Bd. Cardiovasc. Diseases, Nat. Bd. Med. Examiners. Intern, then resident in medicine Johns Hopkins Hosp., 1958-61; clin. assoc. cardiology br., sr. asst. surgeon USPHS, Nat. Heart Inst., NIH, 1961-63, asst. sect. dir. cardiovascular diagnosis, attending physician, sr. investigator cardiology br., 1963-68; prof. medicine, prof. physiology, chief cardiovascular medicine U. Calif. Med. Sch., Davis-Sacramento Med. Center, 1968-82; dir. cardiac ctr. Cedars Med. Ctr., Miami, Fla., 1982-83; physician-in-chief Western Heart Inst., San Francisco, 1983—; chmn. dept. cardiovascular medicine St. Mary's Med. Ctr., 1986-99, hon. med. staff, 2000—. Co-chmn. cardiovascular-renal drugs U.S. Pharmacopeia Com. Revision, 1970-75; mem. life scis. com. NASA; med. rsch. rev. bd. VA, NIH; vis. prof. numerous univs., cons. in field; mem. Am. Cardiovascular Splty. Cert. Bd., 1970-78. Editor-in-chief Am. Heart Jour., 1980-96; author 25 books on cardiovasc. medicine; contbr. numerous articles to med. jours. Recipient rsch. award Am. Therapeutic Soc., 1965; Theodore and Susan B. Cummings Humanitarian award Dept. State-Am. Coll. Cardiology, 1972, 73, 75, 78; Skylab Achievement award NASA, 1974; U. Calif. Faculty Rsch. award, 1978, Award of Honor Wisdom Soc., 1997, Medal of Honor Winston Churchill Soc., 1998, Armand Hammer Creative Genius award, 1998, Dwight D. Eisenhower Admirable Am. of Achievement award, 1998, Eternal Jesus Christ award, 1998, Blessed Lord's Prayer award, 1998, Dean Towle Mason Eminent Physician of Wisdom award, 1999, 2002. Master Am. Coll. Cardiology (pres. 1977-78); fellow A.C.P., Am. Heart Assn., Am. Coll. Chest Physicians, Royal Soc. Medicine; mem. Am. Soc. Clin. Investigation, Am. Physiol. Soc., Am. Soc. Pharmacology and Exptl. Therapeutics (Exptl. Therapeutics award 1973), Am. Fedn. Clin. Research, N.Y. Acad. Scis., Am. Assn. U. Cardiologists, Am. Soc. Clin. Pharmacology and Therapeutics, We. Assn. Physicians, AAUP, We. Soc. Clin. Research (past pres.), Phi Beta Kappa, Alpha Omega Alpha. Clubs: El Marcero Country. Republican. Methodist. Home: 44725 Country Club Dr El Macero CA 95618-1047 Office: Western Heart Inst St Marys Med Ctr 450 Stanyan St San Francisco CA 94117-1079

MASON, DEBORAH, entrepreneur; b. Columbus, Ohio, Oct. 10, 1951; d. Neil E. and Georgia M. (Hargan) M. BFA in Comml. Art Design, Art Therapy, Columbus Coll. Art & Design, 1974. Registered art therapist; cert. profl. child care worker; cert. in RET, PET, RBT, family relations, awareness through movement, parent to parent; cert. instr. N.G. Bur. Art therapist St. Ann's Hosp., Columbus, 1973-76; cmty. rels./edn. and tng. specialist Franklin County 648 Bd., 1976-79; trainer Bank One Columbus N.A., 1981-83; coord. Ctrl. Ohio ADMS Women's Set-Aside Funds, 1987-90; exec. dir. Inst. for Human Awareness, Inc., 1979—; adminstr. Bus. Against Substance Abuse Coalition, 1990—. Cons. ABA, AMA, Am. Hosp. Assn., NIMH, Nat. Inst. Drug Abuse, N.Am. Rockwell, Nationwide Ins., Compuserve, Inc., others, 1979; instr. Ohio State U., Columbus, 1989—; trainer Robert Stutman & Assocs., Inc., Dedham, Mass., 1994—; pres. Working Ptnrs. Sys., Inc., 1997—; adv. bd. Franklin U., Columbus, 1994—; facilitator task force for developing drug-free workplace discount program Ohio Bur. Workers' Compensation, 1997. Founder: The Working Partners Program: Substance-Free Workplace Consultation Program for Small Businesses, 1993 (Trademark award 1996), Psycho-Social Drama: A Training and Education Process, 1976 (trademark 1980); dir.: (videotape) The Ohio State University Drug and Alcohol Prevention Education Tape, 1989 (FIPSE grantee 1989); contbr. articles to profl. jours. Founder Bus. Against Substance Abuse (BASA) Coalition, 1990; bd. comm. chmn. Ctrl. Ohio Red Ribbon Com., Columbus,1991-94; founder Bus. to Bus. Spkrs. Bur., Columbus, 1990. Recipient Ms Executive award Columbus Dispatch Newspaper, 1980, Gov.'s Spl. Recognition award State of Ohio, 1990, Award of Achievement, Franklin County Drug-Free Schs. Consortium, 1993, Extra Mile award Franklin County ADAMH Bd., 1995; named to Outstanding Young Women of Am., 1984; grantee Yassenoff Found., 1979, Columbus Found., 1979, Ohio Dept. Health, 1980. Mem.Inst. for a Drug-Free Workplace, Cmty. Anti-Drug Coalitions Assn. (CADCA). Home: 178 Homestead Dr Pickerington OH 43147-1448 Office: BASA Coalition 700 Bryden Rd Fl 3 Columbus OH 43215-4839

MASON, DERRICK, football player; b. Detroit, Jan. 17, 1974; m. Marci Mason; children: Bailee My-Lin, Derrick Jr. Postgrad in comm., Mich. State Univ. Wide receiver Tenn. Titans, 1997—. Achievements include the ninth player in NFL history to record consecutive seasons with more than 2,000 all-purpose yards. Office: Tn Titans Baptist Sports Park 460 Great Cr Rd Nashville TN 37228*

MASON, DONALD ROGER, protective services official, city official; b. Kalamazoo, June 30, 1942; s. Donald R. and Mary Jane (Anderson) M.; m. Judith Gay Thompson, Feb. 24, 1964 (div. July 1981); children: Chad A., Bredt P.; m. Katherine M. Compton, Nov. 25,1981; children: Meg E. Krueger, Stephanie Shepherd. BS in Criminal Justice, Nazareth Coll., Kalamazoo, 1980; grad., FBI Acad., Quantico, Va., 1988. Cert. EMT, police officer, firefighter, Mich.; lic. bldg. contractor, Mich.; reg. bldg. inspector, Mich. Police officer City of Otsego, Mich., 1966, City of Plainwell, 1977, City of Battle Creek, 1970-71; youth officer Portage (Mich.) Police Dept., 1971-78; chief police City of Mendon, Mich., 1978-80; chief police, dir. emergency med. svcs. City of Belding, 1980-92, dir. pub. safety, 1992—. Advisor criminal justice program Grand Valley State U., Allendale, Mich., 1984—; chmn. Emergency Dispatch Fire and Emergency Med. Svcs. Com., Ionia, Mich., 1990— Trustee Belding Bd. Edn., 1988—; chmn., founder Miss Belding Pageant, 1988—. Sgt. USAF, 1966-70. Recipient Chief's Achievement award City of Belding, 1984, achievement award Mich. Mcpl. League, 1985. Mem. Internat. Assn. Chiefs Police, Mich. Assn. Chiefs Police (rep. 1985), West Mich. Assn. Chiefs Police (chmn. 1987), Mich. Assn. Sch. Bds., Belding Area C. of C. (pres. 1984-85, 87, 92), FBI Acad. Assocs., Masons. Republican. Methodist. Avocations: computer programming, residential building. Home: 13495 12 Mile Rd Greenville MI 48838-8319 Office: Belding Police Dept 120 Pleasant St Belding MI 48809-1644

MASON, DWIGHT NEWELL, foreign and defense policy consultant; b. N.Y.C., Apr. 20, 1939; s. Newell Ormsbee Mason and Eleanor Dwight; m. Sue Elizabeth Wheeler, Apr. 23, 1965; children: Margaret Carleton Mason Richards, Nathaniel Dwight Mason. AB, Brown U., 1961; MA, U. Calif., 1962; postgrad., Woodrow Wilson Sch., 1971-72. Fgn. svc. officer Dept. State, Washington, 1962-91; cons. Dilworth, Paxon, 1991—; U.S. chmn. Permanent Joint Bd. on Def. Can.-U.S., 1994—2002. Mem. Atlantic Coun. of the U.S., Washington, 1992—, Can. Inst. of Strategic Studies, Ottawa, 1993—. Contbr. articles to profl. jours. Asst. in registration Am. Voters Dem. Abroad, Washington, 1992-94. Congrl. fellow Am. Polit. Sci. Assn., 1976-77. Mem. Cosmos Club, Kenwood Club, Am. Fgn. Svc. Assn., Assn. for Can. Studies in the U.S., Can. inst. Strategic Studies, Am. Coun. for Quebec Studies. Democrat. Episcopalian. Office: Dilworth Paxon 1200 19th St NW Washington DC 20036 E-mail: dmason@dilworthlaw.com.

MASON, EARL JAMES, JR. pathologist, educator; b. Marion, Ind., Mar. 26, 1923; s. Earl James and Grace A. (Leer) M.; m. Eileen Gursansky, Dec. 2, 1967. Student, Marion Coll., 1940-41; BS in Medicine, Ind. U., 1944, AB in Chemistry, MA in Bacteriology, Ind. U., 1947; PhD in Microbiology, Ohio State U., 1950; MD, Western Res. U., 1954. Diplomate Am. Bd. Nuc. Medicine; diplomate in anat. and clin. pathology, radioisotopic pathology and dermatopathology Am. Bd. Pathology. Tchg. asst. dept. bacteriology Ind. U., 1945-47; rsch. fellow depts. ophthalmology and bacteriology Ohio State U., Columbus, 1947-48, tchg. asst. dept. bacteriology, 1948-50; Crile rsch. scholar Western Res. U., Cleve., 1951-53; Damon Runyon cancer rsch. fellow dept. pathology Western REs. U.-Cleve. City Hosp., 1951-56; chief dept. pathology USPHS Hosp., San Francisco, 1956-58; fellow pathology U. Tex. Postgrad. Sch. Medicine/M.D. Anderson Hosp, Houston, 1958-59; asst. prof. dept. pathology Baylor U. Coll. Medicine, 1959-60; asst. pathologist Jefferson Davis Hosp., 1959-60, Michael Reese Hosp. and Med. Ctr., Chgo., 1960-61; assoc. dir. dept. pathology, dir. dept. biol. scis. Mercy Hosp., 1960-65; dir. labs. St. Mary Med. Ctr., Gary and Hobart, Ind., 1965-94; cons. pathology and nuclear medicine, 1994—. Assoc. prof. pathology Chgo. Med. Sch., 1966—; clin. prof. pathology Ind. U. Med. Sch., 1976—; clin. prof. Inst. Critical Care Medicine, Palm Springs, Calif., 1996—. Mem. Coll. Am. Pathologists, Am. Assn. Pathologists and Bacteriologists, Am. Soc. Clin. Pathologists, Internat. Acad. Pathologists, Am. Soc. Exptl. Pathology, Am. Assn. Cancer Rsch., Am. Assn. Blood Banks, Am. Soc. Hematology, Am. Acad. Dermatology, Am. Soc. Cytology, Sigma Xi. Achievements include research on cellular origin of antibodies and virus-cell interactions. Home: 7 Summit Rd Portage IN 46368-8714 Office: 1500 S Lake Park Ave Hobart IN 46342-6638 E-mail: emason@dc.rr.com.

MASON, EDWARD EATON, surgeon; b. Boise, Idaho, Oct. 16, 1920; s. Edward Files and Dora Bell (Eaton) M.; m. Dordana Fairman, June 18, 1944; children— Daniel Edward, Rose Mary, Richard Eaton, Charles Henry. BA, U. Iowa, 1943, MD, 1945; PhD in Surgery, U. Minn., 1953. Intern, resident in surgery Univ. Hosps., Mpls., 1945-52; asst. prof. surgery U. Iowa, 1953-55, asso. prof., 1956-60, prof., 1961-91, prof. emeritus, 1991—, chmn. gen. surgery, 1978-91. Cons. VA Hosp.; trainee Nat. Cancer Inst., 1949-52 Author: Computer Applications in Medicine, 1964, Fluid, Electrolyte and Nutrient Therapy in Surgery, 1974, Surgical Treatment of Obesity, 1981; developer gastric bypass and gastroplasty for treatment of obesity; contbr. articles profl. jours. Served to lt. (j.g.) USNR, 1945-47. Fellow ACS; mem. AMA, Am. Surg. Assn., Western Surg. Assn., Soc. Univ. Surgeons, Internat. Soc. Surgery, Ctrl. Surg. Assn., Soc. Surgery Alimentary Tract, Am. Thyroid Assn., Am. Soc. Bariatric Surgery, Sigma Xi, Alpha Omega Alpha. Republican. Presbyterian. Home: 5 Melrose Cir Iowa City IA 52246-2013 Office: University Hosp Dept of Surgery Iowa City IA 52242 *Continuity of interest and planning weaves the daily decisions into a whole cloth that does more than cover one's imperfections.*

MASON, EILEEN B. federal agency administrator; b. N.Y.C. m. Arthur Mason; children: Elizabeth, Laura. BA, Cornell U.; MPA, Am. U. Tchr. math., reading an dhealth Hephzibah High Sch., Ga.; editor Acripolis Books, Washington; music adv. panelist Md. State Arts Coun.; v.p. grants Arts and Humanities Coun., Montgomery County, Md.; mgr. and adminstr. U.S. Nuclear Regulatory Commn.; acting chmn. NEA, Washington, 2001, 2002—. Performer: (violinist) Cornell U. Symphpny, MIT Symphpny, Augusta Symphony, Am. U. Symphony Orchestra. Mem.: Ph Alpha Alpha. Office: NEA 110 Pennsylvania Ave NW Washington DC 20506*

MASON, ELLSWORTH GOODWIN, librarian; b. Waterbury, Conn., Aug. 25, 1917; s. Frederick William and Kathryn Loretta (Watkins) M.; m. Rose Ellen Maloy, May 13, 1951 (div. Oct. 1961); children: Kay Iris Maurice, Joyce Iris Lande; m. Joan Lou Shinew, Aug. 16, 1964; 1 son, Sean David. BA, Yale U., 1938, MA, 1942, PhD, 1948; LHD, Hofstra U., 1973; Diploma, Inst. Children's Lit., 1996. Cert. Christian Writer's Guild, 1997. Reference asst. Yale Library, 1938-42; export license officer Bd. Econ. Warfare, 1942-43; instr. English Williams Coll., 1948-50; instr. humanities div. Marlboro (Vt.) Coll., 1951-52; serials libr. U. Wyo. Libr., 1952-54; reference libr. Colo. Coll. Libr., Colorado Springs, 1954-58; lectr., libr. Colo. Coll., 1958-63; prof., dir. libr. svcs. Hofstra U., Hempstead, N.Y., 1963-72; prof., dir. U. Colo. Librs., Boulder, 1972-76; freelance writer children's lit., 1995—. Adj. prof. U. Ill., Urbana, 1968; pres. Mason Assocs., Ltd., 1977—; rsch. assoc. U. Calif.-Berkeley, 1965; vis. lectr. Northwestern U., 1961, Colo. Coll., 1965, Syracuse U., 1965-68, Elmira Coll., 1966, Columbia U., 1966-68, U. Ill., 1972, Lincoln U., 1969, U. B.C. (Can.), 1969, U. Toronto, 1970, U. Tulsa, 1971, 76, Rutgers U., 1971, Colgate U., 1972, Simmons Coll., 1972, U. Oreg., 1973, Hofstra U., 1974, U. N.C., 1976, U. Ala., 1976, Ball State U., 1977, U. Lethbrige, Can., 1977, U. Ariz., 1981, Ariz. State U., 1981, Victoria U., New Zealand, 1983, U. Canterbury, New Zealand, 1983, U. Nev. Las Vegas, 1992, Remember Pearl Harbor Assn., 1993, 94; libr. cons., 1958—, libr. value engr., 1992—. Editor: (with Stanislaus Joyce) The Early Joyce, 1955, Xerox U.M. edit., 1964, (with Richard Ellmann) The Critical Writings of James Joyce, 1959, 2d edit., 1989, Critical Commentary on A Portrait of the Artist as a Young Man, 1966; translator: Recollections of James Joyce (S. Joyce), 1950, Essais de J. Joyce, 1966, Escritos Criticos de James Joyce, (Portuguese edit.), 1967, (Spanish edit.), 1973, 75, James Joyce's Ulysses and Vico's Cycle, 1973, Kritische Schriften v. James Joyce, 1975, Mason on Library Buildings, 1980, (with Walter and Jean Shine) A MacDonald Potpourri, 1988, The University of Colorado Library and Its Makers, 1876-1972, 1994; contbr. Contemporary Authors, 1988—; editor: Colorado College Studies, 1959-62; editor and compiler: Focus on Robert Graves, 1972-88; adv. editor: Focus on Robert Graves and His Contemporaries, 1988—; editor: The Booklover's Bounty, 1977-82; mem. editl. bd. Serial Slants, 1957-59, The Serials Librarian, 1977-98, Choice, 1962-65, Coll. and Rsch. Librs., 1969-72. Mem. exec. bd. U. Ky. Libr. Assocs., 1991-94; exec. bd. Concerned Christians in Ky., 1993-98. Served with USNR, 1943-46. Recipient Harry Bailly spkr.'s award Assn. Colls. of Midwest, 1975; fellow Coun. on Libr. Resources, 1969-70; grantee Am. Coun. Learned Socs., Edn. Facilities Labs., Hofstra U., U. Colo.; named Ky. Col., 1993. Mem. ALA (councillor-at-large 1961-65), Colo. Libr. Assn. (pres. so. dist. 1960-61), Bibliog. Soc. Am., Libr. Assn. (London), N.Z. Libr. Assn., Pvt. Librs. Assn., Alcuin Soc. Vancouver, Conf. Editors Learned Jours., N.Z. Royal Forest and Bird Protection Soc., Colo. Book Collectors (founder, pres. 1975-86), Inst. Vico Studies, James Joyce Found. (chmn. sect. on translation from Joyce, 2d Internat. James Joyce Symposium, Dublin 1969), Nat. Assn. Scholars, Am. Christian Writers, Black America's PAC, Caxton Club, Archons of Colophon, Ghost Town Club, Alpha Sigma Lambda, Sigma Kappa Alpha (pres. 1969-70). Home: 736 Providence Rd Lexington KY 40502-2267 also: 39 Discovery Dr Whitby New Zealand

MASON, EMANUEL JOEL, psychology educator; b. N.Y.C., Aug. 7, 1943; s. Murray Aaron and Natalie Mason; m. Susan B. Spreiregen, Apr. 9, 1944; children: Sara Beth, Sandra Lisa. BS in Psychology, CCNY, 1965; MEd in Ednl. Psychology, Temple U., 1969, EdD in Sch. Psychology, 1972. Lic. psychologist, Ky.; nat. cert. sch. psychologist. Sch. psychologist Edgewater Twp. Schs., Edgewater Park, N.J., 1969-72; faculty in sch. and ednl. psychology U. Ky., Lexington, 1972-96, chmn. dept. ednl. and counseling psychology, 1988-93; prof. counseling and sch. psychology, dept. chmn. Northeastern U., Boston, 1996—. Co-author: Computers in Schools, 1985, Research in Education and the Behavioral Sciences, 1997; contbr. articles to profl. jours. 2nd lt. to capt. U.S. Army, 1965-67. Fellow APA (editor div. 16 newsletter 1978-81, Lightner Witmer award, div. sch. psychologists 1978), Am. Psychol. Soc., Nat. Assn. Sch. Psychologists (state del. 1977). Office: Northeastern Univ (LA203) Dept Counseling Psychology Boston MA 02115

MASON, FRANK HENRY, III, automobile company executive, leasing company executive; b. Paris, Nov. 16, 1936; s. Frank H. and Dorothy (Carter) M.; children: Robert C., William C. B of Elec. Engring., Vanderbilt U., 1958; MS in Indsl. Mgmt., MIT, 1965. With Ford Motor Co., 1965-71; asst. controller Ford Brazil, Sao Paulo, 1971-74; mgr. overseas fin. dept. Ford Motor Co., Dearborn, Mich., 1974-76, asst. controller engine divsn., 1976-78, mgr. facilities and mgmt. svcs., 1978-81; controller Ford Motor Credit Co., 1981-87; dir. fin. Ford Fin. Svcs. Group, 1987-89; exec. v.p., chief fin. officer U.S. Leasing, Internat., San Francisco, 1989-92; retired, 1992. Lt. USN, 1958-63.

MASON, FRANKLIN ROGERS, retired automotive executive; b. Washington, June 16, 1936; s. Franklin Allison and Jeannette Morgan (Rogers) M.; m. Aileen Joan Larson, July 29, 1961; children: William Rogers, Elisa Ellen. BS in Engring, Princeton U., 1958; MBA, Northwestern U., 1960. With Ford Motor Co., 1960-75, finance mgr., Portugal, 1969-72; fin. analysis mgr. Ford subs. Richier S.A., France, 1972-75; sr. v.p. finance Raymond Internat. Inc., Houston, 1975-86; chief fin. officer Quanex Corp., 1986-87; group v.p., chief fin. officer Gulf States Toyota, Inc., 1987-97; sr. v.p., gen. mgr. Friedkin Bus. Svcs., 1998; ret., 1998. With arty. U.S. Army, 1960. Mem.: Princeton U. Alumni Assn., Houston Racquet Club. Republican. Episcopalian. Home: 5765 Indian Cir Houston TX 77057-1302 E-mail: frmason@earthlink.net. *Business is people, and success is dependent on good communication with people. Effective communication must be accompanied by fairness, consistency, patience, and a willingness to compromise.*

MASON, GEORGE HENRY, business educator, consultant; b. Chgo., Sept. 11, 1929; s. Robert De Main and Dorothy Wills (Belden) M.; m. Constance Eleanor Wolcott, May 14, 1960. AB, Kenyon Coll., 1955; MBA, Cornell U., 1957; MF, Duke U., 1983. CFA. Investment officer Travelers Ins. Co., Hartford, Conn., 1957-88; exec.-in-residence U. Hartford, West Hartford, 1989-98, dir. Bus. Applications Ctr., 1998-2001. Vis. prof. Jagiellonian U., Cracow, Poland, spring 1996, Yang-En U., Quanzhou, Fujian, China, fall 1997; investment adv. coun. State of Conn., 1999—. Co-author: Timberland Investments, 1992. Mem.: Hartford Soc. Fin. Analysts, Assn. Investment Mgmt. and Rsch., Dataw Island Club, Mill Reef Club, Country Club of Farmington. Republican. Avocations: skiing, golf, writing.

MASON, GREG, publishing executive; MBA, U. S.F. Pub. PC Computing (now Smart Bus.), San Francisco; exec. v.p. sales CNET Networks, Inc., 2000—. Office: CNET Networks Inc 235 Second St San Francisco CA 94105*

MASON, GREGG CLAUDE, orthopedic surgeon, researcher; b. Schenectady, N.Y., July 28, 1958; s. George and Maureen (Murphy) M.; m. Dina Marie Sokolowski, June 16, 1990. BS in Chemistry magna cum laude, Allegheny Coll., 1980; MD, U. Pitts., 1984. Diplomate Am. Bd. Orthop. Surgery, Nat. Bd. Med. Examiners. Gen. surgery intern U. Colo./U. Colo. Med. Ctrs., Denver, 1984-85; orthopaedic rsch. fellow U. Pitts., 1985-86, resident in orthopaedic surgery, 1986-89; orthopedic surgeon U.S. Naval Hosp., Okinawa, Japan, 1989-92; pvt. practice, Erie, 1992—. Active staff St. Vincent Med. Ctr., St. Vincent Surgery Ctr., Hamot Med. Ctr., Union City Meml. Hosp.; lectr. in field. Contbr. articles to profl. jours. Comdr. M.C. USNR, 1980—. Recipient Outstanding Student Rsch. award U. Pitt. Sch. Medicine, 1984, Harold Henderson Sankey Orthop. award, 1984; rsch. grantee Competitive Med. Rsch. Fund., Presbyn.-Univ. Hosp. of Pitts., 1986-87, U. Pitts. Rsch. Devel. Fund, 1986-87. Disting. Alden scholar 1977, 78, 79, 80, Sandra Doane Turk scholar, 1979, Armed Svcs. Health Professions scholar, 1981-84. Fellow ACS, Internat. Coll. Surgeons, Mil. Soc. Orthop. Surgeons, Am. Acad. Orthop. Surgeons (tchg. seal 1993); mem. AMA, Pa. Orthop. Soc. (Best Rsch. Paper 1987, 88), Erie Orthop. Soc., U. Pitts. Med. Ctr. Orthop. Alumni., Am. Orthop. Soc. of Sports Medicine (Cabaud award 1988), Ea. Orthop. Assn. (Founders award 1988), Phi Beta Kappa. Office: Orthopaedic Surgeons Inc 204 W 26th St Erie PA 16508-1898

MASON, GREGORY WESLEY, JR. secondary education educator; b. Chgo., Jan. 21, 1963; s. Gregory Wesley and Diana (Burton) M.; m. LaTanya Yvonne Brown, June 8, 1991; children: Gregory Arthur, Timothy Michael. BS, Ill. State U., 1986; MEd, U. Ill., Chgo., 1996. Cert. secondary tchr., gen. adminstr., Ill. Instr. City Coll. Chgo., 1986-89; instr. project alert Roosevelt U., Chgo., 1989-91, counselor project upward bound, 1991-93; tchr. math. Bowen High Sch., 1993-95, chmn. profl. planning adv. com., 1994-95; tchr. math. Whitney M. Young Magnet H.S., 1995-2000, chmn. dept. math., 1997-2000; adminstr. Chgo. Pub. Schs., 2000—. Instr. Ill. Math. and Sci. Acad., Aurora, summers 1993-96; lectr. Coll. Edn., Loyola U., Chgo., 1999—; tchr. coord. Golden Apple Found., 2000-01; mem. nat. adv. bd. Schs. and Scholars Program, Woodrow Wilson Nat. Fellowship Found. Mem. pres.'s coun. edn. com. Mus. Sci. and Industry; mem. Ill. Robotic Competition Adv. Bd. Named Outstanding Young Men of Am., 1985. Mem. ASCD, Nat. Coun. Tchrs. Math., Ill. Coun. Tchrs. Math., Ill. Coun. for Coll. Attendance (bd. dirs. 1993-97), Nat. Assn. Secondary Sch. Prins., Benjamin Banneker Assn., Masons, Phi Delta Kappa. Avocations: swimming, chess, reading, stock trading, computers. Home: 2729 W 84th St Chicago IL 60652-3909 Office: Chgo Pub Schs 1326 W 14th Pl Chicago IL 60608 E-mail: gmason@csc.cps.k12.il.us.

MASON, HERBERT WARREN, JR. religion and history educator, author; b. Wilmington, Del., Apr. 20, 1932; s. Herbert Warren and Mildred Jane (Noyes) M.; m. Jeanine Young, June 25, 1982; children from previous marriage: Cathleen, Paul, Sarah. AB, Harvard U., 1955, AM, 1965, PhD, 1969. English tchr. Am. Sch. Paris, 1959-60; asst. prof. St. Joseph's Coll., Gorham, Maine, 1960-62; vis. lectr. Simmons Coll., Boston, 1962-63; vis. lectr. in Islamic Hist. Tufts U., Medford, Mass., 1965-66; teaching fellow in English Harvard U., Cambridge, 1962-66, teaching fellow in Islamic Hist., 1966-67; translator Bollingen Found., N.Y.C., 1968-72; prof. History and Religion Boston U., 1972-2000, William Goodwin Aurelio prof. history and religious thought, 2000—. Author: Reflections on the Middle East Crisis, 1970, Two Statesmen of Medieval Islam, 1971, Gilgamesh, 1971 (Nat. Book award nomination), The Death of al-Hallaj, 1979, Moments in Passage, 1979, (novel) Summer Light, 1980; translator: La Passion d'al-Hallaj, 4 vols., Bollingen Series (Louis Massignon), 1983, abridged 1 vol., 1994, A Legend of Alexander, 1986, Memoir of a Friend: Louis Massignon, 1988, Testimonies and Reflections, 1989, al-Hallaj, 1995, Haythu Taltaqi al-Anhar (novel in Arabic "Where the Rivers Meet"), 1999, (poems) Disappearances, 1999; co-editor Humaniora Islamica; contbr. articles, essays, reviews, fiction, reviews and poetry to popular fiction mags. Sec. Inter-racial Riverside Assn., Cambridge, Mass., 1965-67; trustee Bd. Charity of Edward Hopkins, Boston Athenaeum. Fellow Soc. for Values in Higher Edn.; mem. PEN (bd. dirs. Delos chpt.), Medieval Acad. Am., Am. Oriental Soc., Am. Acad. Religion, Mark Twain Soc., Inst. Internat. des Recherches Louis Massignon in Paris (dir. edn., v.p.), Am. Acad. Poetry, Japan Poetry Mus. (Iwate-Ken). Home: 30 Common St Phillipston MA 01331-2935 Office: Boston U 745 Commonwealth Ave Boston MA 02215-1401 E-mail: masonh@buiedu.

MASON, J. WILLIAM L. lawyer; b. Kittery, Maine, Apr. 14, 1940; s. Murray Lawrence and Dolores Elizabeth (Laird) M.; m. Mary Elizabeth Jordan; children: Joseph Patrick, Catherine Shannon, Brendan Michael. BA, U. N.H., 1973, MBA, 1979; JD, New Eng. Sch. Law, 1987. Molder Portsmouth (N.H.) Naval Shipyard, 1958-71, with labor rels., 1973-91; rehab. technician State of N.H., Concord, 1971-73; pvt. practice Portsmouth, 1991—. Staff sgt. N.H. Air Nat. Guard, 1974-81. Mem. ABA, Am. Trial Lawyers Assn., N.H. Bar Assn. Congregationalist. Avocation: coins. Home: 27 Old Concord Tpke Lee NH 03824-6729 Office: 5 Greenleaf Woods Dr Ste 301 Portsmouth NH 03801-5442 E-mail: jwlmason@hotmail.com.

MASON, JAMES HENRY, IV, retired surgeon; b. Atlantic City, Nov. 22, 1921; s. James Henry III and Violet French (Shreve) M.; m. Helen Theresa Dempsey, Nov. 22, 1947; children: James H. 5th, Cynthia Louise. AB with high honors, Princeton U., 1943; MD, Columbia U., 1946. Diplomate Am. Bd. Surgeons. Surg. tng. U. Pa. Grad. Sch. medicine, 1949-50; postgrad. med. tng. Atlantic City (N.J.) Med. Ctr., 1946-52, chief attending surgeon, surg. dir., 1954-75, pres. med. staff, 1967; pres. Med. Soc. Atlantic County, 1971-72; v.p. So. N.J. P.S.R.O., Cherry Hill, 1977-82; emergency physician Atlantic City Med. Ctr., 1975-86, mem. governing bd., 1967-2000, ret. Ofcl. local historian Ventnor City, N.J., 1991—; pres. Ventnor City Hist. Soc., 1996—, Ventnor City Cultural Arts Ctr., 1993—, Atlantic County Hist. Soc., 1985-86, 95-97, gen. chmn. Batsto (N.J.) Hist. Site, 1989-90, 98-99. Capt. U.S. Army, 1952-54, Korea. Decorated Bronze Star. Fellow: ACS; mem.: Soc. Surgeons N.J. Avocations: history, philately, art, gardening. Home: 3 S Oxford Ave Ventnor City NJ 08406-2842

MASON, JANE MUSSELMAN, artist; b. Ann Arbor, Aug. 31, 1950; d. Merle McNeil and Dorothy G. Musselman; m. Steve Mason, Feb. 9, 1979; children: Geoff, Graham. BS in Family Sci./Mgmt. and Journalism, U. Nebr., 1972. Creative dir. Jim Raglin Inc., Lincoln, Nebr., 1972-75; v.p. mktg. Commerce Group, 1975-81, Norwest Banks Inc., Mpls., 1981-84; v.p. account svcs. Glennon, St. Louis, 1984-90; v.p. strategic planning Nat. System Inc., 1990-94; pres., owner Jane Mason & Assocs., 1994—. Exec. dir. Merry Merry Art Fest, Ellisville, Mo., 1997. Artist Journey Series 1 (hon. mention in show award 1997, award of recognition 1999, 3rd place St. Louis Watercolor Soc. 1998, hon. mention 1999); exhibited in group show St. Louis Metro Printers Assn., 1999 (2d place award). Vestry mem. St. Martin's Episcopal Ch., Ellisville, Mo., 1989-92; cmty. liaison USPO cmty. panels, Des Peres, 1993-95; vol. costume designer Kirkwood H.S. Drama Dept.; art resource Jewish Ctr. for Aged, Chesterfield, Mo.; sec. North Kirkwood Mid. Sch. PTO, 1999-00. Mem. St. Louis Artists Guild, Greater St. Louis Art Assn. (bd. dirs., exhibits dir. 1996-97, pres. 1998-00), Art St. Louis, St. Louis Watercolor Soc. (pres. 2001-2003), Romance Writers of Am. (by-laws rev. com. Mo. chpt. 1991-92). Avocations: gardening, writing, being thankful. Office: Jane Mason & Assocs PO Box 31877 Des Peres MO 63131-0877

MASON, JOHANNA HENDRIKA ANNEKE, retired secondary education educator; b. Indramajoe, Indonesia, Feb. 17, 1932; came to U.S., 1957; d. Johannes Simon and Hendrika Jacoba (De Vroedt) Vermeulen; m. Alfred Bob Markholt, Feb., 1958 (div. Dec. 1966); children: Bob, Anneke, Joe Ralph, Lee Markholt; m. Rollin Mason, 1968 (div. 1978). French lang. diploma with top honors, Paris Alliance Française, 1952; BA in Philosophy summa cum laude, U. Puget Sound, 1976, MA in Comparative Lit., 1979, BA in Edn., 1988. Cert. pub. sch. tchr. 4-12. Adminstrv. asst. to pres. N.V. Nutricia, Zoetermeer, The Netherlands, 1953-57; pvt. sec. Grad. Sch. Bus. Harvard U., Cambridge, Mass., 1957; adminstrv. asst., lectr. humanities divsn. U. Puget Sound, Tacoma, 1966-88; tchr. English and French h.s. and mid. sch., 1988-94. Mem. pres. staff orgn. U. Puget Sound, Tacoma, 1978-80, budget task force, 1981-86. Author: (poetry compilation) Journey, 1981, A Handfull of Bubbles, 1981, Echoes, Mirrors, Reflections, 1983; contbr. poetry to lit. mags. Mem. city's task force on hate crimes, Tacoma, 1992, translator, 1974-90. Selected to literary pub. art registry, City of Tacoma, 1999. Mem. So. Poverty Law Ctr., Amnesty Internat., Coun. Indian Nations, Phi Kappa Phi (nat. com. on comms. 1991-94, pres. chpt. 1973-77). Avocations: reading, hiking, theater, needlework, poetry.

MASON, JOHN MILTON (JACK MASON), judge; b. Mankato, Minn., Oct. 31, 1938; s. Milton Donald and Marion (Dailey) M.; m. Vivian McFerran, Aug. 25, 1962; children: Kathleen, Peter, Michael. BA cum laude, Macalester Coll., 1960; JD, Harvard U., 1963. Bar: Minn. 1963, U.S. Supreme Ct. 1970. Assoc. Dorsey & Whitney, Mpls., 1963-68, ptnr., 1969-71, 73-95; solicitor gen. State of Minn., St. Paul, 1971, chief dep. atty. gen., 1972-73; U.S. magistrate judge Dist. of Minn., 1995—. Bd. dirs. Macalester Coll., St. Paul, 1971-77, St. Paul Chamber Orch., 1979-88, U. Minn. Hosps. and Clinics, St. Paul, 1979-83, Mpls. Bd. Edn., 1973-80, Minn. Chorale, 1990-95, MacPhail Ctr. for Arts, 1990-96, Ordway Music Theatre, 1990-99, 2000—; mem. nat. adv. bd. Concordia U. Lang. Villages, 1996—, Theatre de la Jeune Lune, 1998-2001. With USAF, 1957, with Res., 1957-65. Mem. Harvard Law Sch. Assn. (pres. Minn. sect. 1980-81) Avocations: classical piano, bicycling, accordion, foreign languages. Home: 2849 Burnham Blvd Minneapolis MN 55416-4331 Office: 610 Federal Cts Bldg 316 Robert St N Saint Paul MN 55101-1495 E-mail: jmmason@mnd.uscourts.gov.

MASON, JOHN GROUARD, political science educator; b. N.Y.C., Oct. 31, 1946; s. Edward Gay and Ruth Loring (Warner) M.; m. Catherine Michele Coufleau, Jan. 8, 1983; children: Julia DeForest, Jonathan Loring. BA in History with honors, NYU, 1972, MA in Polit. Sci., 1977; MA in Sociology, Queens Coll., CUNY, 1989; M Phil in Sociology, Grad. Ctr., CUNY, 1991; PhD in Sociology, CUNY, 1993. Lectr. sociology Ramapo (N.J.) State Coll., 1979-84; lectr. polit. sci. William Paterson Coll., 1980-92, asst. prof. polit. sci., 1993—; lectr. sociology Queens Coll., CUNY, Flushing, 1985-92; press officer Michael Harrington Ctr., Queens Coll., CUNY, 1990-92. Co-chair European Security Workshops NYU Ctr. European Studies, 1992—; lectr. dept. study of English speaking countries U. Paris VIII, 1984-85; corr. La Foundation Pour Les Etudes de la Defense Nat., Paris, 1986-89. Co-editor: Les Syndicats Francais et Americains face aux mutations technologiques, 1984; contbg. author: French Security Policy in a Disarming World, 1989; editorial assoc. polit. quar. TELOS, N.Y.C., 1982-90, quar. Punto de Contacto/Point of Contact, N.Y.C., 1973-76. Mem. internat. affairs commn. Dem. Socialists Am., 1988—; prodr. pub. affairs dept. Sta. WBAI Radio Pacifica, N.Y.C., 1980-92. NIH fellow, 1974-77; resident scholar NYU Inst. for French Studies, 1988-92, NYU Ctr. for European Studies, 1992—; recipient La Bourse Chateaubriand French Govt., 1984-85. Mem. Am. Polit. Sci. Assn. (colloquium on European politics and study), Internat. Studies Assn. Democrat. Episcopalian. Home: 55A Harrison St New York NY 10013-2705 Office: William Paterson Coll NJ Science Hall Wayne NJ 07470

MASON, JOHN LATIMER, engineering executive; b. Los Angeles, Nov. 8, 1923; s. Zene Upham and Edna Ella (Watkins) M.; m. Frances Howe Draeger, Sept. 1, 1950 (dec. June 1951); m. Mary Josephine Schulte, Nov. 26, 1954; children: Andrew, Peter, Mary Anne, John Edward. BS in Meteorology, U. Chgo., 1944; BS in Applied Chemistry, Calif. Inst. Tech., 1947, MS in Chem. Engring., 1948, PhD, 1950. Registered profl. engr., Calif. Engr. AiResearch Mfg. Co., Los Angeles, 1950-60; dir. engring. AiResearch Mfg. Co. div. Garrett Corp., 1960-72; v.p. engring. Garrett Corp., 1972-87; v.p. engring. and tech. Allied-Signal Aerospace Co., 1987-88, cons., 1989-96; chmn. tech. adv. com. Indsl. Turbines Internat., Inc., 1972-81, bd. dirs., 1980-88; adj. prof. engring. Calif. State U., Long Beach, 1992-96. Mem. tech. adv. bd. Tex. Ctr. for Superconductivity, U. Houston, 1989—; chair Calif. Coun. Sci. and Tech. Panel on Transp. R&D Ctr., 1993-94; bd. dirs. Planetary Sci. Inst., 1995—, sec., 1998—; cons. Capstone Turbine Corp., 1994-98; mem. tech. adv. bd. Ceryx Inc., 1998-2001; mem. workshop com. Transp. Rsch. Bd., 1998. Patentee in field. Chmn. energy and environment com. FISITA Coun., 1990-94. 1st lt. USAAF, 1943-45, PTO. Fellow AIAA (assoc.). Soc. Automotive Engrs. (bd. dirs. 1984-87, 90-93, pres.-elect 1989-90, pres. 1990-91), Performance Rev. Inst. (chmn. 1990-91, bd. dirs. 1992-93); mem. AAAS, NRC of NAS (com. on alternative energy R&D strategies 1989-90), Office Sci. and Tech. Policy (Nat. Critical Techs. panel 1992-93), Inst. Medicine of NAS (com. on health effects of indoor allergens 1992-93), Nat. Acad. Engring., U.S. Advanced Ceramics Assn. (chmn. tech. com., bd. dirs. 1985-88), Am. Chem. Soc., Am. Ceramic Soc., Caltech Assocs., Sigma Xi (assoc.). E-mail: JL-Mason@cox.net.

MASON, JOHN OLIVER, freelance journalist, poet, community activist; b. Kingston, Pa., Aug. 1, 1957; s. Oliver B. and Dorothy Mae (Hunter) Mason. BA, Temple U., 1984. Editorial writer Temple News, Phila., 1983-85; writer Phila. Tribune, 1989-95, Irish Edition, Phila., 1990-95, Northeast Breeze, Rockledge, 1993—, Germantown Courier, Phila., 1996—, Phila. Sunday Sun, 1996—, Chestnut Hill Local, 2000—. Sec. Concerned Citizens of Delaware Valley, 1990; rec. sec. A. Philip Randolph Inst., Phila., 2001; mem. Jewish Labor Com., Phila., 1985. Mem. Meridian Writers Collective. Avocations: philately, reading, cultural activities. E-mail: jomason@earthlink.net.

MASON, JOSEPH See BUSHINSKY, JAY

MASON, JUDITH ANN, freelance writer; b. Newark, Dec. 27, 1945; d. Richard Algie and Mary Ann (Beneck) M. Diploma in legal sci., Spencerian Bus. Coll., 1965; BA, Northeastern Ill. U., 1984. Legal sec. Harney B. Stover, Atty., Milw., 1967-69, Robert P. O'Meara, Atty., Waukegan, Ill., 1969-70; sec. to pres. First Midwest Bank, 1970-72, asst. cashier, 1972-76; legal sec. Eugene M. Snarski, Atty., 1976-81; adminstrv. aide Lake County Forest Preserve Dist., Libertyville, Ill., 1981-89; freelance writer Tucson, 1989—; legal sec., asst. Jeffrey H. Greenberg, Atty.; office mgr. Greenberg & Assocs., Tucson, 1989-96; legal asst. Leonard, Felker, Altfeld, Greenberg & Battaile, 1997—; exec. adminstr. JHG Devel. Co. LLC, 1995—, 1998—. Travel rep. Antioch (Ill.) Travel Agy., 1980-89, Advance Travel Agy., Zion, Ill., 1980-89; pub. speaker for various orgns., Lake County, Ill., 1984-89. Author: Why I Remember Yesterday, 1979, Haggadah (play), 1982; editor poetry column: Bank Man Magazine, 1972-75; contbg. article writer Compendum Mag. Tchr. Confraternity Christian Doctrine St. Patrick's Ch., Wadsworth, Ill., 1980-85; lector, eucharistic min. Prince of Peace Ch., Lake Villa, Ill., 1980-89; hospice vol. St. Therese Hosp., Waukegan, 1984; speech writer Grace Mary Stern lt. gubernatorial campaign, Lake County, 1984; voter registrar County of Lake Ill., 1986-89; cons. pub. rels. Lake County Cir. Ct. Judge campaign, 1988, Presdl. Campaign Paul Simon; co-chmn., organizer Women's Exhibit, Evergreen Air Show, 1993. Recipient Brian F. Shehanhan Creative Writing award Am. Inst. Banking, 1972, 1st Place pub. speaking, 1974. Mem. AAUW (pub. rels. chair 1986, pres. Chain O'Lakes br. 1988-89, Ill. Pub. Info. award 1987, pub. rels. chair Tucson br. 1991-92), NAFE, Northeastern Ill. U. Alumni Assn., Soc. Southwestern Authors, Pi Rho Zeta (pres. 1964-65). Democrat. Roman Catholic. Office: PO Box 191 Tucson AZ 85702-0191

MASON, LINDA, physical education educator, softball and basketball coach; b. Indpls., Jan. 29, 1946; d. Harrison Linn and Hazel Marie (Bledsoe) Crouch; divorced; children: Cassandra, Andrew. BS, Ind. U., 1968, MS, 1977. Cert. phys. edn. tchr., K-12, Ind. Tchr. phys. edn. Woodview Jr. H.S., Indpls., 1968-71; tchr. phys. edn., coach Ind. U.-Purdue U. of Indpls., 1972-76; basketball coach Butler U., Indpls., 1976-84; head softball coach, asst. basketball coach Westfield Washington High Sch., Westfield, Ind., 1985; tchr. phys. edn., basketball coach Orchard Park Elementary Sch., Carmel, 1985—; elem. physical edn. tchr. Carmel-Clay Schs., 1985—; asst. varsity coach softball Carmel H.S., 1993-95, head varsity softball coach, 1996-99. Head coach Ind. Girls' H.S. All-Stars Basketball Team, Indpls., 1980. Named Coach of Yr. Dist. 4, Nat. Collegiate Athletic Assn., 1983, Coach of Yr. for softball ICGSA, 1997, coach ICGSA Girls All Stars, 1998. Mem. Delta Psi Kappa. E-mail: lmason@ccs.k12.in.us.

MASON, LINDA ANNE, pre-school administrator; m. Roger Brown; 3 children. BA, Cornell U., 1976; DLCF, Sorbonne U., Paris, 1977; MBA, Yale U., 1980. Relief worker, Cambodian refugee camp CARE, Thailand, 1980; cons. Booz, Allen & Hamilton, N.Y.C., Paris, 1981-82; co-dir. Save the Children, Sudan, 1984-1986; co-founder Horizons Initiative; chmn., co-founder Bright Horizons Family Solutions, 1986—. Bd. dirs. Horizon Initiative, Whole Foods Market, Inc., Boston Globe. Co-author: (book) Rice, Rivalry, and Politics, 1983; author: Working Mother's Guide to Life, 2002. Mem. adv. bd. Sch. Mgmt. Yale U., trustee. Named Entrepreneur of the Yr., Ernst & Young/USA Today, 1996, Cornell U., 1997; named one of Best Entrepreneurs, Bus. Week, 1997; recipient Ten Outstnding Young Leaders award, Boston Jaycees, 1987, Mothers and Shakers award, Redbook, 1998. Office: Bright Horizons Family Solutions 200 Talcott Ave South Watertown MA 02472 Fax: 617-673-8650.

MASON, LOIS E(LAINE) (J. DAY MASON), painter, poet, actress, educator; b. Boston, May 4, 1919; d. Harold Monroe and Orpah Cecil (Smith) Scheibe; m. Lucien Bunce Day, June 21, 1941 (div. 1954); children: Felicity, Christopher, Sarah; m. Frederick Dike Mason, Apr. 27, 1964 (dec.); children: Frederick Dike III, Victoria, Johanna. Student, U. Leiden, Netherlands, 1939; BA, Oberlin (Ohio) U., 1940; postgrad., Cranbrook Acad. Art, Bloomfield Hills, Mich., 1941. Set-up and tchr. art dept. Pingree Sch., Hamilton Mass.; TV, lectr. creative arts and writing, Mass. and Conn., 1949-58. Actress appearing in Alien Corn, Twelfth Night, Crucible, George Washington Slept Here, Philadelphia Story, Auntie Mame, Skin of our Teeth, Spoon River, Anything Goes, Call Me Madame, Seven Keys to Baldpate, Other People's Money, Quilters, Golden Pond, Cat on a Hot Tin Roof, Little Foxes, Lettice and Lovage, Close Ties, Grace and Glorie, others; set designer, decorator Auntie Mame, See How They Run, Tea House of the August Moon, Spoon River, Archie and Mehitable; author: Speaking to Strangers, 1987-88; one-woman shows include New Britain (Conn.) Mus., Am. Ballet, N.Y., Green Mountain Gallery, N.Y.C., Essex (Mass.) Inst., Marblehead Arts, Quadrom, Mast Cove, 6 Deering, Miles Hosp., Atty. Gen.'s Office, Kennebec Valley Art Assn., Chocolate Ch. Art Ctr., Maine Gallery, Kristina's, Oliver's, Islesboro Historic Soc. Ch. ladies com. Hamilton Hall, Salem, Mass., 1975-78; set designer Cmty. Theater, Swampscott, Mass., 1973-78. Recipient C. Law/Watkins fellowship Phillips Gallery, Mus., Washington, 1944-46. Mem. Nat. Assn. Women Painters, Conn. Acad., Silvermine, Maine Gallery, Kennebec Valley Arts, Chocolate Ch. Art Ctr., Marblehead Arts, Conn. Acad., Maine Writers and Publs. Avocations: cooking, sailing, gardening.

MASON, LORETTA ANN, accountant; b. Albertville, Ala., Dec. 14, 1959; d. Robert Dewayne Hudgins and Tassie Marie Strong; div.; 1 child, Shannon David. Asst. acct. NAFECO, Decatur, Ill. Author: (book of poetry) Yesterday's Memories, 1997; contbr. poems to anthologies. Mem. Internat. Soc. Poets (disting. mem.), So. Poetry Assn., Eastern Star. Republican. Avocations: horseback riding, motorcycles, reading, writing. E-mail:. Home: PO Box 522 Arab AL 35016 Office: NAFECO 1515 W Moulton Decatur AL 35601 E-mail: rettaann@mindspring.com.

MASON, LUCILE GERTRUDE, fundraiser, consultant; b. Montclair, N.J., Aug. 1, 1925; d. Mayne Seguine and Rachel (Entorf) M. AB, Smith Coll., 1947; MA, NYU, 1968, 76. Editor ABC, N.Y.C., 1947-51; asst. casting dir. Compton Advt., Inc., 1951-55, dir. and head casting, 1955-65; conf. mgr. Camp Fire Girls, Inc., 1965-66; exec. dir. Assn. of Jr. Leagues of Am. Inc., 1966-68; dir. div. pub. affairs Girl Scouts U.S.A., 1969-71; dir. pub. rels. YWCA of City of N.Y., 1971-73; dir. community rels. and devel. Girl Scout Coun. of Greater N.Y., N.Y.C., 1973-76; dir. devel. Montclair Kimberley Acad., Montclair, N.J., 1976-78, Ethical Culture Schs., N.Y.C. and Riverdale, N.Y., 1978-80; pres. Lucile Mason & Assocs., Montclair, 1980-83; devel. officer founds. Fairleigh Dickinson U., Rutherford, N.J., 1983-85; dir. devel. Whole Theatre, Inc., Montclair, 1985-86, YMWCA of Newark & Vicinity, 1986-88; v.p. adminstrn. and fin. devel. Inst. Religion and Health, N.Y.C., 1988-90; dir. corp. and found. rels. Upsala Coll., East Orange, N.J., 1990-91; pres. Lucile Mason & Assocs., Montclair, 1991—. Vol. bd. counselors Smith Coll., 1964—74, chmn. theatre com., mem. exec. com., 1969—74; trustee Citizens Com. Presby. Meml. Iris Gardens of Montclair, 1992—98; trustee Friends of Barnet, 1994—95; v.p. Neighborhood Coun., Inc. , Montclair, 1987—95, 1997—98, bd. dirs., 2000—01; mem. fund devel. com. Greater Essex County coun. Girl Scouts U.S., 1986—92. Mem.: Pub. Rels. Soc. Am., Assn. Fundraising Profls. (bd. dirs. N.J. chpt. 1983—86, mem. awards com. 1994, co-chair awards com. N.J. Conf. on Philanthropy 1995), Cmty. Agys. Pub. Rels. Assn. (membership chmn. 1973—76), Am. Women in Radio and TV (pres. N.Y.C. chpt. 1955—56), Smith Coll. Club Montclair (bd.dirs. 1986—90). Avocations: collecting pewter, gardening, concerts, plays. Home and Office: 142 N Mountain Ave Montclair NJ 07042-2350

MASON, MARILYN GELL, library administrator, writer, consultant; b. Chickasha, Okla., Aug. 23, 1944; d. Emmett D. and Dorothy (O'Bar) Killebrew; m. Carl L. Gell, Dec. 29 1965 (div. Oct. 1978); 1 son, Charles E.; m. Robert M. Mason, July 17, 1981. BA, U. Dallas, 1966; M.L.S., N. Tex. State U., Denton, 1968; M.P.A., Harvard U., 1978. Libr. N.J. State Libr., Trenton, 1968-69; head dept. Arlington County Pub. Libr., Va., 1969-73; chief libr. program Metro Washington Coun. Govts., 1973-77; dir. White House Conf. on Librs. and Info. Svcs., Washington, 1979-80; exec. v.p. Metrics Rsch. Corp., Atlanta, 1981-82; dir. Atlanta-Fulton Pub. Libr., 1982-86, Cleve. Pub. Libr., 1986-99; writer, cons., 1999—. Trustee Online Computer Library Ctr., 1984-97; Evalene Parsons Jackson lectr. div. librarianship Emory U., 1981; commr. Nat. Commn. Libr. Info. Svcs., 2001-02. Author: The Federal Role in Library and Information Services, 1983, Strategic Management for Today's Libraries, 1999; editor: Survey of Library Automation in the Washington Area, 1977; project dir.: book Information for the 1980's, 1980. Bd. visitors Sch. Info. Studies, Syracuse U., 1981-85, Sch. of Libr. and Info. Sci. , U. Tenn.-Knoxville, 1983-85; trustee Coun. on Libr. Resources, Washington, 1992-2000. Recipient Disting. Alumna award N. Tex. State U., 1979, Herbert and Virginia White award, ALA, 1999; inducted into Ohio Libr. Coun. Hall of Fame, 1999. Mem. ALA (mem. council 1986—90), Am. Assn. Info. Sci., Ohio Library Assn., D.C. Library Assn. (pres. 1976-77) Home and Office: 811 Live Oak Plantation Rd Tallahassee FL 32312-2412

MASON, MARSHALL W. theater director, educator; b. Amarillo, Tex., Feb. 24, 1940; s. Marvin Marshall and Lorine (Chrisman) M. BS in Speech, Northwestern U., 1961. Prof. Ariz. State U., 1994—; chief drama critic New Times, Phoenix, 1994-96. Founder, artistic dir. Circle Repertory Co., 1969-87, guest artistic dir., Ctr. Theater Group, 1988; dir. Broadway prodns. Redwood Curtain, 1993, The Seagull, 1992, Solitary Confinement, 1992, Burn This, 1987, As Is, 1985 (Drama Desk award, Tony nomination), Passion, 1983, Angels Fall, 1983 (Tony nomination), Fifth of July, 1981 (Tony nomination), Talley's Folly, 1980, (Pulitzer Prize, N.Y. Drama Critics Circle award, Tony nomination), Murder at the Howard Johnsons, 1979, Gemini, 1977, Knock Knock, 1976 (Tony nomination); Off-Broadway prodns. Book of Days, 2002, Sympathetic Magic, 1997, Robbers, 1997, Cakewalk, 1996, A Poster of the Cosmos/The Moonshot Tape, 1994, The Destiny of Me, 1992, Sunshine, 1989, Talley and Son, 1985, Childe Byron, 1980, Hamlet, 1979, Serenading Louie, 1976 (Obie award), Knock Knock, 1976 (Obie award), The Mound Builders, 1975 (Obie award), Battle of Angeles, 1974 (Obie award), The Sea Horse, 1974, The Hot L Baltimore, 1973 (Obie award); dir. numerous prodns. including Who's Afraid of Virginia Woolf?, Tokyo, 1985, Talley's Folly, 1982, London, Home Free! and The Madness of Lady Bright, 1968, London, Nat. Tour Sleuth, 1988, L.A. Summer and Smoke, 1988, Whisper in the Mind, 1990, King Lear, 1998, The Elephant Man, London, 1998, Long Day's Journey into Night, 1998, Riga, 1999, Los Alamos, 1999, Ginger, 2000; transl. Pirandello's Enrico IV, 2001, Ghosts, 2001, Private Lives, 2002; dir. numerous TV prodns. including Picnic, 1986, Kennedy's Children, 1982, The Fifth of July, 1983. Recipient Vernon Rice award, 1975, Drama Desk award, 1977, Margo Jones award, 1977, Outer Critics Circle award, 1978, Theatre World award, 1979, Shubert's Vaughan award, 1980, Obie award for Sustained Achievement, 1983, Inge Festival award for lifetime achievement, 1990, Last Frontier award, 1994, award Ariz. Press Club, 1995, Erwin Piscator award, 1996, Millennium Mr. Abbott award, 1999, Creative Achievement award Ariz. State U., 2001. Mem. Soc. Stage Dirs. and Choreographers (pres. 1983-85), Dirs. Guild Am., Actors Equity Assn., Coll. Fellow of Am. Theater. Address: 1948 E Ellis Cir Mesa AZ 85203-5825 E-mail: mwm@asu.edu.

MASON, NAOMI ANN, interior designer; b. Kansas City, Mo., Mar. 11, 1934; d. Hugh Fredrick and Lottie Elizabeth (Granstrom) Guilford; m. Ronald A. Mason, May 28, 1954; children: Teresa Elizabeth, Sheryl Lynn, Christina Marie, Ronald Anthony Jr. AA, Kansas City (Mo.) Jr. Coll., 1954; BA, Calif. State U., Long Beach, 1980. Cert. interior designer, Calif. Owner Design Ctr. Interiors, Orange, Calif., 1985—. Co-host (TV show) A Slice of Orange. Mem. Orange Planning Commn., 1982-86; bd. dirs., 2d v.p. Orange C. of C., 1987-92; bd. dirs. Orange Elderly Svcs., 1987-91, Red Ribbon 100, 1987—; pres., 1st v.p., 2d v.p. Orange Rep. Women Fedn., 1991-2000; bd. dirs. Pacific S.W. dist. Mo. Synod Luth. Ch., 1994-2000. Named Citizen of Yr. City and Chamber, Orange, 1992, Women of Distinction Soroptimist Internat., 1993. Mem. Am. Soc. Interior Designers (bd. dirs. 1986-90), Rotary. Republican. Lutheran. Avocations: golf, reading, tennis, water skiing, gardening. Home and Office: 525 S Arlington Rd Orange CA 92869-5127 E-mail: naomiamason@hotmail.com.

MASON, PAUL MARK, economics educator, researcher; b. Aug. 30, 1955; s. Saul and Evalyn (Katz) Mason; m. Julia Elizabeth Kline, Dec. 23, 1976; children: Jessica Lee, Joshua Aaron, Nathaniel Saul. BA, U. Del., 1977, MA, 1980; PhD, U. Tex., 1984. Math. tchr. Bishop Eustace Prep. Sch., Pennsauken, NJ, 1977—80; asst. prof. econs. Southwest Tex. State U., San Marcos, 1980—84; vis. asst. prof. fin. Clemson U., SC, 1984—85; prof. econs. U. North Fla., Jacksonville, Fla., 1985—, chmn. dept., 2002—. Pres. Holiday Hill Manor Civic Assn., 1987—88; v.p. Radnor Green Civic Assn., Claymont, Del., 1979—80, bd. dirs., 1978—79. Mem.: Western Econ. Assn., So. Econ. Assn., Am. Econ. Assn., Beta Gamma Sigma, Omicron Delta Epsilon, Phi Mu Epsilon. Home: 2755 Scott Mill Pl Jacksonville FL 32223-9133 Office: Univ North Florida St Johns Bluff Rd N Jacksonville FL 32224 E-mail: pmason@unf.edu.

MASON, PERRY CARTER, philosophy educator; b. Houston, Sept. 24, 1939; s. Lloyd Vernon and Lorraine (Carter) M.; m. Judith Jane Fredrick, June 11, 1960; children— Gregory Charles, Nicole Elizabeth BA, Baylor U., Waco, Tex., 1961; B.D., Harvard U., 1964; MA, Yale U., 1966, PhD, 1968. Asst. prof. philosophy Carleton Coll., Northfield, Minn., 1968-73, assoc. prof. philosophy, 1973-80, prof. philosophy, 1980—, v.p. for planning and devel., 1988-89, v.p. for external rels., 1989-91. Contbr. articles to profl. publs. Mem. Minn. Philos. Soc., Am. Philos. Assn. Democrat. Home: 8629 Hall Ave Northfield MN 55057-4884 Office: Carleton College 1 N College St Northfield MN 55057-4044 E-mail: pmason@carleton.edu.

MASON, PHILLIP HOWARD, aircraft company executive, retired army officer; b. Cash, Va., Mar. 13, 1932; s. Phillip Howard and Mary Armisted (Hogg) M.; m. Frances Murray Gallogly, Mar. 3, 1962 (dec. 1995); children: Mary Catherine, Patrick Howard, Susan Frances, Sheryl Ann. BS in BA, magna cum laude, St. Benedicts, 1966; MBA, Shippensburg State Coll., 1976; postgrad., U.S. Army Command and Gen. Staff Coll., 1965-66, U.S. Army War Coll., 1975-76. Enlisted in U.S. Army, 1948, advanced through grades to brig. gen., 1980, bn. comdr. 1st Bn., 1st ADA Gr., 1971-73, sec. gen. staff 32d Army Air Def. Command Ger., 1974, systems coordinator ODCSRDA, Dept Army, 1975; project mgr. AD Command and Control Redstone Arsenal, Ala., 1976-78; comdr. 11th ADA Bde Fort Bliss, Tex., 1978-79; project mgr. STINGER Redstone Arsenal, 1979-83; dir. combat support system ODCS-RDA, Dept. Army Washington; ret. U.S. Army, 1983; v.p. bus. devel. Sanders Assocs., Nashua, N.H., 1984-90; project mgr. Hughes Aircraft Co., 1990—; ret., 1998. Decorated Disting. Svc. medal, Legion of Merit with oak leaf cluster, Bronze star, Meritorious Svc. medal with two oak leaf clusters, Joint Svcs. Commendation medal, Army Commendation medal. Home: 2 Vineyard Ln Methuen MA 01844-3377 E-mail: phmason@attbi.com.

MASON, RAYMOND E., JR. distributing company executive; b. Columbus, Ohio, Mar. 20, 1920; s. Raymond E. and Lula Estella (Potter) M.; m. Margaret E. Edwards, Feb. 6, 1942; children: Raymond E. III, Michael D., Bruce R. BS, Ohio State U., 1941; grad., U.S. Command and Gen. Staff, 1962, U.S. Army War Coll., 1965; DBS (hon.), Ohio State U., 2001. Ops. mgr. Suburban Motor Freight, Columbus, 1946-47; pres., gen. mgr. CFL Lines, 1947-48; pres., chmn. Columbus Truck & Equipment Co., 1949—. Pres., chmn. Bode-Finn Co., Cin., 1966-99, REM Realty, Columbus, 1962—; chmn. Ford Bros. Inc., Ironton, Ohio, 1975-79; mem. distbr. adv. coun. Mack Trucks; mng. dir. J.D. Ranch, Myakka City, Fla. Active Boy Scouts Am.; chmn. bd. trustees emeritus Franklin U.; former trustee Freedoms Found. of Valley Forge, Ohio Hist. Found.; vice-chmn. New Coll. Found.; dir. Mote Marine Lab., Ohio State U. Found. With U.S. Army, 1941-45, maj. gen. Res., ret. Decorated Bronze Star medal with V for Valor, Legion of Merit, Silver Star; recipient Pres. Unit citation; Truck Dealer of Yr. award Time mag., 1972, Good Scout award Cen. Ohio Coun. Boy Scouts Am., Baden-Powell fellow World Scout Found., Silver Beaver award, Silver Antelope award, Boy Scouts Am., Centennial medal Ohio State U., Pacesetters award Coll. Bus. ISU, 1996, Virginia Steckler Internat. Svc. award ARC, 1998, Lifetime Achievement award Ohio State U., 1999, Disting. Citizen of Yr. award Boy Scouts Am., 1999, Harrison Sayre award, 2001, Philanthropist of Yr. Columbus Found., 2001, others; named

State of Ohio Vet. Hall of Fame, 1997, Buckeye Boys State Hall of Fame, 1999, Ohio State U. ROTC Hall of Fame, Jr. Achievement Cen. Ohio Bus. Hall of Fame, 2000. Mem. Am. Truck Dealers, Ohio Truck Assn., U.S. Army Artillery Assn., Armor Assn., Army War Coll. Alumni Assn., Ohio State U. Alumni Assn., Columbus Club, Queen City Club, Masons, Rotary (past dist. gov., Man of Yr., Paul Harris fellow). Office: Columbus Truck Equipment Co PO Box 83250 Columbus OH 43203-0250 Home: 85 Sugar Mill Dr Osprey FL 34229-9067

MASON, REBECCA SUSSA, secondary education educator; b. Knoxville, Tenn., Sept. 21, 1945; d. Max and Greta (Hans) M. BA, SUNY, Fredonia, 1967; MA, Columbia U., 1977. Cert. permanent tchr., N.Y. Tchr. music Kakiat Jr. High Sch., East Ramapo Ctrl. Sch. Dist., Spring Valley, N.Y., 1967-95, head dept., 1985—, condr. All Dist. Band, 1980, 97—, asst. condr., 1989-96; tchr. music Ramapo Sr. H.S., 1995-2001. Bass clarinetist Rockland Suburban Symphony, Spring Valley, 1967-68; 1st clarinet Westchester Pops Band, White Plains, N.Y., 1967-68, South Orange (N.J.) Symphony, 1986-87, Rockland Community Band, Pearl River, N.Y., 1988—. Recipient various plaques, awards and letters of commendation East Ramapo Sch. Dist., 1968—, letter of commendation SUNY, 1990. Mem. Music Educators Nat. Conf., N.Y. State Sch. Music Assn., East Ramapo PTA (life). Democrat. Jewish. Avocations: travel, antiques, collecting autographs and baseball cards, quilting, counted cross-stitch. Home: 31 Briar Ct Cross River NY 10518-1309 Office: East Ramapo Cen Sch Dist 105 S Madison Ave Spring Valley NY 10977-5474

MASON, RICHARD J. lawyer; b. Syracuse, N.Y., June 16, 1951; BA with high honors, U. Ill., 1973; MBA, U. Chgo., 1980; JD, U. Notre Dame, 1977. Bar: Ill. 1977. Ptnr., mem. exec. com. Ross & Hardies, Chgo., 1995—. Adj. prof. law Kent Coll. Law, Inst. Tech., Chgo., 1984—. Bd. dirs. Ill. Farm Legal Assistance Found., 1985-88. Mem. ABA (chmn. bus. bankruptcy subcom. on use and disposition of property under the bankruptcy code 1989—), Am. Bankruptcy Inst., Ill. State Bar Assn. (mem. banking and bankruptcy law sect. coun. 1986-88), Chgo. Bar Assn. (mem. bankrupcty and reorgn. com. 1978—), Comml. Law League. Office: Ross & Hardies 150 N Michigan Ave Ste 2500 Chicago IL 60601-7567

MASON, ROBERT LESTER, engineer, small business computer consultant; b. Urbana, Ill., Oct. 24, 1945; s. Curtis Leonel and Mary Eleanor (Funkhouser) M.; m. Shirley Coggins, June 5, 1971. AS, Va. Commonwealth U., 1973; BA, N.C. State U., Raleigh, 1978; student, Long Ridge Writer's Group, 1996. Cen. office switchman Chesapeake & Potomac Telephone Co., Richmond, Va., 1970-71; asst. engr. Gen. Telephone (GTE), Durham, N.C., 1973-74; design engr. GE, Mebane, 1978-79; application engr. Cornell Dublier Electronics, Sanford, 1980; field support engr. No. Telecom, Inc., Research Triangle Park, 1980-82, customer service rep., 1982-86, technical accounts rep., 1986-87, customer service engr., 1987-88; pres. RLM Enhancers Inc., Chapel Hill, 1989—, pres., CEO, computer cons., 1989—; sales rep. Telecom Solutions, Inc., 1992-93. Vice-chair Northern Telecom Employee Club, Research Triangle Park, 1983; desktop pub. and computer/telecom cons.; Aptiva support tech., IBM, 1996; contractual IS mgr. Elon Homes for Children, 1996-98, contractual computer rollout for Wachovia Bank, 1998. Patentee electronic burglar alarm. Mem. Orange County Econ. Devel. Coun., 1990-92; mem. Good Samaritan coun. Chapel of the Cross Episc. Ch., Chapel Hill, 2000. With USN, 1966-70, Vietnam. Mem. Am. Assn. Individual Investors, No. Telecom Inc. Mgmt. Assn. (facility rep. 1986-87, treas. 1987-88), Nat. Trust for Historic Preservation, Postal Commemorative Soc., Nat. Geog. Soc., World Futurist Soc., Navy League U.S., U.S. Navy Meml., VFW (jr. vice comdr. 1986-87), Chapel Hill-Carrboro C. of C. (bus. and llegis. issues coun. 1992-98), Chapel Hill-Carrboro Kiwanis (bd. dirs., newsletter editor). Avocations: home computers, travel, golf. Fax: (919) 967-2676. E-mail: rmason2@bellsouth.net.

MASON, ROBERT MARION, mathematician, musician; b. Toledo, May 27, 1928; s. Ernest E. and Joanna H. Mason; m. Janet E. Polich, Mar. 31, 1956. BE, U. Toledo, 1950, MA, 1951. Jazz pianist, music tchr. Am. Fedn. Musicians, Toledo, 1949-53, Bach Conservatory, Toledo, 1951; mathematician U.S. Naval Rsch. Lab., Washington, 1953-74, cons., 1961-68, mem. tactical electronic warfare divsn., lead lab staff, 1968-74; cons. Rsch. Computation Ctr., 1961-65, Applied Math. Staff, 1965-68; dir. computer ctr. divsn. U.S. Naval Oceanog. Office, Suitland, Md., 1974-76; math. statistician Dept. Commerce, Washington, 1976-79; cons. CLEF, Peterborough, N.H., 1980—; writer, pub. Schoolhouse Press, 1985—. Advisor math. and info. scis. divsn. Office Naval Rsch., Washington, 1967-68; mem. panel Project LEX Task Force Engrs. Joint Coun., N.Y.C., 1968; spl. agt. U.S. Dept. Census, Suitland, 1979. Co-author: Applied Matrix and Tensor Analysis, 1970; author: Modern Methods of Music Analysis Using Computers, 1985; contbr. articles to profl. jours. Mem. Am. Math. Soc., Am. Musicological Soc., Assn. Computing Machinery (reviewer 1961-74), Math. Assn. Am. Achievements include 2 patents. Avocations: music composition, keyboard improvisation, MIDI programming. Office: CLEF 46 Mountain View Dr Peterborough NH 03458-1325

MASON, ROBERT MCSPADDEN, technology management educator, consultant; b. Sweetwater, Tenn., Jan. 16, 1941; s. Paul Rankin and Ruby May (McSpadden) M.; m. Betty Ann Durrence (div. 1980); children: Michael Dean, Donald Robert; m. Marilyn Killebrew Gell, July 17, 1981. SB, MIT, 1963, SM, 1965; PhD, Ga. Inst. Tech., 1973. Tech. staff mem. Sandia Labs., Livermore, Calif., 1965-68; rsch. scientist Ga. Inst. Tech., Atlanta, 1971-75, sr. rsch. scientist, 1975; prin. Metrics Inc., 1975-80; pres. Metrics Rsch. Corp., 1980-86, Cleve., 1986-98, Tallahassee, 1998—; adj. prof. Weatherhead Sch. Mgmt. Case Western U., 1987-88, vis. prof., 1988-91, prof. for practice of tech. mgmt., 1991-98; dir. Ctr. Mgmt. Sci. and Tech., 1988-96; Sprint prof. mgmt. Coll. Bus. Fla. State U., Tallahassee, 1998—, chair mgmt. info. sys., 1998—2002. Co-author: Library Micro Consumer, 1986; co-editor: Information Services: Economics, Management, and Technology, 1981, Management of Technology V: Technology Management in a Changing World, 1996; co-author: The Impact of Office Automation on Clerical Employment, 1985-2000, 1985; Am. editor Technovation, 1994—; contbr. article series "Mason on Micros" to Libr. Jour., 1983-86, articles to various profl. publs. Mem. Internat. Assn. for Tech. Mgmt. (newsletter editor 1992-93, program chair internat. conf., 1996, pres. 1996-98). Republican. Presbyterian. Avocations: flying, skiing, sailing, scuba diving, photography. Home: 811 Live Oak Plantation Rd Tallahassee FL 32312-2412 Office: Fla State U MIS Dept Coll of Bus Tallahassee FL 32306-1110 E-mail: rmason@alum.mit.edu.

MASON, RODNEY, performing arts educator; b. Phila. Dancer Urban Colors, Portland, Oreg. Instr. hip-hop dance U. Arts Phila. Recipient Bessie Ward award, 2002. Office: Univ Arts Phila 320 S Broad St Philadelphia PA 19102*

MASON, SALLY KAY FROST, biology educator, provost; b. N.Y.C., May 29, 1950; d. Michael and Alberta Viparina; m. John S. Frost, Aug. 1975 (div. Feb. 1982); m. Kenneth Andrew Mason, Mar. 17, 1990. BA in Zoology, U. Ky., 1972; MS in Cell/Devel. Biology, Purdue U., 1974; PhD in Cell/Devel. Biology, U. Ariz., 1978. Rsch. assoc. Ind. U., Bloomington, 1978-80; asst. prof. biology U. Kans., Lawrence, 1981-86, assoc. prof. biology, 1986-91, prof. biology, 1991-2001, chair dept. physiology and cell biology, 1986-89, assoc. dean scis., 1990-95, dean arts and scis., 1995-2001; provost, prof. biology Purdue U., West Lafayette, Ind., 2001—. Bd. mem. Kans. U. Ctr. for Rsch., Lawrence. Mem. editl. bd. Pigment Cell Rsch., 1988-99; contbr. chpts. to books and articles to profl. jours. Dissertation fellow AAUW, 1977-78, Kemper Tchg. fellow U. Kans., Lawrence, 1997; grantee NSF, NIH, Washington, 1981-98; Wesley Found. grantee Welsey Health Found., Wichita, Kans., 1991-93. Mem. Internat. Fedn. Pigment Cell Scis. (coun. mem. 1997-2000), Pan Am. Soc. for Pigment Cell Rsch. (coun. mem. 1988-98, pres. 1996-98), Coun. Colls. Arts and Scis. (bd. mem. 1997-99, pres. elect 1999-2000, pres. 2000-2001). Avocations: travel, reading, writing. Office: Purdue U Office of Provost Hovde Hall West Lafayette IN 47905

MASON, SCOTT MACGREGOR, entrepreneur, inventor, consultant; b. N.Y.C., Feb. 11, 1923; s. Gregory Mason and Mary Louise Turner; m. Mildred Davidson, Mar. 13, 1949 (div. 1970); children: Alan Gregory, Phoebe Louise, Caleb; m. Virginia Frances Perkins, May 5, 1970 (dec. 1990). AB, Princeton U., 1943; MS, NYU, 1947. Control chemist Firestone Tire & Rubber Co., Akron, Ohio, 1943-44; R & D chemist Am. Cyanamid Co. Rsch. Labs., Stamford, Conn., 1948-52; mgr. stearate dept. Warwick Chem. div. Sun Chem. Corp., Wood River Junction, R.I., 1952-58; cons., Stonington, Conn., 1958-59; instr. Williams Meml. Inst., New London, 1959-63; NSF fellow Brown U., Providence, 1963-64; tchr. Moses Brown Sch., 1964-70; owner, mgr. Innoventures, Wakefield, R.I., 1970—. Cons. Greene Plastics Corp., Canonchet, R.I., 1972-80, Deterde Inc., Pawtucket, R.I., 1982-83. Patentee in field. Trustee Pine Point Sch., Stonington, 1956-62, pres. bd., 1959-61. With AUS, 1944-46, ETO. Named Tchr. of Week, Sta. WICE, Providence, 1967; summer rsch. fellow NSF, U. R.I., 1960. Mem. AAAS, N.Y. Acad. Scis. Avocations: tennis, fishing, snorkeling, photography, music. Office: Innoventures PO Box 369 Wakefield RI 02880-0369

MASON, SHERILYN SUE, artist; b. Seattle; d. George Joseph Keiter and Betty Jane Rozear; m. Patrick Jesse Mason, Sept. 22, 1952; children: Kelly Anne Piccolo, Patrick Matthew Mason. BS, U. Maine, 1975. Designer, painter Showstoppers, Ft. Lauderdale, Fla., 1996—. Exhbns. include 35th Ann. competition Mus. Art Ft. Lauderdale, 1993, Lighthouse Point Libr., 1996, Art Serve, Ft. Lauderdale, 1998, Soc. of the Four Arts Nat. Exhbn., 1993, Cornell Mus., Delray, Fla., 2000; co-illustrator: Storyteller's Bible Study, 1992 Precinct chmn. Republican Exec. Com., Ft. Lauderdale, 1996-98; mem. Coral Ridge Presbyn. Ch. Fine Art Guild, 1993-98. Recipient Mary Hulitar prize Soc. of the Fine Arts, 1995. Mem. Broward Art Guild (People's Choice award 1993, 94, Best in Show award 1998), Women in the Visual Arats. Republican. Avocation: home school educator. Home: 4982 NW 91st Ter Sunrise FL 33351-5339

MASON, SIMON JAMES, climatologist; b. Portsmouth, Eng., Dec. 22, 1965; came to U.S., 1997; s. Dennis William and Christine Anne Mason; m. Sonja Pleskova. BA with honors, U. Oxford, Eng., 1988; PhD, U. Witwatersrand, Johannesburg, South Africa, 1992. Jr. rsch. officer Climatology Rsch. Group U. Witwatersrand, 1988-90; rsch. officer, 1991-93; sr. rsch. officer, 1993-94; dep. dir., 1994-97; products cons. numerical algorithms group Polygon Sys., Johannesburg, 1990-91; sole mem. Numerical Solutions, 1991-97; asst. rsch. meteorologist Scripps Instn. Oceanography, La Jolla, Calif., 1997-2001, assoc. rsch. meteorologist, 2001—. Mem. AMS com. on probability and stats., 2001—. Patient care vol. San Diego Hospice, 2000. Mem. Am. Meteorol. Soc. (com. on probability and stats. 2001—). Avocations: piano, classical music, literature, Ancient Greek. Office: Scripps Instn Oceanography U Calif 9500 Gilman Dr La Jolla CA 92093-0230 E-mail: smason@ucsd.edu.

MASON, STEPHEN OLIN, nonprofit association administrator; b. Fresno, Calif., July 11, 1952; s. Olin James and Mary Edna (Moyer) Mason. BA, Bridgewater (Va.) Coll., 1974; MEd, James Madison U., 1979; PhD, Loyola U., Chgo., 1991. Asst. to the dir. student ctr. Bridgewater Coll., 1974-76; guidance counselor Woodlawn Elem. Sch., Sebring, Fla., 1976-77; asst. dean for student devel. Bridgewater Coll., 1977-81; dir. student life Roger Williams Coll., Bristol, R.I., 1981-83; assoc. dean for residential svcs. Dickinson Coll., Carlisle, Pa., 1983-84; v.p., dean student affairs Westmar Coll., LeMars, Iowa, 1984; rsch. assoc. to pres. Elmhurst (Ill.) Coll., 1986-87; v.p. student affairs Felician Coll., Chgo., 1987-88; dean students Huntingdon Coll., Montgomery, Ala., 1988-90; dir. devel. McPherson (Kans.) Coll., 1990-94, v.p. fin. svcs., 1994-97; exec. dir. Assn. of Brethren Caregivers, Elgin, Ill., 1997—. Bd. dirs. Brethren Benefit Trust, 2002—; participant ARC Blood Drive, 1978—79; mem. allocations com. United Way, Carlisle, 1984; adv. bd. mem. LeMars chpt. Siouxland Coun. for Alcoholism and Drug Abuse, 1984; site coord. for coat drive Mental Health Greater Chgo., 1985; dir.-at-large Alumni Bd. Bridgewater Coll. , 1987—93; v.p. McPherson Habitat for Humanity, 1993, 1994, bd. dirs., 1993—96, pres., 1994; bd. dirs. McPherson Mus. and Arts Found., 1992—94, Assn. Brethren Caregivers, 1993—97, Assn. Anabaptist Risk Mgmt., 2000—; governing coun., mem. adv. Bethany Hosp., 2001—02. Mem.: Assn. Forum Chicagoland. Avocation: Avocations: calligraphy, community theatre, barbershop singing, spelunking. Home: 649 N Spring St Elgin IL 60120-3651 Office: Assn Brethren Caregivers 1451 Dundee Ave Elgin IL 60120-1674 E-mail: smason_abc@brethren.org.

MASON, STEVEN GERALD, lawyer; b. Dayton, Ohio, Oct. 24, 1963; s. Robert G. and Pauline (Wise) M. BA in Polit. Sci. and History, U. Cen. Fla., 1985; JD, Nova U., 1989. Bar: Fla. 1990, U.S. Dist. Ct. (mid. dist.) Fla. 1990, U.S. Ct. Appeals (11th cir. 1992). Law clk. to Hon. G. Kendall Sharp U.S. Dist. Ct. for Mid. Dist. Fla., Orlando, 1988; felony divsn. atty. Office Pub. Defender, 1989-91; pvt. practice, 1992—. Contbr. to profl. jours. Bd. dirs. Seminole County Humane Soc., Sanford, Fla., 1991-98. Recipient Franklin Graham Defender award, 1990. Mem.: Ctrl. Fla. Assn. Criminal Def. Lawyers (sec. 1992—93, amicus com.), Orange County Bar Assn., Fla. Assn. Criminal Def. Lawyers, Fla. Bar (cert. criminal trial and criminal appellate specialist). Democrat. Avocation: reading. Office: 1643 Hillcrest St Orlando FL 32803-4809 E-mail: sgmason@bellsouth.net.

MASON, TERENCE K. critical care nurse, emergency nurse practitioner; b. Elgin, Ill., Jun. 10, 1953; s. LeRoy B. and Doris M. (Kelly) M.; m. Cheryl S., Apr. 23, 1989. AA, Phoenix Coll., 1977; BSN, Ariz. State U., 1981, postgrad. RN, Ariz.; cert. critical care nurse; provider and instr. ACLS, BCLS, PALS, AHLS. Staff nurse SCU Valley Luth. Hosp., Mesa, Ariz., 1985-86; freelance nurse, Tempe (Ariz.) St. Luke's Hosp., Phoenix, 1989-90, charge nurse coronary ICU, 1981-85, 86-88, asst. clin. dir. coronary ICU, Ariz., 1988-89, 91-95, staff nurse emergency rm., 1995-98; paramedic coord. Tempe St. Lukes Hosp., 1998-99; emergency med. svc. specialist Mesa Fire Dept., 1999—. Instr. ACLS, BCLS, PALS, AHLS, PEPP. Bd. govs. Ariz. Emergency Med. Sys., 1999-2000. Sgt. U.S. Army, 1971-74. Mem. AACN. Office: Mesa Fire EMS 40 N Center St Ste 105 PO Box 1466 Mesa AZ 85201-1466

MASON, THEODORE W. lawyer; b. June 17, 1943; AB, Yale U., 1965; JD, U. Pa., 1972. Bar: Pa. 1972, Fla. 1987. Shareholder Greenberg Traurig, Phila., 1997—2001. Treas., bd. dirs. Nat. Adoption Ctr., Adoption Ctr. Del. Valley, The Hill Top Preparatory Sch. Mem. Nat. Assn. Bond Lawyers (steering com. workshop, enforcement com.). Office: Greenberg Traurig LLP 2700 Two Commerce Sq 2001 Market St Philadelphia PA 19103 Fax: 215-988-7801. E-mail: masont@gtlaw.com.

MASON, THOMAS ALBERT, lawyer; b. Cleve., May 4, 1936; s. Victor Lewis and Frances (Speidel) M.; m. Elisabeth Gun Sward, Sept. 25, 1965; children: Thomas Lewis, Robert Albert. AB, Kenyon Coll., 1958; LLB, Case-Western Res. U., 1961. Bar: Ohio 1961. Assoc. Thompson, Hine and Flory, Cleve., 1965-73, ptnr., 1973—. Trustee Cleve. YMCA, 1975-94. Capt. USMCR, 1962-65. Mem. ABA, Am. Coll. Real Estate Lawyers, Am. Land Title Assn. (lender's counsel group), Mortgage Bankers Assn. of Met. Cleve., Ohio Bar Assn., Cleve. Bar Assn., Am. Coll. Mortgage Attys., The Country Club. Republican. Episcopalian. Avocations: tennis; golf. Home: 23375 Duffield Rd Cleveland OH 44122-3101 Office: Thompson Hine LLP 3900 Key Ctr 127 Public Sq Cleveland OH 44114-1216 E-mail: tom.mason@thompsonhine.com.

MASON, THOMAS ALEXANDER, historian, educator, author; b. Port Huron, Mich., Oct. 29, 1944; s. Frank Hallgren and Charlotte (Hamilton) M.; m. Christine Huguette Guyonneau, Aug. 11, 1984; 1 child, Charlotte Guyonneau. BA in History with highest honors, Kenyon Coll., 1966; MA, U. Va., 1970, PhD, 1975. Asst. prof. history Pembroke (N.C.) State U., 1976-79; assoc. editor Papers of James Madison, U. Va., 1979-86, acting editor, 1986-87; dir. publs. Ind. Hist. Soc., 1987—2001, v.p. publs., 2001—02; v.p. Ind. Hist. Soc. Press, 2002—. Author: Serving God and Mammon: William Juxon, 1582-1663, 1985; exec. editor: Traces of Indiana and Midwestern History, 1989—; editor: Documentary Editing, 1989-93, Mag. of Albermarle County History, 1984-86; co-editor: Papers of James Madison, congl. series, vols. 14-16, 1983-89, presdl. series, vol. 1, 1984; project dir.: Papers of Lew Wallace, 1992—; mem. editl. bd. Papers of Philander Chase, 1997—, Jour. of the Early Republic, 1991-95, Ency. of Indpls., 1990-94; contbr. articles to encys. and scholarly jours. Served with USMC, 1966-68. Mem. Am. Assn. for State and Local History, Am. Hist. Assn., N.Am. Conf. on Brit. Studies, So. Hist. Assn., Assn. Documentary Editing (councillor-at-large 1999-2002, dir. publs. 1995-98, Disting. Svc. award 1993), Hist. Soc. of the Episcopal Ch. (sec. 1995—, bd. dirs. 1993—), English-Speaking Union U.S. (chmn. region VI 1996-2002, bd. dirs. 1995-2002, pres. Indpls. br. 1989-96, Lily Dabney scholar 1972), Raven Soc., Rotary (Indpls., bd. dirs. 1998-2000), Athletic Club (Indpls.), Colonnade Club (Charlottesville), Royal Commonwealth Soc. (London), Omicron Delta Kappa (faculty sec. Va. Cir. 1984-86), Alpha Delta Phi. Episcopalian. Home: PO Box 20331 Indianapolis IN 46220-0331 Office: Ind Hist Soc 450 W Ohio St Indianapolis IN 46202-3269 E-mail: tmason@indianahistory.org.

MASON, WILLIAM A(LVIN), psychologist, educator, researcher; b. Mountain View, Calif., Mar. 28, 1926; s. Alvin Frank and Ruth Sabina (Erwin) M.; m. Virginia Joan Carmichael, June 27, 1948; children: Todd, Paula, Nicole, Hunter. BA, Stanford U., 1950, MS, 1952, PhD, 1954. Asst. prof. U. Wis.-Madison, 1954-59; research assoc. Yerkes Labs. Primate Biology, Orange Park, Fla., 1959-63; head dept. behavioral sci. Delta Primate Research Ctr., Tulane U., Covington, La., 1963-71; prof. psychology, research psychologist U. Calif., Davis, 1971-91, leader behavioral biology unit Calif. Primate Rsch. Ctr., 1972-96, prof. emeritus, 1991. Bd. dirs. Jane Goodall Inst., 1978-92, Karisoke Rsch. Ctr., 1980-86. Mem. Editorial bd. Animal Learning and Behavior, 1973-76, Internat. Jour. Devel. Psychobiology, 1980-92, Internat. Jour. Primatology, 1980-90; contbr. numerous articles to profl. jours., chpts. to books. With USMC, 1944-46. USPHS spl. fellow, 1963-64. Fellow AAAS, APA (pres. divsn. 6 1982, disting. sci. contbn. award 1995), Am. Psychol. Soc., Animal Behavior Soc.; mem. Internat. Primatological Soc. (pres. 1976-80, 81-84), Am. Soc. Primatologists (pres. 1988-90, disting. primatologist award), Internat. Soc. Devel. Psychobiology (pres. 1971-72, Best Paper of Yr. award 1976), Sigma Xi. Home: 2809 Anza Ave Davis CA 95616-0257 Office: U Calif Regl Primate Rsch Ctr 1 Shields Ave Davis CA 95616 E-mail: wamason@ucdavis.edu.

MASORO, EDWARD JOSEPH, JR. physiology educator; b. Oakland, Calif., Dec. 28, 1924; s. Edward Joseph and Louise Elizabeth (DePaoli) M.; m. Barbara Weikel, June 25, 1947. AB, U. Calif., Berkeley, 1947, PhD, 1950. Asst. prof. physiology Queen's U., Kingston, Ont., Can., 1950-52; asst. prof., then asso. prof. Tufts U. Sch. Medicine, 1952-62; research asso. prof., then research prof. physiology and biophysics U. Wash., 1962-64; prof. physiology and biophysics, chmn. dept. Med. Coll. Pa., 1964-73; prof. physiology, chmn. dept. U. Tex. Health Sci. Center, San Antonio, 1973-91, prof., 1991-96; dir. Aging Rsch. and Edn. Ctr., 1992-96; prof. emeritus, 1996—. Cons. coun. basic sci. Am. Heart Assn., 1965-67; chmn. metabolic discussion group Fed. Am. Soc. Exptl. Biology, 1969-73; mem. aging rev. com. Nat. Inst. on Aging, 1981-84, chmn. bd. sci. counselors, 1985-89; chmn. Gordon Conf. on Biology of Aging, 1983; mem. bd. sci. advisors Human Nutrition Inst., Internat. Life Sci. Inst., 1989-92; mem. rsch. com. Am. Fedn. Aging Rsch., 1988—; vis. prof. U. Pisa, 1993; Wellcome vis. prof. basic med. scis., 1992-93. Author: Physiological Chemistry of Lipids in Mammals, 1967; co-author: Acid-Base Regulation: Its Physiology and Pathophysiology, 1971, 2d edit., 1977, Challenges of Biological Aging, 1999; editor sct. 24 Internat. Ency. Pharmacology and Therapeutics, 1974; mem. editorial bd. Jour. Lipid Rsch., 1967-83, Jour. Gerontology, 1979-91, Exptl. Gerontology, 1984—, Proc. Soc. Exptl. Biol. Medicine, 1986-92, Physiol. Rev., 1988-94; editor Jour. Gerontology: Biol. Scis., 1991-95, Handbook Physiol. Aging, 1995, Handbook of Biology of Aging, 5th edit., 2001; editor for biol. sics. Exptl. Aging Rsch., 1980-88; co-editor: handbook Biology of Aging, 5th edit., 2001, Aging: Clinical and Experimental Research, 1989—; assoc. editor: Encyclopedia of Aging, 3d edit., 2001; contbr. articles to profl. jours. Served with USNR, 1943-46. Recipient Christian R. and Mary F. Lindback Disting. Teaching award Med. Coll. Pa., 1967, Golden Apple award Student Am. Med. Assn., 1966, 71, Achievement award Allied Signal, 1989, Rsch. Achievements in Gerontology, U. Pisa, 1991, Irving Wright award Am. Fedn. Aging Rsch., 1995, Glenn Found. award, 1995. Fellow AAAS (coun. 1970—), Gerontol. Soc. Am. (chmn. biol. sci. sect. 1978-79, v.p. 1978-79, Kleemeir award 1990, pres.-elect 1992-93, pres. 1994-95); mem. AAUP, Am. Physiol. Soc. (chmn. endocrinology and metabolism sect. 1981-82), Soc. Exptl. Biology and Medicine (coun. 1987-91), Am. Soc. Biochemistry and Molecular Biology, N.Y. Acad. Scis., Phila. Physiol. Soc. (pres. 1966-67). Office: U Tex Dept Physiology Health Sci Ctr San Antonio TX 78229-3900 E-mail: masoro@aol.com.

MASOTTI, LOUIS HENRY, finance educator, consultant; b. N.Y.C., May 16, 1934; s. Henry and Angela Catherine (Turi) Masotti; m. Iris Patricia Leonard, Aug. 28, 1958 (div. 1981); children: Laura Lynn, Andrea Anne; m. Ann Randel Humm, Mar. 5, 1988. AB, Princeton U., 1956; MA, Northwestern U., 1961, PhD, 1964. Fellow Nat. Ctr. Edn. in Politics, 1962; asst. prof. polit. sci. Case Western Res. U., Cleve., 1963-67, assoc. prof., 1967-69, dir. Civil Violence Rsch. Ctr., 1968-69; sr. Fulbright lectr. Johns Hopkins U. Ctr. Advanced Internat. Studies, Bologna, Italy, 1969-70; assoc. prof. Northwestern U., Evanston, Ill., 1970-72, prof. polit. sci. and urban affairs, 1972-83, dir. Ctr. Urban Affairs, 1971-80, dir. Program in Pub. and Not-for-Profit Mgmt., Kellogg Sch. Mgmt., 1979-80, prof. mgmt. and urban devel. Kellogg Sch. Mgmt., 1983-94, dir. Real Estate Research Ctr. Kellogg Sch. Mgmt., 1986-88. Cons. to numerous publs, govt. agys., real estate firms, and corps.; vis. assoc. prof. U. Wash., 1969; exec. dir. Mayor Jane Byrne Transition Com., Chgo., 1979; vis. prof. Stanford Sch. Bus., 1989—92, UCLA Sch. Mgmt., 1989—92; prof., dir. real estate mgmt. program U. Calif. Grad. Sch. Mgmt., Irvine, 1992—98; bd. dirs. Mfd. Home Cmtys., inc., Facilities Mgmt. Internat. Author: (book) Educaiton and Politics in Suburbia, 1967, Shootout in Cleveland, 1969, A Time to Burn?, 1969, Suburbia in Transition, 1973, The New Urban Politics, 1976, The City in Comparative Perspective, 1976; co-editor: Metropolis in Crisis, 1968, Metropolis in Crisis, 2d edit., 1971, Riots and Rebellion, 1968, The Urbanization of the Suburbs, 1973, After Daley: Chicago Politics in Transition, 1981, Downtown Development, 1985, Downtown Development, 2d edit., 1971; editor: Edn. and Urban Soc., 1968—71, Urban Affairs Quar., 1973—80; sr. editor: Econ. Devel. Quar., 1986—92, vice chmn. bd.: Ill. Issues Jour., 1986—92, vice chmn. bd.: BOMA Office Mag., 1990—95. Mem. Cleveland Heights Bd. Edn., 1967—69; devel. coord. high tech. State of Ill. - City of Chgo., 1982—83; Rsch. dir. Carl Stokes for Mayor Cleve., 1967; advisor to various congl., gubernatorial and mayoral campaigns, Ill., NJ, Calif.; cons. urban devel. issues corps. developers, govt agys. and news media. Lt. USNR, 1956—59. Recipient Disting. Svc. award, Cleve. Jaycees, 1967; fellow, Homer Hoyt Inst. Advanced Real Estate Studies; grantee Rsch., numerous fed. and found., 1963—2000. Mem.: Coun. Urban Econ. Devel., Nat. Assn. Indsl. Office Properties, Internat. Devel. Rsch. Coun., Internat. Assn. Corp. Real Estate Execs., Nat. Trust Hist. Preservation, Habitat, Urban Land Inst., Lambda Alpha Internat. Office: 915 Sunset Dr Healdsburg CA 95448 E-mail: lmasotti@aol.com.

MASOUREDIS, SERAFEIM PANAGIOTIS, pathologist, educator; b. Detroit, Nov. 14, 1922; s. Panagiotis and Lemonia Masouredis; m. Marion Helen Mykytew, Oct. 1943; children: Claudia, Linus. AB, U. Mich., 1944, MD, 1948; PhD in Med. Physics, U. Calif., Berkeley, 1952. Diplomate Am. Bd. Pathology. Intern U. Calif. Svc./San Francisco Gen. Hosp., 1952-53, asst. resident in medicine, 1954-55; fellow Clinic Hematology/Donner Lab./Univ. Calif., Berkeley, 1953-54; asst. prof., then assoc. prof. pathology U. Pitts. Med. Sch., 1955-59; asst. dir. Cen. Blood Bank Pitts., 1955-59; assoc. prof. preventive medicine U. Calif., San Francisco, 1959-62, assoc. prof. medicine, 1962-67, assoc. prof. clin. pathology, 1966-67; prof. medicine Marquette U., Milw., 1967-69; exec. dir. Milw. Blood Ctr., 1967-69; prof. pathology U. Calif., San Diego, 1969-90, prof. emeritus, 1990—. Cons. WHO, Geneva, 1965-67; bd. dirs. Am. Assn. Blood Banks, Washington,1 981-83. Assoc. editor Jour. Transfusion, Washington, 1981-90; contbr. sci. articles and rsch. papers to various publs. Emily Cooley Meml. lectr. Am. Assn. Blood Banks, 1973, recipient Karl Landsteiner Meml. award, 1979. Mem. Am. Assn. Immunologists, Am. Soc. Clin. Investigation, Am. Soc. Hematology, Brit. Soc. Immunology, Am. Assn. Cancer Rsch., Internat. Soc. Blood Transfusion, Western Assn. Physicians. Avocations: woodworking, travel. Office: U Calif San Diego Dept Pathology Sch Medicine La Jolla CA 92093-0612

MASOVER, GERALD KENNETH, microbiologist; b. Chgo., May 12, 1935; s. Morris H. and Lillian (Perelgut) M.; m. Bonnie Blumenthal, Mar. 30, 1958 (dec. 1992); children: Steven, Laurie, David; m. Lee H. Tower, Mar. 25, 1995. BS, U. Ill., Chgo., 1957, MS, 1970; PhD, Stanford U., 1973. Registered pharmacist, Calif., Ill. Owner, operator Ropert Pharmacy, Chgo., 1960-68; rsch. assoc. Stanford U. Med. Sch., Palo Alto, Calif., 1974-80; assoc. rsch. cell biologist Children's Hosp., Oakland, 1980-83; rsch. microbiologist Hana Biologics, Berkeley, 1983-86; pharmacist various locations, 1970—; quality control sect. head Genentech, Inc., South San Francisco, 1986-90, quality control sr. microbiologist, 1990—. Contbr. articles to profl. jours., chpts. to books. 1st Lt. USAR, 1957-66. NSF predoctoral fellow, 1970-73; Rsch. grant

NIH, 1974-78. Mem. Internat. Orgn. for Mycoplasmology, Parenteral Drug Assn., Am. Soc. Microbiology, Sigma Xi. Jewish. Achievements include patents on triphasic mycoplasmatales detection method, triphasic mycoplasmatales detection device. Home: 6214 Acacia Ave Oakland CA 94618-1821 Office: Genentech Inc 1 DNA Way South San Francisco CA 94080-4990 E-mail: jer@gene.com.

MASQUE, MARIA L. urban planner; b. Habana, Cuba, Oct. 1, 1956; d. Ada R. Garcia-Masque and Jose L. Masque. AA , Santa Fe C.C., 1983; BA Anthropology, U. Fla., 1987, MA Urban & Regional Planning, 1994. Dir. Inst. of Hispanic and Latino Cultures - U. of Fla., Gainesville, 1995—97; prin. planner North Ctrl. Fla. Regional Planning Coun., 1987—2000; sr. planner/project mgr. The Planning Ctr., Tucson, 2000—02. Mem. Santa Cruz River Corridor Study Tech. Adv. Com., City of Marana, 2000—01, So. Ariz. Home Builders Assn. Tech. Adv. Com., Tucson, 2000—02, CANAMEX Trade Corridor Project, Tucson, 2000—02, Arizona/Sonora Mex. Project, Tucson, 2000—02, City of Douglas Focused Future II, 2001—02; member/consultant/facilitator Davis-Monthan AFB Airfield Compatibility Study Steering Com., Tucson, 2001—02. Adv., vol. cons. Hist. Barrio Anita Neighborhood Orgn., Tucson, 2000—02; cons. City of Douglas Housing Authority, 2001—02; mem. El Presidio Neighborhood Orgn., Tucson, 2001—02; cons. Pascua Yaqui Tribe, 2001—02. Mem.: Ariz. Planning Assn. Avocation: writing, traveling, networking, team building, horseback riding. Office: The Planning Center, Tucson 110 South Church St 6320 Tucson AZ 85701 Business E-Mail: mmasque@azplanningcenter.com.

MASRI, MERLE SID, biochemist, consultant; b. Jerusalem, Palestine, Sept. 12, 1927; came to U.S., 1947; s. Said Rajab and Fatima (Muneimné) M.; m. Maryjean Loretta Anderson, June 28, 1952 (div. 1974); children: Kristin Corinne, Allan Eric, Wendy Joan, Heather Anderson. BA in Physiology, U. Calif., Berkeley, 1950; PhD in Mammalian Physiology and Biochemistry, U. Calif. Berkeley, 1953. Rsch. asst. Dept. Physiology, Univ. Calif., Berkeley, 1950-53; predoctoral fellow Baxter Labs., 1952-53; rsch. assoc. hematology Med. Rsch. Inst., Michael Reese Hosp., Chgo., 1954-56; sr. rsch. biochemist Agrl. Rsch. Svc., USDA, Berkeley, 1956-87; supervisory rsch. scientist Agrl. Rsch. Svc., USDA, N.D. State U. Sta., Fargo, N.D., 1987-89; pvt. practice as cons. Emeryville, Calif., 1989—. Lectr. numerous confs. Contbr. articles to profl. jours. and books. Recipient Spl. Svc. and Merit awards USDA, 1966, 76, 77, Superior Svc. award USDA, 1977. Mem. AAAS, Am. Chem. Soc., Am. Oil Chemists Soc., Am. Assn. Cereal Chemists, N.Y. Acad. Scis., Inst. Food Technologists, Commonwealth Club Calif., Internat. Platform Assn., World Affairs Coun. of No. Calif., Sigma Xi. Achievements include patents for detoxification of aflatoxins in agricultural crops and aflatoxin contaminated milk, improved dyeability of cotton fabrics and reduced dye and electrolyte discharge in plant effluent, new closed-circuit raw wool scouring technology to conserve water and energy and control pollution, synthesis and use of polymers and modification of biopolymers for wastewater treatment, and for encapsulation, enzyme immobilization, toxic heavy metals removal and textile finishing treatment, non-polluting new technology for scouring raw wool in a closed circuit with water recycling and re-use and waste effluent control; studied chlorination of water in food processing operations and water re-use and recycle and the generation of mutagens and means of improving disinfection efficiency and reducing mutagen formation, pharmacology, metabolism, and toxicology of natural and synthetic compounds, cereal and baking technology and wheat and durum quality, carbohydrate chemistry, fermentation and enology, confectionery, and ceramic chemistry; discovered new methods and reagents for protein and amino acid residue modification and analysis, new mammalian metabolic pathways; developed other non-polluting textile finishing treatments. Home: 9 Commodore Dr Emeryville CA 94608-1652

MASRI, SAMI F(AIZ), civil and mechanical engineering educator, consultant; b. Beirut, Dec. 9, 1939; came to U.S., 1956; BS in Aerospace Engring., U. Tex., 1960, MS in Aerospace Engring., 1961; MS in Mech. Engring., Calif. Inst. Tech., 1962, PhD in Mech. Engring., 1965. Research fellow Calif. Inst. Tech., Pasadena, 1965-66; asst. prof. civil and mech. engring. U. So. Calif., Los Angeles, 1966-69, assoc. prof., 1969-76, prof., 1976—. Contbr. articles to profl. jours. Research grantee NSF, NASA, NRC Mem. AIAA, ASME, ASCE, IEEE, AAAS, Sigma Xi Office: U So Calif Dept Civil Engring Mc 2531 Los Angeles CA 90089-0001

MASS, MICHAEL D. state legislator; b. McAlester, Okla., Oct. 29, 1951; s. Fred Jr. and Lois M.; m. Suzanne Kline; children: Elena, Angie, Micah, Lucas. Student, Grayson C.C., Sherman, Tex., Ea. Okla. State Coll. Mem. Ho. of Reps., 1991—. Dist. mgr. Pittsburg County Conservation Dist.; chair Okla. Dem. Party. Mem. McAlester C. of C. (exec. dir.), Latimer and Pittsburg County Cattlemen's Assn., Hartshorne C. of C. (v.p.). Office: State Capitol Building 2300.North Lincoln Blvd., Rm 432D Oklahoma City OK 73105*

MASSA, CONRAD HARRY, religious studies educator; b. Bklyn., Oct. 27, 1927; s. Harry Frederick and Josephine W. (Lepold) M.; m. Anna W. Rossi, Aug. 19, 1951; children: Stephen Mark, Barbara Ann. AB with honors, Columbia U., 1951; M.Div., Princeton Theol. Sem., 1954, PhD, 1960; HHD, Lafayette Coll., 1987. Ordained to ministry Presbyn. Ch., 1954. Pastor Elmwood Presbyn. Ch., East Orange, N.J., 1954-57; asst. prof. homiletics Princeton Theol. Sem., 1957-61; sr. pastor Old First Ch., Newark, 1961-66, Third Presbyn. Ch., Rochester, N.Y., 1966-78; dean acad. affairs Princeton Theol. Sem., 1978-94, dean emeritus, 1994—, Charlotte W. Newcombe prof., 1978-95, Charlotte W. Newcombe prof. emeritus, 1995—. 1st moderator Synod of the Northeast, United Presbyn. Ch.; vis. prof. St. Bernard's Roman Cath. Sem., Rochester, 1968-70; keynote speaker 11th ann. conf. Inst. Theology, Yonsei U., Seoul, Republic of Korea, 1991. Author articles and book revs. Trustee Lafayette Coll., Easton, Pa., 1982-93. Served with U.S. Army, 1946-47. Mem. Acad. Homiletics, Am. Acad. Religion, Internat. John Bunyan Soc. Home: 14691 Blackbird Ln Fort Myers FL 33919-8346 *I have learned to try to understand all events and persons in terms of their relationships to other things, persons and events. While it is sometimes fruitful to isolate a particular and study it in its solitude, nothing and no one really exists in such isolation. This has become a guiding principle in my continued research and growth in those areas of greatest interest - religion, education and society.*

MASSA, JAMES, priest, theology studies educator; b. Jersey City, Sept. 3, 1960; s. Andrew Massa, Irene Gilbert. BA, Boston Coll., 1982; MDiv, Yale U., 1985; PhD, Fordham U., 1997. Parochial vicar Our Lady Queen of Martyrs, Forest Hills, NY, 1986—90; campus min. Cath. Diocese of Bklyn., 1990—93; asst. prof. Theology Newman U., Wichita, Kans., 1993—96, Pope John XXIII N Seminary, Weston, Mass., 1996—2001; assoc. prof. Theology Sem. of Immaculate Conception, Huntington, NY, 2001—. Parish priest St. Helen's Roman Cath. Ch., Westfield, NJ, 1998—. Contbr. . Grantee Tchrs.-Scholars grant, Wabash Ctr., 1999. Mem.: Amnesty Internat. (group coord. 1981—82). Roman Catholic. Office: Seminary Immaculate Conception 440 W Neck Rd Huntington NY 11743

MASSA, RICHARD WAYNE, retired communications educator; b. Carona, Kans., May 2, 1932; s. Columbo and Ella (Whitehead) M.; m. Mary Lou Marshall, May 29, 1960 (div. 1969); m. Teresa Rose Ramirez, Mar. 19, 1971; children: Tod, Daphne, Sara. B in Journalism, U. Mo., 1954, MA, 1955; postgrad., U. Ark., 1964-65. Instr. U. Mo., Columbia, 1955, Miss. State Coll. for Women, Columbus, 1957-58; from instr. to assoc.prof. comm. Okla. Coll. for Women/Okla. Coll. Liberal Arts, Chickasha, 1958-69; assoc. prof. Mo. So. State Coll., Joplin, 1972-87, prof., 1987-99, head dept. comm., 1980-99, dir. Inst. Internat. Studies, 1996-99, acting head dept. lang. and lit., 1979-80. V.p. Interpersonal Comm. Consultants, Oklahoma City, 1969-72. Co-author: Principal Ideas of Medieval and Renaissance Man, 1967, Contemporary Man in World Society, 1969; co-editor: Classical Readings for Contemporary Man, 1967, Inquisitive Man; His Quest for Truth, 1970. With U.S. Army, 1955-57. Recipient Gov.'s award for Excellence in Tchg., Mo. Dept. Higher Edn., Jefferson City, 1996. Home: 25399 Demott Dr Joplin MO 64801-6309 E-mail: massa727@aol.com.

MASSA, SALVATORE PETER, psychologist; b. Queens, N.Y., Aug. 5, 1955; s. Joseph and Marie Massa; m. Patricia Louise Kathryn Kelley, Mar. 12, 1979; children: Kathryn Kelley, Kristopher Kelley, KayLynn Kelley, Patrick Kelley, Grace Kellley, Frank Kelley. BA in Psychology, CUNY, 1975; MA, St. John's U., 1978, profl. diploma, 1979, PhD, 1985. Lic. psychologist, N.Y.; cert. sch. psychologist, N.Y.; nat. cert. sch. psychologist. Intern psychologist Sagamore Children's Psychiat. Hosp., Melville, N.Y., 1978-79; habilitation supr. Suffolk Child Devel. Ctr., Smithtown, 1979; staff psychologist Cumberland Mental Health Ctr., Bklyn., 1979-81; asst. program dir., dir. clin. svcs. Rhinebeck (N.Y.) Country Sch., 1981-87; cons. psychologist Brookwood Ctr., 1985-86, Anderson Sch., 1987-89, Renssalaer Columbia Greene BOCES, 1987—97. Sch. psychologist Red Hook Ctrl. Sch. Dist.; cons. psychologist Rhinebeck Ctrl. Sch. Dist., 1986-90; cons. Columbia County Advocacy and Resource Ctr., Rehab. Programs, Inc., 1989; adj. prof. Marist Coll., Poughkeepsie, N.Y., 1989—. Co-author study on relaxation tng. in residential treatment; contbr. papers to profl. confs. Trustee J.A. Coleman Cath. H.S.; head football coach YMCA Winter League, 1979-81; asst. football coach Rhinebeck Country Sch., 1982; coach Germantown Little League, Germantown Winter Basketball League; treas. Red Hood Soccer Club, 1999—. Recipient pub. svc. award for vol. work Middletown State Hosp., 1975, spl. recognition Internat. Coun. Psychology, 1981. Mem. APA, NASP, Ea. Psychol. Assn., Internat. Coun. Psychologists, Hudson Valley Psychol. Assn., Nat. Soc. Autistic Children, Soc. for Personality Assessment. Democrat. Roman Catholic. E-mail: SJU@rhcsd.dcboces.org.

MASS-ACHS, SHARON, social worker, educator; b. Bklyn., Jan. 29, 1945; d. Jack and Rose (Mendelsohn) Mass; m. Samuel Achs, June 16, 1976. BA in English, Bklyn. coll., 1966; MSW, Hunter Coll., 1975; PhD, U. So. Calif., 1986. Diplomate Am. Bd. Examiners; lic. social worker, Calif. Libr. reference Donaldson, Lufkin & Jenerette, N.Y.C., 1966-75; clin. social worker Jewish Hosp. Med. Ctr., Bklyn., 1975-79; corp. dir. social work United We. Med., Santa Ana, Calif., 1979-1990; dir. case mgmt. Cedars Sinai Med. Ctr., L.A., 1991—. Assoc. prof. U. So. Calif., L.A., 1984—. Contbr. (book chpt.) Working With the Dying Patient, 1992, Case Management Patient Focused Care, 1994, Case Management Revisited, 1997, Care Management by Design, 1999. Fellow NASW, Soc. Clin. Social Workers, Am. Case Mgmt. Assn. Democrat. Jewish. Avocation: music. Home: 395 S Old Bridge Rd Anaheim CA 92808-1361 Office: Cedars Sinai Med Ctr 8700 Beverly Blvd Los Angeles CA 90048-1865 E-mail: sharon.mass@cshs.org.

MASSAD, MALEK GEORGE, surgeon, researcher; b. Beirut, Sept. 2, 1957; came to US, 1987; s. George C. and Chamat Issa M.; m. Helene Rubeiz, Oct. 13, 1988; children: Nina, Nicole. BS in Biology-Chemistry, Am. U. Beirut, 1978, MD, 1983. Diplomate Am. Bd. Surgery, Am. Bd. Thoracic Surgery. Acad. surgeon U. Ill., Chgo., 1996—, dir. circulatory support program, 1996—, heart and lung transplant surgeon, 1996—, dir. cardiovascular rsch. labs., 1998—, head thoracic organ transplantation, 1998—; cardiovascular and thoracic surgeon U. Ill. Hosp., 1996—. Cons. thoracic surgeon Westside VA Hosp., Chgo., 1998—; mem. curriculum adv. bd. Osler Inst., Terre Haute, Ind., 1996-98; mem. thoracic organ transplant subcom. Regional Bank Ill., Chgo., 1996—. Recipient Investigator award Am. Coll. Chest Physicians, 1988, 99. Fellow ACS; mem. AAAS, AHA (mem. coun. thoracic and cardiovascular surgery 1995—), Nat. Transplant Soc. (mem. med. adv. bd. 1997—), Internat. Soc. Heart and Lung Transplantation, Ill. State Med. Soc., Soc. Thoracic Surgeons, Karl Meyer Soc., Warren Cole Soc. Avocations: tennis, reading, writing, research. Home: 110 Kraml Dr Burr Ridge IL 60527-0302 Office: U Ill Divsn Cardiothoracic Surg 840 S Wood St Ste 417 Chicago IL 60612-7317

MASSAD, STEPHEN ALBERT, lawyer; b. Wewoka, Okla., Dec. 20, 1950; s. Alexander Hamilton and Delores Jean (Razook) Massad; children: Caroline, Sarah, Margaret. AB, Princeton U., 1972; JD, Harvard U., 1975. Bar: Tex. 1975. Assoc. Baker & Botts, Houston, 1975-82, ptnr., 1983—. Office: Baker & Botts 3000 One Shell Plz 1200 Smith St Ste 1200 Houston TX 77002-4592 E-mail: stephen.massad@bakerbotts.com.

MASSALSKI, THADDEUS BRONISLAW, material scientist, educator; b. Warsaw, Poland, June 29, 1926; came to U.S., 1959; s. Piotr and Stanislawa (Andrukaniec) M.; m. Sheila Joan Harris, Sept. 19, 1953; children: Irena, Peter, Christopher. B.Sc., Birmingham (Eng.) U., 1952, PhD, 1954, D.Sc., 1964; fellow, Inst. Study Metals, U. Chgo., 1954-56; D.Sc. (h.c.), Warsaw (Poland) U., 1973. Lectr. Birmingham U., 1956-59; head. metal physics group Mellon Inst., Pitts., 1959-75, staff fellow, 1961—; prof. metal physics and materials sci. Carnegie-Mellon U., 1968—. Vis. prof. U. Buenos Aires, 1962, Calif. Inst. Tech., 1962, Stanford, 1963, U. Calif., 1964, 66, Inst. Physics, Bariloche Argentina, 1966, 70, Harvard, 1969; exchange prof. Krakow (Poland) U., 1968; vis. scientist Nat. Bur. Standards, 1980-81; NAVSEA prof. Naval Postgrad. Sch., Monterey, Calif; chmn. bd. govs. Acta Metallurgica, Inc., 1992—. Co-author: Structure of Metals, 3d edit, 1966, Advanced Physical Metallurgy, 1965; co-editor Progress in Materials Science, 1969—, Metall. Transactions, 1991—; editor-in-chief ASM/NIST Phase Diagram Program, 1980—; author papers and articles on alloy theory, crystallography, metal physics, meteorites. Guggenheim fellow Oxford U., 1965-66; recipient Alexander von Humboldt prise, 1991. Fellow Am. Soc. Metals (gold medal 1993), Am. Phys. Soc., The Metals Soc. (gold medal 1995), Brit. Inst. Metals, Brit. Inst. Physics, AIME (Hume-Rotherly prize 1989); mem. Polish Acad. Sci. (fgn.), German Acad. Sci. (fgn.), Phys. Soc. Home: 900 Field Club Rd Pittsburgh PA 15238-2127 Office: Carnegie Mellon U 3303 Wean Hall Pittsburgh PA 15213

MASSARO, DOMINIC ROBERT, judge, public official, writer; BS and MPA, NYU; MS, L.I. U.; JD, N.Y. Law Sch.; LLD , LittD (hon.), Mercy Coll.; DJA (hon.), Constantinian U.; LLD, Frederick II U. Bar: N.Y. 1969, U.S. Supreme Ct. 1974, U.S. Dist. Ct. (so. and ea. dists.) N.Y. 1978, U.S. Tax Ct. 1980, U.S. Ct. Appeals (2d cir.) 1986. V.p. indsl. rels. Teledyne-Stillman Mfg. Co., N.Y.C., 1967-71; commr. Com. Human Rights, 1967-70; adminstrv. commr. div. human rights State of N.Y., 1971-75; U.S. reg. dir. ACTION, 1975-77; ptnr. Fiore, Massaro & Vignola, 1977-86; judge N.Y. Ct. Claims, 1986, N.Y. Supreme Ct., N.Y.C., 1987—. Mem. N.Y.S. appeal bd. Selective Svc. Sys., 1972-76. Author: Cesare Beccaria: The Father of Criminal Justice-His Impact on Anglo American Jurisprudence, 1991. Pres. Nat. Com. Social Justice, 1989-91; grand cross Republic of Italy; pres. Gramercy Boys Club of N.Y., 1973-74; dir. Lavelle Sch. Blind, 1976—. Maj. N.Y. Guard. Pontifical knight, Vatican; recipient Internat. Dorso prize, 1991, Gold Collar, Colombian Acad. Internat. Law, Bogota, Acad., Pontifical Tiberian Acad., Rome; vis. fellow Woodrow Wilson Found., Princeton; named Outstanding Young Man Am. U.S. Jaycees, 1965. Mem. ABA, Am. Judges Assn. (rep. to UN 1991—), Justinian Soc. Jurists (bd. dirs.), N.Y. State Bar Assn. Office: 851 Grand Concourse Bronx NY 10451-2937

MASSARO, DONALD JOHN, medical educator, medical researcher; b. N.Y.C., Aug. 7, 1932; s. Angelo G. and Filomena Massaro; m. Gloria De Carlo Massaro, June 15, 1957; children: Julia Marie, Paul Anthony. BA, Hofstra Coll., 1953; MD, Georgetown U., 1957. Asst. prof. medicine Georgetown U., Washington, 1965—67, Cohen prof., 1990—; assoc. prof. medicine Duke U., Durham, NC, 1967—68, George Washington U., Washington, 1969—72, prof. medicine, 1972—76; Sertel prof. U. Miami, Fla., 1976—90. Mem. NHLBI adv. coun. NIH, Bethesda, Md., 1988—92. Editor: Lung Cell Biology, 1989, Oxygen, Gene Expression, Cellular Function, 1998; respiration editor: Ann. Rev. Physiol., 1994—98; editor: Am. Jour. Physiol., 1988—92. Vice chmn. Gordon Rsch. Conf., Maine, 1976, chmn., 1978; adv. coun. Parker B. Francis Found., Kans., 1990—94. Named The Joseph H. Bates vis. prof., U. Ark., 1999; recipient The Stony-Wold Lecture, Cornell U., 1990, Sci. Accomplishment award, Am. Thoracic Soc., 1997. Mem.: Am. Physiol. Soc. (chair respiration section), Am. Soc. Clin. Investigation, Assn. Am. Physicians. Achievements include discovery of all trans-retinoic acid abrogates by features of pulmonary emphysema in rats. Avocation: walking. Office: Georgetown U Sch Medicine 3900 Reservoir Rd NW Washington DC 20007-1481

MASSARO, JAMES C. military officer, government agency administrator; Grad., USAF Acad., 1974. Master navigator, electronic warfare officer. Commd. 2d lt. USAF, 1974, advanced through grades to col., comdr. 67th info. opers. wing., comdr. Air Force Info. Warfare Ctr., comdr. 67th Intelligence Group, chief Combat Crew Tgn. Sch. Nebr., mem. staff hqrs. U.S. Pacific Command, mem. staff Control Warfare Ctr., asst. to vice comdr. Air Intelligence Agy. Tex. Office: Lackland AFB 102 Hall Blvd Ste 201 San Antonio TX 78243-7009*

MASSARO, TRACI LYNN, special education educator; b. Gadsden, Ala., Jan. 16, 1969; d. James Michael Cushing and Sheltie Anna Griffin; m. Thomas Christopher Massaro, Aug. 18, 1992; children: Lorren Elizabeth, Ryan Thomas, Andrew Michael. BS in Spl. Edn., Jacksonville State U., 1992; M, Kennesaw State U., 2000. Tchr. Bartow County Schs., Cartersville, Ga., 1992-93, Douglas County Schs., Douglasville, 1993-99, Etowah County Schs., Gadsden, Ala., 1999—. Recipient Mamie Jo Jones scholarship, 1995, Hope Tchr. scholarship, 1996-98, Outstanding Grad. Student Special Edn. award, 1999, Pledge of Yr. award Gadsden City Coun., 2002. Mem. Coun. Exceptional Children (v.p. 1996-97, pres. 1997—), Kiwanis (Circle K, v.p. 1989-90. pres. 1990-91), Anchor Club (v.p. 1985-86, pres. 1986-87), Beta Sigma Phi (Gadsden City Coun. pledge of Yr. 2002). Republican. Baptist. Avocations: crafting, sewing. Home: 505 Cosby St Gadsden AL 35903-6911

MASSAUA, JOHN ROGER, retail executive; b. N.Y.C., Aug. 7, 1947; s. George John and Dorothy Regina (Coyle) M.; m. Janice Grace Vroom, Mar. 29, 1970; children: Matthew, Andrew, Meghan. BS, Fordham U., 1969; MBA, Fairleigh Dickinson U., 1973. Cert. fasttrack instr. Mem. staff Supermarkets Gen., Woodbridge, N.J., 1964-73; dist. mgr. Courtesy Drug Stores, Port Washington, N.Y., 1973-75; exec. v.p. Motts Shop Rite Supermarkets, East Hartford, Conn., 1975-80; sr. v.p. Imperial Distbrs., Auburn, Mass., 1980-86; group v.p. ops. Staples Inc., Newton, 1986-89; pres. Window Rama, Deer Park, N.Y., 1989-91; exec. v.p. ALP Freddy's Ltd., Rochester, 1991-93; v.p. mdse, and mktg. Nature Food Ctrs., Wilmington, Mass., 1994; sr. v.p. purchasing and merchandising McKesson Corp.: Millbrook Distbn. Svcs., Leicester, 1994-99; bus. mgmt. assistance counselor Coastal Enterprises Inc./Maine Small Bus. Devel. Ctr., Fairfield, Maine, 1999-2001; state dir. Maine Small Bus. Devel. Ctr. U. So. Maine Sch. of Bus., Portland, 2001—. Adj. faculty U. So. Maine, 2000—. Troop com. chmn. Boy Scouts Am., Northborough, Mass., 1979-89; pres. Minnaseroke Community Assn., 1991; bd. dirs. China Village Libr. Recipient Sales and Mktg. Achievement award Sales and Mktg. Mag., 1978; Price-Babson fellow, 2000, Paul Harris fellow, 2000. Mem.: GMDC (bd. dirs. 1996—99), Soc. Econ. Devel. (coun. of Maine), Am. Mgmt. Assn., Waterville C. of C., Rotary. Roman Catholic. Avocations: sailing, hiking, photography. Home: PO Box 6427 China ME 04926-0427 Office: Maine SBCD U So Maine Sch of Bus PO Box 9300 Portland ME 04104 E-mail: jrmassaua@maine.edu.

MASSAY, GLENN FRANK, college administrator; b. New Brighton, Pa., May 17, 1931; s. George Dewey and Florence Hough Massay; m. Catherine Marshall Massay, June 4, 1960 (div. 1987); children: Garth, Holly Anne; m. Donna A. Massay, Aug. 11, 1991; children: Robin Gentry, Chrispin Gentry. BS in Edn., Calif. State Coll., 1959; MA in History, W.Va. U., 1962, PhD in History, 1970. Assoc. prof. Fairmont (W.Va.) State Coll., 1965-71; academic dean Parkersburg (W.Va.) C.C., 1971-73; pres. So. W.Va. C.C., Logan, 1973-74; campus pres. Tanana Valley C.C., Fairbanks, Alaska, 1974-80; dean of instrn. Mat-Su Coll., Palmer, 1980-87, coll. dir., 1988-95, 99-00. Campaign co-chair United Way, Mat-Su Borough, 1996; bd. dirs. Valley Performing Arts, Wasilla, Alaska, 1996-98; Dem. Party candidate for Alaska State Senate, 1998. With U.S. Army, 1954-56. Recipient Outstanding Adminstrv. Svc. award U. Alaska, 1995. Mem.: Palmer C. of C. (bd. dirs. 1999—, pres. 2001—02). Democrat. Presbyterian. Avocations: skiing, photography. Home: PO Box 3096 Palmer AK 99645-3096 Office: Mat-Su Coll PO Box 2889 Palmer AK 99645-2889

MASSÉ, MARK HENRY, journalism educator; b. White Plains, N.Y., Oct. 24, 1952; s. Donald Merton and Peggy Hart Massé; m. Michelle Anne Perdue, June 28, 1997; stepchildren: Robert, John, Mark Dewsnup. BA, Miami U., 1974; MS with honors, U. Oreg., 1994. Prin. Words that Work, 1988—; adj. asst. prof. Sch. Journalism and Comm., U. Oreg., Eugene, 1994-96; asst. prof. dept. journalism Ball State U., Muncie, Ind., 1996—2001, assoc. prof. dept. journalism, 2001—. Cons. Ohio Dept. of Edn., Columbus, 1988-93, Bank One, Cleve., 1989-95, LTV Steel, Cleve., 1989-92. Author: (with others) Writer's Handbook, 1996, From the Heartlands, 1988. Recipient Gold Quill award of Merit IABC, 1983. Mem. Am. Soc. of Journalists and Authors, Soc. of Profl. Journalists, Assn. for Edn. in Journalism and Mass Comm., Kappa Tau Alpha. Democrat. Roman Catholic. Avocations: creative writing, photography, golf, fitness sports. Home: 209 N Bayberry Ln Muncie IN 47304-9319 Office: Dept of Journalism Ball State Univ Muncie IN 47306-0001 E-mail: mhmasse@bsu.edu.

MASSE, WILLIAM BRUCE, archaeologist; b. San Diego, July 10, 1948; s. Gerald John Masse and Viola Hope Bumgarner; m. Judith Lee Peters, Sept. 12, 1971; 1 child, Jeffrey Alan. BA in Anthropology, Stanford U., 1971; MA in Anthropology, U. Ariz., 1977; PhD in Anthropology, So. Ill. U., 1990. Archeologist Nat. Park Svc., Tucson, 1977-79, Ariz. State Mus., Tucson, 1985-86; field archaeologist State Historic Preservation Office, Honolulu, 1988-89; pacific area archaeologist Dept. of Navy, Pearl Harbor, Hawaii, 1990-94; archaeologist Dept. Air Force, Luke Air Force Base, Ariz., 1995-98, Los Alamos (N.Mex.) Nat. Lab., 1999—. Editor: The Protohistoric Period in the North American Southwest, 1981; contbr.: Chaco and Hohokam: Prehistoric Regional Systems in the North American Southwest, 1991, Natural Catastrophes During Bronze Age Civilizations: Archaeological, Geological, Astronomical, and Cultural Perspectives, 1998; editor (spl. issue) Jour. S.W., 1996; contbr. articles to profl. jours. Mem.: AAAS, Soc. Am. Archaeology (repatriation com. 1998—2001), Am. Anthrop. Assn., Sigma Xi. Office: Los Alamos Nat Lab ESH-20 Ecology Group Mail Stop M887 Los Alamos NM 87545 Fax: (505)667-0731. E-mail: wbmasse@lanl.gov.

MASSEL, ELIHU SAUL, lawyer; b. Bklyn., May 3, 1940; s. Ezekiel and Sadie (Sutta) M.; m. Matilda Montefiore, May 15, 1968; children: Morris, Richard, Tracy. BA, Alfred U., 1962; JD, NYU, 1965. Bar: N.Y. 1966, U.S. Dist. Ct. (ea. dist.) N.Y. 1967, (so. dist.) N.Y. 1967, (no. dist.) N.Y. 1970, (we. dist.) N.Y. 1970, U.S. Ct. Appeals (2d cir.), 1967, U.S. Supreme Ct. 1970. Law guardian Legal Aid Soc., Bklyn., 1966-67; assoc. Law Offices of Henry Abrams, N.Y.C., 1967-69; asst. atty. gen. N.Y. State Dept. Law, 1969-72; pvt. practice, 1972—. Lectr. N.Y. County Lawyers Assn., N.Y.C., 1982-96. Vice-pres. Am. Youth Hostels, Inc., Washington, 1970-79; bd. dirs., past pres. Met. N.Y. Coun. Am. Youth Hostels, Inc., 1969-90; trustee N.Y.C. chpt. Leukemia Soc. Am., 1976-96. Recipient Pro Bono award U.S. Dept. Justice, 1997, 98, Pro Bono award Am. Immigration Lawyers Assn., 1998. Mem. ABA, N.Y. State Bar Assn. (Pro Bono award 1996), Assn. Bar City N.Y., Queens County Bar Assn., Am. Immigration Lawyers Assn. (chmn. N.Y.C. chpt. 1976-77, N.Y.C. chpt. Pro Bono award 1996). Jewish. Avocations: hosteling, bicycling, photography, numismatics. Office: 122 E 42nd St New York NY 10168-0002

MASSENGALE, MARTIN ANDREW, agronomist, university president; b. Monticello, Ky., Oct. 25, 1933; s. Elbert G. and Orpha (Conn) M.; m. Ruth Audrey Klingelhofer, July 11, 1959; children: Alan Ross, Jennifer Lynn. BS, Western Ky. U., 1952; MS, U. Wis., 1954, PhD, 1956; LHD (hon.), Nebr. Wesleyan U., 1987; DS (hon.), Senshu U., Tokyo, 1995. Cert. profl. agronomist, profl. crop scientist. Research asst. agronomy U. Wis., 1952-56; asst. prof., assoc. agronomist U. Ariz., 1958-62, assoc. prof., assoc. agronomist, 1962-65, prof., agronomist, 1965-76, head dept., 1966-74, assoc. dean Coll. Agr. assoc. dir. Ariz. Agr. Expt Sta., 1974-76; vice chancellor for agr. and natural resources U. Nebr., 1976-81; chancellor U. Nebr.-Lincoln, 1981-91, interim pres., 1989-91; pres. U. Nebr., 1991-94, pres. emeritus, 1994, found. disting. prof. and dir., 1994—. Chmn. pure seed adv. com. Ariz. Agrl. Expt. Sta.; past chmn. bd., pres. Mid-Am. Internat. Agrl. Consortium; coord. com. environ. quality EPA-Dept. Agrl. Land Grand U.; past chmn. bd. dirs. Am. Registry Cert. Profls. in Agronomy, Crops and Soils; bd. dirs. Ctr. for Human Nutrition; bd. dirs., trustee U. Nebr. Found.; chair bd. dirs. Agronomic Sci. Found., chmn. selection com; dir. devel. Secretariat, Filippo Maseri Florio World Prize for Disting. Rsch. in Agr.; exec. com. U. Nebr. Tech. Park, LLC; bd. dirs. Lincoln Ins. Group., Woodmen Accident & Life Co., LIG, Inc., Am. First, LLC; mem. adv. bd. Nat. Agrl. Rsch., Ext., Edn. and Econs., 1998—, mem. exec. com.; mem. nat. adv. bd. Trees Am., 1998—. Chmn. NCAA Pres.'s Comm., 1988-91; distbn. revenue com., standing com. on appointments North Ctrl. Assn. Schools Commn. on Insts. Higher Edn., 1991; trustee Nebr. Hist. Soc. Found.; bd. dirs. Nebr. Hist. Soc.; bd. govs. Nebr. Sci. and Math. Initiative; mem. Knight Found. Commn. on Intercollegiate Athletics; bd. dirs. Great Plains Funds, IBP; hon. life trustee Nebr. Coun. on Econ. Edn.; hon. lifetime trustee Nebr. Coun. on Econ. Edn. With U.S. Army, 1956-58. Named

Midlands Man of Yr., 1982, to We. Ky. U. Hall of Disting. Alumni, 1992, DeKalb Crop Sci. Disting. Career award, 1996, Outstanding Educator Am., 1970; recipient faculty recognition award Tucson Trade Bur., 1971, Ak-Sar-Ben Agrl. Achievement award, 1986, Agrl. Builders Nebr. award, 1986, Walter K. Beggs award, 1986, Vol. of Yr. award for disting. svc. Nebr. Coun. on Econ. Edn., IANR Team Initiation award, Agri award Triumph of Agr. Expn., 1999, Exemplary Svc. to Agr. award Nebr. AgRels. Coun., 2000, Friend of LEAD award Nat. LEAD Alumni Assn., 2001, Outstanding Pres. award All-Am. Football Found., 2001; hon. state farmer degrees Ky., Ariz., Nebr. Future Farmers Am. Assns. Fellow AAAS (sect. chmn.), Crop Sci. Soc. Am. (past dir., pres. 1972-73, past assoc. editor, pres. western soc., disting. career award 1996), Am. Soc. Agronomy (past dir., vis. scientist program, past assoc. editor Agronomy Jour., Disting. Svc. award 1984); mem. Am. Grassland Coun., Ariz. Crop Improvement Assn. (bd. dirs.), Am. Soc. Plant Physiology, Nat. Assn. Colls. and Tchrs. Agr., Soil and Water Conservation Soc. Am., Ariz. Acad. Sci., Nebr. Acad. Sci., Agrl. Coun. Am. (bd. dirs., issues com.), Coun. Agrl. Sci. and Tech. (bd. dirs. budget and fin. 1979-82, 94—, treas., exec. com. 1997—), Nat. Assn. State Colls. and Land Grant Univs. (chmn. com. on info. tech. 1987-94, exec. com. 1990-92, bd. dirs. 1992-94), Edn. Engring. Professions (mem. commn.), Coll. Football Assn. (chmn., bd. dirs. 1986-88), Am. Assn. State Coll. and Univs. (task force instl. resource allocation), Assn. Am. Univs. Rsch. Librs. (steering com. 1992-94), Nebr. Crop Improvement Assn. (disting. svc. award), Grazing Lands Forum (pres.), Nebr. C. of C. and Industry, Nebr. Diplomats Inc. (hon. diplomate), Nebr. Vet. Med. Assn. (hon.), Sigma Xi, Phi Kappa Phi, Gamma Sigma Delta (Award of Merit), Alpha Zeta, Phi Sigma, Gamma Alpha, Alpha Gamma Rho, Phi Beta Delta, Golden Key Nat. Honor Soc., Innocents Soc. Office: U Nebr 220 Keim Hall Lincoln NE 68583-0953 E-mail: mmassengale1@unl.edu.

MASSENGALE, ROGER LEE, lawyer; b. Somerset, Ky., Mar. 23, 1953; s. Wendell Howard and Norma Jean (Neely) M.; m. Debra Kaye Marcum, Mar. 19, 1978; children: Sarah Anne, Jessica Claire. BA, U. Ky., 1975; JD, Capitol U., 1979. Bar: Ky. 1979, U.S. Dist. Ct. (ea. dist.) Ky. 1980, U.S. Ct. Appeals (6th cir.) 1986. Assoc. Lovelace, Carroll & Peck, Monticello, Ky., 1979-80; asst. county atty. Wayne County, 1979-80; region counsel Ashland (Ky.) Exploration, Inc., 1980-83; atty. Ashland Oil, Inc., 1983-85; assoc. Wells, Porter & Schmitt, Paintsville, Ky., 1985-88, ptnr., 1988-94; pvt. practice Law Offices Roger L. Massengale, 1994—. Bd. dirs. Parents Anonymous Ea. Ky., Ashland, 1984, Tri-State Fair and Regatta, Ashland, 1983-85; past chmn. adminstrv. bd. First United Meth. Ch., Paintsville, lay del. to Ky. Ann. Conf. Mem. ABA, Ky. Bar Assn. (mem. ho. dels. 1991-98), Ky. Acad. Trial Attys., Johnson County Bar Assn., Def. Rsch. Inst. Avocations: fly fishing, backpacking, wood working. Home: 208 4th St Paintsville KY 41240-1150

MASSEY, ALLYN FRANCES, artist, educator; b. Norwood, Mass., Aug. 3, 1949; d. Gordon J. and Gwendolyn M. BFA, Corcoran Sch. Art, 1986; MFA, Md. Inst. Coll. Art, 1989. Prof. U. Md., Coll. Park, 1990-91, Corcoran Sch. Art, Washington, 1992-97, Goucher Coll., Balt., 1997—. Bd. dirs., chair program adv. com. Md. Art Pl., Balt., 1998-2000; mem. adv. bd. Clipper Artists Fire Fund, Balt., 1996; resident Goya Girls Press, 2000; artist residency Jentel Found, Banner, Wyo., 2001, Bemis Ctr. for Contemporary Art, Omaha, 2002; Jesse DuPont, Nat. Humanities Ctr., Raleigh, NC, 2000. Illustrator: Second Person Rural, 1980; sculptor, printmaker, installation artist. Artist, panelist Balt. Mus. Art, 1993, BWI airport commn. Md. Aviation Bd., Linthicum, 1995, 1% for art commn. GSA, Balt./Washington, 1996; mem. pres.'s coun. Md. Inst., Coll. Art, 1998--. Recipient awards for individual artist, new genre Md. Arts Coun., 1992, 95, 97, 2001; Henry A. Walters fellow Md. Inst. Coll. At, 1989. Mem. Internat. Scuplture Ctr., Balt. Mus. Art, School 33 Art Ctr., Sculptors Inc. (sec. 1991-93, editor newsletter 1995-97), Cultural Alliance, Contemporary Mus. Avocations: astronomy, geology. Office: Goucher Coll 1021 Dulaney Valley Rd Baltimore MD 21204-2753 E-mail: amassey@goucher.edu.

MASSEY, ANDREW JOHN, conductor, composer; b. Nottingham, Eng., May 1, 1946; came to U.S., 1978; s. Henry Louis Johnson and Margaret (Park) M.; m. Sabra Ann Todd, May 29, 1982; children: Colin Sebastian, Robin Elizabeth. BA, Oxford U., 1968, MA, 1981, Nottingham U., 1969. Asst. condr. The Cleve. Orch., 1978-80; assoc. condr. New Orleans Symphony, 1980-86, San Francisco Symphony, 1985-88; music dir. Fresno (Calif.) Philharmonic, 1986-93, R.I. Philharmonic, Providence, 1986-91, Toledo Symphony Orch., 1991—2000, also condr. Vis. scholar Brown U., Providence, 1986-91; music dir. Oreg. Mozart Players, 1998—. Composer incidental music (stage prodns.) Murder in the Cathedral, 1968, King Lear, 1971, A Midsummer Night's Dream, 1972. Avocations: trees, computers, astrology, philosophy of Karl Popper. Office: c/o John Gingrich Management Inc PO Box 1515 New York NY 10023 also: Oregon Mozart Players PO Box 11474 Eugene OR 97440*

MASSEY, CHARLES KNOX, JR. advertising agency executive; b. Durham, N.C., Jan. 16, 1936; s. Charles Knox and Louise (Southerl) M.; m. Mary Ann Keith, Aug. 27, 1960; children: Elizabeth, Knox, Louise. BS in Bus. Adminstrn, U. N.C., 1959. Vice pres. C. Knox Massey & Assoc., Inc., advt. agy., Durham, N.C., 1959-64; account exec. Tucker Wayne & Co., advt. agy., Atlanta, 1964-78, pres., 1978-88, Tucker Wayne/Luckie & Co., Atlanta, 1988-95; chmn., CEO West Wayne, Inc., 1996—. Trustee The Lovett Sch., Atlanta, Inst. for the Arts and Scis., U. N.C., Chapel Hill, The Atlanta Opera. Mem. Piedmont Driving Club (pres. 1990-92), Coral Beach and Tennis Club (Bermuda), Highlands (N.C.) Country Club. Episcopalian. Home: 67 Brighton Rd NE Atlanta GA 30309-1518 Office: West Wayne Inc 1100 Peachtree St NE Ste 1800 Atlanta GA 30309-4502

MASSEY, CLINTON EDWARD, neurosurgeon; b. Charlotte, N.C., Oct. 31, 1947; s. Robert Lee and Mary Alice (Grier) M.; m. Carolyn Jean Spaduzzi, May 23, 1970; children: Heather Christine, Lauren Ashley. BS, Presbyn. Coll., 1970; MD, Med. Coll. Ga., 1978. Diplomate Am. Bd. Neurol. Surgery. Intern Med. Coll. Ga., 1978-79, resident, 1979-84; pvt. practice, Augusta, Ga., 1984—. Bd. dirs. Walton Rehab. Hosp., Augusta, St. Joseph Hosp., Augusta. Bd. dirs. March of Dimes, Augusta, 1989-92. 2d lt. U.S. Army, 1970. Mem. AMA, Am. Assn. Neurol. Surgery, Congress Neurol. Surgeons, Ga. Neurosurg. Soc. Republican. Home: 67 Conifer Cir Augusta GA 30909-4508 Office: 2315C Central Augusta GA 30904 E-mail: cemassey@bellsouth.net.

MASSEY, CYNTHIA LEAL, writer, literature educator; b. San Antonio, Mar. 14, 1956; children: Michael, Meghan. BA, St. Mary's U., San Antonio, 1978, MA, 1983. Cert. pastoral lay ministry Oblate Sch. Theology, 93. Editor S.W. Rsch. Inst., San Antonio, 1979—89; freelance writer, 1988—; English instr. San Antonio Coll., 1991—. Author: Fire Lilies, 2001, The Caballeros of Ruby, Texas, 2002; contbr. short stories to lit. publs. Mem.: Writers Friends of the San Antonio Libr. (program chair 2001—02), Women Writing the West (pres.-elect 2001—02). Roman Catholic. Avocations: collecting books, reading, aerobics. Home: PO Box 294 Helotes TX 78023 Office: San Antonio Coll 1300 San Pedro Ave San Antonio TX 78212 Fax: 210-695-5227. E-mail: cmass22@aol.com.

MASSEY, DONALD WAYNE, clergyman, small business owner; b. Durham, N.C., Mar. 7, 1938; s. Gordon Davis and Lucille Alma (Gregory) M.; m. Violet Sue McIlvain, Nov. 2, 1958; children: Kimberly Shan (dec.), Leon Dale, Donn Krichele, Anthony Donn Prestarri. Student, U. Hawaii, 1959, U. Ky., 1965, 66, U. Va., 1970, Piedmont C.C., 1982. Ordained Hookerton Christian Ch., 1999. Head microfilm sect. Ky. Hist. Soc., Frankfort, 1961; dir. microfilm ctr. U. Ky., Lexington, 1962—67; dir. photog. svcs. and graphics U. Va., Charlottesville, 1967—73; pres. Micrographics II, Charleston, SC, 1973—; min. Hookerton (N.C.) Christian Ch., 1999—2001, Bethel Christian Ch., Grifton, 1999—2001, Park St. Christian Ch., Charlottesville, 2002—. Instr. U. Va. Sch. Continuing Edn., 1971—72, Ctrl. Va. Piedmont C.C., 1976; cons. Microform Systems and Copying Ctrs.; owner Massland Farm, Shadwell, Va.; basketball coach Rock Hill Acad., 1975—77; chaplain Cedars Nursing Home, Charlottesville, 1992—94, Colonnades Charlottesville, 1992—, Our Lady Peace Charlottesville, 1996—, Manor House, 1999—, Britthaven, Snow Hill, NC, 1999—2000; vol. chaplaincy program Martha Jefferson Hosp., Charlottesville, 2002—. Pub.: Micropublishing Series, 18th Century Sources for Study of English Lit. and Culture, Women Authors 18th and 19th Centuries, 1993, Va. Colonial History, 1994—, Theology in the 18th and 19th Centuries, 1995; author: Episcopal Churches in the Diocese of Virginia, 1989, A Catechism for Children, 1995, A Guide to Colonial Churches in Virginia, 1996, The Christian Philosophy of Patrick Henry, In Memoriam to the Rt. Rev. William Meade, Third Bishop of Virginia, 1996, Jamestown, the Beginning of the Church in Virginia, 1996, Christ Epsicopal Church, Monticello Parish, Charlottesville, Va.. The First 100 Years, 1924-1924, 1996, Ministry in Nursing Homes and Health Care Centers, 1997, St. John's-Waldrop a Church History, 1845-1997, 1998, Jamestown and the Colonial Churches in Virginia, 1999, Twelve Gates to the Kingdom of God, Apostles of Christ, 1999; contbg. editor Va. Libr., 1970-71; contbr. articles to profl. jours. Introduced and Leader of Fest. of Carols and Liturgy in Retirement and Nursing Homes, 1995—98; with USMCR, 1957—73; rep. Senatorial Inner Cir., 1990, George Bush Rep. Task Force, 1990; chmn. bd. Park St. Christian Ch., 1969—76; mem. Emmanuel Epsic. Ch., Greenwood, Va., Grace Episc. Ch., Cismont; pres. region XV Episc. Diocese Va.; chalice bearer St. Luke's Chapel, Simeon, Christ Ch., Charlottesville, 1992, lay eucharistic min., 1993—; lay reader eucharistic min. Christ Episcopal Ch.; chaplain Cedars Nursing Home, 1991—; eucharistic min. Grace Episc. Ch., Cismont, 1996—; chaplain Comyn Hall, Charlottesville, 2001—; pres. Rock Hill Acad. Aux., 1975—76; pres. bd. Workshop V for handicapped, Charlottesville, 1972—73. Named Ky. Col.; recipient Jey award Workshop V. Mem. ALA, Va. Libr. Assn., Soc. Reprodn. Engrs., Nat. Microfilm Assn. (libr. rels. com. 1973), Va. microfilm Assn. (pres. 1971-72, v.p. 1973-74, program chmn. ann. conf. 1974, Pioneer award 1973, fellow 1976), Ky. Microfilm Assn. (Oustanding award 1967, pres. 1964-67), Assn. Info. and Image Mgmt., Va. Gamebird Assn., Thoroughbred Owners and Breeders Assn., Am. Rose Soc., Thomas Jefferson Rose Soc. (charter), NRA, Nat. Trust Hist. Preservation, Va. Microfilm Assn. (contbg. editor Micro-News 1983-85). Home: 3304 Keswick Rd Keswick VA 22947-2600 Office: Hookerton & Bethel Christian Chs PO Box 186 Hookerton NC 28538-0186 also: Park Street Christian Church 1200 Park Street Charlottesville VA 22901-3915

MASSEY, DOUGLAS S. sociologist, educator; b. Olympia, Wash., Oct. 5, 1952; s. E. Martin and Ruth M. Massey; m. Susan R. Ross, Jan. 8, 1983 (div. Aug. 2001); 1 child Vanessa Ross. BA in Sociology, Psychology, Spanish, Western Wash. U., 1974; MA in Sociology, Princeton U., 1977, PhD, 1978; MA (hon.), U. Pa., 1985. Rsch. assoc. Princeton U., 1978-79; postdoctoral fellow U. Calif., Berkeley, 1979-80; asst. prof. U. Pa., Phila., 1980-85, assoc. prof., 1985-87, Dorothy Swaine Thomas prof., 1994—; prof. U. Chgo., 1987-94. Author: Return to Aztlan, 1987, American Apartheid, 1993 (Am. Sociol. Assn. award 1994), Miracles on the Border (S.W. Book award 1995), Worlds in Motion, 1998. Mem. adv. bd. Russell Sage Found., N.Y.C., 1994—; trustee Leadership Coun., Chgo., 1993-94, nat. adv. bd., 1994—; adv. bd. Chgo. Urban League, 1990-94, Mex. Cultural Ctr., Phila., 1994—. Recipient Merit award NIH, 1987-97, Exemplary Alumnus award Western Wash. U., 2000; Guggenheim fellow, 1990-91. Fellow Am. Acad. Arts and Scis.; mem. Nat. Acad. Sci., Am. Sociol. Assn. (pres. 2000-2001), Population Assn. Am. (pres. 1996, Clogg award 1998), Sociology Rsch. Assn., L.Am. Studies Assn. (nominating com. 1993-94). Democrat. Avocation: collecting Latin American art. Office: Univ of Pennsylvania Population Studies Ctr 3718 Locust Walk Philadelphia PA 19104

MASSEY, GWENDOLYN INEZ, nurse, counselor; b. Greensboro, Ala., Oct. 12, 1929; d. Judson Lyons Kilpatrick and Rubye Hill Kilpatrick-Jacobs; m. James Earl Massey, Aug. 4, 1951. BSN, Wayne State U., 1952; MA, Ball State U., 1978. Sr. pub. health nurse Dept. Pub. Health Nursing, Detroit; supr. patient care and edn., clin. instr. pub. health nsg. Henry Ford Hosp.; coord. of refugee and relief svcs. Missionary Bd. of Ch. of God, Anderson, Ind. Contbr. articles to profl. jours. Recipient Distikng. Svc. award, Commn. on Social Concerns, Ch. of God. Mem. Am. Nursing Assn., Am. Assn. Counseling and Devel. Home: RR 3 Box 475 Greensboro AL 36744-9349

MASSEY, HENRY P., JR. lawyer; b. Montclair, N.J., Sept. 2, 1939; AB, Cornell U., 1961, JD with distinction, 1968. Bar: Calif. 1969. Ptnr. Wilson Sonsini Goodrich & Rosati, Palo Alto, Calif., 1982—. Bd. editors Cornell Law Rev., 1967-68. Mem. ABA (sects. on corp., banking and bus. law, taxation law), State Bar Calif. (mem. corps. com. bus. law sect. 1979-82), Order of Coif, Phi Kappa Phi. Office: Wilson Sonsini Goodrich & Rosati 650 Page Mill Rd Palo Alto CA 94304-1050

MASSEY, JAMES EARL, clergyman, educator; b. Ferndale, Mich., Jan. 4, 1930; s. George Wilson and Elizabeth (Shelton) M.; m. Gwendolyn Inez Kilpatrick, Aug. 4, 1951. Student, U. Detroit, 1949-50, 55-57; BTh, BRE, Detroit Bible Coll., 1961; AM, Oberlin Grad Sch. Theology, 1964; postgrad., U. Mich., 1967-69; DD, Asbury Theol. Sem., 1972, Ashland Theol. Sem., 1991, Huntington Coll., 1994; HumD, Tuskegee U., 1995; DD, Warner Pacific Coll., 1995; LittD, Anderson U., 1995; DD, Wash. and Jefferson Coll., 1997, North Park Theol. Sem., 1999. Ordained to ministry Ch. of God, 1951. Assoc. min. Ch. of God, Detroit, 1951-53; sr. pastor Met. Ch. of God, 1954-76, pastor-at-large, 1976; spkr. Christian Brotherhood Hour, 1977-82; prin. Jamaica Sch. Theology, Kingston, 1963-66; campus min. Anderson Coll., Ind., 1969-77, asst. prof. religious studies, 1969-75, assoc. prof., 1975-80, prof. N.T. and homiletics, 1981-84; dean of chapel and univ., prof. religion and society Tuskegee U., Ala., 1984-89; dean, prof. preaching and bibl. studies Anderson Sch. Theology, 1989-95; dean emeritus and disting. prof.-at-large, 1995—. Chmn. Comm. on Higher Edn. in the Ch. of God, 1968-71; vice chmn. bd. publs. Ch. of God, 1968-78; dir. Warner Press, Inc.; rsch. scholar Christianity Today Inst. Author: When Thou Prayest, 1960, The Worshipping Church, 1961, Raymond S. Jackson, A Portrait, 1967, The Soul Under Seige, 1970, The Church of God and the Negro, 1971, The Hidden Disciplines, 1972, The Responsible Pulpit, 1973, Temples of the Spirit, 1974, The Sermon in Perspective, 1976, Concerning Christian Unity, 1979; gen. editor: Christian Brotherhood Hour Study Bible, 1979, Designing the Sermon, 1980; co-editor: Interpreting God's Word for Today, 1982; editor: Educating for Service, 1984, The Spiritual Disciplines, 1985, The Bridge Between, 1988, Preaching From Hebrews, 1992, The Burdensome Joy of Preaching, 1996, Sundays at The Tuskegee Chapel, 1999, Aspects of My Pilgrimage: An Autobiography, 2002; mem. editl. bd. The Christian Scholar's Rev. Leadership mag.; mem. editl. bd., contbg. editor Vol I New Interpreter's Bible,, 1990—; contbg. editor Preaching mag.; sr. editor Christianity Today mag. Mem. Corp. Inter-Vrsity Christian Fellowship; bd. dirs. World Vision. Served with AUS, 1951-53. Mem. Nat. Assn. Coll. and Univ. Chaplains, Nat. Com. Black Churchmen, Nat. Negro Evang. Assn. (bd. dirs. 1969-86). Office: 367 Beverly Rd Greensboro AL 36744-6034

MASSEY, JEANNE KELLY, music festival producer; b. Charleston, S.C., Oct. 30, 1938; d. Lawrence Lees and Margaret Augusta (Montgomery) Kelly; m. William Massey III, June 25, 1960 (div. 1994); children: Kelly Massey-Carlier, John Gant Massey. BA, Duke U., 1960; advanced libr. cert., William and Mary Coll., 1976. Founding libr. Jamestown Acad., Williamsburg, Va., 1974-77; pres. Va. State Ballet, Newport News, 1978-82; founder, pres. Arts Resale of Williamsburg, 1978-88; pres., gen. mgr. Mid-Atlantic Chamber Orch., Washington, 1985-98; exec. prodr. Benedictinus 2000 Internat. Order of Benedictines, 1977-2000; prodr. Annual World Bank Mozart Festival, 1991—. Commr. Va. Comm. for the Arts, Richmond, 1979-84; nat. exec. com. Children of Am. Revolution, Washington, 1973-76; dir., pres. The Wyo. Condominium, Washington, 1988-91; mem. Arts Adv. Bd., Williamsburg, 1979-81. Recipient Platinum Violin award Festival Williamsburg, 1984. Mem. DAR (pres. 1970-76), Jamestowne Soc., Jane Austen Soc. of N.Am., Phi Beta Kappa, Kappa Delta Pi, Sigma Delta Pi. Republican. Presbyterian. Avocations: walking, reading, concerts, museums, theatre. Office: JKM Inc PO Box 21439 Washington DC 20009-0939 Fax: 202-483-9320. E-mail: jkminc@de.infi.net.

MASSEY, KATHLEEN MARIE OATES, lawyer; b. Chgo., Dec. 2, 1955; d. William Robert Jr. and Ethelyn Rose (Calhoun) Oates. Student, U. Claremont-Ferrand, France, 1976-77; BA cum laude, Kalamazoo Coll., 1978; JD, U. Wis., 1981. Bar: Wis. 1981, Minn. 1981, U.S. Dist. Ct. Minn. 1981, U.S. Dist. Ct. (ea. dist.) Wis. 1983. With Larkin, Hoffman, Daily & Lindgren Ltd., Mpls., 1981-87; ptnr. Habush, Habush & Davis, Milw., 1987-90; asst. gen. counsel A.O. Smith Corp., 1992-97; sr. litigation counsel Motorola Inc., Schaumburg, Ill., 1997—. Mem. ABA, Minn. Bar Assn., Wis. Bar Assn., Phi Beta Kappa, Alpha Lambda Delta, Phi Eta Sigma.

MASSEY, MARY S. emergency nurse practitioner; b. Whitties, Calif., Jan. 13, 1959; d. Jack Lee Hoffa and May Hoffa Parlene; m. Charles Bruce Massey, Apr. 30, 1989; children: Melissa, Danielle. BS in nursing, Calif. State U., Fullerton, Calif., 1983; A, Cypress Coll., Calif., 1981. Paramedic liaison nurse Araheim Meml. Med. Ctr., Anaheim , Calif., 1997—; instr. U. Calif. , Davis, 2002; ops. mgr. critical care Irvine Med. Ctr., 1995—97; ER supr. Western Med. Ctr., Santa Ana , 1985—95; ER nurse St. Jope Med. Ctr., Fullerton, 1980—92. Disaster coord. Anaheim Meml. Med. Ctr., Calif., 1997—; instr. weapons of mass destruction Dept. of Justice, 2002. Contbr. articles to profl. jours. Mem.: Ctrl. Paramedic Adv. Com., Orange County ER Mgrs. Com., Paramedic Coord. of Orange County (chmn. 2002). Office: Anaheim Meml Med Ctr 1111 La Palma Ave Anaheim CA 92801

MASSEY, PATTI CHRYL, elementary school educator; b. Electra, Tex., Nov. 18, 1952; d. Francis Leon and Violet V. (Inabinette) Perry; m. William S. Massey, July 18,1986. BS, Midwestern U., 1974; MEd, Southwest Tex. State U., 1979. Cert. elem. educator, reading specialist, coop. learning trainer, reading recovery tchr. Tchr. East Central Ind. Sch. Dist., San Antonio, 1975-89, San Antonio Ind. Sch. Dist., 1990—. Vol. Tex. Spl. Olympics, San Antonio, 1975—, Jimenez Thanksgiving Sr. Citizens Dinner, San Antonio, 1983—, Amateur Athletic Union Jr. Olympics, San Antonio, 1989, Amateur Athletic Union Nat. Basketball Tournament, San Antonio, 1990, U.S. Olympic Festival, San Antonio, 1993, Alzheimer's Memory Walk, 1992—. Named one of Outstanding Young Women in Am., 1983. Mem. NEA, San Antonio Tchrs. Coun., Tex. State Tchrs. Assn., PTA (hon. life, sec. 1982-84), Alamo Reading Coun., Tex. State Reading Assn., Kappa Delta Pi, Alpha Delta Kappa, Sigma Kappa (Outstanding Alumna 1988, 91, Pearl Ct. award 1990, Outstanding Regional Alumna 1991, alumnae/collegiate rels. coord. 1998-2001). Democrat. Methodist. Avocations: reading, volunteering, aerobic activities, baking. Home: 4527 Black Oak Woods San Antonio TX 78249-1478

MASSEY, RICHARD WALTER, JR. retired investment counselor; b. Birmingham, Ala., May 19, 1917; s. Richard Walter and Elizabeth (Spencer) M.; m. Ann Hinkle, Sept. 4, 1959; children— Richard Walter, Dale Elizabeth. BS, U. Va., 1939; MA, Birmingham-So. Coll., 1954; PhD, Vanderbilt U., 1960. Owner, mgr. Massey Bus. Coll., Birmingham, Ala., 1946—56; asst. to chancellor Vanderbilt U., 1959—60; chmn. dept. econs. Birmingham-So. Coll., 1960—66; investment trust officer 1st Nat. Bank of Birmingham, 1966—67; prof. econs. U. Ala., Tuscaloosa, 1967—68; v.p., dir. investment rsch. Sterne, Agee & Leach, Inc., Birmingham, 1968—75; pres. Richard W. Massey & Co., Inc., Investment Counsel, 1975—2001; ret., 2001. Served to maj. U.S. Army, 1941-46. Mem. Country Club of Birmingham. Home: 1304 Kingsway Ln Birmingham AL 35243-2174 E-mail: rmassey1@netzero.net.

MASSEY, ROBERT UNRUH, physician, university dean; b. Detroit, Feb. 23, 1922; s. Emil Laverne and Esther Elisabeth (Unruh) M.; m. June Charlene Collins, May 28, 1943; children: Robert Scott, Janet Charlene. Student, Oberlin Coll., 1939-42, U. Mich. Med. Sch., 1942-43; MD, Wayne State U., 1946. Intern, resident in internal medicine Henry Ford Hosp., Detroit, 1946-50; assoc. Lovelace Clinic, Albuquerque, 1950-68, chmn. dept. medicine, 1958-68, bd. govs., 1957-68; dir. med. edn. Lovelace Found. for Med. Edn. and Research, 1960-68; clin. assoc. U. N.Mex. Sch. Medicine, 1961-68; prof. medicine U. Conn. Sch. Medicine, Farmington, 1968-92, prof. emeritus, 1992—, assoc. dean for grad edn., 1968-71, dean Sch. Medicine, 1971-84, currently prof. emeritus dept. community medicine and health care, acting univ. v.p. for health affairs, 1975-76. Chief staff Newington (Conn.) VA Hosp., 1968-71; trustee Am. Assn. Med. Clinics, 1966-68; exec. com., regional adv. group Conn. Regional Med. Program, 1971-76; trustee, v.p. Capitol Area Health Consortium, 1974-78, pres., 1980-81. Editor-in-chief Conn. Medicine, 1986-99; editor Jour. of the History of Medicine and Allied Scis., 1987-91. Bd. dirs. Health Planning Coun., Inc., 1974-76; bd. dirs. Hartford Inst. for Criminal and Social Justice, 1976-80, Conn. Easter Seal Soc., 1977-85, Hospice Inst. Edn., Tng. and Rsch., 1979-81. With AUS, 1955-57; maj. Res. Fellow ACP; mem. Am. Group Practice Assn. (accreditation commn. 1968-78), Assn. Am. Med. Colls., Am. Assn. History of Medicine, Hartford County Med. Assn., AMA, Conn., Hartford med. socs., Am. Osler Soc., Beaumont Med. Club, Soc. Med. Adminstrs., Twilight Club (Hartford), Acorn Club, Sigma Xi, Alpha Omega Alpha. Roman Catholic.

MASSEY, STEPHEN CHARLES, rare books and manuscripts appraiser, auctioneer; b. London, May 9, 1946; s. Charles Dudley and Sheila Florence (Browne) M.; divorced; 1 child, Sarah Louise. Grad. high sch., U.K. Cataloguer books and manuscripts Christie's, London, 1964-75, sr. dir. rare books and manuscripts dept. N.Y.C., 1975-96, sr. internat. cons., 1997-99. Fellow Pierpont Morgan Libr.; mem. The Grolier Club, The Old Book Table. Avocations: cinema, reading, running, music, forestry.

MASSEY, THOMAS BENJAMIN, educator; b. Charlotte, N.C., Sept. 5, 1926; s. William Everard and Sarah (Corley) M.; m. Bylee Hunnicutt Massey, July 10, 1968; children: Pamela Ann, Caroline Forest. AB, Duke U., 1948; MS, N.C. State U., 1953; PhD, Cambridge U., 1968. Assoc. dean students Ga. Inst. Tech., Atlanta, 1950-58; lectr. U. Md. Univ. Coll., 1960-66, asst. dir. London, 1966-69, dir. Toyko, 1969-71, dir. Heidelberg (Fed. Republic of Germany), 1971-76, vice chancellor, 1976-78, chancellor, 1978-88, pres., 1988-98, pres. emeritus, 1998—. Served with USN, 1943-46. Mem. APA, Univ. Continuing Edn. Assn., Am. Assn. Higher Edn., Interernat. Confs. on Improving Learning and Tchg. at the Univ. (chair 1975—). E-mail: benmo905@aol.com.

MASSEY, WALTER EUGENE, physicist, science foundation administrator; b. Hattiesburg, Miss., Apr. 5, 1938; s. Almor and Essie (Nelson) M.; m. Shirley Streeter, Oct. 25, 1969; children: Keith Anthony, Eric Eugene. BS, Morehouse Coll., 1958; MA, PhD, Washington U., St. Louis, 1966. Physicist Argonne (Ill.) Nat. Lab., 1966-68; asst. prof. physics U. Ill., Urbana, 1968-70; assoc. prof. Brown U., Providence, 1970-75, prof., dean of Coll., 1975-79; prof. physics U. Chgo., 1979-93; dir. Argonne Nat. Lab., 1979-84; v.p. for rsch. and for Argonne Nat. Lab. U. Chgo., 1984-91; dir. NSF, Washington, 1991-93; sr. v.p. acad. affairs U. Calif. System, 1993-95; pres. Morehouse Coll., Atlanta, 1995—. Cons. NAS, 1973-76; mem. NSB, 1978-84; chair Sec. Energy Adv. Bd., 1997-99; bd. dirs. Mellon Found, Bank Am. Corp., McDonald's Corp., BP Amoco, Gates Millennium Scholars Adv. Coun., Marine Biol. Lab. Coun. Visitors. Contbr. articles on sci. edn. in secondary schs. and in theory of quantum fluids to profl. jours. Bd. fellows Brown U., 1980-90, Mus. Sci. and Industry, Chgo., 1980-89, Ill. Math. and Sci. Acad., 1985-88; bd. dirs. Urban League R.I., 1973-75; mem. Salzburg seminar, 1997—, Atlanta Symphony Orch., 1996—, Woodruf Art Ctr., 1995—, Atlanta Com. Pub. Edn., 1996—, Bd. Project GRAD; chair Atlanta Com. for Pub. Edn., 1996—. Recipient over 25 hon. degrees; NAS fellow, 1961, NDEA fellow, 1959-60, AAAS fellow, 1962. Mem. AAAS (bd. dirs. 1981-85, pres.-elect 1987-88, pres. 1988-89, chmn. 1989-90), Am. Phys. Soc. (councillor-at-large 1980-83, v.p. 1990), Energy Adv. Bd. (chair 1997-99), Mellon Found., Amoco Corp., Motorola, Inc. , Bank of Am. Corp., McDonald's Corp., BP Amoco, Gates Millenium Scholars Adv. Coun., Marine Biol. Lab. Coun. Visitors, Smithsonian Inst. Bd. Regents, Sigma Xi. Office: Morehouse Coll 830 Westview Dr SW Atlanta GA 30314-3773

MASSEY, WILLIAM S. mathematician, educator; b. Granville, Ill., Aug. 23, 1920; s. Robert R. and Alma (Schumacher) M.; m. Ethel Heap, Mar. 14, 1953; children— Eleanor, Alexander, Joan. Student, Bradley U., 1937-39; BS, U. Chgo., 1941, MS, 1942; PhD, Princeton, 1948. Mem. research dept. Princeton, 1948-50; from asst. prof. to prof. Brown U., 1950-60; prof. math. Yale, 1960—, Erastus L. Deforest prof. math., 1964-82, Eugene Higgins prof. math., 1983-91, Eugene Higgins prof. math. emeritus, 1991—, chmn. dept. math., 1968-71. Author: Algebraic Topology: An Introduction, 1967, Homology and Cohomology Theory, 1978, Singular Homology Theory, 1980, A Basic Course in Algebraic Topology, 1991; mem. editorial staff math. jours. Served as officer USNR, 1942-46. Fellow Am. Acad. Arts and Scis.; mem. Am. Math. Soc. Achievements include research in algebraic topology, differential topology, homotopy theory, fibre bundles. Home: 200 Leeder Hill Drive Hamden CT 06517-2729 Office: Yale U Math Dept PO Box 208283 New Haven CT 06520-8283

MASSEY, WILLIAM WALTER, JR. sales executive; b. Lawrenceburg, Tenn., Sept. 21, 1928; s. William Walter and Bess Ann (Brian) M.; m. Virginia Claire Smith, Aug. 16, 1952; children: William Walter III, Laura Ann, Lynn Smith, Lisa Claire. BBA, U. Miami, Fla., 1949; BFA, U. Fla., 1969. Exec. v.p., dir. Massey Motors, Inc., Jacksonville, Fla., 1950—; v.p., dir. Atlantic Discount Co. Inc., 1954-64; pres. Owners Surety Corp., 1959—, General Svcs.

Corp., Jacksonville, 1960-69, Owners Guaranty Life, Phoenix, 1960-64, Securities Guaranty Life, Phoenix, 1961-64, Fla. Properties, Inc., Jacksonville, 1961-66, Chi-Cha, Inc., Jacksonville, 1965-70, Univ. Square Properties, Jacksonville, 1969-80. V.p., bd. dir. Southside Country Day School, Jacksonville, 1963-68; bd. dirs. Southside Atlantic Bank, Jacksonville, 1965-93. Exhibited in group shows at Internat., N.Y., 1970, Ball State U., 1972. Lt. USAF, 1950-1952. Mem. Ponte Vedra Club, River Club, Epping Forest Club, Deerwood Club, Sigma Chi. Methodist. Avocations: music, painting, writing. Fax: (904) 642-8815. E-mail: billmasseyii@prodigy.net.

MASSEY, W(ILMET) ANNETTE, retired nurse, former educator; b. Big Chimney, W.Va., June 30, 1920; d. Robert Lee and Twila Augusta (Pringle) M. Student, Morris Harvey Coll., 1938-39; diploma, Phila. Gen. Hosp. Sch. Nursing, 1943; BS in Edn., U. Pa., 1948; MSN, Yale U., 1959. Nurse cadet instr. U.S. Cadet Nurse Corps. Huntington (W.Va.) Meml. Hosp., 1943-45; nurse instr. St. Mary's Sch. Nursing, Huntington, 1948-51; WHO nurse cons. Govt. Ceylon, 1951-55; staff nurse instr. VA Hosp., Ft. Thomas, Ky., 1955-57; asst. prof. nursing Brighan Young U., Provo, Utah, 1959-61; assoc. prof. nursing W.Va. U., Morgantown, 1961-83, chmn. dept. psychiat. nursing, 1968-72, ret., 1983. Cons. Applachian Regional Hosp., Beckley, W.Va. Dept. Mental Health, Charleston, Valley Cmty. Mental Ctr., Kingwood, W.Va.; group leader med.-nursing group to India, Expt. Internat. Living, Brattleboro, Vt., 1965. Mem. Appalachian Trail, Morgantown Hospice, Rep. Nat. Com., Drummond Chapel United Meth. Ch., United Meth. Women, health adv. com. Coun. Mins., ARC, Nat. Coun. Sr. Citizens, Monongalians Srs., Rails to Trail, W.Va. Highlands Conservancy, W.Va. Citizens Action, Cooper's Rock Found. NIMH grantee, 1964-75. Mem. ANA, League Nursing, Am. Orthopsychiat. Assn., Internat. Transactional Analysis Assn., Am. Counseling Assn. (dir. 1981-82, v.p. 1982), Am. Soc. Profl. and Exec. Women, Environ. Def. Fund, Nat. Parks and Conservation Assn., Nat. Trust for Hist. Preservation, Tarrytown Group, Nat. Registry Psychiat. Nurse Specialists (edn. and resources com.), Internat. Acad. Cancer Counselors and Cons., Nat. Alliance Family Life, Inc. (founding), AAUP, Nat. Hist. Soc., Hastings Ctr., Nat. Wildlife Fedn., Smithsonian Assocs., Phila. Gen. Hosp. Sch. Nursing Alumni, U. Pa., Yale U., W.Va. U. Sch. Nursing (hon.) Alumni Assns., 20/20 Vision Winterthur Guild, Empower Am., Pub. Citizen, Friends of the Earth, W.Va. Pub. Theatre, Am. Rivers, Project Vote Smart, W.Va. Rivers Coalition, World Learning, Wash. Nat. Cathedral, So. Property Law Ctr., Am. Red Cross, Am. Farmland Trust, Sierra Club, Lakeview Resort Club, Appalachian Trail, Sigma Theta Tau. Clubs: Alpine Lake Recreation Cmty. (Terra Alta, W.Va.), Penn (N.Y.C.). Home: # 1 2202 Heritage Pointe Morgantown WV 26505-3065

MASSEY-HOLDEN, SANDRA S(UE), retired insurance executive; b. Hannibal, Mo., Mar. 22, 1938; d. John Thomas and Mary Louise (Rouse) Massey; m. Robert Henry Dumit, 1958 (div. Sept. 1963); m. Sidney K. Holden, Apr. 16, 1966 (div. Mar. 1999); 1 child, Michael Andrew. Student, U. Mo., 1956-58; BS in Mgmt., Ariz. State U., 1963; cert. teaching, U. Mo., 1969, postgrad., 1980. Sec. Ariz. Title & Trust Co., Phoenix, 1958-60; data entry clk. Ariz. Pub. Svc., 1960-63; rsch. staff agrl.-econs. dept. U. Mo., Columbia, 1963-64; adminstrv. asst. electronics dept. Monsanto Co., St. Louis, 1964-69; substitute tchr. Pinellas County Schs., Clearwater, Fla., 1975-79; tchr., coop. edn. coord. Boone County R4 Schs., Hallsville, Mo., 1979-81; asst. credit mgr. Philips & Co. (Wholesale Electric and Plumbing), Columbia, 1981-82; asst. v.p. Boone County Abstract Co., 1982-88; pres. Guaranty Land Title Ins. of Columbia, 1988-97; ret., 1997. Mem. Muleskinners Local Dems., Columbia; trustee Daniel Boone Regional Libr. Bd., Columbia, 1987-89; mem. mgmt. adv. com. City of Columbia, 1991, commn. on arts, 1991; bd. dirs. Am. Cancer Soc., 1991. Personnel Mgmt. Soc. scholar, 1962. Mem. Am. Land Title Assn., Columbia Bd. Realtors (affiliate com. 1993), Women's Coun. Realtors (mem. governing bd. Columbia chpt. 1987-91), Mo. Land Title Assn. (chairperson com. Mexico, Mo. chpt. 1986-88), Women's Network of Columbia C. of C. (Leadership Columbia grad. 1991), Bus. Women Owners (women's network), Mo. State C. of C. (grad. Leadership Mo. 1992, steering com. 1993, edn. com. 1997—). Avocations: genealogy, reading, spectator sports. Office: Guaranty Land Title Ins 4558 Hwy 51 Ste 104 Osage Beach MO 65065 E-mail: susiemh321@aol.com.

MASSICK, JAMES WILLIAM, heavy equipment manufacturing company executive; b. Jan. 19, 1932; s. Peter James and Annetta Jean (Dormaier) M.; m. Joyce Allair Puckey, Apr. 7, 1973; children: Scott, Christopher (dec.), Kit, Timothy, Nina, Sally, John, Jill. BS, U. Wash., 1954; MBA, UCLA, 1966. Constrn. engr. Kaiser Engrs., Oakland, Calif., 1957-60; project mgr. Ralph M. Parsons Co., L.A., 1960-65; engring. mgr. Weyerhauser Co., Tacoma, 1965-68; ops. mgr. Western Gear Corp., Everett, Wash., 1968-70; pres. Truckweld Corp. and subs., Seattle, 1970—. Dir. Truckweld Corp., Truckweld Utilities, Inc., Puget Sound Lease Co., Pacific N.W. Utility & Supply Co.; dir. emeritus Pacific Air Lines, Air West, Hughes Air West, The Budd Corp., Borg Warner Acceptance Corp. Patentee in field. Assoc. chmn. UN Concert and Dinner, Washington, 1975-92; active Nat. UN Day Com., N.Y.C., 1977-95. Rear adm. USNR, 1950, 54-57. Decorated Navy Cross, Silver Star, Legion of Merit, Purple Heart. Mem. ASCE, Soc. Am. Mil. Engrs., Seattle C. of C., Mcpl. League, Chosen Few, Overlake Golf and Country Club, The Harbor Club, The Lakes Club, Theta Delta Chi. Episcopalian. Home: 2131 NW Pacific Yew Pl Issaquah WA 98027-8642

MASSIE, ANNE ADAMS ROBERTSON, artist; b. Lynchburg, Va., May 30, 1931; d. Douglas Alexander and Annie Scott (Harris) Robertson; m. William McKinnon Massie, Apr. 30, 1960; children: Anne Harris, William McKinnon, Jr. Grad., St. Mary's Coll., Raleigh, N.C., 1950; BA in English, Randolph Macon Woman's Coll., 1952. Tchr. English E.C. Glass High Sch., Lynchburg, 1955-60. Juror Am. Watercolor Soc. Ann. Exhbn., 1998, Ctrl. Va. Watercolor Guild, 1996. Represented in permanent collections at Hotel de Ville, Rueil-Malmaison, France, L'Association des Amis de la Grande Vigne, Dinan, France, Randolph Macon Woman's Coll., Lynchburg Coll., Va. Episcopal Sch., Va. Sch. of Arts, Va. State Bar Assn., Richmond, St. John's Episcopal Ch. Bd. dirs. Lynchburg Hist. Found., 1968-81, 91-95, pres., 1978-81; bd. dirs. Lynchburg Fine Arts Ctr., 1992-98; bd. dirs. Point of Honor Mus., 1988-99, chmn. collections com., 1989-99; bd. dirs. Amazement Sq. Children's Mus., 1996—; trustee Va. Episcopal Sch., Lynchburg, 1983-89, Va. Ctr. for Creative Arts, 1999—; pres. Friends of Rivermont, 2000-02. Fellow Artists' Fellowship; mem. Am. Watercolor Soc. (signature, Dolphin fellow 1993, Gold medal of Honor 1993), Nat. Watercolor Soc. (signature, Artist's Mag. award), Nat. League Am. Pen Women (pres. 1987, Best in Show 1994), Knickerbocker Artists (signature, Silver medal Watercolor 1993), Watercolor USA Honor Soc., Watercolor West (signature), Catharine Lorrilard Wolfe Art Club (signature), Allied Artists Am., Inc. (signature), Southern Watercolor Soc. (signature), Va. Watercolor Soc. (artist mem., Best in Show 1992, 97, chmn. exhbns. 1986, pres. 1995-96), Nat. Arts Club (exhibiting artist mem.), Artists' Fellowship, Colonial Dames Am. (chmn. 1987-90), Hillside Garden Club (pres. 1974-76), Jr. League (editor 1953-72), Lynchburg Art Club (bd. dirs. 1995-96, chmn. 1981-4), Antiquarian Club. Episcopalian. Avocations: book club, gardening, tennis. Home: 3204 Rivermont Ave Lynchburg VA 24503-2028

MASSIE, BARRY MICHAEL, cardiologist; b. St. Louis, May 23, 1944; s. Edward and Felice (Ozerovich) M.; m. Ellen Sue Weisberg, May 29, 1970; children: Jennifer Nicole, Rebecca Elizabeth. BA, Harvard Coll., 1966; MD, Columbia U., 1970. Resident Bellevue Hosp., N.Y.C., 1970-74; fellow in cardiology U. Calif. and Cardiovascular Rsch. inst., San Francisco, 1975-78; asst. prof. medicine U. Calif., 1978-83, assoc. prof., 1983-89, prof., 1989—; dir. coronary care unit, chief hypertension unit VA Med. Ctr., 1978—, chief cardiology divsn., 1999—; mem. staff Cardiovascular Rsch. Inst., 1981—. Mem. and chmn. adv. panel FDA, Rockville, Md., 1992-97. Editor-in-chief: Journal of Cardiac Failure, 2001—. Fellow Am. Coll. Cardiology, Am. Heart Assn. (coun. clin. cardiology, coun. blood pressure rsch.); mem. Am. Soc. Hypertension (cert. hypertension specialist), Am. Fedn. Clin. Investigation, Heart Failure Soc. N.Am. (founding mem., chair program com. 2000—), Western Soc. Clin. Rsch., Western Assn. Physicians. Avocations: travel, hiking, camping. Office: VA Hosp Cadiology 111C 4150 Clement St San Francisco CA 94121-1545

MASSIE, MAUREEN TERESA, elementary school educator; b. St. Louis, Apr. 13, 1953; d. James H. and Teresa B. Moran; m. Jim Massie, Feb. 3, 1973; 1 child, Kate. BA in Child Study, Webster Coll., 1977, MAT, 1990. Cert. tchr. K-8, Mo. 1st grade tchr. No. St. Francis County Sch. Dist., Bonne Terre, Mo., 1977-87; 4th grade tchr. Lindbergh Sch. Dist., St. Louis, 1987-89; instr. tchg. methods Ctrl. Meth. Coll. at Mineral Area Coll., Park Hills, Mo., 1991-2001, Farmington (Mo.) Sch. Dist., 1989—, Mineral Area Coll., 2001—; tchr. kindergarten, 1st, 2d, 3d, 5th grades Farmington Sch. Dist., 1998-2001, tchr. gifted edn., 2001—. Asst. youth group leader Teenage Ministry, 1993-2000; resource com. co-chair Habitat for Humanity of St. Francois County, Farmington, Mo., 1997—; bd. dirs. Farmington Soccer Adv. Bd., 1991-93; vol. tchr. Project Head Start, Farmington, 1975-76. Project Aiding Children's Edn. State Incentive grant State of Mo., 1991, Truman Learning Ctrs. Group State Incentive grant, 1994, Learn and Svc. State grant, 1998-2000, How and Why of Sci. grant, 2000, Read to be Ready grant, 2000. Mem. Mo. Nat. Edn. Assn. Home: 770 Market St # 116 Farmington MO 63640-1951 Office: Washington Franklin Elem Sch 104 Murphy St Farmington MO 63640-1370

MASSIE, ROBERT JOSEPH, publishing company executive; b. N.Y.C., Mar. 19, 1949; BA, Yale U., 1970; MBA, JD, Columbia U., 1974; diploma, U. d'Aix en Provence, France, 1969. Bar: D.C. 1974. Assoc. Covington & Burling, Washington, 1975-79; mgmt. cons. McKinsey & Co., N.Y.C., 1979-82; v.p. Harlequin Enterprises, Toronto, Ont., Can., 1982-90; pres., CEO Gale Rsch., Inc., Detroit, 1990-92; dir. Chem. Abstracts Svc., Columbus, Ohio, 1992—. Chmn. bd. dirs. Harlequin Mondadori, Milan, Italy, 1985-88; bd. dirs. Harlequin Hachette, Paris, Cora Verlag, Hamburg, Fed. Republic Germany, Mills & Boon, Sydney, Australia. Contbr. articles to law jours. Bd. dirs. Mindleaders.com. Harlan Fiske Stone scholar, 1974. Office: Am Chem Soc Chem Abstracts Svcs PO Box 3012 Columbus OH 43210-0012

MASSIER, PAUL FERDINAND, mechanical engineer; b. Pocatello, Idaho, July 22, 1923; s. John and Kathryn (Arki) M.; m. Miriam Parks, May 1, 1948 (dec. Aug. 1975); children: Marilyn Massier Schwegler, Paulette Massier Holden; m. Dorothy Hedlund Wright, Sept. 12, 1978. *Grandfather Ferdinand Massier pioneered the Baptist missionary movement in Bukovina and Galicia (Austria) during the late 1800's and early 1900's. Father John Massier, a furniture maker, immigrated to the U.S. from Bukovina in 1903 and in 1951 was elected "Deacon for Life" by the First Baptist Church in Pocatello, Idaho. Mother Katie Arki immigrated from Croatia-Slavonia in 1906 and was an excellent cook and gardener. Daughter Marilyn, a flutist, was awarded "Musician of the Year" at Arcadia, California High School, where daughter Paulette, a violinist, was Concert Mistress of the orchestra. Both toured Europe with the American Youth Symphony Orchestra.* Cert. engring., U. Idaho (so. br.), 1943; BSME, U. Colo., 1948; MSME, MIT, 1949. Engr. Pan-Am. Refining Corp., Texas City, Tex., 1948; design engr. Maytag Co., Newton, Iowa, 1949-50; research engr. Boeing Co., Seattle, 1951-55; sr. research engr., supr. and dep. sect. mgr. Jet Propulsion Lab. Calif. Inst. Tech., Pasadena, 1955-84, task mgr., 1984-88, mem. tech. staff, 1989-94. *More than 40 years of engineering research and supervision led to: concepts and analysis of "far out" rocket propulsion systems such as antimatter, laser, nuclear, and metastable states; evaluation of rocket-engine fuel and oxidizer cooling capabilities including the upper limit of nucleate boiling for numerous liquid propellants such as hydrazine, nitrogen tetroxide, oxygen, alcohol, and many others; experimental determination of fluid mechanics and heat transfer phenomena for high-temperature compressible swirling flows in axisymmetric ducts and convergent-divergent nozzles; identification and evaluation of explanted heart valve prostheses; development of gas turbines for use as engines in trucks and boats and as air compressors.* Contbr. articles to profl. jours. Moderator Arcadia Congl. Ch., 1996-98; mem. Arcadia High Sch. Music Club, 1966-71. With U.S. Army, 1943-46. Recipient Apollo Achievement award NASA, 1969, Basic Noise Rsch. award NASA, 1980, Life Mem. Svc. award Calif. PTA, 1970, Layman of Yr. award Arcadia Congl. Ch., 1971, Mil. Unit Citation award, 1946. Fellow AIAA (assoc., Sustained Svc. award 1980-81); mem. N.Y. Acad. Scis., Planetary Soc., Order of the Engr., Sigma Xi, Tau Beta Pi, Pi Tau Sigma, Sigma Tau. Congregationalist. Achievements include 50% reduction of cooling requirements for rocket engines, experimental evaluation of heat transfer from thermally ionized gases at temperatures up to 13,000 degrees; experimental determination of starting characteristics, shock-wave structures, heat transfer and pressure distributions in supersonic diffusers led to the development of criteria for their design and their use as a means of simulating altitude conditions at ground level for static testing of rocket engines; experimental/analytical determination of the relationships of large-scale turbulent structures, density and temperature fluctuations, inverted velocity profiles, internally generated pure tones, twin jet shielding, and aircraft flight on noise emitted from aircraft supersonic jets; understanding of the formation of cenospheres during the combustion of heavy oils by analysis of electron microscope photo images of droplets and stages of formed globules and cenospheres gathered on slides during combustion experiments. Avocations: travelog and documentary film production and presentations, genealogy and family history research, antiques, collecting sheet music. Home: 764 Lava Falls Dr Las Vegas NV 89110

MASSIMO, MICHAEL J. astronaut; b. Oceanside, N.Y., Aug. 19, 1962; married. BS in Indsl. Engring., Columbia U., N.Y.C., 1984; MS in Tech. and Policy, MIT, Cambridge, Mass., 1988; MS in Mech. Engring., MIT, 1990, PhD in Mech. Engring., 1992. Systems engr. IBM, N.Y.C., 1984—86; fellow MIT Mech. Engring. Dept. Human Machine Systems Lab., 1986—92; rsch. engr. McDonell Douglas Aerospace, Houston, 1992—95; asst. prof. Ga. Inst. Tech. Sch. Indsl. and Systeme Engring., 1995—96; astronaut NASA Johnson Space Ctr., Houston, 1996—. Vis. rschr. .(summer) NASA Office of Aero. and Space Tech., 1988, 89; vis. rsch. engr. German Aerospace Rsch. Establishment, Oberpfaffenhofen, Germany, 1990; adj. asst. prof. Rice U. Mech. Engring. and Materials Sci Dept., Houston, 1992—95. Recipient Best Paper award, 5th IFAC Symposium on Man-Machine Systems, Gold medal (student paper contest), 41st Congress Internat. Astro. Fedn. ; fellow MIT Zakhartechenko fellowship. Mem.: Coumbia U. Alumni Assn., MIT Alumni Assn. Avocations: basketball, camping, running, weightlifting. Office: Astronaut Office Johnson Space Ctr Houston TX 77058

MASSIN, EDWARD KRAUSS, physician; b. Houston, 1939; MD, Washington U., St. Louis, 1965; BA, Rice U., 1961. Intern Barnes Hosp., St. Louis, 1965-66; resident Banres Hosp., 1966-67; with St. Lukes Episcopal. Hosp., Houston. Clin. prof. Baylor Coll. Medicine; clin. prof. cardiology & medicine U. Tex., Houston. Cardiology fellow U. Colo. Med. Ctr., 1969-71. Fellow Am. Coll. Cardiology, Am. Coll. Physicians. Office: Cardiology Cons Houston 6624 Fannin St Ste 2310 Houston TX 77030-2335

MASSING, VIRGINIA REEVES, surgical nurse and administrator; b. Thomaston, Ga., Jan. 15, 1934; d. Joel Farley and Virginia Broughton (Hardy) Reeves; m. Ralph Richard Massing, Oct. 25, 1957 (dec. Mar. 1987); children: Thomas Hardy, Tony Douglas. Diploma in Nursing, Piedmond Sch. Nursing, Atlanta, 1955. CRNA, RN, Ga. Cert. RN anesthetist AA's of Rome, Ga., 1970-72, 76-85; dir. surgery Redmond Regional Med. Ctr., Rome, 1972-76, 85-96. Mem. Assn. of Operating Rm. Nurses, Am. Assn. Nurse Adminstrs., Am. Assn. Nurse Anesthetists. Republican. Methodist. Home: 17 Windrush Dr NW Rome GA 30165-4501

MASSIS, BRUCE EDWARD, library director, media executive, consultant; b. N.Y.C., Jan. 2, 1948; s. Louis and Paula (Cooper) M.; children: Eric John, Heather Lyn. BA in English, CUNY, 1973; MLS, Queens Coll., 1974; MA in English, Adelphi U., 1992. Dir. libr. svcs. JGB Cassette Libr., N.Y.C., 1974—; v.p. In Touch Networks, Inc., 1991—. Adj. libr. faculty, Adelphi U., 1995—; cons. various librs., internationally, 1979—. Author: Voice Painting, 1993; editor: Libraries for the Blind: An International Approach, 1982, International Guide to Large Print, 1985, Interlibrary Loan of Alternative Format Materials, 1993, Serving Print Impaired Library Patrons, 1996. Pres., bd. trustees Deer Park (N.Y.) Pub. Libr., 1991—. 3rd class petty officer USN, 1968-72. Mem. ALA (internat. rels. com. 1986—), Internat. Fedn. Librs. Assns. (sect. pres. 1979-81), Dramatists Guild (assoc.), Authors League (assoc.), Acad. Am. Poets (assoc.). Avocations: writing, music, painting, travel, reading. Office: Jewish Guild for the Blind c/o In Touch Networks Inc 15 W 65th St New York NY 10023-6601

MASSLER, HOWARD ARNOLD, lawyer, corporate executive; b. Newark, July 22, 1946; s. Abraham I. and Sylvia (Botwin) M.; children: Justin Scott, Jeremy Ross. BA, U. Pa., 1969; JD, Rutgers U., 1973; LLM in Taxation, NYU, 1977. Bar: N.J. 1974, U.S. Dist. Ct. N.J. 1974, D.C. 1975, U.S. Ct. Appeals (D.C. cir.) 1975, N.Y. 1977, U.S. Dist. Ct. (we. dist.) N.Y. 1977, U.S. Tax Ct. 1977. Counsel house banking, currency and housing com., chmn. sub-com. U.S. Ho. Reps., Washington, 1974-76; tax atty. Lipsitz, Green, Fahringer, Roll, Schuller & James, N.Y.C. and Buffalo, 1977-79; pvt. practice Mountainside, N.J., 1979-89; pres. Bestway Products Inc., A.A. Records Inc., Servor Corp., 1979-85; pres., chief exec. officer, chmn. bd. Bestway Group Inc., Dover, Del., 1985-91; gen. ptnr. 26/27 Law Drive Assocs., 1988—; ptnr. Shonageri, Pearce & Massler, Hackensack, N.J., 1989-90, Mott, Pearce, Williams & Lee, Hackensack and Washington, 1990-91, Pearce & Massler, Hackensack, N.J., 1991-97. Prodn. staff asst. DECCA House Ltd., London, 1968; chief exec. officer Basura Pub., Inc. (affiliated with BMI), 1974-80; arbitrator U.S. Dist. Ct. N.J., 1985—; adj. prof. law Seton Hall U., Newark, N.J., 1988-89, N.J. Inst. for Continuing Legal Edn., 1986; lectr. N.J. Inst. for Continuing Legal Edn., 1986—; assoc. dir. United Jersey Bank/Franklin State Bank, 1987—; del. adv. com. on indsl. trade and econ. devel. U.S./China Joint Sessions, Beijing, People's Republic of China, 1988. Author: QDROs (Tax and Drafting Considerations), 1986, 2nd. ed., 1987; contbr. West's Legal Forms, Vol. 7., 2d edit., 1987, 3d edit., Domestic Relations with Tax Analysis, Contemporary Matrimonial Law Issues: A Guide to Divorce Economics and Practice; tax author: Matthew Bender, NYCP-Matrimonial Actions and Equitable Distribution Actions, 1988; tax author, tax editor: Matthew Bender, Alimony, Child Support & Counsel Fees-Award, Modification and Enforcement, 1988, 2d edit., 1989, 3d edit., 1991, Matthew Bender, Valuation & Distribution of Marital Property, 1988, 89, 91, 92, 94, 95; contbg. author: How to Make Legal Fees Tax Deductible, 1988, Closely Held Corporations, Forms and Checklists, Buy-Sell Agreement Forms with Tax Analysis, 1988, The Encyclopedia of Matrimonial Practice, 1991, 4th edit., 1995; author: New York Practice Guide: Negligence, Tax Law of Compensation for Sickness and Injury, 2d edit., 1992; contbg. editor Pensions and Ins. Problems, 1984—, Taxation, 1984—, Fair$hare, 1984—, Law & Bus., Inc., 1984—; staff contbr., N.J. Law Jour., 1986—; contbr. articles to law revs. and profl. jours. Bd. dirs., legal counsel western N.Y. chpt. Nat. Handicapped Sports and Recreation Assn., 1977-79; counsel Union County, N.J., 1984-85; candidate Springfield (N.J.) Twp. Commn., 1986. Mem. ABA, N.J. Bar Assn. (vice chmn. taxation comm. family law section 1987—), N.Y. Bar Assn. (taxation com., subcom. on criminal and civil penalties), D.C. Bar Assn., Erie County Bar Assn. (sec. taxation com. 1977-79, continuing edn. lectr. taxation 1977—), Essex County Bar Assn. (tax com. 1981—), Union County Bar Assn. (chmn. tax com. 1984—) Republican. Avocation: Sports Car Club Am. formula Ford racing. Home: 508 Main St PO Box 399 Boonton NJ 07005-0399 Office: 508 Main St Boonton NJ 07005-1716

MASSMAN, RICHARD ALLAN, lawyer; b. Beaumont, Tex., Aug. 19, 1943; s. Irwin Massman and Sylvia (Schmidt) Schwartz; m. Barbara Elaine Kessler; children: Jason Todd, Karen Faye. BS cum laude, U. Pa., 1965; JD cum laude, Harvard U., 1968. Bar: Tex. 1968; cert. in taxation, Tex. Bd. Legal Specialization. Assoc. Coke & Coke, Dallas, 1968-70, Johnson & Wortley, P.C. (formerly Johnson & Gibbs, P.C.), Dallas, 1970-71, ptnr., 1971-88, shareholder, 1988-94; of counsel Johnson & Wortley P.C., 1994-95; sr. v.p., gen. counsel Hunt Consolidated, Inc., 1994—. Lectr. So. Meth. U., Dallas, 1973. Bd. dirs. Martin Luther King Jr. Community Ctr., Dallas, 1979-81, Jewish Fedn. Greater Dallas, 1980-83, 89—, The Dallas Opera, 1999—; mem. exec. com. Dallas regional bd. Anti-Defamation League, 1979—, chmn., 1990-92; chmn. Dallas Civil Svc. Bd., 1983; trustee Greenhill Sch., Dallas, 1985-92, vice chmn., 1990-92. Recipient Jurisprudence award Anti-Defamation League, 2000. Mem. Tex. State Bar (chmn., sec. taxation 1983-84), Dallas Bar Assn. (chmn., sec. taxation 1978), Dallas Petroleum Club, Columbian Club. Office: Hunt Consolidated Inc Fountain Pl 20th Fl 1445 Ross at Field Dallas TX 75202-2785

MASSOF, ROBERT WILLIAM, neuroscientist, educator; b. Minn., Jan. 2, 1948; m. Pat Massof; children: Eric, Allison. BA, Hamline U., 1970; PhD, Ind. U., 1975. Postdoctoral fellow in ophthalmology Johns Hopkins U. Sch. Medicine, Balt., 1975-76, instr. ophthalmology, 1976-78, from asst. prof. to assoc. prof., 1978-91, prof. ophthalmology, 1991—, prof. neurosci., 1994—, prof. computer sci., 1994—, mem. staff applied physics lab., 2000—. Lectr. in field. Mem. editl. bd. Clin. Vision Scis., N.Y.C., 1986-94, Eye Care Technology/Computers in Eye Care, Folsom, Calif., 1992-96; patentee in field (5); contbr. articles to profl. jours. Recipient Manpower award, 1989, Tech. Transfer award NASA, 1993, Popular Mechanics Design and Engring. award, 1994, EyeCare Tech. Lifetime Achievement award, 1995, Richard E. Hoover Svc. award, 1995, Humanitarian award Lions, 2000, Disting. Svc. in Vision award Am. Pub. Health Assn., William Feinbloom award Am. Acad. of Optometry, 2000. Fellow Optical Soc. Am. (chmn. edn. coun. 1993-95, bd. dirs. 1993-95), Am. Acad. Optometry; mem. Assn. for Edn. and Rehab. of the Visually Impaired, Soc. for Info. Display, Am. Congress Rehab. Medicine, Assn. Rsch. in Vision and Ophthalmology. Office: Johns Hopkins Univ Lions Vision Ctr 550 N Broadway Fl 6 Baltimore MD 21205-2007

MASSON, GERALD M. computer science educator; BSEE, Ill. Inst. Tech.; MSEE, PhD, Northwestern U. Staff AT&T; faculty U. Pitts., Carnegie-Mellon U.; prof. computer sci. Johns Hopkins U., Balt., 1986—, dir. Info. Security Inst., 2001—. Tech. advisor Compunetix, Inc., Monroeville, Pa. Contbr. over 100 articles to scientific publs. Fellow IEEE. Office: Johns Hopkins U Info Security Inst Wyman Pk Bldg 406 3400 N Charles St Baltimore MD 21218-2608

MASSON, KNUTE ANDREW, artist; b. Wilkes Barre, Pa., Apr. 14, 1946; s. Newton Lenard Masson and June Ann Davies; m. Patricia Ann Masson, Jan. 21, 1973 (div. June 20, 1981); 1 child Dylan Curtis. AA, Am. River Coll., 1974; BS, Calif. State U., Sacramento, 1976. Clin. dir. New Morning, Inc., Placerville, Calif., 1972—74; asst. quality assurance engr. Bechtel, L.A., 1976—79; sr. counselor St. George Homes, Inc., Berkeley, 1980—86, Sutter Ctr. for Psychiatry, Sacramento, 1989—95; self-employed artist Placerville, 1996—. Stress mgmt. cons. Stress Mgmt. Inc., Sacramento, 1986—88. V.p. El Dorado Arts Coun., Placerville, 1997—98; pres. Gold Country Arts Gallery, 1998. Sgt. U.S. Army, 1967—70, Vietnam. Mem.: VFW. Buddhist. Home: 3516 Suncrest Dr Placerville CA 95667-5214

MASSON, ROBERT HENRY, paper company executive; b. Boston, June 27, 1935; s. Robert Louis and Henrietta Hill (Worrell) M.; m. Virginia Lee Morton, Dec. 28, 1957; children: Linda Anne, Kenneth Morton, Robert Louis, II. BA in Econs. cum laude, Amherst Coll., 1957; MBA, Harvard U., 1964. Fin. staff Ford Motor Co., Dearborn, Mich., 1964-68, mktg. services div. controller, 1968-70; pres. Knutson Constrn. Co., Mpls., 1970-72; v.p. fin., treas. Ellerbe, Inc., Bloomington, Minn., 1972-77; fin. dir. CirTech, Inc., Mpls., 1973-77; v.p. fin. transp. div. PepsiCo., Inc., Tulsa, 1977, corp. v.p., treas. Purchase, N.Y., 1978-80; v.p., treas. Combustion Engring., Inc., Stamford, Conn., 1981-86, v.p. fin. and venture devel., 1986-87, v.p. venture fin. and internat. ops., 1988-90; v.p., CFO Parsons & Whittemore, Inc., Rye Brook, N.Y., 1990—. Mem. adv. bd. Fleet Bank, 1988—. Author: (with others) The Management of Racial Integration in Business, 1964. Pres. North Georgtown Homeowner's Assn., Birmingham, Mich., 1968-70, U.S. Presdl. Advance Man, 1972-76; trustee, chmn. fin. com. Naval Aviation Mus. Found., 1987—; trustee Hebron Acad., 1993-97; elder Presbyn. Ch. of Old Greenwich, 1992—. Served to lt. USN, 1957-62; lt. comdr. Res. Mem. Am. Forest and Paper Assn. (fin. com. 1991—), Fin. Execs. Inst. (com. on corp. fin. 1981—), Fairchester Treas. Group (pres. 1986), Lucas Point Homeowner's Assn. (pres. 1986-87), Theta Delta Chi. Clubs: Wayzata Yacht (dir.-treas. 1973-77), Riverside Yacht (asst. treas. 1985-87). Office: Parsons & Whittemore Inc 4 International Dr Ste 5 Rye Brook NY 10573-1064

MASSURA, EDWARD ANTHONY, accountant; b. Chgo., July 1, 1938; s. Edward Matthew and Wilma C. (Kussy) M.; m. Carol A. Barber, June 23, 1962; children: Edward J., Beth Ann, John B. BS, St. Joseph's Coll., Rensselaer, Ind., 1960; JD, DePaul U., 1963. Bar. Ill. 1963; CPA, Mich., Ill., others. Tax acct. Arthur Andersen LLP, Chgo., 1963-98, ptnr., 1973-98, dir. tax div. Detroit, 1974-84; dep., co-dir. internat. tax Arthur Andersen & Co., 1983-84, ptnr.-in-charge internat. trade customs practice, 1983-88. Co-author: West's Legal Forms, 2d. edit., 1984; contbr. numerous articles to bus. jours. Bd. dirs. Arts Found. of Mich., Detroit, 1982-95, treas., 1982-93; bd. dirs. Ctr. for Internat. Bus. Edn. and Rsch., Wayne State U.; bd. trustees St. Joseph's Coll., Rensselaer, Ind. Mem. AICPA, Internat. Fiscal Assn. (v.p. Eastern Gt. Lakes region), Assn. for Corp. Growth, Mich. Assn. CPAs, Mich. Dist. Export

Coun. (chmn. 1985-92), Detroit Internat. Tax Group (founder,co-moderator), Licensing Exec. Soc., World Trade Club of Detroit, Bus. Assn. Mexico and Mich, Inc., Orchard Lake Country Club, Butterfield Country Club, Lely Golf & Country Club.

MASSURA, EILEEN KATHLEEN, family therapist; b. Chgo., July 25, 1925; d. John William and Loretta (Feil) Stratemeier; m. Edmund Karamanski, July 24, 1948 (dec.); children: John, Kathleen; m. Alfred Massura, Aug. 30, 1963; children: Michael, Kathryn, Mark. BS in Nursing, DePaul U., 1963; MS in Nursing, St. Xavier Coll., 1971. RN; cert. family therapist. Dir. nurses Franklin Blvd. Hosp., Chgo., 1958-62; adminstr. Mich. Ave Hosp., 1962-64; instr. St. Xavier Coll., 1972-74, Joliet (Ill.) Jr. Coll., 1972-81; family therapist Oak Lawn (Ill.) Family Svc., 1978-88; prof. nursing Govs. State U., University Park, Ill., 1981-89; family therapist McCarthy & Assocs., Oak Lawn, 1982-93, Massura & Assocs., Oak Lawn, 1994-99, Chgo., 1999—. Preceptor to grads. St. Xavier Coll., 1980-90, Govs. State U., 1980-89; co-leader Clin. Study Med./Surg. Nursing, Moscow, 1984; presenter Am. Nursing Rev., Ala., Fla., Va., Pa., Tex., Md., 1985-86. Leader Campfire Girls, Oak Lawn, 1964—74; co-leader Orient/Am. Med./Surg. Nursing, 1987; mem. Marist Women's Bd., Chgo., 1978—82, Bro. Rice Women's Bd., Chgo., 1969—72; chmn. evangelization commn. Holy Name Cathedral, 2000—; mem. Luth. Family Svc. Bd. Day Care for Srs., 1988—89. Grantee HEW, 1969-71; named Disting. Nurse Alumnae, St. Xavier Coll., 1985; named Nursing Prof. of Yr., Govs. State U., 1983. Mem. Am. Nurses Assn. (nominating com. 1982-87), Ill. Nurses Assn. (program com. 1980-84), Am. Assn. Marital and Family Therapists, Cath. Order Foresters, Sigma Theta Tau (v.p. 1971-75). Roman Catholic. Avocations: crewel, needlepoint, watercolor, travel. Office: 30 E Huron St Apt 3502 Chicago IL 60611-4714 E-mail: EKM@lopener.net.

MASSY, WILLIAM FRANCIS, education educator, consultant; b. Milw., Mar. 26, 1934; s. Willard Francis and Ardys Dorothy (Digman) M.; m. Sally Vaughn Miller, July 21, 1984; children by previous marriage: Willard Francis, Elizabeth BS, Yale U., 1956; SM, MIT, 1958, PhD in Indsl. Econs., 1960. Asst. prof. indsl. mgmt. MIT, Cambridge, 1960-62; from asst. prof. to prof. edn. and bus. adminstrn. Stanford U., Calif., 1962-96, assoc. dean Grad. Sch. Bus., 1971, vice provost for rsch., 1971-77, v.p. for bus. and fin., 1977-88, v.p. fin., 1988-91, prof. emeritus, 1996—; prof. edn., dir. Stanford Inst. Higher Edn. Rsch., Calif., 1988-96; sr. v.p. P.R. Taylor Assocs., 1995-99; sr. rschr. Nat. Ctr. for Postsecondary Imrprovement, 1996—; pres. The Jackson Hole Higher Edn. Group, Inc., 1996—. Bd. dirs. Diebold, Inc., 1984-; mem. univ. grants com. Hong Kong, 1990—; mem. coun. Yale U., 1980-95; mgmt. cons. Stanford Mgmt. Co., 1991-93. Author: Stochastic Models of Buying Behavior, 1970, Marketing Management, 1972, Market Segmentation, 1972, Planning Models for Colleges and Universities, 1981, Endowment, 1991, Resource Allocation in Higher Education, 1996; mem. editl. bd. Jour. Mktg. Rsch., 1964-70, Harcourt, Brace Jovanovich, 1965-71; contbr. articles to profl. jours. Bd. dirs. Palo Alto-Stanford chpt. United Way, 1978-80, Stanford U. Hosp., 1980-91, MAC, Inc., 1969-84, EDUCOM, 1983-86. Ford Found. faculty rsch. fellow, 1966-67 Mem. Am. Mktg. Assn. (bd. dirs. 1971-73, v.p. edn. 1976-77), Inst. Mgmt. Scis. Office: The Jackson Hole Higher Edn Group Inc PO Box 9849 Jackson WY 83002-9849

MAST, KANDE WHITE, artist; b. St. Louis, Mar. 10, 1950; d. Elliott Maxwell and Mary (Barritt) W. Student, U. Mo., 1968-70, Longview C.C., Kansas City, Mo., 1970-71. Portrait painter, free-lance artist, Albany, N.Y., 1973-74, Kansas City, 1974—; dir., tchr. Studio Kande, Sch. Fine Arts, 1983-86; founder, exec. dir. Art Ctr. Kansas City, 1986-90; behavioral foster parent, 1989—; master foster parent, 1992—. Mem. psychiat. diversion team, mental health rev. team Jackson County Divsn. Family Svcs., 1992-95. Portrait painter and free-lance artist. Pres., bd. dirs. Advocates for Children, Inc., 1996—; vol. Ozanam Home for Boys, Kansas City, 1987—, mem. adv. bd., 1991—; mem. Cmty. Response Team, Jackson County, Divsn. Family Svcs. Named Therapeutic Foster Parent of Yr., 1992. Mem.: Nat. Mus. of Women in Arts (charter). Home and Office: 10243 Cedarbrooke Ln Kansas City MO 64131-4209

MAST, MAE JERENE, nurse; b. Drenthe, Mich., Feb. 13, 1922; d. Henry R. and Hattie (Brouwer) M. Diploma in Nursing, Blodgett Meml. Sch. Nursing, 1953; Diploma, Frontier Nursing Service/Midwifery, 1960. Grad. nurse Blodgett Meml. Hosp., Grand Rapids, Mich., 1953; missionary RN Sudan United Mission Nigeria (West Africa) Christian Reformed Bd. World Missions, 1954-79; staff RN geriatrics nursing home Zeeland, Mich., 1980-98; ret., 1998. Tchr. Spl. Edn. Ministries, Zeeland, 1984—91; vol. Ottawa County Jail Ministries, Grand Haven and Fillmore, 1988—, Zeeland Cmty. Hosp. Sunshine Corner, 1990—, Adult Edn. Program, 1995—2001, Right to Life, Holland, 1999—. Home: Apt 119 230 S State St Bldg 18 Zeeland MI 49464-1646

MAST, RICK, race car driver; b. Rockbridge Baths, Va., Mar. 4, 1957; m. Sharon Mast; children: Ricky, Katie, Sarah. Degree in bus. adminstrn., Blue Ridge C.C. Racecar driver Richard Jackson, 1991—97, Butch Mock Motorsports, 1997—98, Carl Yarborough, 1999, Larry Hedrick, 2000, A.J. Foyt, 2000, Hal Hicks, 2001, Jack Birmingham, 2001, Junie Donlavey, 2002—. Recipient 2d pl., ACDelco 500, 1994. Office: Donlavey Racing 5011 Old Midlothain Pike Richmond VA 23224-1119*

MAST, ROBERT FREDERICK, structural engineer; b. Springfield, Ill., May 20, 1934; BArch, U. Ill., 1957. Registered profl. engr., Wash., Fla., Mo., Tex., Mich., Colo., Ill. Design engr. Anderson, Birkeland, Anderson & Mast, Tacoma, 1959-62, ptnr., 1963-65; exec. v.p. to chmn. bd. ABAM Engrs. Inc., 1966-86, chmn. bd., 1986-97; prin. BERGER/ABAM Engrs. Inc., Federal Way, Wash., 1997—. Contbr. articles to profl. jours. Recipient Boase award Reinforced Concrete Council, 1997, Cons. Engrs. Coun. Washington Engr. of Yr. award, 2001. Mem. Nat. Acad. Engrs., ASCE (TY Lin award 1969, 73, 2002, Opal Design award 2001), Soc. Naval Archs. and Marine Engrs., Marine Tech. Soc., Reinforced Concrete Rsch. Council (Boase award 1997); fellow Prestressed Concrete Inst. (Martin P. Korn award 1992, Medal of Honor 2001), Am. Concrete Inst. (bldg. code com. 318 1984, tech. activity com. 1988-94, v.p. 1993-96, pres. 1997) Office: BERGER/ABAM Engineers Inc 33301 9th Ave S Ste 300 Federal Way WA 98003-2600 Fax: 253-431-2250. E-mail: mast@abam.com.

MAST, STEWART DALE, retired airport manager; b. Kalamazoo, May 10, 1924; s. Virgil S. and S. Louise (Rippey) M.; m. Judy Jo Bolton; children: Peter S., Frances Ann Mast Adams; m. May 20, 1979. Student, U. Mich., 1942-43; grad., Spartan Sch. Aerospace, Tulsa, 1946, Argubright Bus. Coll., Battle Creek, Mich., 1947. Mgr. Mcpl. Airport, Battle Creek, 1948-60; airport dir. Mitchell Field, Milw., 1961-66; mgr. Tampa (Fla.) Internat. Airport, 1966-89; ret., 1989. Pres. Mich. Assn. Airport Mgrs., 1958. Past mem. aviation coun. Milw. C. of C.; past mem. bd. rev. Boy Scouts Am., Milw.; bd. dirs. Sun'n Fun Aviation Found., Inc., Lakeland, Fla., 1992—, Sun'n Fun EAA Fly-in, Inc., Lakeland, Fla., 1994—. 1st lt. USAAF, 1943-45. Recipient Community Leadership award Greater Tampa C. of C., 1979. Mem. Am. Assn. Airport Execs. (past bd. dirs., Pres.'s award 1979), Fla. Assn. Airport Mgrs. Avocations: aviation philately, photography.

MASTER, PETER ANTONY, educator, author, editor; b. Watford, Eng., Jan. 23, 1948; s. Antony Edward and Eva Jana Master. BA, U. Calif., Santa Barbara, 1969; MA, San Francisco State U., 1977; PhD, UCLA, 1987. EFL instr. Berlitz, Zurich, 1970—71; ESL instr., dir. courses ESL Lang. Ctr., Oakland, Calif., 1974-78; supr. U. Calif. Berkeley Extension English Lang. Program, 1980-83; ESL instr. U. Calif., Berkeley, 1978-84; tchg. fellow UCLA, 1984-87; assoc. prof. Calif. State U., Fresno, 1987-95, San Jose (Calif.) State U., 1995-2000, prof., 2000—, dir. Lang. Devel. Ctr., 1996—99. Author: (textbook) Systems in English Grammar, 1996; editor, author: Responses to English for Specific Purposes, 2000; co-editor, author: New Ways in English for Specific Purposes, 1998; ; co-editor: New Ways in Content-Based Instruction, 1997, English for Specific Purposes, 1994—2001. Recipient Daniel M. Horowitz award English for Specific Purposes, 1992, Disting. Tchg. Asst. award UCLA, 1987. Mem. TESOL (column editor 1992-98, presenter), Calif. TESOL (journ. co-editor 1993-97, presenter), Am. Assn. Applied Linguistics (Strand coord., presenter). Democrat. Avocations: piano, running, woodworking, bicycling, rock climbing. Office: San Jose State U One Washington Sq San Jose CA 95192-0093 E-mail: pmaster@sjsu.edu.

MASTERS, ALBERT TOWNSEND, mechanical engineer; b. Cin., Feb. 10, 1925; s. Albert Griffey and Luella Martha (Townsend) M.; m. Ardella Elsie Wise, June 8, 1947; children: Susan Lynn, Barbara Ann. Student, Kent State U., 1946-48; BME, Cleve. State U., 1951. Registered profl. engr., Ohio. Mech. engr. Ramset Inc., Cleve., 1951-55; tech. sales mgr. Ramset divsn. Olin Ind., 5, 1955-61; tchr. mech. engring. Cleve. State U., 1960-62; engring. cons. Nat. Acad. Sci., Washington, 1958-61; engr. Anderson-Bolds, Inc., Cleve., 1961-82, chief engr., 1982-87; ret. Author: Powder-Actuated Fasteners Handbook for Architects and Engineers, 1960 (Prodrs. Coun. award 1961); contbr. numerous articles to profl. jours. 1st lt. USAAF, 1943-46. Recipient Design award Model Airplane News, 1992. Mem. Acad. Model Aviation, Internat. Miniature Aircraft Assn., Westlake R/C Club, Lorain County R/C Club. Avocations: commercial pilot, model aircraft design, writing. Home: 20026 Frazier Dr Rocky River OH 44116-1503

MASTERS, ARLENE ELIZABETH, singer; b. Freeport, Ill., Oct. 6, 1960; d. Elmer and Mary (Green) Masters; m. Douglas Dewayne Burck (div.); 1 child, Douglas. Singer classic rock and blues; with The Blues Transit Band, A. Masters Publishing. Home: PO Box 8221 Rockford IL 61126-8221

MASTERS, BARBARA J. lawyer; b. Denver, July 17, 1933; d. Richard P. and Ruth Ann (Savage) Johnson; children: Eliot, Joan. BA, Middlebury Coll., 1955; JD, U. Conn., 1976. Bar: Conn. 1976, U.S. Dist. Ct. Conn. 1976. Assoc. Maruzo & Lucas, Norwich, Conn., 1976-80; pvt. practice, 1980—; prin. Masters and Benson, 1994—. Mem. Conn. Coun. for Divorce Mediation. Bd. dirs. United Comty. Svcs., Norwich, 1980-87, Women's Ctr. Southeastern Conn., New London, 1983-89, Madonna Pl., Norwich, 1989-93; vice-chmn. Lebanon (Conn.) Bd. Fin., 1984-88; mem. People to People del. women lawyers to China, 1986, Norwich Arts Coun., 1989-93; alt. Old Lyme Zoning Bd. Appeals, 1993-97, Old Lyme Dem. Town Com., 1994-2001; mem. People to People Family Lawyer's Del., Cuba, 2001. Mem. Conn. Bar Assn., New London County Bar Assn. (pres. 1998-99). Unitarian Universalist. Avocations: sailing, walking, third world travel. Home: 2 Point Rd Old Saybrook CT 06475 Office: 199 W Town St Norwich CT 06360-2106 E-mail: norwichlaw@aol.com. *Notable cases include: Mallory v. Mallory, 207 Conn. 48, 539 A 2d 995, 1988, in which the normal civil standard of proof is applicable to the issue of restricted visitation with a child whom the parent has been accused of sexually abusing, where that parent retains some visitation rights.*

MASTERS, BETTIE SUE SILER, biochemist, educator; b. Lexington, Va., June 13, 1937; d. Wendell Hamilton and Mildred Virginia (Cromer) Siler; m. Robert Sherman Masters, Aug. 6, 1960; children: Diane Elizabeth, Deborah Ann. BS in Chemistry, Roanoke Coll., 1959, D.Sc. (hon.), 1983; PhD in Biochemistry, Duke U., 1963. Postdoctoral fellow Duke U., 1963-66, advanced research fellow, 1966-68, assoc. on faculty, 1967-68; mem. faculty U. Tex. Health Sci. Ctr. (Southwestern Med. Sch.), Dallas, 1968-82, assoc. prof. biochemistry, 1972-76, prof., 1976-82, research prof. surgery, dir. biochem. burn research, 1979-82; prof. biochemistry, chmn. dept. Med. Coll. Wis., Milw., 1982-90; Robert A. Welch prof. chemistry, dept. biochemistry U. Tex. Health Sci. Ctr., San Antonio, 1990—. Mem. pharmacology-toxicology rsch. rev. com. Nat. Inst. Gen. Med. Scis., NIH, 1975-79; mem. bd. sci. counselors Nat. Inst. Environ. Health Scis., 1982-86, chmn., 1984-86; mem. adv. com. on biochemistry and endocrinology Am. Cancer Soc., 1989-92, chmn., 1991-92, mem. coun. for extramural grants, 1998—; mem. phys. biochemistry study sect. NIH, 1989-90; vis. scientist Japan Soc. for Promotion Sci., 1978. Mem. editl. bd. Jour. Biol. Chemistry, 1976-81, 96-2001, Archives Biochemistry and Biophysics, 1991-94, Drug Metabolism and Disposition, 1993-, Nitric Oxide, Biology and Chemistry, 1996-, , Internat. Union Biochemistry and Molecular Biology Life, 1999-; contbr. chpts. to books and articles, revs. and abstracts to profl. publs. Mem. coun. extramural grants Am. Cancer Soc., 1998-2000. Recipient Merit award Nat. Heart, Lung and Blood Inst., 1988-97, grantee, 1970—; recipient Excellence in Sci. award Fedn. Am. Socs. for Exptl. Biology, 1992; postdoctoral fellow Am. Cancer Soc., 1963-65, advanced rsch. fellow Am. Heart Assn., 1966-68, established investigator, 1968-73; rsch. grantee NIH, 1970—, Nat. Heart Lung Blood Inst., 1970—, Nat. Inst. Gen. Med. Scis., 1980—, Robert A. Welch Found., 1971-82, 90—; elected to Inst. Medicine of NAS, 1996. Fellow AAAS; mem. NIH (adv. com. to the dir. 2000—), Am. Soc. Biochemistry and Molecular Biology (nominating com. 1983, coun. 1985-86, awards com. 1992-96, fin. com. 1993-98, publs. com. 1994-97, pres.-elect 2001, pres. 2002-), Am. Soc. Pharmacology and Exptl. Therapeutics (exec. com. drug metabolism divsn. 1979-81, chmn. exec. com. 1993-94, bd. publs. trustees 1982-87, Bernard B. Brodie award 2000), Am. Chem. Soc., Assn. Am. Med. Colls. (adv. bd. biomed. rsch. 1995-98), Fedn. Am. Socs. for Exptl. Biology (bd. dirs. 1998—, v.p. 2001-2002), Internat. Union Biochemistry and Molecular Biology (nominating com. 1994-97, chair U.S. nat.com. 1997—), Sigma Xi, Alpha Omega Alpha. Office: U Tex Health Sci Ctr Dept Biochemistry 7703 Floyd Curl Dr MSC 7760 San Antonio TX 78229-3900 E-mail: masters@uthscsa.edu.

MASTERS, CLAUDE BIVIN, lawyer; b. Cleburne, Tex., July 25, 1930; s. Claude Pinkney and Ola Mae (Rollins) M.; m. Jenita Whites, June 1, 1949 (div.); children: C. Thomas, Cl Danette Masters McClanahan, Teresa Masters Lebeck; m. Cynthia McCormack, Nov. 4, 1983. BS, U. Houston, 1953, JD, 1969, LLM, 1985. Bar: Tex. 1969, U.S. Dist. Ct. (so. dist.) Tex. 1972, U.S. Dist. Ct. (we. dist.) Tex. 1972, U.S. Ct. Appeals (5th cir.) 1971, U.S. Ct. Appeals (11th cir.) 1983, U.S. Supreme Ct. 1978. Ptnr. Martin & Masters, Houston, 1971-73; v.p., gen. counsel Summit Ins. Co. N.Y., N.Y.C., 1973-75; sr. atty. Ashland Oil Co., Ky., 1975-78; v.p. Houston Oil and Minerals Co., 1978-84; assoc. Dunnam & Strong, Houston, 1984-85; risk mgmt. cons. Masters & Assocs., 1975—. Bd. dirs. Alford & Assocs., Houston; adj. prof. law U. Houston, 1984—. Dir.-gen. Tex. Safety Assn., Austin, 1959. Served with U.S. Army, 1946-47. Named Outstanding Speaker, Southwest Ins. Info. Svc., Dallas, 1961-62. Fellow Tex. Bar Found.; mem. Jaycees (bd. dirs. Tulsa 1962; named Outstanding Mem. Tex. 1960), Phi Delta Phi. Republican. Mem. Ch. of Christ. Home: 27010 Rock Island Rd Hempstead TX 77445-8848 Office: 5444 Westheimer Rd Ste 1750 Houston TX 77056-5325 E-mail: cmasterspc@excelonline.com., alpaca@abonet.org.

MASTERS, EDWARD E. association executive, former foreign service officer; b. Columbus, Ohio, June 21, 1924; s. George Henry and Ethel Verena (Shaw) M.; m. Allene Mary Roche, Apr. 2, 1956; children: Julie Allene, Edward Ralston. Student, Denison U., 1942-43; BA with distinction, George Washington U., 1948; MA, Fletcher Sch. Law and Diplomacy, 1949. Joined U.S. Fgn. Service, 1950; intelligence research analyst Near East Dept. State, 1949-50; resident officer Heidelberg, Germany, 1950-52; polit. officer embassy Karachi, Pakistan, 1952-54; Hindustani lang. and area tng. U. Pa., 1954-55; consul, polit. officer Madras, India, 1955-58; intelligence research specialist South Asia Dept. State, 1958-60; chief Indonesia-Malaya br. Dept. State (Office Research Asia), 1960-61, officer-in-charge Thailand affairs, 1961-63; grad. Nat. War Coll., 1964; counselor for polit. affairs Am. embassy, Djakarta, 1964-68; country dir. for Indonesia Dept. State, 1968-70; dir. Office East Asian Regional Affairs, 1970-71; minister Am. embassy, Bangkok, 1971-75; ambassador to Bangladesh, 1976-77, to Indonesia, 1977-81; adj. prof. diplomacy Fletcher Sch. Law and Diplomacy, 1981-82; sr. v.p. Natomas Co., 1982-84; pres. Nat. Planning Assn., 1985-92, Edward Masters & Assocs., Washington, 1992—, U.S.-Indonesia Soc., 1994-2000, chmn., 2000—. Adj. prof. Sch. Advanced Internat. Studies, 2000-. Mem. Am. Fgn. Svc. Assn., Phi Beta Kappa, Omicron Delta Kappa, Pi Gamma Mu, Delta Phi Epsilon, Cosmos Club. Home: 4525 Garfield St NW Washington DC 20007-1165 E-mail: mastersdc@worldnet.att.net.

MASTERS, ELAINE, educator, writer; b. Kansas City, Kans., Oct. 6, 1932; d. David Shepherd and Stella Frances (Ragan) M.; m. Donald Ramon Masters, Apr. 27, 1951; children: David, Vicki, Jennifer, Kevin. BS in Edn. with honors, U. Mo., Kansas City, 1968. Cert. tchr., Mo., Va. Tchr. grade 4 Am. Sch., Manila, 1956-57; tchr. grade 5 Escuela Gloria Felix, Caracas, Venezuela, 1960-62; tchr. grade 6 Okinawa Christian Sch., Urasoe, 1968-70; tchr. grade 5 Flint Hill Elem. Sch., Vienna, 1970-73; tchr. Bible Inst. Hawaii, Honolulu, 1991-92; dir. Christian edn. St. Thomas United Meth. Ch., Manassas, Va., 1983-84; tchr. children's ministries Salvation Army, Kaneohe, Hawaii, 1991-94; owner Edon Industries, Quixtar, 1999—. Evangelist, Hong Kong, Malaysia, Nigeria, Thailand, Russia; seminar leader on Bible and Christian living, Hong Kong, Malaysia, Nigeria, Thailand; advisor Pentecostal Assemblies of Tribes, Chiang Mai, Thailand, 1991—; lectr. Christian Writers Workshop, 1993—; writer ednl. measurement, Harcourt Brace, 1998—; workshop leader Conf. on Lit. and Hawaiis Children, 1998—. Author: Ali and the Ghost Tiger, 1967, Teach Us To Pray, 1970, Day Camp and Day Care Handbook, 1989, The Thief in Chinatown, 1998, Footloose the Mongoose and the Jumping Flea, 1999, Malia's Happy Birthday, 2000, Malia and Baby Brother, 2000, Where's Malia's Mama?, 2000, Where's Kimo's Daddy?, 2000, Yumi and Her Best-Forever Friend, 2000, Footloose the Mongoose and His Wonderful Ohana, 2001, Momi The Hawaiian Mermaid, 2001, Kalani and the Night Marchers, 2001, Momi, A Hawaiian Mermaid in the Land of Delight, 2001; contbr. articles to mags. and newspapers; inventor cricket transposer tool for musicians. Mem. spkrs. bur. Alzheimer's Assn., Honolulu, 1991-97; mem. steering com. Children's Lit., Hawaii. Mem. Women's Aglow Fellowship Internat., Soc. Children's Book Writers and Illustrators (regional advisor State of Hawaii 1996-98). Avocations: travel, Hawaiian culture, Thai and hill tribes culture, foreign languages. Home: 2355 Ala Wai Blvd Apt 502 Honolulu HI 96815-3404 E-mail: e.masters@verizon.net.

MASTERS, GARY EVERETT, librarian, educator; b. Fresno, Calif., July 3, 1941; s. Jess Franklin and Lois May (Cain) M.; m. Ella Suzanne Tilson, Dec. 27, 1972. BA, Tex. Tech. U., 1969; MLS, North Tex. State U., 1976, PhD, 1987. Info. specialist CIA, Washington, Vietnam, 1969-75; sci. librarian North Tex. State U., Denton, 1976-87; asst. prof. Uniformed Svcs. U. Health Scis., Bethesda, Md., 1987-93; libr. automated svcs., netware mgr. Tex. A&M Internat. U., Laredo, 1994-2000; sys. libr. FDA, Rockville, Md., 2000—. Systems libr, mgr. web page, online servs., reference libr., data entry supr. Sgt. U.S. Army, 1965-67. Mem. Tex. Libr. Assn. Democrat. Methodist. Avocations: book collecting, photography, computers, electronics. Office: FDA 9200 Corporate Blvd Rockville MD 20850 E-mail: gary4books@yahoo.com.

MASTERS, GEORGE WINDSOR, JR. electrical engineer, educator; b. Annapolis, Md., Mar. 11, 1930; s. George and Ruby Lena (Jess) Masters; m. Barbara Lyons Wilson; children: Barbara Anne, George W. III. BS, MIT, 1952, MS, 1954; PhD, U. Fla., 1966. Mem. tech. staff Instrument Lab., MIT, Cambridge, 1952-55; chief engr. Dynamic Instrument Co., 1955-58; sect. head Electromech. Rsch. Inc., Princeton, N.J., 1958-62; mem. sr. staff, sect. head flight control sect. The Aerospace Corp., El Segundo, Calif., 1962-75; chief engr. airborne sys. dept. USN Test Pilot Sch., Patuxent River, Md., 1975—. Assoc. prof. elec. engring. Fla. Inst. Technology, Melbourne, 1984—. Mem. AIAA, IEEE, US Naval Inst., Elks, Kappa Sigma. Republican. Episcopalian. Home: 47986 Waterview Dr Saint Inigoes MD 20684-3018 E-mail: mastersg@tgci.net., mastersgw@navair.navy.mil.

MASTERS, JEFFREY D. association executive; b. Birmingham, Ala., Feb. 25, 1948; s. J.D. and Laura Linn Masters; m. Diane Sanders. BS, Samford U., Birmingham, 1970. Exec. dir. Assn. Builders and Contractors of Ala., Inc., Birmingham, 1975—; pub. Ala.. Constrn. News Mag., 1994—. Treas. ABC Merit PAC. Mem.: Ala. Coun. Assn. Execs. (bd. dirs., 1st v.p., com. chair 1984—88), Am. Soc. Assn. Execs., Birmingham C. of C., Montgomery C. of C., The Club. Baptist. Avocations: quail hunting, water sports. Office: Assn Builders and Contrs of Ala 1830 28th Ave S Birmingham AL 35209-2606 E-mail: jeff@abc-alabama.org.

MASTERS, JOHN CHRISTOPHER, psychologist, educator, writer; b. Terre Haute, Ind., Oct. 25, 1941; s. Robert William and Lillian Virginia (Decker) M.; m. Mary Jayne Capps, June 6, 1970; children— Blair Christopher, Kyle Alexander. AB, Harvard Coll., 1963; PhD, Stanford U., 1967. Asst. prof. Ariz. State U., Tempe, 1968-69; from asst. prof. to prof. U. Minn., Mpls., 1969-79; assoc. dir. Inst. Child Devel., 1974-79; Luce prof. pub. policy and the family, prof. psychology Vanderbilt U., Nashville, 1979-87, interim chair dept. psychology, 1986-88; pres. Profl. Mgmt. Group, Inc., 1991—; dir. Master Ventures, 1989—, Master Travel, 1989—. Assoc. editor: Child Development, 1973-76, Behavior Therapy: Techniques and Empirical Findings, 1974, 79, 88; editor: Psychol. Bull., 1987-89. Fellow Am. Psychol. Assn.; mem. Soc. for Research in Child Devel., Internat. Soc. for Study of Behavioral Devel., Assn. for Public Policy and Mgmt. Home: 555 Crosswinds Dr Mount Juliet TN 37122-5064

MASTERS, JON JOSEPH, corporate governance consultant; b. N.Y.C., June 20, 1937; s. Arthur Edward and Esther (Shady) M.; m. Rosemary Dunaway Cox, June 16, 1962; children: Brooke Alison, Blake Edward. BA, Princeton U., 1958; JD, Harvard U., 1964. Bar: N.Y. 1965, U.S. Dist. Ct. (so. dist.) N.Y. 1965, U.S. Ct. Appeals (2d cir.) 1965. Cons. asst. to under sec. Dept. Army, 1961; mem. policy planning staff asst. sec. for internat. security affairs Dept. Def. Washington, 1962; mem. Pres. Johnson's Spl. Polit. Research Staff, 1964; assoc. Shearman & Sterling, N.Y.C., 1965-68, 69; mem. staff Bedford-Stuyvesant D & S Corp., Bklyn., 1968-69; v.p., sec., gen. counsel, dir. Baker, Weeks & Co., Inc., N.Y.C., 1969-76; ptnr. Christy & Viener, 1976-96; prin. Lear, Yavitz & Assocs., 1996-2001; mng. prin., 1998—. Mem. bd. dirs. Robb, Peck, McCooey Fin. Svcs. Corp., N.Y.C., 1996-98; vice chmn. Robb, Peck, McCooey Specialist Corp., N.Y.C., 1996-98; mem. SEC adv. com. broker-dealer compliance, 1972-74; legal advisor NACD Blue Ribbon Commn. on CEO and Dir. Performance Evaluation, 1994; chmn. bd. Clear and Present Prodns., 1992-93; bd. dirs. Harris & Harris Group Inc., 1992-98; prin. Mercer Delta Cons., N.Y.C., 2001-2002; chmn. Masters Governance Cons., LLC, 2002—. Mem. implementation com. Econ. Devel. Task Force of N.Y. Urban Coalition, 1968; mem. bd. Internat. Social Service, Am. Br., Inc., 1978-83, pres., 1979-83; bd. dirs. The Arts Connection, 1979-85; mem. steering com. N.Y. Lawyers Alliance for Nuclear Arms Control, 1983-96. Served with USN, 1958-61. Mem. ABA, Assn. Bar City N.Y. (com. mcpl. affairs 1977-80), N.Y. State Bar Assn. Office: 520 E 86th St New York NY 10028 E-mail: mastersjj@aol.com.

MASTERS, JOSEPH HENRY, pathologist; b. Elizabeth City County, Va., Aug. 4, 1923; s. George Henry and Lena (Wright) M.; m. Margaret Lee Masters, Aug. 25, 1947; children: Margo Dianne (dec.), David J., Katherine M. Student, Johns Hopkins U., 1944-46; MD, Va. Commonwealth U., 1949. Diplomate Am. Bd. Pathology, Am. Bd. Forensic Pathology; cert. Nat. Bd. Med. Examiners. 1st lt. U.S. Army, 1954, advanced through grades to maj., chief dept. pathology 98th Gen. Hosp. Fed. Republic Germany, 1954-57, chief dept. pathology Madigan Army Hosp., 1957-58, resigned, 1958; chief dept. pathology Sutter Community Hosps., Sacramento, 1966-75; cons. forensic pathologist County of Sacramento, 1964—. Mem. adv. com. Dept. Lab. Svcs. State of Calif., Berkeley, 1973-75. Fellow Am. Soc. Clin. Pathologists, Coll. Am. Pathologists (sec. 1980-83, Svc. award 1984); mem. N.Y. Acad. Scis. (life), Calif. Soc. Pathologists (bd. dirs. 1969-75, pres. 1975). Republican. Baptist.

MASTERS, ORLAN VINCENT WADE, gynecologist; b. Corona, Calif., Feb. 29, 1920; s. Francis Wakeman and Grace Elizabeth (Wade) M.; m. Marilyn Jean Miss, June 19, 1949 (div. Sept. 1972); children: Michael Vincent Wade, Martin Wakeman, Susan Lynne, Matthew Christian; m. Judy Jay Alves, Aug. 26, 1975. BA, Stanford U., 1949, MD, 1953. Diplomate Am. Bd. Ob-Gyn. Intern L.A. County Gen. Hosp., 1952-53; resident in gen. practice Kern Gen. Hosp., Bakersfield, Calif., 1953-54; resident in ob-gyn. Akron (Ohio) City Hosp., 1954-58; chief res. ob-gyn. Akron City Hosp., 1957-58; resident in ob-gyn. Chgo. Lying-In-Hosp., U. Chgo., 1956; mem. cons. staff St. Mary's Hosp., Ga., 1973—; mem. courtesy staff Athens (Ga.) Regional Med. Ctr., 1973—; asst. clin. prof. ob-gyn. Med. Coll. Ga., Augusta, 1973—; dir. Women's Clinic U. Ga. Health Svc., Athens, 1975-96. Reproductive health cons. Clarke County Health Dept., Athens, 1973—. Bd. dirs. Friends of Ga. State Art Mus., Athens, 1994; dir. Colposcopic clinic, N.E. Ga. Health Dist., Ga., 1996—; active Athens Clarke Heritage Found. Fellow ACOG, ACS; mem. AMA, SMA, Am. Soc. for Colposcopy and Cervical Pathology, Soc. Laparoendoscopic Surgeons. Office: Clarke County Health Dept 345 N Harris St Athens GA 30601-2411

MASTERS, ROBERT EDWARD LEE, psychotherapist, neural researcher, human potential educator; b. Jan. 4, 1927; s. Robert and Katherine (Leeper) Masters; m. Jean Houston, May 8, 1965. BA in Philosophy, U. Mo., 1951; PhD in Clin. Psychology, Humanistic Psychology Inst., 1974. Dir. Libr. of Sex Rsch., N.Y.C., 1962-66, Sensory Imagery Program, 1965-68; dir. rsch. Found. for Mind Rsch., N.Y.C. and Ashland, Oreg., 1965—. Dir. Zarathustra Project, Pomona, 1980—99; co-dir. Human Capacities Tng. Program, Ramapo, NJ, 1982—99; pvt. practice psychotherapy, neural re-edn., aging and geropsychology programs; prin. tchr. Hypnotherapist Tng., Pomona, 1982—99; pres. Human Capacities Corp., Ashland, 1982—. Author: Eros and Evil, 1962, Forbidden Sexual Behavior and Morality, 1964, Mind Games, 1972, Listening to the Body, 1978, Psychophysical Method Exercises, vols. I-VI, 1983, The Goddess Sekhmet, 1987, The Masters Technique, 1987, Neurospeak, 1994, The Way to Awaken, 1997, Sekhmet-Images and Entrances, 2001, Swimming Where Madmen Drown, 2002; co-author (with J. Houston): Varieties of Psychedelic Experience, 1966; contbr. articles to sci. publs., poetry, fiction and essays to profl. jours., lit. and art criticism and book revs. With USN, 1945—46, PTO. Grantee, Erickson Found., 1966, Kleiner Found., 1968, Babcock Found., 1970, Doris Duke Found., 1972. Fellow: Am. Acad. Clin. Sexologists (founder); mem.: AAAS, APA, N.Y. Acad. Scis., Am. Psychotherapy Assn. (diplomate), Assn. Humanistic Psychology, Am. Assn. Sex Educators, Counselors and Therapists, Am. Bd. Sexology (clin. supr.). Office: Found Mind Rsch PMB 501 2305 Ashland St Ste C Ashland OR 97520-3777

MASTERS, ROGER DAVIS, government and neurotoxicology educator; b. Boston, June 8, 1933; s. Maurice and S. Grace (Davis) M.; m. Judith Ann Rubin, June 6, 1956 (div. 1984); children— Seth J., William A., Katherine R.; m. Susanne R. Putnam, Aug. 25, 1984 BA, Harvard U., 1955; MA, U. Chgo., 1958, PhD, 1961; MA (hon.), Dartmouth Coll., 1974. Instr. dept. polit. sci. Yale U., 1961-62, asst. prof., 1962-67; assoc. prof. dept. govt. Dartmouth Coll., Hanover, N.H., 1967-73, prof., 1973-98, John Sloan Dickey Third Century prof., 1980-85, chmn. dept., 1986-89, Nelson A. Rockefeller prof., 1991-98, prof. emeritus, 1998—, rsch. prof., 1999—. Cultural attache Am. Embassy, Paris, 1969-71; chmn. France-Am. Commn. Edni. and Cultural Exch., 1969-71; vis. lectr. Yale U. Law Sch., 1988-89, Vt. Law Sch., 1993, 94; sect. editor Social Sci., Info., 1971; chmn. exec. com. Gruter Inst. Law and Behavioral Rsch., 1995-98; pres. Found. for Neurosci. and Soc., 1998—. Author; The Nation Is Burdened, 1967, The Political Philosophy of Rousseau, 1968, The Nature of Politics, 1989, Beyond Relativism, 1993, Machiavelli, Leonardo, and the Science of Power, 1996, Fortune is a River, 1998; editor: Rousseau's Discourses, 1964, Rousseau's Social Contract, 1978; co-editor: Ostracism: A Social and Biological Phenomenon, 1986, Collected Writings of J.J. Rousseau, 1990—, Primate Politics, 1991, The Sense of Justice, 1992, The Neurotransmitter Revolution, 1994; editor Gruter Inst. Reader in Biology, Law, and Human Social Behavior, 1992. Served with AUS, 1955-57. Fulbright fellow Institut d'Etudes Politiques, Paris, 1958-59; joint Yale U.-Social Sci. Rsch. Coun. fellow, 1964-65; Guggenheim fellow, 1967-68; fellow Hastings Ctr. for Ethics and Life Scis., 1973-78. Mem. AAAS, Am. Polit. Sci. Assn., Assn. Polit. and Life Sci. (coun.), Am. Soc. for Legal and Polit. Philosophy, Internat. Soc. Human Ethology, Human Behavior Evolution Soc. Home: PO Box 113 South Woodstock VT 05071-0113 Office: Dartmouth Coll Dept Govt Silsby Hall HB6108 Hanover NH 03755 E-mail: Roger.D.Masters@Dartmouth.edu.

MASTERSON, CARLIN See GLYNN, CARLIN

MASTERSON, ELLEN HORNBERGER, accountant; b. Ft. Smith, Ark., Feb. 19, 1951; d. Evans Zacharias and Nancy Cravens (Eads) H.; m. Conrad J. Masterson, Jr., Sept. 26, 1987. BA, Emory U., 1973; MBA, So. Meth. U., 1978. CPA, Mass. Staff acct. Coopers & Lybrand, Boston, gen. practice ptnr. Dallas, from 1985; with Am. Gen. Corp., Houston, until 1999; ptnr. PricewaterhouseCoopers, N.Y.C., 1999—. Instr. Sch. Mgmt. and Adminstrv. Scis., U. Tex., Dallas, 1980-81. Bd. dirs. Shakespeare Festival Dallas, 1983-86, Leadership Dallas, 1985-86, USA Film Festival, 1986-88, Dental Health Program, Inc., 1986-88; mem. Jr. League, The 500, Inc.; workshop leader, vol. Cmty. Bd. Inst.; cons. Ctr. for Non Profit Mgmt. Mem. AICPA, Mass. Soc. CPAs, Tex. CPAs, So. Meth. U. MBA Alumni Assn., Kappa Kappa Gamma, Alpha Iota Delta, Beta Gamma Sigma. Presbyterian. Office: PricewaterhouseCoopers 1301 Ave of Americas New York NY 10019

MASTERSON, JAMES FRANCIS, psychiatrist; b. Phila., Mar. 25, 1926; s. James Francis and Evangeline (O'Boyle) M.; m. Patricia Cooke, Jan. 28, 1950; children: James F., Richard K., Nancy. BS, U. Notre Dame, 1947; MD, Jefferson Med. Sch., Phila., 1951. Diplomate Am. Bd. Psychiatry, Am. Bd. Neurology. Intern Phila. Gen. Hosp., 1951-52; resident in psychiatry Payne Whitney Clinic, N.Y. Hosp., N.Y.C., 1952-55, chief resident, 1955-56, dir. adolescent OPD, 1956-66, head adolescent program, 1968-75, asst. attending psychiatrist, 1956-60, assoc. attending psychiatrist, 1960-70, attending psychiatrist, 1970—, dir. The Symptomatic Adolescent Research Project, 1957-67; dir. Masterson Group, P.C. for Study and Treatment Personality Disorders, N.Y.C., 1977—. Author: Psychotherapy of the Borderline Adolescent, Psychotherapy of the Borderline Adult, Countertransference, Narcissistic Personality Disorder, The Real Self, The Psychiatric Dilemma of Adolescence, The Test of Time: From Borderline Adolescent to Functioning Adult; contbr. articles to profl. jours. Fellow Am. Psychiat. Assn., Am. Coll. Psychoanalysts; mem. AMA, Am. Coll. Psychoanalysis, N.Y. Soc. Adolescent Psychiatry (founder, past pres.), N.Y. County Med. Soc. Office: 60 Sutton Pl S New York NY 10022-4168

MASTERSON, JOHN PATRICK, retired English language educator; b. Chgo., Mar. 15, 1925; s. Michael Joseph and Delia Frances (Dolan) M.; m. Jean Frances Wegrzyn, Aug. 18, 1956; children: Mary Beth, Michael, Maureen, Laura. BA, St. Mary of the Lake, 1947; MA, De Paul U., 1952; PhD, U. Ill., 1961. Chmn. English dept. De Paul U., Chgo., 1964-67, head humanities div., 1967-70, prof. English, 1970, dean Coll. Liberal Arts and Scis., 1970-76, prof. mgmt., 1976-80, 82-87, prof. emeritus, 1988—, dean Grad. Sch., 1980-82. Cons. in field. Recipient award Shell Oil Co., 1968, Via Sapientiae award De Paul U., 1987; fellow adminstrn. program Am. Coun. Edn. Roman Catholic. Home: 1922 Belleview Ave Westchester IL 60154-4345

MASTERSON, KLEBER SANLIN, JR. physicist; b. San Diego, Sept. 26, 1932; s. Kleber Sandlin and Charlotte Elizabeth (Parker) M.; m. Sara Ann Cooper, Dec. 21, 1957; children: Thomas Marshall, John Cooper. BS in Engring., U.S. Naval Acad., 1954; MS in Physics, USN Postgrad. Sch., 1960; PhD in Physics, U. Calif., San Diego, 1963; postgrad. Advanced Mgmt. Program, Harvard Bus. Sch., 1981-82. Commd. ensign USN, 1954, advanced through grades to rear adm., 1979; comdg. officer USS Preble, Pearl Harbor, Hawaii, 1969-71; mgr. antiship missile def. project USN, Washington, 1974-77, exec. asst. to sec. of Navy, 1977-79, asst. dep. comdr. Naval Sea Systems Command, 1979-81, chief Studies, Analyses and Gaming Agy., 1981-82, ret., 1982; prin. Booz, Allen and Hamilton, Inc., Arlington, Va., 1982-87, v.p., 1987-92; sr. v.p. Sci. Applications Internat. Corp., 1992-94; pres. The Riverside Group, Ltd., 1994—. Bd. control U.S. Naval Inst., Annapolis, Md., 1971-82; bd. dirs. Mil. Ops. Rsch. Soc., 1984-90, pres., 1988-89; mem. divsn. rev. com. TSA divsn. Los Alamos Nat. Lab., 1996-2001, chmn. 1998-2001. Editor: Book of Navy Songs, 1954; contbr. articles on plasma and theoretical nuclear physics, computer science, radars, ops. rsch. to profl. publs. Mem. Historic Alexandria Resources Commn., 1998—, vice chmn. 2001—. Mem. Am. Phys. Soc., U.S. Naval Acad. Alumni Assn. (pres. Washington chpt. 1989-90), U.S. Naval Acad. Found. (trustee 1991—), Soc. of the Cin. (chmn. edn. com. 1997-2001, v.p. Mass. Soc. 1999-2001, asst. sec. gen. 2001—, pres. Mass. Soc. 2001—), Sigma Xi. Achievements include development of NELIAC computer program and Strategic Simulation Methodology. Home and Office: The Riverside Group Ltd 101 Pommander Walk Alexandria VA 22314-3844 E-mail: skidmasterson@cs.com.

MASTERSON, LINDA HISTEN, medical company executive; b. N.Y.C., May 21, 1951; d. George and Dorothy (Postler) Riddell; m. Robert P. Masterson, March 6, 1982; m. William J. Histen, May 24, 1971 (div. 1979). BS in med. tech., U. R.I., 1973; MS in microbiology, U. Md., 1977; student, Wharton U. Pa., Phila., 1988. Med. technologist various hosps., 1972-78; microbiology specialist Gen. Diagnostics, Warner-Lambert, Morris Plains, N.J., 1978-80; from tech. sales rep. to dir. internat. mktg. Micro-Scan, Baxter Internat., Sacramento, 1980-87; dir. mktg. Ortho Diagnostics, Johnson & Johnson, Raritan, N.J., 1987-89; sr. v.p. mktg/sales GenProbe, San Diego, 1989-92; v.p. mktg./sales Bio Star, Boulder, Colo., 1992-93; exec. v.p. Cholestech Inc., Hayward, Calif., 1994—. Bd. dirs. U.S. Alcohol Testing of Am., Inc., Rancho Cucamonga, Calif. Tribute to women in industry Young Women's Christian Assn., N.J., 1989. Mem. Biomedical Mktg. Assn., Med. Mktg. Assn., Phi Kappa Phi. Avocations: skiing, kayaking, racketball. Office: Cholestech Inc 5347 Investment Blvd Hayward CA 94541-9999

MASTERSON, MARY STUART, actress; b. N.Y.C., June 28, 1966; d. Peter and Carlin Glynn Masterson. Theatre appearances include Alice in Wonderland, 1982, Been Taken, 1985, The Lucky Spot, 1987, Lily Dale, 1987, Three Sisters, 1991; TV movies include Love Lives On, 1985, City in Fear, 1980, Lily Dale, 1996, On the 2nd Day of Christmas, 1997; films: The Stepford Wives, 1975, Heaven Help Us, 1984, At Close Range, 1985, My Little Girl, 1986, Gardens of Stone, 1987, Some Kind of Wonderful, 1987, Mr. North, 1988, Chances Are, 1989, Immediate Family, 1989, Funny About Love, 1990, Married To It, 1990, Fried Green Tomatoes, 1991, Benny and Joon, 1993, Bad Girls, 1994, Radioland Murders, 1994, Heaven's Prisoners, 1996, Bed of Roses, 1996, Digging to China, 1997, Dogtown, 1997, The Postman, 1997, The Florentine, 1998, The Book of Stars, 1999, Black and Blue, 1999; dir., writer for Showtime 2000; TV guest appearances include Amazing Stories, 1985, Inside the Actors Studio, 1994. Office: Creative Artists Agency 9830 Wilshire Blvd Beverly Hills CA 90212-1825

MASTERSON, PETER, actor, director; b. Houston, June 1, 1934; s. Carlos Bee and Josephine Yeager (Smith) M.; m. Carlin Glynn, Dec. 29, 1960; children: Carlin Alexandra, Mary Stuart, Peter Carlos. BA in History, Rice U., 1957. Appeared in Broadway plays Marathon '33, 1963, Blues for Mr. Charlies, 1964; title role in Trial of Lee Harvey Oswald, 1967; appeared in The Great White Hope, 1968, That Championship Season, 1974, The Poison Tree, 1975, (films) The Exorcist, 1972, Man on a Swing, 1973, The Stepford Wives, 1974; playwright The Best Little Whorehouse in Texas, 1978; dir. Broadway prodns. The Best Little Whorehouse in Texas, 1978 (Drama Desk award for Best Dir. of Musical 1978); co-dir., co-writer The Best Little Whorehouse Goes Public, 1994; dir. off-Broadway prodns. The Cover of Life, 1994, The Young Man from Atlanta (Pulitzer prize 1995); screenwriter The Best Little Whorehouse in Texas, 1980; prodr. (TV film) City in Fear, 1980; dir. films The Trip to Bountiful, 1985, Blood Red, 1986, Full Moon in Blue Water, 1987, Night Game, 1988, Convicts, 1989, Arctic Blue, 1993, Lily Dale, 1996, The Only Thrill, 1997, Mermaid, 1999, Lost Junction, 2001. Mem. AFTRA, SAG, Actors Equity Assn., Soc. Stage Dirs. and Choreographers, Writers Guild Am., Actors Studio, Dirs. Guild Am., Seawanhaka Club, Corinthian Yacht Club, Tex. Corinthian Yacht Club.

MASTERSON, WENDY LYNN, choreographer, dance educator; b. St. Charles, Mo., Feb. 19, 1963; d. John Thomas and Lois Jane (Lundmark) M. BFA in Ballet, Point Park Coll., 1984; MFA, U.S. Internat. U., 1986. Tchr. Calif. Ballet, San Diego, 1984; tchr., choreographer San Diego Civic Youth Ballet, 1985-86; ballet mistress Internat. Festival Ballet, San Diego, 1986; assoc. prof. U. Idaho, Moscow, 1986-87; artistic dir. Am. Festival Ballet Jr. Co., 1986-87; tchr., choreographer, ballet mistress Mountain Shadows Sch. of Dance, Great Falls, Mont., 1987-91; dance divsn. adminstr., ballet faculty, choreographer Interlochen (Mich.) Arts Acad., 1991—; adminstrv. asst. DanceAspen, 1992, sch. adminstr., 1993-95. Costume mistress Point Park Coll., Pitts., 1982-84; outreach instr. Ballet Iowa, 1988-90; primary presenter Encore in pub. schs. for Corpus Christi Concert Ballet, 1990-91; rehearsal asst. Corpus Christi Concert Ballet, 1990-91; tchr. Ballet Acad. Corpus Christi, 1990-91; adminstrv. intern Dance Aspen, summer 1991—; dance faculty Interlochen (Mich.) Arts Acad., adminstr. Dance Div., summer adminstr. Vail Internat. Dance Festival, 1997—. Mem. Mont. Dance Arts Assn. (tchr. 1987, scholar 1977), Regional Dance Am. Clubs: Sports Car of Am. Avocations: sewing, reading, languages. Home and Office: Interlochen Arts Acad PO Box 422 Interlochen MI 49643-0422 E-mail: bcm@traverse.net.

MASTERSON, WILLIAM A. retired judge; b. N.Y.C., June 25, 1931; s. John Patrick and Helen Audrey (O'Hara) M.; m. Julie Dohrmann Cosgrove; children: Mark, Mary, Timothy, Barbara. BA, UCLA, 1953, JD, 1958. Bar: Calif. 1959, U.S. Supreme Ct. 1965.. Assoc. Sheppard, Mullin, Richter & Hampton, L.A., 1952-62, ptnr., 1962-79; ptnr. Rogers & Wells, 1979-83, Skadden, Arps, Slate, Meagher & Flom, 1983-87; judge L.A. Superior Ct., 1987-92; justice Ct. Appeal, 1993-2000; ret., 2000. Author, editor: Civil Trial Practice: Strategies and Techniques, 1986. With inf. U.S. Army, 1953-55. Fellow Am. Coll. Trial Lawyers; mem. Order of Coif. Office: PO Box 190 Mendocino CA 95460 E-mail: wmasterson@pobox.com.

MASTERTON, CRAIG WILLIAM, management consultant; b. Rochester, N.Y., Apr. 19, 1948; s. Kay Charles Masterton and Patricia Louise (Pike) Hoelzle; m. Beth Evelyn Austin, Aug. 2, 1969; children: Tara Jeanine, Douglas Austin. BS in Mgmt. and Indsl. Rels., U. Bridgeport, Conn., 1973; MBA in Mgmt. and Orgnl. Theory, U. New Haven, Conn., 1983. Indsl. engr. Warner Lambert Corp., Detroit, 1976-78; prodn. supr. Harrison Radiator Divsn. GM, Lockport, N.Y., 1978-80, Bic Pen Corp., Milford, Conn., 1980-82; corp. indsl. engr. Am. Airlines, Irving, Tex., 1982-83; dep. dir. internat. Gen. Dynamics, Ft. Worth, 1983-91; prin. cons. EDS, Troy, Mich., 1991-93; plant mgr. CTA Acoustics, Corbin, Ky., 1993-94; v.p. consulting svcs. SGMP Performance Analytics, Troy, 1994-96; resultant Thomas Group Inc., Irving, 1996—. Bd. dirs. SGMP Performance Analytics, Troy, 1994-96; mem. exec. mgmt. bd. CTA Acoustics, Corbin, 1993-94. With USAF, 1968-72. Mem. Am. Legion, Moose. Republican. Avocations: fishing, golf, horsemanship. Office: Thomas Group Ste 500 5221 N O'Connor Blvd Irving TX 75039

MASTERTON, LUCINDA CRONIN, lawyer; b. Proctor, Vt., May 18, 1950; d. John Donald and Elsie Lipstein M.; m. Lindsay Morris, Mar. 16, 1998; 1 child: Rachael Leigh. BA, Northwestern U., 1972; JD, W. Va. U., 1981. Bar: Ky. 1982. Law clerk to Hon. K.K. Hall, Charleston, W. Va., 1981-82; law clerk to Hon. Edwin Flowers, 1982; assoc. Goodwin & Goodwin, 1982-83, Lexington, Ky., 1989-93; ptnr., assoc. Vimont & Wills, 1983-89; pvt. practice, 1993—. Trustee Chpt. 7 Bankruptcy, Ea. Dist. Ky., Lexington, 1989—. Mem. Jr. League, Parkersburg, Charleston, W. Va., Lexington, Ky., 1978-90. Mem. Fayette County Bar Assn. Avocations: horseback riding, gardening. Office: 4857 Paynes Mill Rd Lexington KY 40510-9695

MASTIN, WAYNE ALAN, electronic business consultant; b. West Point, N.Y., Jan. 29, 1952; s. John Wayne and Jane Louise (Hahn) M.; m. Kimberly Diane Whalen, Jan. 13, 1978 (div. Mar. 20, 1989); children: Kelly Anne, Bridget Louise; m. Michelle Marie Decoste, Aug. 15, 1993; children: Brian Michael, Sean Patrick. BA in History and Philosophy, N.C. State U., 1976; MA in Philosophy, Kansas U., 1986; postgrad., Boston U., 19925; M in Health Adminstrn., Suffolk U., 1997. Commd. 2d lt. U.S. Army, 1976, advanced through grades to maj., 1987, intelligence officer, 1976-84; asst. prof. U.S. Mil. Acad., West Point, N.Y., 1986-91; tng. mgr. U.S. Army Intelligence Sch., Ft. Devens, Mass., 1991-95; retired U.S. Army, 1995; physician profiles project coord. Bd. of Registration in Medicine, Boston, 1996-98; consumer edn. project coord. Mass. Divsn. of Energy Resources, 1998-99; e-bus. cons. Metro Info. Svcs., Columbia, S.C., 1999-2000; sr. functional cons. Sys. and Computer Tech. Corp., 2000—. Vis. lectr. logic Salem (Mass.) State Coll., 1995; adj. prof. philosophy Mass. Bay C.C., Wellesley Hills, 1995-96. Editl. referee Auslegung, 1984-86; contbr. article to Philosophy and Theology, 1991. Coach youth soccer W. Point (N.Y.) Youth Activities, 1990, Ft. Devens (Mass.) Youth Activities, 1994-95. Mem. Am. Philosoph. Assn., Armed Forces Comms. Electronics Assn., R.G. Collingwood Soc. Kappa Sigma (grandmaster of ceremonies 1974-75), Beta Gamma Sigma. Libertarian. Methodist. Avocations: skiing, rugby, lacrosse, photography, fine scale modelling.

MASTRACCHIO, RICHARD A. (RICK MASTRACCHIO), astronaut; b. Waterbury, Conn., Feb. 11, 1960; s. Ralph and Georgiana Mastracchio(Stepmother), Helen Cooke; m. Candace L. Stolfi; 3 children. BSEE and Computer Sci., U. Conn., 1982; MSEE, Rensselaer Poly. Inst., 1987; MS in Phys. Sci., U. Houston, Clear Lake, Tex., 1991. Engr. sys. design group Hamilton Std., Conn., 1982—87; with Rockwell Shuttle Ops. Co., Houston, 1987—90; engr. flight crew ops. directorate NASA, 1990—93, ascent/entry guidance and procedures officer in mission control, 1993—96; astronaut NASA, Johnson Space Ctr., 1996—. Mem.: IEEE. Achievements include 12 day mission aboard space shuttle Atlantis in Sept. 2000 to prepare International Space Station for arrival of first permanent crew; over 283 hours in space. Avocations: flying, baseball, basketball, swimming, woodworking. Office: Astronaut Office NASA Johnson Space Ctr Houston TX 77058*

MASTRANGELO, LISA SIOBHAN, humanities educator; b. Binghamton, N.Y., Sept. 19, 1971; d. Frank Tracey and Mary Christie (Dann) G.; m. Anthony Michael Mastrangelo. BA, Mt. Holyoke Coll., South Hadley, Mass., 1993; MA, SUNY, Albany, 1995, PhD, 2000. Instr. Sage Jr. Coll. Albany, 1993-96, SUNY, Albany, 1996-99; coord. arts and humanities Empire State Coll. Ctr. Distance Learning, Saratoga Springs, N.Y., 1997-99; instr. Coll. of St. Elizabeth, Morristown, N.J., 1999—. Alumnae admissions rep., alumnae giving rep. Mt. Holyoke Coll., South Hadley, Mass., 1993—. Mem. MLA, NOW, Nat. Coun. Tchrs. English, Coll. Conf. Composition and Communication. Avocations: reading, swimming, gardening.

MASTRINI, JANE REED, social worker, consultant; b. Lincoln, Nebr., July 23, 1948; d. William Scott and Ellen (Daly) Cromwell; m. Charles James Mastrini, July 19, 1969. BA, Western State Coll., Gunnison, Colo., 1970; MSW, U. Denver, 1980. Lic. social worker Colo., Nev.; cert. alcohol counselor Colo. and nat. Tchr. Flandreau (S.D.) Indian Sch., 1970; social worker S.D. Dept. Welfare, Pierre, 1970-75; child care worker Sacred Heart Home, Pueblo, Colo., 1975-76; counselor Fisher Peak Alcohol Treatment Ctr., Trinidad, 1976-77; family therapist West Nebr. Gen. Hosp., Scottsbluff, 1980-81; adolescent coord. St. Luke's Hosp., Denver, 1981-86; exec. dir. New Beginnings At Denver, Lakewood, 1986-90; pres. Counseling Dimensions of Colo., Denver, 1990-92; trainer Mile High Inst., 1987-93; outpatient mgr. Arapahoe House, 1992-94; therapist Kaiser Permanente, Denver, 1994-2000, Human Behavior Inst., Las Vegas, Nev., 2000—02, Nev. State Welfare Dept., 2002—. Cons. Colo. Counseling Consortium, Denver, 1984-90; field work supr. U. Denver, 1983-2000. Lectr., group leader Colo. Teen Inst., Denver, 1984—85, Westminster (Colo.) DARE Bd., 1998—; facilitator Leukemia/Lymphoma Soc. Support Group, 2001—02; sec. Greater House of Prayer Feeding the Homeless Program, 2001—02. Mem. NASW (cert.), P.E.O. (pres. 1984-87, 94-95), Colo. Counseling Consortium, Colo. Assn. Addiction Treatment Programs (v.p. 1991-92), Westminster Dare Bd., 1998-2000. Democrat. Episcopalian. Avocations: hiking, reading. Home: 349 Quiet Harbor Dr Henderson NV 89052-5601 Office: 2740 S Jones Blvd Las Vegas NV 89146-5306

MASTROGIANNIS, DIMITRIOS S. obstetrician/gynecologist, perinatologist; b. Athens, Greece, June 17, 1958; s. Stamatios and Potitsa-Nota M.; m. Marianna Kapsali, Oct. 24, 1986; children: Stamatios-George, Alexander-John, Dimitrios Nicholas. MD, U. Patras, 1983, PhD, 1989. Diplomate Am. Bd. Obstetrics and Gynecology, Maternal and Fetal Medicine. Resident ob/gyn, 1985-89; fellowship in maternal/fetal medicine, 1989-91; dir. perinatal rsch. unit Temple U., Phila., 1991-94; assoc. dir. obstetrics Winthrop U. Hosp., Mineola, N.Y., 1994-95; dir. maternal fetal medicine Good Samaritan Hosp., West Islip, 1996—; clin. prof. obgyn. Coll. Osteopathic Medicine Univ. N.Y. Coll., 1999—. Asst. prof. ob/gyn, Temple U., 1991-94; developer, mem. Am. Inst. Ultrasound in Medicine. Contbr. articles to profl. jours. Recipient award So. Med. Assn., 1990. Fellow Am. Coll. Ob/Gyn.; mem. AMA, Am. Assn. Gynecol. Laparoscopists, Soc. Perinatal Obstetricians. Home: 42 Talisman Dr Dix Hills NY 11746-5323

MASTROIANNI, ANNA CATHERINE, law educator; b. New Haven, Dec. 21, 1960; d. Luigi Mastroianni; m. Gregory M. Shaw, Oct. 16, 1993; children: Ryan Michael Shaw, Ella Catherine Shaw. BA, BS, U. Pa., 1982, JD, 1986; MPH, U. Wash., 1997. Atty. Epstein, Becker and Green, PC, Washington, 1987—88; asst to D.C. fin. dir. Dukakis Bentsen Campaign, 1988—88; legal cons. NRC, 1988—89; atty. Green, Stewart & Farber PC, 1989—92; study dir. Inst. Medicine, NAS, 1992—94; assoc. dir. White Ho. Adv. Com. on Human Radiation Experiments, 1994—95; part time lectr. U. Wash. Sch. Law, Seattle, 1996—98, asst. prof., 1998—. Editor: (book) Women and Health Research: Etical and Legal iIsues of Including Women in Clinical Studies, 1994, Beyond Consent: Seeking Justice in Research, 1998, Ethics of Research with Human Subjects: Selected Policies and Resources, 1998; contbr. articles to profl. jours. Office: Univ Wash Sch Law 1100 NE Campus Pkwy Seattle WA 98105

MASTROIANNI, LUIGI, JR. physician, educator; b. New Haven, Nov. 8, 1925; s. Marion (Dallas) Mastroianni; m. Elaine Catherine Pierson, Nov. 4, 1957; children: John James, Anna Catherine, Robert Luigi. AB, Yale U., 1946; MD, Boston U., 1950, DSc (hon.), 1973; MA (hon.), U. Pa., 1970. Diplomate Am. Bd. Ob-Gyn. and Reproductive Endocrinology and Infertility. Intern, then resident ob.-gyn. Met. Hosp. N.Y., 1950—54; fellow rsch. Harvard Med. Sch. and Free Hosp. for Women, Boston, 1954—55; instr. dept. ob-gyn. Yale U. Sch. Medicine, New Haven, 1955—56; asst. prof. ob.-gyn. dept. Yale U., 1956—61; prof. U. Calif., L.A., 1961—65; chief ob-gyn Harbor Gen. Hosp., 1961—65; William Goodell prof. ob.-gyn., chmn. dept. U. Pa. Sch. of Medicine, Phila., 1965—87, William Goodell prof. ob.-gyn. dept., dir. human reproduction div., 1987—96. Contbr. articles. Recipient Squibb prize, Pacific Coast Fertility Soc., 1965, Christian R. and Mary Lindback award, 1969, Gold medal, Barren Found., 1977, King Faisal prize in medicine, 1989, Pub. Recognition award, Assn. Profls. of Gynecology and Obstetrics, 1990, Disting. Svc. award, Soc. Study Reprodn., 1992, Rector's medal, U. Chile, 1993, Axel Munthe award, 1996, Resolve Svc. award, 1997, medal, Coll. Physicians of Phila., 1998. Mem.: Soc. for Study of Reprodn. (Disting. Svc. award 1992), Endocrine Soc., Soc. for Exptl. Biology and Medicine, Soc. Gynecology Investigation, Inst. of Medicine of NAS, Am. Physiol. Soc., Am. Soc. for Reproductive Medicine, Am. Gynecol. Club, Am. Gynecol. and Obstet. Soc., ACOG, ACS, Chilean Soc. Ob-Gyn. (hon.), Uruguan Soc. Sterility and Fertility (hon.), Israel Soc. Ob-Gyn. (hon.), Soc. Espanola de Fertilidad (hon.), Peruvian Fertility Soc. (hon.), Argentina Fertility Soc. (hon.), Italian Soc. Ob-Gyns. (hon.), Brazilian Fertility Soc. (hon.), Assn. Profs. Ob-Gyn. (hon.), N.C. Gynecol. Soc. (hon.), Tex. Assn. Ob-Gyns. (hon.), Ctrl. Assn. Ob-Gyns. (hon.), Pacific Coast Fertility Soc. (hon.), Alpha Omega Alpha, Sigma Xi. Home: 561 Ferndale Ln Haverford PA 19041-1614 Office: Hosp U Pa 3400 Spruce St Philadelphia PA 19104-4206

MASTROIANNI, THOMAS OWEN, musician, music educator; b. Pitts., Sept. 1, 1934; s. Lawrence Andrew and Julie Agnes Mastroianni; m. MaryAnn Prosser, Jan. 25, 1964; children: Mary Lauren, Michael, Elizabeth. BS, Juilliard Sch., 1957, MS, 1958; MusD, Ind. U., 1969. Chmn. piano, chmn. applied music Tex. Tech U., Lubbock, 1961—72; prof., dean Sch. Music Cath. U. Am., Washington, 1972—81, prof., chmn. piano, 1981—2000, prof. emeritus, 2000—; co-founder, mem. faculty Amalfi Coast (Italy) Music Festival, 1995—. Found. dir. Washington Internat. Competition, 2001—. Contbr. articles to profl. publs.; , musician numerous piano recitals. Choir dir. various chs., Pitts., N.Y., Washington, 1948—73. With U.S. Army, 1958—60. Recipient medal, Hungarian Liszt Soc., 1992. Mem.: World Pedagogy Conf. (wellness com. 2001—), Nat. Assn. Schs. Music (grad. commr. 1975—81), Interam. Friends of Music (treas. 1980—), Music Tchrs.' Nat. Assn., Am. Liszt Soc. (pres. 1999—, exec. sec. 1974—99). Roman Catholic. Avocations: tennis, museums, concerts.

MASTROMARCO, DAN RALPH, lawyer, consultant; b. Saginaw, Mich., Jan. 18, 1958; s. Victor and Helen (Finkbeiner) M. Student, London Sch. of Econs., Eng., 1982; JD, U. Toledo, 1983; LLM, Georgetown U., 1985. Bar: Mich. 1983, D.C. 1984. Counsel U.S. Senate, Permanent Subcom. on Investigations, Washington, 1983-85; trial atty. Tax div. U.S. Dept. of Justice, 1985-86; asst. chief counsel for tax policy U.S. SBA, 1986-92; dir. tax and fiscal policy Jefferson Group, 1992-94; pres., CEO The Argus Group, 1994—. Coord. Nat. Adv. Coun. for Small Bus., Tax Com., 1986-88; hon. mem. tax com. Small Bus. Legis. Coun., 1986-90; adj. prof. internat. mgmt. program U. Md.; exec. dir. Travel Coun. for Fair Competition; pres. The Prosperity Inst.; exec. dir. Small Bus. Regulators Coun. Author: The Art of Lobbying in Poland, 1995, Out by Its Roots, 1999; contbr. author, editor profl. jours., reports. Mem. Nat. Italian Am. Bar Assn. (trustee scholarship fund, counsel, v.p.), U.S. C. of C. (tax policy com.). Roman Catholic. Office: TAG 333 N Fairfax St Alexandria VA 22314-2632 E-mail: drm@prosperity-institute.org.

MASTROMARCO, VICTOR JOSEPH, JR. lawyer; b. Saginaw, Mich., Oct. 29, 1956; s. Victor Joseph Sr. and Helen (Finkbeiner) M.; m. Jill Ann Schmidt, Sept. 12, 1990; 1 child, Victor Joseph III. BA, Albion Coll., 1979; JD, Drake U., 1982. Bar: Mich. 1982, Iowa 1982, U.S. Dist. Ct. (ea. dist.) Mich. 1983. Trial lawyer Cady, Mastromarco & Jahn, Saginaw. Mem. ABA, Mich. Bar Assn., Iowa Bar Assn., Saginaw County Bar Assn. Office: Cady Mastromarco & Jahn PO Box 3197 Saginaw MI 48605-3197

MASTRONARDI, CORINNE MARIE, lawyer; b. Binghamton, N.Y. d. Joseph Daniel and Frances Marie Mastronardi. BS, Liberty U., 1990; JD, Regent U ., 1993. Bar: Fla. 1994, D.C. 1996, Va. 2000. V.p. corp. affairs Va. Metro Protective Svcs., Inc., Virginia Beach, Va., 1995—; atty., pres. corp.

affairs Pro Rep., Inc., Ft. Lauderdale, Fla., 1994—; pvt. practice , 1994—. Treas. Christian Legal Soc. Republican. Office: PO Box 13176 Chesapeake VA 23325-0176 E-mail: corinne@pro-rep.com.

MASUBUCHI, KOICHI, marine engineer, educator; b. Otaru, Hokkaido, Japan, Jan. 11, 1924; s. Yosaku and Tomi (Ota) M.; m. Fumiko Kaneno, Oct. 24, 1949. BS, U. Tokyo, 1946, MS, 1948, PhD, 1959. Rsch. engr. Transp. Tech. Rsch. Inst., 1948-58; vis. fellow, cons. Battelle Meml. Inst., Columbus, Ohio, 1958-62; rsch. assoc., fellow, tech. adviser Battelle Meml. Inst., 1963-68; chief welding mechanics sect., welding div. Ship Rsch. Inst., 1962-63; assoc. prof. naval architecture MIT, Cambridge, 1968-71, prof. ocean engrng. and materials sci., 1971-89, Kawasaki prof. engrng., 1989—. Author: Materials for Ocean Engineering, 1970, Analysis of Welded Structures, 1980; co-author 2 books on residual stresses in weldments; contbr. tech. papers to profl. lit. Recipient Disting. Svc. award Transp. Tech. Rsch. Inst., Ministry Transp., Japan, 1959, Spl. award Min. of Fgn. Affairs, Japan, 1986, Order of Sacred Treasure Gold Raye with Neck Ribbon award Japanese Govt., 1995. Fellow Am. Welding Soc. (life, R.D. Thomas Meml. award 1977, established Prof. Masubuchi/Shinsho Corp. award 1991), Am. Soc. Metals Soc.; mem. Japan Welding Soc. (guest), Soc. Naval Architects and Marine Engrs., Soc. Naval Architects Japan. Home: 34 Hamilton Rd Apt 205 Arlington MA 02474-8277 Office: MIT Rm 5-219 Cambridge MA 02139

MASUCCI, JOHN ANTHONY, chemist, researcher; b. Phila., Aug. 31, 1956; s. Angelo amd America (Marra) M.; m. Jean E. O'Brien, Aug. 25, 1984; children: Jennifer A., Michelle J. BS in Chemistry, Drexel U., 1979; MS in Chemistry, Villanova U., 1988, PhD in Chemistry, 1998. Prin. scientist R.W. Johnson Pharm. Rsch. Inst., Spring House, Pa., 1983—. Contbr. author: Gas Chromatography-Mass Spectrometry, 1995. Mem. Am. Soc. Mass Spectrometry, Chromatography Forum Del. Valley, Del. Valley Mass Spectral Topics Discussion Group, Sigma XI. Roman Catholic. Achievements include discovery of novel interface for coupling capillary electrophoresis with mass spectrometry; development of novel method for coupling thin layer chromatography with mass spectrometry. Office: RW Johnson Pharm Rsch Inst Welsh & McKean Rds Spring House PA 19477

MASUD, ROBERT, lawyer; b. Havana, Cuba, Jan. 2, 1960; came to U.S., 1963; s. Roberto and Olga (Sanchez) M. B in Bus. Adminstrn., U. Miami, 1982, MBA, 1987; JD, Boston U., 1987; postgrad. Program on Negotiation, Harvard Law Sch., 1991-94. Bar: Fla. 1989, Mass. 1989, U.S. Dist. Ct. Mass 1989, U.S. Ct. Appeals (1st cir.) 1989, U.S. Dist. Ct. (so. dist.) Fla. 1991, U.S. Ct. Appeals (11th cir.) 1992, U.S. Supreme Ct. 1993, U.S. Ct. Appeals (D.C. cir.) 1994, fgn. lawyer, Law Soc. of England. Assoc. Kelley, Drye & Warren, Miami, Fla., 1987-88; founder, operating mgr. Masud & Co., LLC (formerly Masud & Assoc.), Boston, 1989—, Miami, 1992—2000; founder, prin. Masud & Co., London, 2001—. Spkr. in field. Contbr. to profl. jours. Dep. gen. counsel Mass. Rep. Party, Boston, 1993-94; co-chmn. exploratory com. Dole for Pres., 1995-96; bd. dirs. Assn. Kepha, The Vatican, Rome, 1998-2001, Fondazione Kepha, The Vatican, 2001—. U. Miami scholar, 1977-82. Mem. ABA (vice chmn. arts entertainment sports law com. 1992-95), Inter-Am. Bar Assn., Fla. Bar Assn., Mass. Bar Assn., Boston Bar Assn., Dade County Bar Assn., Alpha Lambda Delta, Phi Eta Sigma. Avocations: skiing, golfing, traveling, racquetball, magic. Office: Masud & Co LLC 60 State St Ste 700 Boston MA 02109-1800

MASUDA, TAKESHI See ASKA, WARABÉ

MASUR, HENRY, internist; b. N.Y.C., Mar. 8, 1946; s. Jack and Barbara (Forsch) M.; m. Grace Steinacker, Jan. 14, 1979; children: Carrie, Jack, Julia. AB, Dartmouth Coll., 1968; MD, Cornell U., 1972. Diplomate Am. Bd. Internal Medicine, Am. Bd. Infectious Diseases. Intern, resident N.Y. Hosp., 1972-74; resident Johns Hopkins Hosp., Balt., 1974-75; asst. prof. Cornell Med. Coll., N.Y.C., 1978-82; asst. chief critical care medicine NIH, Bethesda, Md., 1982-83, dep. chief critical care medicine, 1983-89, chief critical care medicine, 1989—. Clin. prof. George Washington U. Med. Sch., Washington. Mem. Am. Soc. Clin. Investigation, Assn. Am. Physicians. Office: NIH Rm 7D43 9000 Rockville Pike Bethesda MD 20892-1662 E-mail: hmasur@nih.gov.

MASUREL, JEAN-LOUIS ANTOINE NICOLAS, investment company executive; b. Cannes, France, Sept. 18, 1940; s. Antoine and Anne-Marie (Gallant) M.; children: Anne-Sophie, Aude. Grad., Ecoles des Hautes Etudes Commerciales, 1962; MBA, Harvard U., 1964. With Morgan Guaranty Trust Co., N.Y.C., 1964-80, v.p., gen. mgr. Paris, 1975-78, sr. v.p., 1978-80; sr. exec. v.p. Banque de Paribas, 1980-82; dep. pres. Banque Pays-Bas, 1982-83; mng. dir. Moët-Hennessy, 1983-87, Moët-Hennessy-Louis Vuitton, 1987-89; pres. Arcos Investissement S.A., 1989—, Hediard S.A., 1991-95. Bd. dirs. Peugot S.A., Soc. des Bains de Mer (SBM) Monaco, Banque du Gothard Monaco, Oudart S.A. Bd. govs. Am. Hosp., Paris; hon. chmn., dir. Harvard Bus. Sch. Club France. Address: 31 rue Raynouard 75016 Paris France

MASYS, DANIEL RICHARD, medical school director; b. Columbus, Ohio, Mar. 6, 1949; s. Paul John and Jane Marie (Mollenauer) M.; m. Linda Suzanne Bross, June 2, 1974; 1 child, Christopher. AB in Biochemistry, Princeton U., 1971; MD, Ohio State U., 1974. Diplomate Am. Bd. Internal Medicine. Staff hematologist, oncologist U.S. Naval Hosp., San Diego, 1980-84; chief ICRDB br. NIH, Bethesda, Md., 1984-86; dir. Lister Hill Nat. Ctr. Nat. Libr. Medicine, 1986-94; dir. biomed. informatics, prof. Sch. Medicine U. Calif., San Diego, 1994—. Assoc. editor Acad. Medicine jour., 1988-91. Mem. high performance computing White House Office of Sci., Washington, 1991-94; rep. Fed. Networking Coun., Washington, 1991-94. Capt. USPHS, 1984-94. Fellow: ACP, Am. Coll. Med. Informatics (exec. com. 1989—92); mem.: Nat. Acad. Scis., Inst. Medicine, Am. Med. Informatics Assn. (bd. dirs. 1992—95, assoc. editor jour. 1993—, Pres.'s award 1992), Alpha Omega Alpha. Office: U Calif San Diego Sch Medicine Basic Sci 9500 Gilman Dr La Jolla CA 92093-0602

MATA, DAVID JOSEPH, physician; b. Houston, Feb. 3, 1956; s. José and Josephine M.; m. Judith Symons, Sept. 9, 1978; children: Daniel José, Timothy John. BA in Biology, Point Loma Coll., 1978; postgrad., Calif. State U., L.A., 1978-80; MD, U. Minn., 1987. Diplomate Am. Bd. Family Practice, Nat. Bd. Med. Examiners. Resident in family medicine San Bernardino (Calif.) County Med. Ctr., 1987-90; med. dir. Salud Med. Ctr., Woodburn, Oreg., 1990-96; pvt. practice Hemet, Calif., 1996—. Adj. asst. prof. Oreg. Health Scis. U. Sch. Medicine, Portland, 1991—96; active staff mem. Salem Hosp., Oreg., 1992—96, Silverton Hosp., Oreg., 1992—96, Hemet Valley Med. Ctr., 1997—; vice-chair Family Medicine, 2000—02; cons., steering com. mem. Am. Lung Assn., Salem, 1992—94; med. dir. Ramona Manor Convalescent Hosp., 2002—. Expert witness to U.S. Congress, Oreg. Supreme Ct., 1992; counselor East L.A. Task Force, 1979-80; chaplain Boy Scouts Am., Hemet, 1998—; adv. com. San Jacinto Head Start, 1998—. Geriatric Medicine fellow U. Minn., 1985, Med. Student Rsch. tng. grantee NIH, 1985, scholar Nat. Hispanic Scholarship Found, 1987; named one of 10 Outstanding Young Ams., U.S. Jr. C. of C., 1993, Outstanding Young Person of World, 1993; recipient Golden Aztec award Oreg. Human Devel. Corp., 1993, Citation of Merit award Oreg./Pacific Dist. Ch. of Nazarene, 1993, Mentorship award Dept. Family Medicine Oreg. Health Scis. U., 1993, Disting. svc. award Ch. of the Nazarene, Woodburn, Oreg., 1996; named Family Doctor of the Yr., Oreg., 1995; recipient Congl. Tribute, U.S. Ho. of Reps., 1994. Fellow Am. Acad. Family Physicians; mem. Nazarene Health Care Fellowship, Am. Acad. Family Physicians, Northwest Regional Primary Care Assn. (clinicians com. 1990-93), Riverside County Med. Assn., Calif. Med. Assn. Democrat. Mem. Ch. of the Nazarene. Avocations: drawing, camping, family activities, church activities, public speaking. Office: Bldg B, Ste A 255 N Gilbert St Hemet CA 92543-4066

MATA, ELIZABETH ADAMS, English language educator, land investor; b. Raleigh, N.C., Jan. 11, 1946; d. John Quincy Adams and Beulah Honeycutt; m. Juan Mata, June 21, 1968; children: Laura, Juan, Daniel. Student, Sweet Briar Coll., Paris, 1966-67; BA in French, Randolph-Macon Women's Coll., 1968; tchr. cert. in French and Spanish, N.C. State U., 1981; postgrad., U. Salamanca, Spain, 1983-86; MA in Spanish, NYU, 1986; cert. mentor tchr., N.C. State U., 1989; postgrad., Fordham U., 1994, U. N.C., 1995. Lic. real estate agt., N.C.; cert. ESL tchr. Tchr. ESL, Am. Inst., Madrid, 1968-69; tchr. English, Ay J Garriques, 1968-74, pvt. classes, Madrid, 1975-78; tchr. French, Wake County Schs., Cary, NC, 1982—2002, tchr. Spanish, Apex, 1982—2002; instr. ESL Wake Tech. Coll., Raleigh, 1999—2002; Fulbright tchr. U. del Mar del Plata, Argentina, 2001—. Cons. ETS, 1999—2002. Named Tchr. of Yr., Apex H.S., 1992-93. Mem. Am. Assn. Tchrs. Spanish and Portuguese, Univ. Coun. on Edn., Alpha Kappa Delta (Beta Omicron chpt. historian 1996-98, v.p. 1998-2000). Democrat. Avocations: sculpting, reading, gourmet cooking, restoring antiques, writing. Home: 643 Kings Fork Rd Cary NC 27511-5711

MATA, JOSEFINA, health education coordinator, educator; b. Juarez, Mex., Mar. 28, 1968; came to U.S., 1979; d. Angel and Irma Ulloa; m. Jesus Antonio Mata, Aug. 29, 1989; 1 child, Lizbeth Mata. BS, N.Mex. State U., 1991, MS, 1994, MPH, 1999. News translator Sta. RZOL Radio, El Paso, 1984-86; receptionist aid San Jacinto Sch., Tex., 1985-86; nutritionist La Fe Clinic, summer 1990; gang prevention and intervention counselor Families and Youth Inc., Las Cruces, N.Mex., 1992-93; health educator Adolescent Family Life, 1993-95; health edn. and quality inspection coord. Ben Archer Health Ctr., Truth or Consequences, N.Mex., 1995-98; health edn. coord. La Clinica Familia, Las Cruces, 1998—. Mem. adv. bds. Corp. Extend in Svc., Las Cruces, 1993, Health Sci. Dept. N.Mex. State U., Las Cruces, 1995-98, Sierra County Adv. Sch., 1995-98, Am. Cancer Soc., Sierra County, N.Mex., 1995-98. Mem. cmty. involvement Kellog Found. N.Mex. state U., 1997; mem. Nat. Faculty Comenzando Bien March of Dimes Initiative. Grantee N.Mex. Dept. Health, 1994, 98, N.Mex. Teen Pregnancy Coalition peer edn. program, 1996-98; recipient Marathon Participation award Leukemia Soc. Am., 1996. Mem. MPH Assn., Am. Pub. Health Assn., USA Track & Field Assn., Mesilla Valley Track Club, Tobacco Free Coalition. Roman Catholic. Avocation: road racing. Office: La Clinica Familia 1100 S Main St Ste A Las Cruces NM 88005-2952

MATALON, MARLENE, artist; b. Bronx, N.Y., Sept. 22, 1935; d. Michael and Sonia (Dibner) Friedman; m. Victor Matalon, 1954 (dec. Mar. 1979); children: Jhan Craig, Michele; m. Sidney A. Taylor, Feb. 13, 1981. BFA, U. Houston, 1968; postgrad., Glassell Sch., 1968-70. Instr. art and art history dept. Rice U., 1975; slide reviewer Dorland Mt. Colony residencies. One-woman shows include Brookhaven Coll. Gallery, Dallas, 1990, Dakota Gallery, Houston, 1994, Martin Mus., Waco, Tex., 1994, Autour du Papier, Paris, 1996, Sicardi-Sanders Gallery, 1997, Joan Wich Gallery, 1999, 2001, Two Painters at Morgan Personette, 2000, Summertime Group, 2000, Houston Pub. Art Commn., 2002, prin. works include Compaq Computer Corp., SAP Am., Houston Industries; tech. editor: Gilded Wood, Conservation and History, 1991. Adv. bd. Houston Womens Caucus for Art, 1981—83; visual arts com. reviewing grant applications Cultural Arts Commn. Funding, 1998—2001, co-curator Spanish colonial treasures, 1992. Mem. Am. Inst. for Conservation, Inst. Paper Conservation. Avocations: books, contemporary dance, music, film. Home: 4610 Banning Dr Houston TX 77027-4706

MATAN, LILLIAN KATHLEEN, educator, designer; b. Boston, Aug. 18, 1937; d. George Francis and Lillian May (Herbert) Archambault; m. Joseph A. Matan, Aug. 6, 1960; children: Maria, Meg, Tony, Elizabeth, Joan, Molly. BS, Seton Hall Coll., 1960; MA, San Francisco State U., 1984; EdD, U. San Francisco, 1999. Tchr. St. Jane de Chantal, Bethesda, Md., 1956-60; tchr. home econs. Surrottsville (Md.) H.S., 1960-61; tchr., head home econs. dept. Bruswick (Md.) H.S., 1972-73; designer Dudley Kelley and Assocs., San Francisco, 1976-84; designer (prin.) K. Matan Antiques and Interiors, Ross, 1985-87; designer Charles Lester Assocs., San Francisco, 1987-88; dean of students St. Rose Acad., 1988-90; dir., asst. devel. The Branson Sch., Ross, Calif., 1990-92; prin. St. Anselm Sch., San Anselmo, 1993-94; adminstrv. head Ring Mt. Day Sch., Tiburon, 1995-96; sabbatical, 1997-98. Ednl. cons. Head Start, Frederick County, Md., 1972-73. Pres. Cath. Charities, Marin County, Calif.; mem. Ecumenical Assn. for Housing, Marin County. Mem. KM (dame), Am. Soc. of Interior Designers, Am. Assn. Family and Consumer Scis., Serra Club, Phi Delta Kappa. Democrat. Home: PO Box 1140 Ross CA 94957-1140 E-mail: lmatan6561@aol.com.

MATARAZZO, HARRIS STARR, lawyer; b. Portland, Oreg., July 24, 1957; s. Joseph Dominic and Ruth Wood (Gadbois) M.; m. Judith Grace Hudson, Jan. 2, 1988. AB in Polit. Sci., Brown U., 1979; JD, Northwestern Sch. Law, Portland, 1983. Bar: Oreg. 1986, U.S. Dist. Ct. Oreg. 1986, U.S. Ct. Appeals (9th cir.) 1986, U.S. Supreme Ct. 1992. With Aitchison, Imperati, Paull, Barnett and Sherwood, Portland, 1986; assoc. Parks & Bauer, Salem, Oreg., 1987-88; pvt. practice Portland, 1988—. Sprk. Mental Health and the Law conf. Med. Ednl. Svcs., Inc., 1995, 96. Contbr. to Criminal Law Handbook, 1994, 98. Mem. Hist. Preservation League Oreg., Portland, 1984—, Oreg. State Pub. Interest Rsch. Group, Portland, 1985—, The Old Ch. Soc., Portland, 1986; bd. dirs. Bosco Milligan Found., 1992—, Rape Survivors Inc., 1994, Lincoln H.S. Alumni Assn., 1995—, Morrison Ctr., 1996-2001, Network Housing, Inc., 1998—, Oreg. Advocacy Ctr., 1998, 2000—, Italian Business-men's Club, 1998—, InAct, Inc., 1998—, Rosemont Treatment Ctr. and Sch., 1998-99, Friends of Simon Benson House, 1998—, Parents Anonymous, 2001—; mem. vestry Trinity Episcopal Ch., 1992-95, 2001—; mem. Oreg. Advocacy Ctr. Mental Health Adv. Coun., 1996-2000; mem. planned giving com. Multnomah County Libr., 1997—. Mem. ABA, Fed. Bar Assn., Oreg. State Bar Assn., Oreg. Criminal Def. Lawyers Assn. (spkr. State of Mind. conf. 1990, Property Crimes conf. 1999), Multnomah County Bar Assn. Office: Bank Am Fin Ctr 121 SW Morrison St Ste 1020 Portland OR 97204-3140

MATARAZZO, JOSEPH DOMINIC, psychologist, educator; b. Caiazzo, Italy, Nov. 12, 1925; (parents Am. citizens); s. Nicholas and Adeline (Mastroianni) M.; m. Ruth Wood Gadbois, Mar. 26, 1949; children: Harris, Elizabeth, Sara. Student, Columbia U., 1944; BA, Brown U., 1946; MS, Northwestern U., 1950, PhD, 1952. Fellow in med. psychology Washington U. Sch. Medicine, 1950-51; instr. Washington U., 1951-53, asst. prof., 1953-55; rsch. assoc. Harvard Med. Sch., assoc. psychologist Mass. Gen. Hosp., 1955-57; prof., head med. psychol. dept. Oreg. Health Scis. U., Portland, 1957-96, prof. behavioral neurosci., 1996—. Mem. behavioral medicine study sect. NIH; mem. nat. mental health adv. coun. NIMH; mem. bd. regents Uniformed Svcs. U. Health Scis., 1974-80. Author: Wechsler's Measurement and Appraisal of Adult Intelligence, 5th edit., 1972, (with A.N. Wiens) The Interview: Research on its Anatomy and Structure, 1972, (with Harper and Wiens) Nonverbal Communication, 1978; editor: Behavioral Health: A Handbook of Health Enhancement and Disease Prevention, 1984; editorial bd.: Jour. Clin. Psychology, 1962-96 ; cons. editor: Contemporary Psychology, 1962-70, 80-93, Intelligence: An Interdisciplinary Jour, 1976-90, Jour. Behavioral Medicine, 1977— , Profl. Psychology, 1978-94, Jour. Cons. and Clin. Psychology, 1978-85; editor: Psychology series Aldine Pub. Co, 1964-74; psychology editor: Williams & Wilkins Co, 1974-77; contbr. articles to psychol. jours. With USNR, 1943-47; capt. Res. Recipient Hofheimer prize Am. Psychiat. Assn., 1962 Fellow AAAS, APA (pres. 1989-90, divsn. health psychology 1978-89, mem. coun. reps. 1982-91, bd. dirs. 1986-90, Ann. Disting. Profl. Contbn. award 1991, Annual Gold Medal for Life Achievement in the Application of Psychology 2001); mem. Western Psychol. Assn. (pres. 1986-97), Am. Assn. State Psychology Bds. (pres. 1963-64), Nat. Assn. Mental Health (bd. dirs.), Oreg. Mental Health Assn. (bd. dirs., pres. 1962-63), Internat. Coun. Psychologists (bd. dirs. 1972-74, pres. 1976-77), Am. Psychol. Found. (pres. 1994-2000). Home: 1934 SW Vista Ave Portland OR 97201-2455 Office: Oreg Health Scis U Sch Medicine 3181 SW Sam Jackson Park Rd Portland OR 97201-3011 Fax: 503-494-5972. E-mail: matarazz@ohsu.edu.

MATARAZZO, LINDA MARIE, poet; b. Lynn, Mass., Dec. 28, 1961; d. Richard Carroll Penkul and Nina Ann Gianni. Student, Harvard U., 2000—. Author: The Windham Collection, 2001; contbr. numerous poems to anthologies including the Ever Flowing Stream, 1998, The Long and Winding Rodad, 1999, The Dawn of Inspiration, 1999, From the Mountain Top, 2000, Poetry's Elite, 2000, Natures Echoes, 2001. Grantee Mass. Local Cultural Coun., 1999. Mem. The Acad. of Am. Poets. Avocation: gardening.

MATARÉ, HERBERT F. physicist, consultant; b. Aachen, Germany, Sept. 22, 1912; came to U.S., 1953; s. Josef P. and Paula (Broicher) M.; m. Ursula Krenzien, Dec. 1939; children: Felicitas, Vitus; m. Elise Walbert, Dec. 1983; 1 child, Victor B. BS in Physics, Chemistry and Math., Aachen U. Geneva, 1933; MS in Tech. Physics, U. Aachen, 1939; PhD in Electronics, Tech. U. Berlin, 1942; PhD in Solid State Physics summa cum laude, Ecole Normale Supérieure, Paris, 1950. Asst. prof. physics & electronics Tech. U. Aachen, 1936, 45; head of microwave receiver lab. Telefunken, A.G., Berlin, 1939-46; mgr. semicondr. lab. Westinghouse, Paris, 1946-52; founder, pres. Intermetall Corp., Düsseldorf, Fed. Republic Germany, 1952-56; head semincondr. R & D, corp. rsch. labs. Gen. Telephone & Electronics Co., N.Y.C., 1956-59; dir. rsch. semicondr. dept. Tekade, Nürnberg, Fed. Republic Germany, 1959-61; head quantum physics dept. rsch. labs. Bendix Corp., Southfield, Mich., 1961-64; tech. dir., acting mgr. hybrid microelectronics rsch. labs. Lear Siegler, Santa Monica, Calif., 1963-64; asst. chief engr. advance electronics dept. Douglas Aircraft Co., 1964-66; tech. dir. McDonnell Douglas Missile Div., 1964-69; sci. advisor to solid state electronics group Autonetics (Rockwell Internat.), Anaheim, Calif., 1966-69; pres. Internat. Solid State Electronics Cons., L.A., 1973—. Prof. electronics U. Buenos Aires, 1953-54; vis. prof. UCLA, 1968-69, Calif. State U., Fullerton, 1969-70; dir. Compound Crystals Ltd., London, 1989—; cons. UN Indsl. Devel. Orgn. to 15 Indian insts. and semiconductor cos. with conf. talks at India Inst. Tech., New Delhi and Bombay, 1978. Author: Receiver Sensitivity in the UHF, 1951, Defect Electronics in Semiconductors, 1971, Conscientious Evolution, 1978, Energy, Facts and Future, 1989, (with P. Faber) Renewable Energies, 1993, Bioethics: The Ethics of Evolution and Genetic Interference, 1999; patentee of about 60 patents including first European transistor (1948), first vacuum growth of silicon crystals with levitation, growth of bicrystals, first low temperature transistor with bicrystals, optical heterodyning with bicrystals, first crystal TV transmission link, first color TV transmission over fiber with LEDs and bicrystals, liquid phase epitaxy for LEDs and batch process for III-V-solar cells; contbr. over 100 articles to profl. jours. Fellow IEEE (life); mem. AAAS, IEEE Nuclear Plasma Scis. Soc., IEEE Power Engrng. Soc., Inst. for Advancement of Man (hon.), Am. Phys. Soc. (solid state div.), Electrochem. Soc., Am. Vacuum Soc. (thin film div.), Materials Rsch. Soc., N.Y. Acad. Scis. (emeritus). Avocations: astrophysics, biology, classical music, piano. Office: ISSEC PO Box 2661 Malibu CA 90265-7661 E-mail: hf.matare@verizon.net.

MATARESE, LAUREN A. police officer, lawyer; b. Framingham, Mass., Dec. 15, 1960; BS summa cum laude, Roger Williams Coll., 1991; JD cum laude, New England Sch. Law, 1995. Bar: RI 1996, Conn. 1997, U.S. Dist. Ct. R.I. 1997, U.S. Supreme Ct. 2002. Police officer Westerly (R.I.) Police Dept. Mem. Internat. Brotherhood Police Officers, R.I. Bar Assn., Conn. Bar Assn., Delta Theta Phi. Avocations: softball, bicycling. Office: Westerly Police Dept 5 Union St Westerly RI 02891-2158

MATAS, MYRA DOROTHEA, interior architect, designer, consultant; b. San Francisco, Mar. 21, 1938; d. Arthur Joseph and Marjorie Dorothy (Johnson) Anderson; m. Michael Richard Matas Jr., Mar. 15, 1958; children: Michael Richard III, Kenneth Scott. Cert. interior design, Canada Coll.; cert. interior design, Calif. Owner, operator Miguel's Antiques Co., Millbrae, Calif., 1969-70, Miguel's Antiques & Interiors Co., Burlingame, 1979-79, Country Elegance Antiques and Interiors Co., Menlo Park, 1979-84, La France Boutique Co., 1979-84; owner, operator, interior designer, archtl. designer Myra D. Matas Interior Design, San Francisco, 1984-2000, Lafayette, La., 1994—; mgr. LaFrance Imports, Inc., 1982-92; pres., gen. contractor Artisans 3 Inc., Burlingame, 1988-92; gen. contractor Matas Constr., Millbrae, 1993-98; instr. interior design dept. Canada Coll. Contbr. articles in field to profl. jours. Mem. Calif. Coun. Interior or Design. Office: 1616 Hwy 31 Arnaudville LA 70512 also: 324 rue Jefferson Lafayette LA 70501 E-mail: robinplantation@earthlink.net.

MATASA, CLAUDE GEORGE, researcher, science administrator, educator; b. Romania, Apr. 1, 1930; s. George D. and Marguerite A. (Aurand) M.; m. Eugenia Tonca (div.); m. Netty Matasa. Chem. Engr., Polytechnic U., Bucharest, Romania, 1949-54, Polytechnic U., Timisoara, Romania, 1965-70; D in Tech. Sci., Polytechnic U., Vienna, Austria, 1970-72; D in Chem. Engrng. (hon.), Ecologic U., Bucharest, 1994. Rsch. engr., sr. rsch. engr., head rsch. and devel. Chem. Combine of Craiova and the Synthetic FibersWorks of Savinesti, 1954-70; cons. Chem. Construction Corp., Corpus Christi, Tex., 1970-73; rsch. scientist Unitek Corp., Monrovia, Calif., 1973-76; chief rsch. chem. dept. Consol. Aluminum Corp. Sci. Ctr., St. Louis, 1977-79; chief rsch. Imperial Coatings Corp., New Orleans, 1979-82; pres. Ortho-Cycle Co., 1982—; prof. Univ., Bucharest, Romania, 1990, U. Ill., Chgo., 1995—, Nova Southeastern U., Fla., 1998—. Cons., referee Am. Journal of Orthodontics and Dentofacial Orthopedics, Chgo., 1986—; lectr. M. Richter Courses for the Austrian, German, and Swiss orthodontists, U. Innsbruck, Austria, 1990; guest lectr., rsch. cons. David B. Kriser Dental Ctr., NYU, 1991; internat. cons. Journal of Orthopedics-Orthodontics and Pediatric Dentistry, Caracas, Venezuela, 1995; vis. prof. U. Pa., Phila., 1996-97; hon. vis. prof. Valahia U., Targovista, Romania. Author: 2 books; editor: The Orthodontic Materials Insider, 1987—; contbr. over 100 articles to profl. jours. Mem. AAAS, Am. Chem. Soc., Am. Soc. for Materials, Romanian-Am. Acad., Romanian Acad. Sci., Acad. Medicine of Romania (hon.). Home: 1507 Hollywood Blvd Hollywood FL 33020-5239 Office: Ortho-Cycle Co 2026 Scott St Hollywood FL 33020-2417

MATASAR, ANN B. former dean, business and political science educator; b. N.Y.C., June 27, 1940; d. Harry and Tillie (Simon) Bergman; m. Robert Matasar, June 9, 1962; children— Seth Gideon, Toby Rachel AB, Vassar Coll., 1962; MA, Columbia U., 1964, PhD, 1968; M of Mgmt. in Fin., Northwestern U., 1977. Assoc. prof. Mundelein Coll., Chgo., 1965-78; prof., dir. Ctr. for Bus. and Econ. Elmhurst Coll., Elmhurst, Ill., 1978-84; dean Roosevelt U., Chgo., 1984-92; prof. Internat. Bus. and Fin. Walter E. Heller Coll. Bus. Adminstrn. Roosevelt U., 1992—. Dir. Corp. Responsibility Group, Chgo., 1978-84; chmn. long range planning Ill. Bar Assn., 1982-83; mem. edn. com. Ill. Commn. on the Status of Women, 1978-81 Author: Corporate PACS and Federal Campaign Financing Laws: Use or Abuse of Power?, 1986; (with others) Research Guide to Women's Studies, 1974, (with others) The Impact of Geographic Deregulation on the American Banking Industry, 2002; contbr. articles to profl. jours. Dem. candidate 1st legis. dist. Ill. State Senate, no. suburbs Chgo., 1972; mem. Dem. exec. com. New Trier Twp., Ill., 1972-76; rsch. dir., acad. advisor Congressman Abner Mikva, Ill., 1974-76; bd. dirs. Ctr. Ethics and Corp. Policy, 1985-90. Named Chgo. Woman of Achievement, Mayor of Chgo., 1978. Fellow AAUW (trustee ednl. found. 1992-97, v.p. fin. 1993-97); mem. Am. Polit. Sci. Assn., Midwest Bus. Adminstrn. Assn., Acad. Mgmt., Women's Caucus for Polit. Sci. (pres. 1980-81), John Howard Assn. (bd. dirs. 1986-90), Am. Assembly of Coll. Schs. of Bus. (bd. dirs. 1989-92, chair com. on diversity in mgmt. edn. 1991-92), North Ctrl. Assn. (commr. 1994-97), Beta Gamma Sigma. Democrat. Jewish. Avocations: jogging, biking, tennis, opera, crosswords. Office: Roosevelt U Coll Bus Adminstrn Dept Fin 430 S Michigan Ave Chicago IL 60605-1394 E-mail: amatasar@roosevelt.edu.

MATASEJE, VERONICA JULIA, sales executive; b. St. Ann's, Ontario, Can., Apr. 5, 1949; came to U.S., 1985; d. John and Anna Veronica M. Grad. H.S., Smithville, Can. Clk. typist, typesetter Crown Life Ins. Co., Toronto, Can., 1966-70; typesetter Toronto Life/Calendar Mag., 1970-71; typesetter, exec. sec. Cerebrus Prodns. Ltd., Toronto, 1971-74; pres. Veron Prodns. Ltd., 1975-81, Acclaim Records Inc., Toronto, 1981-88; pvt. health care provider Las Vegas, Nev., 1989-94; retail sales mgr. Top Cats, 1994-00; pres. Abracadabra Music Corp., 2000—. Campaign vol. Dist. Atty., Las Vegas, 1994; vol. pilot Angel Planes, Las Vegas, 1989. Avocations: gardening, interior design, showing cats, travel, music. Home: 4326 Caliente St Las Vegas NV 89119-5801 Office: Top Cats PO Box 61173 Las Vegas NV 89160-1173 E-mail: vm@abracadabramusic.com.

MATASOVIC, MARILYN ESTELLE, business executive; b. Chgo., Jan. 7, 1946; d. John Lewis and Stella (Butkauskas) M. Student, U. Colo. Sch. Bus., 1963-69. Owner, pres. UTE Trail Ranch, Ridgway, Colo., 1967—; pres. MEM Equipment Co., Mokena, Ill., 1979—; sec./treas. Marlin Corp., Ridgway, 1991—, v.p., sec.-treas., 1991—, pres., 1994—; sec.-treas. Linmar Corp., Mokena, 1991-93, pres., 1994—; ptnr. Universal Welding Supply Co., New Lenox, Ill., 1964-90; v.p. OXO Welding Equipment Co, Inc., 1964-90; ptnr. Universal Internat., Mokena, Ill., 1990—; ind. travel agt. Ideal Travel Concepts, 1994—; mgr. Hereford Works Warehouse, 1997—, owner, 2001—, Barnyardblvd.com, 2001—. Co-editor newsletters. U.S. rep. World Hereford Conf., 1964, 68, 76, 80, 84, 96. Recipient Outstanding Hereford Woman award, 1999. Mem. Am. Hereford Aux. (charter, bd. dirs. 1989-94, historian 1990-92, v.p. 1992, pres.-elect 1993, pres. 1994), Am. Hereford Women (charter, pres. 1994, bd. dirs. 1994-96, award 1999), Am. Agri-Women, Colo.

Hereford Aux., Ill. Hereford Aux. (sec. 1969-70, publicity 1970-72), U. Colo. Alumni Assn., Ill. Agri-Women, Las Vegas Social Register. Avocations: showing cattle, computers, travel. E-mail: herefordworks@usa.net.

MATAYOSHI, CORALIE CHUN, lawyer, bar association executive; b. Honolulu, June 2, 1956; d. Peter J. and Daisy (Look) Chun; m. Ronald F. Matayoshi, Aug. 8, 1981; children: Scot, Kelly, Alana. BA, U. Calif., Berkeley, 1978; JD, U. Calif., San Francisco, 1981. Bar: Hawaii 1981, U.S. Dist. Ct. Hawaii 1981. Trial atty. U.S. Dept. Justice Antitrust, Washington, 1981-84; assoc. Chun, Kerr, & Dodd, Honolulu, 1984-86; exec. dir. Hawaii Inst. of CLE, 1987-90, Hawaii State Bar Assn., Honolulu, 1990—. Arbitrator Ct. Annexed Arbitration Program, Honolulu, 1992—; adv. bd. Channel 2 TV Action Line, Honolulu, 1993-96. Contbr. chapters to books. Bd. dirs. Neighborhood Justice Ctr., 1994-97, mediator, 1997—. Office: Hawaii State Bar Assn 1132 Bishop St Ste 906 Honolulu HI 96813-2814

MATCHETT, ANDREW JAMES, mathematics educator; b. Chgo., Jan. 30, 1950; s. Gerald James and Margaret Ellen (Stump) M.; m. Nancy Valentine Stasack, Aug. 7, 1976; children: Gerald Albert, Philip Joseph, Melanie Jeanne. BS, U. Chgo., 1971; PhD, U. Ill., 1976. Grad. teaching asst. U. Ill., Urbana, 1971-76; asst. prof. Tex. A&M U., College Station, 1976-82, U. Wis., La Crosse, 1982-86, assoc. prof., 1986—; grad. teaching asst. U. Ill., Urbana, 1971-76. Dir. Consortium for Core Math. Curriculum, Wis., 1987-88. Contbr. articles to profl. jours. Chmn. troop 18 com. Boy Scouts Am., La Crosse, 1990, charter rep. troop 18, 1992-94, scoutmaster, 1994-97, mem. com., 1997—. Mem. AAAS, Am. Math. Soc., Am. Statis. Assn., Math. Assn. Am. (sec.-treas. Wis. sect. 1989—, admin. 1999—). Unitarian Universalist. Achievements include development of a theory of class group homomorphisms. Avocations: astronomy, skiing, ice skating, backpacking. Home: 327 24th St N La Crosse WI 54601-3850 Office: U Wis Dept Math 1725 State St La Crosse WI 54601 E-mail: matchett@math.uwlax.edu.

MATCHETT, WILLIAM H(ENRY), English literature educator; b. Chgo., Mar. 5, 1923; s. James Chapman and Lucy H. (Jipson) M.; m. Judith Wright, June 11, 1949; children: David H., Katherine C., Stephen C. BA with highest honors, Swarthmore Coll., 1949; MA, Harvard U., 1950, PhD, 1957. Teaching fellow Harvard U., Cambridge, Mass., 1953-54; instr. English lit. U. Wash., Seattle, 1954-56, asst. prof., 1956-61, assoc. prof., 1961-66, prof., 1966-82, prof. emeritus, 1982—. Author: The Phoenix and the Turtle, 1965, Fireweed, 1980; numerous poems and articles; co-author: Poetry: From Statement to Meaning, 1965; editor: Modern Lang. Quar., Seattle, 1964-82. Mem. Soc. Friends. Home: 1017 Minor Ave Apt 702 Seattle WA 98104-1303

MATCHIE, THOMAS FREDERICK, English educator; b. Fargo, N.D., Dec. 16, 1933; s. Timothy Patrick and Agatha Catherine (Dewey) M.; m. Michelle Christian, May 26, 1973; children: James, Mary Pat, Thomas, Michael. BA, St. John's U., Collegeville, Minn., 1957; MA, Moorhead (Minn.) State U., 1967; PhD, U. Wis., 1973. Tchr. English Stanley H.S., Fargo, 1962-67; prof. English N.D. State U., 1971—. Contbr. articles to profl. jours. Rep., sen. N.D. Legis., Fargo, 1976-86. Recipient Outstanding Rsch. and Creativity award Coll. Humanities and Social Svcs., N.D. State U., 1998, Outstanding Educator award, N.D. State U. Alumni Bd., 1999. Mem. AAUP, MLA, Linguistic Cir. of N.D. and Man. Democrat. Roman Catholic. Avocation: tennis. Home: 1218 N 11-1/2 St N Fargo ND 58102-2550 E-mail: tom.matchie@ndsu.nodak.edu.

MATEAS, KENNETH EDWARD, lawyer; b. Aurora, Ill., May 7, 1949; s. Victor Joseph and Lois Rose (Carder) M. BA, U. Ill., 1971; JD, John Marshall Sch. of Law, 1982. Bar: Ill. 1982, D.C. 1982. Assoc. Law Offices of J. Timothy Loats, Aurora, 1982-83, Law Offices of Michael Marsh, Aurora, 1983-84; atty. Kane County States Atty.'s Office, Geneva, 1985; assoc. Law Offices of Gerard Kepple, St. Charles, 1985-89; pvt. practice, Aurora, 1989—. Mem. ABA, Ill. Bar Assn., Nat. Assn. Criminal Def. Lawyers. Lodges: KC. Republican. Roman Catholic. Office: 408 N Lake St Aurora IL 60506-4106

MATEER, DON METZ, lawyer; b. Evanston, Ill., July 29, 1945; s. Bruce DeLoss and Ann M.; m. Dawn Rebecca Hallsten, Oct. 4, 1981; children: Andrew, Alexandra; m. Jacquelyn Susan Henkin, June 7, 1969 (div. Apr. 1981); children: Kristin, Julie. BA, U. Mich., 1967; JD, U. Ill., 1971. Bar: Ill. 1971, U.S. Dist. Ct. (no. dist.) Ill. 1972, U.S. Ct. Appeals (7th cir.) 1974, U.S. Supreme Ct. 1981. Assoc. Gilbert & Powers, Rockford, Ill., 1971-74; ptnr. Gilbert, Powers & Mateer, 1975, Gilbert, Powers, Mateer & Erickson, Rockford, 1976, Mateer & Erickson, Rockford, 1978-90, Mateer & Assocs., Rockford, 1990—. Arbitrator 17th Jud. Cir. State of Ill., 1988—, mediator, 1992—. Precinct and ward coord. mayoral campaign, Rockford, 1980-84; campaign chmn. Rockford Park Dist. Commr., 1989; bd. dirs. Covenant Children's Home, 1987-93, v.p. 1990-91, pres. 1991-93, chair 100 Hole Golf Marathon fundraiser, 1994-98, mem. fund devel. com., 1994-99, investment adv. com., 1996-2001; mem. Protestant Cmty. Svcs., 1986-92, chmn. pers. com. 1987-89, v.p. 1989-90, pres. 1990-92; mem. Bethesda Covenant Ch., chmn. bd. Christian edn., 1986-88, v.p. 1997-99, pres. 1999-2001, chmn. futures task force, 2001-. Mem. ABA (vice-chair trial techniques com. tort and ins. practice sect., judge for final rounds of the nat. appellate adv. competition, 1991), Am. Arbitration Assn. (arbitrator), Winnebago County Bar Assn. (chmn. jud. liaison com. 1986-87), Ill. Bar Assn. (assembly mem. 1988-94), Assn. Trial Lawyers, Am. Def. Rsch. Inst., Ill. Def. Counsel, Union League Club, Forest Hills Country Club, U. Mich. Club (bd. dirs. 1986-92, 98—, v.p. 1989-90, 98-99, pres. 1990-91, 1999-2000). Democrat. Home: 2006 Oxford St Rockford IL 61103-4833 Office: Mateer & Assocs Enterprise Bldg 401 W State St Ste 400 Rockford IL 61101-1240

MATEJA, JOHN FREDERICK, university official, science educator; b. New Castle, Pa., June 3, 1950; s. Frederick Stanley and Dorothy Ann (Simonik) M.; m. Sara Ann King, Dec. 17, 1978; children: John F., Sara J. BS in Physics, U. Notre Dame, 1972, PhD in Nuclear Physics, 1976. Postdoctoral rsch. assoc. Fla. State U., Tallahassee, 1976-78; prof. physics Tenn. Technol. U., Cookeville, Tenn., 1978-88, Murray (Ky.) State U., 1998—; faculty and student program leader Argonne (Ill.) Nat. Lab., 1988-98; dean Coll. Sci., Engring. and Tech. Murray (Ky.) State U., 1998—2001, dir. Undergrad. Rsch. and Scholarly Activities Office, 2001—. Councilor Coun. on Undergrad. Rsch., 1986—, pres., 1993-94; exec. com. Dept. of Energy, Sci. and Engring. Rsch. Semester, Washington, 1988-96; mem. adv. bd. sci. engring. and health Ana G. Mendez U. Sys., 1995—. Contbr. articles to profl. jours. Grantee Dept. Energy, Tenn. Technol. U., 1980-86. Mem. Am. Phys. Soc., Sigma Xi (pres. local chpt. 1984-85), Sigma Pi Sigma, Omicron Delta Kappa. Home: 1311 Fleetwood Dr Murray KY 42071-4705 Office: Murray State U Office of Dean Coll Sci Engring and Tech Murray KY 42071 E-mail: john.mateja@murraystate.edu.

MATEJU, JOSEPH FRANK, hospital administrator; b. Cedar Rapids, Iowa, Oct. 18, 1927; s. Joseph Frank and Adeline (Smid) M. BA, U. N.Mex., 1951; MA, N.Mex. State U., 1957. Sr. juvenile probation officer, San Diego County, 1958-64; adminstr. Villa Solano State Sch., Hagerman, N.Mex., 1965-67; state coordinator on mental retardation planning N.Mex. Dept. Hosps. and Instns., Santa Fe, 1969-70; adminstr. Los Lunas (N.Mex.) Hosp. and Tng. Sch., 1968-69, 70-85. Pres., bd. dirs. Intercare. Bd. dirs. Mountain-Plains region Deaf-Blind Program. Served with USAAF, 1946-47. Fellow Am. Assn. Mental Deficiency; fellow Am. Coll. Nursing Home Adminstrs.; mem. Am. Assn. Retarded Children, Albuquerque Assn. Retarded Citizens, N.Mex. Hosp. Assn., Pi Gamma Mu. Home: 405 Fontana Pl NE Albuquerque NM 87108-1168

MATELAN, MATHEW NICHOLAS, software engineer; b. Stephenville, Tex., Aug. 21, 1945; s. Mathew Albert and Mary Frances (Hardwick) M.; m. Lois Margaret Waguespack, Apr. 5, 1975; children: Evelyn Nicole, Eleanor Gillian. BS in Physics, U. Tex., Arlington, 1969; MS in Computer Engring., So. Meth. U., 1973, PhD in Computer Sci., 1976. Sr. aerospace engr. Gen. Dynamics, Ft. Worth, 1969-75; sys. engr. Lawrence Livermore (Calif.) Labs., 1975-76; group mgr. Gen. Dynamics, Ft. Worth, 1976-78; computer R&D mgr. United Techs./Mostek, Carrollton, Tex., 1978-82; chief sys. arch. Honeywell Comm., Dallas, 1982-83; pres., CEO, chmn., co-founder Flexible Computer Corp., 1983-90; chief arch. Matelan Software Sys., 1991-94; chief engr. Expertware, Santa Clara, Calif., 1991-94; chief tech. officer Learn Techs. Interactive, N.Y.C., 1994—. Cons. Bendix Flight Controls Divsn., Teterboro, N.J., 1974-75; founding dir. Picture Telephone, Boston, 1984-86, Spectrum Digital, Washington, 1984-86; adv. bd. Axavision, N.Y.C., 1993—. Contbr. articles to profl. jours. Libr. automation bd. So. Meth. U., Dallas, 1985-86. Devel. grantee U.S. Energy Dept., 1975, NASA, 1985. Mem. IEEE (sr. mem.), Assn. for Computing Machinery. Avocations: traveling, music, skiing, aviation. Home: 3969 Courtshire Dr Dallas TX 75229-2732 Office: Learn Techs Interactive 3530 Forest Ln Ste 61 Dallas TX 75234-7950

MATELES, RICHARD ISAAC, biotechnologist; b. N.Y.C., Sept. 11, 1935; s. Simon and Jean (Phillips) M.; m. Roslyn C. Fish, Sept. 2, 1956; children: Naomi, Susan, Sarah. BS, MIT, 1956, MS, 1957, DSc, 1959. USPHS fellow Laboratorium voor Microbiologie, Technische Hogeschool, Delft, The Netherlands, 1959-60; mem. faculty MIT, 1960-70, assoc. prof. biochem. engring., 1965-68; dir. fermentation unit Jerusalem, 1968-77; prof. applied microbiology Hebrew U., Hadassah Med. Sch., 1968-80; vis. prof. dept. chem. engring. U. Pa., Phila., 1978-79; asst. dir. rsch. Stauffer Chem. Co., Westport, Conn., 1980, dir. rsch., 1980-81, v.p. rsch., 1981-88; sr. v.p. applied scis. IIT Rsch. Inst., Chgo., 1988-90; proprietor Candida Corp., 1990—. Editor: Jour. Chem. Tech. and Biotech., 1972—; editor: (N.Am. edit.) Biotech., 2001—; editor: Directory of Toll Fermentation and Cell Culture Facilities, 2001—. Penicillin: A Paradigm for Biotechnology, 1998—; contbr. articles to profl. jours. Mem. Conn. Acad. Sci. Engring., 1981—; mem. vis. com., dept. applied biol. sci. MIT, 1980-88; mem. exec. com. Coun. on Chem. Rsch., 1981-85. Fellow Am. Inst. Med. and Biol. Engring.; mem. AICE, AAAS, SAR, Am. Chem. Soc., Am. Soc. Microbiology, Soc. for Gen. Microbiology U.K., Inst. Food Technologists, Soc. Chem. Ind. (U.K.) Union League, Sigma Xi. Home: 150 W Eugenie St Apt 46 Chicago IL 60614-5843 Office: Candida Corp Ste 1310 220 S State St Chicago IL 60604 E-mail: rmateles@candida.com.

MATELIC, CANDACE TANGORRA, museum studies educator, consultant, museum director; b. Detroit, Aug. 21, 1952; d. Paul Eugene and Madeline Marie (Tangora) M.; m. Steven Joseph Mrozek, Sept. 17, 1983 (div. Sept. 1987); 1 child, Madeline Rose. BA, U. Mich., 1974; MA, SUNY, Oneonta, 1977; postgrad. doctoral studies, SUNY, Albany. Interpretive specialist Living History Farms, Des Moines, 1978-80; mgr. adult edn. Henry Ford Mus./Greenfield Village, Dearborn, Mich., 1981-82, mgr. interpretive tng., 1982-84; dir., prof. mus. studies Cooperstown grad. program SUNY, Oneonta, 1985-94; exec. dir. Mission Houses Mus., Honolulu, 1994-96, Historic St. Mary's City, Md., 1997-98; pres./CEO CTM Profl. Svcs., Inc., 1999—; founder, prin. The Cherry Valley Group, 2002—. Cons. history mus., 1979—; lectr., tchr. nat. and regional confs., workshops, seminars, 1979—; grant reviewer NEH and Inst. for Mus. Svc., Washington, 1982—; mem. guest faculty U. Victoria, B.C., 1993, 2000, 02, author distance learning course, 2002—. Author: (with others) Exhibition Reader, 1992; co-author: A Pictorical History of Food in Iowa, 1980, Survey of 1200-Plus Museum Studies Graduates, 1988; contbr. articles and videos on mus. interpretation, tng. and mentoring in mus., 1979—; author conf. proceedings. Trustee Motown Hist. Mus., 1985—; bd. dirs. Hawaii Youth Opera Chorus, 1996. Mem. Am. Assn. State and Local History (sec., bd. dirs. 1988-93, program chmn. ann meeting 1988, mem. edn. com. 1996-99, co-chair task force on edn. and tng. 1994-96, faculty nat. workshop series 2001-03), designed profl. tng. workshop series, 1999-00, Assn. Living Hist. Farms and Agrl. Mus. (bd. dirs. 1980-88, pres. 1985, John T. Schlebecker award Lifetime Disting. Svc. 1996), Midwest Open Air Mus. Coordinating Coun. (founder, bd. dirs., pres. 1978-80), Am. Assn. Museums (mus. studies com. 1986-94), Internat. Coun. Museums, Nat. Trust for Hist. Preservation, Hawaii Museums Assn. (bd. dirs. 1994-96), So. Md. Mus. Assn. (bd. dirs. 1997-98), Historic House Initiative. Democrat. Roman Catholic. E-mail: ctmatelic@aol.com.

MATEMA, ZSUN-NEE KIMBALL (ANNETTE K. MILLER), social sciences educator; b. Washington, Jan. 11, 1944; d. Emmett Robinson Miller and Annette Kimball Brooks; m. John Fitzgerald Payne, Aug. 31, 1963 (div.); children: Kellie Jon, Jaanai Kimball, Myya Machel, Robin Annette. BA, U. D.C., 1982; MMsc, U. Metaphysics. Cert. in clin. hypnosis Am. Hypnosis Tng. Acad.; lic. practitioner of religious sci. Ch. of Religious Sci.; ordained metaphysical min.; cert. in cmty. mediation Fed. Mediation Svcs. Artistic dir. Annette's Theatre of Dance, Inc., Washington, 1968-78; prodr., writer Nat. Broadcast Corp., 1971-74; ednl. counseling cons. Something Better/A.K. Millers & Assocs., Silver Spring, Md., 1979-86; dir. cmty. edn. Am. Digestive Disease Soc., Bethesda, 1986-88; cmty. outreach/arena stage multicult. audience devel. assoc. Washington, 1989-92; founding dir. Intercultural Edn. Exch., 1991—; prof. behavioral scis. Washington Saturday Coll., 1997—; founder, pres. Brannum Robinson Hist. Soc., Inc., 2001—. Native Am. storyteller The Painted Gourd: Red & Black Voices, Washington, 1991—; hist. interpreter Mt. Vernon; colonial and Civil War reenactor D.C. Ladies Contraband Relief Soc., Washington, 1991—; cmty. policing trainer Met. Police Dept., Washington, 1993-97; nat. dir. All Nations Drum, Washington, 1996; pub. rels. coord. The Walk to Can., Silver Spring, Md., 1996; underground railroad historian Nat. Pk. Svc., Washington, 1996—; cmty. mediator Montgomery County Md., 1996—; nat. adv. bd. Trail of Dreams Walk from North to South, Washington, 1999. Contbg. poet: Gurus and Griots, 1986; prodr., writer (cable) Prejudice Picks on Children, 1988, Scripts, 1989, (radio drama) Underground Railroad Traveling Radio Show, 1998; playwright Tales from Tin Cup Alley, 1991; host, prodr. (radio) The Talking Feather, 2000—. Pub. programs chair Afro-Asian Rels. Coun., Washington, 1989-96; past vice chair Com. for Ethnic Affairs, Silver Spring, 1990-96; mem. AFRIASIA founding dir. Cultural Alliance Greater Washington, 1991-94; cmty. mediator Human Rights Commn., Rockville, Md., 1994—; adv. bd. mem. NAACP, Silver Spring, 1996-98, com. mem. multicultural group, 1996-98; Native Am. adv. rep. Montgomery County Sch. Bd., 1996-97; tng. devel. com. mem. Nat. Area Crisis Response Team, Washington, 1997-99. Grantee Nat. Endowment for the Arts, Washington, 1974-76, Hawaii Arts in the Sch., Inc., Owau, Hawaii, 1994. Mem. Zeta Phi Beta. Avocations: colonial reenactment, creative wall art, travel. E-mail: ZSunRise3@aol.com.

MATER, MAUD, lawyer; BA in English, Case Western Reserve U., 1969, JD, 1972. Asst. gen. counsel Freddie Mac, McLean, Va., 1976-78, assoc. gen. counsel, 1978-79, v.p., dep. gen. counsel, 1979-82, v.p., gen. counsel, 1982-84, sr. v.p., gen. counsel, sec., 1984-98, exec. v.p., gen. counsel, sec., 1998—. Mem.: FBA, ABA (com. corp. gen. counsel), Washington Met. Corp. Counsel Assn.; Conf. Bd. Coun. of Chief Legal Officers, DC Bar, Ohio Bar, Am. Arbitration Assn. (dir.), Am. Corp. Counsel Assn. Office: Freddie Mac MS # 200 8200 Jones Branch Dr Mc Lean VA 22102-3110

MATERA, FRANCES LORINE, elementary educator; b. Eustis, Nebr., June 28, 1926; d. Frank Daniel and Marie Mathilda (Hess) Daiss; m. Daniel Matera, Dec. 27, 1973; 2 children. Luth. tchrs. diploma, Concordia U., Seward, Nebr., 1947, BS in Edn., 1956; MEd, U. Oreg., 1963. Elementary tchr. Our Savior's Luth. Ch., Colorado Springs, Colo., 1954-57; tchr. 5th grade Monterey (Calif.) Pub. Schs., 1957-59; tchr. 1st grade Roseburg (Oreg.) Schs., 1959-60; tchr. several schs. Palm Springs (Calif.) Unified Sch. Dist., 1960—93; tchr. 3rd grade Vista del Monte Sch., Palm Springs, Calif., 1973-93; ret., 1993. Named Tchr. of the Yr., Palm Springs Unified Schs. Mem. Kappa Kappa Iota (chpt. and state pres.). E-mail: Franmatera7@aol.com.

MATERA, RICHARD ERNEST, retired minister; b. Hartford, Conn., July 13, 1925; s. Charles Carlo and Philomena Antoinette Cecile (Liberatore) M.; m. Lynn B. Matera; children: Thomas Charles, Nancy Jean Matera Dye. *Former wife Lynn B. Matera is a senior information specialist and operates her own consulting firm, Worldwide Information Research, Chicago. Son, Thomas C. Matera, BA 1974, Colgate University, Hamilton, NY, and his wife, Kate Howell, operate their own human resources consulting firm, Highland Consulting, in Marlborough, MA. Daughter, Nancy Jean Matera Dye and her husband, Lester W. Dye, PhD, Stanford University, operate their own computer software company in Dillon, MT. Nancy is an artist whose works are periodically presented at showings. Lester writes software programs, employs a staff of six PhD's.* Student, Trinity Coll., Hartford, 1943, Biarritz Am. U., France, 1945; BA magna cum laude, Colgate U., 1949; MDiv, Andover Newton Theol. Sch., 1953; DD, Calif. Christian U., 1981. Ordained to ministry Bapt. Ch., 1952. Dir. youth work Quincy Point (Mass.) Congl. Ch., 1949-50; pastor, dir. vacation ch. sch. Panton and Addison (Vt.) chs., 1950; min. Thompson (Conn.) Hill Ch., 1950-51, Waldo Congl. Ch., Brockton, Mass., 1951-54, Cen. Congl. Ch., Orange, 1954-59; sr. min. 1st Congl. United Ch. of Christ, Berea, Ohio, 1959-71, St. Paul Community Ch., Homewood, Ill., 1971-76; interim min. United Ch. Christ, Chgo., 1978-99; min. Immanuel United Ch. of Christ, Bensenville, Ill., 1999—. Pres. Millers River Coun. Chs., 1957-58; mem. dept. ch. world responsibility Mass. Coun. Chs., 1957-59; chmn. internat. affairs com. of state social action com. United Ch. of Christ, 1962-63, del. Gen. Synod, Chgo., mem. peace priority task force Western Res. Assn., 1967-70, mem. commn. on ch. and ministry Ohio conf., 1968-71, chmn. dept. ch. and community Western Res. Assn. Coun., Cleve., 1969-70, peace and internat. rels. com., 1973; mem. ad hoc com. on Vietnam Greater Cleve. Coun. of Chs. of Christ, 1966-68; probation officer DuPage County Probation Dept., Wheaton, Ill., 1985-86; interim min. Chgo. area, 1978—, Sauk Village United Ch. of Christ, 1978-80, Steger 1st Congregation, 1981-83, Forest Park, 1986-88, River Grove Grace, 1989-91, Mont Clare Congregation, 1990-92, St. Nicolai, Chgo., 1992-96. *As a culmination of fifty-five years' ministry with a social conscience, consented to video- taped interview by Survivors of The SHOAH, Steven Spielberg, chairman, which preserves archives documenting WWII Holocaust, as one among the U.S. Army liberators of Buchenwald Concentration Camp, Germany, WWII, 1945. Signer of Greetings from Earth document now on Mars Lnader, as member of the Planetary Society, 1998.WWII/Holocaust.* Contbr. poetry to anthologies including Tears of Fire, 1994, A Break in the Clouds, 1994. Participant Civil Rights March, Selma, Ala., 1965; capt. Cleve. United Fund, 1961-63, Colgate Fund Dr., 1963; trustee Cleve. Union, 1961-63, Berea United Fund, 1963-69; mem. Berea Coun. on Human Rels., 1965-71, U.S. com. Christian Peace Conf., Prague, Czechoslovakia, 1967—. Nat. Arbor Day Found.; del. Action Conf. on Nat. Priorities, Washington, 1969; bd. dirs., mem. ecumenical mission com. Community Renewal Soc., Chgo., 1972-76; bd. dirs. Respond Now, Chicago Heights, Ill., 1972-78; mem. Pres.'s Coun., Chgo. Theol. Sem., 1973-81; pres. Mended Hearts Inc., Downers Grove, Ill., 1989-90. With U.S. Army Med. Corps., 1943-46, ETO. Austen Colgate scholar, 1946-49; recipient Harvard Book prize, 1942; name inscribed on The Wall of Liberty, Battle of Normandy Found., France, 1994. Fellow Profl. Assn. Clergy, Acad. Parish Clergy; mem. Living Bank Internat. (organ donor mem.), Smithsonian Instn., Audubon Soc., Internat. Fellowship of Reconciliation, Internat. Soc. Poets, Nat. Libr.Poetry, Steinway Soc. Chgo., Planetary Soc., Jacques Cousteau Soc., Antique Automobile Club, Hupmobile Club, Cadillac Club, Phi Beta Kappa, Beta Theta Pi. Democrat. Achievements include private interview with Prof. Albert Einstein in 1954. Avocations: drawing, poetry, astronomy, piano, working out at health club. Home and Office: 5 E Memorial Rd Bensenville IL 60106-2541 *From world philosophers, I have gleaned this: While borders stand, we are in prehistory. When all borders are gone, human history will begin.-Yevtushenko A person only has the right to do that which he agrees should become universal law.-Kant Do to others as you want them to do to you.-Hebrew tchg. The human race is now capable of and ready for the above.*

MATERIA, KATHLEEN PATRICIA AYLING, nurse; b. Jersey City, Nov. 7, 1954; d. Donald Anthony and Muriel Cecilia (Joyce) Ayling; m. Francis Peter Materia, June 5, 1983; children: Christopher Michael, Donna Nicole. *Kathleen Materia's son, Christopher Michael, graduated Assumption School in Woodbridge, N.J. in June 2002. He received the President's Award for Academic Excellence, State Science Award Scholarship, Math League Certificate of Merit for Superior Achievement, and an award for being the only student to receive High Honors for all four semesters. Christopher received scholarships for all four high schools that he applied to. He is also a Student Ambassador with the People to People Student Ambassador Program and has traveled with the team to Europe (England, Ireland, Wales) in July 2001. Christopher is now attending the Bergen County Academy for Medical Science Technology (class of 2006).* BSN, Fairleigh Dickinson U., 1976. RN, N.J.. Critical care nurse Palisades Gen. Hosp., North Bergen, N.J., 1976-87; grad. nurse, 1976-77; nurse critical care unit North Hudson Hosp., Weehawken, NJ, 1977-78. Mem. Alpha Sigma Tau. Democrat. Avocations: bowling, dancing.

MATERNA, JOSEPH ANTHONY, lawyer; b. Passaic, N.J., June 13, 1947; s. Anthony E. and Peggy Ann Materna; m. Dolores Corio, Dec. 14, 1975; children: Jodi, Jennifer, Janine. BA, Columbia U., 1969, JD, 1973. Bar: N.Y. 1975, Fla. 1977, U.S. Dist. Ct. (ea. and so. dists.) N.Y. 1977, U.S. Supreme Ct. 1977, U.S. Tax Ct. 1978, U.S. Ct. of Claims 1978. Trusts and estates atty. Chadbourne Parke Whiteside & Wolff, N.Y.C., 1973-76, Dreyer & Traub, N.Y.C., 1976-80, Finley Kumble Wagner Heine Underberg & Casey, N.Y.C., 1980-85; ptnr., head trusts and estates dept. Newman Tannenbaum Helpern Syracuse & Hirschtritt, 1985-90, Shapiro Beilly Rosenberg Aronowitz Levy & Fox LLP, N.Y.C., 1990—. Lectr. in field; expert witness in trusts and estate field ct. litigations, N.Y., 1999—. Contbr. articles to profl. jours. Chmn. planned giving com., mem. bd. govs. Arthritis Found. N.Y. Chpt., N.Y.C., 1980—; mem. bd. trustees, corp. treas. Cath. Interracial Coun., N.Y.C., 1992—; mem. bequests and planned gifts com. Cath. Archdiocese of N.Y., N.Y.C., 1988—; corp. sec. Arthritis Found. N.Y. chpt., N.Y.C., 1997—, mem. budget and fin. com., 2001—; mem. Meml. Sloan-Kettering Nat. Trusts and Estates Assocs. Recipient Planned Giving award Arthritis Found.-N.Y. Chpt., N.Y.C., 1994, Discovery Alliance award Arthritis Found.-N.Y. Chpt., N.Y.C., 1995; named Accredited Estate Planner, Nat. Assn. Estate Planners, Marietta, Ga., 1995. Mem. ABA, Fla. Bar (trusts and estate com.), N.Y. State Bar Assn. (com. on estates and trusts), Bar Assn. of the City of N.Y. (com. on surrogate's ct.), N.Y.C. Estate Planning Coun. (lectr., author), N.Y. County Lawyers Assn. (mem. com. on trusts and estates 1979—, com. on profl. ethics, com. on taxation, 2000—), Queen County Bar Assn. (mem. com. trusts and estates 1990—, mem. com. on taxation, mem. com. on profl. ethics), Am. Judges Assn. (civil ct. arbitrator N.Y.C.), Am. Arbitration Assn. (panel of arbitrators), N.Y. State Trial Lawyers Assn., Richmond County Bar Assn. (com. on surrogates ct.), Columbia Coll. Alumni Assn. of Columbia U. (class pres. 1969—). Republican. Roman Catholic. Home: 155 Johanna Ln Staten Island NY 10309-3604 Office: Shapiro Beilly Rosenberg Aronowitz Levy & Fox LLP 225 Broadway New York NY 10007-3001

MATERNA, THOMAS WALTER, ophthalmologist; b. Passaic, N.J., Oct. 24, 1944; s. Anthony and Ann (Popowich) M.; m. Jorunn Pauline Aronsen, Aug. 18, 1973; children: Richard C., Barbara L. BA, Coll. Holy Cross, Worcester, Mass., 1966; MD, SUNY, N.Y.C., 1971; MBA, Rutgers U., Newark, 1990. Diplomate Am. Bd. Ophthalmology. Intern N.Y. Hosp.-Cornell U. Med. Ctr., N.Y.C., 1971-72; resident N.Y. Eye and Ear Infirmary, 1975-78; pvt. practice ophthalmology San Francisco, 1986; ophthalmologist N.J. Eye Physicians & Surgeons, Newark. V.p. mktg. Biomark Internat., Lviv, Ukraine. Com. mem. N.J. Sch. for the Arts, Montclair, 1991—. Lt. USN, 1972-74, comdr. USNR, 1974—. Fellow ACS, Am. Acad. Ophthalmology; mem. Rotary, Army-Navy Club. Democrat. Roman Catholic. Avocations: coin collecting, rare document collecting, tennis, art history. Home: 87 Lorraine Ave Montclair NJ 07043-2304 Office: NJ Eye Physicians and Surgeons 20 Ferry St Newark NJ 07105-1420

MATERSON, RICHARD STEPHEN, physician, educator; b. Phila., Feb. 11, 1941; s. Alfred Lawrence and June Eileen (Slakoff) M.; m. Rosa Maria Navarro, Aug. 22, 1964; children: Lisa Gail, Lawrence Mark. MD, U. Miami, Coral Gables, Fla., 1965. Diplomate Am. Bd. Phys. Medicine and Rehab. 1966intern Walter Reed Gen. Hosp., Washington, 1965; resident Letterman Gen. Hosp., San Francisco, 1966—68; chief phys. medicine and rehab. Tripler Gen. Hosp., Honolulu, 1968—72; asst. prof. phys. medicine and rehab. Ohio State U., Columbus, 1972—76; assoc. clin. prof. phys. medicine and rehab. Baylor Coll. Medicine, Houston, 1976—93, prof., 1997—; pres. Materson MD, PA, 1976—; sr. v.p. for med. affairs, med. dir. Nat. Rehab. Hosp., Washington, 1990—97; prof. neurology George Washington U. Med. Ctr., 1994—97; med. v.p. Meml. Healthcare Sys., Houston, 1997—; prof. phys. medicine and rehab. U. Tex. Health Sci. Ctr., 1997—; fellow Kaiser Inst., 1999, 2001; chief med. officer Meml. Hermann Continuing Care Corp., 2000—. Med. dir. Dept. Phys. Medicine and Rehab., Meml. Hosp. SE, Houston, 1978-90, Ctr. for Sports Medicine and Rehab., 1987-90, Electromyography Lab., 1978-90; faculty Kaiser Inst., 2000—; bd. dirs. Inst. for Religion and Health, Tex. Med. Ctr., 2002—. Co-author: Physical Medicine and Rehabilitation, 1977, 2d rev. edit., 1980, The Practice of Rehabilitation Medicine, 1982; co-editor: Management of Persons with Stroke, 1993; co-editor, author: The Non Surgical Management of Acute Low Back Pain, 1997, Pain Management, 1998; contbg. author: Practice of Medicine, 1978. Trustee Meml. Hosp. System, Houston, 1986-90, Nat. Rehab. Hosp., Washington, 1990-96; host family Experiment in Internat. Living, 1985, 86, 87. Served to maj. U.S. Army, 1965-72. Fellow Am. Acad. Phys. Medicine and Rehab. (pres. 1986-87, Distng. Pub. Svc. award, 1992, Walter J. Zeiter lectr.,

1994), Am. Assn. Electrodiagnostic Medicine; mem. AMA (del. 1978-93), Phys. Medicine and Rehab. Edn. and Rsch. Found. (founder, pres. 1982-90, bd. dirs. 1983—), Houston Acad. Phys. Medicine and Rehab. (pres. 1979-80), Am. Acad. Pain Mgmt. (chmn. bd. advisors 1989-90, mem. bd. advisors 1990—), Internat. Wine and Food Soc., Knights of Vine (master comdr. 1982—), Confrerie des Chevaliers du Tastevin, Chaine des Rotisseurs. Jewish. Fax: 713-448-6869. E-mail: richard_materson@mhhs.org.

MATES, JAMES MICHAEL, television correspondent; b. Hanover, Germany, Aug. 11, 1961; came to U.S., 1997; s. Michael John and Mary Rosamund (Nevile) M.; m. Fiona Margaret Bennett, May 4 1991; children: Leo, Flora, Charles. BA with honors, Leeds (Eng.) U., 1983. Tokyo corr. Ind. TV News, 1989-90, Moscow corr., 1991-93, diplomatic editor, 1993-96, Washington corr., 1997—. Avocation: bridge. Office: Ind TV News 400 N Capitol St NW Ste 899 Washington DC 20001-1511

MATES, JUDITH ANN LEONG, obstetrician and gynecologist; b. San Francisco, 1944; MD, Tufts U., 1969. Diplomate Am. Bd. Ob-Gyn. Intern Calif. Children's Hosp., San Francisco, 1969-70; resident in ob-gyn. U. Calif. San Francisco Hosps., 1970-75; mem. staff Chinese Hosp., San Francisco, Calif. Pacific Med. Ctr., San Francisco; asst. clin. prof. U. Calif.; mem. staff St. Mary's Hosp. Mem.: AMA (alt. del. governing coun. women physician's congress), San Francisco Med. Soc. (pres. 1995), Calif. Med. Assn. (del. chair 1996—2000), Am. Med. Women's Assn. Office: 929 Clay St Ste 305 San Francisco CA 94108 E-mail: judymates@yahoo.com.

MATES, LAWRENCE A., II, medical company executive, consultant; b. Toledo, Oct. 10, 1954; s. Lawrence A. and Phyllis A. (Thomas) M.; m. Ulrike D. Heermann, Dec. 23, 1977; children: Lawrence A. III, Jessica M. BS in Mktg. cum laude, Princeton U., 1976, MBA, 1977. Sales mgr. Technicare Corp., Cleve., 1977-80; dist. sales mgr. Siemens Med. Systems, Iselin, N.J., 1981-85; regional sales mgr. Digital Equipment Corp., Detroit, 1985-88; nat. sales mgr. Cemax, Inc., Fremont, Calif., 1988-92; exec. v.p. Philips Electronics, Cin., 1992-2000; sr. v.p. Siemens Med. Svcs., 2000—. Bd. dirs. Provident Nat. Bank. Bd. dirs. Cin. City Planners, 1994—, United Way, 1985-86, 92-96, Am. Cancer Soc., 1997-99. Mem. Med. Researchers Assn., Am. Hosp. Assn., Toledo Bus. Assn. (v.p. 1984-85), Ohio Young Men's Bus. Assn. (pres. 1985, chmn. 1992-93), Cin. Profl. Bus. Assn. (v.p. 1993—), Cin. Health Profls. (dir. 1994-95), Cin. Investors Ltd. (dir. 1994-98), Toledo Investors Ltd. (pres. 1986, 92), Cin. Bankers Club, Cin. Club, Univ. Club (v.p. 1993-96, pres. 1998-02), Sycamore Athletic Boosters (pres. 1996-98, bd. dirs. 1996—). Republican. Roman Catholic. Avocations: swimming, travel, wine collecting, automobiles, golf. Home: 8722 Windfield Ln Cincinnati OH 45249-3304 Fax: 573-583-1720. E-mail: LMATES@aol.com.

MATES, ROBERT EDWARD, mechanical engineering educator; b. Buffalo, May 19, 1935; s. Cyril S. and Ruth Elizabeth (Dougan) M.; m. Gail Paxson, June 5, 1960; children: Robert E., Elisabeth, Steven BS, U. Rochester, 1957; MS, Cornell U., 1959, PhD, 1963. Instr. Cornell U., Ithaca, N.Y., 1958-61; asst. prof. SUNY, Buffalo, 1962-65, assoc. prof., 1965-69, chmn. mech. and aero. engring., 1967-70, 79-82, prof. mech. engring., 1969-97, dir. Ctr. Biomed. Engring., 1989-96, prof. emeritus, 1997—. Editor various symposium proceedings; contbr. articles to profl. jours. NIH spl. rsch. fellow, 1970-71, 78-79, H.R. Lissner award Am. Soc of Mechanical Engineers, 1995. Fellow ASME (chmn. winter ann. meeting com. 1989-93, mem.-at-large bd. comm. 1988-93, v.p. bd. comm. 1994-98), Am. Inst. for Med. and Biol. Engring. (founding, chmn. acad. coun. 1996-97); mem. AAUP, Biomed. Engring. Soc. (bd. dirs. 1991-94, chmn. awards com. 1991-92, mem. pub. bd. 1992-94), Am. Soc. Engring. Edn.

MATES, SUSAN ONTHANK, physician, medical educator, writer, violinist; b. Oakland, Calif., Aug. 8, 1950; d. Benson and Lois (Onthank) M.; m. Joseph Harold Friedman, Dec. 10, 1978; children: Rebecca, Deborah, William. Student, Juilliard Sch. Music, 1967-69; BA magna cum laude with distinction, Yale Coll., 1972; MD, Albert Einstein Coll. Medicine, 1976. Cert. Am. Bd. Internal Medicine, Nat. Bd. Med. Examiners. Intern Boston City Hosp., 1976-77; fellow in gen. medicine Coll. of Physicians and Surgeons-Columbia U., N.Y.C., 1977-78; resident/fellow in infectious diseases Montefiore Hosp., Bronx, 1978-82; asst. prof. medicine Brown U., Providence, 1982-85, asst. prof. biochemistry, 1985-86, clin. assoc. prof. medicine, 1993-98; staff mem., former dir. R.I. State Tb Clinic, R.I. Dept. Health, 1986-96, cons. Tb program, 1987-96. Judge short story contest Providence Jour., 1994, 98; mem. jury R.I. Coun. Arts Fellowship; contbg. editor Pushcart Prize, Pushcart Press, 1995, 96, 97, 98, 99. Author: (fiction) The Good Doctor, 1994 (Iowa Short Fiction award 1994); contbr. sci. articles to profl. jours., stories to revs. and jours. and anthologies (Pushcart prize 1994, John Simmons short fiction award). Recipient Recognition award for young scholars AAUW, 1985, Clin. Investigator award NIH, 1984, R.I. Found. award, 1983; McDowell Colony fellow, 1995, Yaddo fellow, 1996; Symposium scholar in lit. and medicine for 21st Century, Brown U., 1997. Mem. Am. Med. Women's Assn., Poets and Writers, Alpha Omega Alpha. Home: 52 Bluff Rd Barrington RI 02806-4314

MATESKY, ELISABETH ANNE, international solo violinist, educator, composer; b. L.A., Oct. 1, 1946; d. Ralph and Betty (Blumberg) M.; m. Allen Leslie Odens, Feb. 18, 1973 (div. Nov. 1979). BMus and spl. degree in violin performance, U. So. Calif., 1964; pvt. study, with Nathan Milstein, London, 1969-71. Artist in residence in violin Syracuse (N.Y.) U., 1971-72; concertmaster Syracuse Symphony Orch., 1971-72; violinist Chgo. Symphony Orch., 1972-73; concertmaster Rockford Symphony Ill., 1981-86; artist tchr. violin, chmn. dept. string Am. Conservatory Music, Chgo., 1986-91; spl. lectr. in violin Chgo. Musical Coll., 1991-93; in residency artist Trinity Coll. Music, London, 1996—. Mistress of ceremonies Stradivari Soc. Concert Series, Chgo., 1993—; entrepreneur young artists concerts, London, 1994—; mem. bd. patrons Sascha Lasserson Meml. Trust, London, 1996—; guest tchr., performer Sibelius Acad. Music, Helsinki, 1999; concertmaster City Symphony Chgo., 2001—. Writer The Strad Mag., Asta Jour., Sun-Scandinavia Newspaper; interviewer Internat. Young Artists; guest artist Ravinia Music Festival; guest soloist Grant Park Music Festival; violinist, student (film) Heifetz Master Class: Elisabeth Matesky in Khachaturian Violin Concerto, 1963; rec. artist BBC of various concertos and recitals, 1967—; solo violinist, artist (TV London film) Grace Under Pressure, 1970-71; dedicatee (PBS TV concert) Bradshaw Violin Concerto, 1981; violinist (TV comml.) Sta. WFMT Radio, 1985 (1st prize N.Y. TV Comml. 1986); guest violinist Salte to My Teachers: Heifetz & Milstein, 1995; artist tchr. (film) Elisabeth Matesky Violin & Chamber Music Master Classes at Trinity College of Music, 1996. Guest violinist at State Dinner with Pres. Jimmy Carter, White House, Washington, 1977. Named Woman of the Yr. Syracuse Jour. Newspaper, 1971; Fulbright scholar Royal Coll. Music, London, 1964-65, 65-66; NEA grantee Sacramento Symphony Orch., 1979-80. Mem. Fulbright Alumni Assn. (honoree 1996), Am. String Tchrs. Assn., Chgo. Symphony Alumni Assn. Home: 215 E Chestnut St Apt 1803 Chicago IL 60611-6712 E-mail: violinplus@yahoo.com.

MATHAVAN, SUDERSHAN KUMAR, nuclear power engineer; b. Muzfrabad, Kashmir, India, Aug. 18, 1945; came to U.S., 1968; s. Kartar Chand and Ram Rakhi (Makoli) M.; m. Alka Rani Ajrawat, Oct. 23, 1979; children: Erik, Sarita, Manika, Ketan. BS, Kasmir U., Srinagar, India, 1967; MS, U. Miami, 1970, PhD, 1977. Registered profl. engr., Fla. Engr. Ground Support Engring., Miami, Fla., 1969-73, Smith, Korach A/E, Miami, 1973-75; cons. engr. U. Miami, Coral Gables, Fla., 1975-77; sr. engr. Duke Power, Charlotte, N.C., 1977-79; prin. engr. Fla. Power & Light Co., West Palm Beach, 1979—. Mem. analysis subcom. Westinghouse Owners Group, Pitts., 1983—. Contbr. articles to profl. jours. Pres. India Soc., Miami, 1984-86; sec. Hindu Temple, Ft. Lauderdale, Fla., 1986—. Mem. Am. Nuclear Soc. Democrat. Achievements include safety analyses of St. Lucie and Turkey Point nuclear power plants. Home: 3004 SW Marco Ln Palm City FL 34990-3186 Office: Fla Power & Light Co Universe Blvd Juno Beach FL 33408

MATHAY, JOHN PRESTON, elementary education educator; b. Youngstown, Ohio, Jan. 27, 1942; s. Howard Ellsworth and Mary Clara (Siple) M.; m. Sandra Elizabeth Rhoades, June 9, 1973 (div. Jan. 1986); children: Elizabeth Anne, Sarah Susannah; m. Judith Anne Matthy, June 19, 1988; 1 child, Andrew Micah. B History, Va. Mil. Inst., Lexington, 1964; Cert. Teaching, Cleve. State U., 1972; postgrad., Mich. State U., 1964-65; MEd, Westminster Coll., New Wilmington, 1986. Cert. asst. supt., elem. tchr., elem. prin., high sch. prin. Cabinet maker Artisian Cabinet, Orwig Cabinets, Cleve. and Howland, Ohio, 1970-72; tchr. Urban Community Sch., Cleve., 1972-73, Pymatuning Valley Schs., Andover, Ohio, 1973—. Cross country coach, 7th and 8th grade track coach, Andover. Bd. mem. Badger Sch. Bd., Kinsman, Ohio; trustee Kinsman Libr.; trustee, elder Kinsman Presbyn. Ch. Capt. U.S. Army Res., 1966-69. Martha Holden Jennings Found. scholar, Cleve., 1976. Mem. ASCD, Pymatuning Valley Edn. Assn. (pres. 1975-76, 91-92, 94-95), Ohio Edn. Assn., Am. Legion, Rotary (pres. 1991-92, sec. 1992-93, treas. 1995-98, Paul Harris fellow), Masons (jr. deacon 1984-85, 32d deg., York Rite commandery), Ashtabula County Antique Engine Club, Phi Delta Kappa. Republican. Presbyterian. Avocations: sailing, skating, ham radio, French and Indian War reenacting, fishing, reading. Office: Pymatuning Valley Schs W Main St Andover OH 44003 Home: PO Box 418 Kinsman OH 44428-0228 E-mail: jamath@suite224.net.

MATHAY, MARY FRANCES, marketing executive; b. Youngstown, Ohio, July 26, 1944; d. Howard E. and Mary C. (Siple) M.; m. Thomas Stone Withgott, Dec. 20, 1969 (div. June 1973). BA in English Lit. and Composition, Queens Coll., 1967; grad. in bus., Katharine Gibbs Sch., 1968. Corp. mktg. mgr., assoc. Odell Assocs., Inc., Charlotte, N.C., 1973-90; dir. pub. rels. and spl. events Charlotte (N.C.)-Mecklenburg Arts and Sci. Coun., 1990-92; pres. Mathay Comm., Inc., Charlotte, 1992-96; pub. rels. mgr. The Mktg. Consortium, 1996—. Speakers bur. chmn. Hospice at Charlotte, Inc., 1980-83; pub. rels. and advt. dir. "Chemical People" program PBS, Charlotte, 1983-84. Author: Legacy of Architecture, 1988; editor: Mint Mus. Antiques Show Mag., 1980, editorial advisor Crier, 1987-92; producer Charlotte's Web, 1977. Vol. tchr. ABLE Ctr. Piedmont C.C., 1987—90; vol. comm. com. Am. Cancer Soc., 1994—96, Charlotte-Mecklenburg Edn. Found., 1992—94, Charlotte-Mecklenburg Sr. Ctrs., 1994—95, bd. dirs., 1998—; v.p. Olde Georgetowne Homeowners Assn., bd. dirs., Jr. League of Charlotte, Inc., 1978—79, ECO, Inc., Charlotte, 1979—86, Arthritis Patient Svcs., 1996—, Learning How Inc., Charlotte, NC, 1988—91; bd. dirs. on adolescent pregnancy Mecklenburg County Coun., 1986—88; bd. dirs. Queens Coll. Alumni, Charlotte, 1984—87, 1997—99, planned giving chmn., 1997—98, class pres., 2001—; bd. dirs. Friends of Libr., 2002—. Mem. Pub. Rels. Soc. Am. (bd. dirs. 1989—, pres. 1995), Charlotte Pub. Rels. Soc. (bd. dirs. 1986-89, 92-93), , Jr. League Charlotte, Olde Providence Racquet Club. Republican. Presbyterian. Avocations: foreign travel, tennis, golf. E-mail: fmamay@aol.com.

MATHAY, WILLIAM LEWIS, metal products executive; b. Greenville, Pa., Dec. 1, 1924; s. Philip Henry and Ivah Ann M.; m. Donna Lee, Apr. 10, 1948; 1 child, Susan Lee Hlebinsky. Cert., Ohio State U., 1945; BS in Chemistry, Thiel Coll., 1947; postgrad., Carnegie Inst. Tech., 1048—1954. Lab. chemist Calgon Corp., Pitts., 1947-54; corrosion supr. U.S. Steel Corp., 1954-64, chief rsch. engr., 1964-66, mktg. mgr., 1966-82, long range planner, 1982-84; metallurg. cons. Nickel Devel. Inst., Toronto, Ont., Can., 1984—. Co-author: nickel Stainless Steels and High-Nickel Alloys for Flue Gas Desulfurization Systems, 1988, 2d edit., 1990; patentee in field; contbr. over 40 articles to profl. jours. Fellow Am. Inst. Chemists; mem. ASME (steel stacks com.), Nat. Assn. Corosion Engrs. (life; nat. dir. 1976-79, chmn. northeast region 1996-97, cert. corrosion specialist, Nat. Disting. Svc. award 1983, Outstanding Svc. award 1985), ASM Internat., Com. Internat. des Cheminees Industrielles (internat. chimney com.), U.S. Figure Skating Assn. (test chair of Yr. 1996). Avocations: ice skating, golfing. Home and Office: 111 Amesbury Dr Pittsburgh PA 15241-2305

MATHEE, KALAI, research scientist, educator; b. Kampar, Perak, Malaysia, Aug. 30, 1959; s. Loganayaki and Kaliaperumal; m. Giri Narasimhan, Apr. 12, 1993. BS, U. Malaya, Kuala Lumpur, 1984, MS, 1986; PhD, U. Tenn., 1992. Elem. sch. tchr., Sitiawan, Perak, Malaysia, 1980; tutor U. Malaya, Kuala Lumpur, Malaysia, 1984-86; postdoctoral fellow Tufts U., Boston, 1992-93, U. Tenn., Memphis, 1993-99; vis. scientist, vis. prof. Danish Tech. U., Lyngby, Denmark, 1997—; rsch. adj. faculty Copenhagen U., Denmark, 1999—; asst. prof. Fla. Internat. U., Miami, 1999—. Participant Genome Annotation Com. Project, Cystic Fibrosis Found., 1999—. Danish Med. Rsch. Coun. grantee, 1998—. Mem. AAAS, Am. Soc. Microbiology, Sigma Delta Epsilon. Avocations: reading, gardening, hiking, camping, travel. Office: Fla Internat U University Park Miami FL 33199-0001 Fax: 305 348-1986. E-mail: matheek@fiu.edu.

MATHEIS, CHERYL, nonprofit association administrator; b. Buffalo, May 15, 1951; d. Charles Wililam and Mary Aileen Matheis; m. Thomas Gillett Goodwin, Sept. 22, 1984; children: John Thomas Mary Claire. BA, Manhattanville Coll., 1973; JD, Cath. U. Am., 1978. Bar: D.C. 1978. Rsch. analyst Civil Rights Divsn. Dept. Justice, Washington, 1973-77; pvt. practice, 1978-86; legis. rep. AARP, 1986-99, dir. state legis., 1999—. Mem. Am. Health Lawyers Assn., Women in Govt. Rels. Office: AARP 601 E St NW Washington DC 20049-0003

MATHELIER, AMEDEE C. obstetrician-gynecologist; b. Gonaives, Haiti, 1934; MD, Sch. Medicine State U., Haiti, 1958. Intern Jewish Hosp., Bklyn., 1962-63; resident in ob.-gyn. Balt. City Hosp., 1963-66, fellow, 1968-70. Pvt. practice. Lt. col. U.S. Army Med. Corps. Mem. AMA, Am. Coll. Ob.-Gyn., CGS, ISMS.

MATHENY, ADAM PENCE, JR. child psychologist, educator, consultant, researcher; b. Stanford, Ky., Sept. 6, 1932; s. Adam Pence and Dorotha (Steele) M.; m. Ute I. Debus, July 10, 1962 (div.); m. Mary P. Tolbert, June 24, 1967 (div.); children— Laura Steele, Jason Gaverick. B.S., Columbia U., 1958; Ph.D., Vanderbilt U., 1962. Sr. human factors engr. Martin Aerospace div., Balt., 1962-63; instr. Johns Hopkins U. Med. Sch., 1963-65; staff fellow Nat. Inst. Child Health and Human Devel., 1965-67; from asst. prof. to prof. pediatrics U. Louisville Med. Sch., 1967-75, assoc. dir. to dir. Louisville Twin Study, 1986—; mem. review panel NIH, 1991-95. Served with USN, 1951-55. Fellow Internat. Soc. Twin Studies, Am. Psychol. Assn., Am. Psychol. Soc., Am. Assn. of Applied and Preventive Psychology; mem. Soc. Research Child Devel., AAAS, Behavior Genetics Assn., Internat. Soc. Behavior Devel., Internat. Soc. Infant Study, Phi Beta Kappa, Sigma Xi. Co-author: Genetics and Counseling in Medical Practice, 1969; contbr. articles to profl. jours.

MATHENY, CHARLES WOODBURN, JR. former army officer, civil engineer, city official; b. Sarasota, Fla., Aug. 7, 1914; s. Charles Woodburn Sr. and Virginia (Yates) M.; m. Jeanne Felkel, July 12, 1942; children: Virginia Ann, Nancy Caroline, Charles Woodburn III. BSCE, U. Fla., 1936; grad., Army Command Gen. Staff Coll., 1944. Lic. comml. pilot, 1952; lic. civil engr., surveyor, Ga. 1939. Sanitary engr. Ga. State Dept. Health, 1937-39; civil engr. Fla. East Coast Ry., 1939-41; commd. 2d lt. F.A., USAR through ROTC U. Fla., 1936; 1st lt. F.A., USAR, 1939; vol. active army svc. F.A., US Army, 1941; commissioned 2d lt. F.A., US Army (Regular Army), 1942; advanced through grades to col. F.A., USAR, 1955; comdr. 351st Field Arty. Bn., 1944-45; commr. 33rd Field Arty. Bn., 1st Infantry Divsn., 1946, artillery staff officer, 1947; gen. staff G-3 Plans Dept. Army, 1948-51; qualified Air Force liaison pilot, 1951; qualified Army aviator airplanes and helicopters, 1952; aviation officer 25th Infantry Divsn., Korea, 1952-53; sr. Army aviation advisor Korean Army, 1953; first dir. combat devel. dept. first dep. commandant Army Aviation Sch., Ft. Sill, Okla., 1954-55; dep. dir. rsch., dep. dir. dept. tactics U.S. Army Field Arty. and Missile Sch., 1955—57; aviation officer 7th U.S. Army, Germany, 1957-58; Munich sub area comdr. So. Area Command, Europe, 1958-59; qualified sr. army aviator, 1959; dep. chief of staff for info. So. Area Command, 1960; Mich. sector comdr. VI Army Corps., 1961-62, ret., 1962; asst. dir. Tampa (Fla.) Dept. Pub. Works, 1963-81, ret., 1981. During World War II, Germany Commd., 351st field artillery Battalion in combat and occupation, 1945, also 33d field artillery battalion, 1st Infantry Divsn., in occupation, 1946. Initiator and originator of tactical use of helicopters in Army, 1949, Army warrant officer helicopter aviator program and organization of first five Army Transp. Helicopter Co. and establishment of a new U.S. Army personnel policy making U.S. Army helicopter pilots warrant officers instead of officers, 1950; 1st to envision army combat units and airphibious army divisions equipped with high performance helicopter mobility capable of land, sea or air warfare operations at 200 mph, 1950; initiated and prepared directive signed by Army chief of staff, Gen. J. Lawton Collins ordering first feasibility tests of Army super-mobile inf. and artillery units equipped with helicopter mobility, 1951; pilot 1st combat observation mission in army helicopter, Korea, 1952; organizer, comdr., helicopter pilot 1st Army combat ops. using helicopter mobility to support inf. and engr. front line combat units 25th Inf. Div., Korea, 1952 proving feasibility of Army helicopter mobility on the battlefield; 1st to advocate, rsch., prepare orgn. plans and design of super-mobile Army combat units equipped with armed and unarmed helicopter mobility, with model designs of helicopters armed with missiles, rockets, etc. to equip proposed combat units, 1955-56; 1st to urge Army to develop a high performance observation and reconnaissance helicopter; development O/R Comanche, RAH-66 reconnaissance helicopter. U.S. Army first to exploit and develop helicopter mobility due to Matheny's devotion to its early beginning; pilot 100 combat observation missions, Korea, 1952-53; author 1st state legis. to establish profl. sch. civil engring. for state of Fla., 1974; mem. U.S. Army's Strategic Planning Com., 1950-51. *Charles W. Matheny, Jr., Colonel U.S., Army Aviator, published the following articles: "What Helicopters Can Do For Us," in combat Forces Journal (now Army), July 1951. "New Flying Vehicle Transportation in our Army," in Military Review, November 1951. "Aerial Vehicle Transport for Combat Units," in Army Aviation Digest, June 1956. As a Professional Civil Engineer and Professional Land Surveyor, he published the following articles: "Effect of Professional Civil engineer School on Professionalism and Ethics" in Report ASCE Education Conference, Ohio State University, 1977. "Creating State Professional School of Civil Engineering" in Issues in Engineering, ASCE, October 1980. "Needed: A State Professional School of Civil Engineering" in Engineering Education, April 1981.* Contbr. numerous articles on tactical use of helicopter aerial vehicles, also need for profl. shc. for civil engring. to mags., 1950-80. Mem. troop com. Boy Scouts Am., 1965-73; active various cmty. and ch. activities; patron Tampa Art Mus., 1965-83, Tampa Cmty. Concert Series, 1979-82; bd. dirs. Tampa YMCA, 1967-71, Fla. Easter Seal Soc., 1978, Easter Seal Soc. Hillsborough County, 1971-84, hon. bd. dirs., 1984-95, treas., 1973-76, pres., 1977. Decorated Bronze Star with oak leaf cluster, Air medal with three oak leaf clusters; recipient of the Eagle Scout award, 1928; Letterman football U.F., 1933, 35; named to U. Fla. Student Hall of Fame, 1936. Mem. ASCE (pres. West Coast br., dir. Fla. sect. 1973, Engr. of Yr. award West Coast br. Fla. sect. 1979, life mem. 1980), Am. Soc. Profl. Engrs., Fla. Engring. Soc., Am. Pub. Works Assn. (pres. West Coast br. Fla. chpt. 1972, exec. com. Fla. chpt. 1972-77, v.p. 1977, pres. 1978), Ret. Officers Assn., Army Aviation Assn., SAR, Fla. Blue Key, Alpha Tau Omega, Sigma Tau. Episcopalian. Home: 4802 W Beachway Dr Tampa FL 33609-4836

MATHENY, EDWARD TAYLOR, JR. lawyer; b. Chgo., July 15, 1923; s. Edward Taylor and Lina (Pinnell) Matheny; m. Marion Elizabeth Shields, Sept. 10, 1947; children: Nancy Elizabeth, Edward Taylor III; m. Ann Spears, Jan. 14, 1984. BA, U. Mo., 1944; JD, Harvard, 1949. Bar: Mo. 1949. Pvt. practice, Kansas City, 1949-91; ptnr. firm Blackwell, Sanders, Matheny, Weary & Lombardi, 1954-91. Pres. St. Luke's Hosp., Kansas City, 1980-95; bd. dirs. Dunn Industries, Inc., Tnemec Co., Inc. Author: The Presence of Care (History of St. Luke's Hospital, Kansas City), 1997, A Long and Constant Courtship (The History of a Law Firm), 1998, The Rise and Fall of Excellence, 2000, The Pursuit of a Ruptured Duck (When Kansas Citians Went to War), 2001. Pres. Cmty. Svc. Broadcasting of Mid-Am., Inc., 1971-72; chmn. Citizens Assn. Kansas City, 1958; chmn. bd. dirs. St. Luke's Found., Kansas City, 1980-95; trustee U. Kansas City, 1980-96, Kansas City Cmty. Found., 1983-94, Eye Found., Kansas City, 1990-2000, H&R Block Found., Kansas City, 1996—, Jacob L. and Ella C. Loose Found., Kansas City, 1996—. Mem. Kansas City Bar Assn., Mo. Bar, River Club, Mission Hills Country Club, Phi Beta Kappa, Sigma Chi (Balfour Nat. award 1944) Episcopalian (chancellor emeritus Diocese West Mo.). Home: 2510 Grand Blvd Kansas City MO 64108-2678 Office: 2300 Main St Kansas City MO 64108-2416

MATHENY, MARY JANE, lawyer; b. Wauchula, Fla., May 29, 1953; d. George W. and Anna Lee (Scarborough) Marsh; m. Charles W. Matheny III, Mar. 30, 1974. BA, Fla. State U., 1974, JD with honors, 1978. Cert. travel counselor, 1990, master cruise counselor, 1992. Personnel aide Office of Gov. State of Fla., Tallahassee, 1974-75; sole practice Sebring, Fla., 1978—; travel agt. Ridge Travel Agy., 1985-94, Paradise Travel, Sebring, Fla., 1994—. Operator Bed and Breakfast, 1989-97. Bd. dirs. Staywell Clinic, 1996—. Named Outstanding Young Woman of Am., 1980-81. Mem. Fla. Bar Assn. (vice chmn. travel com. 1986-87), Highlands County Bar Assn. (pres. 1983-84, treas. 1985—), Fla. Fedn. Bus. and Profl. Women (dist. dir. 1985-86, state resolutions chmn. 1986-87). Young Career Woman, Am. Retail Travel Assn., Phi Delta Phi. Republican. Baptist.

MATHENY, RUTH ANN, editor; b. Fargo, N.D., Jan. 17, 1918; d. Jasper Gordon and Mary Elizabeth (Carey) Wheelock; m. Charles Edward Matheny, Oct. 24, 1960. BE, Mankato State Coll., 1938; MA, U. Minn., 1955; postgrad., Universidad Autonoma de Guadalajara, Mex., summer 1956, Georgetown U., summer, 1960. Tchr., U.S. and S.Am., 1938-61; assoc. editor Charles E. Merrill Pub. Co., Columbus, Ohio, 1963-66; tchr. Confraternity Christian Doctrine, Washington Court House, 1969-70; assoc. editor Jr. Cath. Messenger, Dayton, 1966-68; editor Witness Intermediate, 1968-70; editor in chief, assoc. pub. Today's Cath. Tchr., 1970—2002, editor-in-chief emeritus, 2002—; editor in chief Catechist, 1976-89, Ednl. Dealer, Dayton, 1976-80; v.p. Peter Li, Inc., 1980—. Editorial collaborator: Dimensions of Personality series, 1969— ; co-author: At Ease in the Classroom; author: Why a Catholic School?, Scripture Stories for Today: Why Religious Education? Bd. dirs. Friends Ormond Beach Library. Mem.: 3d Order St. Francis (eucharistic min. 1990—), Nat. Coun. Cath. Women. Home: 26 Reynolds Ave Ormond Beach FL 32174-7043 Office: Peter Li Ednl Group 2621 Dryden Rd Ste 300 Dayton OH 45439 E-mail: chilermat@aol.com. *In a world that is constantly changing, a strong religious faith is a dependable compass through which we are able to stay on a positive, forward course.*

MATHER, BRYANT, consultant; b. Balt., Dec. 27, 1916; s. Leon Bryant and Julia (Ferguson) M.; m. Katharine Selden Kniskern, Mar. 27, 1940 (dec. Feb. 1991). Grad., Balt. City Coll., 1934; AB in Geology, Johns Hopkins, 1936, postgrad., 1936-38, Am. U., 1938-39; D.Sc. (hon.), Clarkson U., 1978. Curator mineralogy Field Mus. Natural History, 1939-41; with U.S. Army Corps Engrs., 1941—; geologist Central Concrete Lab., U.S. Mil. Acad., 1941-42, Mt. Vernon, N.Y., 1942-46; supervisory research civil engr., chief engring. scis. br., concrete lab. Waterways Expt. Sta., Vicksburg, Miss., 1946-65, asst. chief concrete lab., 1965-66, chief, 1966-78, acting chief structures lab., 1978-80, chief lab., 1980-92, dir. structures lab., 1992-98, Waterways Expt. Sta. (now Corps Engrs. Rsch. Devel. Ctr.), 1998-2000, dir. emeritus structures lab., 2000—. Rsch. assoc. Fla. Dept. Agr. and Consumer Svcs., Gainesville, 1968—, Miss. Mus. Natural Scis., 1979—; bd. dirs. Miss. Ent. Mus. Miss. State U., 1985—99, rsch. assoc., 1985—, bd. dirs. emeritas, 1999—; rsch. assoc. Am. Mus. Natural History, N.Y.C., 1979—; mem. Sr. Exec. Assn., 1980—2000; mem. U.S. Com. of Internat. Commn. Large Dams, 1959—; lectr. Purdue U., 1961, Old Master lectr., 91; lectr. U. Notre Dame, 1964, MIT, 1966, Clemson U., 1967; Henry M. Shaw lectr. N.C. State U., 1967; lectr. U. Wis., 1978—, U. Tex., 1987—, Okla. State U., 1987, 99, Johns Hopkins U., 1991, Utah State U., 1995, U. Mo (Rolla), 2002; Stanton Walker lectr. U. Md., 1969; Edgar Marburg lectr. ASTM, 1970; mem. 4th, 5th, 6th and 7th Internat. Symposia Chemistry Cement, Internat. Symposium Movement Water in Porous Bodies, Paris, 1964. Co-author: Butterflies of Mississippi, 1958; Editor: Handbook for Concrete and Cement, 1942, 49, also quar. supplements, 1949-98. Fellow: ASTM (sec. com. C-9 1952—60, chmn. 1960—66, chmn. com. C-1 1968—74, chmn. com. E-39 1973—75, dir. 1970—73, v.p. 1973—75, pres. 1975—76, Award of Merit 1959, Sanford E. Thompson award 1961, Frank E. Richart award 1972, William T. Cavanaugh award 1990, Bryant and Katharine Mather award 1998, 2001), AAAS, NAS-NRC (chmn. concrete divsn. 1963—69, chmn. curing com. 1970—76, hon. mem. concrete divsn. and concrete coms. 1987, Roy W. Crum Disting. Svc. award 1966, 2d Disting. lectr. 1993), Transp. Rsch. Bd., Inst. Concrete Technologists (hon.; U.K.); mem.: NAE, ASCE (hon.), Mencken Soc., Soc. Ky. Lepidopterists, Mining Metall. and Petroleum Engrs. (Legion of Honor), So. Lepidopterists Soc. (John Abbot award 1983), Miss. Gem and Mineral Soc., Miss. Acad. Sci., Lepidopterists Soc., Am. Concrete Inst. (hon.; pres. 1964, Henry C. Turner medal 1973, Charles S. Whitney medal 1974, Delmar L. Bloem award 1990, Robert E. Philleo award 1992, Arthur R. Anderson award 2001), Am. Mus. Natural History (hon.; hon. patron 1974), Orleans County (Vt.) Hist. Soc., Natural Hist. Soc. Md., Meeoritical Soc., Mich. Entomol. Soc., Entomol. Soc. Md., Entomol. Soc. Am., Sigma Xi, Phi Beta Kappa. Home: 213 Mount Salus Dr Clinton MS 39056-5007 Office: US Army Corps of Engrs R&D Ctr Structures Lab 3909 Halls Ferry Rd Vicksburg MS 39180-6133 E-mail:

matherb@wes.army.mil. *The production of hydraulic-cement concrete—a synthetic sedimentary rock, may be the human race's most successful attempt to reproduce an activity previously engaged in only by God; and we have done it better; there are more varieties and there is better uniformity.*

MATHER, ELIZABETH VIVIAN, healthcare executive; b. Richmond, Ind., Sept. 19, 1941; d. Willie Samuel and Lillie Mae (Harper) Fuqua; m. Roland Donald Mather, Dec. 26, 1966. BS, Maryville (Tenn.) Coll., 1963; postgrad., Columbia U., 1965-66. Tchr. Richmond Cmty. Schs., 1963-67, Indpls. Pub. Schs., 1967-68; systems analyst Ind. Blue Cross Blue Shield, Indpls., 1968-71, Ind. Nat. Bank, Indpls., 1971; med. cons. Ind. State Dept. Pub. Welfare, 1971-78, cons. supr., 1978-86; systems analyst Ky. Blue Cross Blue Shield, Louisville, 1988-89; contracts specialist Humana Corp., 1989—. Active Rep. Cen. Com. Montgomery County, Crawfordsville, 1976-86, Centenary Meth. Ch., adminstrv. bd., 1990. Mem. DAR (treas. 1963-66, sec. 1978-86). Avocations: designing and sewing clothes. Home: 6106 Partridge Pl Floyds Knobs IN 47119-9427 Office: 500 W Main St Fl 6 Louisville KY 40202-2946 E-mail: emather@humana.com.

MATHER, GEORGE ROSS, clergy member; b. Trenton, N.J., June 1, 1930; s. Samuel Wooley and Henrietta Elizabeth (Deardorff) M.; m. Doris Christine Anderson, June 28, 1958; children: Catherine Anne Mather-Grimes, Geoffrey Thomas. BA, Princeton U., 1952; MDiv, Princeton Theol. Sem., 1955; DD, Hanover Coll., 1986. Ordained to Ministry, 1955. Asst. pastor Abington (Pa.) Presbyn., 1955-58; pastor 1st Presbyn. Ch. Ewing, Trenton, 1958-71; sr. pastor 1st Presbyn. Ch. Ft. Wayne, Ind., 1971-86; pastor 3d Presbyn. Ch. Ft. Wayne, 1987-95. Author: Frontier Faith: The Story of the Pioneer Congregations, 1992, The Best of Fort Wayne, vol. 1, 2000, vol. 2, 2001; co-editor: On the Heritage Trail, 1994; contbr. articles to profl. jours. Pres. Allen County Libr. Trustees, Ft. Wayne, Allen County Libr. Found., Ft. Wayne, Clergy United for Action, Ft. Wayne; trustee Hanover (Ind.) Coll.; chmn. Bicentennial Religious Heritage Commn., 1994; bd. dirs. Smock Found., 1971-85. Mem. Ind. Religious History Assn. (bd. dirs.), Allen County Ft. Wayne Hist. Soc. (bd. dirs.), The Quest Club (pres.). Avocations: travel, hiking, canoeing. Home: 6726 Quail Ridge Ln Fort Wayne IN 46804-2874

MATHER, JOHN CROMWELL, astrophysicist; b. Roanoke, Va., Aug. 7, 1946; s. Robert Eugene and Martha Belle (Cromwell) Mather; m. Jane Anne Hauser, Nov. 22, 1980. BA, Swarthmore (Pa.) Coll., 1968; PhD, U. Calif., Berkeley, 1974; DSc (hon.), Swarthmore Coll., 1994. NAS/NRC rsch. assoc. NASA/Goddard Inst. for Space Studies, N.Y.C., 1974-76; lectr. in astronomy Columbia U., 1975-76; astrophysicist NASA/Goddard Space Flight Ctr., Greenbelt, Md., 1976—, head infrared astrophysics br., 1988-89, 90-93, sr. scientist, 1989-90, 93—, study scientist Cosmic Background Explorer Satellite, 1976-82, project scientist COBE, 1982—, prin. investigator FIRAS on COBE, 1976—. Chmn. external adv. bd. Ctr. for Astrophys. Rsch. in the Antarctic, U. Chgo., 1992—95; mem. lunar astrophysics mgmt. ops. working group NASA Hdqrs., Washington, 1992; study scientist Next Generation Space Telescope , 1995—; mem. NRC Bd. Physics and Astronomy, 1998—2001. Author: The Very First Light with John Boslough, 1996; contbr. articles to profl. jours. Recipient Nat. Space Achievement award, Rotary, 1991, Laurels award, Aviation Week and Space Tech., 1992, Space Sci. award, AIAA, 1993, John Scott award, City of Phila., 1995, Mark Aaronson Meml. prize, 1998, Franklin medal in Physics, 1999. Fellow: AAAS (Rumford prize 1996), Am. Phys. Soc.; mem.: Nat. Acad. Scis., Internat. Astron. Union, Am. Astron. Soc. (councilor 1998—2001, Dannie Heineman prize astrophysics 1993), Sigma Xi. Democrat. Unitarian Universalist. Achievements include proposed Cosmic Background Explorer Satellite, led team to successful launch in 1989; measured spectrum of cosmic microwave background radiation to unprecedented accuracy. Office: NASA/Goddard Space Flight Code 685 Greenbelt MD 20771-0001

MATHER, JOHN RUSSELL, climatologist, educator; b. Boston, Oct. 9, 1923; s. John and Mabelle (Russell) M.; m. Amy L. Nelson, 1946 (dec. 1994); children: Susan, Thomas, Ellen; m. Sandra F. Pritchard, 1997. BA, Williams Coll., 1945; BS in Meteorology, MIT, 1947, MS, 1948; PhD in Geography-Climatology, Johns Hopkins U., 1951. Rsch. assoc., climatologist Lab. Climatology, Seabrook, N.J., 1948-54, prin. rsch. scientist Centerton, 1954-63; pres. Lab. Climatology, C.W. Thornthwaite Assoc., 1963-72; asst. prof. Johns Hopkins U., 1951-53; assoc. prof. climatology Drexel Inst. Tech., Phila., 1957-60; prof. geography U. Del., Newark, 1963-99, prof. emeritus, 1999—, chmn. dept. geography, 1966-89; state climatologist Del., 1978-92. Vis. lectr. geography U. Chgo., 1957-61; vis. prof. U.S. Mil. Acad., 1989. Author 2 books on applied climatology, 1 book on water resources; co-author biography of C.W. Thornthwaite; U.S. editor joint U.S.-USSR book on global change; contbr. numerous articles to tech. jours. Recipient Lifetime Achievement award in climatology, 1999. Fellow AAAS; mem. Am. Meteorol. Soc., Assn. Am. Geographers (v.p. 1990-91, pres. 1991-92, Lifetime Achievement award 1998), Am. Geog. Soc. (councilor 1981-99, sec. 1982-99, Charles P. Daly medal), Am. Water Resources Assn., Tau Beta Pi, Phi Kappa Phi. Achievements include contributing to concept of potential evapotranspiration, its measurement, use in climatic water balance; moisture factor in climate; application of climatic water balance to studies in agr., hydrology, applied climatology. Home: 13 Roosevelt Way Avondale PA 19311-9337 Office: U Del Dept Geography Newark DE 19716 E-mail: mather@udel.edu.

MATHER, MILDRED EUNICE, retired archivist; b. Washington, July 25, 1922; d. Hollis John and Delpha Irene (Cummings) Whiting; m. Stewart Elbert Mather, Aug. 7, 1955; children: Julie Marie, Thomas Stewart (dec.). Cert. bus sch., Burlington and Des Moines (Iowa), 1941, 1947; cert., Stenotype Inst., 1948. Typist Burlington Willow-Weave, 1941-42, Burlington Basket Co., 1942; clk. typist U.S. Dept. War, Washington, 1942-43; supr. internat. conf. Dept. State, 1949-52; bookkeeper Iowa Wesleyan Coll., Mt. Pleasant, 1952-55; clk. typist Herbert Hoover Presdl. Libr., West Branch, Iowa, 1964-69, archives technician, 1964-72, archivist, libr., 1972-92. WAC, 1943-46. Mem. Order of Eastern Star (worthy matron). Republican. Home: 79 Eisenhower St West Branch IA 52358-9403

MATHER, RICHARD BURROUGHS, retired Chinese language and literature educator; b. Baoding, Hebei, China, Nov. 11, 1913; s. William Arnot and Grace (Burroughs) M.; m. Virginia Marjorie Temple, June 3, 1939; 1 dau., Elizabeth Temple. BA, Princeton U., 1935; B.Th., Princeton Theol. Sem., 1939; PhD in Oriental Langs, U. Calif., Berkeley, 1949. Ordained to ministry United Presbyterian Ch. U.S., 1939; pastor Belle Haven (Va.) Presbyterian Ch., 1939-41; asst. prof. Chinese U. Minn., Mpls., 1949-57, assoc. prof., 1957-64, prof., 1964-84. Mem. Am. Council Learned Socs. Com. on Study of Chinese Civilization, 1979-81 Author: Shih-shuo hsin-yu, A New Account of Tales of the World, 1976, The Poet Shen Yueh (441-513), the Reticent Marquis, 1988, The Age of Eternal Brilliance: Three Poets of the Yung-ming Era, 2001; contbr. articles on medieval Chinese lit. and religion. Guggenheim fellow, 1956-57; Fulbright Hays grantee, 1956-57, 63-64; Am. Council Learned Socs. grantee, 1963-64 Mem. Am. Oriental Soc. (pres. 1980-81), Assn. Asian Studies, Chinese Lang. Tchrs. Assn. Democrat. Home: 2091 Dudley Ave Saint Paul MN 55108-1415

MATHER, ROGER FREDERICK, music educator, writer; b. London, England, May 27, 1917; came to U.S., 1938; s. Richard and Marie Louise (Schultze) M.; m. Dorothea Meinen, Sept. 11, 1943 (div. Sept. 1971); children: Arielle Diane, Christopher Richard; m. Betty Louise Bang, Aug. 3, 1973. BA with honors, Cambridge U., 1938; MSc, MIT, 1940; MA in Metallurgy, U. Cambridge, 1941. Registered profl. engr., Ohio, Mich., Pa. Rsch. metallurgist Inland Steel Co., East Chicago, Ind., 1940-42; chief metallurgist Willys-Overland Motors, Toledo, 1942-46, Kaiser-Frazer Corp., Willow Run, Mich., 1946-50; project mgr. U.S. Steel Corp., Pitts., 1950-61; dir. rsch. engring. Mine Safety Appliances Co., 1961-62; rsch. staff Du Pont Co., Wilmington, Del., 1962-63; chief nuclear power tech. br. NASA, Cleve., 1963-73; adj. prof. music U. Iowa, Iowa City, 1973-96. Instr. pub. speaking and stage fright U. Iowa, 1983-85, Kirkwood C.C., Iowa City, 1983-85; cons. Miyazawa Flutes, U.S.A., Coralville, Iowa, 1985-90; lectr. U. Toledo; Mich. state examiner Registration of Profl. Engrs.; condr. numerous workshops, clinics, classes, and flute recitals regionally, nationally, Europe and Asia. Author: The Art of Playing the Flute, 1980, Vol. 2, 1981, Vol. 3, 1988; contbr. chpts. to several woodwind anthologies; pub., exec. editor The Romney Press, 1980—; contbr. poems to numerous poetry anthologies in US, Eng., numerous articles to sci. and music jours. Mem. Internat. Soc. Poets (Hall of Fame, 1998, Poet of Merit, 2002), Nat. Flute Assn. (life, coms.), The Pa. Assn., Mensa. Episcopalian. Avocations: semi-professional photography, high fidelity sound reproduction contributions, alternative medicine. Home: 715 George St Iowa City IA 52240 E-mail: bangmather@aol.com.

MATHER, RUTH ELSIE, writer; b. Waverly, Wash., Feb. 14, 1934; d. James Orrin and Leona Ezthelda (Mather) Tallman; m. Mike Nicholas Dakis, Apr. 20, 1958 (div. Nov. 1971); children: Cynthia Michelle, Martin Nicholas; m. Fred Junior Morgan, Nov. 20, 1971. BA with highest honors, Brigham Young U., 1961, MA, 1965; postgrad., U. Miss., 1977-78. Cert. secondary tchr., Idaho, cert. elem. tchr. and secondary tchr. grades 7-14, Calif. English tchr. Iglesia Jesucristo Rama Roma, Mexico City, 1955-56, Lemhi County Schs., Leadore, Idaho, 1962-66; English instr. Yonsei U., Seoul, Republic of Korea, 1973-74, U. Md. Far East Divsn., Seoul, 1975-77, Boise (Idaho) State U., 1978-79, Coll. of the Redwoods, Eureka, Calif., 1980-81; writer hist. video scripts History West Pub. Co., Oklahoma City, 1990—; screenwriter Frontier Images, Canyon Country, Calif., 1994—. Cons. on hist. video for PBS, A La Carte, San Francisco, 1994-95; guest expert on Secrets of the Gold Rush-PBS, 1995; cons. Western Mont. Coll. Schmittroth collection of electronically printed Western history books, Dillon, 1997—. Author: Hanging the Sheriff: A Biography of Henry Plummer, 1987, John David Borthwick: Artist of the Gold Rush, 1989, Gold Camp Desperadoes: Study of Crime & Punishment on Frontier, 1990, Vigilante Victims, 1991, Scandal of the West: Domestic Violence on the Frontier, 1998, The Bannack Gallows, 1998, The Cottonwood Murders: Unsolved, 1999; contbr. short stories, book revs., articles to encys. and profl. jours. Local campaign dir. Dem. Party, Arcata, Calif., 1969-70. Mem. Nat. Outlaw and Lawman Assn., Western Outlaw and Lawman Assn., Virginia City Preservation Alliance, People for the Ethical Treatment of Animals, Nat. Anti-Vivisection Soc., Physicians' Com. for Responsible Medicine. Avocations: reading, hiking. Office: History West Pub Co PO Box 23133 Oklahoma City OK 73123-2133

MATHER, STEPHANIE JUNE, lawyer; b. Kansas City, Mo., Dec. 5, 1952; d. Edward Wayne and H. June (Kunkel) M.; m. Miles Christopher Zimmerman, Sept. 23, 1988. BA magna cum laude, Okla. City U., 1975, JD with honors, 1980. Lawyer Pierce, Couch, Hendrickson, Johnston & Baysinger, Okla. City, Okla., 1980-88, Manchester, Hiltgen & Healy, P.C., Okla. City, 1989-90; sr. staff counsel Nat. Am. Ins. Co., Chandler, Okla., 1990-98; atty. Ctr. for Edn. Law, Oklahoma City, 1998—. Asst. v.p. Lagere & Walkingstick Ins. Agy., Inc., Chandler, Okla., 1993-98. Co-chair Lincoln County Dem. Party, 1991-92, 95-97; v.p. Lincoln County Dem. Women, 1992-95, pres., 1995-97; bd. dirs. Lincoln County Partnership for Children, 1994—, Gateway to Prevention and Recovery, 1996-97. Mem. Okla. Bar Assn. (editor, bd. editors, 1992-99), Lincoln County Bar Assn. (mem. libr. bd. 1990—), Nat. Sch. Bds. Assn. (coun. of sch. attys. 1998—, bd. dirs. 2001--), Okla. State Sch. Bds. Assn. (coun. of sch. attys. 1998—, bd. dirs. 2002--), Lincoln County Profl. Women, Alpha Phi (treas. Ctrl. Okla. Alumnae 1997-99). Democrat. Avocations: reading, genealogy, ranching, cooking. Home: PO Box 246 Chandler OK 74834-0246 Office: Ctr for Edn Law 809 NW 36th St Oklahoma City OK 73118-7213 E-mail: smather@cfel.com.

MATHERLEE, THOMAS RAY, health care consultant; b. Dayton, Ohio, Sept. 18, 1934; s. Dennis R. and Eleanor E. Matherlee; children: Michael, Jennifer, Craig, Brent, Brian. BSBA, Findlay Coll., 1958; MBA, U. Chgo., 1960. Adminstrv. resident Shannon Hosp., San Angelo, Tex., 1959-60; asst. adminstr. Richland Meml. Hosp., Olney, Ill., 1960-61; adminstrv. asst., then adminstr. Forsyth Meml. Hosp., Winston-Salem, N.C., 1961-68; exec. dir. Gaston County (N.C.) Hosp., 1968-70, Gaston Meml. Hosp., Inc., Gastonia, 1970-80, pres., 1981-85; sr. v.p. Vols. Hosps. of Am., Inc., Washington, 1986-87, exec. v.p. Irving, Tex., 1987-90; pres. AMA Svcs., Inc., 1990-94; sr. v.p. The Hunter Group, 1994-97; pres. Matherlee Assoc., Banner Elk, N.C., 1997—. Cons. Sch. Pastoral Care N.C. Bapt. Hosp., Winston-Salem, 1967-68; mem. sub-area adv. coun. Health Systems Agy., 1975-80; adj. faculty Sch. Cmty. and Allied Health U. Ala.-Birmingham, 1980-85; bd. dirs. Joint Commn. on Accreditation of Healthcare Orgns., 1986-90, treas., audit and fin. com. chmn., mem. exec. com. Contbr. articles on hosp. adminstrn. to profl. jours. Dir. Olney, Ill. CD, 1960-61; mem. fin. com. Piedmont coun. Boy Scouts Am., 1970; mem. adv. bd. Gastonia Wesleyan Youth Chorus. 1972; mem. joint com. nursing edn. N.C. State Bd. Edn. and Bd. Higher Edn., 1969-71; mem. adminstrv. bd. First United Meth. Ch., Gastonia, 1972-74; bd. dirs. Gaston County Heart Assn., 1968-70, Forsyth County Cancer Soc., 1964-65; trustee N.C. Hosp. Edn. and Rsch. Found., 1966-71, pres. 1970-71; trustee N.C. Blue Cross and Blue Shield, Inc., 1971-77, Southeastern Hosp. Conf., 1971-72, 73-81; mem. edn. com. 1978—, mem. program com., 1975-76. Named Boss of Yr., Nat. Secs. Assn., 1970-71. Fellow Am. Coll. Healthcare Execs.; mem. MGMA, N.C. Hosp. Assn. (life, trustee 1966-72, pres. 1970-71, chmn. coun. govt. liaison 1978-81, Disting. Svc. award 1985), N.C. League Nursing, Am. Hosp. Assn. (ho. of dels. 1973-78, 83-85), spkr. Ho. of dels. 1985, trustee 1975-78, 83-85, chmn. bd. trustees 1984), Gastonia C. of C. (health affairs com. 1969-72), Kiwanis.

MATHERLEY, STEVE ALLEN, cost accountant; b. Hixson, Tenn., July 15, 1954; S Frank Heilman and Shirley Belle (Clements) M.; m. Gina Anne Baker, Jan. 24, 1981; children: Steve Allen Jr., Mekeesha Anne. Student, David Lipscomb Coll., 1972, 73-75, Tenn. Tech. U., 1973, Fla. Atlantic U., 1976; BS in Bus. Adminstrn. and Acctg., U. Tenn., 1978. Cost acct. Cavalier Corp., Chattanooga, 1978-82; pvt. practice bookkeeper, 1982-83, 84-86; contr. Robert M. Davenport Co., 1983-84; sr. staff acct. Carter Ltd., Inc., Fayetteville, Tenn., 1986-88; mgr. acctg. and fin., Ctr. Space Transp. and Applied Rsch. U. Tenn. Space Inst., Tullahoma, 1988-94; cost acct. Tenn. Apparel Corp., 1994-96, Samuel Strapping Systems, Winchester, Tenn., 1996-98; contr. BSG divsn. Wheland Automotive Industries, Chattanooga, 1998—. Ind. cons. Engring. Rsch. & Cons., Inc., 1989-94. Mem. loan policy com. Arnold Eng. Devel. Ctr., Fed. Credit Union, 1989-90; adult vol./leader Boy Scouts Am., 1991-95; preacher Ch. of Christ, 1990—; vol., instr. cmty. CPR and first aid ARC, 1993—. Mem. Inst. Mgmt. Accts. Republican. Avocations: fishing, hiking, hunting, gardening, reading. Office: Wheland Foundry 2800 Broad St Chattanooga TN 37408-3101

MATHERN, TIM, state legislator; b. Edgeley, N.D., Apr. 19, 1950; s. John J. and Christina Mathern; m. Lorene Mathern, Feb. 12, 1971; children: Reba, Tonya, Josh, Zach. BA, N.D. State U., 1971; MSW, U. Nebr., Omaha, 1980; MPA, Harvard U., 2000. Staff Cath. Family Svc., Fargo, N.D., 1973-99; mem. N.D. Senate, Bismarck, 1986—; parish adminstr. Fargo, N.D., 2000—; mem. legis. mgmt. com. N.D. Senate, Bismarck, 1993-99, asst. majority leader, 1991, senate minority leader, 1995-99, also mem. jud. stds. com. Mem. polit. subdivsn. com., N.D., 1995-97, intergovtl. com., 1999-2001, human svcs. com, 2000—, govt. and veterans com., 2000 chmn. Budget Com. on Govt. Adminstrn., 2001—; mem. Kennedy Sch. Student Govt., Cambridge, Mass., 1999-2000. Mem. Fargo-Cass County Econ. Devel. Corp., 1993-99; bd. dirs. Prairieland Home Care, 1993-99, Charism Cmty. Ctr., 1997—; pres., bd. dirs. Kaleidoscope, 2001—; mem. exec. com. N.D. Dem. Nonpartisan League Party, 1995-99; chmn. Budget Com. on Human Svcs., 1997-99; mem. Garrison Diversion Overview Com., 93-99; sch. coun., Martin Luther King Jr., Cambridge, Mass., 1999-00. Recipient N.D. Prairie Peacemaker award, 2000, Pub. Svc. award U. Nebr. Alumni Assn., 2002; named Legislator of Yr., Red River Valley Mental Health Assn., 1989, 91, Legislator of Yr., N.D. Children's Caucus, 1993, 98; Bush Leadership fellow, 1999. Mem. NASW (Social Worker of Yr. award 1987, Lifetime Achievement award 1998), Mental Health Assn. Democrat. Roman Catholic. Home: 406 Elmwood Fargo ND 58103-4315 E-mail: tmathern@state.nd.us.

MATHERS, ALLEN STANLEY, judge, arbitrator, consultant; b. Elmhurst, N.Y., Jan. 20, 1949; s. William Albert and Agnes (Przeniczny) M.; m. Mary Elizabeth Breslin, Oct. 1, 1977; children: Matthew Allen, Sarah Anne, Amanda Mary. BA, St. Francis Coll., 1970; JD, St. John's U., Jamaica, N.Y., 1973. Bar: N.Y. 1974, Conn. 1989, U.S. Dist. Ct. (so. and ea. dists.) N.Y. 1974, U.S. Ct. Appeals (2d cir.) 1974, U.S. Supreme Ct. 1983. Assoc. Israelson & Streit, N.Y.C., 1973-80; dir. labor rels. Trans World Airlines, Inc., 1980-82; dir. legal svcs. fund, local 74 Svc. Employees Internat. Union, AFL-CIO, Long Island City, N.Y., 1982—. Village justice Village of Garden City, N.Y., 1997—. Mayor, Village of Garden City; bd. dirs. Arthritis Found. Col., JAG, N.Y. Guard. Mem. ABA, N.Y. State Bar Assn. (spl. com. prepaid legal svcs.), Nassau County Bar Assn., Am. Arbitration Assn., Atlantic Beach Club, Equestrian Order Knights of Holy Sepulchre. Roman Catholic. Home: 30 Kensington Rd Garden City NY 11530-4241 Office: Service Employees Internat Union Local 74 24-09 38th Ave Long Island City NY 11101-3512

MATHERS, EARL FRANK, economic developer; b. Marietta, Ohio, Mar. 26, 1950; s. Earl Frank and Mildred Augusta (Lunsford) M.; m. Kalie Rea Rademacher, Oct. 6, 1980; children: Jonathan, Joshua, Julie, Jena. BA, U. Mont., 1980; MPA, U. Wyo., 1986. Dir. phys. plant Northwest Coll., Powell, Wyo., 1981-85; dir. vocat. svcs. RENEW, Sheridan, 1986-88; county devel. dir. Fremont County, Lander, 1988-91; exec. dir. Campbell County Econ. Devel. Corp., Gillette, 1991-95; CEO Northeast Wyo. Econ. Devel. Coalition, 1995—. Cons. adminstr. City of Lander, 1989-90; Am. Advisor to Russia, 1994—. Contbr. articles to profl. jours. Mem. Gillette Campus Bd., 1983—, Gillette Adminstrv. Caucus, 1991; del. Rocky Mountain Trade Corridor, Helena, Mont., 1992. Mem. Am. Econ. Devel. Coun., Wyo. Econ. Devel. Assn., Rotary. Republican. Mem. Ch. of Christ. Avocations: outdoor recreation, coaching baseball, phys. fitness. Home: 110 W Lakeway Rd # 1000 Gillette WY 82718-6355 Office: Campbell County Econ Devel PO Box 3948 222 S Gillette Ave #510 Gillette WY 82717-3948

MATHERS, MARGARET, reference librarian, archivist; b. Ada, Okla., Feb. 16, 1929; d. Robert Lee and Josiephine Margaret (Reed) Erwin; m. Coleman F. Moss, Sept. 1956 (div. 1966); children: Carol Lee Gibson-Taylor, Marilyn Frances; m. Boyd Leroy Mathers, Apr. 10, 1967 (div. 1987). BS in Music, Tex. U., 1950. Svc. rep. Gen. Tel. Co., Santa Monica, Calif., 1955-58; tchr. pvt. sch., 1958-60; computer program and data analyst System Devel. Corp., 1961-66; computer programmer Inst. Def. Analyses, Arlington, Va., 1966-70; typist, transcriber Edgewater, Md., 1971-80; sec. People Assisting the Homeless, 1992-94; proofreader, copy editor Farmington Daily Times, 1993-99, mem. editl. bd., libr., office mgr., 1999—. Pres. San Juan Coun. Cmty. Agys., 1986-87, treas., 1987-89, sec., 1989-90; cons. in field. Dir. San Juan Cath. Charities, Farmington, N.Mex., 1984-93, asst. dir., 1993-96, sec. bd. dirs., 1997-2000; chmn. county Libertarian Party N.Mex., San Juan County, 1985-99, sec. ctrl. com., 1988-92, mem. ctrl. com., 1988—; mem. selection com. Habitat for Humanity, 1990; mem. San Juan County Task Force on Housing, 1991, Task Force on Transp., 1991; mem. social justice com. Sacred Heart, Farmington, 1992; mem. adv. bd. San Juan County DNA Legal Aid, 1992, sec., 1993; sec. Cmty. Network Coun., 1992-94, treas., 1994—; treas. Neighborhood Watch, 1998—; minister Secular Franciscan Order, 1997-2001. Roman Catholic. Avocations: puzzles, politics, philosophy. Office: The Daily Times PO Box 450 Farmington NM 87499-0450

MATHERS, THOMAS NESBIT, financial consultant; b. Bloomington, Ind., Apr. 22, 1914; s. Frank Curry and Maud Esther (Bowser) M.; m. Helen M. Curtis, Oct. 23, 1943 (dec.); children: Mary, Abigail. AB, Ind. U., 1936, LL.B., 1939; MBA, Harvard U., 1941. Bar: Ind. 1939. Research asst. No. Trust Co., 1941-43; legal asst. Chgo. Ordnance Dist., 1943-44; employee to ptnr. Woodruff Hays & Co., Chgo., 1944-51; pres. Security Counselors, Inc., 1951-62, Mathers & Co., Chgo., 1962-75, chmn. bd., 1975-85, vice chmn., 1985-91. Bd. dirs. Lincoln Income Fund, 1978-2001, Lincoln Convertible Securities Fund, 1986-2001; pres. Mathers Fund, 1965-75, chmn. bd., 1975-85, vice chmn., 1985-91; v.p., bd. dirs. OFC Corp. Meadowood Project, 1991—. Trustee Beloit Coll., 1970-2001, life trustee, 2001—. Recipient Disting. Alumni Service award Ind. U., 1979 Mem. Ind. U. Disting. Alumni Assn. (past pres.). Clubs: Union League, Econ. of Chgo, Westmoreland Country, Mich. Shores, Investment Analysts Chgo. (past pres.). Republican. Presbyterian. Home: 115 Bertling Ln Winnetka IL 60093-4202

MATHERS, WILLIAM HARRIS, lawyer; b. Newport, R.I., Aug. 27, 1914; s. Howard and Margaret I. (Harris) M.; m. Myra T. Martin, Jan. 17, 1942; children: William Martin, Michael Harris, John Grinnell, Myra Tutt, Ursula Fraser. AB, Dartmouth Coll., 1935; JD, Yale U., 1938. Bar: N.Y. 1940. With Milbank, Tweed & Hope, 1938-48; mem. Milbank, Tweed, Hope & Hadley, 1948-57; v.p., sec., dir. Yale & Towne Mfg. Co., Stamford, Conn., 1957-60; ptnr. Chadbourne & Parke, 1960-75, counsel, 1983—; exec. v.p., gen. counsel, sec., dir. United Brands Co., 1975-82. Mayor, trustee Village of Cove Neck, N.Y., 1950-82; trustee Barnard Coll., 1958-69. Served as pvt. to maj. U.S. Army, 1942-46. Mem. ABA, N.Y. State Bar Assn., Nassau County Bar Assn., Assn. of Bar of City of N.Y., New Eng. Soc. in City of N.Y., Casque and Gauntlet, Corbey Court, Piping Rock Club, Seminole Golf Club, N.Y. Yacht Club, Cold Spring Harbor Beach Club, Phi Beta Kappa, Psi Upsilon. Home: 1389 King George Farm Rd Sutton VT 05867-9623 Office: 30 Rockefeller Plz New York NY 10112-0002

MATHES, DOROTHY JEAN HOLDEN, occupational therapist; b. Paterson, N.J., Mar. 13, 1953; d. Cornelius Fred and Dorothy Johanna (Ferguson) Holden; m. Clayton Derald Mathes, May 26, 1973 (div. Dec. 1984); children: Christy, Carl, Chuck, Chad; m. Elie Youssef Hajjar, Oct. 4, 1989 (dec. Dec. 1996). BS in Occupational Therapy, Tex. Woman's U., Denton, Tex., 1988; MA in Occupational Therapy, Tex. Woman's U., 1995. Lic. occupational therapist, Tex. Occupational therapy cons. Lakes Regional-SOCS Early Childhood Intervention, 1988-97, Denton (Tex.) State Sch., 1997—. Mem. Am. Occupational Therapy Assn., Tex. Occupational Therapy Assn. Avocations: gardening, reading, swimming. Home: 2608 Woodhaven St Denton TX 76209-1340 Office: Denton State Sch PO Box 368 Denton TX 76202-0368 E-mail: djmathes@verizon.net.

MATHES, EDWARD CONRAD, architect; b. New Orleans, Mar. 10, 1943; s. Earl L. and Margaret (Gash) M.; m. Anne M. Ergenbright, Mar. 1, 1964 (div. June 2000); children: Margaret Elizabeth Hughes, Anne Catherine Aboud. BArch, U. Southwestern La., 1968. Registered arch., La., Miss., Fla., Tex., Ala., Ga., Tenn., Ky., N.C., S.C., W.Va., Conn. Tchr. U. Southwestern La., Lafayette, 1968-69; asst. to mng. arch. Rogers, Taliaferro, Kostritsky & Lamb, Balt., 1969; pres. Mathes, Bergman & Assocs., Inc., New Orleans, 1969-82, The Mathes Group, New Orleans, 1982—2000; chmn. MathesBrierre Architects, 2001—. Chmn. Orleans Svc. Ctr., ARC, 1993-94; bd. dirs. City Park Improvement Assn., 1996—, pres. Recipient Am. Sch. and Univ. award, 1983, 1985, Partnership award, ARC, 1998, CEO's award, S.E. La. chpt. ARC, People's Choice award for music., comms., theatre complex, Loyola New Orleans, 1989, People's Choice award for Univ. Libr., 2000. Mem.: AIA (pres. New Orleans chpt. 1989, Inst. scholar 1968—69, Honor award New Orleans Chpt. 1982, 1989, 2000, Honor award La. 1982, 1986, 2001), Constrn. Industry Assn. (pres. 1984—85, Honor award 1993), City Energy Club, Metairie Country Club, Pickwick Club, Rotary (pres. New Orleans 1985—86). Republican. Presbyterian. Avocations: tennis, travel. Home: # 4 Park Island Dr New Orleans LA 70122 Office: MathesBrierre Architects 201 Saint Charles Ave Fl 41 New Orleans LA 70170-4100 E-mail: emathes@mathesbrierre.com.

MATHES, STEPHEN JON, lawyer; b. N.Y.C., Mar. 18, 1945; s. Joseph and Beatrice M.; m. Michele Marshall, Oct. 22, 1972 (div. 1992); children: Aaron, Benjamin; m. Maria McGarry, Dec. 19, 1992; 1 child, Sara. BA, U. Pa., 1967, JD, 1970. Bar: N.Y. 1971, Pa. 1972, U.S. Dist. Ct. (ea. dist.) Pa. 1971. U.S. Ct. Appeals (3d cir.) 1972, U.S. Ct. Appeals (5th cir.) 1985, U.S. Ct. Appeals (4th cir.) 1985, U.S. Ct. Appeals (9th cir.) 2000, U.S. Supreme Ct. 1978. Law clk. U.S. Ct. Appeals (3d cir.), Phila., 1970-71; asst. dist. atty. major felony unit, spl. investigation unit Office of Phil. Dist. Atty., 1975; assoc. Dilworth, Paxson, Kalish & Kauffman, 1971-74, 76-77, sr. ptnr., 1977-91, mem. exec. com., 1987-90, co-chmn. litigation dept., 1987-91; ptnr. Hoyle, Morris & Kerr, 1992—; bd. dirs. The Levitt Found., 1990—, sec., 1991—. Mgmt. com. Hoyle, Morris & Kerr, Phila., 1992-97, 2001—. Bd. dirs., exec. com. Acad. Vocal Arts, 1993-2000, mem. exec. com., chmn. student aid com.; mem. legal and compliance divsn. Securities Industry Assn., 1998—. Mem. ABA, Am. Law Inst., Securities Industries Assn., Pa. Bar Assn., Phila. Bar Assn. (mem. litigation divsn.), Thanatopsis Soc., Racquet Club, Germantown Cricket Club. Home: 199 Lynnebrook Ln Philadelphia PA 19118-2706 Office: Holye Morris & Kerr One Liberty Pl Ste 4900 Philadelphia PA 19103 E-mail: smathes@hoylemk.com.

MATHESON, ALAN ADAMS, law educator; b. Cedar City, Utah, Feb. 2, 1932; s. Scott Milne and Adele (Adams) M.; m. Milicent Holbrook, Aug. 15, 1960; children— Alan, David Scott, John Robert. BA, U. Utah, 1953, MS, 1957, JD, 1959; postgrad. asso. in law, Columbia U. Bar: Utah 1960, Ariz. 1975. Asst. to pres. Utah State U., 1961-67; mem. faculty Ariz. State U., Tempe, 1967—. prof. law, 1970—, dean, 1978-84, 89, 97-98. Bd. dirs. Ariz.

Center Law in Public Interest, 1979-81; bd. dirs. DNA Navajo Legal Services, 1984-97. Pres. Tri-City Mental Health Citizens Bd., 1973-74. Served with AUS, 1953-55. Mem. Utah Bar Assn., Ariz. Bar Assn., Maricopa County Bar Assn., Phi Beta Kappa, Order of Coif. Democrat. Mem. Lds Ch. Home: 720 E Geneva Dr Tempe AZ 85282-3737 Office: Ariz State U Coll Law Tempe AZ 85287

MATHESON, ANN, librarian, writer; b. Lochalsh, Wester Ross, Scotland, July 5, 1940; d. Alexander and Catherine (MacRae) M.; m. T. Russell Walker, Nov. 24, 1973. MA, U. St. Andrews, 1962; Diploma in Scottish Studies, U. Edinburgh, 1968, MLitt, 1970, PhD, 1979; Order of the Brit. Empire, 1998; DLitt, St. And, 1999. Asst. keeper Nat. Libr. Scotland, Edinburgh, 1975—83, keeper, 1983-2000; sec. gen. coun. U. Edinburgh, 2001—. Gen. sec. Ligue des Bibliothèques Européennes de Recherche, 1994-2000; chair lit. com. Scottish Arts Coun., 1997—; chair Consortium of European Rsch. Librs., 2000—, NEWSPLAN 2000, 1999—. Author: (with Mary Ferguson) The Scottish Gaelic Union Catalogue, vol. I, 1984, Theories of Rhetoric in the 18th-century Scottish Sermon, 1995; editor: (with Patrick Cadell) For the Encouragement of Learning, 1989; editor Transactions of the Edinburgh Bibliographical Society, 1973-83; contbr. articles and revs. to profl. jours. Decorated Order Brit. Empire. Mem.: Scottish Libr. Assn. (hon.), Ligue des Bibliothèques Européennes de Recherche (hon.). Home: Yewbank 52 Liberton Brae Edinburgh EH16 6AF Scotland E-mail: a.matheson@tinyworld.co.uk.

MATHESON, GORDON KEITH, neuroanatomist, educator, neuroendocrinologist; b. Chgo., Apr. 22, 1934; s. William John and Dorothy Fletcher (Taylor) M.; m. Linda Nan Olsen, Dec. 19, 1958; children: Mark, Paul, Jan, Jean. BS, Brigham Young U., 1962, MS, 1964; PhD, U. Wash., 1968. Fellow Brain Rsch. Inst. UCLA, 1968-69; asst. prof. Stritch Sch. Medicine Loyola U. Chgo., Maywood, Ill., 1969-74; assoc. prof. Ind. U. Sch. Medicine, Evansville, 1974-88, prof. anatomy, 1987-99, prof. emeritus, 1999—. Contbr. articles to profl. jours. Mem. Am. Assn. Anatomists, Soc. for Neurosci., Soc. for Exptl. Biology and Medicine, Sigma Xi. Avocations: photography, computer imaging and graphics. E-mail address. Office: Ind Univ Sch Medicine 8600 University Blvd Evansville IN 47712-3534 E-mail: matheson@iupui.edu.

MATHESON, JEAN KING, neurologist, educator; b. Boston, Oct. 28, 1949; d. Daniel Nicholson and Isabella (Mills) M.; m. Mark David Aronson, Aug. 17, 1981; children: Alexander, Benjamin. BS, Antioch Coll., Yellow Springs, Ohio, 1972; MD, Harvard U., 1976. Intern in medicine Beth Israel Hosp., Boston, 1976-77; resident in neurology Lonwood Tng. Program in Neurology Harvard Med. Sch., 1977-80, chief resident in neurology, 1979-80; fellow in clin. neurophysiology Brigham and Women's Hosp., 1980-82; neurologist Beth Israel Hosp., 1982—, co-dir. Sleep Disorders Ctr., 1982-98; med. dir. Sleep Disorders Ctr. Beth Israel Deaconess Med. Ctr., 1998—. Asst. prof. neurology Harvard Med. Sch., Boston, 1997—. Contbr. chpts. to books and articles to profl. jours. Fellow: Am. Acad. Sleep Medicine; mem.: Am. Acad. Neurology, Alpha Omega Alpha. Office: Beth Israel Deaconess Med Ctr 330 Brookline Ave Boston MA 02215-5400 E-mail: jmatheso@caregroup.harvard.edu.

MATHESON, JIM, congressman; b. Salt Lake City, 1960; m. Amy; 1 child: Will. BA in govt., Harvard U.; MBA, UCLA. Worked in energy indus., 12 yrs.; founder The Matheson Group, 1998; congressman Utah, second dist. Mem. Congressional coms. House Budget, Transportation and Infrastructure, Sci.; subcom. Transportation and Infrastructure, Highways and Transit, Aviation, Energy; liaison with Rep. for freshman class. Mem. Salt Lake Public Utilities bd., Scott M. Matheson Leadership Forum. Office: 410 Cannon House Office bldg Washington DC 20515*

MATHESON, LINDA, retired clinical social worker; b. Martna, Estonia, Mar. 29, 1918; came to U.S., 1962, naturalized, 1969; d. Endrek and Leena Endrekson; m. Charles McLaren Matheson, Feb. 5, 1955. Diploma, Inst. Social Scis., Tallinn, Estonia, 1944; MS, Columbia U., 1966, D in Social Work, 1974. Diplomate clin. social work. Social work officer UN Rehab. and Resettlement Assn., Germany, 1946-48; social worker Victorian Mental Hygiene, Australia, 1955-62; rsch. assoc., social work project dir. Arthritis Midway House, N.Y.C., 1966-68; rsch. Columbia Presbyn. Med. Ctr., 1971-75; field instr. Columbia U. Sch. Social Work, 1977-79, Columbia Presbyn. Med. Ctr., NYU Sch. Social Work, 1989-90; ret., 1992. Family Found. fellow, 1966, 89-90; grantee NIMH, 1969-72. Mem. Nat. Assn. Social Workers, Nat. Wildlife Fedn., Ctr. for Study of Presidency, Internat. Platform Assn., United Leaders, BATUN, Baltic-Am. Freedom League, Smithsonian Assn., English Spkg. Union, Alliance Francaise, Columbia U. Alumni Assn., Met. Mus. N.Y. Lutheran. Home: 30-95 29th St Astoria NY 11102-2735

MATHESON, SCOTT MILNE, JR. dean, law educator; b. Salt Lake City, July 18, 1953; s. Scott Milne and Norma (Warenski) M.; m. Robyn Kuida, Aug. 12, 1978; children: Heather Blair, Briggs James. AB, Stanford U., 1975; MA, Oxford U., Eng.; JD, Yale U., 1980. Bar: D.C., 1981, Utah 1986. Assoc. Williams & Connolly, Washington, 1981-85; assoc. prof. law U. Utah, 1985-91; dep. atty. Salt Lake County Attys. Office, 1988-89; vis. assoc. prof. JFK Sch. Govt. Harvard U., Cambridge, Mass., 1989-90; assoc. dean law U. Utah, 1990-93, prof. law, 1991—, dean, 1998—; U.S. atty. Dist. Utah, 1993-97. Adv. com. on rules of evidence Utah Supreme Ct., 1987-93, Utah Constitutional Revision Commn., 1987-93, adv. com. on the local rules of practice, U.S. Dist. Ct. Utah, 1993-97. Contbr. articles to profl. jours. Chmn. U.N. Day for State of Utah, 1991; mem. Univ. Com. on Tanner Lectures on Human Values U. Utah, 1993-2000, Honors Program Adv. Com. U. Utah, 1986-88, Adv. Bd. Hinckley Inst. Politics U. Utah, 1990-93; trustee Legal Aid Soc. of Salt Lake, 1986-93, pres., 1987; trustee TreeUtah, 1992-93; campaign mgr. Matheson for Gov., 1976, 1980; vol. state dir. Clinton/Gore '92. Recipient Up'n Comers award Zions Bank, 1991, Faculty Achievement award Burlington Resources Found., 1993, Disting. Svc. to Fed. Bar award Fed. Bar Assn., Utah chpt., 1998, spl. recognition award Utah Minority Bar Assn., 1999; named one of Outstanding Young Men of Am., 1987, 1988; Rhodes scholar. Mem. ABA, Assn. Am. Law Schs. (chair sect. on mass com. law 1993), Utah State Bar, Salt Lake County Bar Assn. (exec. com. 1986-92), Golden Key Nat. Honor Soc. (hon. 1990), Phi Beta Kappa.

MATHESON, WILLIAM LYON, lawyer; b. Coeburn, Va., Dec. 5, 1924; s. Julius Daniel and Ruth Steele Lyon M.; m. Katrina B. Hickox; children: Katherine, William Lyon, Alline, Thornton; m. Marjorie H. Anderson, Nov. 26, 1977. Student, Emory U., 1946-47; AB, Mercer U., 1944; LLB, U. Va., 1950. Bar: N.Y. 1951. Assoc. firm Patterson, Belknap & Webb, N.Y.C., 1950-57; assoc. Wertheim & Co. (investments), 1957-58; ptnr. Webster & Sheffield, 1959-65; pvt. practice, 1965-92; chmn. bd. Mich. Energy Resources Co., Monroe, 1959-89, Mercom Inc. (cable TV), 1984-91. Bd. dirs. Madison Sq. Boys' Club, N.Y.C., 1958-76, assoc. mem. bd. dirs., 1977-91; trustee Police Athletic League, N.Y.C., 1962—. Cold Spring Harbor (N.Y.) Lab. Served to lt. (j.g.) USN, 1942-46. Mem. Links Club (N.Y.C.), Piping Rock Club (Locust Valley, N.Y.), Meadow Brook Club (Jericho, N.Y.), Seminole Golf (North Palm Beach, Fla.), Jupiter Island Club (Hobe Sound, Fla.). Home: 430 S Beach Rd Hobe Sound FL 33455-2702 also: Sunset Hill Heather Ln Mill Neck NY 11765

MATHEU, FEDERICO MANUEL, university chancellor; b. Humacao, P.R., Mar. 17, 1941; s. Federico Matheu-Baez and Matilde Delgado-Vazquez; m. Myrna Delgado-Miranda, May 30, 1963; children: Federico Antonio, Rosa Myrna, Alfredo Javier, David Reinaldo. BS in Chem. Engring, U. P.R., 1962; PhD in Phys. Chemistry, U. Pitts., 1971. Chem. engr. Commonwealth Oil Refining Co., 1962-63; mem. adminstrv. staff and faculty U. P.R., 1963-78, dir. Humacao Coll., 1976-78; chancellor San German campus Inter Am. U. P.R., 1978-91; exec. dir., gen. coun. on edn. Commonwealth of P.R., Hato Rey, 1991-96; chancellor U. Metropolitana-Ana G. Méndez U. System, 1996—. Cons. in field. Author papers, reports in field. Named Disting. Educator P.R. Jaycees, 1974 Mem. Colegio de Quimicos P.R., Am. Chem. Soc., Sci. Tchrs. Assn. P.R. (pres. 1975-76), P.R. Acad. Arts and Scis., Phi Delta Kappa, Phi Tau Sigma. Home: Parque de Villa Caperra No 17 Zuania St Guaynabo PR 00966 Office: UMET PO Box 21150 San Juan PR 00928-1150

MATHEUSSEN, JOHN J. state legislator; b. Jersey City, Jan. 30, 1953; m. Janet M. Reilly, 1977; children: John, Ashley, Joseph. BA, Seton Hall U., 1975; JD, Dayton U. Sch. Law, 1978. Mem. N.J. Senate, Dist. 4, Trenton, 1992—. Mem. N.J. State Rep. Exec. Com., 1987—, co-chair senate health com., mem. judiciary com.; co-chair bd. dirs. Home Port Alliance Battleship USS New Jersey; pvt. practice law. Mem.: Pa. Bar Assn., N.J. Bar Assn. Address: PO Box 8019 Turnersville NJ 08012-8019 E-mail: SenMatheussen@njleg.org.

MATHEW, JAMES, cardiologist; b. Nariyapuram, Kerala, India, Oct. 15, 1954; came to U.S., 1982; s. T. G. and Mariamma Mathew; 1 child, Shanti. BSc, U. Kerala, 1975; MBBS, Med. Coll. Trivandrum, Kerala, 1980. Diplomate Am. Bd. Internal Medicine, Am. Bd. of Internal Medicine Cardiovascular Diseases. Resident in internal medicine Cook County Hosp., Chgo., 1989, fellowship in cardiology, chmn. divsn. adult cardiology, 1990-97, program dir. fellowship in cardiovasc. disease, 1990-97; pres. LaSalle Cardiology Inc., Galesburg, 1997—2001; dir. cardiology Galesburg (Ill.) Cottage Hosp., 1998—; clin. assoc. prof. U. Iowa Coll. of Medicine, Iowa City, 2000—. Contbr. articles to med. jours. Fellow Am. Coll. Cardiology, Am. Coll. Chest Physicians, Am. Coll. Angiology, Am. Heart Assn. Office: Galesburg Cottage Hosp 695 N Kellogg St Galesburg IL 61401-3726

MATHEW, TOM, economics educator; b. Adoor, India, Dec. 10, 1935; came to U.S., 1959; naturalized, 1969; s. Mathen and Sosamma (Chandy) M.; m. Saramma Thomas, Aug. 5, 1963; children— Teki, Thomas, Alexander. B.Sc., Kerala U. (India), 1958; M.A., Howard U., 1967; Ph.D., U. Ga., 1976. Asst. prof. Piedmont Coll., Demorest, Ga., 1969-74; instr. U. Ga., Athens, 1974-76; asst. prof. Albany State Coll., Ga., 1976-80; assoc. prof. Wartburg Coll., Waverly, Iowa, 1980-83; assoc. prof. Troy State U., Montgomery, Ala., 1983— , dir. M.B.A. program, 1983— . Reviewer books in field. Mem. Am. Econ. Assn., So. Econ. Assn., Midwestern Econ. Assn., Mo. Valley Econ. Assn. Eastern Orthodox. Avocations: soccer; tennis; gardening; racquetball. Home: 7018 Mid Pines Dr Montgomery AL 36117-5148

MATHEWS, BARBARA EDITH, gynecologist; b. Oct. 5, 1946; d. Joseph Chesley and Pearl (Ceri) Mathews. AB, U. Calif., 1969; MD, Tufts U., 1972. Diplomate Am. Bd. Ob-Gyn. Intern Cottage Hosp., Santa Barbara, Calif., 1972-73, Santa Barbara Gen. Hosp., 1972-73; resident in ob-gyn Beth Israel Hosp., Boston, 1973-77; clin. fellow in ob-gyn Harvard U., 1973-76, instr., 1976-77; gynecologist Sansum Med. Clin., Santa Barbara, 1977-98; sr. scientist Sansum Med. Rsch. Inst., 1998—; med. dir., gynecologist Women's Health Svcs., Santa Barbara, 1998—. Faculty mem. ann. postgrad. course Harvard Med. Sch.; bd. dirs. Sansum Med. Clinic, 1989-96, vice chmn. bd. dirs., 1994-96; dir. ann. postgrad course UCLA Med. Sch. Bd. dirs. Meml. Rehab. Found., Santa Barbara, Channel City Club, Santa Barbara, Music Acad. of the West, Santa Barbara, St. Francis Med. Ctr., Santa Barbara; mem. citizen's contg. edn. adv. coun. Santa Barbara C.C.; moderator Santa Ba rbara Cottage Hosp. Cmty. Health Forum. Author: (with L. Burke) Colposcopy in Clinical Practice, 1977; contbg. author Manual of Ambulatory Surgery, 1982. Fellow ACOG, ACS; mem. AMA, Am. Soc. Colposcopy and Cervical Pathology (dir. 1982-84), Harvard U. Alumni Assn., Tri-counties Obstet. and Gynecol. Soc. (pres. 1981-82), Birnam Wood Golf Club (Santa Barbara), Phi Beta Kappa. Home: 2105 Anacapa St Santa Barbara CA 93105-3503 Office: 2235 De La Vina St Santa Barbara CA 93105-3815 Fax: 805-687-0012.

MATHEWS, BARBARA JEAN, genealogist; b. Derby, Conn., Mar. 11, 1949; d. Charles Pons and Barbara Louise (Anderson) M.; m. Kent Harold Hoult, Sept. 8, 1984; 1 child, Adelaide Marie. BA in Physics, U. Conn., 1971; M in Human Svcs. Mgmt., Brandeis U., 1981. Cert. genealogist Bd. Cert. Genealogists. Staff dir. Elizabeth Stone House, Jamaica Plain, Mass., 1976-80; tech. writer Boston, 1973-84; mgr. documentation InterSys., Inc., Boston, Cambridge, Mass., 1985-87; dir. corp. comm. DataTree, Inc., Waltham, 1987-91; freelance genealogist Lexington, 1991—; cons. editor Newbury St. Press, Boston, 1996-2000. Verifying genealogist Nat. Soc. Colonial Dames Am., Boston, 1993—; cons. Office for Children, Dept. Social Svcs., Boston, 1981. Author: Philo Hodge (1756-1842) of Roxbury, CT, 1992. Mem. Assn. Profl. Genealogists (trustee 1997-2001), Conn. Profl. Genealogists Coun. (sec.-treas. 1993-95, v.p. 1999, sec. 1999-2001), Conn. Soc. Genealogists (mem. bd. govs. 1992-95), Mass. Soc. Genealogists, Welles Family Assn. (pres. 1993-97, sec. 1997-2001, v.p. 2001--), Descs. of Founders of Ancient Windsor (membership sec. 1989-93).

MATHEWS, CLAYTON JEROME, trucking executive; b. Winfield, Ala., Nov. 12, 1973; s. Clayton Lennox Mathews and Pamela Jane Reynolds. Student, Wallace State Coll. Front mgr. C.P. Pharmacy, Birmingham, Ala., 1998—2002; pres. M.K. Diesel Svcs., Remlap, 2002. Named Adult Edn. Amb., Right to Read Found., Fayette, Ala., 1997. Home: 99 Cedar Lane Remlap AL 35133

MATHEWS, DAVID, foundation executive; b. Grove Hill, Ala., Dec. 6, 1935; s. Forrest Lee and Doris (Pearson) M.; m. Mary Chapman, Jan. 24, 1960; children: Lee Ann Mathews Hester, Lucy Mathews Heegaard. AB, U. Ala., 1958; PhD, Columbia U., 1965; LL.D., U. Ala., 1969, Mercer U., 1976; L.H.D., William and Mary Coll., 1976, Med. U. S.C., 1976, Samford U., 1978, Transylvania U., 1978, Stillman Coll., 1980, Miami U., 1982; H.H.D., Birmingham-So. Coll., 1976, Wash. U., St. Louis, 1984; L.H.D., Ctr. Coll., 1985; L.L.D., Ohio Wesleyan U., 1987, Lynchburg Coll., 1987; L.H.D., U. New Eng., 1988, Hofstra U., 1999; L.L.D., Aquinas Coll. Exec. v.p. U. Ala., 1968-69, pres., 1969-80, prof. history, 1977-81; pres., chief exec. officer Charles F. Kettering Found., Dayton, Ohio, 1981—. Sec. HEW, Washington, 1975-77; dir. Birmingham br. Fed. Res. Bank of Atlanta, 1970-72, chmn., 1973-75; mem. council SRI Internat., 1978-85; chmn. Council Public Policy Edn., 1980— Contbr. articles to profl. jours. Trustee Judson Coll., 1968-75, Am. Univs. Field Staff, 1969-80; bd. dirs. Birmingham Festival of Arts Assn., Inc., 1969-75; mem. Nat. Programming Council for Public TV, 1970-73, So. Regional Edn. Bd., 1969-75, Ala. Council on Humanities, 1973-75; vice chmn. Commn. on Future of South, 1974; mem. So. Growth Policies Bd., 1974-75; mem. nat. adv. council Am. Revolution Bicentennial Adminstrn., 1975; mem. Ala. State Oil and Gas Bd., 1975, 77-79; bd. dirs. Acad. Edni. Devel., 1975— , Ind. Sector, 1982-88, ; chmn. Pres.'s Com. on Mental Retardation, 1975-77; chmn. income security com. aging com. Health Ins. Com. of Domestic Council, 1975-77; bd. govs. nat. ARC, 1975-77; bd. govs., bd. visitors Washington Coll., 1982-86 ; trustee John F. Kennedy Center for Performing Arts, 1975-77, Woodrow Wilson Internat. Center for Scholars, 1975-77; fed. trustee Fed. City Council, 1975-77; bd. dirs. A Presdl. Classroom for Young Americans, Inc., 1975-76; trustee Tchrs. Coll., Columbia U., 1977—85, Nat. Found. March of Dimes, 1977-83, Coun. om Learning, 1977-84, Miles Coll., 1978— ; mem. nat. adv. bd. Nat. Inst. on Mgmt. Lifelong Edn., 1979-84; mem. Ala. 2000, 1980— ; spl. adviser Aspen Inst., 1980-84; mem. bd. trustees Gerald R. Ford Found., 1988—, bd. visitors Mershon Ctr. Ohio State U., 1988-91; bd. dirs. Nat. Civic League, 1996—. Served with U.S. Army, 1959-60. Recipient Nicholas Murray Butler medal Columbia U., 1976, Ala. Adminstr. of Year award Am. Assn. Univ. Adminstrs., 1976, Educator of Year award Ala. Conf. Black Mayors, 1977, Brotherhood award NCCJ, 1979 Mem. Newcomen Soc. Am., Phi Beta Kappa, Phi Alpha Theta, Omicron Delta Kappa, Delta Theta Phi. Home: 6050 Mad River Rd Dayton OH 45459-1508 Office: Charles F Kettering Found 200 Commons Rd Dayton OH 45459-2788 E-mail: jenkyn@kettering.org.

MATHEWS, E. ANNE JONES, library educator and administrator, consultant; b. Phila. d. Edmond Fulton and Anne Ruth (Reichner) Jones; m. Frank Samuel Mathews, June 16, 1951; children: Lisa Anne Mathews-Bingham, David Morgan, Lynne Elizabeth Bietenhader-Mathews, Alison Fulton Sawyer. AB, Wheaton Coll., 1949; MA, U. Denver, 1965, PhD, 1977. Field staff Intervarsity Christian Fellowship, Chgo., 1949-51; interviewer supr. Colo. Market Rsch. Svcs., Denver, 1952-64; reference libr. Oreg. State U., Corvallis, 1965-67; program dir. Ctrl. Colo. Libr. Sys., Denver, 1969-70; inst. dir. U.S. Office of Edn., Inst. Grant, 1979; dir. pub. rels., prof. Grad. Sch. Librarianship and Info. Mgmt. U. Denver, 1970-76, prof., dir. continuing edn., 1977-80, from assoc. prof. to prof., 1977-85; dir. office libr. programs, office ednl. rsch., improvement U.S. Dept. Edn., Washington, 1986-91, cons. mil. installation voluntary edn. rev., 1990—; dir. Nat. Libr. Edn., 1992-94; cons. Acad. Ednl. Devel., 1994—; cons. mil. installation vol. end. rev. Am. Coun. on Edn., 1990—. Cons. Walden U., Mpls., 2001; vis. lectr. Simmons Coll. Sch. L.S., Boston, 1977; cons. USIA, 1984—85, mem. book and libr. adv. com., 1981—91; faculty assoc. Danforth Found., 1974—84; spkr. in field; mem. secondary sch. curriculum com. Jefferson County Pub. Schs., Colo., 1976—78; mem. adv. com. Golden H.S., 1973—77; mem. adv. coun. White House Conf. on Librs. and Info. Svcs., 1991; del. Internat. Fedn. Libr. Assns., 1984—93. Author, editor 6 books; contbr. articles to profl. jours., numerous chpts. to books. Mem. rural librs. and humanities program Colo. planning and resource bd. NEH, 1982—83; bd. mgrs. Friends Found. of Denver Pub. Libr., 1976—82; pres. Faculty Women's Club, Colo. Sch. Mines, 1963—64; bd. dirs. Jefferson County Libr. Found., 1996—, v.p., 1997—2000. Mem.: ALA (visionary leaders com. 1987—89, mem. coun. 1979—83, com. on accreditation 1984—85, orientation com. 1974—77, 1983—84, pub. rels. com.), English Speaking Union, Assn. Libr. and Info. Sci. Edn. (comm. com. 1978—80, program com. 1977—78), Colo. Libr. Assn. (pres. 1974, bd. dirs. 1973—75, continuing edn. com. 1976—80), Mountain Plains Libr. Assn. (profl. devel. com. 1979—80, pub. rels. and publs. com. 1973—75, continuing edn. com. 1973—76), Am. Soc. Info. Sci. (chmn. pub. rels. 1971), Naples Philharm. League, Pelican Bay Women's League Fla., Mountain Rep. Women's Club (v.p. 1997—2000), Mt. Vernon (Colo.) Country Club, Cosmos Club (Washington). Avocations: travel, reading, museum and gallery activities, volunteer work. Home: 492 Mount Evans Rd Golden CO 80401-9626 E-mail: afmathews2@earthlink.net.

MATHEWS, FRED LEROY, librarian; b. New Kensington, Pa., Apr. 20, 1938; s. Fred Lyman and Mabel (Vivola) M.; m. Carolyn Zorn, Dec. 2, 1988; 1 child, Eric. Student, U. Md., European Div., 1968-69; AA, Weber State Coll., Ogden, Utah, 1981, B Gen. Studies, 1983; MSLS, Clarion U. Pa., 1985. Enlisted man USAF, 1957, advanced through grades to master sgt., 1977; coord. subscriber svcs. 1920th Communications Group, Washington, 1970-73; noncommd. officer-in-charge phys. therapy USAF, Bitburg, Fed. Republic Germany, 1976-79, supt. phys. medicine Carswell AFB, Tex., 1979-80; ret., 1980; asst. systems libr. Maxwell AFB, Montgomery, Ala., 1985-86; refrence libr. Hdqrs. Tng. and Doctrine Command Libr., Ft. Monroe, Va., 1986-89; trainer, asst. systems libr. Hdqrs. Tng. and Doctrine Command Libr. and Info. Network, 1989-91; systems adminstr. Strategic Def. Command Libr., Huntsville, Ala., 1991-97; command libr. U.S. Army Space & Strategic Def. Command, 1997—. Recipient U.S. Army Achievement medal Hdqrs. Tng. and Doctrine Command, 1990. Mem. ALA, Assn. U.S. Army, Air Force Sgts. Assn., Beta Phi Mu. Avocations: running, reading, bodybuilding. Office: US Army Strategic Def Command Libr PO Box 1500 Huntsville AL 35807-3801

MATHEWS, GEORGE MEPRATHU, accounting executive; b. Taiping, Perak, Malaysia, Feb. 23, 1960; came to U.S., 1985; s. Mathews and Annamma Chempanal; m. Asha Henry, May 29, 1993; children: Reishma Ann, Raveen Henry, Reena Mable. B of Commerce, U. Kerala, Trivandrum, South India, 1982; MBA, U. Dallas, 1987. Acctg. asst. AGK Acctg. & Mgmt., Butterworth, Penang, West Malaysia, 1982-83; acctg. officer Sabah Rubber Fund Bd., Kota Kinabula, Sabah, East Malaysia, 1984; acctg./LAN mgr. Karol Media, Wilkes-Barre, Pa., 1988-94; mgr. finance southeast asia Amway Corp., Ada, Mich., 1994—. Mem. Am. Mgmt. Accts., Sigma Iota Epsilon. Avocations: hiking, stamp and coin collecting, table tennis, badminton. Office: Amway Corp 7575 E Fulton St Ada MI 49301 E-mail: george_mathews@Amway.com.

MATHEWS, JACK WAYNE, journalist, film critic; b. L.A., Dec. 2, 1939; s. Walter Edwin and Dorothy Helen (Friley) M.; m. Lucinda Lucille Herbert, Nov. 5, 1971; children: Darren Brady, Shelby Kay. BA, San Jose (Calif.) State Coll., 1965; MS, UCLA, 1966. Reporter Riverside (Calif.) Press, 1967-69; mktg. exec. Riverside Raceway, 1969-75; columnist, editor Rochester (N.Y.) Democrat & Chronicle, 1975-78; columnist, film critic Detroit Free Press, 1978-82, USA Today, L.A., 1982-85; columnist L.A. Times, 1985-89, film editor, 1989-91; film critic Newsday, L.I., 1991-99; film critic, movie editor N.Y. Daily News, 1999—. Co-host Cinema, PBS, 1995-98; juror Montreal World Film Festival, 1993. Author: The Battle of Brazil, 1987. Democrat. Office: 450 W 33rd St New York NY 10001-2681 E-mail: jmathews@edit.nydailynews.com.

MATHEWS, JAMES HAROLD, minister; b. Longview, Tex., Nov. 28, 1946; s. James Harold Sr. and Ruth Mildred (Gaines) M.; m. Carol Elaine Hartin, Aug. 2, 1969; children: Katherine Mathews Curlee, Patrick Alan, Suzanne Elaine Mathews Wright. Student, Southwestern Bapt. Theol. Sem., 1984-87. Minister of music and youth, Goldthwaite, Tex., 1973-75, Freeman Heights Bapt. Ch., Garland, 1975-78, N.W. Bapt. Ch., Austin, 1978-81, First Bapt. Ch., Marshall, 1981-85, minister of music West Columbia, 1985-95; assoc. pastor pastoral ministries Glen Meadows Bapt. Ch., San Angelo, 1995—. Pres. bd. Tex. Bapt. Encampment, Palacios, 1989-90. Bd. dirs. Cen. Emergency Med. Svcs., West Columbia, Tex., 1986-91, v.p., 1989-90; pres. Howard Payne U. Alumni bd. dirs., 1992-94. Mem. Soda Lake Assn. (assist team Marshall chpt. 1983-86), Mills Assn. (assoc. music dir. Goldthwaite chpt. 1969-73), Austin Assn. (assoc. music dir. Austin chpt. 1978-80), Rotary (bd. dirs. West Columbia chpt. 1987-90, sec. 1990-91). Home: 4913 Bermuda Dr San Angelo TX 76904-7206 Office: Glen Meadows Bapt Ch 6002 Knickerbocker Rd San Angelo TX 76904-7732 E-mail: h.mathews@gte.net., mathews@gmbc.

MATHEWS, JENNIFER PAULINE, anthropologist, educator, archaeologist; b. Glendale, Calif., Feb. 11, 1969; d. Cynthia Ethel Lowry, Louis Paul Mathews, Alison McIlvane Turner (Stepmother), Gary L. Withrow (Stepfather). PhD in Anthropology, U. Calif., Riverside, 1998. Lectr. U. Calif., Riverside, Calif., 1998—99; asst. prof. Trinity U., San Antonio, 1999—. Co-dir. Yalahau Regional Human Ecology Project , Cancun, Quintana Roo, Mexico, 1998—. Grantee, NSF, 1997, Found. Advancement of Mesoamerican Studies, Inc., 1999—2000, Trinity U., 2000, 2002. Mem.: Alamo Pre-Columbian Soc. (bd. dirs. 2000—02, editor 2000—02), Soc. Am. Archaeology, Am. Anthropological Assn. Avocations: travel, reading, exercising. Office: Depart Sociology and Anthropology 715 Stadium Dr San Antonio TX 78209 Office Fax: 210-999-8509. Business E-Mail: jmathews@trinity.edu.

MATHEWS, JESSICA TUCHMAN, executive, foreign policy expert; b. N.Y.C., July 4, 1946; d. Lester Reginald and Barbara (Wertheim) Tuchman; m. Colin D. Mathews, Feb. 25, 1978 (divorced); children: Oliver Max Tuchman, Jordan Henry Morgenthau. AB magna cum laude, Radcliffe Coll., 1967; PhD, Calif. Inst. Tech., 1973. Congrl. sci. fellow AAAS, 1973-74; profl. staff mem. Energy and Environment subcom. House Com. on Interior and Insular Affairs, Washington, 1974-75; dir. issues and rsch. Udall Presdl. campaign, 1975-76; dir. Office of Global Issues NSC staff, Washington, 1977-79; mem. editorial bd. The Washington Post, 1980-82; v.p., dir. rsch. The World Resources Inst., Washington, 1982-92; dep. to undersec. for global affairs U.S. Dept. State, 1993; sr. fellow Coun. on Fgn. Rels., 1993-97; columnist Washington Post, 1991-97; pres. Carnegie Endowment Internat. Peace, Washington, 1997—. Mem. numerous adv. panels Office Tech. Assessment, NAS, AAAS, EPA; adv. com. Air Products Corp., 1995—99; bd. dirs. Somalogic Inc. Trustee Rockefeller Found., Century Found., Nuc. Threat Initiative, Transp. Policy Project; mem. Coun. Fgn. Rels.; bd. dirs. Joyce Found., Chgo., 1984—91, Inter-Am. Dialogue, 1991—2000, Surface Transp. Policy Project, 1991—, Radcliffe Coll., 1992—96, Carnegie Endowment for Internat. Peace, Washington, 1992—, Rockefeller Bros. Fund, N.Y.C., NY, 1992—96, Brookings Instn., Washington, 1995—2001. Mem.: Inst. Internat. Econs. (adv. com.), Fedn. Am. Scientists (bd. dirs. 1985—87, 1988—92), Trilateral Commn. Democrat. Jewish. Office: Carnegie Endowment Internat Peace 1779 Massachusetts Ave NW Washington DC 20036-2109

MATHEWS, JOAN HELENE, pediatrician; b. Manchester, N.H., Feb. 3, 1940; d. John Barnaby and Helen A. Wlodkoski; m. Ernest Stephen Mathews, June 1, 1965; 3 children. BS, U. N.H., 1961; MD, Columbia U., 1965. Diplomate Am. Bd. Pediatrics. Med. intern Roosevelt Hosp., N.Y.C., 1965-66; pediatric resident Babies Hops. Columbia Presbyn. Med. Ctr., 1966-68, pediatric endocrine fellow Babies Hosp., 1968-70; instr. clin. pediat. Columbia U. Coll. Physicians and Surgeons, 1973-77; asst. prof. pediat. Cornell U. Med. Coll., 1977-81; clin. instr. pediat. Harvard Med. Sch., Boston, 1985—; clin. assoc. children's svc. Mass. Gen. Hosp., 1985—. Fellow Am. Acad. Pediat.; mem. Phi Beta Kappa. Office: 777 Concord Ave Cambridge MA 02138-1053 Fax: (617) 876-5713.

MATHEWS, KENNETH PINE, physician, educator; b. Schenectady, N.Y., Apr. 1, 1921; s. Raymond and Marguerite Elizabeth (Pine) M.; m. Alice Jean Elliott, Jan. 26, 1952 (dec.); children: Susan Kay, Ronald Elliott, Robert Pine; m. Winona Beatrice Rosenburg, Nov. 8, 1975. AB, U. Mich., 1941, MD, 1943. Diplomate Am. Bd. Internal Medicine, Am. Bd. Allergy and Immunology (past. sec.). Intern, asst. resident, resident in medicine Univ. Hosp., Ann Arbor, Mich., 1943-45, 48-50; mem. faculty dept. medicine med. sch. U. Mich., 1950—, assoc. prof. internal medicine, 1956-61, prof., 1961-86, prof. emeritus, 1986—, head div. allergy, 1967-83. Adj. mem. Scripps Clinic and Research Found., La Jolla, Calif., 1986—; past chmn. residency rev. com. for allergy and immunology, past chmn. allergy and immunology rsch. com. NIH. Co-author: A Manual of Clinical Allergy, 2d edit, 1967; editor: Jour. Allergy and Clin. Immunology, 1968-72; contbr. numerous articles in field to profl. jours. Served to capt. M.C. AUS, 1946-48. Recipient Disting. Service award Am. Acad. Allergy, 1976; Faculty Disting. Achievement award U. Mich., 1984 Fellow Am. Acad. Allergy (past pres.), A.C.P. (emeritus); mem. Am. Assn. Immunologists (emeritus), Ctrl. Soc. Clin. Rsch. (emeritus), Am. Fedn. Clin. Rsch., Alpha Omega Alpha, Phi Beta Kappa. Home: 7080 Caminito Estrada La Jolla CA 92037-5714 E-mail: kennona@webtv.net.

MATHEWS, LINDA MCVEIGH, newspaper editor; b. Redlands, Calif., Mar. 14, 1946; d. Glenard Ralph and Edith Lorene (Humphrey) McVeigh; m. Thomas Jay Mathews, June 15, 1967; children: Joseph, Peter, Katherine. BA, Radcliffe Coll., 1967; JD, Harvard U., 1972. Gen. assignment reporter L.A. Times, 1967-69, Supreme Ct. corr., 1972-76, corr. Hong Kong, 1977-79, China corr., 1979-80, editor op-ed page, 1980-81, dep. nat. editor, 1981-84, dep. fgn. editor, 1985-88, editl. writer, 1988-89, editor L.A. Times Mag., 1989-92; corr. Wall Street Jour., Hong Kong, 1976-77; sr. prodr. ABC News, N.Y.C., 1992-93; nat. editor N.Y. Times, 1993-96; editor USA Today, McLean, Va., 1997—. Lectr.; freelance writer. Author (with others): Journey into China, 1982, One Billion: A China Chronicle, 1983. Mem. Women's Legal Def. Fund, 1972-76; co-founder, pres. Hong Kong Montessori Sch., 1977-79; bd. dirs. Ctr. for Childhood. Mem. Fgn. Corrs. Club Hong Kong. Office: USA Today 7950 Jones Branch Dr Mc Lean VA 22108 E-mail: lmathews@usatoday.com., LiMathews@aol.com.

MATHEWS, MARK ROBERT, anesthesiologist; b. Mpls., Oct. 13, 1955; MD, U. Ariz., 1985. Diplomate Am. Bd. Anesthesiology. Intern Tucson Hosps. Med. Edn. Program, 1985-86; resident in anesthesiology U. Minn., Mpls., 1986-88; fellow in neuroanesthesia Barrow Neurol. Inst., Phoenix, 1988-89; staff Scottsdale (Ariz.) Meml. Hosp.; instr. Mayo Med. Sch.; sr. assoc. cons. Mayo Clinic, Scottsdale, 1989-91; pvt. practice, 1991—. Mem. AMA, Am. Soc. Anesthesiologists, Ariz. Med. Assn., Ariz. Soc. Anesthesiologists, Internat. Anesthesia Rsch. Soc. Home: 8711 E Pinnacle Peak Rd # 338 Scottsdale AZ 85255-3517 E-mail: gasdoc@direcpc.com.

MATHEWS, MARSHA ANDERSON, English educator, poet, minister; b. St. Petersburg, FLa., Oct. 29, 1952; d. Allen Conrad and Doris Marsh A.; children: Gena Renee, Gretchen J. BA with high honors, Univ. Fla., 1974; MA, Fla. State Univ., 1980, PhD, 1987; MDiv, Asbury Theol. Sem., 1995. Tchg. asst. Fla. State Univ., Tallahassee, 1978-86; asst. prof. English Va. Intermont Coll., Bristol, 1987-91; adj. prof. Asbury Coll., Wilmore, Ky., 1991-95; pastor United Meth. Ch. Holston conf., 1995-2000; adj. prof. Univ. Va., Wise, 2000, Mountain Empire Cmty. Coll. Big Stone, Dalton, Ga., 2000-01; asst. prof. English Dalton State Coll., 2001—. Dir. Wesley Found. Campus Ministries, United Meth. Ch., 1996-2000. Contbr. to jours. Clown, visits hosp. and nursing homes, 1996—. Mem. MLA, Assoc. Writing Program, Internat.Soc. Humor Studies, Phi Beta Kappa, Theta Phi, Lambda Iota Tau. Avocations: travel, water sports, scrabble, reading. Home: 1009 Park Canyon Dr Dalton GA 30720-4346 Office: Dalton State Coll 1009 Park Canyon Dr Dalton GA 30720-3797

MATHEWS, MARY BETH, nursing education administrator; b. Kansas City, Kans., July 3, 1942; d. Leon Ward and Mary Elizabeth (McManis) Zimmerman; m. Richard H. Strauss, Oct., 1967 (div.); 1 child, Scott Christopher Strauss; m. C. Weldon Mathews, Nov., 1989; stepchildren: Cynthia Elaine, Terri Mathews Ely. BSN, Cornell U., 1965; M in Nursing, U. Wash., 1969; PhD in Higher Edn. Adminstrn., Adult/Continuing Edn., Ohio State U., 1983. Cert. staff devel. and continuing edn., ANCC. Instr. Sch. Nursing U. Pa., 1970-72; dir. continuing edn. Sch. Nursing Boston U., 1975-78; asst. prof. nursing, dir. Office Continuing Edn. Coll. Nursing Ohio State U., Columbus, 1981-90; assoc. prof. nursing, dean Sch. of Nursing Ashland (Ohio) U., 1990-93; dir. nursing edn. devel and rsch. Grant/Riverside Meth. Hosp., Columbus, 1993-98; chair divsn. nursing U. Hartford, West Hartford, Conn., 1999—. Contbr. articles to profl. jours. Mem. ANA (chair coun. continuing edn. 1978-80, chair constituent assembly 1988-90, bd. dirs. 1992-94), Ohio Nurses Assn. (pres. 1985-89), Conn. Nurses Assn., Nat. Nursing Staff Devel. Orgn., Sigma Theta Tau, Phi Delta Kappa, Phi Kappa Phi. E-mail: mbmathews@hartford.edu.

MATHEWS, MARY KATHRYN, retired government official; b. Washington, Apr. 20, 1948; d. T. Odon (dec.) and Kathryn (Augustine) M. Student, Pa. State U., 1966-68; BBA, Am. U., 1970, MBA, 1975. Personnel mgmt. specialist, coordinator coll. recruitment program, GSA, Washington, 1971-75, adminstrv. officer, 1975-78; personnel mgmt. specialist Office of Personnel Mgmt., 1978; employee devel. specialist Office Sec. Transp., 1978-80, dep. chief departmental services and spl. programs div., 1980-81; asst. dir. adminstrv. div. Farm Credit Adminstrn., 1981-84, dir. adminstrv. div. McLean, Va., 1984-86, chief adminstrv. services div., 1987-88; dep. staff dir. for mgmt. U.S. Commn. Civil Rights, Washington, 1988-90, asst. staff dir. for mgmt., 1990-91, asst. staff dir. for congl. affairs, 1991-94, staff dir., 1994-97; ret., 1997. Chief spl. programs staff and homebound handicapped employment program GSA, Washington, 1973-74; mem. task force Presdl. mgmt. intern program U.S. Office Pers. Mgmt., Washington, 1977-78; coord. mgmt. devel. program for women Office Sec. Transp., Washington, 1979-81. Vol. mentor, speaker Alexandria Commn. on Women. Mem. Exec. Women in Govt. (treas. 1993-94, v.p. 1994-95, pres. 1995-96, bd. dirs.), Small Agy. Coun. (exec. com. 1990-91, 94-96, chmn. micro agy. group 1990-91), Internat. Alliance (bd. dirs. 1996-97), Nat. Trust Hist. Preservation, Nat. Assn. Mus. Women in Arts (charter), Delta Gamma (rush advisor 1971-73, pres. bd. dirs. local chpt. house corp. 1972-73). Avocations: antiques, classical music.

MATHEWS, MICHAEL STONE, investment banker; b. Ohio, Oct. 23, 1940; s. Robert Green and Dallas Victoria (Stone) M.; m. Cecilia Aall, May 13, 1967; children: Brandon, Mark, Alexander. AB, Princeton U., 1962; JD, U. Mich., 1965. Bar: N.Y. 1966. Assoc. White & Case, N.Y.C., 1965-69; v.p. Smith Barney Harris Upham & Co., 1969-77; sr. v.p. Scandinavian Securities Corp., 1977-79, DNC Am. Banking Corp., N.Y.C., 1979-89; pres. DNC Capital Corp., 1986-89; ptnr. Bradford Assocs., 1989-92; mng. dir. Westgate Capital Co., 1993—. Bd. dirs. Petroleum Geo-Svcs., Apptix ASA, Telecomputing, ASA, Cedar Creek Fibers. Home: 193 Elm Rd Princeton NJ 08540-2520 Office: 65 E 55th St Ste 3502 New York NY 10022-3219

MATHEWS, PAUL JOSEPH, health educator; b. Washington, Aug. 17, 1944; s. Paul Joseph and Ruth Irene (O'Malley) M.; m. Loretta Jeanne Calvo; children: Heather Marie, Amy Elizabeth, Timothy Hunter. AS, Quinnipiac Coll., 1971, BS, 1975; MPA, U. Hartford, 1978; EdS, U. Mo., Kansas City, 1989, PhD, 1998. Registered respiratory therapist; lic. respiratory therapist, Kans. Instr., clin. coord. New Britain (Conn.) Gen. Hosp., 1971-74; instr. Quinnipiac Coll., Hamden, Conn., 1974-76; chief respiratory therapy dept. Providence Hosp., Holyoke, Mass., 1974-80, dir. cardiology/neurology, 1977-80, asst. dir. planning, 1980-81; asst. prof. U. Kans. Sch. Allied Health, Kansas City, 1981-88, assoc. prof. respiratory care edn., 1988—, chmn. dept. respiratory care edn., 1981-93, assoc. prof. phys. therapy Grad. Sch., 1992—; U. Kans. Adj. assoc. prof. Ctr. on Aging U. Kans. Med. Ctr. , 1987—; hon. prof. U. Costa Rica , San Jose, 1987—, U. Santa Paula, Costa Rica, 2000—; vis. prof. Nat. U. Medicine and Pharmacy, Ho Chi Mihn City , Vietnam, 2001; cons. FDA, 1988, NIH, 1988, 89, SUNY, Stony Brook, 1990, USPHS, 1994, 95, 1997-2001, Singapore Gen. Hosp., 1997-, Coll. Santa Paula, 1998- ; prin. Clin. Legal Cons., 1998—; hon. prof. Nat. U. of Medicine, Ho Chi Miku City, Vietnam, 2001, cons., 01. Mem. editl. bd. Nursing, 1989—, Neonatal Intensive Care, 1990—, Jour. Respiratory Care Edn., 1993—, Respiratory Therapy, 1988—, Respiratory Therapy Intern, 1991—, Respiratory Care Management, 1998—; sect. editor Focus, 1998—; author books, videotapes, and audiotapes in field; contbr. articles to profl. jours., chpts. in books; chair editl. bd. RPN Webzine, 2000. Recipient Creative Achievement award Puritan-Bennett Corp., 1984, 85, A. Gerald Shapiro award N.J. Soc. for Respiratory Care, 1990; internat. fellow Project HOPE, 1987, 92. Fellow: Am. Coll. Chest Physicians, Soc. Critical Care Medicine (chair respiratory care sect. 2001—02), Am. Assn. Respiratory Care (life; bd. dirs. 1984—87, v.p. 1987, pres.-elect 1988, pres. 1989), Coll. Critical Care Medicine; mem.: Midwest Bioethics Ctr., N.Y. Acad. Scis., Philippine Respiratory Care Soc. (hon.), Phi Lambda Theta, Lambda Beta, Sigma Xi. Avocations: scuba diving, reading, travel. Home: 8844 Hemlock Dr Overland Park KS 66212-2946 Office: U Kans Med Ctr 3901 Rainbow Blvd Kansas City KS 66160-0001

MATHEWS, RICHARD BARRETT, English educator, writer; b. Washington, Nov. 16, 1944; s. James Thomas and Martha Anne (Moss) M.; m. Julienne Helen Empric; children: Emily Anne, Joseph Thomas. BA in English, U. Fla., 1966; PhD in English, U. Va., 1973; MA in Info. Studies, U. S.Fla., 1986. Assoc. prof. Eckerd Coll., St. Petersburg, Fla., 1970-79; teaching affiliate Poynter Inst. for Media Studies, 1979-83; adj. lectr. U. S.Fla., Tampa, 1983-84; editor, pub., printer Konglomerati Press., Gulfport, Fla., 1971-86, exec. dir., 1979-86; prof. English U. Tampa, 1986—, chmn. dept. English, Writing and Composition, 1992-94. Examiner Internat. Baccalaureate Program, U. Cardiff, Wales, Eng., 1987—; bd. dirs. Suncoast Writers' Conf., U. So. Fla., 1985—, faculty, 1984; faculty Longboat Key Writers' Conf., U. Mo., Kansas City, 1983, 84; reader ARTS Lit. Competition, ETS, Princeton, N.J., 1982-84; citizens adv. com. Cmty. Devel., Gulfport, Fla., 1979-84; dir. U. Tampa Press, 1993—. Author: The Clockwork Universe of Anthony Burgess, 1978; editor: Tampa Rev., 1987—; (with Rick Wilber) Subtropical Speculations: Anthology of Florida Science Fiction, 1991; author numerous poems. Grantee NEA; recipient So. Book awrd S.E. Librs. Assn., 1978-82, Book awrd Swamp Press, 1979, Honor prize S.E. Fine Print Competition, 1978, CELJ Phoenix award for significant editl. achievement, 1994; hon. fellow Woodrow Wilson Found., Rotary, Ford Found. Mem. AAUP, Soc. Utopian Studies, Am. Printing History Assn., Acad. Am. Poets, Danforth Found. Assocs., Sci. Fiction Rsch. Assn., Fantasy Assn., William Morris Soc., Phi Beta Kappa. Home: 900 Country Club Rd N Saint Petersburg FL 33710-4405 Office: U Tampa English Dept 401 W Kennedy Blvd Tampa FL 33606-1450

MATHEWS, SHARON WALKER, artistic director, secondary school educator; b. Shreveport, La., Feb. 1, 1947; d. Arthur Delmar and Nona (Frye) Walker; m. John William (Bill) Mathews, Aug. 14, 1971; children: Rebecca, Elizabeth, Anna. BS, La. State U., 1969, MS, 1971. Dance grad. asst. La. State U., Baton Rouge, 1969-71, choreographer, 1975-76; 6th grade tchr. East Baton Rouge Parish, 1971-72, health phys. edn. tchr., 1972-74; dance instr. Magnet High Sch., Baton Rouge, 1975—; artistic dir. Baton Rouge Ballet Theatre, 1975—; dance dir. Dancers' Workshop, Baton Rouge, 1971—; choreographer Baton Rouge Opera, 1989-94, Univ. H.S. Musical Theatre, 1998—; choreographer Baton Rouge Gilbert and Sullivan Soc. summer musical La. State U., 2000; choreographer Baton Rouge Little Theater, 2000. Artistic director, secondary school educator; b. Shreveport, La., Feb. 1, 1947; d. Arthur Delmar and Nona (Frye) Walker; m. John William (Bill) Mathews, Aug. 14, 1971; children: Rebecca, Elizabeth, Anna. BS, La. State U., 1969, MS, 1971. Dance grad. asst. La. State U., Baton Rouge, 1969-71, choreographer, 1975-76; 6th grade tchr. East Baton Rouge Parish, 1971-72, health phys. edn. tchr., 1972-74; dance instr. Magnet High Sch., Baton Rouge, 1975—; artistic dir. Baton Rouge Ballet Theatre, 1975—; dance dir. Dancers' Workshop, Baton Rouge, 1971—; choreographer Baton Rouge Opera, 1989-94, Univ. H.S. Musical Theatre, 1998—, Baton Rouge Gilbert and Sullivan Soc., summer musical La. State U., 2000, Baton Rouge Little Theater, 2000. Author: East Baton Rouge Parish Dance Curriculum. Named Dance Educator of Yr., La. Alliance for Health, Physical Edn., Recreation and Dance, 1986-87. Recipient Mayor-Pres.'s award for Excellence in the Arts, 1999. Mem. Southwestern Regional Ballet Assn. (bd. dirs. 1981—, treas., exec. bd. dirs. 1989-92), La. Assn. for Health, Phys. Edn., Recreation and Dance (dance chairperson 1995). Republican. Baptist. Author: East Baton Rouge Parish Dance Curriculum. Mem. Supt.'s Task Force for the Arts in Edn., 1999—; mem. La. Content Standards Com. for Dance, 2001; mem. East Baton Rouge Parish Curriculum Com. for Dance, 1997. Named Dance Educator of Yr., La. Alliance for Health, Physical Edn., Recreation and Dance, 1986-87; recipient Mayor-Pres.'s award for Excellence in the Arts, 1999. Mem. Southwestern Regional Ballet Assn. (bd. dirs. 1981—, treas., exec bd. dirs. 1989-92), La. Assn. for Health, Phys. Edn., Recreation and Dance (dance chairperson 1995). Republican. Baptist. Office: Baton Rouge Ballet Theater 11017 Perkins Rd Baton Rouge LA 70884*

MATHEWS, STEVEN CONRAD, educational company executive; b. Wis., Dec. 15, 1945; BS, U. Wis., Oshkosh, 1968. Trainer hardcore unemployed Manpower Tng., 1969-71; sales rep., mng. editor edn.-coll. divsn. Allyn & Bacon, Boston, 1971-81; exec. editor PRO-ED, Austin, Tex., 1981-83, v.p., 1983—. Co-author: (tests) The Diagnostic Test of Arithmetic Strategies, Children's IQ and Achievement Test, Children's Skills Test, Toddler Devel. Test. Mem. Am. Speech, Lang. and Hearing Assn. (adv. bd.), Coun. for Exceptional Children (past pres. Austin chpt.), Internat. Coun. for Learning Disabled (adv. bd.). Office: PRO-ED 8700 Shoal Creek Blvd Austin TX 78757-6897

MATHEWS, THOMAS JAY, reporter, columnist, writer; b. Long Beach, Calif., , Apr. 5, 1945; s. Thomas Jay and Frances Corcoran Mathews; m. Linda McVeigh McVeigh; children: Joseph, Peter, Katherine. BA, Harvard U., 1967, MA, 1971. Reporter Washington Post, Washington, 1971—. Dir. Editl. Projects in Edn., Bethesda, Md., 1994. Author: One Billion: A China Chronicle, 1983 (Nat. Edn. Reporting award, 1984), Escalante: The Best Teacher in America, 1988, A Mother's Touch, 1992, Class Struggle, 1998 (Benjamin Fine Outstanding Edn. Reporting award, 1999). Specialist 4 U.S. Army, 1967—69, Ft. Lewis, Ft. Ord, Long Binh. Avocations: reading, tennis, rating schools. Office: Washington Post 526 King St Ste 515 Alexandria VA 22314 Home Fax: 703-518-3001; Office Fax: 703-518-3001. E-mail: mathewsj@washpost.com.

MATHEWS, WALTER MICHAEL, educational consultant; b. Phila., Nov. 13, 1942; s. Walter John and Helen Linda Mathews; m. Mary Florence Richardson, June 13, 1964; children: Lisa, Walter John. BA, La Salle U., 1964; MEd, Temple U., 1967; PhD, U. Wis., 1971. Prof. U. Miss., Oxford, 1971-81; prof., adminstr. Hofstra U., Hempstead, N.Y., 1981-84, L.I. U., Brookville, 1984-88, dean acad. affairs, 1988-98, internat. liaison, 1998—. Home: 27 Midway Ave Locust Valley NY 11560-2008 Office: Evaluation Cons Inc 27 Midway Ave Locust Valley NY 11560-2008 E-mail: wmathews13@lycos.com.

MATHEWS, WILLIAM EDWARD, neurological surgeon, educator; b. Indpls. , July 12, 1934; s. Ples Leo and Roxie Elizabeth (Allen) M.; m. Eleanor Jayne Comer, Aug. 24, 1956 (div. 1976); children: Valerie, Clarissa, Marie, Blair; m. Carol Ann. Koza, Sept. 12, 1987; 1 child, William Kyle. BS, Ball State U., 1958; DO, Kirksville Coll. Osteo. Med., 1961; MD, U. Calif., Irvine, 1962; fellow, Armed Forces Trauma Sch., Ft. Sam Houston, Tex., 1967-68. Diplomate Am. Bd. Neurol. and Orthopedic Surgery, Am. Bd. Pain Mgmt., Am. Bd. Indsl. Medicine, Am. Bd. Spinal Surgeons (v.p. 1990-92), Am. Bd. Forensic Medicine, Am. Bd. Traumatic Stress, Am. Bd. Clin. Neurosurgery, Am. Bd. Spinal Surgery. Intern Kirksville (Mo.) Osteo. Hosp., 1961-62; resident neurosurgery Los Angeles County Gen. Hosp., 1962-67; resident in neurosurgery Rancho Los Amigos Spinal Rehab. Ctr., 1964-65; with Brooke Army Hosp., Ft. Sam Houston, 1967-68; with 8th field hosp. U.S. Army Neurosurgeon C.O. & 933 Med. Corp, Vietnam, 1968-69; chief neurosurgery Kaiser Med. Group, Walnut Creek, Calif., 1969-77; staff neurosurgeon Mt. Diablo Med. Ctr., Concord, 1977—. Student rsch. fellow electromyography NIH, 1959—61; asst. prof. biochemistry Kirksville Coll. Osteo. Medicine, 1958—62; asst. prof. neuroanatomy U. Calif. Coll. Medicine, 1962—65; sec. Am. Fedn. Med. Edn., 1997—; chmn. Am. Bd. Spinal Surgery, 1998, Am. Bd. Med. Accreditation, 1999—; assoc. prof. dept. neuroscis. Touro U. Coll. Osteo. Medicine. Author: Intracerebral Missile Injuries, 1972, Intrasellar Chordoma, 1976, Intraoperative Myelography, 1982, Thin Slice Computed Tomography of the Cervical Spine, 1985, Early Return to Work Following Cervical Disc Surgery, 1991, Iatrogenic Tethering of the Spinal Cord, 1998, Operative Treatment of Cervical Spondylotic Myelopathy, 2001, Surgical Treatment of Spondylotic Myelopathy, 2002; contbr. articles to profl. jours. Mem. adv. com. Rep. Presdl. Selection Com. Maj. U.S. Army, 1967-69, Vietnam. Recipient Disting. Svc. award Internat. Biography, 1987; scholar Psi Sigma Alpha, 1957. Fellow Congress Neurol. Surgeons (joint sect. on neurotrauma), Royal Coll. Medicine, Am. Acad. Neurologic and Orthopedic Surgeons (pres. 1981-82, bd. dirs. 1990—), Bay Area Spinal Surgery Soc., Internat. Coll. Surgeons; mem. AMA, Calif. Med. Assn., San Francisco Neurologic, Contra Costa County Med. Soc. Roman Catholic. Avocations: pen and ink art, golf, gardening. E-mail: bayareaneuro@aol.com.

MATHEWS, WILMA KENDRICK, public relations executive; b. Danville, Va., Dec. 23, 1945; d. Clarence Blanchard and Tina Collins (Powell) Kendrick. AA, Stratford Coll., 1966, BA, 1970; student, East Carolina U., 1966-67, U. Md., European divsn., 1967-68, Guilford Coll., 1978-80. Asst. editor The Commonwealth Mag., Richmond, Va., 1970-72; news editor The Comml. Appeal, Danville, 1972-73; pub. rels. mgr. Danville C. of C., 1973-74; publs. officer Bowman Gray Bapt. Hosp. Med. Ctr., Winston-Salem, N.C., 1974-78; sr. pub. rels. specialist Western Electric, 1978-82; mgr. pub. rels. AT&T Internat., Basking Ridge, N.J., 1982-84; media rels. mgr. AT&T Network Systems, 1985-87, mgr. pub. rels. field support, 1987-90, pub. rels. adv. dir., 1990-93, cons., 1993—; dir. pub. rels. Ariz. State U., 1995—. Sr. pub. rels. adv. N.C. Epilepsy Info. Svc., 1979-80. Co-author: On Deadline: Managing Media Relations, 1985, 3d edit., 1999, Inside Organizational Communications, 3d edit., 1999, Marketing Communications, 1987; author: Effective Media Relations: A Practical Guide for Communicators, 1998, 2d edit., 2002. Mem. Danville Bicentennial Commn., 1972-74; bd. dirs. Nat. Tobacco-Textile Mus., 1973-74; mem. Danville City Beautiful Com., 1973-74, Maplewood Cultural Commn., 1986-87. Named to Rowan U. PR Hall of Fame, 2001. Fellow Internat. Assn. Bus. Communicators (dir. 1978-81, 99-01, pres. N.C. chpt. 1977, 78, dir. Found. 1984-87, chmn. Found. 1987-90, accreditation bd. 1983-89, 94-01, bd. chmn. 1990-91, 97-99), Pub. Rels. Soc. Am. (dir. Valley of Sun chpt. 1996-97); mem. Danville Hist. Soc. (dir. 1973-74), N.C. Zool. Soc., Smithsonian Instn., Internat. TV Assn. (sec. N.C. chpt. 1979-80), Internat. Pub. Rels. Assn., Coun. for Communications Mgmt. (bd. dirs. 1987-89), Friends of Maplewood Libr. (pres. 1985-86), Friends of Phoenix Libr., Ahwatukee Foothills C. of C. (bd. dirs. 1994-98, vice chair 1996-98), Stratford Coll. Alumni Assn., Internat. Order Job's Daus. Republican. Baptist. Home: 5150 N 20th St # 202 Phoenix AZ 85016 Office: Ariz State U PO Box 871002 Tempe AZ 85287-1002 E-mail: wkm23@asu.edu .

MATHEWSON, CHRISTOPHER COLVILLE, engineering geologist, educator; b. Plainfield, N.J., Aug. 12, 1941; s. George Anderson and Elsa Rae (Shrimpton) M.; m. Janet Marie Olmsted, Nov. 2, 1968; children: Heather Alexis, Glenn George Anderson. BSCE, Case Inst. Tech., 1963; MS in Geol. Engring., U. Ariz., 1965, PhD in Geol. Engring., 1971. Registered profl. engr., Tex., Ariz., geologist, Oreg., Alaska. Officer, lt. Nat. Ocean Survey, 1965-71; prof. Tex. A&M U., College Station, 1981—. Cons., speaker in field. Author: Engineering Geology, 1981 (C.P. Holdredge award); contbr. articles to profl. publs. Chmn. College Station Planning and Zoning Commn., 1973—81; trustee Geol. Soc. Am. Found., 2001—. Fellow Geol. Soc. Am. (chmn. engring. geology divsn. 1986-87, Meritorious Svc. award 1991); mem. Assn. Engring. Geologists (editor bull. 1981-88, pres. 1988-89, C.P. Holdredge award 1981, F.T. Johnston Svc. award 1995, exec. dir. 1998-2002), Am. Geol. Inst. (pres. 1991-92), Nat. Coal Coun., Internat. Assn. Engring. Geologists (chmn. U.S. nat. com. 1995-98). Office: Tex A&M U Dept Geology And Geophysics College Station TX 77843-0001 E-mail: mathewson@geo.tamu.edu. *Commitment and dedication to the mission will lead to its successful completion regardless of the odds.*

MATHEWSON, GEORGE ATTERBURY, lawyer; b. Paterson, N.J., Mar. 31, 1935; s. Joseph B. and Christina A. (Atterbury) M.; m. Ann Elizabeth, July 31, 1975' 1 child, James Lemuel. AB cum laude, Amherst Coll., 1957; LLB, Cornell U., 1960; LLM, U. Mich., 1961. Bar: N.Y. 1963. Atty office spl. legal assts., trial atty. FTC, Washington, 1963-65; regional atty. N.Y. State Dept. Environ. Conservation, Liverpool, 1972-73; pvt. practice Syracuse, N.Y., 1967-72, 73—. Adj. instr. bus. law Onondaga Community Coll., Syracuse, 1979-84. Bd. dirs. South Side Businessmen, 1971-72, 88-91, v.p., 1992, pres. 1993; elder Onondaga Hill Presbyn. Ch., 1979, 82-85; dir. Manilus C. of C., 1995, v.p., 1997. Mem. ABA, Fed. Bar Assn., N.Y. State Bar Assn. (state and county bar assn. coms.), Kiwanis (bd. dirs. Onondaga club 1988-89, v.p. 1989, pres. 1989-91). Patentee safety device for disabled airplanes. Office: 224 Fayette St Manlius NY 13104-1804

MATHEWSON, HUGH SPALDING, anesthesiologist, educator; b. Washington, Sept. 20, 1921; s. Walter Eldridge and Jennie Lind (Jones) M.; m. Dorothy Ann Gordon, 1943 (div. 1952); 1 child, Jane Mathewson Holcombe; m. Hazel M. Jones, 1953 (div. 1978); children: Geoffrey K., Brian E., Catherine E. Brock, Jennifer A. Jehle; m. Judith Ann Mahoney, 1979 (div. 1990). Student, Washburn U., 1938-39; AB, U. Kans., 1942, MD, 1944. Intern Wesley Hosp., Wichita, Kans., 1944-45; resident anesthesiology U. Kans. Med. Ctr., Kansas City, 1946-48; pvt. practice specializing in anesthesiology Mo., 1948-69; chief anesthesiologist St. Luke's Hosp., 1953-69; med. dir., sect. respiratory therapy U. Kans. Med. Ctr., 1969-92, assoc. prof., 1969-75, prof., 1975-92, prof. anesthesiology emeritus, respiratory care edn., 1992—; examiner schs. respiratory therapy, 1975-95; oral examiner Nat. Bd. Respiratory Therapy; mem. Coun. Nurse Anesthesia Practice, 1974-78; prof. phys. therapy edn., 1993-98. Author: Structural Forms of Anesthetic Compounds, 1961, Respiratory Therapy in Critical Care, 1976, Pharmacology for Respiratory Therapists, 1977; contbr. articles to profl. publs.; mem. editorial bd. Anesthesia Staff News, 1975-84; assoc. editor: Respiratory Care, 1980-90, cons. editor, 1980—, editor-in-chief Respiratory Mgmt., 1989-92. Pres. Overland Park Civic Band, 1997, Overland Park Orch., 1998-2001; trustee Kansas City Mus., Kansas City Conservatory of Music, 1993—. Served to lt. comdr. USNR, 1956. Recipient Bird Lit. prize Am. Assn. Respiratory Therapists, 1976, Spl. Recognition award Am. Assn. Nurse Anesthetists, 1997. Mem. Mo. Soc. Anesthesiologists (pres. 1963), Kans. Soc. Anesthesiologists (pres. 1974-77), Kans. Med. Soc. (council), Phi Beta Kappa, Sigma Xi, Lambda Beta (hon.) Office: Kans Med Ctr 39th And Rainbow Blvd Kansas City KS 66160-0001 E-mail: hmathews@kumc.edu.

MATHEWSON, JUDITH JEANNE, special education educator; b. May 4, 1954; d. Robert Edward and Jeanne Eileen (Parcels) M. AA, Kansas City C.C., 1974; BS in Psychology (Secondary Edn.) and Journalism, Kans. State U., 1976; MS in Psychology and Spl. Edn., Emporia State U., 1979; MEd in Guidance and Counseling, U. Alaska, Anchorage, 2002. Cert. secondary tchr., Alaska; prof. recognized spl. educator. Spl. edn. tchr. grades 1-12 Wichita Pub. Schs., 1978-2001; mediation trainer Chugiak H.S., Anchorage, 1997-2001; bereavement facilitator Clark Jr. H.S., 1995—; tchr. grad. level classes U. Alaska, 2001. Adj. faculty Def. Equal Opportunity Mgmt. Inst., Patrick AFB, Fla., 1989-2002; lead instr. Youth Corps Challenge Program Alaska Nat. Guard, Ft. Richardson, 1993-95; staff trainer disability awareness, school to work. Contbr. articles to newspapers and newsletters. Mem. Nat. Hospice Assn. critical incident stress mgmt. team Alaska Police Chaplains, 1997—. Lt. col. Alaska Air N.G., 1986—. Decorated Air Force Commendation medal, Achievement medal, Cmty. Svc. medal, Jt. Svc. medal for Outstanding Achievement, Alaska Gov. Disting. Unit citation, Alaska Cmty. Svc. award, 1994. Mem. Coun. for Exceptional Children, Alaska N.G. Officers Assn. Roman Catholic. Avocations: computers, travel, teaching, bicycling. Home: 2104 F Scott Ct Montgomery AL 36106 E-mail: jjmathewson@att.net.

MATHEWS-ROTH, MICHELINE MARY, medicine educator, clinical researcher; b. Mineola, N.Y., July 26, 1934; d. John Francis and Micheline Genevieve Mathews; m. Robert Steele Roth, May 13, 1966; 1 child, John Doguereau. BS magna cum laude, Coll. of St. Elizabeth, Convent Station, N.J., 1956; MD with honors, NYU, 1961. Intern pathology Boston City Hosp., 1962-63; from rsch. assoc. to assoc. in microbiology Harvard U. Med. Sch., Boston, 1965-71, prin. rsch. assoc. in medicine, 1974-84, assoc. prof., 1984—; from jr. assoc. in medicine to assoc. physician Peter Bent Brigham Hosp. (now Brigham and Women's Hosp.), 1977-92; physician Brigham and Women's Hosp., 1992—. Assisting physician in med. microbiology Boston City Hosp., 1973-74. Editor: (with N.I. Krinsky and R.F. Taylor) Carotenoids Chemistry and Biology, 1989; also over 100 articles and revs. on carotenoid pigments and their functions and light-sensitive porphyrias. Former mem. bd. dirs. Peabody-Mason Music Found., Boston; pres. Mass. State Sci. Fair, Boston, 1989-92, also former mem. bd. dirs. Mem. Am. Soc. Gene Therapy, Am. Soc. for Microbiology, Am. Fedn. for Clin. Rsch., Am. Soc. for Clin. Investigation, Am. Soc. for Photobiology (assoc. editor Photochemistry and Photobiology 1974-83, councillor 1985-88, pres. 1991-92), Sigma Xi. Avocations: photography, singing. Office: Channing Lab 181 Longwood Ave Boston MA 02115-5804

MATHIA, MARY LOYOLA, parochial school educator, nun; b. Hempstead, N.Y., Sept. 14, 1921; d. Paul John and Laura Marie (Linck) Mathia. BA, Coll. Mt. St. Joseph, 1953; M in Pastoral Studies, Loyola U.-Chgo., 1980. Joined Sisters of Charity of Cin., Roman Cath. Ch., 1941. Tchr. various schs. Ohio and Mich., 1943-62, St. John Bapt. Sch., Chillum, Md., 1962-63; social studies tchr. and dept. chmn. Holy Name High Sch., Cleve., 1963-69; ednl. cons. Diocese of Cleve., 1970-78; dir. edn. St. Benedict Ch., Crystal River, Fla., 1979-86; founding prin. Cen. Cath. Sch. of Citrus County, Lecanto, Fla., 1985-90, v.p. devel. and pub. rels., 1990-91; parish cons. and dir. adult edn., St. Scholastica, 1986—. Recipient Mother Seton award, 1998, St. Jude medal Award for Svc. to St. Scholastic Ch., presented by Rev. Robert Lynch, Bishop of the Diocese of St. Petersburg, 2002; listed in Citrus County Chronicle for outstanding contbns., 2000. Republican. Office: St Scholastica Ch 4301 W Homosassa Trl Lecanto FL 34461-9106 *Society today is crying out for stability and a purpose for life. Only a God-centered education can fill the void created by the noise of external forces and the deadening of creative ideas stemming from a computer, media*saturated environment. As ministers of the Gospel our "quiet whispers" must penetrate the minds of a weary people, inspire them and bring them safely to the harbor of salvation in Christ Jesus Our Lord.*

MATHIAS, ALICE IRENE, business management consultant; b. N.Y.C., Mar. 2, 1949; d. Murray and Charlotte (Kottle) M. BS in Math., Western New Eng. Coll., 1972. Programmer Carnation Co., L.A., 1973-78; programmer/analyst Cedars-Sinai Med. Ctr., 1978-79, Union Bank, L.A., 1979-81; group leader Kaiser Found. Health Plan, Pasadena, Calif., 1981-98; sr. cons. KPMG LLP, L.A., 1998—. Mem. NAFE, Am. Mgmt. Assn., L.A. County Mus. Art (sponsor), Smithsonian Inst., KCET Pub. TV, Choice In Dying, U.S. Holocaust Meml. Mus. (charter mem.), Caithness Collectors Club, Statue of Liberty Ellis Island Found. Home: 4210 Via Arbolada Apt 311 Los Angeles CA 90042-5124 Office: KPMG LLP 725 S Figueroa St Los Angeles CA 90017-5524

MATHIAS, BETTY JANE, communications and community affairs consultant, writer, editor, lecturer; b. Oct. 22, 1923; d. Royal F. and Dollie B. (Bowman) M.; 1 child, Dena. Student, Merritt Bus. Sch., 1941, 42, San Francisco State U., 1941-42. Asst. publicity dir. Oakland (Calif.) Area War Chest and Comty. Chest, 1943-46; pub. rels. Am. Legion, Oakland, 1946-47; asst. to pub. rels. dir. Cen. Bank of Oakland, 1947-49; pub. rels. dir. East Bay chpt. Nat. Safety Coun., 1949-51; propr., mgr. Mathias Pub. Rels. Agy., Oakland, 1951-60; gen. assignment reporter, teen news editor Daily Rev., Hayward, Calif., 1960-62; freelance pub. rels. and writing Oakland, 1962-66, 67-69; dir. corp. comms. Systech Fin. Corp., Walnut Creek, Calif., 1969-71; v.p. corp. comms. Consol. Capital cos., Oakland, 1972-79, v.p. comty. affairs Emeryville, Calif., 1981-84, v.p. spl. projects, 1984-85; v.p., dir. Consol. Capital Realty Svcs., Inc., Oakland, 1973-77, Centennial Adv. Corp., Oakland, 1976-77; comms. cons., 1979—. Cons. Mountainair Realty, Cameron Park, Calif., 1986-87; pub. rels. coord. Tuolumne County Visitors Bur., 1989-90; lectr. in field Editor: East Bay Mag., 1966-67, TIA Traveler, 1969, Concepts, 1979-83; editor, writer souvenir program: Little House on the Prairie Reunion, 1998. Bd. dirs. Oakland YWCA, 1944-45, ARC, Oakland, So. Alameda County chpt., 1967-69, Family Ctr., Children's Hosp. Med. Ctr. No. Calif., 1982-85, March of Dimes, 1983-85, Equestrian Ctr. of Walnut Creek, Calif., 1983-84, also sec.; mem. Women's Ambulance and Transport Corps of Calif., Oakland, 1942-46; active USO and Shrine Hospitality Ctrs., Oakland, USO-Travelers Aid Soc., Oakland, 1942-46; publicist Oakland Area War Bond Com., 1943-46; adult and publs. adv. Internat. Order of the Rainbow for Girls, 1953-78; comms. arts adv. com. Ohlone (Calif.) Coll., 1979-85, chmn., 1982-84; mem. adv. bd. dept. mass comms. Calif. State U.-Hayward, 1985; pres. San Francisco Bay Area chpt. Nat. Reyes Syndrome Found., 1981-86; vol. staff Columbia Actors' Repertory, Columbia, Calif., 1986-87, 89; mem. exec. bd., editor newsletter Tuolumne County Dem. Club, 1987; publicity chmn. 4th of July celebration Tuolumne County C. of C., 1988; vol. children's dept. Tuolumne County Pub. Libr., 1993-97; vol. Ann. Comty. Christmas Eve Dinner, Sonora, Calif., 1988-96; mem. adv. com. Ride Away Ctr. for Therapeutic Riding for the Handicapped, 1995-96, vol. Hold Your Horses Therapeutic Riding Acad., 1997; vol. Tuolumne County Visitors Bur. and Film Commn., 1996-99. Recipient Grand Cross of Color award Internat. Order of Rainbow for Girls, 1955. Mem. Order Ea. Star (life, worthy matron 1952, publicity chmn. Calif. state 1955). Home: 20575 Gopher Dr Sonora CA 95370-9034

MATHIAS, CORDULA, art dealer; b. Constance, Baden, W. Germany, Feb. 18, 1955; came to U.S., 1979; d. Gotthold Bernhard and Mathilde (Eisele) M. BA, U. Constance, Germany, 1979; MA, Columbia U., 1981. Rsch. assoc. Soc. for Renewal of Christian Art, N.Y.C., 1982-83; dept. mgr. Logos Corp., Mt. Arlington, N.J., 1983-87; dir. of ops. John Szoke Graphics, N.Y.C., 1987-88; exhbn. curator Pace U., 1988-89; pres. Mathias Fine Art, Trevett, Maine, 1990—. Exhbn. sponsor Maine Coast Artists, Rockport, 1997-2001. Fulbright scholar, 1979-80. Mem. Boothbay Harbor C. of C. Avocation: chamber music. Office: Mathias Fine Art West Side Rd Trevett ME 04571

MATHIAS, EDWARD JOSEPH, merchant banker; b. Camden, N.J., Nov. 11, 1941; s. Edward Joseph and Zelma (Pollack) M.; m. Ann Robyn Rafferty, Aug. 3, 1968; 1 child, Ellen Susannah. BA, U. Pa., 1964; MBA, Harvard U., 1971. Mng. dir. T. Rowe Price Assocs., Inc., Balt., 1971-93, Carlyle Group Merchant Bank, Washington, 1994—. Spl. ltd. ptnr. Trident Capital. Trustee U. Pa.; trustees coun. Nat. Gallery Art. Lt. USN, 1964—69. Mem. Coun. Fgn. Rels., Harvard Club, Univ. Club (N.Y.C.), Columbia Country Club (Chevy Chase, Md.), Robert Trent Jones Golf Club (Manassas, Va.), Coral Beach Club (Bermuda), The Brook (N.Y.C.), Ctr. Club (Balt.), Met. Club, Georgetown Club, Talbot Country Club (Easton, Md.). Republican. Home: 5120 Cammack Dr Bethesda MD 20816-2902 Office: The Carlyle Group 1001 Pennsylvania Ave NW Washington DC 20004-2505

MATHIAS, JOSEPH MARSHALL, lawyer, judge; b. Frankfort, Ky., Jan. 23, 1914; s. Harry L. and Catherine Snead (Marshall) M.; children: Mark Wellington, Marcia Ann Mathias Wilson, Marilyn Roberta. AB, U. Md., 1935; JD, Southeastern U., 1942. Bar: Md. 1942, U.S. Supreme Ct. 1949, U.S. Dist. Ct. Md. 1963. Ptnr. Moorman and Mathias, 1946-50, Jones, Mathias and O'Brien and predecessor firms, 1950-65; judge Md. Tax Ct., 1959-65; assoc. judge Circuit Ct. of Montgomery County (Md.), 1965-80; chief judge 6th Jud. Circuit of Md., 1980-81; spl. assignments, 1981-83; spl. counsel Beckett, Cromwell & Myers, P.A., 1983-88; of counsel Frank, Bernstein, Conaway and Goldman, 1988-92. Past dir. Nat. Bank Md., Bank So. Md.; former mem. adv. bd. Citizens Bank and Trust Co. Chmn. Bd. Property Rev., Montgomery, Md., 1992—. Served with USN, 1942-46. Recipient cert. of disting. citizenship Gov. of Md., 1981. Mem. ABA, Md. State Bar Assn., Md. Bar Found., Montgomery County Bar Assn., Am. Judicature Soc. Democrat. Roman Catholic. Home: 10011 Summit Ave Kensington MD 20895-3835 E-mail: rwmjmm@erols.com.

MATHIAS, JULIAN ROBERT, investment manager; b. Arundel, Eng., Sept. 7, 1943; s. Anthony Robert Mathias and Cecily Mary Hughes; m. Frances Bone, May 31, 1996. MA, Oxford U., Eng., 1963. Mgr. Hill Samuel & Co. Ltd., London, 1964-71; ptnr. Buckmaster & Moore, 1971-81; dir. Fgn. & Colonial Mgmt. Ltd., 1981-95, BZW Investment Mgmt., London, 1995-96; with Rapael Asset Mgmt., 1996-97. Mem. Boodles, Berkshire Golf Club. Roman Catholic. Avocations: bridge, golf, shooting, wine tasting. E-mail: Julianmathias@onetel.net.uk.

MATHIAS, LESLIE MICHAEL, electronic manufacturing company executive; b. Bombay, Dec. 17, 1935; came to U.S., 1957; s. Paschal Lawrence and Dulcine (D'Souza) M.; m. Vivian Mae Doolittle, Dec. 16, 1962. BSc, U. Bombay, 1957; BS, San Jose (Calif.) State U., 1961. Elec. engr. Indian Standard Metal, Bombay, 1957; sales engr. Bleisch Engring. and Tool, Mt. View, Calif., 1958-60; gen. mgr. Meadows Terminal Bds., Cupertino, 1961-63; prodn. mgr. Sharidon Corp., Menlo Park, 1963-67, Videx Corp., Sunnyvale, 1967-68, Data Tech. Corp., Mt. View, 1968-69; pres. L.G.M. Mfg., Inc., 1969-83; pvt. practice plating cons. Los Altos, Calif., 1983-87; materials mgr. Excel Cirs., Santa Clara, 1987-91, 93-98, acct. mgr., 1991-93, materials mgr., 1993-98, internat. materials mgr., 2000—; buyer Planned Parenthood, San Jose, 1998-2000. Social chmn. Internat. Students, San Jose, 1958-59. Mem. Nat. Fedn. Ind. Bus., Calif. Cirs. Assn., Better Bus. Bur., Purchasing Assn., U.S. C. of C. Roman Catholic. Avocations: electronics, reading, med. jours. Home: 20664 Mapletree Pl Cupertino CA 95014-0449 E-mail: lesliemathias01@msn.com.

MATHIAS, MARGARET GROSSMAN, manufacturing company executive, leasing company executive; b. Detroit; d. D. Ray and Lila May (Skinner) Grossman; children: Deborah, Robert, Lesley, Jennifer, Mary. BA, Mt. Holyoke Coll.; cert., Am. Acad. Art. Artist and co-mgr. Mary Chase Marionettes, N.Y.C.; exec. v.p. Star Five Corp., Elkhart, 1975-88, pres., treas., chmn. bd., 1985-90, sec., chmn. bd. L & J Press Corp., Ind., 1985-91, also chmn. bd. dirs.; chmn., pres., CEO Magland Co., 1986—, Magco Inc., Elkhart, 186—; pres., chmn., CEO Tech Products, Inc., 1992—. Mem. fin. com. United Fund, Elkhart; mem. parents adv. bd. Furman U., Greenville, S.C., 1978-83, mem. art adv. bd. Mt. Holyoke Coll., South Hadley, Mass., 1982—; pres. Tri Kappa Service Orgn., Elkhart, 1965-66; trustee Stanley Clark Sch., South Bend, Ind., 1977-87; bd. dirs. Bridgework Theatre, Goshen, Ind., also Balt., 1996—; mem. adv. bd. Ruthmere 1910 House Mus. designated one of Am.'s castles, 1999—; instr., spkr. etiquette Montessori Schs., Elkhart, Ind., 1998—. Recipient Lawson Top Sculpture Purchase award Midwest Mus. Am. Art, 1990. Mem. Elkhart C. of C. Clubs: Elcona Country (Elkhart), Woman's Athletic (Chgo.), Thursday (Elkhart) (pres. 1976). Republican. Avocations: sculpting, traveling, skiing. Home: 1077 Greenleaf Blvd Apt 101 Elkhart IN 46514-3562 Office: 429 S Main St Elkhart IN 46516-3210

MATHIAS, MERVIN A. retired surgeon; b. Phila., 1917; MD, Temple U., 1942. Diplomate Am. Bd. Surgery. Intern Jewish Hosp., Phila., 1942-43, resident in pathology, 1946-47; resident in surgery West Jersey Hosp., Camden, N.J., 1948-50; surgeon in pvt. practice, to 1982. Mem. Am. Occupl. Medicine Assn., Internat. Med. Assn.

MATHIAS, REUBEN VICTOR (VIC MATHIAS), chamber of commerce executive, real estate investor; b. Copperas Cove, Tex., Mar. 5, 1926; s. Alvin E. and Ella L. (Teinert) M.; m. Helen I. Thoresen, Jan. 28, 1950; children: Mona, Mark, Matt. BBA, U. Tex., 1950. Cert. Chamber Exec. Dist. mgr. W.A. Shaeffer Pen Co., Youngstown, Ohio, 1950-51; mgr. Cen-Tex Fair, Temple, Tex., 1951-52; dir. info. Tex. Assn. Soil Conservation Suprs., 1952-53; mgr. membership dept. Austin (Tex.) C. of C., 1953-56, chief exec. officer, 1956-82; dir. corp. devel. Hardin Corp., Austin, 1983-86; real estate and investments, 1987-92; pres. Tex. Travel Industry Assn., Austin, 1992-96. V.p. Austin Tours, Inc.; sec. Longhorn Caverns, Inc.; chmn. bd., instr. Inst. for Orgn. Mgmt., U. Houston; mgmt. cons. not-for-profit orgns., 1997—. Contbr. monthly editorial Thoughts While Thinking to Austin Mag., 1961-82. Pres. Austin USO Council, 1958-59; v.p. Beautify Tex. Council, 1975-77; founding pres. Discover Tex. Assn., 1969-70; chmn. Central Tex. Blood Donor Fund, 1979. Served with U.S. Army, 1944-46. Mem. Am. C. of C. Execs., Tex. C. of C. Execs. (pres. 1965), Rotary (pres. Austin 1985-86). Lutheran. Home: 3100 Mistywood Cir Austin TX 78746-7861 *You can find happiness only by giving it to others. Much of my life has been devoted to community building through voluntary action. The fact that my career has allowed me to stay in one community has made it possible for me to make and carry out long-term plans, both for the community and personally.*

MATHIESEN, THOMAS JAMES, musicology educator; b. Roslyn Heights, N.Y., Apr. 30, 1947; s. James Christian and Edris Elva (Leatherman) M.; m. Penelope Jay Price, Sept. 11, 1971. Student, Stanford U., 1965, 67; MusB, Willamette U., 1968; MusM, U. So. Calif., L.A., 1970, D. Musical Arts, 1971. Lectr. musicology U. So. Calif., L.A., 1971-72; prof. music Brigham Young U., Provo, Utah, 1972-88, assoc. dean honors, 1986-88; prof. music Ind. U., Bloomington, 1988-96, dist. prof., 1996—, dir. ctr. history of music theory & lit., 1998—, David H. Jacobs chair in music, 1998—. Project dir. Thesaurus Musicarum Latinarum, Ind. U., Bloomington, 1990—, doctoral dissertations in musicology, 1996—. Author: Bibliography of Sources for the Study of Ancient Greek Music, 1974, Aristides Quintilianus on Music, 1983, Ancient Greek Music Theory, 1988 (Duckles award 1989), Greek Views of Music, 1997, Apollo's Lyre: Greek Music and Music Theory in Antiquity and the Middle Ages, 1999 (Kinkeldey, Berry & ASCAP-Deems Taylor awards 2000); editor: Festa Musicologica: Essays in Honor of George J. Buelow, 1995, Music in the Mirror: Reflections on the History of Music Theory and Literature for the 21st Century, 2002; gen. editor Greek and Latin Music Theory, 1982—; editor 10 vols.; contbr. articles to profl. jours., New Grove Dictionary of Music and Musicians, 2d edit. and Die Musik in Geschichte und Gegenwart, 2d edit. Pres. Holiday Hills Assn., Springville, Utah, 1978-84. Grantee Am. Coun. Learned Socs., 1977, NEH, 1992-96; fellow NEH, 1985-86, Guggenheim fellow, 1990-91; recipient Disting. Alumni Citation Willamette U., 1999, U. So. Calif., 2001. Fellow Am. Acad. Arts & Scis.; mem. AAUP, Am. Musicological Soc., Soc. for Music Theory, Music Libr. Assn., Am. Philol. Assn., Theta Alpha Phi, Omicron Delta Kappa, Pi Kappa Lambda, Phi Mu Alpha. Home: 1800 N Valley View Dr Ellettsville IN 47429-9487 Office: Ind U Sch Music Bloomington IN 47405 E-mail: mathiese@indiana.edu.

MATHIESON, GARRETT ALFRED, insurance brokerage executive; b. Bronxville, N.Y., June 12, 1952; s. William Frederick and Susan (Prager) M.; m. Doris King, June 21, 1980; children: Christine, William. BA, Hobart Coll., 1974; MBA, N.Y. U., 1980. Account rep. Marsh & McLennan, N.Y.C., 1974-77; sr. broker Frank B. Hall & Co., 1977-78; risk mgmt. cons. Marsh & McLennan, 1978-80, cons. mgr.-asst. v.p., 1980-82, v.p., mgr. world consulting svcs., 1982-85; mng. cons. Towers Perrin Forster & Crosby, 1985-86; sr. v.p. Jardine Ins. Brokers, 1986-90; exec. v.p. Rollins Burdick Hunter, 1990-92; chmn., CEO, Rollins Hudig Hall Pa., Phila., 1992-94; vice chmn. Aon Risk Svcs., 1994—99; pres., CEO Willis Risk Solutions, N.Y.C., 1999—. Seminar mgr. World Trade Inst., 1982-84, Marsh & McLennan, 1981-85. Contbr. articles to profl. jour. Mem.: N.Y. Choral Soc., Shenorock Shore Club, Siwanoy Country Club. Presbyterian. Avocations: vocal music, theatre, golf, tennis.

MATHIESON, MICHAEL RAYMOND, controller; b. Pontiac, Ill., May 3, 1952; s. Raymond Irving and Dorothy Mae (Yentes) M.; m. Nancy Anne Repa, May 11, 1985; children: Patrick Michael, Brady Raymond. BS in Acctg., U. Ill., 1974. Sr. mgr. Peat, Marwick, Mitchell & Co., Chgo., 1974-80, N.Y.C., 1980-84; v.p. Becker Paribas, Inc., 1984-85, Paine Webber Group, Inc., N.Y.C., 1985-89, Chase Manhattan Bank, N.Y.C., 1989-90; asst. contr. Avon Products, Inc., 1990-95, v.p., contr. N.Y., 1995-98, Fortune Brands, Inc., Lincolnshire, Ill., 1998—. Mem. AICPA, Ill. Soc. CPA's. Conway Farms Golf Club, Financial Exec. Inst., Alpha Delta Phi. Republican. Presbyterian. Avocations: golf, tennis. Home: 208 Brampton Ln Lake Forest IL 60045-4700 Office: Fortune Brands Inc 300 Tower Pkwy Lincolnshire IL 60069-3640

MATHIEU, GEORGES VICTOR ADOLPHE, artist; b. Boulogne, France, Jan. 27, 1921; s. Adolphe Mathieu d'Escaudoeuvres and Madeleine Dupre d'Ausque. Ed., Facultés de droit et des lettres, Lille, France. Tchr. English; mgr. pub. rels. U.S. Lines. Exhbns. include Paris, 1950, N.Y.C., 1952, Japan, 1957, Scandinavia, 1958, Eng., Spain, Italy, Switzerland, Fed. Republic Germany, Austria and S.Am., 1959, Middle East, 1961-62, Can., 1963, Musée Municipal d'Art Moderne, Paris, 1963, Galerie Charpentier, Paris, 1965, Musée Nat. d'Art Moderne, Paris, 1967, Musée de la Manufacture Nat. des Gobelins, 1969, Antibes, 1976, Ostend, 1977, Grand Palais, Paris, 1978, Wildenstien Gallery, N.Y.C., Dominion Gallery, Montreal, Que., Can., 1979, Musée de la Poste, Paris, 1980, Palais des Papes, Avignon, 1985, Galerie Sapone, Nice, 1987, Galerie Protée, Paris, 1988, Abbaye de Chateautoux, France, 1990, Musée de Boulogne Sur Mer, St. Germain en Laye, 1994, Refectoize des Jacobins, Toulouse, 1995, Jeu De Paume, 2002; prin. works include Hommage à la Mort, 1950, Hommage au Marechal de Turenne, 1952, Les Capetiens Partout, 1954, La Victoire de Denain, 1963, Hommage à Jean Cocteau, 1963, Paris, Capitale des Arts, 1965, Hommages aux Freres Boisseree, 1967, Hommages à Condillac, 1968, La prise de Berg op Zoom, 1969, Election de Charles Quint, 1971, Matta-Salums, 1978, La Liberation de Paris, 1980, La liberation d'Orleans par Jeanne d'Arc, 1982, Le Massacre des 269, 1985, Paradis des Orages, 1988, Les enfants de Bogota, 1989, Rumeurs de Paradis, 1991; designed gardens and bldgs. for B.C. transformer factory, Fontenay-le-comte, 1966; 16 posters for Air France; tapestries; 18 medals for Paris Mint, 1971, new 10 F coin, 1974; creater Tachism; author: Audela du Tachisme; Le privilege d'Etre; De la Revolté à Rénaissance; La Réponse de l'Abstraction lyrique; L'Abstraction Prophetique, Les Massacre de la Sensibilité, Desormais, Seul en Face de Dieu; represented in 90 museums and pub. collections. Mem. Acad. Fine Arts.

MATHIEU, MICHELE SUZANNE, medical association administrator; b. Chgo., Mar. 24, 1950; d. Joseph Edward Mathieu and Mary Ellen Fisher; m. Robert Steven Harris, May 1, 1988 (dec. Sept. 2000). BS in Mktg., Regents Coll., Albany, N.Y., 1998; cert. web site design, Columbia Coll., Chgo., 2000. Broadcast coord. Grey-North Advt., Chgo., 1967-71; head drama dept. Patricia Stevens Coll., 1972; instr. beginning acting Ted Liss Sch. Performing Arts, 1973-75; project coord. grants and contracts Am. Dietetic Assn., 1974-81, adminstr. govt. affairs, 1981-86, mgr. licensure comm., 1986-90, adminstr. nutrition svcs. payment systems, 1990-94, team leader, health care fin. team, 1994-97, dir. health care fin. team, 1998-00, dir. mem. web, 2000-01, dir. applications devel., 2001—. Grant proposal cons. various performance arts, Chgo., 1978-2000; med. reporter, writer various internat. clients, 1994—; PC cons., Chgo., 1994—. Editor Legis. Newsletter, 1981-86; contbg. editor Nutrition Forum, 1986, Courier, 1987—; contbr. articles to profl. jours., mags., newspapers. Website project mgr. DigitalEve, Chgo., 2001—. Ill. Arts Coun. grantee, 1981. Mem. Am. Soc. Assn. Execs. (Excellence in Govt. award 1989), Assn. of Internet Profls., Chgo. PHP Users Group. Roman Catholic. Avocations: reading, fitness walking. Office: Am Dietetic Assn 216 W Jackson Blvd Chicago IL 60606-6995 E-mail: mmathie@eatright.org.

MATHIEU, RICHARD GRABER, business educator; b. Bellefonte, Pa., July 1, 1960; s. Richard Detweiler and Doris (Graber) M.; m. Peggy Smith, Oct. 21, 1954; children: Pattie, Richard. BCE, U. Del., 1982; MS in Sys. Engring., U. Va., 1987, PhD in Sys. Engring., 1991. Asst. patent examiner U.S. Patent and Trademark Office, Washington, 1982-83; H.S. tchr., coach Severn Sch., Severna Park, Md., 1983-85; rsclf. and tchg. asst. U. Va., Charlottesville, 1985-91; asst. prof. MIS, U. N.C., Wilmington, 1991-95, assoc. prof., 1995-99, Cameron fellow, 1994-95; assoc. prof. MIS, St. Louis U., 1999—. Author: Manufacturing and the Internet, 1996; mem. editl. rev. bd. Jour. for Info. Sys. Edn., 1993—; contbr. articles to profl. jours. Mem. IEEE (Computer Soc.), INFORMS. Home: 9301 Tea Rose Ln Saint Louis MO 63126-2611 E-mail: prmathieu@aol.com., Mathieur@slu.edu.

MATHIOUDAKIS, MICHAEL ROBERT, life insurance and estate planning executive; b. Indpls., Sept. 3, 1963; s. Robert G. and Annabel M. (Pattison) M.; m. JoLee Katherine Pilarski, Dec. 27, 1986. BBA, U. Notre Dame, 1985. CLU, ChFC. Acct. Price Waterhouse, Indpls., 1985-87; account exec. Anderson Assocs., 1987-88; v.p. Exec. Fin. Group Inc., 1988-94; founder, pres. The GENESIS Group, LLC, 1995—; founder, prin. GENESIS Devel. Group, LLC, 1999—. Sr. mng. dir. The Private Cons. Group. Deacon East 91st St. Christian Ch., Indpls., 1988-90, trustee East 91st St. Christian Ch. Found., 1996-99; bd. dirs. Ind. Fellowship Christian Athletes, 1989-91; mem. adv. bd. Student Venture of Greater Indpls., 1989-92. Mem. Ptnrs. Fin., Million Dollar Round Table (Top of the Table), Nat. Assn. Life Underwriters, Indpls. Estate Planning Coun., Am. Soc. CLU and ChFC (cert.), Indpls. Bus. Connection (founder, pres. 1987-90), Nat. Assn. Philanthropic Planners, Nat. Assn. Family Wealth Counselors. Republican. Home: 10555 Chestnut Hill Cir Fishers IN 46038-9431 Office: The Private Cons Group 10150 Lantern Rd Fishers IN 46038

MATHIS, ALICIA, biologist; b. Meridian, Miss., May 7, 1960; d. Shirley Broadhead. BS, U. So. Miss., 1982, MS, 1985; PhD, U. Southwestern La., 1989. Tchg. asst. U. So. Miss., Hattiesburg, 1983—85; biologist U.S. Army Corps of Engrs., Vicksburg, 1985; tchg. asst. U. Southwestern La., Lafayette, 1985—89; post-doctoral fellow U. Sask., Saskatoon, Canada, 1990—93; assoc. prof. S.W. Mo. State U., Springfield, 1993—. Rev. panel NSF, 2001—01; mem. adv. bd. Ozark Ctr. for Wildlife Rsch., Reeds Spring, Mo., 1994—97. Contbr. articles to profl. jours., chapters to books; assoc. editor: Jour. Herpetology, 1997—2000, assoc. editor: Behavioral Ecology and Sociobiology, 2000—. Fellow, Mountain Lake Biol. Sta., 1988; grantee, U.S. Fish and Wildlife Svc., 2001—, Mo. Dept. Conservation, 1997—99, NSF, 1996, Sigma Xi, 1987, 1988. Mem.: Herpetologists League (councilor 2001—), Am. Soc. of Ichthyologists and Herpetologists (symposium organizer 1997), Soc. for the Study of Evolution, Internat. Soc. for Behavioral Ecology, Animal Behavior Soc. (travel grantee 1993). Avocation: singing. Office: SW Mo State U 901 S National Ave Springfield MO 65807

MATHIS, ANDREW SCOTT, pharmacist; b. Woodbury, NJ, Mar. 23, 1973; s. Albert Driver and Lucretia Mathis; m. Jacqueline S. Cunningham, June 14, 1997. BS in Pharmacy, Phila. Coll. of Pharmacy and Sci., 1996, PharmD., 1997. Registered pharmacist NJ, Pa. Pharmacist Our Lady of Lourdes Med. Ctr., Camden, NJ, 1996—98; resident in pharmacy practice Hahnemann U., Phila., 1997—98; asst. clin. prof. Rutgers U., Piscataway, NJ, 1997—. Peer reviewer various pharmacy and med. jours., 1997—. Contbr. articles to profl. jours. Mem.: Am. Soc. of Health-Systems Pharmacists (Poster Competition Awards from NJ Chpt. 2000, 2002), Am. Coll. of Clin. Pharmacy. Personal E-mail: smathis@rci.rutgers.edu.

MATHIS, CLEOPATRA, English language educator, poet; b. Ruston, La., Aug. 16, 1947; d. James Christopher Walton and Maxine Theodos; m. William Jefferson Mathis, June 20, 1973 (div. June 1984); 1 child, Alexandra Cary; m. William Foster Phillips, July 5, 1987; 1 child, Zachary Constantine Phillips. BA, S.W. Tex. State U., 1970; MFA, Columbia U., 1978. Tchr. English Converse (Tex.) H.S., 1970-72, Austin (Tex.) Pub. Schs., 1972-73, Lawrenceville (N.J.) H.S., 1973-74, Pelletier Day Sch., Trenton, N.J., 1974-76; instr. English Trenton State Coll., 1978; prof. English Dartmouth Coll., Hanover, N.H., 1982—. Author (poetry): What To Tip the Boatman?, 2001; contbg. editor: The Pushcart Press. Recipient NEA award, 1985, Robert Frost award Frost Place, 1982, Pushcart prize Pushcart Press, 1982; fellow in poetry Fine Arts Work Ctr., 1981-82. Mem. PEN Internat., Acad. Am. Poets (Peter Lavin award for younger poets 1985), Poetry Soc. Am., Associated Writing Programs. Democrat. Episcopalian. Office: Dartmouth Coll Dept English HB 6032 Hanover NH 03755

MATHIS, F. JOHN, finance educator; b. Rockford, Ill., Dec. 9, 1941; s. F. John and Jean K. (Vorwald) M.; children: John K., Laura K. BA, U. Calif., Riverside, 1962; MA, U. Iowa, 1964, PhD in Econs., 1966. Asst. prof. U. Ill., Chgo., 1964-66; assoc. prof. SUNY, Brockport, 1966-68; internat. economist Chase Manhattan Bank, N.Y.C., 1968-70; chief internat. economist Continental Bank of Chgo., 1970-83; sr. fin. analyst World Bank, Washington, 1983-85; sr. portfolio mgr. Internat. Fin. Corp., 1986-88; prof. internat. fin. Thunderbird-Am. Grad. Sch. Internat. Mgmt. & Banking, Phoenix, 1988—2000. Exec. dir. Thunderbird Internat. Trade and Fin. Ctr.; mng. dir. Thunderbird Ctr. Bus. Skills Devel., 2002; dir. faculty Thunderbird Am. Grad. Sch. Internat. Mgmt. Editor: Offshore Lending by U.S. Commercial Banks, 1985, First Steps in Treasury Management, 1991. Republican. Office: Thunderbird Am Grad Sch Internat Mgmt 15249 N 59th Ave Glendale AZ 85306-3236 E-mail: mathisj@t-bird.edu.

MATHIS, JACK DAVID, advertising executive, consultant; b. La Porte, Ind., Nov. 27, 1931; s. George Anthony and Bernice (Bennethum) Mathis; m. Phyllis Dene Hoffman, Dec. 24, 1971; children: Kane Cameron, Jana Dene. Student, U. Mo., 1950-52; BS, Fla. State U., 1955. With Benton & Bowles, Inc., 1955-56; owner Jack Mathis Advt., 1956—. (cons.): (films) That's Action, 1977; Great Movie Stunts: Raiders of the Lost Ark, 1981; The Making of Raiders of the Lost Ark, 1981; An American Legend: The Lone Ranger, 1981; Heroes and Sidekicks: Indiana Jones and The Temple of Doom, 1984; The Republic Pictures Story, 1991; The Making of the Quiet Man, 1992; Roy Rogers: King of the Cowboys, 1992; Cliffhangers! Adventures from the Thrill Factory, 1993; The Making of the Sands of Iwo Jima, 1993; Gene Autry: Melody of the West, 1994; Happy Trials: America Honors Roy Rogers and Dale Evans, 2001; author: Valley of the Cliffhangers, Republic Confidential, Valley of the Cliffhangers Supplement, Modern Marvels: Models, 2002. Mem. U.S. Olympic Basketball Com. Named to, Ill. Basketball Hall of Fame; recipient citation, Mktg. Rsch. Coun. N.Y. Mem.: Alpha Delta Sigma. Office: PO Box 3580 Barrington IL 60011-3580 E-mail: dmathis46@aol.com.

MATHIS, JAMES FORREST, retired petroleum company executive; b. Dallas, Sept. 28, 1925; s. Forrest and Martha (Godbold) M.; m. Frances Ellisor, Sept. 4, 1948; children: Alan Forrest (dec.), Lisa Lynn Lambeth.

BSChE, Tex. A&M U., 1946; MS, U. Wis., 1951, PhD, 1953. Rsch. engr. Humble Oil & Refining Co., Baytown, Tex., 1946-49, 53-61, mgr. R & D, 1961-63, mgr. Splty. products planning, 1963-65; v.p. Exxon Rsch. & Engring. Co., Linden, N.J., 1966-68; sr. v.p., dir. Imperial Oil Ltd., Toronto, Ont., Can., 1968-71; v.p. tech. Exxon Chem. Co., Florham Pk., N.J., 1971-80; v.p. sci. and tech. Exxon Corp., N.Y.C., 1980-84; ret., 1984. Cons. Arthur D. Little, 1985-92, ChemShare Corp., 1989-92; chmn. N.J. Commn. Sci and Tech., 1988-96; dir. Laser Recording Systems, Inc., 1989-93, N L Industries, 1985-86, Hanlin Corp., 1989-99, Beaver Lake Realty Co., 1995-98. Bd. dirs. Chem. Industry Inst. Toxicology, 1975-83, treas., 1977-80, chmn., 1980-83; bd. dirs. Tex. Inst. for Advancement of Chem. Tech., 2001--; trustee Wis. Alumni Rsch. Found., 1984—, pres., 1993-97; bd. chem. sci. and tech. of Nat. Rsch. Coun., 1987-89, chem. weapon stockpile demilitarization comn., 1998—. Served with AC, USNR, 1944-45. Recipient Disting. Alumni award Coll. Engring. Tex. A&M U., 1982, Disting. Svc. citation Coll. Engring. U. Wis., 1969. Fellow Am. Inst. Chem. Engrs. (interim exec. dir., sec. 1987-88, Robert L. Jacks award in Mgmt. 1985, Van Antwerpen award for Svc. to Inst. 1989); mem. AAAS, NAE, Am. Chem. Soc. (Earle B. Barnes award for Chem. Rsch. Mgmt. 1984), Sigma Xi, Phi Lambda Upsilon, Tau Beta Pi. Presbyterian. Achievements include 2 patents in field. Home: 2714 S Southern Oaks Dr Houston TX 77068-2600 E-mail: jfmathis@aol.com.

MATHIS, JOHN PRENTISS, lawyer; b. New Orleans, Feb. 10, 1944; s. Robert Prentess and Lena (Horton) M.; m. Karen Elizabeth McHugh, May 31, 1966; children: Lisa Lynne Mathis Kirkpatrick, Andrew P. BA magna cum laude, So. Meth. U., 1966; JD cum laude, Harvard U., 1969. Bar: Calif. 1970, D.C. 1975, U.S. Ct. Appeals (D.C. cir.) 1972, U.S. Ct. Appeals (5th cir.) 1975, U.S. Ct. Appeals (3d cir.) 1980, U.S. Supreme Ct. 1982. Assoc. Latham & Watkins, L.A., 1969-71; spl. asst. to gen. counsel FPC, Washington, 1971-72; gen. counsel Calif. Pub. Utilities Commn., San Francisco, 1972-74; assoc. Baker & Botts, Washington, 1974-76, ptnr., 1976-92, Hogan & Hartson, Washington, 1992-2000; v.p., assoc. gen. counsel regulatory affairs Edison Mission Energy, 2000—. Mem. ABA (litigation sect., chmn. energy litigation com. 1985-89, div. dir. 1989-90, chmn. legis. com. 1990-94, rep. to coord. group energy law 1992-97), Fed. Energy Bar Assn., Harvard U. Law Sch. Assn. D.C. (past pres.), Congl. Country Club, Met. Club (Washington), Talbot Country Club (Easton, Md.). Republican. Methodist. Home: 9400 Turnberry Dr Potomac MD 20854-5447 Office: Edison Mission Energy 555 12th St NW Ste 640 Washington DC 20004

MATHIS, KAREN MCHUGH, artist; b. Alma, Mich., June 13, 1945; d. James Edward and Nelda Ellen (Grubaugh) McHugh; m. John Prentiss Mathis, May 31, 1966; children: Lisa Lynne Mathis Kirkpatrick, Andy Prentiss. BS, So. Meth. U., 1965; BA, George Washington U., 1979. Cert. secondary tchr., Washington. Mem. gen. staff for spl. events Nat. Gallery Art, Washington, 1985-88. Paintings featured in The Best of Watercolor, 1995, 97, 99, Best of the Best, 2002; one-woman shows Landon Gallery, Landen Sch., Bethesda, Md., 1989, 93, Town Ctr. Gallery, Rockville, Md., 1990, Met. Meml. United Meth. Ch., Washington, 1990, Grenleaf Gallery, Nags Head, N.C., 1994, Yellow Barn Gallery, Glen Echo, Md., 1996, Albany (Ga.) Mus. Art, 1991, Gwinnett Fine Arts Ctr., Duluth, Ga., 1996, Howard Mandville Gallery, Kirkland, Wash., 1996, Gallery B.A.I., N.Y.C., 1998, 2002, Spectrum Gallery, Georgetown, Washington. Docent chmn. at Nat. Gallery of Art, Jr. League Washington, 1985, designer spl. exhibit project, 1986. Mem. Art League Washington, Ga. Watercolor Assn., N.W. Watercolor Assn. Democrat. Methodist.

MATHIS, KEVAN EUGENE, journalist; b. Saint Louis, Mo., Oct. 18, 1956; s. Clinton Eugene Mathis and Veda Josephine Harness; m. Pamela Diane Bartlett, Dec. 7, 1991; children: Aubri, Spencer Watson, Ryan Watson. BA, North Ark. Coll., Harrison, AR, 1995. Reporter Harrison Daily Times, Harrison, Ark., 1994—. Humor columnist Harrison Daily Times Newspaper, Harrison, Ark., 1994—; bd. sec. North Ark. Coll. Alumni Assn., Harrison, Ark., 1996—; entertainment editor Harrison Daily Times, Harrison, Ark., 2002—. Recipient Second Pl., Grand Prairie Festival of Arts, 2000; grantee Three-Week Ednl. Adv. Bd. in Japan, U.S. CC Exch. Program, 1995. Baptist. Avocations: ATV riding, photography, hunting, fishing, writing. Home: 7792 Bubbling Springs Road Harrison AR 72601 Office: Harrison Daily Times Newspaper 111 West Rush Avenue Harrison AR 72601

MATHIS, LAURELLE SHEEDY, executive recruiter, volunteer; b. Southampton, N.Y., Aug. 29, 1948; d. Edmund Sheedy and Tatiana (Widrin) Brooks; children: Liliana Sheedy, Bronwyn Trimble, Kane Timberlake. BA, Stephens Coll., Columbia, Mo., 1970; MBA, Harvard U., 1977. Spl. asst. Congressman Ed Foreman, Washington, 1970; staff asst. Senator James L. Buckley, 1971-72; staff asst. to Pres. of U.S., 1973-75; v.p. Blyth Eastman Paine Webber, N.Y.C., 1977-81, Merrill Lynch Capital Markets, N.Y.C., 1981-83; pres. Harris Energy Corp., Greenwich, Conn., 1988-91; CFO Diocese of Mt. Kilimanjaro, Arusha, Tanzania, 1991-93; v.p. TechnoServe, Norwalk, Conn., 1994-96, TMP Exec. Resourcing, N.Y.C., 1997—. Bd. curators Stephens Coll., 1981-83; bd. dirs. Putnam Indian Field Sch., Greenwich, 1986-91, chmn. auction, 1987; chmn. Christ Ch. Antiques Show, 1987, 88, 89; bd. dirs. Episcopal Ch., Women of Christ Ch. Recipient Alumni Achievement award Stephens Coll., 1980. Republican. Episcopalian. Home: 62 N Sound Beach Ave Riverside CT 06878-1231

MATHIS, LOIS RENO, retired elementary education educator; b. Vinson, Okla., June 10, 1915; d. William Dodson and Trudie Frances (Brady) Reno; m. Harold Fletcher Mathis, June 6, 1942 (dec.); children: Robert F., Betty Mathis Sproule. BS, Southwestern Okla. U., 1939; MA, U. Pitts., 1945; PhD, Ohio State U., 1965. Cert. elem. tchr.; cert. elem. supr. Tchr. Okla. Pub. Schs., Tea Cross, 1936-39, Tipton, 1939-42, Ohio County Schs., Wheeling, W.Va., 1944-45, Norman (Okla.) Pub. Schs., 1951-52, Kent (Ohio) State U., 1954-60, Ohio State U., Columbus, 1961-62, Columbus (Ohio) Pub. Schs., 1967-80; ret., 1980. Ednl. cons. in field, 1965—. Mem. Women's Round Table, Columbus, 1986-88; mem. data collection com. 100 Good Schs., Columbus, 1982-84. Mem. AAUW (pres. 1986-88), Ohio State Univ. Women's Club, Phi Delta Gamma (pres. 1980-82), Pi Lambda Theta, Alpha Delta Kappa, Kappa Delta Pi (counselor 1976—, alumni counselor exec. coun. internat. 1990-92, Honor Key 1991). Democrat. Baptist. Avocations: reading, bell collecting and research, entertaining friends, church activities. Home: 4590 Knightsbridge Blvd Apt 242 Columbus OH 43214-4353

MATHIS, LUSTER DOYLE, college administrator, political scientist; b. Gainesville, Ga., May 5, 1936; s. Luster and Fay Selena (Wingo) M.; m. Rheba Burch, June 5, 1958; children— Douglas James, Deborah Jane. AB, Berry Coll., 1958; MA, U. Ga., 1958, PhD (Univ. Alumni Found. fellow), 1966. Asst. prof. polit. sci. Brenau Coll., Gainesville, 1960-61; asso. prof. Calif. Baptist Coll., 1961-62, Belmont Coll., Nashville, 1962-64; asso. prof., head dept. polit. sci. W.Ga. Coll., Carrollton, 1965-68, prof., 1969-75, head dept., 1969-71, chmn. div. grad. studies, 1970-73; assoc. dean, 1972-75; research asso., asst. editor Papers of Thomas Jefferson Princeton U., 1968-69; v.p., dean of coll. Berry Coll., Mt. Berry, Ga., 1975-93, v.p. acad. affairs, 1993-99, provost, 1999-2000, coll. historian, prof. govt., 2000—. Cons. Citizens Com. on Ga. Gen. Assembly. Co-author: Courts as Political Instruments, 1970. Mem. Ga. Democratic Charter Commn., 1974-75; mem. consumer adv. com. Floyd Med. Center, 1978-80. Nat. Hist. Publs. Commn. fellow, 1968-69 Mem. Am. Assn. Higher Edn., Am. Conf. Acad. Deans, Ga. Polit. Sci. Assn. (pres. 1968-69). Democrat. Baptist. Office: Berry Coll Dept Govt Mount Berry GA 30149 E-mail: lmathis@berry.edu.

MATHIS, MARK JAY, lawyer; b. N.Y.C., Aug. 25, 1947; s. Meyer and Beulah (Nechemias) M.; m. Marylin Gail Goodman, Aug. 14, 1971; children: Alison Leigh, Brian Todd. BS, MIT, 1969; JD, U. Pa., 1972. Bar: D.C. 1973. Assoc. Arent, Fox, Kintner, Plotkin & Kahn, Washington, 1972-75; minority counsel Com. on D.C. U.S. Ho. of Reps., 1975-76; atty. Chesapeake & Potomac Telephone Cos., Washington, 1977-81, gen. atty., 1982-83, v.p., gen. counsel, 1984-89; v.p., assoc. gen. counsel Bell Atlantic Network Svcs., 1988-89, v.p., gen. counsel, 1990-91; v.p., dep. gen. counsel, sec. Bell Atlantic Corp., Phila., 1992; v.p., gen. counsel Bell Atlantic NSI, Arlington, Va., 1993-97, sr. v.p. external affairs, 1997, group pres. Mid Atlantic States, 1998, sr. v.p. regulatory, 1999; exec. v.p., gen. counsel Bell Atlantic Corp., N.Y., 2000; sr. v.p. and dep. gen. counsel Verizon, Arlington, Va., 2001—. Office: Verizon 1515 N Court House Rd Fl 5 Arlington VA 22201-2519 E-mail: mark.j.mathis@verizon.com.

MATHIS, MARSHA DEBRA, customer relations manager; b. Detroit, Dec. 22, 1953; d. Marshall Junior and Anita Willene (Biggers) M. BS, Fla. State U., 1978; MBA, Miss. Coll., 1982. With telecommunications dept. Fla. State Dept. Safety, Tallahassee, 1973-76; asst. to chmn. Tallahassee Savs. and Loan Assn., 1976-78; sales engr. Prehler, Inc., Jackson, Miss., 1978-82; mktg. mgr. Norand Corp., Arlington, Tex., 1982-87; v.p. mktg. and sales Profl. Datasolutions, Inc., Irving, 1987-88; v.p. mktg. and sales, ptnr. Target Systems, Inc., 1988-89, also bd. dirs.; v.p. mktg. Profl. Datasolutions, Inc., 1990—2002, Onvance, Atlanta, 2002—. Contbr. articles to industry trade jours. Advisor Am. Diabetes Assn., Jackson, 1983—. Mem. Internat. Platform Assn., Nat. Adv. Group, Nat. Assn. Convenience Stores (Industry Task Force 1987-88). Republican. Roman Catholic. Avocations: SCUBA diving, sailing, reading, coin collecting. Home: 325 Old York Rd Irving TX 75063-4247 Office: Onvance 1230 Peachtree NE Promenade 11 19th Fl Atlanta GA 30309

MATHIS, PATRICK BISCHOF, lawyer; b. Pinckneyville, Ill., Feb. 1, 1952; s. John Archibald and Theresa Ann (Bischof) M.; m. Rosanne Azar; children: Daniel P., Adrienne C. BA in Chemistry, St. Louis U., 1973; MBA, JD, Washington U., St. Louis, 1978, LL.M. in Taxation, 1979. Bar: Mo. 1978, Ill. 1979, U.S. Tax Ct. 1979, U.S. Dist. Ct. (so. dist.) Ill. 1980, U.S. Ct. Appeals (7th cir.) 1980, U.S. Ct. Claims 1980, U.S. Supreme Ct. 1982. Assoc. John J. Vassen, P.C., Belleville, Ill., 1979-84; ptnr. Mathis, Marifian, Richter & Grandy, Ltd., 1984—. Spkr. in field. Contbr. articles to profl. jours. Mem. fin. com. Special Children, Inc. Mamie O. Stookey Sch., 1987-90; parish coun. Blessed Sacrament Parish, 1992-98, pres., 1993-98; chmn. annual fund drive Big Brothers/Big Sisters, St. Clair County, 1994; bd. dirs. Signal Hill Neighborhood Assn., 1989-92, St. Clair County Greenspace Found., 1990-2000, Signal Hill Sch. Edn. Found., 1997-99; mem. Signal Hill Sch. Dist. Bd. Edn., 1999—. Mem. ABA (tax sect. civil and criminal penalties com., domestic rels. tax problems com., vice chmn. subcom. alimony issues, gen. practice sect. chmn. taxation com.), Ill. Bar Assn. (fed. taxation sect. council 1984-85, 89-93, chmn. 1992-93), St. Clair County Bar Assn., Bar Assn. Met. St. Louis, Ill. Inst. Continuing Legal Edn. (chmn. 1996-97, bd. dirs. 1990-98), Am. Coll. Trust and Estate Counsel. Roman Catholic. Mo. Athletic Club, Alpha Sigma Nu, Eta Sigma Phi. Home: 33 Oak Knoll Pl Belleville IL 62223-1880 Office: Mathis Marifian Et Al 720 W Main St Ste 100 Belleville IL 62220-1541 Fax: 618-234-9786. E-mail: pmathis@mmrg.com.

MATHIS, SHARON BELL, author, retired elementary educator and librarian; b. Atlantic City, Feb. 26, 1937; d. John Willie and Alice Mary (Frazier) Bell; m. Leroy F. Mathis, July 11, 1957 (div. Jan. 1979); children: Sherie, Stacy, Stephanie. BA, Morgan State Coll., 1958; M.L.S., Catholic U. Am., 1975. Interviewer Children's Hosp. D.C., Washington, 1958-59; tchr. Holy Redeemer Elem. Sch., 1959-65, Charles Hart Jr. H.S., Washington, 1965-72; spl. edn. tchr. Stuart Jr. H.S., 1972-74; libr. Benning Elem.Sch., 1975-76, Friendship Ednl. Ctr. (now Patricia R. Harris Ednl. Ctr.), 1976-95, ret., 1995. Writer-in-charge children's lit. div. D.C. Black Writers Workshop; writer-in-residence Howard U., 1972-73 Author: Brooklyn Story, 1970, Sidewalk Story, 1971 (Council on Interracial Books for Children award 1970), Teacup Full of Roses, 1972 (Outstanding Book of Yr. award New York Times 1972), Ray Charles, 1973 (Coretta Scott King award 1974), Listen for the Fig Tree, 1974, The Hundred Penny Box, 1975 (Boston Globe-Horn Book Honor book 1975, Newbery Honor Book 1976), Cartwheels, 1977, Red Dog Blue Fly: Football Poems, 1991 (Children's Book of Yr. award Bank St. Coll. 1992), Red Dog Blue Fly: An American Bookseller (Pick of the List 1995), Running Girl: The Diary of Ebonee Rose, 1997, Ray Charles, 2001. Mem. bd. advisers lawyers com. D.C. Commn. on Arts, 1972. Nominated Books for Brotherhood list NCCJ, 1970; recipient D.C. Assn. Sch. Librs. award 1976, Arts and Humanities award Archdiocese of Washington Black Secretariat, 1978; Weekly Reader Book Club fellow Bread Loaf Writers Conf., 1970, MacDowell Colony fellow, 1978. Roman Catholic. *My success is due to the glorious African blood which flows throughout my body— and to the dignity, intelligence, strength, pride, efforts, and faith of my very creative parents and all people who have helped me.*

MATHIS, TERANCE, professional football player; b. Detroit, June 7, 1967; Student, U. N.Mex. Wide receiver, kick returner N.Y. Jets, 1990-93, Atlanta Falcons, 1994—2001; wide receiver Pittsburgh Steelers, 2002—. Named to Sporting News Coll. All-Am. 1st Team, 1989; selected to Pro Bowl, 1994. Office: Pittsburgh Steelers 100 Art Rooney Ave Pittsburgh PA 15212*

MATHIS, WILLIAM LOWREY, lawyer; b. Jackson, Tenn., Dec. 19, 1926; s. Harry Fletcher and Syrene (Lowrey) M.; m. Marilyn Jayne Cason, Sept. 10, 1949; children: Amanda Jayne Miller, Amy Susan Webb, Peter Andrew, Perry Alexander, Anne Lowrey Mandigo. B.M.E., Duke U., 1947; JD, George Washington U., 1951. Bar: D.C. bar 1951, Fla. bar 1972, Va. bar 1977. Examiner U.S. Patent Office, 1947-52; mem. Swecker & Mathis, Washington, 1952-61; of counsel Burns, Doane, Swecker & Mathis, Alexandria, Va., 1961—. Adj. prof. law Georgetown U. Law Center, 1974— Co-author: Trademark Litigation in the Trademark Office and Federal Courts, 1977; also chpt. in Handbook of Modern Marketing, 2d edit., 1986. Mem. Am., D.C. bar assns., Am. Intellectual Property Law Assn., Order of Coif. Roman Catholic. Home: 3709 Chanel Rd Annandale VA 22003-2024 Office: 1737 King St Ste 500 Alexandria VA 22314-2727

MATHISEN, HAROLD CLIFFORD, portfolio management executive; b. East Orange, N.J., Apr. 1, 1924; s. Harold and Ottilie Christine (Nordland) M.; AB, Princeton U., 1943; MBA, Harvard U., 1948; m. Dora Elizabeth Bachtel, Sept. 14, 1946; children: Margaret Bennett, Harold, Elizabeth Mathisen Andersen, Barbara Ramsland. Asst. to controller Kaiser Frazer Corp., Willow Run, Mich., 1948-52; investment analyst Smith Barney & Co., N.Y.C., 1952-61; pres. Alliance Found., N.Y.C., 1961—; treas. AGF Mgmt. Co., N.Y.C., 1969-85; asst. treas., investment mgr. Christian and Missionary Alliance, Nyack, 1978-80; pres. Alliance Growth Fund, N.Y.C., 1968-78; asst. treas. N.Y. Internat. Bible Soc., N.Y.C., 1980-82; portfolio mgr. Legg Mason Wood Walker, Inc., N.Y.C., 1967-78, 82—. Trustee, pres. McAuley Water St. Mission, N.Y.C., 1967—. Lt. USNR, 1944-46. Mem. N.Y. Soc. Securities Analysts, Inst. Chartered Fin. Analysts, Phi Beta Kappa, Sigma Xi. Home: 36 Runnymede Rd Chatham NJ 07928-1374 Office: One Chase Manhattan Plaza New York NY 10005

MATHISEN, HOWARD, psychologist, minister; b. Bklyn., June 3, 1938; s. Olaf and Hjordis K. (Skjaerum) M.; m. Kathleen Ann Poce, Sept. 20, 1980 (dec. Oct. 1987); children: Randi Sue, Lisa Jane; m. Carolynn Anne Burroughs, Aug. 22, 1992. BA, Taylor U., 1960; MDiv, Phila. Theol. Sem., 1963; postgrad., Luth. Theol. Sem., 1964-65; MA in Religion, Concordia Sem., 1967; postgrad., Rutgers U., 1975, Assumption Coll., 1971-76; DMin in Psychology, Andover Newton Theol. Sch., 1976. Lic. psychologist, Mass., marriage and family therapist, Mass.; cert. sex therapist Am. Assn. Sex Educators, Counselors and Therapists; diplomate in marital and sex therapy Am. Bd. Family Psychology; diplomate Am. Bd. Sexology. Pastor Christ Meml. Ch., Phila., 1962-66, Zion Luth. Ch., Webster, Mass., 1967-73; dir. Human Svcs. Ctr. Hubbard Regional Hosp., 1973-81; pvt. practice psychology Boylston, Mass., 1976-81; co-dir. Counseling Affiliates, Worcester, 1981-97; dir. pastoral counseling Boston Road Clinic, 1997—2001; dir. credentialing svcs. Capstan, 1998-99; asst. pastor Concordia Luth. Ch., 1976-98; dir. min. asst. program New Eng. Synod, Luth. Ch., 1991—; psychologist Prescott Health Care, 2002—. Adj. instr. psychology Nichols Coll., Dudley, Mass., 1981, Assumption Coll., Worcester, 1983-86. Dean ctrl. Mass. conf. New Eng. Synod, Luth. Ch., 1988-90; bd. dirs. Luth. Svc. Assn. New Eng., 1973-87, vice chmn., 1983-85, chmn., 1985-87; bd. dirs. Luth. Home of Worcester, 1987-92, chmn., 1987-89; chmn. bldg. com. Luth. Nursing Home, Worcester, 1977-79; chmn. Family Svcs. Com., 1981-83; mem. Mass. Adv. Com. Continuing Edn. for Nursing, 1979-81; bd. dirs. Family Planning Svcs. Ctrl. Mass., 1975-81; mem. tech. adv. subcom. substance abuse Ctrl. Mass. Health Sys. Agy., 1979-80. Fellow Acad. Family Psychology, Am. Acad. Clin. Sexologists; mem. APA, Am. Assn. Marriage and Family Therapy, Mass. Psychol. Assn., Mass. Assn. Marriage and Family Therapy, Acad. Managed Care Providers. Home: 6 Camelot Cir Dudley MA 01571-6110 Office: 130 Elm St Worcester MA 01609 E-mail: mathisen@charter.net.

MATHISEN-REID, RHODA SHARON, international communications consultant; b. Portland, Oreg., June 25, 1942; d. Daniel and Mildred Elizabeth Annette (Peterson) Hager; m. James Albert Mathisen, July 17, 1964 (div. 1977); m. James Albert Mathisen, July 17, 164 (div. 1977); m. James A. Reid Sr., Jan. 1, 1991. BA in Edn., Music, Bible Coll., Mich., 1964. Cmty. rels. officer Gary-Wheaton Bank, Wheaton, Ill., 1971-75; br. mgr. Stiver Temporary Personnel, Chgo., 1975-79; v.p. sales Exec. Technique, 1980-83; prin. Mathisen Assocs., Clarendon Hill., Ill., 1983—. Presenter seminars; featured speaker Women in Mgmt. Oak Brook Chpt., 1988.; cons. Haggai Inst., Atlanta; adv. mem. Nat. Bd. Success Group, 1986. Newsletter editor/publisher: 90th Divsn. Assn. (WWII Vets) 2001—. Mem. Downers Grove Twp. Precinct # 87 Rep. Com., 1998—; pres. chancel choir Christ Ch. Oak Brook, 1985—87; bd. dirs. Career Devel. Inst., Oak Brook, 1992—99, chair operational fin. com., 1997—98; bd. dirs. Crossroads Ministry Internat., 2000—; chmn. 1st Profl. Women's Seminar, 1995; judge Mrs. Ill., USI Pageant, 1994; exec. sec., treas. 90th Divsn. Assn., 2001—. Recipient Denby Steel award, 90th Divsn. Assn., 2001. Mem. Bus. and Profl. Women (charter mem., Woodfield chpt.), Execs. Club Oak Brook, Assn. Commerce and Industry (named Ambassdor of month N.W. suuburban chpt. 1979), Oak Brook Assn. Commerce and Industry (membership com.), Women Entrepreneurs of DuPage County (membership chmn., featured speaker Ja 1988), Art. Inst., Willowbrook/Burr Ridge C. of C., 90th Divsn. Assn. (asst. sec., treas., 2001 Denby Steel award, editor newsletter), US Army WWII Vets. Orgn. (newsletter editor 2001-). Office: Mathisen Assocs 17 Lake Shore Dr Hinsdale IL 60527-2221

MATHISON, IAN WILLIAM, chemistry educator, academic dean; b. Liverpool, Eng., Apr. 17, 1938; came to U.S., 1963; s. William and Grace (Almond) M.; m. Mary Ann Gordon, July 20, 1968; children: Mark W., Lisa A. B. Pharm., U. London, 1960, PhD, 1963, D. Sci., 1976. Lic. pharmacist, Gt. Britain. Research assoc. U. Tenn. Ctr. for Health Scis., Memphis, 1963-65, asst. prof., 1965-68, assoc. prof., 1968-72, prof., 1972-76; medicinal chemistry prof. Ferris State U., Big Rapids, Mich., 1977—, dean, prof., 1977—. External examiner U. Sci., Malaysia, 1978-79; mem. Mich. dept. Mental Health Pharmacy Facilities Rev. Panel, Lansing, 1978-90, Quality Assurance Commn., 1979-90; cons. WHO, 1999; cons. in field. Mem. editorial bd.: Jour. Pharm. Sci., 1981-86 ; contbr. articles to profl. jours.; sr. inventor, patentee in field. Marion Labs. awardee, 1965-74; NSF grantee, 1968-72; Beecham Co. grantee, 1974-79 Fellow Royal Inst. Chemistry, Royal Soc. Chemistry; mem. Am. Pharm. Soc., Am. Chem. Soc., Am. Assn. Coll. Pharmacy (bd. dirs. 1988-90), Nat. Assn. Retail Druggists (edn. adv. com. 1989-94), Royal Pharm. Soc. Gt. Britain, Nat. Assn. Chain Drug Stores (ednl. adv. com. 1993—). Home: 820 Osborn Cir Big Rapids MI 49307-2536 Office: Ferris State U 220 Ferris Dr Big Rapids MI 49307-2295

MATHOG, ROBERT HENRY, otolaryngologist, educator; b. New Haven, Apr. 13, 1939; s. William and Tiby (Gans) M.; m. Deena Jane Rabinowitz, June 14, 1964; children: Tiby, Heather, Lauren, Jason. AB, Dartmouth Coll., 1960; MD, NYU, 1964. Diplomate Am. Bd. Facial Plastic and Reconstructive Surgery. Intern Duke Hosp., Durham, N.C., 1964-65, resident surgery, 1965-66, resident otolaryngology, 1966-69; practice medicine, specializing in otolaryngology Mpls., 1971-77, Detroit, 1977—; chief of otolaryngology Hennepin County Med. Center, Mpls., 1972-77; asst. prof. U. Minn., 1971-74, asso. prof., 1974-77; prof., chmn. dept. otolaryngology Wayne State U. Sch. Medicine, 1977—. Chief otolaryngology Hennepin County Hosp., Mpls., 1972-77, Harper-Grace Hosps., Detroit, 1977—, Detroit Receiving Hosp., 1977-92; cons. staff VA Hosp., Allen Park, Minn., 1977—, Children's Hosp., Detroit, 1977—, Hutzel Hosp., Detroit, 1966, St. Joseph Mercy Hosp., Oakland, Mich., 2001; mem. adv. coun. Nat. Inst. Deaf and Other Communicable Disorders NIH, 1992-96; chief otolaryngology, head and neck surgery June Hosp., 1994-95. Author: Otolaryngology Clinics of North America, 1976, Textbook of Maxillofacial Trauma, 1983; editor in chief Videomed. Edn. Systems, 1972-75; editor: Atlas of Craniofacial Trauma, 1992; contbr. articles to med. jours. Bd. dirs. Bexer County Hearing Soc., 1969-71; adv. coun. WIDCB, 1993. Maj. USAF, 1969-71; chmn. Lens Hearing Ctr. of S.E. Mich. Recipient Valentine Mott medal for proficiency in anatomy, 1961, Recognition award Wayne State Bd. Govs. Faculty, 1993; Deafness Rsch. Found. grantee, 1979-81, NIH grantee, 1986, 92, 96, Lawrence M. Weiner Alumni award Wayne State U. Sch. Med., 1999. Fellow ACS, Am. Acad. Otolaryngology, Head and Neck Surgery (Cert. award 1976, Cert. of Appreciation 1978), Am. Soc. Head and Neck Surgery, Triological Soc. (v.p. 1995-96, mtg. guest of honor 2002), Am. Otol. Soc., Am. Acad. Facial Plastic and Reconstructive Surgery (v.p. 1980), Am. Neurotology Soc.; mem. AMA, Am. Laryngol. Soc. (coun. 1994—), Am. Laryngol. Assn., Mich. Med. Soc., Am. Head and Neck Soc., Soc. Univ. Otolaryngologists (pres. 1995), Assn. Acad. Depts. Otolaryngology, Assn. Rsch. Otolaryngology (pres. 1981). Home: 27115 Wellington Rd Franklin MI 48025-1329 Office: 27177 Lahser Rd Ste 203 Southfield MI 48034-8468 Also: Wayne State U Sch Med 540 E Canfield St Detroit MI 48201-1928

MATHRE, LAWRENCE GERHARD, minister, federal agency administrator; b. Vancouver, B.C., Can., Mar. 24, 1925; s. Lawrence Alfred and Nellie Josephine (Thompson) M.; m. Blanche Kathleen Brudevold, Sept. 2, 1951; children: James Lawrence, Jerome Keigh, John Mark, Joel David. BA, St. Olaf Coll., 1948; MDiv., Luther Sem., 1952; MA, Phillips U., 1962. Ordained to ministry Evang. Luth. Ch. in Am., 1952. Pastor First Luth. Ch., Fargo, N.D., 1952-54, Bethlehem Luth. Ch., Buffalo Center, Iowa, 1952-57; founder, pastor Prince of Peace Luth. Ch., Oklahoma City, 1957-63; chaplain fed. prison system U.S. Dept. Justice, Okla., Wash., Ill. and Calif., 1963-73, chaplain dir. Western and N.C. regions, 1973-83; pastor Hope Luth Ch., San Mateo, Calif., 1984-87, Zion Luth. Ch., Stockton, 1987-91; ret., 1991. Assoc. prof. Pacific Luth. U., Parkland, Wash., 1970-72; chaplain St. Joseph's Regional Med. Ctr. Nat. chaplain Fed. Parson Retirees Assn., 1999—. With AUS, 1943-45, ETO. Decorated Bronze Star. Mem. Am. Protestant Correctional Chaplains Assn. (nat. pres. 1974), Am. Correctional Chaplains Assn. (nat. pres. 1977), Assn. Clin. Pastoral Edn. (regional chmn. 1979-83, v.p. 1977-79, treas. 1984-89), Winnebago Itasc Travelers (chaplain), Lions (chaplain San Mateo club 1985-87). Republican. Home: 2228 Meadow Lake Dr Stockton CA 95207-4528 also: 2228 Meadow Lake Dr Stockton CA 95207-4528 *It is not nearly as important what happens to you as it is what you do about what happens to you. A life lived for oneself is empty; a life lived with and for others is full. You truly find yourself when you are well related—to God and to others.*

MATHUR, DEVESH, chemical engineer, researcher; b. Kanpur, India, Sept. 14, 1969; came to U.S., 1991; s. Gyanesh Narayan and Ranjana M.; m. Priya Mathur, Feb. 15, 1997; 1 child, Dhruv Mathur. BS, Harcourt Butler Tech. Inst., Kanpur, India, 1991; MS, Rensselaer Poly. Inst., Troy, N.Y., 1994, PhD, 1998. Engr. Imperial Chem. Industries, Kanpur, 1990; tchg. asst. Rensselaer Poly. Inst., Troy, 1993-96, rsch. asst., 1992-97; chem. process engr. GE Plastics, Waterford, N.Y., 1998-99, quality engr. Mt. Vernon, Ind., 1999, new product introduction engr., tech. black belt Waterford, 2000—; NPI and product engr. GE-Bayer Silicons, LeverKusen, Germany, 2000. Cons. Rensselaer Poly. Inst., Troy, 1996-97. Contbr. articles to profl. jours. Mem. exec. coun. Nat. Svc. Scheme, Kanpur, 1990-91; mem. organizing com. SPICMACAY, Kanpur, 1989-91, 95-97; active ELFUN, 1998—. Mem. ACS, AAAS, Am. Inst. Chem. Engrs., Soc. Polymer Engrs., Mensa, Sigma Xi, N.Y. Acad. Scis. Achievements include research in optimal particle size in PS/PB blends with compatibilizers, vapor deposition of parylene f, pilot plant design and scale up work, new product commercialization and business growth, quality and six sigma; expertise in silicones, polycarbojnate, polymer, blends and process engineering. Office: GE Silicones 260 Hudson River Rd Waterford NY 12188-1921 E-mail: devpriya97@hotmail.com.

MATHUR, IKE, finance educator; b. Jamshedpur, India, Nov. 22, 1943; came to U.S., 1961; s. Robert William and Ivy (Phillips) M.; children: Rebecca Lynn, Jason Gabriel. BS, Eastern Mich. U., 1965, MBA, 1968; PhD, U. Cin., 1974. Editor Am. Math. Soc., Providence, 1965-69; rsch. asst. U. Cin., 1969-72; instr. U. Dayton, Ohio, 1972-73; asst. prof. U. Pitts., 1973-77; assoc. prof. fin. So. Ill. U., Carbondale, 1977-81, prof., 1981—, chmn. fin., 1979-92, 94-95, dean Coll. Bus., 1992-94. Mgmt. trainer AID, Washington, 1978-81; Fulbright prof., Turku, Finland, 1983-84, Lisbon, Portugal, 1993. Author:

Introduction to Financial Management, 1979, Cases in Managerial Finance, 1984, Personal Finance, 1989, Wealth Creation in Eastern Europe, 1992, Financial Management in Post Europe, 1992. Mem. Am. Fin. Assn., French Fin. Assn., Western Fin. Assn., Midwest Fin. Assn., Fin. Mgmt. Assn. Avocations: running, martial arts, travel. Home: 32 Apple Orchard Rd Carbondale IL 62901-7672 Office: So Ill U Coll Bus Carbondale IL 62901 E-mail: imathur@cba.siu.edu.

MATIA, PAUL RAMON, federal judge; b. Cleve., Oct. 2, 1937; s. Leo Clemens and Irene Elizabeth (Linkert) M.; m. Nancy Arch Van Meter, Jan. 2, 1993. BA, Case Western Res. U., 1959; JD, Harvard U., 1962. Bar: Ohio 1962, U.S. Dist. Ct. (no. dist.) Ohio 1969. Law clk. Common Pleas Ct. of Cuyahoga County, Cleve., 1963-66, judge, 1985-91; asst. atty. gen. State of Ohio, 1966-69, adminstrv. ast. to atty. gen. Columbus, 1969-70; senator Ohio State Senate, 1971-75, 79-83; ptnr. Hadley, Matia, Mills & MacLean Co., L.P.A., Cleve., 1975-84; judge U.S. Dist. Ct. (no. dist.) Ohio, 1991-99, chief dist. judge, 1999—; mem. 6th Cir. Jud. Coun., 1999—. Candidate Lt. Gov. Rep. Primary, 1982, Ohio Supreme Ct., 1988. Named Outstanding Legislator, Ohio Assn. for Retarded Citizens, 1974, Watchdog of Ohio Treasury, United Conservatives of Ohio, 1979; recipient Heritage award Polonia Found., 1988. Mem. Fed. Bar Assn., Club at Key Ctr. Avocations: skiing, gardening, travel. Office: US Dist Ct 201 Superior Ave E Cleveland OH 44114-1201

MATIAS, PATRICIA TREJO, secondary education educator; b. Havana, Cuba; came to U.S., 1967; d. Juan Mario and Maria (Rexach) Trejo; m. Miguel Matias, Mar. 20, 1972; children: Michael George, Mark Patrick. BA in French/Spanish, Ga. Coll., 1973; MAT in Spanish Edn., Ga. State U., 1985, EdS in Fgn. Lang. Edn., 1991, postgrad., 1998. Cert. Spanish tchr., Ga. Spanish lead tchr. Wheeler High Sch., Marietta, Ga., 1980-2000; AP Spanish tchr. Walton High Sch., 2000—. Part-time instr. Kennesaw State Coll., 1991-1998. VIP guest svc. goodwill amb. Olympics Games Com., Atlanta, 1995-96. Mem. Am. Assn. Tchrs. Spanish and Portuguese, Profl. Ga. Assn. Educators, Fgn. Lang. Assn. Ga., Kappa Delta Pi, Sigma Delta Pi (hon.). Avocations: golf, travel, gardening. Office: Walton High Sch 1590 Bill Murdock Rd Marietta GA 30062 E-mail: pmatias@aol.com.

MATIJEVIC, EGON, chemistry educator; b. Otocac, Croatia, Apr. 27, 1922; came to U.S., 1957; s. Grgur and Stefica (Spiegel) M.; m. Bozica Biscan, Feb. 27, 1947. Diploma in chem. engring., U. Zagreb, 1944, PhD in Chemistry, 1948, Dr. Habil. in Phys. Chemistry, 1952; DSc (hon.), Lehigh U., 1977, M. Curie-Sklodowska U., Lublin, Poland, 1990; DSc (hon.), Clarkson U., 1992; DSc (hon.), Zagreb U., Croatia, 1998. Instr. chemistry U. Zagreb, Croatia, 1944-47, sr. instr. phys. chemistry, 1949-52, privat dozent in colloid chemistry, 1952-54, dozent in phys. and colloid chemistry, 1955-56, on leave, 1956-59; rsch. assoc. Inst. Cinematography, Zagreb, 1948; rsch. fellow dept. colloid sci. U. Cambridge, Eng., 1956-57; vis. prof. Clarkson Coll. Tech., Potsdam, N.Y., 1957-59, assoc. prof. chemistry Postdam, 1960-62; prof. Clarkson U., 1962-86, disting. univ. prof., 1986-99, LaMer prof. colloid and surface sci., 2000—; assoc. dir. Inst. Colloid and Surface Sci. Clarkson Coll. Tech., 1966-68; dir. inst., 1968-81; chmn. dept. chemistry, 1981-87; vis. prof. Japan Soc. for Promotion Sci., 1973, U. Melbourne, Australia, 1976, Sci. U. Tokyo, 1979, 84; vis. scientist U. Leningrad, USSR, 1977; Internat. Atomic Energy Agy. adviser Buenos Aires, Argentina, 1978, 80; fgn. guest Inst. Colloid and Interface Sci. Sci. U. Tokyo, 1982; lectr. in field; mem. adv. com. Univs. and Space Research Assn.; referee NATO Advanced Study Inst. Egon Matijevic chair in colloids Clarkson U., 2002. Author: (with M. Kesler) General and Inorganic Chemistry for Senior High Schools, 11 edits., including Croatian, Macedonian, Hungarian, Italian, 1943-63; translator: Einfuhrung in die Stochiometrie (Nylen and Wigern), 1948; editor: (with Alter J. Weber) Adsorption from Aqueous Solution, 1968, Surface and Colloid Science, vols. 1-17, 1969-2002; contbr. numerous articles to profl. publs. Recipient Gold medal Am. Electroplaters Soc., 1976; guest of honor 56th and 63rd Colloid and Surface Sci. Symposiums, Blacksburg, Va., 1982, Seattle, 1989. Mem. Am. Chem. Soc. (councilor div. colloid and surface chemistry 1982-87, chmn. 1969-70, Kendall award 1972, Langmuir Disting. Lectureship award 1985, Ralph K. Iler award 1993), Kolloid Gesellschaft (hon. life, Thomas Graham award 1985), Internat. Assn. Colloid Interface Sci. (pres. 1985-87), Chem. Soc. Japan, Inst. Colloid and Interface Sci. of Sci. of Tokyo (hon.), Phalanx Soc., Croatian Acad. Scis. and Arts (fgn.), Am. Ceramic Soc. (hon.), Materials Rsch. Soc. Japan (hon.), Acad. Ceramics (Italy), Croatian Chem. Soc. (hon., Bozo Tezak medal 1991), Sigma Xi (Clarkson Coll. Tech. chpt. award 1972, nat. lectr. 1987-89). Roman Catholic. Office: Ctr Advanced Materials Proc Clarkson U Dept Chem Potsdam NY 13699-5814

MATIN, A. microbiology educator, consultant; b. Delhi, India, May 8, 1941; came to U.S., 1964, naturalized, 1983; s. Mohd Said; m. Mimi Keyhan, June 21, 1968. BS, U. Karachi, Pakistan, 1960, MS, 1962; PhD, UCLA, 1969. Lectr. St. Joseph's Coll., Karachi, 1962-64; research assoc. UCLA, 1964-71; sci. officer U. Groningen, Kerklaan, The Netherlands, 1971-75; prof. microbiology and immunology Stanford U., Calif., 1975—, prof. Western Hazardous Substances Rsch. Ctr., 1981-98; cons. law offices Swidler Berlin Shereef Friedman, LLP, Washington, 1999—2001. Cons. Engenics, 1982-84, Monsanto, 1984-86, Chlorox, 1992-93; chmn. Stanford Recombinant DNA panel, mem. human subject panel, 2002--; mem. Accreditation Bd. for Engring. and Tech.; mem. internat. adv. com. Internat. Workshop on Molecular Biology of Stress Response: Meml. Found., Banaras U. and German Min. of Rsch., mem. panel Yucca Mountain Microbial Activity, Dept. of Energy, mem. study sect.; NASA study sect.; participant DOE, NABIR program draft panel; mem. study sect. NIH; convenor of microbiol. workshop and confs.; rev. panel DOE environ. mgmt. program; mem. rev. panels DOE NABIR program, mem. Stanford Biosafety Panel; bd. dirs. Chembiotek; keynote spkr., adv. bd. several internat. confs.; ASM Found. lectr. Mem. editl. bd. Jour. Bacteriology, Ann. Rev. Microbiol., Jour. Microbiology; reviewer NSF and other grants; contbr. numerous publs. to sci. jours. Fulbright fellow, 1964-71; recipient rsch. awards NSF, 1981-92, Ctr. for Biotech. Rsch., 1981-85, EPA, 1981—, NIH, 1989-92, U.N. Tokten, 1987, DOE, 1993—, Dept. Agrl., 1995-97, NASA, 1999—. Fellow Am. Acad. Microbiology; mem. AAAS, AAUP, Am Soc. for Microbiology (Found. lectr. 1991-93), Soc. Indsl. Microbiology, No. Soc. Indsl. Microbiology (bd. dirs.), Biophys. Soc., Am. Chem. Soc., Inst. Molecular Medicine (bd. dirs.). Avocations: reading, music, hiking. Home: 690 Coronado Ave Stanford CA 94305-1039 Office: Stanford U Fairchild Sci Bldg Dept Microbiology & Immunology Stanford CA 94305-5124 E-mail: a.matin@Stanford.edu.

MATISOFF, GERALD, geology educator; b. Boston, Apr. 27, 1951; s. David and Corinne Gloria (Price) M.; m. Susan Ilene Meyerson, Oct. 17, 1973; children: Daniel Charles, Lauren Jo. BS, MIT, 1973; MA, Johns Hopkins U., 1975, PhD, 1978. Asst. prof. Case Western Res. U., Cleve., 1977-83, assoc. prof., 1983—. Vis. prof. Cleve. State U., 1985-86; pres. Geosci. Assocs., Inc., 1986—; adj. prof. Oberlin (Ohio) Coll., 1991; panelist NSF and EPA, Washington, 1980—. Contbr., rev. articles for profl. jours. Leader Boy Scouts Am., Cleve., 1988-92; youth softball coach, Cleve., 1992—; mem. tech. com. Cuyahoga Remedial Action Plan, Cleve., 1989—. Grantee NSF, 1980-82, 84-86, 89-90, U.S. EPA, 1975-81, 90-93, NOAA, 1980-83, 84-89, Am. Water Works Assn., 1990-91, U.S. Geol. Survey, 1979-81, 80-82, 93-95, U.S. Army Corps Engrs., 1984, U.S. DOE, 1989-91. Mem. Internat. Assn. Great Lakes Rsch. (assoc. editor jour. 1981—), Geochem. Soc., Am. Soc. Limnologists and Oceanographers, Am. Geophys. Union, Am. Assn. Petroleum Geologists, Assn. Groundwater Scientists and Engrs., No. Ohio Geol. Soc., Sigma Xi. Democrat. Jewish. Avocations: science fiction, photography, golf, jogging, fishing. Office: Case Western Res Univ Dept Geol Sci A W Smith #112 Cleveland OH 44106

MATJASKO, M. JANE, anesthesiologist, educator; b. Harrison Twp., Pa., 1942; MD, Med. Coll. Pa., 1968. Diplomate Am. Bd. Anesthesiology. Resident in anesthesiology Md. Hosp., Balt., 1968-72; prof., chmn. anesthesiology U. Md., 1990—. Mem. Am. Soc. Anesthesiologists, Assn. Univ. Anesthesiologists. Office: U Md Hosp Dept Anesthesiology 22 S Greene St Baltimore MD 21201-1544

MATKIN, JUDITH CONWAY, jewelry designer and manufacturer; b. Ontario, Oreg., Jan. 26, 1943; d. Edward Owen and Lois Lorraine Conway; m. Eltjo Emile Witkop, Feb. 23, 1963 (div. Jan. 1970); children: Gregory Lyn, Joella Monique, Bradley Michael; m. Reuel P. Matkin, Mar. 20, 1995; stepchildren: Chris, Marcie, Ryan. Grad. H.S., Ontario. Designer, sales rep. Jerome I. Silverman, Inc., N.Y.C., 1970-86, Gem East Corp., Seattle, 1986-87; designer Nova Stylings, Van Nuys, Calif., 1987-91, Bagley & Hotchkiss, Santa Rosa, 1991-94; designer, owner Judith Conway, Windsor, 1994—. Design cons. Jade and Gem Corp., Hong Kong, 1986; career fair advisor Gemol. Inst. Am., L.A., N.Y.C., 1990-99. Designer Diamond Internat. Awards, 1990, Jewelers of Am. Awards, 1991, Platinum Guild Internat., 1998. Lobbiest Parents of Blind Children, Oreg., 1978-79; pres. Lambda Chi Alpha Parents Orgn., Oreg. State U., Corvallis, 1983, 84, Lakeridge Parents Music Orgn., Lake Oswego, Oreg., 1984-85. Mem. Womans Jewelers Assn. (chairperson annual dinner 1990, Designer of the Yr. 1998), Jewelry Info. Ctr., Contemporary Design Group, Chaine Des Rotisseurs (dame de la chaine). Avocations: art collecting, wine and food, musical instruments and listening, boating, family activities. Office: Judith Conway Inc PO Box 956 Windsor CA 95492-0956 E-mail: jconway@verio.com.

MATKOWSKY, BERNARD JUDAH, applied mathematician, educator; b. N.Y.C., Aug. 19, 1939; s. Morris N. and Ethel H. M.; m. Florence Knobel, Apr. 11, 1965; children: David, Daniel, Devorah. BS, CCNY, 1960; M.E.E., NYU, 1961, MS, 1963, PhD, 1966. Fellow Courant Inst. Math. Scis., NYU, 1961-66; mem. faculty dept. math. Rensselaer Poly. Inst., 1966-77; John Evans prof. applied math., mech. engring. & math. Northwestern U., Evanston, Ill., 1977—, chmn. engring. sci. and applied math. dept., 1993-99. Vis. prof. Tel Aviv U., 1972-73; vis. scientist Weizmann Inst. Sci., Israel, summer 1976, summer 1980, Tel Aviv U., summer 1980; cons. Argonne Nat. Lab., Sandia Labs., Lawrence Livermore Nat. Lab., Exxon Research and Engring. Co. Editor Wave Motion—An Internat. Jour., 1979-99, Applied Math. Letters, 1987—, SIAM Jour. Applied Math., 1976-95, European Jour. Applied Math., 1990-96, Random and Computational Dynamics, 1991-97, Internat. Jour. SHS, 1992—, Jour. Materials Synthesis and Processing, 1992—; mem. editl. adv. bd. Springer Verlag Applied Math. Scis. Series; contbr. chpts. to books, articles to profl. jours. Fulbright grantee, 1972-73; Guggenheim fellow, 1982-83 Fellow: AAAS, Am. Acad. Mechs.; mem.: Soc. Natural Philosophy, Com. Concerned Scientists, Conf. Bd. Math. Scis. (coun., com. human rights math. scientists), Am. Assn. Combustion Synthesis, Am. Physics Soc., Combustion Inst., Am. Math. Soc., Soc. Indsl. and Applied Math., Eta Kappa Nu, Sigma Xi. Home: 3704 Davis St Skokie IL 60076-1745 Office: Northwestern U Technological Institute Evanston IL 60208-0001 E-mail: b-matkowsky@northwestern.edu.

MATLINS, STUART M. management consultant, publisher; b. N.Y.C., July 25, 1940; s. Louis Karl and Lillian (Keit) M. m. Andrea Cines, June 20, 1960 (div.); children: Seth, Andrew; m. Antoinette Leonard, Oct. 9, 1977. Student, London Sch. Econs., 1958-59; BS, U. Wis., 1960; AM, Princeton U., 1962, postgrad., 1962-63. Internat. economist Bur. Internat. Commerce, U.S. Dept. Commerce, Washington, 1963-66; cons. Booz Allen & Hamilton, Inc., N.Y.C., 1966-67, asst. to pres. internat./adminstrv. dir., 1967-70, v.p. internat. ops., 1970-71, v.p./mng. officer, instl. and pub. mgmt. div., 1971-74; pres., mgmt. cons. Stuart Matlins Assocs., Inc., Woodstock, Vt., 1974—. Chmn. bd. dirs. LongHill Ptnrs., Inc.; publisher Gemstone Press, Jewish Lights Pub., SkyLight Paths Pub. Bd. dirs. Health Edn. Found., Woodstock (Vt.) Area Jewish Cmty.; chmn. emeritus bd. overseers N.Y. Sch., Hebrew Union Coll.-Jewish Inst. Religion; bd. govs. Hebrew Union Coll.; trustee South Woodstock Fire Protection Assn., Inc., Mertens House, Woodstock, Vt.; elected auditor Town of Woodstock; mem. adv. bd. Abraham Geiger Coll., Germany; dir. Jewish Book Coun. Woodrow Wilson fellow, 1960-61, Herbert O. Peet fellow, 1961-62, Phillip A. Rollins fellow, 1962-63. Mem. Princeton Club. Office: LongHill Ptnrs Inc PO Box 237 Woodstock VT 05091-0237 also: Sunset Farm Offices Rt 4 Woodstock VT 05091

MATLOCK, HUDSON, civil engineer, educator; b. Floresville, Tex., Dec. 9, 1919; s. Lee Hudson Sr. and Charlie Mary (Stevenson) M.; m. Harriett Nadine Kidder, Nov. 28, 1942 (dec. Jan. 1996); children: John Hudson, David Kidder; m. Catherine Wahrmund, Mar. 16, 1997. BSCE, U. Tex., 1947, MSCE, 1950. Registered profl. engr., Tex. From instr. to prof. U. Tex., Austin, 1948-78, chmn. dept. civil engring., 1972-76, prof. emeritus civil engring., 1995—; v.p. R & D Earth Tech. Corp., Long Beach, Calif., 1978-85; civil engring. cons. Kerrville, Tex., 1985—. Cons. Shell, Mobil, Chevron, Conoco and others, 1958—. Contbr. numerous tech. papers and sponsored rsch. reports to profl. publs. 1st lt. AC, U.S. Army, 1941-45. Recipient Disting. Achievement award Offshore Tech. Conf., Houston, 1985; named Disting. Engring. Grad. Coll. Engring. U. Tex.-Austin, 1986. Fellow ASCE (J. James R. Croes medal 1968), Tau Beta Pi; mem. NAE. Methodist. Avocations: flying, fishing, gardening. Home and Office: Tierra Linda Ranch 297 Airport Ridge Loop Kerrville TX 78028-1750 E-mail: hmatlock@ktc.com.

MATLOCK, JACK FOUST, JR. diplomat; b. Greensboro, N.C., Oct. 1, 1929; s. Jack Foust and Nellie (McSwain) M.; m. Rebecca Burrum, Sept. 2, 1949; children: James, Hugh, Nell, David, Joseph. AB summa cum laude, Duke U., 1950; MA, Columbia U., 1952; cert., Russian Inst., 1952; LLD (hon.), Greensboro Coll., 1989, Albright Coll., 1992, Conn. Coll., 1993. Instr. Dartmouth, 1953-56; fgn. service officer Dept. State, 1956-91; assigned Washington, 1956-58, Am. Embassy, Vienna, 1958-60; Am. consul. gen. Munich, 1960-61; assigned Am. Embassy, Moscow, 1961-63, Accra, Ghana, 1963-66, Am. Consulate, Zanzibar, 1967-69, Am. Embassy, Dar es Salaam, Tanzania, 1969-70, Sr. Seminar in Fgn. Policy, Dept. State, 1970-71; country dir. for USSR State Dept., 1971-74; minister-counselor, dep. chief mission Am. Embassy, Moscow, 1974-78; diplomat-in-residence Vanderbilt U., Nashville, 1978-79; dep. dir. Fgn. Service Inst., Washington, 1979-80; chargé d'affaires ad interim Am. Embassy, Moscow, 1981; ambassador to Czechoslovakia, 1981-83; spl. asst. to pres., sr. dir. European and Soviet Affairs Nat. Security Council, 1983-87; U.S. ambassador to the Soviet Union, Moscow, 1987-91; sr. rsch. fellow Columbia U., N.Y.C., 1991-93, Kathryn and Shelby Collum Davis prof. Practice Internat. Diplomacy, 1993-96; George F. Kennan prof. Inst. for Advanced Study, Princeton, N.J., 1996-2001; John L. Weinberg/Goldman Sachs and Co. vis. prof. pub. and internat. affairs Princeton U., 2001—02. Author: Autopsy on an Empire: The American Ambassador's Account of the Collapse of the Soviet Union, 1995; compiler, editor: Index to J.V. Stalin's Works, 2d edit., 1971. Mem. Am. Acad. Diplomacy, Coun. on Fgn. Rels., Century Assn. N.Y., Am. Philosophical Soc. Home: 940 Princeton Kingston Rd Princeton NJ 08540-4128 Fax: 609-252-9373. E-mail: ifmatlo@attglobal.net.

MATLOCK, JOHN HUDSON, science administrator, materials engineer; b. San Angelo, Tex., Nov. 23, 1944; s. Lee Hudson Jr. and Harriett (Kidder) M.; m. Kathe Lynne Reep, Sept. 3, 1966; children: Michelle, Joseph. B. Engring. Sci., U. Tex., 1967, MSME, 1969, PhD in Material Sci. and Engring., 1970; MBA, So. Ill. U., Edwardsville, 1976. Registered profl. engr., Mo., Wash., Oreg. Sr. rsch. engr. Monsanto Co., St. Peters, Mo., 1970-72, rsch. specialist, 1972-74, supt. tech. svcs., 1974-79; sr. staff engr. Mostek Corp., Carrollton, Tex., 1979-80, mgr. material tech. group, 1980-83; v.p. tech. SEH Am., Inc., Vancouver, Wash., 1983-90, exec. v.p., 1990-96, Komatsu Silicon Am., Hillsboro, Oreg., 1996, pres., CEO, 1997—. Mem. vis. com. Engring. Coll., U. Wash., Seattle, 1985-94, mem. indsl. adv. bd. Material Sci. and Engring., 1988-2000; mem. engring. adv. bd. Wash. State U., Pullman, 1984-96, adj. lectr., 1985; adj. prof. mech. engring., mem. grad. faculty Oreg. State U., Corvallis, 1985-90; adj. asst. prof. physics So. Ill. U., Edwardsville, 1973-76. Contbr. approximately 40 articles on silicon crystal growing and the effect of silicon properties on electronic devic performance to profl. and trade jours. Mem. bd. trustees 1st Ch. of God, Vancouver, 1988-91, tchr. adult ch. sch., 1986-91, 2001-2002; mem. sch. bd. Kingsway Christian Sch., Vancouver, 1990-91. Mem. Electrochem. Soc., Metall. Soc., AIME, Am. Soc. for Materials, Materials Rsch. Soc., ASTM, Tau Beta Pi, Pi Tau Sigma, Phi Kappa Phi, Beta Gamma Sigma. Home: 787 NE Rogahn St Hillsboro OR 97124-1652 E-mail: jmatlock@komsil.com.

MATLOW, LINDA MONIQUE, photographic agency executive, publishing executive; b. Chgo., July 24, 1955; d. Charles and Milly Matlow. Grad. high sch., Chgo.; student, Sch. Modern Photography, N.Y.C., 1977-79. Promotions and pub. relations staff Jaydee Enterprises, Chgo., 1971-73; mgr. First Venture, Inc., 1973-77; photographer, pub. relations staff Bands & Mags., 1977—; photographer, writer, editor, pres. Pix Internat., 1982—. Pub. variety of monthly mags. on disk including Retro, ARTchive, Prairie Sun (bur. chief). Chgo. Sounds; electronic pub. and image design Internet Pub. Contbr. photographs to publs. including N.Y. Times, Chgo. Tribune, Boston Globe, Harper's Bazaar, Redbook. Vol. telethon Variety Club of Chgo., 1986, Spl. Childrens' Charities, Chgo. Acad. for the Arts, Starlight Found., Literacy Chgo. Named Rock Photographer Night Rock newspaper, Chgo., 1980, 81, one of Chgo.'s Most Successful and Eligible Bachelorettes Today's Chgo. Woman mag., 1989; recipient Hon. mention Internat. Photographer Mag., 1990, winner B&W Print of Ray Charles, 1991; finalist Photographers Forum B&W Print category, 1991, 99, Color Print category, 98. Mem. Nat. Press Photographers Assn., NARAS, Internat. Freelance Photographers Orgn., Chgo. Women in Pub., Chgo. Area Internet Soc. Roman Catholic. Avocations: travel, design, computers, real estate.

MATNEY, EDWARD ELI, financial advisor; b. Salisbury, N.C., Oct. 24, 1927; s. Eli Abraham and Marie (Hanna) M.; m. Herma Lee Wooten, Oct. 1, 1960; children: Marc Edward, David Alan. BS in Gen. Engring., U.S. Mil. Acad., 1951; MBA, U. Ala., 1959. 2d lt. U.S. Army, 1951, advanced through grades to col., 1972, platoon leader, co. exec. officer 82nd Airborne Divsn. N.C., 1951-52, co. comdr. 2d Inf. Divsn. Korea, 1952-53, aide de camp Army Forces Far East Japan, 1953-54, co. comdr. BN ops. officer 82nd Airborne Divsn., 1954-57, pers. and sys. br. mgr. Hdqrs. Continental Army Command Ft. Monroe, Va., 1959-63, contr. North Baden Dist. Heidelberg, Germany, 1964-66, bat. comdr. and G-1 Army Tng. Ctr. Ft. Benning, Ga., 1966-68, sr. mil. advisor Vietnam, 1969-71, chief Southeast Asia tng. br., Pacific Commd., 1971-73, head security assistance dept., dir. support U.S. Inst. Mil. Assistance, 1974-78, ret., 1978; v.p. Pinehurst Airlines, Greenville, S.C., 1979-81; sr. v.p. Wachovia Securities (formerly Wheat First Union), Pinehurst, NC, 1982—. Moderator Cmty. Congl. Ch., Southern Pines, N.C., 1986-88. Decorated Bronze star, Legion of Merit, air medals, Combat Infantry badge; recipient James C. Wheat Cmty. Svc. award Wheat First Butcher Singer, 1991. Mem. Elks, Kiwanis (pres. Sandhills chpt. 1990-91), Phi Gamma Delta, Chi Alpha Phi. Avocations: golf, tennis. Home: 485 Hill Rd Southern Pines NC 28387-6656 E-mail: eematney@sprynet.com., ematney@wachoviasec.com.

MATON, KENNETH I. psychology educator; b. N.Y.C., Jan. 3, 1952; s. Norman Maton and Edith Lang (stepfather Oscar Lang); m. Mary Kay Parkinson; children: Nathan Maton-Parkinson, Tyler Maton-Parkinson. BA, Yale U., 1975; PhD, U. Ill., 1984. Asst. prof. psychology U. Md. Baltimore County, 1984-90; assoc. prof. psychology U. Md., 1990-95, prof. psychology, 1996—. Dir. cmty.-social PhD program in human svcs. psychology, 1984—. Co-author: Beating the Odds, 1998; mem. editl. bd. Am. Jour. Cmty. Psychology, 1998—. Pres. Soc. for Cmty. Rsch. and Action, 1998-99. Recipient Nat. Rsch. award Nat. Assn. for Specialists in Group Work, 1988; Meyerhoff Program Longitudinal Studies grantee NSF, 1999-2001. Avocations: family, camping, movies, reading. Home: 9321 Ocala St Silver Spring MD 20901 Office: Psychology Dept U Md Baltimore County Baltimore MD 21250

MATOS, CRUZ ALFONSO, environmental consultant; b. N.Y.C., Mar. 6, 1929; s. José and Gertrudes (Manzanares) M.; m. Aurelia Santos, Dec. 13, 1963; children: Miguel, Veronica, Monica, Angélica. B in Engring. Sci., Oxford U., 1957, M in Engring. Sci., 1958; DSc (hon.), U. Met., P.R., 1995. Pres., CEO Fischer & Porter de P.R., 1964-69; asst. sec. dept. pub. works Govt. of P.R., 1969-70, exec. dir. Environ. Quality Bd., 1970-73, sec. dept. natural resources, 1973-75, cabinet mem., 1970-75; UN chief tech., dir. Inst. Marine Affairs, Trinidad and Tobago, 1975-79; UN Devel. Program regional rep. Trinidad and Tobago, Barbados, Surinam and Dutch West Indies, 1978-80; UN chief tech. adviser South Pacific, dir. Com. for Coordination of Offshore Prospecting in the South Pacific, Suva, Fiji, 1980-89; ret. Advisor to pres. P.R. Senate for natural resources, the environ. and energy, 1993-97; advisor to exec. dir. UN Environ. Program for L.Am. and Caribbean, 1994-98; mem. various adv. panels and overseas mission U.S. NAS; mem. U.S. Nat. Commn. on Environment, Consejo Consultive Recursos Naturales y Ambientales (apptd. Gov. P.R.), Com. Sobre Política Publica Energetíca P.R., Consejo Asesor Sobre Energia. Contbr. articles to sci. jours. and mags. Trustee Conservation Found., U.S.; bd. dirs. World Wildlife-Fund-U.S.A., Caribbean Environment and Devel. Inst. With U.S. Army, 1952-54. Recipient Boriquen Conservation award, 1971. Office: PO Box 7627 Playa Cerro Gordo Vega Alta PR 00692

MATOS MORALES, GERMÁN JOSEPH, art and antiques dealer, advocate, fundraiser; b. Utuado, P.R., Dec. 18, 1954; s. Orlando Afanador Morales and Regalada Alvarez Matos. Student, Baruch Coll., 1973-74. Dir., owner Herman Joseph Galleries, N.Y.C., 1974-87; pres., owner N.Y. Auction Gallery, Jackson Heights, 1988-91; dir., owner Coldenham Manor Gallery, Newburgh, N.Y., 1992-93, Castle Manor Gallery, Jackson Heights, 1994-95; dir. Chelsea Internat. Gallery, N.Y.C., 1996-97; dir., pres. People's Charitable Found., Queens, N.Y., 1998—. Owner-curator Princess Diana Mus. of N.Y. for AIDS and Cancer, 2001—. Co-author: Touched by a Saint: Mother Teresa of Calcutta, 2000; exhibited N.Y. HIst. Soc., 2000. Founder The People's Auction Ho., world's first charitable auction ho. for catastrophic and terminal illnesses; bd. dirs. Cornell Cmty. Adv. Bd., N.Y.C., 1998—; pres. Jack-Elm Block Assn., Jackson Heights, 1998, 99, 2000; curator/owner The Princess Diana Mus. of N.Y. for Cancer and AIDS, 2001-02. Recipient Cmty. Hero award Assemblyman Joseph F. Lisa, Jackson Heights, 1975. Mem. Holy Name Soc. Roman Catholic. Home: 40-11 79th St Elmhurst NY 11373

MATOVICH, MITCHEL JOSEPH, JR. motion picture producer, executive; b. Watsonville, Calif., Dec. 16, 1927; s. Mitchel Joseph and Mildred Florence (Ingrom) M.; widowed, 1968; divorced, 1983; children: Wayne, Mark, Laura; m. Patte Dee Matovich, 1989 (div. 2000). Student, San Jose State U., 1946-49. Mechanical designer Stanford Rsch. Inst., Menlo Park, Calif., 1955-59; rsch. specialist Lockheed Missiles & Space Co., Sunnyvale, 1959-70; mgr. NASA and Dept. of Def. bus. sect. Engineered Systems Div. FMC Corp., San Jose, 1970-77; pres. and chief exec. officer Morton Co. Div. of Haycor Corp., Hayward, 1977-82; pres. Concept Devel. Co., Newark, 1982-89, Matovich Prodns., Hollywood, 1987—, Stereotronics Inc., Beverly Hills, 1988—. Pres. Matovich Prodns., 1989—, Movietown Pictures, 1997—; co-owner Vagabond Theatre, L.A., 1990-91. Author: The Image Machine, Webville, The Last Discoverer, 2001, others; feature length screenplays, stories for screenplays, short stories; author and artist childrens book series; producer, dir. (feature film) Deadly Delusions, 1999; producer (feature film) Lightning in a Bottle, 1993 (Gold award Houston Film Festival, Award of Excellence Film Adv. Bd.), I Don't Buy Kisses Anymore, 1992 (Best Ind. Feature Houston Internat. Film Festival, Award of Excellence Film Adv. Bd., Angel award Excellence in Media, Top Applause award Santa Clarita Valley Internat. Film Festival 1994); co-producer: Social Suicide; co-inventor stereotronics 3-D video system; patentee in field. Chmn. bd. Santa Clarita Internat. Film Festival, 1995-2001; bd. dirs. Interguild Credit Union. With USN, 1945-46, 51-52, Korea. Mem. ASCAP, Acad. TV Arts and Scis., Soc. Motion Picture and TV Engrs., Dirs. Guild, Producers' Guild (bd. dirs.), Mensa, Intertel. Avocations: flying, scuba diving, writing, travel, art. Home: 21325 Alder Dr #203 Newhall CA 91321 Office: Matovich Prodns Inc PO Box 5744 Beverly Hills CA 90209-5744

MATOVINA, JIM, mathematician, educator; Masters, Purdue U., Hammond, Indiana, 1992—96. Post Baccalaureate Certificate in Statistics Purdue U., 1996. Math. prof. CC of So. Nev., Las Vegas, Nev., 1996—. Mem.: SW Assn. for Devel. Edn. (assoc.), Nev. Math. Assn. of Two-Year Colleges (assoc.; pres./past pres. 1998—2002), Am. Math. Assn. of Two-Year Colleges (assoc.; voting del./affiliate pres. 1998—2002). Achievements include development of Online Mathematics Courses. Office: Community College of Southern Nevada 6375 W Charleston Blvd Las Vegas NV 89146 E-mail: jim_matovina@ccsn.edu.

MATRAY-DEVOTI, JUDITH, pharmaceutical executive, consultant; d. Elizabeth Matray; m. John Devoti, June 1, 1990. BS, Rutgers U., Coll. of Pharmacy, Piscataway, NJ, 1985; PhD, Rutgers U., Piscataway, NJ, 1996—96. Rschr., toxicology Bristol Myers Squibb, New Brunswick, NJ, 1985—92, study dir., toxicology, 1992—98; sr. mgr. med. info. Bristol Meyer Squibb, Plainsboro, 1998—2002. Med. info. Pedagogue Solutions, Princeton, NJ. Mem.: Am. Pharm. Assn., Am. Med. Writers Assn., Drug Info. Assn., Mensa (bd. of directors, local group 1999—2002, Local Publs. award 1997). Avocations: bicycling, knitting, reading, home decorating, remodeling. Office: Pedagogue Solutions 100 Thanet Circle Princeton NJ 08540 E-mail: jmatraydevoti@pedagogue.com.

MATROS, LARISA GRIGORYEVNA, medical philosophy researcher, writer; b. Odessa, Ukraine, USSR, Jan. 30, 1938; d. Grigory Lyvovich and Eva Michailovna (Bulkach) Akselrod; m. Yurii Shaevich Matros, July 25, 1960; 1 child, Elena. M in law, State U., Odessa, 1963; PhD, State U., Novosibirsk, USSR, 1972. Lawyer Roskulttorg Trading Co., Novosibirsk, 1962-64; researcher Inst. Clin. and Exptl. Medicine, 1975-81; researcher, philosophy cons., coordinator Presidium of USSR (Siberian Branch) Acad. Med. Scientists, 1982-88; chief philosophy dept. Siberian Med. Acad., 1988-91; freelance writer, rschr., 1992—. Lectr. in field, Novosibirsk, 1975. Author: Social Aspects of the Problem of Health, 1992, (poetry anthology) And Life, and Tears, and Love, 1999, (novel) Presumption of Guilt, 2000; co-author: The Right to Be Healthy, 1979; contbr. articles, short stories, lit. revs. poems and essays to profl. jours. anthologies including National Library of Poetry, 1997, Best Poems of 1998. Recipient Hon. Diploma Internat. Poetic Competition, 1993, 96, award of excellence 23rd Internat. Congress of Art and Comm., San Francisco, 1996, Am. Biog. Inst. World Lifetime Achievement award, 1996, Editors Choice award for outstanding achievement in poetry Nat. Libr. of Poetry, 1997, 98. Fellow: Internat. Biographical Assn. (life), Soviet Sociol. Assn. (inspection com. chairwoman 1970—78, medicine divsn. sec. 1984—92); mem.: The Russian Writers Club (N.Y.), Internat. Govs. Club (life), P.E.N. Internat. Pushkin Soc., Soviet Philos. Seminars, Internat. Platform Assn., Am. Biographical Inst. Rsch. Assn. (dep. gov. 1995—). Home: 14963 Green Circle Dr Chesterfield MO 63017-7826 E-mail: larisamatros@aol.com.

MATSA, LOULA ZACHAROULA, social services administrator, educator; b. Piraeus, Greece, Apr. 16, 1935; came to U.S., 1952, naturalized 1962; d. Eleftherios Georgiou and Ourania E. (Fraguiskopoulou) Papoulias; m. Ilco S. Matsa, Nov. 27, 1953; 1 child, Aristotle Ricky. Student, Pierce Coll., Athens, 1948-52; BA, Rockford Coll., 1953; MA, U. Chgo., 1955. Diplomate clin. social worker; bd. cert. clin. social workers, N.Y. cert. social orkers, pub. employees fedn. Marital counselor Family Soc., Cambridge, Mass., 1955-56; chief unit II social svc. Queen's (N.Y.) Children's Psychiat. Ctr., 1961-74; dir. social svcs., supr.-coord. family care program Hudson River Psychiat. Ctr., Poughkeepsie, N.Y., 1974-91; supr. social work Harlem Valley Psychiat. Ctr., Wingdale, 1991-93, Hudson River Psychiat. Ctr., 1993—. Field instr. Adelphi, Albany and Fordham univs., 1969—. Contbr. articles to profl. jours.; instrumental in state policy changes in treatment and court representation of emotionally disturbed and mentally ill. Fulbright Exch. student, 1952-53; Talcott scholar, 1953-55. Mem. NASW, Internat. Platform Assn., Internat. Coun. on Social Welfare, Acad. Cert. Social Workers, Assn. Cert. Social Workers, Pierce Coll. Alumni Assn. Democrat. Greek Orthodox. Home: 81-11 45th Ave Elmhurst NY 11373-3553

MATSEN, FREDERICK ALBERT, III, orthopedic educator; b. Austin, Tex., Feb. 5, 1944; s. Frederick Albert II and Cecilia (Kirkegaard) M.; m. Anne Lovell, Dec. 24, 1966; children: Susanna Lovell, Frederick A. IV, Laura Jane Megan. BA, U. Tex., Austin, 1964; MD, Baylor U., 1968. Intern Johns Hopkins U., Balt., 1971; resident in orthopaedics U. Wash., Seattle, 1971-74, acting instr. orthopaedics, 1974, asst. prof. orthopaedics, 1975-79, assoc. prof. orthopaedics, 1979-82, prof., 1982-85, 86—, adjunct prof. Ctr. Bioengring., 1985—, dir. residency program orthopaedics, 1978-81, vice chmn. dept. orthopaedics, 1982-85, acting chmn. dept. orthopaedics, 1983-84, prof., chmn. dept. orthopaedics, 1981—. Mem. Orthopaedic Residency Rev. Com., Chgo., 1981-86. Author: Compartmental Syndromes, 1980; editor: The Shoulder, 1990; contbr. articles to profl. jours., chpts. to textbooks; assoc. editor Clin. Orthopaedics, Jour. Orthopaedic Rsch., 1981—. Lt. comdr. USPHS, 1969-71. Recipient Traveling fellowship Am. Orthopaedic Assn., 1983, Nicholas Andry award Assn. Bone and Joint Surgery, 1979, Henry Meyerding Essay award Am. Fracture Assn., 1974. Mem. Am. Shoulder and Elbow Surgeons (founding, pres. 1991—), Am. Acad. Orthopaedic Surgeons (bd. dirs. 1984-85), Orthopaedic Rsch. Soc., Western Orthopaedic Assn., Phi Beta Kappa. Office: U Wash Dept Orthopaedics RK 10 1959 NE Pacific St Seattle WA 98195-0001

MATSEN, JOHN MARTIN, academic administrator, pathologist; b. Salt Lake City, Feb. 7, 1933; s. John M. and Bessie (Jackson) M.; m. Joneen Johnson, June 6, 1959; children: Marilee, Sharon, Coleen, Sally, John H., Martin K., Maureen, Catherine, Carl, Jeri. BA, Brigham Young U., 1958; MD, UCLA, 1963. Diplomate Am. Bd. Pediatrics, Am. Bd. Pathology, Spl. Competence in Med. Microbiology. Intern UCLA, 1963-65; resident Los Angeles County Harbor/UCLA Med. Ctr., Torrance, Calif., 1965-66; USPHS fellow U. Minn., Mpls., 1966-68, asst. prof., 1968-70, assoc. prof., 1971-74, prof., 1974, U. Utah, Salt Lake City, 1974—, assoc. dean, 1979-81, chmn. dept. pathology, 1981-93, univ. sr. v.p. health scis., dean Sch. Medicine, 1993-98. Pres. Associated Regional and Univ. Pathologists, Inc., Salt Lake City, 1983-93, chmn. bd. dirs., 1993-99. Author over 200 publs. in field. Recipient Sonnenwirth Meml. award Am. Soc. Microbiology, 1993. Mem. Acad. Clin. Lab. Physicians and Scientists (pres. 1978-79), Assn. Pathology Chmn. (pres. 1990-92). Mem. Lds Ch.

MATSEN, JOHN MORRIS, retired engineer; b. Neenah, Wis., May 30, 1936; s. Morris and Bertha Rowena (Witt) M.; m. Sandra Louise Schwartz, May 8, 1971. BS in Engring., Princeton (N.J.) U., 1957; MS, Columbia U., 1959, PhD, 1963. Instr. Columbia U., N.Y.C., 1959-61; engr. Exxon Rsch. & Engring. Co., Florham Park, N.J., 1961-66, sr. engr., 1966-73, engring. assoc., 1973-97; ret., 1997; vis. scientist Lehigh U., 1997—. Mem. tech. com. Particulate Solids Rsch. Inc., Chgo., 1976-97. Editor: Fluidization Technology, 1976, Fluidization, 1980; mem. editorial bd. Advances in Environ. Sci. and Engring., Ency. Environ. Sci. and Tech.; patentee in field; contbr. articles to profl. jours. Active Hunterdon County Agrl. Devel. Bd., N.J., 1982-87, Clinton (N.J.) Twp. Planning Bd., 1976-92, chmn., 1978-82, bd. adjustment, 1992—, chmn., 1998—; allocations com. Hunterdon County Dept. Human Svcs., 1993—; councilman Clinton Twp., 1983-92, mayor, 1986; trustee N.J. Symphony Orch. League, 1966-82, pres., 1973-79; class agt. Phillips Exeter Acad. Class of 1953, 1993-98. NSF fellow, 1959-60. Mem. Am. Inst. Chem. Engrs., Am. Chem. Soc., Raritan Yacht Club, Princeton Club of N.Y., Rolls Royce Owners Club (chmn. Atlantic region 1999—), Phi Lambda Upsilon, Sigma Xi. Republican. Avocations: organology, yachting, historic preservation. Home: 39 Sand Hill Rd Annandale NJ 08801-3111 E-mail: jmatsen@aol.com.

MATSEOANE, CAROL, social worker; b. N.Y.C., July 10, 1944; d. Joseph Daniel Taylor and Nannie Lee Winborne; m. Stephen Matseoane, Jan. 21, 1968; children: Dara, Joyce, Karen. BA, Hunter Coll., 1966, MSW, 1970; PhD, Walden U., 1992. Cert. social worker, N.Y. Social worker Spl. Svcs. for Children Protective Svcs., N.Y.C.; psychotherapist-counselor O. Quentin Hyder MD, N.Y.C.; social work supr. JHMCB Ctr. for Nursing and Rehab./Long Term Home Care Prog., Bklyn.; clin. dir. Lamb's Counseling Ctr., New Hope Counseling Ctr. Recipient Apple Polisher award, Women's Inner Circle of Achievement award. Mem.: NAFE, NASW, Am. Bd. Med. Psychotherapists (life). Home: 159-34 Riverside Dr W New York NY 10032

MATSLER, FRANKLIN GILES, retired education educator; b. Glendive, Mont., Dec. 27, 1922; s. Edmund Russell and Florence Edna (Giles) M.; m. Lois Josephine Hoyt, June 12, 1949; children— Linda, Jeanne, David, Winfield. BS, Mont. State U., Bozeman, 1948; MA, U. Mont., Missoula, 1952; PhD, U. Calif. at Berkeley, 1959. Tchr. Missoula County (Mont.) High Sch., 1949-51, Tracy (Calif.) Sr. Elem. Schs., 1952-53, San Benito County (Calif.) High Sch. and Jr. Coll., 1953-55; grad. asst. U. Calif. at Berkeley, 1955-58; asst. prof. Humboldt State Coll., Arcata, Calif., 1958-62, assoc. prof., 1962-63, asst. exec. dean, 1958-63; chief specialist higher edn. Calif. Coordinating Council for Higher Edn., Sacramento, 1963-68; exec. dir. Ill. Bd. Regents, Springfield, 1968-84; prof. higher edn. Ill. State U., Normal, 1968-96, Regency prof. higher edn., 1984-96; ret., 1996. Chancellor Ill. Bd. Regents, 1995-96. Bd. dirs. Ill. Edn. Consortium, 1972-76; bd. dirs. Central Ill. Health Planning Agy., 1970-76, Springfield Symphony Orch. Assn.; pres. Bloomington/Normal Symphony Soc., 1988-90. Served to 1st lt. AUS, 1943-46. Mem. Nat. Assn. Sys. Heads (exec. v.p. 1985-92), Am. Assn. State Colls. and Univs. Assn. for Instl. Rsch., Phi Delta Kappa, Lambda Chi Alpha. Home: 31 Arbor Ct Bloomington IL 61704-2452 Office: Illinois State U 539 DeGarmo Hall Normal IL 61761 E-mail: fmatsler@ilstu.edu.

MATSON, ROBERT EDWARD, public management educator, leadership consultant; b. Chauncey, Ohio, Dec. 2, 1930; s. William I. and Mary Royal (Rivers) M.; m. Mary Athearn, June 27, 1954; children— Laurie, Jeanne, Scott BS, Ohio U., 1956, M.Ed., 1957; Ed.D., Ind. U., 1961. Dean men Carroll Coll., Wis., 1961-65; v.p. student affairs Kent State U, Ohio, 1965-70; pres. Ricker Coll., 1970-74; sr. prof. Fed. Exec. Inst., Charlottesville, Va., 1974-80, acad. dean, 1980-82, dir., 1982-87, sr. prof., dir. emeritus, 1987-89; prof., dir. leadership edn. program Ctr. Pub. Svc., U. Va., 1989—, dir. Inst. Govt., 1994-96. Served to 1st. lt. U.S. Army, 1953-55; Korea Recipient Sweeney Acad. award Internat. City and County Mgrs. Assn., 1993. Fellow Nat. Acad. Pub. Adminstrn. Methodist. Office: U Va Ctr for Pub Svc 918 Emmet St N Charlottesville VA 22903-4829

MATSON, VIRGINIA MAE FREEBERG (MRS. EDWARD J. MATSON), retired special education educator, author; b. Chgo., Aug. 25, 1914; d. Axel George and Mae (Dalrymple) Freeberg; m. Edward John Matson, Oct. 18, 1941; children: Karin (Mrs. Donald H. Skadden), Sara M. Drake, Edward Robert, Laurence D., David O. BA, U. Ky., 1934; MA, Northwestern U., 1941. Spl. edn. tchr. area high schs., Chgo., 1934-42, Ridge Farm, 1944-45; tchr. h.s. Pub. Schs. Lake County, Ill., 1956-59; founder Grove Sch., Lake Forest, 1958-87, ret., 1987. Instr. evening sch. Carthage Coll., 1965-66. Author: Shadow on the Lost Rock, 1958, Saul, the King, 1968, Abba Father, 1970 (Friends Lit. Fiction award 1972), Buried Alive, 1970, A School for Peter, 1974, A Home for Peter, 1983, Letters to Lauren, A History of the Methodist Campgrounds, Des Plaines, 1985; contbr. many articles to profl. publs. Mem. Friends of Lit. Dem. Recipient Humanitarian award Ill. Med. Soc. Aux. Dem. Home: 4133 Mockingbird Ln Suffolk VA 23434-7186

MATSON, WESLEY JENNINGS, educational administrator; b. Svea, Minn., June 25, 1924; s. James and Ettie (Mattson) Matson; m. Doris Cragg; 1 child James Jennings. BS with distinction, U. Minn., 1948; MA, U. Calif., Berkeley, 1954; EdD, Columbia U., 1960. High sch. tchr. Santa Barbara County Pub. Schs., Santa Maria, Calif., 1948-50; instr. U. Calif., Berkeley, 1950-54, Columbia U., N.Y.C., 1954-55; lectr. Fordham U., 1955-56; asst. prof. U. Md., College Park, 1956-59; prof., asst. dean U. Wis., Milw., 1959-72; dean, prof. Winona (Minn.) State U., 1972-88, emeritus, 1989—. Vis. prof. U. P.R., Rio Peidras, We. Wash. U., Bellingham, San Diego State U., U. Minn., Mpls., U. Hawaii; adj. faculty St. Olaf Coll., Northfield, Minn.; cons. U.S. Dept. Edn., Washington, Ill. State U.; bd. regents Wis. Dept. Pub. Instrn.; examiner Nat. Coun. Accreditation Tchr. Edn. North Ctrl. assn., Chgo. Contbr. Exec. com. Minn. Alliance of Arts, Mpls.; mem. Minn. com. Certification Stds., St. Paul; cons. ARC; bd. dirs. Ft. Snelling Meml. Chapel Found.; apptd. by Minn. Supreme Ct. to Minn. Bd. CLE. Capt. USAF. Decorated Bronze Star; recipient Disting. Svc. award, Wis. Assn. Tchr. Edn., 1972. Mem.: NEA (life), VFW, Minn. edn. Assn., Assn. Higher Edn., Nat. Assn. Tchr. Educators (exec. com.), Minn. Assn. Colls. for Tchr. Edn. (pres. 1983—85, Hon. life Award of Merit), U. Minn. Alumni Soc. (Outstanding Educator award 1984), Am. Legion, Minn. Hist. Soc., Rotary Club, Alpha Sigma Phi, Kappa Delta Pi, Phi Delta Kappa. Home: 6615 Lake Shore Dr S Minneapolis MN 55423-2218

MATSUDA, FUJIO, retired academic administrator; b. Honolulu, Oct. 18, 1924; s. Yoshio and Shimo (Iwasaki) M.; m. Amy M. Saiki, June 11, 1949; children: Bailey Koki, Thomas Junji, Sherry Noriko, Joan Yuuko, Ann Mitsuyo, Richard Hideo. BSCE, Rose Poly. Inst., 1949; DSc, MIT, 1952; DEng (hon.), Rose Hulman Inst. Tech., 1975. Rsch. engr. MIT, 1952-54; rsch. asst. prof. engring. U. Ill., Urbana, 1954-55; from asst. prof. engring. to prof. engring. U. Hawaii, Honolulu, 1955-66, chmn. dept. civil engring., 1960-63; dir. Hawaii Dept. Transp., 1963-73; v.p. bus. affairs U. Hawaii, 1973-74, pres., 1974-84, exec. dir. Rsch. Corp., 1984-94; pres. Japan-Am. Inst. Mgmt. Sci., Honolulu, 1994-96. Dir. Hawaii Dept. Transp., Honolulu, 1963-73; v.p. Park & Lee, Ltd., Honolulu, 1956-58; pres. SMS & Assocs., Inc., 1960-63; pvt. practice structural engring., 1958-60; bd. dirs. C. Brewer & Co., Ltd., First Hawaiian Bank, BancWest Corp., Inc., Rehab. Hosp. of Pacific, Kuakini Health Sys., Japanese Cultural Ctr. of Hawaii; CEO, chmn. bd. dirs. Pacific Internat. Ctr. High Tech. Rsch.; mem. Airport Ops. Coun. Internat., 1968-73; pres. Pacific Coast Assn. Port Authorities, 1969; mem. sci. bd. Dept. Army, 1978-80. Bd. dirs. Aloha United Way, Kuakini Med. Ctr., 1987-89; trustee Kuakini Health Sys., 1973-76, bd. dirs., 1984-89; trustee Nature Conservancy, 1984-89, Hawaiian Cmty. Found. With U.S. Army, 1943-45. Recipient Honor Alumnus award Rose Poly. Inst., 1971, Disting. Svc. award Airport Ops. Coun. Internat., 1973, Disting. Alumnus award U. Hawaii, 1974, 91; named Hawaii Engr. of Yr., 1972. Mem. NAE, NSPE, ASCE (Parcel-Sverdrup Engring. Mgmt. award 1986), Social Sci. Assn., Western Coll. Assn. (exec. com. 1977-84, pres. 1980-82), Japan-Am. Soc. Honolulu (trustee 1976-84, adv. council 1984—), Japan-Hawaii Econ. Coun., World Sustainable Agr. Assn., Sigma Xi, Tau Beta Pi. E-mail: fmatsuda@hawaii.rr.com.

MATSUDA, STANLEY KAZUHIRO, secondary education educator; b. Glendale, Calif., Oct. 10, 1963; s. Shindo and Naoe (Nomura) M.; m. Marjorie Denine Paige, Dec. 17, 1989; children: Keiko Paige, Kimiko Ane. BS, Loma Linda U., 1986; MS, U. So. Calif., L.A., 1993. Cert. tchr. math., elementary and sr. math. Tchr. Glendale Adventist Elem. Sch., 1988-93; tchr. math. Glendale Adventist Acad., 1993-96, sch. bd. rep., 1991-92, tutorial svc. dir., 1993-95, chair math. dept., 1996-99; tchr. Mesa Grande Acad., 1999—. Contr. Sansei Day Camp, L.A., 1991-98; treas. L.A. Ctrl. Japanese-Am. Seventh-day Adventist Ch., 1994-98. Loma Linda U. scholar, 1982, Hughes scholar, 1985. Republican. Home: 13559 Mesa Crest Dr Yucaipa CA 92399-5821 E-mail: mgapclab@netzero.net.

MATSUDA, TAKAYOSHI, surgeon, educator, biomedical researcher; b. Tonan, Japan, 1937; came to U.S., 1965; MD, Keio Gijuku U., Tokyo, 1963. Diplomate Am. Bd. Surgery. Rotating intern Cook County Hosp., Chgo., 1965-66, resident in surgery, 1966-71, dir. burn ctr., 1975-93; asst. prof. surgery Kyorin U., Tokyo, 1971-75; asst. prof. U. Ill., Chgo., 1977—; pres. TM & Assocs., Oak Park, 1994—; CEO, Matsuda Cleen Energy Co. Cons. alternative medicine, cons. leadership devel., fin. freedom. Editl. bd. Jour. Burn Care Rehab., 1987-93; contbr. numerous articles to profl. publs., chpts. to books. Fellow ACS; mem. Internat. Soc. Surgery, Internat. Soc. Burn Injuries, Am. Burn Assn., Am. Assn. Surgery Trauma, Soc. Critical Care Medicine, Chgo. Surg. Soc. Office: TM & Assocs Alternative Medicine Cons 103 Bishop Quarter Ln Oak Park IL 60302-2672 E-mail: takimatsuda@hotmail.com.

MATSUI, DOROTHY NOBUKO, elementary education educator; b. Honolulu, Jan. 9, 1954; d. Katsura and Tamiko (Sakai) M. Student, U. Hawaii, Honolulu, 1972-76, postgrad., 1982; BEd, U. Alaska, Anchorage, 1979, MEd in Spl. Edn., 1986. Clerical asst. U. Hawaii Manoa Disbursing Office, Anchorage, 1974-76; passenger service agt. Japan Air Lines, 1980; bilingual tutor Anchorage Sch. Dist., 1980, elem. sch. tchr., 1980—. Facilitator for juvenile justice courses Anchorage Sch. Dist., Anchorage Police Dept., Alaska Pacific U., 1992-93; mem. adv. bd. Anchorage Law-Related Edn. Advancement Project. Vol. Providence Hosp., Anchorage, 1986, Humana Hosp., Anchorage, 1984, Spl. Olympics, Anchorage, 1981, Municipality Anchorage, 1978, Easter Seal Soc. Hawaii, 1975. Mem. NAFE, NEA, Alaska Edn. Assn., Smithsonian Nat. Assoc. Program, Nat. Space Soc., Smithsonian Air and Space Assn., World Aerospace Edn. Orgn., Internat. Platform Assn., Nat. Trust for Hist. Preservation, Nat. Audubon Soc., Planetary Soc., Cousteau Soc., Alaska Coun. for the Social Studies, Alaska Coun. Tchrs. Math., World Inst. Achievment, U.S. Olympic Soc., Women's Inner Circle Achievement, U. Alaska Alumni Assn., World Wildlife Fund, Japanese-Am. Nat. Mus., Alpha Delta Kappa (treas. Alpha chpt. 1988-92, corr. sec. 1993-96, sgt. at arms 1996-98). Avocations: reading, sports, learning. Office: Anchorage Sch Dist 7001 Cranberry St Anchorage AK 99502-7145

MATSUI, EUGENE PAUL, music educator; b. Chicago, Ill., June 15, 1953; s. Takanobu and Tsuyako M.; m. Gail F. Wilson, Aug. 28, 1982; children: Ryan, Michael, Krista. BS in Music Edn., U. Ill., Urbana, Ill., 1975, MS in Music Edn., 1979. Cert. instrumental music tchr. Instrumental music tchr. Forrestville Valley Schs., Forreston, Ill., 1975—77, A. Vito Martinez Mid. Sch., Romeoville, 1979—. Com. chmn. Cub Scouts pack 83 Boy Scouts Am., Joliet, Ill., 1995—97, asst. scoutmaster troop 19 Plainfield, 1995—2001, com. chmn. troop 19. Mem.: Ill. Grade Sch. Music Assn. (instrumental music adjudicator 1990—), Ill. High Sch. Assn. (instrumental music adjudicator 1992—), Crowther Cougars Baseball Assn., Plainfield Band Boosters, Music Educators Nat. Conf., Ill. Music Educators Assn., Nat. Band Assn., Am. Fedn. Tchrs. Avocation: photography, cooking. Office: A Vito Martinez Mid Sch 590 Belmont Dr Romeoville IL 60446 E-mail: matsuig@vvsd.org.

MATSUI, ROBERT TAKEO, congressman; b. Sacramento, Sept. 17, 1941; s. Yasuji and Alice (Nagata) M.; m. Doris Kazue Okada, Sept. 17, 1966; 1 child, Brian Robert. AB in Polit. Sci, U. Calif., Berkeley, 1963; JD, U. Calif., San Francisco, 1966. Bar: Calif. 1967. Practiced law, Sacramento, 1967-78; mem. Sacramento City Coun., 1971-78, vice mayor, 1977; mem. 96th-107th Congresses from 5th Calif. dist., 1979—; mem. ranking minority, ways and means, s.s. subcom.; dep. chair Dem. Nat. Com., 1995—; bd. regents Smithsonian Inst., Washington, 2000—. Chmn. profl. bus. forum Dem. Congl. Campaign Com.; mem. fin. coun. Dem. Nat. Com.; mem. adv. coun. on fiscal policy Am. Enterprise Inst. Chmn. Profl. Bus. Forum of the Dem. Congl. Co. and Com.; congl. liaison Nat. Fin. Council, Dem. Nat. Com.; mem. Am. Enterprise Inst. Adv. Council on Fiscal Policy. Named Young Man of Yr. Jr. C. of C., 1973; recipient Disting. Service award, 1973 Mem. Sacramento Japanese Am. Citizens League (pres. 1969), Sacramento Met. C. of C. (dir. 1976) Clubs: 20-30 (Sacramento) (pres. 1972), Rotary (Sacramento). Democrat. Office: US Ho Reps 2308 Rayburn Hob Washington DC 20515-0505

MATSUMOTO, GEORGE, architect; b. San Francisco, July 16, 1922; s. Manroku F. and Ise (Nakagawa) M.; m. Kimi Nao, Dec. 15, 1951; children— Mari-Jane, Kiyo-Ann, Kei-Ellen, Kenneth Manroku, Miye-Eileen. Student, U. Calif. at Berkeley, 1938-42; B.Arch., Washington U., 1944; M.Arch., Cranbrook Acad. Art, 1945. Designer Heathers Garden Devel. Co., Calif., 1941-42; designer with George F. Keck, Chgo., 1943-44; sr. designer, planner Saarinen & Swanson, Birmingham, Mich., 1945-46; sr. designer Skidmore, Owings & Merrill, Chgo., 1948; partner Runnells, Clark, Waugh, Matsumoto, Kansas City, Mo., 1946-47; practice architecture Okla., 1948, N.C., 1948-61, San Francisco, 1962-92; pres. George Matsumoto and Assocs., 1992-93; ret., 1993. Instr. U. Okla., 1947-48; prof. N.C. State Coll., 1948-61, U. Calif. at Berkeley, 1961-67 Important works include libraries, office bldgs., schs., recreation ctrs., chs., govt. bldgs., pvt. residences, med. research labs. and offices. Bd. dirs. Young Audiences, Oakland Mus. Assn., Oakland Arts Coun., Friends of Oakland Park and Recreation, East Bay Agy. for Children. Recipient over 50 archtl. awards and prizes. Fellow AIA (dir. chpt.), Internat. Inst. Arts and Letters; mem. Mich. Soc. Architects, Assn. Coll. Sch. Architecture, Raleigh Council Architects, San Francisco Planning and Urban Renewal Assn., Nat. Council Archtl. Registration Bds., Calif. Assn. Architects, Bldg. Research Inst., Japanese-Am. Citizens League. Home: 1170 Glencourt Dr Oakland CA 94611-1405 E-mail: georkimi@aol.com.

MATSUMOTO, HIROYUKI, biochemistry educator, researcher; b. Izuhara, Nagasaki, Japan, May 5, 1948; came to U.S., 1977; s. Masayuki and Yuriko (Heima) M.; m. Makiko Ohnishi; 1 child, Masaomi. BS, Kyoto U., Japan, 1972, PhD, 1977. Jr. rschr. U. Hawaii, Honolulu, 1977-79; ass. rsch. scientist Purdue U., West Lafayette, Ind., 1980-85; from asst. prof. to assoc. prof. U. Okla. Health Sci. Ctr., Oklahoma City, 1985-97; prof. Health Sci. Ctr., U. Okla., 1997—. Mem. study sect. NIH, 1998—; dir. Epscor Okla. biotech. network laser mass spectrometry facility NSF. Contbr. articles to profl. jours. including Nature, Science. Rsch. grantee NSF, 1980-88, NIH, 1985—. Mem. Assn. Rsch. Vision and Ophthalmology, Am. Soc. Biol. Chemists, Protein Soc., Am. Soc. for Mass Spectrometry, Am. Soc. for Photobiology, Japanese Soc. Zoology, Sigma Xi. Achievements include prediction of beta-ionone ring binding pocket in rhodopsin; discovery of phosphorylated homologs of arrestin; research in molecular mechanism of vision, biological mass spectrometry, and ocular proteomics. Home: 1525 Cinderella Ave Norman OK 73072-6030 Office: U Okla Health Sci Ctr 940 Stanton L Young Blvd Oklahoma City OK 73104-5020

MATSUMOTO, SHINICHI, surgeon, researcher; b. Sakai, Osaka, Japan, Mar. 17, 1963; s. Takeshi and Hiroko (Fukai) M.; m. Eriko Amano, Oct. 10, 1991; children: Kyohei, Hana. Bachelor's degree, Kobe (Japan) U., 1988, PhD, 1996. Med. lic., Japan. Physician Kobe U. Hosp., 1988-89, Osaka Red Cross Hosp., 1989-90, Kanzaki (Japan) Hosp., 1991, Kasai (Japan) Citizen Hosp., 1992; with dept. surgery U. Minn. Med. Sch., Mpls., 1997-99, U. Wash. Med. Ctr., Seattle, 1999—; sr. rsch. scientist Puget Sound Blood Ctr., 1999—, 2000—; rsch. assoc. U. Wash. Med. Ctr., Seattle, 2000—, clin. cons., 2001—, rsch. assoc., clin. assoc., 2001—. Vis. scientist U. Wash. Med. Ctr.; rsch. assoc. Puget Sound Blood Ctr.; cons. Islet Isolation Facility. Contbr. articles to med. jours. Mem. Internat. Soc. Surgery, Internat. Pancreas and Istet Transplant Soc., Japanese Surg. Soc., Japanese Gastroenterol. Surgery, Am. Soc. Transplantation. Avocations: golf, skiing. Home: 4236 129th Pl Apt 6 Bellevue WA 98006 Office: 4236 129th Pl SE # 6 Bellevue WA 98006-6706 E-mail: shinichim@psbc.org., shinichimatsumo@hotmail.com., shinichim@mac.com.

MATSUMURA, VERA YOSHI, pianist; b. Oakland, Calif. d. Naojiro and Aguri Tanaka; m. Jiro Matsumura, Aug. 8, 1942; 1 son, Kenneth N. BA in Piano Pedagogy, Coll. Holy Names, Oakland, 1938; pvt. studies with F. Moss, M. Shapiro, L. Kreutzer, P. Jarrett. Mem. staff, pianist Radio Sta. KROW, Oakland, 1938-39. Numerous concert performances in Far East (Japan, Thailand), 1940—; numerous teaching appointments, 1940—; dir. Internat. Music Council, Berkeley, Calif., 1969—. Named to Hall of Fame, Piano Guild, 1968. Mem. Nat. Music Tchrs. Nat. Assn., Music Tchrs. Assn. Calif., Internat. Platform Assn., Alpha Phi Mu. Methodist. Home: 2 Claremont Cres Berkeley CA 94705-2324

MATSUNAGA, GEOFFREY DEAN, lawyer; b. L.A., Sept. 30, 1949; s. Hideo Arthur and Yuri M.; m. Masako Inoue, Aug. 20, 1981; children: Ayako, Hideko, Lisa Fumi. BS, USAF Acad., 1971; MBA, UCLA, 1972; postgrad., Inter U. Ctr. Japanese Lang. Studies, 1979-80; JD, U. Calif., Berkeley, 1982. Bar: Calif. 1982, U.S. Dist. Ct. (cen. dist.) Calif. 1982, N.Y. 1983, U.S. Dist. Ct. (so. dist.) N.Y. 1983. Jud. extern U.S. Dist. Ct. (cen. dist.), L.A., 1981; assoc. Milbank, Tweed, Hadley & McCloy, N.Y.C., 1982-84, Tokyo, 1984-87, Sidley & Austin, Tokyo, 1987-88, L.A., 1988-91; counsel Sheppard, Mullin, Richter & Hampton, 1991-94; ptnr. Kagei & Matsunaga, 1995—2001; sole practice, 2002—. Founding bd. dirs. Futures Industry Assn., Japan, 1987; counsel East West Players, 1992-95. Lt. USN, 1972-78. Japan Found. fellow, Tokyo, 1979-80. Mem. Japan Bus. Assn. Southern Calif., Japan Am. Soc. So. Calif. (adv. bd. South Bay 1992-95). Episcopalian. Avocation: hiking, classical music. Office: Law Offices of Geoffrey D Matsunaga 19191 S Vermont Ave Ste 420 Torrance CA 90502-1051

MATSUNAKA, STANLEY T. state legislator; b. Akron, Colo., Nov. 12, 1953; m. Kathleen Matsunaka; three children. BS, Colo. State U., 1975; JD, U. San Diego. Atty.; mem. Colo. Senate, Dist. 15, Denver, 1994—. Cubmaster, den leader Boy Scouts Pack 190; active Namaqua Sch. Accountability Com. Mem. ABA, Colo. Bar Assn. (former sect. young lawyers sect.), Larimer County Bar Assn. (former sec.), Loveland Sertoma Club (pres.). Democrat. Presbyterian. Home: 2109 S County Road 21 Loveland CO 80537-9052 Office: State Capitol 200 E Colfax Ave Ste 274 Denver CO 80203-1716 also: 2881 N Monroe Ave Loveland CO 80538-3295 E-mail: stanseante@aol.com.*

MATSUO, FUMISUKE, physician, educator; b. Iida, Japan, Dec. 24, 1942; came to U.S., 1969; s. Riichi and Utako (Sasaki) M.; m. Ruth Ann Smith, May 24, 1975; children: Jocelyn, Bryan. MD, Kyoto (Japan) Prefectural U. Medicine, 1968. Asst. prof. U. Iowa, Iowa City, 1975, U. Utah, Salt Lake City, 1975-79, assoc. prof., 1979-87, prof., 1987—. Dir. EEG Lab. Univ. Hosp., Salt Lake City, 1975—. Contbr. articles to profl. jours. Fellow Am. Acad. Neurology, Am. Clin. Neurophysiology Soc.; mem. AMA, Soc. Neuroscis., Am. Epilepsy Soc., Epilepsy Assn. Utah (bd. dirs. 1978-81, 87-89), Western EEG Soc. (bd. dirs. 1983-86, sec.-treas. 1989-90, pres. 1991-92). Home: 1353 S 1900 E Salt Lake City UT 84108-2219 Office: U Utah Med Ctr 50 N Medical Dr Salt Lake City UT 84132-0001

MATSUOKA, ERIC TAKAO, mathematics educator; b. Honolulu, May 9, 1967; s. Kenneth Tamotsu and Hilda Sumie (Hino) M. BA in Math. with distinction, U. Hawaii, 1987, MA in Math., 1994. Acctg. clk. Wayne Choo, CPA, Honolulu, 1987-88; lab. instr. math. Leeward C.C., Pearl City, Hawaii, 1988-91, lectr. math., 1989-94; asst. prof. math. Leward C.C., 1994—; contr. Computronics, Honolulu, 1989-93. Faculty rep. U. Hawaii Profl. Assembly,

1996—2001. Mem. Hawaii Coun. Tchrs. Math. (membership dir. 1999—). Avocations: bowling, gemstones, jewelry, computers, mathematics. Office: Leeward CC 96-045 Ala Ike St Pearl City HI 96782-3366 E-mail: ematsuok@hawaii.edu.

MATSUSHIMA, AKIRA PAUL, international company executive; b. Tokyo, July 7, 1937; came to U.S., 1970; s. Hiromasa and Tomiko (Watanabe) M.; m. Kathleen Sue Rowland, Aug. 18, 1968; children: John Hikaru, Karen Emi, Amy Kathryn. BS, Waseda U., Tokyo, 1961; MSME, Waseda U., 1964; M in Mgmt., Northwestern U., 1981. Registered profl. engr., Calif. Asst. R&D mgr. NOK Corp. (Nippon Oil Seal Industry), Tokyo, 1961—85, mgr. rsch. planning, 1968-70; dir. engring. NOK-USA, Inc., L.A., 1970-72, v.p., 1973-74, exec. v.p. Chgo., 1975-83, sec., 1979-82, dir., 1971-85; dep. gen. mgr. engring. divsn. NOK Corp., Tokyo, 1983-85; with Chgo. Rawhide Mfg. Co. (SKF), Elgin, Ill., 1985—98, sr. v.p., 1995-98; pres. Matsushima Mgmt., Palatine, 1999—. Bd. dirs. K.K. Arai Seisakusho, Tokyo, Hi-Tech Arai, Inc., Madurai, India; bd. dirs., exec. v.p. Koyo-Chgo. Rawhide Co., Ltd., Osaka, Japan, 1986-99; bd. dirs. Chgo. Rawhide-Mexicana, S.A. de C.V., Guadalajara, Mex., 1988-91, 96-98, K.C. Engring., Ltd., Yokohama, Japan, 1989-93, rep. dir., chmn. bd. dirs., 1993-2001; Japanese govt. del. to Internat. Standardization Orgn., 1973-78; del. Motor Equipment Mfr. Assn./Japan Auto Mfr. Assn. Conf., 1990, 92, 94; treas. PLACO Co., Ltd., Saitama, Japan, 2000-02, bd. dirs. 2002—; bd. dirs., pres., sec., treas. ARAI Ams. Inc., Virginia Beach, Va., 2001—; v.p. bd. dirs. NCC, Inc., Virginia Beach, Va., 2002—; comisario PT Arai Rubber Seal Indonesia, Jakarta, 2002—. Contbr. articles to tech. jours.; patentee sealing device; holder numerous Japanese patents in field. Fund dirve chair western divsn. Jr. Achievement, Chgo., 1988—89, mem. governing bd., 1990—98, United Way of Elgin, 1988—96, v.p. planning, 1991—92; pres. Oak Crest Residence, Elgin, 1993—95; commr. to gen. assembly Presby. Ch. U.S.A., 2001. Mem. Soc. Automotive Engrs. (adv. bd. seals com., chmn. various subcoms., Cert. Appreciation 1986), Nat. Soc. Profl. Engrs., Internat. House of Japan. Presbyterian. Office: Matsushima Mgmt 1660 Beaver Pond Rd Palatine IL 60067-4433 E-mail: apmatsu@aol.com.

MATSUSHITA, MARIMI, educator, mathematician; b. Utsunomiya, Tochigi, Japan, Sept. 17, 1963; came to the U.S., 1982; d. Fumikazu and Fusako Matsushita. BS in Physics, Creighton U., 1988, MS in Math., 1992; EdD, Columbia U., 1998. Adj. lectr. CUNY/F.H. La Guardia C.C., L.I., 1995-96; adj. asst. prof. Pace U., N.Y.C., 1997-98, CUNY/Bronx (N.Y.) C.C., 1998; asst. prof. DeVry Inst. Tech., L.I., N.Y., 1999-2000, dir. STAR program, 1999-2000; assoc. prof. DeVry Coll. Inst., New Brunswick, 2001; asst. prof. Hawaii Pacific U., Honolulu, 2002—. Spkr. N.Y. State Engring. Assn.; adj. asst. prof. Medger Evers CUNY, 2001—. Tchg. fellow Creighton U., Omaha, 1990-92. Avocations: ballroom dance, opera, tennis, ping-pong, swimming.

MATSUURA, JOHN HENRY, surgeon; b. Mpls., June 25, 1958; MD, U. Hawaii, 1987. Diplomate Am. Bd. Surgery, Am. Bd. Vascular Surgery. Intern Wright State U. Sch. Medicine, 1987-88, resident in gen. surgery, 1988-92; surgeon 93d Med. Group, Castle AFB, Calif., 1992-94; fellow in vascular surgery Med. Coll. Va., 1994—; pvt. practice. Asst. prof. surgery Med. Coll. Ga., Emory U. Address: 315 Boulevard NE Ste 412 Atlanta GA 30312-1264

MATSUURA, KENNETH RAY, counselor, articulation officer; b. Urbana, Ill., July 17, 1954; s. George Shigeo and Sally Sueko (Kawasaki) M.; m. Peggy Ai Iwata, May 27, 1995. BA, U. Calif., Santa Barbara, 1976; MA, UCLA, 1978, PhD, 1996. Career counselor Calif. State U. Dominguez Hills, Carson, 1984-85; grad. recruitment coord. U. Calif., Irvine, 1985-90; counselor/articulation officer Cerritos Coll., Norwalk, Calif., 1990—. Mem. accreditation teams Western Assn. Schs. and Colls., L.A., 1994, Alameda, 1999, mem. accreditation task force Project Renewal; chair South Coast Higher Edn. Coun.; program reviewer Am. Coll. Pers. Assn. Ann. conf., Washington, 1988; presenter to confs. UCLA grad. advancement program fellow, 1977-78. Avocations: singing, music. Home: 1066 Rocton Dr Pasadena CA 91107-5917 Office: Cerritos Coll 11110 Alondra Blvd Norwalk CA 90650-6298 E-mail: kpmatsu@attglobal.net.

MATTAR, PHILIP, institute director, editor; b. Haifa, Palestine, Jan. 21, 1944; came to U.S. 1961; m. Evelyn Ann Keith, June 20, 1971; 1 child, Christina. MPhil, Columbia U., 1977, PhD, 1981. Exec. dir. Inst. for Palestine Studies, Washington, 1984-2001; assoc. editor Jour. Palestine Studies, 1985-2001; fellow Woodrow Wilson Ctr., 2001—. Adj. lectr. history Yale U., 1981; adj. prof. history Georgetown U., 1990, 91, 94. Author: Mufti of Jerusalem, 1988, 2d edit., 1991; co-editor: Encyclopedia of the Modern Middle East, 1996; editor: Encyclopedia of the Palentinians, 2000; contbr. articles to profl. jours., including Fgn. Policy, Middle East Jour., Middle Ea. Studies. Mem. adv. com. Human Rights Watch/Middle East. Vis. scholar Columbia U., 1984; Fulbright-Hays Rsch. fellow, 1978. Mem. Middle East Studies Assn., Middle East Inst. Avocations: jogging, chess, reading, travel. E-mail: pjmattar@aol.com.

MATTAS, RICHARD FRANK, nuclear energy industry executive; b. Chgo., Sept. 14, 1947; s. Charles Joseph and Lillian (Sebek) M.; m. Loretta Ann Urbaczewski, June 27, 1970. BA, Yale U., 1969; MS, U. Ill., 1971, PhD, 1974. Lab. asst. U. Ill., Champaign, 1969-74; post-doctoral appointee Argonne (Ill.) Nat. Lab., 1974-75, metallurgist, 1975-81, prin. investigator, 1981-85, mgr. fusion blanket tech., 1985-89, assoc. dir. fusion power, 1989-99, sr. scientist, 1999, dir. fusion power, 1999—. Task leader liquid metals tech. Internat. Energy Agy., Vienna, 1993--; chmn. tech. program Internat. Symposium on Fusion Nuclear Tech., L.A., 1995, tech. program com., 2002; nat. coord. Advanced Limiter-Divertor Program, 1998—. Contbr. articles to sci. and profl. jours. Bd. dirs. Galena (Ill.) Territory Assn., 1997—, v.p., 2001—. Recipient Cert. of Appreciation U.S. DOE, 1988, 90. Mem. Am. Soc. for Metals, Fusion Power Assocs, Driftless Area Ptnrship. Natural Resource Conservation Orgn. (vice chmn. 1997-2002, chmn. 2002—), Sierra Club. Avocations: photography, oil painting, bird watching. Home: 1585 Stonebridge Trl Wheaton IL 60187-7112 Office: Argonne Nat Lab 9700 Cass Ave Argonne IL 60439-4803 E-mail: mattas@anl.gov.

MATTATHIL, GEORGE PAUL, communications specialist, consultant; b. Kottayam, India, May 12, 1957; came to U.S., 1985; s. Paul and Annamma M. Bs, U. Kerala (India), 1973-78; MS, Indian Inst. Tech., 1978-82. Project engr. Tekelec, Calabasas, Calif., 1986-89; sr. systems analyst Security Pacific Automation, L.A., 1989-90; sr. design. engr. Telenova, Camarillo, Calif., 1990-91. Cons. Raynet, Menlo Park, Calif., 1991, Larse, Santa Clara, Calif., 1991—, NEC, 1992—, Level One Comm., Sacramento, 1994—, DigitalLink, 1994—, Verilink, San Jose, 1994—, Telebit, Sunnyvale, 1995—, Hitachi, San Jose, 1995—, C-Cor Electronics, Fremont, 1996, Xylan, Calabasas, Calif., 1996—, GoDigital Telecomm., Fremont, 1996—, Diva Systems, Menlo Park, Calif., 1998—. Nat. Sci. Talent scholar, India, 1975-80. Mem. IEEE, Assn. Computing Machinery, Soc. Telecom. Cons., Am. Mktg. Assn. Avocations: photography, biking. Office: PO Box 249 San Bruno CA 94066-0249 E-mail: george.mattahil@ieee.org.

MATTAUCH, ROBERT JOSEPH, electrical engineering educator; b. Rochester, Pa., May 30, 1940; s. Henry Paul and Anna Marie (Mlinarcik) M.; m. Frances Sabo, Dec. 29, 1962; children: Lori Ann, Thomas J. BS, Carnegie Inst. Tech., Pitts., 1962; MEE, N.C. State U., Raleigh, 1963, PhD, 1967. Asst. prof. elec. engring. U. Va., Charlottesville, 1966-70, assoc. prof. elec. engring., 1970-76, prof. elec. engring., 1976-83, Wilson prof. elec. engring., 1983-86, Standard Oil Co. prof. sci. and tech., 1986-89, chmn. dept. elect. engring., 1987-95, BP Am. prof. sci. and tech., 1989-95; Commonwealth prof., founding chair dept. elec. engring. Va. Commonwealth U., Richmond, 1995-99, dean of engring., Commonwealth prof., 1999—. Cons. The Rochester Corp., Culpeper, Va., 1983-88, Milltech Corp., Deerfield, Mass., 1985. Patentee: infrared detector; solid state switching capacitor; thin wire pointing method, whiskerless Schottky diode, controlled in-situ etch back growth technique. Bd. dirs. U. Va. Patent Found., 1989-95, Greater Richmond Technology Coun., 2001—, Va. Bioscis. Devel. Ctr., 2000—. Recipient Excellence in Instruction of Engring. Students award Western Electric, 1980. Fellow IEEE (Centennial medal 1984); mem. Eta Kappa Nu (recipient Oustanding Prof. in Elec. Engring. 1975), Sigma Xi, Tau Beta Pi, Sigma Pi Sigma. Office: Va Commonwealth U Dept Elec Engring PO Box 843068 Richmond VA 23284-3068 E-mail: rjmattau@vcu.edu.

MATTEO, CHRISTINE E. librarian; b. Jersey City, May 26, 1952; d. Peter J.G. and Doris Ella (Stoffel) Dirschauer; m. Joseph A. Matteo, Sept. 9, 1978. BA in Psychology, Washington Coll., Chestertown, Md., 1974; MLS, Rutgers U., 1977. Cert. libr., N.J. Sr. libr., br. mgr. Beachwood (N.J.) br. Ocean County Libr., 1976-78; prin. libr., br. mgr. Jackson br. Ocean County Libr., 1978-86; automation implementation mgr. Ocean County Libr., Toms River, N.J., 1986-89, supervising libr. ctrl. svcs., 1989-91, chief libr. pub. svcs., 1991-95, chief libr. tech., 1995—. Mem. exec. bd., treas. Ctrl. Jersey Regional Libr., Freehold, 1994-96, Customers of Dynix, Inc., Provo, Utah, 1989-91; editor, mem. steering com. Ocean Co. Libr. Master Plan, Toms River, 1984-85, 91-92, 97-98; mem. exec. bd. One Ease-E-Link, Toms River, 1998—. Mem. ALA, ASPCA, Humane Soc. U.S., N.J. Libr. Assn., Toms River Yacht Club, Earthwatch, Greenpeace, Tuckerton Seaport Soc. (charter), Toms River Seaport Soc., Environ. Def. Fund, Monmouth County SPCA. Avocations: sailing, gardening, dog obedience, kayaking, science fiction. Office: Ocean County Libr 101 Washington St Toms River NJ 08753-7688 E-mail: matteo_c@oceancounty.lib.nj.us.

MATTEO, CHRISTOPHER PETER, electronics executive, researcher; b. Bklyn., Feb. 26, 1974; s. Anthony Michael Matteo, Joan Marie Matteo. BA Internat. Rels., U. Pa., 1996. Pres. Silicon Jungle, LLC, N.Y.C., NY, 2001—; dir. Impasse Sys. LLC, 2002—; CEO ru4, 1998—2000; derivatives trader Union Bank of Switzerland, 1996—98. Contbr. ; author (newsletter): Macro Intelligence. Avocation: Avocations: researching, travel, reading, writing, filmmaking. Personal E-mail: matteo@chrismatteo.com.

MATTER, HARRY H. retired wholesale business executive and vice president, reflexologist; b. Lykens, PA, May 23, 1914; s. Homer Calvin and Edith Ellen (Seesoltz) Matter; m. Rita M. De Nicholas Matter, July 24, 1949; children: Robert, Tina. Grad., Air War Coll., Maxwell AFB, Maxwell, AL, 1972. Cert. Am. Reflexology Bd., Internat. Inst. of Reflexology, St. Petersburg, FL, 1992, ARCB, PRA. Salesman Baums Sporting Goods, Sunbury, Pa., 1941—48, vice pres. and treas., 1948—64; sales mgr. Coughlanath Mart, Pottstown, Pa., 1965—78; vice pres. Penna Reflexology Assn., Phila., 1984—99; performer, vocals & guitar Western Music Assn. Festival, Tucson, 1991—99; entertainer Am. Fedn. of Musicians, Pocono Mts., 1965—99. Dir. treas., Baums Sporting Goods, Inc., 1948-60, vice pres., Baums Sporting Goods, Inc., 1958-64, sales mgr., Coughlan Athletic Mart, Pottstown, PA, 1965-78, vice pres. (ret.) Penna Reflexology Assn., Phila., PA, 1980-99. Artist, prodr. The Am. Cowboy Legend (cassette, 1981, compact disc, 1991), The Old Rugged Cross (cassette, 1992), Great COuntry Songs (cassette, 1994). Performs, Selinsgrove Ctr. Home for Mentally Challenged, Selinsgrove, PA, 1986-99. Named to Country Music Hall of Fame, Colo. Country Music. Found., 1985; recipient Nat. Commanders Citation, Civil Air Patrol, USAF, 1973, Top Songwriter, Wyo. Country Music Assn., 1981, Meritorious award, Civil Air Patrol, Pa. Wing, 1983, Exceptional Svc. award, Civil Air Patrol, USAF, Pa. Wing, 1984, Pioneer award, Colo. Country Music. Found., 1985—92, Lifetime Achievement Songwriters award, 2001, Artist Trailblazer Kingeagle award, Nashville, Tenn., 2001, Internat. Star award, Lifetime Achievement Songwriters Divsn., London, 2001, King Earle award, Airplay Internat., Nashville, 2001, Artist Trailblazer award, 2001. Mem. BPO Elks Lodge, Loyal Order of Moose, (vice pres.), Penna Reflexology Assn., 1990-99, Country Music Assn., Western Music Assn. (performer), 1991-99, Officer's Club, Indiantown Gap Mil. Res. Republican. Lutheran. Avocations: walking, music. photography, gardening. Home: 29 Helen St Shamokin Dam PA 17876

MATTER, THEODORE SAYLOR, retired chemical engineer; b. Allentown, Pa., Nov. 25, 1917; s. Guy Earl Matter and Lilla Edna Saylor; m. Margaret Elizabeth Edwards, Oct. 11, 1947; children: Kemble S., Andrew B., Craig E. BS in Chem. Engring., U. Pa., 1939, postgrad., 1947-49. Jr. chem. engr. Am. Viscose Corp., Lewistown, Pa., 1939-42, pilot plant supr. Marcus Hook, 1946-53, sr. process engr. R&D, 1954-60, 69-76; quality control materials and processes GE Missile Space Dept., Valley Forge, 1960-63; sr. engr. tech. svc. Am. Viscose (FMC), Marcus Hook, 1963-69; ret., 1976. Author: Reverend Andrew Bashore Saylor, vol. I, 1996, vol. II, 1997, vol. III, 1998, vol. IV, 1999. Vol. leader, dist. tng. chmn. Boy Scouts Am., Upper Darby, Pa., 1946-59; pres. Elder's Assn. Del. and Montgomery Counties—Presbyn. Ch., 1980-86. Capt. U.S. Army, 1942-46, PTO. Decorated Bronze Star. Republican. Presbyterian. Avocations: tennis, genealogy, ship models, church activities. Home: 510 Netherwood Rd Upper Darby PA 19082-3623

MATTERN, DONALD EUGENE, retired association executive; b. Mapleton Depot, Pa., Feb. 11, 1930; s. John Franklin and Lizzie May (Fiss) M.; m. Anna Mae Bard, Nov. 24, 1951; children: Debra Jeanne, Cynthia Ann, James Franklin. BA, Pa. State U., 1951; MBA, U. Pa., 1955. Exec. trainee Fed. Res. Bank Phila., 1953—55; from asst. cashier to cashier Cumberland County Nat. Bank, New Cumberland, Pa., 1955—63; v.p. 1st Nat. Bank State Coll., 1963—64; asst. v.p., v.p., sr. v.p., sec. Hamilton Bank, Lancaster, 1964—86; sec., v.p. Nat. Cen. Fin. Corp., 1972—83; exec. dir. Mfr.'s Assn. Berks County, 1986—95. Mem. adv. bd. Berks campus Pa. State U., 1987-92. Treas., bd. dirs. Reading-Berks Human Rels. Coun., 1967-70; v.p. bd. dirs. local chpts. Ams. Competitive Enterprise Sys., 1970-92; past bd. dirs., past pres., past gen. campaign chmn. United Way Berks County; trustee, former chmn. bd. Comty. Gen. Hosp., Reading, 1967-98; bd. dirs. Nat. Coun. on Alcoholism, 1967-68, Reading Ctr. City Devel. Fund, 1976-86, Greater Berks Devel. Fund, 1984-89, Reading Mus. Found., 1985-97, Luth. Home Topton, 1990-97, Berkshire Health Plan, 1992-96, Highlands at Wyomissing, 1995-98, Congregation Coun. Advent Luth. Ch., various terms 1965-95, Berk County chpt. ARC, 1999-2001, Reading New Futures Project, Inc., 1988-91, Pub. Edn. Found. for Berks County, 1991-96, Children's Home of Reading, 1997—; mem. adv. exec. bd. Hawk Mountain coun. Boy Scouts Am., 1970—; mem. N.E. Pa. Synod Endowment Investment Fund Com., 1985—, treas., bd. dirs. Housing Opportunities, in Met. Environment, 1968-73. 1st lt. USAF, 1951-53. Mem. Masons, Shriners. Republican. Lutheran. Home: 20 Birchwood Rd Reading PA 19610-1908 Home (Winter): 1075 Andarella Way Vero Beach FL 32963 E-mail: sctchrock@aol.com.

MATTERN, DOUGLAS JAMES, electronics reliability engineer; b. Creede, Colo., May 19, 1933; s. John A. and Ethel (Franklin) Mattern; m. Noemi E. Del Cippo, May 4, 1963. Student, San Jose State U., 1956-58. Reliability engr. Intersil, Sunnyvale, Calif., 1973-80; sr. engr. Data Gen. Corp., 1981-87; staff engr. Apple Computer, Cupertino, Calif., 1987-97; sr. engr. Trimble Navigation, Sunnyvale, 1998-2000. Sec. Gen. World Citizens Assembly, San Francisco, 1975—86; dir. World Citizens Internat. Registry, San Francisco, 1976—, World Citizens Diplomats, Palo Alto, Calif., 1988—; del. Peoples Congress, Paris, 1980—; pres. Assn. World Citizens, San Francisco, 1989—, World Citizens Found., San Francisco, 1991—; chmn. World Citizens Assembly, San Francisco, 1995, Taipei, Taiwan, 2001. Author: Resolution to End the Arms Race; editor: World Citizen Newsmag., 1973—; contbr. Bd. dirs. San Francisco chpt. UN Assn.; bd. dirs. Promoting Enduring Peace. With USN, 1951—55. Recipient Albert Einstein Peace award, Internat. World Educators for World Peace, 2001. Home: 2671 South Ct Palo Alto CA 94306-2462 Office: 55 New Montgomery St Ste 224 San Francisco CA 94105-3421 E-mail: worldcit@best.com.

MATTERN, GERRY A. engineering consultant; b. Attica, Ind., June 16, 1935; s. George Edward and Wanda Mae (McCann) M.; p. Jane Ann Snell, Dec. 27, 1956; children: Kimberly Kaye, Geoffrey Kurtis, Kamala Anne, Kristin Annette. BSEE, Rose Polytech. Instit., 1958. Registered profl. engr., Penn., W.Va., Ind. With Mattern Electric Co., Attica, 1958; draftsman Yeager Architects, Terre Haute, Ind., 1956-58; application engr. W. Penn. Power Co., Greensburg, 1958-60, indsl. power engr. Jeannette, 1960-62; product mgr. Pitts. Reflector Co., Irwin, Penn, 1962-63; owner, operator G.A. Mattern & Assocs., Ligonier, Penn., 1963—; ptnr. Palco, Inc., Greensburg, 1965—; owner, operator Gay 90's Dairy Queen, Ligonier, 1972—. Instr. Profl. Engr's Review, Penn State U., Am. Instit. of Architects Review Class; adj. prof. Carnegie-Mellon U., Pitts., 1982—; design cons. Pitts. Reflector Co. Inventor infra-red electric furnace; designer electric heating equipment, emergency lighting equipment. Bd. dirs. Ligonier Twp. Planning Commn., 1982, Ligonier Twp. Sewerage Authority, 1991, Westmoreland County Coun. Boy Scouts Am., Heritage United Meth. Ch., Ligonier YMCA; pres. Ligonier C. of C., 1974-78. Recipient of Power-up award Westinghouse Electric Co., 1961. Mem. (life) Ligonier Booster's Club, (life) Fire Co. number 1, (arbitrator) Am. Arbitration Assn. Independent. Club: Tall Cedars (Westmoreland County), Lodge: Masons (Ligonier). Avocations: devel. of local YMCA, coaching basketball, orchard farming, antiques, house restoration. Home: 190 Wilpen Rd Ligonier PA 15658-2410 Office: GA Mattern & Assocs 205 N Market St Ligonier PA 15658-1230 E-mail: mattern@andrew.cmu.edu.

MATTERN, JOANNE, writer, educator; b. Nyack, NY, Mar. 5, 1963; d. Robert Frederick and Genevieve Porri Gise; m. James Jude Mattern, June 16, 1990; 1 child Christina Xinwei. BA in English, Hartwick Coll., 1985. Asst. editor Morrow Jr. Books, NYC, 1985—88; sr. editor, writer Troll Comms., Mahwah, NJ, 1988—95; freelance writer, 1995—. Author: (series) Wildlife of North America, 1998, Competing Like a Champion: Gymnastics, 1999, Barbie First-Grade Workbooks, 1999, Fisher-Price Little People Toddler Sticker Workbooks, 2000, Explorers, 2000—01, Working Together, 2001, Animal Geography, 2001, Safety First, 2000, Learning About Cats, 2000—01, Native Peoples, 2001, (children's books) Brer Rabbit in the Briar Patch, 1997, I Can't Believe My Eyes! Extraordinary Photos or Ordinary Things, 1997, Smart Thinking! Clever Ways Animals Make Their Lives Easier, 1997, Telling Time with Goofy, 1997, The Story of Molly Pitcher, 1999, The Trojan Horse, 1999, Big and Small, Homes for All: The Story of Bird Nests, 1999, From Flowers to Honey: The Story of Beekeeping, 1999, Mountain Climb, 1999, A Visit to the Past, 1999, Tower of Stone: The Story of a Castle, 1999, Claws and Wings and Other Neat Things, 2000, Power Rangers Power-Up Skills Learning Pads, 2000, Wishbone Adventures: Curse of Gold, 2000, Teletubbies Fund with Favorite Things Giant Coloring Activity Book, 2000, Animals Animals, 2001, People in the News: Tom Cruise, 2001, Nature's Greatest Hits, 2001, Reading Progress Indicators, 1998, Texas Assessment of Academic Skills, 2000, Reading Workbook, 2001, many others. Mem.: Soc. Children's Book Writers and Illustrators. Roman Catholic. Avocations: choral music, needlecrafts, church activities, reading, travel.

MATTERS, CLYDE BURNS, former college president; b. Fargo, N.D., Nov. 10, 1924; s. Lester H. and Pearl Lila (Burns) M.; m. Anna R. Skeels, Mar. 24, 1948; children— Cynthia (Mrs. Charles V. Carroll), Richard B. BS, Whitworth Coll., Spokane, Wash., 1950, M.Ed., 1951; PhD, U. Wash., 1960; L.H.D. (hon.), Hastings Coll., 1985. Tchr. Spokane Pub. Schs., 1950-51; prof. Whitworth Coll., 1950-57, 70-72; research assoc. U. Wash., 1957-60; asst. supt. schs. King County, Wash., 1960-63; program adviser Ford Found., West Africa, 1963-70; pres. Hastings (Nebr.) Coll., 1972-85. Pres. Nebr. Ind. Coll. Found.; mem. nexus com. Presbyn. Coll. Union; pres. Assn. Ind. Colls. and Univs. Nebr. Resident camp dir. Spokane YMCA, 1952-57, bd. dirs., 1970-72; bd. dirs. United Good Neighbors, Spokane County, 1969-70; trustee Synod of Alaska N.W. Found., 1995-99. With AUS, 1943-46. Decorated Bronze Star Mem. Assn. Ind. Colls. and Univs. (pres. Nebr. 1979-80), Phi Delta Kappa. Presbyterian (elder). Lodge: Kiwanis. Home: 4415 E 51st Ln # 3 Spokane WA 99223-7888

MATTES, BARRY A. lawyer; b. Chgo., Oct. 23, 1953; s. Jerome P. and Shirley (Cooper) M. BA in Econs., U. Rochester, 1975; JD, Chgo.-Kent Coll. Law, 1980. Bar: Ill. 1981, U.S. Dist. Ct. (no. dist.) Ill. 1981. Pvt. practice, Chgo. Democrat. Avocations: musician, tropical fish breeder, record producing. Office: 3320 N Central Ave Chicago IL 60634-4324

MATTES, MARTIN ANTHONY, lawyer; b. San Francisco, June 18, 1946; s. Hans Adam and Marion Jane (Burge) M.; m. Catherine Elvira Garzio, May 26, 1984; children: Nicholas Anthony, Daniel Joseph, Thomas George. BA, Stanford U., 1968; postgrad., U. Chgo., 1968-69, U. Bonn, Fed. Republic Germany, 1971; JD, U. Calif., Berkeley, 1974. Bar: Calif. 1974, U.S. Ct. Appeals (D.C., 5th and 9th cirs.) 1978, U.S. Dist. Ct. (no. dist.) Calif. 1979, U.S. Dist. Ct. (ea. dist.) Calif. 1991. Asst. legal officer Internat. Union Conservation of Nature and Natural Resources, Bonn, 1974-76; staff counsel Calif. Pub. Utilities Commn., San Francisco, 1976-79, legal advisor to pres., 1979-82, adminstrv. law judge, 1983, asst. chief adminstrv. law judge, 1983-86; ptnr. Graham & James, 1986-98, Nossaman Guthner Knox Elliott, LLP, San Francisco, 1998—. Adv. group. Calif. Senate Subcom. on Pub. Utilities Commn. Procedural Reform, 1994. Mng. editor Ecology Law Quar., 1973-74; contbr. articles to profl. jours. Mem. Conf. Calif. Pub. Utility Counsel (treas. 1988-90, v.p. 1990-91, pres. 1991-92), Internat. Coun. Environ. Law, San Francisco Bar Assn., Fed. Comms. Bar Assn., Power Assn. No. Calif. Office: Nossaman Guthner Knox Elliott LLP 50 California St Fl 34 San Francisco CA 94111-4624

MATTESON, CLARICE CHRIS, artist, educator; b. Winnipeg, Man., Can., Sept. 2, 1918; came to U.S., 1922; d. Sergis and Nina (Balter) Alberts; m. D.C. Matteson, 1956 (dec. 1976); children: Kemmer, Gretchen. BA, Met. State U., 1976; MA in Liberal Studies, Hamline U., 1986; PhD in Humanities, LaSalle U., 1995. Mem. Orson Welles' staff, Hollywood, Calif., 1945-46; owner Hilde-Gardes Co., L.A., 1952—56; instr. art North Hennepin C.C., Brooklyn Park, Minn., 1975-81; instr. continuing edn. for women U. Minn. , 1980. Prodr., host TV program Accent on Art , St. Paul, 1979—; instr. art Lakewood C.C., 1979, U. Minn., Bloomington (Minn.) Sch. Dist., 1980-2002, Mpls. Sch. Dist., St. Paul Sch. Dist., 1981-2002; guest artist Montserrat Gallery, Soho, N.Y.C., 1999; appeared as guest artist WCCO-TV, 1998. (one-woman shows) Decathlon Club, 1998, State Capital Rotunda, 1986, Lindbergh Home, 1988, Hamline U., 2002, exhibited (group shows) Mpls. Inst. Art, 1994—98, Art in Bloom, 1999—2002, St. Paul, 2000, Landmark Ctr., Hamline U., St. Paul, 2002, U. Minn. Womens Club, 2002, exhibited Fairmount Hotel, 2002, (represented by) Gov. Ventura's Ofcl. Residence, Montserrat Art Gallery, N.Y.C., Gallery 416, Mpls., Jean Stephen Art Gallery, 1999—2002, Premier Gallery, 2001—02, (corr.) Schaumburg (Ill) Newspapers, 1962—68; prodr.: (TV series, host) Kids Art, 1995—, (series program) Internat. Cafe Internet Arts, 1996—; patentee plastic products; prodr.: Men Aware TV , 2001—02, Print, Pass, or Pie TV, 2001—02; composer: I Want You Near. Active Minn. Orch. (WAMSO), Mpls., 1972—, vol. Recipient award for creative leadership Minn. Assn. for Continuing Adult Edn., 1977, Gold Cup award Bloomington Cable, 1989, Gov.'s Letter of Commendation, 1994; named Outstanding Grad. for past 25 yrs. Met. State U., 1997, Disting. Alumna John Marshall H.S., L.A., 2002, Outstanding Nominee of Grad. Students Met. State U., 2002; Park Cable TV grantee, 1982, Minn. Humanities Commn. grantee, 1985. Qem. ASCAP (award 1997-2001), AAUW (dir. arts com. 1989-90, bd. dirs. 1990-92), Am. Pen Women (Minn. chpt. 1994—, v.p. 1998), Internat. Biog. Assn. (dep. dir. Cambridge, Eng. 2001, participate art and comm. congress, 2001), Am. Composers Forum, Minn. Artists Assn., Minn. Territorial Pioneers (bd. dirs. 1995—, v.p. 1997-99, 1st v.p. 1999-2001, elected Minnesotan of Yr., 1999-2002), Internat. Alliance for Women in Music, St. Paul Neighborhood Network, N.Y. Neighborhood Network, Internat. Platform Speakers (award 1998), Mpls. Telecom. Network, Metro Cable Network, Adelphi Cable, DuLuth-Superior Cable, NDT, Eagan. Avocations: tennis, dancing, writing children's books, composing liturgical music. Home and Office: 2119 Sargent Ave Saint Paul MN 55105-1126

MATTESON, WILLIAM BLEECKER, lawyer; b. N.Y.C., Oct. 20, 1928; s. Leonard Jerome and Mary Jo (Harwell) M.; m. Marilee Brill, Aug. 26, 1950; children: Lynn, Sandra, Holly. BA, Yale U., 1950; JD, Harvard U., 1953. Bar: N.Y. 1954. Clk. to judge Augustus N. Hand U.S. Ct. Appeals, 1953-54; clk. to U.S. Supreme Ct. Justice Harold H. Burton, 1954-55; assoc. firm Debevoise & Plimpton (and predecessors), N.Y.C., 1955-61, ptnr., 1961—98, Debevoise & Plimpton (European office), Paris, 1973-78; presiding ptnr. Debevoise & Plimpton, 1988-93. Lectr. Columbia U. Law Sch., 1972-73, 78-80. Trustee Peddie Sch., Hightstown, N.J., 1968-73, Kalamazoo Coll., 1972-77, Miss Porter's Sch., Farmington, Conn., 1977-83, N.Y. Inst. Spl. Edn., 1981—, Salk Inst., La Jolla, Calif., 1993-96, vice-chair, 1994-96, Statue of Liberty Ellis Island Found., 1996—, Hartford Found., 1996—; active USA Bus. and Industry Adv. Com. to the Orgn. for Econ. Coop. and Devel., Paris, 1986-2000; chmn. Worldwide Bus. and Industry Adv. Com., 1994-96; vice chmn. U.S. Coun. for Internat. Bus., 1990-2000, hon. trustee. Mem. ABA, FBA, Internat. Bar Assn., N.Y. State Bar Assn., Assn. of Bar of City of N.Y. (chmn. securities regulation com. 1968-71), Harvard U. Law Sch. Assn. N.Y.C. (trustee 1968-73), Coun. Fgn. Rels., Union Club, Sky Club, Sankaty Head Club, John's Island Redstick, and Windsor Clubs, N.Y. Yacht Club. Office: Debevoise & Plimpton 919 3d Ave 47th Fl New York NY 10022 E-mail: wbmatteson@debevoise.com.

MATTESSICH, RICHARD VICTOR (RICHARD ALVARUS), business administration researcher; b. Trieste, Venezia-Julia, Italy, Aug. 9, 1922; s. Victor and Gertrude (Pfaundler) M.; m. Hermine Auguste Mattessich, Apr. 12, 1952. Mech. engr., Engring. Coll., Vienna, Austria, 1940; Diplomkaufmann, Hochschule für Welthandel, Vienna, 1944; Dr.rer.pol., Hochschule für Welthandel, 1945; Accademico Ordinario, Accademia Italiana di Economia Aziendale, Bologna, 1980—; corr. mem., Austrian Acad. Scis., Vienna, 1984—; D h.c., U. Complutense, Madrid, 1998. Research fellow Austrian Inst. Econ. Research, Vienna, 1945-47; instr. Rosenberg Coll., St. Gallen, 1947-52; dep. head Mt. Allison U., Sackville, Can., 1953-59; assoc. prof. U. Calif.-Berkeley, 1958-67; prof. econs. Ruhr U., Bochum, W. Ger., 1966-67; prof. indsl. adminstrn. U. Tech., Vienna, 1976-78; prof. bus. adminstrn. U. B.C., Vancouver, 1967-87, Arthur Andersen & Co. Disting. chair, 1980-87, prof. emeritus, 1988—. Vis. prof. Free U., Berlin, 1965, U. Social Scis., St. Gallen, Switzerland, 1965-66, U. Canterbury, 1970, Austrian Acad. Mgmt., 1971, 73, City Univ. Hong Kong, 1992, Chuo U., Tokyo, 1992; mem. bd. nominations Acctg. Hall of Fame, Columbus, Ohio, 1978-87; bd. govs. Sch. Chartered Accountancy, Vancouver, 1981-82; bd. dirs. Can. Cert. Gen. Accts. Research Found., 1984-90; internat. adv. bd. CGA Rsch. Found., 1993—. Author: Accounting and Analytical Methods, 1964, Simulation of the Firm Through a Budget Computer Program, 1964, Instrumental Reasoning and Systems Methodology, 1978, Critiqie of Accounting, 1995, Foundational Research in Accounting: Professional Memoirs and Beyond, 1995, The Beginnings of Accounting and Accounting Thought, 2000; editor: Modern Accounting Research History, Survey and Guide, 1984, 89, 92, Accounting Research in the 1980s and Its Future Influence, 1991, French transl., 1993, others; mem. editl. bd. Theory and Decision Libr., Jour. Bus. Adminstrn., Economia Azlendale, Praxiology, Acctg., Bus. and Fin. History. Sec.-treas. Internat. House, U. B.C., 1969-70; bd. dirs. Can. Cert. Gen. Accts. Research Found., 1984-90. Served to lt. Orgn. Todt., 1944-45. Recipient Lit. award AICPA, 1972, Haim Falk award Can. Acad. Acctg. Assn., 1991;Ford Found. fellow, 1961-62; Disting. Erskine fellow U. Canterbury, 1970; Killam sr. fellow U. B.C., 1971-72. Fellow Accademia Italiana di Economia Aziendale (accademico ordinario 1980—); mem. Am. Acctg. Assn. (lit. award 1972), Schmalenbach Gesellschaft, Verb. d. Hochschullehrer für Betriebswirtschaft (exec. adv. council 1976-78), Inst. Chartered Accts. of B.C. (bd. of govs. 1981-82), Austrian Acad. Scis. (corr.), Acad. Acctg. Historians (life) (hon. prof. Centro Univ. Francesco de Vitoria, U. Madrid). Achievements include pioneering analytical methods in acctg. and the computerized spreadsheet. Office: U BC Dept Bus Adminstrn Vancouver BC Canada V6T 1Z2 *Cautious optimism is the best long-run strategy.*

MATTEUCCI, DOMINICK VINCENT, real estate developer; b. Trenton, N.J., Oct. 19, 1924; s. Vincent Joseph and Anna Marie (Zoda) M.; BS, Coll. of William and Mary, 1948; BS, Mass. Inst. Tech., 1950. Registered profl. engr., Calif.; lic. gen. bldg. contractor, real estate broker; m. Emma Irene DeGuia, Mar. 2, 1968; children: Felisa Anna, Vincent Eriberto. Owner, Matteucci Devel. Co., Newport Beach, Calif.; pres. Nat. Investment Brokerage Co., Newport Beach. Home: 2104 Felipe Newport Beach CA 92660-4040 Office: PO Box 10474 Newport Beach CA 92658-0474

MATTHAEI, GAY HUMPHREY, interior designer; b. N.Y.C., Mar. 13, 1931; d. Robert Lois and Ethel Gladys Humphrey; m. Konrad Henry Matthaei, Nov. 16, 1956; children: Marcella, Leslie, Konrad. BA, Mt. Holyoke Coll., 1952; MIA, MA, cert. Russian Inst., Columbia U., 1954; grad., Parsons Sch. Design, 1970. Lectr., cons. NBC, 1956; dir. Radrick Prodns., Where Time Is a River, 1966-67; cons. N.Y.C. Parks Recreation and Cultural Adminstrn., 1970-72; assoc. Pearl R. Mitchell A.S.I.D., 1972-74, owner, 1974-97; owner, mgr. Gay Matthaei Interiors, N.Y.C., 1976-86. Restorations include Town Farms Inn, 1978, State Capital of Conn., 1977-78, Pres.'s House, Mt. Holyoke Coll., 1982, Samuel Russell House, Wesleyan Coll., 1984, Courtly Manor, Greenwich, Conn., 1987 Buhl Family Found., 1991; author: The Ledgerbook of Thomas Blue Eagle, 1994, 1995, (CD-Rom) The Journey of Thomas Blue Eagle, 1995, Sketchbook of Thomas Blue Eagle (Best Books for Teenagers NY Pub. Libr. 2002). Trustee Mt. Holyoke Coll.; mem. Commn. on State Capital Preservation and Restoration, Conn., 1977-82; active Women's Bd. of Realtors, Greenwich Bd. Realtors. Recipient Christopher award, 1994, Internat. Readers Assn. award, 1995, EMMA award, best CD-Rom award Multimedia Asia, others. Mem.: Asia Soc., Phi Beta Kappa. Home: 710 Riverbank Rd Stamford CT 06903-3514 Office: Weichert Realtors 25 Field Point Rd Greenwich CT 06830-5335 E-mail: tphq@optonline.net.

MATTHAU, CHARLES MARCUS, film director; b. N.Y.C., Dec. 10, 1965; s. Walter and Carol M. BA, U. So. Calif., 1986. Pres. The Matthau Co., L.A., 1987—. Bd. govs. Cedar Sinai Med. Ctr., L.A. Dir. motion picture Doin' Time on Planet Earth, 1990 (Saturn award Coun. Film Orgns., Silver Scroll award Acad. Sci. Fiction); dir., prodr. TV show Mrs. Lambert Remembers Love, 1993 (Golden Angel award Best TV Spl. 1993, Golden Medal award Best Drama Prodn. 1993, Grand award The Houston Internat. Film Festival); dir., prodr. motion picture The Grass Harp, 1996 (recipient Best Dir. Family Film awards 1996); dir. The Marriage Fool, 1998; dir. over 50 feature shorts. Nat. spokesperson Am. Lung Assn., L.A., 1989—; active Action on Smoking and Health, Washington, 1986—. Recipient Cine award, Coun. Non-Theatrical Events, Washington, 1985, Golden Seal award, London Amateur Film Festival, 1986, Platinum Circle award Am. Film Inst. Mem. Dirs. Guild Am.

MATTHEI, EDWARD HODGE, architect; b. Chgo., Dec. 21, 1927; s. Henry Reinhard and Myra Beth (Hodge) M.; m. Mary Nina Hoffmann, June 30, 1951; children: Edward Hodge, Suzanne Marie, Christie Ann, Laura Jean, John William. BS in Archtl. Engring, U. Ill., 1951. Registered arch. 17 states, including Ariz., Fla., Ill., Mich., N.Y., Wis., Calif.; cert. NCARB. Dir. health facilities planning and constrn. Child & Smith (architects and engrs.), Chgo., 1951-60; sr. v.p. health facilities planning Perkins & Will, 1960-74; ptnr. firm Matthei & Colin Assoc., 1974-96; planning and archtl. design cons., 1996—. Com. chmn. Am. Nat. Standards Inst., 1983-89; lectr. 1st Internat. Conf. on Rehab. of Handicapped, Beijing, 1986, Design USA, Novosibirsk and Moscow, USSR, 1990. Editor: Inland Architect, 1956-58; prin. works health facilities projects, med. ctr. master plans including Akron (Ohio) Gen. Hosp., Heritage Hosp., Taylor, Mich., Rose Meml., Denver, Silver Cross Hosp., Joliet, Ill., Shands Tchg. Hosp. & Med. Sch., U. Fla., Gainesville, Mercy Hosp., Davenport, Iowa, Westlake Cmty. Hosp., Chgo., Highland Park (Ill.) Hosp., Ctrl. DuPage Hosp., Winfield, Ill., Nebr. Meth. Hosp., Omaha, Rockford (Ill.) Meml. Hosp., U. Ala. Med. Ctr., Birmingham, U. Calif. Sch. Medicine, Irvine, Kent Hall, U. Chgo., Holy Cross Hosp., Md., West Mich. Cancer Ctr. Second v.p. Nat. Easter Seal Soc., 1978; mem. bd. dirs. St. Scholastica H.S., Chgo., 1973-83, 86-96; mem. Welfare Coun. Greater Met. Chgo., 1965-72; chair profl. adv. coun. Nat. Easter Seal Soc., 1988-89. With AUS, 1946-47. Recipient Leon Chatelain award for barrier-free environ. Nat. Easter Seals Soc., 1979, Disting. Svc. award, 1990, 99, Meritorious Svc. award Am. Nat. Standards Inst., 1987, Speedy award Paralyzed Vets. Am., 1993. Fellow AIA (Disting. Svc. award Chgo. chpt. 1988); mem. Am. Hosp. Assn., Am. Assn. Hosp. Planning, Internat. Hosp. Fedn., Nat. Center Barrier Free Environ. (dir.), Builders Assn. Chgo., Chgo. Assn. Commerce and Industry. Home: 1437 W Glenlake Ave Chicago IL 60660-1801 Office: Matthei & Colin Assocs 332 S Michigan Ave Chicago IL 60604-4434

MATTHEW, BARACLOUGH F, music educator; b. Cortland, NY, Nov. 19, 1966; s. Jean A Baraclough; m. Denna L. Smith, Jan. 12, 1973. MusB Edn., Shenandoah Conservatory of Music, Winchester, Va., 1989. Band dir. Moorefield (W.Va.) H.S., 1990—95, Nelson County H.S., Lovingston, Va., 1995—97, Wilson Meml. H.S., Fishersville, 1997—. Min. of music / worship leader Fishersville Bapt. Ch., Fishersville, Va., 1997—. Recipient Tchr. of the Month, Clear Channel Radio, 2001. Mem.: Music Educators' Nat. Conf., Va. Music Educators Assn.

MATTHEW, LYN, sales and marketing executive consultant; b. Long Beach, Calif., Dec. 15, 1936; d. Harold G. and Beatrice (Hunt) Matthew; m. Wayne Thomas Castleberry, Aug. 12, 1961 (div. Jan. 1976); children: Melanie, Cheryl, Nicole, Matthew. BS, U. Calif., Davis, 1958; MA, Ariz. State U., 1979. Cert. hotel sales exec., meeting profl. Pres. Davlyn Cons. Found., Scottsdale, Ariz., 1979-82; cons., vis. prof. The Art Bus., 1982—; pres., dir. sales and mktg. Embassy Suites, 1987-98; pres., Matthew Enterprises, Inc., 1998—. Trustee Hotel Sales and Mktg. Assn. Internat. Found., 1988-90, chmn., 1991-93, mem. exec. com., 1993-95; mktg. exec. HSMAI, 1998—; vis. prof. Maricopa C.C., Phoenix, 1979—, Ariz. State U., Tempe, 1980-83; cons. Women's Caucus for Art, Phoenix, 1983-88; coun. adminstr. Lynn Andrews Prodns., 2001--. Author: The Business Aspects of Art, Book I, 1979, Book II, 1989, Marketing Strategies for the Creative Artist, 1985, Moxibustion Manual, 1999. Bd. dirs. Rossom House and Heritage Square Found., Phoenix, 1987-88. Recipient Cmty. Bldg. award, 2000. Mem. Women Image Now (Achievement and Contbn. in Visual Arts award 1983), Women in Higher Edn., Nat. Women's Caucus for Art (v.p. 1981-83), Ariz. Women's Caucus for Art (pres. 1980-82, hon. advisor 1986-87), Ariz. Vocat. Edn. Assn. (sec. 1978-80), Ariz. Visionary Artists (treas. 1987-89), Hotel Sales and Mktg. Assn. Internat. (pres. Great Phoenix chpt. 1988-89, regional dir. 1989-90, bd. dirs. 1985-90), CHME (profl. designation tng. chair 1995, cert. commr. 1998-2000), Meeting Planners Internat. (v.p. Ariz. Sunbelt chpt. 1989-91, pres. 1991-92, Supplier of Yr. award 1988, CMP cert. trainer 1995—), Soc. Govt. Meeting Planners (charter bd. dirs. 1987, Sam Gilmer award 1992, nat. conf. co-chair 1993-94), Ariz. Visionary Artists (treas. 1987-88), Ariz. Acad. Performing Arts (v.p. bd. dirs. 1987-88, pres. 1988-89), Am. Orgn. for Bodywork Therapies of Asia (pres., stae dir. 1999-), Coun. Whistling Elk (worldwide coun. adminstr., 2001—).

MATTHEW, NEIL EDWARD, artist, educator; b. Anderson, Ind., Jan. 19, 1925; s. Mark Neil and Mary Bertha (Clifford) M.; m. Jeannette Morrow, Dec. 22, 1963. BA in Edn., Ariz. State U., 1949; MFA, Ind. U., 1955; postgrad., U. Iowa, 1957-58, State Acad. of Fine Arts, Stuttgart, Germany, 1959-60. Tchr., art Covington (Ind.) Jr. H.S., 1949-50, Clay H.S., South Bend, Ind., 1955-57; instr. art Ind. U., Kokomo, 1960-64, instr. to asst. prof. art. Indpls., 1964-71; asst. to assoc. prof. art Herron Sch. Art/Ind. U. Purdue U., 1971-87, assoc. prof. emeritus, 1987—. Art exhbit judge Kokomo Art Assn., Ind., 1970; rschr. for salary studies AAUP, Ind. U. Purdue U., 1970s, others. Painter oils, acrylics, and watercolors, 1945—; printmaker etching and woodcuts, 1953—; photographer; one-man shows include: Lyman-Snodgrass Gallery, Indpls., 1984, Lieber's Gallery, Indpls., 1962, 68, Purdue U. Gallery, 1962, Ind. U. Med. Ctr., Indpls., 1966, Ind. U. at Kokomo, 1967, Ind. U. Purdue U. Archives and Libr., 1996, 98, others; group shows include: Ind. Arts Competition, 1988, Purdue U., 1966, 69, Libr. of Congress, 1956, 58, 59, numerous others; work represented at Lieber's Gallery, Indpls., 1959-73, Assoc. Am. Artists, N.Y.C., 1965-72, Lyman-Snodgrass Gallery, Indpls., 1984-85, Ruschman Gallery, Indpls., 1989—; permanent collections include: U. Ariz. Mus. of Art, Tucson, Ctr. for Creative Photograhy, Tucson, Archives, Ind. U. -Purdue U. at Indpls., Indpls. Mus. Art, others; copper plate included in ednl. show U. Ariz. Mus. Art, 2000. Pvt. first class U.S. Army, 1950-52. Named Outstanding Art Grad., Ariz. State U., Tempe, 1949; recipient tuition scholarship U. Iowa, Iowa City, 1957-58; Fulbright grantee, Stuttgart, 1959-60. Mem. Soc. Ind. Pioneers, Coll. Art Assn., Ctr. for Creative Photography, Assocs. of Art History (bd. dirs. 1991-97), Fulbright Assn. Republican. Presbyterian. Avocations: travel, reading, art history, fiction. Home: 5233 North Via Sempreverde Tucson AZ 85750-5967

MATTHEWS, ALLAN FREEMAN, geologist; b. Wakefield, Mass., May 27, 1916; s. Ralph Freeman Matthews and Mary (Morrill) Hill; m. Shirley Jean Spencer, Dec. 23, 1937 (div. Oct. 1955); children: David Allan, Kim; m. Doris Olive Haignere, June 26, 1962. BA, Carleton Coll., 1937; MS, Antioch Coll., 1939; postgrad., Johns Hopkins U., 1939-40. Tech. editor Ceramic Industry Jour., Chgo., 1940-41; editor, sect. chief U.S. Bur. of Mines, Washington, 1941-51; asst. dir., staff Pres.'s Materials Policy Commn., 1951-52; materials cons. Nat. Security Resources Bd., 1952-53; ops. analyst Johns Hopkins Ops. Rsch. Office, Chevy Chase, Md., 1953-54; program officer U.S. Agy. for Internat. Devel., Washington, 1954-75; editor, pub. Developing Country Courier, McLean, Va., 1978-85. Del. UN Global Modeling Conf., Paris, 1982; initiated citizens transnat. constl. conv., The Hague, Netherlands, 1998; chmn. constn. action group Alliance for Democracy, Waltham, Mass., 1997-99; minerals cons. Global 2000 Project, 1978-80; drafter petition and rationale for nat. initiative and referendum sys.; cons. in field. Author: Sovereigns Peacefully Take Charge, 1997; editor: Minerals Yearbook, 1947-50; contbr. articles to profl. jours. and chpts. to books. Dir. Assn. to Unite the Democracies, Washington, 1957—, former sec.; core planner 20/20 Vision, Washington, 1991-97; a founder The Reston Forum, 1990-92; pres. Waterford Sq. Condominium Assn., Reston, 1992; apptd. adv. bd. Phila. Two Orgn. Direct Democracy, 2001. Lt. (j.g.) USN, 1944-46. Recipient Meritorious award U.S. Agy. for Internat. Devel., 1955, Commendation for Devel. Analysis, 1957; named Fellow in Geology, 1937-39. Mem. AAAS, ACLU, Democratic Socialists Am., Natural Resources Def. Coun., U N Assn., World Federalist Asssn., Unitarian Universalist Assn., Fed. Am. Scientists, Phila. Two Direct Democracy (adv. bd.), Soc. for Internat. Devel. (proposer continental fed. unions at N.Am. regional conf. 2000), Ctr. Defense Info. (Am. vets. com.). Green Party. Achievements include evaluation of mineral resources adequacy and advancement of transnational constitutions. Home: 11500 Fairway Dr Apt 503 Reston VA 20190-4457

MATTHEWS, BRIAN W. molecular biology educator; b. Mount Barker, Australia, May 25, 1938; came to U.S., 1967; s. Lionel A. and Ethlinda L. (Harris) M.; m. Helen F. Denley, Sept. 7, 1963; children: Susan, Kristine. BS, U. Adelaide, Australia, 1959, BS with honors, 1960, PhD, 1964, DSc, 1986. Mem. staff Med. Rsch. Coun., Cambridge, Eng., 1963-66; vis. assoc. NIH, Bethesda, Md., 1967-69; prof. molecular biology U. Oreg., Eugene, 1969—, chmn. dept. physics, 1985-86, dir. Inst. Molecular Biology, 1980-83, 90-92; Drummond lectr. U. Calgary (Can.), 1995. Advisor NSF, Washington, 1975-77; investigator Howard Hughes Med. Inst., 1989—; mem. U.S. Nat. Commn. for Crystallography, Washington, 1980-86, 88-90. Rsch. fellow Alfred P. Sloan Found., 1971, Guggenheim fellow, 1977; recipient Career Devel. award NIH, 1973, Faculty Excellence award Oreg. Bd. Edn., 1984, Discovery award Med. Rsch. Found. Oreg., 1987, Reed Coll. Vollum award, 1994, Stein and Moore award Protein Soc., 2000. Mem. NAS, AAAS, Crystallographic Assn., Am. Chem. Soc., Protein Soc. (pres. 1995-97), Biophysical Soc. (nat. lectr. 2001). Office: U Oreg HHMI Inst Molecular Biology Eugene OR 97403 E-mail: brian@uoxray.uoregon.edu.

MATTHEWS, BRUCE RANKIN, former professional football player; b. Arcadia, Calif., Aug. 8, 1961; BS in Indsl. Engring., U. So. Calif., 1983. Center, guard Houston Oilers, 1983-96, Tenn. Oilers (formerly Houston Oilers), 1996-97; offensive guard Tennessee Titans, 1997—2002. Named NFL All-Pro Team Guard by Sporting News, 1988-90, 92, Leader, 1993. Played in Pro Bowl, 1988-93. Office: Tennessee Titans 460 Great Circle Rd Nashville TN 37228-1404*

MATTHEWS, C(HARLES) DAVID, real estate appraiser, consultant; b. Anniston, Ala., June 15, 1946; s. James Boyd and Emma Grace (McCullough) M.; m. Stephanie Ann Woods, Dec. 28, 1968; children: Alison Paige, Dylan McCullough. BS, U. Tenn., 1968. County appraiser Assessor's Office, Freeport, Ill., 1969-71; staff appraiser Ill. Dept. Highways, Springfield, 1971-72; appraiser, dir. counseling Norman Benedict Assocs., Hamden, Conn., 1972-76; mgr. appraisal dept. Citizens Realty & Ins., Evansville, Ind., 1976-80; owner, mgr. David Matthews Assocs., 1980—. Adj. real estate faculty U. Conn., 1974-76, U. Evansville, 1978-87, Appraisal Inst., 1989—; citizen amb. to Russia on Urban Valuation Team, 1993. Tympanist Chattanooga Symphony; drummer Templeaires Big Band; author: (with others) Downtown Master Plan of Evansville, Indiana, 1984, The Appraisal of Real Estate, 10th edit. Mem. Leadership Evansville, 1982; arbitrator Am. Arbitration Assn., 1986-91; chmn. bd. trustees Meth. Temple, 1994-98, 2001. Recipient merit award Willard Libr. Photog. Contest, 1988. Mem. Am. Inst. Real Estate Appraisers (vice chmn. nat. admissions 1990, state pres. 1987, governing councillor 1989-90), Appraisal Inst. (chmn. gen. appraiser bd. 1991-92, exec. com. 1991-92, 95-96, chmn. pub. rels. 1993, chmn. comm. 1995-96, Percy Wagner award 1992, Y.T. Lum award 1997), Soc. Real Estate Appraisers (local pres. 1981), Evansville Bd. Realtors (pres. 1986, Realtor of Yr. award 1987), Counselors of Real Estate, Evansville C. of C. (chair govt. affairs 1998-99), Mensa, Rotary. Avocations: cinematographer, jazz drummer, travel, golf. Home: 430 S Boeke Rd Evansville IN 47714-1616 Office: 123 NW 4th St Rm 711 Evansville IN 47708-1719 E-mail: dma@evansville.net.

MATTHEWS, CHARLES SEDWICK, petroleum engineering consultant, research advisor; b. Houston, Mar. 27, 1920; s. Charles James and Zadoc Coleman (Sedwick) M.; m. Miriam Loraine Ormerod, June 2, 1945; children— Joan Gail, Wendy Loraine BSChemE, Rice U., 1941, MSChemE, 1943, PhD in Chemistry, 1944. Registered profl. engr., Tex. Engr. Shell Devel. Co., San Francisco, 1944-48, rsch. engr. Houston, 1948-56, dir. rsch., 1967-72; chief reservoir engr. Shell Oil Co., 1965, mgr. engring., 1972-73, sr. petroleum engring. cons., 1973-89. Engring. adv. com. Rice U., Houston, 1973-77; cons. Dept. Energy, Washington, 1974-78, adv. com., 1975-79; spl. asst. Nat. Petroleum Council, Washington, 1981-83; reserves com. Am. Petroleum Inst. Author: Pressure Buildup and Flow Tests in Wells, 1967; contbr. articles to profl. jours.; patentee in field. Chmn. Tex. Engrs. for Conservation, Houston, 1973 Recipient Disting. Alumnus award Rice U., 1994. Mem. NAE, Soc. Petroleum Engrs. (hon. mem., Lester Uren award 1975, disting. author, disting. lectr. 1968, Disting. lectr. emeritus 1986), Phi Beta Kappa, Sigma Xi, Tau Beta Pi, Phi Lambda Upsilon. Clubs: Houston, Meyerland (treas. 1982-85). Republican. Methodist. Avocations: swimming; fishing. Home: 5307 S Braeswood Blvd Houston TX 77096-4149

MATTHEWS, CHRISTIAN WILLIAM, JR. minister; b. Jersey City, Oct. 12, 1934; s. Christian William and Lydia Louise (Weller) M.; m. Elaine Louise Ochs, June 18, 1955; children: Christian William III, Patricia Louise, Judith Ann, Barbara Jean. BA, King's Coll., 1956; MRE, Ea. Theol. Sem., 1960, MDiv, 1962; MEd, U. Del., 1961; ThM, Princeton Theol. Sem., 1965; DD, Grove City Coll., 1988. Ordained to ministry Presbyn. Ch. (U.S.A.), 1962. Dir. Christian edn. United Presbyn. Ch. of Manoa, Havertown, Pa., 1959-62; asst. min. 1st Presbyn. Ch., Norristown, 1962-65; assoc. min. Marble Collegiate Ch., N.Y.C., 1965-68; sr. min. Fox Chapel Presbyn. Ch., Pitts., 1968-79, Christ Presbyn. Ch., Toledo, 1979-2000, 2d Presbyn. Ch., Balt., 2000—. Mem. The Fellowship, Washington, Synod Gen. Coun. Presbyn. Ch. U.S.A.; chmn. Synod Evangelism; leader marriage and family seminars; mem. alumni fund bd. Princeton Theol. Sem.; mem. Kirk coun., Alma Coll.; cons. Presbyn. Ch. in U.S.A., Nat. Com. for Prison Reform, County Human Svc. Commn. Author: Lingering with Luke—A Study of the Life of Christ, 1976, Marriage and Family Study Course, 1983; developer (nat. program for Presbyn. chs.) Risk Evangelism; signer Lausanne Covenant of Internat. Congress on World Evangelization. Chmn. Com. for Ecol. Instrn.; founding pres. Samaritan Counseling Ctr.; sec. The Ability Ctr.; bd. dirs. area coun. Boy Scouts Am., Met. Toledo Chs. United, North Toledo Community Ctr., AASK-Mid Am., Toledo Leadership Found.; mem. Coun. for Religion and Psychiatry. Office: 4835 Turnbridge Rd Toledo OH 43623-2744 E-mail: DrCWMatthews@aol.com. *As I reflect upon life, I believe that God is at work in our world bringing together people of faith to meet the complex challenges confronting us at this time of history. Working together, we are able to encourage, strengthen, and support one another in meeting the needs of our world.*

MATTHEWS, CRAIG GERARD, energy company executive; b. Bklyn., Mar. 8, 1943; m. Carol O. Olsen, Sept. 10, 1971; children: Kenneth C., Bradford P., Melinda M. BCE, Rutgers U., 1965; MS in Indsl. Mgmt., Polytech. Inst. Bklyn., 1971. Trainee Bklyn. Union Gas Co., 1965; vice chmn., COO, KeySpan Corp. (formerly Bklyn. Union Gas Co.), 1996—2002; ret., 2002. Pres., bd. dirs. Bklyn. Philharm.; bd. dirs. Poly. Univ., Salvation Army; bd. mem. Covanta Corp. Republican. Presbyterian. Home: 132 Canterbury Way Basking Ridge NJ 07920

MATTHEWS, CYNTHIA ANN, school administrator; b. Fort Myers, Fla., May 20, 1951; d. Arthur and Rebecca Kitchen; m. Leroy Matthews, Jan. 6, 1976; children: Dionne Griffin, Alicia Matthews, LaRonda, Denise, LeRoy Jr., John. BA, Barry U., 1992; MS, Palm Beach Atlantic, 2000. Cert. tchr., Fla. Office mgr. Martin County Schs., Stuart, Fla., 1975-89; program specialist St. Lucie County Schs., Ft. Pierce, 1989—. Home: 1910 Ave Q Fort Pierce FL 34950

MATTHEWS, DANE DIKEMAN, urban planner; b. Memphis, Dec. 19, 1950; d. Neil Jude and Virginia Ann (Turnbull) Dikeman; m. John Wesley Matthews, Dec. 28, 1971. BA with distinction, U. Okla., 1972, M of Regional and City Planning, 1974. Planner Hudgins, Thompson & Ball, Inc., Tulsa, 1975-76; econ. devel. planner Tulsa Metro. Area Planning Commn., 1976-77; planner II Tulsa Met. Area Planning Commn., 1977-80; prin. regional planner Indian Nations Coun. Govts., Tulsa, 1980—. Project dir. Kendall-Whittier Neighborhood Master Plan, 1992. Bd. dirs., chair house com. Arts and Humanities Coun., Tulsa, 1991—96, 2000—; divsn. chair Tulsa Area United Way, 1988—96; mem. adv. coun. Mobile Outreach and Crisis Svcs., 1995—2002, co-chair, 2000—02; chmn. Tulsa County Long Term Care Authority, 1999—2000, 2002—; Bd. dirs. Met. Tulsa Urban League, 1993—95, Parkside Cmty. Mental Health Ctr., Tulsa, 1986—2000; bd. dirs. Tulsa County Long Term Care Authority, 1995—. Recipient Spl. Recognition award Downtown Tulsa Unltd., 1988. Mem. Am. Inst. Cert. Planners (cert.), Am. Planning Assn. (Okla. chpt. pres. 1988-89, Master Plan award 1992, Outstanding Profl. Planner 1991), Phi Beta Kappa. Democrat. Episcopalian. Avocations: cooking, reading, raising dogs. Office: INCOG 201 W 5th St Ste 600 Tulsa OK 74103-4236 Fax: (918) 583-1024. E-mail: dmatthews@incog.org.

MATTHEWS, DAVID, clergyman; b. Indianola, Miss., Jan. 29, 1920; s. Albert and Bertha (Henderson) M.; m. Lillian Pearl Banks, Aug. 28, 1951; 1 dau., Denise. AB, Morehouse Coll., Atlanta, 1950; student, Atlanta U., 1950, Memphis Theol. Sem., 1965, Delta State U., Cleveland, Miss., 1969, 71, 72; D.D. (hon.), Natchez (Miss.) Jr. Coll., 1973, Morris Booker Meml. Coll., 1988. Ordained minister Nat. Baptist Conv. U.S.A., 1946; pastor chs. in Miss., 1951—. Bell Grove Baptist Ch., Indianola, 1951—. Strangers Home, Greenwood, 1958—. Tchr., chmn. dept. social sci. Gentry H.S., Indianola, 1958-83; moderator Sunflower Bapt. Assn., 1957—; v.p. Gen. Bapt. Conv. Miss., 1958—, former lectr., conv. congress religious edn.; v.p. Nat. Bapt. Conv. U.S.A., 1971-94; del. to Nat. Coun. Chs., 1960, supr. oratorial contest, 1976; pres. Gen. Missionary Bapt. State Conv. Miss., 1974-98. Mem. Sunflower County Anti-Poverty Bd., 1965-71, Indianola Bi-Racial Com., 1965— ; mem. Gov.'s Advisory Com.; col. on staff Gov. Finch, 1976-80; mem. budget com. Indianola United Fund, 1971— ; chmn. bd. Indianola FHA, 1971— ; trustee Natchez Jr. Coll.; mem. Miss. Gov.'s Research and Devel. Council, 1984— ; apptd. mem. So. Govs. Ecumenical Coun. Infant Mortality, 1987. Served with U.S. Army, 1942-45, PTO. Recipient citation Morehouse Coll., 1950, citation Miss. Valley State Coll., 1956; J.H. Jackson Preaching award Midwestern Baptist Laymen Fellowship, 1974; Gov.'s Merit award, 1975 Mem. NEA, Miss., Indianola Tchrs. Assns., Am. Bible Soc. (adv. coun. 1991—, student reform theol. sem. centennial edn. 1990—). Democrat. Home: PO Box 627 Indianola MS 38751-0627 Fax: 662-887-9078. *I have learned not to seek honors and success but to become so involved in worthwhile works that I lose myself and by such actions success and honors have come.*

MATTHEWS, DAVID FORT, career officer; b. Lancaster, N.H., Sept. 25, 1944; s. Clinton Fort and Mabel Sawin (Oaks) M.; m. Eva Mae Horton, Nov. 10, 1990. BA, Vanderbilt U., 1966; MA, Mid. Tenn. U., 1973. Cert. acquisition mgr. Rsch. and devel. officer U.S. Army Rsch. Inst., Washington, 1974-77; exec. officer 194th Maintenence Battalion-Camp Humphreys, Korea, 1978-79; career program mgr. U.S. Army Mil. Pers. Ctr., Washington, 1979-82; logistics staff officer Dep. Chief of Staff Logistics, 1982-83; team chief Chief of Staff Army Study Group, 1983-85; logistics div. chief Multiple Launch Rocket System Project Office, Huntsville, Ala., 1985-88; comdr. Ordnance Program Div., Riyadh, Saudi Arabia, 1988-90; project mgr. Army Tactical Missile System, Huntsville, 1990-94; sr. lectr. weapon systems acquisition Naval Postgrad. Sch., Monterey, Calif., 1994—. Decorated Legion of Merit, Bronze Star; recipient award as project mgr. of yr. Sec. of Army, 1991. Mem. Nat. Def. Indsl. Assn., Assn. U.S. Army. Avocations: spectator sports, water skiing, reading, scuba diving. Home: 83 High Meadow Ln Carmel CA 93923 Office: Naval Postgrad Sch Monterey CA 93943 E-mail: DMatthews@nps.navy.mil.

MATTHEWS, DONALD ROWE, political scientist, educator; b. Cin., Sept. 14, 1925; s. William Procter and Janet Burch (Williams) M.; m. Margie C. Richmond, June 28, 1947 (div.); children: Mary, Jonathan; m. Carmen J. Onstad, July 7, 1970 (div.); children: Christopher, Amy. Student, Kenyon Coll., 1943, Purdue U., 1944-45; AB with high honors, Princeton, 1948, MA, 1951, PhD, 1953; Dr. hon. causa, U. Bergen, 1985. Instr. Smith Coll., Northampton, Mass., 1951-53, asst. prof. govt., 1953-57; lectr. polit. sci. U. N.C., Chapel Hill, 1957-58, assoc. prof., 1958-63, prof., 1963-70; research prof. Inst. for Research in Social Sci., 1963-70; sr. fellow in govtl. studies Brookings Instn., Washington, 1970-73; prof. polit. sci. and research assoc. Inst. for Research in Social Sci., U. Mich., Ann Arbor, 1973-76; chmn. dept. polit. sci. U. Wash., Seattle, 1976-83, prof. polit. sci., 1976-94, prof. emeritus,

1995—. Guest prof. U. Bergen, Norway, 1980; fellow Ctr. for Advanced Study in the Behavioral Scis., 1964-65; cons. to U.S. Commn. on Civil Rights, 1958-60, NBC News, 1966-68, Ford Found., 1967-68, U.S. Ho. of Reps., 1970-72, others; faculty lectr. U. Wash., 1989. Author: The Social Background of Political Decision-Makers, 1954, U.S. Senators and Their World, 1960, (with James Prothro) Negroes and the New Southern Politics, 1966, Perspectives on Presidential Selection, 1973, (with William Keech) The Party's Choice, 1976, (with James Stimson) Yeas and Nays: A Theory of Decision-Making in the U.S. House of Representatives, 1975, (with Henry Valen) Parliamentary Representation: The Case of the Norwegian Storting, 1999; Contbr. articles to profl. jours. Served with USNR, 1943-46. Recipient Sr. Award for Research in Govtl. Affairs Social Sci. Research Council, 1962; Ford Found. fellow, 1969-70; Guggenheim fellow, 1980-81 Fellow Am. Acad. Arts and Scis.; mem. Am. Polit. Sci. Assn. (treas. 1970-72, v.p. 1985-86), Pacific N.W. Polit. Sci. Assn. (pres. 1977-78), Western Polit. Sci. Assn. (pres. 1979-80), So. Polit. Sci. Assn., Midwestern Polit. Sci. Assn., Inter-Univ. Consortium for Polit. Research (exec. com. 1970-72) Democrat. Home: 2125 1st Ave Apt 1301 Seattle WA 98121-2118 E-mail: drm@u.washington.edu.

MATTHEWS, DOUGLAS EUGENE, lawyer, educator, consultant; b. Highland Park, Mich., July 28, 1953; s. Max and Mary Elizabeth (Crane) M. BA with high distinction, Judson Coll., Elgin, Ill., 1982; JD cum laude, U. Wis., 1985, MS in Legal Instns., 1988; LLM, Harvard U., 1991. Bar: Fla. 1986, Ill. 1987, D.C. 1989. Assoc. Gunster, Yoakley, Criser & Stewart, West Palm Beach, Fla., 1986, Zukowski, Rogers, Flood & McArdle, Crystal Lake, 1987; asst. pub. defender McHenry County, Woodstock, Ill., 1988-89; law lectr. No. Ill. U., De Kalb, 1990; asst. prof. St. Thomas U. Sch. Law, Miami, Fla., 1991-94, assoc. prof., 1994-96; adj. prof. law, 1996—; co-founder, v.p. The Grifo Group, Inc., Miami, Fla., 1997—. Past v.p., bd. dirs. Youth Svc. Bur., Woodstock. Mem. Fla. Bar Assn., Ill. Bar Assn., Dade County Bar Assn., Ind. Computer Cons. Assn., Harvard Club of Miami. Democrat. Unitarian Universalist. Avocations: gardening, historic preservation. Office: 686 NE 74th St Miami FL 33138-5114 E-mail: matthews@post.harvard.edu.

MATTHEWS, DREXEL GENE, quality control executive; b. Vanzant, Ky., Feb. 1, 1952; s. Marcus Ivan and Lillia Mae (Lake) M.; m. Roberta June Eby, Oct. 16, 1971; children: Tracie Marie, Marcia Nichole. Student, Brescia Coll., Owensboro, Ky., 1976-79, Morehead State U., 1969-71. Cert. ISO lead auditor. With Nat. Aluminum Divsn., Nat. Steel Corp., Hawesville, Ky., 1971-78, customer svc. mgr., 1977-78; quality control. mgr. Hunter Douglas Bldg. Products divsn., Roxboro, N.C., 1979-81; process engring. mgr., mgr. quality control and specification engring. Mepco-Electra Co., 1981-84; quality assurance sr., mng. engr. Sumitomo Electric Co., Rsch. Triangle Park, 1984-87; quality assurance supplier, quality engring. resource Consolidated Diesel Co. (divsn. Cummins Engine Co.), Whitakers, 1987-95; quality assurance mgr. Fuel Systems Bus., 1987-94; mgr. quality devel. and improvement Consol. Diesel Co., 1994-95; mgr. bus. analysis and audit Cummins Engine Co., Columbus, Ind., 1995—, mgr. bus. process audits fin. dept., 1995-97, mgr. quality info. sys., 1997—. Mem. ASM, SAE (diesel standards com. 1993-95), Am. Soc. Quality Control (sr. mem.; guest speaker 1987, 91), Am. Statis. Assn., Am. Nat. Standards Inst. (fiber optics com. 1986-90). Republican. Baptist. Home: 614 N National Rd Columbus IN 47201-7851 E-mail: drexel.matthews@cummins.com.

MATTHEWS, ELIZABETH WOODFIN, law librarian, law educator; b. Ashland, Va., July 30, 1927; d. Edwin Clifton and Elizabeth Frances (Luck) Woodfin; m. Sidney E. Matthews, Dec. 20, 1947; 1 child, Sarah Elizabeth Matthews Wiley. BA, Randolph-Macon Coll., 1948, LLD (hon.), 1989; MS in Libr. Sci., U. Ill., 1952; PhD, So. Ill. U., 1972; LLD, Randolph-Macon Coll., 1989. Cert. law libr., med. libr. III. Libr. Ohio State U., Columbus, 1952-59; libr., instr. U. Ill., Urbana, 1962-63; lectr. U. Ill. Grad. Sch. Libr. Sci., 1964; libr., instr. Morris Libr. So. Ill. U., Carbondale, 1964-67; classroom instr. So. Ill. U Coll Edn., 1967-70; med. libr., asst. prof. Morris Libr. So. Ill. U., 1972-74, law libr., asst. prof., 1974-79, law libr., assoc. prof., 1979-85, law libr., prof., 1985-92, prof. emerita, 1993—. Author: Access Points to Law Libraries, 1984, 17th Century English Law Reports, 1986, Law Library Reference Shelf, 1988, 4th edit., 1999, Pages and Missing Pages, 1983, 2d edit., 1989, Lincoln as a Lawyer: An Annotated Bibliography, 1991. Mem. AAUW (pres. 1976-78, corp. rep. 1978-88), Am. Assn. Law Librs., Beta Phi Mu, Phi Kappa Phi. Methodist. Home: 811 S Skyline Dr Carbondale IL 62901-2405 Office: So Ill U Law Libr Carbondale IL 62901

MATTHEWS, ESTHER ELIZABETH, education educator, consultant; b. Princeton, Mass., June 20, 1918; d. Ralph Edgar and Julia Ellen (Cronin) M. BS in Edn., Worcester State Coll., 1940; EdM, Harvard U., 1943, EdD, 1960. Tchr. various Mass. schs., 1942-47; guidance dir. Holden (Mass.) Pub. Schs., 1947-53, Wareham (Mass.) Pub. Schs., 1954-57; counselor Newton (Mass.) High Sch., 1957-60, head counselor, 1960-66; assoc. prof. edn. U. Oreg., 1966-70, prof. edn., 1970-80, prof. emerita, 1980—. Vis. prof. U. Toronto, Ont., Can., summer 1971; lectr. on edn. Harvard U., 1963-66; cons. in field; lectr. various colls. and univs. Author book chpts.; contbr. numerous articles to profl. jours. and papers to conf. proc.; featured in spl. issue of Oreg. Counseling Assn. Jour., 1998. Recipient ACD award for contbn. to promote human rights, 1987. Mem. Nat. Vocat. Guidance Assn. (pres. 1974-75, chair nat. com. 1966-67, sec. 1967-68, bd. trustees 1968-71, editl. bd. Vocat. Guidance Quar. 1966-68), Oreg. Pers. and Guidance Assn. (Leona Tyler award 1973, Disting. Svc. award 1979), Oreg. Career Devel. Assn. (Disting. Svc. award 1987, Esther E. Matthews Ann. award established in her honor 1993). Home: 832 Lariat Dr Eugene OR 97401-6438

MATTHEWS, EUGENE EDWARD, artist; b. Davenport, Iowa, Mar. 22, 1931; s. Nickolas Arthur and Velma (Schroeder) M.; m. Wanda Lee Miller, Sept. 14, 1952; children: Anthony Lee, Daniel Nickolas. Student, Bradley U., 1948-51; BFA, U. Iowa, 1953, MFA, 1957. Prof. fine arts grad. faculty U. Colo., Boulder, 1961-96, prof. fine arts emeritus, 1996—, dir. vis. artists program, 1985-96. Vis. artist Am. Acad. Rome, 1989. One-man shows include U. Wis., Milw., 1960, Brena Gallery, Denver, 1963, 65, 67, 70, 74, 76, 78, 80, 83, 88, Colorado Springs Fine Arts Ctr., 1967, Sheldon Art Gallery, U. Nebr., 1968, Denver Art Mus., 1972, James Yu Gallery, N.Y.C., 1973, 77, Dubins Gallery, L.A., 1981, Galeria Rysunku, Poznan, 1983, CU. Art Galleries, U. Colo., Boulder, 1996, Rule Art Gallery, Denver, 1998; exhibited in numerous group shows U.S., Europe, Africa, Asia; internat. watercolor exhbn. New Orleans, 1983, Louvre, Paris, Met. Mus. of Art, N.Y.C., Internat. Art Ctr., Kyoto, Japan, Mus. of Modern Art, Rijeka, Yugoslavia, Taipei Fine Arts Mus., Taiwan, Republic of China, Internat. Watercolor Biennial-East/West, Champaign, Ill., 1997; represented in permanent collections Nat. Mus. Am. Art, Washington, Denver Art Mus., Butler Inst. Am. Art, Chrysler Art Mus., others. Recipient Penello d'Argento award Acitrezza Internazionale, 1958, S.P.Q.R. Cup of Rome, Roma Olimpionica Internazionale, 1959, Gold medal of honor Nat. Arts Club, N.Y.C., 1969, Bicentennial award Rocky Mountain Nat. Watercolor Exhbn., 1976, Am. Drawings IV Purchase award, 1982, others; fellow in painting Am. Acad. Rome, 1957-60, U. Colo. Creative Rsch. fellow, 1966-67. Mem. Watercolor U.S.A. Honor Soc. (charter). Home: 720 Hawthorn Ave Boulder CO 80304-2140

MATTHEWS, FRANK, retired pathologist; b. Chgo., Feb. 13, 1931; s. Warren B. and Martha Nancy (Eakes) M.; m. Elizabeth Jean Wilson, June 13, 1953; children: Susanna Dell, Margaret Ann, Beverly Jean. BS, Emory U., 1951; MD, U. Mich., 1954. Diplomate Am. Bd. Pathology. Intern Boston City Hosp., 1954-55; resident pathology U. Mich., 1955-59; chief pathologist DeKalb Med. Ctr., Decatur, Ga., 1961-97. Courtesy staff Decatur Hosp., Eastside Med. Ctr., DeKalb Med. Ctr., Winder-Barrow Hosp.; pres. PSPA Reg. Lab., Decatur, 1970-78; cons. Ga. Bd. Health, 1967-70, Blood Bank, ARC, 1965—. Contbr. articles to profl. jours. Mem. Coll. Am. Pathologists (bd. govs. 1977-84, pathologist of the yr. 1984), Atlanta Soc. Pathologists (pres. 1963), Ga. Assn. Pathologists (pres., bd. dirs.), DeKalb Med. Soc. (pres. 1987), Rotary (pres. 1987-88). Methodist. Avocation: choral singing. Home: 2544 River Oak Dr Decatur GA 30033-2803

MATTHEWS, GAIL THUNBERG, marketing executive; b. Hartford, Conn., July 29, 1938; d. Harold Einar and Mildred (Wentland) Thunberg; m. Glenn Holbrook Matthews, Aug. 9, 1959; children: Scott Holbrook, Brett Holbrook. Student, Boston U., 1958-59. Hostess show, copywriter Sta. WJDA, Boston, 1956-58; fashion coord. Jordan Marsh, 1958-59, Miller & Rhoades, Richmond, Va., 1959-60, Sage Allen, Hartford, 1960-61; columnist Boston Globe, 1962-63, Hartford Times, 1961-63; freelance writer, contbr. articles to New Englander mag. Christian Sci. Monitor, Yankee, 1961-65; v.p., treas. Coll. Mktg. Group, Inc.(GMGi), Winchester, Mass., 1968-86. Corporator Reading Savings Bank; mem. adv. coun. Baybank Middlesex; coord. Harrods London, New London, 1992, Brit. Isles Festival for Scotland-England, Wales, No. Ireland by Brit. Dept. Trade and Industry for New London, 1994—. Author: Hors'd'oeuvre Cooking, 1966, Gourmet Cooking, 1966, Birthday Fortune Book, 1967, (children's series) The Adventures of a Shih Tzu, The Good Luck Puppy, 1980; co-host TV show Kearsarge Valley Magazine. Choral dir. Barrows Sch., Reading; pres. local PTA; chmn. Heart Fund, Reading; founder, chmn. Reading chpt. Am. Cancer Soc., Love Lights a Tree chpt. New London Am. Cancer Soc.; pres. Kimpton Brook Gardens Restorations; coord. London, Eng.-New London, N.H. Twinning, 1992, anniversary oldest theatre N.H., 1993; founder smart baby program New London Hosp. Birth Ctr., 1999; founder Nurses Appreciation Fund, Lahey Clinic, Burlington, Mass., 2001. Recipient Svc. to Youth award Reader's Digest, 1962, CAP award, 1965, Spl. award Am. Cancer Soc., 1981-82, Citizenship award Reading Tchrs. Assn, 1980; named Citizen of Yr., New London Am. Cancer Soc., 1983-84. Mem.: Women Who Make a Difference (founder), Dartmouth Coll. Women's Assn. (bd. dirs., founder mammography fund for women in need), Antiquarian Soc., Rose Hill Equestrian Club.

MATTHEWS, GEORGE ROBERT, retired radiologist; b. Paoli, Pa., 1915; BA, Ursinus Coll., 1936; MD, Temple U., 1940. Diplomate Am. Bd. Radiology. Intern Reading Hosp., West Reading, Pa., 1940-41, resident in radiology, 1948-51, assoc. in radiology, 1951-69, chief, dept. dir., 1969-80, emeritus mem. staff, 1980—. Mem. AMA, Am. Coll. Radiology.

MATTHEWS, GILBERT ELLIOTT, investment banker; b. Brookline, Mass., Apr. 24, 1930; s. Martin W. and Charlotte (Cohen) M.; m. Anne Lisbeth Barnett, Apr. 20, 1958 (div. 1975); children: Lisa Joan, Diana Kory (dec. 1995); m. Elaine Rita Siegal Pulitzer, Jan. 2, 1978 (div. 1999); 1 child, Jennifer Rachel. AB, Harvard U., 1951; MBA, Columbia U., 1953. Chartered fin. analyst. Dept. mgr. Bloomingdale's, N.Y.C., 1953, 56-60; security analyst Merrill Lynch, 1960; investment banker Bear, Stearns & Co., 1960-95, gen. ptnr., 1979-85; mng. dir. Bear, Stearns & Co. Inc., 1985-86, sr. mng. dir., 1986-95, Sutter Securities Inc., San Francisco, 1995—, chmn. bd. dirs., 1997—. Bd. dirs. Oak Industries, Inc., Waltham, Mass. Served as lt. (j.g.) USN, 1953-56. Mem. N.Y. Soc. Security Analysts. Democrat. Jewish. Office: Sutter Securities Inc One Sansome St Ste 3950 San Francisco CA 94104

MATTHEWS, JAMES SHADLEY, lawyer; b. Omaha, Nov. 24, 1951; s. Donald E. and Lois Jean (Shadley) M.; m. Mary Kvaal, May 3, 1991; 1 child, Katherine. BA cum laude, St. Olaf Coll., 1973; JD, U. Ill., 1976; MBA, U. Denver, 1977. Bar: Minn. 1976, U.S. Dist. Ct. Minn. 1978. With Northwestern Nat. Life Ins. Co., Mpls., 1978-89, v.p., asst. gen. counsel, 1985-89; ptnr. Lindquist & Venum, Mpls., 1990—. Sr. v.p., gen. counsel Washington Square Capital, Inc., 1989; sec. NWNL Health Network, Inc., St. Paul, 1987-89; pub. dir. Minn. Health Reins. Assn., 1992-94; bd. dirs. Northstar Life Ins. Co.; spkr. in field. Mem. ABA, Am. Health Lawyers Assn., Minn. Bar Assn. (chmn. health law sect. 1986-87). Office: Lindquist & Vennum IDS Ctr 80 S 8th St Ste 4200 Minneapolis MN 55402-2274 E-mail: jmatthews@lindquist.com.

MATTHEWS, JAMES MARK, civil engineer, educator; b. Kavali, India, Aug. 12, 1961; came to the U.S., 1986; s. Krishnamurthy and Vara Lakshmi (Kavaturu) Tangella. MS, U. Calif., Berkeley, 1988, PhD, 1989. Registered profl. engr., Pa. Asst. rsch. engr. inst. transp. studies U. Calif., Berkeley, 1989-90; dir. transp. engring. divsn. civil engring. dept. Temple U., Phila., 1991—. Mem. nat. roster on disaster svcs. and human resources ARC, Washington, 1994. Named Phila. Transp. Engr. of Yr., ASCE, 1994, Delaware Valley Young Engr. of Yr., Phila. Club Engrs., 1993, Outstanding Faculty of Coll. of Engring., Temple U. Coll. of Engring. Alumni Assn., 1995. Mem. NSPE (nat. com. on rsch. 1993-94), Pa. Soc. Profl. Engrs. (bd. dirs. Phila. chpt. 1993—). Home: 1914 N Park Ave Apt C Philadelphia PA 19122 Office: Temple U Civil Engring Dept 12 and Norris St Philadelphia PA 19122

MATTHEWS, JOHN FLOYD, writer, educator; b. Cin., Apr. 8, 1919; s. Floyd L. and Helen (Orth) M.; m. Maurine Zollman, Mar. 4, 1945 (dec. 1959); children— Lauralee Alice, Caroline Elaine (dec.); m. Brenda Martin, Aug. 27, 1966. Student, Wooster Coll., 1935-37, Northwestern U., 1937; BA, U. Cin., 1940, postgrad., 1940-41, Columbia U., 1943, New Sch. for Social Research, 1944-45. Lectr. New Sch. for Social Research, 1948-50; lectr., chmn. faculty Dramatic Workshop and Tech. Inst., N.Y.C., 1950-52; lectr. in playwriting CCNY, 1947-63; asst. prof. dramatic lit. and history Brandeis U., 1952-59, assoc. prof., 1959-67, Schulman prof., 1967-71, chmn. dept. theatre, 1955-58, prof. Am. studies, 1971—, chmn. dept. Am. studies, 1973-74, Richter prof. Am. Civilization and Instns., 1972-84, prof. emeritus, 1984—. Vis. critic Yale Sch. Drama, 1965; mem. Seminar in Am. Studies, Circle Cultural de Royaumont, France, 1965; founding mem. Brandeis Creative Arts Awards Commn. Network radio actor, writer, producer, 1939-45, screenwriter, Warner Bros., 1945; author: plays, including The Scapegoat, 1950, Michael and Lavinia, 1956, Barnum, 1962; books The Old Vic In America, 1946, El Greco, 1952, Shaw's Dramatic Criticism, 1959, George Bernard Shaw, 1969, Reflections on Abortion, 1976; contbr. fiction to lit. mags.; cons., play doctor for script and prodn. problems of numerous Broadway and off-Broadway plays and musicals including Anastasia, The First Gentleman, others; TV scriptwriter for maj. networks, 1955-64; screenwriter, MGM, United Artists, Asso. Screen Prodns., Toronto, Ont., Can., 1958-64; Contbg. editor: Library of Living Painters, 1949-51, Dictionary of the Arts, 1946, Ency. World Biography, 1970. Mem. Westport (Conn.) Democratic Town Com., 1959-64; mem. Newton (Mass.) Republican City Com., 1977—, Mass. Rep. Platform Com., 1978; bd. dirs. Newton Taxpayers Assn., 1979-81, 86-91. Recipient Arts of the Theatre Found. award, 1950 Mem. Brit. Drama League, The Nat. Trust, English Speaking Union, Trustees of Reservations. Episcopalian. Home: 5 Tudor Close Dean Court Rd Rottingdean BN1 7DF England

MATTHEWS, KATHLEEN SHIVE, biochemistry educator; b. Austin, Tex., Aug. 30, 1945; d. William and Gwyn Shive; m. Randall Matthews. BS in Chemistry, U. Tex., 1966; PhD in Biochemistry, U. Calif., Berkeley, 1970. Post doctoral fellow Stanford (Calif.) U., 1970-72; mem. faculty Rice U., Houston, 1972—, chair dept., 1987-95, Wiess prof., 1989-96, Stewart Meml. chair, 1996—, dean natural scis., 1998—. Mem. BBCB study sect. NIH, Bethesda, Md., 1980-84, 86-88, BRSG adv. com., 1992-94; mem. adv. com. on rsch. programs Tex. Higher Edn. Coord. Bd., Austin, 1987-92; mem. undergrad. edn. initiative rev. panel Howard Hughes Rsch. Inst., Bethesda, 1991, mem. rsch. resources rev. panel, 1995, mem. predoctoral fellowships rev. panel, 2001. Mem. editl. bd. Jour. Biol. Chemistry, 1988-93, assoc. editor, 1994-99; contbr. 140 reviewed papers. Fellow AAAS; mem. Am. Soc. Biochemistry and Molecular Biology (nominating com. 1993-94, 96-97, fin. com. 2001—), Protein Soc., Biophys. Soc., Pub. Affairs Com. 2001-, Am. Chem. Soc., Phi Beta Kappa. Office: Rice Univ PO Box 1892 6100 Main St MS102 Houston TX 77005-1892 E-mail: ksm@rice.edu.

MATTHEWS, LELAND RAY, obstetrician-gynecologist; b. North Vernon, Ind., June 1, 1941; MD, Ind. U., 1966. Diplomate Am. Bd. Ob-Gyn. Intern Butterworth Hosp., Grand Rapids, Mich., 1966-67, resident in ob-gyn., 1969-72; med. staff Bloomington Hosp., Ind., 1972—; clin. asst. prof. ob-gyn. Ind. U. Med. Sch., 1973—. Mem. Am. Coll. Ob-Gyn., Am. Fertility Soc., Ctr. Assn. of Obs.-Gyn., Ind. State Med. Assn. Office: Aegis Womens Healthcare 421 W 1st St Bloomington IN 47403-2403

MATTHEWS, LEONARD SARVER, advertising and marketing executive; b. Glendean, Ky., Jan. 6, 1922; s. Clell and Zetta Price (Sarver) M.; m. Dorothy Lucille Fessler; children: Nancy, James, Douglas. BS summa cum laude, Northwestern U., 1948. With Leo Burnett Co., Inc., Chgo., 1948-75, v.p., dir., 1958-59, exec. v.p. charge mktg. services, 1959-61, exec. v.p. client svc., 1961-69, pres., 1970-75; asst. sec. commerce for domestic and internat. bus., 1976; pres., exec. com., dir. Young and Rubicam, 1977-78; pres. Am. Assn. Advt. Agys., 1979-89; co-founder Matthews & Johnston, Stamford, Conn., 1989-92; chmn. Next Century Media, 1992—. Mem. adv. bd. Adcom, Carlsbad, Calif., Ambient Capital, Beverly Hills, Calif., Scripps Capital, San Diego, D2 Media, Intuitive Design. Ensign USCGR, 1942-46. Named to Advt. Hall of Fame, 1999. Mem. Advt. Coun. (life bd. dirs.), Sky Club (N.Y.C.), Pine Valley Golf Club (N.J.), Rancho Santa Fe Golf (Calif.), Georgetown Club (Washington), Delta Sigma Pi, Beta Gamma Sigma. Republican. Lutheran. Office: PO Box 2629 Rancho Santa Fe CA 92067-2629

MATTHEWS, MANYALIBO JOSEPH, physicist, researcher; b. Berkeley, Calif., Mar. 14, 1970; s. Kwame Mugodo and Elizabeth Rodriguez. BS, U. Calif., Davis, 1993; PhD in Physics, MIT, 1998. Part-time rsch. asst. Lawrence Berkeley Labs., 1988-91; cons. Lawrence Livermore (Calif.) Nat. Lab., 1994-95; mem. tech. staff Bell Labs., Lucent Technologies, Murray Hill, N.J., 1998—. Tech. cons., Bronx, N.Y., 1998-99; inventor in field. Chmn. Nat. Conf. of Black Physics Students, Cambridge, 1997; physics instr. Interphase Program, Cambridge, 1995; student mentor, advisor U. Calif., Davis, 1990-92. Grad. fellow NSF, 1993; Ronald E. McNair scholar U. Maine, 1992. Mem. Am. Phys. Soc., Materials Rsch. Soc., Alpha Phi Alpha (pres. U. Calif. 1991-93, advisor MIT 1996-98, Exceptional Svc. 1998). Avocations: saxophone, cooking, running, travel. Office: Bell Labs Lucent Technologies 600 Mountain Ave # 1a361 New Providence NJ 07974-2008

MATTHEWS, MILDRED SHAPLEY, scientific editor, freelance writer; b. Pasadena, Calif., Feb. 15, 1915; d. Harlow and Martha (Betz) Shapley; m. Ralph Vernon Matthews, Sept. 25, 1937; children:: June Lorrain, Bruce Shapley, Melvin Lloyd, Martha Alys. AB, U. Mich., 1936. Rsch. asst. Calif. Inst. Tech., Pasadena, 1950-61; bilingual editor, rsch. asst. Astron. Obs. Merate-Milan and Trieste, Italy, 1960-70; rsch. asst. Lunar-Planetary Lab., editor space sci. series U. Ariz., Tucson, 1970-96; retired, 1996. Contbr. articles to Sky and Telescope, Astronomia. Recipient Masursky Meritorious Svc. award div. planetary sci. Am. Astron. Soc., 1993. Avocations: classical music concerts, especially opera, travel. Home: 1600 Milvia St Berkeley CA 94709-2012

MATTHEWS, NORMAN STUART, department store executive; b. Boston, Jan. 13, 1933; s. Martin W. and Charlotte (Cohen) M.; m. Joanne Banks, June 11, 1956; children: Gary S., Jeffrey B., Patricia A. BA, Princeton U.; MBA, Harvard U. Ptnr. Beacon Mktg. and Advt. Assocs., N.Y.C., 1956-71; sr. v.p. Broyhill Furniture Co., Lenoir, N.C., 1971-73, E.J. Korvettes, N.Y.C., 1973-78; chmn., chief exec. officer Gold Circle Stores, Columbus, Ohio, 1978-82; vice chmn. Federated Dept. Stores, Cin., from 1982, pres., chief oper. officer, 1987-88, retail cons., 1988—. Dir. Progressive Corp., Cleve., Sunoco, Phila.; bd. dirs. Finlay Fine Jewelry, N.Y.C., Galyan's Trading Co., Indpls., Toys 'R' Us, Paramus, NJ, Henry Schein, Inc., Melville, NY. Office: 650 Madison Ave New York NY 10022-1029

MATTHEWS, PAUL AARON, lawyer; b. Memphis, May 7, 1952; s. Joseph Curtis and Sarah Rebecca (Barret) M.; m. Roberta Bartow, July 29, 1978; children: Sarah Pierrepont, Elizabeth Barret. AB, Duke U., 1974; JD, Vanderbilt U., 1977. Bar: Tenn. 1977, U.S. Dist. Ct. (we. dist.) Tenn. 1977, U.S. Dist. Ct. (ea. dist.) Mich. 1987, U.S. Dist. Ct. (ea. dist.) Tenn. 1991, U.S. Ct. Appeals (6th cir.) 1991, U.S. Dist. Ct. (ea. and we. dists.) Ark. 1995, U.S. Dist. Ct. (mid. dist.) Tenn. 1998, U.S. Dist. Ct. (no. and so. dists.) Miss. 2000, U.S. Supreme Ct. 1998; cert. in bus. bankruptcy law and consumer bankruptcy law, Am. Bd. Certification and Tenn. Comm. on Cont. Legal Edn. and Specialization. Assoc. Armstrong Allen, PLLC, Memphis, 1977-82, ptnr., mem., 1982—. Chief justice Vanderbilt Law Sch. Moot Ct. Bd., Nashville, 1976-77. Co-author: Passport to Tennessee History, 1996; contbg. editor: Martindale-Hubbell Tenn. Law Digest, 1994—99; contbr. articles to profl. publs. Com. chmn. Memphis-in-May Internat. Festival, 1977-79, Tenn. Hist. Commn., 1987-97; bd. dirs. Davies Manor Assn., Brunswick, Tenn., 1994-99, pres. 1996-97; mem. Leadership Memphis Class of 1987, alumni adv. coun., 2000—; trustee Tenn. Hist. Commn. Found., 1998—, Shelby County Hist. Commn., 1997—, vice-chmn. 1999, chmn., 2000-01; commr. Tenn. Wars Commn., 1994-97; vestry Episcopal Ch. of the Holy Communion, 1995-98; trustee St. Mary's Episcopal Sch., 2001—. Recipient Newman award Memphis Heritage, Inc., 1992. Fellow, Tenn. Bar Found.; mem. ABA, SAR (Isaac Shelby chpt.), Am. Bankruptcy Inst., Tenn. Bar Assn., Memphis Bar Assn. (publs. coun. 1990-98, bd. dirs. 1999-2001, jud. practice and procedures com. 2000—), Memphis and Shelby County Mental Health Assn. (pres. 1984-85), Duke U. Alumni Assn. (pres. Memphis chpt. 1986-88), Descendants of Early Settlers of Shelby County (v.p. 1999—), Sigma Alpha Epsilon. Episcopalian. Home: 4271 Heatherwood Ln Memphis TN 38117-2302

MATTHEWS, ROWENA GREEN, biological chemistry educator; b. Cambridge, Eng., Aug. 20, 1938; (father Am. citizen); d. David E. and Doris (Cribb) Green; m. Larry Stanford Matthews, June 18, 1960; children: Brian Stanford, Keith David. BA, Radcliffe Coll., 1960; PhD, U. Mich., 1969. Instr. U. S.C., Columbia, 1964-65; postdoctoral fellow U. Mich., Ann Arbor, 1970-75, asst. prof., 1975-81, assoc. prof. biol. chemistry, 1981-86, prof., 1986—, assoc. chmn., 1988-92, G. Robert Greenberg disting. univ. prof., 1995—, chair biophysics rsch. divsn., 1996—2001. Mem. phys. biochemistry study sect. NIH, 1982-86; mem. adv. coun. Nat. Inst. Gen. Med. Scis., NIH, 1991-94; adv. bd. NATO, 1994-96; mem. Commn. on Advancement of Women and Minorities in Sci., Engring. and Tech. Devel., 1999; mem. faculty Life Scis. Inst., 2002—. Mem. editl. adv. bd. Biochem. Jour., 1984-92, Arch. Biochemistry, Biophysics, 1992-97, Biochemistry, 1993—, Jour. Bacteriology, 1995—; contbr. articles to profl. jours. Recipient Merit award Nat. Inst. Gen. Med. Scis., 1991-2001; NIH grantee, 1978—, NSF grantee, 1992—. Fellow AAAS, NAS; mem. Am. Soc. Biochem. and Molecular Biology (program chair 1995, chair human resources 1996-98, William C. Rose award 2000), Am. Chem. Soc. (program chair biochemistry divsn. 1985, sec. biochemistry divsn. 1990-92, chair 1994-96, Repligen award 2001), Phi Beta Kappa, Sigma Xi. Avocations: bicycling, snorkeling, cross country skiing, cooking, gardening. Office: U Mich Biophysics Rsch Divsn 4028 Chemistry 930 N University Ave Ann Arbor MI 48109-1001 E-mail: rmatthew@umich.edu.

MATTHEWS, STEPHEN PHILIP, trade association administrator; b. Mar. 17, 1949; BS, East Ctrl. Okla. State U., 1976. Sr. adminstr. asst. Office of Gov., Okla., 1977-86; exec. dir. Okla. Dept. Econ. Edn., 1987-89; spl. asst. U.S. Congress House Appropriations Com., 1989-99; v.p. distilled spirits coun. U.S., Inc., Washington; pres., CEO Govt. Rels., LLC, Va., 1999—. Home and Office: 13106 Brook Mist Ln Fairfax VA 22033 E-mail: gr_llc@msn.com.

MATTHEWS, STEVE ALLEN, lawyer; b. Columbia, S.C., Oct. 11, 1955; s. Philip Garland and Vernecia Neely (Wilson) M.; m. Caroline Elizabeth FitzSimons, Sept. 26, 1987; children: Philip Garland II, Nathalie FitzSimons, Caroline Salley. BA in History, U. S.C., 1977; JD, Yale U., 1980. Bar: S.C. 1980, D.C. 1982. Assoc. Boyd, Knowlton, Tate & Finlay, Columbia, 1980-81, Dewey, Ballantine, Bushby, Palmer & Wood, Washington, 1981-85; spl. counsel to asst. atty. gen. Civil Rights Div. U.S. Dept. Justice, 1985-86, dep. asst. atty. gen. for jud. selection, Office of Legal Policy, 1986-88; exec. asst. to U.S. Atty. Gen., 1988; mem. Haynsworth Sinkler Boyd, PA, Columbia, 1988—, mng. ptnr., 2001—. Mem. Federalist Soc., Nat. Assn. Bond Lawyers (bd. dirs. 1995-96), Am. Coll. Bond Counsel (bd. dirs. 1995-99), Collegiate Network, Inc. (chmn. bd. dirs.), Fed. Comms. Bar Assn., Phila. Soc., St. Andrews Soc. Columbia. Office: Haynsworth Sinkler Boyd PA 1426 Main St Ste 1200 Columbia SC 29201-2843

MATTHEWS, THOMAS MICHAEL, former energy company executive; b. Luling, Tex., May 20, 1943; s. Chester Raymond and Mary Lucille (Stutts) M.; m. Sherry Dianne Klein, May 25, 1968; children: Stephanie Dianne, Leslie Michelle. BSCE, Tex. A & M U., 1965; postgrad., U. Okla., 1967, UCLA, 1975, Stanford U., 1988, Columbia U., 1993. Staff engr. Exxon Co. USA, Houston, New Orleans, 1965-69, project engr. L.A., 1974-76, div. engr. Houston, 1969-74, engring. mgr. Anchorage, 1976-78; v.p. Exxon Gas, Houston, 1978-81, Tenn. Gas/Tenneco, Houston, 1981-86, pres., 1986-89; v.p., gen. mgr. Texaco USA, Houston, 1989—; pres. Texaco Gas, 1990-93; pres., CEO Texaco Refining & Mktg., Inc.; v.p. Texaco, Inc.; pres. NGC Corp., 1996-98; chmn., CEO & pres. Avista Corp., Wash. Power Co., Spokane, 1998—2001; mem. bd. dir. Global Water Tech. Inc., Denver, 2002—. Dir. Offshore Tech. Ctr., Tex. A & M U., 1987-89, adv. coun.; bd. dirs. Inroads, Inc. Contbr. articles to profl. jours.; inventor in field. Pres., chmn. Ponderosa Forest Community Council, Houston, 1980-85; mem. PTO, Scenic Pk. Sch., Anchorage, 1976-78. Mem. NSPE (bd. dirs.), Soc. Petroleum Engrs., Soc. Ga. Assn., Am. Petroleum Inst., Natural Gas Supply Assn., Gas Rsch. Inst., Petroleum Club, Northgate Forest Country Club. Republican. Lutheran. Avocations: snow skiing, golf, reading, running, singing. Office: Global Water Tech. Inc. 1767 Denver W. Blvd. Golden CO 80401*

MATTHEWS, WARREN WAYNE, state supreme court justice; b. Santa Cruz, Calif., Apr. 5, 1939; s. Warren Wayne and Ruth Ann (Maginnis) M.; m. Donna Stearns, Aug. 17, 1963; children: Holly Maginnis, Meredith Sample. AB, Stanford U., 1961; LL.B., Harvard U., 1964. Bar: Alaska 1965. Assoc. firm Burr, Boney & Pease, Anchorage, 1964-69, Matthews & Dunn, Matthews, Dunn and Baily, Anchorage, 1969-77; assoc. justice Alaska Supreme Ct., 1977—, justice, chief justice. Bd. dirs. Alaska Legal Services Corp., 1969-70. Mem. Alaska Bar Assn. (bd. govs. 1974-77), ABA, Anchorage Bar Assn.*

MATTHEWS, WENDY SCHEMPP, psychologist, researcher; b. Bridgeport, Conn., Feb. 4, 1945; d. Harry Edward and Julie Schempp; m. Robert J. Matthews, Aug. 16, 1969 (div. June 1984); 1 child, Avery. BA, Arcadia U., 1966; MA, Cornell U., 1971, PhD, 1975; cert., Université de Paris, 1972. Rsch. assoc. Harvard U., Cambridge, Mass., 1977-78; jr. fellow N.J. Div. Human Svcs., Trenton, 1978; clin. assoc. prof. U. of Medicine & Dentistry of N.J., New Brunswick, 1979—; dir. children's ctr. Contemporary Psychology Inst., Skillman, N.J., 1983-87; pediatric psychologist N.J. Div. Youth & Family Svcs., Trenton, 1987—; pvt. practice Princeton, N.J., 1987—. Author: He & She: How Children Develop Their Sex Role Identity, 1977; contbr. articles to profl. jours.

MATTHEWS, WILLIAM ANDREW, construction equipment rental executive, consultant; b. Dallas, Nov. 24, 1934; s. Irving Eston and Veneda (Hicks) M.; Lourinda Marvourene Harvey, Apr. 10, 1954; children: Terri Dean, Michielle Renee, Martha Jane, Tracy Keith, William Andrew II. Cert. in rental mgmt., U. Tex., 1970. Cert. adminstrv. mgmt. Mgr. Beckman Tool Rental and Supply Co., Dallas, 1951-63; supr., facilitator Strawn Rentals, 1963-98. Lectr. in field. Author: With Water Came Fire, 1983, Alien - The Missing Link; contbr. articles to profl. jours.; inventor mobile robot, 1987. Vol. Tex. Civil Justice League, Austin, 1988. Recipient cert. of award Dallas Sales Exec. Club, 1952, Silver Cup award Tex. L.P. Gas Assn., 1975. Mem. NRA, Am. Rental Assn. (lectr. 1974, 75, 76, 83, 86, 88), Tex. Rental Assn. pres. 1978-79, dir. at large 1979-80, Disting. Rental Man 1980), Dallas County Rental Assn. (pres. 1977). Republican. Baptist. Avocations: study of ancient civilization, geology, aeronautics, astrophysics, astronomy. Home and Office: 300 Lake St Lake Dallas TX 75065-9801 E-mail: billnatthews01@msn.com.

MATTHEWS, WILLIAM D(OTY), lawyer, consumer products manufacturing company executive; b. Oneida, N.Y., Aug. 25, 1934; s. William L. and Marjorie L. (Doty) M.; m. Ann M. Morse, Aug. 4, 1956; children: Judith Anne, Thomas John. AB, Union Coll., 1956; LLB, Cornell U., 1960. Bar: N.Y. 1960, D.C. 1962. Atty. divsn. corp. fin. SEC, Washington, 1960-62; assoc. Whitlock, Markey & Tait, 1962-69; gen. counsel Oneida (N.Y.) Ltd., 1973-98, from v.p. to exec. v.p., 1977-86, also dir., chmn., CEO, 1986-2000. Bd. dirs. Oneida Fin. Corp., Conmed Corp.; trustee Oneida Savs. Bank. Alderman City of Oneida, 1972-79; mem. Madison County Bd. Suprs., 1984-86. Presbyterian. Home: 621 Patio Circle Dr Oneida NY 13421-1820

MATTHEWS, WYHOMME S. music educator, college administrator; b. Battle Creek, Mich., July 22, 1948; d. Woodrow R. and LouLease (Graham) Sellers; m. Edward L. Matthews, Apr. 29, 1972; children: Channing DuVall, Triston Curran, Landon Edward, Brandon Graham. AA, Kellogg C.C., 1968; MusB, Mich. State U., 1970, MA, MusM, Mich. State U., 1972. Cert. elem. and secondary tchr., Mich. Tchr., vocal music dir. Benton Harbor (Mich.) Pub. Schs., 1971-72, dir. vocal music, 1972; dir. edn. head start program Burlington (N.J.) County, 1972-73; pvt. music tchr., 1973-89; tchr. Southeastern Jr. H.S., 1986-87, W.K. Kellogg Jr. H.S., 1987-89; chair visual and performing arts dept. Kellogg C.C., Battle Creek, Mich., 1989-99, dir. Eastern acad. Ctr., 1999—. Part-time instr. Kellogg C.C., 1973-89, dir. Eclectic Chorale, 1973—, dir., organizer Kellogg C.C. Eclectic Chorale Sacred Cultural Festival, 1979—, judge various contests; artistic dir. Battle Creek Sojourner Truth Monument Presentation Day, 1999; presenter in field. Pres. Dudley Elem. Sch., 1981-85; active Battle Creek Pub. Schs. PTA, Pennfield Pub. Schs. PTA, Mt. Zion African Meth. Episc. Ch. Mich. State U. fellow, 1971; recipient Outstanding Cmty. Svc. award, 1975, Sojourner Truth award, 2000, George award City of Battle Creek, 2000. Mem. Mich. Music Tchr. Assn., Nat. Music Tchrs. Assn., Battle Creek Music Tchrs. Assn., Battle Creek Morning Music Club (bd. dirs.), Nat. Leadership Acad., Battle Creek Cmty. Concert Assn. Home: 466 Alton Ave Battle Creek MI 49017-3212 Office: Kellogg CC 450 North Ave Battle Creek MI 49017-3306 E-mail: matthewsw@kellogg.cc.mi.us.

MATTHIAS, GEORGE FRANK, retired educator; b. Aug. 22, 1934; s. George and Marguerite (Blanchard) M.; m. Mary Jo Avery, Aug. 18, 1956; children: Todd Avery, Tara Lynn. BS, SUNY, Cortland, 1957; MS, Syracuse U., 1962; MA, Conn. Wesleyan U., 1970. Tchr. secondary earth sci. Belleville (N.Y.) Acad., 1957-58, Croton-Harmon H.S., Croton-on-Hudson, N.Y., 1961-89; tchr., prin. Raquette Lake (N.Y.) Elem. Sch., 1958-61; ret., 1989. Mem. N.Y. State Earth Sci. Syllabus Revision Writing Commn., 1967-70, 89-91; coord. Bur. of Sci. Edn., N.Y. State Dept. Edn., 1971-72; instr. Finger Lakes Inst., Alfred U., 1970; guest staff Coll. of St. Rose, summers 1984-85, 88-90; freelance cons. earth science edn.; item writer Nat. Testing Service, Nat. Assessment for Ednl. Progress, 1984; cons. in field. Author: (with Berey, Higham, Knabel, Maust) Observation and Interpretation in Earth Science, 1972; (with Daley and Higham) Earth Science: A Study of a Changing Planet, 1986; (with Deacon) Plate Tectonics, 1980; developer: (with Snyder) Individualized Earth Science Program, 1975-89; (with Snyderetal) Prentice-Hall General Science Series, 1986, NYS Student Performance Examination (Ed. Assessment), 1994; contbr. articles to profl. jours. NSF grant, 1963, 67-70; Merit fellow Shell, 1971. Mem. Nat. Assn. Geology Tchrs., Nat. Assn. Rsch. in Sci. Tchg., Sci. Tchrs. Assn. N.Y. State, N.Y. State United Tchrs., Am. Fedn. Tchrs. Home and Office: 143 Dutch St Montrose NY 10548-1505 Fax: 914-739-3489. E-mail: gfmjmatt@mymailstation.com.

MATTHIAS, JOHN EDWARD, English literature educator; b. Columbus, Ohio, Sept. 5, 1941; s. John Marshall and Lois (Kirkpatrick) M.; m. Diana Clare Jocelyn, Dec. 27, 1967; children— Cynouai, Laura. BA, Ohio State U., 1963; MA, Stanford U., 1966; postgrad., U. London, 1967. Asst. prof. dept. English U. Notre Dame, Ind., 1966-73, assoc. prof., 1973-80, prof., 1980—. Vis. fellow Clare Hall, Cambridge U., 1966-77, assoc., 1977— ; vis. prof. dept. English, Skidmore Coll., Saratoga Springs, N.Y., 1975, U. Chgo., 1980. Author: Bucyrus, 1971, Turns, 1975, Crossing, 1979, Five American Poets, 1980, Introducing David Jones, 1980, Contemporary Swedish Poetry, 1980, Bathory and Lermontov, 1980, Northern Summer, New and Selected Poems, 1984, The Battle of Kosovo, 1987, David Jones: Man and Poet: A Gathering of Ways, 1991, Reading Old Friends, 1991, Swimming at Midnight, 1995, Beltane at Aphelion, 1995, Pages: New Poems and Cuttings, 2000. Recipient Columbia U. Transl. award, 1978, Swedish Inst. award, 1981, Poetry award Soc. Midland Authors, 1984, Ingram Merrill Found. award, 1984, 90; Woodrow Wilson fellow, 1963, Lily Endowment fellow, 1993; Fulbright grantee, 1966. Mem. AAUP, PEN, Poets and Writers, Poetry Soc. Am. (George Bogin Meml. award 1990). Office: U Notre Dame Dept English Notre Dame IN 46556

MATTHIAS, JUDSON STILLMAN, civil engineering educator, consultant; b. Scofield Barracks, Hawaii, Oct. 6, 1931; s. Norman Arthur and Charlotte Aleta (Stillman) M.; m. Georgia Stewart, June 9, 1956; children: Mary, Elizabeth, Judson Jr., Anne. BS, grad. U.S. Mil. Acad., 1954; MSCE, Oreg. State U., 1963; PhD, Purdue U., 1967. Commd. 2d lt. U.S. Army, 1954, resigned, 1961; instr. Oreg. State U., Corvallis, 1962-64, Purdue U., West Lafayette, Ind., 1964-67; prof. civil engring. Ariz. State U., Tempe, 1967—. Contbr. articles to profl. jours. Mem. Traffic Accident Reduction Program, Phoenix, 1982-85, Valley Forward, Phoenix, 1972-84. Grantee Fed. Hwy. Administrn., Evanston, Ill., 1980, Washington, D.C., 1982; elected Outstanding Engr. of Yr., Ariz. Soc. Profl. Engrs., 1986. Fellow Inst. Transp. Engrs.; mem. ASCE (hwy. and traffic safety), Am. Rd. and Transp. Builders Assn. (pres. ednl. div. 1984-185, bd. dirs. 1984-85), Transp. Research Bd. of Nat. Acad. of Scis. (univ. rep. 1971—). Home: 2032 E Laguna Dr Tempe AZ 85282-5915 Office: Ariz State U Dept Civil Engring Tempe AZ 85287

MATTHIES, FREDERICK JOHN, architectural engineer; b. Omaha, Oct. 4, 1925; s. Fred. J. and Charlotte Leota (Metz) M.; m. Carol Mae Dean, Sept. 14, 1947; children— John Frederick, Jane Carolyn Matthies Goding BSCE, Cornell U., 1947; postgrad., U. Nebr., 1952-53. Diplomate Am. Acad. Environ. Engrs.; registered profl. engr., Iowa, Nebr. Civil engr. Henningson, Durham & Richardson, Omaha, 1947-50, 52-54; sr. v.p. devel. Leo A. Daly Co., 1954-90; cons. engr., 1990—. Lectr. in field; mem. dist. export coun. U.S. Dept. Commerce, 1981-83. Contbr. articles to profl. publs. Mem. Douglas County Rep. Cen. Com., Nebr., 1968-72; bd. regents Augustana Coll., Sioux Falls., S.D., 1976-89; bd. dirs. Orange County Luth. Hosp. Assn., Anaheim, Calif., 1961-62, Nebr. Humanities Coun., 1988-94, Omaha-Shizuoka City (Japan) Sister City Orgn.; trustee Luth. Med. Ctr., Omaha, 1978-82; mem. adv. bd. Marine Mil. Acad., Harlingen, Tex. 1st lt. USMCR, 1943-46, 50-52, Korea. Fellow ASCE, Instn. Civil Engrs. (London, Euro Engr. European Econ. Commn.); mem. NSPE, Am. Water Works Assn. (life), Air Force Assn., Am. Legion, VFW, The Omaha Club. Lutheran. Home: 337 S 127th St Omaha NE 68154-2309

MATTHIES, MARY CONSTANCE T. lawyer; b. Baton Rouge, Mar. 22, 1948; d. Allen Douglas and Mazie (Poche) Tillman. B.S., Okla. State U., 1969; J.D., U. Tulsa, 1972. Bar: Okla. 1973, U.S. Ct. Appeals (10th cir.) 1974, U.S. Ct. Appeals (8th and D.C. cirs.) 1975, U.S. Supreme Ct. 1976. Assoc., ptnr. Kothe, Nichols & Wolfe, Inc., Tulsa, 1972-78; pres. sr. prin. Matthies Law Firm, P.C., Tulsa, 1978—; guest lectr. U. Tulsa Coll. Law, U. Okla. Sch. Law, Oral Roberts U. Sch. Contbr. articles to profl. jours; mem. staff Tulsa Law Jour., 1971-72. Fellow Am. Coll. of Labor and Employment Lawyers; mem. ABA (mem. spl. subcom. for liaison with EEOC, 1974—, spl. subcom. for liaison with OFCCP, 1979—, mgmt. co-chmn. equal employment law subcoms. on nat. origin discrimination 1974-75, class actions and remedies 1975-80), Okla. Bar Assn. (coun. mem. labor law sect. 1974-80, chmn. 1978-79), Women's Law Caucus, Phi Delta Phi. Presbyterian. Office: Thompson Bldg 20 E 5th St Ste 310 Tulsa OK 74103-4435 Business E-Mail: mattlawfrm@aol.com.

MATTICE, HOWARD LEROY, retired education educator; b. Roxbury, N.Y., Sept. 23, 1935; s. Charles Pierce and Loretta Jane (Ellis) M.; m. Elaine Grace Potts, Feb. 4, 1956; children: Kevin, Stephen. BA, King's Coll., 1960; MA, L.I. U., 1965, NYU, 1969; cert., CUNY, 1972; EdD, NYU, 1978. Cert. tchr. N.Y., clin. educators trainer, Fla. Dept. Edn. Social studies tchr. N.Y.C. Bd. Edn., 1961-90, mid. and jr. H.S. asst. prin., 1970-72, 73-75; assoc. prof. edn. and history Clearwater (Fla.) Christian Coll., 1990-92, chmn. divsn. of edn., prof. edn. and history, 1992-99, ret., 1999. Adj. lectr. history S.I. C.C., CUNY, 1969-75; curriculum writer N.Y.C. Bd. Edn., 1985; program reviewer Fla. Dept. Edn., Tallahassee, 1994—; item writer GED Testing Svc., Washington, 1988-92; mem. So. Assn. Colls. and Schs. Accreditation Team H.S., 1995—. Chmn. bd. New Dorp Christian Acad., S.I., 1973-90; chmn. bd. deacons New Dorp. Bapt. Ch., S.I., 1981-90. Mem. ASCD, Assn. Tchr. Educators, Nat. Coun. Social Studies, So. Assn. Colls. and Schs. (h.s. accreditation review team 1995—). Avocations: reading, traveling, gardening.

MATTILA, ANNA SIRKKU, marketing professional; BS, Cornell U., 1984, PhD, 1995; MBA, U. Hartford, 1986; cert., U. Sorbonne, Paris, 1987. Cons. Horwath & Horwath, Paris, 1987-88; faculty bus. adminstrn. Schiller U., 1988-91; rsch. asst. Cornell U., Ithaca, N.Y., 1991-95; asst. prof. Nat. U. of Singapore, 1995-97, Pa. State U., State College, 1998—. Vis. asst. prof. Cornell U., 1997-98. Contbr. articles to profl. jours. Seed grantee Coll. of Health and Human Devel., Pa. State U., 1998, competitive rsch. grant Nat. U. Singapore, 1996, 97, Cornell U., 1995; recipient Hospitality Mgmt. Studies award Paulon Saatio, 1991. Mem. Cornell Soc. of Hotelmen, Am. Mktg. Assn., Soc. for Consumer Psychology, Coun. on Hotel, Restaurant and Institutional Edn.

MATTILA, DANIEL E. priest, social worker; b. Santa Clara, Ca., Dec. 21, 1968; s. William Richard Mattila and Gloria Mae (Secola) Secola-Mattila. BA, Hamline U., 1991; MDiv, diploma in Anglican studies, Yale U., 1994; MSW, U. Conn., 1997. Cert. social worker N.Y.; Ordained to ministry Episcopal Ch. as priest 1995. Assisting priest St. John's Episcopal Ch., Bridgeport, Conn., 1994—96, priest-in-charge Sandy Hook, 2001—; Chaplain Bridgeport Hosp., 1994—95; priest-in-charge St. George's Episcopal Ch., Bridgeport, 1996—99; supervising therapist Cognitive Therapy Ctr. N.Y., N.Y.C., 1997—. Co-author: Comparative Treatments of Depression, 2002. Scholar N.Am. scholar, Fund for Theological Edn., 1992. Fellow: Acad. Cognitive Therapy (founder); mem.: NASW, Assn. for Clinical Pastoral Edn., Am. Orthopsychiat. Assn., Save the Manatees, Pi Gamma Mu, Psi Chi, Phi Kappa Phi, Phi Beta Kappa. Democrat. Episcopalian. Avocations: automobiles, travel, poetry. Home: 6133 Avalon Gates Trumbull CT 06611 Office: Cognitive Therapy Ctr NY 120 E 56th St Ste 530 New York NY 10022 Office Fax: 212-588-1998. Personal E-mail: dm@schematherapy.com.

MATTILA, MARY JO KALSEM, elementary and art educator; b. Canton, Ill., Oct. 26, 1944; d. Joseph Nelson and Bernice Nora (Milbauer) Kalsem; m. John Peter Mattila, Jan. 27, 1968. BS in Art, U. Wis., 1966; student, Ohio State U., 1972, Drake U., 1981; MS in Ednl. Adminstrn., Iowa State U., 1988. Cert. tchr., prin., supr., adminstr., art tchr., secondary tchr., Iowa. Tchr. 2d grade McHenry (Ill.) Pub. Schs., 1966-67, Wisconsin Hts. Schs., Black Earth, Wis., 1967-69; substitute tchr. Columbus (Ohio) City Schs., 1969-70; elem. art tchr. Southwestern City Schs., Columbus, 1972-73; adminstrv. intern Ames, Iowa, 1984-86; lead tchr. at Roosevelt Sch. Ames Cmty. Schs., 1986-87, art vertical curriculum chair, 1983-89, art educator, elem. and spl. edn., 1973—. Author articles. Active LWV, Ames, 1982—; fundraiser Altrusa, Ames, 1992—. Recipient Very Spl. Svc. award for Disting. Svc. in Very Spl. Arts, Gov. of Iowa, 1984. Mem. ASCD, NEA, Nat. Assn. Elem. Sch. Prins., Nat. Art Edn. Assn. Avocations: collecting old stoneware jugs, growing orchids, reading. Home: 2822 Duff Ave Ames IA 50010-4710 Office: Ames Cmty Schs 120 S Kellogg Ave Ames IA 50010-6719

MATTINGLY, J. VIRGIL, JR. federal lawyer; b. Leonardtown, Md., Oct. 18, 1944; BBA in Acctg., JD, George Washington U. Sr. atty. Fed. Res. Bd., Washington, 1974-79, asst. gen. counsel, 1979-81, assoc. gen. counsel, 1981-85, dep. gen. counsel, 1985-89, gen. counsel, 1989—. With JAGC, U.S. Army, 1970-74. Office: Fed Res Bd Bd Govs 20th & C Sts NW Washington DC 20551-0001

MATTINGLY, MACK FRANCIS, former ambassador, former senator, entrepreneur; b. Anderson, Ind., Jan. 7, 1931; m. Carolyn Longcamp, 1957 (dec.); children: Jane, Anne; m. Leslie Ann Davisson, 1998. BS, Ind. U., 1957. Acct. supr. IND, Arvin, Ind., 1957-59; mktg. mgr. IBM, Ga., 1959-79; owner, pres. M's Inc., 1975-80; U.S. senator from Ga., 1981-87; asst. sec. gen. def. support NATO, Brussels, 1987-90; amb. to Seychelles Dept. State, 1992-93. Spkr./author econ., def., fgn. policy, entrepreneur, 1993—; mem. U.S. Senate Com. Appropriations, chmn. legis and mil. constrn. subcoms.; mem. energy and water devel., agt. rural devel., treasury, postal svc. and gen. govt., mil. constrn. legis. subcoms., U.S. Senate com. Banking, Housing and Urban Affairs, chmn. rural housing, econ. policy subcoms.; mem. select com. ethics, 1981-83, joint econ. com., 1983-87; chmn. Rep. Com. on Coms., mem. Rep. Senate Leadership, 1985-87,, Holocaust Commn.; U.S. del. GATT, Geneva, 1982. Author 40 U.S. Sen. Bills, Amendments and Resolutions. Del. Atl. Sgt.-at-Arms, Rep. Nat. Convs., Del. Georgian Rep. Party Convs., 1964-90; chmn. 8th Dist. Goldwater for Pres., 1964, Ga. 8th Congl. Dist., Cand. U.S. Congress, 8th Dist., 1966; mem. Ga. Rep. Ctrl. Com.; mem. Ga. Exec. Com., vice chmn., 1968-75, chmn., 1975-77; elected 1st Rep. U.S. Senator from Ga. since 1871, 1980; bd. dirs. NOVECON., Cumberland Preservation Soc., Marshall Legacy Inst., Southeastern Legal Found., Compucredit Corp., InsiderAdvantage.com, Bus. Leadership Coun.; hon. mem. bd. dirs. M.L. King Jr. Fed. Holiday Commn., Brunswick Golden Isles C. of C. With USAF, 1951-55. Recipient S.E. Father of Yr. award 1984, Ga. Wildlife Fed. Conservationist of Yr. award 1985, Selective Svc. System Dist. Svc. Gold medal 1985, Watchdog of Treasury award 1981-86, Nat. Taxpayers Union Taxpayers Best Friend award 1981-86, NFIB's Guardian of Small Bus. award 1981-86, Am. Security Coun. award 1981-86, Sec. Def. medal for Outstanding Pub. Svc. 1988. Mem. Am. Legion. Episcopalian.

MATTIS, OLIVIA, musicologist; b. White Plains, N.Y., July 16, 1962; d. Daniel Charles and Noémi (Perelman) Mattis; m. Kenneth Eric Wayne, Sept. 1, 1991; 1 child Gabriel Noah Wayne. BA, Yale U., 1984; PhD, Stanford U., 1992. Rsch. dir. Man Ray Trust, Paris, 1992-94; instr. Stanford-in-Paris, 1992-94; rsch. assoc. U. Md., College Park, 1994-95; lectr. U. N.H., Durham, 1995-98, U. So. Maine, Gorham, 1996; founder, exec. dir. New Music Alliance, 1996—; dir. devel. Bowdoin Summer Music Festival, Brunswick, Maine, 1996-97; chair dept. music history Portland (Maine) Conservatory of Music, 1998-99. Mem. adv. bd. Portland Conservatory of Music, 1996—99; vis. asst. prof. musicology Eastman Sch. Music, Rochester, NY, 1999—2000, SUNY, Buffalo, 2002—. Assoc. editor: Critique Musicale d'Hector Berlioz, 1996; contbr. chapters to books, articles. Organizer Internat. Theremin (Music) Festival, 1997, Moog Fest, 2000. Recipient Deems Taylor award, ASCAP, N.Y.C., 1993; Lurcy fellow, Georges Lurcy Found., N.Y.C., 1988-89; Faculty Rsch. grant Susan B. Anthony Inst. U. Rochester, 1999. Mem. Theremin Enthusiasts Club Internat., Yale Club Western Maine (bd. dirs. 1998-99), Yale Club Western N.Y. Democrat. Jewish. Avocations: art, music, reading, travel. E-mail: omattis@webtv.net.

MATTISON, DONALD ROGER, physician, educator, medical administrator, military officer; b. Mpls., Apr. 28, 1944; s. Milford Zachary and Elizabeth Ruth (Davey) M.; m. Margaret Rose Libby, Jan. 28, 1967; children: Jon, Amy. BA cum laude in Chemistry and Math., Augsburg Coll., Mpls., 1966; MS in Chemistry, MIT, 1968; MD, Columbia U., 1973. Resident in ob-gyn Presbyn. Hosp., N.Y.C., 1973-75, 77-78; commd. rsch. assoc. USPHS, 1975, advanced through grades to comdr., 1984; rsch. assoc. Nat. Inst. Child Health and Human Devel., NIH, Bethesda, Md., 1975-77, med. officer, 1978-84; assoc. prof. ob-gyn. U. Ark., Little Rock, 1984-87; prof. U. Pitts., 1987-90, assoc. prof. toxicology, 1984-88, prof., 1988-90, dean Grad. Sch. Pub. Health, prof., 1990-99; medical dir. March of Dimes, 1998—. Mem. Bd. Environ. Studies and Toxicology, NRC, NAS, 1988—; mem. sci. adv. bd. Hawaii Heptachlor Edn. and Rsch. Found., 1987—; mem. sci. adv. panel Semicondr. Industry Assn., 1987—; mem. portfolio team United Way Allegheny County and Western Pa., 1990—; mem. pre-screening com. Magee-Women's Hosp., Pitts., 1990—; mem. steering com. Pa. Dept. Health, Harrisburg, 1990—; mem. com. Inst. Medicine, NAS, 1989-91, elected mem., 2000; cons. Women's Vietnam Health Study Protocol Devel., New England Rsch. Inst., 1986-90. Mem. editorial bd. Pediatric Pharmacology, 1980-87, Reproductive Toxicology, 1987—, Devel. Pharmacology and Therapeutics, Switzerland, 1987—, Reproductive Scis., The Info. Netork, 1989—, Methods in Toxicology, 1989—; guest editor Jour. Symposium on Reproductive Toxicology, Am. Jour. Indsl. Medicine, 1983; contbr. numerous articles, abstracts, letters and editorials to profl. publs. Recipient Am. Chem. Soc. medal Minn. sect. Am. Chem. Soc., 1966, Assn. Am. Publs. award, 1983. Fellow AAAS, 1997, Mem. APHA, Soc. Risk Analysis (editorial bd. jour. 1988—), Pitts. chpt. Soc. Risk Analysis, Am. Assn. Cancer Rsch., N.Y. Acad. Sci., Am. Coll. Toxicology, Am. Fertility Soc., Soc. Gynecologic Investigation, Soc. Toxicology. Avocations: photography, computer sciences, fly fishing, cross country skiing. Office: March of Dimes 1275 Mamaroneck Ave White Plains NY 10605-5298*

MATTISON, ELISA SHERI, organizational psychologist; b. Grand Rapids, Mich., Apr. 24, 1952; d. Andrew and Loraine R. Wierenga. BS cum laude, Western Mich. U., 1974, MA, 1979; postgrad., Fielding Inst., 1990. Trainer No. Inst., Anchorage, 1980; mgmt. cons., trainer Alaska Assocs. Human Devel. Inc., 1980-82; job devel. specialist Collins, Weed and Assocs., 1982-83; owner, pres., cons. Mattison Assocs. Inc., 1992—; enrollment advisor enrollment svcs. U. Alaska Anchorage, 2000—01; tng. program mgr. workforce and cmty. edn. Cmty. and Tech. Coll., 2001—. Mem. adj. faculty Anchorage Community Coll., 1981-82; work environment and design coord. ARCO Alaska Inc., 1983-86; cons. Employee Assts. Cons. Alaska, Anchorage, 1982; v.p. Human Resource Mgmt. and Mktg. Alaskan Fed. Credit Union, 1986-90; asst. dir. degree completeion program, adult and continuing edn., Alaska Pacific U., 1990-92, adj. faculty, 1990-93. Contbr. articles to profl. publs. Mem. Am. Soc. Tng. and Devel., Soc. Human Resource Mgmt. Office: 3211 Providence Dr Anchorage AK 99508-8046 E-mail: anesm@uaa.alaska.edu.

MATTISON, ROBERT MYRON, consultant, author, researcher; b. Key West, Fla., Nov. 23, 1954; s. Clarence L. and Eleanor (Kelly) M.; m. Brigitte Kilger, Nov. 10, 1979; children: Stephanie, Chris, Dustin, Peter. BS, U. Ill., Chgo., 1984. Cert. office automation prof. Cons. Safeway Tuckpointing, Des Plaines, Ill., 1976-85, AT&T, Skokie, 1985-87, Cap Gemini Am., Westchester, 1987-92, Deloitte & Toucet., Westchester, 1992-94, Sequent Computers, 1995-96, IBM, 1996—. Co-chair Unix Internat. Perfomance Mgmt. Work Group. Author: Understanding DBMS, 1992, Object Oriented Enterprise: Data Warehousing and Strategies, Technologies, Techniques, Data Mining for Telecommunications; contbr. articles to profl. jours. Bd. dirs. ALANO of Des Plaines, 1991—. Mem. IEEE, Assn. for Computing Machinery, Nat. Assn. Systems Programmers, Am. Mktg. Assn., DMA, NCDM. Republican. Avocations: scuba diving, camping, racquetball. Home: 114 Buxton Cir Pleasant Hill CA 94523-2043

MATTOLI, AGOSTINO MARRON, international business projects advisor; b. Rome, Feb. 23, 1938; s. Giorgio Mattoli and Doris Virginia Marron; m. Patrizia Chiavarelli Costa, June 11, 1966; children: Maurizio, Michele, Giorgio, Alessio, Agostino. BA in Arts and Sci., Rutgers U., 1962. Internat. advisor to pres. Fisvina, Rome, 1991-95; cons. Armemise Harva Found. Sci. Rsch. in Medicine, 1995—96; advisor, asst. to chmn. Armemise-Harvard Found. for Rsch. in Medicine, 1996—99; bd. dirs. Orders of the Royal House of Savoy, 2000—. Dir. bus. rels. Africa Ctr./Oil and Mineral Explorations, Rome and London, 1970-78; cons. Fada Pharm. Editor, founder (journal) Cambridge Transcontinental, 1957 (Spl. Fgn. Student award, 1958). Cons. internat. ops. Red Cross, Rome, 1996-2001. Named a knight, officer, Savoy Order SS Maurizio & Lazzaro, knight, Order San Tommaso D'Acre (min. Plemipotenziario for Chile), senator, Sacroromano Impero; recipient award for hunting achievements, Safari Club Internat., 1968—2000. Mem.: Gruppo Savoia, Royal Circolo Canottieri Tevere Remo (life socio senior 1975), Sons of Am. Revolution, Inst. of The Holy Roman Empire. Roman Catholic. Avocations: travel, sailing, yachting, big game hunting. Address: c/o MBE 328 via Lazio 10 00187 Rome Italy E-mail: trailmas@unete.cl.

MATTOON, JAMES RICHARD, biology educator; b. Loveland, Colo., Dec. 9, 1930; s. Arthur Maxwell and Margaret (Scilley) M.; m. Martha Jean McKissick, June 16, 1953; children: Thomas Edward, Jean Ellen. BS in Chemistry, U. Ill., 1953; MS in Biochemistry, U. Wis., 1954, PhD in Biochemistry, 1957. From instr. to asst. prof. chemistry U. Nebr., Lincoln, 1957-62; rsch. assoc. physiol. chemistry Johns Hopkins U. Sch. Medicine, Balt., 1962-64, from asst. to assoc. prof. physiol. chemistry, 1964-79; prof. biology U. Colo., Colorado Springs, 1979—, dir. Biotech Ctr., 1988—. Vis. prof. biochemistry Fed. U. Rio de Janeiro, 1975-77; vis. rsch. prof. Autonomous U. Mex., Mexico City, summer 1971, 74, San Marcos U., Lima, Peru, 1974, faculty of medicine U. Buenos Aires, summer 1980, 84, 93; organizing chmn. Rocky Mountain Microbrewing Symposium, Colorado Springs, 1995—. Contbr. rsch. articles to profl. jours. Fellow in chem. tchg. and rsch. Nat. Acad. Sci., U.S. and Brazil, 1975-77. Mem. Am. Chem. Soc., Am. Soc. for Biochemistry and Molecular Biology, Am. Soc. Brewing Chemists, Genetics Soc. of Am., Nat. Acad. Exact Phys. and Natural Scis. of Argentina (corr. mem.), Sigma Xi. Achievements include patent for enhancing production of hemoproteins. Avocations: gardening, reading, music. Home: 1090 Garlock Ln Colorado Springs CO 80918-3134 Office: Biotech Ctr 1420 Austin Bluffs Pkwy Colorado Springs CO 80918-3733 E-mail: jmattoon@corb.net., jmattoon@mail.uccs.edu.

MATTOON, PETER MILLS, lawyer; b. Bryn Mawr, Pa., Oct. 22, 1931; s. Harold Gleason and Marguerite Jeanette (Mills) M.; m. Mary Joan Henley, June 27, 1953; children: Pamela M. Zisselman, R. Stephen, Peter H., Philip P. AB, Dartmouth Coll., 1953; LLB, Harvard U., 1959; LLD (hon.), Widener U., 2001. Bar: Pa. 1960. Assoc. Ballard Spahr Andrews & Ingersoll, Phila., 1959-67; ptnr. Ballard Spahr Andrews & Ingersoll, LLP, 1967—2001. Mem. adv. bd. PNC Bank, Phila. Emeritus trustee The Episcopal Acad., Merion, Pa., 1970—, former chmn.; trustee, v.p. Widener Meml. Found., Lafayette Hill, Pa., 1972—; trustee Thomas Jefferson U., Phila., 1989—; overseer Widener U. Law Sch., Wilmington, 1979—. Served to lt. USN, 1953-56. Office: Ballard Spahr Andrews & Ingersoll LLP 1735 Market St Fl 51 Philadelphia PA 19103-7599

MATTOS, WILLIAM HAROLD, trade association executive, newspaper publisher; b. Calif., July 4, 1952; s. Irma A. Mattos; m. Susan Elizabeth Coelho, Nov. 11, 1978; children: Antoinette, Natalie. BS in Journalism, Calif. Polytech. State U., 1974; MS, U. Wis., 1975. Pres., pub. Mattos Newspapers, Inc., Newman, Calif., 1976—; pres. Calif. Poultry Fedn., Modesto, 1991—.

Dir. Stanislaus County Fair Bd., Turlock, Calif., 1993, Agrl. Network, Sacramento, Calif., 1994—. Bd. regents Stanislaus State U., Turlock, 1999; bd. govs. Doctor's Hosp., Modesto, Calif., 2001; area 9 coord. Gov. George W. Bush for Pres., Modesto, 2000; dir. Stanislaus County Fair, Turlock, Calif., 1994; campaign cabinet United Way of Stanislaus County, Modesto, 1999; bd. supr. Stanislaus County Bd. Suprs., 1990-91. Recipient John Silveira Meml. Svc. award Newman C. of C., 1990; named Outstanding Young Man of Am. Calif. Jaycees, 1986, Grand Marshall Newman Fall Festival, 1990, Disting. Citizen of Yr. Summer League Bseball, 1980; Paul Harris fellow Newman Rotary Club. Mem. Newman Rotary Club (Paul Harris fellow 1985), Phi Kappa Phi. Avocations: walking, swimming, travel, speaking. Office: Calif Poulty Fed 3117A McHenry Ave Modesto CA 95350

MATTRAN, DONALD ALBERT, management consultant, educator; b. Chgo., July 8, 1934; s. George Charles and Lucille Alice (Boule) M.; m. Betty Elena Flores, July 18, 1953 (div. Mar. 1988); children: Donald, Julie, Kimberly, Guy, Christy; m. Rose Lynn Castellano, May, 1988. B.Mus., U. Mich., 1957, M.Mus., 1960. Tchr. Van Buren Schs., Belleville, Mich., 1957-61; asst. prof. U. N.H., Durham, 1961-65, Boston U., 1965-66; assoc. prof. Hartt Sch. Music, West Hartford, Conn., 1966-82, dean, 1971-80; dir. Syracuse U. Sch. Music, N.Y., 1982-83; dean Sch. Fine and Performing Arts Montclair State Coll, Upper Montclair, N.J., 1983-87; pres. Sales Consultants of Sarasota (Fla.) Inc., 1987—. Cons. Music div. Kaman Corp., Bloomfield, Conn.; cons., evaluator Nat. Assn. Schs. of Music and Joint Commn. Theater and Dance Accreditation; guest condr. Hartford Symphony Orch., Hartt Opera Theatre, All-State Festivals, 1976-83, Soc. New Music, Syracuse, N.J. Sch. Arts Orch., 1985-87. Co-author: (with Mary Rasmussen) A Teacher's Guide to the Literature of Woodwind Instruments, 1966; condr.: rec. Concerto for Cello and Jazz Band, 1972. Chmn. adv. com. Prodigy Inc., Syracuse, 1982-86; trustee Conn. Opera Assn., 1977-80; bd. advs. Watkinson Sch. Creative Arts Program, Hartford, 1977-80; mem. humanities adv. com. N.J. Dept. Higher Edn., 1984—; mem. multi-disciplinary panel N.J. State Council on Arts, 1985-87; mem. adv. com. on auditions Met. Opera Nat. Council, 1984-87; mem. adv. com. Frank and Lydia Bergen Found., 1986-87. Mem. Nat. Assn. Schs. Music (exec. bd., sec. 1978-81). Home: Apt 204 888 Boulevard Of The Arts Sarasota FL 34236-4827 Office: 1343 Main St Ste 600 Sarasota FL 34236-5630

MATTSON, CAROL LINNETTE, social services administrator; b. Frederic, Wis., Oct. 3, 1946; d. Clarence Waldemar and Lucille Anna Mathilda (Bengtson) Hedlund; m. Wesley Harlan Mattson, June 24, 1967; 1 child, Aaron Ray. BS, U. Wis., Menomonie, 1968. Home econs. tchr. Luck (Wis.) High Sch., 1968-72; clk. Daniels Twp., Siren, Wis., 1973-75; family living instr. Wis. Indianhead Tech. Inst., New Richmond, 1974-77; aging program dir. Polk County, Balsam Lake, Wis., 1977—. Treas., bd. dirs. Polk County Transp. for the Disabled and Elderly, Inc., Balsam Lake, 1978—; mem. com. Long Term Support Com., Balsam Lake, 1985—. Mem. Wis. Assn. Nutrition Dirs., Wis. Assn. Aging Unit Dirs. Lutheran. Avocations: reading, needlecraft. Office: Polk County Aging Programs 300 Polk County Plz Ste 20 Balsam Lake WI 54810-9096

MATTSON, CLARENCE RUSSELL, safety engineer; b. Norwood, Mass., Nov. 3, 1924; s. Clarence R. and Jane P. (Dawson) M.; m. Constance W. Towne, June 7, 1953; children: Jennifer Lynn, Sue Ann. AA in Transp., Northeastern U., 1953, BBA, 1956. Cert. safety profl.; registered profl. engr., Calif. Ins. industry safety engr., 1953-62; mgr. accident prevention Dravo Corp., Pitts., 1962-72; corp. mgr. safety and environ. affairs Perini Corp., Framingham, Mass., 1972-84; dir. safety and tng. The Marr Co., South Boston, 1984; mng. dir. Long Beach-L.A. rail project Transit Ins. Adminstrs.-L.A. County Transp. Commn., 1984-86; v.p. tech. svcs. Fred S. James & Co., Short Hills, N.J., 1987-89; pres. Athena Assocs. Ltd., Safety Mgmt. Cons., Sunset Beach, N.C., 1990—. Deacon Scituate (Mass.) Congl. Ch. Recipient Disting. Svc. award Nat. Safety Coun., 1988. Mem. Am. Soc. Safety Engrs., Nat. Safety Coun. (hon. life, past gen. chmn. constrn. exec. com., disting. svc. award 1988), Assn. Gen. Contractors Am. (past chmn. safety and health com., safety engrs. adv. com.), Nat. Constructors Assn., Vets. of Safety, Mass. Safety Coun. (bd. dirs.), Mass. Constrn. Safety Congress (bd. dirs.), Elks. Republican. Home and Office: 655 Kings Ct Sunset Beach NC 28468-5326

MATTSON, FRANCIS OSCAR, retired librarian and rare books curator; b. Boston, Aug. 17, 1931; s. Frans Oscar and Catherine (Carr) M. BA, Boston U., 1957, MA, 1959; MS, Sch. Library Sci., Simmons Coll., 1967. Cert. librarian. Teaching fellow Boston U., 1958-60; instr. Tufts U., Medford, Mass., 1960-64, State Coll. at Salem, 1964-65; librarian Boston Pub. Library, 1965-68, N.Y. Pub. Library, N.Y.C., 1969-95, curator rare books, 1981-88, chief spl. collections cataloging unit, 1988-93, curator Berg Collection of English and Am. Lit., 1991-95. Mem. adv. com. Small Press Ctr., 1984-88; mem. adv. bd. Biblion, 1990-95. Book rev. editor Printing History, 1983-86, contbg. editor Am. Book Collector, 1984-88. Staff sgt. USAF, 1952-56. Mem. Bibliog. Soc. of U. Va. (life), Am. Printing History Assn. (program chmn. ann. confs. 1983, 84, bd. dirs. 1985-90), Manuscript Soc. (trustee 1977-80, 83-86), Assn. Internationale de Bibliophilie, Browning Inst. (sec. bd. dirs. 1975-90), Soc. for Preservation New Eng. Antiquities (life), Grolier Club. Home: 426 Hudson St New York NY 10014-3934

MATTSON, JAMES STEWART, lawyer, environmental scientist, educator; b. Providence, July 22, 1945; s. Irving Carl and Virginia (Lutey) M.; m. Carol Sandry, Aug. 15, 1964 (div. 1979); children: James, Birgitta; m. Rana A. Fine, Jan. 5, 1983. BS in Chemistry, U. Mich., 1966, MS, 1969, PhD, 1970; JD, George Washington U., 1979. Bar: D.C. 1979, Fla. 1983, U.S. Dist. Ct. D.C. 1979, U.S. Dist. Ct. (so. dist.) Fla. 1984, U.S. Ct. Appeals (D.C. cir.) 1979, U.S. Ct. Claims 1985, U.S. Supreme Ct. 1985, U.S. Ct. Appeals (11th cir.) 1985, U.S. Ct. Appeals (5th cir.) 1987, U.S. Ct. Appeals (fed. cir.) 1990. Staff scientist Gulf Gen. Atomic Co., San Diego, 1970-71; dir. R & D Ouachita Industries, Inc., Monroe, La., 1971-72; asst. prof. chem. oceanography Rosenstiel Sch. Marine & Atmospheric Sci., U. Miami, Fla., 1972-76; phys. scientist NOAA, Washington, 1976-78; mem. profl. staff & congl. liaison Nat. Adv. Commn. on Oceans and Atmosphere, 1978-80; ptnr. Mattson & Pave, Washington, Miami, Key Largo, 1980-86, Mattson & Tobin, Key Largo, 1987-2000; founder/CEO Great House of Wine, Inc, Ft. Lauderdale, Fla., 1997—2002, Napa, Calif., 1997—2002. Adj. prof. law U. Miami, 1983-93; cons. Alaska Dept. Environ. Conservation, 1981-91. Author: (with H.B. Mark) Activated Carbon: Surface Chemistry and Adsorption from Solution, 1971; editor (with others): Computers in Chemistry and Instrumentation, 8 vols., 1972-76; The Argo Merchant Oil Spill: A Preliminary Scientific Report, 1977, (with H.B. Mark) Water Quality Measurement: Modern Analytical Techniques, 1981; contbr. articles to profl. jours. Candidate dist. 120 Fla. Ho. of Reps., 1994. Fellow Fed. Water Pollution Control Adminstrn., 1967-68; recipient Spl. Achievement award U.S. Dept. Commerce, 1976-77; Regents Alumni scholar U. Mich., 1963. Mem. ABA, Am. Chem. Soc. (chmn. Symposium on Oil Spill Indentification 1971), Order of Coif. Address: PO Box 586 Key Largo FL 33037-0586 E-mail: mattsonj@bellsouth.net.

MATTSON, JANET MARIE, contracting officer, microbiologist; b. Bozeman, Mont., Mar. 21, 1947; d. Howard Lawrence and Lucille Irene (Cloninger) M.; m. Harry Franklin Baker, May 23, 1981; children: Matthew, David. BS, Mont. State U., 1969; MS, S.D. State U., 1972; postgrad., Georgetown U., 1977; MGA, U. Md., 1984. Cert. profl. contracts mgr. Virologist, vet. rsch. diagnostic lab. S.D. State U., Brookings, 1970-73; microbiologist Meloy Labs., Inc., Springfield, Va., 1973-74, Microbiol. Assocs., Inc., Bethesda, Md., 1974-75; virologist Nat. Inst. Neurol. and Communicable Diseases and Stroke/NIH, 1975-80; tech. info. specialist Nat. Libr. Medicine/NIH, 1980-84; Presdl. mgmt. intern Goddard Space Flight Ctr., Greenbelt, Md., 1984-86, contract specialist, 1986-89; contracting officer divsn. procurement NIH, Bethesda, 1990-93; contracting officer Nat. Cancer Inst./NIH, Rockville, Md., 1993-2000, Nat. Inst. Allergy & Infectious Diseases/NIH, Rockville, 2000—. Fellow Nat Contract Mgmt. Assn., Sigma Xi; mem. Gamma Sigma Delta. Home: 5 Watch Hill Pl Gaithersburg MD 20878-2857 Office: Nat Insts Of Health Bethesda MD 20892-0001

MATTSON, JOY LOUISE, oncological nurse; b. Moline, Ill., Feb. 1, 1956; d. Norman O. and Jeannette (Squier) M.; m. Duncan F. Crannell, Sept. 9, 1988. BA magna cum laude, Bates Coll., 1977; MTS, Harvard U., 1982; BSN magna cum laude, Rutgers U., Newark, 1988; MLS, Rutgers U., 1993. RN, N.J. Staff nurse oncology Muhlenberg Reg. Med. Ctr., Plainfield, N.J., 1987-88; staff nurse St. Lawrence Rehab. Ctr., Lawrenceville, 1988-89; clin. rsch. asst. G.H. Besselaar Assocs., Princeton, 1990-91; med. writer Convatec, Skillman, 1991-92, G.H. Besselaar Assocs., Princeton, 1992-94; sr. clin. safety assoc. Pfizer Inc., N.Y.C., 1994-99, sr. project mgr., antibiotics, 1999-2000, sr. med. writer, 2000—. Mem. Phi Beta Kappa. Home: 11 Hurley Ave North Plainfield NJ 07060-4402

MATTSON, MARGARET ELLEN, health research administrator; b. Phila., May 13, 1947; m. Thomas J. Manuccia Jr., July 17, 1991; 1 child, Allison. BA magna cum laude, Holy Family Coll., 1969; PhD, Cornell U., 1975. Rsch. asst. Ea. Pa. Psychiat. Hosp., 1964-68; pharmacology info. specialist ICI Am., Wilmington, Del., 1969-70; sr. rschr. Enviro Control, Rockville, Md., 1976-78; project officer Nat. Heart, Lung and Blood Inst., Bethesda, 1978-83; program dir. Nat. Cancer Inst., 1983-89; staff collaborator Nat. Inst. Alcohol Abuse and Alcoholism, 1989—. Contbr. over 100 articles to profl. publs. V.p., pres. Grad. Women in Sci., Bethesda. Recipient Recognition award Pub. Health Svc., 1988, PHS Meritorious Achievement award NIH, 1991, NIH Dirs. award, 1994. Mem.: Rsch. Soc. on Alcoholism. Office: Nat Inst on Alcohol Abuse and Alcoholism 6000 Executive Blvd Ste 505 Bethesda MD 20892-0001 E-mail: m.mattson@willco.niaaa.nih.gov.

MATTSON, MARLIN ROY ALBIN, health facility administrator, psychiatry educator; b. Bellingham, Wash., Apr. 25, 1939; s. Conrad Roy and Ruth Viola (Thompson) M. BA, U. Wash., 1961, MD, 1965. Diplomate Am. Bd. Psychiatry and Neurology. Intern and resident in medicine Cornell U. program at Bellevue and Meml. Hosps., N.Y.C., 1965-67; resident in psychiatry Payne Whitney Clin. The N.Y. Hosp., 1969-72, chief resident in psychiatry, 1972-73, asst. med. dir., 1973-89, assoc. med. dir., 1989-99; asst. med. dir. quality assurance Westchester Div. N.Y. Hosp., White Plains, 1979-89, assoc. med. dir. quality assurance, 1989-93, head quality assurance program dept. psychiatry N.Y.C., 1979-94; assoc. med. dir. for quality mgmt. Dept. Psychiatry N.Y. Presbyn. Hosp., Payne Whitney Clinic and Westchester divsn., 1999—2001, assoc. vice chmn. quality mgmt., 2002—. Asst. prof. psychiatry Cornell U. Med. Coll., N.Y.C., 1973-79, assoc. prof. clin. psychiatry, 1979—, sec. gen. faculty coun., 1999-2001, vice chmn. gen. faculty coun., 2001—; bd. visitors Manhattan Psychiat. Ctr., 1991—; bd. dirs. N.Y. County Health Svcs. Rev. Orgn., N.Y.C., 1983-95; mem. stds. com. URAC/Am. Accreditation Health Care Commn., 1996-2000, bd. dirs., 2000—. Editor Manual of Psychiat. Quality Assurance, 1992; contbr. numerous articles to profl. jours. Capt. U.S. Army Med. Corp., 1967-69, Korea. Fellow Am. Psychiat. Assn. (mem. nat. com. on quality assurance 1988-95, chmn. 1992-95, mem. com. champus peer rev. program 1984-86, sec. N.Y. County dist. br. 1987-91, pres.-elect 1991-92, pres. 1992-93, co-pres. 1995-96, assembly rep. 1996—, cons. or mem. nat. com. on stds. and survey procedures 1996—), N.Y. Acad. Medicine (com. pub. health 1984-92, sec. sect. on psychiatry 1993-94, chmn. 1994-95); mem. N.Y. State Psychiat. Assn. (chmn. peer rev. com. 1982-95, mem. com. econ. affairs 1995—), N.Y. County Med. Soc. (bd. dirs. 2002—), Republican. Episcopalian. Avocations: piano, European travel, theater, Swedish-American organizations. Home: 501 E 87th St Apt 4J New York NY 10128-7609 Office: NY Hosp Payne Whitney Psychiat Clinic 525 E 68th St New York NY 10021-4885 E-mail: mmattson@med.cornell.edu.

MATTSON, STEPHEN JOSEPH, lawyer; b. Abilene, Tex., Oct. 11, 1943; s. Joseph Martin and Dorothy Irene (Doyle) M.; m. Lynn Louise Mitchell, Mar. 13, 1965; children: Eric, Laura. BA (hon.), U. Ill., 1965, JD (hon.), 1970. Bar: Ill., 1970, U.S. Dist. Ct. (no. dist.) Ill. 1970. Assoc. Mayer, Brown, Rowe & Maw, Chgo., 1970—77, ptnr., 1978—. Mem. ABA, Ill. State Bar Assn., Chgo. Bar Assn., Order of Coif. Office: Mayer Brown Rowe & Maw 190 S La Salle St Ste 3100 Chicago IL 60603-3441

MATTSSON, AKE, psychiatrist, physician; b. Stockholm, May 30, 1929; came to U.S., 1956, naturalized, 1964; s. Erik H. and Thyra (Bergtsson) M.; m. Margareta Fürst, Jan. 5, 1953; children: Erik, Peter, Nicholas. B.M., Karolinska Inst., Stockholm, 1950, MD, 1955. Intern Vanderbilt U. Med. Sch., Nashville, 1955-56; resident in pediatrics and child psychiatry Karolinska Hosp., Stockholm, 1958-60; fellow in child devel. Case Western Res. U. Med. Sch., 1957-58, resident in psychiatry and child psychiatry, 1960-64, asst. prof. psychiatry, 1964-70; prof. psychiatry and pediatrics U. Va. Med. Sch., 1970-77, U. Pitts Med. Sch., 1977-78; prof. psychiatry and pediatrics, dir. div. child and adolescent psychiatry N.Y. U. Med. Sch., 1978-85, rsch. prof. psychiatry, 1985—; prof. psychiatry U. Va. Med. Sch., 1985-91; prof. psychiatry and pediatrics, dir. div. child and adolescent psychiatry Med. Sch., East Carolina U., Greenville, N.C., 1991-97; med. dir. divsn. mental health V.I. Dept. Health, St. Thomas, 1997—. Contbr. numerous articles to med. jours. Served with Swedish Navy, 1948-59. Fulbright-Hays grantee, 1975 Mem. Am. Psychiat. Assn., Am. Psychoanalytical Assn., N.Y. Psychiat. Soc., Am. Acad. Child Adolescent Psychiatry, N.Y. Acad. Scis., Soc. Biol. Psychiatry, Am. Acad. Psychiatry and the Law. Office: US VI Dept Health Divsn Mental Health Saint Thomas VI 00802

MATTURRO, PETER JOHN, social worker; b. Corona, N.Y., Aug. 4, 1953; s. Anthony Francis and Bridget Anne (Campbell) M.; m. Mary Martha Mahoney, June 10, 1978; children: Elizabeth Mary, David Peter, Laura Elaine. AS, CUNY, 1973, BA, 1976; MPA cert., Marist Coll., Poughkeepsie, N.Y.; M in Social Work, Fordham U., 1980. cert. Social Worker, N.Y. Adoption, social worker St. Cabrini, Inc., West Park, N.Y., 1978-80; program dir. Kingston (N.Y.) Children's Home, 1980-82; psychiatric social worker Rockland Children's Psychiatric Ctr., Newburgh, N.Y., 1982-88; supr. Fordham U., 1987-88; coord. intensive case mgmt. Rockland Children's Psychiat. Ctr., Newburgh, N.Y., 1988—. Ct. apptd. spl. asst., Kingston, N.Y., 1987-88. Avocations: sports, camping, cinema, music. Home: 230 Marcott Rd Kingston NY 12401-8318

MATUANA, LAURENT MALANDA, engineering educator, researcher; BS, U. Laval, Quebec City, Que., Can., 1989, MS, 1991; PhD, U. Toronto, Ont., Can., 1997. Assoc. scientist Noranda Tech. Ctr., Pointe-Claire, Canada, 1997—98; asst. prof. Mich. Technol. U., Houghton, 1998—2001, Mich. State U., East Lansing, 2002—. Mem.: ASME, Forest Products Soc., Soc. Wood Sci. and Tech., Soc. Plastics Engrs. Office: Mich State U Dept Forestry 126 Natural Resources East Lansing MI 48824 Office Fax: 517-432-1143. Business E-Mail: matuana@msu.edu.

MATUG, ALEXANDER PETER, lawyer; b. Chgo., May 25, 1946; s. Alexander J. and Marianne (Paszek) M.; m. Jeanne Marie Buker, Aug. 16, 1969; children: Alexander W., Krista E., Thomas E. BA, St. Mary's Coll., Minn., 1968; JD, Loyola U., Chgo., 1972. Bar: Ill. 1972, U.S. Dist. Ct. (no. dist.) Ill. 1972. Pvt. practice, Palos Heights, Ill., 1972—. Bd. dirs. Am. Heritage, Sertoma, Palos Heights, 1991—; profl. adv. bd. Sertoma Speech and Hearing Ctr., Palos Hills, Ill., 1991—. Mem. Ill. Bar Assn., S.W. Suburban Bar Assn. Roman Catholic. Office: 7110 W 127th St Ste 250 Palos Heights IL 60463-1571

MATUGA, EDWARD ANTHONY, lawyer; b. Chgo., Sept. 3, 1921; s. Joseph John and Michalene Helen (Labiak) M.; m. Pearl Elizabeth Krysiak, Apr. 5, 1948; children: Edward, Janice, Rita, Michael. BS, Loyola U., Chgo., 1943; JD, DePaul U., 1948. Bar: Ill. 1953, U.S. Dist. Ct. (no. dist.) 1948, U.S. Ct. Appeals (4th cir.) 1975. Prosecutor, Westchester, Ill., 1960—, Bellwood, 1961—, Broadview, 1965—. Atty. Westchester Park Dist., 1967—; gen. counsel First Fed. Westchester, 1963—, Proviso Mental Health Commn., Melrose Park, Ill., 1970—. Capt. USAF, 1960-70. Mem. Chgo. Bar Assn., Ill. State Bar Assn., Advocates Soc., West Suburban Bar Assn. (pres. 1982-83). Republican. Roman Catholic. Home: 1651 Westchester Blvd Westchester IL 60154-4331 Office: 1651 Westchester Blvd Westchester IL 60154-4331

MATULEVICIUS, EDWARD, engineering company executive, consultant; b. Montreal, Que., Can., Sept. 4, 1942; s. Vacys and Jule Andrejauskas; m. Mary Lou Quinn; children: Stephen, Susan. B in Engring., McGill U., Mont., 1964; SM, MIT, 1967, ScD, 1970. Ptnr. Fuel Tech. Assocs. , Gilette, NJ, 1999—2002; rsch. assoc. Exxon Rsch. & Engring., Linden, 1978—99. Sect. head Air Products & Chems., Trexlertown, 1974—78; group leader Exxon Rsch. & Engring., Linden, NJ, 1969—74. Bd. dirs. So. Lehigh Pub. Libr., Coopersburg, 1983—86. Mem.: API (com. chmn. 1995—99), ASTM (Award of Appreciation 1998), Coord. Rsch. Coun. (group and panel leader 1990—2002). Avocations: bicycling, reading, music, computer programming. Office: Fuel Tech Assocs LLC 1785 Briar Hill Ln Coopersburg PA 18036 Office Fax: 610-965-6890. Business E-Mail: edmat@ix.netcom.com.

MATULEWICZ, PATRICIA ANN, social worker; b. Rockland, Maine, Aug. 11, 1952; d. Francis Joseph and Rose Ann O'Connor; m. William Matulewicz, June 23, 1974; children: Lauren, Michael. BA, Upsala Coll., 1974; MEd, Xavier U., 1995. Lic. social worker, Ohio; lic. profl. counselor, Ohio. Social worker St. Colman's Home for Children, Watervliet, N.Y., 1974-77; exec. dir. asst. Orange County Dept. Social Svcs., Goshen, 1978-82; med. social worker Franciscan Health Sys., Cin., 1992-97; psychiat. social worker Mercy-Franciscan Behavioral Health, 1996—. Mem. ACA. Avocation: church choir singing, cmty. svc., travel, hiking, bike riding. Office: 2446 Kipling Ave Cincinnati OH 45239-6650

MATULICH, SERGE, accounting educator, author; b. Split, Croatia, June 8, 1933; came to U.S., 1946; s. Daniel M. and Josephine (Schuster) Raseta; m. Margarete Manderscheid, Dec. 7, 1957; children: Alexander Matulich, Erika Matulich. BS in Acctg. with honors, Calif. State U., Sacramento, 1964; PhD in Bus., U. Calif., Berkeley, 1971. CPA, Fla.; cert. cost analyst. Grad. asst. U. Calif., Davis, 1964-65; asst. prof. Calif. State U., Hayward, 1966-67; assoc. in acctg. U. Calif., Berkeley, 1968-71, vis. asst. prof., 1974-75; asst. prof. Sch. Bus. Ind. U., 1971-76; assoc. prof. acctg. Sch. Bus. Tex. Christian U., 1976-84; vis. prof. U. North Tex., spring 1983; prof. Crummer Grad. Sch. Bus. Rollins Coll., Winter Park, Fla., 1984—2001, prof. emeritus, 2002—. Bd. dirs. Marconi Med. Ctr., Inc., Sacramento, 1967-71, Bazeghi Corp., Oakland, Calif., 1968-71, Crescent Gen. Corp., 1969-71 (also v.p.), Fin. Floorplans, Inc., Ft. Worth, 1980—, Way To Go, Inc., Orlando, Fla., 1988-2000, Unicorn Rsch. Corp., Orlando, 1989-2000, Global Ptnrs. Corp., Orlando, 1994-2000 (also sec.). Author number of fin. acctg., mgmt. acct., cost acctg. textbooks, study guides; contbr. many articles to profl. jours. With U.S. Army, 1956-58. Recipient U. Pitts. BEFEE grant, 1993, 94, Ernst & Ernst Acctg. Achievement award, 1967, EMBA Outstanding Prof. award Class of 1986, 88, Delta Sigma Pi Scholarship key, 1964; Fulbright fellowship, 1999; Fulbright Alumni initiatives awards program grant, 2000—. Mem. AICPA, Am. Acctg. Assn., World Future Soc., Fulbright Assn. (founding mem., treas. mid-Fla. chpt. 2002--), Beta Alpha Psi, Beta Gamma Sigma. Avocations: classical music, travel. Home: 4621 N Landmark Dr Orlando FL 32817-1235 Office: Crummer Grad Sch Bus Rollins Coll 1000 Holt Ave Winter Park FL 32789-4499 E-mail: serge@rollins.edu., serge@unicorn.us.com.

MATUS, NANCY LOUISE, artist; b. Wichita, Kans., Jan. 22, 1955; d. Joseph John and Josephine Emily (Kulina) M.; m. Kenneth Lee Walker, Feb. 14, 1990. AA, Phoenix Coll., 1980; student, U. Ariz., 1978, 79, Ariz. State U., 1984, 85. Exhibited in group shows Ariz. Sate Capitol, Phoenix, 1985, Movimento Artistico del Rio Salado Gallery, Phoenix, 1986, 87, 89, 91, 92, Tempe (Ariz.) Arts Ctr., 1987, U. Ariz., Phoenix, 1987, Nat. Acrylic Painters Assn., Long Beach, Calif., 1996, Coos Bay (Oreg.) Art Museum, 1999, Coos Art Mus., 1999, Nat. Acrylic Painters Assn.-Westminster Gallery, London, 1999; represented in numerous pvt. collections, including loan to City of Phoenix, City Hall, 1998; work represented in Best of Acylric Painting, 1996, Creative Inspirations, 1997. Mem. Nat. Acrylic Painters Assn. (signature), Nat. Oil and Acrylic Painters Soc. (assoc.), Cottonwood Country Club, Catharine Lorillard Wolfe Art Club (assoc.). Address: 25802 S Cloverland Dr Chandler AZ 85248-6875

MATUS, WAYNE CHARLES, lawyer; b. N.Y.C., Mar. 10, 1950; s. Eli and Alma (Platt) M.; children: Marshall Scott, Scott Adam. BA, Johns Hopkins U., 1972; JD, NYU, 1975. Law clk. Superior Ct. D.C., 1975-76; assoc. Marshall, Bratter, Greene, Allison and Tucker, N.Y.C., 1976-79, Christy & Viener, N.Y.C., 1979-83, ptnr., 1984—98, Salans Hertzfeld Heilbronn Christy & Viener, N.Y.C., 1999-2001, Leboeuf Lamb Greene & MacRae, N.Y.C., 2001—. Faculty ABA-Am. Law Inst., 1988; neutral mediator Supreme Ct. comml. divsn. 1st jud. dist. State of N.Y. Unified Ct. sys., 1997—; past chmn. global high tech. group Salans Hertzfeld Heilbronn Christy & Viener; co-chmn. intellectual property litigation group LeBoeuf Lamb Greene & MacRae. Mem. Assn. Bar City of N.Y. (com. on computer law 1985-88, chmn. com. on state cts., subcom. on motion practice 1982-84, com. product liability 1994-97), N.Y. State Bar Assn. (com. on class actions and complex civil litigation comml. fed. litigation sect. 1990-99, com. on Internet and litigation 2000—, lectr.), N.Y. Litigators Club (steering com. 1985—), Johns Hopkins U. Alumni Assn. (bd. dirs. met. N.Y. chpt., v.p. 1988—2002, nat. alumni counsel 1996—2002, pres. 2002—). Office: LeBeoeuf Lanb Greene & McRae 125 W 55th St New York NY 10019

MATUSEN, ARMAND MILTON, executive; b. Chgo., June 4, 1934; s. Solomon and Anne (Ballin) M.; m. Virginia Arlene Carr, Aug. 13, 1966 (dec. 1991); 1 child, Darren Edric. AB, U. Chgo., 1956; MEd, U. Mass., 1968. Dept. head A.S. Burg. Co., Salem, Mass., 1974-81; exec. v.p. Lane Fabric Corp., Haverhill, 1981—. Home: 208 High St Newburyport MA 01950-3824 Office: Lane Fabric Corp 175 Ward Hill Ave Haverhill MA 01835-6973 E-mail: matusenkovitch@msn.com., amatusen@aol.com.

MATUS-MENDOZA, MARIADELALUZ, language educator, sociologist; b. Mexico City, Apr. 10, 1961; arrived in U.S., 1991; d. MariadelaPaz Matus-Mendoza; m. Geoffrey Fitch, Sept. 3, 1993. BA in English Lit. and Applied Lang., Mex. Autonoman U., Mexico City, 1984; MA, Temple U., 1993, PhD, 1999. Tchr. Mex. Autonomon U., 1984—91; tchg. asst. Temple U., Phila., 1991—94, adj. instr., 1994—95, LuSulle U., Phila., 1995—98, U. Pa., Phila., 1996—99; asst. prof. Spanish U. Ctrl. Fla., Orlando, 1999—2001, Drexel U., Phila., 2001—. Cons. ETS, Princeton, NJ, 2001—. Mem.: MLA, Am. Assn. Tchrs. of Spanish and Portugese, Nat. Assn. Hispanic and Latino Studies. Roman Catholic. Office: Drexel Univ 229 N 33rd St Philadelphia PA 19104

MATUSOW, NAOMI C. state legislator; b. Nashville, Oct. 31, 1938; m. Gene R. Matusow; children: Gary, Jason. BA cum laude, Vanderbilt U., 1960; MA in Counseling and Guidance, NYU, 1966; JD, Pace U., 1979. Bar: N.Y. 1981. Editl. asst. Golden Press, 1960-62; tchr. math. N.Y.C. Pub. Schs., 1962-65, guidance counselor, 1965-67; pvt. practice as lawyer Armonk, 1981-92, White Plains, 1981-92; mem. N.Y. State Assembly, 1992—, chair librs. and edn. tech. com., mem. assembly coms., econ. devel.. environ. conservation, local govt., transp., consumer affairs, tourism, arts, sports devel., spkrs. steering com. Chmn. Women's Bus. Devel. subcom.; bd. dirs. Juvenile Diabetes Found. Westchester County. Mem. NOW, Nat. Women's Polit. Caucus. Office: NY State Assembly 125-131 Main St Mount Kisco NY 10549-2316 E-mail: matusow@assembly.state.ny.us.

MATUSZEK, JOHN MICHAEL, JR. environmental scientist, educator, consultant; b. Worcester, Mass., Apr. 16, 1935; s. John Michael and Felicia Martha (Shandruk) M.; m. Roberta Eva Coonan, Nov. 30, 1957; children: Debra-Jane Y., John Michael III, Kevin P., Jennifer R. BS in Chemistry with distinction, Worcester Poly. Inst., 1957; PhD in Nuclear Chemistry, Clark U., 1962. Dept. mgr. Teledyne Isotopes, Westwood, N.J., 1964-71; rsch. scientist in nuclear chemistry, radioactive waste mgmt., radiological health, environ. radioactivity and radiation N.Y. State Health Dept., Albany, 1971-2000; cons., owner JMM Cons. Svcs., Delmar, N.Y., 1992—. Adj. prof. Rensselaer Poly. Inst., Troy, N.Y., 1977—; prof. SUNY, Albany, 1996-99. Lt. comdr. USPHS, 1962-64. Mem. Internat. Commn. Radionuclide Metrology. Avocations: skiing, music. Home and Office: JMM Cons Svcs 10 Fieldstone Dr Delmar NY 12054 E-mail: jmatuszek@att.net.

MATUSZKO, ANTHONY JOSEPH, research chemist, administrator; b. Hadley, Mass., Jan. 31, 1926; s. Joseph Anthony and Katherine (Narog) M.; m. Anita Colley, Oct. 26, 1956; children— Martha, Mary, Stephen, Richard. BA, Amherst Coll., 1946; MS in Chemistry, U. Mass., 1951; PhD in Chemistry, McGill U., 1953. Demonstrator in chemistry McGill U., Montreal, Que., Can., 1950-52; from instr. to assoc. prof. chemistry Lafayette Coll., Easton, Pa., 1952-58; head fundamental process div. Naval Propellant Lab., Indian Head, Md., 1958-62; program mgr. in chemistry Air Force Office Sci. Research, Washington, 1962-89; cons., Annandale, Va., 1989—. Contbr. articles to tech. jours. Patentee in field. Pres. Forest Heights PTA, Md., 1967. Served with U.S. Army, 1946-48. Named Hon. Fellow in Chemistry, U. Wis.-Madison, 1967-68, recipient Superior Performance award USAF, Outstanding Career Svc. award U.S. Govt. Fellow AAAS, Am. Inst. Chemists (life); mem. Am. Chem. Soc., Cosmos Club, Sigma Xi. Home: 4210 Elizabeth Ln Annandale VA 22003-3654

MATWICZAK, KENNETH MATTHEW, university educator, consultant; b. Milw., Sept. 26, 1948; s. Matthew T. and Dorothy M. Matwiczak; m. Barbara A. Larsen, June 12, 1971; 1 child, Brynn E. BS, U.S. Mil. Acad., 1971; MS, Purdue U., 1979; MBA, L.I. U., 1982; PhD in Indsl. Engring., Tex. A&M U., 1990. Commd. 2d lt. U.S. Army, 1971, advanced through grades to lt. col., 1990; air def. platoon leader, exec. officer 2 Bn. 56th ADA, Pirmasens, Fed. Rep. Germany, 1971-74; air def. battery comdr. 2/5 ADA, 2nd AD, Ft. Hood, Tex., 1975-76; asst. dean acad. computing U.S. Mil. Acad., West Point, N.Y., 1979-82, assoc. prof., 1989-93; chief studies and analysis Forward Area Air Def. Joint Test Force, Ft. Bliss, Tex., 1982-85; bn. exec. officer staff and faculty battalion U.S. Army Air Def. Sch., 1985-86; adj. assoc. prof. U. Tex., Austin, 1993-99, sr. lectr., 1999—. Statis. cons., 1994—; owner, proprietor Fare Choice Vending Svcs., Austin, 1996-99; guest lectr. Ctr. Pub. Mgmt., San Marcos, Tex., 1997-. Admissions rep. U.S. Mil. Acad.-W. Point, Austin, 1997—. Mem. ASPA (bd. dirs. Centex chpt. 1999—), Inst. Ops. Rsch. and Mgmt. Sci., W. Point Soc. Ctrl. Tex. (pres. 1995-97, bd. dirs.), KC. Repblican. Roman Catholic. Avocations: bowling, traveling, golf, reading, softball. Office: U Tex LBJ Sch Pub Affairs Drawer Y University Sta Austin TX 78713 E-mail: kmat@mail.utexas.edu.

MATYJASZEWSKI, KRZYSZTOF, chemist, educator; b. Konstantynow, Poland, Apr. 8, 1950; came to U.S., 1985; s. Henryk and Antonina (Styss) M.; m. Malgorzata Kowalska, July 15, 1972; children: Antoni, Maria. BS, MS, Tech. U., Moscow, 1972; PhD, Polish Acad. Scis., Lodz, 1976; DSc, Lodz Poly., 1985. Postdoctoral fellow U. Fla., 1977-78; rsch. assoc. Polish Acad. Scis., 1978-84, CNRS, France, 1984-85; asst. prof. chemistry Carnegie Mellon U., Pitts., 1985-89, assoc. prof., 1989-93, prof., 1993—, head dept. chemistry, 1994-98, J.C. Warner prof., 1998—. Invited prof. U. Paris, 1985; vis. prof. U. Freiburg, 1988, U. Paris, 1990, 97, 98, U. Bayreuth, 1991, U. Strasbourg, 1992, U. Bordeaux, 1996, Univ. Ulm, 1999, U. Pisa, 2000; adj. prof., U. Pitts., 2000-, Polish Acad. Scis., 2000-; cons. Dow Corning, Midland, Mich., 1988-89, Arco, Phila., 1990-92, GE, Schenectady, 1992—, Amoco, Naperville, Ill., 1994-97, Reilly Ind., Indpls., 1994—, Air Products, Allentown, Pa., 1994-97. Author 5 books; mem. editorial bd. Macromolecules, Macromolecular Synthesis, Jour. Polymer Sci., Jour. Macromolecular Sci.-Pure and Applied Chemistry, Jour. Inorganic and Organometallic Polymers, Macromolecular Reports, others; editor Progess Polymer Sci.; contbr. chpts. to books, more than 500 articles to profl. jours.; 27 patents in field. Recipient award Polish Acad. Sci., 1981, Presdl. Yount Investigator award NSF, 1989, Humboldt award for Sr. U.S. Scientists, 1999, Pitts. award, 2001. Fellow: ACS (Carl S. Marvel award 1995, Polymer Chemistry award 2002), Internat. Union Pure and Applied Chemistry (corr. mem. polymer nomenclature), Polymer Materials Sci. Engring.; mem.: French Acad. Sci. (ELF chair 1998). Achievements include research in synthesis of well defined macromolecules via living and controlled polymerizations; organometallic polymers. Home: 9 Queens Ct Pittsburgh PA 15238-1519 Office: Carnegie Mellon U 4400 5th Ave Pittsburgh PA 15213-2617

MATYSTIK, WALTER FRANCIS, engineering researcher; b. Yonkers, N.Y., Mar. 20, 1950; s. Walter F. Sr. and Orvilla F. (Collins) M.; m. Deborah J. DeBlassis, Oct. 18, 1975; children: Matthew M., Jennifer J. B of Engring., Manhattan Coll., 1972, M of Engring., 1974; JD, N.Y. Law Sch., 1981. Bar: N.Y. 1982, U.S. Dist. Ct. (so. dist.) N.Y. 1984. Project engr. Manhattan Coll., Riverdale, N.Y., 1974-77, rsch. project mgr., 1978-83, dir. rsch., 1984—. Atty. pvt. practice, 1982—. Bd. dirs. Mt. Pleasant Cen. Sch. Dist., Thornwood, N.Y., 1981-93, pres., 1984, 90, 91; dist. leader Mt. Pleasant Dem. Com., Hawthorne, N.Y., 1989—. Mem. ABA, ASCE, AAAS, CAUSE, Soc. Rsch. Adminstrs., Nat. coun. Univ. Rsch. Adminstrn., Internat. Assn. for Gt. Lakes Rsch., Westchester County Bar Assn., Sigma Xi (sec. Manhattan Coll. chpt. 1995—). Democrat. Roman Catholic. Office: Manhattan Coll 203RLC 4513 Manhattan College Pky Bronx NY 10471-4005

MATZ, DEBORAH, federal agency administrator; m. Marshall Matz; children: Hayley, Peter. BS, Cornell U.; MA, George Washington U. Cmty. devel. rep. U.S. Dept. Housing and Urban Devel.; legis. asst. Congressman Peter Peyser; dir. Office Tech. Assessment, U.S. Congress; economist Joint Econ. Com.; exec. officer Liaison Office N.Am. Food and Agrl. Orgn., UN; numerous positions including deputy asst. sec. adminstrn., chair loan resolution task force, chief of staff adminstrs. Farm Svc. Agy and Farmers Home USDA, 1993—2001; mem. Nat. Credit Union Adminstrn., Alexandria, 2002—. Office: Nat Credit Union Adminstrn 1775 Duke St Alexandria VA 22314-3428*

MATZ, JAMES RICHARD, county official; BA with honors, U. Tex., 1961; postgrad., Mexico city Coll., 1961-62. Mktg. exec. Fluor Corp.; mem. diplomatic corps Dept. of State; commr. City of Harlingen, Tex., Cameron County. Mem. Pres.'s Exec. Interchange Program, Bank of Am. Contbr. articles to profl. jours. Founder Harlingen Proud; founder, chmn. Valley Proud Environ. Coun., 1990; mem. citizen's exec. adv. coun. Rio Grande State Mental Health and Retardation Ctr.; bd. dirs. Harlingen, South Padre Island, San Benito Emergency Med. Svcs.; chmn. Tex. Reg. Cmty. Devel. Grant Rev. Com.; mem. Met. Planning Orgn., Cameron County; mem. exploration com. World Birding Ctr.; bd. dirs. Tex. Urban Forestry Coun.; mem. Tex. Energy Coord. Coun., Govt. Adv. Com. to U.S. Rep. to N.Am. Commn. for Environ. Coop.; past vice chmn. legis. policy com. on utility regulation and environment Tex. Mcpl. League; past chmn. City of Harlingen Utility Rate Rev. Bd., pub. works com. Harlingen Capital Improvement Adv. Bd.; past. bd. dirs. Rio Grande basin Sustainable Devel. Initiative, Border Trade Alliance, Area Health Edn. Ctr. South Tex., Keep Tex. Beautiful; former commr. Cameron County; past exec. com. Rio Grande Valley Emergency Mgmt. Coord. Coun., numerous others. Recipient Rotary Found. Dist. Svc. award, 1990, Svc. Above Self award Harlingen Rotary, 1991, Tex. Urban Forestry Individual Accomplishment award, 1992, Harlingen Proud, Chairman's award, 1992, Outstanding Dist. Gov., Keep Tex. Beautiful, 1995, Leadership award, 1995, Pres.'s Nat. Svc. award, 1995, Outstanding tex. Urban Forester award, 1996, State of Tex. Senate Resolution #989, 1995, Joint Resolution of Appreciation, San Benito City Commn. and San Benito Area C. of C., 1997, others. Mem. Harlingen Area C. of C. (past dir.), Assn. for Local Control of Utility Rates (past officer, dir.). Office: 900 Palm Valley Dr W Harlingen TX 78552

MATZDORFF, JAMES ARTHUR, investment banker, marketing professional; b. Kansas City, Mo., Jan. 3, 1956; BS, U. So. Calif., 1978; MBA, Loyola U., L.A., 1980. Comml. loan officer Bank Am., L.A., 1976-78; mng. dir. James A. Matzdorff & Co., Beverly Hills, 1978—. Mem. Rep. Nat. Com., 1980—. Mem. Am. Fin. Assn., Mercedes Benz Car Club, BMW Motorcycle Internat., Phi Delta Theta. Avocations: tennis, sailing, karate, skiing, sport target shooting. Office: 9903 Santa Monica Blvd Beverly Hills CA 90212-1671 E-mail: James@Projectsfinance.com.

MATZIORINIS, KENNETH N. economist; b. N.Y.C., May 4, 1954; s. Neocles N. and Popi (Gregoratos) Matziorinis; m. Catherine Marina Astrakianakis, July 27, 1985; children: Anna Maria, Angela Ellen Fylitsa. BA, McGill U., 1976, MA, 1979, PhD, 1988. Cert. mgmt. cons. Asst. economist Nat. Bank Greece (Can.), Montreal, 1978-81; lectr. econs. McGill U., 1977—; prof. econs. John Abbott Coll., 1981—. Pres. Canbek Econ. Cons., Inc., Montreal, 1983—; econs. adviser to bd. dirs. Internat. Orgn. Psychophysiology, 1982-89; bd. dirs. Nat. Bank of Greece, Can., Hellenic Bd. of Trade of Met. Montreal; dir. Hellas Capital, Inc. (Canada), 2001—. Author: Introduction to Macro Economics: An Applied Approach, 1988, 2d edit., 1994, 3d edit., 2000, Business Economics: Theory and Practice, 2d edit., 2000, Business Economics: Theory and Practice, 2d edit., 2000; editor: Vital Graphs of Canadian Economy, 1984; contbr. articles to profl. jours. V.p. Westmount Liberal Riding Assn., Montreal, 1975-77; bd. govs. McGill U., 1978-81, John Abbott Coll., 1978-81; chmn. bd. dirs. Cmty. Svc. Ctr. St. Louis, Montreal, 1978-80; bd. trustees Trafalgar Sch. for Girls, 2002—. Mem. Am. Econ. Assn., Am. Hellenic Ednl. and Progressive Assn., Can. Assn. Bus. Economists, Can. Econ. Assn., Que. Inst. Cert. Mgmt. Cons., Nat. Assn. Bus. Economists, St. James Club. Greek Orthodox. Home: Laval 615 67th Ave Montreal QC Canada H7V 3N9 Fax: 450-688-8529. E-mail: canbekeconomics@spint.can.

MATZKA, MICHAEL ALAN, lawyer; b. Newark, Oct. 30, 1954; s. John and Liselotte (Heim) M. BS, MIT, 1976; JD, Boston Coll., 1984. Bar: Mass. 1985, U.S. Dist. Ct. Mass. 1985. Assoc. computer systems Index Systems, Inc., Cambridge, Mass., 1976-81; assoc. Sullivan & Worcester, Boston, 1984-92; ptnr. Sullivan & Worcester LLP, 1992-2000, of counsel, 2000—. Mem. ABA. Office: Sullivan & Worcester LLP 1 Post Office Sq Ste 2300 Boston MA 02109-2129

MATZKE, FRANK J. architect, consultant; b. Akron, Ohio, Jan. 28, 1922; s. Frank G. and Erna (Weibel) M.; m. Shirley Elizabeth Hall, Nov. 27, 1952 (div. Dec. 1966); children: Kim Elizabeth, Karla Jo. Student, State Tchrs. Coll. at Buffalo, 1940-41; B.Arch., Rensselaer Poly. Inst., 1951. Registered architect, N.Y., Md. Field rep., project architect W. Parker Dodge Assos., Rensselaer, N.Y., 1951-54; sr. architect div. architecture N.Y. State Dept. Pub. Works, Albany, 1954-58; assoc. architect State U. N.Y., 1958-62; dep. mgr. planning State U. Constrn. Fund, 1962-68, dep. gen. mgr., 1968-72; assoc. commr. for project mgmt. Pub. Bldgs. Service, GSA, Washington, 1972-75, acting asst. commr. for constrn. mgmt., 1974-75; exec. dir. Ill. Capital Devel. Bd., 1975-76; v.p. for tech. and programs Nat. Inst. Bldg. Scis., Washington, 1978-83; mem. Bldg. Research Adv. Bd., 1976-79; chmn. Mgmt. Resource Council, 1974-75; cons. to pub. agys., colls. and univs. on methods to expedite design and constrn. of phys. facilities. Contbr. articles to profl. jours. Chmn. Johnsburg Planning Bd., 1962-65; nat. ski patrolman, 1953-73, past patrol leader O.C. Ski Club Ski Patrol; bd. dirs. Bldg Rsch. Inst., 1973-75, Town Ctr. Coop., Inc., 1980-82. 1st lt. inf., AUS, 1942-46, PTO. Decorated Bronze Star. Fellow AIA (pres. Ea. N.Y.. chpt 1959-60, dir. 1960-63, mem. nat. commn. on architecture for education 1966-72, chmn. nat. com. on architects in govt. 1975, medal for excellence 1951), N.Y. State Assn. Architects (dir. 1966-69); mem. VFW, Wilderness Soc., Sierra Club, Smithsonian Assocs., Natural Resources Def. Coun., Am. Rivers, Nature Conservancy, Environ. Def. Fund, Mil. Order of Caraboa, Nat. Order of Battlefield Commissions, 31st Inf. "Dixie" Divsn. Soc., 124th Inf. Rgt. Assn., Am. Legion, St. Augustine Shores Men's Golf Assn., Sigma Xi (ret. assoc.), Tau Beta Pi, Sigma Phi Epsilon. Address: 24 Andalusia Ct Saint Augustine FL 32086-7647

MATZKE, GARY ROGER, pharmacist, educator; b. Sturgeon Bay, Wis., July 13, 1950; s. Erwin Walter and Alice (Logerquist) M.; m. Cindy Claire Boxwell, Apr. 11, 1981; children: Megan, Jonathon, Jason, Christina, Alicia. BS in Pharmacy, U. Wis., 1973; PharmD, U. Minn., 1977. Asst. prof. Wayne State U. Sch. Pharmacy, Detroit, 1977-80, U. Minn., Mpls., 1980-84, assoc. prof., 1984-87, prof., 1987-89; prof., vice chmn. U. N.C., Chapel Hill, 1989-91; prof. pharmacy and medicine Ctr. for Clin. Pharmacology, U. Pitts., 1991—. Editor: Pharmacotherapy: A Pathophysiologic Approach, Pharmacotherapy: A Patient Focused Approach; contbr. over 150 articles to profl. jours. Fellow Am. Coll. Clin. Pharmacy, Am. Coll. Clin. Pharmacology; mem. Am. Soc. for Clin. Pharmacology and Therapeutics, Am. Soc. Nephrology, Internat. Soc. Nephrology, Nat. Kidney Found. Avocations: golf, running. Office: U Pitts Sch Pharmacy 724 Salk Hall Pittsburgh PA 15261-1907

MATZKIN, ROSA LILIANA, economics educator; b. Buenos Aires, Argentina, Oct. 30, 1956; d. Jose and Paulina (Rosemberg) M.; m. Emil Moffa, Mar. 24, 1984. BS in Mgmt. and Econs. cum laude, Israel Inst. Tech., Haifa, 1981; PhD in Econs., U. Minn., 1986. Research asst. dept. of banks regulation Bank of Israel, Jerusalem, 1980; teaching asst., assoc. U. Minn., Mpls., 1981-84; econ. cons. Softkey, 1985-86; asst. prof. econs. Yale U., New Haven, 1986—. Grantee U. Tel Aviv, Israel, 1982-83, grantee Nat. Sci. Found., 1987—, Sloan Found. U. Minn., 1984-85. Fellow Silliman Coll.; mem. Am. Econ. Assn., Econometric Soc., Cowles Found., Phi Kappa Phi. Office: Northwestern U Dept Econs 2003 Sheridan Rd Evanston IL 60208-0826

MATZNER, CHESTER MICHAEL, writer; b. N.Y.C. s. Sigmund Simon and Rose (Greenberg) M. BS in Physics, L.I. U., 1949; MA in English, Bklyn. Coll., 1954. Tchr. English N.Y.C. Bd. Edn., 1954-59; jr. chemist Nat Synthetic Rubber Co., Louisville; with S. Matzner & Co., N.Y.C. and Mt. Vernon. Internat. trade cons. N.Y.C.; fgn. and UN corres. Can. Mil. Jour., Montreal, 1959-79; fgn. corres. The Soldier Illustrated, Manhattan, Kans., 1958-59. Author (plays) Whither Youth?, 1987, Mystic Lady, 1988, The Deceased (?) Embezzler, 1989, Ship Aswirl, 1992, (screenplay) A Warrior's Journey, 1992, (songs) On The Road, (musical drama) Henri Christophe, (poetry) The Red-Haired Dancer & Other Poems; producer (documentary films) Margaret Corbin, America's First Heroine, 1989, Caribbeana, 1991, The Pageant of America, 1992, Circus-Time, The World Dances; (short films) Waiting, Beauty's Passing Parade, (song collection) On The Road, Songs You Love To Sing, 1994; (ballets) Dance of the Waters, 1994, The Austrian Officers, 1994; (documentary films) The Cardinal Mindszenty Story, 1994; contbr. various mil. jours. County committeeman N.Y. Dem. County Com., 1991. Mem. Am. Fedn. Tchrs., Dramatists Guild, Inc., Authors League of Am., Song Writers Guild of Am., Mus. of Modern Art, Finnish-Am. C. of C. (charter mem.). Avocations: reading, travel, archaeology, ethnology. Office: c/o Rainbow Prodns Ste 802 208 W 30th St New York NY 10001- E-mail: ChesterMatzner@aol.com.

MATZNER, EGON, economics educator; b. Klagenfurt, Austria, Mar. 2, 1938; s. Heinrich and Josefine (Posautz) M.; m. Monica Siegel, Mar. 2, 1959 (div. 1983); children: Joerg, Robert; m. Gabriele Holzer, Oct. 14, 1984; 1 child, Sissela. M in Econs., U. Econs., Vienna, PhD, 1961; Docent, U. Linz, 1970. Asst. dir. Bank for Labor and Industry, Vienna, Austria, 1962-65; rsch. fellow Internat. Inst., Stockholm (Sweden) U., 1965-67; dean of faculty U. Tech., Vienna, Austria, 1992-95; dir. Sci. Ctr., Berlin, Germany, 1984-89; dir. rsch. unit for socio-econs. Austrian Acad. Sci., Vienna, Austria, 1992-98; fellow Max Weber Coll., 1998—2002. Cons. Fed. Min. Fin., Vienna, 1970-79, OECD, Paris, 1975; coord. Fed. Ministry Tech., Bonn, Germany, 1986-88; vis. prof. U. B.C., Vancouver, 2001—. Author: Monopolar World Order, 2000, The Wasted Republic, 2001; co-editor: Barriers to Full Employment, 1988, Beyond Keynesianism: The Socio-Economics of Production and Full Employment, 1991, The Market Shock, 1992. Mem. German Econ. Assn., SASE, European Assn. Polit. Economy. Avocation: mountaineering. Office: Austrian Acad Scis Rsch Unit of Instnl Charge Eugenstresse 8-A0 A-1040 Vienna Austria E-mail: egon.matzner@aon.at.

MAU, BENJAMIN, artist; b. Sien, China, Dec. 25, 1944; came to U.S., 1962; s. James K. and Sue Y. Mau; m. Sonya Chu Mau, July 14, 1972. AA, Southwest Bapt. U., Bolivar, Mo., 1964; BS, Ouachita Bapt. U., 1967; MS, Memphis State U., 1969. Paintings featured in books, including Artists of Illinois, 1995, The Best of Watercolor, 1995, The Best of Watercolor 2, 1997, Painting Color, 1997, Floral Inspirations, 1997, Landscape Inspirations, 1997, The Watercolor Expressions, 1999. Recipient Permanent Collection awards Ea. Ill. U., Charleston, 1975, Caterpillar, Decatur, Ill., 1975, Carson P. Scott, Quincy, Ill., 1978. Mem. Nat. Watercolor Soc. (signature mem.), Am. Watercolor Soc. (signature mem.). Home: 1 Lateer Dr Normal IL 61761-3925 E-mail: maucorp@aol.com.

MAU, C. S. See SALERNO, CHERIE ANN

MAU, WILLIAM KOON-HEE, financier; b. Honolulu, Apr. 25, 1913; s. Wah Hop and Mau (Ho Shee) M.; m. Jean Lau, Oct. 17, 1936; children—Milton, Cynthia, Lynette, Leighton, Letitia. Ed. pub. schs., Hawaii; LL.D., Pacific U., 1969. Chmn. bd., chief exec. officer Am. Security Bank, Honolulu, 1958-69; pres. Tropical Enterprises, Ltd. and Ambassador Hotel of Waikiki, Honolulu, Top of Waikiki Revolving Restaurant, 1955—; owner, developer Waikiki Bus. Plaza, Waikiki Shopping Plaza, Aloha Motors Properties; pres. Empress Ltd., Hong Kong, 1962-70, Aloha Motors, Inc. Vice chmn. Hawaii Bd. Land Natural Resources, 1959-63; Bd. dirs. Chinese Cultural Found., Hawaii, 1960— , Aloha United Fund, 1966— , Am. Nat. Red Cross, 1965— ; past mem. exec. bd. Boy Scouts Am.; trustee Kauikeolani Children's Hosp., 1959-61. Recipient Golden Plate award Am. Acad. Achievement Bd. Govs., 1969; Wisdom Hall of Fame award of honor, 1969; named Bus. Man of Year Hawaii Bus. and Industry mag., 1966 Mem. Am., Hawaii bank assns., Newcomen Soc. N.Am., Am. Bd. Arbitration, Downtown Improvement Assn., United Chinese Soc., Tsung Tsin Assn., Hawaii Visitors Bur., Hawaii Islanders, Hawaii Pub. Links Golf Assn., Chinese C. of C. (dir., auditor 1959-62) Home: 3938 Monterey Pl Honolulu HI 96816-3922 Office: Waikiki Bus Plaza 2270 Kalakaua Ave Honolulu HI 96815-2519

MAUBERT, JACQUES CLAUDE, retired school superintendent; b. Provins, France, May 19, 1932; s. Jean Pierre and Simone Jeanne (Bocquého) M.; m. Micheline Josephine Lathuille, June 16, 1956; children: Eric, Sandrine. MA, Dakar U., Senegal, 1969; CAPES, U. Bordeaux (France), 1971. Tchr. French Ministry Edn., Morocco, 1952-62, Senegal, 1962-73, councellor Senegal, 1973-75, Togo, 1975-77, headmaster France, 1977-79, headmaster Lycee Francais of San Francisco, 1979-85, headmaster France, 1985-86, headmaster Lyceum Kennedy N.Y.C., 1986-2000; ret., 2000. Mem. presdl. commn. Reform for Tchg. French in Africa, Dakar, 1973—75; pedagogic councellor U. Benin, Togo, 1975—77. Author: French Literature for 11th Grade, 1975. Pres. Union des Francais de l' Etranger, San Francisco, 1983-85. Decorated officer The Acad. Palms (France). Roman Catholic. Avocations: swimming, tennis, classical music, jazz, opera. Home: 80 Longfellow Rd Mill Valley CA 94941-1591 E-mail: jacqmichmaub@home.com.

MAUCH, ROBERT CARL, service industry executive, venture capitalist; b. Cleve., Dec. 7, 1939; s. Otto Herman and Clara (Lapple) M.; m. Rita Marie Szucs, Aug. 25, 1964 (div. Jan. 1980); children: David O., Martin L., Karolyn L.; m. Drusilla Ann Tesch, Feb. 18, 1989. AMP, Harvard U., 1983; MS, U. Calif., Berkeley, 1965; BSChemE, Cleve. State U., 1962. V.p., gen. mgr., LP gas divsn. Amerigas Inc., Valley Forge, Pa., 1978-83; v.p. UGI Corp., 1978-87, sr. v.p., 1987-90; dir. Ansutech, Inc., 1981-82, Matheson Gas Products, Inc., Valley Forge, 1981-82; pres., dir. AP Propane Inc., 1983-90, Amerigas Propane, Valley Forge, 1983-96; pres., CEO, dir. AmeriGas Inc., 1991-96, Petrolane, Inc., Valley Forge, 1993-96, Amerigas, Inc. subs. UGI Corp., Valley Forge, 1990-96, AmeriGas Propane Inc. (gen. ptnr. AmeriGas Ptnrs. L.P.); chmn., CEO Anthem Holdings Corp., Valley Forge, 1997-98, AllianceOne Inc., Exton, 1998—. Bd. govs. Pa. Economy League, Phila., 1985-91; mem. World Affairs Coun., Phila., 1980-95. Mem.: Am. Collectors Assn., Propane Vehicle Coun. (chmn. 1994—), Waynesborough C. of C., Nat. Propane Gas Assn. (bd. dirs., exec. com., pres. 1978—95), Healthcare Fin. Mgmt. Assn. Lutheran. Avocations: tennis, reading, skiing, running, weight training. Office: AllianceOne Inc 690 Stockton Dr PO Box 556 Exton PA 19341-0556

MAUCK, HENRY PAGE, JR. medical and pediatrics educator; b. Richmond, Va., Feb. 3, 1926; s. Henry Page and Harriet Hutcheson (Morrison) M.; m. Janet Garrett Horsley, May 14, 1955; children— Henry Page III, John Waller. BA, U. Va., 1950, MD, 1952. Diplomate: Am. Bd. Internal Medicine. Intern Henry Ford Hosp., Detroit, 1952-53; resident Med. Coll. Va., Richmond, 1953-56, asst. prof. medicine and pediatrics, 1961-66, assoc. prof., 1966-72, prof., 1972—. Fellow in cardiology Am. Heart Assn., 1956-57; cons. cardiology Langley Field Air Force Hosp., Hampton, Va., McGuire's VA Hosp., Richmond. Contbr.: chpt. to Autonomic Control of Cardiovascular System, 1972; contbr. articles to sci. jours. Served with U.S. Army, 1944-46. Fellow ACP, Am. Coll. Cardiology (former gov. Va.); mem. Am. Physiol. Soc., So. Soc. Clin. Investigation, Am. Fedn. Clin. Research, So. Soc. Clin. Research. Presbyterian. Home: 113 Oxford Cir W Richmond VA 23221-3224 Office: Med Coll Va PO Box 281 Richmond VA 23218-0281

MAUCKER, EARL ROBERT, newspaper editor, newspaper executive; b. St. Louis, Sept. 20, 1947; s. Robert Buffem and Linette (Meloy) M.; m. Betsy Ann Johnson, May 21, 1977; children: Eric Robert, Michael Earl. BA in Mass Communications, So. Ill. U., 1972. Reporter Alton (Ill.) Telegraph, 1969-73; reporter, city editor, news editor, asst. mng. editor Rockford (Ill.) Morning Star, 1973-79; mng. editor Springfield (Mo.) Daily News, 1979-80, Ft. Lauderdale (Fla.) Sun-Sentinel, 1990-95, v.p. editorial, 1995—. Sgt. SUAF, 1966-69. Mem. Am. Soc. Newspapers Editors, Fla. Soc. Newspapers Editors, Associated Press Mng. Editors Assn. (bd. dirs. 1989-93). Home: 3511 NE 26th Ave Lighthouse Point FL 33064-8105 Office: Sun-Sentinel 200 E Las Olas Blvd Fort Lauderdale FL 33301-2293

MAUDERLY, JOE LLOYD, pulmonary toxicologist; b. Strong City, Kans., Aug. 31, 1943; s. Joseph Park and Violet May (Cox) M.; m. Cheryl Gaines, Jan. 31, 1965; children: Laurie Jean, Jameson Lynn. BS, Kans. State U., 1965, DVM, 1967. Respiratory physiologist Inhalation Toxicology Rsch. Inst., Albuquerque, 1967-89, supr. pathophysiology group, 1976-89, dir., 1989-96; rsch. prof. medicine U. N.Mex., 1988—, clin. prof. pharmacy, 1990—; sr. scientist, dir. external affairs Lovelace Respiratory Rsch. Inst., 1997-99; v.p., dir. Nat. Environ. Respiratory Ctr., 1999—. Cons. in field; mem. EPA Clean Air Scientific Adv. Com., 1992-96, chair, 1997-2000. Assoc. editor Fundamental Applied Toxicology, 1989-94; contbr. articles to profl. jours., chpts. to books. Served to capt. USAF, 1967-69. Mem. Am. Thoracic Soc. (chmn. assembly of environ. and occupational health 1991-93, long-range planning com. 1991-94, sci. adv. com. 1993-96, editl. bd., exptl. lung rsch.), Am. Physiol. Soc., Am. Vet. Med. Assn., N.Mex. Vet. Med. Assn., Soc. Toxicology. Republican. Home: 4517 Banff Dr NE Albuquerque NM 87111-2829 E-mail: jmauderl@lrri.org.

MAUDLIN, ROBERT V. economics and government affairs consultant; b. Washington, June 8, 1927; s. Cecil V. and Eva Jane (Wright) M.; m. Carole M. Jackson, Sept. 3, 1949; children: Lynda C., David V., Tim W.E. Student, MIT, 1945; BS, Am. U., 1951. Ptnr. C.V. & R.V. Maudlin, Washington, 1952-72, owner, 1972—. Mng. dir. Bur. Applied Econs., Washington, 1960—; sec. Nat. Assn. Scissors and Shears Mfrs., 1970-97; exec. dir. Joint Govt. Liaison Com., 1973-81; mem. Industry Sector Adv. Com. U.S. Dept. Commerce and U.S. Trade Rep., Washingotn, 1975-97; commr. Adv. Neighborhood Commn. of D.C., 1999—. Author econ. and statis. reports. Pres. Forest Hills Citizens Assn., Washington, 1964; chmn. Boy Scouts Am., Washington, 1972. 2d lt. C.E., AUS, 1945-47, USAR, 1947-55. Republican. Home: 2906 Ellicott Ter NW Washington DC 20008-1023 E-mail: maudlin@alum.mit.edu.

MAUE, LETA JO, special education administrator; b. York, Pa., Dec. 7, 1951; d. Wilford Thomas and Helen Louise Myers; m. Frederick Robert Maue, Sept. 24, 1994; children: Frederick C., Patrick P. BS in Elem. Edn., Mansfield U., 1973; MA in Spl. Edn., Shippensburg U., 1979; Cert. in Supervision of Spl. Edn., Bloomsburg U., 1998. Cert. in reality therapy. Elem. tchr. Shikellamy Sch. Dist., Sunbury, Pa., 1973-76, spl. edn. tchr., 1986-90, instrnl. support diagnostician, 1990-97, spl. edn. supr., 1997—; tchr. of gifted York (Pa.) Suburban Sch. Dist., 1976-83. Dir. Camp Pennwood, York County Arc, 1982-83; staff devel. trainer Shikellamy Sch. Dist., 1991—, supt. leadership adv. coun., 1997—. Mem. Local Right to Edn. task force, Danville, Pa., 1997—; vol. Sunbury Revitalization, 1989-95; mem. Northumberland County Hist. Soc.; bd. dirs. Susquehanna Valley Chorale, 1984-92; mem. coun.. Zion Luth. Ch., 1990-94, pres. coun., 1993-94, mem. choir, 1984—. Mem. Coun. for Exceptional Children, William Glasser Inst., SAI Hon. Music Frat. Avocations: playing piano, singing, opera, travel, camping. Home: 168 N 11th St Sunbury PA 17801-2444 Office: Shikellamy Sch Dist 200 Island Blvd Sunbury PA 17801-1028

MAUER, ALVIN MARX, physician, medical educator; b. LeMars, Iowa, Jan. 10, 1928; s. Alvin Milton and Bertha Elizabeth (Marx) M.; m. Theresa Ann McGivern, Dec. 2, 1950; children: Stephen James, Timothy John, Daria Maureen, Elizabeth Claire. BA, State U. Iowa, 1950, MD, 1953. Intern Cin. Gen. Hosp., 1953-54; resident in pediatrics Children's Hosp. Cin., 1954-56; fellow in hematology dept. medicine U. Utah, Salt Lake City, 1956-59; dir. div. hematology Children's Hosp. Cin., prof. dept. hematology, 1959-73; prof. dept. pediatrics U. Cin. Coll. Medicine, 1959-73; prof. pediatrics U. Tenn. Coll. Medicine, Memphis, 1973-97, prof. medicine, 1983-97, prof. emeritus, 1997—; dir. cancer program U. Tenn. Coll. Health Scis.; dir. St. Jude Children's Research Hosp., Memphis, 1973-83. Mem. hematology study sect. NIH; mem. clin. cancer investigation rev. com. Nat. Cancer Inst.; mem. com. on maternal and infant nutrition NRC. Author: Pediatric Hematology, 1969; editor: The Biology of Human Leukemia, 1990. Served with U.S. Army, 1946. Mem. Am. Soc. Hematology (pres. 1980-81), Assn. Am. Cancer Insts. (pres. 1980), am. Acad. Pediatrics (com. on nutrition), Am. Assn. Cancer Edn., Am. Soc. Clin. Investigation, Am. Fedn. Clin. Rsch., Assn. Am. Physicians, Am. Pediatric Soc., Cen. Soc. Clin. Investigation, Cen. Soc. Clin. Rsch., Internat. Soc. Hematology (pres. 1988-90, chmn. 1992-96, bd. councilors 1992-96), Am. Cancer Soc. (pres. Tenn. divsn. 1992-93), Midwest Soc. Pediat. Rsch., N.Y. Acad. Scis., Soc. Pediat. Rsch., Am. Assn. Cancer Rsch., Phi Beta Kappa, Sigma Xi, Alpha Omega Alpha. Democrat. Roman Catholic. Office: U Tenn Ctr for Health Scis Rm 808 910 Madison Ave Memphis TN 38103 E-mail: amauer@utmem.edu.

MAUER, KENNETH RAY, gastroenterologist, educator; b. N.Y.C., Apr. 27, 1957; s. Samuel and Estelle (Miller) M.; m. Fran Sheff, Aug. 17, 1980; 1 child, Elizabeth. BA with honors, Johns Hopkins U., 1979; MD, NYU, 1983. Diplomate Am. Bd. Internal Medicine, Am. Bd. Gastroenterology, Nat. Bd. Med. Examiners; lic. physician, N.Y., Conn. Intern in internal medicine Bronx (N.Y.) Mcpl. Hosp. Ctr., Albert Einstein Coll. Hosp., 1983-84, resident, then chief resident in internal medicine, 1984-87; attending physician emergency rm. Cabrini Hosp., N.Y.C., 1986-89; fellow in gastroenterology Mt. Sinai Med. Ctr., 1987-89, clin. instr., 1989—; adj. instr. N.Y. Med. Coll., Valhalla, 1994—; mem. staff St. Vincent's Med. Ctr., Bridgeport, Conn., 1989—, Bridgeport Hosp., 1989—; clin. instr. Columbia U. P&S, 1999. Author: (ednl. tape series) Clinical Advances in Gastroenterology, 1992; co-contbr. chpt. to: Inflammatory Bowel Disease: Diagnosis and Treatment, 1991; contbr. articles to sci. jours. Elected one of Best Drs. in N.Y. Met. Area., The Castle & Connolly Guide. Fellow ACP, Am. Coll. Gastroenterology (mem. subcom. on abstract selection for colon abstracts 1991); mem. Am. Gastroent. Assn., Am. Soc. Gastrointestinal Endoscopy, Crohn's and Colitis Found. Am. (mem. med. adv. com. Westchester and Fairfield County chpt.). Office: Gastroenterology Assoc Fairfield County 1305 Post Rd Fairfield CT 06430-6016

MAUGANS, JOHN CONRAD, lawyer; b. Miami County, Ind., May 10, 1938; s. Willis William and Evelyn Jeannette (Mills) M.; m. Judith M. Gallagher, Jan. 24, 1960 (dec. June 1984); children: Lisa Denise, Stacy Erin, Kristen Cherie: m. Jo Ella Middlekauff, June 7, 1985. AB, Manchester Coll., 1960; LLB with distinction, Ind. U., 1962, JD, 1969. Bar: Ind. 1962. Assoc. Barnes, Hickam, Pantzer & Boyd, Indpls., 1962-63; atty. pvr. practice, Kokomo, Ind., 1966—; ptnr. Bayliff, Harrigan, Cord & Maugans, 1969—. Guest lectr. Coll. Bus. Manchester Coll., 1966-80 Contbr. articles to profl. jours. Chmn. Howard fund dr. Manchester Coll., 1971; bd. dirs. Tribal Trials coun. Girl Scouts U.S.A., 1977-85, Vols. in Cmty. Svc., 1978-84, Home Health Care of Ctrl. Ind., Inc., 1983-89; trustee Western Sch. Corp., 1986—, pres., 1991-93; bd. dirs. kokomo Park Band, Inc., 1989—; chmn. Christian Edn. com., Main St. Christian Ch., 1993—; mem. asset devel. and mktg. com. Cmty. Found. Howard County, Inc., 1994—. Capt. AUS, 1963-66. Fellow Am. Trial Lawyers Assn. (Roscoe Pound chpt.), Ind. Bar Found.; mem. Assn. Trial Lawyers Am., Ind. Bar Assn., Howard County Bar Assn. (pres. 1989), Ind. Trial Lawyers Assn., Manchester Coll. Alumni Assn. (chmn. area chpt. 1970, 88, 89, 90, 91), Manchester Coll. M. Alumni Assn. (pres. 1972), Am. Legion, Order of Coif, Phi Delta Phi. Home: 3274 Woodhaven Trl Kokomo IN 46902-5062 Office: PO Box 2249 123 N Buckeye St Kokomo IN 46904-2249 E-mail: connie.maugans@bhcmlaw.com.

MAUGHAN, SIR DERYCK, bank executive; Degree earned, King's Coll., Univ. of London, 1969, Stanford U., 1978. With Treasury Dept., United Kingdom, from 1969, Salomon Bros. Inc., 1983—; mng. dir. Salomon Bros. Inc, 1986—91, COO, 1991-92, chmn., CEO, 1992—; vice-chmn. Citigroup, 1998—. Office: Citigroup 399 Park Ave New York NY 10043-0001

MAUGHAN, DONNA See ALLISON, DONNA M.

MAUGHAN, MICHAEL WILLIAM, industrial psychologist, management consultant; b. San Diego, Dec. 29, 1951; s. William Leland and Hope Elene Maughan; m. Onda Lea Maughan, May 28, 1977; children: Kimberly, Mikaela, Rebecca, Daniel. BS in Psychology, No. Ariz. U., 1978, MA in Psychology, 1986; PhD in Indsl. and Orgnl. Psychology, U. Houston, 1989. Patrol officer Coconino County Sheriff's Dept., Sedona, Ariz., 1973-76, Flagstaff, 1976-77, sgt., 1977-83; mgmt. cons. Gehlhausen Ruda & Assocs., Chgo., 1989-2000, Ruda Cohen & Assocs., Chgo., 2000—. Cons. Creating Pride, Chgo., 1987—. Mem. Soc. for Indsl. and Orgnl. Psychology, Am. Psychol. Soc., Oak Brook Assn. Commerce and Industry. Republican. Avocations: rock climbing, bicycling, woodworking, archery. Office: Ruda Cohen & Assocs 303 W Madison 650 Chicago IL 60606 E-mail: mmaughan@rudacohen.com.

MAUGHAN, WILLARD ZINN, dermatologist; b. Riverside, Calif., Apr. 21, 1944; s. Franklin David and Martha Charlotte (Zinn) M.; m. Rona Lee Wilcox, Aug. 20, 1968; children: Julie Anne, Kathryn Anita, Willard Wilcox, Christopher Keith. Student, Johns Hopkins U., Balt., 1962-64; BS, U. Utah, 1968, MD, 1972. Diplomate Am. Bd. Dermatology. Intern Walter Reed Army Med. Ctr., Washington, 1972-73; fellow Mayo Clinic, Rochester, Minn., 1976-79; pvt. practice Ogden, Utah, 1979—. Contbr. articles to profl. jours. Commr. Boy Scouts Am., Weber County, Utah, 1980-84, dist. chmn., 1993-94, assoc. mem. bd. dirs. Trapper Trails coun., 1995-99, v.p., mem. exec. bd., 1999—; pres. Am. Cancer Soc., Weber County, 1985-86. Maj. U.S. Army, 1971-76. Recipient Dist. award of merit Boy Scouts Am., 1985, Silver Beaver award 1994. Fellow ACP, Am. Acad. Dermatology, Royal Soc. Medicine (London); mem. N.Y. Acad. Scis., Kiwanis Club, Alpha Omega Alpha, Phi Sigma Iota. Republican. Mem. Lds Ch. Avocations: woodcarving, camping. Home: 2486 W 4550 S Roy UT 84067-1944 Office: 3860 Jackson Ave Ogden UT 84403-1956

MAUKE, LEAH RACHEL, retired counselor; b. Newport, R.I., Aug. 29, 1924; d. Louis and Annie (Price) Louison; m. Otto Russell Mauke, June 18, 1950. BSBA, Boston U., 1946, MBA, 1948. Teaching fellow Boston U., 1946-48; head advt. dept. Endicott Coll., Beverly, Mass., 1948-66; guidance counselor Vineland (N.J.) Sr. High Sch., 1966-69, Black Horse Pike Regional Sch. Dist., Blackwood, N.J., 1969-86, ret., 1986. Vol. ARC, Vero Beach, Fla., 1988—. Boston U. fellow 1946. Mem. AAUW (life, pres. North Shore br. 1955-59, state fellowship chmn. 1957-58), NEA, N.J. Edn. Assn., Camden County Pers. and Guidance Assn. (sec. 1972). Avocations: reading, travel, crossword puzzles. Home: 2119 E Lakeview Dr Sebastian FL 32958-8519

MAUKE, OTTO RUSSELL, retired college president; b. Webster, Mass., Jan. 26, 1924; s. Otto G. and Florence (Giroux) M.; m. Leah Louison, June 18, 1950. AB, Clark U., 1947, A.M., 1948; PhD (Kellogg fellow), U. Tex., 1965. Tchr. history, acad. dean Endicott Jr. Coll., Beverly, Mass., 1948-65; acad. dean Cumberland County Coll., Vineland, N.J., 1966-67; pres. Camden County Coll., Blackwood, 1967-87, pres. emeritus. Served with U.S. Army, 1943-46, PTO. Home: 2119 E Lakeview Dr Sebastian FL 32958-8519

MAUL, CAROL ELAINE, small business owner; b. Joliet, Ill., Feb. 28, 1953; d. Donald James and Virginia Olive (Wilson) Johnson; m. Richard Kester Maul, June 16, 1979. Student, Met. State Coll., 1971-76. Mgr. So-Fro Fabrics, Elgin, 1976-79; owner, operator Port Arthur Pie Co., Denver, 1985-87; freelance musician, 1987—; owner CAMA Creative Mktg. Bus. Promotion, Profl. Voice Work. Prin. flutist Elgin Symphony Orch., 1976-79; mem. Denver Botanic Gardens. Mem. Colo. Rail Passenger Assn., Nat. Trust Hist. Preservation, Citizens for Classical FM Radio (bd. dirs.). Independent. Episcopalian. Lodge: Job's Daughters (Honored Queen 1970-71). Avocations: needlepoint, calligraphy. Home and Office: 387 S Pontiac Way Denver CO 80224-1335

MAUL, KEVIN JAY, financial consultant; b. York, Pa., Jan. 11, 1968; s. Peter Henry Jr. and Patricia Louise (Young) M. BA, Shippensburg U., 1990; MA, U. Va., 1992. Economist USDA Econ. Rsch. Svc., Washington, 1991-92; fin. cons. Pricewaterhouse Coopers LLP, 1992-99, Resources Connection, McLean, Va., 1999-2000, Deloitte & Touche LLP, Washington, 2000—. Author: The Handbook of Mortgage Banking, 1993. Mem. Am. Econ. Assn. Lutheran. Avocations: music, travel, gardening, stamp collecting. Home: 909 S Rolfe St # A Arlington VA 22204-4545 Office: Deloitte & Touche LLP 555 12th St NW Washington DC 20004-1207

MAUL, TERRY LEE, psychologist, educator; b. San Francisco, May 6, 1946; s. Chester Lloyd and Clella Lucille (Hobbs) M.; m. Gail Ann Retallick, June 27, 1970 (div. Dec. 1986); 1 child, Andrew Eliot. Student, Coll. San Mateo, 1964-65; AB, U. Calif., Berkeley, 1967, MA, 1968, PhD, 1970. Prof. psychology San Bernardino Valley Coll., San Bernardino, Calif., 1970—, chmn. dept., 1979-83, 96—. Rschr. self-actualization. Author: (with Eva Conrad) Introduction to Experimental Psychology, 1981; (with Gail Maul) Beyond Limit: Ways to Growth and Freedom, 1983; contbg. author other psychol. texts. Mem. APA, AAUP (chpt. pres. 1971-73), Audubon Soc., Mensa, Nature Conservancy, Wilderness Soc., Sierra Club. Democrat. Office: San Bernardino Valley Coll 701 S Mount Vernon Ave San Bernardino CA 92410-2705

MAULDEN, JULIA WATSON, volunteer; b. Wilmington, N.C., Sept. 27, 1913; d. Thomas Arnold and Ruby (Piver) Watson; m. Paul Ranzo Maulden, Sept. 18, 1935 (dec. 1963); children: Gilbertine, Kerry, Paul Jr., Timothy. BA in French, U. N.C. Greensboro, 1933; MEd, U. N.C. Charlotte, 1973; DHL (hon.), Queens Coll., 1988. Instr. lang. Nat. U. Zaire, 1974-75; dir. Low-Income Housing Project, Davidson, 1978-80; vol. Holy Cross Hosp., Leogane, Haiti, 1980-81; coord., dir. Summer Work Camp, Croix Fer, Haiti, 1982-84, 86, 91; vol. exec. dir. Habitat for Humanity, Charlotte, 1984-88. Constn. com. mem. World Assn. Girl Guides and Girl Scouts, 1957-66, nat. bd. dirs., 1948-66, chmn. Juliet Low Region VI, 1948-54, troop leader, 1940-74, vol. trainer, 1942-70, coun. pres. 1940-44; instr. in child devel. Coll. of Human Devel. and Learning, U. N.C., Charlotte, 1976-78. Mem. Phi Beta Kappa. Democrat. Presbyterian. Avocations: reading, reviewing books, gardening, horseback riding, tennis. Home: 400 Avinger Ln Apg 247 Davidson NC 28036

MAULDIN, JOHN INGLIS, public defender; b. Atlanta, Nov. 6, 1947; s. Earle and Isabel (Inglis) M.; m. Cynthia Ann Balchin, Apr. 15, 1967 (div. Dec. 1985); children: Tracy Rutherford, Abigail Inglis; m. Linda W. Farmer, Nov. 7, 1998. BA, Wofford Coll., 1970; JD, Emory U., 1973. Bar: S.C. 1974, U.S. Ct. Appeals (4th cir.) 1974, U.S. Dist. Ct. S.C. 1975, U.S. Supreme Ct. 1978. Asst. pub. def. Defender Corp. Greenville County, S.C., 1974-76; ptnr. Mauldin & Allison, Greenville, 1977-92; pub. defender Greenville County, S.C., 1992—. Chair S.C. Commn. on Indigent Def., 1993-96; adj. prof. Greenville Tech. Coll., 1975-80; sec., treas. Def. Corp. Greenville County, 1979-92, bd. dirs. Bd. dirs. Speech Hearing & Learning Ctr., Greenville, 1977-90, pres., 1982; bd. dirs. Save Our Sons, 1995—. Named S.C. Atty. Yr. ACLU, S.C., 1986. Mem. Nat. Assn. Criminal Def. Attorneys, Nat. Legal Aid and Defender Assn. (defender policy bd. 1999—), S.C. Trial Lawyers Assn., S.C. Assn. Criminal Def. Lawyers (bd. dirs. 1997-99), S.C. Pub. Defender Assn. (bd. dirs. 1992—), Rotary, Sigma Delta Phi. Democrat. Methodist. Office: PO Box 10264fs Greenville SC 29603

MAULDIN, RICHARD DANIEL, mathematics educator; b. Longview, Tex., Jan. 17, 1943; s. Stanley Hubert Mauldin and Helen Jane Dowling; stepfather: Cloyd James Dowling; m. Diana Rogers Block, June 24, 1985; children: Christopher, Catherine. BA, U. Tex., 1965, MA, 1966, PhD, 1969. From asst. prof. to assoc. prof. U. Fla., Gainesville, 1969-77; assoc. prof. U. North Tex., Denton, 1977-79, prof., 1979-88, Regents prof., 1988—. Cons. Los Alamos (N.Mex.) Nat. Lab., 1980-92, Ctr. for Comms. Rsch., San Diego, 1999-2001. Editor: Advances in Mathematics, 1994-2001, Real Analysis Exchange, 1994-2001; author: TransAMS, Japan Jour. Math.; contbr. articles to profl. jours. Rsch. grantee NSF, 1978-2001. Mem. Am. Math. Soc. (editor procs. 1988-92), Math. Assn. Am., Inst. Math. Stats., Assn. Symbolic Logic, Sigma Xi. Office: U North Tex Math Dept Box 311430 Denton TX 76203-1430 Fax: 940-565-4805. E-mail: mauldin@unt.edu.

MAULDIN, ROSETTA JOHNSON, dean, social work educator; b. Bedford County, Va. d. Perroneau and Edna Johnson; m. Charles A. Pinder, May 20, 1995; children: Lee, Michael, Adrienne Mauldin Oliver, Mark. BS, Hampton Inst., 1957; MSW, Ohio State U., 1968, PhD, 1990. Lic. ind. social worker, Ohio. Social worker Hamilton County Welfare Dept., Cin., 1959-70; exec. dir. Careers in Social Work, 1970-72; dir. children's svcs. Ctrl. Cmty. Health Bd., 1972-77; prof. social work No. Ky. U., Highland Heights, 1977—, interim dean Coll. Profl. Studies, 1985-87, 98—, assoc. provost, 1994-97. Chairperson dept. social work No. Ky. U., Highland Heights, 1982-85; bd. mem. Counselor and Social Worker Bd., State Ohio, 1990-93; adj. prof. U. Ky., Lexington, 1990—; presenter in field. Contbr. chpt. to book. Mem. bd. regents No. Ky. U., Highland Heights, 1990-93; pres., sec., commr. Nat. Accreditation Coun. for Agys. Serving the Blind and Visually Impaired, N.Y.C., Cin., 1990—; bd. mem. United Way, Cin., 1991—; alumnae Class 17 Leadership Cin., 1994. Recipient Career Woman of Achievement award YWCA, Cin., 1986, Cmty. Svc. award U.S. Postal Svc., 1994, Top Achiever award Successguide, Cin., 1995. Mem. NAACP, NASW (state bd. mem., state sec., state membership chair), Acad. Cert. Social Workers. Baptist. Avocations: reading, singing. Fax: 606-572-6176. E-mail: mauldin@nku.edu.

MAULDON, JANE GILBERT, public policy educator; b. Oxford, Eng., Jan. 5, 1955; d. James Grenfell and Margaret M.; m. Rondi Gilbert, Jan. 5, 1994. BA, Oxford (Eng.) U., 1976; M in Pub. Policy, Princeton U., 1984, PhD, 1989. Asst., then assoc. prof. Goldman Sch. Pub. Policy U. Calif., Berkeley, 1990—.

MAULDON, MARGARET, translator; b. Buenos Aires, Sept. 24, 1929; came to U.S., 1968; d. Arthur Capron and Prudence Trattles Taylor; m. James Grenfell Mauldon, July 11, 1953; children: Jane, Matthew, Maria, Lucy. BA with 1st class honors, Newnham Coll., Cambridge, Eng., 1951; MA, U. Mass., 1975, PhD, 1980. Rsch. officer Russian affairs Brit. Fgn. Office, London, 1952-53; asst. prof. French Mt. Holyoke Coll., South Hadley, Mass., 1979-82; lectr. French Smith Coll., Northampton, 1982-88; freelance translator Oxford (Eng.) U. Press, 1991—. Translator: L'Assommoir (Emile Zola), 1995, The Charterhouse of Parma (Stendhal), 1997, Against Nature (Joris-Karl Huysmans), 1998, Adolphe (Benjamin Constant), 2001, Bel-Ami (Guy de Maupassant), 2001. Recipient Scott Moncrieff prize Soc. Authors, 1999; Grantee Nat. Endowment Arts, 1988. Mem. Translators' Assn. Avocations: travel, creative writing, old movies. Home and Office: 327 Spencer Dr Amherst MA 01002 E-mail: mauldonm@yahoo.com.

MAULE, JAMES EDWARD, law educator, lawyer; b. Phila., Nov. 26, 1951; s. Edward Randolph George and Jennie Elisabeth (Zappone) M.; m. Susan Margaret Noonan, June 26, 1982 (div. May 1988); children: Charles Edward, Sarah Margaret; m. Susan K. Garrison, Apr. 7, 1990 (div. 1991). BS cum laude, U. Pa. Wharton Sch., 1973; JD cum laude, Villanova U., 1976; LLM with highest honors, George Washington U., 1979. Bar: Pa. 1976, U.S. Tax Ct. 1986. Atty.-adv. Office Chief Counsel to IRS Legis. and Regulations Divsn., Washington, 1976-78; atty.-adv. judge U.S. Tax Ct., 1978-80; asst. prof. law Dickinson Sch. Law, 1981-83, lectr. and tax program chmn. continuing legal edn., 1981-83; assoc. prof. Villanova Sch. Law, 1983-86, prof., 1986—. Lectr. continuing legal edn. Pa. Bar Inst. , Harrisburg, Continuing Legal Edn. Satellite Network, Inc., 1988; lectr. state and local taxes Georgetown U. Law Ctr. Inst., 1992; sr. tax and tech. ptnr. Ctr. Info. Law and Policy, 1993—99; owner JEMBook Pub. Co.; owner TaxJEM Inc.; co-owner Starjem LLC ; lectr. continuing legal edn. Phila. Tax Conf., 1996, 2001. Author: Cases and Materials in Federal Income Taxation, 1981, (21st edit.) , 2001, Materials in Partnership Law and Taxation, 1985, (6th edit.) , 1991, Materials in Partnership Taxation, 1987, (20th edit.) , 2001, Materials in Introduction to Taxation, 1987, (2d edit.) , 1988, Cases and Materials in Introduction to the Taxation of Business Entities, 1992, (10th edit) , 2002, Materials in Taxation of Fundamental Wealth Transfers , 1986, (2d edit.) , 1988, Materials in Tax Consequences of Disposition of Property, 1983, (3d edit) , 1985, Materials and Problems in Taxation of Property Disposition I, 1987, Materials in Tax Planning for Real Estate, 1986, Materials in Estate and Gift Tax, 1983, (3d edit) , 1985, Materials in Taxation of Real Estate Transactions, 1986, (3d edit.) , 1992, Taxation of Residence Transactions, 1985, S Corporations: State Law and Taxation, 1989, (supp.edits) , 1989, 1990, 1991, 1992, 1993, Materials and Problems in Computer Applications in the Law, 1990, (6th edit.) , 1995, Materials in Tax Policy, 1990, Materials in Digital Legal Practice Skills, 1996, Materials and Problems in Computer Applications in Tax Law, 1991, (8th edit.) , 1998, Better That 100 Witches Should Live, 1995, Materials in Decedents Estates and Trusts , 1997, (5th edit.) , 2001; author: (with A. Clay) Preparing the 1065 Return, 1992, 1993; author: Continuing Legal Edn. Publs., 1981—; contbg. author: Federal Tax Service, 1989, contbg. author: Tax Practice Series, 1989—; contbr. articles, chapters to books, monographs; author, developer: Computer Assisted Legal Edn. Programs in Taxation, owner, author, editor : computer assisted tax law instruction TaxJEM Inc. , cons., prin. author: ABA Section of Taxation Model S Corporation Income Tax Act and Commentary, 1989, author, editor: Report of the Subcommittee on Comparison of S Corporations and Partnerships, 1990, author, editor: Report of the Subcommittee on Comparison of S Corporations and Partnerships , 1991, case and comment editor: Villanova Law Rev., 1975—76, columnist, mem. editl. bd.: S Corps. Jour., 1987—91, columnist, mem. editl. bd.: Jour. of Ltd. Liability Cos., 1994—98, columnist, mem. editl. bd.: BNA Tax Mgmt., 1994—. Recipient Dist. Author award, BNA Tax Mgmt., 1993; scholar Nat. Merit, 1969—73. Mem. ABA (chair and reporter phaseout Elimination Project, Tax Simplification and Restructuring Com., sect. of taxation, cons., ex-officio mem. subcom. on state law, S Corp. com., chmn. subcom. on comparison of partnerships, mem. task force on pass-through entities, tax sect., former chmn. subcom. manuscripts and unpub. tchg. material, com. tchg. tax), Phila. Bar Assn. (lectr. tax sect. state and local tax CLE program 1991, fed. income taxes 1992—), Ctr. Info. Law and Policy, Order of Coif, Friars Sr. Soc. (Phila), Beta Alpha Psi. Home: 219 Comrie Dr Villanova PA 19085-1402 Office: Villanova U Sch Law Villanova PA 19085 E-mail: maule@law.villanova.edu.

MAULION, RICHARD PETER, psychiatrist, physician, neurolinguist; b. Rosario, Argentina, Sept. 2, 1949; s. Peter Henry and Vivien Ormsby (Gough) M.; divorced; 1 child, Maximillian. BS, Colegio Salesiano San Jose, Rosario, ARgentina, 1967; MD, U. Nacional de Rosario, 1980. Diplomate Am. Bd. Psychiatry and Neurology, Am. Acad. Psychoanalysis, Am. Acad. Addiction Medicine, Am. Acad. Pain Mgmt., Am. Bd. Forensic Examiners, Am. Bd. Quality Assurance and Utilization Rev. Physicians, Am. Bd. Disability Analysts, Am. Acad. Experts in Traumatic Stress; cert. neurolinguistic programming (NLP) master practitioner and trainer. Intern Kans. U., Kansas City, 1981-82; resident in psychiatry Tulane U., New Orleans, 1983-86, fellow in psychoanalytic medicine, 1984-87; pvt. practice gen. psychiatry Covington, La., 1986-87; pvt. practice psychiatry Ft. Lauderdale, 1987—; founder, med. dir. The Rose Inst., Fla., 1988—; founder Integrative Medicine Sch. of Thought, 1999; neurolinguistic programming master practitioner and trainer, 2000—. Sec. med. exec. com., chmn. quality assurance com. The Retreat Hosp., Sunrise, Fla., 1994-95; med. dir. Anxiety and Depression prog., CPC Ft. Lauderdale Hosp., 1989-90; med. dir. Acad. Medicine and Psychology, Ft. Lauderdale, 1988-89, CEPHAS Prog., HSA Greenbrier Neuropsychiat. Hosp., Covington, La., 1986-87, chief med. staff, 1987; clin. instr. psychiatry Tulane U. Med. Ctr., 1986-87; pres. med. exec. com., chief med. staff, chmn. quality assurance com. Retreat Hosp., 1992-96; workshop speaker; radio program host The Rose Institute Hour; lectr. in field; cons. in field. Host ednl.-cmty. svc. radio program The Rose Inst. Hour, 1995-97. Mem. pub. health com. for the Health and Human Svcs. Bd., Dist. 10; mem. alochol, drugs and mental health com.. Fellow Am. Acad. Psychoanalysis, Am. Bd. Forensic Examiners, Interam. Coll. Physicians and Surgeons; mem. AMA, Am. Psychiat. Assn., Am. Acad. Psychoanalysis, Am. Soc. Clin. Hypnosis, Am. Acad. Anti-Aging Medicine, Fla. Med. Assn. (Med. Speaker of Yr. award, 1st pl. radio, 2nd pl. TV, 1990, del. 1993—), Fla. Psychiat. Soc. (coun. mem. 1993-94), Broward County Psychiat. Soc. (med. exec. com., pres. 1994-95), Broward County Med. Assn. (chmn. physicians recovery network com., bd. dirs.), Broward County Psychiat. Soc. (pres. 1993-96), M.I.N.D. Home and Office: 1521 Alton Rd # 332 Miami FL 33139 E-mail: richardmaulion@yahoo.com.

MAULL, ETHEL MILLS, retired special education educator; b. Phila., Mar. 13, 1930; d. William Burley and Ethel (Hallowell) Mills; m. Robert Wallace Maull, June 19, 1954; children: Roger Wallace, William Robert. BS in Edn., West Chester (Pa.) U., 1951, cert. in spl. edn., 1973. Elem. tchr. Hershey (Pa.) Schs., Derry Twp. Sch. Dist., 1951-55, Newark (Del.) Spl. Sch. Dist., 1960-65; tchr. kindergarten pvt. sch., Newark, 1959-60; tchr. lang. devel. George Crothers Meml. Sch., Bethel, Pa., 1967-74; tchr. itinerant learning disabilities, cons. Delaware County Intermediate Unit 25, Media, 1974-80, liaison-spl. edn. resource tchr., 1980-91; ret., 1991. Pvt. cons. to parents of learning disabled children. Author poems, children's stories. Mem. NEA, Coun. for Exceptional Children, Pa. Edn. Assn., Delaware County Intermediate Unit Edn. Assn., PSERS, PASR. Republican. Avocation: creative writing. Home: 105 Barley Mill Rd Wallingford PA 19086-6042

MAULL, GEORGE MARRINER, music director, conductor; b. Phila., Oct. 14, 1947; s. Frederick Dunlap and Helen Norbury (Jordan) M.; m. Marcia Eileen Korn, Aug. 13, 1984. MusB, U. Louisville, 1970, MusM, 1972; postgrad., Juilliard Sch. Music, 1976-78. Condr. Louisville Ballet Co., 1971-75; asst. condr. Opera Orch. N.Y., N.Y.C., 1976-78, N.J. Symphony Orch., Newark, 1979-80; music dir., condr. Bloomingdale Chamber Orch., N.Y.C., 1980-83, N.J. Youth Symphony, Summit, 1979—97, Philharm. Orch. N.J., Warren, 1987—; Condr. Laureate N.J. Youth Symphony, 1997. Conducting debut Carnegie Hall, N.Y.C., 1989; condr. in Eng., Belgium, The Netherlands, Poland, Romania, Hungary, Germany, recordings with Nat. Polish Radio Symphony Orch., 2001, 2002; featured in WNET mini-documentary Art Effects: Young and Noteworthy, 1988. Named Disting. Alumnus, U. Louisville, 1994. Mem. Am. Fedn. Musicians, Am. Symphony Orch. League (conducting fellow 1978, Nat. Cert. Merit 1980), Condr's. Guild. Episcopalian. Home: 79 Stone Run Rd Bedminster NJ 07921-1711 Office: Philharm Orch of NJ PO Box 4064 Warren NJ 07059-0064

MAULSBY, ALLEN FARISH, lawyer; b. Balt., May 21, 1922; AB, Williams Coll., Williamstown, Mass., 1944; LL.B., U. Va., 1946. Bar: Md. 1947, N.Y. 1950. Law clk. to judge U.S. Circuit Ct. Appeals 4th Circuit, 1946-47; assoc. firm Cravath Swaine & Moore, N.Y.C., 1947-57, ptnr., 1958-95. Vestryman St. James' Episcopal Ch., N.Y.C., 1962-68, 80-85, warden, 1986-87; trustee Greer-Woodycrest Child Care, 1961-82; bd. dirs. Episc. Ch. Found., 1973-86. Mem. Am. Bar Found., N.Y. Bar Found., Am. Coll. Trial Lawyers, Am. Bar Assn., N.Y. State Bar Assn., Fed. Bar Assn., Assn. Bar City N.Y., N.Y. County Lawyers Assn. Office: Cravath Swaine & Moore 825 8th Ave New York NY 10019-7475 E-mail: amaulsby@cravath.com.

MAULUCCI, MARY K. computer programmer; b. New Milford, Conn., Oct. 18, 1964; d. Fred Vincent and Eileen Mary (O'Donnell) M. AS, Dutchess C.C., 1984; BS, SUNY, New Paltz, 1986, MS, 1992. Tchg. asst. SUNY, New Paltz, 1987; adminstr. Granada Sys. Design, Inc., East Fishkill, N.Y., White Plains, 1988-95; sys. programmer Fun Ctr. Software, Fishkill, 1995, The Onyx Group, Alexandria, Va., 1996-97; analyst ICF Consulting Group, Inc., Fairfax, 1998—. Regents scholar N.Y. State Bd. Regents, 1982. Democrat. Roman Catholic. Avocations: reading, music, archiving videos, computer. Home: 5375 Duke St Apt 118 Alexandria VA 22304-3037 Office: ICF Consulting Group Inc 9300 Lee Hwy Fairfax VA 22031-1207 E-mail: mmaulucc@icfconsulting.com.

MAUMENEE, IRENE H. ophthalmology educator; b. Bad Pyrmont, Germany, Apr. 30, 1940; MD, U. Gottingen, 1964. Cert. Am. Bd. Ophthalmology, Am. Bd. Med. Genetics. Rsch. asst. U. Hawaii, 1968; vis. geneticist Population Genetics Lab., 1968-69; fellow dept. medicine Johns Hopkins U., 1969-71; ophthalmology preceptorship Wilmer Inst. Johns Hopkins Hosp., 1969-71, from asst. prof. to assoc. prof. Wilmer Ophthalmology Inst., 1972-87; prof. ophthalmology and pediatrics Wilmer Ophthalmology Inst., 1972—; dir. Johns Hopkins Ctr. Hereditary Eye Disease, Wilmer Inst., 1979—. Cons. John F. Kennedy Inst. Visually & Mentally Handicapped Children, 1974—; dir. Low Vision Clinic, Wilmer Inst., 1977-88; vis. prof. French Ophthalmology Soc., Paris & French Acad. Medicine, 1988; advisor Nat. Eye Inst. Task Forces, 1976, 81. Mem. AMA, Am. Soc. Human Genetics, Am. Acad. Ophthalmology, Assn. Rsch. Vision & Ophthalmology, Internat. Soc. Genetic Eye Disease, Am. Ophthal. Soc., Pan Am. Assn. Ophthalmology. Achievements include research in nosology and management of ophthalmic and general medical genetics; population genetics; computer application to genetic analysis; molecular genetics; over 200 publications on human genetics and eye diseases. Office: Johns Hopkins Ctr Hereditary Eye Diseases 600 N Wolfe St # 517 Baltimore MD 21287-0005 E-mail: jhched@jhmi.edu.

MAUMUS, CRAIG W(ALTHER), psychiatrist, consultant; b. New Orleans; m. Priscilla Guderian; 1 child, Michael Fletcher. BS, Tulane U., 1968, MD, 1972. Diplomate Am. Bd. Psychiatry and Neurology. Pvt. practice, Metairie, La., 1976—95; chief day programs VA Med. Ctr., New Orleans, 1995—. Clin. assoc. prof. psychiatry Tulane Med. Ctr. Stadium, basketball and regatta coms. Sugar Bowl, New Orleans, 1971-76. Fellow: Am. Psychiat. Assn. (chair newsletter subcom. 1993—98); mem.: AMA, La. Psychiat. Med. Assn. (exec. com. 1979—98, newsletter editor), La. State Med. Soc., Am. Coll. Psychiatrists, Tulane Psychiatry and Neurology Alumni Assn., So. Yacht Club. Avocations: computers, sailing, writing.

MAUN, CAROLINE CHERIE, writing educator; b. Lansing, Mich., Jan. 14, 1968; d. David Donald and Laurette Marie Maun. PhD, U. Tenn., 1998. Dir. Writing Ctr. Morgan State U., Balt., 1998—. Office: Morgan State U 1700 E Cold Spring Ln Baltimore MD 21251-0001 Office Fax: 443-885-8225. E-mail: cmaun@morgan.edu.

MAUN, MARY ELLEN, computer consultant; b. N.Y.C., Dec. 18, 1951; d. Emmet Joseph and Mary Alice (McMahon) M. BA, CUNY, 1977, MBA, 1988. Sales rep. N.Y. Telephone Co., N.Y.C., 1970-76, comml. rep., 1977-83, programmer, 1984-86; systems analyst Telesector Resources Group, 1987-89, sr. systems analyst, 1990-95; pres. Sleepy Hollow (N.Y.) Techs., Inc., N.Y., 1995—. Corp. chmn. United Way of Tri-State Area, N.Y.C., 1985; recreation activities vol. Pioneers Am., N.Y.C., 1982—; active Sleepy Hollow Hist. Soc.; founder Mary Ellen Maun Philanthropic Found., 1998; Dem. dist. leader for Philipse Manor. Recipient Outstanding Community Service award, Calvary Hosp., Bronx, N.Y., 1984. Mem. N.Y. Health and Racquet Club, Road Runners. Avocations: antique restoration, classical music, skiing, running. Office: Sleepy Hollow Techs Inc 3 Farrington Ave Tarrytown NY 10591-1302

MAUNDER, ADDISON BRUCE, agronomic research company executive; b. Holdrege, Nebr., May 13, 1934; s. Addison Haynes and Marie Sophia (Luebs) M.; m. Katherina Marlene Blum, Sept. 8, 1978; children: Lynda Diane, Christopher Allen. B.Sc., U. Nebr., 1956; M.Sc., Purdue U., 1958, PhD, 1960; DSc (hon., U. Nebr., 1991. With DeKalb AgResearch, Inc., Lubbock, Tex., 1960-96, sorghum breeder, 1960-61, dir. sorghum research, 1961-76, v.p. sorghum research, 1976-78, v.p. rsch., 1978-82; v.p. DeKalb-Pfizer Genetics, DeKalb, Ill., 1982-89; v.p. agronomic research DeKalb Plant Genetics, 1989-91; sr. v.p. DeKalb Genetics Corp., 1991-96; rsch. advisor Nat. Grain Sorghum Prodrs. Assn., 1997—. Bd. dirs. Diversity Mag., Washington, 1984-95; adj. prof. Tex. Tech. U., 1992—. Contbr. 12 chpts. to books and more than 70 articles to profl. jours. Mem. deans adv. com. Tex. Tech. U., Lubbock, 1983-86; chmn. external rev. INTSORMIL of AID, Lincoln, Nebr., 1980-2001; bd. dirs. Tex. Tech. U. Rsch. Found., 1986-92; mem. Nat. Plant Genetic Resources Bd., 1991-92, Nat. Plant Variety Protection Bd., 1991-94. Recipient Gerald Thomas award Tex. Tech. U., 1974, Prodn. award Grain Sorghum Producers Assn., 1985, Genetics and Plant Breeding award for Industry, 1987, Indsl. Agronomy award, 1988, Purdue Disting. Alumni award, 1997, Monsanto Crop Sci. Disting. Career award, 2000, President's Disting Svc. award ASTA, 2001. Fellow AAAS, Am. Soc. Agronomy (bd. dirs. 1991-92), Crop Sci. Soc. Am. (bd. dirs. 1991-92, pres. 1995-96); mem. Am. Seed Trade Assn., Sigma Xi, Alpha Zeta. Republican. Achievements include development of plant products (150 hybrids) emphasizing yield, improved drought and insect resistance as well as nutritional quality. E-mail: ngsp@sorghumgrowers.com.

MAUNDER, JILL ELLEN, consulting executive; b. Hartford, Conn., Oct. 9, 1955; d. David Kenneth and Rhoda Betty (Gofberg) Grossman; m. Richard Lawrence Maunder, Oct. 20, 1984. BA in Social Svcs., U. N.H., 1977. Cons. Robert Kleven & Co., Lexington, Mass., 1979-83; human resources rep. Comml. Union Assurance Co., Boston, 1983-84; sr. human resources rep. Gen Rad, Inc., Concord, Mass., 1984-89; dir. human resources Bull Worldwide Info. Sys., Billerica, 1989-92, Thomson Fin. Svcs., Boston, 1992-93; v.p. cons. Strategic Outsourcing, Inc., Wellesley, Mass., 1993-96; pres., prin. Outsourcing Solutions, Inc., Newton, 1996—. Speaker in field. Mem. Northeast Human Resources Assn. Avocations: art, skiing, travel, decorating. Office: Outsourcing Solutions Inc 1185 Washington St Ste 200 Newton MA 02465-2184 Address: 5 Chestnut Ln Bedford MA 01730-1050

MAUNEY, THOMAS LEE, theater designer; b. Lexington, N.C., May 29, 1967; s. Thomas Pete and Iris Elnita (Washburn) M. BFA, U. N.C., Greensboro, 1990; MFA, U. Mont., 1995. Asst. tech. dir., designer Raleigh (N.C.) Little Theatre, 1989-90; tech. dir. U. Mont., Missoula, 1990-92; designer Big Fork (Mont.) Summer Playhouse, 1994-98; prodn. supr. Raleigh Meml. Auditorium, 1998—. Freelance designer theatre and spl. events.

MAUPIN, A. WILLIAM, state supreme court justice; children: Allison, Michael. BA, U. Nev., 1968; JD, U. Ariz., 1971. Atty., ptnr. Thorndal, Backus, Maupin and Armstrong, Las Vegas, 1976—93; judge 8th Jud. Dist. Clark County, 1993—97; assoc. justice Supreme Ct. Nev., 1997—. Bd. govs. Nev. State Bar, 1991—95. Recipient highest rating for Retention as Dist. Ct. Judge, 1994, 1996, Highest Qualitative Ratings, 1996, Las Vegas Review Jour., Clark County Bar Assn., highest rating as Supreme Ct. Justice, Clark County Bar Assn. and Las Vegas Rev. Jour. judicial poll, 1998, 2000. Mem.: Nev. Supreme Ct. (study com. to review jud. elections, chmn. 1995, alternate dispute resolution implementation com. chmn. 1992—96). Office: Nev Supreme Ct 201 S Carson St Carson City NV 89701-4702

MAUPIN, ARMISTEAD JONES, lawyer; b. Raleigh, N.C., Nov. 10, 1914; s. Alfred McGhee and Mary Armistead (Jones) M.; m. Diana Jane Barton, May 16, 1942 (dec.); children: Armistead Jones, Anthony Westwood, Jane Stuart; m. Cheryl Leigh Erhard, July 31, 1982. AB, U. N.C., 1936; JD, George Washington U., 1940. Bar: N.C. 1939. Ptnr. Maupin, Taylor & Ellis, Raleigh. Pres. Occoneechee coun. Boy Scouts Am., 1962-64; pres. Carolina Charter Corp., 1976-80, 93—; former chancellor Episcopal Diocese of N.C.; former sr. warden Christ Ch. Parish; vice chmn. Am. Battle Monuments Commn., 1981-90. Comdr. USNR, WWII, PTO. Decorated chevalier French Legion of Honor. Fellow Am. Bar Found.; mem. ABA (ho. of dels. 1960-72), N.C. State Bar (coun. 1955-60, pres. 1959-60), Soc. of Cincinnati (v.p. gen. 1968-70, pres. gen. 1971-74, pres. N.C. soc. 1964-67), Carolina Country Club, Circle Club, Triangle Fox Hounds Club. Republican. Episcopalian. Home: 2005 Banbury Rd Raleigh NC 27608-1121 Office: Highwoods Tower One 3200 Beech Leaf Ct Raleigh NC 27604-1085

MAUPIN, STEPHANIE ZELLER, educator, consultant; b. St. Louis, Apr. 16, 1946; d. Robert H. and Pernelle (Santhuff) Zeller; 1 child, Britt. BEd, U. Mo., 1967; MAT in Comm. Arts, Webster Coll., St. Louis, 1977; postgrad., Webster Coll., 1979-87, St. Louis U., 1986—. Cert. tchr., Mo. Tchr. Mehlville Sch. Dist., St. Louis County, 1967-97; tchr. French and English Oakville H.S., Mehlville Sch. Dist., 1971-97. Adj. faculty Webster U., St. Louis, 1980, St. Louis U., 1982-97, mentor tchr., 1988-89, Nat. Louis U., 1992—, U. Mo., St. Louis, 1993-97, St. Louis C.C., 1997; adj. instr. Jefferson Coll., Southwestern Ill. Coll., 1998—; specialist tchr. Springboard to Learning, 1997; cons. Living on the Edge broadcasting series; presenter Mo. State Dept. Edn. Fgn. Lang. Assn. Conf., Nat. Conf. Tchr. English, NE Conf. Tchg. Fgn. Lang., Fulbright Tchr. Exch., 1991, 92; spkr. in field. Dir. in charge exchange program St. Louis-Lyon Sister Cities Corp.; founder St. Louis-St. Louis du Senegal Sister Cities Corp., 1991. NEH fellow, Rockefeller Found. Fgn. Lang. Tchrs. fellow, 1987, Fulbright Exch. Tchr., 1990-91; recipient Agnes Garcia-Ponty Meml. award, 1991. Mem. ASCD, NEA, MLA, NEH Fgn. Lang. Tchrs. Fellowship (advocate for Mo. 1995), Nat. Coun. Tchrs. English, Arts Edn. Coun., African Lit. Assn., French Soc., Am. Assn. Tchrs. French, African Studies Assn. Network Women Adminstrn., Fgn. Lang. Tchrs. Assn. (pres. 1992-94), Internat. Edn. Consortium, NE Conf. Tchg. Fgn. Lang. (adv. bd.), Ctrl. States Conf. Tchg. Fgn. Lang. (adv. bd.), Fgn. Lang. Assn. Mo., Internat. Platform Assn., Webster U. Alumni Assn., Fgn. Lang. Tchrs. St. Louis, Ind. State Fgn. Lang. Conf., African Lit. Assn. Conf., Phi Sigma Iota. Home: 5608 Duchesne Parque Dr Saint Louis MO 63128-4176 E-mail: szmaupin@aol.com.

MAURANDY, JEAN-PIERRE J. sales professional; b. Varese, Italy, May 1, 1965; Diploma, Ecoles de Hautes Etudes Commls. du Nord, Lille, France, 1989; diploma in acctg. and fin., London Sch. Econs., 1989; MBA, UCLA, 1991. Sr. fin. analyst Mattel Toys, El Segundo, Calif., 1991; v.p. internat. instnl. sales Compagnie Financière de CIC, Paris, 1992-94; instnl. salesman, v.p. Sanford C. Bernstein, N.Y.C., 1994—. Brig. French Mountain Rescues, 1985-86.

MAURER, BEVERLY BENNETT, school administrator; b. Bklyn., Aug. 23, 1940; d. David and Minnie (Dolen) Bennett; m. Harold M. Maurer, June 12, 1960; children: Ann Maurer Rosenbach, Wendy Maurer Rausch. BA, Bklyn. Coll., 1960, postgrad., 1961, U. Richmond, 1980-90, Va. Commonwealth U., 1980-90. Cert. tchr., N.Y., Va. Math. tchr. Col. David Marcus Jr. High Sch., Bklyn., 1960-61, Pomona (N.Y.) Jr. High Sch., 1967-68; math. tchr. Hebrew day sch. Rudlin Torah Acad., Richmond, Va., 1969-80, asst. prin., 1980-86, prin., 1986-89; dir. edn. Jewish Community Day Sch. Ctrl. Va., 1990-93; ednl. cons., 1993—; owner East Coast Antiques. Propr. East Coast Antiques. Developed talented and gifted program, pre-admission program for children at Med. Coll. Va., 1982. Bd. dirs. Jewish Cmty. Ctr., Richmond, 1980s, Aux. to Med. Coll. Va., Richmond, 1980s, Aux. to U. Nebr. Med. Ctr., 1994—, Uta Hallee, 1994-97, Met. Omaha Med. Soc. Alliance, 1997—; bd. govs. Joslyn Fine Art Mus., 2000—; founder, exec. bd. dirs. Nebraskans For Rsch., 2001-. Recipient Master Tchr. award Rudlin Torah Acad., 1983. Mem. Jewish Cmty. Day Sch. Network, Anti-Defamation League, Jewish Women's Club, U. Nebr. Med. Ctr. Faculty Women's Club (bd. dirs. 1995—). Avocations: collecting contemporary and art nouveau glass, world travel.

MAURER, DAVID LEO, lawyer; b. Evansville, Ind., Oct. 31, 1945; s. John G. Jr. and Mildred M. (Lintzenich) M.; m. Diane M. Kaput, Aug. 11, 1973; children: Eric W., Kathryn A. BA magna cum laude, U. Detroit, 1967, Cert. in Teaching, 1971; JD, Wayne State U., 1975. Bar: Mich., U.S. Dist. Ct. (ea. and we. dist.) Mich., U.S. Ct. Appeals (6th cir.) Cin. Law clk. Mich. Ct. Appeals, Detroit, 1976, Supreme Ct. Mich., Lansing, 1977-78; asst. U.S. atty. civil div. U.S. Dept. Justice, Detroit, 1978-81; assoc. to ptnr. Butzel, Long, Gust, Klein & Van Zile, 1981-85; ptnr. Pepper, Hamilton & Scheetz (now Pepper Hamilton LLP), 1985—. Guest lectr. Practicing Law Inst., 1988—, Nat. Bus. Inst., 1989—, U. Mich. Law Sch., U. Detroit Law Sch., 1990, Hazardous Waste Super Conf., 1986-87. Co-author: Michigan Environmental Law Deskbook, 1992; contbr. articles to profl. jours. and chpts. in books. Mem. Energy & Environ. Policy Com., 1988—, chairperson, 1989-90; mem. Great Lakes Water Resources Commn., 1986. Mem. State Bar Mich. (environ. couns. 1986-91, sec., treas., chairperson-elect, chairperson 1991-93). Office: Pepper Hamilton LLP 100 Renaissance Ctr Ste 3600 Detroit MI 48243-1101

MAURER, EDWARD LANCE, chiropractor, radiologist; b. Rahway, N.J., June 4, 1937; s. Frank Eugene and Charlotte Marian (Crook) Maurer; m. Jean Carol Outten, Feb. 14, 1960 (dec. Jan. 1995); children: Lance P., Terry L. D of Chiropractic, Lincoln Chiropractic Coll., Indpls., 1958; student, Western Mich. U., 1970-72, Upper Iowa U., 1974-76. Diplomate Am. Chiropractic Bd. Radiology. Pvt. practice, Kalamazoo, 1961—. Past pres. Chiro/Net. Ltd., Chiropractic IPA; chmn. Valhalla Enterprises; mem. postgrad. faculty in radiology Nat. coll. Chiropractice; hon. bd., adv. com. Coll. Human Svcs. Fla. State U.; exec. v.p. Mich. Chiro/Net Corp.; bd. mem. U.S. Bone and Joint Decade, Mich. Bd. Chiropractic, 2002—. Editor (-in-chief): ACA Press Pub.; mem. editl. bd. Jour. Manipulative and Physiol. Therapeutics, Am. Jour. Chiropractic Medicine, D.C. Tracts Periodical, chmn. editl. bd. Jour. Am. Chiropractic Assn.; author: (book) Practical Applied Roentgenology, 1983, Selected Ethics and Protocols in Chiropractic, 1991; contbr. articles to profl. jours., chapters to books. Bd. dirs., chmn. Lincoln Coll. Edn. and Rsch. Fund, others. Fellow: Internat. Coll. Chiropractic, Can. Chiropractic Coll. Radiologists; mem.: Am. Chiropractic Registry Radiol. Techs. (exec. v.p.), Am. Chiropractic Coun. Diagnostic Imaging (past dist bd. dirs. and pres.), Mich. Chiropractic Soc. (past dist. v.p.) (Chiropractor of Yr. 1981), Kalamazoo county Chiropractic Assn. (past pres.), Am.. Chiropractic Assn. (chmn. bd. govs., exec. com., radiol. health cons., state del. (Chiropractor of Yr. 2001). Republican. Office: Kalamazoo Chiropractic Ctr 2330 Gull Rd Kalamazoo MI 49048-1432

MAURER, FREDERIC GEORGE, III, banker; b. Grand Rapids, Mich., May 15, 1952; s. Frederic George and Rhea Marie (Annesser) M. BA, St. Louis U., 1974, MBA, 1977. Dir. residence Marguerite Hall St. Louis U., 1977-79; internat. banking analyst Merc. Trust Co., St. Louis, 1979-80, banking rep. Latin Am., 1980-81, internat. officer, 1981-83, asst. v.p., 1983, Union Bank, L.A., 1983-86; asst. v.p. internat. sect. Centerre Bank, N.A., St. Louis, 1986-87, asst. v.p. portfolio mgmt. sect., 1987-88; with pvt. banking dept. Boatmen's Nat. Bank, 1988-90, v.p., 1990-97, Nations Bank, St. Louis, 1997-99, Bank of Am., St. Louis, 1999-2001, Commerce Trust Co., St. Louis, 2001—. Bd. dirs. Assocs. St. Louis U. Librs., 1975-79, Friends of Forum, St. Louis, NCCJ, 1992—, Franciscan Missionary Union, 1996-2001; mem. dir.'s assn. Mo. Bot. Garden, 1986—; mem. World Affairs Coun., St. Louis, DuBourg Soc. Internat. Bus. fellow, 1975-77. Mem. Ctr. Internat. Banking Studies, U. Va., Charlottesville, Robert Morris Assocs., Alumni Council St. Louis U., Opera Guild, Performing Arts Council-In the Wings, L.A., Japan-Am. Soc., U.S.-Mexico C. of C. (Pacific chpt.), English-speaking Union. Clubs: American (London); Noonday, Mo. Athletic (St. Louis); Los Angeles Athletic. Roman Catholic. Home: 849 Aldan Dr Saint Louis MO 63132-3501 Office: 1 Met Sq 211 N Broadway Saint Louis MO 63102-2733 E-mail: rick.maurer@commercebank.com.

MAURER, GERNANT ELMER, metallurgical executive, consultant; b. Sayre, Pa., May 5, 1949; s. Elmer L. and Joyce F. (Fox) M.; m. Suzanne Walker Berry, Aug. 19, 1972. BES, Johns Hopkins U., 1971; PhD, Rensselear Poly. Inst., 1976. Materials engr. Spl. Metals Corp., New Hartford, N.Y., 1976-80, mgr. R & D, 1981-84, dir. R & D, 1985-87, v.p. tech., 1987—. Founding v.p. Splty. Metals Processing Consortium, pres., 1992-93; chmn. Internat. Symposium on Superalloys, 1984-88. Co-editor: Superalloys, 1980, 2d edit., 1988; contbr. tech. papers to profl. jours.; inventor various superalloys. Dir. devel. com. Munson William Proctor Inst., Utica, N.Y., 1988-89. Fellow Am. Soc. for Metals (trustee 1992-95); mem. The Metall. Soc., Am. Vacuum Soc. (bd. dirs. metall. div. 1988), Utica Area C. of C. (bd. dirs. 1986-89), Wash. State U. (adv. materials engring. adv. bd. 1993—), Yahnundasis Club. Avocations: golf, fly fishing, art, photography, metal working. Home: 27 Sherman Cir Utica NY 13501-5808 Office: Spl Metals Corp Middle Settlement Rd New Hartford NY 13413 E-mail: gmaurer@specialmetals.com.

MAURER, HAROLD MAURICE, pediatrician; b. N.Y.C., Sept. 10, 1936; s. Isador and Sarah (Rothkowitz) M.; m. Beverly Bennett, June 12, 1960; children: Ann Maurer Rosenbach, Wendy Maurer Rausch. AB, NYU, 1957; MD, SUNY, Bklyn., 1961. Diplomate Am. Bd. Pediatrics, Am. Bd. Pediatric Hematology-Oncology. Intern pediatrics Kings County Hosp., N.Y.C., 1961-62; resident in pediatrics Babies Hosp., Columbia-Presbyn. Med. Center, 1962-64; fellow in pediatric hematology/oncology Columbia-Presbyn. Med. Center, 1966-68; asst. prof. pediatrics Med. Coll. Va., Richmond, 1968-71, asso. prof., 1971-75, prof., 1975—, chmn. dept. pediatrics, 1976-93; dean U. Nebr. Coll. Medicine, Omaha, 1993-98; chancellor U. Nebr. Med. Ctr., 1998—. Chmn. Intergroup Rhabdomyosarcoma Study, 1972-98; exec. com. Pediatric Oncology Group; mem. cancer clin. investigation rev. com. NIH, Gov.'s Homeland Security Policy Group. Editor: pediatrics, 1983, Rhabdomyosarcoma and Related Tumors in Children and Adolescence, 1991; mem. editorial bd. Am. Jour. Hematology, Journal Pediatric Hematology and Oncology, Medical and Pediatric Oncology, 1984-99; contbr. articles to profl. jours. Mem. Youth Health Task Force, City of Richmond., Gov.'s Adv. Com. on Handicapped., Gov.'s Homeland Security Policy Group, Nebr., 2002-; mem. nat. com. on childhood cancer Am. Cancer Soc., bd. dirs. Va. div. Served to lt. comdr. USPHS, 1964-66. NIH grantee, 1974-98. Mem. Am. Acad. Pediatrics (com. oncology-hematology), Am. Soc. Hematology, Soc. Pediatric Rsch., Am. Pediatric Soc., Va. Pediatric Sic. (exec. com.), Assn. Med. Sch. Pediatric Dept. Chmn., Internat. Soc. Pediatric Oncology, Am. Soc. Clin. Oncology, Va. Hematology Soc., Am. Assn. Cancer Rsch., Am. Cancer Soc., Am. Soc. Pediatric Hematology-Oncology (v.p. 1990-91, pres. 1991-93), Sigma Xi, Coun. Deans AAMC, Gov.'s Blue Ribbon Commn., Alpha Omega Alpha. Republican. Jewish. Home: 9822 Ascot Dr Omaha NE 68114-3848 Office: U Nebr Med Ctr 986605 Nebraska Med Ctr Omaha NE 68198-0001 E-mail: hmmaurer@unmc.edu.

MAURER, JEFFREY STUART, finance executive; b. N.Y.C., July 9, 1947; s. Herbert and Phoebe Maurer; m. Wendy S. Nemerov. BA, Alfred U., 1969; MBA, NYU, 1975; JD, St. John's U., 1976. With U.S. Trust Co. N.Y., 1970—, pres., 1990; COO U.S. Trust Co., N.Y.C., 1994-2001, CEO, 2001—02, chmn., CEO, 2002—. Bd. dirs. Greater N.Y. Ins. Cos., Charles Schwab Corp., Forbes.com. Trustee Alfred (N.Y.) U., 1984, North Shore L.I. Jewish Health Sys.; bd. dirs., treas. Children's Health Fund, N.Y.C., 1988; bd. dirs. Hebrew Home Aged, Riverdale, N.Y., 1992, Roundabout Theatre Co., U.S. Trust Co. Mem. ABA, N.Y. State Bar Assn., Glen Head Country Club, Harmonie Club. Jewish. Avocations: skiing, golf. Office: US Trust Co NY 114 W 47th St New York NY 10036-1510 E-mail: jmaurer@ustrust.com.

MAURER, PAUL HERBERT, biochemist, educator; b. N.Y.C., June 29, 1923; s. Joseph and Clara (Vogel) M.; m. Miriam Esther Merdinger, June 27, 1948; children— Susan Gail, David Mark, Philip Mitchell. BS, City Coll. N.Y., 1944; PhD, Columbia, 1950. Research biochemist Gen. Foods Corp., Hoboken, N.J., 1944-46; instr. City Coll., N.Y., 1946-51; research asso. Coll. Phys. and Surg., Columbia, 1950-51; asst. research prof. Sch. Medicine, U. Pitts., 1951-54, asso. prof. immunochemistry, 1954-60; asso. prof. microbiology Seton Hall Coll. Medicine, 1960-62; prof. microbiology N.J. Coll. Medicine, 1962-66; prof., chmn. dept. biochemistry Jefferson Med. Coll., Phila., 1966-93, prof. pathology, biochemistry and molecular biology emeritus, 1993—. Mem. allergy and infectious diseases tng. grant com. NIH, 1961-66; mem. commn. on albumin Protein Fedn.; mem. NRC com. on plasma; chmn. Transplantation Biology and Immunology Com. NIAID, 1986—. Asso. editor: Immunochemistry, 1964, Science, 1966; Contbr. profl. jours. Served with USNR 1946-48. Recipient Research Career award Nat. Inst. Allergy and Infectious Diseases, 1962-66, Chemistry medal City Coll. N.Y., 1944 Mem. Am. Chem. Soc., N.Y. Acad. Scis., Biochem. Soc. (London), Harvey Soc., Am. Assn. Immunologists, Am. Soc. Biol. Chemistry, AAAS, Societe de Chimie Biologique (France), Soc. Exptl. Biology and Medicine, Sigma Xi. Home: 8470 Limekiln Pike Apt B517 Wyncote PA 19095-2724 Office: Jefferson Med Coll Dept Pathology 1020 Locust St Philadelphia PA 19107-6731

MAURER, P(AUL) REED, pharmaceutical company executive; b. Minersville, Pa., Sept. 20, 1937; s. Paul Reed and Ruth Lillian (Daniel) M.; m. Beverly Mae Seaman, June 25, 1963 (div. Feb. 1984); children: Paul Reed, Glenn Charles; m. Yuko Arai, June 30, 1984; children: Michelle Aoi, Tricia Haruna, Brett Ken. BS, Kutztown U., 1959; MS, U. Pa., 1962; cert., Stanford U., 1967-68. Fellowship U. Otago, Dunedin, New Zealand, 1961; tchr. Allentown (Pa.) H.S., 1959-60; asst. prof. Bucknell U., Lewisburg, 1963-64; v.p. Eli Lilly, Kobe, Japan, 1970-76, Merck & Co., Tokyo, 1976-86; pres. Metpac, Ltd., Honolulu, 1986-99, Nippon Pharma Promotion K.K., Tokyo, 1995—; mgr. IAL (USA) LLC, Honolulu, 1997—. Dir. Colby Group Internat., Tokyo; pres., dir. Internat. Alliances Ltd., Tokyo, 1989—. Author: Competing in Japan, 1989; editl. bd. Hearing Internat., 1992—. Fellowship Rotary Found., 1961, Paul Harris fellow, 1980. Mem. Pharma Delegates. Avocations: writing, tennis, boating. Home: Arisugawa Park Hills #902 5-6-48 Minami Azabu Minato-ku 106 Japan Office: Internat Alliances Ltd 1-5-12-101 Kita Aoyama Minato-ku Tokyo 107-0061 Japan E-mail: nppial@gol.com.

MAURER, RICHARD HORNSBY, physicist; b. Reading, Pa., Apr. 27, 1942; s. Samuel Forest and Marian E. (Hornsby) M.; m. Marian Ross Harvey, May 3, 1975; children: Jonathan, Andrew. BS, L.I. U., 1964; PhD, U. Pitts., 1970. Postdoctoral fellow Bartol Rsch. Found., Swarthmore, Pa., 1970-73; environ. engr. AMP Inc., Harrisburg, 1973-81; physicist Applied Physics Lab. Johns Hopkins U., Laurel, Md., 1981—, reliability group supr. test and evaluation sect., 1986-94, instr. Whiting Sch. Engring., 1988—. Contbr. chpt. to: Space Systems Reliability and Survivability, 1994; contbr. articles to Jour. IEEE Transactions Nuclear Sci., Jour. Spacecraft and Rockets, Internat. Reliability Physics Symposium. Baseball mgr. Howard County Youth Program, Ellicott City, Md., 1985-97; lector St. John's Episcopal Ch., 1994-98. Mem. IEEE, Am. Soc. Quality Control, Am. Phys. Soc., Sigma Xi. Achievements include patent for fabrication of thermal batteries by multi-layer ceramic of organic printed circuit board methods; research on effects of radiation on electronic devices, on reliability of electronic packaging designs and gallium arsenide devices; development of portable neutron spectrometer. Office: Johns Hopkins U Applied Physics Lab 11100 Johns Hopkins Rd Laurel MD 20723-6005

MAURER, RICHARD MICHAEL, investment company executive; b. Bethlehem, Pa., June 4, 1948; s. Richard Thomas and Anna Theresa (Bold) M.; m. Karen Coe, June 13, 1970; children: Christopher Coe, Mark Emerson. Student, Pa. State U., 1966-68; BS, Point Park Coll., 1971; MBA, U. Pitts., 1982. CPA Pa. Staff acct. Price Waterhouse, Pitts., 1972-74, tac acct., 1974, sr. tax acct., 1974-77, tax mgr., 1977-78; dir. taxes The Hillman Co., 1978-85; pres. Maurer Ross & Co., Inc., 1985—; co-mng. ptnr. Wesmar Ptnrs., 1985—; chmn., CEO Admatic Industries, Inc., 1998—. Bd. dirs. Women's Golf Unlimited, Inc., Admatic Industries, Inc., Maurer Ross & Co., Inc., Maurer & Ross, Inc. Bd. trustees Pa. State McKeesport U. Point Park Coll. Alumni. Mem. AICPA, Assn. Corp. Growth, Pa. Inst. CPAs, Rotary (past dir., past pres.), Oakmont Country Club, Duquesne Club, Lake Nona Golf Club. Office: Three Gateway Ctr Pittsburgh PA 15222 E-mail: rmm@admaticindustries.com.

MAURER, ROBERT DISTLER, retired industrial physicist; b. St. Louis, July 20, 1924; s. John and Elizabeth J. (Distler) M.; m. Barbara A. Mansfield, June 9, 1951; children: Robert M., James B., Janet L. BS, U. Ark., 1948, LLD, 1980; PhD, MIT, 1951. Mem. staff MIT, 1951-52; with Corning Glass Works, N.Y., 1952-89, mgr. physics research, 1963-78, research fellow, 1978-89. Contbr. articles to profl. jours., chpts. to books; patentee in field. Served with U.S. Army, 1943-46. Recipient Indsl. Physics prize Am. Inst. Physics, 1978, L.M. Ericsson Internat. prize in telecommunications, 1979, Indsl. Rsch. Inst. Achievement award, 1988, Optical Soc. Am./IEEE Leos Tyndall award, 1987, Disting. Alumni award U. Ark, 1994, Am. Innovator award U.S. Dept. Commerce, 1995, Nat. Medal of Technology, 2000; decorated Purple Heart. Fellow IEEE (Moris N. Liebmann award 1978), Am. Ceramic Soc. (George W. Morey award 1976), Am. Phys. Soc. (New Materials prize 1989); mem. NAE (Charles Draper prize 1999), Nat. Inventors Hall of Fame. Home: 6 Roche Dr Painted Post NY 14870-1225

MAURER, ROBERT MICHAEL, medical company executive; b. Boston, July 6, 1952; s. Robert Distler and Barbara Anne (Mansfield) M.; m. Jae Young Sim, Oct. 31, 1982; children: Andrew, Joanne, Stephen. BA, Carleton Coll., 1974; MBA, Harvard U., 1980. Sales rep. diagnostic div. Abbott Labs., North Chicago, Ill., 1974-78, area mgr. diagnostic div. Far East, 1980-85, cancer mktg. mgr. diagnostic div., 1985-86, venture mgr. psychiat. and neurology diagnostic div., 1986-90, mgr. bus. planning diagnostic divsn., 1990-91; COO, CFO Molecular Geriatrics, Lake Bluff, 1992; COO, 1993-95; v.p. bus. devel. Avigen Alameda (Calif.) Co., 1996—. Office: Avigen Co 1201 Harbor Bay Pkwy Ste 1000 Alameda CA 94502-6586

MAURER, VIRGINIA GALLAHER, law educator; b. Shawnee, Okla., Nov. 7, 1946; d. Paul Clark Gallaher and Virginia Ruth (Watson) Abernathy; m. Ralph Gerald Maurer, July 31, 1971; children: Ralph Emmett, William Edward. BA, Northwestern U., 1968; MA, Stanford U., 1969, JD, 1975. Bar: Iowa 1976. Tchr. social studies San Mateo (Calif.) H.S. Dist., 1969-71; spl. asst. to pres. U. Iowa, Iowa City, 1976-80, adj. asst. prof. law, 1979-80; affiliate asst. prof. law U. Fla., Gainesville, 1981, asst. prof. bus. law, 1980-85, assoc. prof., 1985-93, prof., 1993—, Huber Hurst prof., 1997—. Dir. Poe Fin. Group Bus. Ethics Program, 1998—, MBA program U. Fla., 1987, chair dept. mgmt., 1994—; dir. Poe Fin. Group ethics program, 1999-; vis. scholar Wolfson Coll., Cambridge, 1994; vis. prof. SDA Bocconi U., Milan, 1994, 95, 96, Helsinki Sch. Econs. and Bus., 1998, U. Catania, Sicily, 1999; cons. Gov.'s Com. on Iowa 2000, Iowa City, 1976-77, Fla. Banker's Assn., Gainesville, 1982. Contbr. articles to profl. jours.; jr. editor Am. Bus. Law Jour., 1989-90, mng. editor, 1990-91, editor-in-chief, 1992-94. Bd. dirs. Gainesville Chamber Orch., 1990-93; mem. fundraising com. Pro Arte Musica, Gainesville, 1980-84; sr. warden, mem. vestry Holy Trinity Episc. Ch., 1991-93, 99—, jr. warden, 2000—; bd. dirs. Holy Trinity Found., Gainesville, 1991-93; mem. com. charter and canon law Episc. Diocese Fla., 1994-96; bd. dirs. Samaritan Ctrs. of North Ctrl. Fla., Inc., 1995-97. Fellow Soc. Advanced Legal Studies (UK); mem. ABA, AAUW, Acad. Legal Studies in Bus. (ho. of dels. 1989-90, exec. com. 1992, sec.-treas. 1998-99, v.p. 1999-2000, pres-elect 2000-01, pres. 2001—), Southeastern Bus. Law Assn. (proc. editor 1984-87, treas. 1985-86, v.p. 1986-87, pres.-elect 1987-88, pres. 1988-89), Iowa Bar Assn., LWV, U. Fla. Athletic Assn. (bd. dirs. 1982-88, v.p. chmn. fin. com.), Gainesville Womens' Forum (bd. dirs. 1988-91), Fla. Women' Network (bd. dirs. 1995-99), Univ. Woman's Club (Gainesville, Fla.), Rotary (bd. dirs. 1989-91, dist. scholarship com. 1997-99, regional scholarship com. 2000, chair 2001), Beta Gamma Sigma, Kappa Alpha Theta, Delta Sigma Pi. Home: 2210 NW 6th Pl Gainesville FL 32603-1409 Office: U Fla Grad Sch Bus Gainesville FL 32611 E-mail: maurer@notes.cba.ufl.edu.

MAURER, YOLANDA TAHAR, publisher; b. Tuuis-Tunisia, North Africa, Oct. 8, 1922; d. Joseph Tahar and Oro (Sidi) Tahar; m. William S. Maurer, Jan. 5, 1966; 1 child, Larry. Columnist Ft. Lauderdale News, 1948-65; pub. Pictorial Life, 1965-71; edtl. writer Ft. Lauderdale News, 1971-80; pub., 1980-86. Author: The Best of Broward, 1986, Ode To the City, 1995. Bd. mem. Miami City Ballet, Performing Arts Ctr., 1985-89, Fla. Philharm. Orch., Opera Guild Ft. Lauderdale. Recipient First Prize Fla. Mag., Fla. Newspaper Assn., 1958, George Washington award Freedoms Found., 1975; named Woman of Yr., Am. Cancer Soc., 1983, Woman of Style and Substance,

Philharm. Soc., 1996, Woman of Yr., Women in Comms., 1967, 83. Republican. Avocations: writing, reading, computers, cooking. Home: 1811 SE 14th St Fort Lauderdale FL 33316-2225 Office: Lauderdale Life 11 NE 12th Ave Fort Lauderdale FL 33301-1603

MAURER RITTEL, KATHLEEN ANN, educator; b. Jamaica, N.Y., Feb. 28, 1951; d. William Michael and Ann Marilyn; m. Donald Russell Rittel, Aug. 10, 2001; 1 child Sophia Anndrina Maria Buterakos. BA in English and Edn., Queens Coll., 1972, MS in Edn., 1977; postgrad., SUNY, Albany, 1978, Brigham Young U., 1978, McPherson Coll., 1978; diploma in ednl. supervision, St. John's U., Jamaica, N.Y., 1982; postgrad., Adelphi U., 1983, U. Mont., 1986, U. N.Mex., 1999, L.I. U., 2000; postgrad. Coll. St. Rose, 2000. Cert. tchr., adminstr., supr., N.Y. Tchr. Elijah Clark Jr. H.S., South Bronx, N.Y., 1972-75, Intermediate Sch. 291, Bklyn., 1975; tchr., dean, asst. prin. Jean Nuzzi Jr. H.S., Queens Village, N.Y., 1975-83; asst. prin. William Cowper Intermediate Sch., Maspeth, 1983-93; asst. prin.-in-charge I.S. 73 Annex, Elmhurst, 1994-97; adminstr.-in-charge 51st Ave. Annex for P.S. 7 and P.S. 71, 1997-99; adminstr.-in charge 51st Ave. Annex for P.S. 7 and I.S. 5, 1999. Doctoral fellow Hofstra U., 1990. Mem. Nat. Sci. Tchrs. Assn., Nat. Coun. Tchrs. English, Internat. Reading Assn. Roman Catholic. Avocations: playing piano, roller skating, ice skating, dancing, travel. E-mail: maurerkat@hotmail.com.

MAURICE, DON, personal care industry executive; b. Peoria, Ill., Aug. 29, 1932; s. Imajean (Webster) Crayton; m. Cindalu Jackson, Aug. 31, 1990. Student, Loma Linda U., 1984-86; cert. paralegal studies, Calif. State U., San Bernardino, 1994. Lic. hair stylist, skin therapist; cert. paralegal, notary pub. Owner 2 schs. in advanced hair designs, San Diego, 1962-64, D & M Enterprises, Advt. Agy., 1964-78; now cons. D&M Enterprises Advt. Agy.; dist. mgr. AqRo Matic Co. Water Purification Systems, San Diego, 1972-75; profl. sales educator Staypower Industries, 1972-76, 3d v.p., 1975-76; regional bus. cons. Estheticians Pharmacology Rsch., Garden Grove, Calif., 1975-81; owner, operator Don Maurice Hair Designs, Hemet, 1980-83; dir., operator Hair Sytles by Maurice, Loma Linda, 1984-88; owner, pres. Grooming Dynamics, Redlands, 1988—. Bus. cons. Yogurt Place, Paradise Valley, Ariz., 1978-79, others; regular guest Channel 6/Channel 8, San Diego, 1968-78; cons. infomercial Pre-Paid Legal Svcs., Inc., 1994—; undercover criminal investigator, 1955-59, 1999—. Author: The New Look For Men, 1967, The Art of Men's Hair Styling, 1968 (accepted by Library of Congress), Baldness, To Be or Not To Be, 1989. Promoter Spl. Olympics, Hemet, 1981. Sgt. U.S. Army, 1950-53, Korea. Decorated Purple Heart, 1952; named Leading Businessman in His Profession, Union and Evening Tribune, 1969. Mem. Internat. Platform Assn., Christian Businessmen's Assn. Avocations: writing, sculpting, art, sports, music. Office: Grooming Dynamics PO Box 1279 Loma Linda CA 92354-1279

MAURICE, PAUL, professional hockey coach; b. Jan. 30, 1967; m. Michelle; 1 child, Sydney. Asst. coach Detroit Jr. Red Wings, 1988-93, head coach, 1993-94, Carolina Hurricanes, 1995—; asst. coach All-Star Game NHL, 1997. Named runner up Coach of Yr. nominamtion OHL, 1995. Mem. Compuware Hockey Orgn. Office: Carolina Hurricanes 500 Aerial Ctr Ste 100 Morrisville NC 27560*

MAURIN, JAMES E. real estate executive; Grad. in aerospace engring., La. State U., 1970; MBA, Tulane U., 1972. Acct. Ernst and Ernst, New Orleans; mng. ptnr. Maurin-Ogden Properties, Covington, 1975—; chmn. Stirling Properties, 1975—. Mem.: Internat. Coun. Shopping Ctrs., World Pres.'s Orgn., Urban Land Inst. Office: Stirling Properties 109 Northpark Blvd Covington LA 70433-5005 E-mail: jmau@stirlingprop.com.

MAURLAND, ANNE ELISABETH, potter; b. Oslo, Apr. 6, 1964; came to U.S., 1984; d. Harald and Unni Elisabeth (Bjanes) M. BA, Luther Coll., 1987; MA, Ill. State U., 1989. Potter Genszler Stoneware Designs, Briggsville, Wis., 1989-94, Decorah, Iowa, 1994—. Recipient Award of Excellence, Plaza Art Fair, 1995, 97, Old Orchard Crafts Fair, 1994, Best of Show award Art Fair on the Square, 1995, Excellence in Clay award Minn. Craft Fair, 1995, 98, Award of Merit Winter Park Sidewalk Art Festival, 1999, 3d place award Cherry Creek Arts Festival, 1999. Mem. Norwegian Assn. Arts and Crafts. Avocations: mountain biking, skiing, reading, piano playing, cooking. Studio: Elisabeth Maurland Studio 411 W Water St Decorah IA 52101-1731

MAURO, GEORGE THEODORE, corporate executive; b. N.Y.C., Mar. 7, 1938; s. Peter Terzo and Bella (Cohn) M.; m. Mary Ann Stoehr, Feb. 15, 1964; children: Mary Patricia, Christine. BA, U. N.H., 1959; MBA, U. Pa., 1972. Sr. cons. Booz, Allen & Hamilton, Inc., Phila., 1972-75, v.p., 1975-77; dir. Asset Value Analysis, U.S. Ry. Assn., Washington, 1977-79; sr. assoc. Temple Barker & Sloane, Inc., Lexington, Mass., 1979-83; dir. transp. FMC Corp., Chgo., 1984-85, dir. logistics, 1985-89, dir. mfg. automotive svcs. equipment divsn., Conway, Ark., 1989-91; v.p. ops. Delta Consol. Industries, Jonesboro, Ark., 1991-92, exec. v.p. ops., Raleigh, N.C., 1994-96; exec. v.p., gen. mgr. So. Case Inc., Raleigh, N.C., 1992-93; v.p. ops. Interpane Glass Co., Clinton, N.C., 1996-97; exec. v.p. Mail Am Comms., Inc., Forest, Va., 1997—. Served with USAF, 1960-70. Decorated Meritorious Service medal Dept. Def., Air Force Commendation medal. Mem. Council Logistics Mgmt., Assn. for Mfg. Excellence, Beta Gamma Sigma, Tau Kappa Alpha, Psi Chi, Pi Kappa Alpha.

MAURO, RICHARD FRANK, lawyer, investment manager; b. Hawthorne, Nev., July 21, 1945; s. Frank Joseph and Dolores D. (Kreimeyer) M.; m. LaVonne M. Madden, Aug. 28, 1965; 1 child, Lindsay Anne. AB, Brown U., 1967; JD summa cum laude, U. Denver, 1970. Bar: Colo. 1970. Assoc. Dawson, Nagel, Sherman & Howard, Denver, 1970-72, Van Cise, Freeman, Tooley & McClearn, Denver, 1972-73, ptnr., 1973-74, Hall & Evans, Denver, 1974-81, Morrison & Forester, Denver, 1981-84; of counsel Parcel & Mauro, P.C., 1984—; pres. Parcel, Mauro & Hultin, P.C., 1988-90; of counsel Parcel, Mauro P.C., 1992-99; pres. Sundance Oil Exploration Co., 1985-88; exec. v.p. Castle Group, Inc., 1992-97, pres., 1998—, Richard F. Mauro, P.C., 1999—; ptnr. Moye, Giles, O'Keefe, Vermeire & Gorrell, 1999—. Adj. prof. U. Denver Coll. Law, 1981-84. Symposium editor: Denver Law Jour., 1969-70; editor: Colorado Corporation Manual; contbr. articles to legal jours. Pres. Colo. Open Space Coun., 1974; mem. law alumni coun. U. Denver Coll. Law, 1988-91. Francis Wayland scholar, 1967; recipient various Am. jurisprudence awards Mem. ABA, Colo. Bar Assn., Denver Bar Assn., Colo. Assn. Corp. Counsel. (pres. 1974-75), Am. Arbitration Assn. (comml. arbitrator), Order St. Ives, Denver Athletic Club (bd. dirs. 1986-89). Home: 2552 E Alameda Ave Unit 128 Denver CO 80209-3330 Office: 1225 17th St Fl 29 Denver CO 80202-5534 E-mail: rfmauro@mgorg.com.

MAURSTAD, DAVID INGOLF, federal agency administrator, insurance company executive; b. North Platte, Nebr., Aug. 25, 1953; s. Ingolf Byron and Marilyn Sophia (Gimble) M.; m. Karen Sue Micek, Sept. 7, 1974; children: Ingolf, Derek, Laura. A. in Fine Arts, Platte Community Coll., Columbus, Nebr., 1973; BSBA, U. Nebr., 1989, MBA, 2000. Asst. golf profl. Country Club of Lincoln (Nebr.), 1973-76; head golf profl. Westward Ho Country Club, Sioux Falls, S.D., 1977; ins. agt. Maurstad/Zimmerman Ins., Beatrice, Nebr., 1978-84; ins. agy. mgr. Maurstad Ins. Svcs., Inc., 1984-90, pres., 1990—; mayor City of Beatrice, 1991-94; mem. Nebr. Senate from dist. 30, 1995—99; lt. gov. State of Nebr., 1998—2001; regional dir. FEMA, 2001—. Pres. Beatrice YMCA, 1982-83, Gage County United Way, Beatrice, 1985, founding trustee, 1st pres. Beatrice Ednl. Found., 1988-96; mem. Nebr. Rep. State Cen. Com., Lincoln, 1985-90, 95-97, elected Bd. Edn. Sch. Dist. #15, Beatrice, 1988-90; candidate Nebr. Legislature, Lincoln, 1986; chmn. Highway 77 Improvement Assn., 1991-94; chair Nebr. Info. Tech. Commn., 1999-2001; trustee Beatrice Libr. Found., 1996-2001; bd. dirs. Madonna Found., 1997-2001. Named Outstanding Young Man of Am., Beatrice Jaycees, 1985, Citizen of Yr. Beatrice C. of C., 1993, Outstanding Amateur Golfer Nebr. Golf Assn., 1981, Harold Sieck Pub. Ofcl. of Yr., Arc of Nebr., 1998; recipient Young Alumnus award U. Nebr. Alumni Assn., 1993, Disting. Svc. award Nat. Fedn. Interscholastic Ofcls. Assn., 1989, Disting. Svc. award League of Nebr. Municipalities, 1998, Outstanding Alumnus award Ctrl. C.C. Platte Campus, Coll. Alumni Assn., 1998, Disting. Alumni award Nebr. C.C. System, 2000. Mem. Ind. Ins. Agts. Nebr. (Young Agt. of Yr. 1985), Blue Valley Life Underwriters (bd. dirs. 1988-94), Beatrice C. of C. (bd. dirs. 1985-87), U. Nebr.-Lincoln Coll. Bus. Adminstrn. Alumni Bd. (bd. dirs. 1989-96, pres. 1994-95, Leadership award 1994), Nebr. Diplomate, Shriners, Rotary, Eagles, Mason. Lutheran. Avocations: golf, reading, spectator sports.

MAURY, NANCY JANE (NANCY JANE GOOCH), realtor, mortgage company executive; b. Ann Arbor, Mich., Dec. 19, 1941; d. Donald B. and Marjorie (Gilchrist) G. BA, Western Mich. U., 1963; MA, Ea. Mich. U., 1987. Lic. real estate broker, Fla., Mich. Tchr. Broward County Schs., Ft. Lauderdale, Fla., 1968-73; v.p. Chinelly Real Estate, Inc., Miramar, 1973-83; closing exec. Cenville Devel. Co., Hollywood, 1983-85; mortgage originator Empire of Am., Southfield, Mich., 1987-90; dir. Am. Mortgage Tng. Co., Garden City, 1990-2000; residential mortgage specialist Wells Fargo Home Mortgage, Portage, Ind., 2000—02; residential mortgage specialist AmeriFirst Fin. Corp., Mich., 2002—. Editor Bridlepath mag., 1983-84, The Saddlebred Mag., 1989-95; contbr. numerous articles to various publs. Pres. Broadway Area Neighborhood Assn., Ann Arbor, 1985-86. Recipient honors S. Fla. Trail Riders Broward County, 1983. Mem. Wayne-Oakland Bd. Realtors, Am. Saddlehorse Assn. (bd. dirs. Mich. chpt. 1990-95, sec. 1994-95, editor The Saddlebred, 1989-95), Women's Econ. Club. Republican. Avocations: equestrian, photographer. Office: AmeriFirst Fin 616 W Ctr Portage MI 49024

MAUS, JOHN ANDREW, computer systems engineer, consultant; b. Whittier, Calif., July 13, 1945; s. Kenneth Waring and Bertha Estella (Eckman) M.; M. Diana Barba, April 16, 1977 (div. May 1, 1983); m. Colette An Moschelle, Nov. 23, 1985; stepchildren: BreAnn, Adam; children: Steven Andrew, Terra An. BA in Physics, U. Calif., Riverside, 1963-67; MS in Physics, San Diego State U., 1967-70. Cert. data processor, 1983. Programmer, analyst San Diego State Found., 1970-72; instr. bus. San Diego State U., 1971-73, systems programmer, 1971-74; data processing mgr. M.H. Golden Co., 1974-79; computer systems engr. Hewlett-Packard Co., Spokane, Wash., 1979-84, sr. systems engr., 1984-86, network systems engr., 1986-89, sr. tech. cons., 1989-93, UNIX high availability cons., 1994—, sr. tech. cons. high availability, 1999-2000; owner, cons. Maus Software Tech. Cons., 2000—. Physics lab. asst. USDA Salinity Lab., Riverside, 1965-67; underwater acoustics programmer Naval Undersea Ctr., San Diego, 1967-70; programmer San Diego Inst. Pathology, 1972-76; adv. com. Computer Sci. Bus. Applications North Idaho Coll., 1989-96; mem. career network U. Calif., Riverside, 1990—; dist. tech. com. Nine Mile Falls (Wash.) Sch., 1994-97. Author: INTEREX Conference Proceedings, 1989; co-author: Chemical Physics Letters, 1971, Electronic and Atomic Collisions, 1971. Merit badge counselor Spokane chpt. Boy Scouts Am., 1983—. Mem. Assn. Computing Machinery (founder Spokane chpt., chpt. chmn. 1980-82, service award 1981). Avocations: internat. travel, skiing, computers. Home and Office: 12417 W Sunridge Dr Nine Mile Falls WA 99026-9311 E-mail: john_maus@mstci.com.

MAUSER, KEVIN EDWARD, finance executive; b. Plattsburgh, N.Y., Nov. 22, 1959; s. Edward Anton and Josie Agnes (Collins) M. BS, Sacramento State U., 1981. Auditor Am. Savs., Sacramento, 1983-84; underwriter United Guaranty Ins., San Ramon, 1984-85, Ticor Investment Securities, L.A., 1985; asst. v.p. Prin. Portfolio Svcs., 1986-97; transaction mgr. Amresco, 1997—98; ind. mortgage cons., 1998—. Cons. in field. Mem. Nat. Assn. Rev. Appraisers (sr.), Mortgage Underwriters. Roman Catholic.

MAU-SHIMIZU, PATRICIA ANN, lawyer; b. Jan. 17, 1953; d. Herbert G. K. and Leilani (Yuen) Mau; 1 child, Melissa Rose. BS, U. San Francisco, 1975; JD, Golden Gate U., 1979. Bar: Hawaii 1979. Law clk. State Supreme Ct., Honolulu, 1979-80; atty. Bendet, Fidell & Sakai, 1980-81; legis. atty. Honolulu City Coun., 1981-83, House Majority Staff Office, Honolulu, 1983-84, dir., 1984-93; chief clk. Hawaii Ho. of Reps., 1993—. Mem. Hawaii Bar Assn., Hawaii Women Lawyers, Jr. League Hawaii. Democrat. Roman Catholic. Home: 7187 Hawaii Kai Dr Honolulu HI 96825-3115 Office: State House Reps 415 S Beretania St Rm 027 Honolulu HI 96813-2407

MAUSKOPF, SEYMOUR HAROLD, history educator; b. Cleve., Nov. 11, 1938; s. Philip and Dora (Trompeter) M.; m. Josephine Mary Album, Aug. 9, 1964; children: Deborah, Philip, Alice. AB, Cornell U., 1960; PhD, Princeton U., 1966. Instr. history Duke U., Durham, N.C., 1964-66, asst. prof., 1966-72, assoc. prof., 1972-80, prof., 1980—, dir. program in sci. tech. and human values, 1979-84, dir. Focus Interdisciplinary programs, 1995—. Author: Crystals and Compounds, Molecular Structure and Composition in Nineteenth Century French Science, 1976, (with M.R. McVaugh) The Elusive Science; Origins of Experimental Physical Research, 1915-1940, 1980; editor: The Reception of Unconventional Science by the Scientific Community, 1979, Chemical Sciences in the Modern World, 1993. Recipient Dexter award for outstanding achievement in history of chemistry, 1998, award Sci. and Religion Course Program, Ctr. for Theology and the Natural Scis., 2002; NSF postdoctoral fellow, 1971-72, Charles Price fellow Chem. Heritage Found., 2000; NSF grantee, 1974, 92-93; Am. Philos. Soc. travel grantee, 1979; Nat. Endowment for Humanities summer stipend, 1982; Edelstein internat. fellow in history chem. scis. and tech. Beckman Ctr. U. Pa. and Hebrew Univ., Jerusalem, 1988-89. Mem. History Sci. Soc. (exec. com. treas. 1979-83, coun. 1993-95). Jewish.

MAUSSER, ALBERT, municipal official; b. Bklyn., Jan. 8, 1963; s. Josef and Helene Mausser; m. Colleen J. Price, Sept. 26, 1988; children: Thomas, Samantha. Cert. indoor environmentalist IAQA, mech. inspector Fla., mech. plans examiner Fla. Tactical comm. chief U.S. Army, Tacoma, 1981—85; animal care specialist Sea World of Fla., Orlando, 1985—88; apprentice City of Orlando, 1988—89, journeyman, 1989—96, energy mgr., 1996—. Sgt. U.S. Army, 1981—85. Mem.: Assn. Energy Engrs. (cert. energy mgr.). Republican. Avocations: scuba diving, travel, woodcrafts. Home: 3417 Ridgemont Rd Orlando FL 32808 Office: City of Orlando 1010 S Westmoreland Ave Orlando FL 32805 Fax: 407-246-3725. Personal E-mail: albert.mausser@ci.orlando.fl.us.

MAUTZ, KARL EMERSON, engineering executive; b. Columbia, Mo., Sept. 30, 1957; s. Wayne Albert Mautz and Imogene (Embrey) Whitten; m. Pamela Dawn Quillen, Mar. 12, 1988; children: Alyssa Mae, Brandon Tyler. BS in Chemistry, U. Tex., El Paso, 1979, BS in Geology, 1983; MS in Chemistry, Ariz. State U., 1985, PhD, 1987. Process engr. Motorola, Inc., Mesa, Ariz., 1980-87, mem. tech. staff Austin, Tex., 1988—. Cons. Motif, Inc., Portland, Oreg., 1994, Semicondr. 300, Dresden, Germany, 1998-2000; chmn. Austin Patent Com., 2000—. Contbr. articles to profl. jours.; patentee in field of semiconductor processes; numerous patents pending; development of 300mm wafer process tool technology. Mem. recycling com. Homeowners Assn., Austin, 1992. Recipient Disting. Innovator award Motorola Inc., 1999, Gold Badge award, 2000. Mem. Electrochem. Soc., Am. Chem. Soc. Achievements include 10 patents for semiconductor processes. E-mail: karl.mautz@motorola.com.

MAUZ, HENRY HERRWARD, JR. retired naval officer; b. Lynchburg, Va., May 4, 1936; s. Henry Herrward and Rene C. (Ball) M.; m. Margaret Catherine O'Neill, June 6, 1959; children: Sheila, David, Lynn, Daniel. BS, U.S. Naval Acad., 1959; BSEE, U.S. Naval Postgrad. Sch., 1965; MBA, Auburn U., 1970. Commd. ensign USN, 1959, advanced through grades to adm., 1992, various ships and shore duty assignments, 1977-80; strategy and concepts officer Office of Chief Naval Ops. Washington, 1980-82; comdg. officer USS England, San Diego, 1980-82, chief of staff Carrier Group One, 1982-83; ops./readiness officer SHAPE Belgium, 1983-85; comdr. Cruiser/Destroyer Group 12 Mayport, Fla., 1985-86; ops./plans officer to comdr. in chief Pacific Fleet, Pearl Harbor, Hawaii, 1986-88; comdr. Seventh Fleet Yokosuka, Japan, 1988-90; dep. chief Office Naval Op.s, Washington, 1991-92; comdr. in chief U.S. Atlantic Fleet, 1992-94; ret. USN, 1994. Pres. Naval Postgrad. Sch. Found. Decorated D.S.M. with four gold stars, Def. Superior Svc. medal, Legion of Merit, Bronze Star with combat V device. Mem. U.S. Naval Inst., U.S. Naval War Coll. Found., Naval Hist. Found., Monterey Peninsula Country Club, Army-Navy Country Club. Avocations: golfing, skiing. Home: 1608 Viscaino Rd Pebble Beach CA 93953-3303

MAUZY, MICHAEL PHILIP, environmental consultant, chemical engineer; b. Keyser, W.Va., Nov. 14, 1928; s. Frank and Margery Ola (Nelson) M.; m. Nancy Shepherd Watson, Mar. 27, 1949; children: Michael P. Jr., Jeffrey A., Rebecca A. BSChemE, Va. Poly. Inst., 1950; MSChemE, U. Tenn., 1951. Registered profl. engr., Va., Ill. With Monsanto Co., St. Louis, 1951-71, dir. engring. and mfg., 1968-71; mgr. comml. devel. Kummer Corp., Creve Coeur, Mo., 1971-72; mgr. labs. Ill. EPA, Springfield, 1972-73, mgr. water pollution control, 1973-74, mgr. environ. programs, 1974-77, dir., 1977-81; v.p. Roy F. Weston, Inc., West Chester, Pa., 1981-88, Vernon Hills, Ill., 1988-93, Albuquerque, 1993-96, also bd. dirs. West Chester, Pa.; mgr. The Pangaea Group, LLC, Albuquerque, 1996—. Bd. dirs. DeTox Internat. Corp., St. Charles, Ill.; provider Congl. testimony, 1974-81; presenter various workshops, symposia and seminars, 1974—. Contbr. articles on environ. mgmt. to profl. publs., 1974—. Mem. Ohio River Valley Water Sanitary Commn., Cin., 1976-81. 1st lt. U.S. Army, 1951-53. Recipient Environ. Quality award Region V, U.S. EPA, Chgo., 1976, Disting. Svc. award Cons. Engrs. Coun. of Ill., 1978, Ill. award Ill. Assn. Sanitary Dists., 1979, Clarence W. Klassen award Ill. Assn. Water Pollution Control Ops., 1984. Mem. Am. Pub. Works Assn., Am. Inst. Chem. Engring., Water Pollution Control Assn., Am. Mgmt. Assn. Avocations: reading, travel, home improvements.

MAVEL, MARY ANN, foundation administrator; b. LeRoy, Wis., June 1, 1935; d. James Joseph and Marie Ann (Bauer) Weinberger; m. Gerald George Davel, June 21, 1958 (dec. 1963); children— Elizabeth, David, Ann, Amy. B.S., St. Norbert Coll., 1957. Traffic coordinator Sta. WTMJ-TV, Milw., 1966-71; ptnr. Maier, Richman & Costello Advt., Inc., Milw., 1971-75; pub. relations specialist Milw. Area Tech. Coll., 1975-77; exec. dir. Milw. Area Tech. Coll. Found., Inc., 1977— . Mem. Nat. Soc. Fund Raising Execs. (Wis. chpt.). Avocations: biking; sailing; cross-country skiing; gardening; needlecraft. Home: 1420 Lone Oak Ln Brookfield WI 53045-7834

MAVES, MICHAEL DONALD, medical association executive; b. East St. Louis, Ill., Oct. 14, 1948; BS, U. Toledo, 1970; MD, Ohio State U., 1973; MBA, U. Iowa, 1988. Lic. physician, Iowa, Mo., Ill., D.C.; diplomate Am. Bd. Otolaryngology. Rsch. fellow Ohio State U. Coll. Medicine, Columbus, 1977; fellow head and neck surgery Columbia-Presbyn. Med. Ctr., N.Y.C., 1978, U. Iowa Hosps. and Clinics, Iowa City, 1980-81; asst. prof. otolaryngology, head and neck surgery Ind. U. Sch. Medicine, Indpls., 1981-84, U. Iowa Hosps. and Clinics, Iowa City, 1984-87, assoc. prof., 1987-88; chmn. dept. otolaryngology St. Louis U. Sch. Medicine, St. Louis, 1988-94; exec. v.p. Am. Acad. Otolaryngology, Head and Neck Surgery, Alexandria, Va., 1994—2001, Am. Medical Assn., Chicago, 2002—. Lectr. in field. Contbr. articles to profl. jours. Capt. U.S. Army, 1974-76. Recipient numerous awards including Honor award and Pres.'s award Am. Acad. Otolaryngology-Head and Neck Surgery; named one of Best 1000 Physicians in U.S., 1992, 94, One of Best 400 Cancer Doctors in Am., Good Housekeeping, 1992. Fellow ACS; mem. AMA (RBRVS update com.), Am. Cancer Soc., others. Office: Am Medical Assn 515 N State St Chicago IL 60610

MAVRIDES, GREGORY, computer scientist, psychoanalyst, computer engineer, computer company executive; b. Flushing, N.Y., Jan. 17, 1955; s. George and Antoinette (Karamanol) M.; m. Nicole Witteboon, Feb. 14, 1977 (div. Jan. 1996); m. Doreen A. Diem, Apr. 25, 1998. BA, SUNY, Stony Brook, 1978; MS, Columbia U., 1980, PhD, 1990; certificate in Sys. Engring., Intense Sch., Ft. Lauderdale, Fla., 2001. Diplomate in clin. social work. Clin. social worker Pride of Judea Mental Health Ctr., Douglaston, N.Y., 1980-84, dir. computer rsch., 1985-89; asst. prof. social work U. S.C., Columbia, 1989-91, chmn. computer com. Coll. Social Work, 1989-91; assoc. prof. social work Barry U., Miami, Fla., 1991-94; clin. social work psychotherapist Emerald Hills Med. Sq., Hollywood, 1994-97; program dir. Am. Family Counseling Ctr., Boca Raton, 1997-98; exec. dir., CEO Lifeskills of Boca Raton, 1998-2000; CEO Elite Compusys., 2000—, microsoft cert. sys. engr., owner, 2001. Mem. Nat. Assn. Social Workers (chmn. clin. issues S.C. chpt. 1990-91), S.C. Soc. for Clin. Social Workers. Republican. Greek Eastern Orthodox. Avocations: chess, bridge, computer technology. Office: Elite Compusystems Ste 3 990 S Congress Ave Delray Beach FL 33445

MAVROS, GEORGE S. clinical laboratory director; b. Adelaide, Australia, Oct. 14, 1957; came to U.S., 1970; s. Sotirios George and Angeliki (Korogiannis) M.; m. Renee Ann Cuddeback, June 24, 1979. BA in Microbiology, U. South Fla., 1979, MS in Microbiology, 1987; MBA, Nova U., 1991; PhD in Health Sci. Mgmt., LaSalle U., 1995. Cert. lab. dir. Nat. Certifying Agy. for Clin. Lab. Pers.; diplomate Am. Coll. Health Care Execs. Med. technologist Jackson Meml. Hosp., Dade City, Fla., 1979-81; microbiology supr. HCA Bayonet Point-Hudson Med. Ctr., Hudson, 1981-82, dir. labs., 1982-88; lab. mgr., adminstrv. and tch. dir. Citrus Meml. Hosp., Inverness, 1988—. Lab. cons. HCA Oak Hill Hosp., Spring Hill, Fla., 1983-84; cons. lab. info. systems Citation Computer Systems, St. Louis, 1983—, Hosp. Corp. of Am., Nashville, 1986; instr. Microbiology Pasco Hernando Com. Coll., New Port Richey, Fla., 1986-88, Inst. Biolog. Scis. Cen. Fla. Community Coll., Lecanto, 1989—; bd. dirs. Gulf Coast chpt. Clin. Lab. Mgrs. Assn., Tampa, Fla., 1987, pres., 1987-89. Parish pres. Greek Orthodox Ch. of West Cen., Inverness, Fla.; chmn. Bayonet Point Hosp. Good Govt. Group, Hudson, 1986-88. Mem. APHA, Am. Mgmt. Assn., Am. Soc. Microbiology, Am. Soc. Clin. Pathologists (cert. in lab. mgmt.), Am. Soc. Med. Technologists (cert.), Fla. Soc. Med. Technologists, Clin. Lab. Mgmt. Assn. (pres. Gulf Coast chpt. 1988-90), Am. Assn. Clin. Chemists, Am. Acad. Microbiology (cert.), Fla. State Bd. Clin. Lab. Pers. (chmn. 1994). Clubs: Greek Orthodox Youth Am. (Clearwater, Fla.). Lodges: Order of DeMolay, Sons of Pericles (sec.). Democrat. Home: 6 Byrsonima Ct W Homosassa FL 34446-4610 Office: Citrus Meml Hosp 502 W Highland Blvd Inverness FL 34452-4754

MAWARDI, OSMAN KAMEL, plasma physicist; b. Cairo, Dec. 12, 1917; came to U.S., 1946, naturalized, 1952; s. Kamel Ibrahim and Marie (Wiennig) M.; m. Betty Louise Hosmer, Nov. 23, 1950. BS, Cairo U., 1940, MS, 1945; A.M., Harvard U., 1947, PhD, 1948. Lectr. physics Cairo U., 1940-45; asst. prof. Mass Inst. Tech., 1951-56, asso. prof., 1956-60; prof. engring., dir. plasma research program Case Inst. Tech., Cleve., 1960-88; dir. Energy Research Office, Case Western Res. U., 1977-82. Pres. Collaborative Planners, Inc.; mem. Inst. Advanced Study, 1969-70; also cons. Contbr. articles to profl. jours. Past trustee Print Club Cleve., Cleve. Inst. Art. Recipient Biennial award Acoustical Soc. Am., 1952; CECON medal of achievement, 1979 Fellow AAAS, Acoustical Soc. Am., IEEE (Edison lectr. 1968-69, Centennial award 1984, Cleve. sect. Engr. of Yr. 1994); mem. N.Y. Acad. Scis., Sigma Xi, Eta Kappa Nu. Home: 15 Mornington Ln Cleveland OH 44106 Office: 2490 Lee Rd Cleveland OH 44118-4125 E-mail: okm@po.cwru.edu. *I never cease to be amazed that the goals I really believe in invariably materialize.*

MAWASHA, P. RUBY, dean, engineering educator; b. Johannesburg, South Africa, Feb. 10, 1966; s. Thimothy B. and Angela Pule Mawasha; m. Joann Cheryl Wright; children: Ishe Timothy, Thando Joshua. B of Mech. Engring.Engineering), CCNY, 1990—90; MSME, U. Akron, 1993, PhD in Engring., 1998. Asst. dean engring. and computer sci. Wright State U., Dayton, Okla., 2001—; asst. dean engring. U. Akron, 1998—2001. Dir. sci., tech., and engring. prep. program Wright State U., Dayton, 2001—. Mem. exec. com. Students Open to Aviation Rsch. (SOAR) Program, Dayton, 2000; Bd. dirs. Summit County Bd. Pub. Stds., Akron, 1999—2001; bd. dirs. Wayne County Career Pathways/Sch.-to-Work Com., Wooster, 1999—2001. Mem.: ASME (assoc.; chair Region V young engrs. program 2000—02, Young Engrs. Program award 2000, Oral Presentation Cert. 1994), Nat. Soc. Black Engrs., Am. Soc. for Engring. Edn. (assoc.; vice chair North Cen. sect. 2000—01), Tau Beta Pi, Pi Tau Sigma, Omicron Delta Kappa, Pi Mu Epsilon. Office: Wright State U 3640 Colonel Glenn Hwy Dayton OH 45435 Office Fax: 937-775-5000. Business E-Mail: mawasha@cs.wright.edu.

MAWBY, COLIN JOHN, musician, composer, writer; b. Portsmouth, Eng., May 9, 1936; s. Bernard John and Enid Dorothy (Vaux) M.; m. Beverley Jane Courtney, July 15, 1987; children: Benedict John, Clement Donald. Student, Royal Coll. Music, London, 1951-54. Choirmaster Plymouth (Eng.) Cathedral, 1955-56, Sacred Heart, Wimbledon, Eng., 1978-81; organist St. Anne's Ch., London, 1957-59; asst. master music Westminster Cathedral, 1959-61, master of music, 1961-78; choral dir. Radio Telefis Eireann, Dublin, 1981-95; dir. Irish Nat. Chamber Choir, 1996—2001. Prof. Trinity Coll. Music, London, 1975-80; short term chorus master BBC, London, 1973; exec. assoc. bd., London, 1978; has conducted BBC Singers, Belgian Radio Choir, Pro Cantione Antiqua, London Mozart Players, The Nash Ensemble; regular spkr. and condr. BBC Radio 3. Composer 23 masses and more than 200 other choral pieces, also 2 operas for young people; recorded with Argo, Naxos, Unicorn, Classics for Pleasure, Oreg. Cath. Press, EMI, Sony, others. Decorated officer of merit Knights of Malta; fellow Guild Ch. Music, 1989. Roman Catholic. Home: Gerrardstown Garlow Cross Navan County Meath Ireland E-mail: colinmawby@eircom.net.

MAWHINNEY, KING, insurance company executive; b. Richmond, Va., Sept. 13, 1947; s. John A. and Ellen E. (King) M.; m. Jeanne Dale Smothers, June 8, 1976 (div. Oct. 1984); m. Cathryn C. Morley, Nov. 15, 1986. AB, Davidson Coll., 1971; MA, Pacific Lutheran U., 1973; MEd, U. Tex., 1992. CLU; ChFC; FLMI; ALHC; fellow life and health claims; ALHC; registered health underwriter, registered employee benefits cons.;assoc. customer svc., health ins. assoc. devel. mgr. Prudential Ins. Co., Newark, 1977-80; sr. sales rep. USAA Life Ins. Co., San Antonio, 1980-81, sales tng. adminstr., 1981-82, dir. procedures and tng., 1983-85, dir. group/bus. sales, 1985-86, sr. dir. USAA Ednl. Services, 1986-88, exec. dir. life sales, FSD Mktg., 1989-90, asst. v.p. life sales, 1990-91; asst. v.p. health sales Life Gen. Agy., 1991-92, asst. v.p. health ins., 1992-94, v.p. health ins., 1994-97, v.p. life sales, 1997—. Mem. choir Alamo Heights Presbyterian Ch., 1981-83, deacon, 1982-83; mem. Univ. United Meth. Ch., 1991—, mem. adminstrv. bd., 1992-93; mem. bd. gov's. San Antonio Estate Planners Coun., 1988-92; with U.S. Olympic Festival, 1993; chmn. Dreams for Youth Project; bd. dirs. Boysville, Inc., 1991—, pres., 1997, trustee, 1998—. Capt. U.S. Army, 1972-77; Korea. Mem. Life Office Mgmt. Assn. (coun. mem. 1988-91, 93-97, chmn. soc. com. 1988-91), Davidson Coll. Alumni Assn. (chpt. pres. 1983-94), San Antonio Chpt. C.L.U. (bd. dirs., v.p. programs, v.p. fin., v.p. adminstrn., pres.-elect, pres.), FLMI Soc. So. Cen. Tex. (chpt. pres. 1986, bd. dirs. 1987-88), Leadership San Antonio (class XVII 1991-92), Phi Kappa Phi, Sigma Nu, Kappa Delta Pi. Republican. Avocations: sports cards, walking. Home: 23744 Up Mountain Trl San Antonio TX 78255-2002 Office: USAA Life Ins Co 9800 Fredericksburg Rd San Antonio TX 78288-0002

MAWHIRTER, BRUCE ROBERT, civil engineer; b. Queens, N.Y., May 6, 1957; s. Quentin Francis Mawhirter and Dorothy Ruth Levy; m. Deborah A. Ambrosio, Oct. 2, 1983. B of Engring., Hofstra U., 1995. Lic. profl. engr., N.Y., Conn. Archtl. designer Rockaway Metal Prodn., Inwood, N.Y., 1979-84; mgr. facilities engring. Fanning, Phillips & Molnar, Ronkonkoma, 1984-93, Law Environ. PE, PC, N.Y.C., 1993-94; project mgr. Bohler Engring., Valley Stream, N.Y., 1994-95; mgr. civil engring. Cameron Engring., P.C., Syosset, 1995—. Mem. ASCE, APWA, N.Y. State Soc. Profl. Engrs. (bd. dirs. Nassau County chpt. 1996-99), Design Profls. Coalition of L.I. (bd. dirs. 1996-99), Phi Theta Kappa. Office: 3 Aerial Way Syosset NY 11791-5501

MAWHOOD, ARISTIDE ROSCOE, mechanical engineer; b. Darjeeling, India, Nov. 18, 1933; parents Brit. citizens; s. Charles Timothy and Thelma Quida (Hollow) M.; m. Mary Bridget McManamon, Dec. 1, 1962; children: Sean Ross, Anton Morgan. BSME, Brit. Inst. Engring. Tech., 1955; postgrad., Imperial Coll. Sci. and Tech. Registered profl. engr., U.S.; profl. engr., U.K. Apprentice engr. Cen. Electricity Generating Bd., 1951-55; dist. engr., mgr., adv. and field engr. Worthington Corp., 1956-63; sr. maintenance engr., maintenance project engr. Hess Oil Virgin Islands Corp., 1970-73; mgr. field engring. svcs. Sam P. Wallace, Internat., 1973; chief engr., chief planning engr., sr. constrn. engr. C.E. Lummus Corp., 1973-75; chief field and resident engr. Pritchard Internat., Inc., 1976-77; engr. 1 mech. (project mgmt. team) Arabian Am. Oil Co., 1977-82; sr. sys. engr. ITT-Fed. Electric Corp., 1985; sr. engr.-cum-cons. Mawhood & Assocs., 1983, 84, 86; sr. mech. engr.-cum-cons. Brown & Root Internat., Inc., 1987-88; sr. engr.-cum-cons. Allis Chalmers Compressor Corp., Appleton, Wis., 1988-89; tech. asst. specialist Corporacion Venezolana de Guayana, S.A., 1989-90, M&H Engring., Inc., Houston, 1990-91; project mgr., engr. Am. Samoa Govt., Pago Pago, American Samoa, 1991-94; sr. program officer, cons. Fed. Emergency Mgmt. Agy. (Pacific), 1994-95; mech. engr., cons. Saudi Arabian Oil Co., Dammam, Saudi Arabia, 1995-96; mech. engr. Dow Chem. Co., Houston, 1996-97; cons. electronic data processing, 1997—. Mech. engr., cons. Saudi Arabian Oil Co., Damman, Saudi Arabia, 1995-96; mech. engr. tech. support unit, engring. and constrn. divsn. Dow Chem. USA, Inc., 1996-97, Engring. and Constrn. Venezuela (Petrozuata) Extra Heavy Crude Oil Engring. Project, Brown & Root USA, Inc., 1997-98; semi-ret. project mgr., engr., tech. cons., 1998—; condr. seminars and revs. Tex. Employment Commn., Houston, 1983-84. Author: Value Engineering, 1975, Role of Gas Turbines, 1978 (IGTI award 1980), Machinery Diseases, 1982 (Vibration Inst. award 1983), Saline Water Conversion, 1987 (Water Inst. award 1988). Active various ch. groups, Houston. Recipient Safety at Constrn. Sites award Constrn. Assn. Can., 1974, Tech. Transfer award Operaciones al Sur del Orinoco, Puerto Ordaz, Venezuela, Value Engring. award Refineria Isla, Curacao, 1987. Fellow Instn. Plant Engrs., India Soc. Mech Engrs., Japan Soc. Mech. Engrs.; mem. ASME (corp.), NSPE, Am. Soc. Metals, Soc. Am. Mil. Engrs., Am. Inst. Plant Engrs., Instn. Mech. Engrs. (assoc.). Republican. Christian Scientist. Achievements include development of solutions for erosion/corrosion problems on pump casings; findings on excess stiffness characteristics in Bendex Diaphragm Couplings for high-speed gas compressors. Avocations: model engineering, photography, philately, world travel, fitness. Home: West Univ PO Box 272562 Houston TX 77277-2562

MAX, BUDDY (BORIS MAX PASTUCH), musician; b. Jan. 25; m. Freda Max; 1 child, John. Musician, performer as America's Singing Flea Market Cowboy: albums include: Many Styles and Sounds of Buddy Max, 1980, The Great Nashville Star, 1984, The Story of Freda and Bud, 1985, Cowboy Junction Stars, 1985, Tribute to Challenger's Crew of 7, 1986, With Our Friends at Cowboy Junction, 1989, Little Circle B, 1990, Together-Our Masterpiece, 1991, The Life to Fame and Fortune, 1992, Orange Blossom Special, 1996, Hall of Fame, Gold Record Award Winning Buddy Max, 1996, Hall of Fame; composer songs include When the Magnolia Tree Blooms in Lecanto, The Story of Barney Clark, Hang My Guitar on the Wall, John F. Kennedy, The Challenger, Where the Maple Syrups Flow, Little Circle B, Way Up on the Mountain, Desert Storm, When Do I Love You, The Pretty Girl on TV. Recipient World Hall of Fame award and gold medallion, 1997, numerous trophies, awards for benefit and non-profit shows Am. Heart Assn., Am. Lung Assn., Girl Scouts Am., Citizens of Citrus County Fla., Deaf Svcs. of Citrus County, Statue of Liberty trophy and coin award Cowboy Junction Opry Country Music Show, 2000 for song I Love Miss America, cert. Young Marines of Citrus County, 2002; named Ky. Col., Gov. Paul E. Patton, 2001. Address: care Cowboy Junction 3949 W Hwy 44 & Jct 490 Lecanto FL 34461-9232

MAX, CLAIRE ELLEN, physicist; b. Boston, Sept. 29, 1946; d. Louis William and Pearl (Bernstein) M.; m. Jonathan Arons, Dec. 22, 1974; 1 child, Samuel. AB, Harvard U., 1968; PhD, Princeton U., 1972. Postdoctoral rschr. U. Calif., Berkeley, 1972-74; physicist Lawrence Livermore (Calif.) Nat. Lab., 1974—; dir. Livermore br. Inst. Geophysics and Planetary Physics, 1984-93, dir. univ. rels., 1993-2000; assoc. dir. Ctr. for Adaptive Optics, U. Calif., Santa Cruz, 2000—. Mem. Math.-Sci. Network Mills Coll., Oakland, Calif.; mem. com. on fusion hybrid reactors NRC, 1986, mem. com. on internat. security and arms control NAS, 1986-89, mem. com. on phys. sci., math. and applications NRC, 1991-94, mem. policy and computational astrophys. panels, astron. and astgrophys. survey NRC, 1989-91; mem. sci. steering com. W.M. Keck Obs., 1992-96, mem. adaptive optics sci. team, 1994—; mem. vis. com. Space Telescope Sci. Inst., 1996-2000, Hubble Space Telescope Second Decade Com., 1998-2000. Editor: Particle Acceleration Mechanisms in Astrophysics, 1979; contbr. numerous articles to sci. jours. Fellow AAAS (coun. rep. physics sect. 2001—), Am. Phys. Soc. (exec. com. divsn. plasma physics 1977, 81-82); mem. Am. Astron. Soc. (exec. com. divsn. high energy astrophysics 1975-76), Am. Geophys. Union, Internat. Astron. Union, Phi Beta Kappa, Sigma Xi. Achievements include rsch. on adaptive optics and laser guide stars for astronomy; astrophys. plasmas. Avocations: violin, skiing. Office: Lawrence Livermore Nat Lab PO Box 808 7000 East Ave # L413 Livermore CA 94550-9516 E-mail: max1@llnl.gov.

MAX, ELIZABETH, educator; b. Fort Worth, Oct. 9, 1924; d. Frederick Ward and Alice Louise (Matthews) Maxwell; m. Herbert Jones McCorkle, Sept. 22, 1945 (div. Oct., 1969); children: Anne McCorkle Moore, Louise Kate McCorkle, Bruce Ward McCorkle, Sallie Matthews McCorkle. BS, Tex. Women's U., 1944; MS in Library Sci., U. North Tex., 1966; PhD in Edn., Okla. State U., 1974. Cert. secondary, elementary tchr., Tex., Okla.; cert. sch. librarian, Tex., Okla. Copy clerk, beginning writer UPI, NBC, N.Y.C., 1944—45; elementary and secondary tchr. various schs., Tex., 1950-69; instr. library sci. Western Ill. U., Macomb, 1969-70; asst. prof., fine arts libr. Okla. State U., Stillwater, 1970-72, asst. prof., coord. Library Sci. Dept., 1972-76, assoc. prof., 1976-82, supervisor, English Edn., 1982-90, prof. emerita, 1990—. Cons. Skelly Oil Co., Tulsa, Okla., 1976, The Ctr. for Local Govt. Tech., 1983-84, Stillwater Library Sys. Bd., 1985. Author (with others): Teaching the Short Story, 1996; mem. reader panel New York Times, 1996—, mem. New York Times Online Panel, 2002; contbr. Pres. Meml. Soc. Central Pa., 1994, 96-99; vol. Nat. Disaster Relief, ARC, 1991-96; women's rights activist. Mem. NEA, ALA, Nat. Women's Studies Assn. (founder), Okla State U. Women's Coun. (founder, 2d chair), Okla. Adult & Continuing Edn., Nat. Collegiate Players, Stillwater Okla. Writer's Club (pres., 1985-89), Greek Sabbatical, Nat. Council Tchrs. of English, Gen. Soc. Mayflower Descs., Parents and Friends of Lesbians and Gays, Phi Delta Kappa, Phi Kappa Phi, Beta Phi Mu. Democrat. Home and Office: 463 Kemmerer Rd State College PA 16801-6408 E-mail: elizabethmax@earthlink.net.

MAX, ERNEST, surgeon; b. Vienna, Austria, Mar. 3, 1936; m. Silvia Neger, Mar. 18, 1964; children: Yvette Rosa, Oliver Fredrick. MD, U. Chile, 1961. Diplomate Am. Bd. Surgery, Am. Bd. Colon and Rectal Surgeons, Am. Bd. Laser Surgery. Intern Hosp. San Borja, Santiago, Chile, 1960-61, resident Chile, 1962-63; fellow in gen. surgery, colon and rectal surgery Lahey Clinic Found., Boston, 1969-70; resident Sinai Hosp., Balt., 1971-72, The Western Pa. Hosp., Pitts., 1972-74; resident in colon and rectal surgery Hermann Hosp., Houston, 1974-75, staff, 1975—, Park Plz. Hosp., 1975—, Meml. Hosp. Southwest, 1975—, Meml. NW Hosp., 1975—, Diagnostic Ctr. Hosp., 1975—, The Methodist Hosp., 1976—, Meml. City Hosp., 1976—, Woman's Hosp., 1976—, HCA Spring Br., 1976—, Houston NW Med. Ctr., 1976—, Sam Houston Meml. Hosp., 1977—, St. Luke's Episcopal Hosp., 1981—, Cypress Fairbanks, 1983—; chief of staff Meml. Hosp., 1983; staff HCA Med. Ctr., 1986—, Meml. Hosp. Southeast, 1994—; CEO Colon and Rectal Clinic PA, 1989—. Clin. assoc. prof. surgery Baylor Coll. Medicine; clin. instr. surgery U. Tex. Med. Sch., Houston. Author: (with others) Current Diagnosis, 1971. Recipient Walter A. Fansler Travel Edn. award Am. Soc. Colon and Rectal Surgeons, 1974, Harriet Cunningham award Tex. Med. Assn., 1988, Best of the Best award Tex. Med. Assc., 1989; The Purdue Fredrick fellow Am. Soc. Colon and Rectal Surgeons, 1974. Mem. Am. Coll. Surgeons, Tex. Med. Soc., Harris County Med. Soc., Tex. Soc. Colon and Rectal Surgeons (pres. 1982-83), Am. Soc. Laser Medicine and Surgery, Internat. Soc. Univ. Colon and Rectal Surgeons, Lahey Clinic Alumni Assn., Am. Soc. Colon and Rectal Surgeons, Tex. Gulf Coast Colon and Rectal Surgical Soc. (sec. treas. 1992—), Colombian Soc. Colo-Proctology (hon. mem.). Office: Colon & Rectal Clinic PA 6550 Fannin St Ste 2307 Houston TX 77030-2723

MAXANER, CATHERINE L. business and political consultant; b. Queens, N.Y., June 26, 1940; d. Charles Middlebury and Dora Hüther Maxaner; 1 child, Madonna Rose. BA in Spanish and Edn., Marymount Coll., 1962; MA in Spanish Lang. and Lit., U. Nat. Autonoma, Mexico City, 1965; diploma in Spanish methodology, Inst. Caro y Cuervo, Bogota, Colombia, 1965; cert. paralegal, Pa. State U., 1988, rural leadership cert., 1989. Caseworker, immigration liaison Internat. Inst., Milw., 1966; tchr. ESL and Spanish, Milw. Tech. Coll., 1966-69; freelance translator Milford, Pa., 1975—. V.P. Pa. Coun. Rep. Women, Harrisburg, 1998-2000, dir. 1994-98, 2001—; Pa. del. Nat. Fedn. Rep. Women, 1998-99, Nat. Women Leaders Forum, 1998-2000; mem. State Bd. Psychology, 2000—; dir. Women's Polit. Network Pa., 1998—. Scholar Colombian Govt., Inst. Caro y Cuervo, 1964; grantee Nat. Def. Edn. Act, N.Y. U., 1967. Mem. Nat. Assn. Legal Assts., Women's Nat. Rep. Club, Pa. Soc., Williams Club. Avocations: travel, languages, power walking, swimming.

MAXCY, SPENCER JOHN, education educator; b. Chgo., June 22, 1939; s. Spencer Thomas and Marian Adele (Davis) M.; m. Doreen Kay Oliver, Sept. 6, 1970; children: Colleen Shivaun, Spencer Oliver. BA in History, Blackburn Coll., 1961; MA in History, Loyola U., 1965; PhD in Philosophy of Edn., Ind. U., 1972. Cert. tchr. social studies, Ill. Substitute tchr. Chgo. Pub. Schs., 1962-63; social studies tchr. Dist. 218, Blue Island, Ill., 1963-67; assoc. instr. Ind. U., Bloomington, 1969-72; asst. prof. La. State U., Baton Rouge, 1972-76, assoc. prof., 1976-85, full prof., 1985—. Author: Educational Leadership, 1991, Democracy, Chaos, and the New School Order, 1995, Ethical School Leadership, 2002; editor: (book) Postmodern School Leadership, 1994; mem. editorial bd. Record in Ednl. Adminstrn. and Supervision, 1981-91, Internat. Jour. of Ednl. Reform, 1992—. Basketball coach YMCA, Baton Rouge, 1993, 94, 95. NDEA fellow U. Chgo., 1966-67, Ind. U. fellow, 1967-68. Fellow Philosophy of Edn. Soc.; mem. Am. Ednl. Rsch. Assn., S.W. Philosophy of Edn. Soc. (pres. 1974-93). Avocations: weightlifting, fishing. Home: 251 E Woodgate Ct Baton Rouge LA 70808-5408 Office: La State U Peabody Hall 111 Baton Rouge LA 70803-0001

MAXEINER, CLARENCE WILLIAM, lawyer, construction company executive; b. Sioux City, Iowa, Mar. 24, 1914; s. Frank A. and Dora A. (Olson) M.; m. Julie Frazer, Sept. 8, 1937; children: Martha Ann, Jay Frank, Mary Katherine, Nancy Carol; m. Rosalie F. Steele, May 29, 1974. Student, Columbia Coll., 1933-34, Columbia U. Law Sch., 1938-39; AB, Grinnell Coll., 1936; JD, U. Calif.-Berkeley, 1941. Bar: Calif. 1941. Ptnr. Thelen, Marrin, Johnson & Bridges, San Francisco and Los Angeles, 1941-60; sr. v.p., gen. counsel, dir. J.H. Pomeroy & Co., Inc. (and affiliated cos.), San Francisco, 1959-65; v.p., gen. counsel Dillingham Corp. (and affiliated cos.), Honolulu, 1966—, sr. v.p., gen. counsel, sec., dir., mem. exec. com., 1968-71, spl. counsel, 1971—. Chmn. equipment fund com. Sonoma State Hosp., 1956-65; bd. overseers Grinnell Coll., 1964; bd. dirs. Del Monte Forest Found., Calif. Autism Found. Mem. ABA, San Francisco Bar Assn., State Bar Calif., Am. Judicature Soc., Hawaii State Bar (assoc.), Columbia, U. Calif. law schs. assns., Phi Beta Kappa, Phi Delta Phi. Clubs: Commonwealth of Calif. (San Francisco), The Family (San Francisco). Congregationalist. Address: 1808 Wildflower Dr Medford OR 97504 Home: 1432 Village Center Dr Medford OR 97504-4502 E-mail: bmaxeiner@rvm.org.

MAXEY, DAVID WALKER, lawyer; b. Scranton, Pa., May 17, 1934; s. Paul Harold and Margaret (Walker) M.; m. Catharine Eglin, June 6, 1968; children: Paul Eglin, Margaret Wilson. AB, Harvard U., 1956, LLB cum laude, 1960. Bar: Pa. 1961, U. S. Dist. Ct. (ea. dist.) Pa. 1961, U.S. Ct. Appeals (3d cir.) 1963. Assoc. Drinker Biddle and Reath LLP, Phila., 1960-66, ptnr., 1967-2000, chmn. real estate dept., 1970-88, mng. ptnr., 1977-91, co-chmn., 1988-91, of counsel, 2000—. Vis. faculty Villanova (Pa.) U. Law Sch., 1987-95. Contbr. articles to profl. jours. Sec., bd. dirs. Greater Phila. Internat. Network, 1981-94; bd. dirs. Young Audiences Ea. Pa., Phila., 1985-95, Libr. Co., Phila., 1993-2000, sec., 1997-2000; chmn. bd. dirs. Hist. Soc. Pa., Phila., 1991-93; chmn. internat. adv. com. Greater Phila. First, 1994-98; bd. dirs. Gladwyne (Pa.) Libr., 1991-98, pres., 1996-98; bd. dirs. Phila. Soc. Preservation Landmarks, 2002-. Recipient Hughes-Gossett award U.S. Supreme Ct. Hist. Soc., Washington, 1991. Mem. ABA, Pa. Bar Assn., Phila. Bar Assn., Am. Coll. Real Estate Lawyers, Harvard Club Phila. (pres. 1970-72), Merion Cricket Club, Sunday Breakfast Club. Avocation: historical research and publication. Home: 829 Black Road Rd Gladwyne PA 19035 Office: One Logan Sq 18th and Cherry Streets Philadelphia PA 19103-6996 E-mail: cdmmax@aol.com., maxeydw@dbr.com.

MAXEY, DIANE MEADOWS, artist; b. Lufkin, Tex., Feb. 26, 1943; d. Warren Gaston and Jackie Meadows; m. William Brant Maxey, Sept. 5, 1964; children: Dananne, Robert Warren. BA in Art and Edn., U. North Tex., 1965; postgrad., U. Tex., Arlington, Tex. Tech U., Lubbock; studied with Al Brouilette, Bud Biggs, Edgar Whitney, Dick Phillips, Robert E. Wood, Rex Brandt, Milford Zornes. Art tchr. Dallas Pub. Schs., 1965-66; substitute tchr. Arlington Pub. Schs., 1969-72; pvt. classes San Angelo, Tex., 1973-77; owner Maxi Watercolor Studio, Paradise Valley, 1978—, Bandanna Tours, Scottsdale, 1988-91. Mem. staff Scottsdale Artist Sch., The Shemer Art Ctr.; tchr. numerous watercolor workshops for different local schs. and internat. tours cos. Exhibited at Gold Nuggett Art Gallery, Wickenburg, Ariz., Long Gallery, Scottsdale, Ariz.; featured artist in Freshening Your Paintings with New Techniques, Fresh Flowers The Best of Flower Painting, The Best of Watercolor 2, The Best of Watercolor Composition, Splash 5, Splash 7, 2002; featured in Internat. Artist Mag., 1998; cover artist Watercolor Magic, spring 2000, Scottsdale Life mag., 2002—, A Valley Virtuoso, Five Outstanding Artist. Dir. visual ministry First So. Bapt. Ch., Scottsdale, 1988-95. Recipient numerous awards including Outstanding Artist Scottsdale Mag., 2002. Mem. Western Fedn. Watercolor Soc. (gen. chmn. 1981-82), Southwestern Watercolor Assn. (signature), Ariz. Artist Guild (hon. life; pres. 1982-83), Ariz. Watercolor Assn., Tex. Watercolor Assn. (signature), 22 x 30 Profl. Critique Group. Avocations: gardening, travel. Home and Office: Maxi Watercolor Studio 7540 N Lakeside Ln Paradise Valley AZ 85253-2857 E-mail: dmaxey.watercolor@worldnet.att.net.

MAXEY, LATANYA, writer; b. Houston, July 23, 1970; d. Lorenzo Edward and Dorothyfay Johnson; m. Brian Keith Maxey, Aug. 3, 1988; children: Elizabeth Paige, Lauren April. Polit. Sci., U. of Houston, Houston, TX, 1988—93. Bookkeeper Raepfeffer Apt., Houston, 1988—90; office mgr. United Advanced Tech., 1990—92; pension consultan Loren D. Stark Co., 1992—95; retirement plans mgr. Morgan Stanley, 1995—2002; freelance writer Self-employed, Missaricity, 2000—. Mem. Nat. Orgn., National, 2000—02, Dem., 2002—02, Al Gore, 2002—02. Democrat-Npl. Methodist. Avocations: writing, reading, school volunteering. Home: 3115 Ivymill Ln Missouri City TX 77459 Home Fax: 281-778-8134. Personal E-mail: latanya__maxey@hotmail.com.

MAXEY, NIGEL AARON, publisher; b. Rock, W.Va., Nov. 29, 1945; s. Aaron Burr and Ruth Aretta (Wiley) M.; m. Linda Sharon Boyd, Oct. 29, 1971. BA, Concord Coll., 1969; MA, W.Va. U., 1987. Reporter Princeton (W.Va.) Times, 1963-64, mng. editor, 1965; editor Mail Order Bus. Mag., Bluefield, W.Va., 1972-77; pub. Small Pub. Mag., Pineville, 1993—. With W.Va. Dept. Human Svcs., Pineville, 1970—. Author: How to Successfully Publish and Market Your Own Book, 1996, Publishing 101, 1996, Government Open for Business-Working People Not Served, 1998. Home: PO Box 1620 Pineville WV 24874-1620 Office: 92 C Cedar Ave Pineville WV 24874

MAXEY, SUSAN MARIE, geology department head; b. Evansville, Ind., July 6, 1946; d. Russell H. and Irene G. (Horn) Wiberg; m. George F. Maxey. BS, U. Tex., 1969, postgrad., 1986—; MA, U. Tex., Dallas, 1976. Tchr. Forest Oaks Mid. Sch., Ft. Worth, 1969-71, Browne Mid. Sch., Dallas, 1971-76; lectr. U. Tex., 1977-78; geology dept. head Brookhaven Coll., 1978—. Mem. editl. rev. bd. Jour. Coll. Sci. Tchg., 1984-87; contbr. articles to profl. jours. Maj. gifts chmn. Sta. KERA-TV Auction, Dallas, 1985-88; grad. Leadership Lewisville, Tex., 1989-90; v.p. Lewisville Edn. Found., 1989-96; bd. dirs. Greater Lewisville Habitat for Humanity, 1995-97; del. Tex. Rep. Convention, 1996, 2000; mem. adv. bd. Lake Lewisville Environ. Learning Area, 1995—. Recipient Master Tchr. award Nat. Inst. for Staff & Organizational Devel., 1987; Kellogg Found. fellow, 1988. Mem. Geol. Soc. Am., Lions (Balloon Festival com. chair 1991—, treas. 1992-96), Delta Kappa Gamma. Avocations: underwater photography, quilt-making. Home: 20 Horseshoe Dr Highland Vill TX 75077-6714 Office: Brookhaven Coll 3939 Valley View Ln Dallas TX 75244-4906

MAXFIELD, FREDERICK ROWLAND, medical educator; b. Bklyn., Oct. 21, 1949; s. Allen F. and Marjorie Grant Maxfield; m. Christine Meredith Kiley, Aug. 21, 1971; children: Laura, Andrew. BS, Union Coll., Schenectady, N.Y., 1971; PhD, Cornell U., 1977. From asst. prof. to prof. pharmacology NYU Sch. Medicine, N.Y.C., 1979—87; prof. pathology and physiology Coll. Physicians and Surgeons Columbia U., 1987—95; prof., chmn. dept. biochemistry Weill Med. Coll. Cornell U., 1995—. Mem.: N.Y. Soc. Exptl. Microscopists (pres. 1996—97), Biophysical Soc., Am. Soc. Cell Biology, Harvey Soc. (pres. 2002—). Office: Cornell U Weill Med Coll 1300 York Ave New York NY 10021 Business E-Mail: frmaxfie@med.cornell.edu.

MAXFIELD, GUY BUDD, lawyer, educator; b. Galesburg, Ill., May 4, 1933; s. Guy W. and Isabelle B. Maxfield; m. Carol Tunick, Dec. 27, 1970; children: Susan, Stephen, Karen. AB summa cum laude, Augustana Coll., 1955; JD, U. Mich., 1958. Bar: N.Y. 1959. Assoc. White & Case, N.Y.C., 1958-63; prof. law NYU, 1963—; of counsel August & Kulunas, P.A. Author: Tennessee Will and Trust Manual, 1982, Federal Estate and Gift Taxation, 8th edit., 2002, Florida Will and Trust Manual, 1984, Tax Planning for Professionals, 1986; contbr. articles to law jours. Trustee Acomb Found., Newark, 1974—. With U.S. Army, 1958-64. Fellow Am. Coll. Tax Counsel; mem. ABA, Am. Law Inst., N.Y. State Bar Assn., Order of Coif, Phi Beta Kappa. Office: NYU Sch Law 40 Washington Sq S New York NY 10012-1099

MAXFIELD, JOHN EDWARD, retired university dean; b. Los Angeles, Mar. 17, 1927; s. Chauncey George and Rena Lucile (Cain) M.; m. Margaret Alice Waugh, Nov. 24, 1948; children— Frederick George (dec.), David Glen, Elaine Rebecca, Nancy Catherine, Daniel John. BS, Mass. Inst. Tech., 1947; MS, U. Wis., 1949; PhD, U. Oreg., 1951. Instr. U. Oreg., 1950-51; mathmatician U.S. Naval Ordnance Test Sta., China Lake, Calif., 1949-56, head computing br., 1956-57, head math. div., 1957-60; lectr. UCLA, 1951-60; head prof. dept. math. U. Fla., 1960-67; prof., chmn. dept. math. Kans. State U., 1967-81; dean Grad. Sch. and univ. research La. Tech. U., 1981-92, dean emeritus, 1992—; ret. La. Tech. U., 1992. Mem. Am. Math. Soc., Math. Assn. Am., Soc. Indsl. and Applied Math., Sigma Xi. Home: 209 E Louisiana Ave Ruston LA 71270-4417

MAXFIELD, MARY CONSTANCE, management consultant; b. Washington, Mar. 16, 1949; d. Orville Eldred and Rose Mary (Stiarwalt) Maxfield; m. Robert Charles Kneip III, Aug. 21, 1971 (div. Apr. 1981); 1 child, Stephanie Alexandra; m. Richard Howard Cowles, May 16, 1981 (dec.); m. Phillip Walker, July 25, 1985 (div. June 1991). BA in History and Spanish, Va. Tech., 1970; MS in Occupl. Tech., U. Houston, 1996. Clk.-typist HEW, Social Security Adminstrn., New Orleans, 1971-72, svc. rep., 1972-73; mgmt. analyst Office Comptroller of Currency Treasury Dept., Washington, 1974-77, dir. mgmt. analysis divsn. U.S. Customs New Orleans, 1978-80, mgmt. analyst Houston, 1980-81, program analyst, 1981-82, chief data processing br., 1982-83, chief mgmt. analysis br., 1983-85; pres. Constance Walker Assocs., Inc., 1985-91, Maxfield Productivity Cons., Inc., 1991—. Co-founder Supplier Registry. Author (with others): Team Approach to Problem Solving, 1991; author: Quality School Facilitator Training, 1992, Interpersonal Communications Skills, 1992, Introduction to Total Quality Schools, 1992, Tex. Leadership Ctr. DuPont LDP Tng., TQM Module, 1999, Total Quality Management, 1999, Strengthening Team Development, 1995, Internal Auditing to ISO 9000 Standards, 1995, Essential Facilitation Skills, 2000, Personnel Management in Food Service, 1995, Successfully Leading Change, 1996, Leading Change Through Site-Based Teams, 1996, Quality Tools 101, 1996, Introduction to ISO 9000, 1999, Benchmarking, 1999, Advanced Facilitation Skills, 2000, Developing and Evaluating Training, 2000, Presentation Skills for Change Agents, 2000, Successfully Managing Projects, 2001, Coaching for Performance, 2001, Everyday Creativity, 2001, Appreciative Inquiry, 2001, Kitchen 101; contbr. Named Customs Woman of Yr., U.S. Customs, 1979, Fed. Exec. Bd. Woman of Yr., 1979, Cora Bell Wesley scholar, UDC, 1969; recipient Outstanding Performance award, 1979—85, Outstanding Svc. award, Office of Sec. of Treasury, 1976, Key to City, New Orleans, 1990. Mem. DAR, ASTD, Assn. Psychol. Type, Am. Soc. Quality, Assn. Quality and Participation (past pres. Houston chpt.), Treasury Hist. Assn., Daus. Rep. of Tex., Daus 1812, UDC, Va. Tech. Alumni Assn., Austin's Old 300 (founding), Delta Zeta. Episcopalian. Home and Office: Maxfield Productivity Cons Inc 8007 Liberty Elm Ct Spring TX 77379-6125

MAXFIELD, PETER C. state legislator, law educator, lawyer; b. 1941; AB, Regis Coll., 1963; JD, U. Denver, 1966; LLM, Harvard U., 1968. Bar: Colo. 1966, Wyo. 1969. Trial atty. Dept. Justice, 1966-67; assoc. Hindry, Erickson & Meyer, Denver, 1968-69; asst. prof. U. Wyo. Coll. Law, 1969-72, assoc. prof., 1972-76, prof., 1976-96, dean, 1979-87, prof. emeritus, 1996—. Vis. assoc. prof. U. N.Mex., 1972-73; Raymond F. Rice Disting. prof. U. Kans., 1984; Chapman Vis. Disting. prof., U. Tulsa, 1987; vis. prof. U. Utah, 1992. Author: (with Garr Houghton) Cases and Materials on the Taxation of Oil and Gas and Natural Resources Transactions, 1990, (with Allen Houghton) Taxation of Mining Operation, 1981, 97; (with Trelease and Dietrich) Natural Resources Law on American Indian Lands, 1977. Coord. Wyo. State Planning 1988-89; spl. asst. Gov. Wyo. 1989-90; Dem. nominee U.S. Ho. Reps., 1990; mem. Wyo. Environ. Quality Coun., 1991-93; mem. Wyo. Senate, Laramie, 1993-97. Mem. Omicron Delta Kappa, Pi Delta Phi. Home: 1159 Escalera St Laramie WY 82070-5020 Office: U Wyo Coll Law PO Box 3035 Laramie WY 82071-3035 E-mail: petemaxfield@earthlink.net., petemax@uwyo.edu.

MAXIM, L. DANIEL, engineer; b. N.Y.C., Feb. 27, 1941; s. Leslie Morgan and Lillian Lester Maxim; m. Karen Angela Dunne, Sept. 29, 1962; children: Lauren Daria, Lysandra Danielle. B of Chem. Engring., Manhattan Coll., 1961; MS, SUNY, 1963, Stevens Tech. inst., 1966; PhD, NYU, 1973. Engr.

Nat. Starch, Plainfield, N.J., 1960-68; v.p. Mathtech, Princeton, 1968-79; pres. Everest Cons., Cranbury, 1980—. Ceramic fiber adv. bd. Unifrax Corp., Niagara Falls, N.Y., 1988—; silicone sci. adv. bd. Dow Corning, Midland, Mich., 1994—. : mem. editl. bd. Regulatory Pharmacology and Toxicology, 1999—; contbr. articles to profl. jours. With. USCG, Aux. Mem. Cosmos Club. Republican. Office: Everest Cons 15 N Main St Cranbury NJ 08512

MAXIMOS, METROPOLITAN (MAXIMOS DEMETRIOS AGHIORGOUSSIS), bishop, metropolitan; b. Callimassia, Chios, Greece, Mar. 5, 1935; s. Evanghelos G. and Lemonia G. (Rythianou) A. Licentiate, Patriarchal Sch. Theology, Halki, 1957; Baccalaureate, Th.D., U. Louvain, Belgium, 1964. Ordained to ministry Greek Orthodox Ch., 1957; chaplain U. Louvain, 1957-64; pastor chs. Brussels, Rome, Brookline, Mass., Manchester and Newport, N.H., 1960-78; observer-del. II Vatican Council, 1964-65; chaplain Holy Cross Sem., Brookline, 1967-76; prof. systematic theology Holy Cross Sch. Theology, 1967-79, Christ Savior Sem., Johnstown, Pa., from 1979; bishop Greek Orthodox Diocese Pitts., 1979-97, metropolitan, 1997—. Mem. Orthodox-Roman Cath. Consultation, from 1967; v.p. Nat. Council Chs. Christ U.S., 1979-81; ecumenical officer Greek Orthodox Archdiocese N. and S. Am., 1978-79, chmn. synodal coms. ecumenical affairs, spiritual renewal and youth, 1979-. Author: In the Image of God, 1998; contbr. articles in field. Mem. Orthodox Theol. Soc. Am., AAUP, Christian Assos. Pitts., Pa. Coun. Chs., W.Va. Coun. Chs., Ohio Coun. Chs. Office: Greek Orthodox Diocese Pittsburgh 5201 Ellsworth Ave Pittsburgh PA 15232-1421 *My ministry is such that it requires a total commitment to its goals, but first of all a total commitment to Christ. In my childhood, I was fortunate to be guided by excellent parents and grandparents, who gave me not only the necessary security and stability, but also the inspiration to imitate their personal commitment to the Lord. I fully trust in the grace of the Lord, but I also have always accepted my responsibility for everything I have done.*

MAXSON, BARBARA KINZIE, clinical social worker, educator; b. Whittier, Calif., July 11, 1948; d. Lester Lewis and Marian Elizabeth (Crawley) Kinzie; children: Jonathan, Christopher, Melissa. BA, Westmont Coll., Santa Barbara, Calif., 1970; MSW, Ariz. State U., 1987. Family therapist Family Svc. Agy., Phoenix, 1987-89; instr. Grand Canyon U., 1987—, dir. Counseling Ctr., 1987-91; therapist Nat. Inst. Drug Abuse, Purdue U., 1991—; pvt. practice family therapy, 1991—. Adj. prof. Ariz. State U., Tempe, 1988-91. Trainer Am. Bapt. Conv., Phoenix, 1985—. Mem. NASW, Acad. Cert. Social Workers, Am. Assn. Marriage and Family Therapists, Nat. Assn. Christian Social Workers, Am. Assn. Christian Counselors, Ariz. Assn. Marriage and Family Therapy (rep. bd. dirs. 1991—). Democrat. Avocations: playing piano, painting, camping. Office: 10220 N 31st Ave Ste 205 Phoenix AZ 85051-9563

MAXWELL, ANDERS JOHN, investment banker; b. San Francisco, Oct. 3, 1946; s. John L. and Deborah A. M.; m. Carlene S. Maxwell, 2000; children by previous marriage: Lauren A., Colin A., Ian W., Erin C., Ryan N. BArch, U. Calif.-Berkeley, 1969; MBA, U. Pa., 1971. Analyst GE, 1971-73; v.p. GE Credit Corp., Stamford, Conn., 1973-83; mng. dir. Dean Witter Reynolds Inc., N.Y.C., 1983-87; v.p. Kidder Peabody & Co., Inc., 1987-88; prin. L.F. Rothschild & Co., 1988; v.p. Smith Barney, Harris Upham & Co., Inc., 1989-91, Lazard Frères & Co., N.Y.C., 1991-92; ptnr. Benedetto, Gartland & Greene, 1992-94; v.p., gen. mgr. GE Capital Corp., Stamford, Conn., 1994-96; dir. Salomon Smith Barney Inc., N.Y.C., 1997-98; mng. dir. Barington Capital Group, 1998, Peter J. Solomon Co., N.Y.C., 1999—. Served to capt. U.S Army, 1971. Office: Peter J Solomon Co 767 5th Ave New York NY 10153-0023 E-mail: amaxwell@pjsolomon.com.

MAXWELL, ARTHUR EUGENE, oceanographer, marine geophysicist, educator; b. Maywood, Calif., Apr. 11, 1925; s. John Henry and Nelle Irene M.; m. Colleen O'Leary, July 1, 1988; children: Delle, Eric, Lynn, Brett, Gregory, Sam Wade, Henry Wade. BS in Physics with honors, N.Mex. State U., 1949; MS in Oceanography, Scripps Instn. Oceanography, 1952, PhD in Oceanography, 1959. Jr. rsch. geophysicist Scripps Instn. Oceanography, La Jolla, Calif., 1950-55; head oceanographer Office Naval Rsch., Washington, 1955-59, head br. geophysics, 1959-65; assoc. dir. Woods Hole (Mass.) Oceanographic Instn., 1965-69, dir. rsch., 1969-71, provost, 1971-81; prof. dept. geol. scis., dir. Inst. Geophysics U. Tex., Austin, 1982-94, prof. emeritus dept. geol. sci., 1994—. Bd. dirs. Palisades Geophys. Inst. Corp.; chmn. bd. govs. planning com. deep earth sampling, 1968-70, chmn. exec. com. deep earth sampling, 1971-72, 78-79, 91-92; mem. joint U.S./USSR com. for coop. studies of the world ocean NAS/NRC, 1973-80, chmn. U.S. nat. com. to Internat. Union Geodesy and Geophysics, 1976-80, vice chmn. outer continental shelf/environ. studies rev. com., 1986-93; chmn. U.S. nat. com. on geology NAS, 1979-83, chmn. geophysics rsch. bd. geophysics study com., 1982-87; nat. sea grant rev. panel NOAA, 1982-85, 90-2000, sci. adv. bd., 1998—; mem. vis. com. Rosenteil Sch. Marine and Atmospheric Studies U. Miami, 1982-86, dept. physics N.Mex. State U., 1986-94; acad. adv. com. Com. Exch. CIA, 1983-96; mem. Gulf of Mexico Regional Marine Rsch. Bd., 1992-96. Editor: The Sea, Vol. 4, Parts I and II, 1970; editorial adv. bd. Oceanus, 1981-92; contbr. articles to profl. jours. Chmn. tech. adv. com. Navy Thresher Search, 1963; mem. Mass. Gov's. Adv. Com. on Sci. and Tech., 1965-71. With USN, 1942-46, PTO. Recipient Meritorious Civilian Svc. award Chief Naval Rsch., 1958, Albatross award AMSOC, 1959, Superior Civilian Svc. award Assn. Sec. of Navy, 1963, Disting. Civilian Svc. award Sec. of Navy, 1964, Disting. Alumni award N.Mex. State U., 1965, Bruun Meml. Lecture award Intergovtl. Oceanographic Commn., 1969, Outstanding Centennial Alumnus award N. Mex. State U., 1988. Fellow Am. Geophys. Union (pres. 1976-78, pres. oceanography sect. 1970-72); mem. Marine Tech. Soc. (charter, pres. 1981-82), Cosmos Club. Achievements include research in heat flow through the ocean floor, in structure and tectonics of the sea floor. Home: 8115 Two Coves Dr Austin TX 78730-3122 Office: Univ Tex Inst Geophysics Bldg 600 4412 Spicewood Springs Rd Austin TX 78759 E-mail: art@utig.ig.utexas.edu.

MAXWELL, DAVID OGDEN, former government official and financial executive; b. Phila., May 16, 1930; s. David Farrow and Emily Ogden (Nelson) M.; m. Joan Clark Paddock, Dec. 14, 1968. BA, Yale U., 1952; LLB, Harvard U., 1955. Bar: Pa. 1955, D.C. 1955. From assoc. to ptnr. Obermayer, Rebmann, Maxwell & Hippel, Phila., 1959-67; from ins. commr. to adminstrn. and budget sec. State of Pa., 1967-70; gen. counsel HUD, Washington, 1970-73; pres., CEO Ticor Mortgage Ins. Co., 1973-81; CEO Fannie Mae, Washington, 1981-91; dir. bus. and non-profit orgns. Bd. dirs. Corp. Ptnrs., L.P., Fin Security Assurance Holdings, Ltd. Bd. dirs. Sta. WETA-TV; trustee Nat. Gallery Art. With USNR, 1955-59. Office: 5335 Wisconsin Ave NW Ste 440 Washington DC 20015-2052

MAXWELL, DIANA KATHLEEN, early childhood education educator; b. Seminole, Okla., Dec. 16, 1949; d. William Hunter and ImoJean (Mahurin) Rivers; m. Clarence Estel Maxwell, Jly 3, 1969; children: Amanda Hunter, Alexandra Jane. BS, U. Md., 1972; M of Secondary Edn., Boston U., 1974; PhD, U. Md., 1980. Cert. tchr., counselor, Tex. Tchr. Child Garden Presch., Adelphi, Md., 1969-71; tchr., dir. PREP Edn. Ctr., Heidelberg, Germany, 1972-74; tchr. N.E. Ind. Schs. Larkspur, San Antonio, 1974-77, 89-90, Headstart, Boyds, Md., 1978; dir., founder First Bapt. Child Devel. Ctr., Bryan, Tex., 1982-84; instr. English lang. Yonsei Med. Ctr., Seoul, Republic of Korea, 1985-87; asst. prof. Incarnate Word Coll., San Antonio, 1987-89; tchr. kindergarten Fairfax County Pub. Schs., Kings Park, Va., 1990-94; tchr. Encino Park, San Antonio, 1994-95; lectr. U. Tex., 1995-96; multi-age tchr., theater arts tchr. Ft. Sam Houston Elem. Sch., 1996—. Cons. Sugar N'Spice Child Devel. Ctr., Kilgore, Tex., 1980-90; bd. dirs. Metro Area Assn. for Childhood Edn. Internat., 1991-93. Author: (book revs.) Childhood Education, 1979, 80, 92. Block chairperson March of Dimes, 1991, 92, 93, , 2000-, 01, 02, Am. Heart Assn., Fairfax, Fa., 1991, 92, San Antonio, 2000, 01, 02, Am. Diabetes Assn., Fairfax, 1992; judge speaking com. Burke Optomists, 1992, 93, judge writing competition N.E. Ind. Sch. Dist., 1996; sec. Cole H.S. Cougar Club, Ft. Sam Houston, San Antonio, 1996-97, v.p., 1997-2002, chair project graduation, 2002—; Bible tchr. 1st Bapt. Ch., Alexandria, Va., 1993-95; tchr. kindergarten Trinity Bapt. Ch., San Antonio, 1995-99, tchr. 1st grade, 2001—. Named one of Outstanding Young Women of Am., 1983; Md. fellow State of Md., 1978, 79; Tech. grantee Tex. Edn. Agy., San Antonio, 1990, State of Va. and Fairfax County, Springfield, 1991; recipient Yellow Rose of Tex. vol. award Gov. of Tex., 1996, Dean's Outstanding Tchg. award U. Tex., San Antonio, 1995-96, Ft. Sam Houston Hero award, 2001, 02. Mem. ASCD, Internat. Reading Assn., Assn. Profl. Tchr. Educators, Edn. Internat., Assn. for Childhood Edn. Internat. (v.p., pres.-elect), Tex. Assn. Childhood Edn., Bexar County and Surrounding Areas Assn. Childhood Edn. Avocations: oriental brush painting, singing, collecting butterflies, children/teacher advocate. Home: 2602 Country Square St San Antonio TX 78209-2235 Office: Ft Sam Houston Elem Sch 3370 Nursery Rd San Antonio TX 78234-1479

MAXWELL, DONALD MALCOLM, clergyman, religious educator; b. Watford, Eng., Apr. 6, 1934; s. Arthur S. and Rachel Elizabeth (Joyce) M.; m. Eileen J. Bolander, Aug. 25, 1955; children: Wendy E. Maxwell Henderson, D. Kevin. BA in Theology and Biblical Langs., Pacific Union Coll., 1956; MA in Systematic Theology, Andrews U., 1958; PhD in Biblical Studies New Testament, Drew U., 1968. Ordained to ministry Seventh-Day Adventist Ch., 1960. Pastor No. Calif. Conf. Seventh-Day Adventists, Oakland, Calif., 1956-64; instr. religion Union Coll., Lincoln, Nebr., 1964-65; prof. religion Walla Walla Coll., College Place, Wash., 1965-78, v.p. acad. affairs, 1978-83; pres. Pacific Union Coll., Angwin, Calif., 1983—2001, pres. emeritus, 2001—. Trustee St. Helena Hosp., Deer Park, Calif., 1983-2001, Rio Lindo Acad., Healdsburg, Calif., 1983-2001; bd. dirs., membership com. Adventist Health/West, Roseville, Calif., 1983-2001. Recipient Charles Elliot Weniger award of excellence, 1996, Edn. award of excellence, 2001; Rockefeller fellow, 1967-68; Drew U. scholar, 1967-68; named Tchr. of Yr., Wash. State Auto Assn., 1971. Mem. Soc. Biblical Lit. Avocations: golf, boating, gardening. Office: Pacific Union Coll 1 Angwin Ave Angwin CA 94508-9713 E-mail: mmaxwell@puc.edu.

MAXWELL, DONALD ROBERT, pharmacologist; b. Paris, Mar. 30, 1929; s. Titus Bonner and Helen Marie-Camille M.; m. Catherine Marie Billon, Aug. 16, 1956; children— Monica, Nicholas, Christopher, Caroline, Denis, Dominic, Marie-Claire, Philip. BA in natural scis. (physics) (rsch. scholar), U. Cambridge, Eng., 1952, MA, 1956, PhD in med., 1955; MA in romance langs. and lit., U. Mich., 1994, PhD in romance langs. and lit., 1998. Attachée de recherches du C.N.R.S. Institut Pasteur, Paris, 1955-56; various appts. May & Baker Ltd., Eng., 1957-74; dir. preclin. research Warner-Lambert Co., Morris Plains, N.J., 1974-77; v.p. preclin. research Warner-Lambert/Parke-Davis, Ann Arbor, Mich., 1977-90, sr. v.p. rsch. and devel.; exec. v.p. sci. affairs Warner-Nambert/Parke-Davis, 1990—. Vis. asst. prof.. lectr. French, U. Mich. Author: The Abacus and the Rainbow: Bergson, Proust and the digital analogic Opposition, 1999, Science or Literature? The Divergent Cultures of Discovery and Creation, 2000; contbr. articles to profl. jours. V.p., pres. Bd. Edn., Gabriel Richard H.S., Ann Arbor, 1981-85; adv. com. Cambridge U., U.S. Office, 1991—. Fellow Inst. Biology (Eng.), Royal Soc. Medicine (London); mem. Brit. Pharmacol. Soc., Physiol. Soc. (U.K.), Am. Soc. Pharmacology and Exptl. Therapeutics, Biochem. Soc., Internat. Coll. Neuro-Psychopharmacology, British Soc. Immunology, British Soc. Allergy and Clin. Immunology, European Soc. Study of Drug Toxicity. Home: 2940 Fuller Rd Ann Arbor MI 48105 Office: Dept Romance Languanges and Literatures U Mich Ann Arbor MI 48109 E-mail: maxwelld@umich.edu.

MAXWELL, DOROTHEA BOST ANDREWS, civic worker; b. Greenville, Ill., Apr. 20, 1911; d. Samuel Washington and Viola Maud (Bost) Andrews; m. Richard Wesley Maxwell, June 1, 1935; children: Andrea Judith Maxwell Platz, Anne Dorothea Maxwell Walsh. BA with honors, diploma in piano, Greenville Coll., 1933; MusM, Northwestern U., 1937. Cert. primary and secondary tchr., music tchr., Mo. Dir. sch. music Spring Arbor (Mich.) Jr. Coll., 1933-34; tutor orthopedic handicapped children St. Louis Pub. Schs., 1950-56. Tour guide Mo. Bot. Garden, St. Louis, 1975—87; pres. The Wednesday Club St. Louis, 1983—85, archivist, 1985—92; guide tours of distinction St. Louis Symphony Soc., 1980—85; pres. Women's Assn., 2d Presbyn. Ch., St. Louis, 1956—58. Mem. Clan Maxwell Soc. U.S.A., Mo. Hist. Soc., St. Louis Genealogy Soc., Piano Club St. Louis, Washington U. Faculty women's Club, Mu Phi Epsilon. Republican. Congregationalist. Home: Peace Village 10300 Village Circle Dr Apt 4104 Palos Park IL 60464

MAXWELL, FLORENCE HINSHAW, civic worker; b. Nora, Ind., July 14, 1914; d. Asa Benton and Gertrude (Randall) Hinshaw; m. John Williamson Maxwell, June 5, 1936; children: Marilyn Maxwell Grissom, William Douglas. BA cum laude, Butler U., 1935. Coord., bd. dirs. Sight Conservation and Aid to Blind, 1962-73, nat. chmn., 1969-73; active various fund drives; chmn. jamboree, hostess coms. North Ctrl. H.S., 1959, 64, Girl Scouts USA, 1937-38, 54-56; mus. chmn. Sr. Girl Scouts USA Regional Coun., 1956-57; scorekeeper Little League, 1955-57; bd. dirs. Nora Sch. Parents' Club, 1958-59, Eastwood Jr. H.S. Triangle Club, 1959-62, Ind. State Symphony Soc. Women's Com., 1965-67, 76-79, Symphoguide chmn., 1976-79; vision screening Indpls. inner city pub. sch. kindergartens, pre-schs., 1962-69, 81—, Headstart, 1967-98; trainer vision screening Jameson Camp for Children, 1987. Asst. Glaucoma screening clinics Gen. Hosp., Glendale Shopping Ctr., City County Bldg., Am. Legion Nat. Hdqrs., Ind. Health Assn. Conf., 1962—73; chmn. sight conservation and aid to blind Nat. Delta Gamma Found., Indpls., Columbus, Ohio, 1969—73; mem. telethon team Butler U. Fund, 1964; symphoguide hostess Internat. Conf. on Cities, 1971, Nat. League of Cities, 1972; mem. health adv. com. Headstart, 1976—98, sec., 1980—98, mem. social svcs. com., 1987—98, coord. vision rescreening and referrals, assessment team of compliance steering com., 1978—79, 1984, 86, 87, 88, 91, 92, 94, 96, 98; founder People of Vision Aux., 1981, bd. dirs., 1981—, v.p., 1990—92, mem. coord. vision and glaucoma screenings and office svcs., 1990—92, sec. emeritus, 1997; initiated vision screening and eye safety edn. Jameson Camp for Children, 1987. Recipient Key to City of Indpls., 1972, Those Spl. People award Women in Comm., 1980, Appreciation award Headstart, 1983, Jefferson award for Disting. Pub. Svc. Indpls. Star, 1991, Cmty. Action Head Start Outstanding Vol. award, 1996, Health/Social Svcs. award Family Devel. Svcs., 1998, Appreciation award Prevent Blindness, 1999. Mem.: People of Vision, Ind. State Symphony Soc. Women's Com. (vol. Indpls. symphony orch.'s discovery concerts, vol. Indpls. noontime concerts, vol. Yuletide, coffee concerts), Jameson Camp Aux., Ind. Soc. to Prevent Blindness (now Prevent Blindness Ind.) (dir. 1962—99, sec. 1971—83, exec. com. 1971—95, v.p. 1983—86, asst. sec.-treas. 1987—92, adv. bd. 1999—, Ind. del. to nat. 3-yr. program planning conf. 1985—, internal analysis task force for svcs. 1987, life hon. v.p. 1983—, Sight Saving award 1974, Svc. Appreciation award 1999, Lifetime Achievement award 2000), Ind. Hist. Soc., Ind. Audubon Soc., Nat. Soc. to Prevent Blindness (now Prevent Blindness Am.), Delta Gamma (chpt. golden ann. celebration decade and comm. chmn. 1975, treas. Alpha Tau house corp. 1975—78, nat. chmn. Parent Club Study Com. 1976—77, instr. province leadership sem. workshop 1989, Cable award 1969, Outstanding Alumna award 1973, Svc. Recognition award 1977, Shield award 1981, scholarship hon. 1981, Stellar award 1986, Oxford award 1992). Republican. Address: 1502 E 80th St Indianapolis IN 46240-2706

MAXWELL, FLOYD DAWSON, research engineer, consultant; b. Athens, Ga., Mar. 12, 1935; s. Archie Lee Maxwell and Samantha Lee Willingham; m. Roberta Marie Runnestrand, Aug. 4, 1975; children: Michael R., Pamela J. BSEE, U. Ariz., 1961; PhD, U. Calif., Riverside, 1974; postgrad., UCLA. Electronic engr. Naval Ordinance Lab., Corona, Calif., 1961-69, br. head, 1967-69; rsch. engr. Forest Fire Lab., Riverside, 1969-74; rsch. assoc. U. Calif., 1971-74; tech. staff The Aerospace Corp., El Segundo, Calif., 1974-75, mgr., sr. engr. specialist, 1975—. Cons. USN, Corona, Justice Dept., Riverside, 1969-74, Atty. Gen., Sacramento, 1979-81, INMARSAT, London, 1994; lectr. grad. studies U. So. Calif., L.A., 1980-83. Planning commr. City of Riverside, 1974-75; pres. South Shores Homeowners Assn., 1977-88; bd. dirs. Palos Verdes (Calif.) Land Conserv, 1988—. Recipient Outstanding Young Men of Am. award Jr. C. of C., 1966. Mem. AAAS, Combustion Inst. (bd. dirs. 1970-80), Sigma Xi. Achievements include patent for near infrared system for imaging forest fires through smoke. Office: The Aerospace Corp 2350 E El Segundo Blvd El Segundo CA 90245-4691

MAXWELL, GEORGE RUSSELL, scenic designer; b. Salt Lake City, Oct. 18, 1951; s. George Henry and LaRae Greathouse Maxwell. BS, Weber State U., 1973. Property master Pioneer Theatre Co., Salt Lake City, 1974-87, resident scenic designer, 1987—; scenic designer Utah Shakespearean Festival, Cedar City, Utah, 1995-2000. Set designer of 100's of prodns., including A Funny Thing Happened on the Way to the Forum, The Count of Monte Cristo, An American Daughter, South Pacific, The Three Musketeers, Camelot, Evita, Cabaret, Peer Gynt, The Grapes of Wrath, Man of La Mancha, Crazy for You, Ain't Misbehavin', The Coronation of Poppea, The Winter's Tale, The Mikado, The Tempest, You Can't Take It With You, Hamlet, Romeo and Juliet, Relative Values, You Never Can Tell, The Lion in Winter, The Ballad of Baby Doe, Dinner With Friends, Phantom, One Flew Over the Cuckoo's NestProof, Peter Pan. Bd. dirs. Salt Lake Arts Coun., Salt Lake City, 1989-93. Mem. United Scenic Artists. Office: Pioneer Theatre Co 300 S 1400 E Rm 205 Salt Lake City UT 84112-0660 E-mail: gmax316@aol.com.

MAXWELL, J. B. financial and marketing consultant; b. Clarksburg, W.Va., Sept. 30, 1944; s. J.B. and Martha (Hornor) M.; m. Valerie Ronson, Oct. 13, 1983; 1 child, Jennifer. BS, Salem (W.Va.) Coll., 1967; M of Mktg., Harvard U., 1970. Lic. in real estate sales, ins., secutities; registered commodity rep.; accredited mgmt. cons. and fin. planner; registered fin. planner, investment adv.; accredited asset mgmt. specialist. Exec. v.p. Textron Inc., Providence, 1968-71; pres. Martech Inc. and 6 other cos., Portland, Maine, 1968—; v.p. E.F. Hutton Co., 1976-83; 1st v.p. fin. planning Dean Witter, Boston, 1983-90; pres. Planning Svcs. Corp., 1990-92; 1st v.p. Gruntal & Co., Inc., 1992—. Author handbooks, booklets and articles. Contbr. Portland Coll. Art, 1980-93. Bd. dirs. Wellness Inst., Boston, 1990-91. Recipient Bronze award Nat. Acad. Scis., 1962. Mem. Internat. Assn. for Fin. Planning, Am. Mgmt. Assns., Am. Mktg. Assn., Inst. Mgmt. Cons., World Affairs Coun., Nat. Assn. Security Dealers (formerly br. office mgr.), Boston C. of C., Rotary Internat. Avocations: golf, woodworking, travel, literature. Home: 6939 McCormack Sta Boston MA 02106-6939 Office: Gruntal & Co Inc One Post Office Sq Boston MA 02109-3400

MAXWELL, JACK ERWIN, manufacturing company executive; b. Cleve., July 17, 1926; s. Fred A. and Gertrude F. (Haug) M.; m. Martha Jane Miller, Dec. 28, 1966; children by previous marriage: Laura Jane, Fredric, Elizabeth Grant, Carla Moore, Linda Hanson. BS, Case Inst. Tech., 1949; MBA, Harvard U., 1952. Indsl. engr. Lincoln Electric Co., Cleve., 1952-53; mgr. purchase analysis Ford Motor Co., Dearborn, Mich., 1953-57; v.p. Booz, Allen & Hamilton, Inc., Detroit, 1957-69; v.p. corp. devel. Am. Motors Corp., 1969-71, v.p. adminstrn., 1971-76, v.p. non-automotive subsidiaries, 1976-79, v.p. diversified ops., 1979-80; chmn., pres. Wheel Horse Products, Inc., South Bend, Ind., 1974-80; chmn., CEO Ingersoll Products Corp., Chgo., 1980-86; pres. Wellmax, Inc., 1976—. Served with USNR, 1944-46. Mem. Case Inst. Tech. Alumni Assn., Harvard Bus. Sch. Alumni Assn., Detroit Athletic Club, Detroit Econ. Club, Chgo. Club, Old Club, Tau Beta Pi, Theta Tau. Address: Wellmax Inc 3541 Bradway Blvd Ste 100 Bloomfield Hills MI 48301-2409 E-mail: wellmaxx@earthlink.net.

MAXWELL, JAMES A. music educator; b. Cameron, Mo., Feb. 6, 1961; s. Willa R. and Charles D. Maxwell; m. Sonya R. Ramsey, June 29, 1985; children: Genee , Allen. B in Music Edn., U. Kans., 1984; M in Music Edn., Wichita State U., 1997. Cert. K-12 vocal and instrumental music tchr. 1984. Instrumental music dir. Wichita (Kans.) West HS, 1994—99; band dir. Rose Hill (Kans.) Pub. Schs., 1999—. Choir dir. First Ch. of Brethren, Wichita, 1992—. Mem.: Music Educators Nat. Conf. Protestant. Avocations: sports, music, reading, movies. Home: 10107 E Skinner Wichita KS 67207 Office: Rose Hill Pub Sch 104 N Rose Hill Rd Rose Hill KS 67133 Business E-Mail: jmaxwell@usd394.com.

MAXWELL, JAMES L. non-profit management executive; b. Bryceland, La., July 11, 1936; s. Hedrick David Jr. and Bessie Dee Maxwell; m. Patricia Ann Ewing, June 5, 1965 (div. Nov. 1970); 1 child, Caroline Coleman Ewing. BA, Ouachita U., 1959; postgrad., La. State U., 1959-61, Johns Hopkins U., 1968-70. Assoc. dir. devel. Johns Hopkins U., Balt., 1965-68; exec. v.p. Nat. Soc. Fund Raising Execs., Washington, 1968-71; dir. devel. Nat. Symphony Orch., 1971-83; cons. Washington and Houston, 1983-97; pres., CEO Downtown Hist. Dist., Houston, 1997—. Internat gen. chmn. Nat. Conf. on Philanthropy, Washington, 1976, Nat. Philanthropy Day, Houston, 1989. Bd. dirs. Ford's Theater, Washington, 1972-74, Escape Family Resource Ctr., Houston, 1985-92, Careen & Recovery Resources, Houston, 1989-98. Named Profl. Fund Raiser of Yr., Nat. Soc. Fund Raising Execs., 1979. Avocations: classical music, opera, art, writing.

MAXWELL, JANE See SMITH, JANE MARILYN DAVIS

MAXWELL, JEROME EUGENE, corporate executive; b. Princeton, Ill., June 2, 1944; s. Emmett Eugene and June (Erickson) M.; m. Cynthia Jane O'Connell, July 30, 1977; children: Eric Vaughn, Christina Dawn, Jeremy Emmett, Jason Daniel, Nicholas Mark. BSEE, So. Meth. U., 1967, MSEE, 1971. Maintainability engr. product support divsn. Collins Radio Co., Richardson, Tex., 1965-67, jr. engr. computer sys. divsn., 1967-70; sr. engr. TRW Electronics Products, Inc., Colorado Springs, Colo., 1970-73, mgr. engring., 1973-79, mgr. program mgmt. office, 1979-81, gen. mgr. space electronics mfg. divsn., 1981-86; pres., CEO G&S Sys., Inc., Bedford, Mass., 1986-87, Atec, Inc., Houston, 1987-91; v.p., divsn. dir. Nat. Sys. & Rsch. Co., Colorado Springs, Colo., 1992-94; pres., chmn. bd. dirs. Tech. Assocs. of Colo., Inc., 1994-96; pres., CEO Advanced Profl. Tng., Inc., 1996—. Patentee in field. Mem. adv. coun. U. Colo., Colorado Springs, 1973-86, U. So. Colo., Pueblo, 1974-78; Webelo leader, asst. pack leader Boy Scouts Am., 1976-77; fin. chmn. Ascension Luth. Ch., 1981-86; cons. to cmty. edn. coord. for computer sys. and equipment, 1980-86; mem. Soli Deo Gloria Choir, 1999—. Mem. AIAA (sr.), Assn. Old Crows (pres. space chpt.), Mesa Sertoma (charter, bd. dirs.). Republican. E-mail: maxsquared@qwest.net.

MAXWELL, JOE EDWIN, lieutenant governor, lawyer; b. Kirksville, Mo., Mar. 17, 1957; s. Robert E. and Molly B. Maxwell; m. Sarah Baker; children: Megan, Shannen. BS in Secondary Edn., Social Studies, U. Mo., 1986, JD, 1990. Farmer, Rush Hill, Mo., 1976-78; ptnr., operator Maxwell Svc., Laddonia, 1978-84; rural mail carrier U.S. Postal Svc., Rush Hill, 1980-84; outstate field coord. Travis Morrison's Campaign for State Auditor, Mo., 1986; Mo. state field coord. Richard Gephardt for Pres., 1986-87; atty. Mexico, Mo., 1992—; mem. Mo. House, 1990-94, Mo. Senate, 1995—. Mem. Senate Appropriations, Judiciary, Labor and Indsl. Rels., Pub. Health and Welfare coms.; vice chair Elections, Corrections, and Vet.'s Affairs coms.; chair Commerce and Environment Com. Assoc. editor-in-chief Mo. Jour. of Dispute Resolution, 1989. Mem. Am. Legion, 1982—, adj. Post 510, 1982-84; mem. Young Dem. Clubs Mo., 1982—, jud. coun. Young Dems. Am., 1985, pres., 1984-87, 9th Congl. Dist. chmn., 1982; mem. Laddonia Bapt. Ch., 1975—, Sunday Sch. tchr., 1990-91, pulpit com.; bd. dirs. Handi-Shop Inc., Mexico, 1981-84, chmn. mfg. and mktg. com., 1982-84; bd. dirs. Boy Scouts Am. Troop 94, 1980-82. Recipient St. Louis Globe Dem. award for outstanding achievement, 1979, Cert. of Appreciation, Troop 94, Boy Scouts Am., 1982, Mo.'s Outstanding Male Young Dem. award, 1987, George B. Freeman award for outstanding svc., 1987, Appreciation award Mo. Bar, 1992, Mo. Ho. of Reps. Resolution # 624 for exceptional svc. Mo., 1987, Mo. State Senate Resolution # 382 for exceptional svc. Mo., 1987; named one of Outstanding Young Men of Am., 1983, 85. Mem. Moose, Jaycees (Laddonia chpt. pres. 1978-79, coord. Laddonia Area Blood Drive, coord. Laddonia City Clean-up Day, chmn. Mexico Soybean Festival 1989, chmn. Lenten Breakfast 1990, Presdl. award of honor 1979), Kappa Delta Pi, Golden Key Nat. Honor Soc. Office: Office of Lt Gov Rm 121 Capitol Bldg Jefferson City MO 65101

MAXWELL, JOHN ALEXANDER, JR. retired newspaper editor, consultant; b. Bridgeport, Ohio, May 14, 1915; s. John Alexander and Mary Lewella (Fox) Maxwell; m. Margaret Wilma Winchell, Aug. 20, 1940 (dec. June 1993); children: Richard Alexander, Roberta Maxwell Young. BA, Coll. of Wooster, 1936. Sportswriter The Repository, Canton, Ohio, 1936-41, reporter, asst. city editor, makeup editor, 1941-44, news editor, 1946-51, editor, 1969-80, The Marion (Ohio) Star, 1953-69. Consult News Serv Office, Col Wooster, Ohio, 1970—80, Canton Regional CofC, Pro Football Hall of Fame Festival, 1984—98. Mem exec bd Buckeye Coun Boy Scouts Am, Canton, 1970—80; mem adv bd Malone Col, 1980—88, Malone Assocs, 1988—; bd dirs Jr Achievement, Stark County, Ohio, 1970—80. Lt USN, 1944—46, PTO, lt USN, 1951—53. Recipient John d McKee Alumni Award, Col Wooster, 1989, Appreciation Award, Canton Regional CofC, 1991. Mem.: Col Wooster Alumni Asn (bd dirs 1980—82), Soc Profl Journalists, Am Soc Newspaper Journalists, Rotary Int (pres Canton 1975—76, gov dist 665 1982—83, pres Marion 1958—59, Paul Harris Fellow 1979). Republican. Methodist. Avocations: reading, golf. Home: 2671-1 Wingate Way NW Canton OH 44708 E-mail: jmax514@aol.com.

MAXWELL, KENNETH ROBERT, historian; b. Wellington, Somerset, U.K., Feb. 3, 1941; s. Kenneth Bruce Maxwell and Jean Anderson. BA, Cambridge U., 1963, MA, 1967, Princeton (N.J.) U., 1967, PhD, 1970. Prof. history Columbia U., N.Y.C., 1976-84, dir. Camoes Ctr., 1988-99; program dir. Tinker Found., 1979-85; sr. fellow Latin Am. Coun. on Fgn. Rels., 1989—, v.p., dir. studies, 1996, Nelson and David Rockefellor sr. fellow, 1995—. Vis. prof. history and L.Am. studies Princeton U., N.J., 1985-86; vis. prof. history Yale U., New Haven, Conn., 1991-92; consultative coun. Luso-Am. Found., Lisbon, Portugal, 1996—; bd. dirs. Spanish Inst. Author: Pombal: Paradox of Enlightment, 1995, The Making of Portuguese Democracy, 1995, Conflicts and Conspiracies: Brazil and Portugal, 1973; co-author: The New Spain, 1994; book reviewer: Foreign Affairs.; contbr. articles to profl. jours. and publs.; columnist no.com.br., 2000-02, Folha de S. Paulo, 2001-, Epoca, 2002-. Bd. trustees Latin Am. Scholarship, Cambridge, Mass., 1991-97; founding mem. Com. for Internat. Grantmakers, Washington, 1981-86; adv. com. Ams. Watch, N.Y.C., 1996—; adv. Dwight D. Eisenhower Exch. Fellowship, Phila., 1996; selection com. Hubert H. Humphery fellowship, 1985. Recipient Grand Cross Order of Merit, 1996; named Comdr. Order of Rio Branco, 1997; Herodotus fellow Inst. for Advanced Study, 1971-75, Guggenheim fellow, 1976-77, hon. fellow Romance Inst. London U., 1993—. Mem. Century Assn., Norfolk Country Club, Am. Hist. Assn., Coun. on Fgn. Rels., Instituto Historico Geografico Brasileiro. Avocations: swimming, drawing. Home: 165 Litchfield Rd Norfolk CT 06058-1279 Office: Coun on Fgn Rels 58 E 68th St New York NY 10021-5953

MAXWELL, LEROY STEVENSON, retired lawyer; b. Chambersburg, Pa., Jan. 12, 1915; s. Levi Houser and Maye (Stevenson) M.; m. Pauline Kauffman, Dec. 28, 1939; children: LeRoy S. Jr., Ann K. AB, Juniata Coll., 1936; JD, U. Pa., 1939. Bar: Pa. 1940, U.S. Supreme Ct. 1953, U.S. Dist. Ct. (mid. dist.) Pa. 1948. Ptnr. Minick & Maxwell, Waynesboro, Pa., 1940-46; pvt. practice law, 1947-52, 57-61; ptnr. Maxwell & Good, 1952-57, Maxwell & Bridgers, Waynesboro, 1962-76, Maxwell & Maxwell, Waynesboro, 1977-78, Maxwell, Maxwell & Dick, Waynesboro, 1978-84, Maxwell, Maxwell, Dick & Walsh, Waynesboro, 1985-90, Maxwell, Maxwell, Dick, Walsh & Lisko, Waynesboro, 1990-94, Maxwell Maxwell Walsh & Lisko, Waynesboro, 1995-97, Maxwell, Maxwell & Walsh, Waynesboro, 1997-98; ptnr Maxwell Law Offices, 1998-2001; ret., 2001. Dir. emeritus First Nat. Bank and Trust Co., Waynesboro, 1990-92, Waynesboro Hosp., 1990-92; dist. atty. Franklin County, Pa., Chambersburg, 1944-48. Trustee Juniata Coll., Huntingdon, 1961-64, 70-81, emeritus, 1981—. ABA, Pa. Bar Assn., Franklin County Bar Assn., Masons. Republican. Ch. of the Brethren. Avocations: golf, gardening. Office: 92 W Main St Waynesboro PA 17268-1563

MAXWELL, MARILYN JULIA, retired elementary education educator; b. Flint, Mich., Apr. 3, 1933; d. Clement Daniel and Gwendoline Mae (Evans) Rushlow; m. Dewey Theodore Maxwell, Apr. 22, 1965; 1 child, Bruce Dewey. Student, Baldwin-Wallace Coll., 1951-53; BS, U. Tenn., 1954-56, MEd, 1962. Cert. elem. edn. tchr.; lang. devel. specialist. Elem. tchr. Guy Selby Sch., Flint, Mich., 1956-58, Henry L. Barger Sch., Chattanooga, 1958-63, Dept. of Def. Sch., Seville, Spain, 1963-65, Loma Vista Elem. Sch., Lompoc, Calif., 1965-66, Crestview Elem. Sch., Lompoc, 1966-68, LaHonda Elem. Sch., Lompoc, 1969—2000, tchr.-in-charge, acting prin., 1998—2000; ret., 2000. Lang. arts mentor tchr. Lompoc Unified Schs., 1985-86. Mem. Calif. Hist. Soc. Mem. Internat. Reading Assn., Assoc. Mems. Libr. of Congress, Nat. Trust for Hist. Preservation, Am. Fedn. Tchrs., Computer Using Educators, Nat. Coun. Tchrs. Math., Calif. Ret. Tchrs. Assn. Home: 4219 Centaur St Lompoc CA 93436-1229 E-mail: dmaxwell@impulse.net.

MAXWELL, NEAL A. religious organization administrator; b. Salt Lake City, July 6, 1926; s. Clarence H. and Emma (Ash), m. Colleen Hinckley; four children. B in Polit. Sci., M in Polit. Sci., LLD (hon.), U. Utah, Brigham Young U.; LittD (hon.), Westminster Coll.; HHD (hon.), Utah State U., Ricks Coll.; BA, U of Utah; HHD (hon.), Salt Lake C.C., 1998; MA, U of Utah; Four Hon. PhD's. Legis. asst. U.S. sen. Wallace F. Bennett, Utah; exec. v.p., Neal A. Maxwell pres. endowed chair pol. theory U. Utah, Salt Lake City; various ch. positions including bishop Salt Lake City's Univ. Sixth Ward, mem. gen. bd. youth orgn., adult correlation com. and one of first Regional Reps. of the Twelve; elder Ch. Jesus Christ Latter Day Sts., Asst. to the Council of Twelve, 1974-76, mem. of Presidency of First Quorum of the Seventy, 1976-81, mem. Coun. of Twelve Apostles, 1981—. Mem. Quorum of the Twelve Ch. of Jesus Christ of Latter-Day Saints, Salt Lake City. Recipient Liberty Bell award Utah State Bar, 1967; named Pub. Adminstr. of Yr. Inst. Govt. Service Brigham Young U., 1973. Office: LDS Church Quorum Twelve 47 E South Temple Salt Lake City UT 84150-0001

MAXWELL, PATRICIA JOY, fund raising executive; b. Belle Plaine, Iowa, Feb. 7, 1937; d. Verne Edwin and Julia Inez (Beem) M. Student, Pepperdine Coll., 1954-55; BS, Iowa State Tchrs. Coll., 1958; MPA, Roosevelt U., 1982. Cert. fund raising exec. Dir. resource devel. Boys Clubs Am., 1978-81; exec. dir. Westlake Health Svcs. Found., 1981-84; assoc. dean devel. and alumni affairs U. Ill. Coll. Medicine, 1984-91; sr. maj. gifts officer U. Ill., 1991-93; v.p. devel. Orlando (Fla.) M.D. Anderson Cancer Ctr., 1993; assoc. dir. nat. hdqrs. Alzheimer's Assn., Chgo., 1994; dir. devel. N.Y. Acad. Scis., N.Y.C., 1997; sr. dir. devel. Calif. State U., Long Beach, 1997—. Cons. Ency. Britannica Ednl. Corp., Prentice Hall Inc., U.S. State Dept. Mem. N.Y. Acad. Scis., Am. Mktg. Assn. (co-founder Acad. of Health Svcs. Mktg. 1980), Chgo. Area Pub. Affairs Group, Univ. Club (Chgo.), Balboa (Calif.) Bay Club, Lake Nona Club (Orlando).

MAXWELL, RAYMOND ROGER, retired accountant; b. Parmer County, Tex., Jan. 7, 1918; s. Frederick W. and Hazel Belle (Rogers) M.; m. Jeanne Hollarn, June 16, 1945 (dec. Dec. 1987); children: Donald R., Bruce Edward, Sabrina G. Ed.B., Western Ill. State Tchrs Coll., 1941; MBA in Acctg., U. Fla., 1949; postgrad., UCLA, 1965-68. CPA, Fla., Calif. Asst. to bus. mgr. Western Ill. State Tchrs. Coll., Macomb, 1939-41; apprentice acct. Charles H. Lindfors, CPA, Ft. Lauderdale, Fla., 1946-48; acct./auditor Frederic Dunn-Rankin & Co. CPA, Miami, 1948-49; CPA staff Charles Costar, CPA, 1951; resident auditor/CPA prin. Raymond R. Maxwell CPA, Ft. Lauderdale, 1951-56; supt. pub. instrn. Broward County, 1956-61; staff asst. in fin. North Am. Aviation, Inc., El Segundo, Calif., 1961-65; acctg. prin. Raymond R. Maxwell, CPA, Whittier, 1968-2000. Part-time rsch. asst. UCLA, 1965, teaching asst., 1966, 67; instr. Calif. Poly., 1967. Active precinct election bds., Whittier, L.A. County, 1989, 98-2000; 1st reader First Ch. of Christ, Scientist, Whittier, 1990-92, 96-98, exec. bd., 1989, exec. bd. chmn., 1993, participant Bible Explorations, 1991-92. 1st lt. USAAF, 1942-46. Republican. Avocations: dancing, swimming, computers. *One, with God, is a majority.*

MAXWELL, RICHARD CALLENDER, lawyer, educator; b. Mpls., Oct. 7, 1919; s. Bertram Wayburn and Blossom (Callender) M.; m. Frances Lida McKay, Jan 27, 1942; children— Richard Callender, John McKay. BSL., U. Minn., 1941, LL.B., 1947; LL.D. (hon.), Calif. Western U., 1983; LLD (hon.), Southwestern U., 1993. Assoc. prof. U. N.D., 1947-49; assoc. prof. U. Tex., 1949-51, prof., 1951-53; counsel Amerada Petroleum Corp., 1952-53; prof. UCLA, 1953-81; dean UCLA (Sch. Law), 1959-69, Connell prof., 1979-81, Connell prof. emeritus, 1981—; Chadwick prof. Duke U. Sch. Law, 1981-89, Chadwick prof. emeritus, 1989—. Vis. prof. Columbia U., 1955; vis. Alumni prof. U. Minn., 1970-71; Fulbright lectr. Queen's U., No. Ireland, 1970; vis. Ford Found. prof. U. Singapore, 1971; Thompson prof. U. Colo., 1982; vis. prof. Hastings Coll. Law, 1976, Duke U., 1979-80, U. Tex., 1985; pres. Minn. Law Rev., 1946; chmn. Council Legal Edn. Opportunity, 1971-72; pres. Assn. Am. Law Schs., 1972; chmn. adv. com. law Fulbright Program, 1971-74, chmn. adv. com. U.K., 1974-77; mem. com. on gas prodn. opportunities NRC, 1977-78; mem. law sch. editorial and adv. bd. West Pub. Co., 1971-94. Author: (with S. A. Riesenfeld) Cases and Materials on Modern Social Legislation, 1950, (with H.R. Williams and C.J. Meyers) Cases on Oil and Gas Law, 1956, 7th edit., (with Stephen F. Williams, Patrick H. Martin, Bruce M. Kramer), 2002, (with S. A. Riesenfeld) California Cases on Security Transactions, 1957, 4th edit. (with S.A. Riesenfeld, J.R. Hetland, W.D. Warren), 1991; West Coast editor Oil and Gas Reporter, 1953— . Mem. Los Angeles Employee Relations Bd., 1971-74; bd. dirs. Constl. Rights Found., 1963-81; trustee Calif. Western U., 1979-81; bd. visitors Duke U. Sch. Law, 1973-79, chmn. bd. Pvt. Adjudication Ctr., 1984-89; bd. visitors Southwestern U. Sch. Law, 1981—. Served to lt. comdr. USNR, 1941-46. Recipient Disting. Tchg. award UCLA, 1977, Duke Law Sch., 1986, UCLA medal, 1982, Clyde O. Martz Tchg. award Rocky Mountain Mineral Law Found., 1994. Mem. ABA (com. on youth edn. for citizenship 1975-79, spl. com. on public understanding about the law 1979-84), Order of Coif. (nat. exec. com. 1980-86) Office: Duke U Sch Law Durham NC 27708-0362 E-mail: rcmaxwell@mindspring.com.

MAXWELL, RICHARD ANTHONY, retail executive; b. N.Y.C., Apr. 1, 1933; s. Arthur William and Mary Ellen (Winestock) M.; m. Jacqueline Ann Creamer, Oct. 27, 1962. Student, NYU, 1957-58, Acad. Advanced Traffic, 1959. Import ops. mgr. Associated Merchandising Corp., N.Y.C., 1950-52, 56-65; v.p. Associated Dry Goods Corp., 1965-86, sr. v.p. mktg., 1980-82, exec. v.p. mktg., 1982-86; pres. A.D.G. Export Mktg., Florence, Italy, 1982-86, Associated Dry Goods Ltd., Hong Kong, 1983-86, Inter Textyle Corp., 1987-89; with Matol Botanical Internat. Ltd.; exec. v.p. Matol World Corp., Montreal, Que., Can., 1992-94; dir. Matol Botannical New Zealand, New Zealand, 1994-96; v.p. internat. ops. L'Aprina Internat. Inc., 1994-96; chief internat. officer Camelot Concept Co., Montreal, 1995-96; CFO Showcase Prodns., Phoenix, 1996; exec. v.p. Harmony House Internat., 1996-97, IGW Trust, Phoenix, 1997-99, Pre-Paid Legal Svcs., Inc., 1999—; pres. Team 39, Inc., Dunedin, Fla., 2000-2001; dir. Presley Promotions Inc., Memphis, 2001—02. Mem. industry sector adv. com. Dept. Commerce, 1984-93. Mem. shippers adv. com. Nat. Maritime Coun. Served with USAF, 1952-56. Recipient Silver medal for contbns. to trade expansion, Republic of China, 1980; appt. to rank of comdr. in Order of Merit in recognition of improvement of trade between Italy and U.S., Republic of Italy, 1985. Mem. Am. Assn. Exporters and Importers (past pres., dir.), Shippers Conf. Greater N.Y. (past pres., dir.), Nat. Retail Mchts. Assn. (vice chmn. fgn. trade com.), Nat. Com. Internat. Trade Documentation (past vice chmn. gen. bus. com.), Transp. Assn. Am., Italy-Am. C. of C. (past pres., dir.), Am. Soc. of Italian Legion of Merit (dir.). Home: 2408 Stag Run Blvd Clearwater FL 33765-1832 E-mail: rmaxwel2@tampabay.rr.com.

MAXWELL, ROBERT EARL, federal judge; b. Elkins, W.Va., Mar. 15, 1924; s. Earl L. and Nellie E. (Rexstrew) M.; m. Ann Marie Grabowski, Mar. 29, 1948; children— Mary Ann, Carol Lynn, Ellen Lindsay, Earl Wilson. LLD (hon.), Davis and Elkins Coll., 1984; LLB, W.Va. U., 1949; LLD (hon.), Davis and Elkins Coll., 1984. Bar: W.Va. 1949. Practiced in, Randolph County, 1949; pros. atty., 1952-61; U.S. atty. for No. Dist. W.Va., 1961-64; judge, then sr. judge U.S. Dist. Ct. (no. dist.) W.Va., Elkins, 1965—; judge Temp. Emergency Ct. of Appeals, 1980-89. Past chmn. budget com. Jud. Conf. U.S.; former mem. exec. com. Nat. Conf. Fed. Trial Judges; former mem. adv. bd. W.Va. U. Mem. bd. advisors W.Va. U., past chmn.; bd. advisors Mary Babb Randolph Cancer Ctr. Recipient Alumni Disting. Svc. award Davis and Elkins Coll., 1969, Religious Heritage Am. award, 1979, Outstanding Trial Judge award W.Va. Trail Lawyers Assn., 1988, Order of Vandalia award W.Va. U., Outstaning Alumnus award, 1992, Tenured Faculty Mem. Recognition award Bd. Govs., Def. Trail Coun., W.Va., 1992, Cert. of Merit, W.Va. State Bar, 1994, Justitia Officium award Coll. of Law, W.Va. U., 1994; fellow W.Va. Bar Found., 1999; Melvin Jones fellow Lions Internat. Found., 2001. Mem. Nat. Conf. Federal Trial Judges, Dist. Judges Assn. 4th Cir. (past pres.), Moose (life), Lions (life), Beta Alpha Beta (merit award), Elkins-Randolph County C. of C. (citizen of yr. 1994). Office: US Dist Ct No Dist PO Box 1275 Elkins WV 26241-1275 E-mail: rmaxwell@neumedia.net.

MAXWELL, ROBERT WALLACE, II, lawyer; b. Sept. 6, 1943; s. Robert Wallace and Margaret Maxwell; m. Mamie Lee Payne, June 18, 1966; children: Virginia, Robert, William. BS magna cum laude, Hampden-Sydney Coll., 1965; JD with hons., Duke U., 1968. Bar: Ohio 1968. Assoc. Taft, Stettinius & Hollister, Cin., 1968—75, ptnr., 1975—88, Keating, Muething & Klekamp, Cin., 1988—. Instr. U. Cin. Sch. Law, 1975—76. Elder Wyoming Presbyn. Ch.; bd. dir. Contemporary Arts Ctr. of Cin., Cin. Ballet Co. Mem.: ABA, Am. Assn. Mus. Trustees. Republican. Home: 535 Larchmont Dr Cincinnati OH 45215-4215 Office: Keating Muething & Klekamp 1 E 4th St Ste 1800 Cincinnati OH 45202-3752

MAXWELL, RUTH ELAINE, artist, interior designer, decorative painter; b. Cleve., Oct. 7, 1934; d. Norman Lee and Katherine Ellen (Hamilton) Brown; m. Clarence L. Maxwell, June 25, 1955; children: Lisa Maxwell Callahan, Lynne Maxwell Quinn, Laura Maxwell Jochem, James Maxwell. BFA, teaching cert., Ohio State U., 1956. Cert. elem. sch. tchr., Ohio. Tchr. Hilliard (Ohio) Elem. Sch., 1956-58; comptr. Callahan Family Golf Ctr., Hilliard, 1989-99. Vol. Columbus Assn. Performing Arts Colleagues, 1981—; mem. Hilliard Arts Coun., 1989-91; vocalist Damenchor of Columbus Maennerchor, 1975—, treas., 1979-81, fin. sec., 1991-94; pres. Canterbury Unit of Columbus Symphony Orch. Women's Assn., 1997-98; treas. Women's Assn. of the Columbus, Symphony Orch., 1995-96; mem. Women's Guild of Opera, Columbus, 1994—, sec., 2000-2001, v.p., 2001—; buyer Ohio Theatre Shop, 1995—. Mem. Gamma Alpha Chi (hon., sec. Ohio State U. chpt. 1954), Gamma Phi Beta. Republican. Avocations: reading, gardening, traveling. E-mail: maxdarbyoaks@aol.com.

MAXWELL, SARA ELIZABETH, psychologist, educator, speech pathologist, director; b. DuQuoin, Ill., Jan. 23; d. Jean A. (Patterson) Green; m. David Lowell Maxwell, Dec. 27, 1960 (div. Mar. 1990); children: Lisa Marina, David Scott; m. James F. Manning, July 19, 1997 (div. Aug. 1998). BS, So. Ill. U., 1963, MS, 1964, MSEd, 1965; MEd, Boston Coll., 1982; attended, Harvard U., 1983; PhD, Boston Coll., 1992. Cert. and lic. speech.-lang. pathologist, early childhood specialist, guidance counselor, sch. adjustment counselor, behavior specialist, EMT. Clin. supr. Clin. Ctr. So. Ill. U., Carbondale, 1964-65, grad. clin. instr., 1965-66; speech/lang. pathologist, sch. adjustment counselor Westwood (Mass.) Pub. Schs., 1967-93; grad. faculty Emerson Coll., Boston, 1979-81; cons. Mass. Dept. Mental Health, 1979-82; grad. clin. supr. Robbins Speech/Hearing Ctr., Emerson Coll., 1979-82; predoctoral intern in clin. psychology South Shore Mental Health Ctr., Quincy, 1985-86, devel. and clin. staff psychologist Hingham and Quincy, Mass., 1989-93, emergency svcs. team and respite house manager Quincy, 1990-93; cons. Westwood Nursery Preschs., 1986-93; pvt. practice Twin Oaks Clin. Assocs., Westwood, Mass, 1986-88, South Coast Counseling Assocs., Quincy, 1989-93. Cons. local collaboratives and preschs., Westwood, 1980-83; profl. workshops presenter Head Start, 1980; program specialist speech, lang., learning Broward County (Fla.) Schs., 1993-96, exceptional student edn. specialist, 1996-98; behavior specialist, 1999—; adj. prof. grad. sch. of psychology Nova Southeastern U., 1995—; presenter Head Start, ASHA, CEC, APSC, IALP and other profl., nat. and state confs., 1980-99; invited del. to Sino-Am. Conf. on Exceptionality, Beijing Normal U., People's Republic of China, 1995. Contbr. articles to profl. jours., chpts. to textbooks. Mem. adv. coun. Westwood (Mass.) Bd. Health, 1977-80; emergency med. technician Westwood Pub. Schs. Athletic Dept., 1981. Vocat. Rehab. fellow So. Ill. U., 1964; Merit scholar Perry County, Ill., 1959-64, Credi meml. scholar So. Ill. U., 1964. Mem. Am. Speech & Hearing Assn. (nat. schs. com., nat. chairperson Pub. Sch. Caucus 1985-87), Am. Psychol. Assn., Assn. Psychiat. Svcs. for Children, Coun. Exceptional Children, Internat. Assn. of Logopedics, Rio Vista Civic Assn., Boston Coll. Alumni Assn., Harvard Club. Episcopalian. Avocations: squash, sailing, skiing. Office: Nova Southeastern U Ctr Psychol Studies Maxwell Maltz Psych Bldg 3301 College Ave Fort Lauderdale FL 33314-7796

MAXWELL, W(ILBUR) RICHARD, retired management consultant; b. Troy, Ohio, June 20, 1920; s. Wilbur D. and Gertrude (McDowell) M.; m. Roberta Mae Kennedy, June 29, 1942; children: Douglas R., Jean Ann. Student, Ohio Wesleyan U., 1938-41; BS, Richmond Profl. Inst. of Coll. William and Mary, 1955. Sec. Troy C. of C., 1948-50, Va. C. of C., 1950-55; asst. to pres./chmn. bd. Reynolds Metals Co., 1955-64; v.p., dir. Reynolds Fgn. Sales Inc., 1964-68; pres. Nat. Better Bus. Bur., 1968-70; pres., chief exec. officer Jr. Achievement, Inc., Stamford, Conn., 1970-82. Instr. Richmond Profl. Inst., part-time 1955-57; sponsor-trustee U. Va. Grad. Bus. Sch., 1963-72. Pres. Lancaster County Libr., 1984-85, Rappahannock Gen. Hosp. Found., 1988-90, Northern Neck Vocat.-Tech. Edn. Ctr., 1991-93; bd. dirs. Rappahannock Gen. Hosp., 1988-90, Richmond (Va.) Cmty. H.S., 1989-91; chmn. Northumberland County (Va.) Econ. Devel. Commn., 1994-97. Civilian specialist USAAC, USN, 1942-46. Recipient Albert Schweitzer award Hugh O'Brien Youth Fedn., 1982; inducted Jr. Achievement Profl. Hall of Fame, 1986. Mem. Indian Creek Yacht and Country Club (v.p., 1991-93, bd. dirs. 1991-93). Home: 4600 Middleton Park Cr E Apt D-562 Jacksonville FL 32224

MAXWELL, WILLIAM LAUGHLIN, retired industrial engineering educator; b. Phila., July 11, 1934; s. William Henry and Elizabeth (Laughlin) M.; m. Judith Behrens, July 5, 1969; children: Deborah, William, Judith, Keely BMechE, Cornell U., 1957, PhD, 1961. Andrew Schultz Jr. prof. dept. indsl. engring. Cornell U., Ithaca, N.Y., 1961-98. Author: Theory of Scheduling, 1967. Recipient Disting. Teaching award Cornell Soc. Engrs., 1968, Ralph S. Watts Tchg. award, 1997. Fellow Inst. Indsl. Engrs.; mem. Ops. Rsch. Soc., Soc. Mfg. Engrs., Nat. Acad. Engring. Home: 106 Lake Ave Ithaca NY 14850-3537

MAXWELL, WILLIAM STIRLING, retired lawyer; b. Chgo., May 2, 1922; s. W. Stirling and Ethel (Bowes) Maxwell Reineke. AB with distinction, U. Mich., 1947, postgrad., 1946-49, JD, 1949. Bar: Ill. 1949, U.S. Ct. Mil. Appeals 1951, U.S. Supreme Ct. 1952. Assoc. Sidley & Austin, Chgo., 1949-60, 61, ptnr., 1962-84; now ret.; sr. legis. counsel U.S. Treasury, Washington, 1960-61. Trustee Mid-North Animal Shelter Found., Chgo., 1971— . Mem. Order of Coif, Phi Beta Kappa Clubs: Lawyers Club. Republican. Episcopalian. Home: PO Box 1839 Brookings OR 97415-0048

MAXWELL-BROGDON, FLORENCE MORENCY, school administrator, educational adviser; b. Spring Park, Minn., Nov. 11, 1929; d. William Frederick and Florence Ruth (LaBrie) Maxwell; m. John Carl Brogdon, Mar. 13, 1957; children: Carole Alexandra, Cecily Ann, Daphne Diana. BA, Calif. State U., L.A., 1955; MS, U. So. Calif., 1957; postgrad., Columbia Pacific U., San Rafael, Calif., 1982-86. Cert. tchr., Calif. Dir. Rodeo Sch., L.A., 1961-64; lectr. Media Features, Culver City, Calif., 1964—; dir. La Playa Sch., 1968-75; founding dir. Venture Sch., 1974—, also chmn. bd. dirs. Bd. dirs., v.p. Parent Coop. Preschools, Baie d'Urfe Que., Can., 1964—; del. to Ednl. Symposium, Moscow-St. Petersburg, 1992, U.S./China Joint Conf. on Edn., Beijing, 1992, Internat. Confedn. of Prins., Geneva, 1993, Internat. Conf., Berlin, 1994. Author: Let Me Tell You, 1973, Wet'n Squishy, 1973, Balancing Act, 1977, (as Morency Maxwell) Framed in Silver, 1985; (column) What Parents Want to Know, 1961—; editor: Calif. Preschooler, 1961-74; contbr. articles to profl. jours. Treas. Dem. Congl. Primary, Culver City, 1972. Mem. NASSP, Calif. Coun. Parent Schs. (bd. dirs. 1961-74), Parent Coop. Preschs. Internat. (advisor 1975—), Pen Ctr. USA West, Mystery Writers of Am. (affiliate), Internat. Platform Assn. Liberatarian. Home: 10814 Molony Rd Culver City CA 90230-5451 Office: Venture Sch 11477 Jefferson Blvd Culver City CA 90230-6115 E-mail: morencee@aol.com.

MAY, ADOLF DARLINGTON, civil engineering educator; b. Little Rock, Mar. 25, 1927; s. Adolf Darlington and Inez (Shelton) M.; m. Margaret Folsom, Dec. 23, 1948; children— Dolf, Barbara, David, Larry. B.Sc. in Civil Engring, So. Meth. U., 1949; M.Sc., Iowa State U., 1950; PhD, Purdue U., 1955. Asst. prof., then assoc. prof. Clarkson Coll. Tech., 1952-56; assoc. prof. Mich. State U., 1956-59; research engr. Thompson-Ramo Wooldridge, 1959-62; project dir. Ill. Div. Hwys., 1962-65; mem. faculty U. Calif., Berkeley, 1965—, prof. civil engring., 1965-91, prof. emeritus, 1991—. Guest prof. numerous univs., 1965— , cons. to industry, 1965— Contbr. to profl. jours., books. Served with USNR, 1944-47. Recipient Disting. Engring. Alumnus award Purdue U., 1978, Transp. Sci. and Ethics Internat. award, 1995; Fulbright scholar to Netherlands, 1977; German Humboldt scholar, 1980. Mem. ASCE (Turner award 1994), Transp. Rsch. Bd. (Disting. Lectr. award 1994), Nat. Acad. Engring. (Matson Transp. Rsch. award 1992), Am. Soc. Engring. Edn. (hon.), Inst. Traffic Engrs. (award 1995), Sigma Xi, Tau Beta Pi. Home: 1645 Julian Dr El Cerrito CA 94530-2011 Office: U Calif Dept Civil Engring 106 Mclaughlin Hall Berkeley CA 94720-1720 E-mail: amay@uclink4.berkeley.edu.

MAY, ALAN ALFRED, lawyer; b. Detroit, Apr. 7, 1942; s. Alfred Albert and Sylvia (Sheer) M.; m. Elizabeth Miller; children: Stacy Ann, Julie Beth. BA, U. Mich., 1963, JD cum laude, 1966. Bar: Mich. 1967, D.C. 1976; former reg. nursing home adminstr., Mich. Ptnr. Map and Map, PC, Detroit, 1979—2001, Kemp Klein, Umphrey and May, Washington, 2001—. Spl. asst. atty. gen. State of Mich., 1970—; pres., instr. Med-Leg Seminars, Inc., 1978; lectr. Wayne State U., 1974; instr. Oakland U., 1969. Chmn. Rep. 18th Congressional Dist. Com., 1983-87, now chmn. emeritus; chmn. 19th Congressional Dist. Com., 1981-83; mem. Mich. Rep. Com., 1976-84; del. Rep. Nat. Conv., 1984, rules com., 1984; del. Rep. Nat. Conv., 1988, platform com., 1988; former chmn. Mich. Civil Rights Commn.; former mem. Mich. Civil Svc. Commn., 1984-88; former trustee, mem. exec. bd., vice chmn. nat conf. for cmty. and justice NCCJ; trustee Temple Beth El Birmingham, Mich., pres. exec. bd.; mem. Electoral Coll.; bd. dirs. ADL, Mich.; bd. dirs. exec. bd., pres., Detroit Region/Nat. Conf. Cmty. and Justice, Charfoos Charitable Found. Mem. Nat. Conf. Cmty. and Justice (exec. bd., vice chmn.), Detroit Bar Assn., Oakland County Bar Assn., Victors Club, Franklin Hills Country Club (past pres., bd. dirs.), President's Club (trustee). Home: 4140 Echo Rd Bloomfield Hills MI 48302-1941 Office: Klein Klein Umphrey Endelman & May PC 201 W Big Beaver Rd Ste 600 Troy MI 48084

MAY, APRIL MICHELLE, lawyer; b. Ft. Worth, June 27, 1968; d. Charles Richard and Sandra (Crouch) M. BBA, Baylor U., 1989, JD, 1991. Bar: Tex. 1992, U.S. Supreme Ct. 1999, cert.: Tex. (bd. cert. family law) 1997. Pvt. practice, Belton, Tex., 1992—97; assoc. Erwin A. Cain, P.C., Dallas, 1997-98, McCurley, Kinser, McCurley & Nelson, LLP, Dallas, 1998—2000, Downs Stanford PC, Dallas, 2000—02, McCurley, Kinsen, McCurley & Nelson LLP, Dallas, 2002—. Mem. ABA, Tex. Bar Assn., Dallas Bar Assn., Bell County Bar Assn. (dir.), Bell County Young Lawyers Assn. (pres.), Dallas Young Lawyers Assn., Tex. Assn. Family Law Specialists. Avocations: geneology, reading. Office: 5950 Sherry Ln Ste 800 Dallas TX 75225 E-mail: michelle@mkmn.com.

MAY, ARTHUR W. retired university president; b. St. John's, Nfld., Can., June 29, 1937; s. William J. and Florence (Dawe), M.; m. Sonia Susan Streeter, Aug. 18, 1958; children— Stephen J., Heather E., Maria S., Douglas W. BSc with honors, Meml. U., St. John's, 1958; MSc, Meml. U., 1964; PhD, McGill U., Montreal, Que., Can., 1966; D of Univ. (hon.), U. Ottawa, 1988; DSc (hon.), Meml. U. Nfld., 1989; LLD (hon.), Brock U., 1992. Sci. adviser internat. fisheries Dept. Fisheries, Ottawa, Ont., Can., 1971-73, dir. Nfld. biol. sta. St. John's, 1973-75, dir. gen. resource services Ottawa, 1975-78; asst. dep. minister Atlantic Dept. Fisheries and Oceans, 1978-82, dep. minister, 1982-86; pres. Natural Sci. and Engring. Rsch. Coun. Canada, 1986-90; pres., vice chancellor Meml. U. Nfld., St. Johns, 1990-99. V.p. Internat. Coun. for Exploration of Seas, Copenhagen, 1977-79; mem. Task Force on Atlantic Fisheries, Ottawa, 1982, Nat. Adv. Bd. Sci. and Tech., 1988-90, 94-95; Canadian rep. to NATO Sci. Com., 1990-97; bd. dirs. Can. Mus. of Nature, 1998-2001, Canadian Millenium Scholarship Found., 1998—. Contbr. articles to profl. jours. Served to sub. lt. Can. Navy, 1955-58 Decorated officer Order of Can.; recipient Gov.-Gen.'s medal Nfld. Dept. Edn., 1954, Meml. U. Nfld., 1958; named Alumnus of Yr., Meml. U. Nfld., 1983. Mem. N.W. Atlantic Fisheries Orgn. (pres. 1977-80) Anglican. Avocations: gardening; philately. Home: 20 Baker St Saint John's NF Canada A1A 5A7 Office: Meml Univ Nfld Office of the Pres Saint John's NF Canada A1C 5S7

MAY, AVIVA RABINOWITZ, music educator, linguist, musician; b. Tel Aviv; naturalized, 1958; d. Samuel and Paula Pessia (Gordon) Rabinowitz (div.); children: Chelley Mosoff, Alan May, Risa McPherson, Ellanna May/Gassman. AA, Oakton C.C., 1977; BA in Piano Pedadogy, Northeastern Ill. U., 1978. Folksinger, educator, musican Aviva May Studio/Piano and Guitar, 1948—; Sunday sch. dir. Canton (Ohio) Synagogue, 1952-54; nursery sch. tchr. Allentown (Pa.) Jewish Cmty. Ctr., 1954-56; Hebrew music tchr. Brith Shalom Cmty. Ctr., Bethlehem, Pa., 1954-62; Hebrew tchr. Beth Hillel Congregation, Wilmette, Ill., 1964-83; tchr. B'nai Mitzva, 1978; music dir. McCormick Health Ctrs., Chgo., 1978-79, Cove Sch. Perceptually Handicapped Children, Chgo., 1978-79; prof. Hebrew and Yiddish, Spertus Coll. Judaica, 1980-89; Hebrew tchr. Anshe Emet Day Sch., 1989—, West Suburban Temple Har Zion, Oak Park, Ill., 1993—; music studio tchr. Cosmopolitan Sch., Chgo., 1992—. Tchr. continuing edn. Northeastern Ill. U., 1978-80, Niles Twp. Jewish Congregation, 1993—, also Jewish Cmty. Ctrs.; with Office Spl. Investigations, Dept. Justice, Washington; music dir. Temple Emanuel Rosenwald Sch. Composer classical music for piano, choral work, folk songs; developer 8-hour system for learning piano or guitar; contbr. articles to profl. jours. Recipient Magen David Adom Pub. Svc. award 1973; grantee Ill. State, 1975-79, Ill. Congressman Woody Bowman, 1978-79. Mem. Music Tchrs.

Nat. Assn. (co-founder), North Shore Music Tchrs. Assn. (charter mem., sec.), Ill. Music Tchrs. Assn., Organ and Piano Tchrs. Assn., Am. Coll. Musicians, Ill. Assn. Learning Disabilities, Sherwood Sch. Music, Friends of Holocaust Survivers, Nat. Yiddish Book Exch., Nat. Ctr. for Jewish Films, Chgo. Jewish Hist. Soc., Oakton C.C. Alumni Assn., Northeastern Ill. U. Alumni Assn. Democrat. Office: Aviva May Studio 410 S Michigan Ave Ste 920 Chicago IL 60605-1471 E-mail: arm801@aol.com.

MAY, BENJAMIN TALLMAN, securities specialist, administrator; b. N.Y.C., Dec. 22, 1957; s. Joseph Leserman and Natalie Maria (McCuaig) M.; m. Kaaren Todd Clark, Sept. 1, 1985; children: Caroline Todd, Emily Applegate, Suzannah Tallman. BA, Yale U., 1980; MBA, NYU, 1985. Corp. bond trader, v.p. Drexel Burnham Lambert, N.Y.C., 1980-84; high yield bond trader, sr. v.p. Dillon Read, Inc., 1984-95; mng. dir. high yield bond dept. 1st Union Corp., Charlotte, N.C., 1995-2000, mng. dir. fixed income sales, trading and rsch., 2000—. Mem. Alexis de Toqueville Soc., United Way, Charlotte, 1997; trustee Charlotte Arts and Sci. Coun. Mem. Yale Club N.Y. (Yale Alumni Recruiter), The Bond Market Assn. (bd. dirs. 2001—). Republican. Jewish. Home: 2420 Lemon Tre Ln Charlotte NC 28211 Office: 1st Union Corp 301 S College St Charlotte NC 28202-6000

MAY, BRIAN CAPERS, customer service administrator, writer; b. Rochester, Pa., Feb. 12, 1971; s. Chester Capers May, Robyn Renee May; m. Veronica Jean Gross; children: Tia Lewis, Samuel. BSc in Comm. Media, Ind.U.of Pa., 1993. Customer solutions rep. Xerox, St Petersburg, Fla., 1994—. Mem. Xerox Cmty. Involvement Program. Personal E-mail: thebrosjones@aol.com.

MAY, CAROL LEE, mechanical engineer; b. Arlington, Va., May 10, 1961; d. Ralph Waldo Jr. and Jane Brownley (Moore) M. BS, Va. Poly. Inst. and State U., 1983; postgrad., U. Göttingen, Germany, 1984-85; MS, Stanford U., 1984. Registered profl. engr., Va. Engring. technician (co-op student) Nat. Park Svc., Wyo., Colo., Alaska, 1980-82; physics instr. Fairfax County Pub. Schs., Oakton, Va., 1985; sr. engr. Cortana Corp., Falls Church, 1986—. Author, co-author over 50 corp. reports on submarine tech., 1986—; contbr. articles to profl. jours. and conf. procs. Stanford U. grad. fellow, 1983-84; Deutsche Akademische Austauschdienst postgrad. fellow in fluid mechs., 1984-85. Mem. AIAA, Naval Submarine League. Achievements include coordinating transfer and documentation of fluid mechanics technology from Russian and Ukrainian institutes; providing design recommendations for U.S. and foreign submarines; investigating influence of boundary layer control techniques on drag and flow noise; managing software development programs, developing business. Home: 7215 Janet Pl Falls Church VA 22046-3724 Office: Cortana Corp 520 N Washington St Ste 200 Falls Church VA 22046-3549

MAY, CECIL RICHARD, JR. academic administrator; b. Memphis, June 13, 1932; BA in biblical langs. magna cum laude, MA in New Testament, MTh, Harding U.; LLD (hon.), Freed-Hardeman U., 1984. Min., Holly Springs, Miss., 1954-57, Ripley, 1957-59, Pine Bluff Ch., Ctrl. Acad. Ch., 1959-60; dist. scout exec. Yocona Area Coun. Boy Scouts Am., Oxford, 1959-60; min. Ashland, 1961, Fulton, 1962-67, Eastside Campus Ch., Portland, Oreg., 1967-69; Bible tchr. Columbia Christian Coll., 1967-69; min. Vicksburg, Miss., 1969-76; dean Internat. Bible Coll., Florence, Ala., 1977-80; pres. Magnolia Bible Coll., Kosciusko, Miss., 1980-97; dean bibl. studies Faulkner U., Montgomery, Ala., 1998—, dir. annual Bible lectureship. Lectr. in field. Editor: Preacher Talk; assoc. editor: Magnolia Messenger; contbr. articles to profl. jours. Elder Vicksburg (Miss.) Ch., 1971-76, South Huntington St. Ch., Kosciusko, 1981-97; active Boy Scouts Am., 1954-76; com. chair Kosciusko-Attala County C. of C., 1992; bd. dirs. Am. Cancer Soc., 1971-74, fin. campaign chmn., 1971; bd. dirs. Miss. Econ. Coun., 1985-86, 89-92, area vice-chmn., 1991-92; chmn. Attala County Med. Study Task Force, 1991-92. Mem. Nat. Assn. Ind. Coll. and Univs., Miss. Assn. Ind. Colls. (bd. dirs.), Evang. Theol. Soc., Miss. Assn. Colls. (bd. dirs.), Rotary Club (bd. dirs. 1983-85, pres. 1985-86). Office: Faulkner Univ 5345 Atlanta Hwy Montgomery AL 36109-3390 E-mail: cmay@faulkner.edu.

MAY, CHRISTOPHER, lawyer; b. Rochester, N.Y., Oct. 22, 1929; s. Arthur James and Hilda Jones May; m. Elisabeth Mary Hawkins, Nov. 13, 1954 (div. July 1972); children: Andrew, Corinna, Brian, Laurence; m. Carolyn M. Stearns, May 23, 1987. AB, Harvard U., 1951; JD, Georgetown U., 1978. Bar: D.C. 1979. Staff officer CIA, Washington, 1951—52, 1955—77; v.p. Mortgage Data Svc., 1979—2001; pvt. practice child abuse and neglect law, 1991—. Founding pres. McLean Gardens Residents Assn., Washington, 1971-73; mem. ManKind project. Lt. (j.g.) USNR, 1952-55. Mem.Soc. for the Preservation and Encouragement of Barber Shop Quartet Singing in Am. Democrat. Avocations: singing, skiing, swimming, men's work. Home: 6039 Melbourne Ave Deale MD 20751-9719 Office: Ste 401 419 7th St NW Washington DC 20004-2236 E-mail: christomay@aol.com.

MAY, DAVID A. dean; b. Buffalo, May 23, 1947; children: Jordan D., Jared R. AAS in Bus. Adminstrn., Niagara County C.C., Sanborn, N.Y., 1983; BS in Pub. Adminstrn., Empire State Coll., 1988; MA in Orgn. Mgmt., U. Phoenix, 1996; PhD in Mgmt., LaSalle U., 1997. V.p. Simpson Security, Inc., Niagara Falls, NY, 1973—78; lt. Niagara Falls (N.Y.) Police Dept., 1986—98; ret., 1998; dean N.Y. Paralegal Sch. Bd. mem. Nat. Conf. Christians and Jews, 1984-90, ARC, 1986-89, Music Sch. of Niagara, 1987-90, Niagara Falls Little Theatre, chmn., 1994; pres. Niagara Cmty. Ctr., Niagara Falls, 1987, Niagara Falls (N.Y.) Sch. Bd., 1988, Niagara Falls (N.Y.) Meml. Day Assn., 1990, 91, 93; lt. gov. N.Y. State Kiwanis, 1989; mem. Niagara Co. Lrgis., 1994. Recipient Svc. award Fellowship House Found., Niagara Falls, 1986; named Civic Leader of Yr., Niagara Cmty. Ctr., Niagara Falls, 1990. Mem. Kiwanis Club North Niagara Falls (pres. 1987, Kiwanian of the Yr. 1991), Lasalle Am. Legion (vice commdr. 1975), Lasalle Sportsmens Club (fin. sec. 1989). Avocations: playing tennis, golfing, amateur historian. Home: 2573 E 18th St 1st Fl Brooklyn NY 11235

MAY, DONALD ROBERT LEE, ophthalmologist, retina and vitreous surgeon, educator, farmer; b. Spring Valley, Ill., Nov. 26, 1945; BS in Liberal Arts & Scis. with high honors and distinction, U. Ill., 1968, MD, 1972. Diplomate Am. Bd. Ophthalmology, Nat. Bd. Med. Examiners. Rsch. fellow dept. ophthalmology U. Ill. Eye and Ear Infirmary, Chgo., 1971—72; intern Northwestern U. Sch. Medicine Meml. Hosps., 1972—73; resident in ophthalmology U. Ill. Eye and Ear Infirmary, 1973—76, instr. dept. ophthalmology, 1974—77, attending surgeon dept. ophthalmology, 1976—77, fellow in diabetic retinopathy study, diabetic retinopathy vitrectomy study, and retina and vitreous surgery, 1976—77; asst. prof. ophthalmology, founder, dir. Retina/Vitreous/Ocular Trauma Svc. U. Calif. Davis Sch. Medicine, Calif., 1979—81; assoc. prof., dir. retina, vitreous and ocular trauma svc. U. Calif. Sch. Medicine, Davis, 1981—84; prof. ophthalmology Tulane U. Sch. Medicine, New Orleans, 1984—89, dir. med. student edn. dept. ophthalmology, 1985—89, dir. ophthalmology Charity Hosp., 1985—89; prof. Tex. Tech U. Health Scis. Ctr., Lubbock, Tex., 1989—2001, chmn. dept. ophthalmology and visual scis., 1989—94; prof. dept. health orgn. mgmt. Tex. Tech U Health Scis. Ctr., 1993—2001; assoc. dean Sch. Medicine Tex. Tech U. Health Scis. Ctr., 1994—96. Co-investigator in the intraocular gentamicin prophylaxis study Govt. Erskine Hosp., Madurai, India, 1975, Dept. Ophthalmology, Audie Murphy VA Hosp., San Antonio, 1977—79, Martinez VA Hosp., Calif., 1979—84, VA Hosp., New Orleans, 1984—89, VA Med. Ctr., Big Spring, Tex., 1989—93, Big Spring, 1996—2001, VA Ctr., Lubbock, Tex., 1989—92, Lubbock, 1996—2001; cons., China, 1980, China, 82, China, 85, China, 96, Japan, 1982—83, Japan, 1985; vis. prof., Germany, 84, Switzerland, 87; 1st v.p. U.S. Eye Injury Registry, 1990—92, pres.-elect, 1992—94, pres., 1994—96; founder, med. dir. Tex. Eye Injury Registry, 1991—2001. Contbg. editor: Outcome/Fragmatome Newsletter, 1978—81; assoc. editor: Vitreoretinal Surgery and Tech., 1989—98, mem. editl. bd.: Jour. Eye Trauma, 1996—2001; contbr. articles to profl. jours.; appeared in numerous TV and radio programs. Com. mem. Sch. Medicine U. Calif., Davis, Tulane U. Sch. Medicine, New Orleans, Sch. Medicine Tex. Tech. U. Health Scis. Ctr.; bd. dirs. Lubbock Internat. Cultural Ctr., Inc., 1997—, chmn. ways and means com., 1998—2000; mem. planning com., chmn. medicine and history com., liaison Vatican Mus. Exhbn. Found., 2002. Maj. USAF, 1973—80. Decorated Air Force Commendation medal. Mem.: AMA, ACS, Patrons Arts Vatican Mus., Ret. Officers Assn., Ill. Farm Bur., Ill. Agrl. Assn., Am. Farm Bur. Fedn., Soc. Med. Cons. Armed Forces, World Eye Found. (bd. dirs. 1982—), Vitreous Soc. (charter), Retina Soc., Pan-Am. Assn. Ophthalmology, Schepens Internat. Soc., Rsch. Prevent Blindness, Tex. Tech. Rsch. Found. (bd. dirs. 1993—96), Tex. Ophtal. Assn. (chair edn. com. 1990—93, coun. 1990—93, nominating com. 1991—93), So. Retina Study Group (steering com. 1987—89), Tex. Med. Assn. (com. continuing edn. 1993—96, bd. dirs. TEXPAC 2000—), So. Med. Assn. (vice-chmn. sec. ophthalmology 1995—96, chmn. sec. ophthalmology 1996—97), Christian Med. Soc., Chinese Am. Opthal. Soc. (charter), Assn. Rsch. Vision and Ophthalmology (pub. rels. com. 1997—2000), Am. Acad. Ophthalmology (bylaws and rules com. 1990—95, com. internat. ophthalmology 1991—95), Sigma Xi (sec. Tex. Tech. chpt. 1990—91, v.p., pres.-elect 1999—2000, pres. 2000—01). Republican. Lutheran. Avocations: travel, photography, cycling, hiking. Home: PO Box 1678 Lubbock TX 79408-1678 Office: The Vatican Mus Exhbn Ste 204 1001 Main St Lubbock TX 79401 *If we are to survive as a free society, we must each accept responsibility. The individual must function on the premise that personal rewards come with the investment of hard, honest work and not as a right mediated by government at the expense of others. Our legislative bodies must enact laws for the common good and not for individual self-interest. Our judicial systems must provide for the just enforcement of our laws. Our leadership must be the watchdog to ensure the indivdual has the opportunity to life without unreasonable danger, the freedom to follow one's dreams, and the ability to pursue happiness through individual achievement. Security comes with the contribution of all who are able.*

MAY, DOUGLAS L. music educator; b. Greenville, Pa., Apr. 17, 1967; s. Harold Leslie and Ardis Rae May; m. Jennifer Marie O'Brien, June 25, 1994; children: Makenzie, Lindsay. BS in Edn. Emphasis on Music, Clarion (Pa) U., , 1989; MusM Emphasis on Edn., Ea. N.Mex U., Portales, 1991. Asst. dir. of bands Hobbs Mcpl. Schools, Hobbs, N.Mex., 1991—92; dir. of bands Lakeview Sch. Dist., Stoneboro, Pa., 1992—; guest lectr. in trombone Grove City (Pa.)Coll., 1995—. Recipient Outstanding Tchr. Award, Sharon Herald, 1997. Mem.: Internat. Trombone Assn., Pa, Music Educators Assn. Office: Lakeview Sch Dist 2482 Mercer St Stoneboro PA 16153

MAY, EDGAR, former state legislator, nonprofit administrator; b. Zurich, Switzerland, June 27, 1929; arrived in U.S., 1940, naturalized, 1954; s. Ferdinand and Renee (Bloch) May. B.J. with highest distinction, Northwestern U., 1957. Reporter, acting editor Bellows Falls (Vt.) Times, 1951-53; reporter Fitchburg (Mass.) Sentinel, 1953; part time reporter Chgo. Tribune, 1955-57; reporter Buffalo Evening News, 1958-61; dir. pub. welfare projects State Charities Aid Assn., 1962-64; mem. President's Task Force on War Against Poverty, 1964; spl. asst. to dir., asst. dir. Office Econ. Opportunity, 1964; spl. adviser to Ambassador Sargent Shriver, 1968-70; cons. Ford Found., 1970-75; mem. Vt. Ho. of Reps., 1975-82, Vt. Senate, 1983-91, chmn. com. appropriations; project dir. Vt. Jud. Mgmt. Study, 1992; COO Spl. Olympics Internat., Washington, 1993-96; cons. New Eng. Culinary Inst., 1996—2001; chmn. So. Vt. Recreation Ctr. Found., 1998—. Author: The Wasted Americans, 1964. With AUS, 1953-55. Recipient Page One award Buffalo Newspaper Guild, 1959, Walter O. Bingham award, 1959; Pulitzer prize for local reporting, 1961; Merit award Northwestern U. Alumni Assn., 1962

MAY, ERNEST DEWEY, university administrator, musician, executive; b. Jersey City, May 8, 1942; s. Ernest Max and Harriet Elizabeth (Dewey) M.; m. Eileen Marie Mayhew, Jan. 29, 1963 (div. 1984); children: Ernest Jr., Elizabeth May Goodell, Katherine May Waite, Caroline, Christopher, Abigail May Robles, Deirdre; m. Mary L. Milkey, June 29, 1985. AB, Harvard U., 1964; MFA, Princeton U., 1968, PhD, 1975. Asst. prof. music Amherst (Mass.) Coll., 1969-75; from asst. prof. to prof. music dept. music and dance U. Mass., Amherst, 1976-88, prof. music, chmn. dept. music and dance, 1988-2000, presiding officer faculty senate, 1997-2000, sec. faculty senate, 2000—. Faculty rep. Bd. Trustees, U. Mass., 1988-97; chair Intercampus Faculty Coun., 2001—; organist, dir. mus. South Congl. Ch., Springfield, Mass., 1983—. Rec.: Music for Trumpet and Organ, 1979, 2001; co-editor: J.S. Bach: Neve Ausgabe Samtlicher Werke Vol. I/20, 1986, J.S. Bach as Organist, 1986; contbr. New Harvard Dictionary of Music, 1986. Mem. Am. Assn. Higher Edn., Nat. Assn. Schs. Music Commn. on Accreditation, Am. Guild Organists, Am. Musicological Soc. (pres. New Eng. chpt. 1988-90). Home: 44 Amherst Rd Pelham MA 01002-9700 Office: U Mass Faculty Senate Amherst MA 01003 E-mail: secretary@senate.umass.edu.

MAY, ERNEST MAX, charitable organization official; b. Newark, July 24, 1913; s. Otto Bernard and Eugenie (Morgenstern) M.; m. Harriet Elizabeth Dewey, Oct. 12, 1940; children: Ernest Dewey, James Northrup, Susan Elizabeth. BA, Princeton, 1934, MA, 1935; PhD in Organic Chemistry, U. Chgo., 1938; LittD (hon.), Montclair State Coll., 1989. With Otto B. May, Inc., Newark, 1938-73, successively chemist, gen. mgr., 1938-52, pres., 1952-73; trustee Youth Consultation Service Diocese of Newark, 1952-59, 61-66, 68-75, pres., 1971-75, hon. trustee, 1975—; dir. Cone Mills Corp., 1961-73, mem. exec. com., 1968-71. Tech. adviser to spl. rep. trade negotiations, 1964-67. Councilman, Summit, N.J., 1963-70; mem. Summit Environ. Com., 1971-75, chmn., 1974-75; pres. Family Svc. Assn. Summit, 1959-61, Mental Health Assn. Summit, 1954, Summit Coun. Chs. Christ, 1962-63; mem. exec. com. Christ Hosp., Jersey City, 1971—, v.p., chmn., 1974-93; chmn. Summit Hwy. Adv. Com., 1976-94; trustee, organizer Summer Organic Chemistry Inst., Choate Sch., Wallingford, Conn.; mem. Union County Mental Health Bd., 1973-76; bd. dirs. N.J. Mental Health Assn., 1974-81; trustee Montclair (N.J.) State Univ., 1975-85, vice-chmn., 1976-80, chmn., 1980-83; adviser applied prof. psychology Rutgers U., 1976—; mem. Nat. commn. on Nursing, 1980-83; adviser dept. music Princeton U.; trustee Assn. for Children in N.J., 1975—, Citizen's Com. on Biomed. Ethics in N.J., 1984-95, N.J. Health Decisions, 1995-97; advisor Nat. Exec. Svcs. Corps Health Care Consulting Group, 1994—; mem. N.J. Early Early Care and Edn. Coalition, 1999—, N.J. Child Care Adv. Coun., 1999—. Fellow Am. Inst. Chemists; mem. Am. Chem. Soc., Synthetic Organic Chem. Mfrs. Assn. (bd. govs. 1952-54, 63-70, v.p. 1966-68, chmn. internat. comml. rels. com. 1968-73, hon. mem.), Vol. Trustees Not-for-Profit Hosps. (trustee 1986-88, 94-98), Chemists Club (N.Y.), Beacon Hill Club (Summit, N.J.), Nassau Club (Princeton), N.J. Hosp. Assn. (coun. on edn. 1990-91), Sigma Xi. Republican. Episcopalian (vestry 1950-60). Home: 57 Colt Rd Summit NJ 07901-3004 also: State Rd Chilmark MA 02535 E-mail: emmay@comcast.net. *To live right and help others live right too, each in his own way.*

MAY, FRANK BRENDAN, JR. lawyer; b. Bronx, N.Y., Oct. 17, 1945; s. Frank Brendan and Margaret May; m. Mary Frances Fitzsimmons, June 19, 1976; children: David Brendan, Brian Christopher. BA in Econs., NYU, 1973, postgrad., 1973-75; JD, John Marshall Law Sch., Chgo., 1978. Bar: Ill. 1979, U.S. Dist. Ct. (no. dist.) Ill. 1979, U.S. Ct. Appeals (7th cir.), 1979, U.S. Supreme Ct. 1995, lic. Ill. real estate broker 1994. Legal intern criminal div. Cook County State's Atty.'s Office, Chgo., 1977-78; legal intern juvenile div. DuPage County State's Atty.'s Office, Wheaton, 1978; sr. assoc. atty. Lillig, Kemp & Thorness, Ltd., Oak Brook, 1978-81; v.p., gen. counsel Coldwell Banker, 1981-90, Prudential Preferred Properties, Des Plaines, Ill., 1991-98, Law Offices, Frank B. May, Jr., Wheaton, 1999-2001; sr. corp. atty., asst. sec. Budget Rent a Car Corp., Lisle, 2001—. Arbitrator 18th Jud. Cir. Ct., Dupage County, Ill., 1993—. Dir. Ray Graham Found. for People with Disabilities, 1999—. Sgt. USAF, 1963-67. NYU Coun. scholar, 1971-73; David Davis Meml. scholar, 1970-71. Mem. Ill. State Bar Assn. (real estate sect.), DuPage county Bar Assn. (real estate law com.), Medinah Country Club (mem. legal/bylaws com. 1998-2000, membership com. 1997—, chmn. PGA credentials com. 1999), Ill. Assn. Realtors (mem. large brokers coun. 1996-98, exec. com., fin. com. 1998-1999, lic. law rewrite task force, nominating com. 1998-99), Realtor Assn. Western Suburbs (legal counsel 1999-2000). Avocations: golf, music, gourmet cooking, wine collector. Home: 2064 Stonebridge Ct Wheaton IL 60187-7177 Office: Budget Rent a Car Corp 4225 Naperville Rd Lisle IL 60532-3662 Fax: 630-665-7456. Business E-Mail: fmay@budgetgroup.com.

MAY, GITA, French language and literature educator; b. Brussels, Sept. 16, 1929; came to U.S., 1947, naturalized, 1950; d. Albert and Blima (Sieradska) Jochimek; m. Irving May, Dec. 21, 1947. BA magna cum laude, CUNY-Hunter Coll., 1953; MA, Columbia U., 1954, PhD, 1957. Lectr. French CUNY-Hunter Coll., 1953-56; instr. Columbia U., 1956-58, asst. prof., 1958-61, assoc. prof., 1961-68, prof., 1968—, chmn., 1983-93, mem. senate, 1979-83, 86-88, chmn. Seminar on 18th Century Culture, 1986-89. Lecture tour English univs., 1965 Author: Diderot et Baudelaire, critiques d'art, 1957, De Jean-Jacques Rousseau à Madame Roland: essai sur la sensibilité préromantique et révolutionnaire, 1964, Madame Roland and the Age of Revolution, 1970 (Van Amringe Disting. Book award), Stendhal and the Age of Napoleon, 1977, Encyclopedia of Aesthetics, 1998, Dictionnaire de Diderot, 1999, French Women Writers, 1991, The Feminist Encyclopedia of French Literature, 1999; co-editor: Diderot Studies III, 1961; mem. editl. bd. 18th Century Studies, 1975-78, French Rev., 1975-86, 98—, Romanic Rev., 1959—, Women in French Studies, 2000—; contbg. editor: Oeuvres complétes de Diderot, 1984, 95; gen. editor: The Age of Revolution and Romanticism: Interdisciplinary Studies, 1990—, extensive essays on Diderot and George Sand in European Writers, 1984, 85, and on Rebecca West, Anita Brookner and Graham Swift in British Writers, 1996, 97, 99; contbr. articles and revs. to profl. jours. Decorated chevalier and officier Ordre des Palmes Acad.; recipient award Am. Coun. Learned Socs., 1961, award for outstanding achievement CUNY-Hunter Coll., 1963; Fulbright rsch. grantee, 1964-65; Guggenheim fellow, 1964-65, NEH fellow, 1971-72. Mem. AAUP, MLA (del. assembly 1973-75, mem. com. rsch. activities 1975-78, mem. exec. coun. 1980-83), Am. Assn. Tchrs. of French, Am. Soc. 18th Century Studies (pres. 1985-86, 2nd v.p. 1983-84, 1st v.p. 1984-85, One of Gt. Tchrs. award 1999), Soc. Française d'Etude du Dix-Huitième Siècle, Soc. Diderot, Am. Soc. French Acad. Palms, Soc. des Etudes Staëliennes, N.Am. Soc. for the Study of Jean-Jacques Rousseau, Soc. des Professeurs Francais et Francophones d'Amérique, Phi Beta Kappa. Office: Columbia U Dept French/Romance Philol 516 Philosophy Hall MC4918 New York NY 10027 E-mail: gm9@columbia.edu.

MAY, GRACE BUCKNER (MRS. MICHAEL HUGO MAY), civic worker; b. Los Angeles; d. Manfred R. and Jean Ann (Naftalin) Buckner; student UCLA, 1946-49; B.A., Los Angeles State Coll., 1955; m. Michael Hugo May, Dec. 23, 1948; children— Carolyn Estherlee, Michael Werner, Jonathan Gustav. Docent, Los Angeles County Mus. Natural History; mem. art council UCLA; tour guide George C. Page Mus. Bd. dirs. Helping Hand, Los Angeles. Home: 4917 San Feliciano Dr Woodland Hills CA 91364-4125

MAY, HAROLD EDWARD, chemical company executive; b. N.Y.C., Oct. 18, 1920; s. Charles Edward and Mollie (Flax) M.; m. Margaret June Hochman, June 27, 1943; children: Charles S., Michael E., Suzanne E. AB, Columbia U., 1941, BS in Mech. Engring, 1942. With E.I. duPont de Nemours & Co., Inc., 1942—, v.p. materials and logistics Del., 1977-82, sr. v.p. corp. staff, 1982-85, ret., 1985. Recipient Illig medal Columbia U., 1942 Mem. Phi Beta Kappa, Tau Beta Pi. Jewish. Home: 36 Southridge Dr Kennett Square PA 19348-2714

MAY, HENRY STRATFORD, JR. lawyer; b. Greensboro, N.C., May 12, 1947; s. Henry Stratford and Doris (Richardson) M. BA, U. Tex., 1969, JD, 1971. Bar: Tex. 1972, U.S. Ct. Appeals (D.C. cir.) 1974, U.S. Supreme Ct. 1977, U.S. Ct. Appeals (5th and 11th cirs.) 1981, U.S. Dist. Ct. (so. dist.) Tex. 1985. Law clk. to judge U.S. Ct. Appeals (D.C. cir.), Washington, 1972-73; assoc. Vinson & Elkins, Houston, 1973-79, ptnr., 1979—, head energy sect., 1990—. Adj. prof. U. Houston Law Sch., 1994—. Author: Natural Gas Contracts. Mem. ABA, Tex. Bar Assn. Republican.

MAY, J. PETER, mathematics educator; b. N.Y.C., Sept. 16, 1939; s. Siegmund Henry and Jane (Polachek) M.; m. Maija Bajars, June 8, 1963; children: Anthony D., Andrew D. BA, Swarthmore Coll., 1960; PhD, Princeton U., 1964. Instr. Yale U., New Haven, 1964-65, asst. prof., 1965-67; assoc. prof. U. Chgo., 1967-70, prof., 1970—, chmn. dept. math., 1985-91, chmn. coun. on teaching, 1991-96. Mem. Inst. Advanced Study, Princeton, 1966; vis. prof. Cambridge U., Eng., 1971-72, 1977. Author: Simplicial Objects in Algebraic Topology, 1967, The Geometry of Iterated Loop Spaces, 1972, E-infinity Ring Spaces and E-infinity Ring Spectra, 1977, Equivariant Homotopy and Cohomology Theory, 1996, A Concise Course in Algebraic Topology, 1999; co-author: The Homology of Iterated Loop Spaces, 1976, H-infinity Ring Spectra and Their Applications, 1986, Equivariant Stable Homotopy Theory, 1987, Rings Modules and Algebras in Stable Homotopy Theory, 1997, A Concise Course in Algebraic Topology, 1999; also numerous articles and monographs. NSF grantee, 1967—; Fulbright fellow, 1971-72; fellow Nat. Research Council, Eng., 1977. Mem. AAUP, Am. Math. Soc. Office: U Chgo Dept Math 5734 S University Ave Chicago IL 60637-1514

MAY, JACKSON CAMPBELL, real estate developer, writer; b. Danville, Ky., June 19, 1936; s. Earl Campbell and Emma Lee (Fleming) May; m. De Lena Inez Courtney, Nov. 26, 1965 (div. Jan. 1981); children: Jackson Campbell(dec.) , Geoffrey Courtney; m. Juanita Lucielee Sarver, June 16, 1984; children: Winston Augustus, Emmalee Annabella. BS, U.S. Mil. Acad., 1958. Commd. 1st lt. U.S. Army, 1958, with airborne, ranger and mountain sects. 82d Airborne Divsn., 1958-61; founder The May Cos., Gainesville, Fla., 1961—. Bd. dirs. First City Bank, Gainesville, Nat. Apt. Devel. Coun.; internat. explorer, safari photographer, mountain climber, 1950—; founder Pub. Partnerships for Infestment. Contbr. Patron Jacksonville Symphony, Hippodrome State Theatre, Performing Arts Ctr. U. Fla., World Wildlife Fund; advisor dept. classics U. Fla. Named to Hon. Order Ky. Cols. Mem.: SAR, Smithsonian, Ducks Unltd., Am. Mus. Nat. History, Gator Boosters U. Fla., Assn. Grads. West Point, Soc. Colonial Wars, Cousteau Soc., Alumni Assn. U. Fla., Circumnavigators Club N.Y., Univ. Club Orlando, Sports Car Club Am., Poinciana Club Palm Beach, Safari Club Internat., Lodge and Bath Club Ponte Vedra Beach, Gator Hunt Club, Explorers Club N.Y., Chevaliers du Tastevin Palm Beach, Gainesville Country Club, Heritage Club Gainesville, River Club Jacksonville, Seminole Club Jacksonville, Societe de Bons Vivants, Mensa. Republican. Baptist. Avocations: photography, writing, mountaineering, arctic and underwater exploration, automobiles. Office: The May Cos PO Box 140600 Gainesville FL 32614-0600

MAY, JEFFREY R. business executive; b. July 21, 1951; BS, Calif. State U., Fullerton, 1973; secondary tchg. credential, C.S.U.F., 1974. Rescue boat capt., ocean lifeboard Calif. Lifeguards, Huntington Beach, 1969-80; tchr., coach Calif. State U., Fullerton, 1973-75; traffic officer Calif. Hwy. Patrol, 1980-87; owner/founder JRM Enterprises Internat., Sisters, Oreg., 1982—. Home and Office: 31402 Lovegren Ln Sisters OR 97759

MAY, JOHN RAYMOND, clinical psychologist; b. Rahway, N.J., Jan. 31, 1943; s. John Y. and Aline (Eichorn) M.; m. Brenda Lee Berg, June 17, 1967; children: Stacey Anne, John Jeffrey. BA in Psychology, Colgate U., 1965; PhD in Clin. Psychology, U. N.C., 1970. Clin. intern U. Wis. Med. Ctr., 1967-68; staff psychologist to chief, clin. svcs. divsn. Nat. Security Agy., Ft. Meade, Md., 1969-72, cons., 1972-92; pvt. practice clin. psychology Columbia, 1972—. Exec. dir. Psychol. Health Svcs., Inc., Columbia, 1976-84, 1993-2001; exec. dir. Columbia Psychol. Services, 1984-91, Cmty. Counseling Assocs., 1991—; co-dir. Columbia Addictions Ctr., 1994-98; adj. prof. Loyola Coll., 1970-72. Co-author films on mental health tng., articles in profl. jours. and manuals. Recipient Wallach award U. N.C., 1969, Humanitarian award Citizens Against Spousal Assault, 1989; USPHS fellow, 1966-69; VA fellow, 1965-66. Mem. APA, Md. Psychol. Assn. (exec. coun., various coms. 1977-91, treas. 1985-88, pres.-elect 1988, pres. 1989-90, past pres. 1990-91, Outstanding Profl. Contbn. to Psychology award 1993), Am. Bd. Sexology (diplomate), Assn. Advancement of Psychology, Am. Soc. Clin. Hypnosis, Am. Assn. Sex Educators, Counselors, and Therapists (cert. sex. therapist), Anxiety Disorders Assn. Am., Howard County Psychol. Soc. (pres. 1975-76). Home: 6264 Cardinal Ln Columbia MD 21044-3802 Office: 10774 Hickory Ridge Rd Columbia MD 21044-3646 E-mail: cca21044@msn.com.

MAY, JOSEPH LESERMAN (JACK MAY), lawyer; b. Nashville, May 27, 1929; s. Daniel and Dorothy (Fishel) M.; m. Natalie McCuaig, Apr. 12, 1957 (dec. May 1990); children: Benjamin, Andrew, Joshua, Maria; m. Lynn Hewes Lance, June 10, 1994. BA, Yale U., 1951; JD, NYU, 1958; postgrad., Harvard Bus. Sch., 1969. Bar: Tenn. 1959. Prodr. Candied Yam Jackson Show, 1947-51; with CIA, 1951-55; pres. Nuweave Socks, Inc., N.Y.C., 1955-59, May Hosiery Mills, Nashville, 1960-83, Athens Hosiery Mills, Tenn., 1966-83; v.p. Wayne-Gossard Corp., Chattanooga, 1972-83; pvt. practice law Nashville, 1984—. Mem. adv. bd. Asian Strategies Group, 1994. Bd. dirs. Vanderbilt Cancer Ctr., 1994-99; pres. Jewish Cmty. Ctr., 1969; chmn. Guardianship and Trust Corp., 1994-96, Campus for Human Devel., 2000-02; mem. AAA panel of neutrals. With USN, 1947-53, U.S. Army, 1954. Mem. Tenn. Bar Assn., Nashville Bar Assn., Am. Arbitration Assn. Panel of Neutrals, Tenn. Hist. Soc. (trustee, pres. 2000-02), Eagle Scout Assn., Belle Meade

Country Club, Shamus Club, Old Oak Club, Yale Club N.Y., Rotary (pres. Nashville 1971). Republican. Jewish. Home: 133 Abbottsford Nashville TN 37215-2442 Office: PO Box 190628 424 Church St Ste 2000 Nashville TN 37219-3304

MAY, KENNETH NATHANIEL, food industry consultant; b. Livingston, La., Dec. 24, 1930; s. Robert William and Mary Hulda (Caraway) M.; m. Patsy Jean Farr, Aug. 4, 1953; children: Sherry Alison (dec.), Nathan Elliott. BS in Poultry Sci., La. State U., 1952, MS in Poultry Sci., 1955; PhD in Food Tech., Purdue U., 1959, DAgr. 1988. Asst. prof. U. Ga., Athens, 1958-64, assoc. prof., 1964-67, prof., 1967-68, Miss. State U., State College, 1968-70; dir. rsch. Holly Farms Poultry, Wilkesboro, N.C., 1970-73, v.p., 1973-85, pres., 1985-88, chmn., CEO, 1989. Adj. prof. N.C. State U., 1975. Contbr. over 60 articles to profl. jours.; patentee treatment of cooked poultry. Bd. trustees Appalachian State U., 1987-94, chmn., 1989-90. Recipient Industry Service award Poultry and Egg Inst. Am., 1971, Meritorious Service award, Ga. Egg Commn., 1964, Disting. Service award Agribus. N.C., 1986; named to Am. Poultry Hall of Fame, 1992. Fellow Poultry Sci. Assn.; mem. Nat. Poultry Hist. Soc. (bd. dirs. 1982-83), Inst. Food Technologists. Methodist. Avocations: reading, stained glass. Office: 113 La Maison Belle Dr Denham Springs LA 70726

MAY, LINDA, delivery business owner; b. Indpls., Feb. 1, 1959; d. Charles F. and Geneva Clark. Grad., Southport H.S., Indpls., 1977. With Spl. Dispatch, Inc., Indpls., 1975—, owner, pres., 1992—. Mem. MCAA, ACCA, Ind. C. of C., Indpls. C. of C., Builders Assn. Greater Indpls. Office: Spl Dispatch Inc 3560 Developers Rd Indianapolis IN 46227-3518

MAY, MARGRETHE, health educator; b. Tucson, Oct. 6, 1943; d. Robert A. and Margrethe (Holm) M. BS in Human Biology, U. Mich., 1970, MS in Anatomy, 1986. Cert. surg. technologist. Surg. technologist Hartford (Conn.) Hosp., 1965-68, U. Mich. Hosps., Ann Arbor, 1968-70; asst. operating room supr. U. Ariz. Med. Ctr., Tucson, 1971-72; coord. operating room tech. program Pima Coll., 1971-76; prof., coord. surg. tech. and surg. first asst. programs Delta Coll., University Center, Mich., 1978-99, coord., surg. first asst. distance edn. program, 1999—. Commr. Commn. on Accreditation of Allied Health Ednl. Programs, Chgo., 1994-97, Coun. Accreditation and Unit Recognition, 1994-96. Editor: Core Curriculum for Surgical Technology, 3d edit., 1990, Core Curriculum for Surgical First Assisting, 1993; contbr. articles to profl. jours. Mem. Assn. Surg. Technologists (bd. dirs. 1987-89, pres.-elect 1989-90, pres. 1990-91, on-site visitor program accreditation 1974—, chmn. exam writing com. 1981, liaison coun. on cert. co-chmn. 1977, chmn. 1978, sec.-treas. 1979, chmn. accreditation review com for edn. in surg. tech. 1994-97, Mich. state assembly AST bd. dirs. 2000—), Am. Soc. Law, Medicine and Ethics, Mich. Assn. Allied Health Professions (sec. 1994-97), Nat. Network Health Career Programs in Two-Year Colls. Avocations: international health care issues and allied health education. Home: 2506 Abbott Rd Apt P-2 Midland MI 48642-4876 Office: Delta Coll Health And Wellness Divsn University Center MI 48710-0001 E-mail: mmay@alpha.delta.edu.

MAY, MARY JO EMILIE, researcher; b. Saginaw, Mich., Feb. 9, 1939; d. John Ernest and Josephine Mary Von Klempnow; m. Richard Charles May, Aug. 15, 1961 (div.); children: Joel, Stephanie, Angela. PhD Philosophy of Learning, U. of Mich., Ann Arbor, MI, 1989—97; MA individualized studies, Ea. Mich. U., Ypsilanti, MI, 1984—88; MA Liberal Arts, Ctrl. Mich. U., Mount Pleasant, MI, 1962—65. Teaching Certificate Mich., 1962. Rschr. self-employed, Ann Arbor, Mich., 2002; english educator Various Colleges And High Schools, Flint, Ypsilanti, Dearborn, Detroit, Ann Arbor, Livonia, 1962—87. Chairperson Edn. Alumni Bd., Ea. Mich. U., Ypsilanti, Mich., 1984—87; exec. bd. info. coord. Midwest Conf. on English, 1980—87. Contbr. literary magazine and journals. Avocation: human nature.

MAY, MARY LOUISE, elementary education educator; b. Highland, Ill., Nov. 9, 1946; d. Cecil S. and Marie (Papp) Harmon; 1 child, Alesia Lovellette. BS, So. Ill. U., Edwardsville, 1973. Elem. tchr. Edwardsville Sch. Dist. 7, 1974—. Presenter math. confs., 1990—. Mem. Ill. Edn. Assn., Edwardsville Edn. Assn. (v.p. 1990-95, pres. 1995—), Illini Tchrs. Whole Lang., Delta Kappa Gamma, Beta Sigma Phi (pres. laureate chpt.). Avocations: reading, writing, golf, counted cross-stitch, walking. Home: 16 Dorset Ct Edwardsville IL 62025-3920 Office: Woodland Sch 59 S State Route 157 Edwardsville IL 62025-3870

MAY, PHILIP ALAN, sociology educator; b. Bethesda, Md., Nov. 6, 1947; s. Everette Lee and Marie (Lee) M.; m. Doreen Ann Garcia, Sept. 5, 1972; children: Katrina Ruth, Marie Ann. BA in Sociology, Catawba Coll., 1969; MA in Sociology, Wake Forest U., 1971; PhD in Sociology, U. Mont., 1976. NIMH predoctoral fellow U. Mont., Missoula, 1973-76; dir. health stats. and rsch. Navajo Health Authority, Window Rock, Ariz., 1976-78; asst. prof. U. N.Mex., Albuquerque, 1978-82, assoc. prof., 1982-89, prof., 1989—, dir. Ctr. on Alcoholism, Substance Abuse and Addictions, 1990-99; co-dir., 2000—; sr. rsch. scientist Ctr. on Alcoholism, Substance Abuse and Addictions, 2000—. Fetal alcohol syndrome study com. Inst. of Medicine/NAS, 1994-96; dir. Nat. Indian Fetal Alcohol Syndrome Prevention Program, Albuquerque, 1979-85; adv. bd. Nat. Orgn. on Fetal Alcohol Syndrome, Washington, 1990—; rsch. assoc. Nat. Ctr. for Am. Indian and Alaska Native Mental Health Rsch., 1986—; mem. U.S. Surgeon Gens. Task Force on Drunk Driving, 1988-89; prin. investigator fetal alcohol syndrome epidemiology rsch. in South Africa, 1997—; com. on pathophysiology and prevention of adolescent and adult suicide Inst. Medicine/NRC/NAS, 2000-02; cons. in field. Contbr. chpts. to books and articles to profl. jours. V.p. Bd. Edn., Laguna Pueblo, N.Mex., 1998—2002, pres., 2002—. Lt. USPHS, 1970—73. Recipient Spl. Recognition award U.S. Indian Health Svc., 1992, award Navajo Tribe and U.S. Indian Health Svc., 1992, Human Rights Promotion award UN Assn., 1994, Program award for Contbns. to Mental Health of Am. Indians, U.S. Indian Health Svc., 1996, O.B. Michael Outstanding Alumnus award Catawba Coll., 2000. Mem. APHA, Am. Sociol. Assn., Population Ref. Bur., Coll. on Problems of Drug Dependence, Rsch. Soc. Alcoholism. Methodist. Home: 4610 Idlewilde Ln SE Albuquerque NM 87108-3422 Office: U NMex CASAA 2650 Yale Blvd Albuquerque NM 87106-3202 E-mail: pmay@unm.edu.

MAY, PHYLLIS JEAN, financial executive; b. Flint, Mich., May 31, 1932; d. Bert A. (dec.) and Alice C. (Rushton) Irvine; m. John May, Apr. 24, 1971 (dec. 1997). Grad., Dorsey Sch. Bus., 1957; cert., Internat. Corr. Schs., 1959, Nat. Tax Inst., 1978; MBA, Mich. U., 1970. Registered real estate agt; lic. life, auto and home ins. agent. Office mgr. Comml. Constrn. Co., Flint, 1962-68; bus. mgr. new and used car dealership, 1968-70; contr. various corps., 1970-75; fiscal dir. Rubicon Odyssey Inc., Detroit, 1976-87, Wayne County Treas.'s Office, 1987-93; exec. fin. office Grosse Pointe Meml. Ch., 1993—. Acad. cons. acctg. Detroit Inst. Commerce, 1980-81; pres. small bus. specializing in adminstrv. cons. and acctg., 1982—; supr. mobile svc. stat., upholstery and home improvement businesses; owner retail bus. Pieces and Things. Pres. PTA Westwood Heights Schs., 1972; vol. Fedn. of Blind, 1974-76, Probate Ct., 1974-76; mem. citizens adv. bd. Northville Regional Psychiat. Hosp., 1988, sec., 1989-90; pres. La'Renaissance Condominium Assn., Atlantic City, N.J., 1996-2000, sec., 2000—. Recipient Meritorious Svc. award Genesee County for Youth, 1976, Excellent Performance and High Achievement award Odyssey Inc., 1981. Mem. NAFE (bd. dirs.), Am. Bus. Women's Assn. (treas. 1981, rec. sec. 1982, v.p. 1982-83, Woman of Yr. 1982), Womens Assn. Dearborn Orch. Soc., Dearborn Community Art Ctr., Mich. Mental Health Assn., Internat. Platform Assn., Guild of Carillonneurs in N.Am., Pi Omicron (officer 1984-85). Presbyterian.

MAY, RICHARD WARREN, writer, consultant, inventor; b. Marlboro, Mass., Mar. 1, 1944; s. Richard and Lavinia (Crane) M. BS in Psychology, U. Mass., 1968; MA in Humanities and Philosophy, Calif. State U., Dominguez Hills, 1991. Lic. real estate broker. Tchr. Boston Pub. Schs., Boston, 1970-89; pres., founder The Aleph (formerly Promethean Pastimes), 1975—. Adv. bd. mem. and rsch. assoc. Point One Adv. Group, Inc., Madisonville, Ky. Author: (games of strategy) Game of the Gods, 1984, Trihex, 1985, Aliens and Amazons, The Game of Tetra, 1994; contbr. (anthology) Thinking on the Edge, 1993; patentee game bd. and pieces TriHex, 1988. Mem. Assn. Advance Ethical Hypnosis, West Orange, N.J., 1974-75, Boston Tchrs. Union, 1984-89, Point One Adv. Group. Fellow Internat. Soc. Philos. Enquiry (asst. historian 1981-82, diplomate); mem. Nat. Coalition of Ind. Scholars, Prometheus Soc. (past first jour. editor, ombudsman 1984-94, pres. 1991-98), Hoeflin Rsch. Group, The Mega Soc., One-in-Million Soc., Triple Nine Soc. (membership officer 1983-84, regent 1987-90), Mensa, Internat. Am. Acad. Religion, Internat. Acad. Philosophy (bd. dirs., founder Found.), The Jewish Geneal. Soc. Office: Point One Adv Group PO Box 1111 Madisonville KY 42431-0022 E-mail: ferdlilac@yahoo.com.

MAY, ROBERT GEORGE, dean, accounting educator; b. Detroit, Nov. 11, 1943; s. George Joseph and Winifred Marie (Donnelly) M.; m. Carol Ann Rogers, June 18, 1965; children: Gregory Charles, Lynn Marie. BBA, Mich. State U., 1965, PhD, 1970. Asst. prof. U. Wash., Seattle, 1970-73, assoc. prof., 1973-79; prof. acctg. U. Tex., Austin, 1979—, chmn. dept. acctg., 1988-92, assoc. dean, 1992-95, interim dean, 1995-2001, dean McCombs Sch. Bus., 2001—. Vis. asst. prof. Stanford U., 1972-73; dir. Fedn. Schs. Accountancy, Athens, Ga., 1982. Co-author: Accounting, 1995, Financial Accounting, 1995, Managerial Accounting, 1995, Corporate Financial Accounting, 1995; assoc. editor: the Accounting Review Recipient Notable Contbn. to Acctg. Lit. award AICPAs, 1976; named Outstanding Alumnus, Mich. State U. Dept. Acctg., 1995. Mem. Am. Acctg. Assn. (chmn. audit sect. 1988-89, pres., adminstrs. of acctg. programs 1993-94, Innovation in Acctg. Edn. award 1991, 93). Home: 7137 Valburn Dr Austin TX 78731-1812 Office: McCombs Sch Bus U Tex Deans Office 21st and Speedway GSB2 104 Austin TX 78712

MAY, ROBERT MCCREDIE, biology educator; b. Sydney, Australia, Jan. 8, 1936; s. Henry W. and Kathleen (McCredie) M.; m. Judith Feiner, Aug. 3, 1962; 1 child Naomi Felicity. BSc, Sydney U., 1956, PhD, 1959; DSc (honoris causa) (hon.) , City U. London, 1989, Uppsala U., 1990; DSc (hon.) (hon.) , Yale U., 1993, Heriot-Watt U., 1994, U. Edinburgh, 1994; DSC (hon.) (hon.) , U. Sydney, 1995. Gordon Mackay lectr. applied math Harvard U., Cambridge, Mass., 1959—61, mem. vis. faculty, 1966; theoretical physics lectr. Sydney U., 1962—64, reader, 1964—69, personal chair, 1969—73; prof. biology Princeton U., NJ, 1973—88; Royal Soc. rsch. prof. U. Oxford, England, 1989—, fellow Merton Coll. England, 1989—. Chief sci. adviser to U.K. Govt., head U.K. Office Sci. and Tech., 1995—2000; vis. faculty Calif. Inst. Tech., 1967; vis. prof. Imperial Coll., England, 1975—, UKAEA Culham Lab., 1971, Magdalen Coll., 1971; pres. Royal Soc., 2000—. Editor: Stability and Complexity in Model Ecosystems, 1973, Population Biology of Infectious Diseases, 1982, Theoretical Ecology: Principles and Applications, 1976, Perspectives in Ecological Theory, 1989, Infectious Diseases of Humans: Dynamics and Control, 1991, Extinction Rates, 1995. Decorated Order of Australia, Knighthood; recipient Crafoord prize, Royal Swedish Acad. Scis., 1996, Life Peerage, Ho. of Lords Appointments Commn., 2001. Fellow Royal Soc., Am. Acad. Arts and Scis.; mem. NAS, Athenaeum Club. Office: Dept. Zoology U. Oxford Oxford OX13PS England also: The Royal Society 6-9 Carlton House Terrace SW1Y 5AG London England E-mail: robert.may@zoo.ox.ac.uk.

MAY, RONALD ALAN, lawyer; b. Waterloo, Iowa, Sept. 8, 1928; s. John W. and Elsie (Finlayson) M.; m. Naomi Gray, Aug. 18, 1950 (div. Feb. 1974); children: Sarah, Jonathan, Andrew, Rachel; m. Susan East Gray, May 9, 1975. BA, U. Iowa, 1950; LL.B., Vanderbilt U., 1953. Bar: Ark. 1953. Atty. Daggett & Daggett, Marianna, 1953-57, Wright, Lindsey & Jennings, Little Rock, 1957-84, sr. ptnr., 1984-96, of counsel, 1996—. Editor: Automated Law Research, 1972, Sense and Systems in Automated Law Research, 1975; contbg. editor Fifty State Construction Lien and Bond Law, 1992, Fifty State Public Construction Contracting, 1996; assoc. editor Jour. Irreproducible Results. Pres. Spl. Com. on Pub. Edn., Ark. Assn. for Mental Health, Friends of Library, Central Ark. Radiation Therapy Inst.; chmn. Ark. Cancer Research Ctr., 1990-92; bd. dirs. Nat. Assn. for Mental Health, Ark. State Hosp., Gaines House, State Bd. Architects; bd. dirs. State Bd. Bar Examiners, chmn. 1987-88, Ark. ethics com., 1991-93; trustee Mus. Sci. and Natural History, Little Rock, chmn., 1973; mem. profl. adv. bd. sch. architecture U. Ark., 1990-96, mem. profl. adv. bd. sch. urban studies and design, 1993—; mem. human rsch. adv. com. U. Ark. for Med. Scis., 2000—. Served with AUS, 1946-47. Mem. ABA (chmn. sci. and tech. sect. 1975-76), Ark., Pulaski County Bar Assns., Internat. Assn. Def. Counsel, Am. Inns of Ct. (Master of the Bench), Assn. for Computing Machinery, Order of Coif, Phi Beta Kappa. Republican. Episcopalian. Home: 821 Ash St Little Rock AR 72205-2051 Office: Wright Lindsey & Jennings 200 W Capitol Ave Ste 2200 Little Rock AR 72201-3699 E-mail: rmay@wlj.com.

MAY, STEPHEN, writer, former government official; b. Rochester, N.Y., July 30, 1931; s. Arthur J. and Hilda (Jones) M. Grad., Wesleyan U., 1953; LL.B., Georgetown U., 1961. Bar: N.Y. 1963. Exec. asst. to Rep. and Senator Kenneth B. Keating, 1955-64; asso., mem., then ptnr. Branch, Turner & Wise, Rochester, 1965-81; city councilman-at-large, 1966-73; mayor, 1970-73; chmn. and commr. N.Y. State Bd. Elections, Albany, 1975-79; asst. sec. for legis. and Congl. relations Dept. Housing and Urban Devel., 1981-88; lectr. and freelance writer for newspapers and mags., 1988—. Vice chmn. Temporary State Commn. on Powers of Local Govt., 1970-73; mem. 20th Century Fund Task Force on Future of N.Y.C., 1979, Nat. Adv. Commn. Higher Edn. for Police Officers, 1977-79, Joint Com. Assn. Bar City N.Y. and Drug Abuse Council on N.Y. Drug Law Evaluation, 1977-78; chmn. Rochester Interfaith Com. on Israel, 1973-81; del.-at-large Republican Nat. Conv., 1972; mem. N.Y. State Crime Control Planning Bd., 1970-73 Contbr. numerous articles on Am. art, culture and hist. preservation to newspapers and periodicals. Bd. dirs. Police Found., 1970-81, Nat. Com. for Labor Israel, 1977-81, Empire State Report, 1974-81, Inst. Mediation and Conflict Resolution, 1973-81. Served with U.S. Army, 1953-55. Mem. Phi Beta Kappa. Home and Office: 4101 Cathedral Ave NW Washington DC 20016-3585 also: 270 Mt Pleasant Rd Union ME 04862-3003

MAY, STEPHEN JAMES, communications educator, writer; b. Toronto, Ont., Can., Sept. 10, 1946; s. Thomas and Claire (Thompson) M.; m. Caroline Casteel, Sept. 27, 1947; 1 child, Trevor. BA, Calif. State U., Carson, 1975; MA, Calif. State U., L.A., 1977; DLitt, Internat. U., London, 1990. Prof. and chair dept. of English and Lit. Pikes Peak C.C., Colorado Springs, Colo., 1980-91; prof. Colo. N.W. C.C., Craig, 1992-98; chair dept. of English and Lit. Pikes Peak C.C., Colorado Springs, Colo., 1998—2001; vis. prof. U. No. Colo., 2001—. Advisor Internat. Biog. Ctr., Cambridge, Eng., 1989-95; vis. prof. U. Colo., 2000—. Author: Pilgrimage, 1987, Fire From the Skies, 1990, Footloose, 1993, Zane Grey, 1997, Maverick Heart, 2000, Rascals, 2002; contbr. to profl. jours. including SouthWest Art, Ohio Review. Mem. Western Writers Am., Colo. Authors League, Zane Grey Soc., Soc. S.W. Authors, C.C. Humanities. Avocations: traveling, writing, drawing. Home: 731 Peregrine Run Fort Collins CO 80524 E-mail: stepkm@msn.com.

MAY, STERLING RANDOLPH, health association executive; b. Muskogee, Okla., Dec. 27, 1946; s. Sterling May William and Mary Catherine (Griffith) May. BA with honors, U. Kans., 1968; MS, U. Mich., 1969, PhD, 1977; M in Bus., Johns Hopkins U., 1995. Coord. Skin Bank St. Agnes Med. Ctr., Phila., 1977-79, assoc. dir. Burn Rsch., 1980, dir. Burn Rsch., 1981-83; dir. Southeastern Burn Rsch. Inst., Augusta, Ga., 1983-87; v.p. LifeCell Corp., The Woodlands, Tex., 1987-91; chief oper. officer ARC Nat. Hdqs., Arlington, Va., 1991-2000. Rsch. asst. prof. Hahnemann U. Sch. Medicine, Phila., 1979-82, rsch. assoc. prof., 1983; assoc. clin. prof. Med. Coll. Ga., 1984-87; adj. prof. U. Tex. Med. Sch., Houston, 1987-91. Editor: Care of the Burn Wound, 1985; author 84 published articles in biomed. lit., 1974—; mem. editorial bd. Jour. Burn Care and Rehab., 1982-90, Burns, 1985-92, Cryobiology, 1987-93. Mem. Soc. for Cryobiology (pres. 1989-91, chmn. 23d ann. meeting, 1986), Am. Burn Assn. (chmn. rsch. com. 1998-2000), Internat. Soc. For Burn Injuries (mem. gen. coun. 1982-90), Am. Assn. Tissue Banks (sec. 1991-93, v.p. 1993-95, pres. 1995-97, bd. govs. 1989-93), Nat. Trust for Hist. Preservation. Avocations: antique furniture, music, archaeology. Home: 1501 Crystal Dr Ste 828 Arlington VA 22202-4125 Office: Health Care Rsch 1501 Crystal Dr Ste 828 Arlington VA 22202-4125 E-mail: srmayphd@aol.com.

MAY, SUE SINGLETON, physical therapist, educator; b. Hattiesburg, Miss., Oct. 8, 1953; d. William Guy and Margret Glynn (Brown) Singleton; m. James M. May Jr., July 26, 1975; children: William Randall, Rebekah Leigh, Jonathan Lewis. BS in Phys. Therapy, U. Med. Ctr., Jackson, Miss., 1975. Registered phys. therapist, Miss.; cert. EMT. Phys. therapy cons. Laird Home Health, Forest, Miss., 1988-89; therapist, tchr. U. So. Miss., Hattiesburg, 1988-89; contract phys. therapist Forest Pub. Schs., 1989-92; staff weekend therapist Riley Hosp., Meridian, Miss., 1991; dir. phys. therapy Medicomp, Magee, 1989-94; clin. instr. Hinds Jr. Coll., Jackson, 1994-96; dir. clinic, hosp. phys. therapy Forest, Morton, 1994-96; dir. clinic, nursing home Rehability Corp., Philadelphia, 1995-96; dir. inpatient phys. therapy Jeff Anderson Med. Ctr., Meridian, 1996—. Mem. Forest Band Boosters, Forest Choral Boosters (bd. dirs., pres. 1998-2000, spl. events com.), Jr. Auxiliary (fundraising com.), Forest United Meth. Ch. (bd. dirs. 1996-97); mem. Dale Mayo Circle. Mem. Am. Phys. Therapy Assn., Miss. Phys. Therapy Assn. Methodist. Avocations: baseball, mud riding, swimming, basketball. Home: 112 1/2 Meadowhill St Forest MS 39074-3800

MAY, TIMOTHY JAMES, lawyer; b. Denver, Aug. 3, 1932; s. Thomas Henry and Helen Frances (O'Conner) M.; m. Monica Anita Gross, Aug. 24, 1957; children: Stephanie, Maureen, Cynthia, Timothy, Anthony. BA, Cath. U. Am., 1954; LLB, Georgetown U., 1957, LLM, 1960. Bar: D.C. 1957, U.S. Supreme Ct. 1961. Law clk. to judge U.S. Ct. Appeals, D.C. Cir., 1957-58; assoc. Covington & Burling, Washington, 1958-61; cons. Exec. Office of Pres. U.S., 1961-62; chief counsel subcom. on stockpile Armed Svcs. Com., U.S. Senate, 1962-63; mng. dir. Fed. Maritime Commn., 1963-66; gen. counsel U.S. Post Office Dept., 1966-69; sr. ptnr. Patton Boggs, L.L.P., 1969—. Bd. dirs. Legal Aid Soc. D.C., 1984—; pres. Coun. for Ct. Excellence, Washington, 1999—, Marine Corps Law Enforcement Found., 1996—; chmn. bd. regents Cath. U. Am., 1988-93, trustee, 1993—; pres. Holy Family of Bethlehem Found., 1997-99. Recipient Servant of Justice award Legal Aid Soc. D.C., 1997, St. Elizabeth Ann Seton award SOAR!, 1998, Caritas award Archdiocese D.C., 1998. Fellow Am. Bar Found. (life); mem. ABA (House of Dels.), Fed. Bar Assn., Bar Assn. of D.C. (pres. 1991-92, Lawyer of the Yr. award 1999), Congl. Country Club (bd. govs. 1992-98, sec. 1994-97), Nat. Christian Leadership Conf. for Israel (mem. exec. com.), Met. Club, Indian Creek Country Club (bd. dirs. 1999—, v.p. 2001—), Bal Harbour Club, Fed. City Coun., Econ. Club D.C. (bd. dirs. 2001—), Knight of Malta, Constantinian Order St. George (knight). Democrat. Roman Catholic. Home: 3828 52nd St NW Washington DC 20016-1924 Office: Patton Boggs LLP 2550 M St NW Washington DC 20037-1350 Address: 286 Bal Bay Dr Bal Harbour FL 33154 E-mail: tmay@pattonboggs.com.

MAY, WALTER GRANT, chemical engineer, educator; b. Saskatoon, Sask., Can., Nov. 28, 1918; came to U.S., 1946, naturalized, 1954; s. George Alfred and Abigail Almira (Robson) M.; m. Mary Louise Stockan, Sept. 26, 1945 (dec. 1977); children: John R., Douglas W., Caroline O; m. Helen Dickerson, 1988. B.Sc., U. Sask., Saskatoon, 1939, M.Sc., 1942; Sc.D., M.I.T., 1948. Registered profl. engr., Ill. Chemist British Am. Oil Co., Moose Jaw, Sask., 1939-40; asst. prof. U. Sask., 1943-46; with Exxon Research & Engring. Co., Linden, N.J., 1948-83; sr. sci. adv., 1976-83; prof. U. Ill., 1983-90, prof. emeritus, 1990—. With Advanced Research Projects Agy., Dept. Def., 1959-60; industry based prof. Stevens Inst. Tech., 1968-74, Rensselaer Poly. Inst., 1975-77 Recipient Process Indsl. Div. award ASME, 1972 Fellow Am. Inst. Chem. Engrs.; mem. Am. Inst. Chem. Engrs. (Chem. Engring. Practice award 1989), Nat. Acad. Engring. Home: 916 W Clark St Champaign IL 61821-3328 Office: U Ill Dept Chem Engring 1209 W California Ave Urbana IL 61801-3705 E-mail: w-may@uiuc.edu.

MAY, WILLIAM FRANCIS, ethicist, educator; b. Chgo., Oct. 25, 1927; s. Harry Stuart and Leontine Frances (Torczynski) M.; m. Beverly Wilson May, June 28, 1952; children: Catherine, Theodore, David, Elisabeth. AB, Princeton U., 1948; BD, Yale U., 1952, PhD, 1962. Ordained minister Presbyn. Ch. From lectr. to assoc. prof. Smith Coll., Northampton, Mass., 1952—66, chmn. dept., 1959-62, 64-66; prof. Ind. U., Bloomington, Ind., 1966—80, chmn., founder religious studies dept., 1971-76; J.P. Kennedy prof. Christian ethics Georgetown U., Washington, 1980-85; Cary M. Maguire prof. ethics So. Meth. U., Dallas, 1985—2001, dir. Cary M. Maguire Ctr. for Ethics and Pub. Responsibility, 1995—98. Founding fellow Hastings Ctr. Author: A Catalogue of Sins, 1967, The Physician's Covenant, 1983, 2d edit., 2000, The Patient's Ordeal, 1991, Testing the Medical Covenant: Active Euthanasia and Health Care Reform, 1996, The Ethics of Giving and Receiving, 2000, Beleaguered Rulers: The Public Obligation of the Professional, 2001. Mem. work group on ethical founds., Clinton task force on health care reform The White House, Washington, 1993; mem. pres.'s coun. on bioethics, White House, 2002—. Lilly open faculty fellow, 1976-77, Guggenheim Found. fellow, 1978-79. Mem. Am. Acad. Religion (pres. 1974-75, Outstanding Tchr. in Religious Studies award 1993), Soc. for Values in Higher Edn., Soc. for Christian Ethics (pres. 2002). Democrat. Presbyterian. Avocations: golf, hiking, music. Home: RR 1 Box 1440 Berlin NH 03570-9716 Office: 9444 Viewside Dr Dallas TX 75231-1504

MAY, WILLIAM FREDERICK, manufacturing executive; b. Chgo., Oct. 25, 1915; s. Arthur W. and Florence (Hartwick) M.; m. Kathleen Thompson, June 14, 1947; children: Katherine Hartwick (Mrs. Edward W. Bickford), Elizabeth Shaw. BS, U. Rochester, 1937; grad. Advanced Mgmt. Program, Harvard, 1950; D in Engring., Clarkson U.; LLD, Okla. Christian Coll.; LHD, Livingstone U.; LLD, Lafayette U. Research worker E.I. Du Pont de Nemours Co., 1937-38; with Am. Can Co., 1940-80, mgr., 1957-58, v.p., 1958-64, exec. v.p., 1964-65, vice chmn. bd. dirs., 1965, chmn. bd. dirs., chief exec. officer, 1965-80, mem. exec. com. Conn., 1960—. Dean Grad. Sch. Bus. Adminstrn., NYU, 1980-84; chmn. and chief exec. officer Statue of Liberty Found., 1984—. Bd. dirs. Lincoln Ctr.; trustee Am. Ditchley Found., Am. Mus. Natural History, Columbia-Presbyn. Hosp., U. Rochester; mem. corp. Poly. Inst. N.Y.; chmn. pub. policy council Advt. Council. Mem. Nat. Order of Merit (France, officier), Econ. Club, Round Hill Club, Meguntícook Golf Club, Phi Beta Kappa, Alpha Delta Phi. Episcopalian. Home: 84 Indian Harbor Dr Greenwich CT 06830-7148 Office: Statue of Liberty Found 292 Madison Ave New York NY 10017-7769 E-mail: w.k.may@aol.com.

MAYA, IVAN DARIO, internist; b. Bogota, Colombia, May 3, 1961; s. Ivan and Agustina (Cortes) M.; m. Patricia Alvarado, Aug. 10, 1985; children: Joanna, Nancy, Jessica. MD, Juan N. Corpas Sch. Medicine, Suba, Colombia, 1983. Diplomate Am. Bd. Internal Medicine. Intern, resident U. Ala. Birmingham, Montgomery, 1994-97; staff Bapt. Med. Ctr., 1997—; instr. medicine internal medicine U. Ala. Birmingham, 1998—. Phys. asst. Dept. Def., Eglin AFB, Fla., 1990-94; med. officer VA Hosp., Montgomery, 1995—; attending physician Bapt. Med. Ctr., Montgomery, 1997—; contract clin. dir. FPC Maxwell, Montgomery, 1997-98; instr. medicine Montgomery internal medicine residency program U. Ala., Birmingham, 1998—. Recipient awards Fed. Bur. Prisons, 1991, 92, 93. Fellow ACP, Am. Soc. Internal Medicine; mem. AMA, Med. Assn. State Ala. Roman Catholic. Avocations: reading, music, family. Office: 4371 Narrow Lane Rd Ste 200 Montgomery AL 36116-2975 Fax: 334 613-6191. E-mail: ivmaya@hotmail.com.

MAYBAY, DUANE CHARLES, recycling systems executive; b. Ft. Dodge, Iowa, Oct. 5, 1922; s. John H. and Florabel (Hibbard) Lungren; m. Mary Trible Parrish, Dec. 18, 1947 (div. Oct. 1972); children: Tina Biggs, Karen Woodward. BA in Mktg., U. Wis., 1948. Product engr. Gates Rubber Co., Denver, 1948-50; asst. dir. sales & mktg. Hi-C divsn. Hi-C and Snow Crop Divsn. Minute Maid Corp., N.Y.C., 1951-63; mktg. dir. Knudsen Foods, L.A., 1963-70; owner Mountain Foods, Altadena, Calif., 1970-76, Maybay Recycling Sys., Irvine, 1976-84; ptnr. Resource Recovery Sys., 1984—. Served to lt. col. U.S. Army Air Corps, 1943-45, Italy. Avocation: antiques. Home: 104 Pergola Irvine CA 92612-1704 Office: Peterson Maybay Inc PO Box 17426 Irvine CA 92623-7426 E-mail: dcmaybay@aol.com.

MAYBERRY, HERBERT SYLVESTER, lawyer; b. Enid, Okla., Jan. 20, 1927; s. Herbert Sylvester and Pearl Wilma (Bridal) M.; m. Gladys Anne Cody, Nov. 21, 1951 (div. Feb. 1974); children: Martha Rebecca, Molly Nanette; m. Joan Wilma Burnette, Dec. 28, 1974. BS in Geology, U. Okla., 1949; JD, U. Denver, 1959. Bar: Colo. 1959, Tex. 1979. Geologist Shell Oil Co., Denver, 1949-58; mgr. Ball Assocs. Ltd., 1958-65; exec. asst. Western Geophys. Co., Shreveport, La., 1965-66; v.p., gen. counsel, sec. McAlester (Okla.) Fuel Co., 1966-81; assoc. gen. counsel Enstar Corp., Houston, 1977-84; v.p., gen. counsel, sec. Ultramar Oil and Gas Co., 1985-89; pvt. practice Grand Junction, Colo., 1989—. With USNR, 1945-46. Mem.: ABA, Am. Assn. Petroleum Geologists. Home: 1701 Cortland Ct Grand Junction CO 81506-5247

MAYBURY, GREG J. academic administrator; b. Hamilton, Ohio, July 23, 1951; s. Edward Charles and Betty Jeanne (Eicher) M.; m. Kathryn Ann Maybury, June 21, 1980; children: Christopher James, Kyle Edward, Kevin Greg. AB, Dartmouth Coll., 1973; MS, U. Ill., 1979. Instr. math. Choate Sch., Wallingford, Conn., 1973-77; mem. math. and computer faculty Parkland Coll., Champaign, Ill., 1980-88, v.p., 1988-90; dir. computing and info. tech. Hope Coll., Holland, Mich., 1990-92, dir. info. systems and adminstrv. svcs., 1992—. Mem. Am. Assn. Computing Machinery, Math. Assn. Am., Educom, Cause. E-mail: maybury@hope.edu.

MAYDA, JARO, lawyer, educator, writer, consultant; b. Brno, Czechoslovakia; came to U.S., 1949, naturalized, 1955; s. Francis and Maria (Hornova) M.; m. Maruja del Castillo, 1967; children by previous marriage: Jaro II, Maria Raquel, Pavel. Dr. Juris Utriusque, Masaryk U., Brno, 1945; JD (Rockefeller fellow 1955-56), U. Chgo., 1957. Legal counsel export div. Skodaworks, Pilsen-Prague, 1946-48; vis. prof. polit. sci. Denison U., Granville, Ohio, 1949-50, Ohio State U., Columbus, 1950-51; asst. prof. law and polit. sci. U. Wis.-Madison, 1951-56; mem. faculty U. P.R., Rio Piedras, 1957-89, prof. law and public policy, 1958-85, research prof., 1985-89; dir. Inst. Policy Studies and Law, 1972-75, spl. asst. to pres., 1972. Fulbright research prof. Inst. Comparative Law, U. Paris, 1967-68; fellow Woodrow Wilson Internat. Ctr. for Scholars, 1971; Bailey lectr. La. State U., 1969; lectr. Am. specialist program Dept. State, 1960, Fed. Office of Environ., Berlin, 1983, UN Ctr. for Formation in Environ. Scis., Madrid, 1983, Grad. Sch. Bus. Adminstn., IESA, Caracas, Venezuela, 1987, U.S. Info. Agy. (German Democratic Republic, Czechoslovakia, Poland), 1988; Fulbright prof. Sch. Applied Econs., Dakar, Senegal, 1980; dep. sec. gen. 42d Conf. Internat. Law Assn., 1947; cons. Internat. Assn. Legal Sci., UNESCO, 1972-85, FAO, 1974-79, UN Environ. Program, 1977-95, UN Econ. and Social Commn. for Asia and Pacific, 1977-78, UN Econ. Commn. for Europe, 1981, World Bank, 1994, Govt. of Columbia, 1974, Govt. of Honduras, 1977, Govt. of St. Vincent and the Grenadines, 1983, AID, Haiti, 1985, Govts. of Mozambique, Guinea-Bissau, 1991, Chile, 1992, China, 1993, São Tomé & Principe, 1994; mem., policy adv. Gov.'s Study Group P.R. and Sea, 1972; research assoc. Ctr. Energy and Environ. Research, U. P.R.-U.S. Dept. Energy, 1977-88; adviser P.R. Environ. Quality Bd., 1984-86; mem. com. environ. policy and law Internat. Union Conservation Nature, 1972-78; mem. adv. com. Internat. Juridicial Orgn., Rome, 1991—; adv. panel on Ecosystem Data Handbook, NSF, 1976-77; mem. Internat. Council Environ. Law, Bonn, Ger., 1974— ; U.S. rapporteur X Internat. Congress Comparative Law, Budapest, 1978; reporter on comparative legislation Congress on Forest Mgmt. and Environment, Madrid, 1984, Environ. Penal Law Internat. Symposium, San Juan, P.R., 1991, Globalization and Environment Conf. on Wider Caribbean, San Juan, 1994, NATO Advanced Rsch. Workshop on integrated assessment, Durham, N.C., 1995, Izmir, 1996; lectr. Academia Istropolitana, Bratislava, 1994, Internat. Seminar on Environ. Impact, Moscow, 1995. Author: Introduction to Law, 1959, 74, Environment and Resources: From Conservation to Ecomanagement, 1967, François Geny and Modern Jurisprudence, 1978, Policy Research and Development: Outline of a Methodology, 1979, UNEP Manual on Environ. Legis., 1979; also articles, manuals; translator: law treatises; mem. editl. bd.: Am. Jour. Comparative Law, 1958-78; dir.: U. P.R. Law Rev, 1958-62; contbr. to Ency. Environ. Law, Berlin, 1987, 93. Home and Office: R Pedro de Ornelas 12-B 9050-069 Funchal Madeira Portugal

MAYDEN, BARBARA MENDEL, lawyer; b. Chattanooga, Sept. 18, 1951; d. Eugene Lester Mendel and Blanche (Krugman) Rosenberg; m. Martin Ted Mayden, Sept. 14, 1986. AB, Ind. U., 1973; JD, U. Ga., 1976. Bar: Ga. 1976, N.Y. 1980. Assoc. King & Spalding, Atlanta, 1976-79, Willkie Farr & Gallagher, N.Y.C., 1980, Morgan Lewis & Bockius, N.Y.C., 1980-82, White & Case, N.Y.C., 1982-89; spl. counsel Skadden, Arps, Slate, Meagher & Flom, 1989-95; mem. Bass, Berry & Sims PLC, Nashville, 1996—; lectr. Vanderbilt U. Sch. Law, 1995-97. Mem. bd. visitors U. Ga. Sch. Law, Athens, 1986—89; mem. Leadership Nashville, 1999—2000; mem. adv. bd. Women's Fund of the Cmty. Found. of Mid. Tenn., 2001—; bd. dirs. YWCA, 2001—, Jewish Cmty. Ctr., 2001—02. Fellow Am. Bar Found. (life); mem. ABA (sec. 2001-2002, vice chmn. 2002-, bus. law sect., chair young lawyers div. 1985-86, house of dels. 1986—, commr. commn. on women 1987-91, commr. commn. opportunities for minorities in profession 1986-87, chmn. assembly resolutions com. 1990-91, select com. of the house 1989-91, membership com. of the house 1991-92, chair com. on rules and calendar 1996-98, bd. govs. 1991-94, chair bd. govs. ops. com., exec. com. 1993-94, mem. task force long range fin. planning 1993-94, com. scope correlation of work 1998—, chair 2001-2002), Nat. Assn. Bond Lawyers (bd. dirs. 1985-86), Bond Attys.' Workshop (chmn. 1986), N.Y. State Bar Assn. (mem. ho. of dels. 1993-95), Assn. of Bar of City of N.Y. (internat. human rights com. 1986-89, 2d century com. 1986-90, com. women in the profession, 1989-92), N.Y. County Lawyers Assn. (com. spl. projects, chair com. rels with other bars), Am. Law Inst. Democrat. Jewish. Home: 4414 Herbert Pl Nashville TN 37215-4544 Office: Bass Berry & Sims PLC 315 Deaderick St Ste 2700 Nashville TN 37238-0002 E-mail: bmayden@bassberry.com.

MAYEDA, AKILA, molecular biologist; b. Kyoto, Japan, Apr. 22, 1958; BS, Saitama (Japan) U., 1983; PhD, U. Tsukuba, Ibaraki, Japan, 1989. Postdoctoral fellow Kyushu U., Fukuoka, Japan, 1989-90, Cold Spring Harbor (N.Y.) Lab., 1990-93, staff assoc., 1993-94, staff rsch. investigator, 1995-98; asst. prof. U. Miami Sch. Medicine, 1998—. Mem. Molecular Biology Soc. Japan, RNA Soc. Office: U Miami Sch Medicine 1011 NW 15th St Miami FL 33136-1019

MAYEKAWA, MARY MARGARET, education counselor; b. Neptune, N.J., Nov. 13, 1941; d. Willis Gilbert and Thelma Anita Virginia (Anderson) Bills; m. Jackie Toshio Mayekawa, Nov. 28, 1970; 1 child, Leland Willis Magokichi. BA, Western Ky. U., 1965; postgrad., U. Va., 1966-68; MEd in Counseling, Coll. of William and Mary, 1971. Educator Fairfax County Schs., Annandale, Va., 1965-68; project transition counselor U.S. Army, Ft. Hood, Tex., 1971-73; student officer wives liason U.S. Army Transp. Sch., Ft. Eustis, Va., 1980-83; guidance counselor U.S. Army Japan IX Corp, Japan, 1983-87, 2nd Infantry Divsn., Korea, 1987-89, USAF, Reese AFB, Tex., 1989—. Vol. Edn. Divsn. Tex. Tech. Mus., Lubbock, 1990—, mem. women's coun., 1990—; vestry Episcopal Ch., Okinawa and Sagamihara City, Japan, 1974, 76, 84-86; counselor Camp Blue Yonder, Reese AFB, Tex., 1989—. Capt. U.S. Army, 1968-71. Mem. Am. Counselor Assn., Mil. Educator Counselor Assn., Tex. Assn. for Counseling and Devel., Tex. Career Guidance Assn. Avocations: Japanese flower arranging, Japanese dollmaking, church activities, reading. Home: PO Box 16233 Lubbock TX 79490-6233

MAYER, ALLAN, media consultant, writer; b. N.Y.C., Mar. 15, 1950; s. Theodore H. and Phyllis (Zwick) M. BA, Cornell U., 1971. Staff reporter Wall Street Jour., N.Y.C., 1972-73; assoc. editor, gen. editor Newsweek mag., 1973-77, fgn. corr. London, 1977-80, sr. editor N.Y.C., 1980-82; editl. dir. Arbor House Pub., 1986-88; sr. editor Simon & Schuster, 1988-89; editor-in-chief Buzz mag., L.A., 1990-95, editor-in-chief, pub., 1996; sr. ptnr. Sitrick and Co., 1997—. Author: Madam Prime Minister, 1980, Gaston's War, 1987; co-author: Spin, 1998. Recipient award Overseas Press Club, 1974, Nat. Mag. award Am. Soc. Mag. Editors, 1978, William Allen White award City and Regional Mag. Assn., 1995-96. Mem. Writers Guild Am. E-mail: allan_mayer@sitrick.com.

MAYER, ALLAN REED, osteopath, gynecologic oncologist; b. Charleroi, Pa., Dec. 12, 1951; s. Martin and Grace Florence (Miller) M.; m. Ellen Graves, June 18, 1989; children: Michael Graves, Sarah Alexandra, David Philip. BA cum laude, Temple U., 1972; DO, Phila. Coll. Osteo. Medicine, 1977. Diplomate Am. Bd. Ob-gyn., Am. Bd. Gynecologic Oncology. Intern Walter Reed Army Med. Ctr., Washington, 1977-78, resident in ob-gyn., 1978-81; fellow in pelvic surgery U. Nairobi (Kenya)/Kenyatta Nat. Hosp., 1984-86; fellow in gynecologic oncology Yale U., New Haven, 1988-91; staff ob-gyn. Nürnberg (Germany) Army Hosp., 1981-83, chief ob-gyn. svc., 1983-84; chief gen. gynecology William Beaumont Army Med. Ctr., El Paso, Tex., 1986-88; divsn. chief gynecologic oncology Brooke Army Med. Ctr., San Antonio, 1991-93, Walter Reed Army Med. Ctr., Washington, 1993-96, chmn. dept. ob-gyn., 1996-99; co-dir. divsn. gynecologic oncology St. Francis Hosp. and Med. Ctr., Hartford, Conn., 1999—. Col. Med. Corps, U.S. Army, 1977-99, ret. 1999. Recipient Nat. Faculty award for Excellence in Resident Edn., 2000, Excellence in Tchg. award assn. of Profs. of Gynecology and Obstetrics, 2001; Lt. Gen. Claire L. Chennault Outstanding Tchr. award Walter Reed Army Med. Ctr., 1998, Legion of Merit medal, 1999; named "A" Proficiency Designator U.S. Army Surgeon Gen., 1995. Fellow ACS, ACOG (Outstanding Exhibit award 1988-89); mem. AMA, Soc. Gynecologic Oncologists, Internat. Assn. Gynecologic Oncologists. Democrat. Jewish. Avocations: art, swimming. Home: 1161 Prospect Ave Hartford CT 06105-1128 Office: St Francis Hosp and Med Ctr Dept Ob-Gyn 1000 Asylum Ave Ste 2110 Hartford CT 06105-1719 Fax: 860-714-8880. E-mail: amayer@stfranciscare.org.

MAYER, ANDREW MARK, librarian, journalist; b. N.Y.C., Feb. 9, 1947; s. Richard J. and Helen A. Mayer; m. Hyacinth P. Franklin, Jan. 19, 1972 (div. May 1976); m. Carmen Mercedes Zapata-Gomez, Feb. 28, 1988; 1 child, Andrew Charles. Student, Hillsdale Coll., 1964-67; BA in History, George Washington U., 1968, MA in History, 1971; postgrad., Georgetown U., 1977; proofreading, copyediting cert., NYU, 1992; MA TESOL, Hunter Coll., 1999. Rschr. Glaverbel S.A., Brussels, 1966; libr. asst. rsch. Washington Post Co., 1969-73, asst. libr. rsch., 1973-87, night coord. rsch. newsroom, 1987-92; rsch. libr. Bituminous Coal Operators Assn., Washington, 1971; rschr., editor to author Donald Neff, 1981-84; pres. cons. Latin Am. Rsch. Assn., 1984; libr., rschr. Ctr. for Strategic Internat. Studies, 1986-87; libr. pub. rels. Sawyer/Miller Group, N.Y.C., 1992; libr. newspaper N.Y. Law Pub. Co., 1994; rsch. analyst Ctr. for Pub. Comm., 1994—. V.p. R.J. Mayer & Co., N.Y.C., 1984—; book reviewer Small Press Pub. (now Ind. Pub.), R.I., 1992—, Army Times Pub. Co., Washington, 1972-75; freelance writer Washington Post Co., 1976—, temp. instr. ESL, Inc., Wagner Coll., S.I., N.Y., 1999, proofreader, S.I. IslandBot. Gardens, Chinese Scholar's Project, Snug H arbor, S.I., 1999; fact checker US Weekly, 2000—. Active McGovern for Pres. campaign, Washington, 1972; rschr. Dem. Nat. Com., Washington, 1971; active U.S. Holocaust Meml. Mus., Washington, 1992—. Mem. Am. Hist. Assn. (writer for hist. convs. 1976—), Modern Hist. Soc., Spl. Librs. Assn., Phi Alpha Theta. Jewish. Avocations: tennis, dramatic arts, music, literature, soccer. Home and Office: 181 Roosevelt Ave Staten Island NY 10314-4152

MAYER, ANTHONY JOHN, investment company executive; b. Milw., Apr. 21, 1936; s. Anton J. and Mary (Plesnk) M. BS, Marquette U., 1958, postgrad., 1965. Pvt. investor, Milw., 1968—; pres. Anthony J. Mayer, Inc., 1994—; mng. dir. Banc One Investment Mgmt. Group, Muskego, 2001—. Chmn. Millionaire Investor Entities Guidance.Com, 2000—. Author: Anthony J. Mayer Investment Bible, 1995, Anthony J. Mayer Investment Parables, 1995; editor (newsletter) Anthony J. Mayer Investment Bible, 1995-98; investment radio personality, 1990-93; country music seminar host, 1995; contbr. articles to fin. mags.. Trustee Anthony J. Mayer Trust, 1991—, Jesuit Ptnrs., 1998—; mem. Ignatius Loyola Inner Circle, 1999—; pres. Pub. Lands Decor Classics, 2000—; bd. dirs. West Allis Food for Milw.; del. Adv. Coun. Nat. Rep. Congl. Com., 2001—; hon. sponsor Pres. Bush victory dinner, 2001. With U.S. Army, 1958-60. Named Successful Investor of Yr. Sta. WGN, 1996, Notable Pulaskian, Milw. Pub. Sys. Sch., 1999; recipient VIP award Speedway-Super Am., 1995, 2000; featured in Reader's Digest mag. article, 1990. Mem. Acad. Country Music, N.Am. Investors Alliance (founder, chair 1993). Roman Catholic. Avocation: reading.

MAYER, CARL JOSEPH, prosecutor, lawyer; b. Boston, Apr. 23, 1959; s. Arno Joseph and Nancy Sue (Grant) M. AB magna cum laude, Princeton U., 1981; JD, U. of Chgo., 1986; LLM, Harvard U., 1988. Bar: N.J. 1986, Mass. 1988, N.Y. 1989, D.C. 1989. Writer for Ralph Nader, Washington, 1981-83; law clk. to presiding justice U.S. Dist. Ct., Wilmington, Del., 1986-87; law assoc., prof. Hofstra Law Sch., Hempstead, N.Y., 1989-94; atty. Milberg, Weiss, Bershad, Hynes and Lerach, N.Y.C., 1995-96; spl. counsel N.Y. State Atty. Gen.'s Office, 1999—. Cons. U.S. Senate Com., Washington, 1988-89. Author: Shakedown, 1998; co-author: Public Domain, Private Dominion, 1985; contbr. articles to profl. jours. Town committeeman, Princeton, N.J., 1995-98. NYU fellow, 1988-89. Mem. ABA, N.Y. Bar Assn., N.J. Bar Assn., Mass. Bar Assn. Avocations: marathon running, squash, tennis. Home: 58 Battle Rd Princeton NJ 08540-4902 Office: NY State Atty Gen Office 120 Broadway New York NY 10271-0002 E-mail: carlmayer@aol.com.

MAYER, CHARLES ARTHUR, management consultant, musician; b. Salt Lake City, Oct. 6, 1949; s. Robert C. and Barbara (Arthur) M.; m. Carolyn Familetti, June 21, 1975 (div. June 1989); 1 child, George. BS in Indsl. Mgmt., Purdue U., 1971; MBA, Temple U., 1978. Cert. mgmt. cons. Systems analyst Burroughs Corp., Detroit, 1972-76; cons. Pinkerton Computer Cons., Phila., 1976-79, Coopers & Lybrand, Phila., 1979-82, Deloitte Haskins & Sells, Phila., 1982-85; prin. Mayer Computer Solutions, Merion Station, Pa., 1985—. Pres. Merion Park Civic Assn., Merion Station, Pa., 1979-80; Uptown String Band, (treas., 1999—). Mem. Inst. Mgmt. Cons. (chpt. pres. 1987-89), Cynwyd Club (treas. 1986-94). Office: PO Box 368 Merion Station PA 19066-0368

MAYER, ELIZABETH BILLMIRE, educational administrator; B.Ed., Nat. Coll. Edn., Evanston, Ill., 1953; M.A. in Liberal Studies, Wesleyan U., 1979. Teaching asst. Hull House, Chgo., 1950-51; teaching scholar Nat. Coll. Edn. Demonstration Sch., 1952-53; pre-sch. tchr. St. Matthew's Sch., Pacific Palisades, Calif., 1959-63, tchr. 2d grade, 1963-67; librarian Chandler Sch., Pasadena, Calif., 1971-72, tchr. 4th grade, 1972-80, curriculum coordinator 1st-8th grades, 1979-80, tchr. 4th-6th grades Inst. for Experimentation in Tchr. Edn., SUNY-Cortland, 1980; asst. prof. edn. SUNY-Cortland, 1980-82; founder, headmistress The Mayer Sch., Ithaca, N.Y., 1982-92, Ariz. State U., Tempe, 1992—, Coll. Edn., 1992-94, faculty liaison Acad. Affairs, 1994—. Mem. Nat. Council Tchrs. Math., Nat. Council Tchrs. English, Nat. Sci. Tchrs. Assn., Rotary Internat. (mem. bd. dirs. 1994-96), Phi Delta Kappa (officer 1980-81, 92-96), Mem. Leadership America, class of 1995. Office: Ariz State U PO Box 870101 Tempe AZ 85287-0101

MAYER, ERNEST, consulting chemical engineer; b. N.Y.C., Jan. 9, 1939; s. Ernst and Theresa (Dosch) M.; m. Irene S. Bogdanowicz, Mar. 19, 1961; children: Sandra, Eric. BSChemE, Columbia U, 1963, MSChemE, 1964; PhDChemE, U. Del., 1969. Chem. engr. E.I. du Pont de Nemours & Co., Wilmington, Del., 1963-75, sr. chem. engring. cons. Newark, 1980—; chem. engr. Pfizer Co., Easton, Pa., 1976-80. Contbr. numerous articles in field of environ. and separation fields to profl. jours. Mem. AIME, Am. Inst. Chem. Engrs., Am. Water Works Assn., Water Pollution Control Fedn., Am. Electroplaters and Surface Finishers Soc., Am. Filtration Soc., N.Y. Acad. Scis., Hazardous Materials Control Rsch. Inst., Tau beta Pi. Achievements include patents on new iron-oxide pigment and nylon salt filtration process. Home: 806 Highfield Dr Newark DE 19713-1104 Office: Dupont 1007 S Market St Wilmington DE 19801-5227

MAYER, EVE ORLANS, retired public relations and marketing consultant, writer; b. Bklyn., Apr. 26, 1930; d. Abraham Salem Orlans and Rose V. Wissotsky; m. Sidney A. Mayer, Jun. 8, 1952; children: Marc Orlans Mayer and Jonathan Orlans Mayer. BA cum laude, Hunter Coll., 1951; MS, Columbia Univ., 1952. Asst. editor Human Interest Mag., N.Y.C., 1952-53; asst. prodr. Channel 5, 1953-54; publicity writer NYU, 1954-57; freelance writer, 1957—; publ. rels. dir. Parsons Sch. of Design, 1970-74, 1979-84; owner, prin. Eve Orlans Mayer, Inc., 1984-92. Contbr. ; ghost writer, speech writer: , interviewer : Steven Spielberg's Survivors of the Shoah Visual History Found., 1993—2000. Bd. dirs., newsletter editor, writer, fundraiser CARING at Columbia, Columbia U. Coll. Phys. and Surg., 1995; mem. alumni exec. com. Columbia U. Grad. Sch. Journalism, Dem. Congl. Campaign Com. Recipient Disting. Svc. medal, Columbia U. Alumni, 2002. Mem. Hadassah Women's Zionist Orgn. Am. (events fundraising cons.), World Jewish Congress, Anti-Defamation League, Am. Jewish Congress, NARAL, NOW, Planned Parenthood, Choice in Dying, Hemlock Soc., Mother's Voices, Emily's List, Phi Beta Kappa, Sigma Tau Delta. Democrat. Jewish. Avocations: theater, travel, friends, books, music. Home: 15 W 81st St Apt 8A New York NY 10024-6022 E-mail: eveomayer@aol.com.

MAYER, FRANK D., JR. lawyer; b. Dec. 23, 1933; BA, Amherst Coll., 1955; student, Cambridge U.; JD, U. Chgo., 1959. Bar: Ill. 1959. Ptnr. Mayer, Brown, Rowe & Maw, Chgo. Mem. ABA, Chgo. Bar Assn., Order of Coif, Phi Beta Kappa. Office: Mayer Brown Rowe and Maw 190 S La Salle St Ste 3100 Chicago IL 60603-3441 E-mail: fmayer@mayerbrown.com.

MAYER, GEORGE MERTON, retired elementary education educator; b. Ellisburg, N.Y., July 11, 1936; s. Carlton Scott and Florence Geraldine (Allen) M.; m. Charlotte Ann Dawley, Aug. 31, 1963; children: Linda Sue Mayer Randall, Brian Keith, Amanda Leanne Hawkins. AA, Erie County Tech. Inst., 1957; BA in Edn., SUNY, Buffalo, 1966, MEd, 1973. Cert. tchr., N.Y. Lab. tech. Sylvania Electric Co., Buffalo, 1957-58; sch. driver, mechanic Ransomville (N.Y.) Bus Lines, 1959-66; coach driver Lockport (N.Y.) and Grand Island Transit Bus Lines, 1966-87; tchr. Thomas Marks Sch., Wilson, N.Y., 1965-82; tchr. remedial math. Wilson Sch. Dist., 1982-96; ret., 1996. Coach wrestling Wilson High Sch., 1977-88, coach jr. varsity football, 1972. Lay leader, mem. choir Ransomville United Meth. Ch., 1960-90; co-chmn. Niagara County Foster Parents, 1980-93; bd. dirs. Town of Porter Recreation Commn. With N.Y. N.G., 1955-58, USAR, 1958-62. Mem. Wilson Tchrs. Assn., N.Y. State United Tchrs. Assn., N.Y. State Foster and Adoptive Assn. Republican. Avocations: music, electronics, sports, woodworking. Home: 2470 Youngstown Lockport Rd Ransomville NY 14131-9644 E-mail: geochar63@adelphia.net.

MAYER, GEORGE ROY, educator; b. National City, Calif., Aug. 28, 1940; s. George Eberly and Helen Janet (Knight) M.; m. Barbara Ann Fife, Sept. 9, 1964 (div. June 1986); children: Kevin Roy, Debbie Rae Ann; m. Jocelyn Volk Finn, Aug. 3, 1986. BA, San Diego State U., 1962; MA, Ind. U., 1965, EdD, 1966. Cert. sch. psychologist; bd. cert. behavior analyst. Sch. counselor, psychologist Ind. U., Bloomington, 1964-66; asst. prof. guidance and ednl. psychology So. Ill. U., Carbondale, 1966-69; profl. edn. Calif. State U., L.A., 1966—. Cons. in field; mem. adv. bd. Dept. Spl. Edn., L.A., 1986—, Alamansor Edn. Ctr., Alhambra, Calif., 1986-90, Jay Nolan Ctr. for Autism, Newhall, Calif., 1975-86; lectr. in field; mem. study group on youth violence prevention Nat. Ctr. for Injury Prevention and Control, Divsn. Violence Prevention of the Ctrs. for Disease Control and Prevention, 1998. Author: Classroom Management: A California Resource Guide, 2000; co-author: Behavior Analysis for Lasting Change, 1991; contbr. articles to profl. jours. Recipient Outstanding Prof. award Calif. State U.-L.A., 1988; U.S. Dept. Edn. grantee, 1996—. Mem. Assn. for Behavior Analysis, Nat. Assn. Sch. Psychologists, Calif. Assn. Behavior Analysis (pres., Outstanding Contbr. to Behavior Analysis award 1997, hon. life), Cambridge Ctr. for Behavioral Studies (adv. bd.), Calif. Assn. Sch. Psychologists (chmn. practitioners conf. 1994—). Avocations: horseback riding, fishing, swimming. Home: 10600 Pinyon Ave Tujunga CA 91042-1517 E-mail: grmayer@aol.com.

MAYER, HALDANE ROBERT, federal chief judge; b. Buffalo, Feb. 21, 1941; s. Haldane Rupert and Myrtle Kathleen (Gaude) Mayer; m. Mary Anne McCurdy, Aug. 13, 1966; children: Anne Christian, Rebecca Paige. BS, U.S. Mil. Acad., 1963; JD, Coll. William and Mary, 1971. Bar: Va. 1971, D.C. 1980, U.S. Ct. Appeals (4th cir.) 1972, U.S. Dist. Ct. (ea. dist.) Va. 1972, U.S. Ct. Mil. Appeals 1973, U.S. Supreme Ct. 1977, U.S. Ct. Claims 1984. Law clk. U.S. Ct. Appeals (4th cir.), Richmond, Va., 1971—72; atty. McGuire Woods & Battle, Charlottesville, 1975—77; spl. asst. to chief justice U.S. Supreme Ct., Washington, 1977—80; atty. Baker & McKenzie, 1980—81; acting spl. counsel U.S. Merit Systems Protection Bd., 1981—82; judge U.S. Claims Ct., 1982—87, U.S. Ct. Appeals (fed. cir.), Washington, 1987—97, chief judge, 1997—. Adj. prof. U. Va. Sch. Law, 1975—77, 1992—94, George Washington U. Law Sch., 1992—96. Bd. dirs. William and Mary Law Sch. Assn., 1979—85. Maj. U.S. Army, 1963—75, ret. lt. col. USAR. Decorated Bronze Star. Mem.: West Point Soc. D.C., Army Athletic Assn., West Point Assn. Grads., Omicron Delta Kappa. Office: US Ct Appeals for Fed Cir 717 Madison Pl NW Washington DC 20439-0002

MAYER, HARVEY ETHAN, educator; b. N.Y.C., Oct. 30, 1936; s. William Mayer and Bess Lewinstein. BA, Stanford U., 1959; MA, Harvard U., 1960, PhD, 1966. Cert. tchr., Calif. Asst. prof. Purdue U., Lafayette, Ind., 1963-68; prof. Calif. State U., Fullerton, 1968-80; tng. instr. Def. Lang. inst., Monterey, Calif., 1982-94. Contbr. articles to profl. jours. Petty officer 1st class USNR, 1979-85. Mem. Assn. for Advancement of Baltic Studies. Home: 800 Pennsylvania Ave Apt 23 Beaumont CA 92223-2460

MAYER, HENRI ANDRÉ VAN HUYSEN, association executive; b. New Haven, Dec. 19, 1946; s. Jean and Elizabeth (Van Huysen) M.; m. Joan Krizack; children: Pierre-André, Eve. AB, Harvard U., 1970; MA, U. Calif., Berkeley, 1971; Candidate in Philosophy, U. Calif., 1974. Sr. editor New England Bd. Higher Edn., Boston, 1981-83; various positions Mass. Bd. Regents, 1983-91; dir. planning Higher Edn. Coordinating Coun., 1991-92; sr. v.p. comm. and rsch. Associated Industries of Mass., 1992—. Adv. bd. mem. Nat. Environ. Tech. Inst., Amherst, Mass., 1995—; ednl. cons. in field. Author: King's Chapel, 1976; co-author: The Crocodile Man, 1982; contbr. articles to profl. jours. Trustee, sec. Cambridge (Mass.) Pub. Libr., 1992—; dir. Continuing Edn. Inst., Watertown, Mass., 1994—; dir. New Eng. Econ. Project, 1999—, pres., 2002. Recipient Commonwealth citation Commonwealth of Mass., 1986. Mem. Am. Hist. Assn., Boston Athenaeum. Avocation: baseball. Office: Associated Industries Mass 222 Berkeley St Boston MA 02116-3748

MAYER, IRA EDWARD, gastroenterologist; b. Bklyn., July 31, 1951; s. Elias M. and Mollie (Taxerman) M.; m. Celeste Ann Sivak, Mar. 13, 1976; children: Madelaine Rose, Amanda Beth. BS, Bklyn. Coll., 1972; MD, N.Y. Med. Coll., 1975. Diplomate Am. Bd. Internal Medicine, Am. Bd. Gastroenterology, Nat. Bd. Med. Examiners. Asst. resident in internal medicine N.Y. Med. Coll., 1975-76; resident in internal medicine Met. Hosp. Ctr., N.Y.C., 1976-78; fellow Digestive Diseases div. Emory U., Atlanta, 1978-80; assoc. attending gastroenterologist Maimonides Med. Ctr., Bklyn., 1980—; clin. instr. medicine SUNY Health Sci. Ctr., 1980-81, instr. medicine, 1981-83, clin. asst. prof. medicine, 1983—, chmn. patient care com., 1984-99. Co-chmn. operative invasive and noninvasive procedures com., Maimonides Med. Ctr. Author: (with others) Digestive Diseases, 1983, Medicine, 1983; contbr. articles to profl. jours. Fellow ACP, Am. Coll. Gastroenterology; mem. Am. Gastroent. Assn., Am. Soc. for Gastrointestinal Endoscopy, N.Y. Acad. Scis., N.Y. Acad. Gastroenterolgy, N.Y. Soc. for Gastrointestinal Endoscopy, Med. Soc. for the State of N.Y. Jewish. Office: 2560 Ocean Ave Brooklyn NY 11229-4521

MAYER, JAMES HOCK, mediator, lawyer; b. Neptune City, N.J., Nov. 1, 1935; s. J. Kenneth and Marie Ruth (Hock) M.; m. Carol I. Keating, Sept. 20, 1958 (div. Feb. 1981); children: Craig, Jeffrey; m. Patrisha Renk, Mar. 28, 1981 (div. July 2001). AB with distinction, Dartmouth Coll., 1957; JD, Harvard U., 1964. Bar: Calif. 1965, U.S. Dist. Ct (no. dist., so. dist.) Calif. 1965, U.S. Ct. Appeals (9th cir.) 1965, U.S. Supreme Ct. 1974. Assoc. Pillsbury, Madison & Sutro, San Francisco, 1964-72, ptnr., 1973—; ind. mediator, 1992—. Rear adm. USNR. 1957-93. Rufus Choate scholar Dartmouth Coll., 1956-57. Mem. Newcomen Soc., Navy League, Naval Order of U.S., Harvard Club. E-mail: just-results@msn.com.

MAYER, JAMES WILLIAM, priest, educator; b. Cleve., Aug. 29, 1965; s. James William Mayer, Sr. and Audrey Therese (Zielinski) Mayer. MDiv, St. Charles Borromeo Sem., Phila., 1991; lic. sacred theology, Lateran Pontifical U., Rome, 1993. Novice master Order of Mercy, LeRoy, NY, 1993—97, parochial vicar Cleve., 1997—2000, educator elem. sch., 1997—2000, hosp. chaplain, 1997—2000, master of students Phila., 2000—, vacation dir., 2000—, editor, 2000—. Editor: (jours.) Mercy Works, 2000—. Republican. Roman Catholic. Avocations: artist, music. Mailing: Monastery Our Lady of Mercy 6398 Drexel Rd Philadelphia PA 19151-2596

MAYER, JOYCE HARRIS, artist; b. N.Y.C., May 7, 1935; d. Harold and Dorothy H.; m. Bernard Charles Mayer, Mar. 15, 1969; 1 child, Robert Charles Mayer. AAS, Inst. of Applied Art & Sci., N.Y.C., 1957. Sketcher Merrylen Cartooning Studio, 1952. Client contact, layout artist Haire Publs., N.Y.C., 1957-59; art dir. Real Estate Forum, N.Y.C., 1959-60, Denhard & Stewart, N.Y.C., 1960-67, self employed N.Y.C., 1967-71. Among first women to have work published in Art Direction, 1964; work exhbns. include N.Y. Inst. of Applied Arts and Sci., Horizon Gallery, Royal Typographers, N.Y., Nat. Arts Club, Tulane U., Dominican Coll., Robinson Gallery, Mario Villa, and Arthur Roger, New Orleans, TWEED Gallery, Plainfield, N.J., Barbara Gillman Gallery, Miami, Contemporary Art Ctr., New Orleans, Bruce Mus., Conn.; co-curator New Orleans Mus. of Art, 1985; paintings and monoprints in numerous museums and pub. and pvt. collections in Europe and U.S. Mem. Bd. Edn., Greenwich, Conn., 1978; art advisor Freeport McMoRan Art Collection, New Orleans, 1985; curator Mario Villa Gallery, New Orleans,

1989; juror Arts Coun., New Orleans, 1990. Coll. Art Assn. Avocations: reading, attending theater, ballet, birdwatching. Home: 325 Audubon Blvd New Orleans LA 70125-4124 Address: 34 Castle Rock Branford CT 06405

MAYER, KENNETH HUGH, physician; b. N.Y.C., Dec. 27, 1950; BA, U. Pa., 1972; MD, Northwestern U., 1977; postgrad., New Eng. Epidemiology Inst., 1991. Diplomate Am. Bd. Internal Medicine, Am. Bd. Infectious Diseases. Intern, jr. and sr. resident in internal medicine Beth Israel Hosp., Boston, 1977-80; clin. fellow in infectious diseases Brigham and Women's Hosp., 1980-81, rsch. fellow in infectious diseases, 1981-83; rsch. fellow dept. microbiology and molecular genetics Harvard Med. Sch., 1981-83; assoc. staff mem. Norwood (Mass.) Hosp., 1980-83; staff physician, rsch. dir. Fenway Community Health Ctr., Boston, 1980; attending physician Beth Israel Hosp., 1981; infectious disease specialist, staff physician Meml. Hosp., Pawtucket, R.I., 1983, assoc. microbiologist, 1983, chief infectious disease divsn. RI, 1984; physician Miriam Hosp., Providence, 2001—. Clin. rsch. assoc. dept. cmty. medicine Northwestern U. Med. Sch., Chgo., 1974-77; adj. asst. prof. microbiology U. R.I., Kingstown, 1988; adj. asst. prof. epidemiology U. Mass., Amherst, 1986-89, adj. assoc. prof., 1989; asst. prof. medicine divsn. biology and medicine Sch. Medicine Brown U., Providence, 1983-88, dir. AIDS Program, 1987, assoc. prof. medicine and community health, 1989-93, prof., 1993—; lectr. continuing edn. Northeastern U., Boston, 1983; lab. instr. infectious disease pathophysiology Harvard Med. Sch., Boston, 1982, clin. instr. medicine, 1983; mem. Mayor's Ad Hoc Com. on AIDS, Boston, 1982-86; cons. R.I. State Dept. of Health Adv. Group on AIDS, 1983, Mass. Dept. Health, 1983, Health AIDS exec. task force NIH, 1986; bd. dirs. Internat. AIDS Prospective Epidemiology Network, 1985; mem. transfusion medicine curriculum rev. com. program in medicine Brown, 1985; mem. HIV program adv. com. R.I. Dept. Health, 1989; vis. scientist Clin. Rsch. Ctr., MIT, 1990; mem. sci. adv. com. Am. Found. for AIDS Rsch., 1990, bd. dirs.; lectr. in field. Mem. editl. bd. Brown U. STD Report, 1987, Case and Consensus, 1988, AIDS Alert, 1990, Jour. Clin. Microbiology, 1991, Opportunistic Infections in HIV Infected Patients, 1992, AIDS Patient Care and STDs, 1996; med. editor AIDS/HIV Treatment Directory, 1992; mem. internat. editl. adv. com. Actualizaciones en Sida, 1994, Atualizacao em AIDS, 1995; mem. editl. adv. com. Clin. Microbiology and Infection, 1995; reviewer various jours.; contbr. articles, abstracts to profl. publs., chpts. to books. Grantee NIH, 1983, 87—, R.I. Found., 1983, 87-88, Schering Corp., 1984, Squibb Pharms., 1984, Miles Pharms., 1985, 86, Commonwealth of Mass., 1985, Ctrs. for Disease Control, 1985, 91, Brown U., 1985, 91, Rhone-Poulenc Pharms., 1986, Warner-Lambert Pharms., 1987, 90, 91, Nat. Inst. Allergy and Infectious Diseases, 1987, Genetic Systems, Inc., 1987-88, Cambridge Biosci. Corp., 1987-88, Searle, Inc., 1988, Health Resources and Svc. Adminstrn., 1988-91, 96-98, Ctrs. for Disease Control, 1988-91, 96—, Abbott Labs., 1989, Bristol-Myers Pharm., 1989, Integra Inst./NIMH, 1989, World AIDS Found., 1990, Am. Found. AIDS Rsch., 1990, 91, Glaxo Pharm., 1993, Upjohn Pharm., 1993, Nat. Inst. Allergy and Infectious Diseases, 1995, 96-97, Immune Response Corp., 1996, Nat. Insts. Drug Abuse, 1997-98, Gilead Scis., 1997-98; recipient Gov.'s Recognition award for AIDS Rsch., Commonwealth of Mass., 1986, Cmty. Recognition award AIDS Action Com., Boston, 1990. Fellow ACP; mem. APHA, AAAS, Am. Fedn. for Clin. Rsch., Am. Soc. for Microbiology, Assn. for Practitioners in Infection Control, Am. Venereal Disease Assn., Infectious Disease Soc. Am. (AIDS com. 1993), Soc. for Epidemiol. Rsch., Internat. AIDS Soc., Internat. Soc. for Infectious Diseases, Internat. Acad. of Sex Rsch., Soc. for Hosp. Epidemiology, Immunocompromised Host Soc., Soc. Hosp. Epidemiologists Am. (AIDS/TB com. 1993). Jewish. Home: 369 Tappan St Apt 18 Brookline MA 02445-5372 Office: Miriam Hosp 164 Summit Ave Providence RI 02906 E-mail: Kenneth_Mayer@brown.edu

MAYER, KLAUS, hematologist, educator; b. Mainz, Germany, May 21, 1924; came to U.S. 1934; s. Stephan Karl Mayer and Caecilie Mueller; m. Vera Strasser, May 6, 1950; children: Rulon, Carla Glasser. BS, Queens Coll., 1945; MD, U. Zurich and Groningen, The Netherlands, 1950. Bd. cert. Am. Bd. Internal Medicine, Nat. Bd. Med. Examiners; lic. physician, Ohio, D.C., Vt., N.Y. Intern in medicine Hosp. St. Raphael, New Haven, 1950-51; resident in medicine Meml. Hosp. for Cancer and Allied Diseases, N.Y.C., 1952-55, spl. fellow in medicine, 1955-56; clin. asst. dept. medicine Meml. Hosp., 1951-60; attending hematologist Hosp. for Spl. Surgery, 1957—, dir. blood bank, 1958—; dir. blood bank and serology lab. dept. medicine Meml. Hosp., 1966-93, dir. hematology labs. dept. medicine, 1971—, attending physician, 1972—; attending hematologist Manhattan Eye, Ear, & Throat Hosp., 1977—; prof. clin. medicine Weil Coll. Medicine, Cornell U., 1977—; clin. assoc. prof. medicine Cornell U. Med. Coll., N.Y.C., 1968-79, prof. clin. medicine, 1979—; dir. bone marrow lab. Meml. Hosp., 1990—. Rsch. fellow divsn. clin. investigation Sloan-Kettering Inst., N.Y.C., 1954-58, rsch. assoc. sect. cancer anemia, 1958-59, asst., 1959-60, assoc., 1960-81, asst. mem., 1981-84; rsch. hematologist Hosp. for Spl. Surgery, N.Y.C., 1958-62; physician to out-patients dept. medicine N.Y. Hosp., N.Y.C., 1958-68; asst. vis. physician dept. James Ewing Hosp., N.Y.C., 1959-64, assoc. vis. physician, 1964-68; asst. vis. physician Meml. Hosp., N.Y.C., 1960-64, assoc. vis. physician, 1964-72; asst. vis. physician Bellevue Hosp., N.Y.C., 1962-68; sr. scientist Hosp. for Spl. Surgery, N.Y.C., 1963-86; rsch. collaborator Brookhaven Nat. Lab., N.Y.C., 1965-66; assoc. attending physician dept. medicine N.Y. Hosp., N.Y.C., 1968-79; assoc. chmn. clin. labs. dept. medicine Meml. Hosp., N.Y.C., 1981-93, assoc. chmn. dept. medicine; clin. mem. Meml. Sloan-Kettering Cancer Ctr., N.Y.C., 1984—. Contbr. numerous articles, abstracts, reports, and book chpts. to profl. pubs. With U.S. Army, 1943-46; col. USPHS, 1955-80; col. M.C., USAR, 1980-86. Damon Runyon Cancer Rsch. fellow, 1955-58. Fellow ACP, Am. Soc. Clin. Pathologists, N.Y. Acad. Medicine; mem. AMA, Internat. Soc. Hematology, Internat. Soc. Blood Transfusions, Am. Assn. Blood Banks (Disting. Svc. award 1976), Am. Coll. Nuclear Physicians, Am. Fedn. for Clin. Rsch., Am. Soc. Hematology, Am. Assn. Blood Banks (pres. 1973-74), N.Y. State Med. Soc., N.Y. County Med. Soc., N.Y. Soc. for Study of Blood, Soc. for Nuclear Medicine, The Harvey Soc. Home: 45 Sutton Pl S Apt 5F New York NY 10022-2445 Office: Meml Sloan-Kettering 1275 York Ave New York NY 10021-6094

MAYER, MARILYN GOODER, steel company executive; b. Chgo. d. Seth MacDonald and Jean (McMullen) Gooder; m. William Anthony Mayer, Nov. 14, 1959; children: William Anthony Jr., Robert MacDonald. Grad., Career Inst., Chgo., 1941; student, Lake Forest Coll., Ill., 1942. Adminstrv. asst. Needham, Louis & Brorby, Chgo., 1949-53; v.p. RMB Corp., 1963-71, Mayer Motors, Ft. Lauderdale, Fla., 1965-74, Gooder-Henrichsen, Chicago Heights, Ill., 1975—. Dir. Barnett Bank, West Palm Beach, Fla. Trustee Gulf Stream (Fla.) Sch.; trustee emeritus St. Andrew's Sch., Boca Raton, Fla.; bd. dirs. Bethesda Hosp. Assn., Boynton Beach, Fla., pres. 1981-82; bd. dirs. Gulf Stream Civic Assn. Mem. Soc. Four Arts, Little Bath and Tennis Club (gov. of Gulf Stream). Avocation: travel. Home: 2925 Polo Dr Delray Beach FL 33483-7331

MAYER, MICHAEL A. lawyer, educator; b. Bellvue, Nebr., Dec. 3, 1965; s. L.A. and Elizabeth S. Mayer. BS, Miami U., Oxford, Ohio, 1988; JD, U. Toledo, 1994. Bar: Ohio 1994. Judicial clk. Toledo (Ohio) Mcpl. Ct., 1993-95; asst. city prosecutor City of Fairborn, Ohio, 1995-98, law dir., 1999—; ptnr. Wolaver Mayer & Cusack, Fairborn, Ohio. Office: Wolaver Mayer & Cusack 510 W Main St Fairborn OH 45324

MAYER, MORRIS LEHMAN, marketing educator; b. Demopolis, Ala., Dec. 14, 1925; s. Lehman M. and Anne (Rochotsh) M.; m. Judith Marian Morton, Dec. 22, 1957; children: Susan Morton, Elizabeth Anne. BS in Bus. Adminstrn, U. Ala., 1949, DHL (hon.), 1994; MS in Retailing, N.Y. U., 1950; PhD in Bus. Orgn, Ohio State U., 1961. Buyer Goldblatts Dept. Store, Chgo., 1951-55; mem. faculty U. Ala., 1955—, prof., 1960—, chmn. dept. mktg., 1969-74, dir. Hess Inst. Retailing, 1985-92, Bruno prof. mktg., 1986-92; Bruno prof. mktg. emeritus, 1992—; instr. Ohio State U., Columbus, 1956-60. Cons. Mgmt. Horizons Co., Columbus, 1966-70, N.C.R. Co., Dayton, Ohio, 1967-75. Co-author: Modern Retailing, 1978, 6th edit., 1993, Retailing, 1981, 5th edit., 1993. Served with AUS, 1944-46, 50-51. Recipient Teaching Excellence award Burlington No. Found., 1986, Distinctive Image award Jewish Childrens Regional Svc. Bd., 1997, Circle of Honor award Direct Selling Edn. Found., 1997; Ford Found. fellow, 1962-63, So. Mktg. fellow, 1986; named to U. Ala. Bus. Faculty Hall of Fame, 1995, Retail Patronage Acad. Hall of Fame, 1995; Morris Mayer Endowed scholarship established 1992; Morris L. Mayer award established U. Ala., 1993; Morris L. Mayer Outstanding Sutdent award established Sales and Mktg. Execs., 1993, others. Mem. Am. Mktg. Assn. (Morris L. Mayer Outstanding Mem. award estab. Birmingham chpt. 1993), So. Mktg. Assn. (pres.), Ala. Retail Assn. (bd. dirs.), Am. Coll. Retail Assn. (pres., Hall of Fame 1992, Mortar Bd., Beta Gamma Sigma, Eta Mu Pi, Pi Sigma Epsilon, Omicron Delta Kappa, Zeta Beta Tau (chpt. trustee). Jewish (temple trustee). Home: 1321 Montclair Cir Tuscaloosa AL 35404-4241 Office: U Ala PO Box 870225 Tuscaloosa AL 35487-0154

MAYER, NEAL MICHAEL, lawyer; b. N.Y.C., Dec. 4, 1941; s. Joseph Henry and Cele (Brodsky) M.; m. Jane Ellen Greenberg, Aug. 24, 1963; children: Andrew Warren, Amy Lynn, Rebecca Ann, Jenny Leigh. BA in History with honors, Kenyon Coll., 1963; JD, Georgetown U., 1966. Bar: D.C. 1967, U.S. Dist. Ct. D.C. 1967, U.S. Ct. Appeals (D.C. cir.) 1967, U.S. Customs Ct. 1967, U.S. Supreme Ct. 1970, U.S. Ct. Appeals (5th cir.) 1975. Assoc. Coles & Goertner, Washington, 1966-71, ptnr., 1971-82; sr. ptnr. Hoppel, Mayer & Coleman, 1982—. Trustee Kenyon Coll., 1995—. Mem. ABA, D.C. Bar Assn., Maritime Adminstrv. Bar Assn. (pres. 1979), Assn. for Transp. Law, Logistics and Policy, Propeller Club of U.S. (Washington), Kenyon Coll. Alumni Assn. (pres. 1993-94). Office: Hoppel Mayer & Coleman 1000 Connecticut Ave NW Washington DC 20036-5302 E-mail: nmayer@hmc-law.com.

MAYER, PATRICIA JAYNE, financial officer, management accountant; b. Chgo., Apr. 27, 1950; d. Arthur and Ruth (Greenberger) Hersh; m. William A. Mayer Jr., Apr. 30, 1971. AA, Diablo Valley Coll., 1970; BSBA, Calif. State U., Hayward, 1975. Cert. mgmt. acct. Staff acct., auditor Elmer Fox Westheimer and Co., Oakland, Calif., 1976; supervising auditor Auditor's Office County of Alameda, 1976-78; asst. acctg. mgr. CBS Retail Stores doing bus. as Pacific Stereo, Emeryville, Calif., 1978-79; contr. Oakland Unified Sch. Dist., 1979-84; v.p. fin., CFO YMCA, San Francisco, 1984-96; v.p. fin. customer segments Charles Schwab & Co., 1996—. Instr. acctg. to staff YMCA, San Francisco, 1984-96, CBS Retail Stores, 1978-79. Draft counselor Mt. Diablo Peace Ctr., Walnut Creek, Calif., 1970-72; dep. registrar of voters Contra Costa County Registrar's Office, Martinez, Calif., 1972-77. Mem. Fin. Execs. Inst. (bd. dirs. San Francisco chpt.), Inst. Mgmt. Accts. (pres.-elect Diablo Valley chpt. 1995—, pres. 1995-96), Dalmatian Club No. Calif., Dalmation Club Am. Democrat. Jewish. Avocations: showing and breeding Dalmatians, playing Tex. Hold 'Em poker tournaments. Office: Charles Schwab & Co 101 Montgomery St Ste 200 San Francisco CA 94104-4175

MAYER, PATRICIA LYNN SORCI, mental health nurse, educator; b. Chgo., July 22, 1942; d. Ben and Adonia (Grenier) Sorci; 1 child, Christopher David Mayer. AGS with high honors, Pima Community Coll., Tucson, 1983; BSN with honors, U. Ariz., 1986, MS in Nursing, 1987. RN, Ariz.; cert. addictions counselor, chem. dependency therapist; lic. pvt. pilot. Nurse educator, dir. CQI risk mgmt. U. Ariz., Tucson. Contbr. articles to profl. jours. Mem. Nat. Nurses Soc. on Addictions, Phi Kappa Phi, Sigma Theta Tau, Pi Lambda Theta.

MAYER, RAYMOND RICHARD, business administration educator; b. Chgo., Aug. 31, 1924; s. Adam and Mary (Bogdala) M.; m. Helen Lakowski, Jan. 30, 1954; children: Mark, John, Mary, Jane. BS, Ill. Inst. Tech., 1948, MS, 1954, PhD, 1957. Indsl. engr. Standard Oil Co., Whiting, Ind., 1948-51; orgn. analyst Ford Motor Co., Chgo., 1951-53; instr. Ill. Inst. Tech., 1953-56, asso. prof., 1958-60; asst. prof. U. Chgo., 1956-58; Walter F. Mullady prof. bus. adminstrn. Loyola U., Chgo., 1960—. Author: Financial Analysis of Investment Alternatives, 1966, Production Management, 1962, rev. edit., 1968, Production and Operations Management, 1975, rev. edit., 1982, Capital Expenditure Analysis, 1978. Served with USNR, 1944-46. Ingersoll Found. fellow, 1955-56; Machinery and Allied Products Inst. fellow, 1954-55; Ford Found. fellow, 1962 Mem. Acad. Mgmt., Am. Econ. Assn., Am. Statis. Assn., Am. Inst. for Decision Scis., Nat. Assn. Purchasing Mgmt., Polish Inst. Arts and Scis. in Am., Alpha Iota Delta, Alpha Kappa Psi, Beta Gamma Sigma. Home: 730 Green Bay Rd Winnetka IL 60093-1912 Office: 820 N Michigan Ave Chicago IL 60611-2147

MAYER, RICHARD EDWIN, psychology educator; b. Chgo., Feb. 8, 1947; s. James S. and Bernis (Lowy) M.; m. Beverly Linn Pastor, Dec. 19, 1971; children: Kenneth Michael, David Mark, Sarah Ann. BA with honors, Miami U., Oxford, Ohio, 1969; MS in Psychology, U. Mich., 1971, PhD in Psychology, 1973. Vis. asst. prof. Ind. U., Bloomington, 1973-75; asst. prof. psychology U. Calif., Santa Barbara, 1975-80, assoc. prof., 1980-85, prof., 1985—, pres., chmn. dept., 1987-90. Vis. scholar Learning Rsch. and Devel. Ctr., U. Pitts., 1979, Ctr. for Study of Reading, U. Ill., 1984. Author: Foundations of Learning and Memory, 1979, The Promise of Cognitive Psychology, 1981, Thinking, Problem Solving, Cognition, 1983, 2d edit., 1992, BASIC: A Short Course, 1985, Educational Psychology, 1987, The Critical Thinker, 1990, 2d edit., 1995, The Promise of Educational Psychology, 1999; editor: Human Reasoning, 1980, Teaching and Learning Computer Programming, 1988; editor jours. Instructional Sci., 1983-87, Educational Psychologist, 1983-89. Sch. bd. officer Goleta (Calif.) Union Sch. Dist., 1981—. NSF grantee, 1975-88. Fellow APA (divsn. 15 officer 1987—, G. Stanley Hall lectr. 1988), Am. Psychol. Soc.; mem. Am. Ednl. Rsch. Assn. (divsn. C officer 1986-88), Psychonomic Soc. Democrat. Jewish. Avocations: computers, hiking, bicycling, reading, dogs. Office: U Calif Dept Of Psychology Santa Barbara CA 93016

MAYER, ROBERT ANTHONY, retired college president; b. N.Y.C., Oct. 30, 1933; s. Ernest John and Theresa Margaret (Mazura) M.; m. Laura Wiley Christ, Apr. 30, 1960. BA magna cum laude, Fairleigh Dickinson U., 1955; MA, NYU, 1967. With N.J. Bank and Trust Co., Paterson, 1955-61, mgr. advt. dept., 1959-61; program supr. advt. dept. Mobil Oil Co., N.Y.C., 1961-62; asst. to dir. Latin Am. program Ford Found., 1963-65, asst. rep. Brazil, 1965-67; asst. to v.p. adminstrn., 1967-73; officer in charge logistical services Ford Found., 1968-73; asst. dir. programs N.Y. Community Trust, N.Y.C., 1973-76; exec. dir. N.Y. State Council on the Arts, 1976-79; mgmt. cons., 1979-80; dir. Internat. Mus. Photography, George Eastman House, Rochester, N.Y., 1980-89, mgmt. cons., 1989-90; pres. Cleve. Inst. of Art, 1990-97; ret., 1997. Mem. editorial adv. bd.: Grants mag., 1978-80; author: (plays) La Borgia, 1971; Alijandru, 1971, They'll Grow No Roses, 1975. Mem. state program adv. panel NEA, 1977-80; mem. Mayor's Com. on Cultural Policy, N.Y.C., 1974-75; mem. pres.'s adv. com. Bklyn. campus, L.I. U., 1978-79; bd. dirs. Fedn. Protestant Welfare Agys., N.Y.C., 1977-79, Arts for Greater Rochester, 1981-83, Garth Fagan's Dance Theatre, 1982-86; trustee Internat. Mus. Photography, 1981-89, Lacoste Sch. Arts, France, 1991-96, sec., 1994-96; mem. dean's adv. com. Grad. Sch. Social Welfare, Fordham U., 1976; mem. N.Y. State Motion Picure and TV Devel. Adv. Bd., 1984-87, N.Y. State Martin Luther King Jr. Commn., 1985-90, Cleve. Coun. Cultural Affairs, 1992-94; chmn. Greater Cleve. Regional Transit Authority Arts in Transit Com., 1992-95; bd. dirs. Friends of Ariz. State U. Ctr. for Latin Am. Studies, 1997-99; pres. bd. dirs. Villa Solana Townhouse Assn., 2000. Recipient Nat. award on advocacy for girls Girls Clubs Am., 1976 Mem. Nat. Assembly State Art Agys. (bd. dirs. 1977-79, 1st vice chmn. 1978-79), Alliance Ind. Colls. Art (bd. dirs. 1983-91, vice chmn. 1986-87, sec. 1987-89), N.Y. State Assn. Museums (bd. councilors 1983-86, pres. 1986-89), Assn. Ind. Colls. Art and Design (bd. dirs. 1991-97, exec. com. 1991-93, 96-97). Home: 2704 N 60th St Scottsdale AZ 85257-1012

MAYER, ROBERT HALL, JR. civil engineer, educator; b. Summit, N.J., Nov. 16, 1945; s. Robert Hall and Muriel Anna (Hinze) M.; m. Donna Lin Foster, Oct. 25, 1980; 1 child, Robert Paul. B.C.E., U. Del., 1967, M. Applied Sci., 1969, Ph.D., 1982. Asst. prof. constrn. U. Colo., Boulder, 1981-82; assoc. prof. ocean engring. U.S. Naval Acad., Annapolis, Md., 1983— ; comdr. Civil Engr. Corps U.S. Naval Res., Washington, 1979— ; pvt. practice cons. and research in constrn. mgmt., Annapolis, 1983— . Co-author: Quantitative Construction Management: Uses of Linear Optimization, 1983. Served to lt. Civil Engrs. Corps USN, 1971-78. Decorated Navy Commendation medal, 1978. Mem. ASCE (assoc.), Ops. Research Soc. Am., Am. Soc. Engring. Edn. Presbyterian. Home: 424 Stanford Ct Arnold MD 21012-1828 Office: US Naval Acad Naval Systems Engring Dept 11- Annapolis MD 21402

MAYER, ROSEMARY, artist; b. Ridgewood, N.Y., Feb. 27, 1943; d. Theodore Albert and Marie Anne (Stumpf) M. AB magna cum laude, U. Iowa, 1964; postgrad., Bklyn. Mus. Art Sch., 1964-65, Sch. of Visual Arts, N.Y.C., 1967-69. Model Raphael Soyer, N.Y.C., 1968-74; writer Arts Mag., 1972-75, Art in Am., N.Y.C., 1974-75. Vis. artist many schs. including Hartwick Coll., Oneonta, N.Y., 1976, Art Inst., Chgo., 1974; guest artist Nat. Endowment Workshop, Tyler Sch. Art, Phila., Mpls. Acad. Art and Design, 1981; adj. lectr. La Guardia C.C., CUNY, 1992—; adj. assoc. prof. L.I. U., 1988—; writer, speaker A.I.R. Gallery, N.Y.C., 1972-74. Translator: Pontormo's Diary 1983; author: Swatches, 1969, Surroundings, 1977. Grantee numerous orgns. including NEA, CAPS, 1976—. Democrat. Home: 55 Leonard St New York NY 10013-2928

MAYER, STEPHAN ANTHONY, neurologist; b. N.Y.C., Sept. 22, 1962; s. Roman Henry Mayer and Karin (Lehmkuhl) Ludewig; m. Elizabeth Alcott Webster, Sept. 11, 1993; children: Philip Brett, Catherine Weld. AB, Brown U., 1984; MD, Cornell U., 1988. Diplomate Am. Bd. Psychiatry and Neurology. Intern Presbyn. Hosp., N.Y.C., 1988-89; resident in neurology Columbia-Presbyn. Med. Ctr., 1989-92; asst. prof. neurology Columbia U. Coll. Physicians & Surgeons, N.Y.C., 1995; dir. neurol. ICU Presbyn. Hosp., 1995—; with Neurol. Inst., 1989—. Co-author: On Call-Neurology, 1997. Rsch. Fellow Nat. Stroke Assn., 1993; Am. Heart Assn. grant, 1997. Fellow Am. Heart Assn. (stroke coun.); mem. Am. Acad. Neurology, Soc. Critical Care Medicine. Office: Neurol Inst 710 W 168th St # 39 New York NY 10032-2603 E-mail: sam14@columbia.edu.

MAYER, SUSAN LEE, nurse, educator; b. N.Y.C., Feb. 10, 1946; d. Hans and Frieda (Schein) Abramson; m. Steven Mayer, June 24, 1973; children: Jason, Stuart, Richard, Deborah. BSN, Hunter Coll., 1968; MA, NYU, 1974; EdD, Columbia U., 1996; postgrad., Yeshiva U., 1986, Adelphi U., 1987. RN, N.Y.; cert. in gerontology; cert. tchr., N.Y. Staff nurse ICU-CCU Montefiore Hosp., Bronx, N.Y., 1968; organizer CCU Jewish Meml. Hosp., N.Y.C., 1968; supr., adminstr. Morrisania City Hosp., 1969-76; instr. Adelphi U., Garden City, N.Y., 1977-78; substitute nurse Great Neck (N.Y.) Pub. Schs., 1980-90; rsch. asst. to dean Adelphi U. Sch. Nursing, 1987-88; dir. ambulatory edn. North Bronx Healthcare Network, 2001—. Staff nurse Winthrop U. Hosp., Mineola, NY, 1987—90, per diem nurse, NY, 1987—90; instr. dept. nursing edn. Bronx Mcpl. Hosp. Ctr. (now Jacobi Med. Ctr.), 1990—96; asst. prof. Helene Fuld Coll. Nursing, 1996—2001; adj. instr. Bronx C.C., 1992, Queensborough C.C., 1987—89; adj. asst. prof. Iona Coll. Sch. Nursing; adj. assoc. prof. Tchrs. Coll./Columbia U., 1997—; field nurse coord. RN Home Care Winthrop U. Hosp., Mineola, 1996—2001; dir. ambulatory edn. N. Bronx Healthcare Network, 2001—; lectr. and presenter in field. Contbr. articles to profl. jours. including Nursing and Health Care. Bd. dirs. Great Neck Synagogue, 1981-91, v.p. Sisterhood, 1978-79, pres., 1979-81; former bd. dirs. Russell Gardens Assn.; founder Work for Share Zedek Hosp., 1977—; past pres., fin. sec. L'Chaim chpt. Hadassah Nurse Coun. N.Y. State Regents scholar, 1963. Mem. ANA, Assn. Orthodox Jewish Scientists, Nat. League for Nursing, N.Y. Counties Registered Nurses Assn., N.Y. State Nurses Assn. (dist. 13 bd. dirs., past chmn. nurse practice com., past treas., past chair coun. ethical practice), Am. Assn. for History of Nursing, Nurses Edn. Alumni Assn. (historian), Sigma Theta Tau, Kappa Delta Pi. Democrat. Home: 28 Laurel Dr Great Neck NY 11021-2827 E-mail: sm192@columbia.edu.

MAYER, SUSAN MARTIN, art educator; b. Atlanta, Oct. 25, 1931; d. Paul McKeen and Ione (Garrett) Martin; m. Arthur James Mayer, Aug. 9, 1953; 1 child, Melinda Marilyn. Student, Am. U., 1949-50; BA, U. N.C., Greensboro, 1953; postgrad., U. Del., 1956-58; MA, Ariz. State U., 1966. Artist-in-residence Armed Forces Staff Coll., Norfolk, Va., 1968-69; mem. art faculty U. Tex., Austin, 1971—. Co-editor: Museum Education: History, Theory and Practice, 1989; author various mus. publs.; contbr. articles to profl. jours. Recipient award Austin Ind. Sch. Bd., 1985. Mem. Nat. Art Edn. Assn. (bd. dirs. 1983-87, award 1987, 91), Tex. Art Edn. Assn. (mus. edn. chair 1982-83, Mus. Educator of Yr. 1986), Tex. Assn. Mus. (mus. edn. chair), Austin Visual Arts Assn., Am. Assn. Mus. Office: U Tex Dept Art History Austin TX 78712

MAYER, THOMAS, economics educator; b. Vienna, Austria, Jan. 18, 1927; s. Felix and Helen (Pollatschek) M.; m. Dorothy JoAnne Harmison, Apr. 7, 1963. BA, Queens Coll., 1948; MA, Columbia U., 1949, PhD, 1953. Economist Treasury Dept., 1951-52, Office of Price Stabilization, 1952, Bur. of Mines, 1953; vis. asst. prof. W.Va. U., 1953—54; asst. prof. U. Notre Dame, 1954-56; from asst. to assoc. prof. Mich. State U., 1956-61; vis. assoc. prof. U. Calif., Berkeley, 1961-62, prof. Davis, 1962-93, prof. emeritus, 1993—. Author: Monetary Policy in the United States, 1968, Permanent Income, Wealth and Consumption, 1972; author: (with D.C. Rowan) Intermediate Macroeconomics, 1972; author: (with others) The Structure of Monetarism, 1978, Money, Banking and the Economy, 1981, 6th edit., 1996, Chinese edit., 1988, Portuguese edit., 1995, Revealing Monetary Policy, 1987, Monetarism and Macroeconomic Policy, 1990, Truth Versus Precision in Economics, 1993, Polish edit., 1996, Doing Economics: Essays on the Applied Methodology of Economics, 1995, Monetary Policy and the Great Inflation in the United States, 1999; editor: The Political Economy of American Monetary Policy, 1990, Monetary Theory, 1990; editor: (with F. Spinelli) Studies in Macroeconomics and Monetary Policy Issues, 1991; editor: (with S. Sheffrin) Fiscal and Monetary Policy, 1995; mem. editl. bd.: Jour. Money, Credit and Banking, 1970—74, mem. editl. bd.: numerous others. Mem. Am. Econ. Assn., Am. Fin. Assn., Internat. Network Econ. Method (chmn. 1993—), Western Econ. Assn. (v.p. 1976-77, pres. 1978-79), Royal Econ. Soc. Home: 3054 Buena Vista Way Berkeley CA 94708-2020

MAYER, VICTOR JAMES, geologist, educator; b. Mayville, Wis., Mar. 25, 1933; s. Victor Charles and Phyllis (Bachhuber) M.; m. Mary Jo Anne White, Nov. 25, 1965; children: Gregory, Maribeth. BS in Geology, U. Wis., 1956; MS in Geology, U. Colo., 1960, PhD in Sci. Edn., 1966. Tchr. Colo. Pub. Schs., 1961-65; asst. prof. SUNY Coll., Oneonta, 1965-67, Ohio State U., Columbus, 1967-70, assoc. prof., 1970-75, prof. ednl. studies, geol. scis. and natural resources, 1975-95, prof. emeritus, 1995—. Co-organizer symposa at 29th and 31st Internat. Geol. Congresses; internat. sci. edn. assistance to individuals and orgns. in Japan, Korea, Taiwan, Russia, and Venezuela; dir. NSF Insts., program for leadership Earth Sys. Edn., 1990-95; dir. Korean Sci. Tchrs. Insts., 1986-88, 95; keynote spkr. U.S.A. rep. Internat. Conf. on Geoscis. Edn., Southampton, Eng., 1993; co-convenor Second Internat. conf. on Geosci. Edn., Hilo, Hawaii, 1997; disting. vis. prof. SUNY, Plattsburg, 1994; vis. rsch. scholar Hyogo U., Japan, 1996; sr. Fulbright rschr. Shizuoka U., Japan, 1998; vis. prof. Korea Nat. U. of Edn., 2000. Contbr. articles to profl. jours. Served with USAR. Recipient Lifetime Disting. Svc. award to the Internat. Earth Sci. Edn. Cmty., 1997; named Disting. Investigator, Ohio Sea Grant Program, 1983. Fellow AAAS (chmn. edn. 1988-89), Ohio Acad. Sci. (v.p. 1978-79, exec. com. 1993-94, outstanding univ. educator 1995); mem. Nat. Sci. Tchrs. Assn. (bd. dirs. 1984-86), Sci. Edn. Coun. Ohio (pres. 1987-88), Sigma Xi, Phi Delta Kappa. Roman Catholic. Avocation: photography. Home: 111 W Dominion Blvd Columbus OH 43214-2607 Office: Ohio State U Dept Geol Scis 125 S Oval Mall Columbus OH 43210-1308 E-mail: mayer.4@osu.edu.

MAYER, WILLIAM DIXON, pathologist, educator; b. Beaver Falls, Pa., Oct. 5, 1928; s. Emil Leroy and Elizabeth (Townsend) M.; m. Donna S. Dashiell; children: Elizabeth Ann, David Dixon, William Dixon, Kathy Dashiell AB, Colgate U., 1951; MD with honor, U. Rochester, 1957; D.Sc. (hon.), U. Osteopathic Medicine and Health Scis., 1988. Intern, then resident pathology Strong Meml. Hosp., Rochester, N.Y., 1957-61; instr., mem. faculty U. Mo. Sch. Medicine, 1961-76, dir. Univ. Med. Center, 1967-74; dean U. Mo. Sch. Medicine (Sch. Medicine), 1967-74, prof. pathology, 1967-76; asst. chief med. dir. for acad. affairs VA, Washington, 1976-79; pres. Med. Coll. Hampton Roads, Norfolk, Va., 1979-87. Assoc. dir. div. regional med. programs NIH, 1966-67; mem. exec. com. Nat. Bd. Med. Examiners, 1969-81, treas., 1975-79, vice-chmn., 1979-81, hon. mem., 1981—, fin. com., 1987-93; bd. regent Nat. Libr. of Medicine, 1980-84, chmn., 1982-84. Bd. dirs., 1st v.p. Future of Hampton Rds., 1983—; bd. dirs. Greater Norfolk Corp., 1987-91—, exec. v.p., 1989-90; founding mem. bd. dirs. Town Point Club, 1983-91. With USMC, 1946-48. Markle scholar acad. medicine, 1962-67 Fellow Coll. Am. Pathologists; mem. AMA, Assn. Am. Med. Colls. (Disting. Service mem.), C. of C. (bd. dirs. 1986-91), Sigma Xi, Alpha Omega Alpha. Episcopalian. Home: Owings Mills, Md. Deceased.

MAYER, WILLIAM EMILIO, investor; b. N.Y.C., May 7, 1940; s. Emilio and Marie Mayer; m. Katherine Mayer, May 16, 1964; children: Kristen Elizabeth, William Franz. BS, U. Md., 1966, MBA, 1967. Pres., CEO First

Boston Corp., N.Y.C., 1967-91; dean Coll. Bus. and Mgmt. U. Md., College Park, 1992-96; ptnr. Devel. Capital, 1996-99, Park Ave. Equity Ptnrs., 1999—. Bd. dirs. Lee Enterprises, Inc., Premier, Inc., WR Hambrecht & Co., Liberty Fund Group, Sunrise Med., Inc., First Health Group Corp. Trustee U. Md., Tulane U.; chmn. Aspen Inst. 1st lt. USAF, 1961—65. Mem. Annapolis Yacht Club, Manhasset Bay Club (N.Y.), Univ. Club (N.Y.C.), Mashomack Fish & Game Club, Met. Club (Washington). Home: 172 Long Neck Point Rd Darien CT 06820-5816 Office: 399 Park Ave Ste 3204 New York NY 10022-1606

MAYERI, BEVERLY, artist, ceramic sculptor, educator; b. N.Y.C., Nov. 2, 1944; d. Bernard and Cora (Wisoff) Howard; m. Earl Melchior Mayeri, Sept. 1, 1968; 1 child, Rachel Theresa. BA, U. Calif., Berkeley, 1967; MA in Art and Sculpture, San Francisco State U., 1976. Tchr. Foothill Coll., Los Altos Hills, 1990, Natsoulas Gallery, 1992, U. Minn., Mpls., 1993, Sonoma Stae U., Rohnert Park, Calif., 1994, Mendocino (Calif.) Art Ctr., 1995, Fresno State U., 1996, CCAC, Oakland, Calif., 1996, Edinboro (Pa.) U., 1997, Scropps Coll., Claremont, Clif., 1999, Cuesta Coll., San Luis Obispo, Calif., 2001, San Diego State U., 2002. Artist: solo exhibitions include Palo Alto (Calif.) Cultural Ctr., 1979, Ivory/Kimpton Gallery, San Francisco, 1981, 83, Garth Clark Gallery, N.Y., 1985, 87, Esther Saks Gallery, Chgo., 1988, 90, Dorothy Weiss Gallery, San Francisco, 1990, 92, 94, 96, 98, 2000, San Jose Inst. Contemporary Art, 1990, Robert Kidd Gallery, Birmingham, Mich., 1993, Perimeter Gallery, Chgo., 1998, Susan Cummins Gallery, Mill Valley, Calif., 2002; group exhibitions include San Francisco Mus. of Art, Northern Calif. Clay Routes: Sculpture Now, 1979, Smithsonian Instn., Renwick Gallery, 1981, Prieto Meml. Gallery, Mills Coll., Oakland, Calif. 1982, Crocker Art Mus., San Francisco, 1983, Euphrate Gallery, De Anza Coll., Cupertino, Calif., 1984, 88, Fisher Gallery, U. So. Calif., L.A., traveled to Pratt Inst., N.Y.C., 1984, Arts Commn. Gallery, San Francisco, 1984, Signet Arts Gallery, St. Louis (two person show), 1984, Garth Clark Gallery, N.Y., 1985, Robert L. Kidd Gallery, Birmingham, Mich., Animals Contemporary Vision, Major Concepts: Clay, 1986, Fresno (Calif.) Arts Ctr. and Mus., 1987, Canton (Ohio) Art Inst., 1991, Soc. for Contemporary Crafts, Pitts., 1992, Triton Mus. of Art, Santa Clara, Calif., 1992, Nat. Mus. of History Taipei, Taiwan, 1993, Lew Allen Gallery, Santa Fe, New Mex., 1993, Perimeter Gallery, 1995, Duane Reed Gallery, St. Louis, 1997, Scripps Coll., 1999, LACMA, L.A., 2000, Calif. State U., Chico, 2001, Clay Studio, Phila., 2001; works in pub. and private collections include: Nat. Mus. History, Taipei, Canton Art Inst., Long Beach (Calif.) Parks and Recreation, L.A. Arts Commn., Mr. and Mrs. Eric Lidow, L.A., Alfred Shands, Louisville, Mrs. Audrey Landy, Atlanta, Karen Johnson Boyd, Racine, Wis., Alan and Esther Saks, Chgo., Gloria and Sonny Kamm, L.A. County Mus. Art. Founder Marin Women Artists, Marin County, Calif., 1974-84. Recipient fellowship visual artist NEA, Washington, 1982, 88; grantee: Marin Arts Coun., 1987, Virgina A. Groot Found., 1991. Avocations: painting, hiking, skiing, gardening, environmentalist. Office: Dorothy Weiss Gallery 3 Indian Gulch Rd Piedmont CA 94611-3527

MAYERS, DANIEL KRIEGSMAN, lawyer; b. Scarsdale, N.Y., July 10, 1934; s. Chauncey Maurice and Helen P. (Kriegsman) M.; m. Karen E. Silverman, Sept. 30, 1956, children: Peter D., Leslie H. Shroyer. AB, Harvard U., 1955, LLB, 1960. Bar: D.C. 1961, U.S. Supreme Ct. 1961. Law clk. to Justice Felix Frankfurter, U.S. Supreme Ct., Washington, 1960-61; spl. asst. U.S. Dept. Justice, 1961-62; assoc. Wilmer Cutler & Pickering, 1962-65, ptnr., 1967-99, of counsel, 2000—; exec. asst. to undersec. U.S. State Dept., 1965-66. Vis. com. Harvard Law Sch., Cambridge, Mass., 1982-89, chmn., 1986-89; chmn. Legal Action Ctr., N.Y.C., 1998—, Washington Ednl. TV Assn., 1993-97, Survivors Fund for Pentagon Victims, 2001--; bd. dirs. Hypres Corp., Netscan, Inc. Pres. Nat. Symphony Orch., Washington, 1987-89; chmn. Sidwell Friends Sch., Washington, 1979-81; mem. Ams. for Peace Now, 1991—, Fed. City Coun., Washington, 1981—; trustee Cmty. Found. for Nat. Capital Area, 1997—; counsel, dir. Ctr. for Nat. Policy, Washington, 1984-93. With U.S. Army, 1955-57. Recipient Sears prize Harvard Law Sch., 1959 Mem. ABA, Met. Club, Woodstock Country Club. Democrat. Jewish. Avocations: tennis; fishing. Home: 3222 Woodland Dr NW Washington DC 20008-3547 Office: Wilmer Cutler & Pickering 2445 M St NW Washington DC 20037-1487

MAYERS, DAVID, political science and history educator; b. El Paso, Tex., Nov. 30, 1951; s. Eugene David and Odette Margaret Julliette (Gilchrist) M.; m. Elizabeth Kirkland Jones, Dec. 4, 1982; 1 child, Peter. BA, Oberlin Coll., 1974; postgrad., Oxford (Eng.) U., 1974-75; MA, U. Chgo., 1976, PhD, 1979. Faculty Kenyon Coll., 1979-80, U. Calif., Santa Cruz, 1980-88; prof. polit. sci. and history Boston U., 1989—, 1999—, dir. undergrad. studies polit. sci., 1991-98, dir. grad. studies polit. sci., 1998-2000, chmn. dept. polit. sci., 2001—. Lectr. in field; active various profl. confs.; mem. numerous profl. panels. Author: Cracking the Monolith: US Policy against the Sino-Soviet Alliance, 1949-55, 1986, Reevaluating Eisenhower; American Foreign Policy in the 1950s, 1987, George Kennan and the Dilemmas of US Foreign Policy, 1988, The Ambassadors and America's Soviet Policy, 1995 (Book prize The Am. Acad. Diplomacy 1995), Wars and Peace: The Future Americans Envisioned, 1861-1991, 1998; contbr. articles to profl. jours., chpts. to books. Vol. ARC; bd. trustees Carnegie Coun. on Ethics and Internat. Affairs. Fellowships from Oberlin Coll., Oxford U., U. Chgo., U. Calif., Santa Cruz, Inst. on Global Conflict and Coop., 1983-89, Inst. for Study of World Politics, 1986, Boston U., Hoover Instn., Stanford U., 1990, Ctr. Internat. Studies at U. So. Calif., 1991, John M. Olin Found., 1991, Gilder Lehrman Inst. Am. History, 2000. Episcopalian. Democrat. Avocations: tennis, swimming, camping, skiing, sailing. Home: 173 Oliver Rd Waban MA 02468-2322 Office: Boston Univ Dept Polit Sci Boston MA 02215 E-mail: dmayers@bu.edu.

MAYERS, EUGENE DAVID, philosopher, educator; b. N.Y.C., July 30, 1915; s. Sylvester and Estelle (Weinstein) M.; m. Odette Julia Marguerite Gilchrest, Dec. 30, 1950; children: David Allan, Marilyn Anne, Judith Odette, Peter Michael. AB, Yale U., 1936, LLB, 1940; PhD, Columbia U., 1956. Bar: N.Y. State bar 1941. With Nat. Bur. Econ. Research, N.Y.C., 1941, Office Gen. Counsel, Navy Dept., 1946; mem. faculty Carleton Coll., Northfield, Minn., 1950-61, Columbia, 1959-60, Mills Coll., Oakland, Calif., 1961-63; prof. philosophy Calif. State U., Hayward, 1963-92, prof. emeritus, 1992—, chmn. dept. philosophy, 1963-73, acting head div. humanities, 1966-67. Adj. prof. Calif. State U., 1996-97. Author: Some Modern Theories of Natural Law, 1957; Contbr. articles to profl. jours. Served to capt. (field artillery) AUS, 1941-46, 51-52; lt. col. judge adv. gen. USAR ret. Fellow Soc. Values in Higher Edn.; mem. AAUP, Am. Philos. Assn. (chmn. conf. dept. chmn. Pacific divsn. 1973-75, Pacific divsn. exec. com. 1976-80, chmn. exec. com. 1978-80), Am. Soc. Polit. and Legal Philosophy, Pacific Coast Theol. Soc. (sec. 1984-86), Internat. Assn. Philosophy Law and Social Philosophy, Am. Acad. Religion, Soc. Advancement Am. Philosophy, Soc. Study Process Philosophies (Pacific Coast rep. 1987-97, jurisprudence 3d internat. Whitehead conf. 1998). Home: 3191 Frye St Oakland CA 94602-4040 Fax: 510-336-0514. E-mail: edmayers@ix.netcom.com.

MAYERS, STANLEY PENROSE, JR. public health educator; b. Phila., Nov. 9, 1926; s. Stanley Penrose and Margaret Amelia (Thorpe) M.; m. Virginia Lee Lytle, Aug. 25, 1951 (dec. Oct. 1990); children: Douglas Lytle, Kenneth Stanley, Daniel John, Andrew William; m. Patricia Ann Harne Hulsey, Mar. 6, 1993. BA, U. Pa., 1949, MD, 1953; MPH, Johns Hopkins U., 1958. Diplomate Am. Bd. Preventive Medicine. Intern Phila. Gen. Hosp., 1953-54; resident Arlington County Health Dept., Va., 1954-55; health dir. Henry-Martinsville-Patrick Health Dist., Martinsville, 1955-57; regional dir. Va. State Health Dept., Richmond, 1958-59; dist. state health officer N.J. State Dept. of Health, Trenton, 1959-62; asst. prof. and asst. dean Johns Hopkins Sch. Hygiene and Pub. Health, Balt., 1962-65; dir. Arlington County Dept. of Human Resources, Arlington, Va., 1965-71; prof. health policy and adminstrn. Pa. State U., University Park, 1971-97, prof. emeritus, 1997—, chmn., 1979-88, assoc. dean undergrad. studies Coll. Health and Human Devel., 1989-92, assoc. dean acad. studies Coll. Health and Human Devel., 1992-95, assoc. dean emeritus, 1997—. Interim dir. internat. edn. programs and studies Pa. State U., 2000-2001; faculty assoc. Johns Hopkins U. Sch. Hygiene and Pub. Health, Balt., 1965-75; clin. assoc. prof. Georgetown U. Sch. Medicine, Washington, 1965-71; cons. VA, 1985—. Contbr. articles to profl. jours. Pres. Arlington Optimist Club, 1970-71; bd. dirs. Centre County Family Planning Svcs., Bellefonte, Pa., 1972-79. With USN, 1945-46. Recipient Outstanding Achievement award Dept. Community Medicine, Georgetown U. Sch. Medicine, 1968, Saubel award Coll. of Human Devel., Pa. State U., 1985, Pioneer Achievement award Frankford H.S., Phila., 1999. Fellow Am. Coll. Preventive Med., APHA (chmn. membership com. health officer's sect. 1968-70, mem. nominating com. health adminstrn. sect. 1970-72, chmn. com. to draft a statement on local health agy. responsibilities 1973-74); mem. AMA, Arlington County Med. Soc. (Wellborn award 1971), Centre County Med. Soc. (pres. 1978), Med. Soc. Va., Met. Washington Health Officers Assn. (sec. 1967-71), Am. Assn. Pub. Health Physicians (pres. Va. chpt. 1970-71), Pa. Med. Soc. (mem. Ho. of Dels. for Centre County 1974-76, 81-97, treas. 1973-74, 85—, sec. 1974-76, v.p. 1976, pres. elect 1977, pres. 1978), Mt. Nittany Soc., Univ. Club (State College, Pa.), Phi Beta Kappa. Episcopalian. Avocations: fishing, boating, hiking. Home: 648 Wiltshire Dr State College PA 16803-1450 Office: Pa State U Human Devel Bldg Rm 115 University Park PA 16802 E-mail: spm1@psu.edu. *Never attempt to promote something or someone that you do not believe in yourself.*

MAYERSDORF, ASSA, neurologist; b. Tel Aviv, Sept. 21, 1937; came to U.S., 1974, naturalized, 1982; s. Bernard and Nettie Mayersdorf; m. Nira Keren, June 8, 1965; 2 children. MD, Hebrew U., 1963. Diplomate Am. Bd. Neurology, Am. Soc. Neurorehab., Israel Bd. Specialization in Neurology. Resident Hadassah-Hebrew U. Hosp., Jerusalem, 1962-63; house officer dept. neurosurgery Tel Hashomer Govtl. Hosp., Israel, 1964-66; asst. resident dept. neurology Balt. City Hosp., 1966-68; fellow dept. neurology Johns Hopkins Hosp., Balt., 1966-69, asst. resident dept. neurology, 1968-69; instr. divsn. neurology, assoc. mem. Ctr. Neurobiol. Scis. U. Fla., Gainesville, 1970; chief sect. neurology Soroka Med. Ctr. in Negev U. Ctr. for Health Scis., Ben-Gurion U. in Negev, Beer Sheva, Israel, 1971-74; asst. prof. dept. neurology U. Minn. Sch. Medicine, Mpls., 1974-80; dir. epilepsy treatment ctr. VA Med. Ctr., 1974-80, chief neurology svs. Milw., 1980-90, dir. EEG lab. Mpls., 1975-80; assoc. prof. dept. neurology Med. Coll. Wis., Milw., 1980-90, vice chmn. dept. neurology, 1989-90, interim chmn. dept. neurology, 1988-89; clin. prof. neurology So. Ill. U. Sch. Medicine, Springfield, 1991—; mem. staff Springfield Clinic Neurosci. Inst., 1992—. Guest lectr. U. Negev, 1971-74; sr. attending staff mem. Foredtert Meml. Luth. Hosp., Milw., 1980-90, Milw. County Med. Complex, 1980-90; attending staff mem. Milw. Psychiat. Hosp., 1987-90, West Allis Meml. Hosp., Milw., 1988-90, St. John's Hosp., Springfield, 1990—, Meml. Med. Ctr., Springfield, 1990—, Doctors Hosp., Springfield, 1990—, Passavant Area Hosp., Jacksonville, Ill., 1990—, Hillsboro (Ill.) Hosp., 1990—, St. Vincent's Hosp., Taylorville, Ill., 1990—, St. Francis Hosp., Litchfield, Ill., 1992—; mem. cons. staff St. Luke's Med. Ctr., Milw., 1988-90, Children's Hosp. of Wis., Milw., 1987-90, St. Michael Hosp., Milw., 1989-90, Abraham Lincoln (Ill.) Meml. Hosp., 1992—; presenter, mem. coms. workshops in field; cons Dist. Ct. of Labor Rels., Beer Sheva. Bd. dirs. Minn. Epilepsy League, 1975-78, sec., exec. com., 1977-78; bd. dirs. Wis. Epilepsy Assn., 1983-90, mem. exec. and fin. coms., profl. adv. bd., 1983-90, chmn. profl. adv. bd. 1985-90; trustee Inst. Islamic Art, Jerusalem, 1988-90. Mem. Israel Def. Armed Forces Res., 1963-83. Hebrew U. scholar, 1955-61; recipient Best Pub. Controlled Clin. Trial award Internat. League Against Epilepsy, 1985. Mem. Am. Epilepsy Soc. (pub. rels. and liaison com. 1975-79), Epilepsy Assn. of Lincoln Land (bd. dirs. 1991—, sec. 1991-93, treas. 1993-95), Am. Acad. Neurology, Epilepsy Found. Am., Am. Electroencephalographic Soc., Am. Med. Electroencephalographic Assn., Am. Soc. Neurorehab., Am. Stroke Assn. (stroke coun.). Office: Springfield Clinic Neurosci Inst 455 W Carpenter St Springfield IL 62702-4903 Fax: (217) 753-1707.

MAYERSOHN, ARNOLD LINN, JR. lawyer; b. Little Rock, Mar. 26, 1955; s. Arnold Linn and Janet (Grundfest) Mayersohn; m. Elizabeth Hardin Rudel, May 31, 1981; children: Sarah K., Veronica R. BS in Bus., U. Colo., 1977; JD, U. Ark., 1981. Bar: Ark. 1981, Mo. 1991. House counsel Sterling Stores Co., Inc., Little Rock, 1981-83; assoc. Prince & Ivester, 1984-86; v.p., sec., counsel Worthen Banking Corp., 1986-90; counsel CenterMark Properties, Inc., St. Louis, 1990-95, Westfield Corp., Inc., St. Louis, 1995—. Bd. dirs. Ark. Epilepsy Soc., Little Rock, 1982—83, Ark. Assn. for Hearing Impaired Children, 1988—90. Mem. Ark. Bar Assn., Mo. Bar, Bar Assn. Met. St. Louis. E-mail: amayersohn@westfield.com.

MAYERSON, HY, lawyer; b. Phila., June 29, 1937; s. Henry and Gertrude Mayerson; m. June 13, 1964 (div. 1973); children: Merrie Joy, Benjamin, Erin Megan, Stephnie Dawn; m. Colleen Koos. BS, Temple U., 1958, JD, 1961. Bar: Pa. 1961, Phila. Ct. Common Pleas 1962, Pa. Supreme Ct. 1968, U.S. Ct. Appeals (3d cir.) 1980, U.S. Ct. Appeals (4th cir.) 1986, U.S. Dist. Ct. (ea. dist.) Pa. Pvt. practice, Phila., 1961-65; sr. ptnr. Hy Mayerson Law Offices, 1965-81, Mayerson, Schniper & Gerasimowicz, Spring City, Pa., 1981-87, Mayerson, Gerasimowicz & Munsing, Spring City, 1987-91, Mayerson, Munsing, Corchin & Rosato, P.C., Spring City, 1991-95; pvt. practice The Mayerson Law Offices, P.C., 1995—. Coord. Nat. Forklift Litigation, 1978-91; lead counsel Agent Orange Product Liability Litigation. Contbr. articles to profl. jours. Mem. ATLA (emeritus chair sect. on Indsl. & Agrl. Eqipment, Product Liability adv.bd.), Pa. Trial Lawyers Assn. Home: Sky Farm Birchrunville PA 19421 Office: Rt 724 Spring City PA 19475 E-mail: hy@mayerson.com.

MAYERSON, PHILIP, classics educator; b. N.Y.C., May 20, 1918; s. Theodore and Clara (Fader) M.; m. Joy Gottesman Ungerleider, Nov. 25, 1976 (dec. Sept. 9, 1995); children: Miriam Mayerson, Clare Mayerson. AB, NYU, 1947, PhD, 1956. With Puritan Fed. Clothing Stores, N.Y.C., 1935-42; instr. NYU, 1948-56, asst. prof., 1956-60, assoc. prof., 1960-66, prof. classics, 1966—, vice dean, 1969-71, acting dean, 1971-73, dean Washington Sq. and U. Coll. Arts and Scis., 1973-78. Author: The Ancient Agricultural Regime of Nessana and the Central Negeb, 1961, Classical Mythology in Literature, Art and Music, 1971, Monks, Martyrs, Soldiers and Saracens, 1994; contbr. articles in field to profl. jours. Served with USN, 1942-45. Rockefeller Found. grantee, 1956-57; Am. Council of Learned Socs. fellow, 1961-62 Mem. Am. Philological Assn., Am. Schs. of Oriental Rsch. Home: 720 Walton Ave Mamaroneck NY 10543-4437 Office: NYU Dept Classics 25 Waverly Pl New York NY 10003

MAYERSON, SANDRA ELAINE, lawyer; b. Dayton, Ohio, Feb. 8, 1952; d. Manuel David and Florence Louise (Tepper) M.; m. Scott Burns, May 29, 1977 (div. Oct. 1978); 1 child, Katy Joy. BA cum laude, Yale U., 1973; JD, Northwestern U., 1976. Bar: Ill. 1976, U.S. Ct. Appeals (7th cir.) 1976, U.S. Dist. Ct. (no. dist.) Ill. 1977, U.S. Dist. Ct. Md. 1989, U.S. Ct. Appeals (5th cir.) 1994. Assoc. gen. counsel JMB Realty Corp., Chgo., 1979-80; assoc. Chatz, Sugarman, Abrams et al, 1980-81; ptnr. Pollack, Mayerson & Berman, 1981-83; dep. gen. counsel AM Internat., Inc., 1983-85; ptnr. Kirkland & Ellis, 1985-87; ptnr., chmn. bankruptcy group Kelley Drye & Warren, N.Y.C., 1987-93; ptnr., chmn. N.Y. bankruptcy group McDermott, Will & Emery, 1993-99; ptnr. Holland and Knight, 1999—. Examiner Interco chpt. 11, 1991. Bd. dirs. Jr. Med. Rsch. Inst. coun. Michael Reese Hosp., Chgo., 1981-86; met. divsn. Jewish Guild for Blind, 1990-92; nat. legal afffairs com. Anti-Defamation League, 1990—; lawyers' exec. com. United Jewish Appeal; chair Holland & Knight Nat. Bankruptcy & Creditors Rights Group, 2001-. Named one of Top 50 Women Litigators, Nat. Law Jour., 2001; fellow, Branford Coll., Yale U., 1993—. Mem. ABA (bus. bankruptcy com. 1976—, sec. 1990-93, chair avoiding powers subcom. 1993-96, chair claims trading subcom. 1997—), Ill. State Bar Assn. (governing council corp. and securities sect. 1983-86), Chgo. Bar Assn. (current events chmn. corp. sect. 1980-81), 7th Cir. Bar Assn., Yale Club (N.Y.C.). Democrat. Jewish. Office: Holland and Knight 195 Broadway Fl 24 New York NY 10007-3100

MAYERSON CANNELLA, RENEE, lawyer; b. N.Y.C., June 3, 1965; d. Seymour Sheldon and Edi (Wellner) Mayerson; m. Anthony Joseph Cannella, Oct. 1, 1994; children: Alex Glen, Samantha Regine. BA in Polit. Sci./Legal Studies, SUNY, Purchase, 1987; JD with honors, U. Conn., 1991. Bar: Conn. 1991, U.S. Dist. Ct. Conn. 1992, U.S. Dist. Ct. (so. dist.) N.Y. 1993. Atty. Casper & de Toledo, Stamford, Conn., 1991—97; ct. adv. Sexual Assault Crisis and Edn. Ctr., 2001—. Advocate Rape and Sexual Abuse Crisis Ctr., Stamford, 1993-96. Contbr. article to profl. jour. Office: Sexual Assault Crisis and Edn Ctr 1 Dock st Stamford CT 06902

MAYES, BRIAN A. toxicologist; b. Margaretville, N.Y., July 24, 1952; s. Murray R. and Bertha C. Mayes; m. Nanette S. Dorman; children: Denise Dingman, Zachary. PhD, Albany Med. Coll., 1979. Diplomate Am. Bd. Toxicology. Asst. rsch. dir. Sterling Rsch. Group, Rensselaer, NY, 1992; sr. toxicologist Gen. Electric Co., Schenectady, 1992—. Leader Boy Scouts Am., Delmar, NY, 1998—2002, Cub Scouts, Selkirk, 1994—98. Fellow, NIEHS, 1975—79. Mem.: Soc. Toxicology. Home: 185 Pictuay Rd Selkirk NY 12158-1820 Office: GenElectric Global Rsch Ctr 1 River Rd Schenectady NY 12301 Business E-Mail: mayes@crd.ge.com.

MAYES, GLENN, social worker; b. Aug. 23, 1955; s. Johnny and Lillie (Hopper) M. BS, Cameron U., 1977; MSW, U. Okla., 1984. Cert. profl. healthcare quality; lic. social worker with clin. and adminstrv. specialties, Okla.; bd. cert. diplomate clin. social worker. Quality improvement dir. Jim Taliaferro Comty. Mental Health Ctr., Lawton, Okla., 1976—. Mem. NASW (S.W. chpt. br. chmn. nominations and leadership com.), Nat. Assn. Healthcare Quality, Acad. Cert. Social Workers. Home: 1801 SW 68th St Lawton OK 73505-4442 Office: 602 SW 38th St Lawton OK 73505-6912 E-mail: glennmayes@hotmail.com., gmayes@odmhsas.org.

MAYES, MAUREEN DAVIDICA, physician, educator; b. Phila., Oct. 16, 1945; d. David and Marguerite Cecilia M.; m. Charles William Houser, Dec. 18, 1976; children: David Steven, Edward Charles. BA, Coll. Notre Dame, 1967; MD, Ea. Va. Med. Sch., 1976; MA in Pub. Health, U. Mich., Ann Arbor, 1994. Diplomate Am. Bd. Internal Medicine, Am. Bd. Rheumatology. Resident in internal medicine Cleve. Clinic Found., 1977-79, fellow in rheumatology, 1979-81; asst. prof. medicine W.Va. U., Morgantown, 1981-85, Wayne State U., Detroit, 1985-90, assoc. prof. medicine, 1990-97, prof. medicine, 1997—2001, U. Tex., Houston, 2002—. Dir. scleroderma unit Wayne State U., Detroit, 1991—; prin. investigator Scleroderma Registry NIH, 1994—; pres. Scleroderma Clin. Trials Consortium, 1998—2000. Author: The Scleroderma Book, 1999; contbr. articles to profl. jours. Pres. bd. United Scleroderma Found., 1988-89, pres. med. adv. bd., 1997—; bd. trustees Arthritis Found., Mich. Robert Wood Johnson scholarship EVMS, 1972, NIH fellow, 1993-94, NIAMS Sr. Rsch. fellowship, 1994; recipient Lower award Cleve. Clinic Found., 1981. Fellow: ACP, Am. Coll. Rheumatology (ctrl. region coun. 1995—97). Office: U Tex Health Sci Ctr 6431 Fannin Houston TX 77030

MAYES, PAUL EUGENE, engineering educator, technical consultant; b. Frederick, Okla., Dec. 21, 1928; s. Robert Franklin and Bertha Ellen (Walter) M.; m. Lola Mae Davis, June 4, 1950; children: Gwynne Ellen, Linda Kay, Stuart Franklin, Patricia Gail, Steven Lee, David Thomas. BS in Elec. Engring., U. Okla., 1950; MS in Elec. Engring., Northwestern U., 1952, PhD, 1955. Rsch. asst. Northwestern U., Evanston, Ill., 1950-54; asst. prof. U. Ill., Urbana, 1954-58, assoc. prof., 1958-63, prof., 1963-93, prof. emeritus, 1994—. Tech. cons. Walter Gee and Assocs., San Jose, Calif. Author: Electromagnetics for Engineers, 1965; contbr. articles to profl. jours.; inventor in field. Fellow IEEE. Avocations: woodworking, hiking, camping. Home: 1508 Waverly Dr Champaign IL 61821-5002 Office: U Ill 1406 W Green St Urbana IL 61801-2918 E-mail: pemayes@ix.netcom.com.

MAYES, RANDALL ELAM, journalist, marketing professional; b. Abingdon, Va., Feb. 18, 1956; s. William H. and Nancy Elan Mayes. BA in biology, Christopher Newport Coll., Va., 1980. Journist Free Lance, Alexandria , Va., 1997—; owner Sports Mag. Co., Alexandria , 1998—2001; sales rep. Xerox, Cannon, Wash., DC, 1989—96. Adv. Global MBIO club, Durham, NC, 1997—, Hope Inc., Rockville, Md., 1998—2000. Author: (guide) Reebok Enclave Media Guide, 2000. Staff Presidential Inaugural , Wash., DC, 1988; vol. George Bush for Pres., 1988. Avocations: running, sailing, chess, kickboxing. Home: 116 Stedwick Pl Durham NC 27712

MAYES, SAMUEL WILLIAM, music educator; b. Lock Haven, Pa., Apr. 20, 1955; s. Donald William and Nora Walizer Mayes; m. Kimberly Dawn Fye, Aug. 5, 1978; 1 child Lindsay. BS in Music Edn., Indiana U. of Pa., 1977, MA in Music Edn., 1979. Cert. permanent tchg. cert. Ohio. Dir. of bands Coventry Local Schs., Akron, Ohio, 1979—82, Wadsworth (Ohio) City Schs., 1982—2001, Cen. Intermediate Sch., Wadsworth, 2001—. Orch. dir. Grace Ch., Norton, Ohio, 2001—; trombone player Cuyahoga Valley Brass Band, Akron, Ohio, 2001—, bd. dirs., Ohio, libr., Ohio, 2002—. Orch. dir. Grace Ch., Norton, 2001—02. Mem.: NEA, North Am. Brass Band Assn., Internat. Assn. of Jazz Educators, Nat. Band Assn., Internat. Trombone Assn., Ohio Music Edn. Assn., Music Educators Nat. Conf.-Nat. Assn. for Music Edn., Phi Mu Alpha. Conservative. Avocations: golf, Harley-Davidson motorcycles, Drum and Bugle Corps, band concerts, travel. Home: 119 Pin Oak Trail Seville OH 44273 Office: Cen Intermediate Sch 151 Main St Wadsworth OH 44281 Personal E-mail: skmayes@bright.net.

MAYES, WENDELL WISE, JR. broadcasting company executive; b. San Antonio, Mar. 2, 1924; s. Wendell Wise and Dorothy Lydia (Evans) M.; m. Mary Jane King, May 11, 1946; children: Cathey, Sarah, Wendell Wise, III. Student, Schreiner Inst., 1941-42, U. Tex., 1942, Daniel Baker Coll., 1946; BS, Tex. Tech. Coll., 1949; BA summa cum laude, St. Edward's U., 2002. Program dir., sta. mgr. Sta. KBWD, Brownwood, Tex., 1949-57; mgr. Sta. KCRS, Midland, 1957-63, pres., 1965-84, chmn., 1984-96; pres. Sta. KNOW, Austin, Tex., 1970-81, Stas. KVIC and KAMG, Victoria, 1970-84, chmn., 1984-98, Sta. KCRS-FM, Midland, 1984-96; pres. Sta. KCSW, San Marcos, 1976-81; sec.-treas. Sta. KSNY-AM-FM, Snyder, 1952-94; mem. bd. mgrs. Sta. KLBJ/KHHT-AM-FM, Austin, 1991-97. Lectr. Coll. Communications, U. Tex., Austin, 1978-81 Chmn. bd. Am. Diabetes Assn., 1974—77; mem. Nat. Diabetes Adv. Bd., 1977—84; v.p. Internat. Diabetes Fedn., 1980—88, pres.-elect, 1988—91, pres., 1991—94, hon. pres., 1997—; pres. Tex. Broadcast Edn. Found., 1973—76, dir., 2002—; mem. Tex. Diabetes Coun., 1983—86, chmn., 1983—86, exec. dir., 1999; bd. regents Tex. Tech U., 1985—91, chmn., 1987—88. With USNR, 1943—46. Recipient Addison B. Scoville award Am. Diabetes Assn., 1977, first Wendell Mayes Jr. award, 1986, Josiah K. Lilly award, 1991, Harold Rifkin award, 1994, Masaji Takeda medal Kobe. Japan Colloquium Med. Sci., 1994; named to Tex. Tech. Mass Comm. Hall of Fame, 1978, Hall of Fame Tex. affiliate Am. Diabetes Assn., 1994; named Disting. Alumnus Tex. Tech. U., 1981, Disting. Engr., 1985. Mem. Tex. Assn. Broadcasters (pres. 1964, named Pioneer Broadcaster of Year 1978), Nat. Assn. Broadcasters (dir. 1969-72), Am. Council on Edn. in Journalism (dir. 1977-80), Broadcast Edn. Assn. (dir. 1973-77), AP Broadcasters (bd. dirs. 1988-91), Tex. Tech. Elec. Engring. Acad. Episcopalian (vestryman 1966-69, 86-88; sr. warden 1988). Home: 2834 Montebello Rd Apt 1 Austin TX 78746-6820 Office: 1907 N Lamar Blvd Austin TX 78705-4992 E-mail: wmayes@swbell.net.

MAYFIELD, J. W. police official; b. Hubbard, Tex., Nov. 5, 1937; s. William L. and Othella (Olsson) M.; m. Alma Louise McMahon, Oct. 10, 1958; children: Jana D., Shari Ann Mayfield Harrison, Joseph R. AA, Abilene Christian U., 1972, BS, 1974, MS, 1978. Licensed peace officer, Tex. Police officer, asst. police chief City of Garland (Tex.) Police Dept., Garland, Tex., 1960-93; chief of police City of Electra, 1993-96. Instr. criminal justice, Abilene Christian U., Garland, 1974-80. With USAF, 1956-60. Named Officer of the Yr., Garland Jaycees, 1976; chmn. awards com. Garland Optimist Club, Garland, 1977-78. Mem. Internat. Assn. Chiefs of Polics, Law Enforcement Officers Tex. (bd. dirs.), Garland Police Officers Assn., Tex. Law Enforcement Intelligence Units Assn., Abilene Christian U. Alumni Assn., Garland Police Assn. (sec. 1978-80), Garland Country Music Assn. Republican. Missionary Baptist. Avocations: playing guitar (country music), fishing, hunting (quail). Home: 718 Eastern Star Dr Garland TX 75040-5178

MAYFIELD, JACQUELINE ROWLEY, finance educator, department chairman; b. Detroit, Feb. 17, 1952; d. Ralph James and Worth Carpenter Rowley; m. Milton Ray Mayfield, Jr., June 2, 1991. BA in French, George Washington U., 1974, MBA in Mktg., 1979; MA in Tchg. (French), U. Chgo., 1975; PhD in Bus. Adminstrn., U. Ala., 1993. Tchr. French D.C. Pub. Schs., Washington, 1975—76; market rsch. analyst, product devel. coord. Blue Cross Blue Shield , 1979—82, product devel. specialist, health industry analyst Jacksonville, Fla., 1982—87; asst. prof. mgmt. Radford U., Va., 1992—95, Tex. A&M Internat. U., Laredo, 1995—99, assoc. prof., 1999—, co-chair dept. mgmt. and mktg., 2001—. Pvt. practice orgnl. cons., Cotulla, Tex., 1992—. Named Outstanding Young Woman of Am., Outstanding Young Ams. Assn., 1983; recipient Best Paper in Orgnl. Behavior, Inst. Behavioral and Applied Mgmt., 1994, Citation of Excellence, Anbar Pub., 1999. Mem.: Assn. Bus. Comm., Acad. Mgmt., Phi Kappa Phi, Beta Gamma Sigma. Avocation: music, films, meteorology. Office: Tex A&M Internat U 5201 Univ Blvd Laredo TX 78041-1900 Office Fax: 956-326-2494. Business E-Mail: jmayfield@tamiu.edu.

MAYFIELD, RICHARD HEVERIN, lawyer; b. Washington, Sept. 29, 1921; s. Robert Edwin and Helen May (Benton) M.; m. Caroline C. Mayfield; children: Elinor D., Nancy L., Anne W. AB, Swarthmore Coll., 1943; LLB, Harvard U., 1948. Bar: D.C. 1948, Md. 1954. Assoc. Craighill, Mayfield, Fenwick, Cromelin & Cobb, Washington, 1948-54, ptnr., 1954—. Editor: Will Forms and Clauses, 1969, Trust Forms and Clauses, 1975. Bd. govs. Beauvoir Sch., 1961-67, chmn., 1967. Served with AUS, 1943-46. Fellow Am. Coll. Trust and Estates Counsel; mem. Washington Estate Planning Coun., Barrister Club (sec. 1959), Lawyers Club, Columbia Country Club, Masons, Shriners. Home: 5 E Kirke St Bethesda MD 20815-4216 Office: Craighill Mayfield Fenwick Cromelin & Cobb 4910 Massachusetts Ave NW Washington DC 20016-4300

MAYFIELD, ROBERT CHARLES, university official, geography educator; b. Abilene, Tex., Oct. 15, 1928; s. Percy Anderson and Fay (Hicks) M.; m. Loraine Poindexter, Sept. 3, 1952; children: Julie Barnes, Jennifer Manley, Mark Stanley, Malcolm Randall. BA, Tex. Christian U., 1952; MS, Ind. U., 1953; PhD, U. Wash., 1961. Chmn. geography dept. Tex. Christian U., Ft. Worth, 1960-64, U. Tex., Austin, 1967-71, Boston U., 1972-77, acad. v.p. external programs, 1977-83, provost, 1979-84. Cons. Coun. for Econ. Action, Boston, 1980—; adj. prof. U. Tex., Austin, 1987—; lectr. U.S. Info. Svc., Bangladesh, 1994; seminar dir. U. Tex. Seminars for Adult Growth and Enrichment, 1995-2002; mem. faculty rev. bd. Bangladesh U. Engring. and Tech., Dacca, 1996—. Editor, contbg. author: Man, Environment and Space, 1972. With USAF, 1946-49. Rsch. fellow Nat. Acad. Sci. No. India, 1957-58, Fulbright-Hays fellow Office Edn., Bangalore, Mysore, India, 1966-67; Rsch. grant Agrl. Devel. Coun., 1968. Mem. Assn. Am. Geographers. E-mail: rmayfield@mail.utexas.edu.

MAYFIELD, RONALD KEITH, endocrinologist, educator; b. Morgantown, W.Va., July 15, 1950; s. Albert Keith and Mary Kathleen (Lemley) M.; m. Karen Elizabeth Gaspar, Dec. 27, 1970; children: Douglas Keith, Cortnie Anne. MD, W.Va. U., 1975. Diplomate Am. Bd. Internal Medicine (cert.), Am. Bd. Endocrinology and Metabolism. Intern W.Va. U. Sch. Medicine, Charleston Area Med. Ctr., 1975-76, resident internal medicine, 1976-78; fellow in endocrinology-metabolism and nutrition Med. U. S.C., Charleston, 1978-80, instr. medicine, 1980-81, asst. prof., 1981-86, asst. prof. lab. medicine, 1983-86, assoc. prof. medicine, pathology and lab. medicine, 1986-92, prof. medicine, pathology and lab. medicine, 1992—. Staff physician, 1980—; cons. in endocrinology Med. U. Hosp., Charleston VA Med. Ctr., Charleston Meml. Hosp.; dir. specialized diagnostic and therapeutic unit VA Med. Ctr., 1984—; assoc. dir. Gen. Clin. Rsch. Med. Ctr. U. So. Calif., 1988-95, dir. fellowship tng. endocrinology, 1995—; bd. dirs. Diabetes Initiative S.C. Contbr. articles to profl. jours. Recipient Spl. Emphasis Rsch. Career award NIH, 1980-85; bd. govs. scholar W.Va. U. Sch. Medicine, 1971-75, Mosby scholar, 1972, Health Scis. Developing scholar Med. U. S.C., 1988. Fellow ACP; mem. Assn. Subspecialty Profs., Am. Diabetes Assn. (rsch.-rev. com. 1986-89, Outstanding Profl. Svc. award S.C. affiliate 1983, bd. dirs. S.C. affiliate 1981-88), Am. Fedn. Med. Rsch., So. Soc. for Clin. Investigation, Endocrine Soc., Alpha Epsilon Delta. Republican. Home: 537 Rice Planters Ln Mount Pleasant SC 29464 Office: 69 Jonathin Lucas St Charleston SC 29425-0001

MAYFIELD, WILLIAM STEPHEN, law educator; b. Gary, Indiana, Mar. 2, 1919; s. William Henry and Elnora Elizabeth (Williams) M.; m. Octavia Smith, Feb. 6, 1949 (dec.); children: Pamela L., William E., Stephanie K. Stokes; m. Mildred G. Harris, May 25, 1991. BA, Detroit Inst. Tech., 1946; JD, Detroit Coll. Law, 1949. Bar: Mich. 1949, U.S. Supreme Ct. 1996. Mem. firm Lewis, Rowlette, Brown, Wanzo and Bell, Detroit, 1949-51; atty. U.S. Office Price Stblzn., 1951-53; referee Friend of the Court, 1953-72; vis. prof. Law Center, La. State Univ., Baton Rouge, summer, 1979; prof. law So. U., 1972—. Mem. com. sci. and tech. in cts. La. Supreme Ct., 1978 Mem. regional bd. Boy Scouts Am., Detroit, 1961-63; Served with U.S. Army, 1942-46. Mem. Am. Bar Assn., Nat. Bar Assn., Wolverine Bar Assn., World Assn. Law Profs., Detroit Coll. Law Alumni Assn., Assn. Henri Capitanti, Comml. Law League Am., Ret. Officers Assn. (pres. Greater Baton Rouge 1985), Am. Legion, Mil. Order of the World Wars, Delta Theta Phi (Outstanding Prof. of Yr. award 1983) Office: 5909 Marina View Ct Prospect KY 40059-8865

MAYGARDEN, JERRY LOUIS, health care foundation executive; b. Pensacola, Fla., Dec. 22, 1948; s. Louis Ameal and Jean (Saxon) Maygarden; m. Rhonda Delene Fosha, June 25, 1977; children: Louis Ameal III, Morgan Lora. AA in Liberal Arts, Pensacola Jr. Coll., 1972; BA in Communications Arts, U. West Fla., 1974, MA in Communication, 1975. V.p. U. West Fla., Pensacola, 1980-83; exec. v.p. Sacred Heart Found., 1983-89; pres. Bapt. Health Care Found., 1989—. Bd. dirs. Bank of Pensacola; mem. Fla. House of Reps., 1994—. City councilman Pensacola City Coun., 1985-92, mayor pro tem, 1989-91, mayor, 1991-94; bd. dirs. C. of C. Com. 100, Pensacola, 1989—. With USN, 1968-74, Viet Nam. Recipient George Washington Honor medal, Freedoms Found. of Valley Forge, 1992, Paul Harris fellow, Rotary Found Internat., 1993; named Cmty. Leader of Yr. C. of C., Pensacola, 1988, Outstanding Young Man Am. U.S. Jaycees, 1977, Nat. Soc. Fund Raising Execs., Assn. for Health Care Philanthropy, Rotary Internat. Mem. Fla. League Cities, Nat. League Cities, Nat. Soc. Fund Raising Execs., Assn. for Health Care Philanthropy, Rotary Internat. Democrat. Methodist. Avocations: tennis, sailing, hiking, biking, fishing. Home: 1240 Tamara Dr Pensacola FL 32504-6622 Office: Bapt Health Care Found PO Box 17500 Pensacola FL 32522-7500

MAYHALL, C. GLEN, internal medicine educator; b. St. Louis, Feb. 17, 1939; s. Orville Green and Mary Beatrice (Trulove) M.; m. Kathryn Ann Rompel, June 12, 1965; children: Lisa, Michelle, Mark. BA, Washington U., St. Louis, 1961; MD, Baylor U., 1966. Diplomate Am. Bd. Internal Medicine, Am. Bd. (Infectious Diseases). Intern in internal medicine Barnes Hosp., St. Louis, 1966-67, resident in internal medicine, 1967-68, fellow in infectious diseases, 1973-75; resident in internal medicine St. Luke's Hosp., 1971-73; asst. prof. Med. Coll. Va., Richmond, 1975-80, assoc. prof., 1980-87, prof., 1987-89, U. Tenn., Memphis, 1990-93; prof. internal medicine U. Tex. Med. Br., Galveston, 1994—. Hosp. epidemiologist Med. Coll. Va. Hosps., Richmond, 1975-89, Regional Med. Ctr., Memphis, 1990-93, U. Tex. Med. Br. Hosps., Galveston, 1994—. Editor: Hospital Epidemiology and Infection Control 2nd Edition, 1999. Maj. U.S. Army, 1968-71. Fellow Infectious Disease Soc. Am.; mem. Soc. for Healthcare Epidemiology of Am. (pres. 1991). Episcopalian. Office: U Tex Med Br 301 University Blvd Galveston TX 77555-0435

MAYHER, WILLIAM EDGAR, III, neurosurgeon; b. Columbus, Ga., Nov. 5, 1938; s. William Edgar Jr. and Frances Hicks (Lummus) M.; m. Jo Anne Mullis, June 9, 1963; children: William Roy, Brant Edgar, Anne Mullis. Student, Tulane U., 1956-58; BS, U. Ga., 1960; MD, Med. Coll. Ga., 1964. Diplomate Am. Bd. Neurol. Surgery. Intern in surgery Grady Meml. Hosp. Emory U., Atlanta, 1964-65; resident in neurosurgery Coll. of Ga., Augusta, 1965-70; practice medicine specializing in neurosurgery Neurosurg. Assocs., Albany, Ga., 1970-98. Chmn. bd. dirs. Blue Cross and Blue Shield of Ga., 1980-90; chmn. bd. dirs. Gray Comms. Sys., Gaston-Loughlin, Inc. Mem. ACS, AMA, Am. Assn. Neurol. Surgeons (bd. dirs.), Congress Neurol. Surgeons, Ga. Neurosurg. Soc. (pres. 1989-90), So. Neurosurg. Soc., Ga. Surg. Soc., Rotary Club Albany, Med. Coll. Ga. Found. (bd. dirs. 1994—, chmn. bd. dirs. 1999—). Republican. Episcopalian. Avocations: flying, hunting, fishing, photography. Home: 2520 E Doublegate Dr Albany GA 31707-9241

MAYHEW, AUBREY, music industry executive; b. Washington, Oct. 2, 1927; s. Aubrey and Verna June (Hall) M.; m. Carol de Onis, May 10, 1962 (div. 1971); children: Lawrence Aubrey, Michael Aubrey, Parris Mitchell, Casey Aran. Student, Wilson Tchs. Coll., 1948. Dir. Sta. WWVA, Wheeling, W.Va., 1947-54, Sta. WCOP, Boston, 1954-56; asst. to pres. MGM Records, N.Y.C., 1957-58; v.p. mktg. Capitol Records, Los Angeles, 1958-60; prodr., dir. Sta. KCAM-TV Prodns., Nashville, 1981—. Pres., founder John F. Kennedy Meml. Ctr., 1968; authority on John F. Kennedy life and memorabilia. Author: (books) Commandants Marine Corps, 1953, World Tribute to John F. Kennedy, 1965; composer (music) Touch My Heart, 1966 (Broadcast Music, Inc. award, 1967); record producer, artist mgmt., 1947—; music pub., 1954—; developed careers numerous entertainers including Johnny Paycheck, Jeannie C. Riley, Bobby Helms. Served to cpl. U.S. Army Signal Corps, 1945-48. Named Govs. Aide, Nashville, 1978. Mem. Country Music Assn., Broadcast Music Inc., Manuscript Soc., N.Y. Numismatic Soc., Gospel Music Assn. Republican. Episcopalian. Avocations: collector, historian, author. Office: Amcorp Music Group 827 Meridian St Nashville TN 37207-5856

MAYHEW, DAVID RAYMOND, political science educator; b. Putnam, Conn., May 18, 1937; s. Raymond William and Jeanie (Nicholson) M. BA, Amherst Coll., 1958; PhD, Harvard U., 1964. Tchg. fellow Harvard U., 1961-63; from instr. to asst. prof. polit. sci. U. Mass., Amherst, 1963-67; vis. asst. prof. Amherst Coll., 1965-66; faculty Yale U., 1968-77, prof. polit. sci., 1977—, chmn. dept., 1979-82, Alfred Cowles prof. govt., 1982-98, Sterling prof. polit. sci., 1998—. Olin vis. prof. Am. govt. Nuffield Coll., Oxford (Eng.) U., 2000-01. Author: Party Loyalty Among Congressmen, 1966, Congress: The Electoral Connection, 1974 (Washington Monthly ann. polit. book award 1974), Placing Parties in American Politics, 1986, Divided We Govern, 1991, America's Congress, 2000, Electoral Requirements, 2002. Recipient Richard E. Neustadt prize 1992, James Madison award, 2002, Yale Grad. Student Mentor award, 2002; Woodrow Wilson fellow, 1958-59, vis. fellow Nuffield Coll., Oxford, 1978, Guggenheim fellow, 1978-79, Hoover Nat. fellow, 1978-79, Sherman Fairchild fellow, 1990-91, fellow Ctr. for Advanced Study in Behavioral Scis., 1995-96. Fellow Am. Acad. Arts and Scis.; mem. Am. Polit. Sci. Assn. (nat. council 1976-78, Congl. fellow 1967-68), So. Polit. Sci. Assn., New Eng. Polit. Sci. Assn. Home: 100 York St Apt 5C New Haven CT 06511-5611 Office: Yale U Polit Sci Dept Box 208301 New Haven CT 06520-8301 E-mail: david.mayhew@yale.edu.

MAYHEW, ERIC GEORGE, medical researcher, educator; b. London, June 22, 1938; came to U.S., 1964; s. George James and Doris Ivy (Tipping) M.; m. Barbara Doe, Sept. 28, 1966 (div. 1976); 1 child, Miles; m. Karen Caruana, Apr. 1, 1978 (div. 1994); children: Ian, Andrea; m. Ludmila Khatchatrian, June 29, 1995. BS, U. London, 1960, MS, 1963; PhD, 1967; DSc, U. London, 1993. Rsch. asst. Chester Beatty Rsch. Inst., London, 1960-64; cancer rsch. scientist Roswell Pk. Meml. Inst., Buffalo, 1964-68, sr. cancer rsch. scientist, 1968-72, assoc. cancer rsch. scientist, 1979-93, dep. dir. exptl. pathology, 1988-93; prin. scientist The Liposome Co., Princeton, N.J., 1993-99, May Pharm Consulting, 2000—. Assoc. rsch. prof. SUNY, Buffalo, 1979-93; ad-hoc mem. NIH study sects., 1982-94; cons. to industry, 2000—. Editor jour. Selective Cancer Therapeutics, 1989-91; contbr. articles to Jour. Nat. Cancer Inst., Cancer Rsch. and many other profl. jours. Grantee NIH, Am. Heart Assn., and pvt. industry, 1972-93. Mem. Am. Assn. Cancer Rsch., N.Y. Acad. Sci. Achievements include development of liposomes for drug delivery and patents for new chemical entities and liposome delivery. Office: May Pharm Consulting 1782 S Seaview Ave Coupeville WA 98239 E-mail: eailkmay@aol.com.

MAYHEW, KENNETH EDWIN, JR. transportation company executive; b. Shelby, N.C., Sept. 27, 1934; s. Kenneth Edwin and Evelyn Lee (Dellinger) M.; m. Frances Elaine Craft, Apr. 7, 1957; 1 dau., Catherine Lynn Prince. AB, Duke U., 1956. CPA, N.C. Sr. auditor Arthur Andersen & Co., Atlanta, 1956-58, 60-63; controller Trendline, Inc., Hickory, N.C., 1963-66; with Carolina Freight Corp., Cherryville, 1966-93; treas., 1969-74; v.p. Carolina Freight Carriers Corp., Cherryville, 1971-72, exec. v.p., 1972-85, pres., chief oper. officer, 1985-89, dir., 1968-93, chmn., pres., CEO, 1989-93. Pres., dir. Robo Auto Wash Shelby Inc., 1967-73, Robo Auto Wash Cherryville, Inc., 1968-73; dir. Cherryville Nat. Bank, Kenmar Bus. Group, Inc. Mem. Bus. Adv. Bd., Fuqua Sch. Bus., Duke U.; bd. dirs., vice-chmn. Gaston Meml. Hosp.; trustee Pfeiffer U. With AUS, 1958-60. Mem. AICPA, Am. Trucking Assn. (dir., v.p.), N.C. Trucking Assn. (dir., chmn.), Gaston County C. of C. (v.p. pub. affairs), Lions (pres. Cherryville 1972-73), Phi Beta Kappa, Omicron Delta Kappa, Phi Eta Sigma. Methodist. Home: 507 Spring St Cherryville NC 28021-3540

MAYHUE, RICHARD LEE, provost, dean, pastor, writer; b. Takoma Park, Md., Aug. 31, 1944; s. J. Richard Mayhue and Myrtle Lorraine (Hartsell) Lee; m. Lois Elaine Nettleingham, June 18, 1966; children: Lee, Wade. BS, Ohio State U., 1966; MDiv, Grace Theol. Seminary, Winona Lake, Ind., 1974, ThM, 1977, ThD, 1981. Ordained pastor. Asst. pastor Grace Brethren Ch. of Columbus (Ohio), 1975-77; asst. prof. New Testament and Greek, Grace Theol. Seminary, Winona Lake, 1977-80; assoc. pastor Grace Cmty. Ch., Sun Valley, Calif., 1980-84, 89—; sr. pastor Grace Brethren Ch., Long Beach, 1984-89; sr. v.p., dean, prof. systematic theology and pastoral mins. The Master's Seminary, Sun Valley, 1989—; sr. v.p., provost The Master's Coll., Santa Clarita, Calif., 2000—. Bd. dirs. Grace Theol. Sem., 1987-89. Author: (booklets) The Biblical Pattern for Divine Healing, 1979, Snatched Before the Storm, 1980, (books) Divine Healing Today, 1983, How to Interpret the Bible for Yourself, 1986, A Christian's Survival Guide, 1987, Unmasking Satan, 1988, (2d edit., 2001), Spiritual Intimacy, 1990, Spiritual Maturity, 1992, The Healing Promise, 1994, What Would Jesus Say About Your Church?, 1995, 2d edit., 2001, Fight the Good Fight, 1999, 1 and 2 Thessalonians, 1999, Seeking God, 2000; contbr., editor: Rediscovering Expository Preaching, 1992, Rediscovering Pastoral Ministry, 1994; contbr. Tim LaHaye Prophecy Study Bible, 2000, A Festschrift In Honor of Homer A. Kent, 1991; contbr., assoc. editor MacArthur Study Bible, 1997; contbr.: The Master's Perspective on Difficult Texts, 1998, The Master's Perspective on Contemporary Issues, 1998; contbr., co-editor: The Master's Perspective on Pastoral Ministry, 2002, The Master's Perspective on Biblical Prophecy, 2002; contbr. articles to profl. jours. Bd. dirs. Capitol Ministries, 1998—, Slavic Gospel Assn, 1993—; bd. elders Grace Cmty. Ch., 1989; mem. bd. of ref. Coun. on Bibl. Manhood and Womanhood, 1991—. Recipient Bronze Star with Combat V USN, 1969. Mem. Evang. Theol. Soc., Nat. Fellowship Grace Brethren Ministers (pres. 1988), Far West Region Evang. Theol. Soc. (pres. 1995), Evang. Homiletics Soc. Avocation: N-gauge model railroading. Office: The Master's Seminary 13248 Roscoe Blvd Sun Valley CA 91352-3739 also: The Master's Coll 21726 Placerita Canyon Rd Santa Clarita CA 91321-1200

MAYLAND, KENNETH THEODORE, economist; b. Miami, Fla., Nov. 17, 1951; s. Herbert and Vera (Bob) M; m. Gail Fern Bassok, Apr. 14, 1984. BS, MIT, 1973; MS, U. Pa., 1976, PhD, 1979. Cons. economist Data Resources, Inc., Lexington, Mass., 1973; economist, then chief economist First Pa. Bank, Phila., 1973-89; sr. v.p., chief economist Soc. Nat. Bank, Cleve., 1989-94; sr. v.p., chief fin. economist Key Corp., 1994-96, sr. v.p., chief economist, 1996-2000; pres. ClearView Econs., LLC, 2000—. Econs. instr., Chartered Fin. Aanalysts Assn., Phila, 1984—; econ. adv. com. Phila. Econ. Devel. Coalition, 1984-86; chmn. econ. adv. com. Pa. Bankers Assn., Harrisburg, 1982-84; mem. Gov.'s Econ. Adv. Com., Ohio, 1989—. Contbr. semi-monthly periodical Money Markets, 1981-85, quar. periodical Regional Report, 1980-89, EconViewpoint/KeyViewpoint biweekly periodical, 1989—, Regional Rev. quar. periodical, 1989-94/ Mem. curriculum adv. com. Widener U., 1986-89. Mem. Am. Bankers Assn. (econ. adv. com. 1990-93), Internat. Econ. Roundtable (vice chmn. 1987-88, chmn. 1988-90), Nat. Assn. Bus. Economists (New Face for the Eighties award 1979), Phila. Coun. Bus. Economists (pres. 1982-84), Cleve. Bus. Economist Club (sec.-treas. 1990-91, v.p. 1991-92, pres. 1992-93). Avocations: fishing, badminton, gardening, camping. Home: 3237 Fox Hollow Dr Cleveland OH 44124-5426 Office: Key Corp 127 Public Sq Cleveland OH 44114-1306

MAYNARD, CHARLES DOUGLAS, radiologist; b. Atlantic City, Sept. 11, 1934; m. Mary Anne Satterwhite; children: Charles D., Deanne, David. BS, Wake Forest U., 1955, MD, 1959. Diplomate Am. Bd. Radiology (trustee 1987-99, sec.-treas., v.p. 1992-94, pres. 1994-96, guest examiner). Intern U.S. Army Hosp., Honolulu, 1959—60; resident N.C. Baptist Hosp., 1963—66; dir. Nuclear Medicine Lab., 1966—77; asst. dean admissions Bowman Gray Sch. Medicine, 1966—71, asso. dean student affairs, 1971—75, prof. radiology, chmn. dept., 1977—2000. Mem. Am. Bd. Med. Specialists; acting dean Wake Forest U. Sch. Medicine, 2001—02. Author: Clinical Nuclear Medicine, 1969; mem. editl. bd.: Academic Radiology, mem. editl. bd.: Yearbook of Diagnostic Radiology, mem. editl. bd.: Contemporary Diagnostic Radiology. Mem. Leadership Winston-Salem, Triad Leadership Network; bd. dirs. Downtown Devel. Corp., 1995—2000, Winston-Salem Bus., Inc., 1995—99. Mem.: AMA, Greater Winston-Salem C. of C. (bd. dirs.), Acad. Radiology Rsch. (pres. 1999—), Soc. Chairmen Radiology Depts. (past pres.), Assn. Univ. Radiologists, Radiol. Soc. N.Am. Rsch. and Edn. Found. (chmn. bd. 1999), Radiol. Soc. N.Am. (pres. 1999—2000), Am. Coll. Radiology (past bd. chancellors, past chmn. commn. on nuc. medicine), Soc. Nuc. Medicine (past pres.). Office: Wake Forest U Sch Medicine Dept Radiology Medical Center Blvd Winston Salem NC 27157-1088

MAYNARD, DONALD NELSON, horticulturist, educator; b. Hartford, Conn., June 22, 1932; s. Harry Ashley and Elsie Frances (Magnuson) M.; 1 child, David Nelson. BS, U. Conn., 1954; MS, N.C. State U., 1956; PhD, U. Mass., 1963. Instr. plant sci. U. Mass., Amherst, 1956-62, asst. prof., 1962-67, assoc. prof., 1967-72, prof., 1972-79, asst. dean, 1974-75, prof. emeritus, 1979—; prof. vegetable crops U. Fla., Gainesville, 1979—, chmn. dept., 1979-85. Cons. Greenleaf, Inc., Hackensack, N.J., SRD Rsch., Logan, Utah. Assoc. editor Jour. Am. Soc. Hort. Sci., 1976-80, 89-91, HortSci, 1975-80, 89—, HortTechnology, 1997—. Recipient Aid to Edn. award Gulf Oil Corp., 1965 Fellow Am. Soc. for Hort. Sci. (Environ. Quality Rsch. award 1975, Marion W. Meadows award 1977, pres. 1996-97, chmn. bd. 1997-98, So. region pres. 1996-97); mem. Sigma Xi, Phi Kappa Phi, Alpha Zeta, Phi Tau Sigma. Republican. Episcopalian. Home: 852 Hudson Ave Sarasota FL 34236-7744 Office: U Fla Gulf Coast Rsch Edn Ctr Bradenton FL 34203 E-mail: dnma@ifas.ufl.edu.

MAYNARD, ELLIOTT, state supreme court justice; b. Williamson, W.Va., Dec. 8, 1942; BS in Psychology, Fla. So. Coll., 1967; JD, W.Va. U., 1974. Judge W.Va. Cir. Ct. 30th Jud. Cir., 1982-97; justice W.Va. Supreme Ct. Appeals, Charleston, 1997—, chief justice, 2000. Prosecuting atty., Mingo County, 1976, 80. Mng. dir. Tug Valley C. of C., 1968-70; active Boy Scouts Am.; dist. chmn. Mingo-Pike Dist., Chief Cornstalk Dist.; bd. dirs. Buckskin Coun. With USAF, 1961-66. Recipient Silver Beaver award Boy Scouts Am. Office: State Capital State Ct Appeals Bldg 1 Rm E306 Charleston WV 25305*

MAYNARD, GEORGE FLEMING, III, financial executive; b. Tupelo, Miss., Mar. 29, 1947; s. George Fleming Jr. and Shirley Lindsey (Russell) M.; m. Janie White, Aug. 16, 1969; children: George Fleming IV, Benjamin Hoyle. BA in Sociology, U. Miss., 1969; MS in Social Work, U. Tenn., 1972. Lic. trainer Covey Leadership Inst. Child welfare supr. Miss. Dept. Pub. Welfare, Pontotoc, 1972-74; exec. dir. Lift, Inc., Tupelo, 1974-77; dir. devel. and pub. relations North Miss. Med. Ctr., 1977-82; v.p. pub. affairs United Health Svcs., Binghamton, N.Y., 1982-87; pres. Orlando (Fla.) Regional Healthcare Found., 1987-98; sr. ptnr. Jerold Panas, Linzy and Ptnrs., 1998-2001; mng. dir. Philanthropy Work, LLC, Longwood, 2001—. Contbr. chpts. to books, articles to profl. jours. Mem. Leadership Miss., 1980, Leadership Orlando, 1988, Econ. Devel. Commn.; mem. exec. com. Bayhill Invitational, Orlando, 1987—96; elder Metro Ch. of Christ; lay missionary Varna, Bulgaria; bd. dirs. Broome County Cmty. Charities, Endicott, NY, 1984—87; Mem. nat. bd. dirs. Water Missions Internat., Inc., Charleston, SC; bd. dirs. Greater Orlando Leadership Found., 2001—, Shepherd's Hope, Inc., 2001—. Recipient MacEachern award Am. Soc. Hosp. Pub. Relations, 1979. Fellow Assn. Healthcare Philanthropy; mem. Health Systems Devel. Network (pres. 1994-97), Planned Giving Coun. Ctrl. Fla. (pres. 1994-95), Rotary (pres. Tupelo chpt. 1980-82). Avocations: racquetball, teaching Bible school. Home and Office: 451 Longmeadow Ln Longwood FL 32779-6011 E-mail: gmaynard@ceoexpress.com.

MAYNARD, JOAN, education educator; b. Louisa, Ky., Oct. 18, 1932; d. Macon Scott and Jeanette (Thompson) Chambers; m. Frank Maynard Jr., June 15, 1951 (dec. Oct. 1988); children: Mark Steven, Julia Beth Maynard McFann, Robert Blake. BA, Wittenberg U., 1977; MEd, Wright State U., 1980, MEd, 1984. Tchr., reading specialist Mechanicsburg (Ohio) Exempted Village Schs., 1976—; pres. TOTT Publs. Inc., Bellbrook, Ohio, 1988—99; ret., 1999. Rep. Career Edn., Mechanicsburg, 1981-88, mem. Thompson Grant Com., Mechanicsburg, 1987-88. Author: Mud Puddles, 1988, Mud Pies, 1989. Vol. Mechanicsburg Schs. Levy, 1980, 82, 88, Congl. Race, Campaign County, Ohio, 1982, 84, 86; cons. Urbana U., Ohio, 1988-90, 91, 92, 93; tutor Laubach Lit. Action, Urbana, 1989-90, 91-93, 94. Recipient Thompson grant, 1982, 88, 92. Mem. AAUW (edn. chmn. Champaign County chpt. 1988-89, treas. 1989-90), Internat. Reading Assn., Champaign County Reading Coun. (treas. 1990-91), Midwestern Assembly Lit. Young People (treas. 1989-93), Kappa Delta Pi. Avocations: collecting children's lit. books, travel, reading. Home: 1546 Parkview Rd Mechanicsburg OH 43044-9779 Office: Exempted Village Schs 60 High St Mechanicsburg OH 43044-1071

MAYNARD, JOHN RALPH, lawyer; b. Mar. 5, 1942; s. John R. and Frances Jane (Mitchell) Maynard Kendryk; m. Meridee J. Sagadin, Sept. 10, 1995; children: Bryce James, Pamela Ann. BA, U. Wash., 1964; JD, Calif. Western U., San Diego, 1972; LLM, Harvard U., 1973. Bar: Calif. 1972, Wis. 1973. Assoc. Whyte & Hirschboeck, Milw., 1973-78, Minahan & Peterson, Milw., 1979-91, Quarles & Brady, Milw., 1991-2000, Davis & Kuelthau, Milw., 2000—. Bd. dirs. Am. Heart Assn., 1979—82, Transitional Living Svcs., Inc., 1999—2001; pres. Milw. Chamber Orch., 2000—01; mem. Wis. Adv. Coun. to U.S. SBA, 1987—89. Mem.: ABA, Milw. Yacht Club, Harvard Club (Wis.). Home: 809 E Lake Forest Ave Milwaukee WI 53217-5377 Office: Davis & Kuelthau 111 E Kilbourn Ste 1400 Milwaukee WI 53202

MAYNARD, JOHN ROGERS, English educator; b. Williamsville, N.Y., Oct. 6, 1941; s. Atherton Rogers and Olive (Fisher) M.; m. Florence Michelson, July 1, 1967 (div. 1980); 1 child, Alex Stevens; m. Ursula Krammer, Oct. 17, 1992 (div. 1995). BA, Harvard U., 1963, PhD, 1970. Asst. prof. Harvard U., Cambridge, Mass., 1969-74, NYU, N.Y.C., 1974-76, assoc. prof., 1976-84, prof. English, 1984—, chmn. English dept., 1983-89. Chmn. Faculty Council NYU, 1983-84; vis. prof. U. Venice, Italy, 1991. Author: Brownings Youth, 1977 (Wilson prize 1977), Charlotte Bronte and Sexuality, 1984, Victorian Discourses on Sexuality and Religion, 1993, Browning Re-Viewed, 1998; editor: Literature and Sexuality, 1991-2002; series of books on sexuality and lit.; editor: (with Lockridge and Stone) Nineteenth Century Lives, 1989, (with Bloom) Shankman's Anne Thackeray Ritchie: Journals and Letters, (with Munich) Victorian Literature and Culture, 1991—. Organizer Concord Sq. Assn., Boston, 1972-74. NEH grantee, 1972-73; Guggenheim fellow, 1979-80. Mem. IAUPE, MLA, PEN, Browning Inst. (bd. dirs.), Signet Soc., Fly Club, Andiron Club (pres. 1983-84), Brooklyn Heights Assn. Democrat. Avocation: bicycling.. Office: NYU Dept of English 19 University Pl New York NY 10003-4556

MAYNARD, KENNETH IRWIN, medical educator, researcher; b. San Fernando, Trinidad, Jan. 17, 1963; Student, Howard U., 1982; BSc with honors, Univ. Coll., London, 1986, MSc, 1987, PhD, 1991. Cert. design and conduct of clin. trials. Postdoctoral rsch. assistantship Univ. Coll., London, 1991; postdoctoral rsch. fellow Stroke Rsch. Lab. Neurosurg. Svc. Mass. Gen. Hosp., Harvard Med. Sch., Boston, 1991-93, postdoctoral rsch. fellow neurophysiology lab. Neurosurg. Svc., 1993-97; tchg. fellow dept. neurobiology Harvard Med. Sch., 1992, instr. in surgery, 1995-98, asst. prof., 1998—2001; asst. neuroscientist Mass. Gen. Hosp., 1998—2001; section head, cerebrovascular disorders Aventis Pharms., Inc., 2000—. Ad hoc reviewer Jour. Vascular Rsch., 1991, Neurosci. Letters, 1995, Vision Rsch., 1996, Neurosurgery, 1998, others; presenter in field; tutor dept. of neurobiology, 1998-2000; asst. prof. surgery, 1998; steering com. Boston Area Neurosci. Group, 1998-2000; ad hoc reviewer Ministry of Health, Internal Grant Agy., Czech Republic, 1998, med. rsch. grant program The Jewish Hosp. Found., 2000; cons. neurosurgery Mass. Gen. Hosp., 2001-02; lectr. Harvard U. Med. Sch., 2001-02. Contbr. articles to med. jours. including Neurosci. Letters, Stroke, Exptl. Neurology, Jour. Neurol. Rsch. Mem. parish pastoral coun. St. Joseph's Cath. Ch., Boston, 1992-95, chmn. stewardship commn., 1996-97; advisor regional com. ctrl. region on stewardship for Archdiocese of Boston, 1995-97. Travel fellow for minority neuroscientists Nat. Inst. Neurol. Disease and Stroke, 1995; scholar Autumn Sch. Caen France, 1996, scholar Tokyo, 1998, travel award FASEB MARC, 1998. Fellow Am. Heart Assn. (mem. stroke coun., minority scientist devel. award 1996); mem. AAAS, Am. Stroke Assn. (mem. affil. brain rsch. peer review group 1999), Am. Heart Assn. (nat. affiliate brain/stroke study sect. 1999—, minority affairs cmty. stroke coun. 2002), N.Y. Acad. Sci., Soc. for Neurosci., Am. Assn. Neurosurg. Surgeons (adj. assoc. mem. joint sect. on cerebrovascular surgery 1995), Congress of Neurosurg. Surgeons, Internat. Soc. of Cerebral Blood Flow and Metabolism (Young Scientist Bursary award 1993), Soc. Neurosci. (mem. steering com., mem. minority neurosci. fellowship program 2000—, minority edn., tng. and profl. advancement com. 2000—, membership cmty. 2002). Office: Aventis Pharm Inc Rte 202-206 JR-2-303A Bridgewater NJ 08807-0800 E-mail: Kenneth.Maynard@aventis.com.

MAYNARD, MICHAEL, librarian; b. Yuma, Ariz., July 8, 1955; s. Ernest Ray and Refugio (Guerrero) M. AAS in Electronic Tech., Phoenix Coll., 1986; BA in German, Ariz. State U., 1989; postgrad., U. Leipzig, 1990, Eberhard-Karls U., Tubingen, Germany, 1990-91; MLS, U. Ariz., 1992. Electronics technician USN, 1977-83; asst. libr. Chapel Libr., Venice, Fla., 1983-84; security officer Anderson Agy., Phoenix, 1984-89; grad. asst. U. Ariz., Tuscon, 1989-90, libr. asst. main libr. acquisitions dept., 1992; asst. libr. Internat. Bapt. Coll., Tempe, Ariz., 1992-94; head libr. Fitch Libr., Mesa, 1994-97; libr. II Ariz. Dept. Corrections, Douglas, 1997-2000, Goodyear, Ariz., 2000—. Author: History of the Debate Over I John 5:7-8, 1995. With USN, 1977-83. Scholar U. Ariz., 1989-90, Herman Weinel scholar, 1990. Mem. Assn. Christian Librs. Baptist. Avocations: foreign languages, lexicology, philology, nutrition, New Testament Biblical studies. Home and Office: Receptus Press PO Box 1625 Tempe AZ 85280-1625 E-mail: receptus@sprynet.com.

MAYNARD, NATALIE RYSHNA, pianist, piano educator; b. Phila., Aug. 21, 1930; d. George Thomas Hook and Helen Agatha Reese; m. Harry Edgar Maynard, Jan. 30, 1960; children: Melanie Dawn, Amie Anne. Degree in piano performance, Juilliard Graduate Sch. of Music, N.Y.C., 1952. Concert pianist Columbia Artists Mgmt., tours in U.S. and Europe, 1963-94; recording artist Contemporary Records and Ambiphon Records, 1957-75; pvt. piano instr., 1985—; project dir. Title III and State Urban Edn. program N.Y.C. Schools. Pres. Performers of Conn., Westport, 1985-91, bd. dirs. 1982—; exec. dir. R.B. Fisher Foun. Composer Awards, 1986-96; v.p. ednl. outreach, Friends of Music of Fairfield County, 1995-99; founder, chmn. edn. com. Sta. WNET/13, N.Y.C., 1973-77. Bd. dirs. Friends of Channel 13, Nat. Friends of Pub. Broadcasting, 1971-82; apptd. to arts adv. com. Town of Westport, Conn., 1998-2000, 2000—, mem. town millenium edn. com. co-chair., 1998; mem. adv. bd. Stamford Symphony Orch. Mem. Nat. Music Tchrs. Assn., Ct. State Music Tchrs. Assn., Schubert Club.

MAYNARD, ROBERT HOWELL, retired lawyer; b. San Antonio, Feb. 15, 1938; s. William Simpson Sr. and Lillian Isabel (Tappan) M.; m. Joan Marie Pearson, Jan. 6, 1962; children: Gregory Scott, Patricia Kathryn, Alicia Joan, Elizabeth Simms. BA, Baylor U., 1959, LLB, 1961; LLM, Georgetown U., 1965. Bar: Tex. 1961, D.C. 1969, Ohio 1973. Trial atty. gen. litigation sect. lands div. U.S. Dept. Justice, Washington, 1964-65; spl. asst. to solicitor U.S. Dept. Interior, 1965-69; legis. asst. U.S. Senate, 1969-73; ptnr., dept. head Smith & Schnacke, Dayton, Ohio, 1973-83; dir. Ohio EPA, Columbus, 1983-85; ptnr., environ. policy and strategy devel., tech. law Vorys, Sater, Seymour and Pease, 1985-2000; ret., 2000; pres. Tappan Woods LLC, 2001—. Trustee Ohio Found. for Entrepren. Edn., Business Technology Ctr., 1994-2000, Episcopal Cmty. Svcs. Found., 1990-96, Industry & Tech. Coun. Ctrl. Ohio, Johnson's Island Preservation Soc. USNR, 1962-65. Episcopalian. Office: Vorys Sater Seymour & Pease PO Box 1008 52 E Gay St Columbus OH 43215-1008

MAYNARD, STEVEN HARRY, writer; b. San Diego, July 4, 1954; s. Harry Clark and Ruby Kristina (Odna). BA in Communications, U. Wash., 1976; MA in Theology, Fuller Theol. Seminary, 1979. Religion writer, gen. news reporter Walla Walla (Wash.) Union-Bulletin, 1979-84; religion writer Houston Chronicle, 1984-87; religion/ethics/values reporter The News Tribune, Tacoma, 1987—. Recipient Mng. Editors award Tex. Associated Press, 1984, Wilbur award Religious Pub. Relations Council, 1981. Mem. Religion Newswriters Assn. Office: 1950 S State St Tacoma WA 98405-2817

MAYNARD, TERRELL DENNIS, minister; b. Paducah, Ky., Dec. 10, 1944; s. Claude and Euda (Finley) M.; m. Mary Jacqueline Chappell, Sept. 3, 1965; children: Terrell Geoffrey, Christopher Dennis. BA, Bethel Coll., 1966; MDiv, Memphis Theol. Sem., 1969. Pastor Cumberland Presbyn. Ch., Searcy, Ark., 1969-72, Hohenwald, Tenn., 1972-76, Swan Cumberland Presbyn. Ch., Centerville, 1972-76, Elliottsville Presbyn. Ch., Alabaster, Ala., 1976-94, 1st Cumberland Presbyn. Ch., Jackson, Tenn., 1994—. Pres. Bd. Christian Edn., Memphis, 1976-85; chair Gen. Assembly's Exec. Com., Memphis, 1987-93. Bd. dirs., pres. Shelby Emergency Assistance, Montevallo, Ala., 1990-94; bd. dirs. Developing Ala. Youth Found., Alabaster, 1989-94, Shelby County Hosp. Authority, Alabaster, 1993-94, Area Relief Ministry, Jackson, 1996—. Recipient Disting. Alumni award Bethel Coll., McKenzie, Tenn., 1992; named Outstanding Vol. Shelby County Chpt. ARC, Alabaster, 1989. Mem. Assn. Cumberland Presbyn. Ch. Educators. Avocations: fishing, golf, huntung, reading, college basketball. Home: 139 Paddock Pl Jackson TN 38305-7718 Office: 1st Cumberland Presbyn Ch 1730 US Highway 45 Byp Jackson TN 38305-4415

MAYNARD, VIRGINIA MADDEN, charitable organization executive; b. New London, Conn., Jan. 29, 1924; d. Raymond and Edna Sarah (Madden) M. BS, U. Conn., 1945; postgrad., Am. Inst. Banking, 1964-66, Cornell U., 1975. With Nat. City Bank (now Citibank), N.Y.C., 1954-79, asst. cashier, 1965-69, asst. v.p., 1969-74, v.p. internat. banking group, 1974-76, comptroller's div., 1976-79; v.p. First Women's Bank, 1979-80; Internat. Fedn. Univ. Women rep. UN, 1982—. Trustee fellowships endowment fund AAUW Ednl. Found., Washington, 1977-80, Va. Gildersleeve Internat. Fund Univ. Women, Inc., pres., 1987-93, bd. dirs., 1994-2000, rep. UN, 1997—; bd. dirs. Conf. Nongovtl. Orgns. Found., Inc., 1997—, treas., 1999—. Mem. AAUW (fin. chmn. N.Y.C. br. 1976-79, bylaws chmn. 1979-83, adminstr. Meml. Fund 1983-92, 2000—, bd. dirs. 1992-94, 96-99, Woman of Achievment 1976). Republican. Congregationalist. Home: 601 E 20th St New York NY 10010-7622 E-mail: vmaynard@mindspring.com.

MAYNE, LUCILLE STRINGER, finance educator, educator; b. Washington, June 6, 1924; d. Henry Edmond and Hattie Benham (Benson) Stringer; children: Patricia Anne, Christine Gail, Barbara Marie. BS, U. Md., 1946; MBA, Ohio State U., 1949; PhD, Northwestern U., 1966. Instr. fin. Utica Coll., 1949-50; lectr. fin. Roosevelt U., 1961-64, Pa. State U., 1965-66, asst. prof., 1966-69, assoc. prof., 1969-70; assoc. prof. banking and fin. Case-Western Res. U., 1971-76, prof., 1976-94, prof. emerita, 1994—, grad. dean Sch. Grad. Studies, 1980-84. Sr. economist, cons. FDIC, 1977-78; cons. Nat. Commn. Electronic Fund Transfer Sys., 1976; rsch. cons. Am. Bankers Assn., 1975, Fed. Res. Bank of Cleve., 1968-70, 73; cons. Pres.'s Commn. Fin. Structure and Regulation, 1971, staff economist, 1970-71; analytical statistician Air Materiel Command, Dayton, Ohio, 1950-52; asst. to promotion mgr. NBC, Washington, 1946-48; expert witness cases involving fin. instns. Assoc. editor: Jour. Money, Credit and Banking, 1980-83, Bus. Econs., 1980-85; contbr. articles to profl. jours. Vol. Cleve. Soc. for Blind, 1979—, Benjamin Rose Inst., 1995—; mem. policyholders nominating com. Tchrs. Ins. and Annuity Assn./Coll. Retirement Equities Fund, 1982-84, chairperson com., 1984; bd. dirs. Women's Cmty. Found., 1994-96. Grad. scholar Ohio State U., 1949; doctoral fellow Northwestern U., 1963-65. Mem. LWV (bd. dirs. Shaker Heights chpt. 1999--), Midwest Fin. Assn. (pres. 1991-92, bd. dirs. 1975-79, officer 1988-93), Phi Kappa Phi, Beta Gamma Sigma. Episcopalian. Home: 3723 Normandy Rd Cleveland OH 44120-5246 Office: Case Western Res U Weatherhead Sch Mgmt U Circle Cleveland OH 44106-7235 E-mail: lsm5@po.cwru.edu.

MAYNE, RUTH E. medical nurse; b. New Castle, Pa., Jan. 16, 1946; d. Robert J. and Dorothy (Whiting) McKnight; m. Robert Mayne (div.); 1 child, Robert A. Diploma, Jameson Meml. Hosp., 1967; postgrad., Pa. State U. RN, Pa.; cert. practitioner of clin. hypnotherapy Nat. Hypnosis Tng. Acad. Head nurse Shenongo Valley Med. Ctr., Farrell, Pa., from 1970, nursing supr., staff vis. nurse, relief supr., until 1992; nurse, staff devel. coord. ABC Home Health Svcs., 1992; staff devel. coord. Hermitage, PA and Boardman, Ohio; clin. supr. 1st Am. Home Care, 1994; corp. quality assurance coord. Acute Care Home Nursing Svcs., Inc., 1997, asst. adminstr., 1998—; with Clinical Hypnotherapy Assocs., 1999; case mgr. DACAS Home Care, 2001—, MVI Home Care, 2002—, Forum Health@Home, 2002. Mem. NAFE, Am. Bus. Womens Assn., Keystone Nurses Assn., Sigma Theta Tau. Home: 744 S Neshannock Rd Hermitage PA 16148-9273

MAYNE, WILEY EDWARD, lawyer; b. Sanborn, Iowa, Jan. 19, 1917; s. Earl W. and Gladys (Wiley) M.; m. Elizabeth Dodson, Jan. 5, 1942; children—Martha (Mrs. F.K. Smith), Wiley Edward, John. S.B. cum laude, Harvard, 1938; student, Law Sch., 1938-39; JD, State U. Iowa, 1939-41. Bar: Iowa bar 1941, U.S. Supreme Ct. 1950. Practiced in, Sioux City, 1946-66, 75—; mem. Shull, Marshall, Mayne, Marks & Vizintos, 1946-66, Mayne and Berenstein, 1975-87, Mayne & Mayne, 1988-99, Mayne, Marks, Madsen and Hirschbach, 1999—. Spl. agt. FBI, 1941-43; Mem. 90th-93d Congresses, 6th Dist. Iowa; mem. judiciary com., agr. com. Commr. from Iowa Nat. Conf. Commrs. Uniform State Laws, 1956-60; chmn. grievance commn. Iowa Supreme Ct., 1964-66; del. FAO, 1973; chmn. Woodbury County Compensation Bd., 1975-80 Chmn. Midwest Rhodes Scholar Selection Com., 1964-66; pres. Sioux City Symphony Orch. Assn., 1947-54, Sioux City Concert Course, 1947-54; vice chmn. Young Republican Nat. Fedn., 1948-50; bd. dirs. Iowa Bar Found., 1962-68. Served to lt. (j.g.) USNR, 1943-46. Fellow Am. Coll. Trial Lawyers; mem. ABA (ho. of dels. 1966-68), Iowa Bar Assn. (pres. 1963-64), Sioux City Bar Assn., Internat. Assn. Def. Counsel (exec. com. 1961-64), Harvard Club (N.Y.C.), Sioux City Country Club, Masons (Scottish Rite/33 deg.). Home: 2728 Jackson St Sioux City IA 51104 Office: Pioneer Bank Bldg 701 Pierce St Ste 300 Sioux City IA 51101 Fax: 712-252-1535. E-mail: maynelaw@pionet.net.

MAYNES, CHARLES WILLIAM, foundation administrator; b. Huron, S.D., Dec. 8, 1938; s. Charles William and Almira Rose (Summers) M.; m. Gretchen Schiele, July 17, 1965; children: Stacy Kathryn, Charles William. BA, Harvard U., 1960; MA, Oxford (Eng.) U., 1962. UN polit. affairs ofcl. Dept. State, Washington, 1962-65; chief monetary economist AID, Laos, 1965-67; econ. officer Am. Embassy, Moscow, 1968-70; sec. Carnegie Endowment Internat. Peace, 1971-76; sr. legis. asst. to Sen. Fred R. Harris, 1972; mem. issues Sargent Shriver's Vice-Presdl. campaign, 1972; mem. Carter-Mondale Transition team, 1976-77; asst. sec. for internat. orgn. affairs Dept. State, 1977-80; editor Fgn. Policy mag., 1980-97; mem. Clinton-Gore Transition team, 1992-93, 96-97; pres. Eurasia Found., Washington, 1997—. Mem. Coun. Fgn. Rels., Washington Inst. Fgn. Affairs, UN Assn., Overseas Devel. Coun., Nat. Acad. Pub. Adminstrn., Internat. Inst. Strategic Studies. Contbr. articles to profl. jours. Recipient Meritorious Service award Dept. State; congl. fellow Rep. F. Bradford Morse, 1971, Sen. Fred R. Harris, 1971; Rhodes scholar. Mem. Phi Beta Kappa. Democrat. Office: Eurasia Found 10th Fl 1350 Connecticut Ave NW Washington DC 20036-1722 Home: 3914 Leland St Chevy Chase MD 20815-5036 E-mail: bmaynes@eurasia.org.

MAYO, CAROLYN, marketing professional, public relations executive; BA in Journalism, La. State U. Pub. rels. mgr. Houston dist. J.C. Penny; pvt. practice; shareholer, pres. Vollmer, 2002—. Supporter arts orgns. , Gulf Coast area. Named 1 of city's top 50 woman bus. owners. Mem.: Pub. Rels. Soc. Am. Counselor's Acad., Pub. Rels. Soc. Am. (accredited mem.). Office: 808 Travis Ste 501 Houston TX 77002-5706*

MAYO, C(ATHERINE) M(ANSELL), writer, editor, economist; b. El Paso, Tex., Mar. 22, 1961; d. Roger and Carolyn (Mayo) M.; m. Agustín Guillermo Carstens, July 19, 1986. BA in Econs., U. Chgo., 1982, MA in Econs., 1985. Economist CBI Casa de Bolsa, Mexico City, 1987; mgr. futures and options analysis EuroAm. Capital Corp., Ltd., 1988-89, chief economist, 1989; prof. econs. Inst. Tecnológico Autónomo de Méx., 1990-95; editor Tameme, Mexico City and Los Altos, Calif., 1995—. Author: (as Catherine Mansell Carstens) Las Nuevas Finanzas en México, 1992, Las Finanzas Populares en México, 1995, (as C.M. Mayo) Sky Over El Nido, 1995 (Flannery O'Connor award for Short Fiction 1994); Miraculous Air: Journey of a Thousand Miles Through Baja California, The Other Mexico, 2002; editor: Liberalización e innovación financiera, 1995, Tameme: Sun and Moon/Sol y Luna, 2001. Fellow MacDowell Colony, 1993, 95, Yaddo, 1995, 98, Sewanee Writers Conf., 1996, Bread Loaf Writers Conf., 1996, Wesleyan Writers Conf., 2000, Va. Ctr. for Creative Arts, 2001; recipient Flannery O'Connor award U. Ga. Press. Mem. The Authors Guild, PEN West, Am. Literary Translators Assn., The Writers Center, Coun. Editors Learned Jours., Nat. Book Critics Cir.

MAYO, CLYDE CALVIN, organizational psychologist, educator; b. Robstown, Tex., Feb. 2, 1940; s. Clyde Culberson and Velma (Oxford) M.; m. Jeanne Lynn McCain, Aug. 24, 1963; children: Brady Scott, Amber Camille. BA, Rice U., 1961; BS, U. Houston, 1964, PhD, 1972; MS, Trinity U., 1966. Lic. psychologist, Tex., La. Mgmt. engr. LWFW, Inc., Houston, 1966-72, sr. cons., 1972-78, prin., 1978-81; ptnr. Mayo, Thompson, Bigby, 1981-83; founder Mgmt. and Pers. Systems, 1983—. Counselor Interface Counseling Ctr., Houston, 1976-79; dir. Mental Health HMO Group, 1985-87; instr. St. Thomas U., Houston, 1979—, U. Houston Downtown Sch., 1972, 2002—, U. Houston, Clear Lake, 1983-88, U. Houston-Central Campus, 1984—; dir. mgmt. devel. insts. U. Houston Woodlands and West Houston, 1986-1991, adj. prof. U. Houston, 1991—, U. Houston, Clear Lake, 1998. Author: Bi/Polar Inventory of Strengths, 1978, LWFW Annual Survey of Manufacturers, 1966-81. Coach, mgr. Meyerland Little League, 1974-78, So. Belles Softball, 1979-80, S.W. Colt Baseball, 1982-83, Friends of Fondren Libr. of Rice U., 1988—; charter mem. Holocaust Mus. Mem. APA, Soc. Indsl. Orgn. Psychologists, Tex. Indsl. Orgnl. Psychologists (founder, bd. dirs. 1995—, pres. 1999-2002), Houston Psychol. Assn. (membership dir. 1978, sec. 1984), Tex. Psychol. Assn., Am. Psychol. Soc., Houston Area Indsl. Orgnl. Psychologists (bd. dirs. 1989-92), Found. Contemporary Theology, Forum Club, Meyerland Club (bd. dirs. 1988-92, pres. 1991). Home: 8723 Ferris Dr Houston TX 77096-1409 Office: Mgmt and Personnel Systems 4545 Bissonnet St Bellaire TX 77401-3121

MAYO, DANA WALKER, chemistry educator; b. Bethlehem, Pa., July 20, 1928; s. Dana Harrat Nickerson and Ethel Marie (Chapman) M.; m. Odile Jeanne d'Arc Mailhiot, Jan. 12, 1962; children: Dana Lawrence, Chapman Scott, Sara Walker. BS, MIT, 1952; PhD, Ind. U., 1959. Asst. prof. chemistry Bowdoin Coll., Brunswick, Maine, 1962-65, assoc. prof. chemistry, 1965-68, prof. chemistry, 1969-70, Charles Weston Pickard prof. chemistry, 1970-91, Charles Weston Pickard rsch. prof. chemistry, 1991—. Pres. Microscale Organic Lab. Co., New Castle., N.H., 1985—. Author: Microscale Organic Laboratory, 1986, 2d edit., 1989, 3d. edit., 1994, 4th edit., 2000, Microscale Techniques for the Organic Laboratory, 1991, 2d edit., 2001; patentee microscale spinning band distillation column. Capt. USAF, 1956-61. Fellow MIT, 1959-62; recipient Charles A. Dana Found. award, N.Y.C., 1986, John A. Timm award New Eng. Assn. Chemistry Tchrs., 1987, Catalyst nat. award Chem. Mfr. Assn., Washington, 1989. Fellow AAAS, mem. Nat. Inst. Chemists (cert.), Am. Chem. Soc. (health and safety award 1987, James Flack Norris award New Eng. sect. 1988, chair Maine sect. 1971-72), Soc. Applied Spectroscopy, Coblentz Soc. (bd. dirs. 1977-79). Avocations: book collecting, genealogical research, forest management, swimming.

MAYO, DAVID WAYNE, sportswriter; b. San Diego, Dec. 28, 1960; s. Derwood Crandle and Shirley Ann (Jester) M. BA, Henderson State U., 1982. Sportswriter The Amarillo (Tex.) Globe-News, 1982-85, The Grand Rapids (Mich.) Press, 1985-87, sports columnist, 1989—; baseball beat writer Detroit Tigers Newhouse/Booth Newspapers, Lansing, Mich., 1987-89. Heisman Trophy elector, 1996—. Contbg. writer: Ring Mag., 1991—. Recipient first place Mich. Sustained Sports Coverage, Mich. AP, Detroit, 1989; named Mich. Sports Feature of the Yr., Mich. Press Assn., Detroit, 1994, 95, 98, Sports Columnist of Yr., Mich. Press Assn., 1998. Mem. Football Writers Assn. Am., Basketball Writers Assn. Am., Phi Sigma Kappa. Democrat. Baptist. Office: The Grand Rapids Press 155 Michigan St NW Grand Rapids MI 49503-2353 E-mail: davidwmayo@yahoo.com.

MAYO, GEORGE WASHINGTON, JR. lawyer; b. Waycross, Ga., Dec. 23, 1946; s. George Washington Sr. and Perrie R. (Ling) M.; m. Katherine Louise Boland, Nov. 15, 1977; children— Regan L.B., Taylor L.B. A.B., Emory U., 1967; J.D., U. Va., 1973. Bar: Va. 1973, D.C. 1974. Assoc., Hogan & Hartson, Washington, 1973-80, ptnr., 1980—. Contbr. articles to prof. jours. Bd. dirs. Vietnam Vets. Meml. Fund, Inc., 1978—, Earth Conservation Corps., 1990—, coll. coun. of advisors Emory U., 1994—, Deafness Rsch. Found., 1997-2001. Served to 1st lt., U.S. Army, 1969-71, Vietnam. Mem. ABA, D.C. Bar Assn., Order of Coif, Met. Club (Washington), City Club (Washington), Congl. Country Club (Washington). Democrat. Methodist. E-mail: gwmayo@hhlaw.com Home: 26 Holly Leaf Ct Bethesda MD 20817-2652 Office: Hogan & Hartson 555 13th St NW Ste 800E Washington DC 20004-1161 E-mail: gwmayo@hhlaw.com.

MAYO, JAMES WATIE (JIM MAYO), publishing executive; b. Fort Smith, Ark., July 17, 1942; s. Richard Wheeler and Florence Marie (Baker) M.; m. Rebecca Ann Boen, July 17, 1965; children: John Robert, Jeffrey William. BAin Journalism, U. Okla., 1964. Assoc. pub., gen. mgr. Sequoyah County TIMES, Sallisaw, Okla., 1968-86, pub., 1986—. Bd. dirs. First Nat. Bank, 1975-91; v.p. Lincoln County Pubs., Chandler, Okla., 1987-99. Author: History of Sallisaw, 1993. Mem., former pres. Sallisaw C. of C., 1968—; mem. Okla. Coun. Judicial Complaints, Okla. City, 1974-77; mem. nominating com. Grand River Dam Authority, Vinita, Okla., 1980; bd. dirs. Okla. Hist. Soc., 1986-88, Higher Edn. Alumni Coun., Oklahoma City, 1993-95; dist. chairman Indian Nations Coun. Boy Scouts Am., Tulsa, 1987-90; coun. bd. Indian Nations Coun. Boy Scouts Am., 1987-90. Lt. (j.g.) USNR, 1964-67. Recipient (with Rebecca Mayo) Beacy Musselman award for outstanding contbn. to newspaper journalism Okla. Newspaper Found., 2002; named to Okla. Journalism Hall Fame The Soc. Profl. Journalists U. Ctrl. Okla., 1993. Mem. Nat. Newspaper Assn., Internat. Soc. Weekly Newspaper Editors, Okla. Press Assn. (pres. 1986-87, H. Milt Phillips award for outstanding contbns. to newspaper industry and pub. svc. 1999), Okla. Newspaper Found (pres. 1993-95), Sallisaw Lions Club (pres. 1972). Democrat. Presbyterian. Avocations: hiking, photography. Office: Sequoyah County TIMES 111 N Oak St Sallisaw OK 74955-4637

MAYO, JOHN SULLIVAN, telecommunications company executive; b. Greenville, N.C., Feb. 26, 1930; s. William Louis and Mattie (Harris) M.; m. Lucille Dodgson, Apr. 1957; children: Mark Dodgson, David Thomas, Nancy Ann, Lynn Marie. BS, N.C. State U., 1952, MS, 1953, PhD, 1955; hon. doctorate (hon.) , Rutgers U., Stevens U., Lehigh U. With AT&T Bell Labs., Murray Hill, N.J., 1955-95, exec. dir. toll electronic switching div., 1973-75, v.p. electronics tech., 1975-79, sr. v.p. network systems and network svcs., 1979-91, pres., 1991-95, pres. emeritus, 1995—. Bd. dirs. Johnson and Johnson, Found. for Nat. Medals of Sci. and Tech., The Kenan Inst. for Engring., Tech. and Sci. at N.C. State U. Contbr. articles to profl. jours.; patentee in field. Trustee emeritus Polytech U., The Kenan Inst. for Engring., Tech. and Sci. at N.C. State U., Liberty Sci. Ctr. Recipient Indsl. Rsch. Inst. medal, 1992, Navy League N.Y. Coun. Roosevelts gold medal for sci., 1993, Engring. Mgr. of Yr. award Am. Soc. for Engring. Mgmt., 1992, N.J. Sci./Tech. medal, 1994; named Outstanding Engring. Alumnus N.C. State U., 1977; Internat. Engring. Consortium fellow, 1994. Fellow IEEE (Alexander Graham Bell award 1978, Simon Ramo medal 1988, C&C prize 1988, Nat. Medal of Tech. 1990), mem. NAE, Royal Swedish Acad. Engring. Scis., Sigma Xi, Phi Kappa Phi. Baptist. Avocations: fishing, gardening, bicycling, jogging.

MAYO, LOUIS ALLEN, corporation executive; b. Durham, N.C., Nov. 27, 1928; s. Louis Allen and Amy Earl (Overton) M.; m. Emma Jean Minshew, Oct. 31, 1953 (div.); children: Louis Allen III, Robert Lawrence, Carolyn Jean; m. 2d, Myrna Ann Smith, Feb. 16, 1980 (div.). Student, Calif. State Poly. Coll., 1948-50; BA in Criminology, Calif. State Coll., Fresno, 1952; MA in Pub. Adminstrn., Am. U., 1960, PhD in Pub. Adminstrn., 1983; postgrad., U. So. Calif., 1960-62. Spl. agt. U.S. Secret Svc., Treasury Dept., L.A., 1956-58, 60-63, White House, Washington, 1958-60, 63-66; program mgr. law enforcement Office Law Enforcement Assistance, Justice Dept., 1967-68; acting chief Rsch. Ctr., rsch. program mgr. Nat. Inst. Law Enforcement and Criminal Justice, 1968-74; alternate assoc. mem. Fed. Coun. on Sci. and Tech., White House, 1973-74; dir. tng. and testing divsn. Nat. Inst. Justice, 1975-87; pres. Mayo, Mayo & Assocs., Alexandria, Va., 1987—. Lectr. criminology Armed Forces Inst. Tech., 1954-55; professorial lectr. Am. U., 1974-82; adj. prof. August Vollmer U., 1990-95. 2d lt. to 1st lt. USAF, 1952-56. Mem. Police Assn. Coll. Edn. (exec. dir., founder), Internat. Assn. Chiefs of Police, Am. Soc. Pub. Adminstrn. (nat. chmn. sect. on criminal justice adminstrn. 1975-76), Am. Soc. for Law Enfocement Tng., Acad. Criminal Justice Scis., Police Exec. Rsch. Forum, Soc. Police Futurists Internat., Pi Sigma Alpha. Methodist. Home and Office: 5200 Leeward Ln # 101 Alexandria VA 22315-3944

MAYO, ROBERT N. computer science researcher; b. Washington, Aug. 23, 1959; s. Robert P. and Marian A. Mayo. BS in Computer Sci., Washington U., St. Louis, 1981; MS in Computer Sci., U. Calif., Berkeley, 1983, PhD of Computer Sci., 1987. Asst. prof. U. Wis., Madison, 1988; staff Digital Equipment Corp./Compaq Computer/Hewlett Packard, Palo Alto, Calif., 1989—. Mem. Assn. Computer Machinery. Home: 407 W Dana St Mountain View CA 94041-1337 Office: HP Labs 1501 Page Mill Rd Palo Alto CA 94304 E-mail: wwbob@bobmayo.com.

MAYO, ROBERT PORTER, banker; b. Seattle, Mar. 15, 1916; s. Carl Asa and Edna Alberta (Nelson) M.; m. Marian Aldridge Nicholson, Aug. 28, 1942; children: Margaret Alice, Richard Carl, Carolyn Ruth (Mrs. Gregory Brown), Robert Nelson. AB magna cum laude, U. Wash., 1937, MBA, 1938. Research asst., auditor Wash. State Tax Commn., 1938-41; economist U.S. Treasury, 1941-47, asst. dir. office of tech. staff, 1948-53, chief debt div. analysis staff, 1953-59; asst. to sec. Treasury Dept., 1959-60; v.p. Continental Ill. Nat. Bank & Trust Co. of Chgo., 1960-69; chmn. Boye Needle Co., 1963-67; staff dir. Pres. Commn. on Budget Concepts, 1967; dir. U.S. Bur. of Budget, 1969-70; counsellor to Pres. U.S., 1970; pres. Fed. Res. Bank of Chgo., 1970-81, 81-95, ret. Trustee No. Trust Benchmark Funds, Goldman Sachs Funds, CNA Income Shares; Duff and Phelps Utilities Income Fund. Trustee YMCA, Chgo.; bd. dirs. Exec. Svc. Corps, Chgo. Mem. Comml. Club Chgo., Econ. Club Chgo., Perico Bay (Fla.) Club, Bartlett-on-the-Greens Homeowner's Assn., Phi Beta Kappa. Presbyterian.

MAYOCK, ROBERT LEE, internist; b. Wilkes-Barre, Pa., Jan. 19, 1917; s. John F. and Mathilde M.; m. Constance M. Peruzzi, July 2, 1949; children: Robert Lee, Stephen Philip, Holly Peruzzi Luff. BS, Bucknell U., 1938; MD, U. Pa., 1942. Diplomate Am. Bd. Internal Medicine. Intern Hosp. U. Pa., Phila., 1943-44, resident in internal medicine, 1944-45, chief med. resident, 1945-46, attending physician, 1946—; chief pulmonary disease Phila. Gen. Hosp., 1955-72, chief pulmonary disease sect., 1959-72, sr. cons. pulmonary disease sect., 1972—; asst. prof. clin. medicine U. Pa., 1949-59, assoc. prof., 1959-70, prof. medicine, 1970-87, prof. emeritus, 1987—. Med. adv. com. for Tb Commonwealth of Pa., 1965-74, med. adv. com. on chronic respiratory disease, 1974-92, chmn. adv. com., 1981-90; mem. subsplty bd. pulmonary disease Am. Bd. Internal Medicine, 1965-76; nat. bd. dirs. Am. Lung Assn., 1983-92, local bd. dirs., 1961, local pres., 1966-69, dir. at large, 1983—. Contbr. articles to profl. jours. Capt. U.S. Army, 1952-54. Robert L. Mayock-David A. Cooper Prof. of Medicine Endowed Chair named in his honor U. Pa. Sch. Medicine, 1997. Fellow ACP, Am. Coll. Chest Physicians (regent 1972-79), Phila. Coll. Physicians; mem. AMA, Am. Thoracic Soc., Am. Fedn. Clin. Rsch., Pa. Lung Assn. (dir. 1976—), N.Y. Acad. Scis., Pa. Med. Soc., Phila. County Med. Soc., Physiology Soc. Phila., Laennec Soc. Phila., Merion Cricket Club, Westmoreland Club, Swiftwater Res., Sigma Xi. Home: 244 Gypsy Ln Wynnewood PA 19096-1113 Office: U Penn Ravdin Bldg 3d Fl Ste F Philadelphia PA 19104

MAYOL, RICHARD THOMAS, advertising executive, political consultant; b. Springfield, Ill., Oct. 30, 1949; s. Richard McFaren and Marjorie (Maddex) M. AA, Springfield Coll., 1969; BS, U. Tulsa, 1972. Co-owner First Tuesday Inc., Phoenix, 1976-85; pres. Mayol and Assocs., 1985—; CEO New West Policy Group, Prescott, Ariz., 1993—; v.p. Winning Directions Inc., San Francisco, 1998—. Cons. Dem. candidates ballot issues, corp. pub. policy Western U.S., Nev. Dem. Party, Ariz. Dem. Party, Nature Conservancy, Proposition 202 Indian Gaming, Proposition 400. Mem. Phoenix Film Commn., 1985—. Mem. Am. Assn. Polit. Cons., Phoenix Grand Prix Commn. Avocations: photography, writing, horseback riding. Home and Office: 348 Moreland Cir Prescott AZ 86303-4035 also: 143 N Mccormick St Ste 101 Prescott AZ 86301-2725 E-mail: newwest@cableone.net.

MAYOR, BABETTE ROBIN, artist, art educator; b. Warwick, R.I., May 27, 1952; d. Adrian Lester and Elfriede Maria (Barwitz) M; m. John Edward Morgan; children: Heidi, Cooper. AA, Chaffey Coll., Alta Loma, Calif., 1972; BA, U. Calif. Riverside, 1974; MFA, Claremont Grad. Sch., 1978. Adj. prof. Chaffey Coll., Alta Loma, Calif., 1977, '79; adj. prof. of art Mt. San Antonio Coll., Walnut, 1978-82; sr. graphic designer U. La Verne, 1981-90, adj. prof. art, 1988-90; assoc. prof. art Calif. State Polytech. U., Pomona, 1990—. Free lance artist/graphic designer Rancho Cucamonga Calif., 1979—; organizer, curator student art exhibitions with Coll. Environ. Design Glass Gallery, Calif. Poly Tech, Pomona, 1994, 95, 96, co-organizer with Patric D. Prince and Patrick Merril digital art exhbns. in Kellogg U. Art Gallery, 1996, 97. Artist: work exhibited at Arco Ctr. for Visual Art, L.A., 1979, Mt. San Antonio Coll. Art Gallery, Walnut, Calif., 1979, Pasadena Festival of Arts 5th ann. Juried Show, Ambassador Coll., 1980 (hon. mention), Villa Senor Art Gallery, San Bernardino, Calif., 1983 (2-person show), Norman F. Feldheym Ctrl. Libr. Art

Galleries, San Bernardino, 1987, U. La Verne Faculty Exhbn., Da Gallery, Pomona, Calif., 1989, W. Keith and Janet Kellogg U. Art. Gallery, 1991, 92, 93, 94, 95, 96, 97, CGS Gallery, Claremont, Calif., 1994, Kohn Turner Art Gallery, L.A., 1995, Brewery Annex Gallery, L.A., 1996, Riverside C.C. Art Gallery, 1996.; designer: Fgn. Lang. Brochure, 1983 (Creativity award 1983). Cons., educator OCCUR, Ontario, Calif., 1995; mem. Calif. Youth Authority Trade Adv., 1990—. Home: 13992 Glendora Dr Rancho Cucamonga CA 91739-2181 Office: Calif State Polytech U 3801 W Temple Ave Pomona CA 91768-2557

MAYOR, HEATHER DONALD, medical educator; b. Melbourne, Victoria, Australia, July 6, 1930; d. Joseph A. L. and Elizabeth Emily (Boyd) Donald; m. Richard Blair Mayor, May 28, 1956; children: Diana Boyd (Mrs. Russell Hawkins), Philip Hastings. BS, U. Melbourne, Australia, 1949; MS, U. Melbourne, 1951, DSc, 1970; PhD, U. London, 1954. Electron microscopist Nat. Inst. for Med. Research, London, 1952-55; postdoctoral fellow Walter and Eliza Hall Inst., Melbourne, 1955-56; post doctoral fellow Harvard U. Med. Sch., Boston, 1956-60; from asst. prof. to prof. Baylor Coll. Medicine, Houston, 1960—, prof., 1970-96, prof. emeritus, 1996—. Cons. AEC, Washington, 1971—, Nat. Cancer Inst., Bethesda, Md., 1975—, U. Tex. Med. Sch., Houston, 1975—. Contbr. articles and papers to profl. jours.; artist, coordinator Life Shapes, Contemporary Arts Mus. Houston, Tex. art exhbn., 1974. Recipient Disting. award Ctr. for Interaction Man-Sci.-Soc., Houston, 1973, Sir Hiram Maxim award, 1990; named Scientist of Yr., Ency. Britannica, 1992; scholar in residence Rockefeller Inst. and Found., Bellagio, Italy, 1983. Mem. Am. Assn. Immunologists, Biophysical Soc. (program chmn.), Am. Soc. for Cell Biology (program chmn.), Doctors Club, Houstonian Club, Houston Harpsichord Soc. (bd. dirs.). Avocations: piano, harpsichord, skiing, jogging. Home: 6 N West Oak Dr Houston TX 77056-2120 Office: Baylor Coll of Medicine 1 Baylor Plz Houston TX 77030-3411 E-mail: hmayor@bcm.thc.edu.

MAYOR, RICHARD BLAIR, lawyer; b. San Antonio, Mar. 27, 1934; s. E. Allan and Elizabeth Ann (Hastings) M.; m. Heather Donald, July 28, 1956; children: Diana Boyd, Philip Hastings. BA, Yale U., 1955; postgrad., Melbourne U., Australia, 1955-56; JD, Harvard U., 1959. Bar: Tex. 1960. Assoc. Butler and Binion, Houston, 1959-67, ptnr., mem. exec. com., 1967-82; founding, sr. ptnr. Mayor, Day, Caldwell & Keeton, L.L.P., 1982—. Trustee, chmn. exec. com. Contemporary Arts Mus., Houston, 1972-78; trustee, mem. exec. com., v.p. govt. affairs Houston Ballet Found., 1983-88; dir. Am. Oncology Resources, 1995—; trustee Houston Grand Opera, 1997—. Fulbright scholar, 1955-56 Fellow Tex. Bar Found.; mem. ABA, Am. Law Inst., Tex. Bar Assn., Coronado Club, Houstonian Club, Houston Club, Phi Beta Kappa. Office: Mayor Day Caldwell & Keeton LLP 700 Louisiana St Ste 1900 Houston TX 77002-2725

MAYORA-ALVARADO, EDUARDO RENE, lawyer, law educator; b. Guatemala, Guatemala, Apr. 20, 1957; s. Eduardo Alfredo Mayora-Dawe and Adelaida (Alvarado) De Mayora; m. Alicia Bascunana, June 18, 1983; children: Javier Eduardo, Santiago, Jose Andres, Sebastian. JD, U. Rafael Landivar, Guatemala, 1980; LLM, Georgetown U., U.S.A., 1982; Diploma (2) in Principles Econ. Sci., U. Francisco Marroquin, Guatemala, 1991, LLD, 1997. Bar: Guatemala, 1980; cert. notary. Assoc. Mayora & Mayora, Guatemala, 1980-81, ptnr., 1982—, mem. tax adminstrn. bd., 1998-2000; prof. bus. law and principles of law U. Francisco Marroquin, 1984-87, prof. bus. law and principles of law Sch. of Econs., 1986-88, prof. constitutional law, dean Sch. of Law, 1989-2000, prof. principles of pvt. and pub. law, 1993; bd. dirs. Financiera de Inversion, S.A., 1988-96. Alt. dir. Seguros Alianza S.A., Guatemala, 1988-94; trustee U. Francisco Marroquin, 1989—; vis. prof. Pontificia U. Catolica, Porto Alegre, Brazil, 1994, Montpellier U. Sch. Law, France, 1995. Co-author: El Desafio Neoliberal, 1992; author: Teoría Constitucional para una sociedad libre Fundación República para una nueva generación, 1997; (essay) El Drama De La Arena Movedisa, 1993 (Charles Stillman award 1993); contbr. to profl. jours. Mem. Guatemala Bar Assn. (author articles Bar Law Jour. 1990—m v.p. ethics bd. 1985-86), Assn. De Amigos Del Pais, Fundacion Para La Cultura (v.p. 1994), Inst. Guatemalteco De Derecho Notarial, Phi Delta Phi, Guatemala Country Club. Roman Catholic. Avocations: reading, sailing, golf. E-mail: mayorae@intelnet.net.gt; mayora&mayora@gua.gbm.net. Office: Mayora & Mayora15 Calle 1-04 Plz Centrica 3er Nivel #301 Zona 10 Guatemala City Guatemala also: PO Box 661447 Miami FL 33266-1447 E-mail: mayorae@intelnet.net.gt.

MAYORAS, DONALD EUGENE, corporate executive, writer, consultant, educator; b. Danville, Ill., Aug. 25, 1939; s. Andrew John and Katherine Ann (Shelato) M.; m. JoAnna Marie Kacmer, June 9, 1962; children: D. Tyler, Stacie J. BS in Edn., Purdue U., 1962; postgrad., Northwestern U., 1968-71; MBA, So. Ill. U., 1977. Regional mgr. Pacific Intermountain Express, Akron, Ohio, 1972-74; v.p. United Van Lines, Fenton, Mo., 1974-78; pres. Bekins Van Lines, L.A., 1978-83; pres., CEO Sun Carriers, Inc., Holliston, Mass., 1983-90, chmn. bd. dirs.; vice-chmn., CEO Builders Transport, Camden, S.C., 1990-91. Chmn., CEO Truckload Holding Inc., Chester, N.Y., 1995-97, Cloverleaf Transp., Inc., Chester, 1997—; spkr. in field. Trustee Ross Ade Found., West Lafayette, Ind., 1962—. Capt. U.S. Army, 1962-68; Europe, Vietnam. Decorated Bronze Star. Mem. Am. Trucking Assn. (v.p. 1983—, trustee Found. 1983-91), Nat. Spkrs. Assn., Nat. Coun. Logistics, Nat. Pvt. Truck Coun., Purdue U. Alumni Assn., Nat. Def. Transp. Assn., Aronomink Golf Club (Newton Sq., Pa.), Orange County Golf Club, Delta Nu Alpha, Beta Gamma Sigma, Omicron Delta Kappa. Republican. Roman Catholic. Avocations: golf, antiques, classic automobiles. E-mail: clor@aol.com., dmayoras@cloverleaftransport.com.

MAYORKAS, ALEJANDRO, lawyer, former prosecutor; b. Cuba; With Patterson, Belknap, Webb & Tyler, L.A., 1986-89; asst. U.S. atty., 1989-99; chief office's gen. crimes sect., 1996-98; U.S. atty. cen. dist. Calif. U.S. Dept. Justice, 1999—2001; ptnr. O'Melveny & Myers, L.A., 2001—. Tchr. trial advocacy Loyola Law Sch., 1997-98. Office: O'Melveny & Myers 400 S Hope St Los Angeles CA 90071-2899*

MAYPOLE, JOHN FLOYD, real estate holding company executive; b. Chgo., May 17, 1939; s. John James and Althea Floyd M.; m. Anne White, 1961; children: Cynthia, John, Kimberly. BA in Econs, Yale U., 1961. With Arthur Andersen & Co., 1961-62, 65-66; mgr. corp. acctg. Interpace Corp., 1966, asst. treas., 1967-68, treas., 1968-70, treas., controller, 1970-73, v.p. fin., 1973-77, sr. v.p., 1977-80, exec. v.p., 1980-81, pres., 1981-83; pres., chief operating officer Clevepak Corp., 1983-84; mng. ptnr. Peach State Real Estate Holding Co., Toccoa, Ga., 1984—. Bd. dirs. Dan River, Inc., Mass. Mut. Life Ins. Co., Meridian Automotive Sys., Inc., Church & Dwight Co., Inc., Nat. Captioning Inst., Inc., Whitehead Inst. for Biomed Rsch. Bd. adjustment Borough of Mountain Lakes, N.J., 1971-81, chmn., 1980-81. Served with USMC, 1962-65. Mem. Yale Club (N.Y.C.), Rockaway River Country Club, Laurel Oak Country Club. Republican. Office: PO Box 1223 Toccoa GA 30577-1421

MAYR, ERNST, retired zoologist, philosopher; b. Kempten, Germany, July 5, 1904; came to U.S., 1931; s. Otto and Helene (Pusinelli) M.; m. Margarete Simon, May 4, 1935; children: Christa E., Susanne. Cand. med., U. Greifswald, 1925; PhD, U. Berlin, 1926; PhD (hon.), Uppsala U., Sweden, 1957; D.Sc. (hon.), Yale U., 1959, U. Melbourne, 1959, Oxford U., 1966, U. Munich, 1968, U. Paris, 1974, Harvard U., 1980, Guelph U., U. Cambridge, 1982, U. Vt., 1984; DSc (hon.), U. Mass., 1993; PhD (hon.), U. Vienna, 1994; DPhil (hon.), U. Konstanz, 1994; DSc (hon.), U. Bologna, 1995, Rollins Coll., 1997; Dr. ner. nat. (hon.), U. Berlin, 2000. Asst. curator zool. mus. U. Berlin, 1926-32; mem. Rothschild expdn. to Dutch New Guinea, 1928, expdn. to Mandated Ty. of New Guinea, 1928-29, Whitney Expdn., 1929-30; research asso. Am. Mus. Natural History, N.Y.C., 1931-32, asso. curator, 1932-44, curator, 1944-53; Jesup lectr. Columbia U., 1941; Alexander Agassiz prof. zoology Harvard U., 1953-75, emeritus, 1975—; dir. Mus. Comparative Zoology, Harvard U., 1961-70. Messenger lectr. Cornell U., 1985; Hitchcock prof. U. Calif., 1987; hon. fellow Ctr. for Philosophy of Sci., U. Pitts. Author: List of New Guinea Birds, 1941, Systematics and the Origin of Species, 1942, Birds of the Southwest Pacific, 1945, Birds of the Philippines, (with Jean Delacour), 1946, Methods and Principles of Systematic Zoology, (with E. G. Linsley and R. L. Usinger), 1953, Animal Species and Evolution, 1963, Principles of Systematic Zoology, 1969, 2d edit., 1991, Populations, Species and Evolution, 1970, Evolution and the Diversity of Life, 1976, (with W. Provine) Evolutionary Synthesis, 1980, Biologie de l'Evolution, 1981, The Growth of Biological Thought, 1982, Toward a New Philosophy of Biology, 1988, One Long Argument, 1991, This is Biology, 1997, What Evolution Is, 2001, The Birds of Northern Melanesia, 2001; editor: Evolution, 1947-49. Pres. XIII Internat. Ornith. Congress, 1962. Recipient Leidy medal, 1946, Wallace Darwin medal, 1958, Brewster medal Am. Ornithologists Union, 1965, Daniel Giraud Elliot medal, 1967, Nat. Medal of Sci., 1970, Molina prize Accademia delle Sci., Bologna, Italy, 1972, Linnean medal, 1977, Gregor Mendel medal, 1980, Balzan prize, 1983, Darwin medal Royal Soc., 1987, Disting. Scientist award UCLA, 1993, Salvin Godman medal, 1994, Japan prize, 1994, Benjamin Franklin medal 1995, 96, Lewis Thomas prize, 1998, Crafoord prize, 1999, Golden Plate Am. Acad. Achievement, 2001; establishment of the Ernst Meyr Lectureship of the Berlin-Brandenburgische Akademie. Fellow Linnaean Soc. N.Y. (past sec. editor), Am. Ornithol. Union (pres. 1956-59), N.Y. Zool. Soc.; mem. NAS, Am. Philos. Soc., Am. Acad. Arts and Scis., Am. Soc. Zoologists, Soc. Systematic Zoology (pres. 1966), Soc. Study Evolution (sec. 1946, pres. 1950); hon. or corr. mem. Royal Soc., Royal Australian, Brit. ornithol. unions, Zool. Soc. London, Soc. Ornithol. France, Royal Soc. New Zealand, Bot. Gardens Indonesia, S. Africa Ornithol. Soc., Linnean Soc. London, Deutsche Akademie der naturforsch Leopoldina, Accad. Naz. dei Lincei, Royal Soc., Academie des Sci., Ctr. for Philosophy of Sci. (Pitts.), Russian Acad. Sci., Berlin - Brandenburgische Akademie. Office: Harvard U Mus Comparative Zoology 26 Oxford St Cambridge MA 02138-2902

MAYR, JAMES JEROME, fertilizer company executive; b. Beaver Dam, Wis., Aug. 19, 1942; s. Alfred A. and Maxine E. (Kuehl) M.; m. Carol Ann Kaufman, Sept. 4, 1965; children: Christin and Carin (twins), Cathy, Conni. BS in Agrl. Econs., U. Wis., 1964. Mgr. trainee Oscar Mayer, Madison, Wis., 1964-65; v.p. Mayr's Seed and Feed, Beaver Dam, 1966-78; product mgr. Chem. Enterprises, Houston, 1978-80; gen. mgr. Coash, Inc., Bassett, Nebr., 1981-88, v.p., 1989; mgr. Blicks Agri-Farm Ctr., Inc., Scott City, Kans., 1990-91; area mgr. Rosen's Inc., Fairmont, Minn., 1992-95, Helena Chem. Co., Rochester, 1995—. Cons. Beaver Dam, 1971-75; speaker fertilizer orgns., Wis. Advisor U. Wis. Coll. Agriculture; mem. com. Upper Elk Horn Natural Resources Dist., Oneill, Nebr., 1985-86. Mem. Wis. Fertilizer Assn. (bd. dirs. 1970-74), Nat. Fertilizer and Solutions Assn., Nebr. Fertilizer and Chem. Assn. Lodges: KC (dep. grand knight 1978-80, 81-85, Man of Yr. 1982). Republican. Roman Catholic. Avocations: target shooting, hunting, fishing, teaching target shooting. Home: 2550 Oak Hills Dr SW Rochester MN 55902-1263 E-mail: jmayrusa@aol.com.

MAYS, GEORGE WALTER, JR. educational technology educator, consultant, tutor; b. Decatur, Ill., July 1, 1926; s. George Walter Sr. and Ida May (Lookabaugh) M.; children: Richard, Steven, John, James. BS in Edn., U. Ill., Champaign, 1950, MS in Edn., 1952; BSEE, U. md., 1960; cert., Calif. State U., Carson, 1987. Tchr. math. and physics Mahomet (Ill.) High Sch., 1950-52, prin., 1952-55; br. chief engring studies Nat. Security Agy., Ft. Meade, Md., 1955-62; sr. engr. Jet Propulsion Lab., Pasadena, Calif., 1962-71; tchr. math.-sci., chair Aviation High Sch., Redondo Beach, 1971-82; tchr. math. and physics, dept. chair Redondo Union High Sch., 1982-89; cons. ednl. tech. Apple Valley, Calif., 1989—; math. coord. Sci. and Tech. Ctr., 1990—. Part-time instr. electronics Pasadena City Coll., 1963-72, Pepperdine U., 1975-76, math. Victor Valley Coll., 1991-97; instr. math. Acad. for Acad. Excellence, Apply Valley, 1998—. Author: Educational Technology Application Notes, 1989-90. With USN, 1944-46. Recipient Appollo Achievement award NASA, 1969. Mem. IEEE (life), Calif. Tchrs. Assn. (WHO award 1988-89), Nat. Coun. Tchrs. of Math., Computer Using Educators, Apple Valley Country Club, Victor Valley Aero Club. Avocations: reading, sports, computer usage, flying. Home and Office: 13458 Sunset Dr PO Box 745 Apple Valley CA 92307-0013

MAYS, JILL DUNCAN, social services administrator, counselor; b. Louisville, Apr. 17, 1966; d. Charles Henry Sr. and Ruth Ella (Bohannon) Duncan; m. Samuel Aaron Mays Sr., Dec. 28, 1991; children: Shelby Amaris, Samuel Aaron Jr., Jayce Allan. BA in Psychology, Emory U., 1988; MS in Cmty. Counseling, Ga. State U., 1992. Lic. profl. counselor, Ga.; master addiction counselor, nat. cert. counselor Nat. Bd. Cert. Counselors, Inc. Rsch. interviewer Emory U. Sch. Pub. Health, Atlanta, 1990-92; evening outpatient coord. Decatur (Ga.) Hosp., 1992-94; counselor The Atlanta Union Mission, 1992-94, dir. women and children's svcs., 1994—. Cons. Intracultural Comm., Decatur, 1993-95, DeKalb County Dept. Youth Svcs., Decatur, 1993; com. mem. Atlanta Summit Against Poverty, 1997. Olympic Force coord. Atlanta Com. for the Olympic Games, 1995—96; mem. Atlanta Women Making a Mark, 2002. Mem.: Coun. Vol. Adminstrs., Assn. Gospel Rescue Missions, Am. Assn. Christian Counselors, Nat. Assn. for the Edn. Young Children, Alpha Kappa Alpha Sorority, Inc. Democrat. Baptist. Avocations: singing, reading, acting/playwriting. Office: The Atlanta Union Mission 3965 Roosevelt Hwy College Park GA 30349-2607 E-mail: samnjam1@prodigy.net.

MAYS, K. J. writer, musician; b. Lake Station, Ind. m. Lee Mays; 1 child Mitchell. AA, Harold Washington, Chgo. Composer: (songs) Plan, Call, Stand Up, 1999. Mem.: Golden Key. Achievements include invention of K.J. Mallet for cymbal, timpani, vibraphone, bells, bass drum, xylophone. Office: JLM Enterprises PO Box 79 West Brooklyn IL 61378-0079

MAYS, LARRY W. civil engineering educator, hydrologist; b. Pittsfield, Ill., Feb. 7, 1948; s. Fred W. and Lola M. Mays; children: Travis, Elyssa, Tyler. BSCE, U. Mo., Rolla, 1970, MSCE, 1971; PhD in Civil Engring., U. Ill., 1976. Registered profl. engr., Ariz., Okla., Calif., Ill., Mo. Ark., La.; registered prof. hydrologist Am. Inst. Hydrology. Asst., then assoc. , then prof. civil engring. U.Tex., Austin, 1976-89, Engring. Found. endowed prof., 1987-89, dir. Ctr. for Rsch. in Water Resources, 1988-89; prof. civil engring. Ariz. State U., Tempe, 1989—, chmn. dept., 1989-96. Cons. to various state and fed. agys., engring. cons. firms, legal firms, and fgn. govts.; lectr. numerous countries, including China, Korea, Japan, Georgia, India, Israel, Turkey, Greece, Portugal, Australia, Taiwan, Mex. and Spain; bd. dirs. Univs. Coun. on Water Resources, 1991-95, pres., 1994. Co-author: Applied Hydrology, 1988, Hydrosystems Engineering and Management, 1992; author: Optimal Control of Hydrosystems, 1997, Water Resources Engineering, 2000; editor-in-chief: Water Resources Handbook, 1996, Water Distribution Systems Handbook, 2000, Hydraulic Design Handbook, 2000, Stormwater Collection Systems Design Handbook, 2001, Urban Water Supply Handbook, 2002. With U.S. Army, 1970-73. Recipient cert. of commendation Nat. Assn. Water Inst. Dirs., 1989, Engr. of Yr. in Edn. award Ariz. Soc. Profl. Engrs., 1992, Quentin Mees rsch. award Ariz. Water Pollution Control Assn., 1993, Disting. Alumnus award dept. civil engring. U. Ill., 1999,. Fellow ASCE, Internat. Water Resources Assn.; mem. Am. Water Resources Assn., Internat. Assn. Hydraulic Rsch., Am. Water Works Assn. Avocations: snow skiing, fly fishing, scuba diving, gardening, photography. Home: 6064 E Cholla St Scottsdale AZ 85254-4905 Office: Ariz State U Dept Civil Engring Tempe AZ 85287

MAYS, STEPHANIE BELLE, social worker; b. San Antonio, Sept. 25, 1971; d. Howard Wright and Lula Belle (Maddox) Mays. B in Social Work, U. Miss., 1994; MSW, Our Lady of the Lake U., San Antonio, 1999. LCSW Washington, lic. master social worker Tex. Customer svc. rep. Dun & Bradstreet, Austin, Tex., 1995—97; crisis response team counselor San Antonio Police Dept., 1997—98; pediat. intensive care social work intern Tex. Children's Hosp., Houston, 1999; social worker counselor U. Tex. MD Anderson Cancer Ctr., 1999—2000; clin. social worker Children's Nat. Med. Ctr., Washington, 2000—. Bereavement program developer Children's Nat. Med. Ctr., Washington, 2000—. Advocate Stand for Children, Washington, 2000—02, Young Profls. for Children, Houston, 1999—2000; bd. dirs. Assn. for Death Edn. and Counseling, 1999—2000, Tex. Alliance for End of Life Care, Houston, 1999—2000. Mem.: NASW, Phi Alpha. Office: Children's Nat Med Ctr 111 Michigan Ave NW Washington DC 20010 Personal E-mail: stephmays@yahoo.com. Business E-Mail: smays@cnmc.org.

MAYS, WILLIAM GAY, II, lawyer, real estate developer; b. Washington, Apr. 8, 1947; s. Frank G. and Geneva Pauline (Brookhart) M.; m. Judith Ann Kriete, Oct. 5, 1974; 1 son, Daniel Brookhart. AB, U. Mo., 1969, JD, 1972. Bar: Mo. 1972, U.S. Dist. Ct. (we. dist.) Mo. 1972. Legis. rschr. State of Mo., 1972; pub. defender 13th Jud. Cir. Mo., 1973-77; ptnr. Holt, Mays & Brady, Columbia, Mo., 1977-98; ptnr. and gen. counsel comml. real devel. firm. Mem. Jud. Planning Commn., Mo., 1977. Served to capt. USAFR, 1969-82. Named Outstanding Young Man of Am., 1974. Mem. Mo. Bar Assn., Boone and Callaway County Bar Assn., Mo. Trial Lawyers Assn., Mo. Pub. Defender Assn. (pres. 1976-77), Assisted Living Fedn. Am., Beta Theta Pi. Clubs: Masons. Republican. Office: Emerald Office Ctr The Mays Bldg PO Box 10013 Columbia MO 65205-4001

MAYSEL, KYLE WAYNE, lawyer; b. Austin, Tex., July 2, 1958; married, Dec. 12, 2000. Bar: Tex. 1984. Sole practice atty., San Marcos, Tex., 1984—. Mem. Buda (Tex.) City Coun., 1994—99, mayor pro tem, 1997—99; bd. dirs. Old Town Buda Assn., 1995—99. Mem.: Hays County Bar Assn. (pres. 1995—). Avocations: gardening, outdoors, fencing. Office: 174 S Guadalupe St Ste 101 San Marcos TX 78666-5567

MAYSENT, HAROLD WAYNE, hospital administrator; b. Tacoma, June 26, 1923; s. Wayne L. Shivley and Esther Pierce M.; m. Marjorie Ellen Hodges, June 13, 1953; children: Jeffrey, Nancy, Brian, Gregory. BA, U. Wash., 1950; MS in Hosp. Adminstrn. with distinction, Northwestern U., 1954. Adminstrv. resident Passavant Meml. Hosp., 1953-54, adminstrv. asst., 1954-55; research asso. hosp. adminstrn. Northwestern U., Evanston, Ill., 1954-55; with Lankenau Hosp., Phila., 1955-72, dir., 1963-67, exec. dir., 1967-72; exec. v.p. Rockford (Ill.) Meml. Hosp., 1972-75, pres., 1975-91, Rockford Meml. Corp., 1983-91, pres. emeritus, 1991—; pres. The Rockford Group, 1983-91. Tchg. assoc. Rockford Sch. Medicine, U. Ill., 1974-89, adj. assoc. prof., 1989-92; mem. Ill. Health Facility Planning Bd., 1980-92; chmn. bd. Ill. Hosp. Joint Ventures, Inc., 1977-78, Vol. Hosps. Am. Midwest Partnership, 1985-89. Contbr. articles to profl. jours. Chmn.-elect Coll. Healthcare Execs., 1988-89, chmn., 1989; coach, adminstr. Broomal (Pa.) Little League, 1962-72; bd. dirs. Community Health Assn., 1964-70, Rockford Med. Edn. Found., 1972-87, Tri State Hosp. Assembly, 1978-80, Rockford Coun. 100, 1987-91, exec. com. 1987-91. With AUS, 1942-46. Recipient Malcolm T. MacEachern award Northwestern U., 1954, Laura G. Jackson Alumni Assn. award, 198, Disting. Svc. award Ill. Hosp. Assn., 1989. Fellow Am. Coll. Hosp. Adminstrs. (life, Ill. regent 1979-84, dist. bd. govs. 1984-88, gov. 1984-88, chmn. elect 1988-89, chmn. 1989-90, past chmn. 1990-91); mem. Am. Hosp. Assn. (com. on vols. 1976-80, coun. patient svcs. 1980-82, ho. of dels. 1977-84, rep. Am. Acad. Pediatrics com. on hosp. care 1983-85), Pa. Hosp. Assn. (bd. dirs. 1965-68), Ill. Hosp. Assn. (trustee 1973-79, sec. 1974-76, chmn. elect 1977, chmn. bd. trustees 1978, named Outstanding Leader in Hosp. Industry 1978, Disting. Svc. award 1989). Office: Rockford Meml 2400 N Rockton Ave Rockford IL 61103-3681

MAYSILLES, DANIEL BRUCE, pharmaceutical services executive; b. Hamilton, Ohio, May 26, 1952; s. Carl A. and Ella Jean (Thorpe) M.; m. Dawn M. Hamilton, Aug. 9, 1975 (div. May 1989); m. Nancy K. Cragg, Feb. 15, 1992; 1 child, Ryan. AA, U. South Fla., 1972; BS in Pharmacy, U. Fla., 1975. Registered pharmacist. Pharmacist Roscoe's Rexall Drugs, New Port Richey, Fla., 1975-77, Eckerd Drugs, Spring Hill, 1977-79; staff pharmacist Cmty. Hosp., New Port Richey, 1979-83; assoc. dir. pharmacy HCA New Port Richey Hosp., 1983-85; dir. pharmacy Cmty. Hosp. New Port Richey, 1985—. Pharmacy adv. com. Hosp. Corp. of Am., Nashville, 1985-93, tech. adv. com., 1991-93, cons. pharmacist 1978—, mem. PACT adv. com., 2002--; care of the patient chairperson Columbia New Port Richey Hosp., 1994-2001, cons. pharmacist; assoc. prof. Pasco/Hernando C.C., New Port Richey, 1987-88; chmn. Care of the Patient, 1994-2000; interim dir. pharmacy HCA Oak Hill Hosp., 2001. Chmn., mem. planning and zoning bd. City of New Port Richey, 1979—; mem. pastors coun. Ch. of God, Tarpon Springs, Fla., 1978-88. Regents scholar Bd. of Regents, 1970. Mem. Pasco/Hernando Pharmacy Assn. (pres. 1995-96, historian 1993-94, John Dunwoody award 1996, Humanitarian award 1993), Am. Soc. of Health Systems, Rotary Internat., Kappa Psi (Pres. award 1975). Republican. Avocations: golf, tennis, fishing, reading, music. Home: 6134 Oak Ridge Ave New Port Richey FL 34653-4235 Office: Cmty Hosp New Port Richey 5637 Marine Pkwy New Port Richey FL 34652-4316

MAYSILLES, ELIZABETH, speech communication professional, educator; b. Sleepy Creek, W.Va. d. Evers and Rose (Scott) M. AB, W.Va. U.; MA, Hunter Coll., 1963; PhD, NYU, 1980. Announcer Radio Sta. WAJR, Morgantown, W.Va.; broadcaster Radio Sta. WGHF-FM, Rural Radio Network, N.Y.C.; group leader GMAC; instr. NYU; adj. prof. speech comm. Pace U., 1978—; exec. adminstr. Am.-Scottish Found., 1980-90; adminstrv. asst. Brit. Schs. and Univs. Found., Inc.; numerous radio and television appearances. Cons., lectr. in field. Vol. counselor Help Line, N.Y.C., 1971-75. Recipient Disting. Svc. award NYU Grad. Orgn., 1970-71. Mem. Internat. Platform Assn. (bd. govs. 1980—), N.Y. Acad. Scis., English-Speaking Union, Caledonian Club N.Y. (bd. dirs. 1994-96, chieftain 2001—). Avocations: reading, swimming, gardening, travel in England and Scotland. Home: 155 E 77th St Apt 6F New York NY 10021-1955 Office: Pace U 41 Park Row New York NY 10038-1508

MAYSLES, ALBERT H. filmmaker; b. Boston, Nov. 26, 1926; s. Philip and Ethel (Epstein) M.; m. Gillian Walker, Sept. 14, 1976; children: Rebekah, Philip, Sara. BA, Syracuse U., 1949; MA, Boston U., 1953. Rsch. fellow in anesthesia Mass. Gen. Hosp., Boston, 1951-52; instr. social rels. Boston U., 1953-55; pres. Maysles Films, Inc., N.Y.C., 1962—. Filmmaker, prodr. Psychiatry in Russia, 1955, (with others) Primary, 1960, Showman, 1963, What's Happening: The Beatles in the USA, 1964, Salesman, 1967, Gimme Shelter, 1970, Christo's Valley Curtain, 1974, (Blue Ribbon award 1975, Acad. award nomination), Grey Gardens, 1976, Running Fence, 1978 (Blue Ribbon award, 1978), Ozawa, 1985, Vladimir Horowitz: The Last Romantic, 1985, Islands, 1986 (Blue Ribbon award, Emmy award), Horowitz Plays Mozart, 1987, Christo in Paris, 1990, Soldiers of Music: Rostropovitch Returns to Russia, 1990 (Emmy award), Abortion: Desparate Choices, 1995 (Peabody award), Letting Go, A Hospice Journey, 1996 (Ace Cable award), Concert of Wills: The Making of the Getty Art Center, 1997. Served as pvt. U.S. Army, 1944-46. Named one of 100 World's Finest Cinematographers, Eastman Kodak, 1999; recipient Career Achievement award, Internat. Documentary Assn., 1994, John Grierson award for Documentary, SMPTE, 1997, Pres.'s award, Am. Soc. Cinematographers, 1998, Vision award, The Boston Film and Video Found., 1998, The Doubletake Career Achievement award, 1998, Lifetime Achievement award, Toronto's Hot Docs, 1999, Flaherty award, 1999, award for documentaries, Sundance Film Festival Cinematography, 2001; fellow Guggenheim, 1965. Mem. The Reality Club. Home: One West 72nd St New York NY 10023 Office: 250 W 54th St New York NY 10019-5515 E-mail: amaysles@mayslesfilms.com.

MAYSON, PRESTON B., JR. retired lawyer; b. Spartanburg, S.C., June 18, 1932; s. Preston Brooks and Sophie Rowena (Morgan) M.; m. Sara Dudley Heaton, June 16, 1955; children: Brooks, James. BS, U.S. Mil. Acad., West Point, 1955; MD, George Washington U., 1962; JD, Washington and Lee U., 1991. Bar: Va. Diplomate Am. Bd. Radiology. Physician Letterman Hosp., San Francisco, 1962-66, 93rd Evacuation Hosp., Vietnam, 1966-67, Walter Reed Army Hosp., Washington, 1967-70, Radiology Assocs., Roanoke, Va., 1970-88; law student Washington & Lee U., Lexington, 1988-91; sr. atty. Woods, Rogers & Hazlegrove, Roanoke, 1991-95; pres. Preston B. Mayson, PC, 1995-2000; ret., 2000. Decorated Bronze Star medal. Mem. ABA, Va. State Bar Assn., Va. Trial Lawyers Assn. Presbyterian. Avocation: oil painting. E-mail: pdoctorlaw@aol.com.

MAYTHAM, THOMAS NORTHRUP, art and museum consultant; b. Buffalo, July 30, 1931; s. Thomas Edward and Margaret (Northrup) M.; m. Daphne Chace, Dec. 30, 1960 (div.); 1 child, T.F. Gifford; m. Gloria Maytham, June 11, 1994. BA in Art History, Williams Coll., Williamstown, Mass., 1954; MA in Art History, Yale U., 1956; cert. in German, Colby Coll., 1954. Intern Wadsworth Atheneum, 1955; rsch. asst. Yale U., 1956; head dept. paintings Boston Mus. Fine Arts, 1957-67; assoc. dir., acting dir. Seattle Art Mus., 1967-74; dir. Denver Art Mus., 1974-83; art cons., pub. Artadvisors LLC, Denver, 1983—. Mus. accreditation program evaluator Am. Assn. Museums; past trustee, mem. exhbns. adv. com. Am. Fedn. Arts, N.Y.; past mem. mus. program panel, grants reviewer Nat. Endowment for Arts, Washington; reviewer Nat. Endowment for Humanities, Washington; mem. adv. panel, grants reviewer Nat. Mus. Act, Smithsonian Instn.; past mem. policy panel and adv. com., econ. impact of arts study Colo. Coun. Arts and Humanities;

co-founder Consortium of Rocky Mountain Regional Conservation Ctr., U. Denver; founder dirs. assn. Denver cultural agys.; del. Inter-Am. Museums Conf., Oaxaca, Mexico; co-founder United Arts Fund, Seattle; mem. art adv. com. Airport Art Program, Port of Seattle; vis. faculty Leadership Denver program, Pres.'s Leadership class U. Colo.; cons. Aspen Ctr. Visual Arts, Sangre de Cristo Arts Ctr., Pueblo, Western States Arts Found., Santa Fe, BBHC, Cody, Wyo.; lectr. museums, colls., corporate groups and art assns. Exhbns. organized include Ernst Ludwig Kirchner Retrospective, Seattle, Pasadena and Boston museums, 1968-69, Am. Painting from the Boston and Met. Museums, Nat. Gallery, St. Louis and Seattle museums, 1970-71; contbr. articles to profl. jours.; presenter TV programs on collections and exhbns. Boston Pub. TV, WGBH-TV. Trustee Internat. Exhbns. Found., Washington. Recipient Gov.'s Arts award Seattle Airport Art Program, 1972, Denver Art mus., award Downtown Denver Inc., 1978. Mem. Assn Art Mus. Dirs. (officer, trustee, ops. com. sec., future directions. com. chmn.) Office: Maytham Artadvisors 3882 S Newport Way Denver CO 80237-1246

MAYTON, CATHY ANN, histotechnician, researcher, small business owner; b. Key West, Fla., Apr. 12, 1954; d. Robert Gary and Cheri Dae S.; m. J.C. Mayton, Jan. 30, 1998; 1 child, Nichole Renee. Grad. h.s., Phoenix, Ariz., 1972. Histology trainee St. Luke's Medical Ctr., Phoenix, 1972-73, histotechnician, 1973-83; histotechnician/rsch. Harrington Arthritis Rsch. Ctr., 1983-87, Emory U., Atlanta, 1987-88, VA Medical Ctr, Salt Lake City, 1988-97; entrepreneur, bus. owner Wasatch Histo Cons. Inc., Winnemucca, Nev., 1997—. Founder, chair hard tissue com. Nat. Soc. Histotech., Bowie, Md., 1989-98, editor, 1992—, vet. indsl. rsch. com., 1989—, health and safety com., 1988-96, mem. ednl. com., 1989-91; owner Wasatch Histo Cons., 1988—. Mem. editl. bd. Jour. Histotechnology, 1993—; contbr. articles to numerous profl. jours. Organizer Neighborhood Watch, West Valley City, Utah, 1993-97; aux. mem. Grass Valley Vol. Fire Dept., 1998-99, Sch. to Careers, 1999-2001. Named Histotechnologist of Yr., Nat. Soc. Histotechnology, 1992; recipient Hacker Instruments; Membership Incentive award, 1991-92, 98, Superior Performance award, 1989-92, 95-97, William J. Hacker award, 1988, 99, Diamond Cover award, 1999, Rsch. Technician of Yr. award, 1989. Mem. Nat. Wildlife Fedn., Am. Assn. Lab Animal Sci. (bd. dirs. 1989-91), The Cousteau Soc., Inc., Nat. Soc. Histotechnology. Achievements include development of Sandersons Rapid Bone Stain and staining protocol for mineralized bone which differentiates mineralized bone from soft tissue and non-mineralized bone.

MAZA, MICHAEL WILLIAM, newspaper editor, columnist; b. Detroit, June 19, 1947; s. Frank Michael and Irene (Boiczuk) M.; m. Cynthia Jeanne Nash, Apr. 8, 1972 (div. Apr. 1985); 1 child, Lydia Anne; m. Jean Ann Zinsmaster, Mar. 1, 1987. BA, U. Detroit, 1969. Reporter, editor Detroit Free Press, 1969-70, Detroit News, 1970-77; film, theater critic, arts editor Ariz. Republic, Phoenix, 1979-87; asst. arts editor Dallas Morning News, 1987-89, 2000—; book columnist "Help Yourself" Dallas Morning News/KRT Newswire, Dallas, Washington, 1989—; mng. editor Dallas Morning News Dallas Life Mag., 1989-95, Dallas Morning News Guide, Dallas, 1995-2000. Ariz. corr. People weekly mag., N.Y.C., 1983-84; Detroit corr. New Times, mag., N.Y.C., 1974-75. Avocations: running, ceramics, travel. Office: Dallas Morning News 508 Young St Dallas TX 75202-4828 E-mail: mmaza@dallasnews.com.

MAZANKOWSKI, DONALD FRANK, Canadian government official; b. Viking, Alta., Can., July 27, 1935; s. Frank and Dora (Lonowski) M.; m. Lorraine Poleschuk, Sept. 6, 1958; children: Gregory, Roger, Donald. Student, pub. schs., 1987; PhD in Engring (hon.), N.S. Inst. Tech.; LLD (hon.), U. Alta., 1993. MP Ho. of Commons, 1968—, chmn. com. transp., 1972-74, mem. com. govt. ops., 1976-77, mem. com. trans. and communication, 1977-79; min. of transp., min. responsible for Can. Wheat Bd. Govt. of Can., 1979-80, min. of transp. (re-drafted Nat. Transp. Act), 1984-86, dep. prime min., 1986—, govt. house leader, 1986-88, pres. Privy Coun., 1986-91, pres. Treas. Bd., 1987-88, min. responsible for privatization and regulatory affairs, 1988-91, min. of agriculture, 1988-91, min. of fin., 1991-93; chmn. Inst. of Health Econs. Former mem. bd. govs. U. Alta; bd. dirs. Power Corp. Can., Power Fin. Corp., Great West Life Assurance, The Investors Group, Shaw Comms. Inc., Weyerhauser Co., IMC Global Inc., Can. Oilsands Trust, ATCO Ltd., London Life Ins.; chmn. Can. Genetic Diseases Network. Apptd. chmn. Premier's Adv. Coun. on Health. Apptd. Officer of Order of Can., 2000; Paul Harris fellow Rotary Internat., 2002. Mem. Royal Can. Legion (life). Clubs: Vegreville Rotary (past dir.). Lodges: KC. Roman Catholic. Fax: 780-632-4737. E-mail: maz1@agt.net.

MAZARIEGOS, GEORGE VINCENT, pediatric transplant surgeon; b. July 24, 1963; BS, Northwestern U., 1984, MD, 1986. General surgery resident Mich. State U. Butterworth Hosp., Grand Rapids, 1986-91; fellow surgical critical care, transplantation U. Pitts. Med. Ctr., 1991-93, asst. prof. surgery, 1994—2001; transplant surgeon Children's Hosp. of Pitts., 1997—; assoc. prof. surgery, anesthesiology & critical care medicine U. Pitts. Med. Ctr., 2001. Fellow ACS; mem. Am. Soc. Transplantation. Office: Children's Hosp Pitts 3705 5th Ave Pittsburgh PA 15213-2524 E-mail: mazarieg@pitt.edu.

MAZE-DAVIS, LAURI, psychiatric mental health nurse; b. N.Y.C., Mar. 1, 1954; d. Oscar and Eva (Fields) M.; m. Warren Lee Davis, Mar. 16, 1987; children: Karen Johnson, Warren Jr., Lea (dec.), Donte. BA, U. Pa., 1976; BSN, Georgetown U., 1980; MS, U. Md., 1983. RN, Md., D.C.; cert. clin. specialist; cert. child adolescent mental health, family therapy. Psychiat. nurse St. Elizabeths Mental Hosp., Washington, 1980, Psychiat. Inst., Washington, 1981-83; diagnostic assessor Georgetown U., 1984-86; family therapist Prince Georges Hosp., Cheverly, Md., 1986; psychiat. nurse, crisis intervention specialist D.C. Govt., Washington, 1988-90; crisis intervention specialist, Mobile Crisis Branch Supr. U.S. Pub. Health Svc., 1990-95; outreach divsn., access bur. HHS, 1992-95; clin. therapist Prince George's County Health Dept., 1996-97, 99—; dir. staff devel., clin. therapist Riverside Treatment Svcs., Inc., 1997-98. Speaker in field. Vol. Parent to Parent Hotline program, 1991.

MAZEL, JOSEPH LUCAS, publications executive, consultant; b. Paterson, N.J., Oct. 1, 1939; s. Joseph Anthony and Anne (Kidon) Mazel; m. Joyce Virginia Kronenberger, Feb. 14, 1992; children from previous marriage: Joseph William, Jeanne Eileen. BME, Newark Coll. Engring., 1960. Mech. engr. Austin Co., Roselle, N.J., 1960-61; engr. We. Electric Co., Newark, Atlanta, 1961-62; asst. assoc., sr. editor Factory Mag. McGraw-Hill Pub. Co., N.Y.C., 1962-71; editor-in-chief, sr. editor 33 Metal Producing mag., Newark, Summit, N.Y.C., 1971-85, chmn. editl. bd., 1980-82; pub. rels. account supr. Hammond Farrell, Inc., N.Y.C., 1985-87; mgr. corp. publs. Siemens Corp., Iselin, N.J., 1987-92; pres. Mazel Editl. Assocs., Fair Lawn, 1992—. Guest lectr. Writers Conf. N.J. Inst. Tech., 1972—83; group editor Inst. Mgmt. and Adminstrn., Inc., N.Y.C., 1983—. Property maintenance com. Borough of Fair Lawn, NJ, 1996—97; employment assistance response network mem. St. Catharine's Ch., Glen Rock, 1993—99. With Nat. Guard, 1963—69. Recipient Apolloneer award, GE Co., 1966, Jesse H. Neal Cert. of Merit, 1977, 1979, 1983, Jesse H. Neal Editl. Achievement award, 1979, Disting. Alumni award for Outstanding Achievement, N.J. Inst. Tech., 1979, Steuben Wise Old Owl award, U.S. Steel Corp., 1981. Mem.: KC (grand knight 1967—68, trustee 1968—71), Inst. Indsl. Engrs., Coun. Logistics Mgmt., Materials Handling and Mgmt. Soc., Am. Prodn. and Inventory Control Soc., Inc., Am. Soc. Engring. Mgmt., Nat. Assn. Purchasing Mgmt., Soc. Profl. Journalists, Sigma Delta Chi. Home: 40-22 Tierney Pl Fair Lawn NJ 07410-5141 E-mail: jmazel@ioma.com.

MAZGALEV, TODOR NIKOLOV, health science association administrator, biomedical engineering educator; b. Munich, Oct. 21, 1942; came to U.S., 1984; s. Nikola D. and Maria Mazgalev; m. Tatiana D. Zheltuhin, Feb. 28, 1972; 1 child, Victoria. BS, Sofia Poly. U., 1964; MS summa cum laude, St. Petersburg Electrotech. Inst., 1969, PhD, 1972. Rsch. assoc. Bulgarian Acad. Scis., Sofia, 1972-84; sr. scientist Lankenau Med. Rsch. Ctr., Phila., 1984-90; rsch. assoc. prof. U. Pitts., 1991-94; dir. basic cardiac electrophysiology rsch., dir. Cleve. Clinic Found., 1994—; assoc. staff in cardiology, 2000—. Editor: Electrophysiology of the Sinoatrial and Atrioventricular Nodes, 1988. Atrial-AV Nodal Electrophysiology, 2000; contbr. more than 50 original manuscripts in profl. jours.; presenter in field. Grantee NIH, 2000—, Fellow Am. Coll. Cardiology; mem. Internat. Cardiac Electrophysiology Assn., N.Am. Soc. Pacing and Electrophysiology, Am. Heart Assn. (grant-in-aid 1998-2000). Achievements include studies on thr prppagation of cardiac electric impulses and arrhythmics, with particular focus on the electrophysiology of the atriventricular mode in worm and pathology. Avocations: short-hand writing. Home: 29149 Bryce Rd Pepper Pike OH 44124-5767 Office: Cleve Clinic Found 9500 Euclid Ave Bldg Ff1-2 Cleveland OH 44195-0001 Fax: (216) 445-4168. E-mail: mazgalt@ccf.org.

MAZO, MARK ELLIOTT, lawyer; b. Phila., Jan. 12, 1950; s. Earl and Rita (Vane) M.; m. Fern Rosalyn Litman, Aug. 19, 1973; children: Samantha Lauren, Dana Suzanne, Ross Elliott, Courtney Litman. AB, Princeton U., 1971; JD, Harvard U., 1974. Bar: D.C. 1975, U.S. Dist. Ct. D.C. 1975, U.S. Claims Ct. 1975, U.S. Ct. Appeals (D.C. cir.) 1976, U.S. Supreme Ct. 1979. Ptnr. Hogan & Hartson, L.L.P., Washington and Paris, 1990—. Contbr. articles to profl. jours. White House intern Exec. Office of Pres., Washington, 1972. Capt. USAR, 1971-79. Mem. ABA, Harvard Law Sch. Assn., D.C. Bar Assn., Columbia Country Club, Princeton Club (N.Y.C.), Colonial Club, City Club, Phi Beta Kappa. Republican. Home: 3719 Cardiff Rd Chevy Chase MD 20815-5943 Office: Hogan & Hartson LLP 555 13th St NW Ste 800E Washington DC 20004-1161 also: Hogan & Hartson Cariddi Mee Rue 12 rue de la Paix 75002 Paris France E-mail: memazo@hhlaw.com.

MAZO, ROBERT MARC, chemistry educator, retired; b. Bklyn., Oct. 3, 1930; s. Nathan and Rose Marion (Mazo) M.; m. Joan Ruth Spector, Sept. 5, 1954; children: Ruth, Jeffrey, Daniel. BA, Harvard U., 1952; MS, Yale U., 1953, PhD, 1955. Research assoc. U. Chgo., 1956-58; asst. prof. Calif. Inst. Tech., 1958-62; assoc. prof. U. Oreg., Eugene, 1962-65, prof. chemistry, 1965-95; prof. emeritus, 1996; head chemistry dept. U. Oreg., 1978-81, dir. Inst. Theoretical Sci., 1964-67, 84-87, assoc. dean Grad. Sch., 1967-71; program dir NSF, 1977-78. Alfred P. Sloan fellow, NSF Sr. Postdoctoral fellow, vis. prof. U. Libre de Bruxelles, Belgium, 1968-69; vis. prof. Technische Hochschule Aachen, Weizmann Inst., Rehovoth, Israel, 1981-82, U. New South Wales, Australia, 1989. Author: Statistical Mechanical Theories of Transport Processes, 1967, Brownian Motion, 2002, also rsch. articles. NSF Postdoctoral fellow U. Amsterdam, Netherlands, 1955-56 Mem. Am. Phys. Soc. Home: 2460 Charnelton St Eugene OR 97405-3214 Office: U Oreg Inst Theoretical Sci Eugene OR 97403 E-mail: mazo@oregon.uoregon.edu.

MAZO, VINCENT ALLEN, registered nurse, artist, poet; b. Stockton, Calif., Feb. 7, 1969; s. Victor Allen and Leila Karene Mazo; m. Roberta Lynn Schramek. Assoc. Bus., San Joaquin Delta Coll., 1992, ADN, 1996. RN, Calif. RN San Joaquin Gen. Hosp., French Camp, Calif., 1997—; author, artist, owner Endymion Publs., Stockton, 1999—. Author, poet: These Poems, 2000. Avocations: writing poetry, sculpting, drawing, art. Home: 3809 Bonnie Ln Stockton CA 95204 Office: Endymion Publs PO Box 692271 Stockton CA 95269-2271 E-mail: endypub@aol.com.

MAZOR, LESTER JAY, law educator; b. Chgo., Dec. 12, 1936; s. Bert William and Mildred (Mazur) Mazor; m. Sondra R. Bernstein, Sept. 2, 1957 (div. July 1981); children: David, Shari, Marya; m. Anne Spier, Apr. 26, 1993. AB, Stanford (Calif.) U., 1957, JD, 1960. Bar: Utah 1963. Law clk. to Hon. Warren E. Burger U.S. Ct. Appeals, Washington, 1960-61; instr. U. Va. Law Sch., Charlottesville, 1961-62; asst. prof. U. Utah, Salt Lake City, 1962-66, assoc. prof., 1966-69, prof., 1969-72; Henry Luce prof. Hampshire Coll., Amherst, Mass., 1970-75, prof., 1975—. Reporter ABA Com. on Prosecution and Def. Functions, 1965-69; project dir. ABF study of law tchg. materials, 1975-80; vis. rsch. scholar Macquarie U., Sydney, Australia, 1997; vis. prof. law Ctrl. European Univ., Budapest, Hungary, 1999, 2000; dir. Hampshire in Berlin, 2001. Co-author: Introduction to Law Study, 1965. Fulbright scholar, Germany and U.K., 1983. Mem. Internat. Soc. Assn. (rsch. com. on sociology of law), Internat. Assn. Legal and Social Philosophy, Am. Legal Studies Assn., Phi Beta Kappa, Order of Coif. Home: 52 Elizabeth St Northampton MA 01060-2320 Office: Hampshire Coll Sch Social Sci Amherst MA 01002 E-mail: lmazor@hampshire.edu., spier-mazor@t-online.de.

MAZUMDAR, RAVI RASENDRA, engineering and mathematics educator; b. Bangalore, India, Apr. 17, 1955; naturalized Can. citizen, 1993; s. Rasendra Indulal and Yamini Kulinchandra (Majmudar) M.; m. Catherine Patricia Rosenberg; children: Claire, Eric. B in Tech., Indian Inst. Tech., Bombay, 1977; MSc, DIC, Imperial Coll., London, 1978; PhD, UCLA, 1983. Mem. tech. staff AT&T Bell Labs., Holmdel, N.J., 1983; vis. asst. prof. UCLA, 1983-84; vis. docent U. Twente, The Netherlands, 1984-85; asst. prof. elec. engring. Columbia U., N.Y.C., 1985-88; prof. Nat. Inst. Sci. Rsch., Montreal, Que., Can., 1988-97; prof. math. U. Essex, Colchester, Eng., 1996-99; prof. Sch. Elec. and Computer Engring. Purdue U., West Lafayette, Ind., 1999—. Vis. prof. Indian Inst. Sci., Bangalore, 1994-95, Nat. Superior Sch. Telecom., Paris, 1995; invited prof. elec. engring. McGill U., Montreal, 1988-96; sci. counselor CNET, France Telecom., Lannion, 1994-97. Contbr. over 75 articles to profl. publs. Fellow Royal Statis. Soc; mem. IEEE (sr.), Soc. Indsl. and Applied Math., Bangalore Club. Avocations: reading, travel, squash, bridge. Office: Purdue U Sch Elec and Computer Engrg West Lafayette IN 47907 E-mail: mazum@ecn.purdue.edu.

MAZUMDER, JYOTIRMOY, mechanical and materials engineering educator; b. Calcutta, India, July 9, 1951; came to U.S., 1978; s. Jitendra Mohan and Gouri (Sen) M.; m. Aparajita, June 17, 1982; children: Debashis, Debayan. B in Engring., Calcutta U., 1973; diploma, PhD, Imperial Coll., London U., 1978. Rsch. scientist U. So. Calif., L.A., 1978-80; asst. prof. mechanical and indsl. engring. U. Ill., Urbana, 1980-84, assoc. prof., 1984-88, prof., 1988-96, co-dir. ctr. laser aided materials processing, 1990-96; Robert H. Lurie Prof. Engring. U. Mich., Ann Arbor, 1996—, dir. ctr. laser aided intelligent mfg., 1996—. Co-dir. ctr. laser aided material processing U. Ill., 1990-96; dir. Quantum Laser Corp., Edison, N.J., 1982-89; pres. Laser Scis., Inc., Urbana, 1988—; dir., CEO POM Inc., Plymouth, Mich.; vis. scholar physics dept. Stanford (Calif.) U., 1990. Author: (with others) Laser Welding; editor and co-editor more than 9 books including co-editor: Laser Materials Processing, 1984, 88; more than 250 technical papers; contbr. numerous articles to profl. jours. Fellow Am. Soc. of Metals and Laser Inst. of Am. (life, pres. 2000, editor-in-chief Jour. Laser Application); mem. Am. Inst. Metallurgical Engrs. (phys. mets. com. 1980—), Optical Soc. Am. Achievements include patent: weld pool visualization system for measurement of free surface deformation, apparatus and method for monitoring and controlling multi-layer cladding. Office: U Mich Dept Mech Engring & Mechs 2041 GG Brown Ann Arbor MI 48109-2125 E-mail: mazumder@umich.edu.

MAZUMDER, SANDIP, engineer, researcher; b. Calcutta, India, Feb. 23, 1969; came to U.S., 1991; s. Satya and Amita Mazumder; m. Srirupa Dhar, Nov. 25, 1998. BTech with honors, Indian Inst. Tech., 1991; MS, Pa. State U., 1993, PhD, 1997. Project engr. CFD Rsch. Corp., Huntsville, Ala., 1997-98, sr. engr., 1999-2000, group leader, 2000—. Reviewer NSF, Arlington, Va., 1999—, Jour. Heat Transfer, 1997—, Numerical Heat Transfer, 1999—. Contbr. over 20 articles to profl. jours. including Internat. Jour. Heat and Mass Transfer, Jour. Heat Transfer, Internat. Jour. Numerical Method Fluids, Numerical Heat Transfer, others. Grantee NSF, 1999—. Mem. ASME, AIAA. Avocations: piano, guitar. Office: CFD Rsch Corp 215 Wynn Dr Huntsville AL 35805 E-mail: sm@cfdrc.com.

MAZUR, ALLAN CARL, sociologist, engineer, educator; b. Chgo., Mar. 20, 1939; s. Joseph and Esther (Markowitz) M.; m. Minnette Albrecht, Jan. 21, 1968; children— Julie Elizabeth, Rachel Lee. BS, Ill. Inst. Tech., 1961; MS, UCLA, 1964; PhD, Johns Hopkins U., 1969. Research engr. North Am. Aviation Co., Los Angeles, 1961-64; instr. polit. sci. Mass. Inst. Tech., 1966-67; ops. research analyst Lockheed Missile & Space Corp., Sunnyvale, Calif., 1967-68; asst. prof. sociology Stanford U., 1968-71; mem. faculty Syracuse U., N.Y., 1971—, prof. pub. affairs, 1992—. Author: Dynamics of Technical Controversy, 1981, Global Social Problems, 1991, A Hazardous Inquiry: The Rashomon Effect at Love Canal, 1998, True Warnings and False Alarms about Technology:1948-1971; co-author: Biology and Social Behavior, 1972; contbr. articles to profl. jours. Fellow AAAS. Jewish. Office: Syracuse U 400 Eggers Maxwell Sch Syracuse NY 13244 Home: Apt 2B 189 E 93rd St New York NY 10128-3700 E-mail: amazur@syr.edu.

MAZUR, DAVID JOHN, psychiatrist, educator; b. Detroit, Mar. 28, 1947; s. John Paul and Flora M.; m. Dorothy E. Mazur, Nov. 3, 1977; children: Sarah, Kate. BA, U. Chgo., 1967; DO, Chgo. Coll. Osteo. Medicine, 1971. Diplomate Am. Bd. Psychiatry and Neurology, Am. Osteo. Bd. Neurology and Psychiatry. Staff psychiatrist C.F. Menninger Meml. Hosp., Topeka, 1975-82, sect. chief, 1982-85; psychiatrist Psychiat. Consultation Svcs., Grand Rapids, Mich., 1985-93; assoc. prof. psychiatry Mich. State U., Lansing, 1987—; pvt. practice Grand Rapids, 1993—. Dir. brain injury program Forest View Hosp., Grand Rapids, 1986-89, chief med. staff, 1988, 94, 00, dir. older adult unit, 1997-99. Contbr. articles to profl. jours. Mem. Am. Psychiat. Assn., Am. Osteo. Assn. Office: 833 Kenmoor Ave SE Grand Rapids MI 49546-2390

MAZUR, DEBORAH JOAN, counselor; b. Highland Park, Mich., Apr. 22, 1958; d. Frank J. and Joan A. (Cader) M.; m. Michael J. Baker, Sept. 20, 1986 (div. Apr. 1997); children: Adam Joseph, John Michael, Ryan Francis. BS, Western Mich. U., 1981; MA, Oakland U., 1989, EdS, 2002. Spl. edn. resources room tchr. Capac Cmty. Schs., Mich., 1981-82; supr. group home Blue Water Developmental Housing, Port Huron, 1982-83; unit adminstr. group home Luth. Social Svcs. Mich., Detroit, 1983-85; mgr. sales Fin. Svcs. Am., Inc., Madison Heights, Mich., 1985-86; clinician, case mgr. Ditty, Lynch and Assocs., Birmingham, 1986-87; spl. edn. tchr. Pontiac (Mich.) Sch. Dist., 1987-96; counselor Warren (Mich.) Consol. Schs., 1996—. Bd. dirs. YMCA, Warren, Mich. Mem.: ASCD, NEA, ACA, Mich. Counseling Assn., Mich. Edn. Assn., Warren YMCA (bd. dirs.), Western Mich. U. Alumni Assn.

MAZUR, EDWARD JOHN, JR. financial planner; b. Lowell, Mass., Mar. 5, 1948; s. Edward John Sr. and Mary Annette (Terry) M.; m. Sheila MacDonald, Dec. 13, 1969 (div. Nov. 1984); 1 child, Kristen Leigh; m. Anna Maria Maia, May 18, 1985; children: Edward John III, Kara Maia Mazur. BA in History, U. Mass., 1969. CLU, Chartered Fin. Cons., Life Underwriters Tng. Coun. Fellow. Agt. John Hancock Mut. Life Ins. Co., Boston, 1973-77, sales supr., 1977-82, field asst., 1982-83, dir. agys., 1983-84, gen. agt. Hartford, 1984-89; established Mazur Fin., Farmington, Conn., 1990-2001; founder Profl. Investors Exch., LLC, 2001—. Treas. HLUA, 1991. Team coord. Team Conn., 1998—. Recipient Raymond T. Wilbur award, Mass. Jaycees, 1982-83; named President of Yr., Mass. Jaycees, 1982-83, Outstanding Young Men of Am., Mass. Jaycees, 1984. Mem. Million Dollar Round Table, Nat. Assn. Ins. and Fin. Advisors (pres. Conn. chpt. 2000-01), Hartford Life Underwriters Assn. (bd. dirs., ednl. chmn. 1987-88, treas. 1991, pres. 1995-96, 96-97), Life Underwriters Tng. Coun. (chmn. 1988-89, bd. dirs.), U.S. Racquetball Assn. (mem. jr. coun. 2001), Conn. Racquetball Assn. (pres. 1985-94). Avocations: racquetball, coaching, hiking. Home: 48 Knollwood Ln Avon CT 06001-2701

MAZUR, JOHN, city administrator; b. Queen Anne, Md., Dec. 31, 1952; AA, Cmty. Coll. Balt., 1974. Call taker City of Balt., 2002—. Contbr. poetry to anthologies, mags., etc. Recipient awards including Editor's award, 1977, Spl. Editor's award, 1976, Third Place award, Honorable Mention, 1992, 93, 94, 99, others. Home: 247 S Ellwood Ave Baltimore MD 21224

MAZUR, LEONARD L. pharmaceutical company executive; b. Ansbach, Germany, Jan. 23, 1945; came to U.S., 1949; s. Walter and Maria (Zatwarnitsky) M.; m. Helena Maria Olijnyk, Nov. 1966; children: Maria, Michael, Irene. BA, Temple U., 1968, MBA, 1975. Mktg. mgr. Cooper Labs., Inc., Fairfield, N.J. and Palo Alto, Calif., 1971-81; dir. product mgmt. Knoll Pharm. Corp. divsn. BASF, Whippany, N.J., 1981-84; v.p. ICN Pharm. Corp., Costa Mesa, Calif., 1984-88; pres., COO Chantal Pharm. Corp., L.A., 1988-89; exec. v.p. Medicis Pharm. Corp., N.Y.C., 1989-93; vice chmn. Cabot Labs., Inc., 1994-96; chmn., CEO Genesis Pharm., Inc., Parsippany, NJ, 1996—. Ptnr. Mazier Ptnrs. LLC, Morristown, N.J., 1995—. Patentee in field. Mem. adv. bd. Manor Coll., Jenkintown, Pa., 1972-78, trustee, 2000—; ind. observer Referendum for Independence, Ukraine, 1991. Roman Catholic. Office: Genesis Pharm Inc 9 Campus Dr Parsippany NJ 07054

MAZUR, MICHAEL, artist; b. N.Y.C., Nov. 2, 1935; s. Burton Boris and Helen (Isaacs) M.; m. Gail Lewis Beckwith, Dec. 28, 1958; children: Daniel Isaac, Kathe Elizabeth. BA, Amherst Coll., 1958; BFA, Yale U., 1959, MFA, 1961; degree (hon.) , Lesley U. Asst. prof. fine arts Brandeis U., Waltham, Mass., 1965-76; instr. RISD, 1962-65. Vis. prof. Yale U. Sch. Art and Arch., 1972, 81, Queens Coll., CUNY, 1973, U. Calif., Santa Barbara, 1974-75, Boston U., 1982, Mass. Coll. Art, 1994, 95; lectr. Mus. Fine Arts, Boston, Brown U., U. Calif., Berkeley, New Sch. for Social Rsch., Bennington Coll., U. Iowa, Boston U., 1994-95, Katonah Mus., N.Y. Studio Sch., 1994; vis. lectr. Carpenter Ctr., Harvard U., 1976, 78, 89, 92, 94, 95, 97, others; illustrator Fleur du Mal, 1984, The Inferno of Dante, Farrar, Strans & Giroux, 1994, Genesis, 1996; co-chair bd. Fine Arts Work Ctr., Provincetown, Mass., 1996—. Exhibited in one-man shows at Kornblee Gallery, N.Y.C., 1960, 63, 66, Boris Mirski, Boston, 1963, 65, Phila. Print Club, 1964, Silvermine Guild, 1964, Fla. State U., 1966, Shoemaker Gallery Juniata Coll., 1966, Alpha Gallery, Boston, 1967, 68, 74, OGL Gallery, Los Angeles, Calif., 1968, Rose Art Mus., Brandeis U., 1969, A.A.A. Gallery, 1969, Inst. Contemporary Art, Boston, 1970, Terry Dintenfass, N.Y.C., 1974, 76, Picker Gallery, Colgate U., 1973, Trinity Coll., 1976, Ohio State U., 1975, Robert Miller Gallery, N.Y.C., 1977, 80, Harkus-Krakow, Boston, 1977, 79, 80, Pace Gallery, N.Y.C., 1980, John Stoller, Mpls., 1981, 85, 88, 91, William and Mary Coll., 1981, Ronald Greenberg, St. Louis, 1981, Janus Gallery, L.A., 1982, 84, 88, Barbara Mathes Gallery, N.Y.C., 1984, 86, Barbara Krakow Gallery, Boston, 1984, 86, 89, 91, 93, 95, 97, 98, 2000, Art Club Chgo., 1985, Beaver Coll., 1985, Joe Fawbush, N.Y., 1987, 88, Jan Turner Gallery, L.A., 1988, Butler Gallery, Houston, 1989, Mary Ryan Gallery, N.Y.C., 1990, 94, 95, 96, 97, 98, 99, 2000, Mus. Fine Arts, Boston, 2000, Cantor Ctr.-Stanford U., 2000, Zimmerli Art Mus., New Brunswick, N.J., 2000, Mus. di Castelvecchio, Verona, Italy, 2000, Am. Acad. Rome, 2000—; exhibited group shows at, Mus. Modern Art, 1964, 75, Bklyn. Mus., 1960, 62, 64, 66, 76, 80, 84, 86, Fogg Art Mus., 1966, 76, 94, Art. Inst. Chgo., 1964, Pa. Acad., 1966, 93, Phila. Mus., 1966, 88, Boston Mus. Fine Arts., 1967, 68, 76, 77, 80, 88, 90-91, 92, DeCordova Mus., Lincoln, Mass., 1965-67, 75, 86, 87, Whitney Mus. Am. Art, 1965, 81, 90, 92, Nat. Inst. Arts and Letters, 1965, 74, 80, 86, Sivermine Guild, 1965, Print Biennial of Americas, Santiago, Chile, 1965, Paris Biennale, 1969, Venice Biennale, 1970, Finch Coll. Mus., 1971-72, 2d and 3d Biennial Graphic Art, Cali, Colombia, N.A.D. Ann., 1974, Butler Inst., Youngstown, Ohio, 1974, Ball State U., 1974, America-1976, Sense of Place, Met. Mus., N.Y.C., 1979, 80, Montreal Mus. Fine Arts, 1977, Palais Royale, Brussels, 1979, Claude Bernard, Paris, 1980, Alan Frumkin, N.Y.C., 1981, 82, Madison Art Ctr., 1989, Nat. Gallery of Art, Washington, 1990, Pratt Mus., N.Y.C., 1990, Nat. Mus. Am. Art, 1997; traveling exhbns. include, Bicentennial Exhbn., 1976, State Arts Councils, Iowa, Kans., Mo., Nebr., 1973, Am. Monotypes, Smithsonian Instn., 1977; represented in permanent collections, Met. Mus., N.Y.C., Mus. Modern Art, Smith Coll. Art Mus., Library Congress, Fogg Art Mus., Art Inst. Chgo., Whitney Mus., Los Angeles County Art Mus., Mus. R.I. Sch. Design, Oreg. Art Mus., U. Maine, Mpls. Inst., Pa. State U., Toledo Art Mus., Phila. Art Mus., U. Ohio Westminster Found., Boston Mus. Fine Arts, Boston Pub. Library, Bklyn. Mus., Addison Gallery, Andover Acad., Yale Art Gallery, Montreal Mus. Fine Arts; commd. Fed. Res. Bank, Boston, 1998, USB-Warburg-Dillon, Stanford, Conn., 1999; (Recipient 2d prize Soc. Am. Graphic Artists 1963, Nat. Inst. Arts and Letters award 1965). Co-founder Artists Against Racism and the War, 1968; bd. dirs. Artists Found., co-chair, 1995—; bd. dirs. Fine Arts Work Ctr., Provincetown, Mass.; mem. Mass. Coun. on Arts and Humanities; mem. Pennell com. Libr. of Congress, 1983-93; founder, dir. Art for Nuc. Weapons Freeze, 1983-84, New Provincetown Print Project, 1990-95; chmn. bd. Provincetown Fine Arts Work Ctr.; overseer Mus. Fine Arts, Boston. Grantee Tiffany Found., 1964, Tamarind Lithography Workshop, 1968; Guggenheim Found. fellow, 1964-65; winner numerous purchase awards. Home: 5 Walnut Ave Cambridge MA 02140-2706 also: 5 Walnut Ave Cambridge MA 02140-2706

MAZUR, PETER, cell physiologist, cryobiologist; b. N.Y.C., Mar. 3, 1928; s. Paul M. and Adolphia (Kaske) M.; m. Drusilla Stevens, May 28, 1953 (dec. May 1982); 1 child, Timothy Stevens; m. Sara Jo Bolling, June 16, 1984. AB magna cum laude, Harvard U., 1949, PhD, 1953; DSc (hon.), Wilson Coll., 1998. NSF postdoctoral fellow Princeton (N.J.) U., 1957-59; rsch. staff biology divsn. Oak Ridge Nat. Lab., 1959-98. Group leader fundamental and applied cryobiology Oak Ridge Nat. Lab., 1966-98, sci. dir. biophysics and cell physiology, biology div., 1974-75, corporate fellow, 1985; chmn. ORNL Corp. Fellows Coun., 1995-96; mem. vis. com. biology Harvard U. Bd. Overseers 1972-77; rsch. prof. dept. biochem. and cellular and molecular biology U. Tenn., 1998—; mem. Space Sci. Bd. of Nat. Acad., 1975-77; Sigma Xi nat. lectr., 1980. Trustee Wilson Coll., Pa., 1984-93; bd. dirs. Meth. Hosp.

Found., Oak Ridge, 1997—. Served to capt. USAF, 1953-57. Recipient Author of Yr. award, Martin-Marietta Energy Sys., 1985, Disting. Svc. award, Am. Assn. Tissue Banks, 1993, R&D 100 award, R&D Mag., 1993, Disting. Achievement award, Am. Soc. Reproductive Medicine, 2000; fellow Lalor fellow, Harvard U., 1952, John Harvard fellow, 1951. Fellow AAAS; mem. Soc. Cryobiology (pres. 1973-74, bd. govs. 1979-96), Rotary Club Oak Ridge, Phi Beta Kappa, Cosmos Club (Washington). Current work includes cryobiology and the mechanisms of freezing injury in living cells and tissues. Subspecialties are cell biology and biophysics. Home: 125 Westlook Cir Oak Ridge TN 37830-3856 Office: Dept of Biochemistry and Cellular and Molecular Biology M407 Walters Life Sci Bldg Knoxville TN 37996-0001

MAZUR, RHODA HIMMEL, community volunteer; b. Bklyn., July 4, 1929; d. Morris and Gussie (Nadler) Himmel; m. Marvin Irwin Mazur, June 7, 1952; children: Jody, Amy, Leslie, Eric. Student, CCNY, CUNY. Bd. dirs. Newport News Social Svcs. Adv. Bd., 1979-84, Gov.'s Commn. Status Women, Richmond, 1981-84, Coun. Jewish Fedns., N.Y.C., 1985-87, Nat. Coun. Christians and Jews, 1985-89, Rodef Sholom Endowment Com., 1996—; v.p. Anti-Defamation League Regional Bd., Richmond, 1983-85, bd. dirs., 1985—; pres. Newport News Hadassah, 1984-85, United Jewish Cmty. Va. Peninsula Inc., Newport News, 1985-88, Rodef Sholom Sisterhood, 1997-98; active Newport News Task Force on Emergency Housing, 1984-85; chair fin. com. Peninsula Peace Edn. Ctr., Newport News, 1984-85; adv. bd. Friends of the Homeless, Inc., 1987-2000, pres., 1993-98, v.p., 1998-99; adv. bd. Associated Marine Inst., 1988-92; mem. social svcs. com. United Jewish Cmty. Va. Peninsula, 1995—, mem. campaign coun., 1999—; chair social action com. Rodef Sholom Temple, 1993-96, endowment com., 1998—; cmty. activist; bd. dirs., Peninsula Camp Fund, 2001—, FEMA. Recipient Young Leadership award Jewish Fedn. Newport News, 1968, Brotherhood citation Nat. Conf. Christians and Jews, 1984, Anti-Defamation Leadership award, 1997. Democrat. Avocations: hand crafts, reading, music, photography. Home: 114 James River Dr Newport News VA 23601-3604

MAZUREK, JOSEPH P. attorney, former state legislator; b. San Diego, July 27, 1948; m. Patty Mazurek; 3 children. BA, U. Mont., 1970, JD, 1975. Bar: Mont. 1975. Atty. Gough, Shanahan, Johnson, and Waterman, Helena, Mont.; mem. Mont. Senate from 23d Dist., 1981—92, pres., 1991—92; atty. gen. State of Mont., 1993—2000; atty. practice, Helena, Mont., 2000—. Mem. Revenue Oversight Com., 1983—92; chmn. Senate Judiciary Com. Mem. editl. bd.: Mont. Law Rev., 1974—75. With U.S. Army, 1970—72. Mem.: ABA, Phi Delta Theta, Phi Delta Phi, Beta Gamma Sigma. Office: PO Box 797 Helena MT 59625-0797 also: 100 N Park Ave Helena MT 59601-6263*

MAZURKIEWICZ, CYNTHIA HALL, geriatrics nurse, nursing administrator; b. Loudoun County, Va., Aug. 31, 1949; d. Otto Gibson and Esther Margaret (Poston) Hall; m. Edward John Mazurkiewicz, Nov. 28, 1970; 1 child, Gibson Edward. Diploma, Alexandria Hosp. Sch. Nursing, 1971. RN, Va.; cert. gerontol. nurse; cert. dir. nursing adminstrn. Charge nurse Loudon Long Term Care Ctr., Leesburg, Va., head nurse, asst. dir. nursing; dir. nursing Oak Springs of Warrenton, Marshall Manor Assisted Living Ctr., CLC Westhampton Health/Rehab. Ctr. Mem. No. Va. Dirs. Nursing Assn. for Long Term Care, Va. Dirs. Nursing Assn. for Long Term Care (chmn. legis. com., pres. 1994-97), No. Va. Alzheimer's Assn. (pub. policy com., edn. com.). Home: 2412 Trefoil Way Richmond VA 23235-3814

MAZZA, BIAGIO, religious studies educator; b. Gioia Del Colle, Bari, Italy, Oct. 2, 1946; came to U.S., 1956; s. Ulderico and Mildred (Giannone) M.; m. Dorothy Elizabeth Collins, Aug. 7, 1976; children: Biagio Dominic, Mary Carol. BA in English, Marist Coll., 1970; MA in English, Fordham U., 1973, MA in Religious Studies, 1979. Cert. ESL instr., N.Y. Secondary sch. tchr. Regis H.S., N.Y.C., 1973-75; dir. religious edn. St. Mary's Ch., Poughkeepsie, N.Y., 1976-81, St. Mary's Parish, Fish Kill, 1981-88; religion educator Cath. Diocese Kans. City-St. Joseph, Mo., 1988—. ESL instr. BOCES, Dutchess County, N.Y., 1975-77; religious edn. cons. Silver Burdett & Ginn, Poughkeepsie, 1983-88; regional coord. religious edn. Archdiocese of N.Y., Poughkeepsie, 1986-87. Author: (with others) Catholic Study Bible - Personal Study Edition, 1993, Call To Leadership, 1993, New Wine, 1994. Mem. Cath. Bibl. Assn., Soc. Bibl. Lit., Am. Acad. Religion, Religious Edn. Assn., Nat. Cath. Edn. Assn. Dem. Roman CAth. Avocations: cooking, reading history, gardening, book collecting. Home: 10513 Cleveland Ave Kansas City MO 64137-1621 Office: Cath Diocese Kansas City 300 E 36th St Kansas City MO 64111-1410 E-mail: mazza@diocesekcsj.org

MAZZA, MARIE GRIMALDI, court clerk; b. Springfield, Mass., Oct. 6, 1936; d. James L. and Lillian G. (Voyik) Grimaldi; m. Joseph S. Mazza, June 14, 1958; children: Rosemarie, James, Joanne, Thomas, Mario, Christine. JD, WNEC Law Sch., 1971. Bar: Mass., 1972. Pvt. practice Superior Ct. Hampden County, Springfield, Mass., 1972-73, asst. city solicitor, 1973-74, asst. clerk, 1974-94, clk. of ct., 1995—. Office: Superior Ct 50 State St Springfield MA 01103-2021

MAZZA, TERILYN MCGOVERN, finance executive; b. Troy, N.Y., Apr. 25, 1952; d. Edward Joseph and Mary Elizabeth (Ryan) McGovern; m. Mario G. Mazza, Oct. 6, 1978. Student, Royal Acad. Dramatic Art, London, U. London Westfield Coll., 1972-73; BA with honors, Marymount Coll., 1974; MA, SUNY, Albany, 1976; MS, Pace U., 1989. Tchg. fellow SUNY, Albany, 1974-76; co. mgr. Cohoes (N.Y.) Music Hall, 1976-78; pub. rels. dir. Lake George (N.Y.) Opera Festival, 1978; promotion/rsch. dir. Capital Newspaper Group, Albany, N.Y., 1979-81; promotion dir., columnist Editor & Pub., N.Y.C., 1981-83; sr. v.p., dir. pub. rels. Am. Bus. Press, 1983-94; pub. adv. bd. Pace U.; adv. bd. Dyson Coll.; mag. adv. bd. Pace U./Fed. Farm Credit Banks Funding Corp., 1995-98, v.p., dir. corp. devel., 1998, cons. corp. devel., 1995—, dist. legis. officer, 1995—. Trustee Co. Bank Pension Plan, 1995-98. Recipient Weyerhauser Craftmanship award Weyerhauser Paper Co., 1980, Design award Strathmore Paper Co., 1980, Design award Strathmore Paper Co., 1980, Telly award Local/Regional TV Comml. Festival, 1982, Pub. award Pace U., 1989, Dyson Fellowship award for excellence Pace U., 1989. E-mail: tmcgovern1@mediaone.net.

MAZZA-DEBLAUWE, TANIA SUE, software engineer, technology educator; b. Belton, Tex., July 14, 1963; d. Anthony Charles and Fronia Irene (Tubbs) Mazza; m. Francis Gilbert George Deblauwe, May 7, 1989; children: Hannah, Anton, Miranda. BA in English, Baylor U., 1985; MEd, Boston U., 1993. Vol., English tchr. Peace Corps, Yemen, 1986-88; lectr. Cambria English Inst., L.A., 1988-90; dir. ESL Program Pacific States U., 1990-91; lectr. U. Md.-College Park, Brussels, 1993-94; assoc. prof. DeVry, Kansas City, Mo., 1994-97; quality assurance engr., software developer, software documentation specialist, 1997—. Mem. Am. Soc. for Quality. Democrat. Unitarian-Universalist. Avocations: writing, Internet, Star Trek memorabilia collecting. Home: 101 E 113th Ter Kansas City MO 64114-5449

MAZZAFERRI, ERNEST LOUIS, physician, educator; b. Cleve., Sept. 27, 1936; s. Joseph and Nanetta (Marinelli) M.; m. Florence Mildred Marolt, Nov. 23, 1957; children: Patricia Marie Atchison, Michael Louis, Sharon Lynne Brown, Ernest Louis. BS cum laude, John Carroll U., 1958; MD, Ohio State U., 1962. Diplomate Am. Bd. Internal Medicine. Intern Ohio State U. Hosps., Columbus, 1962-63, resident, 1963-64, 66-68; asst. prof. medicine Ohio State U., 1968-70, assoc. prof., 1973-76, prof., 1976-79, dir. div. endocrinology and metabolism, 1975-78; acting dean U. Nev., Reno, 1979-81, prof., chmn. dept. medicine, 1978-84, prof. physiology, 1982-84; prof., chmn. dept. medicine, prof. physiology Ohio State U., Columbus, 1984-99, prof. emeritus, 1999—; pres. Dept. of Medicine Found., 1986-99; chmn. bd. Ohio State Practice Group, 1996-99; clin. prof. medicine U. Fla., Gainesville, 2001—. Bd. dirs. The Ohio State U. Hosps., 1997—99; mem. com. on exposure of Am. people to I-B1 from Nev. atomic bomb tests .Nat. Acad. Sci. Inst. of Medicine, 1997—99; mem. com. on health effects assoc. with exposures experienced during the Gulf War, 1999—2000; mem. com. guidelines for thyroid cancer screening Inst. Medicine, 1997—99; chmn. Nat. Cancer Ctr. Network Com. on Thyroid Cancer Guidelines; mem. com. on health effects associated with exposures during the Gulf War Inst. of Medicine Nat. Academies of Sci., 1999—2000. Author: Endocrinology Case Studies, 3d edit., 1985, Internal Medicine Pearls, 1993; editor: Textbook of Endocrinology, 3d edit., 1986, Contemporary Internal Medicine, 1988, 3d edit., 1990, Advances in Endocrinology and Metabolism, Vol. 6, 1995, Endocrine Tumors, 1993, Morning Report, 1999, Yearbook of Endocrinology, 1999—; Endocrine editor Yearbook of Medicine, 1999—; mem. sci. adv. bd. Western Jour. Medicine, 1993; mem. editl. bd. Jour. Lab. Clin. Medicine, 1987-97, Hosp. Practice, Jour. of Clin. Endocrinology and Metabolism, Thyroid, 1999—; contbr. articles to profl. jours. Chmn. Gov.'s Com. on Radiation Fallout in Nev., 1980-84, hosp. ethics com. Ohio State U., 1994-98; mem. Sec. of Energy Dose Assessment Adv. Com., 1980-84, Agy. for Health Care Policy, Rsch. Cataract Guideline Com., 1991-92, Inst. of Medicine Guideline for Thyroid Cancer Screening com., 1997-99; mem. rsch. coun. com. on expense of Am. People to I-131 from Nev. Atomic Bomb Tests: Implications for Public Health, 1997-99. Lt. col. USAF, 1964-72; col. USAR. Recipient Earl N. Metz Disting. Physician award, Ohio State U., 1998, Light of Life award, Light of Life Found. N.Y., 1999, Graves' award, Thyroid Soc. for Rsch. and Edn., 2001. Master: ACP (gov. for Nev. 1984—85, chmn. clin. efficacy assessment program com. 1992—95, edn. policy com. 1992—95, mem. health and pub. policy com.); mem.: AMA, Am. Coll. Clin. Endocrinology (bd. dis. 1995—96, Disting. Clinician award 2002), Ctrl. Soc. Clin. Rsch., Am. Clin. and Climatol. Assn., Endocrine Soc., Am. Diabetes Assn. (pres. Ohio affiliate 1988—89), Am. Thyroid Assn. (Paul Star award), Am. Bd. Internal Medicine (chmn. Endocronology and Metabolism 1996, cert. in endocrinology and metabolism, gen. internal medicine, cert. in geriatrics, continuous profl. devel., bd. dirs. 1999—), Alpha Omega Alpha. Roman Catholic. Achievements include research in thyroid cancer. Home: 4020 SW 93rd Dr Gainesville FL 32608-4653 E-mail: mazz01@bellsouth.net. *Success, like every other human experience, is relative, measured against shifting standards and subject to the scrutiny of time. One must strike a fine balance— self certainty against external review— that permits the full expression of new ideas enriched by the best and time-worn thoughts of others.*

MAZZAFERRI, KATHERINE AQUINO, lawyer, bar association executive; b. Phila., May 14, 1947; d. Joseph William and Rose (Aquino) M.; m. William Fox Bryan, May 5, 1984 (div.); 1 child, Josefa Mazzaferri Bryan. BA, NYU, 1969; JD, George Washington U., 1972. Bar: D.C., 1972. Trial atty. EEOC, Washington, 1972-75; dir. litigation LWV Edn. Fund, 1975-78; dep. asst. dir. for advt. practices FTC, 1978-80, asst. dir. for product liability, 1980-82, asst. dir. for advt. practices, 1982; exec. dir., v.p. pub. svcs. activities corp. D.C. Bar, 1982—. Bd. dir. regulatory analysis project U.S. Regulatory Coun.; mediator D.C. Mediation Svc., 1982; vis. instr. Antioch Law Sch., Washington, 1985; mem. Bd. of Women's Bar Assn. Found., 1990-93; mem. FBA Meml. Found., 1991-96. Bd. dirs. River Rd. Unitarian Ch., 2001—, bd. dir., 2001—. Recipient Superior Service award FTC, 1979 Mem. ABA (rep. of the homeless project steering com. 1988-90), D.C. Bar , Womens Legal Def. (pres. 1972-73, bd. dirs. 1971-75, 76-79), FBA Meml. Found. Home: 5832 Lenox Rd Bethesda MD 20817-6070 Office: DC Bar 1250 H St NW Lbby 6 Washington DC 20005-5906

MAZZAFERRO, JAMES JOSEPH, music educator; b. San Francisco, Apr. 19, 1956; s. James John and Marilyn Jeanne Mazzaferro; m. Anita Marie Piccone, Nov. 27, 1976; children: Cherylyn Mazzaferro, Joseph Mazzaferro, Jeanette Mazzaferro. Bachelors Music Edn., San Francisco State U., San Francisco, CA, 1978; Masters Music Conducting, CSV Sacramento, Sacramento, CA, 1995. San francisco archdiocese Archbishop Riordan H.S., San Francisco, 1979—89; tchr. music Florin H.S. Elk Grove Unified, Sacramento, 1989—97, Sacramento City Coll. Los Rios CC, Sacramento, 1997—2001, Sheldon H.S. Elk Grove Unified, Sacramento, 1997—, Cosumnes River Coll. Los Rios CC, Sacramento, 1999—. Bd. directors Cazadero Performing Arts, Cazadero, Calif., 1995—2001, Calif. Band Directors, Fresno, 1999—2001. Mem.: Calif. Music Educators Assn. (band rep. 1994—98), Musician's Union Local 6, Music Educators Nat. Conf., Phi Kappa Lambada (hon.), Phi Kappa Phi (hon.). D-Liberal. Avocation: music performance. Home: 9068 Shetland Court Elk Grove CA 95624 Office: Sheldon High School 8333 Kingstridge Drive Sacramento CA 95829 Home Fax: 916-681-7505. Personal E-mail: jmazz@cwia.com.

MAZZAFRO, JOSEPH D. international adoption agency executive, web designer; b. Phila., Dec. 26, 1949; s. Joseph E. and Joan Mazzafro; m. Carole Peden, Jan. 5, 1972 (div. Feb. 1985); children: Michael, Tuan, Son, Brandon, Richard, Mikie. BA, Temple U., 1972; MA, Liberty U., Lynchburg, Va., 1994, BS in Theology. Cert. internat. lic. adoption agy. adminstr. Restaurant mgr. Marriott, Phila., 1972-82; restaurant owner Longhorne Ranch, Glenn Mills, Pa., 1982-84; vocat. coord. Applied Skills Industries, Willow Grove, 1984-89; CEO, owner Adoption World, Inc., Phila., 1989—. Author in field. Child advocate Luth. Children and Family Svcs., Phila., 1989-94; advocate for spl. needs children Adoption World, 1990—. Republican. Christian. Avocations: special needs kids, web page building, piano, travel. Office: Adoption World Inc PO Box 16269 Philadelphia PA 19114-0269 E-mail: adoption@adoptionworld.org.

MAZZARELLA, JAMES KEVIN, business administration educator; b. Phila., Sept. 22, 1955; s. Samuel Charles and Rosemary C. (Queenan) M. BA, St. Joseph's U., 1977; MBA, La Salle U., 1981, post MBA cert., 2001; MA, Temple U., 1987; PhD, Columbia-Pacific U., 1987; DBA, Pacific-Western U., 1988; cert. in acctg., Thomas Edison State Coll., 1994; BS, SUNY, 1996. Cert. mgmt. acct.; cert. in fin. mgmt. Asst. mgr. Olney Oil & Burner Co., Phila., 1977-80; data processing Craig Fuel Co., 1980-84; supr. M. Kelley Son's Inc., 1984-86; adj. instr. Holy Family Coll., 1987-88, instr., 1989, asst. prof., 1989—. Adj. instr. Phila. (Pa.) Coll. Textiles, 1984-86, La Salle U., Phila., 1985—, Rosemont (Pa.) Coll., 1988-91. Mem. Acad. Fin. Svcs., Am. Econs. Assn., Am. Fin. Assn., Am. Statis. Assn., Nat. Assn. Bus. Econs., Am. Risk and Ins. Assn., Inst. Mgmt. Accts., Math. Assn. Am., Fin. Mgmt. Assn., Prodn. and Ops. Mgmt. Soc., Midwest Fin. Assn., Western Econs. Assn. Internat., Ea. Econ. Assn., Ea. Fin. Assn., Am. Mgmt. Assn., So. Fin. Assn., Multinat. Fin. Soc., Am. Math. Soc., Am. Law and Econs. Assn., Nat. Coun. Tchrs. Math. Roman Catholic. Home: 5101 N Fairhill St Philadelphia PA 19120-3126 Office: Holy Family College Grant & Frankford Ave Philadelphia PA 19114

MAZZARELLA, ROSEMARY LOUISE, business administration executive; b. Phila., Aug. 20, 1959; d. Samuel Charles and Rosemarie Claire Mazzarella. BA, La Salle U., 1985, MS in Orgnl. Devel. & Mgmt., 1991. Materials mgmt. exec. Sun Refining & Mktg. Co., Phila., 1979-91; purchasing asst. Children's Seashore House, 1992-94; adminstr. FMC Corp., 1994-99, AIG Corp., Phila., 2001—. Mem. Assn. Behavior Analysis (sustaining), Alpha Sigma Lambda.

MAZZARESE, MICHAEL LOUIS, executive coach, consultant; b. S.I., Jan. 25, 1941; s. Louis John and Helen Ermenia (Mazzei) M.; m. Maureen Ann Starace, Oct. 3, 1970 (div. May 1998); children: Lauren, Adrienne BA, St. Joseph's Sem. and Coll., 1962; MS, CUNY, 1971, profl. dipl., 1973; PhD, Fordham U., 1980. Tchr. high sch., N.Y. and Maine, 1963-73; prof. CUNY, 1973-78; asst. dir. med. edn. St. Barnabas Med. Ctr., Livingston, N.J., 1978-79; staff supr. AT&T, Bedminster, 1979-84; mgr. Johnson and Johnson, New Brunswick, 1984-86; dir. EQUICOR, N.Y.C., 1986-87; exec. dir. Dun & Bradstreet, Murray Hill, N.J., 1987-92; v.p. Hoechst Celanese Corp., Somerville, 1992-94; pres. Mazzarese & Assocs., Westfield, 1994—; adjunct prof. bus. ethics N.Y.U. Stern Sch. Bus., 1999—. Translator: Letters from Paris (Teilhard J. Chardin), 1966. Recipient Excellence in Human Resources Devel. award Brigham Young U., 1985. Mem. Am. Psychol. Assn., Am. Soc. Tng. and Devel., Am. Evaluation Assn., Am. Evaluation and Rsch. Assn., Soc. Human Resource Mgmt., Human Resources Planning Soc. Home: 213 Scotch Plains Ave Westfield NJ 07090-4437 Office: Mazzarese & Assocs 213 Scotch Plains Ave Westfield NJ 07090-4437 E-mail: mmazzarese@aol.com.

MAZZARI, LOUIS W. managing editor; b. Miami Beach, Fla., Sept. 14, 1955; s. Dante J. and Betty (Kelahear) M.; 1 child, Dante J. BA in Comm., U. Ctrl. Fla., 1977; MA in English, U. Mass., 1982; postgrad. in history, U. N.H., 1998—. Reporter Cape Cod News, Hyannis, Mass., 1980-81; advt. mgr. Harvard Educational Review Harvard U., Cambridge, 1983-84; mng. editor Orchard House Pubs., Inc., Concord, 1985-88; sr. writer, editor U. N.H., Durham, 1988-97; dir. pubs. Boston U. Coll. Engring., 1997-98. Fieldworker Smithsonian Instn., 1998-2000. Mng. editor: Identities: Global Studies in Culture and Power, 1998-2000; contbg. author: Encyclopedia of New England Culture, 2001-02; author poems and fiction. N.H. Coun. Arts fellow, 1998. Avocations: art, music, film, sports, travel. Home: 17 Wareham St # 2 Medford MA 02155-6221

MAZZE, EDWARD MARK, marketing educator, consultant; b. N.Y.C., Feb. 14, 1941; s. Harry Alan and Mollie (Schneider) M.; m. Sharon Sue Hastings, Sept. 9, 1967; children— Candace, Thomas. BBA, City U. N.Y., 1961, MBA, 1962; PhD, Pa. State U., 1966. Lectr. bus. adminstrn. CCNY, 1961-62; bus. cons., 1961—; pres., dir. JET Corp., East Orange, N.J., 1976-79; instr. bus. Pa. State U., 1963-66; assoc. prof. mktg. U. Detroit, 1966-68; assoc. prof., dir. spl. programs W.Va. U., 1968-70; prof. bus. adminstrn., coordinator mktg. program Va. Poly. Inst. and State U., Blacksburg, 1970-75; v.p. adminstrv. services, dean Sch. Bus., Seton Hall U., South Orange, N.J., 1975-79; dean sch. bus. adminstrn. Temple U., Phila., 1979-86, prof. mktg. and internat. bus., 1979-93; dean Belk Coll. Bus. Adminstrn., prof. mktg. U. N.C.-Charlotte, Charlotte, 1993-98; dean Coll. Bus. Adminstrn., Alfred J. Verrecchia-Hasbro Inc. Leadership chair in bus. U. R.I., Kingston, 1998—. Chmn. bd. William Penn Bank, Phila., 1985-87; bd. dirs. Technitrol, Inc., Washington Trust Bancorp, Inc., Barrett Growth Fund; mem. dist. export coun. U.S. Dept. Commerce, 1978-80, 83-93; mem. panel trustees U.S. Bankruptcy Ct., 1984-96; adv. bd. McGettigan Ptrns., 1997-99, Radiator Specialty Co., 1997-99, Piedmont Venture Ptrns., 1997-98. Author: International Business: Articles and Essays, 1963, Readings in Organization and Management, 1963, Marketing in Action, 1963, Case Histories in Sales Management, 1965, Sales Management: Theory and Practice, 1965, International Marketing Adminstration, 1967, Introduction to Marketing, 1970, Marketing in Turbulent Times: The Challenges and the Opportunities, 1975, Personal Selling: Choice Against Chance, 1976, The Food Marketing Wars: Marketing Triumphs and Blunders, 1998, Specialty Retailers: Marketing Triumphs and Blunders, 2001; mem. editl. bd. Jour. Econs. and Bus., 1976-80, Indsl. Mktg. Mgmt., 1977—, Jour. Internat. Bus. Studies, 1978-82, Jour. Acad. Mktg. Sci., 1980-91, Jour. Mktg. Edn., 1985-94, Jour. Global Mktg., 1987—; contbr. articles to profl. jours. Trustee Phila. Home Care, 1984-89, Manor Coll., 1985-92, Thomas A. Edison State Coll. Found., 1987-89, Delaware Valley Coll. Sci. and Agr., 1991-97, Pa. Inst. Tech., 1992-93; chmn. econ. devel. adv. com. Village South Orange, 1977-80; mem., vice-chmn. Bd. Suprs. Doylestown Twp., 1980-81. Ford Found. fellow, 1962-63 Mem. Am. Mktg. Assn., Acad. Internat. Bus., Nat. Assn. Corp. Dirs., Acad. Mktg. Sci., Beta Gamma Sigma, Alpha Kappa Psi, Pi Sigma Epsilon, Pi Kappa Alpha. Home: 52 Horizon Dr Saunderstown RI 02874-2402 Office: U RI Dept Bus Kingston RI 02881

MAZZELLA, ANTHONY J. minister, psychotherapist, musician; b. Bronx, NY, Dec. 15, 1957; s. Anthony and Angelina Mazzella; m. Beverly A. DellOlio Mazzella, Aug. 30; children: Seth, Jordana. BSMus, Mercy Coll., 1983; MA in Theology, Andrews U., 1985; MSW, Yeshiva U., 1994; cert. pastoral counseling, Blanton Peale Inst. Religion and Health, 1991. LCSW NY. Min. 7th Day Adventist Ch., Manhasset, NY, 1984—; pvt. practice Hartsdale, 1994—, Yonkers, 1994—. Supr. interns Greater NY chpt. 7th Day Adventist Ch., Manhasset, 1999—, exec. com., 1997—2000, multiethnic adv. bd., 1994—. Guitarist (CD) An Alm for the Love of God, 2002. Mem.: NASW, Focus on Family, Am. Assn. Christian Counselors. Avocations: web design, reading, running. Home: 87 Wharton Dr Cortlandt Manor NY 10567 Office: Yonkers 7th Day Adventist Ch 793 N Broadway Yonkers NY 10701 Fax: 914-739-5216. E-mail: ask@pastortonycsw.com.

MAZZEO, ANTHONY R. chemist; b. Buffalo, May 2, 1958; s. George J. and Louise C. M.; m. Darlene Van Eseltine, May 21, 1988; children: Victoria, Seth. BS, SUNY, Brockport, 1980; PhD, Syracuse U., 1991. Chemist DuPont, Aiken, S.C., 1980-84; rsch., tchg. asst. Syracuse (N.Y.) U., 1984-88; mgr. quality assurance/tech. support New Methods Rsch., Syracuse, 1988-93; quality assurance scientist Bayer Corp., Spokane, Wash., 1993-99; sr. quality assurance scientist Hollister-Stier Labs., 1999-2000; R&D stability mgr. DuPont Pharm. Co., Wilmington, Del., 2000—02; rsch. assoc. rsch. and devel. Pfizer Global , 2002—. Contbr. articles to profl. jours. Mem. AAAS, Am. Chem. Soc. (chair Inland N.W. sect. 1998-2000, sec. treas. 1996), Am. Assn. Pharm. Scientists. E-mail: Anthony@R.Mazzeo@dupontphama.com. Home: 25395 Crown Point Ct Farmington Hills MI 48335 Office: Pfizer 2800 Plymouth Rd Ann Arbor MI 48105

MAZZEO, DANIEL PATRICK, aerospace engineer, aviation consultant; b. N.Y.C., Apr. 18, 1949; s. Gennaro and Marie Grace (Mazzei) M.; m. Belva Faye Musick, Sept. 10, 1977; children: Gennaro, Jina Marie. BS in Aerospace Engring., Poly. Inst. Bklyn., 1971; grad. in Aviation Safety, U.S. Naval Postgrad. Sch., Monterey, Calif., 1981. Commd. ensign USN, 1969, advanced through grades to comdr., 1982, aviator, 1969-91; aviation program mgr. BDI Engring., Pensacola, Fla., 1991-95; aviation project mgr. DH Engrs., Sarasota, 1995-99; pres., CEO Aerocomm Group, Pensacola, 1999—. Airline transport pilot rating FAA, 1979; mem. State Aviation Planning Process, Fla., 1990—; completed over 150 major airport improvement projects. Contbr. articles to profl. jours. Tech. advisor in aviation County Govt., Escambia, Fla., 1985, Santa Rosa, Fla., 1987, Tallahassee, Fla., 1994. Decorated Navy commendation medal, Navy expdn. medal, Def. Svc. medal with one bronze star; recipient Sci. grant N.Y.C., 1965, 68, Innovative Environmental award FAA, 1997, Airport of the Year award Fla. Dept. Transp., 1997. Mem. ASCE (section pres.), AIAA, Soc. Am. Mil. Engrs., Aircraft Owners and Pilots Assn. (advisor 1997). Achievements include invention of electrophotographic imaging machine and invention of the respirograph employed in medical research. Home: PO Box 614 Gulf Breeze FL 32562-0614 Office: Aerocomm Group Pensacola FL 32502 E-mail: OneGoodEngineer@aol.com, Aerocomm@aol.com.

MAZZEO-MERKLE, LINDA LOU, legal administrator; b. Washington, Apr. 6, 1947; d. Robert Clifton Shreeves II and Esther A. (Harrison) Shreeves; m. John T. Mazzeo; children: Christina L. Schneider, Regina L. Hodges; stepchildren: John T. Mazzeo Jr., Christina M. Mazzeo. Lic. real estate salesperson, Prince Georges C.C., Largo, Md., 1972. Various secretarial positions, 1964-65, 67-72; real estate saleswoman, 1973-74; divsn. sec. Prince Georges C.C., 1974-75; real estate saleswoman Harvest Realty Inc., Clinton, Md., 1974-75; legal adminstr., property mgr., investment mgr. Tucker, Flyer, Sanger, Reider & Lewis, P.C., Washington, 1975-84; legal adminstr. Anderson, Heibey, Nauheim & Blair, 1984-85; v.p. fin. and adminstrn. Barnes, Morris, Pardoe & Foster, Inc., 1985-93; former CFO, chief adminstrv. officer Barnes, Morris & Pardoe, Inc.; legal adminstr. Payne, Negroni & Winston, Washington, 1994-95, Buckmaster & Assocs., Washington, 1996-98; cert. NIA instr. Vicksburg, Miss., 1998—; designer, owner Instant Ancestor, Jewelry Co., 2000—. Cons. and spkr. in field. Mem. Assn. Legal Adminstrs. (chmn. new adminstrs. and gen. adminstrn. sect. 1984-85). Home: 100 Lakewood Hls Vicksburg MS 39180-5543

MAZZETTI, ROBERT F. real estate manager, retired orthopedic surgeon; b. San Francisco, Sept. 29, 1930; children: Mark, Robert Alan, Michelle. BA, U. Calif., San Francisco, 1952, MD, 1955. Diplomate Am. Bd. Orth. Surgery. Pvt. practice orth. surgeon, Santa Barbara, Calif., 1962-98; owner Mazat, Ltd., 1994—, Brushy Creek, Ltd., 1998. Pres. real estate mgmt. co. Mazat LLC, 1994—. Office: 11615 Angus Rd Ste 104 Austin TX 78759-4064 E-mail: olmazz@aol.com.

MAZZILLI, PAUL JOHN, investment banker; b. White Plains, N.Y., Dec. 4, 1948; s. Philip Joseph and Sara (Bialick) M.; m. Sharon Pickett, May 23, 1986; children: Meredith Paige, Nicholas Parker. BS in Indsl. Engring., Syracuse U., 1970; MBA, Columbia U., 1973. Budget analyst The Pentagon, Washington, 1972; mgr. planning and analysis Xerox Corp., White Plains, 1973-75, Morgan Stanley & Co., Inc., N.Y.C., 1975-78, dir. planning and analysis, 1979-80, exec. asst. to oper. com., 1981-82, new product specialist, 1982-83, v.p. hedging products, 1984-85, prin. pension svcs. group, 1986-87, head strategy group for Employee Stock Ownership Plans, 1988-91, head of Equity Derivatives Corp. Svc. Group, 1992-93, prin. equity capital markets svcs., 1993-97, dir. exchange-traded fund rsch., 1997—. Pres. Wall Street Planning Group, N.Y.C., 1979-80; adj. prof. fin. Mercy Coll., Dobbs Ferry, N.Y., 1977-79; mem. tax rev. bd. Town of Greenburgh, N.Y., 1972-77. Coun. mem. Jr. Achievement N.Y., 1976-78; elected Westchester County Rep. Com., 1970-75. Capt. USAFR, 1970-76. Mem. Nat. Assn. Securities Dealers (registered rep.), Columbia U. Alumni Assn. (rep. 1979-80), Columbia Bus. Sch. Alumni Assn. (bd. dirs., v.p. 1978-81), Sleepy Hollow Country Club, Shattemuc Yacht Club (Ossining, N.Y.), Shelter Harbor Golf Club. Home: Tower Hill Rd Scarborough NY 10510 Office: Morgan Stanley & Co Inc 1585 Broadway New York NY 10036-8200

MAZZIO-MOORE, JOAN L. radiology educator, physician; b. Belmont, Mass., Oct. 26, 1935; d. Frank Joseph and Maria L. Mazzio; children: James Thomas, Edwin Stuart. BA in Chemistry and Theology, Emmanuel Coll., 1957; MA in Genetics and Physiology, Mass. Wellesley Coll., 1961; PhD in Genetics, Bryn Mawr (Pa.) Coll., 1964; MD, Phila. Coll. of Medicine, 1977, MSc in Radiology, 1981. Instr. in biochemistry Gwynedd Mercy Coll., Springhouse, Pa., 1963—65; instr. in genetics Holy Family Coll., Phila., 1965—66; instr. in anatomy Phila. Coll. of Medicine, 1971—77, tchr., 1973—77, asst. prof., 1977—84; prof. W.Va. Sch. of Medicine, 1984—; rotating intern Phila. Coll. of Medicine Hosp., 1977—78, resident in radiology, 1978—81; advanced through grades to maj. USAR, 1984—; med. dir. 91W transition program U.S. Army Med. Corps Reserves, divsn. surgeon, 80th divsn. (IT) Va. Author: (with Dr. DiVirgilito) Essentials of Neuropathology, 1974. Lector St. Ann's Cath. Ch., Phoenixville, Pa., 1981-84; treas. Hist. Soc. of Frankford, Phila., 1968-75, Sch. Mother's Assn., Devon (Pa.) Prep., 1980-81. Col. med. corps U.S. Army, 1992. Mem. AAUP, Am. Acad. Family Physicians, Am. Assn. Women Radiologists, Am. Med. Women's Assn., Am. Osteo. Coll. of Radiology, Am. Soc. Clin. Oncology, Am. Soc. Therapeutic Readiologists, Hist. Soc. of Lewisburg (life), Pa. Osteo. Med. Assn., Pa. Osteo. Gen. Practitioner's Soc., Radiol. Soc. N.Am., Radiation Rsch. Soc., Res. Officers Assn. (life), W.Va. Soc. Osteo. Medicine, Greenbrier River Hike and Bike Trail. Home: RR 1 Box 123 Frankford WV 24938 Office: WVa Sch of Medicine 400 N Lee St Lewisburg WV 24901-1128 Fax: 304-497-2752. E-mail: jmoore@wvsom.edu.

MAZZOCCO, ANGELO, language educator, cultural historian, linguist; b. Cerreto di Vastogirardi, Isernia, Italy, May 13, 1936; came to U.S., 1954, naturalized, 1957; s. Giuseppe and Ida (Rotolo) M.; m. Elizabeth Hunt Davis, Oct. 7, 1990; children: Michael Ray, Marco Angelo. BS, BA, Ohio State U., 1959, MA, 1963; PhD in Romance Langs. and Lits., U. Calif., Berkeley, 1973. Instr. Spanish John Carroll U., Cleve., 1962-65; teaching asst. Italian U. Calif., Berkeley, 1966-69; asst. prof. Italian No. Ill. U., DeKalb, 1970-75; asst. prof. Spanish and Italian Mt. Holyoke Coll., South Hadley, Mass., 1975-78, assoc. prof., 1978-83, prof., 1983—, chair dept., 1981-84, 1993—96, chair Romance langs. and lits., 1989-93, 1999—2002. Assoc. Columbia U. Renaissance Seminar, 1981-90; fellow-in-residence Inst. for Advanced Study, Ind. U., Bloomington, 1998; mem. editl. adv. bd. Renaissance Quart.; interview NPR, 2000. Author: Linguistic Theories in Dante/Humanists, 1993; contbr. numerous chpts. to books, articles and revs. to profl. jours. Travel grantee Am. Coun. Learned Socs., 1985, Gladys Krieble Delmas Found. Rsch. grantee, 1993-94, 96-97; Italian-Am. traveling fellow U. Calif., 1969-70, NEH Italian Humanism summer sem. fellow, 1981, NEH/NSF award, 1995-98. Mem. MLA (exec. com. Medieval and Renaissance Italian Lit. 1981-85, assembly del. 1985-87), Am. Assn. Tchrs. Italian, Dante Soc. Am. (coun. assoc. 1985-90, coun. 1994-97), Medieval Acad., Renaissance Soc. Am. (elected discipline rep. Ital. lit., 2000-2002), Internat. Assn. Neo-Latin Studies, N.Am. Assn. History Lang. Soc., Assn. Internat. Studi di Lingua e Letteratura Italiana, Internat. Soc. Classical Tradition, Am. Boccaccio Assn. (v.p. 1982-83), Am. Assn. Italian Studies, Nat. Assn. Scholars, Nat. Ital. Am. Found. Office: Mt Holyoke Coll Dept Spanish and Italian South Hadley MA 01075 E-mail: amazzocc@mtholyoke.edu.

MAZZOLA, ANTHONY THOMAS, editor, art consultant, designer, writer; b. Passaic, N.J., June 13, 1923; s. Thomas and Jennie (Failla) M.; m. Michele Morgan, Nov. 18, 1967; children: Anthony Thomas II, Marc Eden, Alisa Morgan. Grad., Cooper Union Art Sch., N.Y.C., 1948. Art dir. Street & Smith Publs., N.Y.C., 1948, Town and Country mag. (pub. by Hearst Corp.), N.Y.C., 1948-65, editor-in-chief, 1965-72, Harpers Bazaar, 1972-92; pres. Anthony Mazzola Design Corp., N.Y.C., 1963—; creative cons. Hearst Mags., 1992—. Editorial dir. 125 Great Moments of Harper's Bazaar, 1991-94, Town & Country 150th Anniversary, 1994—; cons. designer United Nations Childrens' Fund, Assn. Jr. Leagues Am., Columbia Pictures Corp., Sells Spltys., Gen. Foods, Paramount Pictures, Princess Marcella Borghese, Inc., Huntington Hartford, Ltd., N.Y. World's Fair, 1965 Exhibited, Art Dirs. Club N.Y., ann. exhbns., 1948— . Served with AUS, 1943-46. Decorated Bronze Star, Knight Officer of Order of Merit Italy; recipient Cert. of Merit awards N.Y. Art Dirs. Club; medal Art Dirs. Club N.Y.C., 1955. Office: Town and Country 1790 Broadway New York NY 10019-1412

MAZZOLA, CLAUDE JOSEPH, physicist, small business owner; b. Newton, Mass., May 24, 1936; s. Gradinola and Anne (Cicconi) M.; m. Helen Alamanos, July 25, 1965; children: Peppina, Jean-Claude. BS in Physics, Boston Coll., 1959; postgrad. in Physics, MIT, 1961-62. Jr. engr. Lab. for Electronics, Boston, 1959-61; scientist AVCO R&D, Wilmington, Mass., 1961-62; engr. Space Scis., Waltham, 1962-63, BBN, Cambridge, 1963-72; staff engr. Edo, College Point, N.Y., 1972-82; engr. Sperry, Great Neck, 1982-89; sole proprietor Namlak, Mamaroneck, 1989—. Author: Active Sound Absorption, 1993; patentee Magnetic Storage Device (floppy disc), 1963; developer sound absorption system for aircraft cabins; contbr. articles to profl. jours., papers to sci. confs. and meetings. Mem. IEEE. Republican. Roman Catholic. Avocations: jogging, skiing, sailing, foreign travel. Home: 106 Lawn Ter Mamaroneck NY 10543-4023 Office: Namlak PO Box 804 Mamaroneck NY 10543-0804 E-mail: namlak@aol.com.

MAZZOLA, JOHN WILLIAM, former performing arts center executive, consultant; b. Bayonne, N.J., Jan. 20, 1928; s. Roy Stephen and Eleanor Burnett (Davis) M.; m. Sylvia Drulie, Mar. 7, 1959; children: Alison, Amy. AB, Tufts U., 1949; LLD, Fordham U., 1952. Bar: N.Y. 1956. Mem. firm Milbank, Tweed, Hadley & McCloy, N.Y.C., 1952-64; sec., exec. v.p. Lincoln Center for Performing Arts, 1964-68, gen. mgr., chief exec. officer, 1969-70, mng. dir., chief exec. officer, 1970-77, pres., chief exec. officer, 1977-84. Cons. performing arts ctrs. in U.S. and abroad, also motion pictures, non-profit orgns. Bd. dirs. various charitable orgns.; mem. adv. bd. U. S.C. Koger Arts Ctr. With CIC, U.S. Army, 1953-55. Decorated cavaliere ufficiale Ordine al Merito della Repubblica Italiana; Ordre des Arts et des Lettres France; Benjamin Franklin fellow Royal Soc. Arts. Mem. Watch Hill Yacht Club, Misquamicut Club (R.I.). Episcopalian. Home: 12 Beekman Pl New York NY 10022-8059

MAZZOLA, MICHAEL, lighting designer; Resident lighting designer Oreg. Ballet Theatre, 1986—. Lighting designer Bebe Miller Co., N.Y.C. Improvisational Festival. Recipient Bessie Ward award, 2002. Office: 742 SW Vista #32 Portland OR 97205*

MAZZONI, BARBARA JEAN, nurse; b. Cumberland, Md., July 23, 1949; d. Robert Taylor and Loretta McLaughlin; m. Robert A. Mazzoni, Feb. 17, 1979; 1 child, Michael. Diploma, Ch. Home/Hosp. Sch. Nursing, 1971; BS in Nursing, U. Md., 1976. Advice nurse Kaiser Permanente, Lutherville, Md., 1989—; clin. mgr. Greater Balt. Med. Ctr., Towson, 1987-89; nurse clinician U. Md. Hosp., 1978-87. Home: 670 Post Ln Rock Hill SC 29730-6028

MAZZUCELLI, COLETTE GRACE CELIA, author, internet multimedia educator; b. Bklyn., Nov. 26, 1962; d. Silvio Anthony and Adeline Marie (De Ponte) M. BA, U. Scranton, 1983; MA in Law and Diplomacy, Tufts U., 1987; PhD, Georgetown U., 1996. Instr. Georgetown U., Washington, 1990-96; rsch. fellow Inst. fuer Europaeische Politik, Deutsche Gesellschaft fuer Auswaertige Politik, Bonn, Deutsch-Franzoesisches Inst., Ludwigsburg; asst. ratification process Treaty European Union, German Fgn. Minstry; cons. Jean Monnet Coun., Washington, 1994-98; dir. internat. programs Budapest Inst. Grad. Internat. and Diplomatic Studies, 1995-97; dir., founder Partnership Initiatives, 1997—; founding dir. internat. peace and conflict resolution grad. program Arcadia U., 1998-99, asst. prof. polit. sci., 1998-99; dir. fiscal affairs and strategic devel. Transatlantic Info. Exch. Svc., 1998-99, Arcadia U., 1998—99; chmn. transatlantic internet seminar Kosovoa-Southea. Europe Inst. Polit. Studies, Paris, 2000—; chmn. transatlantic internet multimedia seminar Southea. Europe (TIMSSE) Rotary Ctr., Scis. Po, 2000—. Program officer, edn. arts NGO rep. UN Carnegie Coun. on Ethics and Internat. Affairs, 2001—02; sr. rsch. fellow Eastwest Inst., 2000—01; lectr. U.S. Info. Svc. Spkrs. Program in Europe, 1994; active IPSA Rsch. Com. on European Unification; instr. in-house tng. in negotiations Hungarian Fgn. Ministry, 1996—97; Hungarian Ministry Def. del. to NATO Accession Talks, 1997; advisor to bd. dirs. Transatlantic Info. Exch. Svc., 1997—98; mem. study group on religion and ethnicity Fgn. Policy Rsch. Inst., 2000—. Author: France and Germany at Maastricht Politics and Negotiations to Create the European Union, 1997, paperback 2d edit., 1999; asst. editor: The Evolution of an International Actor: Western Europe's New Assertiveness, 1990; author: Monnet Case Studies in European Affairs, 1995; contbr.: Dimensions of German Unification, 1994, Redefining European Security, 1999, United Nations Chronicle, 2001; also articles to profl. publs. Swiss U. grantee, 1984-85; Pi Gamma Mu scholar, 1985, Rotary grad. scholar, 1987-88, Fulbright scholar, 1991; Jean Monnet Coun. dissertation fellow, 1991, European Commn. fellow, 1992, Robert Bosch Found. fellow, 1992-93, 2001, Salzburg Seminar fellow, 1997, 21st Century Trust fellow Merton Coll., Oxford (Eng.) U., 2001. Mem. Am. Polit. Sci. Assn., Deutsche Atlantische Gesellschaft, European Cmty. Studies Assn., Robert Bosch Found. Alumni Assn. (mem. exec. com. 1994-96, 97-98, co-pres. 1999-2000), The Fletcher Club of N.Y. (v.p. 1998), Alpha Sigma Nu (student pres. 1984), Pi Gamma Mu (chpt. sec. 1982-84, Frank C. Brown scholarship medal 1984), Phi Sigma Tau (founder Scranton chpt.), Phi Alpha Theta, Pi Sigma Alpha, Alpha Mu Gamma, Delta Tau Kappa. Avocations: chess, swimming, karate, poetry writing, astrology. Home: 1864 74th St Brooklyn NY 11204-5752 Office: Carnegie Coun on Ethics and Internat Affairs 170 E 64th St New York NY 10021-7496 Business E-Mail: cmazzucelli@cceia.org.. E-mail: copres2000@boschalumni.org.

MBADUGHA, LORETTA NKEIRUKA AKOSA, social services administrator, consultant; b. Onitsha, Anambara, Nigeria, Dec. 10, 1957; d. James and Sylvia O. (Asika) Akosa; m. Christian Mbadugha; children: Kristen Ogechi, Kyle Kelechi, Kelsey Odinaka. Assoc., Langham Secretarial Coll., London, 1978; BS, Tex. So. U., Houston, 1981, MS, 1982; PhD, U. New Orleans, 2000, PhD in Higher Edn. Adminstrn., 2001. Program analyst Tex. So. U., Houston, 1982-84; sanitarian City of Houston Health Dept., 1984-85; adj. faculty So. U., New Orleans, 1981-90; asst. to exec. dir. YWCA, 1984-93; family rep. Jefferson Parish Human Svcs. Authority, 1993—2001; CEO Profl. Family Support Svcs., 1994—. Cons., founder, bd. mem. Camelot Providers, New Orleans, 1987—; bd. mem. United Svcs. AIDS Found., 1990-92; trainer Coun. for Early Childhood Profl. Recognition, 1987—; cons., trainer on child devel. State of La., 1987-89; exec. dir. Gilbert Acad.; asst. prof. edn. Dillard U. Sec. Chapel of Praise, 1997. Recipient Mayoral Cert. of Merit, New Orleans, 1991; Grace Hodge fellow YWCA, 1992. Mem. ACA, Nigeria Ebony Club for Women (pres. 1995). Home: 7141 Westhaven Rd New Orleans LA 70126-2132 Office: 7041 Real Ln New Orleans LA 70127

MBAH, CHRIS H.N. business educator; b. May 1, 1956; BBA, Sul Ross State U., 1979, MBA, 1980. Lectr. U. Jos, Nigeria, 1982-89; sr. lectr. U. Tech., South Pacific, 1991-95; adj. prof. Ferris State U., Big Rapids, Mich., 1996-97; assoc. prof. Cornerstone U., Grand Rapids, 1997—. Adj. prof. Ferris State U., Big Rapids, 1996—. Office: Cornerstone U Business Divsn Grand Rapids MI 49505 E-mail: cmbah@cornerstone.edu.

MBAKU, JOHN MUKUM, economics educator; b. Bessi-Awum, Cameroon, Jan. 4, 1950; came to U.S., 1973; s. Fotoh Ba Worifah Mbaku and Lydia Nnah; m. Theresa Thomas, July 27, 1985; children: Vivianne Elizabeth Api, Fotoh Thomas Mukum. BS in Chemistry, Berry Coll., Mt. Berry, Ga., 1977; M. Internat. Bus., U. S.C., 1979; PhD in Econs., U. Ga., 1985. Teaching asst. U. Ga., Athens, 1982-85; asst. prof. econs. Kennesaw State U., Marietta, Ga., 1985-90, assoc. prof. econs., 1990-91, assoc. prof., 1990—2001; assoc. prof. econs. Weber State U., Ogden, Utah, 1990—94, prof. econs., 1994—. External examiner U. Madras, India, 1994—; vis. lectr. Shandong Acad. Social Scis., Qingdao, China, 1993; post-doctoral rsch. fellowship in pub. choice Ctr. Study of Pub. Choice George Mason U., 1995 (summer); lectr. in field. Editl. bd. Jour. Third World Studies, assoc. editor; contbr. over 70 articles to profl. jours. including Pub. Choice, Cato Jour., Studies in Comparative Internat. Devel., Rev. of Black Polit. Economy, Applied Econs. (UK), Applied Econs. Letters (UK), Indian Jour. Social Sci., Indian Jour. Polit. Sci., Southern Econ. Jour., several books on African polit. economy. Mem. Mayor's Econ. Adv. Bd., Ogden, 1993—. Recipient Black History award Def. Depot, Ogden, 1993, Outstanding Faculty award Omicron Delta Epsilon, 1994; Fulbright scholar, China, 1988. Mem. Assn. Third World Studies (pres. 1994-95, sec. 1991-93, Presdl. award 1993), Am. Econ. Assn., Nat. Econ. Assn., So. Econ. Assn., Pub. Choice Soc., Phi Kappa Phi. Democrat. Presbyterian. Avocations: reading, travel, photography, coins, stamp collecting. Home: 2258 E 3500 N Layton UT 84040-2471 Office: Weber State University 3807 University Cir Ogden UT 84408-3807 E-mail: jmbaku@weber.edu.

MCABEE, DOUGLAS DEWITT, biochemistry educator, researcher; b. Moscow, Oct. 21, 1955; s. DeWitt Clinton and Iona Catherine (Gause) McA.; m. Cristy Ann McCarty, Feb. 29, 1984; children: Kathryn Leigh, Douglas Keith. BA, Point Loma Coll., 1979; PhD, Southwestern Med. Ctr., 1984. Post-doctoral fellow U. Tex. Med. Br., Galveston, 1984-89; asst. prof. cell biology U. Notre Dame, South Bend, Ind., 1989-97; asst. prof. biochemistry Calif. State U., Long Beach, 1997-99, assoc. prof., 1999—, chair dept. chemistry and biochemistry, 2002—. Contbr. articles to profl. jours. including Jour. Biol. Chemistry, Biochemistry, Biochem. Jour., Jour. Cellular Physiology. Recipient Alumnus of Point Loma award, 1986; grantee: Am. Heart Assn., South Bend, Ind. 1993-94, NIH, South Bend, 1995-99, Rsch. Corp., Long Beach, 2000—. Mem. AAAS, Am. Soc. Cell Biology, Am. Soc for Biochemistry and Molecular Biology., Cell Stress Soc. Internat., Am. Chem. Soc. Episcopalian. Avocations: music, hiking. Office: Calif State U Dept Biochemistry 1250 N Bellflower Blvd Long Beach CA 90840-0001 E-mail: dmcabee@csulb.edu.

MCABEE, SONJA LOUISE, library administrator; b. Anniston, Ala., Mar. 17, 1955; d. Ralph J. and Thelma Louise Sherman; m. Kenneth Blair McAbee, July 15, 1978; children: Megan Elizabeth, Patrick Ryan. BA in Polit. Sci., Jacksonville State U., 1975; MLS, U. Ala., 1988. Acquisitions libr. Jacksonville (Ala.) State U., 1990-96, head libr. svcs., 1996—. Contbr. articles to profl. jours. Mem. Ala. Libr. Assn. Democrat. Avocations: gardening, reading, home improvement projects. Home: 1837 Noah Valley Rd Jacksonville AL 36265 Office: Jacksonville State U 700 Pelham Rd North Jacksonville AL 36265 Office Fax: 256-782-5872. E-mail: smcabee@jsucc.jsu.edu.

MCABEE, THOMAS ALLEN, psychologist; b. Spartanburg, S.C., Mar. 31, 1949; s. Thomas Walker and Doris Lee (Gillespie) McA. Student, Ga. Inst. Tech., 1967-69; BA, Furman U., 1971; MA, U. S.C., 1975, PhD, 1979. Clin. counselor Adolescent Inpatient Svc. William S. Hall Psychiat. Inst., Columbia, S.C., 1971-73; counselor children's therapeutic camp Columbia Area Mental Health Ctr., 1974; co-dir. cmty. problems survey Eau Claire Cmty. Project, Columbia, 1975; asst. aging svcs. planner Ctrl. Midlands Regional Planning Coun., 1976; instr. U. S.C., 1976; NSF intern S.C. State Legislature, 1978; rsch. dir. S.C. Legis. Gov.'s Com. Mental Health and Mental Retardation, Columbia, 1979-80; co-dir. TV project "Feelings Just Are" Columbia Area Mental Health Ctr., 1980-89; psychologist S.C. Dept. Mental Retardation, 1982-93, S.C. Dept. Disabilities and Spl. Needs, 1993—. Cons. S.C. Protection and Advocacy System for Handicapped Citizens, 1980, 81, S.C. Dept. Mental Health, 1981; mem. deinstitutionalization task force S.C. Developmental Disabilities Coun., 1979-80; mem. subcom. State Commr.'s Ad Hoc Com. to Study and Develop Work/Lodge System for S.C., S.C. Dept. Mental Health, 1979-80; mem. Media Task Force of Gov.'s Adv. Com. on Early Childhood Devel. and Edn., 1980-81; chmn. primary prevention public media com. S.C. Dept. Mental Health, 1979-81. Recipient Palmetto Pictures Photography award, 1977; NIMH fellow, 1976-77. Mem. APA, S.C. Psychol. Assn. Home: 353 Palmer Dr Lexington SC 29072-7476 Office: 8301 Farrow Rd Columbia SC 29203-3245 E-mail: tmcabee@ddsn.state.sc.us.

MCADAM, PAUL EDWARD, retired library administrator; b. Balt., Jan. 30, 1934; s. Joseph Francis Jr. and Irene Cecile (Heineck) McA. BA in Romance Langs., Johns Hopkins U., 1955, MA, 1956; MLS, Drexel U., 1970. Libr. Free Libr. Phila., 1969-81; br. mgr. Phila. City. Inst. Libr., 1974-81; dir. Am. Libr., Paris, 1981-85; libr. collection devel., libr. tech. svcs. Catonsville (Md.) C.C., 1986-89; assoc. v.p. learning resources Carroll C.C., Westminster, Md., 1989-99, assoc. v.p. emeritus, 1999—; adj. libr. C.C. of Baltimore County, Catonsville, 1999—2002, Balt. Internat. Coll., 2000—. Mem. adv. bd. Coop. Librs. Ctrl. Md., Annapolis, 1992-96, State Libr. Resource Ctr., Balt., 1994-95; bd. dirs. Renew, 1995—; del. Internat. Fedn. Libr. Assn, 1993, 95. Vol. MPT, 1989-2000, Walters Art Mus., Md. Fine Arts Festival, 1991-97 AIRS, Drexel U., 2002--. 1st lt. U.S. Army, 1956-58. Mem. ALA (membership com. 1996-98), Coll. Air Consortium, Congress Acad. Libr. Dirs. (treas. 1998-2000), Md. Libr. Assn. (hon.; membership chair 1993-96, awards chair 1996-97, 1999-2000, treas. 1997-99, chair fundraising task force 2001-02), Consortium Md. C.C. Libr. Dirs. (treas. 1998-2000), Beta Phi Mu. Democrat. Home: 524 Academy Rd Baltimore MD 21228-1814 Personal E-mail: PaulMcAd@aol.com.

MCADAM, WILL, electronics consultant; b. Wheeling, W.Va., Oct. 22, 1921; s. Will and Elizabeth Margaret (Wickham) McA.; m. Evelyn Virginia Warren, Sept. 22, 1945; children: Elizabeth Ruth, Margaret Evelyn. BSEE, Case Inst. Tech., 1942; MSEE, U. Pa., 1959. Rsch. technologist Leeds & Northrup Co., Phila., 1945-57, head elec. sect. R&D dept. North Wales, Pa., 1957-68, assoc. dir. rsch. ops., 1968-76, mgr. devel. and engring. adv. devel., 1977-79, prin. scientist rsch. dept., 1979-82, ret., 1982; cons. in electronics, 1982—. Contbr. articles to profl. jours., chpts. to handbooks; 30 patents in field. 1st lt. AUS, 1942-45, ETO. Decorated Bronze Star. Fellow IEEE (life, chmn. subcom. on elec. and high frequency measurements 1957-59, com. indsl. electronic and control instruments 1961-65, Prize Paper award 1958), Eta Kappa Nu, Tau Beta Pi. Republican. Presbyterian. Avocations: amateur radio, woodworking/cabinetmaking. Home: 3321 Twin Silo Dr Blue Bell PA 19422

MCADAMS, A. JAMES, government studies educator; b. Balt., May 22, 1954; m. Nancy O'Connell, June 29, 1980; children: Jacqueline E., Erin E. PhD, U. Calif., Berkeley, 1983. Asst. prof. Hamilton Coll., Clinton, N.Y., 1983-85; Robert K. Root asst. prof. Princeton (N.J.) U., 1985-92; prof., chair U. Notre Dame, Ind., 1992—, William M. Scholl prof. internat. affairs, 2001—. Dir. Nanovic Inst. for European Studies U. Notre Dame, South Bend, 2002—. Author: (books) East Germany and Detente, 1984, Germany Divided: From the Wall to Reunification, 1993 (Choice award for Disting. Book of 1994), Transitional Justice and the Rule of Law in New Democracies, 1997, Judging the Past in Unified Germany, 2001. Apptd. mem. Ind. Adv. Coun., U.S. Commn. on Civil Rights, Washington, 1995-2000. DAAD prize Disting. scholar in German studies DAAD and Am. Inst. for Contemporary German Studies, 1997; rsch. fellow Humboldt Found., 1987-88, sr. rsch. fellow Internat. Rsch. and Exchs. Found., 1988, Bark Nat. fellow Hoover Instn., 1990-91, rsch. fellow Am. Coun. Learned Socs., 1984, 91-92; rsch. grantee in internat. security J.D. and C.T. MacArthur Found., 1996-97. Roman Catholic. Office: U Notre Dame Dept Polit Sci Notre Dame IN 46556 E-mail: a.j.mcadams.5@nd.edu.

MCADAMS, JASON DAVID, mechanical engineer; b. New Orleans, Sept. 13, 1972; s. Thomas David McAdams, Elizabeth Ann McAdams; m. Heather Valentine Wiltshire; 1 child Nathan 1 child Ian. BSME, U. Tulsa, 1994. Profl. engr., 2001. Project engr. Koch Refining Co., Corpus Christi, Tex., 1994—97, reliability engr., 1997—99; tech. develop. engr. John Zink Co., LLC, Tulsa, 1999—. Contbr. articles. Mem.: ASME, Tau Beta Pi (life). Office: John Zink Co LLC 11920 E Apache St Tulsa OK 74116

MCADAMS, JOHN C. political scientist; b. Fayette, Ala., Oct. 26, 1945; s. J.C. and Ellen Stamps McA.; m. Lynda Darlene Winfield, May 31, 1969; children: Laura Vasquez, Amy, John. AB, U. Ala., 1968; AM, Columbia U., 1971; PhD, Harvard U., 1981. Tchr. Kennedy High Sch., Ala., 1968-70; project dir. Lamar County Bd. Edn., Vernon, 1971-73; faculty mem. Marquette u., Milw., 1977—. Mgr. Voter News Svc., Wis., 1982-96. Polit. Sci. grantee NSF, 1983-84. Mem. Am. Polit. Sci. Assn., Midwest Polit. Sci. Assn. Office: Marquette U Box 1881 Milwaukee WI 53201 Fax: 414-288-3360. E-mail: john.mcadams@marquette.edu.

MCADAMS, JOHN P. lawyer; b. Phila., June 5, 1949; s. Eugene P. and Mary (Miller) McA.; m. Anne Christina Connelly, Sept. 5, 1970; children: Emily Lane, Anne Connelly. BA, U. N.C., 1971; JD, Wake Forest U., 1976. Bar: Fla. 1976, N.C. 1976, U.S. Dist. Ct. (mid. dist.) Fla. 1977. Assoc. Carlton, Fields, Ward, Emmanuel, Smith & Cutler, Tampa, Fla., 1976-82, ptnr., 1982—. Contbg. editor: The Developing Labor Law, 1983, Employee Duty of Loyalty, 1995; contbr. articles to profl. jours. Pres. Hillsborough Cmty. Mental Health Ctr., Tampa, 1983; trustee City of Temple Terrace (Fla.) Pension Plan, 1985-89; pres. Hyde Park Preservation, Inc., Tampa, 1993, Child Abuse Coun., Inc., 2001; bd. dirs. Tampa Lighthouse for the Blind, 1997, Child Abuse Coun., Inc., 1998. Mem. ABA, ABA Equal Rights & Responsibilities Com., Fla. Bar Assn. (exec. coun. labor sect. 1987-89). Republican. Episcopalian. Home: 820 S Delaware Ave Tampa FL 33606-2915 Office: Carlton Fields PO Box 3239 Tampa FL 33601-3239

MC ADOO, DAVID JOHN, neurochemist; b. Washington, Aug. 11, 1941; s. Donald Wayne and Helen Louise (Bromely) Mc A.; m. Martha Cole Hervey, May 20, 1967; children: Catherine Lynn, Matthew David. BA in Chemistry, Lafayette Coll., 1963; PhD in Chemistry, Cornell U., 1970. Chemist U.S. Dept. Agr., Phila., 1963-64, Union Carbide, Tarrytown, N.Y., 1966-67; postdoctoral fellow Johns Hopkins U., Balt., 1970-71; sr. scientist Jet Propulsion Lab., Pasadena, Calif., 1971-73; prof. U. Tex., Galveston, 1973—. Contbr. articles to profl. jours. With U.S. Army, 1964-66. Mem. AAAS, Soc. Neurosci., Neurotrauma Soc., Am. Soc. Mass Spectrum, Sigma Xi. Democrat. Avocation: cave exploration. Office: Univ Tex Med Br 301 University Blvd Galveston TX 77555-5302

MCAFEE, I. PAUL, III, editor; b. Denver, Oct. 23, 1955; s. I. Paul Jr. and Shirley Naomi McAfee; m. Aimee Suzanne Kepner, Apr. 9, 1976; children: Harmony, Megan, Tessie. BA in English, Biola U., 1978. City editor S.E. News-Signal, South Gate, Calif., 1983-85; asst. city editor City News Svc., Hollywood, 1986-87, Progress Bull., Pomona, 1988-89; city editor Inland Valley Daily Bull., Ontario, 1990, bus. editor, 1991-95; editor The Business Press, 1996—. Mem. Soc. Profl. Journalists (pres. Inland chpt. 1999-00, Best Bus. Story 1994, Best Feature Story 1996, Best Tech./Sci. Story 1998, Best Legal Affairs Story 1999), Soc. Am. Bus. Editors and Writers. Avocations: Internet research, book writing, competitive rollerskating. Office: The Business Press 3700 Inland Empire Blvd Ste 450 Ontario CA 91764-4914 E-mail: paulmac@linkline.com.

MCAFEE, JOHN WILSON, SR. retired principal; b. Hallsville, Tex., May 17, 1942; s. Howard Lawrence Sr. and Julia (Hart) McA.; m. Ruby Lee Runnels, May 31, 1966 (div.); children: Veronica Michelle, Charlotte Nichelle, John Wilson Jr.; m. Karen Walker, Nov. 23, 1993; children: Christopher Walker, Derrick Walker. BS, Bishop Coll., 1963; MEd, East Tex. State U., 1970, EdD, 1977. Tchr. Terrell (Tex.) Ind. Sch. Dist., 1963-79, prin., 1979-83, head start dir., 1979-83, Midland (Tex.) Ind. Sch. Dist., 1983-86, prin., 1986-98; now ret. Author and presenter video Coun. Minority Students, 1988; spkr. in field. Election judge City of Terrell, 1980-82; co-chairperson Census Redistricting Com., Terrell, 1981; bd. dirs. YMCA, Midland, 1983-90; rep. Dist. Tchr. Com., Midland, 1988-93; mem. distbn. panel United Way, Midland, 1990-93; speaker Achievement Day Wiley Coll., 1994, Baylor U., 1998, Multicultural Achievement Day, 1998. Recipient Helping Hands award Midland Reporter-Telegram, 1995; named Man of Distinction, Austin, Tex., 1990. Mem. NAACP (edn. chmn., chmn. dropout prevention program 1986-89), Tex. Elem. Prins. Assn. (dist. officer), Midland Prins. Assn., Renaissance Club (v.p., Achievement award 1980), Kappa Alpha Psi, Pi Lambda Theta, Phi Delta Kappa (historian 1980-81), Kappa Psi (Achievement award 1978). Mem. Ch. of Christ. Avocations: jazz music, accapella singing. Home: PO Box 9052 Midland TX 79708-9052 Office: Midland Ind Sch Dist 615 W Missouri Ave Midland TX 79701-5017

MCAFEE, PAUL HINDMAN, III, marketing professional; b. Auburn, Ala., Dec. 2, 1948; s. Paul Hindman Jr. and Anne McAfee; m. Anna Laurie McKendree, May 10, 1980; children: Marguerite, Bonnie, Rosaleen. BA, U. Md., 1974; MBA, U. Rochester, 1995. Film courier UPI, NBC, Washington, 1967-68; retail merchandiser Braun N.Am., 1973-74, salesman N.Y. Met. ter., 1974-75; pres. Paul McAfee and Friends, Ltd., 1975-82; product mktg. mgr. Ilford Inc., Paramus, N.J., 1982-83, mktg. comm. mgr., 1983-85, worldwide product mgr. Mobberley, Eng., 1985-88; nat. sales mgr. Ilford Can. Ltd., Markham, Ont., 1988-89; v.p. sales and mktg. Charles Beseler Co., Linden, N.J., 1989-91; pub. rels. mgr. CD Imaging and Consumer Imaging Divsns. Eastman Kodak Co., Rochester, N.Y., 1991-92, dep. dir. consumer profl. and internat. news, 1992-94, dir. corp. media rels., 1994, dir. worldwide photo CD mktg., 1994-95, dir. mktg. process devel., 1995-96; v.p. sales and mktg., 2d v.p. nat. ethnic mktg. Sprint PCS, Boca Raton, Fla., 1996-98; v.p. sales and mktg. Am. Sigma (Danaher), Medina, NY, 1998-99; pres. paulmcafee.com,

Buffalo, 1999—; chief marketing officer Harmonycom, Inc., 2000—. Sgt. U.S. Army, 1968-71, Viet Nam. Mem. Pub. Rels. Soc. Am., Photographic Mfrs. and Distbrs. Assn., Inc. (dir. 1981-91), Mensa (Ireland, Eng., Can., U.S.). Avocations: photography, music, gardening, literature, scuba diving. Office: Harmony Comm Inc 1000 Victors Way Ann Arbor MI 48108 Fax: 716-830-5219. E-mail: paulmcafee@earthlink.net.

MCAFEE, SUSAN JACQUELINE, educator; b. L.A., June 3, 1944; d. Nat and Lillian Dorothy (Taylor) Louis; m. Robert Richard McAfee, Apr. 27, 1965; children: Robert Jack, Lani Laurelle. BA in English, Mont. state U., 1969; M.Ednl. Adminstrn., No. Ariz. U., 1991. Cert. tchr., adminstr., Ariz. Tchr. Lake Havasu (Ariz.) Jr. H.S., 1981-92; vice prin. Bigfork (Mont.) Elem. sch., 1992-93; instr. English Mohave C.C., Lake Havasu City, 1993-96; master tchr. Telesis Ctr. for Learning, 1994-95; tchr. basic edn. and gen. edn. diploma Mohave County Career Ctr., 1995-99; program supr. Mohave County work-force devel. and cmty. svcs. divsns., 1999—. Mem. Humane Soc. U.S. Avocations: reading, writing, music, computer-based instruction. Office: Mohave County Cmty Devel PO Box 7000 Kingman AZ 86402-7000 E-mail: susan.mcafee@co.mohave.az.us.

MC AFEE, WILLIAM, government official; b. Port Royal, Jan. 25, 1910; s. French and Willietta (Anderson) McA. BA, Coll. of Wooster, 1932; MA in Am. History, Pa. State U., 1941; student, Oxford, Eng., summer 1937. Wooster in India rep. on faculty Ewing Christian Coll., Allahabad, India, 1932-35; tchr. pub. high schs. and prep. sch. Pa., 1935-42; joined State Dept., 1946; country specialist (Office Chinese Affairs), 1946-50; coordinator current intelligence (Bur. Intelligence and Research), 1950-56, spl. asst. to dir., 1956-60, dir. ops. staff, 1960-66, asst. dep. dir. coordination, 1966-72, dep. dir. coordination, 1972-80, dep. asst. sec. intelligence coordination, 1980—; dir. (Office of Intelligence Liaison), 1981-86, ret. Adviser Griffin Econ. Aid Mission to S.E. Asia, 1950 Served to lt. col. AUS, 1942-46, CBI. Decorated Legion of Merit; Order Brit. Empire; Precious Tripod Chinese Nationalist Govt.; recipient Superior Honor award State Dept., 1964, Disting. Honor award, 1980 Mem. Am. Fgn. Service Assn., Delta Sigma Rho. Home: 4433 Brandywine St NW Washington DC 20016-4419

MCALEER, JOHN JOSEPH, English literature educator; b. Cambridge, Mass., Aug. 29, 1923; s. Stephen Ambrose and Helen Louise (Collins) McA.; m. Ruth Ann Delaney, Dec. 28, 1957; children: Mary Alycia, Saragh Delaney, Seana Caithlin, John Joseph, Paul Bernard, Andrew Stephen. AB, Boston Coll., 1947, MA, 1949; PhD, Harvard U., 1955. Teaching fellow Boston Coll., 1947-48, English and Latin instr., 1948-50; Dexter fellow in Europe Harvard U., 1952, teaching fellow gen. edn., 1953-55; from asst. prof. to prof. Boston Coll., 1955—. Vis. fellow Durham (Eng.) U., 1988-89. Author: Ballads and Songs Loyal to the Hanoverian Succession, 1962, Theodore Dreiser: A Biography, 1968, Artist and Citizen Thoreau, 1971; (with M. Tjader) Notes on Life: The Philosophical Writings of Theodore Dreiser, 1974, Rex Stout: A Biography, 1977, Justice Ends at Home: The Early Crime Fiction of Rex Stout, 1977; (with others) Rex Stout: An Annotated Primary and Secondary Bibliography, 1980; (with Billy Dickson) Unit Pride, 1981, Royal Decree: Conversations with Rex Stout, 1983, Ralph Waldo Emerson: Days of Encounter, 1984, Queens Counsel: Conversations with Ruth Stout, 1986, Coign of Vantage, 1988; editor-in-chief: Rex Stout Jour., 1979—, Thorndyke File, 1981-95, Best Sellers, 1965-85, Shakespeare newsletter, 1959-71, Arm-chair Detective, 1978-82, The Quarterdeck: The Muster Book of the Patrick O' Brian Society, 1999—; cons. editor: Dreiser Studies, 1971—; mng. editor Crimestalkers Casebook, 1998—. Mem. Boston Athenaeum Libr.; adv. bd. Walden Woods Project, 1990—, Parents Choice, 1980—. Sgt. U.S. Army, 1942-46. Recipient Cath. Press Assn. award, 1969, New Eng. Hist. Soc. award, 1985, Humanities award Boston Coll. Alumni Assn., 1991, Ignatian medal Boston Coll., 1995; permanent mem. Soc. of Fellows, Durham (Eng.) U., 1988—. Mem. Thoreau Soc. (pres., dir. 1971—), Mystery Writers Am. (v.p., dir. 1979-89, Edgar Allan Poe award 1978), R. Austen Freeman Soc. (pres. 1981—), Edith Wharton Soc., Jane Austen Soc. (Burke award 1991), Internat. Dreiser Soc. (founding mem. 1991—), Trollope Soc., Freeman Wills Croft Soc. (1st v.p. 1997—), Irene Adler Soc., Boston Authors Club (pres., dir. 1982-2002), Manuscript Soc., Tavern Club (Boston) (Silver medal 2002), Baker St. Irregulars, Patrick O'Brian Soc. (pres. 1995—). Democrat. Roman Catholic. Avocations: swimming, bibliopoly, genealogy, philately, gardening. Home: 121 Follen Rd Lexington MA 02421-5942

MCALHANY, TONI ANNE, lawyer; b. Decatur, Ind., May 1, 1951; d. Robert Keith and Evelyn L. (Fisher) McA. BA, Ind. U., 1973; JD, Valparaiso U., 1976. Bar: Mich. 1976, Ind. 1982, Ill. 1986, U.S. Dist. Ct. (no. dist.) Ind. 1989. Asst. prosecutor Ottawa County Prosecutor's Office, Grand Haven, Mich., 1976-81; assoc. Hann, Doss & Persinger, Holland, 1981-82, Romero & Thonert, Auburn, Ind., 1982-85; ptnr. Dahlgren & McAlhany, Berwyn, Ill., 1985-88, Colbeck, McAlhany & Stewart, Angola, Ind. & Coldwater, Mich., 1988-98. Atty. Angola Housing Authority, 1989-98. Bd. dirs. Child and Family Svcs., Ft. Wayne, Ind., 1983, Fillmore Ctr., Berwyn, 1986-88, Altrusa, Coldwater, 1989-92. Mem. ATLA, State Bar Mich., State Bar Ind., State Bar Ill., Mich. Friend of the Ct. Assn., Referees Assn. Mich., Branch County Bar Assn., Steuben County Bar Assn. Avocations: traveling, horseback riding. E-mail: tmcalhany@hotmail.com.

MCALISTER, MICHAEL H. architect; b. Calif. s. Doyle R. and Mary E. McAlister. AA, Bakersfield Coll.; BArch, Calif. Polytech. U. Planning technition Bakersfield City Hall, 1963; carpenter Del Webb Corp., Kern City, Calif., 1964; architectural draftsman Goss & Choy Architects, Bakersfield, 1965-67; architect, v.p. D.G.C. & Assocs., 1971-80; dir. architecture, v.p. N.B.A. & Assocs., Architects, 1980-83; architect, pres. Michael H. McAlister, A.I.A., 1983—. Nepthrology design cons. for various treatment groups and hosps., 1987—. Commr., architectural advisor Historic Preservation Commn., Bakersfield, 1986-87; bd. dirs. Camp Fire Coun., Kern County, Calif., 1980-84. Recipient Architectural Pub. Bldg. Hist. award Beautiful Bakersfield Com., City of Bakersfield's City Coun. and Hist. Preservation Commn., 1985, 87, Exterior Environ. Design Excellence Bakersfield C. of C., 1988, Comml. Design Excellence award, 1984, Design Excellence and Beautification award City of Taft, Calif., 1989, Design Excellence award State of Nev., 1992. Mem. AIA (Calif. Coun., Golden Empire chpt.). Avocation: art and sculpture. Office: 5030 Office Park Dr Ste B Bakersfield CA 93309-0612

MCALLISTER, ANN MARIE, social worker, educator; b. Birmingham, Ala., Sept. 5, 1938; d. Ernest and Clara (Graham) Motte; m. Aaron McAllister, Sept. 1, 1962; children: Adrienne, Annette. BA, Birmingham-So. Coll., 1959; MSW, Tulane U., 1961; PhD Tulane U., 2002. LCSW, La. Clin. social worker S.E. La. State Hosp., Mandeville, 1961-63, Ctrl. La. State Hosp., Pineville, 1963-76; prof. La. Coll., 1976—. Mem. NASW, Alpha Kappa Delta, Phi Alpha, Omicron Delta Kappa. Baptist. Avocation: travel. Home: 105 Iris Cir Pineville LA 71360-4422 E-mail: mcallister@lacollege.edu.

MCALLISTER, DEUCE, football player; b. Dec. 27, 1978; s. Carl and Cornelia McAllister. Attended, Morton HS. Football player New Orleans Saints, 2001—. Office: New Orleans Saints 5800 Airline Dr Metairie LA 70003*

MCALLISTER, DONALD LESLIE, priest, writer; b. Norway, Maine, Aug. 21, 1933; s. Donald F. McAllister and Mildred J. Oberg. BA, U. Maine, 1955; degree, U. Helsinki, Finland, 1963; MS, Villanova U., 1966; MA, Wash. Theol. Coalition, 1971. Cert. hospital chaplain. Tchr. world history Waldbur Lynch H.S., Limsburdans, NY, 1958—59; tchr. U. Helsinki, Finland, 1960—64; chaplain St. Mary Hosp. & Med. Ctr., San Francisco, 1971—73, St. Joseph Hosp., Ann Arbor, Mich., 1973—84, Mercy Hosp., Portland, Maine, 1987—. Editor: Norway in the 1840's, 1986, Marriage Returns of Oxford City, Maine to 1892, 1992; author: Bound By Memories Ties Peclorat Heat of Norway Maine, 1988. Chmn. Norway Bicentennial Com., Norway, Maine, 1985—86; pres. Norway Hist. Soc., 1985—87. With U.S. Army, 1956—58. Grantee, Norwegian Am. Found., 1953—54, Fulbright Found., 1961—64. Roman Catholic. Avocations: genealogy, collectables, square dancing. Home: 44 Witner St Portland ME 04102 Office: Diocese of Portland Maine Portland ME 04102

MC ALLISTER, GERALD NICHOLAS, retired bishop, clergyman; b. San Antonio, Feb. 23, 1923; s. Walter Williams and Leonora Elizabeth (Alexander) McA.; m. Helen Earle Black, Oct. 2, 1953; children— Michael Lee, David Alexander, Stephen Williams, Elizabeth. Student, U. Tex., 1939-42, Va. Theol. Sem., 1948-51, DD (hon.), 1977. Ordained to ministry Episcopal Ch. as deacon, 1953, as priest, 1954. Rancher, 1946-48; deacon, priest Ch. of Epiphany, Raymondville, Ch. of Incarnation, Corpus Christi, St. Francis Ch., Victoria, Tex., 1951-63; 1st canon Diocese of West Tex., 1963-70; rector St. David's Ch., San Antonio, 1970-76; consecrated Episcopal bishop of Okla., Oklahoma City, 1977-89, ret., 1989; bishop-in-residence Episcopal Theol. Sem., Austin, Tex., 1990-93. Trustee Episcopal Theol. Sem. of S.W., 1961-2000, adv. bd., 1974—; mem. Case Commn. Bd. for Theol. Edn., 1981-82; pres. Tex. Council Chs., 1966-68, Okla. Conf. Chs., 1980-83; bd. dirs. Presiding Bishop's Fund for World Relief, 1972-77, Ch. Hist. Soc., 1976—; chmn. Nat. and World Mission Program Group, 1973-76; mem. Structure of Ch. Standing Commn., 1979, mem. standing com. on Stewardship/Devel., 1979-85; founder Chaplaincy Program, Bexar County Jail, 1968; mem. governing bd. nat. council Ch. of Christ, 1982-85; chmn. standing commn. on stewardship Episcopal Ch., 1983-85; v.p., trustee The Episc., Episc. Theol. Sem. of Southwest, 1987-93, chmn. bd. trustees, 1993-97. Author: What We Learned from What You Said, 1973, This Fragile Earth Our Island Home, 1980. Bd. dirs. Econ. Opportunity Devel. Corp., San Antonio, 1968-69; mem. exec. com. United Way, 1968-70, vice-chmn., 1970. With U.S. Mcht. Marines, 1942; to 1st lt. USAAF, 1942-45. Recipient Agudas Achim Brotherhood award, 1968. Address: 507 Bluffestates San Antonio TX 78216-7930

MCALLISTER, JEF See MCALLISTER, JOHN FRANCIS OLIVARIUS

MCALLISTER, JOHN FRANCIS OLIVARIUS (JEF MCALLISTER), journalist; b. Syracuse, Feb. 13, 1956; s. John Francis McAllister Jr. and Pauline Bertha Meyer; m. Ann Olivarius, Sept. 5, 1981; children: Chase, Kathryn, Jack. BA in History summa cum laude, Yale U., 1977, JD, 1986; DPhil, U. Oxford, Eng., 1987. Bar: N.Y., Conn., 1988. Law clk. to Hon. Robert Peckham, San Francisco, 1986-87; assoc. Sidley & Austin, N.Y.C., 1987-89; state dept. corr. Time Mag., Washington, 1989-94, diplomatic corr., 1994-95, White Ho. corr., 1995-98, dep. bur. chief, 1998-99, London bur. chief, 1999—. Co-author: The Right Hand of Power, 1984. Henry Luce Found. scholar, 1977-78, Marshall Aid Commemoration Commn. scholar, 1979-82. Mem. Coun. Fgn. Rels. Unitarian Universalist. Avocations: biking, reading, platform tennis. Home: 30 Stamford Brook Rd London W6 0XH England Office: Time Mag Brettenham Ho, Lancaster Pl London WC2E 7TL England

MCALLISTER, KENNETH WAYNE, lawyer; b. High Point, N.C., Jan. 3, 1949; s. John Calhoun and Ruth Welch (Buie) McA.; children: Katherine Owen, Kenneth Grey. BA, U. N.C., 1971; JD, Duke U., 1974. Bar: N.C. 1974, U.S. Dist. Ct. for Middle dist. N.C. 1974, U.S. Ct. Appeals for 4th circuit 1980, U.S. Supreme Ct. 1980. Ptnr. firm Fisher, Fisher & McAllister, High Point, 1974—81; former U.S. atty. for middle dist. N.C. U.S. Dept. Justice, Greensboro, 1981—86; sr. exec. v.p., gen. counsel Wachovia Corp., Winston-Salem, NC, 1988—2001. Bd. of visitors Wake Forest U. Sch. of Law, 1988-96, U. N.C. at Chapel Hill, 1989-93, Duke U. Law Sch., 1996—. Pres. High Point Drug Action Coun., 1977-78; chmn. High Point Rep.Com., 1976-78, 88-89; mem. adv. bd. Salvation Army, High Point, 197-79; bd. dirs. Sch. of Nursing Found., U. N.C., Chapel Hill, 1993-99; vice chair Attys. Gen. Adv. Com. U. S Attys., 1985-86; govs. commn. Bus. Laws and the Economy, 1994—; bd. govs. Presbyn. Homes, 1997—, chmn. 2000—; permanent mem. Fourth Cir. Jud. Conf. John Motley Morehead scholar Morehead Found., 1967; Arthur Priest scholar Phi Delta Theta, 1971 Fellow Am. Bar Found.; mem. N.C. Bar Assn. (bd. govs. 2000—), Piedmont Triad Airport Authority (bd. dirs. 1998-2001), High Point Country Club, Phi Beta Kappa. Republican. Presbyterian. Home: 220 Cascade Dr High Point NC 27265-9685

MC ALLISTER, LESTER BELDEN, economics educator; b. Chgo., Feb. 21, 1921; s. Lester Belden and Bertha (Wulpi) McA.; m. Elaine Schneider, Feb. 17, 1945; 1 child, Margaret. BA, Coe Coll., 1942; MA, Northwestern U., 1947; PhD (Carnegie fellow 1950-52), U. Oreg., 1953. Instr. econs. Coe Coll., 1947-50, Oreg. State Coll., 1952-53; mem. faculty Beloit Coll., 1953-91, prof. econs., 1959-91, prof. emeritus, 1991—, chmn. dept. econs. and bus., 1960-74. Cons.-examiner, 1974-91; vis. prof. econs. U. Wis., 1968; prof. fgn. affairs Nat. War Coll., 1961-62; mem. Wis. Banking Rev. Bd., 1974-79, Beloit Bd. Edn., 1955-58 Author articles, essays. Served to maj. USAAF, 1942-46. Ford Found. fellow U. Wis., 1957 Mem. Phi Beta Kappa. Home: 1400 N Drake Rd Apt 255 Kalamazoo MI 49006-3918

MCALLISTER, WILLIAM HOWARD, III, newspaper reporter, columnist; b. Durham, N.C., Nov. 6, 1941; s. William Howard, Jr. and Dorothy Fisk (Tillett) McA.; m. Rena Catherine Farrell, June 13, 1965; children: William Howard IV, Christopher F., Jonathan T., Benjamin J. BA in Polit. Sci, U. N.C., Chapel Hill, 1964, MA in Journalism, 1966. Cecil Prince research asst. U. N.C., 1965; reporter The Virginian-Pilot, Norfolk, 1964-67; reporter, city editor Virginian-Pilot, 1972-75; reporter Wall St. Jour., San Francisco, 1968-72, Washington Post, 1975-78, Va. editor, 1978-86, nat. reporter, 1986-99, columnist stamp and coin sect., 1987-99, lobbying columnist, 1997-99; Washington bur. chief Denver Post and MediaNews Newspapers, 1999—. TV cons. Ford Found., 1969-72 Capt. USNR, 1966-93. Decorated Navy Commendation medal, Meritorous Svc. medal, Gold Star; recipient Lidman prize for philatelic writing, 1990. Mem. Am. Soc. Newspaper Editors, Kappa Tau Alpha, Nat. Press Club. Presbyterian. Home: 10121 Ratcliffe Manor Dr Fairfax VA 22030-2427 Office: 1255 National Press Bldg Washington DC 20045-2200 E-mail: bmcallister@denverpost.com.

MCALPIN, KIRK MARTIN, lawyer; b. Newark, Sept. 14, 1923; s. Aaron Champion and Margaret (Martin) McA.; m. Sarah Frances Morgan, Dec. 14, 1951; children: Kirk Martin Jr., Philip Morgan, Margaret Champion Margeson. LLB, U. Ga., 1948; postgrad., Columbia U., 1949. Bar: Ga. 1949. Asst. solicitor gen. Ea. Jud. Cir. Ct. Ga., 1951; assoc. Bouhan, Lawrence, Williams, Levy & McAlpin, Savannah, Ga., 1952-53, ptnr., 1954-63; sr. ptnr. King & Spalding, Atlanta, 1963-86; pvt. practice Savannah, 1987-97, Atlanta, 1998—. Chmn. Inst. Continuing Legal Edn., 1980-81, Inst. Continuing Jud. Edn. in Ga., 1981-84, Jud. Council Ga., 1979-82. Pres. Atlanta Legal Aid Soc., 1971. Fellow Am. Bar Found., Am. Law Inst., Am. Coll. Trial Lawyers, Internat. Acad. Trial Lawyers, Internat. Soc. Barristers; mem. ABA (Jr. Bar Conf. chmn. 1958-59, chmn. gen. practice sect. 1972-73, chmn. sr. lawyers div. 1986-87, ho. of dels. 1960-90, state del. 1970-90, bd. govs. 1973-76), State Bar Ga. Assn. (chmn. Young Lawyers 1953-54, bd. govs. 1953-63, pres. 1979-80), Atlanta Bar Assn., Savannah Bar Assn. (v.p. 1960-61), Nat. Conf. Bar Pres. (exec. com. 1981-83), Ga. Def. Lawyers Assn., Ga. Trial Lawyers Assn., Am. Trial Lawyers Assn., Fed. Bar Assn., Am. Judicature Soc., Assn. R.R. Trial Counsel, Soc. of Cin., Sons Colonial Wars, St. Andrews Soc., Capital City Club, Piedmont Driving Club, Oglethorpe Club, Phi Delta Phi, Sigma Alpha Epsilon. Episcopalian. Office: 77 E Andrews Dr NW Apt 352 Atlanta GA 30305-1392 Fax: 404-467-0619. E-mail: kmcasratty@mindspring.com.

MCALPINE, FREDERICK SENNETT, anesthesiologist; b. Monessen, Pa., June 16, 1929; s. Karl Sennett and Kathryn Helen (Schuerhoff) McA.; m. Barbara Ellen Adams, June 23, 1956; children: Christopher, Daniel, Karen. AB with honors, St. Vincent Coll., Latrobe, Pa., 1950; MD, U. Pitts., 1954. Diplomate Am. Bd. Anesthesiology. Rotating intern U.S. Naval Hosp., Bethesda, Md., 1954-55; resident in anesthesia Mass. Gen. Hosp., Boston, 1955-57, chief resident anesthesia, 1957; asst. chief anesthesia Bethesda Naval Hosp., 1957-60; staff anesthesiologist Lahey Clinic, Boston, 1960-95, chmn. dept. anesthesiology, 1971-82, sr. staff anesthesiologist, 1962-95; retired, 1995. Contbr. chpts. to books. Del. Am. Soc. Anesthesiologists, 1970-74. Lt. comdr. USN. Mem. Mass. Med. Soc. (sr. physicians program 1996—), Mass Soc. Anesthesia Med. Malpractice (tribunal mem. 1985—), Mass. Soc. Anesthesiologists (pres. 1971-72, spkrs. bur. 1995—). Republican. Roman Catholic. Home: 49 Arnold Rd Wellesley Hills MA 02481-2819 E-mail: fsmbam@worldnet.att.net.

MCAMIS, EDWIN EARL, lawyer; b. Cape Girardeau, Mo., Aug. 8, 1934; s. Zenas Earl and Anna Louise (Miller) McAmis; m. Malin Eklof, May 31, 1959; 1 child Andrew Bruce ; life ptnr. Gerson Gonzalez. AB magna cum laude, Harvard U., 1956, LLB, 1959. Bar: N.Y. 1960, U.S. Dist. Ct. (so. dist.) N.Y. 1962, U.S. Supreme Ct. 1965, U.S. Ct. Appeals (2d and 3d cirs.) 1964, U.S. Ct. Appeals (D.C. cir.) 1981. Assoc. law firm Webster, Sheffield & Chrystie, N.Y.C., 1959-61, Regan Goldfarb Powell & Quinn, N.Y.C., 1962-65, Lovejoy, Wasson, Lundgren & Ashton, N.Y.C., 1965-69, ptnr., 1969-77, Skadden, Arps, Slate, Meagher & Flom, N.Y.C., 1977-90, spl. ptnr., pro bono, 1990-93; adj. prof. law Fordham U., 1984-85, Benjamin N. Cardozo Sch. Law, N.Y.C., 1985-90. Mem. Lambda Legal and Edn. Fund, 1991—95; bd. dirs. Aston Magna Found. Music, Inc., 1982—93, Cmty. Rsch. Initiative N.Y., 1988—89. With U.S. Army, 1961—62. Mem.: ABA, Selden Soc. Home: 4110 Kiaora St Coconut Grove FL 33133-6350

MCANALLY, ANN, puzzle constructor; b. Sioux City, Iowa, Jan. 13, 1920; d. Walter Peter and Clerce Ellen (Gregoire) Knudsen; m. Paul Edward McAnally, July 12, 1942; children: Kathleen, Thomas P., Gary Edward. AA in Bus., NBT, Sioux City, Iowa, 1937-39. Puzzle constructor Acrostics Network, 1993—. Poems pub. Internat. Soc. Poets.; author: All I Remember: A Memoir. Vol. Red Cross, Family Svcs. Recipient poetry awards, Internat. Soc. Editors Choice, honorable mention, Iliad Lit. Awards, President's award for Literary Excellence, Nat. Authors Registry, 2001. Mem. Internat. Poets Soc., S.W. League of Fine Arts (treas.), So. Az. Watercolor Guild, Mensa, Alpha Iota. Avocations: art, travel, mah jongg. Home: Apt 1102 400 S Broadway Pl Tucson AZ 85710-3700

MCANALLY, JOHNNIE SUE, library director, deceased; b. Decatur, Ala., June 13, 1945; d. Ruth Whitt Gurley; m. David R. McAnally, Mar. 17, 1967; 1 child, Jon David. BS, Auburn (Ala.) U., 1966; MA, U. North Ala., 1975, Cert. in Supervision, 1989. Tchr. Morgan County Schs., Decatur, 1967-72, libr. media specialist, 1967-92, dir. libr. media svcs., 1992—. Recipient Exemplary Sch. Libr. Svc. award Ala. State Dept. Edn., 1990, Exceptional Svc. award Lib. and Media Profls., 1992. Mem. Ala. Libr. Assn., Ala. Instructional Media Assn. (Carrie C. Robinson award 1987, Lois E. Henderson award 1994), DAR (chaplain 1988—), Decatur Bus. and Profl. Women, Phi Delta Kappa. Baptist. Avocations: reading, travel. Office: Morgan County Schools 1325 Point Mallard Pky Decatur AL 35601-6542

MCANANEY, KEVIN GEORGE, lawyer; b. Yonkers, N.Y., Mar. 22, 1949; s. Francis A. and Katherine A. (McClatchy) McA.; m. Catherine R. McCabe, Sept. 9, 1978; children: Sheila, Cara, Patrick. BA, U. N.C., 1971; JD, Columbia U., 1977. Bar: N.Y. 1979, U.S. Dist. Ct. (so. dist.) N.Y. 1979, DC 1990. Assoc. Kelley Drye & Warren, N.Y.C., 1977-80; asst. counsel to Gov. Hugh Carey State of N.Y., Albany, N.Y., 1980-83; assoc. Dewey Ballantine, Washington, 1983-86, ptnr., 1986-97; chief industry guidance br., Office of Counsel to Insp. Gen. U.S. Dept. Health and Human Svcs., 1997—. Bd. dirs. Hosp. Sick Children, Washington, 1992-96. Mem. Am. Health Lawyers Assn., Peter and Adeline Ruffin Found. (trustee 1980—), Phi Beta Kappa. Office: Office Counsel to Insp Gen Cohen Bldg Rm 5527 330 Independence Ave SW Washington DC 20201-0003

MCANARNEY, ELIZABETH R. pediatrician, educator; b. N.Y.C., May 7, 1940; d. Henry Kellers and Kathryn (Blaney) McA. AB, Vassar Coll., 1962; MD, SUNY, Syracuse, 1966. Diplomate Am. Bd. Pediatrics in pediatrics and adolescent medicine. Intern, resident SUNY Upstate Med. Ctr., Syracuse, N.Y., 1966-68; fellow in behavioral pediatrics U. Rochester (N.Y.) Med. Ctr., 1968-70, sr. instr. pediatrics, 1969-71, asst. prof. pediatrics, 1971-77, assoc. prof. pediatrics, 1977-85, prof. pediatrics, 1985—, chair pediatrics dept., 1993—. Adv. com. Fertility and Maternal Health FDA, Bethesda, Md, 1987-92; mem. program adv. bd. Robert Wood Johnson Clin. Scholars Program, Princeton, N.J., 1995—. Editor: (books) Premature Adolescent Pregnancy, 1983, Identifying Social/ Psychological Antecedents of Adolescent Pregnancy, 1984, Textbook of Adolescent Mediciane, 1992. Recipient McNeil Outstanding Achievement award Soc. for Adolescent Medicine, 1989, Job Lewis Smith award Cmty. Pediat., Am. Acad. Pediat., 1990; named to Alumni Honor Roll, SUNY, 1998. Fellow AAAS; mem. Soc. for Pediatric Rsch., Am. Pediatric Soc. (mem. exec. coun. 1998—), Assn. for Med. Sch. Pediatric Chairs (pres. 1999—), Inst. Medicine, Nat. Acad. Sci. Achievements include determination of relationship between young maternal age and maternal/neonatal outcomes. Office: U Rochester Med Ctr Dept Pediatrics 601 Elmwood Ave Rochester NY 14642-0001 E-mail: carole_berger@urmc.rochester.edu.*

MCANDREW, PAUL JOSEPH, JR. lawyer; b. Kalona, Iowa, Mar. 8, 1957; s. Paul Joseph and Virginia (Krowka) McA.; m. Lola Maxine Miller, Mar. 1, 1975; children: Stephanie, Susan, Rose, Paul Joseph III, Bridget. BA with honors, U. Iowa, 1979, JD with high distinction, 1983. Bar: Iowa 1983, U.S. Dist. Ct. Iowa 1985, U.S. Claim Ct. 1985, U.S. Ct. Appeals (8th cir.) 1999, U.S. Supreme Ct. 2000. Law clk. to chief judge U.S. Dist. Ct. (so. dist.) Iowa, Des Moines, 1983-85; ptnr. Meardon, Sueppel, Downer & Hayes, Iowa City, 1985-99, Paul J. McAndrew Law Firm, Coralville, 1999—. Claimant's counsel rep. Iowa Workers' Compensation Adv. Com., 2000—. Recipient Hancher-Finkbine award, 1979. Mem. ABA, ATLA (1st v.p. workers' compensation sect. 2000), Iowa Bar Assn. (chmn. worker's compensation sect. 1993-95), Iowa Trial Lawyers Assn. (rep. bd. govs. 1993—, workers' compensation sect. 1997—), Johnson County Bar Assn., Iowa Assn. Workers Compensation Attys. (rep. bd. govs. 1993—), Work Injury Litigation Group (Iowa rep. to nat. bd. govs. 1997—). Democrat. Roman Catholic. Avocations: jogging, biking, golf, travel. Home: 620 Scott Park Dr Iowa City IA 52245-5140 Office: Paul McAndrew Law Firm 2590 Holiday Rd Ste 100 Coralville IA 52241 Fax: 319 887 1693.

MCANDREW, THOMAS JOSEPH, lawyer; b. Providence, Oct. 19, 1945; s. Joseph L. and Amelia L. (Bonhotel) McA.; m. Luise Mary Fogarty, June 13, 1970; children: John Maxwell, Mercedes, Hope, Marya, Cornelia. BA, Providence Coll., 1968; JD, Georgetown U.-Am. U.-George Washington U., 1971; LLM, Georgetown U., 1973. Bar: R.I., 1971, U.S. Dist. Ct. R.I., 1972, D.C. 1972, U.S. Ct. Claims, 1972, U.S. Tax Ct., 1971, U.S. Custom and Patent Ct., 1971, U.S. Ct. Mil. Appeals, 1971, U.S. Ct. Appeals (1st cir.), 1971, U.S. Ct. Appeals (D.C.), 1971, U.S. Supreme Ct., 1974, Comm. of Mass., 1985. Trial atty. Civil Aeros. Bd., Washington, 1971-72; legal asst. to John H. Fanning NLRB, 1972-73; labor rels. officer dept. edn. State of R.I., Providence, 1973-74, dep. asst. commr. edn., 1974-79, adminstr. labor rels., 1979-80; with Powers & McAndrew, Inc., 1980-87; pvt. practice, 1987—. Adj. prof. law U. R.I., Kingston, 1976; lectr. in field. Contbr. articles to profl. jours. Treas., trustee John E. Fogarty Found., Providence, 1974—; mem. Providence Com. on Fgn. Rels., Providence. Mem. ABA (com. on labor law) FBA, ATLA, Am. Arbitration Assn. (adv. coun.). Avocations: golf, tennis, walking. Home: 6 Wingate Rd Providence RI 02906-4910 Office: Ste 205 One Turks Head Place Providence RI 02903 Fax: 401-455-0882. E-mail: mcalaw@hotmail.com.

MCANDREWS, JAMES PATRICK, lawyer; b. Carbondale, Pa., May 11, 1929; s. James Patrick and Mary Agnes (Walsh) McA.; m. Mona Marie Steinke, Sept. 4, 1954; children: James P., George A., Catherine McAndrews Hazel, Joseph M., Anne Marie, Michael P., Edward R., Daniel P. BS, U. Scranton, 1949; LL.B., Fordham U., 1952; grad., Real Estate Inst., NYU, 1972. Bar: N.Y. 1953, Ohio 1974. Assoc. James F. McManus, Levittown, N.Y., 1955; atty. Emigrant Savs. Bank, N.Y.C., 1955-68; counsel Tchrs. Ins. and Annuity Assn., 1968-73; assoc. Thompson, Hine & Flory, 1973-74, ptnr., 1974-84, Benesch, Friedlander, Coplan & Aronoff, Cleve., 1984-94. Mem. law faculty Am. Inst. Banking, N.Y.C., 1968-69; mem. faculty Lakeland C.C., 1995-97. 1st lt. USAF, 1952-54. Fellow Am. Bar Found. (life); mem. Am. Coll. Real Estate Lawyers (gov. 1983-86, treas. 1986-88, chmn. membership devel. com. 1985-87), Ohio Land Title Assn. (life, trustee 1985-88), Bar Assn. Greater Cleve. (past chmn. real estate sect.), Ohio State Bar Assn. Roman Catholic. Home: 6638 Duneden Ave Cleveland OH 44139-4048

MCANIFF, EDWARD JOHN, lawyer; b. N.Y.C., June 29, 1934; s. John Edward and Josephine (Toomey); m. Jane Reiss, June 11, 1960; children: John E., Maura T., Anne T. Annick, Jane A., Peter J., Kathleen A. AB magna cum laude, Holy Cross Coll., 1956; LLB cum laude, NYU, 1961. Bar: N.Y. 1962, Calif. 1963, D.C. 1976. Law clk. to Justice A.T. Goodwin Supreme Ct. Oreg., Salem, 1961-62; ptnr., of counsel O'Melveny & Myers, L.A., 1962—. Adj. prof. Sch. Law Stanford U., 1974-75, 94-98, Boalt Hall Law Sch., 1992-95, UCLA Law Sch., 1996—; vis. prof. U. Oreg. Law Sch., 1999—; fgn. law counsel Freehill, Hollingdale & Page, Sydney, 1981-82; bd. dirs. Mellon Fin. Corp. Bd. dirs. L.A. Master Chorale, 1979-81, 87—, chmn., 1996—; dir., exec. com. Perf. Art Ctr. Los Angeles County, 1992—; bd. dirs. Music Ctr. Found., 1992—. Capt. USNR, 1956-87. Republican. Office: O Melveny & Myers 400 S Hope St Ste 1717 Los Angeles CA 90071-2899 E-mail: tmcaniff@omm.com.

MCANINCH, JACK WELDON, urological surgeon, educator; b. Merkel, Tex., Mar. 17, 1936; s. Weldon Thomas and Margaret (Canon) McA.; m. Barbara B. Buchanan, Dec. 29, 1960 (div. Aug. 1972); m. Burnet B. Sumner, Dec. 29, 1987; children: David A., Todd G., Brendan J. BS, Tex. Tech U., 1958; MS, U. Idaho, 1960; MD, U. Tex., 1964. Diplomate Am. Bd. Urology (trustee 1991-97, pres. 1996-97). Commd. capt. U.S. Army, 1964-66, advanced through grades to col., 1977, ret., 1977; col. USAR; intern then resident Letterman Army Med. Ctr., San Francisco, 1964-69; chief urol. surgery San Francisco Gen. Hosp., 1977—; prof. urol. surgery U. Calif., San Francisco, 1977—. Editor: Urogenital Trauma, 1985, Urologic Clinics of North America, 1989, Smith's General Urology, 1995; section editor: Early Care of the Injured Patient, 1990, Traumatic and Reconstructive Urology, 1996. Col. US Army, 1964-72. Recipient Disting. Alumnus award Tex. Tech U., 1994; named Disting. Alumnus U. Idaho, 1997. Fellow ACS (gov. 1992-97, regent 1998—); mem. Am. Urol. Assn. (pres. we. sect. 1992-93, bd. dirs. 1990—, pres. 1996-97), Genitourinary Reconstructive Surgeons (pres.), Am. Assn. Surgery Trauma (v.p.), Soc. Univ. Urologists, Am. Bd. Urology (pres. 1996-97). Office: San Francisco Gen Hosp Dept Urology 1001 Potrero Ave San Francisco CA 94110-3594

MCARDLE, BARRY FRANCIS, dentist; b. Boston, Jan. 28, 1958; s. Joseph William and Brigitte Johanna Maria (Block) McA. BS, Boston U., 1980; DMD, Tufts U., 1985. Rsch. assoc. Naval Blood Rsch. Lab., Boston, 1980-81; dentist pvt. practice, Portsmouth, N.H., 1985—. Cons. United Dental Systems, Portsmouth, 1996—; bd. dirs. Priority Dental Health, Inc., Concord, NH; active med. staff in dentistry Concord Hosp., 1998—2002; mem. Seacoast Dental Adv. Bd., 2001—; spkr., lectr. in field. Patentee in field. Mem.: ADA, Bus. Network Internat. (pres. Tri-State Seacoast chpt. 1998—99), Alliance for Optimal Dental Care, Seacoast Esthetic Dentistry Assn. (co-founder), N.H. Dental Soc. (editl. bd. Granite State Dentist newsletter 1999—), New Eng. Dental Soc., Boston U. Alumni Assn., Portsmouth C. of C. Independent. Avocations: fine art, jazz, bodybuilding, hockey. Office: The Captain Moses House 118 Maplewood Ave Ste B-7 Portsmouth NH 03801-3787 E-mail: drmcardle@mcardledmd.com.

MCARDLE, PATRICIA ANNE, security company executive; b. Freeport, N.Y., Oct. 8, 1963; d. John Fergerson and Dorothy Patricia (Williamson) McA.; m. Robert Tyszkowski, Dec. 30, 1995. BBA, Pace U., 1985; MBA, N.Y. Inst. Tech., 1990; postgrad., John Jay Coll., 1993-94. Lic. pvt. detective, Mass., N.Y. Mfg. planner Grumman Aerospace, Milledgeville, Ga., 1981-82, Hazeltine Corp., Commack, N.Y., 1987-89; contracts analyst N.Y.C. Transit Authority, Bklyn., 1989-90, contracts mgr., 1991-92, acting dir. procurement, 1992-93; spl. investigator City of N.Y., 1993-96; prin., CEO, chmn. bd. dirs. P.M.T. Assocs. Inc., Boston, 1996—; CEO, pres., chmn. bd. dirs. Evidaunt Investigations, Inc., 1997—. Author: Handbook of Investigations, 1995. Event vol. U.S. Special Olympics, Hempstead, N.Y., 1992; mem. Redwood Libr. and Athenaeum, Newport, R.I. Recipient Silver Leader award DAV, 1997, 98, 99. Mem. Athenaeum (Boston, Newport, R.I.), Nat. Assn. Investigative Specialists, Tennis and Racquet Club (Boston), Redwood Libr. Republican. Avocations: reading, international travel. Office: Evidaunt Investigations Inc Prudential Ctr PO Box 990067 Boston MA 02199-0067 E-mail: evidaunt@aol.com.

MCARDLE, RICHARD JOSEPH, academic administrator, retired; b. Omaha, Mar. 10, 1934; s. William James and Abby Marie (Menzies) McA.; m. Katherine Ann McAndrew, Dec. 27, 1958; children: Bernard, Constance, Nancy, Susan, Richard. BA, Creighton U., 1955, MA, 1961; PhD, U. Nebr., 1969. Tchr. pub. high schs., Nebr., 1955-65; grad. asst. romance langs. U. Nebr., 1965-66, instr. fgn. lang. methods, 1966-69; chmn. dept. edn. Cleve. State U., 1969-70; chmn. dept. elem. and secondary edn. U. North Fla., 1971-75; dean Coll. Edn. Cleve. State U., 1975-87, prof. edn., 1987-89, spl. asst. to pres. for campus planning, 1989-91, vice provost for strategic planning, 1991-92, acting provost, v.p. for acad. affairs, 1992-94, vice provost for strategic planning, 1994-96, prof. edn., 1996-2001, ret., 2001. Cons. in field. Author articles related to issues in tchr. edn. Mem. World Future Soc., Am. Assn. Higher Edn., Am. Assn. Adult and Continuing Edn., Phi Delta Kappa. Office: CASAL Dept Cleve State U Cleveland OH 44115

MCARTHUR, ELDON DURANT, geneticist, researcher; b. Hurricane, Utah, Mar. 12, 1941; s. Eldon and Denise (Dalton) McA.; m. Virginia Johnson, Dec. 20, 1963; children: Curtis D., Monica McArthur Bennion, Denise McArthur Johnson, Ted O. AS with high honors, Dixie Coll., 1963; BS cum laude, U. Utah, 1965, MS, 1967, PhD, 1970. Postdoctoral rsch. fellow, dept. demonstrator Agrl. Rsch. Coun. Gt. Britain, Leeds, Eng., 1970-71; rsch. geneticist Intermountain Rsch. Sta. USDA Forest Svc., Ephraim, Utah, 1972-75, rsch. geneticist Shrub Scis. Lab., Intermountain Rsch. Sta. Provo, 1975-83, project leader, chief rsch. geneticist, 1983-97, Rocky Mountain Rsch. Sta., USDA Forest Svc., Provo, 1997—. Adj. prof. dept. botony and range sci. Brigham Young U., Provo, 1976-2002, dept. intergrative biology, 2002—. Author more than 330 rsch. papers; contbr. chpts. to books; editor symposium procs. Named USDA Forest Svc. Superior Scientist, 1990, Disting. Scientist, 1996; Sigma Xi grantee, 1970, NSF grantee, 1981, 85, 96, Coop. State Rsch., Svc. grantee, 1986, 91; recipient Eminent Sci. Publ. award Rocky Mtn. Rsch. Station, 2001, New Century of Svc. award 2002. Mem. Soc. Range Mgmt. (pres. Utah sect. 1987, Outstanding Achievement award 1992), Botan. Soc. Am., Soc. Study Evolution, Am. Genetic Assn., Shrub Rsch. Consortium (chmn. 1983—, Disting. Svc. award 2002), Intermountain Consortium for Aridlands Rsch. (pres. 1991—). Mem. Lds Ch. Avocations: hiking, cycling, basketball. Home: 555 N 1200 E Orem UT 84097-4350 Office: USDA Forest Svc Shrub Scis Lab 735 N 500 E Provo UT 84606-1856 E-mail: dmcarthur@fs.fed.us., edmdixie@aol.com.

MC ARTHUR, GEORGE, journalist; b. Valdosta, Ga., July 15, 1924; s. George and Ann (Johnson) McA.; m. Eva Kim, Sept. 17, 1979. BA in Journalism, U. Ga., 1948. With AP, 1948-69, corr. Korea, 1950-54, Paris, 1954-60, bur. chief Cairo, 1960-63, Manila, 1963-65, corr. Saigon, 1966-68, bur. chief, 1968-69; with Los Angeles Times, 1969-83, bur. chief, 1970-75, corr. for Southeast Asia Bangkok, 1975-79; diplomatic corr. U.S. News & World Report, 1983-85. Served with USNR, 1943-45. Recipient citation for fgn. reporting Overseas Press Club, 1973 Mem. Sigma Delta Chi. Clubs: Fgn. Corrs. (Hong Kong); Glen Arven Country (Thomasville, Ga.); River Bend Country (Gt. Falls, Va.). Address: 506 E Creek Ct Vienna VA 22180-3578 E-mail: kimparkcho@aol.com.

MC ARTHUR, JANET WARD, endocrinologist, educator; b. Bellingham, Wash., June 25, 1914; d. Hyland Donald and Alice Maria (Frost) McA. AB, U. Wash., 1935, MS, 1937; M.B., Northwestern U., 1941, MD, 1942; ScD (hon.), Mt. Holyoke Coll., 1962. Diplomate: Am. Bd. Internal Medicine. Intern Cin. Gen. Hosp., 1941-42, asst. resident in medicine, 1942-43; asst. resident, rsch. fellow in medicine H.P. Walcott fellow clin. medicine Mass. Gen. Hosp., Boston, 1943-47, assoc. physician, 1959-84, assoc. children's svc., 1968-84; instr. Harvard U., 1955-57, asst. prof., 1960-64, assoc. prof., 1964-73, prof., 1973-84, prof. emerita, 1984—; clin. prof. medicine Boston U. Sch. Medicine, 1984—. Adj. prof. Sargent Coll. Allied Health Scis. Boston U., 1982—; mem. reproductive biology study sect. NIH, 1974-78, Com. on Population Studies, 1980-84; co-dir. Vincent Meml. Rsch. Lab., 1977-79; sr. scientist U. London, 1985-86. Author: (with others) Functional Endocrinology from Birth Through Adolescence, 1952; editor: (with Theodore Colton) Statistics in Endocrinology, 1970; contbr. articles to profl. jours. Fellow ACP; mem. AMA, AAAS, Endocrine Soc., Am. Soc. Reproductive Medicine, Boston Obstetrical Soc., Phi Beta Kappa, Sigma Xi, Alpha Omega Alpha. Home: 865 Central Ave Apt F505 Needham MA 02492-1348

MCARTHUR, JOHN HECTOR, business educator; b. Vancouver, B.C., Can., Mar. 31, 1934; came to U.S., 1957; s. Hector and Elizabeth Lee (Whyte) McA.; m. Netilia Ewasiuk, Sept. 15, 1956; children: Jocelyn Natasha, Susan Patricia. B in Commerce, U. B.C., 1957, LLD (hon.), 1995; MBA, Harvard U., 1959, DBA, 1962; LLD (hon.), Simon Fraser U., 1982, Queens U., 1985, Middlebury Coll., 1988, U. Navarra, Spain, 1989, U. Western Ont., 1992. Prof. bus. adminstrn. Harvard U., Cambridge, Mass., 1962—79, Sylvan C. Coleman prof. fin. mgmt., 1972—80, George F. Baker prof. bus. adminstrn., 1980—96; dean Harvard Bus. Sch., 1980-96; sr. advisor to pres. World Bank Group, Washington, 1995—. Bd. dirs. AES Corp., Bell Can. Enterprises, Inc., BCE Emergis, Inc., Rohm and Haas Co., Cabot Corp., Glaxo SmithKline Plc, HCA Inc., KOC Holdings A.S., Reuters Founders Share Co. Ltd., Telsat Can.; cons. numerous cos. and govt. agys. in Can., Europe, Asia and U.S. Named to McArthur Hall, Harvard U., 1999; recipient Harvard Statesman award, HBS Club, NYC, Mgmt. Achievement award, McGill U., Can. Bus. Leadership award, HBS Clubs of Can. Mem. Harvard Club, Links Club, Comml. Club, Somerset Club, Willowbend Club. Home: 140 Old Connecticut Path Wayland MA 01778-3202 Office: Harvard Univ Sch Bus Adminstrn Boston MA 02163

MCARTHUR, STEVEN FRANCIS, psychologist, educator; b. Grand Rapids, Mich., Aug. 12, 1954; s. George Harold and Evelyn Theresa McArthur; m. Barbara Louise Duch, Oct. 18, 1975; children: Ryan, Alan. BA in Psychology, Aquinas Coll., Grand Rapids, 1975; PhD in Psychology, So. Ill. U., 1990. Lic. psychologist, Mich. Staff psychologist St. John Hosp. and Med. Ctr., Detroit, 1990-95, Henry Ford Ctr. Human Sexuality, West Bloomfield, Mich., 1991-95; primary care provider VA Med. Ctr., Detroit, 1997—; asst. prof. dept. psychiatry and behavioral neuroscis. Wayne State U. Sch. Medicine. Mem. rev. panel behavior and performance NASA, Washington. Mem. APA, Nat. Register Health Svc. Providers Psychology, Mich. Psychol. Assn., N.Y. Acad. Scis. Office: Detroit Receiving Hosp 3-P 4201 St Antoine Detroit MI 48201 E-mail: smcarthu@med.wayne.edu.

MCARTHUR, WILLIAM SURLES, JR. astronaut, retired military officer; b. Laurinburg, N.C., July 26, 1951; s. William S. and Edith P. McArthur; m. Cynthia Catherine Lovin; 2 children. BS in Applied Scis. and Engring., U.S. Mil. Acad., West Point, N.Y., 1973; MS in Aerospace Engring., Ga. Inst. Tech., 1983; DSc (hon.) , U.N.C., Pembroke. Commd. 2d lt. U.S. Army, 1973, advamced through grades to Col., retired, 2001; 2d lt. U.S. Airborne Divsn., Fort Bragg, 1973—75; student U.S. Army Aviation Sch., 1975—76; aeroscout team leader, brigade aviation sect. commdr. US Army 2nd Infantry Divsn, Republic of Korea, 1976—78; company commdr., platoon leader, ops. officer 24th Combat Aviation Battalion , Savanna, Ga.; asst. prof. dept. mechs. U.S. Mil. Acad. , West Point, 1983—86; student pilot USN Test Pilot Sch., 1986—87; exptl. test pilot U.S. Army, 1987—91; astronaut NASA Space Ctr., Houston, 1991—. Named vis. Green Hons. Prof., Dept. Sci. and Engring. Tex. Christian U.; recipient Order of the Long Leaf Pine, N.C., Ellis Island Medal of Honor. Mem.: MENSA, AIAA, Assn. Space Explorers, U.S. Mil. Acad. Assn. Grads., Assn. United States Army, Army Aviation Assn. Am. (Order of St. Michael (Silver award) 2000, Robert M. Leich award 2000), West Point Soc. Greater Houston, Phi Kappa Phi. Office: Astronauts Office Johnson Space Ctr Houston TX 77058

MCAULIFFE, JANE DAMMEN, religious studies and Islamic studies educator; BA in Classics and Philosophy, Trinity Coll., 1968; MA in Religious Studies, U. Toronto, 1979, PhD in Islamic Studies, 1984. Asst. prof. dept. religious studies U. Toronto, 1981-86, assoc. to full prof. dept. Middle East and Islamic studies, dept. study religion, 1992-99, chair dept. study of religion, dir. Ctr. Study of Religion, 1992-97; from asst. prof. to assoc. prof. history of religions and Islamic studies Candler Sch. Theology Emory U., Atlanta, 1986-92, assoc. dean Candler Sch. Theology, 1990-92; prof. Dept. for the Study of Religion, 1997-99; dean, prof. history and Arabic Georgetown Coll. Georgetown U., Washington, 1999—. Appointed Vatican Commn. for Religious Rels. with Muslims, 1994. Author: Qur'anic Christians: An Analysis of Classical and Modern Exegesis, 1991, 'Abbasid Authority Affirmed: The Early Years of al-Mansur, vol. 28, 1995; editor: Encyclopaedia of the Qur'an, 2001—; contbr. articles to profl. jours. Danforth Found. fellow, 1976-80, NEH Summer fellow, 1979-80, Charles Gordon Heyd fellow, 1980-81, Social Scis. and Humanities Rsch. Coun. doctoral fellow, 1981-84, Postdoctoral fellow, 1984-86, CASA II fellow, 1986, NEH Summer Faculty Travel fellow, 1989, NEH Rsch. fellow, 1992, Mellon fellow, 1994, Guggenheim fellow, 1996. Mem. Am. Soc. Study of Religion, Am. Acad. Religion, Am. Oriental Soc., Can. Soc. Study of Religion, Mid. East Studies Assn. (Thesis award 1985), Soc. Values in Higher Edn. Office: Georgetown Coll Georgetown U PO Box 571003 Washington DC 20057-1003 Home: 1321 36th St NW Washington DC 20007

MCAULIFFE, JOHN ANTHONY, hand surgeon; b. Miami, Dec. 11, 1952; s. William A. McAuliffe and Gertrude A. Rogers; m. Marilyn Wiegand, Dec. 31, 1977; children: Christopher, Jacob, Caitlin. BA, Columbia U., 1977; MD, U. Fla., 1982. Diplomate Am. Bd. Orthopedic Surgeons. Intern in gen. surgery Shands Hosp., U. Fla., 1982-83, orthopedic resident, 1983-88; fellow in hand surgery Jackson Meml. Hosp., U. Miami, 1988-89; assoc. prof. U. Miami, 1989-95; hand surgeon Cleve. Clinic Fla., Weston, 1995—. Contbr. chpts. to books and articles to profl. jours. Fellow Am. Acad. Orthopedic Surgeons; mem. AMA, Am. Soc. for the Surgery of the Hand, New Millennium Hand Study Group (pres. 1994-95), Fla. Hand Soc. (pres. 1994-96), Alpha Omega Alpha. Office: Cleve Clinic Florida 2950 Cleveland Clinic Blvd Weston FL 33331

MCAULIFFE, KEITH WILLIAM, association administrator; b. Wellington, New Zealand, Dec. 26, 1954; s. John William and Doris (Pyke) McA.; m. Margaret Amanda Graham, Nov. 12, 1988; children: Blair, Scott. B in Agrl. Sci., Massey U., Palmeston, New Zealand, 1976, M in Agrl. Sci. with honors, 1978, diploma in bus. adminstrn., 1998. Cons. agronomist New Zealand Sports Turf Inst., 1979; sr. lectr. Massey U., 1980-88; CEO New Zealand Sports Turf Inst., Palmerston North, 1989. Presenter in field. Contbr. more than 200 articles to profl. jours. Mem. Internat. Turfgrass Soc. (dir. 1993—), New Zealand Sports Turf Industry Tng. Orgn. (chair 1993-96), New Zealand Land Drainage Assn., Internat. Soc. for Sports Surface Scis., New Zealand Soc. Assn. Execs. Avocations: golf, soccer, tennis. Office: New Zealand Spts Turf Inst Box 347 Palmerston North New Zealand

MCAULIFFE, STEVEN JAMES, federal judge; b: 1948; BA, Va. Mil. Inst., 1970; JD, Georgetown U., 1973. Capt. appellate coun. U.S. Army Judge Advocate Gens. Corps, 1973-77; asst. atty. gen. Office N.H. Atty. Gen., 1977-80; ptnr. Gallagher, Callahan, Gartrell, P.A., Concord, N.H., 1980-92; fed. judge U.S. Dist. Ct. (N.H. dist.), 1992—. Trustee Univ. System of N.H., 1986-94; bd. dirs. N.H. Med. Malpractice Stabilization Res. Fund Trust, 1987-92, Office Pub. Guardian, 1980-92, Challenger Ctr. for Space Sci. Edn.; active N.H. Dem. Leadership Coun., 1988-92. Capt. U.S. Army, 1970-77, USAR, 1977-80, N.H. Army NG, 1980-88. Fellow N.H. Bar Found.; mem. ABA, N.H. Bar Assn. (pres. 1991-92, pres.-elect 1990-91, v.p. 1989-90, mem. ex-officio N.H. Supreme Ct. com. profl. conduct 1989-90, mem. ethics com. 1984-86), Nat. Conf. Bar Pres., Merrimack County Bar Assn., D.C. Bar Assn., U.S. Supreme Ct. Hist. Soc., N.H. Jud. Coun. (vice-chmn. 1991-92), Aircraft Owners and Pilots Assn., Concord Country Club. Office: US Dist Ct 55 Pleasant St Room 416 Concord NH 03301-3904

MCAUSLAND, RANDOLPH M. N. arts administrator; b. Phila., Oct. 9, 1934; s. John Randolph and Helen (Neal) McA.; m. Marilynn Kemp, July 10, 1965 (div. 1976); children: Andrew, Sean; m. Jan E. Tribbey, May 9, 1986. AB, Princeton U., 1957. Copy editor Wall Street Journal, N.Y.C., 1960-61; editor, publisher Stowe Reporter, 1961-63; consulting editor Interpub. Group Cos., 1963-67; creative dir. The Progress Group, N.Y.C., 1967-70, gen. mgr., 1970-75; dir. mktg. Billboard Pubs., 1975-77; asst. to pres. Macmillan Mag., Stamford, Conn., 1977-80; editor The New Satirist, New Canaan, 1980-82; pres. Design Pubs. Inc., N.Y.C., 1983-89; dir. Design Arts Program, NEA, Washington, 1989-90; dep. chmn. programs NEA, 1990-93; writer, arts cons. Richmond, Va., 1993-94. Founder, dir. Design History Found., N.Y.C., 1988-89; advisor Coll. Design, Arch., Art and Planning, U. Cin., 2000—. Author: Supermarkets: History of an American Institution, 1980; contbr. articles to profl. jours. Bd. dirs. Hand Wodkshop, Richmond, 1993-94, Richmond Choral Soc., 1994, Worldesign Found., 1994—, Fla. Friends Librs., 1995—, Fla. Ctr. for the Book, Broward County Vision Com., 1998-99. With U.S. Army, 1957-60. Recipient Commendation N.Y.C. Police Dept., 1971, Pres. Cup Am. Comedy Club N.Y., N.Y.C., 1974, Bronze Apple award Indsl. Design Soc., 1987, Disting. Svc. award NEA, 1991-92. Mem. Am. Ctr. For Design (hon.), Coalition Ind. Scholars, Ivy Club. Home: 7405 Fair Oaks Dr Cincinnati OH 45237-2925 E-mail: RandyMCA@cinci.rr.com.

MCAUSLIN, VALERIE LYNN TANCREDI, writer; b. Providence, Aug. 31, 1953; d. Arthur and Ruth (Mathews) Tancredi; m. Ronald Vincent McAuslin, Nov. 18, 1983; 1 child, Ashley Mary. AS, Sawyer Coll., Providence, 1974; BA, R.I. Coll., 1993. Probate city clk. City of Warwick (R.I.), 1974-77; legal asst. Connors and Kilguss, Providence, 1979-81; pres. Mex. Interiors Plus, Warwick, 1984-85; with tax office City of Warwick, 1984-85; writer Vantage Press, N.Y.C., 1985—; owner Balloons by Val and More. Author (children's books) Skoinks Advanture, 1992, Skoink the Hero, 1993; songwriter Move Over World, 1994; co-designer Planet Hollywood, San Diego, 1995. Democrat. Avocations: history, singing, parapsychology, art, interior decorator. Home: 475 Woodward Rd N Providence RI 02904-4747

MCAVANEY, THOMAS JOHN, music educator, musician; b. Scranton, Pa., July 1, 1960; s. John Patrick and Mary Joyce McAvaney; m. Margaret Amy Chappell, Oct. 19, 1985; children: John Thomas, Michael Jordan, Matthew Joseph. MusB, Marywood Coll., 1982; MusM, Ithaca Coll., 1985. Cert. K-12 music tchr. NY. Tchr. Quinte Suzuki Sch. for Strings, Belleville, Canada, 1985—88; orch. dir. Ilion (NY) Ctrl. Sch., 1988—97, New Hartford (NY) Ctrl. Sch., 1997—. Musician (violist, violinist, condr.). Bd. of dirs. Utica (NY) Symphony Orch., 2001—02, prin. violist; clinician Suzuki Insts. Recipient Theodore Presser scholarship, Marywood Coll., 1981. Mem.: Pi Kappa Lambda, NY State Untited Teachers, Am. Fedn. of Musicians, Suzuki Assn. of the Americas, Music Educators Nat. Conf./NY State Sch. Music Assn. (zone rep./Herkimer County pres. 1992—99, Svc. 1999). Home: 163 S Third Ave Ilion NY 13357-2011 Office: New Hartford Central School 33 Oxford Rd New Hartford NY 13413 Personal E-mail: tjviola@aol.com.

MCAVINN, JAMES D. communications executive, consultant; b. Buffalo, Nov. 20, 1950; s. Frederick Francis McAvinn, Jean Marie McAvinn; m. Susan Darcel, July 15, 1982 (dec. June 2001); children: Jenna Marie, Kelly Jean. BA, Ind. U., 1972; MS, U. Ill., 1976; MBA, U. Chgo., 1983. Rsch. scientist Kendall Co., Barrington, Ill., 1976—80; mgr. engring., mgr. product, sr. mgr. product Boxter Healthcare, Inc., Deerfield, 1980—89; dir. mktg. Meadux Med., Inc., Oakland, NJ, 1989—95; dir. strategic mktg. Boston Sci. Corp., Wayne, 1995—2000; pres. Informal Comm., Stanhope, 2000—.

MCAVITY, JOHN GILLIS, museum director, association executive, museologist; b. St. John, N.B., Can., Oct. 30, 1950; s. J. Patrick H. and Catharine A. (McNeill) McA. BA, U. N.B., 1972. Cert. assn. exec. Asst. curator Kings Landing Mus., Fredericton, N.B., Can., 1972-73; provincial mus. adviser N.B. Mus., St. John, Can., 1973-76; exec. dir. Ont. Mus. Assn., Toronto, Can., 1976-81, Can. Mus. Assn., Ottawa, Ont., Can., 1981—. Bd. dirs. internat. mus. Mgmt. Com., Internat. Coun. Mus., Can. Soc. of the Decorative Arts; sec. treas. Intercom, 2001—. Editor INTERCOM News, 1997—. V.p. St. John Heritage Trust, 1974-76; exec. com. Can. Club, St. John, 1975, English Speaking Union, St. John, 1974-76; vol. fundraiser Kidney Found., Can.; bd. dirs. Centretown Citizens Corp.; founding dir. Mus. Found. Can., 1994—. Mem. Am. Assn. Museums, Am. Assn. for State and Local History (awards com. 1981-84, nominations com. 1985), Mus. Found. Can. (founding dir. 1994—), Inst. Assn. Execs. (chmn. postal com., bd. dirs. Ottawa chpt., cert.), Assn. Cultural Execs. (bd. dirs. 1988-92, apptd. to senate 1995), Quaco Hist. and Libr. Soc. (hon. life), Tourism Industry Assn. Can. (bd. dirs.), Assn. Museums N.B. (founding mem.), Nat. Mus. Assn. (chair internat. com. 2000—), Ont. Assn. Art Galleries (bd. dirs. 1986-90), Can. Soc. Copyright Consumers, Can. Soc. Assn. Execs. (bd. dirs. 1993-96), Can. Art Mus. Dirs. Orgn., Shefford Heritage Co-op (membership chair 1992-95, 2000—). Anglican. Home: 300 Cooper St Apt 41 Ottawa ON Canada K2P 0G7 Home (Summer): 29 Kingshurst Ln Rothesay NB Canada E2H 1T3 E-mail: jmcavity@museums.ca.

MCAVOY, BRUCE RONALD, engineer, consultant; b. Jamestown, N.Y., Jan. 30, 1933; s. George Harold and Agda Amelia (Martinson) McA. BS in Physics, U. Rochester, 1954. Jr. engr. Westinghouse Air Arm Div., Balt., 1956-57, assoc. engr., 1957-58; rsch. engr. Westinghouse Rsch. Ctr., Pitts., 1958-69; sr. rsch. engr. Westinghouse R & D Ctr., 1969-78, fellow engr., 1978-84, adv. scientist, 1984—. Adv. bd. mem. Nat. Ctr. Physical Acoustics, U. Miss., 1987-88. Editor spl. issue IEEE Trans. Microwave Theory Tech., Ultrasonics Symposium procs., 1976-96; mem. editl. bd. jour. Microwave and Guided Wave Letters, 1990. With U.S. Army, 1954-56. Fellow IEEE (life, awards and recognition com. 1989—, def. R&D policy com. 1989-91, Centennial medal 1984, tech. program com. Internat. Microwave Symposium 1986-99); mem. DAV (life), Ultrasonic, Ferroelectric and Frequency Control Soc. of IEEE (pres. 1986-87, Disting. Svc. award 1999), Electromagnetics Acad., Microwave Theory and Techniques Soc. (chmn. microwave acoustics tech. com. 1988-99). Republican. Lutheran. Home: 926 Ivy St Pittsburgh PA 15232-2651 E-mail: mcavoy12@earthlink.net.

MCAVOY, JOHN JOSEPH, lawyer; b. Worley, Idaho, June 28, 1933; s. Earl Francis and Florence Jewel (Mitchell) McA.; m. Joan Marjorie Zeldon, Sept. 20, 1964; children: Jason, Jon. BA, U. Idaho, 1954, LLB, 1958; LLM, Yale U., 1959. Bar: Idaho 1958, U.S. Supreme Ct. 1962, N.Y. 1963, U.S. Tax Ct. 1969, D.C. 1976. Asst. prof. law George Washington U., Washington, 1959-62; staff atty. stockpile investigating subcom. Armed Forces Com. U.S. Senate, 1962; assoc. White & Case, N.Y.C., 1963-71, ptnr., 1972-95; of counsel Lukas, Nace, Gutierrez & Sachs, Washington, 1995—. Adj. prof. Washington Coll. Law, Am. U., Washington, 1990. Bd. dirs. N.Y. Civil Liberties Union, 1975-77, commr. Uniform State Laws, 2001—; chmn. due process com. ACLU, 1971-75. With U.S. Army, 1954-56. Mem. D.C. Bar Assn. (ethics com. 1982-88, vice chmn. 1986-87, chmn. 1987-88), Phi Beta Kappa, Phi Alpha Delta. Democrat. Avocations: swimming, bicycling, fgn. travel. Office: Lukas Nace Gutierrez & Sachs 1111 19th St NW Washington DC 20036-3603

MCBAY, ARTHUR JOHN, toxicologist, consultant; b. Medford, Mass., Jan. 6, 1919; s. Arthur and Virginia (Davito) McB.; m. Avis Louise Botsford, Aug. 24, 1946; children: John, Robert. BS, Mass. Coll. Pharmacy, 1940, MS, 1942; PhD, Purdue U., 1948. Diplomate Am. Bd. Forensic Toxicology; cert. toxicol. chemist Am. Bd. Clin. Chemistry; registered pharmacist, Mass. Asst. prof. chemistry Mass. Coll. Pharmacy, Boston, 1948—53, 63asst. in legal medicine, dept. legal medicine, 1953; lectr. legal medicine Harvard U.; toxicologist, criminalist, cons. Mass. State Police Chemistry Lab., 1955—63; instr. Northeastern U., 1962—63; assoc. prof. toxicology Law-Medicine Inst. Boston U., 1963—69, assoc. prof. pharmacology Med. Sch., 1963-69; supr. lab. Mass. Dept. Pub. Safety, Boston, 1963—69; assoc. prof. pathology and toxicology U. N.C., Chapel Hill, 1969—73, prof., 1973—89, prof. emeritus pharmacy and pathology, 1989—; chief toxicologist Office Chief Med. Examiner, 1969—89. Mem. task force on alcohol, other drugs and transp. NRC; cons. toxicology resource com. Coll. Am. Pathologists, 1975-95, Bur. Med. Devices and Diagnostic Products, FDA, 1975-91, N.C. Drug Authority, 1971-75; dir. Mass. Alcohol Project, 1968-69. Mem. editl. bd. Jour. Forensic Scis., 1981-95; bd. editors Yearbook of Pathology, 1981-91; contbr. numerous articles on toxicology to profl. jours. Served to capt. USAAF, 1943-45. Fellow Am. Acad. Forensic Scis.; mem. Internat. Assn. Forensic Toxicologists, Nat. Safety Coun. (exec. bd. com. on alcohol and drugs 1981-91), Am. Pharm. Assn. (sec., treas. sci. sect. 1954-57), Soc. Forensic Toxicologists (dir. 1978), Am. Chem. Soc., Sigma Xi, Rho Chi, Phi Lambda Upsilon. Democrat. Roman Catholic. Home: V-306 Carolina Meadows Chapel Hill NC 27517 E-mail: canoe@medunc.edu.

MCBEATH, DON B. health administrator; b. Marlin, Tex., July 25, 1954; s. Hugh M. and Margaret Laverne (McDonald) McB.; m. Beverly O. Bishop, May 22, 1976; 1 child, Brian. BA in Mass. Comm., Tex. Tech U., 1977. News reporter KAMC TV, Lubbock, Tex., 1979-81; office adminstr. Lubbock County Dist. Atty., 1981-90; judge Lubbock County, 1991-98; dir. telemedicine Tex. Tech. U. Health Scis., Lubbock, 1999—. Named Outstanding Alumni Tex. Tech Sch. Mass Comm., 1995; recipient Friend of Reese AFB award, 1995; Eagle Scout, 1972. Mem. Tex. Conf. Urban Counties (chmn. 1996-97), Lions. Republican. Baptist. Home: 7903 Wayne Ave Lubbock TX 79424-3131 Office: Tex Tech U Health Scis Ctr 3601 4th St Lubbock TX 79430-0001

MCBEATH, GERALD ALAN, political science educator, researcher; b. Mpls., Sept. 13, 1942; s. Gordon Stanley and Astrid Elvira (Hjelmeir) McB.; m. Jenifer Huang, June 7, 1970; children: Bowen, Rowena. BA, U. Chgo., 1963, MA, 1964; PhD, U. Calif., Berkeley, 1970. Vis. asst. prof. polit. sci. Rutgers Coll., New Brunswick, N.J., 1970-72; asst. prof. John Jay Coll., CUNY, N.Y.C., 1972-74, 75-76; assoc. prof. Nat. Chengchi U., Mucha, Taipei, Taiwan, 1974-75; prof. polit. sci. U. Alaska, Fairbanks, 1976—, dept. chair, 1980-85, 97—, dir. faculty devel., 1990-92, acting dean coll. liberal arts, 1991-93, dir. faculty devel., 1990-92. Cons. Inst. Social and Econ. Rsch., Anchorage, 1976-77; contract rschr. Alaska Dept. Natural Resources, Alaska Dept. Edn., Nat. Inst. Edn., others; staff dir. task force on internat. trade policy Rep. Conf., U.S. Senate. Sr. author: Dynamics of Alaska Native Self-

Government, 1980; author monograph: North Slope Borough Government and Policymaking, 1981; jr. author: Alaska's Urban and Rural Governments, 1984; sr. editor: Alaska State Government and Politics, 1987; co-author: Alaska Politics and Government, 1994 (Am. Assn. State & Local History Commendation cert. 1995); author: The Alaska State Constitution, 1997, Wealth and Freedom: Taiwan's New Political Economy, 1998; editor: Alaska's Rural Development, 1982. Mem. bd. edn. Fairbanks North Star Borough, 1986-95, pres. 1989-90, 93-94, treas. 1991-93. Recipient Emil Usibelli Disting. Svc. award 1993; Chiang Ching-Kuo Found. fellow, 1995-97; named Outstanding Faculty Mem., Assn. Students U. Alaska, Fairbanks, 1979, Alumni Assn. U. Alaska, Fairbanks, 1981; grantee Nat. Inst. Edn., 1980-83, Alaska Coun. on Sci and Tech., 1982-84, Spencer Found., 1987-88, Chiang Ching-Kuo Found., 1995-97. Bd. mem. Am. Assn. Chinese Studies, 1999—; mem. Asian Studies on Pacific Coast (program chmn. 1983, bd. dirs. 1982-83); Assn. Asian Studies, Western Polit. Sci. Assn. (mem. editl. bd. Western Govtl. Rschr.), Am. Polit. Sci. Assn., Fairbanks N. Star Borough Bd. Edn. Democrat. Home: 1777 Red Fox Dr Fairbanks AK 99709-6625 Office: U Alaska Dept Polit Sci Fairbanks AK 99775 E-mail: ffjam@uaf.edu.

MCBEE, LUCY ARMIJO, retired elementary education educator, administrator, singer, actress, writer; b. Santa Fe, Feb. 26, 1931; d. Jose Alfonso and Celine (Chaves) Armijo; m. Robert Levi McBee, June 13, 1959; children: Martin Christopher, Mark Antony, Mathieu A.C. Music cert., Kansas City Conservatory Music, 1952; BA in Econs., Avila Coll., 1952; postgrad. in theater, U. Mo., Kansas City, 1962; MA in Tchg., Webster Coll., 1974. Cert. Montessori tchr. Sec., translator fgn. dept. Commerce Bank Kansas City, Mo., 1952-53; sec., with econ. rsch. dept. Farmland Industries, Kansas City, 1953-59; sec. Western Electric, 1961-62; drama resident theatre tchr. Jewish Cmty. Ctr., 1962-63; Montessori tchr. Wee Wisdom Sch., Unity Village, Mo., 1964-67; Montessori/Spanish tchr. Montessori Sch., Blue Springs, 1967-68; tchr., dir. St. Peter's Day Sch., Kansas City, 1968-71; tchr., prin./adminstr. Loretto Sch., 1974-83; writer plays San Antonio, 1985—87; comptroller Charles Feldstein Co., Chgo., 1990-94. Drama/voice tchr. Backstage Workshop for profl. actors and singers, 1979-84; theatre tchr. Visitation Sch. Kans. City, 1983 Co-editor: The Clan McBean Register. Mem., cantor Visitation Cath. Ch. Choir, Kansas City, 1948-85; computer consultation, data processing VA, Marion, Ind., 1988; fundraising, data processing, trainer Dukakis/Bentsen Presdl. Campaign, Chgo., 1987-88; fundraising office mgr. Simon for Senate Campaign, Chgo., 1988-89; comptroller Pres. Cook County Bd. Fundraising office, 1989-90; mem. Early Childhood Edn. Com., 1973-78, Holy Name Cathedral Choir, Chgo., 1988-94. Recipient Best Actress award U. Kans. City Theatre, 1958, Silver Tray award, Notre Dame de Sion Montessori Sch., Kans. City, 1971, St. Peter's Annual medal St. Peter's Episcopal Ch., Kansas City, 1974, VA award for svc. during Golden Age Games, Marion, Ind., 1988, 1st place award Irish Cultural Soc. Poetry Awards; named Miss Congeniality Dukakis-Bentsen Presdl. Campaign, Chgo., 1988. Mem. San Antonio Poets Assn., The Clan McBean, Scottish Soc. San Antonio. Roman Catholic. Avocations: acting, singing, writing poetry, plays and music. Home: 7118 Walnut Trace San Antonio TX 78239-3058

MCBEE, SUSANNA BARNES, journalist; b. Santa Fe, Mar. 28, 1935; d. Jess Stephen and Sybil Elizabeth (Barnes) McBee; m. Paul H. Recer, July 2, 1983. AB, U. So. Calif., 1956; MA, U. Chgo., 1962. Staff writer Washington Post, 1957-65, 73-74, 77-79, asst. nat. editor, 1974-77; asst. sec. pub. affairs HEW, 1979; articles editor Washingtonian mag., 1980-81; assoc. editor U.S. News & World Report, 1981-86; news editor Washington Bur., Hearst Newspapers, 1987-89, asst. bur. chief, 1990—; Washington corr. Life mag., 1965-69; Washington editor McCall's mag., 1970-72. Bd. dirs. Washington Press Club Found., 1992-95. Recipient Penney-Missouri mag. award, 1969, Hall of Fame award, Soc. Profl. Journalists, 1996, Sigma Delta Chi Pub. Svc. award, 1969, Hearst Eagle award, 1994. Mem. Nat. Press Club, Cosmos Club. Home: 5190 Watson St NW Washington DC 20016-5329 Office: 1701 Pennsylvania Ave NW Washington DC 20006-5805

MCBETH, DAVID PAUL, fundraiser, consultant; b. Arcadia, Fla., Mar. 4, 1932; s. Paul William and Sarah Esther (McCulloh) McB.; m. Lois Fern Hostetler; children: Carol Jean, Stephen Wesley, Dora Sue, Timothy David. B in Religious Edn., Messiah Coll., 1952; MDiv, Asbury Theol. Sem., 1960; DMin, Fuller Theol. Sem., 1981. Mgr. Welgo Traders, Lexington, Ky., 1958; co-mgr. Asbury Sem. Press, Wilmore, 1958-60; pastor Brethren in Christ Ch., Palmyra, Pa., 1960-63; dir. coll. advancement Messiah Coll., Grantham, 1963-82; exec. dir. stewardship fin. Brethren in Christ Ch., U.S.A., 1982-86; sr. cons. Ketchum, Inc., Pitts., 1986-97; fin. cons. Mechanicsburg, 1997—. Contbg. author: Handbook for Educational Fund Raising, 1981. V.p. Harrisburg Arts Coun., 1971. Mem. Assn. Fundraising Profls. (cert.). Republican. Avocations: travel, reading. Home: PO Box 2015 636 Messiah Vlg Mechanicsburg PA 17055-2015

MCBETH, ELAINE SUSAN, university administrator; b. N.Y., Aug. 5, 1961; m. Michael Steven McBeth, June 6, 1992. AB, Hamilton Coll., 1983; MA in econs., Univ. Va., 1987, PhD, 1988. Instr. Univ. Va., Charlottesville, Va., 1985-88; asst. prof. Coll. William & Mary, Williamsburg, 1988—, assoc. dir., prof. econs. Thomas Jefferson Program, 1993—. Faculty cons. Ednl. Testing Svc., 1989—; adv. bd. Com. on Sprawl Devel. & Livable Communities, Sierra Club, 1997; cons. Va. Dept. Edn., 1993-94, Inst. for Local Gov., 1994-95. Co-author: Encyclopedia of Banking & Finance, 1991; contbr. articles to profl. jours. V.p. League of Women Voters, Va., 1997—, pres. League of Women Voters, Williamsburg, Va., 1996-97. Recipient Leadership Historic Triangle award C. of C., Williamsburg, 1996-97. Mem. Stingray Harbor Yacht Club (treas. 1997-98, rear commodore 1998-99, vice commodore 1999, commodore 2000—). Avocations: sailing, scuba diving, swimming. Office: Coll William & Mary Dept Pub Policy PO Box 8795 Williamsburg VA 23187-8795 E-mail: mcbeth@wm.edu.

MCBREARTY, MICHAEL LEIGH, family physician; b. Ft. Belvoir, Va., Apr. 4, 1947; s. Charles Francis and Margaret Elizabeth McBrearty; m. Cindy Lyn Rutland, Apr. 3, 1953; children: Heather, Lee, Sean, Colin. BS in Chemistry, U. Ala., 1969; MD, U. Ala. Birmingham, 1973. Diplomate Am. Bd. Family Practice. Intern U. Okla. Hosp. and Clinics, Oklahoma City, 1973-74; chief resident Coll. Cmty. Health Svc., Tuscaloosa, Ala., 1974-76; pvt. practice Family Practice Assocs. of Montrose, P.A., Fairhope, 1976—. Med. dir. Thomas Hosp., 1998—; clin. assoc. prof. U. Ala., U. So. Ala.; bd. dirs. Family Practice Rural Health Bd. Fellow Am. Acad. Family Physicians (pres. Ala. chpt. 1982-83, bd. dirs.); mem. Mutual Assurance (bd. dirs.). Republican. Methodist. Avocation: repairing z-cars. Office: Family Practice Assocs of Montrose PA 306 S Greeno Rd Fairhope AL 36532-1905

MCBRIDE, ANGELA BARRON, nursing educator; b. Balt., Jan. 16, 1941; d. John Stanley and Mary C. (Szcpepanska) Barron; m. William Leon McBride, June 12, 1965; children: Catherine, Kara. BS in Nursing, Georgetown U., 1962, LHD (hon.), 1993; MS in Nursing, Yale U., 1964; PhD, Purdue U., 1978; D of Pub. Svc. (hon.), U. Cin., 1983; LittD (hon.), Purdue U., 1998; LLD (hon.), Ea. Ky. U., 1991; DSc(hon.), Med. Coll. of Ohio, 1995; LHD (hon.), U. Akron, 1997. Asst. prof., rsch. asst. inst. Yale U., New Haven, 1964-73; assoc. prof., chairperson Ind. U. Sch. Nursing, Indpls., 1978-81, 80-84, prof., 1981-92, assoc. dean rsch., 1985—91, interim dean, 1991—92, univ dean, 1992—, disting. prof., 1992—; sr. v.p. acad. affairs, nursing Clarian Health Ptnrs., 1997—. Mem. Nat. Adv. Mental Health Coun., 1987—91; mem. adv. com. NIH Office of Women's Health Rsch., 1997—2001; mem. Yale U. Coun., 2000—; ext. acad. advisor dept. nursing Hong Kong Polytechnic U., 2000—. Author: The Growth and Development of Mothers, 1973 (Best Book award 1973), Living with Contradictions, A Married Feminist, 1976, How to Enjoy A Good Life With Your Teenager, 1987; editor: Psychiatric-Mental Health Nursing: Integrating the Behavioral and Biological Sciences, 1996 (Best Book award 1996); compiler: Nursing and Philanthropy, 2000. Recipient Disting. Alumna award Yale U., Disting. Alumna award Purdue U., Univ. Medallion, U. San Francisco, 1993, Hoosier Heritage award, 2000; named Influential Woman in Indpls., Indpls. Bus. Jour./Ind. Lawyer, 1999, Disting. Nurse Educator award Coll. Mt. St. Joseph, Cin., 2000; Kellog nat. fellow; Am. Nurses Found. scholar, Salute to Women award Indpls. YMCA, 1999, Sagamore of Wabash, 1999. Fellow: Nat. Acads. Practice, Am. Acad. Nursing (past pres.), APA (nursing and health psychology award divsn. 38 1995); mem.: Nat. Acad. Scis., Inst. of Medicine, Soc. for Rsch. in Child Devel., Midwest Nursing Rsch. Soc. (Disting. Rsch. award 1985), Sigma Theta Tau (past pres., mentor award 1993, disting. lectr 1995—99, Melanie Dreher award for contbns. as a dean 2001), Chi Eta Phi (hon.). Home: 744 Cherokee Ave Lafayette IN 47905-1872 E-mail: amcbride@iupui.edu.

MCBRIDE, BEVERLY JEAN, lawyer; b. Greenville, Ohio, Apr. 5, 1941; d. Kenneth Birt and Glenna Louise (Ashman) Whited; m. Benjamin Gary McBride, Nov. 28, 1964; children: John David, Elizabeth Ann. BA magna cum laude, Wittenberg U., 1963; JD cum laude, U. Toledo, 1966. Bar: Ohio 1966. Intern Ohio Gov.'s Office, Columbus, 1962; asst. dean women U. Toledo, 1963-65; assoc. Title Guarantee and Trust Co., Toledo, 1966-69; spl. counsel Ohio Atty. Gen.'s Office, 1975; assoc. Cobourn, Smith, Rohrbacher and Gibson, 1969-76; v.p., gen. counsel, sec. The Andersons, Maumee, Ohio, 1976—. Exec. trustee, bd. dirs. Wittenberg U., Springfield, Ohio, 1980-83; trustee Anderson Found., Maumee, 1981-93; mem. Ohio Supreme Ct. Task Force on Gender Fairness, 1991-94, Regional Growth Partnership, 1994—; chmn. Sylvania Twp. Zoning Commn., Ohio, 1970-80; candidate for judge Sylvania Mcpl. Ct., 1975; trustee Goodwill Industries, Toledo, 1976-82, Sylvania Cmty. Svcs. Ctr., 1976-78, Toledo-Lucas County Port Authority, 1992-99, vice chair Fla. CPA; chair St. Vincent Med. Ctr., 1992-99; founder Sylvania YWCA Program, 1973; active membership drives Toledo Mus. Art, 1977-87. Recipient Toledo Women in Industry award YWCA, 1979, Outstanding Alumnus award Wittenberg U., 1981. Fellow Am. Bar Found.; mem. ABA, AAUW, Ohio Bar Assn., Toledo Bar Assn. (pres., treas., chmn., sec. various coms.), Toledo Women Attys. Forum (exec. com. 1978-82), Pres. Club (U. Toledo exec. com.). Home: 5274 Cambrian Rd Toledo OH 43623-2626 Office: The Andersons 480 W Dussel Dr Maumee OH 43537-1690

MCBRIDE, DONALD LOREN, minister, marketing professional; b. The Dalles, Oreg., July 24, 1951; s. Don Carlyle and Edith Elizabeth (Buchanan) McB.; m. Janet I. Hensley, Mar. 19, 1973 (div. Mar. 1993); 1 child, Charles; m. Sherry L. Mower, May 21, 1993 (div. Mar. 1999); m. Donna Sue Shaffer, July 4, 1999. BA in Liberal Studies, Shaw U., 1975; MA in Religion, Western Evang. Sem., 1978; MA in Journalism, U. Iowa, 1982; D in Ministry, United Theol. Sem. Twin Cities, 1988; BLS, U. Iowa, 1995. Asst. prof. comm. Vennard Coll. Iowa, 1979-81, Crown Coll. Minn., 1982-83; asst. prof. journalism S.D. State U., 1983-87; lectr. broadcast writing So. Ill. U., Carbondale, 1987-91; chair dept. mass comm. Wilson Coll., Chambersburg, Pa., 1991-93; writer Bus. Comm. Inst., 1994-96; dir. Pa. Nursing Home Ministry, 1995-97. Announcer KART-AM, Jerome, Idaho, 1967—68, KAIN-AM, Nampa, Idaho, 1969—70, KCRH-FM, Nampa, 1970—71, KLIQ-AM-FM, Portland, Oreg., 1971; news dir. KGEM-AM, Boise, Idaho, 1971—73, KGAY-AM, Salem, Oreg., 1973—75; reporter KWJJ-AM, Portland, 1976—77; feature news reporter KSPO-AM, Spokane, Wash., 1977—79; assoc. min. South Salem Ch. of the Nazarene, Salem, Oreg., 1974—76; min. Ch. of the Nazarene, Deer Park, Wash., 1977—79; supply min. United Meth. Ch., Keswick, Iowa, 1980; min. Calvary Evang. Ch., Mpls., 1981—82, Evang. Congl. Ch., Arlington, SD, 1984—87, Boskydell Bapt. Ch., Carbondale, Ill., 1988—91; supply min. Grace Bapt. Ch., Fairfield, Pa., 1991—92; min. Grace United Ch. Christ, Greencastle, Pa., 1995—98; owner, mgr. Atlantic Book Mktg., Butler, Pa., 1991—. Republican. Baptist.

MCBRIDE, DONNA JANNEAN, publisher; b. Kansas City, Kans., July 3, 1940; d. donald Merle and Hazel Frances (Williams) McBride; life ptnr. Barbara Grier. AB, Central Coll., 1962; MLS, U. Mo., Columbia, 1969. Tchr. Pilot Grove (Mo.) H.S., 1961-62; corr. Bus. Mens Assurance Co., Kansas City, Mo., 1962-66; acctg. clk. Prudential of Eng., Sydney, Australia, 1966-67; head tech. processes Kansas City (Mo.) Pub. Libr., 1967-77; customer rep. C.L. Sys., Inc., Newtonville, Mass., 1977-80; dir. support svcs. Leon County Pub. Libr., Tallahassee, 1980-82; v.p., CFO The Naiad Press, Inc., 1982—. Publisher; b. Kansas City, Kans., July 3, 1940; d. Donald Merle and Hazel Frances (Williams) McBride; life ptnr. Barbara Grier, 1972. AB, Central Coll., 1962; MLS, U. Mo.-Columbia, 1969. Tchr., Pilot Grove (Mo.) H.S., 1961-62; corr. Bus. Men's Assurance Co., Kansas City, Mo., 1962-66; acctg. clk. Prudential of Eng., Sydney, Australia, 1966-67; head tech. processes Kansas City Pub. Library (Mo.), 1967-77; customer rep. C.L. Systems, Inc., Newtonville, Mass., 1977-80; dir. support services Leon County Pub. Library, Tallahassee, 1980-82; v.p., CFO The Naiad Press, Inc., Tallahassee, 1982—; dir. The Naiad Press, 1976—, Sappho's Libr., 1983—. Mem. ALA, Nat. Gay Task Force, Am. Booksellers Assn., Nat. Women's Studies Assn., NOW. Mem. ALA, NOW, Nat. Gay Task Force, Am. Booksellers Assn., Nat. Womens Studies Assn. Home: 1097 Alligator Dr Alligator Point FL 32346-5107 Office: The Naiad Press Inc PO Box 10543 Tallahassee FL 32302-2543 E-mail: naiadpress@aol.com.

MCBRIDE, EILEEN LOUISE, lawyer; b. West Palm Beach, Fla., Aug. 18, 1956; d. Donald William and Theresa Ann (Thiele) McB.; m. Joseph S. Ramirez, June 5, 1982; children: Eric M., Michael A., Daniel J., Gregory S. BS, U. Nebr., Lincoln, 1978, JD, 1981. Bar: Nebr. 1981. Dep. county atty. Lincoln County Atty.'s Office, North Platte, Nebr., 1981-83; assoc. Ruff & Florom, 1983-84, Jewell, Gatz & Collins, Norfolk, Nebr., 1985-86; assoc. gen. counsel Farm Credit Svcs. of. Am., Omaha, 1986—. Bd. dirs. FCE Credit Union, Omaha, 1990—. Officer Madison County Dems., Norfolk, 1991-93; mem. Douglas County Dem. party, Omaha, 1996—; mem. bd. edn. St. Cecilia's Cathedral, 1998-2001, mem. pastoral coun., 2002-. Mem. Nebr. State Bar Assn. (mem. com.), Omaha Bar Assn. (pub. svc. com.), Rotary (bd. dirs., pres.-elect 1991-93). Roman Catholic. Avocation: family. Office: Farm Credit Svcs Am Legal Dept 206 S 19th St Omaha NE 68102-1745 E-mail: mcbridee@fcsamerica.com.

MCBRIDE, ELIZABETH ANNE WILMORE, writer, artist; b. Charlotte, N.C., Nov. 10, 1942; d. John Henry and Frances (Cox) Wilmore; divorced; children: John and Laura. BA in English, Rice U., 1964; MA in English & Creative Writing, U. Houston, 1982; student, Edward Albee Workshops, 1989-92. Instr. U. Houston, 1979—81, 1985—88; editor Lit. Mag., Houston, 1982-83, Domestic Crude, Houston, 1983-84; contbr. editor, columnist Artscene, 1989; editor rsch. papers for Naomi Kraus, U. Tex., Houston, 1990. Reader Houston Festival; judge Southwest Writers' Conf., 1984; bd. dirs. Lawndale Art and Performance Ctr.; panel mem. Seminar on Hispanic Art, U. Ariz., 1987-88. Guest curator Rice U., Houston, 1988, Glassel Sch., Houston, 1993, Houston Art League, 1997; contbr. author: (short stories) Her Work, Common Bonds, The Whole Story, Texas Short Stories II; reviewer The Houston Chronicle, 1980, ARTspace Mag., 1987-92, ARTnews, 1990-95, 2000, Pub. News, 1988-94, Sculpture Mag., 1989-90, Artscene Mag., 1984, and numerous others; poems: Vapor Trails, 1981, Diversions, 1982, Biloxi 1945, 1982, South Pacific Stars and Stripes, 1982, Kwajalein, 1983, Deep Sea Fishing With My Father, 1984, Everyday Places, 1985, Linguistics, 1987, Moctezuma's Headdress, 1992, I Bury My Father, 1993, Corazal, 1993, Inca Doves, 1993, O Corporeal, 1997; editor Ctr. for Big Bend Studies, Gosque Bonito, 2002; contbr. articles and short stories to profl. jours. and mags.; exhibited in group shows at Treebeards, 1995, The New Gallery, 1995, Lawndale Art Ctr., 1995, Diverse Works Alternative Space, 1996, Sally Sprout Gallery, 1996, Houston Pottery Guild and Gallery, 1997, 2000; one woman shows at Westenberg Gallery, Marfa, 2000, Big Bend Setinel, Marfa, 2000, Devin Borden Hiram Butler Gallery, Houston, 2002; represented in pvt. collections, S.I. Assocs., Houston, Playwright, Long Island; writer-in-residence Chinati Found, 1995-96. Vol. tchg. Hartman Jr. High, Roberts Elem. Sch., Valley of Peace, Belize, Marfa Tex. Libr.; mem. literacy events bd. Houston Festival, chmn. lit. arts panel, 1986; bd. dirs. lit. and humanities panel Cultural Arts Coun. Houston, 1987-88; mem. lit. panel Tex. Commn. Arts, 1988-89. Recipient Brazos for fiction prize, 1984; fellow MacDowell Colony, 1986, Edward Albee Found., 1990. Mem. Poets and Writers, League Women Voters (chmn. voters svc.); founding bd. mem. Zocalo Theater. Office: PO Box 8 Marfa TX 79843

MCBRIDE, GORDON SCOTT, lawyer; b. Cleve., Sept. 22, 1961; s. Gordon Charles and Patricia Jo (McCormick) McB.; m. Joyce Marie Gordon, June 20, 1987; children: Alyse Marie, Christine Ann. BA cum laude, Ohio U., 1983; JD, Ohio No. U., 1986. Assoc. Spurlock, Sears, Pry & Griebling, Bucyrus, Ohio, 1986-93; ptnr. Spurlock, Sears, Pry, Griebling & McBride, 1994—. Assoc. editor Ohio No. U. Law Rev. Bd. dirs., cons. Turning Point, Bucyrus, Marion, Upper Sandbury, Ohio, 1994-99, Waycraft, Bucyrus, 1993—, Crawford County Park Dist., Bucyrus, 1995—, Crawford County Law Libr., Buryrus, 1987-96. Mem. Ohio State Bar Assn., Crawford County Bar Assn., Ohio Acad. Trial Lawyers, Moose Lodge. Republican. Lutheran. Avocations: tennis, racquetball, golf. Office: Spurlock Sears Pry Griebling & McBride 120 N Lane St Bucyrus OH 44820-2338

MCBRIDE, GUY THORNTON, JR. college president emeritus; b. Austin, Tex., Dec. 12, 1919; s. Guy Thornton and Imogene (Thrasher) McB.; m. Rebekah Jane Bush, Sept. 2, 1942 (dec. Aug. 1998); children: Rebekah Ann, William Howard, Ellen M. Alsobrooks; m. Cordelia D. Rush, Aug. 7, 1999. BS in Chem. Engring., U. Tex., 1940; Sc.D., MIT, 1948; D.P.S. (hon.), Regis Coll., 1979; D.Engring. (hon.), Colo. Sch. Mines, 1984. Registered profl. engr., Tex. La., N.Y., Colo. Instr. chem. engring. Mass. Inst. Tech., 1942-44, research assoc., 1946-48; job engr. Standard Oil Co. Calif., 1944-46; asst. prof. chem. engring Rice Inst., 1948-55, assoc. dean students, 1950-57, dean, 1957-58, assoc. prof., 1955-58; cons. Tex. Gulf Sulphur Co., 1950-58, asst. mgr. research dept., 1958-59, mgr., 1959-60, v.p., mgr. research, 1960-63; v.p. Tex. Gulf Sulphur Co. (Phosphate div.), 1963-70, gen. mgr., 1966-70; pres. Colo. Sch. Mines, Golden, 1970-84; ret. Dir. Halliburton Co., Kerr-McGee Corp., Hercules, Inc.; hon. dir. Texasgulf Inc. Fellow Am. Inst. Chem. Engrs.; mem. Am. Chem. Soc., Nat. Soc. Profl. Engrs., Sigma Xi, Phi Lambda Upsilon, Tau Beta Pi. Clubs: Mile High (Denver). Home: 2615 Oak Dr Apt 13 Lakewood CO 80215-7182

MCBRIDE, JACK J. financial services executive; b. Orient, Iowa, June 24, 1936; s. Marvin Clair and Ruth (Jones) McB.; m. Mary Ann Garden, June 16, 1957; children: Jeffry J., Beth Ann, Kelley Lynn, Grant G. BA, Simpson Coll., Indianola, Iowa, 1958; postgrad., U. Conn., 1963, U. Ill., 1974. Cert. agy. mgmt., sch. mgmt., LIMRA, 1968; cert. mgmt. devel., Aetna Inst., 1980. Spl. agt. Prin. Fin. Group, Des Moines, 1958-60; agy. supr. Aetna Life and Affiliated Cos. (now INQ Aetna Fin. Svcs., Hartford, Conn., 1960-65; agy. mgr. Equitable Life Iowa and Affiliated Cos. (now INQ Equitable Life Ins.), Omaha, Davenport, Iowa, 1965-72; gen. agt. Springfield, Ill., 1972-77, Milw., 1977-82; supt. personal fin. security divsn. Aetna Inc., Chgo., 1982-84; instr. Life Underwriters Tng. Coun., Quad Cities, 1968-69; ret. Lectr. to various univs. and colls. Contbr. articles to profl. jours. Chmn. friends bd. So. Ill. U. MEd. Sch., 1975-77; charter chmn. stewardship St. Luke's Ch., Omaha, 1966; mem. steering com. devel. coun. Simpson Coll., 1960. Named Outstanding Young Man Am., 1966. Mem. Nat. Assn. Life Underwriters (past co-chmn. edn. com., chmn., dir. Iowa State com.), Springfield Gen. Agts. and Mgrs. Assn. (past pres., dir.), Sangamon Estate Planners Coun. (charter), Brain Injury Assn. Am., Brain Injury Assn. Ill., Adminstrv. Mgmt. Soc., Quad Cities C. of C. (spkrs. bur.), Iowa Pioneer Arledge Farm Family, Masons, Scottish Rite, The Union Ch. of Hinsdale, Rotary.

MCBRIDE, JOHN ALEXANDER, retired chemical engineer; b. Altoona, Pa., Mar. 29, 1918; s. Raymond E. and Carolyn (Tinker) McB.; m. Elizabeth Anne Vogel, Aug. 28, 1942; children: Katherine M. Harris, Susan McBride Malick, Carolyn McBride Nafziger. AB, Miami U., Oxford, Ohio, 1940; M.Sc., Ohio State U., 1941; PhD, U. Ill., 1944. Registered profl. engr., Calif. Various positions in research and devel. dept. Phillips Petroleum Co., 1944-58, 59-65; dir. chem. tech. Phillips Petroleum Co. (Atomic energy div.), 1963-65; chief applications engring. Astrodyne, Inc., 1958-59; dir. div. materials licensing AEC, 1965-70; v.p. E.R. Johnson Assocs., Inc., Fairfax, Va., 1970-92; asst. gen. mgr. Nuclear Chems. & Metals Corp., 1970-71. Adviser U.S. del. 3d Internat. Conf. Peaceful Uses Atomic Energy, 1964 Mem. AIChE (chmn. nuclear engring. divsn. 1986, Robert E. Wilson award 1991), Am. Chem. Soc., Alpha Chi Sigma, Phi Kappa Tau. Achievements include publications and patents on petrochemical products and processes, solid propellant rockets, irradiated fuel reprocessing, radioactive waste fixation and disposal. Home: 1727 Sherman Ave Canon City CO 81212 Address: PO Box 1482 Canon City CO 81215-1482 E-mail: 7grandkids@mymailstation.com.

MCBRIDE, JONATHAN EVANS, executive search consultant; b. Washington, June 16, 1942; s. Gordon Williams and Martha Alice (Evans) McB.; BA, Yale U., 1964; m. Emilie Evans Dean, Sept. 5, 1970; children: Webster Dean, Morley Evans. Account exec. Merrill Lynch & Co., Washington, 1968-72; v.p. dept. mgr. Lionel D. Edie & Co., N.Y.C., 1972-76; v.p., exec. search cons. Simmons Assocs., Inc., Washington, 1976-79; pres. McBride Assocs., Inc., Washington, 1979—. Bd. dirs. Yale U. Alumni Fund, 1974-79; bd. trustees Sidwell Friends Sch., Washington, 1996—. Served to lt. USNR, 1964-68. Clubs: Yale (N.Y.C.); Met. (Washington); Chevy Chase (Md.). Office: 1742 N St NW Washington DC 20036-2907

MCBRIDE, JUDITH, elementary education educator; Art tchr. Slade Elem. Sch., Laramie, Wyo., 1996, Spring Creek Elem. Sch., Laramie, 1996—. Named Wyo. State Tchr. of Yr., 1993. Office: Spring Creek Elem Sch 1203 Russell St Laramie WY 82070-4682

MCBRIDE, MARY E. social worker; b. Ville Platte, La., June 24, 1950; d. Howard Charles and Bernadine (Fontenot) M. BA, U. Southwestern La., 1972; MSW, La. State U., Baton Rouge, 1978. Lic. social worker, Kans., La. Coord. consultation and edn. Acadiana Mental Health Ctr., Lafayette, La., 1978-80; psychiat. social worker Brentwood Hosp., Shreveport, 1980-82; substance abuse counselor Pines Treatment Ctr., 1983-84; psychiat. social worker Western Mo. Mental Health Ctr., Kansas City, 1984-87; psychotherapist Cath. Social Svcs., 1985—; psychiat. social worker Rsch. Psychiat. Ctr., 1987-90. Field intern instr. U. Kans. Sch. of Social Welfare, Lawrence, 1989-90. Mem. NASW, Acad. Cert. Social Workers, Sierra Club (membership com. Shreveport chpt. 1982-83), Phi Mu Alumni Assn. (treas. Kansas City chpt. 1984-85). Democrat. Avocations: walking, gardening, bicycling. Office: Upshaw & Assocs 10680 Barkley St Shawnee Mission KS 66212-1861

MCBRIDE, MILDRED MAYLEA, retired elementary school educator; b. Bowerston, Ohio, Oct. 7, 1922; d. Harry Scott and Mary McGary (Mowl) McB.; 1 adopted child, Marjorie Mi Sang McBride. BS in Music, Baldwin-Wallace Coll., 1944; MA, Columbia U., N.Y.C., 1949. Cert. tchr., Ohio, Hawaii. Traveling music tchr. Tuscarawas County Sch., 1944-45; tchr. elem. music Parma (Ohio) Schs., 1945-48, tchr. jr. h.s. music, 1946-48; tchr. h.s. gen. music, chorus Kamehameha Sch. for Girls, Honolulu, 1949-59; tchr. elem. music Tempe (Ariz.) Schs., 1959-60, Hawaii Pub. Sch. Sys., 1960-86, ret., 1986. Co-founder Elem., Intermediate, Gen. Music Interest Group, Honolulu, 1969-79. Author, editor: (biography) Meg!, 1996, Three Women of Kintail, 2001, 4 hist. novels; writer mus. plays. Helper Bowerston Pub. Libr., 1939, 48, 97—; bd. dirs. Hawaii Habitat for Humanity, Honolulu, 1986-93; mem. Honolulu Symphony Chorus; head soup kitchen, vol. Harris United Meth. Ch., Honolulu, 1990-96, mem. choir, 1975-96; libr. asst. Dormont Presbyn. Ch. Libr. Avocations: golf, travel, singing, cooking, enjoying daughter. Home: 2934 Espy Ave Pittsburgh PA 15216-2017

MCBRIDE, MILFORD LAWRENCE, JR. lawyer; b. Grove City, Pa., July 16, 1923; s. Milford Lawrence and Elizabeth B. (Douthett) McB.; m. Madeleine Coulter, Aug. 6, 1947; children: Marta, Brenda, Trip, Randy, Barry. AB, Grove City Coll., 1944; BS, N.Y.U., 1944; JD, U. Pa., 1949. Bar: Pa. 1949, U.S. Dist. Ct. (we. dist.) Pa. U.S. Supreme Ct. Ptnr., McBride & McBride, Grove City, 1949-77, sr. ptnr., 1992—; ptnr. McBride and McNickle, Grove City, 1977-92; dir. Integra Fin. Corp., 1988-93; trustee Grove City Coll., 1995—. Served to 1st lt. USAAF, 1943-46. Mem. Mercer County Bar Assn. (state treas. 1970-77), ABA, Am. Bar Found. Republican. Clubs: Oakmont Country, University (Pitts.). Office: 211 S Center St Grove City PA 16127-1508

MCBRIDE, ROBERT ALBERT, training services executive; b. Woonsocket, R.I., Mar. 9, 1960; s. Albert and Leonora Anna McB.; m. Kathryn Moore, June 14, 1998; 1 child, Jordan. BA in Psychology, Providence Coll., 1982; MBA in Mgmt., Bryant Coll., 1994. Commd. ensign USN, 1985, advanced through grades to comdr.; sales rep. Aventis Pharms., Providence, 1991—96, regional trainer New England region, 1996—99, area mgr. Pa., 1999—2002; global tng. mgr. Genzyme Corp., 2002—. Mem. adv. bd. Boy's & Girl's Club, Cumberland, R.I., 1995-99; instr. Literacy Vols. Am., Woonsocket, R.I., 1997-99. Decorated Navy & Marine Corp Commendation medal, Navy Achievement medal. Mem. World Affairs Coun., U.S. Naval Res. Assn., Naval Inst. Roman Catholic. Avocations: golf, biking, reading, basketball. Home: 10 Cathedral Ct Cumberland RI 02864 Office: Genzyme Corp One Kendall Sq Cambridge MA 02139 E-mail: rmcbusnr@aol.com.

MCBRIDE, RONALD OWEN, journalism educator, department head; b. Detroit, Sept. 19, 1948; s. Elmer Owen McBride and Doris Emma Morley; m. Deborah Ann Jones, July 1, 1972; children: Stephanie Lee, Melanie Lee. BA in Art Edn., Northwestern State U., Natchitoches, La., 1970, MA in Studio Arts and Design, 1972, MEd in Ednl. Media, 1973; EdD in Media Prodn., Ga. State U., 1982, PhD in Comm. and Media Mgmt., 1990. Dir. media svcs. Dalton (Ga.) Coll., 1973-83; comm. specialist La. Sch. for Math., Sci. and the Arts, Natchitoches, 1983-89, dir. telelearning, 1989-91; dir. office of distance learning Northwestern State U., Natchitoches, 1991-94, head dept. journalism and telecomm., 1994—. Creator, designer La. Instrnl. Satellite and Telecomm. Network, Northwestern State U., 1990; tech cons., La. rep. to S.W. Ednl. Devel. Lab., Austin, Tex., 1990—; tech. cons. Resource Advantage, Inc., Dallas, 1993—; affiliate to Nat. Ednl. Telecomm. Orgn., 1993; staff devel. units instr. State Dept. Edn., Walker and Catoosa Counties, Ga., 1976-83; instr. Profl. Improvement Program, State of La., 1984-87; adj. lectr. Northwestern State U., 1985-91; instr. distance edn. Telelearning Network, 1986-91; presenter numerous confs. in field. Author: Handbook for Distance Learning: Procedures and Regulations for Interactive Satellite Classes, 1993, 94; contbr. articles to profl. jours.; exec. prodr.: Smart Discipline for the Classroom, 1995, 20 interactive satellite classes, 1993—, Technology in the Classroom: Making it Happen, 1993, 64 interactive space sci. classes for mid. schs., 1994, 95, 2 cable classes, 1993, 94, LaSip Teleconf., 1993, 20 programs in econ. devel. series, drug-free forum teleconf., Snap Shots of Natchitoches tourism video, LAAC La. Quiz Bowl, 1993, 93, 94, 95; creator (videocassettes) Photography as Fine Art, 1982, The History of Photography, 1982, Absolute Value, 1987, Arc of a Circle, 1987, Completing the Square, 1987, Introduction to Trigonometric Functions, 1987, Land of Care-a-Lot, 1987, (multi-images) A Ten Year History of Dalton Junior College, 1977, This is the Louisiana School, 1985, Survival of a Lab School, 1987, (16 millimeter films) Looking at Animation, 1982, Wing Service, 1983, (sound/slide program) Making a Slide/Tape Program, 1983, What's Happening in Innovative Education, 1986. Mem. Gov.'s Task Force on Telecomm. Com. on Higher Edn., 1994—; mem. steering com. Project Get-Set, 1993, La. 2000, Natchitoches-Northwestern Folk Festival; mem. Supt.'s Task Force for Distance Edn. K-12, Regents' Task Force for Distance Learning; pres. Parent-Tchr. Orgn. Natchitoches Ctrl. H.S., 1993-96, mem. exec. bd., 1991-93; dir. fine arts North Ga. Fair, Dalton. Recipient Nat. award for outstanding applications of audio graphics/computers in distance learning, Internat. Teleconferencing Assn., 1991, Gold medal for distance learning N.Y. Festivals Internat. Awards, 1994, Silver medal, 1995. Mem. Assn. for Edn. in Journalism and Mass Comm., U.S. Distance Learning Assn., Internat. Soc. for Tech. in Edn., Assn. for Gifted and Talented Students, La. Assn. Computer Users in Edn., La. Assn. Ednl. Comm. and Tech., Rotary (bd. dirs. 1992-93, sec. 1993-94, pres. 1994-95). Republican. Methodist. Avocations: photography, painting, sports. Office: Northwestern State U PO Box 5273 Natchitoches LA 71497-0001

MCBRIDE, SANDRA TEAGUE, psychiatric nurse; b. Corinth, Miss., Sept. 13, 1958; d. Clarence R. and Alice (Ingram) T. AAS, Shelby State Community Coll., 1983; BSN, U. North Ala., 1987; MSN, Union U., 2001. RN, Miss., Tenn. Nurse supr. Alcorn County Care, Inc., Corinth, Miss., 1985-87; staff nurse Bolivar (Tenn.) Community Hosp., 1988-90; staff nurse West Tenn. High Security Facility Tenn. Dept. of Corrections, Ripley, 1990-91; staff nurse U.S. Med. Ctr. for Fed. Prisoners, Springfield, Mo., 1991-92, Western Mental Health Inst., Bolivar, 1992—.

MCBRIDE, SHARON LOUISE, counselor, technical communication educator; b. Peoria, Ill., Dec. 5, 1939; d. Ralph Cannon and Joyce Eliz (Shoff) McB.; m. Armond B. Ciota, Jr., Apr. 23, 1960 (div.); children: Matthew Ciota, Eliz Faron, Thomas Ciota, Nathan Ciota. BA, Bradley U., 1960, MA, 1987. Various positions to undergrad. student adviser Bradley U., Peoria, 1972—; instr. Ill. Ctrl. Coll., East Peoria, 1987—. Chmn. bd. trustees Greater Peoria Mass Transit. Trustee West Peoria Twp., 1984-96; sec.-treas. Ill. Twp. Trustees, 1993-96; chairperson West Peoria Zoning Bd. Appeals; mem. policy com. Peoria Pekin Urbanized Area Transp. Study. Mem.: Am. Assn. Women in C.C., Am. Pub. Transit Assn. (transit bd., Region IV rep.), Am. Soc. Engring. Edn., Rotary Club (Peoria North), Lions (bd. dirs. West Peoria chpt. 1984—97, precinct com.). Republican. Avocations: travel, community volunteer. Home: 2413 W Kellogg Ave West Peoria IL 61604-5011

MCBRIDE, SHARON SUE, artist; b. Houston, Oct. 23, 1947; d. Dickson Leeonard McBride and Laura Francis Owens. One-woman shows include Villa Santa Barbara, 2000, Gallery 113, 2000, Roy, 2000, Faulkner West Gallery, 2001, Soho Music and Dinner Club, 2001, Fresco, 2002, Max's, 2002, exhibited in group shows at Karpeles Manuscript Libr., Mus. and Gallery, 2000. Recipient Jurors Choice award, Goleta Valley Art Assn., 2002. Mem.: ASCAP, Santa Barbara Art Assn. (Hon. Mention 2001), Goleta Valley Art Assn. (Juror's Choice award 2000—02). Avocations: photography, poetry, guitar, songwriting.

MCBRIDE, SYLVIA ELAINE, pharmacist; b. Houston, June 3, 1955; BS in Pharmacy, Tex. So. U., 1979. Registered pharmacist Tex.; cert. tchr. Tex. Pharmacist Tex. State Bd. of Pharmacy, 1980—. Pharmacy preceptor Tex. State Bd. Pharmacy, Houston, 2001. Co-author: (poetry book) An Anthology of Our Love, 1996; author: A Poem for All Seasons, 1998. Recipient Editor's Choice award, Nat. Libr. of Poetry, 1996. Mem.: Houston Writers League, Internat. Soc. Poets. Avocation: writing poetry, drawing, painting, reading.

MCBRIDE, THOMAS DWAYNE, management consultant; b. Brownwood, Tex., Feb. 13, 1947; s. Thomas Alfred and Eula Faye (Harvey) McB.; m. Peggy Anne Kimbrough McBride, Oct. 14, 1967; children: Jeffery Dwayne, Stacy Anne. AS, Crowder Coll., Neosho, Mo., 1967; BS in Mech. Engring., U. Mo., Rolla, 1970; MBA in Mgmt., U. Akron, 1978. Registered profl. engr., Ohio. Engring. supr. Babcock & Wilcox, Barberton, Ohio, 1972-79; mgr. engring. Bendix Corp., South Beloit, Ill., 1979-83; mgr. sales engring. Bendix/Warner & Swasey, Worcester, Mass., 1983-84, mgr. Product Engring., 1984-86; program mgr. Design Tech. Corp., Billerica, 1986-87; mgr. engring. Netco, Inc., Haverhill, 1987-88; dir. engring. The Nelmor Co., North Uxbridge, 1988-95; tech. mgr. Lawrence (Mass.) Pumps Inc., 1995-96, ops. mgr., 1996-2000; pres. Ptnrs. for Creative Solutions, Inc., Shrewsbury, Mass., 2000—. Tech. and bus. cons. Micromation, Inc., Altoona, Pa., 1988-90. Inventor: Granulator Knife, 1991, 94, Bin Deflector, 1991; author: Society of Manufacturing Engineers, 1992, M&A Today, 2000. Mem. Worcester Area C. of C. 1st lt. U.S. Army, 1970-72. Recipient Curator's scholarship U. Mo., 1967. Mem. Soc. Mfg. Engrs., Turnaround Mgmt. Assn., Assn. Corp. Growth, Phi Theta Kappa (chpt. pres. 1966-67). Mem. Trinity Ch. Avocations: golf, bicycling, genealogy, religious history, hiking. E-mail: tmcbride@pcs.-info.com.

MC BRIDE, THOMAS FREDERICK, lawyer, former university dean, government official; b. Elgin, Ill., Feb. 8, 1929; s. Thomas Wallace and Sarah Rosalie (Pierce) McB.; m. Catherine Higgs Milton, Aug. 23, 1975; children: Matthew (dec.), Elizabeth, John, Raphael, Luke. BA, NYU, 1952; LLB, Columbia U., 1956. Bar: N.Y. 1956, D.C. 1966, Calif. 1989, Conn. 2000, U.S. Supreme Ct. 1963. Asst. dist. atty., N.Y. County, 1956-59; trial atty. organized crime sect. Dept. Justice, 1961-65; ofcl. Peace Corps, 1965-68; assoc. spl. prosecutor Watergate, 1973-75; dir. bur. enforcement CAB, 1975-77; insp. gen. U.S. Dept. Agr., Washington, 1977-81, U.S. Dept. Labor, Washington, 1981-82; assoc. dean Stanford Law Sch., Calif., 1982-89; mem. Pres.'s Commn. Organized Crime, 1983-86, Calif. Council on Mental Health, 1986-90; dir. environ. health and safety Stanford U., 1990-92; counselor U.S. Dept. Energy, Washington, 1993-95. Adv. to Home Ministry, Govt. India, 1964. Spl. asst. to pres. Save the Children, 1997-99. With AUS, 1946-47. Mem. D.C. Bar Assn. Home and Office: 4 Anchor Ln Westport CT 06880-3602

MCBRIDE, TIMOTHY DOMINIC, economist, educator; b. Milw., Oct. 25, 1959; s. Raymond Edward and Marian Bernice (Dunne) McB.; m. Shirley Lynn Porterfield, Apr. 30, 1989. BA, U. Wis., Milw., 1981; MS, U. Wis., 1985, PhD, 1987. Statistician The Milw. Bucks, 1977-87; sports reporter The Milw. Jour., 1977-81; rsch. asst. U. Wis., Madison, 1981-87; rsch. assoc. The Urban Inst., Washington, 1987-91; asst. prof. U. Mo., St. Louis, 1991—. Co-author: The Needs of the Elderly in the 21st Century, 1990. Mem. Am. Econ. Assn., Am. Statis. Assn., Gerontol. Soc. Am., Assn. for Pub. Policy and Mgmt. Democrat. Avocations: sports statis., computers, writing. Office: U Mo Dept Econs 8001 Natural Bridge Rd Saint Louis MO 63121-4401 Home: 11638 Holly Springs Dr Saint Louis MO 63146-5434

MCBRIDE, VICKIE DARLENE, geriatrics nurse; b. Tampa, Fla., Jan. 17, 1944; d. Harold Victor Burch and Dorothy June (Higley) Keen; m. Dennis McBride, July 12, 1969 (div. June 1980); m. John Lawrence Petonic Jr., Mar. 20, 1982 (div. Dec. 1993); children: Elizabeth, Christopher. BSN, Marycrest Coll., Davenport, Iowa, 1966; MBA, Baldwin-Wallace Coll., Berea, Ohio, 1986. Cert. rehab. nurse, dir. nursing.; cert. legal nurse cons. Charge nurse Mercy Hosp., Davenport, 1966; staff devel. for critical care Cleve. Clinic, 1969-73; dir., med. svcs. coord. Free Clinic West, Cleve., 1973-74; DON Cuyahoga Falls (Ohio) Gen. Hosp., 1974-76, Kaiser Found. Hosp., Cleve., 1976-79, regional coord. staff devel., 1979-83; DON Forest Hills Nursing Home, 1983-86; sr. cons. Clemens Nelson & Assocs., Worthington, Ohio, 1986-88; corp. cons. Altercare Inc., Navarre, 1988-99; CEO, pres. New Beginnings, Inc., 1996-98; sr. nurse cons. Dart Chart, Milw., 1999-2000; regional dir. compliance Eastern divsn. Healthprime, Alpharetta, Ga., 2000—. Course coord. critical care Cleve. State U., 1973-75; trustee Free Med. Clinics of Cleve., 1972-73; affiliate faculty Capital U., 1976-79. Lt. USN, 1966-69. Fellow Acad. Dir. Nursing LTC; mem. AACN, Nat. Dirs. Nursing Long Term Care, Ohio Dirs. Nursing Long Term Care, Am. Healthcare Assn., Nat. League for Nursing, Am. Rehab. Nurses., Nadona Wis. DON Coun. Roman Catholic. Avocations: bowling, golf. Home: 1603 Woodside Ln Sheboygan WI 53081-8866 Office: Healthprime 950 North Pint Pkwy Ste 100 Alpharetta GA 30005 E-mail: vickie-mcbride@healthprime.com.

MCBRIDE, WILLIAM BERNARD, treasurer; b. N.Y.C., May 22, 1931; s. William and Nora (Hughes) McB.; m. Lorraine Barry, May 27, 1956; children: Mary, William, Stephen, Anne. BS, Fordham U., 1952; MBA, Baruch Sch., 1963. CPA, N.Y. Staff auditor Touche, Ross, Bailey & Smart (CPAs), N.Y.C., 1952-58; asst. v.p. Bankers Trust Co., 1959-67; treas. Kidde, Inc., Saddle Brook, N.J., 1967-87, v.p., 1974-87; cons. Hanson Industries, other cos., Iselin, N.J., 1987—. Mem. AICPA, N.Y. State Soc. CPAs. Home and Office: 243 Sunset Ave Ridgewood NJ 07450-2420

MC BRIDE, WILLIAM LEON, philosopher, educator; b. N.Y.C., Jan. 19, 1938; s. William Joseph and Irene May (Choffin) McB.; m. Angela Barron, July 12, 1965; children: Catherine, Kara. AB, Georgetown U., 1959; postgrad. (Fulbright fellow), U. Lille, 1959-60; MA (Woodrow Wilson fellow), Yale U., 1962, PhD (Social Sci. Rsch. Coun. fellow), 1964. Instr. philosophy Yale U., New Haven, 1964-66, asst. prof., 1966-70, assoc. prof., 1970-73; lectr. Northwestern U., Evanston, Ill., summer 1972; assoc. prof. Purdue U., West Lafayette, Ind., 1973-76, prof., 1976-2001, Arthur G. Hansen disting. prof., 2001—. Lectr. Korcula Summer Sch., Yugoslavia, 1971, 73; Fulbright lectr. Sofia U., St. Kliment Ohridski, Bulgaria, fall 1997. Author: Fundamental Change in Law and Society, 1970, The Philosophy of Marx, 1977, Social Theory at a Crossroads, 1980, (with R.A. Dahl) Demokrati og Autoritet, 1980, Sartre's Political Theory, 1991, Social and Political Philosophy, 1994, Philosophical Reflections on the Changes in Eastern Europe, 1999, From Yugoslav Praxis to Global Pathos, 2001; editor: (with C.O. Schrag) Phenomenology in a Pluralistic Context, 1983, Sartre and Existentialism, 8 vols., 1997, (with M.B. Matustik) Calvin O. Schrag and the Task of Philosophy after Postmodernity, 2002. Decorated chevalier Ordre des Palmes Académiques. Mem. AAUP (pres. Purdue chpt. 1983-86, pres. Ind. conf. 1988-89), Am. Philos. Assn. (chmn. com. on internat. coop. 1992-95, bd. dirs. 1992-95), N.Am. Soc. Social and Polit. Philosophy (v.p. 1997-2000, pres. 2000—), Am. Soc. Polit. and Legal Philosophy, Soc. Phenemonology and Existential Philosophy (exec. co-sec. 1977-80), Sartre Soc. N.Am. (chmn. bd. dirs. 1985-88, 91-93), Am. Soc. Philosophy in the French Lang. (pres. 1994-96), Fed. Internat. Soc. Philosophie (mem. steering com. 1998—). Home: 744 Cherokee Ave Lafayette IN 47905-1872 Office: Purdue U Dept Philosophy West Lafayette IN 47907-1360

MCBROOM, DIANE CRAUN, accountant, horse trainer; b. Gettysburg, Pa., Jan. 2, 1962; d. Edward Kenneth and Suzanne (Catchings) Craun; m. Stephen Cushing, June 3, 1993; children: Emily, Michael Ross. AAS, Piedmont Va. C.C., 1983; BA in Environ. Sci. with distinction, U. Va., 1985, MS in Taxation with distinction, 1990. CPA, Va., Md.; notary public, Va. Rsch. asst. U. Va. Hosp., Charlottesville, 1980-86; instr. The Miller Sch. of Albemarle, 1986-88; adj. prof. U. Va., 1987-90; tax assoc. Deloitte & Touche, N.Y.C., 1990-91, Coopers & Lybrand, Roanoke, Va., 1991-92; acct. Owl Hollow Farm, Floyd, 1992—. Horse trainer Owl Hollow Farm, Floyd, 1980—. Asst. editor: (instrnl. book) Lotus 1-2-3, 1987; editor Blue Ridge Combined Training Assn. Newsletter, 1996-97, United States Combined Training Assn. Area II Newsletter, 1997—. Leader Jr. Achievement, Roanoke, 1991-92; exec. dir. Boy Scouts Am., Charlottesville, 1986-90. Edmund P. Berkely scholar Commonwealth of Va., 1982. Mem. AICPA, Va. Soc. CPAs, U.S. Equestrian Team, U.S. Combined Tng. Assn., U.S. Dressage Fedn., Am. Horse Shows Assn. Republican. Episcopalian. Avocations: riding, reading, hiking, investing, photography. Home and Office: Owl Hollow Farm RR 4 Box 212 Floyd VA 24091-9117

MCBROOM, THOMAS WILLIAM, SR. aviation consultant; b. Atlanta, Mar. 29, 1963; s. William Ralph and Ethel Irene (Bradley) McB.; m. Susan H.; 1 child, Thomas William Jr. B in Mech. Engring., Ga. Tech., 1985, MS in Mech. Engring., 1987; JD, MBA, Ga. State U., 1992; postgrad., Embry-Riddle Aero. U. Registered profl. engr., Ga.; cert. ins. agt.-life, accident and sickness, property, casualty & surety Ga.; bar: Ga. 1993, D.C. 1994, U.S. Tax Ct. 1993, U.S. Supreme Ct. 1996; lic. comml. pilot and flight instr., registered mediator and arbitrator Ga. Mfg. engr. AT & T Techs., Norcross, Ga., 1985-86; energy systems engr. Atlanta Gas Light Co., 1987-89, sales engr., 1989-90, dir. power systems markets, 1991-94, sr. corp. planning analyst, 1994-95, mgr. major accounts, 1995-97, dir. major accts., 1997-99; atty., cons. Newnan, Ga., 1999—; pilot ground instr. Delta Air Lines, Atlanta, 2000—01; project mgr. Aviation Consulting, AIR, Inc., 2001—. Mem. Grad. Leadership Coweta, 1996, Grad. Coverdell Rep. Leadership Inst., 1997. With USAR, 1997—, Capt. JAGC. Mem. Ga. Bar Assn., Coverdell Leadership Inst., Phi Delta Phi (exchequer 1991). Home: 15 Culpepper Way Newnan GA 30265-2217 E-mail: tmcbroom@charter.net.

MCBRYDE, JOHN HENRY, federal judge; b. Jackson, Oct. 9, 1931; m. Betty Vinson; children: Rebecca McBryde Dippold, Jennifer, John Blake. BS in Commerce, Tex. Christian U., 1953; LLB, U. Tex., 1956. Bar: Tex. 1956, U.S. Ct. Appeals (5th cir.) 1958, U.S. Dist. Ct. (no. dist.) 1958, U.S. Dist. Ct. (ea. dist.) 1989, U.S. Supreme Ct. 1972. Assoc. Cantey, Hanger, Johnson, Scarborough & Gooch, Ft. Worth, 1956-62; ptnr. Cantey & Hanger and predecessor firm, 1962-69, McBryde, Bennett and predecessor firms, Ft. Worth, 1969-90; judge U.S. Dist. Ct. (no. dist.) Tex., 1990—. Fellow Am. Bar Found. (life), Tex. Bar Found. (life), Am. Coll. Trial Lawyers. Office: US Dist Ct US Courthouse 501 W 10th St Ste 401 Fort Worth TX 76102-3642

MCBRYDE, NEILL GREGORY, lawyer; b. Durham, N.C., Jan. 11, 1944; s. Angus M. and Priscilla (Gregory) McB., m. Margaret McPherson, Aug. 1, 1970; children: Margaret Courtauld, Neill Gregory Jr. AB cum laude, Davidson Coll., 1966; JD with high honors, U. N.C., 1969. Bar: N.C. 1969., Ga. 1972. Assoc. King & Spalding, Atlanta, 1971-76; ptnr. Fleming, Robinson, Bradshaw & Hinson, Charlotte, N.C., 1977-81, Helms, Mulliss & Johnston, Charlotte, 1981-86, Smith Helms Mulliss & Moore, Charlotte, 1986-90, Moore & Van Allen PLLC, Charlotte, 1990—. Lectr. in field, conducter workshops in field. Author, editor: First Union National Bank of North Carolina Will Book, 1986; contbr. to profl. jours. Elder and Deacon Myers Park Presbyn. Ch., Charlotte, 1980-86, 92-95, 2001-04; dir. sec. Presbyn. Home for Aged, Charlotte, 1978-82; trustee Charlotte Latins Schs., Inc., 1980-86, 87-93; past chmn., trustee Mint Mus. Charlotte. Fellow Am. Coll. Trust and Estate Counsel (past mem. bd. regents, past pres.), Am. Coll. Tax Counsel; mem. ABA, Ga. Bar Assn., N.C. Bar Assn. (probate and fiduciary law sect.), Order of Coif, Phi Beta Kappa, Omicron Delta Kappa. Republican. Avocations: tennis, golf, fishing. Office: Moore & Van Allen PLLC Nations Bank Corp Ctr 100 N Tryon St Fl 47 Charlotte NC 28202-4003

MCBURNEY, ANDREW ELLIOTT, secondary school educator; b. Ann Arbor, Mich., Jan. 8, 1972; s. Terrance McBurney, Lynnea McBurney. BA, U. Tex., Austin, 1994. Cert. Tchr. Tex., 1995. Tchr. Northside Ind. Sch. Dist., San Antonio, 1996—. Bd. dir. North Ctrl. Thousand Oaks Neighborhood Assn., San Antonio, 1997—99. Lutheran. Home: 15306 Mt. Eagle San Antonio TX 78232 Office: Sunset High School (Northside ISD) 8000 Lobo Lane San Antonio TX 78240 Personal E-mail: crm114@texas.net.

MCBURNEY, CHARLES WALKER, JR. lawyer; b. Orlando, Fla., June 6, 1957; s. Charles Walker McBurney and Jeane (Brown) Chappell. BA, U. Fla., 1979, JD, 1982. Bar: Fla. 1982, U.S. Dist. Ct. (mid. dist.) Fla. 1983, U.S. Ct. Appeals (11th cir.) 1984. Assoc. Mathews, Osborne, McNatt, Gobelman & Cobb, Jacksonville, Fla., 1982-84; asst. state's atty. State's Atty.'s Office, 1984-90, civil atty., 1987-88, sr. trial atty., 1988-90; ptnr. Fischette, Owen, Held & McBurney, 1990—. Dir. Serious or Habitual Juvenile Offender Program, 1986. Bd. dirs. Civic Round Table, 1988-92, treas., 1988-89, pres. 1989-90; chmn. com. congl. campaigns, Jacksonville, 1982, 84, 88; mem. Mayor's Bicentennial Constnl. Commn., 1989-91; dir. Internat. Devel. Commn. for Jacksonville, 1993—, treas., 1995-97; bd. dirs. Am. Heart Assn. N.E. Fla., 1990-92. Mem. ABA, Jacksonville Bar Assn. (chmn. bankruptcy sect. 1998-2000, 2002—), Jacksonville Bankruptcy Bar Assn. (bd. dirs. 1999—), Nat. Dist. Attys. Assn., Comml. Law League (So. region exec. coun. 1998—, treas. 2000—), Fla. Jaycees (legal counsel 1987-88, most outstanding local pres. award 1987), Jacksonville Jaycees (pres. 1986, Jaycee of yr. 1984), Jacksonville C. of C. (bd. govs. 1987, govtl. affairs com. 1998—), Summit Civitan (judge adv. 1991-93, 2001-), Masons, Bull Snort Club (pres. 1995-96, 99-2000, chmn. bd. 1996-97, 1998-99), C. of C. (trustee 1996-98, govtl. affairs com. 1998—), N.E. Fla. Alumni Assn. (v.p. 1998-2000), James Madison Inst., Jacksonville Hist. Soc., Phi Beta Kappa, Southeast CPAC (environ. sub-chmn. 2001-). Republican. Presbyterian. Home: 6326 Christopher Creek Rd E Jacksonville FL 32217-2485 Office: Fishette Owen Held & McBurney Riverplace Tower Ste 1916 Jacksonville FL 32207

MCBURNEY, ELIZABETH INNES, physician, educator; b. Lake Charles, La., Dec. 24, 1944; d. Theodore John and Martha (Caldwell) Innes; divorced, 1980; children: Leanne Marie, Susan Eleanor. BS, U. Southwestern La., 1965; MD, La. State U., 1969. Diplomate Am. Bd. Internal Medicine, Am. Bd. Dermatology. Intern Pensacola (Fla.) Edn. Program, 1969-70; resident in internal medicine Boston U. and Carney Hosps., 1970-72; resident in dermatology Charity Hosp., New Orleans, 1972-74; staff physician Ochsner Hosp., 1974-80; assoc. head of dermatology Ochsner Clinic, 1974-80; clin. asst. prof. La. Health Scis., 1976-79, clin. assoc. prof., 1979-90, clin. prof., 1990—; clin. asst. prof. Tulane Health Scis., 1976-88, clin. assoc. prof., 1988-91, clin. prof., 1991—. Mem. courtesy staff Northshore Regional Med. Ctr., Slidell, La., 1985—; mem. staff Slidell Meml. Hosp., 1988—, chmn. CME courses, 1988—, pres.-elect med. staff, 2000-01, pres., 2001—; regional dir. Mycosis Fungoides Study Group, Balt., 1974-94. Contbr. articles to profl. jours. Bd. dirs. Slidell Art Coun., 1988—, Camp Fire, New Orleans, 1979-83, Cancer Assn. New Orleans, 1978-83; juror Art in Pub. Places, Slidell, 1989. Recipient Disting. Woman Physician award AMA, 1999, Samuel Stegman award, 2000. Fellow ACP; mem. Am. Soc. Dermatologic Surgery (treas. 1991-94, bd. dirs. 1988-91, pres. elect 1995-96, pres. 1996-97), Am. Acad. Dermatology (bd. dirs. 1994-98), Am. Bd. Laser Medicine and Surgery (bd. dirs. 1991-96), La. Dermatologic Soc. (pres. 1989-90), St. Tammary Med. Soc. (pres. 1988), Phi Kappa Phi, Alpha Omega Alpha. Avocations: reading, gardening, fine art, music, film. Office: 1051 Gause Blvd Ste 460 Slidell LA 70458-2985

MCBURNEY, MARGOT B. librarian; b. Lethbridge, Alta., Can. d. Ronald Laurence Maness and R. Blanche (Lott) Hart; children: Margot Elisabeth McBurney Lane, James Ronald Gordon. BA with honours, Principia Coll., 1953; M.Sc. in L.S, U. Ill., 1969. Sec. Marshall Brooks Library, Principia Coll., Elsah, Ill., 1966-69, reference librarian, 1969-70; systems analyst trainee in library systems U. Alta. Library, Edmonton, 1970-71, undergrad. reference librarian, 1971-72, editor periodicals holdings list, 1972-73, serials cataloguer, 1973-74, head acquisitions div., 1974-77; chief librarian Queen's U. Library, Kingston, Ont., Can., 1977-90. Editor: Am. Soc. Info. Sci. Western Can. chpt. Proceedings, 1975, 76. Mem. ALA, Am. Soc. Info. Sci. (councilor-at-large 1976-79, past chmn. chpt.), Assn. Research Libraries (dir. 1978-81, chmn. task force on library edn. 1980-83), Can. Assn. Info. Sci., Can. Assn. Research Libraries, Can. Library Assn., Council on Library Resources (PETREL com. 1981-84), Phi Alpha Eta, Beta Phi Mu. E-mail: mbm1@myexcel.ca.

MCCABE, CHRISTOPHER J. state legislator; b. Encino, Calif., Jan. 19, 1956; s. John Joseph and Theresa (Lesso) M.; m. Deidre Nerreau, 1988; children: Caroline, Maura, Colin, Aidan. BBA, U. Notre Dame, 1978; MBA, Fairleigh Dickinson U., 1980. Fin. analyst Exxon Rsch. and Engring. Co., 1978-81; with Contel Tech. Svc. Divsn., 1981-87; devel. officer Johns Hopkins Hosp. and Med. Sch., Balt., 1987—; senator Dist. 14 Md. State Senate, 1991—, mem. econ. and environ. affairs com., 1991—. Mem. adminstrv. exec. legis. review com., exec. nominations com., Md. State Senate; chmn. Howard Co. Senate Delegation; task force charter schs., edn. equity and finance. Mem., treas. Howard County Rep. State Ctrl. Com., 1984—86; mem. Howard County Foster Care Rev. Bd., 1982—86; mem. citizen's adv. bd. Howard County Bd. Edn., 1988—90; fin. chmn. Mothers Against Drunk Driving, 1990; co-chmn. First Tee of Balt.; alt. del. Rep. Nat. Conv., 1984; del. Repub. Nat. Conv., 2000, mem. platform com., 2000; mem. Md. Commn. on Criminal Sentencing Policy; Gov.'s Adoption Oversight Com.; hon. chair Md. Cath. Leadership Council; mem. Marylanders Against Casinos; pres., mem. Md. Commn. of Fatherhood, 2000—. Named Rep. of Yr., Howard County Rep. Club, 1984; recipient Humanitarian award, Adoptions Together, Inc., 1994, Christian Svc. award, Ctrl. Md. Ecumenical Coun., 1996, Pro-Life award, Md., 2001, Repub. Legis. of Yr., Nat. Repub. Legis. Assn., 2001. Mem. Jaycees, KC. Address: 429 Miller Senate Bldg 11 Bladen St Annapolis MD 21401-1991 E-mail: christopher_mccabe@senate.state.md.us.

MCCABE, DONALD JAMES, educational research director; b. Flint, Mich., Oct. 4, 1932; s. Lemuel Cicero and Bernice Agnes (Webb) McCabe; m. Ann Louise Smith; children: Robert James, Linda Carol. AA, Flint Jr. Coll., 1950-52; PhB, U. Detroit, 1954, MA, 1962. Tchr. L'Anse Creuse Schs., Mt. Clemens, Mich., Mt. Morris (Mich.) Bd. Edn., 1959-61; tchr. reading Flint Bd. Edn., 1962-74; research dir. AVKO Dyslexia Rsch. Found., Birch Run, Mich., 1974—, pres., 1974-76. Advisor Decade of Progress com. Mich. Dept. Edn., 1980. Author: Reading Via Typing, 1980, (series) Sequential Spelling I-VII, 1982, (dictionary) Word Families Plus, 1984, For Adults Only, 1986, AVKO Spelling "Difficulty" Dictionary, 1988, Helping Anyone Overcome Reading/Spelling Problems, 1988, The Patterns of English Spelling, 1990, To Teach A Dyslexic, 1995; contbr. numerous articles to profl. jours. Served as sgt. U.S. Army, 1954-57. Recipient Mary Scott award AVKO Ednl. Research Found. Inc., 1982, Disting. Leadership award ABI, 1988. Mem. Internat. Reading Assn., Correctional Edn. Assn., Coalition of Literacy, Orton Dyslexia Soc. Clubs: Clio (Mich.) Golf; Flint Duplicate Bridge. Lodges: Rotary, Lions. Roman Catholic. Home: PO Box 83 Birch Run MI 48415-0083 Office: AVKO Dyslexia Rsch Found Inc 3084 W Willard Rd Clio MI 48420-7801 E-mail: avkoemail@aol.com.

MCCABE, EDWARD OWEN, photoprocessing executive; b. N.Y.C., Mar. 30, 1947; s. Edward James McCabe Jr. and Ethel Gertrude Corrigan; m. Julianne Susan Moneagle, June 25, 1969; children: Rachel Arnold, Edward James III, Michael Owen, Benjamin Moneagle. BA in Econs., Cornell U., 1969; MBA in Mktg., U. Conn., 1980. Sr. product mgr. Grolier Enterprises, Danbury, Conn., 1973-79; group product mgr. Xerox Publs., Middletown, 1979-83; dir. mktg. Carol Wright Sales, Stanford, 1983-85; v.p., mgmt. supr. Wunderman Worldwide, N.Y.C., 1985-88; v.p. mktg. BMG Music Svc., 1988-92; pres., CEO Numa Corp., Akron, Ohio, 1993-96, Mystic (Conn.) Color Lab, Inc., 1997—. Mem. adv. bd. Direct Mktg. Days in N.Y., N.Y.C., 1999. Bd. dirs. Quiambaug Fire Dist., Stonington, 1998-2002, pres., 2000-01; chmn. Mystic Outdoor Art Festival, 1999-2001. Mem. Direct Mktg. Assn., Photo Mktg. Assn. (wholesale/mail order com. 1998—), Mystic C. of C. (bd dirs. 1998—, v.p. 2000—), NPG/Buck Rogers. Avocations: motorcycling, skiing, photography. Office: Mystic Color Lab Inc PO Box 144 Masons Island Rd Mystic CT 06355-0144 E-mail: edmccabe@mysticcolorlab.com.

MCCABE, EDWARD R. B. academic administrator, educator, physician; b. Balt., Mar. 26, 1946; BA in Biology, Johns Hopkins U., 1967; PhD in Pharmacology, U. So. Calif., 1972, MD, 1974. Diplomate Am. Bd. Pediatrics. Resident in pediatrics U. Minn. Hosps., Mpls., 1974-76; pediatric metabolism fellow Sch. Medicine U. Colo., Denver, 1976-78, instr., asst. prof., assoc. prof. pediatrics Sch. Medicine, 1978-86; from assoc. prof. to prof. genetics, pediatrics Baylor Coll. Medicine, Houston, 1986-94; prof., chmn. dept. pediatrics Sch. Medicine UCLA, 1994—. Physician-in-chief Mattel Children's Hosp. at UCLA, 1995—; mem. med. genetics residency rev. com. Accreditation Coun. Grad. Med. Edn., 1993-97; chmn. conf. gaucher disease NIH, Bethesda, Md., 1994-96, mem. NICHD coun., Bethesda, 1995-99. Editor Biochem. and Molecular Medicine, 1990-97, Molecular genetics and Metabolism, 1998—. Chair sci. adv. bd. Hereditary Disease Found., L.A., 1998-99; chmn. Basil O'Connor Award March Dimes, White Plains, N.Y., 1997-99. Mem. Am. Acad. Pediatrics (chmn. com. genetics Elk Grove Village, Ill. 1987-91, co-founder, chmn. sect. genetics Elk Grove, 1990, 93-95), Am. Bd. Med. Genetics (diplomate, bd. dirs. 1992-97, pres. Bethesda 1995-96), Am. Soc. Human Genetics, Am. Fedn. Clin. Rsch., Am. Pediatric Soc., Am. Soc. Biochemistry and Molecular Biology, Am. Coll. of Med. Genetics (pres.-elect 1999-00; co-chair newborn screening task force, maternal and child health bur. 1999-2000; chair sec.'s adv. com. ge netic testing 1998—), Soc. Pediatric Rsch. (E. Mead Johnson award, 1993), Phi Kappa Phi (L.A.), Sigma Xi (L.A.), Alpha Omega Alpha (L.A.), Inst.Medicine. Achievements include first to describe the Continguous Gene Syndrome, Complex Glycerol Kinase Deficiency; first to extract DNA from blood in newborn screening blotters; first to set up molecular genetic diagonosis for sickle cell disease as part of newborn screening; developement of concept of molecular genetic triage of bacterial infection. Office: UCLA Sch Medicine Dept Pediatrics 22 412 MDCC 10833 Le Conte Ave Los Angeles CA 90095-3075*

MC CABE, GERARD BENEDICT, retired library administrator; b. N.Y.C., Jan. 22, 1930; s. Patrick Joseph and Margaret Irene (McDonald) McC.; m. Jacqueline L. Maloney, Aug. 3, 1963 (dec. 1987); children: Theresa Marie, Rebecca Mary. BA in English, Manhattan Coll., 1952; A.M. in Library Sci. (scholar), U. Mich., 1954; MA in English, Mich. State U., 1959. Asst. acquisitions dept. U. Nebr. Library, Lincoln, 1954-56; chief bibliog. acquisitions dept. Mich. State U. Library, East Lansing, 1956-58; librarian Inst. Community Devel. and Service, Mich. State U., 1958-59; acquisitions librarian U. S. Fla., Tampa, 1959-66, asst. dir. planning and devel., 1967-70; assoc. dir. U. Ark. Library, Fayetteville, 1966-67; dir. univ. libraries Va. Commonwealth U., Richmond, 1970-82; dir. libraries Clarion U. of Pa., 1982-95; ret., 1995; libr. cons., Wilmington, N.C., 1995—. Editor: The Smaller Academic Library: A Management Handbook, 1988, Operations Handbook for Small Academic Library, 1989, Academic Libraries in Urban and Metropolitan Areas, 1992; co-editor ann. pub. Advances in Libr. Adminstrn. and Orgn., vols. 1-12, Insider's Guide to Libr. Automation: Essays of Practical Experience, 1993, Acad. Librs.: Their Rationale and Role in Am. Higher Edn., 1995, Introducing and Managing Academic Library Automation Projects, 1996, Leadership for Academic Librarians, 1998, Planning for a New Generation of Public Library Buildings, 2000, The Modern Public Library Building, Managing Planning, 2002; contbr. articles to profl. jours. Mem. ALA, Southeastern Library Assn., Bibliog. Soc. Am. Home and Office: 408 Waveland Rd Baltimore MD 21228-4222 E-mail: bldlib@aol.com. *Consideration for others is a guiding principle for my personal and professional behavior. I, as a librarian, must have concern for those I serve. Their needs are my first and only interest, not success, not notoriety, only their service and their satisfaction.*

MC CABE, JOHN CHARLES, III, writer; b. Detroit, Nov. 14, 1920; s. Charles John and Rosalie (Dropiewski) McC.; m. Vija Valda Zarina, Oct. 19, 1962 (dec. 1984); children— Linard Peter, Sean Cahal and Deirdre Rose (twins); m. Rosina Lawrence, June 8, 1987 (dec. June 1997); m. Karen Jackson, Apr. 16, 1998. Ph.B., U. Detroit, 1947; M.F.A. in Theatre, Fordham U., 1948; PhD in English Lit, Shakespeare Inst., U. Birmingham, Eng., 1954. Instr. theatre Wayne State U., 1948-51, CCNY, 1955; mem. faculty N.Y. U., 1956-68, prof. dramatic art, chmn. dept., 1962-68; chmn. dept. drama and theatre arts Mackinac Coll., Mackinac Island, Mich., 1968-70. Founder The Sons of the Desert (group devoted to works Laurel and Hardy), 1963 Profl. actor, 1928—, producer-dir., Milford (Pa.) Playhouse, summers, 1948-53, prodr., N.Y.U. Summer Theatre, Sterling Forest, N.Y., 1963-65, author-in-residence, Lake Superior State Coll., Sault Ste. Marie, Mich., 1970-86; author: Mr. Laurel and Mr. Hardy, 1961, rev. edit., 1986, George M. Cohan: The Man Who Owned Broadway, 1973, The Comedy World of Stan Laurel, 1974, Laurel & Hardy, 1975, (with G.B. Harrison) Proclaiming the Word, 1976, Charles Chaplin, 1978, Grand Hotel: Mackinac Island, 1987, Babe: The Life of Oliver Hardy, 1990, The High, 1992, Cagney, 1997; ghostwriter James Cagney's autobiography, Cagney by Cagney, 1976. Served with USAAF, 1943-45, ETO. Mem. Shakespeare Assn. Am., Actors Equity Assn., Catholic Actors Guild Am., Baker St. Irregulars. Clubs: The Players (N.Y.C.), The Lambs (N.Y.C.). Home: PO Box 363 Mackinac Island MI 49757-0363 *At fourteen I learned from the Jesuits that one who knows both the function and beauty of an English sentence will be blessed life-long.*

MCCABE, JOHN L. lawyer; b. Chgo., Oct. 17, 1941; BA, U. Notre Dame, 1963; LLB, Harvard U., 1966. Bar: Ill. 1967, Colo. 1967. Ptnr. Davis, Graham & Stubbs, Denver. Office: Davis Graham & Stubbs 1550 Seventeenth St Ste 500 Denver CO 80202 E-mail: john.mccabe@dgslaw.com.

MCCABE, MARGARET CLARK, family nurse practitioner; b. Washington, Feb. 21, 1956; d. Philip R. and Jeanne M. (Cushing) C. ADN, Marymount Coll. Va., 1981; BSN, Cath. U. Am., 1986; MSN, FNP, Wilmington Coll., 1999. RN, D.C., Del.; cert. CPR instr.; cert. family nurse practitioner. Staff nurse, charge nurse med.-surg. unit Providence Hosp., Washington, 1981-84, staff nurse CCU, 1984-86; staff nurse critical care unit Beebe Med. Ctr., Lewes, Del., 1986-88, asst. nurse mgr., 1988-89, nurse mgr., 1989-91, edn. specialist patient/community staff edn., 1991-94; nurse Millville (Del.) Family Health Ctr. & Beebe Home Health Agy., 1995-98; clin. coord. Beebe Physician Network Inc., 1998-99, family nurse practitioner, 2000—. V.p. Cape unit Am. Heart Assn., Del., 1990-92; chair pub. edn. com. Ea. unit Am. Cancer Soc., Sussex County, 1989-95; family nurse practitioner migrant worker program Delmarva Rural Ministries; mem. Planned Parenthood of Del., 1999—, Delmarva Rural Ministries, Dover, Del. Mem. NAN, Am. Coll. Nurse Practitioners, Am. Acad. Nurse Practitioners, Am. Assn. Nurse Practitioners, Am. Hosp. Assn., Internat. Patient Edn. Coun., Am. Soc. Healthcare Edn. and Tng., Del. Nurses Assn., Del. Soc. Healthcare Edn. and Tng. (pres. 1992-94), Sigma Theta Tau. Home: 203 Banks Rd Millville DE 19970-9795 Office: Delmarva Rural Ministries 26 Wyoming Ave Dover DE 19904-6922

MCCABE, MARY WILLIAMSON, computer systems analyst; b. Memphis, Aug. 8, 1934; d. Edwin Lacey and Mary Maxine (Maners) Williamson; m. Henry Arthur McCabe, Sept. 22, 1973; stepchildren: Patrick, Anne, Kevin, Cathleen, John. BA, Rhodes Coll., 1956. Math. tchr. Bolton (Tenn.) High Sch., 1956-57; programmer/analyst Mallory AF Sta., Memphis, 1957-61; sr. systems specialist computer dept. GE, Huntsville, Ala., 1961-66; sr. systems specialist Honeywell Info. Systems, Phoenix, 1966-78, Honeywell Bull, Mpls., 1979-88. Pres. McCabe & Assocs., Inc., Minnetonka, Minn., 1990-91, v.p. 1992. Vol. Am. Cancer Soc., Minnetonka, 1980-91. Mem. Paradise Rep. Women's Club (cmty affairs chair 2001-02), Alpha Omicron Pi (v.p. Kappa Omicron chpt. 1955-56). Republican. Episcopalian. Avocations: reading, photography. Home: 15193 N 102d Way Scottsdale AZ 85255

MCCABE, MATTHEW CLARK, lawyer, forensic economist; b. New Hartford, N.Y., Nov. 22, 1958; s. Kenneth Ethan and Caroline Ruth McC.; m. Gayle Marie Grimaldi, June 6, 1981; childre: Catherine, Alexander, Jonathan, Matthew, Ethan. BA in Econs., SUNY, 1983; MBA, JD, Syracuse U., 1986. Bar: N.Y. 1988. Economist, assoc. atty., investment advisor Blitman & King, Syracuse, N.Y., 1986-88; forensic economist, investment advisor J.P. Jeannret Assocs., 1988-94; forensic economist North Main Cons., Jordan, 1994—. Presenter in field. Chmn. Village Jordan Planning Bd., 1989—. Mem. Nat. Assn. Forensic Econs., Am. Acad. Econ. and Fin. Experts, N.Y. State Bar Assn., Onondaga County Bar Assn., Ea. Econ. Assn., Home: 20 N Main St PO Box 298 Jordan NY 13080-0298 Office: North Main Cons 20 N Main St PO Box 921 Jordan NY 13080-0921

MCCABE, MICHAEL JOSEPH, JR. environmental scientist, educator; b. N.Y.C., June 17, 1962; s. Michael Joseph and Kaye Lorraine McCabe; m. Deborah Daigneault, Aug. 23, 1986; children: Conor, Evan. BS, Siena Coll., 1984; MS, Albany Med. Coll., PhD, 1990. Rschr. Dept. Toxicology, Stockholm, 1990—92; asst. prof. Wayne State U., Detroit, 1992—2000; asst. prof. dept. environ. med. U. Rochester, NY, 2000—. Mem.: Soc. Toxicology (Young Investigator award Immunotoxicology Specialty Sect. 2000). Roman Catholic. Home: 1495 Chigwell Ln N Webster NY 14580 Office: U Rochester 575 Elmwood Ave Rochester NY 14642 Business E-Mail: michael_mccabe@urmc.rochester.edu.

MCCABE, MONICA JANE, oncological nurse; b. Anaheim, Calif. d. Thurman Huston and Marcia Diane (Gandy) Walker; m. Roger Alan McCabe, July 27, 1985; children: Justin Robert, Sarah Jane. Assoc. Nursing, N.Mex. State U., Alamogordo, 1993. RN N.Mex., Ariz., cert. oncology nurse. Med.-surg. nurse Meml. Med. Ctr., Las Cruces, N.Mex., 1993-94; oncology nurse Dr. Bishnu Rauth, 1994-95; oncology and bone marrow transplant nurse Univ. Med. Ctr., Tucson, 1995-98, mem. reengring. core team, 1996; nurse clinician Nat. Med. Care Homecare, 1995-96; oncology nurse specialist Ariz. Oncology Assocs. divsn. U.S. Oncology, 1998-2000; sr. rsch. nurse Ariz. Cancer Ctr., U. Ariz., 2000—02; clin. rsch. monitor Protein Therapeutics, Inc., 2001—. Unit asst. liaison Univ. Med. Ctr., 1996—98, clin. practice com. cost containment com., 1997, Keystone computer trainer, 97, lectr. in oncology, 1997—98; computer cons. Meml. Med. Ctr., Las Cruces, 1994; mem. Caring Environ. Patient Edn. Team U. Med. Ctr., 1996; mem. Spkrs. Bur. for Better Bone Health for Breast Cancer Survivors, 1999—; mem. spkrs. bur. Omni Network, 2001—; clin. rsch. assoc., registry coord. Gaucher Registry, Boston, 1998—; lectr. in field. Mem.: ANA, So. Ariz. Oncology Nursing Soc. (pres.-elect 1999, pres. 2000, nominating chair 2001), N.Mex. Nurses Assn., Ariz. Nursing Assn., Oncology Nursing Soc. (cert. Oncology Nursing Cert. Corp. subs.). Avocations: ceramics, outdoor activities, computers. Home: 1018 W Placita Camillia Tucson AZ 85704-

MCCABE, NANCY G. English educator, writer; b. Wichita, Kans., Nov. 10, 1962; d. Bill J. McCabe and Frances Lucille West; 1 child, Sophie McCabe. BA, Wichita State U., 1984; MFA, U. Ark., Fayetteville, 1989; PhD, U. Nebr., 1995. Instr. U. Nebr., Lincoln, 1992-96; asst. prof. English Presbyn. Coll., Clinton, S.C., 1996-2001; dir. writing program U. Pitts., Bradford, 2001—. Author: Making Poems: Writing Exercises for the Classroom, 1988; contbr. essays, articles and short fiction to mags. and profl. jours. (Best Am. Essays Notable Essay 1998, 99, Pushcart Prize Best of Small Presses, 2000, numerous other awards). Home: 23 Sanford St Bradford PA 16701 Office: U Pitts Bradford 300 Campus Dr Bradford PA 16701 E-mail: ngm@pitt.edu.

MCCABE, RICHARD LEE, real estate developer; b. Cheyenne, Wyo., June 9, 1943; s. Thomas Junior and Alice May (Vernon) McC.; m. Janet Ann Lefkow (div.); children: Bradley Samuel, Kevin Ira; m. Julianne Clements, Dec. 22, 1979; children: Thomas Durant, Claire Angela Kim. BArch., U. Colo., 1967. V.p., sec. McSan Enterprises, Inc., Boulder, 1968-72; pres. Boulder (Colo.) Design & Tool Group, Inc., 1972-74; pvt. practice R.L. McCabe & Assocs., Boulder, 1974-77; pres. R.L.M. Inc., 1977-80, Cubit Corp., Boulder, 1980-84, Centermark Corp., Boulder, 1984-87, Cubit Constrn. Corp., Boulder, 1987-88, Core Corp., Boulder, 1988—. Dir. Boulder Builders Group, 1988-89, Nat. Fastpitch Assn., Mpls., 1990—; pres. Boulder County Builders Assn., 1990-91. Co-author: (mcpl. legislation) Community Housing Assistance Plan, 1991. Mem. Affordable Housing Task Force, Boulder, 1989, Thistle Community Housing Corp., Boulder, 1991; mem. steering com. North Boulder Subcmty., 1994. Recipient Svc. award Assn. Student Chpts. of AIA, 1966, award of appreciation City Boulder Housing Authority, 1989, cert. award Dept. Housing and Human Svcs., Boulder, 1990, cert. appreciation Boulder County Safehouse, 1991. Mem. Boulder County Chpt. of the Met. Denver Home Builders Assn. (pres. 1991-92), Congress for New Urbanism. Avocations: sailing, fishing, camping, hiking, river floating. Home: 526 Arapahoe Ave Boulder CO 80302-5827 Office: Core Corp 2041 Broadway St Fl 2 Boulder CO 80302-5202

MCCABE, ROBERT HOWARD, college president; b. Dec. 23, 1929; s. Joseph A. and Kathryn (Greer) McC.; m. Arva Moore Parks, June 1992. BEd, U. Miami (Fla.), 1952; MS, Appalachian State U., Boone, N.C., 1959; PhD, U. Tex., Austin, 1963; LLD (hon.), Barry U., 1986, U. Miami, 1990, Fla. Internat. U., 1990. Asst. to pres. Miami Dade C. of C., Fla., 1963-65, v.p., 1965-67, exec. v.p., 1969-80, pres., 1980-95, Essex County Coll., Newark, 1967-69; sr. fellow League for Innovation in the C.C., 1995—; Disting. fellow Edn. Commn. of the States, 2000—. Exec. com. So. Regional Edn. Bd., Atlanta, 1981-83; trustee Coll. Bd., chmn., 1988-90; vice chair The Miami Coalition for a Drug-Free Cmty., 1989-93, chair, 1991—. Author: Man and Environment, 1971, No One to Waste, 2000, Yes We Can, 2002, several monographs; contbr. ; editor: Jour. Environ. Edn.; cons. editor Change Mag., 1980—98. Bd. dirs. Nat. Ctr. Pub. Policy and Higher Edn., 1998—. Recipient Disting. Svc. award Fla. Congl. Del., 1983, Spirit of Excellence award The Miami Herald, 1988, Harold W. McGraw Jr. prize in Edn., 1991, The Coll. Bd. medal, 1995; named Outstanding Grad., Coll. Edn., U. Tex., 1982, named one of the 18 Most Effective Chief Exec. Officer in Am. Higher Edn. Bowling Green U., 1988; Disting. Svc. award Dade County, Fla., 1983; Kellogg fellow, 1962-63, MacArthur fellow John D. and Catherine T. MacArthur Found., 1992. Fellow League for Innovation in the C.C. (sr. fellow, dir. exec. com. 1985—, disting. svc. award 1995); mem. Am. Assn. C.C. (bd. dirs. 1991—, disting svc. award 1995), Am. Assn. Higher Edn. (dir. on Higher Edn. Issues, Higher Edn. Consortium), Am. Coun. Edn (dir. 1973-75), Am. Assn. for Environ. Edn. (pres. 1970-73), Am. Coun. on Edn. (bd. dirs. 1983-85, 92—), Southeast Fla. Edn. Consortium (chmn. bd. 1981-83). Episcopalian. Home: 1601 S Miami Ave Miami FL 33129-1103 E-mail: mccabe@telocity.com.

MCCABE, ROBERT JOHN, automotive industry executive; b. Cambridge, Mass., May 28, 1943; s. Francis Thomas and Luberta Marie (Harden) McC; m. Maureen Anne Miller (div. Jan. 1985); m. Susan Lynn Morton; children: Christa A., Kasey M., Kami J., John F., Katherine L. BS, Cornell U., 1967, MBA, 1970. Small bus. owner, Cambridge, 1961-63; with fin. mgmt. dept. Borg Warner Morse Chain, Ithaca, N.Y., 1965; from mid-mgmt. level to dir. treas. office GM, N.Y.C. and Detroit, 1970-81, asst. comptr., spl. asst. to group v.p. internat., 1981-82, asst. comptr. assembly divsn. Warren, Mich., 1982-84; asstr. comptr. Detroit Diesel Corp., Redford, 1984-86; chmn. bd. dirs., CEO Terex Equipment Ltd., Scotland, 1986-88; dir. fin. Packard Electric (now Delphi), Warren, Ohio, 1988-92; group dir. finance powertrain group GM, Pontiac, Mich., 1992-97, gen. dir. fin., svc. parts ops. Grand Blanc, 1997—. Bd. dirs. Flint-Genesee Econ. Growth Alliance, 1998—, Flint Area Conv. and Visitors Bur., 1998—, chmn. elect, 2001—. Mem. Flint-Genesee C. of C. (bd. dirs. 1998—, chmn. elect 2001—). Roman Catholic. Avocations: SCUBA diving, ice skating, skiing, sky diving, travel. Office: GM PO Box 6020 6200 Grand Pointe Dr Grand Blanc MI 48439-5501

MCCABE, STEVEN LEE, structural engineer; b. Denver, July 11, 1950; s. John L. and M. Leora (Shaw) McC.; m. Ann McCabe, Aug. 10, 1974; 1 child, Stephanie A. BSME, Colo. State U., 1972, MSME, 1974; PhD in Civil Engring., U. Ill., 1987. Registered profl. engr., Colo., Kans., Okla. Engr. Pub. Svc. Co. of Colo., Denver, 1974-77; sr. engr. R.W. Beck and Assocs., 1977-78; engr., project engr. Black & Veatch Cons. Engrs., Kansas City, Mo., 1978-81; asst. prof. civil engring. U. Kans., Lawrence, 1985-91, assoc. prof., 1991-98, prof., 1998—, chmn. dept. civil and environ. engring., 1998—2001, tchg. fellow, 1994—, chmn. dept. civil and environ. engring., 2001—. Vis. prof. structural engring. Norwegian Inst. Tech., Trondheim, 1995-96. Contbr. articles to profl. jours. Named Fulbright scholar U.S. Govt. to Norway, 1995-96, Ill. fellow, 1981-82; grantee Am. Inst. Steel Constrn., 1990-91, NSF, 1989-91, 91—, Civil Engring. Rsch. Found., 1991—; recipient Mech. Coupler Industry Testing Consortium Funding, 1992-95, Structural Rsch. Paper award Am. Concrete Inst., 1996. Fellow ACI (pres. Kans. chpt. 1992, reinforced concrete rsch. coun. 1999—, bldg. code com. 2002-); mem. ASME (pressure vessels and piping divsn. honor paper award 1989, cert. of recognition for svc. 1993), ASTM, ASCE (assoc. editor Jour. Structural Enging. 1992-94, chair com. concrete masonry structures, 2000—), Concrete Reinforcing Steel Inst., Am. Soc. Engring. Edn., Earthquake Engring. Rsch. Inst., Com. Euro-Internat. du Beton, Sigma Xi, Sigma Tau, Pi Tau Sigma, Phi Kappa Phi, Chi Epsilon. Republican. Roman Catholic. Achievements include development of relationships for bond and anchorage of reinforcing bars in concrete, industry specifications for headed reinforcing bars, improved damage mechanics techniques for prediction of earthquake effects on structures, seismic design criteria for power plants; research on inelastic cyclic behavior of reinforcing bars and mechanical splices, on structural dynamics and earthquake engineering as well as computational mechanics, on the evaluation of response and damage and predictions of reserve capacity in structures and members subjected to earthquake strong ground motion, on use of finite element analysis for the response of structures and machines to various types of loading. Office: U Kans 2006 Learned Hall Lawrence KS 66045-7526 E-mail: slmccabe@ku.edu.

MCCABE, THOMAS EDWARD, lawyer, business consultant; b. Washington, Jan. 22, 1955; s. Edward Aeneas and Janet Isabel McCabe; m. Kelly Marie McCarthy; children: Edward Charles, Benjamin Patrick, Adrienne Marie, Therese Eileen, Luke Stevens, Nicholas Joseph, Maximilian Karol. AB, Georgetown U., 1977; MBA, JD, U. Notre Dame, 1981. Bar: D.C. 1982, U.S. Dist. Ct. D.C. 1983, U.S. Ct. Appeals (D.C. cir.) 1983, Va. 1989, U.S. Supreme Ct. 1990. Law clk. U.S. Dist. Ct. Judge Hon. Charles R. Richey, Washington, 1981-82; assoc. Reavis & McGrath, 1982-84, Venable Baetjer Howard & Civiletti, Washington, 1984-85, McCarthy & Durrette, Washington, 1985-88; ptnr. McCarthy & Burke, 1988-91; sr. v.p., dir. corp. devel., gen. counsel, sec. GRC Internat., Inc., Vienna, 1992—2001; pres., CEO MicroBankx Sys., LLC, Bethesda, Md., 2000—. Republican. Roman Catholic. E-mail: tmccabe@tmccabe.net., tmccabe@microbanx.com.

MCCADDEN, JOSEPH A. lawyer; b. Mass., May 25, 1963; m. Kelly McCadden. BA, Northeastern U., Boston, MA, 1986; JD, Suffolk U., 1994. Bar: (Mass.) 1994. V.p. optics divsn. Acton (Mass.) Rsch. Corp., 1998—2001, v.p. fin. and adminstrn., 2001—. Office: Acton Rsch Corp 530 Main St Acton MA 02056 Business E-Mail: mccadden@acton-research.com.

MCCAFFERTY, JAMES ARTHUR, sociologist; b. Columbus, Ohio, Jan. 1, 1926; s. James A. and Marjorie Agatha (Gilchrist) McC.; m. Jane Roush, June 13, 1948 (dec. Oct. 1984); children: Lucinda Jane Martin, James Stanley Thomas, Bridget Anne Roush Green; m. Carolyn Ring Bradley, Nov. 7, 1987 (div. Apr. 1992); m. Irma Mae Prosser Nicholson, May 28, 1993 (dec. Nov. 1996). BS, Ohio State U., 1948, MA, 1954; postgrad., Am. U. Social rsch. analyst Ohio State Dept. Pub. Welfare, 1948-51; criminologist U.S. Bur. Prisons, Washington, 1951-63; ast. chief divsn. info. sys. Adminstrv. Office of U.S. Cts., 1963-77, chief statis. analysis and reports divsn., 1977-86; ret. Vis. lectr. Am. U., 1959, 62-64; adj. instr. Fordham U., 1978-89. Editor: Capital Punishment, 1972; contbr. articles on criminology and correctional stats. to profl. jours. Life mem. Md. State PTA; past pres. Potomac area coun. Camp Fire Girls of U.S., 1966-67; v.p. Prince George's County (Md.) Coun. PTAs, 1964-65; chmn. Prince George's County Youth Commn., 1970-72; past pres. Hypoglycemia Assn., past pres. Interfaith Cmty. Action Coun., Inc., 1991-93. Cpl. USAAF, 1944-46. Recipient Vol. award Prince George's Co., Md., 1992. Mem. AAUP, NSSAR (v.p. gen. MidAtlantic dist. 2002-), Md. Soc. SAR (life, past pres., trustee), Am. Sociol. Assn., Am. Correctional Assn. (life), Assn. Correctional Rsch. and Info. Mgmt. (life, past pres., Ronald H. Beattie award 1997), Nat. Geneal. Soc., Nat. Assn. Retired Fedl. Employees (life), Am. Statis. Assn., Prince George's County Geneal. Soc. (life, past pres.), Ohio Geneal. Soc. (life), Nat. Capital Buckeye chpt., former editor newsletter), Judicature Soc., Md. State Beekeepers Assn. (life), DAV (life), Sons of Union Vets. Civil War (life, past camp comdr., former editor), Am. Legion (life), Army Airways Com. Sys. (life), Gallia County (Ohio) Hist. Geneal. Soc. (life), Nat. Congress Patriotic Orgns. (life, recorder), Germany Soc. SAR (sec. 2001—). Presbyterian. Home: 613 Rosier Rd Fort Washington MD 20744-5554 E-mail: jirma@aol.com.

MCCAFFERTY, OWEN EDWARD, accountant, dental-veterinary practice consultant; b. Cleve., Sept. 5, 1952; s. Owen James and Ann Theresa (Barrett) McC.; m. Colleen Maura Mullen, Aug. 3, 1974; children: Owen Michael, Hugh Anthony, Maura Kathleen, Bridget Colleen. AB, Xavier U., 1974. CPA, Ohio, Ga., S.C., Tex., Nev.; diplomate Am. Coll. Forensic Acctg.; cert. vet. practice mgr. Mem. staff to sr. accountant Deloitte, Haskins, & Sells, Cleve., 1974-78; ptnr., pres. Douglas, McCafferty & Co., Inc., Rocky River, Ohio, 1978-86; pres. Owen E. McCafferty, CPA, Inc., North Olmsted, 1986—, McCafferty/Beach Devel., Inc., North Olmsted, 1989—, Anicare N.Am., Inc., 1994—, McCafferty/Beach Devel., Inc., North Olmsted, 1989—, Anicare N.Am., Inc., 1994—. Lectr. various vet. and dental assns.; cons. in field; mng. ptnr. McCafferty/Beach Real Estate Ventures, 1988—; pres. Virtual Profl. Publ. Inc., 1997—; mng. unit holder Prescott/McCafferty Initiative, LLC; asst. treas. Vet. Study Groups, Inc. Co-author: The Business of Veterinary Practice, 1993; mem. editl. adv. bd. Vet. Econs. Mag., 1977-97, Vet. Bus., 1999—; contbr. articles to acctg. and vet. jours.; co-author audiotape vet. practice mgmt. series, 1997; mem. editl. bd. Vet. Bus. Jour., 1999—. Mem. fin. com. St. Richard Parish, 1987-95, chmn. budgeting com., 1991-95. Recipient Meritorious Service award Ohio Vet. Med. Assn., 1986, Am. Animal Hosp. Assn. award, 1988. Mem. AICPA (pvt. cos. practice sect., mgmt. cons. divsn., tax divsn.), Ohio Soc. CPAs (chmn. mgmt. adv. svcs. com. Cleve. chpt. 1987-89), mem. liaison com.), Vet. Hosp. Mgrs. Assn. (pres. 1993), Vet. Practice Mgrs. Assn. Gt. Britain and Republic of Ireland (hon. life), Am. Soc. Appraisers (candidate), Am. Coll. Forensic Examiners. Democrat. Roman Catholic. Office: PO Box 819 North Olmsted OH 44070-0819 E-mail: omccaffert@aol.com.

MCCAFFERTY, ROBERT HENRY, computer scientist; b. Wilmington, Del., July 8, 1956; s. Robert Henry and Mary Cecelia (O'Connor) McC.; m. Diane Elaine Czop, June 6, 1981; children: James Daniel, Elaine duRoss. BS in Mech. Engr., U. Va., 1979, MS in Mech. Engring., 1980, MCS, 1982. Research project engr. Scott Paper Co., Phila., 1979-80; research asst. Rotating Machinery and Con. Labs., Charlottesville, Va., 1980-81; sr. assoc. engr. IBM, Burlington, Vt., 1981-87, staff engr., 1988—. Contbr. articles to profl. jours. Served with USN, 1974-76. Polish National Catholic. Avocations: scuba diving, cross country skiing, antique Mercedes restoration. Home: 404 Meadowood Dr Jericho VT 05465

MCCAFFREY, BARRY RICHARD, federal official, retired army officer; b. Taunton, Mass., Nov. 17, 1942; s. William Joseph and Mary Veronica (Curtin) McC.; m. Jill Ann Faulkner, June 8, 1964; children: Sean, Tara, Amy. BS, U.S. Mil. Acad., 1964; MA, Am. U., 1971; postgrad., Command and Gen. Staff Coll., Ft. Leavenworth, Kans., 1976, Army War Coll., Carlisle Barracks, Pa., 1982. Commd. 2d lt. U.S. Army, 1964, advanced through grades to full gen., 1994; co. comdr. 7th Cav. Div., Vietnam, 1968-69; assoc. prof. dept. social sci. U.S. Mil. Acad., West Point, NY, 1972-75; from chief ops. br. to comdt. 2d battalion 3d Inf. Div., Germany, 1976-81; from chief staff to comdt. 3d brigade 9th Inf. Div., Ft. Lewis, Wash., 1982-86, comdr. 3d brigade, 1984-86; asst. comdt. U.S. Army Inf. Sch., Ft. Benning, Ga., 1986-88; dep. U.S. mil. rep. NATO, Brussels, 1988-89; div. comdr. 24th Inf. Div., Ft. Stewart, Ga., 1990-92; asst. to chmn. Joint Chiefs of Staff, Washington, 1992-93; dir. strategic plans and policy directory The Joint Staff, 1993-94; comdr. in chief U.S. So. Commd., Quarry Heights, Panama, 1994-96; dir. White Ho. Office Nat. Drug Control Policy, Washington, 1996—2001; Olin disting. prof. nat. security studies U.S. Mil. Acad., 2001—; pres. B.R. McCaffrey Assocs., LLC, Alexandria, Va., 2001—. Contbr. articles to mil. publs. Decorated D.S.C. with oak leaf cluster, D.M.S. with oak leaf cluster, Silver Star with oak leaf cluster, Def. Superior Svc. Medal. Mem. NAACP, Assn. of U.S. Army, Coun. of Fgn. Rels., Inter-Am. Dialogue, Legion of Valor of U.S. Avocations: hunting, reading military history. Office: BR McCaffrey Assocs Ste 600 1800 Diagonal Rd Alexandria VA 22314

MCCAFFREY, JOHN ANTHONY, brokerage house executive; b. Bklyn., June 16, 1944; s. Bernard and Ann Florence (Sweeney) McC.; m. Cynthia Elizabeth Bushek, Nov. 6, 1965; children: Tara, Heather. BBA, Pace U., 1975. Asset liability mgr. Bank of Montreal, N.Y.C., 1964-77; mgr., corp. bond trader Midland Doherty, Inc., 1977-78; corp. bond trader Burns, Fry & Timmons, 1978-81; 1st v.p. Cantor, Fitzgerald, Inc., 1981-87; exec. v.p. Brokerage Corp. of Am., 1987-89; 1st v.p. Cantor, Fitzgerald, Inc., 1989-97. Mem. Vols. for Wildlife, Cold Spring Harbor, N.Y., 1985—, The Nature Conservancy, 1988—. Cpl. USMC, 1965-67, Vietnam. Mem. Am. Legion. Roman Catholic. Avocations: travel, gardening. Home: 32 Marilyn Blvd Plainview NY 11803-1945

MCCAFFREY, JOHN P. protective services official; b. Hornell, N.Y., Feb. 23, 1949; AAS in Criminal Justice, Erie C.C., Buffalo, 1970. With N.Y. State Police, 1970-94, sr. investigator, 1994; U.S. marshal U.S. Ct., Western dist. N.Y., 2nd cir., Rochester, 1994—. Office: Office of US Marshal US Courthouse 100 State St Rochester NY 14614-1350

MCCAFFREY, JUDITH ELIZABETH, lawyer; b. Providence, Apr. 26, 1944; d. Charles V. and Isadore Frances (Langford) McC.; m. Martin D. Minsker, Dec. 31, 1969 (div. May 1981); children: Ethan Hart Minsker, Natasha Langford Minsker. BA, Tufts U., 1966; JD, Boston U., 1970. Bar: Mass. 1970, D.C. 1972, Fla. 1991. Assoc. Sullivan & Worcester, Washington, 1970-76; atty. FDIC, 1976-78; assoc. Dechert, Price & Rhoads, 1978-82, McKenna, Conner & Cuneo, Washington, 1982-83; gen. counsel, corp. sec. Perpetual Savs. Bank, FSB, Alexandria, Va., 1983-91; ptnr. Powell, Goldstein, Frazer & Murphy, Washington, 1991-92, McCaffrey & Raimi, P.A., 1992—. Contbr. articles to profl. jours. Mem. Leadership Collier, 1998. Mem. ABA (chairperson subcom. thrift instns. 1985-90), Fed. Bar Assn. (exec. com., banking law com. 1985-91), D.C. Bar Assn. (bd. govs. 1981-85), Fla. Bar Assn. (chmn. fin. svcs. com. 1999-2000), Women's Bar Assn. D.C. (pres. 1980-81), Collier County Women's Bar Assn. (pres. 1997-98). Episcopalian. Avocations: golf, travel, sailing, reading. Home: PO Box 2081 Naples FL 34106-2081 Office: McCaffrey & Raimi PA 5811 Pelican Bay Blvd Ste 206-A Naples FL 34108-2710

MCCAFFREY, ROBERT HENRY, JR. retired manufacturing company executive; b. Syracuse, N.Y., Jan. 20, 1927; s. Robert Henry and May Ann (McGuire) McC.; m. Dorothy Anne Evers, Sept. 22, 1956; children: Michael Robert, Kathleen Mary. BS, Syracuse U., 1949. Sales asst. Sealright Corp., Fulton, N.Y., 1949-50; with TEK Hughes div. Johnson & Johnson, Metuchen, N.J., 1950-67, gen. sales mgr., 1958-59, v.p. sales, 1959-62, pres., 1962-67; gen. mgr. med. div. Howmet Corp., N.Y.C., 1967-70; group v.p. Howmedica, Inc., 1970-73, sr. v.p., 1973-74, exec. v.p., also bd. dirs., 1974-76; pres., CEO C.R. Bard, Inc., Murray Hill, N.J., 1976-78, chmn. bd. dirs., CEO, 1978-89, chmn. bd., 1989-91, also bd. dirs., chmn. exec. com., 1991—. Bd. dirs. Summit and Elizabeth Trust, Summit Bancorp, Thomas & Betts Corp. Trustee Found. for Univ. Medicine and Dentistry N.J., 1987-90, Syracuse U., 1979—, chmn. corp. adv. council, 1974-75. With AUS, 1945-46. Mem. Orthopedic Surg. Mfrs. Assn., Health Industry Mfrs. Assn. (bd. dir., chmn. 1982-83), N.Y. Sales Execs. Club, Algonquin Club (Boston), Baltusrol Golf Club (Springfield, N.J.), Oyster Harbors Club (Osterville, Mass.), Sigma Chi. Republican. Roman Catholic. Avocations: reading, skiing, golf. Office: C R Bard Inc 730 Central Ave New Providence NJ 07974

MCCAGHY, CHARLES HENRY, sociology educator; b. Eau Claire, Wis., Apr. 29, 1934; s. Elmer and Anna Josephine (Soha) McC.; m. M. Dawn Ysebaert, June 10, 1961 BBA, U. Wis., 1956, MS, 1962, Ph.D, 1966. Instr. sociology U. Conn., 1964-66; asst. prof. sociology Case Western Res. U., Cleve., 1966-70; assoc. prof. sociology Bowling Green State U., Ohio, 1970-76, prof., 1976-94, prof. emeritus, 1994—. Vis. scholar Australian Inst. Criminology, 1984 Author: Deviant Behavior: Crime, Conflict and Interest Groups, 1976, 5th edit., 2000, Crime in American Society, 1980, 2d edit., 1987. Lt. (j.g.) USN, 1956-59 Mem. Am. Soc. Criminology (treas. 1978-82), Popular Culture Assn. Home: 221 Williams St Bowling Green OH 43402-3259

MCCAIG, JEFFREY JAMES, transportation company executive; b. Moose Jaw, Sask., July 5, 1951; s. John Robert and Anne Shorrocks (Glass) McC.; m. Marilyn Graves, July 7, 1983; children: Robbert Angus, Scott Thomas, Christa Mae. Student, Can. Jr. Coll. Lausanne, Switzerland, 1970; AB, Harvard Coll., 1973; LLB, Osgoode Hall Law Sch., Can., 1976; MSc in Mgmt., Leland Stanford Jr. U., 1984. Assoc. MacKimmie Matthews, 1976-81; owner, sr. officer Jeffrey J. McCaig Profl. Corp., 1981-83; v.p. planning and corp. devel. Trimac, Calgary, Canada, 1983—87, exec. v.p., 1987—90, pres., 1990—94, pres., CEO, 1994—. Bd. dirs. Bovar, Inc., Trimac Corp., Potash Corp. of Sask, EnerVest Group, Seamans Drilling Inc.; adv. bd. Weldwood of Can. Ltd. Mem. Law Soc. Alta., Young Pres.'s Orgn., Calgary Golf and Country Club, Calgary Petroleum Club, Glencoe Club, 400 Club. Home: 708 Riverdale Ave SW Calgary AB Canada T2S OY3 Office: Trimac Corp 800 5 Ave SW Ste 2100 Calgary AB Canada T2P 5A3

MCCAIN, DAVID B. lawyer; b. 1961; AB, Brown U., 1983; JD, U. Miami, 1986. Bar: Fla., 1986. V.p., gen. counsel Lennar Corp., Miami, Fla. Mem. ABA. Office: Lennar Corp 700 NW 107th Ave Ste 400 Miami FL 33172-3154 E-mail: dmccain@lennar.com.

MCCAIN, JOHN SIDNEY, III, senator; b. Panama Canal Zone, Aug. 29, 1936; s. John Sidney and Roberta (Wright) McC.; m. Cindy Hensley, May 17, 1980; children: Doug, Andy, Sidney, Meghan, Jack, Jimmy, Bridget. Grad. U.S. Naval Acad., 1958; grad., Nat. War Coll., 1973-74. Commd. ensign U.S. Navy, 1958, capt., navy pilot, 1977; prisoner of war Hanoi, Vietnam, 1967-73; dir. Navy Senate Liaison Office, Washington, 1977-81; mem. U.S. Ho. Reps. 98th-99th Congress from 1st Ariz. Dist., 1982-86; senator from Ariz. U.S. Senate, 1986—, mem. armed svcs. com., chmn. commerce, sci. and transp. com. chmn., Indian affairs com. Decorated Legion of Merit; decorated Silver Star, Bronze Star, Purple Heart, D.F.C., Vietnamese Legion of Honor Mem. Am. Legion, VFW Republican. Episcopalian. Office: US Senate 241 Russell Office Bldg. Washington DC 20510*

MCCAIN, LYNNE ANNETTE, counselor; b. St. Augustine, Fla., July 13, 1961; d. Robert George and Mildred (Cone) McC. BSN, Duke U., 1983. Cert. BCLS, RN, Ga. Nurse hemotology/oncology to nurse plastic surgery Emory Clinic, Atlanta, 1985-86, patient counselor, educator, 1986-97; clin. coord. PIP USA, Miami, 1997-98, v.p. clin. studies, 1998-2000; dir. clin. ops. Sebbin Labs., Atlanta, 2000—01; clin. rsch. assoc. Kendle Internat., 2002—. Founder, coord. Image Reborn, 1988—. Contbr. articles to profl. jours. Founder, coord. Image Reborn Nat. Support Group, 1988—. Recipient 2d place writing award Plastic Surgery Nursing Jour. Mem. Am. Soc. Plastic and Reconstructive Surgery Nurses (co-chmn. southeastern dist. 1990, exec. bd. 1995, 96, Nurse of Yr. 1994).

MCCAIN, MARVIN ENLOE, real estate developer; b. Lineville, Ala., Nov. 9, 1923; s. Reuben Glover and Annie Martin McCain; m. Lenda Haynes McCain, May 19, 1949; children: Eleanor Annie, Allen Haynes. BA, Vanderbilt U., 1950, MA, 1953. Tchr., prin. Bill Arp Elem. Sch., Douglasville, Ga., 1951—52; tchr., asst. prin. Midway Elem. Sch., Rome, 1952—53; asst. prin. Jinks Jr. H.S., Panama City, Fla., 1953—61; prin. West Bay Sch., 1961—62, Callaway Elem. Sch., Panama City, 1962—70, Mosley H.S., Panama City, 1975—85; asst. supt. Bay County Schs., 1970—75; pres. Marlen Developers, 1985—. Cpl. U.S. Army, 1942—46, ETO. Mem.: Sons Confederate Vets., SAR (pres.), Lynn Haven Rotary Club (pres.). Republican. Presbyterian. Avocations: golf, hunting, fishing, travel. Home: 712 W Pierson Dr Lynn Haven FL 32444 Office: Marlen Developers 712 W Pierson Dr Lynn Haven FL 32444 Fax: 850-265-1924. E-mail: Marvinm923@aol.com.

MCCAIRNS, REGINA CARFAGNO, pharmaceutical executive; b. Phila., Dec. 23, 1951; d. Carmen Augustus and Regina Mary (Yost) Carfagno; m. Robert Gray McCairns Jr., Nov. 6, 1982. BS, Marymount Manhattan Coll., 1973; MS, Villanova U., 1976; cert. bus., U. Pa., 1982; MS, Temple U., 2001. Rsch. asst. Temple U. Med. Coll., Phila., 1975-77; mfg. supr. William H. Rorer, Ft. Washington, 1977-79; from mgmt. trainee, tech. asst. to validation coord. SmithKline & French Labs., Phila., 1979-87; mgr. validation svcs. SmithKline Beecham, 1987-96; quality assurance investigator pharm. tech. Glaxo Smith Kline, Upper Providence, 1996—99. Trustee Country Day Sch. of the Sacred Heart, 1993—99, PDA Sci. Found., 1997—. Mem. Parenteral Drug Assn. (bd. dirs. 1985-92, chmn. spring program 1988, 90, chmn. tng. com. 1986-88, chmn. nat. program com. 1990-93), Jefferson Med. Coll. Faculty Wives Club (v.p. 1988-90, program chmn., 1988-90, pres.-elect 1990-92, pres. 1992-94). Democrat. Roman Catholic. Avocations: golf, books. Office: Glaxo Smith Kline 1250 S Collegeville Rd Collegeville PA 19426-9100 E-mail: regina_c_mccairns@gsk.com.

MCCALEB, ANNETTE WATTS, executive secretary; b. Darbfork, Ky., Dec. 11, 1931; d. Benjamin Taylor and Suzanna Elizabeth (White) Watts; m. John Henry McCaleb, Oct. 23, 1962; children: Jonathan Jeffrey, Suzanna Elizabeth McCaleb Woodhead, Sarah Leslie McCaleb James. BS, U. Ky., 1954. Med. technologist Good Samaritan, Lexington, Ky., 1953-54; lab. supr. Charleston (W.Va.) Meml., 1954-58; chief med. technologist Meml. Hosp., Indpls., 1958-63; assoc. prof. UAMC, Little Rock, 1963-66; sec., treas., co-owner John H. McCaleb Constrn., Inc., 1966—. Justice of the peace Pulaski County Quorum Ct., Ark., 1989—; state bd. dirs. F.L.A.G., 1989-98. Mem. S.W. Kiwanis (pres.-elect 1997—), Pulaski County Property Owners Assn. (pres. 1990-92). Democrat. Baptist. Avocations: reading, crossword puzzles, gardening, sewing, swimming. Home and Office: 3900 Annette Ct Little Rock AR 72206-5357 Fax: 501-888-3462. E-mail: annmccaleb@msn.com.

MCCALEB, GARY DAY, university official; b. Anson, Tex., Nov. 2, 1941; s. Victor Earl and Vivian (Day) McC.; m. Sylvia Ravanelli, June 5, 1964; children: Cara Lee Cranford, Bryan Day. BA, Abilene Christian Coll., 1964; MBA, Tex. A&M U., 1975, PhD, 1979. Asst. dir. alumni rels. Abilene (Tex.) Christian U., 1964-65, dir. alumni rels., 1965-69, dir. coll. rels., 1969-73, asst. acad. dean, 1978-80, v.p. pub. rels., 1980-83, v.p., dean campus life, 1983-91, v.p., 1991—, exec. dir. Ctr. for Bldg. Cmty., 1999—; asst. dir. devel. Tex. A&M U., Bryan, 1973-75. Leader internat. travel and goodwill groups; U.S. rep. to world exec. com. Internat. Union Local Authorities, 1996-99. Author: Community, The Gift of Community. Coun. mem. City of Abilene, 1985-90, mayor, 1990-99; bd. dirs. Taylor County Am. Cancer Soc., 1972-73; mem. adv. bd. United Way of Abilene, 1979-83, dir. pub. svc. divsn., 1987, chmn. consortium on drug and alcohol abuse, 1989; bd. dirs. Civic Abilene, Inc., 1981-83; treas. Abilene Task Force on Drug and Alcohol Abuse, 1984-86; active March of Dimes; mem. Tex. Sci. and Tech. Coun., 1997-2000. Recipient Polit. Courage award John Ben Shepperd Pub. Leadership Forum, Austin, Tex., 1993, Tex. Urban Leadersip award U. Tex.-Arlington Sch. Urban and Pub. Affairs, 1995. Mem. Nat. League Cities (nat. steering com. on fin., adminstrn. and intergovtl. rels. 1989-90, adv. bd. 1994, bd. dirs. 1992-94), U.S. Conf. Mayors, Internat. Mcpl. Consortium (chmn. 1994-95), Tex. Mcpl. League (legis. policy com. Houston 1986, resolutions com. Dallas 1988, v.p. region 6 1988-89, bd. dirs. 1989-90, pres. 1992), Abilene C. of C. (aviation com. 1981, 94). Republican. Mem. Ch. of Christ. Avocations: art, baseball, jogging. Office: Abilene Christian Univ PO Box 29136 Abilene TX 79699-0001 E-mail: mccalebg@acu.edu.

MCCALEB, JOE WALLACE, lawyer; b. Nashville, Dec. 9, 1941; s. J.W. McCaleb and Majorie June (Hudson) DePriest; m. Glenda Jean Queen, June 26, 1965. BA, Union U., 1964; JD, Memphis State U., 1970; MSEL cum laude, Vt. Law Sch., 1995. Bar: Tenn. 1971, U.S. Dist. Ct. (mid. dist.) Tenn. 1977, U.S. Ct. Appeals (6th cir.) 1984, U.S. Supreme Ct. 1978. Law clk. to presiding justice Tenn. Supreme Ct., Memphis, 1970-71; staff atty. Tenn. Dept. of Pub. Health Bur. Environ. Svcs., Nashville, 1971-77; pvt. practice Hendersonville, Tenn., 1977-94, 96—. Chmn. Hendersonville Recycling Com., 1990-91. Mem. ATLA, Tenn. Bar Assn., Sierra Club (chmn. local chpt. 1980-81, chmn. mid.-Tenn. group 1989-90, 93-94, chmn. water quality com., co-chmn. forestry com.), Tenn. Environ. Coun. (v.p. 1987-88, conservation adv. 1991-92), Defenders of Wildlife, Tenn. Forest Def. Coun., Save Our Cumberland Mountains. Democrat. Avocations: wilderness backpacking, photography, forestry, environmental protection. Home and Office: 100 Colonial Dr Hendersonville TN 37075-3205

MCCALEB, MALCOLM, JR. lawyer; b. Evanston, Ill., June 4, 1945; BA, Colgate U., 1967; JD, Northwestern U., 1971. Bar: Ill. 1971. Atty. McCaleb, Lucas & Brugman, Chgo., 1970—85; ptnr. Keck, Mahin & Cate, 1985—95, Foley & Lardner, Chgo., 1995—2000, Barack Ferrazzano Kirschbaum Perlman & Nagelberg, LLC, Chgo., 2000—. Chmn. Northfield (Ill.) Village Caucus, 1981-82, active, 1977-82, Northfield Zoning Commn., 1985-88; pres. bd. dirs. Vols. Am., 1977-79; active Northfield Sch. and Park Bd. Caucus, 1980-87. Mem. Chgo. Bar Assn., Bar Assn. 7th Fed. Cir., Patent Law Assn. Chgo., Internat. Trademark Assn. Office: Barack Ferrazzano Kirschbaum Perlman & Nagelberg LLC 333 W Wacker Dr Chicago IL 60606 Business E-Mail: mac.mccaleb@bfkpn.com.

MCCALEB, NEAL, federal agency administrator; b. Oklahoma City; m. Georgann McCaleb; 4 children. BS in Civil Engring., Okla. State U. Sec. transp. Dept. Transp., Okla., 1987—91, 1995—2001; asst. sec. Bur. Indian Affairs, U.S. Dept. Interior, Washington, 2001—. Mem. Okla. Ho. of Reps., minority floor leader, 1978. Office: US Dept Interior Bur Indian Affairs 1849 C St NW Washington DC 20240*

MCCALL, BRIAN PATRICK, industrial relations educator; b. Evanston, Ill., Apr. 19, 1959; s. John Joseph and Kathleen Dorothy (Arvidson) McC.; m. Toni A. McCall, Aug. 25, 1984; children: Megan, Conor. BA, UCLA, 1981; MA, Princeton U., 1986, PhD, 1988. Asst. prof. dept. indsl. rels. Carlson Sch. Mgmt., U. Minn., Mpls., 1988—. Contbr. articles to profl. jours. Mem. Phi Beta Kappa. Avocations: baseball card collecting, running. Office: U Minn Indsl Rels Ctr 271 19th Ave S Minneapolis MN 55455-0430 Home: 1902 Highland Pkwy Saint Paul MN 55116-1327

MC CALL, CHARLES BARNARD, health facility executive, educator; b. Memphis, Nov. 2, 1928; s. John W. and Lizette (Kimbrough) McC.; m. Carolyn Jean Rosselot, June 9, 1951; children: Linda, Kim, Betsy, Cathy. BA, Vanderbilt U., 1950, MD, 1953. Diplomate: Am. Bd. Internal Medicine (pulmonary diseases). Intern Vanderbilt U. Hosp., Nashville, 1953-54; clin. assoc., sr. asst. surgeon USPHS, Nat. Cancer Inst., NIH, 1954-56; sr. asst. resident in medicine U. Ala. Hosp., 1956-57, chief resident, 1958-59; fellow chest diseases Nat. Acad. Scis.-NRC, 1957-58; instr. U. Ala. Med. Sch., 1958-59; asst. prof., then assoc. prof. medicine U. Tenn. Med. Sch., 1959-69, chief pulmonary diseases, 1964-69; mem. faculty U. Tex. System, Galveston, 1969-75, prof. medicine med. br., 1971-73; assoc. prof. medicine Health Sci. Center, Southwestern Med. Sch., Dallas, 1973-75, also assoc. dean clin. programs, 1973-75; dir. Office Grants Mgmt. and Devel., 1973-75; dean, prof. medicine U. Tenn. Coll. Medicine, 1975-77, Oral Roberts U. Sch. Medicine, Tulsa, 1977-78; interim assoc. dean U. Okla. Tulsa Med. Coll., 1978-79; clin. prof. medicine U. Colo. Med. Sch., Denver, 1979-80; prof. medicine, assoc. dean U. Okla. Med. Sch., 1980-82; exec. dean and dean U. Okla. Coll. Medicine, 1982-85; v.p. patient affairs, prof. medicine U. Tex. M.D. Anderson Cancer Ctr., 1985-94; chief of staff VA Med. Center, Oklahoma City, 1980-82. Exec. dir. Worldwide Healthcare Svcs., Inc., Waco, Tex., 1998—2002; clinic dir. Claremore Family Medicine, 2002, cons., 02; bd. dirs. Amigos Internacionales, Inc. Contbr. articles to med. jours. Fellow ACP, Am. Coll. Chest Physicians; mem. AMA, Am. Thoracic Soc., So. Thoracic Soc. (pres. 1968-69), Am. Fedn. Clin. Rsch., Sigma Xi, Alpha Omega Alpha. Baptist. Home: 1011 Douglas Dr Claremore OK 74017-6626 Office: 1402 N Florence Claremore OK 74017 E-mail: mccallcharles@msn.com.

MCCALL, DAVID WARREN, retired chemistry research director, consultant; b. Omaha, Dec. 1, 1928; s. H. Bryron and Grace (Cox) McC.; m. Charlotte Marion Dunham, July 30, 1955; children: William Christopher, John Dunham BS, U. Wichita, 1950; MS, U. Ill., 1951, PhD, 1953. Mem. tech. staff AT&T Bell Labs, Murray Hill, N.J., 1953-62, head dept. phys. chemistry NJ, 1962-69, asst. chem. dir., 1969-73, dir. chem. rsch. lab., 1973-91, dir. environ. chemistry rsch. N.J., 1991-92. Chmn. bd. trustees Gordon Rsch. Confs.; mem. adv. bd. Chem. Abstract Svcs.; chmn. Nat. Commn. on Super-conductivity; chmn. panels on advanced composites, electronic packaging, fire suppression for USN, and shipboard pollution control NRC; mem. Naval Studies Bd. Fellow: AAAS, Royal Soc. Chemistry London, Am. Phys. Soc.; mem.: AICE, NAE (chmn. materials engring. sect., chmn. membership com.), Am. Chem. Soc. (com. on chemistry and pub. affairs, Barnes award 1992). Home: 12 Polo Club Rd Far Hills NJ 07931-2467 E-mail: D1MCCALL@AOL.COM.

MCCALL, DAVY HENDERSON, economics educator, consultant; b. Cleve., June 30, 1922; s. James Henderson and Rachel Jane (Kennedy) McC.; m. Alice J. Bacon, June 1949 (div. Nov. 1950). AB, Kenyon Coll., 1944; MA, Harvard U., 1948, PhD, 1962. Instr. Western Res. U., Cleve., 1949-50; internat. affairs officer Dept. of State, Washington, 1950-53; internat. economist Fgn. Ops. Adminstrn., 1953-56, Phnom Penh, Cambodia, 1958-60; asst. mgr. Brownell-Lane Internat., Saigon, Republic of Vietnam, 1956; instr. San Francisco State Coll., 1957-58; budget examiner U.S. Bur. of Budget, Washington, 1960-65; internat. economist U.S. Agy. Internat. Devel., 1965-68, loan officer Damascus, Syria, 1976-84, World Bank, Washington, 1968-76; chmn. dept. econs. Washington Coll., Chestertown, Md., 1984—93. Team leader evaluation project Integrated Rural Devel., Burkina Faso, 1984; chmn. Low Income Housing Fund, Chestertown, 1986—91, Episcopal Diocese Low Income Housing Task Force, Easton, 1986—88; v.p. Preservation, Inc., Chestertown, 1985—; vestryman St. Paul's Ch. Kent County, 1985—88, Emmanuel Ch., 1998—2000. With U.S. Army, PTO. Mem.: Md. Club (Balt.), DACOR Club (Washington). Home: 109 S Queen St Chestertown MD 21620-1521

MCCALL, DUKE KIMBROUGH, clergyman; b. Meridian, Miss., Sept. 1, 1914; s. John William and Lizette (Kimbrough) McC.; m. Marguerite Mullinnix, Sept. 1, 1936 (dec. 1983); children: Duke, Douglas H., John Richard, Michael W.; m. Winona Gatton McCandless, Feb. 2, 1984. BA, Furman U., Greenville, S.C., 1936; MDiv, So. Bapt. Sem., Louisville, 1938; PhD, So. Bapt. Sem., 1943; LLD (hon.), Baylor U.; DD (hon.), Furman U., U. Richmond, Stetson U.; LittD, Georgetown Coll. Ordained to ministry, Bapt. Ch., 1937. Pastor Broadway Bapt. Ch., Louisville; pres. New Orleans Bapt. Theol. Sem., 1943-46; exec. sec. So. Bapt. Exec. Com., Nashville, 1946-51; pres. So. Bapt. Theol. Sem., Louisville, 1951-82, chancellor, 1982-92. Pres. Bapt. World Alliance, Washington, 1980-85; chmn. bd. dirs. Covenant Life Ins. Co., 1989-90. Author: God's Hurry, 1948, Passport to the World, 1951, Broadman Comments, 1957, 2nd edit., 1958, A Story of Stewardship, 1996; editor: What is the Church, Duke K. McCall: An Oral History, 2001. Recipient E.Y. Mullins Denominational Svc. award. Avocations: golf; boating. Home: 3534 Lantern Bay Dr Jupiter FL 33477-1312 E-mail: dukemccall@mindspring.com.

MCCALL, EDITH SANSOM, writer; b. Charles City, Iowa, Sept. 5, 1911; d. William John and Mary Catherine (May) Sansom; m. Merle Rederick McCall, June 7, 1935 (div. Jan. 1963); children: Constance Anita, Mary Edith. MA, U. Chgo., 1949. Cert. elem. educator, Ill. Tchr. Elmhurst (Ill.) Pub. Schs., 1930-35; tchr. Western Springs (Ill.) Pub. Schs., 1943-48; reading cons. LaGrange (Ill.) Pub. Schs., 1949-55; writer, 1953—. Author: Conquering the Rivers, 1982, Sometimes We Dance Alone, 1994, 53 other books for young readers; co-author: 30 textbooks; contbr. articles to profl. jours.; monthly column. Recipient Maritime Journalism award Inland Waterways Libr., St. Louis, 1992, Honor Book award Children's Reading Round Table, Chgo., 1989; named Disting. Alumnus U. Wis. Stevens Point, 1988; named to Mo. Writers' Hall of Fame, Springfield, 1996. Mem. Mo. Writers Guild (hon., life, pres. 1970, 2000, Best Book award 4 times 1960-89), Western Writers Am. (finalist non-fiction award 1985), Ozark Writers League (v.p.), Authors Guild, Inc. Home: Apt 308 500 Paisano St NE Albuquerque NM 87123-1476

MCCALL, JACK HUMPHREYS, JR. lawyer; b. Nashville, Jan. 10, 1961; s. Jack Humphreys Sr. and Patricia Jean (Holmes) McC.; m. Jennifer Lynn Ashley, Oct. 4, 1992; 1 child, Margaret Ashley. BA, Vanderbilt U., 1983; JD, U. Tenn., 1991. Bar: Tenn. 1992, U.S. Ct. Appeals (10th cir.) 1993. Clk. Hon. Gilbert S. Merritt, Chief Judge U.S. Ct. Appeals 6th Cir., Nashville, 1991-92; assoc. Farris, Warfield & Kanaday, 1992-94; counsel Hunton & Williams, Knoxville, 1994—. Adj. prof. U. Tenn. Coll. Law, Knoxville, 1997—; bd. dirs. Legal Aid of East Tenn., 2001--. Contbr. chpt. to book and articles to profl. jours. Mem. alumni adv. coun. U. Tenn. Coll. Law, Knoxville, 1992-95. Capt. U.S. Army, 1983-88. Recipient Loevinger prize ABA Sect. of Sci. and Tech., 1992, Bruno Bittker award ABA Standing Com. World Order Law, 1993, Pro Bono Lawyer award Knoxville Legal Aid Soc., 1999, 2000. Mem. Nashville Bar Assn. (elder law com. chair young lawyers divsn. 1993-94), Knoxville Bar Assn. Barristers (com. chair young lawyers sect. 1995-97, bd. govs. 2001--), Nat. Assn. Real Estate Investment Trusts. Lutheran. Avocations: history, writing, genealogy, languages, travel. Office: Hunton & Williams 900 S Gay St Ste 2000 Knoxville TN 37902-1861 E-mail: nmccall@hunton.com.

MC CALL, JERRY CHALMERS, retired government official; b. Oxford, Miss., June 30, 1927; s. E. Forrest and Mariada (Huffaker) McC.; m. Margaret Denton, Nov. 28, 1952; children: Betsy, Lynn, Kim. BA, MA, U. Miss., 1951; MS, U. Ill., 1956, PhD, 1959. Tchg. asst. dept. math. U. Miss., 1950-51, instr. math., 1952-53, prof. math., 1973-76, exec. vice chancellor, 1973-76; rsch. assoc. U. Ill., 1953-57; applied sci. rep. IBM, Springfield, Ill., 1957-58, mgr. Bethesda, Md., 1966-68, Huntsville, Ala., 1968-71, Owego, N.Y., 1971-72; exec. v.p. Midwest Computer Service, Inc., Decatur, Ill., 1958-59; mem. sci. staff computation lab. Army Ballistic Missile Agy., Huntsville, 1959-60; asst. to dir. Marshall Space Flight Ctr., NASA, 1960-63; dep. dir. rsch. and devel. ops. Marshall Space Flight Ctr. NASA, 1963-66, dir. info. rsch. NASA Miss. Test Facility Bay St. Louis, 1972-73; pres. 1st State Bank and Trust Co., Gulfport, Miss., 1976-77; dir. Nat. Data Buoy Ctr., 1977-99; pres. McKool, Inc., Gulfport, 1982-94, Am. Mini Storage, Gulfport, 1985—, Am Crane Rentals, Inc., 1985-89, Cool-Power, Inc., 1988-93; ret., 1999; cons. EG & G Corp., 1999—2000. Head math. dept. St. Bernard Coll., Cullman, Ala., part-time, 1960-65; asso. prof. math. U. Ala., Huntsville, 1960-62; pub. speaker, 1960-63; chmn. incorporators First State Bank & Trust Co., Gulfport, Miss., 1973-76; tech. cons. Gen. Electric Co., 1974-75 Editor: (with Ernst Stuhlinger) Astronautical Engineering and Science, 1963, From Peenemunde to Outer Space, 1963. Mem. Miss. Criminal Justice Standards Commn., 1974-75; mem. Miss. Marine Resources Council, 1974-76; bd. dirs. U. Miss. Found.; bd. advisers Sch. Engring., U. Miss., 1965-73; mem. indsl. advisors U. New Orleans; chmn. founders U. Ala. Research Inst., Huntsville, 1960-62. Mem. U.S. Dept. Commerce Sr. Exec. Assn. (bd. dirs.), Am. Judicature Soc. (lay mem.), U. Miss. Alumni Assn. (dir. 1966-73) Home: PO Box 7092 Gulfport MS 39506-7092

MCCALL, JOHN CLARK, JR. interior designer; b. Vidalia, Ga., Sept. 6, 1949; s. John Clark McCall and Carolyn Elizabeth Kay. BA, Ga. State U., 1972, MPA, 1980. Program coord. dept. music Ga. State U., Atlanta, 1972-73, adminstrn. supr. dept. music, 1973-78, asst. to dir. office acad. assistance Coll. Arts and Scis., 1978-81; dir. Ctr. for Career Devel. Winthrop U., Rock Hill, S.C., 1981-83, dir., founder Office Campus Planning and Design, 1983-85, asst. prof. interior design, 1985-89; pres. John Clark McCall, Jr. Design Cons., Inc., Rock Hill, S.C., Hahira, Valdosta, Moultrie, Ga., 1983—. Acting chair dept. interior design Winthrop U., Rock Hill, 1985-86. Author: (foreword) Frank McCall: A Complete Designer in the Class Tradition, 1985, (monograph) Atlanta Fox Album: Mecca on Peachtree Street, 1975; designer interiors for residential and non-residential projects. Dir. Friends of Albany (Ga.) Theatre, 1998-99; bd. trustees Valdosta (Ga.) Symphony Orch.; vol. Save the Atlanta Fox, 1974-80; project dir. Rylander Theatre Moller Pipe Organ Donation, Americus, Ga., 1998-99. Mem. Am. Soc. Interior Designers (allied mem., D. Brahms H. Presv. award 1985, Pres.'s award 1987), Am. Theatre Organ Soc., Theatre Hist. Soc., Found. for Interior Design Edn. Rsch. (bd. visitors), Lincoln Continental Owners Club, Packard Club. Episcopalian. Avocations: antique automobiles, theater and theater organ history and research, watercolor painting. Office: John Clark McCall Jr Design Cons Inc 1415 Crescent Dr Moultrie GA 31768 E-mail: jcmdc@alltell.net.

MCCALL, JOHN PATRICK, college president, educator; b. Yonkers, N.Y., July 17, 1927; s. Ambrose V. and Vera E. (Rush) McC.; m. Mary-Berenice Morris, June 15, 1957; children: Claire, Anne, Ambrose, Peter. AB, Coll. of Holy Cross, 1949; MA, Princeton U., 1952, PhD, 1955; DHL, Knox Coll., Galesburg, Ill., 1993. Instr. Georgetown U., 1955-57, asst. prof. English, 1957-62, asso. prof., 1962-66; prof. U. Cin., 1966-82, head dept. English, 1970-76, sr. v.p., provost, 1976-82; pres. Knox Coll., 1982-93, pres. emeritus and prof. emeritus English, 1993—; vol. Peace Corps, Turkmenistan, 1993-95. Vis. prof. Turkmen State U., 1994-95; vice chmn. Gov.'s Task Force on Rural Ill., 1986; pres. Associated Colls. Ill., 1986-88; chmn. Associated Colls. of M.W., 1991-92; mem. edn. com. Ill. Bd. Higher Edn., 1985, 90; mem. rural libr. panel, State of Ill., 1992. Author: Chaucer Among the Gods: the Poetics of Classical Myth, 1979; contbr. articles to profl. jours.; research in medieval lit. and Chaucer's poetry. Exec.-in-residence Xavier U. La., 1997—. With Signal Corps, U.S. Army, 1952-54. Am. Coun. Learned Socs. fellow, 1962-63; John Simon Guggenheim Meml. Found. fellow, 1975; Fulbright grantee, 1962. Mem. Medieval Acad. Am. MLA, AAUP, World Affairs Coun. New Orleans. Democrat. Roman Catholic. Bus. Home: 1404 3rd St New Orleans LA 70130-5746 Office: Xavier U La 1 Drexel Dr Box 66A New Orleans LA 70125-1098 E-mail: jmccall@xula.edu.

MC CALL, JULIEN LACHICOTTE, banker; b. Florence, S.C., Apr. 1, 1921; s. Arthur M. and Julia (Lachicotte) McC.; m. Janet Jones, Sept. 30, 1950; children: Melissa, Alison Gregg, Julien Lachicotte Jr. BS, Davidson Coll., 1942, LLD (hon.), 1983; MBA, Harvard U., 1947. With First Nat. City Bank, N.Y.C., 1948-71, asst. mgr. bond dept., 1952-53, asst. cashier, 1953-55, asst. v.p., 1955-57, v.p., 1957-71; 1st v.p. Nat. City Bank, Cleve., 1971-72, pres., 1972-79, chmn., 1979-85, chief exec. officer, from 1979, also bd. dirs.; pres. Nat. City Corp., 1973-80, chmn., chief exec. officer, 1980-86, also bd. dirs., cons. Mem. fed. adv. coun. Fed. Res. Bd., 1984-87. Trustee St. Luke's Found., United Way Services, Boy Scouts Am., Playhouse Sq. Found., Cleve. Mus. Natural History. Served with AUS, 1942-46, Africa, ETO. Mem. Pepper

Pike Club, Chagrin Valley Hunt Club, Mountain Lake Club (Lake Wales, Fla.), Rolling Rock Club (Ligonier, Pa.). Home: Arrowhead 115 Quail Ln Chagrin Falls OH 44022 Office: 30195 Chagrin Blvd Ste 104W Pepper Pike OH 44124-5703

MCCALL, LOUISE HARRUP, artist; b. Oklahoma City, July 8, 1925; d. Paul Louis and Lucile (Martin) Harrup; m. Robert Theodore McCall, July 20, 1945; children: Linda Louise, Catherine Anne. Student, Okla. State U., 1943-44, U. N.Mex., 1944-45, Art Inst., 1946; pvt. study, N.Y., 1955-65. Freelance artist, Chgo., 1946-48, Tarrytown, N.Y., 1949-53, Chappaqua, 1953-67, 68-71, London, 1967, Paradise Valley, Ariz., 1971—; owner McCall Studios, Inc., 1986—. Exhibitions include Ariz. State U., 1999, Grace Mus., Abilene, Tex., 1999, Sky Harbor Millenium Traveling Show, 1999—2000, Ariz. State U. Club, 1999, Women Artists of Ariz., Wickenburg, 2001; artist with husband (murals) Air and Space Mus., Washington, 1975—76, Johnson Space Ctr., Houston, 1978, Disney Epcot Ctr., L.A., 1983, Phoenix Indsl. Commn., 1987, designed with husband windows of Valley Presbyn. Chapel, Scottsdale, Ariz. , 1984, 2002, window of Sky Harbor Airport, Phoenix, 1998, artist (paintings in pvt. collections) H.R.H. Prince Fahd Bin Salman and H.R. Prince Sultan Bin Salman of Saudi Arabia, Mayo Clinic Collection, Scottsdale, 1997, designer meditation chapel for new cancer ctr., 2001; exhibitions include West Valley Art Mus., Phoenix. Fundraiser Crisis Nursery, Phoenix, 1984, Ariz. Hist. Soc., Phoenix, 1986, Scottsdale Cultural Ctr. 1990-92, Phoenix Art Mus., 1993-94, Scottsdale Art. Sch., 1996, 1994 Art Show O'Brien's Gallery, 1995 Art Show Peoria Sch. Dist.; ann. fund raiser Hospice Phoenix, 1983-92, Bot. Gardens Phoenix. Winner 1st Prize, State of Tex., 1943, 1st Prize, Jr. League Artists No. Westchester and N.Y., 1961. Mem. NASA Permanent Art Collection, Nat. Mus. Women in the Arts, Jr. League of Phoenix, Paradise Valley Country Club. Republican. Presbyterian. Avocation: speaking. Home and Office: 4816 E Moonlight Way Paradise Valley AZ 85253 Fax: (480) 991-2099. E-mail: robtmccall@cox.net.

MCCALL, LWW, race car driver; Chief mechanic Jerry Mayfield driver NASCAR, NC, 2000—01; crew chief Chip Ganassi Racing, Mooresville, 2001—. Office: Chip Ganassi Racing 114 Meadowhill Cir Mooresville NC 28115

MCCALLA, BRIAN CLARK, engineering executive; b. Manassas, Va., Nov. 14, 1970; s. William Clark and Giselle McCalla; m. Jennifer Lee Ford, June 15, 2000. BS Mech. Engring., U. Pitts., 1994; BS Physics, U. of Pitts., 1994; MS Mech. Engring., Gannon U., 2000. Cert. Professional Engineer (PE), State of Ohio, Ohio, Pa. Asst. mech. projects engr. Wash. Steel Corp., Washington, 1991—94; plant mech. engr. Erie Malleable Iron (EMI), Erie, 1994—95; staff engr. Rabe Environ. Systems, Inc., 1995—97; energy engr. Johnson Controls, Inc., Cleve., 1997—98, Ohio area project devel. mgr., 1999—2001, mgr. programs and svc. engring. Milw., 2001—. Engring. cons., Cleve., 2000; adj. prof. of engring. U. Pitts., Titusville, Pa., 1996—98. Mem.: The Assn. of Energy Engineers, NSPE, Am. Soc. of Heating, Refrigeration, and Air - Conditioning Engineers, ASME (exec. com. 1996—97). Conservative. Roman Catholic. Avocation: skiing, math and science education, home automation, computers, electronic music. Home: 1461 Sherman Dr Parma OH 44134 Office: Johnson Controls Inc 9797 Midwest Ave Cleveland OH 44125 Home Fax: 440-888-8426; Office Fax: 216-587-2256. Personal E-mail: brian2@aol.com. E-mail: brian.mccalla@jci.com.

MCCALLA, SANDRA ANN, educational administrator; b. Shreveport, La., Nov. 6, 1939; d. Earl Gray and Dorothy Edna (Adams) McC. BS, Northwestern La. State U., 1960; MA, U. No. Colo., 1968; EdD, Tex. A&M U., 1987. With Caddo Parish Sch. Bd., Shreveport, 1960-88; asst. prin. Capt. Shreve H.S., 1977-79, prin., 1979-88, 94—; dir., dean divsn. edn. Northwestern State U., Natchitoches, La., 1988-94; instr. math. La. State U., 1979-81. Mem. adv. bd. Sta. KDAQ Pub. Radio, 1985-89, Shreveport Women's Commn., 1983-89. Named Educator of Yr. Shreveport Times-Caddo Tchrs. Assn., 1966, La H.S. Prin. of Yr., 1985, 87; recipient Excellence in Edn. award Capt. Shreve H.S., 1982-83; Danforth fellow, 1982-83. Mem. nat. Assn. Secondary Sch. prins., La. Assn. Prins. (Prin. of Yr. 1985), La. Assn. Sch. Execs. (Disting. Svc. award 1983), Times-Caddo Educators Assn. (Educator of Yr. 1984), Phi Delta Kappa, Kappa Delta Pi. Republican.

MCCALLISTER, MICHAEL B. managed health care executive; BA, La. Tech. U.; MBA, Pepperdine U. Fin. specialist Humana Inc., 1974—, v.p. for integrated ops. health plans and hosps. Ariz., 1989—92, Tex., 1992—96, pres. divsn. 1 with responsibility for Tex., Fla. and P.R., 1996—97, mem. Office Chmn., sr. v.p. health plan divsn., 1997—2000, pres., CEO, 2000—. Office: Humana Inc Humana Bldg 500 W Main St Ste 300 Louisville KY 40202-4268*

MCCALLISTER, RICHARD ANTHONY, business consulting company executive; b. Newark, Apr. 10, 1937; s. Ward C. and LeDema Mc.; m. Trina D. Gordon, Sept. 1, 1979; children: Todd, Mark. BS, Ill. State U., 1960; postgrad., U. So. Calif., 1960-62. Indsl. cons. Sci. Rsch. Assocs., 1964-66; v.p. Mgmt. Psychologists, Inc., Chgo., 1966-68; dir. Price Waterhouse & Co., 1968-75; pres. William H. Clark Assocs., Inc., 1975-89; sr. v.p., dir. Boyden Internat., 1989-91; mng. dir. Boyden Midwest, 1991—. Mng. dir., bd. dirs. Boyden World Corp.; chmn. WHCA Ptnrs., 1986—; bd. dirs. sec., pres. Mid Am.; bd. dirs. Spirian Techs.; mem. adv. bd. Fiduciary Management, Inc., Lionheart Trust Co., 1988-93. Former pres. Dist. 113 Bd. Edn., Deerfield, Ill.; bd. dirs., exec. com. Grant Hosp., Chgo., House of Vision, 1975-82. Mem. Glen View Club, Racquet Club, Chgo. Club, Mid-Am. Club (bd. dirs., treas., pres. 1998—). Office: 180 N Stetson Ave Chicago IL 60601-6710

MC CALLUM, CHARLES ALEXANDER, university official; b. North Adams, Mass., Nov. 1, 1925; s. Charles Alexander and Mabel Helen (Cassidy) McC.; m. Alice Rebecca Lasseter, Dec. 17, 1955; children: Scott Alan, Charles Alexander III, Philip Warren, Christopher Jay. Student, Dartmouth Coll., 1943-44, Wesleyan U., Middletown, Conn., 1946-47; DMD, Tufts U., 1951; MD, Med. Coll. Ala., 1957; DSc (hon.), U. Ala., 1975, Georgetown U., 1982, Tufts U., 1988, Chulalongkorn U., Thailand, 1993, U. Medicine and Dentistry, N.J., 1993. Diplomate Am. Bd. Oral Surgery (pres. 1970). Intern oral surgery Univ. Hosp., Birmingham, Ala., 1951-52, resident oral surgery, 1952-54, intern medicine, 1957-58; mem. faculty U. Ala. Sch. Dentistry, 1956-96, prof., chmn. dept. oral surgery, 1959-65, dean sch., 1962-77; prof., dept. surgery U. Ala. Sch. of Medicine, 1965-96; v.p. for health affairs, dir. U. Ala. Med. Center, Birmingham, 1977-87; pres. U. Ala., 1987-93, chief sect. oral surgery Sch. Dentistry, 1958-65, 68-69; prof., 1959-93; disting. prof., 1992-2000; disting. prof. emeritus, dean emeritus, 2000—. Mem. nat. adv. dental rsch. coun. NIH, 1968-72; mem. Joint Commn. on Accreditation of Hosps., 1980-91, vice chmn., 1985, chmn., 1986-88. Fellow Am. Coll. Dentists, Internat. Coll. Dentists; mem. ADA (council on dental edn. 1970-76), Am. Assn. Dental Schs. (pres. 1969), Ala. Acad. of Honor, AMA, Am. Soc. Oral Surgeons (trustee 1972-73, pres. 1975-76), Southeastern Soc. Oral Surgeons (pres. 1970), Inst. of Medicine of Nat. Acad. of Scis., Assn. Acad. Health Ctrs. (chmn. bd. dirs. 1984-85), Omicron Kappa Upsilon, Phi Beta Pi. Home: 2328 Garland Dr Birmingham AL 35216-3002 Office: Univ Ala Birmingham 617 Sdb Birmingham AL 35294-0001

MC CALLUM, CHARLES EDWARD, lawyer; b. Memphis, Mar. 13, 1939; s. Edward Payson and India Raimelle (Musick) McC.; m. Lois Ann Gowell Temple, Nov. 30, 1985; children: Florence Andrea, Printha Kyle, Chandler Ward, Sabra Nicole Temple. BS, MIT, 1960; JD, Vanderbilt U., 1964. Bar: Mich., Tenn. 1964. Assoc. Warner Norcross & Judd LLP, Grand Rapids, Mich., 1964-69, ptnr., 1969—, mng. ptnr., 1992-97. Rep. assemblyman State Bar Mich., 1973-78; dir. TerraLex, 2001—, Rsch. and Tech. Inst. West Mich., 1986-96, chmn., 1989-91; lectr. continuing legal edn. programs; chmn., bd. dirs. Butterworth Ventures, 1987-96; mem. West Mich. World Trade Week Com., 1988-99, chmn., 1990-91; mem. Mich. Dist. Export Coun., 1990-99, chmn., 1992-97. Chmn. Grand Rapids Area Transit Authority, 1976-79, mem., 1972-79; regional v.p. Nat. Mcpl. League, 1978-86, mem. coun., 1971-78; pres. Grand Rapids Art Mus., 1979-81, 96-98, trustee, 1976-83, 94-99; chmn. Butterworth Hosp., 1979-87, trustee, 1977-87; chmn. Butterworth Health Corp., 1982-89, dir., 1982-97, vice chmn., 1989-91, sec., 1991-97; vice chmn. Citizens Com. for Consolidation of Govt. Svcs., 1981-82; mem. nat. alumni bd. Vanderbilt U. Sch. Law, 1998-2001; chmn. Priority Health, 1995—, bd. dirs., 1995—. Woodrow Wilson fellow, 1960-61; Fulbright scholar U. Manchester, Eng., 1960-61. Fellow Coll. Law Practice Mgmt.; mem. ABA (chmn. com. on law firms 1994-98, coun. mem. bus. law sect. 1998-2002, mem. fed. regulation of securities com., mem. internat. bus. law com., commr. on multijurisdictional practice 2000-2002, com. profl. conduct 1996-, co-chair com. profl. conduct 2002-), Am. Bar Found., Am. Law Inst., Tenn. Bar Assn., Mich. Bar Assn. (mem. coun. bus. law sect. 1983-89, sect. chmn. 1988-89, ex-officio coun. bus. law sect. 1989—, chmn. takeover laws subcom. 1986-88, co-chmn. internat. bus. law com., internat. law sect. 1988-89), Grand Rapids Bar Assn., Internat. Bar Assn., Grand Rapids C. of C. (pres. 1975, bd. dirs. 1970-76), Univ. Club, Order of Coif, Sigma Xi. Home: 110 Bittersweet Ln NE Ada MI 49301-9552 E-mail: mccallce@wnj.com.

MCCALLUM, RICHARD WARWICK, medical researcher, clinician, educator; b. Brisbane, Australia, Jan. 21, 1945; came to U.S., 1969; MD, BS, Queensland U., Australia, 1968. Rotating intern Charity Hosp. La., New Orleans, 1969-70; resident in internal medicine Barnes Hosp., Washington, 1970-72; fellow in gastroenterology Wadsworth VA Hosp., L.A., 1972-74, chief endoscopic unit, dept gastroenterology, 1974-76; dir. gastrointestinal diagnostic svcs. Yale-New Haven Med. Ctr., New Haven, 1979-85; asst. prof. medicine UCLA, 1974-76, Yale U., New Haven, 1977-82, assoc. prof., 1982-85; prof., chief div. gastroenterology, hepatology and nutrition U. Va., Charlottesville, 1985-95; dir. GI Motility Ctr. U. Va. Health Sci. Ctr., 1990-96; Paul Janssen prof. medicine U. Va., 1987-96; prof. medicine and physiology U. Kans. Med. Ctr., Kansas City, 1996—, chief div. gastroenterology and hepatology, 1996—, dir. Ctr. for Gastrointestinal Motility Disorders, 1996—. Patentee catheter for esophageal perfusion, gastrointestinal pacemaker using-phased multipoint stimulation, esophageal protection by mastication. Fellow ACP, Am. Coll. Gastroenterology (gov. Kans. 1998—), Royal Australasian Coll. Physicians, Royal Australian Coll. Surgeons; mem. Australian Gastroenterology Soc., Am. Fedn. Clin. Rsch., Am. Assn. Study Liver Diseases, Am. Soc. Gastrointestinal Endoscopy, Am. Soc. for Clin. Investigation, Am. Gastroenterology Assn., Am. Motility Soc. (host-organizer 11th biennial meeting Kansas City 2000), So. Soc. for Clin. Investigation (pres. 1997-98), Internat. Electrogastrography Soc. (pres. 1998-2000), So. Med. Assn. (chmn. gastrointestinal 1996-97). Office: U Kans Med Ctr Dept Internal Medicine 3901 Rainbow Blvd Kansas City KS 66160-0001 E-mail: rmccallu@kumc.edu.

MCCALLUM, ROBERT D. federal agency administrator; Grad., JD, Yale U.; Masters Degree, Oxford U. Ptnr. Alston & Bird, Atlanta, 1973—2001; asst. atty. gen. civil divsn. U.S. Dept. Justice, Washington, 2001—. Scholar Rhodes scholar. Office: US Dept Justice Civil Divsn 950 Pennsylvania Ave NW Washington DC 20530-0001*

MCCALLUM, RODERICK EUGENE, dean, microbiologist; b. Denver, Aug. 14, 1944; s. Thomas H. and Elizabeth M. (Matheson) McC.; m. Cheryl A. Ortmann, Aug. 20, 1967; children: Christopher, David. BA, U. Kans., Lawrence, 1967, PhD, 1970; postdoctoral study, U. Tex., 1970-72. Instr. U. Tex., Austin, 1970-72; asst. prof. microbiology U. Okla., Oklahoma City, 1972-75, assoc. prof., 1975-84, prof., 1984-92; prof., head dept. med. microbiology and immunology Health Sci. Ctr. Tex. A&M U., College Station, 1992-97, dir. Inst. Molecular Pathogenesis and Therapeutics, 1993—; assoc. dean for rsch., dir. rsch. Ctrl. Tex. Vets. Health Care System, 1997—; interim dean, v.p. academic affairs Texas A&M Univ. Health Sci. Center, 1999—2000, assoc. dean for research and grad studies, 2000—02; interim dean Texas A&M Univ. Health Sci. Center Coll. of Med., 2002—. Guest prof. U. Heidelberg, Germany, 1980, 85; reviewer BM-2 study sect. NIH, Bethesda, Md., 1986-90; lectr. Mid-Am. States Univ. Assn., 1988. Contbr. articles to profl. jours. Coalition mem. Shots Across Tex., College Station, 1993—. Fellow Am. Acad. Microbiology; mem. AAAS, Am. Soc. Microbiology (editor Infection and Immunity 1992—), Internat. Endotoxin Soc., Tex. Infectious Disease Soc., Soc. Leukocyte Biology, Shock Soc. Democrat. Lutheran. Avocations: woodworking, gardening, golf, travel. Office: Tex A&m U Health Sci Ctr College Station TX 77843-0001*

MCCALLUM, SCOTT, governor; b. Fond du Lac, Wis., May 2, 1950; m. Laurie McCallum; children: Zachary, Rory, Cara. BA, Macalester Coll., 1972; MA in Internat. Studies, Johns Hopkins U., 1974. Property developer, Fond du Lac; mem. Wis. State Senate, 1976-87; lt. gov. State of Wis., 1987-2001, gov., 2001—. Dir. Workplace Child Care Clearinghouse; chair Repeat Offenders Task Force State of Wis., Trauma and Injury Prevention Task Force; coord. Gov.'s Conf. on Small Bus.; presdl. appointee to Internat. Trade Policy Adv. Com.; past chair Nat. Conf. of Lt. Govs.; gov.'s appointee to Nat. Aerospace States Assn. Office: 115 E State Capitol PO Box 7863 Madison WI 53702*

MCCALLY, CHARLES RICHARD, construction company executive; b. Dallas, Oct. 5, 1958; s. Richard Holt and Elizabeth Ann (Webster) McC.; m. Shirley Elizabeth Avant, Aug. 18, 1979 (div.); children: Charles Richard Jr., Meredith Holt; m. Judy Lynn Tackett, June 24, 1993. BSME, So. Meth. U., 1981. Engr. McCally Co., Dallas, 1977-83; owner, v.p. DRT Mech. Corp., 1983-95; owner McCally Svc. Co., Inc., 1995-97; pres. C.R. McCally & Assocs., Inc., 1997—. Active Young Reps., Dallas, 1980—. Mem. NSPE, ASME, ASHRAE, Am. Soc. Plumbing Engrs. (membership com. 1983-89), Tex. Soc. Profl. Engrs., So. Meth. U. Alumni Assn., SMU Mustang Club, Bent Tree Country Club (Dallas), Oaktree Country Club (Garland, Tex.) (bd. dirs. 1986-89), Sigma Chi. Avocations: tennis, boating, traveling, camping. Home: PO Box 29701 Dallas TX 75229-0701

MCCALLY, JOHN FRANK, healthcare executive, writer; b. Niles, Mich., June 29, 1935; s. Frank Dile and Beatrice (Phillips) McC.; m. Marcia Kierland, June 28, 1958 (div. Nov. 1975); children: Lisa K., Cray R., John Jr.; m. Elaine Olson, Apr. 7, 1979. BA in Econs., Mich. State U., 1959; postgrad., Mankato State U., 1974, Luther Seminary, 1997-99. Adminstrn. Mayo Clinic, Rochester, Minn., 1959-74; adminstr. San Jose (Calif.) Med. Group, 1974-75; hosp. adminstr. Am. Med. Internat., Anaheim, Calif., 1976-77; sr. adv. Ernst & Young, Minneapolis, 1986-88; pres., CEO Detroit Med. Ctr. Healthcare Ctrs., 1989-90; nat. dir. healthcare reform McGladrey and Pullen, Mpls., 1991-95; v.p. managed care cons. Summit Med.—BSM Cons. Group, 1996-98; pres., CEO Physician's Cons. Svcs. Am. Ltd., North Oaks, Minn., 1998-2000. Mem. adj. faculty Carlson Sch. Mgmt. U. Minn., 1998-2000. Author numerous books including Economic Security for Healthcare Providers, 1999; contbr. over 50 articles to profl. jours. Bd. dirs. Minn. Found. Student Orgns., treas. 1998-99. With U.S. Army, 1955-56. Mem. Rotary (program chmn. 1999). Republican. Lutheran. Avocations: photography, travel, music, golf. Home: 15778 73rd Cir No Maple Grove MN 55311

MCCAMBRIDGE, JOHN JAMES, civil engineer; b. Bklyn., Oct. 27, 1933; s. John Joseph and Florence Josita (McDonnell) McC.; m. Dorothy Antoinette Cook, Mar. 17, 1962; children: Sharon J., John S., Patrick J., Kathleen C. BCE, Manhattan Coll., 1955; MS, Vanderbilt U., 1958; postgrad., UCLA, 1963-66. Civil engr. Raymond Concrete Pile Co., N.Y.C., 1955; commd. 2d lt. USAF, 1955, advanced through grades to col., 1972; exec. sec. Defense Com. On Rsch., Washington, 1971-73, DOD-NASA Supportive Rsch. Tech. Panel, Washington, 1972-74; asst. dir. Def. Rsch. and Engring. (for Life Scis.) Office Sec. Def., 1974-75; dir. Air Force Life Support Systems Program Office, Wright Patterson AFB, Ohio, 1975-79; ret. USAF, 1979; prin. Booz, Allen & Hamilton, Inc., Bethesda, Md., 1979-86; v.p. Espey, Huston & Assoc., Inc., Falls Church, Va., 1986-90; mng. prin. JMC Cons. Group, McLean, 1990—. Chmn. air panel on NBC Def., NATO, Evere, Belgium, 1970-71; def. dept. rep. to physics survey com., Nat. Acad. Scis., Washington, 1971. Contbr. articles to profl. jours. Decorated Legion of Merit with oak leaf cluster. Fellow Aerospace Med. Assn. (exec. coun. 1972-73), Inst. Hazardous Materials Mgmt. (Disting. Diplomate, dir. 1984—, chmn. 1988-94); mem. Coun. Engring. and Sci. Splty. Bds. (dir., exec. com. 1995—, v.p. 2000, pres. 2001), Acad. Cert. Hazardous Materials Mgrs. (pres. 1984-86), Survival and Flight Equipment Assn. (nat. sec. 1977-78), Air Force Ret. Officers' Cmty. (dir. 1997—), The Washington Assembly, (treas. 2002--), River Bend Golf and Country Club, Black Tie Club, Tower Club, KC, Sigma Xi, Chi Epsilon. Republican. Roman Catholic. Office: JMC Cons Group 9200 Falls Run Rd Mc Lean VA 22102-1028 E-mail: jjmccambridge@earthlink.net.

MC CAMERON, FRITZ ALLEN, retired university administrator; b. Nacogdoches, Tex., Oct. 8, 1929; s. Leland Allen and Gladys (Turner) Mc C.; m. Jeannine Young, June 11, 1957; 1 child, Mary Hartley. BBA, Stephen F. Austin State Coll., 1950, MA, 1951; PhD, U. Ala., 1954. C.P.A., La. Asso. prof. La. State U., 1959-62, prof., 1962-67, chmn. dept. accounting, 1967-71, asst. vice chancellor, 1971-73, dean continuing edn., 1973-95; ret., 1995. Cons. in field. Author: FORTRAN Logic and Programming, 1968, Cobol Logic and Programming, rev. edit, 1970, 5th edit., 1985, FORTRAN IV, 1970, rev. edit., 1974, 3d edit., 1977. Mem. numerous civic and charitable bds. including Salvation Army, Womens Hosp., Computer Rehab. Tng. and others. Mem. Am. Inst. C.P.A.'s, La. Soc. C.P.A.'s, Am. Accounting Assn. Home: 930 Rodney Dr Baton Rouge LA 70808-5867

MCCAMMAN, JOHN WILLIAM, federal official; b. Ventura, Calif., May 26, 1953; s. Kenneth Taylor and Mary Gertrude (Wachob) McC.; m. Joan Rae Guissi, May 1, 1982; children: Meaghan Anne, Sarah Kathleen, Michael John. BA in Politics and Philosophy, U. Calif., Santa Barbara, 1975; MA in Politics, Calif. State U., Sonoma, 1982. Adminstrv. analyst IV-I County of Sonoma, Santa Rosa, Calif., 1978-87; county adminstrv. officer County of Mariposa, 1987-93; county adminstr. County of Shasta, Redding, 1993-95; chief of staff Office of Congressman G. Radanovich, Washington, 1995—. Campaign dir. Radanovich for Congress, Fresno, Calif., 1996, 98, 2000. Bd. dirs. Mariposa Rotary, 1988-94; sec. United Way Yosemite, Mariposa, 1990-94; asst. scoutmaster Boy Scouts Am. Troop 1916, McLean, Va., 1999—. Recipient fellowship John. C. Stennis Ctr., 1997-98. Mem. House Adminstrv. Assts. Assn. (bd. dirs., v.p., pres. 1996-2001). Avocations: camping, golf. Office: Office Congressman George Radanovich 123 Cannon House Office Bld Washington DC 20515-0001 Fax: 202-225-3402. E-mail: john.mccamman@mail.house.gov.

MCCAMMON, JAMES ANDREW, chemistry educator; b. Lafayette, Ind., Feb. 8, 1947; s. Lewis Brown and Jean Ann (McClintock) McC.; m. Anne Elizabeth Woltmann, June 6, 1969. BA magna cum laude, Pomona Coll., 1969; MA, Harvard U., 1970, PhD, 1976. Research fellow Harvard U., Cambridge, Mass., 1976-78; asst. prof. U. Houston, 1978-81, M.D. Anderson prof. chemistry, 1981-94, dir. Inst. for Molecular Design, 1987-94, prof. biochemistry, 1989-94, adj. prof. chemistry, 1995—. Adj. prof. molecular physiology and biophysics Baylor Coll. Medicine, Houston, 1986-94, adj. prof. biochemistry, 1992-94; Joseph E. Mayer chair theoretical chemistry U. Calif., San Diego, 1995—, prof. pharmacology, 1995—; investigator Howard Hughes Med. Inst., 2000—. Author: Dynamics of Proteins and Nucleic Acids, 1987. Recipient Tchr.-scholar award Camille and Henry Dreyfus Found., George H. Hitchings award Burroughs-Wellcome Fund, 1987, Computerworld Smithsonian Info. Tech. Leadership award for Breakthrough Computational Sci., 1995; named Alfred P. Sloan Rsch. fellow, 1980. Fellow AAAS, Am. Phys. Soc., Biophys. Soc.; mem. Am. Chem. Soc., Protein Soc., Phi Beta Kappa. Achievements include development of the molecular dynamics simulation method for proteins and nucleic acids, of the thermodynamic cycle perturbation method for studying molecular recognition, and of the Brownian dynamics method for simulating diffusion-controlled reactions. Office: U Calif San Diego Dept Chemistry La Jolla CA 92093-0365

MCCAMY, CALVIN SAMUEL, optics scientist; b. St. Joseph, Mo., Sept. 22, 1924; s. Benjamin Samuel and Della Emma (Cervenka) McC.; m. Mabel Alice Bellerud, Nov. 4, 1945; children: Susan, Nicholas, Carter. BSChemE, U. Minn., 1945, M in Physics, 1950. Instr. math. U. Minn., Mpls., 1947-50; instr. physics Clemson (S.C.) U., 1950-52; chief image optics and photography Nat. Bur. Standards, Gaithersburg, Md., 1952-70; v.p. for rsch. Macbeth, Newburgh, N.Y., 1970-89; pvt. practice cons. in color sci. Wappingers Falls, 1990—. Leader in nat. and internat. standardization; adj. prof. chemistry Rensselaer Poly. Inst., Troy, N.Y., 1980-85; mem. adv. bd. Munsell Color Sci. Lab., Rochester (N.Y.) Inst. Tech., 1985—; pres. Kollmorgen Found., Hartford, 1979-89; photog. analyst Ho. of Reps. investigation of shooting of Pres. John F. Kennedy, Washington, 1978. Editor: Papers on Image Optics from National Bureau of Standards, 1973; contbr. over 100 articles to profl. jours., books and encys. Lt. (j.g.) USN, 1943-47. Fellow Optical Soc. Am. (chmn. color com. 1978), Soc. Photographic Scientists and Engrs. (v.p. sci. 1968-72, vis. lectr. 1986), Royal Photographic Soc. Gt. Britain, Soc. Motion Picture and TV Engrs., Washington Acad. Scis., N.Y. Acad. Scis., Inter-Soc. Color Coun. Unitarian Universalist. Achievements include improving Munsell color system; development of new principle of absolute radiometry, the compensated variable aperture; discovery of cause of redox blemishes threatening federal microfilm records; design of color test chart used internationally. Home: 44 All Angels Hill Rd Wappingers Falls NY 12590-1828 E-mail: c.mccamy@att.net.

MCCAMY, SHARON, English educator; b. Fredericksburg, Va., May 31, 1961; d. Howard E. and Vivian R. Grove; m. Michael D. McCamy, Jan. 10, 1986; 1 child, Katherine Howard. BA in English, U. Va., 1983; MA in English, George Mason U., 1994. Devel. asst. Corcoran Gallery of Art, Washington, 1983-84; coord. individual giving Nat. Parks Conservation Assn., 1984-87; dir. devel. Piedmont Environ. Coun., Warrenton, Va., 1991-94; lectr. in English Mary Washington Coll., Fredericksburg, 1996-99. Elected Fauquier County Bd. Suprs., 2000—; mem. bd. Fauquier County Water and Sewer Authority, 2000—01; mem. com. Fauquier Rep. Com., 1997—; bd. dirs. Fauquier County Pub. Libr., Warrenton, 1996—2000, Libr. Va., 1998, Libr. Va. Found., 1999—2002, Va. Ctr. Book Bd., 2000—. Mem.: Va. Libr. Assn., Nat. Coun. Tchrs. English, Piedmont Rep. Women's Club (sec. 1998—2000). Home: PO Box 10 Sumerduck VA 22742-1722 E-mail: mccamy@infi.net.

MCCAN, JAMES LAWTON, education educator; b. Plymouth, Ind., Aug. 10, 1952; s.Jean F. and Mildred P. (Hayn) McC.; m. Carolyn G. Splain, Jan. 16, 1971; children: Kendra, Brittany. B of Phys. Edn., Purdue U., 1974; MS in Edn., 1981, PhD, 1983. Tchr. reading and English Waynetown (Ind.) Mid. Sch., 1974-75, Yorkville (Ill.) H.S., 1979-80; reading specialist Purdue U., West Lafayette, Ind., 1983-89; program chair Basic Skills Advancement Ind. Voc-Tech. Coll., Lafayette, 1989-91; asst. prof., coord. student teaching Hillsdale (Mich.) Coll., 1991-95; dir. Student Achievement Zone, South Bend, Ind., 1995-96; assoc. prof. Nova Southeastern U., Ft. Lauderdale, Fla., 1996—. Contbr. articles and poetry to jours. Mem. Internat. Reading Assn., Fla. Reading Assn. Avocations: reading, music. Home: 1024 St Croix Ave Apopka FL 32703 Office: Nova Southeastern U Dept Edn Fort Lauderdale FL 33314

MCCANDLESS, CAROLYN KELLER, retired human resources executive; b. Patuxent River, Md., June 6, 1945; d. Stevens Henry and Betty Jane (Bethune) Keller; m. Stephen Porter McCandless, Apr. 22, 1972; children: Peter Keller, Deborah Marion. BA, Stanford U., 1967; MBA, Harvard U., 1969. Fin. analyst Time Inc., N.Y.C., 1969-72, mgr. budgets and fin. analysis, 1972-78, asst. sec., dir. internat. adminstrn., 1978-85, v.p., dir. employee benefits, 1985-90; v.p human resources and adminstrn. Time Warner, Inc., 1990—2001. Bd. dirs. Friends and Relatives of Institutionalized Aged; mem. adv. bd. Booker T. Washington Learning Ctr. Democrat. Mem. Unitarian Ch.

MCCANLESS, CHRISTEL LUDEWIG, library consultant, researcher; b. Peenemuende, Germany, Nov. 20, 1939; came to U.S. 1953. d. Hermann Richard R. and Emmy Jaglitz Ludewig; m. George F. McCanless, Jr., July, 11, 1963; 1 child, Katherine W. BA in English, U. Montevallo, 1961; MSLS, U. N.C., 1966. Libr. dir. U. Ala., Huntsville, 1963-68, bookstore cons., 1968-76; libr. cons. Huntsville-Madison County Pub. Libr., 1975-78, Huntsville Times, 1985-89, Huntsville Mus. Art, Huntsville, 1999-2000, Ala. Libr. Exch., Inc., 1991-99, Rsch. Inst. of Paper Hist. and Tech., Brookline, Mass., 2000—. Bd. dirs. Huntsville Libr. Assn., 1970-75, Friends Huntsville Pub. Libr., 1960s. Author: Fabergé & His Works, 1994; co-author: Fabergé Eggs: A Retrospective Encyclopedia, 2001; editor: Faberge Arts Foundation Newsletter, 1997—. Bd. dirs Monte Sano Sch. PTA, 1978-84, Burritt Mus. Park, Huntsville, 1980-94, Monte Sano Civic Assn., Huntsville, 1987-89, bd. dirs. Huntsville Lit. Assn., 1970-75, Friends Huntsville Pub. Libr., 1960s; vol. instr. ARC, Huntsville, 1970's, 80's; vol. bookkeeper Monte Sano Pool Assn, Huntsville, 1980's. Recipient Libr. Volunteer of the Year, Women's Guild Huntsville Mus. Art, 1999. Mem. Ala. Libr. Assn., Ala. Mus. Assn., Huntsville Literary Assn. (bd. dirs. 1965-75)), Friends of WLRH, Friends of Huntsville-Madison County Libr., Art Librs. Assn. North Am., Beta Phi Mu, Mu Alpha Theta. Avocations: swimming, sailing, traveling, colored pencil drawing. Home and Office: PO Box 6261 Gulf Shores AL 36547-6261

MCCANLESS, LAURI LYNN, neonatal and pediatrics nurse; b. Mpls., Jan. 23, 1953; d. Alden Wood and Carolyn (Kreitlow) McC. BSN, U. Mo., 1974; MS in Child Nursing, U. Ariz., 1985. Cert. neonatal intensive care nurse AWHONN, cert. pediatric nurse ANA, cert. nursing staff devel. ANA. Staff nurse pediat. ICU U. Mo. Med. Ctr., Columbia, 1974-75; staff nurse neonatal

ICU/pediat. ICU Univ. Med. Ctr., Tucson, 1975-79; rsch. asst. U. Ariz. Coll. Nursing, 1977; nursing instr. Jefferson Coll., Hillsboro, Mo., 1979-85; clin. nurse educator pediat.-nurseries U. Med. Ctr., Tucson, 1985-87, pediat. clin. nurse specialist-nurse mgr. infant-toddlers, 1987-91, clin. nurse educator NICU-newborn nursery, 1991-94; clin. nurse educator Women and Childrens Svcs., 1994—. Facilitator, instr. nursing U. Phoenix, Tucson, 1991—, area chairperson clin. practice, 1992-94, asst. dept. chair nursing Tucson Campus, 1994-96, area chairperson sci. and gen. studies, 2001—; adj. clin. asst. prof. nursing U. Ariz. Coll. Nursing, Tucson, 1986—. Mem. AACN, AWHONN, ANA (bd. dirs. parent-child chpt. 1992-93), Assn. Care Children's Health (pres. Ariz. affiliate 1989-90, bd. dirs. at large 1995-96), Nat. Assn. Neonatal Nurses, So. Ariz. Assn. Neonatal Nurses (treas. 1989-90), Ariz. Nurses Assn. (continuing edn. program approval panel 1992—, Tucson panel facilitator 1997—), Soc. Pediat. Nurses, Sigma Theta Tau (co-chair nominating com. Beta Mu chpt. 1995-97), Ariz. Hosp. Assn. (staff devel. network), Sigma Theta Tau (Omicron Delta chpt., mem. steering com. 1995-96, eligibility counselor 1998-2000). Office: Univ Med Ctr PO Box 245100 Tucson AZ 85724-5100 E-mail: lmccanless@umcaz.edu.

MCCANN, BERNARD THOMAS, lawyer; b. Lackawannna, N.Y., June 28, 1943; s. Francis Daniel Sr. and Catherine Louise (Moran); m. Melanie A.; children: Kelly, Casey, Brigid. BA cum laude, Niagara U., 1965; JD, Union U., 1968; MA in Edn., SUNY Albany, 1996. Bar: N.Y. 1969, U.S. Dist. Ct. (no. dist.) N.Y. 1969. Assoc. McPhillips, Fitzgerald & Meyer, Glens Falls, N.Y., 1970-72; city atty. City of Glen Falls, 1973-77; sole practice Glens Falls, 1973-81, Lake George, NY, 1982—96; social studies tchr. North Warren H.S., Chestertown, 1996—; assoc. atty. Hinman Straub Pigors & Manning PC, Albany. Assoc. dir. legis. program rep. N.Y. State Nurses Assn., Guilderland, 1982-89; atty. Minerva Cen. Sch., Olmstedville, N.Y. 1974—. Bd. dirs. Glens Falls Housing Authority, 1972; exec. sec. Glens Falls Indsl. Devel. Agy., 1975-77; bd. dirs. Adirondack chpt. ARC, Glens Falls, 1974—; active Warren County Dem. Com., Glens Falls, 1974-79. Served as capt. U.S. Army, 1968-70. Mem. ABA, Indsl. Labor Relations Research Assn. Clubs: Glens Falls Figure Skating (bd. dirs. 1985—). Roman Catholic. Avocations: golf, reading, travel, coaching basketball and softball. Home: 89 Gurney Ln Queensbury NY 12804-8249 Office: NY State Nurses Assn 89 Gurney Ln Queensbury NY 12804-8249 E-mail: btmccann@adelphia.com.

MCCANN, CHRIS (CHRISTIAN DAVID MCCANN), software engineer, educator; b. Springfield, Mass., June 5, 1929; s. James Millard and Helen (Joblin) McC.; children: Nicole Fitzgerald, Adrienne Bashe, Gary McCann. Grad., GE Fin. Mgmt. Program, Schenectady, N.Y. With GE, Schenectady, 1947-66, indsl. educator in stats., probability, math., computers, 1966-80, work effectiveness instr., 1969-83, designer employee incentive programs, 1970-80, software designer, 1966-87; ret., 1987. Prodr., dir., stage mgr., performer, playwright, adminstr., treas. various cmty. theatre groups including Schenectady Light Opera Co., 1949-52, 61-67; founder Merrimoppets Children's Theater, Schenectady, exec. dir. 1968-71; author: Master Pieces-The Art History of Jigsaw Puzzles, 1998; contbr. articles to antiques and collectibles mags.; designer computer database for golden age of jigsaw puzzles. Pres. Schenectady Civic Ballet Co., 1965-68; mem., officer Schenectady Young Adult Civic Coun., 1951-57; pres. N.Y. State Young Adult Civic Coun., 1952-54; mem. Schenectady GE/United Way liaison bd., 1974-77, chmn., 1976; stage mgr. U.S. Bicentennial celebration Schenectady County, 1976. Named to Schenectady honor roll of outstanding citizens, 1990. Avocation: research on jigsaw puzzle artists. Home: 658 Macelroy Rd Ballston Lake NY 12019-2202

MCCANN, CLARENCE DAVID, JR. special events coordinator, museum curator and director, artist; b. Mobile, Ala., Apr. 30, 1948; s. Clarence David and Theresa (Pope) McC.; m. Brenda Clemens (div. 1979); 1 child, Nathan; m. Robin Chiavaroli, 1980; children: Angela, John. BFA, U. South Ala., 1970; MFA, U. Cin., 1972; grad. cert., Mus. Mgmt. Inst., Berkeley, Calif., 1982. Art instr. Spring Hill Coll., Mobile, 1972-75, U. South Ala., Mobile, 1975-76; mem. staff, asst. registrar Fine Arts Mus. of South, 1977-78, registrar, 1978-81, curator collection, 1981-84, asst. dir., 1985-86, 88-91, acting dir., 1986-88, mus. curator, 1988-91; asst. mgr. spl. events coord. City of Mobile, 1991—. Adj. lectr. U.S. Ala., 1990-91, adj. lectr. Bishop State Community Coll., 1991-2000, 2002--; adj. art instr. U. South Ala., 1999—. Author: (catalogues) The Ripening of American Art: Duveneck and Chase, 1979, The Artists of Barbizon: The Boone Collection, 1983, Enisled Visions: The Southern Nontraditional Folk Artist, 1987, The Acquisitive Eye: Selections From The Collection of James M. Younger, 1990. Pres. Contemporary Artists Consortium of Mobile, 1979-81, Mobile Art Assn., 2002--; bd. dirs. Very Spl. Arts, Ala., 1997—. Recipient various painting awards Allied Arts Coun., Mobile, 1974; U. Cin. fellow, 1972. Mem. Am. Assn. Mus., Ala. Mus. Assn., Southeastern Mus. Assn. Democrat. Home: 9080 Rawhide Ct Semmes AL 36575-7275 Office: Office of Spl Events 2900 Dauphin St Mobile AL 36606-2420 E-mail: david.mccann@ci.mobile.al.us., cdmccann@msn.com.

MCCANN, DERVILLA MAIRIN, physician, consultant; b. N.Y.C., Nov. 18, 1955; d. B. Cairbre and Eithne Carmel (Madden) McC.; m. Stephen Joseph Meister, Aug. 11, 1979; children: Liam Cairbre, Aiden Stephen. BS, Bates Coll., 1977; MD, Tufts U., 1984. Cert. internal medicine and cardiovasc. disease. Staff internist USN Naval Hosp., San Diego, 1987-90; staff physician, lt. comdr. USN Camp Pendleton (Calif.) Naval Hosp., 1993-94; staff physician, comdr., dir. CCU USN Bethesda (Md.) Naval Hosp., 1994-96; cons. in pvt. practice Kennebec Valley Med. Ctr., Augusta, Maine, 1996-99; cons. pvt. practice Ctrl. Maine Med. Ctr. and St. Mary's Hosp., Lewiston, 1999—. Spkr. Am. Heart Assn., Bethesda, 1994-96; spkr., cons. Merck, Bethesda, 1996—. Spkr. Soc. for Advancement Rsch. on Women, Washington, 1995, 97. Comdr. USN, 1987-96. Fellow Am. Coll. Cardiology; mem. Am. Soc. Nuc. Cardiology. Roman Catholic. Avocations: sking, horseback riding. Office: Two Great Falls Plaza Auburn ME 04210

MC CANN, FRANCES VERONICA, physiologist, educator; b. Manchester, Conn., Jan. 15, 1927; d. John Joseph and Grace E. (Tuttle) Mc C.; m. Elden J. Murray, Sept. 20, 1962 (dec. Nov. 1975). AB with distinction and honors, U. Conn., 1952, PhD, 1959; MS, U. Ill., 1954; MA (hon.), Dartmouth Coll., 1973. Investigator Marine Biol. Lab., Woods Hole, Mass., 1952-62; instr. physiology Dartmouth Med. Sch., Hanover, N.H., 1959-61, asst. prof. NH, 1961-67, assoc. prof., 1967-73, prof., 1973—98; adj. prof. biol. scis. Dartmouth Coll., 1974—80, prof. emerita. Mem., cons. physiology study sect. NIH, 1973-77, mem. biomed. rsch. devel. com., 1978-82, chmn, 1979; cons. Hayer Inst., 1979—; cons. staff Hitchcock Hosp., Hanover, 1980—, sr. staff rsch. Norris Catton Cancer Ctr., 1980—; mem. NRC, 1982-86; chmn. Symposium on Comparative Physiology of the Heart, 1968; course leader, mem. curriculum com. Inst. Lifelong Edn., Dartmouth Coll., 2000--. Editor: Comparative Physiology of the Heart: Current Trends, 1965; contbr. numerous articles to profl. jours. Trustee Lebanon Coll., 1970-73, Montshire Mus. Sic., Hanover, 1975-80, Hanover Health Coun., 1976, Lebanon Coll., 1978-80; incorporator Howe Libr., 1975—; active LWV, 1980—, Conservation Coun., 1983—, Hist. Soc., 1975—, N.H. Lakes Assn., 1992—; pres. Armington Lake Assn., 1991-93. Nat. Heart Inst. fellow, 1959; NIH rsch. grantee, 1959-98, Nat. Heart Inst., 1960, N.H. Heart Assn., 1964-65, Vt. Heart Assn., 1966-68. Mem. AAAS, Am. Assn. Advancement of Lab. Animal Care, Am. Physiol. Soc., Soc. Gen. Physiologists, Biophys. Soc., Am. Heart Assn. (coun. basic sci., exec. coun. Dallas chpt. 1982-86), Soc. Neurosci. Marine Biol. Lab., LWV, Sigma Xi, Phi Kappa Phi. Avocations: sailing, hiking, reading, keyaking, skiing. Office: Dartmouth Med Sch Lebanon NH 03756

MCCANN, GAIL ELIZABETH, lawyer; b. Boston, Aug. 25, 1953; d. Joseph and Ruth E. (Lagerquist) McC.; m. Stanley J. Lukasiewicz. AB, Brown U., 1975; JD, U. Pa., Phila., 1978. Bar: R.I. 1978, Mass. 1984, U.S. Dist. Ct. R.I. 1978, U.S. Dist. Ct. Mass. 1990. Ptnr. Edwards & Angell, LLP, Providence, 1978—. Bd. dirs. Caritas House, Inc.; mem. R.I. adv. coun. New Eng. Legal Found.; mem. exec. com. Brown U. Ann. Fund; mem. Mass. adv. coun. AAA So. New Eng. Mem. R.I. Bar Assn., Brown U. Alumni Assn. (past pres.). Avocations: hiking, travel, yoga. Office: Edwards & Angell LLP 2800 Financial Plz Providence RI 02903

MCCANN, JEAN FRIEDRICHS, artist, educator; b. N.Y.C., Dec. 6, 1937; d. Herbert Joseph and Catherine Brady (Ward) Friedrichs; m. William Joseph McCann, May 14, 1960; children: Kevin, Brian, Maureen McCann Breslin, William, James, Denis Gerard, Kathleen. Student, Caton-Rose Inst. Fine Arts, 1955-57; AAS, SUNY, Farmingdale, 1959; BS, SUNY-Empire State Coll., Binghamton, 1986; MA summa cum laude, Marywood Coll., 1987, MFA in Art summa cum laude, 1989; completed Kellogg Leadership Progam, Sch. Mgmt., SUNY, Binghamton, 1992; PhD, Nova Coll., 1995. Designer Patton Corp., N.Y.C., 1959-66; sub. art tchr. Owego-Apalachin Sch. Dist., 1968-88; tutor, evaluator Empire State Coll. SUNY, 1987—; dir. ArtSpace Gallery, Owego, N.Y., 1992-94. V.p. bd. dirs. Tioga County Coun. on Arts, 1990—91, pres., 1992—95; tchr. design and drawing Diàn Dà Shui Coll., Guiyang, Guizhou, China, 2001; demonstrator for various schs., ednl. TV and county museums. One-woman shows include IBM, Owego, 1972, Tioga County Hist. Soc. Mus., Owego, 1975, Nat. Hist. Ct. House, 1982, Visual Arts Ctr., Scranton, Pa., 1989-90, ArtSpace Gallery, 1991, Coll. Misericordia MacDonald Art Gallery, Dallas, Pa., 1992, Plaza Gallery, Binghamton, 1992, Krembs Gallery, Binghamton, 1993, 2000, Wilson Gallery, Johnson City, N.Y., 1994, 2001, Countryside Gallery, Owego, N.Y., 1996, 2002, Meml. Gallery, SUNY, Farmingdale, 1998; exhibited in group shows at IBM, Owego, 1970, Roberson Ctr., Binghamton, 1972, Arnot Art Mus., Elmira, 1974, 89, 92, Nat. Exhibits at Arena, Binghamton, 1974-76, Riise Gallery, St. Thomas, 1975-78, Pennino's Gallery, Burlington Vt., 1975-77, Wilson Gallery, Johnson City, N.Y., 1977, 1999-2000, Visual Arts Ctr., Scranton, Pa., 1987, Grand Concourse Gallery, Albany, N.Y., 1987, Tioga County Hist. Soc. Mus., 1990, ArtSpace Gallery, 1990, Contemporary Gallery, Scranton, 1992, 96, Meml. Gallery, SUNY, Farmingdale, 1997, Artists Guild Gallery, 1993, 1999-2000, Krembs Gallery, Binghamton, N.Y., 1999, 2001, Schweinfurth Meml. Art Ctr., Auburn, N.Y., 2002; represented in pvt. collections including Pres. George Bush, Congressman Matt McHugh, Senator Tom Libous, Gov. George Pataki. Bd. dirs. Birthright of Owego, 1993—. Recipient N.Y. State Artisans award, 1982, Nat. Strathmore Silver award, 1989, 1st pl. in Graphic Arts award Jericho Arts Coun., 1994. Mem. Nat. Mus. Women in Arts (charter), Kappa Pi (pres. Zeta Omicron chpt. 1987-89, life), Artists Guild. Avocations: travel, read, visit museums. Home: 23 Paige St Owego NY 13827-1617

MCCANN, JOYCE JEANNINE, retired elementary education educator; b. Council Bluffs, Iowa, Dec. 15, 1926; d. Clyde Oliver and Reva Arleta (Myers) Tisher; m. Daniel Steven McCann, Aug. 14, 1960 (div. 1968); children: Marianne Rose, Daniel Patrick. BA, UCLA, 1955. Elem. tchr. L.A. Unified Sch. Dist., 1968-92. Recipient grant L.A. Bd. Edn., 1986-87. Mem.: Profl. Educators L.A., PEO Sisterhood, Delta Kappa Gamma (pres. Zeta Xi chpt. 2000—01). Republican. Avocation: violinist.

MCCANN, LAWRENCE ALTON, music educator; b. Sikeston, Mo., Jan. 11, 1951; s. William Alton and Billie Sue (Thomas) McC.; m. Vickie Dean Brown, Apr. 14, 1979; children: Luke Adam, Mollie Elizabeth. B Music Edn., Southeast Mo. State U., 1976. Cert. tchr. vocal music, K-12, Mo. Music/youth dir. First Bapt. Ch., Gideon, Mo., 1974-77, Red Star Bapt. Ch., Cape Girardeau, 1977-78; news dir., announcer KPBM-FM, Poplar Bluff, 1979; elem. music tchr. Doniphan (Mo.) Elem. Sch., 1979—; pvt. guitar tchr. Three Rivers C.C., Poplar Bluff, 1979-86; music/youth dir. Calvary Bapt. Ch., Dexter, Mo., 1982-87; music dir. Temple Bapt. Ch., Poplar Bluff, 1987—. Profl. devel. chmn. Doniphan R-I Sch. Dist., 1993—; owner Luke and Mollie Music (ASCAP affil.). Composer/lyricist: (sacred music) Opus One, 1988, Choral Praise, 1989, Sacred Music Quarterly/Hong Kong, 1993, (conservation songs), Mo. Conservation Melodies, 1982, (ednl.) Luke and Mollie Music, Dare to Live, 1993, We Teach the Children, 1992. Commr. planning and zoning, City of Poplar Bluff, 1982; team coach/youth soccer Optimist Soccer League, Poplar Bluff, 1988-96; team coach/youth baseball, Park and Recreation Dept., Poplar Bluff, 1993; bicentennial choir dir., Gideon (Mo.) Bicentennial Com., 1976. Recipient Cmty. Svc. award Mo. N.G., 1991; Outstanding Contbr. DARE and Drug Consortium, Ripley County, Mo., 1993. Mem. Mo. State Tchrs. Assn. (state exec. bd. 1994-2000, pres. S.E. dist. 1992-93, CTA pres. 1984-85, 91-92, Medium Sized Sch. Outstanding Leadership award for state, dist. and local svc., SE Region meritorious svc. edn. award 2001), Music Educators Nat. Conf., Mo. Music Educators Assn. Baptist. Avocations: photography, sports card collecting, record collecting, ornament collecting. Office: Doniphan Elem Sch 603 E Summit St Doniphan MO 63935-1142

MCCANN, LEE I. psychology educator; BS, MS, PhD, Iowa State U. Prof. psychology U. Wis., Oshkosh, assoc. vice chancellor, 1992-97. Co-author: Recruiting Good College Faculty, 1996; co-editor: Lessons Learned: Practical Advice for the Teaching of Psychology, 1999.

MCCANN, LOUISE MARY, paralegal; b. Bklyn., Apr. 12, 1949; d. James Joseph and Edith Dorothea (Wubbe) McC. AAS, Elizabeth Seton Coll., 1967; BS, N.Y. Inst. Tech., 1981; paralegal cert., Adelphi U., 1987. Cert. ind. adjustor, motor vehicle and casualty, N.Y. Adminstrv. asst. J.P. Stevens & Co., Inc., N.Y.C., 1969-86; para-legal asst. Congdon, Flaherty, O'Callaghan, Reid, Donlon, Travis & Fishlinger, Garden City, N.Y., 1986—. Capt. tng. divsn. Aux. Police Force, N.Y.C. Police Dept., 1975-92; trooper Boots & Saddles Civil War Re-enactment Unit, 10th N.Y. Cavalry Co. C; contbg. sponsor U.S. Equestrian Team, Gladstone, N.J., 1980; trustee Inc. Village of Roslyn. Master sgt. USAR, 1979—. Decorated Meritorious Svc. medal, Nat. Def. Svc. medal, Army Achievement medal, Army Commendation medal, Armed Forces Res. medal, Outstanding Vol. Svc. medal, Component Achievement medal U.S. Army Res. Mem. Nassau Suffolk (L.I.) Horseman's Assn. Republican. Roman Catholic. Avocations: horseback riding, swimming, needlepoint, crocheting, golf. Home: 305 Main St Roslyn NY 11576-2114 Office: 377 Oak St Garden City NY 11530-6553

MCCANN, MARTHA SUE POWERS, education educator; b. Imlay City, Mich., Sept. 28, 1935; d. Donald Franklin and Virginia (Matthews) Bade; m. Russell L. Powers, Dec. 21, 1957 (div. Apr. 1983); children: Jeffrey, Michael; m. Lyle J. McCann, Aug. 3, 1992. BS, Ea. Mich. U., 1960, MA, 1966; EdS, Oakland U., Rochester, Mich., 1983. Tchr. Imlay City Schs., 1956-60, pub. schs., Niles, Ill., 1960-61, Lakeville Sch., Battle Creek, Mich., 1961-63, Davison (Mich.) Cmty. Sch., 1963-91, elem. chmn., 1973-79, coord. Chpt. I reading and math., 1979-91; ret., 1991; instr. Ea. Mich. U. Ext., Ypsilanti, 1984—. Cons. on reading and lang. arts, tutor, Davison, 1965-91; instr. U. Mich., Flint, 1992; presenter lang. and reading workshops to various Mich. sch. dists., 1982—. Mem. various coms. Davison United Meth. Ch., 1965—; bd. dirs. Davison br. Genesee County Libr., 1993—. Recipient 1st Ann. Outstanding Tchr. award Davison Edn. Assn., 1986. Mem. Nat. Coun. Tchrs. English, Internat. Reading Assn., Mich. Reading Conf. (speaker 1984-86), Mich. Assn. Ret. Pers., Flint Area Reading Coun. (past pres.), Davison Schs. Ret. Tchrs. Club, Beta Sigma Phi (various offices 1975—). Home: 334 Rosemore Dr Davison MI 48423-1616

MCCANN, MARY CHERI, medical technologist, horse breeder and trainer; b. Pensacola, Fla., July 29, 1956; d. Joseph Maxwell and Cora Maria (Underwood) McCann; m. John Coleman Riggs, July 3, 1999 (div. 2002). AA, Pensacola Jr. Coll., 1975; student, U. Md., 1977-78; BS in Biology, Troy State U., 1979; postgrad., U. Fla., 1979. Med. technologist Cape Fear Valley Med. Ctr., Fayetteville, N.C., 1981-85, Doctors Diagnostic Ctr., Fayetteville, 1985-86; sales rep. Waddell & Reed, 1985-86; med. technologist Roche Biomed. Lab., Burlington, N.C., 1986-87; lab. dir. Cumberland Hosp., Fayetteville, 1987-89, Naval Hosp., Pensacola, 1989-90, chemistry supr., 1990-96, night shift supr., 1996—2001; med. technologist Andalusia Regional Hosp., Andalusia, Ala., 2001—. With U.S. Army, 1976-77. Mem. NAFE, Am. Soc. Clin. Pathologists (registrant), Am. Quarter Horse Assn., Japan Karate Assn., Arabian Horse Assn. Am. Republican. Avocations: karate, guns, oil painting. Home: 300 Dogwood Dr Pensacola FL 32505-5323 Office: Cheri's Tack Shack 300 Dogwood Dr Pensacola FL 32512 E-mail: C5horses@yahoo.com.

MCCANN, MAURICE JOSEPH, lawyer; b. St. Louis, July 26, 1950; s. James M. and Marie V. (Del Commune) M.; m. Suzanne Marie Grob, Dec. 29, 1990; 1 child, Mathew Maurice. BS, So. Ill. U., 1972, MA, 1974, PhD, 1976, JD, 1986. Bar: Ill. 1986, Mo. 1987, U.S. Dist. Ct. (ea. dist.) Mo. 1987, U.S. Dist. Ct. (so. dist.) Ill. 1988, U.S. Ct. Appeals (7th cir.) 1998. Teaching asst. So. Ill. U., Carbondale, 1972-76; asst. dir. Vermillion County Comprehensive Employment and Tng. Act, Danville, Ill., 1976; prof. John A. Logan Coll., Carterville, 1977; adj. prof. St. Louis U., 1977-78; exec. dir. Jackson County Comprehensive Employment and Tng. Act, Murphysboro, Ill., 1978-81, Jackson County YMCA, Carbondale, 1982-83; ptnr. McCann & Foley, Murphysboro, 1986-88; pvt. practice law, 1988—. Atty. Murphysboro Fire Protection Dist., Jackson County, 1988—; instr. dept. fin. So. Ill. U., 1988—, instr. dept. higher edn., 1994-96. Author: A Prelude to McCarthyism, 1974, Truman Administration and Federal Aid to Education, 1976, The Black Sox Scandal, 1986. Mem. Found. for Restoration of Ste. Genevieve, Mo., 1984; bd. dirs. So. Ill. Spl. Olympics, Carbondale, 1983-86; commr. Murphysboro Pk. Dist., 1990-92. Harry S. Truman scholar Truman Libr., Independence, Mo., 1975. Mem. ABA, Ill. Bar Assn., St. Louis Bar Assn., Mo. Bar Assn., Jackson County Bar Assn. Roman Catholic. Home: 42 Brian Ave Murphysboro IL 62966-6189 Office: 1331 Walnut St Murphysboro IL 62966-2026

MCCANN, MICHAEL F. industrial hygienist; b. Toronto, Jan. 19, 1943; s. Jack Francis McCann and Bertha Alice (Singleton) Maher; m. Lois Kaggen, Sept. 26, 1984. BSc with honors, U. Calgary, 1964; PhD in Chemistry, Columbia U., 1972. Cert. in comprehensive practice in indsl. hygiene. Sci. tchr. St. Anne's Episc. Sch., Bklyn., 1971-72; sr. technical writer, product safety coord. GAF Corp., N.Y.C., 1973-75; dir. Art Hazards Resource Ctr. Found. for Community of Artists, 1975-77; founder, pres., exec. dir. Ctr. for Safety in Arts (formerly Ctr. Occupational Hazards), 1977-96; indsl. hygiene cons., 1975—. Adj. faculty N.Y. State Sch. Indsl. and Labor Rels., Cornell U. , N.Y.C., 1978, N.Y.C., 79; lectr. environ. scis. Sch. Pub. Health, Columbia U., N.Y.C., 1981—92; instr. U. Man. , Winnepeg, Canada, 1982, Winnepeg, 83; adviser, task force on toxicity of art materials ASTM, 1980—82; mem. ad hoc com. on heal hazards of arts and crafts materials Can. Dept. Nat. Health and Welfare, 1981—84; mem. adv. bd. Mt. Sinai Occupational Health Clinic, N.Y.C., 1987—99; dir. N.Y. State Health and Safety Project, Comms. Workers Am. Dist. 1, 1997—99; dir. ergonomics and safety Ctr. to Protect Workers' Rights, 1999—; adj. asst. prof. environ. occupl. health George Washington U. Sch. Pub. Health and Health Svcs., 2000—. Author: Health Hazards Manual for Artists, 1975, 4th edit., 1994, Artist Beware, 1979, 2d edit., 1992, Lights! Camera! Safety, 1991, Art Safety Procedures for Art Schools and Art Departments, 1992, School Safety Procedures for Art and Industrial Art Programs, 1994; sr. assoc. editor ILO Ency. of Occupational Health and Safety, 1995-97; writer, narrator videotape Art Safety: Hazards and Precautions, 1988; contbr. articles on art materials hazards to various publs.; editor profl. publs. Presenter testimony on labeling of art materials, U.S. Ho. of Reps., 1980, N.Y. State Assembly, 1981. Mem.: N.Y. Com. Occupl. Safety and Health (exec. bd. 1977—87, 1994—99, treas. 1980—85), IEEE, Am. Soc. Safety Engrs., Am. Indsl. Hygiene Assn., Am. Acad. Indsl. Hygiene, APHA. Avocations: science fiction, computers. Office: Ctr to Protect Workers' Rights 8484 Georgia Ave Silver Spring MD 20910-1461 E-mail: michael.mccann@att.net.

MCCANN, NESSAN, physiatrist; b. Dublin, Ireland; came to U.S., 1959; s. John James and Margaret (Hession) McC.; m. Betty Edythe Cahail, Sept. 22, 1961. MBChB, Nat. U., Dublin, 1949; MD, Yale U., 1966. Diplomate Am. Bd. Phys. Medicine and Rehab. Intern St. Vincent's Hosp., Dublin, 1949-50; resident New Haven Hosp., 1965-66; postdoctoral fellow Yale U., New Haven, 1965-66; physician East Side Med. Clinic, Ocala, Fla.; pvt. practice phys. medicine and rehab., 1970-82; chief phys. medicine and rehab. VA Med. Ctr., Washington, 1982-7; pvt. practice phys. medicine and rehab. pediat., Ocala, Fla., 1987—. Assoc. prof. George Washington U., Georgetown U., Med. U. S.C., Charleston. Author: A Doctor's Odyssey, 1999. Office: East Side Med Clinic 2139 NE 2nd St Ocala FL 34470-8264

MCCANN, PETER PAUL, biology researcher, educator; s. Peter F. and Kathleen (Burnett) McC.; m. Danielle Soury, July 31, 1971. AB in Zoology, Columbia U., 1965; PhD, Syracuse U., 1970. Fellow NIH, Bethesda, Md., 1970-73; sr. scientist Ctr. of Rsch. Merrell Internat., Strasbourg, France, 1973-79; sr. biochemist Merrell Dow Rsch. Ctr., Cin., 1979-82; rsch. assoc. scientist Merrell Dow Rsch. Inst., 1982-84, dir. scientific and acad. liaison, 1984-90, dir. sci. adminstrn., 1988-90; prof. U. Cin. Coll. Medicine, 1981—; sr. dir., ctr. dir. Marion Merrell Dow Inc., Indpls., 1990-93; pres. Brit. Biotech Inc., Annapolis, Md., 1993-98; interim pres. U. Md. Biotech. Inst., College Park, 1998-99; pres., CEO Oncostasis, Inc., 1999—2001, Mymetics Corp., 2001—; GG. Co-vice chmn. Gordon Rsch. Conf. on Polyamines, 1987, co-chmn., 1989. Chief editor, co-author Inhibition of Polyamine Metabolism, 1987; co-editor, co-author: Enzymes as Targets for Drug Design, 1989; contbr. articles to profl. jours. Mem. Am. Soc. Cell Biology, Am. Soc. Tropical Medicine and Hygiene, Am. Soc. Biochemistry and Molecular Biology, Biochem. Soc. (editorial adv. bd. 1986-92, editor 1992-99), Soc. of Protozoologists (editorial bd. reviewers 1989-95), Am. Philat. Congress, Inc. (pres. 1990-95), Am. Philat. Soc. (v.p. 1995-99, pres. 1999—). Achievements include patents for method of inhibiting the growth of protozoa, method of controlling phytopathogenic fungus. E-mail: 103226.706@compuserve.com.

MCCANN, RICHARD EUGENE, lawyer; b. Billings, Mont., Aug. 14, 1939; s. Oakey O. and Edith May (Miller) McC.; m. Mona N. Miyagishima, Apr. 27, 1964; children: Tami, Todd (dec.), Jennifer. BA magna cum laude, Rocky Mountain Coll., 1965; JD with highest honors, U. Mont., 1972. Bar: Mont. 1972, Washington 1977, Alaska 1982. Law clk. to Judge W. Jameson U.S. Dist. Ct., Billings, 1972-73; assoc. Crowley, Haughey, Hansen, Toole & Dietrich, 1973-77, Perkins Coie, Seattle, 1977-80, ptnr., 1981—. Contbr. articles to profl. jours. Trustee Rocky Mountain Coll., Billings., 1973-77. Served with USMC, 1957-61. Mem. ABA, Mont. Bar Assn., Wash. Bar Assn., Alaska Bar Assn. Office: Perkins Coie 1201 3rd Ave Fl 40 Seattle WA 98101-3029 E-mail: mccar@perkinscoie.com.

MCCANN, RICHARD STEPHEN, lawyer; b. Wilmington, Del., Dec. 26, 1938; s. Francis E.B. and Naomi H. (Riley) McC.; m. Gloria M. Baum (div. 1973); 1 child, Heather Marie; m. Sharon R. Cannon. BA, Georgetown U., 1960, JD, 1963; M in City Planning, U. Pa., 1965. Bar: Del. 1964. Alderman City of Newark, Newark, 1964-66, pvt. practice law, 1970—; city planner Dover, Del., 1966-70. Atty. Del. Police Chief's Coun., Dover, 1971—, Del. Police Chief's Found., Dover, 1983—. Atty. Aetna Hose, Hook & Ladder Co., Newark, 1975—. Mem. ABA, Del. Bar Assn. Avocations: Skiing, gardening, cannons. Home: 19 Carriage Ln Newark DE 19711-2637 Office: 125 E Delaware Ave Newark DE 19711-4644 E-mail: rsmccannesq@aol.com.

MCCANN, SUSAN LYNN, elementary education educator; b. Forest Hills, N.Y., Feb. 11, 1947; d. Henry August and Frances Susan (Kleist) Kupsch; m. Kevin Daniel McCann, June 28, 1970; children: Christopher, Megan. BS in Edn., St. John's U., 1968, MS in Edn., 1971. Elem. tchr. Bellmore (N.Y.) Schs., 1968-76, Massapequa (N.Y.) Schs., 1987—. Pvt. tutor, Massapequa, 1968—; mem., chair N.Y. State Sch. Com., Massapequa, 1990—; chair Shared-Decision-Making, Massapequa, 1994-96, Ptnrs. in Reading, Massapequa, 1992-93. Chmn. cultural arts Birch Lane PTA, Massapequa, 1986-90; chmn. Earthday com. Unqua Sch., Massapequa, 1991—; vol. Am. Heart Assn., Bohemia, N.Y., 1991—, Nancy Waters Meml. Run, Seaford, N.Y., 1982-92; cmty. outreach chmn. Massapequa Fedn. Tchrs., 1995—. Recipient Cmty. Svc. Merit cert. Massapequa Bd. Edn., 1995, Nat. Lifetime award PTA, 1995, Disting. Svc. award Unqua PTA, 1997. Mem. Am. Fedn. Tchrs., N.Y. State United Tchrs. (gifts of the heart award 1994, cmty. svc. award 1995), Massapequa Fedn. Tchrs. (chair sch. holiday fundraisers 1993—, coord. pub. rels. 1996-98, outreach chmn. 1995-97). Avocations: cooking, baking, cross-country skiing, reading. Office: Massapequa Schs Merrick Rd Massapequa NY 11758 E-mail: skmteach@aol.com.

MCCANN, THOMAS RYLAND, JR. minister; b. Columbus, Miss., May 28, 1944; s. Thomas Ryland and Shirley Elizabeth (Jones) McC.; m. Beverly Jane Marshall, Nov. 26, 1966; children: Jane, Thomas Scott, Stephen. Student, U. Hawaii, 1962-64; BA in Polit. Sci., U. Richmond, 1966; MPA, U. N.C., Chapel Hill, 1971; MDiv, Southeastern Sem., 1985, DMin, 1990. Ordained to ministry So. Bapt. Conv., 1983. Pastor Wakefield Cen. Bapt. Ch., Zebulon, N.C., 1983-86, 1st Bapt. Ch., Dunn, 1986-91, Martinsville, Va., 1991—. Mem. gen. bd. Bapt. State Conv., Cary, N.C., 1990, mem. coun. on Christian life and pub. affairs, 1990, svcs.-rendered com., 1990; sec. Dunn Ministerial Assn., 1989—; v.p. Mcpl. Advisors, Inc., Virginia Beach, Va., 1975-82; county adminstr. James City County, Va., 1973-75; budget dir. Alexandria, Va., 1970-73; dep. dir. Model Cities, Winston-Salem, N.C., 1967-70; mem. strategy planning com. Bapt. Gen. Assn. Va., 1996-97, mem. com. on bds. and coms., 1998—, pres., 2000-01; trustee Bapt. Theol. Sem., Richmond, Va., 1993-2000; chair, chair exec. com. Va. Bapt. Mission Bd., 2000—, chair Nat. Ministry Ptnrs. Study com.; mem. coord. coun. Coop. Bapt. Fellowship,

2001-. Co-chmn. Evening in the Park Com., Dunn, 1987—; mem. City Planning Bd., Dunn, 1989—; chmn. Dunn (N.C.) Drug Abuse Task Force, 1989—; mem., chmn. City Planning Commn., Martinsville, 1993—; bd. dirs. Piedmont Arts Assn., Martinsville, Va. Mem. Pi Sigma Alpha. Office: 1st Bapt Ch 23 Starling Ave Martinsville VA 24112-2921

MCCANTS, CLYDE TAFT, retired clergyman; b. Jan. 9, 1933; s. Edwin Clyde and Mary Rachel (Taft) McC. AB, Erskine Coll., 1954; MA, Duke U., 1956; MDiv, Erskine Theol. Sem., 1970; D of Ministry, Columbia Theol. Sem., 1987. Ordained to ministry, 1970. English faculty Elon Coll., N.C., 1955-60, Erskine Coll., Due West, S.C., 1960-65; faculty English, dept. chmn. Gaston Coll., Gastonia, N.C., 1965-67; pastor Lauderdale Ch., Lexington, Va., 1970-73; dir. ch. ext. Gen. Synod, Assoc. Ref. Presbyn. Ch., 1973-77; pastor 1st A.R. Presbyn. Ch., Burlington, N.C., 1977-78; asst. and assoc. prof. ministry Erskine Theol. Sem., 1978-82; pastor Greenville (S.C.) A.R.P. Ch., 1982-93, Bethel A.R.P. Ch., Winnsboro, S.C., 1993-98. Trustee Erskine Coll., 1973-78; moderator Gen. Synod of Assoc. Ref. Presbyn. Ch., 1978-79; chmn. Presbyn. Coun. on Chaplains and Mil. Personnel, Washington, 1983-84; chmn. bd. Friends of Fairfield County Libr., 1995-96, sec. 1997-99, Fairfield County Libr. Bd., 1996—, chmn., 1997—; vice-chmn. Friends of S.C. Libraries, 1998-99, chmn., 1999-2000; adv. coun. Palmetto Book Alliance, 1998—. Author: The God Who Makes History, 1976, David, King of Israel, 1978; contbr. articles to profl. jours. Democrat. Home: 120 Walnut St Winnsboro SC 29180-1040

MCCARBERG, BILL HAROLD, physician; b. Seattle, Apr. 4, 1948; s. Harold Carl and Elizabeth Ann Mehlberg; m. Peggy J. McCarthy McCarberg. BA summa cum laude, U. Calif., Berkeley, 1972; MD, Northwestern U., Chgo., 1976. Diplomate Am. Bd. Family Practice, Am. Coll. Pain Medicine; cert. in geriatrics. Residency Highland Hosp., Rochester, N.Y., 1979; physician in charge Kaiser Permanente, Escondido, Calif., 1982—; asst. clin. prof. U. Calif. Sch. Medicine, San Diego, 1983—; coord. of pain svcs. Kaiser Permanente, 1974—, dir. chronic pain mgmt. program, 1984—; founding mem. managed care task force Am. Pain Soc., 1990—; program chair Western Pain Soc., 1999—. Adv. bd. Knoll Pharma, Olive Mt., N.J., 1998—. Author: (monograph) Chronic Pain Management: Perspective for Primary Care Physicians, 1998, (book chpt.) A Sample of Existing Managed Care Organizations Pain Programs, 1999; contbr. articles to profl. jours. Recipient K Star for Outstanding Svc., Kaiser Permanente, San Diego, 1985, 92, Award of Excellence Southern Calif. Cancer Pain Initiative, L.A., 1999. Mem. Am. Acad. Pain Medicine, Am. Pain Soc. (chair managed care com. 2000—, bd. dirs. 2000—), Western Pain Soc., Appraisal of Physician Svcs., Phi Beta Kappa. Avocations: running, guitar, golf. Office: Kaiser Permanente 732 N Broadway Escondido CA 92025-1870 Fax: 760-839-7096. E-mail: bill.h.mccarberg@kp.oag.

MCCARDELL, HARRIETT WYNN See STAMBAUGH, HARRIETT MCCARDELL

MCCARDELL, JAMES ELTON, retired naval officer; b. Daytona Beach, Fla., Jan. 22, 1931; s. J. Elton and Margaret Almira (Payne) McC.; m. Nancy Ann Chandler, July 9, 1955; children: Jenise, Patrick. Student, U. Fla., 1948-50; BA, U.S. Naval Postgrad. Sch., 1965. Commd. ensign U.S. Navy, 1952, advanced through grades to rear adm., 1980; exec. officer USS Forrestal, 1972-73; dep. chief of staff Air Readiness Staff, Chief Naval Res., New Orleans, 1973-76; comdg. officer NAS, Key West, Fla., 1976-78; chief of staff Staff of Chief Naval Res., New Orleans, 1978-80; def. and naval attache U.S. Embassy, Brasilia, Brazil, 1981-83; dir. Inter-Am. Def. Coll., Fort L.J. McNair, Washington, 1983-85; ret., 1985. Decorated Legion of Merit with cluster, Bronze Star medal, Air medal with 12 clusters, Def. Disting. Service medal, Def. Superior Performance medal Republican. Roman Catholic. Home: PO Box 719 Pass Christian MS 39571-0719 *The absolute measure of successful leadership has always been reflected by performance of subordinates in the achievement of unit goals.*

MCCARDELL, JOHN MALCOLM, JR. college administrator; b. Frederick, Md., June 17, 1949; s. John Malcolm Sr. and Susan (Lane) McC.; m. Bonnie Greenwald, Dec. 30, 1976; children: John Malcolm III, James Benjamin Lee. AB, Washington and Lee U., 1971; postgrad., John Hopkins U., 1972-73; PhD, Harvard U., 1976; Litt.D., Washington and Lee U., 1997. Asst. prof. history Middlebury (Vt.) Coll., 1976-80, assoc. prof. history, 1982-87, dean for academic devel., 1985-88, prof. history, 1987—, dean facuty, 1988-89, provost, v.p for academic affairs, 1989-91, acting pres., 1991-92, pres., 1992—; sr. rsch fellow U. S.C., Columbia, 1980-81, 96. Bd. dirs. Nat. Bank Middlebury. Author: The Idea of a Southern Nation, 1979 (Allan Nevins award 1977); editor: A Master's Due, 1985. Sgt. USAR, 1971-77. Recipient Algernon Sydney Sullivan prize Washington and Lee U., 1971, Charles Eliot medal Eliot House Harvard U., 1976; Nat. Endowment for Humanities fellow, 1980; Am. Philosophical Soc. fellow, 1979. Mem. Am. Hist. Assn., Orgn. Am. Historians, So. Hist. Assn., Am. Studies Assn., Vt. Hist. Soc., Omicron Delta Kappa, Phi Beta Kappa, Lambda Chi Alpha. Office: Middlebury Coll Old Chapel Bldg Middlebury VT 05753

MCCARDELL, KEENAN, football player; b. Jan. 6, 1970; Attended, Univ. Las Vegas. Wide receiver Tampa Bay Buccaneers , 2002—, Jacksonville Jaguars, 1996—2001, Cleveland Browns, 1992—95. Office: Tampa Bay Buccaneers 1 Buccaneer Pl Tampa FL 33607*

MCCARGAR, ELEANOR BARKER, portrait painter; b. Presque Isle, Maine, Aug. 30, 1913; d. Roy and Lucy Ellen (Hayward) Barker; m. John Albert McCargar, Feb. 18, 1947; children: Margaret, Lucy, Mary. Cert. elem. sch. tchg., Aroostook State Normal Sch., Presque Isle, 1933; student, Acadia U., 1935-36; B of Sociology, Colby Coll., 1937; summer student, Harvard U., 1939; and, Cambridge Sch. Art, 1939; studied portrait painting with Kenneth Washburn, Thomas Leighton, Maria von Ridelstein, Jean Henry, 1957-67. Ltd. svc. credential in fine and applied arts and related techs. Calif. C.C. Tchr. sci. and geography Limestone (Maine) Jr. H.S., 1937-41; ins. claim adjuster Liberty Mut. Ins. Co., Boston, 1941-42, Portland, Maine, 1943; ARC hosp. worker 20th Gen. Hosp., Ledo, Assam, India, 1944-45; portrait painter Burlingame and Apple Valley, Calif., 1958—. Commns. include more than 800 portraits in 10 states and 4 fgn. countries. Recipient M. Grumbacher Inc. Merit award for outstanding contbn. to arts, 1977; named Univ. of Maine Disting. Alumnus in Arts, 1981. Avocations: canoeing, camping, travel, studying.

MCCARGAR, JAMES GOODRICH, diplomat, writer; b. San Francisco, Apr. 20, 1920; s. Jesse B. and Addie May (Goodrich) McC.; m. Geraldine Claudia Cooper-Key, Aug. 2, 1948 (div. 1954); m. Emanuela Butculescu, Dec. 22, 1973. BA, Stanford U., 1942. Commd. Fgn. Svc. Officer, 1942; Dept. State, Moscow, 1942, 43; Vladivostok, 1942-43; Santo Domingo, 1943-44; sec. of legation, chief polit. sect. Budapest, Hungary, 1946-47; vice consul Genoa, Italy, 1948; chief div. Southeastern European Affairs Office of Policy Coordination, Washington, 1948-50; sec. of embassy, mem. U.S. Del. to Allied Coordinating Com., Paris, 1950-53; asst. to v.p. Free Europe Com., Inc., N.Y.C., 1955, European dir. polit. ops. Paris, 1956-58, cons. to pres., 1959-60, 71-76; spl. asst. to chmn. NEH, Washington, 1978-82; U.S. del. UNESCO confs., 1978, 80, 82; alt. rep. U.S.-Japan Friendship Commn., 1979-82; U.S. del. U.S.-Mexico Commn. on Cultural Coop., 1980, Sem. on Funding of Culture, Madrid, 1982; cons. BBC-TV, London, 1984, Nat. Dem. Inst. Internat. Affairs, Washington, 1984, African-Am. Labor Ctr., Washington, 1984-85, Am. Inst. Free Labor Devel., Washington, 1985, Dept. Internat. Affairs, AFL-CIO, Washington, 1986-95, Free Trade Union Inst., Washington, 1993-95, U.S. Info. Agy., Washington, 1998; editl. advisor Interco Press, 1988-96. Panelist internat. conf. Hungary and the World 1956, Budapest, 1996; bd. dirs. Ams. for Universality of UNESCO, Washington. Author: A Short Course in the Secret War, 1963, rev. edit., 1988, 4th edit., 2001, El Salvador and Nicaragua: The AFL-CIO Views on the Controversy, 1985, Ferenc Nagy: Smallholder or Statesman?, 1995; co-author: Three-Cornered Cover, 1972, Lost Victory, 1989; contbr. articles and book revs., 1940-70; ghostwriter, 1964-96. Co-founder, sec. Ams. Abroad for Kennedy, Paris, 1960. Ensign USNR, 1944-46. Recipient Cert. of Appreciation Internat. Ctr. for Free Trade Unions in Exile, 1958, Fed. Outstanding Performance award NEH, 1979, 81; decorated Knight First Class Royal Norwegian Order St. Olav, 1983, Silver Medallion of the Hungarian Parliament, 1991, Officer's Cross Order of the Hungarian Republic, 1992, Officer's Cross Order of Merit of the Rep. of Poland, 1993. Mem. Polish Inst. Arts and Scis. Am. (elected), Diplomatic and Consular Officers Retired, Oss Soc. (hon.), Authors' Guild, Cosmos Club (Washington). Democrat. Home and Office: 4201 Cathedral Ave NW Washington DC 20016-4948

MCCARGAR, REX, music educator; BME, NE La. U., Monroe, 1977. Band dir. Catahoula Parish Schls., Jonesville, La., 1977—87; band dir. Eldon R-1 Schools, Eldon, Mo., 1987—. Mem.: Mo. Music Educators' Assn., Mo. Bandmasters Assn., Music Educators' Nat. Conf., Catahoula Tchrs. Assn. (pres.), Mo. State Tchrs. Assn., Phi Beta Mu.

MCCARL, HENRY NEWTON, economics and geology consultant, venture capitalist; b. Balt., Jan. 24, 1941; s. Fred Henderson and Mary Bertha (Yaeger) McCarl; m. Louise Becker Rys, June 8, 1963 (div. May 1986); children: Katherine Lynne(dec.) , Patricia Louise, Fredrick James; m. Mary Frederica Rhinelander, Jan. 31, 1987; 1 stepchild Francesca C. Morgan. BS in Earth Sci., MIT, 1962; MS in Geology, Pa. State, 1964, PhD in Mineral Econ., 1969. Lic. profl. geologist Ala., N.H. Market rsch. analyst Vulcan Materials Co., 1966-69; asst. prof. econs., asst. prof. geology U. Ala., Birmingham, 1969-72, assoc. prof. econs., 1973-77, assoc. prof. econs. and geology, 1978-91, prof. econs. and geology, 1991-95, prof. econs., edn. and geology, 1995-2001, prof. emeritus, 2001—, dir. Ctr. for Econ. Edn., Sch. Bus., 1987-2001; chief econs. div. Ala. Energy Mgmt. Bd., Montgomery, 1973-74; sr. lectr. in energy econs. Fulbright-Hays Program, Bucharest, Romania, 1977-78; ret., 2001. Mng. dir. McCarl & Assocs., Gloucester, Mass., 1969—; vis. fellow Grad. Sch. Arts and Scis. Harvard U., Cambridge, Mass., 1987; v.p., ptnr. Economagic, 1999—. Co-author: Energy Conservation Economics, 1986, Introduction to Energy Conservation, 1987; contbr. articles to profl. jours. Mem. Birmingham Planning Commn., 1974—86, chmn., 1980—86; dist. commr. Boy Scouts Am., Birmingham, 1988—94, asst. coun. Com. Greater Ala. Coun., 1999—2001; mem. edn. coun. MIT, 1974—. Recipient George B. Morgan award, MIT Alumni Assn., 1999. Mem.: SAR (life, treas. gen. 2000—, nat. trustee 1996-97, nat. soc. sec. fin. com. 1995-97, chmn. GWEF dist. com. 1997-99, GWEF bd., Ins. com. 1997—, St. Andrews Soc. Mid-South (life, sec. 1996, 97), Nat. Assn. Econ. Educators, Ala. Geol. Soc., Mineral Econs. and Mgmt. Soc. (pres. 1992-93), Am. Inst. Profl. Geologists (reg. profl. geologist, sect. pres. 1981-83), Soc. Mining Engrs. of AIME (disting. award 2000, bd. dirs. 1978-80). Republican. Episcopalian. Avocations: amateur radio, woodworking, collections, model railroading. Home: 28 Old Nugent Farm Rd Gloucester MA 01930-3167 Office: 112 Eastern Ave Gloucester MA 01930

MCCARLEY, GEORGE DAVID, management executive; b. Franklin, Ga., Oct. 25, 1953; s. Earl Robertson and Almadge Elizabeth (Barnes) McC. BBA, Jacksonville State U., 1975; cert. in design engring., U.S. Army, 1976. Supr. Milliken & Co. Inc., La Grange, Ga., 1976-79; mgmt. engr. Ops. Mgmt. Group, Atlanta, 1979-83; mgmt. cons. Kerry Meg, Inc., Gulf Shores, Ala., 1983-86; pres. McCarley & Assocs., Inc., Roanoke, 1986—. Cons. Dow Badische, Anderson, S.C., 1979, GE, 1981, Carrier Corp., 1982, DuraCell, 1983, Woolworths Australia Ltd., Sydney, 1983—, Steel Warehouse Cos., South Bend, Ind., 1985—, Walker Machine and Foundry, Roanoke, Va., 1985—, Steel Joist Ind., Lafayette, La., 1986—, Wilson Mktg., Inc., 1990—, Murray Ohio Mfg. Co., 1990—, Ciba Geigy, Inc., 1991—, Bapt. Hosp. Systems, Birmingham, 1994—, Jim Walter Resources, 1996—; affiliated with Ga. Tech. Southea. Inst. of Tech.; acting gen. mgr. Fairmont Foundry Co., Inc., 1989. Trumpeter 16 classical music recordings La Grange Symphony Orch., 1989—; contbr. writer Voice of the People, featured performer Ga. Musician of the Year Award Banquet; software developer Beta Testor, Datastream Software Sys., Microsoft. Mgr., pres. La Grange Symphony Orch., 1983; active ARC, United Way; founder, chmn. Ronald Hyche Scholarship Found., 1992—, Randolph County Ala. Indsl. Devel. Bd.; foreman Fed. Jury, 1994; mem. exec. com. Rep. Presdl. Roundtable, 1998; life mem. Rep. Nat. Com., 1998. 1st lt. C.E., USAR, 1975-83. Mem. NRA (life), Jacksonville State U. Nat. Alumni Assn. (gov. 1987—, chmn. athletic status com. 1990-91), Nat. Geog. Soc., Quail Unltd., Grey Echelon (ret. col. 1982), Gun Owners of Am. Washington, No. Am. Hunting Club, Gamecock club. Republican. Baptist. Avocations: music, tennis, running, outdoor sports, wildlife habitat management. Home and Office: 105 Chestnut St Roanoke AL 36274-1301

MCCARLEY, ROBERT EDWARD, real estate executive, real estate appraiser; b. Memphis, Apr. 19, 1943; s. Bernie Bryant and Mildred (Clark) McC.; m. Anne Weatherford Hyatt, Oct. 23, 1971; children: Hyatt, Clark, John. BS in Bus. Adminstrn., U. Ark., 1965. Pres. McCarley & Co., West Memphis/Little Rock, Ark., 1966—; v.p. The Hathaway Group, Little Rock, 1986-89. Sec.-treas. The Title Co., West Memphis, 1992—. Dir. Bank of West Memphis, Ark., 1973-86. Mem. Appraisal Inst. (regional committeeperson 1990—, pres. Ark. chpt. 1989), Country Club of Little Rock. Presbyterian. Avocations: golf, travel. Home: 5614 Edgewood Rd Little Rock AR 72207-5314

MCCARNEY, WILLIAM CHRISTOPHER, music educator; b. Fairfax, Va., June 30, 1972; s. William Lee and Silvia Hange McCarney; m. Andrea Leigh Sheetz. MA Ednl. Adminstrn., George Wash. U., 2002. Dir. of bands Chesterfield County Pub. Schs., Va., 1995—. Recipient Commonwealth of Va. Honor Band, Va. Band and Orch. Director's Assn., 1999—2001. Mem.: Va. Music Educator's Assn. Office: Manchester High School 12601 Bailey Bridge Road Midlothian VA 23112

MCCARRICK, THEODORE EDGAR, archbishop; b. N.Y.C., July 7, 1930; s. Theodore Egan and Margaret (McLaughlin) McC. Student, Fordham U., 1950-52; AB, St. Joseph's Sem., 1954, AM, 1958; MA, Cath. U., 1960, PhD, 1963; LLD, Mt. St. Vincent Coll., 1967; STD, Inter-Am. U., 1969; STD (hon.), Niagara U., 1982; LHD (hon.), St. John's U., 1974, St. Peter's Coll., 1987. Ordained priest Roman Cath. Ch., 1958. Asst. chaplain Cath. U. Am., Washington, 1959-61, dean students, 1961-63, asst. to rector, dir. univ. devel., 1963-65, instr. dept. sociology, 1961-65; domestic prelate, 1965; pres. Cath. U. P.R., 1965-69; assoc. dir. edn. Archdiocese of N.Y., 1969-71; sec. to Cardinal-Archbishop N.Y., 1971-77; titular bishop of Rusubisir, aux. bishop N.Y., 1977-81; 1st bishop Diocese of Metuchen, N.J., 1981-86; 4th archbishop Newark, 1986-2000; archbishop Washington, 2000—; elevated to cardinal, 2001; cardinal Ch. of Sts. Nereus and Achilleus, 2001—. Mem. policy bd. Washington Consortium, Peace Corps, 1962-63, Pontifical Commn. for Migrants and Refugees, 1987—; chmn. U.S. Bishops Com. on Migration, 1986-89, 92-95; mem. Nat. Coun. for Spanish-Speaking People, 1961-65; chmn. Gov.'s Commn. for Higher Edn. in P.R., 1968, P.R. Adv. Coun. on Tech. and Vocat. Edn., 1968-69. Mem. Fed. Commn. for Study of Migration and Econ. Devel., 1989; Episcopal promoter Apostleship of the Sea, 1989-92; chmn. com. aid to ch. in Ctrl. and Ea. Europe, Nat. Conf. Cath. Bishops, 1992-96, chmn. internat. policy com., 1996-99; sec.-treas. Papal Found., 1988-96, pres., 1997—; mem. U.S. Sec. of State's Adv. Com. on Religious Freedom Abroad, 1996—, U.S. Com. for Internat. Religious Freedom, 1999—; invited to visit China to discuss religious freedom in that country, 1998; mem. U.S. Synod for Am. and Post Synod Coun. Named officer, knight grand cross Holy Sepulchre, Order of Cedars of Lebanon, Lebanese Govt., 2000 Mem.: KC, Am. Assn. Knights Malta (chaplain 1978-82). Office: Washington Archdiocesan Pastoral Ctr PO Box 29260 Washington DC 20017-0260

MCCARROLL, EARL, educator, director; b. Memphis, Aug. 20, 1939; s. Earl Lucas and Helen (Shannon) McC. BA, Duke U., 1961; MA, U. Ark., 1963. Actor, dir. Champlain Shakespeare Festival, Burlington, vt., 1966-68; dir. theatre Duke U., Durham, N.C., 1970-71; artistic dir. Shakespeare Theatre of Maine, Monmouth, 1973-76; full prof. Ithaca (N.Y.) Coll., 1971-2001. Guest dir. Columbia U., N.Y.C., 1968; speech coach IBM, N.Y.C., 1968-69; Shakespeare coach pvt. studio, N.Y.C., 1979; guest dir. Champlain Shakespeare Festival, Burlington, Vt., 1988; lectr. Am. Coll. Theatre Festival, Ithaca, 1987; guest dir., lectr. Nat. Shakespeare Conservatory, 1989. Appeared on Broadway as Chaucer in Canterbury Tales, 1980; other appearances include (film) Agee (Acad. Award nominee 1981), (PBS series) Your Future Is Now, 1972, To Render a Life, 1992; translator, dir. L'Histoire du Soldat and The Miser, N.Y.C., 1982; dir. plays including Julius Caesar, 1973, Comedy of Errors, 1974, King Lear, 1975, Antony & Cleopatra, 1976, Loose Ends, 1980. Writer, actor Ithaca Centennial celebration, 1987; dir., writer fundraising campaigns Cornell U., Yale U., 1991-93. Recipient study grant Oxford U., England, 1989; named Dana Outstanding Tchr., 1982, Best Actor U. Ark., 1963, State Winner Voice of Democracy, 1956. Mem. AFTRA, SAG, Actors Equity Assn., Soc. Stage Dirs. and Choreographers, Theta Alpha Phi. Home: 203 W High St Milford PA 18337 Office: Ithaca Coll Dept Theater Arts Ithaca NY 14850 E-mail: emccarroll@ithaca.edu., earlmc@pikeonline.net.

MCCARROLL, KATHLEEN ANN, radiologist, educator; b. Lincoln, Nebr., July 7, 1948; d. James Richard and Ruth B. (Wagenknecht) McC.; m. Steven Mark Beerbohm, July 10, 1977 (div. 1991); 1 child, Palmer Brooke. BS, Wayne State U., 1974; MD, Mich. State U., 1978. Diplomate Am. Bd. Radiology. Intern/resident in diagnostic radiology William Beaumont Hosp., Royal Oak, Mich., 1978-82, fellow in computed tomography and ultrasound, 1983, dir. divsn. emergency radiology, 2001—; radiologist, dir. radiologic edn. Detroit Receiving Hosp., 1984-2001, vice-chief dept. radiology, 1988-96, chief dept. radiology, 1996-2001. Pres.-elect med. staff Detroit Receiving Hosp., 1992-94, pres., 1994-96; mem. admissions com. Wayne State U. Coll. Medicine, Detroit, 1991-2001; trustee Detroit Med. Ctr., 1996-2001, dir. med. staff consolidation, 1996-97, mem. consol. med. exec. com., 1998-2001, chmn. credentials com., 1998-99, joint conf. com., 1998-99; officer bd. dirs. Dr. L. Reynolds Assoc., P.C., Detroit, 1991-94, 96-2001; presenter profl. confs.; assoc. prof. radiology Wayne State U. Sch. Medicine, Detroit, 1995—; health care cons./med. staff affairs, 1998—. Editor: Critical Care Clinics, 1992; mem. editorial bd. Emergency Radiology; contbr. articles to profl. publs. Named to Crain's Bus. Detroit, Detroit's 100 Most Influential Women, 1997. Mem.: AMA, Wayne/Oakland County Med. Soc., Mich. State Med. . Soc., Am. Soc. Emergency Radiologists (bd. dirs. 1996—2001, mem. exec. com. 1998—2001, bylaws com. 2001—), Am. Roentgen Ray Soc., Assn. Univ. Radiologists, Radio. Soc. N.Am., Am. Coll. Radiology (Mich. chpt. sec. 1995—98, alt. councilor 1999—2000, councilor 2002—), Phi Beta Kappa. Avocations: travelling, skiing, reading. Office: Wm Beaumont Hosp Dept Diag Radiology 3601 W 13 Mile Rd Royal Oak MI 48073

MCCARRON, JEFFREY BALDWIN, lawyer; b. Bryn Mawr, Pa., Mar. 7, 1961; s. John R. and Bette R. McC.; m. Kathryn Gilmour, Oct. 18, 1982; children: Sarah Jane, Jacqueline Lillian. BA, Hampshire Coll., 1983; JD, Temple U., 1987. Bar: Pa. 1987, N.J. 1987, U.S. Dist. Ct. N.J. 1987, U.S. Dist. Ct. (ea. dist.) Pa. 1989, U.S. Ct. Appeals (3d cir.) 1990; diplomate Am. Bd. Profl. Liability Attys. Atty. maj. trial divsn. Defender Assn. Phila., 1987-90; ptnr. Swartz, Campbell & Detweiler, Phila., 1990—. Contbr. articles to law jours. Mem. ABA, Pa. Bar Assn. (vice chmn. profl. liability com. 1997-98), Phila. Bar Assn. Office: Swartz Campbell & Detweiler 1601 Market St Fl 34 Philadelphia PA 19103-2397 E-mail: mccarron@scdlaw.com.

MCCARRON, JOHN FRANCIS, editor; b. Providence, Jan. 20, 1949; s. Hugh Francis and Katherine Anne (Brooks) McC.; m. Janet Ann Velsor, Sept. 3, 1971; children: Veronica, Catherine. BS in Journalism, Northwestern U., 1970, MS in Journalism, 1973. Gen. assignment reporter Chgo. Tribune, 1973-80, urban affairs writer, 1980-91, fin. editor, 1991-92, editorial bd. columnist, 1992-2000; v.p. strategy and comms. Met. Planning Coun. Chgo., 2000—02; vis. prof. Roosevelt U., 2002—. Contbr. to Planning mag., World Book Ency., Preservation mag. Lt. USNR, 1970-72. Recipient Editors award AP, 1983, 84, Ann. Journalism award Am. Planning Assn., 1983, Heywood Broun award Am. Newspaper Guild, Washington, 1989, Peter Lisagor award Soc. Profl. Journalists, 1994. Home: 1425 Noyes St Evanston IL 60201-2639 Office: MPC 25 E Washington St Ste 1600 Chicago IL 60602 E-mail: j.mccarron@att.net.

MCCARRON, ROBERT FREDERICK, II, orthopedic surgeon; b. Hot Springs, Ark., Oct. 31, 1952; s. Robert Frederick and Irene (Shanks) McC.; m. Vicki Lynn Nichols, June 10, 1977; children: Elizabeth, Jennifer. BS, La. Tech. U., 1974; MD, U. Ark., 1977. Diplomate Am. Bd. Orthopedic Surgery; cert. clin. densitometrist.. Intern U. Ark., Little Rock, 1977-78; resident Tex. Tech U., Lubbock, 1978-82, instr. dept. orthopedics, 1983-84, asst. prof., 1984-88; trauma fellow Kantonspittal, Basel, Switzerland, 1982; spine fellow St. Vincent's Hosp., Melbourne, Australia, 1983; pvt. practice orthopedic surgery Conway (Ark.) Orthopaedic and Sports Medicine Clinic, P.A., 1988—. Cons. physician U. Ctrl. Ark., Conway, 1989; chief of surgery Conway Regional Med. Ctr., 1991-94; presenter, exhibitor in field. Contbr. articles to profl. publs. Bd. dirs. Clifton Day Care Ctr., chmn. 1994-95; bd. dirs. Conway Regional Health Sys., Conway Regional Health Found., Instnl. Svcs. Corp., 2000—; pres. Conway Regional Physician Hosp. Orgn., 1996, sec., 1995. Fellow Am. Acad. Orthopedic Surgeons, Am. Orthopedic Foot and Ankle Soc.; mem. Ark. Med. Soc., Faulkner County Med. Soc., Ark. Orthopedic Soc., Conway Area C. of C., Sigma Nu. Republican. Presbyterian. Avocations: reading, racquetball, basketball, computering, trumpet. Office: Conway Orthopaedic Clinic 525 Western Ave Ste 202 Conway AR 72034 E-mail: McCarron@conway.corp.net., rmcortho@conwaycorp.net.

MC CARTAN, PATRICK FRANCIS, lawyer; b. Cleve., Aug. 3, 1934; s. Patrick Francis and Stella Mercedes (Ashton) Mc Cartan; m. Lois Ann Buchman, Aug. 30, 1958; children: M. Karen, Patrick Francis III. AB magna cum laude, U. Notre Dame, 1956, JD, 1959. Bar: Ohio 1960, U.S. Ct. Appeals (6th cir.) 1961, U.S. Ct. Appeals (3rd cir.) 1965, U.S. Ct. Appeals (DC cir.) 1980, U.S. Ct. Appeals (5th cir.) 1981, U.S. Ct. Appeals (4th cir.) 1989, U.S. Ct. Appeals (7th cir.) 1992, U.S. Supreme Ct. 1970. Law clk. to Hon. Charles Evans Whittaker, U.S. Supreme Ct., 1959; assoc. Jones, Day, Reavis & Pogue, Cleve., 1961—65, ptnr., 1966—93, mng. ptnr., 1993—. Trustee U. Notre Dame, 2000—, chair, 2000—; trustee Cleve. Clinic Found.; chair Greater Cleve. Roundtable; mem. standing com. on rules of practice and procedure Jud. Conf. of U.S. Fellow: Internat. Acad. Trial Lawyers, Am. Coll. Trial Lawyers; mem.: ABA, Bar Assn. Greater Cleve. (pres. 1977—78), Ohio Bar Assn., 6th Cir. Jud. Conf. (life), U.S.-Japan Bus. Coun., Coun. on Fgn. Rels., Greater Cleve. Growth Assn. (chmn. 1997—2000), Musical Arts Assn. (trustee). Roman Catholic. Office: Jones Day Reavis & Pogue North Point 901 Lakeside Ave E Cleveland OH 44114-1190 E-mail: pmccartan@jonesday.com.

MCCARTER, CHARLES CHASE, lawyer; b. Pleasanton, Kans., Mar. 17, 1926; s. Charles Nelson and Donna (Chase) McC.; m. Clarice Blanchard, June 25, 1950; children— Charles Kevin, Cheryl Ann. BA, Principia Coll., 1950; JD, Washburn U., 1953; LLM, Yale U., 1954. Bar: Kans. 1953, U.S. Supreme Ct. 1962, Mo. 1968. Asst. atty. gen. State of Kans., 1954-57; lectr. law sch. Washburn U., 1956-57; appellate counsel FCC, Washington, 1957-58; assoc. Weigand, Curfman, Brainerd, Harris & Kaufman, Wichita, 1958-61; gen. counsel Kans. Corp. Commn., 1961-63; ptnr. McCarter, Frizzel & Wettig, Wichita, 1963-68, McCarter & Badger, Wichita, 1968-73; pvt. practice law St. Louis, 1968-76; ptnr. McCarter & Greenley, 1976-85; mng. ptnr. Gage & Tucker, 1985-87, Husch and Eppenberger, St. Louis, 1987-89, McCarter & Greenley, LLC, St. Louis, 1990—. Prof. law, assoc. dir. law sch. Nat. Energy Law and Policy Inst. Tulsa U., 1977-79; prof. law, coach nat. moot ct. coll. of law Stetson U. Coll., St. Petersburg, Fla., 1980-84; mem. govtl. adv. coun. Gulf Oil Corp., 1977-81 ; legal com. Interstate Oil Compact Commn.; mem. adv. bd. Allegiant Bank Trust Divsn., 1997—. Co-author: Missouri Lawyers Guide; assoc. editor Washburn U. Law Rev., 1952-53; contbr. articles to profl. jours. Chmn. Wichita Human Rels. Devel. Adv. Bd., 1967-68; bd. dirs. Peace Haven Assn.; active St. Louis estate planning coun., 1987—, bequests and endowment com. Salvation Army, 1995—, YMCA endowment com., 1996—. With USNR, 1944-46. Recipient Excellent Prof. award U. Tulsa , 1979; vis. scholar Yale U., 1980 Mem. ABA (sect. real property, probate and trust law, bus. law sect.), Kans. Bar Assn., Mo. Bar Assn. (probate and trust com., tax com.), Am. Legion, VFW, Native Sons and Daus. Kans (pres. 1957-58), Kappa Sigma, Delta Theta Phi, Principia Dads Club (bd. dirs.) Republican. Office: One Metropolitan Sq Ste 2100 Saint Louis MO 63102-2797 E-mail: cmccarter@mccartergreenley.com.

MCCARTER, DANIEL G. music educator, composer; b. Abington, Pa., Aug. 12, 1976; s. George T. and Kathryn A. McCarter; m. Natalie Margaret Noyes, Jan. 16, 1977. BMus, Ithaca (N.Y.) Coll., 1999. Dir. of orchestras Suffern (N.Y.) H.S., z, 1999—; cello instr. Acad. Music Ramapo Coll., Nyack, NY, 2000—; freelance cellist, bassist, and guitarist Suffern, 1999—. Composer: (orchestral and vocal works) Crux fidelis, Concerti grosso, song cycles, 2002. Mem.: NY State Sch. Music Assn. Office: Suffern HS 49 Viola Rd Suffern NY 10901 Personal E-mail: daniel.mccarter@verizon.net. E-mail: mccarterd@ramnet.k12.ny.us.

MCCARTER, JAMES PHILIP, biotechnology company executive, researcher; b. Chgo., Aug. 27, 1967; s. John Wilbur and Judith (West) McC.; m. Rosalie M. Truong, Oct. 19, 1996. AB in Biology, Princeton U., 1989; MD, PhD in Devel. Biology, Washington U., St. Louis, 1998. Pres., chief sci. officer Divergence Inc., St. Louis, 1998—; postdoctoral fellow, group leader parasitic nematode project Washington U. Genome Sequencing Ctr., 1998—2002, rsch. instr. genetics, 2002—. Co-founder young scientist program and www.mad-sci.org, St. Louis. Contbr. articles to sci. jours., including Devel. Biology, Jour. Cell Biology, Jour. Molecular Evolution, Jour. Nematology. Olin predoctoral fellow Washington U., 1997-98, postdoctoral fellow Nat. Human Genome Rsch. Inst., NIH, 1998-99, Merck postdoctoral fellow Helen Hay Whitney Found., 1999-2002, Henry Crown fellow Aspen Inst., 2002; named one of 40 Under 40 Bus. Leaders, St. Louis Bus. Jour., 2002. Mem. AAAS, Soc. Nematology, Am. Soc. Parasitologists, Am. Soc. Tropical Medicine and Hygiene, Internat. Soc. for Computational Biology, Sigma Xi. Avocations: science education, urban restoraton, basketball, rowing. Office: 4444 Forest Park Blvd PO Box 8501 Saint Louis MO 63126-0501 E-mail: mccarter@genetics.wustl.edu.

MC CARTER, JOHN WILBUR, JR. museum executive; b. Oak Park, Ill., Mar. 2, 1938; s. John Wilbur and Ruth Rebecca McC.; m. Judith Field West, May 1, 1965; children: James Philip, Jeffrey John, Katherine Field. AB, Princeton U., 1960; postgrad., London Sch. Econs., 1961; MBA, Harvard U., 1963. Cons., assoc., v.p. Booz Allen and Hamilton, Inc., Chgo., 1963-69; White House fellow Washington, 1966-67; dir. Bur. Budget and Dept. Fin., State of Ill., Springfield, 1969-73; v.p. DeKalb AgResearch, Ill., 1973-78, dir., 1975-86, exec. v.p., 1978-80, pres., 1981-82; pres., chief exec. officer DeKalb-Pfizer Genetics, 1982-86; pres. DeKalb Corp., 1985-86; sr. v.p. Booz Allen & Hamilton Inc., 1987-97; pres., CEO Field Mus., Chgo., 1996—. Bd. dirs. A.M. Castle & Co., Divergence LLC, W.W. Grainger, Inc., Harris Insight Funds. Trustee Chgo. Pub. Television, 1973—, chmn., 1989-96, trustee Princeton U., 1983-87, U. Chgo., 1993—. Office: Field Museum 1400 S Lake Shore Dr Chicago IL 60605-2496

MCCARTER, KATHERINE SAUTER, association executive; b. Nyack, N.Y., Nov. 12, 1942; d. William Charles and Josephine Rosina (Schoenle) Sauter; B.A. in Biology, Cedar Crest Coll., Allentown, Pa., 1964; M.H.S. (EPA trainee), Johns Hopkins U., 1973; m. Robert James McCarter, Dec. 6, 1969; 1 dau., Emily Katherine. Chmn. sci. dept. Arundel (Md.) Jr. High Sch., 1964-68; assoc. career devel. program Am. Lung Assn., N.Y.C., 1968; air conservation cons. Mass. Lung Assn., 1968-69; exec. dir. Met. Boston Citizen's Coalition Clean Air, 1968-69; community health educator Environ. Health Adminstrn., Md. Dept. Health, 1971-76; dir. govt. relations Am. Public Health Assn., Washington, 1976-80, asst. exec. dir., 1980-83, assoc. exec. dir., 1984-97; bd. dirs. Nat. Coalition Health and Environ., 1980-82; bd. dirs. Coalition for Health Funding, 1983—, treas., 1983-86 , v.p. 1987-88, pres. 1989-94, past pres., 1994—; mem. nat. air pollution manpower devel. adv. com. EPA, 1973-76; exec. dir. Ecol. Soc. Am., 1997—. Editorial adv. bd., The AIDS Reference Guide, 1987. Mem. Nat. Environ. Health Assn., Am. Public Health Assn., Ecol. Soc. Am. Home: 9027 Billow Row Columbia MD 21045-2343 Office: 1015 15th St NW Washington DC 20005-2605

MCCARTER, THOMAS NESBITT, III, investment counseling company executive; b. N.Y.C., Dec. 16, 1929; s. Thomas N. Jr. and Suzanne M. (pierson) McC. Student, Princeton U., 1948-51. Chartered investment counselor. Sales exec. Mack Trucks, Inc., N.Y.C., 1952-59; ptnr. Kelly, McCarter, D-Arcy Investment Counsel, 1959-62; v.p., sec., dir. D-Arcy McCarter & Chew, 1962-66; v.p., dir. Trainer, Wortham & Co., Inc., 1967-71, exec. v.p., 1971-75; chmn. bd., dir. Island Security Bank Ltd., 1976-78; pres. Knottingham Ltd., N.Y.C., 1976-84; gen. ptnr. W.P. Miles Timber Properties, New Orleans, 1974—; exec. v.p. Yorke McCarter Owen & Bartles, Inc., N.Y.C., 1985-89. Cons. Laidlaw Holdings, Inc., 1990—92; pres. Mentor Mgmt. Group, Inc., N.Y.C., 1986—90; chmn. bd. dirs. Ramapo Land Co., Slotasburg, NY, 1990—, Stillrock Mgmt., Inc., N.Y.C., 1992—96, Pendragon Tech., 1996—98. Dir Anker Coal Group Inc., Hyseq, Inc.; bd. advisors Knowledge Delivery Sys. Inc.; vice chair Runnymede Capital Mgmt., Inc. Chmn. bd. trustees Christodora Found., Inc., N.Y.C., 1970-93; charter trustee Dalton Sch., N.Y.C., 1969-76, v.p., 1972-76; pres., trustee Civil War Libr. and Mus., Phila., 1985-92; chmn. bd. trustees ASPCA, 1984-95; chmn. loyal Legion Found., N.Y.C.; trustee Children's Aid Soc. N.Y.C., 1973-94, Joffrey Ballet, Found. for Am. Dance, 1973-77; pres., trustee N.Y.C. Marble Cemetery Assn., 1990-2002; mem. Nat. Com. for Preservation of U.S. Treasury Bldg., 1988-92; trustee Nat. Symphony Orch., Washington, 1990-94; chmn. Gibraltar Am. Coun., 1998—; bd. assocs. Whitehead Inst., Cambridge, Mass., 2000—. Mem. Loyal Legion U.S. (comdr. N.Y. State 1964-66, nat. comdr. in chief 1977-81), Racquet and Tennis Club, Brook Club, Links Club, River Club, St. Nicholas Soc., Pilgrims of U.S. (N.Y.C.), Meadow club (Southampton, N.Y.), Ivy Club (Princeton, N.J.). Republican. Home and Office: 188 E 64th St New York NY 10021-7451

MCCARTHY, ALBERT HENRY, executive recruiter, consultant; b. Worcester, Mass., May 17, 1944; s. Albert H. and Rosemary (Sheehan) McCarthy; m. Ann F. Arseneault, 1965; children: Erin Marie, Caitlin Ann. BA in Sociology, Coll. Holy Cross, Worcester, Mass., 1968, cert. indsl. rels., 1975; postgrad., Assumption Coll., Worcester, Mass. Recruiter Data Gen. Corp., Southborough, Mass., 1972-73, personnel adminstr., 1973-74, personnel supr., 1974-76; New Eng. dist. personnel mgr. Digital Equip. Corp., Waltham, 1976-78; mgr. staffing systems and programs Honeywell Info. System, Inc., 1978-80; dir. human resources NEC Info. Systems, Inc., Boxborough, 1980-84, v.p. human resources, 1984-93, Simplex Time Recorder Co., Gardner, 1993-97; founder, pres. Sexton Reed, North Andover, 1997-2000, 01—; prin. Heidrick and Struggles, Lexington, 2000-01; pres. Sexton Reed, Osterville, 2002—. Spkr., panelist Japan External Trade Orgn./Bus. Wk. Symposium, 1989. Author: (book) Personal Journal, 1989, 1991, Bureau of Business Practice, Sales Manager's Guide, 1993, NEHRA Insights, 2001. Trustee Mt. Wachusett C.C., 1996—. Recipient Best Practice Recruitment award, Human REsource Exec. mag., 1992. Mem.: VFW, Human Resource Exec. Forum (founding mem.), Boxborough Bus. Assn., New Eng. Human Resources Assn. (founding mem.), New Eng. Exec. Resources Coun. (founding mem. 1997), Internat. Assn. Corp. and Profl. Recruiters (co-pres. Boston chpt. 1992—95, bd. dirs. 1994—95), Soc. Human Resource Mgmt. (Yoder Heneman Creative Application award 1990, nominee profl. excellence award 1993), Employment Mgrs. Assn., Cape Cod Tech. Coun., Japan Soc. Boston, Greater Gardner C. of C. (bd. dirs. 1996—97), Am. Legion. Home: 63 Osterville-W Barnstable Osterville MA 02655-2504 Office: Sexton Reed PO Box 676 Osterville MA 02655-0676 E-mail: ahm@tiac.net.

MCCARTHY, ANN LOREE, communications executive; b. Iowa; m. Joseph Milton Strout. BS, Iowa State U., 1973; MBA, U. Wis., Oshkosh, 1983; postgrad., Webster U., 1996. CPA, Iowa, Tex. Auditor Peat Marwick Mitchell & Co., Des Moines, 1973-74; mgr. promotions Kimberly Clark Corp., Neenah, Wis., 1974-84; owner McCarthy Cons., San Antonio, 1984-85; dir. strategic comms. Ralston Purina Co., St. Louis, 1985—. Named Corp. Woman of Yr. Women in Mgmt., 1983. Avocations: child devel. golf, reading. Office: Ralston Purina Co Checkerboard Sq Saint Louis MO 63164-0001

MCCARTHY, ANNE MARIE, strategic management educator, researcher; b. Chgo., Aug. 28, 1958; d. Casimir Francis and Michaeleen M. (Kimmey) Derwinski; m. Paul John McCarthy, May 3, 1986. BA, Georgetown U., 1980; MBA, U. Conn., 1986; PhD, Purdue U., 1992. Owner, mgr. Derwinski & Assocs., urban renovation, Hartford, Conn., 1981-84; researcher The Traveller's, 1984; teaching asst. U. Conn., Storrs, 1984-86; grad. asst. Purdue U., West Lafayette, Ind., 1986-90; asst. prof. strategic mgmt. Ind. U., Bloomington, 1990—. Bd. dirs. Ctr. Entrepreneurship & Innovation, Bloomington, Ind.; presenter, speaker to profl. meetings and bus. orgns., conductor of entrepreneurial workshops and seminars in U.S. and Eastern Europe. Contbr. articles to profl. jours. Rsch. grantee Ind. Ctr. for Global Bus., 1991. Mem. Strategic Mgmt. Soc., Acad. Mgmt. Assn., Beta Gamma Sigma. Avocations: gardening, sailing, music.

MCCARTHY, BERNARD FRANCIS, lawyer; b. Butte, Mont., Aug. 20, 1955; s. John Joseph and Helen Patricia (Ryan) McC.; m. Helen Jean Waldbillig, Sept. 1, 1990; children: Sean Michael, Patrick Nicholas. BA, Carroll Coll., 1977; JD, U. Mont., 1983. Bar: Mont. 1983, U.S. Dist. Ct. Mont. 1983. Mgmt. analyst Mont. Supreme Ct., Helena, 1978-79; ptnr. O'Leary & McCarthy, 1983-85; justice of peace Lewis and Clark County, 1984-89; clk. U.S. Bankruptcy Ct., Butte, Mont., 1990—. Chair edn. com. Fed. Jud. Ctr., Washington, 1994—; mem. law practice com. State Bar Mont., Helena, 1994—; v.p., pres.-elect, pres. Nat. Conf. Bankruptcy Clks., Dayton, Ohio, 1996-98, pres., 1998-2000; mem. Nat. Integrated Bankruptcy System user group Adminstr. Office U.S. Cts., Washington, 1996—. Pres. bd. Big Bros. and Sisters, Helena, 1985-86. Mem. KC, Lions (pres./sec. 1992—). Democrat. Roman Catholic. Avocations: horse riding, fishing, reading, traveling, ranching. Home: PO Box 523 176 Paul Gulch Rd Whitehall MT 59759 Office: US Bankruptcy Ct PO Box 689 Butte MT 59703-0689

MCCARTHY, BILL DARCY, sociologist, criminologist; b. Guelph, Ont., Can., July 4, 1958; HBA, U. Guelph, 1979; BEd, U. Western Ontario, 1981; MA, U. Toronto, 1984, PhD, 1990. From asst. prof. to assoc. prof. sociology U. Victoria, 1989-95, assoc. prof. sociology, 1995-98, U. Calif., Davis, 1998—. Co-author: Mean Streets: Youth Crime and Homelessness, 1997 (C. Wright Mills award 1998, Michael J. Hindelang award, 1998). Office: U Calif Davis Dept Sociology 1 Shields Ave Davis CA 95616-5270

MCCARTHY, CAROL A. pediatric nurse practitioner; b. Phila. d. Leo B. and Pauline (Carney) McCarthy; m. Richard Grayev (div.); children: Allison, Matthew, Brian. AD, Gwynedd Mercy Coll., Gwynedd Valley, Pa., 1965; BSN, U. Pa., 1971, MS in Nursing, 1986; postgrad., Widener U. ANA cert. pediatric nurse pracitioner. Pediatric nurse practitioner Perinatal Coop., Camden, N.J., Pa. Hosp., Phila., Sch. Dist. Phila., Temple Children's E.D., Phila. Mem. Nat. Assn. Pediatric Nurse Assocs. and Practitioners, Nat. Assn. Sch. Nurses, Pa. Assn. Sch. Nurses and Practitioners, Sigma Theta Tau. Home: 713 Kincaid Mills Ln Wallingford PA 19086-6785

MCCARTHY, CAROLYN, congresswoman; LPN. Mem. U.S. Congress from 4th N.Y. dist., 1997—. Mem. edn. and workforce com., budget com.; subcom. postsecondary edn., tng., and life-long learning, employer-employee rels. Recipient numerous awards, including being named one of Newsday's 100 L.I. Influentials, Congl. Quarterly's 50 Most Effective Legislators in Congress, one of nine Redbook Mag.'s "Mothers and Shakers", Ladies' Home Jour. list of America's 100 Most Important Women, and Advertising Age's list of Most Impact by Women in 1999; also honored by U.S. Women's Soccer Team and Oprah Winfrey. Office: US Ho of RepsS 1224 Longworth Ho Office Bldg Washington DC 20515-0001 : 1 Fulton Ave Ste 30 Hempstead NY 11550*

MCCARTHY, CHARLES FRANCIS, JR. lawyer; b. Springfield, Mass., Dec. 9, 1926; s. Charles Francis and Maude Veronica (Clayton) McC.; m. Dorothy Bray, June 14, 1952 (dec. June 1987); children: Richard J., Linda A. Moylan, Robert P. AB, St. Michael's Coll., 1949; JD, Boston Coll., 1951. Bar: Mass. 1952, U.S. Dist. Ct. Mass. 1953. Assoc. Ganley, Crook & Smith, Springfield, Mass., 1954-67, Laming, Smith & Auchter, Springfield, 1967-80; of counsel Bacon & Wilson, P.C. and predecessor firms, 1980-94; ret., 1994. Clk. Ellis Title Co., Inc., Springfield, 1988-94. Democrat. Roman Catholic. Home: 48 Palmyra St Springfield MA 01118-2027

MCCARTHY, CHARLES R. bioethicist, consultant; b. St. Paul; s. Frederic D. and Florence Ruth (Milton) McC.; m. Estelle Rountree, July 23, 1971. BA, U. St. Thomas, St. Paul, 1947; MA, U. Toronto, 1956, PhD, 1961. Ordained priest, 1956. Priest Paulist Fathers; tchr. St. Paul's Coll., Cath. U. Am., George Washington U., Washington; program analyst NIH Divsn. Legis. Analysis, Bethesda, Md., 1971-74, chief legis. devel. br., 1975-78; dir. Office for Protection from Rsch. Risks NIH, 1978-92; sr. rsch. fellow Kennedy Inst. Ethics Georgetown U., Washington; cons. to rsch. instns., 1992—; dir. Office Rsch. Compliance Va. Commonwealth U., 2000. Fellow Hastings Ctr. Ethics, 1987—; bd. dirs. Pub. Responsiblity in Medicine and Rsch. Contbr. articles to profl. jours., chpts. to books; mem. editl. bd. Inst. Lab. Animal Rsch. Nat. Acad. Scis., 1995-99, issue editor, 1998. Group leader No. Ireland Peace Missions, Belfast, 1993, 96; mem. State of N.Y. Dept. Health Adv. Group on Human Subjects Rsch. Involving Protected Classes, N.Y.C., 1997-98. Recipient Exptl. Achievement award Asst. Sec. for Health, 1983, Pub. Health Superior Achievement award Surgeon Gen. of U.S., 1989, Spl. citation for 15 yrs. of leadership in protection of humans Commr. FDA, 1992, Outstanding Achievement award Sec. HHS, 1991, Harry C. Rowsell award Scientists Ctr. for Animal Welfare, 19999, Lifetime Achievement award ARENA, 2000. Mem. Nat. Acad. Scis. Inst. Medicine (com. on legal and ethical issues relating to the inclusion of women in rsch. 1993-94), Scientists Ctr. for Animal Welfare (bd. trustees, v.p., 1993—), Am. Fertility Soc. (mem. ethics com. 1989-94), Acad. Medicine, Kiwanis Internat. North Ctrl. Richmond (charter), Roman Catholic. Avocations: fishing, golf, carpentry, travel. Home: 3613 Hawthorne Ave Richmond VA 23222-1823 Fax: 804-321-6478. E-mail: chamcc@erols.com.

MCCARTHY, DANIEL WILLIAM, management consultant; b. Syracuse, N.Y., Apr. 15, 1952; s. William Cornelius and Ruth Francis (Geller) McC.; m. Mary Coleen Kisil, Jan. 17, 1987; children: Katherine M., Kevin D., Patrick W. BA in Polit. Sci., SUNY, Geneseo, 1974; MBA, NYU, 1982. Asst. buyer Abraham & Straus, Bklyn., 1976-78; buyer Lord & Taylor, N.Y.C., 1978-80; cons. Touche Ross, Newark, 1982-87; sr. mgr. Deloitte & Touche, N.Y.C., 1987-93; dir. Coach Leatherware, 1993-94; prin. Greenvale Consulting Group, Poughkeepsie, N.Y., 1994-2000; pres. Retex Cons. Group, N.Y.C., 2000—, Greenvale Cons. Group, LLC, 2002—. Author: Point of Sale - Current Trends and Beyond, 1986; contbr. articles to profl. jours. Mem. Town of Poughkeepsie Hist. Planning Commn. Mem. Nat. Retail Fedn., Inst. Mgmt. Cons. Roman Catholic. Avocations: wine collecting, ballet, fencing, architecture, investing. E-mail: dwmccarthy@att.net.

MCCARTHY, DAVID BRUCE, minister; b. Owatonna, Minn., Mar. 8, 1955; s. Harold Charles and Barbara Susan (Kaercher) McC.; m. Joan Christina LaFollette, Oct. 12, 1986. BA cum laude, Carleton Coll., 1977; AM, Duke U., 1979; MDiv with distinction, Harvard U., 1985. Ordained to ministry Presbyn. Ch., 1986. Pastor John Hus Presbyn. Ch., Binghamton, N.Y., 1986-93; mem. staff Grad. Inst. Duke U., 1993-2000; interim pastor Cross Roads Presbyn. Ch., 1994-96; asst. prof. religion, chaplain to coll. Hastings (Nebr.) Coll., 2001—. Mem. 1st Ward Clergy, Binghamton, 1986-93, convener, 1987-89; dir. Metro Interfaith, 1988-93; moderator Broad Ave.-North Presbyn. Ch., Binghamton, 1989-91; moderator Permanent Jud. Commn., Presbytery of Susquehanna Valley, 1986-92, mem. com. on preparation for ministry, 1986-92, bills and overtures com., 1988-91, presbytery coun., 1990-91; mem. ecumenical and worship com. Broome County Coun. Chs., N.Y., 1989-92; mem. planning, evaluation and rev. com. Synod of N.E., 1990-91, presbytery rep. synod mission coun., 1990-91, commr., 1990, mem. synod permanent jud. commn., 1992-98; mem. faculty Ghost Ranch, Abiquiu, N.Mex., 1991, 96; vis. instr. Duke U., 1999-2001. Editor Report from Susquehanna Valley Presbytery, 1989-90; contbr. author: The Organizational Revolution, 1991, Concise Encyclopedia of Preaching, 1995, Dictionary of Heresy Trials in American Chrisianity, 1997, Enclyclopedia of Religious Controversies in the United States, 1997, American National Biography, 1999. Capt. Unitd Way Appeal, Broome County, 1990—91; chair CPM Presbytery of Ctrl. Nebr., 2001—, moderator PJC, 2001—, mem. presbytery coun., 2001—. Mem. Am. Soc. Ch. History, Am. Acad. Religion, Soc. for Scientific Study Religion, Witherspoon Soc. (editorial asst. 1989-93), Presbyn. Hist. Soc., So. Assn. Women Historians. Office: Hastings Coll 800 Turner Ave Hastings NE 68901

MCCARTHY, DAVID MURRAY, cardiologist, educator; b. Morristown, N.J., Dec. 12, 1945; s. John Murray and Mary Francis (Apgar) McC.; m. Linda Elena Frisa, Aug. 30, 1969; 1 child, Alice Leslie. BA, Yale U., 1967; MD, Columbia U., 1971. Diplomate Am. Bd. Internal Medicine, Am. Bd. Cardiovascular Diseases. Intern U. Chgo., 1971-72; resident St. Luke's Hosp., N.Y.C., 1974-75; cardiology fellow Columbia-Presbyn. Hosp., 1975-79; instr. Columbia U., 1977-79; asst. prof. U. Pa., Phila., 1979-87, assoc. prof., 1987—; dir. outpatient cardiac svcs. Hosp. U. Pa., 1991—, chmn. cardiac svcs. quality improvement com., 1996—. Sr. asst. surgeon USPHS, 1972-74. Rsch. fellow N.Y. Heart Assn., 1977-79. Fellow Am. Coll. Cardiology; mem. ACP, Am. Heart Assn. Coun. on Clin. Cardiology. Avocations: bicycling, antiques, gardening, travel. Office: U Pa Med Ctr 3400 Spruce St Philadelphia PA 19104-4206 E-mail: davidmcc@mail.med.upenn.edu.

MCCARTHY, DESMOND FERGUS, English literature educator; b. Boston, Oct. 18, 1959; s. Desmond Christopher and Agnes McCarthy. BA, Framingham State Coll., 1981; MA, Brandeis U., 1984, PhD, 1992. Lectr. Brandeis U., Waltham, Mass., 1987-88; instr. Simmons Coll., Boston, 1989-91, Northeastern U., Boston, 1990; asst. prof. English Framingham (Mass.) State Coll., 1991-99, assoc. prof. English, 1999—. Adviser The Gatepost, Framingham, 1992—. Author: Reconstructing the Family in Contemporary American fiction, 1997, 2d edit., 1998. Recipient 1997 Disting. Four Yr. Coll. Newspaper Advisor, presented by CMA. Office: Framingham State Coll 100 State St Framingham MA 01702-2460 E-mail: dmccart@frc.mass.edu.

MC CARTHY, EUGENE JOSEPH, writer, former senator; b. Watkins, Minn., Mar. 29, 1916; s. Michael John and Anna (Baden) McC.; m. Abigail Quigley, June 1945; children— Ellen, Mary, Michael, Margaret. AB, St. John's U., Collegeville, Minn., 1935; A.M., U. of Minn., 1939. Tchr. pub. schs., 1935-40, 45; prof. econ. edn. St. John's U., 1940-42; civilian tech. work with Mil. Intelligence Div., War Dept., 1944; instr. sociology and econs. St. Thomas Coll., St. Paul, 1946-48; mem. 81st-85th Congresses from 4th Minn. dist., 1949-59, mem. ways and means com.; U.S. senator from Minn., 1959-70; mem. senate finance, fgn. relations and govt. ops. coms.; Adlai Stevenson prof. polit. sci. New Sch. for Social Research, 1973-74; syndicated columnist, 1977—. Dir. Harcourt Brace Jovanovich, Inc. Author: Frontiers in American Democracy, 1960, Dictionary of American Politics, 1962, A Liberal Answer to the Conservative Challenge, 1964, The Limits of Power, 1967, The Year of the People, 1969, Other Things and The Aardvark, 1970, Up 'Til Now, 1987; also, The Hard Years, 1975, Mr. Raccoon and His Friends, 1977, America Revisited, 1978, Ground Fog and Night, 1979, The Ultimate Tyrany, 1980, Gene McCarthy's Minnesota, 1982, Complexities and Contraries: Essays of Mild Discontent, 1982, The View from Rappahannock, 1984; co-author: A Political Bestiary, 1978, Up 'Til Now, 1987, Required Reading, 1988, 89, The View from Rappahannock II, 1989, Up Til Now, 1991, Colony of the World, 1993, Required Reading, 1994, Selected Poems, 1997, No Fault Politics, 1999, Am. American Bestiary, 1999. Roman Catholic. Office: 271 Hawlin Rd Woodville VA 22749-1721

MC CARTHY, FRANK MARTIN, oral surgeon, surgical sciences educator; b. Olean, N.Y., Aug. 27, 1924; s. Frank Michael and Joan (Quinn) McC.; m. Julia Richmond, Nov. 24, 1949; children: Robert Lee, Joan Lee. BS, U. Pitts., 1943, D.D.S., 1945, MD, 1949; MS in Oral Surgery, Georgetown U., 1954; Sc.D. (hon.), St. Bonaventure U., 1956. Med. intern Mercy Hosp., Pitts., 1949-50; practice oral surgery L.A., 1954-75; teaching fellow Georgetown U., 1952-53; rsch. fellow NIH, 1953-54; prof. oral surgery U. So. Calif. Sch. Dentistry, 1966-75, prof., chmn. sect. anesthesia and medicine, 1975-90, prof. emeritus, 1990—, chmn. dept. surg. scis., 1979-84, assoc. dean adminstrv. affairs, 1977-79, asst. dean hosp. affairs, 1979-84. Dir. anesthesiology U.So. Calif. oral surgery sect. L.A. County Hosp., 1958-89; clin. supr., lectr. dental hygiene program Pasadena City Coll., 1992—; v.p. Am. Dental Bd. Anesthesiology, 1984-89; lectr. in field; mem. adv. panel on dentistry sect. anesthesizing agts. Nat. Fire Protection Assn., 1971-79; mem. Am. Nat. Standards Com., 1974-86, 95—; cons. in field. Author: Emergencies in Dental Practice, 1967, rev., 1972, 79, Medical Emergencies in Dentistry, 1982, Safe Treatment of the Medically Compromised Patient, 1987, Essentials of Safe Dentistry for the Medically Compromised Patient, 1989; mem. editorial bd.: Calif. Dental Assn. Jour; contbr. articles to profl. publs. Bd. councilors Sch. Dentistry, U. So. Calif., 1972-75. Served as lt., M.C. USNR, 1950-52. Fellow Internat. Assn. Oral Surgeons (founder), Am. Coll. Dentists, Internat. Coll. Dentists; mem. ADA (editorial bd. jour.), Am. Dental Soc. Anesthesiology (Heidbrink award 1977), Am. Assn. Oral-Max Surgeons (chmn. anesthesia com. 1971), So. Calif. Soc. Oral Surgeons (pres. 1974), Calif., Los Angeles County dental assns., Delta Tau Delta, Psi Omega, Phi Rho Sigma, Omicron Kappa Upsilon. Home and Office: 480 S Orange Grove Blvd Apt 11 Pasadena CA 91105-1720

MCCARTHY, FREDERICK WILLIAM, investment banker; b. Boston, Nov. 25, 1941; s. Frederick William and Josephine Leona (Pannier) McC.; children: Daniel Arthur, Frederick William III, Kathryn Elizabeth. BA magna cum laude, Harvard U., 1963, MBA with high distinction, 1967. Mgmt. cons. Booz Allen & Hamilton, Inc., Chgo., 1967-70; 1st v.p. investment banking Shearson, Hammill & Co., Inc., N.Y.C., 1970-72, Chgo., 1972-74; mng. dir. Drexel Burnham Lambert, Inc., Boston, 1974-90; chmn. bd. dirs. Triumph Capital Group Inc., 1990—; mng. dir. Triumph Corp. Fin. Group Inc., Palm Beach, 1990—. Bd. dirs. Fairchild Corp., Seminole Kraft Corp., Rexnord Holdings Inc., NutraMax Products Inc., RC/Arby's Corp. 1st lt. U.S. Army, 1963-65. Home: 222 Lakeview Ave # 160-26 West Palm Beach FL 33401-6145 Office: 512 N Flagler Dr 8th Fl West Palm Beach FL 33401

MCCARTHY, G. DANIEL, lawyer; b. Butte, Mont., Mar. 23, 1949; s. George Denis and Mary Agnes (Kiely) McC.; m. Carolyn M. Scully, June 19, 1976; children: Brendan, Katie, Kelly, Sean. BA, U. Dayton, 1971; JD, U. Notre Dame, 1974; AMP, Harvard U., 1994. Bar: Md. 1974, D.C. 1975, U.S. Ct. Appeals (D.C. cir.) 1976, Pa. 1977, N.Y. 1985, U.S. Ct. Appeals (10th cir.) 1985. Assoc. Bilger & Blair, Washington, 1974-77, 79-80; asst. U.S. atty. U.S. Dist. Ct. (ea. dist.) Pa., Phila., 1977-78; assoc. Abourezk, Shack & Mendenhall, Washington, 1980-83; atty. AT&T, N.Y.C., 1983-85; sr. v.p., gen. counsel and sec. AT&T Credit Corp., Morristown, N.J., 1985-89; sr. v.p., gen. counsel, sec., chief risk mgmt. officer. AT&T Capital Corp., 1990-96; v.p., gen. counsel, sec. Compaq Fin. Svcs. Corp., Murray Hill, NJ, 1996—2002; v.p. govt. affairs, dep. gen. counsel Compaq Computer Corp., Houston, 2001—02; v.p., gen. counsel, sec. Hewlett-Packard Fin. Svcs. Co., Murray Hill, 2002—. Vis. lectr. Marymount Coll., Arlington, Va., 1979-83; bd. dirs. Compaq Fin. Svcs. Europe, LLC, Compaq Capital A/P, LLC, Computer Ins. Co., Compaq Fin. Svcs. Can. Corp.; mem. adv. coun. U. Dayton, Coll. of Arts and Scis., 1993-97, chmn., 1994-96. Mem.: ABA, DC Bar Assn., Fairmount Country Club (Chatham, NJ) (bd. dirs. 2002—). Avocation: golf, fly fishing. Office: HP Fin Svcs Co 420 Mountain Ave New Providence NJ 07974-0006 E-mail: dan.mccarthy@compaq.com.

MCCARTHY, HAROLD CHARLES, retired insurance company executive; b. Madelia, Minn., Dec. 5, 1926; s. Charles and Merle (Humphry) McC.; m. Barbara Kaercher, June 24, 1949; children: David, Susan. BA, Carleton Coll., Northfield, Minn., 1950; postgrad. With Federated Mut. Ins. Co., Owatonna, Minn., 1950-67; with Meridian Mut. Ins. Co., Indpls., 1967-91, exec. v.p., then exec. v.p., gen. mgr., 1972-75, pres., 1975-90, bd. dirs., past chmn. bd., 1990-91; past pres. North Meridian Bus. Group; past pres., chmn. bd. Meridian Ins. Group, Inc. Chmn. bd., dir. Meridian Life Ins. Co.; past chmn., exec. com., bd. dirs. Ind. Ins. Inst.; mem. adv. bd. Harbor Fed. Savs. Bank. Former mem. Met. Devel. Commn., Corp. Community Council; bd. dirs. Meth. Health Found., Family Services Assn., Boy Scouts Am.; trustee Butler U.; mem. adv. bd. Harbor Fed. Bank. With USNR, 1944-46. Named Sagamore of the Wabash. Mem. Govs. Club of the Palm Beaches, Indian River Golf Club. Republican. Congregationalist. Office: 2955 N Meridian St Indianapolis IN 46208-4714

MCCARTHY, J. THOMAS, lawyer, educator; b. Detroit, July 2, 1937; s. John E. and Virginia M. (Hanlon) McC.; m. Nancy Irene Orrell, July 10, 1976 BS, U. Detroit, 1960; JD, U. Mich., 1963. Bar: Calif. 1964. Cassoc. Julian Caplan, San Francisco, 1963—66; prof. law U. San Francisco, 1966—. Founding dir. McCarthy Inst. Intellectual Property and High Tech. Law; mem. Trademark Rev. Commn., 1986—88; cons. in field. Author: McCarthy on Trademarks and Unfair Competition, 6 vols., 4th edit., 1996, McCarthy on Rights of Publicity and Privacy, 1987, 2d edit., 2000, McCarthy's Desk Encyclopedia of Intellectual Property, 2d edit., 1995; mem. editl. bd. Trademark Reporter. Recipient Jefferson medal N.J. Intellectual Property Assn., 1994, Ladas award Brand Names Ednl. Found., 1997, Pattishall medal Brand Names Found., 2000. Mem. Am. Intellectual Property Law Assn. (Watson award 1965, Centennial award in Trademark law 1997), Internat. Assn. for Advancement of Teaching and Rsch. in Intellectual Property, Am. Law Inst. (adv. com. on restatement of law of unfair competition), IEEE.

MCCARTHY, JEAN JEROME, retired physical education educator; b. St. Paul, Sept. 11, 1929; s. Joseph Justin and Florence (Quirin) McC.; m. Norma Louise Shermer, July 30, 1955; children: Patrick J., Anne L., Kevin M. BS, U. Minn., 1956, PhD, 1986; MS, Wash. State U., 1958. Tchg. asst. Wash. State U., 1956-57, U. Minn., 1957-59, adminstrv. asst., 1959-60; asst. prof. phys. edn. U. South Fla., 1960-62, Mankato State U., 1962-71, assoc. prof., 1971-86, prof., 1986-91, ret., 1991, baseball coach, 1962-77. Cons. AAU. Contbr. articles to profl. jours. Mem. Minn. Gov.'s Phys. Fitness Adv. Com. With USAF, 1950-54. Recipient Outstanding Faculty award Mankato State U., 1979; named Region 2 Coach of Yr., NCAA, 1971, Outstanding Educators Am., 1970; named to Mankato State U. Athletic Hall of Fame, 1993; U. Minn. Grad. Sch. fellow, 1959-60; Lilly Found. scholar, 1974—; Rsch. Consortium fellow. Mem. AAPHER, Minn. Assn. Health, Phys. Edn., Recreation and Dance, Mensa, Phi Delta Kappa, Phi Epsilon Kappa (scholarship award 1972), Phi Kappa Phi. Roman Catholic.

MCCARTHY, JEFFREY MATHES, English educator; b. June 15, 1965; BA, Wesleyan U., Middletown, Conn., 1989; MLitt., U. Edinburgh, Scotland, 1992; PhD, U. Oreg., 1997. Grad. rsch. fellow Oreg. Humanities Inst., U. Oreg., Eugene, 1996; rsch. fellow Calgary (Alta., Can.) Inst. for Humanities, U. Calgary, 1997; fulbright fellow to Can. Whyte Mus., Banff, Alta., Can., 1997-98; chair English, Westminster Coll., Salt Lake City, 1998—. E-mail: j-mccart@wcslc.edu.

MCCARTHY, JOHN, computer scientist, educator; b. Boston, Sept. 4, 1927; s. Patrick Joseph and Ida McCarthy; children: Susan Joanne, Sarah Kathleen, Timothy Talcott. BS, Calif. Inst. Tech., 1948; PhD, Princeton U., 1951. Instr. Princeton U., 1951—53; acting asst. prof. math. Stanford U., 1953—55; asst. prof. Dartmouth Coll., 1955—58; asst. and assoc. prof. communications scis. M.I.T., Cambridge, 1958—62; prof. computer sci. Stanford U., 1962—, Charles M. Pigott prof. Sch. Engring., 1987—94. Served with AUS, 1945-46. Recipient Kyoto prize, 1988, Nat. Medal of Sci., NSF, 1990. Mem.: NAE, NAS, Am. Assn. Artificial Intelligence (pres. 1983—84), Am. Math. Soc., Assn. for Computing Machinery (A.M. Turing award 1971), Am. Acad. Arts and Scis. Home: 885 Allardice Way Stanford CA 94305-1050 Office: Stanford U Dept Computer Sci Stanford CA 94305 E-mail: mccarthy@stanford.edu.

MCCARTHY, JOHN ALOYSIUS, language educator, literature educator; b. St. Clair, Mich., Jan. 9, 1942; s. Raymond Aloysius and Angela Julia McCarthy; m. Mechthild Irmgard Buening, Nov. 26, 1965; children: Brian Peter, Monika Kerry, Kristin Aileen. BA, Oakland U., Rochester, Mich., 1964; MA, SUNY, Buffalo, 1967, PhD, 1972; MA (hon.), U. Pa., 1979. Instr., asst. prof. German Oakland U., Rochester, 1969—72; asst., assoc., full prof. German and comparative lit. U. Pa., Phila., 1972—91; prof. German and comparative lit. Vanderbilt U., Nashville, 1991—. Vis. prof. German and comparative lit. U. Munich, 1993—; vis. prof. German Swarthmore (Pa.) Coll., 1986—; vis. prof. German and comparative lit. Rutgers U., New Brunswick, NJ, 2001. Author: C.M. Wieland: The Man and his Work, 1979, Crossing Boundaries: A Theory and History of Essay Writing in German 1690-1815, 1989; mem. editl. bd.: Internat. Forschungen zur allgemeinen und vergleichenden Literaturwissenschaft, 1993—, adv. editor: Ency. of the Essay, 1995—97; contbr. articles to profl. jours. Recipient NDEA, Title IV award, Nat. Endowment for the Humanities, 1964—66; fellow summer fellow, Am. Philos. Soc., 1977, 1983, German Acad. Exch. Svc., 1978, 1979, sr. Fulbright rsch. fellow, Fulbright Commn., 1993, Spence & Rebecca Webb Wilson fellow in the humanities, Ctr. for the Humanities, Vanderbilt U., 1994—95. Mem.: MLA (exec. com. divsn. on 18th and 19th Century German lit. 1989—93, mem. selection com. for Scaglione Book prize in German studies 2000—), Deutsche Schillergesellschaft, Internat. Herder Soc., Deutsche Gesellschaft fur die Erforschung des 18 Jahrhunderts, Goethe Soc. N.Am., Am. Comparative Lit. Assn., Am. Soc. for Eighteenth-Century Studies (editl. bd. Studies in Eighteenth-Century Culture 1994—96), Am. Assn. Tchrs. German (editl. bd. mem. The German Quarterly 1998—), German Studies Assn. (exec. com. 1995—98), Lessing Soc. (v.p. 1994—96, pres. 1996—99, sr. editor Lessing Yearbook 2000—). Democrat. Roman Catholic. Avocations: house renovations, travel, plumbing. Home: 1100 Beech Grove Rd Brentwood TN 37027-8916 Office: Vanderbilt Univ Dept Germanic & Slavic Box 1567 Nashville TN 37235

MCCARTHY, JOHN DAVID, mathematician, educator; b. Salem, Mass., June 12, 1955; s. James Joseph and Joanne McCarthy; m. Catherine Rose McCarthy; children: David Michael, Steven Matthew, Ethan Joseph, Colin Patrick. BS, Stevens Inst. Tech., Hoboken, N.J., 1977; PhD, Columbia U., 1983. Moore instr. MIT, Cambridge, Mass., 1983—85; asst. prof. math. Mich. State U., East Lansing, 1985—90, assoc. prof. math., 1990—98, prof. math., 1998—. Rsch. visitor Max Planck Institut fur Mathematik, Bonn, Germany, 1984, Univerite de Louis Pasteur, Strasbourg, 1986, Max Planck Institut fur Mathematik, Bonn, 1988, Universite de Louis Pasteur, Strasbourg, 1996. Co-author: (book) Casson's invariant for oriented homology 3-spheres. An exposition, 1990; contbr. Grantee, NSF, 1986—88, 1993—95. Avocation: outdoor sports (e.g. orienteering). Home: 4943 Holt Rd Holt MI 48842-1033 Office: Mich State U A228 Wells Hall East Lansing MI 48824-1027 Home Fax: 517-432-1562; Office Fax: 517-432-1562. Personal E-mail: mccarthy@math.msu.edu. Business E-Mail: mccarthy@math.msu.edu.

MCCARTHY, JOHN ROBERT, real estate firm officer; b. Carlisle, Pa., May 29, 1945; s. James Francis and Eleanor Marie (Harrington) McC.; m. Cathleen Ann Rice, Oct. 25, 1975; children: Kevin James, Michael John. BA in Bus. & Polit. Sci., St. Leo Coll., Fla., 1969. Mktg. rep. R.H. Donnelley Corp., N.Y.C., 1969-70; employee benefits rep. Marsh & McLennan Corp., 1970-73; overseas sales rep. AMF, Inc., White Plains, N.Y., 1973-79; ptnr., sr. v.p. Rostenberg-Doern Co., 1979-90; ptnr. pres. McCarthy-O'Callaghan Co Inc, 1990—. Mem. Con Edison Sports Hall of Fame Com., White Plains, 1981—, St. Agnes Hosp. Children's Com., 1983-90; bd. dirs. Am. Diabetes Assn. Westchester, 1987-94, adv. bd. St. Vincents Hosp., Harrison, N.Y., 1998—, Lighthouse West County, 1999—; mem. Cardinals Com. of Laity, Westchester; pres. Archbishop Stepinac H.S. Crusader Mens Club, 1998-2000; fund raising chmn. Gt. Hunger Meml. Westchester County, 1999-2001; Grand Marshal White Plains St. Patrick's Parade, 2000; mem. St. Patrick's Parade Com., 1997--. Mem. Exch. Club (hon., past pres. Downtown chpt.), Friendly Sons St. Patrick (officer Westchester chpt. 1984-91, pres. 1990-91, bd. stewards 1990—), Orienta Beach Club (chmn. children's com. 1987-92, bd. dirs. 1992-98, pres. 1995-98), Winged Foot Golf Club. Roman Catholic. Avocation: sports, charitable fund raising. Home: 16 Ridgeway Cir White Plains NY 10605-4119 Office: 1 N Broadway White Plains NY 10601-2310 E-mail: john@mcoc.com., jrmcc222@aol.com.

MC CARTHY, JOHN ROBERT, tax consultant, hospital consultant; b. N.Y.C., Mar. 27, 1923; s. James Anthony and Gertrude Madeline (Casey) Mc C.; m. Helen Ruth House, Aug. 16, 1950; children: William, Anne, Elizabeth, Christopher, Margaret, John Jr., Michael. AB, Holy Cross Coll., 1943; MA, George Washington U., 1980. Diplomat U.S. Info. Agy., Washington, 1951-78; hosp. cons. Peterborough, N.H., 1980—; English tchr. Franklin Pierce Coll., Rindge, 1982-92; tax practitioner Peterborough, 1992—. Dir. Monadnock Chorus, 1979—, Monadnock Lyceum, 1993-95; trustee Peterborough Hist. Soc., 1992-95, Peterborough Pub. Libr., 1996—. 1st lt. USAAF, 1943-46, CBI. Mem. Chevalier du Tastevin. Democrat. Roman Catholic. Avocations: writing novels, reading Latin. Home: 22 Pine St Peterborough NH 03458-1535

MCCARTHY, JONATHAN PAUL, economist; b. Britt, Iowa, Dec. 8, 1957; s. Henry Felix and Lucille McC.; m. Diana Marie Shaw, Aug. 23, 1997. BS summa cum laude, U. Wis., Parkside, 1980, MS, 1991; PhD, U. Wis., Madison, 1992. Teaching asst. U. Wis., Madison, 1986-87, rsch. asst., 1987-90, lectr. Whitewater, 1990-91; economist Fed. Res. Bank, N.Y.C., 1992—. Vis. economist Bank Internat. Settlements, Basel, Switzerland, 1997-98 Contbr. articles to profl. jours. Mem. Am. Econ. Assn., Nat. Assn. Bus. Economists. Avocations: running, basketball, softball. Home: 395 S End Ave Apt 14E New York NY 10280-1029 Office: Fed Res Bank 33 Liberty St New York NY 10045-1003

MCCARTHY, JOSEPH HAROLD, consultant, former retail food company executive; b. Derby, Conn., Dec. 21, 1921; s. Joseph Harold and Kathryn (Feeley) McC.; m. Jean K. Ryan, June 7, 1947; children: Timothy J., Maureen, Barbara, Richard, Joseph Harold. BS in Econs., Villanova U., 1944. Sr. v.p. First Nat. Stores Inc., Boston, 1947-76, Grand Union Co., Elmwood Park, N.J., 1976-80; exec. v.p., chief oper. officer Great Atlantic and Pacific Tea Co., Inc., Montvale, 1980-90, ret., 1990, cons. North Chatham, Mass., 1990-92. Served to capt. USMC, 1943-46, PTO; served to capt. USMC, 1951-52, Korea. Named to Villanova Football Hall of Fame, 1989. Home: 2030 Imperial Golf C Blvd Naples FL 34110 Office: 2030 Imperial Golf Course Blvd Naples FL 34110-1025

MCCARTHY, JUSTIN MILTON, marketing professional; b. St. Paul, Feb. 9, 1924; s. Frederic Donough and Florence Ruth (Milton) McC.; m. Inez Victoria Jensen, June 25, 1949; children: Patricia E. McCarthy Graham, Daniel V., John D., Anne Marie McCarthy Brosko. B in Med. Sci., U. Minn., 1949, MA, 1954; DO (hon.), Am. Coll. Gen. Practice, Arlington Heights, Ill., 1982. With Wyeth Labs., 1950-94; dir. profl. rels. Wyeth-Ayerst Labs., Radnor, Pa., 1979-94; pres. McCarthy & Assocs., Saint Davids, 1994—. Cons. Group for the Advancement of Psychiatry, 1994—, Am. Women's Health, Obstetrics and Neonatal Assn., 1994—, Am. Coll. Family Physicians Found., 1995—. Co-author: Job Loss, 1981; contbr. numerous articles to profl. jours. Bd. dirs., past chmn. Nat. Osteo. Found., Chgo., 1963-2001; past pres. Del. County chpt. Am. Heart Assn.; co-founder A Better Change, Radnor Twp., 1998; campaign chmn. Rep. Com., Radnor, 1979, 83, 87, 91, 95; mem. Bd. Health, Radnor, 1994—, pres., 1996—; pres. Main Line Serra Club, 1997-2001; chair Let Freedom Ring, Wayne, Pa., 2001—. Pfc. Med. Svc., U.S. Army, 1943-46. Decorated equestrian knight comdr. Holy Sepulchre of Jerusalem; recipient Hon. Citizenship, City of New Orleans, 1964; named Main Line Person of Yr., Lions, Wayne, 1971, Man of Yr., Pa. Police Chiefs, Harrisburg, 1970. Mem.: ACOG (cons. task force on cancer 1985—94, first spl. recognition award 2001), Nat. Assn. Local Bds. Health (tobacco control fellow 1999—2000, mem. tobacco control com.), Exhibit Industry Edn. Found. (dir. U.S. trade show bur. 1986—94, bd. dirs. 1988—), Found. for Advances in Clin. Medicine (bd. dirs.), Healthcare Conv. and Exhibitors Assn. (bd. dirs., past pres.), Am. Acad. Family Physicians Found. (trustee 1986—95, Merit award 1984), Am. Cancer Soc. (bd. dirs., past pres. Delaware County unit), Harris County Med. Soc. (hon.). Republican. Roman Catholic. Home: 125 Cornwall Ln Saint Davids PA 19087-4439

MCCARTHY, KAREN P. congresswoman, former state legislator; b. Mass., Mar. 18, 1947; BS in English, Biology, U. Kans., 1969, MBA, 1985; MEd in English, U. Mo., Kansas City, 1976. Tchr. Shawnee Mission (Kans.) South High Sch., 1969-75, The Sunset Hill (Kans.) Sch., 1975-76; mem. Mo. House of Reps., Jefferson City, 1977-94; cons. govt. affairs Marion Labs., Kansas City, Mo., 1986-93; mem. U.S. Congress from 5th Mo. dist., Washington, 1995—; mem. commerce com. Rsch. analyst pub. fin. dept. Stearn Bros. & Co., 1984-85, Kansas City, Mo.; rsch. analyst Midwest Rsch. Inst., econs. and mgmt. scis. dept., Kansas City, 1985-86. Del. Dem. Nat. Conv., 1992, Dem. Nat. Party Conf., 1982, Dem. Nat. Policy Com. Policy Commn., 1985-86; mem. Ho. Commerce Com. Energy and Power, Telecom., Trade and Consumer Protection; co-chair Dem. Caucus Task Health Care Reform. Recipient Outstanding Young Woman Am. award, 1977, Outstanding Woman Mo. award Phi Chi Theta, Woman of Achievement award Mid-Continent Coun. Girl Scouts U.S., 1983, 87, Annie Baxter Leadership award, 1993; named Conservation Legislator of Yr., Conservation Fed. Mo., 1987. Fellow Inst. of Politics; mem. Nat. Inst. of Politics; mem. Nat. Conf. on State Legis. (del. on trade and econ. devel. to Fed. Republic of Germany, Bulgaria, Japan, France and Italy, mem. energy com. 1978-84, fed. taxation, trade and econ. devel. com. 1986, chmn. fed. budget and taxation com. 1987, vice chmn. state fed. assembly 1988, pres.-elect 1993, pres. 1994), Nat. Dem. Inst. for Internat. Affairs (instr. No. Ireland 1988, Baltic Republics 1992, Hungary 1993). Office: US House Reps 1330 Longworth HOB Washington DC 20515-2505*

MC CARTHY, KATHRYN A. physicist; b. Lawrence, Mass., Aug. 7, 1924; d. Joseph Augustine and Catherine (Barrett) McCarthy. AB, Tufts U., 1945, MS, 1946; PhD, Radcliffe Coll., 1957; DSc (hon.), Coll. Holy Cross, 1978; DHL (hon.), Merrimack Coll., 1981. Instr. physics Tufts U., 1946-53, asst. prof., 1953-59, assoc. prof., 1959-62, prof., 1962-95, emerita, 1995—, dean Grad. Sch., 1969-74, provost, sr. v.p., 1973-79. Rsch. fellow in metallurgy Harvard, 1957-59, vis. scholar, 1979-80; rsch. assoc. Baird Assocs., 1947-49, 51, Boston U. Optical Rsch. Lab., summer 1952; assoc. rsch. engr. U. Mich., summer 1957-58; dir. Mass. Electric Co., State Mut. Assurance Co.; chmn. Hallmark Health Systems, 1997—. Trustee Southeastern Mass. U., 1972-74, Merrimack Coll., 1974-83, Coll. Holy Cross, 1980-97; corporator Lawrence Meml. Hosp., 1975-97, dir., 1978-97. Fellow Optical Soc. Am., Am. Phys. Soc.; mem. Soc. Women Engrs. (sr.), Phi Beta Kappa, Sigma Xi. Roman Catholic. Home: 1580 Massachusetts Ave Apt 5D Cambridge MA 02138-2926 Office: Tufts U Dept Physics 4 Colby St Medford MA 02155-6013 E-mail: kmccar6694@aol.com.

MCCARTHY, KEVIN BART, lawyer; b. Washington, May 7, 1948; s. Frank Jeremiah and Frances Patricia (Bilderback) McC.; m. Patrice Borders, Apr. 3, 1971; children: Kevin Patrick, Charles Ryan, Molly Virginia, Bridget Louise, Moira Patrice. BBA, U. Notre Dame, 1970; JD, Ind. U., Indpls., 1973. Bar: Ind. 1973, U.S. Dist. Ct. (so. dist.) Ind. 1973, U.S. Ct. Appeals (7th cir.) 1974, Ill 1976, U.S. Dist. Ct. (cen. dist.) Ill. 1985, U.S. Ct. Appeals (6th cir.) 1985. Bail commr. Mcpl. Ct. Marion County, Indpls., 1972-73; asst. regional counsel Fed. Hwy. Adminstrn., Homewood, Ill., 1973-75; 1st asst., chief counsel Ill. Dept. Transp., Springfield, 1975-77; counsel com. on interstate and fgn. commerce, subcom. on transp. and commerce Ho. Reps., Washington, 1977-79, asst. counsel com. on pub. works and transp., 1979-82, counsel com. on pub. works and transp., 1982; pvt. practice law Springfield, 1982-87; acting U.S. trustee Dept. Justice, 1987-88, U.S. trustee Indpls., 1988—. Pvt. practice Indpls. and Springfield. Mem. Ill. State Bd. Agrl. Advisors, 1987-88. Home: 5619 Surrey Hill Rd Indianapolis IN 46226-1561

MCCARTHY, KEVIN JOHN, lawyer; b. N.Y.C., Apr. 8, 1941; s. Vincent Patrick and Mary (H.) McC.; m. Marianne Pitts, Nov. 5, 1966; children: Mary Rita, Kevin, Colin. BS, U. Md., 1963; JD, U. Md., Balt., 1966. Bar: Md. 1966, U.S. Dist. Ct. Md. 1966, U.S. Ct. Appeals (4th cir.) 1966, U.S. Supreme Ct. 1972, D.C. 1976, U.S. Dist. Ct. D.C. 1976, U.S. Ct. Appeals (D.C. cir.) 1976, Fla. 1998. Law clk. Cir. Ct. for P.G. County, Upper Marlboro, Md., 1964-66; assoc., ptnr. Sasscer, Clagett & Channing, 1966-76; ptnr. O'Malley, Miles & McCarthy, 1976-86, McCarthy, Bacon & Costello, Landover, 1986—. Arbitrator Am. Arbitration Assn., Washington, 1972—. Contbg. author: Maryland Civil Patter Jury Instructions, 1975, 2d edit., 1984, 3d edit., 1993. Named The Best Lawyers in Am., Woodward/White. Fellow Am. Bar Found., Md. Bar Found.; mem. Internat. Assn. Ins. Counsel, Fedn. Ins. and Corp. Counsel, Def. Rsch. Inst., Am. Trial Lawyers Assn., Md. Trial Lawyers Assn., Assn. Def. Trial Attys., Million Dollar Advocates Forum, Trial Lawyers for Pub. Justice. Avocations: golf, racquetball, coaching soccer and lacrosse. Office: McCarthy & Costello 4640 Forbes Blvd Lanham Seabrook MD 20706-4323 E-mail: Kevin@McCarthyCostello.com.

MCCARTHY, LAURENCE JAMES, physician, pathologist; b. Boston, Aug. 11, 1934; s. Theodore Clifford and Mary Barrett (Moran) McC.; m. Cynthia Marion DeRoch, Aug. 28, 1978; children: Laurence J. Jr., Jeffrey A., Karen E., Patrick K., Ryan N. BA, Yale U., 1956; student, Georgetown U. Sch. Med., 1956-58; MD, Harvard U., 1960; MS, U. Minn., 1965. Cert. Am. Bd. Pathology, 1965. Intern Boston City Hosp., 1960-61; resident in pathology Mayo Clinic, Rochester, Minn., 1961-65; pathologist Honolulu Heart Program, 1965-67; chief pathology Kelsey-Seybold Clinic, Houston, 1967-68; clin. asst. pathologist M.D. Anderson Hosp., 1967-68; chief pathology Straub Clinic, Honolulu, 1968-72; assoc. pathologist Wilcox Hosp., Lihue, Hawaii, 1972-74; chief pathology A.R. Gould Hosp., Presque Isle, Maine, 1975-78; assoc. pathologist Kuakini Med. Ctr., Honolulu, 1978—. Med. dir. USPHS, 1965-67. Fellow Coll. Am. Pathologists, Am. Soc. Clin. Pathologists; mem. AMA, Hawaii Soc. Pathologists (pres. 1970), Am. Acad. Forensic Sci., Hawaii Med. Assn., Honolulu County Med. Soc. (del. 1982-83). Roman Catholic. Home: 249 Kaelepulu Dr Kailua HI 96734-3311 Office: Kuakini Med Ctr 347 N Kuakini St Honolulu HI 96817-2306

MCCARTHY, LEE HOLLEMAN, secondary school teacher; b. Jonesboro, Ark., Dec. 21, 1938; d. Eugene Joseph and Vivian Mae (Burton) H.; 1 child, Cullen Chase. BA, U. Tenn., 1960; MA, San Francisco State U., 1969. Clk.-typist Walter F. Bennett & Co., Chgo., 1961-62; tchr. Albin (Wyo.) Sch. Dist., 1963-64, Lyman (Wyo.) Sch. Dist., 1965-66, McFarland (Calif.) H.S., 1966-68, Wasco (Calif.) Union H.S., 1969-94; tchr. at-risk students Independence H.S., Wasco, 1994-2001. Adj. lectr. Calif. State U., Bakersfield, 1976-77, 92, Bakersfield C.C., 1973, 82, 83, 91. Author: Desire's Door, 1991 (Roerich award, 1991), Combing Hair..., 1992 (Ion Books award, 1992), Good Girl, 2002. Stegner fellow Stanford U., 1974-75, NEH Seminar grantee Yale U., summer 1983, SUNY-Geneseo, summer 1988, U. So. Miss., Hattiesburg, summer 1995; recipient Arts Educator award Arts Coun. of Kern, Bakersfield, 1993, Calif. Assembly Resolution of Commendation, Assemblyman Dean Florez and Sen. Jim Costa, Sacramento, 2000.

MCCARTHY, LYNN COWAN, professional genealogist; b. Panama City, Panama, Mar. 18, 1940; d. John Linus and Rose (Cowan) McC. BA, Mary Washington Coll., 1961; MSW, Va. Commonwealth U., 1969. Pub. asst. social worker Social Svc. Bur., Norfolk, Va., 1961-62; grad. resident advisor U. Ky., Lexington, 1962-63, head resident, 1963-64; child welfare worker Commonwealth of Ky., 1964-67; asst. tng. specialist Commonwealth of Ky. Cabinet for Human Resources, Frankfort, 1969-71, tng. adminstr., 1971-74, child protective svcs. cons., 1974-81, employer svcs. supr., 1981-83; grants and contracts adminstr. Commonwealth of Ky. Dept. Librs. and Archives, 1983-94; profl. genealogist, 1994—. Sec., exec. bd. Friends of Ky. Pub. Archives, Frankfort, 1994. Rschr. (TV prodn.) The Hatfields and McCoys: An American Feud, 1996; prodr. (video) The Family of Rose and Jack McCarthy, 1998. Vol. Habitat for Humanity, Inc., Ky., 1997-2000. Named Col. Hon. Order of Ky. Cols., 1994, Outstanding Profls. in Human Svcs., Am. Acad. Human Svcs., 1973. Mem. NASW, Nat. Geneal. Soc., Ky. Hist. Soc., Ky. Geneal. Soc., Va. Geneal. Soc., N.C. Geneal. Soc., Friends of Ky. Pub. Archives, Ky. Pub. Retirees, Acad. Cert. Social Workers, Assn. Profl. Geneaologists, Ky. Network Profl. Genealogists (co-founder 1999). Democrat. Methodist. Avocations: travel, bird-watching, photography, landscaping, spectator sports. Home and Office: 929 Brookhaven Dr Frankfort KY 40601-4439 E-mail: Lcmccarthy@aol.com.

MCCARTHY, M. JULIANN, school psychologist; b. Lewistown, Mont., Jan. 5, 1957; d. John Joseph and Helen Patricia (Ryan) McC. BA, Carroll Coll., 1979; MA, U. Mont., 1983, 84; EdD, No. Ariz. U, 2002. Cert. tchr., sch. psychologist, Ariz.; nat. cert. sch. psychologist. English tchr. Garfield County H.S., Jordan, Mont., 1979-81; sch. psychologist Cassia County Joint Sch. Dist., Burley, Idaho, 1984-85, Ednl. Svc. Dist. #112, Vancouver, Wash., 1985-92, Chandler (Ariz.) Unified Sch. Dist., 1992-94, Fountain Hills (Ariz.) Unified Sch. Dist., 1994-98, Flagstaff Unified Sch. Dist., 1998-99, Paradise Valley Unified Sch. Dist., 1999—. Del. Wash. Dem. Party Clark County, Olympia, 1992. Mem. Nat. Assn. Sch. Psychologists. Roman Catholic. Avocations: music, theater, golf, cooking, hiking. Home: 6789 W Rowel Rd Peoria AZ 85383-7036 Office: Paradise Valley High Sch 3950 E Bell Rd Phoenix AZ 85032-2113 E-mail: jumccarthy@pvusd.k12.az.us.

MCCARTHY, MARK FRANCIS, lawyer; b. Boston, July 8, 1951; s. William Alfred and Martha Louise (Blodgett) McC.; m. Karen Marie Umerley; children: Kevin Francis, Daniel Henry. AB in Theology, Georgetown U., 1973, JD, 1976. Bar: Ohio 1976. Assoc. Sweeney, Mahon, & Vlad, Cleve., 1976-80; ptnr. Arter & Hadden, 1980—. Atty. asst. to bd. pres. Bd. Cuyahoga County Commrs., Cleve., 1976-80; adj. prof. Case Western Reserve Law Ctr., Cleve., 1986—. Active Greater Cleve. Growth Assn. Leadership Cleve., 1979-80; trustee Parmadale, Parma, Ohio, Western Res. Hist. Soc., 1978-80, Cath. Charities Found.; chmn. Cath. Charities Svcs. Corp. Mem. Ohio Assn. Civil Trial Attys. (chmn. product liability sect. 1989—), Fedn. Ins. & Corp. Counsel, Ct. of Nisi Prius, Rowfant Club. Democrat. Roman Catholic. Avocations: book collecting, fly fishing, upland shooting. Home: 363 Britannia Pky Avon Lake OH 44012-2180 Office: Arter & Hadden 1100 Huntington Bldg 925 Euclid Ave Ste 1100 Cleveland OH 44115-1475 E-mail: mark.mccarth@arterhadden.com.

MCCARTHY, MARY FRANCES, medical foundation administrator; b. Washington, Apr. 16, 1937; d. Joseph Francis and Frances (Oddi) McGowan; m. Charles M. Sappenfield, Dec. 14, 1963 (div. June 1990); children: Charles Ross, Sarah Kathleen; m. Daniel Fendrich McCarthy, Jr., Aug. 25, 1990 (dec. Apr. 1999). BA, Trinity Coll., Washington, 1958; cert. in bus. adminstrn., Harvard U.-Radcliffe Coll., 1959; MA, Ball State U., Muncie, Ind., 1984. Systems engr. IBM, Cambridge, Mass., 1959-61; editl. asst. Kiplinger Washington Editors, 1961-63; feature writer pub. info. dept. Ball State U., 1984-85, coll. editor Coll. Bus., 1985-86, coord. alumni and devel., 1986-88, dir. major gift clubs and donor rels., 1988-90; dir. devel. Sweet Briar (Va.) Coll., 1990-91; adminstr. St. Mary's Hosp. and Med. Ctr. Found., Grand Junction, Colo., 1991—. Editor: A History of Maxon Corporation, 1986, Managing Change, 1986, Indiana's Investment Banker, 1987; assoc. editor Mid-Am. Jour. Bus., 1985-86. Participant Leadership Lynchburg, 1990, Jr. League; regional dir. IX Assn. for Healthcare Philanthropy, 1996—98, found. bd., 1997—; bd. dirs. Sr. Companions, Grand Junction, 1992—; mem. steering com. Mesa County Health Cmtys., 1992—; bd. dirs. Grand Junction Musical Arts, 1997—; trustee Women's Found. of Colo., 2000—; bd. dirs. Grand Valley Hospice, 2002—; mem. Mesa County Health Assessment, 1994—. Recipient Golden Broom award Muncie Clean City, 1989; svc. of distinction award Ball State U. Coll. Bus., 1990. Mem. Coun. for Advancement and Support of Edn., Assn. of Healthcare Philanthropy (regional 9 cabinet 1992—, bd. dirs. 1997—), Nat. Soc. Fundraising Execs. (cert., Colo. chpt. bd. dirs. 1994—), Rotary. Republican. Avocations: biking, walking, cross-country skiing, gardening. Office: St Marys Hosp/Med Ctr Found 2635 N 7th St Grand Junction CO 81501-8209

MCCARTHY, MICHAEL FITZMICHAEL, business executive; b. Boston, May 5, 1944; s. Michael Fitzmichael and Stella Mary (Krajewski) McC. BA in Comm., Harvard U., 1963; MS in Psychology, U. Miami, 1972. Audio engr. Scripps-Howard Broadcasting, Palm Beach, Fla., 1972-73; field svc. engr. Xerox Corp., West Palm Beach, 1973-84; mng. broker Croton Plaza Realty, Palm Beach, 1984-88; dep. clk. of cts. Palm Beach County, West Palm Beach, 1989-93; ptnr. G2 Resources, Inc., North Palm Beach, Fla., 1993—. State vice chmn. Teen Dems. for Kennedy, West Palm Beach, 1960; del. at large Dem. Nat. Conv., Chgo., 1968. Lt. col. USAF, 1963-68. Mem. Soc. for Tech. Commn., Poinciana Club of Plam Beach, Govs. Club, Palm Beach Yacht Club, Masons, Mensa. Democrat. Anglican. Avocations: humorist, photography, antique cars, clocks and watches. Home: 5200 Poinsettia Ave Apt 2105 West Palm Beach FL 33407-2775 Office: G2 Resources Inc 47097 Glenaire Ct Sterling VA 20165-7521

MCCARTHY, MICHAEL JAMES, military intelligence officer; b. Columbus, Ohio, July 29, 1962; s. James Patrick and Alice Marie (Gartner) McC.; m. Muriel Ruth Levine, Oct. 8, 1987. BA, Ohio State U., 1984; diploma, Pushkin Inst., Moscow, 1984; MA, Cath. U. Am., Washington, 1996; M in Mil. Sci. with distinction, USMC Command and Staff Coll., Quantico, Va., 2000. Commd. 2d lt. USAF, 1986, advanced through grades to lt. col., 2002; staff intelligence officer 31st Tactical Fighter Wing, Homestead AFB, Fla., 1987, chief intelligence sect., 1987-89, chief target intelligence, 1989-90; watch officer Hdqrs. US Air Forces in Europe, Ramstein AB, Germany, 1990, command briefer, 1990-93; sr. analyst Nat. Air Intelligence Ctr., Washington, 1993-95; plans and requirements officer Hdqrs. U.S. Air Force, 1995-96, exec. officer, 1996-97; ops. officer Joint Intelligence Ctr. Ctrl., MacDill AFB, Fla., 1997-98, team chief Ctrl. Asia Analysis, 1998—99; detailed to US Marine Corps Command and Staff Coll., 1000—2000; ops. officer 23d Info. Ops. Squadron, Kelly AFB, Tex., 2000—02; UN mil. observer Tbilisi, Georgia, 2001—02; country dir. Office of Internat. Affairs, Hdqrs. USAF, Washington, 2002—. Contbr. articles to mil. publs. Vol. Alexandria (Va.) Animal Shelter, 1994-96, Carpenter's Lodging, Alexandria, 1995-97; lectr. Civic Air Patrol, Falls Ch., Va., 1995-97, Jr. ROTC, Brandon, Fla., 1997-98. Mem. Am. Assn. Advancement Slavic Studies, Nat. Mil. Intelligence Assn., Air Force Assn. Republican. Roman Catholic. Avocations: running, weightlifting, travel, military history. Office: SAF/IARE 1500 Wilson Blvd Ste 801 Rosslyn VA 22209

MCCARTHY, MICHAEL SHAWN, health care company executive, lawyer; b. Evergreen Park, Ill., May 16, 1953; s. Martin J. and Margaret Anne (McNeill) McC.; m. Jane F. Alberding, Oct. 28, 1988; children: Caroline Margaret, Nicholas Michael, Claire Patricia. BA, Georgetown U., 1975; MS, U. Ill., 1976; JD, Loyola U., 1980. Bar: Ill. 1980, U.S. Dist. Ct. (no. dist.) Ill. 1980. V.p., sec., gen. counsel Luth. Gen. Health Care System, Park Ridge, Ill., 1980-85, sr. v.p., sec., gen. counsel, 1985-91, sr. v.p. corp. svcs., sec., gen. counsel, 1990-93; chmn., CEO Parkside Sr. Svcs., LLC, Skokie, 1993—. Chmn. bd. trustees Lake Forest Acad., 1995-98. Mem. ABA, ASHA (exec. bd.), Ill. Hosp. Assn., Ill. Pub. Health Assn., Chgo. Bar Assn., ALFA

Leadership Coun. Roman Catholic. Avocations: golf, travel. Home: 1026 Pine St Winnetka IL 60093-2024 Office: Parkside Sr Svcs LLC 5215 Old Orchard Rd Skokie IL 60077-1035 E-mail: McCarthy@parkside-sr.com.

MCCARTHY, PATRICIA BENNETT, social worker; b. N.Y.C., Feb. 28, 1936; d. Walter William Konvalinka and Alice Marsh (Waterman) Bennett; m. Franklin L. McCarthy, Aug. 8, 1964; children: Heather, John. BA, Hood Coll., 1958; MA, U. Chgo., 1962. Diplomate ACSW; lic. social worker, Pa. Psychiat. social worker Univ. Settlement Child Guidance Clinic, N.Y.C., 1962-64, Wilder Child Guidance Clinic, St. Paul, 1964-66, Lane County Mental Health Clinic, Eugene, Oreg., 1966-69; coord. Halfway House for State Mental Patients, 1970-72; vol. counselor alcohol program Puget Sound Hosp., Tacoma, 1976-77; vol. counselor, psychiat. cons. Parents Anonymous, Pitts., 1977-79; vol. outpatient counselor Alcohol Treatment Ctr. St. Francis Hosp., 1981-83; drug and alcohol counselor Whale's Tale, 1988-92; inpatient psychiat. social worker St. Francis Hosp., 1992-97. Bd. dirs. All of Us Care, group leader Grandparents Raising Children because Parent are Addicted, Pitts; mem. Com. for Abolition of Nuclear Weapons; deacon East Liberty Luth. Ch.; vol. Riding for Handicapped of Western Pa. Mem. AAUW. Lutheran.

MCCARTHY, PATRICK, magazine publishing executive; Joined Women's Wear Daily, 1977, reporter D.C., bur. chief, Paris, editor N.Y.C., 1985-88, exec. editor, 1988-92; editor W, 1985-88, exec. editor, 1988-92; exec. v.p. Fairchild Publs., 1992-97; chmn., editl. dir., 1997—. Recipient Eugenia Sheppard award for fashion journalism CFDA, 1994. Office: Fairchild Publs Seven West 34th St New York NY 10001

MCCARTHY, PAUL FENTON, aerospace executive, former naval officer; b. Boston, Mar. 3, 1934; s. Paul Fenton and Jane Gertrude (O'Connor) McC.; m. Sandra Williams, June 20, 1959; children: Paul Fenton III, Susan Stacy. BS in Marine and Elec. Engring., Mass. Maritime Acad., 1954; MS in Mgmt., U.S. Naval Postgrad. Sch., 1964; D of Pub. Adminstrn. (hon.), Mass. Maritime Acad., 1987. Commd. ensign U.S. Navy, 1954, advanced through grades to vice adm., 1985; 7 command tours have included Aircraft Carrier USS Constellation, Carrier Group One, Task Force Seventy; commdr. U.S. 7th Fleet, 1980-82; dir. R & D USN, Washington, 1980-83; negotiator Naval Air, Incidents at Sea Agreement, Moscow, 1980; ret., 1990; cons. in field Alexandria, Va., 1990-92; pres. McCarthy and McCarthy, Ltd.; v.p., chief engr., dep. gen.mgr. McDonnell Douglas Aerospace/Boeing, St. Louis, 1992-95; v.p. processes and sys. integration McDonnell Douglas Aerospace, 1995-97, dir. naval systems integration, 1997-2000; vis. disting. prof. Peter Conrad Chair Naval Post Grad. Sch., 2000-02. Mem. engring adv. coun. Fla. State U. Trustee Naval Mus., 1990; bd. visitors Mass. Maritime Acad., 1993. Decorated D.S.M., Legion of Merit, D.F.C., also by govts. of South Vietnam, Korea, Japan. Mem. Mass. Maritime Acad. Alumni Assn., Soc. Exptl. Test Pilots, Naval Inst., Nat. Soc. Profl. Engrs. (mem. industry adv. group). Episcopalian. Avocations: research, development and acquisition, aircraft and missile systems, financial management. E-mail: mcandmc@aol.com.

MCCARTHY, PAUL LOUIS, pediatrics educator; b. Springfield, Mass., Aug. 9, 1941; s. Alfred Lawrence and Minnie Josephine (Vivian) McC.; m. Barbara Jean Burns, Nov. 30, 1963; children: Paul, Scott, Brian. BA, Dartmouth Coll., 1963; MD, Georgetown U., 1969; MA (in privatum), Yale U., 1982. Diplomate Am. Bd. Pediatrics, Am. Bd. Pediatric Rheumatology. Pediat. intern Children's Hosp., Buffalo, 1969-70, pediat. resident, 1970-72; fellow in ambulatory pediatrics Children's Hosp. Med. Ctr., Boston, 1972-74; asst. prof. pediat. Yale U. Sch. Medicine, New Haven, 1974-78, assoc. prof., 1978-82, prof., 1982—, head gen. pediat., 1985—. Morrison lectr. Geisinger Clinic, Danville, Pa., 1990. Author: Evaluation and Management of Febrile Children, 1985; author 4 monographs; contbr. numerous articles to med. jours., chpts. to books. Fellow Am. Acad. Pediatrics (chmn. com. pediat. rsch. 1996-2000); mem. Ambulatory Pediatric Assn. (pres. 1989-90, Armstrong award 1991, rsch. award 1999), Soc. for Pediatric Rsch., Am. Pediatric Soc., Assn. Am. Med. Colls. (exec. coun. 1998-2001, chair, coun. acad. socs. 1999-2000). Achievements include research in clinical judgment in acute illnesses in children. Avocations: reading, walking. Office: Yale U Sch of Medicine 333 Cedar St New Haven CT 06510-3289

MCCARTHY, ROBERT EMMETT, lawyer; b. Bklyn., May 26, 1951; s. John Joseph and Leona Mary (Hart) McC.; m. Elizabeth Anne Naumoff, May 20, 1978; children: John Philip, Emily Jane. BS in Fgn. Studies, Georgetown U., 1973, MS in Fgn. Studies, JD, 1978. Bar: N.J. 1978, U.S. Dist. Ct. (ea. and so. dists.) N.Y. 1979. Assoc. Patterson, Belknap et al, N.Y.C., 1978-84; gen. counsel MTV Networks Inc., 1984-86; v.p., counsel/communications Viacom Internat., 1986-87; exec. v.p. Nelson Vending Tech., Ltd., 1987-89; exec. v.p., gen. counsel Cateret Savs. Bank FA, Morristown, N.J., 1989-91; cons. McCarthy Comms., Elizabeth, 1991-95; sr. v.p., gen. counsel Time, Inc., N.Y.C., 1996—. Cons. UN Ctr. on Transnat. Corps., N.Y.C., 1979; exec. dir. Spl. Master Reapportionment of N.Y., 1982; term mem. Council Fgn. Relations, N.Y.C., 1980-84. Founder, pres. Elizabeth (N.J.) Dem. Assn., 1980; coordinator Florio for Gov., Union County, N.J., 1981. Mem. ABA, N.Y. State Bar Assn., N.J. State Bar Assn., Assn. Bar City N.Y. Roman Catholic. Home: 3 Woods Ln Chatham NJ 07928-1760 Office: Time Inc 33rd Fl 1271 Avenue Of The Americas New York NY 10020-1300 E-mail: RobertMcCarthy1@aol.com.

MCCARTHY, ROGER LEE, mechanical engineer; AB in Philosophy with high distinction, BSME summa cum laude, U. Mich., 1972; MS in Mech. Engring., MIT, 1973, MechE, 1975, PhD in Mech. Engring., 1977. Registered profl. engr., Calif., Ga., Ariz. Project engr. machine design and devel. engring. div. Proctor & Gamble, Inc., Cin., 1973-74; program mgr. Spl. Machinery Group Foster-Miller Assocs., Inc., Waltham, Mass., 1976-78; prin. design engr. Failure Analysis Assocs., Inc. (became Exponent Failure Analysis Assocs., Inc. in 1998), Menlo Park, Calif., 1978—; chmn. bd. dirs., 1988—; CEO The Failure Group, Inc., Menlo Park, 1988-96, chief tech. officer, 1996-98; chmn. Exponent Failure Analysis Assocs., Inc., Calif., 1998—. Co-contbr. numerous articles to profl. jours. Mem. Pres.' Commn. on Nat. Medal of Sci., 1992-94. Recipient Outstanding Civilian Svc. Gold medal U.S. Army, 1998; NSF fellow, 1972-75. Mem. Am. Soc. Metals, ASME, Soc. Automotive Engrs., Am. Welding Soc., Am. Soc. for Testing and Materials, Human Factors Soc., ASHRAE, Nat. Fire Protection Assn., Phi Beta Kappa, Sigma Xi (James B. Angell scholar). Office: Exponent Failure Analysis Assn Inc 149 Commonwealth Dr Menlo Park CA 94025

MCCARTHY, STEVEN MICHAEL, lawyer; b. Morristown, N.J., May 2, 1949; s. George Doane and Frances (Jones) McC. BA in Philosophy, U. Va., 1971; MA in Philosophy, Calif. State U., San Francisco, 1975; JD, Golden Gate U., 1978. Diplomate Nat. Inst. for Trial Advocacy; bar: Calif. 1979, U.S. Dist. Ct. (no. dist.) Calif. 1979, U.S. Ct. Appeals (9th cir.) 2002; cert. tchr. secondary school law, philosophy, religion, Calif.; cert. diver rescue specialist, instr. Law clk. United Farm Workers Union, 1973, San Francisco Lawyers' Com. on Urban Affairs, 1975, San Francisco Pub. Defender, 1975, Bayview Hunters' Point Cmty. Defender, 1976-77; pvt. practice, 1979—2002; ptnr. McCarthy & Wakeley, Oakland, Calif., 1988-91. Judge pro tempore Contra Costa Superior Ct. Judge Pro Tem Panel and EASE program evaluator, 1993—; domestic violence emergency protective order judge Solano County Superior Ct., 1994—; arbitrator Solano County Mcpl. Ct., 1994—, Alameda County Bar Assn. Fee Arbitration Panel, 1989—; judge pro tem small claims and traffic, Alameda County Mcpl. Ct., 1981—, others. Bd. dirs. Mental Health Assn. of Alameda County, 1994-97; pres. bd. dirs. Elms Homeowners Assn., 1992-94; treas. bd. dirs. Oaks Homeowners Assn., 1989-90; lectr. Alameda H.S. Spkrs. Program; vol. mounted patrol East Bay Regional Parks Dist., 1999—; mem. Alameda County Sheriff's Posse, 1999-2002. Mem. NRA, Calif. State Bar Assn. (spl. master), Alameda County Bar Assn., Solano County Bar Assn., Back Country Horsemen of Calif., Calif. Rifle and Pistol Assn., Tri Valley Trailblazers, Alameda Divers, Ctrl. Calif. Coun. Dive Clubs, Chabot Gun Club. Avocations: scuba diving, horseback riding, bicycling, sailing, spearfishing. Office: 2100 Embarcadero Ste 100 Oakland CA 94606-5309 E-mail: caractacus@aol.com.

MCCARTHY, SUSAN STACY, company executive; b. China Lake, Calif., Aug. 8, 1962; d. Paul Fenton Jr and Sandra Sue (Williams) McCarthy. BA in Econs. and Chinese Studies, U. Calif., San Diego, 1986; M of Pub. Fin. Mgmt., Am. U., 1992; postgrad., Naval War Coll., 1993-95, Webster U., 1995—. Exec. v.p. Calif. Designers Delivery, Vernon, Calif., 1986-88; fin. mgr. office of comptr. U.S. Dept. Navy, Washington, 1988-91; fin. analyst def. subcom., appropriations com. U.S. Senate, 1991-92; fin. mgt. strategic nuclear forces and sealift Office of Navy Comptroller, 1992-93; head fin. analyst for procurement USMC/USNG and Res. Equipment, 1993-95; v.p. Quarterdeck Investment Ptnrs., 1995-96; mgr. strategic bus. devel. McDonnell Douglas Corp., St. Louis, 1996-97; dir. strategic planning The Boeing Co., 1997-98, exec. devel. program, 1998-99, dir. investor rels., 1999—2001. Active Habitat for Humanity; sponsor World Visions, Sponsor Plan Int. Lt. comdr. USNR, 1990. Republican. Episcopalian. Avocations: travel, athletics, reading, music, language study.

MCCARTHY, THOMAS JAMES, JR. lawyer; b. Pulaski, Va., Nov. 24, 1943; s. Thomas James and Jane (Osborne) McC.; m. Sally Stockdale, July 25, 1987. BA in Econs., Washington and Lee U., 1967; JD, U. Va., 1970. Bar: Va. 1970, U.S. Dist. Ct. (we. dist.) Va. 1974, U.S. Supreme Ct. 2000. Asoc. Gilmer, Sadler, Ingram Sutherland & Hutton, Pulaski, 1970-75, ptnr., 1975—; county atty. Pulaski County, 1983—. Adminstrv. hearings officer Commonwealth of Va., 1983—; commr. of accts. Pulaski County, 1989—. Bd. dirs. New River C.C., 1980-88, 96—, vice-chair, 1981-88, 2000-02, chair 2002—, found. bd., 1989-91. Col. JAGC, U.S. Army Res., ret., 1997. Decorated Legion of Merit, Meritorious Svc. medal, Army Commendation medal. Mem. Va. Bar Assn., 27th Jud. Cir. Bar Assn. (pres. 1978-81), Pulaski County Bar Assn., Sigma Chi, Phi Alpha Delta. Democrat. Episcopalian. Home: PO Box 818 Pulaski VA 24301-0818 Office: Gilmer Sadler et al 65 E Main St Pulaski VA 24301-5013

MCCARTHY, THOMAS ANTHONY, philosophy educator; b. Springfield, Mass., Mar. 6, 1940; s. Alfred Lawrence and Minnie Josephine (Vivian) McC.; m. Patricia Perry, Aug. 3, 1963; children: Jennifer, Justin. BS in Math., Holy Cross Coll., 1961; MA in Philosophy, U. Notre Dame, 1963, PhD in Philosophy, 1968. Instr. U. Munich, Germany, 1968-72; from asst. to assoc. prof. Boston U., 1972-85; prof. philosophy Northwestern U., Evanston, Ill., 1985—, John Shaffer Disting. prof. in the Humanities, 1992—. Dir. NEH summer seminar, Boston, 1982, 84. Author: The Critical Theory of Jurgen Habermas, 1978, Ideals and Illusions, 1991; co-author: Critical Theory, 1994; editor (series) Studies in Contempory German Social Thought, 1981—. Fellow Guggenheim Found., 1985, Alexander von Humboldt Found., Germany, 1975-76, Am. Coun. Learned Socs., 1989-90; grantee NEH, 1989-90. Mem. Am. Philos. Assn., N.Am. Kant Soc., Soc. for Phenomenology and Existential Philosophy. Office: Northwestern U Dept Philosophy 1818 Hinman Ave Evanston IL 60208-0810 E-mail: t-mccarthy@nwu.edu.

MCCARTHY, THOMAS EDWARD, retired telecommunications executive; b. Sacramento, July 18, 1925; s. James Daniel and Lorene Margaret McCarthy; m. Joyce Elaine Reilly, June 28, 1952 (dec. Nov. 1987); children: Thomas E. Jr., Sharon E., Lisa A. McCarthy Harding; m. Gloria Adair Radford, Dec. 30, 1989. BS in Journalism with distinction, Northwestern U., 1950. Cert. Pub. Rels. Soc. Am. Reporter UP, San Francisco, 1951-54, Wall St. Jour., N.Y.C., 1954-56; pub. rels. project mgr. Sylvania Electric, 1956-62; mgr. pub. info. GTE Corp., 1962-72, dir. pub. info. Stamford, Conn., 1972-80, v.p. pub. affairs, 1980-86; ret., 1986. Cons. in field. Author: The History of GTE Corp., 1990 (Assn. Bus. Comms. award 1991), Irish Jubilee, 1997. With USAAC, 1943-46. Mem. Sigma Delta Chi, Kappa Tau Alpha, Zeta Psi. Roman Catholic. Avocations: reading, writing, travel, walking, history. Home: 9885 Mill Station Rd Sebastopol CA 95472-9662

MCCARTHY, THOMAS O. lawyer; b. Denver, Aug. 3, 1947; s. Thomas E. and Edna D. (Davis) McC.; m. Sharon K., June 22, 1974; children: Jennifer, Julianne. BSEE cum laude, U. Mo., 1970, JD, 1972. Bar: Mo. 1973, U.S. Supreme Ct. 1994, U.S. Ct. Appeals (8th cir.) 1974, U.S. Dist. Ct. (ea. dist.) Mo. 1974. Mng. ptnr. McMahon, Berger, Hanna, Linihan, Cody & McCarthy, St. Louis. Bd. dirs. BJC Healthsys., St. Louis, 1997—, Mo. Bapt. Med. Ctr., St. Louis, 1996—, Humane Soc. Mo. Mem. St. Louis Bar Assn. (chmn. labor law com. 1985-86, labor and employment sect., litigation sect.). Avocations: hunting, skiing. Home: 13522 Weston Park Dr Saint Louis MO 63131-1044 Office: McMahon Berger Hanna Linihan Cody & McCarthy 2730 N Ballas Rd Ste 200 Saint Louis MO 63131-3039

MCCARTHY, VINCENT PAUL, lawyer; b. Boston, Sept. 25, 1940; s. John Patrick and Marion (Buckley) McC.; children: Vincent, Sybil, Hope. AB, Boston Coll., 1962; JD, Harvard U., 1965. Bar: Mass. 1965. Ptnr. Hale and Dorr LLP, Boston, 1965—; sr. ptnr. Hale and Dorr, 1976—. Bd. dirs., sec. Robert F. Kennedy Action Corps, Inc.; bd. dirs. Boston Alcohol Detoxification Project, Inc.; mem. Mass. Gov.'s Adv. Coun. on Alcoholism, Boston, 1984-94, Gov.'s Jud. Nominating Com., 1991—; chmn. Mass. Housing Partnership Fund, 1991—; past chmn. Boston Ctr. for Arts; mem. adv. coun. Harvard Internat. AIDS Inst.; trustee, sec. Franklin Square House; past pres. Mass. Assn. for Mental Health; bd. dirs., past sec.-treas. Human Rights Campaign Found.; chmn. Gov.'s Commn. on Gay and Lesbian Youth, 2001—. Recipient Vols. of Am. Outstanding Svc. award, 1989. Mem. ABA (Pro Bono Publico award 1987), Mass. Bar Assn., Boston Bar Assn. (mem. jud. nominating com. 1991-99, Pub. Svc. award 1995). E-mail: vincent.mccarthy@haledorr.com.

MC CARTHY, WALTER JOHN, JR. retired utility executive; b. N.Y.C., Apr. 20, 1925; s. Walter John and Irene (Trumbl) McC.; m. Linda Lyon, May 6, 1988; children by previous marriage: Walter, David, Sharon, James, William. B.M.E., Cornell U., 1949; grad., Oak Ridge Sch. Reactor Tech., 1952; D.Eng. (hon.), Lawrence Inst. Tech., 1981; D.Sc. (hon.), Eastern Mich. U., 1983; LHD, Wayne State U., 1984; LLD, Alma (Mich.) Coll., 1985. Engr. Public Service Electric & Gas Co., Newark, 1949-56; sect. head Atomic Power Devel. Assos., Detroit, 1956-61; gen. mgr. Power Reactor Devel. Co., 1961-68; with Detroit Edison Co., 1968-90, exec. v.p. ops., 1975-77, exec. v.p. divs., 1977-79, pres., chief operating officer, 1979-81, chmn., chief exec. officer, 1981-90. Bd. dirs. Energy Conversion Devices Inc. Author papers in field. Past chmn., bd. dirs. Inst. Nuclear Power Ops.; past pres. Monterey County Symphony Orch. Fellow Am. Nuc. Soc., Engring. Soc. Detroit; mem. ASME, NAE. Methodist.

MCCARTHY, WILLIAM ROBERT, minister; b. Tacoma, Nov. 17, 1941; s. Denward Sylvester and Florence Elizabeth (Lohan) McC.; m. Bernice Bigler, Apr. 22, 1962; children: Brian Edward Earl, Sean David. BS, Oreg. State U., 1966; MDiv, Nashotah House, 1975. Ordained deacon Episcopal Ch., 1975, priest, 1975. Curate St. Michael's Ch., Barrington, Ill., 1975-77; vicar St. Anselm's Ch., Park Ridge, 1977-81; rector Christ Ch. Parish, Waukegan, 1981-89, Ch. of Good Samaritan, Corvallis, Oreg., 1989—. Diocesan cursillo officer Diocese Chgo., 1975—85; spiritual dir. Ecumenical Cursillo Cmty. , Chgo., 1977—83; mem. steering com. Happenings in Christianity, Chgo., 1978—80; chmn. Bishop's Adv. Commn. on Renewal & Evangelism, Chgo., 1983—85; mem. diocesan coun. Diocese of Oreg., 1991—93, 2000—; bd. dir. Oreg. Episcopal Clergy Assn.; standing com. Diocese of Oreg., 1994—97; bd. dir. Intercmty. HealthNetwork. Contbr. articles to profl. jours. Bd. mem. Waukegan Area Crime Stoppers, 1982-85; founder, chmn. FOCUS 90 Com. for Downtown Devel., 1988-89; charter bd. dirs. Waukegan Downtown Assn., 1983-89, v.p., 1986-87, pres., 1987-88; founder, exec. dir. Share/Food Waukegan Area, 1985-89; bd. dirs. YMCA of Lake County, 1985-89; trustee Good Samaritan Hosp., Corvallis, 1989—; vice chair bd. Samaritan Health Svcs., 1998-2000, chmn. bd. dirs., 2001—. With USNR, 1962-65. Mem. Assn. for Psychol. Type, Rotary, Masons, Phi Sigma Kappa. Office: Ch of the Good Samaritan 333 NW 35th St Corvallis OR 97330-4908 E-mail: rector@goodsamchurch.com., BernieBill@aol.com.

MCCARTIN, BRIAN JAMES, mathematician, educator; b. Providence, Aug. 26, 1951; s. James Dominic and Dorothy Frances (Kelly) McC.; 1 child, Sean Colin. BS in Applied Math. with highest distinc., U. R.I., 1976, MS in Applied Math., 1977; PhD in Applied Math., NYU, 1981; BMus in Music Theory summa cum laude, U. Hartford, 1994. Sr. rsch. mathematician United Technologies Corp., East Hartford, Conn., 1977-89; prof. computer sci. Rensselaer Poly. Inst., Hartford, 1989-92; prof. applied math. Kettering U., Flint, Mich., 1993—. Vis. lectr. high schs., 1997—. Contbr. articles to profl. jours., chpts. to books. Named Disting. Vis. Prof., N.J. Inst. Tech., 1997. Mem. Math. Assn. Am. (dept. liaison), Soc. Indsl. and Applied Math. (founder spl. interest group on numerical methods for partial differentiation equations Great Lakes sect. 1997-98, sec. 1998-2000, v.p. 2000-02), Kappa Mu Epsilon (faculty advisor 1997-98), Pi Kappa Lambda, Phi Kappa Phi, Alpha Chi, Pi Mu Epsilon (Kettering U. Outstanding Rschr. award 2000, Kettering U. Outstanding Tchg. award 2001). Avocation: classical pianist. Home: 2310 Crestbrook Ln Flint MI 48507-2209 Office: Kettering Univ Applied Math 1700 W 3d Ave Flint MI 48504-4832 E-mail: bmccarti@kettering.edu.

MCCARTIN, THOMAS JOSEPH, advertising executive; b. Rockville Centre, N.Y., Sept. 6, 1957; s. John Francis and Agnes (Farrell) McC.; m. Louise Ann Cuccurullo, Mar. 10, 1990; children; Thomas Joseph, Sean Cody. BS in Mktg., N.Y. Inst. Tech., 1979. Bus. devel. officer Mfrs. Hanover Trust, N.Y.C., 1981-83; asst. sec. Dollar Dry Dock Savs. Bank, 1983-84; sr. v.p. IMC Mktg. Group, 1984-86; pres. McCartin & Kunin, Inc., 1986-95, M&K West, Phoenix, 1993-95; exec. v.p. Lipman, Richmond, Greene Advt., N.Y.C., 1995-2000, Warren, Kremer, Paino, N.Y.C., 2001—. Bd. dirs. Delta Dental of N.Y., N.Y.C. Mem. NRA, Distributive Edn. Clubs Am. (life), Direct Mktg. Assn., Bus. Coun. N.Y. State, Sierra Club, Vet. Corps of Arty. Conservative. Roman Catholic. Avocations: hunting, camping. Office: Warren Kremer Paino 2 Park Ave New York NY 10016 E-mail: tmccartin@hotmail.com.

MCCARTNEY, CHARLES PRICE, retired obstetrician-gynecologist; b. Barnesville, Ohio, Aug. 18, 1912; s. Jesse Thomas and Carrie (Price) McC.; m. Phyllis Helen Graybill, Sept. 27, 1940; children— Marilyn B., Ann E. BS, U. Chgo., 1942, MD, 1943. Diplomate: Am. Bd. Obstetricians and Gynecologists. Intern U. Chgo. Clinics, 1943-44, resident, 1947-50; mem. faculty U. Chgo. Med. Sch., 1950-71, prof. obstetrics and gynecology, 1960-71, Mary Campeau Ryerson prof., 1967-71; clin. prof. obstetrics and gynecology U. Ill., 1971-80, prof. emeritus, 1980—. Attending gynecologist and obstetrician Chgo. Lying-In Hosp., 1950— Mem. Cook County Com. Maternal Welfare, 1965— . Served to maj., M.C. AUS, 1944-46. Fellow Am. Gynecol. Soc.; mem. Am. Gynecol. and Obstetrical Soc., Chgo. Gynecol. Soc. (pres. 1967), Chgo. Med. Soc. (councillor 1960—, pres. 1973, chmn. bd. trustees 1973), Am. Coll. Obstetricians and Gynecologists (chmn. Ill. sect. 1965—), Cen. Assn. Obstetricians and Gynecologists. Home: 916 Thornwood Dr Saint Charles IL 60174-5018

MCCARTNEY, ELAINA, space mission planner; b. Ithaca, N.Y., May 23, 1944; d. John R. and Dorothy (Wilson) McC.; children: John F. Carr, Kelly C. Zitzmann, Jennie M. Jeddry. BA, Cornell U., 1967, M in Engring., 1993. Computer scientist Cornell U., Ithaca, 1984-98; planetary space mission planner NASA/Cornell U., 1998—; spacecraft sequencer Near Earth Asteroid Rendezvous Mission, 1998—; mission planner APEX, Athena and MER Missions to Mars, Cassini Mission to Saturn, 1998—. Rsch. scientist/KC-135 microgravity aircraft, NASA/Cornell, 1996—; instr. transcendental meditation, 1977--. Contbr. articles to profl. jours. Field vol., mastodon excavation, Cornell-Gilbert Mastodon, Ithaca, 1999. Mem. AAAS. Avocations: writing poetry, bicycling, sailing, flying trapeze, residential architecture. Office: Cornell U 427 Space Sciences Ithaca NY 14850 E-mail: emm5@cornell.edu.

MCCARTNEY, JAMES HAROLD, newspaper columnist, educator, journalist; b. St. Paul, July 25, 1925; s. Floyd Allen and Cora Jeanette (Heilig) McC.; m. Jule Ann Graham, Jan. 19, 1952 (div. 1983); children: Robert, Sharon; m. Molly Kathleen Bowers, Sept. 8, 1984. BA, Mich. State U., 1949; MSJ, Northwestern U., 1951. Reporter South Bend (Ind.) Tribune, 1949-50, Chgo. Daily News, 1952-60, Washington corr., 1960-66, city editor, 1966-68; Washington corr. Knight-Ridder Newspapers, Miami, Fla., 1968-90, columnist, 1985-96, Bradenton (Fla.) Herald, 2000—; lectr. Georgetown U., 1990—. With U.S. Army, 1943-45, ETO. Mem. Nat. Press Club, Gridiron Club (pres. 1987). Avocation: golf. Home: 419 Spring Lk Rehoboth Beach DE 19971-1735 E-mail: jamesmccartney76@aol.com.

MCCARTNEY, JAMES ROBERT, psychiatrist; b. Elmira, N.Y., Jan. 6, 1932; s. James L. and Edith T. (Tufs) McC; m. Lois McCartney; 4 children. BA, Ohio Wesleyan U., 1952; MD, Columbia U., 1955; MA (Ad Eundem-)(hon.), Brown U., 1989. Diplomate Nat. Bd. Med. Examiners, Am. Bd. Pscyhiatry and Neurology, Am. Bd. Geriatric Psychiatry. Intern Boston City Hosp. for Medicine, 1955-56; resident in psychiatry Elizabeth's Hosp., Washington, 1958-59, Inst. Living, Hartford, Conn., 1959-61; assoc. attending psychiatrist then attending psychiatrist North Shore U. Hosp., 1964-80, dir. tng. and edn. dept. psychiatry, 1972-79, chief of liaison svcs., 1973-80, assoc. dir., 1978-80; attending psychiatrist Meadowbrook Hosp., 1961-64; assoc. attending psychiatrist Nassau Hosp., 1964-71; on staff Butler Hosp., 1980—; psychiatrist-in-chief The Miriam Hosp., Providence, 1980-97; dir. geropsychiatry Life Span Acad. Med. Ctr., 1998; ret. Adv. bd. Mental Health Assn. of Nassau County, 1972-80; cons. impaired physician com. R.I. Med. Soc., 1981—; asst. prof. psychiatry Brown U., Providence, 1980-88, assoc. prof., 1988-98, assoc. prof. emeritus, 1998—. Contbr. articles to profl. jours. Capt. U.S. Army, 1956-58. Fellow ACP, Am. Psychiat. Assn., Acad. of Psychosomatic Medicine; mem. R.I. Med. Soc., Assn. for Acad. Psychiatry, Providence Med. Assn., Am. Assn. Gen. Hosp. Psychiatrists. E-mail: james_mccartney@brown.edu., mccartney@ids.net.

MCCARTNEY, N. L. investment banker; b. Jameson, Mo., Oct. 12, 1923; m. Helen M. Walsh, Feb. 11, 1950; children: Patricia, Deborah, Patrick. BS, U. Md., 1956; MBA, Syracuse U., 1959; MPA, George Washington U., 1963. Enlisted U.S. Army, 1944, advanced through grades to col., ret., 1972; dir. S.W. Mo. Health Care Foun., Springfield, 1974-88; pres. Resource Mgmt. Co., 1988-96; exec. v.p. Spencer and Assocs., 1990-94, Mo. Adv. Capital, 1995-99; pres. DMS, Inc., 1999—. Instr. Southwest Mo. State U., Springfield, 1972-82, Crescent Capital, 1999-2000. Pres. S.W. Mo. Adv. Coun. Govts., Ozarks Crime Prevention Coun., 1983-93, Vis. Nurse Assn.; mayor of Springfield, 1993-95. Mem. Rotary. Methodist. Home: 1233 E Loren St Springfield MO 65804-0041 Office: 330 N Jefferson Springfield MO 65806

MC CARTNEY, RALPH FARNHAM, lawyer; b. Charles City, Iowa, Dec. 11, 1924; s. Ralph C. and Helen (Farnham) McC.; m. Rhoda Mae Huxsol, June 25, 1950; children: Ralph, Julia, David. JD, U. Mich., 1950; B. Sci., Iowa State U., 1972. Bar: Iowa 1950. Mem. firm Miller, Heuber & Miller, Des Moines, 1950-52, Frye & McCartney, Charles City, 1952-73, McCartney & Erb, Charles City, 1973-78; judge Dist. Ct. Iowa, 1978-87; chief judge 2d Judicial Dist., 1987-92; sr. judge Ct. Appeals, 1992—. Mem. jud. coordinating com. Iowa Supreme Ct. Chmn. Supreme Ct. Adv. Com. on Adminstrn. of Clks. Offices; mem. Iowa Ho. of Reps., 1967-70, majority floor leader, 1969-70; mem. Iowa Senate, 1973-74. Bd. regents U. Iowa, Iowa State U., U. No. Iowa, Iowa Sch. for Deaf, Iowa Braille and Sight Saving Sch. Served with AUS, 1942-45. Mem. Iowa Judges Assn. No e-mail. Home: 1828 Cedar View Dr Charles City IA 50616-9129 Office: Cty Chambers Courthouse Charles City IA 50616

MCCARTNEY, RHODA HUXSOL, farm manager; b. Floyd County, Iowa, June 30, 1928; d. Julius Franklin and Ruth Ada (Carney) Huxsol; m. Ralph Farnham McCartney, June 25, 1950; children: Ralph, Julia, David. AA, Frances Shimer, 1948; BA, U. Iowa, 1950. Mng. dir. McCartney-Huxsol Farms, Charles City, Iowa, 1969—; prin. trustee J.F. Huxsol Trusts, 1984—. Pres. Nat. 19th Amendment Soc., Charles City, 1991-2002, past pres., 2002—; mem. Terace Hill Commn., Des Moines, 1988-94; bd. dirs. Iowa Children and Family Svcs., Des Moines, 1963-68; mem. Iowa. Arts Coun., Des Moines, 1974-78. Named Woman of Yr., local C. of C., 2000. Mem. AAUW, Iowa LWV, PEO. Congregationalist. Avocations: church work, gardening, travel. Home: 1828 Cedar View Dr Charles City IA 50616-9129 Office: McCartney-Huxsol Farms 1000 S Grand Charles City IA 50616-2002

MCCARTNEY, ROBERT CHARLES, retired lawyer; b. Pitts., May 3, 1934; s. Nathaniel Hugh and Esther Mary (Smith) McC.; m. Janet Carolyn Moore, June 16, 1956; children: Ronald K., Sharon S., Carole J. AB, Princeton U., 1956; JD, Harvard U., 1959. Bar: D.C. 1959, Pa. 1960, U.S. Dist. Ct. (we. dist.) Pa. 1960, U.S. Ct. Appeals (3d dist.) 1960, U.S. Supreme Ct. 1966. Assoc. Eckert Seamans Cherin & Mellott, LLC, Pitts., 1959-64, ptnr., 1965-93, mem. exec. com., 1991-93, of counsel, 1993—. Sec., gen. counsel Ryan Homes, Inc., 1969-93; bd. dirs. United Meth. Found. of Western Pa., 1971— v.p., 1981-85, chmn., 1985-86; sec., gen. counsel Rimoldi of Am., Inc., 1989-99. Solicitor North Pitts. Cmty. Devel. Corp., 1968-76, alt. dir., 1968-80; mem. McCandless Twp. Govt. Study Commn., 1973-74; solicitor, asst. sec. McCandless Indsl. Devel. Authority, 1972-98; mem. exec. com. Princeton U. Alumni Coun., 1966-70, 76-85, vice chmn., 1981-83, chmn., 1983-85, co-chair Spl. Com. for 250th Anniversary of Princeton U., 1994-97; nat chmn., class planned giving chair program Princeton U., 2000—; trustee

Otterbein Coll., 1975-83, Pa. S.W. Assn., 1992-96, Pitts. Cultural Trust, 1992-99; chmn. conf.-wide endowment program United Meth. Conf. Western Pa., 1985-87; bd. dirs. Pitts. Civic Light Opera Assn., 1986—, v.p., 1987-92, pres., 1992-99; dir. The Ireland Inst. Pitts., 1991—, vice chmn., 1996—; mem. No. Ireland Partnership, 1991—; bd. dirs. Pitts. Concert Chorale, 1998—, Pitts. Irish and Classical Theater, 1999—. Princeton fellow Harvard U., 1956-59. Mem. Princeton U. Alumni Assn. West Pa. (pres. 1976-78), Duquesne Club, Nassau Club. Republican. Home: 9843 Woodland Rd N Pittsburgh PA 15237-4347 Office: Eckert Seamans Cherin Et Al 600 Grant St Ste 42D Pittsburgh PA 15219-2703

MCCARTNEY, TIMOTHY OSBORNE, finance educator, psychologist; b. Nassau, The Bahamas, Apr. 27, 1933; s. Timothy Osborne and Cora Eliza (Culmer) McCartney; m. Pauline Elizabeth Moysten Silvera, Dec. 16, 1962; children: Lawrence Clive Silvera, Angela Forrest, Lorraine Williams, Sean-(dec.). Bachelors, St. John's U., 1957; PhD, U. Strasbourg, France, 1967; cert. in rational behavior therapy, U. Ky., 1980. Rsch. asst. clin. psychology St. Cloud State Coll., Minn., 1957—58; intern in psychoanalysis U. Strasbourg, 1963—67; clin. asst. to chief psychiat. unit Stephansfeld Hosp., Brumath, France, 1965—67; clin. psychologist Ministry Health, Nassau, 1967—93; prof. Sch. Bus. and Entrepeneurship Nova Southeastern U., Ft. Lauderdale, Fla., 1993—. Lectr. extramural dept. U. West Indies, Jamaica, The Bahamas, 1968—73; adj. prof. St. John's Coll., St. Benedicts, The Bahamas, 1968—90; cons. cmty. mental health U. Miami, 1975—78; specialist, bd. dirs. IPARC, Brazil, 1980—93; cons. Bahamas Psychol. Assn., 1st chmn., 1990. Author: Neurosis in the Sun, 1969, Bahamian Sexuality, 1971; editor: Jour. Bahamas Mental Health Assn., 1969—71. Mem. Bahamas Cath. Sch. Bd., Nassau, 1970—93; mem. Commn. for Prerogative of Mercy Bahamas Govt., 1970—84; mem. nat. task force on AIDS Ministry Health, The Bahamas, 1987—93. Recipient Golden Heart award, Sir Victor Sassoon Heart Found., The Bahamas, 1969, Travel Lectr. award, Republic of China, 1973, award, U.S. State Dept., 1978, Gold Medal of Excellence award, Brazil, 1980, bldg. named in his honor, Ministry Health, The Bahamas, 1999. Fellow: Internat. Inst. Integral Human Scis. Roman Catholic. Avocations: gourmet cooking, wine collecting, music. Home: 476 Lakeview Dr #106 Weston FL 33326 Office: Nova Southeastern U 3100 SW 9th Ave Fort Lauderdale FL 33315 E-mail: mccartne@huizenga.nova.edu.

MCCARTOR, SHEILA SMITH, b. Raymondville, Tex., May 4, 1941; d. M.D. Smith and Mae (Sansom) Jessie; m. Gary Don McCartor, July 20, 1999; m. Ira Yale Levanthal, Aug. 5, 1966; 1 child Adam Yale. BS, N. Tex. State U., 1963, MEd, 1965; postgrad., Nova U., 1972, MIT, 1979. Elem. tchr. Grapevine (Tex.) Pub. Schs., 1963—65; tchr., team leader Lamplighter Sch., Dallas, 1965—. Task force for diversity Lamplighter Sch., 2002, mem. steering com., computer staff, 1979—84, sci. com., 1990—, chair, sci. com., 1993—94; presenter Internat. Conf. Tech. in Edn., U. London, 1994; pub. Internat. Conf. Tech. in Edn., 1993—94; staff Ind. Sch. Assn. of S.W. Beginning Tchr. Inst., 1993—94; presenter Internat. Coop. Learning Conf., Columbus, Ohio, 1996; pub. Dallas Opera Instrl. Series. Staff mem. Episc. Sch. Spirituality, Dallas, 1983, dir., 1989—. Mem.: Women of St. Francis (v.p. Dallas 1983, mem. task force diversity 2002). Office: Lamplighter Sch 11611 Inwood Rd Dallas TX 75229-3098

MCCARTY, DARREN, professional hockey player; b. British Columbia, Canada, Apr. 1, 1972; With Detroit Red Wings, 1993—. Office: Detroit Red Wings Joe Louis Arena 600 Civic Center Detroit MI 48226*

MCCARTY, DORAN CHESTER, religious organization administrator; b. Bolivar, Mo., Feb. 3, 1931; s. Bartie Lee and Donta Marian (Russell) McC.; m. Gloria Jean Laffoon, June 14, 1952; children: Gaye, Risë, Marletta, Leslie. AA, Southwest Bapt. Coll., 1950; AB, William Jewell Coll., 1952; BD, So. Bapt. Theol. Sem, 1956, PhD, 1963. Pastor 1st Bapt. Ch., Switz City, Ind., 1956-62, Pleasant Hill, Mo., 1962-65, Susquehanna Bapt. Ch., Independence, 1965-67; prof. Midwestern Bapt. Theol. Sem., Kansas City, 1967-81, Golden Gate Bapt. Theol. Sem., Mill Valley, Calif., 1981-87; coord. Northeastern Bapt. Sch. Ministry, N.Y.C., 1987-94; exec. dir. Sem. Ext., Nashville, 1988-94; pres. McCarty Svcs., 1994—. Cons. Bapt. Home Mission Bd., 1981—; assoc. dean So. Bapt. Theol. Sem., Louisville, 1989; pres. McCarty Svcs., St. Augustine. Author: Rightly Dividing trhe Word, 1973, Teilhard de Chardin, 1976, The Supervision of Ministry Students, 1978, The Supervision of Mission Personnel, 1983, The Inner Heart of Ministry, 1985, Working With People, 1987, Leading the Small Church, 1991, Supervision: Developing and Directing People on Mission, 1994, Making the Most of Your Time, 1996, Making the Most of Conflict, 1997, Making the Most of Change, 1998, Making the Most if Empowerment, 1999, Making the Most of Coping, 2000, Making the Most of Pastoral Leadership, 2002, Hallowed Be Thy Name, 2002; editor: Key Resources, 5 vols., Broadman Leadership Series, 16 vols., The Practice of Ministry: A Sourcebook, 1995. Recipient Life Service award Southwest Bapt. U., Bolivar, 1973, William Jewell Coll. Achievement citation, 1987. Mem. Assn. for Theol. Field Edn. (chairperson 1979-81), Inst. Theol. Reflection (exec. dir. 1978-86), Fellowship In Service Guidance Dirs. (pres. 1986-87, Lewis Newman award 1988). Home: 116 Del Lago Ln Saint Augustine FL 32080 *As I have experienced life, grace affords priviledge, priviledge calls forth duty, duty depends on transcendence and transcendence provides enrichment.*

MCCARTY, FREDERICK BRIGGS, electrical engineer, consultant; b. Dilley, Tex., Aug. 11, 1926; s. John Frederick Briggs and Olive Ruth (Snell) Briggs McCarty; m. Doris Mary Cox, May 3, 1950 (div. 1970); children: Mark Frederick, David Lambuth, Jackson Clare; m. Nina Lucile Butman, Aug. 17, 1973. BSEE, U. Tex., 1949. Registered profl. engr., Calif. Design engr. GE, Schenectady, N.Y., 1949-51; sr. design engr. Convair, Ft. Worth, 1951-55; sr. engr. Aerojet Gen., Azusa, Calif., 1955-61; sr. engring. specialist Garrett Corp., Torrance, 1961-91; v.p., founder Patio Pacific, Inc., 1973-84; owner, operator Textiger Co., 1980-91; cons., 1991—. Author computer software, Textiger word processor, Tiger Tools, Big Mag and Roundrot generator synthesizers; designer (superconducting acyclic motor for) U.S. Navy and various high speed elec. machines for aerospace and transp. Served with USNR, 1944—46, PTO. Mem.: IEEE (sr.), Eta Kappa Nu, Tau Beta Pi. Democrat. Achievements include patents in field of 15 patents in field. Home and Office: 1366 Stonewood Ct San Pedro CA 90732-1550

MCCARTY, JOHN ALBERT, advertising and marketing educator, consultant; b. Nashville, May 28, 1951; s. Justin Hunter and Emily Lavender (Lacy) McC. BA, Vanderbilt U., 1973; MA, U. Ill., 1979, PhD, 1986; MA, U. Chgo., 1981. Rsch. assoc. Needham Harper Worldwide Advt., Chgo., 1983-85; asst. prof. dept. advt. and bus. adminstrn. U. Ill., Urbana, 1986-93; asst. prof. dept. mktg. Am. U., Washington, 1993—. Vis. lectr. dept. advt. U. Ill., 1985-86. Contbr. chpts. to books: Advances in Non Profit Marketing, 1990, Global and Multi-National Advertising, 1994, Marketing and Consumer Research in the Public Interest, 1996, also articles to profl. jours.; reviewer Jour. of Advt., 1988—. Lt. (j.g.) USN, 1973-76. Mem. Am. Mktg. Assn. (workshop coord. 1987-88), Assn. for Consumer Rsch., Am. Acad. Advt. Office: American Univ Kogod Coll of Business 4400 Massachusetts Ave NW Washington DC 20016-8200

MCCARTY, JOHN EDWARD, medical clinic administrator; b. Cleve., July 16, 1951; s. John Charles and Dorothy McC.; m. Patricia Ann Witten, Aug. 31, 1973; children; Phillip, Kourtney. BA, U. Wis., Green Bay, 1991; M.Physician Asst. Studies, U. Nebr., 2001. Physician asst. Marshfield (Wis.) Clinic, 1974-81, adminstrv. asst. med. edn., 1981-85, asst. dir. med. edn., 1985-2000, adminstrv. dir. med. edn., 2000—. Exec. dir. Accreditation Rev. Commn. Edn. Physician Asst., Marshfield, 1991—. Pres. Marshfield Tiger Booster Club. Fellow Am. Acad. Physician Assts., Wis. Acad. Physician Assts.; mem. Nat. Inst. Farm Safety, Farm Health and Safety Coun. Wis., Boondocks Med. Soc. Avocation: golf. E-mail: mccartyj@mfldclin.edu. Office: Marshfield Clinic 1000 N Oak Ave Marshfield WI 54449

MCCARTY, LEANN CHRISTINE, counselor; b. Toledo, Oct. 11, 1954; d. Leo J. Slater and Joan K. (Allen) Johnson; m. Dennis Daniel McCarty, Apr. 7, 1990. BA in Psychology, U. Mo., St. Louis, 1989; MA in Counseling, Webster U., 1995. Lic. counselor, Nat. Bd. Cert. Counselors. Therapist Comtrea, Inc., Festus, Mo., 1995—. Mem. ACA. Home: 12920 W Watson Rd Saint Louis MO 63127

MCCARTY, MACLYN, medical scientist; b. South Bend, Ind., June 9, 1911; s. Earl Hauser and Hazel Dell (Beagle) McC.; m. Anita Alleyne Davies, June 20, 1934 (div. 1966); children: Maclyn, Richard E., Dale, Colin; m. Marjorie Steiner, Sept. 3, 1966. AB, Stanford U., 1933; MD, Johns Hopkins U., 1937; ScD (hon.), Columbia U., 1976, U. Fla., 1977, Rockefeller U., 1982, Med. Coll. Ohio, 1985, Emory U., 1987, Wittenberg U., 1989; MD (hon.), U. Cologne, Germany, 1988; LHD (hon.), Mount Sinai Sch. of Medicine, 1995; DMS (hon.), Thomas Jefferson U., 1999; ScD (hon.), Harvard U., 2000; LHD (hon.), Johns Hopkins U., 2001. House officer, asst. resident physician Johns Hopkins Hosp., 1937-40; assoc. Rockefeller Inst., 1946-50, prof., 1957-81, v.p., 1965-78, physician in chief to hosp., 1961-74, prof. emeritus, 1981—. Cons. USPHS, NIH. Author: The Transforming Principle: Discovering That Genes are Made of DNA, 1985 Mem. distbn. com. N.Y. Cmty. Trust, 1966-74; chmn. Health Rsch. Coun. City N.Y., 1972-75; Mem. bd. trustees Helen Hay Whitney Found; chmn. bd. dirs. Pub. Health Rsch. Inst. of N.Y., 1985-92. Served with Naval Med. Rsch. Unit, Rockefeller Hosp. USNR, 1942-46. Fellow medicine N.Y. U. Coll. Medicine, 1940-41; NRC fellow med. scis. Rockefeller Inst., 1941-42; Recipient Eli Lilly award in bacteriology and immunology, 1946, 1st Waterford Biomed. Rsch. award, 1977, Wolf Found. prize in medicine, Israel, 1990, Lasker Spl. Pub. Health award, 1994. Mem. Am. Soc. for Clin. Investigation, Am. Assn. Immunologists, Soc. Am. Bacteriologists, Soc. for Exptl. Biology and Medicine (pres. 1973-75), Harvey Soc. (sec. 1947-50, pres. 1971-72), N.Y. Acad. Medicine (Acad. medal 1979, John Stearns award for lifetime achievement in medicine 1993), Assn. Am. Physicians (Kober medal 1989), Nat. Acad. Scis. (Kovalenko medal 1988), Am. Acad. Arts and Scis., N.Y. Heart Assn. (1st v.p. 1967, pres. 1969-71), Am. Philos. Soc. Home: 400 E 56th St New York NY 10022-4147 Office: Rockefeller U 66th St and York Ave New York NY 10021 E-mail: mccartm@rockvax.rockefeller.edu.

MCCARTY, PERRY LEE, civil and environmental engineering educator; b. Grosse Pointe, Mich., Oct. 29, 1931; s. James C. and Alice C. (Marsom) McC.; m. Martha Davis Collins, Sept. 5, 1953; children: Perry Lee, Cara L., Susan A., Kathleen R. BSCE, Wayne State U., 1953; MS in Sanitary Engring., MIT, 1957, ScD, 1959; DEng (hon.), Colo. Sch. Mines, 1992. Field engr. Edwin Orr Co., Dearborn, Mich., 1951-52; engr. Pate & Hirn, Detroit, 1952-53; field engr. Hubbell, Roth & Clark, 1953; instr. civil engring. Wayne State U., 1953-54; field engr. George Jerome & Co., Detroit, 1954; engr. Civil Engrs., Inc., 1956; assoc. Rolf Eliassen Assocs., Winchester, Mass., 1958-61; asst. prof. sanitary engring. MIT, 1958-62; mem. faculty Stanford U., 1962—, prof. civil engring., 1967-75, Silas H. Palmer prof., 1975-99, Silas H. Palmer prof. emeritus, 1999—, chmn. dept. civil engring., 1980-85; dir. Western Region Hazardous Substance Rsch. Ctr., 1989—. Chmn. Gordon Rsch. Conf. Environ. Scis., 1972; vice chmn. environ. studies bd. NRC-NAS, 1976-80, mem. com. on phys. scis., math. and resources, 1985-88, bd. on radioactive waste mgmt., 1989-96, mem. com. geoscis., environment, resources, 1994-97. Co-author: Chemistry for Environmental Engineering, 4th edit., 1994, Environmental Biotechnology Principles and Applications, 2001. Served with AUS, 1954-56. Recipient Tyler Prize for Environ. Achievement, 1992, Clarke Prize Outstanding Achievement Water Sci. and Tech., 1997; NSF faculty fellow, 1968-69. Fellow AAAS, Am. Acad. Microbiology, Am. Acad. Arts and Scis.; mem. ASCE (Walter L. Huber Rsch. prize 1964, Simon W. Freese Environ. Engring. award 1979, James R. Croes medal 1995), NAE, Am. Water Works Assn. (hon. 1981, life 1987, chmn. water quality divsn. 1972-73, trustee rsch. divsn. 1980-85, Best Paper award 1985, A.P. Black Rsch. award 1989), Am. Soc. for Microbiology, Water Environment Fedn. (hon. 1989, Harrison P. Eddy award 1962, 77, Thomas Camp award 1975), Assn. Environ. Engring. Profs. (Disting. Faculty award 1966, Oustanding Publ. award 1985, 88, 98, Founders award 1992), Am. Soc. Engring. Edn.(vice chmn. environ. engring. divsn. 1968-69), Internat. Assn. on Water Quality, Am. Chem. Soc., Sigma Xi, Tau Beta Pi (fellow 1957-58). Home: 823 Sonoma Ter Stanford CA 94305-1024 Office: Stanford U Civil Environ Engring Dept Stanford CA 94305-4020 E-mail: mccarty@ce.stanford.edu.

MCCARTY, RICHARD CHARLES, psychology educator, university dean; b. Portsmouth, Va., July 12, 1947; s. Constantine Ambrose and Helen Marie (Householder) McC.; m. Sheila Adair Miltier, July 12, 1965; children: Christopher Charles, Lorraine Marie, Ryan Lester, Patrick James. BS in Biology, Old Dominion U., 1970, MS in Zoology, 1972; PhD in Pathobiology, Johns Hopkins U., 1976. Rsch. assoc. NIMH, Bethesda, Md., 1976-78; asst. prof. U. Va., Charlottesville, 1978-84, assoc. prof., 1984-88, prof., 1988-2001, chair psychology, 1990-98, chair Coun. of Grad. Depts. Psychology, 1996-97; exec. dir. sci. directorate APA, Washington, 1998-2001; dean arts and sci. Vanderbilt U., Nashville, 2001—. Co-editor: Development of the Hypertensive Phenotype, vol. 19, Handbook of Hypertension, 1999; editor: Am. Psychologist, 2000—01. Lt. comdr. USPHS, 1976-78. Recipient Rsch. Scientist Devel. award NIMH, 1985-90; sr. fellow Nat. Heart Lung Blood Inst., NIH, 1984-85. Fellow AAAS, APA, Soc. Behavioral Medicine, Acad. Behavioral Med. Rsch., Am. Psychol. Soc., Am. Inst. Stress, Coun. for High Blood Pressure Rsch., AHA; mem. Internat. Soc. for Investigation of Stress (exec. bd. 1996-2001). Roman Catholic. Avocations: sports, gardening. Office: Office of the Dean Vanderbilt U Coll Arts and Sci 301 Kirkland Hall Nashville TN 37240

MCCARTY, ROBERT CLARKE, mathematician; b. Mountain View, Calif., Apr. 29, 1922; s. John Emmet and Eldora Lydia (Freeman) McC.; m. Netta Cassen, July 29, 1945 (div. Oct. 1968) 1 child, Stephanie Ann; m. Rita Ransier, July 29, 1969; children: Michael Wayne, Teresa Kay, Kathleen Gail. BA in Math., San Jose Sate U., 1950; MS in Math. and Statistics, U. Wash., 1957; PhD in Math., Pacific Western U., 1990. Staff mathematician Boeing Rsch. Labs., Seattle, 1952-59; rsch. mathematician Stanford Rsch. Inst., Menlo Park, Calif., 1959-70; pres., cons. McCarty and Assocs., Gilroy, 1976—; sr. staff scientist ESL-TRW Corp., Sunnyvale, 1984-87; prin. staff scientist ARGO Systems, 1987-93. Cons. in math., orchard mgmt.; sci. advisor to Congresswoman Zoe Lofgren, sci. com. US Congress, 1994—; rsch. proxy for Prof. A.S. Paulraj, Dept. Elec. Engring., Info. Scis., Stanford U., 1993-95; sr. rsch. mathematician Ares Corp., Arlington, Va., 1994-96. Contbr. articles to profl. jours. Lt. USCGR, 1941—52, ret. lt. USCGR-Ret 3, 1965—. Mem. Sigma Xi. Avocations: HAM radio, rifle and pistol marksmanship, swimming. Home and Office: 9425 Marcella Ave Gilroy CA 95020-9085

MCCARTY, ROGER LELAND, chemical company official; b. Coos Bay, Oreg., Apr. 6, 1953; s. James Cleo and Dorothy Jean (Beach) McC.; m. Marsha Lee Peterson, Dec. 18, 1976; children: Margie, Heather, Aura Lee, Becky, Allison, Katy, Chelsea, Lori. BSChemE, Brigham Young U., 1977; MBA, Keller Grad. Sch. Mgmt., Chgo., 1981. Registered engr.-in-tng., Mich. Missionary LDS Ch., Washington, 1972-74; with mktg. devel. program Dow Chem. Co., Denver, 1977-78, sales rep. organic chems. Chgo., 1978-82, from sr. sales specialist to mgr. product mktg. Houston, 1982-88, mgr. product mktg. Midland, Mich., 1988-89, mgr. bus. rsch. chems. and performance products dept., 1989-92, group mktg. mgr. new ventures, strategy facilitator, 1989-92, sr. econ. planning assoc. value-based mgmt., 1992-95, sr. VBM strategy devel. mgr., 1995-96, bus. devel. mgr. specialty chems. new bus., 1997-99, staffing and devel. dir. new bus. devel., 1999—2001, strategic devel. leader, 2001—. Sales trainer Dow Chem. Co., Houston, 1987-88; presenter in mktg. strategy field. Author: Value Based Strategy Development Guide Book, 1989-94; contbr. articles to profl. jours. Mem. Coos Bay Mayor's Adv. Coun., 1970-71; pres. men's group LDS Ch., Elgin, Ill., 1979-82; mem. stake high coun., Houston, Ill., 1979-82, 89-94, mem. Midland State Presidency, 1995—; explorer leader Boy Scouts Am., Houston, 1985-87; exec. bd. dirs. Lake Huron Area coun. Boy Scouts Am., 1998; mem. Music Soc. Chorale, 1993-96, Camarata Singers, 1995, LDS choir dir., 1992-94; music and computer vol. elem. sch., Midland, 1989-90; parks and recreation commr., Midland, Mich., 1999—. Mem. AIChE (sec.-treas. mktg. divsn. 1989-90, bd. dirs. 1986-89, nat. program dir. 1985-89, mem. nat. program com. 1985-89), Gas Processors Assn. (mem. com. 1987-88). Republican. Avocations: music, drama, sports, dancing, reading. Home: 1200 Wakefield Dr Midland MI 48640-2733 Office: Dow Chem Co Larkin Ctr Midland MI 48674-0001

MCCARTY, SALLY F. educational consultant, entrepreneur; b. San Antonio, June 11, 1948; d. Charles and Edyth McCarty; 1 child, Ryan Shane. BS in Edn., Howard Payne U., 1969. Cert. tchr., Tex. Tchr. San Antonio Ind. Sch. Dist., Birdville Ind. Sch. dist., Haltom City, Tex., N.E. Ind. Sch. Dist., San Antonio, 1969-80; instr. adult edn. Wackenhut Corrections Corp., Kyle, Tex., 1989-91; instr., curriculum developer, field trainer analyst U. Tex., Austin, 1991-94; CEO K-Mc Etc. Ednl. Tng. Corp., 1995—. Curriculum designer. Co-author: The Competitive Edge, 1993; author: Employability Refresher Course, 1997. Vol. Act-Teen. Scholar Howard Payne U., PTA. Mem. NEA (Student Tchr. of Yr.), NAFE, Nat. Assn. Civilian Cons. Corps Alumni, Phi Theta Kappa, Kappa Delta Pi, Alpha Chi, Gamma Beta Phi. Office: 7631 W Highway 290 Apt 114 Austin TX 78736-3602

MCCARTY, THOMAS JOSEPH, publishing company executive; b. Waltham, Mass., June 10, 1938; s. Raymond Anthony and Mary Agatha (Riley) McC; m. Colette Ann Koechley, Aug. 3, 1963; children: Matthew Thomas, Brendan James, Sarah Katherine. BA, Holy Cross Coll., 1960; cert., Harvard U., 1961. Various mgmt. positions Oxford U. Press, N.Y.C., 1960-71, mgr. ops., 1971-79, dir. distbn., 1980-81, v.p. distbn., 1982-84, v.p. distbn. and info. systems, 1985-88, sr. v.p., 1988-90; sr. v.p., gen. mgr. Oxford U. Press, Cary, N.C. ops., 1990-98, spl. cons. to pres., 1998-2000. Chmn., bd. advs. Carolina Pub. Inst. U. N.C., Chapel Hill, 1995-98. Trustee N.C. Symphony Found., v.p., 1998—; mem. adv. bd. Sch. Info. and L.S., U. N.C., Chapel Hill; mem. City of Cary Unified Devel. Ordinance Adv. Commn., 1999—; mem. bd. advisors Open Mind Publ. Group, 2000; mem. N.C. Mus. Art; bd. dirs. Shakti for Children Found., 1994—98, English Speaking Union of Research Triangle, pres., 1998—2002. Mem.: Exec. Svc. Corps., Fine Arts League Cary, Am. Mgmt. Assn., Svc. Corps Ret. Execs., Am. Assn. Pubs., U. N.C. Faculty Club (Chapel Hill), Carolina Club, McGregor Downs Country Club (Cary). E-mail: tjm2@mindspring.com.

MCCARTY, VIDA FINCH, small business owner; b. Atlantic City, Feb. 27, 1945; d. Walter G. and Mary Adele (Roberts) m. Thomas B. McCarty Esq., June 26, 1970. AA, Catonsville Community Coll., Balt., 1965; BS, U. Md., 1968. Exec. trainee Hutzlers, Balt., 1968-69, asst. buyer, 1969-70; employment counselor Guilford Persolnal, 1970-72; interior designer Hochschilds, 1972-75; office mgr., bookkeeper McCarty & McCarty Law Firm, Catonsville, 1976-2000; owner Vida's Vintage Valuables, 1993—. Program, hospitality, involvement in action com. Catonsville Presbyn. Ch., 1990—, deacon, sec., bd. good samaritan, Sunday sch. tchr. Recipient Tri-Color award Landscape Design Critic Sch., 1999-2001. Mem. Parliamentary Edn. Assn., Catonsville C.C. Alumni Assn. (bd. dirs., pres. 1975-76), Bent Twig Federated Garden Club (pres. 1989-91, 98-99, gardening cons. 1995), Federated Women's Club Catonsville (1st v.p., 2d v.p., contbn. chmn., chmn. fine arts, forward plan chmn., yearly rental chmn.), Camellia Soc. (corr. sec. 1998-99, sec. 1999-2000). Avocations: painting, gardening, antique jewelry and collectibles, travel, raising schnauzers. Office: McCarty & McCarty 401 Frederick Rd Baltimore MD 21228-4622

MCCARTY, V.K. publisher, chaplain, librarian; b. Boston, June 26, 1948; d. Charles Osner and Dorothy June (McAlister) Long. BM, Mich. State U., 1969; MM, U. Louisville, 1972; cert. in theatre arts, U. London, 1972; clin. pastoral edn., St. Luke's Roosevelt Hosp., N.Y.C., 1988, 95. Advt. asst. Lansing (Mich.) State Jour., 1968-69; market rsch. cons. Sta. WKLO, Louisville, 1969-70; libr. Louisville Free Pub. Libr., 1970-72; v.p. assoc. pub. Gen. Media Inc., N.Y.C., 1979-2000; acquisitions libr. Gen. Theol. Sem. St. Mark's Libr., 2000—. Bd. dirs. B.F.T., Inc., N.Y.C. Dance editor Saturday Review Mag. Online, 1993-95. Master of ceremonies St. Ignatius, N.Y.C., 1984-98; chaplaincy coord. St. Luke's Roosevelt Hosp., N.Y.C. Mem. N.Y. Liturgical Music Found. (steering com. 1982-84), N.Y. Ch. Club. Avocations: riding, ballet, preservaton of Benedictine monasticism. Office: Gen Theol Sem St Mark's Libr 175 9th Ave New York NY 10011-4977

MCCARTY, WILLIAM MICHAEL, JR. lawyer; b. Trenton, N.J., 1938; AB, Am. U., Dickinson Coll., 1964; JD, Dickinson Sch. Law, 1967. Bar: Vt. 1967, U.S. Dist. Ct. Vt. 1967, U.S. Ct. Appeals (2d cir.) 1973, U.S. Supreme Ct. 1978. Assoc. Fitts & Olson, Brattleboro, Vt., 1967-71; sole practice, 1971-76; ptnr. McCarty & Rifkin, Brattleboro, Wilmington, Vt., 1976-80; sr. ptnr., pres. McCarty Law Offices, P.C., 1980—. Presenter in various fields; dir. various corps. Mem. Brattleboro Zoning Bd. Adjustment, 1968-75; trustee Vt. Legal Aid, 1970-82, pres., 1979-80; pres. Brattleboro Winter Carnival, 1971-72; rep. Windham Regional Planning & Devel. Com., 1968-70, chmn. ch. coun., bench bar com., 1992-97, moderator Congl. Ch., 1990-94. With USMC, 1956-60. Mem. ABA, ATLA, Am. Bd. Trial Advocates, Vt. Bar Assn., Windham County Bar Assn. (pres. 1991-93, chair bench bar com. 1989-97), Am. Jud. Soc., Am. Law Student Assn. (nat. v.p., bd. govs. 1966-67), Nat. Coun. Sch. Attys., Vt. Trial Laywers Assn. (outstanding litigation achievement award 1994), Am. Bd. Trial Advocates (advocate, Vt.), Inns of Ct., Vt. Criminal Def. Attys. Assn., Brattleboro C. of C. (bd. mgrs. 1971-72), U.S. Supreme Ct. Hist. Soc. (Vt. state chair 1999-). Republican. Office: 76 High St Brattleboro VT 05301-6074

MCCASKEY, MICHAEL B. professional football team executive; b. Lancaster, Pa., Dec. 11, 1943; s. Edward B. and Virginia (Halas) McCaskey; m. Nancy McCaskey; children: John, Kathryn. Grad., Yale U., 1965; PhD, Case Western Res. U. Tchr. UCLA, 1972-75, Harvard U. Sch. Bus., Cambridge, Mass., 1975-82; pres., chief exec. officer Chgo. Bears (NFL), 1983-99, chmn. bd., 1999—. Author: The Executive Challenge: Managing Change and Ambiguity. Named Exec. of Yr. Sporting News, 1985. Office: Chgo Bears Halas Hall 250 Washington Rd Lake Forest IL 60045-2459 also: 1000 Football Dr Lake Forest IL 60045-4829*

MC CASKEY, RAYMOND F. insurance company executive; b. 1942; With Continental Assurance Co., Chgo., 1963-73, Health Care Svc. Corp., Chgo., 1976—, now pres., CEO. Office: Health Care Service Corp 300 E Randolph St Chicago IL 60601-5014*

MCCASKILL, RODERICK BURNS, engineer; b. Boston, May 31, 1933; s. Daniel and Margaret H. (Burns) M.; m. Margaret Elizabeth Tait; children: Susan, Malcolm. BS in Engring., Letourneau Coll., 1960. Registered profl. engr., Calif. Engr. Stanley Aviation Corp., Denver, 1960-62, Emerson Elect. Co., Colorado Springs, Colo., 1962-66, Coors Porcelain Co., Golden, 1966-71, Storage Technology Corp, Louisville, 1971-84, McData Corp., Broomfield, 1985—. Cpl. U.S. Army, 1953-55, Germany. Mem. Internat. Facilities Mgmt. Assn., Toastmasters, Denver (area gov. 1982-84). Avocations: beekeeper, bicycling.

MCCASLIN, F. CATHERINE, consulting sociologist; b. Chattanooga, Feb. 21, 1947; d. John Jacob and Elizabeth Dorothy (Johnson) McC. AB, Hollins Coll., Roanoke, Va., 1969; MA, Ga. State U., 1972; PhD, UCLA, 1979. Assoc. dir. Ga. Narcotics Treatment Program, Atlanta, 1972-73; research assoc., dir. research Health Care Delivery Services, Inc., Los Angeles, 1974-76; sr. survey analyst Kaiser Found. Health Plan, 1978-80; program officer The Robert Wood Johnson Found., Princeton, 1980-84; faculty U. Pa. Sch. Medicine, Phila., 1984-86; ptnr. Schuhmacher & McCaslin Assocs., 1986—; exec. dir. The H.F. Lenfest Found., Pottstown, Pa., 1988-89; dir. rsch. Beaufort (S.C.) County Sch. Dist., 1992—. Adj. faculty sociology U. S.C., Beaufort, 1992—; mem. adv. bd. Nat. Childhood Asthma Project, NHBLI, Washington, 1982-84; adv. com. mem. Statewide Adolescent Pregnancy, New Brunswick, 1981-84; trainee NIH, 1973-79; cons. in field. Mem. editorial bd. Jour. Health & Social Behavior, 1988—; editor Med. Sociology newsletter, 1984—; contbr. articles to profl. jours. Fellow NIMH, 1975; grantee Spl. Action Office for Drug Abuse Prevention, 1972, Robert Wood Johnson Found., 1984. Mem. Am. Sociol. Assn. (nat. coun. med. sociology sect. 1984—), Am. Assn. Sch. Adminstrs., Am. Pub. Health Assn., Sociologists for Women in Soc. Democrat. Episcopalian. Avocations: skiing, swimming, classic car restoration. Home: 802 London Ave Port Royal SC 29935-2408 Office: Beaufort County Sch Dist PO Box 309 Beaufort SC 29901-0309 E-mail: mccaslin@islc.net.

MCCASLIN, JOHN LARSON, political columnist; b. Alexandria, Va., Oct. 31, 1957; s. Robert William and Wanda (Larson) McC.; m. Catharine Gohn, June 15, 1985 (div. Apr. 1992); 1 child, Kerry Elizabeth. BA in Speech Comm., Old Dominion U., Norfolk, Va., 1980. News dir. KOFI Radio, Kalispell, Mont., 1980-82, KJJR-KBBZ FM, Whitefish, 1982-84; corr. UPI, Helena, 1980-84; White House corr. The Washington Times, 1984-85, met. editor, 1989-91, polit. columnist Inside the Beltway, 1992—; column syndicated by L.A. Times, 2000—. Columnist Chgo. Tribune Media Svc., 2001. Bd. dirs. Stop Child Abuse Now, Alexandria, 1996-99. Recipient column writing awards Nat. Soc. Newspaper Columnists, 1999, Blinded Am. Vets., Washington, 1999. Mem. Nat. Soc. Newspaper Columnists (chmn. 2000 conf.), Old

Dominion U. Alumni Assn. (bd. dirs. 1997—). Roman Catholic. Avocations: travel, photography, raising my daughter. Office: Washington Times 3600 New York Ave NE Washington DC 20002-1996 E-mail: jmccaslin@washingtontimes.com.

MCCASLIN, KATHLEEN DENISE, child abuse educator; b. Poughkeepsie, N.Y., Aug. 4, 1962; d. Nancy Ann Gosselin; m. David Wayne McCaslin, Sept. 27, 1986 (dec. Oct. 1990); 1 child LeAnn ; m. Larry Thomas Ward, July 14, 1998. BA, Adelphi Coll., 1984. Pub. speaker Impact Seminars, Littlestown, Pa., 1987-96; exec. dir. McCaslin Internat., Guffey, Colo., 1994—; pub. speaker The Family Advocate, 1997—. Founder We the People, Colorado Springs, Colo., 1982; vol. counselor/facilitator Beginning Experience, Harrisburg, Pa., 1991-94. Author: (books) Trusting in God, 1993, Respecting Yourself, 1993, Loss and Recovery, 1992, (cd audio) One Child's Journey to Freedom, 1998. Troop leader Girl Scouts U.S., Guffey, Colo., 1998-2000. Recipient Outstanding Grad. award Adelphi Coll., Colorado Springs, 1984. Mem. ASCPA, World Wildlife Fedn., Arbor Day Found., S.W. Indian Found. Avocations: reading, hiking, needlework, gourmet cooking, gardening. Office: McCaslin Internat PO Box 100 Guffey CO 80820

MCCASLIN, RICHARD BRYAN, history educator; b. Atlanta, Feb. 21, 1961; s. Jerry L. and Ann Elizabeth (Sharman) McC.; m. Jana Dawn Maryovich, Apr. 5, 1979; 1 child, Christina Michele. BA, Delta State U., 1982; MA, La. State U., 1983; PhD, U. Tex., 1988. Tchg. asst. La. State U., 1982-83, grad. asst. La. Bus. Rev., 1983; tchg. asst. U. Tex., Austin, 1983-87, rsch. assoc., 1984-87; rsch. asst. prof. U. Tenn., Knoxville, 1988-90; asst. prof. history High Point (N.C.) U., 1990-94, assoc. prof., 1994-2000, prof., 2000—. Instr. Pellissippi State C.C., 1988-89, Roane State C.C., 1989; adj. prof. Corpus Christi (Tex.) State U., 1989; lectr. East Tenn. Hist. Soc., 1990; rsch. cons. Tex. Senate, 1986-89, Nat. Pk. Svc., 1989-90, Tex. State Historical Assn., 2000—; assoc. historian Futurepast: History Co., Spokane, Wash., 1987-89; presenter Southwestern Social Sci. Assn., AAAS, Soc. for Mil. History. Author: (with Earnest F. Gloyna) Commitment to Excellence: One Hundred Years of Engineering Education at The University of Texas at Austin, 1986, Andrew Johnson: A Bibliography, 1992, Portraits of Conflict: A Photographic History of South Carolina in the Civil War, 1994, Tainted Breeze: The Great Hanging at Gainesville, Texas, October 1862, 1994 (Tullis prize Tex. State Hist. Assn., commendation Am. Assn. for State and Local History), Remembered Be Thy Blessings: High Point University—The College Years, 1924-1991, 1995, Portraits of Conflict: A Photographic History of North Carolina in the Civil War, 1997, Lee in the Shadow of Washington, 2001, The Last Stronghold: The Fort Fisher Campaign, 2002; contbr. chpt. to: 100 Years of Science and Technology in Texas: A Sigma Xi Centennial Volume, 1986; columnist Greensboro News and Record, 1993-94; referee Southwestern Hist. Quar., La. State U. Press, U. Nebr. Press, U.S.C. Press, Tex. A&M U. Press; asst. editor, then assoc. editor Papers of Andrew Johnson, U. Tenn., 1988-90; contbr. articles and book revs. to various profl. publs. U. Tex. dissertation fellow, 1987-88, Clara H. Driscoll fellow in Tex. history Daus. of Republic of Tex., 1985-87; James H. and Minnie M. Edmonds Ednl. Found. scholar, 1983-85, Colonial Dames Am. grad. scholar, 1987; Slatten award Va. Hist. Soc., Laney prize Austin Civil War Roundtable. Mem. So. Hist. Assn. (presenter), Soc. Civil War Historians (presenter), Tex. State Hist. Assn. (presenter), Hist. Soc. N.C. (treas. 2000). Episcopalian. Home: 221 Pine Ridge Dr High Point NC 27262-8204 Office: High Point Univ Dept History and Polit Sci High Point NC 27260 E-mail: rmccas@acme.highpoint.edu.

MCCASLIN, TERESA EVE, human resources executive; b. Jersey City, Nov. 22, 1949; d. Felix F. and Ann E. (Golaszewski) Hrynkiewicz; m. Gary A. McCue. BA, Marymount Coll., 1971; MBA, L.I. U., 1981. Adminstrv. officer Civil Service Commn., Fed. Republic Germany, 1972-76; personnel dir. Oceanroutes, Inc., Palo Alto, Calif., 1976-78; mgr., coll. relations Continental Grain Co., N.Y.C., 1978-79, corp. personnel mgr., 1979-81, dir. bus. redesign, internal cons., 1981-84; dir., human resources Grow Group, Inc., 1984-85, v.p. human resources, 1985-86, v.p. adminstrn., 1986-89; corp. v.p. human resources Avery Dennison Corp., Pasadena, Calif., 1989-94; v.p. human resources Monsanto Co., St. Louis, 1994-97; sr. v.p. human resources and pub. rels. Conti Group Cos. (formerly Continental Grain Co.), N.Y.C., 1997—, exec. v.p. human resources & info. systems, 1999—. Mem. Am. Mgmt. Assn. (fin. and exec. com., chair compensation com.), Human Resources Coun. Roman Catholic. Avocations: skiing, tennis, traveling, golf. Office: Conti Group Cos 277 Park Ave New York NY 10172-0003

MCCAUGHAN, DELLA MARIE, retired science educator; b. Pass Christian, Miss., Apr. 10, 1928; d. John Jeff and Nora Bell (Tullos) Sims; m. Finley Brandt McCaughan, Aug. 2, 1952; children: Leona Grace McCaughan Clawson, Diana Kay McCaughan Rodwig. Assocs. Degree, Miss. Gulf Coast C.C., Perkinston, Miss., 1949; BS, U. So. Miss., 1951, MS, 1959, specialist degree in sci. edn., 1979. Cert. elem. and secondary edn. in sci. Miss. Sci. educator Biloxi (Miss.) Pub. Schs., 1951—58, chairperson dept. sci., educator, 1959—95; ret., 1995. Adj. instr. biology for gifted secondary students Johns Hopkins U., Balt., 1988—91; ind. contractor Miss.-Ala. Sea Grant Consortium, Biloxi, 1980—84; edn. advisor U.S. Senate (Office Senator Thad Cochran), Washington, 1991—92; ind. contractor, author Miss. Dept. Marine Resources, Biloxi, 1996—99. Author: Guide to Federal Programs for Mississippi Educators, 1992; editor: Marine Resources and History of the Mississippi Gulf Coast (vols. 1-4), 1998. Finalist Nat. Tchrs. Hall of Fame, 2002; named Congl. Einstein fellow, U.S. Senate, Washington, 1991—92; named to Miss. Hall of Master Tchrs., 1991; recipient Presdl. award for excellence in sci. and math. tchg., Washington, 1984, Tandy Tech. Scholars award, Tandy Corp., L.A., 1991. Mem.: Nat. Sci. Tchrs. Assn. (Nat. Disting. Svc. citation 1976), Assn. Presdl. Awardees in Sci. Tchg., Benevolent Protective Order of Elks. Avocations: reading, traveling. Home: 134 St Jude St Biloxi MS 39530

MCCAUL, JOSEPH PATRICK, chemical engineer; b. N.Y.C., May 11, 1952; s. Joseph and Marion (Sheehan) McC.; Kathleen Anne Crowley, Aug. 3, 1974 (div.); children: Kenneth, Christine; m. Nancy Marie Powell, May 28, 2000. BSChemE, Poly. Inst. Bklyn., 1973, M in Polymer Sci. and Engring., 1977; MBA, Case Western Res. U., 1987. Registered ofcl. baseball umpire Ill. H.S. Assn. Prodn. supr. Mobay Chem. Corp., Bayonne, NJ, 1973—77; process engr. Borg Warner Chems., Parkersburg, W.Va., 1977—78, process control engr. Ottawa, Ill., 1978—79, process control mgr. Linmar plant, 1979—82; mgr. tech. svc. Standard Oil Co., Cleve., 1982—87; mgr. internat. sales and tech. svc. Barex Group BP Chems., 1987—96, dir. sales and licensing, 1996—98; group v.p. sales and mktg. EVAL Co. Am., Lisle, Ill., 1988—2001, v.p. rsch. and bus. devel., 2001; founder, pres. Joseph Assoc. Internat., Inc., Naperville, 2002—. Bd. dirs. EVAL Co. Am. Contbr. articles to profl. jours., mags., ency.; patentee in field. Exec. bd. dirs. Mentor Lake Area Baseball, Mentor on the Lake, Ohio, 1988-89, pres. Mentor McMinn Area Baseball League, 1989-91; trustee Pinegate Homeowners Assn., Mentor, Ohio, 1988-89. Mem. Soc. Plastics Engrs. (award 1987), Pinegate Homeowners Assn. (past trustee), Am. Mensa, Naperville C. of C., Bus. Brokers Network. Republican. Roman Catholic. Avocations: fishing, boating, fitness, baseball, travel. Home: 1612 Pennsylvania Ct Naperville IL 60563-2600 Office: Joseph Assoc Internat. Inc PO Box 72 Naperville IL 60566-0072

MCCAULEY, BARBARA LYNNE, language educator; b. Kansas City, Mo., Mar. 2, 1951; d. J. C. and Rebecca Ernestine (Alley) McCauley. BSE, Ctrl. Mo. State U., 1973, MA, 1976; PhD, Fla. State U., 1993. Instr. Macon (Ga.) Coll., 1979-83; asst. prof. Gainesville (Ga.) CC, 1987-88; English instr. North Fla. CC, Madison, 1993—, divsn. chmn. humanities divsn., 2001—. Adj. prof. Fla. State U., Tallahassee, 1983—86, Tallahassee, 1989—93, vis. prof., 1988—89; adj. prof. Tallahassee CC, 1989—93. Contbr. articles to profl. jours. Bd. dirs. Northland Symphony, Kansas City, 1978—79, Macon Balllet, 1980—83. Mem.: Medival Soc. Am., Fla. Coll. English Assn., Internat. Assn. Found. Arts, Mythopoeic Soc., Internat. Arthurian Soc., Internat. Assn. Fantastic Arts, Alpha Pi Omega, Kappa Delta Pi, Sigma Tau Delta, Phi Kappa Phi. Avocation: art. Office: North Fla CC 1000 Turner Davis Dr Madison FL 32340 E-mail: mccauleyb@nfcc.edu.

MCCAULEY, BRUCE GORDON, financial consultant; b. St. Louis; s. William Maurice and Evylin Adele (Halbert) McC.; m. Barbara Allen Stevens, Mar. 16, 1945 (dec.); children: David S., Sharon; m. Gwen Crumpton Cummings, Nov. 25, 1967. Student, U. Mo., 1939-41, Yale U., 1944; BS in Engring., U. Calif., Berkeley, 1948, MBA, 1949, MS in Indsl. Engring., 1952. Registered profl. engr., N.Y., Calif., Hawaii. Asst. purchasing agt. Curtis Mfg. Co., St. Louis, 1941—43; teaching asst. U. Calif., Berkeley, 1948—49, asst. prof. mech. engring., 1950—56, chmn. indsl. engring. inst., 1954—55; design engr. Standard Oil Co. of Calif., 1949—50; sr. ptnr. McCauley & Dunmire, San Francisco, 1952—56; v.p. Shand & Jurs Co., Berkeley, 1956—58, exec. v.p., 1958—60; asst. to pres. Honolulu Star-Bulletin, 1960—62; gen. mgr. Christian Sci. Pub. Soc., Boston, 1962—69; gen. mgr., sec. N.Y. Daily News Inc., N.Y.C., 1969—74, v.p., 1971—76, sr. v.p., 1973—75, asst. to pres., 1974—75, dir., 1971—75; v.p. Daseke & Co. Inc., Westport, Conn., 1975—77, sr. v.p., 1977—86, mgr. West Coast office, 1978—86; vis. scholar Principia Coll., Elsah, Ill., 1988—91; pres. Rossmoor Mut. 48 Corp., Walnut Creek, 1994—97. Bd. dirs. Better Bus. Bur., N.Y.C., 1973-77, N.Y.C. Conv. and Visitors Bur., 1974-77, Albert Baker Found., 1979-90, Asher Found., 1983-93, Sopac Energy Corp., 1986-92. Capt. USAAF, 1943-46, PTO. Mem. ASME (life), NSPE (life), Am. Inst. Indsl. Engrs. (life), Nat. Assn. Accts. (life), U. Calif. Alumni Assn., Principia Alumni Assn., Rossmoor Golf Club, Masons (32 degree), Kiwanis, Sigma Xi, Tau Beta Pi, Beta Gamma Sigma, Pi Mu Epsilon. 16536519n Scientist. $D Christian Scientist. Home: 3266 Ptarmigan Dr Apt 3B Walnut Creek CA 94595-3149 E-mail: bgmccauley@attbi.com.

MCCAULEY, CLEYBURN LYCURGUS, lawyer; b. Houston, Feb. 8, 1929; s. Reese Stephens and Elizabeth Ann (Burleson) McC.; m. Elizabeth Kelton McKoy, June 7, 1950; children: Stephens Francis, Lillian Elizabeth, Cleyburn, Lucy Annette. BS, U.S. Mil. Acad., 1950; MS in Engring. Econ., Statistical Quality Control and Indsl. Engring., Stanford U., 1959; JD, Coll. William and Mary, 1970. Bar: D.C. 1971, Va. 1970, Tex. 1970, U.S. Ct. Claims 1971, U.S. Tax Ct. 1971, U.S. Supreme Ct. 1973. Commd. 2d lt. U.S. Air Force, 1950, advanced through grades to lt. col., 1971, ret., 1971; pvt. practice law, Washington, 1975—. Mem. Fed. Bar Assn., Va. Bar Assn., Tex. Bar Assn., D.C. Bar Assn., IEEE, AIAA, Am. Soc. Quality Control, Phi Alpha Delta. Home: 402 S 3rd St Wilmington NC 28401-5102

MCCAULEY, DAN PAUL, dentist; b. Pittsburg, Tex., Nov. 13, 1949; s. Loyd Cecil McCauley and Claudia Aletha Moore; m. Sandra Scott Kraemer, Sept. 14, 1974; children: Jennifer, Rebecca, Crissy. BA in Psychology, So. Meth. U., 1974; DDS, U. Tex., 1977. Pvt. practice, Mt. Pleasant, Tex., 1977—. Sec. N.E. Tex. C.C., 1994-2001. Trustee N.E. Tex. C.C., Mt. Pleasant, 1989—; deacon First Bapt. Ch., Mt. Plesant, 1977—; chmn. Titus County Rep. Party, Mt. Pleasant, 1980; bd. dirs. Red River Girl Scouts, 1986-89; active Boy Scouts Am., 1977—. Recipient Optimist Lifetime Achievement North Tex. Dist. Optimist Internat., 1995, Fraternal Achievement award Psi Omega Dental Fraternity, 1976. Mem. ADA, Tex. Dental Assn. (del. 1995—), 1st Dist. Dental Soc. (pres. 1986-87, v.p., pres. 2002), North Tex. Optimists (gov. 1985-86, Lifetime Achievement 1999), N.E. Tex. C.C. Found. (pres. 1989-2001), Acad. Gen. Dentistry; fellow Pierre Fauchard Soc. Republican. Baptist. Avocations: tennis, travel, skiing. Home: 1403 S Florey Ave Mount Pleasant TX 75455-5813 Office: 1603 N Jefferson Ave Mount Pleasant TX 75455-2366 E-mail: drdansmu@hotmail.com.

MCCAULEY, FLOYCE REID, psychiatrist; b. Braddock, Pa., Dec. 30, 1933; d. John Mitchel and Irene (Garner) Reid; m. James Calvin McCauley, July 15, 1955; children: James Stanley, Lori Ellen. BS in Nursing, U. Pitts., 1956; D.O., Coll. Osteopathic Medicine, Phila., 1972. Diplomate Am. Bd. Forensic Medicine, Am. Bd. Forensic Examiners; bd. eligible in child and adult psychiatry. Intern Suburban Gen. Hosp., Norristown, Pa., 1972-73; resident in adult psychiatry Phila. State Hosp. and Phila. Mental Health Clinic, 1973-75; fellow Med. Coll. of Pa. and Ea. Pa. Psychiat. Inst., Phila., 1975-78; Chief child psychiatry inpatient unit Med. Coll. Pa., 1978-80; med. dir. Carson ValleySch., Flourtown, 1980-82; dir. outpatient psychiat. clinic Osteopathic Med. Ctr. Phila., 1980-86; staff psychiatrist Kent Gen. Hosp., Dover, Del., 1986-89; psychiat. cons. Del. Guidance Svcs. for Children, 1986-91; clin. dir. children's unit HCA Rockford Ctr., Newark, 1991-93; with Kid's Peace Nat. Hosp. for Kids in Crisis, 1993-95; staff psychiatrist St. Lukes Quakertown Hosp., 1996-98; cons. Interact Phila., 1996-98; staff psychiatrist Del. Guidance Svcs. for Children and Youth, Dover, 1998—2001. Mem. Mental Health Code Rev. Com. for Del., 1991; inducted into the Chapel of Four Chaplains, Phila., 1983; psychiat. cons. Seaford (Del.) Br. of New Eng. Fellowship for Rehab., 1991-93, Cath. Charities Day Treatment Program for 3-6 Yr. Olds, Dover, Del., 1990—; cons. Del. Guidance Day Treatment Program, 1990-2002; staff psychiatrist Kids Peace Nat. Hosp. for Kids in Crisis, 1993-95, Penn Found., 1995-98; cons. psychiatrist Valley Day Sch., 2000—, Children's Svcs., Inc., 2002—. Mem. Mayor's Com. for Mental Health, Phila., 1983. Mem. Am. Osteopathic Assn. Democrat. Methodist. Avocations: sewing, decorating, playing classical guitar, drawing, singing with Copper Penny Players.

MCCAULEY, HELEN NORA, civic worker; b. Modesto, Ill., Mar. 4, 1913; d. Raymond R. and Dena (Dohrs) Hills; m. Joseph James Nora, June 28, 1940 (dec. 1968); children: James J., Lonnie L., Ruth Nora Rader, Louise; m. Dannis H. McCauley, Apr. 19, 1980 (dec. 1991). BA with honors, Ill. Coll., Jacksonville, 1934. Cert. elem. and secondary tchr., Ill. Tchr. elem. sch., Franklin, Ill., 1934-36, high sch., Tiskilwa, 1936-40; receptionist, bookkeeper med. office, 1956-68. Mem. Bureau County (Ill.) Med. Aux., 1940-90; past pres. Woman's Club, Tiskilwa, numerous times; past treas. Altar and Rosary Soc., St. Mary's Cath. Ch.; bd. dirs. Perry Meml. Hosp., Aux., Princeton, Ill., 1970-76; charter mem. bd. dirs. Children's Home Aux., Princeton, 1972-80, Bureau County In-Home Care, 1977-83; bd. dirs. Twp. Libr., Tiskilwa, 1975—, treas., 1975-88; chmn. Tiskilwa Student Loan Assn., 1960—. Mem. Investment Club (past treas. Tiskilwa and Buda, Ill.). Home: 400 W Main St Tiskilwa IL 61368-9419

MCCAULEY, H(ENRY) BERTON, retired public health dentist; b. Duluth, Minn., Dec. 20, 1913; s. Henry Berton and Flora Agnes (Bourassa) McC.; m. Claire Ann Wolff, Dec. 20, 1937. DDS, U. Md., 1936. Lic. dentist, Md. Instr. oral roentgenology U. Md., Balt., 1936-40; Carnegie fellow in dentistry U. Rochester, N.Y., 1940-43, asst. prof. dentistry, cons. Manhattan Project, 1943-45; dir. dental care Balt. City Health Dept., 1949-75; health advisor Office of Mayor, Balt., 1975-77, gen. health adminstr., 1977-80; pres. North Balt. (Mental Health) Ctr., 1980. Bd. visitors Balt. Coll. Dental Surgery, U. Md., 1997-2002. Contbr. more than 50 articles to profl. jours. Dir. Cooley's Anemia Found. Md., 1977-93. With USPHS, Nat. Inst. Dental Rsch., 1945-49. Fellow APHA, AAAS, Am. Coll. Dentists (J. Ben. Robinson award 1991), Internat. Coll. Dentists, Pierre Fauchard Acad.; mem. ADA (life, coun. on dental therapeutics 1943-48, chmn. sect. on pub. health 1968), Internat. and Am. Assn. Dental Rsch., Am. Acad. Pediat. Dentistry for Children (Disting. Svc. award 1978), Am. Assn. Pub. Health Dentistry, Am. Acad. History of Dentistry (Hayden-Harris award 1988, pres. 1990-91), Md. Soc. Dentistry for Children (pres. 1954-55), Md. State Dental Assn. (historian 1959-87, Disting. Svc. award 1986), Md. Pub. health Assn. (pres. 1967-68), Balt. City Dental Soc. (pres. 1973), Nat. Mus. Dentistry (bd. visitors 1997—), Md. Hist. Soc., Walters Art Mus., Balt. Mus. Art, Mil. Order World Wars (comdr. chpt. 1986-87, dept. 1994-95), Sigma Xi, Omicron Kappa Upsilon, Psi Omega. Roman Catholic. Avocations: history, travel, photography, gardening. Home and Office: 3804 Hadley Sq E Baltimore MD 21218-1807 E-mail: wilmabert@mailbug.com.

MCCAULEY, JAMES WEYMANN, ceramics engineer, educator; b. Phila., Mar. 21, 1940; s. Edward Joseph and Emily Marie (Weymann) McC.; m. Mary Ann Malone, June 6, 1964; children: Patrick, Kathleen, Daniel. BS, St. Joseph's Coll., 1961; MS, Pa. State U., 1965, PhD, 1968. Rsch. asst. solid state sci. Pa. State U., University Park, 1966-68; rsch. scientist MATS Tech. Lab. U.S. Army, Watertown, Mass., 1968-74; group leader MATS Tech. Lab. U.S. Army, 1974-81; div. chief Tech. Lab. U.S. Army, 1981-90; liaison scientist Far East Rsch. Office U. S. Army, Tokyo, 1988; dean N.Y. State (SUNY) Coll. Ceramics Alfred (N.Y.) U., 1990-95; prof. ceramic engring. Alfred U., 1995—. Adj. prof. Boston U., 1984-86; bd. dirs. Alfred Tech. Resources Inc.; mem. Army Sci. Bd.; mem. Los Alamos Nat. Lab. Ext. rev. com. Editor books; contbr. articles to sci. and profl. jours.; patentee in field. Vice chmn. Wakefield Cable TV Com., Mass., 1970-80; chmn. Wakefield Conservatin Com., 1980-90. Emeritus fellow Army Rsch. Lab. Fellow Am. Ceramic Soc. (trustee 1988-91, 92-95, treas. 1995-96, v.p. 1987-91, F. H. Norton award 1987, J. Mueller award 1988). Home: HC 64 Box 64L Hillcrest Ext Wellsville NY 14895 Office: Alfred U Coll of Ceramics Alfred NY 14802

MCCAULEY, JANE REYNOLDS, journalist; b. Wilmington, Del., Oct. 22, 1947; d. John Thomas and Helen (Campbell) McC. BA, Guilford Coll., 1969. Editor, sr. writer Nat. Geographic Soc., Washington, 1970-90; freelance writer, editor, artist, 1990-96; exec. editor AM Quilter's Soc., 1996-97; freelance editor, writer, cons., profl. quilt restorer, 1997—. Former owner Unique Native Crafts. Author of 15 children's books; co-author award-winning travel books. Mem.: Children's Book Soc. Am. E-mail: ritstuff4u@aol.com.

MCCAULEY, NORMA ELIZABETH, volunteer, advocate; b. Mpls., June 20, 1905; d. George Arthur Hunt and Mollie Elizabeth Eide; m. Earl Dale McCauley, Nov. 30, 1930; children: Hunt, Mollie. BA, U. Minn., 1923. Pres. YWCA, Sioux City, Iowa; founder Sioux City Planned Parenthood. Recipient 1st Margaret Sanger award in Iowa. Mem. AAUW. Democrat. Congregationalist. Avocations: music, gardening, singing. Home: 4101 Glenrose St Kensington MD 20895

MC CAULEY, R. PAUL, criminologist, educator; b. Highspire, Pa., Jan. 13, 1943; s. Paul Herbert and Frances Vaden (Harper) McC.; m. Gail Lee Gummo, Jan. 30, 1965; 1 child, Brent Clayton. A.S., Harrisburg Area Community Coll., 1968; BS, Va. Commonwealth U., 1969; MS, Eastern Ky. U., 1971; PhD (fellow), Sam Houston U., 1973; certificate Home Office Detective Tng. Course, Eng., 1967. Diplomate Am. Coll. Forensic Examiners, Am. Bd. Law Enforcement Experts. Police officer Highspire Police, 1964-69; adminstr. Burns Internat. Security Services Inc., 1969-71; prof. police sci. and adminstrn., dir. grad. studies in adminstrn. of justice U. Louisville, 1973-82; prof., chmn. dept. criminology Indiana U. of Pa., 1982—; co-founder Sempas Security and Safety Technologies, 1980; advisor Reagan Presdl./Congressional Task Force on Criminal Justice, 1980; mem. staff So. Police Inst., 1973-82, Nat. Crime Prevention Inst., 1973-82. Researcher, ptnr. McShan Assocs., 1974-85; cons. U.S. Congress Com. on Emergency Communications, 1967. Co-author: The Criminal Justice System, 1976, 3d edit., 1984; co-founder, editor: Criminal Justice Policy Rev., 1984-86; contbr. chpts. to books, articles to profl. jours.; patents. Active Metro Child Abuse Program, Crime Clinic of Greater Harrisburg, 1965-74; mem. Lower Swatara Twp. Police Civil Service Commn., 1967-69. Served with USMC, 1962-66 Recipient Mayor's Citation, City of Louisville, 1982, Gold medal Educator of the 1980's; honoree Silliman Coll., Yale U., 1984; Fulbright scholar, lectr., Australia, 1987. Mem. Acad. Criminal Justice Scis. (exec. bd. 1980-83, pres. 1985), Navy League (award for disting. community service) Home: 4620 Lucerne Rd Indiana PA 15701-6003 Office: Indiana U of Pa G-1 McElhaney Hall Indiana PA 15705-0001 E-mail: mccauley@grove.iup.edu. *One's philosophy, spirit, and drive contributes more to his relative success than do economic resources, social position, planning, or timing.*

MCCAULEY, WILLIAM ALBERT, business executive; b. Lexington, Ky., Feb. 18, 1934; s. William Albert McCauley and Olive Gertrude (Snowden) Barkhau; m. Julia Ann Bauer, June 5, 1940; children: Kristi Jo, Kelly Dawn, Kevin Jay. BSBA, U. Cin., 1959. Sales rep. Trailmobile Inc., Cin. and Columbus, 1959-66; gen. mgr., v.p. Summer & Co., Columbus, 1966-78; pres., COO Beasley Industries, 1978-82, Borror Corp., Columbus, 1982-85; cons. WAM, 1985—. Bd. dirs. George Igel & Co., Inc, Contract Sweepers; cons., mgr. over 25 different industries. Chmn. Franklin County Zoning, Columbus, 1972-80; bd. dirs. Franklin County Childrens Svcs., Columbus, 1980-83, Mt. Carmel Health System, Columbus, 1982-92, Col. Zool. Assn., Columbus, 1966-82; active Mid Ohio Emergency Planning Commn., Mid Ohio Regional Planning Commn., Franklin County Rural Zoning Commn., Columbus Waterway Task Force, Columbus Waterway Commn., Drug and Alcohol Abuse Prevention Bd., Cmty. Ch. Bd., Coalition for Cost Effective Health Care, Goodman Guild. Avocations: photography, boating, bicycling. Home and Office: 2996 Leatheralips Trl Dublin OH 43017-3597

MCCAW, JOHN E., JR. professional sports team executive; Co-founder, bd. dirs. McCaw Comm., McCaw Cellular Comm., Inc.; owner, bd. dirs. Seattle Mariners, 1992; co-chmn. Orca Bay Sports and Entertainment, Vancouver, B.C.; chmn., gov. Vancouver Canucks. Office: Vancouver Canucks 800 Griffiths Way Vancouver BC Canada V6B 6G1*

MCCAW, VALERIE SUE, civil engineer; b. Kansas City, Kans., Aug. 8, 1960; BS, Okla. State U., 1982, MS, 1994. Profl. engr. Okla. Suvey lab instr. Okla. State U., Stillwater, 1981-82; civil engr. U.S. Corps. Engrs., Tulsa, Okla., 1982-83; asst. city engr. City of Broken Arrow, 1983-87; civil engr. The Benham Group, Tulsa, 1987-91, project mgr., 1991-93, City of Tulsa, 1993-95; v.p. NAI, Tulsa, 1995-97; assoc, office mgr. Tulsa office Burns & McDonnell Engring. Co., 1997—. Grad. Leadership Broken Arrow, 1985-86; participant Discover "E", Tulsa, 1991-92. Dir. Pride in Tulsa, 1990-91. Okla. State U. scholar, 1978-82. Mem. Nat. Soc. Profl. Engrs. (state v.p., pres. 1998-99, named Young Engr. of Y r. 1992), Am. Soc. Civil Engrs., Assn. State Dam Safety Officials. Office: Burns & McDonnell 6450 S Lewis Ave Ste 220 Tulsa OK 74136-1059 E-mail: vmccaw@burnsmcd.com.

MCCAWLEY, AUSTIN, psychiatrist, educator; b. Greenock, Scotland, Jan. 17, 1925; arrived in U.S., 1954; s. Austin and Anna Theresa (McBride) McC.; m. Gloria Klein, Feb. 15, 1958; children: Joseph, Tessa. MBCHB, U. Glasgow, 1948. Diplomate Am. Bd. Psychiatry and Neurology; DPM Royal Coll. London. Intern Glasgow Royal Infirmary, Scotland, 1948; resident Inst. Living, Harford, Conn., 1954-57, clin. dir., 1960-66; med. dir. Westchestor br. St. Vincent's Hosp., N.Y.C., 1966-72; dir. psychiatry St. Francis Hosp., Hartford, 1972-88; prof. psychiatry U. Conn. Med. Sch., Farmington, 1983-93; pvt. practice, West Hartford, Conn., 1988—. Dir. psychiatry Kaiser Permanente of Conn., 1996-99. Co-author: The Physician, 1983; contbr. articles to profl. jours. Chmn. Bd. Mental Health, State of Conn., 1981-84, Search Com. for Commr. Mental Health, Conn., 1981; mem. Gov.'s Spl. Task Force on Mental health Policy, Conn., 1982. With RAF, 1948-50. Fellow: Am. Coll. Psychiatry (charter fellow, founder), Am. Psychiat. Assn.; mem.: Conn. Psychiat. Soc. (pres. 1978—79). Democrat. Roman Catholic. Avocations: music, golf. Home and Office: 20 Worthington Dr Farmington CT 06032

MCCAWLEY, WILLIAM DALE, II, accountant, writer, ethnohistorian; b. Long Beach, Calif., Nov. 26, 1952; s. William Dale and Antoinette Gertrude (Wolke) M.; children: Michael Breier, Jonathan William. BA, Calif. State U., Long Beach, 1974. Cert. elem. tchr., Calif. CFO, dir. finance and adminstrn. McDonnell Douglas Physician Sys. Co., Gardena, Calif., 1981-88; dir. adminstrn. U. Phoenix, Fountain Valley, 1988-89; sr. accountant Robert-John Industries, Huntington Beach, 1989-91; controller Tallon Termite & Pest Control, Long Beach, 1991-95; cons. LSA Assoc. Inc., Irvine, 1995-96; acctg. mgr. Microage Computer Ctr., Fountain Valley, 1997-01; asst. controller Paragon Ptnrs., Ltd., Huntington Beach, 01—. Cons. Channel Islands Nat. Park, Ventura, Calif., 1991—, Rancho Los Alamitos Historical Ranch and Gardens, Long Beach, 1993—. Author: The First Angelinos: The Gabrielino Indians of Los Angeles, 1996 (cert. commendation Am. Assn. State and Local History 1997). Recipient Donald H. Pflueger Local History award Hist. Soc. So. Calif., 2000. Avocations: photography, hiking, reading, astronomy. Home: 14672 Monroe St Midway City CA 92655-1051 E-mail: billmccawley@hotmail.com.

MCCAY, THURMAN DWAYNE, university official; b. Wynne, Ark., Sept. 2, 1946; s. Thurman Ellis and Vetra Marcella (Jones) McC.; m. Mary Helen Johnston, Oct. 3, 1985; children: Audra Lee, Leesa Marie. BS in Physics, Auburn U., 1968, MS in Engring., 1969, PhD in Engring. and Math., 1974; postgrad. mgmt. sci. program, Air Force Inst. Tech., Wright-Petterson AFB, Ohio, 1985. Rsch. engr. gas diagnostics sect. aerospace projects br. ARO, Inc., Arnold Air Force Station, Tenn., 1973-78; sr. rsch. phys. scientist, plume tech. br. Air Force Rocket Propulsion Lab., Edwards AFB, Calif., 1978-81; sr. aerospace engr., br. chief, chief propulsion divsn. NASA, George G. Marshall Center, Ala., 1981-86; prof. engring. sci. and mechanics, adj. prof. engring. U. Tenn. Space Inst., Tullahoma, 1986—, v.p., 1993-00; v.p. rsch. & info. tech. U. Tenn. , Knoxville, 2000—. Tchr. Auburn U., 1970-72, Calif. State U., Fresno, 1980, U. Ala., Huntsville, 1985, U. Tenn. Space Inst., 1986—; chmn. Tenn. Valley Aerospace Region; mem. rev. bd. NASA Lewis Rocket Thruster Rsch. Program, Dept. of Def. Fellowship Program, Indsl. Laser Handbook; mem. nat. adv. bd. NASA Enring. Rsch. Ctr. for Propulsion, Pa. State U., NASA Ctr. for Advanced Space Propulsion, U. Tenn. Space Inst./Calspan. Reviewer Jour. Spacecraft and Rockets, Jour. Propulsion and Power, Jour. Thermophysics and Heat Transfer, Jour. Heat Transfer; contbr. articles to profl. jours.; patentee in field. Maj. U.S. Army, 1972-73. NRC rsch. fellow, 1980-84. Assoc. fellow

AIAA (liquid propulsion tech. com. 1984-88, assoc. editor Jour. Propulsion and Power 1988-91); mem. Am. Soc. Metals, Am. Welding Soc., Laser Inst. Am. (chmn. ICALEO 1994), Am. Soc. Engring. Edn. Roman Catholic. Avocations: tennis, private pilot (instrument rated). Office: Univ Tenn Office of VP Rsch/Info Tech 527 Andy Holt Tower Knoxville TN 37996-0150 E-mail: dwayne-mccay@tennessee.edu.

MCCHESNEY, CHARLES E. retired marketing professional; b. Springfield, Mass., July 14, 1939; s. Herbert L. and Charlotte W. (Miller) McC.; m. Ann S., Dec. 30, 1961 (dec.); children: Charles E. II, Matthew H., Daniel D.; m. Ruth Ann McChesney, Feb. 20, 2000. BChE, Cornell U., 1962; MA, Princeton U., 1967, PhD, 1973. Registered profl. engr., N.J. Devel. engr. Film Divsn. 3M Co., Hastings, Minn., 1962-64; rsch. assoc. Am. Can Co. Rsch. Lab., Princeton, N.J., 1968-76; sr. devel. engr. Union Carbide Corp., Bound Brook, 1976-78; sr. applications engr. Celanese Plastics and Specialities Co., Summit, 1978-83; staff engr. Celanese Engring. Resins Co., 1983-86, group leader applications devel., 1986-89, mgr. E/E applications devel., 1989-92; mgr. E/E programs Hoechst Celanese Advanced Materials Group, 1992-93, mktg. profl., 1993-97. Mgr. auto market, Vectra Bus. Line, Ticona, Summit, 1998-2000. Patentee in field; contbr. articles to profl. jours. Mem. South Brunswick Twp. Environ. Commn., 1982-86. Mem. Soc. Plastics Engrs. Home and Office: 311 Scenic Ridge Ter Mars PA 16046-2349 E-mail: charlie1939@hotmail.com.

MCCHESNEY, MARGARET LEE, clinical social worker; b. St. Paul, Oct. 14, 1937; d. Lloyd Harold Berg and Erma Evelyn (Swant) Berg Baker; m. James Reid McChesney, Jr., June 7, 1956; children: Cynthia Louese Lundeen, Stephen Reid McChesney. BA in Communications summa cum laude, Augsburg Coll., 1980; MSW, U. Minn., 1982. Cert. IMAGO-conscious relationship therapy, lic. independent clin. social worker, Minn., Wis., marital and family therapist, integrative therapist. Therapist Family Sexual Abuse Prog./Fairview Southdale Hosp., Mpls., 1981-82; dir. social svcs. Stevens Square Residence for Women, 1982-86; psychiat. social worker St. Mary's Hosp., 1986-87; psychotherapist, pvt. practice St. Paul, 1987-88; instr. Carthage Coll., Kenosha, Wis., 1988; psychotherapist Lakeside Family Therapy Svcs., Racine, 1989-98. Speaker in field. Mem. NASW, AIRT, IIRT, NAMI, Internat. Breathwork Found. (IBF) Network. Methodist. Avocations: world travel, family time, reading, writing, hiking. Home: 3025 Simpson St Saint Paul MN 55113-1650

MCCHESNEY, ROBERT MICHAEL, SR. educator; b. Effingham, Ill., Oct. 5, 1942; s. J.D. and Helen Grace (Russell) McC.; m. Laraine Freeman, Aug. 28, 1965; children: Robert M. Jr., Todd Patrick, Jennifer Laraine, Grant Russell, Brent Steven. BA, U. La., Lafayette, 1964; MA, U. Va., 1967, PhD, 1969. Asst. instr. U. Va., Charlottesville, 1967-68; chmn. dept. polit. sci. U. Ctrl. Ark., Conway, 1971-76, dean coll. scis. and humanities, 1976-82, v.p. for acad. affairs, 1982-89, disting. prof., 1989-90; provost U. Montevallo, Ala., 1990-92, pres., 1992—. V.p. Survey Rsch., Inc., Conway, 1989-92; spl. cons. U. Ark. System, Little Rock, 1989. Mem. Carmichael Found., Conway, 1975-79; exec. bd. Quapaw coun. Boy Scouts Am., Little Rock, 1982-88; Greater Ala. Area Coun., 1995—; chair Ala. Higher Edn. Partnership, Pres. Adv. Coun., 1999-2001. Capt. Med. Svc. Corps U.S. Army, 1968-71. Grantee State Justice Inst./Adminstrv. Office of Cts., Ark., 1989. Mem. Ala. Coun. Univ. and Coll. Pres. (chmn. 1993-95), So. Com. Colls. and Schs. (exec. coun. 1996-99), Birmingham C. of C., Montevall C. of C., Rotary (pres. Conway Club 1987-88, Paul Harris fellow 1986), Phi Beta Kappa, Phi Kappa Phi, Alpha Chi, Golden Key, Phi Alpha Theta, Phi Eta Sigma, , Omicron Delta Kappa, Blue Key, Kappa Alpha Delta. Mem. Lds Ch. Avocations: hunting, fishing, golfing. Office: U Montevallo Station 6001 Montevallo AL 35115

MCCHESNEY, ROBERT PEARSON, artist; b. Marshall, Mo., Jan. 16, 1913; s. John and Ruby (Pearson) McC.; m. Mary Ellen Fuller, Dec. 17, 1949. Student, Sch. Fine Arts, Washington U., 1931-34, Otis Art Inst., Los Angeles, 1936-37. Represented by Annex Galleries, Santa Rosa, Calif., Robert Green Fine Arts, Mill Valley, Thomas McCormick Gallery, Chgo., Claire Carlevaro Art Exchange, San Francisco. Instr. art Calif. Sch. Fine Arts, San Francisco, 1949-51, Santa Rosa Jr. Coll., 1957-58; trustee San Francisco Art Inst., 1965-67. One-man shows include San Francisco Mus. Modern Art, 1949, 53, San Francisco Art Inst., 1957, 20th Century West, 1965, Bolles Gallery, N.Y., 1962, Nev. Mus., 1994, also others; one-man retrospective Fresno (Calif.) Mus. Art, 1996, Calif. State U., Fresno, 1999, City Visions Gallery, Santa Rosa, Calif., 2000, Art Exch., San Francisco, 2002; group shows include Art Inst. Chgo., 1947, 3d Biennial Sau Paulo, Brazil, 1955, Whitney Annual, 1955, Corcoran, 1957, Provincetown, 1957, Chgo., 1959, Osaka, Japan, 1970, Whitney, 1980, Robert Green Fine Arts, Mill Valley, Calif., also others; represented in permanent collections, Fresno Art Mus., Art Inst. Chgo., Worcester (Mass.) Art Mus., Whitney Mus., N.Y., San Francisco Mus. Modern Art, Utah State Mus., Nev. Art Mus., Laguna Beach Art Mus., Cleve. Art Mus., others; executed mural San Francisco Social Svcs. Bldg., 1978; author: (photo biography) Robert McChesney-An American Painter, 1996. Address: 2955 Sonoma Mountain Rd Petaluma CA 94954-9559 ***The desert wilderness, which I truly love to be in as much as possible, has influenced me a great deal. Of course, the artist is no different from anyone else in that he is influenced by everything around him visually and psychologically, but he has the ability to digest this, you might say, and then transform it into art.***

MCCHESNEY, SAMUEL PARKER, III, real estate executive; b. Oakland, Calif., July 30, 1945; s. Samuel Parker and Edna Margaret (McCorkle) McC.; m. Vicki Storrie, June 21, 1969; children: Nathan, Amanda, Jed. BA, Washington and Lee U., 1967; JD, Case Western Res. U., 1970. Lic. real estate broker, Mo., Kans. Urban intern and multifamily housing rep. HUD, Chgo., 1970-71; project loan mgr. 1st Home Investment Corp., Overland Park, Kans., 1971-72; v.p. devel. Northland Bldg. Corp., Gladstone, Mo., 1973-74; cons. Urban Equities, Kansas City, 1975; pres., co-owner McChesney Devel. Co., Inc., Edwardsville, Kans., 1976-78; pres., owner McChesney, Inc., Kansas City, 1978—; Managed Maintenance Inc., 1990-97. Pres. Lake Quivira (Kans.) Homeowners Assn. Inc., 1983-85; mem. planning and zoning com. City of Lake Quivira, 1983, mem. planning commn., 1992—; mem. real estate com. Quivira, Inc., 1986, nominating com., 1987-88, 90, restrictions & covenants update com., 1993-95; mem. patron's com. Tom Watson Golf Classic, Kansas City, 1984-85; mem. Lake Quivira Long Range Planning Com., 1987-88. Recipient cert. Nat. Assisted Housing Profl. Exec. Level. Mem. Johnson County Bd. Realtors, Affordable Housing Mgrs. Assn. (dir. region 7 1995—, v.p. region 7, mem. fin. com. 1995-96, chmn. 1995-96, mem. membership com. 1997—, mem. edn. com. 1997—), Lake Quivira Country Club (pres. 1983-85), Saddle and Sirloin Club. Avocations: golf, reading, gardening, travel, horseback riding. Home: 510 Hillcrest Rd E Lake Quivira KS 66217-8781 Office: 6870 W 105th St Overland Park KS 66212 E-mail: sam@mcchesneyinc.com.

MCCLAIN, CURTIS KEITH, JR. religious studies educator, minister; b. Muskogee, Okla., Sept. 10, 1955; s. Curtis Keith Sr. and Dorothy Lee Scarborough McClain; m. Patsy Marlene Cater, Aug. 23, 1980; children: Elisabeth Ruth, Meredith Lee. BA, Howard Payne U., 1977; MDiv, Southwestern Bapt. Theol. Sem., 1980; PhD, Mid-Am. Bapt. Theol. Sem., 1995. Asst. tchr. Dean's Sch., Ft. Worth, 1980-81; adj. instr. Mid-Am. Bapt. Theol. Sem., Memphis, 1984-87; prof. Bible, chair humanities divsn. Mo. Bapt. Coll., St. Louis, 1988—. Preacher various chs., Mo., 1988—. Contbr. articles to profl. jours. Trustee Christian Civic Found., St. Louis; chmn. steering com. So. Bapt. Founders Conf. Midwest, St. Louis. Named Parkway Disting. prof. Parkway Bapt. Ch., 1991. Mem. Evangelical Theol. Soc., His Way Evangelistic Assn. (bd. dirs. 1995—). Baptist. Avocations: computers, cross-stitch. Home: 2813 Mcclay Valley Blvd Saint Peters MO 63376-7136 Office: Mo Bapt Coll 1 College Park Dr Saint Louis MO 63141-8660 Fax: (314) 434-7596. E-mail: mcclain@mobap.edu.

MCCLAIN, EDWARD FIFER, JR. retired physicist; b. Carrolton, Mo., Aug. 22, 1921; s. Edward Fifer and Corrine Carrie (Rahmoeller) McC.; m. Louise Cherry Shelby, Dec. 9, 1943; children: Deanna Louise, William Edward, Robert Jay. BSEE, George Washington U., 1950. With Naval Rsch. Lab., Washington, 1942-68, head radio astronomy br., 1956-68; ret., 1968. Past chmn. commn. radio astronomy Internat. Scientific Radio Union; past adv. com. Nat. Radio Astronomy Obs.; cons. Nat. Acad. Sci., Interdept. Radio Adv. Com., Nat. Radio Astronomy Obs.; astronomy panel NSF. Contbr. articles to profl. jours.; patentee in field. Fellow AAAS, Washington Acad. Scis.; mem. IEEE (life), Internat. Astron. Union, Am. Astron. Soc., Scientific Rsch. Soc. Am., Sigma Tau. Achievements include conducting sea trials ST periscope radar in submarine; designed AN/APN67 self-contained doppler automatic navigator for aircraft; determined correct distance to radio source Cass A using galactic hydrogen absorption. Avocation: sound reproduction. Home: 4133 Maple Rd Morningside MD 20746-3514

MCCLAIN, GEORGE NELSON, economist, lawyer; b. New Haven, Aug. 10, 1952; s. James and Trina (George) McC.; m. Lisa Crossley, May 5, 1982. BS in Econs., U. Conn., 1975; JD, Yale U., 1978. Pres. McClain Internat., Washington, 1990—. Office: 5325 85th Ave Apt 103 Hyattsville MD 20784

MCCLAIN, GREGORY DAVID, minister; b. Anderson, S.C., June 6, 1957; s. Lemuel David and Mary Josephine (Hawkins) McC.; m. Anne Leigh Blackwell, May 21, 1983; children: Jonathan David, Sean Gregory. AS, Anderson Coll., 1977; BA, Erskine Coll., 1979; MDiv, Southeastern Bapt. Theol. Sem., Seminary, Wake Forrest, N.C., 1982; D of Ministry, Wesley Theol. Sem., Washington, 1996. Ordained Boulevard Bapt. Ch., 1983. Chaplain extern Bapt. Med. Ctr., Columbia, S.C., 1982; assoc. pastor First Bapt. Ch., South Boston, Va., 1983-86; minister Corrottoman Bapt. Ch., Lancaster, 1986-93, Colonial Beach (Va.) Bapt. Ch., 1993-98, Neill's Creek Bapt. Ch., Angier, NC, 1998—2002; chaplain Duke U. Med. Ctr., Durham, 2002—. Pres. Dan River Bapt. Pastors, Halifax, Va., 1984-85; preacher-jr. high weekend, Va. Bapt. Gen. Assn., 1986, faculty youth week, 1984-88; v.p. Lancaster Ministerial Assn., 1987-88; v.p. Little River Bapt. Pastor's Conf., Lillington, N.C., 2000. Active CROP walk, South Boston, Va., 1984-85; coach youth soccer, South Boston, 1985, Westmoreland County, Va., 1995-97, Buics Creek, N.C., 1998; merit badge counselor Boy Scouts Am., Lancaster, 1990-93; mem. Lancaster Ednl. Task Force, 1988. Mem. Ruritan Club (chaplain 1990-93). Office: Duke U Box 3112 Durham NC 27708 *The Kingdom of God exists wherever God is king.*

MCCLAIN, JUANITA, library director; b. Montgomery County, Ala., Oct. 6, 1949; BS, Ala. State U., 1972, MEd, 1979; MLS, Atlanta U., 1984. Dir. pub. libr. Macon-Tuskegee County, Macon, Ala., 1978-88, br. head, 1989-94; dir. Montgomery City-County Pub. Libr., 1994—. Recipient Black Role Model award Montgomery-Tuskegee Times, 1996; Ala. Pub. Libr. Svc. scholar, 1984, Atlanta U. fellow, 1983. Mem. ALA, Ala. Libr. Assn. (sec. 2001-02, pres.-elect 2002—). Office: Montgomery City-County Pub Libr PO Box 1950 Montgomery AL 36102-1950

MCCLAIN, LENA ALEXANDRIA, protective services official; b. Toledo, Aug. 15, 1966; d. Lee Earl McClain, Mattie May Roberts-McClain; m. David Angelo Neyland, Aug. 4, 1990 (div. July 1995). AAS in Criminal Justice Adminstrn., Pikes Peak C.C., Colorado Springs, Colo., 1994; postgrad., U. Colo., 1994—95; BS in Criminology, U. So. Colo., 1996; postgrad., Spring Arbor U., Mich., 2001—02. Corrections officer Colo. Dept. Corrections, Colorado Springs, 1994—96, sgt., 1996—97, case mgr./lt., 1997—99; sr. resident specialist coord. N.W. Cmty. Corrections Ctr., Bowling Green, Ohio, 1999—2000; shift supr. Lucas County Dept. Wk. Release, Toledo, 2000—. Employee counsel, bd. dirs. Delta Correctional Ctr., 1998—99. Mem. Colo. Grievance Team, 1998; bd. dirs. Pub. Arts Commn., Delta, Colo., 1999; bd. dirs., liaison Nat. Assn. Blacks in Criminal Justice, 1998. With U.S. Army, 1987—90. Mem.: Am. Correctional Assn., Correctional Peace Officers Found., Phi Theta Kappa. Democrat. Avocations: golf, basketball, softball, chess, writing.

MCCLAIN, MARILYN RUSSELL, counseling administrator; b. Laurelton, N.Y., Aug. 18, 1956; d. Russell H. and Lillian A. (Yarbrough) McClain; 1 child Amy Lynne Roberts White. BS in Social Work, Harding U., 1977; MA in Adult Edn., Okla. State U., 1997. Career counselor Foothills Vo-Tech Sch., Searcy, Ark., 1977-78; social worker Dept. Social Svcs., Tulsa, 1978-79; owner, operator, instr. Spl. Deliveries Childbirth Preparation Ctr., 1980-85; mgr. One Hour Moto Photo, 1986-89; area mgr. Mervyn's, 1989-92; admissions counselor Rogers State U., Claremore, 1992-96, student counselor for health scis., 1996—. Primary advisor Adult Students Aspiring Prosper, Claremore, 1993—; pres. Rogers U. Staff Assn., 1995—97, mem. staff senate, 1995—, CASA adv., 1997—; parent educator Parenting Ptnrs., Claremore, 1994—95. Mem. Oologah PTA, 1990—97; sec. Oologah-Talala Sch. Found., 1994—95, pres., 1995—99, trustee, 1994—2001; mem. statue and hotel com. Rogers County Hist. Soc., Claremore, 1994—. Mem.: Am. Assn. Adult and Continuing Edn., Okla. Acad. Advising Assn., Sertoma. Republican. Baptist. Avocations: needlepoint, reading, piano. Home: 18021 Oaklawn Dr Claremore OK 74017-3681 Office: Rogers State Univ 1701 W Will Rogers Blvd Claremore OK 74017-3259 E-mail: mmcclain@rsu.edu.

MCCLAIN, MICHAEL H. writer; b. Middletown, Ohio, Aug. 30, 1940; s. Thomas H. and Blanche (Hamilton) McC. BA in History, U. Miami; MA in History, U. Granada, Spain. Staff columnist El Correo Gallego, Santiago de Compostela, Spain, 1974-84. Spkr. in field. *Perhaps the most interesting aspect of Michael McClain's professional life is the fact that he was staff columnist for the newspaper El Correo Gallego of Santiago de Compostela, Spain, from September 1974 to October 1984. In 1984 he was invited to attend a conference on Buddhism in New Delhi, India. During his time in India he gave speeches on Muslim Spain at the tomb of the Sufi holy man Nizamuddin Aluliya in Delhi, after which he was honored with a lesi of marigolds. The Iranian Embassy in Madrid contracted Mr. McClain to write a book on Persian influences in Medieval Spain, both Muslim and Christian. The Khomeini regime cancelled the publication and recently, the University of London has shown interest in publishing Mr. McClain's book as part of The Curzon Series on Persian Art and Culture.* Author: Spain & Persia: Aryium & Iran, numerous essays; contbr. articles to Cath. and Islamic jours. internationally. With U.S. Army, 1963-67. Mem. Nat. Assn. Scholars, Nat. Alumni Forum, Am. Muslim Coun. (nat. adv. bd. 1994—), Assn. Art History, Caths. United for the Faith (sec. Dayton chpt. 1990—), Coun. of Shia Islamic Orgn., Valaam Soc. Am., Ameer Khusro Soc. Am., Assn. of Literary Scholars and Critics, Great War Soc., Am. Tradition Family and Property, The 1745 Assn., Order of the White Rose, Archconfraternité du Archange St. Michel, ComuniÓn Tradicionalista, Mensa. Avocations: hunting, fishing, travel. Home: 4518 Bonita Dr Apt 130 Middletown OH 45044-6759

MCCLAIN, PAULA DENICE, political scientist, educator; b. Louisville, Jan. 3, 1950; d. Robert Landis and Mabel (Molock) McC.; stepdau. of Annette Williams McClain; m. Paul C. Jacobson, Jan. 30, 1988; children: Kristina L., Jessica A. BA, Howard U., Washington, 1972; MA, Howard U., 1974, PhD, 1977; postgrad., U. Pa., 1981-82. Asst. prof. dept. polit. sci. U. Wis., Milw., 1977-82; assoc. prof. and prof. pub. affairs Ariz. State U., Tempe, 1982-91; prof. govt. and fgn. affairs U. Va., Charlottesville, 1991-2000, chair govt. and fgn. affairs, 1994-97; prof. dept. polit. sci. Duke U., Durham, N.C., 2000—. Co-author: Can We All Get Along? Racial and Ethnic Minorities in American Politics, 1995, 2d edit., 1998, 3d edit. 2001, Race, Place and Risk: Black Homicide in Urban America, 1990; editor: Minority Group Influence, 1993; co-editor: Urban Minority Administrators, 1988. Mem. Nat. Conf. Black Polit. Scientists (pres. 1989-90), Am. Polit. Sci. Assn. (exec. coun. 1985-87, v.p. 1993-94), So. Polit. Sci. Assn. (exec. coun. 1992-95, v.p.-elect 2000-01), Internat. Polit. Sci. Assn. (exec. com. 1997—, v.p. 1997-), Midwest Polit. Sci. Assn. (v.p. 2002-). Office: Duke U Dept Polit Sci Perkins Libr PO Box 90204 Durham NC 27708-0204 E-mail: pmcclain@duke.edu.

MCCLAIN, RICHARD DOUGLAS, lawyer; b. Lincoln, Nebr., June 28, 1927; s. Leo LeRoy and Laura Thelma McC.; s. Donna J. Burbach, July 25, 1949; children: Daniel Douglas, Laurie Lynn. BA, U. Nebr., 1951; JD, U. So. Calif., 1959. Bar: Calif. 1960, Nebr. 1970, Oreg. 1991, U.S. Dist. Ct. Nebr. 1970, U.S. Supreme Ct. 1978. Atty. Union Pacific R.R., L.A., 1960-64, Hindin, Sterling, McKittrick & Powsner, Beverly Hills, Calif., 1964-67, Carnation Co., L.A., 1967-68, Atlantic Richfield Co., L.A., 1968-69; dep. county atty. County Atty., Lincoln, 1970-74; pvt. practice, 1974—. Pres. Exec. Toastmasters 412, L.A., 1967, Res. Officers Assn., Lincoln, 1990—, pres. Nebr. dept. 1993—; counsellor Footprinters, Lincoln, 1990—. Lt. USNR, 1951-55. Republican. Avocations: sailing, skating, shooting. Home: 3235 W Pershing Rd Lincoln NE 68502-4844 Office: 1919 S 40th St Ste 111 Lincoln NE 68506-5247

MCCLAIN, RICHARD STAN, cinematographer; b. Los Angeles, Oct. 7, 1951; m. Kim Girard, Nov. 7, 1987. Founder Pasadena Camera Sys., Inc., Expendol.com. Aerial cameraman: (feature films) On Any Given Sunday, The Client, Contact, Man on the Moon, I Love Trouble, Tombstone, Falling Down, Heart and Soul, So, I Married an Axe Murderer, The Good Son, Made in America, This Boy's Life, Fearless, Passenger 57, Wind, At Play in the Fields of the Lord, The Iceman, Rambo, Firebirds, Wind, Basic Instinct, Innerspace, U2 Rattle and Hum, Crazy People, The Hunt for Red October, The Doors, Flatliners, Nell, Murder in the First, Drop Zone, Get Shorty, The Money Train; (TV shows) Magnum P.I., Airwolf; editor: Operating Cameraman Mag. Recipient Best Cinematography award London Internat. Advt. Awards, 1993, Telly award (2), 1993, (1), 1994. N.Y. Festival Silver award, 1993, Telly award (2) 1994, (4) 1995, (2), 1996. Mem. Internat. Cinematographers Guild, Screen Actors Guild, Dirs. Guild Am., Soc. Operating Cameramen (past pres.).

MCCLAIN, SYLVIA NANCY (NANCY JO GRIMM), voice educator, classical vocalist; b. Worthington, Minn., July 16, 1943; d. Walter Deming and Naomi Leona (Deters) Grimm.; m. Joseph T. McClain (div. Feb. 1994); children: Raimund, Hermine. MusB with honors, Ind. U., 1966, MusM with honors, 1969; D of Musical Arts with commendation, U. Tex., Austin, 1989. Apprentice artist Santa Fe (N.Mex.) Opera, 1968-69; performing singer various concert and opera venues, Germany, 1970-78; asst. prof. dept. music Howard Payne U., Brownwood, Tex., 1980-82; asst. prof. voice dept. fine arts Southwestern U., Georgetown, 1986-91; assoc prof., chair voice dept. sch. music Hardin-Simmons U., Abilene, 1992-98; assoc. prof. music, coord. voice and opera U. Conn., Storrs, 1998—. Performer: (recital) Portraits of Women in Songs of Hugo Wolf. Vol. cons. Leadership of Edn. in Arts Professions, Austin, 1990-92, Austin Lyric Opera, 1983-92. Fulbright scholar, Stadtliche Hochschule für Musik, Stuttgart, Germany, 1969-70. Mem. Nat. Assn. Tchrs. of Singing, Phi Kappa Lambda, Mu Phi Epsilon. Avocations: exercise, reading, travel. Home: 76 England Rd Chaplin CT 06235-2403

MCCLAIN, THOMAS EMERSON, communications executive; b. East Liverpool, Ohio, July 26, 1950; s. Thomas E. and Helen Marie (Polinski) McC. BA, Case Western Reserve, Cleve., 1972; MA, Kans. State U., 1973. With intergovtl. rels. Ohio EPA, Columbus, 1974-77; legis. liaison Ohio Consumers Counsel, 1977-80, dep. dir., 1980-81; press sec. Ohio Atty. Gen., Columbus, 1982-83; asst. dir. Pub. Utilities Commn., 1983; with instnl. rels. dept. Battelle Project Mgmt. Div., Chgo., 1983-84, mgr. instl. rels., 1984-86; mgr. comms. Battelle, Columbus, 1986-88, dir. corp. comm., 1989-95, v.p. corp. comms., 1995—. Sec. devel. bd. Children's Hosp., Columbus, 1990-91. Vol. Ohio Youth Commn., Columbus, 1975-76; active ARC-Cen. Ohio chpt., 1986-87; mem. design rev. com. Ohio State U. Sci. and Tech. Park; active Colo. Energy Sci. Ctr. Bd.; amb. USAR Program; mem. Ohio State Bd. of Edn. Mem. Rotary (chmn. program com. 1991-93, bd. dirs. 1994-95, 2d v.p. 1996-97). Presbyterian. Avocations: basketball, golf. Home: 2689 Camden Rd Upper Arlington OH 43221-3221 Office: Battelle 505 King Ave Columbus OH 43201-2693

MCCLAIN, TIM S. federal agency administrator; Grad., U.S. Naval Acad., 1970; JD, Calif. We. Sch. Law, San Diego, 1978. Commd. Navy JAG Corps USN, ret., 1990, mil. def. counsel Navy Legal Svc. Office, head claims officer Navy Legal Svc. Office, head legal assistance officer Navy Legal Svc. Office, staff judge adv. for the commanding officer Naval Air Station Miramar, 1981—83, dept. head, instr. Naval Justice Sch. RI, 1981—86, gen. court-martial mil. judge Navy-Marine Trial Judiciary, S.W., 1986; joined litigation law firm, San Diego, 1990, internat. mgmt. cons. firm, dir. opers.; gen. counsel Dept. Vet. Affairs, Washington, 2001—. Office: US Dept Vet Affairs Gen Counsel 810 Vermont Ave NW Washington DC 20420*

MCCLAIN, WILLIAM ANDREW, lawyer; b. Sanford, N.C., Jan. 11, 1913; s. Frank and Blanche (Leslie) McC.; m. Roberta White, Nov. 11, 1944. AB, Wittenberg U., 1934; JD, U. Mich., 1937; LLD (hon.), Wilberforce U., 1963, U. Cin., 1971; LHD, Wittenberg U., 1972. Bar: Ohio 1938, U.S. Dist. Ct. (so. dist.) Ohio 1940, U.S. Ct. Appeals (6th cir.) 1946, U.S. Supreme Ct. 1946. Mem. Berry, McClain & White, 1937-58; dep. solicitor, City of Cin., 1957-63, city solicitor, 1963-72; mem. Keating, Muething & Klekamp, Cin., 1972-73; gen. counsel Cin. br. SBA, 1973-75; judge Hamilton County Common Pleas Ct., 1975-76; judge Mcpl. Ct., 1976-80; of counsel Manley, Burke, Lipton & Cook, Cin., 1980—; adj. prof. U. Cin., 1963-72, Salmon P. Chase Law Sch., 1965-72. Mem. exec. com. ARC, Cin., 1978—; bd. dirs. NCCJ, 1975—. Served to 1st lt. JAG, U.S. Army, 1943-46. Decorated Army Commendation award; recipient Nat. Layman award, A.M.E. Ch., 1963; Alumni award Wittenberg U., 1966; Nat. Inst. Mcpl. Law Officers award, 1971, Ellis Island Medal of Honor, 1997. Fellow Am. Bar Found.; mem. ABA, FBA, Am. Judicature Soc., Cin. Bar Assn., Ohio Bar Assn., Nat. Bar Assn., Friendly Sons St. Patrick, Bankers Club, Masons (33d degree), Alpha Phi Alpha, Sigma Pi Phi. Republican. Methodist. Home: 2101 Grandin Rd Apt 904 Cincinnati OH 45208-3346

MCCLANAHAN, LELAND, university director; b. Hammond, Ind., Mar. 14, 1931; s. Alonzo Leland and Eva (Hermanson) McC.; m. Lavaughn Adell Meyrer, June 5, 1954; children: Lindel, Loren. Diploma, Ctrl. Bible Coll., 1954; PhBB, Nat. Postgrad. Bible Acad., 1969; BA, Southwestern Coll., 1973; MA, Fla. State Christian Coll., 1964, ThD, 1970; PhD, Faith Bible Coll. and Sem., Ft. Lauderdale, Fla. and Marina, Lagos, Nigeria, 1969; MA, Bapt. Christian U., 1988; PhD, Freedom U., 1989; ThD, Bapt. Christian U., 1989, DLitt, 1990, PsyD, 1991; PhD, Hawaii U., 1995; DEd, Bapt. Christian U., 1992, D in Bus. Adminstrn., 1993; DD (hon.), Internat. Evangelism Crusades, 1969, Trinity Union Coll., 1991; LLD, La. Bapt. U., 1994; StD, PhD, Trinity Internat. U., 1994; HHD (hon.), La. Bapt. U., 1995; LittD (hon.), Cambridge Theol. Sem., 1995; PhD, LittD, PsyD, DBA, LLD, EdD, U. Hawaii, 1995; LittD(hon.), The Messianic Coll. of Rabbinical Studies; MA, Am. Bible Coll. & Sem., 1998; MDiv, Chapel Christian U., 1991; PhD, Midwestern U., 1998; D in Min., Am. Bible Coll. and Sem., 1999. Diplomate Nat. Bd. Christian Clin. Therapists; ordained pastor, Christian Ch., 1950; archbishop Hierarchical Christian Ch., 2000. Founder, pastor Evangel Temple, Griffith, Ind., 1954-73, Abundant Life Temple, Cocoa, Fla., 1974-77; mgr. ins. divsn. United Agys., 1979-81; assoc. pastor Merritt Assembly of God, Merritt Island, 1982-85, Palm Chapel, Merritt Island, 1987-89, 1990-93; founder Hawaii U., Merritt Island Offices, Fla., 1990-97; chancellor Hawaii U. Merritt Island Offices, 1995-97; dir. Fla. Hawaii U. Schs., 1994-97, Chapel Christian U., Merritt Island, FL, 1990—; founder People's Ch. Internat., Inc., 2000—. Founder, dir. Griffith Youth Ctr., 1960-70, Todd Nursery Sch., Griffith, 1971-73; founder, chancellor Ind. Bible Coll., Griffith, 1971-73; dir. Chapel Counseling Ctr., Merritt Island, 1990-94; mem. national accreditation com. Hawaii U. Author: Is Divine Healing For Today?, 1989, Truths From the Gospel of St. John, 1991, An Outline of the Revelation, 1993, Numbers in the Bible, 1994, An Outline of the Acts of the Apostle, 1995, An Outline of the Book of Proverbs, 2000; author 142 coll. courses and books. Recipient Disting. Svc. award U.S. Jaycees, 1966; named Hon. Lt. Col., Gov. Guy Hunt, 1988, Archbishop, Hierarchical Christ Ch., 2000. Fellow Am. Biog. Inst. (life); mem. Internat. Platform Assn., Order of Internat. Fellowship (life), Am. Inst. Clin. Psychotherapists, Am. Assn. christian Counselors, Nat. Christian Counseling Assn. (assoc., lic.), Internat. Assn. Pastoral Psychologists (lic.), Order of St. John, Knight of Malta (comdr. 1990). Republican. Avocations: reading, walking, watching sports, watching television adventures, weight lifting. Office: Chapel Christian Univ 870 Australian St Merritt Island FL 32953-4676

MCCLANAHAN, MICHAEL NELSON, systems analyst; b. Cin., Oct. 28, 1953; s. Roland Nelson and Jeanne Ann (Stevens) McC.; m. Tina Rosanne Swiecki, Mar. 8, 1986; 1 child, Sean Gabriel. Student, U. Cin., 1972-73, Goldenwest Coll., 1979-80, Riverside Community Coll., 1980-83, 90-92. Pres. Riverside (Calif.) Mktg., 1983-88; digital systems analyst Wyle Labs., Norco, Calif., 1988-93; systems analyst Ctr. for Environ. Rsch. and Tech. U. Calif., Riverside, 1993—. Author: (software) SDAS, 1989, HCSS DAS System, 1990, (book) HCSS Systems Operation, 1990, (manual) Software Quality Assurance, 1991. Recipient Svc. award Wyle Labs., 1991. Mem. IEEE, Assn. Computing Machinery, Instrument Soc. of Am., Soc. Automotive Engrs. Achievements include design of numerous software systems and integration of these with data acquisition hardware systems for the purposes of acquiring rsch. data from unique test systems in environ., aerospace, nuclear and def. industries; rsch. in ULEV hydrogen-powered vehicle devel. Office: U Calif Riverside CE-CERT 1200 Columbia Ave Riverside CA 92507-2129

MCCLANAHAN, PATSY HITT, women's health nurse practitioner; b. Pasadena, Tex., Sept. 17, 1954; d. Clifton Lee and Doris Allene (Edwards) Hitt; m. George Terrell McClanahan, Nov. 26, 1980; children: Terry Lee, Jennifer Allene. BSN, N.E. La. U., 1976; Ob/gyn. Nurse Practitioner Cert., U. Tex., Dallas, 1987; MSN, Northwestern State U., 1990. RN RN/advanced nurse practitioner, ob-gyn, sonography, NAACOG. Nurse dir. Columbia (La.) State Sch., 1976-77; staff nurse Caldwell Meml. Hosp., Columbia, La., 1977-79; instr. N.E. La. U., Monroe, 1979; staff nurse Schumpert Med. Ctr., Shreveport, La., 1979; dir. nurses Citizens Med. Ctr., Columbia, 1980-84; pub. health nurse III Caldwell Parish Health Unit, 1984-88; nurse II E.A. Conway Hosp., Monroe, 1988; regional pub. specialist Regional Pub. Health, 1988-89; instr. dept. ob/gyn La. State U. Med. Ctr. , 1989—; asst. prof. dept. ob/gyn La. State U. Med. Ctr., 2001—. Mem. La. Bd. Nursing, 1996—; mem. com. on prescriptive authority for Advanced Practice RN (APRN), 1996—97; alt. officer, 1998; v.p., 1999—2000; pres. La. Bd. Nursing, 2000—; bd. dirs. Maternal Child Coalition, 2001—; mem. Commn. for Anesthesia Assts., 2001—. Dir. youth Music Fellowship Bapt. Ch., Columbia, 1990-92; youth Sunday sch. tchr. Fellowship Bapt. Ch., 1995-96, softball coach Caldwell Parish Dixie Youth, Columbia, 1989-90. Mem. ANA, La. Nurse Practitioners (N.E. regional rep. 1990-95, prescriptive task force 1992-94, treas. 1995-97), Assn. Women's Health, Obstet. and Neonatal Nurses, Am. Inst. Ultrasound Medicine, Am. Acad. Nurse Practitioners (State award for Excellence 1991, state rep. 1995), La. Coalition for Maternal and Infant Health, Sigma Theta Tau. Democrat. Baptist. Avocations: fishing, swimming, camping, bowling, volleyball. Home: 1780 Blankston Rd Monroe LA 71202-9681 Office: La State U Med Ctr E A Conway Divsn 4864 Jackson St Monroe LA 71202-6400 E-mail: pmccla@lsuhsc.edu.

MCCLANE, ROBERT SANFORD, former bank holding company executive, entrepreneur; b. Kenedy, Tex., May 5, 1939; s. Norris Robert and Ella Addie (Stochton) McC.; m. Sue Nitschke, Mar. 31, 1968; children: Len Stokes McClane Brown, Norris Robert. BS in Bus. Adminstrn., Trinity U., San Antonio, 1961. With Ford Motor Co., Detroit, 1961-62; with Frost Nat. Bank, San Antonio, 1962-97, mem. staff, 1962-68, v.p., 1968-78; exec. v.p. Cullen/Frost Bankers, Inc., 1976—85, pres., 1985-97, dir., 1985—, Benefit Planners, Inc., 1997-2001; advisor, dir. Ellison Grandchildren Trust, 1996—; pres., owner McClane Ptnrs., LLC, 1997—; dir., vice chmn. Tobin Internat., 1998—. Bd. dirs. Frost Nat. Bank, San Antonio, Princeton eCom, Prism Acquisition Corp., Prodigy Comm. Corp. Crusade chmn. Bexar County chpt. Am. Cancer Soc., 1974; bd. dirs. Bexar County ARC, 1969-72; sr. warden St. Luke's Episopal Ch., San Antonio, 1980; trustee Alamo Pub. Telecomms. Coun., San Antonio, 1981-88, Trinity U., 1990, chmn., 2001—; chmn. San Antonio Econ. Devel. Found., 1987-89, exec. com. 1985-91. Mem. Greater San Antonio C. of C. (chmn. leadership San Antonio 1975-76, bd. dirs. exec. com. 1994-97, chmn. 1996), Trinity U. Alumni Assn. (pres. 1968-69, disting. alumnus 1987), Free Trade Alliance San Antonio (bd. dirs., exec. com. 1997—, chmn. 1998-2000), Southwest Rsch. Inst. (trustee 1997—), San Antonio German Club, Order Alamo, Tex. Cavaliers, Argyle Club, Club Giraud, Plaza Club (bd. dirs. 1973-92). Episcopalian. Office: 1616 Frost Bank Tower 100 W Houston St San Antonio TX 78205-1414 E-mail: bmcclane@frostbank.com.

MCCLARD, JACK EDWARD, lawyer; b. Lafayette, La., May 13, 1946; s. Lee Franklin and Mercedes Cecile (Landry) McC.; m. Marilyn Kay O'Gorman, June 3, 1972; 1 child, Lauren Minton. BA in Hist., Rice U., 1968; JD, U. Tex., 1974. Bar: Va. 1974, D.C. 1981, N.Y. 1985, Tex. 1996, U.S. Dist. Ct. (ea. and we. dists.) Va. 1974, U.S. Dist. Ct. D.C. 1981, U.S. Dist. Ct. (so. and ea. dists.) N.Y. 1985, U.S. Dist. Ct. (ea. dist.) Tex. 1998, U.S. Ct. Appeals (4th cir.) 1978, U.S. Ct. Appeals (D.C. cir.) 1980, U.S. Ct. Appeals (5th cir.) 1993, U.S. Ct. Appeals (7th cir.) 2001. Assoc. Hunton & Williams, Richmond, Va., 1974-81, ptnr., 1981—. Contbr. articles to profl. jours., books. Served to lt. (j.g.) USN, 1968-71. Mem. ABA, Va. Bar Assn., Richmond Bar Assn., Assn., 5th Cir. Bar, John Marshall Inns of Ct. Democrat. Episcopalian. Avocations: bridge, gardening, wine. Home: 100 Trowbridge Rd Richmond VA 23233-5724 Office: Hunton & Williams Riverfront Plz E Tower 951 E Byrd St Richmond VA 23219-4074 E-mail: jmcclard@hunton.com.

MC CLARREN, ROBERT ROYCE, librarian; b. Delta, Ohio, Mar. 15, 1921; s. Dresden William Howard and Norma Leona (Whiteman) Mc Clarren; m. Margaret Aileen Weed (dec. Oct. 2001); children: Mark Robert(dec.) , Todd Adams. Student, Antioch Coll., 1938-40; AB, Muskingum Coll., 1942; MA in English, Ohio State U., 1951; MS in L.S., Columbia, 1954; DLitt (hon.), Rosary Coll. (now Dominican U., 1989. Registration officer VA, Cin., 1946-47; instr. English Gen. Motors Inst., 1949-50; head circulation dept. Oak Park (Ill.) Pub. Libr., 1954-55, acting head librarian, 1955; head librarian Crawfordsville (Ind.) Pub. Libr., 1955-58, Huntington Pub. Libr., Western Counties Regional Pub. Libr., W.Va., 1958-62; dir. Ind. State Libr., 1962-67; system dir. North Suburban Libr. System, 1967-89, system dir. emeritus, 1990—; cons. libr. Chgo. Pub. Libr. Found., 1990. Del. White House Conf. on Librs., 1979; instr. U. Wis., summer 1964, Rosary Coll., 1968-80, U. Tex., summer 1979, 82, No. Ill. U., 1980; pres. W.Va. Libr. Assn., 1960, Ill. Libr. Assn., 1975; mem. Gov. Ind. Commn. Arts, 1964-65, Ill. State Libr. Adv. Com., 1972-79, 87-89, chmn., 1975-79, vice chmn., 1988-89; bd. dirs. Ill. Regional Libr. Coun., 1972-82, pres., 1977; chmn. adv. commn. Nat. Periodical System, Nat. Commn. on Librs. and Info. Sci., 1978-81; treas. Ill. Coalition Libr. Advs., 1982-89. Contbr. articles to profl. jours. Served to 1st lt. AUS, 1942-46, 51-52; maj. Res. Named Ill. Librarian of Yr., 1978; recipient Sagamore of Wabash (Ind.), 1966. Mem. ALA (councilor 1966-68, 74-78, treas. 1968-72, endowment trustee 1972-78, mem. publ. bd. 1972-75, pres. reference and adult svc. div. 1975-76, Joseph-Towne Wheeler award 1954, Melville Dewey award 1989, Nat. Libr. Advocacy Honor Roll 2000), Assn. State and Coop. Libr. Agys. (prs. 1972), Beta Phi Mu. Home: 1560 Oakwood Pl Deerfield IL 60015-2014 Office: 200 W Dundee Rd Wheeling IL 60090-4750

MCCLARY, JAMES DALY, retired contractor; b. Boise, Idaho, July 19, 1917; s. Neil Hamaker and Myrtle (Daly) McC.; m. Mary Jane Munger, Feb. 2, 1939; children: Pamela, John. Student, Boise Jr. Coll., 1934-36, AA, 1957; AB, Stanford U., 1938; LLD, Gonzaga U., 1976. Laborer to supt. Morrison-Knudsen Co., Inc., Boise, 1932-42, project mgr., asst. dist. mgr., 1942- 47, gen. mgr. Mexican subs., 1947-51, asst. to gen. mgr., 1951-53, asst. gen. mgr., 1953-60, dir., 1955-78, v.p., 1956-60, exec v.p., 1960-72, chmn. bd., 1972-78. Mem., vice chmn. Idaho Permanent Bldg. Fund Adv. Council, 1961-64, chmn., 1964-71 Treas. Idaho Rep. Cen. Com., 1964-70; presdl. elector, 1968; trustee Boise Jr. Coll., 1960-83, vice chmn., 1967-73, chmn., 1973-83; bd. dirs. Boise State U. Found., Inc., 1964-91, pres., 1970-81; bd. dirs. AGC Edn. and Rsch. Found., 1974-91, pres., 1974-90; elector Hall of Fame for Great Ams., 1976—; trustee St. Alphonsus Regional Med. Ctr., 1976-82, vice chmn., 1981-82. Recipient George Washington medal of honor Freedoms Found., Valley Forge, Pa., 1977, Disting. Alumnus award Boise State U., 1988, Silver medallion, 1996; decorated Chevalier and Legion of Honor, Order of DeMolay; named Disting. Alumnus of Yr. Boise State U. Alumni Assn., 1971. Fellow ASCE, Am. Inst. Constructors; mem. Internat. Rd. Fedn. (bd. dirs. 1972-78, vice chmn. 1977-78), Soc. Am. Mil. Engrs., Assoc. Gen. Contractors Am. (bd. dirs., exec. com. 1961-78, pres. 1972), Cons. Constructors Coun. Am., Newcomen Soc., Conf. Bd. (sr.), Idaho Assn. Commerce and Industry (bd. dirs., chmn. 1974-77, Harwood award 1994), Moles (hon., award for Outstanding Achievement in Constrn. 1976, Mem. award 1978), Hillcrest Country Club (bd. dirs. 1965-67, 69, pres. 1967), Arid Club (exec. com. 1966), Ariz. Club (Scottsdale), Ariz. Country Club (Phoenix), Univ. Club (Mexico City), Stanford Club (Washington). Episcopalian. Home: 4903 Roberts Rd Boise ID 83705-2805

MCCLARY, JIM MARSTON, accounting executive, consultant; b. Nashville, Feb. 26, 1949; s. Joseph Patrick and Daisy Wynell (Marston) McC.; m. Billie Sue Gwinn, Feb. 27, 1970; children: Traci Gwinn, Matthew Ryan. BSBA with honors, U. Tenn., 1974. CPA, Tenn.; cert. personal fin. specialist. Staff acct. Price Waterhouse & Co. CPAs, Nashville, 1974-76; sr. acct. Bradley & Crenshaw, CPAs, 1976-77; controller Holder & No. Lumber Sales, Inc., 1977-78; pres. Retirement Plans, Inc., 1978-80; ptnr. McClary, Yeary & Howell, CPAs, Brentwood, Tenn., 1980-85; cons. Franklin, 1985—; pres. Employee Benefit Svcs. Inc., Brentwood, 1985—. Ops. prin. Thoroughbred Fin. Svcs., LLC, Brentwood, 1985—, cons. 1985—. Served with USAF, 1968-69. Mem. AICPA, Tenn. Soc. CPAs, U.S. C. of C. Republican. Avocation: athletics. Office: Employee Benefit Svcs Inc 5038 Thoroughbred Ln Brentwood TN 37027-4225 E-mail: jmcclary@thoroughmedfinalcial.com.

MCCLARY, LORETTA M. accounting educator; b. Boston, July 18, 1957; d. Loretto J. and Mary L. (Rufo) Salvucci; m. Richard E. McClary, May 17, 1980 (dec. Apr. 1997); children: Loretta, Robert, Gina. BA, Regis Coll., 1979; MA, Boston U., 1980; MBA, Suffolk U., 1984; MS in Taxation, advanced taxation cert., Bentley Coll., 1990. CPA, Mass. With fin. dept. GSA, Boston, 1979-84; acct. Feeley & Driscoll PC, 1986-97; prof. acct. LaSell Coll., Newton, Mass., 1996—. Mem. fin. com. Our Lady's Parish, Waltham, Mass., 1996-97. Mem. AICPA, Mass. Soc. CPA's. Avocation: golf. Home: 438 Main St Waltham MA 02452-6129 Office: LaSell Coll Dept Bus 1844 Commonwealth Ave Auburndale MA 02466-2709

MCCLATCHY, J. D. editor, writer, educator; b. Bryn Mawr, Pa., Aug. 12, 1945; s. J. Donald and Mary Jane (Hayden) McC. BA summa cum laude, Georgetown U., 1967; PhD, Yale U., 1974. Instr. English dept. LaSalle Coll., Phila., 1968-71; asst. prof. English dept. Yale U., New Haven, 1974-81, lectr. English dept., 1983, 86-87; writer-in-residence CCNY, 1982; writer-in-residence Poetry Ctr. 92d St. YMCA, N.Y.C., 1983-84, workshop leader Poetry Ctr., 1982-91; lectr. Creative Writing program, English dept. Princeton U., 1981-87, 89-93; editor The Yale Rev., New Haven, 1991—. Poet-in-residence Southampton Writers Conf., 1988; lectr. MFA Parsons/New Sch., 1989, English dept. Rutgers U., 1989, writing divsn. Columbia U., 1989, 92; vis. prof. English dept. UCLA, 1990, 92; selection com. Conn. Poetry Cir. Author: (poetry) Scenes from Another Life, 1981, (London 1983), Lantskip, Platan, Creatures Ramp'd, 1983, Stars Principal, 1986, Kilim, 1987, The Rest of the Way, 1990, (poetry) Ten Commandments, 1998; librettist: A Question of Taste, 1989, Mario and the Magician, 1994, Orpheus Decending, 1994, Emmeline, 1996; editor: The Yale Review, 1991—, (books) Anne Sexton: The Artist and Her Critics, 1978, For James Merrill: A Birthday Tribute, 1986, Recitative: Prose by James Merrill, 1986, Poets on Painters: Essays on the Art of Painting by Twentieth Century Poets, 1988, The Vintage Book of Contemporary American Poetry, 1990, Woman in White: Selected Poems of Emily Dickinson, 1991, The Vintage Book of Contemporary World Poetry, 1996, Twenty Questions, 1998, Christmas Poems, 1999, On Wings of Song, 2000, The Magic Flute (translation) 2000, Longfellow, Selected Poetry and Prose, 2000, Poems of the Sea, 2001, Love Speaks its Name, 2001, Bright Pages: Yale Writers, 1701-2001, 2001, James Merrill: Collected Poems, 2001, James Merrill: Collected Novels and Plays, 2002, Hazmat, 2002, Horace: The Odes, 2002, Division of Spoils, 2002; translator Carmen, 2001; assoc. editor Four Quarters, 1968-71; contbg. editor Am. Poetry Review; poetry editor The Yale Review, 1981-91; trans. articles, contbr. poems, stories, articles, reviews to various jours. Fellow Am. Acad. Arts and Scis., 1998—; mem. Am. Acad. Arts and Ltrs., 1999—; bd. dirs. Ingram Merrill Found., 1986-99; chancellor The Acad. of Am. Poets, 1996—. Recipient gold medal Vergilian Acad., 1967, O. Henry award, 1972, prize Am. Acad. Poets ,1972, Chase Going Woodhouse Poetry prize, 1976, Michener award, 1982, Gordon Barber Meml. award Poetry Soc. Am., 1984, Eunice Tietjens Meml. prize Poetry Mag., 1985, Witter Bynner Poetry prize Am. Acad. and Inst. Arts and Letters, 1985, award in lit., 1991, Oscar Blumenthal prize Poetry Mag., 1988, Levinson prize, 1990, Melville Cane award Poetry Soc. Am., 1991, Literary Lion N.Y. Pub. Libr., 1992; grantee Ingram Merrill Found., 1979, Conn. Commn. Arts, 1981; fellow NEA, 1987, John Simon Guggenheim Meml. Found., 1988; fellow lit. Acad. Am. Poets, 1991; artist resident Djerassi Found., 1988; Woodrow Wilson fellow 1967-68; Yale U. fellow, 1971-72; Ethel Boise Morgan fellow, 1972-74; artist's fellow N.Y. Found. Arts, 1986; artist resident Yaddo, 1991, MacDowell Colony, 1991. Mem. Am. Acad. Poets (chancellor 1996), Phi Beta Kappa, Alpha Sigma Nu. Home: 15 Grand St Stonington CT 06378-1340 Office: The Yale Review Yale Univ PO Box 208243 New Haven CT 06520-8243

MCCLATCHY, KEVIN S. professional sports team executive; b. Sacramento, Jan. 13, 1963; Diploma in Polit. Sci., U. Calif., Santa Barbara. Sport producer WPLG-TV, Miami; mktg. profl. Knight-Ridder Newspapers; nat. sales mgr. Newspaper Network (subs. McClatchy Newspapers); CEO, mng. gen. ptnr. Pittsburgh Pirates, 1996—; bus. opers. mgr. Amador Ledger-Dispatch, Calif., 1990. Co-owner Modesto A's, Oakland Athletics. Trustee Trinity-Pawling H.S., Pawling, N.Y., U. Calif. Santa Barbara; active United Way, Roberto Clemente Found., Extra Mile Found., U. Pitts. Cancer Inst., also Catholic charities. Office: Pittsburgh Pirates 115 Federal St Pittsburgh PA 15212*

MCCLAUGHERTY, JOE L. lawyer, educator; b. June 1, 1951; s. Frank Lee and Elease (Terrell) McC. BBA with honors, U. Tex., 1973, JD with honors, 1976. Bar: Tex. 1976, N.Mex. 1976, U.S. Dist. Ct. N.Mex. 1976, U.S. Ct. Appeals (10th cir.) 1976, U.S. Supreme Ct. 1979, Colo. 1988. Assoc. Rodey, Dickason, Sloan, Akin & Robb, P.A., Albuquerque, 1976-81, ptnr., dir., 1981-87, resident ptnr. Santa Fe, 1983-87, mng. ptnr., 1985-87; ptnr. Kemp, Smith, Duncan & Hammond, P.C., 1987-92, mng. ptnr., 1987-92; ptnr. McClaugherty & Silver, P.C., Santa Fe, 1992—. Adj. prof. law U. N.Mex., Albuquerque, 1983—; faculty Nat. Inst. Trial Advocacy, so. regional, So. Meth. U. Law Sch., 1983—, Rocky Mt. regional, U. Denver Law Sch., 1986—, nat. session U. Colo. Law Sch., 1987; faculty Hastings Ctr. for Trial and Appellate Advocacy, 1985—; bd. dirs. MCM Corp., Raleigh, N.C., Brit.-Am. Ins. Co., Ltd., Nassau, The Bahamas, 1985-91. Mem. N.Mex. Bar Assn. (bd. dirs. trial practice sect. 1976-85, chairperson 1983-84, dir. young lawyers divsn. 1978-80), N.Mex. Assn. Def. Lawyers (pres. 1982-83, bd. dirs. 1982-85). Office: McClaugherty & Silver PC PO Box 8680 Santa Fe NM 87504-8680

MCCLAUGHERTY, JOHN LEWIS, lawyer; b. Bluefield, W.Va., Feb. 13, 1931; s. William N. and N. Louisa (Shelton) McC.; m. Sallie M. Fredeking, June 27, 1953; children: Martha M. Nepa, John W. BS, Northwestern U., 1953; LLB, W.Va. U., 1956. Bar: W.Va. 1956, U.S. Dist. Ct. (so. dist.) W.Va. 1956, U.S. Ct. Appeals (4th cir.) 1956, U.S. Supreme Ct. 1975, U.S. Ct. Mil. Appeals 1957. Assoc. Jackson & Kelly, Charleston, W.Va., 1959-65, ptnr., 1965-86; mng. mem. Jackson & Kelly Pllc, 1986—. Mem. com. Nat. Conf. Commrs. on Uniform State Laws, Chgo., 1977—, pres. 1999-01; pres. Ea. Mineral Law Found., Lexington, Ky., 1983-84; bd. dirs., Wesbanco Bank, Inc., Charleston. Contbr. articles to profl. jours., chpts. to books. Pres. W.Va. Symphony Orch., Charleston, 1982—; vice-chmn. Am. Symphony Orch. League, Washington, 1991-00, W.Va. Wesleyan Coll., Buckhannon, 1989-94; bd. dirs. Charleston Renaissance Corp., Fund for Arts; mem. exec. com. Arts Advocacy Com. of W.Va., Inc.; former trustee United Meth. Charities of W.Va., Inc.; vice chmn. Clay Ctr. for Arts and Scis. of W.Va. 1st lt. USAF, 1956-59. Recipient Mayor's award for Arts Vol., 1990, Individual Art Patron of Yr. award Coll. of Creative Arts of W.Va. U., 1998, YMCA's Spirit of Valley award, 1998, Professionalism award U.S. Ct. Appeals (4th cir.), 1999, James R. Thomas II Outstanding Vol. award Charleston Renaissance Corp., 1999, Sam Walton Bus. Leader award Sam's Club and Wal-mart, 1999, Disting. Reader award Read Aloud W.Va., 1999, Outstanding Vol. Fund Raiser award W.Va. chpt. Nat. Soc. Fund Raising Execs., 2000, Disting. W.Va. award Gov. W.Va. Fellow Am. Bar Found. (life); mem. ABA, W.Va. Bar Found. (pres. 1994-98, Lawyer Citizen of Yr. award 1998), Am. Judicature Soc., W.Va. Bar Assn. (pres. 1995-96), Kanawha County Bar Assn. (pres. 1980-82, Outstanding Achievement award for meritorious svc. to the legal profession and the cmty. 1995), 2nd Cent. Leadership award, W.V. State Coll. Found., W.Va. State C. of C. (chmn. workers compensation and unemployment compensation com., chmn., bd. dirs., exec. com.), Kiwanis, Masons, Shriners, Order of Coif. Democrat. Methodist. Home: 3 Bendcrest Pl Charleston WV 25314-1510 Office: Jackson & Kelly PLLC PO Box 553 Charleston WV 25322-0553 E-mail: jmcclaugherty@jacksonkelly.com.

MCCLAVE, DONALD SILSBEE, professional society administrator; b. Cleve., May 7, 1941; s. Charles Green and Anne Elizabeth (Oakley) McC.; m. Christine Phyllis Mary Tomkins, Feb. 19, 1966; children: Andrew Green, Susan Elizabeth (dec.). BA, Denison U., 1963. Mktg. rsch. officer Bank of Calif., San Francisco, 1968-70; v.p. Cen. Nat. Bank, Chgo., 1970-75, First Interstate Bank, Portland, Oreg., 1975-77, sr. v.p., 1977-79, exec. v.p., 1979-86; pres., CEO Portland Met. C. of C., 1987—2002; asst. to pres. Portland State U., 2002—. Instr. Grad. Sch. Mktg. and Strategic Planning, Athens, 1982-84, Pacific Coast Sch. Banking, Seattle, 1976-78. Pres. Oreg. Episc. Sch. Bd., Portland, 1983-84; pres. Assn. Oreg. Industries Found., Salem, 1984-85; pres., co-chmn. Japan-Am. Conf. Mayors and C. of C., Portland, 1985, trustee, 1991—, exec. com., 1992-97; trustee YMCA of Columbia-Willamette, 1990-92, Portland Student Svcs. Corp., 1991-93; mem. METRO Urban Growth Mgmt. Adv. Com., 1989-92; mem. adv. com. Downtown Housing Preservation Partnership Adv. Com., 1989-94; mem. City of Portland Mayoral Transition Team, 1992, Mayor's Bus. Roundtable, 1993—; bd. dirs. Oreg. Trail chpt. ARC, 1994-95, Tri-Met, 1994—, chair fin. com., 1995—; dir. United Way Columbia Willamette, 1978-83, 2000-01; dir. Urban League Portland, 2000-01. Capt. USAF, 1963-68. Mem. Oreg. Chamber Execs. Assn. (pres. 1998-2002). Avocations: reading, travel, golf, model building. Office: Portland State U PO Box 751 Portland OR 97207-0751

MCCLAY, HARVEY CURTIS, data processing executive; b. Houston, Jan. 2, 1939; s. Clarence and Agnes E. McC.; m. Patricia Lott, Jan. 8, 1961; children: James, John, Susan, Robert. BA in Math., Rice U., 1960. Field engr. Western Electric Co., Marysville, Calif., 1960-62; analyst math. Litton Data Systems Co., Canoga Park, 1962-63; mgr. programming Lockheed Electronics Co., Houston, 1967-75; systems mgr. City of Houston, 1975-77; project mgr. fin. systems devel. Brown & Root, Houston, 1977-81; mgr. data processing Nat. Supply, 1981-84; project mgr. Computer Scis. Corp., 1984-92, Grumman Tech. Svcs., Houston, 1992-95; exec. dir., applications Houston Ind. Sch. Dist., 1996—. Instr. data processing and mgmt. Houston Community Coll. Home: 2911 Huckleberry Ln Pasadena TX 77502-5409 E-mail: hmcclay@houstonisd.org.

MCCLEARY, BENJAMIN WARD, investment banker; b. Washington, July 9, 1944; s. George William and Nancy (Grim) McC.; m. Dierdre Marsters, May 6, 1967 (div. 1977); children: Benjamin, Katherine; m. Jean Muchmore, Oct. 15, 1983. AB, Princeton U., 1966. With Chemical Bank, N.Y.C., 1969-81, trainee, asst. sec., asst. v.p., v.p.; sr. v.p. Lehman Bros. Kuhn Loeb, N.Y.C., 1981-83; mng. dir. Shearson Lehman Bros., 1983-87, Shearson Lehman Hutton Internat., London, 1987-88, Shearson Lehman Hutton, Inc., N.Y.C., 1988-89; ptnr. McFarland Dewey & Co., LLC, 1989—. Dir. Detrex Corp., Detroit, Harvel Plastics, Easton. Lt. (j.g.) USN, 1966-69. Office: McFarland Dewey & Co LLC 230 Park Ave Rm 1450 New York NY 10169-1450 E-mail: mccleary@mcfd.com.

MCCLEARY, BERYL NOWLIN, civic worker, travel agency executive; b. Ft. Worth, Feb. 22, 1929; d. Henry Bryant and Phyllis (Tenney) Nowlin; m. Henry Glenn McCleary, May 29, 1950; children: Laura Gail, Glenn Nowlin, Neil Ray, Paul Tenney. BS in Zoology, Tex. Tech U., 1950. Owner, mgr. Beryl McCleary Travels, Chicago, 1975-81, Denver, 1981-84. Treas. Kappa Alpha Theta Ednl. Found., Tex. Christian U., Ft. Worth, 1958-61; pres. study club Jr. Woman's Club, Ft. Worth, 1959-60; pres. Symphony League, Ft. Worth, 1961-62; v.p., dir. Ft. Worth Symphony Orch. Assn. Inc., 1961; treas. Jr. Pro-Am Tarrant County, 1961-62; corr. sec. Ft. Worth Children's Mus. Guild, 1961; sec. Tarrant County (Tex.) Democratic Exec. Com., 1956-62; pres. guild, bd. dirs. Maadi Community Ch., Cairo, 1964-66; mem. women's bd. Lincoln Park Zool. Soc., Chgo, 1976-81; mem. Episcopal Ch. Women's Diocesan Bd., Chgo., 1976-79; pres., charter mem. Rainbow Investment Club, London, 1970-71, travel dir. Over the Hill Gang Ski Team Internat., Denver, 1982-84. Mem. AAAS, DAR, Geol. Geophys. Aux., Service Club Chgo., Jr. League Denver, Denver Symphony Guild, Central City Opera Guild, Houston Symphony League, Alpha Epsilon Delta, Kappa Alpha Theta (charter mem. Gamma Phi chpt. 1953). Home: 232 Warrenton Dr Houston TX 77024-6226 E-mail: berylmcc@juno.com.

MCCLEARY, ELLIOTT HAROLD, magazine editor; b. Dixon, Ill., Sept. 12, 1927; s. Harold Elliott and Ruth C. (LieVan) McC.; m. Ann Roberts Morgan, Aug. 18, 1962 (div. 1976); children: Bryan, Heather; m. Patricia Mary Sherburne McCabe, Feb. 10, 1996. BA in English, Beloit Coll., 1952. Asst. editor Popular Mechs. mag., Chgo., 1952-56, Rotarian Mag., Evanston, Ill., 1956-65; editor-in-chief Today's Health mag., Chgo., 1966-69; freelance writer, editor Evanston, 1969-78, 81-82; sr. editor Rand McNally, Skokie, Ill., 1978-81, Consumers Digest mag., Chgo., 1983-85, exec. editor, 1986-98, contbg. editor, 1998-99. Author: New Miracles of Childbirth, 1974; co-author: American Medical Association Book of Heartcare, 1982. With U.S. Army, 1946-48. Mem. Am. Soc. Journalists and Authors (pres. Midwest chpt. 1980, 93-95). Avocation: photography. Home: 2747 Meadowlark Ln Evanston IL 60201-4937

MCCLEARY, HENRY GLEN, geophysicist; b. Casper, Wyo., June 4, 1922; s. Raymond and Wyoma N. (Posey) McCleary Grieve; m. Beryl Tenney Nowlin, May 28, 1950; children: Gail, Glenn, Neil, Paul. Geol. Engr., Colo. Sch. Mines, 1948. From geophysicist to party chief seismic Amoco, various locations, 1948-53; exploration mgr. Woodson Oil Co., Fort Worth, 1953-60; resident mgr. NAMCO, Tripoli, Libya, 1961-62; chief geophysicist to staff geophys. assoc. Amoco Internat. Oil Co., 1963-86, Cairo, London and Buenos Aires, 1963-73, Chgo., 1973-84, Denver, 1983-84, Houston, 1984-86; internat. geophys. cons., 1986—. Served with USN, 1943-46. Named Hon. Admiral Tex. Navy, 1968. Mem. Soc. Exploration Geophysicists, Soc. Petroleum Engrs., AAAS, Houston Gem and Mineral Soc., Profl. Oil People, Sigma Alpha Epsilon, Theta Tau. Clubs: Adventurers, Meml. Forest (Houston). Republican. Episcopalian. Home: 232 Warrenton Dr Houston TX 77024-6226

MCCLEARY, LLOYD E(VERALD), education educator; b. Bradley, Ill., May 10, 1924; s. Hal and Pearl McC.; m. Iva Dene Carter, June 13, 1971; children: Joan Kay, Victoria Lea, Karen Ann. Student, Kans. U., 1941-42; BS, U. Ill., 1948, MS, 1950, D.Ed., 1956; postgrad., Sorbonne, Paris, 1946. Tchr., asst. prin. Portland (Oreg.) Public Schs., 1949-51; asst. prin. Univ. High Sch., Urbana, Ill., 1951-52, prin., 1953-56; asst. supt. Evanston Twp. (Ill.) High Sch., 1956-60; assoc. Roosevelt U., 1957-69; mem. faculty U. Mich., summers, 1958-59; prof. ednl. adminstrn. U. Utah, 1969—, chmn. dept., 1969-74. Assoc. CFK Ltd. Found., 1971-76; dir. projects in Latin Am. for AID, World Bank, Ford Found., Bolivian Govt.; dir. Nat. Sch. Prin. Study, 1976-79, 86-89, res. project Families in Edn., 1992-94; edn. rep. to Utah People to People Program; Keynoter Asian Conf. Edn., 1985; edn. adviser Office of the Queen, Jordan, 1985-86; advisor Nat. Commn. on Standards in the Principalship; U.S. del. Conf. on Status Children, Senegal, 1992, Yr. of the Family, Malta, 1993; J. Lloyd Trump lectr., New Orleans, 1994. Author: Organizational Analysis X-Change, 1975, Politics and Power in Education, 1976, The Senior High School Principalship, 1980, Educational Administration, Today, 1984, High School Leaders and Their Schools, vols. 1 and 2, 1990, Leadership, 1996; editor Western Hemisphere Edn. Sch. Orgn., 1989—. Served with inf. AUS, 1941-46. Decorated Bronze Star with oak leaf cluster, Army Commendation medal; S.D. Shankland fellow, 1956; Grantee Ford Found., 1968, 72, AID, 1966, 67, 70, 72, 74, 76, CFK Ltd., 1970-74, Rockefeller Family Found., 1979-80, U.S. Dept. State, 1981, 86-87, U.S. Dept. Def., 1986—; recipient Hatch Prize, 1988-89. Mem. Nat. Assn. Secondary Sch. Prins. (cert. of merit 1978, scholar-in-residence fall 1989, grantee 1969, 77, 86—), Assn. Supervision and Curriculum Devel., Nat. Assn. Elem. Sch. Prins., Phi Delta Kappa, Kappa Delta Pi. Methodist. Home: 1470 Wilton Way Salt Lake City UT 84108-2549 Office: U Utah 339 MBH Salt Lake City UT 84112

MCCLEARY, PAUL FREDERICK, voluntary agency executive; b. Bradley, Ill., May 2, 1930; s. Hal C. and Pearl (Aeicher) McC.; AB, Olivet Nazarene U., Kankakee, Ill., 1952; MDiv, Garrett-Evang. Sem., Evanston, Ill., 1956; MA, Northwestern U., 1972; DD, MacMurray Coll., Jacksonville, Ill., 1970; m. Rachel Timm, Jan. 26, 1951; children— Leslie Ann, Rachel Mary, John Wesley, Timothy Paul. Ordained to ministry United Methodist Ch., 1956; missionary in Bolivia, 1957-68; exec. sec. structure study commn. United Meth. Ch., 1969-72, asst. gen. sec. to Latin Am., 1972-75; exec. dir. Ch. World Service, N.Y.C., 1975-84; assoc. gen. sec. for research Gen. Council on Ministries, United Meth. Ch., 1984-87; exec. v.p. Save the Children, Westport, Conn., 1987-88; pres. Christian Children's Fund Inc., 1988-95, For Children, Inc., 1995—; cons. World Bank, Interam. Devel. Bank; mem. adv. coun. Overseas Devel. Council; mem. adv. com. on economic matters World Council Chs.; mem. com. on African Devel. Strategies; mem. Com. on Dialogue and Devel., Nat. Leadership Commn. on Health Care, Bretton Woods Com.; pres. NGO com. on UNICEF, CODEL, Christian Century Found.; mem. Mattell Ind. Monitoring Coun.; vis. prof. Johns Hopkins Sch. Advanced Internat. Studies. Mem. AAAS, Acad. Polit. Sci., Latin Am. Studies Assn., Masons,

Rotary, Alpha Kappa Lambda. Democrat. Author: Global Justice and World Hunger, 1978; co-author: Quality of Life in a Global Society, 1978; contbr. articles to mags. E-mail: pmccfc@aol.com. Office: For Children Inc 20 Malanga Ct Scotch Plains NJ 07076-1642 Home: 20 Malanga Ct Scotch Plains NJ 07076-1642

MCCLEARY, SCOTT FITZGERALD, lawyer; b. Oak Park, Ill., Nov. 19, 1962; s. John Mark and Beverly Jane (Stange) McC.; m. Kelly Elizabeth Shaff, Sept. 5, 1987; children: Ian Fitzgerald, Kara Hope. BA in Polit. Sci. and History, North Ctrl. Coll., 1984; JD, Northwestern U., 1987. Bar: Ill. 1987. Assoc. Moses and Heimsoth, Aurora, Ill., 1988-89; asst. city atty. City of Aurora, 1989-92, exec. asst. to mayor, 1992-97, asst. corp. counsel, 1997, 1999—, budget analyst, 1997-99. Mem. Villa Park (Ill.) Pub. Libr. Bd., 1983-89, pres., 1985-88, v.p., 1988-89, sec., 1989; mem. Villa Park Hist. Preservation Commn., 1985-89, vice chmn., 1985-87, chmn., 1987-89; mem. Aurora Pub. Libr. Bd., 1991-98, DuPage Libr. Sys. Bd., Geneva, Ill., 1992-98, pres., 1996-98; sec., mem. Cmtys. in Schs. Bd., Aurora, 19 96—; mem. Big Bros./Big Sisters Resource Bd., Aurora, 1997-98, Family Counseling Svcs. Bd., Aurora, 1997—, treas., 1999—; bd. dirs. Fox Valley Girl Scout Coun., 2002—. Mem. Ill. State Bar Assn., Kane County Bar Assn. Avocations: reading, walking, traveling, stamps. Home: 206 S Gladstone Ave Aurora IL 60506-4838 Office: City of Aurora 44 E Downer Pl Aurora IL 60505-3302

MCCLEERY, WINSTON THEODORE, computer consulting company executive; b. Mobile, Ala., Sept. 6, 1935; s. Robert Alton and Theadora K. (Kiebel) McC.; m. Sandra Thoss, Dec. 28, 1958; children: Winston T., Jacqueline McCleery McNeely. BS, Springhill Coll., 1957; postgrad., U. Ala., 1957-58. Logic design engr. Autonetics N.Am. Aviation, Anaheim, Calif., 1960-63; dirt. info. sys. Litton Industries, L.A., 1963-69; founder, owner Winston T. McCleery, Cons., 1969—; pres., CEO Mgmt. Software Systems, Inc., Mobile, 1979—. Patentee in field. With U.S. Army, 1958-60. Recipient Cert. for Heroism Boy Scouts Am., 1949. Mem. Data Processing Mgmt. Assn., Assn. Computer Machinery, Am. Mgmt. Assn., Ind. Computer Cons.'s Assn., Optimists (pres. 1972). Republican. Achievements include contributions to the design and development of the U.S. Army Field Artillery's first digital fire direction computer; member of design team of the centaur missile's guidance system that made the first soft landing on the moon; design and development of the first seamless, integrated, on-line and instant-time computer application system for main frame class computers; inventor of computer power and temperature enviroment control system, development of first automatic documentation system used to document computer programs written in the Cobol language. Home: 5213 Janekyn Dr Mobile AL 36693-4142 Office: PO Box 9365 Mobile AL 36691-0365

MCCLELLAN, BARRY DEAN, city manager; b. Parsons, Kans., Sept. 20, 1946; s. Don Leonard and Doris Elaine (Hamsher) McC.; m. Marshal Ellen Neuber, May 14, 1978 (div. Apr. 1990); children: Yvette, Scott, Jennie, Brian. BS, U. San Francisco, 1986; MPA, Calif. State U., San Bdrnardino, 1994. Registered engr., Calif. Assoc. engr. City of Riverside, Calif., 1969-78; mng. engr. Kicak & Assocs., Redlands, 1978-80; pub. works dir. City of Palm Desert, 1980-85; regional mgr. Neste, Brudin & Stone, Inc., Palm Springs, 1985-86; pub. works dir. City of Irvine, 1995-96, City of Moreno Valley, 1986-95, asst. city mgr., 1996—. Curriculum advisor U. Calif. Extension, Riverside, 1993-94. Chair regional steering com. United Way of Inland Valley, Riverside, 1997-2000, bd. dirs., 2000—; dir. Riverside County Regional Med. Ctr. Found., program adv. bd. pub. adminstrn. dept. Calif. State U., San Bernardino. Served with USAF, 1964-68. Named Outstanding Campaign Vol., United Way, 1998-99, 99-2000. Mem. Am. Soc. Pub. Adminstrn., Internat. City Mgmt. Assn., Rotary (bd. dirs. 1998-2001), Victoria Club, Moreno Valley Rotary Club (pres. 2000-2001). Republican. Avocations: exercise, travel, reading, golf. org. Home: 15600 Oliver St Moreno Valley CA 92555 Office: City of Moreno Valley PO Box 88005 Moreno Valley CA 92552-0805 E-mail: barrym@moval.

MC CLELLAN, CATHARINE, anthropologist, educator; b. York, Pa., Mar. 1, 1921; d. William Smith and Josephine (Niles) McClellan; m. John Thayer Hitchcock, June 6, 1974. AB magna cum laude in Classical Archaeology, Bryn Mawr Coll., 1942; PhD (Anthropology fellow), U. Calif. at Berkeley, 1950. Vis. asst. prof. U. Mo. at Columbia, 1952; asst. prof. anthropology U. Wash., Seattle, 1952-56; anthrop. cons. USPHS, Arctic Health Research Center, Alaska, 1956; asst. prof. anthropology, chmn. dept. anthropology Barnard Coll., Columbia U., 1956-61; asso. prof. anthropology U. Wis. at Madison, 1961-65, prof., 1965-83, prof. emeritus, 1983—, John Bascom prof., 1973. Vis. lectr. Bryn Mawr (Pa.) Coll., 1954; vis. prof. U. Alaska, 1973, 87. Assoc. editor: Arctic Anthropology, 1961; editor, 1975-82; assoc. editor: The Western Canadian Jour. of Anthropology, 1970-73. Served to lt. WAVES, 1942-46. Margaret Snell fellow AAUW, 1950-51; Am. Acad. Arts and Scis. grantee, 1963-64, Nat. Mus. Can. grantee, 1948-74 Fellow Am. Anthrop. Assn., Royal Anthrop. Inst. Gt. Britain and Ireland, AAAS, Arctic Inst. N.Am.; mem. Am. Ethnol. Soc. (sec.-treas. 1958-59, v.p. 1964, pres. 1965), Kroeber Anthrop. Soc., Am. Folklore Soc., Am. Soc. Ethnohistory (exec. com. 1968-71), Sigma Xi. Achievements include rsch. in archaeol. and ethnographic field investigations in Alaska and Yukon Territory in Can.

MCCLELLAN, CRAIG RENE, lawyer; b. Portland, Oreg., June 28, 1947; s. Charles Russell and Annette Irene (Benedict) McC.; m. Susan Armistead Nash, June 7, 1975; children: Ryan Alexander, Shannon Lea. BS in Econs., U. Oreg., 1969; JD magna cum laude, Calif. We. U., 1976. Bar: Calif. 1976, U.S. Dist. Ct. (so. dist.) Calif. 1976, U.S. Dist. Ct. (ea., ctrl., no. dists.) Calif. 1991, U.S. Supreme Ct. 1991. Compliance specialist Cost of Living Coun. and Price Commn., Washington, 1972-73, dir. Oil Policy subcom., 1973; ptnr. Luce, Forward, Hamilton & Scripps, San Diego, 1976-87; owner McClellan & Assocs., 1987—. Chmn. annual fundraising auction KPBS, 1984. Capt. USMC, 1969-72. Fellow Am. Coll. Trial Lawyers; mem. Assn. Trial Lawyers Am., Am. Bd. Trial Advocates, Am. Inns of Ct. (master), Calif. State Bar Assn., San Diego County Bar Assn., Calif. Trial Lawyers Assn. (bd. govs. 1985-87), San Diego Trial Lawyers Assn. (bd. dirs. 1983-90), Nat. Forensics League, Phi Gamma Delta, Phi Alpha Delta. Presbyterian. Avocations: reading, running, tennis, chess, civic activities. Office: McClellan & Assocs 1144 State St San Diego CA 92101-3529 E-mail: McClellansLaw@aol.com.

MCCLELLAN, DIXIE, secondary education educator; b. Freeburn, Ky., Dec. 4, 1940; d. Albert Eugene and Pauline (Lusk) McC.; m. Edward Lee Jessee, June 13, 1969 (div. Apr. 1975); m. Richard Joel McDuffee, July 2, 1996. BS in Edn., Concord Coll., Athens, W.Va.; MA in Polit. Sci., W.Va. U., 1972. Cert. secondary edn. tchr. Tchr. Roanoke County Schs., Salem, Va., 1959-62, Wyoming County Schs., Pineville, W.Va., 1962-64, Garrett County Schs., Oakland, Md., 1964-69, Preston County Schs., Kingwood, W.Va., 1969-72; Appalachian edn. specialist Appalachian Reigonal Com., Washington, 1972-77; rural devel. dir. Tenco Devel., Shelbyville, Tenn., 1977-81; exec. dir. Tenn. Export Devl. Assn., Nashville, 1982-85; pvt. cons., 1985-89; tchr. Williamson County Schs., 1989—. Chmn. Bedford County Adult Activity Ctr., Shelbyville, 1977-81; mem. Balance of State CETA Bd., Nashville, 1980-81; bd. dirs. Clan McClellan in Am., 1980-83. Writer monograph, grants, articles. Named to Outstanding Young Women of Am., 1979. Mem. Am. Polit. Sci. Assn., Profl. Educators Tenn. Republican. Episcopalian. Avocations: reading, gourmet cooking. Home: 2936 Spanntown Rd Arrington TN 37014-9123 Office: Centennial HS 5050 Mallory Ln Franklin TN 37067-1398 E-mail: McDuffee@mindspring.com.

MCCLELLAN, DONALD WILLIAM, JR. lawyer; b. Salem, Ohio, Nov. 5, 1960; s. Donald William and Doris Louis (McGhee) McC.; m. Bonnie Lynn Bailey, Aug. 9, 1986. BA, Kent State U., 1983; JD, Catholic U. Am., 1986. Bar: Ohio 1986, D.C. 1988, U.S. Ct. Appeals (D.C. cir.) 1988, U.S. Dist. Ct., D.C., 1989, U.S. Supreme Ct. 1989. With FCC, Washington, 1986-89, spl. asst. office of Chief Mass Media Bur., 1986-87, legal asst. to commr., 1987, spl. asst. office div. chief, policy div. Mass Media Bur., 1987-89; legis. counsel Office of U.S. Senator Conrad Burns, 1989-93; telecom. lawyer, policy mgr. Intel Corp., 1993-94; sr. comm. counsel U.S. Senate Com. on Commerce, Sci., and Transp., 1994-97; sr. fellow comm. legal and policy issues The Progress & Freedom Found., 1997-98; dir. govt. rels. Gateway Inc., Washington, 1998-99, v.p. govt. rels., 2000—. Mem. Fed. Communications Bar Assn., ABA (forum com. communications law), Ohio Bar Assn., Fed. Bar Assn., D.C. Bar Assn., Young Republicans Fedn. (pres. coll. republicans), Phi Alpha Delta, Omicron Delta Kappa, Alpha Lambda Delta, Blue Key, Alpha Kappa Mu, Alpha Epsilon Rho, Pi Sigma Alpha. Avocations: music, movies, golf, politics, television. Home: 5984 Wescott Hills Way Alexandria VA 22315-4746 Office: Gateway Inc 707 D St NW Washington DC 20004-2810 Fax: 202-737-2688. E-mail: donald.mcclellan@gateway.com.

MCCLELLAN, JOAN C. OSMUNDSON, retired art educator, artist; b. Milw., Jan. 5, 1934; d. Henry and Alma (Oyaas) Osmundson; m. Robert J. McClellan, Apr. 2, 1955 (dec.); children: Michael J., Linda A., Katherine M., Mary M. BS, SUNY, Buffalo, 1956; MA, Adelphi U., 1968; postgrad., SUNY, Buffalo, 1961, Hofstra U., 1966. Tchr. Harris Hill (N.Y.) Elem. Sch., 1957; art specialist Huth Rd. Sch., Grand Island, N.Y., 1958-59; art educator Prospect Ave Sch., East Meadow, 1959-89, W.T. Clarke High Sch., East Meadow, 1959-89. Exhibited in group shows including Sarasota Art Assn., 1989, Art League of Manatee County, 1989, Federated Woman's Club, 1990, Englewood Artisan Guild, 1990 (Best of the Best award). Vol. English tchr. to Spanish immigrants, L.I., N.Y., 1987-88; vol. soup kitchen, Wyndauch, L.I., 1987-88. Mem.: AAUW, Sarasota Art Assn., Nat. Mus. Women in Arts, Englewood Artisan Guild (rec. sec. 1989—90, chair publicity com. 1997—98, bd. dirs.), Nat. League Pen Women (chair S.C. art com.), Venice Art League, Sea Grape Gallery, Charlotte County Art Guild, Rotonda West Federated Woman's Club (past pres., arts chmn. 1989—). Republican. Roman Catholic. Avocations: travel, cooking, gardening, computers, painting. Home and Studio: 8229 Palmview Ct Englewood FL 34224-7698 E-mail: artisjoan@earthlink.net.

MCCLELLAN, LARRY ALLEN, educator, writer, minister; b. Buffalo, Nov. 3, 1944; s. Edward Lurelle McClellan and Helen (Denison) Greenlee; m. Diane Eunice Bonfoey, Aug. 19, 1973; children: Kara E., Seth C. Student, U. Ghana, 1964-65; BA in Psychology, Occidental Coll., 1966; MTh, U. Chgo., 1969, D Ministry, 1970. Ordained to ministry Presbyn. Ch. (U.S.A.), 1970. Prof. of sociology and community studies Govs. State U., University Park, Ill., 1970-86; interim pastor Presbyn. Ch. (U.S.A.), Chgo. area, 1980-86; sr. pastor St. Paul Community Ch., Homewood, Ill., 1986-96; adj. prof. Govs. State U., University Park, 1987-96; dir. South Met. Regional Leadership Ctr., Govs. State U., 1996—2001; cmty. rels. dir. Northeastern Ill. Planning Commn., 2001—. Newspaper columnist Star Publs. Chgo., 1993—; trustee Internat. Coun. Community Chs., 1989-91, pres., 1991-93. Author: Local History South of Chicago, 1988; developer social simulation games; contbr. articles to profl. publs. Mayor Village of Park Forest South (name now University Park), Ill., 1975-79; co-organizer S. Region Habitat for Humanity, Chgo. area, 1989; pres. S. Suburban Heritage Assn., Chgo. area, 1988-91. Fellow Layne Found., 1966-70, NEH, 1979. Mem. Urban Affairs Assn., Assn. for Sociology of Religion, Am. Assn. State and Local History, Ill. State Hist. Soc. (Spl. Achievement award 1989). E-mail: larryamcclel@msn.com.

MCCLELLAN, MARK B. federal agency administrator; Grad., U. Tex.; MPA, MD, Harvard U.; PhD, MIT. Dep. asst. sec. Treasury Dept., 1998—99; attending physician Stanford U. Health Svcs.; dir. program on health outcomes rsch. Stanford Med. Sch.; assoc. prof. dept. econs. and dept. medicine Stanford U.; mem. Coun. of Econ. Advisors Exec. Office of the Pres., Washington, 2001—.*

MCCLELLAN, MARY ANN, pediatrics nurse, educator; b. Mar. 29, 1942; BS, Tex. Woman's U., 1964; MN, U. Wash., 1968-69; cert., U. Tex., Arlington, 1997. Cert. family life educator, CPNP, pediatric nurse procationer; advanced RN practitioner, Okla. Charge nurse Baylor U. Med. Ctr., Dallas, 1964-65; pub. health staff nurse Dallas County Health Dept., 1965-68; supervising nurse Okla. State Dept. Health, Oklahoma City, 1969-70, maternal-child health nurse cons., 1971; asst. prof. U. Okla. Coll. Nursing, 1971-72; from instr. to asst. prof. Harris Coll. Nursing Tex. Christian U., Ft. Worth, 1972-75; asst. prof. continuing edn. U. Okla. Coll. Nursing, Oklahoma City, 1976-79, asst. prof. baccalaureate program, 1979—96, mem. grad. faculty, 1991—. Cons. and lectr. in field. Contbr. chpts. to books, articles to profl. jours. Mem. Nat. Coun. on Family Rels., Okla. Family Resources Coalition, Nat. Assn. Pediatric Nurse Assocs. and Practitioners (Okla. chpt.), Assn. Faculty of Pediat. Nurse Practitioner Programs, So. Early Childhood Assn., Okla. Coun. on Family Rels., Early Childhood Assn. Okla., Sigma Theta Tau., Phi Kappa Phi. Office: U Okla Coll Nursing PO Box 26901 Oklahoma City OK 73126-0901

MCCLELLAN, RICHARD AUGUSTUS, small business owner; b. Gainesville, Fla., Sept. 13, 1930; s. Marion Theodore Sr. and Cornelia (Hampton) McC.; m. Thelma Watson, May 19, 1947 (dec. Mar. 1980); children: Richard A., Wayne Theodore, Viola Patricia, Michael Ray; m. Betty Lee Snow, Dec. 12, 1980 (div. July 1991); children: Claranell Y., Juanita F., Johnnie C.; m. Geraldine C. Williams, Aug. 14, 1993. Diploma, Nat. Inst. Drycleaning, 1975, Napoleon Hill Found., 1994. Drycleaner S & S Cleaners, Gainesville, 1958-97; ret., 1997. Mem. Am. Soc. Notaries (govt. relations com. 1984, pub. relations com. 1989), Notary Pub. Assn. State Fla., Nat. Notary Assn., Internat. Order St. Luke the Physician. Democrat. United Methodist. Avocations: reading, radio, jazz music. Home and Office: 625 SE 15th St Gainesville FL 32641-3123

MCCLELLAN, ROBERT EDWARD, civil engineer; b. Atlanta, Feb. 27, 1922; s. Robert Edward and Maria Elizabeth (Ameln) McC.; m. Mary Margaret Billetter, Oct. 21, 1944; children: Kathleen Mary, Mary Elizabeth, Patricia Maura, Eileen Mary, Robert Edward III, Mary Margaret, Thomas Francis. BCE, U. So. Calif., 1947, MSCE, 1956, PhD in Engring., 1970. Registered profl. civil and structural engr., Calif. Gen. supr. design Rocketdyne, Canoga Park, Calif., 1959-62; mem. tech. staff The Aerospace Corp., El Segundo, 1962-69, mgr. strategic studies, 1980-85; chief tech. staff The Ralph M. Parsons Co., Pasadena, 1969-80; v.p. research and devel. Apollo Systems Tech., Canyon Country, 1985-88, also bd. dirs. Served to lt. (j.g.) USN, 1943-46, PTO. Recipient Outstanding Civil Engring. Grad. award U. So. Calif., 1977. Mem. AIAA, Am. Def. Preparedness Assn., AAAS, N.Y. Acad. Scis., L.A. Athletic Club, Sigma Xi, Tau Beta Pi, Chi Epsilon. Republican. Roman Catholic.

MCCLELLAN, ROGER ORVILLE, toxicologist; b. Tracy, Minn., Jan. 5, 1937; s. Orville and Gladys (Paulson) McC.; m. Kathleen Mary Dunagan, June 23, 1962; children: Eric John, Elizabeth Christine, Katherine Ruth. DVM with highest honors, Wash. State U., 1960; M of Mgmt, U. N.Mex., 1980. diplomate Am. Bd. Vet. Toxicology, cert. Am. Bd. Toxicology. From biol. scientist to sr. scientist Gen. Electric Co., Richland, Wash., 1957-64; sr. scientist biology dept. Pacific N.W. Labs., 1965; scientist med. research br. div. biology and medicine AEC, Washington, 1965-66; asst. dir. research, dir. fission product inhalation program Lovelace Found. Med. Edn. and Research, Albuquerque, 1966-73; v.p., dir. research adminstrn., dir. Lovelace Inhalation Toxicology Research Inst., 1973-76, pres., dir., 1976-88; chmn. bd. dirs. Lovelace Biomedical and Environ. Research Inst., 1988-96; pres., CEO Chem. Industry Inst. Toxicology Research, Triangle Park, N.C., 1988-99, pres. emeritus, 1999—; pvt. advisor Toxicology and Human Health Risk Analysis, 1999—. Mem. research com. Health Effects Inst., 1981-92; bd. dirs. Toxicology Lab. Accreditation Bd., 1982-90, treas., 1984-90; adj. prof. Wash. State U., 1980-95, U. Ark., 1970-88; clin. assoc. U. N.Mex., 1971-85, adj. prof. toxicology, 1985—; adj. prof. toxicology and occupational and environ. medicine Duke U., 1988—; adj. prof. toxicology U. N.C. Chapel Hill, 1989—; adj. prof. toxicology N.C. State Univ., 1991—; regents lectr. U. Calif., L.A., 1999—; mem. dose assessment adv. group U.S. Dept. Energy, 1980-87, mem. health and environ. research adv. com., 1984-85, 1999—, Particulate Matter Panel, 1993-97, 99—; mem. exec. com. sci. adv. bd. EPA, 1974-95, mem. environ. health com., 1980-83, chmn., 1982-83, chmn. radionuclide emissions rev. com., 1984-85, chmn. Clean Air Sci. Adv. Com., 1987-92, Diesel Exhaust Panel, 1996-2001, chmn. rsch. strategies adv. com., 1992-94; mem. com. on toxicology NAS-NRC, 1979-87, chmn., 1980-87; mem. com. risk assessment methodology for hazardous air pollution NAS-NRC, 1991-94, com. biol. effects of Radon NAS NRC, 1994-98, com. rsch. priorities for airborne particulate matter, 1998—; mem. Environ. Roundtable, Inst. Medicine, 1998—; mem. com. on environ. justice Inst. of Medicine, 1996-99; pres. Am. Bd. Vet. Toxicology, 1970-73; mem. adv. council Ctr. for Risk Mgmt., Resources for the Future, 1987-2001; council mem. Nat. Council for Radiation Protection, 1970-2001, hon. mem., 2002—; bd. dirs. N.C. Assn. Biomedical Rsch., 1989-91, N.C. Vet. Medical Found., 1990-95, pres., 1993-94; bd. govs. Rsch. Triangle Inst., 1994-2001; mem. adv. com. alternative toxicol. methods Interagy. Ctr. Evaluation Alternative Methods, Health and Human Svcs., 1998-2001; mem. sci. adv. bd. strategic environ. rsch. strategies program Dept. Def./Dept. Energy/EPA, 1997-99. : mem. editl. bd. Jour. Toxicology, 1984—89, : assoc. dir., 1987—89; editor: CRC Critical Revs. in Toxicology, 1987—; : mem. editl. bd. Regulatory Toxicology and Pharmacology, 1993—, : mem. editl. bd. Risk Analysis, 1998; contbr. articles to profl. jours. Recipient Herbert E. Stokinger award Am. Conf. Govtl. Indsl. Hygienists, 1985, Alumni Achievement award Wash. State U., 1987, Disting. Assoc. award Dept. Energy, 1987, 88, Arnold Lehman award Soc. Toxicology, 1992; co-recipient Frank R. Blood award Soc. Toxicology, 1989; Internat. Aerosol fellow Internat. Aerosol Rsch. Assembly, 1998; named Disting. Vet. Medicine Alumnus Wash. State U., 1999, Disting. Alumnus R.O. Anderson Sch. Mgmt. U. N.Mex., 2002. Fellow: AAAS, Health Physics Soc. (chmn. program com. 1972, Elda E. Anderson award 1974), Soc. Risk Analysis, Am. Acad. Vet. and Comparative Toxicology; mem.: NAS, Gesellschaft fur Zerosolforschung, Am. Vet. Med. Assn., Internat. Soc. Aerosols in Medicine (Thomas Mercer Joint prize for Aerosol Rsch. 1997), Am. Assn. Aerosol Rsch. (bd. dirs. 1982—94, treas. 1986—90, v.p. to pres. 1990—93), Toxicology Edn. Found. (founding pres. 1990—91), Internat. Congress Toxicology VII (treas. 1995), Soc.Toxicology (chmn. 1983—85, inhalation splty. sect. v.p. tp pres. 1983—86, bd. publs. 1983—86, v.p.-elect to pres. 1987—90), Am. Conf. Govtl. Indsl. Hygienists, Internat. Regulatory Pharmacology and Toxicology (Internat. Achievement award 1999), Am. Assn. Cancer Rsch., Am. Thoracic Soc., Radiation Rsch. Soc. (chmn. fin. com. 1979—82, sec.-treas. 1982—84), Inst. Medicine (chair other health professions sect. 1999—2001, elected 1990), Am. Chem. Soc., Phi Zeta, Phi Kappa Phi, Sigma Xi. Republican. Lutheran. E-mail: roger.o.mcclellan@att.net.

MC CLELLAN, WILLIAM MONSON, library administrator, retired; b. Groton, Mass., Jan. 7, 1934; s. James Lewis and Ruth Caldwell (Monson) McC.; m. Jane Muir, Sept. 3, 1955; children— Jennifer, Anne, Margaret, Amy. BA, Colo. Coll., 1956, MA, 1961; A.M. in L.S, U. Mich., Ann Arbor, 1959. Music librarian U. Colo., Boulder, 1959-65; dir. Music Library, U. Ill., Urbana, 1965-97. Cons. music library resources and services to colls. and univs.; co-dir. Inst. Music Librarianship, Kent State U., 1969 Editor: Music Library Assn. Notes, 1977-82; Contbr. articles to profl. jours. Council on Library Resources fellow, 1976-77 Mem. Internat. Assn. Music Librs., Music. Libr. Assn. (pres. 1971-73, conf. panelist, chmn. stats. subcom. 1990-93). Home: 451 Boardwalk Dr Apt 1306 Fort Collins CO 80525-3230 E-mail: muirmack@verinet.com. *To commit myself daily to giving and opening myself to others in all professional and other contexts.*

MCCLELLAND, HAROLD FRANKLIN, economics educator; b. Omaha, Mar. 8, 1918; s. Frank Melanchthon and Nellie (Hawthorne) McC.; m. Marion Lois Ludlow, July 3, 1941; children— Donald G., Nancy J., Jeanne L. BA, Hastings Coll., 1939; MA, U. Nebr., 1940; MS, Denver U., 1942; PhD, Harvard, 1959. Research asso. Govtl. Research Inst., St. Louis, 1942-43; treas. McClelland-Rose Motors, Inc., Hastings, Neb., 1946-55; from instr. to prof. econs. Claremont (Calif.) McKenna Coll. and Claremont Grad. Sch., 1958-65, James G. Boswell prof. econs., 1976-88, ret., 1988; dean faculty Claremont (Calif.) Men's Coll., 1963-70. Author: State and Local Finance, Nebraska, 1962, (with others) Essays in Federalism, 1961, The American Property Tax, 1965; also articles. Mem. Calif. Constn. Revision Commn., 1969-72. Served to lt. USNR, 1943-46. Mem. Am. Econ. Assn., Western Econ. Assn., Nat. Tax Assn. (bd. dirs. 1978—) Clubs: Commonwealth of Calif, University. Republican. Presbyterian. Home: 845 E Bonita Ave # 14 Pomona CA 91767-2055

MCCLELLAND, HELEN, music educator; b. Chgo., Dec. 5, 1951; d. Leon Leroy and Willie Jo (Darnell) McC.; (div. Sept. 1981); 1 child, Tasha Renee. Diploma in arts, Kennedy-King Coll., 1971; cert. in voice, Sherwood Music Coll., 1971-73; BS, Chgo. State U., 1975, MA in Adminstrn., 1983; D in Adminstrn. and Supervision, U. Calif., 1993. Tchr. Faulkner Sch., Chgo., 1975-78; tchr. music Harvey (Ill.) Pub. Sch. Dist. 152, 1978—. Dir. music Pleasant Green Missionary Bapt. Ch., Chgo., 1971—; mem. sch. bd. New World Christian Acad., Chgo., 1988—; bd. dirs. South Shore Drill Team, Chgo. Author: operetta So You Want to Be a Star, 1987. Cmty. worker People United to Save Humanity, Chgo., 1973, Harold Washington Orgn., Chgo., 1987; cmty. educator Chgo. Planned Parenthood, 1988; cmty. counselor Lincoln Cmty. Ctr., Chgo., 1975; mem. sch. bd. Dist. 160, 1994, now v.p.; mem. Ill. State Sch. Bd., 1997-98; bd. dirs. Operation P.U.S.H.; vice chmn. Ill. Assn. Sch. Bds., Ill. State Assn. Bd.; v.p. Sch. Dist. #160; ; mem. Grace M.B. Ch. Named Tchr. of the Yr., Faulkner Sch., 1976. Mem. Ill. Edn. Assn., NEA, Harvey Edn. Assn., Tennis Club, Traveling Club, Phi Delta Kappa, Pi Lambda Theta. Democrat. Baptist. Avocations: singing, bowling, piano. Home: 18029 Ravisloe Ter Country Club Hills IL 60478-5169

MCCLELLAND, JAMES LLOYD, psychology educator, cognitive scientist; b. Cambridge, Mass., Dec. 1, 1948; s. Walter Moore and Frances (Shaffer) McC.; m. Heidi Marsha Feldman, May 6, 1978; children: Mollie S., Heather Ann. BA in Psychology, Columbia U., 1970; PhD in Cognitive Psychology, U. Pa., 1975. Asst. prof. dept. psychology U. California, San Diego, 1974-80, assoc. prof., 1980-84, Carnegie-Mellon U., Pitts., 1984-85, prof. psychology, 1985—, prof. computer sci., 1987—, acting head psychology, 1989-90, co-dir. Ctr. for Neural Basis of Cognition, 1994—, univ. prof., 2001—. Adj. prof. neurosci. U. Pitts., 1995—; vis. scientist dept. psychology and Ctr. Cognitive Sci., MIT, 1982-84; vis. scholar dept. psychology Harvard U., 1982-84; mem. com. on basic rsch. in behavioral and social scis. NRC, 1985, rev. panel for cognition, emotion and personality NIMH, 1983-87, behavioral scis. rsch. br. assessment panel, 1987-88, Cognitive Functional Neurosci., 1995—, chair 1997—; co-organizer NSF workshop on connectionism and cognitive sci., 1986; assoc. Neurosci. Rsch. Program, Nat. Adv. Mental Health Coun., 2000—. Author: (with others) Parallel Distributed Processing: Explorations in the Microstructure of Cognition, Vols. I, II, 1986; co-author: A Handbook of Models, Programs, and Exercises, 1988; contbr. numerous articles, reports, book chpts. to profl. publs.; sr. editor Cognitive Sci., 1988-91; sect. editor (Cognitive Neuroscience), Internat. Ency. of The Social and Behavioral Sciences; mem. numerous jour. edit. bds. Co-recipient Growemeyer prize in psychology, Columbia U., 2002; recipient William W. Cumming prize, 1970, Rsch. Scientist Career Devel. award, NIMH, 1981—86, 1987—97; fellow, NSF, 1970—73; grantee, 1976—79, 1980—84, 1986—87, 1988—, Office Naval Rsch., 1982—87. Fellow: APA (Disting. Sci. Contbn. award 1996), AAAS, Am. Psychol. Soc.; mem.: NAS, Soc. Exptl. Psychologists (Warren medal 1993), Internat. Assn. for Study Attention and Performance (governing bd. 1986—94, lectr. 1986), Psychonomics Soc., Cognitive Sci. Soc. (governing bd. 1988—93, chmn. 1991), Phi Beta Kappa (assoc. neurosci. rsch. program). Office: Ctr Neural Basis of Cognition 115 Mellon Inst 4400 5th Ave Pittsburgh PA 15213-2617 E-mail: jlm@lnbl.cmu.edu.

MCCLELLAND, JAMES RAY, lawyer; b. Eunice, La., June 21, 1946; s. Rufus Ray and Homer Florene (Nunn) McC.; m. Sandra Faye Tate, Feb. 6, 1971; children: Joseph Ray, Jeffrey Ross. BS, La. State U., 1969, MBA, 1971, JD, 1975. Bar: La. 1975, U.S. Ct. Appeals (5th cir.) 1976, U.S. Dist. Ct. (ea. dist.) La. 1976, U.S. Dist. Ct. (we. dist.) La. 1976, U.S. Dist. Ct. (mid. dist.) La. 1994. Assoc. Aycock, Horne & Coleman, Franklin, La., 1975-78, ptnr., 1978—; dir. Bayou Bouillon Corp., Cotten Land Corp. Mem. exec. com. Democratic Party, St. Mary Parish, 1980-88; del. La. Dem. Party, 1982, 84. Mem. La. State Bar Assn. (ho. of dels. 1982-95, 98-99, law reform com. 1984-86, bd. govs. 1995-98, 99-2002), St. Mary Parish Bar Assn. (pres. 1978-79), Order of Coif, Rotary (pres. 1981-82). Home: PO Box 268 Franklin LA 70538-0268 Office: PO Box 592 Franklin LA 70538-0592

MCCLELLAND, KAMILLA KURODA, news reporter, proofreader, book agent; b. Bozeman, Mont., June 16, 1964; d. Yasumasa and Alice (Kassis) Kuroda; m. Craig Alexander McClelland, June 25, 1989. BA in Asian Studies, U. Calif., Berkeley, 1987; MS in Print News, U. Ill., Champaign-Urbana, 1989. Legis. aide Hawaii State Ho. of Reps., Honolulu, 1987; grad. asst. U. Ill. Dept. Journalism, Champaign, 1987-89; asst. op-ed editor The Daily Illini, 1988-89; reporter AP, Seattle, 1989, Tacoma News Tribune, 1989-90; bus. news reporter The Olympian, Olympia, Wash., 1990-97; editor-in-chief Friday edit. N.Am. Post (formerly N.W. Nikkei), Seattle, 1997-98; asst. editor South Sound Bus. Examiner, Tacoma, 1998—. Proofreader Minerva Rsch., Inc., Honolulu, 1982-1996. Vol. Am.-Arab Anti Disc Com., Berkeley, Calif., 1984-87, Capital City Marathon, Olympia, 1993-95, Olympia Symphony, 1996, Black Hills Triathalon, 1993—, Olympia Chamber Orch., 1996; judge

Soc. Profl. Journalists Best of Ind. Contest, 2000. Recipient Recognition awards for newswriting Gannett, 1991, 92, 95, 1st Pl., Best of Gannett award for bus. and consumer reporting, 1994, Well Done Bus. Reporting Gannett award, 1995, 2nd place bus. and consumer reporting Best of Gannett award, 1995. Mem. Asian Am. Journalists Assn. (Seattle chpt.), Soc. Profl. Journalists (western Wash. chpt 2d pl. award Bus. Features Pacific Northwest Excellence Journalism comp. 1996, judge Best of Ind. competition 2000). Avocations: hiking, camping, martial arts, raising rabbits, backpacking. Office: 203 4th Ave E Ste 307 Olympia WA 98501-1188 E-mail: kamilla@businessexaminer.com.

MCCLELLAND, MARLEEN IANNUCCI, physical therapist, educator; b. Warren, Ohio, Aug. 28, 1952; d. Anthony Armond and Rose (Fittipaldo) Iannucci; m. Michael Ernst McClelland, Mar. 3, 1951; children: Michael Iannucci, Adam Iannucci. BA, Kent State U., 1973; BS, Marquette U., 1979; MS, Ohio State U., 1986, PhD, 1990. Phys. therapist N.W. Gen. Hosp., Milw., 1979-80, Nathaniel Witherall, Greenwich, Conn., 1980-82, Riverside Hosp., Columbus, Ohio, 1986-90; asst. prof. Ohio U. Sch. Phys. Therapy, Athens, 1991-97; assoc. prof. Youngstown State U., Ohio, 1997—, dept. chairperson, 1999—. On-site evaluator Commn. on Accreditation for Phys. Therapy edn., Alexandria, Va., 1996. Contbr. ; co-author (with Roberta G. Sands): Interprofessional & Family Discourses: Voices, Knowledge, and Practice, 2002. Recipient Doctoral Rsch. award, Found. for Phys. Therapy, 1990; grantee, Ohio U. Rsch. com., 1995. Mem.: Am. Phys. Therapy Assn. (cons. edn1. cons. pool 1996), Am. Ednl. Rsch. Assn., Phi Kappa Phi. Office: Youngstown State U Dept Phys Therapy B86 Cushwa Hl Youngstown OH 44555-0001

MCCLELLAND, PATRICIA G. minister; b. Warsaw, July 12, 1944; d. Gail Raymond and Martha Carolyn (Lewis) Easton; m. Lester E. McClelland, Aug. 18, 1974; 1 child, Melody. BS, U. Mo., 1968; MA, Drury Coll., 1972. Cert. tchr., Mo., Kans., Ill.; lic. counselor; ordained to ministry Unity Ch., 1986. Instr. U. Mo., Kansas City, 1968, 71-74, Park Coll., Parkville, Mo., 1968-70; spl. cons. Kansas City Pub. Schs., 1970-71; author edn. materials, 1975-78; instr. U. Wis., 1978-79; min. Milw., 1979-81; instr. Sem. Unity Sch. Christianity, 1983-85; co-min. Unity Ch. Pitts., 1985-86; sr. min. Unity Ch., Anderson, Ind., 1986-87, sr. minister Warren, Ohio, 1987-88, Massillon, 1988-90; dir. housing Southwestern Coll., Winfield, Kans., 1990-91; min. specializing in ministry to women, cons., Lincoln, Nebr., 1991-93; co-min. Lindenwood Union Ch., Rockford, Ill., 1993—. Founding min. Council Bluffs Unity Ch.; tchr. pub. schs., Rochelle, Ill., 1994—2000; instr. Rockford (Ill.) Coll.; tchr., facilitator Skylight grad. program Rock Valley Coll. , Janesville, Wis., 2002—; tchr. Belvidere CUSD #100, 2002—, St. Xavier U., 2002—. Mem. NAFE, Nat. Assn. Self-Employed, Internat. New Thought Alliance, Internat. Platform Assn. Methodist/Unity. Home and Office: 7399 Bermuda Dr Rockford IL 61108-4486 E-mail: revpatmmcl@yahoo.com. *Our inheritance as Children of God is a world where everything necessary is available for every human being to live a happy, healthy, peaceful, abundant life. The choice to do so, as well as the work to fulfill that choice, is up to us both individually and collectively.*

MCCLELLAND, RICHARD LEE, dentist; b. Pitts., May 18, 1927; s. William Noble and Pauline Elizabeth (Lee) McC.; m. Elizabeth Anne Michon, Dec. 6, 1958; children: Richard Scott, William Alfred, Robert Craig. BA, Princeton U., 1950; DDS, U. Pa., 1954. Pvt. practice, Princeton, N.J., 1958-92. Clin. instr. U. Pa. Dental Sch., Phila., 1958-62; mem. exec. com. Med. Ctr. Princeton, 1971-72, past chmn. dental dept.; elected Nat. Dental Surgeon Res. Officers Assn. of U.S., 1972-73. With USN, 1945-46, WWII, lt. Dental Corps, USNR, 1954-57, capt., ret. Fellow: Acad. Gen. Dentistry, Internat. Coll. Dentists, Am. Coll. Dentists; mem.: ADA, Fedn. Dentaire Internat., Res. Officers Assn., Princeton Club (N.Y.C.), Nassau Club, Rotary (pres. Princeton 1978—79). Republican. Episcopalian. Avocations: sailing, photography. Home: 58 Governors Ln Princeton NJ 08540-3671

MC CLELLAND, ROBERT NELSON, surgeon, educator; b. Gilmer, Tex., Nov. 20, 1929; s. Robert Hilton and Verna Louise (Nelson) McC.; m. Connie Logan, May 5, 1958; children: Robert Christopher, Alison, Julie. BA, U. Tex., Austin, 1952; MD, U. Tex., Galveston, 1954. Diplomate Am. Bd. Surgery. Rotating intern U. Kans. Med. center, 1954-55; resident in gen. surgery Parkland Hosp., Dallas, 1957-59, 60-62; instr. surgery Southwestern Med. Sch., U. Tex., 1962-63, asst. prof., 1963-67, asso. prof., 1967-71, prof., 1971—, Alvin Baldwin prof. surgery, 1977—. Examiner Nat. Bd. Med. Examiners Editor Audio Jour. Rev. Gen. Surgery, 1971-82, Selected Readings in Gen. Surgery, 1974— ; contbr. numerous articles to profl. jours., chpts. to books. Served to capt. M.C. USAF, 1955-57. Fellow ACS (mem. grad. edn. com.); mem. AMA, Am. Surg. Assn., Western Surg. Assn., Soc. Surgery of Alimentary Tract, Am. Gastroent. Assn., Southwestern Surg. Soc., So. Surg. Assn., Dallas Soc. Gen. Surgeons (pres. 1987-88), Tex. Surg. Soc., Tex. Med. Assn., Dallas Country Med. Soc., Soc. Internatale de Chiurgie (bd. dirs. Am. chpt.), Phi Beta Kappa, Alpha Omega Alpha. Republican. Lutheran. Home: 3601 Potomac Ave Dallas TX 75205-2110 Office: 5323 Harry Hines Blvd Dallas TX 75390-7208

MCCLELLAND, SHEARWOOD JUNIOR, orthopaedic surgeon; b. Gary, Ind., Aug. 1, 1947; s. Shearwood and Zenobia McClelland; m. Yvonne Shirley Thornton, 1974; children: Shearwood III, Kimberly. AB, Princeton U., 1969; MD, Columbia U., 1974; MPH, 1996. Diplomate Am. Bd. Orthopaedic Surgery. Intern St. Luke's Hosp., N.Y.C., 1974-75; resident, 1975-76; asst. resident in orthopaedic surgery N.Y. Orthopaedic Hosp., 1976-79; commd. lt. USNR, 1979-82; staff orthopaedic surgeon Nat. Naval Med. Ctr., Bethesda, Md., 1979-82; asst. prof. surgery Uniformed Svcs. U. Health Scis., 1980-82; acting chief orthopaedic surgery Harlem Hosp. Ctr., 1983-84; assoc. dir. orthopaedic surgery, 1985-92; acting dir., 1992-94; dir., 1994—; asst. prof. clin. orthopaedic surgery Columbia U., 1983-94; assoc. prof. clinic, 1994—. Oral examiner Am. Bd. Othopaedic Srgery; mem. N.Y. State Bd. of Profl. Med. Conduct, 1989-98. Annie C. Kane fellow in orthopaedic surgery, 1978-79; fellow in total joint implant surgery Ohio State U., 1982. Pres. Columbia P&S Alumni Assn., 2002—. Fellow ACS, Am. Acad. Orthopaedic Surgeons, N.Y. Acad. Medicine; mem. Assn. Mil. Surgeons of U.S., Am. Coll. Phys. Execs., N.Y. Orthopaedic Hosp. Alumni Assn., Mensa, No. N.J. Princeton Alumni Assn., Columbia P&S Alumni Assoc., pres. 2002-03. Office: Harlem Hosp Ctr KP-9101 506 Lenox Ave New York NY 10037-1802

MCCLENAHAN, MARY TYLER FREEMAN, civic and community volunteer; b. Richmond, Va., Apr. 6, 1917; d. Douglas Southall and Inez Virginia (Goddin) Freeman; m. Leslie Cheek Jr., June 3, 1939 (dec. Dec. 1992); children: Leslie III, Richard Warfield, Elizabeth Cheek Morgan; m. John Lorimer, Aug. 14, 1993. AB, Vassar Coll., 1937; LHD (hon.), St. Paul's Coll., 1977, Washington and Lee U., 1983, Va. Commonwealth U., 1993, Hollins Coll., 1993; HHD (hon.), U. Richmond, 1985; LHD (hon.) (hon.) , Va. Union U., 2002. Author: (booklet) Death, The Key to Life, 1982, (with Alonzo T. Dill) A Visit to Stratford and the Story of the Lees, 1986, Douglas Southall Freeman: Reflections By His Daughter, His Research Associates and a Historian, 1986; contbr. articles to popular mags. Active Robert E. Lee Meml. Assn., Stratford, Va., 1964-95, hon. dir., 1995—; dame, bd. govs. Order of Hosp. St. John, N.Y.C., 1984—; bd. dirs. Maymont Found., 1982—, Va. Cmty. Devel. Corp., 1989—, Trees for Richmond, 1991—, Caucus for Future Ctrl. Va., 1992—, (hon.) Va. League Planned Parenthood (Outstanding Svc. award), 1952—; bd. dirs., exec. com. Richmond Renaissance, 1982-96; former bd. dirs., chair, adv. bd. Coun. Am.'s First Freedom; trustee Va. Union U., Richmond, 1985—, Va. Hist. Soc. (hon.), Black History Mus. and Cultural Ctr. of Va., Hist. Richmond Found.; chair, founder Richmond Better Housing Coalition, 1989—; vice-chair Conserve Va.; pres.'s coun. So. Environ. Law Ctr.; adv. bd. ARC, 1992—, Christian Children's Fund, 1993-95; adv. com. Girl Scouts U.S., Va; nat. com. Jefferson Poplar Forest Fund. Recipient Mary Mason Anderson Williams Preservation award Assn. Preservation Va. Antiquities, 1977, Barbara Ransome Andrews disting. vol. award Jr. League Richmond, 1982, Fair Housing award Housing Opportunities Made Equal, 1983, Brotherhood award Nat. Conf. Christians and Jews, 1983, Human Rels. award, 1984, Ten Outstanding Women award YWCA-Richmond, 1986, Sallie Wilson Peake Meml. award Housing Opportunities Made Equal, 1987, Charlotte J. Washington cmty. svc. award Richmond Urban League, 1988, Archtl. medal Am. Inst. Architects, 1991, Liberty Bell award Richmond Bar Assn., 1991, Faith in Action award Va. Coun. Churches, 1992, Outstanding Citizen award Civitan Club, 1992, Hope award Nat. Multiple Sclerosis, 1994; named Richmonder of Yr. STYLE mag., 1990, Va. Women Hall Fame Va. Coun. on Status Women, 1991, Flame Bearer of Edn. award United Negro Coll. Fund, 1995, Local Initiatives Support Corp. award, 1997, Lifetime Achievement award Urban League of Greater Richmond, 1999, Ne Plus Ultra award Va. Assn. Fund Raising Execs., 1999, Good Citizenship award SAR, 2000, Lettie Pate Whitehead Evans award Va. Theol. Sem., 2000, Mary Tyler McClenahan cmty. award, Richmond Cmty. Develop. Alliance, 2000, Lifetime Achievement in Philanthropy award, Assn. of Fund Raising Execs., 2001. Mem. Richmond Urban Forum (founder, chair, hon.), AIA (hon.) Women's Club of Richmond, Cosmopolitan Club, The Acorn Club of Phila., Hroswitha Club, James River Garden Club, Va. Writer's Club, Richmond First Club (Good Govt. award, 1987), Omicron Delta Kappa, Phi Beta Kappa. Democrat. Episcopalian. Avocations: writing, literature, hist. preservation, gardening, urban devel. Home: 4703 Pocahontas Ave Richmond VA 23226-1720

MCCLENDON, EDWIN JAMES, health science educator; b. Troy, Okla., Dec. 3, 1921; s. Charles Wesley and Mattie (Reed) McClendon; m. Ruby Wynona Scott, May 5, 1950 (dec. Apr. 8, 2001); children: Edwin James Jr., Melody Jan, Joy Renee. BS, Okla. East Ctrl. State U., 1946; MEd, U. Okla., 1954; EdD, Wayne State U., 1964; hon. DrPH, Seoul Nat. U., 1989. Instr. U. Okla., Norman, 1946-47; head speech dept., tchr. Wewoka High Sch., Okla., 1947-49; assoc. dir. Tb Control, Oklahoma City, 1949-51; dir. sch health project Okla. Dept. Health and Edn., 1951-54; assoc. dir. Tb Control, Wayne County, Mich., 1954-56; dir. sch. health, 1956-63; dir. secondary edn. Wayne County Intermediate Sch., Detroit, 1963-67; supt. schs. Highland Park, Mich., 1967-68; v.p. Highland Park Coll., 1968-69; asst. supt. health Mich. Dept. Edn., Lansing, 1969-71; prof., chmn. health edn. U. Mich., Ann Arbor, 1971-88, prof. health behavior and pub. health, 1971-88, prof. emeritus, 1988—; cons. pub. health care WHO, 1985—. Cons. WHO, 1978-89, dir. field study for Western Pacific, 1981; health field study of Arabic states, 1979-80; cons., Papua, New Guinea, Japan, Korea, Philippines, 1983-84, Fiji and Malaysia, 1987-88; vis. prof. U. Okla., 1965, Okla U. Liberal Arts, 1966, U. Wis., Madison, Kent U., Ohio, Wayne State U., Mich. State U., U. Mich., Flint and Dearborn, 1979-97. Author: Drug Education-A Teacher's Guide, 1969, Maxi Minds in Mini Cages, The Gifted, 1972, Healthful Living for Today and Tomorrow, 1981, Health and Wellness, 1987, Evaluation Study of Growing Healthy, 1993; contbg. author: Practical Stress Management, 2000; editor: Michigan Tenth Largest, A History of Plymouth-Canton Schools, 1986; contbr. 60 articles to profl. publs. Chmn. bd. dirs. Am. Cancer Soc., Detroit, 1977-78, mem. nat. pub. edn. com., 1969-83, hon. life mem., 1980—; mem. adv. coun. alcohol abuse NIH, 1976-80; pres. Plymouth-Canton Sch. Bd., 1974-78, 82-91; Tax Rev. Bd., Plymouth, Mich., 1980-85; chmn. Jr. Red Cross S.E. Mich., 1969-73; chmn., cons. Polio Plus immunization campaign, WHO, Rotary Internat; bd. dirs. ARC S.E. Mich., 1992-98, exec. com., 1993—, mem. health, safety, youth and internat. coms, chair HIV/AIDS com.; Choctaw Tribal rep. Served with USN, 1942-46. Decorated Bronze Star with V for Valor, others; recipient Disting. Health Edn. award Cen. Mich. U., 1978; adminstrn. bldg. Plymouth-Canton (Mich.) schs. dedicated E.J. McClendon Edn. Ctr., 1992, Inductee Hon. Hall of Fame Plymouth Culture Ctr., 2002. Fellow APHA, Am. Sch. Health Assn. (pres. 1970-71, Disting. Service award 1962, William A. Howe award 1976), Am. Cancer Soc. (hon. life mem., bd. dirs.), Am. Social Health Assn. (dir. 1978-86), Royal Soc. Health (London); mem. NEA (hon. life), AAUP, VFW (life), Mich. Sch. Health Assn. (hon. life mem., Disting. service award 1967, Golden Anniversary award 1985), Nat. Assn. Curriculum and Devel., Am. Venereal Disease Assn., Alliance Advancement Health Edn., Soc. Pub. Health Edn., Soc. Sex Educators and Counselors, Nat. Coun. for Internat. Health, Am. Assn. for WHO, Tcgh. Prof. Alumni Wewoka and Seminole (life, disting. svc. award, 50 Yr. Svc. award), Soc. Native Am. Indians, Rotary (pres. 1989-91, chair dist. polio plus campaign, elected to Plymouth Hall of Fame), Phi Delta Kappa. Democrat. Methodist. Home and Office: 40664 Newport Dr Plymouth MI 48170-4704

MCCLENDON, FRED VERNON, real estate professional, business consultant, equine and realty appraiser, financial consultant; b. Vernon, Tex. s. Guy C. and Lexie M. (Johnson) Mc C.; m. Dorothy J. Seibert, June 1943 (div. 1953); children: Cathy, Kent, Tracy; m. Ethel R. Cherry, Sept. 15, 1959; children: Tess, Rob, J.T. Assoc. in Commerce, Hannibal La Grange Coll., 1947; BBA, Baylor U., 1949; MBA, postgrad. in law, Harvard U., 1951; postgrad. in banking, Colo. U., 1951-52; postgrad., Denver U., 1951-52. Lic. ins. agt., Tenn.; cert. real estate broker, Tenn.; cert. internat. financier. Asst. cashier U.S. Nat. Bank, Denver, 1951; gen. mgr. Nat. Paper Band Co., 1952-53; personnel mgr. Houston Fire & Casualty Co., Ft. Worth, 1954-56; gen. sales mgr. City Lincoln/Mercury, Dallas, 1957-58; owner INS-Bank Personnel Agy., 1959-61; mng. ptnr. Allen & Mc Clendon Ins., 1959-63; owner, broker Mc Clendon Real Estate, 1959-63; pres. Mc Clendon Realty Co., Hampton, Tenn., 1961-2001; gen. mgr. Eagle Nest Ranch, Roan Mountain, 1963-88, Mile High Ranch, Roan Mountain, 1988-99; pres. FMV Appraisal Co., Hampton, 1988-99, Amerifund Ventures, Internat., Tex., 2000—. Cons. Gen. Adjustments Bur., 1981—, Debourdieux Corp., 1985—, Wachesaw Corp., 1985—, Hidden Lakes Devel. Corp., various ins. cos. and law firms in U.S. and Can., IRS, U.S. Marshals Svc., U.S. Customs, 1993—, Heartland Presbyn. Ctr.; exec. cons. El Dorado Ranch, 1991-98; cons. IRS; lectr. to lodges and assns.; gen. ptnr. Flexnet Investments, Ltd., Dallas, 1988-91; pres. Bus. Realty Internat. Cons., Hillsboro, Tex., 2000-2001; exec. v.p. OmniVue, Inc., S.C., 1992-95; chmn. AmeriFund Ventures, Internat., Tex., 1995-99, Tex., 2000—; pres. U.S. Med-Am. Bus. Svcs., 1995—. Contbr. articles to profl. jours. Recipient W.T. Grant fellow Harvard U., 1950-51. Mem. Am. Quarter Horse Assn. (life), Australian Appaloosa Assn., Appaloosa Horse Club U.S., Tenn. Walking Horse Breeders Assn., Am. Paint Horse Assn., Am. Soc. Equine Appraisers, Am. Horse Coun., Am. Soc. Appraisers (Accredited sr. appraiser, bd. examiners 1990—), Internat. Real Estate Inst., Nat. Assn. Real Estate Appraisers, Environ. Assessment Assoc. (cert. insp. 1991—), Appraisers Assn. Am. (cert. sr. appraiser), Internat. Soc. Financiers (cert. internat. financier). Republican. Mem. Seventh Day Adventists. Avocations: boating, travel, fishing, swimming. Home: Eagle Nest West Ranch 1580 Hwy 77 N Hillsboro TX 76645 Office: Amerifund Ventures Internat PO 1209 Hillsboro TX 76645-1209 E-mail: fmcclendon@juno.com.

MCCLENDON, IRVIN LEE, SR. office services and computer consultant, writer and editor; b. Waco, Tex., June 12, 1945; s. Irvin Nicholas and Evelyn Lucile (Maycumber) McC.; divorced; children: Michael Boyd, Irvin Lee Jr., Laura Ann, Paul Nicholas, Richard Lester. Student, El Camino Coll., 1961-63, U. So. Calif., 1962-66; BA in Math., Calif. State U., Fullerton, 1970, postgrad. in bus. adminstrn., 1971-76; cert. nat. security mgmt., Indsl. Coll. Armed Forces, 1974; postgrad. in religion, Summit Sch. Theology, 1982-84. Engring. lab. asst. Rockwell Internat. Corp., Anaheim, Calif., 1967-68, test data analyst, 1968-70, mem. tech. staff, 1970-82; systems programmer A-Auto-trol Tech. Corp., Denver, 1982-84; sr. tech. writer, editor Colo. Data Systems, Inc., Englewood, Colo., 1986-87; engring. writer III CalComp subs. Lockheed Co., Hudson, N.H., 1987; sr. tech. writer CDI Corp., Arvada, Colo., 1987-88; staff cons. CAP GEMINI AM., Englewood, 1989; sr. tech./instrnl. writer & editor TTS Inc., Aurora, Colo., 1990-96, sr. multimedia developer, 1996-97; gen. mgr., chief editor The Berkeley Group, LLC, Denver, 1997-99; writer Am. Resume Ctr., Northglenn, Colo., 1997-98; info. processing technician County of Orange, Calif., 1998—. Sec. of governing bd. Yorba Linda Libr. Dist., 1972-77; mem. First United Meth. Ch. of Orange, 1998—; mem. Cypress Masterworks Chorale, 1999—; trustee Ch. of God (Seventh Day), Bloomington, Calif., 1979-81, treas., 1980-81, mem. Calif. State U. and Coll. Statewide Alumni Coun., 1976-77; 2d v.p. Orange County chpt. Calif. Spl. Dists. Assn., 1976, pres., 1977; mem. Adams County Rep. Ctrl. Com., 1984-90, Denver County Rep. Ctrl. Com., 1992-95; tech. support adviser to chmn. Colo. Rep. Com., 1997-98. With USAFR, 1967-71. USAF Nat. Merit scholar, 1963-67. Mem. Calif. Assn. Libr. Trustees and Commrs. (exec. bd., So. Calif. rep. 1976-77), Nat. Eagle Scout Assn. (life), Bible Sabbath Assn. (life), Calif. State U.-Fullerton Alumni Assn. (dir. 1975-77). Republican. Office: 7342 Orangethorpe Ave Ste A212 Buena Park CA 90621-4542 E-mail: lmcclendon@hca.co.orange.ca.us., LeeSrTBG@aol.com.

MCCLENDON, MAXINE CLARA, artist; b. Leesville, La., Oct. 21, 1931; d. Alfred Harry and Clara (Jackson) McMillan; m. Edward Edson Nichols, Mar. 28, 1967; children: Patricia Ann, Joan Terri, Christopher, Jennifer. Student, Tex. U., 1948-50, Tex. Woman's U., 1950-51, Pan Am. U., 1963-64. Instr. McAllen Internat. Mus., 1987-90; artist, owner in studio, Mission, Tex., 1991—; pvt. practice drawing tchr., 1990—. Artist: one woman shows include: Art Mus. S. Tex., Corpus Christi, 1971, McAllen (Tex.)Internat. Mus., 1976, Amarillo (Tex.) Art Ctr., 1982, U. Tex., Pan American, 1994; group shows in Wichita, Kans., 1972, Marietta, Ohio, 1975, Dallas, 1977, represented in permanen collections: Mus. Internat. Folk Art, Santa Fe, Ark., Mus. Fine Art, Little Rock, McAllen Internat. Mus., Lauren Rogers Mus., Laurel, Miss.; commns.: Caterpiller Corp., Peoria, Ill., Union Bank Switzerland, N.Y.C., Crocker Bank, L.A., Tarleton U., Tex., Hyatt Regency, Ft. Worth, Forbes, Inc., San Francisco, First Savs. & Loan, Shreveport, La., Continental Plaza, Ft. Worth.; curator folk art McAllen Internat. Mus., 1974-80. Recipient judges' award 4th Nat. Marietta, 1975, numerous others. Mem. World Crafts Coun., Am. Crafts Coun. (Tex. rep. 1976-80), Tex. Designer/Craftsmen (pres. 1973-74). Christian Scientist. Home: 2018 Sharyland St Mission TX 78572 E-mail: nichols@hiline.net.

MC CLENDON, WILLIAM HUTCHINSON, III, lawyer; b. New Orleans, Feb. 19, 1933; s. William H. and Eleanor (Eaton) McC.; m. Eugenia Mills Slaughter, Feb. 6, 1960; children: William Hutchinson, IV, Virginia Morris, Eleanor Eaton, Bryan Slaughter. BA, Tulane U., 1956, LLB, 1958. Bar: La. 1958, U.S. Supreme Ct. 1964. Atty. Humble Oil & Refining Co., 1958-60; with firm Taylor, Porter, Brooks & Phillips, Baton Rouge, 1960—, ptnr., 1966-2001, mem. exec. com., 1987-2001; mediator, assoc. Mediation Arbitration Profl. Sys., Inc., 1999—. Instr. comml. law and negotiable instruments Am. Inst. Banking, 1963-74; lectr. movable Property La. Bar Assn. Bridging the Gap Inst., 1965; lectr. La. State U. LAw Sch. and Real Estate Seminar chmn., 1972, 74, 76, 80, 82, 85, 87, 95, La. Soc. of Profl. Surveying, 1989, La. Soc. CPA's, 1991, Banking Seminar, 1995; adj. prof. La. State U. Legal Negotiation, 1983—; mem. faculty Profl. Edn. Group, Inc. Contbr. articles to legal jours. Bd. dirs. Cancer Soc. Baton Rouge, 1968-71; trustee Episcopal High Sch., 1976-78; mem. Dean's council Tulane U. Law Sch., 1984-88. Served to capt. AUS. Recipient Preservation award Found. for Hist. La., 1997. Mem. ABA, Am. Judicature Soc., La. Bar Assn. (chmn. sect. trust estates, probate and immovable property law 1969-70, Meml. award article 1987), Baton Rouge Bar Assn. (chmn. title standards com. 1968-69), Tulane Alumni Assn. Greater Baton Rouge (pres. 1968-69), Baton Rouge Green (bd. dirs. 1991-93), Hilltop Aboretum (bd. dirs. 1993-95), La. Civil Svc. League (pres. 1992-94), La. Tulane Law Alumni (treas., 2d v.p. 1964-65), Baton Rouge Assembly (treas. 1983, ball chmn. 1997, chmn. 1999), Toastmasters (pres. 1970), Baton Rouge Country Club, Camelot Club, Pickwick Club, Rotary (bd. dirs. Baton Rouge club 1972), Kappa Alpha, Baton Rouge Symphony (bd. dir. 2001—). Republican. Episcopalian (vestry, sr. warden 1975, 81, 84, diocesan standing com. 1985-89). Home: Oakland at Gurley 6165 Highway 963 Ethel LA 70730-3615 Office: 451 Florida St Fl 8 Baton Rouge LA 70801-1700 E-mail: william@tpbp.com.

MCCLENNEN, CRANE, judge; b. July 31, 1946; s. Louis McClennen and Dorothy (Petrovich) Johnson; m. Deborah Ann Hass, Feb. 19, 1995. BS, Ariz. State U., 1968, JD cum laude, 1972. Bar: Ariz. 1972, U.S. Dist. Ct. (Ariz.) 1972, U.S. Ct. Appeals (9th cir.) 1977, U.S. Supreme Ct. 1977. Atty. Snell & Wilmer, Phoenix, 1972-75; asst. atty. gen. Ariz. Atty. Gen.'s Office, 1975-97; judge Ariz. Superior Ct., Maricopa County, 1997—. Lectr. State Bar of Ariz., 1987—, continuing legal edn. commn., 1987—, chair, 1996-97, appellate handbook com., 1985—, criminal jury inst. com., 1996—, bd. legal specialization, 1991-96, chair, 1993-95, peer review com., 1992-95, criminal rules com., 1990-94, alternative dispute resolution com., 1984-86, criminal justice sec., 1980-87, chair, 1984-86; editl. bd. Ariz. Atty., 1987-98; spkr. in field. Author: Arizona Courtroom Evidence Manual, 3rd edit., 1998, Arizona Legal Forms, Criminal Procedure, 1990. Named Disting. Public Lawyer, State Bar Ariz., 1991, Mem. of Yr. State Bar of Arizona, 1995. Fellow Ariz. Bar Found.; mem. Phi Delta Theta. Office: 201 W Jefferson St SPC 47 Phoenix AZ 85003-2244

MC CLENNEN, LOUIS, lawyer, educator; b. Cambridge, Mass., May 29, 1912; s. Edward F. and Mary (Crane) Mc C.; m. Miriam Jacobs, Apr. 25, 1969; children by previous marriage: Adams, James, Helen, Persis, Crane, Emery. AB cum laude, Harvard U., 1934, JD, 1937. Bar: Mass. 1937, Ind. 1940, Ariz. 1947. Pvt. practice, Boston, 1937-39, Indpls., 1940-42, Phoenix, 1946-95; pres. McClennen & Fels, P.C., 1974—; adj. prof. law fed. taxation Ariz. State U., 1974-80, pres. Law Soc., 1981-83. Author: (with others) Arizona Estate Tax, 1953, (with J.T. Melczer Jr.) Arizona Income Tax Regulations, 1954; contbr. articles to profl. jours. Pres. Ariz. Bd. Edn., 1965-69; trustee No. Ariz. Mus.; past pres., bd. dirs. Maricopa County Legal Aid Soc., Phoenix Symphony Assn.; v.p., bd. dirs. Phoenix United Fund; founder, sec., bd. dirs. Phoenix Country Day Sch.; bd. dirs. Ariz. Acad.; regional dir. Harvard Alumni Assn. Maj. USAAF, 1942-46. Mem. ABA, Am. Law Inst., Ariz. Bar Assn., Maricopa County Bar Assn. (dir., past v.p.), Harvard Law Sch. Assn. (v.p.) Lawyers Club Phoenix (pres.), Phoenix Country Club, Eastward Ho Country Club (Chatham, Mass.). Unitarian Universalist. Home and Office: 5311 N La Plaza Cir Phoenix AZ 85012-1415

MCCLENNEN, MIRIAM J. former state official; b. Seattle, Sept. 16, 1923; d. Phillip and Frieda (Golub) Jacobs; m. Louis McClennen, Apr. 25, 1969; stepchildren: Peter Adams, James C.A., Helen, Persis, Crane, Emery. BA, U. Wash., 1945; MBA, Northwestern U., 1947. Exec. trainee Marshall Field & Co., Chgo., 1945-47; buyer Frederick & Nelson (subs. of Marshall Field), 1949-57; adminstrv. asst. to pres. Ariz. State Senate, Phoenix, 1973-76; dir. publs. Office of Sec. of State, 1976-87. Chairwoman legis. subcom. adminstrv. procedure Ariz. State Legislature, Phoenix, 1984-85. Original compiler, codifier, editor publ. Ariz. Adminstrv. Code, 1973-87, Ariz. Adminstrv. Register, 1976-87. Bd. dirs., mem. Phoenix Art Mus. League, 1972-90; bd. dirs., mem. exec. bd. Phoenix Symphony Guild, 1969-88; bd. dirs., sec. Combined Met. Phoenix Arts and Scis., 1974-90, mem. adv. bd., 1990-95; bd. dirs. Phoenix Art Coun., 1973-78, Master Apprentice Programs, 1980-83; bd. dirs., mem. exec. com. Heard Mus., 1982-88, 90—; mem. adv. bd. Ariz. State Hist. Records, 1987-90, Ariz. Commn. on Arts, 1989-96, Phoenix Art Mus., 1966—; bd. dirs. Arizonans for Cultural Devel., 1996—; mem. Cape Mus. of Fine Arts, 1996—. Recipient Disting. Svc. award Atty. Gen. Ariz., 1987, Outstanding Svc. to People, Ariz. State Senate, 1987, Nat. Assn. Secs. of State award, 1987. Mem.: Ariz. Club, Phoenix Country Club, Charter 100 (bd. dirs. 1981—85). Home: 5311 N La Plaza Cir Phoenix AZ 85012-1415 also: 5311 N La Plaza Cir Phoenix AZ 85012-1415

MC CLENNEY, BYRON NELSON, community college administrator; b. San Antonio, Dec. 14, 1939; s. Thomas B. and Lorene Holley McC.; children: Mark Nelson, Don Alan; m. Kay McCullough, May 17, 1986. BS, U. Tex., 1961, MEd, 1963, EdD, 1969. Asst. dean evening divsn. San Antonio Coll., 1966-68; dean instrn. McLennan C.C., Waco, Tex., 1968-70, Eastfield Coll., Dallas County, 1970-71, pres., 1971-78, Parkersburg (W.Va.) C.C., 1978-81, San Antonio C.C. Dist., 1981; chancellor Alamo C.C. Dist., 1982-86; pres. C.C. Denver, 1986-2000, Kingsborough C.C., 2000—. Author: Management for Productivity, 1980. Mem. steering com. Pres. Clinton's Am. Reads Challenge, 1997-2000. Recipient PBS O'Banion prize, 2002; NDEA fellow, 1965-66; recipient Disting. Alumni award U. Tex. Coll. Edn., 1982-83, Thomas J. Peters Nat. Leadership award League for Innovation, 1989. Mem. Am. Assn. Cmty. and Jr. Colls. (chmn. pres.'s acad. 1983-84, mem. urban commn. 1987-90), Commn. on Instns. of Higher Edn. Clubs: Rotary (past dist. gov.). Presbyterian. Office: 2001 Oriental Blvd Brooklyn NY 11235

MCCLENON, JOHN RAYMOND, chemistry educator; b. Grinnell, Iowa, May 1, 1937; s. Raymond Benedict and Erika (Weber) McC.; m. Mary Alice Thornton, June 7, 1959; children: Anne Jeanette, Marca Kay, Maureen. BA, Grinnell Coll., 1959; PhD, UCLA, 1964. Asst. prof. Milton Coll., Wis., 1963-65; asst. prof. chemistry Sweet Briar (Va.) Coll., 1965-72, assoc. prof., 1972-76, prof., 1976-82, Charles A. Dana prof., 1982—2002. Head FBN Microcomputing, Lynchburg, Va., 1980— , Johnny McClenon Big Band, Lynchburg, Va., 1978— Editor: (newsletter) Macintosh User's Group, Sweet Briar Coll. Chmn. ACLU local chpt., 1966-75; prin. clarinettist Lynchburg Symphony, Va., 1976—. Mem. AAUP (chmn. Sweet Briar chpt. 1982-83) Democrat. Unitarian Universalist. Home: 712 Riverside Dr Lynchburg VA 24503-1327 E-mail: mcclenon@cstone.net.

MCCLESKEY, JERRY MICHAEL, retired chemical company executive; b. Ft. Worth, July 3, 1933; s. Ray Emmett McCleskey and Nelle Ileta Canuteson; m. Margaret Elaine Milton, July 19, 1957; children: Claire McCleskey Dubit, Catherine McCleskey Gassman. BA, Rice U., 1955,

BSChE, 1956. Chief engr. Conoco, Inc., Ponca City, Okla., 1960-67; plant mgr. Conoco Chems., Balt., 1967-72, mgr. mfg. Saddle Brook, N.J., 1972-74, v.p. Houston, 1974-80; pres. Conoco Coal Devel. Co., Stamford, Conn., 1980-82; dir. chems. dept. EI Du Pont de Nemours, Wilmington, Del., 1982-92; ret., 1992. Trustee, chmn. fin. com. Kosciuszko Found., N.Y.C., 1984-94; bd. govs. Rice U., Houston, 1985-89, gov. advisor, 1990—; mem. fine arts com. U. Del., 1988-92. Lt. USN, 1956-60. Avocation: woodworking. Home: 211 Heritage Oaks Ln Houston TX 77024 Fax: 713-977-1951. E-mail: jmcc33@swbell.net.

MCCLIMON, TIMOTHY JOHN, lawyer; b. Clinton, Iowa, July 17, 1953; s. Leonard James and Celeste Margaret (Borman) McC.; m. Suzanne Berman, Jan. 30, 1994. BA magna cum laude, Luther Coll., 1975; MS, St. Cloud State U., 1976; JD, Georgetown U., 1986. Bar: N.Y. 1987. Asst. dir. student activities St. Cloud (Minn.) State U., 1975-76; performing arts coordinator Western Ill. U., Macomb, 1976-79; program specialist Nat. Endowment for the Arts, Washington, 1979-82, program adminstr., 1982-86, law clk., 1985-86; assoc. Webster and Sheffield, N.Y.C., 1986-88; v.p. AT&T Found., 1988-96, exec. dir., 1996—. Adj. prof. NYU, 1990—; bd. dirs. Coun. on Founds., Washington, N.Y. Regional Assn. Grantmakers, N.Y.C., Merce Cunningham Dance Found., N.Y.C., Second Stage Theatre, N.Y.C., BBB Found., N.Y.C., New Vision Pub. Schs., N.Y.C., Field Papers, Inc., N.Y.C.; spkr. confs. on arts mgmt., fundraising and nonprofit mgmt., 1979—; cons. NEA, Washington, 1986—; mem. mayor's cultural affairs adv. commn. City of N.Y.C., 1992-94. Author: (textbook chpt.) Audiences and the Arts, 1981; contbr. articles to Jour. of Law and the Arts, 1986, other publs., 1989—. Recipient Eagle Scout award Boy Scouts Am., 1967, Faculty award Blue Key Nat. Honor Frat., 1979. Mem. N.Y.C. Bar Assn. (com. mem. 1987-92), ABA (com. mem. 1986-88), N.Y. State Bar Assn., Vol. Lawyers for the Arts. Avocations: photography, bicycling, traveling, reading. Home: 222 Riverside Dr Apt 14A New York NY 10025-6809 Office: AT&T Found 32 Ave of Americas 6th Fl New York NY 10013

MCCLINTIC, HOWARD GRESSON, foundation executive; b. Pitts., Feb. 27, 1951; s. Stewart and Pamela Mary (Gresson) McC.; m. Katherine Davis Foss, Sept. 14, 1948; children: Margaret Gresson, Katherine Davis, Henry Stewart. BA in Polit. Sci./Econs., George Washington U., 1973. Legis. asst. U.S. Sen. Howard H. Baker, Washington, 1973-75; assoc. cons. Energy Decisions, Inc., 1975-78; energy policy analyst Chem. Sys., Inc., N.Y.C., 1978-80; sr. cons. Coal Use Group, Inc., Washington, 1980-83; staff officer NAS, 1983-87; exec. dir. The Jefferson Energy Found., 1987—. Spl. cons. NAS, 1973-74, Law Offices of Dudley & Warner, N.Y.C., 1979, Internat. Bus. Counsellors, Washington, 1982, Japan Nat. Oil Co., Washington, 1983. Co-editor: NAS Com. Rept., Oceans in Year 2000, 1974, staff coord. reprts., 1984, 86; exec. prodr. energy films, 17-part PBS series, 1997—, Clean Cities: The Future of Alternatively Fueled Vehicles, sponsored by U.S. Energy Dept. and GM; Everything Starts with Energy, Energy Policy on Trial, Future Energy Sources, Double Jeopardy, Access to Public Lands and Waters, Nuclear Waste and the West, What Price Cheap Oil?, The Emerging National Energy Strategy. Co-founder Decade Soc., Washington, 1979-83; coord. Washingtonians for Bush, 1983; chmn. subcom. U.S. Dept. Energy, 1988; assoc. mem. Naval War Coll. Found. Mem. Am. Energy Assurance Coun. (advisor 1988—), Internat. Assn. Energy Economists, Atlantic Coun. U.S. (participant energy study 1989), Rolling Rock Club, Mid-Ocean Club (Bermuda), Chevy Chase Club, Potomac Boat Club. Republican. Episcopalian. Avocations: skiing, golf, tennis, sailing. Home: 5115 Palisade Ln NW Washington DC 20016-5337 Office: The Jefferson Energy Found 12th Fl 1300 Pennsylvania Ave NW 2nd Fl Washington DC 20004-3016

MCCLINTOCK, DONNA MAE, social worker; b. Confluence, Pa., Aug. 4, 1954; d. Everett and Mayalene (Newcomer) McC. AA, Garrett Community Coll., 1974; BS, Frostburg State U., 1976; MSW, W.Va. U., 1983. ACSW; lic. clin. social worker, Md. Dir. job readiness program, vocat. counselor Western Md. Consortium, Oakland, 1979-83; social worker Thomas B. Finan Ctr., Cumberland, 1983-84; coord. geriatric edn. svcs., social worker/program adminstr. Garrett County Health Dept., Oakland, 1984—. Group leader Alzheimer's/Dementia Support Group, Oakland, 1987—. Mem. NASW, We. Md. Geriatric Social Workers, Garrett and Allegany County Social Work Caucus, Garrett County Bus. and Profl. Women's Club, W.Va. U. Alumni Assn. Lutheran. Avocations: travel, reading. Office: Garrett County Health Dept 1025 Memorial Dr Oakland MD 21550 E-mail: dmcclintock@dhmh.state.md.us.

MCCLINTOCK, GEORGE DUNLAP, retired lawyer; b. Pocatello, Idaho, Nov. 30, 1920; s. George Dunlap and Jessie (McCabe) McC.; m. Aileen McHugh, Sept. 19, 1945 (dec. Jan. 2000); children— Jessie Kelly, Catharine, George, Jane Wyatt, Michael, Anne AB cum laude, Dartmouth Coll., 1942; LLB, Harvard U., 1948. Bar: Minn. 1948. Ptnr. Faegre & Benson, Mpls., 1948-90. Dir. Merchants Bank, Rugby, N.D.; trustee Douglas Rees Trust, 1966—, Paul R. Held Testamentary Trusts, 1980—. Trustee, mayor City of Woodland, Minn., 1970-79; exec. bd., Viking council Boy Scouts Am., Mpls., 1959-74, pres., 1966-67; gen. campaign chmn. United Way of Mpls., 1972, bd. dirs., 1973-81, pres., 1976; trustee Convent of Visitation Sch., St. Paul, 1975-81; trustee North Meml. Med. Ctr., Robbinsdale, Minn., 1959-75; trustee, sec. Minn. Med. Found., Mpls., 1982-90. Served to lt. USNR, 1942-46 Recipient Disting. Eagle Scout award Boy Scouts Am., 1982 Mem. Mpls. Club (governing com. 1983-89, pres. 1987), Woodhill Country Club (trustee 1985-94). Republican. Presbyterian. Avocations: golf; waterfowl hunting.

MCCLINTOCK, JANE, sculptor, painter; b. Oakland, Calif., July 13, 1937; d. John and Virginia (Gamon) McC. BA, Marymount Coll., Tarrytown, N.Y., 1959; student, Sch. Painting and Sculpture, Skowhegan, Maine, 1960; MFA, Columbia U., 1961; student, Villa Schifanoia, Florence, Italy, 1963. Pres. bd. dirs. Amos Eno Gallery, N.Y.C., 1997—. Exhibited in solo shows at Pacem in Terris Gallery, N.Y.C., Central Arts Gallery, N.Y.C., Amos Eno Gallery, Marymount Coll., YWCA Gallery, Bklyn.; group exhbns. include NAD, N.Y.C., Cathedral of St. John the Divine, N.Y.C., Bank St. Coll., N.Y.C., The Sculpture Ctr., N.Y.C., The Heckscher Mus., Huntington, N.Y., Foundry Gallery, Washington, Columbia U., N.Y.C., The Adobe Art Gallery, Lake City, Colo., ARC Gallery, Chgo., Michael Ingbar Gallery, N.Y.C., Gallery Oscar, Toronto, Salena Gallery, L.I. U., 750 Gallery, Sacramento; represented in collections McKinsey and Co., Museo de Presepios, São Paulo, Brazil, Pepsi Co., U. Va. Art Mus., Towers Perin, Mus. of City of N.Y., numerous others. Studio: 195 Plymouth St Brooklyn NY 11201-1133

MCCLINTOCK, JANET MARIE, interior designer, consultant; b. Dearborn, Mich., Dec. 7, 1947; d. Gailard and Julie (Skorina) McCarty; m. Douglas Cove McClintock, Aug. 2, 1969; children: Coleen, William, Margaret. BS in Design, U. Mich., 1969. Cert. interior designer, Mich. Asst. designer interior design svcs. U. Mich., Ann Arbor, 1968-69; interior designer KMM Assocs., 1969-70, Sperry Rand/Libr. Bur., Inc., Plymouth, Mich., 1971-76; dir. design Libr. Design Assocs., Inc., 1976. Cons. various library projects, Mich., Ohio, Ky., Ill., 1971—. Recipient 2d Place award ASID/DuPont Corian Nat. Design, 1989. Mem. Am. Soc. Interior Designers (profl. mem., Presdl. Citation, 1983, Mich. Designer of Distinction award Mich. Chpt., 1983), Inst. Bus. Designers (profl. mem.). Roman Catholic. Avocations: quilting, painting. Office: Libr Design Assocs Inc 1149 S Main St Plymouth MI 48170-2213

MCCLINTOCK, MARTHA K. biologist, educator; David Lee Shillinglaw Distinguished Service Prof. Psychology U. Chgo., dir., Inst. Mind & Biology. Chair com. on biopsychology, com. human devel., com. neurobiology, com. evolutionary biology; elected mem., Inst. of Medicine, 1999. Contbr. articles to profl. jours. Office: U Chgo 5730 S Woodlawn Ave Chicago IL 60637*

MCCLINTOCK, MICHAEL SCOTT, music educator; b. Medina, Ohio, 1976; s. Carman Neil and JoAnne Marie McClintock; m. Cynthia Casde Humpal McClintock; children: Abigail Lindsay. Bachelors in Music (bm), Bowling Green State U., Bowking Green,Ohio, 1998; H.S. Diploma, Medina Sr. H.S., Medina, Ohio, 1994. Band dir. grade (5-12) Medina City Sch., Medina, Ohio, 2000; band dir. grade(5-8) North R oyalton City Sch., North Royalton, 1998—2000. Assistance chancel chior dir. Medina United Mehhodist Ch., Medina, Ohio, 2001; vice -pres. Medina County Chorus, Medina, Ohio, 1999—2000. Recipient Mark S,KellyFuture Outstanding, Bowling Green State University,Ohio, 1998. Mem.: Nat. Ednl. Assn. (assoc.), Music Edn. Nat. Conf. (assoc.), Ohio Music Edn. Assn. (assoc.). Office: Medina Senion High School 777E Union Street Medina OH 44256 E-mail: mclintockmicheal@hotmail.com.

MCCLINTOCK, RICHARD POLSON, dermatologist; b. Lancaster, N.H., Dec. 16, 1933; s. Richard P. and Dorothy Grace McClintock; m. Barbara Wyatt, June 1959 (div. Mar. 1970); children: Peter, Pamela; m. Mary Joy Fitzgerald, Mar. 21, 1970; children: Wayne, Patrick. BA, Dartmouth Coll., 1956; MD, Harvard U., 1960. Diplomate Am. Bd. Dermatology, Am. Bd. Dermatopathology. Intern in medicine U. N.C., Chapel Hill, 1960-61; resident in dermatology Stanford U., Palo Alto, Calif., 1964-67; pvt. practice Ukiah, 1967—; clin. instr. dermatology Stanford U., Palo Alto, 1967-78, clin. asst. prof., 1978-86, assoc. clin. prof., 1986-92, lectr., 1992-98, assoc. clin. prof., 1998—. Mem. hosp. staff Ukiah Valley Med. Ctr., chief of staff, 1974; bd. dirs. IPA and Found. Med. Care Mendocino and Lake Counties. Contbr. articles to profl. jours. Trustee Found. for Med. Care for Mendocino and Lake Counties, 1990-94, pres., 1992-94. Lt. Med. Corps, USN, 1961-64. Mem. San Francisco Dermatol. Soc., Pacific Dermatol. Assn., Am. Acad. Dermatology, Calif. Med. Soc., Mendocino Lake County Med. Soc., Internat. Soc. Dermatopathology. Office: 723 S Dora St Ukiah CA 95482-5335 E-mail: fitzmac@pacific.net.

MCCLINTOCK, ROBERT OLIVER, history and education educator; b. N.Y.C., Aug. 17, 1939; s. Franklin T. and Margot (DeBruyn Kops) McC.; m. Jean Gardner, June 30, 1962 (div. 1976); 1 child, Moira; m. Maxine Bookstaber, July 4, 1981. AB with honors, Princeton U., 1961; MA, Columbia U., 1963, PhD, 1968. Asst. prof. edn. Johns Hopkins U., 1965-67; instr. dept. philosophy and social scis. Columbia U., N.Y.C., 1967-68, asst. prof. history and edn., 1968-70, assoc. prof., 1970-82, prof., 1982—; co. dir. University Seminars Univ. Seminar on Innovation in Edn., 1980—; prof. dept. communication, computing, tech. Tchrs. Coll. Columbia U., 1984—, chmn. dept., 1985-88. Vis. scholar Philipps U., Marburg, Fed. Republic Germany, 1970, Goethe U., Frankfurt am Main, 1974-75; project dir. JHM Corp., Palm Beach Gardens, Fla., 1988-90; spl. asst. for policy studies HEW, 1976; cons. Am. History Workshop, 1987, Smithsonian Instn., 1987; sr. advisor strategic initiatives Office of Pres. Cooper Union for Advancement of Sci. and Art, 1990; dir. Inst. Learning Techs., N.Y.C., 1985—; co-dir. New Lab. for Teaching and Learning, The Dalton Sch., N.Y.C., 1991—. Author: Man and His Circumstances: Ortega as Educator, 1971 (Sch. and Soc. Outstanding Edn. Book 1971), Power and Pedagogy: Transforming Education Through Information Technology, 1992; editor: Henry Barnard's School Architecture, 1970, Computing and Education: The Second Frontier, 1988; contbr. articles, reviews to profl. jours. Fellow Columbia U., 1963-64. Mem. Computer Soc. IEEE, Am. Ednl. Rsch. Assn., Assn. Computing Machinery, Am. Hist. Assn., Am. Political Sci. Assn., Soc. History Tech., Conf. on Political Thought, Soc. Scholarly Pub., Internat. Communication Assn., Internat. Interactive Communication Soc., Am. Soc. Info. Sci. Office: Tchrs Coll Box 136 525 W 120th St New York NY 10027-6625

MCCLINTOCK, WILLIAM THOMAS, skilled nursing administrator; b. Pittsfield, Mass., Oct. 23, 1934; s. Ernest William and Helen Elizabeth (Clum) M.; m. Wendolyn Hope Eckerman, June 22, 1963; children: Anne Elizabeth, Carol Jean, Thomas Daniel. BA, St. Lawrence U., Canton, N.Y., 1956; MBA, U. Chgo., 1959, MHA, 1962. Prodn. planner Corning (N.Y.) Glass, 1959-60; adminstrv. resident Alameda County Med. Instns., Oakland, Calif., 1961-62; adminstrv. asst. Univ. Hosps. of Cleve., 1962-65; asst. adminstr. Presbyn. Hosp., Whittier, Calif., 1965-68; regional asst. Kaiser Found. Hosps., Oakland, 1968-70; assoc. dir., exec. dir. Conn. Hosp. Planning Commn., New Haven, 1970-75; project dir., lectr. sch. health studies U. N.H., Durham, 1975-77; regional mgr. Tex. Med. Found., Austin, 1977-81; adminstr. Schick Shadel Hosp., Ft. Worth, 1981-87; mgmt. cons. George S. May Internat. Co., Park Ridge, Ill., 1987-88; mgr. Nat. Ctr. Rsch. Programs Am. Heart Assn., Dallas, 1988-89; adminstr. Ambulatory Svcs. Health Care of Tex., Ft. Worth, 1990-92; CEO Boundary Cmty. Hosp., Bonners Ferry, Idaho, 1992-2000; healthcare cons., 2000—02; exec. dir. Oceanview Convalescent Ctr., Long Beach, Wash., 2002—. 1st lt. U.S. Army, 1957. Fellow Am. Coll. Health Care Execs. (life; Sr.-Level Healthcare Exec. Regent's award 2000); mem. Am. Hosp. Assn. (life), Am. Heart Assn. (bd. dirs. Idaho/Mont. affiliate 1993-95), Idaho Hosp. Assn. (bd. dirs. 1995-2000, sec.-treas. 1998, chmn. elect 1998, chmn. bd. dirs. 1999, immediate past chmn. 2000, Recognition of Retirement award 2000), Masons (Unity Lodge No. 9). Republican. Presbyterian. Avocations: book collections, gardening, photography, fly fishing. Home: County Rd 62C PO Box 1226 Long Beach WA 98631-1221 E-mail: wtmcclintock@centurytel.net.

MCCLINTON, DONALD GEORGE, retired diversified holding company executive; b. Pitts., June 30, 1933; s. Donald K. and Ethel M. McC.; m. Jane Ann Knoebel, Apr. 12, 1958; children: Catherine, D. Scott. BS, Miami U., Oxford, Ohio, 1955. Audit mgr. Arthur Andersen & Co., Cleve., 1955-62; mgr. accounting E. Ohio Gas Co., 1962-66; exec. v.p. Nat. Industries, Inc., Louisville, 1966-79; pres. Yellow Cab Co., 1979-94; owner, chmn. bd. Interlock Industries, Inc., 1982-94; pres. Skylight Thoroughbred Tng. Ctr., Inc., 1994—. Bd. dirs. Almost Framily, Clifton Ctr.; trustee Jewish Hosp. Health Care Systems, Inc., 1983—. Mem. Louisville-Jefferson County Bicentennial Commn., 1976-77; mem. coun., treas. Old Kentucky Home. coun. Boy Scouts Am., 1976-94; mem. Citizens at Large Jefferson County Budget Com., 1978-84; bd. overseers Bellarmine Coll., 1978-84; bd. dirs. Ky. Derby Festival, 1978—, Jewish Hosp., Louisville, 1980-86; trustee Spalding U., 1985-91, U. Med. Ctr. Found. Mem. Fin. Execs. Inst. Office: Skylight Thoroughbred Tng Ctr Inc PO Box 4 Goshen KY 40026-0004 Home: Apt A26 8410 Abbington Cir Naples FL 34108-7728

MCCLINTON, DOROTHY HARDAWAY, former business educator; b. Seguin, Tex., Jan. 4, 1925; d. George Washington and Rosetta (Hodge) Hardaway; m. Marion N. Hopkins Sr., Oct. 27, 1951 (div. Dec. 1982); 1 child, Marion N. Jr.; m. Elmer McClinton, Aug. 12, 1986; children: Thomas, Evelyn M., Nathaniel. BS, Huston-Tillotson Coll., 1947; MBEd, Tex. So. U., 1960. Tchr. Ball Elem. Sch., Seguin, 1947-49, Ball Mid. Sch., Seguin, 1949-54; clk., typist Kelly AFB, San Antonio, 1956-57; tchr. Ball High Sch., Seguin, 1957-64; tchr., dept. chair St. Philips Community Coll., San Antonio, 1964-86, prof. emeritus, 1986—. Audio visual tutorial cons. Media Systems Corp. subs. Harcourt Brace Jovanovich, Inc., 1978-86; mem. nat. rsch. rev. panel Ohio State U., 1983-84. Chair telethon United Negro Coll. Fund, San Antonio, 1990-92, 98; trustee Huston-Tillotson Coll., 1990—. Recipient Bus. Tchr. of Yr. award Tex. Bus. Edn. Assn., Austin, 1981-82, Acad. Achievement award Huston-Tillotson Coll., 1990-91; Inst. for Ednl. Leadership fellow St. Philip's Coll., San Antonio, 1984-85, Lifetime Achievement award San Antonio Black Achievement Awards, 1996; named Woman of Yr. St. Paul UMC, 1991; inductee Educators' Hall of Fame, Gamma Tau chpt. Phi Delta Kappa, 1993-94. Mem. Alamo Community Coll. Retirees, Top Ladies of Distinction (sgt.-at-arms 1987-92), Huston-Tillotson Coll. Alumni (pres. 1982-91, nat. pres. 1985-87) Delta Sigma Theta, Inc. (pres. 1972-74). Home: 1639 Lone Oak St San Antonio TX 78220-4223

MCCLINTON, JAMES LEROY, city administrator; b. Longview, Wash., Oct. 14, 1949; s. James Delmer and Norma Jean (Ammons) McC.; m. Carmen Lassaphine Amador, Nov. 7, 1983; children: James Andrew, Ian Tyler, Kevin Riley. AA, SUNY, Albany, 1973; BA, Upper Iowa U., 1974; MA, Calif. State U., Carson, 1984; PhD, Calif. Coast U., 1985. Cert. mgr. Inst. Cert. Profl. Mgrs. With USCG, 1967-89, commd. officer, 1981-83, advanced through grades to comdr., 1987, ret., 1989; bur. mgr. adminstrv. svcs. Charleston (S.C.) County Sheriff's Office, 1989—. Spkr. pro tem S.C. Criminal Justice Acad., Columbia, 1989—; mem. auditor selection com. Charleston County Govt., 1989—, computer users action com., 1989—; mem. various coms. County Govt. and Sheriff's Office, Charleston, 1989—. Editor (newsletter) The Badge, 1989—; newspaper columnist; contbr. articles to profl. jours. and mags. Mem. Charleston Police Pipes and Drums, 1994—; grad. Leadership S.C., 1993, Leadership Charleston, 1997. Recipient Achievement award Nat. Assn. Counties, Washington, 1993, 96, Golden Pen award The Post and Courier Newspaper, Charleston, 1996. Mem. ASPA, S.C. Law Enforcement Officers Assn., Rotary Internat. (bd. dirs. North Charleston). Republican. Avocations: bagpipes, writing.

MCCLINTON, WENDELL C. religious organization administrator; b. Waco, Tex., Jan. 10, 1933; s. Clyde E. and Gertrude (Cotton) McC.; m. Beverly A. Harrison, Oct. 19, 1954; children: Kent, Jana, Lori, Meg. BBA, Baylor U., 1960. Exec. dir. Gideons Internat., Nashville, exec. dir. emeritus, 1997—.

MCCLISH, JERRY FRANKLIN, artist; b. Windfall, Ind., July 15, 1920; s. Walter and Alpha May McClish; m. Charlotte Estelle Klekamp, Apr. 15, 1960. Student, Gallups Island Sch., 1939-41. Adj. prof. Nova U., Ft. Lauderdale, Fla., 1978. Tchr. numerous art classes and workshops, 1980—; radio engr., owner RADCO, Chgo., 1955-64; pvt. charter pilot, Bahamas, 1965-75. Editor: A Gallery of Marine Art, 1999; contbg. editor to art publs., show critiques for newspapers; executed murals at Art League of Manatee County Bldg., City of Bradenton bldg., Las Vegas; represented in permanent collections at Barnett Bank, Port Manatee, County Commn. offices, also 5 mus.; illustrator for history books, book covers. Prodr. art in edn. program Manatee Edn. TV, Bradenton. Deck officer Maritime Svc., 1939-43. Mem. Art League Manatee County (bd. dirs. 1997-98), Am. Artist Profl. League (hon.), Internat. Soc. Marine Painters (pres. 1989—), Am. Merchant Marine Soc. Lutheran. Home: 1011-51 Ave East Bradenton FL 34203-4872 Fax: 941-758-1042. E-mail: mcclish@pcsonline.com.

MCCLISTER, MICHAEL, writer; b. Bristol, Va., July 9, 1941; s. Cecil McClister and Pauline McNeil; divorced; 1 child Porter 1 child Jennifer Howard. BA, U. N.C., Chapel Hill, 1962; MA, Rutgers U., New Brunswick, N.J., 1963. Adminstr. asst. Dem. Nat. Com., Washington, 1963—66; campaign mgr. Jay Rockefeller Campaign, Charleston, W.Va., 1966—68; exec. v.p. Matt Reese and Assocs., Washington, 1970—72. Dir. Campaign Mgmt. Inst., Washington, 1977—83. Author: (novels) Victim's Choice, 1999, Double Deal, 2000, (polit. tng. manual) Campaign Manual Series -- Democratic National Committee, 1976, Grassroots Campaigning -- National Education Association, 1981. Mem.: Authors Guild, Phi Beta Kappa. Home: PO Box 3279 Placida FL 33946-3279 Office: PO Box 3279 Placida FL 33946-3279 Home Fax: 941-697-1868; Office Fax: 941-697-1868. Personal E-mail: McClisterM@aol.com. Business E-Mail: McClisterM@aol.com.

MCCLORY, ROBERT J. television producer, director, columnist; b. Kokomo, Ind., Sept. 29, 1952; s. Fritz Lee and Wanda Lee (Bagby) McC.; m. Mary Ellen Mead, Mar. 31, 1978; children: Aric Robert, Andrew. AA, Palm Beach C.C., Lake Worth, Fla., 1976; BA in Journalism, Fla. Atlantic U., 1982; grad., South Tech. Sch., 1991. Advtsg. sales rep. Lake Worth (Fla.) Herald, 1976-84, columnist, 1976—; advtsg. sales rep. Palm Beach Newspapers, Inc., W. Palm Beach, Fla., 1984-88; tv prodr., dir. Palm Beach County Ch. 20, 1992—. Asst. scout master troop 204 Boy Scouts Am., Lake Worth. Served with USAF, 1971-74. Recipient Govt. Comm. award, 1993. Mem. Internat. TV Assn. (sec. Palm Beach chpt. 1994—, News First Place award 1995), Fla. Motion Picture and TV Assn. Home: 3840 Dorrit Ave Boynton Beach FL 33436-2736 Office: Palm Beach County Pub Affairs Ch 20 301 N Olive Ave West Palm Beach FL 33401-4705

MCCLOSKEY, DONNA WEAVER, business educator; BSBA, U. Del., Newark, 1990; MBA in Fin./MIS, Widener U., Chester, Pa., 1992; PhD in MIS, Drexel U., Phila., 1997. Prof. bus. Widener U., Chester, 1998—. Office: Widener Univ-SBA One University Pl Chester PA 19013

MCCLOSKEY, J(OHN) MICHAEL, retired association administrator; b. Eugene, Oreg., Apr. 26, 1934; s. John Clement and Agnes Margaret (Studer) McC.; m. Maxine Mugg Johnson, June 17, 1965; stepchildren: Claire, Laura, James, Rosemary Johnson. BA, Harvard U., 1956; JD, U. Oreg., 1961. N.W. rep. Sierra Club, Eugene, 1961-65, asst. to pres. San Francisco, 1965-66, conservation dir., 1966-69, exec. dir., 1969-85, chmn. Washington, 1985-99, acting exec. dir., 1986-87; vice-chmn. Commn. on Environ. Law and Policy (Internat. Union for Conservation of Nature), Gland, Switzerland, 1978-88; mem. Pres.'s Commn. on Agenda for 1980's, Washington, 1979-80; co-chmn. OSHA-Environ. Conf., 1983-87; vice chmn. Am. Com. on Internat. Conservation, 1988-90; mem. Internat. Union for Conservaton of Nature World Commn. on Protected Areas, 1988—. Mem. adj. faculty Sch. Natural Resources, U. Mich., 1988—; chmn. Mineral Policy Ctr., 1998-2001; co-chmn. environ. policy task force Pres.'s Coun. Sustainable Devel., 1997-99; pres. Fedn. of Western Outdoor Clubs, 2000—. Contbr. articles to profl. jours. Bd. dirs. Nat. Resources Coun. Am., 1988-94, vice chmn., 1989-91, chmn., 1992-93, chmn. Advocacy Forum, 1989-91; bd. dirs. Ind. Sector, 1990-96, Mineral Policy Ctr., 1988-2001, Coalition for Environmentally Responsible Economies, 1989-99, OMB Watch, 1998—; bd. trustees Sierra Club Found., 2000—; mem. steering com. Blueprint for Environ., 1987-88; nominated candidate Oreg. Ho. of Reps., 1962. Recipient award Calif. Conservation Coun., 1969, John Muir award Sierra Club, 1979, UN Environ. Program Global 500 award, 1992, Lifetime Achievement award Wild Found., 1998, Honor award Natural Resources Coun. Am., 1999. Mem. Univ. Club (Portland, Oreg.), Explorers Club (N.Y.C.). Democrat. E-mail: jmmccloskey@aol.com.

MCCLOSKEY, LAURA ANN, medical educator; b. Boston, Nov. 9, 1953; d. Robert Green and Helen Stueland McCloskey. PhD, U. Mich., 1986. From asst. to assoc. prof. U. Ariz., Tucson, 1988-99; assoc. prof. mternal and child heealth Harvard U., Boston, 1999—. Contbr. rsch. articles to profl. jours. Rsch. grantee Nat. Inst. Mental Health, 1995-2000, Agy. for Healthcare Rsch. Quality, 2000-2005, Agy. for Children, Youth and Families, 1989-92, Ariz. Ctr. for Disease Control, 1994-97. Democrat. Avocations: swimming, cooking Italian cuisine, playing piano. Office: Harvard U HSPH 677 Huntington Ave Boston MA 02115 Home: 113 Concord Ave Lexington MA 02421 Fax: (781) 432-3755. E-mail: lmcclosk@hsph.harvard.edu.

MCCLOSKEY, MARK, educator; b. N.Y.C., Feb. 1, 1938; s. John McCloskey and Adele Bernard; m. Bernadette Jeanne Maron, Aug. 15, 1961 (div.); children: Daria, Adrian. BA, Iona Coll., 1961; MA, Ohio U., 1963. Instr. Ohio U., Athens, 1963-64, asst. editor, 1964-66; asst. prof. SUNY, Cortland, N.Y., 1966-70, U. So. Calif., L.A., 1970-73, Calif. State U., Chico, 1973-77; instr. U. So. Calif., 1977-90, Occidental Coll., L.A., 1977-90, Glendale (Calif.) Coll., 1990-91, Portland C.C., 1993, Patten Coll., Oakland, Calif., 1996-99. Author: Goodbye, But Listen; Poems, 1968; author, translator: The Latin Poetry of George Herbert, 1965; author of poems. Recipient Theodore Roethke prize Poetry Northwest, Seattle, 1976, Bullis prize, 1974. Mem. Assoc. Writing Programs. Avocation: walking. Home: 5631 Valley Oak Dr Los Angeles CA 90068-2556

MCCLOSKEY, ROBIN ANN, artist, educator; b. Camden, N.J., Mar. 26, 1955; d. John William and Anita Isabel (Morales) McC.; m. Keith W. Hartman, Dec. 27, 1954; 1 child, Isaac Hartman. BA, U. N.C., Charlotte, 1977; MFA, Pa. State U., 1984. Instr. art Cabrillo Coll., Aptos, Calif., 1994-95; Dayton-Hudson vis. artist Carleton Coll., Northfield, Minn., 1995; instr. art City Coll. San Francisco, 1996-99. Recipient Gold prize 8th Internat. Print & Drawing Biennial, 1997. Mem. Calif. Soc. Printmakers, Women's Caucus for Art.

MCCLOUD, ANECE FAISON, academic administrator; b. Dudley, N.C., May 29, 1937; d. J.D. Faison and Nancy Jane (Simmons) Faison-Cole; m. Verable Lancaster McCloud, June 1, 1959; children: Aja Siobhan, Carla Danette. BS, Bennette Coll., Greensboro, N.C., 1959; MA, U. Nebr., Omaha, 1989; Basic Mediations Skills, Ea. Mennonite Coll., 1994. Tchr. Lincoln Jr. High Sch., Greensboro, N.C., 1959-60, Woodbridge Airforce Base (Eng.), 1961-62; resident advisor and ednl. coord. Child Saving Inst., Omaha, 1967-71; asst. registrar for acad. records U. Nebr. Med. Ctr., 1972-76, first dir. minority student affairs, 1976-85; assoc. dean of students Washington and Lee U., Lexington, Va., 1985—. Cons. Deans Forum on Revitalizing Health Profl. Edn., Dept. of Health and Human Svcs., 1985, Campus Alcohol Initiative, N.C. Gov.'s Inst. Alcohol and Substance Abuse, 1999—, Peer Rev., Health Careet Opportunity Program, 1982, 1984; cons. on simulated minority admissions Assn. Am. Med. Colls., Washington, 1979. Bd. mem., v.p. Rockbridge Area Housing Corp., Lexington, 1988-95; mem. Va. adv. com. U.S. Commn. on Civil Rights, 1995—; mem. Va. Identification Program for Advancement of Women in Higher Edn., 1995-96; treas. Mayor's Commn. on Status of Women, Omaha, 1977-78. Recipient Plaque for Outstanding Svc. to Washington and Lee Comty., 1994, Cert. Acknowledgement of Contbn. to Edn., Omaha Pub. Schs., 1984, Cert. Black History Month Spkr., VA Hosp.,

Omaha, 1983, Vol. Program award Girls Club of Omaha, 1977; grantee Health Career Opportunity, Disadvantaged Assistance Office, Dept. Health and Human Svcs., 1976, 80, 83. Mem. Am. Assn. for Higher Edn., Nat. Assn. For Women in Edn., Am. Coll. Personnel Assn., Assn. of Am. Med. Colls., Am. Assn. of Counseling and Devel., Nebr. Assn. for Non-White Concerns (past sec.), Nebr. Assn. of Collegiate Registrars and Admissions Officers (chairperson sub.-com. on minority affairs 1978-89), Nat. Assn. of Med. Minority Educators (vice coord. 1982-83). Democrat. Avocations: social research, writing, interior decorating. Office: Washington & Lee U Payne Hall 3 Lexington VA 24450

MCCLOUD, MELODY THERESA, obstetrician-gynecologist, surgeon; b. N.Y.C., Sept. 11, 1955; d. William and Eva McC. BA, Boston U., 1977, MD, 1981. Intern Emory U. Affiliated Hosps., Atlanta, 1981-82, resident in ob-gyn., 1982-85; pres., founder, CEO Atlanta Women's Health Care, 1985—. Bd. dirs. Vis. Nurses Health Sys., Atlanta; med. cons. Greeley Co., Wis., 1994—; spkr. Nat. Dental Assn.-Atlanta Bus. League, 1995, Women-On-Tour Conf., Nat. Coalition 100 Black Women, Congl. Black Caucus-Women, others; cons. health WXIA-TV, Atlanta, 1995, 99. Author: Medical Bloopers!! Amusing, Amazing Stories, 1994, The Health Diary for Women, 1999, Blessed Health, 2002; med. advisor Body and Soul, 1994; health columnist: Women Looking Ahead, 1995—. Mem. med. support group Com. Olympic Games, Atlanta, 1996; chair selection com. YWCA Acad., Atlanta, 1999; bd. dirs. Positive Alternatives, Decatur, Ga., 1996—. Inductee Leadership Atlanta, 1992, YWCA Acad. for Women Achievers, 1992; named Bus. Woman of Yr. Am. Bus. Women's Assn., 1994; recipient Cmty. Health Svc. award Black Pages. Mem. Med. Assn. Ga., Ga. Ob-Gyn Soc., Med. Assn. Atlanta, Atlanta Med. Assn., Soc. Laparoendoscopic Surgeons. Baptist. Avocations: tennis, bowling, water sports, theatre, travel. Office: Melody T McCloud MD PO Box 344 Roswell GA 30077-0344 E-mail: newlfpubl@aol.com.

MCCLOUD, PAUL DUANE, chemical engineer; b. Akron, Ohio; s. Paul Richard and Martha McCloud; m. Mary Elizabeth Wojcik, July 6, 1985. BS in Chem. Engring., U. Akron, Ohio, 1982. Registered profl. engr., Ohio. Engr. II mech. engring. divsn. Am. Electric Power, Columbus, Ohio, 1982-90; plant engr. Del. Ranch plant Magna Power Co., Calipatria, Calif., 1990-91, asst. plant supt. Vulcan/Hoch, 1991-94; sr. project engr. Cal Energy Co.l, Pasadena, 1995-97; project mngr. FLP Energy Inc., Juno Beach, Fla., 1997—. Mem. ASTM (com. D-5 1988-90), AIChE. Avocations: fishing, snow skiing, camping, wine, bassoon. Office: FPL Energy 700 Universe Blvd Juno Beach FL 33408-2657 E-mail: duane_mccloud@fpl.com.

MCCLOUD, ROBERT OLMSTED, JR. lawyer; b. Chgo., Dec. 7, 1951; s. Robert Olmsted and Suzanne (Eyerly) McC.; m. Kathryn Bartholomees, June 3, 1978; children: Lyle Olmsted, Stewart Wilcox, Kathryn Suzanne. Student, U. Ga., 1970-72; AB, Duke U., 1974; JD, U. Ga., 1977. Bar: Ga. 1977, U.S. Dist. Ct. (no. dist.) Ga. 1977, U.S. Ct. Appeals (5th and 11th cirs.) 1977. Assoc. Webb, Young, Daniel & Murphy, Atlanta, 1977-80, Jones & Van Gerpen, Atlanta, 1980-82, Carter & Ansley, Smith & McLendon, Atlanta, 1982-84; ptnr. Carter & Ansley, 1985-2000, mng. ptnr., 1991-94; shareholder Davis, Matthews & Quigley P.C., 2000—. Bd. dirs. Wildwood Civic Assn., Atlanta, 1984-86. Mem. ABA, Atlanta Bar Assn., Lawyers Club Atlanta (treas. 1988-89, exec. com. 1988-90), Cherokee Town and Country Club. Republican. Presbyterian. Home: 3137 Rockingham Dr NW Atlanta GA 30327-1234 Office: Davis Matthews & Quigley PC 14th Fl Lenox Towers II 3400 Peachtree Rd NE Atlanta GA 30326 Fax: 404-261-0159. E-mail: rmccloud@dmqlaw.com.

MCCLOW, ROGER JAMES, labor lawyer; b. St. Johns, Mich., July 23, 1947; s. Jack Gordon and Madalene V. (Mahaffy) McC.; m. Suzanne Terese Posler, July 13, 1978. BA in Polit. Sci. with distinction, U. Mich., 1969; JD magna cum laude, Wayne State U., 1976. Bar: Mich. 1977, U.S. Dist. Ct. (ea. dist.) Mich. 1977, U.S. Ct. Appeals (6th cir.) 1985, U.S. Ct. Appeals (8th cir.) 1987, U.S. Supreme Ct. 1988. Assoc. Miller, Cohen, Martens & Sugerman, Detroit, 1977-81, Klimist, McKnight & Sale, P.C., Southfield, Mich., 1981-83; ptnr. Klimist, McKnight, Sale, McClow & Canzano, P.C., 1983—. Bd. dirs. Hemid (Sr. Citizen's Agy.), Detroit, 1982-2002; tutor Children's Ctr., Detroit, 1990-93; vol. Hospice Legal Aid, Detroit, 1991—, Patient Advocate Found., 1998—; mem. gun safety com. Alliance for Greater, Safer Detroit, 1993-95. Recipient Outstanding Vol. Svc. award Children's Ctr. Detroit, 1993. Mem. State Bar Mich. (coun. mem., labor law and employment sect. 1992-96), Detroit Bar Assn., Oakland County Bar Assn., Assn. Trial Lawyers Am., Mich. Trial Lawyers Assn., Indsl. Rels. Rsch. Assn., Phi Sigma Alpha. Democrat. Avocations: antiques, tennis, historic home restoration, landscaping. Office: Klimist McKnight Sale McClow & Cazano 400 Galleria Officentre Ste 117 Southfield MI 48034-2161 E-mail: rjmcclow@aol.com.

MCCLUNE, MICHAEL MARLYN, real estate executive; b. Denver, July 12, 1950; s. Raymond Earl and Lorraine Elva (Bohm) McC.; m. Elizabeth Ann Butler, Sept. 18, 1982; children: Kristin Elizabeth, Michael Ryan. BSCE magna cum laude, U. So. Calif., 1972, MBA, 1974. Lic. real estate broker, Calif. Real estate investment broker Vistar Fin., Marina del Rey, Calif., 1979-81; program bus. mgr. Hughes Aircraft Co., El Segundo, 1981-85; v.p. LaSalle Ptnrs. Ltd., L.A., 1985-93; pres., CEO, New Am. Asset Mgmt. Svcs., Long Beach, Calif., 1993-97; pres. New Am. Cons. Svcs., 1993-97; regional v.p. LaSalle Ptnrs. Mgmt. Svcs., Inc., 1998; nat. dir. real estate svcs. EPS Solutions, Newport Beach, Calif., 1999-2000; CEO MKC Mgmt. Svcs., Long Beach, 2000-2001; sr. mng. dir. Newmark of Calif., 2001—. Capt. USAF, 1974-79. Mem. Bldg. Owners and Mgrs. Assn. Greater L.A. (exec. com. 1994—, bd. dirs. 1994—, chmn. bd. dirs. 1995-96, President's award 1993), Long Beach Mgrs. Assn. (v.p. 1988-90), Rotary, Tau Beta Pi. Avocations: family, tennis, golf. Office: Newmark of Calif 400 Oceangate Ste 210 Long Beach CA 90802-2614

MCCLUNEY, ROSS (WILLIAM MCCLUNEY), research physicist; b. Cape Girardeau, Mo., Dec. 26, 1940; s. William Jones and Luella Benjamin McCluney; m. Judith McCluney, June 15, 1969 (div. Jan. 1984); children: Alan Michael, Kevin Elliot. BA in Physics, Rhodes Coll., 1963; MS in Physics, U. Tenn., 1966; PhD in Physics, U. Miami, 1971. Devel. engr. Eastman Kodak Co., Rochester, N.Y., 1966-67; rsch. scientist NASA/Goddard Space Flight Ctr., Greenbelt, Md., 1971-76; prin. rsch. scientist Fla. Solar Energy Ctr., Cocoa, 1976—. Author: Daylighting-- Natural Light for passive Design, 1986, Introduction to Radiometry and Photometry, 1994; author, editor: The Environmental Destruction of South Florida, 1971. V.p. Floridians for a Sustainable Population, Fla., 1998—. Mem. AAAS, Optical Soc. Am., Internat. Optical Engring. Soc. Avocations: tennis, swimming. Office: Fla Solar Energy Ctr 1679 Clearlake Rd Cocoa FL 32922-5703

MCCLUNG, A(LEXANDER) KEITH, JR. retired lawyer; b. Gallipolis, Ohio, Sept. 13, 1934; s. Alexander Keith and Florence (Juhling) McC.; m. Sandra B. Foley, Aug. 17, 1957; children: Alexander Keith III, Martha E. AB, W.Va. U., 1956; JD, Harvard U., 1959. Bar: W.Va. 1959, Md. 1970, Mich. 1972. Assoc. Jackson, Kelly, Holt & O'Farrell, Charleston, W.Va., 1959-69; assoc. counsel Comml. Credit Corp., Balt., 1969-70; v.p., counsel McCullagh Leasing, Inc., Roseville, Mich., 1970-73, Comml. Credit Corp., Balt., 1973-82, gen. atty., 1982-85; sr. gen. atty. Comml. Credit Co., 1985-89, sr. v.p., gen. counsel, 1989-98. V.p., counsel McCullagh Leasing, Inc., Roseville, Mich., 1970-73; bd. dirs. Traelers Bank; trustee Roland Park Found.; mem. adv. coun. Coll. Arts and Sci., W.Va. U. Lt. U.S. Army, 1961-62. Mem. ABA (subcom. uniform comml. code, com. equipment leasing). Democrat. Home: 13 Devon Hill Rd Baltimore MD 21210-1044 Office: Comml Credit Co 300 Saint Paul St Baltimore MD 21202-2120

MCCLUNG, HUGO JUHLING, pediatrician, educator; b. Gallipolis, Ohio, Feb. 27, 1941; s. A. Keith and Florence E. (Juhling) McC.; m. Helen K. Peters, Aug. 22, 1964; children: William J., Andrew P., Matthew A. BA, W. Va. U., 1963, MD, 1967. Diplomate Am. Bd. Pediatrics in Gen. Pediatrics, Pediatric Gastroenterology. Intern, then resident U. Wis.; rsch. fellow Hosp. for Sick Children, Toronto, Canada, 1972—74; chief pediatric gastroenterology Ohio State U., Columbus, Ohio, 1974—; assoc. med. dir. Columbus Children's Hosp., 1985—; prof. pediatrics Ohio State U., Columbus, 1992—2000. Med. dir. Children's Homecare Svcs., 1992—. Elder Presbyn. Ch., Blacklick, Ohio. Maj. U.S. Army, 1969-72. Mem. Am. Gastroenterology Assn., N. Am. Soc. Pediatric Gastroenterology and Nutrition, Pediatric Acad. Assn. (pres. 1992—). Avocation: genealogy. Home: 6470 Havens Rd Blacklick OH 43004-9671 Office: Columbus Children's Hosp 700 Childrens Dr Columbus OH 43205-2664

MCCLUNG, J(AMES) DAVID, corporate executive, lawyer, academic administrator; b. Lamesa, Tex., July 16, 1943; s. Jack Weldon Sr. and Ruby (Brown) McC.; m. Linda Nelson, Feb. 12, 1966; children: LeEtta McClung Felter, Dennis, Pamela McClung Frazier, Jennifer McClung Panicker. Student, N.E. La. State Coll., 1961-62, McNeese State Coll., 1963; BSBA cum laude, Bethany Nazarene Coll., 1965; postgrad., U. Okla., 1967-68; JD cum laude, Baylor U., 1973. Bar: Tex. 1973, U.S. Dist. Ct. (no. dist.) Tex. 1975, U.S. Ct. Appeals (5th cir.) 1974. Assoc. Jackson & Walker, Dallas, 1973-76; exec. v.p. Austin Industries, Inc., 1976-88; pres., chief exec. officer, chmn. bd. Green Internat., Inc., Denver, 1988—; owner NazNet.Com, 1999—. Arbitrator Am. Arbitration Assn., 1978—; bd. dirs. Green Holdings, Inc., Denver; chmn. bd. Green Construction Co., Green Mining, Inc., Green Alaska, Inc., GEM Investors, Inc., Green Overseas Corp., Northland Maintenance Co., Northland Alaska, Inc., Green Investments, Inc., Denver, 1988—; pres. Triton Marine Cons., 1994-2000; chmn. Triton Marine Cons., 2000—; pres. Ea. Nazarene Coll., 2002—. Contbr. articles to profl. jours. Trustee So. Nazarene U., Bethany, Okla., 1978—; mem. gen. bd. Ch. of the Nazarene, Kansas City, 1985-89, sec. Commn. Report, 1989. Capt. USAF, 1965-71, Vietnam. Decorated 6 Air medals; recipient Young Grads. award of merit Baylor U., 1983, Outstanding Alumni award So. Nazarene U., 1989, Disting. Svc. award Ch. of the Nazarene, 1989. Mem. ABA, Tex. Bar Assn., The Beavers. Republican. Avocations: digital photography, fishing. Home: 3504 C St NW Gig Harbor WA 98335-7801 Office: Ea Nazarene Coll 23 E Elm Ave Quincy MA 02170-1663 E-mail: mcclung@naznet.com.

MCCLUNG, KENNETH AUSTIN, JR. training executive, performance consultant; b. Decatur, Ga., Apr. 11, 1947; s. Kenneth Austin Sr. and Marianne (Conklin) McC.; m. Christina June Palensar, Mar. 21, 1975. BA, North Ga. Coll., 1969; MS, EdD, U. So. Calif., 1976. Commd. 2d lt. U.S. Army, 1969, advanced through grades to maj., 1980; col. USAR; sr. ptnr. Instrl. Design Group, Inc., Morristown, N.J., 1981-99; v.p., nat. learning dir. Jack Morton Worldwide, 1999-2000, nat. learning dir., 2000—02; ptnr. McClung, McClung & Assoc., Hertford, NC, 2002—. Bd. dirs. Nat. Productivity Ctr., Boulder, Colo., Price Waterhouse Learning Bd.; author/mgr. over 150 mgmt., sales, and tech. tng. programs; cons. in field. Author: Microcomputers for Medical Professionals, 1984, Microcomputers for Legal Professionals, 1984, Microcomputers for Investment Professionals, 1984, Microcomputers for Insurance Professionals, 1984, Personal Computers for Executives, 1984, French edit. 1985; co-author: Sales Training Handbook, 1989. Mem. ASTD, Internat. Soc. for Performance Improvement (pres. N.J. chpt. 1986-88, N.E. regional cons. 1989-90, nat. nomination chmn. 1990-91, nat. emerging tech. chmn. 1991-92). Avocations: sailing, tennis, bicycling, running, skiing. Home: 128 Back Creek Dr Hertford NC 27944 Office: McClung McClung & Assoc 128 Back Creek Dr Hertford NC 27944

MCCLUNG, L. BRUCE, electronics executive; b. Rupert, W.Va., June 26, 1937; BSEE, W.Va. U., 1960. Registered profl. engr., W.Va. With Union Carbide Corp., 1960; prin. engr. energy sys. engring. and tech. group Union Carbide, South Charleston, W.Va.; now vice chmn. Elec. Safety Con. Svcs. Inc., Charleston. Contbr. articles to profl. jours. Fellow: IEEE (Stds. Medallion award 1990, Charles Proteus Steinmetz award 1995, medal for engring. excellence); mem.: Nat. Fire Protection Assn. (mem. elec. sect., nat. elec. code and elec. safety requirements for employee workplace), Am. Petroleum Inst. (subcom. on elec. equipment), Chem. Mfrs. Assn. (elec. codes nad stds. task group), Dielectrics and Elec. Insulation Soc., Power Engring. Soc., Indsl. Application Soc. Office: Elec Safety Cons Svcs 656 Whittington Dr Charleston WV 25312 Business E-Mail: mcc-escs@worldnet.att.net.*

MCCLUNG, MERLE STEVEN, lawyer; b. Montevideo, Minn., June 30, 1943; BA, Harvard U., 1965, JD, 1972; AB, MA, Oxford U., Eng., 1967. Bar: Mass. 1973. Instr. Miles Coll., Birmingham, Ala., 1969-70; staff atty. Harvard Ctr. Law & Edn., Cambridge, Mass., 1972-79; dir. law and edn. ctr. Edn. Commn. States, Denver, 1979-81; gen. counsel Pendleton Land & Exploration, Inc., 1981-94, Accelerated Cos., Englewood, 1994—2001; owner and mgr. McEdlaw LLC, 2001—. Legal cons. Conn. Dept. Edn., Hartford, 1974-77, Calif. Dept. Edn., Sacramento, 1978-81. Contbr. articles to profl. jours. Rhodes scholar Oxford U., Eng., 1965. Mem. ABA, Mass. Bar Assn., Phi Beta Kappa. Avocations: biking, books. Home: 6048 S Locust Cir Englewood CO 80111-4465 Office: Accelerated Companies 5295 Dtc Pkwy Centennial CO 80111-2752

MCCLUNG, WILLIAM ALEXANDER, foundation administrator, educator; b. Norfolk, Va., Jan. 22, 1944; s. William Alexander and Winifred (Boggs) McC. BA, Williams Coll., 1966; AM, Harvard U., 1967, PhD, 1972. Asst. prof. English, Miss. State U., Mississippi State, 1971-76, assoc. prof., 1976-84, prof., 1984-2001; exec. dir. Theta Delta Chi Ednl. Found., Inc. Vis. assoc. prof. Conn. Coll., New London, 1980; vis. prof. Ga. Tech, 1986, UCLA, 1989, Meisei U., Tokyo, 1990-91. Author: The Country House in English Renaissance Poetry, 1977, The Architecture of Paradise, 1983, Landscapes of Desire, 2000 (L.A. Times Best Nonfiction book award 2000); contbr. numerous articles on architecture and lit. to profl. jours. Mem.: Williams Club NY, Harvard Faculty Club (Cambridge, Mass.), Harvard Club N.Y.C., Theta Delta Chi (editor 1967—88, 1998—, trustee Ednl. Found. 1984—). Avocation: photography. Office: 214 Lewis Wharf Boston MA 02110 E-mail: execdir@tdx.org.

MCCLURE, ALLAN HOWARD, materials engineer, space contamination specialist, space materials consultant; b. Phila., Mar. 29, 1925; s. C. Howard and Edda Cherry (Speirs) McC.; m. Jean Florence Hall, May 31, 1947; children: Joyce Ann, Allan Hall. BS, Widener U., 1949; postgrad., Command & Gen. Staff Coll., 1972. Chemist Am. Cyanamid, Pitts., 1950-52; materials engr. Piasecki/Vertol Helicopter Co., Morton, Pa., 1952-59; lead engr. Boeing Aerospace Co., Seattle, 1959-71, sr. specialist engr. Kent, Wash., 1974-85; tech. cons. Adhesive Engring. Co., San Carlos, Calif., 1971-74. Author, investigator spacecraft contamination control documents and govt. reports. Pres. Seattle Crime Prevention League, 1974-84. Served to maj. U.S. Army, 1943-46, ETO, PTO; sec. Boeing Employees Amateur Radio Soc., 1984; membership chmn. Amateur Radio Emergency Services, 1984-85. Recipient Silver Beaver award and William H. Spurgeon III award Boy Scouts Am., Seattle, 1964. Mem. Am. Chem. Soc., Soc. for Advancement of Material and Process Engring. (nat. dir., pres. Seattle chpt.), Rainier C. of C., Res. Officers Assn. (life). Republican. Avocations: amateur radio, hiking, coin collecting, canoeing, photography. Home: 12015 Marine Dr Unit 454 Marysville WA 98271-9325

MCCLURE, ALVIN BRUCE, technical consultant; b. Cin., Mar. 2, 1953; s. Alphonso Bruce McClure and Jewel Lee (Smith) Yates; m. Katherine Shenkar, Nov. 7, 1979; children: Jaina, Randi; m. Penny Bliss, July 7, 2000. Student, U. Mich., 1971-73, 76-77, Fanshawe Coll., London, Ont., Can., 1974-75, Coll. of St. Thomas, 1989-91. Programmer Mfg. Data Systems, Ann Arbor, Mich., 1978-79; systems software specialist Mpls. Star and Tribune, 1979-81; systems analyst NCR COMTEN, Inc., Roseville, Minn., 1981-84; software systems support programmer INTRAN Corp., Bloomington, 1984-85; programmer/analyst Minn. Dept. Natural Resources, St. Paul, 1985-97; local area network adminstr. Minn. Pollution Control Agy., 1997-98; network mgr. Minn. Dept. Health, Mpls., 1998; info. sys. mgr. Van Wagenen Co., Eden Prairie, 1998-99; sr. tech. cons. Database/Network/WEB Lawson Software, St. Paul, 1999-2000; tech. cons. Productive Solutions Group, Mpls., 2000—01; pres. Reality Bytes, Inc., Elk River, 2001—. Mem. mgmt. info. services tech. com., St. Paul, 1987-97. Community adv. bd. Sta. WCAL-FM, 1988-90. Mem. IEEE, Am. Inst. Physics, Audio Engring. Soc., Internat. Platform Assn., Mgmt. Info. Svcs., Aikido Yoshinkai Mpls.-St. Paul (5th degree black belt, head instr.). Avocations: chess, photography, audiophile, sailing, aquaria. Home: 14348 96th St NE Elk River MN 55330-7376 Office: Reality Bytes Inc 14348 96th St NE Elk River MN 55330-7376 E-mail: alvin@heisei.com.

MCCLURE, ANN CRAWFORD, judge, lawyer; b. Cin., Sept. 5, 1953; d. William Edward and Patricia Ann (Jewett) Crawford; m. David R. McClure, Nov. 12, 1983; children: Kinsey Tristen, Scott Crawford. BFA magna cum laude, Tex. Christian U., 1974; JD, U. Houston, 1979. Bd. cert. in family law and civil appellate law Tex. Bd. Legal Specialization. Assoc. Piro and Lilly, Houston, 1979-83; pvt. practice El Paso, Tex., 1983-92; ptnr. McClure and McClure, 1992-94; justice 8th Ct. of Appeals, 1995—. Past mem. Tex. Bd. Law Examiners, Bd. Disciplinary Appeals; mem. Family Law Specialization Exam Com., 1989—93; mem. civil appellate law adv. com. Tex. Bd. Legal Specialization; mem. Tex. Jud. Coun. Contbr. articles to profl. jours.; past editor The Family Law Forum; past contbg. editor: Texas Family Law Service; mem. editl. bd. Tex. Family Law Practice Manual, 1982-93; editl. cons. Matthew Bender Tex. Family Law Practice and Procedure. Mem.: El Paso Bar Assn. (sec. 2002—), Tex. Acad. Family Law Specialists (past dir.), State Bar Tex. (appellate divsn. jud. sect. chair 2000—01, family law sect. chair 1997—98). Democrat. Presbyterian.

MCCLURE, BROOKS, management consultant; b. N.Y.C., Mar. 8, 1919; s. Walter Harsha and Angelica (Mendoza) McClure; m. Olga Beatrice Gallik, Oct. 15, 1949; 1 child Karen (dec.). AB summa cum laude, U. Md.; disting. grad., U.S. Naval War Coll. N.Y. corr. Western Press Ltd., Australia, 1939-42; copy editor Washington Eve. Star, 1946-51; joined U.S. Fgn. Service, 1951; information officer, attache embassy Copenhagen, 1951-53; press attache embassy Vienna, 1953-55; information officer, attache embassy Cairo, 1956-57, Seoul, 1957-60, Bonn, 1960-63; policy officer Europe USIA, 1963-66; pub. affairs officer 1st sec. embassy, Copenhagen, 1967-72; spl. asst. policy plans and nat. security council affairs, internat. security affairs Dept. Def., 1972-76; internat. security adviser USIA, 1976-77; program coordinator Crisis Assessment Staff, Dept. Commerce, 1977-78; dir. ops. Internat. Mgmt. Analysis and Resources Corp., 1978-81, v.p., 1982—; sec. Cross-Continent Assocs. Ltd., 1994-99. Various spl. assignments Europe, Mid. East, Asia, Africa; detailed to Vietnam, 1967, 70; lectr. FBI Acad., Fgn. Svc. Inst., Inter-Am. Def. Coll., Army War Coll., Navy War Coll. Contbg. author: book Modern Guerrilla Warfare, 1962, contbg. author: book Dynamics of Terrorism, 1977, contbg. author: book International Terrorism in Contemporary World, 1978, contbg. author: book Corporate Vulnerability and How to Assess it: Political Terrorism and Business, 1979, contbg. author: book Business and the Middle East, 1981, contbg. author: book Political Terrorism and Energy, 1981; contbr. articles to profl. jours.; author: report to Senate Judiciary Com. on internat. terrorism and hostage def. measures; testifier on internat. security, hostage behavior, def. of Alaskan pipeline, FBI charter U.S. Senate, 1975—79. With AUS, 1942—46, ETO. Mem.: DACOR, Nat. Press Club, Assn. Diplomatic Studies, Am. Fgn. Svc. Assn., Alpha Sigma Lambda, Phi Kappa Phi. Home: 6204 Rockhurst Rd Bethesda MD 20817-1756 Office: IMAR Corp PO Box 34528 Bethesda MD 20827-0528 E-mail: imarmgtsvcs@mindspring.com., b-kmcclure@mindspring.com.

MCCLURE, CONNIE DIANE, elementary school educator; b. Huntsville, Tex., July 4, 1956; d. Albert Joseph and Alpha Lee (Ash) Davis; m. Ronnie Preston McClure, May 20, 1978; children: Micah Lindsay, Matthew Christopher. BS in Edn., Howard Payne U., 1978; MS in Art Edn., U. North Tex., 1996. Cert. elem. tchr., Tex. Tchr. Brownwood (Tex.) Ind. Sch. Dist., 1980-82; interviewer Tex. Employment Commn., Ft. Worth, 1983-85, investigator, 1985-87, job search tng. seminar facilitator, 1987-89; elem. art tchr. Ft. Worth Ind. Sch. Dist., 1989-97; workshop leader North Tex. Getty Inst. Visual Arts Edn., 1992-94; tchr. elem. art Hurst-Euless-Bedford Ind. Sch. Dist., 1997—. Vol. Brownwood Community Cultural Affairs Commn., 1980-82; coord. Tex. Rangers Baseball Club Summer Acad., 1997-99. Marcus fellow Sch. Visual Arts, U. North Tex., 1995-96. Mem. NEA, NAEA, Tex. Classroom Tchrs. Assn., Alpha Rho Tau (sec. 1976-77). Republican. Baptist. Avocations: ceramics, drawing, writing, reading, sewing. Office: 1809 NE 36th St Fort Worth TX 76106-4607

MCCLURE, DANIEL M. lawyer; b. Enid, Okla., Feb. 5, 1952; s. Larry M. and Marie Dolores (Sarver) McC.; m. Judy Lynn Pinson, Jan. 3, 1976; children: Andrew Mead, Mark William, Kathleen Claire. BA with highest hons., U. Okla., 1974; JD cum laude, Harvard U., 1978. Bar: Tex. 1978, U.S. Dist. Ct. (so. dist., ea. dist.) Tex. 1979, U.S. Ct. Appeals (5th cir., 11th cir.) 1981. Assoc. Fulbright & Jaworski, LLP, Houston, 1978-86, ptnr., 1986—. Fellow Tex. Bar Found.; mem. ABA, Nat. Health Lawyers Assn., Nat. Assn. R.R. Trial Counsel, Tex. Bar Assn., Houston Bar Assn. (cert. civil trial law), Harvard Law Sch. Assn. Avocation: tennis. Home: 2 Long Timbers Ln Houston TX 77024-5445 Office: Fulbright & Jaworski LLP 1301 McKinney St Houston TX 77010-3031 E-mail: dmcclure@fulbright.com.

MCCLURE, DAVID H. utilities company analyst; b. Kennesaw, Ga., Apr. 29, 1948; s. Benjamin H. and Katherine E. (Reece) McC.; m. Judy King McClure; children: Christina Aldridge, John Robert Aldridge, Lori K. Aldridge, Charissa Diane Thomas. B in Indsl. Engring. Tech., So. Poly. U., 1976. Assoc. engr. Western Electric Co., Atlanta, 1972-75; jr. acct. Jack McPherson, CPA, Acworth, Ga., 1975-76; div. materials planner Southwire Co., Carrollton, 1976-78, indsl. engr., 1978-79; process engr. Alcan Cable, Tucker, 1979-82; rsch. specialist Ga. Power Co., Forest Park, 1982-86, staff rep., 1986-87, staff services engr., 1987-91, head of quality assurance sect., 1982-91, mgr. quality and support, 1991-94; bus. cons., 1994-96; bus. analyst, 1996—. Chmn. bd. dirs. Am. Diabetes Assn. Ga. Affiliate, Inc., Atlanta, 1985-87, nat. bd. dirs., 1988-91, mem. nat. com. on affiliate assocs., 1986-89, vice chmn., 1988-89, chmn. 1991-92, nat. So. region liaison, 1987-89; chmn. Nat. Com. on Fund Raising, 1989-91; nat. bd. mentor, 1989—, chmn. nat. bd. dirs., 1995-96, chmn. nat. strategic planning steering com., 1994-95, chmn. nat. nominating com., 1996-97, chmn. nat. alumni assn., 1996-97, ctr. for quality excellence adv. coun., 1987-92, chmn., 1989-90; chmn. Southeastern Quality Conf. Program, 1989, 90, 91, chmn. arrangements, 1992; mem. Ga. Dept. Human Resources Diabetes adv. com., 1989-92; chmn. bd. dirs. Am. Diabetes Rsch. Found., 1997-98, chmn. rsch. found. nominating com., 1998-99; nat. bd. dirs. Combined Health Appeal of Am., 1993-99, chmn. agy. rels., 1996-99. Staff sgt. USAF, 1968-72. Named Vol. of Yr., Am. Diabetes Assn. Ga. Affiliate, Inc., 1983-84, 84-85; recipient Ga. Power Co. R.W. Scherer award for leadership in cmty. svc., 1991, Am. Diabetes Assn. Charles H. Best award for disting. svc., 1996. Mem. Inst. Indsl. Engrs. (sec. 1976-77, v.p. seminars 1977-78), Am. Soc. Quality Control (cert. quality engr. 1983—, chmn. bd.-elect Greater Atlanta sect. exec. bd. 1989-92), Nat. Mgmt. Assn. (LDR chpt., profl. devel. com. 1989-91), Capital Area Kiwanis Club (bd. dirs. 1989—, pres. elect 1990-91, pres. 1991-92). Baptist. Home: 706 Singley Dr Lawrenceville GA 30044-5972

MCCLURE, DONALD STUART, physical chemist, educator; b. Yonkers, N.Y., Aug. 27, 1920; s. Robert Hirt and Helen (Campbell) McC.; m. Laura Lee Thompson, July 9, 1949; children: Edward, Katherine, Kevin. BChem, U. Minn., 1942; PhD, U. Calif., Berkeley, 1948. With war rsch. divsn. Columbia U., 1942-46; mem. faculty U. Calif., Berkeley, 1948-55; group leader, mem. profl. staff RCA Labs., 1955-62; prof. chemistry U. Chgo., 1962-67, Princeton (N.J.) U., 1967-91, prof. emeritus, 1991—, sr. rsch. assoc. Vis. lectr. various univs.; cons. to govt. and industry. Author: Electronic Spectra of Molecules and Ions in Crystals, 1959, Some Aspects of Crystal Field Theory, 1964; also articles. Guggenheim fellow Oxford (Eng.) U., 1972-73; Humboldt fellow, 1980; recipient Irving Langmuir prize, 1979 Fellow Am. Acad. Arts and Scis., Nat. Acad. Scis., Am. Phys. Soc.; mem. Am. Chem. Soc. Home: 23 Hemlock Cir Princeton NJ 08540-5405 E-mail: d.s.mcclure@att.net., dmcclure@princeton.edu.

MCCLURE, EVELYN SUSAN, historian, photographer; b. Milw., Mar. 11, 1940; d. Henry F. and Blanche E. Schuster; m. John C. McClure, Oct. 26, 1967; 1 child, Heather. BS, U. Wis., 1964. Cert. fine art photography, U. Calif. Adminstrv. asst. Northwestern U., Chgo., 1964-66, KGO-TV, San Francisco, 1966-70, Crocker Bank, San Francisco, 1980-86, Wells Fargo Bank, San Francisco, 1986-93; pub. Belle View Press, Sebastopol, Calif., 1993—. Author, photographer: Sebastopol, California - History, Homes & People 1855-1920, 1995 (Historic Scholarship award Sonoma County Hist. Soc. 1997), Sebastopol's Historic Cemetery, 2000; columnist Sonoma West Times and News, Sebastopol, 1998—. Exhbn. com. Sebastopol Ctr. Arts, 1995-97; bd. mem., publicity chair, newsletter editor, vol. Western Sonoma County Hist. Soc., Sebastopol, 1996; dir. W. Co. Mus., 1999—. Roman Catholic. Avocation: gardening. E-mail: belleview@monitor.net.

MCCLURE, GROVER BENJAMIN, management consultant; b. Houstonia, Mo., Oct. 15, 1918; s. Grover B. and Sue F. (Cook) McC. BA, U. Richmond, 1939. Pres. internat. div. Richardson-Merrell, N.Y.C., 1954-62; pres. Europe and Africa divs. Paris, 1960-81; exec. v.p., dir. Richardson-Vicks, Inc., Wilton, Conn., 1981-85; cons. New Canaan, 1985—. Bd. dirs., co-chmn. Silvermine Art Guild. Served to lt. comdr. USNR, 1941-46. Mem. Silver Springs Club (Ridgefield, Conn.). Republican. Presbyterian. Avocations: tennis, golf, travel, yachting. Home: 1321 Meadow Ridge Redding CT 06896

MCCLURE, HAL H. travel film producer; b. Indpls. s. Harold Alonzo and Betty (Zemah Hays) McC.; m. Dorothea Vernell Millar, Jan. 15, 1949 (dec. 1994). AA, L.A. City Coll., 1941. Journalist various newspapers, Calif., 1949-56; newsman AP, L.A., 1956-58, N.Y.C., 1959-60, fgn. corr. S.E. Asia and Middle East, 1961-76, bur. chief N.J., 1976-77; prin., travel film producer Hal McClure Prodns., Laguna Woods, Calif., 1978—. Adj. asst. prof. journalism Seton Hall U., S. Orange, N.J., 1976-77. Contbr. (book) Lightning Out of Israel, 1967; editor: Fire Over Suez, 1971; prodr. 13 travel films including Istanbul—Travels in Turkey, 1990, Land of Legend—England Scotland and Wales, 1993, Adventure Holland, 1994, Mystery Tales of Europe, 1996, Dracula-Travels in Transylvania, 1997, Story Book England, 1999, Magic of Malaysia, 2001; editor, co-owner Travel Adventure Cinema mag., 1978—; prodr. live electronic cinema for theater audience, 1994; leader in Travelogue Field's move to digital prodn. Capt. USAFR, 1942-56. Recipient Rising Star award Program mag., 1978, Travelogue Hall of Fame award, 1994; Ogden Reid Found. fellow, 1959. Mem. Travel Adventure Cinema Soc. Home and Office: 686 Avenida Sevilla # C Laguna Woods CA 92653-3838

MCCLURE, HOWARD JEAN, JR. advocate; b. High Point, N.C., June 15, 1959; s. Howard Jean McClure Sr. and Mary Elizabeth McClure. Author: Conflict Of Interest, 1999. Chmn. polit. action com. Carolina Advocates for Legal Reform, Charlotte, NC, 2001—02, v.p., 2001—02; rels. com. Charlotte Mecklenburg Cmty., 2002—. Mem.: NAACP (mem. legal redress com. 1999—, edn. com. 2001—, labor & industry com. 2001—). Conservative. Avocations: music, writing, fishing, travel, football. Home: 3621 B Central Ave Charlotte NC 28205 Office: Charlotte Mecklenburg NAACP Post Office Box 25774 Charlotte NC 28229-5774 Personal E-mail: theebonysaint@webtv.net.

MCCLURE, JAMES FOCHT, JR. federal judge; b. Danville, Pa., Apr. 6, 1931; s. James Focht and Florence Kathryn (Fowler) McC.; m. Elizabeth Louise Barber, June 14, 1952; children: Holly McClure Kerwin, Kimberly Ann Pacala, Jamee McClure Sealy, Mary Elizabeth Hudec, Margaret McClure Persing. AB, Amherst Coll., 1952; JD, U. Pa., 1957. Bar: D.C. 1957, Pa. 1958, U.S. Dist. Ct. D.C. 1957, U.S. Dist. Ct. (ea. and mid. dist.) Pa. 1958, U.S. Ct. Appeals (3d cir.) 1959. Atty., advisor Dept. State, Washington, 1957-58; assoc. Morgan, Lewis & Bockius, Phila., 1958-61; atty. Merck & Co., Inc., N.Y.C., 1961-65; ptnr. McClure & McClure, Lewisburg, Pa., 1965-77, McClure & Light, Lewisburg, 1978-84; pres., judge Ct. Common Pleas, 17th Jud. Dist. Pa., 1984-90; sr. dist. judge U.S. Dist. Ct. (mid. dist.) Pa., Williamsport, Pa., 1990—. Dist. atty. Union County, Lewisburg, 1974-75. Pres. bd. sch. dirs. Lewisburg Area Sch. Dist., 1969-74. Cpl. U.S. Army, 1952-54. Mem. Pa. Bar Assn., Union County Bar Assn., Bucknell U. Golf Club, Susquehanna Valley Chorale, Order of Coif, Phi Beta Kappa. Republican. Presbyterian. Office: US Dist Ct 240 W 3rd St Ste 406 Williamsport PA 17701-6466 E-mail: gary_palmer@unc.edu.

MCCLURE, JAMES JULIUS, JR. lawyer, former city official; b. Oak Park, Ill., Sept. 23, 1920; s. James J. and Ada Leslie (Baker) McC.; m. Margaret Carolyn Phelps, Apr. 9, 1949; children: John Phelps, Julia Jean, Donald Stewart. BA, U. Chgo., 1942, JD, 1949. Bar: Ill. 1950. Ptnr. Gardner, Carton & Douglas, Chgo., 1962-91, of counsel, 1991—; mem. Oak Park Plan Commn., 1966-73, Northeastern Ill. Planning Commn., 1973-77, pres., 1975-77, Village of Oak Park, 1973-81, Oak Park Exch. Congress Inc., 1978—2002. Mem. Bus. Leaders for Transp., 1998—. Pres. United Christian Cmty. Svcs., 1967-69, 71-73, Erie Neighborhood House, 1953-55, Oak Park-River Forest Cmty. Chest, 1967; moderator Presbytery Chgo., 1969; mem. Gov.'s Spl. Com. on MPO, 1978-79; bd. dirs. Leadership Coun. of Met. Open Cmtys., 1981-2002, sec., 1990-98; bd. dirs. Met. Planning Coun., 1982-93, hon. dir., 1993—; bd. dirs. Cmty. Renewal Soc., 1982-91, v.p., 1984-88, treas. 1988-91; chmn. Christian Century Found., 1981—; bd. trustees McCormick Theol. Sem., 1981—, chmn. bd. 1987-90. hon. trustee, 1990—; mem. ch. vocations unit, 1987-92, vice chair 1990; mem. gen. assembly coun. Presbyn. Ch. U.S.A., 1987-90, mem. gen. assembly Permanent Jud. Commn., 1997—; bd. dirs. Oak Park Edn. Found., 1991-96, Oak Park River Forest Cmty. Found., 1991-2002; mem. Vision 2000 (Oak Park) Coordinating Com., 1995. With USNR, 1942-46. Recipient Disting. Citizen award Oak Park, 1976; Silver Beaver award; Disting. Eagle Scout award Boy Scouts Am., Carl Winters Cmty. Svc. award Oak Park Rotary Club, 1996, William Staczak award Oak Park Edn. Found., 1997, Rita Johnson award Oak Park Family Svc. and Mental Health Ctr., 1997, Public Svc. award U. Chgo. Alumni Assn., 1997, Tradition of Excellence award Oak Pk. River Forest H.S., 1998. Mem. ABA, Am. Coll. Trust and Estate Counsel, Ill. State Bar Assn., Chgo. Bar Assn., Am. Law Inst., Order of the Coif, Lambda Alpha. Clubs: Univ. (Chgo.). Home: One Calvin Cir # C 309 Evanston IL 60201 Office: Gardner Carton & Douglas 321 N Clark St Ste 3200 Chicago IL 60610-4719 *Love of God, love of family, awareness of both the uniqueness and the contribution of every other human being, a sense of the wholeness of life with my religious faith, my profession of law, my family and my community service each playing an important part and complimenting each other.*

MCCLURE, KENNETH HUFFMAN, import/export executive; b. Chattanooga, Apr. 26, 1919; s. Alexander Ewart and Mary Jeanette (Huffman) McC.; m. Mary Lily Rule, July 28, 1942; children: Pamela Weyeneth, Diane Holsenbeck, Wendy Rule Thomson. BS, U. Pa., 1940; honorary degree in engring., Worcester Poly. Inst., 1990. Sales rep. Am. Airlines, Inc., N.Y.C., 1940-41, supr. purchasing, 1945-47; dir. purchasing CARE, Inc., 1947-51; dir. purchasing and v.p. overseas ops. E.J. Brach & Sons, Chgo., 1951-55; pres., chief exec. officer K.H. McClure & Co., Stamford, Conn., 1955-66; chmn. K.H. McClure & Co. and affiliates, 1966-79; mng. dir. Coco Co. de Mexico S.A., Campeche, Mexico, 1967-79; cons. Novo Mundo Devel. Corp., Charlottesville, Va., 1979—. Chmn. Crown Cocoa Corp., S.A., Caracas, Venezuela, 1957-79; bd. dirs. Deerfield Groves, Inc., Vero Beach, Fla., fgn. divsn. State Nat. Bank Conn. Elder Presbyn. Ch. Comdr. USN, 1941-45. Mem. Rotary (pres. Stamford chpt. 1973-74). Republican. Home: 625 Worthington Dr Apt 103 Charlottesville VA 22903-4659

MCCLURE, ROGER JOHN, lawyer; b. Cleve., Nov. 22, 1943; s. Theron R. and Colene (Irwin) McClure. BA, Ohio State U., 1965, JD cum laude, 1972; MA, Northwestern U., 1966. Bar: Va. 1973, Md. 1973, U.S. Ct. Appeals (D.C. cir.) 1974, U.S. Supreme Ct. 1978, Ohio, U.S. Ct. Appeals (4th, 5th & 10th cirs.). Asst. atty. gen. State of Ohio, Columbus, 1972; trial atty. FTC, Washington, 1972-76; sr. assoc. Law Offices of A.D. Berkeley, 1976-81; pvt. practice Alexandria, Va., 1981—; pres. Roger J. McClure, PC, 1987—; del. Va. Gen. Assembly, 1992—2002, co-chmn. militia and police com., 1998—2002. Adj. prof. Acad. Multidisciplinary Practice Mich. State U., Lansing, 2001—; host talk show Sta. WRC Radio, 1987—93, 1999—2001, Sta. WPGC, 1993—94. Co-author: (book) Winning the Syndication Game, 1988, Advanced Estate Planning in Virginia, 2001, Virginia Elder Law, 1988, Family Limited Partnerships and LLCS, 1999, Asset Protection in Virginia, 1999, Estate and Wealth Strategies Planning, 2000, Choice of Entity in Virginia, 2000; contbg. reviewer ; contbr. articles to profl. jours. Bd. dirs. No. Va. Cmty. Found., 1995—. With U.S. Army, 1967—69. Decorated Bronze Star; fellow Masters, Espertis Peterson Inst., 1996—. Mem.: Dulles Area Transp. Assn. (bd. dirs.), Nat. Network Estate Planning Attys., No. Va. Apt. Assn. (bd. dirs. 1988—92, 1st v.p. 1987—88, pres. 1988—89), D.C. Bar Assn. (real estate steering com. 1982—84, chmn. antitrust divsn. 1975—76), Washington Nat. Cathedral, Wolf Trap Found. (adv. coun.). Avocation: sailing. Office: 500 N Washington St Alexandria VA 22314-2314 E-mail: rmcclure@ix.netcom.com.

MCCLURE, THOMAS ALLAN, physician; b. San Diego, May 7, 1953; s. Irvin Leslie and Virginia Anne McC.; m. Christina Morgan, Sept. 4, 1983; children: Max Allan, Kelsey Morgan. BS in Biology, Stanford U., 1976; MD, U. Cin., 1981. Diplomate Am. Bd. Occupl. Medicine, Am. Bd. Preventive Medicine. Med. dir. dept. occupl. health Calif. Pacific Med. Ctr., San Francisco, 1994—. Mem. Am. Coll. Occupl. and Environ. Medicine. Office: Calif Pacific Med Ctr Dept Occupl Health Ste 160A Castro and Duboce San Francisco CA 94114

MCCLURE, THOMAS JAMES, lawyer; b. Chgo., Feb. 19, 1955; BA in Humanities cum laude, St. Norbert Coll., 1977; JD, Marquette U., 1980. Bar: Wis. 1980, U.S. Dist. Ct. (we. dist.) Wis. 1980, U.S. Dist. Ct. (ea. dist.) Wis. 1981, U.S. Ct. Appeals (7th cir.) 1984. Asst. dist. atty. Washington County, West Bend, Wis., 1980-81, Milwaukee (Wis.) County, 1982, Rock County, Janesville and Beloit, Wis., 1982-85; assoc. deVries, Vlasak & Schallert, Milw., 1985-88, McLario Law Offices S.C., Menomonee Falls, Wis., 1988-92; ptnr. Osinga & McClure, Milw., 1992-97; pres. McClure Law Offices, S.C., Delafield, Wis., 1997—. Instr. Am. jurisprudence Am. Inst. Paralegal Studies Alverno Coll., Milw., 1986; legal counsel city of Delafield Promotional and Tourism Coun., Inc. Elder, bd. dirs. Kettle Moraine Evang. Free Ch., Delafield, Wis., 1987—; mem. police fire commn. City of Delafield, 1988, planning commn., 1988-90; alderman city coun. City of Delafield, 1988-90, pres. city coun., 1989-90. Named One of Outstanding Young Men in Am. U.S. Jaycees, 1984. Mem. Milw. County Bar Assn., Assn. Trial Lawyers Am., Wis. Acad. Trial Lawyers, Wis. State Bar (young lawyers div. subcom. mem. and presenter, Law Day for Clergy 1991), The Rutherford Inst.(Wis. state coord., 1993—), Delafield C. of C., Waukesha County Bar Assn. Home: W318 737 Partridge Run Delafield WI 53018-2820 Office: McClure Law Offices SC 15 Crossroads Ct Delafield WI 53018-2035

MCCLURE, WILLIAM OWEN, biologist; b. Yakima, Wash., Sept. 29, 1937; s. Rexford Delmont and Ruth Josephine (Owen) McC.; m. Pamela Preston Harris, Mar. 9, 1968 (div. 1979); children: Heather Harris, Rexford Owen; m. Sara Joan Rorke, July 27, 1980. BSc, Calif. Inst. Tech., 1959; PhD, U. Wash., 1964. Postdoctoral fellow Rockefeller U., N.Y.C., 1964-65, rsch. assoc., 1965-68; asst. prof. U. Ill., Urbana, 1968-75; assoc. prof. U. So. Calif., L.A., 1975-79, prof. biology, prof. neurology, 1979—; v.p. sci. affairs Nelson Rsch. & Devel. Co., Irvine, Calif., 1981-82, acting v.p. rsch. & devel., 1985-86; dir. program. neurol. info. sci. U. So. Calif., 1982-92, dir. program in psychobiology, 1991—. Dir. cellular biology U. So. Calif., 1979-81, dir. neurobiology, 1982-88, dir. prog. psychobiology, 1991—; cons. in field; dir. Marine & Freshwater Biomed. Ctr., U. So. Calif., 1982-83; co-dir. Baja Calif. Expedition of the R/V Alpha Helix, 1974, others; chmn. Winter Conf. on Brain Rsch., 1979, 80, others; lectr. in field; sci. adv. bd. Nelson R & D, 1972-91; mem. bd. commentators Brain and Behavioral Scis., 1978—. Co-editor: Wednesday Night at the Lab, 1972; patentee in field; mem. editl. bd. Neurochem. Rsch., 1975-81, Jour. Neurochemistry, 1977-84, Jour. Neurosci. Rsch., 1980-86; contbr. over 150 articles to profl. jours. Bd. dirs. San Pedro and Peninsula Hosp. Found., 1989-95, Faculty Ctr., U. So. Calif., 1991-95, San Pedro Health Svcs., 1992-97. Recipient John R. Hubbard award Univ. Assoc., 1993, Assocs. award for outstanding tchg., 1994; Scripps Inst. fellow, 1958, NIH fellow, 1959-65, Alfred P. Sloan fellow, 1972-76, , West Coast Coll. Biol. Psychiatry fellow, 1983, Intersci. Rsch. Inst. fellow, 1989, others; recipient numerous rsch. grants. Mem. AAAS, Am. Soc. Neurochemistry, Soc. for Neurosci., Am. Soc. Biol. Chemistry and Molecular Biology, Internat. Soc. Neurochemistry, Assn. Neurosci. Depts. and Programs, Univ. Park Investment Group, Bay Surgical Soc., N.Y. Acad. Scis, Phi Beta Kappa, Phi Kappa Phi. Republican. Presbyterian. Avocations: computing, travel, photography. Home: 30533 Rhone Dr Palos Verdes Peninsula CA 90275-5742 Office: U So Calif Dept Biol Scis Los Angeles CA 90089-0101

MCCLURE, WILLIAM EARL, financial advisor; b. Tuscaloosa, Al, Mar. 26, 1946; s. James William and Julie Savanna McC.; m. Alison Todd, Apr. 17, 1971; children: Guerin James, Summer Scripps, Elizabeth Hope, Georgia Ann. Student, U. Ala., 1964-66; BA cum laude, Harvard U., 1970, MBA, 1976. Lending officer Inter-Am. Devel. Bank, Washington, 1971-74; sr. v.p. Royal Trust Bank, Miami, 1976-77; pres. Macdavin Internat., 1977-78, Synervest Corp., Champaign, Ill., 1978-80; sr. v.p. Roe, Martin & Neiman, Atlanta, 1980-85; pres., chief exec. officer Carnegie Securities Corp., 1986-90, McClure Capital Strategies, Atlanta, 1986-90; dir. Inter-Am. U.S. Peace Corps, 1989-92, assoc. dir. internat. ops., 1992-93; chief of staff Office of Senator Paul Coverdell, 1993-94; mng. dir. Internat. Projects Group, Inc., Washington, 1994—. Mem. editorial bd. The Wall St. Digest, Princeton, 1985-89. Trustee Atlanta Internat. Sch. Served with USAR, 1970-76. Mem. Internat. Assn. Fin. Planners, Airplane Owners and Pilots Assn., Harvard Club Washington, Harvard Bus. Sch. Club Washington, Univ. Club Washington, Harvard Club N.Y.C. Home: 1803 Briar Ridge Ct Mc Lean VA 22101-4203 Office: Internat Projects Group Inc 1655 Fort Myer Dr Ste 700 Arlington VA 22209-3199

MCCLURE, WILLIAM PENDLETON, lawyer; b. Washington, May 25, 1925; s. John Elmer and Helen Newsome (Pendleton) McC.; children: Marilyn Alexander, Helen Pendleton, Elizabeth Ruffin, Melinda Geoghegan. BS, U. Pa., 1949; JD, George Washington U., 1951, LLM, 1954; postgrad., The Hague (Netherlands) Acad. Internat. Law, 1952. Bar: D.C. 1951. Sr. ptnr. McClure & Trotter, Washington, 1952-91, McClure, Trotter & Mentz, Washington, 1991-93, McClure, Trotter & Mentz, chartered, Washington, 1993-95; ptnr. White & Case, 1995—. Chmn. D.C. div. Crusade Against Cancer, Am. Cancer Soc., 1966, 67. Served from pvt. to 1st lt., inf. U.S. Army, 1943-46, PTO. Mem. Am. Bar Assn., Bar Assn. D.C., Am. Judicature Soc., Order of Coif, Phi Delta Phi, Phi Delta Theta. Clubs: Metropolitan (Washington), Columbia Country (Washington), Nat. Press (Washington). Office: 601 13th St NW Ste 600 S Washington DC 20005-3807

MCCLURE-BIBBY, MARY ANNE, former state legislator; b. Milbank, S.D., Apr. 21, 1939; d. Charles Cornelius and Mary Lucille (Whittom) Burges; m. D.J. McClure, Nov. 17, 1963 (dec. Apr. 1990); 1 child, Kelly Joanne Kyro; m. John E. Bibby, May 1, 1993. BA magna cum laude, U. S.D., 1961; postgrad., U. Manchester, Eng., 1961-62; M of Pub. Adminstrn., Syracuse (N.Y.) U., 1980. Staff asst. U.S. Senator Francis Case, Washington, 1959-61; sec. to lt. gov. State of S.D., Pierre, 1963, with budget office, 1964; exec. sec. to pres. Frontier Airlines, Denver, 1963-64; tchr. Pub. High Schs., Pierre and Redfield, S.D., 1965-66, 68-70; mem. S.D. State Senate, Pierre, 1975-89, pres. pro tem, 1979-89, vice chmn. coun. of state govts., 1987, chmn. coun. of state govts., 1988; spl. asst. to Pres. Bush for intergovernmental affairs, 1989-92; exec. dir. S.D. Bush-Quayle Campaign, 1992. Vice chmn. sch. bd. Redfield Ind. Sch. Dist., 1970-74. Fulbright scholar, 1961-62, Bush Leadership fellow, 1977-80. Mem. Phi Beta Kappa. Republican. Congregationalist. Home: 822 8th Ave Brookings SD 57006-1314

MCCLURG, ROBERT JAMES, emergency nurse practitioner, educator; b. Warsaw, Sept. 5, 1958; s. Robert and Elizabeth (Castiglia) McC.; m. Tina Marie Crawford, July 15, 1984; 1 child, Rose Marie. AAS, SUNY, Morrisville, 1978; ASN, SUNY, Albany, 1987; AAS, C.C. of the Air Force, Maxwell AFB, Ala., 1988; BSN, Brockport State coll., 1996; MS, U. Buffalo, 1999. RN, N.Y.; cert. paramedic. Enlisted USAF, 1980, advanced through grades to maj., 2000; med. technician 390 Tactical Fighter Squadron, Mountain Home AFB, Idaho, 1981-83; supr., shift leader David Grant USAF Med. Ctr., Travis AFB, Calif., 1983-84, USAF Hosp., Kirtland AFB, N.Mex., 1984-85; ind. duty med. technician USAF Survival Sch., Spokane, Wash., 1985-86, supr., field med. br., 1986-88; staff nurse St. Luke's Hosp., 1987-88, Wyo. County Cmty. Hosp., Warsaw, 1988-89; flight nurse, med. crew dir. USAFR, Niagara Falls, 1989—; EMS coord. St. Jerome Hosp., Batavia, 1989-96; emergency nurse practitioner Strong Meml. Hosp., Rochester, 1999—; clin. assoc. faculty U. Rochester, N.Y., 2000—; family nurse practitioner Wyo. County Cmty. Health Sys., 2000—. Chmn. prehosp. adv. com. Western Regional EMS System, Buffalo, N.Y., 1993-95; mem. Wyo.-Erie Regional EMS Coun. Buffalo, 1993—; vice-chmn. Genesee County EMS Coun., Batavia, 1994-96; EMS coord. World Univ. Games, Buffalo, 1994; alternate rep. to N.Y. State EMS Coun.; mem. legis. com., regional activities com. N.Y. State EMS Coun. Vol. paramedic Perry Emergency Ambulance, N.Y., 1978-79, 88—; mem. Wyo. Co. Paramedic Task Force. Mem. Res. Officer Assn. (life), Air Force Assn. (life). Avocations: pvt. pilot, kayak instr., backpacking/camping, computers. Office: Strong Meml Hosp Emergency Dept 601 Elmwood Ave Rochester NY 14642-0002 E-mail: robert_mcclurg@urmc.rochester.edu.

MCCLURKEN, JAMES BARTHOLOMEW, surgeon; b. Pottstown, Pa., Sept. 28, 1950; married; 3 children. BA, Washington U., St. Louis, 1972; MD, Temple U., 1976. Diplomate Am. Bd. Surgery, Am. Bd. Thoracic Surgery. Thoracic surgeon Abington (Pa.) Hosp., 1982-85, chief thoracic surgery, 1985—; asst. prof. cardiothoracic surgery Temple U. Hosp., Phila., 1985-92, assoc. prof. surgery, 1992-99, assoc. dir. cardiopulmonary transplant., 1991-99, prof. surgery, 1999—. Cons. HIT Investigation, Tex. Biotech., Houston, 1995—97, SmithKline, Phila., 1998, Am. Bd. Surgery, Phila., 1996—. Contbg. articles to profl. jours., chpts. to books. Career day spkr. Upper Dublin Schs., Ft. Washington, Pa., 1996, 97, 98, Color Day award spkr. Pottsgrove Schs., Pa., 1992, 2002. Fellow Am. Coll. Surgeons, Am. Coll. Cardiology, Am. Coll. Chest Physicians, Phila. Coll. Physicians; mem. Soc. Thoracic Surgeons, Internat. Soc. Heart/Lung Transplant, Alpha Omega Alpha. Avocations: skiing, bicycling, sailing, fishing, golf. Office: Temple Univ Hosp Dept of Cardiothoracic Surg 3401 N Broad St Philadelphia PA 19140-5189 also: Levy Med Plz 1235 Old York Rd Ste G28 Abington PA 19001-3800 E-mail: mcclurjb@tuhs.temple.edu.

MCCLUSKEY, CHARLES JAMES, JR. physician assistant; b. Rockville Center, N.Y., Oct. 16, 1947; s. Charles James McCluskey Sr. and Genevieve Ann (Reaves) Murphy; children: Charles James III, Christopher James. Student, Broward Jr. Coll., 1967, Weber State Coll., 1971; cert. physician asst., Med. U. S.C., 1975. Cert. physician's asst., Fla., cert. procurement transplant coord. Am. Bd. Transplant Coords. Staff physician asst. George L. Timmons, MD, P.A., Hartsville, S.C., 1975-76; physician asst. U.S. Dept. Justice, Washington, 1977-80, supervisory physician asst., health svc. adminstr., 1980-82; organ procurement coord. U. Fla., Jacksonville, 1982-86, exec. dir. organ procurement ops. Gainesville, 1986—. Cons. Japanese Transplant Orgn., Kobe, Osaka, 1989—; cons. in organ procurement Japan Kidney Transplant Network, 1997—; pres. bd. dirs. Nat. Coalition on Organ and Tissue Donation, 1999, pres., 2001—. Contbr. articles to profl. jours. State dir. S.C. Jaycees, Hartsville, 1975—77; bd. dirs., v.p. Nat. Kidney Found., Jacksonville, 1983—87, bd. trustee, 1996—; pres. Nat. Coalition Donation, 2000—02; bd. dirs. Nielsen Organ Transplant Found., Jacksonville, 1983—; chairperson Fla. Coalition on Organ and Tissue Donation, 1998. Fellow Am. Acad. Physician's Assts. (liaison transplantation 1975—), N.Am. Transplant Coord. Orgn. (chair edn. 1982—, liaison to Japan 1986-88, Appreciation award 1986); mem. S.E. Organ Procurement Found. (chair procurement presentation 1982—, organ procurement orgn. com. 1997—, Appreciation award 1991), United Network for Organ Sharing, Coalition on Organ and Tissue Donation (chairperson Fla. 1998-99, bd. dirs. 1999). Avocations: skiing, diving, boating, golf. Home: PO Box 142584 Gainesville FL 32614-2584 E-mail: cjmcc@ufl.edu.

MCCLUSKEY, GAYLA JACQUE, health, safety and environmental executive; b. Apr. 5, 1955; d. Jack and S. Andrea (Matthiesen) McC.; m. David McClure Humphrey. BS in Engring. Tech., Okla. State U., 1977; MBA in Engring. Mgmt., U. Dallas, 1984. Diplomate Am. Acad. of Indsl. Hygiene; cert. safety profl.; registered occupl. hygienist; qualified environ. profl.; grad. Pa. State master gardener. Indsl. hygienist Exxon Nuclear Co., Richland, Wash., 1978-79, OSHA, Dept. Lab., Irving, Tex., 1979-81, United Techs.-Mostek, Carrollton, 1981-82; cons. risk mgmt. Sun Exploration and Prodn. Co., Dallas, 1982-88; mgr. health, safety and security Interchem Inc., Louisville, 1988-91; dir. health safety and environ. affairs Rhone-Poulenc Rorer, Phila., 1991-94; mng. cons. Sun Co., 1994-95; prin. Global Environ. Health Svcs., Radnor, Pa., 1995—. Mem. editl. bd. Indsl. Safety and Hygiene News, 1993—. Chmn. Responsible Citizenship Program, 1984-86, Dallas Women's Coalition, Dallas, 1984-86, Leadership Dallas, 1987-88; grad. Leadership Dallas Alumni Assn., 1988—, Leadership Inc., 200001; active Leadership Louisville, 1988-91; co-chair auction Louisville Jaycees. 1989-90; mem. priority programs com. Metro United Way, Louisville, 1990-91; founding mem. Louisville Network, 1990-91; pres., bd. dirs. Women's Ctr. of Dallas, charter supporter fund for women; dir. Women in Search of Exec. Responsibilities, 1988; mem. Ctr. for Women and Families, 1990-94, vice-chair Nat. Endowment Campaign, 1995-99; trustee, pres.-elect Am. Indsl. Hygiene Found., 1991—; mem., v.p. bd. health Radnor Twp., 1994-2002, bd. dirs., pres. Women's Resource Ctr., 1994-2000, chair search com., 1995, chair adv. bd. com., 1996-97, pres., 1996-97, chair strategic plan com., 1996-2000, bylaws com., 1996, adv. bd., 2002—, charter mem., pres., v.p. environ. adv. coun., Radnor Twp., 1997, chmn. devel. com., 1997—, vice-chair, 1997—; bd. trustees Wayne Presbyn. Ch., 2000—. Named to Hon. Order of Ky. Cols., 1990. Mem. AAUW, LWV (dir. 1994—), Am. Mgmt. Assn., Am. Soc. Safety Engrs., Am. Acad. Indsl. Hygiene (profl. conf. com. 1994-99, nominating com. 1995, 97), Chm. Mfrs. Assn. (responsible care com. 1990-91), Pharm. Mfrs. Assn. (water com. 1993-94), Dallas C. of C. (natural resources adv. coun.), Am. Indsl. Hygiene Assn. (nat. conf. com. 1989-94, chair mgmt. com. 1990-92, pub. rels. com. 1990-94, internat. task force 1992, internat. com. 1992-94, nat. bd. dirs. 1994—, treas. 1997-2000, v.p. 2000-01, pres.-elect 2001—, NAFTA task force 1993-94, health care reform task force 1994—, cons. task force 1994-97, chair OSHA Program task force 1997—, chmn. AIHA/ASSE coop. task force 1997—), Network of Career Women (officer Irving chpt. 1980-88), Leadership Louisville Alumni, Radnor League of Women (voters bd. 1997—), Third Century (bus. and econ. devel. com. 1990-92), Soc. of St. Patrick, Thorobreds (Ky. Derby festival com. 1991-92), Main Line Women's Caucus, Nat. Soc. Daus. of Am. Revolution (Jeptha Abbott chpt. 1994—, ann. luncheon chair 2000-02), Tau Iota Epsilon, Omicron Delta Kappa, Sigma Iota Epsilon (officer U. Dallas chpt. 1984-88), Alpha Chi Omega (officer Louisville chpt. 1990-91). Methodist. Home: 6 Harford Ln Radnor PA 19087-4529 Office: Global Environ Health Svcs 6 Harford Ln Radnor PA 19087-4529

MCCLUSKEY, JEAN ASHFORD, nursing educator, retired; b. Phila., Apr. 27, 1926; d. Charles Robert and Susanna Myers (Smith) Ashford; m. Robert C. McCluskey, June 28, 1947 (dec. Sept. 2000); children: David C., Robert C., Jean Alyce Loux. RN, Jewish Hosp., Phila., 1947; BS in Edn., West Chester (Pa.) State Coll., 1965; EdM, Temple U., PHila., 1970. Coord. practical nursing prog. North Montco AVTS, Lansdale, Pa., 1967-70; dir. dipl. LPN-RN Sch. Nursing Bucks County Grand View Hosp., Sellersville, 1970-77; dir. Sch. Practical Nursing Sacred Heart Hosp., Norristown, 1977-93; nursing edn. cons., 1993-2001. Coord. evening/weekend part time practical nursing program Ea. Ctr. for Arts and Technology, Willow Grove, Pa., 1995-2001; chmn. Healthcare Corp., 1998—, mem., 1995—. Contbr. articles to profl. jours. Mem. mgmt. bd. Luth. Cmty. at Telford, 1993-99; congl. del. to assembly Southeastern Pa. synod Evang. Luth. Ch. in Am., 1996, 97, 98, 99, 2000. Recipient Disting. Svc. award, S.E. Pa. League for Nursing, 1984; named Ky. Col., 1980, others. Mem. Nat. League Nursing (bd. dirs. 1983-87, bd. rvs. CPNP 1987-93).

MCCLUSKEY, JOHN ASBERRY, JR. literature educator, writer; b. Middletown, Ohio, Oct. 25, 1944; s. John Asberry and Helen Mildred (Harris) McC.; m. Audrey Louise Thomas, Dec. 24, 1969; children: Malik Douglass, Jerome Patrice, John Toure. BA in Social Rels., Harvard U., 1966; MA in English, Stanford U., 1972. Lectr. Miles Coll., Birmingham, Ala., 1967-68, Valparaiso (Ind.) U., 1968-69; from lectr. to asst. prof. Case-Western Res. U., Cleve., 1969-77; from assoc. prof. to prof. Ind. U., Bloomington, 1977-85, prof., 1985—, assoc. dean Grad. Sch., 1983-88, chair Afro-Am. studies, 1995-2000. Dir. Com. Instl. Cooperation Minorities Fellowship, Bloomington, 1983-88. Author: (novels) Look What They Done to My Song, 1974, Mr. America's Last Season Blues, 1983; editor: (story collection by Rudolph Fisher) City of Refuge, 1987; co-editor: Black Men Speaking, 1997. Mem. Bd. Pub. Safety, Bloomington, 1983-88; life mem. Monroe County NAACP. Named one of Outstanding Educators of Am., 1976; Yaddo fellow, 1984, 86. Mem. MLA, Am. Studies Assn., Midwest MLA, Authors' Guild. Avocations: master swimmer, jogging, mini-triathlons, gardening. Home: 3300 E Moores Pike Bloomington IN 47401-7102 Office: Ind U Afro-Am Studies Memorial Hall E-28 Bloomington IN 47405 E-mail: mccluske@indiana.edu.

MCCLUSKEY, LOIS THORNHILL, photographer; b. Boston, Apr. 7, 1945; d. Fred S. and Mary (Evans) Thornhill; m. Edward J. McCluskey, Feb. 14, 1981. BA, Middlebury Coll., 1966; postgrad., U. St. Thomas, Houston, 1967-69; MA, NYU, 1971; cert. in graphic design, U. Calif., Santa Cruz, 1983. Rsch. technician dept. virology Baylor Sch. Medicine, Houston, 1966-68; with Kelly Girls, Palo Alto, Calif., 1971-72; slide curator dept. art Stanford (Calif.) U., 1972-80; founder, pres. Stanford Design Assocs., Palo

Alto, 1981—. Cons. copy and museum photography; graphic designer. Mem. Smithsonian Assocs. Home: 895 Northampton Dr Palo Alto CA 94303-3434 Office: Stanford Design Assocs PO Box 60451 Palo Alto CA 94306-0451 E-mail: loispt@earthlink.net.

MCCLUSKEY, MALCOLM MURRAY, marketing professional; b. N.Y.C., Sept. 26, 1943; s. Thomas Patrick McCluskey and Mary Violet Murray; m. Veronica Cecila Vangreen, May 13, 1967 (div. June 1985); children: Joseph, Mary Catherine, Daniel; m. Angela Loretta Carbonaro, Apr. 2, 1994. Student, Pace U., 1964-67. Sales mgr. Better Homes & Gardens, N.Y.C., 1966-74; v.p. mktg. Yield House, North Conway, N.H., 1974-77; pres. Qualified List Corp., Armonk, N.Y., 1977-80; pres., CEO List Svcs. Corp., Bethel, Conn., 1980—. With USN, 1960-64. Mem. Direct Mktg. Assn. Avocations: hiking, running, swimming, traveling. Office: List Svcs Corp 6 Trowbridge Dr Bethel CT 06801-2858

MCCLUSKEY, NEIL GERARD, gerontologist, educator, literary agent; b. Seattle, Dec. 15, 1920; s. Patrick John and Mary Genevieve (Casey) McC.; m. Elaine Lituchy, June 5, 1977. AB, Gonzaga U., 1944, MA, 1945; Lic. in Sacred Theology, Gen. Theol. Union, Berkeley, 1952; PhD, Columbia U., 1957. Assoc. editor Am. (Nat. Cath. Weekly), N.Y.C., 1955-60; dean sch. edn. Gonzaga U., Spokane, 1960-62, dir. hons. program, 1963-65, v.p. acad., 1963-66; prof. U. Notre Dame, South Bend, Ind., 1966-71, dean, dir. Inst. Studies in Edn., 1968-71; prof., dean profl. studies Lehman Coll. CUNY, 1971-75; dir. Ctr. Gerontol. Studies CUNY Grad. Sch., 1975-81; exec. dir. BHRAGS Social Svcs. Ctr., Bklyn., 1981-84; sr. cons. Retirement Advisors, Inc., N.Y.C., 1985—. Pres. Westchester Lit. Agy., 1991—. Author: Public Schools and Moral Education, 1958, Catholic Viewpoint on Education, 1959, Catholic Education Faces Its Future, 1969; author, editor: Aging and Society, 1980, Aging and Retirement, 1981. Bd. dirs. Cath. Big Bros. N.Y., 1985—. Home: 2533 Egret Lake Dr West Palm Beach FL 33413-2161 E-mail: neilagency@adelphia.net.

MCCLUSKY, LAURA J. university educator; b. Utica, N.Y., Mar. 3, 1963; d. Joseph Walter and Phylis Emma McClusky; m. Michael I. Niman. BA, SUNY Buffalo, Amherst, 1985, MA, 1988, PhD, 1998. Adj. asst. prof. Erie C.C., Williamsville, NY, 1993—2001, SUNY Buffalo, Amherst, 1998—2001, Buffalo (N.Y.) State Coll., 1999—2001; asst. prof. Wells Coll., Aurora, 2001—. Author: Here, Our Culture is Hard: Stories of Domestic Violence From a Mayan Village, 2001. Office: Wells Coll Main St Aurora NY 13026 Home: 46 St James Pl Buffalo NY 14222-1411

MCCLYMONDS, JEAN ELLEN, marketing professional; b. Richmond, Calif. d. Rollin John Lepley and Doris Ellen Baughman; m. Gareth Lynn McClymonds, Sept. 18, 1981. BS in Edn., U. Calif., Berkeley, 1970; M Bus. Communications, San Jose State U., 1987. Adminstr. sales Dohrmann Div. Envirotech, Santa Clara, Calif., 1970-74; supr. order processing Molectron Corp., Sunnyvale, 1974-79; mgr. mktg. svcs. Gould-Biomation, Santa Clara, 1979-84; dir. corp. communications Madic Corp., 1984-86; dir. mktg. nat. accounts Skyway Freight Systems, Inc., Watsonville, Calif., 1986-89; pres. Just Mktg., Scotts Valley, 1989—. Pub. speaker various local orgns., 1984—. Contbr. articles industry jours., 1986—. Mem. Am. Trucking Assn. (outstanding svc. award 1997), Bus. Profl. Advt. Assn., Nat. Assn. Quality Control, Peninsula Mktg. Assn., Coun. Logistics Mgmt., San Jose Women in Bus. Republican. Avocations: speaking, dancing, skiing. Office: 2365 Weston Rd Scotts Valley CA 95066-2509 E-mail: justmktng@aol.com.

MCCLYMONT, ELEANOR JEAN, educational administrator, pathologist; b. Newark, July 5, 1938; d. Michael Joseph and Selena (Gilchrist) Gargan; m. William James McClymont, June 20, 1959 (dec. May 1995); children: Scott William, Lisa Eleanor McClymont Chowansky. BA, Montclair State Coll., 1960, MA, 1975; prin.-supr. cert., Kean Coll., 1982. Speech and lang. pathologist Saddle Brook (N.J.) Bd. Edn., 1960-61, Vis. Nurse Assn., Plainfield, N.J., 1963-65, Scotch Plains (N.J.) Fanwood Bd. Edn., 1969-83, chair dept. speech and lang., 1983-86, supr. spl. edn., 1986-90; dir. spl. edn., 1990—. Mem. Jaycetts, Scotch Plains, 1968-72; v.p. Fanwood Jr. Women's Club, 1964-65; mem. bd. deacons 1st Bapt. Ch., Somerville, N.J., 1988-89, chair presch. com., 1980-90, choir mem., 1975—, sec. bd. trustees, 1993—. N.J. State Dept. Edn. grantee, 1986, 87-88, 88. Mem. Assn. for Supervision and Curriculum Devel., N.J. Prins. and Suprs. Assn., N.J. Speech and Hearing Assn., Coun. for Exceptional Children. Republican. Home: 29 Mallard Dr Hackettstown NJ 07840-2821 Office: Office of Pupil Svcs 721 Westfield Rd Scotch Plains NJ 07076-2156

MCCOBB, ALLAN PAUL, not-for-profit organization executive; b. Russell, Kans. s. Boyden and Doris Marie (Marsh) McC.; m. Ursula Fox, June 25, 1983 (div. Sept. 1991). BS in Phys. Edn., Kans. State U., 1967, BS in Bus. and Acctg., 1971; MS in Exercise Sci., Ft. Hays State U., 1986. Staff acct. Arthur Young & Co., Kansas City, 1972-74; gen. mgr., part owner McCobb Inc., Russell, Kans., 1974-80; grants mgr. N.W. Kans. Area Agy. on Aging, Hays, 1980-81; exec. dir. S.W. Kans. Area Agy. on Aging, Dodge City, Kans., 1981-85; grants mgr. N.W. Area Agy. on Aging, Hays, 1985-86; exec. dir. United Way of Enid and N.W. Okla., Enid, 1990—. Exec. dir. Wheatbelt Girl Scout Coun., Hutchinson, Kans., 1987-90; presenter, group facilitator Meth. Divorce Support Group and Workshop, Enid, 1993—; youth coord. Enid Cmty. Children's Choir, 1994—; mem. initial bd. Enid Cmty. Free Health Clinic, Enid, 1996-99, Enid Cmty. Found., 1998-, Gar. County Child Advocacy Coun., 1997--; small claims mediator N.W. Okla. Early Settlement, Fairview, 1998—; bd. dirs./sec. Eudi Cmty. Found., 1998—. With U.S. Army, 1968-70, Vietnam. Decorated Bronze Star U.S. Army, 1970; inductee Lake Atwood 10 Mile Hall of Fame, 1984. Mem. Okla. Assn. United Ways (bd. dirs., treas. 1994-96), Garfield County Area C. of C., Fellowship of Christian Athletes. Methodist. Avocations: running, genealogy, youth work. Home: PO Box 771 Enid OK 73702-0771 Office: United Way Enid NW Okla 321 W Cherokee Ave Ste C Enid OK 73701-5603

MCCOBB, JOHN BRADFORD, JR. lawyer; b. Orange, N.J., Oct. 14, 1939; s. John Bradford and Dorothea Joyce (Hoffman) M.; m. Maureen Kelly, Oct. 6, 1973; 1 dau., Carrie Elizabeth. A.B., Princeton U. cum laude, 1961; J.D., Stanford U., 1966; LL.M., NYU, 1973. Bar: Calif. 1967. Assoc., IBM, Armonk, N.Y., 1966-1974, gen. counsel, Tokyo, 1974-77, lab. counsel, Endicott, N.Y., 1977-79, sr. atty., White Plains, N.Y., 1979-81, regional counsel, Dallas, 1981-83; counsel, sec. IBM Instruments, Inc., Danbury, Conn., 1983-87; area counsel European Labs, Hursley, England, 1987-90; counsel govtl. programs IBM, Washington, 1990-97. Trustee Princeton-in-Asia, Inc., 1970-86 . Princeton-in-Asia-teaching fellow at Chinese Univ. of Hong Kong, 1963-65. Mem. ABA, State Bar of Calif., Phi Beta Kappa. Contbr. articles to profl. jours.

MCCOID, DONALD JAMES, bishop; b. Wheeling, W.Va., Dec. 31, 1943; s. Roy Conrad and Alberta Virginia (Sturm) McC.; m. Saundra Ernette Piisila, Oct. 20, 1973; children: Kimberly, Elizabeth. AB, West Liberty (W.Va.) State Coll., 1965; MDiv, Luth. Theol. Sem., Phila., 1968; DD (hon.), Thiel Coll., 1983. Ordained to ministry Evang. Luth. Ch. in Am., 1968. Pastor St. Luke's Luth. Ch., Monessen, Pa., 1968-72; assoc. pastor St. John's Luth. Ch. Highland, Pitts., 1972-74; area Luth. coord. Western Pa.—W.Va. synod, Luth. Ch. Am., Clarksburg, W.Va., 1974-77; sr. pastor Trinity Luth. Ch., Latrobe, Pa., 1977-87; bishop Southwestern Pa. synod, Evang. Luth. Ch. in Am., Pitts., 1987—. Bd. dirs. Pa. Coun. Chs., Harrisburg, Inst. for Mission, 1997—, chair 1997—; co-chair Luth.-Orthodox Nat. Dialogue, 1997—; del. Luth. World Fedn. Assembly, 1997. Bd. dirs. Religious Leadership Forum, Pitts., 1998—, Luth. Svcs. in Am., 1997—; mem. exec. com. Christian Assocs. S.W. Pa., Pitts., 1988—, chair coun., 1994-96; chair Conf. Bishops, Evangel. Luth. Ch. Am., 1999—. Office: Evang Luth Ch in Am SW Turn Pa Synod 9625 Perry Hwy Pittsburgh PA 15237-5555 E-mail: donald.mccoid@ecunet.org.

MC COIN, JOHN MACK, social worker; b. Sparta, N.C., Jan. 21, 1931; s. Robert Avery and Ollie (Osborne) McC. BS, Appalachian State Tchrs. Coll., Boone, N.C., 1959-60; MS in Social Work, Richmond (Va.) Profl. Inst., 1962; postgrad., U. N.C., 1959-60; PhD, U. Minn., 1977. Lic. master social worker; cert. social worker, N.Y. Social svc. worker Broughton State Hosp., Morganton, N.C., 1958-59, John Unstead State Hosp., Butner, 1960-61; clin. social worker Dorothea Dix State Hosp., Raleigh, 1962-63; child welfare case worker Wake County Welfare Dept., 1963-64; psychiat. social worker Toledo Mental Hygiene Clinic, 1964-66; sr. psychiat. social worker N.Y. Hosp.-Cornell U. Med. Ctr. Westchester divsn., White Plains, 1966-68; social worker VA Hosp., Montrose, N.Y., 1968-73; also vol. mental health worker Westchester County Mental Health Assn. and Mental Health Bd., White Plains; seminar instr. Grad. Sch. Social Work U. Minn., Mpls., 1973-74; social worker F.D.R. VA Health Care Facility, Montrose, 1975-77; asst. prof. social work U. Wis., Oshkosh, 1977-79, chmn. dept. cmty. liaison com., 1978-79; assoc. prof. social work Grand Valley State Colls., Allendale, Mich., 1979-81; social worker VA Med. Ctr., Battle Creek, 1981-83, supr. social worker dept. Leavenworth, Kans., 1983-94. Cons. 44th Gen. Hosp., USAR, Menasha, Wis., 1978-79, 5540th Support Command, USAR, Grand Rapids, Mich., 1979-83; cons. in field; adj. faculty mem. social scis. dept. Kansas City C.C., 1985-89, St. Mary Coll., 1984, Kellogg C.C., Battle Creek, 1981-83; adj. faculty mem. sch. social welfare U. Kans., Lawrence, 1992; presenter in field. Author: Adult Foster Homes: Their Managers and Residents, 1983; founder (with Human Scis. Press), editor Adult Foster Care Jour., 1987-88, Adult Resdl. Care Jour., 1989-91, ind. jour., 1992-96; contbr. articles to profl. jours. With USMC, 1948-52, USMCR, 1957-72; lt. col. USAR, 1972-91. Recipient Outstanding Performance award VA, 1971, 83, Superior Performance award, 1982; grantee NIMH, 1974. Mem. NASW (social action com. West Mich. br. 1980-81), Alpha Delta Mu. Democrat. Baptist. Home and Office: 4913 Colonial Way Lawrence KS 66049-3599

MCCOLL, HUGH LEON, JR. bank executive; b. Bennettsville, S.C., June 18, 1935; s. Hugh Leon and Frances Pratt (Carroll) McC.; m. Jane Bratton Spratt, Oct. 3, 1959; children: Hugh Leon III, John Spratt, Jane Bratton. BS in Bus. Adminstrn, U. N.C., 1957. Trainee NCNB Nat. Bank, Charlotte, 1959-61, officer, 1961-65, v.p., 1965-68, sr. v.p., 1968, div. exec., 1969, exec. v.p., 1970-73, vice chmn. bd., 1973-74, pres., 1974-83, also dir.; CEO Bank of Am. (formerly NationsBank Corp.), 1983—; CEO,pres. Barnet Banks, Miami, Fla., 1998-; Pres., CEO, chmn. Bank of America Corp., Charlotte, NC, 1983—2001, Chmn. Emeritus, 2001—. Bd. dirs. Sonoco Products Inc., Hartsville, S.C. Trustee Heineman Found., Charlotte, 1976—, Queens Coll., Charlotte; bd. visitors Grad. Sch. Bus. U. N.C. at Chapel Hill; chmn. Charlotte Uptown Devel. Corp., 1978-81, 85. 1st lt. USMCR, 1957-59. Mem. Bankers Roundtable (mem. trialateral commn.), Am. Bankers Assn., N.C. Bankers Assn. (pres. 1974). Democrat. Presbyterian. Office: Bank of Am 100 N Tryon St Charlotte NC 28255-0001*

MCCOLLAM, MARION ANDRUS, consulting firm executive, educator; b. New Orleans, Feb. 8, 1931; d. Gerald Louis and Lucile Gordon (Isacks) Andrus; m. Andrew McCollam, Jr., Jan. 29, 1955 (div. 1978); children: Andrew III, Gerald Andrus, Marion Cage. BA, Tulane U., 1952; M. Urban and Reg. Planning, U. New Orleans, 1978. Human affairs coord. Office of the Mayor, City of New Orleans, 1978, arts coord., 1978-80; dir. planning, prin. cons. Duncan Plaza Design Project, New Orleans, 1978-80; dir. planning Downtown Devel. Dist., 1980-81; pres. Andrus and Roberts Inc., Phoenix, New Orleans, 1980-84; exec. dir. Arts Coun. New Orleans, 1981-90, Cultural Arts Coun. of Houston and Harris County, 1991-98; pres. McCollam Cons., LLC, 1998—. Cons. in field; adj. lectr. in arts adminstrn. Goucher Coll., 1998—. Mem. nat. adv. com. Working Capital Fund, Mpls., 1995-99, Nat. Arts Stabilization, Balt., 1998—; adv. panel design Nat. Endowment for the Arts, Washington, 1995, adv. and chair local arts agencies, 1992-94; bd. dirs., sr. fellow Am. Leadership Forum, Houston, 1994-2000; mem. cmty. assessment com. United Way of Tex. Gulf Coast, 1995-99; bd. dirs. Urban League of New Orleans, 1984-89; pres. Jr. League of New Orleans, 1969-70. Recipient Arts Adminstr. of Yr. award Arts Mgmt. Inst./Nat. News Svc., 1987, Award for Sustained Mgmt. Excellence, Greater New Orleans Found., 1989. Mem. Am. Inst. Cert. Planners, AIA (hon.), U.S. Urban Arts Fedn. (pres. 1988), Nat. Assembly of Local Arts Agencies (vice chmn. bd. dirs. 1988-94, Chairman's award 1992). Avocations: music, art, reading, travel, family activities. Office: 1914 Bissonnet St Houston TX 77005-1645

MCCOLLAM, WILLIAM, JR. utility company executive; b. New Orleans, Mar. 15, 1925; s. William and Marie (Mason) McC.; m. Hope Flower Joffrion, Apr. 20, 1947; children: Ellendale McCollam Hoffman, William Cage, Stephen Mason. BS, La. State U., 1943; BS in Engring., U.S. Mil. Acad., 1946; MS in Civil Engring., MIT, 1954. Registered profl. engr., N.Y. Commd. 2d lt. U.S. Army, 1946; advanced through grades to lt. col. U.S Army; resigned U.S. Army, 1961; with Ark. Power and Light Co., Little Rock, 1961-70, exec. asst., 1961-64; v.p. Ark Power and Light Co., 1964-68; sr. v.p. Ark. Power and Light Co., 1968-70; exec. v.p. New Orleans Pub. Service, 1970-71, pres., 1971-78, Edison Electric Inst., Washington, 1978-90, pres. emeritus, 1990—. Cons. energy mgmt., Washington, 1990—; bd. dirs. Burns and Roe Group, Inc., Oradell, NJ; trustee Thomas Alva Edison Found., Detroit, 1978—89; past chmn. S.W. Power Pool, Little Rock, 1973—74, Nat. Elec. Reliability Coun., Princeton, NJ, 1975—78; bd. dirs., exec. com. U.S. Mem. Com., World Energy Coun., Washington, 1978—94; bd. dirs. McDermott Internat., Inc., 1990—99. Past pres. Greater New Orleans area C. of C., 1974-75; former dir. Loyola U., New Orleans, 1975-78; pres.'s council Tulane U., 1982-86. Named to La. State U. Alumni Hall of Distinction, 1985; recipient U.S. Energy award in recognition of outstanding contbn. to world energy coun., 1991. Mem. La. Soc. Profl. Engrs. (A.B. Paterson award 1975) Clubs: Chevy Chase, Metropolitan (Washington); Boston, New Orleans Country. Republican. Episcopalian. Home: 2411 Tracy Pl NW Washington DC 20008-1628 Office: Edison Electric Inst 701 Pennsylvania Ave NW Fl 3 Washington DC 20004-2696

MCCOLLEY, ROBERT MCNAIR, history educator; b. Salina, Kans., Feb. 2, 1933; s. Grant and Alice Elizabeth (McNair) McC.; m. Diane Laurene Kelsey, Aug. 30, 1958; children: Rebecca, Susanna, Teresa, Margaret, Carolyn, Robert Lauren. BA, Harvard U., 1954, MA, 1955; PhD, U Calif.-Berkeley, 1960. Instr. to prof. history U. Ill., Urbana, 1960-97. Mem. Com. for Advanced Placement Test in Am. History, 1987-90, chmn. 1988-90. Author: Slavery and Jeffersonian Virginia, 1964 (Dickerson award 1964); editor: Federalists, Republicans and Foreign Entanglements, 1969; editor: Henry Adams, John Randolph, 1995; co-editor: Refracting America, 1993; mem. editorial bd. Jour. Early Republic, 1981-85, Va. Mag. of History and Biography, 1994-98; editor Jour. Ill. State Hist. Soc., 1998-2002, editl. bd., 2002—; classical recs. reviewer Fanfare mag., 1989—. Mem. Soc. Historians of Early Republic (pres. 1982), Orgn. Am. Historians, Va. Hist. Soc., Ill. Hist. Soc. (bd. dirs. 1978-81, 92-95, pres. 1997-99), Chgo. Hist. Soc., Cliff Dwellers. Episcopalian. Home: 503 W Illinois St Urbana IL 61801-3927 Office: U Ill Dept History 810 S Wright St Urbana IL 61801-3644 E-mail: rmccolle@uiuc.edu.

MCCOLLEY, RUTH ANN, music teacher, band director; b. DuQuoin, Ill., Mar. 9, 1953; d. Robert Lester and Clara Louise Marchino; m. Stephen Ray McColley, May 21, 1988; 1 child, Matthew Michael. BS, St. Joseph's Coll., Rensselaer, Ind., 1975; MS, Ind. State U., Terre Haute, 1979; cert. in Music Therapy, St. Mary-of-the-Woods Coll., Ind., 1989. Music tchr., band dir. Clinton Ctrl. Schs., Michigantown, Ind., 1975-87; band dir., music tchr. Triton Schs., Bourbon, 1995-98; music tchr., band dir. Culver (Ind.) Cmty. Schs., 1998—2002. Image cons. BeautiControl Cosmetics, Dallas, 1998—. Home-care vol. Hospice of Marshall County, Plymouth, Ind., 1998—2001. Schropschire scholar, 1987, Alpha Rho scholar, 1987, Guerin scholar, 1987-88, Epsilon scholar, 1987. Mem. Ind. Music Educators Assn., Music Educators Nat. Conf., Am. Assn. for Music Therapy. Avocations: cross-stitch, reading, drum and bugle corps. Home: 6605 N Brindale Dr Muncie IN 47304

MC COLLISTER, JOHN CHARLES, writer, clergyman, educator, executive producer; b. Pitts., June 1, 1935; s. John Charles and Caroline Jesse (Hall) Mc C.; m. Beverly Ann Chase, Aug. 6, 1960; children: Beth Ann, Amy Susan, Michael John. BA, Capital U., 1957; MDiv, Luth. Theol. Sem., Columbus, Ohio, 1961; PhD, Mich. State U., 1969. Ordained to ministry Luth. Ch., 1961. Pastor Zion Luth. Ch., Freeland, Mich., 1961-65, Bethlehem Luth. Ch., Lansing, 1965-71; prof. religion and Greek Olivet (Mich.) Coll., 1970-74; prof. religion and philosophy Bethune-Cookman Coll., Daytona Beach, Fla., 1974-76, Embry-Riddle Aero. U., 1976-82, dir. profl. programs, 1979-80, cons. to pres., 1980-82. Pres. Wright Advt. Co., Daytona Beach, 1975-76; CEO New Arran Prodns., Inc., Daytona Beach, 1993—, Yongestreet Prodns., Ormond Beach, Fla., 1986; arbitrator Fed. Mediation and Conciliation Svc., 1978; spl. master Fla. Pub. Employees Rels. Commn., 1975—; mgmt. cons. Hoover Ball and Bearing, Charlotte, Mich.; pres. Am. Writers Inst., 1982—. Host Open Phone Forum, radio sta. WROD, Daytona Beach, 1974—76; author: A Philosophy of Flight, 1981, So Help Me, God, 1981, The Christian Book of Why, 1983; ; author: The Sky is Home, 1986; co-author: The Sunshine Book, 1979, Day by Day, 1990; editor and compiler A Child is Born, 1972, Portraits of the Christ, 1974, Writing for Dollars, 1995, The Story of the Pittsburgh Pirates, 1998, The Tigers and Their Den, 1999, The Best Baseball Games Ever Played, 2002; contbr. articles to various mags. Vol. probation officer, Mich., 1961-71, hearing officer, 1970-74; commr. Mich. Dept. Commerce, 1969-72; speaker Nat. Lincoln Day Observance, Washington, 1982; internat. adviser Han Nam U., Taejon, Republic of Korea, 1989. Recipient Outstanding Am. award Daytona Beach Jaycees, 1974. Mem. Am. Arbitration Assn. Home and Office: 26 Lazy Eight Dr Daytona Beach FL 32128-6775

MCCOLLOCH, JAMES F. minister; b. McAlester, Okla., Aug. 9, 1945; s. Ira E. and Lolala McColloch; m. Annie J. Ecker; children: Jana Rae, Jina Rae. Adult Bible Studies Cert., Moody Bible Inst., Chgo., 1993; B of Bible Studies, Christian Bible Coll. and Sem., Independence, Mo., 1996; ThD, ThM, Andersonville Bapt. Sem., Camilla, Ga., 1999. Pastor 1st Bapt. Ch., Hermann, Mo., 2001—. Owner Jimmy Mac Music Co. - BMI, Tulsa, 1978—; editor, pub. Dist. 2 Voice, Osage County, 1986—90. Author: (book) Understanding The Apocalypse, 1995, composer mus. titles. Founding pres. Native Am. C. of C., Tulsa, 1977; chmn. Precinct 204, Osage County, 1988. With U.S. Army, 1966—68, Vietnam. Democrat. Southern Baptist. Avocations: writing music, publishing, Web author. Office: 1st Bapt Ch 1409 Market St Hermann MO 65041 Personal E-mail: jimmy.mac@att.net. Business E-Mail: jimmy.mac@att.net.

MCCOLLOUGH, W. ALAN, electronics retail executive; Gen. mgr. corp. ops. Circuit City Stores Inc., Richmond, Va., 1988, asst. v.p., 1989-91, pres. ctrl. operating divsn., 1991-95, sr. v.p. merchandising, 1995-97, pres., COO, 1997—2000, chmn., pres., CEO, 2000—. Office: Circuit City Stores Inc 9950 Maryland Dr Richmond VA 23233*

MCCOLLUM, ALVIN AUGUST, consultant, real estate company executive; b. L.A., Jan. 20, 1920; s. Nile Clarkson and Ida Martha (Kuhlman) McC.; m. Maxine Eleanor Seeberg, July 29, 1944; children: Robert Michael, James Alan, Patricia Kathleen. BA, UCLA, 1941; postgrad., U.S. Naval Acad., 1946, Southwestern U., 1949-50. Exec. v.p., dir. Strout Realty, N.Y.C., 1948-61, Del E. Webb Corp., Phoenix, 1961-67; pres., dir. Sahara Nev. Corp., Las Vegas, 1964-67, Devel. Svcs., Inc., Scottsdale, Ariz., 1967-69; pres., chmn. Recreation Leisure Land, Inc., 1969-71; asst. pres., dir. A.J. Industries, Inc., L.A., 1971-74; pres., dir. Carefree (Ariz.) Ranch, Inc., 1974-76; pres., bd. dir. Cons. Internat., Scottsdale, 1976—; chmn. CEO Greenway Environ. Svs., Inc., Gilbert, Ariz., 1992—. Pres., bd. dirs. Combined Assets, Inc., Westlake Village, Calif., First Realty Fin., Inc., L.A., Corp. Capital Resources, Inc., Westlake Village. Bd. dirs. Admiral Nimitz Found., Fredericksburg, Tex., 1970—, Boys Club Las Vegas, 1964-68, United Fund, Las Vegas, 1966; co-chmn. NCCJ, Las Vegas, 1966; elder Presbyn. Ch. USA, 1954—. Lt. USN, 1943-48, PTO. Mem. Masons, Shriners, Am. Legion, Mt. Shadows Country Club (bd. dirs. 1962-64). Republican. Avocations: golf, swimming, camping, sailing. Home: 215 N Power Rd Unit 180 Mesa AZ 85205-8442

MCCOLLUM, BETTY, congresswoman; b. July 12, 1954; m. Douglas McCollum; 2 children. BS in Edn., Coll. St. Catherine. Retail store mgr., Minn.; mem. Minn. Ho. Reps., 1992-2000, mem. edn. com., environ. and natural resources com., mem. gen. legis. com., vet. affairs and elections com., mem. transportation and transit com., asst. majority leader, chair legis. commn. on econ. status of women, mem. rules and adminstrv. legis. com.; mem. U.S. Congress from Minn. 4th Dist., Washington, 2001—; mem. edn. and workforce com., resources com. Mem. St. Croix Valley Coun. Girl Scouts. Mem. VFW Aux., Am. Legion Aux. Democrat. Office: US Ho of Reps 1029 Longworth HOB Washington DC 20515 Home: Ste 17 165 Western Ave N Saint Paul MN 55102-4613*

MCCOLLUM, CLIFFORD GLENN, college dean emeritus; b. South Gifford, Mo., May 12, 1919; s. William Henry and Aultie V. (Westfall) McC.; m. Alice Elizabeth Erickson, Aug. 18, 1940; children: Eric Edward, Lisa Buren. Student, Central Coll., 1935-37; BS, U. Mo., 1939, MA, 1947, EdD, 1949. Tchr. pub. schs., Monett, Mo., 1938-39, Poplar Bluff, 1939-41, Boonville, 1941-42; asst. prof. sci. U. No. Iowa, 1949-55, assoc. prof., 1956-59, prof., 1959-84, prof. emeritus, 1984—, head dept. sci., 1957-68; dean U. No. Iowa (Coll. Natural Scis.), 1968-84, dean emeritus, 1984—. Prof. State U. N.Y. at Oneonta, 1955-56; Dir., instl. rep. Central States Univs., Inc.; cons. Coronet Instrnl. Films; cons. on sci. curricula to pub. schs. and colls.; speaker in field. Contbr. articles to profl. jours. Served with USAAF, 1943-46. Fellow AAAS (nat. committeeman 1964-67), Iowa Acad. Sci. (pres. 1979-80); mem. Am. Inst. Biol. Scis., Nat. Assn. Biology Tchrs. (regional dir. 1963-65), Nat. Assn. Research in Sci. Teaching, Nat. Sci. Tchrs. Assn., Sigma Xi, Phi Delta Kappa. Home: 6511 N Revere Ave Kansas City MO 64151-3989 E-mail: cmccollumi@kc.rr.com. *My personal response to the philosophical conditions in which we live today is one of preparing to live rather consistently with crises. It is my conviction that the mood of our time is toward a growing pessimism, and much of this is associated with the concomitants of a galloping technology. Yet we are not willing at this point to give up our human condition to the natural evolution that would result from basic environmental mechanisms. We will still try to condition that destiny.*

MC COLLUM, IRA WILLIAM, JR. (BILL MC COLLUM), former congressman; b. Brooksville, Fla., July 12, 1944; s. Ira William and Arline Gray (Lockhart) McC.; m. Ingrid Mary Seebohm, Sept. 25, 1971; children: Douglas Michael, Justin Randolph, Andrew Lockhart. BA, U. Fla., 1965, JD, 1968. Bar: Fla. 1968, D.C. 2001. Ptnr. Pitts, Eubanks & Ross (P.A.), Orlando, Fla., 1973-80; mem. 97th-102nd Congresses from 5th Dist. Fla., 1981-92, 103d-106th Congresses from 8th Dist. Fla., 1993-2001; former vice chmn. banking/fin. svcs. com.; former chmn. judiciary subcom. on crime; former mem. select com. on intelligence; ptnr. Baker & Hostetler LLP, Orlando, Fla. and Washington, D.C., 2001—. Vice chair House Rep. Conf. 101st-103d Congresses. Chmn. Rep. Exec. Com. Seminole County, Fla., 1976-80; county chmn.'s rep. 5th Dist. Fla. State Rep. Exec. Com., 1977-80; co-chmn. rep. platform com., 1992. With USN, 1969-72. Mem. Fla. Bar, Naval Res. Assn., Res. Officers Assn., Orange County Bar Assn. (exec. coun. 1975-79), Am. Legion, Mil. Order World Wars, Fla. Blue Key, Phi Delta Phi, Omicron Delta Kappa, Kiwanis. Episcopalian.

MCCOLLUM, JEAN HUBBLE, medical assistant; b. Peoria, Ill., Oct. 21, 1934; d. Claude Ambrose and Josephine Mildred (Beiter) Hubble; m. Everett Monroe Patton, Sept. 4, 1960 (div. Jan. 1969); 1 child, Linda Joanne; m. James Ward McCollum, Jan. 2, 1971; 1 child, Steven Ward. Student, Bradley U., Ill. Cen. Coll. Stenographer Caterpillar Tractor Co., Peoria, 1952-53, supr. stenographer pool, 1953-55, adminstrv. sec., treas., 1955-60, sec., asst. dept. mgr., 1969-71; med. staff sec. Proctor Cmty. Hosp., 1978-82; med. asst. Drs. Taylor, Fox and Morgan, 1982-84; freelance med. asst. Meth. Hosp. and numerous physicians, 1984-89; office mgr. Dr. Danehower, McLelland and Stone, 1989—. Vol. tutor Northmoor Sch., Peoria, 1974-78; bd. dirs., mem. exec. com., com. chmn. Planned Parenthood, Peoria, 1990-92. Recipient Outstanding Performance award Proctor Hosp., 1981, also various awards for svc. to schs., ch. and hosps. for mentally ill. Mem. Nat. Wildlife Fedn., Mensa Internat. (publs. officer, editor 1987-89), Mothers League (treas. 1977), Willow Knolls Country Club (social com. 1989-90), Nature Conservancy (Seasons of the River event com. 2000—), World Wildlife Fund, Forest Park Found., Jacques Cousteau Soc., Wilderness Soc., Nat. Trust for Historic Preservation. Methodist. Avocations: socializing, reading, travel, theatre, yoga. Home: 6501 N Brookwood Ln Peoria IL 61614-2401

MCCOLLUM, JOHN MORRIS, tenor; b. Coalinga, Calif., Feb. 21, 1922; s. Fay James and Ingabord Telette (Mason) McC.; m. Mary Margaret Wilson, Jan. 23, 1944; children: Kristi Elizabeth, Timothy James. Student, Coalinga Coll., 1939-40; BA in Journalism, U. Calif. at Berkeley, 1947; student voice and acting, Am. Theatre Wing, 1951-53. Reporter, city editor Coalinga Record, 1947-50; editor agrl. news U. Calif. Coll. Agr., 1950-51. Prof. music and chmn. voice faculty U. Mich.; dir. U. Mich. div. Nat. Music Camp; faculty Aspen Music Festival and School, 1963-76 Concert and opera singer, 1951—, soloist, Fifth Ave. Presbyn. Ch., N.Y.C., 1953-56, debut, Town Hall, N.Y.C., 1952, with, Boston Symphony Orchestra, Tanglewood, Mass., summer 1952, engagements with Symphony Orchestras in, N.Y.C., Chgo., Phila., San Francisco, Cleve., Washington, St. Louis, Detroit, New Orleans, Toronto, London, Mexico; with opera companies of, Boston, Washington, Toronto, Ft.

Worth, Central City, Colo., also, NBC-TV, music festivals and oratorio societies, European debut, Festival of Two Worlds, Spoleto, Italy, summer 1958, Santa Fe Opera Co., leading tenor, N.Y.C. Opera Co., performing mem., Music Assos. of Aspen. (Recipient award Atwater Kent Auditions 1950, Am. Theatre Wing award 1952). Mem. Rep. Ctrl. Com., Fresno County, Calif., 1950; pres. Ann Arbor Civic Theatre, 1987-88; mem. Sarasota County Rep. exec. com.; mem., bd. dirs. Sarasota Concert Assn.; bd. dirs. Univ. Mich. Alumni Club. Served with U.S. Navy, 1942-49. Mem. U. Calif. Alumni Assn., Nat. Assn. Tchrs. Singing, Am. Acad. Tchrs. Singing, Alpha Tau Omega, Sigma Delta Chi, Pi Kappa Lambda. Episcopalian (lay reader). Clubs: Rotary (pres. 1977, Paul Harris fellow), Ann Arbor Golf and Outing (pres. 1979), The Meadows Country Club (Sarasota, Fla.). Home: 3380 W Chelmsford Ct Sarasota FL 34235-0947

MCCOLLUM, ROBERT WAYNE, physician, educator; b. Waco, Tex., Jan. 29, 1925; s. Robert Wayne and Minnie (Brown) McC.; m. Audrey Talmage, Oct. 16, 1954; children: Cynthia, Douglas Scott. AB, Baylor U., 1945; MD, Johns Hopkins, 1948; DPH, London Sch. Hygiene and Tropical Medicine, 1958; MA (hon.), Yale U., 1965, Dartmouth Coll., 1985. Intern in pathology Columbia-Presbyn. Med. Center, N.Y.C., 1948-49; intern in internal medicine Vanderbilt Hosp., Nashville, 1949-50; asst. resident in internal medicine Yale-New Haven Med. Center, 1950-51; faculty Yale Sch. Medicine, 1951-81, prof. epidemiology, 1965-81, chmn. dept. epidemiology and public health, 1969-81; dean Sch. Medicine Dartmouth Coll., Hanover, N.H., 1982-90, prof. epidemiology, 1982-95, dean emeritus, 1990—; prof. emeritus, 1995—. Assoc. physician Yale-New Haven Hosp., from 1954; v.p. Dartmouth-Hitchcock Med. Ctr., 1983-90, acting v.p. for devel., 1999; cons. WHO, 1962-79; surgeon gen. U.S. Army, from 1960. Contbr. articles on epidemiology and control infectious diseases to profl. jours. Bd. sci. advisers Merck Inst., 1981-85; trustee Mary Hitchcock Meml. Hosp., Hanover, 1982-90. Capt. M.C., AUS, 1952-54. Mem. Assn. Tchrs. Preventive Medicine, Am. Epidemiological Soc., Internat. Epidemiological Assn., Infectious Diseases Soc. Am., Conn. Acad. Sci. and Engring., Am. Coll. Epidemiology Office: Dartmouth Med Sch Dartmouth-Hitchcock Med Ctr Lebanon NH 03756

MCCOLLUM, WILLIAM FRANKLIN, JR. sociology educator, private investigator; b. Wichita Falls, Tex., Apr. 2, 1942; s. William F. and Edna Marie McCollum; div.; children: Chris, Jeff. BBA, Midwestern State U., 1964; MA, U. Houston, 1996. Cert. rec. agt., Tex.; lic. pvt. investigator, Tex.; commd. security officer, Tex. V.p. Moody Nat. Bank, Galveston, Tex., 1965-80, Bank of the West, Galveston, 1980-81; pres. Bank of Sierra Blanca, 1981-82; ins. agt. McCollum Ins., Dickinson, 1982—; pvt. investigator Eagle Security Investigators, 1991—; instr. sociology Coll. of Mainland, Texas City, 1996—; assoc. dean, retention dir. ITT Tech. Inst., Houston, 1997—. Sec.-treas. Galveston City Nat. Corp., 1970-78; dir. McCollum Inst. Criminology, Dickinson, 1999—. Newspaper columnist (religion page) Galveston Daily News, 1970-75. Dir., former pres. Noon Optimist Club, Galveston, 1967—; dir. Big Bros.-Big Sisters, Galveston, 1968-70; res./spl. dep. sheriff Galveston County Sheriff Dept., 1969-81. With N.G., 1965-67. Recipient Father of Yr. award Galveston County, 1972. Mem. AAUP, Am. Sociol. Assn., Tex. Assn. Lic. Investigators (jour. reporter 1992—), Tex. Jr. Coll. Tchrs. Assn. Republican. Baptist. Avocations: Sherlock Holmes Society, Galveston Gun Club. Home: PO Box 1901 Dickinson TX 77539-1901 Office: ITT Tech Inst 2222 Bay Area Blvd Houston TX 77058-2070 E-mail: bmccollum@itt-tech.deu.

MCCOLM, GEORGE LESTER, international agricultural consultant, journalist; b. Colby, Kans., Aug. 2, 1911; s. Theodore Harrison and Jane (Speirs) McC.; m. Emma Victoria Davis, Aug. 9, 1936 (dec. Sept. 1959); children: Carol Ann, Patricia Alice; m. Elizabeth Jane Gunder Funderburg, May 1, 1975. BS in Agr., Kans. State U., 1935; postgrad., U. Ariz., 1961-64. Cert. profl. agronomist Am. Soc. Agronomy. Various soil conservation and agrl. positions, 1935-41; dir. crop. prodn. War Relocation Authority, Topaz, Utah, 1942-43; chief agrl. officer planning invasion and occupation Japan Joint Chief's of Staff, 1944-45; officer in charge civilian govt. of Ponape Island USN, 1946; soil conservationist Bur. Indian Affairs, Window Rock, Ariz., 1947—48, dir. nursery Shiprock, N.Mex., 1953-57; dir. B Square Ranch Expt. Sta., Farmington, 1958-61; educator U. Ariz., 1961-64; with U.S. Dept. State, India, 1964-66, tech. rep. internat. Mekong River devel. com. Vietnam, 1966—67; agrl. advisor CORDS, Vietnam, 1968—72; rancher Lewiston, Calif., 1973-87; owner Lewiston Nursery, 1987-95. Part-time agrl. advisor Mex. Govt., 1976-81; with Office Strategic Svcs. in WWII conf., Washington, D.C., 1991. Contbr. articles to sci. jours. Bd. dirs. Trinity County Fair Assn. Lt. USNR, 1944-46, PTO; USN officer directing civilian govt. Ponape Island, 1946. Mem. NRA, CAST, Am. Soc. Agronomy and Soil Sci., Calif. Soc. Agronomy and Soil Sci., Am. Asst. Ret. Persons, Am. Legion, Alpha Gamma Rho, 4-H Club (Edison medal). Republican. Methodist. Achievements include direction of first U.S. Soil survey made with aerial photographs, 1936; development of method of taking water from a flowing stream without a diversion dam in stream channel, 1939; perfection of method of constructing a stable roadbed or airfield through a swampy area, without limiting movement of ground water, 1939; wrote original draft of Japanese Land Reform Law, 1945. Avocations: fishing, fly tying, history research. Home: 760 Kerryjan Ct Redding CA 96002

MCCOMAS, DAVID JOHN, science administrator, space physicist; b. Milw., May 22, 1958; s. Harrold James and Hazelyn (Melconian) McC.; m. Richelle Wolff, May 30, 1981; children: Random A., Koan I., Orion G. BS in Physics, MIT, 1980; MS in Geophysics and Space Physics, UCLA, 1985, PhD in Geophysics and Space Physics, 1986. Mem. staff Los Alamos (N.Mex.) Nat. Lab., 1980-91, sect. leader space plasma and planetary physics, 1991-92, NASA program mgr., group leader space and atmospheric scis., 1992-98, group leader for space and atmospheric scis., 1992-98, founding dir. Ctr. for Space Sci. and Exploration, NASA prog, 1998-2000; exec. dir. space sci. and engring. divsn. S.W. Rsch. Inst., 2000—. Mem. strategic planning com. earth and space scis. divsn. Los Alamos Nat. Lab, 1986; mem. advanced composition explorer phase A study team NASA, 1988-89, mem. space physics data system steering com., 1990-91, mem. inner magnetosphere imaging study team, 1991-94, prin. investigator Ulysses Solar Wind Observations Over the Poles of the Sun Experiment, Two Wide-Angle Imaging Neutral-Atom Spectrometers, Explorer Mission-of-Opportunity, Solar Wind Electron Proton Alpha Monitor (instrument on the Advanced Composition Explorer, co-investigator Medium Energy Neutral Atom instrument on IMAGE Midsized Discovery Mission, plasma instrument for Cassini mission to Saturn, GENESIS Discovery mission, ISTP Polar Spacecraft's Thermal Ion Dynamics Experiment, Cluster plasma electron instrument, team mem. New Millennium Plasma Experiment for Planetary Exploration, mem. Space Sci. Adv. Com., chmn. Sun-Earth Connections Adv. Subcom.; mem. com. solar-terrestrial rsch. Nat. Rsch. Coun., 1991-94, mem. com. space sci. tech. planning Aeronautics and Space Engring. Bd./space studies bd., 1992, mem. task group rsch. prioritization future space sci. space studies bd., 1994—; former prin. investigator series of 10 magnetospheric plasma analyzer instruments at geosynchronous orbit Dept. Energy; mem. coms. and panels Nat. Acad. Sci.'s Nat. Rsch. Coun., U. Calif., State of N.Mex., others. Assoc. editor Jour. Geophys. Rsch.-Space Physics, 1993-94; contbr. over 300 sci. papers to profl. jours.; patentee in field. Grad. fellow Inst. Geophysics and Planetary Physics, 1983-84. Fellow Am. Geophys. Union (James B. Macelwane award 1993): Office: SW Rsch Inst PO Drawer 28510 San Antonio TX 78228-0510

MCCOMAS, RICHARD CARROLL, economist; b. Baltimore, Sept. 23, 1945; s. Louis Gough and Mary Elizabeth (Rainsford) M.; B.S., Loyola Coll., Baltimore, 1968; M.A., U. Pitts., Pa., 1970; M.A., Princeton U. (N.J.), 1974. Sec.-treas. H.C. McComas Fuel Co., Balt., 1970-72; asst. in instruction Princeton U., 1974-76; lectr. in econs., Rutgers Coll., New Brunswick, N.J., 1976-78; cons. in econs., 1978— ; dir. H.C. McComas Fuel Co., Balt. Mem. Md. Hist. Soc. Republican. Roman Catholic. Club: Princeton (N.Y.C.). Home: 915 Breezewick Cir Baltimore MD 21286-3302

MCCOMB, DAVID GLENDINNING, history educator; b. Kokomo, Ind., Oct. 26, 1934; s. John Floyd and Jennie (Glendinning) McC.; m. Mary Alice Collier, Sept. 6, 1957; children: Katherine, Susan, Joseph. BA, So. Meth. U., 1956; MBA, Stanford U., 1958; MA, Rice U., 1962; PhD, U. Tex., 1968. Purchasing agt. McRan Co., Houston, 1958-60; instr. South Tex. Jr. Coll., 1962, U. Houston, 1966-68; asst. prof. San Antonio Coll., 1962-66; rsch. assoc. U. Tex., Austin, 1968-69; asst. prof. history Colo. State U., Ft. Collins, 1969-72, assoc. prof., 1972-77, prof., 1977—2002, chmn. dept., 1975-80, emeritus prof., 2002—. Interviewer, dir. Oral History of Colo. Project, 1973-77, Big Thompson Disaster Oral History, 1976-78, Olympic Tng. Ctr. Oral History, 1983-87. Author: Houston, a History, 1969, rev. edit., 1981 (Tullis award 1969), Galveston, a History, 1986 (Tex. history 1987), Texas, a Modern History, 1989, Texas, an Illustrated History, 1995, Historic Seacoast of Texas, 1999, Travels with Joe, 2001, also others; editor: World History Ann. Edits., 1987, 89, 92, 96, 98, 2000, 01; contbr. articles to hist. jours. Recipient award of merit Am. Assn. for State and Local History, 1980, Disting. Svc. award Colo. State U., 1986; Danforth Found. grantee, 1978, Sigma Xi, 2001, also others, 1966-85. Fellow Tex. Hist. Assn.; mem. Oral History Assn. (program chmn. 1980), N.Am. Assn. for Sports History, World History Assn. (exec. coun. 1997-99), Western History Assn. (program chmn. 1979), Rocky Mountain World History Assn. (chmn. 1988-92). Democrat. Unitarian Universalist. Avocation: master swimming competition. Office: Colo State U Dept History Fort Collins CO 80523-0001 E-mail: david.mccomb@colostate.edu.

MCCOMB, RONALD GRAEME, filmmaker; b. Burns, Oreg., Jan. 6, 1938; s. Oliver Graham and Melba Viettta (Oard) McC.; m. Annie Bernice Duggan, Nov. 1968 (div.); 1 child, Siobhan Ariel Duggan Student, Portland Art Mus. Sch., 1957-61; Cert., Rolf Inst., Boulder, Colo., 1971. Cert. rolfer. Artist, 1961-66; film maker Union Light Co., N.Y.C., 1966-70, Am. Film Inst., Hollywood, Calif., 1970; rolfer pvt. practice Portland, Seattle, 1971—. Contbr. articles to profl. jours. Mem. Rolf Inst.

MCCOMBIE, SUSAN CAROLE, anthropologist; b. East Orange, N.J., Dec. 8, 1955; BA, Montclair State Coll., 1979; MA, U. Ariz., 1980, PhD, 1986. Instr. U. Ariz., Tucson, 1982-83; epidemiologist Pima County Health Dept., 1983-88; rsch. dir. U. Pa., Phila., 1988—. Researcher AIDSCORT-AIDS rsch. in Africa, 1988—. Author: (with others) Culture and AIDS, 1990; contbr. articles to profl. jours. Grantee Ariz. Disease Control Rsch. Commn., 1986. Mem. Am. Anthrop. Assn. (AIDS task force 1988—), Soc. for Med. Anthropology, Am. Anthrop. Assn. Office: U Pa 3620 Walnut St Philadelphia PA 19104-6220

MCCOMBS, BILLY JOE (RED MCCOMBS), professional football team executive; m. Charlene McCombs; 3 daughters. Founder, dir. Clear Channel Communications, Inc, 1972—; former owner, chmn. bd. Denver Nuggets, 1982—86, San Antonio Spurs; chair. bd of trustees Southwestern Univ.; owner, chair., pres. Minnesota Vikings, Eden Prairie, 1998-. Chmn. bd. trustees Southwestern U.; former chmn. United Way of San Antonio, Hemis-Fair World's Fair '68. Named to Bus. Hall of Fame. Mem. San Antonio C. of C. (former chmn.), Nat. Ford Dealers, U. Tex. Longhorn Club. Office: Winter Park Admin. Office 9520 Viking Dr Eden Prairie MN 55344-3898*

MCCOMBS, KELLY FRITZ, dietitian; b. Flemington, N.J., Sept. 23, 1968; d. John Frederick Fritz III and Joy Elaine Gallagher; m. Timothy Ronald McCombs, Aug. 31, 1996. BS, Ohio State U., 1997, MS, 1999. Cert. pharmacy technician. Pharmacy technician Riverside Meth. Hosp., Columbus, Ohio, 1989-99, med. rsch. asst., 1996-99; oncology pharmacy technician St. Anthony Regional Oncology Ctr., 1990-91; intern Ohio State U., 1998—99; family and consumer sci. agt. N.C. Coop. Ext., Elizabeth City, 1999—. Co-author: Jour. Food Quality. Recipient Florence Hall award, 2000, Early Career award, 2002. Mem.: Coastal Diabetes Educators Assn., N.C. Extension Assn. Family and Consumer Scis., Soc. Nutrition Educators, N.C. Dietetic Assn., Am. Dietetic Assn., Phi Upsilon Omicron Alumni Assn., Elizabeth City Jr. Women's Club, Phi Upsilon Omicron. Avocations: gardening, cooking. Office: NC Coop Ext PO Box 1608 Elizabeth City NC 27906-1608

MCCOMBS, MARK JAMES, lawyer; b. Blue Island, Ill., Sept. 28, 1959; s. James Marren and Yolanda Rose (Spinazzola) McCombs; m. Kathryn Anne Crivolio, May 28, 1994; children: James John, Thomas Michael. BS, Am. U., 1981; JD, Northwestern U., 1984. Bar: Ill. 1984, U.S. Dist. Ct., no. dist., Ill., 1984. Assoc. Jerome H. Torshen, Ltd., Chgo., 1984-87, Arnstein & Lehr, Chgo., 1987-88; assoc., ptnr. Wildman, Harrold, Allen & Dixon, 1998—. Village atty. Village of Sauk, Ill., 1988—, Village of Phoenix, Ill., 1999—; adminstrv. hearing officer Village of Calumet Park, Ill., 1998—. Contbr. articles to profl. jours. Mem.: South Suburban Mayors and Mgrs. Assn. (assoc. mem., chmn. attys.com.). Democrat. Roman Catholic. Office: Wildman Harrold Allen & Dixon 225 W Wacker Dr Ste 3000 Chicago IL 60606-1229 Business E-Mail: mccombs@wildmanharold.com.

MC COMIC, ROBERT BARRY, real estate development company executive, lawyer; b. Selmer, Tenn., Nov. 6, 1939; s. Richard Donald and Ila Marie (Prather) McC.; children: Thomas Christopher, Robert Geoffrey. BS, Union U., 1961; LLB, Tulane U., 1964; postgrad. in law, U. Freiburg, W. Ger., 1964-65, Hague (Netherlands) Internat. Acad. Law, 1965. Bar: Tenn. 1964, N.Y. 1966, Calif. 1971. Assoc. Donovan Leisure Newton & Irvine, N.Y.C., 1965-68; assoc. gen. counsel Avco Corp., Greenwich, Conn., 1968-70; exec. v.p., pres., CEO Avco Cmty Developers, Inc., 1973-82; chmn., CEO R.B. McComic, Inc., 1982-92, McComic Consolidated, Inc., 1992—; CEO Trans West Housing, Inc., 1994—, Globelink, LLC, 1995—; chmn. Price Smart Travel, San Diego, 2000—. Chmn. bd. dirs. Price Smart Travel. Pres. emeritus U. Calif. San Diego Found.; bd. dirs. World Affairs Coun. Honoree Human Relations Inst. Am. Jewish Com., 1981, Kellog's Celebrity Tribute, 1988. Mem. ABA, Calif. Bar Assn., San Diego County Bar Assn., Assn. of Bar of City of N.Y., San Diego Bldg. Industry Assn., San Diego Yacht Club, Order of Coif, Sigma Alpha Epsilon, Omicron Delta Kappa, Lambda Alpha. Office: McComic Consolidated Inc 9968 Hibert St Ste 102 San Diego CA 92131 Home: 7180 Fairway Rd La Jolla CA 92037-5623 E-mail: bMcComic@Yahoo.com.

MCCONATHY, JAMES LESLIE, SR. cattle farmer, insurance agent, retired; b. Gibsland, La., Dec. 19, 1927; s. Oliver Leslie and Mattie Marie (Cole) McC.; m. Mary Ernestine Lane, Oct. 6, 1950; children: Mary Melissa, James Leslie, Jr., Thomas Lane. BS, Northwestern La. U., 1949; MEd, U. Ark., 1955. Tchr., athletic coach Tensas Parish Sch. Bd., St. Joseph, La., 1949-50, 53-59, Newenkon H.S., Tensas Parish, St. Joseph, 1959-64; prin. Davidson H.S., Tensas Parish, 1964-68; tchr., athletic coach Bienville Parish Sch. Bd., Arcadia, La., 1950-51; supt. Tensas Parish, St. Joseph, 1968-74, Richland Parish Sch. Bd., Rayville, La., 1974; salesman N.Y. Life Ins. Co., N.Y.C., 1974-95; farmer Westlane farms, Inc., Rayville, 1995—. Republican. Baptist. Office: Ste 100 67 McConathy Dr Rayville LA 71269-6460

MCCONAUGHY, BENNET ALAN, lawyer; b. Des Moines, Mar. 5, 1954; s. Willis D. McConaughy and Joan M. Whitney; m. Dawn M. Thiry, July 1, 1988; children: Kate, Joe. BS, U. Washington, 1976, JD, 1979. Bar: Wash. 1979, Alaska 1980. Judicial law clk. U.S. Dist. Ct. Wash., Seattle, 1979-81; assoc. Roberts & Shefelman, 1981-85, ptnr., 1985-87, Foster, Pepper & Shefelman, P.L.L.C., 1987-97; mng. mem. Sandler Ahern & McConaughy PLLC, Seattle, 1997—. Contbr. articles to profl. jours. Trustee Fed. Bar Assn., 1997-2000. Office: Sandler Ahern & McConaughy PLLC 1200 5th Ave Ste 1900 Seattle WA 98101-3135 E-mail: ben@sandlaw.com.

MCCONKEY, JAMES RODNEY, English educator, writer; b. Lakewood, Ohio, Sept. 2, 1921; s. Clayton Delano and Grace (Baird) McC.; m. Gladys Jean Voorhees, May 6, 1944; children: Lawrence Clark, John Crispin, James Clayton. BA, Cleve. Coll., 1943; MA, Western Res. U., 1946; PhD, U. Iowa, 1953. Teaching fellow, instr. Cleve. Coll., 1945-46; teaching asst. U. Iowa, Iowa City, 1949-50; asst. prof. Morehead State Coll., Ky., 1950-54, assoc. prof., 1954-56; asst. prof. Cornell U., Ithaca, N.Y., 1956-62, assoc. prof., 1962-67, prof., 1967-87, Goldwin Smith prof. English lit., 1987-92; Goldwin Smith prof. emeritus, 1992—. Dir. Morehead Writers Workshop, 1951-56, Antioch Seminar in Writing and Pub., Yellow Springs, Ohio, 1957-59 Author: The Novels of E.M. Forster, 1957, Night Stand, 1965, Crossroads, 1968, Journey to Sahalin, 1971, The Tree House Confessions, 1979, Court of Memory, 1983, To a Distant Island, 1984, Kayo: The Authentic and Annotated Autobiographical Novel From Outer Space, 1987, Rowan's Progress, 1992, Stories From My Life With the Other Animals, 1993; editor: The Structure of Prose, 1963, Chekhov and Our Age, 1984, The Anatomy of Memory, 1996. Served with U.S. Army, 1943-45. Guggenheim fellow, 1970; Eugene Saxton Meml. Trust Fund fellow, 1962; recipient Nat. Endowment of Arts essay award, 1968, Am. Acad. and Inst. Arts and Letters award in lit., 1979 Democrat. Home: 402 Aiken Rd Trumansburg NY 14886-9733 Office: Cornell Univ Goldwin Smith Hall Dept English Ithaca NY 14853 E-mail: jrm9@cornell.edu.

MCCONKIE, GEORGE WILSON, educational psychology educator; b. Holden, Utah, July 15, 1937; s. G. Wilson and Mabel (Stephenson) McC.; m. Orlene Carol Johnson, Sept. 6, 1962; children: Lynnette Mooth, Heather Usevitch, April Rhiner, Faline Coffelt, George Wilson, Bryce Johnson, Camille Howard, Elissa, Esther, Bryna, Ruth, Anna May Cox, Cynthia, Thomas Oscar. AA, Dixie Jr. Coll., 1957; BS, Brigham Young U., 1960, MS, 1961; PhD, Stanford U., 1966. Missionary LDS Ch., 1957-59; asst. prof. edn. Cornell U., 1964-70, asso. prof., 1970-75, prof., 1975-78, chmn. dept. edn., 1977-78; prof. U. Ill., Champaign, 1978—, chmn. dept. ednl. psychology, 1993-94, 95-97. Sr. scientist Ctr. for Study of Reading, 1978-95, Beckman Inst., 1989—; rsch. fellow Cath. U. Louvain, Belgium, 1991-92; vis. prof. Nat. Yang Ming U., Taiwan, 1998, Beijing Normal U., 1999. Contbr. articles to profl. jours. Recipient Outstanding Sci. Contbn. award Soc. for Sci. Study of Reading, 1995; NIMH spl. fellow, 1971-72, NIH Fogarty Internat. fellow, 1991-92; grantee U.S. Office Edn., 1970-73, Nat. Inst. Edn., 1974-77, NIMH, 1974-84, NICHHD, 1983-89, 91-95, AT&T, 1986-89, NSF, 1989-91, 2000—, CIA, 1991-97, Army Rsch. Lab., 1996-2001, Yamaha Motor Corp., 1997-99, GM, 2002-; Fulbright scholar, Taiwan, 1998, Sr. scholar Chiang Chung Kuo Found., 1998-99. Fellow APA; mem. Am. Ednl. Rsch. Assn., Psychonomic Soc., Cognitive Sci. Soc. Mem. Lds Ch. Home: 2605 Berniece Dr Champaign IL 61822-7225 Office: Beckman Inst for Advanced Sci and Tech 405 N Mathews Ave Urbana IL 61801-2300 E-mail: gmcconk@uiuc.edu.

MCCONKIE, OSCAR WALTER, lawyer; b. Moad, Utah, May 26, 1926; s. Oscar Walter and Margaret Vivian (Redd) M.; m. Judith Stoddard, Mar. 17, 1951; children: Oscar III, Ann, Daniel, Gail, Clair, Pace Jefferson, Roger James, Edward. BS in Polit. Sci., U. Utah, 1949, JD, 1952. Bar: Utah 1952, U.S. Ct. Appeals (10th cir.) 1952, U.S. Supreme Ct. 1981, U.S. Ct. Appeals (8th cir.) 1994. County atty. Summit County (Utah), 1959-63; instr. bus. law Stevens Henager Coll., Salt Lake City, 1952-67; ptnr. Kirton & McConkie, 1967—. Author: The Kingdom of God, 1962, God and Man, 1963, The Priest in the Aaronic Priesthood, 1964, Angels, 1975, Aaronic Priesthood, 1977, She Shall Be Called Woman, 1979. Mem. Utah Ho. of Reps., 1955-57; pres. Utah State Senate, 1965-66; chmn. Utah Bd. Edn., 1983-85. With USN, 1944-46. Mem. Utah Bar Assn., Salt Lake City County Bar Assn. Democrat. Mem. Lds Ch. Home: 1954 Laird Dr Salt Lake City UT 84108-1823 Office: 1800 Eagle Gate Tower 60 E South Temple Salt Lake City UT 84111-1004 E-mail: omcconkie@kmclaw.com.

MCCONNAUGHEY, FREDA RAYNOR, accountant, retired; b. Sandpoint, Idaho, Aug. 24, 1937; d. Frederick William Raynor and Billie Chilcote Harper; m. John Terrence McConnaughey, Mar. 21, 1958; children: Daniel, Traci. BBA, U. Alaska, 1984. Acct. Seattle First Nat. Bank, Spokane, Wash., 1956-59, Idaho First Nat. Bank, Sandpoint, 1961-63, Sykes Logging Co., Wrangell, Alaska, 1966-67, Conley Acctg., Palmer, 1968-70, Sheldon Jackson Coll., Sitka, 1972-75, Tyonek Timber Corp., Anchorage, 1976-79, Martech Internat., Anchorage, 1979-80, ret., 1980. Co-editor: Morton Valley Memories, 1996; author: Freda M—A Life Story, 1997. Vol. Bonner Hist. Mus., Sandpoint, 1995-97. Mem. AAUW. Republican. Avocations: quiltmaking, reading, traveling. Home: PO Box 644 Sandpoint ID 83864-0644

MCCONNAUGHEY, GEORGE CARLTON, JR. retired lawyer; b. Hillsboro, Ohio, Aug. 9, 1925; s. George Carlton and Nelle (Morse) McC.; m. Carolyn Schlieper, June 16, 1951; children: Elizabeth, Susan, Nancy. BA, Denison U., 1949; LL.B., Ohio State U., 1951, JD, 1967. Bar: Ohio 1951. Sole practice, Columbus; ptnr. McConnaughey & McConnaughey, 1954-57, McConnaughey, McConnaughey & Stradley, 1957-62, Laylin, McConnaughey & Stradley, 1962-67, George, Greek, King, McMahon & McConnaughey, 1967-79, McConnaughey, Stradley, Mone & Moul, 1979-81, Thompson, Hine & Flory (merger McConnaughey, Stradley, Mone & Moul with Thompson, Hine & Flory), Cleve., Columbus, Cin., Dayton and Washington, 1981-93; ret. ptnr. Thompson Hine LLP, Columbus, 1993—. Bd. dirs. N.Am. Broadcasting Co. (Sta. WMNI, WBZX and WEGE Radio); asst. atty. gen. State of Ohio, 1951-54. Pres. Upper Arlington (Ohio) Bd. Edn., 1967-69, Columbus Town Meeting Assn., 1974-76; chmn. Ohio Young Reps., 1956; U.S. presdl. elector, 1956; trustee Buckeye Boys Ranch, Columbus, 1967-73, 75-81, Upper Arlington Edn. Found., 1987-93; elder Covenant Presbyn. Ch., Columbus. With U.S. Army, 1943-45, ETO. Fellow Am. Bar Found., Ohio Bar Found., Columbus Bar Found.; mem. ABA, Ohio Bar Assn., Columbus Bar Assn., Am. Judicature Soc., Scioto Country Club, Athletic Club, Rotary, Masons. Home: 1993 Collingswood Rd Columbus OH 43221-3741 Office: Thompson Hine LLP One Columbus 10 W Broad St Ste 700 Columbus OH 43215-3435

MCCONNEL, RICHARD APPLETON, aerospace company official; b. Rochester, Pa., May 29, 1933; s. Richard Appleton Sr. and Dorothy (Merriman) McC.; m. Mary Francis McInnis, 1964 (div. 1984); children: Amy Ellen, Sarah Catherine; m. Penny Kendzie, 1993. BS in Naval Engring., U.S. Naval Acad., 1957; MS in Aerospace Engring., USN Postgrad. Sch., 1966. Commd. ensign USN, 1957; naval aviator Operation ASW, 1959-63, 68-71, 75-79; asst. prof. math. U.S. Naval Acad., 1966-68; program mgr. P3C update Naval Air Devel. Ctr., 1971-75; range program mgr. Pacific Missile Test Ctr., 1979-82; ret. USN, 1982; program mgr. Electromagnetic Systems div. Raytheon Co., Goleta, Calif., 1982-87; sr. engr. SRS Techs., Inc., Camarillo, 1987-92, High Tech. Solutions, Inc., Camarillo, 1992—. Mem. Internat. Test and Evaluation Assn., Assn. Old Crows. Republican. Office: High Tech Solutions 1317 Del Norte # 200 Camarillo CA 93010 Personal E-mail: r.mcconnel@earthlink.net. Business E-Mail: dmcconnel@htshg.com.

MCCONNELL, ALBERT LYNN, county official; b. Springfield, Ohio, Oct. 20, 1946; s. Jack Pershing and Betty Ann (Venema) McConnell; m. Rannette Oledge, Dec. 21, 2001; 1 child Ciara Lynn 1 stepchild Joshua Hooper. BA, Ctrl. State U., 1969; MA, Webster U., 1983; MS, USACGSC, 1984. Commd. 2d. lt. U.S. Army, 1969, advanced through grades. to maj., 1980; ret., 1989; served as inf. bn. intelligence officer Schofield Barracks, Hawaii, 1970-71; inf. co. comdr., asst. ops. officer, inf. bn., 1971; intelligence analyst and briefer U.S. Mil. Assistance Command, 1972-73; instr. U.S. Army Intelligence Sch., Ft Huachuca, Ariz., 1973-77; served in 3rd Armored Divsn., Frankfurt, Germany, 1980-81; project officer Combined Arms Ctr., Ft. Leavenworth, Kans., 1981-83, comdr. spl. security detachment, 1981-83; dir. intelligence, asst. chief staff for intelligence U.S. Army South, Ft. Clayton, Panama, 1984-85, mng. exec. officer Ft. Davis, Panama, 1985-86; tactical intelligence officer, chief adminstrv. svcs. U.S. Army Air Def. Arty. Sch., Ft. Bliss, Tex., 1986-87, dep. directorate chief, 1987-88, sr. intelligence officer, dept. divsn. chief, 1988-89; ops. analyst RAM Inc., Sierra Vista, Ariz., 1989-92; prof. bus. adminstrn. and mgmt. So. Ohio Coll., Columbus, 1992, Bliss Coll., Columbus, 1993; store mgr. Circle K Corp., Yuma, Ariz., 1993-94; tchr. Glendale (Ariz.) Union H.S., 1994-95; mgr. Dexter Book Store, 1995-96; dean students Ariz. Inst. Bus. and Tech., Phoenix, 1996-98, campus dir. Mesa, 1998-2000; dir. edn. High Tech Inst., Phoenix, 2000—02; voter registration official Maricopa County, 2002—. Instr. Mansfield Bus. Sch., El Paso, Tex., 1987-89; adj. prof. Chapman U., Sierra Vista, 1990-92; tax preparer H&R Block, Sierra Vista, 1990-92. Treas. Antioch Missionary Bapt. Ch., Huachuca City, Ariz., 1991-92. Decorated Bronze Star. Mem. Assn. U.S. Army, Air Force Assn., Ret. Officers Assn., Assn. Old Crows, Scabbard and Blade, Phi Alpha Theta, Iota Beta Sigma. Republican. Baptist. Avocations: photography, reading, coaching youth football and baseball.

MCCONNELL, BRUCE WILLIAM, information technology executive; b. Washington, Oct. 26, 1949; s. John Paul McConnell and Sally Dean McConnell Breul; m. Margaret Reagan Anderson. BS, Stanford U., 1971; MPA, U. Wash., 1985. Registered professional engr., Wash. Engr. Austin-Mac, Inc., Seattle, 1980—83; analyst U.S. Office of Mgmt. and Budget, Washington, 1985—92, chief info. policy and tech., 1992—99; dir. Internat. Y2K Cooperation Ctr., 1999—2000; co-chair encryption policy com. U.S. Nat. Security Coun., 1996—2000; pres. McConnell Internat. LLC, 2000—. Mem. bd. visitors RH Smith Sch. of Bus., U. Md., College Park, 2000—; mem. policy group on network-enabled svcs. and govt. Harvard U. Kennedy Sch. Government, Cambridge, Mass., 1997—. Tenor Thomas Cir. Singers, Washington, 1990—. Recipient Eagle award, Fed. Computer Week, 2000, Elmer B. Staats award for accountability in govt., Am. Soc. Pub. Adminstrn., 2000. Mem.: Nat. Press Club. Office: McConnell Internat LLC 1341 G St NW Ste 1100 Washington DC 20005 Office Fax: 202-347-7446. Business E-Mail: mcconnell@mcconnellinternational.com.

MCCONNELL, DAVID KELSO, lawyer; b. N.Y.C., July 12, 1932; s. David and Caroline Hanna (Kelso) McC.; m. Alice Schmitt, Dec. 26, 1953; children: Elissa Anne McConnell Henebry, Kathleen Anne, David Willet. BCE, CCNY, 1954; LLB, Yale U., 1962. Bar: Conn. 1962, U.S. Dist. Ct. Conn. 1963, U.S. Ct. Appeals (2d cir.) 1964, U.S. Ct. Appeals (3d cir.) 1966, U.S. Sup. Ct. 1970, U.S. Dist. Ct. (ea. dist.) Pa. 1971, Pa. 1975, N.Y. 1986. Asst. counsel N.Y.N.H. & H. R.R., New Haven, 1962-65, counsel, 1966-68; asst. atty. gen. U.S. V.I., 1965-66; asst. gen. atty. Pa. Cen. Transp. Co., New Haven, 1969-70, asst. gen. counsel Phila., 1970-71, sr. reorganization atty., 1971, adminstrv. officer, spl. counsel to trustees, 1971-76, gen. atty., 1977-78; asst. to chmn., CEO The Penn Cen. Corp., N.Y.C., 1979-80, corp. sec., 1980-82; v.p., gen. counsel Gen. Cable Co., Greenwich, Conn., 1982-85; pvt. practice Stamford, 1985-86, Pelham, N.Y., 1989-91, Greenwich, Conn., 1991-98. Of counsel McCarthy, Fingar, Donovan, Drazen & Smith, White Plains, N.Y., 1986-89. Dep. supr., councilman Town of Pelham, N.Y., 1986-90, budget officer, 1996; dep. mayor, trustee Village of Pelham, 1992-95, village atty., 1995-96; clk. of session, elder, trustee, deacon Huguenot Meml. Ch., Pelham N.Y. With U.S. Navy, 1954-59, USNR, 1959-79. Mem.: Yale Law Sch. Assn. (exec. com. 1988—91, dir. New Eng. 2001—), Assn. Bar City NY, NY Bar Assn., Conn. Bar Assn., St. Andrews Soc. NY (bd. mgrs. 1986—89, 1996—99, chmn. bd. mgrs. 1988—89), The Corinthians (mem. afterguard, dir. The Corinthians Assn., fleet capt. New Eng. fleet, trustee, pres., treas. The Corinthians Endowment Fund), Rotary Club of Newport RI (dir. 2001—), Rotary Club of Pelhams NY (pres. 1993—94). Home: 68 1/2 Roseneath Ave Newport RI 02840-3849 E-mail: david.mcconnell.law.62@aya.yale.edu.

MCCONNELL, E. HOY, II, advertising/public policy executive; b. Syracuse, N.Y., May 14, 1941; s. E. Hoy and Dorothy R. (Schmitt) McC.; m. Patricia Irwin, June 26, 1965; children: E. Hoy, III, Courtney. BA in Am. Studies magna cum laude, Yale U., 1963; MBA in Mktg. Harvard Bus. Sch., 1965. With Foote, Cone & Belding, 1965-76, v.p. account supr., 1971-72, 74-76, Phoenix, 1972-74; with D'Arcy-MacManus & Masius, Chgo., 1976-85, sr. v.p., dir. client services, then vice chmn., 1978-80, pres., 1980-84, chmn., 1984-85; mng. dir. D'Arcy Masius Benton & Bowles, 1986-96, also bd. dirs.; sr. v.p., account dir. Leo Burnett Co., 1996-98; exec. dir. Bus. and Profl. People for the Pub. Interest, 1999—. Bd. dirs. Evanston (Ill.) United Way, 1980-83, Evanston Youth Hockey Assn., 1980-89, pres. 1981-83; bd. dirs. Off-the-Street Club, 1980-90, Bus. Profl. People for Pub. Interest, 1981-83, 96—, v.p. 1984-89, pres. 1990-95; bd. dirs. Harvard Bus. Sch. Club, 1990-92, The Cradle Soc., 2000—; mem. Chgo. Coun. on Fgn. Rels., 1989-95. Mem. Am. Assn. Advt. Agys. (gov.-at-large Chgo. coun. 1984, sec. 1986, vice chmn. 1987, chmn. 1988-89), BBB Chgo. (mem. advt. rev. bd.), Glen View Country Club (bd. dirs. 1992-96), Dairymen's Country Club, Chgo. Club (membership comm. 1994-96), Yale Club Chgo. (bd. dirs. 1996-99). Democrat. Unitarian Universalist. Home: 2703 Colfax St Evanston IL 60201-2035 Office: BPI 25 E Washington St Ste 1515 Chicago IL 60602-1804 E-mail: hmcconnell@bpichicago.org.

MCCONNELL, EDWARD BOSWORTH, legal organization administrator, lawyer; b. Greenwich, Conn., Apr. 3, 1920; s. Raymond Arnott and Anna Bell (Lee) McC.; m. Jeanne M. Rotton (dec. 1984); children: Annalee, Marilyn, Edward, Barbara, William; m. Florence M. Leonard, (dec. 1991); stepchildren: Susan L. Little, William R. Leonard, Molly M. Leonard. AB, U. Nebr., 1941, LLB, 1947; MBA with distinction, Harvard U., 1943. Bar: Nebr. 1947, N.J. 1950. Mem. faculty Rutgers U. Sch. Bus. Adminstrn., Newark, 1947-53; assoc. firm Toner, Speakman and Crowley, 1949-50; adminstrv. asst. and law sec. to Chief Justice of N.J., 1950-53; adminstrv. dir. Cts. of N.J., Trenton, 1953-73; also standing master Supreme Ct., 1953-73; pres. Nat. Center for State Cts., Williamsburg, 1973-90, bd. dirs., 1980-90, pres. emeritus, 1990—, cons. on ct. mgmt., 1990—. Mem. U.S. Dept. Justice Coun. on Role of Cts. in Am. Soc., 1978-83; mem. adv. com. Dispute Resolution Policy Study, Social Sci. Rsch. Inst., U. So. Calif., 1975-79, Civil Litigation Rsch. Project, U. Wis. and U. So. Calif., 1979-83, nat. judg. edn. program to promote equality for men and women in the cts., 1980—; mem. Nat. Inst. Criminal Justice Task Force, Urban Consortium, 1979-83; participant Access To Justice Colloquium, European Univ. Inst., Florence, Italy, 1979; nat. adv. coun. Ctr. Adminstrn. Justice, Wayne Stae U., 1973-77; nat. project com. State Jud. Info. Sys. Project SEARCH Group, 1973-76; lectr. Inst. of Local and State Govt. Wharton Sch. U. Pa., 1955-65, Appellate Judges Seminar, Inst. Jud. Adminstrn., NYU, 1962-75; vis. expert UN Asia and Far East Inst., Tokyo, 1971; mem. Cts. Task Force Nat. Adv. Commn. Criminal Justice Standards and Goals, 1971-73; nat. adv. com. D.C. Ct. Mgmt. Project, 1966-70; trustee Inst. Ct. Mgmt., 1969-73, 84-86; chmn. Nat. Conf. Ct. Adminstrv. Officers, 1956; mem. nat. task force on gender bias in cts. Nat. Assn. Women Judge's 1985-90; mem. adv. bd. Nat. Ctr. for Citizen Participation in Adminstrn. of Justice, 1984-90; mem. Nat. Commn. Trial Ct. Performance Standards, 1991-95. Mem. adv. com. on article III Commn. on the Bicentennial of the Constitution, 1989-91; adv. com. Judicary Leadership Coun., 1990-95. Maj. C.E., AUS, 1943-46. Decorated Bronze Star medal; recipient Warren E. Burger award for greatest contbn. to improvement of ct. adminstrn. Inst. for Ct. Mgmt., 1975, Herbert Lincoln Harley award for efficient adminstrn. justice Am. Judicature Soc., 1973, Glenn R. Winters award for outstanding service in jud. adminstrn. Am. Judges Assn., 1974, Tom C. Clark award for outstanding contbns. to field of ct. adminstrn. Nat. Conf. Met. Cts., 1983, Award of Merit Nat. Assn. Ct. Mgmt., 1987, Spl. award, Nat. Assn. Women Judges, 1989, Paul C. Reardon award for disting. svc. Nat. Ctr. for State Cts., 1991, Alumni Achievement award U. Nebr., 1991, Robert B. Yegge award ABA Jud. Divsn. Lawyers Conf., 1997. Fellow Nat. Acad. Pub. Adminstrn. (mem. panel on evaluation budget decentralization project of fed. cts. 1989-91, chmn. panel long range planning in fed. cts. 1991-92, mem. panel for study of fed. trial ct. adminstrv. structure 1995-96); mem. ABA (fellow-at-large, coun. mem. 1960-66, 71-80, house of dels., 1977-80, chmn. com. on oversight and goals 1975-76, chmn. com. on jud. compensation jud. adminstrn. div. 1984-89, chmn. jud. adminstrn. div. 1976-77, sect. of litigation task force on excess litigiousness in Am. 1986-88, task force on reduction of litigation cost and delay, jud. adminstrn. dir. 1984-94, chmn. 1991-94, mem. long range planning com. 1989-94), N.J. Bar Assn., Nebr. Bar Assn., Warren E. Burger Soc., Kingsmill (Va.) Golf, Tennis and Yacht Clubs (pres. 2001), Order of Coif (hon.), Delta Upsilon, Sigma Delta Phi, Phi Delta Phi. E-mail: ebm80@aol.com.

MCCONNELL, GREGORY JAMES, biologist, educator; b. Kingsport, Tenn., Apr. 25, 1960; s. Frank Darrell and Pia (Rieden) McConnell. BS, East Tenn. State U., Johnson City, 1983; MS, East Tenn. State U., Johnson City, 1989. Instr. biology Emory and Henry Coll., Emory, Va., 1993—; prof. tropical biology La Suerte Biol. Sta., Pococi, Costa Rica, 2001—. Chair Mt. Rogers Naturalist Rally, Damascus, Va., 1997—; field trip leader Roan Mountain (Tenn.) Naturalist Rally, 1989—. Democrat. Roman Catholic. Avocations: hiking, skiing, canoeing, writing, travel. Home: 19432 Midwest Cir # 21 Abingdon VA 24211 Office: Emory and Henry Coll Dept Biology PO Box 947 Emory VA 24327 Office Fax: 276-944-6695. E-mail: gjmcconn@ehc.edu.

MCCONNELL, HARDEN MARSDEN, biophysical chemistry researcher, chemistry educator; b. Richmond, Va., July 18, 1927; s. Harry Raymond and Frances (Coffee) McConnell; m. Sophia Milo Glogovac, Oct. 6, 1956; children: Hunter, Trevor, Jane. BS, George Washington U., 1947; PhD, Calif. Inst. Tech., 1951; DSc (hon.) (hon.) , U. Chgo., 1991, George Washington U., 1993. NRC fellow dept. physics U. Chgo., 1950—52; research chemist Shell Devel. Co., Emeryville, Calif., 1952—56; asst. prof. chemistry Calif. Inst. Tech., 1956—58, prof. chemistry and physics, 1963—64; prof. chemistry Stanford U., Calif., 1964—79, Robert Eckles prof. chemistry, 1979—, chmn. dept., 1989—; founder Molecular Devices Corp., 1983—. Cons. in field. Contbr. Pres. Found. for Basic Rsch. in Chemistry, 1990—96; hon. assoc. Neurosci. Rsch. Program. Named Sherman Fairchild Disting. scholar, 1988; recipient Calif. sect. award, Am. Chem. Soc., 1961, award in pure chemistry, 1962, Harrison Howe award, 1968, Irving Langmuir award in chem. physics, 1971, Pauling medal, Puget Sound and Oreg. sects., 1987, Peter Debye award in phys. chemistry, 1990, Am. Achievement award, George Washington U., 1971, Disting. Alumni award, Calif. Inst. Tech., 1982, Dickson prize for sci., Carnegie-Mellon U., 1982, Wolf prize in chemistry, 1984, ISCO award, 1984, Wheland medal, U. Chgo., 1988, Nat. Medal Sci., 1989, Brucker prize, 1995, Gold medal, Internat. ESR Soc., Zavoisky award, 2000. Fellow: AAAS, Biophys. Soc.; mem.: NAS ((award in chem. scis. 1988), Serbian Acad. Scis. and Arts (fgn. mem.), Am. Chem. Soc (award in Surface Chemistry 1997, Welch award in Chemistry 2002), Am. Soc. Biol. Chemists, Am. Acad. Arts and Scis., Am. Phys. Soc., Internat. Acad. Quantum Molecular Scis. Achievements include patents for in field. Office: Stanford U Dept Chemistry Stanford CA 94305

MCCONNELL, JAMES JOSEPH, internist; b. Lynchburg, Va., Sept. 4, 1946; s. Willis Samson and Hope (Lewis) McC.; m. Pamela Marie Sabatino, Apr. 7, 1979. BS, Lynchburg Coll., 1968; MD, Med. Coll. Va., 1972. Diplomate Am. Bd. Internal Medicine. Intern USN, Portsmouth, Va., 1972-73; dir. occupational medicine Norfolk Naval Shipyard, 1973-75; resident internal medicine USN, 1975-78; dir. internal medicine clinic Naval Amphibian Base, Virginia Beach, 1978-79; physician internal medicine Wythe Med. Assn., Wytheville, 1979-80; private practice, 1981—. Bd. dirs. Spl. Care Svcs., Wytheville, Echo Vascular Lab., Advanced Cardiac Life Support. Recipient Outstanding Citizenship award M.T. Rodgers, 1982, Woodsmen of World, 1984. Mem. AMA, Am. Coll. Physicians, Am. Soc. Internal Medicine, Am. Heart Assn. (Va. faculty). Avocations: model railroading, stamp collecting. Home: 625 S 9th St Wytheville VA 24382-3213 Office: 365 W Ridge Rd Wytheville VA 24382-1008 E-mail: jmcconnell@naxs.com.

MCCONNELL, JOHN EDWARD, electrical engineering company executive; b. Minot, N.D., July 28, 1931; s. Lloyd Waldorf and Sarah Gladys (Mathis) McC.; m. Carol Claire Myers, July 4, 1952 (dec. Feb. 1989); children: Kathleen Anne, James Mathis, Amy Lynn; m. Heidi Banziger, Sept. 29, 1990. BSME, U. Pitts., 1952; MS, Drexel Inst. Tech., 1958. Registered profl. engr., Pa. With mktg. and design depts. for turbomachinery Westinghouse Electric Corp., Lester, Pa., 1954-60, 63-67, Pitts., 1960-63; mgr. power generation equipment activities in U.S. ASEA, Inc., White Plains, N.Y., 1967-79, regional mgr. power equipment activities Middle Atlantic and Southeastern U.S. regions, 1967-79, mgr. turbine generator dept., 1979-83, mgr. internat. ops. Power Sys. divsn., 1983-84, mgr. transmission substas. dept., 1984-85; mgr. Ea. U.S. ops. ASEA Power Sys., Inc., 1985-86, mgr. ea. ops. measurement divsn. GEC, 1986-91; mgr. ea. region Protection and Control divsn. GEC Alsthom T&D Inc., 1991-98; prin. JEMTECH Co., 1998—; v.p. ATG Exodus, 2000—. Adviser on energy matters to U.S. congressman 1968-74; bd. dirs. SoftStuf, Inc.; spkr. in field. Contbr. articles on energy and electric power to profl. jours. 1st lt. C.E., U.S. Army, 1952-54. Mem. IEEE (life, sr., energy com., past chmn. subcom. cogeneration, hon. mem. power sys. relay com.), IEEE Power Engring. Soc. (sr., past chmn. chpts. pub. affairs subcom.), ASME. Republican. Achievements developer analytical techniques for power systems performance characteristics and economics of cogeneration systems. Home: 173 Remington Rd Ridgefield CT 06877-4324 Office: JEMTECH PO Box 229 Ridgefield CT 06877-0229 *1) If it doesn't produce revenue, is it worthwhile? 2) Problem solving begins with careful listening. 3) Keep people informed. If they don't know, they'll assume the worst. 4) The truth is the most credible explanation you'll find.*

MCCONNELL, JOHN THOMAS, newspaper executive, publisher; b. Peoria, Ill., May 1, 1945; s. Golden A. and Margaret (Lyon) McC.; 1 child, Justin. BA, U. Ariz., 1967. Mgr. Fast Printing Co., Peoria, 1970-71; mgmt. trainee Quad-Cities Times, Davenport, Iowa, 1972-73; asst. gen. mgr., then v.p., gen. mgr. Peoria Jour. Star, 1973-81, pub., 1981—, pres., 1987—; v.p. The Copley Press, Inc., Peoria, 1997—. Bd. dirs. Peoria Downtown Devel. Council, Peoria Devel. Corp.; past trustee Methodist Hosp., Peoria. Served with USAR, 1967-69. Named Young Man of Year Peoria Jaycees, 1979 Mem. Peoria Advt. and Selling Club, Peoria C. of C. Clubs: Peoria Country. Congregationalist. Office: Peoria Jour Star Inc 1 News Plz Peoria IL 61643-0001 E-mail: mac@pjstar.com.

MCCONNELL, JOHN HENDERSON, metal and plastic products manufacturing executive, professional sports team executive; b. New Manchester, W.Va., May 10, 1923; s. Paul Alexander and Mary Louise (Mayhew) McC.; m. Margaret Jane Rardin, Feb. 8, 1946; children— Margaret Louise, John Porter BA in Bus., Mich. State U., 1949; Dr. Law (hon.), Ohio U., 1981. Sales trainee Weirton Steel Co., W.Va., 1950-52; sales mgmt. Shenango-Steel Co., Farrell, Pa., 1952-54; founder, chmn. bd. Worthington Industries, Inc., Columbus, Ohio, 1955—, also past CEO; bd. dirs. Pitts. Pirates; owner, NHL Franchise Columbus Blue Jackets, Worthington, Ohio, 1998—. Dir. Alltel Corp., Hudson, Ohio, Anchor Hocking, Lancaster, Ohio, Nat. City Corp., Cleve. Bd. dirs. Children's Hosp., Columbus; trustee Ashland Coll., Ohio. Served with USN, 1943-46 Recipient Ohio Gov.'s award Gov. State of Ohio, 1980; Horatio Alger award Horatio Alger Assn., 1983; named Outstanding Chief Exec. Officer, Fin. World Mag., 1981 Mem. Columbus Area C. of C. (chmn. 1978) Clubs: Golf (New Albany, Ohio) (pres. 1983—); Brookside Country (Columbus) (pres. 1964-65). Lodges: Masons. Republican. Presbyterian. Avocations: flying; golf. Address: Columbus Blue Jackets 150 E Wilson Bridge Rd Ste 235 Columbus OH 43085-2328 Office: Worthington Industries Inc 1205 Dearborn Dr Columbus OH 43085-4769*

MCCONNELL, JOHN HOWARD, personnel management consultant, writer; b. Highland Park, Mich., June 18, 1933; s. Melvin William and Dorothy Marie (Miller) McC.; m. Dolores Ann Cooper, Oct. 29, 1955; children: Keith Ernest, Brian Howard, Eric William. BS, Wayne State U., 1957, MEd, 1963. Tchr. Detroit Bd. Edn., 1957-59, Highland Park Bd. Edn., 1959-60; personnel mgr. Wolverine Tube Co., Allen Park, Mich., 1960-69; personnel dir. Garan, Inc., N.Y.C., 1970-71; cons. Morristown, N.J., 1971-74; cons. human resource mgmt., pres. McConnell, Simmons & Co., Inc., 1974—. Bd. dirs. Circus Royale, Inc., Morristown. Author: How To Audit, 8 vols., 1974-85, Introduction to Human Resources, 1982, A Ring, A Horse and A Clown, 1994, Shrine Circus, 1998, Hunting Heads, 1999, Auditing the Human Resources Department, 2000, How to Identify Training Needs, 2002; prodr. Player's Theater in Concert, 1989, 90, London Follies, 1994, 96; contbr. articles to various publs. Pres. Morristown Civic Assn., 1980. Mem. Am. Psychol. Assn., Am. Mgmt. Assn., Acad. Magical Arts, Magic Castle Club (L.A.), Circus Hist. Soc. (bd. dirs.), Masons. Democrat. Methodist. Avocation: producing entertainment events. Home: 1 Skyline Dr Morristown NJ 07960-5146 Office: 73 E Hanover Ave Morristown NJ 07960-3161 E-mail: johncircus@sprynet.com.

MCCONNELL, JOHN WILLIAM, JR. lawyer; b. Bessemer, Ala., Apr. 17, 1921; s. John W. and Elizabeth (Sheridan) McC.; m. Margaret B. Snider, Jan. 7, 1944; children— Margaret E. (Mrs. John Evans), Rebecca L. (Mrs. A.D. Braden), Catherine L., John W. III. AB, U. Ala., 1942, MA, 1946; LL.B., Yale, 1948. Bar: Ala. 1948, D.C. 1977. Atty. Inge, Twitty, Armbrecht & Jackson, Mobile, Ala., 1948-56, Armbrecht, Jackson, McConnell & DeMouy, 1956-65; dir. U.S. Peace Corps, Nigeria, 1965-68; v.p. legal Sea-Land Service, Inc., Menlo Park, N.J., 1968-76; also dir., of counsel Haight, Gardner, Poor & Havens, Washington, 1977-94. Atty. for Reynolds v. Sims on legislative reapportionment, U.S. Supreme Ct., 1963-64 Mem. Ala. Dem. Exec. Com., 1963-65. Served to capt. AUS, 1943-46, 50-52. Mem. ABA, Ala. Bar Assn., D.C. Bar Assn., Maritime Law Assn. Methodist. Home: 926 Sea Gull Dr Mount Pleasant SC 29464-4145

MCCONNELL, LORELEI CATHERINE, retired library director; b. Port Jefferson, N.Y., Dec. 5, 1938; d. Alvin and Mary (McConnell) Philibert; m. Thomas McConnell, Jan. 20, 1962; children: Catherine, Michael. BA, Drew U., 1960; MLS, Rutgers U., 1963. Reference libr. Irvington (N.J.) Pub. Libr., 1963-90, dir., 1990-99; founder Irvington Literacy Program, 1986, dir., 1986-90; ret., 1999; cons., 2000—. Mem. exec. bd. Infolink, 1998-99. Mem. ALA, N.J. Libr. Assn. (mem. exec. bd. 1990-93, N.J. Libr. of Yr. 1993-94), Irvington (N.J.) C. of C. (exec. bd. 1992—, Civic award 1996), Beta Phi Mu. Home: 563 Park St Montclair NJ 07043-2027 *The world would be a better place if we could find ways to reward and honor every single person who works hard and does the right thing.*

MCCONNELL, MARY JOAN, civil service; b. McCormick, S.C., Oct. 3, 1946; d. John Leslie and Annie Ruby (White) McConnell; m. Akhilesh Kumar, Dec. 15, 1979 (div. Dec. 1999). BA in English, Lander Coll., 1976. Civil service Randolph Air Force Base, San Antonio, 1983—.

MCCONNELL, MICHAEL ARTHUR, lawyer; b. Ft. Worth, Jan. 15, 1947; BA, Loyola U., New Orleans, 1969; JD, U. Tex., 1975. Bar: Tex. 1976, U.S. Dist. Ct. (no. dist.) Tex. 1976, U.S. Dist. Ct. (ea. dist.) Tex. 1981, U.S. Dist. Ct. (we. dist.) Tex. 1982, U.S. Dist. Ct. (so. dist.) Tex. 1989, U.S. Ct. Appeals (5th cir.) Tex. 1980, U.S. Ct. Appeals (10th cir.) 1987. Briefing atty. U.S. Dist. Ct. Hon. Eldon B. Mahon, Ft. Worth, 1976-77; assoc. atty. Cantey, Hanger, Gooch, Munn and Collins, 1977-81, ptnr., 1981-83; judge no. dist. U.S. Bankruptcy Ct., 1983-86; ptnr. Kelly, Hart & Hallman, 1986-88, Jackson & Walker, Ft. Worth, 1988-95, McConnell & Goodrich, Ft. Worth, 1995-2000, Winstead, Sechrest, and Minick, P.C., Ft. Worth, 2000—. Sgt. USAF, 1969-73. Mem. Nat. Conf. Bankruptcy Judges. Office: Winstead Sechrest & Minick PC 777 Main St Ste 1100 Fort Worth TX 76102

MCCONNELL, MICHAEL THEODORE, lawyer; b. San Francisco, June 18, 1954; s. Lawrence V. and Ann McConnell. BS, U. Oreg., 1977; JD, U. Denver, 1980. Bar: Colo., Wyo., U.S. Dist. Ct. Colo., U.S. Ct. Appeals (10th cir.), U.S. Supreme Ct., U.S. Dist. Ct. Wyo. Ptnr. Long & Jaudon, Denver, 1980—2001; founding mem., CEO McConnell Siderius Fleischner Houghtaling & Craigmile, LLC, 2002—. Fellow Am. Coll. Trial Lawyers; mem. ABA, Colo. Bar Assn., Denver Bar Assn., Colo. Def. Lawyers Assn. Office: McConnell Siderius et al 2401 15th St Ste 300 Denver CO 80202 E-mail: mmcconnell@msfhc.com.

MCCONNELL, MITCHELL, JR. (MITCH MCCONNELL JR., ADDISON MITCHELL MCCONNELL JR.), senator, lawyer; b. Tuscumbia, AL, Feb. 20, 1942; s. Addison Mitchell and Julia (Shockley) McC.; children: Eleanor Hayes, Claire Redmon, Marion Porter; m. Elaine Chao, Feb. 6, 1993. BA with honors, U. Louisville, 1964; JD, U. Ky., 1967. Bar: Ky. 1967. Chief legis. asst. to Senator Marlow Cook, Washington, 1968-70; sole practice Louisville, 1970-74; dep. asst. U.S. atty. gen. Washington, 1974-75; judge Jefferson County, Louisville, 1978-85; U.S. Senator from Ky., 1985—; chmn. Nat. Republican Senatorial Com. 105th and 106th Congress. Mem. agr., nutrition, and forestry com., appropriations com., rules and adminstrn. com. Chmn. Jefferson County Republican Com., 1973-74; co-chmn. Nat. Child Tragedies Coalition, 1981; chmn., founder Ky. Task Force on Exploited and Missing Children, 1982; mem. Pres.'s Partnership on Child Safety Recipient commendation Nat. Trust on Hist. Preservation in U.S., 1982, Conservationist of Yr. award League Ky. Sportsmen, 1983, cert. of appreciation Am. Correctional Assn., 1985 Mem. Ky. Assn. County Judge Execs. (pres. 1982), Nat. Inst. Justice (adv. bd. 1982-84) Republican. Baptist. Avocations: fishing; cooking. Office: Russell Office Bldg # 361A Washington DC 20510-0001

MCCONNELL, PATRICIA LYNN, vocational consultant; b. Denver, Feb. 20, 1956; d. James Donald and Joyce Clemence (Wortman) McC.; m. Roger Tribble, 1989. BS, U. No. Colo., 1979. Mental health worker Arapahoe Mental Health Ctr., Littleton, Colo., 1977-79; work adjustment cons. recycling ctr. City of El Cerrito (Calif.), 1980-83; job developer, ind. contractor with Dept. of Rehab., Pleasant Hill, Calif., San Pablo, Vallejo, Calif., 1983-87; vocat. rehab. cons. Guitterez & Co., Oakland, 1987-89; owner, vocat. cons. JobPerfect, Berkeley, 1989—; owner, fundraiser Community Svcs. Mktg., Oakland. Workshop leader Calif. Dept. of Rehab., Pleasant Hill, 1983-87, San Pablo, 1989. Author: (workbook) Job Search for the Disabled, 1985, JobPerfect Job Search manual Datebook and Organizer, 1999; dir., producer (video) JobPerfect, 1992, How To Improve Your Communication and Interview Skills, 1994, JobPerfect Job Search, 1995, Legacies, 1995, JobPerfect JobSearch Organizer, 1998; creator, producer (cable show) A Good Book to Live In, 1996, Homecare, 1996, HomeTours, 1996, CMO, 1996. Mem., fundraiser No. Calif. Recyclers Assn., Berkeley, 1982-87, Calif. Marine Mammal Ctr., Marine Headlands, Calif., 1987-90, Bay Area Cmty. Svcs., 1993-97. Recipient Dance award Englewood High Sch., Colo., 1974, Appreciation award Regional Occupational Program, San Pablo, 1989. Mem. Calif. Assn. for Rehab. Profls., Nat. Rehab. Assn. (bd. dirs. 1983-85). Avocations: filmmaking, video production, graphics, marine mammals, dance. Office: JobPerfect at BFTI 1440 Broadway Ste 202 Oakland CA 94612-2022

MCCONNELL, ROBERT EASTWOOD, architect, educator; b. Spokane, Wash., July 15, 1930; s. Robert Ervie and Alma (Eastwood) Mc C.; m. Beverly Ann Vincent, Sept. 12, 1953; children: Kathleen Ann, Karen Eileen, Terri Lynn. B in Archtl. Engring., Wash. State U., 1952; MArch, Mass. Inst. Tech., 1954. Project architect John W. Maloney (Architect), Seattle, 1956-62; asst. prof. architecture Ariz. State U., Tempe, 1962-66, asso. prof., 1966-67; prof. U. Kans., Lawrence, 1967-69; prof., head dept. art and architecture U. Idaho, Moscow, 1969-71; prof. U. Ariz., Tucson, 1971-92, dean Coll. Architecture, 1971-77, prof. emeritus, dean emeritus, 1992—, acting assoc. dean, 1994; partner McConnell & Peterson, Architects, Tempe, 1963-66; pvt. practice architecture, 1962-96. Author, project dir.: Land Use Planning for Ariz., Ariz. Acad, 1974; Contbr. articles to profl. jours. Chmn. Idaho Gov.'s Awards Program in Arts and Humanities, 1970; project dir. Rio Salado Conceptual Study, Phoenix, 1966; bd. dirs. Tucson Regional Plan, 1972-79. Served with USAF, 1954-56. Fellow AIA (awards 1969, 76, pres. So. Ariz. chpt. 1975-76, bd. dirs. 1971-77); mem. AIA Ariz. (mem. coun. of dels. 1971-77, chmn. honor awards jury 1975), Phi Kappa Phi, Scarab, Tau Beta Pi, Sigma Tau. Home: 930 East Camino Corrida Tucson AZ 85737-7652

MCCONNELL, SARAH STACEY, film producer, French language educator; b. Missoula, Mont., Aug. 24, 1972; d. Robert Ronald and Janet Louise (Stacey) M. BA in French and English, Ball State U., 1995; Interdisciplinary MA in English, U. of York, Eng., 1997. Video prodr. R.M. Prodns., Muncie, Ind., 1993—; instr. French Ind. Acad., 1997—; instr. English Ball State U. Producer: (video documentaries) The Real France, 1993, Noel En France, 1995, Dining in France, 1995, Un Jour D'ecole Avec Richard, 1997, Richard's School Day, 1997, Notes From Russia, 1999, (books), Robert's Rules Simplified and Applied, 1998. Literacy tutor Project READ, Ind., 1992—. Mem. DAR. Avocations: painting, writing poetry, archery, travelling. Office: AT&T Wireless Svcs Bothell Office Bothell WA 98012-0001 E-mail: sarah.mcconnell@attws.com.

MCCONNELL, TIMOTHY IRVIN, music educator, physical education educator; b. Duluth, Minn., Dec. 9, 1953; s. Lois Mae Marshall and Paul Edward McConnell; m. LeeAnn Marie Doyle, Dec. 31, 1954; 1 child Devon 1 child Ryan. BA, St Scholastica Coll., Duluth, Minn., 1976. Vocal music dir. Floodwood (Minn.) Sch. Dist., Floodwood, Minn., 1977—79, Jackson County Ctrl. Sch. Dist., Jackson, 1979—. Pres. Edn. Minn. Tchr. Union/Jackson County Ctrl., Jackson, Minn., 1999—2001. Mem.: Am. Choral Director's Assn. (sw chair 1995—97). Home: 612 Cherry Lakefield MN P.O. Office: Jackson County Central School 1128 North Highway Jackson MN P.O.

MCCONNELL, WILLIAM THOMPSON, commercial banker; b. Zanesville, Ohio, Aug. 8, 1933; s. William Gerald and Mary Gladys McC.; m. Jane Charlotte Cook, Aug. 25, 1956; children: Jennifer Wynne, William Gerald. BA, Denison U., 1955; MBA, Northwestern U., 1959. Pres. Park Nat. Bank, Newark, 1979-83, pres., chief exec. officer, 1983-93, chmn., chief exec. officer, 1993-98, also bd. dirs., chmn., 1999—; pres., chief exec. officer Park Nat. Corp., 1987-94, chmn., CEO, 1994-98, chmn., 1999—. Mem. Newark Area C. of C. (past pres., dir. 1977-83), Ohio Bankers Assn. (pres., chmn. 1981-83), Am. Bankers Assn. (pres. 1997-98). Office: Park Nat Bank PO Box 3500 Newark OH 43058-3500

MCCONNICO, NANCY MANN, civic worker; b. Memphis, Aug. 31, 1933; d. John Davis and Pauline (Hilton) McConnico; m. Dean Carlton DuBois, Aug. 19, 1950 (div. Nov. 1963); children: Denise DuBois Taylor, Dean Carlton; m. Earl Crafton Beck, Jr. (div. 1987); 1 son, John Beck McConnico. Grad., So. Sem. and Jr. Coll., 1949. Asst. buyer sportswear John Gerber Co., Memphis, 1949-50; fashion coordinator J. Hilton McConnico, Designer, Paris, 1963-65; buyer, mgr. Bridal Salon Goldsmiths, Memphis, 1965-72, buyer, mgr. French Room, 1970-72. Owner NMM Art Assocs. Exec. dir. Germantown Arts Alliance, 1992-98; mem. Grace St. Luke's Episcopal Ch., Memphis; v.p. West Memphis Fine Arts Ctr.; chmn. Crittenden County-Memphis, regional chmn. Mid-South Billy Graham Crusade, May 1978; chmn. Children's Art Day, Memphis, 1976-78, chmn. Memphis Symphony Ball, 1981; bd. dirs. Crittenden Fine Arts Center, 1979-82, Memphis Orchestral Soc., 1981-86, Memphis Arts Council; bd. dirs. Am. Symphony Orch. League, 1985-88, v.p., conf. chmn. vol. council, 1974-75; bd. dirs. Memphis Symphony League, 1977-78; dir. devel. St. George's Day Sch., Germantown, Tenn., 1987—, pres., 1980-81, chmn. of ball 1981; trustee So. Sem. Coll., Buena Vista, Va., 1982-87; chmn. Maestro Vincent De Frank Tribute Com., 1984-85; bd. dirs. Ark. Gov.'s Mansion Assn., 1986-88, Shelby State C.C. Found. Bd., 1987-90; mem. Memphis Bd. Edn. Tchr. Initiative Grants Com., 1987—; mem. devel. com. 1st Tenn. Young Artist Competition, 1988; bd. dirs.

Marguerite Piazza Gala St. Jude Hosp.; mem. Gov.'s Alliance Regional Excellence. Recipient Nat. Ednl. award for Children's Arts Day, 1978, Tenn.-Ark.-Miss. Girl Scout Council award, 1986-87, Memphis Hebe award, 1986. Mem. Episc. Churchwomen (pres. 1983-85), Josephine Circle (pres. 1963-64), Salvation Army (auxiliary bd. dirs., chmn., 2001). Episcopalian. Home: 4400 Poplar Ave Apt 16 Memphis TN 38117-3707

MCCONOMY, JAMES HERBERT, lawyer; b. Pitts., Mar. 24, 1937; s. Murray Michael and Catherine Elizabeth (Herbert) McC.; m. Jeanne Margaret Cronin, Sept. 3, 1960 (div. Apr. 1989); children: Margaret Jeanne, Michael Murray; m. Roberta L. Cavanaugh, June 30, 1989. AB cum laude, Harvard U., 1959, LLB, 1962. Bar: Pa. 1963, U.S. Ct. Appeals (3d cir.) 1972, U.S. Supreme Ct. 1977. Ptnr. Reed, Smith, Shaw & McClay, Pitts., 1962-92; mng. ptnr. Titus & McConomy, 1992—. Fellow Am. Coll. Trial Lawyers; mem. ABA, Pa. Bar Assn. Allegheny County Acad. Trial Lawyers. Clubs: Duquesne, Harvard-Yale-Princeton (Pitts.). Roman Catholic. Avocations: photography, travel. Home: 1117 Harvard Rd Pittsburgh PA 15205-1726 Office: Titus & McConomy Four Gateway Ctr 20th Fl Pittsburgh PA 15222

MCCOOK, KATHLEEN DE LA PEÑA, university educator; b. Chgo. d. Frank Eugene and Margaret L. (de la Peña) McEntee; m. Philip G. Heim, Mar. 20, 1972 (div.); 1 child, Margaret Marie; m. William Woodrow Lee McCook, Oct. 12, 1991; stepchildren: Cecilia, Billie Jean, Nicole. BA, U. Ill., Chgo.; MA, Marquette U., U. Chgo.; PhD, U. Wis.-Madison. Reference librarian Elmhurst Coll. Libr., Ill.; dir. pub. svcs. Dominican U., River Forest; lectr. U. Wis., Madison; asst. prof. library sci. U. Ill., Urbana; dean, prof. La. State U. Sch. Libr. and Info. Sci., Baton Rouge; dean grad. sch. La. State U.; dir. Sch. Libr. and Info. Sci., U. South Fla., 1993-99, prof., 1993—, coord. cmty. outreach, 2000—02, disting. rsch. prof., 2002—. Author: (wth K. Weibel) Role of Women in Librarianship, 1978, (with L. Estabrook) Career Profiles, 1983, (with William E. Moen) Occupational Entry, 1989, Adult Services, 1990, (with Gary O. Rolstad) Developing Readers' Advisory Services, 1993, Toward a Just and Productive Soc., 1994, Opportunities in Library and Information Science, 1997, (with B. Ford) Global Reach: Local Touch, 1998, Women of Color in Librarianship, 1998, (with B. Immroth) Library Services to Youth of Hispanic Heritage, 2000, A Place at the Table, 2000; contbr. essays to books, articles to profl. jours. Chmn. Equal Rights Amendment Task Force, Ill., 1977-79. South Count Coalition for Comty. Concerns, 2001—; mem. Eugene McCarthy campaign, U. Ill., Chgo., 1968; mem. La. Gov.'s Commn. for Women, 1985-88; bd. dirs. La. Endowment for Humanities, 1991-92; mem. exec. bd. Rural Social Svcs. Partnership, Hillsborough County, 1998-2001; mem. dem. exec. com., Hillsborough County, 2001-; dem. del. Fla. State Convention, 2002 Recipient Disting. Alumnus award U. Wis., 1991, award of merit Trejo Foster Found., 1999; named Bradshaw scholar Tex. Woman's Univ., 1994. Mem. ALA (com. chmn. 1980—, editor RQ jour. 1982-88, Pub. Librs. Jour. 1989-90, Am. Librs. adv. com. 1994-96, contbg. editor Am. Librs. 1999-2001, column editor RUSQ 2000—, Equality award 1987, Adult Svc. award 1991, Futas Catalyst for Change award 1998), Assn. for Libr. and Info. Sci. Edn. (com. chmn. 1981—, pres. 1987-88, Pres. award 1997), Fla. Libr. Assn. (bd. dirs. 1995-98, Transformer award 1996), Tampa Bay Libr. Consortium (bd. dirs. 1994-97), Women Libr. Workers, Ruskin Civic Assn. (sec. 1997-99), Ill. Libr. Assn. (treas. 1981-83), Beta Phi Mu (50th Anniversary Disting. Mem. 1999, Dist. Lectr. award 2002). Democrat. Roman Catholic. Avocation: reading. Office: U South Fla Sch Libr and Info Sci 4202 E Fowler Ave Stop Cis1040 Tampa FL 33620-7800 E-mail: kmccook@chuma.cas.usf.edu.

MCCOOK, TERRY L. business executive, consultant; b. Jacksonville, Fla., Aug. 17, 1946; s. Vernon L. and Frances H. (Ulrich) McCook; m. Eileen Marie Hutchin, Sept. 22, 1979; children: Clare Marie, Theresa Renee, Mary Catherine. BA, N.C. State U., 1968; MA, postgrad., Am. U., 1978. Asst. buyer Thalheimer Bros., Richmond, Va., 1969-70; grad. teaching asst. Am. U., Washington, 1971-73, asst. dir. admissions, 1973-77; sys. analyst Solite Corp., Richmond, 1978-81; corp. br. ops. coord. United Va. Bank, 1981-83; mktg. rep. Decimus Corp., Pitts., 1984-85; area sales mgr. Systeme Corp., Orlando, Fla., 1985-86; v.p., mktg. dir. The Citizens Banking Co., Salineville, Ohio, 1986-90; v.p., dimension sales Kirchman Corp., Orlando, 1992-94; CEO Profl. Asset Mgmt., Inc., 1990—. Mng. dir. Rad-Health Internat., Pitts., 1991-92. Author book revs. and article. Past nat. treas., provincial minister of Secular Franciscan Order. With USAR, 1968-74. Named to Outstanding Young Men in Am., 1978. Mem. Bank Mktg. Assn. (pres. tri-state chpt. 1990-91), Kiwanis Internat. Club (pres. 1988-90), Sigma Phi Epsilon, Omicron Delta Kappa, Phi Alpha Theta. Roman Catholic. Avocations: golf, fishing. Home: 266 Katherine Blvd Apt 7112 Palm Harbor FL 34684-5614

MCCOOL, CHASTITY MARIE, real estate manager; b. Waterloo, Iowa, Mar. 20, 1975; d. Jerry Ray Cagley and Renee Sue Cagley-Card; m. Joseph William McCool, Oct. 2, 1999 (div. Jan. 2001); children: Ocean, Noah. AA, Hawkeye C.C., Waterloo, 1998. Team leader Hardees, Waterloo, 1991—95; supr. Sams Club Whse., 1995—2000; property mgr. Coll. Sq. Apts., Cedar Falls, 1999—. Author: (poetry) Pathway's-Illiad Press, 1998. With U.S. Army, 1997—. Decorated Army Achievement medal. Avocations: reading, painting. Home: 116 W Wellington St Waterloo IA 50701-2508

MCCOOL, DEBORAH JOYCLYN, science educator; b. Johnstown, Pa., June 17, 1953; d. Paul Eugene and Delores June (Gilliland) Butler; children: Bryan K. Spiker, Jeffrey S. Spiker, Eric T. Spiker, Sean R. McCool. BS, U. Pitts., 1974; MEd, St. Francis Coll., Loretto, Pa., 1990. Secondary tchr., Pa. Tchr., biology and chemistry Penn Cambria H.S., Cresson, 1984—; instr., anatomy and physiology Mt. Aloysius Coll., 1990-95, 2001—; instr. chemistry St. Francis Coll., 1996-98; instr. healthcare mgmt. Cambria County Area C.C., 1996—; instr. biology Pa. State U., Altoona, 2000—. Mem. NSTA, NEA, Am. Chem. Soc. (edn. divsn.), Ctrl. Pa. Assn. Chemistry Tchrs., Pa. Edn. Assn., Pa. Sci. Tchrs. Assn. Republican. Baptist. Avocations: reading, piano, building computers, needlework. Office: Penn Cambria High School 401 Linden Ave Cresson PA 16630-1359 E-mail: debjmccool@netscape.net.

MCCOOL, WILLIAM C. astronaut, military officer; b. San Diego, Sept. 23, 1961; married. BS in Applied Sci., USN Acad., Annapolis, 1983; MS in Computer Sci., U. Md., 1985; MS in Aero. Engring., USN Postgrad. Sch., 1992. Student pilot USN Flight Tng. Sch., 1983—86; trainee Squadron 129, Whidby Island, Wash., 1986; pilot Tactical Electronic Warfare Squadron 122, USS Coral Sea in Mediterranean, 1986—89; student Test Pilot Sch., Calif., 1989—92; test pilot USN Flight Systems Dept., Patuxent River, Md., 1992—94; adminstrv. and ops. officer Tactical Electronic Warfare Squadron 132 aboard USS Enterprise, 1992—96; astronaut NASA Johnson Space Ctr., Houston, 1996—. Mem.: US Naval Acad. Alumni Assn. Office: Astronaut Office Johnson Space Ctr Houston TX 77058

MCCORD, DON LEWIS, surgeon; b. Vernon, Tex., Aug. 25, 1929; s. Thomas Garfield and Dola (Cavender) McC.; m. Gayle McCord, Mar. 4, 1972; children: Daniel Lindsey, Elizabeth Ann, Melissa Ann Mares, Nicole Pryor. BS in Chemistry, Abilene Christian U., 1949; MD, U. Tex., 1953. Diplomate Am. Bd. Surgery. Intern U. Hosp., Ann Arbor, Mich., 1953-54; resident in surgery U.S. Naval Hosp., Oakland, Calif., 1955-59, asst. chief of surgery Corpus Christi, Tex., 1959-62; pvt. practice Hamilton, 1962-74; group practice Clifton, 1974-86; pvt. practice Med. City, Dallas, 1986—, sect. chief gen. surgery, 1990-92. Cons. in surgery Hamilton (Tex.) Gen. Hosp., 1988-96, De Leon (Tex.) Hosp. Lt. comdr. USN, 1954-62. Fellow ACS; mem. AMA, Tex. Med. Assn., Dallas County med. Soc., Dallas Soc. Gen. Surgeons, Flying Physicians Assn., Alpha Omega Alpha. Republican. Avocation: flight instructor. Office: 7777 Forest Ln Ste C-608 Dallas TX 75230-2517

MCCORD, GLORIA DAWN HARMON, music educator, choral director, organist; b. Jacksonville, Fla., June 14, 1949; d. Earl H. and C. Grace (Lupo) Harmon; m. Mark L. McCord, Sr., Aug. 7, 1971; children: M. Lance, Ian H. BMus in Edn., Fla. State U.; MMus in Choral Conducting, La. State U.; postgrad., U. New Orleans, U. Ga. Cert. tchr., Ga. Classroom music tchr. Nassau County (Fla.) Bd. Edn., 1971, Orange County (Fla.) Bd. Edn., 1971-74; choral dir., gen. music tchr. Fulton County (Ga.) Bd. Edn., 1974-75; dir. music Aldersgate United Meth. Ch., Slidell, La., 1978-86; tchr. for gifted and talented in music St. Tammany Parish Schs., 1988-91; asst. prof. arts and scis. Brenau U., Gainesville, Ga., 1991—; registrar, pub. rels. dir., choral dir. Firespark Summer Sch. for Students Gifted in Arts, 1992—; organist Riverside Mil. Acad., 1994—. Presenter, adjudicator North Gwinnett Piano club, 1992, North Gwinnett Federated Festival, 1993, 95, 96, Ga. Music Educators Edn. Piano Festival, 1993; choir dir. Ga. Music Educators Dist. IX Honor Choir, 1993, others; series dir. radio broacast Panorama; adjudicator West Gwinnett Fed. Piano, 1995. Interim organist 1st United Meth. Chancel Choir, 1993, other positions; evaluator United Meth. Ch.; sec. Gainesville H.S. Band Boosters, Gainesville H.S. PTA, 1992-94. Recipient Lake Como (Orange county, Fla.) NEA Tchr. of the Yr., 1973. Mem. Am. Choral Dirs. Assn., United Meth. Am. Guild of Organists, Music Educators Nat. Assn (seminar facilitator 1993), Music Tchrs. Nat. Assn., Ga. Music Tchrs. Assn., Ga. Music Educators, Sigma Alpha Iota. Office: Brenau Univ 1 Centennial Cir Gainesville GA 30501-3697

MCCORD, GUYTE PIERCE, JR. retired judge; b. Tallahassee, Sept. 23, 1914; s. Guyte Pierce and Jean (Patterson) McC.; m. Laura Elizabeth Mack, Dec. 1, 1939; children: Florence Elizabeth, Guyte Pierce III, Edward LeRoy. Student, Davidson Coll., 1933-34; BA, JD, U. Fla., 1940. Bar: Fla. 1940. Summer ranger Yosemite Nat. Park, 1936-39; rsch. aide Fla. Supreme Ct., summer 1940; pvt. practice Tallahassee, 1940-48; dep. commr. Fla. Indsl. Commn., 1946-47; pros. atty. Leon County, 1947-48; asst. gen. counsel Fla. Pub. Svc. Commn., 1949-60; judge 2d Jud. Cir. Fla., Tallahassee, 1960-74, Ct. Appeals 1st Dist. Fla., 1974-83, chief judge, 1977-79. Mem. Fla. Senate Pres.'s Council on Criminal Justice 1972; mem. appellate ct. rules com. Fla. Supreme Ct., 1977-78, mem. appellate ct. structure commn. 1978-79. Pres. Murat House Assn., Inc., 1967-69; bd. dirs. Fla. Heritage Found., 1969-70, mem. exec. com., 1965-69; mem. Andrew Jackson staff of Springtime Tallahassee, 1973-74, 84-86, Andrew Jackson, 1987. Comdr. USNR, 1942-46, 52-53. Mem. ABA, Ret. Officers Assn., Fla. Bar, Fla. Conf. Cir. Judges (sec.-treas. 1970, chmn. 1972), Fla. State U. Pres. Club, Kiwanis (dir. 1958-59). Presbyterian (elder 1960—, ch. trustee 1981-86). Home: Apt 511 Oaks South 4425 Meandering Way Tallahassee FL 32308-5745

MCCORD, JAMES RICHARD, III, chemical engineer, mathematician; b. Norristown, Ga., Sept. 2, 1932; s. Zachariah Thigpen Houser Jr. and Neilie Mae (Sumner) McC.; m. Louise France Manning, Oct. 1956 (div. 1974); children: Neil Alexander, Stuart James, Valerie France, Kent Richard. Student, Abraham Baldwin Agrl. Coll., Tifton, Ga., 1949-50; BChE with honors, Ga. Inst. Tech., 1955; postgrad., U. Pitts., 1955-56, Carnegie Inst. Tech., 1956-57; MS, MIT, 1959, PhD in Math, 1961. Asst. chem. engr. TVA, Wilson Dam, Ala., 1951-54; assoc. engr. Westinghouse Electric Corp., Pitts., 1955-57; rsch. asst. ops. rsch. MIT, Cambridge, Mass., 1957-59, tchg. asst. dept. math., 1959-61, rsch. assoc. dept. math., 1961-62, asst. prof., postdoctoral fellow dept. chem. engring., 1962-64; sr. engr., project analyst Esso Research and Engring. Co., Florham Park, N.J., 1964-68; asst. prof. Emory U., Atlanta, 1968-71; pvt. practice math. cons., 1971-80; instr. in math. Ga. So. Coll., Statesboro, 1980-81; inventory control Lovett & Tharpe, Inc., Dublin, 1981-84; Norristown-Adrian; farmer, businessman, 1984—. Contbr. numerous articles to sci. and math. jours. WEBELOS den leader Boy Scouts Am., Dunwoody, Ga., 1969-70; mem., vol. worker Key Meml. Found., Adrian-Norristown, Ga., 1965—. Mem. AIChE, Ga. Tech. Alumni Assn., MIT Alumni Assn., Sigma Xi, Tau Beta Pi. Republican. Methodist. Avocations: music, fishing, gardening, mathematical puzzles. Home and Office: RR 1 Box 58C Adrian GA 31002-9461

MCCORD, JEAN ELLEN, secondary art educator, coach; b. Ilion, N.Y., Oct. 20, 1952; d. Harold Shepard and Marian Alice (Bernier) Shepard; m. Colin McCord, May 10, 1977 (div. Sept. 1993). AA, Mohawk Valley C.C., Utica, N.Y., 1972; BA, SUNY, New Paltz, 1975, postgrad., 1976-77; student, Coll. Santa Reparata Sch. Art, Florence, Italy, 2001. Cert. art educator, N.Y. Jr. kindergarten tchr. Norfolk (Va.) Naval Base, 1978-79; jr. kindergarten and art tchr. Sunnybrook Day Sch., Virginia Beach, Va., 1979-81; tchr. art Fisher Elem. Sch., Mohawk, N.Y., 1982-84, Mechanicstown Sch., Middletown, N.Y., 1984-88, Middletown (N.Y.) Start Ctr., 1986-87, tchr. synergetic edn., Middletown Tchr. Ctr., 1986-87; pvt. portfolio tutor Middletown, 1989-91; tchr. art Middletown Elem. Summer Sch., 1989—, Middletown H.S., 1987-97; tchr. Maple Hill Elem., 1997—. Sec. of policy and exec. bds. Middletown Tchr. Ctr., 1988-91, chmn. policy and exec. bds., 1991-92; mem. Bicentennial of Edn. com.; advisor Nat. Art Honor Soc., 1989-97; coord. After Sch. Program for Youth at Risk, 1995—, tchr., 1992-94. Actress, vocalist; designer in regional theatre, 1970—; artistic designer sch. plays and Creative Theatre Group; writer, dir. for local cabarets and charities; local muralist and portraitist, 1990—; designer sets for Off Broadway prodns. in N.Y.C. incl. Mother Posture, Seedless Grapes, The Pelican, New Village Prodns. benefit for AIDS, marquee 1st Theatre Mus. Village, Monroe, N.Y.; performer for Cancer Soc. fundraiser, 1997; producer/dir. Follies/Toys for Tots Campaign, 1997; performer for John Brigham Meml. Scholarship fundraiser, Ruthie Dino Marshall fundraiser, others; exhibited in shows in Lisbon, Portugal, 2001, Paramount Theatre, Middletown, N.Y., Cambridge, Eng., 2001, Vancouver, B.C., Can., 2002. County svc. coord. Orange County Youth-In-Govt. (adv. 1988—), Goshen, N.Y., 1991-93; Odyssey of the Mind Coach, 1984-92; chairperson edn. and cultural sem., Lisbon, Portugal, 1999. Named for outstanding set design Times Herald Record, 1994; honored by Bd. Edn. Outstanding Educator, 1992, Apple award, 1999; tchg. excellence award S.W. Arts Mag., 2001. Mem. Marine Corps League (hon.), NJROTC (hon. cadet 1997). Episcopalian. Avocations: theatrical design, singing, calligraphy. Home: PO Box 4429 Middletown NY 10941-8429 Office: Middletown City Schs Wisner Ave Middletown NY 10940

MCCORD, JOAN, sociologist, educator, rsearcher; b. N.Y.C., Aug. 4, 1930; d. Robert and Mildred Lucile (Stern) Fish; m. William Maxwell McCord, Mar. 17, 1951 (div. 1965); children: Geoffrey Sayre McCord, Robert Maxwell McCord; m. Carl Avrom Silver, June 24, 1970 (dec. July 1998). BA, Stanford U., 1952, PhD, 1968. Tchr. Concord (Mass.) Pub. Schs., 1952-55; rsch. asst. Harvard U., Cambridge, Mass., 1955-56; rsch. assoc. Stanford (Calif.) U., 1959-65; from asst. prof. to prof. Drexel U., Phila., 1968-87; prof. criminal justice Temple U., 1987—. Sr. assoc. U. Montreal, Quebec, 1987—, Johns Hopkins U., Balt., 1986-97; co-chair NRC Panel on Juvenile Crime: Prevention, Treatment and Control. Contbg. author: Straight and Devious Pathways From Childhood to Adulthood, 1990, At the Treshold: The Developing Adolscent, 1990, Ency. Marriage and the Family, 1995, Understanding Aggressive Behavior in Children, 1996, Nebraska Symposium on Motivation, 1997, Ency. Mental Health, 1998, Where and When: Historical and Geographical Aspects of Psychopathology, 1999, Social Dynamic of Crime and Control: New Theories for a World in Transition, 2000, Handbook of Law and Social Science: Youth and Justice, 2001; editor: Facts, Frameworks and Forecasts: Advances in Criminological Theory, 3, 1992; editor: Coercian and Punishment in Long-Term Perspectives, 1995, Violence and Childhood in the Inner-City, 1997; co-editor: Juvenile Crime/Juvenile Justice, 2001; contbr. articles to profl. jours. Recipient Josiah Royce fellow Harvard U., 1957, Stanford Wilson fellow Stanford U., 1962-63, fellow NIMH, 1965-68, Am. Soc. Criminology, 1982, Internat Soc. for Rsch. on Aggression, 1984. Mem. NSF (adv. bd. 1987-91), NAS (vice-chair NRC law and justice com. 1990-96), Internat. Soc. Criminology (bd. dirs. , v.p. 1995—, Prix Emile Durkheim award 1993), Am. Soc. Criminology (pres. 1988-89, Herbert Block award 1991, Edwin L. Sutherland award 1994), Am. Sociol. Assn. (chmn. sect. on crime law and deviance 1989-90), Soc. for Life History Rsch. (chair 1990-92). Home: 623 Broad Acres Rd Narberth PA 19072-1510 Office: Temple U Philadelphia PA 19122 E-mail: mccord@astro.temple.edu.

MC CORD, JOHN HARRISON, lawyer, educator; b. Oceanside, N.Y., Dec. 22, 1934; s. John Francis and Elsie (Powers) McC.; m. Maureen Ursula Maclean, Dec. 30, 1961; children: John F.X., Paul V., David G., Maureen E. AB, Fordham Coll., 1957; JD magna cum laude, St. John's U., 1960; LLM, U. Ill., 1965. Bar: N.Y. 1960, Ill. 1964. Atty. U.S. Dept. Justice, Washington, 1960-61; mem. faculty U. Ill. Coll. Law, Champaign, 1964—, prof. law, 1965—, assoc. dean for acad. affairs., 1990-92; of counsel Meyer Capel PC, 1998—; auditor/notary Cath. Diocese of Peoria, 2000—. Acad. cons. Ill. Inst. Continuing Legal Edn., 1968-72; vis. prof. law U. N.C., 1975, U. Hawaii, 1976 Author: (with Keeton and O'Connell) Crisis in Car Insurance, 1967, Buying and Selling Small Businesses, 1969, (with O'Byrne) Deskbook for Illinois Estate Planners, 1969, Closely Held Corporations, 1971, (with O'Neill, Pearlman and Stroud) Buying, Selling and Merging Businesses, 1975, (with Lowndes and Kramer) Estate and Gift Taxes, 3d edit, 1974, (with McKee) Federal Income Taxation-A Summary Analysis, 1975, (with Kramer) Problems for Federal Estate and Gift Taxes, 1976, Estate and Gift Tax Reform, 1977, Estate and Gift Tax Summary, 15th edit. 1993, Estate, Gift and Generation-Skipping Taxes, 1999; editor: Dimensions and Academic Freedom, 1969, With All Deliberate Speed: Civil Rights Theory and Reality, 1969, Ill. Law Forum, 1965-69; contbr. articles to profl. jours.; author computer programs for estate planning, 1984—. Served to capt. JAGC, USAF, 1961-64. St. Thomas More fellow St. John's U., 1960. Fellow Am. Coll. Trust and Estate Counsel; mem. ABA (com. CLE and chief reporter for study outline on buying, selling and merging businesses sect. fed. tax 1969-73, com. estate and gift taxes 1973-84, chmn. subcom. gross estate issues 1976-78, subcom. tax reform 1978-84), Ill. Bar Assn. (exec. coun. fed. tax sect. 1966-73, chmn. sect. 1971-72, exec. coun. bus. planning sect. 86-91), Champaign County Bar Assn., Am. Arbitration Assn. (nat. panel arbitrators 1969-90), Eastern Ill. Estate Planning Coun. (pres. 1970-71), U. Miami Inst. Estate Planning (adv. coun. 1979-87), Assn. Am. Law Schs. (fed. taxation roundtable coun. 1969-72), Ill. Inst. CLE (bd. dirs. 1991-2000, estate planning adv. com. 2000—), U.S. Navy League, Order of Coif. Home: 104 E Sherwin Dr Urbana IL 61802-7133 Office: U Ill Coll Law Champaign IL 61820 E-mail: jmccord@law.uiuc.edu.

MCCORD, MICHAEL DAVID, anesthesiologist; b. Gary, Ind., Mar. 22, 1959; BS in Pharmacy, Purdue U., 1984; MD, Ind. U., 1989. Diplomate Am. Bd. Anesthesiology; cert. pharmacist. Intern Mayo Clinic, Rochester, Minn., 1989-90, resident, 1990-93; staff mem. St. Elizabeth Hosp., Beaumont, Tex., 1993—, Bapt. Hosp. (now Meml. Hermann Bapt. Hosp.), Beaumont, 1993—. Mem. Am. Soc. Anesthesiologists, Tex. Soc. Anesthesiology, Tex. Med. Assn. Office: 6440 Wellington Pl Beaumont TX 77706-3206

MCCORISON, MARCUS ALLEN, librarian, cultural organization administrator; b. Lancaster, Wis., July 17, 1926; s. Joseph Lyle and Ruth (Mink) McC.; m. Janet Buckbee Knop, June 10, 1950 (dec. 1998); children: Marcus Allen II, Judith McC. Gove, Andrew Buckbee, Mary McC. Rosenbloom (dec. 2001), James Rice, Peter Gardner. AB, Ripon Coll., 1950; MA, U. Vt., 1951, LittD (hon.), 1992; MS, Columbia U., 1954; LHD (hon.), Assumption Coll., Worcester, Mass., 1987, Coll. of the Holy Cross, 1992; LittD (hon.), Clark U., 1992. Librarian Kellogg-Hubbard Library, Montpelier, Vt., 1954-55; chief of rare books dept. Dartmouth Coll. Library, Hanover, N.H., 1955-59; head spl. collections dept. State U. Iowa Libraries, 1959-60; libr. Am. Antiquarian Soc., Worcester, Mass., 1960-91, editor Procs., 1960-67, dir., 1967-89, pres., 1989-92, pres. emeritus, 1993—; cons. Christie, Manson & Woods, Internat., 1993-96, N.Y. Hist. Soc., 1994-95, Libr. Congress, Hist. Soc. of Pa., 1996, U. Kans., 1998-99. Mem. N.Am. steering com. 18th Century Short Title Catalogue, 1977—; mem. Com. for a New Eng. Bibliography, 1968-90, treas., 1970-77; mem. adv. com. Eleutherian Mills-Hagley Found., 1971-74, 87-89; chmn. Ind. Rsch. Librs. Assn., 1972-73, 78-80; mem. adv. coun. Princeton U. Libr., 1988-92; bd. govs. Rsch. Librs. Group, 1980-91, chmn. preservation com., 1982-85, chmn. governance com., 1989-91, chmn. Writings of James Fenimore Cooper, 1991-2002. Author: Vermont Imprints 1778-1820, 1963, The 1764 Catalogue of the Redwood Library, 1965; contbr.: The Pursuit of Knowledge in the Early American Republic, 1976, Publishing and Readership in Revolutionary France and America, 1993; editor: History of Printing in America by Isaiah Thomas, 1970. Trustee Fruitlands Mus., 1978-89, Old Sturbridge Village, 1981-92, Hist. Deerfield, Inc., 1991—; mem. bd. mgrs. Lewis Walpole Libr., Yale U., 1995—; nat. trustee Newberry Libr., 1995—; mem. Cultural Commn. City Worcester, Mass., 1999—, Mass. Hist. Commn., 1999—; mem. com. of mgmt. Wm. L. Clements Libr., U. Mich., 2001—. Recipient Samuel Pepys medal Ephemera Soc., London, 1980, Disting. Alumni award Ripon Coll., 1989, Columbia U. Sch. Libr. Svc., 1992. Fellow Pilgrim Soc.; mem. Am. Antiquarian Soc., Mass. Hist. Soc., Coll. and Rsch. Librs. Assn. (chmn. rare books sect. 1965-66), Bibliog. Soc. Am. (pres. 1980-84, del. to ACLS 1985—), Am. Printing Hist. Assn. (trustee 1998—, laureate 1998), Vt. Hist. Soc. (trustee 1956-66), Worcester Hist. Mus. (exec. com. 1967-80), Ctr. for Rsch. on Vt. (assoc.), N.E. Am. Soc. 18th Century Studies (pres. 1978-79), Colonial Soc. Mass., Club of Odd Vols., Grolier Club (councillor 1979-82, 83-84), Zamorano Club (hon.), Roxburghe Club (San Francisco), Century Assn. Democrat. Congregationalist. Home and Office: 3601 Knightsbridge Close Worcester MA 01609-1161

MCCORKINDALE, DOUGLAS HAMILTON, lawyer, publishing company executive; b. N.Y.C., June 14, 1939; s. William Douglas and Kathleen (Miles) McC.; m. Nancy Walsh, Dec. 24, 1991; children by previous marriage: Laura Ann, Heather Jean. BA, Columbia U., 1961, LLB cum laude (Harlan Fiske Stone scholar), 1964. Bar: N.Y. 1964. Assoc. Thacher Proffitt & Wood, N.Y.C., 1964-70, ptnr., 1970-71; gen. counsel, sec. Gannett Co., Inc., Arlington, Va., 1971-72, v.p., gen. counsel, sec., 1972-77, sr. v.p. fin. and law, 1977-79, sr. v.p., chief fin. officer, 1979-83, pres. diversified media div., 1980-83, exec. v.p., 1983, vice chmn., CFO, 1984—, chief adminstrv. officer, 1986—, vice chmn., pres., 1997—, CEO, 2000—, chmn., pres., CEO, 2001—. Bd. dirs. Continental Airlines Inc., Lockheed Martin Corp., The Global Govt. Plus Fund Inc., Prudential Global Genesis Fund Inc., Prudential Natural Resources Fund Inc., Prudential Multi-Sector Fund Inc.; trustee Prudential Equity Income Fund, Prudential Allocation Fund, Prudential Mcpl. Bond Fund, Mut. Ins. Co. Ltd. Mem. ABA (chmn. com. Exch. Art of 1934 1971-73), Newspaper Assn. Am., Pine Valley Golf Club, Mid Ocean Club, Burning Tree Club. Office: Gannett Co Inc 7950 Jones Branch Dr Mc Lean VA 22102

MCCORKLE, CONSTANCE MARIE, anthropology educator; b. Kansas City, Nov. 23, 1948; d. Burford L. and Martha Marie (Hall) McC.; m. Harry Robert Silver, Sept. 18, 1973 (div. 1981). BA, Rice U., 1971; MA in Anthropology, Stanford U., 1972, MA in Linguistics, 1979, PhD in Anthropology, 1983. Rsch. asst. U. Sci. and Tech., Kumasi, Ghana, 1973-74; rsch. affiliate Centro de Investigacion de Linguistica Aplicada, Lima, Peru, 1976-77; rsch. assoc. U. Mo. at Cuzco, Peru, 1980, Am. Inst. Rsch. in Behavioral Scis., Palo Alto, Calif., 1981-83; rsch. sci., project anthropologist Internat. Agrl. Programs U. Wis., Madison, 1983-84; dir. CMC Consulting, Falls Church, Va., 1985—; rsch. asst./assoc. prof. U. Mo., Columbia, 1985-90; prin. rsch. scientist, dir. USAID staff environ. tng. prog. Inst. for Internat. Rsch., Washington, 1990-92; dir. rsch. and evaluation Gender in Econ. and Social Sys. project, sr. assoc. The Futures Group, 1992-93; dir. Results Ctr., U.S. Agy. Internat. Devel./Mali, 1997—98; pres. CMC Cons., 1993—2001, sr. tech. advisor for monitoring and evaluation, 2001—. Instr. Argentine Consulate, Houston and Lenguas Athikas, Madrid, Spain 1967-69, pvt. tour guide Mex. and Peru 1966-71; vis. lectr. Bridgewater (Mass.) State Coll., 1978; vis. asst. prof. Met. State Coll., Denver, 1979; adj. asst. prof. U. Denver, 1978-81; adj. prof. dept. anthropology U. Tenn., Knoxville, 1993—; cons., lectr. in field. Editor: The Social Scis. in Internat. Agrl. Rsch., 1989, Plants, Animals & People, Agropastoral Systems Research, 1992, Ethnoveterinary R&D, 1996; contbr. chpts. to books, articles to profl. jours. NSF fellow, 1971-73, OAS fellow, 1976-77, NDMFL fellow 1977-78; Stanford L.Am. Studies grantee, 1972; Colo. Humanities scholar, 1980, Fulbright Faculty scholar, 1987-88. Fellow Soc. Applied Anthropology; mem. AAAS, NAFE, Am. Anthropol. Assn., Nat. Assn. Practice of Anthropology, Internat. Assn. Impact Assessment, Wash. Assn. Practicing Anthropologists, Internat. Commn. on Anthropology of Food and Food Problems, Coun. Anthropology and Nutrition, Culture and Agrl. Soc., Rural Sociol. Soc., Soc. Econ. Anthropology, Am. Ethnol. Soc., Agrl. Food and Human Values Soc., Union of Concerned Scientists, World Wildlife Soc., Assn. Farming Systems Rsch. Ext. (charter). Avocations: equitation, international gourmet cuisine, science fiction. Home and Office: 7767 Trevino Ln Falls Church VA 22043-3501 E-mail: mccorkle@boo.net.

MCCORKLE, MICHAEL, electrical engineer; b. Americus, Ga., Mar. 7, 1957; s. Charles Harold and Marjorie Marie (Hamilton) McC. BSEE, Ga. Inst. Tech., 1981. Mgr. Powers Ferry Bottle Shop, Atlanta, 1978-81; product specialist Yokogawa Corp. Am., Shenandoah, Ga., 1981-84; application engr. Gould, Inc., Norcross, 1984-86, sales engr., 1986-92, product sales mgr., 1993-95; sales rep. maj. elec. digital test equipment mfrs., 1995-2000, sales rep. major microwave equipment and component mfrs., 2000—. Roman Catholic. Avocations: photography, computers, aquarium, scuba diving.

MCCORKLE, ROBERT ELLSWORTH, agribusiness educator; b. Salinas, Calif., Apr. 3, 1938; s. Stanley Harold and Muriel Eugenia (Vosti) McC.; m. Mary E. McCorkle, June 26, 1965; children: Bonnie Kathleen, Robyn Krystyna. BSc in Farm Mgmt., Calif. Poly. State U., San Luis Obispo, 1960; MSc in Agrl. Econs., U. Calif., Davis, 1962; postgrad., U. Wis., 1969, Oreg.

State U., 1966. Rsch. statistician U. Calif., Davis, 1960-62; asst. prof. agrl. bus. Calif. Poly. State U., San Luis Obispo, 1962-66, dir. internat. edn., 1970-74, assoc. prof. agrl. mgmt., 1969-76, prof. agribus., 1976—; chief farm mgmt. officer Ministry Agr., Lusaka, Zambia, 1967-69; dir., owner McCorkle Farms, Inc., Willows, Calif., 1970—. Vis. prof. Mich. State U., U.S. AID, Washington, 1984-85; dir., owner McCorkle Trucking, Glenn, Calif., 1988—; agrl. economist U.S. AID-Redso ESA, Nairobi, Kenya, 1984-85. Author: Guide for Farming in Zambia, 1968. Pres. Cabrillo Property Owners Assn., Los Osos, Calif., 1976-78; vol. Atty. Gen.'s Adv. Com., Calif., 1972-74. U.S. Peace Corps strategy grantee, Washington, 1976-2000. Mem. Am. Agrl. Econs. Assn., Am. Soc. Farm Mgrs. and Rural Appraisers, Western Agrl. Econs. Assn., Calif. Poly. Farm Mgmt. Club, Calif. Poly. Alumni Assn., Blue Key, Alpha Zeta (founding mem., sr. advisor Delta chpt., nat. high coun. chronicler, sec.-treas., bd. dirs.), Nat. Alpha Zeta Found. (bd. dirs.). Republican. Episcopalian. Avocations: hunting, fishing. Office: Calif Poly State U San Luis Obispo CA 93407 E-mail: rmccorkl@calpoly.edu.

MC CORMAC, JOHN WAVERLY, judge; b. Zanesville, Ohio, Feb. 8, 1926; s. Samuel D. and Phyllis (Murray) McC.; m. Martha Ann Cunningham, June 22, 1952; children: Michael Paul, John Mark, James Samuel. BS, Muskingum Coll., 1951; JD, Capital U., 1961. Bar: Ohio 1961. Fire protection engr. Ohio Insp. Bur., 1951-60; pvt. practice Columbus, 1961-65; prof. law Capital U., 1965-66, 71-74, dean Law Sch., 1966-71; judge 10th Dist. Ct. Appeals, 1975-92; prof. law Ohio State U., Columbus, 1993—. Mem. staff cons. rules adv. com. Supreme Ct. Ohio; chmn. adv. bd. Vols. in Probation, 1972-74; chmn. ohio Jud. Conf., 1982-84; commr. Ohio Dispute Resolution Com., 1989-96, chmn., 1993-95; chief justice Ohio Ct. Appeals Assn., 1989-91. Author: Ohio Civil Rules Practice, 1970, 2nd edit., 1992, Anderson's Ohio Civil Practice, Vol. 1, 1971, Vol. 2, 1976, Vol. 3, 1977, Wrongful Death in Ohio, 1982. Served with USNR, 1943-46. Fellow Ohio Bar Assn. Found.; mem. League Ohio Law Schs. (pres. 1969-70), ABA, Ohio Bar Assn. (council of dels. 1973-77), Columbus Bar Assn. (bd. govs. 1968-72, sec.-treas. 1973-74, pres. 1975-76), Am. Judicature Soc., Phi Alpha Delta. Clubs: Masons (33 deg.). Republican. Home: 395 Longfellow Ave Columbus OH 43085-3024 E-mail: johnmccormac@hotmail.com.

MC CORMAC, WESTON ARTHUR, retired educator, retired career officer; b. Tacoma, Mar. 5, 1911; s. Jesse Carney and Jessie (Myron) McC.; m. Mary Jeanne Rapinac, Sept. 5, 1941. BA, Golden Gate U., MBA, 1968; diploma, Nat. War Coll., 1956; MPA, U. So. Calif., 1972; MA, Calif. Poly. State U., 1975. Acct. exec. Merrill, Lynch, Pierce, Fenner & Beane, Tacoma, Seattle, 1929-40; commd. lt. U.S. Army, 1940, advanced through grades to col., 1946, comdg. officer 35th F.A. Group Germany, 1958, dep. chief staff V Corps, 1958-60, asst. chief staff G 1 Pacific, 1962-65, ret., 1966; prof. bus., dept. chmn. Calif. Poly. State U., San Luis Obispo, 1968-80, ret., 1980. Decorated Legion of Merit with 2 oak leaf clusters, Silver Star, Bronze Star medal, Commendation medal with oak leaf cluster. Fellow Fin. Analysts Fedn.; mem. L.A. Soc. Fin. Analysts. Home: 16732 Lew Allen Cir Riverside CA 92518-2909 E-mail: fivone@aol.com.

MCCORMACK, BRIAN JEROME, political science educator; b. Yankton, S.D., July 23, 1958; s. Richard Joseph and Leona Julianna McC.; m. Justine Mary Doorn, Dec. 14, 1991. BS in Polit. Sci., BA in Internat. Studies, U. Nebr., 1989; BA (hons.) in Polit. Sci., Australian Nat. U., Canberra, 1990; MA in Polit. Sci., Ariz. State U., 1993, PhD in Polit. Sci., 2000. Grad. tchg. assoc. Ariz. State U., Tempe, 1997-2000, lectr., acad. coord. Bachelor Interdisciplinary Studies, 2000—. Vis. acad. Australian Nat. U., Canberra, 1995-96. Contbr. articles to profl. jours. Co-organizer World Hello Day, 1978—. Recipient fellowship Henry Luce Found., 1995-96, fellowship Nat. Security Edn. Program, 1995-96. Mem. Am. Polit. Sci. Assn., Assn. for Asian Studies, Internat. Studies Assn., Crazy Horse Grass Roots Club, Assn. Integrated Studies. Roman Catholic. Avocation: music composition. Office: Ariz State U Bachlor of Interdisciplinary Studies Tempe AZ 85287-3801

MCCORMACK, DONALD PAUL, newspaper consultant; b. Brockton, Mass., Jan. 15, 1926; s. Everett G. and Esther (Lufkin) McC.; m. Petronella Ruth Seger, Apr. 28, 1951; 1 son, Christopher Paul. BA, U. Pitts., 1949. Corr. U.P.I., 1949-52; asst. city editor Pitts. Sun-Telegraph, 1952-56; pub. relations exec., 1956-64; copy reader N.Y. News, 1964-67, editorial writer, 1967-72, chief editorial writer, 1972-82; cons., 1982—. With USAAF, 1944-46, Pa. N.G., 1952-57. Home and Office: PO Box 3539 Westport CT 06880-8539

MCCORMACK, EMILY ANNA, writer; b. Chgo., Feb. 27, 1922; d. Michael Joseph and Ellen Agnes (Kelly) Sammon; m. Thomas Peter McCormack, Oct. 2, 1954 (dec. Feb. 1982); children: Joseph, Anne Marie, Thomas, Eileen. BA, Ohio U., 1992. Bookkeeper Fed. Res. Bank, Chgo., 1940-43; corp. sec. Ill. Agrl. Assn., 1943-55; amanuensis Coop. League USA, 1955-70; instr. Morton Coll., Berwyn, Ill., 1972-74; co-office mgr. Florsheim Shoe Co., Chgo., 1978-82; sec. 1st Nat. Bank, 1982-84; tchr. Coll. DuPage, Glen Ellyn, Ill., 1998—. Author: (fiction) Never a Teardrop, 2000, (nonfiction) Mostly About Books, 2001; author of poems. Vol. People's Resource Ctr., Wheaton, Ill., 1997, Dem. Party, Riverside, Ill., 1968. Recipient 1st Pl Poetry award Ill. Coun. Fine Arts, Chgo., 1983. Avocations: music, reading, writing. Home: 6340 Americana Dr Apt 317 Willowbrook IL 60527

MC CORMACK, FRANCIS XAVIER, lawyer, former oil company executive; b. Bklyn., July 9, 1929; s. Joseph and Blanche V. (Dengel) Mc C.; m. Margaret V. Hynes, Apr. 24, 1954; children: Marguerite, Francis Xavier, Sean Michael, Keith John, Cecelia Blanche, Christopher Thomas. AB cum laude, St. Francis Coll., Bklyn., 1951; LLB, Columbia U., 1954. Bar: N.Y. 1955, Mich. 1963, Calif. 1974, Pa. 1975. Assoc. Cravath, Swaine & Moore, N.Y.C., 1956-62; sr. atty. Ford Motor Co., 1962-64, asst. gen. counsel, 1970-72; v.p., gen. counsel, sec. Philco-Ford Corp., 1964-72; v.p., gen. counsel Atlantic Richfield Co., 1972-73, sr. v.p., gen. counsel, 1973-94. Editor Columbia U. Law Rev., 1954. Decorated commendatore Ordine al Merito (Italy); Stone scholar Columbia U., 1954. Mem. Calif. Club, Chancery Club, Annandale Golf Club. Home and Office: 975 Singingwood Dr Arcadia CA 91006-1924

MCCORMACK, GRACE LYNETTE, civil engineering technician; b. Dallas, Nov. 2; d. Audley and Janice Meredith (Metcalf) McC. Tech. degree, Durham's Coll., 1958; grad. in civil engring., El Centro Coll., 1972; grad. in advanced surveying, Eastfield, 1975. Cert. sr. engr. technician. Contract design technician various engring firms, Dallas, 1958-70; sr. design engr. technician City of Dallas Survey Div., 1970-80, street light div., 1980-95, ret. 1995. Mem. Unity Ch. Avocations: numerology, astrology, metaphysics, Egyptian-Arabian horses, lighting and designing black and white portrait photography. Home: 1428 Meadowbrook Ln Irving TX 75061-4435

MCCORMACK, HOWARD MICHAEL, lawyer; b. Bklyn., Aug. 26, 1932; s. Michael Francis and Sarah Catherine (Russell) McC.; m. Patricia Anne Riley, Aug. 24, 1957; children: Sean M., Maureen A. MacDougall. AB cum laude, Coll. Holy Cross, Worcester, Mass., 1954; LLB, Fordham U., N.Y.C., 1961; LLM in Internat. Law, NYU, 1965. Bar: N.Y. 1962, U.S. Dist. Ct. (so. and ea. dists.) N.Y. 1963, U.S. Ct. Appeals (2d cir.) 1964, U.S. Ct. Appeals (4th cir.) 1977, U.S. Supreme Ct. 1966, U.S. Dist. Ct. Md. 1975, U.S. Dist. Ct. (so. dist) Tex. 1983, U.S. Ct. Appeals (5th cir.) 1984, U.S. Ct. Mil. Appeals 1994. Acct. exec. C.R. Black Jr. Corp., N.Y.C., 1958-61; ptnr. Zock, Petrie, et al., 1961-71; maritime counsel Bethlehem Steel Corp., 1972-79; ptnr. Healy & Baillie LLP, 1979—; adj. prof. law Fordham U. Adj. prof. law Touro Law Sch. Contbr. articles to profl. publs. Lt. (j.g.) USN, 1954-57; comdr. JAGC, USNR, ret. Mem.: Average Adjusters Assn. U.S. (chmn.), Maritime Law Assn. U.S. (pres. 1998—2000). Avocations: tennis, golf, wine studies. Office: Healy & Baillie LLP New York NY 10006 E-mail: hmccormack@healy.com.

MCCORMACK, JOANNE MARIE, lawyer; b. Evanston, Ill., Apr. 11, 1967; d. Joseph Robert and Audrey Helene (Gineman) Taylor; m. Colin Patrick McCormack, Jan. 2, 1993. BA, Loyola U., 1989, JD, 1994. Bar: Ill., 1994, Wis., 1995. Atty. Godfrey, Neshek, Worth, Elkhorn, Wis., 1994-95, Oliver, Close, Worden, Lake Geneva, 1995-97, 99-01, Hinshaw & Culbertson, Lake Geneva, 1997-99. Office: 325 Center St Lake Geneva WI 53147-1903

MCCORMACK, JOHN BRENDAN, bishop; b. Winthrop, Mass., Aug. 12, 1935; s. Cornelius and Eleanor (Noonan) McC. Student, Cardinal O'Connell Sem. Coll., Brighton, Mass., St. John's Sem.; MSW, Boston Coll., 1969. Ordained priest Roman Cath. Ch., 1960, consecrated bishop, 1995. Exec. dir. North Shore Cath. Charities Ctr., Peabody, Mass., 1967-81; pastor Immaculate Conception Parish, Malden-Medford, 1981—85; cabinet sec., vicar for religious and priests Archdiocese of Boston, 1984-94; pastor St. Francis Xavier Parish, South Weymouth, Mass., 1995; consecrated aux. bishop, 1995; regional bishop so. region Archdiocese of Boston, 1995-98; bishop Diocese of Manchester, N.H., 1998—. Office: PO Box 310 153 Ash St Manchester NH 03105

MCCORMACK, JOHN JOSEPH, JR. insurance executive; b. Morristown, N.J., Aug. 22, 1944; s. John Joseph and Marion Loretta (Smith) McC.; m. Judith Gail Harvey, July 20, 1968; children: Brendan, Matthew, Margaret BBA, St. Bonaventure U., 1966. From group underwriter to exec. v.p. Tchrs. Ins. and Annuity Assn.-Coll. Retirement Equities Fund, N.Y.C., 1966-98; pres. TIAA-CREF Enterprises, 1998-99, group pres., 1999-2001. Trustee Am. Psychol. Assn. Ins. Trust, Washington, 1980-90, chmn., 1985-86, trustee investment com., 1990-98, 2001—; trustee Employee Benefit Research Inst., Washington, 1983—, treas., 1986-90, vice-chmn., 1997-98, chmn., 1999-2001; mem. adv. bd. Andrew W. Mellon Found., N.Y.C., 1997-2001. Pres.'s coun. St. Bonaventure U., 1986—, chmn., 1986-89, trustee, 1996—, chmn. investment com., 1999—; bd. visitors Ctr. for Study Future Mgmt. U. Md., 1987-92; trustee Coll. and Univ. Pers. Assn. Found., 1992-94; bd. govs. Investment Co. Inst., 1994-98. Roman Catholic. Office: PO Box 432 New Vernon NJ 07976-0432 E-mail: jmccsbu@aol.com.

MCCORMACK, KATHERINE MCGRATH, nursing administrator; b. Waterbury, Conn., Sept. 6, 1949; d. Francis John and Katherine (Kelly) McGrath; m. Robert James McCormack, Sept. 30, 1972; divorced; 1 child, Patrick Ryan. BS in Nursing, Russell Sage Coll., 1971; MPH, Yale U., 1981. RN, Conn. Staff nurse New Eng. Deaconess Hosp., Boston, 1971-72; pub. health nurse Dept. Health, Waterbury, 1972-77, supr. nursing, 1977-80, dir. nursing, 1980-94; clin. mgr. ambulatory svcs. St. Francis Hosp. and Med. Ctr./Mt. Sinai Hosp., hartford, Conn., 1994-95; acting health dir. City of Hartford, 1995, health dir., 1996—. Mem. profl. adv. com. interim Health Care INc., New haven, 1985-96. Bd. dirs. Am. Cancer Soc., Waterbury, 1981-89, urban League, Hartford, 1997—, Mayors Child Abuse Prevention Campaign, 1996—, Cmty. Health Partnership, 1996—, Collaboration for Prevention of Child Abuse and Neglect, Waterbury, 1981-83, Alcohol and Drug Coun., Waterbury, 1984-90, sec. 1987-90; shelter mgr. City of Waterbury Disaster Planning, 1986-94; mem. Maternal Child Health Adv. Com., 1987-94; v.p. Waterbury Adminstrs. Assn., 1988-89, exec. bd., 1989-94; active Teenage Pregnancy Prevention, 1989-94; mem. CSAP adv. bd., 1990-94, HIV Initiative, 1996—, healthy Conn. Coalition, 1991—, allocations com. United Way, 1991, Urban League Greater Hartford Cmty. Health Adv., 1996—. Named MS Corp. Achiever, Conn. chpt. Nat. MS Soc., 2001; recipient Socoptimist Tng. award, 1980, Recognition award, Child Guidance, Inc., 1994. Mem. ANA, APHA, Conn. Pub. health Assn., Conn. Nurses Assn., Yale U. Alumni Assn. (honor roll 2001). Democrat. Roman Catholic. Avocations: reading, sports. Office: Hartford Health Dept 131 Coventry St Hartford CT 06112-1548 E-mail: kmccormack@ci.hartford.ct.us.

MCCORMACK, MARK HUME, advertising executive, lawyer; b. Chgo., Nov. 6, 1930; s. Ned and Grace (Wolfe) McC.; m. Nancy Ann Breckenridge, Oct. 9, 1954 (div.); children: Breck, Todd, Leslie; m. Betsy Nagelsen, 1986; 1 child, Maggie. BA, William and Mary Coll., 1951; LLB, Yale U., 1954; PhD (hon.), St. Lawrence U., 1991; LHD, Coll. William and Mary, 1997. Assoc. Arter and Hadden, Cleve., 1957-63, ptnr., 1963—; pres., CEO IMG, The Mark McCormack Group of Cos., Cleve., 1964—. Editor: The World of Professional Golf, 1967-2000, 2002; author: Arnie, The Evolution of a Legend, 1967, Arnie, The Man and the Legend, 1967 (British edit.), Arnie, What They Don't Teach You at Harvard Business School, 1984, The Terrible Truth About Lawyers, 1987, What They Still Don't Teach You at Harvard Business School, 1989, The 110% Solution, 1991, Hit the Ground Running, 1993, Getting Results for Dummies, 2000, Staying Street Smart in the Internet Age, 2000, Never Wrestle with a Pig, 2002. With U.S. Army, 1955-56. Decorated Order of the Polar Star (Sweden). Mem. Cleve. Bar Assn., Author's Guild, Royal and Ancient Club (St. Andrews, Scotland), Union Club, Pepper Pike Club, The Club (Cleve.), Isleworth Club, Deepdale Club, All England Club, Theta Delta Chi. Office: IMG 1360 E 9th St Ste 100 Cleveland OH 44114-1730

MCCORMACK, MICHAEL, state supreme court justice; b. Omaha, July 20, 1939; JD, Creighton U., 1963. Asst. pub. defender, Douglas County, Nebr., 1963-66; pvt. practice Omaha, 1966-97; justice Nebr. Supreme Ct., 1997—. Office: State Capitol Bldg Rm 2218 Lincoln NE 68509 also: PO Box 98910 Lincoln NE 68509*

MCCORMACK, PATRICIA SEGER, independent press service editor, journalist; b. Pitts., June 11, 1927; d. Arthur John and Anne Irene (McCaffrey) Seger; m. Donald P. McCormack, Apr. 28, 1951; 1 son, Christopher Paul. BA, U. Pitts., 1949; certificate, A.P. Inst. Seminar, 1967. News editor weekly newspapers, Mt. Lebanon, Pa., 1950-52; med. editor Pitts. Sun Telegraph, 1952-57; med. sci. editor INS, N.Y.C., 1958-59; columnist, family, health and edn. editor UPI, 1959-84, sr. editor, 1987-90. Mem. Boy of Year selection com. Boys Clubs Am., 1966; mem. Coty Fashion award jury, 1965-72, nat. selection com. Century III Leader Scholarship Competition Nat. Assn. Secondary Sch. Prins., 1986. Recipient Biennial Media award Family Service Assn. Am., 1965, Freedom Found. medal; 1st place Sci. Writing award Am. Dental Assn., 1976; Nat. Media award United Negro Coll. Fund, 1977; John Swett award for disting. educating reporting Calif. Edn. Assn., 1981 Mem. Nat. Assn. Sci. Writers (life), Edn. Writers Assn., Women's Forum Inc. (N.Y.C.), Nat. Fedn. Press Women (Comm. Achievement medal 1993), Conn. Press Club (v.p., Communicator of Achievement 1993), Conn. Women's Forum., N.Y. Acad. Scis. Home and Office: PO Box 3539 Westport CT 06880-8539

MCCORMACK, RICHARD THOMAS FOX, government official, former ambassador; b. Bradford, Pa., Mar. 6, 1941; s. C.H. and Ruth N. (Fox) McC.; m. Karen L. Hagstrom, Oct. 18, 1980; children: Charlotte Louise, Justin Randall, Elizabeth Caroline. BA, Georgetown U., 1963; PhD, U. Fribourg (Switzerland), 1966. With Peace Corps, 1966-67; sr. staff mem. Pres.' Adv. Council on Exec. Orgn., White House, Washington, 1969-71; with Am. Enterprise Inst., 1975-77; dep. asst. sec. for internat. econ. affairs Dept. Treasury, 1974; mem. staff U.S. Senate, 1979-81; asst. sec. state for econ. and bus. affairs U.S. Dept. State, Washington, 1982-85, ambassador Orgn. Am. States, 1985-89, undersec. of state for econ. affairs, 1989-91. Candidate in primary elections for U.S. Congress, 1972, 74; cons. Office Telecommunications Policy, 1971, Coun. on Internat. Econ. Policy, 1972, Office Spl. Trade Rep., 1975, Exec. Office of the Pres., Washington; guest scholar Woodrow Wilson Ctr. Smithsonian Instn., Washington, 1991-92; bus. advisor Am. companies, cons. U.S. Govt. on Internat. Econ. Affairs, 1992—. Author: Asians in Kenya, 1971, The Twilight War, 1979, Microeconomic Reforms for Israel, 1991, Managing Japan's Financial Crisis, 1992. Recipient Superior Honor award Dept. State, 1987, Sec. of State's Disting. Svc. award, 1991; decorated Legion of Honor (France). Mem. Internat. Inst. Strategic Studies, Econ. Club N.Y. Republican. Home: 1601 Walden Dr Mc Lean VA 22101-3160 Office: Ctr for Study of Presidency 1020 19th St NW Ste 250 Washington DC 20036

MCCORMACK, ROBERT CORNELIUS, investment banker; b. N.Y.C., Nov. 7, 1939; m. Mary Lester, Dec. 14, 1963; children: Robert Cornelius Jr., Walter, Scott. BA, U. N.C., 1962; MBA, U. Chgo., 1968. V.p. Dillon Read & Co. Inc., 1968-81; mng. dir. Morgan Stanley & Co., Inc., Chgo., 1981-87; dep. asst sec. def. prodn. support U.S. Dept. Def., Washington, 1987-88, dep. under sec. def. indsl. and internat. programs, 1988-89, acting dep. under sec. of def. acquisition, 1989-90, asst. sec. Navy fin. mgmt., 1990-93; founding ptnr. Trident Capital L.P., Chgo., 1993—. Served to lt. USNR, 1963-66. Office: Trident Capital LP 272 E Deerpath Rd Ste 304 Lake Forest IL 60045-1947

MCCORMACK, STANLEY EUGENE, financial consultant; b. Olney, Ill., Oct. 15, 1949; s. Donald Eugene and Patricia Louise (Dickerson) McC.; m. Janis Eileen Bush; m. Jeffrey Daniel, Erin Louise, Evan Stuart. Student, DePauw U., 1967-68, Ohio State U., 1968-71; MS in Fin. Svc., The Am. Coll., 1991, MS in Mgmt., 1996. CLU; chartered fin. cons. Ins. agt. Art Holtzman Assocs., Rochester, N.Y., 1973-75, ins. sales mgr., 1975-82; fin. cons., pres. Assoc. Fin. Cons., 1983—. Instr. Am. Coll., Rochester, 1988, Empire State Coll. Moderator Webster (N.Y.) Bapt. Ch., 1985-88, mem. fin. com., 1994-2000; com. mem. Webster Rep. Com., 1978-81; mem. fin. com. Webster Swim Assn., 1993-95, treas., 1989-91. Mem.: Estate Planning Coun. Rochester, Internal Assn. Fin. Planners (bd. dirs. 1989—95, v.p. chmn. symposium 1990, pres. 1993—94, pres. adv. bd. 1994—96), Am. Soc. Chartered Life Underwriters and Charterred Fin. Cons., Phi Delta Theta (pres. Beta West 1999—2001). Avocations: voice, bridge. Home: 622 Fairmont Dr Webster NY 14580-8967

MCCORMACK, THOMAS JOSEPH, retired publishing company executive; b. Boston, Jan. 5, 1932; s. Thomas Joseph and Lena Carolyn (Allen) McC.; m. Sandra Harriet Danenberg, Aug. 21, 1964; children: Daniel Aaron, Jed Charles (dec.), Jessie Ann. Student, U. Conn., 1950-51; AB summa cum laude (James Manning scholar), Brown U., 1954; postgrad. (G.H. Palmer scholar, Woodrow Wilson fellow), Harvard U., 1956. Writer radio news WSTC, Stamford, Conn., 1957-59; editor Doubleday & Co., Inc., N.Y.C., 1959-64, Harper & Row, N.Y.C., 1964-67; edn. editor New Am. Library, 1967-69; dir. trade dept. St. Martin's Press, 1969-70, pres., 1970-87, chief exec. officer, editorial dir., 1970-96, chmn., 1987-97. Pres., chmn. bd. St. James Press, Ltd., London, 1973-79; v.p., treas. Sandra D. McCormack, Inc. (Interior Designer); chmn., chief exec. officer Tor Books, N.Y.C., 1987-96; exec. com. Holtzbrinck GmbH, Stuttgart, Germany, 1995-97. Author: Afterwords, Novelists on Their Novels, 1969, The Fiction Editor, the Novel and the Novelist, (plays) American Roulette, 1969, Endpapers, 2002; columnist: The Cheerful Skeptic, 1997—99. Mem. Play Devel. Coun., Manhattan Theater Club, 1995—, Dramatists Gild, 1997—. With AUS, 1954-56. Mem. Assn. Am. Pubs. (dir. 1973-76, freedom to read com. 1974-77, Curtis Benjamin award 1997, LMP Lifetime Achievement award 1997), Phi Beta Kappa. Clubs: The Players (N.Y.C.), Century Assn. (N.Y.C.). Home: 50 Central Park W New York NY 10023-6028 E-mail: cheerskep@aol.com.

MCCORMACK, WILLIAM ARTHUR, lawyer; b. Rochester, N.Y., Sept. 18, 1951; s. Austin Francis and June Ann (Doyle) McC. AB in Polit. Sci. magna cum laude, St. Louis U., 1973; cert., Sorbonne, Paris, 1974; JD, Georgetown U., 1977. Bar: Tex. 1978, D.C. 1979. Assoc. Crutcher, Hull, et al., Dallas, 1978-82, Hughes & Luce, Dallas, 1982-83, ptnr., 1983—, mem. mgmt. com., exec. com., sect. head, 1993-97, mgn. ptnr., chm., 1997—. Bd. dirs. Engles Capital Corp., McCormack Corp.; speaker and author on legal topics. Contbr. articles to profl. jours. Bd. dirs. Alliance Francaise Found., Dallas, Jesuit Found., Dallas Epilepsy Found., pres., 1992, Dallas Citizens Coun.; bd. advisors Jesuit Prep., Bishop Dunne H.S., Bus. Com. for the Arts, Dallas; coun. mem., exec. comm. circle ten coun. Boy Scouts Am.; leadership coun. Dallas Chamber. Mem. ABA, State Bar Assn. Tex. (chmn. minority com.), Dallas Bar Assn. (chmn. legal ethics com., mem. minority commn.), Pi Sigma Alpha, Alpha Sigma Nu. Roman Catholic. Office: Hughes and Luce 1717 Main St Ste 2800 Dallas TX 75201-4685

MCCORMICK, BARNES WARNOCK, aerospace engineering educator; b. Waycross, Ga., July 15, 1926; s. Barnes Warnock and Edwina (Brogdon) McC.; m. Emily Joan Hess, July 18, 1946; 1 dau., Cynthia Joan. BS in Aero. Engring, Pa. State U., 1948, MS, 1949, PhD, 1954. Research assoc. Pa. State U., University Park, 1949-54, assoc. prof., 1954-55, prof. aero. engring., 1959-92, Boeing prof. aero. engring., 1985-92, prof. emeritus, cons., 1992—, head dept. aerospace engring., 1969-85. Assoc. prof., chmn. aero. dept. Wichita U., 1958-59; chief aerodynamics Vertol Helicopter Co., 1955-58; mem. Congl. Adv. Com. Aeros., 1984-86; U.S. coord. flight vehicle integration panel Adv. Group for Aerospace R&D, 1988—; cons. to industry. Author: Aerodynamics of V/Stol Flight, 1967, Aerodynamics, Aeronautics and Flight Mechanics, 1979, 2d edit., 1995; co-author: (with M.P. Papadakis) Aircraft Accident Reconstruction and Litigation, 1996; contbr. articles to profl. jours.; patentee in field. Served with USNR, 1944-46. Recipient joint award for achievement in aerospace edn. Am. Soc. Engring. Edn.-Am. Inst. Aeros. and Astronautics, 1976 Fellow Am. Inst. Aeros. and Astronautics; mem. ASEE, Am. Helicopter Soc. (hon. fellow), Sigma Xi, Sigma Gamma Tau, Tau Beta Pi. Clubs: Masons. Home: 611 Glenn Rd State College PA 16803-3475 Office: Pa State U Coll Engring University Park PA 16802 E-mail: bwmaer@engr.psu.edu.

MCCORMICK, DAVID ARTHUR, lawyer; b. McKeesport, Pa., Oct. 26, 1946; s. Arthur Paul and Eleanor Irene (Gibson) McC. BA, Westminster Coll., 1967; JD, Duquesne U., 1973; MBA, U. Pa., 1975. Bar: Pa. 1973, D.C. 1978, U.S. Ct. Appeals (3d cir.) 1977, U.S. Ct. Appeals (4th and D.C. cirs.) 1980, U.S. Supreme Ct. 1980. Asst. commerce counsel Penn Cen. R.R., Phila., 1973-76; assoc. labor counsel Consol. Rail Corp., 1976-78; atty. Dept. Army, Washington, 1978—. Author various geneal. and hist. works; contbr. articles to profl. jours. Mem. ATLA, Pa. Bar Assn., Phila. Bar Assn., D.C. Bar Assn., Assn. Transp. Practitioners, Soc. Cin. (Del. chpt.), SAR (Pitts. chpt.), Am. Legion, Res. Officers Assn., Masons, Phi Alpha Delta, Theta Chi. Presbyterian.

MCCORMICK, DONALD BRUCE, retired biochemist, educator; b. Front Royal, Va., July 15, 1932; s. Jesse Allen and Elizabeth (Hord) McC.; m. Norma Jean Dunn, June 6, 1955; children: Susan Lynn, Donald Bruce, Michael Allen. BA, Vanderbilt U., 1953, PhD, 1958; postdoctoral fellow, U. Calif., Berkeley, 1958-60. Asst. prof. Cornell U., 1960-63, assoc. prof., 1963-69, prof. nutrition, biochemistry and molecular biology, biol. scis., 1969-79, Liberty Hyde Bailey prof. nutritional biochemistry, 1978-79; chmn. dept. biochemistry Emory U., Atlanta, 1979-94, Fuller E. Callaway prof. biochemistry, 1979-99; prof. emeritus, 1999—; exec. assoc. dean sci. Emory U. Sch. Medicine, 1985-89. Vis. lectr. U. Ill, 1963; Wellcome vis. prof. U. Fla., 1986, Med. Coll. Pa., 1989; Hurley lectr. U. Calif., Davis, 1992; O'Dell lectr. U. Mo., Columbia, 1993; biochem. cons. Interdeptl. Com. on Nutrition for Nat. Def., Spain, 1958; mem. and chmn. nutrition study sect. NIH, 1977-81; mem. diet and health com., dietary guidelines implementation com., vice chmn. food and nutrition bd. NRC, Inst. Medicine, NAS; exec. com., chmn. dept. med. biochemistry, Coun. Acad. Soc., Am. Assn. Med. Colls., 1984-87; mem. biology panel U.S. Civilian R&D Found., 1998-2001. Author: (with others) Spain: Nutrition Survey of the Armed Forces, 1958, Molecular Associations in Biology, 1968, Flavins and Flavin Enzymes, 1968, Flavins and Flavoproteins, 1980, 82, 84, 88, 89, 91, Comprehensive Biochemistry, Vol. 21, 1971, Riboflavin, 1974, Metal Ions in Biological Systems, Vol. 1, 1974, Present Knowledge in Nutrition, 1976, 84, 90, 2001, Natural Sulphur Compounds, 1979, Vitamin B6, Metabolism and Role in Growth, 1980, Ann. Rev. of Nutrition, Vol. 1, 1981, Vol. 9, 1989, Mechanisms of Enzymatic Reactions: Stereochemistry, 1986, Chemical and Biological Aspects of Vitamin B6 Catalysis, Part A, 1984, Biochemistry of Vitamin B6, 1987, Biochemistry and Molecular Biology of Vitamin B6 and PQQ-Dependent Proteins, 2000, Tietz Textbook of Clinical Chemistry, 1986, 94, 99, Fundamentals of Clinical Chemistry, 1987, 95, 2000, Vitamins and Biofactors in Life Science, 1992, Encyclopedia of Food Science, 1993, Encyclopedia of Molecular, Biology and Molecular Medicine, 1996, 97, Modern Nutrition in Health and Disease, 1988, 94, 99, New Trends in Biological Chemistry, 1990, Chemistry and Biochemistry of Flavins, 1991, Encyclopedia of Human Biology, 1991, 97, Liver, 1994, Molecular Biology and Biotechnology, 1995, Biochemical and Physiological Bases of Human Nutrition, 2000, Nutrition in Space Flight and Weightlessness Models, 1999; editor: Vitamins and Hormones, Vitamins and Coenzymes, Ann. Rev. of Nutrition, Handbook of Vitamins. Recipient award Bausch and Lomb, 1950, award Mead Johnson, 1970, award Osborne and Mendel, 1978, award Ga. Nutrition Coun., 1989, award Bristol-Myers Squibb/Mead Johson, 1999; Westinghouse Sci. scholar, 1950; fellow NIH, 1957-58, 58-60; Guggenheim fellow, 1966-67. Fellow AAAS, Am. Inst. Nutrition (now Am. Soc. Nutrition Sci., pres. 1991); mem. Am. Soc. Biochemistry and Molecular Biology, Soc. Exptl. Biology and Medicine, Am. Chem. Soc., Am. Inst. Biol. Sci., Biophysics Soc., Fedn. Am. Socs. Exptl. Biology (bd. dirs., LSRO scientific steering group), Microbiol. Soc., Photobiol. Soc., N.Y. Acad. Sci., Protein Soc., Sigma Xi. E-mail: biocdbm@emory.edu.

MCCORMICK, DONNA LYNN, social worker; b. Austin, Minn., Aug. 13, 1944; d. Raymond Alois and Grace Eleanor (Hayes) Schrom; m. James Michael McCormick, Jan. 15, 1972. BA in Psychology, Coll. St. Catherine, 1966. Caseworker Phila. County Bd. Pub. Assistance, 1968-70; sr. social worker San Francisco Dept. Human Svcs., 1986-97; interviewer dept. epidemiology and biostats. U. Pa., Phila., 1998-2000. Mem. The Nature Conservancy, Consumer's Union, Emily's List. Mem. AAUW, Coll. St. Catherine

Alumnae Assn., Nat. Trust Hist. Preservation, Nat. Mus. Women in Arts, Met. Opera Guild. Democrat. Avocations: reading, walking, wine tasting, letter writing, opera. Home and Office: 909 Deland Ave Cherry Hill NJ 08034-3925 E-mail: jdcormick@msn.com.

MC CORMICK, EDWARD ALLEN, foreign language educator; b. Fairfax County, Va., July 1, 1925; s. Jesse Allen and Elizabeth (Hord) McC.; m. Diana Festa, Mar. 1, 1952 (div. Aug. 1973); children: Allen Sergio, Marco Kevin, Carlo Brian; m. Marie Parrice, Apr. 2, 1974 (div. Apr. 1980); m. Phyllis van Slyck, June 10, 1980 (div. May 1985); 1 son, Andrew Stuart; m. Ping Tsai, Mar. 19, 1993. AB, Randolph-Macon Coll., 1948; PhD, U. Berne, Switzerland, 1951; MA (hon.), Dartmouth, 1965. Instr. German Princeton U., 1952, asst. prof. German, 1954-58; instr. German U. Mich., 1952-53, Harvard U., 1953-54; asst. prof. German Brown U., 1958-59; mem. faculty Dartmouth, 1959—; prof. German, German and comparative lit., dir. comparative lt. Queens Coll., CUNY, 1966-70; prof. German and comparative lit. Queens Coll., CUNY (Grad. Ctr.), 1970—, exec. officer comparative lit., 1970-74, exec. officer German, 1980-92; retired, 1992. Author: Whitman's Leaves of Grass in deutschen Übertragung, 1953, (with F.G. Ryder) Lebendige Literatur, 1960, 2d edit., 1974, 3d edit., 1986, Theodor Storm's Novellen, 1964; editor: Lessing's Laokoon, 1962, (J.E. Schlegel) On Imitation, 1965, Germans in America, 1983; gen. editor: Studies in European Thought, 1990—; also articles in jours., encys. Served with 82d Airborne Div. AUS, 1943-46, ETO. Recipient Princeton Bicentennial Preceptorship, 1954-58; Dartmouth Faculty fellow, 1963 Mem. MLA, Am. Comparative Lit. Assn., Am. Assn. Tchrs. German. Home: 309 Calzada de Bougainville Marathon FL 33050

MCCORMICK, ELAINE ALICE, fundraising executive, retired medical/surgical nurse; b. Jersey City, Nov. 19, 1943; d. Johannes and Anna (Gantenberg) Kratz; m. Thomas A. McCormick, Oct. 1, 1966; 1 child Thomas John. Diploma, Mt. Sinai Sch. Nursing, 1964; BA summa cum laude, Georgian Ct. Coll., 1982. RN N.Y., N.J. Staff nurse Holy Name Hosp., Teaneck, NJ, 1964-65, 69-70; office nurse Drs. Higdon, Beaugard and Fox, 1965-67; indsl. nurse Dun & Bradstreet, Inc., N.Y.C., 1967-69; camp nurse, ski area dir. Camp Arrowhead, Cmty. YMCA, Marlboro, NJ, 1974-78; adminstrv. asst. DeJesse Advt., Woodbrige, 1982-83; staff writer Georgian Ct. Coll., Lakewood, 1983-84, dir. pub. rels., 1984-92, asst. v.p. for coll. advancement, 1992-94, v.p. for coll. advancement, 1994-97; ret., 1997. Cons. in field. Mem. adv. bd. Ret. Sr. Vol. Program Ocean County, Toms River, NJ, 1987—94, mem. bd. advisors, 1994—97; mem. adv. coun. Eldermed Scan Ocean County; mem., chairwoman, bd. advisors, mem. exec. bd. Sr. Citizen Activities Network Monmouth County; mem. Mercy Higher Edn. Colloquium, Monmouth Ocean Devel. Coun., Nat. Bd. Med. Coll. Pa., 1987—97; pres., bd. dirs. Preserve Homeowners Assn., 2002—; vol. Hope Rural Sch., Indiantown, Fla., 2002—; chairwoman boutique com. St. Martin de Porres Roman Cath. Ch., Jensen Beach, 1998—2001; bd. dirs. Friends of the Jensen Beach Libr. Mem.: Sigma Tau Delta. Republican. Roman Catholic.

MCCORMICK, FLOYD GUY, JR. agricultural educator, college administrator; b. Center, Colo., July 3, 1927; s. Floyd Guy and Gladys (Weir) McC.; m. Constance P. Slane; children: Angela Lynn, Craig Alan, Kim Ann, Robert Guy. BS, Colo. State U., 1950, MEd, 1959; PhD, Ohio State U., 1964. Tchr. vocat. agr. State of Colo., 1956-62; asst. prof. agrl. edn. Ohio State U., 1964-67; mem. com. agr. edn. com. edn. in agr. and natural resources Nat. Acad. Scis., 1967-69; prof. agrl. edn., head dept. U. Ariz., 1967-89, prof. emeritus, dept. head emeritus, 1990—. Cons. in-svc. edn., div. vocat. edn. Ohio Dept. Edn., 1963-64; vis. prof. Colo. State U., 1973, U. Sierra Leone, Njala Univ. Coll., 1989; external examiner U. Sierra Leone, 1984, 85, 87; adv. trustee Am. Inst. Cooperatives, Washington, 1985-88; mem. Nat. Coun. Vocat. and Tech. Edn. in Agr., Washington, 1985-88. Co-author: Teacher Education in Agriculture, 1982, Supervised Occupational Experience Handbook, 1982; author: The Power of Positive Teaching, 1994, also instrl. units, tech. bulls., articles in profl. jours.; spl. editor: Agrl. Edn. mag., 1970-74. Trustee Nat. FFA Found. Served with USNR, 1945-46. Named hon. state farmer Colo., 1958, Ariz., 1968, Am. farmer, 1972; recipient Centennial award Ohio State U., 1970, E.B. Knight award NACTA Jour., 1980, Regional Outstanding Tchr. award Nat. Assn. Coll. Tchrs. Agr., 1989, also fellow, 1988, VIP citation Nat. FFA Assn., 1990, Diamond Anniversary award Ohio State U., 1992. Mem. Am. Vocat Assn. (mem. policy com. agrl. edn. divsn. 1976-79, v.p. divsn. 1985-88, chmn. membership com. 1980-83, sec. agrl. edn. divsn. 1983-86, pres. 1985-88, outstanding svc. awrd 1989), Nat. Vocat. Agr. Tchrs. Assn. (life, Outstanding Svc. award Region I 1974, 83, 96), Am. Assn. Tchr. Educators in Agr. (disting. lectr. 1984, editor newsletter 1975-76, pres. 1976-77, Disting. Svc. award 1978, 88, Rsch. award western region rsch. 1988), Alpha Zeta, Alpha Tau Alpha (hon.), Gamma Sigma Delta, Phi Delta Kappa, Epsilon Pi Tau. Home: 6933 E Paseo San Andres Tucson AZ 85710-2203

MCCORMICK, HOMER L., JR. lawyer; b. Frederick, Md., Nov. 11, 1928; s. Homer Lee McCormick and Rosebelle Irene Biser; m. Jacquelyn R.; children: Deidre Ann and Thomas Lee. Student, George Washington U., 1946-48; AB, San Jose State U., 1951; JD, U. Calif., San Francisco, 1961. Bar: Calif. 1961, U.S. Dist. Ct. Ctrl. Dist. Calif. 1972, U.S. Dist. No. Calif. 1961, U.S. Dist. Ct., So. Dist. Calif. 1976, U.S. Dist. Ct. of Appeals (9th cir. 1961), U.S. Tax Ct. 1977, U.S. Ct. Claims 1977, U.S. Supreme Ct. 1977. Atty. Holiway Jones State of Calif., 1961-63; atty. assoc. Rutan & Tucker, Santa Ana, Calif., 1963-66, atty. ptnr., 1966-70, atty., sr. ptnr. Costa Mesa, 1970-88, dept. head pub. law, 1974-88, mng. ptnr., 1984-88; founding ptnr., sr. ptnr. McCormick, Kidman & Behrens, 1988—. Arbitrator Am. Arbitration Assn., 1966-88; judge pro tem Orange County Superior Ct., 1975, 81, 84; spkr., lectr. Cal. Continuing Edn. of the Bar, 1976-88; profl. designation Internat. Right of Way Assn.; elected mem. Cal. Condemnation Lawyers, 1994—. Contbg. author: Real Property Remedies, 1982; contbr. articles to profl. jours. Mem. bd. govs. Bus. Com. Arts, Orange County Philharm. Soc. Lt. USMCR, 1951-56; pilot, Korea. Named Alumnus of Year Hastings Law Sch., 1992. Mem. ABA (com. chair 1991), Am. Bd. Trial Adv. (pres. O.C. chpt. 1973), Orange City Atty. Assn. (pres. 1972), Fed. Bar Assoc., Consumer Attys. Calif., Am. Judicature Soc., Orange County Bar Assn. (com. chair 1991-92), Orange County Bus. Trial Lawyers, Order Coif, Thurston Soc., Hastings Alumni Assn. (pres. 1973), Springs Country Club, Delta Theta Pi. Republican. Episcopalian. Avocations: boating, fishing, flying, golf, foreign travel.

MCCORMICK, HUGH THOMAS, lawyer; b. McAlester, Okla., Nov. 24, 1944; s. Hugh O. and Lois (McGucken) McC.; m. Suzanna G. Weingarten, Dec. 5, 1975; 1 child, John B. BA, U. Mich., 1968; JD, Rutgers U., 1977; LLM in Taxation, Georgetown U., 1980. Bar: N.Y. 1977, D.C. 1979, Maine 1981. Atty. office chief counsel interpretative divsn. IRS, Washington, 1977-81; assoc. Perkins, Thompson, Hinkley & Keddy, Portland, Maine, 1981-83, LeBoeuf, Lamb, Leiby & MacRae, N.Y.C., 1983-88, counsel, 1989-91; ptnr. LeBoeuf, Lamb, Greene & MacRae, L.L.P., 1992—. Dir. Ins. Tax. Conf., 1993—, sr. v.p., 2000—. Mem. bd. contbrs. and advisors Jour. of Taxation of Investments; contbr. articles to profl. jours. Trustee U.S. Team Handball Found., N.J., 1985-95. Fellow Am. Bar Found.; mem. ABA (chmn. com. on taxation of ins. cos. 1989, chmn. subcom. sect. of taxation 1989-96, mem. torts and ins. practice sect., sect. on taxation), D.C. Bar Assn. Democrat. Home: 555 Pelham Manor Rd Pelham NY 10803-2525 Office: LeBoeuf Lamb Greene MacRae LLP 125 W 55th St New York NY 10019-5369 E-mail: hmccormi@llgm.com.

MC CORMICK, JOHN HOYLE, lawyer; b. Pensacola, Fla., July 30, 1933; s. Clyde Hoyle and Orrie Brooks (Frink) McC.; m. Patricia McCall, Dec. 27, 1974. BS, U. Fla., 1955; JD, Stetson U., 1958. Bar: Fla. 1958. Ptnr. McCormick, Drury & Scaff, Jasper, Fla., 1958-74; county atty., 1973—; sr. ptnr. McCormick, Drury & Scaff, Jasper, 1974-91; pvt. practice, 1991—. County judge, Hamilton County, Fla., 1960-72; local counsel So. Ry. System, 1968—, CSX, Ry., 1972—; atty. Hamilton County Devel. Authority, 1970-91; bd. dirs. 1st Fed. Savs. Bank Fla.; bd. dirs., v.p., atty. Hamilton County Bank. Mayor City of White Springs, Fla., 1959; pres. Hamilton County C. of C., Jasper, 1961. Mem. Phi Delta Phi. Lodges: Masons. Democrat. Methodist. Avocations: gardening, motorhome camping, college football. Home: 403 2nd Ave NW Jasper FL 32052-6687 Office: 215 2nd St NE Jasper FL 32052-6616 Address: PO Drawer O Jasper FL 32052-0695

MCCORMICK, JOHN OWEN, retired comparative literature educator; b. Thief River Falls, Minn., Sept. 20, 1918; s. Owen Charles and Marie Antoinette Beauchemin (Smith) McC.; m. Helen Manuel, 1942; m. Mairi Clare MacInnes, 1954; children: Jonathan, Peter, Antoinette, Fergus. BA magna cum laude, U. Minn., 1941; MA, Harvard U., 1947, PhD, 1951. Dean, lectr. Salzburg Seminar in Am. Studies, 1951-52; lectr., prof. Free U., Berlin, 1952-59; prof. comparative lit. Rutgers U., 1959-87, prof. emeritus, 1987—. Vis. prof. Nat. U. Mexico, 1961-62, Hachioji (Tokyo) seminar, 1979; Christian Gauss Seminar lectr. Princeton, 1969; resident fellow Sch. Letters of Ind. U., 1970 Author: The Middle Distance: a Comparative History of American Imaginative Literature, 1919-32, 1971, The Complete Aficionado, 1967, 2d edit., 1998, (with Mairi MacInnes McCormick) Versions of Censorship, 1962, Der moderne amerikanische Roman, 1960, Amerikanische Lyrik, 1957, Catastrophe and Imagination, 1957, 2d edit., 1998, Fiction as Knowledge, 1975, 2d edit., 1999, George Santayana: A Biography, 1987, Wolfe, Malraux, Hesse, 1987, American and European Literary Imagination: 1919-1932, 2000; editor: (with G. Core) Sallies of the Mind: Essays of Francis Fergusson, 1998, Seagoing: Essay-Memoirs, 2000. With USNR, 1941-46. Recipient prize for non-fiction Longview Found., 1960, Am. Acad. and Inst. Arts and Letters award, 1988; Gugenheim fellow, 1964-65, 79-80, Bruern fellow Leeds (Eng.) U., 1975-76, NEH fellow, 1983-84, hon. fellow U. York, 1992. Mem. Taurino Club, Harvard Club.

MCCORMICK, KENNETH JAMES, education educator; b. Toledo, Sept. 11, 1937; s. Joseph Kenneth McCormick and Dorothy Rose Bostwick; m. Nancy Lee Kellett, June 15, 1963 (dec. Nov. 1999); children: Kevin, Cathleen, Maureen. BS, U. Toledo, 1959; MS, U. Mich., 1962, PhD, 1965. From instr. to assoc. prof. Baylor Coll. Medicine, Houston, 1965—75; assoc. lab. dir. St. Joseph's Hosp./Lab. for Cancer Rsch., 1975—80; rsch. scientist, co-dir. Head and Neck Oncologic Therapy Lab. U. Iowa, Iowa City, 1980—84; rsch. assoc. prof. U. Chgo., 1984—89. Adj. assoc. prof. Baylor Coll. Medicine, Houston, 1975—85. Contbr. chapters to books, articles to profl. jours. Fellow HH Rackham fellow, U. Mich., Ann Arbor, 1959, USPHS fellow pathogenesis, NIH-U. Mich., Ann Arbor, 1960—63, FG Novy fellow, U. Mich., Ann Arbor, 1964. Mem.: C.G. Jung Inst. Chgo. (cert. in analytical psychology). Roman Catholic. Avocations: music, reading. Home: 5555 S Everett Ave Chicago IL 60637

MCCORMICK, MARIE CLARE, pediatrician, educator; b. Haverhill, Mass., Jan. 7, 1946; d. Richard John and Clare Bernadine (Keleher) McC.; m. Robert Jay Blendon, Dec. 30, 1977. BA magna cum laude, Emmanuel Coll., 1967; MD, Johns Hopkins Medical Sch., 1971; ScD, Johns Hopkins, 1978; MA, Harvard, 1991. Diplomate Am. Bd. Pediatrics. Pediatric resident, fellow Johns Hopkins Hosp., Balt., 1971-75, rsch. fellow, 1972-75; asst. prof. U. Ill. Schs. Medicine & Pub. Health, Chgo., 1975-76; pediatrics instr. Johns Hopkins Medical Sch., Balt., 1976-78; asst. prof. healthcare orgn. Johns Hopkins Sch. Hygiene & Pub. Health, 1978-81; asst. prof. pediatrics U. Pa., Phila., 1981-86, assoc. prof. pediatrics, 1986-87, Harvard Medical Sch., Boston, 1987-91; prof., chair. maternal & child health Harvard Sch. Pub. Health, 1992—; prof. pediatrics Harvard Medical Sch., 1992—, 1st Sumner and Esther Feldberg prof. maternal/child health, 1996—. Adj. assoc. prof. pediatrics U. Pa., 1987-92; active attending physician, Johns Hopkins Hosp., 1976-81, asst. physician Children's Hosp. Phila., 1981-84, assoc. physician, 1984-86, sr. physician, 1986-87, assoc. pediatrician Brigham & Women's Hosp., 1987—; sr. assoc. in medicine Children's Hosp., 1987—; sr. assoc. in pediatrics Beth Israel Deaconess Med. Ctr., 1987—; vis. prof. Wash. U., St. Louis, 1993; editorial bds. Health Svcs. Rsch., 1985-94, Pediatrics in Review, 1986-91, Pediatrics, 1993-99; assoc. editor Jour. Ambulatory Pediatric Assn., 1999—; adv. coun. Ctr. Perinatal & Family Health Brigham & Women;s Hosp., 1991—; cons. to numerous coms., orgns. and bds. Contbr. articles to profl. jours. Adv. The David and Lucile Packard Found., 1993-95; bd. dirs. Family Planning Coun. S.E. Pa., 1984-87; chair com. child health Mayor's Commn. Phila., 1982-83. Named Henry Strong Denison scholar Johns Hopkins Sch. Medicine, 1971, Leonard Davis inst. Health Econs. fellow U. Pa. 1984, First Sumner and Esther Feldberg prof. maternal and child health, 1996; recipient Johns Hopkins U. Soc. Scholars award, 1995, Ambulatory Pediat. Assn. Rsch. award, 1996. Fellow Am. Acad. Pediatrics; mem. AAAS, Inst. Medicine-Nat. Acad. Sci., Ambulatory Pediatrics Assn. (Rsch. award 1996), Soc. Pediatric Rsch. (sr.), Am. Pediatric Soc., Am. Pub. Health Assn., Internat. Epidemiological Assn., Assn. Health Svcs. Rsch., Eastern Soc. Pediatric Rsch., Soc. Pediatric Epidemiologic Rsch., Assn. Tchrs. Maternal and Child Health, Mass. Med. Soc., Norfolk Dist. Med. Soc., Mass. Pub. Health Assn., Johns Hopkins U. Soc. Scholars, Inst. Medicine of Nat. Acad. Scis. (elected; nat. assoc.). Office: Harvard Sch Pub Health 677 Huntington Ave Boston MA 02115-6096 E-mail: mmccormi@hsph.harvard.edu.

MCCORMICK, MICHAEL JERRY, judge; b. Fort Lewis, Wash., Oct. 17, 1945; s. Thaddeus Charles and Geraldine (Fogle) McC.; m. Katleen Karen Kelley, Sept. 2, 1967; children: Patrick Kelley, Karen Michelle. BA, U. Tex.-Austin, 1967; JD, St. Mary's U., 1970. Bar: Tex. 1970. Briefing atty. Tex. Ct. Criminal Appeals, 1970-71; asst. dist. atty. Travis County, Tex., 1971-72; exec. dir. Tex. Dist. and County Attys. Assn., Austin, 1972-80; judge Tex. Ct. Criminal Appeals, 1981—, chief presiding judge, 1988-2000, sr. judge, 2001—; of counsel Law Office Kelley McCormick, Lockhart, Tex., 2002—. Dir. Tex. Ctr. for Judiciary, 1983; vice-chmn. Tex. Commn. on Sentencing, 1984; mem. Tex. Jud. Budget Bd., 1983; co-chair Tex. Jud. Coun., 1997—. Author: Branch's Annotated Penal Code, 3d edit., Criminal Forms and Trial Manual, 10th edit., Tex. Justice Court Deskbook, Tex. Constables Civil Process Handbook. Pres. Joslin (Tex.) P.T.A., 1981-82. Served with U.S. Army, 1966-72. Named Rosewood Gavel Outstanding Jurist, St. Mary's U. Sch. Law, 1984, Disting. Law Grad., 1992. Mem. State Bar Tex., Tex. Dist. and County Attys. Assn. Office: 119 W San Antonio St Lockhart TX 78644

MCCORMICK, PAMELA ANN, artist, sculptor; b. Grand Rapids, Mich., Jan. 7, 1948; d. William Albert McCormick and June (Wente) Schuster; m. William K. Scarvie, Mar. 19, 1965 (div. Jan. 1972); children: Will, Jeffrey. BA in Art, San Jose (Calif.) State U., 1972, MA in Art Sculpture, 1974; postgrad., Stanford U., 1975-76. Instr. art Am. River Coll., Sacramento, 1976; dir. Children's Art Studio, N.Y.C., 1981-84; prodn. mgr. Precision Imaging Corp., 1986-88; cons. desktop pub. various pub. cos., 1988-90. Set design Color Story Chaparral, N.Y., 1992, Living Theatre prodn. Sixth Book, N.Y., 1991; solo exhbn. sculpture and photography Mus., N.Y., 1991. One person exhbn. includes Artopia Gallery, N.Y.C., 1995; other exhbns. include Artopia Gallery, N.Y.C., 1995, Bonni Benrubi Gallery, N.Y.C., 1000, Elaine Benson Gallery, East Hampton, N.Y., 1998, 2001; prin. works include Quatrain sculpture Cen. Park, N.Y.C., 1986-89, Flying Light Flushing Park, Queens, N.Y., 1986, Channeling, Erie Barge Canal, Lockport, N.Y., 1988, numerous floating sculptures for Cen. Park, N.Y.C., 1989, set design for Ice Theatre of N.Y., 1989, set and costume design Carmen Beuchat Dance Co., N.Y., 1990, Sixth Book, Living Theater, 1991, Ice Theater of N.Y., 1991, Living Theater, 1991, Color Story, Chaparral, N.Y., 1992; one-person exhbn. of sculpture and photography N.Y.C. Mus. 1991, D&H Canal Rail Trail, Accord, N.Y., 1994; author, photographer: A Walk Around the Block, New Yorkers on Their Home Turf, 1998-2002. Recipient Distinction award Audubon Naturalist Soc., 1986; NEA fellow, 1974; grantee Pollock Krasner Found., Inc., 1990, N.Y. State Coun. for Arts, 1994, Lila Wallace Reader's Digest Arts Internat. grantee, 1994. Mem. Artists Representing Environ. Art, Internat. Sculpture Orgn. Democrat. Avocations: computers, dance. Studio: 97 Wooster St New York NY 10012-3848

MCCORMICK, RICHARD LEVIS, academic administrator; b. New Brunswick, N.J., Dec. 26, 1947; s. Richard Patrick and Katheryne Crook (Levis) McC.; m. Suzanne Dee Lebsock, Aug. 30, 1984; children: Elizabeth, Michael. BA in Am. Studies, Amherst Coll., 1969; PhD in History, Yale U., 1976. From asst. prof. to prof. Rutgers U., New Brunswick, N.J., 1976-92, dean Faculty Arts and Scis., 1989-92; exec. vice chancellor, provost, vice chancellor acad. affair U. N.C., Chapel Hill, 1992-95; pres. U. Wash., Seattle, 1995—. Author: From Realignment to Reform: Political Change in New York State, 1893-1910, 1981, The Party Period and Public Policy: American Politics from the Age of Jackson to the Progressive Era, 1986. Rsch. fellow Am. Coun. Learned Socs., 1978-79, fellow John Simon Guggenheim Meml. Found., 1985. Mem. Phi Beta Kappa. Home: 806 36th Ave E Seattle WA 98112-4320 Office: U Wash Seattle WA 98195-0001*

MC CORMICK, RICHARD PATRICK, history educator; b. N.Y.C., Dec. 24, 1916; s. Patrick Austin and Anna (Smith) McC.; m. Katheryne Crook Levis, Aug. 25, 1945; children: Richard Levis, Dorothy Irene. BA, Rutgers U., 1938, MA, 1940, LittD (hon.), 1982; PhD, U. Pa., 1948. Historian, Phila. Q.M. Depot, 1942-44; instr. U. Del., 1944-45; mem. faculty Rutgers U., 1945—, univ. historian, 1948—; dean Rutgers Coll., 1974-77, Univ. prof. history, 1977-82, Univ. prof. emeritus, 1982—. Research adviser Colonial Williamsburg, 1953-61; Fulbright lectr. Cambridge (Eng.) U., 1961-62; Commonwealth lectr. U. London, 1971; chmn. N.J. Hist. Commn., 1967-70 Author: Experiment in Independence, 1950, History of Voting in N.J, 1953, N.J. From Colony to State, 1964, Second American Party System, 1966, Rutgers: a Bicentennial History, 1966, The Presidential Game, 1982, The Black Student Protest Movement at Rutgers, 1990; co-author: The Case of the Nazi Professor, 1989. Mem. N.J. Tercentenary Commn., 1958-60, Am. Revolution Bicentennial Commn., 1971-74. Social Sci. Research Council fellow, 1956-57 Mem. Am. Hist. Assn., Soc. Historians of Early American Republic (pres. 1988-89), N.J. Hist. Soc. (pres. 1950-57), Phi Beta Kappa. Home: 938 River Rd Piscataway NJ 08854-5504

MCCORMICK, ROBERT JUNIOR, company executive, former government official; b. Boone, Iowa, Aug. 1, 1929; s. Ivyl Robert and Darlene Adel (Bowes) McC.; m. Shirley May Zerbe, Dec. 24, 1950; children: Elaine McCormick Newland, Kathleen, Michael, Tara McCormick Wieting, Tammy McCormick Kirby. Grad., Flying Sch., Williams Field, Ariz., 1951, Parachute Jump Sch., 1964, Armed Forces Staff Coll., Norfolk, Va., 1966, Def. Systems Mgmt. Coll., Ft. Belvoir, Va., 1975; BS, Tex. Tech. U., 1963; cert., Harvard U. Def. Studies Program, 1984. Served as enlisted man USAF, 1948-51, commd. 2d lt., 1951, advanced through grades to col., 1971, pilot U.S., Japan, Korea, Europe, Vietnam; exec. officer to Gen. George Brown 7th Air Force, Saigon, Vietnam, 1969-70; mil. asst. to asst. sec. of Air Force for research and devel. USAF, Washington, 1970-74, ret., 1975; exec. officer NASA, Washington, 1976-80; adminstrv. asst. to sec. of Air Force USAF, 1980-94; mem. U.S. Sr. Exec. Service, 1979-94; pres. McG, Ltd., Fairfax, Va. Mem. transition team Dept. of Def., 2001. Decorated Air Force Legion of Merit, Bronze star, Air medal, Meritorious Svc. medal, Air Force Exceptional Civilian Svc. medal; recipient Presdl. Meritorious Rank, 1989, Disting. Civilian Svc. medal Dept. Def., 1994, Commendation medal State of Calif., 2001. Mem. ASME, DAV, Air Force Assn., Nat. Def. Indsl. Assn., Order of Daedalians, St. Andrews Soc. Washington, Mil. Order of Carabao, Chevaliers du Testevin. Clubs: Army-Navy Country (Fairfax, Va.). Office: 4035 Hadley Ln Fairfax VA 22032-1308 Fax: 703-978-1035. E-mail: mcgltd1@aol.com.

MCCORMICK, ROD, sculptor, art educator; b. Battle Creek, Mich., Sept. 2, 1952; s. Rodney Lawrence and Joan (Kaminsky) McC.; m. Barbara Mail, Dec. 29, 1985; children: Anna, Sonya. BFA, Tyler Sch. Art, 1974; MFA, RISD, 1978. Sculptor and metalsmith, Phila., 1974—; vis. prof. Kent State U., Ohio, 1978-79; prof. U. Arts, Phila., 1981—, chmn. crafts dept., 1993-94, 95-96. One-man shows include Owen Patrick Gallery, Phila., 1990, U. Arts, 1993, John Elder Gallery, N.Y.C., 1998, Design Arts Gallery, Drexel U., Phila., 1999; exhibited in group shows at Phila. Mus. Art, 1990, Pa. State U., 1991, Meredith Gallery, Balt., 1991, Leo Kaplan Modern Gallery, N.Y.C., 1992, Paley Design Ctr., Phila., 1993, Peter Joseph Gallery, N.Y.C., 1994, Md. Art Place, Balt., 1996, Pentimenti Gallery, Phila., 1996, Stedman Gallery-Rutgers, Camden, N.J., 1997, James Michener Art Mus., Doylestown, Pa., 1997, Art in City Hall, Phila., 1997, Ellipse Art Ctr., Arlington, Va., 1998. Recipient Young Americans Metal exhbn. award Am. Craft Mus., 1980; grantee Nat. Endowment Arts, 1990, Pa. Coun. Arts, 1991. Mem. Soc. N.Am. Goldsmiths, Internat. Sculpture Ctr. Home: PO Box 29578 Philadelphia PA 19144-0578 Office: University of the Arts 320 S Broad St Philadelphia PA 19102-4994

MCCORMICK, STEVEN A. pathologist; b. Logan, W.Va., June 2, 1959; s. Clarence Okey and Ernestine (Estep) McC.; m. Suzanne Ursula Stucki, Aug. 16, 1981. BS cum laude, Duke U., 1980; MD, W.Va. U., 1984. Asst. prof. W.Va. Sch. Medicine, Morgantown, 1988-89; assoc. prof. N.Y. Med. Coll., Valhalla, 1989—. Dir. pathology and lab. medicine The N.Y. Eye & Ear Infirmary, 1989—. Fellow Am. Coll. Pathologists; mem. Assn. for Rsch. in Vision & Opthalmology (chmn. anatomy/pathology 1993—), Ea. Ophthalmic Pathology Assocs., Am. Acad. Ophthalmology, Am. Assn. Ophthalmic Pathologists. Republican. Episcopalian. Avocations: pianist, organist. Home: 239 Fuller Mountain Rd Kent CT 06757-1014 Office: The NY Eye/Ear Infirmary 310 E 14th St New York NY 10003-4201

MCCORMICK, STEVEN THOMAS, insurance company executive; b. Phila., Dec. 18, 1955; s. Howard C. and Ruth Marion (Stahl) McC.; m. Helene Mary Trommler, Nov. 21, 1981; children: Matthew Thomas, Bria Helene. BBA, U. Ky., 1978; gen. ins cert., Ins. Inst. Am., 1980. Cert. adminstrv. mgr., purchasing mgr., ins. agt., Ky., 1980. Supr. trainee Ky. Farm Bur. Ins. Cos., Louisville, 1978-79, supr. micrographics dept., 1979-83, supr. adminstrv. svcs., 1983-85, mgr. adminstrv. svcs., 1985-89; asst. v.p. ops., 1989—. Named to Hon. Order Ky. Cols., Outstanding Employee of Yr., Nat. Assn. of Mut. Ins. Cos., 1986; recipient Cert. of Excellence, Jefferson County Bd. Edn. Mem. Adminstrv. Mgmt. Soc. (internat. top recruiter 1985, chpt. pres. 1988, internat. dir. area 7 1990-91, internat. v.p. profl. devel. 1992-93), Acad. Adminstrv. Mgmt. (mem. bd. regents 1991-92, internat. v.p. 1992-93, internat. pres. 1993-94), U. Ky. Alumni Assn., Sigma Nu. Republican. Home: 706 Elsmere Cir Louisville KY 40223-2764 Office: Ky Farm Bur Ins Cos PO Box 20700 Louisville KY 40250-0700

MCCORMICK, TERESA D. accountant; b. Winamac, Ind., July 26, 1970; d. Mark Gregory Whitaker and Joyce Lillian White; m. James Martin McCormick, Sept. 28, 1996; children: Sarah Noel, Emma Grace, John Gregory. BS, Ball State U., 1992. From acctg. clk. to gen. acct. Wabash Nat. Corp., Lafayette, Ind., 1992—. Mem. Inst. Mgmt. Accts. Office: Wabash Nat Corp 1000 Sagamore Pkwy S Lafayette IN 47905-4727

MCCORMICK, THOMAS JAY, infosystems engineer; b. Pitts., Nov. 23, 1946; s. Thomas Jay and Marion (Smith) McC.; m. Patricia Michelle McCormick, Dec. 1, 1990; 1 child, Randall James. BA, Dickinson Coll., 1968; MS, Troy State U., 1976; MA, Boston U., 1985. Tech. officer U.S. Army Units, various cities, 1968-78; army research & devel. coord. BETA Joint Program Office, Washington, 1978-80; student officer Armed Forces Staff Coll., Norfolk, Va., 1981; branch exec. officer Defense Intelligence Agy., Washington, 1981-83; ground forces branch chief Defense Liaison Detachment, Bonn, Germany, 1983-86; army operational test officer Army Operational Test and Evaluation Agy., Washington, 1986-87; chief, intelligence systems branch Army Operational Test and Evaluation AGy., 1987-88; intelligence systems specialist GTE Govt. Systems Corp., Chantilly, Va., 1988-92; spl. programs bus. devel. mgr., 1992—. Co-author: Notes and Cases in Military Management, 1976; author/co-author more than 15 specialized info. systems analyses. Council pres. St. Thomas More Parish, Bonn, Germany, 1985-86. Recipient Disting. Svc. award Crofton Civic Assn., 1983. Mem. Internat. Test and Evaluation Assn., Armed Forces Communications Electronics Assn., Nat. Mil. Intelligence Assn., Kiwanis (sec. 1982-83), Theta Chi. Republican. Methodist. Avocations: skiing, golf. Home: 14206 Hartwood Ct Centreville VA 20121-5023

MCCORMICK, TIMOTHY BRIAN BEER, arbitrator; b. Northampton, Mass., May 16, 1959; s. Brian Beer and Margaret Ann McCormick; m. Lee Hillary Kadis, Sept. 2, 1979 (div. June 1991); m. Virginia Lee Kostner, June 30, 1991 (div. May 1995); 1 child, Cameron A.; m. Jill Ann Knowland, Apr. 23, 1997; 1 child, Britton K. BA, U. Calif., Berkeley, 1984; JD, Am. U., 1987. Bar: Calif. 1987, U.S. Dist. Ct. (no. dist.) Calif. 1987, U.S. Ct. Appeals (9th cir.) 1987, U.S. Dist. Ct. (ea. dist.) Calif., 1991, U.S. Dist. Ct. (ctrl. dist.) Calif. 1994. Staff asst. Office of Lt. Gov., Sacramento, 1982-83; cons. Calif. Rep. Party, 1984; rsch. asst. Nat. Right to Work Found., Springfield, Va., 1985-86; assoc. Graham & James, San Francisco, 1987-93, McPharlin & Mahl, San Jose, 1993-94; ptnr. McPharlin & Sprinkles, 1994-95; v.p., assoc. coun. Fidelity Nat. Title Ins. Co., Walnut Creek, Calif., 1995-2000; prin. McCormick Dispute Resolution Svcs., Piedmont, 1996—2000; prin. cons. Libris Solutions, Oakland, 2000—; gen. mgr. Kono Cons., Inc., 2001—02. Judge pro tem Santa Clara County Superior Ct., 1993—. Comments editor Adminstrv. Law Jour., 1986-87. Treas., Hom for Mayor, San Francisco, 1995; mem. Rep. State Cen. Com. of Calif., 1983-85, 2000—, assoc. mem., 1985-2000, mem. exec. com., 1983-84; gen. coun. Asian Am. Polit. Edn. Found., 1992—; mem. Alameda

County Rep. Ctrl. Com., 2000-2002; Rep. candidate 16th Dist. Assembly, 2000. Mem.: ABA, Engring. and Utility Contractors Assn. (legis. com. 1991—95, co-chair 1994—95). Avocations: skiing, bicycling, cooking, scuba diving. Home: 235 Park View Ave Piedmont CA 94610-1041 E-mail: din3500psi@scubadiving.com.

MCCORMICK, WALTER BERNARD, JR. lawyer; b. Kansas City, Mo., Feb. 8, 1954; s. Walter Bernard and Dorothy Ann (Power) M.; m. Mary Lou Edlefsen, Jan. 3, 1987; children: Walter Patrick, Megan Boutin. Student, Georgetown U., 1975; BJ, U. Mo., 1976, JD, 1979. Bar: Mo. 1979, D.C. 1980. Assoc. Leighton, Conklin, Lemov & Jacobs, Washington, 1980-81, Pepper, Hamilton & Scheetz, Washington, 1981-82; legis. asst. U.S. Senate, 1982-84; gen. counsel U.S. Senate Com. Commerce, Sci. and Transp., 1985-87, minority chief counsel, staff dir., 1988-92; gen. counsel U.S. Dept. Transp., 1992-93; partner Bryan Cave LLP, 1993—. Mem. City Club, Washington, 1993—. Republican. Roman Catholic. Avocation: skiing. Office: United States Telecom Association 1401 H Street, N.W., Suite 600 Washington DC 20005-2164

MCCORMICK, WILLIAM THOMAS, JR. electric and gas company executive; b. Washington, Sept. 12, 1944; s. William Thomas and Lucy Valentine (Offutt) McC.; m. Ann Loretta du Mais, June 13, 1969; children: Christopher, Patrick. BS, Cornell U., 1966; PhD, M.I.T., 1969. Mem. staff Inst. for Def. Analysis, Arlington, Va., 1969-72; mem. staff Office of Sci. and Tech., Exec. office of the Pres., Washington, 1972-73; sr. staff mem. Energy Policy Office, The White House, 1973-74; chief sci. and energy tech. br. Office Mgmt. and Budget, Exec. Office of the Pres., 1974-75; dir. commercialization U.S. Energy Research and Devel. Adminstrn., 1975-76; v.p. policy and govt. relations Am. Gas Assn., 1976-78; v.p., asst. to chmn. Am. Natural Resources Co., Detroit, 1978-80; exec. v.p. Mich. Wis. Pipeline Co., Am. Natural Resources System, 1980-82; pres. Am. Natural Resources Co., 1982-85; chmn., chief exec. officer Consumers Power Co., Jackson, 1985-92, chmn., 1992—2002; chmn., CEO CMS Energy Corp., 1985—2002. Bd. dirs. Bank One Corp., Rockwell Inst., Schlumberger Ltd. Prin. author, editor: Commercialization of Synthetic Fuels in the U.S, 1975. Bd. dirs. McGregor Fund, St. John Hosp. Alfred P. Sloan scholar, 1962-66 Mem. Econ. Club Detroit (bd. dirs.), Detroit Athletic Club, Country Club Detroit, Detroit Club. Roman Catholic.*

MCCORQUODALE, J. ALEXANDER, civil and environmental engineer, educator; BA, U. Western Ont., Can.; MA in Fluid Mechanics, U. Glasgow, Scotland; PhD in Hydraulics, U. Windsor. With H.G. Acres Ltd., Niagara Falls, N.Y., 1964-66; prof. dept. civil and environ. engring. U. Windsor; FMI prof. dept. civil engring. Univ. New Orleans, 1996-. Recipient Harrison Prescott Eddy medal Water Environment Fedn., 1998. Fellow Can. Soc. Civil Engring. (past chair hydrotechnical divsn., Camille A. Dagenais award 1995). Office: Univ New Orleans Coll of Engring Dept Civil Engring 2000 Lakeshore Dr New Orleans LA 70122-3520

MCCOTTER, SUZANNE SCHWARZ, education educator; b. Teaneck, NJ., Dec. 6, 1967; d. Samuel Shalom (Stepfather) and Grace Magee Lewin, Paul Schwarz; m. Keith McCotter; children: Ryan, Will. BA, Rutgers Coll., 1990; MLS, Rutgers U., 1992; PhD, U. Ga., 1999. Asst. prof. Ednl. Founds. Millersville (Pa.) U., 1999—. Office: Millersville Univ PO Box 1002 Millersville PA 17603 Business E-Mail: suzanne.mccotter@millersville.edu.

MCCOUBREY, R. JAMES, advertising and broadcast executive; b. Grand Mere, Que., Can., Sept. 1, 1944; s. James Addison and Margaret G. F. (Scarratt) McC.; m. Annette L. Hebert, Sept. 16, 1972; children: James Andrew, Matthew Alexander. B. of Commerce, McGill U., 1966, MA, 1967. With brand mgmt. Procter and Gamble, Toronto, Ont., Can., 1967-69; asst. mgr. Young and Rubicam, Montreal, Que., 1969-72, dir. client svcs. Toronto, 1972-74, mgr., 1974-77, pres., 1977-80, area dir. Americas N.Y.C., 1980-82, gen. mgr. Europe London, 1982-83, group and area dir. N.Y.C., 1983-85, chmn. Toronto, 1985-90, exec. v.p. N.Y.C., 1984, area dir. Africa, Australia, New Zealand and Can., 1984-90; pres., chief exec. officer Telemedia Inc., North York, Ont., Can., 1990-97, Telemedia Communications USA Inc, Charlotte, Vt., 1991-97; pres. Scotch Block Investments Inc., 1993—; exec. v.p., COO Canadian Broadcasting Corp., Can., 1997-2001. Chmn. Inst. Can. Advt., Toronto, 1981-82; bd. dirs. The Parent Kit Corp. Chmn. regional divsn. McGill Univ. Twenty-First Century Fund, Reitmans Inc.; mem. internat. adv. bd., faculty of mgmt. McGill U. Mem. Can. Assn. Broadcasters (bd. dirs., past chmn.), Inst. of Can. Advt. (past chmn.), Young Pres. Orgn. (past chmn.), Mag. Assn. Can. (chmn. 1992-94), Royal Can. Yacht Club (Toronto), Mt. Royal Club (Montreal). Anglican. Home: 54 Bernard Ave Toronto ON Canada M5R 1R5 Office: 10459 Third Line Halton Hills ON Canada L9T 2X9 E-mail: james_mccoubrey@hotmail.com.

MCCOURT, JOYCE ELISE, lawyer; b. Framingham, Mass., Jan. 31, 1949; d. Paul Joseph and Joyce Loraine McCourt; m. Ronald Richard Perry, June 29, 1980 (dec. July 1997). BA in Psychology, U. Mass., 1971; JD, Boston Coll., 1976. Bar: Mass. 1977 (1st and 2d cirs.). Asst. regional counsel Dept. HHS, Boston, 1976—. Home: 291 Lions Mouth Rd Amesbury MA 01913-5426 Office: Dept HHS Rm 2250 JFK Bldg Boston MA 02203 E-mail: JMcCourt@os.dhhs.gov.

MCCOURT, LISA, writer; b. Jacksonville, Fla., Sept. 2, 1964; d. Michael Lee and Bettye Jean McCourt; m. Gregory Vincent Combs; 1 child Lily-Kate Combs 1 child Tucker Combs. BS, Drew U., Madison, N.J., 1986. Author: (children's book) I Love You, Stinky Face, 1997 (National Parenting Publication Award (Nappa) Honors Award, 1998), The Rain Forest Counts!, 1997, The Long and Short of It , 1998 (chosen for The Original Art by the Society of Illustrators, 1998), Raptors!, 1997, Deadly Snakes, 1998, I Miss You, Stinky Face, 1999 (a PBS "Between the Lions" selection, 2001), Candy Counting, 1999, Rocket to the Moon, 1999, Construction Buddies; Dozer to the Rescue!, 1999, It's Time for School, Stinky Face, 2000, Construction Buddies; Dozer's Wild Adventure, 2000, Chicken Soup for Little Souls; The Best Night Out with Dad, 1997, Chicken Soup for Little Souls; The Never-Forgotten Doll, 1997 (Storytelling World Award; Honor Title, 1998), Chicken Soup for Little Souls; The Goodness Gorillas, 1997, Chicken Soup for Little Souls; The Braids Girl, 1998, Chicken Soup for Little Souls, A Dog of My Own, 1998 (IRA/CBC Children's Choice Award, 1998), Chicken Soup for Little Souls; The New Kid and the Cookie Thief, 1998, Chicken Soup for Little Souls; Della Splatnuk, Birthday Girl, 1999 (Storytelling World Award, Honor Title, 2000), Chicken Soup for Little Souls Family Collection, 1999, Chicken Soup for the Little Souls; 3 Colorful Stories to Warm the Hearts of Children, 2000, Love You Until. . . , 1999, (parenting book) 101 Ways to Raise a Happy Baby, 1999, (preteen book) Attitude--How to Be the Coolest Girl You Know, 2000, (children's book) Weird in the Wild; Wet 'n' Weird, 2000, Weird in the Wild; Hairy 'n' Weird, 2000, (parenting book) 101 Ways to Raise a Happy Toddler, 2000, (children's book) Good Night, Princess Pruney Toes, 2001, I Love You, Stinky Face board book, 2002, Merry Christmas, Stinky Face, 2002, (children's book) What's Inside My Body?, 2000, (children's book) Mysterious Space, 2000. Personal E-mail: lisa@lisamccourt.com.

MCCOVEY, WILLIE LEE, former professional baseball player; b. Mobile, Ala., Jan. 10, 1938; s. Frank and Ester (Jones) McC. Minor league baseball player, 1955-59; first baseman San Francisco Giants, 1959-73, 77-80, active in pub. rels., 1981-86, spl. asst. to pres., 1986-94; mem. San Diego Padres, 1974-76, Oakland Athletics, 1976-81. Named Nat. League Rookie of Year, 1959, Most Valuable Player, 1969; Home Run Champion, 1963, 68, 69; Runs Batted In Leader, 1968, 69; Comeback Player of Year, 1977; 10th on All-Time Major League List of Career Home Runs (521); All-Time Nat. League leader in grand slam home runs (18); mem. Nat. League All-Star Team, 1963, 66, 68-71; inducted into Baseball Hall of Fame, 1986 Office: c/o San Francisco Giants 3 Compark at Candlestick Pk San Francisco CA 94124 also: Baseball Hall Fame PO Box 590 Cooperstown NY 13326-0590

MCCOWAN, OTIS BLAKELY, mathematics educator; b. Monterey, Tenn., June 17, 1934; s. Burton and Martha Catherine (Phipps) McC. BS, Tenn. Tech. U., 1959; MA, La. State U., 1966; PhD, Vanderbilt U., 1975. Mathematician Missile Devel. Ctr., Holloman AFB, N.Mex., 1962-63; math. tchr. Rhea Ctrl. H.S., Dayton, Tenn., 1963-65; math. instr. Kilgore (Tex.) Coll., 1966-67; asst. prof. math. Belmont U., Nashville, 1967-72, assoc. prof. math., 1972-75, prof. math., 1975—. With U.S. Army, 1959-62. Named Outsting Young Educator in Rhea County, Dayton C. of C., 1964. Mem. Nat. Coun. Tchrs. Math., Math. Assn. Am., Tenn. Math. Tchrs. Assn., Kappa Delta Pi, Kappa Mu Epsilon, Pi Mu Epsilon, Omicron Delta Kappa, Alpha Chi (Region III v.p. 1980-82, pres. 1982-84, nat. v.p. 1991-93). Democrat. Baptist. Avocations: traveling, gardening, reading, attending concerts and theatre. Home: 2205 18th Ave S Nashville TN 37212-5001 Office: Belmont Univ Dept Math and Computer Sci Nashville TN 37212 E-mail: mccowano@mail.belmont.edu.

MCCOWEN, ALEC, actor; b. Tunbridge Wells, May 26, 1925; s. Duncan and Mary (Walkden) McC. , Ed. Skinners Sch., Tunbridge Wells, and Royal Acad. Dramatic Art. Appeared as Touchstone, Ford, Richard II, Mercutio, Malvolio, Oberon at Old Vic Theatre, 1959-60; appeared with R.S.C. as Fool in King Lear, 1964, Hadrian VII, 1968, The Philanthropist, 1970, The Misanthrope, 1972, as Dr. Dysart in Equus, 1972, as Henry Higgins in Pygmalion, 1974, as Ben in The Family Dance, 1976, Someone Who'll Watch Over Me, 1992, as Prospero in The Tempest, 1994, as Gaev in The Cherry Orchard, 1995; appeared with Prospect Co. as Antony in Antony and Cleopartra, 1977, in solo performance of St. Mark's Gospel, 1978, 81, as Frank in Tishoo, 1979, as Malvolio in Twelfth Night (TV), 1980, of Kipling, 1984, as Reilly in The Cocktail Party, 1986, as Nicolai in Fathers and Sons, 1987, as Vladimir in Waiting for Godot, 1987; appeared with Nat. Theatre and Abbey Dublin as Jack in Dancing at Cughnasa, 1990; appeared with Nat. Theatre as Crocker-Harris in The Browning Version, Arthur in Harlequinade, Capt. Corcoran in H.M.S. Pinafore, 1981, Adolf Hitler in The Portage to San Cristobal of AH, PTO, 1982, Reginald, in 2000 Quartet; films: Frenzy, 1971, Travels with My Aunt, 1973, Stevie, 1978, Personal Services, Cry Freedom, 1987, The Age of Innocence, 1992, Gangs of New York, 2000; TV: Private Lives, 1976; author: Young Gemini,1979, Double Bill, 1980, Personal Mark, 1984. Named Best Actor, Evening Standard (now New Standard), 1968, 73, 82, Variety Club Stage Actor, 1970. Office: care Conway Van Gelder 18-21 Jermyn St London SW1 Y6HB England

MCCOWN, HALE, retired judge; b. Kansas, Ill., Jan. 19, 1914; s. Ross S. and Pauline (Collins) McC.; m. Helen Lanier, July 15, 1938; children: Robert B., William L., Mary Lynn. AB, Hastings Coll., 1935; LLB, Duke U., 1937. Bar: Oreg. 1937, Nebr. 1942. With firm Carey, Hart, Spencer & McCulloch, Portland, 1937-42; pvt. practice Beatrice, Nebr., 1942-65; ptnr. McCown, Baumfalk & Dalke; justice Supreme Court Nebr., 1965-83. Author articles in legal jours. Served to lt. USNR, 1943-45. Recipient Disting. Alumnus award Hastings Coll., 1981, Charles S. Murphy award Duke U., 1986, Legal Pioneer award Nebr. Bar Found., 1996, Alumni Appreciation award Duke U., 1981. Fellow Am. Coll. Trial Lawyers, Am. Coll. Trust and Estate Counsel; mem. ABA (legal ethics com. 1957-62), Nebr. Bar Assn. (chmn. ho. dels. 1955-56, pres. 1960-61), Am. Law Inst. (mem. council 1969—2000, emeritus 2000—), Am. Judicature Soc. Presbyterian.

MCCOWN, JOE DUANE, document coder/data entry operator; b. Bakersfield, Calif., May 15, 1942; s. Joe and Ruth Elizabeth McC. AA, Bakersfield Coll., 1962; BA, U. Calif., Santa Barbara, 1964; MA, San Jose State, 1968. Co. driver Slate & Leoni , L.A., 1970—72; asst. to gen. mgr. Kirkeby Ctr. Restaurant, Westwood, Calif., 1972-74; title searcher Title Ins. & Trust Co., 1977, Safeco Title Ins. Co., 1978; customer svc. rep. Calif. Land Title Co., 1980—81; sec. United Temporary Svcs., 1981—82; group sec. Rocketdyne, Canoga Park, Calif., 1985-86; typist RC Remodeler Inc., Sierra Madre, 1988; office asst. Glenn Shellcross, Bakersfield, 1989-90; office asst., word processor EWCL Global Enterprises Inc., L.A., 1993; asst. paralegal, asst. office mgr. United Profl. Svcs., Inglewood, Calif., 1993-94; coder O'Melveny and Myers, L.A., 1997; document coder Temp. Solutions, 1997—99; coder Latham & Wartins, 1998—2000; document coder Quorum Staffing Group, 2000. With U.S. Army, 1968—70. Republican. Methodist. Home: 2208 W 8th St Apt 511 Los Angeles CA 90057-4004

MCCOWN, JOHN J, chemist, researcher; b. C leveland, Ohio, 1929; s. Herbert Louis and Cathrine J McCown; m. Barbara Lou Elmer McCown; children: Michael J McCown, Gary J McCown, Patrick J McCown, Sherry Ann McCown. BS Chemistry, Drury Coll., Springfield, MO, 1947—51; MS ,Chemistry, U. of Tenn, Oak Ridge & knoxville,TN, 1953—56; MS, Chemistry, U. of Idaho, Idaho Falls,Ext, 1960—62. Chemist gs-5 USDA Bur of Entonocogy, Orlando, Fla., 1951—52; analytical chemist Oak Ridge Nat. Lab, Oak Ridge, Tenn., 1952—56. Author: of scientific articles in more than 30 publs. Avocations: tennis, golf, hunting, fishing, water & snoe sking. Home: 812 NE Sunrise Street Prineville OR 97754 Home Fax: 541-447-8693.

MCCOWN, LINDA JEAN, medical technology educator; b. Pitts., Mar. 18, 1953; d. William Ernest and Mary Elizabeth McC. BS, Pa. State U., 1975; MS, U. Pitts., 1979. Cert. med. technologist, clin. lab. scientist. Microbiology aide Pa. State U., University Park, 1973-74; med. technologist, asst. supr., rsch. technologist Children's Hosp. of Pitts., 1975-80; asst. prof. med. tech., assoc. program dir. Ctrl. Wash. U., Ellensburg, 1980-99; asst. prof. clinilab. sci. Jewish Hosp. Coll. of Nursing and Allied Health at Wash. Univ. Med. Ctr., 1999—; affiliate asst. prof. U. Mo., St. Louis, 2000—. Critiquer, insp. Nat. Accreditation Agy. for Clin. Lab. Scis., Chgo., 1984—; test item writer Nat. Cert. Agy., Lenexa, Kans., 1989—; recruiter Am. Soc. Clin. Pathologists, Chgo., 1988-98; guest lectr. physician asst. program U. Wash., Seattle, 1996-99. Contbr. articles to profl. jours. Stephen ministry, deacon First Presbyn. Ch., Yakima, Wash., 1992-98; bd. dirs. The Campbell Farm, Wapato, Wash., 1990-95; rally chmn. Heifer Project Internat., Wapato, 1991-94; profl. affairs com. chairperson Mo. Orgn. for Clin. Lab. Sci., 1999-01; host com. Clin. Lab. Educators' Conf., 2001; identity com. Second Bapt. Ch., St. Louis, 2001—. Recipient Key to the Future award Mo. Orgn. Clin. Lab. Sci., 2000. Mem. Am. Soc. for Med. Tech. (mem. commn. on accreditation 1988-91), Wash. State Soc. for Clin. Lab. Sci. (conv. chair 1992, edn. chair 1986-94, 95-96, Pres.'s award 1992, convention hospitality chair and cons. 1998), Mo. orgn. for Clin. Lab Sci. (chmn. hematology sci. assembly 2001—), Columbia Basin Soc. Clin. Lab. Sci. (pres.-elect 1993, pres. 1994-95), Omicron Sigma. Avocations: photography, tennis, travel, music. Home: 646 W Canterbury Rd Apt C Saint Louis MO 63132-4639 Office: Jewish Hosp Coll Mail Stop 90-30-625 306 S Kingshighway Blvd Saint Louis MO 63110-1028 E-mail: lmccown@bjc.org.

MCCOWN, MARJORIE ELAINE, costume designer; b. Tuscola, Ill., Feb. 5, 1955; d. Harrison J. and Helen Esther McCown. BA in Theater, U. Va., 1977; AAS in Fashion Design, Fashion Inst. Tech., N.Y.C., 1978. Costume designer film/TV Firehouse (CBS pilot), Close to Danger, Romeo and Juliet (TV-PBS); asst. costume designer film/TV Wag the Dog (feature), Ed-TV (feature), My Favorite Martian (feature), Father's Day (feature), Kazaam (feature), House Arrest (feature), Apollo 13 (feature), Forrest Gump, The Firm, Clean Slate, A Bronx Tale, Hero, The Marrying Man, The Addams Family, George Vidal's Lincoln (TV miniseries), That 70's Show (sitcom-Fox); costume designer opera/theater East of the Sun/N.Y.C. Opera, West of the Moon (N.Y.C. Opera), Turn of the Screw (N.Y.C. Opera), Don Giovanni (Minn. Opera Co.), The Pearl Fishers (N.Y.C. Opera), The Postman Always Rings Twice (Ft. Worth Opera Assn.), Cosi Fan Tutte (Greater Miami Opera Assn.), Anoush (Mich. Opera Theater), I Pagliacci (N.Y.C. Opera), Tartuffe (Ala. Shakespeare Festival), The Pajama Game (N.Y.C. Opera), Guys and Dolls (Theater Virginia), Noises Off (Theater Virginia), One Touch of Venus (Goodspeed Opera House), A Wireless Christmas (Theater Virginia), The Man (The Apple Corps, N.Y.), Festivities (No Smoking Playhouse, N.Y.), La Turista (Westbeth Theater Ctr. N.Y.), The Great rime (Charlottesville Children's Theater). Author: Death by Design, 2000. Mem.: Mystery Writers of Am., United Scenic Artists, Costume Designers Guild. Home: 1806 Lucretia Ave Los Angeles CA 90026

MCCOY, CAROL P. psychologist, training executive; b. Bronxville, N.Y., June 14, 1948; d. Rawley Deering and Jane (Wiske) McC.; m. Lanny Gordon Foster, Nov. 29, 1975 (div. 1985). BA, Conn. Coll., 1970; MS in Psychology, Rutgers U., 1974, PhD in Psychology, 1980. Adj. instr. psychology Rutgers U., New Brunswick, N.J., 1974-75; faculty chair dept. social sci. Misericordia Hosp. Sch. Nursing, Bronx, N.Y., 1976-79; tng. and devel. cons. Chase Manhattan Bank N.A., N.Y.C., 1980-85, tng. mgr. internat. consumer banking div., 1985-88, tng. mgr. individual banking, 1988-91; dir. corp. tng. UNUM Life Ins. Co. Am., Portland, Maine, 1991-97, mgr. tng. quality assurance, 1997-99; pres. McCoy Trng./Devel. Resources, Falmouth, Maine, 1999—. Author: Managing a Small HRD Department, 1993; editor: Managing the Small Training Staff, 1998. Mem. Am. Soc. Tng. and Devel., Am. Psychol. Assn. Avocations: genealogy, music, baseball cards. Home and Office: McCoy Tng/Devel Resources 11 Johnson Rd Falmouth ME 04105-1408 E-mail: cmccoy3333@aol.com.

MCCOY, CHARLES SHERWOOD, university president, former theology educator; b. Laurinburg, N.C., June 27, 1923; s. Clarence Latimer and Lutie Heber (Walker) McC.; m. Marjorie Louise Casebier, Dec. 28, 1971 (dec. Feb. 1985); children: Carroll, Marsha, Priscilla, Celia, Stephanie, Elizabeth. AS, Presbyn. Jr. Coll., Maxton, N.C., 1942; BA, U. N.C., 1943; MDiv, Duke U., 1945; PhD, Yale U., 1957; LHD (hon.), U. Hawaii, 1966; DLitt (hon.), St. Andrews Coll., Laurinburg, N.C., 1996. Ordained to ministry Meth. Ch., 1945. Pastor Creedmore (N.C.) United Meth. Ch., 1946-47; dir. Wesley Found., Raleigh, N.C., 1947-49; assoc. prof. religion U. Fla., Gainesville, 1954-59; Sproul prof. theol. ethics Grad. Theol. Union, Berkeley, Calif., 1967-98, Sproul prof. emeritus, 1998—; organizer, pres. Pan Pacific U., Oakland, 1999—. Vis. prof. U. N.C.,, Chapel Hill, Fresno (Calif.) State U., U. Calif., Santa Cruz, U. Tübingen, Germany, U. Münster, Germany; lectr. numerous univs., colls., including Danforth lectr. Assn. Am. Colls., Washington, 1963-64, 66-67; Fulbright sr. lectr., Germany, 1977-78; also U. Pacific, U. Puget Sound, Harvard U., Colo. State U., Syracuse U., Calif. State U., Bakersfield, San Francisco Theol. Sem., Kent State U., John Carroll U., U. Heidelberg and Bremen, Germany, Basel and Bern, Switzerland, also in Czech Republic, Japan, China, Republic of Korea; mem. exec. com. Fellowship So. Churchmen, Chapel Hill, N.C., 1944-52; founding exec. sec. Christian Action, New Haven, 1951-52; founder, sr. fellow dir. Ctr. for Ethics and Social Policy, Berkeley, 1974-81, Trinity Ctr. for Ethics and Corp. Policy, N.Y.C., 1981-90. Author: When Gods Change: Hope for Theology, 1980, Management of Values, 1985, Fountainhead of Federalism, 1991, The Greatness of America: People, Promise, Dream, 1994, also others; co-author: Ethics in the Corporate Policy Process, 1975. Frederick Buechner: Novelist/Theologian of the Lost and Found., 1988, also tohers; contbr. over 150 articles to theol. jours., chpts. to books. Pres. coun. on Human Rels., Gainesville, Fla., 1956-59; chmn. (with M.L. King, Jr.) Mission to Miss., Jackson, 1961; mem. Robert Kennedy Campaign Com., Calif.,1 968. Lt. USN, 1943-46, 52-54. Recipient Univ. medal U. Pacific, 1988; Lilly fellow Duke U., 1958. Mem. Am. Acad. Religion, Soc. Christian Ethics (sect. chmn. 1987), Pacific Coast Theol. Soc. (chmn., sec. 1979-81), Polanyi Soc. (co-founder, Centennial lectr. 1991). Democrat. Avocations: tennis, golf, chess, reading. Home: 1191 Glen Ave Berkeley CA 94708 Office: Pan Pacific U 2362 Bancroft Way Berkeley CA 94704 E-mail: aenglert@psr.edu.

MCCOY, DOUGLAS MICHAEL, social services administrator, clergyman; b. Altadena, Calif., Jan. 29, 1945; s. Burton Douglas and Margaret Ellen (Ledbetter) McC.; m. Edna Catherine DeChambeau, Mar. 23, 1968; children: Douglas Arthur, Robert Carl, Lewis Aaron. AA, Sacramento City Coll., 1964; BA in Am. History, Literature, Univ. Calif., 1966; MDiv., Pacific Sch. Religion, 1969. Ordained elder Meth. Ch. Youth dir. First United Meth. Ch., Redwood City, Calif., 1967-68; assoc. pastor 1st United Meth. Ch., 1968-69; pastor Cmty. United Meth. Ch., Georgetown, Calif., 1969-71, Christ United Meth. Ch., Sacramento, 1971-73; assoc. pastor 1st United Meth. Ch., Reno, 1973-82; exec. dir. Kairos Outreach, Inc., 1982-88, Nome (Alaska) Cmty. Ctr., Inc., 1988-2000; pastor Susanville (Calif.) United Meth. Ch., 2000—. Founder, spiritual dir. Nev. Kairos Prison Ministry, Reno, 1981-87. Pres. No. Nev. Sponsoring Com., Reno, 1975-78, AGENET, 1998-99; pres. Planned Parenthood, Reno, 1981-85, Mental Health Adv. Com., Nome, 1988-91, Nome Visitor's Assn., 1990-94; chmn. Interagy. Child Advocates, Nome, 1988-91; mem. Action for Alaska Children, 1990-97; chmn. exec. com., Alaska Food Coalition, 1999-2000. Democrat. Office: Susanville United Meth Ch 70 S Lassen St Susanville CA 96130 E-mail: divenome@aol.com.

MCCOY, EDAIN, writer; b. South Bend, Ind., Aug. 11, 1957; d. Donald Byron Taylor, Billie Doralyn Mitchell; m. R. Wagoner (div.); m. M. Shapiro (div.). Bachelor of Arts, University of Texas, Austin and San Antonio, 1985—90. Stockbroker, finl. advisor various cos., Ind., 1992—2002. Author: (book) Witta, 1992, A Witch's Guide to Faery Folk, 1993, The Sabbats, 1994, How To Do Automatic Writing, Magick and Rituals of the Moon, 1994, Entering the Summerland, 1995, Mountain Magick, 1995, Celtic Myth and Magick, 1995, Making Magick for Witches and Pagans, 1996, Inside A Witches' Coven, 1997, Celtic Women's Spirituality, 1998, Bewitchments, 1999, Enchantments, 2001, Ostara, 2002, SpellWork for Covens, 2002; contbr. articles. Mem.: Ctrl. Ind. Profl. Writers (pres. 1996, media chair 1997), Authors Guild, Romance Writers Am., Clan Eieannach Wittan Tradition (elder 1996—), Clan Eiernnach Coven S. Tex. (priestess of Brighid 1987—). Avocations: reading, ballroom dancing, showing dogs, piano. Personal E-mail: edainmccoy@yahoo.com.

MCCOY, EILEEN CAREY, academic dean; b. Jersey City; d. James Bernard and Nan (Dalton) Carey; m. Thomas James McCoy (dec.); children: Thomas James III, Mary Eileen McCoy Whang. BA, Coll. St. Elizabeth, Convent Station, N.J., 1954; MA, Fairleigh Dickinson U., 1969, EdD, 1983; postgrad., Harvard U., 1985. Mem. faculty County Coll. Morris, Dover, N.J., 1970-75; dir. cmty. rels. Raritan Valley Community Coll., Somerville, 1977-79, dean continuing, community edn. and svcs., 1979-95; dean Evening Coll. and Extension Site, 1995-2000. Author: The Community Education Component of the Community College: New Jersey in Comparative Perspective, 1983. Mem. Morris County Bd. Freeholders, 1975-77, Branchburg Twp. Rep. Mcpl. Com., 1996—; founding chmn. Somerset County Commn. on Women, 1985-88; mem. adv. coun. Somerset County Office on Aging, 1987—; bd. dirs. Rolling Hills Girl Scout Coun., 1991-93, Irish Am. Pub. Action Com., 1993-, pres., 1994—; bd. advisors Somerset County United Way; mem. twp. com. Montgomery Twp., 1993-96, dep. mayor, 1994-95; bd. dirs. Edn. Found. Bridgewater-Raritan, 1993-2000; mem. Elizabeth Ministry Immaculate Conception Ch., Somerville, N.J., 1997—; bd. dirs. Montgomery Arts Coun., 1998-2000, pres., 1998, chmn. lecture com. 2000-2002. Recipient Righteous Gentile award Jewish Fedn. Somerset, Hunterdon and Warren Counties, 1989, Somerset County Tercentennial award, 1989, Woman of Achievement award Rolling Hills Girl Scout Coun., 1991, Irish Person of Yr., 2002. Mem. Nat. Coun. Continuing Edn. and Community Svc. (bd. dirs. and region rep. 1987-90, Person of Yr. region 2 1989), Greater Somerset County C. of C. (v.p. and bd. dirs. 1988-92, Outstanding Woman in Business and Industry 1982), Rotary (pres. Branchburg, N.J., club 1989-90), Raritan Valley Art Assn., N.J. Watercolor Soc., Inc., Garden State Watercolor Soc. (Juror's Merit award Third Annual Assoc. Member Juried Exhibn. 1999), Somerset Art Assn. (Art collector show 1999—), Montgomery Ctr. Arts, 1860 House (chmn. lecture com.). Republican. Roman Catholic.

MCCOY, EUGENE LYNN, civil engineer; b. Ridgefield, Wash., Apr. 9, 1926; s. Eugene Victor McCoy and Thelma Lucinda (Ayres) Martin; m. Marcia Helen Schear, Sept. 14, 1955 (div. 1974); children: Thomas Edwin, Susan Lynn, Molly Kay (dec.). AS, Lower Columbia Coll., 1948; BS, Wash. State U., 1950; MS, U. Wash., 1955. Registered profl. engr., Wash. Successively civil engr. soils, chief soils engr. sect., chief geotech. br. Portland (Oreg.) dist., chief geotech. br. North Pacific div. U.S. Army Corps. Engrs., 1955-85; staff cons. Shannon and Wilson, Portland, 1985-88, Cornforth Cons. Inc., Tigard, Oreg., 1988—. Tech. specialist delegation for design of Longtan Dam, U.S. Army Corps. Engrs., Beijing, 1981, People to People's delegation Dams and Tunnels, 1987. Contbr. articles to profl jours. Active camp com. Campfire Girls, 4-H Clubs, Oregon City; vol. Loaves and Fishes, Oreg. State U. Ext., AARP Tax Aid. Radio officer U.S. Merchant Marine, 1944-46; with U.S. Army, 1950-52. Mem. ASCE, U.S. Com. Large Dams, Oreg. Master Gardener. Democrat. Unitarian Universalist. Avocations: gardening, hiking, skiing, forestry. Home: 20551 S Fischers Mill Rd Oregon City OR 97045-9646 Office: Cornforth Cons Inc 10250 SW Greenburg Rd Ste 111 Portland OR 97223-5460 *Personal philosophy: To be an honest, caring, gentle person dedicated to caring for family, community and country.*

MCCOY, FREDERICK JOHN, retired plastic surgeon; b. McPherson, Kans., Jan. 17, 1916; s. Merle D. and Mae (Tennis) McC.; m. Mary Bock, May 17, 1972; children: Judith, Frederick John, Patricia, Melissa, Steven. BS, U. Kans., 1938, MD, 1942. Diplomate Am. Bd. Plastic Surgery (dir. 1973-79, chmn. 1979). Intern Lucas County Hosp., Toledo, 1942-43; resident in plastic surgery U. Tex. Med. Sch., Galveston, 1946; preceptorship in surgery Grand Rapids, Mich., 1947-50; practice medicine specializing in plastic and reconstructive surgery Kansas City, Mo., 1950-93; staff St. Mary's Hosp., 1950-83, St. Joseph's Hosp., 1950—, N. Kansas City Meml. Hosp., 1955—; mem. staff, chief plastic surgery Kansas City Gen. Hosp. and Med. Center, 1952-72, Children's Mercy Hosp., 1954-93, Research Hosp., 1950—, St. Luke's Hosp., 1951—, Baptist Hosp., 1958—, Menorah Hosp., 1950—; chief div. plastic surgery Truman Med. Ctr., 1972-91; chmn. maxillo-facial surgery U. Kansas City Sch. Dentistry, 1950-57; assoc. prof. surgery U. Mo. Med. Sch., Kansas City, 1964-69, clin. prof. surgery, 1969—; pres. McCoy Enterprises, Kansas City, Mo. Contbr. articles to, profl. jours.; editor: Year Book of Plastic and Reconstructive Surgery, 1971-88. Bd. govs. Kansas City Mus., 1959-93, pres., 1973-74. Served to maj. M.C. U.S. Army, 1943-46. Mem. ACS (pres. Mo. chpt. 1973), AMA, Am. Acad. Pediatrics, Am. Soc. Plastic and Reconstructive Surgeons (sec. 1969-73, dir. 1973-76, pres. 1976, chmn. bd. 1977, Spl. Achievement award 1988), Am. Soc. Pediat. Plastic Surgeons, Pan Pacific Surg. Soc., Singleton Surg. Soc. (v.p. 1965), Am. Assn. Plastic Surgeons (founder plastic surgery rsch. coun.), Internat. Soc. Aesthetic Plastic Surgery, Am. Soc. Aesthetic Plastic Surgery, Jackson County Med. Soc. (pres. 1964-65), Kansas City Southwest Clin. Soc. (pres. 1971), Mo. Med. Assn. (v.p. 1975), Internat. Coll. Surgeons (v.p. 1969), Royal Soc. Medicine (London), U. Tex. Sys. Chancellors Coun., Kansas City C. of C., Conservation Fedn. Mo., Natural Sci. Soc. (founder, chmn. 1973), Citizens Assn. Kansas City, Explorer's Club, Mission Hills Country Club, Boone and Crocket Club, Phi Delta Theta, Nu Sigma Nu. Republican. Mem. Christian Ch. Home: 5814 Mission Dr Shawnee Mission KS 66208-1139 Office: 801 W 47th St Ste 421 Kansas City MO 64112-1253

MCCOY, JAMES NEAL, II, accountant; b. L.A., Dec. 11, 1964; s. James Neal Sr. and Sandra Lee (Songer) McC.; m. Sydney VonSchriltz, Dec. 4, 1988; 1 child, James Neal III. BSBA in Acctg., Oreg. State U., 1987. Cert. mgmt. acct. Sr. acctg. coord. Champion Internat. Corp., Roseburg, Oreg., 1988-90, staff acct. Camden, Tex., 1990-91, sr. acct., 1991-92, acctg. mgr., 1992-94, regional ops. acctg. mgr., 1994-95, bus. unit ops. analyst Stamford, Conn., 1995—. Mem. Hoo-Hoo Internat. (treas. 1994-95). Avocations: computers, music, reading, skiing, hunting. Office: Champion Internat Corp One Champion Plz Stamford CT 06921 E-mail: mccoyj@champint.com.

MCCOY, JEANIE SHEARER, analytical chemist, consultant; b. Mancelona, Mich., May 27, 1921; d. Theophil R. and Goldie Margaret (Halladay) Schroeder; m. Theodore R. Shearer, June 14, 1958 (div. 1964); 1 child, Blair Barnett; m. George Altha McCoy, July 23, 1966. AA, North Pk. coll., 1941; BS, Northwestern U., 1944; MS, No. Ill. U., 1970. Jr. analytical chemist Buick Motor divsn. GM, Melrose Park, Ill., 1944-45; asst. rsch. chemist Hodson Oil Corp., Chgo., 1945-47; asst. analytical chemist Internat. Harvester Co., Melrose Park, 1947-49, analytical chemist, 1949-60, prin. chemist, 1960-74, supr. metal process control, 1974-82; cons. cutting fluid mgmt. divsn. JMT, Inc., Lombard, Ill., 1983—. Author: (monograph chpt.) Metalworking Fluids, 1993; editor: Lubrication Engring. Mag., 1979-2000. Fellow Soc. Tribologists and Lubrication Engrs. (Allan Mantafel award Chgo. sect. 1987, P.M. KU award, 1991, Internat. award 2000); mem. AAUW, Soc. Automotive Engrs., Am. Chem. Soc., Abrasive Engring. Soc., Soc. Mfg. Engrs. Avocations: shell and stamp collecting, fitness activities. Office: JMT Inc Cutting Fluid Mgmt Divsn 654 N West Rd Lombard IL 60148-1547 E-mail: j10mccoy@aol.com.

MCCOY, JERRY JACK, lawyer; b. Pitts., Aug. 4, 1941; s. Norris and Martha (Jack) McC.; m. Alexandra Armstrong; children: MadeleineRena, Allison Norah, Jonathan Howard. BS, W.Va. U., 1963; LLB, Duke U., 1966; LLM in Taxation, N.Y.U., 1967. Bar: D.C. 1968, N.Y. 1967. Assoc. Silverstein & Mullens, Washington, 1968-72, ptnr., 1973-92; of counsel Reid and Priest, N.Y.C., Washington, 1992-94; sole practitioner Washington, 1994—. Adj. law faculty U. Miami, Fla., 1983—, Law Ctr. Georgetown U., 1996—. Co-author: Family Foundation Handbook, 2001; exec. editor Tax Management, Estates Gifts and Trusts series, Washington, 1972—92, co-founder, co-editor Charitable Gift Planning News, Dallas, 1983—, Family Foundation Advisor, 2002; contbr. Mem. ABA, Am. Law Inst., Am. Coll. Trust and Estate Counsel (chair com. on charitable planning and exempt orgns.), Am. Coll. Tax Counsel. Democrat. Jewish. Home: 3560 Winfield Ln NW Washington DC 20007-2368 Office: PO Box 66491 Washington DC 20035-6491

MCCOY, JOHN BONNET, retired banker; b. Columbus, Ohio, June 11, 1943; s. John Gardner and Jeanne Newlove (Bonnet) McC.; m. Jane Deborah Taylor, Apr. 21, 1968; children: Tracy Bonnet, Paige Taylor, John Taylor. BA, Williams Coll., 1965; MBA, Stanford U., 1967; LLD (hon.), Williams Coll., 1991; D of Bus. Adminstrn. (hon.), Ohio State U., 1993; LLD (hon.), Kenyon Coll., 1994. With Banc One Corp., Columbus NA, Columbus, Ohio, 1970—, banking officer, 1970-73, v.p., 1973-77, pres., 1977-83; pres., COO Banc One Corp., 1983-84, pres., CEO, 1984-87, chmn., CEO, 1987-99, also bd. dirs., now chmn., CEO Chgo., 1999. Pres., COO Banc One Corp., Columbus, Ohio, 1983-84, pres., CEO, 1984-87, chmn. CEO, 1987—, also bd. dirs.; pres. Bank One Trust Co., 1979-81; bd. dirs. Cardinal Health, Inc., Fed. Nat. Mortgage Assn., Ameritech Corp., Tenneco Inc.; fed. adv. coun. Fed. Res. Sys., 1991-93. Active Boy Scouts Am.; trustee, chmn. bd. dirs. Kenyon Coll.; trustee Stanford U., Battelle Meml. Inst.; bd. dirs. Sr. PGA Tour; pres. Columbus Area Growth Found.; chmn. Capitol South Urban Redevel. Corp. Capt. USAF, 1967-70. Recipient Ernest C. Arbuckle award Stanford U., 1994. Mem. Columbus C. of C. (past chmn., trustee), Am. Bankers Assn., Bankers Roundtable (bd. dirs. 1989-94), Assn. Bank Holding Cos., Young Pres. Orgn. (chmn. Columbus chpt. 1982-83), Cypress Point Club, Seminole Golf Club, Links Club N.Y.C. Episcopalian. Office: Banc One Corp 1st National Plz Ste 0895 Chicago IL 60670-0001

MCCOY, JOHN DENNY, artist; b. Columbus, Ohio, Dec. 13, 1945; s. Robert William and Dorothy Louise (Denny) McC.; children: Melinda Rene, Nathan Robert. Cert. of Grad., Columbus Coll. Art and Design, 1967; MFA, Washington U., St. Louis, 1969. Instr. Columbus Coll. Art and Design, 1969-73; program dir. Presidio of Monterey, Calif., 1975-78; gallery dir. Richard Danskin Gallery, Carmel, 1978-79, Bleich Gallery West, Carmel, 1979-80. One person shows include: Brunswick Gallery, Columbus, 1973, Seaside (Calif.) City Hall, 1978, Bleich Gallery, Carmel, 1980, Angles Gallery, Santa Monica, Calif., 1987, Hagger Gallery, Dallas, 1999, Flatbed Gallery, Austin, Tex., 2000; exhibited in group shows at Columbus Mus. Art, 1965, Laclede Town Gallery, St. Louis, 1967, Merton Boyd Gallery, Columbus, 1970, Changing Scene Gallery, 1971, 72, Gallery Five, Columbus, 1972, Monterey Peninsula Mus. Art, 1976, 77, Angles Gallery, Santa Monica, 1989, Richard/Bennett Gallery, L.A., 1991, Arlington Mus. Art, 1998, Meridian Internat. Ctr., Washington, Vietnam, China, Singapore, Indonesia, 1999-2000, Haggerty Gallery, Dallas, 2000. Columbus Coll. Art and Design scholar, 1963; Ford Found. grantee, 1966; Washington U. fellow, 1968, 69. Home: 4606 Ave C Austin TX 78751-3026

MCCOY, JOHN JOSEPH, lawyer; b. Cin., Mar. 15, 1952; s. Raymond F. and Margaret T. (Hohmann) McC. BS in Math. summa cum laude, Xavier U., 1974; JD, U. Chgo., 1977. Bar: Ohio 1977, D.C. 1980. Ptnr. Taft, Stettinius & Hollister, Cin., 1977—. Lectr. Greater Cin. C. of C., 1984. Pro bono rep. Jr. Achievement Greater Cin., 1978; fund raiser Dan Beard coun. Boy Scouts Am., 1983; fund raising team leader Cin. Regatta, Cin. Ctr. Devel. Disorders, 1983; account mgr. United Appeal, Cin., 1984; mem. green areas trust adv. com. Village of Indian Hill, 1994-98. Mem. ABA, Ohio State Bar Assn. (banking, comml. and bankruptcy law com., corp. law com., fed. ct. practice com.), Cin. Bar Assn. (fed. cts., common pleas cts. and negligence law coms., trustee Vol. Lawyers for the Poor Found. 1994—, chmn. 1996-97), Cin. Inn. of Ct. (barrister 1984-86), Cin. Athletic Club (pres. bd. trustees 1986-89, nominating com. 1989—), Rhodesian Ridgeback Club of the U.S. (bd. dirs. 2000—).

MCCOY, LEE BERARD, paint company executive; b. Ipswich, Mass., July 27, 1925; d. Damase Joseph and Robena Myrtle (Bruce) B.; student U. Ala., Mobile, 1958-60; m. Walter Vincent de Paul McCoy, Sept. 27, 1943; children: Bernadette, Raymond, Joan, Richard. Owner, Lee's Letter Shop, Hicksville, L.I., N.Y., 1950-56; mgr. sales adminstrn. Basila Mfg. Co., Mobile, Ala., 1957-61; promotion mgr., buyer Mobile Paint Co., Inc., Theodore, Ala., 1961-2002; owner Lee McCoy Comms., 2002—. Curator, Shepard Meml. Libr., 1972—; bd. dirs. Monterey Tour House, Mobile, 1972-78, Old Dauphin Way Assn., 1977-79, Friends of Mus., Mobile, 1978—, Miss Wheelchair Ala., 1980—; del. Civic Roundtable, 1977-78, bd. dirs., 1980-81, 1st v.p., 1980-81, pres., 1981-82; pres.'s Com. Employment of Handicapped, 1981—; chmn. Mobile, Nat. Yr. Disabled Persons, 1982; chmn. Mobile, Internat. Decade Disabled Persons, 1983—; mem. Nat. Project Adv. Bd., 1983—, Nat. Community Adv. Bd., 1983—, World Com. for Decade of Disabled Persons, 1983—; v.p. Bristol Sister City Soc.; active Mobile Area Retarded Citizens, Am. Heart Assn.; mem. City of Mobile Cultural Enrichment Task Force, 1985—, lifetime mem., Internatl. Fellowship; Mobile United Recreation and Culture Com.; deputy dir. General; dir. Culture Mobile, 1986—; v.p., bd. dirs. Joe Jefferson Players, 1986; co-chmn. Brit. Faire, 1983; chmn. Mobile Expo, 1990, Culture & Recreation Com. Mobile United, 1989, steering com., 1990. Recipient Honor award Civic Roundtable, 1979, 80; Service award Women's Com. of Spain Rehab. Center, State of Ala., 1980; award Nat. Orgn. on Disability, 1983, Gayfer's Outstanding Career Woman award, 1988; Golden Rule award JC Penney, 1993. Mem. Spectromatic Assos., Nat. Paint Distbrs., Hist. Preservation Soc., Color Mktg. Group, English Speaking Union (v.p., pres. 1992, 94, 95, 96, 97), U.S. C. of C. (chmn. local cultural enrichment task force 1986), Toastmasters (pres. 1995-96, area gov. 1997), The Nat. Mus. of Women of the Arts, Washington (charter), Internat. Platform Assn. Methodist. Republican. Clubs: Quota (charter mem. Mobile chpt., dir. 1977—, pres. 1978-80, chmn. numerous coms., recipient Service award Dist. 8, 1979, Internat. award for serving club objectives, 1980, editor Care-Gram, Weekly newsletter for nursing homes 1980—), Bienville; writer 10 books; lectr., worldwide traveler.

MCCOY, LINDA KORTEWEG, audio-visual specialist; b. Passaic, N.J., Oct. 12, 1948; d. Christian Adrian and Irene (Morse) Korteweg; m. Rudolph William, Aug. 1, 1970; children: Jill Ann, Lori Lynn. BA in Math. Edn., William Paterson, 1970, BA in Acctg., 1987, MA in Ednl. Media, 1993. Cert. math. tchr. grades 7-12, media specialist grades K-12, supr., N.J. Math. tchr. Woodrow Wilson Middle Sch., Clifton, N.J., 1970-71; media specialist Schs. 5, 11, 13, 1971-78, Schs. 2, 5, Clifton, 1984-93, Clifton H.S., 1993-2000, network coord., 2000—01; dist. supt. media svcs. K-12 Clifton Pub. Schs., 2002—. Webmaster, Clifton Pub. Sch. Dist., 1998—; adj. math. tchr. Tombrock Coll., West Paterson, N.J., 1970-72; adv. bd. Grove Hill Nursery Sch., Clifton, 1984-86; tchr's adv. bd. Clifton Bd. Edn., 1992-93. Treas. Advs. for Quality Edn., Clifton, 1990-93; exec. bd. Clifton (N.J.) Concert Choir Parents, 1992-96; mem. Middlestates Evaluation Com., 1995; chair Task Force for Coll. Preparation, 1996-97, tech. com. dist., 1995—, youth week advisor, 1996-2001; tchr. internet training Passaic County Ednl. Tech. Tng. Ctr., 1998-99; trustee Clifton Pub. Libr., 2000—. Recipient NSF computer study grant St. Peter's Coll., 1970-71, tel cable grant for tech. study at Sparkman Ctr., Colo., Internet Access for H.S. Media Ctrs. grant, 1995, N.J. Gov.'s Tchr. Recognition award N.J. State Bd. Edn., Trenton, 1992, Project NEAT (Internet) grant, 1998. Mem. NEA, Nat. Assn. Ednl. Tech. Specialists, N.J. Edn. Assn., Clifton Suprs.' Assn., N.J. Prins. and Suprs. Assn., N.J. Libr. Assn., Ednl. Media Assn. N.J., Assn. for Ednl. Comm. and Tech., N.J. Assn. Ednl. Technology, Pi Lambda Theta, Kappa Delta Pi. Avocations: computers, sewing. Home: 82 Mountainside Ter Clifton NJ 07013-1177 Office: Clifton High Sch 333 Colfax Ave Clifton NJ 07013-1701 E-mail: webspinner@eudoramail.com., llmccoy@cybernex.net.

MCCOY, LOIS CLARK, emergency services professional, retired county official, magazine editor; b. New Haven, Oct. 1, 1920; m. Herbert Irving McCoy, Oct. 17, 1943; children: Whitney, Kevin, Marianne, Tori, Debra, Sally, Daniel. BS, Skidmore Coll., 1942; student, Nat. Search and Rescue Sch., 1974. Asst. buyer R.H. Macy & Co., N.Y.C., 1942-44, assoc. buyer, 1944-48; instr. Mountain Medicine & Survival, U. Calif., San Diego, 1973-74; cons. editor Search & Rescue Mag., 1975, Rescue Mag., 1988-97, editor, 1992-94, Press On Newsletter, 1992—. Coord. San Diego Mountain Rescue Team, La Jolla, Calif., 1973-75; exec. sec. Nat. Assn. for Search and Rescue, Inc., Nashville, La Jolla, 1975-80, comptr., 1980-82; disaster officer San Diego County, 1980-86, Santa Barbara County, 1985-91, ret.; pres. Nat. Inst. Urban Search & Rescue, Inc., 1987—. Author: Search and Rescue Glossary, 1974; contbr. editor Rescue Mag., 1989-97; editor-in-chief Response! mag., 1982-86; editor Press On! Electronic mag., 1994—; mem. adv. bd. Hazard Monthly, 1991-99; contbr. articles to profl. jours. Cons. law enforcement divsn. Calif. Office Emergency Svcs., 1976-77; pres. San Diego Com. for L.A. Philharm. Orch., 1957-58; bd. dirs. Search and Rescue of the Californias, 1976-77, Nat. Assn. for Search and Rescue, Inc., 1980-87, pres., 1985-87, trustee, 1987-90, mem. Calif. OES strategic com., 1992-96; CEO Nat. Inst. for Urban Search, 1989—; mem. Gov.'s Task Force on Earthquakes, 1981-82, Earthquake Preparedness Task Force, Seismic Safety Commn., 1982-85. Recipient Hall Foss award for outstanding svc. to search and rescue, 1982, Diamond Safety award for outstanding work in emergency svcs., 1996. Mem. IEEE, Armed Froces Comm. and Electronics Assoc., Nat. Assn. for Search and Rescue (life, Svc. award 1985), San Diego Mountain Rescue Team (hon. life), Santa Barbara Amateur Radio Club. Episcopalian. Office: PO Box 91648 Santa Barbara CA 93190-1648 E-mail: niusr@ix.netcom.com.

MCCOY, MARILYN, university official; b. Providence, Mar. 18, 1948; d. James Francis and Eleanor (Regan) McC.; m. Charles R. Thomas, Jan. 28, 1983. BA in Econs. cum laude, Smith Coll., 1970; M in Pub. Policy, U. Mich., 1972. Dir. Nat. Ctr. for Higher Edn. Mgmt. Systems, Boulder, Colo., 1972-80; dir. planning and policy devel. U. Colo., 1981-85; v.p. adminstrn. and planning Northwestern U., Evanston, Ill., 1985—. Trustee One Group Funds. Co-author: Financing Higher Education in the Fifty States, 1976, 3d edit., 1982. Bd. dirs. Evanston Northwestern HealthCare, 1988—, Mather Found., 1995—. Mem. Am. Assn. for Higher Edn., Soc. for Coll. and Univ. Planning (pres., v.p., sec., bd. dirs. 1980—), Assn. for Instnl. Rsch. (pres., v.p., exec. com., publs. bd. 1978-87), Chgo. Network (chmn. 1992-93), Chgo. Econ. Club. Home: 1100 N Lake Shore Dr Chicago IL 60611-1070 Office: Northwestern U 633 Clark St Evanston IL 60208-0001

MCCOY, MARY ANN, state official; b. Duluth, Minn., Oct. 13, 1924; d. Homer Burke and Avis (Woodworth) Hursh; m. Charles Ramon McCoy, June 11, 1949; children: Jeffrey, Mary, Jeremy. BA, Grinnell Coll., 1946; postgrad., Laval U., 1946, Mankato State U., 1964-65. Cert. neutral mediator Minn. Supreme Ct. 1996—. Exec. trainee Younkers, Inc., Des Moines, 1946; advt. copywriter Des Moines Register & Tribune, 1947; field dir. Duluth (Minn.) Girl Scout Coun., 1947-49; with merchandising dept. Dayton's Inc., Mpls., 1966-75; dir. election and legis. manual divsn. Office of Sec. of State of Minn., St. Paul, 1975-81; exec. dir. Minn. State Ethical Practices Bd., 1981-95, cons., 1996—. Mem. Minn. Supreme Ct. Bd. for Continuing Legal Edn., 1981-87; sec. State Rev. Bd. for Nominations to Nat. Register, 1976-89. Editor Minn. Legis. Manual, 1975-81. Mem. Minn. Hist. Soc. (life, hon. coun., exec. coun. 1972-81, 82-90), Coun. on Govt. Ethics Laws (steering com. 1986-89, treas. 1987-88, hon. life), Minn. Assn. Pub. Adminstrs., Am. Judicature Soc., Internat. Assn. Facilitators, Women Historians of Midwest, Am. Assn. State and Local History. E-mail: mamccoy@juno.com.

MCCOY, PATRICIA A. clinical special educator, writer, art and culture critic; b. Seattle, Dec. 20, 1951; d. Robert Wilson and Barbara (Foss) McC. BS, U. Nev., 1974; MA, NYU, 1983; postgrad. in psychoanalysis, Ctr. for Modern Psychoanalytic, Studies, N.Y.; postgrad. in applied linguistics, NYU. Lectr. in English CUNY, N.Y.C., 1984-88, John Jay Coll. of Criminal Justice, N.Y.C., 1988-91; clin. educator August Aichhorn Resdl. Treatment Ctr., 1991-93, St. Vincent's Hosp. Psychiatry Inpatient, N.Y.C., 1993-95; with spl. edn. dist. 75 N.Y.C. Bd. Edn., 1995—. Lectr. contemporary art New Arts Program and others, east coast, 1991—; ind. curator, 1987—; instr. NYU. Editor: N.A.P. Texts jour., 1993—; contbr. Grantee N.Y. State Found. for the Arts, 1987, Pa. Coun. for the Arts, 1991, Mid-Atlantic, 1991, Nat. Endowment for the Arts, 1992, Pew Charitable Trust, 1993. Mem. Nat. Soc. Modern Psychoanalysts, Assn. Internat. des Critiques d'Art, Am. Orthopsychiatric Assn., N.Y. State Coun. Humanities.

MCCOY, REAGAN SCOTT, oil company executive, lawyer; b. Port Arthur, Tex., Nov. 25, 1945; s. William Murray and Elizabeth (Gilbert) McC.; m. Pat Kowalski, June 21, 1969; 1 child, Traci. BCE, Ga. Inst. Tech., 1968; JD, Loyola U., 1972. Bar: Tex. 1972, La. 1978; registered profl. engr., Tex., La. Structural engr. McDermott Inc., New Orleans, 1966-72, data processing mgr. London, 1972-76, cons. engr. New Orleans, 1976-79; adminstrv. mgr. Concord Oil Co., San Antonio, 1979-81, v.p., 1981—. Mem. World Affairs Coun., Tex. Luth. U. Bus. Sch. Adv. Com. Treas. Countryside San Pedro Recreation Club, 1981-82; bd. dirs. Countryside San Pedro Homeowners Assn., 1984-86; v.p. Bluffview Homeowners Assn., 1998-99, pres., 1999—; pres. San Antonio Baylor U. Parents League, 1995-96; mem. Tex. State Bd. Pub. Accountancy, 1997—; bd. dirs. Consumer Credit Counseling Svc. Greater San Antonio, 2000—. Fellow Tau Beta Pi; mem. ABA, NSPE, ASCE, Am. Assn. Profl. Landmen (San Antonio chpt. treas. 1990-91, v.p. 1991-93, pres. 1993-94), La. State Bar Assn., Tex. State Bar, San Antonio Bar Assn. (natural resources com. treas. 1986-87, vice chmn. 1987-88, chmn. 1988-89), Tex. Soc. Profl. Engrs., La. Soc. Profl. Engrs., So. Tex. Assn. Divsn. Order Analysts (v.p. 1993, pres. 1994, 98, bd. dirs. 1999—), Fin Execs. Inst. (treas. 1991-92, sec. 1992-93, v.p. 1993-94, pres. 1994-95, bd. dirs. 1995-97), Soc. Mining Engrs., Real Estate Fin. Soc. (bd. dirs. 1986-89, v.p. 1987-88, pres. 1988-89, 98-2000, pres. coun.), Adminstrv. Mgmt. Soc. (pres. 1985-86, 89-90), Plz. Club, Sonterra Club, Tex. Ind. Producers and Royalty Owners Assn., Am. Petroleum Inst. (South Tex. chpt. pres. 1997-2000). Presbyterian. Avocations: water sports, reading, woodworking. Home: 14103 Bluff Manor Dr San Antonio TX 78216-7976 Office: Concord Oil Co 105 S Saint Marys St Ste 1500 San Antonio TX 78205-2898

MCCOY, STUART SHERMAN, manufacturing executive; b. Little Rock, Dec. 16, 1958; s. Gene Guy and Idella Maria Theresa (Brown) McC.; m. Juliet Kathryn Goens, Sept. 9, 1977 (div. Apr. 1986); children: Ashley Nicole, Christopher Sean. Student, U. Ark., Little Rock, 1976, 78. Various positions Ad Craft Ark., Inc., Little Rock, 1976-80, prodn. supr., 1980-82, v.p. prodn., 1982-86, v.p. ops., 1986-93, exec. v.p., 1993—. Bd. dirs. Subiaco Acad. Alumni Assn. Photojournalist. Team mgr. Red Elk Motorsports, 1990-93, pres., 1991—; v.p. Ark. Dirt Riders, 1991-92, pres., 1992-93. Mem. Am. Advt. Fedn. (10th dist Addy award com. 1989-96, 10th dist. student competition com. 1994—, Nat. Addy com., 1994-96, constrn. and bylaws com. 1991—), Screen Print Assn. Internat., Ark. Advt. Fedn. (bd. dirs. 1992—), Jaycees (state dist. bd. dirs. Ark. chpt. 1983, state bd. dirs. pub. rels. com. 1984-85), Masons., Sabiaco Acad. Alumni Assn. (bd. dirs. 1991-95). Republican. Episcopalian. Avocations: sports, computers, photography, writing short stories, camping, hunting, motorcycle riding. Home: 11940 Southridge Dr Little Rock AR 72212-1740 Office: Ad Craft Ark Inc 1122 W 3rd St Little Rock AR 72201-2008

MCCOY, SUE, surgeon, biochemist; b. Charlottesville, Va., Nov. 14, 1935; d. Hulburt Christopher and Evelyn (Savage) McC. AB, Radcliffe Coll., 1957; PhD, Johns Hopkins U., 1964; MD, U. Va., 1980, postgrad., 2001—. Diplomate Am. Bd. Surgery. Fellow in physiol. chemistry Johns Hopkins U., Balt., 1964-67; asst. prof. chemistry U. South Fla., Tampa, 1967-69; asst. prof. orthopedics U. Va., Charlottesville, 1969-73, asst. prof. surgery, 1973-78; resident in surgery Hosp. U. Pa., Phila., 1980-83; resident in surgery Cooper Hosp. Rutgers U. Med. Sch., Camden, N.J., 1983-85, asst. prof. surgery, 1985-86, East Tenn. State U., Johnson City, 1986-91, assoc. prof., 1991-2000, prof., 2000—01. Mem. ACS, Am. Chem. Soc., N.Y. Acad. Sci., Royal Soc. Chemistry, Assn. for Acad. Surgery, Shock Soc., Internat. Soc. Oxygen Transport to Tissue, Am. Fedn. Clin. Rsch., Tenn. Med. Assn., Southeastern Surg. Congress, Assn. for Surg. Edn., Assn. for Women Surgeons, Tenn. Geriatric Assn., Am. Soc. for Parenteral and Enteral Nutrition, Sigma Xi. Achievements include research in hemorrhagic shock, aging, oxygen transport. Home: 8658 Batesville Rd Afton VA 22920

MC COY, TIDAL WINDHAM, former government official; b. Gainesville, Fla., Apr. 25, 1945; Grad., U.S. Mil. Acad., 1967; MA in Bus. Fin, George Washington U., 1975. Officer U.S. Army, 1967-72; mem. long-range planning and net assessment group Office of Sec. Def., Washington, 1972-73; mem. staff Nat. Security Council, 1973; staff asst. and then dep. asst. to Sec. Def., 1973-77; sci. asst. to asst. sec. for research, engring. and systems Dept. Navy, 1977-78; dir. policy research, office of under sec. for policy Dept. Def., 1978-79; asst. for nat. security affairs to Sen. Jake Garn, 1979-81; asst. sec. for manpower, res. affairs and installations Dept. Air Force, Washington, 1981-87; asst. sec. for readiness support USAF, 1987-88, acting sec. and undersec., 1981-88; sr. assoc. Hecht, Spencer & Assocs., 1988-89; v.p. govt. rels. Thiokol Corp., 1989—2002. Chmn. Washington Capital Ptnrs., 1998—. Recipient DOD Outstanding Civil Svc. medal, USAF Exceptional Civilian Svc. medal. Mem. Space Transp. Assn. U.S.A. (dir., chmn. 1996—), Def. Forum Found. (vice-chmn.).

MCCOY, WESLEY LAWRENCE, musician, conductor, educator; b. Memphis, Jan. 27, 1935; s. Harlan Eftin and Gladys (Coggin) McC.; m. Carolyn June Noble, Aug. 26, 1960; children: Jill Laurene McCoy Kurtz, Scott Edward. B.Music Edn., La. State U., 1957, PhD, 1970; M of Music Edn, U. Louisville, 1958; M Sacred Music, So. Bapt. Theol. Sem., 1960. Minister of music Beechmont Bapt. Ch., Louisville, 1959-62; also instr. music So. Bapt. Theol. Sem.; asst. prof. music, dir. bands Carson Newman Coll., Jefferson City, Tenn., 1962-67; asst. prof. music U. S.C., Columbia, 1969-72; asso. prof. music U. Ark., Little Rock, 1972-77, prof., 1977-80, asst. dean for public service Coll. Fine Arts, 1978-79; condr. Wind Ensemble, River City Community Band, 1972-80, Oklahoma City Youth Symphony, 1985-89; chmn. dept. music Phillips U., Enid, Okla., 1980-82, chmn. fine arts div., 1982-84. Minister music 1st United Meth. Ch., Edmond, Okla., 1983-00; owner Carlson Wagonlit Travel, Oklahoma City. French horn player, Knoxville (Tenn.) Symphony Orch., 1962-67, Columbia Philharm. Orch., 1969-72, Ark. Symphony Orch., 1972-80, Enid-Phillips Symphony, 1980-84; contbr. to Ch. Musician, 1974-76, 85-86 Co-chmn. Jefferson County (Tenn.) Com. for Goldwater for Pres., 1962; mem. Pulaski County (Ark.) Republican Com., 1977-81; mem. Oklahoma County Rep. xec. Com., 1995-97; pres. Ctrl. Okla. LSU Alumni, 1997-98. Mem. S.C. Music Educators Assn. (pres. coll. div. 1971-73), Ark. Music Edn. Assn. (chmn. rsch. 1975-80), Phi Mu Alpha, Pi Kappa Lambda, Phi Delta Kappa, Alpha Tau Omega. Republican. Baptist. Home: PO Box 16391 Oklahoma City OK 73113-2391 Office: 447 SW 59th St Oklahoma City OK 73139 E-mail: wesleymccoy@yahoo.com.

MCCOY, WILLIAM EARL, JR. economic development training consultant; b. Grand Rapids, Mich., Nov. 19, 1953; s. William Earl and Evelyn (Duke) McC.; m. Allene Denise Garrett, Aug. 20, 1977; children: Erin Nicole, Shannon Michele. BA, Alma Coll., 1975; MPA, Am. U., 1977; CID/CED, Am. Econ. Devel. Coun., 1989. Cert. indsl. and econ. developer; cert. violence interruption educator. Dep. city mgr. City of Benton Harbor, Mich., 1977-79; resident fellow Acad. Contemporary Problems, Columbus, Ohio, 1979-82; country dir. Peace Corps, Maseru, Lesotho, 1982-84, spl. asst. to Africa region dir. Washington, 1984-85; pres. The McCoy Co., Columbus, 1985—; v.p. Econ. Devel. Council, Lima, Ohio, 1986-89; project dir. Columbus Found., 1989-91; planning, econ. devel., and tng. cons. in pvt. practice Columbus, 1985—; instr. Phoenix Coll. and South Mountain C.C., 1996—. Cons. on rsch. Joint Ctr. Polit. Studies, Washington, 1976-77; cons. on small cities Nat. League Cities, Washington, 1978; cons. on urban affairs Ohio State U., Columbus, 1980-81; strategic planning, econ. devel. and tng. cons. City of Dayton, Ohio, 1985—, City of Lima, City of Kettering, Montgomery County, Ohio Commn. on Minority Health, Dayton Pub. Schs., Nat. Black Programming Consortium, Nat. Coun. Black Studies, Nat. Urban Policy Inst., Ctr. for Violence Interruption, Ohio Dept. Alcohol and Drug Addiction Svcs., Ohio Dept. Health, Nat. Women's Resource Ctr., NFL, others. Co-author: Managing Fiscal Retrenchment in Cities, 1980, Housing Problems of Black Mayor Cities, Planning Needs of Small Cities, Black Crime: A Police View. Dir. city drive United Way, Benton Harbor, 1978, Godman Guild, Columbus, 1980, ARC, Lima, 1987, Coun. for Arts Greater Lima, Lima Area Food Bank, 1988; chmn. bd. Lima-Allen County Full Employment Commn.; mem. fin. roundtable U.S. Econ. Devel. Adminstrn., Washington, 1980; mem. econ. devel. com. City of Lima, 1989; mem. Coun. on Urban Econ. Devel. Recipient Econ. Devel. Excellence award Ohio Devel. Assn., 1988, Jobs for Columbus Grads., 1991, PHA Cmtys. United, 1995. Mem. Am. Econ. Devel. Coun., Am. Soc. Pub. Affairs and Adminstrn., Nat. Bus. League, Internat. Traders, Internat. Downtown Assn., Am. Entrepreneurs Assn., Internat. City Mgmt. Assn., Nat. Main St. Network, Rotary, Pi Alpha Alpha. Home: 12 Westerville Sq Westerville OH 43081-2919 Office: The McCoy Co 5918 Sharon Woods Blvd Ste 200 Columbus OH 43229-2665

MCCOY, WILLIAM KEITH, library director; b. Cambridge, Mass., Jan. 17, 1954; s. William Charles McCoy and Irene Medeiros; ptnr. Brian Axness Shaw. AB, Harvard U., 1976; MLS, Drexel U., 1978. Ordained deacon Episcopal Ch., 1985. Libr. E. Brunswick (N.J.) Pub. Libr., 1978-81; prin. libr. Plainfield (N.J.) Pub. Libr., 1981-85; dir. Dowdell Libr., S. Amboy, N.J.,

1985-93, Rahway (N.J.) Pub. Libr., 1993-2000, Roselle (N.J.) Pub. Libr., 2000—. Pres. LINX/INFOLINK, Piscataway, N.J., 1989-92, 94. Author: Mission at Harvard Lawn, 1981, (monograph) Deacon as Para-Cleric, 1998; contbr. articles to profl. jours. Deacon Christ Episcopal Ch., New Brunswick, N.J., 1985-87, Grace Episcopal Ch., Plainfield, 1987-2000; sec. Plainfield Symphony Soc., 1994-97, pres., 1998—. Mem. ALA, N. Am. Assn. Diaconate (chair guidelines com. 1995—), N.J. Libr. Assn. (chair pub. rels. com. 1999-2001—), Diocese N.J. (chair com. on diaconate 1994—), Kwanis Club (treas. 1998—). Democrat. Episcopalian. Avocation: postcard collector. Office: Roselle Pub Libr 1175 Saint Georges Ave Roselle NJ 07203-2631 Home: 266 Horizon Dr Edison NJ 08817-5771 E-mail: keithmccoy12@home.com.

MCCOY, WILLIAM ULYSSES, journalist; b. Earle, Ark., May 19, 1921; s. Samuel David and Carrie Mabel (Hinson) McC.; m. Janice King, Jan. 23, 1943; 1 child, William Mark. BA, Ark. State Coll., 1942. Feature writer Western News Svc., Amarillo, Tex., 1946; news editor, writer Memphis Democrat, Memphis, 1946-47; reporter Pampa (Tex.) Daily News, 1947-48; state editor, writer Amarillo Times, Amarillo, Tex., 1948-51; writer, editor The Daily Oklahoman, Oklahoma City, 1955-81; writer national magazines, 1941—. Author: Performing and Visual Arts, 1992; author short stories; contbr. articles to profl. jours. Bd. dirs. Chamber Mus. in Okla, 1982—, Arts at St. Luke's, Oklahoma City, 1995—. Avocations: choir singer, orchestral violinist. Home: 200 S Lexington Way Edmond OK 73003-4222

MCCRACKEN, ANTHONY VEKONY, SR. land use planner, environmental scientist; b. N.Y.C., Apr. 9, 1953; m. Barbara McCracken; children: Anthony Jr., Brian. BS in Environ. Sci., Rutgers U., 1979. Lic. profl. planner, N.J. Adminstrv. planner Somerset County Planning Divsn., Somerville, N.J., 1982—; pres. N.J. sect. Am. Water Resource Assn., 1988-90. Mem. various state bds. and commns., N.J. Mem. Am. Inst. Cert. Planners (cert.), Am. Planning Assn., Nat. Assn. Environ. Profls. Avocations: golf, travel, family. Office: Somerset County Planning Divsn 20 Grove St Somerville NJ 08876

MCCRACKEN, CARON FRANCIS, computer company executive, consultant; b. Detroit, Jan. 12, 1951; d. WIlliam Joseph and Constance Irene (Kramer) McC. AS, Mott C.C., 1971; BS, Ctrl. Mich. U., 1973; MA, U. Mich., 1978; postgrad., Wayne State U., 1979-81, 93—. Tchr. Elkton, Pigeon, Bayport (Mich.) High Sch., 1973-74, Davison (Mich.) Jr. High Sch., 1974-75; instr. Mott C.C., Flint, Mich., 1974-78; planning and rsch. specialist Flint Police Dept., 1977-79; campus coord., programmer Systems & Computer Tech. Corp., Detroit, 1981-82, acad. specialist computing systems, 1982-83, mgr. acad. computing systems, 1983-84, mgr. adminstrv. computing systems, 1984-85; communications analyst Fruehauf Corp., 1985-86, sr. comms. analyst, 1986-87; account cons. US Sprint Communications Co., 1987-89; account mgr. US Sprint Communications Corp., 1989-90; sr. mgr. Technology Specialists, Inc., Phila., 1990-91, Digital Mgmt. Group, Detroit, 1991—92; sr. cons. info. tech. practice, tech. delivery svcs. PriceWaterhouseCoopers LLP, 1992—. Adv. bd. CONTEL Bus. Networks, Atlanta, 1987. Contbr. articles to profl. jours. Vol. charitable and homeless orgns. including Coalition on Temporary Shelter, Core Cities, Paint the Town; undergrad. computer lab. cons., student mgr. computer sci. dept. Wayne State U., 1993-95, vol. computer cons. Bus. Sch., 1997-98; vol. tech. advisor on 1992 elections project City of Detroit; vol. St. Joseph's Mercy Hosp., Pontiac, Mich., 1995; chair of bd., pres., treas. Bloomfield Hills Condominium Assn., 1996-98; vol. Pub. TV WTVS, Detroit, 1996-99, vol., Pub. Radio Sta. WDET, Detroit, 1996-98; elected precinct del., 2002-. Named to Beta Gamma Sigma MBA Hon. Soc., 2001. Mem.: Detroit Zool. Soc., Detroit Inst. Arts, Assn. Computing Machinery, Data Processing Mgmt. Assn., Alumni Assn. Wayne State U., Smithsonian Instn. (assoc.), Alumni Assn. U. Mich., Adventure Cycling Assn. (Missoula, Mont.), Women's Econ. Club of Met. Detroit (fin. com. 1999), Beta Gamma Sigma. Avocations: reading, athletics, personal research, international travel. Home: 100 W Hickory Grove H4 Bloomfield Hills MI 48304-2169 Office: PriceWaterhouseCoopers LLP 400 Renaissance Ctr Ste 780 Detroit MI 48243-1501

MCCRACKEN, INA, business executive; b. Highland Park, Mich., Oct. 7, 1939; d. James Howard and Lodaskia (Smoot) Smith; children: Michalene, Colet, Paulet, Pauleta. BA, Mich. State U., 1961, MEd, 1980; Edn. Specialist cert., Wayne State U., 1982, EdD, 1994. Cert. tchr., adminstr., supt., Mich. Pres. Career Mgmt. Systems, Inc., Detroit; instr. Highland Park Bd. Edn. Bus. trainer Detroit Self-Employment Project; chmn. pre-fundamental bus. seminars Svc. Corps. Retired Execs, 1998—. Mem. Minority Bus. Inc. (corr. sec.), Nat. Alliance of Black Sch. Educators, Wayne State U. Coll. Edn. Alumni (chmn. bd. govs.), Phi Delta Kappa. Office: PO Box 04721 Detroit MI 48204-0721

MCCRACKEN, JOHN DAVID, education educator; b. Fairfield, Iowa, Sept. 17, 1939; s. W. Clyde and Marjorie A. (Bonnett) McC.; m. Jacqueline M. Ball, June 3, 1961; children: Diane M. McCracken Kephart, Stephen J. BS, Iowa State U., 1961, MS, 1962; PhD, Ohio State U., 1970. Cert. secondary tchr., Iowa. Statis. analyst Iowa State U., Ames, 1960-61, rsch. asst., 1961-62; tchr. agr. Charles City (Iowa) Sch. Dist., 1964-68; rsch. assoc., specialist, asst. dir. Ctr. Vocat. Edn. Ohio State U., Columbus, 1968-73, from asst. prof. to assoc. prof., 1970-79, prof., 1979-95; prof. emeritus, 1995—. Vis. prof. U. Putra, Malaysia, 1995-98, external assessor, 1983-95, external examiner, 1983-86; external advisor U. Teknologi, Malaysia, 2000—; adj. prof. U. Ariz., 2001—. Author: Methods of Teaching Agriculture, 1986, Ency. of Ednl. Rsch., 1982, 92, Ency. of Agrl. Sci., 1994; editor Jour. Vocat. Edn. Rsch., 1979; contbr. articles to profl. jours. Bd. dirs. Beulah Beach Corp., Vermillion, Ohio, 1990-94; advisor Malaysian Student Assn., Columbus, 1989-92, Thai Student Assn., Columbus, 1986-92, Indonesian Christian Fellowship, Columbus, 1994-95; chair com. rural edn. USDA, 1994-95. 1st lt. U.S. Army, 1962-64, Fulbright scholar, 1985-86. Fellow Am. Assn. Agrl. Edn. (life, pres. 1979, disting. lectr. 1982, Disting. Svc. award 1990, Outstanding Teaching award 1990); mem. Am. Vocat. Edn. Rsch. Assn. (life, pres. 1990). Avocations: golfing, construction. Home: 4951 S View Ridge Dr Green Valley AZ 85614-5817 Office: Ohio State U 2120 Fyffe Rd Rm 208 Columbus OH 43210-1067

MCCRACKEN, KENNETH DONALD, retired education educator; b. Hiattville, Kans., Feb. 18, 1930; s. Joseph Andrew and Elinor Nellie (Paelle) McC.; m. Janis Erline Houghton, Dec. 24, 1961 (dec. Sept. 2000); children: Schuyler Lowe, Vance. BS, Pittsburg, Kans., 1955, MS, 1956; EdD, Fayetteville, Ark., 1966. Prof. edn. U. Tenn., Martin, 1962-99; ret., 1999. Contbr. chpts. to books and articles to profl. jours. With U.S. Army, 1952-54. Mem. Phi Delta Kappa. Home: 119 Elm Martin TN 38237 E-mail: dmccrack@utm.edu.

MCCRACKEN, LINDA, librarian, commercial artist; b. Rochester, N.Y., Apr. 13, 1948; d. Frederick Hugh Craig and Shirley Betty (Shacter) Bickford; m. Alan Cheah, June 13, 1972 (div. 1978); m. Bruce E. McCracken, Sept. 23, 1978 (div. 1985); 1 child, Karen Elizabeth. BA in History, MLS, SUNY, Geneseo, 1970. Reference libr. Northeastern U., Boston, 1971-72; asst. libr. Burlington (Mass.) Pub. Libr., 1972-74; rsch. asst. Data Resources, Inc., Lexington, Mass., 1974-76; comml. artist McCracken's, Wolfeboro, NH, 1983—85; asst. libr. N.H.. Vocat.-Tech. Coll., Manchester, 1985-87; libr. N.H. Hosp., Concord, 1987-99; med. libr. New London (N.H.) Hosp., 1999, info. svcs. specialist, 1972—. Participant paintings Horseheads Mall Art Show (3d pl. award 1968); graphic artist Rare Coin Rev. mag., 1983; layout artist Market Media Guide, 1979; market rschr. Delahaye Group, Newington, N.H., 1993-94; author Burlington Times-Union, 1973, Pleasant News, 1987-88, Breene Briefings, 1998-99. Treas. Village Players, Wolfeboro, 1982-83; mem. pub. rels. com. Gov.'s Arts Coun., Wolfeboro, 1982. Mem. State Employees Assn. N.H., Mensa. Avocations: reading, hiking, kayaking, theater. Home and Office: PO Box 235 Marlow NH 03456

MC CRACKEN, PAUL WINSTON, retired economist, business educator; b. Richland, Iowa, Dec. 29, 1915; s. Sumner and Mary (Coffin) McC.; m. Emily Ruth Siler, May 27, 1942; children— Linda Jo, Paula Jeanne. Student, William Penn Coll., 1937; MA, Harvard U., 1942, PhD, 1948. Faculty Found. Sch., Berea Coll., Ky., 1937-40; economist Dept. Commerce, Washington, 1942-43; fin. economist, dir. research Fed. Res. Bank of Mpls., 1943-48; assoc. prof. Sch. Bus. Adminstrn., U. Mich., 1948-50, prof., 1950-66, Edmund Ezra Day Univ. prof. bus. adminstrn., 1966-86, prof. emeritus, 1986—, ret. Dir. emeritus Nat. Bur. Econ. Rsch.; trustee Earhart Found. Author: monographs Can Capitalism Survive?; articles on financial, econ. subjects. Fellow Am. Statis. Assn.; mem. Am. Econ. Assn., Am. Finance Assn., Royal Econ. Soc., Harvard Grad. Soc. (coun.). Clubs: Cosmos (Washington); Harvard (N.Y.C.). Presbyterian. Home: 2564 Hawthorne Rd Ann Arbor MI 48104-4032

MC CRACKEN, PHILIP TRAFTON, sculptor; b. Bellingham, Wash., Nov. 14, 1928; s. William Franklin and Maude (Trafton) McC.; m. Anne MacFetridge, Aug. 14, 1954; children— Timothy, Robert, Daniel. BA in Sculpture, U. Wash., 1954. Asst. to Henry Moore, Eng., 1954. One-man shows: Willard Gallery, N.Y.C., 1960, 65, 68, 70, Seattle Art Mus., 1961, Wash. State Capitol Mus., Olympia, 1964, Art Gallery of Greater Victoria, B.C., 1964, LaJolla (Calif.) Mus. Art, 1970, Anchorage Hist. and Fine Arts Mus., 1970, Tacoma Art Mus., 1980, Kennedy Galleries, N.Y.C., 1985, Lynn McAllister Gallery, Seattle, 1986, 89, Valley Mus. N.W. Art, La Conner, Wash., 1993, Whatcom Mus., Bellingham, Wash., 1994, Schneider Mus. Art, 1994, So. Oreg. State Coll., 1994, Monterey Mus. Art, 1999, others; group shows include: Mus. Art, Ogunquit, Maine, 1957, Chgo. Art Inst., 1958, Detroit Inst. Arts, 1958, Pa. Acad. Fine Arts, 1958, Contemporary Art Gallery, Houston, 1958, DeYoung Meml. Mus., San Francisco, 1960, Los Angeles Mcpl. Art Mus., 1960, Galerie Claude Bernard, Paris, 1960, Phillips Gallery, Washington, 1966, Corcoran Gallery, 1966, Mus. Art, Akron, 1967, Finch Coll., N.Y.C., 1968, Rutgers U., 1968, Whitney Mus. Art, 1978, Portland Art Mus., 1976, Mont. State U., Bozeman, 1979, Brigham Young U., 1980, Bellvue (Wash.) Art Mus., 1986, Lynn McAllister Gallery, 1986, Am. Acad. Arts and Letters, N.Y.C., 1986, Schmidt Bingham Gallery, N.Y.C., 1987, Wash. State Capital Mus., 1987, 89, Cheney-Cowles Mus., Spokane, Wash., 1988, Smithsonian Instn., 1991—, Nat. Mus., Ottawa, Can., 1991-92, Gallery Three-Zero, N.Y.C., 1993, Seattle Art Mus., 1994, SA Gallery Christ Ch., New Zealand, 1996, Art and Cultural Ctr., Fallbrook, Calif., 2002, others; sculptures represented: Norton Bldg., Seattle, Kankakee (Ill.) State Hosp., Swinomish Indian Tribal Center, LaConner, UN Assn., N.Y.C., King County King Dome, Seattle, City Hall, Everett, Wash., others. (Recipient numerous prizes, awards). Address: 5029 Guemes Island Rd Anacortes WA 98221-9039

MCCRACKEN, STEVEN R. pharmaceutical executive; b. Tacoma, 1953; m. Judy McCracken; children: Morgan, Kelsey. BS in Mech. Engring., Rose-Hulman Inst. Tech. Field engr. DuPont, Nonwovens-Tyvek, 1978—79, fin. mgr., 1981—84, mktg. dir. apparel, 1984—89; mng. dir. Lycra, Geneva, 1989—93, DuPont Corian, 1993—97, v.p., gen. mgr., 1997—2001; group v.p., gen. mgr. DuPont Apparel & Textile Scis., 2001—02; group v.p. DuPont Textiles & Interiors, Wilmington, Del., 2002—. Office: DuPont Corp Info Ctr Barley Mill Plz PIO Wilmington DE 19880-0010*

MCCRACKEN, THOMAS JAMES, JR. lawyer; b. Chgo., Oct. 27, 1952; s. Thomas J. Sr. and Eileen (Brophy) McC.; m. Peggy A. Jamrok; children: Catherine, Michael, Amanda, Quinn. BA, Marquette U., 1974; JD, Loyola U., 1977. Bar: Ill. 1977, U.S. Dist. Ct. (no. dist.) Ill., U.S. Ct. Appeals (7th cir.) 1984. Asst. state's atty. DuPage County State's Atty.'s Office, Wheaton, Ill., 1977-81; assoc. atty. McCracken & Walsh, Chgo., 1981-84; ptnr. McCracken, Walsh deLaVan & Hetler, 1984—. Commr. Nat. Conf. of Commns. on Uniform State Laws, 1989—; bd. dirs. Oak Trust and Savs. Bank, Chgo. Contbr. articles to profl. jours. State rep. Ill. Gen. Assembly, Springfield, Ill., 1983-93, state senator, 1993; chmn. Regional Trans. Authority, Chgo., 1993—. Named Top Ten Legislators Chgo. Mag., 1990. Mem. Chgo. Bar Assn., Ill. State Bar Assn. Avocations: skiing, fishing, hunting, coaching children's sports. Office: McCracken Walsh deLaVan & Hetler 134 N La Salle St Ste 600 Chicago IL 60602-1079

MCCRADY, JAMES DAVID, veterinarian, educator; b. Beaumont, Tex., June 26, 1930; s. James Homer and Lucyle (Ward) McC.; m. Mary Elizabeth McDougald, Sept. 8, 1951; children— David, Diane, Darla. BS, Tex. A. and M. Coll., 1952, D.V.M., 1958; PhD, Baylor U., 1965. Instr., then asst. prof. Tex. A. and M. Coll., 1958- 62; dir. animal rsch., instr. Baylor U. Coll. Medicine, 1962-64; mem. faculty Tex A&M U., 1964—; prof., head dept. vet. physiology and pharmacology Tex. A. and M. Coll., 1966-90, prof., dir. spl. programs, 1990—. Dir. Russian-Am. Tng. Partnership, 1995—; adj. prof. Baylor Coll., Medicine, M.D. Anderson Hosp. and Tumor Inst. Served with USAF, 1952-54. Mem. AVMA, Tex. Acad. Sci., Am. Physiol. Soc., Sigma Xi, Phi Kappa Phi, Phi Zeta. Achievements include research on comparative cardiovascular and respiratory physiology. Home: 511 Olive St Bryan TX 77801-3506 Office: Tex A&M U College Station TX 77843-0001

MCCRAIN, MICHAEL WILLIAM, accountant, financial advisor; b. Bklyn., Apr. 25, 1952; s. William Joseph Sr. and Penelope (Malarios) McC.; m. Kathleen Jean O'Donnell, June 9, 1974; children: Michael Walter, Kevin O'Donnell, Christopher William. AS in Computer Sci. with honors, Suffolk County C.C., Selden, N.Y., 1973; BBA in Pub. Acctg. cum laude, Hofstra U., 1975; MS in Bus., Columbia U., 1988. CPA, N.Y. Supervising sr. acct. Peat, Marwick, Mitchell Co., Jericho, N.Y., 1974-79; corp. acctg. mgr. Pall Corp., Glen Gove, 1979-81; v.p. CFO North Atlantic Industries, Inc., Hauppauge, 1981-88; v.p. fin. Loral Fairchild Sys., Syosset, 1988-89; pres. MKC Assocs., Inc., Islandia, NY, 1989—. Trustee Sachem Schs. Dist., Lake Ronkonkuma, N.Y., 1992-93; v.p. Sachem Athletic Booster Club, Lake Ronkonkuma, 1993-94, pres., 1994-95; vice chairperson Sachem Cmty. Adv. Coun., Lake Ronkonkuma, 1994-95, chairperson, 1995-97. Mem. AICPA, N.Y. Soc. CPAs, Beta Gamma Sigma. Avocations: racquetball, skiing, golfing, computers, coaching lacrosse. Office: 1747 Veterans Hwy Ste 12 Central Islip NY 11749-1537

MCCRARY, EUGENIA LESTER (MRS. DENNIS DAUGHTRY MC-CRARY), civic worker, writer; b. Annapolis, Md., Mar. 23, 1929; d. John Campbell and Eugenia (Potts) Lester; m. John Campbell Howard, July 15, 1955 (dec. Sept. 1965); m. Dennis Daughtry McCrary, June 28, 1969; 1 child, Dennis Campbell. AB cum laude, Radcliffe Coll.-Harvard U., 1950; MA, Johns Hopkins U., 1952; postgrad., Harvard U., 1953, Pa. State U., 1953-54, Drew U., 1957-58, Inst. Study of USSR, Munich, 1964. Grad. asst. dept. Romance langs. Pa. State U., 1953-54; tchr. dept. math. The Brearley Sch., N.Y.C., 1954-57; dir. Sch. Langs., Inc., Summit, N.J., 1958-69, trustee, 1960-69. Co-author: Nom de Plume: Eugenia Campbell Lester, (with Allegra Branson) Frontiers Aflame, 1987; film script adaptation (with John Gallagher) Frontier, 1998. Dist. dir. Ea. Pa. and N.J. auditions Met. Opera Nat. Coun., N.Y.C., 1960-66, dist. dir. publicity, 1966-67, nat. vice chmn. publicity, 1967-71, nat. chmn. public rels., 1972-75, hon. nat. chmn. pub. rels., 1976-99; bd. govs., chmn. Van Cortlandt House Mus., 1985-90. Mem. Nat. Soc. Colonial Dames Am. (bd. mgrs. N.Y. 1985-90), Met. Opera Nat. Coun., Soc. Mayflower Desc. (former bd. dirs. N.Y. soc., chmn. house com. 1986-89), Soc. Daus. Holland Dames (bd. dirs. 1982-87, 96—, 3d directress gen. 1987-92, directress gen. 1992-96), L'Eglise du St.-Esprit (vestry 1985-88, sr. warden 1988-90), Huguenot Soc. Am. (governing coun. 1984-90, 2000—, asst. treas. 1990-91, sec. 1991-95, 2d v.p. 1995-2000), Colonial Dames Am., Daus. of Cin., Colony Club (bd. govs. 1988-96), Causeries du Lundi. Republican. Episcopalian. Home: 24 Central Park S New York NY 10019-1629 E-mail: elmccrary@aol.com.

MCCRARY, JUDY HALE, education educator; b. Tuscaloosa, Ala., Oct. 16, 1955; d. Rogene Bae and Berta Inez (Smelley) Hale. BA, David Lipscomb U., 1978; MEd, Ala. A&M U., 1989; PhD, Miss. State U., 1994. Art tchr. grades 7-8 Scottsboro (Ala.) Jr. High, 1978-81; headstart tchr. Bridgeport (Ala.) Elem. Sch., 1983-84, tchr. grade 1, 1984-87; migrant tchr. grades K-6 Stevenson (Ala.) Elem. Sch., 1987-89, kindergarten tchr., 1989-91; tchg. asst. Miss. State U., Starkville, 1991-94; asst. prof. Jacksonville (Ala.) State U., 1994—. Owner, operator The Art Studio, Scottsboro, 1981-83; presenter in field. Mem. beautification coun. C. of C., Scottsboro, 1983; mem., v.p. Doctoral Student's Assn., Starkville, 1991-94. Faculty Rsch. grantee Jacksonville State U., 1994-96. Mem. AAUW (sec. 1987-89, pres. 1989-91), DAR, Am. Assn. for Edn. Young Children, Mid South Ednl. Rsch. Assn., Ala. Assn. for Young Children, Beta Phi, Delta Kappa Gamma, Phi Delta Kappa (historian 1993-94). Avocations: traveling, home decorating, gardening, creative arts, racquetball. Office: Jacksonville State Univ Ramona Wood Bldg 700 Pelham Rd N Jacksonville AL 36265-1623 E-mail: jhale@jsucc.jsu.edu.

MCCRAVEN, EVA STEWART MAPES, health service administrator; b. L.A., Sept. 26, 1936; d. Paul Melvin and Wilms Zech (Ziegler) Stewart; m. Carl Clarke McCraven, Mar. 18, 1978; children: David Anthony, Lawrence James, Maria Lynn Mapes. ABS magna cum laude, Calif. State U., Northridge, 1974; MS, Cambridge Grad. Sch. Psycholoy, 1987, PhD, 1991. Dir. spl. projects Pacoima Meml. Hosp., 1969-71, dir. health edn., 1971-74; ast. exec. dir., v.p. Hillview Cmty. Mental Health Ctr., Lakeview Terrace, Calif., 1974-99, exec. dir., 1999—, former dir. clin. svcs. Past dir. dept. consultation and edn. Hillview Ctr., developer, mgr. long-term residential program, 1986-90; former program mgr. crisis residential program, transititional residential program and day treatment program for mentally ill offenders, past dir. mentally ill offenders svcs.; former program dir. Valley Homeless Shelter Mental Health Counseling Program; dir. Integrated Svcs. Agy., Hillview Mental Health Ctr., Inc., 1993-98, dir. clin. programs, 1996-99, exec. dir. 1999—. Former pres. San Fernando Valley Coordinating Coun. Area Assn., Sunland-Jujunga Coordinating Coun.; bd. advisors Pacoima Sr. Citizens Multi-Purpose Ctr.; bd. dirs. N.E. Valley Health Corp., 1970-73, Golden Gate Cmty. Mental Health Ctr., 1970-73. Recipient resolution of commendation State of Calif., 1988, commendation award, 1988, spl. mayor's plaque, 1988, commendation awards for cmty. svcs. City of L.A., 1989, County of Los Angeles, 1989, Calif. Assembly, 1989, Calif. Senate, 1989, award Sunland-Tujunga Police Support Coun., 1989, Women of Achievement award Sunland-Tujunga Bus and Profl. Women, 1990. Mem. Health Svcs. Adminstrn. Alumni Assn. (past v.p.), Sunland-Jujunga Bus. and Profl. Women, LWV, Valley Philharm. Soc. Office: Hillview Cmty Mental Health Ctr 11500 Eldridge Ave Lake View Terrace CA 91342-6523

MCCRAW, KATHY, elementary education educator, special education educator; b. Spartanburg, S.C., Dec. 30, 1954; d. Perry Robert and Lillie Belle Stevens; children: Brooke Kathryn, Courtney Nicole. BA with highest honor, Clemson U., 1977; MA, Converse Coll., 1984. Tchr. spl. edn. Lugoff-Elgin Mid. Sch., Camden, S.C., 1977-80; resource tchr. Spartanburg H.S., 1980-97; resource tchr. and tchr. earth and phys. sci. Houston Elem. Sch. and McCracken Jr. H.S., Spartanburg, 1998; tchr. modified lang. arts Whitlock Jr. H.S., 1999—, tchr. lang. arts, 2002—. Mem. com. writing state stds. for alternative diploma program and developing curriculum and materials. Mem. Coun. for Exceptional Children. Republican. Baptist. Avocation: painting. Home: 14 Somersett Dr Spartanburg SC 29301-6532

MCCRAY, DOROTHY WESTABY, artist, printmaker, educator; b. Madison, S.D., Oct. 13, 1915; d. Robert Spencer and Annie Mary (Otter) Westaby; m. Francis F. McCray, Aug. 6, 1938 (dec. Jan. 1960); 1 child, Peter Michael. BA, State U. Iowa, 1937, MA in Painting, 1939; MFA in Printmaking, Calif. Coll. Arts and Crafts, Oakland, 1955; DHL (hon.), We. N.Mex. U., 2001. Prof. art Western N.Mex. U., Silver City, 1948-81, prof. emeritus, 1981—; profl. painter/printmaker McCray Studios. Solo exhbns. include Mezzanine Gallery, Oakland, Calif., Art Directions Gallery, N.Y.C., Lebanon Valley Coll., Pa., Coralles Art Assn., N.Mex., Richard Levy Gallery, Albuquerque, numerous others; group exhbns. include Art Inst. Chgo., 1940-41, Phila. Acad., 1941, Kansas City Art Inst., 1941, 42, Smithsonian Inst., Washington, 1941, 58, Am. Fine Arts Gallery, N.Y.C., 1943, Joslyn Meml. Art Mus., Omaha, 1947, Mus. Fine Arts, Santa Fe, 1950, 51, 52, 53, 54, 56, 57, 58, 59, 63, 66, Oakland (Calif.) Art Mus., 1955, Cin. Art Mus., 1956, 58, NAD, Newton, Kans., 1956, Dallas Mus. Fine Arts, 1956, 58, Roswell (N.Mex.) Art Mus., 1958, Bradley U., Peoria, Ill., 1960, Highlands U., Las Vegas, 1960, Bklyn. Mus., 1961, Pa. Acad. Art, Phila., 1965, Museo de Arte Historia, Juarez, Mexico, 1978, The Shellfish Collection, Silver City, N.Mex., 1990, 91, Deming (N.Mex.) Ctr. for Arts, 1991, Grant County Art Guild, Pinos Altos, N.Mex., 1991, 92, Carlsbad (N.Mex.) Mus. and Art Ctr., 1992, Richard Levy Gallery, Albuquerque, 1992, Jonathon Green Gallery, Naples, Fla., numerous others; represented in pvt. and mus. collections throughout the United States. Named Hon. Citizen of S.D., 1983; Western N.Mex. U. Art Building named Dorothy McCray Art Building, 1982; recipient N.Mex. Gov.'s Award for Excellence and Contbns. to the Arts, 1992, numerous art awards in exhbns. Office: PO Box 322 Silver City NM 88062-0322

MC CRAY, EVELINA WILLIAMS, librarian, researcher; b. Plaquemine, La., Sept. 1, 1932; d. Turner and Beatrice (Gordon) Williams II; m. John Samuel McCray, Apr. 7, 1955; 1 child, Johnetta McCray Russ. BA, So. U., Baton Rouge, 1954; MS in Libr. Sci., La. State U., 1962. Libr. Iberville H.S., Plaquemine, 1954-70, Plaquemine Jr. High, 1970-75; proofreader short stories, poems Associated Writers Guild, Atlanta, 1982-86. Libr. cons. Evaluation Capitol H.S., 1964, Iberville Parish Educators Workshop, 1980, Tchrs. Core/Iberville Parish, 1980-81. Contbr. poetry New Am. Poetry Anthology, 1988, The Golden Treasury of Great Poems, 1988, Acres of Diamonds: A Collection of Poetry, The Power and the Glory: A Collection of Poetry, Favorite Poems Southern Poetry Assn., 1996. Vol. Allen J. Nadler Libr., Plaquemine, 1980-82; libr. Local Day Care Ctr., Plaquemine, 1978-79; mem. adv. bd. Iverville Parish Project Independence, 1992—; active Arts and Cultural Devel. Coun. Iberville, 1997—. Recipient Citation of Meritorious Achievement, Dictionary of Internat. Biography for Svcs. to Edn., 1998. Mem. ALA, La. Libr. Assn., Nat. Ret. Tchrs. Assn., La. Ret. Tchrs. Assn. (cons. ann. workshops 1986—, state appointee to informative and protective svcs. com. 1988-92), Iberville Ret. Tchrs. Assn. (info. and protective svcs. dir. 1981—), Internat. Soc. Poets, So. Poetry Assn. (Blue Ribbon award 1989, SPA's Finest award 1992). Democrat. Baptist. Home: PO Box Q Plaquemine LA 70765-0220

MCCRAY, RICHARD ALAN, astrophysicist, educator; b. L.A., Nov. 24, 1937; s. Alan Archer and Ruth Elizabeth (Woodworth) McC.; m. Sandra Broomfield; children: Julia, Carla BS, Stanford U., 1959; PhD, UCLA, 1967. Rsch. fellow Calif. Inst. Tech, Pasadena, 1967-68; asst. prof. astronomy Harvard U., Cambridge, Mass., 1968-71; assoc. prof. astrophysics U. Colo., Boulder, 1971-75, prof., 1975—, chmn. Joint Inst. Lab. Astrophysics, 1981-82, chmn. Ctr. for Astrophysics and Space Astronomy, 1985-86, George Gamow prof. astrophysics, 1998—; corr. prof. astronomy Nanjing (China) U., 1996—. Contbr. articles to profl. jours. Guggenheim fellow, 1975-76; NSF Disting. Tchg. scholar, 2002. Mem. NAS, Am. Astron. Soc. (councilor 1980-83, chmn. high energy astrophysics div. 1986-87, Heineman Prize for Astrophysics, 1990), Internat. Astron. Union Office: U Colo Joint Inst Lab Astrophysics Boulder CO 80309-0001 E-mail: dick@jila.colorado.edu.

MCCREA, JUDITH K. BURNS, artist, educator; b. Wichita, Kans. d. Dean Clinton and Hazel Ira (Thomas) Burns. Student, Emporium State U., 1962-64; BFA, Wichita State U., 1967, MFA, 1970. Artist-in-residence Kans. Arts Commn./Butler, El Dorado, 1984-87; asst. prof. Bethany Coll., Lindsborg, Kans., 1987-89, dir. Mingenback Gallery, 1988-89; vis. lectr., instr. Salina (Kans.) Arts Ctr., 1989-90; asst. prof. U. Kans., Lawrence, 1990-93, assoc. prof., 1993-98, chairperson art dept., 1993-97. Dir. Sch. Visual Arts, instr. Wichita Ctr. Arts, 1989-90; vis. instr. U. Nacional Asuncion, Paraguay, 1997; curriculum cons. art dept. Haskell Indian Nations U., Lawrence, 1997; chula vista Sch. Architecture, Kans. U., Lawrence, 1997; juror Riverben 97, Atchison, Kans., 1997; vis. artist Inst. Superior Arte, Asuncion, Paraguay, 1997. Exhibitions include Dinnerware Contemporary Gallery, Tucson, 2001, Santa Reparata Sch. Art, Florence, Italy, 2002, Artemisia Gallery, Chgo., 2002. Fellow Kans. Arts Commn. fellow, 1996; grantee Lithography commn., Nelson-Atkins Mus./Print Soc. grantee, 1993, faculty travel grantee, Kans. U., 1994, U.S. Spkr. and Specialist grantee, U.S. Info. Agy., 1997. Office: U Kans 300 Art And Design Bldg Lawrence KS 66045-0001

MCCREA, PHILIP JAMES, secondary school and college science educator; b. Chgo., Sept. 22, 1948; s. James Patrick and Angela Mary (Scalzitti) McC.; m. Mary Jane T. DiVita, June 20, 1970; children: Sean Patrick, Kristin Ann. MS in Behavioral Genetics, U. Ill., Chgo., 1974, BS in Biology, 1970. Tchr. sci. New Trier H.S., Winnetka, Ill., 1971—; instr. Coll. of Lake County, Grayslake, 1993—. Driver Chgo. Transit Authority; tour guide Chgo. Hort. Soc., Glencoe, Ill.; cons. sci. Ency. Britannica, Chgo., Compton's Ency., Chgo., Rand McNally Corp., Skokie, Ill. Named One of Tandy Corp. Tech. Outstanding Tchrs., 1994-95; recipient Bronze award Brit. Film Assn., 1986. Mem. Nat. Assn. Biology Tchrs. (regional coord., state rep., Outstanding Biology Tchr. award 1980, pres.-elect 1999, pres. 2000), Ill. Edn. Assn., Ill. Sci. Tchrs. Assn., Ill. Assn. Biology Tchrs. (exec. sec.). Avocations: singing, playing guitar. Office: New Trier HS 385 Winnetka Ave Winnetka IL 60093-4238 E-mail: mccreap@newtrier.k12.il.us.

MCCREADY, GUY MICHAEL, lawyer; b. Tulsa, Mar. 21, 1960; s. John McCready and Patsy Ann (Xander) Ryman; children: Sean, Loren. BA, Ft. Hays State U., 1984; JD, Washburn Law Sch., 1987; diploma, Nat. Inst. for

Trial Advocacy, 1992. Bar: Colo. 1987, U.S. Dist. Ct. Colo. 1989, U.S. Ct. Appeals (10th cir.) 1990. Pvt. practice, Colorado Springs, 1987—. Prof. ethics U. So. Colo., Colorado Springs, 1991; mem. jud. com. to reform juvenile ct. procedure, 2000. Author: Manitou, 2002; author: (asst.) Yearbook of School Law, 1987; contbr. articles to profl. jours. Vol. Pikes Peak Legal Svcs., Colorado Springs, 1987—. Mem. Assn. Trial Lawyers Am., Colo. Trial Lawyers Assn., Colo. Bar Assn., El Paso County Bar Assn., Order of Barristers. Avocations: skiing, hiking, jogging. Office: Ste 1100 2 N Cascade Ave Colorado Springs CO 80903

MCCREADY, KENNETH FRANK, past electric utility executive; b. Edmonton, Alta., Can., Oct. 9, 1939; s. Ralph and Lilian McCready; children: John, Janet, Brian. BSc, U. Alta., 1963. Supr. data processing and systems Calgary (Alta.) Power Ltd., 1965-67, supr. rates and contracts, 1967-68, adminstrv. asst. to exec. v.p., 1968-72, asst. mgr. mgmt. cons. div., 1972-75; mgr. mgmt. systems dept., gen. mgr. Montreal Engring. Co., Calgary, 1975-76; v.p. adminstrn. Calgary (Alta.) Power Ltd., 1976-80; sr. v.p. ops. TransAlta Utilities, Calgary, 1980-85, pres., COO, 1985-89, also bd. dirs., 1988-96; pres., CEO TransAlta Corp., 1989-96; CEO TransAlta Energy Corp., 1989-96; pres. K. F. McCready & Assocs. Ltd., Calgary, 1996—. Past mem. environ. adv. bd. ABB Asea Brown Boveri, Zurich; bd. dirs. Colonia Corp., Calgary; adv. bd. Airborne Techs. Inc., Calgary; bd. dirs. Computer Modelling Group, Calgary, Can. Environ. Tech. Advancement Corp., Calgary, Internat. Inst. Sustainable Devel., Winnipeg; past chmn. Conf. Bd. Can.; past chmn. bd. Advanced Computing Techs., Inc.; mem. adv. bd. Tata Energy Rsch. Inst. , Washington; past mem. World Bus. Coun. for Sustainable Devel.; past chair Conf. Bd. Can.; past moderator Premier's Forum, Govt. of Alta.; pres., CEO Ethopower Corp, Kelowna, Biosphere Refineries Corp., Calgary, Canada; adv. bd. NRCan, Ottawa, Canada; bd. dir. Encana Corp., Calgary, Biosphere Technologies, Inc., Edmonton, Canada. Past dep. chmn. bd. govs. So. Alta. Inst. Tech.; past chair Alta. Round Table on Environment and Econ.; past mem. com. on trade and environment Govt. Can. Internat. Trade Adv.; past pres. Western Electric Power and Light Assn.; past chair environ. task force Bus. Coun. Nat. Issues. Mem. Assn. Profl. Engrs., Geologists and Geophysicists of Alta., Ranchmen's Club. Avocations: computers, cycling, photography. E-mail: ken.mccready@cadvision.com.

MCCREADY, SAM, theatre educator, actor, director, writer; b. Belfast, No. Ireland, Nov. 22, 1936; s. David James and Sarah Elizabeth (Howlett) McC.; m. Joan Carslake, Mar. 16, 1962; children: Marcus Diarmuid Julian, Richard Alastair. MA, U. N. Wales, U.K., 1976. Advt. mgr. Berkshire Internat., No. Ireland, 1961-63; head dept. theatre Orangefield Boys Sch., Belfast, 1963-67, head English dept., 1967-69; lectr. U. North Wales, Bangor, 1969-78; artistic dir. Lyric Theatre, Belfast, 1980-81; head dept. theatre Stranmillis Coll., 1978-83; assoc. prof. theatre U. Md., Catonsville, 1984-99, prof., 1999—2001; artistic dir. Shakespeare On Wheels, 1985-96. Examiner Guildhall Sch. Music and Drama, London, 1969—; trustee Lyric Theatre, Belfast, 1978-82; adjudicator Hong Kong Speech and Drama Festival, 1980, 84, 87, 93, 96, 2001; actor Tartuffe, Md. Stage Co., Ctr. Stage, Balt., 1997, 98, Serebriakov,Round House Theatre, Washington, 1997, Songs of Wandering Aengus, N.Y.C., Sligo, Ireland, 1999, 2000, Krapp's Last Tape, Trinity Coll., Hartford, Conn., 1999, That Time, 2000, Early Memories, N.Y., 2001; lectr. Yeats Internat. Summer Sch., Sligo, Ireland, 1998, 99, 2000. Author: Lucille Lortel: The Queen of Off-Broadway, 1993, Yeats Encyclopedia, 1997, Theatre in the North of Ireland, 1969-99, 2000; adaptor, dir. play: Spring's Awakening, 1987 (Best Dir. award 1987), No Country for Old Men, 1985, Picture of Dorian Gray, 1988, Salome, 1989, The Tutor, 1992, The Widening Gyre, 1994, The Shadow of a Gunman, 1995, Diary of a Scoundrel, 1996 (Best Dir. award 1997), On the Verge, 1997, Deirdre, 1997, What the Butler Saw, 1998, Yerma, 2000, Macbeth, 2001; contbr. articles to profl. jours. Named Outstanding Dir. Am. Coll. Theatre Festival, 1986, 87, 93, 97. Mem. Brit. Actors Equity, Am. Actors Equity, East Ctrl. Theatre Conf., Am. Conf. Irish Studies, Phi Kappa Phi. Episcopalian. Avocations: painting, music, photography, reading, gardening. E-mail: mccready@umbc.edu.

MCCREARY, DEBORAH DENNIS, oncology nurse; b. Washington, Oct. 6, 1952; d. Eldon Hugh Dennis and Janice Sylvia (North) Saunders; m. James Leo McCreary, May 21, 1988. BSN, Ohio State Sch. Nursing, 1976. Nurse Ohio State U. Hosp., Columbus, 1976-77; asst. head nurse Riverside Meth. Hosp., 1977-80; nurse Good Samaritan Hosp., San Jose, Calif., 1980-82; asst. head nurse Valley West Hosp., 1982; outpatient oncology nurse Southbay Med. Oncology, 1982-88; oncology nurse specialist, office mgr. Menlo Med. Clinic, Menlo Park, Calif., 1988-98. Cons. Schering Corp., Dallas, 1991, Berlix, Menlo Park, 1992, spkr., 1994, Ortho Biotech, San Francisco, 1995. Mem. Oncology Nursing Soc. (Santa Clara chpt. sec. 1982-84, membership chair 1984-85, cert. oncology nurse). Republican. Avocations: classical music, piano, gourmet cooking, hiking, travel. Home: 23750 Ravensbury Ave Los Altos CA 94024-6341 E-mail: debbiemccreary@hotmail.com.

MC CREARY, JAMES FRANKLIN, lawyer, mediator; b. Farmington, Mo., June 15, 1942; s. Frank J. and Bernice E. (Dugal) McCreary; m. Martha Jean Tucker, June 30, 1962; children: James Franklin, III, Jason Tucker, Josh Adam. BSBA, U. Evansville, 1964; JD, Nashville Law Sch., 1969; MBA, Vanderbilt U., 1980. Bar: Tenn. 1969, rule 31 listed mediator: Tenn. With Old Nat. Bank, Evansville, Ind., 1960-64; with First Am. Corp., Nashville, 1972-80, exec. v.p., corp. sec., gen. counsel, 1974-80; with First Am. Nat. Bank Nashville (N.A.), 1964-72, 80-86, exec. v.p., 1980-86; ptnr. Borod & Huggins Attys., Memphis, 1986-87, Gerrish & Mc Creary, Memphis, 1988, of counsel, 1988-92, dir., 1993—. Pres. Met. Fed. Bank, 1988-91; vis. prof. bus. law David Lipscomb U., 1975-77; instr. law and banking Am. Inst. Banking, 1969-75. Mem. Beta Gamma Sigma Mem. Ch. of Christ. Office: Gerrish & Mc Creary PC 222 2nd Ave N Nashville TN 37201-1646 E-mail: fmccreary@gerrish.com.

MCCREDIE, JAMES ROBERT, fine arts educator; b. Chgo., Dec. 31, 1935; s. William and Mareta (Black) McC.; m. Marian Lucille Miles, Sept. 3, 1960; children: Miles William, Meredeth Black Winter. AB in History and Literature summa cum laude, Harvard U., 1958, AM, 1961, PhD, 1963; student, Am. Sch. Classical Studies, Athens, Greece, 1958-59, 61-62. Instr. NYU, 1963-64, asst. prof., 1965-66, assoc. prof., 1967-70, prof., 1970, 78-88, Sherman Fairchild prof. fine arts, 1988—2002, Sherman Fairchild prof. emeritus fine arts, 2002—, dep. dir. Inst. Fine Arts, 1967-69, acting dir., 1982-83, dir., 1983—2002, asst. field dir. Excavations in Samothrace, 1962, field dir., 1963-65, dir. excavations, 1966—. Dir. Am. Sch. Classical Studies at Athens, Greece, 1969-77, chmn. mng. com., 1980-90, trustee, 1980—, pres. 2001—; vis. mem. Inst. Advanced Study, Princeton, N.J., 1977-78; mem. vis. com. dept. classical and near eastern Archeology Bryn Mayr Coll., 1982, dept. european paintings Met. Mus. Art, 1983—, Ctr. Old World Archaeology and Art Brown U., Providence, 1985; mem. adv. bd. Alexander S. Onassis Ctr. for Hellenic Studies NYU, 1990-97; cons. in field. Author: Fortified Military Camps in Attica, Hesperia, 1966, Samothrace, 7, The Rotunda of Arsinoe, 1992; mem. adv. bd. Am. Jour. Archaeology, 1969-81; contbr. articles to prof. jours.. Bd. dirs. Hellenic-Am. Union, Athens, 1973-77, vice chmn., 1974-77, U.S. Ednl. Found., Greece, 1969-75; active Pres. Adv. Com. on Cultural Property, 1992-95. Charles Norton fellow, 1961-62; named hon. citizen Community of Samothrace, 1976. Mem. Am. Philos. Soc., Archaeol. Inst. Am. (life, trustee 1972-75, mem. exec. com. 1978-81), Archaeol. Soc. Athens (hon.), Deutsches archaeologisches Inst. (corr.). Home: 30 Battle Rd Princeton NJ 08540-4902 also: Palaiopolis GR-680 02 Samothrace Greece Office: NYU Inst Fine Arts 1 E 78th St New York NY 10021-0119 E-mail: jrm1@nyu.edu.

MCCREDIE, JOANN MARY REZNY (JO MCCREDIE), artist; b. East St. Louis, Ill., Apr. 22, 1934; d. James and Anna Ruth (Heveroh) R.; m. William Thomas McCredie, Oct. 2, 1958; children: Kim Diane Elmore, Dawn Renee Collins, Terri Ann Hummel. BFA, U. Ill., 1957; MA, Webster U., 1979. Art tchr. Windsor H.S., Imperial, Mo., 1968-70, Fox H.S., Arnold, 1973-79; asst. prof. art Jefferson Coll., Hillsboro, 1979-85, assoc. prof. art, 1985-90, prof. art, 1990-95; artist, 1995—. Chmn. Jefferson Fair, Hillsboro, 1982-89; curator Jefferson Coll. Fine Arts Theater Gallery, 1979-95; dir. study tours to Europe, 1982, 85, 89, 94. Mem.: St. Louis Water Color Soc. (signature mem.), Mo. Water Color Soc. (signature mem.), Art St. Louis and Women's Caucus for Art, St. Louis Artists Guild (art sect. exec. bd. 1996—98, 2001—03, chair art sect. exec. bd. 2002—03, disting. mem.). Home: 1274 Whispering Winds Dr Arnold MO 63010-3034 E-mail: bjmccredie@earthlink.net.

MCCREE, PAUL WILLIAM, JR. systems design and engineering company executive; b. St. Louis, Oct. 27, 1926; s. Paul William and Hazel Elfrieda (Wilson) McC.; m. Carolyn Williams, Sept. 7, 1955; children: Brian, Paula, Ross. BS in Biochem. Scis., Harvard U., 1950. Mem. tech. staff System Devel. Corp., Santa Monica, Calif., 1956-62, Mitre Corp., Bedford, Mass., 1966-67; prin. engr. equipment divsn. Raytheon Co., Sudbury, 1963-66, 67-72; mem. tech. staff MIT Lincoln Labs., Lexington, 1972-76; mgr. Aerospace Systems divsn. Input Output, Waltham, 1976-79, tech. dir., 1979-80; mem. tech. staff Mitre Corp., Bedford, 1980-82; founder, pres. BPR Co., Profl. Cons. Svcs., 1981—. Sr. mem. tech. staff, mgr. subsystem design and devel. dept. GTE Strategic Systems Div., 1982-84; tech. dir. HH Aerospace and Design Co. Inc., Bedford, 1984-86; prin. engr., mem. tech. staff Raytheon equipment div. Software Systems Lab., Sudbury, 1986-87; v.p. HH Aerospace and Design Co. Inc., Bedford, 1986-91. Mem. NAACP, Urban League. Served with U.S. Army, 1944. Recipient Black Achiever award, Greater Boston YMCA, 1977. Mem. AAAS, IEEE, Math. Assn. Am., Am. Math. Soc., N.Y. Acad. Scis. Democrat. Home: 173 Goodman's Hill Rd PO Box 77 Sudbury MA 01776-0077 E-mail: pmccree@worldnet.att.net., pmccreejr@cs.com.

MCCREEDY, EDWIN JAMES, lawyer; b. Atlanta, Dec. 29, 1939; s. Harold D. McCreedy and Annette Raymond (Denton) Chapman; m. Linda Jandora, Mar. 20, 1965; children: James M., Matthew B. BA, Columbia U., 1961; JD, Fordham U., 1968. Bar: N.J. 1968, U.S. Supreme Ct. 1982, cert. civil trial atty. N.J. Supreme Ct. 1982. Ptnr. McCreedy & Cox, Cranford, NJ, 1984—. Pres. Richard J. Hughes Inn of Court, 1991-92; mem. civil practice com. Supreme Ct. N.J., 1985-96. Fellow ABA, Internat. Soc. Barristers, Internat. Acad. Trial Lawyers, Am. Coll. Trial Lawyers (chair state com, 1995-97); mem. N.J. State Bar Assn. (trustee 1997-2001, chmn. jud. adminstrn. com. 1994-96, treas. 2001, 1st v.p. 2002), Trial Attys. N.J. (trustee), Union County Bar Assn. (pres. 1987). Avocations: golf, travel. Office: McCreedy & Cox 6 Commerce Dr Ste 13 Cranford NJ 07016-3551

MCCREERY, JAMES ALLAN, retired business services company executive; b. Muncie, Ind., Nov. 21, 1933; s. Herman and Margaret Allena (McKinley) McC.; m. Carolyn Henderson, Dec. 18, 1954; children: Lynn, Julie. BS, Ball State U., 1956. Asst. buyer Ball Stores, Muncie, 1956-59; asst. sales svc. mgr. closure divsn. Ball Corp., 1959; salesman Stecks Inc., 1959-61; terr. sales mgr. Western AutoSupply Co., Ft. Wayne, Ind., 1961-63, customer svc. mgr., 1964-65, mgr. new store sales, 1965-66, mktg. analyst Kansas City, Mo., 1965, mgr. wholesale sales Ft. Wayne, 1966-68; v.p. sales Straton Baldwin Hardware Co., New Orleans, 1969-70; v.p. mktg. Klumb Cos., Biloxi, Miss., 1970-78; dir. Klumb Lumber Co., 1976-78; owner, operator Western Auto Store, 1978-80; Midwest sales mgr. So. Importers, Greensboro, N.C., 1980-83; sales mgr. Millburn Peat Co., LaPorte, Ind., 1983-84, Klumb Co., Jackson, Miss., 1984-86, v.p., gen. mgr., 1987-88, pres., COO Miss., 1989-97; ret., 1998. Elder Presbyn. Ch.; chmn. Downtown Franklin Improvement Com.; packmaster Cub Scouts; scoutmaster Boy Scouts Am., Eagle Scout; United Fund; bd. dirs. Timbers II Homeowners Assn., Brandon, 1994-99; vol. Miss. Sports Hall of Fame and Mus., 2001. Recipient Packaging award Greater Jackson Area Advt. Club, 1971, Nat. Bark Mktg. award Forest Products Rsch. Soc., 1972; named to Honorable Order of Ky. Cols. Mem. Franklin Mchts. Assn., Nat. Bark Prodrs. Assn. (membership chmn. 1973-76, program chmn. ann. conv. 1974, 76, pres. 1976-78, bd. dirs. 1974-78, packaging award 1972, membership award 1972), Franklin C. of C. (bd. dirs.), Rotary (bd. dirs. North Jackson 1977-78), Masons, Shriners. Conservative. Home: 208 Old Oak Cir Brandon MS 39042-2611

MCCREIGHT, JOHN A. management consultant; b. Phila., Jan. 29, 1938; s. John A. and Marion R. (Vetter) McC.; m. Kim Amet Healey; children: Laura, Cindy, Brian, Kimberly. BS in Mgmt. Scis., Northeastern U., 1968. Cert. mgmt. cons. Chief systems devel. AVCO Apollo Systems, Boston, 1964-68; sr. mgmt. cons. Touche, Ross & Co., Detroit, 1968-72, ptnr. Detroit and N.Y.C., 1972-80, nat. dir., mem. exec. com. N.Y.C., 1980-83; mng. dir. Hayes Hill, 1983; pres. McCreight & Co., Inc., Phila. and New Canaan, Conn., 1983-85; mng. dir. Hay Group, Inc., N.Y.C., 1985-91; chmn. McCreight & Co., Inc., New Canaan and Wilton, Conn., 1991—. Mem. Presdl. Task Force to Reduce Cost and Improve Effectiveness of USN; advisor Dept. Sec. Def.; dir. officer Inst. Mgmt. Cons. Adv.; Carnegie Hall Bd. Trustee NIH, N.Y. Mayor's Office, Salvation Army; past chmn. N.Y. Corp. Fund Raising, NIMH; mem. N.Y. Ireland U.S. Coun. With USNR, 1955-63. Mem. University Club (N.Y.C.). Office: McCreight & Co Inc Rsch & Opers Ctr 163 Old Field Rd Fairfield CT 06824

MCCREIGHT, SUSAN BUCKLEY, human resources executive; b. Oakland, Calif., Feb. 19, 1946; d. Milton Chester and Virginia Jean (Kincaid) Buckley. BS in Social Sci. summa cum laude, Fordham U., 1983. Mgr., adminstrn. and spl. projects ABC, Inc., N.Y.C., 1979-81, mgr. fair employment practices, 1981-84; dir. personnel Chilton Co., Radnor, Pa., 1984-85; dir. human resources Cahners Pub. Co., N.Y.C., 1987-89; v.p. human resources Warner Pub. Svcs., 1990-95, AmeriChoice Health Svcs., N.Y.C., 1995-99; sr. dir. human resources Weill Med. Coll. of Cornell U., 1999—. Mem. Soc. for Human Resources Mgmt., Slow Food, Phi Kappa Phi (life). Episcopalian. Avocations: cooking, reading, needlework, hiking, travel. Home: 600 W 111th St # 10F New York NY 10025-1813 Office: 445 E 69th St New York NY 10021-5664

MCCRERY, JAMES (JIM MCCRERY), congressman; b. Shreveport, La., Sept. 18, 1949; m. Johnette Hawkins, Aug. 3, 1991; children: Claiborne Scott, Otis Clark. BA, La. Tech. U., 1971; JD, La. State U., 1975. Bar: La. 1975. Pvt. practice, Leesville, La., 1975-78; asst. city atty. City of Shreveport, 1979-80; staff U.S. Rep. Buddy Roemer, 1981-84; regional mgr. Ga.-Pacific Corp., 1984-88; mem. U.S. Congress from 4th La. dist., 1988-93, 97—. U.S. Congress from 5th La. dist., 1993-97; mem. ways and means com. Office: US Ho of Reps 2104 Rayburn House Ofc Bldg Washington DC 20515-1804*

MCCREVAN, ROSEMARY ANN, contingency planning consultant; b. Boston, Aug. 1, 1952; d. George Patrick and Mary (Joyce) McC. BS in Mgmt., Boston State Coll., 1981; MBA, Babson Coll., 1988. With Hawaii Nat. Bank, Honolulu, 1973, U.S. Trust Co., Milton, Mass., 1973-78, Shawmut Bank, Boston, 1978-88, Bank of Boston, 1988-89, Strohl Systems, Tampa, Fla., 1989-90; ind. cons. Milton, Mass., 1990-91; pres. Bus. Continuation Svcs., Inc., 1991—. Mem. No. New Eng. Disaster Recovery Info. X-Change. Mem. Info. Systems Security Assn., Contingency Planning Exchange, DECUS, Psi Chi. Avocations: interior design, travel. Home: 50 Saint Agatha Rd Milton MA 02186-4364 Office: Bus Continuation Svcs Inc PO Box 145 Milton MA 02186-0005

MCCRIE, ROBERT DELBERT, editor, publisher, educator; b. Sarnia, Ont., Can., Oct. 8, 1938; s. Robert Newton and Evelyn May (Johnston) McC.; m. Fulvia Madia, Dec. 22, 1965; children: Carla Alexandra, Mara Elizabeth. BA, Ohio Wesleyan U., 1960; MS, U. Toledo, 1964; postgrad., U. Chgo., 1962-63; MA, Hunter Coll., 1994; MPhil, CUNY, 1994, PhD, 1995. Cert. protection profl. Researcher Connective Tissues Research Lab., Copenhagen; 1963; copywriter numerous advt. agys., 1965-70; owner, editor Security Letter, N.Y.C., 1970—; editor, pub. HBJ Publs., 1973-76; pres. Mags. for Medicine, Inc., 1972-81. Faculty John Jay Coll. Criminal Justice, 1985—, adj. to full prof., chair Law, Police Sci. and Criminal Justice Adminstrn., 1997—; cons. in field; spkr. at numerous meetings. Editor: Behavioral Medicine, 1978—81, Security Letter Source Book, 1983—, Security Jour., 1989—98; author: Security Operations Management, 2001, Readings in Security Management, 2002; contbr. books and articles on security and urban crime and policing. Mem. AAUP, Am. Hist. Assn., Am. Correctional Assn., Am. Soc. Indsl. Security (pres.'s cert. of merit 1990), Nat. Coun. Investigation and Security Svcs. (Duffy Meml. Achievement award 1992), Internat. Security Mmgt. Assn. (Brennan award 1993), Urban History Assn., Internat. Assn. of Profl. Security Cons. Disting. Svc., Accolade, Union League Club, Alpha Tau Omega, Delta Sigma Rho, Pi Delta Epsilon. Presbyterian. Home: 49 E 96th St New York NY 10128-0782 Office: 166 E 96th St New York NY 10128-2565 also: John Jay Coll Criminal Justice 899 10th Ave New York NY 10019-1069 E-mail: rmccrie@mindspring.com.

MCCRIMMON, BARBARA SMITH, writer, librarian; b. Anoka, Minn., May 3, 1918; d. Webster Roy and Jessie (Sargeant) Smith; m. James McNab McCrimmon, June 10, 1939; Children: Kevin Mor, John Marshall. BA, U. Minn., 1939; MSL.S., U. Ill., 1961; PhD, Fla. State U., 1973. Asst. librarian Ill. State Nat. Hist. Survey, Champaign, Ill., 1961-62; research assoc. Bur. Community Planning, U. Ill., Champaign, 1962-63; librarian Ill. Water Survey, Champaign, 1964-65, Am. Meterol. Soc., Boston, 1965-67; edit. asst. Jour. Library History, Tallahassee, 1967-69, 73-74. Adj. asst. prof. Sch. Library Sci., Fla. State U., Tallahassee, 1976-77. Author: Power, Politics and Print, 1981, Richard Garnett: The Scholar as Librarian, 1989; editor: American Library Philosophy, 1975; contbr. articles to profl. jours. Mem. ALA, Pvt. Libraries Assn., Beta Phi Mu, Manuscript Soc. Democrat. Home: The Colonnades C30 2600 Barracks Rd Charlottesville VA 22901

MCCROHAN, KEVIN FRANCIS, business educator; b. N.Y.C., Apr. 7, 1944; s. Francis Howard and Edith Mary McCrohan; m. Veronica Joan, May 28, 1966; children: Tara Marie, Kenneth Francis. BS, NYU, 1967; MBA in Internat. Bus., CUNY, 1971, MBA, 1974, PhD, 1978. Contract adminstr. Ametalco, Inc., N.Y.C., 1966-69; lectr., instr. mktg. Baruch Coll., 1971-75; assoc. prof. mktg. U. New Haven, West Haven, Conn., 1975-80; chief economist IRS, Washington, 1980-81, chief economist, cons., 1981-86; assoc. prof. mktg. George Mason U., Fairfax, Va., 1981-84, chmn. mktg., 1987-90, prof. mktg., 1984—; sr. Fulbright scholar Trinity, Dublin, Ireland, 1988, Kathmandu (Nepal) U., 1998. Cons. in field. Contbr. over 100 articles and papers to profl. jours. and nat. and internat. confs. Bd. dirs. Friends of Children Vietnam, N.Y., 1973-76. Col. USAR, 1968-2000, ret. Decorated Legion of Merit; Am. Assembly Collegiate Schs. of Bus. fed. faculty fellow, 1981. Mem. Am. Mktg. Assn., Am. Statis. Assn., Assn. for Consumer Rsch., Beta Gamma Sigma. Avocations: hiking, climbing, gardening. Office: George Mason U 4400 University Dr Fairfax VA 22030-4444

MCCROHON, CRAIG, lawyer; b. Harvey, Ill., Oct. 17, 1961; s. Maxwell and Nancy McCrohon. BA, Harvard U., 1984; postgrad., London Sch. Econs., 1988; JD, MBA, U. Pa., 1989. Bar: Ill. 1989, U.S. Dist. Ct. (no. dist.) Ill. 1989. Partner McBride, Baker & Coles, Chicago. Editor: Let's Go: USA, 1983. Mem. Cook County Transition Team-Econ. Devel., 1995. Mem.: Tech. Execs. Roundtable (pres. 1996—2001), Ill. C. of C. (working group econ. devel. com. 1992), Chgo. Bar Assn. (chmn. com. on consumer fin. svcs. 1991—92). Home: 2 E 8th St Apt 2708 Chicago IL 60605-2134 Office: 500 W Madison St Chicago IL 60661-4544

MCCRONE, ALISTAIR WILLIAM, retired university president; b. Regina, Can., Oct. 7, 1931; BA, U. Sask., 1953; MSc, U. Nebr., 1955; PhD, U. Kans., 1961. Instr. geology NYU, 1959-61, asst. prof., 1961-64, assoc. prof., 1964-69, prof., 1969-70, supr. Rsch. Ship Sea Owl on L.I. Sound, 1959-64, asst. dir. univ. program, 1965-66, resident master Rubin Internat. Residence Hall, 1966-69, chmn. dept. geology, 1966-69, assoc. dean Grad. Sch. Arts and Scis., 1969-70; prof. geology, acad. v.p. U. Pacific, 1970-74, acting pres., 1971; prof. geology, pres. Calif. State U. Sys. Humboldt State U., Arcata, 1974—2002. Mem. sys. exec. coun. Calif. State U. Sys., 1974-2002, acad. senate Humboldt State U., 1974-2002, mem. chancellor's com. on innovative programs, 1974-76, trustees' task force on off-campus instrn., 1975-76, exec. com. Chancellor's Coun. of Pres., 1976-79, Calif. state del. Am. Assn. State Colls. and Univs., 1977-80; mem. Commn. on Ednl. Telecomm., 1983-86; chair Calif. State U. Statewide Task Force on Earthquake and Emergency preparedness, 1985-88, 95; chmn., mem. accreditation teams Western Assn. Schs. and Colls.; chair com. on energy and environ. Am. Assn. State Colls. and Univs., 1980-84; chair program com. Western Coll.Assn., 1983-84, panelist, 1983; mem. bd. dirs. Assn. Am. Colls., 1989-93, chair, 1992-93. Contbr. articles to profl. jours.; lectr. on geology Sunrise Semester program CBS Nat. Network, 1969-70; various appearances on local TV stas. Bd. trustees Presbyn. Hosp.-Pacific Med. Ctr., San Francisco, 1971-74; mem. Calif. Coun. for Humanities, 1977-82; mem. local campaign bd. United Way, 1977-83; mem. Am. Friends Wilton Park, 1980—; bd. dirs. Humboldt Convention and Visitors Bur., 1980-87, Redwood Empire Assn., 1983-87; bd. dirs. Calif. State Automobile Assn., 1988—, Am. Automobile Assn., 1990-93; bd. trustees Calif. State Parks Found., 1994-2000. Shell fellow in geology U. Nebr., 1954-55; Danforth assoc. NYU, 1964. Fellow Calif. Acad. Scis.; mem. AAAS, Geol. Soc. Am., Am. Assn. U. Adminstrs. (nat. bd. 1986-89, 96-99, 2001-2002), St. Andrews Soc. N.Y. (life), Rotary, Sigma Xi (pres. NYU chpt. 1967-69), Phi Kappa Phi. Avocation: golf. Office: Humboldt State U Univ Campus Arcata CA 95521

MCCRORY, JOHN BROOKS, retired lawyer; b. St. Cloud, Minn., Oct. 23, 1925; s. John Raymond and Mary Lee (Rutter) McC.; m. Margaret Joan Dickson, Sept. 4, 1954 (dec. Apr. 1957); 1 child, William B.; m. Elizabeth Ann Quick, June 27, 1959; children— John B., Ann Elizabeth BA, Swarthmore Coll., 1948; JD, U. Pa., 1951. Bar: N.Y. 1952, D.C. 1985. Assoc. Donovan, Leisure, Newton, Lumbard & Irvine, N.Y.C., 1951-52, Nixon, Hargrave, Devans & Doyle, Rochester, N.Y., 1952-62, ptnr., 1963-92; ret., 1992. Author: Constitutional Privilege in Libel Law, 1977-90. Served to lt. comdr. USNR, 1943-47, PTO Fellow Am. Coll. Trial Lawyers; mem. ABA, Monroe County Bar Assn., N.Y. State Bar Assn., D.C. Bar Assn. Republican. Presbyterian. Home: 25 Kendal Dr Kennett Square PA 19348-2321 Office: Nixon Peabody LLP Clinton Sq PO Box 31051 Rochester NY 14603-1051

MCCRORY, MICHAEL ELLIOTT, radiologist; b. Coral Gables, Fla., Jan. 9, 1947; s. Seaborn Montgomery and Helen (Faires) McC.; m. Joellyn Lewis, May 26, 1973; children: Michael Conor, Lindsay Shea. AB in Biology, Princeton U., 1969; MD, Tufts U., 1973. Diplomate Am. Bd. Radiology. Resident in radiology Med. Coll. Wis., Milw., 1973-77; staff radiologist Durham (N.C.) VA Hosp., 1977-79; asst. prof. radiology Duke U. Med. Ctr., Durham, 1977-79; radiologist/ptnr. Durham Radiology Assocs., 1979—. Mem. AMA, Am. Coll. Radiology, Radiol. Soc. N.Am. Office: Durham Radiology Assocs 4323 Ben Franklin Blvd Durham NC 27704-2177

MCCRORY, PATRICK, mayor; b. Columbus, Oct. 17, 1956; m. Ann Gordon. BA in Polit. Sci. and Edn., Catawba Coll., 1978. With Duke Power Co., N.C., 1978—, now mgr. bus. rels.; mem. Charlotte City Coun., 1989—, mayor protem, 1993-95, mayor, 1995—. Co-chmn. Charlotte's Fighting Back Commn.; mem. Children Svcs. Network; hon. chmn. Cystic Fibrosis Found., Arthritis Found.; former chmn. United Way Corp. Campaign; former mem. U. N.C.-Charlotte Bus. Adv. Com., Charlotte Bond Campaign, ARC Pers. Recruitment Com.; H.S. basketball ofcl.; former bd. dirs. Drug Free Workplace Alliance Com.; founder Uptown Crime Prevention Coun. Office: Office of the Mayor Govt Ctr 600 E 4th St Charlotte NC 28202-2816*

MC CRORY, WALLACE WILLARD, pediatrician, educator; b. Racine, Wis., Jan. 19, 1920; s. Willard L. and Beulah (St. Clair) McC.; m. Sylvia E. Hogben, Feb. 6, 1943; children— Pamela, Michael, Christine. BS, U. Wis., 1941, MD, 1944. Diplomate: Am. Bd. Pediatrics. Rotating intern Phila. Gen. Hosp., 1944-45; resident pediatrics Children's Hosp., Phila., 1945-46, chief resident physician, 1948-49, asso. pediatrician, 1953-55, sr. pediatrician, 1955-58; provisional asst. pediatrician to out-patients, Lewis Cass Ledyard, Jr. fellow pediatrics N.Y. Hosp., 1949-50, pediatrician-in-chief, 1961-80, sr. pediatrician, chief pediatric nephrology, 1980—. Chief pediatric service Univ. Hosp., Iowa City, 1958-61; instr. pathology U. Wis. Med. Sch., 1942-43; instr. pediatrics U. Pa. Sch. Medicine, 1948-49, instr., research fellow pediatrics, 1950-53, asst. prof., 1953-55, asso. prof., 1955-58; prof. pediatrics, chmn. dept. State U. Iowa Coll. Medicine, 1958-61; prof. pediatrics Cornell U. Med. Coll., 1961— Pres. Nat. Kidney Found., 1964-66. Served to capt., M.C. AUS, 1946-48. Fellow N.Y. Acad. Medicine, Royal Soc. Medicine; mem. Am. Pediatric Soc., Am. Acad. Pediatrics, Soc. Pediatric Research, Am. Soc. Nephrology, Am. Soc. Pediatric Nephrology, AAAS, Sigma Xi, Alpha Omega Alpha. Home: 61 Carrs Tavern Rd Clarksburg NJ 08510-1506 Office: NY Hosp Cornell Med Ctr 525 E 68th St New York NY 10021-4885 E-mail: wallacemccrory@msn.com.

MCCRUM, ROBERT TIMOTHY, lawyer; b. Pitts., Nov. 4, 1958; s. Robert Terrence and Gertrude Callanan McCrum; m. Andrea Nourie, Mar. 19, 1960; children: Megan, Kelsey, Brian, Colleen, Shane. BA in Geology, Franklin & Marshall Coll., 1980; JD, Lewis & Clark Coll., 1983. Atty. U.S. Dept. Interior, Washington, 1984-86; ptnr. Crowell & Moring LLP, 1986—, vice chmn. natural resources and environ. group. Co-author: RCRA Hazardous Waste Handbook, 1996, Superfund Manual, 1997, Natural Resources Law Manual, 1995. Mem. Bush-Cheney Transition Adv. Com., 2000-2001. Mem. ABA (chmn. mining com. sect. environment, energy and resources 1997-99), Rocky Mt. Mineral Law Found. (bd. trustees). Republican. Roman Catholic. Avocation: prestidigitation. Office: Crowell & Moring LLP 1001 Pennsylvania Ave NW Washington DC 20004-2505

MCCRYSTAL, ANN MARIE, community health nurse, administrator; b. Jersey City, Jan. 5, 1937; d. Robert W. and Sybilla M. (Koenig) Bouse; m. Hugh K. McCrystal, Sept. 14, 1963; children: Carolyn, Hugh K., Kelly Ann. BSN, U. Miami, 1959. Office mgr., sec.-treas. Indian River Urology Assocs., P.C., Vero Beach, Fla.; chmn. bd. Vis. Nurse Assn. of the Treasure Coast. Chmn. Vis. Nurse Assn. Treasure Coast Found., 1991, adv. coun. Vis. Nurse Assn. of Am., 1994; chmn. bd. dirs. Vis. Nurse Assn./Hospice Found. Named Indian River County Woman of Distinction, Girl Scouts Am., 1998, Vol. Fundraiser of Yr., Treasure Coast Nat. Soc. Fundraising Execs., 1999, Book of Golden Deeds award Exch. Club Vero Beach, 2000; recipient C. of C. Cmty. Svc. award, 2000. Mem. Fla. Nurses Assn., Am. Urol. Assn. Allied, Am. Cancer Soc. (life hon.), Vis. Nurse Assn. Am. (chmn. bd. dirs. 1995—, adv. coun., edn. com., Vol. of Yr. 1991), Sigma Theta Tau. Home: 511 Bay Dr Vero Beach FL 32963-2163

MCCUAIG, IAN CARRUTHERS, fundraising consultant; b. Orillia, Ont., Can., Mar. 5, 1962; came to U.S., 1992; s. Alan Hayes and Elizabeth Louise (Bonnell) McC.; m. Sarah Elizabeth Robertson, July 2, 1994. Student, Royal Conservatory of Music, Toronto, Ont., 1983; BA in Internat. Rels., U. Toronto, 1990; CSPG, Calif. State U., 1997. Cert. specialist planned giving. Devel. cons. UN Assn., Toronto, 1988-89; account exec. Gordon L. Goldie Co., Ltd., 1989-92; cons. Marts & Lundy, Inc., San Francisco, 1992-96; sr. dir. Devel. Goodwill, 1996—. Contbr. articles to profl. publs. Nat. sec. Amnesty Internat. Can., Ottawa, Ont., 1986-88; chair human rights com. UN Assn., Toronto, 1988-89; elder Timothy Eaton Meml. Ch., Toronto, 1984-92; deacon Calvary Presbyn. Ch., San Francisco, 1992-96; mem. Dem. Nat. Com. Mem. World Affairs Coun., Nat. Soc. Fundraising Execs. (cert., v.p. Golden Gate chpt., mem. nat. acad.), Internat. Diplomacy Coun., Nat. Com. on Planned Giving Can.-Am. C. of C., St. Francis Yacht Club, Commonwealth Club of Calif. Avocation: sailing. Office: Goodwill 1500 Mission St San Francisco CA 94103-2513

MCCUAN, WILLIAM PATRICK, real estate company executive; b. Muskogee, Okla., Oct. 28, 1941; s. Lee L. and LaRee A. (Beverage) McC.; m. Jill Pamela Thomas, May 5, 1982; children: LaRee, Megan. Student, U. Tulsa, 1961-62; BA in Psychology, Baylor U., 1965; MRE, So. Sem., Louisville, 1967; MS, U. Louisville, 1969; postgrad., U. Md., 1971-73. Prof., asst. dean grad. sch. U. Md., Balt., 1969-73; lobbyist, cons. Washington, 1973-76; CEO KMS Group, Inc., Columbia, Md., 1976-84, MDG Cos. of Md., 1984—, MDG-Capital Corp., Naples, Fla., 1992—, MDG Cos. of W.Va., Berkeley Springs, 1991—, Place McCuan Found. Adj. prof. Cmty. Coll., Balt., 1969-72, U. Md. College Park, 1969-71; lectr. Univ. Coll.-Univ. Md., Balt., 1970-71, Howard C.C., Columbia, 1987-88; CEO Pet Holiday, Inc., Toledo, 1973-94; CEO Uniglobe Columbia Travel Ctr., 1986-94; non-lawyer mem. Atty. Grievance Commn., Md., 1990-96. Contbr. to numerous publs. Chmn., bd. dirs. Concert Soc. Md., 1988-98; chmn. United Way, Howard County, Md., 1984, Am. Presdl. Inaugural Com., Md., 1988, Howard County Cmty. Partnerships; fin. chmn. Rep. Ctrl. Com., Howard County, 1988-92; trustee Columbia Found.; mem. Pres.'s Commn. on Food, Nutrition and Health, Washington, 1970, Howard County Environ. Affairs Bd.; mem. bus. adv. coun. Howard C.C.; bd. dirs. Congl. Commn. on Mental Health of Children, Washington, 1973-75, Human Svcs. Inst. for Children and Families; pres., trustee McCuan Family Found., 1997—. Recipeint Alumni Fellows award U. Louisville, 1996. Mem. Nat. Assn. Home Builders (bd. dirs. 1979-87, fed. govt. affairs com.), Md. Builders Assn. (pres. 1981-82), Home Builders Assn. Md. (bd. dirs. 1977-82, Award of Honor 1979, Award of Excellence 1980, Presdl. award 1982), Howard County Home Builders Assn. (pres. 1978-80), Howard County C. of C. (pres. bd. dirs. 1984-86). Home: 4256 Snowberry Ln Naples FL 34119-8513 also: 11838 Farside Rd Ellicott City MD 21042-1526 Office: MDG Bldg 5550 Sterrett Pl Columbia MD 21044-2611 E-mail: pmccuan@aol.com.

MCCUBBIN, SHARON ANGLIN, elementary school educator; b. Fullerton, Calif., Nov. 20, 1948; d. Floyd Calvin and Grace Ann Anglin; m. David Paul White (div. 1990); children: Julie, Adrian, Matthew; m. Robert Patrick McCubbin, July 13, 1991. BA, U. Calif., 1973; MEd, Cleve. State U., 1993. Cert. clear multiple subject profl. pre-K, Calif., elem. Montessori tchr., early childhood edn.; cert. mid. childhood generalist, early childhood generalist Nat. Bd. Cert. Tchrs.; cert. Clear Crosscultural, Lang. and Acad. Devel. Tchr. Primanti Montessori, Orange, Calif., 1977-81; tchr., adminstr. Montessori of Orange, 1981-83, Tustin Hills Montessori, Santa Ana, Calif., 1983-89; tchr., cons. for Montessori programs Irvine (Calif.) Unified Sch. Dist., 1990—; Montessori elem. mentor tchr., 1990—. Cons. title VII programs Irvine Unified Sch. Dist., 1990—, GATE adv. bd. mem.; cons. for early childhood programs to local corps. Asst. Jr. Disabled Programs, Orange, 1988—. SBD fellow Johns Hopkins U., 1999. Mem. ASCD, AAUW, Assn. Montessori Internat., Assn. Montessori Internat./U.S.A., Assn. Montessori Internat. Elem. Alumni Assn. (regional rep. 1984), Am. Montessori Soc., N.Am. Montessori Tchrs. Assn., Pvt. Sch. Adminstrs., U. Calif.-Irvine Alumni Assn., Calif. Tchrs. Assn., Irvine Tchrs. Assn., Nat. Coun. Tchrs. Math., Nat. Coun. for Social Studies, Nat. Assn. for Edn. of Young Children. Home: PO Box 616 Tustin CA 92781-0616 Office: Irvine Unified Sch Dist 5050 Barranca Pkwy Irvine CA 92604-4698 also: Santiago Hills Elem 29 Christamon W Irvine CA 92620-1836 E-mail: smccubbi@iusd.k12.ca.us., smccubbi@aol.com.

MCCUE, ARTHUR HARRY, artist, educator; b. N.Y.C., Sept. 27, 1944; s. Raymond Noel and Alice (Cassidy) McC.; m. Lorraine Havel Bingham, Nov. 18, 1989. BFA, Pratt Inst., N.Y.C., 1967; MFA, U. Colo., 1969. Instr. art SUNY, Geneseo, 1969-72; instr. printmaking and drawing Ithaca (N.Y.) Coll., 1973-77, assoc. prof., 1987-2001, chmn. dept. art, 1977—, prof., 2001—. Guest speaker sch. supt.'s seminar Ithaca Coll., 1990; guest artist N.Y. State Pastel Artists Assn., Cooperstown, 1990, 92, Schweinfurth Meml. Art Ctr., 1990; cons., interpreter on wheelwrighting Onondaga County Parks, Salt Mus., Liverpool, N.Y., 1989-90; guest lectr. dept. art Tompkins Cortland Community Coll., 1987. One-man shows include Univ. Club, Boulder, Colo., 1968, David Gallery, Rochester, N.Y., 1973, Ithaca Coll., 1977, 79, 97, Art Gallery Adelphi U., Garden City, N.Y., 1980, Wagner Gallery, Lodi, N.Y., 1983, Ithaca House Gallery, 1984, 85, Schwein Furth Meml. Mus., Auburn, N.Y., 1986, Johnson Mus. Art, Ithaca, 1987, Upstairs Gallery, Ithaca, 1992, Lamoreaux Landing Wine Cellars Gallery, Lodi, N.Y., 1993, 97, 99, Trumanburg Conservatory Fine Arts, 1993, Wells Coll., Aurora, N.Y., 1995; exhibited in two-person shows at Harry McCue/David Smyth, Ithaca House, 1980, Hackworth/McCue, U. Pa., Edinboro, Grippi/McCue, Handwerker Gallery, Ithaca, McCue/Licht, Upstairs Gallery, Ithaca; exhibited in group shows at Internat. Gallery, Denver, 1969, Double U. Gallery, N.Y.C., 1977, Handwerker Gallery, 1980, 82, 84, 85, 86, 87, 89, 90, 91, 92, 93, 94, 95, 97, 98, 99, Upstairs Gallery, 1983—, Everson Mus., Syracuse (2d prize printmaking 1987), New Visions Gallery, Ithaca, 1987-90, Elmira Coll., 1991, Cazenovia Coll., 1993, Cooperstown Nat., 1993, 96, 97, 01, Old Forge Art Assn., 1992, West End Gallery, Corning, N.Y., 1996, 97, 2001; nat. exhbns.: Fall River Art Show, Mass., 1973, 74, 76, Marietta (Ohio) Coll., 1974, 76, Arnot Mus., Elmira, N.Y., 1977, 96, 2001, Ft. Hays State U., 1984, U. Maine, 1985, 92, 93, 96-99, Everson Mus., 1985; included in book The American History Supply Catalogue, 1983, N.Y. Art Rev., 3d edit.; invited spl. guest at spl. showing Christie's Auction House, N.Y.C., 1984, Roch Meml. Art Gallery, 1991; commd. by Cornell U./Statler Hotel to design art work for hotel, 1988. Lodestar grantee, 1984. Home: 2423 Skinner Rd Lodi NY 14860-9739 Office: Ithaca Coll Dept Art Danby Rd Ithaca NY 14850-5736

MCCUE, DAVID J. information systems specialist, entrepreneur; b. Phila., Mar. 28, 1956; s. Earl E. and A. Kathleen McCue; m. Nicole E. Schumacher, Aug. 16, 1981; 1 child, Christopher D. BSc, Rider U., 1978; MBA, NYU, 1980. Cons. Human Sys. Inc., New Vernon, N.J., 1980-81; from cons. to regional dir. tech. Andersen Consulting, 1981-93; chief info. and resource officer Am. Practice Mgmt., Inc., N.Y.C., 1993-96; chief info. officer Computer Scis. Corp., 1996-2001; corp. dir. global applications Computer Scis. Corp. Worldwide, 2001—. Mem. adv. bd. Coll. Edn., Rider U., Lawrenceville, N.J., 1997-99. Mgr. Somerset County 4-H Fair, 1998—99; mem. Air Safety Found.; bd. dirs. Rider U. Alumni Assn., 1984—. Mem. Inst. Mgmt. Cons. (cert.), Assn. MBA Execs., Am. Prodn. and Inventory Control Soc. (cert. prodn. and inventory mgr.). Am. Soc. Indsl. Security, Aircraft Owners and Pilots Assn., Exptl. Aircraft Assn., NRA. Republican. Roman Catholic. Avocations: commercial aviation pilot, equestrian sports. Home: 465 Church Rd Bridgewater NJ 08807-1982 Office: CSC Corp Office VTC-C 348 MC 320 3170 Fairview Park Dr Falls Church VA 22042 E-mail: djmccue@mccue.org.

MCCUE, DENNIS MICHAEL, management consultant; b. Pitts., July 28, 1952; s. Stephen J. and Mary (Maddalon) McC. BA, U. Dayton, 1974. Dist. exec. Allegheny Trails Coun., Boy Scouts Am., Pitts., 1974-77; area mgr. The Nestle Co., 1977-79; account mgr. So. Pacific Communications, 1979-82; dir. sales and mktg. Amertel Co., 1982-84, ITT Bu. Communications, Newport Beach, Calif., 1985-86; dir. mktg. Damac Products, Santa Fe Springs, 1986-87; ptnr. Hunter-McCue Mgmt. Cons., Newport Beach, 1987-89; pres. McCue Assocs., Costa Mesa, 1989—2002, Dynamic Firm Mgmt., Newport Beach, 2002—. Instr. computer info. sys. Cerritos Coll., Norwalk, Calif., 1996—. Contbr. articles to profl. jours. Grad. Leadership Tomorrow, 1988, program chmn., bd. dirs., 1993-95. Mem. Nat. Assn. Corp. Dirs., Nat. Bur. Profl. Mgmt. Cons. (cert. profl. mgmt. cons.), Inst. Mgmt. Cons. (cert. mgmt. cons.), Lew Epstein Men's Club (mgr. 1986-90). Avocations: travel, PC computing, dog showing and training. Office: Dynamic Firm Mgmt 1500 Quail St # 550 Newport Beach CA 92660

MCCUE, HOWARD MCDOWELL, III, lawyer, educator; b. Sumter, S.C., Jan. 4, 1946; s. Howard McDowell and Carolyn Hartwell (Moore) McC.; m. Judith Weiss, Apr. 3, 1972; children— Howard McDowell IV, Leigh AB, Princeton U., 1968; JD, Harvard U., 1971. Bar: Mass. 1971, Ill. 1975, U.S. Tax Ct. 1977. Assoc. Hale and Dorr, Boston, 1971-72; assoc. Mayer, Brown & Platt, Chgo., 1975-77, ptnr., 1977—. Adj. prof. law master in tax program Chgo. Kent Coll. Law, 1981— Author: (with others) Drafting Wills and Trust Agreements, 1979, 82, 85, 87, 90; mem. editorial adv. bd. Trusts and Estates mag., 1981-2000; contbr. articles to profl. jours. Bd. dirs. Art Inst. Chgo., Lawrence Hall Youth Svcs., chmn. bd. govs. Northwestern U. Libr. Coun.; bd. dirs., past vice-chmn. Ravinia Festival Assn. Lt. USN, 1972-75. Princeton U. scholar, 1965 Mem. ABA, Ill. Bar Assn., Chgo. Bar Assn. (fed. tax com., past chmn., exec. coun.), Chgo. Bar Found. (past pres.), Am. Coll. Tax Counsel, Am. Coll. Trust and Estate Counsel, Harvard Law Soc. Ill., Internat. Acad. Estate and Trust Law, Chgo. Club, Phi Beta Kappa.

MCCUE, JUDITH W. lawyer; b. Phila., Apr. 7, 1948; d. Emanuel Leo and Rebecca (Raffel) Weiss; m. Howard M. McCue III, Apr. 3, 1971; children: Howard, Leigh. BA cum laude, U. Pa., 1969; JD, Harvard U., 1972. Bar: Ill. 1972, U.S. Tax Ct. 1984. Ptnr. McDermott, Will & Emery, Chgo., 1995—. Dir. Schawk, Inc., Des Plaines, Ill.; past pres. Chgo. Estate Planning Coun. Trustee Chgo. Symphony Orch., 1995—, vice chair, 1998—2001. Fellow Am. Coll. Trust and Estate Counsel (com. chair 1991-94, 98—, regent 1992-2000, treas. 2002—); mem. Chgo. Bar Assn. (chmn. probate practice com. 1984-85, chmn. fed. estate and gift tax divsn. fed. tax com. 1988-89). Office: McDermott Will & Emery 227 W Monroe St Ste 3100 Chicago IL 60606-5096 E-mail: jmccue@mwe.com.

MCCUEAN, OCTAVIA COPENHAVER, foundation administrator; b. Pensacola, Fla., Jan. 18, 1956; d. Lawrence Luther and Ida (Wolfe) Copenhaver; m. Douglas Clifton McCuean, Aug. 20, 1983. BA in Polit. Sci., Auburn (Ala.) U., 1978. dir., bd. dirs. Preservation Action, Inc., Washington, 1986—. Pub. info. officer Northwest Fla. Water Mgmt. Dist., Tallahassee, 1978-83; exec. dir. Fla. Trust for Hist. Preservation, 1983-88; with The Nature Conservancy, Atlanta, 1988—. Mem. Sec. of State's Columbian Quincentenary Co., Tallahassee, 1986, 87. Mem. altar guild St. John's Episcopal Ch., Tallahassee, 1980-85; active Leadership Tallahassee, 1984; v.p. Leadership Tallahassee Alumni, 1986-87, pres., 1987-88; bd. dirs. Vol. Ctr., Tallahassee, 1986. Named one of Outstanding Young Women in Am., 1982-83. Mem. Fla. Soc. Assn. Execs., Tallahassee Soc. Assn. Execs., Auburn Alumni Club (3d v.p. 1980), Tallahassee Phi Mu Alumnae Club (pres. 1980-81). Clubs: Jr. League of Tallahassee (chmn. pub. relations bd. 1984-85, corr. sec., exec. com. 1986-87). Democrat. Avocations: painting, swimming, skiing, gardening. Office: The Nature Conservancy PO Box 53131 667 Timm Valley Rd NE Atlanta GA 30305-4710

MCCUEN, JOHN JOACHIM, business executive, columnist and lecturer; b. Washington, Mar. 30, 1926; s. Joseph Raymond and Josephine (Joachim) McC.; m. Gloria Joyce Seidel, June 16, 1949; children: John Joachim Jr., Les Seidel. BS, U.S. Mil. Acad., 1948; M of Internatl. Affairs, Columbia U., 1961; grad., U.S. Army War Coll., 1968. Commd. 2d. lt. U.S. Army, 1948, advanced through grades to col.; dir. internal def. and devel. U.S. Army War Coll., Carlisle Barracks, Pa., 1969-72; chief U.S. Def. Liaison Group, Jakarta, Indonesia, 1972-74; chief field survey office U.S. Army Tng. and Doctrine Command, Ft. Monroe, Va., 1974-76; ret. U.S. Army, 1976; mgr. tng. Chrysler Def., Center Line, Mich., 1977-82; mgr. modification ctr. Land Systems div. Gen. Dynamics, Sterling Heights, 1982-83, mgr. field ops. Warren, 1983-94; pres. Mich. Econ. Devel. Corp., Birmingham, 1994—, The Magic Christmas Tree, Inc., Birmingham, 1994—; pres., CEO Laminar, Inc., Southfield, Mich., 1996—; owner Adventure and Exotic Travel Outfitters, Inc., Birmingham, 1995—; past pres. First Internat. Corp., 1995-97. Ptnr. East West Connection, Birmingham, Mich.; past pres. Energy Resource Mgmt. Sys., Inc., Birmingham; armor advisor 3d Royal Thai Army, Utaradit, 1957-58; U.S. rep. users' com. NATO Missile Firing Installation Crete, Paris, 1964-66; advisor Vietnamese Nat. Def. Coll., Saigon, 1968-69; columnist Army Times; spkr. on terrorism and counter insurgency. Author: The Art of Counter Revolutionary War-The Strategy of Counter Insurgency, Faber 1966, Stackpole, 1967, Circulo Militar, 1967; columnist Army Times, 2002-. Pres. Troy (Mich.) Cmty. Concert Assn., 1985—, bd. dirs., 1982—; past pres. Mich. Oriental Art Soc., Birmingham; pres. Grander View Found. Sr. Housing and Nursing, Milford, Mich., 1984-89; 1st reader First Ch. of Christ Scientist, Birmingham, 1989-92, chmn. bd. dirs. 2000-01; past chmn. region VI N.E. unit Detroit United Way Campaign. Mem. Soc. Logistics Engrs., Nat. Mgmt. Assn., Assn. U.S. Army, Oriental Art Soc. Republican. Avocations: oriental antiques, national security, writing. Home: 32863 Balmoral St Beverly Hills MI 48025-3008 Office: Laminar Inc 802 S Worth St Birmingham MI 48009-6929 also: Mich Econ Devel Corp 802 S Worth St Birmingham MI 48009-6929

MCCUEN, JOHN FRANCIS, JR. lawyer; b. N.Y.C., Mar. 11, 1944; s. John Francis and Elizabeth Agnes McCuen; m. Christine McCuen; children: Sarah, Mary, John. AB, U. Notre Dame, 1966; JD, U. Detroit, 1969. Bar: Mich. 1970, Fla. 1970, Ohio 1978. Legal counsel Kelsey-Hayes Co., Romulus, Mich., 1970-77; corp. counsel Sheller-Globe Corp., Toledo, 1977-79, v.p., gen. counsel, 1979-86, sec., 1982-87, sr. v.p. gen. counsel, 1986-89; ptnr. Marshall & Melhorn, Toledo, 1989-92; pvt. practice Law Offices John F. McCuen, 1992-93; counsel Butzel Long, Ann Arbor, Mich., 1994; v.p. legal Kelsey Hayes Co., Livonia, 1994-98, v.p., gen. counsel, 1998-99; of counsel Butzel Long, 1999—2001. Trustee Kidney Found. N.W. Ohio, 1979-88, pres., 1984-86. Mem. ABA, Fla. Bar, Mich. Bar, Forest Lake Country Club. Home: 1668 Trading Post Ln Bloomfield Hills MI 48302-1868

MCCUISTION, PEG OREM, hospice administrator; b. Houston, July 28, 1930; d. William Darby and Dorothy Mildred (Beckett) Orem; m. Palmer Day McCuistion, Sept. 4, 1949 (div. 1960); 1 child, Leeanne E. BBA, Southwest Tex. State, 1963; MBA, George Washington U., 1968; EdD, Wayne State U., 1989. Patient care adminstr. Holy Cross Hosp., Silver Spring, Md., 1968-79; exec. dir. Hospice of S.E. Mich., Southfield, 1979-86, Hospice Austin, Tex., 1987-94; CEO EMBI, Inc., Arlington, 1994—98; gen. mgr. Hospice Home Care, San Antonio, 2001—. Bd. dirs. Cmty. Home for the Elderly, Austin, 1989-92. Fellow Am. Coll. Health Care Execs. (membership com.); mem. Internat. Hospice Inst. (assoc.), Nat. Hospice Orgn. (chair standards and accreditation com.), Tex. Hospice Orgn. (pres. 1993-94), exec. com., standards and ethics com., edn. com., chair legis. com.), Mich. Hospice Orgn. (chair edn. com., bd. dirs.). Office: Hospice Home Care 10122 Desert Sands San Antonio TX 78216 E-mail: pegomc@wimberley-tx.com.

MCCUISTION, ROBERT WILEY, hospital administrator, management consultant, lawyer; b. Wilson, Ark., June 15, 1927; s. Ed Talmadge and Ruth Wiley (Bassett) McC.; m. Martha Virginia Golden, June 11, 1949 (dec. Nov. 1991); children: Beth, Dan, Jed.; m. Sudola M. Getz, Feb. 12, 1994. AB in History and Polit. Sci, Hendrix Coll., Conway, Ark., 1949; JD, U. Ark., 1952. Bar: Ark. 1952, U.S. Dist. Ct. (we. dist.) Ark. 1953. Practice in, Dermott, Ark., 1952-57; dep. pros. atty. 10th Jud. Dist. Ark., 1952-57; bus. mgr. St. Mary's Hosp., Dermott, 1953-56, asst. adminstr., 1956-57; adminstr. Stuttgart (Ark.) Meml. Hosp., 1957-60, Forrest Meml. Hosp., Forrest City, Ark., 1960-68; assoc. adminstr. St. Edward Mercy Hosp., Ft. Smith, 1968-70; pres. Meml. Med Center, Corpus Christi, Tex., 1970-79; adminstr. Methodist Hosp., Mitchell, S.D., 1979-85, cons., 1985-86; mgmt. cons., owner Creative Leadership Concepts, Arlington, Tex., 1985—; adminstr. Cen. United Meth. Ch., Fayetteville, 1986-91. Sec. Ark. Hosp. Adminstrs. Forum, 1958-59, pres., 1959-60; pres. Ark. Hosp. Assn., 1964-65, Areawide Health Planning, 1970; pres. Ark. Conf. Cath. Hosps., 1970; chmn. Twin City Hosp. Coun. West Ark., 1968; v.p. Ark. Assn. Mental Health, 1966-70. Div. chmn. Forrest City United Community Svcs., 1961, Corpus Christi United Way Community Svcs., 1972, DeSoto coun. Boy Scouts Am., Explorer advisor, 1954-57. With USAAF, World War II. Recipient Eminent Leadership award DeSoto Area council Boy Scouts Am., 1956 Mem. Am. Assn. Hosp. Accountants (pres. Ark. chpt. 1957), S.D. Hosp. Assn. (dist. chmn. 1980-81), Mid-West Hosp. Assn. (trustee 1963-65), Am. Coll. Health Execs. (life). Methodist (vice chmn., sec. ofcl. bd. 1957, lay del. S.D. ann. conf. 1980-85). Lodge: Rotary (pres. Forrest City 1964-65). Home and Office: 1101 Briarcreek Dr Arlington TX 76012-1824 E-mail: bobsue@airmail.net., bobandsue@sbcglobal.net.

MCCULLAGH, GRANT GIBSON, architect; b. Cleve., Apr. 18, 1951; s. Robert Ernest and Barbara Louise (Grant) McC.; m. Suzanne Dewar Folds, Sept. 13, 1975; children: Charles Weston Folds, Grant Gibson Jr. BArch, U. Ill., 1973; MArch, U. Pa., 1975; MBA, U. Chgo., 1979. Registered architect, Ill. Dir. mktg. The Austin Co., Chgo., 1977-83, asst. dist. mgr., 1983-84, dist. mgr., 1984-88, v.p., 1987-88; chmn., CEO McClier Corp., 1988—; chmn. Holmes & Narver, Orange, Calif., 1997-2001; exec. v.p. AECOM, L.A., 2000—. Contbr. articles to various indsl. publs. Bd. dirs. Friends of Prentice Hosp.; trustee Newberry Libr. Fellow: AIA; mem.: Design/Build Inst. Am., Indian Hill Country Club, Univ. Club, Casino Club, Chgo. Comml. Club, Econ. Club. Republican. Episcopalian. Home: 43 Locust Rd Winnetka IL 60093-3725 Office: AECOM 555 S Flower Ste 3700 Los Angeles CA 90071-2300

MCCULLAGH, JAMES CHARLES, publishing executive; b. London, Oct. 22, 1941; s. James Christopher and Violet Anne (Smith) McCullagh; children: Declan, Deidre. BS, Ind. U. Pa., 1968; MA, Lehigh U., 1970, PhD, 1974. Tchr. Holidaysburg (Pa.) Area H.S., 1968; teaching asst. Lehigh U., Bethlehem, 1968-71, doctoral fellow, 1971-73; vis. poet Pa. Coun. Arts Inc., Harrisburg, 1974-78; editor Rodale Press Inc., Emaus, 1979-83, pub., editor dir., group v.p., 1984—; pub. Novii Fermer, USSR, 1991—; pub. dir. Scuba Diving, 1992; sr. v.p. Internat. Mag. Devel.; mng. dir. Rodale Press, Inc., Russia, 1996—, DeSilva & Phillips, 1997—; dir. acquisitions Hachette Filipacchi Mags., N.Y.C., 1998-99, v.p. corp. strategy, 1999—; mng. dir. Sci. Am., 2000—. Author: (book) Bicycle Fitness Book, 1984, Bicycling for Health and Fitness, 1995, Cycling for Health, Fitness and Well-Being, 1995, The Mad Cow Culture Book, 1999, (poetry) That Kingdom Coming Business, 1984, Magazines and Culture, 2002; pub.: Mountain Bike, 1994. With USN, 1960—64. Recipient Man of the Yr. award, Bicycle Mfrs. Assn. Am., 1983. Mem.: Bicycle Inst. Am. (pres. 1993—), Bicycle Fedn. (bd. dirs. 1980—), Mag. Pubs. Assn., Am. Assn. Mag. Editors. Democrat. Roman Catholic. Home: 1952 Chancellor St Hellertown PA 18055-2802 E-mail: cmccullagh@sciam.com.

MCCULLAR, BRUCE HAYDEN, oral and maxillofacial surgeon; b. Memphis, June 19, 1953; s. Robert Hayden and Virginia Maria (Daniel) McC; m. Jennifer Hunt, Feb. 15, 1974 (div.); 1 child, Michael. BS in Vertebrate Zoology with honors, Memphis State U., 1976; DDS with honors, U. Tenn., 1979. Diplomate Am. Bd. Oral and Maxillofacial Surgery. Intern then resident U. Tenn. Hosp., Memphis, 1980-82; pvt. practice oral and maxillofacial surgery, 1983—. Assoc. prof. dept. oral and maxillofacial surgery U. Tenn., Memphis, 1987—; dept. head for oral and maxillofacial surgery LeBonheur Children's Med. Ctr. Mem. editorial adv. panel Jour. Dental Econs., 1988. Instr. ACLS, Am. Heart Assn., 1982—. Capt. USNR, 1985—. Fellow Am. Assn. Oral and Maxillofacial Surgeons, Am. Soc. Dental Anesthesiology, Am. Coll. Oral and Maxillofacial Surgeons, Southeastern Soc. Oral and Maxillofacial Surgeons; mem. ADA, Tenn. Dental Assn., Memphis Dental Soc. (Outstanding New Mem. 1987), Tenn. Soc. Oral and Maxillofacial Surgeons (sec.-treas. 1990-92, v.p. 1993-95, pres. 1996-97), Memphis Soc. Oral and Maxillofacial Surgeons (pres. 1991-92, sec.-treas. 1990-91), Naval Res. Assn., Assn. Mil. Surgeons of U.S., Memphis C. of C., Rotary Club (East Memphis br.), Chickasaw Country Club, Mensa, Intertel, Psi Omega, Omicron Kappa Upsilon. Republican. Episcopalian. Avocations: photography, scuba diving, physical fitness. Home and Office: 805 Estate Pl Ste 2 Memphis TN 38120-0647

MCCULLEN, JOSEPH T., JR. venture capitalist; b. Phila., Mar. 15, 1935; s. Joseph Thomas and Sara Ellen (Berryman) McC.; m. Eleanor Joan Houder, July 5, 1958; children: Geoffrey, Jennifer, Justin. BA, Villanova U., 1957, PhD (hon.), 1976. Mgr. planning & acquisitions Merck & Co., Inc., Rahway, N.J., 1961-65; sr. v.p., ptnr. Spencer Stuart & Assocs., N.Y.C., 1965-71; spl. asst. to Pres. Richard M. Nixon, Washington, 1971-73; asst. sec. of The Navy, 1973-77; sr. v.p., sec. New Eng. Mut. Life, Boston, 1977-80; pres. McCullen Ptnrs. Inc., 1980—; mng. dir. OneLiberty Ventures, 1986-99, Whitney & Co., Boston, 1999—2002; sr. advisor Key Bank, Cleve., 2002—; mng. dir. McCullen Capital, 2002—. Bd. dirs. MetroPCS, Inc., Dallas, EXTRAPRISE Group, Boston, Atlantis Wireless, Inc., Washington; bd. advisors Ctr. for Photonics, Boston U., 2002; sr. adviser Key Prin. Ptnrs. and Key Bank, 2002—; adviser Carrot Capital, Atlanta, 2002—, Transistion Team, Mass., (chmn. 2002). Mem. selection com. White House Fellows Program, 1979-96; bd. dirs. World Affairs Coun., 1977-95, Boston Ballet, 1978-85, chmn., 1980-85; bd. trustees Goodwill Industries, 1979-95, Boston Biomed. Rsch. Inst., 1989-95; assoc. dir. Pres. Reagan Transition Team, 1980; advisor Pres. Bush Transition Team, 1988. Served with U.S. Navy, 1952-53; lt. U.S. Army, 1958-61. Recipient Disting. Pub. Svc. medals Exec. Office of Pres., 1973, U.S. Dept. Def., 1977. Home: 97 Essex Rd Chestnut Hill MA 02467-1316 Office: 1 Liberty Sq Fl 12 Boston MA 02109-4825

MCCULLEN, MICHAEL JOHN, advertising executive; b. Phila., Aug. 12, 1937; s. Joseph Thomas and Sara Ellen (Berryman) McC.; m. Kathleen Carol Flynn, Sept. 14, 1968; 1 child, Kelly Ann. BS in Mktg., Temple U., Phila., 1963. Creative liaison Phila. Inquirer, 1963-66; artist/writer The Phila. Bull., 1966-71; pres. Creative Creatures, Inc., Phila., 1971-79; advt. mgr. Eckerd Drug Co., Newark, 1979-83; advt./sales promotion mgr. Eljo Products, Inc., Pennsauken, N.J., 1983-93; pres. McCullen & Assocs., Marlton, 1993—. Mem. Rep. Nat. Com., Washington, 1985-86. With USN, 1957-59. Mem. Am. Soc. Advt. and Promotion, Nat. Assn. Desktop Pubs., Mktg. Color Group, Phila. Advt. Club. Republican. Roman Catholic. Avocations: drawing, painting, reading, sports. Home: 268 Grisscom Ct Marlton NJ 08053-2011 Office: McCullen & Assocs 1 Eves Dr Ste 111 Marlton NJ 08053-3125

MCCULLOCH, ANNA MARY KNOTT, pharmacy technician; b. Riverdale, Md., Aug. 29, 1964; d. Samuel Eugene and Jean M. (Schildt) Knott; m. Richard Sears, Nov. 6, 1988; children: John Austen II, Anna Rebecca. Student, W.Va. U., 1982-84; cert., Children's Inst. Lit., 1987. Pharmacy technician Montgomery Gen. Hosp., Olney, Md., 1981-92; med. asst., sec. Dr. Arthur Lomant, Eldersburg, 1986-87; pharmacy technician Frederick (Md.) Meml. Hosp., 1991-95. Mem. Assn. Pharmacy Technicians, Stringband Am., Inc. (v.p. Eldersburg chpt. 1989-90). Roman Catholic. Avocation: teaching music. Home: 6320 Debold Rd Sabillasville MD 21780-9315

MCCULLOCH, ANNE MERLINE JACOBS, college dean; b. L.A., Mar. 20, 1948; d. Merlin Lee and Edna (Rammell) J.; m. Arlyn Cecil McCulloch, Sept. 17, 1977 (div. Mar. 1993); children: Justin Jacobs, Caroline Ranawn. BA, Coll. of Charleston, 1971; D of Arts, Idaho State U., 1975. Cert. secondary tchr., Idaho; cmty. coll. cert., Calif. Caseworker Dept. Social Svcs., Newport News, Va., 1970-71; asst. prof., then assoc. prof. polit. sci. Idaho State U., Pocatello, 1975-86, prof., 1986-89, grad. dir. polit. sci. dept., 1977-87; prof. Columbia (S.C.) Coll., 1989—, chmn. dept. history and polit. sci., 1991-98, interim dir. Leadership Inst., 1990-91, dean evening coll. and external programs, 1998—. Cons. Shoshone/Bannock Tribes, Ft. Hall, Idaho, 1986-87, 97; cons. S.C. ednl. TV film Snowbird Cherokee, 1993-95. Contbg. author: Native Americans and Public Policy, 1992; editor Native Am. Policy Network Newsletter, 1995—; assoc. editor Ency. Minorities in American

Politics, 1999; contbr. articles to profl. jours. Mem. Idaho Gov.'s Blue Ribbon Econ. Commn., 1982-83; co-program chmn. Elizabeth Cady Stanton Conf., Columbia, 1995. Mem. Am. Polit. Sci. Assn. (coord. Native Am. studies 1995-96), So. Polit. Sci. Assn., So. Polit. Sci. Assn., Phi Kappa Phi, Pi Sigma Alpha, Phi Alpha Theta. Democrat. Mem. Lds Ch. Avocations: gardening, running, home remodeling. Home: 437 Southlake Rd Columbia SC 29223-6601 Office: Columbia Coll Evening Coll Columbia SC 29203 E-mail: amcculloch@colacoll.edu.

MC CULLOCH, ERNEST ARMSTRONG, physician, educator; b. Toronto, Ont., Can., Apr. 27, 1926; s. Albert E. and Letitia (Riddell) McC.; m. Ona Mary Morganty, 1953; children: James A., Michael E., Robert E., Cecelia E., Paul A. MD with honors, U. Toronto, 1948. Intern Toronto Gen. Hosp., 1949-50, sr. intern, 1951-52; NRC fellow dept. pathology U. Toronto, 1950-51; asst. resident Sunnybrook Hosp., Toronto, 1952-53; pvt. practice specializing in internal medicine, 1954-67; clin. tchr. dept. medicine U. Toronto, 1954-60, asst. prof. dept. med. biophysics, 1959-64, assoc. prof., 1964-66, prof., 1966, asst. prof. dept. medicine, 1967-68, assoc. prof., 1968-70, prof., 1970—, univ. prof., 1982-91, univ. prof. emeritus, 1991—; mem. grad. faculty U. Toronto (Inst. Med. Sci.), 1968—; dir. Inst. Med. Sci. U. Toronto, 1975-79, asst. dean Sch. Grad. Studies, 1979-82. Physician Toronto Gen. Hosp., 1960-67; sr. scientist, sr. physician Ont. Cancer Inst., 1957-91, head divsn. biol. rsch., 1982-89, head divsn. cell and molecular biology, 1989-91, sr. scientist emeritus, 1991-93; vis. prof. U. Tex. Med. Ctr. Anderson Cancer Ctr., Houston, 1992-93, adj. prof., 1993-98; cons. Nat. Cancer Plan, 1972—; mem. standing com. on health rsch. and devel. Ont. Coun. Health, 1974-82. Author numerous articles on research in hematology; editorial bd.: Blood, 1969-80, Biomedicine, 1973, Clin. Immunology and Immunopathology, 1972-76; assoc. editor: Jour. Cellular Physiology, 1966-68; editor, 1968-91. Trustee Banting Rsch. Found., 1975-84, hon. sec.-treas., 1958-74, v.p., 1977-79. Decorated officer Order of Can., 1988; recipient William Goldie prize U. Toronto, 1964, Ann. Gairdner award Internat. Gairdner Found., 1969, Starr Medallist award Dept. Anatomy U. Toronto, 1957; Thomas W. Eadie Medal, 1991, Royal Soc. Canada, Nat. Cancer Inst. Can. fellow, 1954-57. Fellow Royal Soc. Can. (pres. Acad. Sci. 1987-90, Thomas W. Eadie Medal 1991), Royal Coll. Physicians and Surgeons Can., Royal Soc. London, Can. Acad. Sci.; mem. Am. Soc. Exptl. Pathology, Am. Assn. Cancer Rsch., Can. Soc. Cell Biology, Can. Soc. Clin. Investigation, Am., Internat. socs. hematology, Internat. Soc. Exptl. Hematology, Inst. Acad. Medicine (charter mem.). Clubs: Badminton, Racquet. Home: 480 Summerhill Ave Toronto ON Canada M4W 2E4 Office: 610 University Ave Toronto ON Canada M5G 2M9 E-mail: mcculloch@oci.utoronto.ca. *Research success depends on associating with agreeable and talented people.*

MCCULLOCH, GEORGE MCQUILLAN, retired foundation executive, fundraiser; b. Glasgow, Scotland, Aug. 22, 1931; came to the U.S., 1949; s. William John and Margaret (McQuillan) McC.; m. Marian Gabriel, Jan. 19, 1954; children: William, David, Clifford, George. Student, Seton Hall U. Asst. credit mgr. Kraft Food Corp., Hillside, N.J., 1950-53; acctg. dept. staff FYR-Fyter Corp., Newark, 1953-64; scout exec. Boy Scouts Am., Rutherford and Elizabeth, N.J., 1965-75; exec. dir. United Cerebral Palsy, East Orange, 1975-80; exec. housekeeper various hotels, N.J./Mich., 1980-86; dir. housekeeping North Caldwell Bd. of Edn., 1986-91; pres. Scotty's Janitorial, Bloomfield, N.J., 1991-94. Cons. McQuillan and Apgar, Elizabeth; fund raising cons. Rahway (N.J.) Food Bank. Mem. Young Reps., Elizabeth, 1954-64; state chmn. N.J. Conservative Party, State of N.J., 1964-66; mem. Rep. Nat. Com., Washington, 1994-96. Mem. Free and Accepted Masons, Friends of Nat. Pks., Assn. Preservation Civil War, Libr. Congress Assn., Civil War Trust, Hospitalized Vets. Avocations: civil war buff, golf, travel, politics. Home: 107 Franklin St Bloomfield NJ 07003-5757

MCCULLOCH, JAMES CALLAHAN, corporate executive; b. Pittsfield, Mass., Aug. 20, 1947; s. G. Robert and Marion Elizabeth (Callahan) McC.; m. Patricia A. Greene, Dec. 28, 1970; children: William Brennan, Patrick Callahan, Daniel Daly, Peter Brennan, James Callahan II. BS in Commerce, St. Louis U., 1969, MS in Commerce, 1970. With Ford Motor Co., 1970-72; group contr. Chemetron Corp., 1972-80; corp. contr. Six Flags Corp., L.A., 1980-82; v.p. fin. and planning Indsl. Controls Group Allen-Bradley Co., Milw., 1982-86; v.p., chief fin. officer and treas. Sybron Corp., Saddle Brook, N.J., 1986-87, also bd. dirs.; pres. McCulloch Investments, Madison, 1987-98. Pres. McCulloch Investments, Madison, NJ, 1987—98; bd. dirs. Summit Industries, Chgo., Fraud-Check, Inc. Mem. Fin. Exec. Inst., Morris County Golf Club. Republican. Office: Fraud-Check Inc 70 W Red Oak Ln White Plains NY 10604 E-mail: JMcCulloch@fraud-check.com.

MCCULLOCH, J(AMES) HUSTON, economist, educator; b. Carmel, Calif., Oct. 9, 1945; BS in Econs., Calif. Inst. Tech., 1967; MA in Econs., U. Chgo., 1969, PhD in Econs., 1973. Asst. prof. Boston Coll., Chestnut Hill, Mass., 1973-79; assoc. prof. Ohio State U., Columbus, 1979-83, prof., 1983—. Author: Money and Inflation, 1982; editor Jour. Money, Credit and Banking, 1983-91; contbr. articles to profl. jours. 1st lt. U.S. Army, 1970-71, Vietnam. Rsch. fellow Nat. Bur. Econ. Rsch., 1976-77. Mem. Am. Econs. Assn., Am. Fin. Assn., Epigraphic Soc. Mem. Libertarian Party. Avocations: epigraphy, tennis, aerobics, bicycling. Office: Ohio State U Econs Dept 1945 N High St Columbus OH 43210-1120

MCCULLOCH, RACHEL, economics researcher, educator; b. Bklyn., June 26, 1942; d. Henry and Rose (Offen) Preiss; m. Gary Edward Chamberlain; children: Laura Meressa, Neil Dudley. BA, U. Pa., 1962; MA in Teaching, U. Chgo., 1965, MA, 1971, PhD, 1973; student, MIT, 1966-67. Economist Cabinet Task Force on Oil Import Control, Washington, 1969; instr., then asst. prof. Grad. Sch. Bus. U. Chgo., 1971-73; asst. prof., then assoc. prof. econs. Harvard U., Cambridge, Mass., 1973-79; assoc. prof., then prof. econs. U. Wis., Madison, 1979-87; prof. Brandeis U., Waltham, Mass., 1987—, Rosen Family prof., 1989—, dir. Lemberg Program in Internat. Econs. and Fin., 1990-91, dir. PhD program Grad. Sch. Internat. Econs. and Fin., 1994—2001. Mem. Pres.'s Commn. on Indsl. Competitiveness, 1983-84; mem. adv. coun. Office Tech. Assessment, U.S. Congress, 1979-88; cons. World Bank, Washington, 1984-86; mem. com. on internat. rels. studies with People's Republic of China, 1984-91; rsch. assoc. Nat. Bur. Econ. Rsch., Cambridge, 1985-93; mem. adv. com. Inst. for Internat. Econs., Washington, 1987—; faculty Advanced Mgmt. Network, La Jolla, Calif., 1985-92; mem. com. examiners econs. test Grad. Record Exam. Ednl. Testing Svc., 1990-96, chair, 1992-96; mem. discipline adv. com. for Fulbright scholar awards in econs. Coun. Internat. Exch. Scholars, 1991-93, chair, 1992-93; mem. adv. com. for Fulbright Chairs Program, 1997; cons. Global Economy Project, Edn. Film Ctr., 1993-94; mem. study group on pvt. capital flows to developing and transitional economies Coun. Fgn. Rels., 1995-96, acad. adv. panel, Fed. Reserve Bank of Boston, 1999—; faculty assoc. Harvard Inst. for Internat. Devel., 1997-2000; fellow Internat. Leadership Forum, 2001-. Author: Research and Development as a Determinant of U.S. International Competitiveness, 1978; contbr. articles to profl. jours. and books. Grantee NSF, 1975-79, Hoover Inst., 1984-85, German Marshall Fund of U.S., 1985, Ford Found., 1985-88, U.S. Dept. Edn., 1990-91, Schulhof Found., 2001-02. Mem. Am. Econ. Assn. (dir. summer program for minority students 1983-84, mem. executive com., 1997-2000), Internat. Trade and Fin. Assn. (bd. dirs. 1993-95). Home: 10 Frost Rd Lexington MA 02420-1904 Office: Brandeis U Dept Econs MS 021 Waltham MA 02454 E-mail: mcculloch@brandeis.edu.

MC CULLOCH, SAMUEL CLYDE, history educator; b. Ararat, Australia, Sept. 3, 1916; came to U.S., 1936, naturalized, 1944; s. Samuel and Agnes Almond (Clyde) McC.; m. Sara Ellen Rand, Feb. 19, 1944; children: Ellen (Mrs. William Henry Meyer III), David Rand, Malcolm Clyde. AB with highest honors in History, UCLA, 1940, MA (grad. fellow history), 1942; PhD, U. Calif. at Los Angeles, 1944. Asst. U. Calif. at Los Angeles, 1943-44; instr. Oberlin Coll., 1944-45; asst. prof. Amherst Coll., 1945-46; vis. asst. prof. U. Mich., 1946-47; mem. faculty Rutgers U., 1947-60, prof. history, assoc. dean arts and scis., 1958-60; dean coll., prof. history San Francisco State Coll., 1960-63; dean humanities, prof. history U. Calif. at Irvine, 1963-70, prof., 1970-87, prof. emeritus, 1987—, coordinator Edn. Abroad Program, 1975-85, dir. Australian Study Ctr., 1986, 87. Vis. summer prof. Oberlin Coll., 1945, 46, U. Calif. at Los Angeles, 1947, U. Del., 1949; Fulbright Research prof. Monash U., Melbourne (Australia) U., 1970; Am. Philos. Soc. grantee, 1970 Author: British Humanitarianism, 1950, George Gipps, 1966, River King: The Mc Culloch Carrying Company and Echura, 1865-1898, 1986, Instant University: A History of U.C.I., 1957-1993, 1995, William McCulloch, 1932-1909, 1997, A Collection of Book Reviews, 1948-93, 2000; contbr. numerous articles, revs. to profl. jours.; assoc. editor Jour. Brit. Studies, 1960-68, bd. advisors, 1968-70; bd. corrs. Hist. Studies: Australia and New Zealand, 1949-83. Mem. Calif. Curriculum Commn., 1961-67, Highland Park (N.J.) Bd. Edn., 1959-60. Grantee Am. Philos. Soc., Social Sci. Research Council and Rutgers U. Research Council to Australia, 1951; Fulbright research fellow U. Sydney, Australia, 1954-55; grantee Social Sci. Research Council to Eng., summer 1955 Fellow Royal Hist. Soc.; mem. Am. Hist. Assn., Church, Royal Australian hist. socs., A.A.U.P., Conf. Brit. Studies (exec. sec. 1968-73, pres. 1975-77), English Speaking Union (pres. New Brunswick 1957-59), Phi Beta Kappa, Pi Gamma Mu. Episcopalian (vestry). Home: 2121 Windward Ln Newport Beach CA 92660-3820

MCCULLOCH, WILLIAM LEONARD, trade association administrator; b. Providence, Mar. 11, 1921; s. William Fraser and Elsie Cornelia (Westeberg) McC.; m. Dolores Ione Collier, July 26, 1952; children— William Fraser, II, Bruce Collier. BS, U.S. Naval Acad., 1945; MA in Internat. Relations, Georgetown U., 1958. Commd. 2d lt. USMC, 1944, advanced through grades to brig. gen., 1971; service in Okinawa, China, Korea and Vietnam; comdg. gen. (1st Marine Div.), 1974-75; congl. aide, 1975-76; exec. dir. Am. Assn. Orthotists and Prosthetists, Washington, 1976-86; pres. nat. office Orthotics and Prosthetics, 1986-88; pres. Assn. Communications and Mktg. Svcs., Washington, 1988—. Bd. dirs. Hanger Orthopedic Group. Decorated Legion of Merit with 2 stars, Bronze Star. Mem. Am. Soc. Assn. Execs., U.S. Naval Acad. Class of 1945 Assn. (pres. 1979-80), U.S. Naval Acad. Athletic Assn., Ret. Officers Assn., Capitol Hill Club (Washington), Army-Navy Country Club (Arlington, Va.), Marine Meml. Club (San Francisco), Army and Navy Club (past pres.), Washington Club. Republican. Presbyterian. Home and Office: 528 Ft Williams Pky Alexandria VA 22304-1849 E-mail: acms-mcculloch@erols.com.

MCCULLOH, JUDITH MARIE, editor; b. Spring Valley, Ill., Aug. 16, 1935; d. Henry A. and Edna Mae (Traub) Binkele; m. Leon Royce McCulloh, Aug. 26, 1961. BA, Ohio Wesleyan U., 1956; MA, Ohio State U., 1957; PhD, Ind. U., 1970. Asst. to dir. Archives of Traditional Music, Bloomington, Ind., 1964-65; asst. editor U. Ill. Press, Champaign, 1972-77, assoc. editor, 1977-82, sr. editor, 1982-85, exec. editor, 1985—, dir. devel., 1992—; asst. dir., 1997—. Advisor John Edwards Meml. Forum, Los Angeles, 1973—. Mem. Editorial Bd. Jour. Am. Folklore, Washington, 1986-90; co-editor Stars of Country Music, 1975; editor (LP) Green Fields of Ill., 1963, (LP) Hell-Bound Train, 1964, Ethnic Recordings in America, 1982; gen. editor Music in American Life series. Trustee Am. Folklife Ctr., Libr. of Congress, Washington, 1986-2004, chair, 1990-92, 96-98. Fulbright grantee, 1958-59; NDEA grantee, 1961, 62-63; grantee Nat. Endowment for the Humanities, 1978; recipient Disting. Achievement citation Ohio Wesleyan U. Alumni Assn., Disting. Svc. award Soc. for Am. Music. Fellow: Am. Folklore Soc. (exec. bd. 1974—79, pres. 1986—87, exec. bd. 2001—); mem.: Am. Anthropol. Assn., Women in Scholarly Pub., Soc. Am. Music (1st v.p. 1989—93), Soc. for Ethnomusicology (treas. 1982—86). Democrat. Office: U Ill Press 1325 S Oak St Champaign IL 61820-6903 E-mail: jmmccull@uillinois.edu.

MCCULLOUGH, COLLEEN, author; b. Wellington, N.S.W., Australia, June 1, 1937; m. Ric Robinson, Apr. 13, 1984. Student, U. Sydney, Australia, London U.; LittD (hon.), Macquarie U., Sydney, 1993. Neurophysiologist Sydney, London, Yale U. Sch. Medicine, 1967-77. Author: Tim, 1974, The Thorn Birds, 1977, An Indecent Obsession, 1981, Cooking with Colleen McCullough and Jean Easthope, 1982, A Creed for the Third Millennium, 1985, The Ladies of Missalonghi, 1987, The First Man in Rome, 1990, The Grass Crown, 1991, Fortune's Favorites, 1993, Caesar's Women, 1996, Caesar, 1997, The Song of Troy, 1998, Roden Cutler, V.C. (The Biography), 1998, Morgan's Run, 2000. Office: PO Box 333 Norfolk Island Australia Fax: (6723) 23313.

MCCULLOUGH, DAVID L. urologist; b. Chattanooga, 1938; MD, Bowman Gray, 1964. Intern U. Hosps. Case Western Reserve U., Cleve., 1964-65, resident in surgery, 1965-66; fellow urology Baylor U. Coll. Medicine, Houston, 1968-69; resident in urology Mass. Gen. Hosp., Boston, 1969-72; chief urologist N.C. Bapt. Hosp., Winston-Salem, 1983—; prof., chmn. urology Wake Forest U. Coll. Medicine. Past pres. Am. Bd. Urology. Mem. ACS, AMA, Am. Urol. Assn. (past pres. southeastern sect., past pres., bd. dirs.), Am. Assn. Genitourinary Surgeons (sec.-treas.), Clin. Soc. Urol. Surgeons., Halsted Soc.

MCCULLOUGH, EDWARD EUGENE, patent agent, inventor; b. Baldwin, N.D., June 4, 1923; s. Elmer Ellsworth and Emma Izelda (Nixon) McC. BA, U. Minn., 1957; postgrad., Utah State U., 1965. Machine designer Sperry Rand Corp., Mpls., 1952-58; patent adminstr. Thiokol Corp., Brigham City, Utah, 1958-86, patent cons., 1986; pvt. practice, 1986—. Patentee 34 U.S. patents including instruments for making perspective drawings, apparatus for forming ignition surfaces in solid propellant motors, passive communications satellite or similar article, flexible bearings and process for their manufacture, rocket nozzel support and pivoting system, cavity-shaping machine, others. Pianist Aldersgate Meth. Ch., Brigham City, 1959—. Staff Sgt. U.S. Army, 1949-52. Decorated two battle stars, Korean War Svc. medal. Avocations: philosophy, music composition, hiking in the mountains. E-mail: ed@burgoyne.com.

MCCULLOUGH, FRANK WITCHER, III, lawyer; b. New Orleans, Dec. 13, 1945; s. Frank Witcher Jr. and Kathleen Elizabeth (Van Pelt) McC.; m. Barry Jean Bock, Mar. 7, 1981; children: William David Oat, Frank Witcher IV, Elizabeth Layton. BA, Stetson U., 1967; JD, W.Va. U., 1970. Bar: W.Va. 1970, Tex. 1970, U.S. Dist. Ct. (so. dist.) W.Va. 1970, U.S. Dist. Ct. (so. dist.) Tex. 1972, U.S. Ct. Appeals (5th cir.) 1972, U.S. Supreme Ct. 1980, U.S. Dist. Ct. (no. dist.) Calif. 1983, U.S. Dist. Ct. (we. dist.) Tex. 1987, U.S. Dist. Ct. (ea. dist.) Tex. 1993. Indsl. rels. specialist Continental Oil Co., Houston, 1970-72; asst. U.S. atty. U.S. Atty.'s Office, 1972-75; assoc. Baker & Botts, 1975-76, Austin, 1985-89; ptnr. Weiner Strother & Lamkin, Houston, 1983-85; regional counsel GATX Leasing Corp., 1976-78; ptnr. Walsh Squires Tompkins & McCullough, 1978-82; shareholder Sheinfeld, Maley & Kay, Austin, 1989-2001, Diamond McCarthy Taylor & Finley, Austin, 2001—. Spl. commr. Harris County, Houston, 1982; mem. Bellaire (Tex.) Bd. Adjustment, 1982; bd. dirs. Big Bros. and Big Sisters of Austin, 1991-94. Mem. State Bar Tex. (grievance com. 1979-87, 95—), chmn. unauthorized practice law com. 1984-87), Austin Country Club, SAR. Republican. Episcopalian. Home: 6707 Bridge Hill Cv Austin TX 78746-1338 Office: Diamond McCarthy Taylor & Finley Ste 400 6504 Bridgepoint Pkwy Austin TX 78730 *Notable cases include: Univ. Savs. Assn. vs. Springwoods Shopping Ctr., 1982, in which the Tex. Supreme Ct. created significant exception to the rule of law that the terms and provisions of deed of trust must be strictly followed in foreclosure proceeding.*

MC CULLOUGH, J. LEE, industrial psychologist; b. Bryn Mawr, Pa., Oct. 3, 1945; s. Leo Francis and Margaret Mary (Hart) McC.; m. Bonnie R. Goldberg, Jan. 14, 1979. AB, Villanova U., 1967; MA, Ohio State U., 1968, PhD, 1971. Tchg. asst. Ohio State U., 1967-68, rsch. assoc., 1968-69; assoc. O.P.S. Assocs., Columbus, 1970-71; assoc., sr. assoc., sr. prin., v.p Hay Group, N.Y.C., 1971-90, v.p., dir. fin. svcs. cons., 1990-94; prin. William M. Mercer, Inc., 1994—. Adj. prof. Fordham U. Grad. Sch. Bus., 1984-89. Served with AUS, 1972. NSF fellow, 1969; NDEA Title IV fellow, 1970; Univ. Disseration Year fellow, 1971. Mem. Am. Psychol. Soc., Met. Psychol. Assn., Am. Psychol. Soc. Home: 6 Hereford Dr Princeton Junction NJ 08550-1514 Office: 30th Fl 1166 Avenue Americas New York NY 10036-2708

MCCULLOUGH, JOHN PHILLIP, management consultant, educator; b. Lincoln, Ill., Feb. 2, 1945; s. Phillip and Lucile Ethel (Ornellas) McC.; m. Barbara Elaine Carley, Nov. 29, 1968; children: Carley Jo, Ryan Phillip. BS, Ill. State U., 1967, MS, 1968; PhD, U. N.D., 1971. Adminstrv. mgr. McCullough Ins. Agy., Atlanta, 1963-68; ops. supr. Stetson China Co., Lincoln, 1967; asst. mgr. Brandtville Svc., Inc., Bloomington, Ill., 1968; instr. in bus. Ill. Ctrl. Coll., 1968-69; rsch. asst. U. N.D., Grand Forks, 1969-71; assoc. prof. mgmt. West Liberty State Coll., 1971-74, prof., 1974—. Chmn. dept. mgmt., West Liberty State Coll., 1974-82, dir. Sch. Bus., 1982-86, dean, 1986—, provost, 1998—, interim pres., 2001, dir. Small Bus. Inst., 1978—; mgmt. cons., Triadelphia, W.Va., 1971—; instr. Am. Inst. Banking, 1971—; lectr. W.Va. U., 1971—; adj. prof. MBA program Wheeling Coll., 1972—, U. Steubenville, 1982—; lectr. Ohio U., 1982—; profl. assoc. Inst. Mgmt. and Human Behavior, 1975—; v.p. West Liberty State Coll. Fed. Credit Union, 1976—; rep. W.Va. Bd. Regents Adv. Coun. of Faculty. Author: (with Howard Fryette) Primer in Supervisory Management, 1973; contbr. articles to profl. jours. Team leader Wheeling divsn. Am. Cancer Soc.; coord. Upper Ohio Valley United Fund, 1972-74; instr. AFL-CIO Cmty. Svcs. Program, Wheeling; project dir. Ctr. for Edn. and Rsch. with Industry; bd. dirs. Family Svc.-Upper Ohio Valley, Ohio Valley Indsl. and Bus. Devel. Corp., Inc., Labor Mgmt. Inst. Wheeling Salvation Army, Progress, Inc., Ohio Valley Health Svcs. and Edn. Corp. Recipient Svc. award Bank Adminstrn. Inst., 1974, United Fund, 1973, Acad. Achievement award Harris-Casals Found., 1971. Mem. Soc. Humanistic Mgmt. (nat. chmn.), ORgn. Planning Mgmt. Assn. (exec. com.), Spl. Interest Group for Cert. Bus. Educators (nat. dir.), Soc. Advancement Mgmt. (chpt. advisor), Acad. Mgmt., Adminstrv. Mgmt. Soc. (cert.), Am. Soc. Pers. Adminstrn. (cert.), Nat. Bus. Honor Soc. (Excellence in Tchg. award 1976, dir. 1974—), Alpha Kappa Psi (Dist. Svc. award 1973, Civic award 1977, chpt. advisor 1971—), Merit Found. W.Va. (Ednl. Excellence award), Delta Mu Delta, Delta Pi Epsilon, Delta Tau Kappa, Phi Gamma Nu, Phi Theta Pi, Pi Gamma Mu, Pi Omega Pi, Omicron Delta Epsilon. Home: 68 Elm Dr Triadelphia WV 26059-9620

MCCULLOUGH, JOHN PRICE, retired oil company executive; b. Dallas, May 10, 1925; s. John A. and Alta (McGee) McC.; m. Mary Ann Calvert, Aug. 5, 1946; children: Sherri, Cathryn, Patricia. Student, U. Denver, 1942-43; BS in Chem. Engring, U. Okla., 1945; MS, Oreg. State U., 1948, PhD in Chemistry, 1949. With U.S. Bur. Mines, Bartlesville, Okla., 1949-63, phys. chemist, 1949-57, chief thermodynamics br., 1958-63; mgr. central research div. Mobil Oil Corp., Princeton, N.J., 1963-69, mgr. applied research and devel. Paulsboro, 1969-71; gen. mgr. research and devel. Mobil Chem. Co., Edison, 1971-78; v.p. environ. health and safety Mobil Research & Devel. Corp., Princeton, 1978-89. Adj. prof. chemistry Okla. State U., Stillwater, 1961-63; vis. fellow Woodrow Wilson Found., 1991-95; dir. Internat. Petroleum Industry Environ. Conservation Assn., 1981-89, chmn., 1985-88; dir. Mobil Found., Inc., 1987-89. Co-author: (with Donald Scott) Experimental Thermodynamics, Volume I: Calorimetry of Non-reacting Systems, 1968; contbr. 90 articles on thermodynamics, molecular structure and energetics, environ. and health policy to profl. jours. Mem. adv. com. Mercer County (N.J.) C.C., 1968-69; bd. dirs. Chem. Industry Inst. Toxicology, 1977-89, chmn., 1986-88; bd. dirs. United Cmty. Fund, Princeton, 1963-69, Middlesex-Somerset-Mercer Regional Study Coun., 1968-69, 86-89, World Environ. Ctr., 1986-89; mem. adv. bd. Georgetown U. Inst. Health Policy Analysis, 1986-89; trustee Stony Brook-Millstone Watershed Assn., 1989-95, vice chmn., 1991-93, adv. bd., 1996-99; trustee Friends of Art Mus. Princeton U., 1994-2000, treas., 1997-2001; elder Nassau Presbyn. Ch. Lt. (j.g.) USNR, 1943-54. Recipient Meritorious Svc. award U.S. Dept. Interior, 1959, Disting. Svc. award, 1962; DuPont fellow, 1947-48. Mem. AAAS, Gordon Rsch. Conf. (trustee, chmn. bd. trustees, mem. coun.), Am. Chem. Soc. (editl. bd. Jour. Chem. and Engring. Data, Jour. Phys. Chemistry, mem. coun. com. on chemistry and pub. affairs 1984-92, chmn. 1987-89, award for petroleum chemistry 1963, Chemtech. award 1977), Internat. Calorimetry Conf. (chmn. 1960, Huffman award 1963), Am. Inst. Chemists, Sigma Xi. Home: 7 Fringe Tree Ct Princeton NJ 08540-5061 E-mail: jmccullough55@comcast.net.

MCCULLOUGH, JOSEPH, college president emeritus; b. Pitts., July 6, 1922; s. Joseph Phillip and Margaret (List) McC.; m. Elizabeth Cramer, Mar. 31, 1945; children— Marjorie Ann, Warren BFA, Yale U., 1949-50, MFA, 1951; Diploma, Cleve. Sch. Art, 1948; DFA (hon.), U. Evansville, Ind., 1980; DA (hon.), Cleve. Inst. Art, 1996. Instr. San Jose State Coll., Calif., 1948-49; asst. instr. Yale U., New Haven, 1949-51; asst. dir. Cleve. Inst. Art, 1952-54, dir., 1954-74, pres., 1974-88. Artist paintings, nat. regional and local exhbns., 1948— Chmn. Fine Arts Adv. Com., Cleve. Planning Commn., 1963-91; trustee Mpls. Coll. of Art and Design, 1988-98, Sculpture Ctr. Cleve., 1990-98; trustee, sec. Access to the Arts, Cleve., 1991-95. Capt. USAAF, 1943-46, ETO. Recipient Cleve. Arts prize Women's City Club, 1971, Centennial medal John Carroll U., 1987, medal for excellence Cleve. Inst. of Art, 1997. Mem.: Coll. Art Assn. ((past dir.)). Home: 20101 North Park Blvd Cleveland OH 44118-5006

MCCULLOUGH, KATHRYN T. BAKER, social worker; b. Trenton, Tenn., Jan. 5, 1925; d. John Andrew and Alma Lou (Wharey) Taylor; m. John R. Baker, Sept. 30, 1972 (dec. Oct. 1981); m. T.C. McCullough, May 14, 1988. BS, U. Tenn., 1945, MSW, 1954; postgrad., U. Chgo., 1950, Vanderbilt U., 1950-51. Lic. social worker, Tenn.; emeritus diplomate in clin. social work Am. Bd. Examiners. Home demonstration agt., agrl. extension svc. U. Tenn., Hardeman County, 1946-49; Dyer County, 1949-50; dir. med. social work dept. Le Bonheur Children's Hosp., Memphis, 1954-57; chief clin. social worker clinic mentally retarded children U. Tenn. Dept. Pediatrics, 1957-59; clin. social worker Children's Med. Ctr., Tulsa, 1959-60; dir. med. social work dept. Coll. of Medicine U. Tenn., Memphis, 1960-69; dir. community svcs. regional med. program Coll. of Medicine, 1969-76; dir. regional clinic program Child Devel. Ctr. Coll. of Medicine, 1976-85; mem. faculty Coll. of Medicine, Coll. of Social Work U. Tenn., Memphis, 1960-85; social worker admissions rev. bd. Arlington Devel. Ctr., 1976-98. Cons. Tenn. Dept. Children's Svcs., 1999—. Author 14 books. Commr. Dist. I, Gibson Utility Dist., 1990—98; former bd. dirs. Am. Heart Assn., Am. Cancer Soc., Am. Lung Assn., United Cerebral Palsy, Goodwill Industries, AGAPE Child and Family Svcs., Health and Welfare Planning Coun., Shelby County Head Start, Greater Memphis Day Care Assn.; advisor AGAPE Child and Family Svcs., 1998—; mem. bd. visitors U. Tenn. Coll. Social Work, Knoxville, 2000—; active Gibson County Fedn. Dem., 1985—98, Dem. Party orgns., 1946—. Fellow: Am. Assn. Mental Retardation (life); mem.: AAUP, Tenn. Conf. on Social Welfare, Acad. Cert. Social Workers, Sigma Kappa Alumni Found. (life). Mem. Ch. of Christ. Avocations: piano, organ, symphony. Home: 627 Riverside Yorkville Rd Trenton TN 38382-5917

MCCULLOUGH, KENNETH DOUGLAS, writer, educator; b. Staten Island, Ny, July 18, 1943; s. Robert Erwin and Barbara Marie McCullough; children: Galway, Orion. BA, Univ. Del., Newark, DE, 1961—66; MFA, Univ. Iowa, Iowa City, IA, 1966—68. Asst. prof., english Mont. State Univ., Bozeman, Mont., 1970—75; writer-in-residence S.C. Ednl. TV, Columbia, 1975—79; union laborer Local 1238, Iowa City, 1979—83; academic advisor Univ. Iowa, 1983—96; adjuct asst. prof. St. Mary's Univ. of MN, Winona, 1996—98; lectr. Winona State Univ., 1998—. Judge, fiction New Rivers Press, Minneapolis, Minn., 1999; panelist SE Mpls. Arts Coun., Rochester, Minn., 1997—2002, Iowa Arts Coun., Des Moines, 1987—95. Author: (book) Travelling Light (Capricorn Book Award, 1987), Sycamore-Oriole, Obsidian Point. Bd. mem. Human Rights Bd., Winona, Minn., 1998—2000. Recipient New Millennium Poetry Award, New Millennium Mag., Tenn., 2000; fellow NEA Fellowship, Nat. Endowment for the Arts, Wash., DC, 1974. Home: 2490 Garvin Heights Road Winona MN 55987 Personal E-mail: flintmc@hbci.com.

MCCULLOUGH, M. BRUCE, judge; b. Princeton, N.J., July 26, 1944; s. Malcolm S. and Ruth S. (Strandness) McC.; m. Kathleen M. Ryan, Apr. 12, 1985. BA in Polit. Sci. and Econs., Whitworth Coll., 1966; JD, U. Mich., 1969. Bar: Pa., Fla., D.C. Ptnr. Buchanan Ingersoll P.C., Pitts., 1969-95; judge U.S. Bankruptcy Ct., 1995—. Chmn. ARC (southwest Pa., 1994-96). With USAR, 1969-75. Mem. Chartiers Country Club, Duquesne Club. Avocations: golf, boating, hunting. Office: US Bankruptcy Ct 600 Grant St Pittsburgh PA 15219-2702

MCCULLOUGH, RALPH CLAYTON, II, lawyer, educator; b. Daytona Beach, Fla., Mar. 28, 1941; s. Ralph C. and Doris (Johnson) McC.; m. Elizabeth Grier Henderson, Apr. 5, 1986; children from previous marriage: Melissa Wells, Clayton Baldwin. BA, Erskine Coll., 1962; JD, Tulane U., 1965. Bar: La. 1965, S.C. 1974. Assoc. Baldwin, Haspel, Maloney, Rainold and Meyer, New Orleans, 1965-68; asst. prof. law U. S.C., 1968-71, assoc. prof., 1971-75, prof. 2, 1975—, chair prof. of advocacy, 1982—, asst. dean Sch. Law, 1970-75, instr. Med. Sch., 1970-79, adj. prof. law and medicine Med. Sch., 1979—; adj. prof. medicine Med. U. S.C., 1984—; of counsel Finkel & Altman, 1978—. Adj. prof. pathology Med. U. S.C., 1985—; asst. dean U. S.C. Sch. Law 1970-75. Author: (with J.L. Underwood) The Civil Trial Manual, 1974, 7th supplement, 1987, The Civil Trial Manual II, 1984,

87, (with Myers and Felix) New Directions in Legal Education, 1970, (with Finkel) S.C. Torts II, 1986, III, 1990, IV, 1995; co-reporter S.C. Criminal Code, 1977, S.C. Study Sentencing, 1977. Trustee S.C. dist. U.S. Bankruptcy Ct., 1979— ; exec. dir. S.C. Continuing Legal Edn. Program.; bd. visitors Erskine Coll.; reporter S.C. Jury Charge Commn., 1991-95. Mem. ABA, La. Bar Assn., S.C. Bar (sec. 1975-76, exec. dir. 1972-76, award of service 1978), New Orleans Bar Assn., Am. Trial Lawyers Assn., Am. Law Inst., Southeastern Assn. Am. Law Schs. (pres.), S.C. Trial Lawyers Assn. (bd. govs. 1984-88), Phi Alpha Delta. Clubs: Forest Lake. Republican. Episcopalian. Home: PO Box 1799 Columbia SC 29202-1799 Office: U SC Sch Law Columbia SC 29208-0001

MCCULLOUGH, RICHARD LAWRENCE, advertising agency executive; b. Chgo., Dec. 1, 1937; s. Francis John and Sadie Beatrice McCullough; m. Julia Louise Kreimer, May 6, 1961; children: Stephen, Jeffery, Julie. BS, Marquette U., 1959. Commd. U.S. Army, 1959, advance through grades to sgt., 1966; account exec. Edward H. Weiss Advt., Chgo., 1960-66; account supr. Doyle Dane Bernbach, N.Y.C., 1966-68; sr. v.p. J. Walter Thompson Co., Chgo., 1969-86; pres. E.H. Brown Advt., 1986-97; exec. v.p. Space-Time Media Mgmt., 1997—; ptnr. Callahan Group, 2000—. Developer Mktg. with Country Music nat. seminar, 1996. Author: Building Country Radio, 1986, A New Look at Country Music Audiences, 1988, (video) Country Music Marketing, 1989. Bd. dirs. Gateway Found., Chgo., 1976—, chmn., 1988-91; bd. dirs., chmn. mktg. com. Cath. Charities, Chgo. Mem. Country Music Assn. (Nashville bd. dirs. 1979—, pres. 1983-85, Pres.'s award 1987, elector Country Music Hall of Fame), NARAS (Nashville chpt.), North Shore Country Club (Glenview, Ill.), Dairymen's Country Club (Boulder Junction, Wis.), Quail Creek Country Club (Naples, Fla.). Roman Catholic. Home: 2720 Lincoln St Evanston IL 60201-2043 Office: Space-Time Media Mgmt Inc 35 E Wacker Dr Chicago IL 60601-2103 Home: 2720 Lincoln St Evanston IL 60201-2043 E-mail: dick@spacetimemedia.com., relchar@aol.com.

MCCULLOUGH, ROBERT DALE, II, osteopath; b. Tulsa, June 2, 1937; s. Robert Dale and Roberta Maud (Purdy) McC.; m. Lindell Arlene Wilcox, Sept. 28, 1963; children: Robert Mark, Lori Lindell. Student, Wheaton (Ill.) Coll., 1955-57; BS, N.E. Mo. State U., 1958; DO, Kansas City (Mo.) Coll. Osteopathy, 1958-62. Cert. Am. Osteo. Bd. Internal Medicine, Internal Medicine and Med. Oncology. Gen. practice McCullough Clinic, Tulsa, 1963-68; internal medicine resident Detroit Osteo. Hosp., 1968-71; internal medicine Baker-Todd-McCullough-Sutton, Tulsa, 1971-74; fellow med. oncology M.D. Anderson Hosp., Houston, 1974-75; internal medicine-med. oncology Baker-Todd-McCullough-Sutton, Tulsa, 1975-90; pvt. practice, 1990-93; attending staff mem. VA Outpatient Clinic, 1993-94; assoc. med. dir. Blue Cross/Blue Shield of Okla., 1994—. Trustee Tulsa Regional Med. Cttr., 1983-88, 90-93; bd. dirs. Okla. Blue Cross Blue Shield, Tulsa, 1983-92, vice chmn., 1991-92; mem. adv. coun. Okla. State U. Coll. Osteo. Medicine, 1988-94, chmn., 1988-90. Mem. bd. of editors Patient Care Magazine, Montvale, N.J., 1988-93. Mem. Okla. State Bd. Health, Oklahoma City, 1983-87, Tulsa City/County Bd. Health, 1988-95, chmn., 1993. Mem. Am. Coll. Phys. Execs., Nat. Osteo. Found. (trustee 1993-2000, treas. 1998-2000), Am. Osteo. Assn. (vice speaker Ho. of Dels. 1986-92, trustee 1993-2000), Am. Coll. Osteo. Internists, Am. Soc. Clin. Oncology, Okla. Osteo. Assn. (pres. 1982-83), Tulsa Downtown Lions Club, Soc. for Preservation and Encouragement of Barbershop Quartet Singing in Am. Republican. Southern Baptist. Avocation: barbershop quartet singing. Home: 2300 Riverside Dr 10F Tulsa OK 74114-2404 Office: 1400 S Boston Ave Tulsa OK 74119-3613 E-mail: rmccullough@bcbsok.com., RMccull207@aol.com.

MCCULLOUGH, ROSS A., JR. messenger service executive; b. Decatur, Ill., Mar. 18, 1966; s. Ross A. and Laura K. McCullough; m. Cindy E. Mullinax, June 11, 1992; children: Ross, III, Gracie. MBA, Emory U., Atlanta, 1996; BS in Indsl. Tech., Ea. Ill. U., 1987. Mgr. strategic planning UPS, Atlanta, 1994—96, v.p. electronic commerce, 1996—2001, v.p. corp. strategy Brussels, 2001—. Mem.: Coun. Logistics Mgmt. Office: UPS Avenue Ariane 5 Brussels 1050 Belgium

MCCULLOUGH, V. BETH, pharmacist, educator; b. Harrison, Ark., May 15, 1953; d. A. G. and Willene L. (McLain) McC.; m. David Mark Pearson, Oct. 25, 1980; children: Colin McCullough-Pearson, Emily McCullough-Pearson. BS in Edn. cum laude, Southwest Mo. State U., 1976; BS in pharmacy, U. Mo., 1981. Registered Pharmacist, Mo. Chief pharmacist Mt. Vernon Park Pharmacy, Springfield, Mo., 1981-89; dir. pharmacy Foster Health Care Group, 1989-96; chief pharmacy ops. Balanced Care Corp./Foster Health Care Group, 1996-97; cons. pharmacist Managed Healthcare Pharmacy divsn. Omnicare Corp., 1997-2001; owner Med. Park Pharmacy, Eureka Springs, Ark., 2001—. Long term care pharmacy cons. Foster Health Care Group, Springfield, 1981-83, Managed Healthcare Pharmacy, Springfield, 1997-2001. Mem. NOW, Springfield, 1982—, assoc. mem. Animal Shelter League of the Ozarks, Nixa, Mo. Mem. Am. Soc. Cons. Pharmacists, Southwest Mo. Humane Soc., Mo. Equine Coun., Mo. Pharmacy Assn., Long Term Care Acad., Biokinetics (instnl. rev. bd. 1999-2001). Avocations: watercolor painting, jewelry making, horse breeding and showing. Office: 146 Passion Play Rd Eureka Springs AR 72632-9495 Home: 146 CR 238 Berryville AR 72616

MCCULLOUGH, WILLIAM LAWRENCE, medical readiness consultant; b. Norfolk, Va., Mar. 18, 1951; s. William Lawrence, Jr. and Anne Laurie McC.; m. Marilyn Jane Greer, Sept. 5, 1971 (div. Nov. 1974); m. Carolyn Elizabeth Buckley, Oct. 9, 1976; children: Ross, Mark, Jena. BBA in Personnel Mgmt., St. Mary's U., San Antonio, Tex., 1973; MS in Healthcare Adminstrn., Trinity U., San Antonio, 1977. Cert. med. adminstr. Commd. 2d lt. U.S. Army, 1974; exec. officer/detachment comdr. U.S. Army dental activity, Ft. McLellan, Ala., 1978-81; commd. lt. USN, 1981; various to head, deployable med. systems Chief of Naval Ops., Washington, 1990-92; head, med. strategic plans and policies The Joint Staff, 1992-96; chief, med. plans and policies Chief of Naval Opers., 1996-97; ret. USN, 1997; sr. rsch. scientist Battelle Meml. Inst., Falls Church, Va., 1997-2000; with Integrated Mgmt. Svcs., Inc., 2000—. Vestry mem. Aquia Episc. Ch., Stafford, Va., 1999; com. chmn. Cub Scout Pack 324, Boy Scouts Am., Stuttgart-Vaihingen Germany, 1987-90, cubmaster Pack 840, Stafford, 1991-93, com. mem. 1992-94. Decorated Def. Meritorious Svc. awards (2) Dept. of Def., Meritorious Svcs. awards (3) USN, Army Commendation medal; named to Outstanding Young Men of Am., 1990. Mem. Am. Assn. Med. Adminstrs. Episcopalian. Avocations: sports cars, sailing. Office: Naval Medical Info Mgmt Ctr Bethesda MD 20889-5605 E-mail: wlmccullough@us.med.navy.mil.

MCCULLOUGH-DIETER, CAROL MAE, database administrator; b. Niagara Falls, N.Y., July 5, 1956; d. Earl Samuel McCullough and Evelyn Mae Doud; m. Thomas Frederick Taylor, May 3, 1975 (div. Apr. 1991); children: Dustin Thomas, Jesse John; m. Patrick Lee Dieter, Jan. 2, 1997; 1 child: Blue Skyler-Mercury. BBA, U. Wis., 1982. Project leader CUNA Mut. Ins., Madison, Wis., 1982-86; database asst. TDS Computing Svc., 1986-89; computer cons. Omni Resources, Inc., 1989-95, McCullough Cons., Kihei, Hawaii, 1995—; database adminstr. Pacific Disaster Ctr., 1996-99. Author: Oracle 7 for Dummies, 1997, Oracle 8 for Dummies, 1998, Oracle 8 Bible, 1998, Oracle 8 Developer's Guide, 1999, Oracle 8i for Dummies, 2000, A Day with Joshua, 2002, Oracle 9i for Dummies, 2002. Vol. Kamalii Elem. Sch., Kihei, 1997; exhbn. chair Wis. Women's Art Caucus, Madison, 1995. Mem. Oracle Devel. Tools User's Group, Grad. Sch. PSI Seminars. Avocations: watercolor painting, art classes for children, silk painting. Home and Office: 4134 SE 32nd Ave Portland OR 97202 E-mail: carolmdieter@yahoo.com.

MCCULLY, BRUCE CALVIN, videographer, director; b. Evanston, Ill., July 8, 1952; Student, Coll. Lake County, 1973. Cert. in TV prodn. 2nd shift computer ops. supr., 1st shift lead operator Americana Interstate, Mundelein, Ill.; computer problem solver, schedular AllState Ins., Northbrook; sound engr. Cheyenne Winter (Country Rock Band), Vancouver, Can., 1979-85; videographer Cabac Prodns. Inc., Waukegan, Ill., 1986-97; dir. Reid Prodns., Evanston, 1988-92; videographer MainStream Prodns. Inc., Lindenhurst, Ill., 1988-2000; freelance videographer Chgo., 2000—. Avocations: travel, music, art, hiking. Office: PO Box 6173 Lindenhurst IL 60046-6173

MCCULLY, CLINTON PAXTON, economist, federal agency administrator; b. Nashville, Nov. 1, 1947; s. Edward Nichol and Eloise (Simmons) McC.; m. Jennifer Rowe Sandberg, May 1, 1982; children: Linnea Christine, Ian Patrick. BA, Ripon Coll., 1969; MA, Rutgers U., 1976. Tchr. Croydon Hall Acad., Atlantic Highlands, N.J., 1971-74; rsch. asst. Joseph Froomkin Inc., Washington, 1976-77; economist Bur. Econ. Analysis, U.S. Dept. Commerce, 1977-82, sr. economist, 1982-87, chief consumption br., 1987—. Unitarian Universalist. Avocations: golf, softball. Office: Bur Econ Analysis 1401 K St NW Washington DC 20005-3418 Home: 2621 Lake Ridge Ct Oakton VA 22124-1510

MCCULLY, EMILY ARNOLD, illustrator, writer; b. Galesburg, Ill., 1939; d. Wade E. and Kathryn (Maher) Arnold; m. George E. McCully, 1961 (div. 1975); children: Nathaniel, Tad. BA, Brown U., 1961; MA, Columbia U., 1964; LittD (hon.) , Brown U., 2002. Author: How's Your Vacuum Cleaner Working? O'Henry Collection, 1977, A Craving, 1982, (novel) Picnic, 1984 (Christopher award), First Snow, 1985, (novel) Life Drawing, 1986, The Show Must Go On, 1987, School, 1987, You Lucky Duck!, 1988, New Baby, 1988, The Grandma Mix-up, 1988, The Christmas Gift, 1988, Zaza's Big Break, 1989, Grandma's at the Lake, 1990, The Evil Spell, 1990, Speak Up, Blanche!, 1991, Mirette on the Highwire, 1992 (Caldecott medal 1992), Grandma's at Bat, 1993, The Amazing Felix, 1993, My Real Family, 1994, Crossing The New Bridge, 1994, Little Kit, or: The Industrious Flea Circus Girl, 1995, The Pirate Queen, 1995, The Ballot Box Battle, 1996, The Bobbin Girl, 1996, Popcorn at the Palace, 1997, Starring Mirette and Bellini, 1997, an Outlaw Thanksgiving, 1998, Beautiful Warrior, 1998, Mouse Practice, 1999, Monk Camps Out, 2000, The Orphan Singer, 2001, Four Hungry Kittens, 2001; illustrator: Sea Beach Express, 1966, The Seventeenth Street Gang, 1966, Rex, 1967, Luigi of the Streets, 1967, That Mean Man, 1968, Gooney, 1968, Journey From Peppermint Street, 1968 (Nat. Book award 1969), The Mouse and the Elephant, 1969, The Fisherman, 1969, Tales from the Rue Brocca, 1969, Here I Am, 1969, Twin Spell, 1969, Hobo Toad and the Motorcycle Gang, 1970, Slip! Slop! Gobble!, 1970, Friday Night is Papa Night, 1970, Maxie, 1970, Steffie and Me, 1970, The Cat and the Parrot, 1970, Gertrude's Pocket, 1970, Go and Hush the Baby, 1971, Finders Keepers, 1971, Ma n Da La, 1971 (Bklyn. Mus. award 1976, N.Y. Pub. Libr. award 1976), Hurray for Captain Jane!, 1971, Michael Is Brave, 1971, Finding Out With Your Senses, 1971, Henry's Pennies, 1972, Jane's Blanket, 1972, Grandpa's Long Red Underwear, 1972, Girls Can Too!, 1972, The Boyhood of Grace Jones, 1972, Black Is Brown Is Tan, 1973, Isabelle the Itch, 1973, When Violet Died, 1973, That New Boy, 1973, How To Eat Fried Worms, 1973, Jenny's Revenge, 1974, Her Majesty, Grace Jones, 1974, Tree House Town, 1974, I Want Mama, 1974, Amanda, the Panda and the Redhead, 1975, The Bed Book, 1976, My Street's A Morning Cool Street, 1976, Professor Coconut and the Thief, 1977, Martha's Mad Dog, 1977, That's Mine, 1977, Where Wild Willie, 1978, No Help At All, 1978, Partners, 1978, The Twenty-Elephant Restaurant, 1978, What I Did Last Summer, 1978, The Highest Hit, 1978, I and Spraggy, 1978, Edward Troy and the Witch Cat, 1978, My Island Grandma, 1979, Whatever Happened to Beverly Bigler's Birthday?, 1979, Last Look, 1979, Ookie-Spooky, 1979, The Black Dog Who Went Into the Woods, 1980, How I Found Myself at the Fair, 1980, How We Got Our First Cat, 1980, Oliver and Allison's Week, 1980, Pajama Walking, 1981, The April Fool, 1981, I Dance in My Red Pajamas, 1982, The Halloween Candy Mystery, 1982, Go and Mush the Baby, 1982, Mitzi and the Terrible Tyrannosaurus Rex, 1983, Best Friend Insurance, 1983, Mail-Order Wings, 1984, Gertrude's Pocket, 1984, Fifth Grade Magic, 1984, The Ghastly Glasses, 1985, Fourth of July, 1985, The Explorer of Barkham Street, 1985, Wheels, 1986, Lulu and the Witch Baby, 1986, Richard and the Vratch, 1987, Molly, 1987, Molly Goes Hiking, 1987, Jam Day, 1987, The Boston Coffee Party, 1988, The Take-Along Dog, 1989, Selene Goes Home, 1989, The Magic Mean Machine, 1989, It Always Happens to Leona, 1989, The Grandpa Days, 1989, Dinah's Mad, Bad Wishes, 1989, Stepbrother Sabotage, 1990, Lulu Goes to Witch School, 1990, The Day Chubby Became Charles, 1990, The Christmas Present Mystery, 1990, Sky Guys to White Cat, 1991, Meatball, 1991, Leona and Ike, 1991, The Butterfly Birthday, 1991, Yankee Doodle Drumsticks, 1992, One Very Best Valentine's Day, 1992, Meet the Lincoln Lions Band, 1992, Jingle Bells Jam, 1992, In My Tent, 1992, Anne Flies the Birthday Bike, 1993, Amzat and His Brothers, 1993, Leo the Magnificent, 1996, Old Home Day, 1996, The Divide, 1997, Rabbit Pirates, 1999.

MCCULLY, KILMER SERJUS, pathologist; b. Daykin, Nebr., Dec. 23, 1933; s. Cyrus Harold and Lula Viola (Litwinenco) McC.; m. Annina Elena Jacobs, Aug. 14, 1955; children: Michael Kilmer, Martha Elizabeth. AB (magna cum laude), Harvard Coll., 1955; MD (cum laude), Harvard Med. Sch., 1959; MA, Brown U., 1983. Diplomate Nat. Bd. Med. Examiners, Am. Bd. Pathology, Anatomic and Clinical Pathology. Intern Mass. Gen. Hosp., Boston, 1959-60, fellow, 1962-63, resident, 1965-68; biochemist NIH, Bethesda, Md., 1960-62; rsch. assoc. genetics Glasgow (Scotland) U., 1963-64; rsch. fellow biology Harvard U., Cambridge, Mass., 1964-65; pathologist Mass. Gen. Hosp., Boston, 1968-79; vis. prof. lab. medicine U. Conn., Farmington, 1980-81; chief pathologist VA Med. Ctr., Providence, 1981-2001; dir. Boston Area VA Labs., 2001—. Asst. prof. pathology Harvard Med. Sch., Boston, 1970-79, assoc. clin. prof. pathology, 2001--; assoc. prof. pathology Brown U., Providence, 1981-88, 97--; editorial bd. Rsch. Communications in Chem. Pathology and Pharmacology, 1983—. Author: Homocysteine Theory of Arteriosclerosis, 1983, The Homocysteine Revolution, 1997, The Heart Revolution, 1999; contbr. articles to profl. jours. and chpt. to book. Violinist First Congl. Ch., Winchester, Mass., 1965—; mem. Harvard Pierian Found., Cambridge, 1983-86. Sr. asst. surgeon USPHS, 1960-62. Recipient Rsch. fellowship NIH, 1962, Faculty Rsch. award Am. Cancer Soc., 1963-68, Career Devel. award NIH, 1971-76. Mem. AAAS, Am. Soc. Investigative Pathology, Harvard Mus. Assn. (pres. 1994-97), Alpha Omega Alpha, Phi Beta Kappa. Democrat. Achievements include research and development of homocysteine theory of arteriosclerosis; discovery of abnormal homocysteine thiolactone metabolism in cancer; patents for antineoplastic homocysteine thiolactone compounds. Office: VA Med Ctr 1400 VFW Pky West Roxbury MA 02132

MCCULLY, WILLIAM CRAIG, library administrator; b. Richmond Heights, Mo., Sept. 15, 1947; s. William Craig and Amelia Agnes (Kearns) McC.; m. Nancy Louise Buddenbaum, June 19, 1976; children: Claire Louise, Edward William. BA in History, U. Notre Dame, 1969, MA in Modern European History, 1970, PhD, 1973; MLS, U. Ill., 1975. Dir. Everett M. Dirkson Congressional Leadership Rsch. Ctr., Pekin, Ill., 1975-78, Pekin (Ill.) Pub. Lib., 1975-82; exec. librarian Park Ridge (Ill.) Pub. Lib., 1982-2000. Chmn. dir.'s adv. coun. Ill. Valley Lib. Sys., Pekin, 1980-81; chmn., Ill. State Lib. Adv. Com. and Subcoms., Springfield, 1982-88; sec., Regional Adv. Coun., North Suburban Lib. Sys., Wheeling, Ill., 1988-89; pres., Coop. Computer Svcs., Arlington Heights, Ill., 1991-92, 2002-; study com. lib. fin., Ill. Gen. Assembly, Springfield, 1993-96; pres. Libr. Cable Network, 1996-2000. Book reviewer: Library Journal, 1980-92. Literature adv. panel, Ill. Arts Coun., Springfield, 1984-87; exec. dir. Prospect Heights (Ill.) PLD, 2000—. Capt. USAR, 1973-74. Mem. ALA, Ill. Lib. Assn. Home: 1321 N Peachtree Ln Mount Prospect IL 60056-1825 E-mail: billmccully@aol.com., wmccully@phl.alibrary.com.

MC CUNE, BARRON PATTERSON, retired federal judge; b. West Newton, Pa., Feb. 19, 1915; s. James Patterson and Lyda Barron (Hammond) McC.; m. Edna Flannery Markey, Dec. 23, 1943; children: Edward M., James H., Barron Patterson. AB, Washington and Jefferson Coll., 1935; LLB, U. Pa., 1938. Bar: Pa. bar 1939. Practiced in, Washington, 1939-64; judge 27th Jud. Dist. Ct. Common Pleas, 1964-71, U.S. Dist. Ct., Western Dist. Pa., Pitts., 1971-95, sr. fed. judge; ret., 1995. Trustee emeritus Washington and Jefferson Coll.; bd. dirs. emeritus Washington (Pa.) Hosp. Served with USNR, 1942-45. Home: 144 Lemoyne Ave Washington PA 15301-3636

MCCUNE, BARRY LYNN, minister; b. Bluffton, Ind., Feb. 23, 1952; s. Harold Kenneth McCune and Jeanette Allebelle (Lantz) Johnson; m. Andrea Lee Sprunger, June 13, 1975; children: Holly Marie, Shauna Leigh, Carmen Joy. Student, Ind. U.-Purdue U., Ft. Wayne, Ind., 1971-72; BA, Taylor U., Ft. Wayne, 1978; grad., Grace Theol. Sem., Winona Lake, Ind., 1981-82; M in Christian Ministry, Huntington (Ind.) Coll., 1993. Lic. to ministry Missionary Ch. Inc., 1987, ordained 1989. Ordained to ministry Ch. of United Brethren in Christ, 1999. Pastor Petroleum (Ind.) United Meth. Ch., 1984-87, Trinity Missionary Ch., Burton, Mich., 1987-93, South Liberty Christian Ch., Poneto, Ind., 1997-98, First United Brethren In Christ Ch., Van Wert, Ohio, 1998—. Dir. Wells County Migrant Ministry, Bluffton, Ind., 1985-85. With USAF, 1970-76. Republican. Home: 509 S Race St Van Wert OH 45891-2169 E-mail: bearnandi@earthlink.net. *One of the greatest challenges the Christian faces today is to stand on the solid ground of God's Holy Word, the Bible, against all evil and the evil powers of darkness, so that people will see the truth about the Lord Jesus Christ - that He is their only hope.*

MCCUNE, ELLIS E. retired university system chief administrator, higher education consultant; b. Houston, July 17, 1921; s. Ellis E. and Ruth (Mason) McC.; m. Hilda May Whiteman, Feb. 8, 1946; 1 son, James Donald. Student, Sam Houston State U., 1940-42; BA, UCLA, 1948, PhD, 1957; LHD, Golden Gate U., 1994. Teaching asst. UCLA, 1949-51; from instr. to assoc. prof. polit. sci. Occidental Coll., Los Angeles, 1951-59, chmn. applied politics and econs. curriculum, 1951-56; asst. prof. Calif. State U., Northridge, 1959-61, assoc. prof., chmn. dept. polit. sci., 1961-63, prof., 1963, dean letters and sci., 1963; dean acad. planning Calif. State Univs. and Colls., 1963-67; pres. Calif. State U., Hayward, 1967-90, pres. emeritus, 1991—; acting chancellor The Calif. State U. System, 1990-91, ret., 1991. Cons. govtl. units and agys.; lectr., panelist; mem. Calif. State Scholarship and Loan Commn., 1964-68, chmn., 1967-68; pres. Govtl. Adminstrn. Group Los Angeles, 1959; chair planning com., mem. exec. com., bd. dirs. Eden Med. Ctr. Found., 1994—, pres.-elect, 1995-97, pres., 1997-99. Chmn. univs. and colls. div. United Bay Area Crusade, 1969-70, 73-74; bd. dirs. Oakland (Calif.) Museum Assn., 1974-77, 86-88, Hayward Area Hist. Soc., 1998—; vice chmn. higher edn. div., East Bay United Way, 1989-90; mem. arts adv. council, 1986-87, devel. com., 1988-89, Bay Area Urban League, bd. trust Calif. Coun. Econ. Edn. No. sect., Emergency Shelter Program Adv. Coun., Hayward Area Hist. Assn., NAACP Hayward chpt.; trustee Calif. Council Econ. Edn.; sec. bd. dirs. Eden Community Found., 1978-79; rsch. fellow Haynes Found, 1957. With US-AAF, 1942-46. Mem. Am. Coun. Edn. (adv. com. 1970-72, inst. coll. & univ. adminstrs. 1973-74, bd. dirs. 1985-86), Western Assn. Schs. and Colls. (accrediting commn. sr. colls. and univs. 1974-78, chmn., 1978-82, pres. 1979-81), N.W. Assn. Schs. and Colls. (commn. colls. 1974-80), Assn. Am. Colls. (bd. dirs. 1972-75, vice chmn. 1975-76), Assn. Western Univs. (bd. dirs.), Coun. Postsecondary Accreditation (bd. dirs. 1977-88, exec. com. 1979-88, chmn. 1985-87, immediate past chmn., 1988-89, chmn. com. recognition 1982-84), Am. Assn. State Colls. and Univs. (chmn. accreditation com. 1983-86, com. acad. pers. and acad. freedom 1987-88, com. on acad. affairs 1988-91), Calif. Coun. Edn. (trustee), Western Polit. Sci. Assn. (exec. coun. 1958-61), Hayward C. of C. (dir. 1968-71, 73-76, 77-80, 82-85, 86-90), Regional Assn. East Bay Colls. and Univs. (exec. com. 1974-90, sec. 1975-76, 87-88, vice chmn. 1976-77, 84-85, chmn. 1977-79, 85-86), Rotary, Phi Beta Kappa, Pi Gamma Mu, Pi Sigma Alpha. Clubs: Bohemian (San Francisco). Home: 22012 Sevilla Rd # 85 Hayward CA 94541-2735 Office: Calif State U Pres Emeritus LI 3167 Hayward CA 94542-3053 Fax: 510-537-3581. E-mail: EMcCune@worldnet.att.net.

MC CUNE, JOHN FRANCIS, III, retired architect; b. New Castle, Pa., Oct. 23, 1921; s. John Francis and Alice (Miles) McC.; m. Jeanne Ramsay, Sept. 28, 1946; children— Morgan R., Martha (Mrs. Dennis L. Maddox), David M., William S. Student, Vanderbilt U., 1938-40; BS in Architecture, U. Mich., 1943. Draftsman firm Walter E. Bort (Architect), Clinton, Iowa, 1946-47; firm Pope & Kruse (Architects), Wilmington, Del., 1947-54, asso., 1955-60; partner firm Pope, Kruse & McCune (Architects), Wilmington, 1961-72; owner McCune Assos. (Architects), 1972-81; v.p., prin. architect Diamond/McCune (Architects & Engrs.), 1981-88. Projects include Gander Hill Correctional Facility; renovation of Wilmington Public Bldg, all Wilmington; historic preservation projects include Presbyn. Ch, New Castle, Old Court House, New Castle, Barrett's Chapel, Frederica, Del., Old State House, Dover, Del., Loockerman Hall, Dover. Mem. Hist. Area Commn., New Castle, Del., 1974-88. Mem. AIA (pres. Del. chpt. 1970-71, mem. nat. com. historic resources 1975-88, state preservation coordinator Del. 1975-88), Soc. Archtl. Historians, Assn. for Preservation Tech., ASTM (com.), Nat. Trust Hist. Preservation, Del. C. of C., Nat. Fire Protection Assn. (com. libraries, museums and hist. bldgs. 1975-88), Kappa Sigma. Home: 1386 Northridge Dr Prescott AZ 86301

MCCUNE, LINDA WILLIAMS, artist, educator; b. Dyersburg, S.C., Sept. 29, 1950; d. Willard Charles and Margie Harrison Williams; m. William Derryman McCune II, Dec. 30, 1972; children: Nova Lauran, Tayce Caitlin. BFA, U. Tenn., 1974, postgrad., 1974-77; MFA, U. S.C., 1982. Cert. tchr. Tenn., S.C. Artist-illustrator U. Tenn., Knoxville, 1970-72; art history commentator Sta. WSJK-TV, 1971-72; artistic designer Morristown (Tenn.) Theatre Guild, 1971-78; artist in residence Morristown City Sch. Sys., 1972-77; asst. prof. art Walters State C.C., Morristown, 1973-77; display designer Laminite-Laminall Corp., Tenn., 1975-76; co-owner Upstairs Gallery, 1976-78; art cons. Allendale (S.C.) County Sch. Sys., 1979-80; co-owner Studio III Frame Shop, Allendale, 1979-86; grad. asst. U. S.C., Columbia, 1980-82, teaching assoc. Allendale, Walterboro, 1980-86; dir. Summer Art Series for Youth, Tryon, N.C., 1987-89; artist in residence S.C. Arts Commn. Residency Program, Columbia, 1987-89; mem. art faculty Greenville (S.C.) Technical Coll., 1989—; grad. student advisor Vt. Coll., Montpelier, 1996—. Mem. fine arts com. Morristown C. of C., 1974—79, bicentennial com., 1975—76; sec. visual and environ. design panel Tenn. Arts Commn., Nashville, 1975—79; mem. fine arts com. Cmty. Devel. Bd., Allendale, 1980, downtown renovations com., 80; chmn. exhbns. com. Allendale County Arts Gallery and Mus., Allendale County Arts Coun., 1984—; mem. bd. Southeastern Art Assn., New Art Examiner Mag., Chgo., 1989—90; guest lectr. S.C. Gov.'s Sch. Arts, 1997, U. S.C., Spartanburg, 1997, Coastal Carolina U., Myrtle Beach, 1997, others. One person shows include Archtl. Bldg. Gallery, U. Tenn., Knoxville, 1970, Morristown-Hamblen Libr., 1971, Walters State C.C., Morristown, 1974, 78, Jonesboro (Tenn.) Gallery, 1975, Appalachia State U., Boone, N.C., 1976, Emory and Henry Coll., Bristol, Va., 1976, Kingsport (Tenn.) Fed., 1977, Rose Cultural Ctr. Mus., Morristown, 1978, U. S.C., Allendale, 1979, Weekend Gallery, Columbia Mus., 1980, Barnwell (S.C.) County Mus., 1982, Copland Wahl House, Columbia, 1982, Columbia Mus. Arts and Scis., 1983, Nexus Contemporary Arts Ctr., Atlanta, 1986, Asheville (N.C.) Art Mus. Civic Ctr., 1990, Converse (S.C.) Coll., 1995, 291 Gallery, Greenville, 1996, Taylors (S.C.) First Bapt. Ch., 1997, Coastal Carolina U., Myrtle Beach, S.C., 1997, U. S.C., Spartanburg, 1997, S.C. Archives and History Ctr., Columbia, 1998, Pickens Mus., 2000, North Greenville Coll., 2002, Fine Arts Ctr. Xershaw, conn., 2001; exhibited in group shows at Dublin Art Mus., Knoxville, 1974, Austin Peay State U., Nashville, 1976, Dock St. Theatre, Charleston, S.C., 1979, Beaufort (S.C.) Art Assn., 1980, 81, Miss. Mus. Art, Jackson, 1981, Tampa (Fla.) Mus., 1982, Roanoke (Va.) Mus. Fine Arts, 1982, McKissick Mus., Columbia, 1982, 93, 95, 96, 98, 2000, Tucson Mus., 1983, Spartanburg (S.C.) Arts Ctr., 1985, Allendale County Mus., 1986, Columbia Mus. Arts and Scis., 1986, The Upstairs Gallery, Tryon, N.C., 1987, 88, Furman U., Greenville, 1988, 93, 99, S.C. State Mus., Columbia, 1990, 92, 94, 99, 2000, 2001, U. Ky., Lexington, 1990, Vista Arts Gallery, Columbia, 1991, Ownesboro (Ky.) Mus. Fine Arts, 1991, Havens Gallery, Columbia, 1992, Asheville Art Mus., 1993, Greenville County Mus., 1990, 93, 2001, 2002, Lee Hall Gallery, Clemson (S.C.) U., 1995, Greenville Tehnical Coll., 1996, 97, 99 U. S.C., Spartanburg, 1996, Columbia, 1996, Mobile (Ala.) Mus. Art, 1996, NationsBank Plz., Columbia, 1997, Rocky Mount (N.C.) Art Ctr., 1997, Fayetteville (N.C.) Mus. Art, 1997, Koller Gallery, Washington, 1997, The White House, Washington, 1998, 2001, Greensboro (S.C.) Cultural Art Ctr., 1998, Zone One Contemporary Gallery, Asheville, 1998, Lander U., Greenwood, S.C., 1998, North Charleston (S.C.) City Gallery, 1999, Wachovia Bank Bldg. Gallery, Greenville, 1999, S.C. State Mus., 2000, Ashville, N.C., Arboretum, 2000, Burroughs-Chapin Mus., Myrtle Beach, S.C., 1999, Longwood Ctr. in the Visualr Arts Farmville, Virginia, 2001, Brevard Coll., Brevard, N.C., Hartz Vistener and Allery, Charlotte, N.C., 2001, Wingate U., Wingate, N.C., 2001, Accessibility, Sumpter, S.C., 2001, Moore Coll. Art and Design, Phila., Pa., 2002, many others; contbr. articles to various publs. Tchr. Taylors (S.C.) First Bapt. Ch., 1988—; active PTA Bd., Buena Vista Elem., Greer, S.C., 1991-92. Recipient award, Tenn. Water Color All-State Show, 1974, Beaufort Art Assn. Exhbn., 1979, 1980, 1981, McKissick Mus. Exhbn., 1982, Sandoz SCRA Regional Exhbn., 1986, Seneca County Art Coun. Exhibit, 1998, 1999, Upstate Visual Arts Millenium Exhbn., 2000, Andenson Arts Coun., 1999, 100 yrs. 100 artist award, S.C. State Mus., 2000; grantee, S.C. Visual Arts, 2001—02, S.C. Visual Arts Commn., 2001. Mem. Southeastern Coll. Art Assn., Upstate Visual Artists, Tri State Sculptors (S.C. state rep.), Metropolitan Arts Council.

Avocations: traveling, visiting antique shows, collecting vintage broaches. Office: Greenville Technical Coll Visual Arts Dept PO Box 5616 Greenville SC 29606-5616 E-mail: sculp999@bellsouth.net., mccunelwm@gultec.edu.

MCCUNE, MARY JOAN HUXLEY, microbiology educator; b. Lewistown, Mont., Jan. 14, 1932; d. Thomas Leonard and Anna Dorothy (Hardie) Huxley; m. Ronald William McCune, June 7, 1965; children: Anna Orpha, Heather Jean. BS, Mont. State Coll., 1953; MS, Wash. State U., 1955; PhD, Purdue U., 1965. Rsch. technician VA Hosp., Oakland, Calif., 1956-59; bacteriologist U.S. Naval Radiol. Def. Lab., San Francisco, 1959-61; tchg. assoc. Purdue U., West Lafayette, Ind., 1961-65, vis. asst. prof., 1965-66; asst. prof. Occidental Coll., L.A., 1966-69; asst. rsch. bacteriologist II UCLA, 1969-70; affiliate asst. prof. Idaho State U., Pocatello, 1970-80, from asst. prof. to prof. microbiology, 1980—2001; prof. emeritus, 2001. Instr. U. Calif., Davis, 1964. Contbr. articles to profl. jours. Pres. AK chpt. PEO, Pocatello, 1988-89; chair faculty senate Idaho State U., 1994-95. David Ross fellow Purdue U., 1964; named Outstanding Alumna, Assn. Women Students, Mont. State U., 1975. Mem. AAAS, N.Y. Acad. Sci., Idaho Acad. Sci. (trustee 1989-95, v.p. 1992-93, pres. 1993-94), Am. Soc. for Microbiology (v.p. Intermountain br. 1988-89, pres. 1989-90, sec.-treas. 2000—), Idaho Edn. Alliance for Sci. (bd. dirs.), Sigma Xi, Sigma Delta Epsilon. Presbyterian. Home: 30 Colgate St Pocatello ID 83201-3459 Office: Idaho State U Dept Biol Scis Pocatello ID 83209-0001 E-mail: mccujoan@isu.edu.

MCCUNE, PHILIP SPEAR, lawyer; b. Spokane, Wash., Sept. 14, 1965; s. Calmar A. McCune and Katrina Y. Spear; m. Joey Leigh Hankins, Jan. 15, 1993; children: Emma Sophia, Jackson Spear. BA magna cum laude, Dartmouth Coll., 1987; JD cum laude, U. Mich., 1991. Law clk. Hon. John C. Coughenour chief judge U.S. Dist. Ct. (we. dist.) Wash., Seattle, 1991—93; with Heller, Ehrman, White and Maculliffe, 1993—97; ptnr., founder Summit Law Group, 1997—. Author: The Forest Practices Act, Washington Environmental Law and Practice, 1997; sr. editor U. Mich. Jour. Law Reform, 1989-91; contbr. articles to profl. jours. Bd. dirs. Cmty. Svc. for the Blind, Seattle, Friends of Ind. Schs. and Better Edn., Seattle Repertory Theater; pres. bd. dirs. Am. Friends St. Michaels U. Sch. Named Washington Law and Politics Rising Star, 2002. Mem. ABA, Washington State Bar Assn., King County Bar Assn., Wash. Athletic Club, U. Mich. Law Sch. Barristers. Avocations: hiking, running. Office: Summit Law Group 1505 Westlake Ave N Ste 300 Seattle WA 98109-6211 E-mail: philm@summitlaw.com.

MCCUNNEY, ROBERT JOSEPH, physician; b. July 4, 1948; s. Robert H. McCunney; m. Marilyn Stanton, Nov. 7, 1987; children: Robby, Kelsey. BSCE, Drexel U., 1971; MS in Environ. Health, U. Minn., 1972; MD, Jefferson Med. Coll., 1976; MPH in Occupl. Health, Harvard U., 1981. Intern, resident Northwestern U. Med. Ctr., Chgo., 1976-78; occupl. medicine fellow Harvard Sch. Pub. Health, Boston, 1979-81; emergency rm. physician Choate Meml. Hosp., Woburn, Mass., 1979-80, Sancra Maria Hosp., Cambridge, 1979-80; med. dir. occupl. health svc. Sturdy Meml. Hosp., Attleboro, 1981-83; med. dir. Goddard Occupl. Health Svcs., Stoughton, 1982-90; chief occupl. & environ. medicine, dir. occupl. med. residency program Boston U. Med. Ctr., 1983-94; corp. med. dir. Cabot Corp., Boston, 1983—; dir. environ. med. svc. med. dept. MIT, Cambridge, 1994—. Instr. anatomy Thomas Jefferson U., 1973; instr. medicine Brown U., Providence, 1982-85; adj. asst. prof. pub. health Boston U., 1983—; clin. asst. prof. Med. Coll. Wis., Milw., 1989—; lectr. medicine Harvard Med. Sch., Boston; staff physician Mass. Gen. Hosp., Boston. Editor: Handbook of Occupational Medicine, 1988, A Practical Approach to Occupational and Environmental Medicine, 1994, A Manager's Guide to Occupational Health Services, 1995, Occupl. & Environ. Medicine Report, Medical Center Occupational Health and Safety, 1999, Occupational and Environmental Medicine Self Assessment Guide, 1998; co-editor Health & Safety Manual, 1992; contbr. chpts. to books and articles to profl. jours. Fellow Am. Occupl. Medicine Assn., Am. Coll. Preventive Medicine; mem. AMA, APHA, Am. Conf. Govtl. Indsl. Hygienists, Am. Coll. Occupl. & Environ. Medicine (bd. dirs. 1991-94, 95—, chair pubs. com. 1985-88, house dels. 1983-89, govt. affairs com. 1989-93, past pres. New Eng. chpt. 1984-86, dir. residency sect. 1988-93), Tau Beta Pi, Phi Beta Upsilon. Roman Catholic. Avocations: athletics, photography, boating. Office: MIT Ctr for Environ Health Scis 77 Massachusetts Ave 76-743 Cambridge MA 02139-4307

MCCURDY, GARY DEAN, dist. judge, educator; b. Tulsa, Sept. 22, 1952; s. Carl Leon and Helen (Manthus) McC.; m. Janie Marie Fischer, May 31, 1975; children: Christopher John, Elizabeth Kay. BA in Polit. Sci., Okla. State U., 1974; JD, U. Tulsa, 1980. Bar: Okla. 1980, U.S. Dist. Ct. (no. dist.) Okla. 1980. Asst. dist. atty. Tulsa County (Okla.) Dist. Atty.'s Office, Tulsa, 1980-84; pvt. practice, 1984-86; asst. dist. atty. Kingfisher County (Okla.) Dist. Atty.'s Office, Kingfisher, 1986-88, Can. County Dist. Atty.'s Office, El Reno, Okla., 1988—2001, spl. dist. judge, 2001—. Adj. faculty criminal justice Redlands C.C., 1998—2001; spkr. in field. Mem. Okla. Bar Assn. (chmn. criminal law com. 1997—), Kingfisher county Bar Assn. (pres. 1987), Okla. Dist. Attys. Assn. Democrat. Office: Canadian County Courthouse 301 N Choctaw Ave Ofc El Reno OK 73036-2468

MCCURDY, GILBERT GEIER, retired retailer; b. Rochester, N.Y., May 25, 1922; s. Gilbert J.C. and Virginia (Geier) McC.; m. Katherine W. Babcock, Nov. 9, 1946; children— Gilbert Kennedy, Lynda Babcock (Mrs. Hotra). BA, Williams Coll., 1944. With McCurdy & Co., Inc., Rochester, 1946—, controller, asst. treas., 1953-55, v.p., 1956-59, exec. v.p., 1959-62, pres., gen. mgr., 1962-80, chief exec. officer, 1969-80, chmn. bd., chief exec. officer, 1980-92, chmn. exec. com. of bd., 1993—. Chmn. bd. Frederick Atkins, 1968-70. 1st Leut. Signal Corps., Austria, 1943—46; bd. dirs. Pathway Houses of Rochester, Boys and Girls Club, Rochester; former mem. bd. dirs. United Way of Greater Rochester; life trustee U. Rochester. 1st lt. Signal Corps AUS, 1943—46. Mem. Rochester C. of C. (pres. 1975) Baptist. Home: 1 Whitney Ln Rochester NY 14610-3551 Office: 1465 Jefferson Rd. Rochester NY 14623

MCCURDY, HARRY WARD, otolaryngologist; b. Branchton, Pa., Aug. 15, 1918; s. Adam Oscar and Sarah Fern (Hindman) McC.; m. Joan Jacqueline Talty, Dec. 10, 1955; children: Bridget Elizabeth, Peter Adam. AB, Allegheny Coll., 1940; MD, U. Pa., 1943. Diplomate: Am. Bd. Otolaryngology. Intern Geisinger Meml. Hosp., Danville, Pa., 1944, resident in otolaryngology, 1944-45, 48-49; resident in pathology Hamot Hosp., Erie, Pa., 1945-48; mem. staff Geisinger Med. Center, Danville, 1948-50; commd. 2d lt. U.S. Army, 1945, advanced through grades to col., 1962-74; mil. cons. Surgeon Gen., U.S. Army, 1964-74; ret., 1974; exec. v.p. Am. Acad. Otolaryngology-Head and Neck Surgery, Washington, 1974-84; mem. staff Walter Reed Army Hosp. Mem. resources council Gallaudet Coll., 1975-80; mem. nat. adv. council Sertoma Found., 1976-84; chmn. FDA Panel on Otolaryngologic Med. Devices, 1974-78, cons., 1978-84 Mem. ACS, AMA, Royal Soc. Medicine (U.K.), Am. Acad. Otolaryngology, Mil. Surgeons Assn., Am. Soc. Assn. Execs., Soc. Med. Consultants to Armed Forces, AAAS, Am. Soc. Facial Plastic Surgery, Soc. Mil. Otolaryngologists, Am. Acad. Facial Plastic and Reconstructive Surgery, Am. Laryngol., Rhinol. and Otol. Soc., Anglo-Am. Med. Soc., Am. Audiology Soc., Royal Soc. Health, Osler Med. Soc., Acad. Medicine, Soc. Univ. Otolaryngologists, Am. Council Otolaryngology, Pan-Am. Soc. Bronchoesophagology., Internat. Fedn. Otolaryngol. Socs. (sec. gen. 1981—), Soc. Mil. Cons. to Armed Forces (sec. 1993—). Clubs: Army Navy, Press, Mil. Attaches of London, Les Chevaliers du Tastevin. Republican. Methodist. Home and Office: 6006 Dellwood Pl Bethesda MD 20817-3812

MCCURDY, JOHN DENNIS, biochemist, toxicologist; b. Irvington, N.J., Aug. 17, 1942; s. Harris John and Emma Grace (Lang) McC.; m. Diane Jena Espinoza, Oct. 3, 1981; children: Kristina Marie, Michael John Daniel. BS, Fairleigh Dickinson U., 1966; MS, Am. U., 1972; PhD, 1974. Diplomate Am. Bd. Toxicology. Assoc. rsch. scientist Am. U., Washington, 1969-74, rsch. scientist, 1976-90; FDA scientist Ctr. Vet. Medicine, Rockville, Md., 1974—. Vis. scientist Howard U., Washington, 1982-83. Instr. Greater Balt. YMCA, Howard county, 1978, Towson, 1985. Capt. U.S. Army, 1966-69. Fellow Am. Inst. Chemists; mem. Am. Chem. Soc. (bd. mgrs. Washington chpt. 1974), Assn. Ofcl. Analytical Chemists, Washington Kendo (Columbia, Md.), Am. Ju-Jitsu Assn. (bd. dirs., no. regioanl dir.). Roman Catholic. Avocations: martial arts, Ju Jitsu, Judo, Kendo, Iaido. Home: 3949 Sugarloaf Dr Monrovia MD 21770-9113

MCCURDY, KURT BASQUIN, real estate corporation officer; b. Portsmouth, Ohio, Dec. 24, 1952; s. Robert Kurt and Sue Ann (Basquin) McC.; m. Eileen Wirtz, May 21, 1977; children: Andrew Kurt, Patrick Robert, Meghan Eileen. Student, Ohio No. U., Ada, 1971-72; BA, Ohio State U., 1976. Cert. residential specialist; accredited buyers rep. Sales assoc. HER Realtors, Inc., Columbus, Ohio, 1975—, also bd. dirs. Appraiser Franklin County Probate Ct., Columbus, 1978—; guest lectr. Ohio State U., 1981, Franklin U., 1982-83. Contbr. articles to real estate mags. Mem. Realtors Polit. Action Com., Columbus, 1978—, Chmn.'s Club, Rep. Party, Franklin County, 1980-85; v.p., bd. dirs. Culver (Ind.) Mil. Summer Schs., 1979-84. Named nat. sales winner The Dozen, 1984-2000; recipient The Dozen award, 1995. Mem. Ohio Assn. Realtors Assn. (trustee 2002, Profl. of Yr. award 1979, 83, 84, president's sales award 1986-99, Pinnacle Sales award 2000, 01), Bldg. Industry Assn. (15 Million Dollar Club, bd. dirs. 1994—, panelist Floyd Wickman Master Sales Acad. 1995, 96, Realtor of Yr. award 1992), Columbus Bd. Realtors (bd. dirs. 2002, 25 Million Dollar Club), Delaware County Bd. Realtors (75 Million Dollar Club), Westerville Athletic Club, Lakes Golf and Country Club, Medallion Golf and Country Club. Avocations: golf, tennis, boating, fishing, hunting. Home: 3295 Glen Oaks Ct Lewis Center OH 43035-9344 Office: HER Realtors Inc 413 N State St Westerville OH 43082-8276 E-mail: kurt.mccurdy@herrealtors.com.

MCCURDY, LARRY WAYNE, automotive parts company executive; b. Commerce, Tex., July 1, 1935; s. Weldon Lee and Eula Bell (Quinn) McC.; m. Anna Jean Ogle, June 2, 1956; children: Michael, Kimberly, Laurie. BBA, Tex. A&M U., 1957. Jr. acct. Tenneco Inc., Houston, 1958-60; sr. acct. Tenneco Oil Co., 1960-64; acctg. supr. Tenneco Chems., 1964-69, from divsn. controller to v.p. fin. Saddle Brook, N.J., 1970-78; sr. v.p. fin. Tenneco Automotive, Deerfield, Ill., 1978-80; pres. Walker Mfg. Co., Racine, Wis., 1980-81; exec. v.p. N.Am. ops. Tenneco Automotive, Deerfield, 1981-82; v.p. fin. Echlin Inc., Branford, Conn., 1983; pres., COO Echlin, Inc., 1983-85, pres., 1997—; pres., CEO Moog Automotive Inc., St. Louis, 1985-94; exec. v.p. ops. Cooper Industries, Houston, 1994-97; chmn. bd., pres., CEO Echlin, Inc., Branford, Conn., 1997-98; pres. Dana Automotive Aftermarket Group, 1998-2000; ret., 2000. Bd. dirs. Lear Corp., Mohawk Industries, Inc., Breed Tech., Inc., Am. Axle and Mfg. Co., Gen. Parts, Inc. Trustee Somerset County Coll., Somerville, N.J., 1974-78, Millikin U., Decatur, Ill., 1991-97; former mem. bd. dirs. Jr. Achievement, Chgo.; bd. dirs. Sam Houston coun. Boy Scouts Am., 1995-97; mem. adv. coun. Tex. A&M U. Engring. Sch., 1995-97. Mem. Fin. Execs. Inst., Nat. Assn. Accts., Motor Equipment Mfrs. Assn. (chmn. bd. dirs. 1989). E-mail: larrywmccurdy@aol.com.

MCCURDY, LAYTON, medical educator; b. Florence, S.C., Aug. 20, 1935; m. Gwendolyn A. McCurdy, 1958; children: Robert Jr., David Barclay. BS, U. N.C., 1956; MD, Med. U. S.C., 1960. Dimplomate Am. Bd. Psychiatry and Neurology (bd. dirs. 1983-91, pres. 1990); lic. psychiatrist, S.C., N.C., Md., Ga., Pa. Resident in psychiatry N.C. Meml. Hosp., Chapel Hill, 1961-64; with psychiatry tng. br. NIMH, Bethesda, Md., 1964-66; asst. prof. dept. psychiatry Sch. Medicine Emory U., Atlanta, 1966-68; prof., chmn. dept. psychiatry and behavioral scis. Med. U. S.C., 1968-82, v.p. med. affairs, dean, 1990—2001, dean emeritus, prof. psychiatry, exec. dir. Cardiovasc. Inst., 2001—; prof. psychiatry Sch. Medicine U. Pa., Phila., 1982-90; psychiatrist-in-chief Inst. of Pa. Hosp., 1982-90. Vis. colleague Inst. Psychiatry, U. London, 1974-75; nat. adv. mental health coun. NIMH, 1980-83; apptd. Pa. Adv. Com. for Mental Health and Mental Retardation, 1984-87; chmn. consensus panel on panic disorder NIH, 1991. Recipient Disting. Alumnus award Med. U. S.C., 1988, George C. Ham. Soc., 1990; rsch. fellow NIMH, 1974-75. Fellow Am. Coll. Psychiatrists (bd. regents 1987-90, v.p. 1990-93, pres. 1993-94, Bowis award 1997), Am. Psychiat. Assn. (joint commn. pub. affairs 1981-84, chmn. com. on diagnosis and assessment 1988-94), So. Psychiat. Assn. (bd. regents 1977-80, chmn. bd. regents 1979-80), Royal Coll. Psychiatrists (U.K.); mem. AMA, Assn. for Acad. Psychiatry (pres. 1970-72), S.C. Med. Assn., Waring Libr. Soc. (pres. 1979-80, exec. com. 1991-99), Cosmos Club (Washington)., Alpha Omega Alpha. Office: Med U SC Coll Medicine 135 Rutledge Ave Rm 1255 Charleston SC 29425-0001 E-mail: mccurdy@musc.edu.

MCCURDY, MICHAEL CHARLES, illustrator, author; b. N.Y.C., Feb. 17, 1942; s. Charles Errett and Beatrice (Beatson) McC.; m. Deborah Lamb, Sept. 7, 1968; children: Heather, Mark. BFA, Tufts U., 1964, MFA, 1971. Dir. Penmaen Press, Lincoln, Mass., 1968-85; instr. Concord (Mass.) Acad., 1972-75, Wellesley (Mass.) Coll., 1976. Illustrator: The Man Who Planted Trees, 1985, American Tall Tales, 1991, American Buffalo, 1992, The Way West: Journal of a Pioneer Woman, 1993, Giants in the Land, 1993, The Gettysburg Address, 1995, The Seasons Sewn, 1996; author, illustrator: Hannah's Farm, 1988, Trapped by the Ice, 1997, The Sailor's Alphabet, 1998, An Algonquian Year: The Year According to the Full Moon, 2000; editor, illustrator: Escape From Slavery: The Boyhood of Frederick Douglass in His Own Words, 1994, American Fairy Tales, 1996, War and the Pity of War, 1998, Tarzan, 1999, The Wizard of Oz, 1999, Iron Horses, 1999, The Signers: The 56 Stories Behind the Declaration of Independence, 2002. Mem. Great Barrington (Mass.) Housing Authority, 1990-93. Small press grantee Nat. Endowment Arts, 1978, Mass. Arts and Humanities, 1978. Mem. Soc. Printers, St. Botolph Club. Democrat. Episcopalian.

MC CURDY, PATRICK PIERRE, editor, consultant; b. Angers, France, Sept. 14, 1928; s. Joseph Alexander and Constance Yolande (Hillairet de Boisferon) McC.; m. Eiko Yamada, May 30, 1953; children: Alan J., Wendy C., Alec J., Jeffrey R. BS in Chem. Engring., Carnegie Inst. Tech., 1949. Chem. engr. tech. service dept. Humble Oil & Refining Co., Baytown, Tex., 1949-50; chem. engr. Callery Chem. Co., Pa., 1954-56; sr. chem. engr. U.S. Army Engr. R & D Labs., Ft. Belvoir, Va., 1956-60; asst. editor Chem. & Engring. News, Washington, 1960-61, N.Y.C., 1961-62, bur. head Frankfurt, Germany, 1962-64, Tokyo, 1964-67, mng. editor Washington, 1967-69, editor, 1969-73; editor in chief Chemical Week, 1973-80, 84-87, editor-in-chief, assoc. pub., 1987-88; dir. communications Am. Chem. Soc., 1988-91, dir. industry rels., 1991-93, founding editor Today's Chemist at Work, 1989-97; cons. American Chemical Soc., 1993-97; pub. issues mgr. Dow Chem. Co., Midland, Mich., 1980-82, dir. tech. communications, 1982-84. Cons. in field, 1997—; editl. cons. Chem. Heritage mag., 1997—. Served to 1st lt. C.E. AUS, 1950-54. Recipient Jesse H. Neal award, 1979, finalist 1985; recipient Carnegie Mellon Univ. Alumni Merit award, 1988. Mem.: AIChE, Societe de Chimie Industrielle (past pres. Am. sect.), Chemists Club, Fgn. Corrs. Club Japan, Am. Chem. Soc., Tokyo Am. Club, Tau Beta Pi, Phi Kappa, Theta Tau, Phi Kappa Phi. Home and Office: 11717 Chauncey Ln Mason Neck VA 22079-4140 E-mail: mccurdypp@aol.com.

MCCURLEY, MARY JOHANNA, lawyer; b. Baton Rouge, Oct. 3, 1953; d. William Edward and Leora Elizabeth (Block) Trice; m. Carl Michael McCurley, June 6, 1983; 1 stepchild, Melissa Reneé Rockenbach. BA, Centenary Coll., 1975; JD, St. Mary's U., 1979. Bar: Tex. 1979; cert. family law. Assoc. Martin, Withers & Box, Dallas, 1979-82, Raggio & Raggio, Inc., Dallas, 1982-83; ptnr. Bruner, McColl, McColloch & McCurley, 1983-87; assoc., ptnr. Selligson & Douglass, 1987-90; jr. ptnr. Koons, Fuller, McCurley & VanderEykel, 1990-92; ptnr. McCurley, Kinser, McCurley & Nelson, 1992—. Contbr. articles to profl. jours. Adv. Women's Service League, Dallas, 1993—. Mem.: Dallas Bar Assn., Tex. Acad. Family Law Specialist, Tex. State Bar Assn. (family law coun., sec. 2001, treas. 2001, vice-chair 2001), Dallas Bar Assn. (chair family law sect. 1985), Am. Acad. Matrimonial Lawyers (treas. Tex. chpt. 1993—95, sec. 1995—96, pres. 1997, nat. bd. dirs., bd. govs. 2000, nat. sec. 2000—01, pres. Tex. chpt. 1997—98). Methodist. Avocations: golf, travel, jogging, horseback riding. Home: 4076 Hanover Ave Dallas TX 75225-7009 Office: McCurley Kinser McCurley & Nelson LLP 5950 Sherry Ln Ste 800 Dallas TX 75225-6533 Fax: 214-273-2470. E-mail: marjo@mkmn.com.

MCCURLEY, ROBERT LEE, JR. lawyer, educator; b. Gadsden, Ala., Sept. 7, 1941; s. Robert Lee and Nellie Ruth McC.; m. Barbara; 1 child, Allison Leah. BS, U. Ala., 1963, JD, 1966. Bar: Ala. 1966, D.C. 1973, U.S. Ct. Mil. Appeals 1966, U.S. Supreme Ct. 1970, U.S. Ct. Appeals (5th cir.) 1972, U.S. Ct. Appeals (11th cir.) 1973, U.S. Ct. Appeals (fed. cir.) 1981. Asst. to dir. Fed. Savs. & Loan Ins. Corp., Washington, 1966-67; partner firm Rains, Rains, McCurley & Wilson, Gadsden, Ala., 1967-75; city judge Southside, 1970-75; dir. Ala. Law Inst., 1975—; assoc. dir. U. Ala. Center Public Law and Service, 1981-82; asst. dean Sch. Law U. Ala., 1978-81. Panelist White House Conf. on Volunteerism; pres. Gadsden Jaycees, 1972; mem. White House Fifty States Project; Henry Toll fellow Coun. State Govt., 1992. Editor: Divorce, Alimony and Child Support Custody, 3d edit., 1993, Land Laws of Alabama, 7th edit. rev., 2001, The Legislative Process, 7th edit., 1999, Alabama Law Office Practice Deskbook, 9th edit., 2000, Federally Mandated State Legislation, 1990, Alabama Legislation, Cases and Statutes, 4th edit., 1998, Alabama Election Handbook, 10th edit., 2002. Pres. Gadsden Boys Club, 1971, Kiwanis Internat. Found., 1998-2000; mem. Nat. Dem. Charter Commn., 1974. Mem. ABA, Am. Law Inst. (life), Order of Coif, Scribes, Farrah Law Soc., Commn. Uniform State Laws, Kiwanis (pres. Tuscaloosa club 1976, gov. Ala. dist. 1984, internat. v.p. 1991-92), Indian Hills County Club, Univ. Club. Baptist.

MCCURN, NEAL PETERS, federal judge; b. Syracuse, N.Y., Apr. 6, 1926; LL.B., Syracuse U., 1952, JD, 1960. Bar: N.Y. 1952. Ptnr. Mackenzie Smith Lewis Mitchell & Hughes, Syracuse, 1957-79; judge U.S. Dist. Ct. (no. dist.) N.Y., 1979-88; chief judge U.S. Dist. Ct. (no. dist.), N.Y., 1988-93; sr. judge, 1993—. Del. N.Y. State Constl. Conv., 1976; mem. 2d Cir. Jud. Council, 1987-93. Pres. Syracuse Common Coun., 1970-78. Mem. ABA, N.Y. State Bar Assn. (chmn. state constn. com.), Onondaga County Bar Assn. (past pres.), Am. Coll. Trial Lawyers, Am. Judicature Soc. (bd. dirs. 1980-84). Office: US Dist Ct 100 S Clinton St Rm 344 Syracuse NY 13261-6100

MCCURRY, JAMES PATRICK, philosophy and literature educator, poet, artist; b. Hawthorne, Calif., Oct. 3, 1943; s. Arlie Leford and Kathleen Alegra McCurry. BA, Knox Coll., 1965; MA, Colo. State U., 1974; PhD, U. Denver, 1985. Instr. Carl Sandburg Coll., Galesburg, Ill., 1980—. Cons., contbr. Archetypes of Wisdom, 2000, Logical Self-Def., 1994; sec., steering com. Carnegie-Mellon project Knox Coll., Galesburg, 1986. Author: CTA, 1977, Happy Nightmares, 1977; editor, pub. (mag.) Delirium v.1-5, 1975-78 (CCLM grant 1978); editl. bd. Farmer's Market, 1989-93. Spkr. Spkrs. Bd. Carl Sandburg Coll., 1991—, chmn. Tenure Commn., 2001. Woodrow Wilson fellowship Woodrow Wilson Found. Yale U., 1965-66; recipient First prize Acad. of Am. Poets, 1977, Gerard Manley Hopkins award Writer's Forum mag., 1999; grantee Ill. Arts Coun., 1991. Mem. NEA, Ill. Edn. Assn. Buddhist. Avocations: painting and collage, writing poetry and essays. Office: Carl Sandburg Coll Humanities Divsn Galesburg IL 61401

MCCURRY, MARGARET IRENE, architect, interior and furniture designer, educator; b. Chgo., Sept. 26, 1942; d. Paul D. and Irene B. McC.; m. Stanley Tigerman, Mar. 17, 1979. BA, Vassar Coll., 1964. Registered architect, Ill., Mass., Mich., Tex., Wis., Pa., Ind., Fla.; registered interior designer, Ill. Design coord. Quaker Oats Co., Chgo., 1964-66; sr. interior designer Skidmore, Owings & Merrill, 1966-77; pvt. practice architect Margaret I, 1977-82; ptnr. Tigerman, McCurry, 1982—. Vis. studio critic Art Inst. Chgo., 1985-86, 88, 98, lectr., 1988, 98; vis. studio critic U. Ill., Chgo., Miami U., Oxford, Ohio, 1990; juror Internat. furniture awards Progressive Architecture mag., N.Y.C., 1986, advt. awards, 1988; juror design grants Nat. Endowment for Arts, Washington, 1983; NEA Challenge Design Rev., 1992; peer reviewer design excellence program Gen. Svcs. Adminstrn., 1992—; juror, Wis., Minn., Calif., Va., Washington, Pitts., Ky., Ga. Conn. Soc. Architects, Detroit, N.Y.C., Memphis, Austin, L.A. chpts. AIA, Am. Wood Coun., AIA Students Design Competition, 1993. Author: Margaret McCurry: Constructing 25 Short Stories, 2000; contbr. Chgo. Archtl. Club Jour.; designer, contbr. archtl. exhibit Art Inst. Chgo., 1983-85, 93, 99, Chgo. Hist. Soc., 1984, Gulbenkian Found., Lisbon Portugal, 1989, Chgo. Athenaeum, 1990, Gwenda Jay Gallery, 1992, Women of Design Traveling Exhbn., 1992-96; archtl. drawings and models in permanent collection Art Inst. Chgo. and Deutsches Architektur Mus., Frankfurt. Chmn. furniture sect. fundraising auction Sta. WTTW-TV, PBS, Chgo., 1975-76; mem. Chgo. Beautiful Com., 1968-70; pres. alumni coun. Grad. Sch. Design, Harvard U., 1997-2000; bd. dirs. Architecture and Design Soc. Art Inst. Chgo., 1988-97, mem. textile adv. bd. textile dept. Loeb fellow Harvard U., 1986-87; recipient Builders Choice Grand award Builders Mag., 1985, Interior Design award Interiors Mag., 1983, Dean of Architecture award Chgo. Design Source and the Merchandise Mart, 1989; inducted into Interior Design Hall of Fame, Interior Design Mag., 1990. Fellow AIA (v.p. bd. dirs. Chgo. chpt. 1984-89, chair 1993, nat. design com., lectr. Colo. chpt. 1985, nat. conv. 1988, 97, 98, Monterey Design Conf. 1989, Washington Design Ctr. 1989, Nat. Honor award 1984, Nat. Interior Architecture award 1992, 98, Disting. Bldg. award Chgo. chpt. 1984, 86, 91, 94, 99, 2000, Disting. Interior Architecture award 1981, 83, 88, 91, 97; product display Neocon award 1985, 88, gold award best of Neocon 1998), Coll. of Fellows AIA, Internat. Interior Design Assn., Chgo. Network, Am. Soc. Interior Designers (Nat. Design award 1992, 94, Ill. chpt. Design award 1994, Ill. chpt. Merit award 1994,v.p. bd. dirs. Chgo. chpt.), Chgo. Archtl. Club, Arts Club Chgo., Womens Athletic Club, Harvard Alumni Assn. (dir. 2000—). Episcopalian. Avocations: drawing, writing, travel, golf, gardening. Office: Tigerman McCurry Archs 444 N Wells St Chicago IL 60610-4501 E-mail: mimccurry@tigerman-mccurry.com.

MCCUSKER, WILLIAM LAVALLE, lawyer; b. Mpls., July 27, 1918; s. John Thomas and Emma Ernestine (Helfmann) McC.; m. Phyllis E. Kischel, June 19, 1943; children: Patricia, Barbara, Marcia (dec.), William James, Nancy. BS, U. Wis.-Superior, 1941; postgrad. U. Minn. Law Sch., 1943-44; JD, U. Wis., 1946. Bar: Wis. 1946, U.S. Dist. Ct. (ea and we. dists.) Wis. 1946, U.S. Ct. Appeals (7th cir.) 1970, U.S. Supreme Ct. 1974. Assoc. Hill, Beckwith & Harrington, Madison, Wis., 1945-48; dep. dist. atty. Dane County, Wis., 1948-50; ptnr. Wilkie, McCusker and Wilkie, Madison, 1950-53; ptnr., pres., sr. mem. McCusker and Robertson, SC., Madison, 1953-94; prin. William L. McCusker Law Offices, Madison, 1994—; spl. asst. atty. gen., Wis., 1955; instr. seminars. Kellogg scholar, 1943-44. Recipient jud. achievement award Wis. Acad. Trial Lawyers. Fellow Internat. Soc. Barristers; mem. ATLA, State Bar of Wis., Dane County Bar Assn., Wis. Acad. Trial Lawyers (pres. 1977-78), Elks Club. Home: 3018 Pelham Rd Madison WI 53713-3468

MCCUTCHAN, GORDON EUGENE, retired lawyer, insurance company executive; b. Buffalo, Sept. 30, 1935; s. George Lawrence and Mary Esther (De Puy) McC.; m. Linda Brown; children: Lindsey, Elizabeth. BA, Cornell U., 1956, MBA, 1958, LLB, 1959. Bar: N.Y. 1959, Ohio 1964. Pvt. practice, Rome, 1959-61; atty., advisor SEC, Washington, 1961-64; ptnr. McCutchan, Druen, Maynard, Rath & Dietrich, 1964-94; mem. office of gen. counsel Nationwide Mut. Ins. Co., Columbus, Ohio, 1964-94, sr. v.p., gen. counsel, 1982-89, exec. v.p., gen. counsel, 1989-94; exec. v.p. Law and Corp. Svcs., Nationwide Ins. Enterprise, 1994-98; ret., 1998. Trustee, bd. govs. Franklin U., 1992-97; trustee Ohio Tuition Trust Authority, 1992-97. Mem. Columbus Bar Assn., Ohio Bar Assn., Am. Corp. Counsel Assn., Assn. Life Inst. Counsel (bd. govs. 1990-94), Fedn. Ins. and Corp. Counsel, Am. Coun. Life Ins. (chair legal sect. 1992-93). Home: 2376 Oxford Rd Columbus OH 43221-4011 E-mail: tunkpa@columbus.rr.com.

MCCUTCHAN, WILLIAM M. banker; b. Evansville, Ind., Apr. 10, 1954; s. Harold O. and Carol A. (Blackman) McC.; m. Donna D. Mushrush, Aug. 11, 1984 (div. July 1990); 1 child, William A; m. Tatyana Tkachenko, Sept. 15, 1999. BS, Ind. U., 1976; diploma comml. lending, Am. Inst. Banking, 1986; loan rev. cert., Bank Adminstrn. Inst., 1990. Mgmt. trainee Citizens Nat. Bank, Evansville, 1977-79; with Old Nat. Bank, 1979-86, loan review officer, 1984-86; dir. loan review, asst. v.p. Old Nat. Bancorp, 1986-96; mgr. loan rev., v.p. Fidelity Fed. Bancorp, 1997-98; br. mgr., comml. loan officer CSB State Bank, Cynthiana, Ind., 2000—. Trustee, treas. Willard Libr., Evansville, 1986-99; sec.-treas. McCutchanville (Ind.) Cemetery Assn., 1980—; bd. dirs. So. Ind. Higher Edn.; mem. McCutchanville United Meth. Ch. Mem. Am. Mensa Ltd., Evansville Kennel Club. Republican. Methodist.

MCCUTCHEN, TOMMY DEE, federal agency administrator; Grad., Western Ill. U., Northwestern U. Assoc. Skadden, Arps, Slate, Meagher and Flom, Chgo., 1992—95, Matkov, Salzman, Madoff anf Gunn, 1995—99; assoc. sr. counsel Hershey Foods Corp., 1999—2001; adminstr. wage and hour divsn. U.S. Dept. Labor, Washington, 2001—. Office: US Dept Labor 200 Constitution Ave NW Washington DC 20210*

MCCUTCHEN, WILLIAM WALTER, JR. management educator; b. Hamlet, N.C., Aug. 26, 1940; s. William Walter and Edith Wall (Rucker) McC.; m. Irene Katherine Lilly, June 16, 1962; 1 child, William Walter III. BS in Civil Engring., Duke U., 1962; MBA, Harvard U., 1967; PhD, Ind. U., 1988. Sales rep. Eli Lilly and Co., San Francisco, 1967-69, analyst econ. studies Indpls., 1969-70, mgr. econ. studies, 1970-72, mgr. personnel (mktg.), 1972-73; dir. nat. sales Elizabeth Arden, N.Y.C., 1973-76; mng. dir. Lilly Industries Pty.

Ltd., Sidney, Australia, 1976-79; dir. corp. communications Eli Lilly & Co., Indpls., 1980-83; assoc. prof. mgmt. Zicklin Sch. of Bus., Baruch Coll., CUNY, N.Y.C., 1988—, dep. chmn. dept. mgmt., 1995—. Capt. USMC, 1962-65. Mem. Acad. Mgmt., Am. Econ. Assn., Woodstock Club, Univ. Club, Phi Delta Theta, Beta Gamma Sigma. Congregationalist. Office: CUNY Baruch Coll Zicklin Sch of Bus 17 Lexington Ave New York NY 10010-5518

MCCUTCHEON, ALLAN LEE, sociology educator; b. Clarinda, Iowa, Mar. 15, 1950; s. Merle Marvin and Margaret Lucille (Larabee) McC.; m. Nancy Ann Cooper, June 13, 1970 (div. May 1975); 1 child, Jennifer; m. Elisabeth Jean Crockett, May 25, 1985. BS, Iowa State U., 1972; MA, U. Chgo., 1977, PhD, 1982. Asst. prof. sociology U. Del., Newark, 1982-88, assoc. prof. sociology, 1988-96, assoc. chair dept. sociology, 1989-95; Donald O. Clifton disting. prof. survey rsch. U. Nebr., Lincoln, 1996—, dir. Gallup Rsch. Ctr., 1996—; sr. scientist Gallup Orgn., 1996—. Cons. Disaster Rsch. Ctr., Newark, 1986-88; vis. scientist Max Planck Inst., Freiburg, Germany, 1988-89; dozent U. Cologne (Germany), 1989; instr. European Consortium for Polit. Rsch. U. Essex (Eng.), 1990—; mem. sci. adv. coun. German Ctr. for Survey Rsch. and Methodology, 1998—. Author (book) Latent Class Analysis, 1987; editor (newsletter) States and Societies, 1988-95; contbr. articles to profl. jours. Resource cons. Leadership Del. United Way, Wilmington, 1991-92. U. Chgo. rsch. fellow, 1974-77; Deutscher Akademischer Austauschdienst scholar, 1990; Fulbright scholar, The Netherlands, 1995-96. Mem. World Assn. for Pub. Opinion Rsch., Coun. for European Studies, Am. Assn. for Pub. Opinion Rsch., Am. Statis. Assn., Am. Sociol. Assn., Sigma Xi. Avocations: German culture, literature. Office: U Nebr Gallup Rsch Ctr 200 N 11th St Lincoln NE 68508-1406 E-mail: AMcCutcheon1@unl.edu.

MCCUTCHEON, JAMES EDWARD, III, lawyer; b. San Antonio, Aug. 7, 1968; s. James Edward McCutcheon Jr. and Barbara Letitia Rogers; m. Elizabeth Jean Cooper, Aug. 21, 1992; children: Davis, Ashley Grace. BA in Econs., Dartmouth Coll., 1990; JD, U. Tex., 1994. Bar: Tex. 1994, U.S. Tax Ct. 1995, Wash. 1998, U.S. Ct. Appeals (5th cir.) 1999, U.S. Dist. Ct. (we. dist.) Wash. 2002. Assoc. Gresham, Davis Gregory, Worthy & Moore, San Antonio, 1994-97, of counsel, 1997—, Vander Wel, Jacobson and Bishop, Bellevue, Wash., 2002—. Chmn., exec. dir. N.W. Christian Legal Found. Mem.: Wash. Bar Assn., Tex. Bar Assn., Order of the Coif Chancellors, Phi Beta Kappa. Office: 10500 NE 8th St Ste 1900 Bellevue WA 98004-4358 E-mail: jim@mccutcheonlaw.com.

MC CUTCHEON, JOHN TINNEY, JR. retired journalist; b. Chgo., Nov. 8, 1917; s. John Tinney and Evelyn (Shaw) McC.; m. Susan Dart, Feb. 1, 1943; children: Anne McCutcheon Lewis, Mary, John Tinney III. BS, Harvard U., 1939. Reporter City News Bur., Chgo., 1939-40, Chgo. Tribune, 1940-51, editor column A Line O' Type or Two, 1951-57, editorial writer, 1957-71, editor editorial page, 1971-82, columnist, 1967-70. Pres. Lake Forest (Ill.) Libr., 1970-72. Served with USNR, 1941-46. Mem. Soc. Midland Authors, Am. Soc. Newspaper Editors, Nat. Conf. Editorial Writers, Geog. Soc. Chgo. (pres. 1955-57), Chgo. Zool. Soc. (hon. trustee), Chgo. Hist. Soc. (life trustee), Inter Am. Press Assn. (dir., freedom of press com. 1978-87), Sigma Delta Chi. Clubs: Tavern (Chgo.), Wayfarers (Chgo.), Tryon (N.C.) Country. Home: 10 Fox Paw Ln Saluda NC 28773-9527

MCCUTCHEON, STEVEN CLIFTON, environmental and ecological engineer, hydrologist; b. Decatur, Ala., Oct. 29, 1952; s. Bernard Clifton and Rosa May (Askenburg) McC.; m. Sherry Lynn Sharp; children: Michael Ian, Alexander Tavis. BS, Auburn U., 1975; MS, Vanderbilt U., 1977, PhD, 1979. Hydrologist U.S. Geol. Survey, Bay St. Louis, Miss., 1977-86; rsch. environ. engr. U.S. EPA, Athens, Ga., 1986—. Adj. asst. prof. Tulane U., New Orleans, 1984-85; panel mem. Nat. Rsch. Coun., Washington, 1989-92; adj. prof. Forestry U. Ga., Athens, 1994—; asst. prof. Clemson (S.C.) U., 1990-97; program evaluator Accreditation Bd. Engrng. & Tech., 1992—. Author: Water Quality Modeling, vol. 1, 1989, (with others) Fate and Transport of Sediment-Associated Contaminants, 1989, Water Quality, Handbook of Hydrology, 1993; editor and author: (with others) Manual for Performing Estuarine Waste Load Allocations, 1990, Hydrodynamics and Transport for Water Quality Modeling, 1999; editor Jour. Environ. Engrng., 1992-94; mem. editl. bd. Ecol. Engrng., 1995—, Internat. Jour. Phytoremediation, 2000—; vice-chair editl. bd. Hazardous Toxic and Radioactive Waste Mgmt., 1996-97. Mem. Zoning Commn., St. Tammany Parish, La., 1984-85; vice=chmn. Planning Adv. Bd., St. Tammany Parish, 1985; asst. den leader Cub Scouts Am., Athens, pack 83, 1991-92, pack 96, 1998-99, den leader, 1999-2001. Recipient medal and plaque Korea Soc. Water Pollution Rsch. and Control, Seoul, 1986, Engr. of Yr. award in EPA, NSPE, 1992, Richard R. Torrens award ASCE, 1994; co-recipient EPA Sci. Achievement award in Waste Mgmt. Air and Waste Mgmt. Assn., 1995, EPA Sci. Achievement award in Chemistry Am. Chem. Soc., 1997, Sci. and Tech. Achievement award EPA, 1999, Bronze medal EPA, 2001, 2002. Mem. ASCE (br. pres. 1983-84, sect. dir. 1984-85, 95-2001, v.p. 2001-2003, Young Civil Engr. of Yr. award 1984, Torrens award 1994), Am. Ecol. Engrng. Soc. (charter), Am. Geophys. Union, Internat. Soc. Environ. Ethics (charter), Internat. Water Assn., Internat. Assn. Hydrologic Scis., Water Environ. Fedn., Sigma Xi (chpt. sec. 1982-84, membership com. 1984-85), Phi Kappa Phi, Phi Theta Kappa. Achievements include development of phytoremediation and ecological engineering to clean up federal facilities and response to Exxon Valdez oil spill. Home: 147 Spalding Ct Athens GA 30605-3716 Office: US EPA Nat Exposure Rsch Lab 960 College Station Rd Athens GA 30605-2720 E-mail: EnvironHyd@aol.com., McCutcheon.Steven@epa.gov.

MCDADE, JAMES RUSSELL, management consultant; b. Dallas, Jan. 15, 1925; s. Marion W. and Jeannette (Reneau) McD.; m. Elaine Bushey, Sep. 10, 1955. BSEE, So. Meth. U., Dallas, 1947; MBA, Northwestern U., Evanston, Ill., 1950. Asst. to pres. Davidson Corp., Chgo., 1951-52, Mergenthaler Linotype Co., Bklyn., 1952-53, comml. works mgr., 1953-56; chief indsl. engr. Tex. Instruments, Inc., Dallas, 1956-57, product gen. mgr., 1958-60, v.p., 1961-64; chmn. bd. McDade Properties Co., Aspen (Colo.), Denver, Dallas, 1964—. Bd. dirs. Pitkin County Bank, Aspen; chmn. bd. dirs. Harley-Davidson Tex., Westec Security of Aspen, Aspen Security, Inc. Founding mem. Aspen Art Mus., 1980; mem. Ballet Aspen, 1980—; pres. club Aspen Valley Hosp., 1984—. Served to 1st lt. USAF, 1943-46. Mem. Rep. Senatorial Inner Circle, Am. Mgmt. Assn., Presidents Assn. Avocations: skiing, horseback riding, camping, swimming.

MCDAID, ELIZABETH WASSON, social worker, consultant; b. Tonawanda, N.Y., Aug. 30, 1941; d. Wales W. and Genevieve Wasson; m. Edward B. McDaid, May 30, 1966. BA, Alfred U., 1963; MSS, Bryn Mawr Coll., 1972. Lic. social worker, Pa. Social worker Erie County Dept. Social Svcs., Buffalo, 1962-64, Fla. dept. Pub. Welfare, Deland, 1964-66; intake supr. Cumberland County Children and Youth, Carlisle, Pa., 1966-69; program rep. Pa. Dept. Pub. Welfare, Phila., 1969-72; assoc. regional commr. U.S. HEW, 1972-74; asst. exec. dir. Youth Svc., Inc., 1974-79; dir. Regional Adoption Resource ctr., 1979-80; supr. children's ops. U.S. HHS, Washington, 1980-81; exec. dir. Phila. Citizens for Children and Youth, 1981-86; assoc. The Conservation Co., Phila., 1986-88; pres. Capital Consultants, 1988—. Chair grant rev. panel U.S. Community Rels. Svc., Washington, 1985-95; mem. Child Abuse Prevention Adv. Coun., Temple U., Phila., 1989-92; mem. Pa. Child Abuse Prevention Com., Harrisburg, 1988-95; founder, pres. Prevent Child Abuse Pa., 1995—. Contbr. to profl. publs. bds. Mem. Phila. Citizens for Children and Youth, Women in Transition (sec. 1988-92), Devel. Coun. Alfred U. Office: 117 S 17th St Ste 1000 Philadelphia PA 19103-5009 Home: Apt 8C 2301 Cherry St Philadelphia PA 19103-1042

MCDANIEL, BARRY LYNN, educational association administrator; b. Baton Rouge, Apr. 19, 1956; s. Shelton D. and Charline (Westmoreland) McD.; m. Kay Humphrey; children: Michael Scott, Jacob Waid. BS, Baylor U., 1978, MS, 1979; PhD, La. State U., 1989; postgrad., Vanderbilt U., 1995. Cert. tchr., La. Speech therapist Livingston (La.) Parish Schs., 1979-80; cons. assessment St. Helena Parish Schs., Greensburg, La., 1981-83; cons. edn. Hunt Correctional Ctr., St. Gabriel, 1983-84; cons. edn. assessment Tangipahoa Parish Schs., Amite, 1984-89; counselor, instr. La. Job Link Ctr. La. State U., Baton Rouge, 1989-90; mgr. program La. State Dept. Edn., 1991-92; assessment tchr. Saint James Parish Sch., Lutcher, 1992-94; ednl. diagnostician, vision con. La. Sch. for the Visually Impaired, Baton Rouge, 1994—. Mem.: La. Vocat. Assn., Coun. Exceptional Children, Kappa Delta Pi, Delta Chi, Phi Delta Kappa. Democrat. Baptist. Avocations: piano, organ, gardening, racquetball, birobics. Home: 6542 Peggy St Baton Rouge LA 70808-4248 Office: La Sch Visually Impaired 1120 Government St Baton Rouge LA 70802-4802

MCDANIEL, CAROLYN MARIE (LYNN), secondary education educator; b. Nevada City, Calif., Jan. 25, 1951; d. Robert Carl and Mary Anne Peterson; m. William Charles McDaniel, July 16, 1972; children: James Robert, John William Michael Charles, Robert Carl. AA in Liberal Arts, Sierra Jr. Coll., Rocklin, Calif., 1971; BA, Calif. State U., Sacramento, 1973. Tchg. credential K-9, high sch. credential, Calif. Tchr. English, chair dept. English Nevada Union H.S., Grass Valley, Calif., 1985—, journalism adviser, 1986—. Adviser Calif. Scholrship FEdn., Grass Valley, 1985—. Contbg. writer journalism curriculum guide. Registrar Gold County Soccer League, Grass Valley, 1983-93; pres. women's aux. Grass Valley Little League, 1985-92; charter mem., Nevada Union coord. Nevada County Peer Ct., Nevada City, 1995—, bd. dirs., 1995—. Named Educator of Yr., Ptnrs. in Edn., 1999. Mem. Nat. Coun. Tchrs. English, Calif. Tchrs. Assn., Journalism Education Assn. No. Calif. (sec. 1993—, v.p. 1996—, pres. 2000—, Newspaper Adviser of Yr. award 1997), Nevada Union H.S. Tchrs. Assn. Avocations: reading, writing, bridge, walking, travel. t. Home: 11671 Cathy Dr Grass Valley CA 95949-6559 Office: Nevada Union HS 11761 Ridge Rd Grass Valley CA 95945-5025 E-mail: lmcdaniel@jps.ne.

MCDANIEL, CHARLES-GENE, journalism educator, writer; b. Luxora, Ark., Jan. 11, 1931; s. Charles Waite and Edith Estelle (Kelly) McD. BS, Northwestern U., 1954, MS in Journalism, 1955. Reporter Gazette and Daily, York, Pa., 1955-58; sci. writer Chgo. bur. A.P., 1958-79; assoc. prof. journalism dept. Roosevelt U., Chgo., 1979-83, prof., 1984-96, chmn. dept., 1979-93, head faculty of journalism and communication studies, 1993-95, prof. emeritus, 1996—. Contbg. editor Libido; contbr. to anthologies, poems, Ency. Britannica, World Book Ency.; contbr. articles to profl. jours.; Chgo. corr. The Med. Post, Toronto, 1979-2000; columnist www.libidomag.com. Trustee Roosevelt U., 1985-94; bd. dirs. Internat. Press Ctr. Chgo., 1993-96. Recipient writing awards Erikson Inst. for Early Edn., 1972, writing award AMA, 1974, writing awards Chgo. Inst. for Psychoanalysis, 1971, 73, writing awards Ill. Med Soc., 1972, 73, writing awards ADA, 1975, Am. Psychol. Assn., 1982. Mem. ACLU, Fellowship of Reconciliation, War Resisters League, Art Inst. Chgo. (life), Mus. Contemporary Art (charter), Ill. Arts Alliance, Handgun Control Inc., Hemlock Soc., Ptnrship in Caring. Home and Office: 5109 S Cornell Ave Chicago IL 60615-4215 *That which we achieve for ourselves is for naught unless we have at the same time contributed to a world in which peace and justice prevail.*

MCDANIEL, CHARLOTTE, health care ethics professional; b. Mo. d. Charles T. II. and Rose (Metz) McD.; children: Kris, Kirk. BA, Washington U., St. Louis, 1965; BSN, Vanderbilt U., 1967; MEd, Columbia U., 1971; PhD, U. Conn., 1985. Assoc. prof., dir. supr. program Yale Div. Sch., New Haven; faculty, Yale U.; dir. family svc. program Conn. Mental Health Ctr.; grad. faculty nursing, med. ethics U. Pitts. Med. Ct.; exec. dir. Ctr. for Bus., Ethics and Professions, Pitts. Theol. Sem.; dir. contextual studies Candler Sch. Theology, Emory U., Atlanta. Vis. scholar Hastings Ctr. Recipient Celella Rsch. award, Postdoctoral Rsch. award Columbia U., Alumni award, 1996, Alumni award Vanderbilt U., 1997; fellow Inst. Theol. Reflections; Fulbright awardee, 2002--; numerous grants. Mem.: Am. Soc. Bioethics and Humanities, Am. Assn. Marriage and Family Therapy, Sigma Theta Tau.

MCDANIEL, DANA IRENE, linguistics educator; b. N.Y.C., May 26, 1959; d. Glenn Otrell and Sonja McD.; m. Kelley Irene Frank, Apr. 24, 1993; children: Otrell Loren Irene, Aedin Toby Irene. BA, SUNY, Binghamton, 1980; PhD, CUNY, 1986. Tchr. German Hunter Coll. H.S., N.Y.C., 1986—87; asst. prof. linguistics U. So. Maine, Portland, 1990—95, assoc. prof. linguistics, 1995—2002, prof. linguistics, 2002—. Adj. asst. prof. linguistics CUNY, N.Y.C., 1986-88; vis. asst. prof. linguistics U. Ariz., Tucson, 1988-89, U. Mass., Amherst, 1989-90. Editor: Methods for Assessing Children's Syntax, 1996; contbr. articles to profl. jours. NSF Rsch. grantee, 1991-93, 95-99. Mem. Linguistic Soc. Am. Avocation: cello. Office: U So Maine Linguistics Dept PO Box 9300 Portland ME 04104-9300

MCDANIEL, DAVID HENRY, physician; b. Clarksburg, W.Va., May 12, 1952; s. Hubert Harold and Ada Virginia (Henry) McD.; m. Sheila Marie Travis, Sept. 17, 1994. BS in Chemistry cum laude, W.Va. U., Morgantown, 1974, MD, 1978. Diplomate Am. Bd. Dermatology, 1983. Emergency physician Monongalia Gen. Hosp., Morgantown, 1979-82; dir. Laser Ctr. of Va., Virginia Beach, Va., 1982—; asst. prof. clin. dermatology Ea. Va. Med. Sch., Norfolk, 1991—, asst. prof. clin. plastic surgery, 1992—; command cons., Dept. Plastic Surgery Naval Med. Ctr., Portsmouth, Va., 1994—. Adj. asst. prof. dept. biol. scis. Old Dominion U., 2001-; pres. The Ctr. for Disfigurement, Virginia Beach, 1993—; adv. coun. mem. Disfigurement Guidance Ctr., Scotland, 1994—; pres. David H. McDaniel Cons., Internat., Virginia Beach, 1995—. Contbr. numerous articles to sci. jours. Fellow Am. Acad. Dermatology, Am. Soc. Laser Medicine and Surgery, Am. Soc. Dermatologic Surgery (com. practice mktg. and pub. rels. 1993-96, chair 1996), Internat. Soc. Dermatologic Surgery; mem. Tidewater Dermatology Soc. (pres. 1987-88), Space Dermatology Found. (founding), Va. Space Bus. Roundtable (charter), Phi Lambda Upsilon. Avocations: nature and wildlife photography, bicycling, gardening, hiking, church and charitable activities. Office: Laser Ctr of Va 933 First Colonial Rd Ste 113 Virginia Beach VA 23454-3172

MCDANIEL, DOLAN KENNETH, oil exploration service company executive; b. Clarksville, Ark., June 9, 1935; s. Lowell William and Dana Estelle (Kinney) McD.; m. Letha Patricia Craven, Jan. 2, 1957; children: Laurie McDaniel Holgate, David. BS, Kans. State U., 1957. Field ops. Geophys. Service Inc., various locations, 1957-66, mgr. Rocky Mountains region Denver, 1966-70, mgr. N. Latin Am. Bogota, Colombia, 1970-72, mgr. land data collection Dallas, 1973-77, mgr. marine exploration, 1977, pres., 1977-88; cons. geophys. industry, 1989—. V.p. Tex. Instruments, Dallas, 1978-88. Mem. Soc. Exploration Geophysicists, Dallas Geophys. Soc., Internat. Assn. Geophys. Contractors (bd. dirs. 1982-89) Home and Office: 213 Crooked Creek Dr Richardson TX 75080-2024

MCDANIEL, DONALD HAMILTON, lawyer; b. Washington, Apr. 26, 1948; s. Roy Hamilton and Mildred Dean (Borden) McD.; m. Eva Styron, Dec. 29, 1973; children: Sharon, Michelle. BS, La. State U., 1970; JD, U. Miss., 1973. Bar: Miss. 1973; bd. cert. tax atty., 1987—; bd. cert. estate planning & adminstrn. atty. Atty. IRS, Washington, 1974-77; tax law specialist Bourgeois Bennett Thokey, New Orleans, 1977-81; ptnr. McCloskey Dennery Page, 1981-85, Lemle & Kelleher, New Orleans, 1985—. Author: Estate Planning in Louisiana, 1991. Trustee St. Martins Episcopal Sch., New Orleans, 1993, East Jefferson Hosp. Found., New Orleans, 1995, United Meth. Found., New Orleans, 1995. Mem. ABA, La. State Bar Assn. (chmn. com. on trusts, estates and immovable property 1997—), Miss. State Bar Assn., New Orleans Estate Planning Coun. Avocations: golf, fishing. Office: Lemle & Kelleher LLP 601 Poydras St Ste 2100 New Orleans LA 70130-6021

MCDANIEL, IVAN DALE, literature educator; b. Denham Springs, La., Dec. 1, 1948; s. Ripley Stennis and Frankie Bonnie McDaniel. BA, Southeastern La. U., 1970; MA, U. New Orleans, 1989; PhD, Tulane U., 1998. Revenue tax auditor La. Dept. Revenue, New Orleans, 1971-89; instr. Tulane U., 1989-98, asst. prof. English, 1998—. Home: Apt E 4231 Coliseum St New Orleans LA 70115 Office: Tulane U 6823 St Charles Ave New Orleans LA 70118

MCDANIEL, JAMES, actor; b. Washington, Mar. 25, 1958; Actor (movies): Rocket Gibraltar, 1988, Alice, 1990, Strictly Business, 1991, Malcolm X, 1992, Heading Home, 1995, Truth or Consequences, N.M., 1997, Sunshine State, 2002, (TV movies) Adventures of Huckleberry Finn, 1985, Internal Affairs, 1988, Murder in Black and White, 1990, Old Man and the Sea, 1990, Murder times Seven, 1990, Scam, 1993, Murder in Mind, 1996, Unforgivable, 1996, The Defenders: Choice of Evils, 1998, Silencing Mary, 1998, Out of Time, 2000, Deliberate Intent, 2000, Livin' for Love: The Natalie Cole Story, 2000; actor in TV series: Cop Rock, 1990, NYPD Blue, 1993-2001; TV guest appearances include: Hill Street Blues, 1981, Crime Story, 1986, Law & Order, 1990, Talk Soup, 1993, Fantasy Island, 1998. Nominated for Emmy award for outstanding supporting actor in a drama series, 1996, Image award, 1998, 99. Office: Innovative Artists 1999 Avenue Of The Stars Los Angeles CA 90067-6022*

MCDANIEL, JAMES EDWIN, lawyer; b. Dexter, Mo., Nov. 22, 1931; s. William H. and Gertie M. (Woods) McD.; m. Mary Jane Crawford, Jan. 22, 1955; children: John William, Barbara Anne. AB, Washington U., St. Louis, 1957, JD, 1959. Bar: Mo. 1959. Assoc. firm Walther, Barnard, Cloyd & Timm, 1959-60, McDonald, Barnard, Wright & Timm, 1960-63, ptnr., 1963-65; ptnr. firm Barnard, Timm & McDaniel, St. Louis, 1965-73, Barnard & Baer, St. Louis, 1973-82; ptnr. Lashly & Baer, 1982—2002, of counsel, 2002—; pros. atty., 1968—. City atty. City of Glendale, Mo., 1996—; bd. dirs. Eden. Theol. Sem.; lectr. Latvian U., Riga, Inst. Fgn. Rels., Banking in Am., 1992-93. Leader legal del. Chinese-Am. Comparative Law Study, People's Republic China, 1988, Russian-Am. Comparative Law Study, USSR, 1990; trustee, past chmn., past treas. 1st Congl. Ch. St. Louis. With USAF, 1951-55. Fellow Am. Bar Found. (life), St. Louis Bar Found. (life); mem. ABA (bd. govs. 1997-2000, ho. of dels. 1976-80, 84-92, 97-2000, state del. 1986-92, chmn. lawyers conf., jud. adminstrn. divsn. 1992-95, 8th cir. rep. standing com. on fed. jud. 1995-98, mem. standing com. on jud. qualification, tenure and compensation 1996-97), The Mo. Bar (pres. 1981-82, bd. govs. 1974-83), Mo. Assn. Def. Counsel, Bar Assn. Met. St. Louis (pres. 1972), Internat. Assn. Ins. Counsel, Assn. Def. Counsel St. Louis (past pres.), Phi Delta Phi. Home: 767 Elmwood Ave Saint Louis MO 63122-3216 Office: Lashly & Baer 714 Locust St Saint Louis MO 63101-1699

MCDANIEL, JARREL DAVE, lawyer; b. Clovis, N. Mex., Oct. 17, 1930; s. Raymond Lee and Blanch (Booth) McD.; m. Anne Louise McAllister; children: Jarrel Dave Jr., Julia Anne. AA, Riverside Coll., 1951; BA, U. Tex., 1956, LL.B., 1957. Bar: Tex. 1957. Assoc. Vinson & Elkins, Houston, 1957-69, ptnr., 1969-96; of counsel Sheinfeld, Maley & Kay, 1997-2001; sr. counsel Akin, Gump, Strauss, Hauer & Feld, L.L.P., 2001—. Author, lectr. in field. Served with USAF, 1950-54. Mem. ABA, Am. Coll. Bankruptcy, State Bar Tex., Am. Bankruptcy Inst., Tex. Bd. Legal Specialization in Bankruptcy (mem. adv. com. 1976-99, chair 1999—). Clubs: Houston Ctr. Roman Catholic. Home: 1217 Potomac Dr Houston TX 77057-1919 Office: Akin Gump Strauss Hauer & Feld LLP 711 Louisiana St Ste 1900 Houston TX 77002 E-mail: jmcdaniel@akingump.com.

MCDANIEL, JOHN MARK, lawyer; b. Decatur, Ala., Nov. 5, 1951; s. John Lester and Helen Juanita McD.; m. Henri Butler, Jan. 19, 1973; children: Henri Jo, John Benjamin. BS, Athens Coll., 1972; JD, Birmingham Sch. of Law, 1976. Bar: Ala. Ptnr. McDaniel & McDaniel, Huntsville, Ala., 1976—; prosecuting atty. Town of New Hope, 1976-83. Pres. McDaniel Media, Inc., Huntsville, 1995—; legal counsel Congressman Cramer, Huntsville, 1991—; trial counsel Gov. Hunt, Montgomery, Ala., 1994; spl. atty. gen., Montgomery, 1984, 90; legal advisor to dir. emergency mgmt., State of Ala., Montgomery, 1984-87; assoc. prof. Faulkner U., Huntsville, 1976—; instr. People's Law Sch., Huntsville, 1993—, Athens State Coll., 1998; adv. bd. Jones Sch. of Law, Montgomery, 1984-87. Bd. dirs. Boys Club, Huntsville, 1994-97, Huntsville Stars, 1995—, Indsl. Devel. Named to County Sports Hall of Fame, Huntsville, 1996, Alumni of Yr., Athens State Coll., 1993. Mem. ABA, Ala. State Bar (pres. criminal law sect. 1985-86), Madison County Bar, Mensa. Mem. Ch. of Christ. Avocations: jogging.

MCDANIEL, JOYCE L. artist, educator; b. Oklahoma City, Feb. 5, 1936; d. Harry L. and Ora Lea (Little) Kirchner; m. Paul R. McDaniel, Apr. 5, 1958 (div. Feb. 1997); children: Alysa, Kyle. BBA, U. Okla., 1958; BA in Fine Arts, Boston Coll., 1973; MA in Art History, Wellesley Coll., 1976; MFA in Sculpture, Tufts U., 1982. Instr. art history U. Lowell, Mass., 1977-79; instr. sculpture Emmanuel Coll., Boston, 1984, R.I. Sch. Design, Providence, 1984; sculpture faculty Sch. Mus. Fine Arts, Boston, 1981—. Founder, organizer BostonSculptors at Chapel Gallery, Newton, Mass., 1992—. One-woman shows include Hess Gallery, Chestnut Hill, Mass., 1981, Gallery NAGA, Boston, 1982, Gallery Eleven, Medford, Mass., 1982, Gallery 410, Lowell, Mass., 1982, Clark Gallery, Lincoln, Mass., 1983, Immig Gallery, Boston, 1983, Crapo Gallery, New Bedford, Mass., 1985, Clark Gallery, Lincoln, Mass., 1986, 87, Art Complex Mus., Duxbury, Mass., 1988, Boston Sculpture at Chapel Gallery, 1994, 96; group exhbns. include Boston Ctr. for Arts, 1979, 410 Gallery, Lowell, 1978, 79, Mus. Sch. Gallery, Boston, 1979, 80, Silvermine Guild Art, New Canaan, Conn., 1977, 79, 80, Nesto Gallery, Milton, Mass., 1980, Boston Visual Artists Union, 1980, 82, Bostin City Hosp., 1980, Boston Ctr. for Arts, 1980, Monteserrat Sch. Visual Art, Beverly, Mass., 1981, Art Complex Mus. Duxbury, Mass., 1983-84, Danforth Mus., Framingham, Mass., 1983-84, Brockton Art Mus., 1984, Boston Mus. Fine Arts, 1986, Alchemie Gallery, Boston, 1987, Mass. Coll. Art, 1987, Johnson Atelier, Mercerville, N.J., 1987, Stockbridge, Mass., 1988, A.I.R. Gallery, N.Y., 1988, Art Complex Mus., 1988, Northeastern U. Gallery, Boston, 1989, Erector Square Gallery, New Haven, Conn., 1989, Boston Ctr. for Arts, 1989, La Galerie d'Art Lavalin, Montreal, Que., Can., 1989, Cooper Union Gallery, N.Y., 1990, Washington Square East Galleries, N.Y., 1990, Boston Gallery, 1990, Sites 1 and 2, Boston, 1990, 91, Rose Art Mus., 1992, Cape Cod Cmty. Gallery, West Barnstable, Mass., 1992, Starr Gallery, Newton, Mass., 1993, Inst. Contemporary Art, Boston, 1994, Ctr. Book Arts, N.Y.C., 1996, Fuller Mus. Art, Brockton, Mass., 1996-97. Recipient fellowship in sculpture Nat. Endowment for Arts, 1984, grant Dieudonne Papermill, 1993, fellowship in sculpture New Eng. Found. for Arts, 1995. Home: 516 E 2nd St Boston MA 02127-1463 E-mail: joymcdan@aol.com.

MCDANIEL, LARRY SCOTT, microbiology and surgery educator; b. Baton Rouge, June 18, 1953; s. Richard Newton and Willie Mae (McElveen) McD.; m. Dalikeh Olga Farhadnejad, Dec. 29, 1978; children: Kori Yerivan, Sevanna Megan. BS, Southeastern La. U., Hammond, 1974; MS, U. Southwestern La., 1978; PhD, U. Okla., 1981. Postdoctoral fellow U. Ala., Birmingham, 1981-85, rsch. assoc., 1985-87, rsch. instr., 1987-89, rsch. asst. prof. microbiology, 1989-95; assoc. prof. microbiology and surgery U. Miss. Med. Ctr., Jackson, 1995-2001, prof., 2001—. Contbr. articles to profl. jours., chpts. to books. NIH grantee, 1989—. Mem. Am. Soc. Microbiology, Am. Assn. Immunologists, Am. Reticuloendothelial Soc. Office: U Miss Med Ctr 2500 N State St Jackson MS 39216 E-mail: lmcdaniel@microbio.umsmed.edu.

MCDANIEL, MICHAEL CONWAY DIXON, bishop, retired theology educator; b. Mt. Pleasant, N.C., Apr. 8, 1929; s. John Henry and Mildred Juanita (Barrier) McD.; m. Marjorie Ruth Schneiter, Nov. 26, 1953; 1 son, John Robert Michael. BA, U. N.C., 1951; B.D., Wittenberg U., 1954; MA, U. Chgo., 1969, PhD, 1978; D.D. (hon.), Lenoir-Rhyne Coll., 1983; LL.D., Belmont Abbey Coll., 1984. Ordained to ministry United Lutheran Ch. in America, 1954. Pastor Faith (N.C.) Luth. Ch., 1954-58, Ch. of the Ascension, Savannah, Ga., 1958-60; assoc. dir. evangelism United Luth. Ch. in Am., N.Y.C., 1960-62; sr. pastor Edgebrook Luth. Ch., Chgo., 1962-67; pastor, guest lectr. Wittenberg U., Springfield, Ohio, 1970-71; prof. Lenoir-Rhyne Coll., Hickory, N.C., 1971-82, Raymond Morris Bost disting. prof., 1982, founding dir. Ctr. for Theology, 1991-99, emeritus, 1999—; bishop N.C. Luth. Ch. in Am., Salisbury, 1982-87, Evang. Luth. Ch. Am., Salisbury, 1988-91. Chmn. humanities div. Lenoir-Rhyne Coll., 1973-82; cons., grant coord. NEH, 1977-79; master tchr. Hickory Humanities Forum, 1981—; chmn. task force on ecumenical and interfaith relationships Commn. Forming a New Luth. Ch., 1983-87; rep. Luth. Orthodox Dialogue In U.S.A., 1983-89;, chmn., cons. bishops governing coun. Evang. Luth. Ch. Am., 1987-89. Author: Welcome to the Lord's Table, 1972. Mem. Englewood Human Rels. Coun., N.J., 1959-60; pres., trustee Edgebrook Symphony, Chgo., 1965-67; sec. Chgo. Astron. Soc., 1966-67; pres. Cmty. Concerts Assn., Hickory, N.C., 1977-80, Western Piedmont Symphony Soc., 1993-94. Served to sgt. U.S. Army, 1946-48, Korea. Luth. World Fedn. fellow, 1967-69, Mansfield Coll. fellow U. Oxford, 1989; recipient Disting. Alumnus award Trinity Luth. Sem., 1990. Home: 125 42nd Avenue Cir NE Hickory NC 28601-9012 E-mail: mcd2@twave.net. *Since Christian faith is a joyous relationship with God, Christian hope is courageously counting on God's promises, and Christian love a daily adventure, the Christian approaches each aspect of life as An Adventure in Courageous Joy.*

MCDANIEL, MIKE, former political association executive; b. Muncie, Ind., Feb. 11, 1951; m. Gail McDaniel, 1978. BS, Ball State U., 1973, MPA, 1979. Legis. intern Rep. Caucus Ind. State Senate, 98th Session, Ind. Gen. Assemply; rsch. dir. City County Coun., Indpls., 1974-75; adminstrv. asst. to Pres. ProTem Ind. State Senate, 1975-76, minority caucus adminstr., 1977-78, spl. asst. to majority caucus, 1978-79; campaign dir. Rep. State Senate Campaign com., 1978; campaign mgr. John Mutz for Lt. Gov. campaign, 1980, 87-88; asst. to gov.-elect Hon. Judge Robert D. Orr, Ind.; chief of staff Lt. Gov. Ind., Hon. John M. Mutz, 1981-87; chmn. Ind. State Rep. Party; pub. rels. account exec. Caldwell Van Riper, Indpls. Instr. polit. sci. Ball State U., 1984—; exec. asst. to v.p. for bus. affairs, 1988-94, dir. govt. rels., 1994-95; exec. dir. Ind. State Election Bd., 1988; writer, producer, dir., editor video module series Ind. Gen. Assempty, 1990; bd. dirs. Bowen Inst. for Practical Politics. Recipient Sagamore of Wabash prize Gov. Otis R. Bowen, 1979, Gov. Robert D. Orr, 1981.*

MCDANIEL, MYRA ATWELL, lawyer, former state official; b. Phila., Dec. 13, 1932; d. Eva Lucinda (Yores) Atwell; m. Reuben Roosevelt McDaniel Jr., Feb. 20, 1955; children: Diane Lorraine, Reuben Roosevelt III. BA, U. Pa., 1954; JD, U. Tex., 1975; LLD, Huston-Tillotson Coll., 1984, Jarvis Christian Coll., 1986. Bar: Tex. 1975, U.S. Dist. Ct. (we. dist.) Tex. 1977, U.S. Dist. Ct. (so. and no. dists.) Tex. 1978, U.S. Ct. Appeals (5th cir.) 1978, U.S. Supreme Ct. 1978, U.S. Dist. Ct. (ea. dist.) Tex. 1979. Asst atty. gen. State of Tex., Austin, 1975-81, chief taxation div., 1979-81, gen. counsel to gov., 1983-84, sec. of state, 1984-87; asst. gen. counsel Tex. R.R. Commn., 1981-82; gen. counsel Wilson Cos., San Antonio and Midland, Tex., 1982; assoc. Bickerstaff, Heath & Smiley, Austin, 1984, ptnr., 1987-96; mng. ptnr. Bickerstaff, Heath, Smiley, Pollan, Kener & McDaniel, 1996—2000. Mem. asset. mgmt. adv. com. State Treasury, Austin, 1984-86; mem. legal affairs com. Criminal Justice Policy Coun., Austin, 1984-8, Inter-State Oil Compact, Oklahoma City, 1984-86; bd. dirs. Austin Cons. Group, 1983-86; mem. Jud. Efficiency Coun., Austin, 1995-96; lectr. in field. Contbr. articles to profl. jours., chpts. to books Del. Tex. Conf. on Librs. and Info. Sci., Austin, 1978, White House Conf. on Librs. and Info. Scis., Washington, 1979; mem. Libr. Svcs. and Constrn. Act Adv. Coun., 1980-84, chmn., 1983-84; mem. long range plan task force Brackenridge Hosp., Austin, 1981; clk. vestry bd. St. James Episcopal Ch., Austin, 1981-83, 89-90; bd. visitors U. Tex. Law Sch., 1983-87, vice chmn., 1983-85; bd. dirs. Friends of Ronald McDonald House Ctrl. Tex., Women's Advocacy, Inc., Capital Area Rehab. Ctr.; trustee Episcopal Found. Tex., 1986-89, St. Edward's U., Austin, 1986—, chmn. acad. com., 1988-2002, vice chair, 2002-; chmn. divsn. capital area campaign United Way, 1986; active nat. adv. bd. Leadership Am.; trustee Episcopal Sem. S.W., 1990-96, Assn. Governing Bds. Univs. and Colls., Leadership Edn. Arts Program, 1995—; adv. bd. mem. Women Basketball Coaches Assn., 1996-99; bd. dirs. U.Tex. Law Sch. Found., 1997-98, Wells Fargo Cmty. Bd., Ctrl. Tex., 2000—; trustee Episcopal Health Charities, 1997—. Recipient Tribute to 28 Black Women award Concepts Unltd., 1983; Focus on women honoree Serwa Yetu chpt. Mt. Olive grand chpt. Order of Eastern Star, 1979, Woman of Yr. Longview Metro C. of C., 1985, Woman of Yr. Austin chpt. Internat. Tng. in Communication, 1985, Citizen of Yr. Epsilon Iona chpt. Omega Psi Phi, Lone Star Girl Scout Coun. Women of Distinction, 1997, Profiles in Power Austin Bus. Jour., 1999, Silent Samaritan award Samaritan Counseling Ctr., 2000. Master Inns of Ct.; mem. ABA, Am. Bar Found., Tex. Bar Found. (trustee 1986-89), Travis County Bar Assn., Travis County Women Lawyers' Assn., Austin Black Lawyers Assn., State Bar Tex. (chmn. Profl. Efficiency & Econ. Rsch. subcom. 1976-84), Golden Key Nat. Honor Soc., Longhorn Assocs. for Excellence in Women's Athletes (adv. coun. 1988—), Order of Coif (hon. mem.), Omicron Delta Kappa, Delta Phi Alpha. Democrat. Office: Bickerstaff Heath Smiley Pollan Keever & McDaniels 1700 First Bank Plz 816 Congress Ave Austin TX 78701-2443

MCDANIEL, NORWOOD ALLAN, insurance broker; b. Pitts., Dec. 16, 1928; children: Norwood Jr., Cherie Suzanne, Thomas Cavin. Student, Washington and Lee U., 1948-50; PhD (hon.), C.C. Allegheny County. Gen. ins. broker, Pitts., 1949—. Adv. bd. Union Nat. Bank, Pitts. Asst. treas. C.C. Allegheny County, 1980-90. Recipient citation Pa. Senate, 1987, Pa. Ho. of Reps., 1987, tribute Congl. Record, Pres. Ronald Reagan, 1987; inducted into Pa. Sports Hall of Fame, 1973. Mem. Fellows Club (pres.), City Club, Ins. Club Pitts., Profl. Ins. Agts. Assn., Amen Corner (pres.), Masons, Shriners (potentate Syria Temple Shrine 1978), Variety Club (chief barker), The Shrine Treas. Assn. N.Am. (sec.-treas. 1985-98). Home and Office: 425 Greentree Rd Pittsburgh PA 15220-5248 Fax: 412-928-0850. E-mail: woodymcdaniel@worldnews.att.net.

MCDANIEL, OLA JO PETERSON, social worker, educator; b. Hot Springs, Ark., Sept. 17, 1951; d. Milton Paul and Ella Floyd (Dickerson) Peterson; m. Daniel Tillman McDaniel, June 11, 1994; 1 child, Cadra Peterson. B Music Edn., Henderson State Coll., Arkadelphia, Ark., 1973; MA in Edn., Lindenwood Colls., St. Charles, Mo., 1983, cert. in social studies, 1977. Cert. tchr., Mo., Ark. Faculty Sch. Dist. St. Charles, 1974-84; adj. faculty Garland County C.C., Hot Springs, 1988-90; social worker Ark. Dept. Human Svcs., 1990-94; substitute tchr. Hot Springs Sch. Dist., 1994-95; tutor St. Michael's Sch., Hot Springs, 1995—; substitute tchr. Mt. Pine (Ark.) Sch. Dist., 1997-98. Substitute tchr. Mt. Pine Sch. Dist., 1997-98; soloist Congr. House of Israel, Hot Springs, 1965-73; cons. scholarships Hot Springs Music Club, 1988; const. student performance Garland County C.C., Hot Springs, 1988. Author, contbr. (learning activities) 3 R's for the Gifted: Reading, Writing, Research, 1982. Vol. Hot Springs Mayorial Campaign, 1993, Dem. Gubernatorial campaign, Hot Springs, 1990; hon. mem. Nat. Steering Com. to Reelect the Pres., Washington, 1995; mem. Dem. Nat. Com., Washington, 1994-00; mem. Pres.' Second Term Com., Washington, 1997; active Hot Springs Mid. Sch. PTO, 1996-98; vol. Dem. campaign U.S. Congress Dist. 4, 2000; vol. Hot Springs H.S. Recipient Certs. of Appreciation, St. Chrysostom's Am. Episcopal Ch., Hot Springs, 1990, Nat. Mus. Am. Indian, Washington, 1995, Alpha Chi, Nat. Mus. Women in the Arts, 1997, Hot Springs Mid. Sch., 1998, Gov.'s Vol. Excellence award, 1997, 98, Parent Vol. award Hot Springs Mid. Sch., 1998. Mem. AAUW, Nat. Mus. Am. Indian, Nat.Mus. Women in Arts, Mid-Am. Sci. Mus., Henderson Alumni Assn., Lindenwood Alumni Assn. Democrat. Roman Catholic. Avocations: advocate of welfare reform, museum volunteer, reading, music. Home: 102 Woodberry St Hot Springs National Park AR 71913-2806

MCDANIEL, RANDALL CORNELL, retired professional football player; b. Phoenix, Dec. 19, 1964; BPE, Ariz. State U., 1988. Offensive guard Minn. Vikings, 1988-98, Tampa Bay Buccaneers, 1998—2002. Named NFL All-Pro Team Guard by Sporting News, 1991-93. Achievements include playing in Pro Bowl, 1988-93. Office: Tampa Bay Bucs 1 W Buccaneer Pl Tampa FL 33607-5701*

MCDANIEL, ROBERT STEPHEN, technical professional; b. Nashville, Sept. 26, 1946; s. Robert Stephen and Dorothy (Leahy) McD.; m. Katherine Wood Johnson, May 26, 1972; 1 child, Benjamin C. BS in Chemistry, U. Notre Dame, 1968; PhD in Organic Chemistry, U. Mo., Rolla, 1974. Sr. rsch. chemist Armak Co., McCook, Ill., 1975-79, sect. head process devel., 1979-80; mgr. new products R&D A.E. Staley Mfg. Co., Decatur, 1980-88; sr. scientist Henkel Corp., Ambler, Pa., 1988-91; mgr. R&D durable spltys. divsn. FiberMark Inc., Quakertown, 1992-2000; technical dir. Custom Bldg. Products, Bell, Calif., 2000—. Author: Essentially Soap, 2000, Essentially Candles, 2001; contbr. articles to profl. jours. Mem. Tree Bd., Decatur, 1986-88. U. Chgo. Ben May Lab. for Cancer Rsch. fellow, 1974-75. Fellow Sigma Xi; mem. TAPPI (splty. coated papers com. 1994—), Am. Chem. Soc., Pa. Guild Craftsmen (juried). Roman Catholic. Achievements include 14 patents. Avocations: golf, fencing, soap making. Office: Custom Bldg Products 6515 Salt Lake Ave Bell CA 90201-2126 E-mail: bobmc@cbpmail.net.

MCDANIEL, RODERICK ROGERS, petroleum engineer, consultant; b. High River, Alta., Can., 1926; s. Dorsey Patton and Daisy (Rogers) McD.; m. Trudy Ethier, Apr. 15, 2000; children: Nancy, Leslie. BS, U. Okla., 1947. Petroleum reservoir engr. Creole Petroleum Corp., 1947, Imperial Oil Ltd., 1948-52, chief reservoir engr., 1952-55; founder McDaniel Cons., Calgary, 1955—; chmn. Can. Airlines Ltd., 1974-91, Can. Regional Airlines, Calgary, 1991-92. Bd. dirs. Prudential Steel Ltd. Hon. dir. Calgary Exhbn. and Stampede, 1979-88, hon. bd. dirs., 1988—; dir. Calgary Stampeder Football Team, 1988, Corp. Commissionaires S.A.B. Mem. Assn. Profl. Engrs. Alta (hon. life), Can. C. of C. (bd. dirs. 1973), Calgary C. of C. (past pres.), Calgary Petroleum Club (past pres.), Calgary Highlanders (hon. col. ret.), Ranchmen's Club, Calgary Golf and Country Club, Outrigger Club (Honolulu), Mission Hills Country Club. Mem. Progressive Conservative Party. Home: # 2200 255 5 Ave SW Calgary AB Canada T2P 3G6 Office: McDaniel & Assoc 2200 255 5th Ave SW Calgary AB Canada T2P 3G6

MCDANIEL, SUE POWELL, cultural organization administrator; b. Jefferson City, Mo., Mar. 13, 1946; d. Ernest Gayle and Ruth Angeline (Raithel) Powell; m. Walter Lee Zimmerman, Aug. 14, 1966 (div. 1980); m. Olin Cleve McDaniel, June 23, 1985. BS in Edn., U. Mo., 1968, MEd in Edn., 1977, EdS, 1980, PhD, 1985. Cert. tchr., Mo. Tchr. Jefferson City Pub. Schs., 1968-80; fiscal assoc. Mo. Coordinating Bd. for Higher Edn., Jefferson City, 1980-90; exec. dir. Mo. Women's Coun., 1990-99; pres. Alternatives, Mo., 1999—. Co-author: Missouri Women Today, 1993, Status of the Women, 1994, (with L.Dixon) Learning, Changing, Leading: Keep to Success in the 21st Century, 1998. Mem. Zonta Internat., Lincoln Women in Devel. (pres. 1993—). Avocations: reading, music, drawing, flower garden, photography.

MCDANIEL, THOMAS ROBB, academic administrator, educator; b. Washington, Jan. 30, 1941; s. Noble Ashby and Emilie (Robb) McD.; m. Suzanne H. McDaniel, June 12, 1965; children: Robb Ashby, Kathryn Noble. BA, Hampden-Sydney Coll., 1963; MAT, Johns Hopkins U., 1964, MLA, 1968, PhD, 1971. Tchr. The Gilman Sch., Balt., 1964-65; adminstr. Johns Hopkins U., 1965-71; prof. Converse Coll., Spartanburg, S.C., 1971—, dean Coll. Arts and Scis., 1986-90, v.p. for acad. affairs, 1990-93, interim pres., 1993-94, provost, 1994—2002, sr. v.p., 2002—. Author: At Home in South Carolina, 1991, rev. edit., 2000, Dr. Luke's Prescriptions for Spiritual Health, 2000; author, editor: Public Education in South Carolina, 1984; exec. editor The Clearing House, 1999—; cons. editor Acad. Leader, 1999—. Chmn. Spartanburg County Bd. Edn., 1981-83; pres., bd. dirs. Charles Lea Ctr., Spartanburg, 1979-81, 89-91; chmn. policy bd. dirs. S.C. Ctr. for Tchr. Recruitment, Rock Hill, S.C., 1994-96; elder First Presbyn. Ch., Spartanburg, 1977—; chmn. Spartanburg County Commn. on Excellence in Edn., Spartanburg, 1984; mem. Spartanburg Human Rels. Commn., 1996-2000; chmn. Weekday Sch. First Presbyn. Ch., 1978—. Mem. Spartanburg C. of C. Phi Beta Kappa (pres. Piedmont chpt. 1998-2001), Phi Delta Kappa (pres. Greenville-Spartanburg chpt. 1989-90, Svc. award 1992). Avocations: reading, writing, consulting, golf. Home: 169 Mills Ave Spartanburg SC 29302 Office: Converse Coll 580 E Main St Spartanburg SC 29302 E-mail: tom.mcdaniel@converse.edu.

MCDANIEL, TIMOTHY ELTON, mathematics, statistics and business educator; b. Excelsior Springs, Mo., Sept. 21, 1961; s. Everett Duncan and Leila Lynette McDaniel; m. Kathleen Marie Armato, June 23, 1984; children: Molly Lyn, Megan Marie, Anna Armato. BS in Math., Polit. and Computer Sci., Rockhurst Coll., 1983; MS in Math. Stats., Northwestern U., 1985; MA in Polit. Sci., U. Mich., 1993. Asst. prof. math., stats. Buena Vista U., Storm Lake, Iowa, 1993—. Instr., cons. in quantitative methods U. Mich., Ann Arbor, summers 1987—. Home: 515 Larchwood Dr Storm Lake IA 50588-3011 Office: Buena Vista U 610 W 4th St Storm Lake IA 50588-1713 E-mail: mcdaniel@bvu.edu.

MCDANIEL, WILLIAM HOWARD TAFT, JR. computer information systems educator; b. Ballinger, Tex., Sept. 28, 1941; s. William Howard Taft and Alta Mae (Broadstreet) McD.; m. Betty Jane Johnson, Aug. 16, 1958; children: William H.T. III, Barry Glenn, Bryan Keith. BS summa cum laude, MBA, Miss. State U., 1968; postgrad., Nova U., 1986. Cert. computer profl. Commd. 2d lt. U.S. Army, 1962, advanced through grades to maj., 1981, computer specialist, 1962-72, systems mgr. Va., 1973-83, ret., 1983; planning dir. Electronic Data Systems, Balt., 1983; assoc. prof. computer infosystems No. Va. C.C., Alexandria, 1983-88, head computer infosystems, 1988—. Instr. Angelo State U., San Angelo, Tex., 1972-73; computer cons. various orgns., 1983—; adj. faculty George Mason U., Annandale, Va., 1990—; mem. computer history adv. com. Smithsonian Instn., 1977-78. Del. Tex. Rep. Conv., San Angelo, 1973; election judge, Prince Georges County, Md., 1984-92; v.p. Skyline Citizens Assn., Prince Georges County, 1985. Decorated Legion of Merit. Mem. SAR, Data Processing Mgmt. Assn. (pres. 1978-79), Mensa, Masons, Sons of Rep. of Tex., Toastmasters Internat. (area gov. 1979-80), Phi Kappa Phi, Beta Gamma Sigma, Alpha Kappa Psi. Republican. Methodist. Achievements include development of computer information system curriculum materials. Home: 6100 Skyline Ter Suitland MD 20746-3752 Office: No Va CC 3001 N Beauregard St Alexandria VA 22311-5050

MCDANIELS, AUDREY EVELYN, microbiologist; b. Grants Pass, Oreg., Feb. 11, 1928; d. Charles Pixley and Ruby Clark Best; divorced; 1 child, David Douglas. BS in Microbiology, Oreg. State U., 1950; BS in Edn., U. Wash., 1964; MS in Gen. Scis., Oreg. State U., 1965; PhD in Environ. Sci., U. Mich., 1980. Jr. scientist GE, Hanford, Wash., 1950-53; microbiologist City of Seattle, 1954-57, Wash. State Pub. Health, Seattle, 1957-60; 4th grade tchr. Amity (Oreg.) Elem., 1965-68; biology tchr. Rainier (Oreg.) H.S., 1968-72; microbiologist EPA, Cin., 1980—. Home: 1029 Fashion Ave Cincinnati OH 45238 Office: US EPA 26 W Martin Luther King Dr Cincinnati OH 45268

MCDANIELS, JOHN LOUIS, retired mathematics educator; b. Alton, Ill., Oct. 3, 1933; s. John Clarence and Carrie Elizabeth (Kortkamp) McD.; m. Betty Lou Verble, June 20, 1964. BS, U. Mo., Rolla, 1960; MS, So. Ill. U., 1977. Registered profl. engr., Ill., Mo. Engr. McDonnell Douglas Corp., St. Louis, 1960-74; prof. Lewis and Clark Community Coll., Godfrey, Ill., 1975-96. Dist. TEAMS competition coord. Ill. Jr. Engring. Tech. Soc., Lewis and Clark C.C., 1987-96, pre-enging. coord., 1975-96, water tech. coord., 1975-92. Bd. dirs. Alton (Ill.) Mus. History and Art, 1984-86. With U.S. Army, 1954-56. Mem. Ill. Math. Assn. Cmty. Colls., Kiwanis (Alton-Godfrey pres. 1989-90, Alton-Godfrey sec. 1997—, Disting. Pres. award 1990), Sigma Pi Sigma, Tau Beta Pi, Kappa Delta Pi. Presbyterian. Home: 3208 Greenwood Ln Godfrey IL 62035-1815 E-mail: jlmcdaniels@charter.net.

MCDANIELS, WILLIAM E. lawyer; b. Needham, Mass., July 1, 1941; BA, Williams Coll., 1963; JD, Georgetown U., 1966. Bar: D.C. 1967, Md. 1983. Grad. fellow criminal law, litigation U. Pa., Phila., 1966-68; pub. defender Phila. Pub. Defender's Office, 1966-68; adj. prof. evidence, criminal law, advanced criminal procedure Georgetown U. Law Ctr., Washington, 1970-87; mem. Williams & Connolly, 1968—. Instr. Nat. Inst. Trial Advocacy, 1975—. Fellow Am. Coll. Trial Lawyers; mem. ABA, Md. State Bar Assn, D.C. Bar. Office: Williams & Connolly 725 12th St NW Washington DC 20005-5901

MC DANNALD, CLYDE ELLIOTT, JR. management consultation company executive; b. June 29, 1923; s. Clyde E. and Evelyn (Tunison-Morgan) McD.; m. Virginia Washington, Apr. 25, 1953; children: Leslie Ann McDannald Malarchick, Clyde Elliott III, Bruce Robert, Bonnie Washington McDannald Jefferis, Brian Christopher (dec.), Laura Leigh. Market rsch. analyst J. Walter Thompson Co., N.Y.C., 1948-50; asst. dir. market rsch. Nat. Lead Co., 1950-51; product rsch. supr., account exec. Foote, Cone & Belding, Inc., 1951-52; product mgr., asst. advt. mgr. Am. Safety Razor Corp., 1953-54; account exec., account supr. Meldrum & Fewsmith, Inc., Cleve., 1954-56; sr. account exec. Young & Rubicam, N.Y.C., 1956-58; exec. asst. to v.p., advt. mgr. Brown & Williamson Tobacco Corp. subs. Brit.-Am. Tobacco Co., Ltd., Louisville, 1959-63; dir. advt. and mktg. svcs., dir. mktg. Miller Brewing Co., Milw., 1963-65; divsn. gen. mgr., v.p. consumer products, corp. v.p. Revere Copper & Brass Inc., N.Y.C., 1966-71; pres., COO H.H. Pott Distillers Ltd. U.S. subs. H.H. Pott NFGR, 1972-80, also bd. dirs.; pres., CEO Oxbridge Cons., Inc., 1981—; ptnr. Hilbert, Peers and Young, Inc., 1984—. Bd. dirs. West Indies Distillers, Ltd., Distilled Spirits Inst., Washington, McFrank & Williams Inc. and Cooperating Cons. Corp., N.Y.C.; vis. prof. mktg. Fairfield U. Sch. Bus., 1975-77. Apptd. to staff Col. Ky. Govs., 1959-63, 92—; mem. Ky. Hwy. Commn., 1960-63, N.Y. Gov.'s Indsl. Com., 1967-72; bd. govs. N.Y. Mil. Acad., 1970-76, trustee, 1975-92. Capt. Inf. USAAF, 1942-45, ETO. Decorated D.F.C., Air medal with 4 oak leaf clusters; recipient Conspicuous Svc. Cross State of N.Y. with 5 oak leaf clusters, Valor medal UDC, Knickerbocker Greys City of N.Y., War Cross, Sons of Confederate Vets., Medaille de la France Liberee, Croix de Guerre (Belgium, France), Roi Leopold III, Battle of Britain, Knight Mil. Order of Malta, Knight Sovereign Mil. Order Temple Jerusalem. Mem. SAR, SR (bd. mgrs. 1988—), Alumni Fedn. Columbia U., Am. Mgmt. Assn., NAM (mktg. com.), Audit Bur. Circulation, Navy League, St. Andrews Soc. State of N.Y., Am. Revolution Round Table, Am. Legion, VFW, N.Y. Soc. Mil. and Naval Officers World Wars, Sons of Confederate Vets., Soc. Colonial Wars, St. George Soc., Soc. Mayflower Descendants, Nat. Huguenot Soc., Columbia U. Club, Explorers Club, Univ. Club, Sigma Chi (life), Alpha Chi Sigma. Democrat. Presbyterian. Home: Clarendon Gardens 5 Red Fox Run Pinehurst NC 28374 E-mail: cmcdann398@aol.com.

MCDARBY, MICHAEL B. biologist, educator; b. Hudson, N.Y., Sept. 28, 1953; s. Harold F. McDarby, Laura M. Norton; m. Sara J. Sobel; children: Kieron. BS, SUNY, Albany, 1981; MS, U. Memphis, 1984. Asst. prof. Fulton-Montgomery C.C., Johnstown, NY, 1990—; fencing coach FMCC Fencing Club, 1991—. Regional head fencing coach N.Y. Empire State Games, Albany, 1988—. Mem.: AAUS, U.S. Fencing Coaches Assn. (divsn. officer Colorado Springs 1986—2002), N.Y. Acad. of Sci., Sigma Xi. Office: Fulton-Montgomery Community College Rte 67 Johnstown NY 12095

MCDARRAH, FRED WILLIAM, photographer, editor, writer, photography reviewer; b. Bklyn., Nov. 5, 1926; s. Howard Arthur and Elizabeth (Swahn) McD.; m. Gloria Schoffel, Nov. 5, 1960; children: Timothy Swann, Patrick James. BA in Journalism, NYU, 1954. Mem. staff Village Voice Newspaper, N.Y.C., 1959—, picture editor, 1971—; book reviewer ASMP Infinity Mag., 1972-73, Photo Dist. News, 1985-88, The Picture Profl., 1990—. Exhibited in Soho Photo Gallery, 1973, Whitney Mus., 1974, 76-77, Dallas Mus. Art, 1974, San Francisco Mus. Art, 1975, Wadsworth Atheneum, 1975, Sidney Janis Gallery, 1976, Basel (Switzerland) Art Fair, 1976, Alfred Stieglitz Gallery, 1976, Empire State Mus., Albany, N.Y., 1978, Lightworks Gallery, Syracuse, N.Y., 1981, Cape Cod Gallery, Provincetown Mass., 1982, Galleria di Franca Mancini, Pesaro, Italy, 1983, Musée du Quebec, 1987, Anita Shapolsky Gallery, N.Y.C., 1988, Hartnett Gallery U. Rochester, N.Y., 1989, G. Ray Hawkins Gallery, L.A., 1989, Read Gallery Antioch (Ohio) Coll., 1989, Mus. Art/Sci./Industry, Bridgeport, Conn., 1989, N.Y.C. Gallery Queens Mus., 1989, Ctr. Photography, Woodstock, 1989, Frumkin/Adams Gallery, 1990, Musée d'Art Moderne De La Ville de Paris, 1990, Musée d'Art Contemporain, Montreal, 1990, Pollack-Krasner Mus., East Hampton, N.Y., 1990, Found. Cartier, Paris, 1990, Marty Carey Pictures Gallery, Woodstock, N.Y., 1992, Galerie Gilles Ringuet, Belfort, France, 1992, Galerie Contre Jour, Belfort, France, 1992, Galleria La Pescheria, Cesena, Italy, 1994, Whitney Mus. Am. Art, 1995—, Nat. Portrait Gallery, 1996, Candice Perich Gallery, 1996; exhbns. include Jack Kerouac Visions of the Road, Les Rencontres D'Arles, Arles, France, 1991, Jack Kerouac Travelling Writers, Saint-Malo (France) Internat. Festival, 1991, 97, Images of Greenwich Village N.Y. Camera Club, 1992, Walker Art Ctr., Mpls., 1996, M.H. de Young Meml. Mus., San Francisco, 1996, Whitney Mus. Am. Art, 1997-98, New York Stories, Chiostro del Bramante, Rome,, 1999, Detroit Inst. Arts, 2000, Great Modern Pictures, N.Y., 2000, MOCA, Wexner Ctr., Parrish Mus., 2000, Mus. Nat. Modern Art 2001, others; author: The Beat Scene, 1960, The Artist's World in Pictures, 1961, rev. edit. 1988, Greenwich Village, 1963, New York, New York, 1964, Sculpture in Environment, 1967, Museums in New York, 1973, French edit., 1979, 5th edit., 1990, Photography Marketplace, 2d edit., 1977, Stock Photo and Assignment Source Book, 1977, 2d edit., 1984, Kerouac and Friends: A Beat Generation Album, 1984, Japanese edit, 1990, Frommer's Atlantic City and Cape May, 4th edit., 1991, 5th edit., 1993; co-author: The New Bohemia, 1967, 2d edit., 1990 Guide for Ecumenical Discussion, 1970, Greenwich Village Guide, 1992, Frommer's Virginia, 1992, 2d edit. 1994, Gay Pride: Photographs from Stonewall to Today, 1994, LA Pop Art Negli Anni '60 Chiostro del Bram Ante, 1999, Glory Days: The Beat Generation, Bayly Art Mus., 1998; The Beat Generation: Glory Days in Greenwich Village, editor, 1996; The Photography Encyclopedia, 1999; Saturday Rev. Executive Desk Diary, 1962-64; photographer: Personality Posters, Fotofolio (post cards) (polit. and social figures); contbr. articles, picture features to various publs. including N.Y. Mag., Vanity Fair, Entertainment Weekly, Vogue. With U.S. Army, 1944-47. Recipient numerous photography awards including 1st place spot news photo award. N.Y. Press Assn., 1964, 68; recipient 1st place feature photo award N.Y. Press Assn., 1967, 1st place picture story award N.Y. Press Assn., 1969, 2nd place spot news photo award N.Y. Press Assn., 1967, 70, 3d place spot news photo award N.Y. Press Assn., 1965, 3d place feature photo award N.Y. Press Assn., 1965, 3d place picture story award N.Y. Press Assn., 1970, 1st place Best Pictorial Series Nat. Newspaper Assn., 1966, Page One award Newspaper Guild N.Y., 1971, 80; Guggenheim fellow in photography, 1972 Mem. Nat. Press Photographers Assn., N.Y. Press Photographers Assn., Am. Soc. Mag. Photographers, Soc. Photog. Edn., Photog. Hist. Soc. N.Y., Authors Guild, N.Y. Press Club, Am. Soc. Picture Profls., Photog. Soc. Am. Office: 36 Cooper Sq New York NY 10003-7118

MCDARRAH, GLORIA SCHOFFEL, editor, author; b. Bronx, N.Y., June 22, 1932; d. Louis and Rose Schoffel; m. Fred W. McDarrah, Nov. 5, 1960; children: Timothy, Patrick. BA in French, Pa. State U., 1953; MA in French, NYU, 1966. Editorial asst. Crowell-Collier, N.Y.C., 1957-59; exec. asst. to pub. Time Inc., 1959-61; libr., tchr. N.Y.C. Pub. Schs. and St. Luke's Sch., 1972-76; exec. asst. to pres. Capital Cities Communications Inc., N.Y.C., 1972-76; analyst N.Y.C. Landmarks Preservation Commn., 1976-79; project editor Grosset & Dunlap Inc., N.Y.C., 1979-80; sr. editor Prentice Hall trade div. Simon & Schuster Inc., 1980-88; pres. McDarrah Media Assocs., 1988—. Author: Frommer's Guide to Virginia, 1992, 2d edit., 1994-95, Frommer's Atlantic City and Cape May, 1984, 4th edit., 1991, 5th edit., 1993-95, The Artist's World, 2d edit., 1988, Photography Encyclopedia, 1999; co-author: Museums in New York, 5th edit., 1990, Photography Marketplace, 1975 (book rev. sect.), The Beat Generation: Glory Days in Greenwich Village, 1996; co-editor Exec. Desk Diary Saturday Rev., 1962-64; contbg. editor quar. Dollarwise Traveler, Fodor's Cancun, Cozumel, Yucatan Peninsula, Fodor's Arizona; editor book rev. The Picture Profl., 1989—; book reviewer Pub.'s Weekly, 1994—. Fax: 212 254-5547.

MCDAVID, DOUGLAS WARREN, systems consultant; b. San Francisco, Feb. 25, 1947; s. James Etheridge and Elizabeth Rae (Warren) McD.; m. Nancy Kathleen Somers, June 1968 (div. 1982); 1 child, Amy Kemp; m. Carleen Ann Richmond, Feb. 14, 1987; 1 child, Amanda Claire. BA in Sociology, U. Calif., Santa Cruz, 1969; MA in Libr. Sci., San Jose State U., 1972. Libr. Palo Alto (Calif.) City Libr., 1969-81; systems analyst Tymnet (Tymshare), Cupertino, Calif., 1981-84; mgr. systems architecture Tymnet McDonnell Douglas, San Jose, 1984-86; data modeling cons. Fireman's Fund Ins., Terra Linda, 1986-87, Bank of Calif., San Francisco, 1988; systems cons. Pacific Bell, San Ramon, Calif., 1989-93; prin. Integrated Info., 1993—; exec. cons. IBM Global Svcs., 1995—. Mem. IBM Acad. Tech., 2000—; spkr. Entity/Relationship Conf. Internat., Burlingame, Calif., 1991, DAMA Internat. Conf., 1994—; sr. cons. in bus. semantic modeling for object oriented applications IBM Corp., 1994—; 1996 spkr. Bus. Rules Conf. OOPSLA, IBM Object Technology Conf., Ind. Labor & Mgmt. Coun.; cons. IBM, 1994-98, mgr. knowledge devel., 1999—; spkr. in field. Assoc. editor: Handbook of Object Technology. Mem. IEEE, Assn. for Computing Machinery, Data Adminstrn. Mgmt. Assn. (San Francisco bd. dirs. 1987-91, Sacramento bd. dirs. 1992, speaker 1991, 92), Data Processing Mgmt. Assn. (speaker 1992), Am. Assn. Artificial Intelligence (speaker 1993). Avocations: golf, gardening, creative writing, investing, swimming. Home and Office: 8611 Kingslynn Ct Elk Grove CA 95624-3135 E-mail: mcdavid@us.ibm.com.

MCDAVID, GEORGE EUGENE (GENE MC DAVID), retired newspaper executive; b. McComb, Miss., June 30, 1930; s. O.C. and Inez S. McDavid; m. Betty Ernestine Tinsley, Sept. 24, 1949; children: Carol McDavid, Martha Gene Newman. BBA cum laude, U. Houston, 1965. Owner, pub. Wilk Amite Record, Gloster, Miss., 1949-58; with Houston Chronicle, 1958—, prodn. mgr., 1967-74, v.p. ops., 1974-85, v.p., gen. mgr., 1985-90, pres., 1990-98, ret., 1998. Mem. adv. bd. Am. Press Inst.; past pres. bd. dirs. S.W. Sch. Printing Mgmt. Chmn. Greater Houston chpt. ARC, nat. bd. govs., 1st vice-chmn.; pres.'s counsel Houston Bapt. U.; vice-chmn. Sam Houston Boy Scouts Am., United Negro Coll. Fund, Asia Soc. Goodwill Industries, YMCA; bd. dirs. Greater Houston Partnership, Nat. Conf. Christians and Jews, chmn. Houston Forum, Houston region Am. Cancer Soc.; bd. dirs., pres. Houston Symphony; bd. dirs., v.p. Books of the World; vice-chmn. devel. bd. U. Houston, bd. regents, 1997—, chmn.; spl. deacon Second Bapt. Ch., Houston. Recipient Franklin award U. Houston, 1961, Disting. Alumnus award, 1990, 97, Taggart award Tex. Newspaper, 1992, Man of Yr. award NCCJ, 1993; named Outstanding Ex-Citizen Gloster, 1973, Hon. Father of Yr., 1996; named to Miss. Jour. Hall of Fame, 2002. Mem. Am. Newspaper Pubs. Assn. (chmn. newsprint com.), So. Newspaper Pubs. Assn. (pres.) Tex. Daily Newspaper

Assn. (pres.), Houston C. of C. (Houston Citizen's Cmty. Svc. award 1993, named Houston Cultural Leader of Yr., 1998), Houston Club, Houstonian Club, Coronado Tex. Club, Pine Forest Country Club, Phi Kappa Phi, Beta Gamma Sigma. Home: 403 Hunters Park Ln Houston TX 77024-5438 Office: 801 Texas St Houston TX 77002-2904

MCDAVID, JANET LOUISE, lawyer; b. Mpls., Jan. 24, 1950; d. Robert Matthew and Lois May (Bratt) Kurzeka; m. John Gary McDavid, June 9, 1973; 1 child, Matthew Collins McDavid. BA, Northwestern U., 1971; JD, Georgetown U., 1974. Bar D.C. 1975, U.S. Ct. Appeals (fed. cir.) 1975 (D.C. cir. 1976), U.S. Supreme Ct. 1980, U.S. Ct. Appeals (5th cir.) 1983, (9th cir.) 1986. Assoc. Hogan & Harston, Washington, 1974-83, ptnr., 1984—. Gen. counsel ERAmerica, 1977-83; mem. antitrust task force Dept. Defense, 1993-94, 96-97; mem. antitrust coun. U.S. C. of C., 1994—; advisor Bush adminstrn. transition team, 2001. Contbr. articles to profl. jours. Participant Clinton and Bush adminstrn. transition team FTC. Mem. ABA (antitrust sect., vice chmn. civil practice com. 1986-89, sect. 2 com. 1989-90, chmn. franchising com. 1990-91, coun. mem. 1991-94, program officer 1994-97, vice chair 1997-98, chair-elect 1998-99, chair 1999-2000, immediate past chair, governing com. of forum on franchising 1991-97), ACLU, U.S. C. of C. (antitrust coun. 1995—), Washington Coun. Lawyers, D.C. Bar Assn., Fed. Bar Assn., Womens Legal Def. fund. Democrat. Office: Hogan & Hartson 555 13th St NW Ste 800E Washington DC 20004-1161

MCDAVID, SARA JUNE, librarian; b. Atlanta, Dec. 21, 1945; d. William Harvey and June (Threadgill) McRae; m. Michael Wright McDavid, Mar. 20, 1971. BA, Mercer U., 1967; MLS, Emory U., 1969. Head librarian Fernbank Sci. Ctr., Atlanta, 1969-77; dir. rsch. libr. Fed. Res. Bank of Atlanta, 1977-81; mgr. mem. services SOLINET, Atlanta, 1981-82; media specialist Parkview High Sch., 1982-84; ptnr. Interncontinental Travel, 1984-85; librarian Wesleyan Day Sch., 1985-86; mgr. info. svcs. Internat. Assn. Fin. Planning, 1986-90; dir. rsch. Korn Ferry Internat., 1990-95; Atlanta rsch. coord. Lamalie Amrop Internat., 1995-98; dir. practice splty. teams LAI Ward Howell, 1998; prin. McDavid Rsch. Assocs., Atlanta, 1998-99; sr. info. specialist The Boston Consulting Group, 1999—. Bd. dirs. Southeastern Library Network, Atlanta, 1977-80, vice chmn. bd., 1979-80. Editor: Libr. Mgmt. Quarterly, 1996-98; contbr. articles to profl. jours. Pres., mem. exec. com. Atlanta Humane Soc., 1985-86, bd. dirs. aux., 1978-90. Mem. Ga. Libr. Assn. (v.p. 1981-83), Spl. Librs. Assn. (treas. libr. mgmt. divsn. 1998-2000, editor Libr. Mgmt. Quar. 1996-98). Home: 1535 Knob Hill Dr NE Atlanta GA 30329-3206 Office: Boston Consulting Group Inc 600 Peachtree St NE Ste 3800 Atlanta GA 30308-2218 E-mail: mcdavid.sara@bcg.com.

MCDERMID, ALICE MARGUERITE CONNELL (MRS. RALPH MANEWAL MCDERMID), civic and political worker, lecturer; b. Sterling, Ill., May 25, 1910; d. William Hayes and Margaret (Durr) Connell; m. Ralph Manewal McDermid, Nov. 28, 1931; children: Ralph Manewal, Jane Dillon (Mrs. Anders Wiberg), Michael Metcalf, John Fairbanks. AB, U. Ill., 1931. Bd. dirs. Scarsdale (N.Y.) Woman's Exchange, 1953-60; mem. social service bd. N.Y. Infirmary, 1960-76, vice chmn., 1964-76; trustees team United Hosp. Fund, 1965-75; case policy bd. Spence-Chapin Adoption Service, from 1960; fund raising Greer Sch., 1958-73, Vis. Nurses Assn., 1960-64; co-chmn. UN Program, Westchester County; founder Jane Todd Meml. Scholarship, 1966; mem. adv. council Morse Gallery of Art, Winter Park, Fla., from 1974. Sec. exec. com. Morse Gallery Art Assocs., 1977-78, v.p., 1978-80, pres., 1980-82; bd. dirs. Council Arts and Scis. Central Fla., 1975-86, v.p., 1976-78; bd. dirs. Charles Hosmer Morse Found., 1980-82. Sec., Young Republicans Ill., 1930-31; bd. dirs. Scarsdale (N.Y.) Women's Rep. Club, 1961-67, pres., 1965-67, legis. chmn., 1981—; del. Washington Conf. Nat. Fed. Rep. Women, 1965-72; mem. council Fedn. Women's Rep. Clubs N.Y. State, 1967-76; Rep. dist. leader, 1967-75; del. Rep. Jud. Conv., 1969-71; vice chmn. Rep. Town Com., 1969-75, mem. Rep. Presidents Club, Scarsdale; mem. N.Y. State Rep. Com., 1970-72; N.Y. Rep. committee woman 90th Assembly Dist., 1970-72. Recipient Rep. Woman of Yr. award, Scarsdale, 1974, other awards. Mem. Women's Rep. Federated Club of Winter Park (pres. 1978-80), Lock Haven Art Center, Friends of Winter Park Library, Winter Park Hist. Soc., English Speaking Union U.S., Town Club Winter Park, Morse Mus. Am. Art, Morse Mus. Art Assocs., Friends of Cornell Fine Arts, Lock Haven Arts Soc., Alpha Xi Delta. Clubs: Scarsdale Women's, Ladies Harvard, Women's Nat. Rep. (N.Y.C.); Women's of Winter Park (dir. 1977-79), Racquet (Winter Park). Episcopalian. Died. Home: Winter Park, Fla. Deceased.

MCDERMITT, EDWARD VINCENT, lawyer, educator, writer; b. Hagerstown, Md., Nov. 29, 1953; s. Edward Bernard and Genevieve Natalie (Gallo) McD.; m. Jane Langmead Springmann, June 28, 1986; children: Edward S., Maureen K. BA, Georgetown U., 1975, MA, 1978; JD, U. Santa Clara, 1980; LLM, U. Pa., 1984. Bar: D.C. 1981, U.S. Dist. Ct. D.C. 1981. Rsch. asst. U. Santa Clara, Calif., 1980; pvt. practice Washington, 1981—; assoc. Law Offices of Miller & Loewinger, 1982; rsch. asst. U. Pa., Phila., 1983-84. Adj. asst. prof. Yale Gordon Coll. Liberal Arts, U. Balt., 1991—, vis. asst. prof., 1996, adj. assoc. prof. U. Md. Univ. Coll., 1998—, lectr. law Columbus Sch. Law, Cath. U. Am., 1999—; mng. ptnr. J-L-S Svcs., Washington, 1985—, Early and Valuable Memorabilia, Md., 1985—; congl. intern to rep. Pat Schroeder, Washington, 1975; vol. atty. ACLU Nat. Capital area, Washington, 1982—; lectr. writing The Writer's Ctr., 1987—; participant program instrn. lawyers Harvard Law Sch., 1989—; session chair Conf. of the Assn. for Practical & Profl. Ethics, 2002. Author: Overruled, Mr./Ms. Writer: An Argument in Favor of Accuracy in Depiction, How to Write an Uncommonly Good Novel, 1990, Return to Berlin, 1996, Toward a New Social (Democratic) Contract, 2000, John Marshall: Farmer Extraordinaire and the Seeds of Corporate Capitalism, 2001. Vol. McGovern for Pres. campaign, Washington and Md., 1972, United Farmworkers Union, Washington, 1973-77, Urban Coalition Basketball League, Washington, 1977-78, Sarbanes re-election campaign, Md., 1982. Mem. D.C. Bar (cons., mem. lawyer/tchr. partnership program 1987—), Superior Ct. Trial Lawyers Assn., Washington Writers Group, Internat. Platform Assn., Assn. for Practical & Profl. Ethics, Pi Sigma Alpha. Roman Catholic. Avocations: photography, poetry, fiction writing, military history, bridge. Home and Office: 8000 Wildwood Dr Silver Spring MD 20912-7425

MCDERMOTT, AGNES CHARLENE SENAPE, philosophy educator; b. Hazelton, Pa., Mar. 11, 1937; d. Charles G. and Conjetta (Ranieri) Senape; children: Robert C., Lisa G., Jamie C. BA, U. Pa., 1956, PhD, 1964; postgrad., U. Calif.-Berkeley, 1960-61, U. Amsterdam, Netherlands, 1965, U. Wis., 1967-69. Instr. math. Drexel Inst. Tech., Phila., 1962-63; asst. prof. philosophy SUNY-Buffalo, 1964-65, Hampton Inst., Va., 1966-67; asst. prof. U. Wis.-Milw., 1967-70; assoc. prof. philosophy U. N.Mex., Albuquerque, 1970-80, prof., dean grad. studies, 1981-86; dean in residence Council of Grad. Schs., Washington, 1985-86; provost, v.p. acad. affairs CUNY, CUNY, 1986-89; prof. philosophy CUNY, 1986-91; dean for acad. and student affairs, cons. Albuquerque Acad., 1991-93; ind. cons. Corrales, N.Mex., 1993—. Vis. assoc. prof. U. Wash., Seattle, 1974, U. Calif.-Berkeley, 1973-74, U. Hawaii, Honolulu, 1975; vis. prof. U. Calif.-Berkeley, 1980; vis. prof. Semester at Sea, U. Pitts., fall 1994; lectr., panelist Author: An Eleventh Century Buddhist Logic of 'Exists', 1969, Boethius' Treatise on the Modes of Signifying, 1980; compiler, editor anthology: Comparative Philosophy: Selected Essays, 1983; rev. editor Phil. East West, 1986—; contbr. articles and stories to profl. and literary jours. Active Albuquerque Care Alliance, 1988-2000. AAUW postdoctoral fellow, 1965-66; NEH Younger Humanist fellow, 1971-72; faculty rsch. fellow U. N.Mex., 1978, 79, 80; U. Pa. grad. fellow, 1961-62; S. Fels Found. fellow, 1963-64;U. Pa. tuition scholar; Pa. Hist. Soc. scholar Mem. N.Y. Acad. Scis., Am. Philos. Soc., Am. Philos. Assn. (exec. com. 1977-80), Assn. Asian Studies (exec. com. 1977-80), Am. Oriental Soc., Western Assn. Grad. Schs. (pres. 1986-87), Phi Beta Kappa, Pi Mu Epsilon. Democrat. Avocations: skiing, fly-fishing.

MC DERMOTT, ALBERT LEO, lawyer; b. Lowell, Mass., Jan. 21, 1923; s. John Thomas and Josephine (Rohan) McD. AB, Boston Coll., 1944; LLB, Georgetown U., 1949. Bar: Mass. 1950, D.C. 1950, U.S. Supreme Ct. 1972. Practice of law, Washington, 1950-54; asso. Ingoldsby & Coles, 1950-52, partner, 1952-54; spl. asst. to Sec. Labor, 1954-61; ptnr. law firm McDermott & Russell (and predecessor), 1961-92; Washington rep. Am. Hotel and Motel Assn., 1963-88. Adv. bd. Maritime Cargo Transp. conf., Fed. Svc. Impasses Panel, 1972-78; alt. rep. Pres. Nixon's Pay Bd., 1971-73; staff dir. Senate Rules Com., 1994-95, Senate Com. on Govtl. Affairs, 1995-96; sr. counsel senate appropriations com., 1997-98. Served as lt. USNR, World War II. Mem. Nat. Acad. Sci. (mem. research council 1957-60), ABA, Bar Assn. D.C. Clubs: Congl. Country, Capitol Hill (Washington); Tavern (N.Y.C.); Rehoboth Country (Del.). Home: 4813 Van Ness St NW Washington DC 20016-2353

MCDERMOTT, ALICE, writer; b. Bklyn., June 27, 1953; married; 3 children. BA, SUNY, Oswego, 1975; MA, U. N.H., 1978. Instr. U. Calif., San Diego, Am. U., Washington; lectr. in English U. N.H.; writer-in-residence Lynchburg Coll., Va., Hollins Coll., Johns Hopkins U., Balt. Author: A Bigamist's Daughter, 1982, That Night, 1987 (Pulitzer Prize finalist, Nat. Book Award finalist, L.A. Times Book Prize finalist), At Weddings and Wakes, 1992, Charming Billy, 1998 (Nat. Book Award); contbr. short stories to numerous profl. publs. Recipient Whiting Writers award. Office: Farrar Straus and Giroux 19 Union Sq W New York NY 10003*

MCDERMOTT, CECIL WADE, mathematics educator, educational program director; b. Parkin, Ark., Aug. 19, 1935; s. Joe E. and Myrtle L. (Davis) McD.; m. Nelda Grace Lyons, June 4, 1961; children: Kevin Scott, Stephen Kyle. BS in Math., U. Ark., 1957; MS in Stats., Purdue U., 1962; EdD in Math. Edn., Auburn (Ala.) U., 1967. Cert. tchr. math., gen. sci., phys. sci., curriculum specialist supr., designated ind. fee appraiser, rsch. analyst. Instr. math. Sikeston (Mo.) H.S., 1957-59; state math. supr. Ark. Dept. Edn., Little Rock, 1959-65; ednl. cons. Auburn U., 1965-67; chmn., prof. math. Hendrix Coll., Conway, Ark., 1967-83; program dir. IMPAC Learning Sys., Inc., Little Rock, 1983—. Co-dir. NSF Inst. Tulane U., New Orleans, summers 1967-71; residential appraiser Morrilton (Ark.) Savs. & Loan, summers 1977-82; cons. Okla. Legis. Coun., Oklahoma City, 1987, America 2000 Project, Dallas, 1991; mem. tchr. tng. panel Office Tech. Assessment, 1994; pres. Ark. Intercoll. Conf. Faculty Rep., 1974-84. Author: (audio-tutorial film) Primary School Mathematics, 1975; co-author: Modern Elementary Mathematics, 1978, Landmarks, Rudders and Crossroads, 1993, Modern Job, 1999, Essay on Jesus, 1999, Discourse on Educaton, 1999, Inner Thoughts and Outer Reflections, 2000, Riding the Waves of Change the Impac Story, 2000; designer: (computer courseware) Mathematics/Basic Skills, 1989, 93. Plan coord. Gov.'s Task Force on Telecomm. Planning, 1991-95; mem. Murphy Commn. Tech. Panel, 1997; bd. dirs. Hendrix Coll. Hall of Honor, 1993—. Rsch. grantee U.S. Office Edn., Washington, 1972-73, Rockefeller Found., Little Rock, 1983-85, Ross Found., 1997; recipient Cert. of Merit award Electronic Learning, 1987, Endowment Scholarship Hendrix Coll., Conway, Ark., 1987, Disting. Svc. award Nat. Tech. Leadership Coun., 2000; state honoree Nat. Gov.'s Assn., 1997; inductee Hendrix Coll. Sports Hall of Honor, 2000. Mem. Ark. Amateur Union (chmn. state long distance running program 1969-72), Ark. Coun. Tchrs. Math. (chmn. regional conf. 1970), Am. Math. Soc., Math. Assn. Am. (pres. Okla./Ark. 1976-77), Phi Delta Kappa, Phi Kappa Phi, Pi Mu Epsilon. Episcopalian. Avocations: long distance running, creative writing, farming. Home: 1204 Hunter St Conway AR 72032-2716 Office: IMPAC Learning Sys Inc 3901 Mccain Park Dr Ste 113 North Little Rock AR 72116-7849

MCDERMOTT, DAVID (JOHN), artist, writer, photographer; b. Wrangell, Alaska, Apr. 8, 1958; s. A.W. and Margaret (Price) McD.; m. Rebeca Reyna, Dec. 29, 1978; children: Amy, Rachel, Kelly. Student, Seattle Pacific Coll., 1976-77. Nat. registered and cert. emergency med. technician; cert. instr. NRA; lic. 3rd class boiler operator. Pres., owner Mut. Devel. Co., Ketchikan, 1980—; facilities supr. U. Alaska, 1995—. Fireman, emergency med. technician Ketchikan Vol. Fire Dept., 1989-91; contbg. cons. bodybldg. books and mags., 1986—; feature article Musclemag Internat. mag., 1990. Artist ltd. edit. art print series, 1977—. Recipient Expert Rifleman award U.S. Govt., 1973, 1st, 2d & 3d Profl. Painting prizes Arts Guild Show, 1995. Mem. NEA (del. state/nat. governing assemblies), Ketchikan Edn. Assn. (exec. bd. 1992-94, pres. 1994—), Nat. Assn. EMTs, Nat. Soc. EMT-Paramedics, Nat. Soc. EMS Adminstrs., Soc. EMT Tech. Instr./Coords. Avocations: weightlifting, motorcycling, target shooting. Home and Office: PO Box 70 Soddy Daisy TN 37384-0070

MCDERMOTT, DENNIS MICHAEL, trade association executive; b. Akron, Ohio, Jan. 9, 1947; s. Gerard Joseph and Irene Cathryn McDermott; m. Margaret Mary Hayden, Dec. 14, 1968 (div. July 1981); children: Martin Jerome, Kathleen Marie; m. Margaret Amberg Egan, Apr. 30, 1983; 1 stepson, Michael Amberg. BS in Journalism, Kent (Ohio) State U., 1969; postgrad. in edn., Chapman Coll., 1972; postgrad. in pub. rels., Kent (Ohio) State U., 1975. Reporter Akron Beacon Jour., 1967-69; conv. mgr. Am. Sch. of Health, Kent, 1973-74, asst. exec. dir., 1974-77; exec. dir. Emergency Dept. Nurses Assn., Chgo., 1977-80; exec. v.p. Oakland (Calif.) Bd. Realtors, 1980-83; v.p. Calif. Assn. of Realtors, L.A., 1983-87; exec. v.p. Mo. Assn. of Realtors, Columbia, 1988—. Vis. lectr. journalism Kent State U., 1973-77; cons. 30 trade assns., 1977-87. Contbg. editor Jour. of Sch. Health, 1973-77; exec. editor Jour. of Emergency Nursing, 1977-80, Oakland Realtor mag., 1980-83, Missouri Realtor mag., 1988—. Life mem. Realtors Polit. Action Com., Washington, 1984—. Sgt. USAF, 1969-73. Scholar Knight Found., 1965-69. Mem. Am. Soc. of Assn. Execs., Pub. Rels. Soc. of Am. Avocations: travel, photography. Home: 3812 Barrington Dr Columbia MO 65203-4453 Office: Mo Assn of Realtors PO Box 1327 Columbia MO 65205-1327

MCDERMOTT, ELAINE CLAIRE, financial analyst; b. Bklyn., Oct. 2, 1940; d. James Michael Burke and Marie Alice McElroy; m. Michael Dennis McDermott, Jan. 18, 1964 (div. Oct. 1968); 1 child, Michael David. BA, The City Coll., 1995. Clk. U.S. Pub. Housing Adminstrn., N.Y.C., 1960-64, U.S. Dept. Housing and Urban Devel., N.Y.C., 1966-75, mgmt. analyst, 1975-85, fin. analyst, 1985-97. Democrat. Roman Catholic.

MCDERMOTT, FRANCIS OWEN, retired lawyer; b. Denver, Feb. 25, 1933; s. Paul Harkins and Agnes (Clark) McD.; divorced; children: Diana, Daniel, Christopher, Anthony, Justine; m. Estella Marina Idiaquez, June 6, 1986; stepchildren: Bernard, Michael, Nicole, Marie, Steven. JD, Am. U., 1960. Bar: D.C. 1960, U.S. Dist. Ct. D.C., 1960, U.S. Ct. Appeals (D.C. cir.) 1960, u.S. Tax Ct. 1961, U.S. Supreme Ct. 1964. Trial atty. office regional counsel IRS, Washington, 1961-65; mem. profl. staff com. on fin. U.S. Senate, 1965-68; tax counsel Assn. Am. R.R.s, 1968-73; assoc. Hopkins & Sutter, 1973-76, ptnr., 1976-98, of counsel, 1999—2001; ptnr. Foley & Lardner, 2001—02, ret., 2001. Gen. counsel Inst. Ill., Washington, 1987-96. Mem. ABA, Fed. Bar Assn., Nat. Def. Transp. Assn. (v.p., gen. counsel 1974—). Roman Catholic. Avocation: tennis. Home: 1 S Montague St Arlington VA 22204-1007 E-mail: fmcdermott@foleylaw.com.

MCDERMOTT, FRANK CLARK, lawyer; b. Bklyn., Sept. 1, 1926; s. Charles Paul and Florence (Ferris) McD.; m. Margot Schinzel, Aug. 27, 1955; children: Charles, Michele, Stacie, Steven. LLB, Bklyn. Law Sch, 1951. Bar: N.Y. 1952, U.S. Dist. Ct. N.Y. 1953, U.S. Supreme Ct. 1957. Pvt. practice law, Bklyn., 1952-55, 56-60; assoc. Copans & Kanon, N.Y.C., 1955-56. Adj. prof. N.Y. City Tech. Coll., 1962-92. Pres. Madison Marine Civic Assn., Bklyn., 1990-96; mem. Community Bd. #15, Bklyn., 1975—, Bishop's Lay Com. of Cath. Charities, Bklyn., 1978—. With U.S. Army, 1944-46. Mem. Bklyn. Bar Assn. (trustee 1984-90), Cath. Lawyers Guild (bd. dirs. 1981-82, pres. 1979-80), Lawyers Club Bklyn., Friendly Sons of St. Patrick in City of N.Y., Bklyn. Club, St. Patricks Soc. Bklyn., Ancient Order Hibernians. Democrat. Roman Catholic. Avocations: golf, antiques. Office: 26 Court St Brooklyn NY 11242-0103

MCDERMOTT, FRANK XAVIER, lawyer, lobbyist; b. N.Y.C., Oct. 15, 1924; s. Peter Joseph and Helen (Gildea) McD.; m. Patricia Mary Keogh, Sept. 11, 1954; children: Gregory Sean, Colleen Maura, Marita Patricia, Matthew Peter, Brendan Xavier. BA, Columbia Coll., 1948, JD, 1949; MPA, NYU, 1953, LLM in Trade Regulation, 1962. Bar: N.Y. 1949, N.J. 1962, D.C. 1981, U.S. Supreme Ct. 1969. Claims adjuster Aetna Casualty & Surety, N.Y.C., 1949-52; asst. dir., indsl. rels. N.J. Mfg. Assn., Trenton, 1952-57; labor rels. Am. Bakeries Co., N.Y.C., 1957-59; exec. dir. N.J. Orgn. for a Better State, Trenton, 1959-73; atty. Seifert, Frisch & McDermott, New Brunswick, N.J., 1963-64; sr. ptnr., of counsel Apruzzese, McDermott, Mastro & Murphy, Liberty Corner, 1964—. Co-adj. staff Inst. Mgmt. and Labor Rels. Rutgers U., 1956-68. Author: New Jersey Labor Laws-Synopsis of Then-Current Laws, 1954. Assemblymen N.J. Gen. Assembly, 1964-67, 76-78; senator N.J. Senate, 1968-74, pres. senate, 1969; acting gov. State of N.J., 1969; del. White House Conf. Edn., 1955; chmn. Union County Rep. Com., 1989-2000, N.J. Turnpike Authority, 1994—. With USAF, 1943-46. Recipient Outstanding Young Legislator award Carnegie Found., 1965. Mem. County Chmns. Assn. N.J. (chmn.), Army and Navy Club, Baltusrol Golf Club. Roman Catholic. Avocations: golf, politics. Home: 940 Wyandotte Trl Westfield NJ 07090-3733 Office: Apruzzese McDermott Et Al PO Box 112 Liberty Corner NJ 07938-0112

MCDERMOTT, JAMES A. congressman, psychiatrist; b. Chicago, Ill., Dec. 28, 1936; children: Katherine, James. BS, Wheaton Coll., 1958; MD, U. Ill., 1963. Intern Buffalo Gen. Hosp., 1963-64; resident in adult psychiatry U. Ill. Hosps., Chgo., 1964-66; resident in child psychiatry U. Wash. Hosps., Seattle, 1966-68; asst. clin. prof. dept. psychiatry U. Wash., 1970-83; mem. Wash. Ho. of Reps., 1971-72, Wash. Senate, 1975-87; regional med. officer U.S. Fgn. Svc., 1987-88; mem. U.S. Congress from 7th Wash. dist., 1989—; former chmn. standards of ofcl. conduct com.; mem. ways and means com., budget com. Mem. exec. and edn. com. Nat. Conf. State Legislatures, chair ethics com.; co-chmn. congressional task force internat. HIV/AIDS, Congl. Caucus on India and Indian Ams., Africa Trade and Investment Caucus, Congl. Kidney Caucus. Mem. Wash. State Arts Commn., Wash. Coun. for Prevention Child Abuse and Neglect; Dem. nominee for gov., 1980. Lt. comdr. M.C., USN, 1968-70. Mem. Am. Psychiat. Assn., Wash. State Med. Assn., King County Med. Soc. Democrat. Episcopalian. Office: US Ho Reps 1035 Longworth Ho Office Bldg Washington DC 20515

MCDERMOTT, JOHN ARTHUR, lawyer; b. Rochester, N.Y., Nov. 23, 1944; s. David E. and Doris L. McDermott; m. Gail Ann Van Putte, Sept. 24, 1965; children: Shawn, Ashley, Wendy. BA, U. Fla., 1966, JD with honors, 1968. Bar: Fla. 1969, U.S. Ct. Mil. Appeals 1969, Colo. 1973, U.S. Dist. Ct. Colo. 1973, U.S. Ct. Appeals (10th cir.) 1981. Rsch. asst. to chief judge Fla. Ct. Appeals, Lakeland, 1969; pvt. practice, Canon City, Colo., 1973—; county atty. Fremont County, 1987-89. City atty. Canon City, Colo., 1989—90; bd. dirs. Fremont Cmty. Found., 2000—01. Pres. Fremont Re1 Sch. Bd., 1977-81, mem. 1975-81; bd. dirs. West Cen. Mental Health Clinic, Canon City, 1973-75. Capt. U.S. Army, 1969-73. Mem. Colo. Bar Assn. (v.p. 1984-85), Colo. Trial Lawyers Assn. (bd. dirs. 1987-89, 91-97, exec. com. 1988-89), Colo. Bar Found., 11th Jud. Dist. Bar Assn. (pres. 1980-82, mem. jud. nominating com. 1980-81), Assn. Trial Lawyers Am., Lions (prs. 1985-86), Elks. Democrat. Avocations: skiing, motorcycling, amateur radio. Home: 715 Pisgah St Canon City CO 81212-4340 Office: PO Box 1040 Canon City CO 81215-1040

MC DERMOTT, JOHN FRANCIS, JR. psychiatrist, physician; b. Hartford, Conn., Dec. 12, 1929; s. John Francis and Camilla R. (Cavanaugh) McD.; m. Sarah N. Schemm, Dec. 27, 1958; children: Elizabeth C., John Francis III. AB, Cornell U., 1951; MD, N.Y. Med. Coll., 1955. Diplomate in psychiatry and child psychiatry Am. Bd. Psychiatry and Neurology. Intern Henry Ford Hosp., Detroit, 1955-56; resident in psychiatry U. Mich. Med. Center, 1956-58, resident in child psychiatry, 1960-62; practice medicine, specializing in psychiatry and child and adolescent psychiatry Honolulu, 1969-95; instr., asst. prof., asso. prof. psychiatry U. Mich. Sch. Medicine, 1962-69; prof., chmn. dept. psychiatry U. Hawaii Sch. Medicine, 1969-95, prof. emeritus, 1995—; scholar-in-residence Rockefeller Found. Study Ctr., Bellagio, Italy, 1985, 92. Chmn. com. cert. in child psychiatry Am. Bd. Psychiatry and Neurology, 1974-78, bd. dirs., 1983-91, chmn. R&D com., 1985-91; sr. vis. scientist dept. exptl. psychology Oxford (Eng.) U., 1993; vis. fellow Inst. Criminology Cambridge U., Eng., 1998, 2000; vis. prof. numerous univs.; cons. numerous mental health clinics and orgns. Author: Psychiatry for the Pediatrician, 1970, Childhood Psychopathology, 1972, Mental Health Education in New Medical Schools, 1973, Roles and Functions of Child Psychiatrists, 1976, Psychiatric Treatment of the Child, 1977, New Directions in Childhood Psychopathology, vol. I, 1980, vol. II, 1982, Raising Cain (and Abel Too), 1980: People and Cultures of Hawaii, 1980, Culture Mind and Therapy: An Introduction to Cultural Psychiatry, 1982, Japanese edit., 1984, The Complete Book on Sibling Rivalry, 1987, German edit., 1991; editor Jour. Am. Acad. Child and Adolescent Psychiatry, 1987-97; contbr. over 150 articles to profl. jours.; mem. editorial bds. numerous psychiat. jours. Served with USN, 1958-60. Named Disting. Alumnus N.Y. Med. Coll., 1976; life mem. Clare Hall, Cambridge (Eng.) U. Fellow Am. Psychiat. Assn. (life, Agnes Purcell McGavin award 1998), Am. Orthopsychiat. Assn., Am. Acad. Child and Adolescent Psychiatry (life), Am. Coll. Psychiatrists, World Psychiat. Assn. (chmn. child and adolescent psychiatry 1977-89), Benjamin Rush Soc. (sec.-treas. 2000-02, v.p. 2002—), Cosmos Club, Chaine Des Rotisseurs. Clubs: Outrigger Canoe, Cosmos. Home: 67-1003 N Alulike Rd Kamuela HI 96743-6840

MCDERMOTT, JOHN H(ENRY), lawyer; b. Evanston, Ill., June 23, 1931; s. Edward Henry and Goldie Lucile (Boso) McD.; m. Ann Elizabeth Pickard, Feb. 19, 1966; children: Elizabeth A., Mary L., Edward H. BA, Williams Coll., 1953; JD, U. Mich., 1956. Bar: Mich. 1955, Ill. 1956. Assoc. McDermott, Will & Emery, Chgo., 1958-64, ptnr., 1964-99, of counsel, 2000—. Bd. dirs. Patrick Industries Inc. 1st lt. USAF, 1956-58. Mem. ABA, Chgo. Bar Assn. Clubs: Commerical of Chgo., Econ. of Chgo., Legal Chgo. (pres. 1981-82), Law Chgo. (pres. 1986-87). Home: 330 Willow Rd Winnetka IL 60093-4130 Office: McDermott Will & Emery 227 W Monroe St Ste 3100 Chicago IL 60606-5096 E-mail: mcdermott330@cs.com.

MCDERMOTT, KEVIN J. engineering educator, consultant; b. Teaneck, N.J., Nov. 21, 1935; s. Francis X. and Elizabeth (Casey) McD.; m. Ann McDermott, Aug. 3, 1959; children: Kathleen, Kevin, Donna, Michael. BSEE, N.J. Inst. Tech., 1965; MS Indsl. Engrng., Columbia U., 1970; EdD, Fairleigh Dickinson U., 1975. Registered profl. engr., N.J. With Bell Telephone Labs., Murray Hill, N.J., 1960-65, Westinghouse Electic, Newark, 1965-67, Columbia U., NASA, N.Y.C., 1967-70, RCA Corp., N.Y.C., 1970-76, Ramapo (N.J.) Coll., 1976-80; prof. N.J. Inst. Tech., Newark, 1980—, chmn. engrng. dept., 1983—. Dir. Computer Aided Design/Computer Aided Manufacture Robotics Consortium. Contbr. more than 50 articles to tech. jours. IBM fellow, 1987. Fellow IEEE, Soc. Mech. Engrs.; mem. Inst. Indsl. Engrs. Achievements include research in industrial robot work cells, manufacturing systems, expert systems, analysis of industrial robotics, flexible manufacturing systems, expert and vision systems in computer aided design and manufacturing.

MCDERMOTT, KEVIN R. lawyer; b. Youngstown, Ohio, Jan. 26, 1952; s. Robert J. and Marion D. (McKeown) McD.; m. Cindy J. Darling, Dec. 11, 1976; children: Ciara, Kelly. AB, Miami U., Oxford, Ohio, 1974; JD, Ohio State U., 1977. Bar: Ohio 1977, U.S. Dist. Ct. (so. dist.) Ohio 1978, U.S. Dist. Ct. (no. dist.) Ohio 1988, U.S. Dist. Ct. (we. dist.) Mich. 1993, U.S. Supreme Ct. 1990, U.S. Ct. Appeals (3rd cir.) 1996, U.S. Ct. Appeals (6th cir.) 1988. Assoc. ptnr. Murphey Young & Smith, Columbus, Ohio, 1977-88; ptnr. Squire Sanders & Dempsey, 1988-90, Schottenstein Zox & Dunn, Columbus, 1990—. Adv. bd. mem. Capitol U. Legal Asst. Program, Columbus, Ohio, 1988—. Bd. pres. Easter Seal Soc. Ctrl. Ohio, Columbus, 1992-94, bd. mem. 1988-92; pres. Upper Arlington Civic Svc. Commn., Columbus, Ohio, 1988-93. Office: Schottenstein Zox & Dunn 41 S High St Ste 2600 Columbus OH 43215-6109

MCDERMOTT, LUCINDA MARY, ecumenical minister, teacher, philosopher, poet, author, psychologist; b. Lynwood, Calif., June 3, 1947; d. R. Harry and Cathrine Jaynne (Redmond) Boand. BA, U. So. Calif., L.A., 1969; MS, Calif. State U., Long Beach, 1975; PhD, Saybrook Inst., San Francisco, 1978. Pres. Environ. Health Systems, Newport Beach, Calif., 1976-90; founder, pres. Forerunner Publs., 1985—, Life-Skills Learning Ctr., Newport Beach, 1985—; founder, dir. Newport Beach Ecumenical Ctr., 1993—. Founder, dir., Tri Delta Mgmt.; pres. bd. dirs., The Boand Family Found. Author: Bridges to Another Place, 1972, Honor Thy Self, Vol. I and II, 1973, Hello-My-Love-Good Bye, 1973, Life-Skills for Adults, 1982, Au Courants, 1983, Life-Skills for Children, 1984, Myrika-An Autobiographical Novel, 1989, White Knights and Shining Halos: Beyond Pair Bonding, 1996, (musical screen play) The Good Life, 1997. Mem. APA, Calif. Psychol. Assn., Truthsayer Minstrels (founder, dir. 1996—), Alpha Kappa Delta, Kappa Kappa Gamma. E-mail: Dr.McD@sbcglobal.net.

MCDERMOTT, MARY ANN, nursing educator; b. La Junta, Colo., June 23, 1938; d. George O. and Alice Agnes (Nohelty) Kelley; m. Dennis J. McDermott; children: Dennis, Michael, Sarah, William. BSN, Loyola U., 1960, MSN, 1969; EdD, No. Ill. U., 1980. RN Ill. Staff nurse Evanston (Ill.)

Vis. Nurse Assn., 1960-63, St. Francis Hosp., Sch. Nursing, Evanston, 1963-67; nurse, tchr. Head Start, Chgo. Bd. Edn., 1967-68; faculty mem. Niehoff Sch. Nursing Loyola U., Chgo., 1969—. Dir. Ctr. Faith and Mission, Loyola U., Chgo., 1998—2002; bd. dirs. Park Ridge Ctr. Study Health, Faith and Ethics; mem. adv. coun. Chgo. Dept. Aging, 1995—99. Co-editor: Parish Nursing: The Developing Practice, 1990, Parish Nursing: Promoting Whole Person Health Within Faith Communities, 1998. Mem. adv. bd. St. Scholastica Acad., Chgo., 1996-2002; mem. adv. coun. Chgo. Schweizer Urban Fellows, 1996-99.—. Recipient Ill. Nurse Leader/Power of Nursing award, 2002. Fellow: Am. Acad. Nursing; mem.: ANA, Health Ministries Assn. (adv. bd. 1989—99), Ill. Nurses Assn., Nat. League Nursing, Am. Hosp. Assn. (nominating com. 1995—97). Democrat. Roman Catholic. Office: Loyola U Sch Nursing Damen Hall 6525 N Sheridan Rd Chicago IL 60626-5344

MCDERMOTT, MOLLY, lay minister; b. Cloquet, Minn., Aug. 19, 1932; d. Harry W. McD.; children: Elizabeth Sanders Hellenbrand, Sarah Sanders, Mary Sanders Day, Margaret Kathleen Sanders Lorfeld. Student, Oreg. State Coll., 1951, U. Minn., Duluth, 1953. Claims specialist Cuna Mut. Ins. Soc., Madison, Wis., 1975-2001. Propr. Molly's Garden. Vol. RSVP Babes; storyteller, ventriloquist St. Bernard's Parish. Mem.: SAS, Univ. League. Roman Catholic. Home: 1724 Parmenter St Middleton WI 53562-3153

MCDERMOTT, PATRICIA ANN, nursing administrator; b. Bklyn., July 10, 1943; d. John J. and Lillian E. (Sweeney) Skelly; m. Joseph Kevin McDermott, Oct. 5, 1963; children: Colleen Mary, John Joseph. Diploma, Kings County Hosp Sch. Nursing, Bklyn., 1963; BS in Health Care Adminstrn., St. Francis Coll., Bklyn., 1979. Staff nurse Kings County Hosp., Bklyn., 1963-66, head nurse outpatient dept., 1966-74; evening supr. Park Nursing Home, Rockaway Park, N.Y., 1974-83; day supr. Hyde Park Nursing Home, Staatsburg, NY, 1984-85, DON, 1985—96, Victory Lake Nursing Ctr., Hyde Park, N.Y., 1996-97. Nurse aide evaluator PRI assessor, MDS, coord. N.Y. State. Active local Girl Scouts U.S.A., 1971-78, Boy Scouts Am., 1978-82, Stella Maris Parents Club, 1978-82, St. Francis de Sales Altar and Rosary Soc., 1970-83; active St. Francis de Sales Little League, 1978-80, also softball coach, 1974-77; elected tax collector Town of Clinton, N.Y., 1999—. Dutchess County Salute to Women honoree, 1997. Home: 184 Shadblow Ln Clinton Corners NY 12514-2834

MCDERMOTT, RAYMOND, JR. physician; b. Chgo., Apr. 20, 1924; s. Raymond A. and Helen (Furlong) M.; m. Audrey H. Bergt, Feb., 1995; children: Kathy, Mary Anne, Raymond III, Thomas, Laura, Sharon, Jean, Michael, Trish. MD, Loyola U., 1947. Bd. cert. Obstertrics and Gynocology. Assoc. attending Cook County Hosp., Chgo., 1954-61; asst. prof. obgyn. Northwestern U. Med. Sch., 1958—; med. reviewer Healthcare Compare, Oakbrook, Ill., 1978-88, CIMRO, Champaigne, 1988—; med. dir. Wellmark (Health Network), Oakbrook, 1992—. Staff pres. Grant Hosp. Chgo., 1976-78, staff v.p., 1974-76. Lt. U.S. Navy, 1941-53. Avocation: sailing. Home: 3950 W Bryn Mawr Ave Chicago IL 60659-3156

MCDERMOTT, RENÉE R(ASSLER), lawyer; b. Danville, Pa., Sept. 26, 1950; d. Carl A. and Rose (Gaupp) Rassler; m. James A. McDermott, Jan. 1, 1986. BA, U. So. Fla., 1970, MA, 1972; JD, Ind. U., 1978. Bar: Ind. 1978, N.C. 1999, U.S. Dist. Ct. (so. and no. dists.) Ind. 1978, U.S. Ct. Appeals (7th cir.) 1979, U.S. Ct. Appeals (9th cir.) 1985. Law clk. to presiding judge U.S. Dist. Ct. (no. dist.) Ind., Ft. Wayne, 1978-80; assoc. Barnes & Thornburg, Indpls., 1980-84, ptnr., 1985-93; pvt. practice, Nashville, 1994-99, Tryon, N.C., 1999—. County atty. County of Brown, Ind., 1994-98. Editor in chief Ind. U. Law Jour., 1977-78. Bd. visitors Ind. U. Law Sch., Bloomington, 1979—; bd. dirs. Pacolet Area Conservancy, 1999—, v.p., 2000—; bd. dirs. Foothills Equestrian Trail Assn., 1999-2002. Fellow Ind. Bar Found. (chair 1998-99), Am. Bar Found. (life); mem. ABA (bus. sect. coun. 1995-98, chmn. environ. controls com. 1991-95, liaison to standing com. on environ. law bus. law sect. 1991-98), Ind. State Bar Assn. (chmn. young lawyers sect. 1985-86, chmn. environ. law sect. 1989-91), Fellows of Ind. Bar. Found. (chair 1998-99), Polk County Cmty. Found. (bd. dirs., chair exceptional distbns. com. 2000—), Order of Coif. Avocations: scuba diving, horseback riding, music, reading, hiking. Home and Office: 845 Fox Run Ln Tryon NC 28782-9758 E-mail: rmcdermott@alltel.net.

MCDERMOTT, ROBERT B. lawyer; b. Washington, June 16, 1927; s. Edward H. and Goldie Lucile (Boso) McD.; m. Julia Wood, Nov. 16, 1950; children: John, Jeanne, Charles; m. Jane S. Whitman, July 31, 1973; m. Sarah Jaicks, Jan. 6, 1996. AB, Princeton U., 1948; LL.B., Harvard U., 1951. Bar: D.C. 1951, Ill. 1955. Atty. Office Gen. Counsel, Navy Dept., Washington, 1951-52; assoc McDermott, Will & Emery, Chgo., 1954-60, ptnr., 1961-92, chmn., 1986-91, of counsel, 1992—. Bd. dirs. Maynard Oil Co., Dallas. Trustee Ill. Inst. Tech., Chgo., 1985—, The Mather Found., Evanston, Ill., 1988—; bd. dirs. Ct. Theatre. Lt. USNR, 1945-46, 52-54. Mem. Chgo. Bar Assn. Clubs: Chicago, Economic, University (Chgo.). Home: 990 N Lake Shore Dr Apt 31E Chicago IL 60611-1386 E-mail: bobmcder61@aol.com.

MCDERMOTT, ROBERT P. finance and tax services company executive; b. Bklyn., Feb. 6, 1939; s. John Henry and Marie Margaret (Geenen) McD.; m. Maureen T. Mannion, Aug. 29, 1964 (dec. Aug. 1999). Student, NYU, 1974. Enrolled agent IRS; registered rep. Owner RPMcDermott Fin. and Tax Svcs., Cedarhurst, N.Y. Office: RP McDermott Fin & Tax Svc 568 W Broadway Cedarhurst NY 11516-1730

MCDERMOTT, SUSAN JEAN CASSI, fundraising and development consultant; b. Astoria, N.Y., Mar. 1, 1953; d. Walter George and Jean Louise (Krivicich) Cassi; m. Michael I. McDermott, Apr. 13, 1980; children: Ian Walter, Marielle Leigh. AA in Liberal Arts and Spanish, Nassau Community Coll., Garden City, N.Y., 1973; BA in Speech and Communications, SUNY, Oneonta, 1975; postgrad. bus. law and stats., Hofstra U. With advt. sales dept. N.Y. Daily News, N.Y.C., 1975-78, mgr. circulation dept., 1978-82; sales rep. Radio Relay, Hicksville, N.Y., 1983; with circulation ops. dept. USA Today, Bayside, 1983-85; exec. dir. AHHS Neighborhood Press Coalition, Rockaway, 1985-86; dir. devel. Threshold Svcs. Inc., Kensington, Md., 1989-94; founder, pres. S&M Devel. Resources, Silver Spring, 1994—. Contbg. editor Newspix mag., 1982. Adv. com. Montgomery County Pub. TV Network; mem. cmty. adv. com. Visions Montgomery County, Md., 1993-94, bd. dirs., 1995; mem., bd. dirs. Silver Spring Cmty. Visions Homeless Project, 1994-96. Mem. Silver Spring C. of C. (bd. dirs. 1993-96). Democrat. Roman Catholic. Home and Office: S&M Devel Resources 226 Castle Hayne Dr Apex NC 27502-9213 Fax: 919-462-8070. E-mail: McDermott4@aol.com.

MCDERMOTT, THOMAS JOHN, JR. lawyer; b. Santa Monica, Calif., Mar. 23, 1931; s. Thomas J. Sr. and Etha Irene (Cook) McD.; m. Yolanda Amante Jatap; children: Jodi Friedman, Kimberly E., Kish S. BA, UCLA, 1953, JD, 1958. Bar: Calif. 1959. Ptnr. Gray, Binkley and Pfaelzer, L.A., 1964-67, Kadison, Pfaelzer, Woodward, Quinn and Rossi, L.A., 1967-87, Rogers & Wells, L.A., 1987-93, Bryan Cave, L.A., 1993-95, Manatt, Phelps & Phillips, LLP, L.A., 1995-99, Shanks and Herbert, San Diego. Served with U.S. Army, 1953-56, Korea. Fellow Am. Coll. Trial Lawyers; mem. ABA, Assn. Bus. Trial Lawyers (pres. 1980-81, mem. exec. com. 9th cir. jud. conf. 1993—, chair 1997), State Bar Calif. (chair litigation sect. 1993-94), UCLA Law Alumni Assn. (pres. 1961-62), Order of Coif. Office: Shanks & Herbert Ste 330 4350 La Jolla Village Dr San Diego CA 92122

MCDERMOTT, WILLIAM THOMAS, accountant, lawyer; b. New Orleans, Jan. 3, 1945; s. William Thomas and Delia Ethel (Belden) McD.; m. Geraldine Dorothy Constantine, Nov. 20, 1965; children: Lisa Anne, Shannon Marie. BSBA, Am. U., 1969, MBA, 1971; JD (with hon.), George Washington U., 1974; grad. exec. mgmt. program, J.L. Kellogg Grad. Sch. CPA, Va.; cert. mgmt. acct.; fellow Life Mgmt. Inst. Ptnr. for tax Ernst & Young, Richmond, Va., 1969—. Co-chmn. U. Va. Fed. Tax Conf., Charlottesville, 1981—; apptd. by Gov. of Va. to Commn. on Competitive and Equitable Tax Policy, 1996. Contbr. articles to profl. jours. Past chmn. bd. dirs. Richmond br. Tuckahoe YMCA, 1984; mem. citizens promotion bd. Henrico County Police Dept., Richmond, 1985; bd. dirs. Greater Richmond YMCA, 1983-84, Theater Va., Richmond, 1982-97; treas., bd. dirs., mem. exec. com. Arts Coun. of Richmond, 1988-96, Children's Home Soc., Richmond, 1987-97/ Recipient Cert. Appreciation award Henrico County Police Dept., 1985, Karl B. Wagner Service award Tuckahoe YMCA, 1986. Mem. ABA, AICPA (individual tax com. 1990-93, chmn. interest expense task force 1993-96), Inst. Mgmt. Accts. (nat. v.p. 1991-92, nat. dir. 1987-89, 95-97, chmn. nat. ethics com., prin. Va. Coun. 1987-88), Va. Soc. CPAs, D.C. Inst. CPAs, Bull and Bear Club, Hermitage Country Club. Roman Catholic. Home: 1701 Locust Hill Rd Richmond VA 23233-4149 Office: Ernst & Young 901 E Cary St Richmond VA 23219-4057

MCDEVITT, BRIAN PETER, history educator, educational consultant; b. Jersey City, Dec. 29, 1944; s. Bernard Aloysius and Veronica Sabina (Decker) McD.; m. Dorothy Helen Gilligan, Oct. 19, 1968; children: Peter David, Timothy Bernard. BS, Seton Hall U., 1966; MA, Columbia U., 1971; DLitt, Drew U., 2001. Tchr. history St. Patrick's High Sch., Elizabeth, N.J., 1966-68, Vail Deane High Sch., Elizabeth, 1968-70; fed. grant writer Alexian Bros. Hosp., 1970-72, Union County Coll., Cranford, 1972-76; prin., owner Ednl. Svcs., Westfield, 1976—. Adj. prof. history Union County Coll., Cranford, N.J., 1976—; adj. prof. classics Montclair (N.J.) State U., 1990—. Author: The Irish Librists, 1988, The Irish Librists and the Scrolls of Aristotle, 1993, A Historian's Thematic Study of Western Civilization, 1994, Evidence of an Ancient Greek Navigation System, 1995, The Irish Librists and The Vatican Library Mystery, 1996, A Definition of Western Civilization, 1997, Ancient Greeks: First Navigators, 2000, Ten Historical Odes, 2001, Twenty-Five Sonnets, 2001, Arthur Brooke's Poem: The Tragic HIstory of Rome and Juliet, revised, 2002, (video) The Minoans According to Sir Arthur Evans; contbr. articles to profl. jours. N.J. Dept. Higher Edn. grantee. Mem. Trireme Trust U.S.A. (internat. rowing team 1990), Friends of Trireme (London), Soc. Naval Architects and Marine Engrs., Assn. Ancient Historians, Soc. Ancient Greek Philosophy, Assn. Muslim Social Scientists, Classical Assn. of Atlantic States, Keats-Shelley Meml. Assn. (London and Rome), Am. Soc. Naval Engrs., Westfield United Fund, Westfield P.A.L., Westfield Basketball Assn., Westfield Baseball Assn., Boy Scouts Am. Roman Catholic. Avocations: golfing, rowing, basketball, playing piano, stamp collecting. Home: 607 S Chestnut St Westfield NJ 07090-1369

MCDEVITT, CHARLES FRANCIS, retired state supreme court justice, lawyer; b. Pocatello, Idaho, Jan. 5, 1932; s. Bernard A. and Margaret (Hermann) McD.; m. Virginia L. Heller, Aug. 14, 1954; children: Eileen A., Kathryn A., Brian A., Sheila A., Terrence A., Neil A., Kendal A. LLB, U. Idaho, 1956. Bar: Idaho 1956. Ptnr. Richards, Haga & Eberle, Boise, 1956-62; gen. counsel, asst. sec. Boise Cascade Corp., 1962-65; mem. Idaho State Legislature, 1963-66; sec., gen. counsel Boise Cascade Corp., 1965-67, v.p. sec., 1967-68; pres. Beck Industries, 1968-70; group v.p. Singer Co., N.Y.C., 1970-72, exec. v.p., 1973-76; pub. defender Ada County, Boise, 1976-78; co-founder Givens, McDevitt, Pursley & Webb, 1978-89; justice Idaho Supreme Ct., 1989-97, chief justice, 1993-97; ptnr., founder McDevitt & Miller, LLP, 1997—. Served on Gov.'s Select Com. on Taxation, Boise, 1988-89; mem. State Select Com. on Campaign Ethics and Campaign Finances, State Select Com. on Legis. Compensation. Chair Idaho Jud. Coun., 1993-97, Cts. Advisors Coun., 1994-98; mem. Multi-State Tax Com. Home: 4940 Boise River Ln Boise ID 83716-8816 Office: McDevitt & Miller LLP 537 W Bannock St Ste 215 Boise ID 83702-5759 E-mail: chas@McDevitt.org.

MCDEVITT, HUGH O'NEILL, immunologist, educator; b. Cin., Aug. 26, 1930; MD, Harvard U., 1955. Diplomate: Am. Bd. Internal Medicine. Intern Peter Bent Brigham Hosp., Boston, 1955-56, sr. asst. resident in medicine, 1961-62; asst. resident Bell Hosp., 1956-57; research fellow dept. bacteriology and immunology Harvard U., 1959-61; USPHS spl. fellow Nat. Inst. Med. Research, Mill Hill, London, 1962-64; physician Stanford U. Hosp., Calif., 1966—; assoc. prof. Stanford U. Sch. Medicine, 1969-72, prof. med. immunology, 1972—, prof. med. microbiology, 1980—2001, Burt and Marian Avery Prof. Immunology, 1990—. Cons. physician VA Hosp., Palo Alto, Calif., 1968— Served as capt. M.C., AUS, 1957-59. Mem. NAS, AAAS, Am. Fedn. Clin. Rsch., Am. Soc. Clin. Investigation, Am. Assn. Immunologists, Transplantation Soc., Inst. Medicine, Royal Soc. (fgn.). Office: Sherman Fairchild Bldg Stanford U Sch of Medicine 299 Campus Dr MC5124 Stanford CA 94305-5124 E-mail: hughmcd@stanford.edu.

MCDIARMID, ROBERT CAMPBELL, lawyer; b. N.Y.C., July 13, 1937; s. Norman Hugh and Dorothy (Shoemaker) McD.; m. Ruth Sussman, 1963 (div. 1996); children: Jennifer, Alexander Samuel; m. Frances Enseki Francis, 1996. BS in Mech. Engring., Swarthmore Coll., 1958; MS in Engring. Physics, Cornell U., 1960; LLB, Harvard U., 1963. Bar: D.C. 1964, Va. 1964, U.S. Supreme Ct. 1967, U.S. Ct. Appeals (4th, 6th and 9th cirs.) 1965, U.S. Ct. Appeals (3d, 5th and 10th cirs.) 1966, U.S. Ct. Appeals (7th, 8th and D.C. cirs.) 1967, U.S. Ct. Appeals (2d cir.) 1970, U.S. Ct. Appeals (1st cir.) 1979, U.S. Ct. Appeals (11th cir.) 1981. Assoc. Weaver & Glassie, Washington, 1963-64; trial atty. civil divsn. appellate sect. Dept. Justice, 1964-68; asst. to gen. counsel Fed. Power Commn., 1968-70; assoc. Law Office of George Spiegel, 1970-73; ptnr. Spiegel & McDiarmid, 1973—. Mem. alumni coun. Swarthmore Coll., 1986-89. Mem. ABA, Va. State Bar, Bar Assn. D.C., D.C. Bar, Energy Bar Assn. (exec. com. 1982-83, bd. dirs. 1997-2000). Democrat. Mem. Soc. Of Friends. Home: 3625 Fulton St NW Washington DC 20007-1452 Office: Spiegel & McDiarmid 1350 New York Ave NW Ste 1100 Washington DC 20005-4798 E-mail: robert.mcdiarmid@spiegelmcd.com.

MCDILL, THOMAS ALLISON, minister; b. Cicero, Ill., June 4, 1926; s. Samuel and Agnes (Lindsay) McDill; m. Ruth Catherine Starr, June 4, 1949 (dec. Aug. 2001); children: Karen Joyce, Jane Allison, Steven Thomas; m. Doris E. McDill, July 27, 2002. Th.B., No. Baptist Sem., Oakbrook, Ill., 1951; BA, Trinity Coll., 1954; M.Div., Trinity Evang. Div. Sch., 1955, DD, 1989; D.Ministries, Bethel Theol. Sem., 1975. Ordained to ministry Evang. Free Ch. Am., 1949. Pastor Community Bible Ch., Berwyn, Ill., 1947-51, Grace Evang. Free Ch., Chgo., 1951-58, Liberty Bible Ch., Valparaiso, Ind., 1959-67, Crystal Evang. Free Ch., Mpls., 1967-76; v.p., moderator Evang. Free Ch. of Am., 1973-74, chmn. home missions bd., 1968-72, chmn. exec. bd., 1973-90, pres., 1976-90, ret., 1990; min. at large Evang. Free Ch. Am., 1991—. Contbr. articles to publs. Chmn. bd. Trinity Coll., Deerfield, Ill., 1974-76; bd. govs. Trinity Western U.; bd. dirs. Trinity Evang. Divinity Sch. Mem. Evang. Free Ch. Ministerial Assn., Evang. Ministers Assn., Nat. Assn. Evangelicals (bd. adminstrn. 1976— , mem. exec. com. 1981-88), Greater Mpls. Assn. Evangelicals (bd. dirs., sec. bd. 1969-73) Home: 3790 Lawndale Ln #313 Plymouth MN 55446 Office: 901 E 78th St Bloomington MN 55420-1334

MC DONAGH, EDWARD CHARLES, sociologist, university administrator; b. Edmonton, Alta., Can., Jan. 23, 1915; came to U.S., 1922, naturalized, 1936; s. Henry Fry and Aletta (Bowles) McD.; m. Louise Lucille Lorenzi, Aug. 14, 1940 (dec.); children: Eileen, Patricia. AB, U. So. Calif., 1937, A.M., 1938, PhD, 1942. Asst. prof. So. Ill. U., Carbondale, 1940-46, asst. to pres., 1942-44; asst. prof. U. Okla., Norman, 1946-47, U. So. Calif., L.A., 1947-49, assoc. prof., 1949-56, prof., 1956-69, head dept., 1958-62, chmn., acad. univ. affairs com., 1963, assoc. dean divsn. social scis. and comms., 1960-63; head dept. sociology U. Ala., 1969-71; chmn. dept. sociology Ohio State U., Columbus, 1971-74, acting dean Coll. Social and Behavioral Scis., 1974—, dean Coll. Social and Behavioral Scis., 1975-78, chmn. coordinating coun. deans Colls. Arts and Scis., 1977-78, prof. emeritus Colls. Arts and Scis., 1981—. Smith-Mundt prof., Sweden, 1956-57; vis. prof. U. Hawaii, summer 1965; cons. Los Angeles and related sch. dists.; mem. Region XV Woodrow Wilson Selection Com., 1961-62 Author: (with E.S. Richards) Ethnic Relations in the U.S, 1953, (with J.E. Nordskog, M.J. Vincent) Analyzing Social Problems, 1956, (with Jon Simpson) Social Problems: Persistent Challenges, 1965, rev., 1969; Assoc. editor: Sociology and Social Research, 1947-69; editorial cons.: Sociometry, 1962-65; Contbr. articles to profl. publs. Served with AUS, 1944-46. Fellow Am. Sociol. Assn. (co-chmn. nat. conf. com. 1963, budget and exec. office com. 1975-78); mem. AAUP, AAAS, Am. Assn. Pub. Opinion Rsch., Alpha Kappa Delta (pres. united chps. 1965-66), Phi Beta Kappa (chpt. pres. 1959-60), Humanist, Blue Key, Skull and Dagger. Democrat. Home: 201 Spencer Dr Amherst MA 01002-3362

MCDONAGH, THOMAS JOSEPH, physician; b. N.Y.C., Feb. 29, 1932; s. John and Delia (Lee) McD.; m. Helen Marie Drury, May 18, 1957; children: Kevin T., Eileen D., Thomas J., Brian P., Patricia M. BS, CCNY; MD, Columbia U. Diplomate Am. Bd. Internal Medicine, Am. Bd. Preventive Medicine-Occupational Medicine. Intern Bronx Mcpl. Hosp., N.Y., 1957-58, resident, 1958-60; fellow in medicine, trainee in gastroenterology Albert Einstein Coll. Medicine, Bronx, 1960-62; pvt. practice internal medicine Coatesville, Pa., 1962-64; sr. physician Exxon Corp., N.Y.C., 1964-69, asst. med. dir., 1969-79; dir. medicine and environ. health Exxon Chem. Co., Darien, Conn., 1979-80, dir. medicine and environ. affairs, 1980-81; v.p. medicine and occupational health Exxon Corp., Dallas, 1981-97; dir. medicine and environ. health Exxon Co. Internat., Florham Park, N.J., 1983-97; bd. dirs. Nat. Assn. Drug Abuse Problems, N.Y.C., 1981-92. Bd. dirs. Nat. Fund Med. Edn., San Francisco, 1983-95. Contbr. articles to med. jours. Chmn. bd. appeals Inc. Village of Bellerose, N.Y., 1977-84, trustee, 1965-77, dep. mayor, 1975-77. Fellow ACP, Am. Coll. Occupational and Environ. Medicine (bd. dirs. 1989-92)); mem. AMA. Roman Catholic.

MCDONALD, ALAN ANGUS, federal judge; b. Harrah, Wash., Dec. 13, 1927; s. Angus and Nell (Britt) McD.; m. Ruby K., Aug. 22, 1949; children: Janelle Jo, Saralee Sue, Stacy. BS, U. Wash., 1950, LLB, 1952. Dep. pros. atty. Yakima County, Wash., 1952-54; assoc. Halverson & Applegate, Yakima, 1956—85; ptnr. Halverson, Applegate & McDonald, 1956-85; judge U.S. Dist. Ct. (ea. dist.) Wash., 1985-95, sr. judge, 1995—. Fellow Am. Coll. Trial Lawyers; Yakima C. of C. (bd. dirs.). Clubs: Yakima Country, Royal Duck (Yakima). Office: US Dist Ct PO Box 2706 Yakima WA 98907-2706

MCDONALD, ALAN THOMAS, lawyer; b. Aug. 16, 1949; s. James Francis and Jennie Eloise (Thomits) McDonald; m. Joyce Ann Martin, Feb. 28, 1981. BSCE, Rutgers U., 1971; JD, U. Houston, 1973; LLM in Patent and Trade Regulation Law, George Washington U., 1976. Bar: Tex. 1974, Pa. 1977, Va. 1980, U.S. Ct. Customs and Patent Appeals 1974. Patent examiner U.S. Patent and Trademark Office, Arlington, Va., 1974—75; patent atty. PPG Industries, Inc., Pitts., 1975—78, Reynolds Metals Co., Richmond, Va., 1978—97, Honda of Am. Mfg., Inc., 1998—. Mem. adminstrv. bd. Dutilh United Meth. Ch., Cranberry, Pa., 1977—78; sunday sch. tchr. Providence United Meth. Ch., Chesterfield County, Va., 1981—84, mem. adminstrv. bd., 1985—, chmn. fin. com., 1988—90; mem. coun. on ministries Reveille United Meth. Ch., 1994—95. Mem.: Am. Intellectual Property Law Assn., ABA, Mensa (vice local sec. Richmond chpt. 1981—82, adminstr. 1980—81), Phi Delta Phi. Republican. Achievements include patents for method for producing slubbed yarn. Home: 23920 N Darby Coe Rd Milford Center OH 43045-9775

MC DONALD, ANDREW JEWETT, securities firm executive; b. Cin., Sept. 7, 1929; s. Matthew Arnold and Jane (Jewett) Mc D. Grad., Hotchkiss Sch., 1947, Yale U., 1951. With Paine, Webber, Jackson & Curtis Inc., Boston, 1955—; dir. Paine, Webber, Jackson & Curtis Inc. (New Eng. region), 1972-73; sr. v.p., dir. Paine, Webber, Jackson & Curtis Inc. (Eastern div.), 1973—; dir. F. W. Paine Found., 1973—. Pvt. trustee and investor, 1985—; allied mem. N.Y. Stock Exch., 1971—. Mem. Flight Safety Found., 1971— . Served with USAF, 1951-55. Mem. Am. Farmland Trust (life), Am. Aviation Hist. Soc. (life). Clubs: Aero of New Eng. (Boston), Fed. (Boston), Down Town (Boston), Yale (Boston). Home: 5 Stonehill Dr Stoneham MA 02180-3927

MCDONALD, ANGUS WHEELER, farmer; b. Washington, Apr. 21, 1927; s. John Yates and Dorothy Helen (Bosworth) McD.; m. Mary Joan Montgomery, May 8, 1952 (div. Sept. 1958); children: Mary Ann Hetzer, Paul Yates. BA, Columbia Union Coll., 1974. Farmer, owner Pleasant View Farm, Charles Town, W.Va., 1953—. Presdl. candidate Democratic Party, 1987-88, 92, 2000. With U.S. Army, 1946-47. Mem. AARP, Jefferson County Farm Bur., W.Va. State Hort. Soc., No. W.Va. Automobile Club, Am. Legion, The Moose. Avocations: photography, travel, attending historical events. Home and Office: Pleasant View Farm RR 3 Box 142 Charles Town WV 25414-9413

MCDONALD, ANNE LEGGETT, mathematics educator; b. Columbus, Ohio, May 28, 1947; d. Ernest William Leggett and Esther Irene Wilson; m. Gerard McDonald, Jan. 9, 1982. BA, Ohio State U., 1969; PhD, Yale U., 1973. Instr. MIT, Cambridge, 1973-75; asst. prof. U. Tex., Austin, 1975-79; assoc. prof. Western Ill. U., Macomb, 1979-83, Loyola U., Chgo., 1983—. Contbr. articles to profl. jours. Fellowship NSF, 1974-76. Mem. Assn. for Women in Math. (newsletter editor 1977—, Award for Disting. Svc. 1993). Democrat. Avocations: genealogy, computer multimedia, hiking. Office: Math Dept Loyola Univ 6525 N Sheridan Rd Chicago IL 60626-5344

MCDONALD, ARTHUR BRUCE, physics educator; b. Sydney, N.S., Canada, Aug. 29, 1943; s. A. Bruce and Valerie M. (DeRoche) McD.; m. Janet Catherine MacDonald, July 16, 1966; children: Bruce, Heather, Ross, Fraser. BSc in Physics, Dalhousie U., 1964, MSc in Physics, 1965, LLD honoris causa, 1997; PhD, Calif. Inst. Tech., 1969; LLD honoris causa, Univ Coll. of Cape Breton, 1999; DSc honoris causa, Royal Mil. Coll., 2001. Postdoctoral fellow Chalk River (Ont., Can.) Nuclear Labs., 1969-70, rsch. scientist, 1970-82; prof. physics Princeton (N.J.) U., 1982-89, Queen's U., Kingston, Ont., Can., 1989—, dir. Sudbury Neutrino Obs. Inst. Can., 1989—. Mem. nuclear sci. adv. com. Dept. Energy, NSF, 1987-89; adv. com. Triumf Experiment, 1987-89; mem. subatomic physics rev. com. Natural Sci. and Engring. Rsch. Coun. Can., 1987-89; mem. adv. com. nuclear sci. divsn. Lawrence Berkeley Lab., 1992-95; mem. rsch. coun. Can. Inst. for Advanced Rsch., 1997—, chair adv. bd. CIAR Cosmolgy Program, 2000—; mem. IVPAP Commn. 19, 1998-, mem. PANAGIC com., 1998-. Contbr. over 100 articles to profl. jours. Killam Rsch. fellow, 1998-2000. Fellow Am. Phys. Soc., Royal Soc. Can.; mem. Can. Assn. Physicists (bd. dirs. 1978-80). Avocations: skiing, skating, swimming. Office: Queens U Stirling Hall Dept Physics Kingston ON Canada K7L 3N6 Fax: 613-533-6813. E-mail: mcdonald@sno.phy.queensu.ca.

MCDONALD, BARBARA ANN, retired psychotherapist; b. Mpls., July 15, 1932; d. John and Georgia Elizabeth (Baker) Rubenzer; m. Lawrence R. McDonald, July 27, 1957 (dec. Sept. 1993); children: John, Mary Elizabeth. BA, U. Minn., 1954; MSW, U. Denver, 1977. Diplomate Am. Bd. Social Work; lic. psychotherapist. Day care cons. Minn. Dept. Pub. Welfare, St. Paul, 1954-59; social worker Cmty. Info. Ctr., Mpls., 1959-60; exec. dir. Social Synergistics Co., Littleton, Colo., 1970—. Cons. to cmty. orgns., Indian tribes; family therapist, 1979—. Author: Selected References on the Group Day Care of Pre-School Children, 1956, Helping Families Grow: Specialized Psychotherapy with Hearing Impaired Children and Their Families, 1984. Bd. dirs. Vol. Bur. Sun Cities, Ariz., 1988, 89, 90. Named 1 of 8 Women of Yr. and featured on TV spl. Ladies Home Jour., 1974; Clairol scholar, 1974; Am. Bus. Women's Assn. scholar, 1974; Alpha Gamma Delta scholar, 1974. Mem. Minn. Pre-Sch. Edn. Assn. (hon. life), NASW, Ariz. Assn. Social Workers, Assn. Clin. Social Workers, Am. Bus. Women's Assn., Alpha Gamma Delta (Disting. Citizen award 1975), Altrusa Club (hon.). Office: 3921 W Meadow Dr Glendale AZ 85308-4122

MCDONALD, BRENDA DENISE, librarian; b. Waco, Tex., Feb. 15, 1954; d. William Dale and Ella Mae (Parrott) Maness; m. Jeffrey L. McDonald, May 26, 1979; 1 child, Sean Thomas. BA in History, William Jewell Coll., 1975; MLS, U. Okla., 1976; MA in History, U. Tex., El Paso, 1988. Libr. govt. documents and periodicals Hardin Simmons U., Abilene, Tex., 1977-79; head documents and maps library U. Tex., El Paso, 1979-84; law libr. Scott Hulse Marshall Feuille Finger and Thurmond, 1984-88; govt. documents libr. St. Louis Pub. Library, 1988-90, coord. info. svcs., 1990-95, dir. ctrl. pub. svcs., 1995-98, dir. ctrl. and regional svcs., 1999—. Jamestown Soc. fellow, 1988. Mem. ALA, Am. Law Library Assn., Spl. Libraries Assn., Beta Phi Mu. Office: St Louis Pub Library 1301 Olive St Saint Louis MO 63103-2389

MCDONALD, BRONCE WILLIAM, community activist, advocate; b. Dayton, Ohio, Mar. 21, 1949; s. Lawrence and Pauline Elizabeth (Macknight) McD. Student, Wright State U., 1968-71, U. Dayton, 1971, Dayton Art Inst., 1967-68. Trainer, cons. Nat. Assn. Youth Orgns. United, Washington, 1971-73; program assoc. Dayton (Ohio) Model Cities, 1973-74; child care worker II Montgomery County Children's Svcs. Bd., Dayton, 1974-78; inventory control Mark Morris Tires, San Francisco, 1979-82; office mgr. Bio-Feedback Internat., 1978-84; speaker, bd. dirs. Dayton Area AIDS Task Force, 1987—, AIDS Found. Dayton, 1988-92; community activist People With AIDS, Dayton, 1987—. Co-chair Dayton HIV Prevention Cmty. Planning Group Montgomery County Combined Health Dist.; com. mem. Direct Svcs. Dayton Area AIDS Task Force, 1987-92, speaker bur., 1987-92, edn. com., 1987-92, AIDS Found. Miami Valley, 1992—, speaker bur., 1992—, edn. com., 1992—, Pub. Policy and Conflict Mgmt., Ohio Statewide HIV Prevention Cmty. Planning Group, Ohio Dept. Health, The Prevention Summit: HIV Prevention Cmty. Planning Co-chairs meeting, Ctr. for Disease Control and Prevention, Nat. Alliance of State & Territorial AIDS Dirs., Nat. Minority AIDS Coun.,

Atlanta, 1995—; hotline vol. Dayton Lesbian & Gay Ctr., 1988—; mem. minority AIDS coalition Montgomery County Health Dept., Dayton, 1987—, minority health and social issues coalition, 1988—; bd. dirs. The African Am. Forum on AIDS, Dayton, 1990—, nat. AIDS awareness program So. Christian Leadership Conf., Dayton, 1993—; speaker numerous orgns. on AIDS; bd. dirs. Miami Valley AIDS Partnership, mem. membership, outreach, and needs assessment coms., 1995—. Founding mem., treas. Dayton Area People with AIDS Coalition, 1987—92, Men of All Colors Together, Dayton, 1988—90; co-chair Regional Cmty. Prevention Coord. Com., 1996—, AIDS Prevention Coun., Dayton; mem. bd. State of Ohio HIV Prevention Cmty. Planning Group, mem. cmty. info. com., 1996—; mem. membership com., mktg. com. Dayton AIDS Prevention Group; mem. exec. com. Consumer Adv. Coun.; exec. dir. Positive People Organized with Every Resource, 1990—2002, bd. chmn., CEO, 1995—2002; bd. dirs. Ohio AIDS Coalition, 1997, mem. healing com. the leadership tng. program com., 1996—; bd. dirs. Dayton Ryan White Consortium, mem. fin. com., promotion evaluation com., 1994—. Recipient Pres.'s Citation, 1989, Ohio AIDS Svc. award Ohio Dept. Health, 1990, Cert. of Merit Ohio Dept. Health, Columbus, 1994, Plaque of Vol. Outstanding Merit Montgomery County Combined Health Dist., Dayton, 1995, Outstanding Vol. Svc. Plaque Ohio Dept. Health, 1995, Man of Yr. award Met. Cmty. Ch., Cmty. Unity Health and Wholeness Project, Dayton, 1995; named Miami Valley Hero, 1998. Mem. Nat. Assn. Black and White Men Together. Avocations: drawing, painting, writing, col. work. Home: 4301 Riverside Dr #A-1 Dayton OH 45405-1332

MCDONALD, CAPERS WALTER, biomedical engineer, corporate executive; b. Georgetown, S.C., Nov. 29, 1951; s. WalBern and Cecilia (Lockwood) McD.; m. Marion E. Kiper, Aug. 23, 1975; child, Adam Capers. BS in Engring. magna cum laude, Duke U., 1974; MS in Mech. Engring., MIT, 1976; MBA, Harvard U., 1983. Registered profl. engr., N.C. Dir. mktg. dept. Becton Dickinson Co., Sunnyvale, Calif., 1978-81; cons. Booz, Allen & Hamilton, San Francisco, 1982-84; v.p. Siegen Corp., Mountain View, 1984, HP Genenchem, S. San Francisco, 1984-87; bio-analytic systems mgr. Hewlett-Packard Corp., Palo Alto, 1987; v.p. Orion Instruments, Inc., Redwood City, 1987-89, Spectroscopy Imaging Systems, Fremont, 1989-90, pres., 1990-92; pres., CEO, bd. dirs. BioReliance Corp., Rockville, Md., 1992—; pres., CEO MAGENTA Corp., 1993—2000; chmn., dir. MAGENTA Svcs., Ltd., Stirling, Scotland, 1994-2000. Bd. dirs. EXPION, Inc., Olney, Md., 1999—, Greater Washington Bd. Trade; chmn., bd. dirs. BioReliance Holding GmbH, Heidelberg, Germany, 1996-2001; guest lectr. Weizmann Inst., Rehovot, Israel, 1977, All-Union Cardiology Ctr., Moscow, 1978, Inst. Hematology Munich, 1978, Christ Church (New Zealand) Clin. Sch., 1980, U. Edinburgh, Scotland, 1981; co-founder, chmn. Md. Biosci. Alliance, 1995-98; bd. visitors U. Md. Biotech. Inst., 1996-2000; bd. advisors Md. Partnership for Workforce Quality, 1996-98; vice chmn. High Tech. Coun. Md., 1998-2001; chmn. Tech. Coun. Md., 2001—; mem. industry adv. bd. Chesapeake Bay Area chpt. ISPE, 1998-2000. Author: chpt. Flow Cytometry and Sorting, 1979; patentee flow microfluorometer; contbr. articles to profl. jours. Asst. scoutmaster Boy Scouts Am., Georgetown, 1965-66; trustee Bethesda Acad. Performing Arts, 1998-2000; mem. oversight bd. advanced tech. consortium Montgomery Coll., 1998-2001; mem. steering com. Biotech. Industry Orgn., 2003 Ann. Meeting, 2002—; mem. econ. adv. coun. Montgomery County, 1998—; mem. founding exec. bd. Greater Washington Regional Partnership, 1998-2001; bd. dirs. Md. Health Care Products Devel. Corp., Columbia, Md., 2001—; bd. visitors Duke U. Sch. Engring., 2001—. Duke U. scholar, 1970-74, MIT scholar, 1974-76; NSF (hon.) fellow, 1974; recipient High Tech. Firm of Yr. award Md. High Tech. Coun., 1995, Leadership in Tech. award Md. High Tech. Coun., 1996, Employer of Yr. award Md. Pvt. Industry Coun., 1996, Region's Most Admired Bosses award Washington Techway Mag., 2000, Good Scout award Nat. Capital Area Coun., Nat. Disting. Eagle Scout award Boy Scouts Am., 2001, Emerging Firm of Yr. award Montgomery C. of C., 2001; named Greater Washington Entrepreneur of Yr. in Life Scis., 2002.. Mem. N.C. Acad. Scis., Md. C. of C. (bd. dirs. 1996-2000), Harvard U. Alumni Assn., Duke U. Alumni Assn., MIT Alumni Assn., Rotary, Sigma Xi, Tau Beta Pi, Phi Eta Sigma, Pi Mu Epsilon, Congl. Country Club. Methodist. Avocations: fresh and salt water fishing, travel. Office: 14920 Broschart Rd Rockville MD 20850-3349

MCDONALD, CASSANDRA BURNS, lawyer; b. Aberdeen, Md., Aug. 28, 1963; d. Charles Franklin and Elizabeth (Connor) Burns; 1 child, Christopher. AB, Dartmouth Coll., Hanover, N.H., 1985; JD, Cornell U., 1990. Bar: Conn. 1991, U.S. Dist. Ct. Conn. 1992, U.S. Dist. Ct. (ea. and so. dists) N.Y. 1992. Atty. Cummings & Lockwood, Stamford, Conn., 1990-94, 96—. 1st v.p. The Links, Inc., Fairfield County, 2000—; mem. Women's Leadership Conf., Conn., 1998—; bd. dirs. Waveny Care Ctr., New Canaan, 2000—, Fairfield Co. Cmty. Found., Wilton, 2001—, Waveny Care Ctr., New Canaan, 2000—, Fairfield County Cmty. Found., 2001—. Mem.: ABA, Dartmouth Lawyers Assn., Lawyers for Children Am., Inc., Stamford/Norwalk Bar Assn., Conn. Bar Assn., Nat. Bar Assn., Black Alumni Dartmouth, Dartmouth Club of Fairfield County, Delta Sigma Theta. Baptist. Avocations: travel, reading, tennis. Office: 4 Stamford Plz Stamford CT 06902-3834 E-mail: cmcdonald@cl-law.com.

MCDONALD, CHARLES EDWARD, lawyer; b. El Paso, Tex., Nov. 13, 1957; s. Carlos and Armida (Adauto) McD.; 1 child, Miranda Lee. BA in Philosophy, U. St. Thomas, Houston, 1980; JD, South Tex. Coll. Law, 1985. Bar: Tex. 1985, U.S. Ct. Appeals. (5th cir.) 1991, U.S. Supreme Ct. 1992. Prin. Law Office Charles E. McDonald, El Paso, 1985-2000, McDonald and Assocs, El Paso, 2000—. Comms. liaison Coleman Re-election Congl. Campaign, El Paso, 1984, 86. Mem. ATLA, Tex. Trial Lawyers Assn., State Bar Tex., El Paso County Bar Assn. (ethics com. 1997-98, rules com. 1997-98, clin. law coun. 1997-98), Nat. Assn. Cave Divers. Roman Catholic. Avocations: cave diving, chess, traveling, foreign language (Spanish). Office: 4150 Rio Bravo St Ste 136 El Paso TX 79902-1013 E-mail: charles.mcdonald@prodigy.net.

MCDONALD, CRAYDON DEAN, psychologist; b. Denver, Dec. 22, 1946; s. Donald D. and Irene (Dunlavy) McD.; children: Ian, Brendan, Tavis, Morgynne. BFA, Parsons Sch. Design, N.Y.C., 1970; MDiv cum laude, St. Paul Sch. Theology, Kansas City, Mo., 1979; D of Ministry, Wesley Theol. Sem., Washington, 1982; PhD, Boston U., 1987. Diplomate Am. Bd. Profl. Psychology; lic. psychologist, Mass., Wis., Ill., Ariz.; approved supr. Am. Assn. Marriage & Family Therapy; ordained to ministry United Meth. Ch., 1982. Psychologist Worcester (Mass.) Pastoral Counseling Ctr., 1982-87; assoc. prof., asst. program dir. Loyola U., Chgo., 1987-88; clin. psychologist Lake Geneva, Wis., 1987-93. Psychology faculty No. Ariz. U., 1993—; chief psychologist Dr. McDonald & Assocs., Inc., 1982—; examiner Am. Bd. Profl. Psychology. Author: Personality and Cognitive Theology, 1982, Type A Coronary Prone Behavior and Narcissism, 1987. Fellow The Acad. Family Psychology (bd. dirs.); mem. APA (program com. divsn. 43), Human Factors Soc., Am. Assn. Pastoral Counselors. Democrat. Office: 1100 N San Francisco St Ste C Flagstaff AZ 86001-3260 *I have seldom found what a person does to be as significant as the motivation for doing it.*

MCDONALD, DAVID EUGENE, package car driver; b. Decatur, Ill., July 6, 1956; s. Robert Alexander McDonald and Ida Jane (Varvil) Crowell; m. Lynda Jean Christensen McDonald, Apr. 23, 1983; children: Melanie Ann, Joshua Glen and Jordan David (twins). BS in History, Ill. State U., Normal; student, Parkland C.C., Champaign, Ill. Asst. mgr. Gen. Cinema Corp., Decatur, Champaign, Chgo., 1978-81; mgr. Classic Cinemas, Elmhurst, Ill., 1981-83, World Mgmt. Inc., Downers Grove, 1983-87; driver UPS, Addison, 1987—. Active Jr. Achievement, 1971-75, Dupage County Rep., Wheaton, Ill., 1993—; treas. Local Luth. Laymans League, 2000—. Named Mr. Exec. Jr. Achievement, Decatur, Ill., 1975; recipient Internat. Literary award Manuscripts Internat., Dayton, Wash., 1988. Republican. Lutheran. Avocations: politics, photography, reading, writing. Home: 841 Prospect Ave Elmhurst IL 60126-4862 Office: UPS 150 S Lombard Rd Addison IL 60101-3020

MCDONALD, DONALD, civil engineer, educator; b. Montgomery, Ala., Oct. 16, 1930; s. John Fairley and Juliet Ruth (Burke) McD.; children: John Bruce, Katheryn Ann, Emily Ferrell. BCE, Auburn U., 1952; MS, U. Ill., 1957, PhD, 1959. Bridge design engr. Ala. Highway Dept., 1954-55; research asst. U. Ill., 1955-57; sr. research engr., research specialist Lockheed Missiles and Space Co., Sunnyvale, Calif., 1959-62; asst. prof. N.C. State U., 1962-65, assoc. prof., 1965-67; mgr. structures and mechanics dept. Lockheed Missiles and Space Co., Huntsville, Ala., 1967-72; prof. civil engring. Tex. A&M U., College Station, 1973-90, exec. dir. Koriyama, Japan, 1990; pres. Am. U. in Cairo, N.Y.C., 1990—; provost, v.p. acad. affairs Tex. A&M U., College Station, 1986-89, exec. dir., interim dean engring., assoc. dep. chancellor, 1983-84; pres. Am. U., Cairo, 1990—. Cons. Koriyama, Japan, 1990, also various industries. Contbr. articles to profl. jours. Served to 1st lt. USAF, 1952-54. Standard Oil N.J. fellow, 1957-58, univ. grad. fellow U. Ill., 1958-59. Fellow ASCE (chmn. com. on electronic computation 1974-77, chmn. structural div. exec. com. 1983-84), AIAA (assoc.); mem. NSPE, Am. Soc. Engring. Edn., Tex. Soc. Profl. Engrs., Cosmos Club (Washington), Sigma Xi, Tau Beta Pi, Chi Epsilon, Phi Kappa Phi. Clubs: Cosmos Washington. Republican. Episcopalian. Office: Am U in Cairo 866 United Nations Plz Rm 517 New York NY 10017-1822

MCDONALD, DOUGLAS ROBERT, non profit agency executive; b. San Francisco, May 27, 1949; s. Robert Angus and Shirley Anne (Beine) McD.; m. Karen Bachanas, June 24, 1978; children: Jennifer, Cameron. AB, Stanford Univ., 1971; MBA, Santa Clara Univ., 1974. Dist. exec. Boy Scouts Am., San Mateo, Calif., 1971-74, exec. Palo Alto, 1974-76; regional sales mgr. Baron Data Systems, San Leandro, 1976-81; field dir./COO Boy Scouts Am., San Mateo, 1981-86, assoc. reg. dir. Sunnyvale, 1986-88, Scout exec./CEO Stockton, 1988-92, San Jose, 1992-99, scout exec./CEO Sacramento, 1999—. Recipient Paul Harris fellow Rotary Internat., 1990, St. George award Roman Cath. Diocese of Sacramento, 2000; James E. West fellow Boy Scouts Am., 1993. Mem. Nat. Soc. Fund Raising Execs., Sigma Alpha Epsilon, Alpha Phi Omega, Silicon Valley Planned Giving Coun., Rotary Internat., Scouting Heritage Soc. Republican. Roman Catholic. Avocations: travel, computers, investments. Office: Boy Scouts of Am PO Box 13558 251 Commerce Circle Sacramento CA 95853

MCDONALD, DOUGLASS WAYNE, museum executive; b. Marshalltown, Iowa, July 22, 1953; s. Wayne Eldon and Miriam Gertrude (Thurber) McD.; m. Kay Louise Stangeland, Sept. 14, 1974; 1 child, Timothy. BA, William Penn Coll., 1974. Pastor Friends Ch., Indpls., 1974-83; dir. of ops. Conner Prairie, 1983-95; pres., CEO Genesee Country Village & Mus., Rochester, N.Y., 1995-99, Cin. Mus. Ctr., 1999—. CEO. Presenter seminars Mus. and Entrepreneurial Endeavors, 1996, Codes of Ethics, 1993. Mem. City Coun., Noblesville, Ind., 1980-95; bd. govs. Legacy Fund, Carmel, Ind., 1991-95. Mem. Am. Assn. Mus. (v.p. 1992-95), Mid-Atlantic Assn. Mus. (bd. dirs. 1996-99), Mid-West Mus. Conf. (life, exec. v.p. 1994-95). Mem. Soc. Of Friends. Home: 3200 Dry Run View Ln Cincinnati OH 45244-3280 Office: Cin Mus Ctr 1301 Western Ave Cincinnati OH 45203-1130

MCDONALD, FORREST, historian, educator; b. Orange, Tex., Jan. 7, 1927; s. John Forrest and Myra (McGill) McD.; m. Ellen Shapiro, Aug. 1, 1963; children from previous marriage: Kathy, Forrest Howard, Marcy Ann, Stephen, Kevin. BA, MA, U. Tex., 1949, PhD, 1955; MA (hon.), Brown U., 1962; LHD (hon.), SUNY, Geneseo, 1989. Exec. sec. Am. History Research Ctr., Madison, Wis., 1953-58; assoc. prof. history Brown U., Providence, 1959-63, prof., 1963-67, Wayne State U., Detroit, 1967-76, U. Ala., Tuscaloosa, 1976-87, disting. univ. rsch. prof., 1987—2002, prof. emeritus, 2002—. James Pinckney Harrison prof. Coll. of William and Mary, Williamsburg, Va., 1986-87; presdl. appointee Bd. Fgn. Scholarships, Washington, 1985-87; mem. fellowship selection com. Richard M. Weaver Fellowships, Bryn Mawr, Pa., 1980—. Author: We The People, 1958, Insull, 1962, E Pluribus Unum, 1965, Alexander Hamilton, 1979 (Frances Tavern Book award 1980), Novus Ordo Seclorum, 1985, Requiem, 1988, The American Presidency: An Intellectual History, 1994, States Rights and the Union, 2000. Trustee Phila. Soc., North Adams, Mich., 1983-86, 87-90, pres. 1988-90; co-chmn. New Eng. for Goldwater, 1964. Served with USN, 1945-46. Recipient George Washington medal Freedom's Found., Valley Forge, Pa., 1980, Best Book award Am. Revolution Round Table, N.Y., 1986, Richard M. Weaver award Ingersoll Found., 1990, First Salvatori award Heritage Found., 1992, Salavatori Book award Intercollegiate Studies Inst., 1994; Guggenheim fellow, N.Y., 1962-63; Jefferson lectr. NEH, 1987. Republican. Avocations: horticulture, tennis.

MCDONALD, FRANCIS MICHAEL, judge trial referee, retired state supreme court justice; b. Waterbury, Conn., Jan. 22, 1931; s. M. Francis and Margaret (Kelly) McD.; m. Mary Kelly, Jan. 28, 1956; children: Michael, Mary Ann, John K. AB, Holy Cross Coll., 1953; LLB, Yale U., 1956. Bar: Conn. 1956. Spl. agt. FBI, Washington, 1956-57; asst. U.S. atty. Dist. of Conn., New Haven, 1958-60; asst. prosecutor Cir. Ct., Waterbury, 1961-68; state's atty., 1968-84; judge Superior Ct., 1984-96; assoc. justice Conn. Supreme Ct., Hartford, 1996-99, chief justice, 1999-2001, judge trial referee Conn., 2001—. Avocations: fishing, skiing, fly tying. Home: 257 Christian Rd Middlebury CT 06762-2908 Office: Superior Ct 400 Grand St Waterbury CT 06702-1900*

MC DONALD, FRANK BETHUNE, physicist; b. Columbus, Ga., May 28, 1925; s. Frank B. and Lucy (Kyle) McD.; m. Virginia Ballew, June 15, 1951 (dec. 1977); children: Kyle Louise McDonald Jossi, Robert Kyle, Douglas Frank; m. Irene Negosh Kelejian, Nov. 7, 1987. BS, Duke U., 1948; MS, U. Minn., 1951, PhD (AEC fellow), 1955. Rsch. assoc. State U. Iowa, Iowa City, 1953-56, asst. prof. physics, 1956-59; chief lab. for high energy astrophysics Goddard Space Flight Ctr. NASA, Greenbelt, Md., 1959-82, mem. phys. scis. com. space program adv. coun., 1974-76; the NASA chief scientist, 1982-87; assoc. dir., chief scientist Goddard Space Flight Ctr. NASA, 1987-89; sr. policy analyst Office Sci. and Tech. Policy, Exec. Office of Pres., Washington, 1982; sr. rsch. scientist Inst. for Phys. Sci. and Tech. U. Md., College Park, 1989—. Part-time prof. U. Md., College Park, 1963-82; mem. Geophysics Rsch. Forum, 1985-88; Internat. Union Pure and Applied Physics mem. Internat. Commn. on Cosmic Rays, 1981-84, sec. to commn., 1984-87, chmn., 1987-90; NASA rep. to NASA Adv. Coun., 1984-89. Editor: High Energy Particles and Quanta in Astrophysics, 1974; assoc. editor: Jour. Geophys. Research, 1964-67; mem. editorial bd.: Space Sci. Revs.; Research in cosmic ray physics With USNR, 1942-45. Recipient Exceptional Sci. Achievement award NASA, 1964, 78, 86, Outstanding Leadership medal, 1981; Presdl. Mgmt. Improvement cert., 1971; Presdl. rank of meritorious exec. Sr. Exec. Service, 1980, 89, W. Randolph Lovelace II award Am. Astronautical Soc., 1986. Fellow Am. Phys. Soc. (chmn. div. cosmic physics 1973-74, mem. council 1982—, mem. exec. com. 1983), Am. Geophys. Union; mem. Am. Inst. Physics (council, governing bd. 1983-86), Washington Philos. Soc., Am. Astronom. Soc., Nat. Acad. Sci., Sigma Xi, Phi Beta Kappa. Office: U Md IPST Rm 3245 Computer Sci Spc Bui College Park MD 20742-0001

MC DONALD, GAIL FABER, musician, educator; b. Jersey City, Oct. 24, 1917; d. Samuel and Jennie (Weiss) Faber; m. George Walther, Nov. 17, 2000; children from previous marriage: Lora McDonald Ferguson, Charles McDonald, Henry McDonald. Diploma, Mannes Music Sch., N.Y.C., 1938; BA, U. Md., 1962; MusM, Cath. U., 1968; DMus Arts, U. Md., 1977. Legis. asst. Capitol Hill, 1943-46; pvt. tchr. piano and music theory Washington and Md., 1950—. Piano soloist Nat. Gallery Art, 1977; rec. artist Educo Records; lectr., performer Bach Sinfonias and Mendelssohn's Complete Songs Without Words; recorded complete solo piano works of Daniel Gregory Mason. Author: Muzio Clementi and the Gradus Ad Parnassum, 1968. Mem. D.C. Music Tchrs. Assn., Md. Music Tchrs. Assn. (pres. 1977—), D.C. Fedn. Music Clubs, Nat. Guild Piano Tchrs. (performing mem.), Friday Morning Music Club (adjudicator 1972—2000). Address: 801 N Monroe St Apt 602 Arlington VA 22201-2372

MCDONALD, GLENA JUNE, school counselor; b. Lubbock, Tex., Aug. 26, 1947; d. Glen Armstrong Egan Jr. and June Eve (Malouf) Welman; m. John Freeman McDonald, June 24, 1967; 1 child, Elizabeth Clare. BA, Albertus Magnus Coll., 1969; MEd, U. Ill., Chgo., 1976; cert. advanced studies, Concordia Coll., River Forest, Ill., 1989. Cert. elem. edn., sch. counselor; nat. cert. counselor.; lic. clin. prof. counselor, Ill. Tchr. Chgo. Pub. Schs., 1973-89, sch. counselor, 1989—. Adj. prof. psychology, Concordia U., River Forest, Ill., 1994—. Mem. Oak Park-River Forest (Ill.) Infant Welfare Soc., 1989—. Recipient Gov.'s Master Tchr. award State of Ill., 1984, Oppenheimer Recognition award Oppenheimer Family Found., 1997; named Finalist for Human Devel. award Oppenheimer Family Found., 1991. Mem. ACA, Am. Sch. Counselor Assn., Ill. Counseling Assn., Ill. Sch. Counselor Assn., Phi Delta Kappa. Episcopalian. Home: 1443 Lathrop Ave River Forest IL 60305-1119

MCDONALD, GREGORY CHRISTOPHER, author; b. Shrewsbury, Mass., Feb. 15, 1937; s. Irving Thomas and Mae (Haggerty) M.; m. Susan Aiken, Jan. 12, 1963 (div. Oct. 1990); children: Christopher Gregory, Douglas Gregory; m. Cheryle Higgins, May 25, 2001. BA, Harvard U., 1958. Bd. dirs. Camaldon Corp. Novelist, critic Boston Globe, 1966-73; author: (novels) Running Scared, 1964, Fletch, 1974, Confess, Fletch, 1976, Flynn, 1977, Love Among the Mashed Potatoes, 1978, Fletch's Fortune, 1978, Fletch Forever, 1978, Who Took Toby Rinaldi?, 1980, Fletch and the Widow Bradley, 1981, The Buck Passes Flynn, 1981, Fletch's Moxie, 1982, Fletch and the Man Who, 1983, Carioca Fletch, Flynn's In, 1984, Fletch Won, Safekeeping, 1985, Fletch, Too, 1986; (non-fiction) The Education of Gregory Mcdonald, 1985, Fletch Chronicle, Vol. 1, Bull's Eye (drama), 1986, A World Too Wide, 1987, Fletch Chronicle, Vol. 2, 1987, Exits and Entrances, 1988, Fletch Chronicle, Vol. 3, 1988, Merely Players, 1988, The Brave, 1991 (trophees in France 813-Best Fgn. Novel, 1997), Son of Fletch, 1993, Fletch Reflected, 1994, Skylar, 1995, Skylar in Yankeeland, 1997; editor: Last Laughs, 1986; dir. Bach Cantata Singers, 1973-80. Mem. vis. com. Boston Mus. Fine Arts, 1970-73, 85—; mem. Lincoln Recreation Com., 1977, 78; mem. Winthrop House Sr. Commons Harvard Coll. 1982—. Recipient Humanitarian of Yr. award Tenn. Assn. Fed. Execs., 1989, Citizen of Yr. award Nat. Assn. Social Workers, 1990, Roger William Straus award NCCJ, 1990, Alex Haley award, 1992. Mem. Authors Guild, Dramatists Guild, Mystery Writers Am. (dir. 1977— , pres. 1985-86, Poe award 1975, 77), Crime Writers Eng., Writers Guild Am., Mass. Chiefs Police Assn., Giles Countians United, Mid-Tenn. Harvard-Radcliffe Assn. Clubs: Harvard (Boston); Overseas Press (N.Y.C.); Hillcrest Country (Pulaski, Tenn.). Office: care Arthur Greene Esq 101 Park Ave New York NY 10178-0002

MCDONALD, JACQUELINE BERNARD, retired radiologist; b. San Diego, Mar. 18, 1925; MD, Marquette Sch. Medicine., 1950. Diplomate Am. Bd. Radiology. Intern French Hosp., San Francisco, 1950-51; resident in internal medicine Franklin Hosp., 1951-52; resident in radiology VA Hosp., 1952-54, Childrens Hosp., San Francisco, 1954-55; fellow jr. rsch. radiology U. Calif. Hosp., 1955-56; pvt. practice, 1956-73; asst. prof. radiology U. N.Mex. Sch. Medicine, Albuquerque, 1973-87; acting chief radiology VA Med. Ctr., 1986-87. Mem. AMA, Am. Coll. Radiology, Assn. Univ. Radiologists, N.Mex. Radiology Soc., Radiol. Soc. N.Am.

MCDONALD, JAMES BOTT, economics educator; b. Logan, Utah, Apr. 16, 1942; s. Leonard Webb and Arola (Bott) McD.; m. Kathleen Thomas, Dec. 28, 1966; children: Jan, Michael, Jonathan, Robert. BS, Utah State U., 1964, MS, 1967; PhD, Purdue U., 1970. Asst. prof. Utah State U., Logan, 1970-72, Brigham Young U., Provo, Utah, 1972-73, assoc. prof., 1974-79, prof., 1980—, assoc. dean honors of gen. edn., 1993—. Contbr. articles to profl. jours; referee for profl. jours. Recipient rsch. award NSF, 1986-87. Mem. Econometric Soc., Am. Statis. Assn., Am. Econ. Assn., Am. Fin. Assn. Achievements include research in econometrics and statistical distributions. Home: 4058 Quail Run Provo UT 84604-5219 Office: Brigham Young U Provo UT 84602

MCDONALD, JINX, interior designer; b. Kingston, Jamaica, Aug. 5, 1946; d. Leonard Fraser and Norma Dawn (Phillips) McConnell; m. C. John McDonald, Dec. 20, 1965 (div. Nov. 1993); children: Sarah, Minka. Interior design/journalism, St. Godric's Coll., Hampstead, Eng., 1967; interior design, Tuxedo Ctr., Atlanta, 1986. Owner/pres. Internat. Accents, Inc., Atlanta, 1986—91; interior designer Style, Inc., Naples, 1991—95, Forum Design group, Inc., Naples, Fla., 1995—2000; prin., owner Jinx McDonald Designs, Inc., 2000—. Cons. interior design. Recipient Sand Dollar award, Collier Bldg. Industry Assn., 1999, 2002, Design of Distinction, Naples Illustrated, 2002. Mem. Am. Soc. Interior Design (allied mem.), Interior Design Soc. Democrat. Anglican. Home and Office: c/o Jinx McDonald Designs Inc 7536 San Miguel Way Naples FL 34109-7162 Office: 5603 Naples Blvd Naples FL 34109-2023 Fax: 941-598-4174. E-mail: jinxmcdonald@yahoo.com.

MCDONALD, JOANNE, business executive; b. San Diego, June 10, 1947; d. Paul and Dolores (Paganucci) McD. BA, U. Md., 1970. High tech. exec. ENSCO, Inc., Springfield, Va., 1981—. v.p. adminstrn. and human resources, 1992—, bd. dirs., 1997—, v.p., 1999—. Office: ENSCO Inc 5400 Port Royal Rd Springfield VA 22151-2312

MCDONALD, JOEL MATTHEWS, lawyer; b. Tylertown, Miss., Nov. 13, 1962; s. William Irvin and Emma Jean McD. BS in Acctg., U. Ala., 1984; JD, U. Va., 1987. Bar: D.C., Ga. Assoc., King & Spalding, Washington, 1987-89, Gibson, Dunn & Crutcher, London N.Y.C. Washington, 1990-93; deputy dir. U.S. Treasury Tax Adv. Program, Moscow, 1994-95; resident dir. Harvard U., Russian Tax Reform Project, 1996-97; of counsel Salans, Herzfeld & Heilbronn, 1998, ptnr., 1999—. Contbr. articles to profl. jours., chpts. to books. Methodist. Office: Salans Hertzfeld Heilbronn 14-18 Gresham St London EC2V 7NN England

MCDONALD, JOHN BARRY, JR. lawyer; b. Fall River, Mass., Aug. 22, 1970; s. John Barry Sr. and Gabrielle Marie (Pires) McD. BA summa cum laude, Boston Coll., 1992; JD, U. Chgo., 1995. Assoc. Goodwin, Procter & Hoar LLP, Boston, 1995-2000, Edwards & Angell LLP, Providence, 2000; candidate Mass. State Senate, 2000; v.p., assoc. counsel State St. Bank and Trust Co., Boston, 2001—. Campaign coord. Citizens for Silber, Fall River, 1990; candidate Mass. State Senate, 2000. Mem. Phi Beta Kappa, Alpha Sigma Nu. Home: 2022 Highland Ave Fall River MA 02720-4311 E-mail: jbmcdonald@statestreet.com.

MCDONALD, JOHN CECIL, lawyer; b. Lorimor, Iowa, Feb. 19, 1924; s. Cecil F. and Mary Elsie (Fletcher) McD.; m. Barbara Joan Berry, May 8, 1943; children: Mary Elisabeth (Mrs. Dell Richard), Joan Frances (Mrs. Andrew Ackerman), Jean Maurine. Student, Simpson Coll., 1942, So. Ill. U., 1943; JD, Drake U., 1948. Bar: Iowa 1948, U.S. Ct. Mil. Appeals 1956, U.S. Supreme Ct. 1956. Practiced in, Dallas Center, Iowa, 1948—; sr. ptnr. McDonald, Brown & Fagen and predecessor firms, 1971—; county atty. Dallas County, 1958-62; asst. county atty., 1963-69; city atty. Dallas Center, 1956-80. Mem. Simpson Coll. Alumni Council, pres., 1977-80; legal adviser Dallas Community Bd. Edn., 1953-69, pres., mem., 1968-76; nat. adv. com. Cen. Coll.; alt. del. Iowa Coordinating Council for Post-High Sch. Edn.; finance chmn. Dallas County Rep.Cen. Com., 1954-63, chmn., 1963-68; chmn. Iowa 7th Congl. Dist. Rep. Cen. Com., 1968-69, Iowa Rep. Cen. Com., 1969-75; mem. Rep. Nat. Com., 1969-88, mem. exec. com., 1973— ; mem. Rule 29 com., com. on reform; mem. Gov. Iowa's inaugural com., 1969, 71, 73, 75, 79; del. Rep. Nat. Conv., 1964, 72, 76, 80, 84, chmn. com. on contests, 1976, 80, 84, 88, chmn. com. on credentials, 1976, 80, 88, mem. com. on arrangements and exec. com. of com. on arrangements, 1976, 80, 84, mem. rules rev. com., 1977-84; chmn. Midwest Rep. State Chairmen's Assn., 1973-75, Nat. Rep. State Chairmen's Adv. Com., 1973-75; hon. co-chmn. Vice Pres.'s Inaugural, 1981; trustee Dallas County Hosp., Perry, Iowa; bd. visitors U.S. Air Force Acad., 1975-78, chmn., 1977-78; trustee Simpson Coll., 1978— ; bd. dirs. Iowa Student Loan Liquidity Corp., 1987-99; mem. Iowa Coll. Aid Commn., 1989—; mem. Iowa Bd. Regents, 1981-87, pres., 1985-87; bd. dirs. Iowa Public Broadcasting Network, 1981-85; U.S. commr. Am. Battle Monuments Commn., 1982-94. Served with USAAF, 1942-46; Col. USAF, 1951-52, ret. Recipient Alumni Achievement award Simpson Coll., 1974; Disting. Service award Drake U., 1978 Mem. ABA, Iowa Bar Assn. (past chmn. spl. com. on mil. affairs, mem. mil. affairs com.), Dallas County Bar Assn. (past pres.), Am. Legion, Farm Bur., Blackfriars, Drake U. Law Sch. Alumni Assn. (class officer), Comml. Club (past pres.) (Dallas Ctr.), Hillcrest Country Club (past pres.) (Adel, Iowa), Des Moines Club, Masons (32 degree), Shriners, Rotary (past pres. Dallas Ctr.), Alpha Tau Omega, Delta Theta Phi, Alpha Psi Omega. Clubs: Des Moines. Lodges: Masons (32 deg.), Shriners, Rotary (pas pres. Dallas Ctr.). Presbyterian. Home: 1006 13th St PO Box 250 Dallas Center IA 50063-0250 Office: McDonald Brown Fagen & Flanders PO Box 250 Dallas Center IA 50063-0250 E-mail: dalctlaw@miindspring.com.

MCDONALD, JOHN CLIFTON, surgeon; b. Baldwyn, Miss., July 25, 1930; s. Edgar Hone and Ethel (Knight) McD.; m. Martha Dennis, Sept. 9, 1956; children: Melissa Lee, Karen Ann, Martha Knight. BS, Miss. Coll., 1951; MD, Tulane U., 1955. Diplomate Am. Bd. Surgery. Intern Confederate Meml. Med. Ctr., Shreveport, La., 1955-56; asst. resident Meyer Meml. Hosp., Buffalo, 1958-62, resident, 1962-63; from asst. attending surgeon to attending surgeon, 1963-68, assoc. dir. surg. research lab., 1965-68; from asst. attending surgeon to attending surgeon Deaconess Hosp., 1965-69, head sect. transplantation, 1966-68; dir. transplantation Charity Hosp. of La., New Orleans, 1969-77, vis. surgeon, 1969-77; clin. asst. surgeon Touro Infirmary, 1969-77; med. staff So. Bapt. Hosp., 1969-77; assoc. dept. surgery Hotel Dieu Hosp., 1969-77; surgeon in chief La. State U. Med. Ctr., Shreveport, 1977-2000, prof., chmn. dept. surgery, 1977-2000, chancellor, dean, 2000—. Buswell rsch. fellow in immunology SUNY-Buffalo, 1963-65, instr. surger, 1963-65, assoc. prof., 1965-68; asst. prof. surgery SUNY-Buffalo, 1965-68; cons. surgeon various La. Hosps., 1969-77; dir. La. Organ Procurement Program, 1971-77; cons. N.W. La. Emergency Med. Services, 1977— ; assoc. prof. surgery Tulane U. Sch. Medicine, 1969-72, prof., 1972-77, assoc. prof. microbiology and immunology, 1969-77, dir. surg. research labs., 1969-77, dir. transplantation labs., 1969-77, dir. Med. Ctr. Histocampatability Testing Lab., 1969-77. Contbr. articles to med. jours. Served to capt. USAF, 1956-58. Recipient Owl Club award for outstanding teaching Tulane U., 1977; grantee Kidney Found., 1966-67, NIH, 1969— , Schlieder Found., 1970-73, Cancer Assn. Greater New Orleans, 1971-72, La. Regional Med. Program, 1971-73. Mem. AMA, ACS, Am. Assn. Clin. Histocompatability Testing (founding), Am. Assn. Immunologists, Am. Soc. for Artificial Internal Organs, Am. Soc. Transplant Surgeons (founding, pres. 1987), Buffalo Surg. Soc. (sec. 1968, Roswell Pk. medal 2002), So. Surg. Assn. (Arthur H. Shipley award 1972, treas. 1988-91, sec. 1991-3, pres. 1993-94), Surg. Assn. La. (dir. 1977—, pres. 1983), Am. Assn. for Surgery of Trauma, Transplantation Soc., Southeastern Surg. Congress, Am. Surg. Assn., Halsted Soc. (pres. 1991), Soc. U. Surgeons, La. Med. Soc., Shreveport Med. Soc., United Network for Organ Sharing (pres. 1986-88), Am. Assn. Endocrine Surgeons, Am. Hepato-Pancreato-Biliary Assn., Internat. Liver Transplantation Soc., Soc. Critical Car Medicine, Soc. Laparoendoscopic Surgeons. Office: La State U Health Scis Ctr Shreveport Office of Chancellor Shreveport LA 71130 E-mail: jmcdon@isuhsc.edu.

MCDONALD, JOHN FRANCIS PATRICK, electrical engineering educator; b. Narberth, Pa., Jan. 14, 1942; s. Frank Patrick and Lulu Ann (Hegedus) McD.; m. Karen Marie Knapp, May 26, 1979. BSEE, MIT, 1963; MS in Engring., Yale U., 1965, PhD, 1969. Instr. Yale U., New Haven, 1968-69, asst. prof., 1969-74; assoc. prof. Rensselaer Poly. Inst., Troy, N.Y., 1974-86, prof., 1986—. Founder Rensselaer Ctr. for Integrated Electronics, 1980—. Contbr. more than 225 articles to profl. publs.; patentee in field. Recipient numerous grants, 1974—. Mem. ACM, IEEE (sr., assoc. editor Transactions on VSLI Design 1995—), Optical Soc., Acoustical Soc., Vacuum Soc., Materials Rsch. Soc. Office: Rensselaer Poly Inst Ctr for Integrated Electronics Troy NY 12181

MCDONALD, JOHN GREGORY, financial investment educator; b. Stockton, Calif., 1937; m. Melody McDonald. BS, Stanford U., 1960, MBA, 1962, PhD, 1967. Mem. faculty Grad. Sch. Bus. Stanford U., Calif., 1968—, now The IBJ prof. fin. Grad. Sch. Bus. Vis. prof. U. Paris, 1972, Columbia Bus. Sch., 1975, Harvard Bus. Sch. 1986; gov., vice chmn., bd. govs. NASD/NASDAQ Stock Market, 1987-90; mem. adv. bd. InterWest Venture Capital; dir. Investment Co. of Am., New Perspective Fund, Inc., Scholastic Corp., Varian Inc., EuroPacific Growth Fund. Contbr. articles to profl. jours. Bd. overseers vis. com. Harvard U. Bus. Sch., Cambridge, Mass., 1994-2000. Fulbright scholar, Paris, 1967-68. Office: Stanford U Grad Sch Bus 518 Memorial Way Stanford CA 94305

MC DONALD, JOHN JOSEPH, electronics executive; b. N.Y.C., Apr. 18, 1930; s. John J. and Margaret (Shanley) McD.; m. Tessa de R. Greenfield, Aug. 22, 1956; children: Kathryn, Elizabeth, Andrew. BA, Bklyn. Coll., 1951. With Sperry Rand Corp., Blue Bell, Pa., 1954-75, v.p., 1972-75; mng. dir. Casio Electronics Ltd., London, 1975-78, pres. Casio Europe, 1975-78; pres., CEO Casio, Inc., Dover, N.J., 1978-99, also bd. dirs.; chmn. Casio Can. Ltd., 1988-90, pres., CEO, 1990-99; pres. McDonald Assocs., Dover, NJ, 1999—2002; pres., CEO Instant Power Corp. subs. Electric Fuel Corp., 2002—. Bd. dirs. Casio Mfg. Corp., Casio de Mex. S.A. Chmn. Electronics Industries Found., 1998; trustee Bklyn. Coll., CUNY, 1997—. Served with U.S. Army, 1952-54. Mem. Electronic Industries Assn. (bd. govs.), Electronic Industries Found. (trustee 1987—), Consumer Electronics Mfrs. Assn.(dirs.). Home: PO Box 322 Hope NJ 07844-0322 Office: 570 Mount Pleasant Ave Dover NJ 07801-1620

MC DONALD, JOHN RICHARD, lawyer; b. Connersville, Ind., Aug. 8, 1933; s. Vernon Louis and Thelma (Venham) McD.; m. Mary Alice Boyd, Aug. 17, 1957; children: Anne Elizabeth, John Richard, Colleen Lynn. BA, U. Ariz., 1957, LL.B., 1960. Bar: Ariz. 1960. Since practiced in, Tucson; assoc. Richard N. Roylston, 1961-62; pvt. practice, 1963-65; ptnr. McDonald & Rykken, 1965-68, DeConcini & McDonald (now DeConcini, McDonald, Yetwin, Lacy, P.C.), 1968—. Mem. adv. bd. Dependable Nurses, Inc., 1994—. Mem. Ariz. Law Rev. Pres., bd. dirs. emeritus Comstock Children's Hosp. Found.; v.p. Ariz. Sch. Bds. Assn., 1979, pres., 1981; v.p. All Ariz. Sch. Bd., 1981; v.p., bd. dirs. Tucson Assn. for Blind, 1966-86; trustee Catalina Foothills Sch. Dist., 1976-82; bd. dirs. Tucson Unified Sch. Dist. Ednl. Enrichment Found., 1994—, Ariz. Acad., 1981-89, Tucson Symphony Soc., 1997—, Catalina Foothills Sch. Dist. Found.; mem. Am. Park Svcs. Mem. Ariz. Bar Assn., Ariz. Law Rev. Assn. (pres. 1994), Pima County Bar Assn. (dir. 1978-86, pres. 1984-85), Nat. Coun. Sch. Attys. (dir. 1992-96), Delta Chi. Republican. Presbyterian. Home: 6151 N Camino Almonte Tucson AZ 85718-3729 Office: 2525 E Broadway Blvd Tucson AZ 85716-5398 E-mail: jmcdonald@dmyl.com., mjr44@qwest.net.

MC DONALD, JOHN WARLICK, diplomat, global strategist; b. Coblenz, Germany, Feb. 18, 1922; s. John Warlick and Ethel Mae (Raynor) McD.; m. Barbara Jane Stewart, Oct. 23, 1943 (div.); children: Marilyn Ruth, James Stewart, Kathleen Ethel, Laura Ellen; m. Christel Meyer, Oct. 24, 1970. AB, U. Ill., 1943, JD, 1946; D (hon.), Mt. Mercy Coll., 1989, Teikyo Marycrest U., 1991, Salisbury State U., 1993. Bar: Ill. 1946, U.S. Supreme Ct. 1951. With legal div. Office Mil Govt., Berlin, 1947; asst. dist. atty. U.S. Mil. Govt. Cts., Frankfort, Germany, 1947-50; with Allied High Commn., Bonn, Germany, 1950-52; U.S. mission to NATO and OEEC, Paris, 1952-54; fgn. affairs officer Dept. State, Washington, 1954-55; exec. sec. to dir. ICA, 1955-59; U.S. econ. coord. for CENTO affairs Ankara, Turkey, 1959-63; chief econ. and comml. sect. Am. Embassy, Cairo, 1963-66; student Nat. War Coll., Washington, 1966-67; dep. dir. office econ. and social affairs Bur. Internat. Orgn. Affairs, Dept. State, 1967-68, dir., 1968-71; coord. UN Multilateral Devel. Programs, Dept. State, 1971-74, acting dep. asst. sec. econ. and social affairs, 1971, 73; dep. dir. gen. ILO, Geneva, 1974-78; pres. INTELSAT Conf. Privileges and Immunities, 1978; U.S. coord. Tech. Coop. among Developing Countries, 1978; rep. with rank of amb. to UN Conf., 1978—. Sec. gen. 27th Colombo Plan Ministerial Meeting, 1978; U.S. coord. UN Decade on Drinking Water and Sanitation, 1979; U.S. coord., amb. Third World Conf. on Indsl. Devel., 1979, World Assembly on Aging, 1980-82; chmn. fed. inter-agy. com. Internat. Yr. of Disabled Persons, 1980-81; U.S. rep. Internat. Youth Yr., 1981-83; coord. multilateral affairs Ctr. Study of Fgn. Affairs, 1983-87; profl. lectr. in law George Washington U. Nat. Law Ctr., 1987-88, lectr. in conflict resolution, multilateral diplomacy and art of negotiation; pres. Iowa Peace Inst., Grinnell, 1988-92; prof. polit. sci. Grinnell Coll., 1989-92; Disting. vis. prof. George Mason U., Fairfax, Va., 1992-93; chmn. Inst. for Multi-Track Diplomacy, Washington, 1992—; mem. Fgn. Affairs Res. Corps., 1993—; adj. prof. Union Inst., 1993-94, 97-98. Author: The North-South Dialogue and the UN, 1982, How to Be a Delegate, 1984, 2nd edit., 1994; co-editor: International Negotiation, 1985, Perspectives on Negotiation, 1986, Conflict Resolution: Track Two Diplomacy, 1987, 2nd edit., 1995, U.S. Soviet Summitry, 1987, US Bases Overseas: Negotiations with Spain, Greece and The Philippines, 1990, Multi-Track Diplomacy, 1991, revised, 1993, 3rd edit., 1996, Defining A U.S. Negotiating Sytle, 1996; contbr. articles on aging, terrorism, water conflict resolution. Bd. dirs. Global Water, 1982—, Touchstone Theatre, 1982-88, World Com.-UN Decade of Disabled Persons, 1987—, Countdown 2001, 1987-93, People-to-People Com. on Disability, 1987—, Am. Impact Found., 1987-89, chmn. bd., 1988-89; dir. Am. Assn. Internat. Aging, 1983—, chmn., 1983—; v.p. nat. capital area UN Assn., 1993-98, mem., 1978—. Recipient Superior Honor award, State Dept., 1972, Presdl. Meritorious Service award, State Dept., 1984; named Patriot of Yr., Kansas City, 1987. Mem. ABA, Am. Fgn. Svc. Assn., U.S. Assn. for Club of Rome, Soc. Profls. in Dispute Resolution, Consortium of Peace Rsch., Edn. and Devel., Cosmos Club, Delta Kappa Upsilon, Phi Delta Phi. Office: IMTD 1819 H St NW Ste 1200 Washington DC 20006-3629 E-mail: imtd@imtd.org.

MCDONALD, JOSEPH ANDREW, information services director, consultant, writer; b. Buenos Aires, July 10, 1942; came to the U.S., 1955; s. Joseph Andrew and Vera Ruth (Brown) McD.; m. Julianna Sue Adams, Oct. 11, 1962 (div. Nov. 1995); children: J. Andrew, Timothy Robert, Jonathan David; m. Kathryn Jean Baehr, Dec. 9, 1995; children: Gabriel Joseph, William Joseph, Peter Joseph. AB, Ea. Coll., 1963; MS, Drexel U., 1966, PhD, 1987. Asst. dir. librs. Stockton State Coll., Pomona, N.J., 1972-75; edn. materials adminstr. Triton Coll., River Grove, Ill., 1975-77; libr., asst. dir. univ. librs. SUNY, Albany, 1978-80; dir. univ. librs. L.I. U., Bklyn., 1981-85; dir. libr. svcs. Holy Family Coll., Phila., 1985-89; dir. univ. librs. Pepperdine U., Malibu, Calif., 1989-92; v.p. info. svcs. Dordt Coll., Sioux Center, Iowa, 1992-93; ind. cons., author St. Louis, 1994-97; dir. libr. Fontbonne Coll., 1997-98; head info. & learning svcs. Benedictine Coll., Atchison, Kans., 1998—. Rschr. Pa. Hist. and Mus. Commn., Harrisburg, 1971-89; cons., coll. visitor Middle States Assn., Phila., 1989-92; cons. City of Thousand Oaks, Calif., 1991, Impact Technologies, St. Louis, 1995—. Author: Public Library Architecture, 1967, Academic Libraries, 1994; contbr. articles to profl. jours. Cons. LWV, Harrisburg, 1967-70; pres. PTO, Vineland, N.J., 1973-74; mem., WEB site adv. com. Luth. Ch.-Mo. Synod, 1997—. Rsch. grantee Drexel U., Phila., 1980-81, Coun. on Libr. Resources, Washington, 1985-89, Pa. Hist. and Mus. Commn., Harrisburg, 1987-89. Mem. ALA (bldgs. for coll. and univ. librs. com. 1979-81), Cath. Libr. Assn. (bd. dirs., fin. com. 1987-89), Tri-State Libr. Coop. (bd. dirs. 1985-89), Consortium for Health Info. (bd. dirs. 1985-89), Acad. Librs. Bklyn. (bd. dirs. 1981-85). Avocations: sailing, hiking, music, painting. Office: Benedictine Coll 1020 N 2d St Atchison KS 66002

MCDONALD, JOSEPH F., III, lawyer; b. Rockville Centre, N.Y., Feb. 6, 1956; s. Joseph F. Jr. and Rita M. McD.; m. Laurie Hurd, Nov. 24, 1978; children: Geoffrey, Ryan, Molly. BA, St. Anselm's Coll., 1978; JD, Suffolk U., 1983; LLM, Boston U., 1987. Bar: N.H., U.S. Dist. Ct., U.S. Tax Ct. Dir., shareholder Cleveland, Waters & Bass, Concord, N.H., 1988-92, 94-98; v.p. trust New London (N.H.) Trust Co., 1992-94; ptnr. McDonald & Kanyuk, PLLC, Concord, 1998—. Dir. AAA No. New England, Portland, Maine, 1997—. Fellow Am. Coll. Trust and Estate Counsel. Office: McDonald & Kanyuk PLLC 7 Hills Ave Concord NH 03301-4804

MCDONALD, JOSEPH LEE, insurance broker; b. Bremerton, Wash., Aug. 15, 1931; s. Joseph Okane and Ida Elizabeth (Finholm) McD.; m. Glorietta Maness, Jan. 22, 1954 (dec. 1984); children: Holly Ann Chaffin, Andrew Lee McDonald; m. Beverly Mae Falkner, June 22, 1986. BS, U. Wash., 1954. Various mgmt. positions AT&T, 1956-62; broker, ptnr. McDonald & McGarry Co., Seattle, 1962-84; ptnr., exec. McDonald Ins. Group, Kirkland, Wash., 1984—. V.p., bd. dirs. Chimayo Inc., Seattle, 1990-94, Santa Fe Food Corp., Seattle, 1991-96. City councilman City of Bellevue, 1971-75; commr. Water Dist. #97, Bellevue, 1967-71, Lake Hills Sewer Dist., Bellevue, 1965-71; pres. Wash. State Assn. of Sewer Dists., Seattle, 1969. With U.S. Army, 1954-56. Mem. Coll. Club of Seattle, Overlake Golf and Country Club, Western Assn. of Ins. Brokers, Ind. Ins. Agts. Assn., Seattle Master Builders Assn., Nat. Wildlife Fedn., Nature Conservancy, Apt. Assn. of Seattle and King County, Roche Harbor Yacht Club, Chi Phi. Avocations: skiing, sailing, tennis. Home: 7235 91st Pl SE Mercer Island WA 98040-5803 Office: McDonald Ins Group 416 6th St S Kirkland WA 98033-6718 E-mail: jlm@mcdonaldins.com.

MCDONALD, JOSEPH VALENTINE, neurosurgeon; b. N.Y.C., June 7, 1925; m. Carolyn Alice Patricia Petersen, Apr. 30, 1955; 5 children. AB, Coll. Holy Cross, 1945; MD, U. Pitts., 1949. Intern St. Vincent's Hosp., N.Y.C., 1949-50; rsch. fellow neuroanatomy Vanderbilt U., 1950-51; gen. surgery asst. resident Cushing VA Hosp., Boston, 1951-52; neurology extern Lenox Hill Hosp., 1952; asst. resident neurosurgery Johns Hopkins Hosp., 1953-55, resident neurosurgeon, 1955-56; practice medicine specializing in neurol. surgery Rochester, N.Y., 1956—; emeritus prof. neurosurgery U. Rochester Med. Sch. Mem. Soc. Neurol. Surgeons, A.C.S., Am. Assn. Neurol. Surgeons, Congress Neurosurgeons. Home: 800 Allens Creek Rd Rochester NY 14618-3412

MCDONALD, JOSH WILLIAM, surgical pathologist; b. Phila., Mar. 5, 1965; s. John William and Barbara McD.; m. Pamela Karen Woodard, Apr. 24, 1993. AB in Chemistry with high honors, Princeton U., 1986; MD, Duke U., 1990. Diplomate Am. Bd. Pathology in anatomic and clin. pathology. Resident in anatomic and clin. pathology Duke U. Med. Ctr., Durham, N.C., 1990-95; asst. prof. pathology St. Louis U. Med. Ctr., 1995—. Contbr. articles to profl. jours. Recipient award NIH rsch. festival, 1992. Fellow Coll. Am. Pathologists; mem. Am. Soc. Clin. Pathology.

MCDONALD, JULIE JENSEN, writer, educator; b. Fiscus, Iowa, June 22, 1929; d. Alfred Julius Jensen and Myrtle Petra Faurschou; m. Elliott Raymond McDonald, Jr., May 6, 1952; children: Beth Pearson, Elliott Raymond, III. BA, U. Iowa, 1951; LLD, St. Ambrose Coll., 1972. Women's editor Rockford (Ill.) Newspapers, 1951—52; feature writer, reviewer Quad-City Times, Davenport, Iowa, 1963—83; lectr. journalism St. Ambrose Coll., 1974—2000; feature writer, reviewer, columnist Dispatch, Argus, Leader, Gold Book, Quad Cities, Iowa, 1983—; bd. dirs. Midwest Writing Ctr. Author: (11 novels and 18 nonfiction books, including) Amalie's Song, 1970 (Press Women's Nat. contest winner, 1970). Trustee Davenport Mus. Art, 1986—; mem. lit. com. Quad City Arts, Rock Island, Ill., 1999—; precinct chair Rep. Party, Davenport, 1955—60; elder St. Andrew Presbyn., 2000—. Recipient Johnson Brigham award, Iowa Libr. Assn., 1983, Isabel Bloom award for arts, Women's Achievement Bd., 1989, Author Achievement award, Friends of the Libr., 1994. Mem.: Iowa Press Women, Nat. Fedn. Press Women. Presbyterian. Avocations: playing clarinet, yoga, swimming. Home: 2802 E Locust St Davenport IA 52803 E-mail: jmcdonald@saunix.sau.edu.

MCDONALD, LARI, secondary education educator, small business owner; b. Oak Forest, Ill., June 16, 1928; d. Haskell Laramie and Rose Veverka Laramie-Key; m. William J. McDonald, June 4, 1949 (div.); children: William James, Samuel Ellis, Arthur Thomas, Marianne Scott, Katherine Stuart. BS in Health and Phys. Edn., Ind. U., 1949; MA in Tchg., Phys. Edn. and Counseling, U. N.C., 1964-66, postgrad., 1966-74. Grad. asst., instr. health and phys. edn. U. N.C., Chapel Hill, 1964-74; sales rep. Nat. Fedn. Ind. Bus., 1980-89; rsch. dir. Family Adv. Coun. on Edn., Greensboro, N.C., 1992-98; tchr. Nat. Heritage Acad., 1998—, Greensboro Acad.-Battleground, 1998—. Rep. candidate N.C. Ho. of Reps., Greensboro, 1994, 96. Avocation: gardening.

MCDONALD, LARRY WILLIAM, neuropathologist educator; b. Louisville, May 25, 1928; s. Clifford Marion and Tessie Margaret (Higgens) McD.; m. Dorothy Ann Baumgartner, Dec. 26, 1955; children: Laura Ann (dec.), Susan Helen, Lawrence Clifford. BA, U. Calif., Berkeley, 1950; MD, Northwestern U., 1955. Resident Chgo. Wesley Meml. Hosp., 1956; resident in pathology Pondville State Hosp., Walpole, Mass., 1959-60; instr. Harvard U. Med. Sch., Boston, 1961-62; rsch. assoc. U. Calif., Berkeley, 1963-67, assoc. prof. of pathology Davis, 1968-74; prof. Wright State U., Dayton, Ohio, 1975-77; prof. neuropathology U. Ill., Chgo., 1978-94, ret., 1994, prof. emeritus, 1994—. Contbr. articles to Jour. of Neurosurgery, Lab. Investigation, Exptl. and Molecular Pathology, Am. Jour. Pathology. Capt. USAF, 1957-58. Recipient 1st place award Electron Micro Exhibit, Electron Microscopy Soc. of N.Am., 1967. Mem. Internat. Acad. Pathology, AMA (Gold Medal Hektoen award 1968), Am. Assn. Neuropathologists, Coll. Am. Pathologists. Achievements include demonstration that blood in space around the brain causes permanent reduction of internal diameter of arteries, that late effects of radiation on the brain produce changes in the walls of small blood vessels of the brain. Office: Univ Ill Dept Pathology M/C 847 1819 W Polk St Rm 446 Chicago IL 60612-7331

MCDONALD, MALCOLM WILLIS, real estate company executive; b. Mpls., Nov. 17, 1936; s. Malcolm Blanchard and Ruth Virginia (Stees) McD.; m. Judy Glynn Ballard, Aug. 22, 1959; children: Malcolm Scott, Margaret Alice, Philip Brian. BA magna cum laude with high honors and high orations, Yale Coll., 1958; MBA, Harvard U., 1960. V.p First Nat. Bank of St. Paul, 1960-77; dir., sr. v.p., trustee Space Center, Inc., St. Paul, 1977—. Adj. prof. grad. programs in mgmt. U. St. Thomas, St. Paul, 1975—94; mem. adv. bd. Firstar Bank of Minn., St. Paul, 1999—2001; bd. dirs. Scherer Bros. Lumber Co., Mpls.; vice chair adv. coun. Minn. State Bd. of Investment, St. Paul, 1982—; mem. adv. bd. Sherbrooke Capital, 2002—, Hill Monastic Manuscript Libr., St. John's U., Collegeville, Minn., 1980—97; bd. dirs. Minntech, Inc., Plymouth, 1998—2001. Mem. North Oaks Home Owners Assn., 1996; trustee, sec., chmn. audit com., investment com. Amherst H. Wilder Found., St. Paul, 1971—; trustee Bigelow & FR Bigelow Found., St. Paul, 1967-98, Lee and Rose Warner Found., 1990—, Manitou Fund, 1990—, Adelaide and Harry G. McNeely Found., St. Paul, 1980-98, Minn. State Fair Found., 2002; trustee, treas. mem., Grotto Found., St. Paul, 1980—; pres. Minn. Taxpayers Assn., 1994-96; former bd. dirs. Guthrie Theater, Minn. Orchestral Assn.; bd. dirs. Minn. State Fair Found., 2002- Mem. Mpls. Club (bd. ogvs. 2002-), Minn. Landmarks, North Oaks Golf Club, White Bear Racquet & Swim Club, Yale Club of N.Y.C., St. Paul C. of C. (Bravo awards), Colony Found., U. Club of St. Paul, Mpls. Club (bd. govs.), Phi Beta Kappa, Phi Beta Kappa Assocs., Phi Gamma Delta. Republican. Episcopalian. Avocations: physical fitness, gardening, travel, encouraging 3rd graders to read. Home: 21 E Oaks Rd North Oaks MN 55127-2527 Office: Space Center Inc 2501 Rosegate Saint Paul MN 55113-2717 E-mail: mmcdonald@spacecenterinc.com.

MCDONALD, MARIANNE, classicist; b. Chgo., Jan. 2, 1937; d. Eugene Francis and Inez (Riddle) McD.; children: Eugene, Conrad, Bryan, Bridget, Kirstie (dec.), Hiroshi. BA magna cum laude, Bryn Mawr Coll., 1958; MA, U. Chgo., 1960; PhD, U. Calif., Irvine, 1975; doctorate (hon.), Am. Coll. Greece, 1988; diploma (hon.), Am. Archaeol. Assn.; DLitt (hon.), U. Athens, 1994, U. Dublin, 1994, Aristotle U., 1997, U. Thessalonika, 1997, Nat. U. Ireland, 2001. Instr. Greek, Latin, English, mythology, cinema U. Calif., Irvine, 1975-79; founder, rsch. fellow Thesaurus Linguae Graecae Project, 1975-97. Tchg. asst. U. Calif., Irvine, 1974; vis. prof. U. Ulster, Ireland, 1997, U. Dublin, 1990--, Univ. Coll. Dublin, 1999, 2002; adj. prof. theatre U. Calif., San Diego, prof. theatre and classics, 1994--; bd. dirs. Centrum. Author: (novels) Terms for Happiness in Euripides, 1978, Semilemmatized Concordances to Euripides' Alcestis, 1977, Cyclops, Andromache, Medea, 1978, Heraclidae, Hippolytus, 1979, Hecuba, 1984, Hercules Furens, 1984, Elecra, 1984, Ion, 1985, Trojan Women, 1988, Iphigenia in Taurus, 1988, Euripides in Cinema: The Heart Made Visible, 1983; translator The Cost of Kindness and Other Fabulous Tales (Shinichi Hoshi), 1986, (chpt.) Views of Clytemnestra, Ancient and Modern, 1990, Classics and Cinema, 1990, Modern Critical Theory and Classical Literature, 1994, A Challenge to Democracy, 1994, Ancient Sun/Modern Light: Greek Drama on the Modern Stage, 1990, Star Myths: Tales of the Constellations, 1996, Sole Antico Luce Moderna, 1999, Mythology of the Zodiac: Tales of the Constellations, 2000, Antigone by Sophocles, 2000, Mythology of the Zodiac, 2000, Sing Sorrow: Classics, History, Heroines in Opera, 2001; translator: (with Michael Walton) Euripides Andromache, 2001; editor: (with M. McDonald and Michael Walton) Six Greek Tragedies, 2002; editor(with Michael Walton): Amid Our Troubles: Irish Versions of Greek Tragedy, 2002. Bd. dirs. Am. Coll. of Greece, 1981-90, Scripps Hosp., 1981, Am. Sch. Classical Studies, 1986—; mem. bd. overseers U. Calif., San Diego, 1985—; nat. bd. advisors Am. Biog. Inst., 1982—; pres. Soc. for the Preservation of the Greek Heritage, 1990—; founder Hajime Mori Chair for Japanese Studies, U. Calif., San Diego, 1985, McDonald Ctr. for Alcohol and Substance Abuse, 1984, Thesaurus Linguarum Hiberniae, 1991—, Hiroshi McDonald Mori Performing Arts Ctr. Recipient Ellen Browning Scripps Humanitarian award, 1975, Disting. Svc. award U. Calif.-Irvine, 1982, 2001, Irvine medal, 1987; named one of the Cmty. Leaders Am., 1979-80, Philanthropist of Yr., 1985, Headliner San Diego Press Club, 1985, Philanthropist of Yr. Honorary Nat. Conf. Christians and Jews, 1986, Woman of Yr. AHEPA, 1988, San Diego Woman of Distinction, 1990, Woman of Yr. AXIOS, 1991; recipient Bravissimo gold medal San Diego Opera, 1990, Gold Medal Soc. Internationalization of Greek Lang., 1990, Athens medal, 1991, Piraeus medal, 1991, award Desmoi, 1992, award Hellenic Assn. of Univ. Women, 1992, Acad. of Achievement award AHEPA, 1992, Woman of Delphi award European Cultural Crr. Delphi, 1992, Civis Universitatis award U. Calif., San Diego, 1993, Hypatia award Hellenic U. Women, 1993, Am.-Ireland Fund Heritage award, 1994, Contribution to Greek Letters award Aristotle U. Thessaloniki, 1994, Mirabella Mag. Readers Choice One of 1000 Women for the Nineties, 1994, citations from U.S. Congress and Calif. Senate, Alexander the Gt. award Hellenic Cultural Soc., 1995, made hon. citizen of Delphi and gold medal of the Amphiktuonon, Del. Bus. award for Fine Arts San Diego Bus. Jour., 1995, Vol. of Decade Women's Internat. Ctr., 1994, 96, Gold Star award San Diego Arts League, 1997, Golden Aeschylus award Inst. Nat. Drama Antkg. Siracusa, 1998, Women Who Mean Bus., Fine Arts award San Diego Bus. Jour., 1998, Fulbright award, 1999, Ellis Island award, 1999, Spirit of Scripps award 1999; Theatre Excellence award KPBS Patte, 2001, Laud and Laurels, U. Calif. Disting. Alumni award. Mem. MLA, AAUP, Am. Philol. Assn. (disting. svc. award 1999), Soc. for the Preservation of the Greek Heritage (pres.), Libr. of Am., Am. Classical League, Philol. Assn. Pacific Coast, Am. Comparative Lit. Assn., Modern and Classical Lang. Assn. So. Calif., Hellenic Soc. (coun. award 2000), Calif. Fgn. Lagn. Tchrs. Assn., Internat. Platform Assn., Royal Irish Acad., Greece's Order of the Phoenix (commdr. 1994), KPBS Producers Club, Hellenic Univ. Club (bd. dir.). Avocations: karate, harp (medieval), skiing, diving. Home: PO Box 929 Rancho Santa Fe CA 92067-0929 Office: U Calif at San Diego Dept Theatre La Jolla CA 92093 E-mail: mmcdonald@ucsd.edu.

MCDONALD, MARK DOUGLAS, electrical engineer; b. Princeton, N.J., Aug. 3, 1958; s. James Douglas and Jacquelyn (Milligan) McD.; m. Patricia Joann Watson, Sept. 12, 1980. BSE, Duke U.; MS, N.C. State U. Product engr. Exide Electronics, Raleigh, N.C., 1981-84; rsch. asst. N.C. State U., 1985-86; mem. tech. staff Avantek (Hewlett Packard), Newark, 1987-90; prin. engr. Nat. Semiconductor, Santa Clara, 1990-92, engring. project mgr., 1992-95; design engring. mgr. Linear Tech. corp., Milpitas, 1995—2001; dir. RF/Analog Bermai Inc, Palo Alto, 2001—. Session chmn. Wireless Symposium, Santa Clara, 1993—, RF and Microwave Applications Conf., Santa Clara, 1992; mem. com. Symposium on VLSI Circuits Program, 1995-97. Contbr. articles to profl. jours. Precinct capt. various polit. campaigns, Fremont, Calif., 1988. Mem. IEEE (sr.), Cairn Terrier Club of No. Calif. (asst. chairperson 1995, specialty show chairperson 1996-97, bd. govs. 1996-99), Cairn Terrier Club Am., Cairn Terrier Club Ctrl. Calif., No. Calif. Terrier Assn. (bd. govs. 2002--). Achievements include U.S. and foreign patents in area of high-speed analog circuits; designed front-end integrated circuits in first wireless digital European cordless telecomm. transceiver (DECT) for voice comm.; design of first selective frequency trip circuit for parallel uninterruptible power supplies; ownership of # 1 Cairn Terrier in the world. Office: Bermai 410 Cambridge Ave 2d Fl Palo Alto CA 94306

MCDONALD, MARY ANN MELODY, investment management executive; b. Sandwich, Ill., Apr. 30, 1944; d. Theodore Harvey and Sarah Elizabeth (Irving) Larson; m. John G. McDonald, June 19, 1973. MusM, New England Conservatory, 1970; studied with Nadia Boulanger, Paris, 1971; MusD, Stanford U., 1975; MBA, Harvard U., 1986. Credit analyst Wells Fargo Bank, San Francisco, 1976-77, loan officer, 1977-79, asst. v.p., 1979-80; chmn. bd. dirs. Cornwall Corp., Stanford, Calif., 1980-84; dir. client svcs. RCM Capital Mgmt., San Francisco, 1986-92, ptnr., 1988-98, mng. dir., 1998—. Active Ill. Youth Commn., 1963-66. Recipient Rockefeller grantee Oberlin (Ohio) Coll. 1967; winner Miss Boston-Miss Am. Pageant, 1968. Mem. Senatorial Inner Cir. (life), Stanford Alumni Assn., Harvard Alumni Assn., Lincoln Club, Sigma Alpha Iota, Kappa Delta (Telford Cup). Republican. Lutheran. Office: DRCM Capital Mgmt 4 Embarcadero Ctr Ste 3100 San Francisco CA 94111-4106

MCDONALD, MARY HELEN, special education educator; b. Killeen, Tex., Jan. 21, 1953; d. Eugene W. and Shirley A. (Clem) Toifl; m. Randy C. McDonald, Feb. 26, 1972; children: Brent McDonald, Mistie McDonald Boyle. BA, U. Tex. San Antonio, 1980; MA, Incarnate Word U., 1990. Cert. tchr. spl. edn. adminstrn., Tex. Tchr. Concordia Luth., San Antonio, 1980-88; tchr., adminstr. Northside Ind. Sch. Dist., 1989-97; spl. edn. adminstrn. N.E. Ind. Sch. Dist., 1997—, asst. prin., 1998—. Vol. Conservation Soc., San Antonio, 1985—. Mem. Zonta (mem. chair 1995—), Phi Delta Kappa (historian 1989—). Republican. Christian. Avocations: walking, reading, skydiving. Home: 23 Greens Clf San Antonio TX 78216-7879

MCDONALD, MARY M. retired lawyer; b. 1944; BA, D'Youville Coll., 1966; JD, Fordham U., 1969. Bar: NY. 1969. With Merck & Co., 1974-99, asst. gen. counsel, 1986-91, v.p., gen. counsel, 1991-99. Home: PO Box 40 Clayton NY 13624-0040

MCDONALD, MICHAEL DENNIS, health products executive; b. New Haven, Dec. 22, 1955; s. Vincent Paul and Zaida (McKenzie) McD.; m. Barbara Story, July 4, 1986; children: Mikayla Zaida, Kenzie Marijka. BA, U. Calif., San Diego, 1981; MPH, U. Calif., Berkeley, 1983, DrPH, 1995. Bus. mgr. Softshell Surfboards, San Diego, 1977-80; exec. prodr. Video Echo, Berkeley, 1982-84; pres., prodr., developer, designer, rschr. Windom Health Enterprises, 1982-99; chmn. bd. Health Ctrl., 1999—; pres. Global Health Initiatives, Inc., 1995—. Bd. dirs. Comms. and Computer Applications in Pub. Health, Berkeley, 1984-86; dir. health and human ecology div. Environ. Scis. and Policy Inst., 1987-92; cons. Nat. Cancer Inst., Nat. Rsch. and Edn. Network, U.S. Office Disease Prevention and Health Promotion, 1985-89, Pub. Health Leadership Inst., Sun Microsystems, City and County of San Francisco, Macro Internat., Birch & Davis; dir. health and telecomms. Koop Found., Inc., 1994-97. Patentee in plastics and hydrodynamics. Primary health care worker Berkeley Community Health Project, 1982-87. Recipient Future of Health Tech. award, 1998; grantee U. Calif. Grad. Assembly, 1982, Pacific Bell, 1988. Mem. Am. Assn. for Med. Systems and Informatics, Am. Pub. Health Assn., Calif. Pub. Health Assn. (bd. dirs. 1983-84), Soc. for Prospective Medicine, Videotex Industry Assn., U. Calif. Alumni Assn., Cosmos Club. Avocations: surfing, tennis, aquaculture, boating. Office: Global Health Initiatives Inc 10604 Crossing Creek Rd Potomac MD 20854-4205

MCDONALD, MICHAEL LEE, clinic administrator, retired naval officer; b. Salt Lake City, Oct. 23, 1949; s. Jack Alex and Dorothy Elsie (Mantle) McD.; m. Celia McKean Smoot, June 23, 1975; children: Sarah Lynn, Michelle Elise, AnnMarie, Jeffrey Michael, Matthew David, Emily Jane. BA, U. Utah, 1973; MA, U. Iowa, 1977. Commd. ensign USN, 1975; advanced through grades to comdr., 1991; patient adminstr. Naval Hosp., Great Lakes, Ill., 1977-80, Oakland, Calif., 1980-82; med. recruiter Navy Recruiting Dist., San Francisco, 1982-84; adminstr. Navy Environ. and Preventative Medicine Unit # 7, Naples, Italy, 1984-87; staff officer Navy Med. Commd. Europe, London, 1987-89; healthcare advisor U.S. Naval Forces Europe, 1989-91; exec. officer Naval Med. Clinic, Seattle, 1991-93, commdg. officer, 1993-94; officer in charge Branch Med. Clinic, Everett, Wash., 1994-96; ret., 1996; clinic adminstr. Medalia Healthcare, 1996—, Providence Med. Group, 1999—. Coach Northshore Little League, Bothell, Wash., 1992-93; scoutmaster Boy Scouts Am., Dublin, Calif., 1981-85, instl. sponsor, Naples, Italy, 1985-87; bd. dirs. North Bothell Little League, 1998—. Fellow Am. Coll. Healthcare Execs. Mem. LDS Ch. (bishop). Avocations: golf, basketball, English literature, cycling. Home and Office: 19225 4th Dr SE Bothell WA 98012-7013 E-mail: michael.mcdonald@swedish.org.

MCDONALD, MICHAEL SCOTT, lawyer; b. Ft. Stockton, Tex., Feb. 6, 1962; s. Roland R. and Harriett L. McD.; m. Sara; children: Matthew, Michael. BA, U. Tex., El Paso, 1984; JD, U. Tex., Austin, 1987. Bar: Tex. 1987, U.S. Ct. Appeals (5th and 10th cirs.), U.S. Dist. Ct. (all dists.) Tex. With Littler Mendelson, Dallas; shareholder Littler, Mendelson. Co-author, editor: Chapter 9, The 1999 National Employer; The Texas Employer; contbg. editor Covenants Not to Compete-A State by State Survey, 1995—, Employee Duty of Loyalty, 1995—, Trade Secrets - A State by State Survey, 1998—; contbr. articles to profl. jours. Mem. ABA (litigation sect., labor and employment law sect.), Tex. Bar Assn. (labor and employment law sect.), Tex. Assn. Bus., Dallas Bar Assn. (employment law sect., chmn. 2000, exec. com. 1994-2001). Office: Littler Mendelson 2001 Ross Ave Ste 2600 Dallas TX 75201-2931

MCDONALD, PATRICK ALLEN, lawyer, arbitrator, educator; b. Detroit, May 11, 1936; s. Lawrence John and Estelle (Maks) Mc D.; m. Margaret Mercier, Aug. 10, 1963; children: Michael Lawrence, Colleen Marie, Patrick Joseph, Timothy, Margaret, Thomas, Maureen. PhB cum laude, U. Detroit, 1958, JD magna cum laude, 1961; LLM (E. Barrett Prettyman Trial scholar, Hugh J. Fegan fellow), Georgetown U., 1962. Bar: D.C. 1961, Mich. 1961, Colo. 1993. Case worker Dept. Pub. Welfare, Detroit, 1958; field examiner NLRB, 1961; practiced in Washington, 1961-62; trial cons. NIH, Bethesda, Md., 1962; staff judge adv. USAF, France, 1962-65; ptnr. Monagham, LoPrete, Mc Donald, Yakima & Grenke, Detroit, 1965—. Bd. dirs., past chmn. Delta Dental Plan of Mich.; past chmn. Delta Dental Plan of Ohio; bd. dirs., v.p. Guest House, Lake Orion, Mich., Rochester, Minn., Detroit Athletic Club, Brighton Hosp.; instr. polit. sci. and law U. Md., 1963-65, U. Detroit Law Sch., adj. prof., 1965—. Co-author: Law and Tactics in Federal Criminal Cases, 1963. Mem. Detroit Bd. Edn., 1966-76, pres.; sec., trustee Mt. Elliott Cemetary Assn.; mem. U. Detroit Sports Hall of Fame; mem. adv. bd. Providence Hosp., Southfield, Mich.; exec. bd. U. Detroit Pres.'s Cabinet. Named one of Five Outstanding Young Men of Mich., Outstanding Young Man of Detroit. Mem. ABA, Detroit Bar Assn., State Bar Mich. (commr.), U. Detroit Alumni Assn. (bd. dirs.), Mensa, Blue Key, Alpha Phi Omega (pres. Eta Pi chpt. 1955), Alpha Sigma Nu (v.p. 1960). Home: 13066 Lashbrook Ln E Brighton MI 48114-6002 Office: 40700 Woodward Ave Bloomfield Hills MI 48304-2211 *In the field of law, as an attorney, professor and arbitrator, I have prayed and attempted to be able in argument, accurate in analysis, correct in conclusion, candid with clients, honest with adversaries, and responsible for obligations assigned to me. I have advocated moderation in all things with the exception of my love for Him who created me.*

MCDONALD, PAUL KIMBALL, lawyer, investment executive; b. Worcester, Mass., June 8, 1932; s. Irving Thomas McDonald and Marie Agnes Haggerty; m. Sally Lou Kirkendall, Oct. 26, 1957; children: Katrina Louise Greenly, Linda Marie Bennett, Heidi Ann Bishop. AB, Harvard U., 1953, LLB, 1956, JD, 1957. Asst. to pres. W.R. Grace & Co., N.Y.C., 1956-65; pres. Paul McDonald & Co., 1965-89. Bd. dirs. several corps. Trustee St. Vincent's Hosp., N.Y.C., 1967-74, N.Y. Foundling Hosp., 1967-74, others. Home: 128 Cutler Rd Greenwich CT 06831-2511

MCDONALD, PEGGY ANN STIMMEL, retired automobile company official; b. Darbyville, Ohio, Aug. 25, 1931; d. Wilbur Smith and Bernice Edna (Hott) Stimmel; m. George R. Stich, Mar. 7, 1953 (dec.); 1 child, Mark Stephen (dec.); m. Joseph F. McDonald Jr., Feb. 1, 1986 (dec.). Missionary diploma with honor, Moody Bible Inst., 1952; BA in Econs. cum laude (scholar), Ohio Wesleyan U., 1965; MBA with distinction, Xavier U., 1977. Lic. capt. USCG. Missionary in S.Am. Evang. Alliance Mission, 1956-61; cost acct. Western Electric Co., 1965-66; acctg. mgr. Ohio Wesleyan U., 1966-73; fin. specialist NCR Corp., 1973-74, systems analyst, 1974-75, supr. inventory planning, 1975, mgr. material planning and purchasing control, 1976-78; materials mgr. U.S. Elec. Motors Co., 1978; with Gen. Motors Corp., 1978-92, shift supt. materials Ga., 1979-80, gen. ops. supr. material data base mgmt. Ctrl. Office Warren, Mich., 1980, dir. material mgmt. GM Truck and Bus divsn. Balt., 1980-91; dir. edn. and tng. GM Truck and Bus, Linden, N.J., 1991-92; ret., 1992. Founder Creaciones Peggy Sport Jeans Mfg., Venezuela, 1993; vis. lectr. Inst. Internat. Trade, Jiao Tong U., Shanghai, China, 1985, Inst. Econs. and Fgn. Trade, Tianjin, China, 1986-87; part time instr. Towson (Md.) State U., 1986-87. Founder, pres. Capt.'s Challenge Corp., Global Christian Ministry of Econ. Devel., 1998; mem. 1st United Meth. Ch., Dunedin, Fla.; vol. missionary/tchr. Susana Wedey Instn. with Missionary Meth. Ch., Bogota, Colombia, 2000-2001. Mem. AAUW, Am. Prodn. and Inventory Control Soc., Am. Soc. Women Accts., Balt. Exec. Women's Network, Balt. Coun. on Fgn. Rels. Methodist. Avocation: sailing. Home: PO Box 884 Sarasota FL 34236 E-mail: jpmcdonald@ozline.net.

MCDONALD, PEYTON DEAN, brokerage house executive; b. Kansas City, Kans., Feb. 6, 1936; s. Charles H. and Myra (Miller) McD.; m. Frances B. Beighley, June 14, 1958; children: Peyton D., Todd B. BS, Bucknell U., 1958. Sales rep. Sprout Waldron and Co., Inc., Muncy, Pa., 1958-67; v.p. Blair & Co., Williamsport, 1967-69; v.p., mgr. Hugh Johnson, 1969-77, E.F. Hutton & Co. Inc., Williamsport, 1977-87; sr. v.p. Smith Barney, 1987—. Mem. N.Y. Stock Exchange; pres. Hope Enterprises. Pres. United Way, Williamsport, 1977-80, Pa. Coll. Found., 1985-86; campaign chmn. Heinz for Senator, Lycoming County, Pa., 1978, 96; bd. dirs., treas. Divine Providence Hosp., chmn.; mem. Susquehanna Health Care Bd. 1st lt. U.S. Army, 1958-59. Mem. Ross Club, Williamsport Country Club, Farmington Country Club, Masons. Republican. Presbyterian. Avocation: golf. Home: 1545 Grampian Blvd Williamsport PA 17701-1917

MCDONALD, REGINALD ADRIAN, musician, educator; b. Columbus, Ohio, Mar. 16, 1968; s. Charlie Alf McDonald, Jr. and Muriel Paulette McDonald; m. Coretta Craddock, July 14, 2000; m. Mia Rochelle Bell, Sept. 7, 1991 (div. Sept. 22, 1995). BA Music Ed., Ala. State Univ., Montgomery, AL, 1991; M. Music, State Univ. West Ga., Carrollton, GA, 1997. Cert. Education Specialist Clark Atlanta Univ., 2002. Band dir. McNair Mid. Sch., College Park, Ga., 1991—96; band dir./music dept. chair SW DeKalb H.S., Decatur, 1996—2001; assoc. dir. of bands/asst. music prof. Tenn. State Univ., Nashville, 2001. Saxophone/clarinet clinician Precision Camp, Inc., Atlanta, 1996—2001; band cons. Milestone, Inc., Atlanta, 1996—2001; band adjudicator/clinician Ga. Music Educators Assn., Atlanta, 1995—; assoc. condr. Tenn. State Univ., Nashville, 2002—. Pres. student govt. Albama State Univ., Montgomery, Ala., 1990; saxophonist/mem. Ga. Afro-American All-Star Band, Atlanta, 1994—99. Recipient Tchr. of the Yr., McNair Mid. Sch., Coll. Pk., GA, 1996-1997, Expert Tchr. Citation, Fulton County Bd. of Edn., Atlanta, GA, 1996, Medal of Excellence, Coll. Pk. Bus. Cmty. Mem.: Alpha Phi Alpha, Inc., Music Educators Nat. Conf., Phi Mu Alpha Sinfonia (pres. delta beta 1988—90). Democrat-Npl. Methodist. Avocations: golfing, golfing. Home: 1420 Brentwood Terrace Nashville TN 37211 Office: Tennessee State Univ 3500 John A Merritt Blvd Nashville TN 37209 Home Fax: 615-963-5351. Personal E-mail: mcdonaldreginald@hotmail.com.

MCDONALD, ROBERT DELOS, manufacturing company executive; b. Dubuque, Iowa, Jan. 30, 1931; s. Delos Lyon and Virginia (Kolck) McD.; m. Jane M. Locher, Jan. 16, 1960 (div. Jan. 1970); children: Jean, Patricia, Maria, Sharon, Rob; m. Marilyn I. Miller, July 4, 1978. BA in Econs., U. Iowa, 1953. With A.Y. McDonald Mfg. Co., Dubuque, 1956—, salesman, 1956-60, sales mgr., 1961-64, mgr. Dubuque wholesale br., 1965-72, v.p., 1971-72, v.p., corp. sec., 1972-83, sr. v.p., corp. sec., 1983-85, pres., 1985-95, chmn. bd., 1987—, CEO, 1987-2001, also bd. dirs., 1964—. Bd. dirs. Brock-McVey Co., Lexington, Ky.; sr. v.p., bd. dirs. A.Y. McDonald Industries, Inc., Dubuque, 1983—; chmn. bd., A.Y.M. Inc., Albia, Iowa, 1988—; pres., CEO, 1988-2001. Trustee, bd. dirs. A.Y. McDonald Mfg. Co. Charitable Found., 1978—, pres., 1982—; bd. dirs. Stonehill Care Ctr., Dubuque, 1984-92, chmn. bd., 1991-92; mem. Stonehill Renovation and Financing Task Force, 1994-97; bd. dirs. Boys and Girls Club of Greater Dubuque, 1989—, Dubuque Bank & Trust Co., 1994—, Save Iowa's Civil War Monument Restoration Fund, 1995—, Dubuque County Hist. Soc., 1996—, Grand Opera House Found., 1997—, Terrace Hill Found., 1997—; bd. govs. Iowa Coll. Found., 1997-2001; trustee United Way Svcs., Inc., Dubuque, 1989—; bd. dirs. Stonehill Benevolent Found., Dubuque, 1998-2000, vice chmn., 1989-92; mem. regional adv. coun. SBA, Cedar Rapids, 1984-89; mem. adv. bd. Jr. Achievement Tri-States, Inc., 1991—, Iowa State Fair Blue Ribbon Found., 1993—. Lt. USNR, 1953-56, Korea. Mem. Am. Mgmt. Assn., Am. Supply Assn., Am. Water Works Assn., Nat. Assn. Mfrs., Dubuque Area C. of C., Am. Legion, Dubuque Shooting Soc., Dubuque Golf and Country Club, Sigma Alpha Epsilon. Republican. Roman Catholic. Home: Fountain Hill 3399 Eagle Point Dr Dubuque IA 52001-8320 Office: AY McDonald Mfg Co PO Box 508 Dubuque IA 52004-0508

MCDONALD, ROBERT IRVING, secondary education mathematics and science educator; b. Lakeland, Fla., Jan. 16, 1958; s. William Lee and Mary Frances (Emerson) McD. BS in Animal Industries, Clemson U., 1980. Cert. secondary tchr., S.C., metric specialist. Tchr., chmn. math. dept. Timmonsville (S.C.) High Sch., 1985—, also former chmn. governing bd. Mem. sch. improvement coun., mem. of writing team for Pee Dee Math. Curriculum, Grades K-8; also sports coach. Mem. Nat. Coun. Tchrs. Math., Math. Assn. Am., S.C. Sci. Coun. Avocations: fishing, golf, photography. Home: PO Box 701 Lamar SC 29069-0701 Office: Timmonsville High Sch Market St Ext Timmonsville SC 29161

MCDONALD, ROBERT WAYNE, cardiac sonographer; b. Butte, Mont., Dec. 16, 1958; s. Clyde Wayne and Stella Mary (Radonich) McD.; m. Mary Jo Rice, Aug. 9, 1986. AAS, Spokane C.C., 1983. Registered cardiovascular technologist. Staff cardiac sonographer Oreg. Health Scis. U., Portland, 1983-88, supr., cardiac sonographer, 1988-91, sr. cardiac sonographer, 1991—. Cons. Oreg. Regional Primate Rsch. Ctr., Beaverton, 1991—; cons., adj. faculty, clin. preceptor, Spokane C.C., 1984—; instr., clin. preceptor Seattle U., 1984-95. Editor-in-chief Pediat. Ultrasound Today, 1995-2001; editl. bd./reviewer Jour. Am. Soc. Echocardiography, 1994-98. Mem. dist. coun. Boy Scouts Am., Portland, 1991—, advancement chmn. Pioneer dist., 1994-97, process and rev. vice chmn. Cascade Pacific coun., 1995-98, dist. commr., 1997—. With U.S. Army, 1978-81. Decorated Army Commendation medal with oak leaf cluster, good conduct medal; recipient Dist. Award of Merit, Boy Scouts Am., 1993, Silver Beaver award, 2000. Mem. Am. Soc. Echocardiography (bd. dirs. 1996-99), Am. Registry of Diagnostic Med. Sonographers (registered, pediat. echo exam rep. 1996-2002), Willamette Valley Soc. Echocardiography (pres. 1991-95). Office: Oregon Health Scis Univ 3181 SW Sam Jackson Park Rd Portland OR 97201-3011 E-mail: mcdonaro@ohsu.edu.

MCDONALD, ROSA NELL, engineering executive; b. Boley, Okla., Feb. 12, 1953; d. James and Beatrice Irene (Hayes) McDonald. BS, Calif. State U., Long Beach, 1975; MBA, Calif. State U., Dominquez Hills, 1980, postgrad., 1988; BS in Computer Info. Sys., Chapman Coll., 1988. Acct. Aerospace Corp., El Segundo, Calif., 1976-77, analytical acct., 1977-79, budget analyst, 1979-81, sr. budget analyst, 1981-84, budget adminstr., 1984-86, mgr. indirect budgets, 1986-91, head budgets and pricing dept., 1991-95, dir. budgets, pricing and fin. planning, 1996—2001, ops. bus. mgr., 2001—. Vol. Youth Motivation Task Force, El Segundo, 1980—, Holiday Project, El Segundo, 1984, 1985, Recording for the Blind and Dyslexic. Named Woman of Achievement, NAACP Legal Def. Fund, 1988. Mem.: NAFE, Am. Bus. Women's Assn., Beta Gamma Sigma. Democrat. Avocations: dancing, aerobics, reading, contests. Office: 2350 E El Segundo Blvd # M1 400 El Segundo CA 90245-4609

MCDONALD, SHARON HOLLIDAY, special education educator; b. Farmington, Mo., Jan. 15, 1948; d. Charles Douglas and Edythe Murriel Holliday; m. Gayle Dean McDonald, Feb. 14, 1969; children: Leslie Douglas, Mry Elizabeth. BS in Edn., U. Mo., 1969; MS in Edn., Kans. State U., 1973. Cert. K-9 tchr., learning disabilities, behavioral disabilities, mental retardation, social studies, composition, Kans. Tchr. spl. edn. Ottumwa (Iowa) Pub. Schs., 1969, Washington (Iowa) Cmty. Schs., 1969-71, Unified Sch. Dist. 336, Holton, Kans., 1971-75, 80-81, 82—. Mem. student improvement team Jackson Heights Elem. Sch., Holton, 1999—. Sunday sch. tchr. 1st United Meth. Ch., Holton, 1991-95, mem. Lady Belles, 1993—, chmn. adminstrv. coun., 1995, del. ann. conf., 1996. Named Outstanding Nutrition Educator, Midland Dairy Coun., 1994. Mem. NEA, Coun. for Exceptional Children (cert. profl. recognized spl. educator), Kans. Edn. Assn., Holton Edn. Assn., Pilot Club (pres. Holton 1980, 2000), Delta Kappa Gamma (membership com. Holton 1998-00). Republican. Avocations: music, needlework, reading. Home: 15587 222nd Rd Holton KS 66436-1406 Office: Jackson Heights Elem Sch 12763 266th Rd Holton KS 66436-8717

MC DONALD, STEPHEN LEE, economics educator; b. Arkadelphia, Ark., Aug. 8, 1924; s. Claud Bethel and Ruth Jane (Gresham) McD.; m. Elizabeth Gene Brewer, Aug. 14, 1945; children: Martha Elizabeth Mc Donald Worchel, Kathryn Ann Mc Donald McGlothlin. BA, La. Poly. Inst., 1947; MA, U. Tex., 1948, PhD, 1951. Asst. prof. U. Tex., Austin, 1950-56, prof. econs., 1961—, Josey prof. in energy studies, 1983-85, Duncan prof. econs., 1985-94, chmn. dept., 1972-76, 78-79, 88-89, emeritus, 1997. Sr. fellow Bur. Bus. Rsch., 1990-97; economist Humble Oil & Refining Co., 1956-57; assoc. prof., prof., chmn. dept. La. State U., 1957-61; mem. faculty Stonier Grad. Sch. Banking; staff assoc., Brookings Instn., 1961-63; mem. econs. adv. panel NSF, 1962-64; cons. to govt. and industry, 1957—. Author: Federal Tax Treatment of Income from Oil and Gas, 1963, Petroleum Conservation in the United States, 1971, The Leasing of Federal Lands for Fossil Fuels Production, 1979; mem. editorial bds.: So. Econ. Journal, 1961-64, Energy Jour., 1979-86; contbr. articles to profl. jours. Served with USNR, 1943-46. Recipient Citation for Excellence Am. Bankers Assn.; Ford Found. grantee, 1964; Resources for Future grantee, 1967, 76; Pres. Assocs. award teaching excellence, 1982 Mem. Am. Econ. Assn., So. Econ. Assn. (v.p. 1969-70), Southwestern Econ. Assn. (pres. 1964-65), Internat. Assn. Energy Econs., Gamma Epsilon, Phi Kappa Phi. Democrat. Methodist. Home: 4002 Sierra Dr Austin TX 78731-3914

MCDONALD, SUSAN F. business executive, county official; b. Rockford, Ill., Jan. 18, 1961; d. John August and Jeanne (Reitsch) Floberg; m. Robert Arthur McDonald, June 19, 1981; children: Molly Jeanne, Amanda Elizabeth. AAS in Bus. Mgmt., Colo. Mountain Coll., Glenwood Springs, 1981. Teller, bookkeeper Alpine Bank, Glenwood Springs, 1981-82; teller Macktown State Bank, Rockford, 1982-83; treas., mgr., owner Roscoe (Ill.) Movie House, 1984-94; sales cons. Lou Bachroot, Inc., Rockford, 1992-93; mem. bd. suprs. Winnebago County Bd., 1992—; exec. v.p., owner Corp. Svc. Alliance, Machesney Park, Ill., 1993-95; leasing and fleet mgr. Budweiser Motors, Inc., Beloit, Wis., 1994-95; bus. mgr. Finley Oldsmobile GMC, South Beloit, Ill., 1995—. V.p. Roscoe Bus. Assn., 1989, pres., 1990, 91; chair, founder Roscoe Beautification Assn., 1991; mem. county bd. dirs. Winnebago County, 1992—, vice chmn. econ. devel. com., 1993-94, chmn. zoning com., 1997—, exec. com. mem., 1993—; chmn. econ. devel. environ. com. Winnebago County Bd., 1994—; commr. Winnebago County Forest Preserve, Rockford, 1992—, chmn. exec. com., 2001—; co-founder, bd. dirs. Very Important Pregnancy, Rockford Meml. Hosp.; bd. dirs. Family Advocate Aux., Rockford, 1987-88; bd. dirs. U. Ill. Extension Svc./Winnebago County, 1994—. Nominated Video Retailer of Yr., Am. Video Assn., 1989, Leadership award, Stateline YWCA, 1989. Mem. Assn. Fin. and Ins. Profls. (cert.) Republican. Methodist. Avocations: horseback riding, hunting and jumping equestrian activities, golfing, skiing. Office: Finley Oldsmobile GMC 1790 Gardner St South Beloit IL 61080-1424

MCDONALD, TANNY, actress; b. Princeton, Ind. d. Douglas Hewitt and Irene Elizabeth (Codding) McD.; m. Robert D. Currie, Mar. 5, 1966 (div. Mar., 1986). BA cum laude, Vassar Coll., 1958. Actress Am. Savoyards, N.Y.C. and Tour, 1961—. Actress: (film) Hercules in New York, 1970, (plays) Broadway: Fiddler on the Roof, 1964, The Lincoln Mask, 1972, Clothes for A Summer Hotel, 1980, Macbeth (First Witch and Nurse), 1988, Man of La Mancha, 1992 and nat. tour, 1996-97, Medea (Woman of Corinth), 1994; Off-Broadway: Chelsea Theater Ctr. - the Beggar's Opera, 1972, Total Eclipse, 1974, Gorky, 1975, N.Y. Shakespeare Festival - Temptation, 1989, Titus Andronicus, 1989, Hamlet (Player Queen) also Great Performances, 1995; L.O.R.T. maj. roles (select): A Little Night Music, 1977, Three Penny Opera, 1979, Pal Joey, 1980, Tintypes, 1982, A Lesson From Aloes, 1982, Cloud Nine, 1984, Heartbreak House, 1986, The Bakkhai, 1995, Orpheus Descending, 1995, House of Bernarda Alba, 1997, Vassar to Vassar Cabaret, Road to Mecca, Long Day's Journey Into Night, 1998, WIT=NYC, Jekyll & Hyde, 1999, NYC: Sitting Pretty, La Bonne Dame (George Sand) 2001; Nat. Tour Copenhagen, 2002; CBS Kate and Allie, NBC The Doctors, 1973, NCB spl. Duty Bound (Emmy award 1973). Reid Hall fellow, Paris, 1958, 59; recipient Frances Walker Prize for Excellence, Vassar Coll., 1958; named Best Actress Richmond (Va.) News Leader in 1978.

MCDONALD, THERESA BEATRICE PIERCE (MRS. OLLIE MCDONALD), church official, minister; b. Vicksburg, Miss., Apr. 11, 1929; d. Leonard C. Pierce and Ernestine Morris Templeton; m. Ollie McDonald, Apr. 23, 1966. Student, Tougaloo Coll., 1946-47, U. Chgo. Indsl. Rels. Ctr., 1963-64; BA in Sociology with deptl. honors, Roosevelt U., 1997; student, Chgo. Theol. Sem., 1997—. Ordained to Gospel Ministry, 1997. Vol. rep. Liberty Bapt. Ch., Am. Legion Aux., VA West Side Hosp., Chgo., 1971-73; nat. instr. ushers dept. Prog. Nat. Bapt. Conv. Inc., Washington, 1973-75, nat. sec. ushers dept., 1975-76, v.p. at large, 1980-82, chmn. pers. com., 1982-84; mem. faculty Congress of Christian Edn., 1978-85; mem. pub. rels. staff Liberty Bapt. Ch., Chgo., 1973-79, trustee, 1987-91; asst. Christian edn. dir. Maryland Ave. Bapt. Ch., 1995-99; assoc. min. Md. Ave. Bapt. Ch., 1997—, dir. Christian edn., 2000—. Cons., lectr. in field; guest speaker TV and radio programs. Participant White House Regional Confs., 1961. Recipient Christian Svc. award Prog. Nat. Bapt. Conv. Inc., 1986, 92, 94, Disting. Svc. award, 1990-94, Dedicated Svc. award, 1998. Mem. VFW (life mem. Hunt aux. 2024), Bethlehem Bapt. Dist. Assn. Chgo. (asst. sec. 1982-84), Ch. Women United in Greater Chgo. (Ecumenical Actions com. 1981-83), Am. Legion (Outstanding Svc. award 1972, 73), Bapt. State Conv. Ill. (life), Order Ea. Star. Address: 9810 S Calumet Ave Chicago IL 60628-1432

MCDONALD, THOMAS EDWIN, JR. electrical engineer; b. Wapanucka, Okla., June 19, 1939; s. Thomas Edwin and Rosamond Bell (Enoch) McD.; m. Myrna Kay Booth, Sept. 10, 1961; children: Stephen Thomas, Jennifer Kay, Sarah Lynn. BSEE, U. Okla., 1962, MSEE, 1963; PhDEE, U. Colo., 1969. Registered profl. engr., N.Mex. Asst. prof. elec. engring. U. Okla., Norman, 1969-70; planning engr. Okla. Gas and Electric Co., Oklahoma City, 1970-72; staff mem. Los Alamos (N.Mex.) Nat. Lab., 1972—, group leader, 1974-80, program mgr., 1980-92, program mgr. Centurion program, 1986-90, dep. program dir. inertial confinement fusion program, 1990-92, program coord. mine detection and laser tech., 1992-93; project mgr. Nat. Ctr. for Advanced Mfg. Tech., 1993-96, project leader high-speed electronic imaging tech. devel., 1996—. Adj. prof. elec. engring. U. Okla., 1970-72; cons. Los Alamos Tech. Assocs., 1980—, mgr. design sect., 1980-81. Rschr. in inertial confinement fusion, high-speed electronic imaging and neutron radiography; contbr. articles to profl. jours. Bd. dirs., mem. United Ch. Los Alamos, 1987— (chmn. fin. bd.), chmn. bd. elders, 1992. Served to capt. U.S. Army, 1963-67. Mem. IEEE (chmn. Los Alamos sect.), AAAS, Soc. for Info. Display, Soc. Photo-Optical Instrumentation Engrs., Los Alamos Gymnastics Club (treas., bd. dirs. 1980-88), Rotary (sec. Los Alamos, pres. 1999), Sigma Xi, Eta Kappa Nu. Republican. Avocation: computer science. Home: 910 Circle Dr Los Alamos NM 87544 Office: Los Alamos Nat Lab PO Box 1663 Los Alamos NM 87544-0600 E-mail: tomonridgeway@aol.com.

MCDONALD, THOMAS PAUL, controller; b. Williamsport, Pa., Aug. 13, 1949; s. Paul Tripp and Ethel Mary (Cowden) McD.; m. Debra Ann Rosamilia, July 17, 1976; children: Kevin, Gail. BS in Acctg., U. Scranton, 1971. CPA, N.Y. Auditor Coopers & Lybrand, N.Y.C., 1971-79; internal audit dir. Ward Foods, 1979-81; contr. Mallory Randall Corp., 1981-83, Sullivan & Cromwell, N.Y.C., 1983—. Mem. AICPA, N.Y. State Soc. CPAs. Avocations: golf, coaching recreational sports. Home: 34 Dawson Dr West Caldwell NJ 07006-8128 Office: Sullivan & Cromwell 125 Broad St Fl 28 New York NY 10004-2489

MCDONALD, TREVY ANN, communications educator, writer; b. Chgo., Aug. 6, 1969; d. Thomas Leonard Sr. and Juanita (Ford) McD. BA, U. Wis., Oshkosh, 1990; MA, U. N.C., Chapel Hill, 1992, PhD, 1995. Asst. prof. N.C. Ctrl. U., Durham, N.C., 1996-99. Vis. asst. prof. N.C. State U., Raleigh, 1996; announcer, prodr. Sta. WNCU-FM, Durham, 1996-99. Author: (novel) Time Will Tell, 1999; author: (with others) Getting In and Gaining Trust, 1999; co-editor: Nature of a Sistuh: Black Women's Lived Experiences in Contemporary Culture, 1999, Building Diverse Communities: Applications of Communication Research, 2000; newsletter editor Black Caucus-Nat. Comm. Assn., 1998-99. Dir. media ministry St. Joseph's A.M.E. Ch., Durham, 1993-99. Recipient Outstanding Young Alumna award U. Wis.-Oshkosh Alumni Assn., 1997. Mem. Nat. Comm. Assn., Internat. Commn. Assn., Assn. for Edn. in Journalism and Mass Comm., Am. Women in Radio and TV, Delta Sigma Theta (journalist Durham alumnae chpt. 1998-99). Methodist. Avocations: singing, film, travel, cooking. Office: PO Box 43255 Chicago IL 60643-0255 E-mail: trevy9230@aol.com.

MCDONALD, WARREN GEORGE, accountant, former savings and loan executive; b. Oakland, Calif., Feb. 14, 1939; s. George Daniel and Barbara (Sainsot) McD.; m. Roberta Anne Peterson, Apr. 27, 1968; children: Edward Bruce, Deborah Lynn. BA, San Francisco State Coll., 1962. CPA, Calif. Ptnr. Main Lafrentz & Co., CPAs, San Francisco, 1969-74; v.p., treas. Imperial Corp. Am., San Diego, 1975-80; v.p. fin. No. Calif. Savs. & Loan, Palo Alto, 1980-82; sr. v.p. fin. Unified Mortgage Co., Santa Clara, Calif., 1982-85; pres. Saratoga Savs., 1985-89; pvt. practice cons. San Francisco, 1989—. Co-author: Power Above The Law, 1990. Served to capt. USCGR. Mem. AICPA, Calif. Soc. CPAs, Inst. Mgmt. Accts., Res. Officers Assn., Naval Inst., Navy League. Home: 1430 Wendy Way Menlo Park CA 94025-6022

MCDONALD, WILLIAM BRICE, educational association administrator; b. Greenville, Ky., June 16, 1957; s. James Marlin and Joyce Rudale (Cox) M. BS in Polit. Sci., Loyola U., Chgo., 1976, MA in Internat. Rels., 1973; MA in Media, Northeastern U., Chgo., 1985; postgrad., Northwestern U., 1993; DD, St. Johns, Saskatchewan, 1995. Tchr. Chgo. Pub. Schs., 1967-69, libr., 1969-85; coordinator Edn. Service Ctr. 6, 1986-92; coord. Bur. of Librs. Chgo.

Pub. Schs., 1992—; CEO Pax Vobiscum, Inc., 1993—. Cons. bd. examiners Chgo. Pub. Schs., 1987; judge, participant Ill. Young Authors, Chgo., 1987-99; advisor Chgo. Tchrs. Libr. Assn., 1988; advisor High Sch. Libr. Media Assn., 1988, treas., 1992—; treas. Chgo. Libr. Club, 1992—; bd. dirs. No. Ill. U. Children's Lit. Inst., 1992-99; edn. cons., 2001—. Author: Alliance for Progress, 1981, Library Networking, 1985, Illinois School Library Media Program Guidelines, 1992. Del. Chgo. Tchrs. Union, 1968-81; bd. dirs. McDonald Charitable Trust, 2002—. George M. Pullman Found. scholar, Chgo., 1966, Kiwanis Internat. scholar, Chgo., 1974, State of Ill. scholar, Chgo., 1978; grantee Northeastern U., Chgo., 1984. Mem. Oriental Inst. Chgo., Breasted Soc., Am. Rsch. Ctr. Egypt (life), Citizens Sch. Com., Friends Chgo. Pub. Libr., Newberry Libr. Assocs., Soc. Sch. Librs. Internat. (nominating com.), Ill. Libr. Assn. (bd. dirs. 1990-92, north cen. evaluation team 1992), Ill. Coalition Libr. Advisors, Assn. Supervision and Curriculum Devel. (Midwest authors selection com. 1993, Chgo. Pub. Libr.-Chgo. Pub. Schs. task force com. 1992—), Children's Reading Roundtable (bd. dirs. 1992—). Avocations: bibliophile, archeology, philately. Home: 3750 N Lake Shore Dr Apt 9D Chicago IL 60613-4233 Office: CPS Bur Libr 1819 W Pershing Rd Chicago IL 60609-2300 also: Pax Vobiscum Inc 1820 Campbell La Salle IL 61301

MCDONALD, WILLIAM HENRY, financial executive; b. Ottawa, Ont., Can., Sept. 8, 1924; s. Joseph and Constance Mary (Gordon) McD.; m. D. Gwen Selkirk, July 8, 1950; 1 child, Barbara Elaine. Grad. high sch. Credit and operating mgr. B.F. Goodrich Co., Winnipeg, Man., Can., 1945-49; fin. adminstrn. officer Govt. Can., Ottawa, 1949-55; asst. gen. mgr. mortgages Bank of N.S., 1955-66; mng. dir. Boyd Stott & McDonald Ltd., Toronto, Ont., 1966-79; exec. v.p., dir. Morguard Trust Co., 1966-74; chmn. bd. Can. Comml. Bank, Toronto, 1976-81, chmn. exec. com., 1981-84; chmn. bd. Can. Comml. Bank Mortgage Investment Corp., 1983-84; pres., CEO, dir. Boyd Stott and McDonald Techs., Ltd., 1984—. Pres. Thornton McDonald Assocs., Inc. Mem. bd. govs. J. Douglas Ferguson Hist. Research Found., 1971—. Served with RCNVR, 1943-45. Mem. Can. Paper Money Soc. (hon. pres.), Internat. Bank Note Soc. (life), Can. Credit Inst., Classical & Medieval Numismatic Soc. (exec. sec.). Conservative. Anglican. Office: PO Box 956 Sta B Willowdale ON Canada M2K 2T6 E-mail: billmcdo@idirect.com.

MCDONALD, WILLIAM HENRY, lawyer; b. Niangua, Mo., Feb. 27, 1946; s. Milburn and Fannie M. McDonald; m. Janice E. Robinson, July 13, 1968; children: Melissa L., Meghan M. BS in Pub. Adminstrn., Southwest Mo. State U., 1968; JD, U. Mo., 1971. Bar: Mo. 1971, U.S. Dist. Ct. (we. dist.) Mo. 1973, U.S. Supreme Ct. 1978, U.S. Ct. Appeals (8th cir.) 1982. Ptnr., pres. Woolsey, Fisher, Whiteaker & McDonald, PC, 1973-95; pres. William H. McDonald & Assocs., PC, Springfield, Mo., 1995—. Chmn. blue ribbon task force on Delivery of Mental Health Services to Southwest Mo., Mo. Commn. Continuing Legal Edn.; pres. Tan Oaks Homeowners Assn.; mem. fin. com. Child Adv. Council, Rep. Nat. Com., Mo. Rep. Com., Greene County Nat. Com.; active various Southwest Mo. State U. Clubs; bd. dirs. Greene County div. Am. Heart Assn., Ozarks regional Am. Athletic Union Jr. Olympics; pres., bd. dirs. Springfield Little Theatre; v.p. pub. affairs Springfield Area C. of C., bd. dirs., 1995-98. Capt. U.S. Army, 1971-73. Named one of Outstanding Young Men Am., 1978, 81, Outstanding Young Men Springfield, 1980. Fellow ABA (life, antitrust and litigation and torts and ins. sects.); mem. ATLA, Fed. Bar Assn., Mo. Bar Assn. (chmn. spol. com. on mandatory continuing edn., various coms., Pres.'s award 1986), Mo. Assn. Trial Attys. (bd. govs. 1998-2001), Springfield Met. Bar Assn. (bd. dirs., chmn. pub. edn. speakers bur.), Met. Bar Assn. St. Louis, Def. Rsch. Inst., Am. Judicature Soc., Am. Bd. Trial Advs. (state coord.), Nat. Bd. Trial Advs., Am. Coll. Barristers, Million Dollar Forum, 31st Jud. Cir. Bar Com. (chmn.), Supreme Ct. Hist. Soc., U. Mo.-Kansas City Sch. Law Found., Springfield Claims Assn. (pres.), U.S. Cavalry Assn., Am. Legion, 1st Inf. Divsn. Soc., K.T., Beta Omega Tau, Kappa Epsilon. Presbyterian. Home: 4857 E Royal Dr Springfield MO 65809-2425

MCDONALD, WYLENE BOOTH, former nurse, pharmaceutical sales professional; b. Kinston, N.C., Sept. 29, 1956; d. Wiley Truett and Hilda Grey (Brinson) Booth; m. Robert H. McDonald; stepchildren: Stephanie Lynn, Robin Leigh. BSN, Barton Coll., 1979; MSN, East Carolina U., 1984. Pub. health nurse Sampson Co. Health Dept., Clinton, N.C., 1979-81; pub. health coord. New Hanover Co. Health Dept., Wilmington, 1981-83; med. ctr. liaison Cape Fear Valley Med. Ctr., Fayetteville, 1984-85; profl. sales rep. Merck, Human Health Div., West Point, Pa., 1985-88; hosp. specialist sales rep. Human Health divsn. Merck, 1988-90, sr. prostate health specialist rep., 1990-94, exec. cardiovascular specialist, 1995—. exec. specialty rep., 1997-98, exec. hosp. specialist, 1998-2001, bus. mgr., 2001—. Speaker Coastal Area Perinatal Assn., 1983, Career Week, U. N.C. Sch. Bus., Wilmington, 1987, 88, 89, 93. Fundraiser March of Dimes, Fayetteville, 1987, Wilmington, 1991, Am. Heart Assn., Wilmington, 1991-93. Named one of Outstanding Young Women of Am., 1981. Mem. ANA, AAUW, N.C. Nurses Assn., N.C. Pub. Health Assn., Sigma Theta Tau. Avocations: exercising, biking, reading, traveling. Home and Office: 108 Seapath Est Wrightsville Beach NC 28480-1964

MCDONALD RACKLEY, COLLETTE LYNN, management consultant; b. N.Y.C., Nov. 21, 1966; d. Robert Louis and Catherine L. (Morris) McD.; m. Richard Rackley, Jr., Sept. 2, 1989; 1 child, Richard III. Student, U. Tenn., 1984, Ga. State U., 1985, 87. Account mgmt. coord. Hutchenshutze Advt., Atlanta, 1987-89; office mgr., exec. asst. to pres., CEO ACT III Broadcasting, Inc., 1989-92; mktg. asst. Price Waterhouse, LLP, 1992, mktg. programs specialist, 1992-93; market rsch. analyst Coopers & Lybrand LLP, 1993, sr. assoc., mktg. rsch. and programs, 1994-96; sr. assoc. new bus. devel. and mktg. comms. Hartsfield Group, 1996; project mgr., sr. cons. Innovative Search Group, LLP, 1996; dir. of rsch. Egon Zehnder Internat., 1996—. Cons., advisor B&C Travel, Inc., College Park, Ga., 1995—, RCR Cons., Atlanta, 1996—. Mem. Nat. Black MBA Assn., Am. Mktg. Assn., Soc. Human Resource Mgmt., Soc. Competitive Intelligence Profls., Exec. Search Roundtable, NAFE. Democrat. Mem. World Changers Ch. Internat. Avocations: Internet, travel, non-fiction. Office: Egon Zehnder Internat 3475 Piedmont Rd NE # 1900 Atlanta GA 30305-2987 E-mail: cmrackley@mailexcite.com.

MCDONALD-WEST, SANDI MACLEAN, headmaster, consultant; b. Lowell, Mass., May 8, 1930; d. Walter Allan and Celina Louise (Lalime) MacLean; m. Thomas D. McDonald, Sept. 8, 1951 (div.); children: Todd F., Brooke Goodfriend, Ned M., Reid A., Heather McDonald McLean. BA, DePauw U., 1951; MA, Fairleigh Dickinson U., 1966; MEd, North Tex. State U., 1980. Cert. in Montessori teaching. Tchr., adminstr. Hudson (Ohio) Montessori Sch., 1966-68, Berea (Ohio) Montessori Sch., 1968-70, Creative Learning Ctr., Dallas, 1970-71; tchr., head of lower sch. The Selwyn Sch., Denton, Tex., 1971-83; tchr., headmaster Cimarron Sch., Enid, Okla., 1983-87; cons. Corpus Christi (Tex.) Montessori Sch., 1987-89, Azlann-Eren Horn Montessori Sch., Denton, 1989-95, Highland Meadow Montessori Acad., Southlake, Tex., 1994-2001. Ednl. dir., pres. Southwestern Montessori Tchg. Ctr., Inc., Denton, 1974—; adj. prof. North Tex. State U., Denton, 1979-80; cons., lectr. Am. Montessori Soc., N.Y.C., 1970—, Japanese Montessori Soc., 1978—, also pub. and pvt. schs., 1972—; chair commn. for accreditation Montessori Accreditation Coun. Tchr. Edn., 1991-97, chair emerita, 1997—. Developer various Montessori materials; contbr. articles to profl. jours. Mem. Am. Montessori Soc. (life), No. Ohio Montessori Assn. (pres. 1968-70), Assn. Montessori Internat., N.Am. Montessori Tchrs. Assn., LWV, Concerned Scientists. Avocations: ecology, golf, reading, travel. Home: 2005 Marshall Rd Denton TX 76207-3316 E-mail: swest4smtc@aol.com.

MCDONELL, EDWIN DOUGLAS, information systems executive, consultant, writer; b. Johnson City, N.Y., Aug. 16, 1953; s. Alexander Edwin and Loretta Arlene (Terry) McD; m. Katherine A. Mandusic (div. 1994); m. Lizabeth L. Marks, Feb. 14, 1998; children: Elizabeth Ashley, Stephanie Allyn. BA in English Lit., U. Cin., 1976; MSLS in Info. Sci., Case Western Reserve U., 1978; MBA in Mgmt. Info. Systems, Ind. U., 1983. Assoc. Crowe Chizek & Co., CPAs, Indpls., 1983-88, prin., 1989-92; dir. office automation USA Group, Fishers, Ind., 1992-95; ind. cons. and writer, 1995—. Com. chairperson Fin. Mgrs. Soc., Chgo., 1989-92; cons., spkr. Lafferty Group Confs., London, 1992-2000; writer Trade Press Svcs., Thousand Oaks, Calif., 2000—. Author: (books) Creating a Customer-Driven Retail Bank, 1991, Rebuilding the Retail Bank, 1992, Document Imaging Technology, 1993; contbg. author procs., reports in field; contbg. editor Bank Adminstrn. Inst., Chgo., 1989-91; contbr. articles to profl. jours. Trustee Sunrise United Meth. Ch. at Geist, 1998—. Mem. Inst. Mgmt. Cons. (cert.), Beta Gamma Sigma, Sigma Iota Epsilon. Home and Office: 8403 La Habra Ln Indianapolis IN 46236-8832 E-mail: edmcdonell@juno.com.

MCDONELL, HORACE GEORGE, JR. instrument company executive; b. N.Y.C., Sept. 23, 1928; s. Horace Gustave and Anabel (Armstrong) McD.; m. Eileen Romar, Sept. 6, 1952; children: Victoria (dec.), Diane, Horace. AB, Adelphi Coll., 1952; postgrad., Harvard U., 1962. Engr. Sperry Gyroscope Co., N.Y.C., 1952; with Perkin-Elmer Corp., Norwalk, Conn., 1963—, mgr. instrument group, 1967-77, v.p., 1966-69, sr. v.p., 1969-77, exec. v.p., 1977-80, pres., 1980-85, chmn., 1985-90, ret., 1990. Bd. dirs. Perkin Elmer, Ltd., U.K. UniRoyal, Inc., Perkin Elmer Internat., Inc., Harvey Hubbell, Inc., Ethan Allen Inc.; Mem. adv. task force on export controls U.S. Def. Sci. Bd., 1975— , chmn. instrumentation subcom., 1975— Mem. Bd. Edn., Ridgefield, Conn., 1969; Bd. dirs. Conn. Sci. Fair.; Trustee, bd. dirs. Danbury (Conn.) Hosp.; trustee Adelphi U.; bd. dirs. Danbury Health Svcs. With AUS, 1946-48. Mem. Sci. Apparatus Maker Assn. (dir., chmn. analytical instrument sect.), Am. Inst. Physics, AAAS, Instrument Soc. Am., Am. Electronics Assn. (bd. dirs. 1984-89, chmn. 1987) Home: 94 School St Chatham MA 02633-2437 E-mail: chatham28@aol.com.

MCDONELL, NEIL EDWIN, lawyer; b. Johnson City, N.Y., May 30, 1952; s. Alexander Edwin McDonell and Loretta Arlene Terry; m. Margaret Lynn Moline, June 18, 1978; children: Adam, Aaron. AB in Philosophy and English Lit., U. Mich., 1974; PhD in Philosphy, Harvard U., 1979; JD, Columbia U., 1983. Bar: N.Y. 1984. Asst. prof. philosophy Middlebury (Vt.) Coll., 1979-80; assoc. Battle Fowler, N.Y.C., 1983-89, Marks & Murase, N.Y.C., 1989-92, ptnr., 1992-96, Dorsey & Whitney LLP, N.Y.C., 1996—. Editor-in-chief Columbia Jour. Tranational Law, 1982-83, bd. dirs., 1989—; contbr. articles to profl. jours. Mem. ABA (internat., sci., tech., and antitrust sects.), N.Y. State Bar Assn., Internat. Trade Commn. Trial Lawyers Assn., Harvard Club, Phi Beta Kappa. Avocations: literature, history, poetry. Office: Dorsey & Whitney LLP 250 Park Ave New York NY 10177-0001

MCDONELL, ROBERT TERRY, magazine editor, novelist; b. Norfolk, Va., Aug. 1, 1944; s. Robert Meinard and Irma Sophronia (Nelson) McD.; m. Joan Raffeld Hitzig, June 15, 1981; Robert Nicholas Campbell, Thomas Hunter Campbell. Student, U. Calif., Berkeley, 1962-63, San Jose State U., 1963-64; BA in Art, U. Calif., Irvine, 1967. With AP, N.Y.C., 1970-72; reporter Los Angeles Weekly, 1972-73; asso. editor San Francisco mag., 1974-76, City mag., San Francisco, 1976-77; sr. editor San Francisco mag., 1977, Outside mag., San Francisco, 1978-79; founding editor Rocky Mountain mag., Denver, 1979-80; mng. editor Rolling Stone mag., N.Y.C., 1980-83; asst. mng. editor Newsweek Mag., 1983-86; founder Smart mag., 1986-90; editor-in-chief Esquire mag., 1990-93; editor-in-chief, pub. Sports Afield Mag., 1994-97; editor Men's Journal, 1997-99; v.p. Wenner Media, 1997—; editor-in-chief US Weekly, N.Y.C., 2000—. Author: California Bloodstock, 1980, paperback edit., 1989; screenwriter: Miami Vice, China Beach. Office: US Weekly 1290 Avenue Of The Americas Fl 2 New York NY 10104-0298

MCDONNEL, ANNA C. biologist; b. Boulder, Colo., Oct. 17, 1976; d. Gerald and Annette McDonnel. AB in Biology, Brown U., 1999; student in Reproductive Biology, U. of Wyo., 1999—. Grantee Grad. Student stipend, Nat. Western Stock Show, 2001, EPSCOR/BRIN, 2002. Mem.: Animal Sci. Grad. Student Assn. (pres. 2001—02). Home: 403 E Lewis 4 Laramie WY 82072 Personal E-mail: amcdonn@uwyo.edu.

MCDONNELL, ARCHIE JOSEPH, environmental engineer; b. N.Y.C., June 3, 1936; s. Patrick and Margaret (O'Reilly) McD.; m. Nancy Carol Schaeffer, June 18, 1966; children: Patrick, Sean. BS in Civil Engring., Manhattan Coll., 1958; MS in Civil Engring., Pa. State U., 1960, PhD in Civil Engring., 1963. Prof. Pa. State U., University Park, 1963-96; asst. dir. Water Resources Rsch. Ctr., Pa. State U., 1969-82; dir. Inst. for Rsch. on Land and Water Resources, Pa. State U., 1982-86, Environ. Resources Rsch. Inst., Pa. State U., 1986—. Bd. dirs. Pa. Environ. Coun., 1989-92, Nat. Assn. State Univs. & Land Grant Colls., 1990-92, chmn. water resources com., 1985-91; mem. rsch. & modeling subcom. EPA Chesapeake Bay Program, 1984-86, sci. & tech. adv. com., 1984—, exec. com., 1988-92; U.S. rep. Internat. Joint Commn., 1976-79, 87-89; mem. Pa. State Conservation Com., 1988-89, water resources policy adv. com. Pa. Dept. Environ. Resources, 1979-82, air & water quality tech. adv. com., 1983—, chmn. water quality subcom., 1986-88; chmn. Northeast Assn. Water Inst. Dirs., 1973-74; mem. exec. com. Nat. Assn. Water Inst. Dirs., 1975-78. Contbr. articles to profl. jours. Fellow U.S. Pub. Health Svc., 1961-62; recipient Commendation cert. Internat. Joint Commn., Conservationist of Yr. award Chesapeake Bay Found., Washington, 1986, Outstanding Rsch. award Pa. State U. Engring. Soc., 1988, Outstanding Profl. Rsch. award Water Pollution Control Assn. Pa., 1990, Karl M. Mason medal Pa. Assn. Environ. Profls., 1991, Gabriel Narutowicz medal Ministry Environ. Protection and Natural Resources, Poland, 1991. Mem. ASCE (chmn. 1972-73, exec. com. 1976-80, J. James R. Croes Rsch. medal 1976, Outstanding Svc. award 1981), Water Environ. Fedn. (co-chmn. 1991—), Fed. Water Pollution Control Fedn., Internat. Assn. Water Pollution Rsch., Am. Soc. Limnology and Oceanography, Chi Epsilon, Sigma Xi, Phi Kappa Phi. Achievements include demonstration of low cost treatment method for renovation of acidmine waters. Office: Pa State U 100 Land Water Research University Park PA 16802-4900

MCDONNELL, LEO FRANCIS, engineer, consultant; b. Edmonton, Alta., Can., May 10, 1926; arrived in U.S., 1948; s. Alexander J. McDonnell and Mary M. Bettin; m. Donna M. Callahan; children: Alexander, Timothy, Donald, Douglas, Sarah. BSChemE, U. Alta., 1948; MS, Lawrence U., 1955, PhD, 1959. Rsch. engr. Minn. and Ont. Paper Co., International Falls, Minn., 1948—53; tech. dir. Scott Paper Cup Divsn., Phila., 1958—61, Scott Paper Co., Marinette, Wis., 1961—73, sr. brand tech. mgr. Phila., 1965—73, internat. tech. devel. mgr., 1973—80, chief devel. mgr., 1980—87; pvt. cons. Media, 1987—. Home: 1999 Kimberwick Rd Media PA 19063

MC DONNELL, LORETTA WADE, lawyer; b. San Francisco, May 31, 1940; d. John H. and Helen M. (Tinney) Wade; m. John L. McDonnell, Jr., Apr. 27, 1963 (div.); children: Elizabeth, John L. III, Thomas. BA, San Francisco Coll. for Women, 1962; MA, Stanford U., 1963; grad., Coro Pub. Affairs Tng. Program for Women, 1976; JD, Golden Gate U., 1989. Bar: Calif. 1990. H.S. tchr. East Side Union H.S. Dist., San Jose, Calif., 1962-63; project coord. Inter Agy. Collaboration Effort, Oakland, 1977; legal asst. Pacific Gas and Elec. Co., San Francisco, 1980-89, coord., 1989-90. Assoc. editor The Antiphon, 1971-74. Chmn. spkrs. panel Focus on Am. Women, 1973-74; bd. dirs. Alameda County Vol. Bur., 1973-74, St. Paul's Sch., 1974-75, Carden Redwood Sch., 1975-77; budget panelist United Way of Bay Area, 1975-77; cmty. v.p. Jr. League, 1976-77, nat. conv. del., 1976. Mem. Jr. League Oakland-East Bay, Inc., Stanford Alumni, Stanford San Francisco Luncheon Club, Commonwealth Club. Democrat.

MCDONNELL, MARY THERESA, travel service executive; b. N.Y.C., Nov. 9, 1949; d. John J. and Mary B. (Lunney) McD.; m. Robert T. Barber, Oct. 7, 1989 (dec. Nov. 7, 1999). Mgr. Kramer Travel Agy., White Plains, N.Y., 1967-79; owner, mgr. New Trends Travel, Rye, 1979-90, Honey Travel Inc., Rye, 1990—. Office: Honey Travel Inc 11 Elm Pl Rye NY 10580-2918 E-mail: mtbarber@att.net., honeytravel@yahoo.com.

MCDONNELL, MICHAEL T., JR. lawyer; b. Phila., June 30, 1936; s. Michael T. and Florence (Mulligan) McD.; m. Ellen Meisner, June l6, 1962; children: Michael, Patrick, Ellen, Theresa, Andrew. BS, Villanova U., 1958, JD, 196l. Bar: Pa. U.S. Dist. Ct. (ea. dist.) Pa., U.S. Claims Ct., U.S. Ct. Appeals (3d cir.), U.S. Supreme Ct. Pvt. practice, Yeadon, Pa., 196l-68; ptnr. McDonnell & McDonnell, P.A., l968-75, pres. Drexel Hill, Pa., 1978—; pvt. practice Yeadon, l. Instr. law Temple U., Phila., 1963-65, Drexel U., Phila., l964-65, Widener U., Wilmington, Del., 1964-66; lectr. in field. Counel Delaware County Coun. Retarded Citizens, Media, Pa., 1975%, Assn. Ret. Mems. Army, Yeadon, l970—; pres. Yeadon Profl. Assn., l975, 85; del. Joint Commn. China-Am. Law, 1987. Fellow Pa. Bar Assn.; mem. Assn. Trial Lawyers Am., Pa. Trial Lawyers Assn., Llanerch Country Club. Office: 4750 Township Line Rd PO Box 395 Drexel Hill PA 19026-0395

MCDONNELL, SANFORD NOYES, aircraft company executive; b. Little Rock, Oct. 12, 1922; s. William Archie and Carolyn (Cherry) McD.; m. Priscilla Robb, Sept. 3, 1946; children: Robbin McDonnell MacVittie, William Randall. BA in Econs., Princeton U., 1945; BS in Mech. Engring., U. Colo., 1948; MS in Applied Mechanics, Washington U., St. Louis, 1954. With McDonnell Douglas Corp. (formerly McDonnell Aircraft Corp.), St. Louis, 1948—, v.p., 1959-66, pres. McDonnell Aircraft div., 1966-71, corp. exec. v.p., 1971, corp. pres., from 1971, chief exec. officer, from 1972, chmn., 1980-88, chmn. emeritus, 1988—. Active St. Louis United Way; mem. exec. bd. St. Louis and nat. councils Boy Scouts Am.; trustee, elder Presbyn. Ch.; chmn. bd. Character Edn. Partnership, Washington, 1993—. Fellow AIAA; mem. Navy League U.S. (life), Tau Beta Pi. Office: McDonnell Douglas Corp PO Box 516 Saint Louis MO 63166-0516

MCDONOUGH, BRIDGET ANN, music theatre company director; b. Milw., June 19, 1956; d. James and Lois (Hunzinger) McD.; m. Gregory Paul Opelka, Sept. 20, 1986 (div. Aug. 1993); m. Robert Markey, Feb. 29, 2000. BS, Northwestern U., 1978. Bus. mgr. Organic Theater Co., Chgo., 1979-80; mng. dir., founder Light Opera Works, Evanston, Ill., 1980—. U.S. rep. European Congress Musical Theatre, 1995. Founder, mem. Chgo. Music Alliance, 1984—, pres., 1995-98; mem. Ill. Arts Alliance; bd. dirs., Nat. Alliance for Musical Theatre, 2001—; bd. dirs. Evanston Convention Visitors Bur.; mem. alumni adv. bd. Northwestern U. Sch. Speech. Recipient Women on the Move award Evanston YWCA, 1991. Mem. Evanston C. of C. (bd. dirs., 1993-99), Rotary (pres. Evanston chpt. 1999-2000). Avocation: birding. Office: Light Opera Works 927 Noyes St Evanston IL 60201-6206

MCDONOUGH, JAMES FRANCIS, civil engineer, educator; b. Boston, June 7, 1939; s. John Joseph and Blanche Cecelia (Murphy) McD.; m. Kathryn Ann Hilvert, Mar. 9, 1985; children by previous marriage: John, James, Jennifer. BS in Civil Engring., Northeastern U., 1962, MS in Civil Engring., 1964; PhD, U. Cin., 1968, MBA, 1981. Registered profl. engr., Ohio. Project engr. Fay, Spofford & Thorndike, Boston, 1962; teaching asst. Northeastern U., 1962-64, U. Cin., 1965, instr. civil engring., 1965-68, asst. prof., 1968-74, assoc. prof., 1974-78, William Thoms prof. civil engring., chmn. dept. civil and environ. engring., 1978-86, assoc. dean acad. affairs, 1986-95; interim dean Clermont Coll., 1996-97, dean, 1997—. Vis. prof. faculty engring. Kabul U., Afghanistan, 1969-71; vis. prof. N.C. State U., 1971 Contbr. articles to profl. jours. Pres. Greenhills Winton Sports Assn., 1981-83, treas., 1977-81; bd. dirs. United Way, 1997—, 2001 Bd., 1998—. Recipient Teaching Excellence award U. Cin., 1973-75; Dow Chem. Outstanding Young Faculty award Am. Soc. for Engring. Edn., 1975; Outstanding Engring. Educator award Am. Soc. Engring. Edn.-Western Electric, 1977; Profl. Accomplishment award Acad.-Tech. and Sci. Council Cin., 1979 Fellow Am. Soc. Engring. Edn. (v.p. 1984-86, chmn. sect. 1982-83, v.p. membership affairs 1992—); mem. ASCE (zone sec. 1983, sect. pres. 1982), NSPE (chmn. Ohio state bd. registration for engrs. and surveyors 1987-90), Ohio Soc. Profl. Engrs., Tech. Socs. Coun. Clin. (Disting. Engr. of Yr. award 1993), ASEE (Centennial medal 1993, George Wadlin Disting. Svc. award 1993), Clermont County C. of C. (bd. dirs. 1998—), Nat. Coun. Examiners for Engring. and Surveying (Profl. Accomplishment award 1993), Sigma Xi, Tau Beta Pi, Chi Epsilon, Beta Gamma Sigma. Home: 5304 Belfast Owensville Rd Batavia OH 45103-9630 Office: 4200 Clermont College Dr Batavia OH 45103-1748

MCDONOUGH, JAMES MICHAEL, engineer, educator; b. Springfield, Ohio, Dec. 10, 1945; s. James Michael and Marjorie Ann (Brandle) McD.; m. Mei Tsuo Huang, Feb. 19, 1983. BS in Aero. and Astronautical Engring., Ohio State U., 1968; MA in Applied Math., UCLA, 1975, PhD in Engring., 1980. Engr./scientist McDonnell-Douglas Co., Santa Monica, Calif., 1968-72; staff mathematician Prose, Inc., L.A., 1973-76; mem. tech. staff Aerospace Corp., El Segundo, Calif., 1980-87; adj. asst. prof. UCLA, 1980-90; assoc. prof. U. Ky., 1990—99, prof., 1999—. Assoc. editor Internat. Jour. Fluid Mechanics Rsch.; contbr. Acad. Press Ency. Phys. Sci. Tech.; reviewer numerous profl. jours., contbr. articles to profl. jours. Mem. AAAS, AIAA, ASME, Am. Math. Soc., Am. Phys. Soc., Soc. Indsl. Applied Math., N.Y. Acad. Scis. (organizing com. internat. confs.), Combustion Inst. Avocations: piano, basketball, model railroading. Home: 4053 Palmetto Dr Lexington KY 40513-1344

MCDONOUGH, JOHN MICHAEL, lawyer; b. Evanston, Ill., Dec. 30, 1944; s. John Justin and Anne Elizabeth (O'Brien) McD.; m. Susan J. Moran, Sept. 19, 1981; children: John E., Catherine Anne. AB, Princeton U., 1966; LLB, Yale U., 1969. Bar: Ill. 1969, Fla. 1991. Assoc. Sidley & Austin, Chgo., 1969-75, ptnr., 1975—. Bd. dirs. Met. Planning Coun., 1978—, pres., 1982-84; bd. dirs. Ctr. Am. Archeology, 1980-85, chmn., 1982-84; bd. dirs. Leadership Greater Chgo., 1984-90, sec.-treas., 1987-90; bd. dis. Brian Rsch. Found., 1985—, pres., 1989-94. With JAGC, USAR, 1969-75. Mem. ABA, Ill. Bar Assn., Chgo. Bar Assn., Racquet Club, Saddle & Cycle Club, Commonwealth Club, Econ. Club, Phi Beta Kappa. Democrat. Episcopalian. Home: 1407 N Dearborn St Chicago IL 60610-1505 Office: Sidley & Austin 425 W Surf St Apt 605 Chicago IL 60657-6139

MC DONOUGH, JOHN RICHARD, lawyer; b. St. Paul, May 16, 1919; s. John Richard and Gena (Olson) McD.; m. Margaret Poot, Sept. 10, 1944; children— Jana Margaret, John Jacobus. Student, U. Wash., 1937-40; LLB, Columbia U., 1946. Bar: Calif. 1949. Asst. prof. law Stanford U., 1946-49, prof., 1952-69; asso. firm Brobeck, Phleger & Harrison, San Francisco, 1949-52; asst. dep. atty. gen. U.S. Dept. Justice, Washington, 1967-68, assoc. dep. atty. gen., 1968; of counsel and ptnr. firm Keatinge & Sterling, L.A., 1969-70; ptnr. Ball, Hunt, Hart, Brown and Baerwitz, 1970-90, Calsmith Ball Wichman Case & Ichiki, L.A., 1990-96, of counsel, 1996-98, Carlsmith Ball, L.A., 1998—. Exec. sec. Calif. Law Revision Commn., 1954-59, mem. commn., 1959-67, vice chmn., 1960-64, chmn., 1964-65. Served with U.S. Army, 1942-46. Mem. State Bar Calif., Am. Coll. Trial Lawyers. Democrat.

MCDONOUGH, JOSEPH CORBETT, former army officer, aviation consultant; b. N.Y.C., Sept. 30, 1924; s. Joseph Walter and Catherine Loretta (Corbett) McD.; m. Mary Patricia Aaron, June 10, 1945; children— Joseph Corbett, Thomas Michael, Robert Timothy. BS, U.S. Mil. Acad., West Point, N.Y., 1945; MA, Georgetown U., Washington, 1957; grad., U.S. Command and Gen. Staff Coll., 1954, Brit. Staff Coll., Camberly, 1958, U.S. Army War Coll., 1965. Commd. 2d lt. U.S. Army, 1945, advanced through grades to maj. gen., 1973, served in Philippine Scouts, 1945-47, served with 82d Airborne Div., 1948-51, served with 40th Inf. Div. Korea, 1952-53; instr. U.S. Naval Acad., 1954-57; staff and command U.S. Army, Europe, 1958-61; with Office Personnel Mgmt., Dept. Army, Washington, 1961-64; mem. staff Office Under Sec. Army, 1965-67; bn. and brigade comdr. 1st Calvary Div. U.S. Army, Vietnam, 1967-68; with Joint Chiefs of Staff, Washington, 1968-71; brigade and asst. div. comdr. Vietnam, 1971-72; chief of staff CENTO, Turkey, 1972-73; comdg. gen. 8th Inf. Div. U.S. Army, Germany, 1973-75; U.S. Comdr. Berlin, 1975-78; ret. U.S. Army, 1978; cons. numerous govt. agys., 1978-79; v.p., gen. mgr. Butler Aviation, BWI Airport, Md., 1980-83; v.p. ops. Butler Aviation Internat., 1983-86; cons., 1986-88; exec. v.p. Butler Aviation Internat., 1988-90; cons., 1990—. Decorated D.S.M. with oak leaf cluster, Silver Star, Legion of Merit with oak leaf cluster, D.F.C., Bronze Star, Air medal with 32 oak leaf clusters, Army Commendation medal with 2 oak leaf clusters. Mem. Assn. U.S. Army, Army Aviation Assn. Address: Apt 704 16531 Heron Coach Way Fort Myers FL 33908-5520

MCDONOUGH, KENNETH LEE, pharmaceutical company medical administrator; b. Buffalo, Apr. 7, 1953; s. Sidney Lee and Jeanne Francis (Sheets) McD.; children: Jameson, Laurel, Meghan; m. Connie Kay Staley; stepchildren: Audrey, Kelsie. BS, U. Minn., 1975, MD, 1979, MS, 1986. Diplomate Am. Bd. Quality Assurance and Utilization Rev. Physicians. Resident in occupl. medicine U. Calif., San Francisco, 1984; v.p. Indsl. Health and Hygiene Group, Mpls., 1982-86; pvt. practice occupl. medicine, 1985—92; v.p. Am. Gen. Ins., Dallas, 1986-88, Mut. of Omaha Ins., Omaha, 1988-91, sr. v.p., 1991-95; med. dir. Stuart Disease Mgmt. Svcs. Inc., Wilmington, Del., 1995-98; asst. clin. prof. dept. preventive medicine and pub. health Creighton U. Sch. Medicine, 1994—; med. dir. AstraZeneca Pharms., Wilmington, Del., 1998—. Instr. nursing Gustavus Adolphus Coll. Nursing, St. Paul, 1984-86; instr. astronomy Met. State U ., St. Paul, 1982-83; prin. rsch. into cost effectiveness of Dr. Dean Ornish's coronary reversal program in collaboration with Harvard Med. Sch., 1992-95. Author and designer of computer software. Instr. Sci. Mus. of Minn., St. Paul, 1982. Recipient Design Excellence award

Seako, Inc., 1987, 3M Creativity award Minn. Mining & Mfg., 1971; recipient acad. scholarships. Mem. Am. Coll. Med. Quality, Am. Coll. Occupl. and Environ. Medicine, Nat. Assn. Managed Care Physicians, Gt. Plains Occupl. Medicine Assn. (nominating com. 1990-91), Am. Lung Assn. Nebr. (bd. dirs. 1995—), Disease Mgmt. Assn. Am., Phi Kappa Phi. Avocations: genealogy, travel, astronomy, medical informatics, ancient history. Home: 9 Devonshire Ct Greenville DE 19807 Office: Astrazeneca Pharmaceuticals 1800 Concord Pike Wilmington DE 19803-2902

MCDONOUGH, MARK, neuropsychologist, forensic consultant; b. Balt., July 6, 1954; BA in Sociology and Psychology, Lynchburg Coll., 1976; MA in Clin. Psychology, Loyola Coll., Balt., 1985; PhD in Clin. Psychology, Calif. Sch. Prof. Psychology, 1992; postgrad., Vanderbilt U., 1994. Diplomate Am. Bd. Forensic Medicine, Am. Bd. Forensic Examiners. Postdoctoral fellow Med. Ctr. Vanderbilt U., Nashville, 1992-94; neuropsychologist, clin. coord. Children's Specialized Hosp., Mountainside, N.J., 1994; assoc. clin. dir. Neurobehavioral Inst. N.J., Somerville, 1994-95, dir. clin. svcs., 1995-99; pvt. practice, San Diego, 1999—. Cons. staff psychiatry Muhlenberg Med. Ctr., Plainfield, N.J., 1996—; cons. staff pediats. U. Med. and Dentistry N.J., Newark, 1995—. Contbr. articles to profl. jours. Grantee Md. Psychol. Assn., 1985. Mem. APA, Nat. Head Injury Assn. (peer reviewer 1995—), Am. Coll. Forensic Examiners (subcom. for diplomatic cert. 1997—), Nat. Acad. Neuropsychology, Internat. Neuropsychol. Soc. Office: Ste 215 4540 Kearny Villa Rd San Diego CA 92123 Office Fax: 858-538-1276.

MCDONOUGH, RICHARD ALOYSIUS, IV, investment banker; b. Ann Arbor, Mich., Oct. 20, 1966; s. Richard Aloysius McDonough III and Mary (Carlin) Camp; m. Gerda-Marie Kenyon, 1995; 1 child, Eliza Lily. AB, Dartmouth Coll., 1988; MBA, Harvard U., 1993. Fin. analyst Merrill Lynch & Co., N.Y.C., 1988-90, L.A., 1990-91; with corp. devel. RJR Nabisco, Inc., N.Y.C., 1992; dir. The Bridgeford Group, 1993-97; mng. dir. The Beacon Group, 1997-2000; mng. dir., group head So. Calif. group J.P. Morgan H&Q, 2001—. Merrill Lynch chmn. Fin. Analyst Fundraiser for N.Y. Times Neediest Cases Fund, N.Y.C., 1988-90 Mem. The Met. Club, Harvard Bus. Club Greater N.Y., Harvard Club of N.Y., Yale Club of N.Y.C., Dartmouth Club of N.Y. Republican. Roman Catholic. Avocations: creative writing, traveling, recreational sports. Office: JP Morgan H&Q 10877 Wilshire Blvd Los Angeles CA 90024 Address: 253 26th St Santa Monica CA 90402-2545

MC DONOUGH, RICHARD DOYLE, retired paper company executive; b. St. Stephen, N.B., Can., May 8, 1931; s. Kenneth Paul and Mary (Doyle) McD.; m. Caroline Wilkins, July 7, 1956; children: Elizabeth Wilkins, Richard David, Philip Bradford. AB, Dartmouth Coll., 1952. Mgmt. trainee Gen. Electric Co., Lynn, Mass., 1953-56, various fin. positions lamp div. Monterrey, Mex., 1956-59, controller Mexican subs. Mexico City, 1959-63; cost supr. Singer Co., N.Y.C., 1964, fin. dir. Clydebank, Scotland, 1965-66, controller Eur. div. London, 1967-69; v.p. ops. Home Furnishings Group, 1969; v.p., corp. contr. Singer Co., N.Y.C., 1970-73, corp. v.p., pres. mail order div. Hanau, Fed. Republic of Germany, 1973-76, v.p. London, 1976-79; sr. v.p., CFO, dir. Bowater Inc., Darien, Conn., 1979-92, vice chmn., CFO, 1992-93, vice chmn., 1993-94, ret., 1994. Dir. Xylem Investments. Mem. Am. Forest and Paper Assn. (fin. com. 1980-94, steering com. 1987-94, vice chmn. 1989-91, chmn. 1991-93), Fin. Execs. Inst., Greenwich Country Club, Harbour Ridge Yacht and Country Club. Republican. Episcopalian. Avocations: scuba, opera. Office: Barons Mead 25 E Point Ln Old Greenwich CT 06870-2403 E-mail: RDM080531@aol.com.

MCDONOUGH, RICHARD MICHAEL, philosophy educator; b. Pitts., Jan. 29, 1950; s. Walter and Marilyn (Duman) McD.; m. Mary Lau, July 26, 1991. BA summa cum laude, U. Pitts., 1971; MA, Cornell U., 1974, PhD, 1975. Asst. prof. philosophy Bates Coll., Lewiston, Maine, 1975-82; sr. lectr. Nat. U. Singapore, 1982-91; asst. prof. philosophy U. Tulsa, 1991—; assoc. prof. philosophy, psychology U. Putra Malaysia, Selangor, 1997-98; prof. philosophy Overseas Family School: The College, Republic of Singapore, 1999—, lectr., 1999—. Author: The Argument of the Tractatus, 1986; contbr. articles to profl. jours. Woodrow Wilson fellow, 1971-72, NSF fellow, 1971-74; postdoctoral rsch. grantee NEH, Ind. U., 1980-81. Mem. Australasian Debating Fedn. (hon. life, adjudicator 1991—), Phi Kappa Phi. Achievements include prodn. of original interpretation of Wittgenstein's logical-metaphys. sys., original application Kantian Copernican Revolution to philosophy of lang.; significant interdisciplinary work logic, linguistics, psychology & philosophy. Office: Dept Philosophy OFS Coll 25F Paterson Rd Singapore 238515 Singapore

MCDONOUGH, RUSSELL CHARLES, retired state supreme court justice; b. Glendive, Mont., Dec. 7, 1924; s. Roy James and Elsie Marie (Johnson) McD.; m. Dora Jean Bidwell, Mar. 17, 1946; children: Ann Remmich, Michael, Kay Jensen, Kevin, Daniel, Mary Garfield. JD, George Washington U., 1949. Bar: Mont. 1950. Pvt. practice, Glendive, Mont., 1950-83; judge Gen. Jurisdiction State of Montana, 1983-87; justice Mont. Supreme Ct., Helena, 1987-93, ret., 1993. City atty. City of Glendive, 1953-57; county atty. Dawson County, Mon., 1957-63; del. Mont. Constl. Conv., Helena, 1972. 1st lt. AC, U.S. Army, 1943-45, ETO. Decorated DFC. Mem. Mont. Bar Assn. Roman Catholic. Home: 441 W Paseo Solana Green Valley AZ 85614-2727

MCDONOUGH, WILLIAM J. banker; b. Chgo., 1934; married. BS, Coll. of Holy Cross, 1956; MA, Georgetown U., 1962. With Dept. of State, 1961-67, 1st Nat. Bank of Chgo., 1967-89, asst. v.p. internat. banking dept., 1967-70, v.p., gen. mgr., 1970-72, area head, Europe, Middle East and Africa, 1972-73, sr. v.p., head internat. banking dept., 1973-75, exec. v.p., 1975-86, CFO, 1982-89, chmn. asset and liability mgmt. com., until 1989; vice chmn. 1st Chgo. Corp. and 1st Nat. Bank Chgo., 1986-89; exec. v.p., head markets group Fed. Res. Bank of N.Y., N.Y.C., 1992-93, pres., CEO, 1993—. Vice chmn. fed. open market com. Fed. Res. Sys.; bd dirs. Bank for Internat. Settlements, Inst. Internat. Econ.; chmn. Basle com. on banking supervision. Bd. dirs. N.Y. Philharm. Orch., Fgn. Policy Assn., Coun. on Fgn. Rels., Inst. for Internat. Econs.; mem. Trilateral Commn. of the Group of Thirty; trustee Carnegie Corp. of N.Y. Mem.: Americas Soc. (bd.dirs.), Fgn. Policy Assn. (bd.dirs.), Coun. Fgn. Rels. (bd.dirs.), N.Y. Acad. Scis. (bd. govs.), Group of Thirty. Office: Fed Res Bank of NY 33 Liberty St New York NY 10045-0001

MCDONOUGH-TREICHLER, JUDITH DIANNE, medical educator, consultant; b. L.A., Aug. 15, 1938; d. William Charles and Eleanor (Lewis) Anderson; m. Raymond Milan McDonough, Mar. 2, 1957 (div. Oct. 2, 1974); children: Joyce Churchill, Steven McDonough, Jill Cannon; m. John Rex Treichler, June 2, 1985. BS in Health Edn., Calif. State U., Long Beach, 1978; MS in Health Care Adminstrn., U. LaVerne, Calif., 1981; PhD in Pub. Health, Loma Linda U., Calif., 1991. Cert. registered nurse, Calif., health edn. specialist nat. Commn. for Health Edn. Credentialing. Dir. health edn. Nat. Med. Enterprises, Lakewood, Calif., 1972-80, Taif, Saudi Arabia, 1980-82, health educator Manila, Philippines, 1983; dir. health promotion and edn. Med. Ptnrs. US Family Care, Montclair, Calif., 1992-97; adj. faculty prof. U. LaVerne, 1986—, U. Phoenix, Ontario, 1996—, Crafton Hills Coll., Yucaipa, 1997—; owner, exec. v.p. JJS Health Edn. Cons., Rancho Cucamonga, 1996—. Rsch. asst. Loma Linda (Calif.) U., 1995-97; adv. bd. mem. Cerritos (Calif.) Coll., 1975-80, U. LaVerne, Calif., 1996—. Contbr. articles to profl. jours. Contbg. mem. La Liga Flying Samaritans, Rosario Mex., 1978-80, Friendship For Animals, Rancho Cucamong, Calif., 1995—. Recipient Dean's fellowship Loma Linda (Calif.) U., 1988. Mem. APHA, Calif. Scholarship Fedn., Nat. Coun. Against Health Fraud, World Clowns Assn., Clowns of Am. Internat., Calif. State U. Alumni Assn., Alpha Gamma Sigma. Avocation: clowning. Office: U LaVerne Dept Health Svcs Mgmt 1950 3d St La Verne CA 91750

MCDOUGAL, ALFRED LEROY, publishing executive; b. Evanston, Ill., Feb. 12, 1931; s. Alfred L. and Mary (Gillett) McD.; m. Gudrun Fenger, May 7, 1960 (div. 1982); children: Thomas, Stephen; m. Nancy A. Lauter, Mar. 1, 1986. BA, Yale U., 1953; MBA, Harvard U., 1957. Asst. to pres. Rand McNally & Co., Skokie, Ill., 1962-65, mgr. sch. dept., 1965-69; pres. McDougal, Littell & Co., Evanston, 1969-91, chmn., CEO, 1991-94; dir. Houghton Mifflin Co., Boston, 1994-2001; CEO Alm Corp., 1994—. Chmn. McDougal Family Found.; gov. Yale U. Press, 1995—. Trustee Hadley Sch. for Blind, Winnetka, Ill., 1980-83; chmn. budget com. Evanston United Fund, 1974-76, bd. dirs.; bd. dirs. Evanston YMCA, 1988-94, Youth Job Ctr., 1987-93, chmn., 1989-91, Opportunity Internat., 1994-2000, Literacy Chgo., 1992-98, treas., 1994-96, Hubbard St. Dance, Chgo., 1995—. With U.S. Army, 1953-55. Mem. Assn. Am. Pubs. (exec. com. sch. divsn. 1981-94, chmn. 1988-89, 92-94, dir. 1987-89), No. Ill. Assn. (1st v.p. 1984, chmn. 1985). Office: ALM Corp 400 N Michigan Ave Ste 300 Chicago IL 60611-4130 E-mail: alfredmcdougal@yahoo.com.

MCDOUGAL, MARIE PATRICIA, retired educator, freelance writer and editor; b. Mt. Clemens, Mich., Apr. 10, 1946; d. Allan Charles and Dorothy Nadine (Berger) Ling; m. Douglas Stevens McDougal, Aug. 23, 1969. BA, Cen. Mich. U., 1968; MA, Antioch U., 1997. Lic. tchr., Mich. Tchr. L'Anse Creuse High Sch., Harrison Twp., Mich., 1969-97; retired, 1997. Mem. L'Anse Creuse High Crisis Team, 1988-93, S.A.F.E. Task Force, Harrison Twp., 1986-98; spkr. in field. Author: Mount Clemens: Bath City U.S.A. in Vintage Post Cards, 2000; columnist: The Jour. Newspaper, 1983—90, writer: Interospective Mag., 1996—98, writer, editor : Antiquities Guide, 1997—98; author: Harrison Township, Michigan, 2002. Mem. L'Anse Creuse Athletic Boosters; chair Harrison Twp. Hist. Commn. Recipient Appreciation award Macomb County Hist. Soc., 1989, Pres. award for lit. excellence The Nat. Authors Registry, 1994. Mem. Soc. Children's Book Writers and Illustrators, Romance Writers Am., Venice Shores Property Owners (bd. dirs. 1994-2000, corr. sec. 1994-98), Detroit Women Writers, L'Anse Creuse Public Schs. Alumni Assn. (steering com. 1996-98), Am. Auto Immune-Related Diseases Assn. Lutheran. Avocations: boating, crafts, reading. E-mail: ratisboat@aol.com. *Personal philosophy: Strive for the pinnacles, but stop to pick up any stragglers along the way.*

MCDOUGAL, STUART YEATMAN, comparative literature educator, author; b. L.A., Apr. 10, 1942; s. Murray and Marian (Yeatman) McD.; m. Menakka Weerasinghe, Apr. 29, 1967 (div. 1977); children— Dyanthe Rose, Gavin Rohan; m. Nora Gunneng, Aug. 4, 1979; children— Angus Gunneng, Tobias Yeatman BA, Haverford Coll., 1964; MA, U. Pa., 1965, PhD, 1970. Lectr. U. Lausanne, Switzerland, 1965-66; asst. prof. Mich. State U., East Lansing, 1970-72; from asst. prof. to prof. English, comparative lit. and film /video U. Mich., Ann Arbor, 1972-85; dir. program in comparative lit. U. Mich., 1981-97, asst. to dean spl. projects, 1997-98; Dewitt Wallace prof. English, chair English Dept. Macalester Coll., St. Paul, 1998—. Vis. prof. film Aegean Inst., Greece, 1994; vis. scholar Senapulli, Brazil, 1996. Author: Ezra Pound and the Troubadour Tradition, 1972 (Bredvold prize 1973), 1973; Made into Movies: From Literature to Film, 1985,; editor: Dante Among the Moderns, 1985; co-editor: Play It Again, Sam: Retakes on Remakes, 1998; contbr. articles to profl. jours. Am. Council of Learned Socs. fellow, 1974-75; U. Mich. Rackham Research grantee, 1975-76; Fulbright Assn. sr. lectr., Italy, 1978; recipient Faculty Recognition award, U. Mich., 1987. Fellow Dirs. Guild Am. (summr workshop, 1993); mem. MLA, Am. Comparative Lit. Assn. (sec.-treas. 1983-89, v.p. 1989-91, pres. 1991-93), Internat. Comparative Lit. Assn., Soc. Cinema Studies. Democrat. Office: Macalester Coll English Dept 1600 Grand Ave Saint Paul MN 55105-1801

MCDOUGAL, WILLIAM GEORGE, civil engineering educator; b. Chico, Calif., Oct. 27, 1951; s. George Alvin and Donna Louise (Staffelbach) McD.; m. Joan Florence Davis, Dec. 30, 1972; children: Tobbie Anna, Ryan Marie. BS in Oceanography, BS Environ. Engring., Humboldt State U., 1976; MCE, U. Del., 1979; PhD in Civil Engring., Oreg. State U., 1982. Oceanographer EPA, Corvallis, Oreg., 1978-79; asst. prof. civil engring. Oreg. State U., 1981-85, chmn. ocean engr., 1984-85, assoc. prof., 1985—. Cons. 1980-85. Contbr. articles to profl. jours. Mem. steering com. Philomath (Oreg.) Rodeo, 1983-85. Mem. ASME, ASCE (assoc., mem. pubs. com. 1983—, research com. 1985—), Am. Geophys. Union, Sigma Xi. Republican. Office: Oreg State U Dept Civil Engring Corvallis OR 97331

MCDOUGAL, WILLIAM SCOTT, urology educator; b. Grand Rapids, Mich., 1942; s. William Julian and Verna Wilma (Pasma) McD.; m. Mary Stuart Logan, Sept. 19, 1992; 1 child, Molly Katherine. AB, Dartmouth Coll., 1964; MD, Cornell U., 1968. Intern in surgery U. Hosps., Cleve., 1968-69, resident in surgery, 1969-75, attending urologist, 1977-80; postdoctoral fellow in physiology Yale U., New Haven, 1971-72; postdoctoral fellow in surgery Case-Western Res. U., Cleve., 1972-75; chief, burn study div. Inst. Surg. Rsch. Brooke Army Med. Ctr., Ft. Sam Houston, 1975-77; instr. surgery U. Tex., San Antonio, 1975-77; asst. prof. urology Case Western Res. U., Cleve., 1977-78, assoc. prof., 1978-80, Dartmouth Coll., Hanover, N.H., 1980-84, chmn. dept. urology, 1982-84; prof., chmn. dept. urology Vanderbilt U., Nashville, 1984-90; Walter S. Kerr Jr. prof. urology Harvard Med. Sch., 1991—; chief urology Mass. Gen. Hosp., Boston, 1991—. Office: Mass Gen Hosp Dept Urology Fruit St Boston MA 02114

MCDOUGALL, ALAN B. retired oil company executive; b. Newark, Oct. 30, 1933; s. Archibald and Margaret Frances (Wright) McD.; m. Joan Livingston Woods, June 15, 1957; children: Steven Woods, Anne Sarah, John David. BSCHe, Princeton U., 1955; postgrad., Yale U., 1955-57; MPA, Columbia U., 1992. Exec. Exxon Corp., Irving, Tex., 1956-86; v.p. Mutual of Am. Found., N.Y.C., 1987-89; cons. Nat. Exec. Svc. Corps., 1989—. Trustee Helene Fuld Coll. of Nursing, N.Y.C., 1991—. Presbyterian. Avocations: travel, economic and urban history. Home: 73 Cedar Hill Rd Bedford NY 10506-2016 E-mail: alan55@optonline.net.

MCDOUGALL, DONALD BLAKE, retired government official, librarian; b. Moose Jaw, Sask., Can., Mar. 6, 1938; s. Daniel Albert and Donela (McRae) McD.; m. Norma Rose Peacock, May 19, 1962. BA, BEd, U. Sask., 1966; BLS, U. Toronto, 1969; MLS, U. Alta., 1983, cert. pub. adminstrn., 1990. Classroom tchr. Regina Bd. Edn., Sask., 1960-63, vice prin., 1963-68; asst. chief libr. Stratford Pub. Libr., Ont., Can., 1969, chief libr. Can., 1970-72; supr. info. svcs. Edmonton Pub. Libr., Alta., Can., 1972, head pub. svcs. Can., 1973-74; legislature libr. Province of Alta., Edmonton, Can., 1974-87; asst. dep. min., legis. libr. Legis. Assembly Alta., 1987-93, ret., 1993. Editor microfilm: Alberta Scrapbook Hansard, 1906-1964, 1976; editor: A History of the Legislature Library, 1979; author: Princess Louise Caroline Alberta, 1988, Premiers of the Northwest Territories and Alberta, 1876-1991, 1991; co-author, editor: Lieutenant-Governors of the Northwest Territories and Alberta, 1876-1991; (pamphlet) Canadian Parliamentary Libraries, 1989; mem. editl. bd. Sask. Hist. Baseball Rev., 1998—. Govt. Sask. scholar, 1965; recipient Queen's Silver Jubilee medal Govt. Can., 1977; named Hon. Clk.-At-The-Table, Legis. Assembly Alberta, 1987-93. Mem. Alta. Govt. Librs. Coun. (chmn. 1975), Assn. Parliamentary Librs. in Can. (pres. 1980-82), Edmonton Libr. Assn., Hist. Soc. Alta. (v.p. Edmonton chpt. 1987), Libr. Assn. Alta., Can. Libr. Assn., Edmonton Jaguar Drivers Club, Edmonton Scottish Soc., Can. Vintage Motorcycle Assn., Beta Phi Mu. Presbyterian.

MCDOUGALL, DUANE C. manufacturing executive; Grad., Ohio State U. With Willamette Industries, exec. v.p. bdlg. materials group, pres., COO. Past pres. Portland Rotary Charitable Trust Found. Office: Willamette Industries Inc 1300 SW 5th Ave Ste 3800 Portland OR 97201-5671 Home: 15067 SW Cabernet Dr Tigard OR 97224*

MCDOUGALL, GERALD DUANE, lawyer; b. Hammond, Ind., Sept. 18, 1931; s. John and Carol Maxine (Lind) McD.; m. Ingrid Rosina Kempf, Jan. 26, 1960 (dec. 2000); children: Manfred, James. JD, Mercer U., 1971. Bar: U.S.V.I. 1972, Colo. 1973, Germany 1973, Tex. 1985. Atty. US V.I. Dept. Labor, St. Thomas, 1971-72; pvt. practice, Denver, 1972-74, 76-84, Heilbronn, Neckar, Germany, 1974-76, Amarillo, Tex., 1985—. Precinct committeeman Rep. Ctrl. Com., Denver, 1978-84. Sgt. U.S. Army, 1951-54, ETO, 61-67, Vietnam. Mem. Tex. Bar Assn., Tex. Criminal Defense Lawyers Assn., Amarillo Bar Assn., State Bar Coll. Home: 7910 Merchant Dr Amarillo TX 79121-1028 Office: PO Box 50898 Amarillo TX 79159-0898

MCDOUGALL, IAIN ROSS, nuclear medicine educator; b. Glasgow, Scotland, Dec. 18, 1943; came to U.S., 1976; s. Archibald McDougall and Jean Cairns; m. Elizabeth Wilson, Sept. 6, 1968; children: Shona, Stewart. MB, ChB, U. Glasgow, 1967, PhD, 1973. Diplomate Am. Bd. Nuclear Medicine (chmn. 1985-87), Am. Bd. Internal Medicine (gov. 1984-86). Lectr. in medicine U. Glasgow, 1969-76; fellow Harkness-Stanford Med. Ctr., 1972-74; assoc. prof. radiology and medicine Stanford (Calif.) U., 1976-84, prof. radiology and medicine, 1985—. Contbr. numerous articles to sci. jours. Fellow Royal Coll. Physicians (Glasgow), Am. Coll. Physicians; mem. Am. Thyroid Assn., Soc. Nuclear Medicine, Western Assn. for Clin. Research. Office: Stanford U Med Ctr Divsn Nuclear Medicine Stanford CA 94305

MCDOUGALL, JASON JAMES, physiologist; b. South Shields, England; s. Robert and Margaret Rose McD.; m. Kristy Elinor Knight, Mar. 4, 1995. BS, U. Glasgow, Scotland, 1992, PhD, 1995. Asst. prof. U. Calgary, Canada, 2000—. Vis. scientist U. Wurzburg, Germany, 1999-2000. Co-author: (chpts.) Neurological Derived Pathological Hyperameia in ARticular Tissues, 1999, Animal Models of Ligament Repair, 2000; contbr. articles to profl. jours. Postdoctoral fellow Alberta Heritage Found. Med. Rsch., 1996-99, U. Calgary, 1996-2000, Joint Injury & Arthritis Rsch. fellow Ernst & Young, 1999—. Mem. Am. Physiol. Soc., European Neuropeptide Club (assoc.). Office: U Calgary 3330 Hosp Dr NW Calgary AB Canada T2N 4N1 E-mail: medougaj@ucalgary.ca.

MCDOUGALL, JENNIFER FECIO, writer; b. Buffalo, Aug. 19, 1971; d. John Paul Jr. and Maureen Leary Fecio; m. Alexander J. McDougall, June 3, 1995; 1 child, Maeve. BA in English, Polit. Sci. & Urban Studies, Canisius Coll., 1993, MPA, 1998. Legis. asst. Buffalo (N.Y.) Common Coun., 1996-98; sr. legis. asst., chief of staff Coun. Mem. Kevin Helfer, Buffalo, 1998-99; sr. staff writer Nonprofit Adminstrv. Svcs., Rochester, N.Y., 1999—. Pro-bono freelance writer. Mem. Belfast Summer Relief Program, Di Gamma. Roman Catholic. Avocations: reading, cooking, Irish cultural activities, creative writing.

MCDOUGALL, JOHN ROLAND, civil engineer; b. Edmonton, Alta., Can., Apr. 4, 1945; s. John Frederick and Phyllis Eirene (Sladden) McD.; m. Susan Carley, July 2, 1971 (div. 1995); children: John Christopher, Jordan Page, Michael Tait; m. Irene Makar, May 15, 1996. BSCE, U. Alta., Edmonton, 1967. Registered profl. engr., Alta. Engr. Imperial Oil Ltd., Calgary, Alta., 1967-69, sr. engr. Edmonton, 1969-75; treas. McDougall & Secord, 1969-85; v.p. McDougall & Secord, Ltd., 1975-90, pres., 1990—; pres., chief exec. officer Dalcor Cos., Edmonton, 1975-91; chmn. Trade Innoventures, Inc., 1992—; chair engring. mgmt. U. Alta., Edmonton, 1991-98. Chmn. D.B. Robinson & Assocs., Edmonton; CEO Alberta Rsch. Coun., 1997—; chmn. World Trade Centre, Edmonton, 1994-98; mem. adv. bd. Royal Trust Corp., 1984-94, Royal Glenora Club, Faculty Club; dir. PFB Corp. Chmn. Edmonton Civic Govt. Assn., 1975-77; mem. Premiers Coun. on Sci. and Tech., 1990. Fellow Can. Acad. Engrs. (bd. dirs. 1992—); mem. Can. Coun. Profl. Engrs. (pres. 1990-91), Assn. Profl. Engrs. Alta. (hon. life, pres. 1980-81), Can. Engring. Manpower Bd. (chmn. 1985-88), Edmonton C. of C. (pres. 1989), Loyal Edmonton Regiment (hon.), Edmonton Club (pres. 1983-84), 8 Field Engring. Regiment (hon. col.). Anglican. Avocations: skiing, travel, cycling, philately, railroad modeling. Office: Alberta Rsch Coun 250 Karl Clark Rd Edmonton AB Canada T6N 1E4

MCDOUGALL, RODERICK GREGORY, lawyer; BBA in Econs., JD, U. Ariz. Bar: Ariz. 1965, U.S. Ct. Claims 1965, U.S. Supreme Ct. 1970, U.S. Dist. Ct. Airz. 1972, U.S. Ct. Appeals (9th cir.) 1972. Law clk. Ariz. Supreme Ct., 1964, Ariz. Ct. Appeals, 1965; dep. county atty. Maricopa County, 1965-67; staff atty. Ariz. State Senate, 1967; asst. atty. gen., 1967-74; chief asst. Atty. Gen., Ariz., 1974-84; city atty. City of Phoenix, 1984-2000. Advisor Ariz. Supreme Ct. Mem. ABA, Internat. Mcpl. Lawyers Assn. (bd. dirs. 1994-2000), Ariz. Bar Assn., Maricopa County Bar Assn.

MC DOW, JOHN JETT, agricultural engineering educator; b. Covington, Tenn., Jan. 6, 1925; s. Robert Simpson and Lucy Ann (Cocke) McD.; m. Dorothy Virginia Glass, Dec. 22, 1946; children: Ronald Allan, Jane Virginia. Student, Franklin and Marshall Coll., 1944-45; BS, U. Tenn., 1948; MS, Mich. State U., 1949, PhD, 1957. Registered profl. engr., Tenn., La. Instr. Mich. State U., 1949; instr. Okla. State U., 1949-51, asst. prof. agrl. engring., 1951; assoc. prof. La. Poly. U., 1951-57, prof., 1957-62, head agrl. engring. dept., 1953-62; prof., head dept. agrl. engring. U. Tenn., Knoxville, 1962-73, dean admissions and records, 1973-83, prof. agrl. engring., 1983-92, prof. emeritus, 1992—. Cons./collaborator Agrl. Research Service, U.S. Dept. Agr., 1970-76; leader Rotary Internat. Found. Group Study Exchange Team to Philippines, 1984; mem. scholarship selection com. N.Am. Philips Corp., 1976-88. Contbr. articles to profl. jours. Mem. La. Engring. Coun., 1955-56; bd. dirs. Tenn.-Venezuela-Amazonas Partners, 1977-80; vol. Internat. Centennial Olympic Summer Games, Atlanta, 1996. Served with USN, 1943—46, comdr. USNR, to 1977. So. Fellowship grantee, 1957 Mem. Am. Soc. Agrl. Engring. (dir. 1973-75), Am. Soc. Engring. Edn. (sec. agrl. engring. div. 1971-72, vice chmn. 1972-73, chmn. 1973-74), Sigma Xi, Tau Beta Pi, Pi Mu Epsilon, Omicron Delta Kappa, Gamma Sigma Delta, Phi Kappa Phi (v.p. 1971-77, nat. pres. elect 1977-80, pres. 1980-83, pres. found. 1974-78). Lodges: Rotary (pres. 1989-90, chmn. dist. scholarship selection com., 1982-87, 88-91). Presbyterian. Home: 2008 Walnut Hills Dr Knoxville TN 37920-2946

MCDOWELL, ANNIE R. retired counselor; b. Lawtey, Fla., Sept. 12, 1934; d. Elbe and Rebecca (Strong) Hamilton; m. John D. Buckhanon, July 12, 1953 (div. June 1962); 1 child, Levon Buckhanon. BA, Fla. A&M U., Tallahassee, 1967; MEd, U. Ctrl. Fla., 1972; M in Guidance Counseling, Rollins Coll., 1975. Tchr. Orange County Pub. Schs., Orlando, Fla., 1967-73; equal opportunity counselor, coord. Valencia C.C., 1973-97; ret., 1997. Mem. Valencia Black Adv. Bd., Orlando, Fla., 1973—, President's Status of Women, 1989—, Sisters Alive, Orlando, 1993—, Orlando Partnership, 1994—. Recipient Appreciation award African-Am. Cultural Soc./Valencia Coll., 1995. Mem. Mem. Nat. Hook-Up of Black Women (Honors ward 1988, pres. 1989), Friendship Club, Negro Coun. Women, Gamma Delta Pi. Democrat. Baptist. Home: 1549 Lawndale Cir Winter Park FL 32792-6160

MCDOWELL, CHARLES E. state agency administrator; b. Milw., Aug. 16, 1949; s. Charles and Ovuida McDowell; m. Candace M. Stone McDowell; children: Monte, Vanessa. B in Edn., U. Wis., 1977. Pers. specialist Wis. Dept. Adminstrn., Madison, 1977—79, divsn. adminstr., 1996—; classification and compensation specialist Wis. Dept. Employment Rels., 1979—80, 1982—84, dir., bur. classification and occupl. surveys, 1984—87, employment rels. specialist, negotiator, 1987—88; pers. dir. Wis. Ct. Sys., 1980—82; divsn. adminstr. Wis. Dept. Revenue, 1988—96. Exec. bd. mem. Wis. Alumni Assn., Madison, 1992—2002; bd. mem. State Employees Combined Campaign, 1998—2002; mem. Govs. Commn. on Minority Participation in Vocat.-Tech. Edn., 1990—91. Named Adminstr. of Yr., Am. Soc. Profl. Adminstrs., 1998; recipient Volunteerism award, Chancellor, U. Wis., Madison, 1997. Mem.: Internat. Pers. Mgmt. Assn. (cert.), Nat. Forum for Black Pub. Adminstrs., Wis. Assn. Black Pub. Sector Employees (pres. 1999—2000, Pres. award 1998). Avocation: golf. Office: Wis Dept Adminstrn 9th Fl 101 E Wilson St Madison WI 53702 Office Fax: 608-264-9500. Business E-Mail: charles.mcdowell@doa.state.wi.us.

MCDOWELL, CHARLES EAGER, lawyer, retired military officer; b. Manchester, N.H., Sept. 9, 1923; s. Joseph Curry and Mildred (Eager) McD.; m. Carolyn A. Gibbons, June 21, 1947; children— Robin, Patricia. AB, Dartmouth Coll., 1947; JD, U. Va., 1950. Bar: Tex. 1950, Va. 1981, D.C. 1981. With land div. Shell Oil Co., Houston, 1950; commd. lt. (j.g.) USN, 1951, advanced through grades to rear adm., 1976; staff legal officer Comdr. Service Force, U.S. Pacific Fleet; staff judge adv., head internat. law div. Naval War Coll., 1963-66; staff legal officer, comdr. 7th Fleet, 1966-68; sr. Navy mem. ad hoc com., dep. asst. judge adv. gen. Office Judge Adv. Gen. Dept. Def., Washington, 1968-72; staff judge adv. on staff comdr. in chief U.S. Naval Forces, Europe, London, 1972-75; comdg. officer Naval Justice Sch., Newport, R.I., 1975-76; dep. judge adv. gen. Navy Dept., Washington, 1976-78, judge adv. gen., 1978-80; pvt. practice Dumfries, Va., 1981-96. Served to 2d lt. AUS, 1943-46. Decorated D.S.M., Bronze Star, Joint Service Commendation medal, Navy Commendation medal with Combat V, Purple Heart, Combat Inf. badge. Mem. FBA, Tex. Bar Assn., Va. Bar Assn., Judge Advs. Assn., Order of Coif, Chi Phi, Square Dancer Club. Methodist. Home: 1106 Croton Dr Alexandria VA 22308-2008

MCDOWELL, DAVID JAMISON, clinical psychologist; b. Pitts., Jan. 11, 1947; s. David Emerson and Auleene Marley (Jamison) McD.; m. Nancy Annis, Jan. 13, 1973; children: Sasha, Christopher. BA, Princeton U., 1968; PhD, U. Maine, 1980. Predoctoral intern clin. psychology Worcester (Mass.) State Hosp., 1976-77, admissions officer, 1979-82; instr. dept. psychology Coll. Holy Cross, Worcester, 1977-78; lectr. dept. psychology and edn. Assumption Coll., 1978-79; clin. dir. Milford (Mass.) Assistance Program, 1978-80; asst. prof. psychiatry and pediatrics U. Mass. Med. Ctr., Worcester, 1980-83; clin. dir. Newton-Wellesley-Weston-Needham (Mass.) Multi-Service Ctr., 1983-84; dir. Lancaster (Mass.) Assocs., 1987—. Ptnr. Worcester County

Counseling Assocs., Bolton, Mass., 1980—87; allied profl. staff St. Vincent Hosp. , Worcester, 1985—88; clin. cons. Mass. Dept. Youth Svcs. , Worcester, 1986—87, 1989—90, 1994—95; assoc. med. dir. psychiat. disability claims Paul Revere Ins. Co., Worcester, Mass., 1996—97, The Provident Cos., 1997—2002, best practice leader psychiat. impairments, 2002—; clin. cons. disability ins. industry and health ins. cos., lectr. in field. Author: (with others) The Mental Health Industry, 1978; contbr. articles to profl. jours. Trustee Westborough State Hosp., 1996-99. Mental Health fellow U. Maine, 1973-75. Fellow: Mass. Psychol. Assn. (legis. com. 1985—86); mem.: APA. Avocations: walking, music, reading. Office: Unum Provident Corp 18 Chestnut St Worcester MA 01608

MCDOWELL, DAVID LYNN, mechanical engineering educator; b. Red Oak, Iowa, Dec. 20, 1956; s. Leland Lee and Wilma McD.; m. Kathryn M. McDowell, May 26, 1979; children: Matthew Todd, Andrew Joel, James Neal. BSME, U. Nebr., 1979; PhDME, U. Ill., 1983. Asst. prof. mech. engring. Ga. Inst. Tech., Atlanta, 1983-87, assoc. prof., 1987-92, prof., 1992—, regents prof., 1996—, Carter N. Paden Jr. Disting. chair in metals processing, 1998—. Dir. Mech. Properties Rsch. Lab., 1992—. Mem. editl. adv. bd. Internat. Jour. Plasticity, Fatigue and Fracture of Engring. Material Structure, Internat. Jour. Damage Mechs., (regional edit.) Internat. Jour. Fracture; contbr. articles to profl. jours. Recipient Alfred Noble prize ASCE, 1986, Ralph R. Teetor award Soc. Automotive Engrs., Outstanding Young Faculty award Dow Chem. Soc., 1990, Presdl. Young Investigator award NSF, 1986. Fellow ASME (Henry Hess award 1988, Nadai award 1997, editor Jour. Engring. Material Tech. 1997-2002); mem. ASTM, Am. Soc. Metals Internat., Materials Rsch. Soc., Am. Acad. Mechanics, Am. Soc. for Engring. Edn., Soc. Engring. Sci. (v.p. 2001, pres. 2002), Pi Tau Sigma (Gold medal 1987). Home: 4275 Cedar Bluff Way SW Lilburn GA 30047-3185 Office: Ga Inst Tech GWW Sch Mech Engring Atlanta GA 30332-0405

MCDOWELL, DONNA SCHULTZ, lawyer, educator; b. Cin., Apr. 23, 1946; d. Robert Joseph and Harriet (Parronchi) Schultz; m. Dennis Lon McDowell, June 20, 1970; children: Dawn Megan, Donnelly Lon. BA in English with honors, Brandeis U., 1968; MEd, Am. U., 1972; CASE with honors, Johns Hopkins U., 1979; JD with honors, U. Md., 1982; MS, Hood Coll., 1995. Bar: Md. 1982. Instr. Anne Arundel & Prince George's C.C., Severna Park and Largo, Md., 1977-78; coll. adminstr. Bowie State Coll. (Md.), 1978-79; assoc. Miller & Bortner, Lanham, Md., 1982-83; sole practice, 1983-87, Gaithersburg, Md., 1987—; sci. tchr. D.C. Pub. Schs., 1999-2000; chair dept. English Montgomery County Pub. Schs., 2000—. Ednl. cons. Chmn. Housing Hearing Com., Bowie, 1981-83; trustee Unitarian-Universalist Ch., Silver Spring, Md., 1979-83; bd. dirs. New Ventures, Bowie, 1983, Second Mile (Runaway House), Hyattsville, Md., 1983; officer Greater Laytonsville Civic Assn., 1989—; founding mem. People to Preserve, Laytonsville; mem. Solid Waste Adv. Com., Montgomery County, Md.; election judge. Recipient Am. Jurisprudence award U. Md., 1981. Mem. Montgomery County Bar Assn., Prince George's Bar Assn., Phi Kappa Phi. Democrat. Avocations: gardening, reading, bluebirds, movies. Home: 24308 Hipsley Mill Rd Gaithersburg MD 20882-3132 Office: PO Box 5205 Laytonsville MD 20882-0205 E-mail: DonnaSMcD@aol.com.

MCDOWELL, EDWARD R. H. chemical engineer; b. Cleve., Aug. 13, 1932; s. Blake and Lois (Held) McD.; m. Joyce Patricia Dudley, June 18, 1955; children: Edward R. H. Jr., James D. BSChemE, Cornell U., 1955; MS, Calif. Inst. Tech., 1960, PhD, 1964. Registered prof. chem. engr., Calif. Instr. Cornell U., Ithaca, N.Y., 1955; assoc. rsch. engr. Calif. Rsch. Corp., El Segundo, 1955-59; instr. Calif. Inst. Tech., Pasadena, 1959-63; rsch. engr. Chevron Rsch. Corp., La Habra, Calif., 1963-66, sr. rsch. engr., 1966-68; sr. engring. assoc. Chevron Oil Field Rsch. Co., 1968-74, mgr., 1974-86; gen. ptnr. C. Blake McDowell Ltd. Partnership, Akron, Ohio, 1986—95. NSF fellow Calif. Inst. Tech., 1961-63; recipient Engring. Merit award Orange County Engring. Coun., 1985. Fellow Am. Inst. Chem. Engrs. (pres. 1989, v.p. 1988, dir. 1982-84, Civic Achievement award 1983, F.J. & Dorothy Van Anwepen award 1992), Inst. for Advancement of Engring.; mem. Soc. Petroleum Engrs., Am. Assn. Engring. Socs. (bd. govs.), King Harbor Yacht Club (commodore 1990, vice commodore 1989, rear commodore 1988), St. Francis Yacht Club (San Francisco), Transpacific Yacht Club (Long Beach, Calif.), Assn. Santa Monica Bay Yacht Clubs (commodore 1989, vice commodore 1988, rear commodore 1987), Nawiliwili Yacht Club (Lihue, Hawaii), Magic Castle Club, Manhattan Country Club, The Cornell Club (N.Y.C.). Avocations: offshore sailboat racing (winner ULDB70 Season Sailing Championship 1990, 92), magic. Home: 2510 The Strand Hermosa Beach CA 90254-2553

MCDOWELL, ELAINE, retired federal government executive, educator; b. Balt., June 28, 1942; d. McKinley and Lena (Blue) McDowell; children: Nathan H. Jr. Murphy, Michael W. Murphy. BA, Morgan State U., Balt., 1965; MSW, U. Md., 1971, PhD, 1988. Drug abuse adminstr., acting regional dir. State Md. Drug Abuse Adminstrn., Balt., 1971-72; social sci. analyst, pub. health advisor Nat. Inst. Drug Abuse, Rockville, MD, 1972-76, dep. dir., dir. div. community assistance, 1976-82, dep. assoc. dir. for policy devel., 1981-82, dir. div. prevention and communications, 1982-85; exec. asst. to adminstr. Alcohol, Drug Abuse & Mental Health Adminstrn., Md., 1985; dep. dir. Nat. Inst. on Drug Abuse, MD, 1985-88; dir. Ctr. for Substance Abuse Prevention, 1988-96; acting adminstr. Alcohol, Drug Abuse and Mental Health Adminstrn., Rockville, Md., 1992, Substance Abuse and Mental Health Svcs. Adminstrn., Rockville, 1992-94. Expert cons. in substance abuse, treatment, and mental health fields; prof. Morgan State U., Balt. Chmn. non-alcoholic internat. gen. svc. bd. Alcoholics Anonymous, 2001—; active Presbyn.. Ch. U.S.A., Balt., 1998—; bd. dirs. Rosalynn Carter Inst. for Human Devel. Recipient Outstanding Leadership in Improving Health Care in Black Cmty. award Nat. Med. Assn., 1989, Secretary's commendation HHS, 1989, Disting. Svc. award, 1990, Nat. Coun. on Alcoholism and Drug Dependence Ind., Pres. award for outstanding fed. leadership, 1991, Presdl. Meritorious Exec. Rank award, 1991, Presdl. Meritorious Disting. Rank award, 1993. Mem.: NASW, Sr. Execs. Assn.

MCDOWELL, EUGENE CHARLES, systems analyst, bioethicist; b. Washington, Jan. 13, 1940; s. Charles Jacob and Voilet Marie (Brown) McD.; m. Jill Perry Huntley, May 4, 1986 (dec. 1989); m. Hendrika Maria Ram, Mar. 21, 1992; step-daughter, Deepa Maria Long. BA, Am. U., 1962; MA, U. Chgo., 1966, 76; adv. cert. in Pub. Adminstrn., U.S. Dept. of Agr. Grad. Sch., 1973; grad. cert., Mastery U., 1995. Rsch. asst. ops. rsch. office Johns Hopkins U., Bethesda, Md., 1958-61; rsch. asst. Rsch. Analysis Corp., McLean, Va., 1961-66, ops. rsch. analyst, 1966-71, Nat. Bur. Standards, Gaithersburg, Md., 1971-80, mgmt. analyst, 1980-82; ops. rsch. analyst Nat. Oceanic and Atmospheric Adminstrn., Rockville, 1982-87, computer systems analyst, 1987—; mem. bioethics com. and policy subcom. Washington Hosp. Ctr., Washington, 1996—. Mem. U.S. Fed. pub. key infrastructure steering com., 1999—, mem. legal/policy working group, 1999—, chmn., 2001–, mem. tech. working group, 2000—, others; convenor Symposium on Legis. for Physician-Assisted Suicide, Bethesda, Md., 1996; mem. bioethics adv. panel Superior Ct. of D.C., 1997—; mem. rsch. working group Md. Atty. Gen., 1997-98; mem. Info. Assurance Tech. Framework Forum, 2000—; mem. customer adv. bd. Gen. Svcs. Adminstrn. ACES, 2000—. Student condr. Nat. Symphony Orch., Washington, 1960. Pres. Hemlock Soc. Nat. Capital Area, Washington, 1991-93, mem. bd. dirs., 1990-97, Nuclear Free Am., Balt., 1991-94, mem. bd. dirs., 1989—, Garrett Park (Md.) Citizens Assn., 1982-84; originator nuclear-free zone movement in U.S., Garrett Park, Md., 1982; auditor North Bethesda Congress of Citizens Assn., 1982-84; active U. Chgo. Profl. Achievement Award com., Washington, 1977—, chmn. 1982-84. Recipient Spl. Svc. citation Nat. Oceanic and Atmospheric Adminstrn., 1991, U.S. Dept. of Commerce Bronze medal, 1995, Govt. Computer News citation, 1995. Mem. Hemlock Soc. USA (life), AAAS (life), Philos. Soc. Washington (life, bd. dirs. 1996-98), Azalea Soc. Am., Metropolitan Washington Bioethics Network (bd. dirs. 1996—), Standards Engring. Soc. (chmn. bd. govs. 1983-84, sr. 1982). Democrat. Unitarian Universalist. Avocations: gardening, reading. Home: PO Box 92 Garrett Park MD 20896-0092

MCDOWELL, FLETCHER HUGHES, physician, educator; b. Denver, Aug. 5, 1923; married BA, Dartmouth Coll., 1943; MD, Cornell U., 1947. From instr. to prof. neurology Cornell U. Med. Coll., N.Y.C., 1968—, assoc. dean, 1970-95, Winifred Masterson Burke prof. rehab. medicine; pres. Winifred Masterson Burke Rsch. Inst., White Plains, 1992—. Mem. Am. Acad. Neurology, Am. Neurol. Assn., Am. Fedn. Clin. Research Office: Burke Rehab Ctr 785 Mamaroneck Ave White Plains NY 10605-2523

MCDOWELL, FREDERICK PETER WOLL, retired English educator; b. Phila., May 29, 1915; s. Samson McDowell and Elma Pennypacker; m. Margaret Louise Blaine, May 29, 1953; children: Steven Frederick, Gloria Catherine, Lawrence Robert, Katherine Anne, Elizabeth Mary. BS in Edn., U. Pa., 1937, MA in English, 1938, Harvard U., 1947, PhD, 1949. Instr. English Washington and Jefferson Coll., Washington, 1938-39, U. Del., Newark, 1939-41, U. Iowa, Iowa City, 1949-51, asst. prof., 1951-58, assoc. prof., 1958-63, prof., 1963-85, prof. emeritus, 1985—. Author: Ellen Glasgow and the Ironic Art of Fiction, 1960, Elzabeth Madox Roberts, 1962, Caroline Gordon, 1966, E.M. Forster, 1968, revised 1982; editor: E.M. Forster: An Annotated Bibliography of Writings About Him, 1976; ; mem. editl. staff English Lit. in Transition, U. N.C., Greensboro, 1960—, Shaw, Pa. State Press, University Park, 1965—, Conradiana Tex. Tech. U., Lubbock, 1975-88. Pvt. to Maj. U.S. Army, 1941-46; lt. col. USAR, 1946-61. Sr. fellow Nat. Endowment for the Humanities, 1973-74, Fulbright fellow U.S. Fulbright Commn., 1980-81. Mem. MLA, Bernard Shaw Soc., Virginia Woolf Soc., Ellen Glasgow Soc. (pres. 1977), D.H. Lawrence Soc., Joseph Conrad Soc., Am. Hemerocallis Soc., Iris Murdoch Soc. Democrat. Avocations: gardening, opera, reading, classical music, performing arts. Home: 3801 Grand Ave Apt 301 Des Moines IA 50312-2845 E-mail: fnmmcdowell1@home.com.

MCDOWELL, JENNIFER, sociologist, composer, playwright, publisher; b. Albuquerque; d. Willard A. and Margaret Frances (Garrison) McD.; m. Milton Loventhal, July 2, 1973. BA, U. Calif., 1957; MA, San Diego State U., 1958; postgrad., Sorbonne, Paris, 1959; MLS, U. Calif., 1963; PhD, U. Oreg., 1973. Tchr. English Abraham Lincoln H.S., San Jose, Calif., 1960-61; free-lance editor Soviet field, Berkeley, 1961-63; editor, pub. Merlin Papers, San Jose, 1969-80, Merlin Press, San Jose, 1973—; rsch. cons. sociology, 1973—; music pub. Lipstick and Toy Balloons Pub. Co., 1978—; composer Paramount Pictures, 1982-88. Tchr. writing workshops; poetry readings, 1969-73; co-producer radio show lit. and culture Sta. KALX, Berkeley, 1971-72. Author: (with Milton Loventhal) Black Politics: A Study and Annotated Bibliography of the Mississippi Freedom Democratic Party, 1971 (featured at Smithsonian Inst. Spl. Event 1992), Contemporary Women Poets, 1977; co-author: (plays off-off Broadway) Betsy and Phyllis, 1986, Mack the Knife Your Friendly Dentist, 1986, The Estrogen Party To End War, 1986, The Oatmeal Party Comes to Order, 1986, (plays) Betsy Meets the Wacky Iraqi, 1991, Bella and Phyllis, 1994; contbr. poems, plays, essays, articles, short stories, and book revs. to lit. mags., news mags. and anthologies; rschr. women's autobiog. writings, contemporary writing in poetry, Soviet studies, civil rights movement, and George Orwell, 1962—; writer: (songs) Money Makes a Woman Free, 1976, 2002, 3 songs featured in Parade of Am. Music, 1976-77; co-creator mus. comedy Russia's Secret Plot To Take Back Alaska, 1988, (CD) Our Women Are Strong, 2002, Music Collected by the Smithsonian, 2002. Recipient 8 awards Am. Song Festival, 1976-79, Bill Casey Award in Letters, 1980; doctoral fellow AAUW, 1971-73; music collected by Smithsonian, 2002; grantee Calif. Arts Coun., 1976-77. Mem. AAUW, Am. Assn. for Advancement of Slavic Studies, Soc. Sci. Study of Religion, No. Calif. Songwriters Assn., Am. Sociol. Assn., Dramatists Guild, Phi Beta Kappa, Sigma Alpha Iota, Beta Phi Mu, Kappa Kappa Gamma. Democrat. Achievements include music from Intern Girl collected by the Smithsonian in 2002. Office: c/o Merlin Press PO Box 5602 San Jose CA 95150-5602

MC DOWELL, JOHN B. bishop; b. New Castle, Pa., July 17, 1921; s. Bernard A. and Louise M. (Hannon) McD. BA, St. Vincent Coll., 1942, MA, 1944, Catholic U. Am., 1950, PhD, 1952; Litt.D. (hon.), Duquesne U., 1962; grad., St. Vincent Sem., Latrobe, Pa. Ordained priest Roman Catholic Ch., 1945, consecrated as titular bishop of Tamazuca and aux. bishop of Pitts., 1966—; asst. pastor St. Irenaeus Ch., Oakmont, 1945-49; asst. supt. schs. Diocese of Pitts., 1952-55, supt. schs., 1955-70, vicar for edn., 1970-85; vicar gen.; pastor Epiphany Parish, Pitts., 1969-96; ret., 1996. Papal chamberlain to Pope Pius XII, 1956, to Pope John XXIII, 1958; domestic prelate to Pope Paul VI, 1964; chmn. ad hoc com. on moral values in our soc. Nat. Conf. Cath. Bishops, from 1973, Bishops Com. for Pastoral on Moral Values, from 1976; mem. Internat. Council for Catechesis, from 1975 Author: Water, Death, and Grace: The Life of Hugh C. Boyle, 6th Bishop of Diocese of Pittsburgh, 1999, Catholic Schools, Public Education, and American Culture, 2000, Giants Were On the Earth in Those Days, The Life of John Francis Regis Canevin, 5th Bishop, Diocese of Pittsburgh, 2000, Blessed Are the Poor in Spirit, For Theirs is the Kingdom of Heaven, the Life of Vincent Martin Leonard, the 9th Bishop of Diocese of Pittsburgh, 2001; c o-author elem. sch. religions series, jr. high sch. lit. series, elem. sci. series and elem. reading series; contbr. ednl. articles to various publs.; former editor: Cath. Educator Mag. Bd. dirs. Allegheny County Community Coll.; bd. dirs. Western Pa. Safety Council, Duquesne U. Named Man of Yr. in Religion Pitts., 1970, 93, Educator of Yr., United Pvt. Acad. Schs. Assn., 1978, Man of Yr., Pitts. chpt. KC, 1989. Mem. Nat. Cath. Ednl. Assn., Cath. Ednl. Assn. Pa., Omicron Delta Kappa Gamma Circle (hon.) Address: Chancery Office 111 Blvd Of The Allies Pittsburgh PA 15222-1613

MCDOWELL, JOHN EUGENE, lawyer; b. Toledo, Nov. 22, 1927; s. Glenn Hugh and Evelyn (Millspaugh) McD.; m. Jean Ann Hepler, June 18, 1950; children: Jane Lynn McDowell Thummel, Sheila Lorraine McDowell Laing. BS, Miami U., Oxford, Ohio, 1949; JD, U. Mich., 1952. Bar: Ohio 1952. Assoc. Dinsmore & Shohl, Cin., 1952-59, ptnr., 1959-97, of counsel, 1997—. Bd. dirs. Structural Dynamics Rsch. Corp., Milford, Ohio. Mem. solicitation coms. United Appeal, Cin., NCCJ, Cin., Boy Scouts Am., Cin. Mem. ABA, Ohio Bar Assn., Cin. Bar Assn., Cin. Country Club, Queen City Club, Order of Coif, Sawgrass Country Club. Democrat. Episcopalian. Office: Dinsmore & Shohl 1900 Chemed Ctr 255 E 5th St Cincinnati OH 45202-4700

MCDOWELL, KAREN ANN, lawyer; b. Ruston, La., Oct. 4, 1945; d. Paul and Opal Elizabeth (Davis) Bauer; m. Gary Lee McDowell, Dec. 22, 1979. BA, U. La., Monroe, 1967; JD, U. Mich., 1971; diploma, John Robert Powers Sch., Chgo., 1976, Nat. Inst. Trial Advocacy, 1990. Bar: Ill. 1973, Colo. 1977, U.S. Dist. Ct. (so. dist.) Ill. 1973, U.S. Dist. Ct. Colo. 1977. Reference libr. assoc. Ill. State Library, Springfield, 1972-73; asst. atty. gen. State of Ill., 1973-75; pvt. practice Boulder, Colo., 1978-79, Denver, 1979—. Mem. So. Poverty Law Ctr.; mem. hate violence task force Colo. Lawyers Com.; foster mom for young kittens Recycled Critter Rescue. Mem.: DAR, ABA, Colo. Women's Bar Assn. (editor newsletter 1982—84), Denver Bar Assn., Colo. Bar Assn. (legal fee arbitration com.), Am. Assn. Retired Persons, Survivors United Network (legal coord. 1992—93), Ams. of Royal Descent, Toastmasters Internat. (Able Toastmaster Bronze 1992), Colonial Dames, Survivors United Network Profls. (exec. com. 1992), Mensa (local sect. Ann Arbor, Mich. 1968), Nat. Soc. Magna Carta Dames, Colonial Order of Crown, Sovereign Colonial Soc., Alpha Lambda Delta, Sigma Tau Delta, Phi Alpha Theta. Avocations: philately, chess, needlework, dinosaurs, Horatio Alger stories. Office: 1525 Josephine St Denver CO 80206-1406 E-mail: kamcdowell@qwest.net.

MCDOWELL, LUCY JANE, allergist, immunologist, pediatrician; b. Balt., Apr. 18, 1950; d. Fletcher Warren and Lucy Walker (Gray) McD. MD, Ind. U., 1974. Diplomate Am. Bd. Allergy and Immunology, Am. Bd. Pediat. Resident in internal medicine Duke U. Hosp., Durham, 1974-75; resident in pediat. Vanderbilt U. Hosp., Nashville, 1975-77; fellow in allergy and immunology Thomas Jefferson U. Hosp., Phila., 1983-85; staff Jackson (Tenn.) Madison County Gen. Hosp., 1977-83, 85-86, Ball Meml. Hosp., Muncie, Ind., 1986—. Mem.: Delaware Blackford County Med. Assn. (pres. 1997—99), Ind. Allergy, Asthma and Immunology Soc. (pres. 1997—98), Am. Coll. Chest Physicians, Am. Coll. Allergy, Asthma and Immunology (bd. regents 2001—), Am. Acad. Pediat., Am. Acad. Allergy, Asthma and Immunology, Alpha Omega Alpha. Office: Muncie Allergy Ctr 4505 N Wheeling Ave Muncie IN 47304-1284 E-mail: janemcdowell@yahoo.com.

MCDOWELL, MAGGIE, biologist, biochemist, educator; b. Ronceverte, W.Va., Mar. 31, 1928; d. William Hemrick McDowell and Mabel May McDowell Perry; m. Thomas Roger Adams, Dec. 15, 1950 (div. Sept. 1961); children: Mabel Newtina, George Robert, Mary V. BS in Secondary Edn., Bluefield (W.Va.) State Coll., 1950. Lab. technician Jefferson Hosp., Phila., 1952-59; biochemist Phila. Gen. Hosp., 1959-66; cytotechnician Med. Arts Lab., Willow Grove, Pa., 1967-68; med. rsch. technician Norristown (Pa.) State Hosp., 1970-72, lab. technician, 1972-81. Active Haws Ave. United Meth. Ch., 1971—; cmty. block party food chmn. West End Ch., Norristown, 1998—, mem . ch. coun., 1989-, fin. team 1996-. Mem. AAUW (co-v.p. Valley Forge br.), Internat. Fedn. Univ. Women, Bluefield State Coll. Alumni Assn., Am. Assn. U. Women, Delta Sigma Theta Sorority, Inc. Democrat. Methodist. Achievements include development of diet for renal insufficiency. Avocations: reading, baking, cooking. Home: 1151 Sterigere St Apt B-25 Norristown PA 19401-3646

MCDOWELL, MARILYN MOOD, interior designer; b. El Campo, Tex., Oct. 3, 1950; d. Rene Lafayette and Gladys Vera (Trojack) Mood; m. Robert Todd McDowell, Apr. 8, 1978; 1 child, Austin Lee. AA, San Jacinto Coll., 1983; BS, U. North Ala., 1972. Adminstrv. asst. Phila. Life Ins. Co., Houston, 1978, supr., 1978-80, cons. methods, 1980-81; designer Interior Looks, Crosby, Tex., 1983-84, McDowell Interiors, Houston, 1984— . Docent Mus. Fine Art, Houston, 1984, 85. Mem. Am. Soc. Interior Designers (assoc.), Nat. Home Fashions League (v.p., mem. com.). Republican. Methodist. Office: McDowell Interiors 3752 Elmora St Houston TX 77005-3712

MCDOWELL, ORLANDO, secondary education educator; b. Chgo., Sept. 4, 1963; s. Willis and Attie (McDowell) Newsome. AA, Olive-Harvey Coll., 1985; BA, Chgo. State U., 1992. Cert. tchr., Ill. Tchr. math. Chgo. Bd. Edn., 1992—; exec. mgr. Mid-West Mktg., Chgo., 1995-96. Spkr. in field. Mem., leader Nat. Rep. Com., Washington, 1995—; mem. Dem. Senate Com., Washington; candidate for U.S. Congress, 1996. Recipient Black Achievement award Harold Washington Jr. Coll., 1994. Mem. AAAS, ACLU (hon.), Internat. Coun. Fgn. Relationships, Acad. Sci., Chgo. Archtl. Found., Chgo. Hist. Soc., Chgo. State U. Alumni Bd., Chicagoland C. of C., Hon. Profs. Soc., Phi Theta Kappa. Home: 9034 S Essex Ave Chicago IL 60617-4051

MCDOWELL, RICHARD LOUIS, academic administrator; b. Battle Creek, Mich., Oct. 22, 1938; s. Louis Dwight and Jane (Shoults) M.; m. Wendy Hsieh, May 20, 2000; children: Vincent, Jason, Nelson, Alison. SB, MIT, 1960, SM, 1966; PhD, Tufts U., 1974. Asst. dir., dir. Boston Area Seminar for Internat. Students, 1963-71 summers; asst. to Dean Student Affairs and Admissions MIT, Cambridge, 1960-66; teaching and rsch. asst. polit. sci. Tufts U., Medford, Mass., 1966-68; instr. Bentley Coll., Waltham, 1968-70, asst. prof. govt., 1970-73; assoc. prof. pub. adminstrn. Suffolk U., Boston, 1973-74, dean and prof. bus. and pub. adminstrn. Sch. of Mgmt., 1974-91; dean, prof. Angyros Sch. Bus. and Econs. Chapman U., Orange, Calif., 1991-2001; provost, v.p. acad. affairs, prof. U. of LaVerne, 2001—. Bd. dirs. South Boston Savs. Bank, Boston Bancorp. Sect. chmn. United Way, Boston, 1982—84, 1986; mem. adv. com. to Sec. of Elder Affairs Commonwealth of Mass., 1962—86; bd. dirs. Mass. Halfway House, Inc., 1984—91, Orange County Forum, 1992—2001, Family Solutions, 1993—, Pacific Symphony, 1999—. Mem. Am. Soc. Pub. Adminstrn. (nat. coun. 1977-80), Am. Assembly Coll. Schs. of Bus. (bd. dirs. 1987-89), Nat. Assn. Schs. Pub. Affairs and Adminstrn. (exec. com. 1979-81). Home: 723 Nicholas Ln Arcadia CA 91006-4449 Office: U LaVerne La Verne CA 91750 E-mail: mcdowell@ulv.edu.

MCDOWELL, ROBERT CONVERSE, retired transportation engineer, writer; b. Dover, Del., June 2, 1930; s. Edwin Spencer and Cecile Fuller McDowell; m. Ruth Hedwig Schwarz, Feb. 12, 1966; 1 child Spencer. BSCE, Drexel Inst. Tech., 1958. Registered profl. engr., Del. Designer New Castle County Dept. Pub. Works, Wilmington, Del., 1954—58; divsn. resident engr. Del. State Hwy. Dept., 1958—64, asst. divsn. engr., 1964—71, dist. maintenance engr., 1971—72; state bridge engr. Del. Dept. Transp., Christiana, 1972—82, state constrn. engr. Dover, 1982—91. Cons. Greenman Pederson, Babylon, NY, 1992—. Author: Basic Concepts of Mathematics, 9 hist. fiction novels. Pres. Bd. Adjustments, Middletown, Del., 1988—; mem. New Castle County Planning Bd., 1995—, Gov.'s Com. on Recycling, Dover, 2000; driver Am. Cancer Soc.; committeeman 9th Dist. Dem. Com., Odessa, Del., 1991—; elder Forest Presbyn. Ch., Middletown, 1964—. Cpl. U.S. Army, 1950—52, Korea. Mem.: VFW (life), Friends of Old Dawyers, Inc. (trustee), Masons. Avocations: antiques, antique cars, Civil War books, furniture restoration. Home: 111 N Broad St Middletown DE 19709

MCDOWELL, ROBERT L. information technology executive; BS in Econs., Va. Mil. Inst.; MS in Bus. Adminstrn., Boston U. Info. tech. staff U.S. Dept. Def.; info. systems mgr. fin. svcs. industry; ptnr., mngr. Strategic Bus. Systems practice Ernst & Young; with Microsoft, 1990—, v.p. enterprise customer unit Wash., 1995—96, v.p. Enterprise Bus. Relationships, 1996—2000, corp. v.p., worldwide svcs., 2000—. Bd. dirs. Visio Corp., Entevo Corp.; mem. Va. Commn. on Info. Tech. Contbr. articles to profl. jours. and mags.; author: Driving Digital. Bd. dirs. Va. Mil. Inst. Found. Office: One Microsoft Way Redmond WA 98052-6399*

MCDOWELL, ROBERT MICHAEL, management consultant; b. Dubuque, Iowa, Mar. 19, 1961; s. James Patrick and Barbara Jean (Bradley) McD. BS in Indsl. Engring., Iowa State U., 1983. Indsl. engr. 3M Corp., Knoxville, Iowa, 1984-86; chief exec. officer, pres. McDowell Enterprises, Cudahy, Wis., 1986—. Pres., chief exec. officer McAid, Ltd., Cudahy, 1986—; cons. McGraw-Edison, Milw., 1987—. Advisor Knoxville Jr. Achievement, 1984, v.p. 1985; active Ams. for Legal Reform. Recipient Citizenship award ABA, 1979. Mem. Inst. Indsl. Engrs. Avocation: reading. Home and Office: PO Box 6115 Sun City West AZ 85376-6115

MCDOWELL, ROBERT WILLIAM, pathologist, internet engineer; b. Muncie, Ind., Sept. 20, 1951; s. Fletcher Warren and Lucy Walker (Gray) McD.; m. Lynda Joan Farnell, May 14, 1977; children: Gullaume, Jean, Luc. BA in Chemistry, Depauw U., 1973; MD, Ind. U., 1977; MSIE, Marlboro Coll., 2001. Diplomate Am. Bd. Pathology. Resident in pathology Ball Meml. Hosp., Muncie, Ind., 1977-78, Berkshire Med. Ctr., Pittsfield, Mass., 1979-80, chief resident pathology, 1980-81; pathologist North Country Hosp., Newport, Vt., 1981—, bd. trustees, 1989-91, pres. med. staff, 1990-91. Adj. asst. prof. pathology Dartmouth Med. Sch., Hanover, N.H., 1991-94. Mem. Evangelical Free Ch. Am. Fellow Am. Soc. Clin. Pathologists, Coll. Am. Pathologists; mem. Vt. Med. Soc., Christian Med. and Dental Soc. (del. 1995), Orleans County Med. Soc. (pres. 1994-95), Vt. Soc. Pathologists (v.p. 1995—). Republican. Evangelical. Avocations: winter sports, boating, religious activities. Office: North Country Hosp 189 Prouty Dr Newport VT 05855-9820

MCDOWELL, SHERRIE LORRAINE, secondary education educator; b. Manchester, Ky., Apr. 20, 1948; d. Alonzo and Madge Loudean (Christensen) Garrison; m. Gary Lynn McDowell, July 11, 1970; 1 child, Marc Ryan. BA, U. No. Colo., 1970; MA, Lesley Coll., 1989; postgrad., U. Wyo. Cert. tchr., Wyo.; nat. bd. cert. tchr. adolescence and young adulthood English lang. arts, 2000. Tchr. English St. Mary's Cath. Sch., Cheyenne, Wyo., 1971-72; instr. homebound program Laramie County Sch. Dist., 1978-84; English instr. Cen. High Sch., 1984—, nat. bd. cert. tchr. adolescence and young adulthood/English lang. arts, 2000. Wyo. coach Nat. Tournament of Acad. Excellence, 1988-90. Mem. NEA (Assembly rep. 1993-2002, cadre trainer state level women's leadership tng. program 1995—), AAUW (sec. 1975-77), Wyo. Edn. Assn. (chair profl. standards and practices comm. 1995-1999, chair summer Inst. 1996-99, co-chmn. local activities Read Across Am. 1999, rep. for del. assembly 2001-2002), Nat. Coun. Tchrs. English (recorder Boston Conv. 1996), Cheyenne Tchrs. Edn. Assn. (edn. assn. del. 1992-2000, chair instrnl. issues 1995, co-chair pub. rels. 1988-90, editor ACCENTS 1988-90, sec. 1995-96, at-large rep. 2000-01), Wyo. Assn. Tchrs. English (presenter), Wyo. Chautauqua Soc. (pres. 1985-86, bd. dirs. 1984-85), Delta Kappa Gamma (state scholarship chair 1989-90, pres. chpt. 1988-90). Home: 100 Grandview Ct Cheyenne WY 82009-4912 Office: Ctrl H S 5500 Education Dr Cheyenne WY 82009

MCDOWELL, W. STUART, producer, composer, playwright, university department chair; b. St. Louis, Jan. 18, 1947; s. W. Davidson and Stacey (Wiley) McD.; m. Gloria Skurski, Aug. 20, 1983; 1 child, Claire Ellen. BA in Theatre, Macalester Coll., 1969; MA, U. Calif., Berkeley, 1974, PhD, 1994. Founder Riverside Shakespeare Co., N.Y.C., 1977, artistic dir., 1977-85; exec. producer McDowell/Scripps Prodns., 1985-92; artistic dir. Grove Shakespeare, Orange County, Calif., 1992-93; chair, dept. theatre, dance and motion pictures Wright State U., Dayton, Ohio, 1994—. Lectr. German theatre & theatre of Bertolt Brecht, Columbia U., Sch. Arts NYU, Goethe Insts., Middlebury, Coll.,

Macalester Coll.; ptnr. Wordsworth Devel. Corp. Dir. plays Romeo and Juliet, 1977, Hamlet, 1978, Henry IV, 1979, Twelfth Night, 1980, Winter's Tale, 1982, Caesar, 1984, King Lear, 1985, A Christmas Carol (with Len Cariou, Mary Elizabeth Mastrantonio, Carole Shelly, Fritz Weaver, Raul Julia and Helen Hayes), 1985, A Tribute to Joseph Papp (with Donna McKechnie, Harris Yulin and Loretta Swit), 1992, Private Lives, 1993, Secret Garden, 1995, Cyrano de Bergerac, 1996, Love Letters (with Martin Sheen and Samantha Langevin), 1997, prodn. over 40 plays and benefits in N.Y.C., including The Mandrake (with Tom Hanks), 1979, Merry Wives of Windsor (with Anna Devere Smith), 1982, Christmas Readings (with Roger Rees, Edward Petherbridge and Emily Richards), 1982, The Shakespeare Center Dedication (with Joseph Papp and Helen Hayes), 1982, The Shakespeare Project (with mem. Royal Shakespeare Co.), 1982, A Christmas Benefit (with Jeremy Irons and Sinead Cusack), 1983, Your Dinner with Andre (with Andre Gregory, Jim Dale and Nicol Williamson), 1984, A Christmas Carol at the Marquis Theatre, N.Y.C. (with Helen Hayes, F. Murray Abraham, Rex Smith, June Havoc and Ossie Davis), 1986; dir., translator Bertolt Brecht's Edward II, 1983, Three-Penny Opera, 1972, Arturo Ui, 1973, 79, (NY premiere) Bertoit Brecht's Downfall of the Egotist Johann Fatzer, 1977; author: (play) The Brothers Booth, 1990 (produced at Bristol Riverside Theatre, Phila. 1992); author, dir.: 1913: The Great Dayton Flood (with narration by Martin Sheen, Ossie Davis and Ruby Dee), 1996-97, Show Boat, 1998, The Crucible, 1999, Romeo and Juliet, 2000, dir., composer, 1903: The Wings of Dreams, 2000; broadcast on PBS Lost In Yonkers, 2001, The Philadelphia Story, 2002; patentee in field of computer design. Fulbright scholar, Berlin, Munich, 1974-76; Dewitt Wallace grantee Reader's Digest, Berlin, 1969; winner Los Angeles Drama-Logue award for Outstanding Directing, 1993, Kennedy Ctr.'s Am. Coll. Theatre Festival Direction and Playwriting award, 1996-97. Democrat. Avocations: tennis, jogging, composition, carpentry. Office: Dept Theatre Dance and Motion Pictures Wright State University Dayton OH 45435 E-mail: stuart.mcdowell@wright.edu.

MCDOWELL-LOUDAN, ELLIS VIRGINIA EBAUGH, anthropologist, educator; b. Rome, July 13, 1938; d. Cameron Duncan Ebaugh and Edith Mable Escott Ebaugh; m. Gary Lee Loudan, Aug. 23, 1976; children: Suzanne Virginia McDowell Lyon, James Cameron McDowell. PhD in Anthropology, The Am. U., Washington, District of Columbia, 1963—72. Register of Professional Archaeologists Register of Profl. Archaeologists, 2002. U. of md., coll. pk. Anthropology Dept., College Park, Md., 1968—72; instr. U. of Va., No. Va. Ctr., Alexandria & Arlington, Va., 1968—72. Asst. prof. to prof. SUNY Coll. at Cortland, Cortland, NY, 1972—. Author: (book) Archaeology: Introductory Guide for Classroom and Field. Organizer & worker Wheels of Love/Habitat for Humanity, Cortland-McGraw, NY, 1993—2002. Grantee Dissertation Improvement Grant, NSF, 1971-1972. Fellow: Am. Anthrop. Assn. Achievements include research in On-going prehistoric archaeological survey-Central New York. Avocations: swimming, travel & walking, native american pow wow volunteer & participant, gardening & wildlife studies. Home: 3 West Academy Street Mc Graw NY 13101-0502 Office: SUNY College at Cortland Prospect Terrace Cortland NY 13045 Home Fax: 607-753-5973; Office Fax: 607-753-5973. Personal E-mail: loudane@cortland.edu. E-mail: loudane@cortland.edu.

MCDUFFIE, KEITH A. literature educator; b. Spokane, Wash., Feb. 12, 1932; s. Clair L. and Helen Marie (Yaeger) McD.; m. Helen E. Ferry, June 5, 1965 (div. July 1995); children: Anne Leslie, Andrew Keith; m. Pamela Philips Bacarisse, Aug. 10, 1995 (dec. Mar. 1996). BA in English, Gonzaga U., Spokane, 1954; MA in Spanish, Middlebury (Vt.) Coll., 1960, Univ. Complutense, Madrid, Spain, 1960; PhD in Hispanic Lit., U. Pitts., 1969. Prof. U. Mont., 1969-74; Mellon postdoctoral fellow U. Pitts., 1974, prof., chair dept. Hispanic lit., 1975-92, prof. Hispanic lit., 1975-99, ret., 1999. Editor Revista Iberoamericana, Pitts., 1991-96; pres. Univ. Senate, 1995-97. Co-author: Co-Textes: Cesar Vallejo, 1987; co-editor: Texto y Contexto-Actas 19 Congreso del IILI, 1980, En Este Aire de America: Homenaje a Alfredo Roggiano, 1990. With U.S. Army Security Agy., 1954-56. Mellon Predoctoral fellow U. Pitts., 1965, Title VI fellow U.S. Govt., 1966; Spanish Govt. scholar Spanish Govt., 1959-60. Mem. Instituto Internacional de Literatura Iberoamericana (contbg., bd. dirs. 1991-96, exec. dir. 1991-96). Democrat. Home: 220 N Dithridge St Apt 1001 Pittsburgh PA 15213-1425 E-mail: kamcd@pitt.edu.

MC DUFFIE, MALCOLM, oil company executive; b. San Francisco, Nov. 14, 1915; s. William Chester and Mary (Skaife) McD.; m. Mary Sutherland de Surville, Dec. 8, 1951; children: Cynthia de Surville, Duncan de Surville. AB in Econs, Stanford U., 1940. With O.C. Field Gasoline Corp., 1940-41, Wilmington Gasoline Corp., 1941-42; with Mohawk Petroleum Corp., 1945-80, pres., dir., 1969-80; dir. Res. Oil & Gas Co., 1973-80, sr. v.p., 1977-80; sp. asst. to pres. Getty Oil Co., Los Angeles, 1980-82. Bd. overseers Huntington Library, Art Gallery and Bot. Gardens, 1972-98; bd. dirs. Calif. Inst. Tech. Assos., 1976-82. Mem. Nat. Petroleum Refiners Assn. (Dir. 1970-80), Ind. Refiners Assn. Calif. (pres. 1967-69, 77-78, dir. 1950-80), Rancheros Visitadores. Clubs: California (Los Angeles); Bohemian (San Francisco); Valley Hunt (Pasadena, Calif.), Annandale Golf (Pasadena, Calif.); Birnam Wood (Santa Barbara, Calif.), Valley (Montecito, Calif.). Republican. Episcopalian. Home and Office: 457 Eastgate Ln Santa Barbara CA 93108-2249

MCDUFFIE, MINNIE, nursing administrator, community health nurse; b. Waverly, Ala., Feb. 13, 1949; d. David and Minnie (Buchannon) Pitts; m. Artis McDuffie, Dec. 6, 1969; children: Pamela Yvette, Artis Glendale Jr. AAS, N.Y.C. Community Coll., Bklyn., 1969; BS in Cmty. Health Edn. cum laude, York Coll., Queens, N.Y., 1987; MA in Health Adminstrn., Hofstra U., 1991; M in Nursing, Pace U., 2001. RN N.Y., cert. basic cardiac life support instr. LPN Unity Hosp., Bklyn., 1967-69, charge nurse, 1969-78; hemodialysis nurse St. John's Episcopal Hosp., 1978-80; clinic conf. nurse Queens Hosp. Ctr., Jamaica, 1980-87, head nurse, 1987-90, supr./instr., 1990—2001; med. surg. instr. Wyckoff Heights Med. Ctr., 2001—01; asst. prof. Medgar Evers Coll., Bklyn., 2002—. Recipient LPN Nursing award, Rudia Scholars award, 1998—99. Mem.: ANA (cert. cmty. health nurse N.Y. chpt.), Am. Lung Assn. (mem. Queens chpt. nursing adv. com.). Office: Medgar Evers Coll Nursing Dept Rm 200B 1150 Carroll St Brooklyn NY 11225

MCEACHEN, RICHARD EDWARD, banker, lawyer; b. Omaha, Sept. 24, 1933; s. Howard D. and Ada Carolyn Helen (Baumann) McE.; m. Judith Ann Gray, June 28, 1969; children: Mark E., Neil H. BS, U. Kans., Lawrence, 1955; JD, U. Mich., 1961. Bar: Mo. 1961, Kans. 1982. Assoc. Hillix, Hall, Hasburgh, Brown & Hoffhaus, Kansas City, Mo., 1961-62; sr. v.p. First Nat. Bank, 1962-75; exec. v.p. Commerce Bank Kansas City, 1975-85, Centerre Bank of Kansas City N.A., 1985-87, Security Bank Kansas City, Kans., 1987-88; exec. v.p., trust officer UMB Overland Park Bank, 1988-93; atty. Ferree, Bunn, O'Grady & Rundberg, Chartered, Overland Park, 1994—. Gov. Am. Royal Assn., Kansas City, Mo., 1970—, amb., 1980—, com. mem., 1995—; bd. dirs. Harry S. Truman Med. Ctr., Kansas City, 1974-86, mem. fin. com., 1975-86, treas., 1979-84, bd. govs., 1986—, mem. bldg. and grounds com., 1993—, mem. pension com., 1976-93, 96-2000; trustee Clearinghouse for Midcontinent Founds., 1980-87; bd. dirs. Greater Kansas City Mental Health Found., 1963-69, treas., 1964-69, v.p., 1967-69; adv. bd. urban svcs. YMCA, Kansas City, 1976-83; cubmaster Kanza dist. Boy Scouts Am., 1982-83, dist. vice chmn., 1982-83, troop com., 1983-90, treas., 1986-88; bd. dirs. Scout Booster Club, Inc., 1989-94; mem. planned gift com. William Rockhill Nelson Gallery Art, Children's Mercy Hosp. Planned Gift Coun., 1991; mem. adv. com. Legal Assistance Program Avila Coll., 1978-80, adv. coun. Future Farmers Am., 1972-82; mgr. Oppenstein Bros. Found., 1979-85; trustee Village Presbyn. Ch., 1987-90, chmn., 1989-90, elder, 1994-97; found. com. Am. Royal Charitable Found., 1995—; bd. dirs. Village Presbyn. Ch. Found., 1987-89, 94-97, chmn., 1996-97, mem. adv. bd., 1997-2001; bd. dirs. Estate Planning Coun., 1984-86; mem. Kansas City Fed. Estate Planning Symposium Com., 1992-98; bd. dirs. Shawnee Mission Med. Ctr. Found., 1988—, fin. com., 1989-92, mem. planned giving com., 1996-, mem. investment com. Mem. Nat. Assn. Securities Dealers Inc. (bd. arbitrators 1994—), Am. Arbitration Assn. (panel arbitrators 1994-96), Estate Planning Soc. Kansas City, Mo. Bar Assn., Kans. Bar Assn., Johnson County Bar Assn., Estate Planning Assn. (pres. 1974-75), Kansas City Jr. C. of C. (v.p. 1964-66), Ea. Kans. Estate Planning Coun., 40-Yrs. Ago Column Club (program com. 1999-2000, pres. 2001, bd. trustees 2001-), Indian Hills Club, Delta Tau Delta Alumni (v.p. Kansas City chpt. 1978-80). Republican. Home: 9100 El Monte St Shawnee Mission KS 66207-2627 Office: One Glenwood Pl 9300 Metcalf Ave Ste 300 Shawnee Mission KS 66212-6319

MCEACHERN, ALLAN, lawyer; b. Vancouver, B.C., Can., May 20, 1926; s. John A. and Blanche L. (Roadhouse) McE.; m. Gloria, July 17, 1953 (dec. Sept. 1997); children: Jean Williams, Joanne Evans. BA, U. B.C., Vancouver, 1949; LLB, U. B.C., 1950, LLM (hon.), 1990. Assoc., sr. ptnr., barrister, solicitor Messrs. Russell & DuMoulin, Vancouver, B.C., 1950-78; chief justice Supreme Ct. B.C., 1979-88, Ct. Appeals B.C., Vancouver, 1988—2001; assoc. counsel Faskin Martineaes, Canada, 2001—. Pres. Kats Rugby Club, Vancouver, 1953-64, B.C. Lions Football Club, Vancouver, 1967, 68. 69, We. Football Conf., 1964, Can. Football League, 1967-68, commr. 1967-68. Mem. Can. Bar Assn. (bd. dirs.), Vancouver Bar Assn. (bd. dirs.), Legal Aid Soc. (pres. 1977-78), Law Soc. B.C. (bencher 1971-79). Avocations: sailing, gardening, walking, summer cottage. Office: Faskin Martineaes 1075 W George St Vancouver BC V6E 3G2 Canada

MCEACHERN, JOAN, medical association administrator; b. East Los Angeles, Calif., Feb. 28, 1937; d. Chester Manwell Biffi and Doris May Horrocks; m. Wayne Emery McEachern, Sept. 8, 1961 (dec. Mar. 1992); children: Marc Alan, David Wayne, Eric John. AA, East Los Angeles Coll., 1957. Sec. Flour Corp., City of Commerce, Calif., 1957-61; volunteer art tchr. Yorkville Schs., Yorkville, IL, 1975-1983; office supr. McKeoun-Dunn Ambulance, Oswego, Ill., 1992-97. Author: Illinois Association for Home and Community Education—An Aim for the Homemaker: 75 Years of Education and Outreach, 1999. Mem. Kendall County 4-H, various coms., 1975-2000, mem. Ill. 4-H Found., 1988-97, sec. exec. com. 1990-97; mem. various state coms. in 4-H, 1979-94, developed 4-H project books; ext. adv. coun. U. Ill., 1994-97; pres. Kendall County Homemakers Ext. Assn., 1982-84; adv. coun. Yorkville Schs. Curriculum Com., 1974-76, pres. 1975-76; started Picture Person Art Appreciation program, Yorkville Schs., 1976, chmn., 1975-81; vol. art tchr., 1975-83, others. Recipient Yorkville Area Humanitarian award City of Yorkville Human Svcs. Com., 1983, Disting. Svc. award award Kendall County Homemakers Ext. Assn., 1985, Kendall County Friend of 4-H award, 1989, numerous others. Mem.: Am. Women for Internat. Understanding (bd. dirs. 2002—), Associated Country Women of the World (pubs. and promotions com. 2001—04), Ill. Assn. Home and Cmty. Edn. (pres. 1994—97), Nat. Vol. Outreach Network (pres. 1998—), Kendall County Hist. Soc. (newsletter editor 1992—), Yorkville Women's club. Avocations: water color painting, skiing, photography, travel, reading. Home and Office: 137 Riverside Dr Yorkville IL 60560-9471 E-mail: mcskikat@hotmail.com.

MCEACHRAN, ANGUS, newspaper editor; b. Memphis, Aug. 24, 1939; s. Angus G. and Maxine (Taylor) McE.; m. Ann Blackwell; children: Angus G. 111, Amanda Simmons. Student, George Washington U., 1958-59, Memphis State U., 1959-61. Reporter The Comml. Appeal, Memphis, 1960-63, asst. city editor, 1963-65, metro editor, 1965-69, asst. mng. editor, 1969-77; exec. editor Birmingham (Ala.) Post-Herald, 1977-78, editor, 1978-82; exec. editor The Pitts. Press., 1982-83, editor, 1983-92, The Commercial Appeal, Memphis, 1993-94, editor, pres., 1994—. Corr. N.Y. Times, Wall St. Jour., Newsweek, The Nat. Observer. Mem. Am. Soc. Newspaper Editors, Pa. Soc. Newspaper Editors (bd. dirs.), Sigma Delta. Roman Catholic. Avocations: fishing, hiking, reading, racquetball. Home: 872 River Park Dr Memphis TN 38103-0804 Office: Commercial Appeal 495 Union Ave Memphis TN 38103-3221*

MCELDOWNEY, RENE, health care educator, consultant; b. Denver, Mar. 31, 1956; d. Raymond James and Barbara Louise (McNeal) Polanis; m. George Adams McEldowney Jr., June 1, 1984. AB, Morris Harvey Coll., Charleston, W.Va., 1977; BS, W.Va. State Coll., 1983; MBA, Marshall U., 1987; PhD, Va. Tech. U., 1994. X-ray technologist Charleston Area Med. Ctr., 1977-79, nuc. medicine technologist, 1979-84; asst. to v.p. acad. affairs Marshall U., Huntington, W.Va., 1984-87, mgmt. instr., 1987-89; asst. prof. Auburn (Ala.) U., 1992—. Rsch. cons. Netherland Sch. Govt., Das Hagg, Holland, 1990—; physics cons. Health Physics & Assocs., Roanoke, Va., 1991-92. Founder Food Search, Charleston, 1987-89; mem. Score, Huntington, 1988-89; literacy vol. Ala. Literacy Coun., Montgomery, Ala., 1993—; mem. Montgomery Jr. League, 1992—. Recipient scholarship Oxford U., 1991. Mem. ASPA, Am. Acad. Mgmt., Mortar Bd., Kappa Kappa Gamma. Avocations: book collecting, tennis, jogging, classical music. Office: Auburn U 1224 Haley Ctr Auburn AL 36849

MCELDOWNEY, ROLAND CONANT, gold mining company executive, photographer; b. Newton, Mass., Nov. 14, 1940; s. Richard Lancaster and Virginia Davis (Conant) McE.; m. Barbara Lynn Read, Mar. 26, 1966; children: Richard Read, Scott Roland, Kathryn Ramsay. AB in Geology, Franklin & Marshall Coll., 1963; MS in Geology, San Diego State U., 1971. Cert. geologist, Maine. Vol. geologist U.S. Peace Corps, Ghana, 1963-66; geologist U.S. Army C.E., San Francisco, 1966-68; sr. geologist Geodata Systems Inc., Orange, Calif., 1969-71; assoc. sr. geologist Dames & Moore, Denver, 1972-79; v.p. Apache Energy and Minerals Co., Lakewood, Colo., 1979-84; pres., owner Wolf Creek Exploration Co., Evergreen Colo., 1984—; sr. v.p. Internat. Gold Resources Corp., Houston, 1985-96; owner Image of Africa, Evergreen, Colo., 1999—. Mng. dir. Internat. Gold Resources, Inc., Bibani, Ghana, 1990-96 (discovered Bibani Open Pit Gold Deposit). Artist, producer silver proof coin World Cup Skiing, Breckenridge, Colo., 1991-92; contbr. numerous articles to profl. geol. and engring. jours. Mem. Soc. Econ. Geologists, Soc. for Mining, Metallurgy and Exploration, Geol. Soc. Am., Kiwanis (past mem. bd. dirs. Blue Spruce). Republican. Avocations: artist, hunting, fishing, skiing, biking. Home: 29434 Greenwood Ln Evergreen CO 80439-7446 E-mail: auexplore@aol.com.

MCELHANEY, JAMES WILLSON, lawyer, educator, author, trial consultant; b. N.Y.C., Dec. 10, 1937; s. Lewis Keck and Sara Jane (Hess) McE.; m. Maxine Dennis Jones, Aug. 17, 1961; children: David, Benjamin. AB, Duke U., 1960; LLB, 1962. Bar: Wis. 1962. Assoc. Wickham, Borgelt, Skogstad & Powell, 1966; asst. prof. U. Md. Law Sch., 1966-69, assoc. prof., 1969-72; vis. prof. So. Meth. U. Sch. of Law, Dallas, 1973-74, prof., 1974-76; Joseph C. Hostetler prof. trial practice and advocacy Case Western Res. U. Sch. of Law, Cleve., 1976—2002, Baker & Hostetler Disting. scholar in trial practice, 2002—; mem. faculty Nat. Inst. Trial Advocacy, Boulder, Colo., 1975—; Fred Parks Disting. lectr. in trial advocacy South Tex. Coll. Law, Houston, 2002—. Vis. prof. U. Tulsa Coll. Law, summer 1977, 79, Ind. U. Law Sch., summer 1980; cons. to U.S. Atty. Gen. on Justice Dept. Advocacy Tng. Programs, 1979— ; lectr. in field; litigation cons.; spl. cons. U. S.C. Sch. of Law Nat. Advocacy Ctr., 1998. Author: Effective Litigation: Trials, Problems and Materials, 1974, Trial Notebook, 1981, 3rd edit., 1994, Trial Notebook on Tape: The Basics, 1989, Mc Elhaney's Trial Notebook on Tape: Advanced Techniques, 1991, Mc Elhaney's Trial Notebook on Tape: Evidence, Foundations and Objections, 1992, Mc Elhaney's Trial Notebook on Tape: Winning Tactics, 1994, Mc Elhaney's Litigation, 1995, Mc Elhaney on Cross-Examination on Tape, 1997, Mc Elhaney on Depositions and Trial Preparation on Tape, 1999; editor-in-chief Litigation mag., 1984-86, sr. editor, 1986—; columnist Trial Notebook, Litigation; contbr. articles to profl. jours. Mem. ABA (mem. coun. on litigation 1987—, author jour. column Litigation), Assn. Am. Law Schs. (chmn. sect. on trial advocacy 1974-76, chmn. sect. on evidence 1978). Home and Office: PO Box 367 Chama NM 87520-0367 Fax: 505-756-1820. *The lamp of doctrine is a flickering and unsteady guide; we are led more by facts than obtuse theory.*

MC ELHANEY, JOHN HESS, lawyer; b. Milw., Apr. 16, 1934; s. Lewis Keck and Sara Jane (Hess) McE.; m. Jacquelyn Masur, Aug. 4, 1962; children— Scott, Victoria. BBA, So. Meth. U., 1956, JD, 1958. Bar: Tex. bar 1958. Pvt. practice law, Dallas, 1958—; pntr. Locke, Liddell & Sapp, L.L.C., 1976—. Lectr. law So. Meth. U., 1967-76 Contbr. articles to legal jours. Trustee St. Mark's Sch. Tex., 1980-86. Fellow Am. Coll. Trial Lawyers; mem. Am. Bd. Trial Advs., ABA, Tex. Bar Assn., So. Meth. U. Law Alumni Assn. (pres. 1972-73, dir. 1970-73), Town and Gown Club (pres. 1981-82). Presbyterian. Home: 5340 Tanbark Dr Dallas TX 75229-5555 Office: Locke Liddell & Sapp 2200 Ross Ave Ste 2200 Dallas TX 75201-6776

MCELHENY, ANNA CONNER, family therapist; b. St. Petersburg, Fla., Nov. 14, 1967; d. Ann Conner Davis; m. Carl William McElheny, Jan. 8, 1994. BS in Polit. Sci., Charleston So. U., 1990; MEd in Clin. Counseling, Citadel, 1993. Social worker Dept. Social Svcs., Charleston, S.C., 1990-93; guidance counselor Vance County Schs., Henderson, N.C., 1994-95; family therapist Area Mental Health, 1995—. Coord., creator PAL to pal Vol. program, Henderson, 1994—; mem. Vance Against Substance Abuse, 1994-95, Task Force Sch. Violence, 1994-95. Vol. Friends Youth Program, Henderson, 1994-95. Mem. Youth Svcs. Adv. Coun. Democrat. Avocations: reading, travel. Home: 120 Pointer Dr Summerville SC 29485-5124 Office: Area Mental Health 303 S Garnett St Henderson NC 27536-4537

MCELHINNEY, JAMES LANCEL, artist, educator; b. Abington, Pa., Feb. 3, 1952; s. James and Joan Howland (Carpenter) McE.; m. Victoria Maria Dávila, Sept. 12, 1981 (div.). Scholarship student, Skowhegan (Maine) Sch. of Art, 1973; BFA, Temple U., 1974; MFA, Yale U., 1976. Asst. prof. Moore Coll. Art, Phila., 1977-78, Skidmore Coll., Saratoga Springs, N.Y., 1979-87; adj. instr. UCLA, 1983, Moore Coll. Art, 1983, Tyler Sch. Art, Phila., 1983-86, U. of Arts, Phila., 1985-89; instr. Milw. Inst. Art and Design, 1991-93; vis. artist East Carolina U., Greenville, N.C., 1994-98; head painting and drawing program visual arts dept. U. Colo., Denver, 1998—; dir. study abroad program Feltre, Italy, 2000—. Artist in residence Harper's Ferry Nat. Hist. Park, 1999; lectr. USAF Acad., 2001. One-man shows include Peninsula Ctr. for the Fine Arts, Newport News, Va., 1993, Danville (Va.) Mus., 1993, Second Street Gallery, Charlottesville, Va., 1995, F.A.N. Gallery, Phila., 1995, 1998, Greenville (N.C.) Mus. Art, 1996, Lee Hansley Gallery, Raleigh, N.C., 1996, 1998, 1999, Ashville (N.C.) Art Mus., 1996, William Havu Gallery, Denver, 2002, exhibited in group shows at Chrysler Mus., Norfolk, Va., 1999, Allen Sheppard Gallery, N.Y.C., 1999, Ucross Found., 2000, Nicolayseu Mus., 2000. Vol. Richmond (Va.) Nat. Battlefield Park, 1991—. Grantee (painting) NEA, 1987—88, Ptnrs. int he Arts, Richmond Arts Coun., 1995, rsch., U. Colo., 2000. Mem. Coll. Art Assn. Home: 5984 S Milwaukee Way Littleton CO 80121-2815 Office: U Colo Coll Arts Media Box 177 PO Box 173364 Denver CO 80217-3364

MCELHINNEY, SUSAN KAY (KATE ECHEVERRIA) (KATE MCELHINNEY), executive assistant; b. Greeley, Colo., May 20, 1947; d. Glenn Eugene and Maxine (Filkins) McE.; m. Ben Echeverria, 1997. Student, U. N.C., 1965-67, U. Kans., 1969, U. Colo., 1971-72, 80. Adminstrv. sec. Colo. Pub. Defender, Denver, 1970-74; clk. Colo. Dist. Ct., Boulder, 1974-80; legal asst., office mgr. Law Office Ben Echeverria, San Marcos, Calif., 1986-97; exec. asst. Palomar (Calif.) C.C., 1997—. Mem. black tie fund raising com. Palomar C.C., 1991-92. Republican. Avocations: reading, golf, travel, animal advocate, gardening.

MCELHINNY, HAROLD JOHN, lawyer; b. San Francisco, Jan. 5, 1947; s. Harold James and Margaret I. (Mahoney) McE.; m. Mary Ellen McElhinny, June 22, 1968; children: Hannah, Jennifer, William. BA in Polit. Sci., U. Santa Clara, 1970; JD, U. Calif., Berkeley, 1975. Bar: Calif. 1976, U.S. Supreme Ct. 1983. Vol. Peace Corps., Tripoli, Libya, 1968-69; juvenile counselor Santa Clara County (Calif.) Juvenile Hall, 1969-72; law clk. U.S. Dist. Ct., Hartford, Conn., 1975-76; ptnr. Morrison & Foerster, San Francisco, 1976—. Mem. ABA, Calif. Bar Assn., State Bar Calif. (rev. dept. 1986-89, chmn. 1988), San Francisco Bar Assn., Am. Intellectual Property Law Assn., Assn. Bus. Trial Lawyers (bd. govs. 1992-97, pres. 1997). Democrat. Roman Catholic. Office: Morrison & Foerster 425 Market St Fl 30 San Francisco CA 94105-2482 E-mail: hmcelhinny@mofo.com.

MCELLIGOTT, JAMES PATRICK, JR. lawyer; b. Chgo., Jan. 11, 1948; s. James Patrick and Helen Cecelia (Hogan) McE.; children: Michael Sean, Andrew David; m. Trina Reff, Aug. 25, 1985. BA, U. Ill., Urbana, 1970; JD, Harvard U., 1973. Bar: Va. 1974, U.S. Dist. Ct. (ea. and we. dists.) Va. 1974, U.S. Ct. Appeals (4th cir.) 1974, U.S. Supreme Ct. 1979. Research asst. U. Ill., 1970; assoc. McGuire, Woods & Battle, Richmond, 1973-79; ptnr. McGuire Woods, 1979—. Mem. exec. com. Va. Home for Boys, Richmond, 1976-92, pres. bd. govs., 1981-83; mem. Leadership Metro Richmond-Met. C. of C., 1984-85; bd. dirs. ARC Greater Richmond Chpt., 1990-96, chmn., 1994-95. Recipient Clara Barton award ARC Richmond Chpt., 1997. Mem. ABA, Va. Bar Assn. (exec. com., chmn. pub. rels. com. 1978-82, producer pub. svc. message 1973, Hot Spot award 1973), Coll. of Labor and Employment Lawyers, Richmond Bar Assn., Fed. Bar Assn. (pres. Richmond chpt. 1986), Nat. Sch. Bds. Assn., Coun. of Sch. Attys., Coll. Labor and Employment Lawyers, Phi Beta Kappa, Phi Kappa Phi, Omicron Delta Epsilon. Home: 203 Cyril Ln Richmond VA 23229-7740 Office: McGuire Woods LLP One James Ctr Richmond VA 23219-3229 E-mail: jmcelligott@mcguirewoods.com.

MC ELRATH, RICHARD ELSWORTH, retired insurance company executive; b. Thompsontown, Pa., Oct. 11, 1932; s. Clayton Ellsworth and Jane Elizabeth (Shoop) McE.; m. Donna Gail Booher, Aug. 18, 1952; children—Leslie Jo, Jennifer Jo, Josie Arlene Elizabeth, Rebekah Clare. *My parents, descended from Eighteenth Century immigrants, raised twelve children on a hard-scrabble, Appalachian farm along the Juniata River in Pennsylvania during the Depression. With little but courage and tenacity, by example they instilled the desire to make something of life, regardless of conditions. Both are now dead but their children and grandchildren have included ministers, teachers, business executives, professional musicians, West Point & Harvard graduates, and other worthy vocations. However, they would have eschewed any triumphalism to remember other descendants who did not find the twentieth century hospitable for their personal and moral development.* BS cum laude, Elizabethtown (Pa.) Coll., 1955; MBA cum laude, Harvard U., 1961. Research asst. Harvard U., 1961-62; asst. to pres. Callaway Mills Co., LaGrange, Ga., 1963-65; with Irving Trust Co., N.Y.C., 1965-73, v.p., 1969-73; treas. Tchrs. Ins. Annuity Assn. and Coll. Retirement Equities Fund, 1973-81; v.p. Met. Life Ins. Co., 1982-95. Pres., dir. MetLife Funding, Inc., MetLife Credit, Inc., 1984-95. Author articles, case studies. Trustee Elizabethtown Coll.; mem. Society Valley Hosp., Ridgewood, N.J.; mem. Boston Rep. Com., 1961-63, Troup County (Ga.) Rep. Com., 1964-65; bd. dirs. Family Counseling Svc., Ridgewood, 1986-92. Lt. comdr. USNR, 1956-59. Mem. Assn. Gov. Bds. Univs. and Colls. Clubs: Harvard (N.Y.C.). Methodist. Home: 17 Cedar St Glen Rock NJ 07452-1608

MCELROY, ANNIE LAURIE, nursing educator, administrator; b. Quitman, Ga., Dec. 30, 1945; d. Frank H. Sr. and Ina Mae (Carpenter) McElroy; children: Laurie, Matt. Grad., Ga. Bapt. Sch Nursing, 1966; BS, Valdosta State U., 1988, MEd, 1989, postgrad., 1991; PhD, Ga. State U., 1994. Health aid, then head nurse Presbyn. Home, Quitman, 1966-68, 68-70; owner, bookkeeper Maddox Drugstore, 1970-80; instr. health occupations Brooks County High Sch., 1981-88, instr. nurses aides, 1983; instr. health occupations Lowndes High Sch., Valdosta, Ga., 1988-89; instr. dept. vocat. edn. Valdosta State U., 1989-92; dir. practical nursing program S.W. Ga. Tech. Coll., Thomasville, 1992—, coord. Allied Health diploma program, 1992—, dean Allied Health, 2002—. Recipient Most Disting. Alumna Ga. Bapt. Coll. Nursing, 2000. Mem. ASCD, NEA, AAUW, Ga. Edn. Assn., Nat. Assn. Educators, Ga. Assn. Educators, Assn. for Career and Tech. Edn., Assn. Indsl. and Tech. Tchr. Educators, Internat. Tech. Edn. Assn., Ga. Nurses Assn., Phi Delta Kappa, Phi Kappa Phi. Avocations: piano, saxophone, bassoon, walking. Home: 607 N Laurel St Quitman GA 31643-1221 E-mail: amcelroy@swgtc.net.

MCELROY, BARBARA WOODS, educator, consultant; b. Canton, OH, Sept. 4, 1953; d. John Alvah Woods, Leila June Woods; m. Joseph William McElroy; children: Michelle, Amie. PhD, The Pennsylvania State University, State College, PA, 1991—96; MBA, Kent State University, Kent, OH, 1989—91; BGS, Ohio University, Athens, OH, 1987—89; AAB, Stark Technical College, Canton, OH, 1976—79; MBA, Kent State University, Kent, Ohio, 1989—91; BGS, Ohio University, Athens, Ohio, 1987—89; AAB, Stark Technical College, Canton, Ohio, 1976—79. Assistant Bruner, Cox, Lotz, Syler, and Graves, CPAs, Canton, OH, 1981—83; Staff Accountant R G Santos and Company, CPAs, 1983—84; Instructor Stark Technical College, 1983—90; Owner Barbara McElroy, CPA, 1984—91; Visiting Faculty University of Akron, Akron; Teaching Assistant Kent State University, Kent, 1989—90; Research Assistant The Pennsylvania State University, State College, PA, 1991—96; Assistant Professor Berry College, Rome, 1996—2002. Board of Directors Canton Natural Foods Co-Op, Canton, OH, 1988—91; Board of Advisors Executive Round Table, Rome, 2000—02; Public Awareness Committee Georgia Society of CPAs, Atlanta, 1999—2002; Treasurer American Association of University Women, Rome, 1998—2000, Nominating Committee, 2001—01. Author: (article) New Accountant, 2000, Journal of the American Academy of Business, 2001 (Best Author, 2001), (articles) World Association for Case Method Research and Application publications, 1997, (article) , 1999. Volunteer Habitat for Humanity, Cartersville, GA, 2001—02. Mem.: Georgia Society of CPAs. Avocation: Gardening, reading, sewing. Office: Berry College Box 5024 Mount Berry GA 30162-5024 Business E-Mail: bmcelroy@campbell.berry.edu.

MCELROY, HOWARD CHOWNING, lawyer; b. Shreveport, La., Mar. 26, 1946; s. Charles Imogene and Verna Mae (Snow) McE.; m. Heidi Margot Hansen, June 17, 1970; children: Andrew, Christopher, Karen. BS, U.S. Mil. Acad., 1968; JD, Georgetown U., 1977. Bar: Va. 1977, U.S. Dist. Ct. (we. dist.) Va. 1977, U.S. Ct. Appeals (4th cir.) 1977. Ptnr. Bundy McElroy Hodges, Abingdon, Va., 1995—. Mem. mandatory continuing legal edn. bd. Va. State Bar 1986-89, professionalism course faculty, 1991-94. Capt. M.I. U.S. Army, 1968-72, Vietnam. Fellow Am. Bar Found., Va. Law Found.; mem. ABA, Am. Bd. Trial Advocates (Va. chpt.), Def. Rsch. Inst., Va. Bar Assn. (exec. com. 1991-95, sec. 1993-95), Va. Assn. Def. Attys. (pres. 1995-96), Internat. Assn. Def. Counsel, Assn. Def. Trial Attys., Rotary (pres. local club 1983-84, Paul Harris fellow). Episcopalian. Home: 160 Crestview Dr NE Abingdon VA 24210-2010 Office: Bundy McElroy Hodges 330 Cummings St Abingdon VA 24210-3208 E-mail: hmcelroybmhlaw@naxs.net.

MCELROY, JACK, editor; B in English, Journalism, U. Ariz.; M in Mgmt., U. N.Mex. Mng. editor The Albuquerque Tribune; reporter Douglas (Ariz.) Daily Dispatch , 1976; mng. editor Rocky Mountain News, editor, assoc. mng. editor, asst. mng. editor, dep. mng. editor, mng. editor, spl. projects editor, 1991, gen. mgr. combined internet ops., 1999; gen. mgr. combined Internet ops. Boulder's Daily Camera, Denver, 1999; editor Knoxville News Sentinel, 2001—. Office: Knoxville News Sentinel 208 W Church Ave Knoxville TN 37902 Office Fax: 865-342-6400. Business E-Mail: letters@knews.com.*

MCELROY, JEROME LATHROP, economics educator; b. St. Louis, Sept. 14, 1937; s. King Gerard and Audrey (Lathrop) McE.; m. Birdie Maria Rossow; children: Jacqueline, Christopher. BA, St. Louis U., 1961, PhL, 1962, MA in Econs., 1965; PhD in Econs., U. Colo., 1972. Instr. St. John's Coll., Belize City, Belize, 1962-65; grad. assoc. U. Colo., Boulder, 1971-72; asst. prof. econs. Coll. of V.I., St. Thomas, 1972-75, assoc. prof. econs., 1975-79; dir. planning Govt. of V.I., St. Thomas, 1979-80; assoc. prof. econs. U. Notre Dame, Ind., 1980-82, St. Mary's Coll., South Bend, 1982-86, prof. econs., 1986—, chmn. dept. bus. and econs., 1990-93. Rsch. fellow Island Resources Found., Washington, 1980—; expert adv. panel Office Tech. Assessment, U.S. Congress, 1985-86; econ. cons. U.S. AID, 1987-89, Govt. V.I., 1974-79, 89. Author: Consumer Expenditure Patterns, 1980, USVI Status Options, 1989; contbr. articles to profl. jours., poems to lit. mags. Mem. adv. bd. Ea. Caribbean Ctr., U. V.I., 1993-95. Recipient Maria Pieta Tchr. award, St. Mary's Coll., 1989, Tchr. of the Yr., Coll. of V.I., 1973, Spes Unica Svc. award, 1997. Mem. Am. Econ. Assn., Caribbean Studies Assn., So. Reg. Sci. Assn., Midwest Assn. Latin Americanists, Internat. Sci. Coun. for Island Devel. (founding mem.), Inst. for Devel. of Insular Economies and Socs. (founding mem.), Island Environ. Inst. (founding mem.). Democrat. Roman Catholic. Avocations: swimming, writing poetry. Home: 2036 Portage Ave South Bend IN 46616-2033 Office: Saint Mary's College 1 Madeleva Notre Dame IN 46556

MC ELROY, JOHN HARLEY, electrical and industrial engineering educator; b. Marion, Ohio, June 27, 1936; s. Francis and Alice Marie McElroy; m. Eleonore Hildegard Schmidt, Mar. 18, 1957. BS in Elec. Engring, U. Tex., Austin, 1966; M.E.E., Cath. U. Am., 1973, PhD, 1978. Instr. guided missles Air Defense Sch. U.S. Army, 1957-63; rsch. asst. Quantum Electronics rsch. Lab U. Texas, Austin, 1963-66; staff Goddard Flight Center, Greenbelt, Md., 1966-79, 80-82, chief communications tech. div., 1978-79, dep. dir. center, 1980-82; dir. communications programs NASA Hdqrs., Washington, 1979-80; asst. adminstr. NOAA, 1982-85; dir. spl. projects Hughes Aircraft Co., Los Angeles, 1985-86; v.p. tech. Hughes Communications, Inc., 1986-87; dean Coll. Engring., prof. elec. engring. U. Tex., Arlington, 1987-96, vice provost for rsch. and grad. studies, 1996-97, prof. elec. and indsl. engring., 1997-2000, dean emeritus Coll. Engring.; chair space studies bd. Nat. Rsch. Coun., 2000—. Cons. satellite communications and earth observations. Contbr. articles to profl. jours. Served with AUS, 1954-63. Recipient Apollo Achievement award NASA, 1969, Applications Tech. Satellite award, 1975, Earth Resources Satellite award, 1973, Internat. Coop. in Space Sci. medal AIAA, 1997; named Wernher von Braun Meml. Lectr. Smithsonian Instn., Disting. Hon. Alumnus U. Tex., Arlington, 1998. Fellow AIAA, IEEE, Washington Acad. Scis.; mem. Nat. Acad. Engring. Home: 5687 Wild Olive St Las Vegas NV 89118-1956 Office: Space Studies Bd 2101 Constitution Ave NW Washington DC 20418-0007 E-mail: jhmcelroy@worldnet.att.net.

MCELROY, JUNE PATRICIA, sales consultant; b. Atlantic City, Sept. 26, 1929; d. Edmund N. and Dorothy R. (McDowell) Ricchezza; m. Ottavio Gelmi, Dec. 16, 1954 (div. 1964); 1 child, Alessandra; m. Robert Joseph McElroy, Oct. 16, 1970 (dec. May 1974). Student, Temple U., 1947-48, Georgetown U., 1951-53. Staff mem. Am. Consulate Gen., Milan, 1954; legis. asst. U.S. Senate, Washington, 1956; social sec. Amb. of Finland, 1958; adminstrv. asst., translator, interpreter Roosevelt and Clark Lobbyists, 1958—59; legis. asst. to congressman Washington, 1960-65; sr. assoc. Gillmore M. Perry Co., 1965-76; sales exec., cons., 1980-87; ptnr. Mfrs. Representatives Internat., Washington, 1987-97; ret. Pres. Spanish Portuguese Study Group, 1994-95. Mem.: AAUW, Pan Am. Round Table, Equestrian Order Holy Sepulchre of Jerusalem (Lady), Georgetown U. Alumni Assn., John Carroll Soc., Army Navy Club (Washington). Republican. Roman Catholic. Home: 4000 Cathedral Ave NW Apt 208B Washington DC 20016-5254

MCELROY, LEO FRANCIS, communications consultant, journalist; b. Los Angeles, Oct. 12, 1932; s. Leo Francis and Helen Evelyn (Silliman) McE.; m. Dorothy Frances Montgomery, Nov. 3, 1956 (div. 1981); children: James, Maureen, Michael, Kathleen; m. Judith Marie Lewis, May 30, 1992. BS in English, Loyola U., L.A., 1953. News dir. KFI, KRLA, KABC Radio, L.A., 1964-72; pub. affairs host TV Sta. KCET, 1967-74; v.p. Sta. KROQ AM/FM, 1972-74; polit. editor Sta. KABC-TV, 1974-81; pres. McElroy Comm., Sacramento, 1981—. Pres. sec. Lt. Gov.'s Office, Sacramento, 1982-84; chmn. Calif. AP Broadcasters, 1972-74; cons. State Office Migrant Edn., Sacramento, 1974, Californians for Water, L.A., 1982, Calif. Water Protection Coun., Sacramento, 1982, Planning and Conservation League, Sacramento, 1984—, Common Cause, Sacramento, 1988—. Author: Uneasy Partners, 1984; author plays: Mermaid Tavern, 1956, To Bury Caesar, 1952 (Christopher award), Rocket to Olympus, 1960, The Code of Whiskey King, 1995. State del. Western Am. Assembly on Prison Reform, Berkeley, Calif., 1973; chmn. State Disaster Info. Task Force, Calif., 1973-74; campaign media cons. statewide issues, various candidates, Sacramento, L.A., 1981—; bd. dirs. Vols. in Victim Assistance, Sacramento, 1984, Rescue Alliance, Sacramento, 1987-92, Mental Health Assn., Sacramento, 1985-89, Leukemia Soc., 1992-97. Recipient Gabriel award Cath. Archdiocese, L.A., 1972, Golden Mike award Radio-TV News Assn., L.A., 1973; Hon. Resolution, Calif. State Assembly, Sacramento, 1981. Mem. ASCAP, AFTRA, Screen Actors Guild, Am. Assn. Polit. Cons. Roman Catholic. Home: 2262 Swarthmore Dr Sacramento CA 95825-6608 Office: McElroy Comm 2410 K St Ste C Sacramento CA 95816-5002 E-mail: McELCOM@pacbell.net.

MCELROY, MARY M. (MICKIE MCELROY), educational writer; b. Ft. Worth, June 29, 1944; d. Kennedy King and Maurine (Davenport) McElroy; m. James William Salterio Jr., Aug. 24, 1966 (div. Aug. 1968); m. Michael John Waters, Dec. 13, 1975 (div. Aug. 1983). BA, U. Tex., 1966, MA, 1970; M in Ednl. Adminstrn., Western Wash. U., 1989. Cert. secondary sch. adminstr., classrm. tchr. math., Latin, history. Classrm. tchr. various schs., Wash. and Tex., 1970-78, 80-89; instrnl. cons. in math. Region XIII Ednl. Svc. Ctr., West Tex., 1979-80; asst. prin. Stevens Mid. Sch., Port Angeles, Wash., 1989-90; bus. owner Office on Call, Seattle, 1991-96; dir. edn. Tex. Soc. Profl. Engrs., Austin, 1996-98; curriculum developer Tchg. Tech., Inc., 1998-99, corp. trainer, 1998-99; devel. editor Thinkwell, 1999—2001; editor, writer Kamico Instrnl. Media, 2001—. Dir. Regional Math. Competition, Everett, Wash., 1981-84; chair Com. to Improve Comm., Everett, 1986-87. Author: Powerpoint for Educators, 1998, The Internet and Social Studies in the Classroom, 1999, Designing Web Pages for Libraries, 1998. Dir. Magnolia Summerfest, Magnolia C. of C., Seattle, 1992-94; bd. dirs. Big Bros., Big Sisters, Port Angeles, Wash., 1989-90. Named Networker of Yr., Western Wash. Entrepreneurs Assn., 1992. Mem. Nat. Coun. Tchrs. Math., Wild Bunch. Democrat. Episcopalian. Avocations: painting, reading, travel, photography. Home: 2712 Deeringhill Dr Austin TX 78745-5112 E-mail: mickiemc@alumni.utexas.net.

MCELROY, MAURINE DAVENPORT, financier, educator; b. Eastland, Tex., Sept. 28, 1913; d. William Fred and Mary Ewell (Johnson) Davenport; m. Kennedy King McElroy, Aug. 9, 1937 (dec. Mar. 1996); children: Mary M., Kennedy King Jr. BA, Tex. Tech U., 1937; MA, Hardin-Simmons U., 1941; PhD, U. Tex., 1964. Tchr. Eastland West Ward Elem. Sch., 1933-39, Eastland H.S., 1939-41, Miller H.S., Corpus Christi, Tex., 1951-54, Ray H.S., Corpus Christi, 1954-57; instr. Del Mar Coll., 1957-59; prin. Birdville H.S., Ft. Worth, 1942-43; feature writer Ark. Dem.-Gazette, Little Rock, 1948-51; assoc. prof. emeritus dept. English U. Tex., Austin, 1964—. Cons. in field. Contbr. articles to profl. publs. Patron art museums, theatrical orgns., hist. preservation; sponsor Shelter for Abused Women and Children; fin. mgr. trusts. Mem. AAUW, Am. Assn. Colls. Tchg. English, Coll. English Assn. (life), Renaissance Soc. Am. Avocations: travel, reading, theatre, horticulture. Home: 3215 Gilbert St Austin TX 78703-2221 Office: U Tex Austin Dept English Parlin Hall 108 Austin TX 78712

MCELROY, MICHAEL ROBERT, lawyer; b. Providence, Feb. 7, 1951; s. Gerald Robert and Jeannette (Belanger) McE.; m. Christine Anne O'Donnell, June 5, 1976; children: Brian Robert, Dianne Elizabeth, Erin Christine. BA with highest distinction, U. R.I., 1973; JD cum laude, Boston U., 1976; MS in Taxation cum laude, Bryant Coll., 1987. Bar: Tenn. 1976, Mass. 1985, U.S. Dist. Ct. (ea. dist.) Tenn. 1977, U.S. Ct. Appeals (5th cir.) 1977, U.S. Supreme Ct. 1979, U.S. Ct. Appeals (6th cir.) 1980, R.I. 1981, U.S. Dist. Ct. R.I. 1981, U.S. Ct. Appeals (1st cir.) 1981, U.S. Dist. Ct. Mass. 2000. Trial atty. TVA, Knoxville, 1976-81; counsel R.I. Pub. Utilities Commn., Providence, 1982-83; spl. asst. atty. gen. Office Atty. Gen., 1982-83; ptnr. O'Leary & McElroy, 1981-85; sole practice, 1985-87; ptnr. Schacht & McElroy, 1987—. Pres. Utility Cons., Inc., Providence, 1983; ptnr. McElroy, Lawrence, Edge & Assocs., Providence, 1983-85. Legal counsel for candidate Congl. campaign, Providence, 1982; legal counsel Pawtuxet Valley Preservation and Hist. Soc., West Warwick, R.I., 1983—; chief speech writer for candidate gubernatorial campaign, R.I., 1984; chief legal counsel for candidate gubernatorial campaign, R.I., 1988, Gov. Bruce Sundlun's successful gubernatorial campaign, 1990; legal counsel to R.I. Pers. Appeal Bd., 1991—; arbitrator Superior Ct. R.I., 1992—; spl. master/commr., 1993—; mediator Superior Ct., 1999—; spl. legal counsel to R.I. Ethics Commn., 2000—. Danforth Found. hon. fellow, 1973; Rhodes scholar nominee, 1973; honoree for life-saving CPR, TVA, 1980; nominated for judgeship Jud. Nom. Commn. Superior Ct., 1994. Mem.: ATLA, Million Dollar Advs. Forum, Assn. Trial Lawyers RI, RI Bar Assn. (mem. Supreme Ct., fed. ct. and superior ct. bench/bar coms.). Democrat. Roman Catholic. Home: 345 Sharon St Providence RI 02908-2220 Office: PO Box 6721 Providence RI 02940-6721 E-mail: mcelroymik@aol.com.

MCELROY, MICHELLE MARIE, physician; b. Atchison, Kans., Jan. 25, 1968; d. James Patrick and Victoria Jane (DeGreeff) McE. BS, Mich. State U., 1990; DO, Kirksville Coll. Osteo., 1994. Intern Riverside Osteo. Hosp., Trenton, Mich., 1994-95, resident in ob-gyn., 1995-98; with Women's Health Assocs. of Middle Ga., Dublin, 1998—2000, Cynthia J. Caputo, MD, PC, Blue Springs, Mo., 2001—. Clin. instr. dept. osteo. medicine Mich. State U., East Lansing, 1995-98. Mem. Am. Osteo. Assn., Am. Coll. Osteo. Obstetricians and Gynecologists, Mo. Assn. Osteo. Physicians and Surgeons. Roman Catholic. Avocations: aerobics, jogging, family and friends. Home: 25800 E 30th Terrace S Blue Springs MO 64015-1114 Office: Cynthia J Caputo MD PC 1900 NW Copper Oaks Circle Bldg 1 Blue Springs MO 64015 E-mail: mobdo@aol.com.

MCELROY, TOM, collage artist, art gallery owner; b. Lowell, Mass., Nov. 1, 1954; s. David Edwards McElroy and Mary Elizabeth Sinclaire; m. Patricia Warren, Apr. 2, 1977 (div.); children: Heather E., Sara L.; life ptnr. Lisa Michelle Sargent, Dec. 31, 1991; 1 child Tristan. Theatre artist, Colo., 1976—86; dir. of performing arts Colorado Springs Fine Arts Ctr., 1986—90; artistic dir. Open Egg Gallery and Theatre, 1990—92, Open Egg Theatre, San Francisco, 1992—94; owner, dir. Egg Studio Theatre, Colorado Springs, 1994—98, CHAOS Studios, Colorado Springs, 1998—. Lectr. Colo. U. at The Springs, Colorado Springs, 2001; lectr./guest artist Colorado Springs Fine Arts Ctr., 2001—02. Video art (Best of Show, 2002). Precinct chair Dem. Party, Colorado Springs, 1988. Mem.: IATSE. Taoist. Office: CHAOS Studios 802 N Weber St. Colorado Springs CO 80903 Personal E-mail: atomic54@yahoo.com.

MCELVAIN, DAVID PLOWMAN, retired manufacturing company financial executive; b. Chgo., Oct. 16, 1937; s. Carl R. and Ruth P. (Plowman) McE.; m. Mary Rosalind Hysong, Dec. 20, 1961; children: Jana, Jodi. BBA, U. Ariz., 1961, MBA, 1962. Cert. mgmt. acct. Consolidation acct., exec. divsn. Dresser Industries, Inc., Dallas, 1962-67, corp. fin. controller, 1973-76, dir. fin. svcs., 1976-78, staff v.p. fin. svc. and risk mgmt., 1978-82, exec. v.p. fin. svcs. group, 1982-83, pres. fin. svcs. group, 1984-86, v.p. fin., CFO, 1987-93; owner McElvain Oil Co., 1993—. Controller crane, hoist & tower div., Muskegon, Mich., 1967-73. Mem. Nat. Assn. Accts., Beta Gamma Sigma, Phi Delta Theta. Episcopalian. Home: 14828 Bellbrook Dr Dallas TX 75254-7647

MCELVEEN, ALLEN RAYMOND, protective services official; b. Florence, S.C., Nov. 18, 1966; s. Johnny Ray and Patsy Ann McElveen. Security law enforcement col. United Artist, Florence, 1988—91; security law enforcement lt. Fed. Security, 1991; security guard Anderson Armor Car, 1991—94; security law enforcement sgt. PPM Security Inc., 1994—99; law enforcement profl. Darlington (S.C.) County Sheriff Dept., 2000—. Author: (novels) Dragon Master Revenge, 1996, Return of the Dragon Master, 1997; songwriter: albums Songs of Allen R. McElveen. Decorated Medal of Valor, Purple Heart. Avocation: martial arts training. Home: 2505 Sage Rd Effingham SC 29541-4443

MCELVEEN, JOSEPH JAMES, JR. journalist, author, educator, mass media executive; b. Sanford, Fla., Feb. 23, 1939; s. Joseph James Sr. and Genevieve (Stoll) McE.; m. Mary Louise Young, Aug. 18, 1979; 1 child, Ryan Leighton. BA, Furman U., 1961; MA, U. S.C., 1968. Editor, pub. West Ashley News, Charleston, S.C., 1951-57; reporter, photographer Charleston Post, 1955-57; tchr. English and journalism St. Andrew's Parish High Sch., Charleston, 1961-65; dir. info., prof. journalism Columbia Coll., S.C., 1965-68; prof. journalism U. S.C., Columbia, 1968-79; sr. pub. affairs specialist FCC, Washington, 1979-81; dir. pub. affairs adminstrn. Nat. Cable TV Assn., 1981-87; dir. internal communications Corp. for Pub. Broadcasting, 1987-92, dir. program adminstrn., 1992-96, sr. program officer, 1996-99; media/comms. cons. Vienna, 1999—. Ombudsman, columnist Alexandria Gazette, Va., 1981—88; pres. McElveen Seminars, Vienna, 2000—. Author: Introduction to Creative Writing, 1963, Modern Communications, 1964; contbr. chpt. to Dictionary of Literary Biography (Mencken), 1986, Words, Words, Words: A Journalist's Memoir, 1997, Effective Writing and Editing, 2000, 1940s: Decade on the Threshold, 2000. Mem. Orgn. of News Ombudsmen, Soc. Profl. Journalists, Mencken Soc. Episcopalian. Avocations: photography, reading, desktop pub. Office: 1807 Hursley Ct Vienna VA 22182-2105 E-mail: jjmcelveen@aol.com.

MCELVEEN, JUNIUS CARLISLE, JR. lawyer; b. Rogersville, Tenn., Feb. 17, 1947; s. Junius Carlisle and Martha Kathleen (Harrison) McE.; m. Mary Wallace Pyles, Sept. 22, 1973; children: Kathryn Carlisle, Sarah Elizabeth. BA cum laude, U. Va., 1969, JD, 1972. Bar: Va. 1972, Calif. 1975, U.S. Dist. Ct. (ea. dist.) Va. 1976, D.C. 1978, U.S. Ct. Appeals (4th cir.) 1978, U.S. Ct. Appeals (Fed. cir.) 1986, U.S. Ct. Appeals (11th cir.) 1990. Rsch. assoc. Atlantic Richfield, Washington, 1972; assoc. Pender & Coward, Norfolk, Va., 1976-77, Seyfarth, Shaw, Washington, 1977-80, ptnr., 1981-83, Jones, Day, Reavis & Pogue, Washington, 1983—. Mem. adv. com., reproductive hazards in the workplace Office of Tech. Assessment, Washington, 1984-86; mem. adv. council Ctr. Environ. Health, U. Conn., 1986-95; mem. editorial bd. The Occupational and Environ. Medicine Report, 1986—, Human and Ecol. Risk Assessment, 1998—. Contbr. articles to legal jours. Elder Kirkwood Presbyn. Ch., Springfield, Va., 1984-86. Served as lt. USN, 1972-75. Mem. ABA, Va. State Bar, State Bar Calif., Phi Beta Kappa, Phi Delta Phi (sec. local chpt. 1971-72, Outstanding Grad. award 1972). E-mial. Home: 318 S Pitt St Alexandria VA 22314-3712 Office: Jones Day Reavis & Pogue 51 Louisana Ave NW Washington DC 20001 E-mail: jcmcelveen@jonesday.com.

MCELVEEN, WILLIAM LINDSAY, broadcasting executive, lecturer; b. Columbia, S.C., Sept. 20, 1950; s. Henry Moody and Dorothy Butler (Sligh) McE.; m. Laurie Wells Boyle, Sept. 8, 1969 (div. 1976); 1 child, Earle Sligh; m. Catharine Elizabeth McCaslin, Aug. 13, 1992; 1 child, Kerry Elizabeth McCaslin. BA in English, U. of South, 1972. Acct. exec. Sta. WNOK-FM, Columbia, S.C., 1972-73, mng. dir., 1973-79; v.p., gen. mgr. Stas. WNOK-AM-FM, 1979-84; pres. Audubon Broadcasting Co., 1984-89, Radio South Carolina, Columbia, 1989—. Exec. dir. Bloomington Broadcasting Corp., 1998-2000; lectr. Internat. Media Fund, Washington, 1993—; v.p. s.e. region Citadel Broadcasting, 2000—. Chmn. bd. dirs. Columbia Urban League, 1983-85; bd. dirs. Crimestoppers of Midlands, 1984-88, S.C. Law Inst., Columbia, 1985-88, Helpline of Midlands, 1986-90; gen. campaign chair United Negro Coll. Fund, Columbia, 1985-86; mem. exec. com. United Way of Midlands, Columbia, 1987-88. Mem. Nat. Assn. Broadcasters (bd. dirs. 1988-92, 96—, v.p. 1997-98, chmn. 1998-2000), S.C. Broadcasters Assn. (exec. com., bd. dirs. 1980-87, pres. 1988-92, Hall of Fame inductee 1996), Columbia Advt. Fedn. (pres. 1980-81), Media Club of Columbia (bd. dirs., pres. 1983-84). Presbyterian. Avocations: golf, tennis, travelling. Home: 263 Tombee Ln Columbia SC 29209-0804 Office: Radio SC 1801 Charleston Hwy Cayce SC 29033-2019

MCELVEEN-COMBS, GAIL MARIE, middle school educator; b. Houston, May 16, 1954; d. William Conlee and Evelyne Lily (Brautigam) McE. BS in Biology, Sam Houston State U., Huntsville, Tex., 1977, cert. in teaching, 1982; ThM, Logos Bible Coll., 1991. Cert. biology and English tchr., Tex. Tchr. biology Harlandale Ind. Sch. Dist., San Antonio, 1984-93, tchr. comparative religions, 1989-90; sponsor, tchr. El Shaddai Bibl. Studies Club, 1990-91, writer life sci. curriculum, 1989-91; tchr. 6th grade sci. Page Mid. Sch., 1993—, sci. dept. chairperson, 1997-98, writer mid. sch. sci. curriculum, 1996-98, mentor tchr., 1997-98; 7th grade sci. 1 tchr. Randolph Field Middle Sch., Randolph AFB, 1998—, middle sch. sci. curriculum writer, 1998—; sci. dept. chairperson Randolph Field Middle and High Schs., 1999—. Recipient Outstanding Sci. Educator award Sigma Xi, 1991, Christa McAuliffe Meml. award Air Force Assn., 2001, Outstanding Tchr. award KENS5-Excel, 2001. Republican. Charismatic Christian. E-mail: combsg@randolph-field.k12.tx.us., combs417@earthlink.net.

MCELVEIN, THOMAS IRVING, JR. lawyer; b. Buffalo, Apr. 19, 1936; s. Thomas I. and Edith Marian (Bowen) McE.; m. Ernesta F. McElvein, June 26, 1965; children: Christopher, Andrew, Kathryn. BA, Antioch Coll., 1959; JD, Yale U., 1962. Bar: N.Y. 1962, U.S. Dist. Ct. (we. dist.) N.Y. 1969. Atty. Village Akron, N.Y., 1963-99, spl. project atty., 2000—. Mem. N.Y. State Bar Assn., Erie County Bar Assn. Home: 295 Nottingham Ter Buffalo NY 14216-3125 Office: 1500 Liberty Bldg Buffalo NY 14202-3612

MCELWAIN, EDWINA JAY, elementary education educator; b. Wheeling, W.Va., Dec. 23, 1936; d. Edgar F. and Myrtle L. Buchanan; m. David Ray McElwain, Nov. 22, 1956; children: Diane Louise, David Alan. BS, Steubenville U., 1973. Cert. tchr., Ohio. Tchr. Springfield Local Sch. Dist., Amsterdam, Ohio, 1956-61; substitute tchr. Edison Local Sch. Dist., Bergholz, 1973-77; tchr. Gregg Elem. Sch., 1977-97, ret., 1997. Tutor, Hammondsville, Ohio. Adult adviser 4-H Club, Jefferson County, 1970-81. Martha Holden Jennings Found. scholar, 1981-82. Mem. NEA, Ohio Edn. Assn., Jefferson County Ret. Tchrs. Assn., Ohio Ret. Tchrs. Assn., Edison Local Edn. Assn., Amsterdam Women's Club (v.p. 1999-2000, pres. 2002-), Delta Kappa Gamma. (corr. sec. 1986-90, v.p. 1994-96, chmn. rsch. com. 1992-94, pres. 1996-2000, parliamentarian 2000—). Avocations: reading, stamp collecting, horses. Home: 1899 County Highway 59 Bergholz OH 43908-7928

MC ELWAIN, JOSEPH ARTHUR, retired power company executive; b. Deer Lodge, Mont., Nov. 13, 1919; s. Lee Chaffee and Johanna (Petersen) McE.; m. Mary Cleaver Witt, Mar. 8, 1945 (dec. June 1992); m. Mary E. McLaughlin, Oct. 9, 1996 (dec. Sept. 1998); children— Lee William and Lori Louise (twins). BA, U. Mont., 1943, LL.B., 1947. Bar: Mont. 1947. Individual practice law, Deer Lodge, 1947-63; Washington legis. counsel Mont. Power Co., Butte, 1954-63, counsel, 1963-65, asst. to pres., 1965-67, v.p., 1967-70, exec. v.p., dir., 1970, then chmn., chief exec. officer, now ret. Dir. Mont. Power Co., First Bank System 1975-84, Devel. Credit Corp. Mont.; MHD Devel. Corp. 1986—; mem. U.S. nat. com. World Energy Conf.; Mont. dir. for U.S. Savs. Bonds, 1980-81; cons. in field Mem. Mont. Pub. Land Law Rev. Adv. Com. City atty. Deer Lodge, 1950-57, 60-63; mem. Mont. Ho. of Reps., 1949-55, majority floor leader, 1951; mem. Mont. State Senate, 1962-64; state chmn. Republican Central Com., Mont., 1952-54; mem. adv. com. Edison Electric Inst., U. Mont. Found., Missoula, Rocky Mountain Coll., Billings; bd. dirs. Mont. Internat. Trade Commn. Served with AUS, World War II and Korea. Recipient Judstin Miller award, 1947 Mem. Mont., Am. bar assns. Clubs: Masons, Shriners, Kiwanis. Episcopalian. Home: 307 Aspen Way Butte MT 59701-3992 Office: 40 W Broadway St Butte MT 59701-9222

MCELWAINE, THERESA WEEDY, academic administrator, artist; b. Culver City, Calif., Nov. 15, 1950; d. Victor Louis and Doris Yvonne Weedy; m. James William McElwaine, Jan. 1, 1989. BA, Calif. State U., Fullerton, 1972, cert. secondary tchr., 1974; MFA in Photography, San Francisco Art Inst., 1981. Bookstore mgr., 1978-81; asst. dir. San Francisco Camerawork, 1981-83; exec. dir. Collective for Living Cinema, N.Y.C., 1984-85; dir. mktg. Am. Internat. Artists Mgmt., 1986-87; asst. dean cont. edn. SUNY, Purchase, 1987-97, dir. comm., 1997—. Cons. Parabola Arts Foun., N.Y.C., 1985-86, Clarity Ednl. Productions, San Francisco, 1983, N.Y. State Coun. on Arts, 1986-91. Exhibited in group and solo shows at San Francisco Camerawork, Inc., Foto Gallery, N.Y.C., U. Calif., Berkeley, San Francisco Mus. Modern Art, Plymouth (England) Arts Ctr., Ariz. State U., Tempe, Vanderbilt U., Nashville, Floating Found. Photography, N.Y.C. Bd. dirs. San Francisco Camerawork, 1977-81; bd. advisors Collective of Living Cinema, 1985-87, Parabola Arts Found., 1986-92. Recipient Excellence awards Am. Inst. Graphic Arts, 1982-83. Avocations: Latin American travel and studies. Home: 64A Valley Rd Cos Cob CT 06807-2533

MCELWEE, BERNARD, management educator; b. Newark, May 12, 1947; s. James Joseph and C. Irma (Kinney) McE.; m. JoAnn Tanski, Apr. 5, 1975; 1 child, Timothy A. BSBA, Montclair State Coll., 1976; MPA, Seton Hall U., 1994. With Fireman's Fund Am. Ins., Newark, 1971-74, AFIA Worldwide Ins., Wayne, N.J., 1974-77, Am. Reinsurance Co., Inc., N.Y.C., 1977-80, The Chubb Ins. Group, Warren, N.J., 1983, Am. Internat. Group, N.Y.C., 1980-87, Thomas A. Greene & Co., Inc. (div. Alexander & Alexander), N.Y.C., 1987-88; cons. in field, 1988-90, 92—; acct. Seton Hall U., 1990-92; adminstrv. asst. Bd. Mem. Inst. N.J., 1993; adj. instr. bus. mgmt. Bramson Ort Tech. Inst., 1994-95; svc. officer and vets. advocate N.J. Vietnam Vets of Am. N.J. Svc. Office, Newark, 1994-2000. Recreation Adv. Com. Parsippany-Troy Hills, N.J., 1992—. Served in U.S. Army, 1966-69, Vietnam. Mem. VFW (N.J. State Svc. Officer 2000—), Vietnam Vets. of Am., Am. Legion. Home: 29 Huron Ave Lake Hiawatha NJ 07034-2901 Office: 20 Washington Pl Fl 5 Newark NJ 07102-3110

MCELWEE, DENNIS JOHN, lawyer, former pharmaceutical company executive; b. New Orleans, July 30, 1947; s. John Joseph and Audrey (Nunez) McE. BS, Tulane U., 1970; JD, U. Denver, 1992. Clean room and quality control analyst Sci. Enterprises Inc., Broomfield, Colo., 1975-76; analytical chemist in toxicology Poisonlab. Inc., Denver, 1977; analytical chemist, then dir. quality control program Colo. Sch. Mines Rsch. Inst., 1977-79; dir. quality control, then dir. compliance Benedict Nuclear Pharms. Co., Golden, Colo., 1979-84; pres. MC Projections Inc., Morrison, 1985-86; dir. regulatory affairs Electromedics Inc., Englewood, 1986-89; pvt. practice, 1992—. Author: Mineral Research Chemicals, Toxic Properties and Proper Handling, 2d edit., 1979; mem. editl. bd. CF Network Mag.; contbr. articles to profl. jours. Bd. dirs. Denver chpt. Cystic Fibrosis Found., 1996, Assn. of Vols. for Children's Hosp., Denver, 1999. Recipient Sutton prize in internat. law U. Denver Sch. Law, 1991, Finest award Denver Charities, 1999. Mem. Colo. Bar Assn., Colo. Criminal Def. Bar, Denver Bar Assn., 1st Jud. Dist. Bar Assn. Office: 2009 Wadsworth Blvd Ste 200 Lakewood CO 80215-2031 E-mail: dionysius@prodigy.net.

MCELWEE, DORIS RYAN, psychotherapist; b. Calif., Feb. 15, 1931; d. Dennis M. and Emma A. (Klockau) Ryan; m. Charles B. McElwee, Feb. 6, 1959; children: Brent, Gregg, Cynthia; m. Craig A. Thomson, May 6, 1988. BA, Millikin U., Decatur, Ill.; MA, U. Ariz.; PhD, U. S.C., UCLA, Temple U. Sr. therapist Am. Inst. Family Rels., Burbank, Calif., 1969—; psychotherapist in pvt. practice Burbank and Arcadia, 1970—; grad. faculty Chapman Coll., L.A., 1973-75, Pepperdine U., L.A., 1975-78, Am. Inst. Family Rels., Burbank, Calif., 1972-85; psychotherapist Calif. Fam. Study Ctr., 1985-90. Guest expert Phil Donahue Show. Contbg. author Ladies Home Jour., Techniques of Marriage and Family Counseling, Suicide Prevention for College Students, A Place to Rest Your Heart. Mem. Arcadia Assistance League, Las Alas Orgn.; bd. dirs. NOW, Pasadena, Calif. Recipient Merit award Millikin U., Decatur, Ill., 1983. Mem. Group Psychotherapy Assn. So. Calif. (v.p., exec. bd. dirs.), Am. Assn. Marriage and Family Therapy, Calif. Assn. Marriage and Family Therapists, Southern Calif. Assn. Marriage and Family Therapy, Soc. Scientific Study of Sex., Self Esteem Task Force, Panhellenic Assn., Pi Beta Phi, Psi Chi. Republican. Lutheran. Avocations: travel, gardening.

MCELYEA, JACQUELYN SUZANNE, accountant, real estate consultant; b. Dallas, July 19, 1958; d. Owen Clyde and Mary Lou (Cockerill) Harvey; m. James E. McElyea, June 11, 1983. BBS, Tex. A&M U., 1980. CPA, Tex. Acctg. mgr. Oxford Tex. Devel., Dallas, 1980-81; staff to dir. PriceWaterhouseCoopers, 1981—. Pres. Nat. Assn. Corp. Real Estate, Dallas. Co-author: Real Estate Accounting Reporting, 1995. Bd. dirs. Am. Diabetes Assn., Dallas, 1996-97. Mem. AICPA, Nat. Assn. Real Estate Cos., Tex. Soc. CPAs. Presbyterian. Avocations: animals, cooking. Office: PriceWaterhouse Coopers 2001 Ross Ave Ste 1800 Dallas TX 75201-2933 E-mail: smcelyea@home.com.

MCELYEA, MONICA SERGENT, lawyer; b. Pennington Gap, Va., Jan. 15, 1967; d. Birg Eugene and Lana Kay (Turner) Sergent; m. Jeffrey Earl McElyea, Dec. 16, 1994. BA, Randolph-Macon Woman's Coll., Lynchburg, Va., 1988; JD, Mercer U., 1991. Bar: Ga. and Va. 1991, Tenn. 1993, U.S. Dist. Ct. (no. dist.) Ga. 1991, U.S. Dist. Ct. (we. dist.) Va. 1992, U.S. Dist. Ct. (ea. dist.) Va. 1995, U.S. Dist. Ct. Colo. 1998, U.S. Ct. Appeals (4th cir.) 1992, U.S. Supreme Ct. 1995, Colo. 1997, U.S. Dist. Ct. Colo., 1998. Law clerk U.S. Magistrate Judge Cynthia D. Kinser, Abingdon, Va., 1991-92; assoc. atty. Birg E. Sergent Atty. at Law, Pennington Gap, 1992-93; asst. Commonwealth's atty. Lee County, Jonesville, 1993-94; pvt. practice Pennington Gap, 1993-94; asst. atty. gen. Office of Atty. Gen., Richmond, 1994-97; assoc. Law Offices David A. Helmer, Frisco, Colo., 1997—. Methodist. Office: Law Offices David A Helmer PO Box 868 611 Main St Frisco CO 80443 E-mail: monica@helmerlaw.com.

MCELYEA, ULYSSES, JR. veterinarian; b. Ft. Collins, Colo., Oct. 29, 1941; s. Ulysses and Hazel (Hall) McE.; m. Rexanna Bell, Dec. 29, 1975 (div. 1980); m. Natalia B. Zarzosa, Apr. 29, 2000. BS in Pharmacy, U. N.Mex., 1963; DVM, Colorado State U., 1967, MS, 1968. Diplomate Am. Bd. Vet. Practicioners; cert. in companion animals. Owner Alta Vista Animal Clinic, Las Cruces, N.Mex., 1970—; attending vet. N.Mex. State U., 1995—. Bd. dirs. N.Mex. Acad. Vet. Practice, Albuquerque, bd. dirs. state of N.Mex. Bd. Vet. Examiners, v.p., 1988-98, vice chair, 1992, chair, 1992-96, Bank of the Rio Grande; adj. prof. N.Mex. State U., 1998—. Pres. Las Cruces Community Theater, 1974; founder, bd. dirs. Dona Ann Arts Coun., Las Cruces, 1976-80. Capt. U.S. Army, 1968-70. Mem. AVMA, Am. Pharm. Assn., Am. Assn. Feline Practitioners, Am. Soc. Vet. Ophthalmologists, N.Mex. Vet. Med. Assn. (bd. dirs. 1976-82), So. N.Mex. Vet. Assn. (pres. 1974, 84), N.Mex. State U. Athletic Assn. 9bd. dirs. 1976—, pres.-elect 1992-93, pres. 1993-94), N.Mex. State U. Pres.'s Assn. 9bd. dirs. 1988-91), U. N.Mex. Alumni Assn. (bd. dirs. 1976-80). Republican. Home: 2635 Fairway Dr Las Cruces NM 88011-5044 Office: Alta Vista Animal Clinic 725 S Solano Dr Las Cruces NM 88001-3244 E-mail: umcelyea@zianet.com.

MC ENALLY, TERENCE E. electrical engineer, educator; b. Richmond, Va., Apr. 21, 1927; s. Terence Ernest and Ellen Elizabeth McEnally; m. Marie Ann Gianino McEnally, June 28, 1964; children: Terence Deirdre McEnally. BS, Va. Poly. Inst., Blacksburg, VA, 1950, MS, 1955; PHD, Mass. Inst. Tech., Cambridge, Massachusetts, 1966. Electronic engr. Norfolk Naval Shipyard, Norfolk, Va., 1950—52; instr. Va. Poly. Inst., Blacksburg, 1952—55; elec. engr. instr. NC State U., Raleigh, NC, 1961—63; instr. Mass. Inst. Tech., Cambridge, Mass., 1966—67; physiscs educator East Carolina U., Greenville, NC, 1967—. Mem. Bord Adjustment, Greenville, NC, 2001. Etm US Naval Reserue, 1945—46, Usa. Mem.: Am. Phys. Soc. (assoc.), Sigma XI (Sci. Rsch. Soc. N.Am.) (assoc.). Avocations: tennis, jogging. Home: 113 North Woodlawn Ave Greenville NC 27858

MCENARY, JOHN WALTER, music educator; b. Minneapolis, Dec. 7, 1952; s. David Nye and Marilynn Sahlin M.; m. Allison Roberts, Mar. 25, 1988. BFA, U. Minn., Minneapolis, 1975; MFA, U. Minn., 1977. Cert. Calif. Cmty. Coll. Instr. Music. prof. Orange Coast Coll., Costa Mesa, Calif., 1978—, music dept. chair, 1984—2001, program coord., 1986—. Software developer Sound Source Unlimited, Agoura Hills, Calif., 1989-92, Midiman, Arcadia, Calif., 1989-98; content developer Coda Music Tech., Eden Prairie, Minn., 1992-94; midi cons. Roland Corp., L.A., 1990-96. Author: (books) Guide to Sequencers, 1992, Computers in Music, 2002, (software) Proteus Sound Manager, 1988, Interval, 1998. Mem. Bowers Mus., Santa Ana, Calif., 1999—; subscriber Globe Theatre, San Diego, 1991-98. Recipient Regents fellowship, U. Calif. San Diego, 1975. Mem. Music Assn. Calif. Cmty. Colls., (life) Orange Co. Guitar Cir. (pres. 1984-86). Avocations: reading, movies, theatre, tech., music. Office: Orange Coast Coll 2701 Fairview Rd Costa Mesa CA 92626-5563 E-mail: jmcenary@mail.occ.cccd.edu.

MCENIRY, ROBERT FRANCIS, education educator, researcher; b. Milw., Feb. 22, 1918; s. Frank Michael and Mary (Brown) McE. BA, St. Louis U., 1941, Philosophiae Licentiatus cum laude, 1944, Theologiae Licentiatus cum laude, PhL, ThL cum laude, St. Louis U., 1953; PhD, Ohio State U., 1972. Elem. sch. inst., 1938-40; tchr. Howdershell Grade Sch., 1939-40; radio announcer Sta. WOW, St. Louis, 1941-43; instr. classics St. Louis U. High Sch., 1944-47, Creighton Prep. Sch., Omaha, 1947-48; asst. prof., chmn. classics Rockhurst Coll., Kansas City, Mo., 1953-58; retreat dir. White House Retreat, St. Louis, 1958-68; assoc. research prof. Creighton U., Omaha, 1972-89; ret., 1989. Dir., facilitator Growth for Couples, 1975-89; lectr. Creighton Natural Family Planning Ctr.; facilitator groups Adult Children of Alcoholism and Dysfunctional Families, 1989-93; vis. lectr. San Francisco Sch. Theology, San Anselmo, Calif., 1985; more than 800 presentations (lectrs., papers, workshops and seminars) in 175 cities, 22 states and 12 fgn. countries on value decisions during high anxiety and stress in marriage, family, teaching and learning; exec. dir. Studies Adult Survivors of Abuse, 1993—; tchr., counselor in marriage and family issues. Editor and pub. Interaction Review, 1982-89; editor Scholar and Educator, 1974-76; mem. editorial bd. Counseling and Values, 1976-82; editor (book) Pastoral Counseling, 1977, Premarriage Counseling, 1978; contbr. over 180 articles to profl. jours.; literary agent, 1992-98. Mem. Bd. of Pastoral Ministry, Omaha, 1972-78. Research grantee Council for Theol. Reflection, 1975-77; recipient Research award Creighton U., 1977; 1st prize for "Pro and Con" in Queen's Work Play contest, 1945. Fellow Nat. Acad. Counselors and Family Therapists (editor book rev. 1979-91); mem. APA, Am. Assn. for Religious Values in Counseling (editor newsletter 1982-89, Outstanding Svc. award 1985, Meritorious Svc. award 1989, Edgar Dale award 1995), Phi Delta Kappa (exec. com. 1977-83, del. 1981-83). Avocations: barbershop quartets, photography, Civil War sites, yoga. Home: 3030 S 60 St #231 Omaha NE 68124-3263

MCENTEE, ROBERT EDWARD, management consultant; b. Franklin, N.J., Mar. 22, 1932; s. William J. and Marie C. (Gorman) McE.; m. Ruth M. Kathalynas, Sept. 29, 1956; children: Kathleen, Susan, Jane, Robert, Christopher. BS, Villanova U., 1953. CPA, N.J. With Price Waterhouse, 1955-63; sr. fin., adminstrv. exec. Beecham Inc., West Paterson, N.J., 1963-88, pres. fin. div., 1974-88; pres., chief oper. officer Russ Berrie & Co., Inc., Oakland, N.J., 1988-90; pvt. practice cons., 1990—. Bd. dirs. Valley Nat. Bancorp, Wayne, N.J. Trustee Archdiocese of Newark, mem. pension bd.; mem. fin. com. Diocese of Venice. With U.S. Army, 1953-55. Mem. AICPAS, N.J. Soc. CPAs. Roman Catholic. Home: 2225 First Ave Spring Lake NJ 07762 E-mail: mrobert849@aol.com.

MCENTIRE, JEAN REYNOLDS, music educator; b. Farmville, Va., Oct. 11, 1943; d. Thomas Pierce and Nancy Noel Reynolds; m. Dennis Pierce McEntire, July 30, 1966; children: Ann-Janette M. Lacatell, David Glenn, Jeremy Reynolds. BS in Music Edn., U. Richmond, 1966; MusM, Va. Commonwealth U., 1996. Tchr. music Itasca (Tex.) Independent Sch. Dist., 1966-68, Jefferson County (Ky.) Pub. Schs., 1968-70; fgn. missionary Fgn. Mission Bd., Richmond, Va., 1970-93; pvt. music tchr. Highland Springs, 1992—; dir., owner Talent Developing Studio, 1992—; min. music Hillcrest Bapt. Ch., Mechanicsville, 1994—2000; wellness cons. Nikken, Highland Springs, 1999—. Workshop instr. Richmond Bapt. Assn., 1996, 98, 99. Paul Harris fellow, Rotary, 1997. Mem. Am. Coll. Musicians, Nat. Fedn. Music Study Clubs, Music Tchrs. Nat. Assn., Kindermusik Educators Assn., Early Childhood Music and Movement Assn. Avocations: music, internet, pets, family. Home: 120 Beauregard Ave Highland Springs VA 23075-1114 Office: Talent Developing Studio PO Box 1598 Mechanicsville VA 23116 E-mail: jeanmc1@excite.com.

MCERLANE, JOSEPH JAMES, insurance company executive; b. Phila., Mar. 5, 1948; s. Joseph Leo and Theophila Mary (Szymanski) McE.; m. Florence Mary Myhasuk; children: Joan Reardon, Rebecca Ann, Megan Diane, Erin Moira, Joseph James Jr. BA, Villanova U., 1970. CLU; cert. employee benefit specialist. Group sales asst. Metro. Life Ins. Co., Phila., 1970-72; mgr. group bus. svcs. Investors Diversified Svcs., Valley Forge, 1972-74, from mgr. to dir. to v.p. and divisional mgr. group ins. sales Mpls., 1974-84; CEO Nat. Benefit Resources Group Svcs., Inc., 1984—. Mem. sch. bd. Annunciation Sch., Mpls., 1984-87, chmn., 1986-87. Mem. Mass. Mktg. Inst., Self-Insured Inst. Am. (bd. dirs. 1993-96), Sertoma (Mpls. Sertoman of Yr. 1982). Office: Nat Benefit Resources Inc 5402 Parkdale Dr Minneapolis MN 55416-1608

MCEVERS, DUFF STEVEN, lawyer; b. L.A., Apr. 21, 1954; s. Milton Stoddard and Virginia Mary (Tongue) McE.; m. Jeannine Marie Matthews, July 14, 1984; children: Tay Colleen, Reily Maureen. BA, U. So. Calif., 1976; JD, Western State U., 1980. Bar: Calif. 1981, U.S. Dist. Ct. (so. dist.) Calif. 1993, U.S. Dist. Ct. (ctrl. dist.) Calif. 1982, U.S. Ct. Appeals (9th cir.) 1988. Assoc. Donald B. Black Inc., Laguna Beach, Calif., 1981-85; pvt. practice Laguna Beach and Newport Beach, 1985-88, Assoc. Law Office of Terry J. Coniglio, Inc., Long Beach, 1988-89; with Barclay Law Corp., 1989-91; pvt. practice Newport Beach and Sonoma, Calif., 1992-2000; of counsel Walker Law Firm, P.C., Newport Beach, 1992-2000; assoc. Cooksey, Toolen, Gage Duffy & Wood, Costa Mesa, Calif., 2000—02; atty. Law Office of Duff S. McEvers, 2002—. Editor: Law Review, 1979. Mem. Calif. Bar Assn., Assn. Bus. Trial Lawyers, St. Timothy's Men's Club. Office: 535 Anton Blvd Fl 10 Costa Mesa CA 92626-1977

MCEVILLY, JAMES PATRICK, JR. lawyer; b. Phila., July 30, 1943; s. James P. and Virginia Frances (Madden) McE.; m. Joan Elizabeth O'Connor; children: James III, Christopher (dec.), Sara, Michael. BS, St. Joseph's U., 1965; JD, Temple U., 1971. Bar: Pa. 1971, U.S. Dist. Ct. (ea. dist.) Pa. 1972, U.S. Ct. Appeals (3d cir.) 1975, U.S. Supreme Ct. 1982. Law clk to president judge Phila. Mcpl. Ct., 1971-73; assoc. Galfand, Berger, Lurie & March, Phila., 1973-76; asst. dist. atty. Phila. Dist. Atty., 1976-79; prin. McEvilly & Assocs., Feasterville, Pa., 1979—. Editor Temple U. Law Rev., 1971. Mem. Pa. Trial Lawyers Assn., Phila. Bar Assn., Trial Lawyers Am. Home: 1401 Silo Rd Yardley PA 19067-4240 Office: 1200 Bustleton Pike Ste 1B Trevose PA 19053-4108

MCEVOY, LORRAINE KATHERINE, oncology nurse; b. S.I., N.Y., Mar. 24, 1950; d. Edward Donald and Josephine (Boyle) McMahon; children: Kelly Ann, Kevin Michael. RN, St. Vincent's Sch. Nursing, 1970; BSN, Seton Hall U., 1994; MSN, Kean U. N.J., 1997. RN, N.J. Staff nurse St. Joseph's Hosp. and Med. Ctr., Paterson, N.J., 1981-88, nurse mgr. oncology, bone marrow transplant, 1988—, cons., educator devel. bone marrow, stem cell and cord blood transplant programs, 1995-98. Adj. prof. Kean U., 1997-98. Recipient Disting. Alumni award Kean U., 1999; Susan G. Komen Breast Cancer Found. grantee, 1997, 98, 99. Mem. Oncology Nursing Soc., Transcultural Nursing Soc., Tri-State Bone Marrow Transplant Nurses Assn., Breast Cancer Connection, Sigma Theta Tau. Office: St Joseph's Hosp and Med Ctr 703 Main St Paterson NJ 07503-2621

MCEVOY, MICHAEL JOSEPH, economist; b. Cork, Ireland, Feb. 16, 1963; came to U.S., 1991. s. Patrick Joseph and Pauline (Heffernan) McE. BA, Univ. Coll., Cork, Ireland, 1984, M in Econ. Sci., 1987; MBA, U. Penn., 1996. Rsch. economist Irish Export Bd., Dublin, 1986-87; sr. analyst economist Fixpoint Ltd., London, 1987-91; rsch. assoc. Micra, Inc., Washington, 1991-92; chief economist Embassy of France, 1992-96; dir. The Tower Group, Boston, 1996—2002; CEO Nechtain LLC, 2002—. Dir. Fixpoint Ltd., 1989-91. Co-author: (quarterly pub.) European Business: Forecasts, Strategies, Tactics, 1989-91. Mem. Nat. Assn. Bus. Economists, Soc. Govt. Economists, Nat. Economists Club, Am. Film Inst., U.S. Holocaust Meml. Mus., Smithsonian Inst. Roman Catholic. Avocations: tennis, walking. E-mail: mcevoy@attbi.com., mcevoy@attbi.com.

MCEVOY, SHARLENE ANN, law educator; b. Derby, Conn., July 6, 1950; d. Peter Henry Jr. and Madaline Elizabeth (McCabe) McE. BA magna cum laude, Albertus Magnus Coll., 1972; JD, U. Conn., West Hartford, 1975; MA, Trinity Coll., Hartford, 1980, UCLA, 1982, PhD, 1985. Bar: Conn., 1975. Pvt. practice, Derby, 1984—; asst. prof. bus. law Fairfield (Conn.) U. Sch. Bus., 1986—; adj. prof. bus. law, polit. sci. Albertus Magnus Coll., New Haven, 1978-80, U. Conn., Stamford, 1984-86; acting chmn. polit. sci. dept. Albertus Magnus Coll., 1980; assoc. prof. law Fairfield U., 1992-98, prof. bus. law, 1998—. Chmn. Women's Resource Ctr., Fairfield U., 1989-91. Staff editor Jour. Legal Studies Edn., 1989-94; reviewer Am. Bus. Law Assn. jour., 1988—, staff editor, 1995—; sr. articles editor N.E. Jour. of Legal Studies in Bus., 1995-96. Mem. Derby Tercentennial Commn., 1973—74; justice of the peace City of Derby, 1975—83; alt. mem. Parks and Recreation Commn., Woodbury, 1995—99; v.p. N.E. Acad. Legal Studies in Bus., 2001—02, 2001—02, pres.-elect, 2002—; mem., treas. Woodbury Dem. Town Com., 1995—96, corr. sec., 1996—98; bd. dirs. Valley Transit Dist., Derby, 1975—77. Recipient Best Paper award N.E. Regional Bus. Law Assn., 1990, Best Paper award Tri-State Regional Bus. Law Assn., 1991; Fairfield U. Sch. Bus. rsch. grantee 1989, 91, 92, Fairfield U. rsch. grantee, 1994. Mem. ABA, Conn. Bar Assn., Acad. Legal Studies in Bus., Mensa (coord. SINISTRAL spl. interest group 1977—). Democrat. Roman Catholic. Avocations: running, chess, tennis, swimming. Office: 198 Emmett Ave Derby CT 06418-1258 E-mail: samcevoy@mail.fairfield.edu.

MCEVOY-JAMIL, PATRICIA ANN, English language educator; b. Butler, Pa., June 26, 1955; d. Joseph Lawrence McEvoy and Janet Ann (McConnell) Beier; m. M. Jamal Jamil, Nov. 23, 1977; 1 child, Amirah M. *Husband M. Jamal was an assistant professor in the Middle Eastern School at the Defense Language Institute. After a post-doctoral fellowship at Harvard University in 1978, he served as Deputy Minister of Foreign Affairs at the Yemeni President's Office until his appointment as Director General of Public Relations at the Yemen Oil and Mineral Resources Corporation. He was employed with the federal government of the United States from 1981 until his retirement in 1998.* MA in TESOL, Monterey Inst. Internat. Studies, 1984; MA in English, U. Notre Dame de Namur, 1995; EdD, U. San Francisco, 1996. Calif. C.C. credential for life. Instr. ESL City Coll. San Francisco, 1989-98, Canada Coll., Redwood City, Calif., 1989-98; lectr. ESL U. Notre Dame de Namur, 1989-97, Coll. Notre Dame, Belmont, Calif., 1991-98; co-owner, v.p. bd. MPA Co. Investments, Inc., Houston, 1998—. Presenter in field; vis. prof. EFL, Georgetown U., Washington, summer 1999; adj. ESL instr. U. Houston-Downtown, 2000—. *Patricia McEvoy-Jamil's academic research has primarily focused on the qualitative investigation of the second language acquisition issues associated with the education of international college students. The findings of some of this qualitative research resulted in the integration of community-based projects in the English as a Second Language classrooms at the College of Notre Dame and the City College of San Francisco.* Mem. leadership coun. So. Poverty Law Ctr.; ptnr. mem. Habitat for Humanity Internat. Recipient ELITE Patron of Honor award ELITE Stanford (Calif.) Hosp., 1989, 90. Mem. AAUW, Nat. Coun. Tchrs. English, Tchrs. English to Speakers of Other Langs., Nat. Mus. Women in the Arts, Phi Delta Kappa. Avocations: tennis, swimming, bicycling. Address: PO Box 22150 Houston TX 77227-2150 E-mail: docpamjam@hotmail.com.

MCEWAN, EWAN DUNCAN, management consultant; b. London, Apr. 15, 1960; s. John Alexander and Ishbel Margaret McEwan; m. Laura Miranda Hollingworth, Dec. 3, 1983; children: Molly, Josey. Diploma in leisure and mgmt. studies, 1989; MBA, Manchester (Eng.) Bus. Sch., 1991. Instr. Bosman Sea Sch., Chichester, Eng., 1980-81, Nat. Sailing Ctr., Southampton, Eng., 1981-84; rigger Yacht Haven, 1984-85; instr. Sports Coun. for Wales, Cardiff, 1985-89; cons., 1991-2000, FT Knowledge, Manchester, 2000—. Bd. dirs. Sailcoach Assocs., Belfast, No. Ireland. Vol. bus. advisor Prince's Trust, 1993—; internat. umpire Internat. Sailing Fedn., 1995. Mem. Assn. MBAs, Brit. Quality Found., Royal Anglesey Yacht Club. Avocations: sailing, match racing, international sports officiating, coaching. Office: FT Knowledge Portland Tower Portland St Manchester M1 3LD England E-mail: ewan.mcewan@ftknowledge.com.

MCEWEN, ALEXANDER CAMPBELL, cadastral studies educator, former Canadian government official, land administration consultant; b. Ryde, Isle of Wight, Eng., Aug. 22, 1926; emigrated to Can., 1949; s. Walter Scott and Florence Lilian (Goodall) McE.; m. Patricia Stuart Richards, July 27, 1956 (div. 1988); m. Sherry Lee Wilson, June 13, 1993; children: Ann Florence, Sheila Jean, Laura Susan. LL.B., U. London, 1966, PhD, 1979; LL.M., U. East Africa, 1970. Sr. surveyor H. Wheeler Assocs., Toronto, Ont., Can., 1961-62; sec. treas. Assn. Ont. Land Surveyors, 1963-64; prin. Survey Tng. Centre, Dar es Salaam, Tanzania, 1964-70; survey cons. Ottawa, Ont., Can., 1970-72; dir. lands and surveys Govt. Nfld., St. John's, 1972-76; commr. Internat. Boundary Commn., Ottawa, Ont., 1976-90; survey adviser Govt. Can., Jesselton, North Borneo, 1954-56, Lagos, Nigeria, 1989-90; tech. expert UN, Victoria, Seychelles, 1958-61; survey cons. Can. Exec. Service Orgn., Kingston, Jamaica, 1981, Quito, Ecuador, 1986; prof. cadastral studies, dept. geomatics engring. U. Calgary, Alta., Can., 1991-96. Author: International Boundaries of East Africa, 1971 In Search of the Highlands, 1988; contbr. articles to profl. jours. Served with Royal Armoured Corp. Mem. Can. Inst. Geomatics (mem. coun. 1977-81, 97—, Jim Jones award 1967, 83, 90, 99, Presdl. citation 1981), Western Can. Bd. Examiners for Land Surveyors (registrar, bd. dirs. 1991-96), Assn. Ont. Land Surveyors (sec.-treas. 1963-64), Assn. Nfld. Land Surveyors (bd. examiners 1975-76), Writer's Union Can. Home: 2129 2d Ave NW Calgary AB Canada T2N OG8 E-mail: amcewen@agt.net.

MCEWEN, BRUCE S. neuroendocrinology educator; Prof., head Lab. Neuroendocrinology, Rockefeller U., N.Y.C. E-mail: mcewen@mail.rockefeller.edu.

MCEWEN, GERALD NOAH, JR. bio-scientist executive; b. Washington, 1943; s. Gerald Noah and Kathryn Lyle (Kimes) McE.; m. Carol Sue Edwards, Aug. 27, 1966; children: Jennifer Lyle, Kathleen Schofield. BS in Life Sci., Ind. State U., Terre Haute, 1966; MA in Life Sci., Ind. State U., 1968; PhD in Physiology and Biophysics, U. Ill., Urbana, 1973; JD, George Washington U., 1989. Vis. lectr. U. Ill., Urbana, 1973-74; research assoc. NASA-Ames Research Ctr., Moffett Field, Calif., 1974-76; research physiologist SRI-Internat., Washington, 1976-77; mgr. Biosci. Group SRI Internat., 1977-78; sr. bioscientist and dir. health hazard info. program, 1978-80; ingredient safety coordinator Cosmetic, Toiletry and Fragrance Assn., Washington, 1980-82, dir., 1982-86, v.p. sci., 1986—. Mem. tech. com. on cosmetics Health Can.; bd. dirs. Environ. Sensitivities Rsch. Inst. Industry liaison representive to cosmetic ingredients review expert panel and to the US FDA dental product panel. Contbr. Editor to several texts, frequent speaker at national and internat. seminars on personal care product safety regulation; Contbr. articles to profl. jours. Recipient Tech. Achievement award NASA, 1976, Superior Achievement award SRI Internat., 1978; NRC research grantee, 1974-76. Mem. FASEB, Am. Physiol Soc., Am. Acad. Dermatology, Am. Contact Dermatitis Soc., Va. Bar Assn., Theta Alpha Phi. Lodges: Masons. Methodist. Home: 2799 N Quebec St Arlington VA 22207-5212 Office: 1110 Vermont Ave NW Washington DC 20005-3544 E-mail: gnmcewen@hotmail.com.

MCEWEN, IRENE RUBLE, physical therapy educator; b. Columbus, Ohio, May 19, 1943; d. John Mitchell and Isabel (Ruble) McE. BS in Phys. Therapy, U. Wash., 1965, MEd in Ednl. Psychology, 1973; PhD in Spl. Edn., Purdue U., 1989. Cert. pediatric clin. specialist Am. Bd. Phys. Therapy Spltys. (pediatric splty. coun.); lic. phys. therapist, Okla., Wash. Phys. therapist St. Vincent Hosp., Portland, Oreg., 1965-69; head phys. therapist Lowell Sch., Seattle, 1970-76; physiotherapist Spastic Centre of New South Wales, Mosman, Australia, 1976-77; head phys. therapist Seattle Sch. Dist., 1977-84; phys. therapist Mesa (Ariz.) Pub. Schs., 1984, Roosevelt Sch. Dist., Phoenix, 1984-86; rsch. fellow Purdue U., West Lafayette, Ind., 1986-89; tech. specialist Ind. Augmentative and Alternative Communication Tech. Team, 1988-89; assoc. prof. phys. therapy U. Okla. Health Scis. Ctr., Oklahoma City, 1989-97, prof. phys. therapy, 1997—, Presbyn. Health Found. Presdl. prof., 1998. Researcher, presenter in field. Mem. editl. bd., dep. editor, editor: Case Reports Phys. Therapy; co-editor: Physical and Occupational Therapy in Pediatrics; contbr. Mem.: Rehab. Engring. and Assistive Tech. Soc. N.Am., Internat. Soc. Augmentative and Alternative Comm., Coun. Exceptional Children, Assn. for Persons with Severe Handicaps, Am. Phys. Therapy Assn. (Margaret L. Moore Outstanding New Acad. Faculty mem. award 1992, Dorothy Briggs Sci. Inquiry award 1993, sect. on pediat. rsch. award 1998, sect. on pediat. Bud DeHaven Svc. award 2001), Am. Assn. Mental Retardation, Am. Acad. Cerebral Palsy and Devel. Medicine, Alpha Eta, Sigma Xi, Phi Kappa Phi. Office: U Okla Dept Rehab Sci PO Box 26901 Oklahoma City OK 73190-1090 E-mail: irene-mcewen@ouhsc.edu.

MCEWEN, MARK, anchor; b. San Antonio, Sept. 16, 1954; Student, U. Md. Co-host WNEW-FM Radio, N.Y.C.; weather reporter CBS News' The Morning Program, 1987; with This Morning, N.Y.C., 1987-99, entertainment editor, 1992-96, co-anchor, 1996-99, CBS The Early Show, N.Y.C., 1999—. Contbr. to CBS News' 48 Hours; reporter CBS Sports' coverage of 1992, 94 Olympic Winter Games, Albertville, France and Lillehammer, Norway; host CBS News' acclaimed Class of 2000, 1997, 1996 Emmy award-winning spl. Tony Bennet: Live by Request. Named one of country's Ten Most Trusted TV News Personalities, TV Guide survey, 1995; recipient Electronic Media Journalist of the Yr. award Country Music Assn., 1992. Office: CBS The Early Show 524 W 57th St New York NY 10019-2924*

MCEWEN, RUTH, foundation administrator; b. Kieghley, Kans., Dec. 29, 1912; d. Henry Kennedy and Mary Estelle (Erdley) Shaffer; m. Theodore Reginald McEwen, Aug. 1, 1942 (dec. Apr. 1976). BMus, Colo. Women's Coll., Denver, 1933; BA, Colo. State Coll. Edn., 1936; MA, U. So. Calif., L.A., 1940. Tchr. music Arvada (Colo.) H.S., 1937-42. Author: Poems From a Couch, 1995. Pres. Rocky Ridge Music Ctr. Found., Estes Park, Colo., 1955-67, Denver Symphony Guild, 1972-79; trustee Golden (Colo.) Symphony, 1950-56, Denver Symphony, 1970-72, Young Musicians of Colo. Found., 1987—; tchr. sr. citizens art YMCA, 1990—; adv. bd. Coll. Music, U. Colo., Boulder, 1980-95; advisor Met. Opera Auditions, 1980—, Young Musicians Found., Denver, 1989—; founder, advisor Young Musicians Competition, Denver Symphony, 1972-76; clinician, adjudicator master classes, 1950—; pres. Lakewood Woman's Club, 1960-62; bd. govs. Jefferson Family YMCA, Lakewood, 1990-93; founder Jefferson Youth Symphony, 1950. Recipient Svc. award Golden Symphony, 1955, Disting. Svc. award Coll. Music, U. Colo., 1988, Eiber St., 1988. Mem. Colo. State Music Tchrs. Assn., Music Tchrs. Nat. Assn., Silver and Gold Soc., Century Club, Mu Phi. Republican. Methodist. Avocations: travel, fishing, swimming. Home: 9650 W 11th Ave Lakewood CO 80215-4602

MCEWEN, WILLARD WINFIELD, JR. lawyer, judge; b. Evanston, Ill., Dec. 26, 1934; s. Willard Winfield Sr. and Esther (Sprenger) McE.; children: Michael, Elizabeth, Allison. BS, Claremont Men's Coll., 1956; LLB, U. Calif., San Francisco, 1959. Bar: Calif. 1960, U.S. Dist. Ct. (no. and so. dists.) Calif. 1960, U.S. Supreme Ct. 1974. Commd. U.S. Army, 1956, advanced through grades to capt., 1965, resigned, 1968; dep. legis. counsel. City of Sacramento, Calif., 1960-61; asst. city atty. City of Santa Barbara, 1961-62; sole practice Santa Barbara, 1962—; judge U.S. Magistrate Ct., Santa Barbara County, 1973—; atty. Goleta Water Dist., 1986-87. Lectr. Santa Barbara Adult Edn. Program. Founder, bd. dirs., officer, gen. legal coun. Santa Barbara Coun. for Retarded, 1962-72; active WORK Workshop for Handicapped, Assn. Retarded

Citizens, Santa Barbara City Landmarks Adv. Com., 1967-73; v.p. Santa Barbara Harbor Pageants and Exhibits Com., 1964; chmn. Citizens Save our Shoreline Com., 1964, Citizens Cmty. Master Plan Com., 1964, YMCA Membership Drive, 1964, Citizens Adv. Com. on Sch. Dist. Tax Needs, 1965; commr. Santa Barbara City Water Commn., 1965, City of Santa Barbara Recreation Commn., 1970-73; elected to founding bd. dirs. City Commerce Bank. Recipient Disting Svc. award Santa Barbara Jaycees, 1965; named Santa Barbara's Young Man of Yr. Sanata Barbara C. of C. 1983. Mem. Am. Heart Assn. (pres. Santa Barbara County chpt. 1981-82), Santa Barbara Heart Assn. (bd. dirs., pres. bd. dirs. 1981-82, chmn. Heart Sunday 1973, 75), Santa Barbara Malacological Soc., Santa Barbara Kiwanis (pres. 1967), C. of C. (com. on local govt., state legisaltion com., bd. dirs., past v.p. bd. dirs., pres. bd. dirs. 1981-82, chmn. several coms.). Republican. Roman Catholic. Avocations: golf, skiing. Office: US Courthouse 8 E Figueroa St Ste 210 Santa Barbara CA 93101-2745 E-mail: imannieo@aol.com.

MCFADDEN, BRIAN, communications executive; married; 2 children. BSEE, U. Waterloo, 1977. From sys. engring. to pres. optical long haul networks Nortel Networks , Brampton, Canada, 1980—. Office: Nortel Optical Long Haul Networks 8200 Dixie Rd Ste 100 Brampton L6T 5P6 Canada

MCFADDEN, DANIEL LITTLE, economics educator; b. Raleigh, N.C., July 29, 1937; s. Robert S. and Alice (Little) McF.; m. Beverlee Tito Simboli, Dec. 15, 1962; children: Nina, Robert, Raymond. BS, U. Minn., 1957, PhD, 1962; LLD, U. Chgo., 1992. Mellon fellow U. Pitts., Pa., 1962-63; asst. prof. U. Calif., Berkeley, 1963-65, assoc. prof., 1965-67, prof., 1967-77; research prof. Yale U., New Haven, 1977-78; prof. MIT, Cambridge, Mass.; E. Morris Cox Chair, prof. of econ. Coll. of Letters & Sci., U. Calif., Berkeley, 1990—; dir. Econometrics Lab., U.Calif., 1991—95; chmn. dept. of econ. U. of Calif., 1995—96; dir. Econometrics Lab., U.Calif., 1996—. Mem. econs. adv. panel NSF, 1969-71, Universities Nat. Bur., 1974-77, rev. com. Calif. Energy Com. Forecasts, 1979, Sloan Found. Book Com., 1977-79, NAS Com. on Basic Research in Social Scis., 1982-1987, NAS Com. on Energy Demand Modeling, 1983-84; chmn. AEA Awards Com., 1981-84, NSF-NBER Conf. on the Econs. of Uncertainty, 1970—; bd. dirs. Nat. Bur. Econ. Research, 1976-77, 1980-83; mem. NAS Commn. Behavioral and Social Scis. and Edn., 1989-1994. Editor: Jour. Statis. Physics, 1968-70, Econometric Soc. monographs, 1980-83; bd. editors: Am. Econ. Rev., 1971-74, Jour. Math. Econs., 1973-77, Transp. Research, 1978-80; assoc. editor: Jour. Econometrics, 1977-78. Mem. adv. com. Transp. Models Project, Met. Transp. Commn., 1975, City of Berkeley Coordinated Transit Project, 1975-76; exec. com. Transp. Research Bd., 1975-78. Recipient John Bates Clark medal, 1975, Outstanding Teacher award MIT Econ. Dept., 1981, Frisch medal, 1986, Nobel Prize in Economics, 2000, Nemmers Prize in Economics, Northwestern U., 2000. Mem. Am. Acad. Arts and Scis., Nat. Acad. Sci., Am. Econ. Assn. (exec. com. 1985-87, v.p. 1994), Econometric Soc. (fellow, 1969, exec. com. 1983-86, v.p. 1984, pres. 1985, Fisher-Schultz Lecture, 1979), Am. Statis. Assn., Math. Assn. Am., Transp. Rsch. Bd. Democrat. Avocations: biking, tennis, squash, sailing, skiing. Home: 1370 Trancas St # 152 Napa CA 94558-2912 Office: U Calif-Berkeley Dept Economics 549 Evans Hall # 3880 Berkeley CA 94720-1775*

MCFADDEN, DAVID REVERE, museum curator; b. Aug. 28, 1947; BA, U. Minn., 1972; MA, 1978. Assoc. curator Mpls. Inst. Arts, 1976-78; curator, 1978; asst. dir collections and rsch., curator decorative arts Cooper-Hewitt Nat. Mus. Design, N.Y.C., 1978-95; exec. dir. Millicent Rogers Mus., Taos, N.Mex., 1995-97; chief curator, v.p. Am. Craft Mus., N.Y.C., 1997—. Adj. prof. art Cooper-Hewitt-Parsons M.. program, N.Y.C., 1983-95; gov. Decorative Arts Trust; pres. applied arts com. Internat. Coun. Mus., 1993-95, 98-2001; mem. exhbn. com. Am. Fedn. Arts. Author: Scandinavian Modern Design (Wittenborn award 1984), 1983, L'Art de Vivre: Decorative Arts and Design in France 1789-1989, 1989. Decorated knight 1st class Order of the Lion (Finland), 1984; knight commdr. Order of No. Star (Sweden); chevallier des l'Ordre des Arts et des Lettres (France); recipient Awards of Merit Smithsonian Instn., 1981, 88, 89, Presdl. Design award, 1994, 95, 98; fellow Kress Found., 1973-74. Mem. Worshipful Co. Goldsmith London. Office: Am Craft Mus 40 W 53rd St New York NY 10019-6106 E-mail: mcfadden99@aol.com.

MCFADDEN, DENNIS, experimental psychology educator; b. Oakland, CA, Oct. 2, 1940; s. Samuel John and Evelyn (Dinnerson) McF.; m. Nancy L. Wilson, Dec. 28, 1960; children: Tracie Ann, Devin James. BA, Sacramento State Coll., Calif., 1962; PhD, Ind U., 1967. Asst. prof. U. Tex., Austin, 1967-72, assoc. prof., 1972-77, prof., 1977—. Contbr. articles to profl. jours. Recipient Jacob K. Javits Neurosci. Investigator award, 1984-89, Claude D. Pepper award, 1989-91; named Piper Prof., Minnie Stevens Piper Found., 1987, named Ashbel Smith Prof., 1998—. Fellow AAAS, Acoustical Soc. Am.; mem. Am. Psychol. Soc., Assn. for Rsch. Otolarynology, CHABA (NAS-NRC com. on hearing, bioacoustics and biomechanics), Soc. Neurosci., Soc. for Behavioral Neuroendocrinology, Internat. Acad. for Sex Rsch. Avocation: Jogging, Biking, Birding, Travel. Office: U Tex Dept Psychology Seay Bldg Austin TX 78712-1189 E-mail: mcfadden@psy.utexas.edu.

MCFADDEN, EMILY JEAN, social work educator, consultant; b. Chgo., Oct. 31, 1938; d. Robert Morse and Elsie M. (Hobson) McF.; children: Linda, Reese, Karen, Gail, Robert Schaumann. BA, Western Mich. U., 1970; MSW, U. Mich., 1976. Caseworker Mich. Dept. Social Svcs., Holland, 1970-74; therapist Western Wayne (Mich.) Counseling, 1976-77; program mgr. foster parent tng. Ea. Mich. U., Ypsilanti, 1978—, mem. faculty social work dept., 1979-90, assoc. dir. nat. foster care edn., 1981-86, assoc. dir. analyzing abuse, 1986-87, assoc. dir. ind. living project, 1987-88, master trainer nat. foster care resource ctr., 1990—, prof. social work, 1991—; prof. Sch. Social Work Grand Valley State U., Grand Rapids, Mich., 1993—. Speaker, presenter in field; mem. editorial bd. Child Welfare, Community Alternatives: The International Jour. Foster Care; expert witness Children's Def. Fund., Balt. Legal Aid, 1987; co-chair practice com. Nat. Commn. on Family Foster Care, Washington, 1990; bd. dirs. Kinship Care Project, 1992, Practice in Permanence Planning, 1992-93. Author: Counseling Abused Children, 1987, Fostering the Child Who Has Been Sexually Abused, 1986; contbr. articles to profl. publs. Sec. Mich. Citizen's Action Com. for Foster Children, 1978-79; mem. nat. adv. bd. Child Welfare League Am., 1981; mem. adv. com. Army foster care needs assessment Dept. Army, 1982; mem. supervised ind. living program com. Youth Living Ctrs., 1983; chair bd. dirs. United Ministries in Higher Edn., Ea. Mich. U., 1990. Mem. N.Am. Assn. Treatment Foster Care (adv. bd. 1990), Nas. Assn. Social Workers, Coun. Social Work Edn., Acad. Cert. Social Workers, Nat. Foster Parent Assn., Network Foster Parent Educators, Internat. Foster Care Orgn. Avocations: guitar, horseback riding, reading, historic homes. Office: Grand Valley State U Sch Social Work 25 Commerce Ave SW Grand Rapids MI 49503-4100

MCFADDEN, FRANK HAMPTON, lawyer, business executive, former judge; b. Oxford, Miss., Nov. 20, 1925; s. John Angus and Ruby (Roy) McF.; m. Jane Porter Nabers, Sept. 30, 1960; children— Frank Hampton, Angus Nabers, Jane Porter. BA, U. Miss., 1950; LL.B., Yale U., 1955. Bar: N.Y. 1956, Ala. 1959. Assoc. firm Lord, Day & Lord, N.Y.C., 1955-58, Bradley, Arant, Rose & White, Birmingham, Ala., 1958-63, partner, 1963-69; judge U.S. Dist. Ct. No. Dist. Ala., 1969-73, chief judge, 1973-81; sr. v.p., gen. counsel Blount, Inc., Montgomery, Ala., 1982-91, exec. v.p. adminstrn. and govt. affairs, 1991, exec. v.p. legal affairs, 1991-93, exec. v.p., gen. counsel, 1993-95; mem. Capell & Howard, P.C., 1995—. Chmn. Blount Energy Resource Corp., Montgomery, 1983-88. Mem. jud. panel CPR Inst. for Dispute Resolution, 1985—. Served from ensign to lt. USNR, 1944-49, 51-53. Fellow Am. Coll. Constrn. Lawyers; mem. Am. Corp. Counsel Assn. (bd. dirs. 1984-93, chmn. 1989). Office: Capell & Howard PC 150 S Perry St Montgomery AL 36104-4227

MCFADDEN, FRED LEE, publishing executive; b. Dallas, Aug. 12, 1942; m. E. J. Caluwaert; children: Amy, Ryan. B in journalism, U. Tex., Austin, 1964; MBA, Stanford Grad. Sch. Bus., 1971. Dir. new products Ency. Britannica Ednl. Corp., Chgo., 1971-76; pres., founder Mosaic Media, Inc., FlipTrack Learning Systems, OneOnOne Computer Tng., Addison, 1976—; pub. Profl. Tng. Assocs. newsletters, 2001—. Publ. Working Smarter tng. bulletins, 1994—; v.p. Village Theatre Guild, Ltd., 2000—. Capt. USAF, 1965-69. Mem. Newsletter and Electronic Pubs. Assn., Glen Oak Country Club. Office: Mosaic Media Inc 2055 W Army Trail Rd Ste 100 Addison IL 60101-1493

MC FADDEN, GEORGE LINUS, retired army officer; b. Sharon, Pa., Oct. 16, 1927; s. George Linus and Frances Jane (Byrne) McF.; m. Floretta Theresa McFadden, Nov. 20, 1948; children: Kenneth William, Mark Edward (dec.), Mary Kathleen, Robert Bernard, George Linus, William. B.E., U. Omaha, 1961; MS, George Washington U., 1967; grad., Advanced Mgmt. Program, Harvard U., 1971. Pvt. U.S. Army, 1946, advanced through grades to maj. gen., 1976; comdg. officer (7th inf. div. arty.), Korea, 1969-70; dep. comdg. gen. U.S. Army Security Agy., Arlington, Va., 1972-74; dep. dir. for field mgmt. and evaluation, dep. chief central security service Fort George G. Meade, Md., 1975-78; dep. dir. ops. Nat. Security Agy., 1978-79; comdg. gen. U.S. Army So. European Task Force, Vicenza, Italy, 1979-82; corp. v.p. CompuDyne Corp., 1986-89; sr. v.p. The Abbott Group, Inc., Annapolis, Md., 1989-90; dir. Washington Studies and Analysis Group McDonnell Douglas Corp., 1985-86; dir. security affairs Dept. Energy, 1990-97, cons., 1999—. Pres., chmn. bd. Met. Washington chpt. Arthritis Found., 1986-95. Decorated D.F.C., D.S.M., Silver Star, Bronze Star, Purple Heart, others. Roman Catholic.

MCFADDEN, GLORIA ARLENE RUTH, poet; b. Washington, Jan. 7, 1951; d. John Henry Nelson and Gloria Lee Pinkney; m. Clarence Richard Reed, Feb. 23, 1968 (div. Apr. 4, 1975); children: Stacy Renee Reed, Clarence Richard Reed, Damon Curtis Reed, Sheena Lynn Stewart; m. Larry Donell McFadden, Dec. 17, 1976 (div. Mar. 29, 1983); 1 child ARlene Takisha. Student, Detroit Bus. Inst., 1977, Am. Career Acad., 1987. Nurse asst. Highland Park (Mich.) Gen. Hosp., 1971; cashier Medicine Chest, Detroit, 1974; freelance writer Internat. Libr. POetry, Owing Mills, Md., 1995—. Composer: (songs) Read and Weep, 1994, Here's to You, 1994, (short stories) There Are Stages, 1994; author: (screenplays) You Can Cry on My Shoulder, 1994. Baptist. Home: 76 Carolane Dr Apt B Jackson TN 38305-4472

MCFADDEN, IRENE FRANCES, medical and surgical nurse, nursing educator, consultant; b. Bklyn., Apr. 5, 1957; d. Francis J. and Irene P. (O'Sullivan) Scahill; m. Francis J. McFadden, Sept. 10, 1983; children: Irene Mary, Maureen, Bridget, Kevin. BSN magna cum laude, Mt. St. Mary Coll., Newburgh, N.Y., 1979; MA, NYU, 1983. Cert. med.-surg. nurse. Asst. head nurse NYU Med. Ctr., N.Y.C.; clin. instr. Brookdale C.C., Lincroft, NJ, 1987-2000; med.-legal cons. McAloon and Friedman, PC, N.Y.C., 2000—.

MCFADDEN, JAMES FREDERICK, JR. surgeon; b. St. Louis, Dec. 5, 1920; s. James Frederick and Olivia Genevieve (Imbs) McF.; m. Mary Cella Switzer, Sept. 15, 1956 (div. Sept. 1969); children: James Frederick, Kenneth Michael, John Switzer, Mary Cella, Joseph Robert; m. Deanne Nemec Puls, Apr. 29, 1989. AB, St. Louis U., 1941, MD, 1944. Intern Boston City Hosp., 1944-45; ward surgeon neorsurg. and orthopedics McGuire Gen. Hosp., Richmond, Va., 1945; ward surgeon in internal medicine Regional Hosp., Fort Knox, Ky., 1946; ward surgeon plastic surgery Valley Forge Gen. Hosp., Phoenixville, Pa., 1946-47; intern St. Louis City Hosp., 1947-48; resident in surgery VA Hosp., St. Louis, 1948-52; clin. instr. surgery St. Louis U., 1952-62; gen. practice medicine specializing in surgery St. Louis, 1952—; mem. staff St. Mary's Hosp., 1952-77, St. John's Mercy Hosp., 1952-74, St. Louis U. (Desloge) Hosp., 1952-62; Cardinal Glennon Children's Hosp., 1952-62; mem. staff Frisco RR Hosp., 1953-64, DePaul Hosp., 1954—, Christian Hosp., 1955-66, 83-91. Mem. St. Louis Ambassadors, 1979-81; officer St. Louis County Aux. Police, 1973-75. Served to capt. AUS, 1945-47. Recipient Eagle Scout award, Order of the Arrow Honor award Boy Scouts Am. Fellow ACS, Royal Soc. Medicine, Internat. Coll. Surgeons; mem. St. Louis Med. Soc., Am. Coll. Occupl. and Environ. Medicine, Am. Soc. Clin. Hypnosis, Internat. Soc. Hypnosis, Am. Assn. RR Surgeons, St. Louis U. Student Conclave, Alpha Sigma Nu, Phi Beta Pi. Roman Catholic. Avocations: hypnosis, photography. Home: PO Box 411933 Saint Louis MO 63141-1933 Office: 11500 Olive Blvd Saint Louis MO 63141-7143

MCFADDEN, JOHN VOLNEY, retired manufacturing company executive; b. N.Y.C., Oct. 3, 1931; s. Volney and Mary Lucile (McConkie) McF.; m. Marie Linstead, June 27, 1953; children— Deborah, John Scott, David. BS in Commerce and Fin, Bucknell U., 1953; JD, Detroit Coll. Law, 1960. Pres., vice chmn. MTD Products, Inc., Cleve., 1960-92; pres. MTD Products Inc., 1980-91, vice chmn., 1990-92; gen. ptnr. Camelot Ptnrs.; pres. Parkside Acquisition Ptnrs. Ltd., 1997—. Dir. C.E. White Co.; bd. dirs. Fusion Inc., Flambeau Corp.; bd. dirs. Guarantee Spltys. Inc., Hinkley Lighting, Inc.; past chmn. financing adv. bd. State of Ohio Devel.; past pres. Cleve. World Trade Assn.; chmn. Parkside Acquisition Ptnrs. Ltd.; vice chair Chemitrol Chem. Co., Inc. Trustee Fairview Health Svcs, Cleve. Clinic. Lt. Supply Corps, USN. Mem. Cleve. Yachting Club. Office: Parkside Acq Ptnrs Ltd 20160 Parkside Dr Cleveland OH 44116-1347

MC FADDEN, JOSEPH MICHAEL, history educator; b. Joliet, Ill., Feb. 12, 1932; s. Francis Joseph and Lucille (Adler) McF.; m. Norma Cardwell, Oct. 10, 1958; children: Timothy Joseph, Mary Colleen, Jonathan Andrew. BA, Lewis Coll., 1954; MA, U. Chgo., 1961; PhD, No. Ill. U., 1968. Tchr. history Joliet Cath. High Sch., 1957-60; mem. faculty history dept. Lewis Coll., Lockport, Ill., 1960-70, asso. prof., 1967-70, v.p. acad. affairs, 1968-70; prof. history, dean sch. Nat. and Social Sci., Kearney (Nebr.) State Coll., 1970-74; prof. history, dean Sch. Social and Behavioral Scis., Slippery Rock (Pa.) State Coll., 1974-77; pres. No. State Coll., Aberdeen, S.D., 1977-82, U. S.D., Vermillion, 1982-88, U. St. Thomas, Houston, 1988-97, pres. emeritus, prof. history, 1997—. Served with USNR, 1954-56. Roman Catholic. Office: U St Thomas Office of Pres 3812 Montrose Blvd Houston TX 77006-4626 E-mail: mcfadden@stthom.edu.

MCFADDEN, JOSEPH TEDFORD, retired neurosurgeon, writer; b. Oxford, Miss., Oct. 7, 1920; s. John Angus and Ruby (Roy) McF.; divorced; children: Joseph T. Jr., Ellen Walker McFadden Snead, John Angus II, Ann Reeves McFadden Lewis. BS, U. Miss., 1942; MD, U. Va., 1944. Prof. neurosurgery Eastern Va. Sch. Medicine, Norfolk, 1974-86, chmn. dept. neurosurgery, 1974-86, dir. resident tng. neurosurgery Grad. Sch., 1974-86, prof. emeritus, 1986—. Author: (book) Hermes' Viper, 2000, The Wafer, Fulton's Monkey, others; inventor McFadden intracranial aneurysm chip, operating room head rest for cranial surgery; contbr. articles to profl. jours. Lt. USNRMC, WWII, Korean War. Fellow ACS; mem. Am. Assn. Neurol. Surgeons (founder devices and drugs standards com.), Congress Neurol. Surgeons (founder devices and drugs standards com.), Soc. Neuro Surgeons, So. Neurosurg. Soc., Norfolk Yacht and Country Club, Town-Point Club, Harbor Club (Norfolk). Avocations: skiing, bicycling, hiking. Home: Treetops II-2D 450 E Lionshead Cir Vail CO 81657-5228 E-mail: tedmcfaddes@msn.com.

MCFADDEN, MARY JOSEPHINE, fashion industry executive; b. N.Y.C., Oct. 1, 1938; d. Alexander Bloomfield and Mary Josephine (Cutting) McF.; m. Philip Harari; 1 child, Justine. Ed., Sorbonne, Paris, France, Traphagen Sch. Design, 1957, Columbia, 1959-62; DFA, Internat. Fine Arts Coll., 1984. Pub. relations dir. Christian Dior, N.Y.C., 1962-64; merchandising editor Vogue South Africa, 1964-65, editor, 1965-69; polit. and travel columnist Rand (South Africa) Daily Mail, 1965-68; founder sculptural workshop Vukutu, Rhodesia, 1968-70; spl. projects editor Vogue U.S.A., 1973; pres. Mary McFadden, Inc., N.Y.C., 1976—; ptnr. MMcF Collection by Mary McFadden, 1991—. Bd. dirs., advisor Sch. Design and Merchandising Kent State U., Eugene O'Neill Meml. Theatre Ctr.; mem. profl. com. Cooper-Hewitt Mus., Smithsonian Inst., Nat. Mus. of Design. Fashion and jewelry designer, 1973—. Advisor Nat. Endowment for Arts; active local Police Athletic League, We Care About N.Y., CFDA-Vogue Breast Cancer Initiative, Beth Israel Hosp., The Chemotherapy Found. Recipient Am. Fashion Critics award-Coty award, 1976, 78, 79, Audemars Piguet Fashion award, 1976, Rex award, 1977, award More Coll. Art, 1977, Pa. Gov.'s award, 1977, Roscoe award, 1978, Pres.'s Fellows award RISD, 1979, Neiman-Marcus award of excellence, 1979, Design Excellence award Pratt Inst., 1993, award N.Y. Landmarks Conservancy, 1994, NU Breed Fashion award, 1996, Marymount Coll. Fashion award, 1996, Legends award N.Y., 2001, Lifetime Achievement award South Am. Press Assn., Miami, Fla., 2002, Pratt Legions award, 2002; named to Fashion Hall of Fame, 1979; fellow RISD. Mem. Fashion Group (bd. dirs. 1981-82), Council of Fashion Designers Am. (past pres., current v.p. bd. dirs.). Office: Mary McFadden Inc 525 E 72nd St New York NY 10021

MCFADDEN, MILLIDENE KATHLEEN, nurse educator; b. Alburtis, Pa., Mar. 3, 1925; d. Fred A. and Helen Daisy (Heintzelman) Grim; m. Robert John McFadden, June 19, 1948; children: Robert William, James Patrick. RN with honors, St. Lukes Hosp. Sch. Nursing, 1948; BS, Kutztown (Pa.) State Coll., 1963; MS, East Stroudsburg (Pa.) U., 1984; Nurse Practioner, U. Pa., 1987. NP, Pa. Project assoc. Pa. Dept. Health, Reading; exec. dir. Am. Cancer Soc., Lansford, Pa.; sch. NP Pleasant Valley Sch. Dist., Brodheadsville. Recipient Citation, Pa. Dept. Health. Mem. Monroe County Sch. Nurse Practitioners of Pa. (rep.), Lioness (bd. dirs. western Pocono chpt. 1990-92).

MCFADDEN, PETER WILLIAM, retired mechanical engineering educator; b. Stamford, Conn., Aug. 2, 1932; s. Kenneth E. and Marie (Gleason) McF.; children: Peter, Kathleen, Mary. BSME, U. Conn., 1954, MS, 1956; PhD, Purdue U., 1959. Registered profl. engr., Ind. Asst. instr. U. Conn., 1954-56, prof. mech. engring., 1971-98, dean Sch. Engring., 1971-85, dir. devel., 1985-88, provost, v.p., 1988, exec. asst. to pres., exec. sec. to bd. trustees, 1989-98; mem. faculty Purdue U., 1956-71; prof. mech. engring., head Purdue U. (Sch. Mech. Engring.), 1965-71; postdoctoral research Swiss Fed. Inst., Zurich, 1960-61. Cons. to industry, 1959-98. Achievements include research in cryogenics, heat transfer, mass transfer.

MCFADDEN, ROBBYN KILBANE, interior designer, public policy specialist; b. Chgo., Oct. 5, 1951; d. Robert Harrison and Adrienne Fay (Seyring) Kilbane; m. James E. McFadden Jr., Dec. 20, 1975; 1 child, Ryan James. BFA, U. Ill., 1969-74; Diploma in Interior Design, Harper Coll., Chgo., 1976. Designer Euromarket Designs, 1978-83; project cons. Volo Interiors, 1983-90; educator, art and design dept. Coll. of Lake County, 1981-83; owner, prin. Design Perspectives, 1983—. Design cons. Law Offices of Patricia Hogan, Monadnock Bldg., Chgo., 1989; project designer retail space Historic Harbor House, Waukegan, Ill., 1988, others. Pub. design commns. include Hunterdon Art Ctr. Archival Print System, 1994, Cleve. Edn. Fund. Historic Dallas Bldg., 1998, Kids First Festival, Lake County, Ill., 1998, numerous others; pvt. commns. include residences in Ill., N.J., Ohio. Mem. adv. com. to internat. programs LWV USA, Washington, 1994—; nat. bd. dirs. UNIFEM/UN Devel. Fund for Women, N.Y.C., 1999—; fundraiser, pub. policy advocate Ctr. for the Humanities and Environment, Jackson Hole, Wyo., 1992-95; adv. mem., cons. Com. for Pub. Art, Cleve., 1995-97 Recipient Carrie Chapman Catt award LWV, Cleve., 1998. Mem. LWV (bd. dirs. Ill. chpt. 2001—), Am. Soc. Interior Designers (allied mem.), Interior Design Soc./Nat. Home Furnishings Assn., PEO. Avocations: painting, golf. E-mail: indezyn@aol.com.

MCFADDEN, ROBERT DENNIS, reporter; b. Milw., Feb. 11, 1937; s. Francis Joseph and Violet (Charleston) McF.; m. Judith Marian Silverman, June 20, 1971; 1 son, Nolan Seth. BS cum laude, U. Wis., 1960. Reporter Wisconsin Rapids (Wis.) Daily Tribune, 1957-58, Wis. State Jour., Madison, 1958-59, Cin. Enquirer, 1960-61; sr. writer, reporter N.Y. Times, 1961—. Mem. adv. coun. St. John's U. dept journalism, 1996—. Co-author: No Hiding Place, 1981, Outrage: The Story Behind the Tawana Brawley Hoax, 1990. With U.S. Army, 1960-61, Res. 1961-68. Recipient Pulitzer Prize for Spot News Reporting (N.Y. Times team), 1994, (individual) 1996; Byline award N.Y. Press Club, 1973, 74, 80, 87, 89, 92, Page One award Newspaper Guild N.Y., 1978, Spot News award Uniformed Firemen's Assn., 1967, Spot News award L.I. Press Club, 1984, 95, Chancellor's award for Disting. Svc. U. Wis., 1987, Man of Yr. award Alumni N.Y., 1997, Excellence in Local Reporting award N.Y. Newspaper Publ. Assn., 1988, Spot News award N.Y. Newspaper Publ. Assn., 1988, Spot News award N.Y. State Associated Press, 1989, 91, Continuing Coverage award, 1995, 99, In Depth Reporting award, 1989, 91, Feature Writing award, 1996, Ochs Prize in Journalism, 1989, Best News/Feature Story award Internat. Assn. Fire Fighters, 1991, Nat. Spot News award Asian-Am. Journalists Assn., 1994, Comprehensive Reporting award, N.Y. Uniformed Fire Officers Assn., 1995. Mem. N.Y. Soc. Silurians (Spot News Story award 1977, 2001, Peter Kihss award 1987, Investigative reporting award 1989, Excellence in Journalism award 1994, gov. 1988—). Office: NY Times 229 W 43rd St New York NY 10036-3959

MCFADDEN, ROBERT STETSON, hepatologist; b. Houston, Mar. 29, 1951; s. David Barnett and Phyllis Reed (Gowell) McFadden; m. Lesa McFadden, Apr. 29, 2000; 1 child Jonathan ;children from previous marriage: William Gordon, Elizabeth Stetson. BS in Biology, Baylor U., 1973; MD, U. Tex., Galveston, 1977. Diplomate Am. Bd. Internal Medicine; cert. gastroenterology Am. Bd. Internal Medicine. Intern in internal medicine La. State U. Med. Sch., New Orleans, 1977-78, resident in internal medicine, 1978-81; staff physician clinic Pub. Health Hosp., 1981; fellow gastroenterology U. Ala., Birmingham, 1981-83; fellow hepatology U. Miami, Fla., 1983-84; gastroenterologist Diagnostic Clinic Houston, 1984-87, Oklahoma City Clinic, 1987-92; hepatologist Okla. Transplantation Inst., Oklahoma City, 1993-2000; chief of hepatology Liver Disease Ctr., Good Samaritan Regional Med. Ctr., Phoenix, 2000-01; med. dir. liver transplantation and chronic liver disease program Tex. Transplant Inst., San Antonio, 2001—. Cons. gastroenterology Diagnostic Clinic of Houston, 1984-87, Oklahoma City Clinic, 1987-92; cons. liver diseases and liver transplant medicine Okla. Transplant Inst., Oklahoma City, 1993-99. Contbr. articles to profl. jours. Mem. ACP, AMA, Am. Assn. for Study of Liver Diseases, Internat. Liver Transplantation Soc., Okla. State Med. Assn. Republican. Baptist. Avocations: Victorian antiques, gardening. Address: 519 Bluffview Estates San Antonio TX 78209

MCFADDEN, ROSEMARY THERESA, lawyer, mercantile exchange executive; b. Oct. 1, 1948; came to U.S., 1951, naturalized, 1967; d. John and Winifred (Quinn) McFadden; m. Brian Doherty, May 26, 1973. BA, Rutgers U., 1970, MBA, 1974; JD, Seton Hall U., 1978; hon. doctorate, St. Elizabeth's Coll., Convent Station, N.J., 1985. Bar: N.J. 1978, U.S. Dist. Ct. N.J. 1978. Spl. asst. Office of the Mayor, Jersey City, 1973-76; exec. dir. Hudson Health Sys., 1976-81; assoc. legal counsel N.Y. Merc. Exch., N.Y.C., 1981-82, exec. v.p., 1982-84, pres., 1984-89, spl. policy advisor to bd. dirs., 1989-91; of counsel Shulman, Hanlon and Doherty, Jersey City and N.Y.C., 1989-97; sr. mgr. Price Waterhouse Internat. Practice Group, 1993-97; sr. v.p. Donaldson Lufkin & Jenrette/Pershing, Jersey City, 1997-98; mng. dir. global devel. CSFBdirect, 1999—. Mem. deans adv. coun. Rutgers U. Grad Sch. Mgmt., Newark, 1985. Bd. dirs. Jersey City Med. Ctr., 1985-87, UNICEF, 1989-92, Futures Industry Assn., 1989-90. Named Alumna of Yr., Rutgers U., 1985, Seton Hall U. Mem. ABA, N.J. Bar Assn., Futures Industry Assn., Securities Industry Assn., Rutgers U. Alumni Assn. Roman Catholic. Avocations: travel, antiques. Office: CSFBdirect Harborside Plz II 5th Fl Jersey City NJ 07311 E-mail: RMcFadden@CSFBdirect.com.

MCFADIN, HELEN LOZETTA, retired elementary education educator; b. Tucumcari, N.Mex., Sept. 7, 1923; d. Henry J. and LaRue Altha (Ford) Stockton; m. John Reece McFadin, July 3, 1946; 1 child, Janice Lynn McFadin Koenig. AB in Edn./Psychology, Highlands U., Las Vegas, N.Mex., 1956; MA in Teaching, N.Mex. State U., 1968; postgrad., U. N.D., 1965, St. Leo's Coll., St. Leo, Fla., 1970. Cert. tchr., K-12 reading/psychology specialist, N.Mex. Tchr. 1st and 2d grades Grant County Schs., Bayard, N.Mex., 1943-44; tchr. 4th grade Durango (Colo.) Pub. Schs., 1946-48; tchr. 2d grade Artesia Pub. Schs., Loco Hills, N.Mex., 1955; tchr. 3d grade Alamogordo (N.Mex.) Pub. Schs., 1957-66, h.s. reading specialist, 1966-72, elem. reading specialist, 1972-77, tchr. 4th grade, 1977-82, reading tchr. 7th grade, dept. chair, 1982-87; ret. N.Mex. State U., Alamogordo, 1987, instr. edn., 1987-90. Organizer reading labs. h.s., elem. schs., Alamogordo, 1966-77, designer programs and curriculum, 1957-89; presenter/cons. in field; cons. Mary Kay Cosmetics; rep. Excel Telecomms., Inc. Contbr. articles to profl. jours. Local and dist. judge spelling bees and sci. fairs Alamogordo Pub. Schs., 1987-98. Recipient Literacy award Otero County Reading Coun., 1986; inducted in Women's Hall of Fame, Alamogordo Women's Clubs, 1989. Mem. Am. Bus. Women's Assn. (pres. 1986-87, v.p. local chpt. 1999-00, Woman of the Yr. 1988), NEA (del. 1957-87, Dedicated Svc. award 1987), N.Mex. Edn. Assn., Internat. Reading Assn. (mem. Spl. League of the Honored 1985, pres. 1975-76), N.Mex. Reading Assn. (bd. dirs. 1988-94, del. to 1st Russian reading conf. 1992, Dedicated Svc. award 1994), Tularosa Basin Hist. Soc., Beta Sigma Phi (pres. local chpt. 1998-99, formed new master chpt. 1999), Kappa Kappa Iota (local pres. Kappa Conclave 1998-00, state officer, nat.

com., co-chair nat. conv. 2000-02, Disting. Educator Emeritus Cert. of Merit 1988, VIP award 2000, 2002). Republican. Baptist. Avocations: reading, fashion modeling. Home: 2364 Union Ave Alamogordo NM 88310-3848

MCFALL, CATHERINE GARDNER, poet, critic, educator; b. Jacksonville, Fla., July 10, 1952; d. Albert Dodge and Joan (Livingston) McF.; m. Peter Forbes Olberg, Oct. 21, 1978; 1 child, Amanda Olberg. Baccalaureat, U. Paris, 1973; AB magna cum laude, Wheaton Coll., Norton, Mass., 1974; MA, Johns Hopkins U., 1975; PhD, NYU, 1990. Editorial asst., short story editor Ladies' Home Jour., N.Y.C., 1975-77; adminstrv. dir. Poetry Soc. Am., 1981-83; instr. writing NYU, 1983-87, asst. dir. Poetics Inst., 1984-86; asst. prof. humanities Cooper Union, 1990-98. Author: Jonathan's Cloud, 1986, Discovery, 1989 (Nation award), Naming the Animals, 1994, The Pilot's Daughter, 1996; editor: Made with Words, 1998; contbr. poetry and revs. to mags. including Paris Rev., Atlantic Monthly, N.Y. Times, others. MacDowell Colony fellow, 1980, 86, Yaddo fellow, 1981, 84, 91, 93, 97, 99, Nat. Arts Club Poetry scholar Bread Loaf Writers Conf., 1983. Mem. MLA, Poets and Writers, Poetry Soc. Am., Nat. Book Critics Circle. E-mail: cathgm@aol.com.

MCFALL, DONALD BEURY, lawyer; b. Charleston, W.Va., Aug. 2, 1941; s. Henry Tucker and Elizabeth Katharine (Beury) McF.; m. Donna Glenn Binion, May 27, 1972; children: Katharine Atkinson, Mary Crawford. BA, Washington and Lee U., 1964, JD, 1969. Bar: Va. 1969, Tex. 1969, U.S. Supreme Ct. 1979, U.S. Dist. Ct. (we., no., so. and ea. dists.) Tex. 1969. Asst. U.S. atty. U.S. Dept. Justice, Houston, 1970-71; assoc. Butler & Binion, 1971-77, ptnr., 1977-85, McFall, Sherwood & Sheeny, Houston, 1985-2000; shareholder McFall Sherwood & Breitbeil, 2000—. Trustee Humana Hosp., Shaprstown, Houston, 1984-85; bd. dirs. Planned Parenthood of Houston and S.E. Tex., 1978-88; trustee Woodberry Forest Sch., Orange, Va., 1984-90, Washington and Lee U., 1997—. Capt. U.S. Army, 1964-66. Fellow Tex. Bar Found., Am. Coll. Trial Lawyers, Internat. Soc. Barristers; mem. Internat. Assn. Def. Counsel, Va. State Bar Assn., Tex. State Bar Assn., Fedn. Ins. and Corp. Counsel, Am. Bd. Trial Advocates (advocate). Office: McFall Sherwood & Breitbeil 4800 Chevron Texaco Heritage Plz 1111 Bagby St Houston TX 77002 Fax: 713-590-9399. Personal E-mail: dbmcf@aol.com. Business E-Mail: dmcfall@msblaw.net.

MCFALL, JOHN, artistic director; b. Kansas City, Mo. Studies with Tatiana Dokoudovska, Conservatory of Music; student, San Francisco Ballet Sch., 1964-65. Formerly with San Francisco Ballet, prin. dancer, 1969; artistic dir. BalletMet, Columbus, Ohio, 1986-94; artistic dir., CEO Atlanta Ballet Co., 1994—. Choregrapher works for Nat. Ballet Can., Am. Ballet Theatre, Dance Theatre Harlem, San Francisco, Hubbard St. Dance Co., Atlanta Ballet, others; for artists including Mikhail Baryshnikov, Cynthia Gregory. Commd. choreographer 2 world premieres for 1996 Olympic Arts Festival; recently staged 10 Atlanta prodns., including The Nutcracker. Ford Found. scholar San Francisco Ballet Sch., 1964; Nat. Endowment for Arts fellow, 1978, 80, 85. Office: Atlanta Ballet 1400 Peachtree St NW Atlanta GA 30309-2906*

MCFALL, SARA WEER, lawyer; b. Balt., Oct. 17, 1953; d. James Edward and Anna Mary (Gumpert) Weer. BFA, U. Hawaii, 1989; JD, U. Okla., 1992. Bar: Okla. 1992, U.S. Dist. Ct. (we. dist.) Okla. 1992. Legal intern Okla. County Pub. Defender, Oklahoma City, 1990—92; assoc. Talley & Perrine, Norman, 1993—95, Rodney D. Watson & Assoc., Norman, 1995—97; contract pub. defender Cleveland County, 1997—2002; chief capital trial divsn. Okla. Indigent Def. System, Norman, 2002—. Mem. Okla. Bar, Cleve. County Bar, Okla. Criminal Def. Lawyers Assn., Order of Barristers. Office: 216 E Eufaula St Norman OK 73069-6019

MCFARLAN, FRANKLIN WARREN, business administration educator; b. Boston, Oct. 18, 1937; s. Ronald Lyman and Ethel Warren (White) McF.; m. Margaret Karen Nelson, Dec. 17, 1971; children: Andrew, Clarissa, Elizabeth. AB, Harvard Coll., 1959, MBA, 1961, D.BA, 1965. Asst. prof. Harvard Bus. Sch., Boston, 1964-68, assoc. prof., 1968-73, prof. bus. adminstrn., 1973—, sr. assoc. dean, dir. rsch., 1991-95, sr. assoc. dean external rels., 1995-2000, sr. assoc. dean, dir. Asia Pacific, 2000—. Dir. Providian Fin. Corp., San Francisco, Li and Fung Corp., HOng Kong, Computer Sci. Corp., L.A. Author: (with Richard Nolan) Information Systems Administration, 1973; (with Linda Applegate and James L. McKenney) Corporate Information Management, 5th edit., 1999, (with Linda Applegate and Robert Austin) Creating Business Advantages in Information Age, 2002; editor; (with Richard Nolan) Information Systems Handbook, 1973, Information Systems Research Challenge, 1984; sr. editor MIS Quar., 1986-88. Bd. dirs., pres. Belmont (Mass.) Day Sch., 1982-86; bd. dirs. Dana Hall Sch., Wellesley, Mass., 1982-94, chmn. bd., 1990-93; trustee Mt. Auburn Hosp., 1991-99, ch mn. bd., 1995-98, trustee care group, 1996—; trustee Winsor Sch., 1994-2000, Milton Acad., 2001--. 1st lt. U.S. Army, 1962-67. Mem.: The Country (Brookline, Mass.). Republican. Episcopalian. Home: 37 Beatrice Cir Belmont MA 02478-2657 Office: Harvard Bus Sch Soldiers Field Rd Boston MA 02163-1317 E-mail: fmcfarlan@hbs.edu.

MCFARLAND, ANDREW GEORGE, analytical chemist, researcher; b. Orange, N.J., Jan. 6, 1947; s. Andrew William and Doris Marie (Nelson) McF.; m. Louise Zimmerman, June 21, 1969; children: Andrew James, Heather Anne. BS in Chemistry, Seton Hall U., 1969; PhD in Analytical Chemistry, Purdue U., 1974. Analytical chemist Squibb Inst. for Med. Rsch., New Brunswick, N.J., 1974-76, Air Products & Chems., Marcus Hook, Pa., 1976-78; group leader analytical chemistry Lonza Inc. (and predecessor co. Glyco Inc.), Williamsport, 1978-89; mgr. analytical and info. svcs. Elf Atochem N.Am., Buffalo, 1989-97; mgr. analytical and sys. rsch. Atofina Chems. (formerly Elf Atochem N.Am.), King of Prussia, Pa., 1997—. Presenter ann. sci. meeting Soc. Cosmetic Chemists, 1983, S.W. sect. meeting Am. Oil Chemists, 1984, 14th Internat. Fedn. Soc. Cosmetic Chemists, 1986. Vol. United Way, Williamsport, Buffalo, 1987-89, bd. dirs., Williamsport, 1989. Mem. ASTM (subcom. chmn. 1995, vice chmn. com. E-15, 1996-99, chmn. 2000—, cert. of appreciation 1995), Am. Chem. Soc., Analytical Lab. Mgrs. Assn. (sec. 1996--, pres. 2002). Office: Atofina Chems 900 1st Ave King Of Prussia PA 19406 E-mail: andy.mcfarland@atofina.com.

MCFARLAND, DAVID E. university official; b. Enid, Okla., Sept. 25, 1938; s. Eugene James McF. and Lydia May (Catlin) Lawson; m. Marcia Ruth Lake, Nov. 27, 1958 (div. 1978); children: Jennifer, Jeffrey, Jon, Julie; m., Susan Kaye Siler, Mar. 3, 1979 (div. 1994); 1 child, Matthew Chapple; m. Barbara Ambrogio, Oct. 1994. BS, Wichita State U., 1961, MS, 1964; PhD, U. Kans., 1967. Stress analysis engr. Boeing Co., Wichita, Kans., 1957-64; instr. U. Kans., Lawrence, 1964-67; asst. v.p., dean Wichita State U., 1967-81; dean. sch. tech., Pittsburgh State U., Kans., 1981-85; provost, v.p. acad. affairs Cen. Mo. State U., 1985-88; pres. Kutztown U. of Pa., 1988—. Author: Mechanics of Materials, 1977; Analysis of Plates, 1972. Contbr. articles to tech. jours. Office: Kutztown U of Pa Office of Pres Kutztown PA 19530

MCFARLAND, DONALD JOE, hardware engineer; b. Oak Creek, Colo., Dec. 8, 1932; s. Donald Coleman McFarland and Barbara (Yirsa) Schwabe; m. Betty Irene Johnson, Nov. 17, 1951; children: Donald J. Jr., Diana D., Cheryl R. BSEE, Okla. State U., 1958. Elec. engr. Rockedyne divsn. N.Am. Aviation, Canoga Park, Calif., 1958-60, elec. engr. space and info. divsn. Lakewood, 1964-66; elec. engr. Lockheed Missile & Space, Van Nuys, 1960-64; sys. engr. Northrip Space Lab., Hawthorn, 1964-66; sr. elec. engr. MTS Jet Propulsion Lab., Pasadena, 1966—. Cpl. USMC, 1952-54. Achievements include design and testing of rocket engine test bed controls; prodn. of various items of surveillance satellite and polaris missile operational support equipment, mariner and voyager attitude control subsy. operational support equipment, drop dynamics module for Spacelab Three, drop physics module for U.S. Microgravity Lab. One, tempus incandescence measuring instrument for Internat. Microgravity Lab. One; design of a Martian surface seismometer prototype design, production and testing of Apollo and Lunar Exploration Module factory and launch Automatic Checkout Equipment. Office: Jet Propulsion Lab 4800 Oak Grove Dr Pasadena CA 91109-8001 Home: 298 Rosevale Rd Grand Jct CO 81503-1774

MCFARLAND, ELLA MAE GAINES, secondary school educator; b. Laneview, Va., July 27, 1938; s. Charles Brown and Estelle Grace Hundley, Preston Hundley (Stepfather); m. Alfred Jr., Feb. 9, 1957 (div. May 1974); children: Alfred III, Barrett, Jeffrey, Kyra, Forrest, Estelle, Carter, Robin. AA, Delaware County C.C., Media, Pa., 1971; BS Elem. Edn., West Chester State U., 1973; MEd, Widener U., 1983. Instrnl. II masters equivalent Pa. Dept. Edn. Elem. sci. tchr. Title 1 Chester-Upland Dist., Chester, Pa., 1973—76; elem. tchr. Chester Upland Sch. Dist., 1973—2001; coord. women's sch. Women's Sch. , Phila., 1985—91; focus adult edn. Delaware County C.C., Chester, 1992—95, coord. GED grant, 1999—; dir. nursery sch. Mount Pleasant Bapt. Ch., Twin Oaks, 1982—83; tchr. pregnant teens GED Project Pride Girls Inc., Wilmington, Del., 2000—. Tng. for GED Pa. Dept. Edn. Active Women's Commn. Delaware County, Media, Pa., 1985—89, Friends to the Women's Commn., Media, 1994—2001; sec. Nova Vista Civic Assn., Chester, 1993—2001; active Bethany Bapt. Ch. Recipient Cmty. Svc. award, Fine Arts Ctr., Chester, Pa., 1998, Outstanding Cmty. Svc. award, Spencer A.M.E. Ch., Chester, Pa., 1999, Mother's Club Bethany. Mem.: NAACP (life), Phi Delta Kappa (epistoles 1990—95). Avocations: worshops, seminars, religious learning, reading. Home: Box 248 215 Gingko Ln Chester PA 19016-0248 Office: Delaware County CC 2600 W 9th St Rm 200 Chester PA 19013 E-mail: emcfar38@aol.com.

MC FARLAND, H. RICHARD, food company executive; b. Hoopeston, Ill., Aug. 19, 1930; s. Arthur Bryan and Jennie (Wilkey) McF.; m. Sarah Forney, Dec. 30, 1967. BS, U. Ill., 1952. With Campbell Soup Co., Camden, N.J., 1957-67, mgr. purchasing, 1961-67; dir. procurement Keebler Co., Elmhurst, Ill., 1967-69; v.p. purchasing and distbn. Ky. Fried Chicken Corp., Louisville, 1969-74, v.p. food svcs., sales and distbn., 1974-75; pres., dir. Mid-Continent Carton Co., Louisville, 1974-75, Ky. Fried Chicken Mfg. Corp., Nashville, 1974-75; owner, pres., dir. McFarland Foods Corp., Indpls., 1975—. Chmn. processed foods com. World's Poultry Congress, 1974; mem. exec. coun., nat. franchise coun. Ky. Fried Chicken, 1979-85; dir. nat. advt. coun. Ky. Fried Chicken, 1985-91, exec. com., 1988-90, chmn., 1989-90; mem. devel. com. U. Ill., 1989—. Mem. U. Ill. Found., 1992—, bd. dirs., 1993—, vice chmn., 2001—;chmn. U. Ill. Nat. Advocates, 1994-2001; life pres. U. Ill. Sr. Class of '52; bd. dirs. Ind. Fedn. Children and Youth, 1983-84; Ind. bd. dirs. Fellowship Christian Athletes, 1997-98, Ind. bd. advisors, 1998—; chmn. campaign Ind. Ky. Fried Chicken March of Dimes, 1978-87; nat. trustee McCormick Theol. Sem., 1993-97, mem. adv. coun., 1998—. 1st lt. USAF, 1952-54, Korea. Recipient Award of Merit U. Ill. Coll. Agr., 1988, Achievement award U. Ill. Alumni Assn., 1996. Mem. Ky. Restaurant Assn. (bd. dirs. 1970-75), Nat. Broiler Coun. (bd. dirs. 1971-74), Ind. Restaurant Assn., Am. Shorthorn Breeders Assn., Great Lakes Ky. Fried Chicken Franchise Assn. (bd. dirs. 1975-91, 1st v.p. 1978-79, pres. 1979-80), Delta Upsilon. Clubs: Main Line Ski (Phila.) (pres. 1964); Hillcrest Country. Presbyterian. Home: 10720 Compass Ct Indianapolis IN 46256-9532

MCFARLAND, JAMES WILLIAM, real estate development company executive; b. Montgomery, Ala., Sept. 7, 1948; s. Ward Wharton and Frances Adelia (Morrow) McF.; B.S., U. Ala., 1970; m. Miriam Melinda Webster, Feb. 20, 1971; children— James William, Mimi Morrow. Dir. real estate for Ky., Ind. and Tenn., Winn-Dixie Stores, Inc., Louisville, 1970-72; v.p. Ward McFarland, Inc., Tuscaloosa, Ala., 1972—, also dir. Mem. Coun. for Devel. of French in La., 1976—, Friends of Libr., 1975—; commr. Dept. Mental Health, 1987-89; ; Rep. nominee U.S. Congress Ala. 7th Dist., 1986; young churchmen adviser Episcopal Diocese Ala., 1976—, conv. del.; charter investor, chair of real estate U. Ala.; chmn. Ala. Rapid Rail Transit Commn.; vice chmn. La.-Miss.-Ala. Rapid Rail Transit Commn., 1983-84, chmn., 1984—; state advisor Congl. Adv. Com., Am. Security Coun.; sr. warden Christ Episc. Ch., 1984; bd. dirs. Tuscaloosa Kidney Found.; mem. Rep. State Exec. Com., 1991—; commr. Dept. Mental Health State of Ala.; chmn. Tuscaloosa County Reps., 1991—; flotilla staff officer USCG Aux., 1994—, dist. staff officer, 1997—. Named hon. citizen of Mobile and New Orleans, hon. mem. mayor's staff, Mobile. Mem. Nat. Assn. Realtors, Tuscaloosa Bd. Realtors, Nat. Small Bus. Assn., U. Ala. Commerce Execs. Soc., U. Ala. Alumni Assn., Nat. Assn. R.R. Passengers, Ala. Assn. R.R. Passengers (pres. 1982, 90, 91), North River Yacht, Kiwanis of Greater Tuscaloosa, Delta Sigma Pi. Flotilla comdr., dists. pub. affairs officer U.S. Coast Guard Aux., 1997. Home: 8714 Forrestal Dr NE Tuscaloosa AL 35406-3404 Office: 325 Skyland Blvd E Tuscaloosa AL 35405-4030

MCFARLAND, JON WELDON, retired county commissioner; b. Wenatchee, Wash., Aug. 23, 1938; s. Charles Edward and Maud Elizabeth (Brennan) McF.; m. Kay Annette Erbes, Apr. 5, 1956; children: Colleen, Michael, Heather. BS in Edn., Eastern Wash. State U., 1961; MS in Personnel Adminstrn., George Washington U., 1966; Grad., Command and Gen. Staff Coll., Fort Leavenworth, Kans., 1970, U.S. Army War Coll., Carlisle Barracks, Pa., 1980. Commd. U.S. Army, 1961, advanced through grades to col., 1981, retired, 1988, ops. officer European Hdqtrs. Fed. Republic Germany, 1980-83, commdr. 16th mil. police brigade Fort Bragg, N.C., 1983-85, provost marshal 18th Airborne Corps, 1983-85; asst. commandant, commdr. of troops U.S. Army Mil. Police Sch., Fort McClellan, Ala., 1985-88; county commr. Columbia County, Wash., 1989-96; ret., 1996; dir., owner Mr. Mc's Direct Mktg. Svcs., 1992—; owner, dir. Spectro-Optics of Ea. Wash., Dayton, 1994—; Wash. staff for courthouse security, 1995-96. Wash. gov. appointee bd. trustees Dist. 20 Cmty. Colls.; vice chmn. Southeastern Emergency Med. and Trauma Coun., Wash., 1990-94, chmn., 1995—; chmn. Columbia County Bd. Commrs., 1990, 96; bd. dirs. Emergency Mgmt. Svcs., Columbia County. Author: History of Civil Disturbance 1960-68, 1969. Bd. dirs. Columbia County Pub. Health Dist., Dayton, 1989-96, chmn., 1995-96; bd. dirs. Project Timothy Pub. Svcs., Columbia County Health Found., 1989—, Inland Counseling Network; vice chmn. Palouse Econ. Devel. Corp., 1990-92, chmn., 1993-95; bd. trustees Walla Walla C.C., 1998—. Decorated Legion of Merit, Bronze Star, numerous others. Mem. Assn. U.S. Army, Wash. State Assn. Counties, U.S. Army War Coll. Found., Kiwanis (bd. dirs. Dayton 1990—, treas. 1998—). Democrat. Roman Catholic. Avocations: woodworking, pottery, fishing, hunting, travel. Home: 150 S Touchet Rd Dayton WA 99328-8741 Office: Columbia County 205 S 4th St Dayton WA 99328-1411

MCFARLAND, KAY ELEANOR, state supreme court chief justice; b. Coffeyville, Kans., July 20, 1935; d. Kenneth W. and Margaret E. (Thrall) McF. BA magna cum laude, Washburn U., Topeka, 1957, JD, 1964. Bar: Kans. 1964. Sole practice, Topeka, 1964-71; probate and juvenile judge Shawnee County, 1971-73; dist. judge, 1973-77; assoc. justice Kans. Supreme Ct., 1977-95, chief justice, 1995—. Mem. Kans. Bar Assn., Women Attys. Assn. Topeka. Office: Kans Supreme Ct Kans Jud Ctr 301 W 10th St Topeka KS 66612 Fax: (785) 291-3274.

MCFARLAND, KEVIN JOHN, foundation administrator; b. Mt. Clement, Mich., Mar. 18, 1958; s. Chuck Paul and Myrna (Bell) McFarland; m. Betty Ann Bolton, Nov. 26, 1976; children: Michelle, Michael, Melinda. BS in Bibl. Studies magna cum laude, Abilene Christian U., Tex., 1980; postgrad., Tex. Tech. U., 1980-81, Stanford U., 1982-83. Resident asst. Abilene (Tex.) State Sch., 1976-78; pvt. landscaping bus. Abilene, 1978-80; research assoc., home and family life dept. Tex. Tech. U., Lubbock, 1980-81; youth and family minister Redwood City (Calif.) Ch. of Christ, 1981-84; pres. Manna Internat. Relief and Devel. Corp., Redwood City, 1984—. Mem. Amnexty Internat., Bread for the World; bd. dirs. Am. Coun. Voluntary Internat. Action. Mem.: Internat. Devel. Network, Acad. Polit. Sci., Inst. Cultural Affairs, Inst. Coop. Interant. Devel. (bd. dirs., founder, exec. dir.), Soc. Internat. Devel. Global Affairs Coun., Evang. for Social Action, Cultural Survival, Nat. Assn. Scholars, Nat. Honor Soc., Alpha Chi. Home: 1193 Hudson St Redwood City CA 94061-2208 Office: Manna Internat PO Box 3507 Redwood City CA 94064-3507

MCFARLAND, M. LANE, human resources educator; b. Bryan, Tex., Jan. 12, 1952; d. Frank Eugene and Trudy (Lively) McF. BA in Journalism, Baylor U., 1974; MS in Counseling and Student Affairs, Okla. State U., 1990; PhD in Counseling and Student Affairs Adminstrn., U. Ga., 1995. Unit asst. to dean Coll. Vet. Medicine Okla. State U., Stillwater, 1985-87, tchg. profl. Coll. Edn., 1989-90, unit asst. to dean, acad. advisor Coll. Bus. Adminstrn., 1987-91; doctoral rsch. asst. dept. counseling and human svcs. U. Ga., Athens, 1991-94, doctoral rsch. asst. Coll. Edn., 1994-95; asst. prof. dept. human resources East Ctrl. U., Ada, Okla., 1997—. Mem. East Ctrl. U. Honors Bd., 1997—, chmn., 1998—. Mem. editl. rev. bd. Ga. Jour. Coll. Student Affairs, Athens, 1994-96, co-editor, 1991-94; mem. editl. reb. bd. Jours. Coll. Student Retention, 1998—); contbr. articles to jours. Polit. campaign vol. State Ho. of Reps. Election, Stillwater, 1996; vol. Athens Area Human Soc., 1994, Ada Area Domestic Violence Svcs., 1997—; blood donor ARC, 1973—. Recipient Outstanding Doctoral Student award Ga. Coll. Personnel Assn., 1995. Mem. Am. Coll. Pers. Assn., Nat. Assn. Student Pers. Adminstrs., Okla. Coll. Student Pers. Assn., Baylor U. Alumni Assn., Okla. State U. Alumni Assn., U. Ga. Alumni Assn., Phi Delta Kappa, Kappa Delta Pi. Avocations: creative writing, reading, music, aerobics. Office: East Ctrl U E 14th St Ada OK 74820

MCFARLAND, MARK DOUGLAS, broker, financial adviser, educator; b. Warren, Mich., Dec. 10, 1967; s. Edward Claude and Frances (Sepulver) McF. BA in Fin. Adminstrn., Mich. State U., 1991; postgrad., Wayne State U., 1991. Lic. broker, Mich. With sale staff St. Clair Paint and Wallpaper, St. Heights, Mich., 1983-87; bartender Mich. Athletic Club, East Lansing, 1989-90; dist. mgr. Fin. Svcs. Am., Utica, Mich., 1991; planning coord., dir. mktg., and v.p. ednl. network Assured Investment Planners, 1991—. Market analyst Timing Svcs., Utica, 1991—. Producer: (videotape) Tax-Deferred Investing, 1991. Avocation: tennis. Home: 13960 24 Mile Rd Shelby Township MI 48315-2406

MCFARLAND, MICHAEL C. academic administrator; b. Boston, 1948; AB in Physics, Cornell U., 1969; M in Elec. Engring., Carnegie M in Elec. Engring., PhD in Elec. Engring., Carnegie Mellon U.; MDiv, ThM in Social Ethics, Weston Sch. Theology. Joined Jesuits, 1975, ordained priest, 1984. Cons. AT&T Bell Labs., 1985-86; assoc. prof. computer sci. Boston Coll., 1986-96, dept. chair; prof. computer sci., dean Coll. Arts and Scis. Gonzaga U., Spokane, 1996—2000; pres. Coll. of the Holy Cross, Worcester, Mass., 2000—. Bd. dirs. U. Scranton. Avocation: running. Office: Coll of the Holy Cross 1 College St Worcester MA 01610-2395

MC FARLAND, NORMAN FRANCIS, bishop; b. Martinez, Calif., Feb. 21, 1922; student St. Patrick's Sem., Menlo Park, Calif.; J.C.D., Cath. U. Am. Ordained priest Roman Catholic Ch., 1946, consecrated bishop, 1970; titular bishop of Bida and aux. bishop of San Francisco, 1970-74; apostolic adminstr. Diocese of Reno, 1974-76; bishop Diocese of Reno-Las Vegas, 1976-87, Diocese of Orange, Calif., 1987-98. Office: 200 W La Veta Ave Orange CA 92866-1936

MCFARLAND, PATRICK E. federal agency administrator; b. St. Louis; m. Kathy McFarland; 4 children. BS, St. Louis U., 1965; MPA, Am. U., 1986. Police officer, detective St. Louis Met. Police Dept.; spl. agt. Fed. Bur. Narcotics, Chgo.; with U.S. Secret Svc., Washington; inspector gen. Office Personnel Mgmt., 1990—. Mem. alumni adv. bd. Key Exec. Program Am. U. Mem.: Assn. Govt. Accts., Internat. Assn. Chiefs of Police, Fed. Investigators Assn. Office: OPM 1900 E St NW Washington DC 20415-1100*

MCFARLAND, PHILIP JAMES, educator, writer; b. Birmingham, Ala., June 20, 1930; s. Thomas Alfred McFarland and Alice Lucile Sylvester; m. Patricia Katherin Connors, July 23, 1960; children: Philip James Jr., Joseph Thomas. BA, Oberlin Coll., 1951; MA, Cambridge U., 1957. Textbook editor Houghton Mifflin Co., Boston, 1958-64; tchr. English Concord (Mass.) Acad., 1965-95. Author: A House Full of Women, 1960, Sojourners, 1979, Seasons of Fear, 1984, Sea Dangers, 1985, The Brave Bostonians, 1998. Lt. j.g. USN, 1951-55. Mem. Mass. Hist. Soc. Democrat. Avocations: bicycling, trekking. Home: 18 Independence Ave Lexington MA 02421-5939

MCFARLAND, RICHARD, engineering educator, pilot; b. Cleve., Jan. 20, 1929; s. Jesse Burrell and Flossie Genevieve McFarland; m. Norma Jean McFarland; children: David R., Jeanne Anne Houpes, Lori Lynn Williams. BS, Ohio U., 1950, MS, 1957, PhD, 1961. Registered profl. engr., Ohio. Russ prof. emeritus Ohio U., Athens, 1962—. 1st lt. USAF, 1951—55. Recipient Hays award, ION, 2001, Disting. Svc. award, FAA. Fellow: IEEE. Avocation: aviation. Home: 80 Briarwood Dr Athens OH 45701-1355 Office: Avionics Engring Ohio Univ 214 Stocker Athens OH 45701-2979

MCFARLAND, RICHARD M. executive recruiting consultant; b. Sept. 10, 1923; s. George Fiske and Phyllis C. (Macomber) McF.; m. Virginia Fitz-Randolph Ripley, Dec. 6, 1947; children: Richard Macomber, Kirk, Jane. BChemE, Rensselaer Poly. Inst., 1944; postgrad., U. Mich., 1946-47. Prodn. supr. E. I. duPont, 1947-51; mgr. agrl. chem. market rsch. Brea Chem. (Calif.) subs. Union Oil Co., 1953-55; product mgr. chem. divsn. FMC Corp., N.Y.C., 1955-59; mgr. mktg. devel. Tex. Butadiene & Chem., 1959-60; pres. Cumberland Chem. Corp., 1960-67; gen. mgr. inorganic divsn. Wyandotte Chem. Co., Mich., 1967-69; assoc. Heidrick & Struggles, Inc., N.Y.C., 1969-72, v.p., 1972-81; founder, pres. Brissenden, McFarland, Wagoner & Fuccella, Inc. and predecessors, Stamford, Conn., 1981-94. Patentee in field. Ensign USNR, 1943-46, lt. comdr., 1951-53. Mem. Cedar Point, Yacht Club, Lambda Chi Alpha. Home: 16 Clover Ln Westport CT 06880-2626

MCFARLAND, RICHARD MACKLIN, retired journalist; b. Blockton, Iowa, Mar. 27, 1922; s. William Harold McFarland and Elsie (Sisson) McFarland Chavannes; m. Jacquelyn Jean Folske, Mar. 22, 1955; children: Bethany Rose, Scott Macklin, Elizabeth Ann McFarland Heyda, Kathryn Belle. BA, U. Iowa, 1944. Newsman UPI, Des Moines, 1944, Chgo., 1945, 46-47, bur. mgr. Bismarck, N.D., 1944-45, Herrin, Ill., 1945, Sioux Falls, S.D., 1947-49, Milw., 1949-51, legis. reporter Des Moines, 1947, Pierre, S.D., 1949, Iowa mgr. Des Moines, 1951-54, NW mgr. Mpls., 1954-55, Wis. mgr. Milw., 1956-57, regional exec. sales, 1958-59, bur. mgr. Chgo., 1960-61, Minn. mgr. Mpls., 1961-69, Mich. editor Detroit, 1969-71, Minn. editor Mpls., 1971-84, bur. mgr.-capitol reporter St. Paul, 1985-89. Bd. dirs. Minn. Press Club, 1981-84. Former deacon, Advent Luth. Ch., Roseville, Minn., 8 yrs; coun. mem. Redeemer Luth. Ch., Bradenton, Fla., 1996-98, pres. coun., 1998-99, coun. mem. 2001-. Served with USN, 1943-44 Avocations: reading, music, fishing, backpacking, golf. Home: 7312 5th Ave NW Bradenton FL 34209-1522 E-mail: rmmcf612@aol.com.

MCFARLAND, ROBERT EDWIN, lawyer; b. St. Louis, July 25, 1946; s. Francis Taylor and Kathryne (Stephens) McF.; m. Jeannine M. Ghekiere, Feb. 26, 1982. BA, U. Mich., 1968, JD, 1971. Bar: Mich. 1971, U.S. Dist. Ct. (ea. dist.) Mich. 1971, U.S. Ct. Appeals (6th cir.) 1974, U.S. Supreme Ct. 1975, U.S. Ct. Appeals (D.C. cir.) 1978, N.Mex. 2001. Law clk. to chief judge Mich. Ct. Appeals, 1971-72; assoc. William B. Elmer, St. Clair Shores, Mich., 1972-74, James Elsman, Birmingham, 1974-75; ptnr. McFarland, Schmier, Stoneman & Singer, Troy, 1975-77; sr. ptnr. McFarland & Bullard, Bloomfield Hills, 1977-90, McFarland & Niemer, Farmington Hills, 1990-91; shareholder Foster, Swift, Collins & Smith, P.C., 1992—, mem. exec. com., 1995—. Chmn. bd. govs. Transp. Law Jour., U. Denver Coll. Law, 1981-83. Mem. bd. control Intercollegiate Athletics, U. Mich., 1966-68; mem. rulemaking study com. Mich. Pub. Svc. Commn., 1983-84, Motor Carrier Adv. Bd., 1984-88. Capt. USAR, 1971-80. Mem. ABA, Transp. Lawyers Assn. (officer 1998—, Disting. Svc. award 1997, pres. 2002-), Assn. Transp. Law, Logistics and Policy, State Bar Mich. (vice-chmn. transp. law com. adminstrn. law sect. 1990—, sect. coun. adminstrv. law sect. 1994, 99), Am. Judicature Soc. Office: Foster Swift Collins & Smith PC 32300 Northwestern Hwy Ste 230 Farmington MI 48334-1571 E-mail: rmcfarland@fosterswift.com.

MC FARLAND, ROBERT HAROLD, physicist, educator; b. Severy, Kans., Jan. 10, 1918; s. Robert Eugene and Georgia (Simpson) McF.; m. Twilah Mae Seefeld, Aug. 28, 1940; children: Robert Alan, Rodney Jon. BS and BA, Kans. State Tchrs. Coll., Emporia, 1940; Ph.M. (Mendenhall fellow), U. Wis., 1943, PhD, 1947. Sci. instr., coach high sch., Chase, Kans., 1940-41; instr. navy radio sch. U. Wis., Madison, 1943-44; sr. engr. Sylvania Elec. Corp., 1944-46; faculty Kans. State U., 1947-60, prof. physics, 1954-60, dir. nuclear lab., 1958-60; physicist U. Calif. Lawrence Radiation Lab., 1960-69; dean Grad. Sch., U. Mo., Rolla, 1969-79, dir. instnl. analysis and planning, 1979-82; prof. physics U. Mo., 1969-84, prof. emeritus physics dept., 1985—; v.p. acad. affairs U. Mo. System, 1974-75; Intergovtl. Personnel Act appointee Dept. Energy, Washington, 1982-84; vis. prof. U. Calif., Berkeley, 1980-81. Mem. Grad. Record Exams. Bd., 1971-75, chmn. steering com., 1972-73; cons. Well Surveys, Inc., Tulsa, 1953-54, Argonne Nat. Lab., Chgo., 1955-59, Kans. Dept. Pub. Health, 1956-57, cons. in residence Lawrence Radiation Lab., U. Calif., 1957, 58, 59, med. physics U. Okla. Med. Sch., 1971, grad. schs., PhD physics program, Utah State U., 1972; physicist, regional counselor Office Ordnance Research, Durham, N.C., 1955. Contbr. over 110 articles to profl. jours.; patentee in field of light prodn., vacuum prodn., controlled thermonuclear reactions. Active Boy Scouts Am., 1952—, mem. exec. bd. San Francisco Bay Area council, 1964-68, Ozark Council, 1986—; chmn. Livermore (Calif.) Library Bond drive, 1964. Mem. Kans. N.G., 1936-40. Recipient Silver Beaver award Boy Scouts Am., 1968, Community Service award C. of

C., 1965, Disting. Alumnus award Kans. State Tchrs. Coll., 1969. Fellow AAAS, Am. Phys. Soc., Kiwanis Internat.; mem. AAUP (chpt. pres. 1956-57), Am. Assn. Physics Tchrs., Mo. Acad. Sci., Mo. Assn. Phys. Sci. Tchrs., Am. Soc. Engring. Edn., Kiwanis (lt. gov. Mo.-Ark. dist. 1984-85, internat. accredited rep. 1985-92, Disting. Lt. Gov. 1985, Tablet of honor award 1997), Sigma Xi, Lambda Delta Lambda, Xi Phi, Kappa Mu Epsilon, Kappa Delta Pi, Pi Mu Epsilon, Gamma Sigma Delta, Phi Kappa Phi. Home: 309 Christy Dr Rolla MO 65401-4073 Office: U Mo Dept Physics Rolla MO 65401 *Continuation of the last hundred years of major progress in the quality of life for the human race will not only require the best of our educational systems and technological talents but a sincere interest in all of us to contribute positively toward our collective well-being.*

MCFARLAND, SAMUEL P., JR. psychologist; b. Atlanta, Oct. 16, 1957; s. Samuel P. and Gladys Blake (Pepper) McF. BA in Psychology, Mercer U., 1983; MA in Gen. and Exptl. Psychology, Fla. Atlantic U., 1987; MS in Clin. Psychology, Nova U., 1993; PhD in Clin. Psychology, Nova Southeastern U., 1998. Store mgr. Reeds Drugs Inc., Atlanta, 1973—81; mental health technician C.P.C. Parkwood Hosp., 1982—84; mental health asst. C.P.C. Ft. Lauderdale Hosp., Fla., 1985, N.M.E. Fair Oaks Hosp., Delray Beach, 1985-87; peer acad. advisor Fla. Atlantic U., Boca Raton, 1986-87; clin. counselor/supr. Henderson Mental Health Ctr./New Vistas, Ft. Lauderdale, 1987-88; adj. faculty instr. Art Inst. Ft. Lauderdale, 1992-93; case mgr., psychologist Bradley Ctr. of St. Francis, Columbus, Ga., 1993—. Therapist Biofeedback Clinic/Nova Clinic, Davie, Fla., 1992, The Family Ctr./Nova U., 1991-92, Child & Adolescent Anxiety Disorders Clinic/Nova Clinic, Coral Springs, 1989-90. Co-sponsor Al-Ateen Group, Atlanta, 1975-76. Mem. APA (nat. treas. 1988-90, mem. divsns. 12 and 37 1994—), APAGS, Am. Psychol. Soc., Columbus Psychol. Assn. Office: Bradley Ctr St Francis 2000 16th Ave Columbus GA 31901 E-mail: sampsy@mindspring.com.

MC FARLAND, TERRY LYNN, construction company executive; b. Knoxville, Tenn., July 8, 1947; s. Jacob E. and Virginia Kay (Allen) McF.; m. Hazel C. Davis, Nov. 1, 1975. Student, Ind. U., 1969-70, Wickes U., 1977-79. Prodn. control staff R.R. Donnelley & Sons, Warsaw, 1965-68; insp. Bendix Corp., South Bend, 1968-69; mgr. Wickes Bldgs. divsn. Wickes Corp., Argos, Inc., 1970-71, Crawfordsville, Ind., 1971-73, Macon, Ga., 1973-76, dist. mgr. Midwest, 1976-78, regional mgr., 1978-80; v.p., gen. mgr. Douglass Bldg. divsn. Stanley Smith & Sons, Columbia, S.C., 1980-81; ter. mgr. Butler Mfg. Co., Kansas City, Mo., 1981-84, southeastern area mgr., 1984-89; dist. mgr. Varco-Pruden Bldgs. divsn. United Dominion Industries, Memphis, 1989-96; dist. sales mgr. Nucor Bldg. Sys. divsn. Nucor Corp., Charlotte, N.C., 1996-98, Ga. ACI Bldg. Sys., Inc., 1998-99; S.E. area sales mgr. Ga. divsn. Nationwide Homes, Inc., 2000—. Served with U.S. Army, 1966-68, Korea. Mem. NRA, Am. Legion, Nat. Geog. Soc., Moose, Masons (Scottish Rite), Shriners. Home and Office: 741 Springdale Woods Dr Macon GA 31210-1530

MCFARLAND, THOMAS, language educator, literature educator; AB, Harvard U., 1949; AM, Yale U., 1951, PhD, 1953; postgrad., Eberhard-Karls-Universität, Tübingen, Germany, 1953-54; MA status (hon.), Oxford U., Eng., 1986. Instr. in English Oberlin Coll., 1954-56, U. Va., 1956-58; asst. prof. Western Res. U., Cleve., 1958-62, assoc. prof., 1962-64, prof., 1964-67, Grad. Ctr. CUNY, 1967-73, disting. prof. English lit., 1973-78; prof. Princeton U., N.J., 1978-81, Murray prof. English lit., 1981-89, Murray prof. English lit. emeritus, 1989—. Vis. prof. U. Colo., 1968, U. Va., 1972, Yale U., 1975; vis. fellow All Souls Coll., U. Oxford, Eng., 1986-87, Humanities Rsch. Ctr., Australian Nat. U., Canberra, 1992, Lechter Inst. for Lit. Rsch., Bar-Ilan U., Ramat Gan, Israel, 1989, U. Otago, Dunedin, New Zealand, 1992; The Ida Beam Lectures U. Iowa, 1985; mem. adv. bd. Bull. Rsch. in Humanities, 1978—, Studies in Romanticism, 1982—, Nineteenth-Century Lit., 1986—, Works of Thomas De Quincey, 1990, Romanticism, 1995—; hon. fellow Ctr. for European Romanticism, 1997—; mem. supervising com. English Inst., 1971-74, chmn. 1974; ; assoc. trustee The Dove Cottage Trust, The Lake Dist., Eng., 1982—; bd. advisors Milton and the Romantics, 1975—; seminar assoc. Columbia U., 1971—, 76—, 97—; cons., spkr. in field. Author: Tragic Meanings in Shakespeare, 1966, Coleridge and the Pantheist Tradition, 1969, Shakespeare's Pastoral Comedy, 1972, Romanticism and the Forms of Ruin: Wordsworth, Coleridge and Modalities of Fragmentation, 1981, Originality and Imagination, 1985, Shapes of Culture, 1987, Romantic Cruxes: The English Essayists and the Spirit of the Age, 1987, William Wordsworth; Intensity and Achievement, 1992, Romanticism and the Heritage of Rousseau, 1995, Paradoxes of Freedom; The Romantic Mystique of a Transcendence, 1996, The Masks of Keats: The Endeavor of a Poet, 2000; editor: The Opus Maximum of Samuel Taylor Coleridge, 2002; mem. editl. bd. Comparative Criticism, 1977—, European Romantic Rev., 1989—; contbr. articles to profl. jours. Fulbright scholar, 1953-54; fellow Guggenheim Found., 1964-65, 74-75, Am. Coun. Learned Socs., 1973-74, Ctr. for Advanced Study in Behavioral Scis., 1981-82, NEH, 1981-82, 86-87. Mem. MLA (exec. com. English 9 1970-73, chmn. 1974), Sydney Soc. for Literature and Aesthetics (hon. life). Home: 711 N O St Lake Worth FL 33460

MCFARLAND, WALTER GERARD, management consultant; b. Chicago Heights, Ill., June 28, 1952; s. Walter Louden and Rosemary (Voelker) McF. BA in Psychology, So. Ill. U., 1976, MPA, 1978; MA in Nat. Security, Georgetown U., 1991; EdD in Human Resource Devel., George Washington U., 1999. Program analyst USAF, San Antonio, 1978-82; program monitor CIA, Washington, 1982-85; spl. asst. to sec. of def. Dept. of Def., 1985-88; mgmt. cons. Hay Mgmt. Consultants, 1988-97; prin. rsch. scientist Am. Insts. Rsch., 1997—. Guest lectr. CIA, 1985-88, Georgetown U., 1995, Johns-Hopkins U., Washington, 1996. Elder Great Falls (Va.) Bible Ch., 1988-90; mem. Wakefield H.S. PTA, Arlington, Va., 1992-96. Mem. ASPA (nat. chpt. head 1985-86, chpt. dir. 1987), Acad. Mgmt. Republican. Baptist. Home: 2214 N Scott St Arlington VA 22209-1012

MCFARLAND, WILLELLYN SHAW, artist, educator; b. Compton, Calif., Nov. 14, 1934; d. William Bruce Shaw and Brenda Marguerite McKee; m. Jim McFarland, Apr. 9, 1960; children: Craig, Robin, Shawn. BFA, U. So. Calif., L.A., 1956; tchg. credentials, Calif. State U., Long Beach, 1978. Lifetime credentials in spl. secondary art, gen. jr. h.s., Calif. Tchr. elem. edn. Montebello Sch. Dist., 1972-92; adult sch. tchr. El Rancho Unified Sch. Dist., 1982-98; tchr. Downey (Calif.) Sch. Dist., 1983—. Advisor Artists Mag., 1996; tchr. adult sch. El Rancho Unified Sch. Dist., 2002-03. Featured in books Artists of California, 1993, The Artistic Touch 3, 1999, The Artists mag., 1999. Mem. Nat. Watercolor Soc. (pres. 1991-92, 96-97, exhbn. dir. 1991-92, 96-97, chmn. selection jury 1998 Ann. Exhbn. 1998, exhibited in juried art exhbns. 1995, corr. sec., advisor 1997-98), Women Painters West (exhibited in juried exhbns. 1986) Avocations: golf, painting on location.

MCFARLANE, BETH LUCETTA TROESTER, former mayor; b. Osterdock, Iowa, Mar. 9, 1918; d. Francis Charles and Ella Carrie (Moser) Troester; m. George Evert McFarlane, June 20, 1943 (dec. May 1972); children: Douglas, Steven (dec.), Susan, George. BA in Edn., U. No. Iowa, 1962, MA in Edn., 1971. Cert. tchr. Tchr. rural and elem. schs., Iowa, 1936-50, 55-56; elem. tchr. Oelwein Cmty. Schs., 1956-64, jr. high reading tchr., 1964-71; city council Oelwein, 1981-82; mayor of Oelwein, 1982-89. Evaluator North Cen. Accreditation Assn. for Ednl. Programs; mem. planning team for confs. for Iowa Cities, N.E. Iowa, 1985; v.p. N.E. Iowa Regional Coun. Econ. Devel., 1986-89; mem. Area Econ. Devel. Com. N.E. Iowa, 1985, Legis. Interim Study Com. on Rural Econ. Devel., 1987-88; mem. policy com. Iowa League Municipalities, 1987-88. V.p. Fayette County Tourism Coun., 1987-88; mem. Iowa State steering com. on road use tax financing, 1988-89; chmn. bd. govs. Oelwein Cmty. Ctr., 1990-94, bd. govs., 2001—; chmn. bldg. and fin. com. Reorganized LDS Ch. Bldg., 1980—, dist. ch. fin. com., 1992-2001, dist. ch. revolving loan com., 1982-00. Named Iowa Reading Tchr. of Yr., Internat. Reading Assn. Iowa, 1978; recipient Outstanding Contbn. to Reading Coun. Activities award Internat. Reading Assn. N.E. Iowa, 1978, State of Iowa's Gov.'s Leadership award, 1988. Mem.: Oelwein Area C. of C. (bd. dirs. 1986—89, Humanitarian award 1987), Oelwein Area Ret. Sch. Pers. (pres. 1994—96), Oelwein Bus. and Profl. Women (Woman of Yr. 1983), MacDowell Music and Arts Orgn. (pres. 1978—80), N.E. Iowa Reading Coun. (pres. 1975—77), Area Univ. Women (pres. 1999—2000), Delta Kappa Gamma (pres. 1980—82). Republican. Mem. Reorganized Ch. of Jesus Christ of Latter Day Sts. Avocations: hiking, refinishing antiques, gardening, walking, creative sewing. Home: 512 7th Ave NE Oelwein IA 50662-1326

MCFARLANE, DONOVAN ANTHONY, writer, poet, researcher; b. Manchester, Jamaica, Apr. 19, 1978; came to U.S., 1997; s. Merceline Agatha Wright. Numerous certs., deCarteret Coll., Jamaica, 1995, Church Tchrs. Coll., 1997; diploma in fitness and nutrition, Harcourt Learning Direct, Scranton, Pa., 1999; restaurant and hotel mgmt. diploma, Profl. Career Devel. Inst., Atlanta, 2000; diploma in bus. mgmt. with highest honor, Stratford Career Inst., Washington, 2000; diploma in small bus. mgmt., Lifetime Career Sch., Archbald, Pa., 2000; BS in Geog. Sci., Bernadean U., North Hollywood, Calif., 2000; PhD in Metaphysics, Am. Coll. Metaphys. Theology, Golden Valley, Minn., 2000, PhD in Comparative Religion, 2002; cert. in paralegal studies, Blackstone Sch., 2002; BS in Parapsychic Sci., MS in Parapsychic Sci., Am. Inst. Holistic Theology, 2002; MBA, Frederick Taylor U., 2002. Cert. in secondary edn. Tchr. trainee in Spanish and social studies Comprehensive H.S., Jamaica, 1997; tutor gen. sci. Church Tchrs. Coll., Jamaica; curriculum planner pvt. orgn., Fla., essayist, cons., 1998—; clk. Phillips and Phillips, Fort Lauderdale, 1997-98; supr. inventory and warehouse Lord's Supermarket, Oakland, 1999; Corp. Edu. Rsch., 2001—. Contbr. poetry to various publs. With USMC, 2000. Recipient cert. excellence in spanish, social studies, geography, math., history, cert. diligence in spanish, religious edn., cert. outstanding achievement in social studies, cert. outstanding achievement in spanish; named hon. alumni Oglata Lakota Coll., S.Dak., 2000. Mem. Nat. Libr. Poetry (Disting. Membership cert. and plaque 1998), Internat. Soc. Poets (Editor's Choice award 1998). Avocations: dancing, oratory, martial arts, singing, writing.

MCFARLANE, JAMES L. artist, educator; b. Phila., Nov. 8, 1939; s. James Harold and Maria Janson McFarlane. BFA, Phila. Coll. Art, 1961; MEd, Temple U., 1968. Freelance illustrator, Phila., 1962-65; home furnishing coord. Sears Roebuck Co., Wayne, 1965-67; tchr. Spring Ford Sch. Dist., 1967-97; artist, tchr. Greater Norristown (Pa.) Art League, 1995—, Wayne Art Ctr., 1995—2001, Woodmere Art Mus., Phila., 1995—. Pres. Greater Norristown Art League, 1970-93. One-man shows include Greater Norristown Art League, Hill Sch. Ctr. for Arts Gallery; exhibited in group shows at Am. Watercolor Soc. Internat. Ann. Exhbns., 1994, 2000, Phila. Watercolor Club Exhbns., Berman Mus., Woodmere Mus., Port of History Mus., Iaccoca Ctr-Lehigh U., Art Inst., Atlantic City Art Ctr., Am. Coll., Jane Law Gallery, Mid-Atlantic Regional Watercolor Exhbns., Johns Hopkins U., N.E. Watercolor Soc. Nat. Ann., Red River Art Assn., N.D., Adirondacks Nat. Exhbn., Greater Norristown Art League, Wayne Art Ctr., Perkiomen Valley Art Ctr., Doylestown Art League, Bethlehem Palette Club Exhbns., Hist. Yellow Springs, Phillips Mill Art Assn., Haverford Coll., Camphill-Soltane, Soroptomist Club, Immaculate Coll., Notre Dame de Namur Exhbns., Gronendahl Gallery, Louisa Melrose Gallery, 4th St. Gallery, Riverbank Gallery, Hardcastle Gallery, Hagley Mus., Allentown Art Mus., Salmagundi Club, N.Y.C.; represented in permenant collections Blue Cross Corp., Subaru Corp., ARA Corp., Spring-House Estates Corp., Clark Ladner Firm, Montgomery County Bar Assn. Mem. Am. Watercolor Soc., Pa. Watercolor Soc., Phila. Watercolor Soc. (bd. dirs., pres. 1994).

MC FARLANE, KAREN ELIZABETH, concert artists manager; b. St. Louis, Jan. 2, 1942; d. Nicholas and Bonita Margaret (Fults) Walz; m. Ralph Leo McFarlane, Nov. 30, 1968 (div.); children: Sarah Louise.; m. Walter Holtkamp, June 19, 1982. B.Mus.Ed. (Presser Music Found. scholar), Lindenwood Coll., 1964. Public sch. music tchr., St. Louis County, 1964-66; music asst. Riverside Ch., N.Y.C., 1966-70; dir. music Park Ave. Christian Ch., 1974-81; also pres. Murtagh/McFarlane Artists, Inc., Cleve., 1976-88; pres. Karen McFarlane Artists, 1989-2000. Mem. Am. Guild Organists, Nat. Assn. Performing Arts Mgrs. and Agts., Inc., Internat. Soc. Performing Arts Adminstrn. Democrat. Presbyterian. Office: 2385 Fenwood Rd Cleveland OH 44118 E-mail: karen@concertorganists.com.

MCFARLANE, STEPHEN C. dean, researcher; BS, MS, Portland State U.; PhD, U. Wash. Chmn. dept. speech pathology and audiology, vice dean U. Nev. Sch. Medicine, 2001, dean, 2002—. Rschr. in field. Author: The Voice and Voice Therapy, 2000; contbr. articles to profl. jours. Office: Manville Bldg Mailstop 357 Reno NV 89557*

MCFARLANE, WALTER ALEXANDER, lawyer, educator; b. Richlands, Va., May 4, 1940; s. James Albert and Frances Mae (Padbury) McF.; m. Judith Louise Copenhaver, Aug. 31, 1962. BA, Emory and Henry Coll., 1962; JD, U. Richmond, 1966. Bar: Ba. 1966, U.S. Supreme Ct. 1970, U.S. Ct. Appeals (4th cir.) 1973, U.S. Ct. Appeals (D.C. cir.) 1977, U.S. Dist. ct. (ea. dist.) Va. 1973. Asst. atty. gen. Office Va. Atty. Gen., Richmond, 1969-73, dep. atty. gen., 1973-90; exec. asst., chief counsel, dir. policy Gov.'s Office Commonwealth of Va., 1990-94, supt. Dept. Correctional Edn., 1994—. Acting dir. Dept. Juvenile Justice, 1997; prof. adj. staff U. Richmond, 1978—; chmn. transp. law com. Transp. Rsch. Bd., Nat. Rsch. Bd. Nat. Acads. Sci. and Engring., Washington, 1977-85, 88-94, chmn. legal affairs com., 1978-85, chmn. environ., archeological and hist. com., 1985-90; mem. State Water Commn., 1994-96, mem., Coun. of State Govts. Henry Toll Fell., 1988; Legal Task Force, 1988—. Contbr. articles to profl. jours. Mem. exec. com., bd. govs. Emory and Henry Coll., 1985-98; pres. Windsor Forest Civic Assn., Midlothian, Va., 1975-76; bd. dirs. Greater Midlothian Civic League, 1980-86, v.p., 1980; instr. water safety ARC, 1962-87; chmn. bldg. com. Mt. Pisgah United Meth. Ch., 1980-85, pres. men's club, 1980-81; bd. dirs. cen. Va. chpt. Epilepsy Assn. Va., 1988-91, Woodland Pond Civic Assn., 1988-89; mem. State Criminal Justice Svcs. Bd., 1994—. Capt. JAGC, USAF, 1966-69. Recipient J.D. Buscher Disting. Atty. award Am. Assn. State Hwy. and Transp. Ofcls., 1983, John C. Vance legal writing award Nat. Acads. Sci. and Engring., 4th ann. outstanding evening lectr. award Student Body, U. Richmond, 1980. Mem. Chesterfield Bar Assn., Richmond Bar Assn. (bd. dirs. 1989-93), Richmond Scottish Soc. (bd. dirs. 1980-82), Emory and Henry Coll. Alumni Assn. (chpt. pres. 1971-73, regional v.p. 1974-77, pres. 1981-83), Meadowbrook Country Club (bd. dir. 2001-). Home: 9001 Wildgoose Way Chesterfield VA 23838-5274 Office: 101 N 14th St Richmond VA 23219-3684

MCFARLANE, WILLIAM JOHN, management consultant; b. Edinburgh, Scotland, Nov. 27, 1949; came to U.S., 1985; s. David Duncan and Doreen (Penney) McF.; children: Robert William, Aran James, Duncan Ewan; m. Isae Wada, Apr. 8, 1998. Grad., Dundee Coll. Tech., 1980; MBA, U. Edinburgh, 1984. V.p. Associated Travel Network, Chgo., 1985-86; gen. mgr. Corp-Net Internat., Libertyville, 1986-88; v.p. Galileo N.Am., Rosemont, 1988-90; prin. Bill McFarlane & Assocs., Norcross, Ga., 1990-93; pres., CEO AQUA Software Products, Inc., Santa Ana, Calif., 1993-96; prin. Bill McFarlane & Assocs., Inc., Mill Valley, 1997—; pres., CEO Travelstore.com, London, 1999-2000, Travelstore.com.; with Bill McFarlane & Assocs., San Geronimo, Calif., 2001—. Contbr. articles to trade mags. Republican. Avocations: travel, computers, world events. Address: 16690 Mission Way Sonoma CA 95476-3079 E-mail: bill@billmcfarlane.com.

MCFARLIN, DIANE HOOTEN, publisher; b. Lake Wales, Fla., July 10, 1954; d. Ruffie Denton Hooten and Anna Loraine (Peeples) Huff; m. Henry Briggs McFarlin, Aug. 28, 1976 (div. 1993). BS, U. Fla., 1976. Reporter Sarasota (Fla.) Jour., 1976-77, asst. news editor, 1977-78, city editor, 1978-82; asst. mng. editor Sarasota (Fla.) Herald Tribune, 1983-84, mng. editor, 1985-87; exec. editor Gainesville (Fla.) Sun, 1987-90; from exec. editor to assoc. publ. Sarasota Herald-Tribune, 1990-99, publ., 1999—. Adv. bd. U. Fla. Coll. Journalism and Comm., 1987—; Pulitzer juror Columbia U., 1995-96, 2001-02. Mem. accrediting coun. Edn. in Journalism and Mass Comms., 1994-96. Recipient Alumna of Distinction award U. Fla., 1999. Mem. Am. Soc. Newspaper Editors (com. chair 1992, 94, 96, 2000, bd. dirs. 1994—, treas., sec., v.p. 2001, pres. 2002), Fla. Soc. Newspaper Editors (sec.-treas. 1993, v.p. 1994, pres. 1995). Office: Sarasota Herald-Tribune PO Box 1719 Sarasota FL 34230-1719 also: 801 S Tamiami Trail Sarasota FL 34236-7824

MCFARLIN, RICHARD FRANCIS, retired industrial chemist, researcher; b. Oklahoma City, Oct. 12, 1929; s. Loy Lester and Julie Mae (Collins) McF.; m. Clare Jane Burroughs, Apr. 4, 1953; children: Robin Sue McFarlin Godwin, Richard Prescott, Rebecca Lynn McFarlin Bray, Roger Whitsitt. BS, Va. Mil. Inst., 1951; MS, Purdue U., 1953, PhD, 1956. Rsch. chemist Monsanto Chem. Co., St. Louis, 1956-60; supr. inorganic rsch. Internat. Minerals and Chems., Mulberry, Fla., 1961; mgr. Agr. Rsch. Ctr. Armour Agrl. Chem. Co., Atlanta, 1962; v.p. rsch., ops., devel. & adminstrn. div. agri-chems. U.S. Steel, 1986; tech. dir. Lester Labs. Inc., 1986-88; exec. dir. Fla. Inst. Phosphate Rsch., Bartow, 1988-96; ret., 1996. Mem. bd. advisors engring. coun. U. South Fla., Lakeland, 1990—, U. Fla., Gainesville, 1991—; mem. bd. advisors Inst. Recyclable Materials La. State U., Baton Rouge, 1990—. Capt. USAR, 1951-61. M. M. Cohn Found. scholar, 1947, L. D. Wall scholar, 1949, O. M. Baldinger scholar, 1950. Presbyterian. Achievements include eight U.S. and foreign patents for selective organic reducing agents, fertilizer processes and selective biocides. Home: 3239 Bridgefield Dr Lakeland FL 33803-7903 E-mail: rfmcf@juno.com.

MCFARREN, FREDDY E. military career officer; b. Cleburne, Tex., Oct. 13, 1943; s. Aubrey McFarren; children: Preston, William. BS, U.S. Mil. Acad., 1966; MEd, Duke U.; grad., Armed Forces Staff Coll., U.S. Army War Coll. Commd. 2d lt. U.S. Army, 1966, advanced through grades to maj. gen., various positions, comdr. 18th Field Artillary Brigade, XVIII Airborne Corps, bn. comdr. 1st Bn. 319th Airborne Field Artillery 82d Divsn., exec. officer 155mm bn. 8th Inf. Divsn. Europe; tactical officer U.S. Mil. Acad.; advisor to Vietnamese Rangers U.S. Army, Vietnam, field arty. battery comdr. XVIII Airborne Corps Arty., asst. chief staff ops. G3 XVIII Airborne Corps N.C., asst. divsn. comdr. 24th Inf. Divsn. (Mechanized) Ft. Stewart, Ga.; comdt. of cadets U.S. Mil. Acad., West Point, N.Y.; dir. tng. Office of the Dep. Chief Staff for Ops. and Plans U.S. Army, Washington, chief Office Mil. Cooperation Cairo, commdg. gen. Ft. Riley Kans., 1998—. Decorated Silver Star, Def. Superior Svc. medal, Legion of Merit with four oak leaf clusters, Bronze Star with V device and three oak leaf clusters, Purple Heart, Meritorious Svc. medal with two oak leaf clusters, Air medal, Army Commendation medal with oak leaf cluster, French Croix de Guerre with Gold Star, The Republic of Vietnam Cross of Gallantry with two Palms and the Honor medal first class. Office: Fort Riley-US Army Fort Riley KS 66442

MCFARREN, NAZA, artist; b. Santa Cruz do Piaui, Brazil, Apr. 19, 1955; d. Jose Cortez and Guiomar Maia Rufino; m. Stuart McFarren, June 22, 1984 (div. Aug. 1991); children: Daniel, Guiomar Silva. Tchr. art Fayetteville (N.C.) Mus. Art, 1990-93; owner, pres. Naza Art Studio, Boca Raton, Fla., 1993—. Exhibited in Sao Paulo Mus. Art, Fayetteville (N.C.) Mus. Art, Cornell Mus. Art and History, Delray, Fla., Parish Gallery, Washington, Ardel Gallery, Washington, Vila Riso Gallery, Rio de Janeiro, Patrimony Gallery, Recife, Brazil, Arte Maior Gallery, Recife, Galerie J.L.T., Paris, Gallery Two, Wooster, 93 South Art Gallery, Nyack, N.Y.; represented in permanent collections West Point Acad., Pres. Clinton, Pres. Fernando H. Cardoso, Ivana Trump, Brigite Bardot, Airton Senna Found., also pvt. collections. Recipient Merit award Fayetteville Mus. Art, 1991; decorated Croix d'Argent, Le Merite et Devouement Francaise (France), Comenda Renacenca-Piaui (Brazil); N.C. Arts Coun. Emerging Artist grantee, 1991. Mem. Women in Visual Arts, Profl. Artists Guild, Boca Raton Mus. Art, Soroptimists Internat. (Woman of Distinction). E-mail: naza@naza.com.

MCFATE, KENNETH LEVERNE, trade association administrator; b. LeClaire, Iowa, Feb. 5, 1924; s. Samuel Albert and Margaret (Spear) McF.; m. Imogene Grace Kness, Jan. 27, 1951; children: Daniel Elliott, Kathryn Margaret, Sharon Ann. BS in Agrl. Engring., Iowa State U., 1950; MS in Agrl. Engring., U. Mo., 1959. Registered profl. engr., Mo. Agrl. sales engr. Ill. No. Utility Co., Aledo, 1950-51; extension agrl. engr. Iowa State U., Ames, 1951-53, rsch. agrl. engr., 1953-56; prof. agrl. engr. U. Mo., Columbia, 1956-86, prof. emeritus, 1986; dir. Mo. Farm Electric Coun., 1956-75; exec. mgr. Nat. Farm Electric Coun., 1975-86; pres. Nat. Food and Energy Coun., 1986-91, pres. emeritus, 1991; mgr. Electrotechnology Rsch., 1991-93. Bd. dirs. Internat. Congress Agrl. Engrs., Brussels, 1989-94. Editor, author: (with others) Handbook for Elsevier Science, Electrical Energy in World Agriculture, 1989; mem. editl. bd. Energy in Agriculture for Elsevier Sci., Amsterdam, The Netherlands, 1981-88. 2d lt. USAAF, 1943-45. Recipient Outstanding Svc. awards Nat. Safety Coun., 1975, MOFEC, 1976, Nat. 4-H Coun., 1982, Nat. Hon. Extension Frat., 1984, Hon. Am. Future Farmers Assn. degree, 1991. Fellow Am. Soc. Agrl. Engrs. (George Kable elec. award 1974, Spl. Svc. award, 2000); mem. Alpha Epsilon, Gamma Sigma Delta. Republican. Presbyterian. Avocations: technical writing, gardening, woodworking.

MCFATE, PATRICIA ANN, foundation executive, scientist, educator; b. Detroit, Mar. 19, 1936; d. John Earle and Mary Louise (Bliss) McF.; m. Sidney Norman Graybeal, Sept. 10, 1988. BA (Alumni scholar), Mich. State U., 1954; MA, Northwestern U., 1956, PhD, 1965; MA (hon.), U. Pa., 1977. Assoc. prof. English, asst. dean liberal arts and scis. U. Ill., Chgo., 1967-74, assoc. prof. English, assoc. vice chancellor acad. affairs, 1974-75; assoc. prof. folklore Faculty Arts and Scis., U. Pa., Phila., 1975-81; prof. tech. and soc. Coll. Engring. and Applied Sci., 1975-81, vice provost, 1975-78; dep. chmn. Nat. Endowment for Humanities, Washington, 1978-81; exec. v.p. Am.-Scandinavian Found., N.Y.C., 1981-82, pres., 1982-88; sr. scientist Sci. Applications Internat. Corp., Mc Lean, Va., 1988—, program dir. Ctr. for Nat. Security Negotiations, 1988—; cons. UN, 1994-95. Vis. assoc. prof. dept. medicine Rush U., Chgo., 1970-85; bd. dirs. First Union Corp.; mem. sr. adv. panel Dept. Def., 1998—. Author: The Writings of James Stephens, 1979, Uncollected Prose of James Stephens, 1983; exec. producer Northern Stars, 1985, Diego Rivera: I Paint What I See, 1989, The Bear in the Skies, 1998; contbr. articles in fields of sci. policy and lit. to various jours. Mem. Arms Control and Non-Proliferation Adv. Bd., Dept. of State, 1995-2001; mem. disting. adv. panel Sandia Nat. Labs.; bd. dirs. Raoul Wallenberg Com. of U.S., Swedish Coun. Am., Santa Fe Cmty. Found., Santa Fe Opera, Lensic Performing Arts Ctr. Decorated officer Order of Leopold II Belgium, comdr. Order Icelandic Falcon, comdr. Royal Order of Polar Star (Sweden), comdr. Order of Lion (Finland), comdr. Royal Norwegian Order Merit, Knight 1st class Royal Order Dannebrog (Denmark); U. Ill. Grad. Coll. faculty fellow, 1968; Swedish Bicentennial Fund grantee, 1981 Fellow N.Y. Acad. Scis.; mem. AAAS (chmn. com. on sci., engring. and pub. policy 1984-87, com. on sci. and internat. security 1976-79, 88-93), Coun. on Fgn. Rels., Acad. Scis. Phila. (founding mem., corr. sec. 1977-79), Theta Alpha Phi, Omega Beta Pi, Delta Delta Delta. E-mail: patricia.a.mcfate@saic.com.

MCFEATTERS, ANN CAREY, journalist; b. Colorado Springs, Colo., June 27, 1944; d. Norman Cromer and Mildred Harriet Carey; m. Dale B. McFeatters, Sept. 27, 1969; children: Dale C., Matthew C., Kirsten C. BA, Marquette U., 1966. Reporter Evansville (Ind.) Press, 1966-68, Pitts. Press, 1969, Washington Daily News, 1969-70, Scripps Howard News Svc., Washington, 1970-99; Washington bur. chief The Pitts. Post-Gazette and The Toledo Blade, 1999—. Named to Hall of Fame Soc. Profl. Journalists, 1998; recipient Disting. Svc. award Scripps Howard News Svc., 1999. Mem. Nat. Press Found. (chmn. 1996-98), Washington Press Club (pres. 1980-81), The Gridiron Club. Office: Block News Alliance 549 14th St NW Ste 955 Washington DC 20045 E-mail: amcfeatters@nationalpress.com.

MCFEE, ARTHUR STORER, physician; b. Portland, Maine, May 1, 1932; s. Arthur Stewart and Helen Knight (Dresser) McF.; m. Iris Goeschel, May 13, 1967. BA cum laude, Harvard U., 1953, MD, 1957; MS, U. Minn., 1966, PhD, 1967. Diplomate: Am. Bd. Surgery. Intern U. Minn. Hosp., 1957-58, resident in surgery, 1958-65; asst. prof. surgery U. Tex. Med. Sch., San Antonio, 1967-70, asso. prof., 1970-74, prof., 1974-2001, ret., 2001. With Univ. Health Sys., Bexar-County, 1968-2001; spl. cons. on emergency med. care text to AAOS. Contbr. articles to profl. jours. Served with USNR, 1965-67. Fellow ACS; mem. AMA, Am. Assn. History of Medicine, Assn. Acad. Surgery, Tex. Med. Assn., Bexar County Med. Soc., Tex. Surg. Soc., Western Surg. Assn., San Antonio Surg. Soc., Soc. Surgery Alimentary Tract, So. Med. Assn., N.Y. Acad. Scis., Royal Soc. Medicine, So. Surg. Assn., Internat. Surg. Soc., Halsted Soc., J. Bradley Aust Surg. Soc., Am. Surg. Assn. Home: 131 Brittany Dr San Antonio TX 78212-1721 Office: 7703 Floyd Curl Dr San Antonio TX 78229-3900 *Most of my life has been spent in training surgeons. It has been an informative experience.*

MCFEE, RICHARD, electrical engineer, physicist; b. Pitts., Jan. 24, 1925; s. William and Beatrice (Allender) McF.; m. Anne Stauffer, June 26, 1947 (div. 1960); m. 2d., Joanellen Lewis, Dec. 31, 1974. BEE, Yale U., 1947; MS in Physics, Syracuse U., 1949; PhDEE, U. Mich., 1955. Rsch. asst. Syracuse U. Med. Sch., 1947-48; instr. Syracuse U. elec. engring. dept., 1948-49; rsch. assoc. U. Mich. Med. Sch., 1949-51; engr. Electro-Mech. Rsch. Inc., Ridgefield, Conn., 1951-52; mem. tech. staff Bell Telephone Labs., Whippany, N.J., 1952-57; prof. elec. engring. Syracuse U., 1957-82; ind. researcher Union Springs, N.Y., 1982-86, Hawi, Hawaii, 1986—. Cons. Arthur D. Little Inc.,

Cambridge, Mass., 1960-61, cardiovascular study sect. NIH, GE Inc., Crouse Hinds Inc., Syracuse, N.Y., 1970, Stanford U. physics dept., 1974-75. Contbr. articles on electronics, electrocardiography, magnetocardiography, superconductivity, circuit theory, thermodynamics, elec. measurements; patentee in field. Sgt. U.S. Army, 1943-46. Sci. Faculty fellowship NSF, Stanford U., 1970. Fellow IEEE; mem. AAAS, Sigma Xi. Home and Office: PO Box 989 Kapaau HI 96755-0989 E-mail: jermcfee@aol.com.

MC FEE, THOMAS STUART, retired government agency administrator; b. Delafield, Wis., Nov. 19, 1930; s. Leon Worrick and Margurette Ella (Morris) McFee; m. Mary Virginia Butler, June 7, 1952; children: Richard Stuart, John Worrick, Charles Paxton. BS, U. Md., 1953, postgrad., 1956-60. Mathematician math. computation divsn. David Taylor Model Basin, Navy Dept., Washington, 1956-58, dir. sys. analysis br. ops. rsch. divsn., 1958-62; project leader weapons sys. evaluation group U.S. Dept. Def., 1962-65; tech. asst. to dir. Sci. and Tech. Office, Exec. Office of Pres., White House, 1965-66; dir. sys. devel. HEW, 1967-69, dep. asst. sec. for program sys., planning and evaluation, 1969-71, dep. asst. sec. for mgmt. planning and tech., 1971-77, dep. asst. sec. for mgmt., 1977-78; asst. sec. for pers. adminstrn. HHS, 1978-95. With USAF, 1954-56. Mem. Am. Soc. Pub. Adminstrn., Am. Consortium for Internat. Pub. Adminstrn., Nat. Acad. Pub. Adminstrn. (elected). E-mail: TomMcfee@aol.com.

MCFEE, WILLIAM WARREN, soil scientist; b. Concord, Tenn., Jan. 8, 1935; s. Fred Thomas and Ellen Belle (Russell) McF.; m. Barbara Anella Steelman, June 23, 1957; children— Sabra Anne, Patricia Lynn, Thomas Hallie. BS, U. Tenn., 1957; MS, Cornell U., 1963, PhD, 1966. Mem. faculty Purdue U., 1965—, prof. soil sci., 1973—, dir. natural resources and environ. sci. program, 1975-91, head dept. agronomy, 1991-2001. Vis. prof. U. Fla., 1986-87; cons. U.S. Forest Svc., Desert Rsch. Inst. Author articles in field, chpts. in books. Served with USAR, 1958-61. Alpha Zeta scholar, 1957; named Outstanding Agr. Tchr. Purdue U., 1972; recipient Am. Educator award Soil Sci. Soc., 1987. Fellow: Soil Sci. Soc. Am. (pres. 1991—92), Am. Soc. Agronomy (pres. 1996—97, resident edn. award 1989); mem.: Purdue Agrl. Alumni Assn. (cert. of distinction 2002), Ind. Seed Trade Assn. (hon.), Sigma Xi. Presbyterian. Home: 708 Mccormick Rd West Lafayette IN 47906-4915 Office: Purdue U Dept Agronomy West Lafayette IN 47907 E-mail: wmcfee@purdue.edu.

MC FEELEY, JOHN JAY, chemical engineer; b. Bklyn., Aug. 15, 1945; s. John Joseph and Maude May (Irvine) McF.; m. Jacquelyn Anne Ratzin, Oct. 30, 1971; children: Christine, John Jay. BS, Poly. Inst. Bklyn., 1966, MS, 1967, PhD, 1972. Engr. Polaroid Corp., Cambridge, Mass., 1971-72, sr. engr., 1972-74, sr. scientist, 1974-77, prin. engr. R&D, 1977-79, tech. mgr. chem. engring. devel., 1979-83, sr. mgr. chem. engring., 1983-99; tech. mgr. ArkWright, Inc., Fiskeville, R.I., 1998-2000. Bd. dirs. Lithium Tech. Corp. Contbr. articles to profl. jours. Mem. water supply study com. Town of Norfolk, Mass., 1976-77, mem. adv. bd., 1979-81, mem. bicentennial com., 1975-76, chmn. adv. bd., 1980-81, selectman, 1981-84, 99—, chmn., 1983-84; registrar of voters, 1991-97, chmn., 1993-97; mem. Dem. Town Com., 1981—, vice-chmn., 1988—; mem. Norfolk Cmty. TV, 1989-98, pres., 1992-94, 95-98; mem. Norfolk Cable Adv. Com., 1998-99. NDEA fellow, 1969-71; NSF fellow, 1968-69, tchg. fellow, 1967-68, rsch. fellow, 1966-67. Mem. AAAS, Am. Chem. Soc., Am. Inst. Chem. Engrs., N.Y. Acad. Scis., Lions (pres. 1977-78, 89-90), Tau Beta Pi, Sigma Xi, Omega Chi Epsilon, Phi Lambda Upsilon. Democrat. Roman Catholic. Home: 10 Chicatabut Ave Norfolk MA 02056-1164 Office: 538 Main St Fiskeville RI 02823

MCFEELY, CLARENCE EDWARD, consultant; b. Oak Park, Ill., May 12, 1929; s. Clarence Edward and Ann (Minarik) McF.; m. Margaret Scott, June 13, 1953; children: Thomas E., Scott G., Elizabeth A. Susan C., Carolyn G. BS, Bradley U., 1951. Pers. supr. Campbell Soup Co., Chgo., 1953-55; employee rels. mgr. The Budd Co., Newark, 1955-59; rep. Dansk Designs Inc., Miami, Fla., 1959-60; prin. A.T. Kearney & Co., Chgo., 1960-69; ptnr. William H. Clark & Assoc., 1969, McFeely Wackerle Shulman, Chgo., 1969—. Pres. AESC, 1980-82. 1st lt. USMC, 1951-53. Republican. Methodist. Avocations: golf, travel, history, theatre, classical music. Office: McFeely Wackerle Shulman PO Box 2741 Homewood IL 60430-7741

MCFEELY, WILLIAM DRAKE, publishing company executive; b. Port Chester, N.Y., July 15, 1954; s. William Shield and Mary (Drake) McF.; m. Karen Gail Eliason, Aug. 12, 1978; children: Matthew Bensen, Eric Daniel, Laura Mae. BA cum laude, Amherst Coll., 1976. Coll. traveler W.W. Norton & Co., Inc., N.Y.C., 1976-80, asst. sales mgr., 1980-82, editor, 1982—, v.p., 1990-94, bd. dirs., 1990—, pres., 1994—. Dir. W.W. Norton & Co., Ltd., chmn., 2000—. Mem. Pubs. Lunch Club (pres. 1998-99), Seven Bridges Field Club (pres. 1989). Home: 106 Seven Bridges Rd Chappaqua NY 10514-1121 Office: WW Norton & Co 500 5th Ave Fl 6 New York NY 10110-0054

MC FEELY, WILLIAM SHIELD, historian, writer; b. N.Y.C., Sept. 25, 1930; s. William C. and Marguerite (Shield) Mc F.; m. Mary Drake, Sept. 13, 1952; children: William Drake, Eliza, Jennifer. BA, Amherst Coll., 1952, L.H.D., 1982; MA, Yale U., 1962, PhD, 1966; LD, Washington Coll., 1986. Asst. prof. history and Am. studies Yale U., 1966-69, assoc. prof., 1969-70; dean faculty Mount Holyoke Coll., 1970-73, prof. history, 1970-80, Rodman prof. history, 1980-82, Andrew W. Mellon prof. humanities, 1982-86; Richard B. Russell prof. Am. history U. Ga., Athens, 1986-94, Abraham Baldwin prof. humanities, 1994-97, prof. emeritus, 1997—; Cardozo vis. prof. history Yale U., 2001—. Tchr. Yale-Harvard-Columbia intensive summer studies program, 1967-69; vis. prof. history Univ. Coll. London, 1978-79, Amherst Coll., 1980-81, U. Mass., 1984-85, John J. McCloy prof., 1988-89 ; cons. to com. on judiciary U.S. Ho. of Reps., 1974 Author: Yankee Stepfather: Gen. O.O. Howard and the Freedmen, 1968, Grant: A Biography, 1981, Frederick Douglass, 1991, Sapelo's People, 1994, Proximity to Death, 1999. Recipient Pulitzer Prize in biography, 1982, Francis Parkman prize, 1982, Lincoln prize, 1992, Avery O. Craven award, 1992; Morse fellow, 1968-69, fellow Am. Coun. Learned Socs., 1974-75, Huntington Library, 1976, 83, Guggenheim fellow, 1982-83, assoc. fellow Charles Warren Ctr., 1991-91, fellow Libr. Co. of Phila., 2002-03, vis. scholar W.E.B. Du Bois Inst., Harvard U., 1992—; NEH grantee, 1986-87 Mem. Am. Hist. Assn., So. Hist. Assn., Soc. of Am. Historians, Org. Am. Historians, PEN Ctr., Century Assn., Authors Guild. Home: 35 Mill Hill Rd Wellfleet MA 02667-7441

MC FERON, DEAN EARL, mechanical engineer, educator; b. Portland, Oreg., Dec. 24, 1923; s. Wallace Suitor and Ruth Carolyn (Fessler) McF.; m. Phyllis Grace Ehlers, Nov. 10, 1945; children: David Alan, Phyllis Ann, Douglas Dean, Donald Brooks. Student, Oreg. State Coll., 1942-43; BSME with spl. honors, U. Colo., 1945, MSME, 1948; PhD, U. Ill., 1956. Instr. U. Colo., Boulder, 1946-48; assoc. prof. U. Ill., 1948-58; rsch. assoc. Argonne (Ill.) Nat. Lab., 1957-58; prof. mech. engring., assoc. dean U. Wash., Seattle, 1958-82, prof. emeritus, 1983—. Cons. to industry, 1959-80 Served with USNR, 1942-46, to comdr. Res., 1946-72. Co-recipient Outstanding Tech. Applications Paper award ASHRAE, 1974; Ednl. Achievement award Soc. Mfg. Engrs., 1970; NSF faculty fellow, 1967-68 Mem. ASME, Am. Soc. Engring. Edn., U.S. Naval Inst. (life), Sigma Xi (nat. dir. 1972-80, nat. pres. 1978), Tau Beta Pi, Sigma Tau, Pi Tau Sigma. Home: 4008 NE 40th St Seattle WA 98105-5422 Office: U Wash Dept Mech Engring Seattle WA 98195-0001 *What matters most in life is what you can do for others.*

MCFERREN, CARL DAVIS, II, retired army officer, risk management consultant; b. Columbus, Ga., July 3, 1946; s. Carl Davis and Mary Homer McFerren; children: Carl Davis III, Mary Anne, Colleen. BA in Polit. Sci., The Citadel, 1968; MS in Counselling, L.I. U., 1978; MBA, Auburn U., 1981; grad., USAF Command and Staff Coll., 1981, Nat. War Coll., 1991. Comml. pilot's license FAA. Commd. 2d lt. U.S. Army, 1968, advanced through grades to col., 1991, brigade exec. officer Aviation Brigade Kans., 1986-88, bn. commdr. 9th U.S. Inf. Ft. Wainwright, Alaska, 1988-90; chief environ. inspections U.S. Army Inspector Gen., Washington, 1991-93; ret., 1993; program mgr. Sys. Rsch. Applications, Arlington, Va., 1993-94; ITAM program mgr. U.S. Army Environ. Ctr., Aberdeen Proving Ground, Md., 1994-98, program mgr. green ammo, 1998-2000; program mgr. Innovative Emergency Mgmt., Salt Lake City, 2000—. Editor: The U.S. Army, 1981; contbr. articles to profl. jours. Commr. Boy Scouts Am., Ft. Riley, 1984. Decorated Silver Star medal Dept. of the Army, 1970, Legion of Merit award Dept. of the Army, 1993; recipient Hammer award Partnership for Reinventing Govt., 2000. Mem. Assn. Citadel Men, Assn. U.S. Army, Nat. War Coll. Alumni Assn., Am. Legion. Republican. Avocations: running, skiing. Home: 2192 E Country View Ln Salt Lake City UT 84121 Office: Innovative Emergency Mgmt Ste 2D 515 South 700 East Salt Lake City UT 84102 E-mail: dave.mcferren@ieminc.com.

MCFERREN, MARTHA DEAN, writer, librarian; b. Henderson, Tex., Apr. 25, 1947; d. Manley Edward McFerren and Emma Lou Turner; m. Dennis Scott Wall, May 22, 1977. BS, North Tex. State U., 1969, M of Libr. Svcs., 1971; MFA, Warren Wilson Coll., 1988. Cert. secondary tchr., Tex. Libr. San Jacinto Coll., Pasadena, Tex., 1971-76, Jefferson Parish Librs., Metairie, La., 1976-81, New Orleans Schs., 1984-85; instr. Dillard U., New Orleans, 1991. Poetry instr. Slidell (La.) Pub. Schs., 1989. Author: Delusions of a Popular Mind, 1983, Get Me Out of Here!, 1984, Contours for Ritual, 1988, Women in Cars, 1992 (Marianne Moore prize 1992); assoc. editor New Laurel Rev., 1980-88. Recipient Moore prize Helicon Nine, 1992, Poetry prize Deep South Conf., 1985, creative writing fellowship Yaddo Colony, 1985, writer's fellowship NEA, 1991, Artist fellowship La. Endowment for the Arts, 1983. Mem. New Orleans Poetry Forum (publicity dir. 1976-90), Poetry Soc. of Am. Home: 2679 Verbena St New Orleans LA 70122-6037

MCGAFFEY, JERE D. lawyer; b. Lincoln, Nebr., Oct. 6, 1935; s. Don Larsen and Doris McG.; m. Ruth S. Michelsen, Aug. 19, 1956; children: Beth, Karen. BA, BSc with high distinction, U. Nebr., 1957; LLB magna cum laude, Harvard U., 1961. Bar: Wis. 1961. Mem. firm Foley & Lardner, Milw., 1961—, ptnr., 1968—. Dir. Smith Investment Co., Northwestern Mut. Trust Co., Lord Balt. Corp., Wis. Gas Co., 1978-2000. Author works in field. Chmn. bd. dirs. Helen Bader Found.; vice chmn. legis. Milw. Met. Assn. Commerce; former chmn. Wis. Taxpayers Alliance, sec.-treas., 1994—; former chmn. bd. dirs. Aurora Health Care, 1986—; chmn. bd. advisors U. Wis. Nursing Sch., Milw. Mem. ABA (chmn. tax sect. 1990-91, ho. dels. 1995-2000), AICPA, Wis. Bar Assn., Wis. Inst. CPAs, Am. Coll. Tax Counsel (chmn. 1996-98), Am. Coll. Trust and Estate Counsel (chmn. bus. planning com. 1994-97, regent 2000—), Am. Law Inst., Univ. Club (Milw.), Milw. Club, Milw. Country Club, Harvard Club N.Y.C., Univ. Club Washington, Phi Beta Kappa, Beta Gamma Sigma, Delta Sigma Rho. Home: 12852 NW Shoreland Dr Mequon WI 53097-2304 Office: Foley & Lardner 777 E Wisconsin Ave Ste 3600 Milwaukee WI 53202-5302 E-mail: jmcgaffey@foleylaw.com.

MCGAFFIGAN, EDWARD, JR. federal agency administrator; widowed; 2 children. AB in Physics summa cum laude, Harvard U., 1970; MS in Physics, Calif. Inst. Tech., 1974; M in Pub. Policy, Harvard Kennedy Sch. Govt., 1976. With RAND Corp, 1974; with Arms Control and Disarmament Agy., Washington, 1975; mem. fgn. svc. U.S. Dept. State, 1976-1983; sci. attache U.S. Embassy, Moscow, 1978-80; sr. policy analyst, asst. dir. Office Sci. and Tech. Policy White House, Washington, 1981-83, nat. security coun. staff, 1982-83; sr. policy advisor Sen. Jeff Bingaman (D-N.Mex.), 1983-96; commr. Nuc. Regulatory Commn., 1996—. Harvard Nat. scholar; Sheldon Traveling fellow, NSF fellow, Woodrow Wilson Found. fellow, Millikan fellow, Harvard Nat. Grad. fellow. Office: Nuc Regulatory Commn 11555 Rockville Pike Rockville MD 20852-2738 E-mail: exm@nrc.gov.

MCGAGH, WILLIAM GILBERT, financial consultant; b. Boston, May 29, 1929; s. Thomas A. and Mary M. (McDonough) McG.; m. Sarah Ann McQuigg, Sept. 23, 1961; children: Margaret Ellen, Sarah Elizabeth. BSBA, Boston Coll., 1950; MBA, Harvard U., 1952; MS, MIT, 1965. Fin. analyst Ford Motor Co., Dearborn, Mich., 1953-55; mem. staff treas. office Daimler-Chrysler, Detroit, 1955-64, compt., treas. Canadian divsn. Windsor, 1965-67, staff exec.-fin. Latin Am. ops. Detroit, 1967-68, asst. treas., 1968-75, treas., 1975-76, v.p., treas., 1976-80; sr. v.p. fin., dir. Northrop Grumman Corp., L.A., 1980-88; owner McGagh Assocs., Beverly Hills, Calif., 1988—. Chmn. bd. dirs. Pacific Am. Income Shares, Inc., Western Asset Premier Bond Fund. Mem. bd. regents Mt. St. Mary's Coll.; chmn. bd. dirs. L.A. Orthop. Hosp., John Tracy Clinic, 1998—. Sloan fellow MIT, 1965. Mem. Fin. Execs. Inst. (pres. Detroit chpt. 1979-80), Harvard Club (N.Y.C. and Boston), Beach Club (Santa Monica, Calif.), L.A. Country Club, Calif. Club (L.A.), Eastward Ho Country Club (Chatham, Mass.). Home: 2189 Century Hl Los Angeles CA 90067-3516 Office: McGagh Assocs 9601 Wilshire Blvd Ste 600 Beverly Hills CA 90210-5208

MCGAHAN, SHARON HELEN ROCHELLE, human resources administrator; b. Hastings, Mich., Feb. 1, 1943; d. William Junior Hecker and Helen Margaret (Scobey) Kozar; children: Christopher Shawn, Helen Rochelle. AA, Northwestern Mich. Coll., 1963; mktg. diploma, modeling cert., PS Career Coll., Milw., 1964; BA, U. Mich., 1968; cert. travel counselor, Breech Acad.-TWA, Kansas City, Kans., 1979. Dir. women's events Sta. WWOM, Wagonvoord Broadcasting Co., New Orleans, 1964-66; writer, mktg. mgr. TV Facts mag., Kalalmazoo, 1975-77; internat. adminstrv. asst. CCDC div. Clark Equipment Co., 1980-81; mgr. Profl. Pers./Staff Leasing, Battle Creek, Mich., 1981-83; project mgr. BOC-GM, Lansing, 1983-85; pers. dir. Imperial Design Svc., Inc., Grand Rapids, 1987—. Speaker, judge Western Mich. U., Kalamazoo, 1986; cons. Gt. Lakes Leadership Coun., Kalamazoo, 1986-87, mentor Aquinas Coll., Grand Rapids, 1990-91. Author children's books, 1971-77. Tutor, storyteller Otsego (Mich.) Pub. Elem. Sch., 1976-77. Mem. Assn. for Human Resource Mgmt., Grand Rapids Pers. Assn. Republican. Avocations: reading, music, travel, swimming, snow skiing. Office: Imperial Design Svc Inc 1958 Wilson Ave SW Grand Rapids MI 49544-2196

MCGAHREN, RICHARD GEORGE, lawyer; b. Bayonne, N.J., June 18, 1928; s. Eugene Dewey and Cecelia (Paulsen) McG.; m. Marjorie J. Waterhouse, Jan. 29, 1994; stepchildren: Lawrence Waterhouse III, Kevin Waterhouse, Patrick Waterhouse, Christine Waterhouse Krizman, Jennifer Waterhouse Pacchiana. AB, Columbia U., 1952, LLB, 1959. Bar: N.Y. 1960, U.S. Dist. Ct. (so. and ea. dists.) N.Y. 1961, U.S. Ct. Appeals (2nd cir.) 1962. Assoc. LeBoeuf Lamb Leiby & MacRae, N.Y.C., 1960-71; ptnr. D'Amato Costello & Shea, 1971-78; founding ptnr. D'Amato & Lynch, 1978-94, counsel, 1994—. With U.S. Army, 1946-47. Mem. ABA. Avocations: skiing, sailing. Office: D'Amato & Lynch 70 Pine St Fl 41 New York NY 10270-0110

MCGANN, JEROME JOHN, English language educator; b. N.Y.C., July 22, 1937; s. John Joseph and Marie Violet (Lecouffe) McG.; m. Anne Patricia Lanni, July 26, 1938; children: Geoffrey, Christopher, Jennifer. BS, Le Moyne Coll., 1959; MA, Syracuse U., 1962; PhD, Yale U., 1966; LHD (hon.), U. Chgo., 1996. From asst. prof. to prof. U. Chgo., 1966-75; prof. Johns Hopkins U., Balt., 1975-80; Dreyfuss prof. humanities Calif. Inst. Tech., Pasadena, 1980-86; John Stewart Bryan univ. prof. U. Va., Charlottesville, 1987—. Author: Swinburne: An Experiment in Criticism, 1972 (Melville Cane award 1972), The Romantic Ideology, 1983, The Beauty of Inflections, 1985, Social Values and Poetic Acts, 1987, Towards a Literature of Knowledge, 1989, The Textual Condition, 1991, Black Riders: The Visible Language of Modernism, 1993; editor: The New Oxford Book of Romantic Period Verse, 1993, Poetics of Sensibility: A Revolution in Literary Style, 1996, Byron: Complete Poetical Works, 7 vols., 1980-93, Dante Gabriel Rossetti and the Game That Must Be Lost, 2000, The Complete Writings and Pictures of Dante Gabriel Rosetti: A Hypermedia Research Archive, 2000—, Radiant Textuality, Literature after the World Wide Web, 2001, Byron and Romanticism, 2002; author, editor 24 scholarly books and 4 poetry books. Fulbright fellow, Fels Found. fellow, Eng., 1965-66; Guggenheim fellow, Eng., 1970-71, 74-75; NEH fellow, Eng. and Europe, 1975-76, 87-88. Fellow Am. Acad. Arts and Scis.; mem. MLA. Address: English Department Bryan Hall U VA Charlottesville VA 22903

MCGANN, JOHN MILTON, real estate executive; b. Omaha, Mar. 18, 1948; s. John Byron and Donna M. (Rehnquist) McG.; m. Barbara June Scott, June 2, 1978. BSBA, cert. real estate, U. Nebr., Omaha, 1971. Property mgr. Boetel & Co., Omaha, 1971-73; asst. office bldg. mgr. The Irvine Co., Newport Beach, Calif., 1973-74; property mgr. Harbor Investment Co., Corona Del Mar, 1974-76, Robert A. McNeil Corp., Santa Ana, 1976-78; gen. mgr. Daon Mgmt., Newport Beach, 1978-80; v.p. August Mgmt. Inc., Long Beach, Calif., 1980-82, Calif. Fed. Asst. Mgmt., L.A., 1982-83; pres. Wespac Mgmt. Realty Corp., Newport Beach, 1983-87; v.p., dir. asset mgmt., pres. CalFed Asset Mgmt. Co., L.A., 1987-90; v.p. com. ops. Pinnacle Realty (formerly Sovereign/Ring), Santa Monica, 1990-95; pres., ptnr. Churchill McGann, LLC, 1995-97; pres. McGann Enterprises Inc. dba Churchill McGann & Round Table Pizza, Lakewood, Long Beach, Calif., 1997—. Mem. Inst. Real Estate Mgmt. (L.A. chpt., cert. property mgr.), Internat. Coun. Shopping Ctrs. (cert. shopping ctr. mgr.), Lambda Chi Alpha, Delta Sigma Pi, Rho Epsilon (pres.). Republican. Mem. Christian Sci. Ch. Home: 3834 Pine Ave Long Beach CA 90807-3234 Office: McGann Asset Mgmt Inc 4201 Long Beach Blvd Ste 306 Long Beach CA 90807-2021 also: McGann Enterprises Inc DBA Round Table Pizza 5250 Faculty Ave Lakewood CA 90712-2508 Address: 1175 Baker St Costa Mesa CA 92626 E-mail: jbmcgann@earthlink.net.

MCGANN, LISA B. NAPOLI, language educator; b. West Hartford, Conn., Sept. 07; d. James Napoli; m. Edward Harrison McGann, Jr. BA, Vassar Coll., 1980; MA, Columbia U., 1983, postgrad., 1991-95; MA, Middlebury Coll., 1987. Cert. tchr. French, ESL and Italian, Conn. Cmty. English program coord. Tchrs. Coll. Columbia U., N.Y.C., 1982-83; mgr. English tchg. com. Jr. League N.Y., 1983-84; asst. dir. ESL Fordham U., 1988-89; ESL instr. Laguardia C.C., CUNY, Long Island City, N.Y., 1983—, Columbia U., 1983-96. ESL instr. Yale U., 1988, 89; ESL specialist, tchr. UN, N.Y.C., 1990. Big sister Highland Hts., New Haven, 1976-77; ESL tchr. Boys and Girls Club, Astoria, N.Y., 1992. Recipient awards and scholarships. Mem. Nat. TESOL Soc., Am. Assn. Tchrs. Italian, Italian-Am. Hist. Soc., Nat. Italian Am. Found. (coun.), The Statue of Liberty-Ellis Island Found., Inc. Roman Catholic. Avocations: ballet, reading, travel, real estate, tennis.

MCGANN, MICHAEL GEYER, martial arts instructor, protection expert; b. Lafayette, La., Sept. 17, 1952; s. Robert Fred and Georgia Marie (Geyer) McG. M in Clin. Psychology, Internat. U., Athens, Greece, 1981, degree in oriental philosophy, 1985; D in Martial Arts, World Martial Arts Hall of Fame, Cleveland Heights, Ohio, 1995. Security supr. Don Cesar Beach Resort, St. Pete Beach, Fla., 1985—90; dir. security Sandpiper Beach Resort, 1990—97; CEO, pres. Wa No Michi Ryu Karate/Kobudo, Clearwater, Fla., 1995—; dep. dir. Police Tactics Instrs. Am., St. Petersburg, 1995—; exec. adminstr. Sokeship coun. Universal Martial Arts Hall of Fame, Clearwater, 1995—. Spl. dep. Pinellas County (Fla.) Sheriff's Dept., 1990-96; tech. advisor Isle of Man Karate Assn., Eng., 1977—. Editor Journey, 1995; contbr. poetry to lit. publs. (Grand award of honor 1990). Mem. WAR (Work Against Rape), St. Petersburg, 1985—. With U.S. Army, 1975-79. Recipient Pioneer/Founder award Fla. Hall of Fame Brotherhood of Martial Artists, 1998; named Nat. Master of Karate, Presdl. Coun. Sports and Phys. Fitness, Washington, 1988, Grandmaster of the Year Self Defense, 2000, 2001, Hon. Grandmast of Yr. Fla. Hall of FAme Brotherhood of Martial Artists, 2001; inducted into Universal Martial Arts Hall of Fame. Fellow Soc. of Black Belt (tech. advisor 1977—); mem. Internat. Union Martial Artists (v.p. Am. 1990—, tech. advisor 1981—, Merit award 1996), World Kung Chung Do Self Defense Instn. (pres. 1977-79, Twain P. Marx Meml. award 1980). Democrat. Avocations: haiku poetry, sumie painting, chess, bonsai, iai jitsu. Home: 6100 150th Ave N Clearwater FL 33760-2138 E-mail: soke143@yahoo.com.

MCGANNEY, THOMAS, lawyer; b. San Mateo, Calif., Mar. 12, 1938; s. Daniel James and Mary Irene (West) McGanney; m. Mildred Kalik McGanney; children: Jennifer, Abigail, Melanie, Juliana. BA, Stanford U., 1959; LLB, Harvard U., 1962. Bar: N.Y. 1963, U.S. Dist. Ct. (so. and ea. dists.) N.Y. 1965, U.S. Ct. Appeals (2d cir.) 1966, U.S. Ct. Appeals (3d cir.) 1969, U.S. Ct. Appeals (10th cir.) 1970, U.S. Supreme Ct. 1971, U.S. Ct. Appeals (9th cir.) 1990. Law clk. U.S. Dist. Ct., So. Dist. N.Y., 1962—64; assoc. White & Case, N.Y.C., 1964—72, ptnr., 1973—. Adj. prof. NYU Law Sch., 1984—86. Mem.: ABA, Assn. Bar City of N.Y., Fed. Bar Coun., N.Y. State Bar Assn., Am. Coll. Trial Lawyers. Office: White & Case Bldg Ll 1155 Avenue Of The Americas New York NY 10036-2787 E-mail: tmcganney@whitecase.com.

MCGARR, CHARLES TAYLOR, accountant; b. Greenwood, Miss., Nov. 5, 1956; s. William Ithamar and Mary (Taylor) McG.; m. Kathryn Augusta Reed, July 21, 1979; children: Charles Taylor II, Annie Flynn. BSBA, La. State U., 1978. CPA, Tex., La. Acct., auditor Arthur Andersen and Co., Houston, 1979-82, audit mgr., 1985-86, acct., auditor Lafayette, La., 1982-85; sec., treas. L.A. Frey and Sons, Inc., 1986-87; asst. sec., controller Waste Mgmt. Baton Rouge, 1987-88; asst. treas., tax mgr. Copolymer Rubber and Chem. Corp., Baton Rouge, 1988-93; divsn. v.p., contr. Waste Mgmt. La., Walker, 1993-97; fin. contr. La. Casino Cruises, Inc., Baton Rouge, 1997-99; dir. treasury and credit Borden Chems. and Plastics, Geismar, 1999—2002; dir. fin. Eatel, Gonzalez, L.A., 2002—. Mem. Am. Inst. CPA's, La. Soc. CPA's, Delta Tau Delta (treas. 1976-77). Republican. Baptist. Office: Eatel Gonzalez 913 S Burnside Gonzales LA 70737

MCGARR, FRANK JAMES, retired federal judge, dispute resolution consultant; b. Feb. 25, 1921; married; 6 children. BA cum laude, Loyola U., Chgo., 1942; JD, Loyola U., 1950. Bar: Ill. 1950. Assoc. Dallstream Schiff Stern & Hardin, Chgo., 1952—54; asst. U.S. atty., chief criminal divsn. No. dist. of Ill., 1954—55, first asst. U.S. atty., 1955—58; ptnr. McKay Solum & McGarr, Chgo., 1958—68; first asst. atty. gen. State of Ill., 1969—70; judge U.S. Dist. Ct. for No. Ill., 1970—88, chief judge, 1981—86, sr. judge, 1986—88; of counsel Phelan Cahill & Quinlan, Chgo., 1988—96, Foley & Lardner, Chgo., 1996—2001; pvt. practice, 2001—. Instr. Eng. and pub. speaking Loyola U., 1946—48, administrv. asst. to pres., 1948—52; instr. law Loyola U. Law Sch., 1950—52, instr. criminal law, 1953—57, prof. admiralty and maritime law, 1953—57; instr. legal ethics John Marshal Law Sch., 1985—86. Chmn. law observance com. Chgo. Crime Comm., v.p., bd. dirs.; chmn. Law Enforcement Week Com.; pres. Constl. Rights Found., 1994; chmn. Ill Gov.'s Comm. on Death Penalty, 2000. With USN, 1942—45, Pacific Fleet. Named Man of Yr., Cath. Lawyers Guild Chgo., 1985; recipient Alumni Medal of Excellence, Loyola Law Alumni, 1964, Mother Cabrini award, Columbus-Cuneo-Cabrini Med. Ctr., 1978, Dei Gloriam award, St. Ignatius Coll. Prep, 1984. Fellow: Am. Coll. Trial Lawyers; mem.: Soc. Trial Lawyers, Chgo. Bar Assn., Fed. Bar Assn. (pres. chgo. chpt. 1962—63, mem. exec. com.), 7th Cir. Bar Assn. Office: 4146 Venard Rd Downers Grove IL 60515-1908

MCGARRELL, JAMES, artist, educator; b. Indpls., Feb. 22, 1930; s. James and Gretchen (Heermann) McG.; m. Anna Harris, June 24, 1955; children: Andrew Rider, Flora Raven. BA, Ind. U., 1953; MA, UCLA, 1955. Artist-in-residence Reed Coll., Portland, Oreg., 1956-59; prof. fine arts, dir. grad. painting Ind. U., Bloomington, 1959-80; prof. fine arts Washington U., St. Louis, 1981-93, prof. emeritus, 1993—; artist in residence Dartmouth Coll., 1993, Roswell (N. Mex.) Found., 1999. One man exhbns. include Frumkin/Adams Gallery, N.Y.C., 1961, 64, 66, 68, 71, 73, 77, 80, 84, 86, 88, 89, 90, 91, 93, 95, George Adams Gallery, N.Y.C., 1997, 2000, Galerie Claude Bernard, Paris, 1967, 70, 74, Galleria Il Fante de Spade, Rome and Milan, 1967, 71, 72, 74, 76, 79, Galeria Gian Ferrari, Milan, 1981, 83, Galerie Simonne Stern, New Orleans, 1989, 91, 94, 95, 98, 2000, Struve Gallery, Chgo., 1988, 90, More Gallery, Phila., 1987, 89, Utah Mus. Art, Salt Lake City, 1972, Art Mus. U. N.Mex., Albuquerque, 1982, St. Louis Art Mus., 1985, Art Mus. U. Ariz., Tucson, 1998, The Art Gallery U. N.H., Durham, 1998; represented in permanent collections at Mus. Modern Art, Met. Mus. Art, Whitney Mus. Am. Art, Pa. Acad., Phila., Santa Barbara Mus. Art, San Francisco Art Mus., Art Inst. Chgo., Joseph Hirshhorn Mus., Washington, St. Louis Art Mus., Hamburg (Germany) Mus. Art, Centre Georges Pompidou, Paris, Rose Art Mus. Brandeis U. Bd. govs. Skowhegan Sch. Painting and Sculpture. Recipient Am. Acad. Arts and Letters Lifetime Achievement award, 1995; Fulbright fellow, 1955-56; Guggenheim Found. fellow, 1965; Nat. Endowment for Arts grantee, 1967, 85. Mem. Coll. Art Assn. (bd. dirs. 1969-73), Academie des Beaux Arts de L'Institut de France, Nat. Acad. Design. Home: PO Box 39 Newbury VT 05051-0039 E-mail: bluedeuce@charter.net.

MCGARRY, CARMEN RACINE, historian, artist; b. Plattsburgh, N.Y., Dec. 15, 1941; d. Allyre Joseph and Annette Cecile (Roy) Racine; sep.; children: Suzanne, John Jr., Annette, Patrick. BA, Coll. St. Rose, 1962. Tchg. cert. Ill.; lic. real estate broker, Ill.; cert. interior designer, Ill. Tchr. Chgo. Bd. Edn., 1962-69; comptr., mgr., broker K&G Bldg. Mgmt., Chgo., 1969-90; rsch. asst. U. Chgo., 1985-89. Author: Magnificent Mile: A History of Hillsboro Beach, 1998; designer and creator stained glass windows St. Anne's Shrine, Isle La Motte, Vt., 1995. V.p. Women's History Coalition, Broward County, Ft. Lauderdale, Fla., 1993—; com. mem. County Health Fair, Broward County, 1994—; bd. dirs. Hillsboro Lighthouse Com., 1994—, Broward 2000, Broward County League of Cities; chmn., bd. mem. adv. coun. Area Agy. on Aging, Ft. Lauderdale, 1996—, chmn., 1997-98; mem. nominating com. for women's hall of fame Broward County, 1996-98; rep. for srs.

on transp. Disadvantaged Coord. Bd. Broward County; town commr. Hillsboro Beach, 1999—. Recipient Cmty. Svc. award Cystic Fibrosis Found., 1999, First Lady of Broward County award 2000; named to Women's Hall of Fame Broward County, 2001. Mem. ASID, Stained Glass Assn. Am., Women's League Hillsboro (bd. mem. 1993—), Broward County Hist. Commn., Palm Beach Hist. Soc., Hillsboro Beach Hist. Commn. (founder, pres.), Deerfield Beach Hist. Soc., Deerfield Beach Rotary (dir. 1996—, pres. 1999—, Cooper-Kirk award for hist. rsch. and preservation 1999), First Ladies of Broward County. Avocations: traveling, writing. Home: 1073 Hillsboro Mile Hillsboro Beach FL 33062-2139 E-mail: ctlm@aol.com.

MCGARRY, CHARLES WILLIAM, lawyer; b. Mt. Kisco, N.Y., June 23, 1957; m. Lori J. Voss. BA in Philosophy, SUNY, Binghamton, 1979; JD, U. Tex., 1982. Bar: Tex. 1983. Law clk. Atty. Gen. of Tex., Austin, 1980-82; briefing atty. Tex. Ct. of Appeals, Dallas, 1982-83; pvt. practice, 1984-93, 95—; chief justice Tex. Ct. Appeals, 1993-94. Mediator Dallas County Juvenile Dept., 1984-93; arbitrator Better Bus. Bur., Dallas, 1985-93. Editor: Aviation Litigation, 1986. Chmn. Irving (Tex.) Dems., 1987-91; pres. Dallas Jazz Orch., 1990-92. Mem. Tex. Bar Assn., Dallas Bar Assn., Irving Bar Assn. Democrat. Roman Catholic. Home: 4324 Twin Post Rd Dallas TX 75244-6743 Office: Ste 1200 1200 Main St Dallas TX 75202-4460 E-mail: cmcgarry@ix.netcom.com.

MCGARRY, DOROTHY, librarian; b. Omaha, May 1, 1929; d. Moore and Ruth (Gorelick) Lasher. AB, UCLA, 1949, MLS, 1971. Catalog libr. UCLA, 1971-76, head cataloging divsn. phys. scis. and tech. librs., 1976-93, emerita, 1993—. Mem. vocabulary task force for revision GeoRef Thesaurus 4th-9th edit. Am. Geol. Inst. Fellow Spl. Librs. Assn. (Hall of Fame 2000—); mem. AAAS, ALA (resources and tech. svcs . divsn., catalog form and function com. 1986-90), Assn. for Libr. Collections and Tech. Svcs. (orgn./by-law com., 1999—, cataloging and classification sect. chair com. on cataloging desc. and access 1985-86, policy and rsch. com. 1988-92, subject analysis com. 1993-96, mem.-at-large cataloging and classification sect. 1993-96, chair cataloging and classification sect. 1997-98), Map and Geography Round Table (cataloging and classification com., 1999—), Am. Math. Soc. (libr. com. 1989-98), Am. Phys. Soc., Am. Soc. for Info. Sci. (L.A. chpt., chair by-laws com. 1986-89, 99-2001, sec. 1987-88, Outstanding Mem. Yr. award 1990, 94, other coms.), Assn. Coll. Rsch. Librs. (sci.-tech. sect., chair ad hoc com. designing conf. proc. style sheet 1984-87, other coms.), Spl. Librs. Assn. (chair com. on cataloging 1983-89, 97-99, rep. CIP adv. group 1983-88, rep. Internat. Fedn. Libr. Assns. and Instns. sect. on classification and indexing 1988-95, rep. to sect. on cataloguing 1995—, chair physics astronomy-math. divsn. 1982-83, chair sci.-tech. divsn. 1991-92, rep. of the SLA geography and map divsn. Anglo-Am. Cataloging com. for Cartographic Materials, 1988—, internat. rels. com. 1989-97, bd. dirs. 1995-97, SLA del. to the Internat. Fedn. of Libr. Assns. and Instns., 1993-97, treas. So. Calif. chpt. 1991-93, rep. other coms., pres. So. Calif. Chpt. 1994-95, SLA John Cotton Dana award 1991, chair by-laws com. 2000-2002), Calif. Acad. and Rsch. Librs., Calif. Libr. Assn., Geosci. Info. Soc., Internat. Fedn. Libr. Assns. and Instns. (chair sect. on classification and indexing 1989-93, sec. 1993-95, sect. cataloging 1995—), Math. Assn. Am., N.Am. Serials Interest Group, Online Audiovisual Catalogers, South Calif. Tech. Processes Group. Office: UCLA Sci & Engring Libr 8251 Boelter Hl Los Angeles CA 90095-1598 E-mail: dmcgarry@library.ucla.edu.

MCGARRY, FREDERICK JEROME, civil engineering educator; b. Rutland, Vt., Aug. 22, 1927; s. William John and Ellen (Dunn) McG.; m. Alice M. Reilly, Oct. 7, 1950 (dec. Jan. 1971); children: Martha Ellen, Alice Catherine, Joan Louise, Carol Elizabeth, Susan Elizabeth, Janet Marian. AB, Middlebury (Vt.) Coll., 1950; S.B., Mass. Inst. Tech., 1950, S.M., 1953. Faculty MIT, 1950—, prof. civil engring., 1965—, prof. materials sci. and engring., 1974—, head materials div., 1964—, dir. materials research lab., 1964—, assoc. dir. inter-Am. program civil engring., 1961—, dir. summer session, 1983—. Contbr. numerous articles to profl. jours. Recipient Best Paper award Soc. Plastics Industry, 1968, 91. Mem. AAAS, ASTM, Soc. Rheology, Soc. Plastics Engrs., Am. Soc. Metals, Sigma Xi. Home: 90 Bakers Hill Rd Weston MA 02493-1774 Office: Mass Inst Tech 77 Massachusetts Ave Cambridge MA 02139-4301

MCGARRY, JOHN PATRICK, JR. retired advertising agency executive; b. Elizabeth, N.J., Nov. 22, 1939; s. John Patrick and Elizabeth (Weber) McG.; m. Gilda R. Spurio, Oct. 24, 1964; children: Victoria Elizabeth, John Patrick, III. BS in Mktg. Econs, Villanova U., 1961. Salesman Exxon Corp., Elizabeth, 1961-64; advt. exec. Young and Rubicam Inc., N.Y.C., 1965-69, sr. v.p., mgmt. supr., 1969-87, pres., mem. ops. com., advt. exec. com., 1987—; vice chmn. Young and Rubicam Advt. Worldwide, 1990—; chmn. Client Svcs. Worldwide, 1987—; pres., CEO Young and Rubicam N.Am., 1992-94; pres. Young & Rubicam Inc., 1996-98; ret., 1998. Bd. dirs. Caramoor; mem. corp. exec.'s com. Young and Rubicam, 1992. Bd. dirs. New Youth Performing Theatre, Bedford, N.Y., Regional Rev. League, Westchester, 4 A's, Louisville Opera Assn., 1981-83, Dominican Coll., Drop-out Prevention Fund, United Negro Coll. Fund, 1994—; bd. dirs. N.Y. coun. Boy Scouts Am., 1992; head parents fund St. Lawrence U. Mem. Internat. Advt. Assn. (pres. U.S. and Can.), Proprietory Assn. (bd. dirs.), Bedford Club, Golf and Tennis Club, N.Y. Athletic Club, The Roundabout Theater (adv. bd. 1994—). Democrat. Roman Catholic. Office: Young & Rubicam Inc 285 Madison Ave New York NY 10017-6486 Home: PO Box 445 Bedford Hills NY 10507-0445

MCGARRY, KELLY JO, social worker, case manager, therapist, consultant; b. Johnstown, Pa., Feb. 13, 1971; d. Joseph Nicholus Onder and Elizabeth L. Crum. BS, St. Francis Coll., Loretto, Pa., 1993; MA, Liberty U., 2000. Counselor So. Allegheny Acad., Portage, Pa., 1993-94; social worker Valley View Nursing Home, Altoona, 1994-98; geriatric social worker Garvey Manor, Hollidaysburg, 1998-2001; therapist Family Svcs. Blair, Altoona, 1999-2000; mobile family therapist Children's Paraclete, Johnstown, Pa., 2000—. Mem. Am. Psychotherapy Assn. (diplomat), Am. Counseling Assn., Am. Assn. Christian Counselors, Assn. Spiritual Ehtical Religious Values Counseling, Pa. Counselor Assn., Pa. Geriatric Interest Network. Office: Childrens Paraclete 134 Gazebo Park Johnstown PA 15901 Home: 1404 Spruce St Hollidaysburg PA 16648-2340

MCGARRY, MARCIA, retired community service coordinator; b. Washington, Dec. 9, 1941; d. Emil Sylvester and Bernice B. (Bland) Busey. BS, Morgan State U., 1964. Cert. tchr., law enforcement officer, Fla. Payroll clk., jr. acct. U.S. Dept. Labor, Washington, 1964-65; English tchr. Taiwan, 1968-70; tchr. Monroe County Sch. Bd., Key West, Fla., 1971-81; exec. dir. Monroe Assn. Retarded Citizens, 1977-79; dep. sheriff Monroe County Sheriff's Dept., 1979-83, 86-90; probation/parole officer Fla. State Dept. Corrections, 1983-91; law enforcement instr. Fla. Keys C.C., 1983-91; cmty. svc. coord. City of Bradenton, 1991-2000; domestic violence specialist II Broward County Sheriff Dept., 2001—. Mem. rev. bd. City of Bradenton Police Dept., 1996—2000, mem. cmty. rels. com., 1996—2000. Active local polit. campaigns; co-founder day schs. for under-privileged children; former mem. Big Bros./Big Sisters Am., mem. com., 1985-86, former bd. dirs., Spouse Abuse, former bd. dirs.; bd. dirs. Adv. Coun. Orange-Ridge Elem., 1991-93; bd. dirs. mayor's com., chmn. task force Drug Free Cmtys., 1991-94, bd. dirs., 1996-2001; bd. dirs. Human Rels. Commn., 1991-93, Drug Free Schs. and Cmty. Adv. Coun., 1991-98, T.O.T.S. (These Our Tots), Inc., 1998-2000; former mem. adv. coun. Byrd Edn. Found., Sweet Adelines Internat., 1992-94, commr. 12th Jud. Nominating Commn., 1992-99, cons., facilitator Cultural Diversity Conflict Resolution Workshops, Manatee County High Schs. and Bradenton Police Dept.; attendance adv. com. Bayshore High, 1993, multicultural com., 1994, former rep. Women's Forum; former dir. choir Luth. Ch.; founding mem. Comprehensive Neighborhood Support Network; mem. adv. bd. Manatee County Sheriff's Dept., 1994-2000, mem. hiring rev. bd., 1997-2000. Recipient Appreciation cert., Lions Club, 1978, 1979, Career Week award, Harris Elem. Sch., 1981, Glynn Archer Elem. Sch., 1989, Trainers award, Probation/Parole Acad., 1987, Cert. of Acknowledgement for Cmty. Svc., AAUW, 1995, awadrd, Vol. Army for the War on Drugs, 1989. Mem. NAFE, Fla. Police Benevolent Assn., Fla. Women in Govt. (mem. Manatee County chpt.), Ecumanical Luth. Ch. of Am. (elected consultation conm. Fla. Synod 1989), Key West Profls., Luth. Ch. Women, Delta Sigma Theta (v.p. 1990-91, corr. sec. 1993-95). E-mail: marciadnc@aol.com.

MCGARRY, RICHARD LAWRENCE, lawyer; b. Flushing, N.Y., Jan. 12, 1960; s. Richard J. and Loretta (McCarthy) McG.; m. Lynda R. Jones, Dec. 21, 1987; children: Abraham A. Eichelberger, Chelsea Eichelberger St. Clair, David B. Eichelberger. BS, Hampden Sydney Coll., 1982; JD, Washington and Lee U., 1989. Bar: Va. 1989, U.S. Dist. Ct. (we. dist.) Va., U.S. Supreme Ct., 1993. Assoc. Jeffrey H. Krasnow and Assocs., Roanoke, Va., 1989-93; ptnr. Johnson & McGarry, P.C., Charlottesville, 1993-94; pvt. practice Roanoke, 1994—. Bd. dirs. Roanoke Valley SPCA. Mem. Va. Trial Lawyers Assn., Assn. Trial Lawyers Am., Roanoke Bar Assn., Va. Bar Assn. Office: PO Box 21565 2320 Electric Rd SW Roanoke VA 24018 E-mail: rick.mcgarry@att.net.

MCGARRY, ROBERT ALAN, university administrator; b. Passaic, N.J., Dec. 23, 1965; s. Thomas R. and Irene (Crawford) McG. MusB, Bucknell U., 1988; M. Music Edn., Hartt Sch. Music, Hartford, Conn., 1990. Cert. tchr. music. Assoc. dir. student affairs The Juilliard Sch., N.Y.C., 1993—. Mem. Mid Atlantic Assn. Coll. and Univ. Housing Officers (presenter 1992), Am. Coll. Pers. Assn. (presenter 1990—). Avocation: solo singing. Home and Office: The Juilliard Sch Office of Student Affairs 60 Lincoln Center Plz New York NY 10023-6500

MCGARTLAND, STEVEN ROSS, secondary education music educator; b. Quincy, Ill., Mar. 6, 1951; s. Howard William and Mary Ellen (Appenbrink) McG.; m. Susan Steinmeyer, June 5, 1977; children: Kori Lynn, Erin Kate, Chad Steven. BA in Music Edn., Ill. Wesleyan U., Bloomington, 1973. Music dir. Hillsboro (Ill.) Community Unit Sch., 1973-75; instrumental/vocal dir. grades 6-8 Carlinville (Ill.) Community Unit Dist. #1, 1975-79; music dir. Kincaid (Ill.) Elem./High Sch., 1980-81; instrumental music dir. 5-12 Moweagua (Ill.) Community Unit Sch. # 6A, 1988-92; dir. instrumental music Ctrl. A & M Community Unit Sch. Dist. # 21, Ill., 1992-98, Virden Community Unit Sch. Dist. #4, 1998—. Band dir. Blackburn Coll., Carlinville, 1979-80; choir dir. United Meth. Ch., Carlinville, 1980-89, 91-94, Federated Ch., 1996—; ednl. rep. Macon Music Inc., Decatur/Carlinville, 1981-85; dist. sales dir. Instl. Fin. Svcs., Benicia, Calif., 1985-88. Music dir. Carlinville Mcpl. Band, 1984—; playing mem. Gillespie (Ill.) Mcpl. Band, 1977—. Mem. ACD, Am. Fedn. Musicians, Ill. Edn. Assn., Ill. Music Educators Assn., Moweaqua Edn. Assn. (treas. 1990-91), Ctrl. A&M Edn. Orgn. Methodist. Avocations: woodworking, camping. Office: Virden H S 231 W Fortune St Virden IL 62690-1228

MCGARVEY, JOSEPH F. X., SR. cardiologist; b. Darby, Pa., Sept. 8, 1936; MD, U. Pa., 1962. Diplomate Am. Bd. Internal Medicine, Am. Bd. Cardovasc. Disease. Intern Fitzgerald Mercy Hosp., Darby, 1962-63; resident Hahnemann U., Phila., 1963-66; fellow in cardiology Cin. Gen. Hosp., 1968-69; mem. staff Doylestown (Pa.) Hosp.; pvt. practice, Doylestown, 1969—. Fellow ACP, Am. Coll. Cardiology. Office: 14 Memorial Dr Ste B Doylestown PA 18901-3529

MCGARVEY, MARY HEWITT, writer; b. Phila. s. Raymond John and Beatrice (Hewitt) McG. BA summa cum laude, Hunter Coll., 1983; MA summa cum laude, New Sch. for Social Research, 1986. Author: (books) Walking to Camden, 1984, Floating to Broadway, 1987. Mem. Classical Assn. of the Empire State, Internat. Soc. Dramatists, Am. Mus. Natural History, N.Y. Classical Club. Roman Catholic. Avocations: painting. Home and Office: 319 E 14th St New York NY 10003-4242

MCGARY, BETTY WINSTEAD, minister, counselor, individual, marriage, and family therapist; b. Louisville, June 21, 1936; d. Philip Miller and Mary Jo (Winstead) McG.; married, 1960 (div. 1979); children: Thomas Edward, Mary Alyson Griffith, Andrew Philip Pearce. BS, Samford U., 1958; MA, So. Bapt. Theol. Sem., 1961; EdD, U. Louisville, 1988. Ordained to ministry Bapt. Ch., 1986; cert. secondary tchr., Ky., Ga.; lic. profl. counselor, marriage and family therapist, Tex. Min. to youth Broadway Bapt. Ch., Louisville, 1958-60; learning disability and behavior disorders specialist Jefferson County Schs., Muscogee Schs., Cobb County Schs., Louisville, Columbus, Ga., Atlanta, 1964-88; min. to adults South Main Bapt. Ch., Houston, 1986-90; assoc. pastor Calder Bapt. Ch., Beaumont, Tex., 1991-96; psychotherapist pvt. practice, 1996—. Marriage enrichment cons. Pastoral Inst., Columbus, 1973-76; co-founder and coord. Ctr. for Women in Ministry, Louisville, 1983-86, exec. bd. dirs., 1983-90; cons. Tex. Christian Life Commn., Ft. Worth, 1989-93; co-therapist pvt. practice, Houston, 1989—. Author: (with others) The New Has Come, 1988, A Costly Obedience: Sermons by Women of Steadfast Spirit, 1994; co-editor nat. newsletter Folio: A Newsletter for Southern Bapt. Women in Ministry, 1983-86. Vice-chairperson exec. bd. dirs. handicapped Boy Scouts Am., Houston, 1986-90; mem. leadership coun. Triangle Interfaith Project, Beaumont, 1995-97; mem. Leadership Houston, 2000—. Recipient citation for Disting. Svc. So. Bapt. Theol. Sem., 1984, Dean's citation Outstanding Achievement U. Louisville, 1988. Mem. The Alliance of Baptists (exec. bd. dirs. 1988-90, v.p. 1990-91), So. Bapt. Women in Ministry (pres. 1988-90, treas. 1995-96, archivist 1998—), Bapt. Gen. Conv. of Tex. (exec. bd. dirs. 1996—, adminstrv. com. 1998—), Leadership Beaumont. Avocations: gardening, interior design, travel. Home: 4112 Meyerwood Dr Houston TX 77025 Office: 2002 N Lucas Beaumont TX 77706 E-mail: mcwingary@aol.com. *All around us there are new opportunities for creating, ordering, liberating and healing our world. It is our calling and our challenge to be God's partners in this holy purpose.*

MCGARY, CHARLES WESLEY, polymer chemist; b. New Castle, Pa., Dec. 12, 1929; s. Charles Wesley and Pearl I. (Ferree) McG.; m. Deloris Maxine Glasser, Nov. 24, 1949; children: Chris W., Susan E., Diane L., Lynn M., Jeffrey S. BS in Chemistry, Westminster Coll., 1951; PhD in Phys. Organic Chemistry, Purdue U., 1954. Chemist, group leader Union Carbide corp., Charleston, W.Va., 1954-64, assoc. dir., 1964-73, product mgr. N.Y.C., 1973-80; v.p. R & D Riverain Corp., Dayton, Ohio, 1980-82, 86-90; dir. R & D Deseret Div. Warner Lambert Co., 1982-86, dir. R & D Novon Product Div. Basle, Switzerland, 1990-91. Contbr. articles to profl. jours. Mem. Am. Chem. Soc., Soc. Plastics Engrs. Achievements include 75 patents. Office: Warner Lambert Co 182 Tabor Rd Morris Plains NJ 07950-2597

MCGARY, RITA ROSE, social worker; b. Frenchville, Me., Sept. 18, 1927; d. Joseph N. and Lula (Labbe) Babin; m. Lawrence E. McGary; children: Philip, Robert, Kathleen. BA in Sociology, Rivier Coll., 1949; MEd, U. Va., 1978; MSW, U. Nev., 1994. Lic. social worker, Nev., nat. cert. counselor, clin. mental health counselor. Tchr. Fort Kent (Me.) H.S., 1949-51; dir., tchr. Nursery Sch., Palembang, Indonesia, 1954-56; tchr. Am. Sch., Asunción, Paraguay, 1963-66; tchr. for homebound Fairfax County Pub. Schs., Fairfax, Va., 1971-74, presenter workshop, cons., case mgr., vis. tchr., 1980-92, sch. social worker, conflict mediator, 1990-92; case mgr. Washoe County Sch. Dist., Reno, 1994—. Mediator Fairfax County Family Ct., Fairfax, Va.,1 991-92; mediator, trainer, dir. peer mediation program Pine Mid. Sch., Reno, Nev.; case mgr., dir. Miguel Ribera Family Resource Ctr., Reno, 1996; social work intern Nev. State Prison, Nev. Women's State Prison, 1993, VA Med. Ctr. and Vet. Ctr., Reno, Nev., 1994, 1994; dir. Miguel Ribera Family Resource Ctr., Reno, 1998; adj. prof. U. Nev., Reno; presenter in field. Contbr. article to profl. jour. Election worker Dem. Party, Va., Nev., 1984; sch. rep. Hisp. Multidisciplinary Team Child Protective Svcs., Fairfax, Va., 1990-92; coord. V.A. Day of Svc. for Homeless, 1994; field exec. Girl Scout Coun. Nation's Capital, Washington, 1975-79; mem. adv. bd. Washoe County, Nev. Social Svcs., 1998-99; trustee Child Abuse and Neglect Task Force; bd. dirs. Girl Scouts of Sierra, 2002—. Recipient Excellence in Edn. Dept. of Cmty. Action, Fairfax, Va., 1991; named Peacemaker of Yr. Nev. Dispute Resolution Coalition, 2001. Mem. AAUW (membership v.p. 2001—), NASW, NOW, Sch. Social Work Assn. Am., Nev. Sch. Social Work Assn., So. Poverty Law Ctr. (v.p. 1998, pres. 2000), Western Alliance of Sch. Social Work Assns. (Nev. women's fund, mem. adv. bd., treas.), Phi Kappa Phi. Home: 1539 Foster Dr Reno NV 89509-1211

MCGAUGHEY, ALBERT WAYNE, retired mathematics educator; b. Russellville, Ind., July 16, 1914; s. Walter Lee and Belvia Jane (Harbison) McG.; m. Margie V. Silverthorn, July 11, 1940; children: Stanley W., Dennis M., Lynn D. McGaughey Kearney, Donna J. McGaughey Defenbaugh. AB in Liberal Arts, Wabash Coll., 1935; MS in Physics, State U. Iowa, 1937; PhD in Math., U. Cin., 1940. Instr. math. Purdue U., West Lafayette, Ind., 1940-41; asst. prof. U.S. Naval Acad., Annapolis, Md., 1941-46; prof., chmn. dept. Westminster Coll., New Wilmington, Pa., 1946-48, Bradley U., Peoria, Ill., 1948-79, dir. NSF Summer Inst., 1961-66; ret., 1979. Part-time prof. Eureka (Ill.) Coll., 1954-81; tchr.-trainer Indian high sch. math. tchrs. AID Summer Inst., Burdwan U., 1967; assoc. dir. secondary edn. dept. NSF, Washington, 1968-69. Mem. Ctrl. Ill. Agy. on Aging, 1970—, also past coun. chmn. and dept. chmn.; bd. dirs., vol., treas., com. chmn. Common Place, 1970—. Mem. Phi Beta Kappa, Sigma Psi, Math Assoc. America (sec. treas. Ill. sect.). Republican. Mem. Christian Ch. (Disciples Of Christ). Avocation: volunteering. Home: 2703 N Kingston Dr Peoria IL 61604-2142

MCGAUGHEY, CHARLES GILBERT, retired research biochemist; b. San Diego, Sept. 8, 1925; s. Gilbert Arthur and Louisa Ellen (Inskeep) McG. BA, U. Calif., Berkeley, 1950; MA, U. So. Calif., 1952. Diplomate Am. Inst. Oral Biology. Scientist radiol. hazards evaluation U.S. Naval Radiol. Def. Lab., San Francisco, 1952; rsch. biochemist VA Med. Ctr., Long Beach, Calif., 1953-81; prin. investigator studies dental caries and oral cancer Oral Diseases Rsch. Lab., 1978-81. Contbr. articles to profl. jours. Grantee Nat. Inst. Dental Rsch., 1965. Mem. AAAS. Republican. Home: 337 N Winnipeg Pl Long Beach CA 90814-2564

MCGAUGHRAN, ALAN L. family physician; b. Abington, Pa., Feb. 18, 1959; BS in Biology, Albright Coll., Reading, Pa., 1981; MD, Pa. State U., 1985. Diplomate Am. Bd. Family Practice. Intern/resident St. Vincent Health Ctr., Erie, Pa.; family physician Agape Family Health Ctr., DuBois, 1991-96, St. Vincent Health Ctr., Edinboro, 1997-98; emergency room physician DuBois Reg. Med. Ctr., 1996-98; family physician Blairsville (Pa.) Family Health Ctr., 1998—, Latrobe Area Hosp., Pa., 1998—. Instr. family medicine Latrobe Area Hosp. Family Practice Residency. Maj. USAF, 1988-91. Mem. Am. Acad. Family Physicians, Christian Med. and Dental Soc., Christian Cmty. Health Fellowship. Home: RR 3 Box 431 Blairsville PA 15717-9181 E-mail: amcgaughran@lah.com.

MC GAUGHY, JOHN BELL, civil engineer; b. Norfolk, Va., Nov. 5, 1914; s. John Bell and Frances Vivian (Coleman) McG.; m. Charlotte Edna Schwartz, Jan. 20, 1940 (dec. Dec. 1978); 1 child, John Bell; m. Page Cook Axson, Sept. 26, 1981. Student, U. Va., 1933-35; BS in Civil Engring, Duke U., 1938. Asst. to project engr. U.S. Dept. Agr., Farmville, Va., 1936-37; tech. asst. civil engring. sect. U.S. Coast Guard, Norfolk, 1939—41; civil engr. constrn. q.m. U.S. Army, Albrook Field, Panama, 1941—44; chief mil. design sect. U.S. Engrs. Office, Norfolk, 1941-44; sr. partner McGaughy, Marshall & McMillan (architects and cons. engrs.)(formerly Lublin, McGaughy & Associates), 1945-65; pres. MMM Design Group (formerly McGaughy, Marshall & McMillan), 1965-81, chmn. bd., chief exec. officer Norfolk, Washington, 1981—. Spl. cons. Office Coal Research U.S. Dept. Interior; mem. Va. Gov.'s Met. Areas Study Commn.; chmn. faculty Norfolk extension U. Va., 1943-46 Named Va. Engr. of Yr., 1970 Fellow ASCE; mem. Am. Concrete Inst., ASTM, Am. Road Bldg. Assn. (bd. dirs. engring. div. 1966-68), Nat. Soc. Profl. Engrs. (v.p. 1957-59), Va. C. of C., Norfolk C. of C. (bd. dirs. 1960-63), Va. Soc. Profl. Engrs. (past pres.), Engrs. Club Hampton Roads (past pres.), Soc. Am. Mil. Engrs., Va. Engring. Found. (bd. dirs. 1970-72, 90—), Cedar Point Golf Club (Suffolk), Harbor Club (Norfolk), Norfolk Yacht and Country Club, Phi Delta Theta, Thelta Tau. Home: 5905 Studeley Ave Norfolk VA 23508-1030 Office: 229 W Bute St PO Box 269 Norfolk VA 23501-0269

MCGAUGHY, RICHARD WAYNE, nuclear consultant; b. Hamilton, Ohio, Mar. 7, 1930; s. William Leigh and Lyda (Sellars) McG.; m. Sue Ellen Eyler, July 1, 1961; children: Ellen Lynn, David Leigh. BS, U.S. Naval Acad., 1952. Commd. ensign USN, Washington, 1952, advanced through grades to capt., 1972, ret., 1976; sect. chief U.S. Nuclear Regulatory Commn., King of Prussia, Pa., 1976-80; v.p. IES Utilities, Cedar Rapids, Iowa, 1980-93; nuclear cons., 1993—. Indsl. adv. bd. Iowa State U., Ames, 1988—; safety com. chair DAEC Power Plant, Palo, Iowa, 1990-2000. Bd. dirs. Cedar Rapids Symphony, 1988-94; Sinclair Soc., United Way, Cedar Rapids, 1990—; docent Presdl. Mus., West Branch, Iowa, 1993—. Decorated Bronze Star. Mem. ASME (vice chmn. concensus com. 1987-93), Am. Soc. for Quality Control, Am. Nuclear Soc. Avocations: sailing, woodworking, photography, music.

MCGAVICK, MICHAEL S. insurance and financial services company executive; b. Seattle; BA, U. Wash., 1983. V.p. The Rockey Comp., Wash. Round Table, 1986—88; chief of staff for Sen. Slade Gorton, 1989—91; ptnr. The Gallatin Group, Seattle, 1991—92; dir. Superfund Improvement Project, Am. Insurance Assn., 1992—95; pres. & COO CNA Fin. Corp., Chicago, 1995—2001; CEO, pres., bd. dirs. SAFECO Corp., 2001—. Office: 4333 Brooklyn Ave NE Seattle WA 98185*

MCGAVRAN, FREDERICK JAEGER, lawyer; b. Columbus, Ohio, Apr. 24, 1943; s. James Holt and Marion (Jaeger) McG.; m. Elizabeth Dowlig, Jan. 5, 1980; children: Sarah Ann, Marian Katherine. BA, Kenyon Coll., 1965; JD, Harvard U., 1972. Bar: Ohio 1972, U.S. Supreme Ct. 1984, Ky. 1992. Assoc. Kyte, Conlan, Wulsin & Vogeler, Cin., 1972-78, Frost & Jacobs, Cin., 1978-2000, Frost, Brown & Todd, LLC, Cin., 2000—. Editor-in-chief Sixth Circuit Federal Practice Manual, 1999. Lt. USN, 1965-69. Mem. Fed. Bar Assn. (pres. Cin. chpt. 1984-85, mem. exec. com. Cin. chpt. 1985—), Ohio State Bar Assn. (chmn. com. on fed. cts. 1982-85), Univ. Club of Cin., The Literary Club. Home: 2560 Perkins Ln Cincinnati OH 45208-2723 Office: Frost Brown & Todd LLC 2200 PNC Ctr Cincinnati OH 45202 E-mail: fmcgavran@fbtlaw.com.

MCGEADY, KATHLEEN BIRMINGHAM, grant administrator; b. Oceanside, N.Y., Aug. 27, 1949; d. James Joseph and Doris Martha (Fraser) Birmingham; m. Dennis J. McGeady, June 14, 1970; children: Kelly, Lauren. Student, Mercer County C.C., Mercer County Vocat. Tech. Sch, 1976-77. Office asst. Madison Square Garden, N.Y.C., 1967-69, PICA, N.Y.C., 1969-70; exec. sec. Pubs. Distbg. Corp., 1970-74; grant adminstr. Law Sch. Admission Coun., Newtown, Pa., 1990-99; proposal mgmt. assoc. Robert Wood Johnson Found., Princeton, 1999—. Mem. animal care com. Princeton U., 1974-90. Vol. Plainsboro Free Pub. Libr., 1982-86; co-dir. Plainsboro Founders Day, 1982-87; co-coord. bicycling portion Liberty to Liberty Triathlon, Plainsboro, 1983-86; founder, dir. Bookworm Five Mile Race, Plainsboro, 1984-85; elected councilman Plainsboro Town Coun., 1986-89, chair, 1988-89; mem. Plainsboro-Cranbury Juvenile Conf. Com., 1988-95, chair, 1992-95; vice-chair Plainsboro Dem. Mcpl. Com., 1990-92, mcpl. com., 1994-99; v.p. Plainsboro Dem. Club, 1991-92; bd. dirs. Teen League Softball, 1993-95; vol. and database adminstr. Millstone Basin Affiliate of Habitat for Humanity, 1996-98, bd. dirs., sec., 1997-98; mentor EnvironMentors, 1999—. Avocations: gardening, gourmet cooking, collecting cookbooks and antique silver, bicycling. Home: 50 Linden Ln Plainsboro NJ 08536-2521

MCGEADY, LEON JOSEPH, engineer, educator; b. Freemansburg, Pa., July 5, 1921; s. Gerald and Elda (Smock) McG.; m. Anne Peters, Sept. 5, 1949. BS in Metall. Engring, Lehigh U., 1943, MS, 1946, PhD, 1950. Research asso. Lehigh U., 1943-49; faculty Lafayette Coll., 1949-87, prof. metall. engring., chmn. dept., 1957-87, dir. engring., 1975-87, prof. emeritus, 1987. Researchers Welding Research Council, 1955—; ind. metall. cons., 1953—; engring. cons. 1987—. Contbr. articles to profl. jours. Mem. Am. Soc. Metals (chmn. Lehigh Valley 1957), Am. Welding Soc., Am. Soc. Engring. Edn., Am. Inst. Mining, Metall. and Petroleum Engrs. Home: 404 Center St Bethlehem PA 18018-6003

MCGEADY, SISTER MARY ROSE, religious organization administrator, psychologist; b. Hazelton, Pa., June 28, 1928; d. Joseph James and Catherine Cecilia (Mundie) McG. BA in Sociology, Emmanuel Coll., 1955; MA in Clin. Psychology, Fordham U., 1961; DHL (hon.), St. John's U., Queens, N.Y., 1982, Coll. New Rochelle, N.Y., 1991, Fordham U., 1991, Niagara U., 1991, Coll. St. Rose, Albany, N.Y., 1991, DePaul U., 1991. Joined Daus. of Charity St. Vincent De Paul, Roman Cath. Ch., 1946. Dir. Astor Home Clinics, Rhinebeck, N.Y., 1961-66; exec. dir. Nazareth Child Care Ctr., Boston, 1966-71; dir. mental health Cath. Charities Bklyn., 1971-79, assoc. exec. dir., 1987-90; dir. Kennedy Child Study Ctr., N.Y.C., 1979-81; provincial supr. Daus. of Charity St. Vincent DePaul, Albany, 1981-87; pres., chief exec. officer Covenant House, N.Y.C., 1990—. Bd. dirs. Cardinal Cooke Health Care Ctr., N.Y.C., Meninger Found., Kans., Ctr. for Human Devel., Washington. Author: Catholic Special Education, 1979. Mem. N.Y. State Mental Health Svcs. Coun., Albany, 1983-90, N.Y. State Mental Health Planning Coun., Albany, 1986-91, Cath. Charities USA, 1966—. Recipient svc. award N.Y.C. Dept. Mental Health, 1988, Encouragement award Cath. U. Am., 1991. Home: 75 Lewis Ave Brooklyn NY 11206-7015 Office: Covenant House 346 W 17th St New York NY 10011-5089

MCGEARY, CLYDE MILLS, artist, educator, advisor; b. New Kensington, Pa., Oct. 31, 1930; s. Charles Everett and Martha Harriet (Mills) McG.; m. Barbara Joyce Conner, Aug. 25, 1954; children: Melinda, Martha, Marilee, Clyde. BS, Ind. U. Pa., 1954; MFA, Carnegie-Mellon U., 1962. Tchr. North Allegheny Schs., Pitts., 1954-61; prof., instr. U. Pitts., 1961-64; fine art advisor Pa. Dept. Edn., Harrisburg, 1964-68, sr. fine art advisor, 1968-75, chief arts & scis., 1975-91; exec. dir. Susquehanna Art Mus., 1991-94, advisor, 1994—. Mem. adv. bd. J. Paul Getty Ctr. Edn. in Arts, L.A., 1984-90, Binney & Smith Corp., Easton, Pa., 1982-93, J.D. Rockefeller 3rd Fund, N.Y.C., 1972-76; trustee, bd. dirs. Marketvest, 1995-98. Author: My World of Art, 1963, Cultural Enrichment, 1968, Learning Through Art, 1973; numerous one-man shows, 1962-95. Bd. dirs. Preservation Pa., Harrisburg, 1997—, Harrisburg Choral Soc., 1994-97; exec. com. Pa. Heritage Soc., Harrisburg, 1995—; chmn. com. Camp Hill (Pa.) Borough, 1996—; chmn. fine arts Cumberland County 250th Anniversary Com., Carlisle, Pa., 1996; bd. dirs. Pa. state affiliate Am. Diabetes Assn., 1995-97, Perry County Coun. on Arts, 1999—, pres. bd. dirs.; steering com. Perry County Libr. Sys. 1st lt. C.E., U.S. Army, 1954-57. Recipient Harrisburg Cmty. award for disting. svc. in arts, 1995, Disting. Alumni award Ind. U. of Pa., 1995. Mem. ASCD (Disting. Educator award 1989), Nat. Art Edn. Assn.(Disting. fellow 1985, Outstanding Educator award 1987), Nat. Asn. State Suprs. of Art, Pa. Art Edn. Assn. (Disting. fellow 1985), Cosmopolitan Internat. (pres. 1982, 99), Masons (Master Mason). Republican. Presbyterian. Avocations: fly fishing, poetry, antiques. Home and Office: 248 Willow Ave Camp Hill PA 17011-3652 E-mail: cbmcgeary@aol.com.

MCGEE, DAN(IEL) W. state representative; b. Shreveport, La., Sept. 30, 1947; m. LaRae McGee; 3 children. BS, La. State U. Land surveyor, geologist; mem. Mont. Ho. of Reps., 1995—, speaker, 2001—. Lt. USAF. Republican. Home: 1925 Pinyon Dr Laurel MT 59044 Office: Speaker of the House State Capitol Helena MT 59620*

MCGEE, DEBRA DIANE, interior designer, consultant; b. Johnson City, Tenn., Dec. 30, 1959; d. Robert Guy and Lula Janette (Rose) McG. BS, U. N.C., Greensboro, 1981. Interior designer Carolina Office Equipment, Hickory, N.C., 1981; salesperson, interior designer Miller Services, Charlotte, 1981—; project designer Joseph T. Ryerson & Son, Charlotte, 1983-84; space planner Internat Paper Co., Charlotte, 1984-85. Mem. Inst. Bus. Designers, Am. Soc. Interior Designers, Nat. Assn. Female Execs. Republican. Baptist. Club: Charlotte Contact Exchange (v.p. 1983). Avocations: golf, tennis, water skiing. Home: 7324 Lake Front Dr Unit 8 Charlotte NC 28278-6538 Office: 100 E Park Ave Charlotte NC 28203-4748

MCGEE, DENNIS EMMETT, research technologist; b. Klamath Falls, Oreg., Feb. 1, 1956; s. Donald Leonard and Roberta S. (Burnbaum) McG.; m. Dorothy L. Kapitan, June 21, 1980; children: Joseph, Benjamin, Levi. BA, U. Oreg., 1978; PhD, Calif. Inst. Tech., 1983. Rsch.chemist Unocal Sci. and Tech. Divsn., Brea, Calif., 1982-91; technologist Mobil Chem., Macedon, N.Y., 1991—. Author: Messages from God, 1999; contbr. articles to profl. jours.; patentee in field. Oreg. scholar, 1974. Mem. Phi Beta Kappa. Avocations: Bible study, writing, fishing. Office: Mobil Chem 729 Pittsford Palmyra Rd Macedon NY 14502-9179 E-mail: iampublishing@juno.com.

MCGEE, DONNA LOUISE, artist, educator; b. Chgo., Dec. 2, 1952; d. Owen Dominic and Marilyn (McDonald) McG.; m. James Frederick Crowell, Oct. 12, 1980; 1 child, Robin Mae. BS, So. Ill. U., 1974; postgrad., Jacob Cramer Ctr. for the Arts, Leeds, Yorkshire, Eng., 1997. Artist, Newton, Mass., 1978-82, Hadley, 1982—. Ceramics instr. The Guild Studio Sch., Northampton, Mass., 1996—, Elms Coll., Chicopee, Mass., 1995. One-woman shows include Ferrin Gallery, 1991, 1997, Am. Hand Gallery, 1992, Mass. Coll., 1999, exhibited in group shows at NCECA, Columbus, Ohio, 1999, Lincoln Arts, Calif., 1994, 2001, 2002. Grantee Mass. Cultural Coun., 1998, 2000, 01; recipient award Heritage Tile Found., 1995, Dr. and Mrs. Crimeas award for ceramics Wadsworth Atheneum, 1994. Mem. Nat. Coun. Edn. in Ceramic Arts, Am. Crafts Coun., Asparagus Valley Potters Guild. Unitarian Universalist. Avocations: bicycling, cross-country skiing, gardening, meditation, reading. Studio: 47 East St Ste 3 Hadley MA 01035-9723 E-mail: donnamcgee@attbi.com.

MCGEE, DOROTHY HORTON, writer, historian; b. West Point, N.Y., Nov. 30, 1913; d. Hugh Henry and Dorothy (Brown) M. Ed., Sch. of St. Mary, 1920-21, Gren Vale Sch., 1921-28, Brearley Sch., 1928-29, Fermata Sch., 1929-31. Asst. Historian Inc. Village of Roslyn, N.Y., 1950-58; historian Inc. Village of Matinecock, 1966—. Author: Skipper Sandra, 1950, Sally Townsend, Patriot, 1952, The Boarding School Mystery, 1953, Famous Signers of the Declaration, 1955, Alexander Hamilton-New Yorker, 1957, Herbert Hoover: Engineer, Humanitarian, Statesman, 1959, rev. edit., 1965, The Pearl Pendant Mystery, 1960, Framers of the Constitution, 1968; author booklets, articles hist. and sailing subjects. Chmn. Oyster Bay Bicentennial Revolution Commn., 1971—, historian Town of Oyster Bay, 1982—, mem. Nassau County Am. Revolution Bicentennial Commn., hon. dir. The Friends of Raynham Hall, Inc., treas. Family Welfare Assn. Nassau County, Inc., 1956-58, dir. Family Svc. Assn. Nassau County, 1958-69. Recipient Cert. of award for outstanding contbn. children's lit. N.Y. State Assn. Elem. Sch. Prins., 1959, award Nat. Soc. Children of Am. Revolution, 1960, award N.Y. Assn. Supervision and Curriculum Devel., 1961, hist. award Town of Oyster Bay, 1963, Cert. Theodore Roosevelt Assn., 1976, Franklin D. Roosevelt award, Local Govt. Historian's Prof. Achievement award Office of State Historian and Assn. Pub. Historians N.Y. State, 1999. Fellow Soc. Am. Historians, mem. Soc. Preservation L.I. Antiquities (hon. dir.), Nat. Trust Hist. Preservation, N.Y. Geneal. and Biol. Soc. (dir., trustee), Oyster Bay Hist. Soc. (hon. pres. 1971-75, chmn. 1975-79, trustee), Theodore Roosevelt Assn. (trustee), Townsend Soc. Am. (trustee). Republican. Address: PO Box 142 Locust Valley NY 11560-0142

MCGEE, HAROLD JOHNSTON, former academic administrator; b. Portsmouth, Va., Apr. 13, 1937; s. Harold Valentine McGee and Clara Mae (Johnston) Webber; m. Mary Frances Eure, Mar. 22, 1959; children: Harold Johnston, Mary Margaret, Matthew Hayden; m. Linda Gayle Stevens, Apr. 3, 1976; 1 child, Andrew Meade. BS, Old Dominion U., 1959; MEd, U. Va., 1962, EdD, 1968. Tchr. Falls Church (Va.) City Schs., 1959-62; asst. dean, then dean of admissions Old Dominion U., Norfolk, Va., 1962-65; field rep., program officer, sr. program officer U.S. Office Edn. Bur. Higher Edn., Charlottesville, 1965-70; provost Tidewater Community Coll., Portsmouth, 1970-71; founding pres. Piedmont Va. Community Coll., Charlottesville, 1971-75; various offices including dean grad. sch., asst. to pres., v.p. student affairs, v.p. adminstrv. affairs, sec. bd. visitors James Madison U., Harrisonburg, Va., 1975-86; pres. Jacksonville (Ala.) State U., 1986-99, pres. emeritus, 1999—. Bd. dirs. Marine Environ. Scis. Consortium, Dauphin Island, Ala., Gulf South Conf., chmn., 1990—92, Ala. Coun. Univ. Pres., 1991—92; bd. dirs. Trans America Athletic Conf., chmn., 1998—99. Author: Impact of Federal Support, 1968, The Virginia Project, 1976. Mem. United Way Calhoun County Ala., 1986—92, Knox Concert Series Adv. Bd., Anniston, Ala., Leadership Ala., Anniston Mus. Natural History Found.; bd. dirs. Southland Athletic League. Mem. NCAA (coun. 1991-95), ACA, Soc. Coll. and Univ. Planning Am. Assn. Higher Edn., Capital City Club (Montgomery, Ala.), Rotary, Phi Delta Kappa. Episcopalian.

MCGEE, JAMES SEARS, historian, educator; b. Houston, July 12, 1942; s. William Sears and Mary Elizabeth (Peterson) McG.; m. Mary Arnall Broach, Aug. 20, 1966; children: Elizabeth, Claude. BA, Rice U., 1964; MA, Yale U., 1966, M in Philosophy, 1968, PhD, 1971. Asst. prof. Ga. So. Coll., Statesboro, 1969-71; asst. prof. history U. Calif., Santa Barbara, 1971-78, assoc. prof., 1978-84, prof., 1984—, chmn. dept., 1990-95. Pres. Pacific Coast Conf. on Brit. Studies, 1998-2000. Author: The Godly Man in Stuart England, 1976; co-author: The West Transformed, 2000; editor: The Miscellaneous Works of John Bunyan, Vol. 3, 1987. Named Disting. Tchr. in Soc. Scis., U. Calif., Santa Barbara, 1989; fellow Abraham Found., 1962-63; Woodrow Wilson fellow, 1964-65; recipient summer stipend NEH, 1975. Fellow Royal Hist. Soc.; mem. Am. Soc. Ch. History, Am. Hist. Assn., N.Am. Conf. on Brit. Studies. Democrat. Episcopalian. Avocation: gardening. Office: U Calif Dept History Santa Barbara CA 93106

MCGEE, JANE MARIE, retired educator; b. Paducah, Ky., Nov. 3, 1926; d. William Penn and Mary Virginia (Martin) Roberts; m. Hugh Donald McGee, Oct. 11, 1946; children: Catherine Jane McGee Bacon, Nancy Ann McGee McManus. BS in Elem. Edn., Murray State U., 1948; cert. in gifted edn., Nat. Coll. Edn., 1976. Tchr. Hazel (Ky.) Pub. Schs., 1948-49, Pittsford (Mich.) Pub. Schs., 1949-50, Leal Elem. Sch., Urbana, Ill., 1950-53, Cleveland Elem. Sch., Skokie, 1953-57; pvt. tutor, pre-sch. tchr., 1953-61; tchr. Woodland Park Elem. Sch., Deerfield, Ill., 1968-83; ret., 1983; beauty and skin care cons. Mary Kay Cosmetics, Gunnison, Colo., 1984—; co-owner Eagles Nest B&B, 1996—. Soprano Western State Coll. and Cmty. Chorus, Gunnison, 1986-97, European concert tour, 1990. Mem. AAUW, Top o' the World Garden Club (sec. 1984—, winner first place at numerous garden club shows). Republican. Baptist. Avocations: flower arranging, crafts, knitting, bird watching, rock collecting. Home: 109 San Juan Dr Sequim WA 98382-9326

MCGEE, JOHN PAUL, JR. lawyer; b. Portsmouth, N.H., Feb. 21, 1950; s. John P. and Louise (Flynn) McG.; m. Diane O'Leary, Aug. 19, 1972. BA, Yale U., 1972; JD, William and Mary Coll., 1975. Bar: N.H. 1975, U.S. Dist. Ct. N.H. 1975. Assoc. Flynn, McGuirk & Blanchard, Portsmouth, N.H., 1975-83; ptnr. Flynn & McGee, 1984-85, Flynn, McGee & Sanderson, Portsmouth, 1986-91; pvt. practice Flynn & McGee, P.A., 1991—. Proprietor, sec. Portsmouth Athenaeum, 1985-92, v.p., 1992-95, pres. 1995-98. Ward moderator, Portsmouth, 1985-89; chmn. Portsmouth Rep. City Com., 1985-87; chmn. N.H. Labor Bd. Appeal, 1978-79; instr. St. Catherine's Religious Edn. Program, 1977-93. Mem. Elks (presiding justice 1982-86). Republican. Roman Catholic. Avocations: reading, archaeology, history. Office: Flynn & McGee PA 222 Court St Portsmouth NH 03801-4416

MC GEE, JOSEPH JOHN, JR. former insurance company executive; b. Kansas City, Mo., Dec. 2, 1919; s. Joseph J. and Margaret (Cronin) McG.; m. Anne Cunningham, Apr. 30, 1949; children: Sally, Peter, Mary, John, David, Julie, Simon. Attended, Rockhurst Coll., Kansas City, Georgetown U. Asst. sec. Old Am. Ins. Co., Kansas City, Mo., 1939-45, v.p., 1946-51, exec. v.p., 1952-55, pres., 1956-87; ins. cons. Kansas City, Mo., 1987-91. Bd. dirs. Truman Med. Ctr., Truman Libr. Inst. for Nat. and Internat. Affairs; trustee emeritus Rockhurst Coll.; pres. McGee Found. Office: 1045 W 54th St Kansas City MO 64112

MCGEE, LYNDA PLANT, guidance counselor; b. L.A., Nov. 22, 1960; d. Larry Earle and Dolores (Balin) Plant; m. William Granville McGee, Dec. 21, 1996; 1 child, Roman Earle. BA in English Edn. cum laude, Xavier U., 1984; MEd in Counseling Psychology, U. Ill., 1986; cert. in coll. counseling, UCLA, 1997. Pupil personell svcs. credential in counseling. English tchr., decathalon coach Dorsey H.S., L.A., 1986-94; English tchr. St. Monica Cath. H.S., Santa Monica, Calif., 1994-98, Electronic Info. H.S., L.A., 1998-2000; guidance counselor Downtown Magnets H.S., 2000—. Instr. Crenshaw-Dorsey Adult Sch., 1988-89; ind. coll. counselor, L.A., 1999—. Author: Active Learning Through Teacher Research, 1997. Mem. sch. decision making coun. Downtown Magnets H.S., L.A., 1998-99; bd. dirs. urban schs. com. UCLA, mem. h.s. initiative com., 2000. Fellow Nat. Endowment, 1994, 2000, UCLA, 1996, 97. Mem. Nat. Assn. Coll. & Admission Counselors, West of Westwood Homeowners Assn. (bd. mem.), Multiracial Americans of So. Calif. (bd. mem.), Western Assn. Coll. & Admission Counselors, Zeta Phi Beta. Democrat. Avocations: reading, traveling, acting. Office: Downtown Magnets HS 1081 W Temple St Los Angeles CA 90012-1513 E-mail: sisofe@aol.com.

MCGEE, LYNNE KALAVSKY, principal; b. Jersey City, July 25, 1949; d. Michael V. and Ann (Fedowitz) Kalavsky; m. Thomas Robert McGee, Aug. 12, 1972; children: Todd Michael, Ryan Thomas. BS, St. Francis Coll., Loretto, Pa., 1971; MEd, Seton Hall U., 1972; EDS, Fla. Atlantic U., 1978, EdD, 1986. Cert. tchr., Fla., N.J., prin., Fla. Asst. prin. for curriculum Palm Beach County (Fla.) Bd. Edn., 1980-82, asst. prin. for student svcs., 1982-86, asst. prin. for adminstrn., 1986-91; prin. Belle Glade (Fla.) Elem. Sch., 1991-94, New Horizons Elem. Sch., Wellington, Fla., 1994-99, Binks Forest Elem. Sch., Wellington, 1999—. Adj. prof. grad. Nova U., 1991—. Mem. Phi Kappa Phi. Office: Binks Forest Elem Sch 15101 Bent Creek Rd Wellington FL 33414-6390

MCGEE, M. KEVIN, economics educator; b. Columbus, Ohio, Dec. 7, 1950; s. Manley L. and Elizabeth M. (Cummins) McG.; m. Barbara J. Hatem, Apr. 16, 1977; children: Megan, Jennifer, Padraic, Conor. BA in Math., Ohio Dominican Coll., 1972; MA in Econ., Ohio State U., 1978, PhD in Econ., 1983. Instr. U. Wis., Oshkosh, 1982-84, asst. prof. econs., 1984-90, assoc. prof., 1990—. Contbr. articles to profl. jours. Mem. Univ. Area Commn., Columbus, Ohio, 1975-82; mem., chair Bd. Zoning Appeals, Oshkosh, 1984-90 Mem. Am. Econ. Assn., Nat. Tax Assn.-Tax Inst. Am. Avocations: soccer referee, coach, theatre, gardening. Office: U Wis Dept Econs Oshkosh WI 54901

MCGEE, MICHAEL JAY, protective services official, educator; b. Ft. Worth, June 9, 1952; s. Cecil Carl McGee and Helen Ruth (Peeples) McGee-Furrh; m. Carol Lee Garbarino, Sept. 18, 1982; children: Megan Rose, John Michael, Molly Caitlin. Student, U. Tex., 1970-73, Western Oreg. State U., 1983; AAS in Fire Protection Tech., Colo. Mountain Coll., 1990. Lic. fire suppression systems insp., Colo., vocat. educator, Colo.; cert. hazardous materials technician, Colo., 1992, EMT, Colo.; cert. fire investigator, 2002, fire safety hazardous materials instr., evaluator. Driver Massengale Co., Austin, Tex., 1970-73; gen. mgr. Sundae Palace, 1973-74; staff mem. Young Life, Colorado Springs, Colo., 1970-75; mgr. Broadmoor Mgmt. Co., Vail, 1974-76; technician Vail Cable Communications, 1976-77; fire marshal, dep. chief fire marshal Vail Fire Dept., 1977—, fire sci. coord., 1995—, emergency med. program coord., 1996—2002; v.p. HAZPRO (Hazardous Materials and Fire Safety Consulting Firm), 1996—; pres. Fire Protection Tng. & Consulting, Inc., 1999. Dist. rep. Joint Coun. Fire Dist. Colo., 1983-85; co-chmn. Eagle County Hazardous Materials, 1984-85, mem. planning com., 1987-90; mem. accountability com. Eagle County Sch. Dist., 1991-96, mem. budget rev. com., 1991-93, vice chair accountability com. 1992-93, chmn. accountability com., 1993-96; mem. policy rev. com., 1993-96, bldg. coord., team coach Odyssey of the Mind at Eaglevalle Elem. Sch., 1995; invited dir. workshops Colo. Dept. Edn. Dist. Accountability Convention, Colo. Springs, 1995; pres. Fire Protection Tng. and Cons., Inc.; instr., trainer EMP Am. Inc. Chmn. Eagle County chpt. ARC, 1980-83, disaster chmn., 1977-80; tng. officer Eagle Vol. Fire Dept., 1988-90; mem. parish coun. St. Mary's Parish, Eagle County, 1989-90; mem. citizen's adv. com. Colo. Mountain Coll., 1990-91, bd. dirs. 1990; bldg. coord., team coach Odessey of the Mind, Eagle Valley Elem. Sch., 1994-95, 97-98, 98-99, coach Destination Imagination, 1999-2000; mem. facilities master planning com. Engle County Sch. Dist., 1996-97; mem. planning com. 1999 World Alpine Ski Championships; program coord. Eagle County Driver's Edn. Named Alumnus of the year, Co. Mountain Coll., 2001. Mem. Internat. Assn. Arson Investigators (Colo. chpt.), Internat. Platform Assn., Nat. Fire Protection Assn., Colo. State Fire Marshals Assn., Colo. State Fire Chiefs Assn. Office: Vail Fire Dept 42 W Meadow Dr Vail CO 81657-5000 E-mail: mmcgee@ci.vail.co.us.

MCGEE, PATRICK EDGAR, postal service clerk; b. Chgo., Jan. 13, 1944; s. Ralph and Minnie Odelia (Crutcher) McG. Machine clk. U.S. Postal Svc., Chgo., 1977—. Author of poems. Mem. The Art Inst. Chgo., Mus. Sci. & Industry, Chgo. Mem. Internat. Soc. Poets. Democrat. Roman Catholic. Avocations: painting, jazz, walking, jogging.

MCGEE, ROBERT MERRILL, oil company executive; b. Laramie, Wyo., Dec. 15, 1946; s. Gale William and Loraine (Baker) McG.; m. Mary Louise Lehman, July 26, 1969; children: Kirk Lehman, Scott Baker. BA in Polit. Sci., Allegheny Coll., 1969. Bus. assoc. B.F. Goodrich Co., Akron, Ohio, 1969-70; dir. of info. Nat. Petroleum Coun., Washington, 1970-73; asst. dir. pub. rels. Occidental Internat. Corp., 1973-74, exec. asst. to pres., 1974-76, v.p., 1976-78, exec. v.p., 1978-82, sr. exec. v.p., 1982-91, pres., 1991—; v.p. Occidental Petroleum Corp., 1994—. Mem. Pres.'s Commn. on White House Fellowships, Washington, 1993—2001, Meridian Internat. Ctr., Washington, 1994—98; mem. bd. advisors Pan Am. Devel. Found., 1985, pres., 1991—93; bd. govs. Ford's Theatre, Washington, 1991—; bd. govs. Karl Landegger Program in internat. bus. diplomacy Sch. Fgn. Svc., Georgetown U., 1991—2000; bd. dirs. Decatur House, 1998, vice chmn. bd., 2000, chmn. bd. dirs., 2001—. Mem. The Econ. Club of Washington, Met. Club Washington, Nat. Press Club, Robert Trent Jones Golf Club. Office: Occidental Internat Corp Ste 400 1717 Pennsylvania Ave NW Washington DC 20006-4614

MCGEE, WILLIAM HOWARD JOHN, librarian, administrator; b. Rochester, N.Y., May 15, 1942; s. William Peter and Cecilia Matilda (Kuhn) McG.; m. Sheila Anne Drumm, Sept. 4, 1965; children: Kathleen Moira, Margaret Frances. BA with honors, U. Toronto, Ont., Can., 1965; MEd, U. Toronto, 1973; MLS, U. Western Ont., London, 1980. Tchr. Mimico (Ont.) High Sch., 1966-67; tchr., libr. Applewood Secondary Sch., Mississauga, Ont., 1967-71; libr. Crestwood Secondary Sch., Peterborough, 1971-74; libr. cons. Cayman Islands Edn. Dept., Grand Cayman, B.W.I., 1975-79; adminstrv. asst. Lake Erie Regional Libr., London, 1980-83; chief libr. Ft. Erie (Ont.) Pub. Libr., 1983-86; asst. dir. McAllen (Tex.) Pub. Libr., 1986-89; coord. Hidalgo County Libr. System, McAllen, 1989—; now libr. circulation supr. Lark Cmty. Ctr. Library. Cons. Grand Ct. Libr., Grand Cayman, 1974-79; mem. Tex. State Libr. Task Force, Austin, Tex., 1991-93; adv. coun. Libr. Svcs. Tech. Act, Austin, 1993—. Editor InTraLogue jour., 1980-83; assoc. editor Can. Jour. Info. Sci., 1980. Bd. dirs. C-ME-CU Credit Union, 1994-99, chmn., 1999. Mem. ALA, Ont. Libr. Assn., Tex. Libr. Assn. (chmn. dist. 4 1994-95, 96-97, intellectual freedom com. 1995-96, profl. rights, responsiblities, and recruitment, 1996—, centennial celebration com. 2000—), Bibliothecaires Francophones Internat. Roman Catholic. Avocations: gourmet cooking, music, travel, reading. Office: Lark Cmty Ctr Libr 2601 Lark Ave Mcallen TX 78504 E-mail: billmcgee@mcallen.lib.tx.us., liam_magee@hotmail.com.

MCGEE, WILLIAM TOBIN, intensive care physician; b. Port Chester, N.Y., May 23, 1957; s. James R. and Mary (Delzotto) McG.; m. Sarah McGrath; children: Erin, Kelly, Mary, Kate. BA in Physics, Dartmouth Coll., 1979; MD, N.Y. Med. Coll., 1983; M in Health Adminstrn., Clark U., 1997. Diplomate Am. Bd. Internal Medicine with spl. qualifications in Critical Care. Resident in internal medicine Baystate Med. Ctr., Springfield, Mass., 1983-86, intensivist, acting dir. surg. ICU, 1990-95; fellow in critical care St. Louis U./St. John's Mercy Med. Ctr., St. Louis, 1986-88; intensivist critical care divsn. Baystate Med. Ctr., Springfield, MA, 1990-98, dir. ICU quality improvement, 1998—. DeWitt Wallace fellow rehab. medicine Rusk Inst. NYU Med. Ctr. Fellow Coll. Chest Physicians (Cecile Lehman Mayer award 1993); mem. AMA, Soc. Critical Care Medicine (presdl. citation 2000, internal medicine specialty award 2000), Am. Soc. Parenteral and Enteral Nutrition. Roman Catholic. Avocations: skiing, biking, hiking, sailing, windsurfing. Office: Baystate Med Ctr 759 Chestnut St Springfield MA 01199-1001 E-mail: william.t.mcgee@bhs.org.

MCGEER, EDITH GRAEF, neurological science educator; b. N.Y.C., Nov. 18, 1923; d. Charles and Charlotte Annie (Ruhl) Graef; m. Patrick L. McGeer, Apr. 15, 1954; children: Patrick Charles, Brian Theodore, Victoria Lynn. BA, Swarthmore Coll., 1944; PhD, U. Va., 1946; DSc (hon.), U. Victoria, 1987, U. B.C., 2000. Research chemist E.I. DuPont de Nemours & Co., Wilmington, Va., 1946-54; research assoc. div. neurological sci. U. B.C., Vancouver, Can., 1954-74, assoc. prof., 1974-76, prof., acting head, 1976-83, prof., head., 1983-89, prof. emerita, 1989—. Author: (with others) Molecular Neurobiology of the Mammalian Brain, 1978, 2d. edit., 1987; editor: (with others) Kainic Acid as a Tool in Neurobiology, 1978, Glutamine, Glutamate, and GABA, 1983; contbr. articles to profl. jours. Decorated officer Order of Can.; recipient Citation Am. Chem. Soc., 1958, Rsch. Prize in Psychiatry Clarke Inst., 1992, Lifetime Achievement spl. award Sci. Coun. B.C., 1995, Hon. Alumnus award, 1996. Fellow Can. Coll. Neuropsychopharmacology; mem. Can. Biochemical Soc., Internat. Brain Research Orgn., Internat. Soc. Neurochemistry, Soc. Neuroscience, Am. Neurochemical Soc. (councilor 1979-83), North Pacific Soc. Neurology and Psychiatry (hon. fellow), Lychnos Soc., Sigma Xi, Phi Beta Kappa Office: U BC Divsn Neurol Scis 2255 Wesbrook Mall Vancouver BC Canada V6T 1Z3 E-mail: mcgeer@interchange.ubc.ca.

MCGEEVER, KATHLEEN MARIE, theater studies educator; b. Bakersfield, Calif., June 14, 1959; d. Thomas Michael McGeever and Dorothy Lorraine Scanlon; life ptnr. Gregory Robert Hales, Sept. 5, 1987. BA, San Diego State U., 1981; MFA, Humboldt State U., 1996. cert. tchr. Tchr. drama, English, sci. Chins Up Youth Care Facility, Colorado Springs, 1986-87; tchr. drama, sci. and English Imogene Garner Hook Jr. H.S., Victorville, Calif., 1987-89; tchr. drama Hesperia (Calif.) H.S., 1989-93; dir. Calif. Arts Project/Redwood Arts Project, Arcata, Calif., 1994-96; asst. prof. theater and directing U. Montevallo, Ala., 1998—. Vis. asst. prof. theater No. Ariz. U., Flagstaff, 1996-98. Dir.: (theatrical performances) The Beauty Queen of Leenane, 2000, The Dumb Waiter, 1995, Really Angry Persons Eavesdrop, 1994, Lil Abner, 1993, Our Town, 1993, Bye Bye Birdie, 1992, Lilly the Felons Daughter, 1991, The Imaginary Invalid, 1990, Up the Down Staircase, 1989, The Legend of Sleepy Hollow, 1988, A Flea in Her Ear, 2001, Ernies Incredible Illucinations, 1987, Jungalbook, 1999, The Virtual play Development Workshop, 1998, Defying Gravity, 2000, A Streetcar Named Desire, 1998, Androcles and the Lion, 1998, Lysistrata, 1997, Tartuffe, 1996, Apron Strings, 1995, The Art of Dining, 2001, Montana Love Story, 1997, Apron Strings, 1995, Wiley and the Hairy Man, 2002, Sticks and Bones, 2002; actor: (theatrical performances) Taking Leave, 1994, Dandelion Wine, 1982, The Bride of Halloween, 2000, Farenheit 451, 1981, Hamlet, 1980, Androcles and the Lion, 1978 (Sybil Eliza Jones scholar 1978), Out LIke a Light, 1999, Manbingo Enterruptus, 2002; contbr. articles and presentations to profl. publs. Bd. dirs. Taoist Tai Chi Soc., Flagstaff, 1986-89. Mem. Ala. Conf. Theatre and Speech (sec. 1989-2001, v.p., pres. 2002), Ariz. Theatre Assn. (NAU rep. 1997-98), Calif. Ednl. Theatre Assn. (DTASC rep. 1985-93), South Eastern Theatre Conf. Assn., So. Calif. Ednl. Theatre Assn., Assn. Theatre in Higher Edn., Alpha Psi Omega (hon. mem., advisor), Phi Kappa Phi (life mem.).

MC GEHEE, H(ARRY) COLEMAN, JR. bishop; b. Richmond, Va., July 7, 1923; s. Harry Coleman and Ann Lee (Cheatwood) McG.; m. June Stewart, Feb. 1, 1946; children: Lesley, Alexander, Harry III, Donald, Cary. BS, Va. Poly. Inst., 1947; JD, U. Richmond, 1949; MDiv, Va. Theol. Sem., 1957, DD, 1973. Bar: Va. 1949, U.S. Supreme Ct. 1954; ordained to ministry Episcopal Ch., 1957. Spl. counsel dept. hwys. State of Va., 1949-51, gen. counsel employment svc., 1951, asst. atty. gen., 1951-54; rector Immanuel Ch.-on-the-Hill, Va. Sem., 1960-71; bishop Diocese of Mich., Detroit, 1971-90. Adv. bd. Nicaraguan Network, Ctr. for Peace and Conflict Studies, Wayne State U.; bd. dirs. Mich. Religious Coalition for Abortion Rights, 1976-84; trustee Va. Theol. Sem., 1978-93; pres. Episc. Ch. Pub. Co., 1978-85. Columnist: Detroit News, 1979-85; weekly commentator pub. radio sta. WDET-AM, Detroit, 1984-90. Mem. Gov.'s Commn. on Status of Women, 1965-66, Mayor's Civic Com., Alexandria, 1967-68; sponsor Nat. Assn. for ERA, 1977-85; pres. Alexandria Legal Aid Soc., 1969-71; bd. dirs. No. Va. Fairhousing Corp., 1963-67; pres. Mich. Coalition for Human Rights, 1980-89; chmn. Citizens' Com. for Justice in Mich., 1983-84; sponsor Farm Labor Orgn. for Children, 1983-85; bd. dirs. Pub. Benefit Corp., Detroit, 1988-90, Mich. Citizens for Personal Freedom, 1989-92, Poverty and Social Reform Inst., Detroit, 1989—, Bread for the World, 1990-94, Ams. United for Separation of Ch. and State, 1990, ACLU Oakland County, Mich., 1991-94; co-chair Lesbian-Gay Found. Mich., 1991—. 1st lt. C.E., U.S. Army, 1943-46. Named Feminist of Yr., Detroit NOW, 1978, Person of Yr., Econ. Justice Commn. Mich., 1997; recipient Humanitarian award Detroit ACLU, 1984, Phillip Hart medal Mich. Women's Studies Assn., 1984, Sayre award for justice and peace Episc. Peace Fellowship, 1988, Spirit of Detroit award, 1989, Archbishop Romero award Mich. Labor Com., 1990, Brotherhood award AME Ch., Detroit, 1993, Ira Jayne award Detroit br. NAACP, 1993, Martin Luther King, Jr. award United Ch. of Christ, 1995, William Scarlett award Episc. Ch. Pub. Co., 1997. Mem.: Detroit Econ. Club (bd. dirs.). Home: 1496 Ashover Dr Bloomfield Hills MI 48304-1215 Office: Diocese of Mich 4800 Woodward Ave Detroit MI 48201-1399

MCGEHEE, LARRY THOMAS, university administrator; b. Paris, May 18, 1936; s. George Eugene and Margaret Elizabeth (Thomas) McG.; m. Elizabeth Hathhorn Boden, Aug. 26, 1961; children: Elizabeth Hathhorn, Margaret Thomas. BA, Transylvania Coll., 1958; BD, Yale U., 1963, MA, 1964, PhD, 1969. Dir., asst. v.p. for univ. relations U. Ala., 1966-68, exec. asst. to pres., 1968-69, exec. v.p., 1969-71; lectr., assoc. prof. dept. Am. studies, 1969-71, acad. v.p., 1971; chancellor U. Tenn., Martin, 1971-79; spl. asst. to pres. U. Tenn. Sys., Knoxville, 1979-82; v.p. coll., prof. religion Wofford Coll., Spartanburg, S.C., 1982—. Syndicated columnist Southern Seen, 1982—.

Danforth fellow Yale U., 1960-66. Home: 1047 Woodburn Rd Spartanburg SC 29302-2867 Office: Wofford Coll 429 N Church St Spartanburg SC 29303-3663 E-mail: mcgeheelt@wofford.edu.

MCGEORGE, RONALD KENNETH, hospital executive; b. Fredericton, N.B., Can., June 7, 1944; s. Hubert Oswald and Ruth Johanna (Kolding) McG.; m. Gail F. Mitchell, July 17, 1970; children: Ronald Millard, Scott, Dacia Gail. BS, Houghton Coll., 1966; diploma in hosp. adminstrn., U. Toronto, Ont., Can., 1969. Adminstrv. counsellor N.S. Hosp. Ins. Commn., Halifax, 1969-70; asst. exec. dir. Izaak Walton Killam Hosp. for Children, 1970-72; v.p. Greater Niagara Gen. Hosp., Niagara Falls, Ont., 1972-74; chmn. Council Teaching Hosps.; exec. dir. Halifax Infirmary, 1974-79, Kingston Gen. Hosp., Ont., 1980-90; CEO Dr. Everett Chalmers Hosp., 1990-92; pres., CEO Region 3 Hosp. Corp., Fredericton, N.B., Can., 1992-95; exec. pastor Moncton Wesleyan Ch., 1995-97; Atlantic Provinces dir. Promise Keepers, 1995; nat. coord. Promise Keepers Can., 1997-98; exec. dir. hosp. svcs. br. New Brunswick Dept. Health & Cmty. Svcs., 1998-2000; CEO Red Lake Margaret Cochenour Meml. Hosp., 2001—. Preceptor hosp. adminstrn. U. Ottawa, U. Toronto; chmn. Ont. Council Adminstrn. Teaching Hosps.; cons. in field. Contbr. articles to profl. jours. Chmn., pres. Wesleyan Men, 1st Wesleyan Ch. Named Bus. Alumnus of Yr., Houghton Coll., 1987. Mem. Can. Coll. Health Services Execs. (pres. 1979-80), Assn. Hosp. Adminstrs. N.S. (pres.-elect 1972), N.S. Assn. Health Orgns. (dir.), Ont. Council Adminstrs. of Teaching Hosps. (pres.), Ont. Hosp. Assn. (mem. exec. com., chmn. exec. com. 1989-90), Alumni Assn. of Bethany Bible Coll. (pres.). Home: PO Box 1057 Red Lake ON Canada P0V 2M0 Office: PO Box 5005 Red Lake ON Canada P0V 2MO

MCGERVEY, TERESA ANN, technical information specialist; b. Pitts., Sept. 27, 1964; d. Walter James and Janet Sarah (Donehue) McG. BS in Geology, Calif. U. Pa., 1986, MS in Earth Sci., 1988; MLS, Cath. U. Am., 1998. Phys. sci. technician U.S. Geol. Survey, Reston, Va., 1989-90; editor, indexer Am. Geol. Inst., Alexandria, 1990-91; cartographer Def. Mapping Agy., Reston, 1991-93; tech. info. specialist Nat. Tech. Info. Svc., Springfield, Va., 1993-2000, Dept. of Def., Arlington, 2000—. Intern Dept. Mineral Scis., Smithsonian Instn., summers 1985, 1986. Mem. ALA, AAUW, Geosci. Info. Soc.

MCGETTIGAN, CHARLES CARROLL, JR. investment banker; b. San Francisco, Mar. 28, 1945; s. Charles Carroll McGettigan and Molly (Fay) McGettigan Pedley; m. Katharine Havard King, Nov. 1, 1975 (div. 1981); m. Meriwether Lewis Stovall, Aug. 6, 1983; 1 child, Meriwether. AB in Govt., Georgetown U., 1966; MBA in Fin., U. Pa., 1969. Assoc., asst. v.p., v.p. Blyth Eastman Dillon, N.Y.C., 1970-75, 1st v.p., 1975-78, sr. v.p. San Francisco, 1978-80, Dillon, Read & Co., San Francisco, 1980-83; gen. ptnr. Woodman Kirkpatrick & Gilbreath, 1983-84; prin. corp. fin. Hambrecht & Quist, Inc., 1984-88; mng. dir., founder McGettigan, Wick & Co., Inc., 1988—; gen. ptnr., founder Proactive Ptnrs., L.P., 1990—, Proactive Investment Mgrs., L.P., San Francisco, 1991—. Gen. ptnr Fremont Proactive Ptnrs., 1991-2001; bd. dirs. Cuisine Solutions, Inc., Alexandria, Va., Tanknology-NDE Corp., Austin, Tex., PMR Corp., San Diego, Modtech, Inc., Perris, Calif.; chmn. Onsite Energy Corp., Carlsbad, Calif.; adv. dir. Chesapeake Ventures, Balt., 1984-94. Trustee St. Francis Meml. Hosp., San Francisco, 1980-86; mem. United San Francisco Rep. fin. com., 1983—, steering com., 1986—; adv. bd. dirs. Leavey Sch. Bus. Adminstrn., Santa Clara U., Calif., 1984-90. With USN, 1966. Named Confrerie des Chevaliers du Tastevin, 1991. Mem. Soc. Calif. Pioneers, The Brook, Racquet and Tennis Club (N.Y.), The Pacific Union Club, Bohemian Club (San Francisco), San Francisco Golf Club, Burlingame Country Club (Hillsborough, Calif.), Boston (New Orleans), White's (London). Republican. Roman Catholic. Home: 3375 Clay St San Francisco CA 94118-2006 Office: McGettigan Wick & Co Inc 50 Osgood Pl San Francisco CA 94133-4622 E-mail: Chas@McGettigan-Wick.com.

MCGHEE, ANNETTE BOOKER, educator; b. Gloucester, Va., Apr. 3, 1938; d. Calvin Roane and Carrie (Eastwood) Booker; m. Craig McGhee, May 30, 1987. BA in Econs., Hollins Coll., 1960; MA in Edn., U. Va., 1964. Surp. elem. edn. Va. State Dept. Edn., Richmond. Participant SALT II talks White House, Washington. Mem. Richmond chpt. Friendship Force. Fulbright grantee to India, 1976, to China, 1986; Kettering fellow. Mem. Am. Symphony Orch. League (vol. coun. 2000—), Richmond Symphony Orch. League (pres. 1998-2000), Delta Kappa Gamma (pres. 1987-89). Episcopalian. Avocations: ikebana, antiques, Asian geopolitical issues, Asian archaeology. Home: One Brockenbrough Ln Richmond VA 23221

MCGHEE, LORI JEAN VOTE, medical/surgical nurse; b. Sac City, Iowa, Nov. 22, 1958; d. Bud Lee and Joanne Kay (Brouchous) V.; m. Wayne McGhee, June 30, 1990. Diploma, Allen Meml. Hosp. Sch. Nursing, Waterloo, Iowa, 1980; student, U. No. Iowa, 1978. Staff nurse in orthopedics Allen Meml. Hosp., 1980-85; charge nurse in orthopedics/renal nursing Humana Hosp. Med. City, Dallas, 1985-88; med. reviewer Blue Cross and Blue Shield of Tex., Inc., Richardson, 1988-89, unit coord., trainer, 1989-90, supr. dept. precert., 1990-93; dir. nursing Integrated Health Svcs. Richardson (Tex.) Manor, 1994; quality case mgr. Baylor Richardson Med. Ctr., Richardson, Tex., 1995—.

MCGIFF, JOHN C(HARLES), pharmacologist, department chairman; b. N.Y.C., Aug. 6, 1927; s. John Francis and Rose (Rieger) McG.; m. Sara Leighton Babb, Feb. 8, 1958 (dec.); children: John, Katharine, Sara, Jeremiah, Elizabeth. BS, Georgetown U., 1947; MD, Columbia U., 1951; Doctorate Honoris Causa, Copernicus Acad. Medicine, Cracow, Poland, 1987. Diplomate: Am. Bd. Internal Medicine. Intern U. Cin., 1951-52; resident in medicine U. Va. Med. Center, 1952-53; tng. in physiology and pharmacology Columbia Presbyn. Hosp., N.Y.C., 1957-58; mem. faculty U. Pa. Med. Sch., 1961-66; dir. cardiovascular sect. St. Louis U. Med. Sch., 1966-71; dir. clin. pharmacology Med. Coll. Wis., Milw., 1971-75; prof., chmn. dept. pharmacology U. Tenn. Center Health Scis., 1975-79, N.Y. Med. Coll., Valhalla, 1979—. Vis. scientist Wellcome Rsch. Labs., Beckenham, Eng., 1975-76; adv. bd. Am. Heart Assn., Kidney Found.; mem. nat. vis. coun. for health sci. faculties Columbia U. Coll. Physicians and Surgeons, 1987; mam. arteriosclerosis hypertension and lipid adv. com. NIH, 1987; cons. in field; chmn. cardiovascular renal study sect. Nat. Heart, Lung and Blood Inst. NIH, 1994. Author articles in books; contbr. articles to profl. jours. Pres. sch. bd. St. Louis Cathedral Sch., 1970. Served as flight surgeon M.C. USMCR, 1955-57, Korea. Recipient Medal of Achievement Copernicus Acad. Medicine, Cracow, Poland, 1984; Terence Cardinal Cooke medal for Disting. Service in Health Care, 1985; CIBA award Am. Heart Assn., 1986, Merit award Nat. Heart, Lung, and Blood Inst. of NIH, 1990; Burroughs Wellcome Fund scholar, 1971-74, Richard Bright award Am. Soc. Hypertension, 1997. Mem. Am. Physiol. Soc., Am. Soc. Pharmacology and Exptl. Therapeutics (Otto Krayer award 1997), Council High Blood Pressure Research (med. adv. bd. 1968), Am. Soc. Clin. Investigation, Brit. Pharmacology Soc., Trabucchi Lecturer, chm. of the Com. of the Am. Soc. of Hypertension. Roman Catholic. Home: 5 Bay Rd East Patchogue NY 11772-6201 Office: NY Med Coll Dept Pharmacology Valhalla NY 10595

MC GIFFERT, DAVID ELIOT, lawyer, former government official; b. Boston, June 27, 1926; s. Arthur Cushman and Elizabeth (Eliot) McG.; m. Enud De Kibedi-Varga, Jan. 21, 1966; children: Laura, Carola.; m. Nelse Greenway, Apr. 9, 1983. Student, U. Calif.-Berkeley, 1944; BA, Harvard U., 1949, LL.B., 1953; postgrad., Cambridge (Eng.) U., 1950. Bar: D.C. 1954. With firm Covington & Burling, Washington, 1953-55, 57-61, ptnr., 1969-77, 81—. Lectr. law U. Wis., 1956; asst. to sec. def. for legis. affairs Dept. Def., 1962-65, undersec. army, 1965-69, asst. sec. for internat. security affairs, 1977-81 Served with USNR, 1944-46. Mem. Am. Bar Assn., Council Fgn. Relations, Alpha Delta Phi. Clubs: Metropolitan (Washington). Home: 3819 Veazey St NW Washington DC 20016-2230 Office: Covington & Burling PO Box 7566 1201 Pensylvania Ave NW Washington DC 20044-7566

MCGIFFERT, MICHAEL, retired history educator, editor; b. Chgo., Oct. 5, 1928; s. Arthur Cushman and Elisabeth (Eliot) McG.; m. Genevieve White Mischel, Aug. 13, 1960; m. Elizabeth Eastman, June 19, 1949 (div. 1960). BA, Harvard Coll., 1949; B.D., Yale U., 1952, PhD, 1958; postgrad., Union Theol. Sem., N.Y.C., 1949-50. Instr. history Colgate U., Hamilton, N.Y., 1954-55, 56-60, U. Md., College Park, 1955-56; asst. prof. history U. Denver, 1960-64, assoc. prof., 1964-69, prof. history, 1969-74; editor William and Mary Quar., Inst. Early Am. History and Culture, prof. history, Coll. William and Mary, Williamsburg, Va., 1972-97; ret. Author: The Higher learning in Colorado, 1964; editor: The Character of Americans, 1964 (rev. edit.), 1969, Puritanism and the American Experience, 1969, (with Robert A. Skotheim) American Social Thought, 1972, God's Plot: The Paradoxes of Puritan Piety, 1972, God's Plot: Puritan Spirituality in Thomas Shepard's Cambridge, 1994. Faculty rsch. grantee U. Denver, 1970, Coll. William and Mary, 1981-82, 89; rsch. fellow NEH, 1977-78. Mem. Am. Hist. Assn., Orgn. Am. Historians, Confr. of Hist. Jours. (pres.1987-89), Am. Antiquarian Soc. Home: 102 Old Glory Ct Williamsburg VA 23185-4914 E-mail: mcgiff@widomaker.com.

MC GILL, ARCHIE JOSEPH, venture capitalist; b. Winona, Minn., May 29, 1931; s. Archibald Joseph and Anne (Lettner) McG.; m. Jeanne Sullivan, Mar. 17, 1974; children: Archibald Joseph, III, Mark E., Gregory P., Debora, Susan, Brian. BA in Econs., St. Mary's Coll., Winona, 1956. With IBM Corp., 1956-69, v.p. market ops. N.Y., 1956-69; founder, pres. McGill Assocs., 1970-73; dir. market mgmt. AT&T Co., 1973-78, v.p. bus. mktg., 1978-83; pres. Advanced Info. Systems Am. Bell, Inc., 1983; pres., chief exec. officer Rothschild Ventures, Inc., 1983; now pres. Chardonnay, Inc. Dir. various cos. Bd. dirs. Steadman/Hawkins Found. With USAF, 1951-54. Named Mktg. Statesman of Year Sales Execs. Club, 1978

MCGILL, CAROL ANN MICHALSKI, medical, surgical and psychiatric nurse, writer, poet; b. Balt., Feb. 21, 1955; d. John B. Rassa and Genevieve J. Ryncewicz; m. Martin Joseph Michalski, June 21, 1976 (div. 2000); children: Matthew Michalski, Nathan Michalski, Robin Michalski, Shara Michalski1 stepchild Jason Michalski ; m. Shawn L. McGill, Nov. 22, 2000. RN, Grand View Hosp., Sellersville, Pa., 1976; BS in Health Care Adminstrn., Pacific Western U., 1986, PhD in Religious Studies/Ministry, 1987, MS in Nursing, 2000. RN; ordained to ministry Christian Ch., 1983. Staff nurse Md. Gen. Hosp., Balt., 1974-75, Union Meml. Hosp., Balt., 1975-77; head nurse Levindale Chronic Hosp., 1977-79; charge staff nurse Franklin Sq. Hosp. Ctr., 1979—, pain mgmt. liaison, 1993—, admission triage nurse supervisor, 1998-2000. Head procedure com. Levindale Chronic Hosp., Balt., 1978-79; admission triage nurse/supr. Franklin Square Hosp. Ctr.; min. Faith Seed Ministries, Balt., 1983—; Bible Coll. adminstr. L.W. Christian Ctr., Balt., 1987-89. Author: Don't Blame God-Making Sense Out of Tragedy and Suffering, 1995; contbr. articles and poetry to profl. jours. and anthologies. Asst. youth activities Ridgeleigh Cmty. Assn., Balt., 1980; block capt. Woodcroft Civic Assn., Balt.; coord. Churchville Christian Sch., 1993-94; group coord. Christian Home Educator's Network, 1995-99, Teen Boys Group, 1995-97; yearbook coord. Chen H.S., 1998-99. Recipient Nursing Achievement award Johnston Sch.-Union Meml. Hosp., 1974, Ministry Recognition Certs. Gospel Tabernacle Balt., 1990, 91, poetry awards. Mem. Md. League Nursing, Nat. Author's Registry, Internat. Soc. Poets. Avocations: art, crafts, writing, hiking, water sports.

MCGILL, CATHY BROOME, gifted and talented education educator; b. Gastonia, N.C., Sept. 26, 1945; d. Harold Beeler and Christine (Hicks) Broome; m. Paul Furman McGill, July 5, 1969; children: Paul Bryan, Harold Marcus. BA, Mars Hill Coll., 1967; MA, Appalachian State U., 1968. Tchr. 6th grade Victory Elem. Sch., Gastonia, N.C., 1968-69; lang. arts, social studies and music tchr. Northside Mid. Sch., West Columbia, S.C., 1969-71, Fulmer Mid. Sch., West Columbia, 1972-76; tchr. Pine View Elem. Sch., 1978-81; tchr. sci. and lang. arts Heiskell Sch., Atlanta, 1981-82; tchr. lang. arts and gifted Fulmer Mid. Sch., 1982-85; itinerant gifted tchr. Lex II, West Columbia, 1985—. In-svc. presenter Lex II, 1992-95. Pianist Holland Ave. Baptist Ch., Cayce, S.C., 1970—2000, Pianist Lexington Presbyterian Ch., 2001-, vacation Bible sch. dir., 1982-93, youth choir dir., 1982-85; neighborhood solicitor Arthritis Found., Columbia, S.C., 1993-95. Mem. Nat. Assn. for Gifted Children, Palmetto State Tchrs. Assn., Alpha Delta Kappa (chaplain 1993—). Republican. Avocations: music, reading. Home: 1404 Martins Crossing Ct Gilbert SC 29054-8672

MCGILL, DAN MAYS, insurance business educator; b. Greenback, Tenn., Sept. 27, 1919; s. John Burton and Jane (Mays) McG.; m. Elaine Kem, June 22, 1952; children: Douglas Russell, Melanie Mays BA, Maryville Coll., 1940, LLD (hon.), 1982; MA, Vanderbilt U., 1941; PhD, U. Pa., 1947. Assoc. prof. fin. U. Tenn., Knoxville, 1947-48; Julian Price assoc. prof. ins. U. N.C., Chapel Hill, 1948-51; assoc. prof. ins. U. Pa., Phila., 1952-56, Frederick H. Ecker prof. life ins., 1959-90. Trustee N.W. Mut. Life Ins. Co., Milw., 1978-90; bd. dirs. NRG Life Reassurance Corp., Phila., 1984-94, Phila. Reins. Corp., 1990—, Independence Blue Cross, 1990—; exec. dir. S.S. Huebner Found., 1954-75, 78-86, chmn., 1965-94; dir. rsch. Pension Rsch. Coun., 1952-90; chmn., mem. governing bd. Leonard Davis Inst. Health Econs., 1967-90; 1st chmn. adv. commn. Pension Benefit Guaranty Corp., 1975-78, mem. 1978-81. Author: An Analysis of Government Life Insurance, 1949, The Fundamentals of Private Pensions, 7th edit., 1996, Legal Aspects of Life Insurance, 1959, Fulfilling Pension Expectations, 1962, Life Insurance, 1967, Preservation of Pension Benefit Rights, 1972, others; editor: (with others) World Insurance Trends, 1959, others. Trustee Presbyn. Med. Ctr., Phila., 1987—96; chmn. Boettner Inst. Fin. Gerontology, 1993—; mem. retirement bd. Mass. Bay Transp. Authority, 1980—96; chmn. bd. pensions Presbyn. Ch. U.S.A., 1977—88; trustee Presbyn. Found. for Phila., 1996—2001. Maj. USAAF, 1942—46, Maj. USAAF, 1951—52. Recipient Disting. Alumni award Maryville Coll., 1962, Huebner Gold medal award Am. Coll., 1977, Gold medal Internat. Ins. Soc., 1987. Mem.: Am. Risk and Ins. Assn. (pres. 1959, Elizur Wright award 1955, 1981), Merion Cricket Club, Union League. Republican. Presbyterian. Avocations: music, travel, sports. Home: 50 Belmont Ave Bala Cynwyd PA 19004-2437

MCGILL, GRACE ANITA, retired occupational health nurse, case manager; b. Lawrence, Mass., Mar. 8, 1943; d. Joseph John and Tina Mary (Sicurella) Tabacco; m. Howard L. McGill, Jr., Feb. 28, 1965; children: Cynthia, Deborah, David. RN, Mass. Gen. Hosp., 1963; BS, Lesley Coll., 1987; MS in Mgmt., Lesley Grad. Sch., 1990. Cert. occupl. health nurse Am. Bd. Occupl. Health Nurses, Inc. Nurse Phillips Acad., Andover, Mass., 1963-65, 97th Gen. Hosp., Frankfurt, Germany, 1966, Highsmith-Rainey Hosp., Fayetteville, N.C., 1968, Lawrence (Mass.) Gen. Hosp., 1969-78, Baldpate Psychiat. Hosp., Georgetown, Mass., 1978-79; nursing staff St. Joseph's Hosp., Lowell, 1980-81, head nurse, 1981-83; occupl. health nurse Wang Labs., Inc., 1983-87, corp. safety specialist, 1987-90; health svcs. adminstr. Loral Infrared and Imaging Sys., Inc., Lexington, Mass., 1990-93; supr. health svcs. Osram Sylvania, Inc., Danvers, 1993-95; occupl. health nurse Occupl. Health Strategies, Inc., Chelmsford, 1995-98; ret.; ret., 1998. Contract instr. Sch. Pub. Health Harvard U.; occupl. health nurse Sts. Meml. Med. Hosp. ; past chair Am. Bd. Occupational Health Nurses, 1997—99. Pres. Cape Cod Hosp. Aux.; dir. Cape Cod Healthcare Found. Bd. Recipient MA Medique Leadership grant, 1999. Mem. Am. Assn. Occupl. Health Nurses, Mass. Gen. Hosp. Nurses Alumnae Assn., Lesley Coll. Alumnae. Episcopalian. Avocations: music, piano, organ. Home: 30 Marsh Side Dr Yarmouth Port MA 02675

MCGILL, HENRY COLEMAN, JR. pathologist, educator, researcher; b. Nashville, Oct. 1, 1921; s. Henry Coleman and Thursa (Lowry) McG.; m. Cloace Laurite Ferguson, Sept. 12, 1945; children: Margaret Ann, Laurilynn, Elizabeth Gail. BA, Vanderbilt U., 1943, MD, 1946. Intern Vanderbilt Hosp., Nashville, 1946-47; asst. prof. pathology La. State U. Med. Ctr., New Orleans, 1950-55, assoc. prof., 1955-61, prof., chmn. dept., 1961-66; prof. patholoyg U. Tex. Health Sci. Ctr., San Antonio, 1966-92, chmn. dept., 1966-72; sci. dir. S.W. Found. for Biomed. Rsch., 1978-92, sr. scientist, 1992-96, sr. scientist emeritus, 1996—. Contbr. articles to med. jours. Capt. M.C., U.S. Army, 1948-50. Mem. Phi Beta Kappa, Sigma Xi, Alpha Omega Alpha. Home: 4102 Fawnridge Dr San Antonio TX 78229-4212 Office: PO Box 760549 San Antonio TX 78245-0549 E-mail: hmcgill@icarus.sfbr.org.

MCGILL, JOHN J. radiologist; b. Denver, Nov. 26, 1965; BA, U. Calif., Berkeley, 1988; MD, Creighton U., Omaha, Nebr., 1992. Diplomate Am. Bd. Radiology. With Associated Radiologists, Ltd., Scottsdale, Ariz. Office: Associated Radiologists Ltd 1125 E Southern Ave # 300 Mesa AZ 85204-5011

MCGILL, JOHN KNOX, lawyer; b. Charlotte, N.C., Aug. 25, 1956; s. John Charles and Mabel (Hamilton) Mc.; m. Elizabeth Roxanne Bondurant. BS in Bus. cum laude, Erskine Coll., 1978; MBA, JD, U. N.C., 1982. Bar: N.C. 1983; CPA, N.C. Ptnr., tax atty. Garland & Alala, P.A., Gastonia, N.C., 1982-86; tax atty., pub. Blair, McGill & Co., Inc., Charlotte, 1986—. Chmn., bd. dirs. Blair, McGill & Co., Inc., Charlotte; bd. dirs., founder, Advanced Pension Systems, Inc., Charlotte. Tax editor: Dental Economics Mag., 1982—; editor-in-chief: (newsletter) The Blair, McGill Advisory; contbr. editor: (textbook) Contemporary Marketing (4th edition, 1983. Bd. trustees Erskine Coll., 1998—; treas. 1st Assoc. Reformed Presbyn. Ch., Gastonia, N.C., 1989-94, deacon, 1989-94, elder, 1995-98. Recipient Tax Law scholarship, Touche, Ross & Co., CPA's, 1982. Mem. ABA, N.C. Bar Assn., Am. Inst. CPA's, N.C. Assn. CPA's, Sertoma Club (Disting. Svc award, Kings Mt. N.C., 1983). Republican. Avocations: jogging, basketball, baseball, snow skiing, card/stamp collecting. Home: 905 Cloister Dr Gastonia NC 28056-6629 Office: Blair McGill & Co Inc 2810 Coliseum Centre Dr Ste 360 Charlotte NC 28217-4622

MCGILL, JUDY ANNELL MCGEE, early childhood and elementary educator; b. Kosciusko, Miss., Oct. 16, 1949; d. Reeves and Martha Lee (Thompson) McGee; m. Ronald Eugene McGill, June 5, 1971; 1 child, Thomas Eugene. Student, U. Colo., 1979, James Madison U., 1974; BS, Miss. State U., 1971; MEd, Northeast La. U., 1984. 4th grade tchr. Harrison County Schs., Gulfport, Miss., 1971; 1st and 2d grade tchr. Oktibbeha County Schs., Starkville, 1971-72; 4th grade tchr. Natchez-Adams (Miss.) County Schs., 1972-74; 2d and 3d grade tchr. Shenandoah County Schs., Woodstock, Va., 1974-78; elem. tchr. Jefferson County Schs., Lakewood, Colo., 1980-81; 7th and 8th grade tchr. Ouachita Parish Schs., Monroe, La., 1982; elem. sch. tchr. Union Parish Schs., Farmerville, 1982-85; early childhood and elem. tchr. Ouachita Parish Schs., Monroe, 1985-95; master tchr., intern assessor Ouachita Parish Schs., 1993-95; elem. tchr. Scottsboro (Ala.) City Schs., 1995—, Hands-On Activity Sci. Program lead tchr. and insvc. instr., 1998—. In-svc. instr. Natchez-Adams County Schs., 1972-74, Shenandoah County Schs., 1974-78; trainer Sci. Rsch. Assocs., Woodstock, 1978; chairperson curriculum revision Ouachita Parish Schs., 1986-92, staff devel. trainer, 1990-92. Den leader Boy Scouts Am., West Monroe, La., 1986-88; sponsor Young Astronauts Coun., 1995--. Grantee La. Quality in Sci. and Math., 1994-95, Jr. League Monroe, 1994-95, MEAD, 1997-98. Mem. NEA, ASCD, La. Assn. on Children Under Six (Jane Herrin grantee 1987, v.p., program chair 1988-94), N.E. La. Reading Coun. (chair grants 1987-88, Reading Tchr. of Yr. 1987-88). Methodist. Avocations: downhill skiing, target shooting, sourdough baking. Home: 2185 July Mountain Blvd Scottsboro AL 35768-7502 E-mail: jamcgill@scottsboro.org.

MCGILL, KENNETH, JR. mental health services professional; b. Paterson, N.J., Aug. 22, 1965; s. Kenneth and Shirley A. McG.;m. Barbara Joan, Dec. 27, 1989; children: Megan Elizabeth, Shannon Eileen BA, William Paterson Coll., 1989; MA in Edn., Seton Hall U., 1995; Ednl. Specialist, 1999. Social Worker N.J., cert. Hypnotherapist Am. Bd. Clin. Hypnotherapy, lic. Marriage and Family Therapist. Mental health worker Wayne (N.J.) Gen. Hosp., 1989-90; case supr. N.J. Superior Ct. Essex County, Newark, 1990-95; adj. prof. psychology William Paterson U., Wayne, 1995—; asst. dir. admissions, evalns., 1996-99; marriage and family therapist St. Mary's Counseling Svcs., Pompton Lakes, N.J., 1998—; owner, pres., therapist Bergen-Passaic Psychol. Assocs., LLC, North Haledon, 1999—. Bd. dirs. Apraxia Network Bergen County, Paramus, N.J., 2000—. Reviewer books. Asst. soccer coach North Haledon Soccer Assn., 2000. Mem. APA, ACA, Am. Assn Marriage and Family Counselors, Mental Health Assn. Passaic County (bd. dirs. 1993-96, 2000—), Assn. Christian Counselors, KC (1st, 2nd degree 1995, 3rd degree 1996, Knight of the Month 1997), Ancient Order Hibernians, Psi Chi. Democrat. Roman Catholic. Avocations: mountain biking, hiking, sketching, writing. Office: Bergen-Passaic Psychol Assocs LLC 552 High Mountain Rd North Haledon NJ 07508-2660 E-mail: mcgillkb@bellatlantic.net.

MCGILL, LAWRENCE DAVID, veterinary pathologist; b. Waverly, Nebr., Mar. 24, 1944; s. Stanley Raymond and Phyllis Roylene (Quick) McG.; m. Cheryl Lynn Nelson, 1966 (div. Jan. 1974); m. Marilyn Sue Nyren, June 15, 1975; children: Marchelle Elizabeth, Mark Stanley-John. Student, U. Nebr., 1962-64; BS, Okla. State U., 1966, DVM, 1968; PhD, Tex. A&M U., College Station, 1972. Diplomate Am. Coll. Vet. Pathologists. Asst. prof. U. Minn., St. Paul, 1971-72, U. Nebr., Lincoln, 1972-77; vet. pathologist Vet. Reference Lab., Salt Lake City, 1977-81, chief pathologist, 1981-85, med. dir. San Leandro, Calif., 1985-88; dir. contract rsch. Animal Reference Pathology, Salt Lake City, 1988-91, asst. v.p., 1991-93; v.p., 1993—. Mem. fed. reg. com. Am. Coll. Vet. Pathologists, 1993—. Contbr. articles to profl. jours. Singer, bd. dirs. Utah Symphony Chorus, Salt Lake City, 1979—; bd. dirs. Iron Blosum Lodge, Snowbird, Utah. NIH postdoctoral fellow, 1968-71; named Veterinarian of Yr., Utah, 1990. Mem. Am. Vet. Med. Assn., Utah Vet. Med. Assn. (chair pub. rels. 1988-90, pres.-elect 1995), Salt Lake Vet. Med. Assn. (pres.-elect 1992, pres. 1993), Masons, Order Ea. Star. Republican. Methodist. Avocations: fishing, carpentry, wood working, gardening, reading. Home: 8288 Top Of The World Dr Salt Lake City UT 84121-6032 Office: Animal Reference Pathology 500 Chipeta Way Salt Lake City UT 84108-1221

MCGILL, MAURICE LEON, financial executive; b. Malden, Mo., Aug. 22, 1936; s. William Howard and Iris (Phillips) McG.; m. Wanda Coral Wirt, Feb. 2, 1957; children— Melany, Melinda, William Shannon BS, U. Mo., 1958, MA, 1959. C.P.A., Mo., Iowa, Ariz. Mgr. Touche, Ross, Bailey & Smart, Kansas City, Mo., 1959-64; fin. v.p., treas. Iowa Beef Packers, Inc., Dakota City, Nebr., 1964-69; exec. v.p., treas. Spencer Foods, Inc., Iowa, 1969-71, also dir.; sr. v.p. Diamond Reo Trucks, Inc., Lansing, Mich., 1971-72; fin. v.p. Ariz. Colo. Land & Cattle Co., Phoenix, 1972-75; ptnr. Touche Ross & Co., 1975-81; exec. v.p. fin. and adminstrn., treas., bd. dirs. IBP, Inc., Dakota City, Nebr., 1981-89; pres., bd. dirs. Wirmac Corp., Garland, Tex., 1989—. Bd. dirs. Bluebonnet Savs. Bank, Dallas, Premium Std. Farms, Kansas City, Mo., Prodeo Techs. Inc., Phoenix. Mem. AICPA, Iowa Soc. CPAs. Home: 3318 S Country Club Rd Garland TX 75043-1314 E-mail: mandwmcgill@msn.com.

MCGILL, MICHAEL JOHN, computer/information scientist; b. Detroit; s. Jack Arthur and Margaret Mary (Woodcock) McG.; m. Jennifer Joan Kuehn, Dec. 2, 1977; children: Erin Kuehn, Andrew Kuehn. BA, Syracuse U., 1968, PhD, 1973. Asst. prof. SUNY, Oswego, 1972-74; assoc. prof. Syracuse U., 1974-80; sr. info./computer advisor U.S. EPA, Washington, 1980-81; program dir. NSF, 1981-83; v.p. OCLC Inc., Dublin, 1983-90; v.p. ind. mktg. Ameritech Info. Systems, 1990-92; chief info. officer U. Mich., Ann Arbor, 1992-98; v.p., chief info. officer Henry Ford Health Sys., Detroit, 1998—. Author: Modern Information Retrieval, 1983; contbr. articles to profl. jours. Author: Modern Information Retrieval, 1983; contbr. articles to profl. jours. Bd. dirs. Arthritis Found. Cen. Ohio, Columbus, 1988—. NSF grantee, 1976—. Fellow AAAS (coun. mem. 1990—); mem. ACM (Spl. Interest Group for Info Retrieval, editor, treas., vice chmn.). Home: 8055 Golfview Ct Columbus OH 43235-1230 Office: Henry Ford Health Sys 1 Ford Pl Fl 2E Detroit MI 48202-3450

MCGILL, ROBERT ERNEST, III, retired manufacturing company executive; b. San Francisco, Apr. 30, 1931; s. Robert Ernest and Madeleine Melanie (Ignace) McG.; m. Daphne Urquhart Driver, Apr. 26, 1958; children: Robert Ernest, Meredith Louise, Christina Elizabeth, James Alexander. BA, Williams Coll., 1954; MBA, Harvard U., 1956. With Morgan Stanley & Co. (investment bankers), N.Y.C., 1956-63; mem. fin. staff Air Products & Chems., Inc., Allentown, Pa., 1963-64, dir. corp. planning and devel., 1964-68; v.p. Gen. Interiors Corp., N.Y.C., 1968-70, exec. v.p., 1970-73; v.p. fin. Ethan Allen, Inc., Danbury, Conn., 1973-75; v.p. fin., sec. Dexter Corp., Windsor Locks, 1975-83, sr. v.p. fin. and adminstrn., 1983-88, exec. v.p., 1989-94; pres. Kettlebrook Ins. Co. Ltd., 1983-93, chmn., 1993-94; pres. Dexter Credit Corp., 1982-88; mng. ptnr. The Berkshires Capital Investors, L.P. Bd. dirs. Lydall, Inc.; bd. mgrs. Travelers Funds for Variable Annuities; trustee Travelers Mut. Fund. Trustee Assn. des Amis L'Abbaye Valmont, Williamstown Arts Conservation Ctr., Atlanta Art Conservation Ctr. Home: 295 Hancock Rd Williamstown MA 01267-3005

MCGILL, WILLIAM JAMES, JR. university official, writer; b. St. Louis, Mar. 25, 1936; s. William James Sr. and Ethel (Williams) McG.; m. Ellen Buck, June 18, 1960; children: Sara Louise, Susan Elizabeth, Alison Marcia. BA, Trinity Coll., 1957; MA, Harvard U., 1958, PhD, 1961, grad. Inst. Ednl. Mgmt., 1989; LLD, Lebenon Valley Coll., 1998. Instr. history Western Md. Coll., Westminster, 1960-62; asst. prof. history Alma (Mich.) Coll., 1962-68, assoc. prof., 1968-72; dean of coll. Washington & Jefferson Coll., Washington, 1972-75, prof. history, 1972-84; asst. dir., div. edn. programs NEH, 1984-86; v.p., dean faculty Lebanon Valley Coll., Annville, Pa., 1986-98, acting pres.,

1987-88. Author: Maria Theresa, 1972, The Rock Springs Chronicles, 1999; contbr. 65 articles to profl. jours., 46 book revs., 15 short stories, numerous poems; poetry editor Spitball Mag., 1993—, mng. editor, 2000—. Assoc. to rector St. Luke's Episc. Ch., Lebanon, Pa., 1986-98; priest-in-charge St. George's Episc. Ch., Waynesburg, Pa., 1974-83; actor Washington Theater Wing, 1984-86, Gretna Playhouse, Mt. Gretna, Pa., 1987-90; bd. dirs. Lebanon County United Way, 1987-95, Gretna Prodns., Mt. Gretna, 1986-90, 91-92, Concertante, 1999-2001; trustee Penn Sch. Art and Design, 1992—. Mem. Phi Beta Kappa. Avocations: sailing, writing, acting. Home: PO Box 682 Cornwall PA 17016-0682 E-mail: wjmcgill@earthlink.net.

MCGILL, WILLIS ALEXANDER, anesthesiologist; b. Cairo, July 1, 1941; s. Willis Alexander and Anne (McAuley) M.; m. Robin Louise Blake, Aug. 2, 1965; children: Margaret Anne McGill Mantz, Leslie Marie McGill Dale, Erin Suzanne. MD, U. Pitts., 1967. Cert. anesthesiology. Intern York Hosp., 1967-68; resident in anesthesiology Naval Hosp., Phila., 1970-73; fellow in pediatric anesthesiology Children's Hosp., 1973; attending anesthesiologist Children's Nat. Med. Ctr., Washington, 1976—, chmn., 1985-97. Prof. anesthesiology George Washington U. Sch. Medicine, 1990—; pres. Children's Faculty Assocs., Washington, 1987-88. Fellow Am. Acad. Pediatrics; mem. AMA, Am. Soc. Anesthesiologists, MDDS CA, Acad. Anesthesiology (pres. 1991-92). Office: Childrens Nat Med Ctr 111 Michigan Ave NW Washington DC 20010-2916 E-mail: wmcgill@cnmc.org.

MCGILLICUDDY, JOAN MARIE, psychotherapist, consultant; b. Chgo., June 23, 1952; d. James Neal and Muriel (Joy) McG. BA, U. Ariz., 1974, MS, 1976; PhD, Walden U., 1996. Cert. nat. counselor. Counselor ACTION, Tucson, 1976; counselor, clin. supr. Behavioral Health Agy. Cen. Ariz., Casa Grande, 1976-81; instr. psychology Cen. Ariz. Coll., 1978-83; therapist, co-dir. Helping Assocs., Inc., 1982—, v.p., sec., 1982—; cert. instr. Silva Method Mind Devel., Tucson, 1986—. Mem. Mayor's Com. for Handicapped, Casa Grande, 1989-90, Human Svcs. Planning, Casa Grande, 1985-95. Named Outstanding Am. Lectr. Silva Mind Internat., 1988-99. Mem. ACA. Avocations: jogging, singing. Office: Helping Assocs Inc 1901 N Trekell Rd Casa Grande AZ 85222-1706

MC GILLICUDDY, JOHN FRANCIS, retired banker; b. Harrison, N.Y., Dec. 30, 1930; s. Michael J. and Anna (Munro) McG.; m. Constance Burtis, Sept. 9, 1954; children: Michael Sean, Faith Burtis Benoit, Constance Erin Mc Gillicuddy Mills, Brian Munro, John Walsh. AB, Princeton, 1952; LL.B., Harvard, 1955. With Mfrs. Hanover Trust Co. subs. Mfrs. Hanover Corp., N.Y.C., 1958-91, v.p., 1962-66, sr. v.p., 1966-69, exec. v.p., asst. to chmn., 1969-70, vice chmn., dir., 1970, pres., 1971-79, chmn., chief exec. officer, 1979-91; chmn. bd., chief exec. officer Chem. Banking Corp., 1992-93, ret., 1994. Bd. dirs. USX Corp. (now USSteel Corp), So. Pero Copper Co., Kelso, Inc., Empire Blue Cross and Blue Shield Bd. dirs. Nat. Multiple Sclerosis Soc.; life trustee, chmn. emeritus N.Y. Presbyn. Hosp., N.Y. Pub. Libr.; trustee emeritus Princeton U.; pres. Boy Scouts Am., Greater N.Y. Couns. Lt. (j.g.) USNR, 1955-58. Mem. Bus. Coun., Westchester Country Club (Rye, N.Y.), Blind Brook Club (Port Chester, N.Y.), Princeton Club (N.Y.C.), Augusta Nat. Golf Club (Ga.), Pine Valley Golf Club (N.J.), Laurel Valley Golf Club (Ligonier, Pa.), Seminole Golf Club (north Palm Beach, Fla.), Links Club (N.Y.C.), Sky Club (N.Y.C.). Roman Catholic. Office: JP Morgan Chase Corp 270 Park Ave New York NY 10017-2014

MCGILLIVRAY, DONALD DEAN, seed company executive, agronomist; b. Muscatine, Iowa, Aug. 28, 1928; s. Walter C. and Pearl E. (Potter) McG.; m. Betty J. Anderson, June 24, 1951; children: Ann E., Jean M. BS in Agronomy, Iowa State U., 1950. Asst. mgr. Iowa, Minn., Wis. sect. Funk Seeds Internat., Belle Plaine, Iowa, 1965-69, mgr., 1969-70, mgr. hybrid corn ops. Bloomington, Ill., 1970-75, v.p. ops., 1976-82, pres., 1982-88; assoc. Smart Seeds, Inc., 1989—. Dir. U.S. Grains Coun., Washington, 1984-87. Bd. dirs. Ill. Agrl. Leadership Found., Macomb, 1985—, chmn. bd., 1990-2000; bd. dirs. Ill. Wesleyan Assocs., 1986-89, Ill. 4-H Found., 1996—; mem. adv. bd. Bro-Menn Hosp., 1985—, pres., 1989-90. Sgt. U.S. Army, 1951-53. Mem. Am. Seed Trade Assn. (bd. dirs. 1986-, divsn. chmn. 1978-79, 2d v.p. 1986-87, 1st v.p. 1987-88, pres. 1988-89), Am. Seed Rsch. Found. (bd. dirs. 1982-95, pres. 1984-87), Exch. Club, Masons.

MCGILLIVRAY, KAREN, retired elementary school educator; b. Richland, Oreg., Aug. 24, 1936; d. Kenneth Melton and Catharina (Sass) McG. BS in Edn. cum laude, Ea. Oreg. State U., 1958; MRE, Pacific Sch. Religion, 1963. Cert. tchr., Oreg. 4th grade tchr. Salem (Oreg.)-Keizer Pub. Schs.; ret., 1995. Contbr. articles, stories to ednl. mags. U.S. Govt. grantee. Mem.: NEA (rep. assembly), Salem Edn. Assn. (officer), Oreg. Ret. Educators Assn. (officer), Oreg. Edn. Assn. (rep. assembly), NEA-Ret. Oreg. (state officer), Wash. State Scottish Terrier Club, Cascade Scottish Terrier Club, Scottish Terrier Club Am., Phi Delta Kappa (officer), Delta Kappa Gamma (officer). Methodist. Home: 325 SW Cedarwood Ave Mcminnville OR 97128-5813

MC GIMSEY, CHARLES ROBERT, III, anthropologist; b. Dallas, June 18, 1925; s. Charles Robert, Jr. and Ellen Randolph (Parks) McG.; m. Mary Elizabeth Conger, Dec. 20, 1949; children— Charles Robert, Brian Keith, Mark Douglass. Student, Vanderbilt U., 1942-43, U. of South, 1943-44; BA, U. N.Mex., 1949; MA, Harvard U., 1954, PhD, 1958. Instr. U. Ark., Fayetteville, 1957, asst. prof., 1958-62, assoc. prof., 1962-67, prof. anthropology, 1967-90, prof. emeritus, 1990—, chmn. dept., 1969-72; asst. curator U. Ark. Mus., 1957-59, dir., 1959-83, Ark. Archeol. Survey, 1967-90, dir. emeritus, 1990—. Cons. archeology U.S. GAO, 1979-87, U.S.-Internat. Com. on Monuments and Sites; Rep. to Internat. Com. on Archeol. Heritage Mgmt., 1988-95. Author: (with G.R. Willey) Monagrillo Culture of Panama, 1954, Mariana Mesa, 1980, Indians of Arkansas, 1969, Public Archeology, 1972, Archeology and Archeological Resources, 1973, (with H.A. Davis) The Management of Archeological Resources, 1977; assoc. editor Am. Antiquity, 1972-80; Co-editor (with H. A. Davis) Southeastern Museums Conf., 1964-73; Contbr. articles to profl. jours. Mem. Ark. Rev. Com., Historic Preservation Program, 1968-76; collaborator Nat. Park Service, 1971-74, adviser, 1974-77; mem. Com. on Recovery Archeol. Remains, 1971-78; mem. adv. bd. dirs. Red River Mus., 1975-76; mem. adv. bd. Am. Indian Archeol. Inst., 1975-80, Ark. Natural and Cultural Heritage Dept., 1976-90. Served to lt. (j.g.) USNR, 1943-47. Recipient Cert. Recognition State of Ark., 1990; rsch. grantee Am. Philos. Soc., Am. Acad. Arts and Scis., Andean Rsch. Inst., Nat. Park Service, NSF, Smithsonian Instn., Wenner-Gren Found.; rsch. fellow dept. archaeology U. Cambridge, 1985-86, assoc. mem. Darwin Coll., 1985— Fellow: Am. Anthrop. Assn.; mem.: Am. Assn. State and Local History (award of merit 1985), Am. Assn. Mus., Soc. Profl. Archeologists (founder, bd. dirs. 1976—79, pres. 1983—84, emeritus, life, Seiberling 1989, presidential recognition award 1997), Am. Soc. Conserv. Archeology (founding, outstanding contrib. 1980), Southeastern Mus. Conf. (coun. 1962—71, editor 1964—77), Ark. Archeol. Soc. (editor 1960—83, Preservationist 1989), Soc. Am. Archeology (pres. 1974—75, Distinguished Serv. 1975, excellence in cultural resource mgt. 1995), Registered Prof. Archeologists. Home: 435 W Hawthorn St Fayetteville AR 72701-1935 Office: Ark Archeol Survey 2475 N Hatch Ave Fayetteville AR 72704-5590

MCGING, NOREEN MARIE, health services professional; b. Chgo. d. John Francis and Nora Philomena (Barnicle) McG. BSN, Loyola U., Chgo., 1981. Cert. med.-surg. nurse, ANA. Staff nurse surg. unit St. Joseph Hosp. and Health Care Ctr., Chgo., 1981-86, dir. staffing support svcs., 1986-89; project dir. Cath. Health Alliance for Met. Chgo., Ill., 1989-95; dir. quality mgmt. Transitional Hosp. Corp., 1995—. Active Art Inst. Chgo., Ill., 1980—, Chgo. Coun. on Fgn. Rels., 1991—. Mem. Am. Orgn. Nurse Execs. (exec. mem.), Ill. Orgn. Nurse Execs. (exec. mem.), Nat. Assn. for Healthcare Quality (exec. mem.), Ill. Assn. for Healthcare Quality (exec. mem.).

MCGINLEY, EDWARD STILLMAN, II, retired military officer, engineering executive; b. Allentown, Pa., June 9, 1939; s. Edward Stillman and Dorothy Mae McGinley; m. Connie Lee Mayo, July 1, 1962; children: Amanda Lee, Edward Stillman III. BS, U.S. Naval Acad., 1961; advanced degree in naval architecture, MIT, 1970; MSA, George Washington U., 1972; cert. exec. program, U. Va., 1981. Commd. ensign USN, 1961, advanced through grades to rear adm., 1990, various positions in submarine engring., 1962-76, repair officer S.C., 1976-83; ops. mgr. Mare Island Naval Shipyard, Vallejo, Calif., 1983-87; comdr. Norfolk Naval Shipyard, Portsmouth, Va., 1987-90; maintenance officer U.S. Pacific Fleet, Honolulu, 1990-93; comdr. Naval Surface Warfare Ctr., Washington, 1993-94; vice-comdr. Naval Sea Sys. Command, 1994-96; sr. engring. duty officer USN, 1994-96; ret., 1996; v.p. project direction Fluor Daniel, Hanford, Wash., 1997-98; dir. govt. svcs. Fluor Corp., Washington, 1999-2000, cons. to DOD, 2001—02; cons. Inst. Def. Analyses Flour Corp., Hunt Corp., 2002—. Contbr. articles to profl. jours. Decorated Navy Disting. Svc. medal; recipient Envrion. award, Sec. of Navy, 1987, Productivity Improvement award, Inst. Indsl. Egnrs., 1988, Quality Improvement award, Office Mgmt. and Budget, 1989, Productivity award, U.S. Senate, 1990. Mem.: U.S. Naval Inst., Am. Soc. Naval Engrs., Capital Hill Exch. Club (bd. dirs.), Tau Beta Pi, Sigma Xi. Republican. Mem. United Ch. Of Christ. Avocations: art, running.

MCGINLEY, JOHN REGIS, JR. lawyer; b. Pitts., Nov. 26, 1943; s. John R. and Marie E. (Rooney) McGinley. BS, St. Bonaventure U., 1965; JD, Duquesne U., 1968. Bar: Pa. 1968, U.S. Dist. Ct. (we. dist.) Pa. 1968, U.S. Ct. Appeals (3d cir.) 1973, U.S. Supreme Ct. 1983. Asst. dist. atty. Allegheny County, Pa., 1968-70; ptnr. Eckert Seamans Cheein & Mellott; assoc. Duff Grogan & Doyle & Duff, Grogan Graffam, Pitts., 1970—71; chmn. Grogan, Graffam, McGinley, 1971—2002; ptnr. Eckert Seaman Cherin & Mellott, 2002—. Mem. disciplinary bd. Pa. Supreme Ct.; mem., chmn. Pa. Ind. Regulatory Rev. Commn.; adj. prof. law Duquesne U. Sch. Law. Contbr. . Trustee Mercy Hosp. Found.; former trustee St. Bonaventure U., mem. exec. com. Fellow: Am. Coll. Trial Lawyers; mem.: ABA, Duquesne U. Law Alumni (pres. 1998), Acad. Trial Lawyers, Allegheny County Bar Assn., Pa. Bar Assn. Office: 4th Fl US Steel Tower 600 Grant St Pittsburgh PA 15219

MCGINLEY, JOSEPH PATRICK, brokerage house executive; b. Phila., Mar. 17, 1947; s. Joseph Robert and Kathaleen (Brennan) McG.; m. Linda L. Irvin, May 15, 1970 (div. 1981); children: Lisa C., Andrew S.; m. Sharon A. Malloy, Sept. 7, 1984; 1 child, Christopher J. BSBA, Villanova U., 1965-69. Sr. v.p. Morgan Stanley, Phila., 1974—. Bd. dirs. Tara Investments Ltd., Phila., Florence Ave. Corp., Phila. Co-founder A Better Chance of Lower Merion; bd. dirs. Phila. City Sail; pres. Friends of the Maya Pa. Mus. Mem. Union League Yacht Club (past commodore), Union League of Phila., Cynwyd Club, Corinthian Yacht Club (Phila.). Republican. Roman Catholic. Avocation: yachting. Office: Morgan Stanley Dean Witter 2 Logan Sq Philadelphia PA 19103-2707

MCGINN, BERNARD JOHN, religious educator; b. Yonkers, N.Y., Aug. 19, 1937; s. Bernard John and Catherine Ann (Faulds) McG.; m. Patricia Ann Ferris, July 10, 1971; children: Daniel, John. BA, St. Joseph's Sem., Yonkers, N.Y., 1959; Licentiate in Sacred Theology, Gregorian U., Rome, 1963; PhD, Brandeis U., 1970. Diocesan priest Archdiocese N.Y., N.Y.C., 1963-71; prof. U. Chgo., 1969—, Naomi Shenstone Donnelly Prof., 1992—. Program coord. Inst. for Advanced Study of Religion, Divinity Sch., U. Chgo., 1980-92. Author: The Calabrian Abbott, 1985, Meister Eckhart, 1986, Foundations of Mysticism, 1991, Growth of Mysticism, 1994, Antichrist, 1994, Flowering of Mysticism, 1998; editor: (series) Classics of Western Spirituality, 1978, (book) God and Creation, 1990. Fellow Medieval Acad. Am., Am. Acad. Arts and Scis. Home: 5701 S Kenwood Ave Chicago IL 60637-1718 Office: U Chgo Divinity Sch 1025 E 58th St Chicago IL 60637-1509 E-mail: bmcginn@midway.uchicago.edu.

MCGINN, CHERIE M. secondary education educator; b. Oil City, Pa., Feb. 5, 1949; d. Rendall Baxter amd Helen Joyce (Kunselman) Agnew; 1 child from previous marriage, Joshua Edward; m. Stephen James McGinn, Jan. 1, 1983; 1 child, Kathleen Erin. BS, Clarion State Coll., 1971. Cert. secondary tchr., Md. Grad. asst. Clarion (Pa.) State Coll., 1971-72; tchr. Montgomery County Pub. Schs., 1972—. Chmn. Montgomery Blair H.S., Silver Spring, Md., 1994—; cons. curriculum, Upper Marlboro, Md.; panelist Odyssey 1984, Excellence in Edn., Md. Humanities Con., Balt., 1984; vol. reader grant proposal Coun. for Basic Edn., fellow, 1983, 91, NIH, Washington, 1984—. Fellow NEH, 1989, 92, 95, 2000. Mem. ASCD, NEA, Nat. Coum. for Social Studies, U.S. Capitol Hist. Soc., Md. Social Studies Assn., Montgomery County Social Studies Coun., Md. Tchrs. Assn., Montgomery County Educators Assn. Democrat. Unitarian Universalist. Home: 14228 Rutherford Rd Upper Marlboro MD 20774-8564 Office: Montgomery Blair HS 51 University Blvd E Silver Spring MD 20901-2451 E-mail: Cherie_McGinn@fc.mcps.k12.md.us.

MCGINN, DANIEL G. public relations executive; B in Congl. Studies, Georgetown U. Staff mem. for 2 W.Va. congressmen House Ways and Means Com.; founder Ryan McGinn, 1987—98; dep. chmn. Weber Pub. Rels. Worldwide, Cambridge, 1998; pres. & CEO The McGinn Group, 2001—. Founder, "Cause for Celebration," provides birthday parties to homeless and needy children. Office: The McGinn Group 2300 Clarendon Blvd., Ste. 901 Arlington VA 22201*

MCGINN, DENNIS VINCENT, career officer; b. Attleboro, Mass. m. Kelly Harris; children: Susan, John, David, Daniel. Grad., U.S. Naval Acad., 1967. Commd. ensign USN, 1967, advanced through grades to vice adm., 1998; served in combat deployments USS Ranger; landing signal officer, weapons officer Squadron 113; ops. & maintenance officer Attack Squadron 146 USS Constellation; exec. officer USS Coral Sea; air warfare officer VX-5, China Lake, Calif.; chief test pilot strike directorate Naval Air Test Ctr., Patuxent River, Md.; chief naval ops. fellow Strategic Studies Group; chief info. sys., chief negotiator Supreme Hdqs. Allied Powers, Europe, Casteau, Belgium; commdg. officer Light Attack Weapons Sch., Attack Squadron 27, F/A-18 Replacement Air Group Strike Fighter Squadron 125, USS Ranger, 1991-93; commdr. Carrier Group 1 Pacific Fleet Carrier Battle Groups; dir. Air Warfare Divsn. Office Chief Naval Ops., 1996-98; comdr. U.S. Navy Third Fleet, 1998-2000, DCNO Warfare Requirements and Programs, 2000—02. Decorated Def. Superior Svc. Medal, 2 Legion Merit awards, DFC, DSM, others. Office: OPNAV N7 2000 Navy Pentagon Washington DC 20350-2000

MCGINN, HOWARD FRANCIS, library director, educator; b. Pitts., Sept. 14, 1943; s. Howard Francis and Sarah Louise (Briggs) McG.; m. Mary Louise Keim (div. Nov. 1994); children: Kristin Louise, Kevin Christopher; m. Jane Florez Moore, Sept. 2, 1995; 1 child, Samantha Haley. BA, Villanova U., 1966; MS in Libr. Sci., Drexel U., 1970; MBA, Campbell U., 1985. Editor Cath. Periodical Index, Cath. Libr. Assn., Haverford, Pa., 1966-68; asst. dir. Ryan Libr., St. Charles Sem., Phila., 1968-71; mktg. coord., mgr. audiovisual sales J.B. Lippincott Pub. Co., 1972-78; mng. editor, gen. mgr. N.Y. Times Co.'s Microfilming Corp. Am., Sanford, N.C., 1978-83; from network cons. to state libr. State of N.C., Divsn. State Libr., Raleigh, 1985-92; dir. Emporia (Kans.) Pub. Libr., 1992-97; exec. dir. Portland (Oreg.) Area Libr. Network, 1995-97; city libr. New Haven (Conn.) Free Pub. Libr., 1997-2000; dean univ. librs. Clarion U. of Pa., 2000—. Mem. network adv. com. Libr. of Congress, Washington, 1990-92. Contbr. chpts. to books and articles to profl. jours. Gubernatorial appointee N.C. 2000, Raleigh, 1992; bd. dirs. Friends of Grove St. Cemetery, New Haven, 1998-2000; sec. bd. dirs. Hill Youth Coop., Inc., New Haven, 1998—; bd. dirs., Pa. Acad. Libr. Consortium, Inc.; mayoral appointee Greater New Haven Cable Adv. Bd., 1998-2000; minority recruiting coun. State of Ct. Dept. Children and Families, 1999-2000. Recipient Dir. of Yr. award N.C. Pub. Libr. Dir.'s Assn., 1990, Annual Achievement award Fiesta de Loisa, Conn., 2000. Mem. ALA (Exceptional Achievement award 1989, Edwards Trust award 1993, mem. black caucus), Pa. Libr. Assn., Rotary, Phi Kappa Phi. Democrat. Roman Catholic. Avocations: track and field, travel. Home: PO Box 46 Clarion PA 16214 Office: Carlson Library Clarion University Clarion PA 16214 E-mail: hmcginn@clarion.edu.

MCGINN, JAMES THOMAS, writer, producer; b. Evanston, Ill., Feb. 19, 1932; s. John Thomas and Mary (Kidney) McG.; m. Patricia Kay McMurtry, Apr. 4, 1959; children: Shannon, Michael, Sean. BS, Northwestern U., 1953, MA, 1958. Floor dir. Sta. WGN-TV, 1956-57; writer, dir. Ency. Britannica Films, Wilmette, Ill., 1957-58; pres. McGinn TV Prodns., Chgo., 1958-62; exec. producer Sta. WBBM-TV, 1962-63; gen. program exec. Young and Rubicam, N.Y.C., 1963-69; dir. programming Bristol-Myers Squibb Co., Pacific Palisades, Calif., 1969-94; pres. Palisades Prodns., Inc., 1994—. Bd. dirs. Paulist Prodns., Pacific Palisades; faculty U. So. Calif. Sch. Cinema & TV. Producer: In Search Of...; writer: (TV film) Nadia, 1984, (TV spl.) Perry Como's Christmas in San Antonio, (TV series) Julia, Capital Cities Family Spls., Insight; playwright: Before You Go, The Singing Weatherman, Star Billing (with Alex Cohen), Viola: Seven Days in Selma, Vinnie, Replacing Pamela. Mem. Writers Guild Am., Dramatists Guild. Office: Palisades Prodns Inc 15219 W Sunset Blvd Ste 202 Pacific Palisades CA 90272-3607

MCGINN, MARY J. lawyer, insurance company executive; b. St. Louis, Apr. 9, 1947; d. Martin J. and Janet McGinn; m. Bernard H. Shapiro, Sept. 6, 1971; children: Sara, Colleen, Molly, Daniel. BA, Dominican U., River Forest, Ill., 1967; JD, St. Louis U., 1970. Bar: Mo. 1970, Ill. 1971. Atty. tax div. U.S. Dept. Justice, Washington, 1970-73; atty. Allstate Ins. Co., Northbrook, Ill., 1973—, v.p., dep. gen. counsel, 1980—. Mem. ABA, Am. Coll. Investment Counsel, Assn. Life Ins. Counsel. Roman Catholic. Home: 155 N Buckley Rd Barrington IL 60010-2607 Office: Allstate Ins Co 3075 Sanders Rd Ste G5A Northbrook IL 60062-7127 E-mail: mmcginn@allstate.com.

MCGINN, TERENCE JAMES, business consultant, minister; b. Rochester, N.Y., Oct. 18, 1950; s. James Edward III and Diane Edwina (Jewell) Ging; m. Kathie Jo Stirk, June 26, 1976 (div. 1984); 1 child, John F. Terris. BA, St. John Fisher Coll., 1972; MDiv, Colgate Rochester Div. Sch., 1975; PhD, U. Mich., 1986, MBA, 1995. Ordained to ministry Am. Bapt. Ch., 1976. Campus min. Am. Bapt. Campus Found., Ann Arbor, Mich., 1980-84; Employee Assistance Prog. mgr. NBD Bank, Detroit, 1988-90, regional mgr. human resources, 1991-93; adj. faculty U. Mich., Ann Arbor, 1990—; pastor Northside Cmty. Ch., 1992—2001; cons. Career Directions, 1994—, Orion Internat., Ann Arbor, 1996—. Bd. dirs. Eden Found., Fairmount, Ind. Avocations: vocal performance, Gaelic studies. Home: 300 Briarcrest Dr Apt 147 Ann Arbor MI 48104-6762 Office: Orion Internat 101 N Main St Ste 850 Ann Arbor MI 48104-1491

MCGINNIES, ELLIOTT MORSE, psychologist, educator; b. Buffalo, Sept. 19, 1921; s. Elliott Morse and Mabel Christina (Hussong) McG.; m. Bessie Yeh, Jan. 27, 1967; children: Michelle, Lisa, Amy. BA, SUNY-Buffalo, 1943; MA, Brown U., 1944; PhD, Harvard U., 1948. Teaching fellow Harvard U., 1944-47; asst. prof. U. Ala., 1947-52; assoc. prof., then prof. U. Md., 1952-70; prof., chmn. dept. psychology Am. U., 1970-86, prof. emeritus, 1987— ; vis. scholar U. Calif., Berkeley, 1987-88; Fulbright prof. Nat. Taiwan U. With AUS, 1943. Fellow Am. Psychol. Assn.; mem. Eastern Psychol. Assn., Psychonomic Soc., Sigma Xi. Author: Social Behavior: A Functional Analysis, 1970, The Reinforcement of Social Behavior, 1971, Attitudes, Conflict and Social Change, 1972, Perspectives on Social Behavior, 1994. Office: The Am Univ Dept of Psychology 4400 Massachusetts Ave NW Washington DC 20016-8001

MCGINNIS, CHARLES IRVING, civil engineer; b. Kansas City, Mo., Jan. 31, 1928; s. Paul Sherman and Sidney (Bacon) McG.; m. Shirley Ann Meyer, Nov. 5, 1955; children: Gail B., Ann K., James P. BS, Tex. A & M Coll., 1949, M.Engring., 1950; grad., Army Engr. Sch., 1955, Command and Gen. Staff Coll., 1959, Armed Forces Staff Coll., 1962, Army War Coll., 1969. Registered profl. engr., Tex., Mo. Enlisted as pvt. U.S. Army, 1945, advanced through grades to maj. gen., 1976; area engr. Ethiopia and Somalia, 1962-65; dist. engr. St. Paul, 1969-71; dir. engring. and constrn. bur. Panama Canal Co., 1971-72, v.p., 1972-74; lt. gov. C.Z., 1972-74; div. engr. southwestern div. C.E., Dallas, 1974-77; dir. civil works Office Chief of Engrs. U.S. Army, Washington, 1977-79; civil engr., 1979—; exec. v.p. Fru-con Corp.; pres. Fruco Engrs., Inc., 1983-87; assoc. dir. Constrn. Industry Inst. U. Tex., 1987-93, sr. lectr. civil engring. dept., 1992-97; vice chmn. chem. weapons stockpile com. NRC, 2000—. Mem. vis. com., dept. civil engring. M.I.T., 1978-81; mem. Mississippi River Commn., 1975-77, Bd. Engrs. for Rivers and Harbors, 1975-77; chmn. water policy task force NSPE, 1979-81. Chmn. Combined Fed. Campaign coordinating com., C.Z., 1972-74; pres. C.Z. coun. Boy Scouts Am., 1973-74; mem. exec. bd. St. Louis area coun., 1983-87, Capitol area coun., 1987-90, Stonewall Jackson area coun., 1999—; mem. com. mgmt. Balboa YMCA, 1973-74; trustee C.Z. United Way, 1972-74. Decorated D.S.M., Legion of Merit with oak leaf cluster, Joint Svcs. Commendation medal, U.S. Army Commendation with oak leaf cluster, Chuong My medal 1st class Vietnam; named Disting. Grad. Civil Engring. Dept., Tex. A&M U., 2002. Fellow ASCE, Soc. Am. Mil. Engrs. (past pres. Twin Cities post and Panama post); mem. Assn. U.S. Army, Mil. Order of the World Wars, Tau Beta Pi, Chi Epsilon. Episcopalian. Address: 50 Gooseneck Ln Charlottesville VA 22903-9712 *The simple four-part philosophy that has well served three generations of my family requires an uncompromising commitment to honesty in all things, industry, concentration on the job and on personal objectives, and economy of all resources, both natural and man-made.*

MCGINNIS, COLIN PATRICK, federal official; b. Morris, Minn., Sept. 14, 1961; s. Patrick John and Barbara Ann McGinnis; m. Claire Regester Mathews, 1991. BA in English Lit., Carleton Coll., 1984; MDiv, Yale U., 1990. Legis. asst., legis. dir. U.S. Rep. James Oberstar, Washington, 1985-88; comm. dir. U.S. Rep. Martin Sabo, 1990-91; sr. policy advisor U.S. Senator Paul Wellstone, 1991-97, chief of staff, 1997—. Democrat. Roman Catholic. Office: US Senator Paul Wellstone 136 Hart Sob Washington DC 20510-0001 Fax: 202-224-8438. E-mail: Colin_McGinnis@Wellstone.Senate.Gov.

MCGINNIS, DAVE, professional football coach; b. Kansas, Aug. 7, 1951; Attended, Tex. Christian U. Coach Ariz. Cardinals, 2000—, defense coord.; linebackers coach Chgo. Bears, 1986—95; defensive ends, linebackers coach Kansas State U., 1983—85; defensive backfield coach Tex. Christian U., 1982; secondary coach Ind. State U., 1978; freshmen coach Tex. Christian U., 1973—74. Avocations: travel, golf, jazz, reading. Office: Ariz Cardinals 8701 S Hardy Dr Tempe AZ 85284*

MCGINNIS, DAVID EARL, urologist, educator; b. LaMesa, Calif., June 22, 1960; s. Robert Earl and Jane Ann McGinnis; m. Doretta Massardo, June 15, 1985; 1 child, Holden. AB, Harvard U., 1982; MD, U. Tex., 1987. Diplomate Am. Bd. Urology. Intern in surgery Thomas Jefferson U. Hosp., Phila., 1987-89, resident in urology, 1989-93; instr. surgery U. Medicine and Dentistry N.J., Camden, 1993-97; asst. prof. Thomas Jefferson U., Phila., 1997—; pvt. practice, 1997—2001; with Bryn Mawr, 2001—. Mem. Am. Urology Assn. Office: 101 S Bryn Mawr Ave Ste 220 Bryn Mawr PA 19010 Fax: 610-525-3664. E-mail: demcginnismd@hotmail.com.

MCGINNIS, HARRILL COLEMAN, humanities educator; b. Richmond, Va., Aug. 11, 1943; s. Harrill and Elizabeth Coleman McGinnis. BA, U. of the South, Sewanee, Tenn., 1965; MA, Tulane U., 1967; PhD, U. Va., 1971. Instr. U. of the South, Sewanee, Tenn., 1967—68; asst. prof. Ga. State U., Atlanta, 1970—72; asst. then assoc. prof. U. Tenn., Nashville, 1972—79; assoc. prof. Tenn. State U., 1979—. Dir. Atlanta Urban Obs., 1971. Contbr. articles to profl. jours. State bd. dirs. Tenn. Common Cause, Nashville, 1974—75, ACLU Tenn., Nashville, 1974—78; pres. dist. 10 Am. Contract Bridge League. Home: 21 Vaughns Gap Rd #18A Nashville TN 37205-4321 Office: Tenn State U 3500 John Merritt Blvd Nashville TN 37209 Office Fax: 615-963-5497. Business E-Mail: emcginnis@tnstate.edu.

MCGINNIS, JAMES MICHAEL, physician; b. Columbia, Mo., July 12, 1944; s. Leland Glenn and Lillian Ruth (Mackler) McG.; m. Patricia Anne Gwaltney, Aug. 4, 1978; children— Brian, Katherine AB, U. Calif., Berkeley, 1966; MA, MD, UCLA, 1971; M.P.P., Harvard U., 1977. House officer in internal medicine Boston City Hosp., 1971-72; internat. med. officer HEW, 1972-74; dir. Office for Asia and Western Pacific, 1974-75; state coordinator smallpox eradication program WHO, India, 1974-75; fellow Harvard Center for Community Health and Med. Care, Boston, 1976-77; cons. to sec. HEW, Washington, 1977, dep. asst. sec. for health, dir. office disease prevention, 1977-95, asst. surgeon gen., 1980-95, acting dir. office of rsch. integrity, 1992-93; scholar-in-residence NAS, Washington, 1995-99; sr. cons. Robert Wood Johnson Found., Princeton, 1996-99, sr. v.p., dir. Health Grp., 1999-. Instr. medicine George Washington U. Med. Sch., 1973-75; adj. prof. pub. policy Duke U., 1979-81, 99—; chair, sec. task force on smoking and health; chair exec. com. HHS Environ. Health Policy Com.; mem. U.S. Japan Leadership program; chair World Bank/European Commn. Task Force on Reconstrn. of Health Sector, Bosnia, 1996-97; sr. scholar Assn. of Acad. Health Ctrs., 1997-99; sr. v.p., dir. Health Group Robert Wood Johnson Found, 1999—. Mem. editl. bd. Jour. Med. Edn., 1975-78, Jour. Preventive Medicine, 1987—, Jour. Health Promotion, 1992-98; editor-in-chief: Healthy People, Healthy People 2000, Surgeon General's Report on Nutrition and Health, Determining Risks to Health. Served with USPHS, 1972-75, 77-95. Recipient Arthur S. Flemming Pub. Svc. award, 1979, USPHS Disting. Svc. medal,

1989, Surgeon Gen.'s medallion, 1995, Fed. Profile in Leadership award, 1989, Wilbur Cohen award, 1995, award for excellence APHA, 1995, Health Leader of Yr. award, 1996. Fellow Am. Coll. Epidemiology, Am. Coll. Preventive Medicine; mem. Inst. Medicine/Nat. Acad. Scis. Office: 330 C St SW Washington DC 20201-0001

MCGINNIS, LAMAR SCOTT, JR. surgeon; b. Waco, Tex., Oct. 17, 1930; BS, U. Ga., 1950; MD, Med. Coll. Ga., 1954. Diplomate Am. Bd. Surgery. Intern Royal Victoria Hosp., Montreal, Que., Can., 1954-55; resident John Sealy Hosp., Galveston, Tex., 1955-56, 57-59, Bellevue Hosp. Ctr., N.Y.C., 1956-57; chief of surgery USAF, 1959-63; pvt. practice. Mem. staff De Kalb Med. Ctr., Atlanta; clin. prof. Emory U. Sch. Medicine. Fellow ACS; mem. AMA, So. Surg. Assn., Soc. Surg. Oncology, Southeastern Surg. Congress, So. Soc. of Clin. Surgs., Alpha Omega Alpha. Office: 2665 N Decatur Rd Ste 730 Decatur GA 30033-6131 E-mail: lsm2045@aol.com., lmcginni@cancer.org.

MCGINNIS, M. SEAN, lawyer; b. Springfield, Mo., May 30, 1959; s. Michael R. and Donna J. McGinnis. BA Bus. Adminstrn./ Econs./ Polit. Sci., Drury Coll, 1981; JD, U. Mo., 1984. Bar: Mo. 1984. Ptnr. Turner & Reid, Springfield, 1984-97, Newberry Haden Cowherd Bullock Keck & McGinnis, Springfield, 1998—. Commr. Mo. State Fair, Sedalia, 1996—; gen. counsel Mo. Dem. Party, Jefferson City, 1996—; mem. bd. curators U. Mo., Columbia, 1999—; bd. dirs. Boys and Girls Clubs, Springfield, 1999—. Mem. Christian Ch. (Disciples Of Christ). Home: 1500 S Fairway Ave Springfield MO 65804-1309 Office: Newberry Haden Cowherd Bullock Keck & McGinnis 2135 E Sunshine St Ste 203 Springfield MO 65804-1862 E-mail: nhcbkm@dialnet.net.

MCGINNIS, MICHAEL BOYD, chemistry educator; b. Balt., Mar. 3, 1970; s. Phyllis Lee (Miller) McG.; m. Maryann Lampart, Oct. 23, 1993. BS in Chem., Elizabethtown Coll., 1992; PhD in Organic Chemistry, U. Tenn., 1997. Postdoctoral rsch. assoc. U. Tenn., Knoxville, 1997, instr. chemistry, 1997; assoc. prof. chemistry, faculty assoc. Ga. Coll. and State U., Milledgeville, 1997—. Contbr. to profl. jours. Instr. ARC, Milledgeville, 1997—; active in various sci. fairs; bd. dirs., exec. dir. Ga. Jr. Acad. of Sci. Hoechst Celanese Sci. Outreach award Hoechst Celanese Corp., 1996. Mem. Am. Chem. Soc. (pub. outreach, mid. Ga. chair younger chemists com.), Sigma Xi. Democrat. Methodist. Avocations: whitewater canoeing, kayaking. Home: 1307 Clack Rd Madison GA 30650-4812 Office: Ga Coll and State U Dept Chemistry and Physics Milledgeville GA 31061 E-mail: mmcginni@mail.gcsu.edu.

MCGINNIS, RENEE, artist; b. Morris, Ill., Mar. 14, 1962; d. Thomas Vincent McGinnis and Myrna Gail Sandeno. BFA, Ill. Wesleyan U., 1984. Artist Cedar Rapids (Iowa) Gazette, 1984-86, Sta. KGAN-TV, Cedar Rapids, 1986-87; artist, broadcast designer Sta. WMAQ-TV, Chgo., 1987-88, Sta. WBBM-TV, Chgo., 1988-89, Sta. WGN-TV, Chgo., 1989—; artist, 1980—. One-woman show Elmhurst (Ill.) Art Mus., 1999; exhibited in group shows, including Gang Gallery, N.Y.C., 1996, 97, 98, David Barnett Gallery, Milw., 1998, ARC Gallery, Chgo., 1997, Artemesia Gallery, Chgo., 1995, Wood St. Gallery, Chgo., 1995; represented in pvt. and pub. collections including Pres. Bill and Hillary Clinton, Hedge Fund Rsch., East Bank Club, Nicholas Fin., Schopf & Weiss; work reviewed in newspaper and arts publ. Membership chair ARC Gallery and Ednl. Found., Chgo., 1996-97. Recipient Broadcast Emmy award, 1991, Best of Show award No. Ind. Arts Assn., 1996, Art on the Walk, 1998; Nat. bronze award Broadcast Designers Assn., 1987, Grumbacher award McLean County Art Assn., 1984, hon. mention Whitney Mus., N.Y.C., 1997, Hyde Park Arts Ctr., 1998. Avocations: reading. Home: 2654 W Medill Ave Apt 308 Chicago IL 60647-3067 Office: WGN-TV 2501 W Bradley Pl Chicago IL 60618-4718

MCGINNIS, ROBERT EARL, lawyer; b. Caldwell, Ohio, May 1, 1931; s. Earl Peregoy and Mary Ethel (Richner) McG.; m. Jane Ann Lindenmeyer, Sept. 12, 1953; children: Sharon Ann, David E. BA, Ohio Weslayan U., 1952; JD summa cum laude, Ohio State U., 1954. Bar: Ohio 1954, Calif. 1956. Asst. judge advocate USAF, 1954-56; sr. ptnr. Luce, Forward, Hamilton, & Scripps, San Diego, 1956—. Counsel to pub. utilities, pub. agys., savs. and loan instns., ins. cos. and contractors. Trustee Wesley Meth. Ch., San Diego, Fine Arts Soc., First Meth. Ch., La Mesa, Calif.; counsel Kensington Community Ch.; dir. San Diego Opera Assn., corp. sec., v.p. Mem. Order of Coif. Republican. Mem. United Ch. Christ. Office: Luce Forward Hamilton & Scripps 600 W Broadway Ste 2600 San Diego CA 92101-3372 E-mail: rmcginnis@luce.com.

MCGINNIS, ROBERT WILLIAM, electronics company executive; b. Modesto, Calif., Oct. 31, 1936; s. George Crawford and Lola May (Provis) McG.; m. Sondra Elaine Hurley, Mar. 1, 1964; children: Michael Fredrick, Traci Anne, Patrick William. BSEE with highest honors, U. Calif., Berkeley, 1962; postgrad., NYU, 1962-63. Mem. tech. staff Bell Tel. Labs., Murray Hill, NJ, 1961—63; devel. engr., engring. mgr., product mgr., ops. mgr. Motorola Semicondr. Group, Phoenix, 1963—73, ops. mgr. for hybrid circuits group comm. divsn. Ft. Lauderdale, Fla., 1973—76, solar ops. mgr., 1976—79; v.p., gen. mgr. Photowatt Internat., Inc., Tempe, Ariz., 1979—83; gen. mgr. SAFT Electronic Sys. Divsn., 1983—85; pres. Safe Power Sys., Inc., 1985—88; gen. mgr. advanced energy sys. Acme Electric Corp., 1988—93; product mgr. energy products divsn. Motorola Worldwide, Plantation, Fla., 1993—97, Motorola, Lawrenceville, Ga., 1993—97; quality dir. computer group Motorola Computer Group, Tempe, 1997—2002; CEO Nanodielectrics Corp., Middleburg Heights, Ohio, 2002—. Mem. Ariz. Solar Energy Commn., 1977-83; chmn. photovoltaic subcom. Am. Nat. Stds. Inst., 1978-83; mem. coordinating coun. Solar Energy Rsch. Inst. Stds., 1977-82. Contbr. articles to profl. jours. Chmn. bd. Ctr. for Habilation, Tempe, 2001—. With USNR, 1955-58. Mem. IEEE, Phi Beta Kappa, Tau Beta Pi, Eta Kappa Nu. Republican. Methodist. Home: 4031 E Fox St Mesa AZ 85205-5017 Office: Nanodielectrics Corp 18683 Sheldon Rd Middleburg Heights OH 44130 E-mail: rmcginnis2002@yahoo.com.

MCGINNIS, THOMAS J. governmemt agency administrator, pharmacist; b. Newark, Apr. 6, 1954; s. Thomas G. and Nellie J. (Jerrytone) M.; m. Diane M. DeMichele, Sept. 10, 1979; (div. Feb. 8, 1989); m. Linda B. Dubroof, July 13, 1989. BS, Rutgers U., 1977; Cert. in Gen. Adminstrn., U. Md., 1991. Registered pharmacist, Md., D.C., N.J. Pharmacy intern Overlook Hosp., Summit, N.J., 1977-78; drug info. specialist divsn. OTC drug evaluation FDA, Rockville, Md., 1978-81, team leader divsn. drug evaluation, 1981-84, acting dir. divsn. drug info., 1984-85, br. chief. divsn. drug info., 1984-87, exec. asst. to dir. office drug standards, 1987-89, exec. asst. to dir. office generic drugs, 1989-91, assoc. dir. pharmacy affairs, 1991-97; hosp. pharmacy assoc. George Washington U. Hosp., Washington, 1980-97. Dep. assoc. commr. for health affairs FDA, 1997—; fed. drug law exam. com., Nat. Assn. Bd. Pharmacy, Chgo, 1993—; mem. pharmacy law com. Food and Drug Law Inst., Washington, 1993—; USPHS alt. del. U.S. Pharmacopeial Conv., Rockville Md. 1995—; adv. assoc. Ruthgers U. Coll. Pharmacy, 2001—; presenter in field. Contbr. articles to profl. jours. Bd. dirs. USPHS Healthy Beginnings Child Devel. Ctr. Capt., USPHS, 1977—. Recipient Commendation medal, USPHS, 1986, 92; named Alumnus of the Yr., Rutgers Univ., 1994. Mem. Commd. Officers Assn. USPHS, Am. Soc. Health Sys. Pharmacists, Am. Pharm. Assn., Drug Info. Assn., Rutgers Club Washington, Assn. Mil. Surgeons U.S., Res. Officers Assn. Roman Catholic. Avocations: tennis, running, physical fitness, golf, scuba-diving. Home: 5106 Wilson Ln Bethesda MD 20814-2420 Office: FDA 5600 Fishers Ln Rm 14-101 Rockville MD 20852-1750 E-mail: tmcginni@oc.fda.gov.

MCGINTY, BRIAN DONALD, lawyer, author; b. June 22, 1937; s. Donald Bruce and Natalia Vallejo (Haraszthy) M. AB, U. Calif., Berkeley, 1959, JD, 1962. Bar: Calif. 1963. Assoc. Twohig, Weingarten & Haas, Seaside, Calif., 1962-63; ptnr. Weingarten & McGinty, 1963-70; sole practice Monterey, 1970-73, San Francisco, 1973-83; writer, editor Matthew Bender & Co., San Francisco, Oakland, Calif., 1984-93. Author: Haraszthy at the Mint (Famous Calif. Trials Series), 1975, The Palace Inns, 1978, We the People, 1987, Strong Wine: The Life and Legend of Agoston Haraszthy, 1998; contbg. author: The Craft of the Essay, Historical Times Illustrated Encyclopedia of the Civil War, Portrait of America, 5th edit., 1990, California Real Estate Law and Practice, California Forms of Pleading and Practice, California Legal Forms, California Insurance Law, California Probate Law and Practice, California Public Agency Law and Practice, California Wills and Trusts; editor: Napa Wine (Rounce and Coffin Club award 1975), 1974; contbr. numerous articles to profl. jours. Recipient Excellence in Writing award Nat. Hist. Soc., 1976, Editor's award for Hist. Scholarship, Sonoma County Hist. Soc., 1999. Mem. Calif. Hist. Soc.

MC GINTY, JOHN MILTON, architect; b. Houston, Apr. 24, 1935; s. Milton Bowles and Ruth Louise (Dreaper) McG.; m. Juanita Jones, May 4, 1957; children: Christopher Harold, Jacqueline Ruth McGinty Carlson. BS, Rice U., 1957; M.F.A., Princeton U., 1961. With archtl. firm Barnes, Landes & Goodman, Austin, Tex., 1957-58, Ingram & Harris, Beaumont, 1958-59; prin. McGinty Partnership, Architects, Inc., Houston, 1961-89, City Assos., Inc., 1979-91, Bovay-McGinty, Inc., engrs. & architects, Houston, 1989-91; founder, pres. Am. Constrn. Investigations Inc., 1991-2000. Instr. archtl. design U. Houston, 1965-67; White House fellow, asst. to Sec. of Interior, 1967-68; vis. prof. architecture Rice U., 1969-70 Named Disting. Alumnus Rice U., 1986. Fellow AIA (mem. U.S. delegation to USSR 1972, pres. Houston chpt. 1973, nat. pres. 1977) Home: 1650 County Rd 312 Palacios TX 77465 Office: Am Constrn Investigations Ste 200 602 Sawyer St Houston TX 77007-7510 E-mail: jmginty@acico.com.

MCGIRR, DAVID WILLIAM JOHN, internet telephone executive; b. Glasgow, Scotland, May 19, 1954; came to U.S., 1991; s. Edward McCombie and Diane Curzon (Woods) McG.; m. Margaret Joslin Richardson, May 9, 1981; children: William David, Katherine Joslin, Lucy Ann, Elizabeth Margaret. BSc with honors, U. Glasgow, 1976; MBA, U. Pa., 1978. Assoc. S.G. Warburg & Co. Ltd., London, 1978-80, exec. dir., 1981-86; mng. dir. S.G. Warburg & Co. Inc., N.Y.C., 1991-95, CFO, 1992-95; assoc. Warburg Paribas Becker Inc., 1980-81; exec. dir. S.G. Warburg Securities, London, 1986-87; CEO S.G. Warburg Securities Ltd., Toronto, Ont., Can., 1987-89; COO, CFO Bunting Warburg Inc., 1989-91; pres. GAB Robins North Am. Inc., Parsippany, N.J., 1996-99, CEO, 1997-99; COO hippo, Inc., New Haven, 1999-2001, pres., 2001—. Selection com. Thouron Scholarship. Thouron scholar, 1976-78. Mem. Apawamis Club (Rye, N.Y.). Avocations: collecting cars, family, golf. Office: Hippo Inc 205 Orange St New Haven CT 06510-2014 E-mail: dwjmcgirr@aol.com.

MCGIVERIN, ARTHUR A. former state supreme court chief justice; b. Iowa City, Nov. 10, 1928; s. Joseph J. and Mary B. McG.; m. Mary Joan McGiverin, Apr. 20, 1951; children: Teresa, Thomas, Bruce, Nancy. BSC with high honors, U. Iowa, 1951, JD, 1956. Bar: Iowa 1956. Pvt. practice law, Ottumwa, Iowa, 1956; alt. mcpl. judge, 1960-65; judge Iowa Dist. Ct. 8th Jud. Dist., 1965-78; assoc. justice Iowa Supreme Ct., Des Moines, 1978-87, chief justice, 1987-2000, sr. judge, 2000—. Mem. Iowa Supreme Ct. Commn. on Continuing Legal Edn., 1975. Served to 1st lt. U.S. Army, 1946-48, 51-53. Mem. Iowa State Bar Assn., Am. Law Inst. Roman Catholic. Avocation: golf. Office: Iowa Supreme Court State Capitol Building Des Moines IA 50319-0001*

MCGIVNEY, JOHN JOSEPH, lawyer; b. Boston, Oct. 31, 1956; s. William A. and Mary Angela (Wall) McG. AB magna cum laude, Boston Coll., 1978, JD cum laude, 1981. Bar: Mass. 1981, U.S. Dist. Ct. Mass. 1982, U.S. Ct. Appeals (1st cir.) 1983, U.S. Supreme Ct. 1990. Assoc. Burns & Levinson, Boston, 1981-87, ptnr., chief appellate sect., 1988-96; ptnr. Rubin and Rudman, 1997—. Sec. Lynnfield (Mass.) Dem. Town Com., 1974-75, chmn., 1976-77. Mem. Mass. Acad. Trial Attys., Mass. Def. Lawyers Assn. (bd. dirs.), Algonquin Club of Boston. Home: 47 Doncaster Cir Lynnfield MA 01940-2255

MC GLAMERY, MARSHAL DEAN, crop scientist, weed science educator; b. Mooreland, Okla., July 29, 1932; s. Walter Gaiford and Bernice (Gardner) McG.; m. Marilyn Hudson, June 2, 1957; children: Paul, Steve. BS, Okla. State U., 1956, MS, 1958; PhD, U. Ill., 1965. Instr. Panhandle A. and M. Coll., 1958-60; agronomist Agribus. Co., Lawrence, Kans., 1960-61; teaching asst. U. Ill., 1961-63, research fellow, 1963-65, asst. prof. weed sci., 1965-70, assoc. prof., 1970-76, prof., 1976-2000, ext. crop scientist, 1965-2000; ret., 2000. Served with U.S. Army, 1953-55. NSF fellow, 1963 Mem. Weed Sci. Soc. Am., Coun. Agr. and Tech. Baptist. Home: 35 Lange Ave Savoy IL 61874-9705 Office: 1102 S Goodwin Ave Urbana IL 61801-4730 E-mail: mmcglame@uiuc.edu.

MCGLAMRY, MAX REGINALD, lawyer; b. Wilcox County, Ga., Sept. 12, 1928; s. Edgar Lee and Allie Bea (Faircloth) McG.; m. Jean Louise Hilyer, Dec. 28, 1950; children: Sharon Kay McGlamry Hendrix, Michael Lee. BS, Auburn U., 1948; LLB cum laude, Mercer U., 1952, JD cum laude, 1970. Bar: Ga. 1953, U.S. Dist. Ct. (mid. dist.) Ga. 1954, U.S. Ct. Appeals (5th cir.) 1964, U.S. Supreme Ct. 1972, U.S. Ct. Appeals (11th cir.) 1981, U.S. Ct. Appeals (4th cir.) 1985, U.S. Dist. Ct. (no. dist.) Calif. 1988, U.S. Dist. Ct. (no. dist.) Ga. 1989. Pvt. practice, Columbus, Ga., 1953-64; from ptnr. to officer Swift, Pease, Davidson & Chapman (name changed to Page, Scrantom, Harris, McGlamry, & Chapman, P.C.), 1964-85; ptnr. Pope, Kellogg, McGlamry, Kilpatrick & Morrison, 1985-90, Pope, McGlamry, Kilpatrick & Morrison, LLP, Columbus, 1990-2000; pres. Max R. McGlamry, P.C., 2000—. Exec. com. Muscogee County Dem. Orgn., Columbus, 1956-60; bd. dirs. Columbus Jr. C. of C. Ens. USN, 1948-49. Am. Coll. Trust & Estate Counsel fellow, 1973, Lawyers Found. Ga. fellow, 1983. Mem. ABA, ATLA, State Bar Ga., Ga. Trial Lawyers Assn., Assn. U.S. Army, Ga. Golfers Sr. Assn., Urban League of Greater Columbus, Inc., Columbus Lawyers Club (pres. 1964-65), Lions (Columbus chpt. pres. 1967-68), Chattahoochee River Club, Green Island Country Club, Phi Kappa Phi, Alpha Epsilon Delta, Phi Alpha Delta, Pi Kappa Alpha. Democrat. Methodist. Avocations: golf, fishing. Home: 6941 Wethersfield Rd Columbus GA 31904-3317 Office: Max R McGlamry PC PO Box 4481 Columbus GA 31904-0481

MCGLATHERY, JAMES MELVILLE, foreign language educator; b. New Orleans, Nov. 22, 1936; s. Samuel Lyon and Mary Jackson (Garrott) McG.; m. Nancy Judith Beyer, June 1, 1939; children: Samuel Lyon, Daniel Beyer, Andrew James, Benjamin Kim. AB, Princeton U., 1958; AM, Yale U., 1959, PhD, 1964. Instr. German Phillips Andover (Mass.) Acad., 1959-60; lectr. German Harvard U., 1963-64, instr. German, 1964-65; from asst. prof. to assoc. prof. U. Ill. at Urbana-Champaign, 1965-84, prof. German, 1984-2000, prof. emeritus, 2000—, acting dept. head, spring 1985, dept. head, 1985-95. Instr. Colby Coll. Summer Lang. Sch., 1964, Harvard U. Summer Lang. Sch., 1965-66, 70, U. Ill., Urbana-Champaign, 1972, 74, 76, 78, 80, 82, 87, 90, U. Göttingen, Germany, 1993-94, 2001; lectr., presenter in field. Author: Mysticism and Sexuality: E. T. A. Hoffmann, Part One: Hoffmann and His Sources, 1981, Desire's Sway: The Plays and Stories of Heinrich von Kleist, 1983, Mysticism and Sexuality: E. T. A. Hoffmann, Part Two: Interpretations of the Tales, 1985, Fairy Tale Romance: The Grimms, Basile, Perrault, 1991, Grimms' Fairy Tales: A History of Criticism on a Popular Classic, 1993, E.T.A. Hoffmann, 1997, Wagner's Operas and Desire, 1998; editor: German Source Readings in the Arts and Sciences, 1974, Journal of English and Germanic Philology, 1976, The Brothers Grimm and Folktale, 1988, 91, Music and German Literature: Their Relationship since the Middle Ages, 1992; contbg. author: Reader in German Literature, 1969, Moliére and the Commonwealth of Letters: Patrimony and Posterity, 1975, Fairy Tales as Ways of Knowing: Essays on Märchen in Psychology, Society, and Literature, 1981, Reflection and Action: Essays on the Bildungsroman, 1991, A Companion to the Nibelungenlied, 1998; mng. editor: Jour. English and Germanic Philology, 1972-2000; contbr. articles and book revs. to profl. jours. Princeton U. scholar, 1954-58; undergrad. rsch. assistantship Princeton U., 1956-58; Woodrow Wilson Nat. fellow Yale U., 1958-59, Jr. Sterling fellow Yale U., 1960-61, Nat. Def. Edn. Act fellow in Russian, Yale U., 1961-63; grad. rsch. bd. grantee U. Ill. Urbana-Champaign, 1975, 79-80, 86, 89, 92. Mem.: N.Am. Heine Soc., E.T.A. Hoffmann Assn. Home: 1204 Thomas Dr Champaign IL 61821-1632 Business E-Mail: mcglath@uiuc.edu.

MCGLAUCHLIN, TOM, artist; b. Turtle, Wis., Sept. 14, 1934; s. Charles Orion and Frances Lenore (Cadman) McG.; m. Patricia Ann Smith, Aug. 5, 1961; children: Christopher, Jennifer (dec.), Patrick (dec.). BS in Art, U. Wis., 1959, MS in Art, 1960; studied pottery with James McKinnell, 1962. Instr. dept. art and art edn. U. Wis., Madison, 1960-61; instr. art dept. Cornell Coll., Mt. Vernon, Iowa, 1961-64, asst. prof. art dept., 1964-68, assoc. prof., chmn. art dept. N.Y., 1968-71; instr. Toledo Mus. Art, 1971-82, prof., dir. glass program, 1982-84. One-man exhbns. include Habatat Gallery, Dearborn, Mich., 1979, Glass Art Gallery, Toronto, 1981, 85, Glass Gallery, Bethesda, Md., 1981, 85, 87, 91, Heller Gallery, N.Y.C., 1983, B.Z. Wagman Gallery, St. Louis, 1983, Running Ridge Gallery, Santa Fe, 1990; selected group exhbns. include Toledo Mus. Art, 1972, 88, Glasmuseum Frauenau, Franenau, Germany, 1977, Habatat Gallery, 1980, 84, The Hand and the Spirit Gallery, Scottsdale, Ariz., 1980, Gallery of Contemporary Crafts, Detroit, 1980, The Naples (Fla.) Art Gallery, 1981, The Craftsman's Gallery, Scarsdale, N.Y., 1981, 84, The Nat. Mus. Modern Art, Kyoto and Tokyo, 1981, Perception Gallery, Houston, 1985, The AirLoft Gallery, Honolulu, 1986, The Corning (N.Y.) Mus. Glass, 1987; selected competitive exhbns. include Everson Mus. Art, Syracuse, N.Y., 1961, 62, Mus. Contemporary Crafts, N.Y.C., 1962, Corning Glass Mus., Met. Mus. Art, N.Y.C., Victoria and Albert Mus., London, Musee Ars Decoratif, Paris; public collections include Toledo Mus. Art, The Smithsonian Collection, Washington, Portland (Oreg.) Art Mus., New Orleans Mus. Art, Mus. Contemporary Crafts, Musee des arts decoratifs de la Ville de Lausanne, Switzerland, Minn. Mus. Art, St. Paul, Kunstmuseum, Dusseldorf, Germany, Corning Glass Mus. Grantee Associated Colls. Midwest, 1966-67; recipient First Jury award Toledo Glass Nat. II, 1968. Mem. Am. Crafts Coun., Internat. Sculpture Soc., Ohio Designer-Craftsmen, Glass Art Soc. Office: The Glass Studio 1940 W Central Ave Toledo OH 43606-3944 E-mail: meglauc@accesstoledo.com.

MCGLAUGHLIN, THOMAS HOWARD, publisher, retired naval officer, marine surveyor; b. Cin., Jan. 12, 1928; s. George Godden and Cordelia (Herrlinger) McG.; m. Moana Maharam-Stone, Jan. 4, 1984. BS in Elec. Engring., U.S. Naval Acad., 1950. Lic. master mariner. Commd. ensign U.S. Navy, 1950, advanced through grades to capt., 1970; White House aide to Pres. John F. Kennedy, Washington, 1960-63; exec. officer USS Prichett, Long Beach, Calif., 1963-65; comdg. officer USS Maddox, 1965-67; exec. officer USS Boston, Boston, 1967-70; chief naval ops. Comdr.-in-Chief, Pacific, Honolulu, 1970-74; chief of staff Mil. Sealift Command, N.Y.C., 1974-79; ret. U.S. Navy, 1979; pres. Falmouth Press, Honolulu, 1983—. Marine surveyor R.W. Dickieson Internat., Inc., Honolulu, 1982—; master Motor Vessel Rella Mae, Honolulu, 1981-90, Royal Taipan, Cebu, Philippines, 1990. Hon. police chief Boston Police Dept., 1969. Decorated Bronze Star, Navy commendation medal with combat "v", combat action ribbon, Vietnamese Disting. Svc. order; recipient medal for Outstanding Svc., Am. Legion, Pitts., 1942. Mem. Nat. Def. Transp. Assn., VFW (life), U.S. Naval Acad. Alumni Assn. (life), The Retired Officers Assn. Republican. Presbyterian. Avocations: flying, scuba diving, tennis, golf. Home: 118 Kiionioni Pl Honolulu HI 96816-4248 Office: RW Dickieson Internat Inc 46-208 Kahuhipa St Kaneohe HI 96744-3905 E-mail: thmcg@juno.com.

MCGLOCKTON, CHESTER, professional football player; b. Whiteville, N.C., Sept. 16, 1969; Student, Clemson U. Defensive tackle Oakland Raiders, 1992-97, Kansas City Chiefs, 1998—2000, Denver Broncos, 2001—. Named to Sporting News NFL All-Pro Team, 1994, to NFL Pro Bowl Team, 1994. Office: Denver Broncos 13655 Broncos Pkwy Englewood CO 80112*

MCGLOTHLIN, KAREN LEAH, science educator; b. Kingsport, Tenn., July 27, 1966; d. Philip Morris and Audrey Mariece McGlothlin. BS, East Tenn. State U, Johnson City, TN, 1987, MS, 1990; PhD, Clemson U, Clemson, SC, 1998. Asst biology prof U of the South, Sewanee, Tenn., 1997—. Co-editor (book series) Exploring Environmental Challenges; contbr. articles to profl. jours. Recipient Tchr. of the Yr., Soc. of Sewanee Scholars, 2002, Advisor of the Yr., Sewanee Student Assembly, 2002. Mem.: Assn of Southeastern Biologists, Tenn. Acad. of Sci., Am. Microscopical Soc. Democrat-Npl. Achievements include discovery of 2 Species Of Organism (Phylum Tardigrada) New To Science. Avocations: scuba diving, walking, reading. Office: U of the South 735 University Ave Sewanee TN 37383 E-mail: kmcgloth@sewanee.edu.

MC GLYNN, SEAN PATRICK, physical chemist, educator; b. Dungloe, Ireland, Mar. 8, 1931; came to U.S., 1952, naturalized, 1957; s. Daniel and Catherine (Brennan) McG.; m. Helen Magdalena Salacz-von Dohnanyi, 4Apr. 11, 1955; children: Sean Ernst, Daniel Julian, Brian Charles, Sheila Ann, Alan Patrick; m. Maureen G. Potts, Oct. 23, 1985; children: Shane Joseph, Brennan John, Colin Patrick. BS, Nat. U. Ireland, 1951, MS, 1952; PhD, Fla. State U., 1956. Fellow Fla. State U., 1956, U. Wash., 1956-57; mem. faculty La. State U., 1957—, prof. chemistry, 1964—, Boyd prof. chemistry, 1967—, dean Grad. Sch., 1981-82, vice chancellor for research, 1981-91. Assoc. prof. biophysics Yale U., 1961; Humboldt prof. physics U. Bonn, W.Ger., 1979-80; cons. to pvt. cos. Author: (with others) Molecular Spectroscopy of the Triplet State, 1969, Introduction to Applied Quantum Chemistry, 1971, Photophysics and Photochemistry in the Vacuum Ultraviolet, 1985, The Geometry of Genetics, 1988; editor Wiley-Interscience Monographs in Chem. Physics; contbr. over 400 articles and chpts. to profl. pubs. Fellow Research Corp., 1960-63; Sloan fellow, 1964-68; recipient award Baton Rouge Council Engring. and Sci. Socs., 1962-63; Sr. Scientist award Alexander von Humboldt Found., 1979; Disting. Research medal U. Bologna, Italy, 1979 Mem. Am. Chem. Soc. (S.W. regional award 1967, Fla. sect. award 1970, Coates award 1977), AAAS, Am. Phys. Soc. Achievements include research in molecular electronic spectroscopy, electronic structure, energy transfer, molecular genetics, bioenergetics, mathematical biology, optoacoustics, optogalvanics. Home: 1056 E Lakeview Dr Baton Rouge LA 70810-4621 E-mail: chspm@lsu.edu., maureen.potts@worldnet.att.net.

MCGLYNN, WILLIAM CHARLES, brokerage house executive; b. Hazelton, Pa., Apr. 4, 1944; s. William Charles and Mary McGlynn; m. Phyllis Marie Fotia, May 28, 1967; children: William Jason, Devon Laura, Robert Ryan, Kirsten Ann. BS in Bus. Mgmt., Farleigh Dickenson U., Madison, N.J., 1968, postgrad. studies in Fin. and Econs., 1968-69. V.p. William D. Witter, Inc., N.Y.C., 1970-75, Dillon Read & Co., Inc., N.Y.C., 1975-79, Tucker Anthony R. L. Day, N.Y.C., 1979-81; mng. dir. L.F. Rothschild, Inc., 1982-88, Bear, Stearns & Co., Inc., N.Y.C., 1988—2002, sr. mng. dir., 2002—. Fundraiser Wall St. Charity Fund, N.Y.C., 1971—75; benefits com. Cath. Charities Home Bur., 1980—90; trustee, exec. com. mem. Oak Knoll Sch. Holy Child, Summit, NJ, 1989—; fundraiser, mem. Fathers and Friends Delbarton Sch., 1993—98, Morristown Bearcd Sch. Assn., 1998—99; advisor, mem. Oak Knoll Fathers Bd., 1989—; trustee, chmn. fin. com. Chubb Found., 2001—. Republican. Roman Catholic. Avocations: skiing, tennis, boating, reading. Home: 151 Deer Run Watchung NJ 07069-6255 Office: Bear Sterns & Co Inc 245 Park Ave New York NY 10167-0002

MCGOLDRICK, JOHN LEWIS, lawyer; b. Plainfield, N.J., Mar. 2, 1941; s. John Leslie and Sarah (Walker) McG.; m. Ann Chapman Puffer, Oct. 1, 1966; children: Scott Runyon, Jennifer Winslow. BA cum laude, Harvard U., 1963, LLB, 1966. Bar: N.J. 1966, N.Y. 1985. Assoc. McCarter & English, Newark, 1966-73, ptnr., 1974-95; exec. v.p. Bristol-Myers Squibb Co., N.Y.C., 1995—. Vice-chmn., bd. dirs. N.J. Transit Corp., Newark; bd. dirs. Bristol-Myers Squibb Found., Zimmer Holdings, Inc., HealthCare Inst. N.J. Chmn. zoning bd. Borough of Princeton, N.J.; trustee Essex-Newark Found. Legal Svcs. N.J.; mem. com. to visit The Coll.., mem. com. to visit Sch. Pub. Health, Harvard Bd. Overseers. Fellow Am. Coll. Trial Lawyers, Am. Bar Found., Am. Acad. Appellate Lawyers; mem. ABA, World Econ. Forum, Legal Svcs. N.J. (bd. dirs.), N.J. Bar Assn., N.Y. Bar Assn., Assn. Bar City of N.Y., Assn. Fed. Bar N.J. (former pres., mem. adv. bd.), Am. Law Inst., Assn. Gen. Counsel, Chief Legal Officers Roundtable, Coun. of Chief Legal Officers (The Conf. Bd. Inc.), CPR Inst. for Dispute Resolution (mem. exec. com.), Aspen Inst. on the World Economy, Regional Plan Assn. (dir.), Coun. on Fgn. Rels., Harvard Law Sch. Assn. N.J. (former pres.). Home: 25 Vandeventer Ave Princeton NJ 08542-6937 Office: Bristol-Myers Squibb Co 345 Park Ave New York NY 10154-0004

MCGOLDRICK, KATHRYN ELIZABETH, anesthesiologist, educator, writer; b. Worcester, Mass., 1946; MD, Cornell U., 1970. Diplomate Am. Bd. Anesthesiology. Intern N.Y. Hosp.-Cornell Med. Ctr., 1970-71; resident anesthesiology Peter Bent Brigham Hosp., Boston, 1971-73, Children's Hosp. Med. Ctr., Boston, 1973-74; prof. anesthesiology Yale U., New Haven, 1992—2001; prof., chmn. dept. anesthesiology N.Y. Med. Coll., Valhalla, 2001—. Med. dir. ambulatory surgery Yale-New Haven Hosp., 1991—2001. Editor-in-chief Survey of Anesthesiology; mem. editl. bd. Anesthesia Web, 1999—. V.p., trustee Wood Libr.-Mus. Anesthesiology, 1998—2001, pres., 2001—. Fellow Am. Coll. Anesthesiology; mem. AMA, Am. Soc. Anesthesiologists, Conn. State Soc. Anesthesiologists (pres. 1998-2000), Assn. Univ. Anesthesiologists, Acad. Anesthesiology. Office: Dept Anesthesiology NY Med Coll Valhalla NY 10595

MCGOLDRICK, WILLIAM PATRICK, educational consultant; b. N.Y.C., Nov. 17, 1946; s. William Patrick and Mary Margaret (Flanagan) McG.; m. Elizabeth Margaret Coyne, July 5, 1969; 1 child, Margaret. BA, Siena Coll., Loudonville, N.Y., 1968; MA, Syracuse U., 1973. Dir. pub. rels. Harrisburg (Pa.) Area Community Coll., 1971-74; asst. to pres. for pub. rels. SUNY, Oswego, 1974-77; dir. of major gifts Coll. of William and Mary, Williamsburg, Va., 1977-80; dir. of devel. Rensselaer Poly. Inst., Troy., N.Y., 1980-85, v.p. inst. rels., 1985-95; ptnr. Washburn & McGoldrick, Inc., Latham, 1995—. Trustee Coun. Advancement and Support Edn., Washington, 1993-95. Bd. dirs. Big Bros., Albany, N.Y., 1980-83, Harrisburg Boy's Club, 1971-74, Oswego C. of C., 1974-77, Samaritan Hosp., Troy, N.Y., 1989-96, St. Anne Inst., Albany, N.Y., 1993-96, Unity House, Troy, 1993-99, pres., 1996-98; mem. Siena Coll. Bd. Assoc. Trustees, 1999—; trustee Cath. Charities of The Diocese of Albany, N.Y., 2001—. Mem. Siena Coll. Alumni Assn. (bd. dirs. 1983-85). Roman Catholic. Home: 16 Carriage Hill Dr Latham NY 12110-4947 Office: Washburn & McGoldrick 8 Century Hill Dr Ste 1 Latham NY 12110-2116 E-mail: mcgold@wash-mcg.com.

MCGOLRICK, J. EDWARD, JR. retired lawyer; b. N.Y.C., June 23, 1932; s. James Edward and Emily May (Venezia) McG.; m. Jean Marie MacInnis, Nov. 10, 1956; children: Elizabeth Anne McGowan, Ellen Marie Rowan, James Edward III, William John. BA, Coll. of Holy Cross, Worcester, Mass., 1954; JD, Georgetown Law Ctr., Washington, 1961. Bar: Va. 1961, U.S. Dist. Ct. D.C. 1961, U.S. Ct. Appeals (D.C. cir.) 1961, U.s. Dist. Ct. (ea. dist.) Va. 1961, U.S. Supreme Ct. 1971, Fla. 1973; diplomate Nat. Bd. Trial Advocacy. Pvt. practice, Manassas, Va., 1961-2000; ret., 2000. Served as capt. USMCR, 1954-58. Mem. ABA, Fla. Bar Assn., Prince William County Bar Assn. (past pres.), Va. State Bar Assn., Assn. Trial Lawyers Am., Congl. Country Club (Bethesda, Md.), Wild Dunes Club (Isle of Palms, S.C.). Roman Catholic. Home: 9502 Nelson Ln Manassas VA 20110-4310

MCGONAGLE, DUNCAN FRANCIS, mental health nurse, substance abuse counselor; b. Brooklyn, N.Y., May 6, 1939; s. John and Kathleen (Rooney) McGonagle; m. Gloria Maria Carrubba, Dec. 5, 1987. AA, Allan Hancock, 1964; AAS in Nursing, CUNY, 1992. Cert. psychiat. and mental health nurse, addictions RN. Substance abuse counselor Pritikin Longevity Ctr., Santa Monica, Calif., 1978-84; paramedic N.Y.C. Emergency Med. Svc., 1987-92; psychiatric nurse Bellevue Hosp. Ctr., N.Y.C., 1992-99; adminstr. MMTP St. Barnabas Hosp., Bronx, NY, 1999—2001; nurse mgr. MMTP Beth Israel Med. Ctr., N.Y.C., 2001—. Founder Methadone Anonymous, N.Y. Aux. police officer N.Y.C. Police Dept., 1985—. With USN, 1956-60, 1961-62, Vietnam. Recipient Nat. award for Clin. Excellence in Nursing, Nat. Nurses Soc. on Addictions, 1995. Mem. Blue Knights, Knights of Life, Rolls Royce Owners Club, Harley Owners Group. Roman Catholic. Avocations: computers, sailing, motorcycling, antique autos. Home: 73 Verona St Brooklyn NY 11231-1612 Office: Beth Israel Med Ctr 215 Park Ave S New York NY 10003 E-mail: duncan73@aol.com.

MCGONIGLE, JAMES GREGORY, financial consultant; b. Bklyn., Nov. 17, 1945; s. William John and Helen Bernadette (Dennin) McG.; m. Francine Anne Falango, May 27, 1972; children: MarieElena, Lauren Anne. AAS in Acctg., CUNY, 1972; BS in Fin. summa cum laude, L.I. U., 1980. Cert. fin. planner Internat. Bd. Cert. Fin. Planners. Account exec. Coburn Credit Corp., Rockville Centre, N.Y., 1965-66; asst. credit mgr. UNI-CARD, Greatneck, 1966-68; accounts receivable mgr. Granite Leasing Corp., Garden City, 1968-73; v.p. Citicorp., N.Y.C., 1973-88; cons. O/E Learning, Inc., Detroit, 1988-90; regional dir. Ednl. Techs., Inc., Troy, Mich., 1989—. Adj. faculty Coll. for Fin. Planning, Denver. Vol. Family Svc. Assn., Nassau, N.Y., 1981-84, Better Bus. Bur., Farmingdale, N.Y., 1987—; vol., career advisor L.I. U., Brookville, N.Y., 1990—; treas. W. Tresper Clarke Friends of Arts, 1988-89. Mem. ABA (assoc.), Fin. Mgmt. Assn., Internat. Assn. Fin. Planning, Adelphi Soc. Cert. Fin. Planners, Internat. Assn. Registered Fin. Planners (speaker's bur.), Nat. Assn. Life Underwriters, Nat. Panel Consumer Arbitrators, Nat. Ctr. for Fin. Edn., Inst. Cert. Fin. Planners (bd. dirs. L.I. 1989-92), N.Y. State Assn. Cert. Fin. Planners, Delta Mu Delta. Republican. Roman Catholic. Avocations: bicycling, public speaking, traveling, writing, gardening. Home: 2167 Plum Tree Rd N Westbury NY 11590-6029 Office: 33 Willis Ave Mineola NY 11501-4423

MCGONIGLE, JOHN LEO, JR. retired civil engineer; b. Pitts., May 2, 1921; s. John L. and Marie (Cannon) McG.; m. Mary Frances McInerney, Oct. 10, 1953; children: Loretta, John III, Maureen, Charles, Thomas, Robert. BS in Civil Engring., Lehigh U., 1942. Registered profl. engr. N.Y., Pa., Conn. Field engr. Bethlehem Steel Corp., N.Y., Boston, 1947-50, resident engr., 1950-57, constrn. mgr. San Francisco, 1957-67, mgr. estimates Bethlehem, Pa., 1967-78; project mgr. C. F. Braun, Berkeley Heights, N.J., 1978-83; prin. resident engr. Berger-Lehman Assocs., Rye, N.Y., 1983-93; self-employed project mgmt. cons., 1993-2001; ret., 2001. Com. mem. Am. Inst. Steel Constrn., Pitts., 1970-73. Mem. Hanover Twp. (Pa.) Planning Commn. Fellow ACSE (life); mem. Lehigh U. Alumni Assn. (pres. San Francisco 1960). Republican. Roman Catholic. Achievements include resident engineer for high level bridges over Passaic River, N.J., Rappahonnock, Va., Missouri River, Annisquam River, Mass., Raritan River, N.J., and Newark Bay; also high rise buildings in Detroit, N.Y., S.I. Ferry Terminal, John Hancock, Boston.

MCGOUGH, BRIAN EDWARD, investment banker, lawyer; b. N.Y.C., Feb. 18, 1964; s. George V. McGough Sr. and Mary Elizabeth (Keaveny) Covell; m. Tamra Ann Pearce, Aug. 1, 1987; children: Michael Christopher, Christopher Thomas, Matthew Steven. BS, Bradley U., 1986; JD, No. Ill. U., 1990. Bar: Ill. 1990, U.S. Dist. Ct. (no. dist.) Ill. 1990, U.S. Tax Ct. 1993, U.S. Ct. Appeals (7th cir.) 1991, U.S. Supreme Ct. 1993. Ptnr. Katten Muchin & Zavis, Chgo., 1990-96; v.p. JP Morgan & Co., 1996-98; sr. mng. dir. Bank One Capital Markets, 1998—. Spl. asst. atty. gen. State Ill., Chgo., 1992-96. Bd. dirs. Naperville (Ill.) Cmty. Outreach, 1990—; trustee No. Ill. U., DeKalb, 1993, mem. law sch. adv. bd., 1993. Recipient Disting. Alumnae award No. Ill. U., DeKalb, 1998.

MCGOUGH, DUANE THEODORE, economist, consultant, retired government official; b. Rice Lake, Wis., Aug. 3, 1932; s. James Patrick and Josephine Margaret (Huerth) McG.; m. Donna Mae Jones, June 13, 1959 Student, Wis. State Coll., Eau Claire, 1950-52, U. Wis., 1952-54, 56-60, BS in Light Constrn. Industry, 1959, MBA in Urban Land Econs., 1962; postgrad., U. So. Calif., 1968-69. Housing mgmt. officer Pub. Housing Adminstrn. Atlanta, 1960-62; program planning analyst Pub. Housing Adminstrn. Phila., 1962-67; program analyst HUD, Washington, 1967-68, 69-70, industry economist, 1970-73, supervisory economist, 1973-77, dir. housing and demographic analysis, 1977-97, govt. tech. rep. ann. housing survey, 1977-83; govt. tech. rep. Am. Housing Survey, 1984-97; acting dep. asst. sec. for econ. affairs (chief economist) HUD, Washington, 1977, 82, 84-85, ret., 1997. U.S. rep housing subcom. UN Econ. Commn. for Europe, Geneva, 1976, 79, 82; HUD rep. Interagy. Com. on Population Rsch., 1978-97, Interagy. Forum on Aging-Related Stats., 1986-97; mem. Fed. Task Force on Household Survey Redesign, 1988-97; mem. policy com. Year 2000Census; coord. PRSC Ctr. U.S./Mex. Sem. Housing Stats., Mexico City, 1997. Editor: President's Report on Housing Goals, 1974-78, Nat. Housing Prodn. Report, 1980, 82; U.S. Housing Market Conditions Report, 1994-97, FEMA National Emergency Management Program, 1967-97, Housing Consultant, 1997—. With U.S. Army, 1954-56; saxophonist 7th Army Band. Fellow NAt. Inst. Pub. Affairs, 1969; recipient Outstanding Performance award Pub. Housing Adminstrn., Phila., 1966, HUD, 1984, 92, 97, Career Edn. award Nat. Inst. Pub. Affairs, 1968-69, Cert. Spl. Achievement, HUD, 1978, 83, 84, 96, Cert. Superior Svc., HUD, 1988, 95, Cert. Appreciation, Bur. Census, 1990. Mem. Am. Econ. Assn., Am. Real Estate and Urban Econ. Assn., Lambda Alpha Internat. (v.p. programs 1987-89, chmn. real estate and fin. com. George Washington chpt. 1990-92, dir.-at-large 1992-93), Lambda Chi Alpha. Avocations: music, gardening, rockhounding, web-surfing. E-mail: duanetm@aol.com.

MCGOUGH, WALTER THOMAS, JR. lawyer; b. Pitts., Nov. 7, 1953; s. Walter Thomas and Jane (Fitzpatrick) McG.; m. Rebecca Gai Frazier, June 24, 1978; children: Emily Ann, Walter Thomas III. BA, Princeton U., 1975; JD, U. Va., 1978. Bar: Pa., D.C., U.S. Dist. Ct. (we. dist.) Pa. 1980, U.S. Ct. Appeals (3d cir.) 1983, U.S. Ct. Appeals (6th cir.) 1984, Pa. Supreme Ct. 1978, U.S. Supreme Ct. 1983. Law clk. to judge U.S. Ct. Appeals 3d Cir., Wilmington, Del., 1978-79; law clk. to Hon. William H. Rehnquist U.S. Supreme Ct., Washington, 1979-80; asst. U.S. atty. We. Dist. Pa., 1980-82; assoc. Reed, Smith, LLP, Pitts., 1982-86; ptnr. Reed, Smith, Shaw & McClay, 1987—, head of litigation dept., 1999—. Assoc. counsel Sen. Select Com. on Secret Mil. Asst. to Iran and the Nicaraguan Opposition, Washington, 1987; mem. lawyers adv. com. U.S. Ct. Appeals (3d cir.), 1987-89, chmn., 1989; atty. Fed. Criminal Justice Def. Panel West Dist. Pa., 1983—; mem. appellate rules com. U.S. Jud. Conf., 1998—. Co-author: federal Appellate Procedure, 3rd Circuit, 1996; contbr. articles to profl. jours. Trustee Sta. WQED, Pitts., 1996—, vice chmn,, 1997-99, chmn., 1999—; mem. 3d Cir. Task Force on Rule 11, 1987-89. Mem. Am. Coll. Trial Lawyers, Allegheny County Bar Assn. (ethics com. 1983-86, bd. govs. 1994—, pres. 1999-2000), Allegheny County Acad. Trial Lawyers, Duquesne Club, Ross Mountain Club, World Affairs Coun. Office: Reed Smith LLP 435 6th Ave Ste 2 Pittsburgh PA 15219-1886

MCGOVERN, JAMES, author; BA in Journalism and Polit. Sci., postgrad., U. Minn. Radio talk show host "Let's Talk Turkey" WDGY, Mpls., 1950; news dir., TV news anchor, newscaster, reporter WDGY, KGTV, KSTP, KMSP-TV, WISN-CBS, SUN Newspapers; local news feed corres. NBC, CBS, ABC; instr. journalism Lakewood Jr. Coll., 1967-68. Polit. advisor, speechwriter, nat. presdl. campaign advance man.; former speechwriter, news, pub. rels., mktg., video prodr. and orgnl. cons. various Minn. businesses and CEO's, including 3M, Honeywell, Control Data, others; trumpeter and leader Jim McGovern Swing Band. Writer, prodr., narrator PURSUIT series of tv documentarie; author 3 dramatic plays, 2 novels; contbr. articles to profl. jours. Mem. Twin Cities Musicians Union (local 30-73); hon. mem. Chinese (Nationalist) Air Force. With USAF. Decorated DFC with one oak leaf cluster, Air Medal with 2 oak leaf clusters; winner Nat. Headliners award for best pub.affairs documentary in U.S., 1963; recipient Award of Merit, Minn. Coll. Radio Network for outstanding leadership in radio news reporting through the "Behind the Parade" radio series on KSTP, 1960. Mem. ASCAP (assoc.), Am. Soc. Composers, Artists and Pubs., DFC Soc. (charter), 14th AAF Flying Tigers, Hump Pilots Assn., U. Minn. Alumni Assn., Irish Nat. Caucus (charter). Home: Saint Paul, Minn. Died June 27, 2002; Ft. Snelling Nat. Cemebery.

MCGOVERN, JAMES RICHARD, historian; b. West Chester, Pa., Aug. 22, 1928; s. James Francis and Catherine Teresa (Crowley) McG.; m. Joan Millon; children: James, Michael, Susan. BS, Villanova (Pa.) U., 1950; MA, U. Pa., 1951, PhD, 1957. From instr. to asst. prof. Loyola U., Chgo., 1954—58; asst. prof. Merrimack Coll., North Andover, Mass., 1958—61; assoc. to prof. Emmanuel Coll., Boston, 1961—69; prof. U. West Fla., Pensacola, 1969-98, prof. emeritus, 1999—. Chair faculty of history U. West Fla., Pensacola, 1969-79, 85-90. Author: Anatomy of a Lynching, 1982 (Patrick Rembert award 1982), Black Eagle: The Life of General Daniel "Chappie" James, 1985-87 (Valley Forge award for books 1986), And A Time for Hope: Americans in Great Depression, 2000. Bicentennial com. Dir. of Transp. Planning Action 76, 1976. Mem.: Am. Hist. Assn. Avocations: mountain climbing, sailing, gardening. Home: 6446 Scenic Hwy Pensacola FL 32504

MCGOVERN, JAMES P. congressman; b. Worcester, Mass., Nov. 20, 1959; m. Lisa Murray. BA, Am. U., 1981, MA in Pub. Administration, 1984. Aide U.S. Senator George McGovern (Dem. South Dakota); spokesman, legis. dir., sr. aide U.S. Congressman Joe Moakley (Dem. South Boston); mem. U.S. Congress from 3rd Mass dist., 1997—; elected regional whip, mem. transp. & infrastructure com. Mgr. George McGovern for Pres., 1984; delivered McGovern presdl. nomination speech Dem. Nat. Convention, San Francisco, 1984; leader Congressional Investigation on El Salvador, 1989 Candidate for U.S. Congress, 1996; vol. Mt. Carmel House; bd. dirs. Jesuit Internat. Vols. Home: 34 Mechanic St Worcester MA 01608-2424 Office: Ho of Representatives 416 Cannon House Office Bldg Washington DC 20515-0001*

MCGOVERN, MICHAEL BARBOT, lawyer; b. N.Y.C., Mar. 6, 1947; s. Michael Malachy and Annette (Barbot) McG.; m. Christine Anne Beaudet, Sept. 2, 1972; children: Kathleen, Ellen, Maura. AB, Georgetown U., 1969, JD, 1972; LLM (Taxation), George Washington U., 1987. Bar: D.C. 1973, Md. 1978. From assoc. to ptnr. Wilkes & Artis, Washington, 1973-79; sole practice, 1980, 84-87; ptnr. Lambert, Griffin & McGovern, 1981-84, Venable, Baetjer, Howard & Civiletti, Washington, 1987-93, Montedoninco, Hamilton & Altman, Washington, 1994-98, Hanson & Molloy, Washington, 1998—. Bd. dirs. Hist. Soc. Washington, 1984-93; co-founder, vice-chair, bd. dirs. Greater Bethesda-Chevy Chase Coalition Inc., 1986—; pres. Westmoreland Citizens Assn. Inc., 1988-90; mem. Leadership Washington, 1987—. Capt. USAFR, 1969-82, bd. dirs., Montgomery Co. Historical Soc., 1997—. Recipient Distinguished Service award Fed. Bar Assn., 1978. Mem. Columbia Country Club (Chevy Chase), Met. Club (Washington), Barristers, John Carroll Soc. Republican. Roman Catholic. Home: 5414 Albemarle St Bethesda MD 20816-1825 Office: Hanson & Molloy 1250 Eye St NW Ste 701 Washington DC 20005-5980

MCGOVERN, RUSSELL DANIEL, artist; b. Great Falls, Mont., Apr. 19, 1922; s. Daniel Cornelius and Electa Margarite (Young) McG.; m. Nancy Ann McGovern, Sept. 8, 1945; children: Russell D. Jr., John W., William E., James Y. BS, U.S. Mil. Acad., 1945; MS, U. Miami, 1961. Commd. U.S. Army, 1945-75, advanced through grades to col., ret., 1975; program mgr. Dalmo Victor Electronic Sys., Belmont, Calif., 1979-88. Recipient numerous awards for paintings in exhbns. Sequoia Art Group, Redwood City, Calif., 1980-97, Burlingame (Calif.) Art Soc., 1995-97. Mem. Soc. Western Artists, Sequoia Art Group (v.p. 1985, 86, 87), Burlingame Art Soc. (treas. 1995-97, Artist of the Yr. 1996). Avocations: golf, world travel. Home: 1812 Hunt Dr Burlingame CA 94010-5726

MCGOVERN, THOMAS AQUINAS, retired utility executive; b. N.Y.C., Mar. 2, 1933; s. Thomas Aquinas and Helen Frances (Carroll) McG.; m. Miriam Anne Howley, July 16, 1955; children: Cecilia, Louise, Pamela. BS in History, Coll. of the Holy Cross, 1954; MA in Econs., L.I. U., 1965. Dep. asst. Consol. Edison Co. of N.Y., N.Y.C., 1958-61, supts. asst., 1961-66, asst. supt., 1967-68, supt., 1968-69, staff dir., 1969-70, asst. to exec. v.p., 1970-72, exec. dir., 1972-82, asst. v.p., 1982-89, v.p., 1989-95; sr. assoc. John Hall Co., Danbury, Conn., 1995—. Mem. Edison Elec. Inst. Sec. Commn., Washington, 1976-90, Mailers' Tech. Adv. Com., Washington, 1990-91; vice-chmn. Nat. Postal Coun., Washington, 1982—; pres. D.C.K. Mgmt. Corp., N.Y.C., 1982-94; mem. Real Estate Bd. N.Y., N.Y.C., 1988-94. Mem. N.Y.C. (N.Y.) Health and Hosps. Security Adv. Com., 1985; pres. Westchester County Police Meml., White Plains, N.Y., 1987—. With U.S. Army, 1954-56. Recipient Svcs. to Nation and FBI award FBI, N.Y.C., 1984, Svc. to Law Enforcement Community award N.Y. State Chiefs of Police, Albany, N.Y., 1989, Appreciation for Svc. award N.Y. State Fedn. of Police, Briarcliff Manor, N.Y., 1989, Svc. to Orgns. award FBI Marine Corps Assn., Cresskill, N.J., 1989, Svc. to Orgns. award N.Y.C. Honor Legion, Richmond Hill, N.Y. Mem. KC, VFW, Am. Legion, Assn. of U.S. Army, U.S. Naval Inst., FBI Marine Corps Assn., Friendly Sons of St. Patrick, VFW, Holy Cross Varsity Club (dir.), Pi Gamma Mu. Roman Catholic. Avocations: U.S. mil. history, post card collecting, toy soldier collecting, Royal Doulton china collecting. Office: John Hall & Co PO Box 187 Glen Ridge NJ 07028-0187

MC GOVERN, WALTER T. federal judge; b. Seattle, May 24, 1922; s. C. Arthur and Anne Marie (Thies) McG.; m. Rita Marie Olsen, June 29, 1946; children: Katrina M., Shawn E., A. Renee. BA, U. Wash., 1949, LL.B., 1950. Bar: Wash. 1950. Practiced law in, Seattle, 1950-59; mem. firm Kerr, McCord, Greenleaf & Moen; judge Municipal Ct., Seattle, 1959-65, Superior Ct., Wash., 1965-68, Wash. Supreme Ct., 1968-71, U.S. Dist. Ct. (we. dist.) Wash., 1971-87, chief judge, 1975-87, sr. judge, 1987—. Mem. subcom. on supporting personnel Jud. Conf. U.S., 1981-87, chmn. subcom., 1983, mem. adminstrn. com., 1983-87, chmn. jud. resources com., 1987-91. Mem. Am. Judicature Soc., Wash. State Superior Ct. Judges Assn., Seattle King County Bar Assn. (treas.), Phi Delta Phi. Clubs: Seattle Tennis (pres. 1968). Office: US Dist Ct US Courthouse 5th Fl 1010 5th Ave Ste 215 Seattle WA 98104-1189

MCGOWAN, BRENDA GAY, social work educator, consultant; b. Boston, Sept. 28, 1941; d. John Gay and Dorothy Frances (Mullin) McG. BA, Wellesley Coll., 1963; MSW, Boston Coll., 1966; DSW, Columbia U., 1974. Lic. ind. clin. social worker, Mass. Caseworker Cath. Charitable Bur. of Boston, 1963-68, supr., dir. family home program, 1968-69; project dir., rsch. assoc. Child Advocacy Rsch. Project Columbia U. Sch. Social Work, N.Y.C., 1971-73, asst. prof., 1976-78, assoc. prof., 1978-85, prof., 1985-99, Ruth Harris Ottman prof. family and child welfare, 1999—. Vis. lectr. U. Maine, Portland-Gorham, summers 1973, 74, Smith Coll. Sch. Social Work, summer 1980, Pontifica Universidade Catolica do Rio de Janeiro, Brazil, summers 1984, 85; rsch. assoc. Children's Def. Fund, Washington Rsch. Project, N.Y.C., 1974-76. Co-author: Child Advocacy: Report of a National Baseline Study, 1973, Why Punish the Children: A Study of Children of Women Prisoners, 1978, Children Without Homes, 1978, Nurturing the One, Supporting the Many: The Center for Family Life in Sunset Park, 2002; co-editor: Child Welfare: Current Dilemmas, Future Directions, 1983, author monographs, articles, and chpts. in books. Mem. adv. com. Fahs-Beck Fund for Rsch. and Demonstration, N.Y. Community Trust, 1992—; N.Y. state del. White House Conf. on Families, 1980; mem. N.Y.C. youth bd. Office of the Mayor, 1984-90, numerous other civic activities. Mem. NASW (nat. com. on inquiry 1993—, bd. dirs. N.Y.C. chpt. 1979-81, 88-90, chair child welfare com. 1974-75, co-chair com. on profl. standards 1983-85, co-chair task force on svcs. to families and children 1984-87), Acad. Cert. Social Workers, Coun. on Social Work Edn., Am. Orthopsychiat. Assn. Home: 225 E 79th St New York NY 10021-0855 Office: Columbia U Sch Social Work 622 W 113th St New York NY 10025-7982

MCGOWAN, CHARLOTTE ACORD, anthropologist; b. Ridgefarm, Ill., Feb. 19, 1930; d. Ira Patrick Acord, Edythe Mae Minerva (Lewis) Acord; m. James Patrick McGowan Jr., June 4, 1949; children: James Patrick McGowan III, Lauren Louise. BA Honors, San Diego State U., 1967, MA Honors, 1969. Tchg. asst., dir. phys. anthropology lab., prof. anthropology San Diego State U., 1967—69; prof. anthropology San Diego Evening Coll., 1969—71, Southwestern Coll., Chula Vista, Calif., 1971—99; ret., 1999. Prof. anthropology San Diego Adult Sch., 1967—69, North Shores Adult Sch., San Diego, 1968—71, Patrick Henry Adult Sch., San Diego, 1970—71, Univ. Ams., Puebla, Mexico, 1978; cons. Environ. Impact Studies, San Diego, 1975—2000, Calif. Dept. Transp., 1995—98, Native Am. Groups, San Diego, 1994—, Campo Band of Mission Indians, Campo, Calif., 1995—; dir., liaison Nat. Am. Interface, 1995—. Author: Inventory of Artifacts from Archaeological Excavation, 1995, Final Report on Excavation, 1997; contbr. , articles to profl. jours. Scholar Fulbright, Peru, 1982, Taiwan, 1996. Mem.: Congress of Hist. of San Diego and Imperial Counties, Calif., San Diego Natural Hist. Mus., San Diego Mus. of Man, SW Missions Rsch. Ctr., SW Anthropol. Assn., Archaeol. Inst. Am. Avocations: travel, reading, writing, embroidery. Office: Southwestern College 900 Otay Lakes Rd Chula Vista CA 91910

MCGOWAN, GERALD S. diplomat; b. Birmingham, Mich., 1946; married Susan Anne Brophy; seven children. BSBA, Georgetown U., 1968, JD, 1974. Bar: D.C.; U.S. Ct. Appeals (D.C.), U.S. Dist. Ct. D.C., U.S. Supreme Ct. Founding prin. Lukas, McGowan, Nace & Gutierrez, Washington; amb. to Portugal U.S. Dept. of State, 1998—. Founder Integrated North Coast, Inc; developer cellular system ea. Ohio, 1992; bd. dirs. Overseas Pvt. Investment Corp. 1st It. U.S. Army, Vietnam, 1970-71. Mem. D.C. Bar, Fed. Comms. Bar Assn. Office: Avenida das Forcas Armadas Psc 83 APO AE 09726-9998

MCGOWAN, HAROLD, real estate developer, investor, scientist, author, philanthropist; b. Weehawken, N.J., June 23, 1909; s. Sylvester and Grace (Kalbfleish) McG.; m. Anne Cecelia McTiernan, Jan. 15, 1938; children—Linda Anne, Harold Charles, Janice Marie. Ed., Bklyn. Poly. U., Pratt Inst., N.Y. U.; student, N.Y. Tech.; ed., Hubbard U. (Eng.); D.Sc., Coll. Fla. Chmn. bd. Atomic Rsch. Inc.; pres. Harold McGowan Builders; owner, developer Central Islip Shopping Center, Central Islip Indsl. Center; developer, builder Brinsley Gardens, Rolling Green, Slater Park, Clover Green, Maple Acres, Wheeler Acres; owner-donor Little League Baseball Pks., 1950—. Sculptures include: Bless Them; Victory, Eternity, Love and Hate, Triumph; author: Green Flight, (originator) The Thoughtron Theory of Life and Matter, Race with Death across the Sahara, The Incorrigibles, The Frigid Trap, The Shah's Swiss Secret, Another World for Christmas, The Spirit of Christmas in Words and Sculpture, The Making of a Universalist, The Journeyman, $800,000 for Love, Beyond the Visible, Shock after Shock, Christmas Stories, Short Stories, Born Again, You Are Forever, Black Shroud Over Bagdad, The Gold Mine; mural Back to Creation; holder U.S. patent to form one-piece plywood corner units, U.S. patent apparatus for forming one-piece plywood corner units. Hwy. commr., Suffolk County; chmn. Recreation & Parks-Islip; past dir. Suffolk County Girl Scouts; land donor St. John of God R.C. Ch., The Episcopal Ch. of the Messiah, Ctrl. Islip Sch. Dist. Recipient Winston Churchill Medal of Wisdom, 1986, Wisdom Hall of Fame, Beverly Hills, Calif., 1970; Churchill fellow, 1989. Mem. AAAS, IEEE, Explorers Club, Mensa Internat. Avocations: sculpture, art, philanthropy. Address: 28 2nd Ave Central Islip NY 11722-3012 *To become a really whole and successful person, one should recognize the efforts and good will of those living and dead who developed the culture, the fruits of which he enjoys, and repay his benefactors by contributing more to that society than he takes and also by doing good deeds to make the society better than he found it. He must also strive to understand the world and his relationship to it and know that the universe is neither capricious nor mysterious, that miracles do not happen. Everything and every action can only occur within the bounds of the laws of physics, chemistry, biology and communication. He must further realize that he is eternal and the basic purpose of human life is to become aware of and to live by these universal laws. The acme of a person's accomplishments would be his comprehension of the structure of the physical universe, the processes of life, and the nature of his mind. When he comprehends the Universe, Life and Mind, he will understand his own immortality.*

MCGOWAN, IAN DUNCAN, librarian; b. Liverpool, Eng., Sept. 19, 1945; s. Alexander and Dora (Sharp) McG.; m. Elizabeth Ann Weir, Oct. 30, 1971; children: Catherine, Margaret. BA, Exeter Coll., Oxford, 1967. FRSA, 1999. Asst. keeper Nat. Libr. of Scotland, Edinburgh, 1971-78, keeper, 1978-88, sec. of libr., 1978-90, libr., 1990—2002. Chmn. U.K. Nat. Preservation Adv. Com., 1995-96; chmn. Britain-Russia Ctr., Scotland, 1999-2002. Mem. Scottish Libr. Assn. (v.p. 1996-97, pres. 1998). Office: Nat Libr of Scotland George IV Bridge Edinburgh EH1 1EW Scotland

MCGOWAN, JOAN YUHAS, development researcher; b. Trenton, N.J., Feb. 13, 1955; d. Bernard Joseph and Estelle (Gray) (dec.) Yuhas; children: Matthew Sheehan, Allison Joo Ok. BA summa cum laude, Trenton State Coll., 1977. Cert. tchr., N.J. Tchr. Blessed Sacrament Sch., Trenton, 1977; intake officer Mercer County Juvenile Ct, 1978-82; rsch. dir. Audits and Surveys, Princeton, N.J., 1982-85; project dir. The Gallup Orgn., 1985-86, Hase/Schannen Rsch. Assocs., Princeton, 1986; devel. researcher Coll. NJ, 1986—. Guest lectr., Thomas Jefferson U., Rutgers U., Helene Fuld Sch. Nursing; guest speaker local television programs. Author: Waiting: The Hopes and Frustrations of a Childless Couple, 1983; contbr. articles to various publs. Pres. Resolve, Inc., Phila, 1982; mem. Holt Internat. Children's Svcs., Trenton, 1984-85, Incarnation Altar Rosary Soc., Trenton, 1988—, Holy Name Soc., Trenton, 1989—; treas, area contact, Homeward Bound, Inc., 1996—. Recipient Think and Suggest award State of N.J., 1977, Meritorious award Trenton State Coll., 1989. Mem.: New Eng. Devel. Rschrs. Assn. (mentor), Assn. Profl. Rschrs. for Advancement, Am. Fedn. Tchrs., Villa Park Civic Assn., Operation Scarlet (assoc.). Democrat. Roman Catholic. Avocations: reading, family activities, rescue dogs, piano, music. Home: 941 Lyndale Ave Trenton NJ 08629-2409 Office: The Coll NJ PO Box 7718 Ewing NJ 08628-0718 E-mail: mcgowanj@tcnj.edu.

MCGOWAN, JOHN EDWARD, JR. clinical epidemiology educator, microbiologist, infectious diseases specialist; b. Poughkeepsie, N.Y., June 30, 1942; s. John Edward and Doris Robinson (Wearne) McG.; m. Linda Kay Hudson, May 28, 1967; 1 child, Angela Kay. BMS, Dartmouth Coll., 1965; MD, Harvard U., 1967. Diplomate Am. Bd. Internal Medicine, Am. Bd. Infectious Diseases, Am. Bd. Pathology in Med. Microbiology. Intern, resident Harvard Svc., Boston City Hosp., 1967-69; rsch. fellow Thorndike Lab., Harvard Med. Sch., 1971-72; instr. Harvard Med. Sch., Boston, 1972-73; asst. prof. Emory Med. Sch., Atlanta, 1973-76, assoc. prof., 1977-81, prof. pathology and medicine, 1982—; prof. epidemiology Rollins Sch. Pub. Health, Emory U., 1992—. Dir. microbiology Grady Meml. Hosp., Atlanta, 1982-98; chmn. panel on microbial devices FDA, 1992-94. Assoc. editor Infection Control and Hosp. Epidemiology, 1980-92; contbr. some 250 sci. articles to profl. jours. Mem. governing bd. Young Singers of Callanwolde, Decatur, Ga., 1981-86; treas. Leafmore Creek-Park Club, Decatur, 1982-84. Sr. surgeon USPHS, 1969-71. Fellow Infectious Diseases Soc. Am. (governing bd. 1995-97), Am. Coll.

Epidemiology; mem. Am. Soc. for Microbiology (divsn. chair 1982-84, governing bd. 1984-87), Soc. Hosp. Epidemiologists Am. (pres. 1981), Am. Hosp. Assn. (panel on infections in hosps. 1989-95), Nat. Com. for Clin. Lab. Standards, Am. Acad. Microbiology. Office: Emory U Rollins Sch Pub Health Dept Epidemiology (442-GCR) 1518 Clifton Rd NE Dept 442 Atlanta GA 30322-4201

MCGOWAN, KEITH RICHARD, environmental planner; b. Shreveport, La., Jan. 7, 1955; s. Garrett P. and Lucille T. McGowan; m. Lise T. McGowan, 1981; 2 children. BS in Forestry, La. State U., 1977; MS, U. Oreg., 1982, M of Urban Planning, 1988. Cert. planner. Rsch. scientist U.S. Forest Svc., PNW Forest Experiment Sta., Seattle, 1982-86; v.p. Shapiro and Assocs., Inc., 1987-96; pres. McGowan Environmental, Inc., 1996—. Treas., bd. dirs. Alpine Edn. Found., Seattle, 1997—; bd. trustees Bayview Manor, Seattle, 1989-90; bd. dirs. Ctr. for Ethics and Urban Policy, Seattle, 1988-90; chmn. adminstrv. bd. First United Meth. Ch., Seattle, 1988-90. Named Outstanding Young Men of Am. U.S. Jaycees, 1982, Eagle Scout of Gold Palm Boy Scouts Am., 1971. Mem. Am. Inst. of Cert. Planners, Am. Planning Assn. (transp. planning divsn.), Nat. Assn. of Environtl. Profls., Womens Transp. Seminar, Nat. Eagle Scout Assn., Xi Sigma Pi (Alpha chpt.).

MCGOWAN, PATRICK FRANCIS, lawyer; b. N.Y.C., July 23, 1940; s. Francis Patrick and Sonia Veronica (Koslow) M.; m. Patricia Neil, June 6, 1964; children: Susan Claire, Kathleen Anne. BA, Rice U., 1962; JD, U. Tex., Austin, 1965. Bar: Tex. 1965, U.S. Ct. Appeals (5th cir.) 1969, U.S. Tax Ct. 1972, U.S. Supreme Ct. 1970, U.S. Ct. Appeals (11th cir.) 1981, U.S. Ct. Appeals (fed. cir.) 1993. Briefing atty. Tex. Supreme Ct., Austin, 1965-66; ptnr. Strasburger & Price, Dallas, 1966-98, Akin, Gump, Strauss, Hauer & Feld, Dallas, 1998—. Pres., chmn. bd. Tex Lex, Inc., 1991-98; faculty I.P. Law Instit. Ctr. Am. and Internat. Law, 2001. Contbr. numerous articles on interent trademark, copyright and franchise law. Bd. advisors Dallas Ft. Worth Sch. Law. Fellow Coll. State Bar Tex. (faculty Franchising Inst. 1987, Intellectual Property Inst. 1992, S.W. Legal Found. Patent Law Inst. 1992, Practising Law Inst. 1996, Ctr. for Am. and Internat. Law I.P. Inst. 2001); mem. ABA (forum com. on franchising, trademark and unfair competition com., patent, trademark and copyright law sect.), State Bar Tex. (intellectual property sect., com. continuing legal edn.), Dallas Bar Assn. (dir. intellectual property law sect. 1994—, chmn. I.P. Basics seminar 1999, sect. vice chmn. 2001, chmn. 2002), ALFA Internat. Tel. Symposium, Internat. Anti-Counterfeiting Assn., Tex. Law Rev. Editors Assn., Phi Delta Phi. Office: Akin Gump 1700 Pacific Ave Ste 4100 Dallas TX 75201-4675 E-mail: pmcgowan@akingump.com.

MCGOWAN, RICHARD STEPHEN, lawyer; b. N.Y.C., Feb. 4, 1954; s. Richard Allen and Ann (Bellner) McG.; m. Arline Rita Finnerty, May 17, 1980; children: Richard J., Matthew S., Michael J. BA in History, SUNY, Stony Brook, 1976; JD, U. Boston, 1979. Bar: Mass. 1979, N.Y. 1980, U.S. Dist. Ct. (so. and ea. dists.) N.Y. 1980, U.S. Dist. Ct. (no. dist.) N.Y., 1988, U.S. Dist. (no. dist.) Calif. 1990, U.S. Dist. Ct. Conn. 1997, U.S. Ct. Appeals (2d cir.) 1982. Assoc. D'Amato & Lynch, N.Y.C., 1980-81, Barry T. McTierman & Moore, N.Y.C., 1981-83, Bower & Gardner, N.Y.C., 1983-85; shareholder Rheingold & McGowan, P.C., 1985-95; of counsel Weitz & Luxenberg, P.C., 1995—. Contbr. articles to profl. jours. Instr. Intensive Trial Adv. Program/Cardoza Law Sch., 1986—. Mem. ATLA, N.Y. State Trial Lawyers Assn. (dir. 1992—, chair product liability com. 1992-94, vice-chair legis. ctr. 1993—, Pres. award 1996), N.Y. State Bar Assn., N.Y. County Lawyers Assn. (co-chair tort sect. 1995-97). Office: Weitz & Luxenberg PC 180 Maiden Ln Fl 17 New York NY 10038-4937

MCGOWAN, SCOTT WAYNE, music educator; b. Bremenhaven, Germany, July 29, 1972; s. Wayne Lester McGowan, June Blanche McGowan. B in Music Edn., U. No. Iowa, 1997. Asst. dir. band Air Acad. H.S., Colorado Springs, Colo., 1997—99; instr. saxophone Adams State Coll., Alamosa, 1999—2000; dir. band Air Acad. H.S., Colorado Springs, 2000—. Musician Little London Winds, Colorado Springs, 2001—; guest condr. All-Star Band Pike's Peak Jazz Festival, 2001, 02; dir. Pike's Peak Jazz Messengers, Colorado Springs, 2000. Mem.: Music Educators Nat. Conf., Internat. Assn. Jazz Educators. Home: 4882 C Sonata Dr Colorado Springs CO 80918 Office: Air Academy HS 6910 Carlton Dr Colorado Sprigns CO 80840

MCGOWAN, THOMAS RANDOLPH, retired religious organization executive; b. Balt., Apr. 19, 1926; s. Robert and Mary (Miller) McG.; m. Bernice A. Bernard, May 20, 1967 (dec. Nov. 1981); children: Howard, James, Terry; m. Roedean Olivia Oden, Feb. 9, 1985; children: Karen White, Kevin, Kurt. AA, Oakland Jr. Coll., 1964; postgrad., San Francisco State Coll., 1964-68; BS, U. Md., 1978. Lt. security police Oakland (Calif.) Army Base, 1955-60; chief motor pool San Francisco Procurement Agy., Oakland, 1960-64, contract specialist, 1964-68, Harry Diamond Labs., Washington, 1968-79, br. chief procurement divsn., 1972-79; chief procurement directorate Yuma (Ariz.) Proving Ground, 1979-82; dir. ecumenism Roman Cath. Diocese of Oakland, 1983—. Dir. African Am. Cath. Pastoral Ctr., Diocese of Oakland, 1991—. Convenor Interreligious Coun. of Oakland, 1988—; trustee Greater Oakland Interfaith Network, 1989-92; mem. East Oakland Renewal Task Force, 1990—; bd. dir. Columbia (Md.) Found., 1972-74, chmn., 1975-79; div. Bd. Cons., Graymoor, N.Y., 1990—; bd. dirs. Thea Bowman Manor, Oakland, 1989—, St. Mary's Ctr. With U.S. Army, 1944-46. Mem. Knights of Peter Claver, Rotary. Democrat. Avocations: tennis, woodworking. Home: 139 Pinto Dr Vallejo CA 94591-8451

MCGOWAN, WILLIAM ANDREW, lawyer; b. N.Y.C., Apr. 29, 1918; s. Andrew J. and Kathryn A. (Sweeney) McG.; m. Manuela Marie Corey, July 11, 1946; children— Susan C. McGowan Turner, Andrew J., Mary Louise McGowan Manifold, William E. B.A., Manhattan Coll., 1938; LL.B., Bklyn. Law Sch., 1941. Bar: N.Y. 1942, Ind. 1958, D.C. 1964. Sole practice, N.Y.C., 1946-48; atty. NLRB, 1948-54; asst. gen. counsel United Brotherhood of Carpenters and Joiners Am., Washington, 1954-69, gen. counsel, 1969— . Served with AUS, 1942-46; World War II. Democrat. Roman Catholic.

MCGOWEN, GERALD ELLIS, biologist; b. Muskegon, Mich., Dec. 27, 1946; s. Gerald Edward and Helen Lorraine McGowen. BS in Biology, San Diego State U., 1970, MS in Biology, 1977; PhD in Biology, U. So. Calif., L.A., 1987. Assoc. environ. specialist Occidental Coll., L.A., 1974-78; rsch. assoc. U. So. Calif., 1978-80; asst. rsch. curator Natural History Mus. L.A. County, 1978-92; lectr. Calif. State U., Long Beach, 1990; water biologist environ. monitoring divsn. City of L.A., 1992—2001, water biologist regulatory affairs divsn., 2001—. Cons. Tenera, San Francisco, 1996-2000. Author: (book chpts.) Ontogeny and Systematics of Fishes, 1984; contbr. articles to books and profl. jours. Mem. Soc. Environ. Toxicologists and Chemists (mem., bd. dirs. So. Calif. chpt. 1999-2002), So. Calif. acad. Scis., So. Calif. Toxicity Assessment Group. Avocations: fishing, hiking, camping, diving, shooting pool. a.us. Office: City of LA Regulatory Affairs 12000 Vista del Mar Playa Del Rey CA 90293 Office Fax: 310-648-5114. E-mail: gem1440@adelphia.net., gem@san.lacity.org.

MCGOWEN, SANDRA GRANT, interior designer; b. Shreveport, La., Dec. 4, 1942; d. Ellis Elva and Mary Lou (McMahen) Grant; m. Norman Douglas McGowen, Mar. 14, 1964 (dec. 1972); children: Amanda Laine, Norman Douglas Jr. BS in Home Econs., La. Tech. U., 1965; BVA in Interior Design, Ga. State U., 1978. Interior designer Rich's, Atlanta, 1978-85; dir. design Comml. Interior Designs, 1985; pres. McGowen Interiors Inc., 1985—. Adj. prof., Brenau Univ., 1995—. Elder Presbyn. Ch., 1986; bd. dirs. Niskey Lake, Atlanta, 1986; design judge March of Dimes, Birmingham, Ala., 1987. Mem.: Am. Soc. Interior Designers (newsletter editor 1986, 87, treas. 1987, 88, pres. Ga. chpt. 1990-91, nat. bd. 1991-93, Presdl. citation 1981, 87), Nat. Trust for Hist. Preservation, Mercedes Benz Club Am. (sec. Peachtree sect.), High Mus. Art., Ga. Trust for Hist. Preservation, Atlanta City Sales Club, Gamma Phi Beta (pres. Mother's Club. U. Ga. 1987-88). Republican. Presbyterian. Home: # 1709 1280 W Peachtree St NW Atlanta GA 30309-3434 Office: 1720 Peachtree St NW Ste 140 Atlanta GA 30309-2439 E-mail: mcgowenint@mindspring.com.

MCGOWIN, PAMELA ROWE, speech-language and hearing pathologist; b. Chgo., Oct. 11, 1942; d. Charles Parker and Martha M. (Vial) Rowe; m. Charles Richard McGowin; children: Brent William Haerle, Derek Parker Haerle. BS with honors, U. Wis., 1964. Cert. gen. and spl. teaching credential, Calif.; basic clin. cert. Am. Speech and Hearing Assn. Speech-lang.-hearing pathologist L.A. City Unified Sch. Dists., 1964-65, San Francisco Unified Sch. Dist., 1965-67; dir. Improvibe Inter-Arts Sch. for Children, San Francisco, 1971-73; dir., tchr., lang. specialist pvt. presch., San Mateo, Calif., 1973-78; program specialist for communicatively handicapped San Mateo City Sch. Dist., 1981-87, speech-lang.-hearing pathologist, 1978-97, ret., 1997. Mem. eligibility and exit criteria task force State of Calif., 1981-82; chmn. Task Force on Delivery Svcs. to Ltd. Intellectual Functioning Children, 1985. Bd. dirs. Monterey County Symphony Assn., Friends of Monterey County Symphony, pres. 1998-2000. Mem. ASCD, NEA, Calif. Tchrs. Assn., Calif. Assn. Program Specialists, Calif. Speech-Lang.-Hearing Assn., San Mateo County Speech-Lang.-Hearing Assn., San Mateo Elem. Tchrs. Assn., Am. Symphony Orch. League, Assn. Calif. Symphony Orchs. E-mail: cmcgpmcg@aol.com.

MC GOWIN, WILLIAM EDWARD, artist; b. Hattiesburg, Miss., June 2, 1938; s. William Edward and Emily (Ratliff) Mc G.; m. Claudia DeMonte, May 28, 1977; children: Leah, Jill. BS, U. So. Miss., 1961; MA, U. Ala., 1964. Prof. art SUNY, Old Westbury, 1978— , Coll. Old Westbury; mem. faculty Corcoran Gallery Art, 1966-77, head sculpture dept., 1967-74; lectr. in field. One-man shows include Corcoran Gallery Art, Washington, 1962, 71, 75, Martha Jackson Gallery, N.Y.C., 1968, Am. Cultural Ctr., Paris, 1974, Mus. Modern Art, Paris, 1978, Brooks Jackson Gallery, Iolas, N.Y.C., 1978-80, Fendrick Gallery, Washington, 1977-80, U. Colo., New Orleans Contemporary Art Ctr., 1982, Project Studios 1, L.I., N.Y., Cranbrook Acad., Bloomfield Hills, Mich., 1983, Art Park, Lewiston, N.Y., 1984, Gracie Mansion Gallery, N.Y.C., 1985, 86, 89, Mus. Fine Arts, Miami, Jones, Troyer Gallery, Washington, 1987, 89, 91, Boca Raton (Fla.) Mus., 1991, Margulis-Taplin Gallery, Miami, 1993, Paris-New York-Bangkok Gallery, Bangkok, Thailand, 1994, Grey Art Gallery, NYU, 1995, Siipakorn U., Bangkok, 1997, Genkan Gallery, Tokyo, 1997, Miss. Mus. Art, 2000; group shows include Contemporary Mus., Houston, Miss. Mus. Art, Whitney Mus., N.Y.C., Detroit Inst. Art, Guggenheim Mus., Speed Mus., Ky., Cologne (Germany) Art Fair, Zurich (Switzerland) Art Fair; represented in permanent collections Phillips Collection, Washington, Indpls. Mus. Art, Addison Mus. Art, Andover, Mass, Corcoran Gallery Art, Nat. Collection Fine Arts, Washington, New Orleans Mus. Art, Whitney Mus. Am. Art, N.Y.C., Guggenheim Mus., N.Y.C., Hirshorn Gallery and Sculpture Garden; permanent commn. U.S. Gen. Svc. Adminstrn., 1979, VA, Indpls., 1985, Percent for Art, N.Y.C., 1992, City of Jubai, Saudi Arabia, 1993, Dallas Rapid Transit Authority, 1994, Queens Co. N.Y. Supreme Ct., 1996, Art in Pub. Places, Socorro, N.Mex., 1997, Met. Transit Authority State of N.Y., Bayside, 1998. Recipient Oscar for painting, 1977, Painting prize 9th Internat. Painting Festival, Cagnes-sur-Mer, France, 1977, Miss. Arts and Letters award for visual arts, 1980, Art Commn. Design award N.Y.C., 1998; Nat. Endowment for Arts grantee, 1967-68, 79-80, pub. outdoor sculpture grantee, 1977, Cassandra Found. grantee. Home and Office: 96 Grand St New York NY 10013-2633

MCGRADY, CORINNE YOUNG, design company executive; b. N.Y.C., May 6, 1938; d. Albert I. and Reda (Bromberg) Young; m. Michael Robinson McGrady; children: Sean, Siobhan, Liam. Student, Bard Coll., Annandale-on-Hudson, N.Y., 1960, Harvard U., 1968-69. Founder, pres. Corinne McGrady Designs; designer Corinneware (joint venture of Corinne McGrady Designs and Boston Warehouse Trading Corp. 1990), East Northport, N.Y., 1970—. Acrylic works exhibited in group shows at Mus. Contemporary Crafts, N.Y.C., 1969-70, Smithsonian Instn., 1970-71, Pompidou Ctr., Paris, 1971, Mus. Sci. and Industry, 1970; sculpture exhibited at Guild Hall Show, Southampton, N.Y., 1968, Hecksher Mus., 1968. Vice pres. Woman's Internat. League for Peace and Freedom, Huntington, N.Y., 1971; mem. bldg. com. Timberland Lib Hoodsport, 1996-97. Recipient Design Rev. award Indsl. Design, 1969, 70; Instant Supergraphic Indsl. Design Rev. award, 1971. Patentee cookbook stand. Home and Office: PO Box 27 Lilliwaup WA 98555-0027

MCGRADY, JONATHAN L. lawyer; b. Knoxville, Tenn., Oct. 29, 1969; s. Joseph Harry and Ann Abate McG.; m. Jennifer Blackmon, Aug. 5, 1995. BA, Hampden-Sydney Coll., 1991; JD, Coll. William & Mary, 1995. Bar: Va. 1995, U.S. Dist. Ct. (we. dist.) Va. 1995, U.S. Ct. Appeals (4th cir.) 1995. Ptnr. McGrady & McGrady, LLP, Hillsville, Va., 1996—. Chmn. Carroll County Dem. Party, 1996—; deacon Hillsville Christian Ch. Mem. Va. Trial Lawyers Assn., Va. Bar Assn., Carroll Bar Assn., Hillsville Masonic Lodge. Home: 149 Camelot Ln Hillsville VA 24343-1676 Office: McGrady & McGrady LLP 127 Mill St Hillsville VA 24343-1314

MCGRAIL, JEANE KATHRYN, artist, educator, poet, curator; b. Mpls., May 1, 1947; d. Robert Vern and Mary Virginia (Kees) McGrail. BS, U. Wis.-River Falls, 1970; MFA, Cranbrook Acad. Art, 1972; postgrad., Sch. of Art Inst. of Chgo., 1985, Ill. Inst. Tech., 1993. Group exhbns. include Saginaw Art Mus., Mich., 1972, Met. Mus. Art, Miami, Fla., 1974, Lowe Mus. Art, Coral Gables, Fla., 1974, 76, Miller Galleries, Coconut Grove, Fla., 1978, 80, Cicchinelli Gallery, N.Y.C., 1980-82, Harper Coll., 1984, Contemporary Art Ctr. Arlington, Arlington Heights, Ill., 1984, 85, 86, 94, Evanston Art Ctr., 1985, South Shore Cultural Ctr., Chgo., 1990, N.A.M.E. Gallery, 1990, Artemisia Gallery, Chgo., 1991, 92, 93, 94, North Lakeside Art Ctr., Chgo., 1991, 94, 95, Ceres Gallery, N.Y.C., 1992, Harper Coll., Ill., 1993, Environ. Concerns, Chgo., 1993, North Pk. Coll., Chgo., 1993, Franklin Square Gallery, Chgo., 1994, 95, 96, Space 900 Gallery, Chgo., 1994, 95, 96, 97, 98, 99, Chuck Levitan Gallery, N.Y.C., 1995, Riverwest Art Ctr., Milw., 1995, Nat. Mus. Women in the Arts, Washington, 1996, Gallery 1040, 1997—, "Red", Chgo., 1998, Oakton Coll. Gallery, Ill., 1999—, Women's Works, Woodstock, Ill., 1999, "Paint It Siver", ARC Gallery, Chgo., 1999, Past/Present, Chgo., 1999, "Blue", Northeastern Ill. U.,Chgo., 2000, Then and Now, Chgo., 1999, Norris Cultural Ctr., St. Charles, Ill., 1999, others; represented in permanent collections at Chgo. Mus. Sci. and Industry, U. Chgo., Mus. Photography, Chgo., Miami-Dade Pub. Libr., U. Wis.-River Falls, MacGregor Found., Printmakers Workshop, N.Y.C., Norman R. Eppnik Art Gallery Emporia State U., Kans., 2000, Mini Print Internat. Exhbn., Binghamton, N.Y., 2000, Yale U. Med. Libr., 2000, Columbia U. Med. Ctr., 2000, Mini Print Internat. of Cadaques, Spain, Macy Gallery, Providence, R.I., 2000, Brickton Gallery, Park Ridge, Fla., 2001, Mini Print Internat. of Cadaques, Spain, 2001, 02, others; solo exhbns. include Gallery at the Commons, Chgo., 1982, Truman Coll. Gallery, Chgo., 1991, C.G. Jung Inst., Evanston, Ill., 1992, Carlson Tower Gallery, Chgo., 1994, Olcott Ctr. Gallery, Theosophical Soc. Am., Wheaton, Ill., 2001; pub. "Mosaic", 1992, The Best of Printmaking, 1997; contbr. publs. to profl. jours. Cranbrook Acad. Art scholar, 1971; CAAP grantee Dept. Cultural Affairs City Chgo, 1992; recipient Poster Competition award Vizcaya Mus., 1974; Print award Auction WPBT, 1979. Mem. Coll. Art Assn., Chgo. Women's Caucus for Art (bd. dirs. 1992-95, sec.), Chgo. Artists Coalition. Democrat. Studio: 1040 W Huron St LL5 Chicago IL 60622-6591 E-mail: mcgrail@jeanemcgrail.com.

MCGRAIL, SUSAN KING, travel agency executive, accountant; b. Richmond, Va., Mar. 7, 1952; d. William Jr. and Anne Winn (Gibson) King; m. John Patrick McGrail, Jr., June 2, 1979; children: Katharine Anne, Patricia Lynn, John Patrick III. BBA, Coll. William and Mary, 1974. CPA, Va., Ohio. Employment counselor Avante Gard of Richmond, Inc., 1970-73; staff acct. Touche Ross & Co., Washington, 1974-75, Richmond, 1975-78; contr. Continental Cablevision, Richmond, 1978-81; v.p. fin. Warner Amex Cable Communications, Cin., 1981-85; prin. Travel Agts. Internat., Cin., 1985-92; sec., treas. Warner Amex Minority Loan Fund, Cin., 1981-85. Alumni career advisor Coll. William and Mary, Williamsburg, Va., 1982—, fund raiser, 1984—. Fellow Am. Inst. CPA's, Va. Soc. CPA's; mem. Am. Soc. Travel Agts., Cruise Lines Internat. Assn., Greater Cin. C. of C. (chief exec. officer roundtable), Pi Beta Phi, Blue Ash-Montgomery Exchange Club (pres. 1989-90). Republican. Episcopalian. Avocations: scuba diving, snorkeling, reading. Home: 840 Oak Ridge Rd Dyersburg TN 38024-6518

MCGRAIN, JOHN WILLIAM, JR. county government official; b. Balt., Sept. 25, 1931; s. John W. and Teresa Loretta (Dolan) McG. BA, Loyola Coll., 1953. Tech. writer Bendix Radio Corp., Towson, Md., 1955-57, Tech. Svc. Corp., Glen Burnie, 1958-69; market forecast editor DMS Internat., Balt., 1969-70; contract writer various state and fed. agys., Balt., Washington, 1970-76; historic sites planner County of Balt., Towson, Md., 1976—. Author: Grist Mills of Baltimore County, 1980, From Pig-Iron to Cotton Duck, 1985, An Agricultural History of Baltimore County, Maryland, 1990; co-editor: History Trails, 1972. Cpl. U.S. Army, 1953-55. Mem. Balt. County Hist. Soc. (pres. 1970), Soc. for Indsl. Archaeology, Soc. Archtl. Historians, Md. Hist. Soc. Democrat. Roman Catholic. Avocation: photography. Home: 34 Willow Ave Towson MD 21286-5226 Office: Office of Planning 401 Bosley Ave Towson MD 21204-4420 E-mail: jmcgrain@co.ba.md.us.

MCGRATH, ANNA FIELDS, retired librarian; b. Westfield, Maine, July 4, 1932; d. Fred Elber and Nancy Phyllis (Tarbell) Fields; m. Bernard McGrath (div.); children: Timothy, Maureen, Patricia, Colleen, Rebecca. BA, U. Maine, Presque Isle, 1976; MEd, U. So. Maine, 1979; MLS, U. R.I., 1982. Libr. U. Maine, Presque Isle, 1976-86, assoc. libr. dir., 1986-89, interim libr. dir., 1989-92, dir., 1992-94, spl. collection libr., 1994-97, ret., 1997. Editor: County: Land of Promise, 1989. Mem. Friends of Aroostook County Hist. Ctr. at Libr., U. Maine-Presque Isle; mem. Plymouth (Mass.) Spiritualist Ch. Mem. Inst. Noetic Scis., Am. Mensa, Sierra Club. E-mail: amcgrath@maine.edu.

MCGRATH, CHERYL JULIA, elementary education educator; b. Milw., Feb. 17, 1947; d. Elmer William and Marjorie (Bleiler) Scherkenbach; m. Robert Edward McGrath, July 25, 1970; children: Edward, Erin, Molly. BA in Edn., Alverno Coll., Milw., 1969. Cert. tchr., Wis. Tchr. grade 1 Greenfield (Wis.) Pub. Schs., 1969-72, St. Lawrence Sch., Wisconsin Rapids, Wis., 1972-80; tchr. grades 7-8 Our Lady Queen of Heaven, 1980-85; substitute work Wisconsin Rapids (Wis.) Pub. Schs., 1987-88, tchr. grade 2, 1988—. Bd. mem. Girl Scouts Samoset Coun., Stevens Point, Wis., 1979-84; com. Math Their Way, 1992-94, Report Card, 1990-93, Able Learner, 1990-92, Peer Tutoring, 1989-91, Wisconsin Rapids Pub. Schs. Recipient Advance Religious Cert. award Diocese of Lacrosse, Wis., 1978. Mem. NEA, Wis. Rapids Edn. Assn., Wis. Edn. Assn., Alverno Coll. Alumnae Assn. Republican. Roman Catholic. Avocations: reading, boating, early childhood development, travel, computer programming. Home: 294 15th Ave Nekoosa WI 54457-8063 Office: Wisconsin Rapids Pub Schs 510 Peach St Wisconsin Rapids WI 54494-4663

MCGRATH, CHRISTOPHER THOMAS, lawyer; b. Inwood, N.Y., Nov. 25, 1958; s. John J. and Dolores Marie McG.; m. Monica Jean DiPalma, Sept. 15, 1984; children: Kristin Marie, Kelli Anne, Katelynn. BS cum laude, St. John's U., Jamaica, N.Y., 1980; JD, U. Dayton, 1983. Bar: N.Y. 1984, U.S. Dist. Ct. (so. and ea. dists.) N.Y. 1984, U.S. Supreme Ct. 1987; bd. cert. civil trial advocacy Nat. Bd. Trial Advocacy. Assoc. Sullivan & Liapakis, N.Y.C., 1983-89, ptnr., 1989-99, Sullivan, Papain, Block, McGrath & Cannavo P.C., N.Y.C., 1999—. Lectr. N.Y. State Bar Assn., N.Y. State Trial Lawyers Assn., Assn. Trial Lawyers Am. Chmn. humanitarian award Nassau County 4th Precinct Police, 1985—. Mem. Assn. Trial Lawyers Am., N.Y. State Trail Lawyers Assn., Nassau County Bar Assn. (bd. dirs., chair med. legal com. 1997-98, chair jud. com. 1999—), N.Y. State Bar Assn., Kiwanis (pres.-elect Hewlet, N.Y., disting. past pres. Peninsula chpt. 1988-89). Republican. Home: 1348 Hewlett Ln Hewlett NY 11557-2208 Office: Sullivan Papain Block McGrath Cannavo PC 120 Broadway New York NY 10271-0002 also: 55 Mineola Blvd Mineola NY 11501-4220 E-mail: cmcgrath@traillaw1.com.

MCGRATH, DON JOHN, banker; b. Springfield, Ill., June 15, 1948; s. Donald John and Wilma P. (Beck) McG.; m. Patriaia Ratti, May 7, 1983. BS in Mktg., U. Ill., 1970; MBA, Boston U., 1973. Investment officer Banque Nationale de Paris, San Francisco, 1975-76, treas. San Francisco and L.A., 1976-78, v.p., treas., 1978-80, Bank of the West, San Francisco, 1980, v.p., CFO, 1980-81, sr. v.p., CFO, 1981-84, sr. exec. v.p., CFO, 1984-87, sr. exec. v.p., COO, 1987-91, pres., COO, 1991-95, pres., CEO, 1996—; pres., COO, dir. BancWest Corp., 1998—. Bd. dirs. Commonwealth Club Calif., Nature Conservancy Calif., Dominican Coll. San Rafael, Calif. Mem. Calif. Bankers Assn., Univ. Club, St. Francis Yacht Club (San Francisco), Diablo (Calif.) Country Club. Office: BancWest Corp 1450 Treat Blvd Walnut Creek CA 94596-7579

MCGRATH, EDWARD GERARD, retired military officer, journalist; b. Boston, May 26, 1921; s. Edward Clement McGrath and Mary Elizabeth Boggie; m. Eileen Patricia Walsh, Mar. 3, 1945 (dec. June 1979); children: Edward, Patricia Papps, Peter, John; m. Annette Bader Conners, June 20, 1981; stepchildren: John Conners, Brian Conners, Charleen Lee, Kim Abt, Michael Conners, Laura Kern. BS in Bus. Adminstrn., Boston Coll., 1942. Reporter, photographer Portsmouth (N.H.) Herald, 1948-49; feature writer, news editor Boston Post, 1949-55; columnist, fgn. corr., editl. writer Boston Globe, 1955-68; chief info. Allied Forces NATO So. Europe, Brussels, Naples, Italy, 1968-72; editor-in-chief Stars and Stripes Europe, Darmstadt, Germany, 1972-75; asst. chief info. USN, Washington, 1975-77; chief info. NATO Supreme Allied Command Atlantic, Norfolk, Va., 1977-80; spkr.-cons. in field. Westbury, N.Y., 1982—. Pub. rels. dir. Deaconess Hosp., Boston, 1956-65; New Eng. corr. Newsweek, N.Y.C., 1963-67; news panelist Pub. Broadcasting, Boston, 1964; lectr. in field. Author syndicated articles N.Am. Newspaper Alliance, 1956-60. Capt. USN, 1942-46, PTO, 1950-52, 68-82. Decorated Legion of Merit, USN, 1972, 82; recipient Best News Writing awards AP, 1949, 60, 63, Amasa Howe award Newspaper Guild, Boston, 1962, UPI Editor award, 1963; named Outstanding News Corr., Boston U. Sigma Delta Chi, 1965. Mem. Ret. Officers Assn., Am. Legion, N.Y. Yacht Club. Roman Catholic. Achievements include invented wopaco code for U.S. subs in wolf pack attack WWII. Avocations: sailing, skiing, foreign traveling. Home: 36 Pinecone Ln Westbury NY 11590

MCGRATH, EDWARD LEO, banker; b. N.Y.C., Apr. 5, 1947; s. Edward Philip McGrath and Mary M. (Kiley) Dennehy; m. Margaret M. Hart, Dec. 16, 1989; children: Philip B., Theresa F. BS, Fordham U., 1969; MBA, Columbia U., 1974. Chartered fin. analyst. With U.S. Peace Corps, Managua, Nicaragua, 1971-73; sr. fin. analyst Mellon Bank, N.A., Pitts., 1974-75, comptroller Tokyo, 1975-78, dep. gen. mgr. Hong Kong, 1978-80, mgr. internat. credit divsn. Pitts., 1980-82, chief internat. fin. officer, 1982-85, country mgr. Mexico City, 1985-89, comptroller trust dept., 1990-91, mgr. internat. mktg. and planning global asset mgmt. Pitts., 1991-93, dir. internat. planning, 1994-95, mgr. wholesale banking-Can., 1995-98; pres. Can. Mellon Asset Mgmt., 1996-98, group head, metals, 1999-2001, credit recovery, 2001—, mgr. fin. instns. group, 2002—. Panelist ann. gen. meeting Investment Co. Inst., 1995. Author: Offshore Assembly Operations in Nicaragua, 1973. Dir., mem. fin. com. Braddock Gen. Hosp., Pitts., 1991-95; dir. Planning Forum, Pitts., 1993-95; dir., mem. exec. and fin. coms. Am. Brit. Cowdray Hosp., Mexico City, 1987-89. Mem. Assn. for Investment Mgmt. and Rsch., Assn. Insolvency and Restructuring Advisors, The Nat. Club Toronto, Princeton Club N.Y., Duquane Club Pitts., Am. Club Hong Kong, Fgn. Corrs. Club Hong Kong, Aircraft Owners and Pilots Assn., Nat. Assn. Rocketry, Asiatic Soc. of Japan. Democrat. Roman Catholic. Avocations: sports cars, sailing, scuba diving, flying. Office: One Mellon Bank Ctr Rm 1525 Pittsburgh PA 15258

MCGRATH, EILEEN MARIE, pediatric nurse; b. N.Y.C., June 13, 1961; d. Patrick J. and Bridget K. (Dolphin) McG. BS in Nursing, Coll. New Rochelle (N.Y.), 1983, M in Nursing Adminstrn., 1990. Cert. pediatric nurse. Staff pediatric nurse Montefiore Med. Ctr., Bronx, N.Y., 1983-86; lic. practical nurse med./surg. New Rochelle Hosp., 1982-83; pvt. duty nurses aide Kingsbridge Jewish Nursing Home, Bronx, N.Y., 1978-80; patient care coord. Montefiore Med. Ctr., 1986—; exec. dir. Am. Med. Women's Assoc, Alexandria, Va., 2001—02, exec. v.p., CEO, 2002—. Mem. Am. Assn. Nurses Network, Inc., N.Y. State Nurses Assn.*

MCGRATH, ELEANOR BURNS, editor, writer; b. Gloucester, Mass., July 28, 1952; d. Edward James and Julia Ann (Holloran) McG.; m. Paul Allen Witteman, May 5, 1984; 1 child, Katharine McGrath Witteman. AB magna cum laude, Mt. Holyoke Coll., 1974. Rschr. Time-Life Books, N.Y.C., 1974-76; reporter, staff writer, edn. editor Time Mag., 1976-86; sr. editor Women's Sports and Fitness Mag., San Francisco, 1986-87; spl. corr. Time Mag., 1988; sr. editor, articles editor Self Mag., N.Y.C., 1991-98; editor Time Mag./Princeton Rev. Coll. Guide, 2000—. Journalist-in-residence U. Mich., Ann Arbor, 1984-85. Author: My One and Only: The Special Experience of the Only Child, 1989; editor: One Earth, 1990. Trustee Mt. Holyoke Coll., South Hadley, Mass., 1976-79; pres. Greater N.Y. Athletic Assn., N.Y.C. 1980-84. Time fellow Duke U., 1981. Mem. N.Y. Rd. Runners Club. Avocation: distance running. Home: 110 Riverside Dr New York NY 10024-3715 E-mail: elliemcgrath@timemagazine.com.

MCGRATH, EUGENE R. utility company executive; b. N.Y.C., 1942; BSME, Manhattan Coll., 1963; MBA, Iona Coll., 1980. With Consol. Edison Co. N.Y., N.Y.C., 1963—, v.p., 1978-82, exec. v.p., 1982-89, pres., COO, 1989-90, chmn. pres., CEO, 1990—, also bd. dirs. Mem. NAE. Office: Consol Edison Co NY Inc 4 Irving Pl New York NY 10003*

MCGRATH, J. NICHOLAS, lawyer; b. Hollywood, Calif., Feb. 12, 1940; children: Nicholas Gerald, Molly Inez. BA with honors, Lehigh U., 1962; LLB magna cum laude, Columbia U., 1965. Bar: D.C. 1966, Calif. 1969, U.S. Supreme Ct. 1970, Colo. 1971. Law clk. U.S. Ct. Appeals (D.C. cir.), 1965-66; law clk. to assoc. justice Thurgood Marshall U.S. Supreme Ct., Washington, 1967-68; pvt. practice Aspen, 1971—. Chmn. grievance com. Colo. Supreme Ct., 1989, mem. 1984-89. Mem. bd. editors Columbia Law Review, 1964-65. Mem. planning commn. Town of Basalt, Colo., 1992—93, town trustee, 1993—94; lectr. nat. and state CLE programs on ethics, litigations, and land use subjects; pres. Basalt Children's Recreation Fund, Inc., 1994—, Basalt Soccer Club, 1997—99. Mem. Colo. Bar Assn. (v.p. 1991-92), Pitkin County Bar Assn. (pres. 1977). Democrat. Home: 415 Elk Cir Basalt CO 81621-8202 Office: 600 E Hopkins Ave Ste 305 Aspen CO 81611-2933 E-mail: jnm@jnmpc.com.

MCGRATH, JAMES CHARLES, III, financial services company executive, lawyer, consultant; b. Davenport, Iowa, May 25, 1942; s. James Charles and Genevieve (Clarke) McG.; m. Sherbourne Everett, Apr. 11, 1970. BA, U. Notre Dame, 1964; JD, U. Iowa, 1967. Bar: Iowa 1967, U.S. Supreme Ct. 1970, D.C. 1971, U.S. Ct. Appeals (D.C. cir.) 1971, U.S. Ct. Mil. Appeals 1974. Spl. agt. FBI, Balt., N.Y.C., 1967-71; trial atty. Dept. Justice, Washinton, 1971-75; dir. investigations Am. Express Co., N.Y.C., 1975-77, v.p. corp. security, 1978-82, sr. v.p. security, 1982-89; pres. McGrath Internat., Inc., 1989—. Overseas security adv. coun. U.S. State Dept., 1985-88. Mem. Soc. Former Spl. Agts. FBI, Am. Soc. Indsl. Security (chmn. white collar crime com. 1985-88), Internat. Assn. Credit Card Investigators (exec. adv. bd. 1985-88), Iowa State Bar Assn., D.C. Bar Assn., U.S. C. of C. (white collar crime adv. panel 1979—), Debordieu Club (Georgetown, S.C.), Phi Delta Phi. Office: McGrath Internat Inc PO Box 1384 Georgetown SC 29442-1384

MCGRATH, JAMES THOMAS, real estate investment company executive; b. N.Y.C., Nov. 10, 1942; s. Thomas James and Mary Ita (Finnegan) McG.; m. Paulette L. Franck, Aug. 16, 1980; 1 child, Tara (dec.). BS in Acctg., Providence Coll., 1964. CPA, N.Y. Sr. auditor Coopers & Lybrand, N.Y.C., 1968-72, mgmt. cons., 1972-74; group contr. IU Internat. Corp., Phila., 1974-77; v.p. fin. Taylor Engring. Corp. subs. IU Internat., Detroit, 1977-78; controller Pool Co. subs. Enserch Corp., Houston, 1978-85; sr. v.p. fin., treas. Lone Star Gas Co. subs. Enserch Corp., Dallas, 1985-91; pres. McGrath & Assocs., Inc., 1991—. Bd. dirs. ARC, Dallas chpt., 1990-93. Lt. USN, 1964-68. Mem. AICPA, Dallas Athletic Club, St. Vincent de Paul Soc. Libertarian. Roman Catholic. Avocations: golf, cooking, skiing, scuba diving, sailing. Home and Office: 2838 Colleen Dr Garland TX 75043-1215 E-mail: pjmcgrath2@attbi.com.

MCGRATH, JANE LEE, education educator, writer; b. Evansville, Ind., Oct. 4, 1945; d. Alva and Mildred (Hutson) Williams; m. Larry W. McGrath, Dec. 22, 1969. BA, Ariz. State U., Tempe, 1967, MA, 1969, EdD, 1972. Reading specialist K-12 Wilson Elem. Dist., Phoenix, 1967-69; mem. fculty Maricopa Colls., 1970—. Author: Building Strategies for College Reading, 1995. Chair Mayor's Com. on Employment of Handicapped, Tempe, 1980-83; mem. Gov.'s Com. on Employmnet of Handicapped, State of Ariz., 1980-87. Named Outstanding Citizen, City of Phoenix, 1981, City of Tempe, 1982; named Innovator of Yr., League for Innovation/Maricopa Colls., 1991. Mem. Nat. Assn. for Devel. Educators, Coll. Reading and Learning Assn. Office: Paradise Valley CC 18401 N 32nd St Phoenix AZ 85032-1210

MCGRATH, JOHN FRANCIS, utility executive; b. Freeport, N.Y., May 4, 1925; s. John Francis and Catherine Frances (Maune) McG.; m. Catherine Elizabeth Zainor, June 22, 1946; children— Joseph R., Susan M., Martha J., Thomas J. BS, U.S. Mcht. Marine Acad., 1944; AB, Muhlenberg Coll., Allentown, Pa., 1948; JD, St. John's U., Bklyn., 1952; grad. bus. exec. program, U. Minn. Grad. Sch., 1973. Bar: N.Y., 1952, Minn., 1958, Fla.-Emeritus, 1991. Atty. firm Casey, Lane & Mittendorf, N.Y.C., 1953-58; jud. inquiry asst. counsel N.Y. State Supreme Ct., 1957-58; atty. U.S. Steel Corp., Duluth, Minn., 1958-64; with Minn. Power & Light Co., 1964-83, sr. v.p., 1978-83, gen. counsel, 1975-83, sec., 1979-84; v.p., dir. USICO Ins. Co., Bermuda. Adj. prof., gen. counsel Coll. St. Scholastica, Duluth; vol. atty. Bay Area Legal Svcs., Tampa, Fla. Bd. dirs. emeritus Duluth Cathedral H.S., 1972, St. Anne's Residence, Duluth, 1963-83; commr. Seaway Port Authority, Duluth, 1966-76, pres., 1970, 75; bd. dirs., sec. Good Samaritan Fund Greater Sun City Center, Fla.; mem. Hillsborough County Bd. Zoning Adjustment, 1992-94. With Merchant Marines, 1943-46, USNR, 1943-68, lt. ret. Mem. Minn. Bar Assn., St. Louis County Bar Assn. Democrat. Roman Catholic. Home: 2036 Hampstead Cir Sun City Center FL 33573-7350 E-mail: cjm2036@aol.com.

MCGRATH, JUDITH, broadcast executive; b. Scranton, PA, 1952; BA, Cedar Crest Coll., Allentown, PA. Former fashion copywriter Mademoiselle; co-exec. prod. MTV Movie Awards; former sr. v.p., creative dir. MTV; pres. MTV Networks Music Group, NY, 1993—. Recipient Cable Ace Award, 1993. Office: MTV 1515 Broadway Fl 25 New York NY 10036-8901*

MCGRATH, KATHRYN BRADLEY, lawyer; b. Norfolk, Va., Sept. 2, 1944; d. James Pierce and Kathryn (Hoyle) Bradley; children: Ian M., James D. AB, Mt. Holyoke Coll., 1966; JD, Georgetown U., 1969. Ptnr. Gardner, Carton & Douglas, Washington, 1979-83; dir. div. investment mgmt. SEC, 1983-90; ptnr. Morgan Lewis , 1990—2002, Crowell & Moring, LLP, Washington, 2002—. Named Disting. Exec. Pres. Reagan, 1987. Mem. Fed. Bar Assn. (exec. council securities law com.). Office: Crowell & Moring LLP 1001 Pennsylvania Ave NW Washington DC 20004 E-mail: kmcgrath@crowell.com.

MCGRATH, MARY HELENA, plastic surgeon, educator; b. N.Y.C., Apr. 12, 1945; d. Vincent J. and Mary M. (Manning) McG.; children: Margaret E. Simon, Richard M. Simon. BA, Coll. New Rochelle, 1966; MD, St. Louis U., 1970; MPH, George Washington U., 1994. Lic. surgeon, Ill. Resident in surg. pathology U. Colo. Med. Ctr., Denver, 1970-71, intern in gen. surgery, 1971-72, resident in gen. surgery, 1971-75, chief resident in gen. surgery, 1975-76; resident in plastic and reconstructive surgery Yale U. Sch. Medicine, New Haven, 1976-77, chief resident plastic and reconstructive surgery, 1977-78; fellow in hand surgery U. Conn.-Yale U., 1978; instr. in surgery divsn. plastic and reconstructive surgery Yale U. Sch. Medicine, 1977-78, asst. prof. plastic surgery, 1978-80; attending in plastic and reconstructive surgery Yale-New Haven Hosp., 1978-80, Columbia-Presbyn. Hosp., N.Y.C., 1980-84, George Washington U. Med. Ctr., Washington, 1984-2000, Children's Nat. Med. Ctr., Washington, 1985-2000, Loyola U. Med. Ctr., 2000—, Hines Veterans Adminstrn. Hosp., 2001—; asst. prof. plastic surgery Columbia U., N.Y.C., 1980-84; assoc. prof. plastic surgery Sch. Medicine, George Washington U., Washington, 1984-87, prof. plastic surgery, 1987-2000, Loyola U. Med. Ctr., 2000—. Attending physician VA Hosp., West Haven, Conn., 1978-80; attending in surgery Hosp. Albert Schweitzer, Deschapelles, Haiti, 1980; historian., bd. dirs. Am. Bd. Plastic Surgery, 1991-95; guest examiner certifying exam., 1986-88, 95-2001; specialist site visitor Residency Rev. Com. for Plastic Surgery, 1985, 87, 91, 94; presenter, cons. in field; senator med. faculty senate George Washington U., bd. govs. Med. Faculty Assocs. Co-editor: (with M.L. Turner) Dermatology for Plastic Surgeons, 1993; assoc. editor: The Jour. of Hand Surgery, 1984-89, Annals of Plastic Surgery, 1984-87, Plastic and Reconstructive Surgery, 1989-95, Contemporary Surgery, 1999—; contbr. book chpts.: Problems in General Surgery, 1985, Human and Ethical Issues in the Surgical Care of Patients with Life-Threatening Disease, 1986, Problems in Aesthetic Surgery, Biological Causes and Clinical Solutions, 1986; guest reviewer numerous jours.; contbr. articles to profl. jours. Recipient numerous rsch. grants, 1978—2001. Fellow ACS (bd. govs. 1995-98, exec. com. 1996-97, chmn. adv. coun. for plastic surgery 1995-98, chmn. adv. coun. chmns. surgical specialists 1996-98, regent 1997—); mem. AAAS, Am. Surg. Assn., Am. Assn. Hand Surgery (rsch. grants com. 1983-86, chmn. edn. com. 1983-88, exec. sec. 1988-90, 1st prize ann. resident contest 1978, other coms., D.C. chpt. program ann. meeting chmn. 1992, pres. 1994-95), Am. Assn. Plastic Surgeons (trustee 1997-2000), Am. Burn Assn., Am. Soc. for Aesthetic Plastic Surgery, Am. Soc. Maxillofacial Surgeons, Am. Soc. Plastic and Reconstructive Surgery (chmn. ethics com. 1985-87, chmn. device/tech. evaluation com. 1993-94, chmn. workforce task force 1997-2000, bd. dirs. 1994-96, chmn. endowment bd. dirs. 2000—, ednl. found. bd. dirs. 1985-96, treas. 1989-92, v.p. 1992-93, pres.-elect 1993-94, pres. 1994-95), Am. Soc. Reconstructive Microsurgery (edn. com. 1992-94), Am. Soc. Surgery of Hand (chmn. 1987 ann. residents' and fellows conf. 1986-87, rsch. com. 1988-90), Assn. Acad. Chmn. Plastic Surgery (bd. dirs. 1999—), Assn. Acad. Surgery, Chgo. Soc. Plastic Surgeons (treas. 2001-), Midwestern Soc. Plastic Surgeons, Chgo. Surgical Soc., Internat. Soc. Reconstructive Surgery, Met. D.C. Soc. Surgery Hand (pres. 1995-97), N.Y. Surg. Soc., Northeastern Soc. Plastic Surgeons (chmn. sci. program com. 1991, chmn. fin. com. 1992-93, treas. 1993-96, pres. 1997-98), Plastic Surgery Rsch. Coun. (chmn. 1990), Surg. Biology Club III, The Wound Healing Soc. Office: Loyola U Med Ctr Divsn Plastic Surgery 2160 S 1st Ave Maywood IL 60153-3304 E-mail: mmcgra4@lumc.edu.

MCGRATH, MIKE, lawyer; b. Rapid City, S.D., Aug. 22, 1947; s. John E. and Jean F. (Funk) McG.; m. Joy L. Rasmusson, May 22, 1971; children— Patrick John, Christopher Paul. B.S., U. Mont., 1970; J.D., Gonzaga U., 1975. Bar: Wash. 1975, Mont. 1977, U.S. Ct. Appeals (9th cir.) 1980, U.S. Supreme Ct. 1980. Reginald Heber Smith cmty. lawyer fellow; atty. Washoe County Legal Services, Reno, Nev., 1975-76; asst. atty. gen. State of Mont., Helena, 1977-82; county atty. Lewis and Clark County, Helena, 1983—2001; atty. gen. State of Mont., 2001- ; pres. Mont. Legal Services Assn., 1984-85, 95-96, bd.dirs. 1980—; bd. dirs. Mountain chpt. Nat. Com. for Prevention of Child Abuse, 1985-90, Big Bros. and Sisters, Helena, 1977-83; bd. dirs. Friendship Ctr. Helena, 1989—, pres., 1995-97; bd. dirs. Conf. of Western Attys. Gen., 2001—, exec. com. Served with USAF, 1970-72. Mem. Mont. Bar Assn., Nat. Dist. Attys. Assn., Mont. County Attys. Assn. (pres. 1996-97). Democrat. Home: 514 Hayes Ave Helena MT 59601-6106 Office: 215 N Sanders 3d Fl PO Box 201401 Helena MT 59620

MCGRATH, PETER, editor; b. Macclesfield, Eng., Aug. 19, 1944; came to U.S., 1947; s. Hugh P. and Barbara W. (Collins) McG.; m. Susan Seliger, June 17, 1972; children: Alexander S., Evan S. BA, Amherst Coll., 1966; MA, U. Chgo., 1971, PhD, 1974. Press, legis. asst. Congressman Timothy E. Wirth, Washington, 1975-77; founding editor Washington Journalism Rev., 1977; sr. editor Washingtonian mag., Washington, 1977-81; spl. corr. The Economist, 1979-81; gen. editor Newsweek, N.Y.C., 1981-83, sr. editor, 1983-86, fgn. editor, 1986-92; mng. editor Newsweek Internat., 1992-95; editor new media Newsweek, 1995—; editor Newsweek e-Life, 1999—. Contbr. articles to profl. jours. Office: Newsweek 251 W 57th St New York NY 10019-1802

MCGRATH, RICHARD, lawyer; b. Chgo., Aug. 10, 1929; s. John Francis and Helen Leone (Hoyer) M.; m. Luisa Sacco y Artze, Aug. 12, 1956; children: Lisa, Deborah, Holly. BA magna cum laude, Georgetown U., 1951; JD cum laude, Harvard U., 1954. Bar: D.C. 1954, N.Y. 1955, Mass. 1957, Conn. 1960, U.S. Supreme Ct. 1965. Assoc. Hughes, Hubbard, Blair and Reed, 1954-57; corp. counsel Raytheon Co., 1957-60; assoc. Cummings & Lockwood, Stamford, Conn., 1960-63, ptnr., 1963—. Gen. counsel, corp. sec. Internat. Exec. Svc. Corps, 1990—. Mem. editl. bd. Harvard Law Rev., 1952-54; contbr. articles to profl. jours.; panelist law seminars. Past pres. Fairfield County Coun. Boy Scouts Am. Mem.: Conn. Bar Assn. (chmn. corp. law com. 1984—86, fee disputes arbitration com. 1980—84), Woodway Country Club (Darien, Conn.) (bd. govs., sec. 1983—91, chmn. nominating com. 2000), Stamford Rotary Club (past pres.), Gold Key Soc., Eta Sigma Phi, Pi Gamma Mu. Avocations: golf, trap, chess. Office: Cummings & Lockwood 4 Stamford Plz Stamford CT 06902-3834 E-mail: rmcgrath@cl-law.com.

MCGRATH, RICHARD N. statistician, educator; b. Pittsburgh, Pa., June 20, 1961; s. Robert G. McGrath, Luella O. McGrath; m. Valerie A. Wertman; children: Maxwell. BS in Indsl. Engring., Pa. State U., 1983; MS in Stat., Rutgers U., 1996; PhD in Stat., Pa. State U., 2000. Quality mgr. AT&T, Bedminster, NJ, 1995—96; mem. tech. staff AT&T Bell Labs., Piscataway, 1988—95; product assurance engr. AT&T Fed. Sys., Greensboro, NC, 1986—88; quality engr. AT&T , Reading, Pa., 1983—86; asst. prof. Bowling Green State U., Bowling Green, Ohio, 2000—. Contbr. articles. Mem.: Am. Soc. Quality, Am. Statis. Assn., Penn State Alumni Assn. (life). Office: Applied Stats and Ops Rsch Bowling Green State Univ Bowling Green OH 43404 Business E-Mail: rnmcgra@cba.bgsu.edu.

MCGRATH, THOMAS J. lawyer, writer, film producer; b. N.Y.C., Oct. 8, 1932; m. Mary Lee McGrath, Aug. 4, 1956 (dec.); children: Maura Lee, J. Connell; m. Diahn Williams, Sept. 28, 1974; 1 child, Courtney C. BA, NYU, 1956, JD, 1960. Bar: N.Y. 1960. Assoc. Milbank, Tweed, Hadley & McCloy, N.Y.C., 1960-69; ptnr. Simpson, Thacher & Bartlett, 1970-95; retired, 1995. Lectr., writer Practicing Law Inst., 1976—, Am. Law Inst. ABA, 1976-81. Author: Carryover Basis Under Tax Reform Act, 1977; contbg. author: Estate and Gift Tax After ERTA, 1982; producer: feature film Deadly Hero, 1977. Bd. dirs. N.Y. Philharm.; pres. Am. Austrian Found. With U.S. Army, 1953-54, Korea. Fellow Am. Coll. Trust and Estate Coun.; mem. ABA, N.Y. State Bar Assn., Assn. Bar City N.Y. Home: 988 5th Ave New York NY 10021-0143 Office: Simpson Thacher & Bartlett 425 Lexington Ave New York NY 10017-3954 E-mail: mcgrathtwf@aol.com., mcgraththomasj@aol.com.

MCGRAW, BRYAN KELLY, financial company executive; b. Ironton, Mo., Sept. 10, 1962; s. Robert Lee and Francine Clara McGraw; m. Elizabeth Adair Keck, Jan. 24, 1987; children: Kaitlyn Adair, Brendan Kelly. BS, S.E. Mo. State U., 1984; MPA, U. Okla., 1990; postgrad., St. Louis U., 1996—. Lic. residential contractor, N.C. Commd. 2d lt. USAF, 1984, advanced through grades to maj., 1998, svcs. officer, mgr. N.H., 1985-87, Kadena AB, Okinawa, Japan, 1987-91; dep. chief svcs. K.I. Sawyer AFB, Mich., 1991-92; v.p. McGraw Builders, Inc., Goldsboro, N.C., 1992-95; exec. officer USAFR, Mitchell ARS, Wis., 1995-96; mgr. total quality Deutsche Fin. Svcs., St. Louis, 1998-99, dir. quality and process innovation, 1999—. Mem. urban planning and real estate com. St. Louis U., 1997-98; coach U.S.A. Youth Hockey, St. Louis, 1998-2000; mem. Heritage Found., Washington, 1996—. Recipient Young Alumni merit award S.E. Mo. State U., 1999. Mem. DAV, Assn. for Quality and Participation (bd. dirs. 1998—), Am. Soc. for Quality, Nat. Geog. Soc., Res. Officers Assn., U.S.A. Hockey. Republican. Roman Catholic. Avocations: hockey, racquetball, music, outdoors, military history. Home: 5346 Old Lemay Ferry Rd Imperial MO 63052-1919 E-mail: bkmgraw@swbell.net.

MC GRAW, DARRELL VIVIAN, JR. state attorney general; b. Mullens, W.Va., Nov. 8, 1936; s. Darrell Vivian and Julia (ZeKany) Mc Graw; m. Jorea Marple; children: Elizabeth, Sarah, Darrell, Elliott. AB, W.Va. U., 1961, JD, 1964, MA, 1977. Bar: W.Va. 1964. Gen. atty. Fgn. Claims Settlement Commn., U.S. Dept. State, 1964; counsel to gov. State of W.Va., 1965—68; pvt. practice Charleston, Shepherdstown and Morgantown, 1968—76; judge W.Va. Supreme Ct. Appeals, Charleston, 1977—88, chief justice, 1982—83; atty. gen. State of W.Va., 1993—. With U.S. Army, 1954—57. Fellow, W.Va. U., Nat. Ctr. Edn. in Politics/Ford Found. Fellow: Am. Polit. Sci. Assn., Rotary. Democrat. Office: Office of Atty Gen 1900 Kanawha Blvd E Rm E-26 Charleston WV 25305-0009

MCGRAW, DONALD JESSE, biologist, science historian, writer; b. Altadena, Calif., Oct. 27, 1943; s. Jesse E. and Mary L. (Hajostek) McG.; m. Laura Lee Hansen, July 13, 1968; children: Adrienne, Holly, Rachel. BS in Biol. Scis., Calif. State Poly. Coll., 1965; MS, Utah State U., 1967; PhD, Oreg. State U., 1976. Registered microbiologist Am. Acad. Microbiology. Research asst. microbiology Utah State U., 1965-66, teaching asst. food and aquatic microbiology, 1966-67; grad. teaching asst. gen. biology Oreg. State U., 1970-72, instr., 1972-73; tchr. phys. and biol. scis. U.S. Bur. Indian Affairs Boarding Sch., Shonto, Ariz., 1974-75; asst. prof. biology Franklin Coll., Ind., 1975-78; adj. asst. prof. biology Ind. Central U., Indpls., 1977-78; adj. asst. prof. Ind. U.-Purdue U., Columbus, 1978; mem. faculty Yavapai Community Coll., Prescott, Ariz., 1978-79; assoc. dir. Ute Research Lab., Ft. Duchesne, Utah, 1980-81, dir., 1981-82; vis. prof. biology Coll. St. Thomas, Minn., 1985-87; asst. prof. biology U. San Diego, 1988—2001, assoc. provost, 2001—. Adj. prof. biology U. San Diego, 2001—; summer ranger, naturalist U.S. Nat. Park Svcs., 1970—79, 1983—86. Author: (scholarly work (book) Andrew Ellicott Douglass and the Role of the Giant Sequoia in the Development of Dendrochonology, 2001; contbr. articles. Commr. San Diego County Columbian Quincentenary Commn., 1990-93, chmn. edn. com., 1990-93; mem. pres.'s adv. com. San Diego Zool. Soc., 1995-97; trustee Quail Bot. Gardens Found., 1995-98. Recipient Disting. Alumnus award, Calif. State Poly. U., 1991, Monrovia High Sch., 1991; Eli Lilly doctoral grantee Oreg. State U., 1973-74; NSF grantee, 1998. Mem. AAAS, Cabrillo Hist. Assn. (bd. dirs. 1989-94, vice chair 1992, chair 1993, 94), Alpha Scholastic Honor Soc. of Franklin Coll. (pres. 1976-78), Sigma Xi (sec. San Diego chpt. 1996-97, v.p. 1997-98, pres. 1999-2000, assoc. dir. S.W. region 2000-02, Silver medal of achievement 2002), Beta Beta Beta. Office: U San Diego Office Provost 5998 Alcala Park San Diego CA 92110-2429

MCGRAW, HAROLD WHITTLESEY, JR. publisher; b. Bklyn., Jan. 10, 1918; s. Harold Whittlesey and Louise (Higgins) McG.; m. Anne Per-Lee, Nov. 30, 1940; children: Suzanne, Harold Whittlesey III, Thomas Per-Lee, Robert Pearce. Grad., Lawrenceville (N.J.) Sch., 1936; AB, Princeton U., 1940. With G.M. Basford (advt. agy.), N.Y.C., 1940-41, Brentano's Bookstores, Inc., 1946; with McGraw-Hill Book Co., Inc., N.Y.C., 1947—, successively promotion mgr., dir. co. advt. and trade sales, 1947-55, dir., v.p. charge trade book, indsl. and bus. book depts., co. advt., 1955-61, sr. v.p., 1961-68, pres., 1968-74, McGraw-Hill, Inc., 1974-81, CEO, 1975-83, chmn., 1976-88; chairman emeritus, 1988—. Bd. dirs. McGraw Hill, Inc., 1954-88. Founder, pres., bd. dirs. Bus. Council Effective Literacy and Bus. Press Ednl. Found. Served as capt. USAAF, 1941-45. Mem.: Bent Pine (Vero Beach, Fla.); Blind Brook (Purchase, N.Y.); Wee Burn (Darien, Conn.). Home: Watch Tower Rd Darien CT 06820 Office: The McGraw-Hill Cos 1221 Avenue Of The Americas New York NY 10020-1095

MCGRAW, JACK WILSON, federal agency administrator; b. Balt., May 19, 1943; s. P.W. and Nina (Gwinn) McG.; m. Nancy F. Foster, Aug. 31, 1974; children— David, Mark BA, Morris Harvey Coll., 1964; B.Div., Tex. Christian U., 1967. Ordained minister Christian Ch. (Disciples of Christ). Dir. temporary housing HUD, Washington, 1979-82; asst. assoc. dir. Fed. Emergency Mgmt. Agy., 1982, dep. asst. dir., 1982-83; dep. asst. adminstr. EPA Office Solid Waste and Emergency Response, 1983-88, acting asst. adminstr.; dep. regional adminstr. EPA Regional Office, Denver, 1988—. Nominee William H. Jump award HUD, 1972; recipient Presdl. Meritorious award, Presdl. Disting. Exec. award. Presbyterian. Avocation: skiing. Home: 8074 S Oneida Ct Englewood CO 80112-3128 Office: EPA Regional Office 8074 S Oneida Ct Englewood CO 80112

MCGRAW, LAVINIA MORGAN, retired retail company executive; b. Detroit, Feb. 26, 1924; d. Will Curtis and Margaret Coulter (Oliphant) McG. AB, Radcliffe Coll., 1945. Mem. Phi Beta Kappa. Home: 2501 Calvert St NW Washington DC 20008-2620

MCGRAW, PATRICK ALLAN, lawyer; b. Radford, Va., Aug. 26, 1942; s. Delford Armstrong and Virginia Elizabeth (Ramsey) McGraw; m. Martha Jane Schrock, June 22, 1968; children: Katherine Martha, Michael Patrick. AB, Kenyon Coll., 1963; JD, Harvard U., 1966. Bar: Ohio 1966, US Dist Ct (no dist) Ohio 1967, US Supreme Ct 1978, US Ct Appeals (6th cir) 1983. Assoc. Fuller and Henry, Toledo, 1967-72, ptnr., 1972-84; prin. The Toledo Group, Inc., 1985-96; supr. Ohio Civil Rights Comn., 1996—. Asst atty gen State of Ohio, 1992—95. Trustee Bell and Beckwith Liquidation, Toledo, 1983—97, Knoxville Col, Tenn., 1981—83. With USAR, 1966—72. Mem.: ABA, Kenyon Col Alumni Asn (pres 1980), Toledo Bar Asn, Cleveland Bar Asn, Ohio State Bar Asn, Am Judicature Soc, Phi Beta Kappa. Democrat. E-mail: mpmcgraw@att.net.

MCGRAW, PATRICK JOHN, judge; b. Detroit, Feb. 3, 1956; s. John William and Elizabeth Kay (Foley) McG.; m. Susan Elaine Borowiak, Jan. 14, 1978; children: Kelly Elizabeth, Ryan Patrick, Brandon David, Kyle Elaine. BS, Cen. Mich. U., 1979; JD, Cooley Law Sch., 1982. Bar: Mich. 1982. Ptnr. McGraw, Martin & Heyn, P.C., Saginaw, Mich., 1982-99; judge Probate Ct. 10th Jud. Cir., 1999—. Instr. Ctrl. Mich. U., Mt. Pleasant, Mich., 1986-90. Atty. Sch. Program, Saginaw, 1986—; mem. YMCA; bd. trustees Saginaw Twp., 1988-1999; sch. coun. mem. Saginaw Nouvel Cath. Ctrl. H.S., 1988—; apptd. Mich. Bd. of Counseling, 1994—, apptd. probate judge by Gov. Engler, 1999; elected probate judge, 2000. Mem. ABA, ATLA, Nat. Coll. Probate and Juvenile Judges, Mich. Bar Assn., Saginaw County Bar Assn., Mich. Probate Judges Assn., Phi Alpha Delta. Avocations: black belt karate, hunting, fishing, racquetball. E-mial. Home: 5220 Overhill Dr Saginaw MI 48603-1727 Office: Saginaw County Govtl Bldg 111 S Michigan Ave Saginaw MI 48602-2019 E-mail: pmcgraw@saginawcounty.com.

MCGRAW, WARREN RANDOLPH, state supreme court chief justice; b. Wyoming County, W.Va., May 10, 1939; m. Peggy Shufflebarger; children: W. Randolph, H. Suzanne, Rebecca L. AB, U. Charleston, 1960; postgrad., W.Va. U.; JD, Wake Forest U., 1963. Bar: W.Va. 1963. Trial atty. U.S. Dept. Justice, Washington; legal svc. atty.; elected W.Va. Ho. of Dels., 1968, 70, W.Va. Senate, 1972, 76, 80; elected prosecuting atty. Wyoming County, 1996; justice W.Va. Supreme Ct. Appeals, 1998—, chief justice, 2001—. Instr. W.Va. U. Ext. Agy.; W.Va. del. Dem. Nat. Conv., 1972, 74; mem. Del. and Senatorial Dist. Exec. Coms.; del. State Dem. Jud. Conv. and State Dem. Conv.; elected pres. W.Va. Senate, 1980, 82; co-chmn. Crime Commn.; mem. Nat. Conf. Lt. Govs. Featured on Nat. Pub. TV series Bill Moyers Journal. Trustee 1st United Meth. Ch., Pineville; participant Marshall U.'s Taft Lectr. Series; elected W.Va. del. Dem. Nat. Conv., 1972, 74, Wyo. County Bd. Edn., 1986, 44th pres. W.Va. Sen., 1980, 82; del. State Dem. Jud. Conv., State Dem. Conv.; past pres. Jaycees; mem. Nat. Conf. Lt. Govs., Heart Fund, Wyoming County Cancer Fund, Del. and Sen. Dist. Exec. Coms.; past chmn. Wyoming County Dem. Exec. Com.; co-chmn. Crime Commn. Named one of nation's Outstanding Legislators, Rutgers U.; recipient Friend of Edn., Margaret Baldwin award W.Va. Edn. Assn. Mem. Wyo. Bar Assn., Raleigh County Bar Assn., Rotary Internat. Office: Bldg 1 Rm E-302 Capitol Complex Charleston WV 25305*

MCGRAW-LEWICKI, M(ARJORIE) LEE, small business owner; b. Englewood, N.J., Jan. 18, 1957; d. John L. and Marjorie (Peddy) McGraw; m. Matthew E. Lewicki, Oct. 1, 1983. BBA, Stetson U., 1979; postgrad., Fairleigh Dickinson U., 1982-83. Promotion asst. McGraw-Hill, Inc., N.Y.C., 1979-81, mktg. comm. assoc., 1981-82, mktg. comm. mgr., 1982-85; pres., owner The Gift Basket, Inc., Waltham, Mass., 1987—. Mem. bd. advisors Stetson U. Sch. Bus., Deland, Fla., 1984—, trustee, 1996—2000, 2002—, sec., 1998—2000; sec. bd. Lupus Found. Mass., 2000—; mem. bd. overseers Boston Ballet bd. overseers, 1998—; bd. trustees Boston Ballet , 2002—; mem., bd. dirs. Lupus Rsch. Inst., N.Y.C., 2000—; bd. dirs. Lupus Found. Mass., 1998—. Mem. Nat. Fedn. Bus. and Profl. Women (pres. Sudbury, Mass. chpt. 1997-99). Episcopalian.

MCGREAL, JOSEPH A., JR. publishing company executive; b. Bklyn., Mar. 6, 1935; s. Joseph A. and Aresta (Noon) McG.; m. Margaret A. Molloy, June 6, 1959; children— Patrick, Pegeen, Joseph. BBA, St. Francis Coll., 1962. Pres. Med./Pharm. Pub. Co., Inc., Port Washington, NY, 1995—. Served with U.S. Army, 1955-57. Home: 71 Willow Ln Spring Lake NJ 07762-2188 Office: Med/Pharm Pub Co Inc 22 Hilltop Rd Port Washington NY 11050

MCGREAL, RORY PATRICK, university official; b. Pontefract, Eng., Dec. 21, 1950; came to Can., 1957; s. Thomas and Ellen McGreal; m. Kathleen Fay, Jan. 13, 1975; children: Donal, Seamus, Sean. BA, McGill U., Montreal, Que., Can., 1975; BEd, Dalhousie U., Halifax, N.S., Can., 1977; cert., Pushkin Inst., Moscow, 1977; MA, Concordia U., Montreal, 1984; PhD, Nova Southeastern U., 1999. Tchr. Knob Lake Sch., Schefferville, Que., 1977-79; union pres. Ea. Que. Tchr.'s Assn., Quebec, 1979-80; tchr. Nat. Youth Svcs., Seychelles Islands, 1980-83; lectr. U. Petroleum & Minerals, Dhahran, Saudi Arabia, 1984-86; dir. tech. studies Bahrain U., Manama, 1986-88; profl. officer Meml. U. Nfld. Faculty Assn., St. John's, Can., 1989-90; sch. liaison supr. Contact North, Sudbury, Ont., 1990-93; exec. dir. TeleEdn. and TeleCampus N.B., Fredericton, Canada, 1993—2001; gen. mgr. N.B. Distance Edn. Inc.; assoc. v.p. rsch. Athabasca U., Canada, 2001—. Mem. exec. com. TeleLearning—Nat. Ctrs. of Excellence. Co-author: WWW Instructor's Manual, 1995; contbr. articles to profl. publs., chpt. to book. Mem. edn. com. Can. Network for Advancement of Rsch., Industry and Edn., 1995-96; mem. adv. coun. Learning and Tng. Working Group of Info. Hwy., 1994-95; bd. dirs. Ctr. Internat. Devel. Info. Highway in French 1996—; mem. Premier's Task force Info. Hwy., 1994—. Russian study scholar Can. Office External Affairs,

1977, Killam scholar, 1983. Mem. Can. Assn. Distance Edn., U.S. Distance Learning Assn. Roman Catholic. Avocation: web surfing. Office: Athabasca U 1 University Rd Athabasca AB Canada T9S 3A3 E-mail: rory@teleeducation.nb.ca.

MCGREEVEY, JAMES E. governor; b. Jersey City, Aug. 6, 1957; m. Kari Schutz; 1 child, Morag Veronica. BA, Columbia U., 1978; JD, Georgetown U., 1981; MEd, Harvard U., 1982. Assembly mem. 19th dist., Middlesex, NJ, 1990—91; state sen. dist. 19, 1994—97; gov. of N.J. Trenton, 2002—. Atty., regional mgr. Merck & Co., Rahway, N.J., 1987-91. Campaign com. vol. State Legis. Campaigns, 1983, 85, 87; campaign vol. Middlesex County Freeholder reelection campaigns, 1983-88; atty., policy counsel Assembly Dem. Majority Office, 1983-84; campaign vol. speaker for Congressman Bernard J. Dwyer, 1984, 86, 88, Senator Frank R. Lautenberg, 1988, 94; former chmn. Ctrl. Jersey chpt. ARC. Mem. Nat. Conf. Christians and Jews (former chmn.), Middlesex County Cult and Heritage Commn. (former chmn.), N.J. League Nursing (former trustee), Diocese of Metuchen Cath. Lawyers Guild (past pres.). Office: Office of the Governor 125 West State St., PO Box 001 Trenton NJ 08625*

MCGREGOR, DOUGLAS HUGH, pathologist, educator; b. Temple, Tex., Aug. 28, 1939; s. Harleigh Heath and Joyce Ellen (Lambert) McG.; m. Mizuki Kitani, July 6, 1969; children: Michelle Sakuya, David Kenji. BA, Duke U., 1961, MD, 1966; postgrad., U. Edinburgh, Scotland, 1961-62. Diplomate Am. Bd. Pathology. Intern, chief resident in pathology UCLA Med. Ctr., 1966-68; surgeon, lt. comdr. Atomic Bomb Casualty Commn., Hiroshima, Japan, 1968-71; chief resident in pathology Queens Med. Ctr., Honolulu, 1971-73; asst., assoc. prof. pathology U. Kans. Med. Ctr., Kansas City, 1973-82, prof., 1982—. Dir. anat. pathology VA Med. Ctr., Kansas City, Mo., 1975-94, chief pathology and lab. medicine, 1994—. Contbr. numerous articles to profl. jours., chpts. to books. Leader YMCA Indian Princess Program, Overland Park, Kans., 1977-79, Indian Guide Program, 1978-80, Cub Scout Am., Overland Park, 1980-82, Boy Scouts Am., Leawood, Kans., 1982—. Lt. comdr. USPHS, 1968-71, Japan. Grantee Merck, Sharp and Dohme, 1980. Fellow Coll. Am. Pathologists, Am. Soc. Clin. Pathologists; mem. Am. Assn. Pathologists, Internat. Acad. Pathologists, Soc. Exptl. Biology and Medicine, N.Y. Acad. Scis., AAAS, Kansas City Soc. Pathologists (sec.-treas. 1982-83, pres. 1983-84), Leawood Country Club. Achievements include research in ultrastructure and pathobiology of neoplasms, radiation carcinogenesis, and morphogenesis of atherosclerosis. Home: 9400 Lee Blvd Shawnee Mission KS 66206-1826 Office: VA Med Ctr 4801 E Linwood Blvd Kansas City MO 64128-2226

MCGREGOR, JAMES HARVEY SPENCE, comparative literature educator; b. Frostburg, Md., Oct. 1, 1946; s. James Harvey and Mary (Twigg) McG.; 1 child, Raphael Harvey Gais; m. Sarah Spence, May 25, 1985; 1 child, Edward Isham Spence. BA, Princeton U., 1968, PhD, 1975. Prof. dept. comparative lit. and assoc. head U. Ga., Athens, 1980—. Vis. prof. dept. English Colgate U., Hamilton, N.Y., 1979-80; vis. prof. dept. Italian U. Calif., Berkeley, 1984-85. Author: Image of Antiquity, 1991, Shades of Aeneas, 1991; editor, translator: Sack of Rome, 1993; editor: Approaches to Teaching Boccaccio's Decameron, 2000. Rome Prize fellow in post-classical humanistic studies Am. Acad. in Rome, 1981-82. Mem. MLA, Am. Assn. Italian Studies, Internat. Assn. for Study of Italian Lang. and Lit. (past pres.), Am. Boccaccio Assn. Office: U Ga 232 J Brown Hall Athens GA 30606-6204

MCGREGOR, JOHN JOSEPH, lawyer; b. Fort Knox, Ky., Nov. 18, 1946; s. Arden Durham and Ruth Marguerite (Funkner) McG.; m. Rebecca Lounsbury, 1989. AB, U. San Francisco, 1968; JD, U. Calif. Hastings Coll. Law, 1971; LLM, NYU, 1974. Bar: Calif. 1972, U.S. Dist. Ct. (no. dist.) Calif. 1972, U.S. Ct. Appeals (9th cir.) 1979, U.S. Dist. Ct. (ea. dist.) Calif. 1988; cert. specialist in taxation law. Sports info. dir. U. San Francisco, 1966-68; staff atty. Community Legal Svcs., San Jose, Calif., 1972-73; cons. IRS Project, Washington, 1974-75; assoc. Thomas, Snell, Jamison, Russell, Williamson & Asperger, Fresno, Calif., 1975-78; shareholder Thomas, Snell, Jamison, Russell & Asperger, 1978-91, McGregor, Dahl, Sullivan & Klug, Fresno, 1991—. Asst. sec., gen. counsel The Vendo Co., Fresno, 1985-88; mem. Fresno County Assessment Appeals Bd., 1993-98. Author: Taxation of Real Property Transfers, 1981. Bd. dirs. Fresno (Calif.) Storyland, 1976-81; mem. Fresno Ski Patrol, 1976-93, Sierra Summit Ski Patrol, Lakeshore, Calif., 1985-93, The Acad., Fresno, 1981—. Named Vol. Atty. of the Year Fresno County Bar Assn., 1983. Mem. Am. Law Inst., Calif. State Bar Assn. (dir. taxation sect., exec. com. 1983-86, chair standards of tax practice com. 1995, 98), Fresno County Bar Assn. (dir. 1982-86). Roman Catholic. Avocations: skiing, golf, reading. Home: 4774 N Wishon Ave Fresno CA 93704-3144 Office: McGregor Dahl Sullivan & Klug 7080 N Whitney Ave Fresno CA 93720-0154 E-mail: jmcgregor@mdsklaw.com.

MCGREGOR, MICHAEL N. writer, educator; b. Seattle, Jan. 23, 1958; s. Norman L. and Doris E. McGregor; m. Sylvia Farkas, Nov. 27, 1993. BA in Journalism, U. Oreg., 1980; MFA in Writing, Columbia U., 1997. Editor World Concern Mag., Seattle, 1981-84, Back Door Travel, Seattle, 1985-88; editor-in-chief Columbia: A Jour. of Lit. and Art, N.Y.C., 1995-96; instr. Columbia U., 1995-97, asst. to composition dir., 1996-97; lectr. So. Ill. U., Carbondale, 1997-2000; asst. prof. Portland (Oreg.) State U., 2000—. Judge, Charles Johnson award, Carbondale, 1998-99; lectr., guide, European cultural tours, Europe Through the Back Door, Seattle. Contbr. short stories, poems and essays to profl. publs. Pres., Fremont Neighborhood Coun., Seattle, 1993-94; election observer and voter registrar, Wash. State, Seattle, 1992-94. Walden Residency fellow, So. Oreg. U., 2001. Mem. MLA, Associated Writing Programs. Office: Portland State U Box 751 Portland OR 97207-0751

MCGREGOR, RUTH VAN ROEKEL, state supreme court justice; b. Le Mars, Iowa, Apr. 4, 1943; d. Bernard and Marie Frances (Janssen) Van Roekel; m. Robert James McGregor, Aug. 15, 1965. BA summa cum laude, U. Iowa, 1964, MA, 1965; JD summa cum laude, Ariz. State U., 1974. Bar: Ariz. 1974, U.S. Dist. Ct. Ariz. 1974, U.S. Ct. Appeals (9th cir.), U.S. Supreme Ct. 1982. Assoc. Fennemore, Craig, von Ammon, Udall & Powers, Phoenix, 1974-79, ptnr., 1980-81, 82-89; law clk. to justice Sandra Day O'Connor U.S. Supreme Ct., Washington, 1981-82; judge Ariz Ct. Appeals, 1989-98, vice chief judge, 1993-95, chief judge, 1995-98; justice Ariz. Supreme Ct., 1998—, vice chief judge, 2002—. Mem. disciplinary commn. Ariz. Supreme Ct., 1984-89, City of Mesa jud. adv. bd., 1997—. Mem., newsletter editor Charter 100, Phoenix, 1981—; bd. dirs., mem. Ctr. for Law in Pub. Interest, Phoenix, 1977-80. Mem. ABA (chmn. state memberships 1985—), Ariz. Bar Assn. (disciplinary com. 1984—), Ariz. Judges Assn. (exec. com. 1990—, sec. 1991-92, v.p. 1992-93, pres. 1993-94), Nat. Assn. Women Judges (chair first time attendees com. 1990-91, 1994 conv. com.; exec. com. 1995—). Lodges: Soroptomists. Democrat. Lutheran. Office: Arizona Supreme Court 1501 W Washington St Phoenix AZ 85007-3231*

MCGREGOR, THEODORE ANTHONY, chemical company executive; b. Detroit, Mar. 28, 1944; s. Lorraine Guyeveve Guyette; m. Bonny-Joan Beach, Sept. 14, 1963; children: Todd, Timothy, Amy. Student, Henry Ford Coll., 1961-63. Mem. sales staff Gen. Binding Corp., GBC Sales and Service, Oak Brook, Ill., 1965-69; with indsl. chem. divsn. Diversey Chem. Corp., Chgo., 1967-69; with Detrex Corp., Detroit, 1969-75, regional mgr. indsl. chem. specialties divsn., 1975-77, asst. gen. mgr., 1977-81, gen. mgr. indsl. chem. specialties divsn., 1981-85, corp. v.p., gen. mgr., 1985-89; group v.p. indsl. chem. specialties divsn. Wayne Chem., RTI, Seibert-Oxidermo, 1987-93; exec. v.p., also bd. dirs. Wayne Chem.; exec. v.p. Asian Rim and Internat. Mktg. Seibert Oxiderno, 1989-90; pres. TAM Consulting Svcs., Redford, Mich., 1993—; exec. v.p. Harbor Group, 1993—; U.S. dir. comm. devel. Novamax Techs., 1994-96; v.p. Automotive Texo Corp., Cin., 1996—2001; pres. IOM Tech., Southfield, Mich., 2001—. Mem. Wire Inst., Am. Electroplaters Soc., Porcelain Enameling Inst., Detroit Socs. Coating Tech. Avocations: reading, chess, boating. Home: 26111 Harbour Pointe Dr N Harrison Township MI 48045-3209

MCGREGOR, THEODORE STANLEY, court administrator; b. Spokane, Wash., Feb. 9, 1938; s. Archie Elester and Hilda Marie McG.; m. Alice Jeanne McGregor, July 25, 1964; children: Theodore Stanley Jr., Piper Anneliese, Joseph Jeremy, Nathan Christopher. BA, St. Martins Coll., 1960; JD, U. San Franscisco, 1969. Bar: Wash. Priv. prac. attorney, Spokane, 1972-79; clerk of court U. S. Bankruptcy Court Eastern Dist. Wash., 1979—. Capt. USNR, 1961—91. Home: PO Box 928 Spokane WA 99210-0928

MCGREGOR, WALTER, medical products company designer, inventor, consultant, educator; b. Kyiv, Ukraine, Nov. 2, 1937; came to U.S., 1957; s. William and Lydia (Aplass) McG.; m. Helen McGregor, July 18, 1965; children: Roxanne, Walter Jr. BS, Fairleigh Dickinson U., 1973, MBA in Pharm. Mktg., 1975. Sect. leader Ethicon Inc., Somerville, N.J., 1965-68, supr., 1968-76, mgr., 1976-83, dir. surg. products devel. and materials engring., 1983-92, dir. of tech., 1992-94; pres., CEO Biomark Tech. Inc., Flemington, 1994—; sr. v.p. Global Med. Countertrade Corp., 1994—; pres. Global Med. Countertrade Svcs., Inc., 1994—; CEO Primatech USA, Inc., 1996—. Guest cons. Wilmer Inst., Johns Hopkins Hosp. Rsch. Lab., Balt., 1965-70; guest lectr. dept. plastic surgery U. Va. Med. Sch., Charlottesville, 1986—. Contbr. articles to profl. jours. Patentee surg. instruments. Life mem. Rep. Presdl. Task Force, Washington, 1984—; mem. Rep. Nat. Com., 1991. Fellow Soc. for Advancement of Med. Instrumentation; mem. Am. Med. Informatics Assn. (founding), Am. Mktg. Assn. (profl.), Med. Mktg. Assn. Avocations: stamp collecting, fishing, reading in surgical developments. Home: 104 Hoffman Rd Flemington NJ 08822-7023 Office: Biomark Tech Inc 104 Hoffman Rd Flemington NJ 08822-7023

MCGREGORY, JERRILYN, English educator; b. Gary, Ind., Jan. 23, 1949; d. Jerry and Henrietta McG.; children: William, Keith, Julian. BA, Ill. Wesleyan U., 1971; MPS, Cornell U., 1985; PhD, U. Pa., 1992. Vis. lectr. Rutgers U., New Brunswick, N.J., 1988-89; scholar-in-residence Franklin & Marshall Coll., Lancaster, Pa., 1989-90; asst. prof. U. Ga., Athens, 1990-93, Fla. State U., Tallahassee, 1993-97, assoc. prof., 1998—. Folklorist Phila. Folklore Project, Phila., 1987-90. Author: Wiregrass County, 1997. Mem. Am. Folklore Soc., Fla. Folklore Soc. (pres. 2000—). Avocation: onomastics. Office: Fla State U Dept English Tallahassee FL 32306

MCGUCKIN, JOHN HUGH, JR. lawyer; b. Bryn Mawr, Pa., Nov. 8, 1946; AB magna cum laude, Harvard Coll., 1968, JD, 1971. Bar: Mass. 1971, Calif. 1973. Assoc. Orrick, Herrington, Rowley & Sutcliffe, 1972-79; sr. counsel legal divsn. Bank Am., 1979-81; exec. v.p., gen. counsel, corp. sec. UnionBanCal Corp./Union Bank Calif., N.A., San Francisco, 1981—. Adj. instr. Hastings Coll. Law U. Calif., 1980-82; judge pro tem San Francisco Superior Ct. Contbr. articles to profl. jours. Mem. ABA, State Bar Calif. (v.p., treas., bd. govs., chmn. subcom. duties and liabilities trustees probate and trust law sect. 1985-86, legal svcs. trust fund commn. 1989-90, minimum CLE com.), Calif. Bankers Assn. (legal affairs com. 1988-90), Bar Assn. San Francisco (chmn. probate and trust law sect. 1985, exec. com., vice chmn. corp. law dept. sect. 1985-87), Phi Beta Kappa. Office: Union Bank Calif NA 16th Fl 400 California St San Francisco CA 94104-1320

MCGUFFEY, CARROLL WADE, JR. lawyer; b. Decatur, Ga., Dec. 1, 1951; s. Carroll Wade and Dorothy (Landers) McG.; m. Virginia Elizabeth Miller, Aug. 12, 1972; children: Carroll Wade, III, Michelle Elizabeth, Jennifer Lanier. BBA, U. Ga., 1973, JD cum laude, 1976. Bar: Ga. 1976, Fla. 1977, U.S. Dist. Ct. (mid. dist.) Ga. 1976, U.S. Supreme Ct. 1980. Capt. Chief Claims Tort Litigation Div. USAF, Eglin AFB, Fla., 1976-80; assoc., ptnr. Savell and Williams, Atlanta, 1980-90; mng. ptnr., CEO Goodman McGuffey Aust & Lindsey LLP, 1990—. Lectr. in field. Editor: Employers Guide to Workers Compensation in Georgia, Employee Leasing: An Employer's Guide. Ward capt. Athens Mayoral Campaign (Ga.), 1975; commr., dir. Stone Mountain Dixie Youth Baseball, 1982-87; cubmaster Boy Scouts Am., 1986-88, scoutmaster, 1988-90, troop chmn., 1991-92, dist. chmn., 1993-95; mgr., coach Murphy Candler Girls Softball Assn., 1996—. Recipient Dist. Award of Merit, Boy Scouts Am., 1995. Mem. ABA, Fla. Bar Assn., Atlanta Bar Assn. (workers compensation seminar chmn. 1993, 97, fundraising chmn. Kid's Chance Found. Race, 1992, workers compensation section, bd. dirs. 1994-01, sec.-treas. 1997, chair-elect 1998, chair 1999), Ga. Def. Lawyers Assn. (trial acad. instr. 1987), Def. Rsch. Inst., Ind. Ins. Agts. of Ga. (hon. life, young agents com.), Ga. Mental Health Assn. (bd. dirs. 1987). Clubs: Athens Boat (dir. 1982-90), Lawyers (Atlanta), UGA Pres. Club. Methodist. E-mail: wmcguffey@gmail.com.

MCGUIGAN, CHARLES JAMES, rehabilitation therapist; b. Maple Shade, N.J., May 8, 1944; s. Charles J. and Frances G. (Abbott) McG.; divorced; 1 child, Richard Holmes. AA, Atlantic C.C., 1977; student, Montclair State Coll., 1977-78, Glassboro State Coll., 1981-83, 88; BA in Social Sci. and History, Thomas A. Edison Coll., 1983; MEd, U. Maine, 2001. Cert. elem. tchr. N.J., computer specialist Fla., CPR, first aid, team tng., rehab. therapist; ordained Universal Life Ch., 2001. Tchr. 4th and 5th grades, track coach St. Nicholas Sch., Atlantic City, 1978-84; tchr. 5th grade, track coach St. Michaels Sch., 1984-88; security guard Securex, Inc., Tampa, Fla., 1988; resident tng. instr. Upper Pinellas Assn. for Retarded Citizens, Clearwater, 1988-89; rehab. therapist Gulf Coast Ctr., Ft. Myers, 1989-95, resdl. counselor, 1995-96; edn. tech III Sch. Union 92, 1996-97, Hermon (Maine) Elem. Sch., 1997-2000; grad. asst., rschr. U. Maine, 2000—. Track coach Camden (N.J.) Diocese Office, 1983-88. Author poetry; contbr. to anthologies; composer: (song) Once Upon a Dream, 1998, Silent Whispers, 1998. Singer with barbershop quartet, musical shows; tchr. creative writing Unity Ch., Ft. Myers, Fla.; bd. dirs. Unitarian Universalist Ch., Bangor, v.p. N.E. dist. bd., 1999-2000, 2000-01. Recipient Outstanding Citizen award Equal Opportunity Fund, 1975, Liberty Bell award City of Phila., 1976, Outstanding Counselor award Atlantic Human Resource, 1984; named Golden Poet of Yr. World of Poetry, 1991; 95 Presidential Poetry award Iliad Press; Nat. Writing Project fellow U. Maine, 1999. Mem. Kappa Delta Pi. Republican. Avocations: creative writing, travel, reading, computers, raising chows. Home and Office: 687 State St Meadville PA 16335-2264 E-mail: chows91@hotmail.com.

MCGUIGAN, PATRICK BRUCE, editor; b. Corpus Christi, Tex., Aug. 18, 1954; s. Bruce Frederick and Bonnie Fay McGuigan; m. Pamela E. Henzel; children: Josef, Stefan, Erin, Andrew. BA in History, Okla. State U., 1976, MA in Medieval History, 1979, tchr. cert., 1980; student, Villanova U., Italy. Grad. tchg. asst. Okla. State U., Stillwater, Okla., 1976—80; reporter family protection report Free Congress Found., Washington, 1980—88, editor initiative and referendum report, 1980—88, editor family law and democracy report, 1988—90, dir. Ctr. for Law and Democracy, 1985—90; chief editl. writer The Oklahoman, Oklahoma City, 1990—95, editor editl. page, 1995—. Bd. dirs. Edn. and Employment Ministry, Oklahoma City, Nat. Inst. Devel. Delays, Shawnee, Okla.; guest lectr. numerous elem. and secondary schs. Editor: Law, Economics and Civil Justice, 1994; author: Ninth Justice: The Fight for Bork, 1990, The Politics of Direct Democracy, 1985; contbr. ; editor: A Blueprint for Judicial Reform, 1981, Criminal Justice Reform, 1983, Crime and Punishment in Modern America, 1986, The Judges War: The Senate, Legal Culture, Political Ideology and Judicial Confirmation, 1987. Mem. steering com. Kids Project Oklahoma City Pub. Schs. Found., 1998—; com. chmn. pack 10 Cub Scouts Am., Oklahoma City, 1999—, cubmaster pack 12, 1993—99. Named Cubmaster of Yr., Last Frontier coun. Cub Scouts, 1998; recipient Edn. Journalism award, Assn. Oklahoma City Pub. Schs. Found., 1998—, Internat. Comm. award, Taiwan, 1998, 1st pl. editl./writing award, AP/Okla. News Execs., 1993, 1995. Mem.: Soc. Profl. Journalists (contest judge Okla. chpt.), Am. Polit. Sci. Assn., Nat. Press Club (libr. and archives chmn. 1989—90), KC (past Faithful Navigator 4th deg. 1983—). Home: PO Box 54955 Oklahoma City OK 73154 Office: The Oklahoman PO Box 25125 Oklahoma City OK 73125 Fax: 405-475-3971 .

MCGUINESS, JAMES D. chemist; b. Evansville, Ind., June 23, 1930; s. Donald A. and Jeannette H. McGinness; m. Mary D. McGinness; children: James E. McGinness, John R. McGinness, Carol R. Flin, Michael E. McGinness, Katie R. St. John. AB Chemistry, Evansville Coll., Evansville, Indiana, 1952. Dir. analytical rsch. Sherwin-Williams Co., Chicago, Ill., 1952—72, mgr. quality assurance Cleveland, Ohio, 1972—74, automotive mgr. Chicago, Ill., 1974—77; bus. machine mgr. Red Spot Paint and Varnish, Evansville, Ind., 1977—80, exterior mgr., 1980—97, analytical sciences mgr., 1997—99; mgmt. and coatings sci. cons. self, 2000—. Chmn. edn. com. EVL Internat. Mgmt. Coun., Evansville, Ind., 1998—99. Contbr. articles to profl. jours. Mem.: Fedn. Societies for Coatings Tech., Soc. of Applied Spectroscopy, Am. Chem. Soc. Avocations: gardening, home remodeling, home building, auto touring. Home: 1420 Saint Phillips Road South Evansville IN 47712 Personal E-mail: jim_mcginess@dynasty.net.

MCGUINN, MICHAEL EDWARD, III, retired army officer; b. Spartanburg, S.C., Feb. 22, 1925; s. Michael Edward Jr. and Margaret Cordelia (Shackleford) McG.; m. Betty Gay Corn, 1948 (div. 1951); m. Phyllis Fryer, Oct. 7, 1952 (dec. July 1997); children: Michael Edward IV, Carol Anne McGuinn Branch. Student, Clemson U., 1941-43, 46, Coll. William and Mary, 1962-63. Served with U.S. Navy, PTO, 1943-46; commd. 2d lt. U.S. Army, 1949, advanced through grades to col., 1971; asst. mil. attache Am. Embassy, Copenhagen, 1958-61; posted to svc. British Army, Longmoor, Eng., 1964-66; served on U.S. Dept. Army Gen. Staff, Washington, 1966-68; comdr. 10th Transp. Bn. U.S. Army, Vietnam, 1968-69; chief transp. div. U.S. Readiness Command, MacDill AFB, Fla., 1969-72; ret. U.S. Army, 1972; state govt. svc. various locations, 1972-82; chief of staff Ga. State Def. Force, an Agy. of the State of Ga., Atlanta, 1987-95; orgnl. cons. Ga. Dept. Def. Decorated Legion of Merit (2), Army Commendation medal (2), Naval Commendation medal. Mem.: U.S. Army Transp. Mus. Avocations: military history, photography, home workshop. Home and Office: 6420 Tanacrest Ct NW Atlanta GA 30328-2837 E-mail: sdftrooper@aol.com. *Since boyhood when a young cadet,I have lived by one code "Duty, Honor and Country". In good times and bad, it has kept me faithful to principles of personal responsibility, personal integrity, and the importance of service to something greater than oneself. The code has never failed our nation nor has it ever failed me.*

MCGUINNESS, AIMS CHAMBERLAIN, JR. higher education policy analyst; b. Phila., Feb. 19, 1940; s. Aims Chamberlain and Margaret Alexander (Hatfield) McG.; m. Susan Norton, Aug. 28, 1965; children: Aims C. III, Alexander W. BA, U. Pa., 1965; MBA, George Washington U., 1970; PhD, Syracuse U., 1979. Adminstrv. resident New Eng. Med. Ctr. Hosps., Boston, 1965-66, Thayer Hosp., Waterville, Maine, 1966-67; asst. dir. Health Facilities Planning Coun., Augusta, 1967-68; health professions coord. Office of Pres. U. Maine, Orono, 1968-69, exec. asst. to chancellor Portland, 1969-73; asst. dir. Project on Statewide Planning for Higher Edn. Edn. Commn. of the States, Denver, 1975-77, asst. exec. dir., 1977-84, dir. higher edn. policy, 1984-93; sr. assoc. Nat. Ctr. for Higher Edn. Mgmt. Systems, Boulder, Colo., 1993—. Team mem. rev. of edn. policy in Russian Fedn., Orgn. for Econ. Cooperation and Devel., Paris, 1996-97, rev. of tertiary edn. and rsch. in the Russian Fedn., 1997-98, rapporteur rev. of nat. edn. policies in the Baltic States, 1999-2001; cons. on edn. in Russian Fedn., World Bank, Washington, 1998-99; mem. internat. strategic experts group to Russian Ministry Edn., 2002-. Author: State Postsecondary Education Structures Sourcebook, 1984, 88, 92, 94, 97; columnist Assn. Governing Bds. of Univs. and Colls., 2000; contbr. articles ot profl. jours., chpts. to books. Mem. bd. edn. Littleton (Colo.) Pub. Schs., 1983-91, pres. bd. edn., 1987-91; trustee Adams State Coll., Colo., Western State Coll., Colo., Mesa State Coll., Colo., Met. State Coll., Colo., 1989-97; chmn. bd. trustees State Colls. in Colo., 1995-97. With USNR, 1959-61. Mem. Am. Assn. Higher Edn., European Higher Edn. Soc. Episcopalian. Avocations: organ, bicycling. Home: 4988 W Fair Ave Littleton CO 80123-6716 Office: NCHEMS PO Box 9752 Boulder CO 80301-9752 Fax: (303) 497-0338. E-mail: aims@nchems.org.

MCGUINNESS, BARBARA SUE, food products executive; b. Lansing, Mich., Feb. 8, 1947; d. William Harrison and Gertrude Esther (Parker) Coleman; m. Michael L. Mueller, Aug. 12, 1965 (div. June 1973); children: Meredith Sue, Matthew Parker; m. John McGuinness, Dec. 8, 1978. Student, Meramec Community Coll., 1975-77, Florissant Valley Community Coll., 1984-87. Instr. Lindbergh Sch. Dist., St. Louis, 1975-77; surp. Velvet Freeze Ice Cream Co., 1977-81, v.p., 1981—. Chmn. Fin. Com. Chesterfield (Mo.) Transition Com., 1988—, campaign chmn. Chesterfield Inc. Com., 1988—, chmn. Chesterfield Planning & Zoning Commn., 1988-95, chmn. Chesterfield Inaugural Commns., 1988; rep. State Mo. Electoral Coll. U.S., 1988; apptd. vice chmn. Selective Svc. System Draft Bd. #20, 1981-, chmn., 1991--; state parliamentarian Mo. Fedn. Women's Dem. Clubs, 1989-91, 93-95; del. Dem. Nat. Conv., 1972, 80, 92; mem., grad. Leadership St. Louis, 1991-92, St. Louis County Pvt. Industry Coun., 1991-92, St. Louis County DARES Bd., 1991-94, Mayor's Chesterfield Valley Flood Recovery Task Force, 1993-94, Chesterfield Valley Rebuilding Task Force, 1993-94, St. Louis County Boundary Commn., 1995-2000, chmn., 1995; mem. Chesterfield Intergovernmental Rels. Com., 1993-94; campaign mgr. St. Louis County Pros. Atty. Robert McCulloch, 1990-94, Howard Wagner Mo. Sec. of State, 1992; mem. Chesterfield Econ. Devel. Coun., 1990-91; chmn. St. Louis County Inaugural Commn., 1991. Recipient Key to City award City Govt. Crestwood, Mo., 1974, Key to City Chesterfield, 1988, Disting. Svc. award, 1988, St. Louis County Dem. of Yr. award, 1986, Planning Commr. of Yr. award Dwight Davis Am. Planning Assn., 1993, Excellence in Cmty. Devel. award Chesterfield Civic Progress, 1993, Humanitarian award 1993, End Hunger award U.S. Mayors, 1993, Disting. Svc. award Mid-East Area Agy. on Aging, 1994, Excellence in Cmty. Devel. award Chesterfield Civic Progress, 1997; named Chesterfield Citizen of Yr., 1989. Mem. Am. Planning Assn., Area Ice Cream Retailers Assn. (pres. 1979-84), Chesterfield C. of C. (Civic award 1988). Democrat. Baptist. Avocation: politics. Home: 95 River Bend Dr Chesterfield MO 63017-2671 Office: Velvet Freeze Ice Cream Co 7355 W Florissant Ave Saint Louis MO 63136-1348

MCGUINNESS, GERARD JOHN, priest, educator; b. Glasgow, Scotland, Jan. 6, 1929; s. James Gerard McGuinness and Ann McGroarty. BA with honors, Birkbeck Coll., London, 1950, BA with honors, 1955; degree in Theology, Salesian Pontifical U., Rome, 1960. Classics educator Salesian Coll., London, 1950—55; philosophy & classics educator Salesian Sem., Beckford, England, 1960—65, theology profl. Bethlehem, Jordan, 1968—70; pastor various chs. Roman Catholic. Home: 27931 Murriet Rd Sun City CA 92586-2320

MCGUINNESS, ROSAMOND ZEIGLER, music educator; b. Bridgeport, Conn., Dec. 4, 1929; arrived in Eng., 1957; d. S. Howard and Adelaide (Zeigler) Cohan; m. Bernard Francis McGuinness (div. 1969); children: Catherine, Sara, Patrick, Lucy; m. George Charles Biddlecombe (div. 1981); 1 child, Elizabeth. BA in Music, Vassar Coll., 1951; MA, Smith Coll., 1952; postgrad., Harvard U., 1955, Cornell U., 1956-57; PhD in Music History, Oxford (Eng.) U., 1964. Lectr. music dept. Vassar Coll., 1955-57; tutor in music history Brasenose, Queen's, St. Peter's and St. Anne's/Oxford U., 1964-72; lectr. music dept. Royal Holloway Coll., London U., 1969-82, sr. lectr., 1982—, prof., personal chair, 1990, emeritus prof., 1995—, project dir. computer register musical data, 1987—. Vis. lectr. Royal Acad. Music, 1969-70,, Imperial Coll. Sci. and Tech., 1976-81, King's Coll., London U., 1979-82, Royal Coll. Music, 1999; mem. coun. Royal Hollow and Bedford New Coll., 1992; quality auditor Higher Edn. Quality Coun., Higher Edn. Funding Coun. for Eng.; alt. mem. Standing Conf. on Univ. Entrance Com. of Vice Chancellors and Prins., U.K., 1997, mem., 1998; chief external examiner Brunel U., West London Inst. Author: English Court Odes 1660-1820, 1971; contbr. articles to profl. jours., chpts. to books; project dir. register musical data London newspapers, 1660-1750. Chair Camden Lay Visitors Panel, Borough of Camden, London, 1990-95; dep. chair North-East London Lay Observers, 1996; mem. Cmty. and Camden Policy Consultative Coun., London, 1989-95. Harriet Boyd Hawes scholar, 1951-52; Louise Hart van Loon fellow, 1955-56, 60-61, Benjamin White Whitney fellow, 1955-56, Fredericka Schepp fellow, 1955-56, Leopold Schepp Found. fellow, 1956-57, Eliza Buffington fellow, 1957-58, Vassie James Hill fellow AAUP, 1958-59, Mary Richardson and Lydia Pratt Babbott fellow, 1960-61, Joanna Randall-MacIver rsch. fellow, 1967-69; named to Great Britain Women of Yr., 1996; recipient Hon. Mention John Lowell Osgood Meml. prize Oxford U., 1963; grantee Ctrl. Rsch. Fund U. London, 1977, Brit. Acad., 1977, Leverhulme Trust, 1978-79, Am. Coun. Learned Socs., 1978-79, Social Sci. Rsch. Coun., 1980-83. Fellow Royal Soc. Arts, mem. Brit. Soc. 18th Century Studies (pres. 1994-96), Am. Musicol. Soc., Royal Musical Assn., Am. Soc. 18th Century Studies, Sharp Studies, Royal Soc. Musicians. Avocations: walking, reading, the arts. Home: 23 Alma St London NW5 3DJ England E-mail: r.mcguinness@rhul.ac.uk.

MCGUIRE, BRIAN LYLE, educator, health science facility consultant; b. Mobile, Ala., June 13, 1959; s. Frank Ludlow, Jr. and Mary Lyle (Davidson) McG.; m. Jean Ellen Marler, June 18, 1983. BS in Acctg., U. S. Ala., 1982,

MBA, 1990; PhD, U. Ctrl. Fla., 1996. CPA, Ala.; cert. mgmt. acct. Staff acct. Smith, Dukes & Buckalew, CPA's, Mobile, 1983-86; corp. acct. So. Med. Health Systems, 1986, dir. corp. ops, 1987-88; exec. dir. Med. Arts Clinic, Inc. subs. So. Med. Health Systems, Foley, Ala., 1986-88; adminstr. Mobile Heart Ctr., 1988-91; acctg. instr. U. Ctrl. Fla., Orlando, 1991-95; asst. prof. acctg. U. So. Ind., Evansville, 1995—. Unit commr. Boy Scouts Am., Buffalo Trace Coun., 1996-97, pack com. chair, 1995-98. Recipient Eagle Scout Order of Arrow Boy Scouts Am., 1977; named one of Outstanding Young Men of Am., 1982. Mem. AICPA, Inst. Mgmt. Accts. (chpt. bd. dirs. 1983-85, pres. 1987-88, nat. bd. dirs. 1989-91, 92-93, 98—, pres. regional coun. 1992-93, 98-99, Award of Excellence 1993, 99, chair regional ops. com. 1998-00, chair com. on ethics 2000—). Episcopalian. Avocations: travel, camping, fishing, golf. Office: U So Ind Dept Acctg and Bus Law 8600 University Blvd Evansville IN 47712-3534

MCGUIRE, CATHERINE FRANCES, elementary education educator; b. New Brunswick, N.J., Sept. 19, 1945; d. Milton and Regina (Zolandz) Ptaszynski; 1 child, Robert J. Jr. BS in Elem. Edn., Seton Hall U., 1970, MA in Edn., 1974, Ed.S., 1999. Cert. pre-sch. tchr. K-8, supr. K-12. Tchr. grade 1 Our Lady of Fatima Sch., Piscataway, N.J., 1965-68, Middlesex (N.J.) Public Schs., 1970-93, tchr. grade 3, 1993-2000; dir. recruitment, admissions Benedictine Acad., Elizabeth, 2000—01; reading specialist Oak Knoll Sch. of the Holy Child, Summit, NJ, 2001—. Devel. tutor, 1971—; dist. adv. coun. Middlesex Pub. Schs., 1996—99, pupil assistance com., 1994—96, dist. lang. arts com., 1995—96, lang. arts curriculum com., 1994—96, math. curriculum com., 1994—95, instructional coun., 1992—98, lang. arts com., 1989, dist. curriculum com., 87, dist. holistic scoring com. for K-12 writing sample assessments, 1987—98; mem. elem. edn. praxis nat. adv. com. Ednl. Testing Svc., Princeton, NJ, 1999—; tutor Somerset Learning Ctr., Raritan, NJ, 2000—01. Masonic scholarship 2000—. Mem. Internat. Dyslexia Assn., N.J. Edn. Assn. (ret.), N.J. Assn. of Tchrs. Educators., Kappa Delta Pi (Zi Gamma chpt.). Roman Catholic. Avocation: family. Home: 1111 Hazelwood Ave Middlesex NJ 08846-1222 Office: Oakknoll Sch of the Holy Child 44 Blackburn Rd Summit NJ 07901 E-mail: cathteach@aol.com., catherine.mcguire@oakknoll.org.

MCGUIRE, EDWARD DAVID, JR. lawyer; b. Waynesboro, Va., Apr. 11, 1948; s. Edward David and Mary Estelle (Angus) McG.; m. Georgia Ann Charuhas, Aug. 15, 1971; children: Matthew Edward, Kathryn Ann. BS in Commerce, U. Va., 1970; JD, Coll. William and Mary, 1973. Bar: Va. 1973, D.C. 1974, Md. 1990, Pa. 1995, U.S. Dist. Ct. (ea. dist.) Va. 1974, U.S. Dist. Ct. D.C. 1974, U.S. Dist. Ct. Md. 1990, Ct. Appeals (4th cir.) 1974, U.S. Ct. Appeals (D.C. cir.) 1974, U.S. Supreme Ct. 1993. Assoc. Wilkes and Artis, Washington, 1973-78; gen. corp counsel Mark Winkler Mgmt., Alexandria, Va., 1978-80; sr. contracts officer Amtrak, Washington, 1980-81; sr. real estate atty., asst. corp. sec. Peoples Drug Stores, Inc., Alexandria, 1981-88; of counsel Cowles, Rinaldi & Arnold, Ltd., Fairfax, Va., 1989-91; sr. assoc. Radigan, Rosenberg & Holmes, Arlington, 1991; pvt. practice, Annandale, 1992-97; sr. assoc. Stein, Sperling, Bennett, DeJong, Driscoll, Greenfeig Metro, Rockville, Md., 1997-99; of counsel Hodes, Ulman, Pessin & Katz, P.A., Annandale, 1999-2000; atty. pvt. practice, Alexandria, Va., 2000—; mng. dir., personal trust adminstr. Riggs Bank, N.A., Washington, 2000—. Co-author: Legacy: Plan, Protect and Preserve Your Estate, 1995, Generations: Planning Your Legacy, 1998. Bd. dirs. Dist. XVI Va. Student Aid Found., 1978-85, George Washington dist. Boy Scouts Am., 1986; active William and Mary Law Sch. Assn., bd. dirs., 1983-96, pres., 1987-88, treas., 1990-91. Capt. JAGC, USANG, 1973-79. Mem. ABA, Va. Bar Assn., Va. State Bar, D.C. Bar, Md. State Bar Assn., Fairfax Bar Assn., Am. Trial Lawyers Am., Arlington County Bar Assn., Va. Trial Lawyers Assn., No. Va. Estate Planning Coun., William and Mary Alumni Soc. (bd. dirs. D.C. chpt. treas. 1992-94), U. Va. Club of Washington (schs. com. chmn. 1995—, v.p. outreach 1997-99, pres.-elect 1998-99, bd. dirs. 1996-99), Rotary (treas. Springfield chpt. 1985-86, sec. 1986-87, pres.-elect 1987, chmn. World Affairs Conf. 1985-88, bd. dirs. 1984-88, 96-97, Dist. 7610 youth leadership awards chmn. 1994-97, Outstanding Rotarian award 1985). Greek Orthodox. Avocations: racquetball, coaching youth sports. Home and Office: 31 W Myrtle St Alexandria VA 22301-2422

MCGUIRE, JAMES CHARLES, aircraft company executive; b. St. Louis, Aug. 8, 1917; s. John Patrick and Anna Beulah (Erbar) McG.; m. Eunice Leota Sloop, Mar. 21, 1942 (div. June 1948); 1 child, Judith Lynn; m. Ingrid Elisabeth Getreu, Sept. 16, 1954. AB, Washington U, St. Louis, 1949, MA (Univ. fellow), 1953, PhD, 1954. Rsch. assoc. Ohio State U., 1953-56; rsch. psychologist Aeromed. Lab., Wright-Patterson AFB, Ohio, 1956-59; group supr. Boeing Airplane Co., Seattle, 1959-61; mgr. Internat. Electric Corp., Paramus, N.J., 1961-62; sr. human factors scientist System Devel. Corp., Santa Monica, Calif., 1962-67; v.p. Booz-Allen Applied Rsch., Saigon, Vietnam, 1967-72, Assoc. Cons. Internat., Saigon, 1972-75, Bethesda, Md., 1977-78; br. chief Human Factors System Tech. Devel., 1978-82; prin. staff engr. tech. modernizaton methodology Douglas Aircraft Co., Long Beach, Calif., 1982-85; program mgr. cockpit automation tech. program Northrop Aircraft divsn., Hawthorne, 1985-87; sect. mgr. aircraft programs human factors engring. dept. Douglas Aircraft Co., Long Beach, 1987-90; sr. staff engr. Crew Systems Tech., 1990-93; prin. engr. tech. McDonnell Douglas Aerospace Transport Aircraft, 1993-94; prin. engr., scientist, crew sys. tech. Phantom Works, Boeing Co., 1995—, DeltaIV Rocket, Robotics Verification Internat. Space Sta. Lectr. Nat. Def. Coll., Vietnamese Armed Forces, Saigon, 1971. Served with AUS, 1940-46. Decorated Bronze Star medal with oak leaf cluster; recipient Tech. Svc. First Class medal Republic South Vietnam Armed Forces, 1968. Mem. APA, IEEE, Computer Soc. of IEEE, Human Factors and Ergonomics Soc., Am. Assn. Artificial Intelligence, Phi Beta Kappa, Sigma Xi. Republican. Home: 23201 Mindanao Cir Dana Point CA 92629-3625 Office: Boeing Co Phantom Works M/C H013-B319 5301 Bolsa Ave Huntington Beach CA 92627 E-mail: mcguirejc@earthlink.net., james.c.mcguire@boeing.com.

MCGUIRE, JAMES GRANT, lawyer; b. Ashland, Ky., Nov. 9, 1955; s. Everett Earl and Martha Lou McGuire; m. P. Kheng Yap-McGuire, Dec. 29, 1984; children: Forrest, Loy. AB, Duke U., 1980; JD, Washington and Lee U., 1984. Bar: W.Va. 1984, Ky. 1985, D.C. 1984, Va. 1997. Adminstr. UN High Commn. for Refugees, Kuala Lumpur, Malaysia, 1980-81; mem. Campbell, Woods, Huntington, W.Va., 1984—. Bd. dirs. 1st Nat. Bank, Grayson, Ky., Guaranty Bank, Huntington. Chmn. bd. dirs. Teubert Found. for Blind, Huntington, 1990—; mem. Huntington Area Devel. Coun., 1995—2001, Huntington Devel. Authority, 1999—. With U.S. Army, 1975-78. Luce scholar Henry Luce Found., N.Y.C., 1980. Mem. City Club, Guyan Country Club, Gypsy Club, Huntington C. of C. (bd. dirs. 1998-2001), W.Va. Bar (bd. govs. 1998-2001), W.Va. State C. of C. (bd. dirs. 1997—). Avocations: golf, reading. Home: 123 Ridgewood Rd Huntington WV 25701-4857 Office: Campbell Woods 517 9th St Ste 1000 Huntington WV 25701-2033 E-mail: grant11955@aol.com., gmcguire@campbellwoods.com.

MCGUIRE, JOHN FRANCIS, JR. construction company executive; b. N.Y.C., May 28, 1941; s. John Francis and Ann Helena (Hoey) McG.; m. Dorann Rastetter (dec. July 1968); 1 child, Sean Philip; m. Jan Barbara Close, Oct. 18, 1969; 1 child, Seth Adrian. Student, Marist Coll., Poughkeepsie, N.Y., 1976, Dutchess C.C., Poughkeepsie, 1976, 90-97, 99—. Founder, owner, mgr., pres. McGuire Constrn. Co., Rhinebeck, N.Y., 1966—; pres., owner Olde Mill Wine & Spirits Inc., NY, 1994-99. Mem. Rhinebeck Town/Village Shared Svcs. study com., 1991. Co-author Rhinebeck and Hyde Park Fire Codes. Trustee Rhinebeck Theater Soc., asst. treas., chmn. fin. com.; bd. dirs., 1987-98, v.p. 1990-93, pres. 1994-98, mem. fin. com., chmn. phys. plant & grounds Wilderstein Preservation Inc.; coach, instr., referee, umpire Rhinebeck Little League Baseball, Jr. League Baseball, Girls Softball League; co-founder, coach Rhinebeck Soccer League, 1972-85; former vice chmn. sch. bldg. needs com. Rhinebeck Cen. Sch. Dist.; chief fire officer Hillside Fire Dist., 1963-75; asst. to mgr. Dutchess County Fair, 1976-85; past pres., past bd. mem. Rhinebeck Alumni Assn.; co-chmn. Rhinebeck Bicentennial, 1974-77; mem. Rhinebeck Rep. Com., 1977—, vice chmn., 1984-88, chmn., 1989-95; mem. Dutchess County Rep. Com., mem. exec. com.; mem. coord. coun. Dutchess County Criminal Justice; mem. Friends of Clermont, Mills Mansion Hist. Sites; mem. merger study com. No. Dutchess Hosp., Kingston Hosp. and Benedictine Hosp., 1997-99; mem. sales tax rev. com. Dutchess County, 1998-99. Named to Hall of Fame, Dutchess County Sports Mus., Poughkeepsie, 1989; recipient Life Saving award Hillside Fire Dist. Mem.: Quitman Hist. Resource Ctr., Rhinebeck C. of C. (bd. dirs. 1968—92, mem. Blue Ribbon com. 2000—02), Huguenot Hist. Soc., Rotary, Alpha Beta Gamma, Phi Theta Kappa. Avocations: basketball, tennis, cross-country skiing, running, reading. Home and Office: 42 Ackert Hook Rd Rhinebeck NY 12572-2605

MCGUIRE, JOHN FRANCIS, retired English educator, consultant; b. Staples, Minn., Mar. 31, 1921; s. Charles and L. Maude (Bennett) M.; m. Betty Mraz, Nov. 23, 1948; children: Mark, Daniel, Mary Kay, Laurie, John, Joseph. BA, St. John's U., 1943; MA, Univ. Notre Dame, 1948; student, U. Iowa, 1956-63. Prof. English St. Ambrose U., Davenport, Iowa, 1946-52, 55-86, ret., 1986; cons. on edn. General Mills, Inc., Mpls., 1952-55. Ednl. cons., instr. Dept. of Army, Rock Island, Ill., 1963-95; comms. cons. Iowa-Ill. Power Co., Davenport, 1954-60, Eagle Signal Corp., Davenport, 1960-61; adv. bd. Advocates for Mental Health, Davenport, 1976-81. Author: Words in Action, 1984. Avocations: reading, writing, swimming, working with mentally disabled. Home: 1822 West Lombard Davenport IA 52804

MCGUIRE, JOHN LAWRENCE, pharmaceuticals executive; b. Kittanning, Pa., Nov. 3, 1942; s. Lawrence F. and Florence G. (Jones) McG.; m. Pamela Hale, Aug. 2, 1969; children: Megan L., Christa H. BS, Butler U., 1965; MA, Princeton U., 1968, PhD, 1969; postgrad., Columbia Sch. Bus., 1981. Asst. in instrn. Princeton U., N.J., 1967-69; pharmacologist Ortho Pharm. Corp., Raritan, 1969-72, sect. head molecular biology, 1972-75, exec. dir. research, 1975-80, v.p. preclinical research and devel., 1980-88, bd. dirs., 1988-93; sr. v.p. global rsch. and devel., bd. dirs. R.W. Johnson Pharm. Rsch. Inst., 1988-92; corp. v.p. bus. devel., pharm./diagnostics group Johnson & Johnson, New Brunswick, 1992—. Adj. assoc. prof. dept. medicine M.S. Hershey Sch. Medicine Pa. State U., 1978—; adj. prof. dept. animal sci. Rutgers U., 1983-92; adj. prof. ob-gyn. East Va. Med. Sch., 1987—; adj. prof. ob-gyn. and reproductive endocrinology U. Medicine and Dentistry of N.J., 1988—; cons. NASA, 1985-87; cons. Nat. Tech. Transfer Ctr., 1997—. Mem. editorial bd. Ullman's Ency. Indsl. Chemistry, 1987—; contbr. articles to profl. jours.; patentee in field Exec. bd. Keystone Area coun. Boy Scouts Am., Harrisburg, Pa., George Washington Coun., Boy Scouts Am., Trenton, NJ, 1980—86, 1995—99, Ctrl. N.J. coun. Boy Scouts Am., Princeton, 1999—, pres., 2000—; trustee August Found., 1997—, pres., 1997—; trustee Raritan Valley C.C., NJ, 1986—, vice chmn., 1990—; bd. dirs. United Way of Hunterdon County, 1983—97, pres., 1985—87; trustee Hunderdon Med. Ctr., Flemington, 1978—, vice chmn., 1984—86, chmn., 1988—98; trustee Hunterdon Health Care Sys., 1986—, chmn., 1989—; trustee Atlantic Health Sys., Morristown, 1991—93, vice chmn., 1992—93; bd. dirs. Tri-State United Way, NY, 1987—94, Hunterdon County YMCA, 1982—87, Mid Jersey Health Corp., 1986—88, chmn., 1986—88; trustee The Pennington (N.J.) Sch., 1995—, pres., CEO, 1996—; trustee N.J. Hosp. Assn., 2002—. Named N.J. Hosp. Trustee of Yr., 2001; recipient Silver Beaver award, Boy Scouts Am., 1984, Disting. Eagle Scout award, 2000, Johnson medal for rsch. and devel., 1990; grantee Population Coun. fellow, 1969. Mem. Am. Soc. Pharmacology and Exptl. Therapeutics, Soc. Exptl. Biology and Medicine, Am. Physiol. Soc., Endocrine Soc., Am. Coll. Ob-Gyn, Am. Soc. Clin. Pharmacology and Therapetics, Soc. Gynecol. Investigation, Licensing Execs. Soc., Biochemistry Soc. Great Britain, Royal Soc. Medicine (U.K.), Am. Chem. Soc. Clubs: Princeton (N.Y.C.). Home: 10 Club House Dr Whitehouse Station NJ 08889-3378 Office: Johnson & Johnson New Brunswick NJ 08933-0001

MCGUIRE, JOHN THOMAS, lawyer, educator; b. Bronx, N.Y., Oct. 12, 1966; s. Thomas John and Irene McGuire. BA in History magna cum laude, MA in History, U. Scranton, 1988; JD cum laude, U. Buffalo, 1991; PhD in Am. History, Binghamton U., 2001. Bar: N.Y. 1991. Trial atty. U.S. Dept. of Justice, Washington, 1991-95; atty. AARP, 1996-97; pvt. practice Vestal, N.Y., 1997—; adj. prof. SUNY-Oneonta, 2000—, Broome C.C., 2001—. Bd. dirs. Broome and Chenango Legal Aid, Inc., Binghamton. Reviewer American Jewish History, 1998, Left History, 2001; editor: Binghamton Jour. of History, 1998—99; author: A Catalyst for Reform: The Women's Joint Legislative Conference and Its Fight for Labor Legislation in New York State, 1918-1933, Making the Democratic Party a Partner: Eleanor Roosevelt the WJLC and the Women's Division of the New York State Democratic Party, 2001, A Sense of Shame, 2001, From Union Station to Plowshares: The Catholic Worker Movement 1933-2000, 2002. Del. Grad. Student Employee's Union, Vestal, N.Y., 1999—; bd. dirs. Broome County Peace Action, Binghamton, 1999—; negotiator GSEU, 2000-01. James A. Finnegan fellowship, 1987. Mem. N.Y. State Bar Assn., Am. Hist. Assn., Orgn. of Am. Historians, Phi Alpha Theta (pres. 1999-01), Alpha Sigma Nu Home: 422 Clubhouse Rd Vestal NY 13850-3727 E-mail: johnmcguireus@yahoo.com.

MCGUIRE, JOHN W., SR. advertising executive, marketing professional, author; b. Chgo., May 12, 1952; s. Eugene H. Sr. and Marjorie (Bolger) McG.; m. Mary Sue Roper, June 17, 1972 (div. 1977); 1 child, John William Jr.; m. Lynn L. Rembos, June 21, 1984 (div. April 1991); children: Kelly Lynn, Ryan Michael. AA, Chgo. City Colls., 1972; BA, Northeastern Ill., Chgo., 1974. Janitor Bd. of Edn., Chgo., 1970-74; sales rep. Motorola Comms., Inc., Schaumburg, Ill., 1974-76, Pattis Group, Chgo., 1976-77; midwest sales mgr. Harcourt Brace Jovanovich Pub. Co., N.Y.C., 1977-79; account sales mgr. Cosmopolitan Mag. Hearst Pub. Co., 1979-81; midwest acct. mgr. Psychology Today Mag. Ziff-Davis Pub. Co., 1981-82; midwest regional mgr. Pennwell Pub. Co., Tulsa, Okla., 1982-84; western regional sales mgr. Nursing Mgmt. Mag. SN Pub. Co., West Dundee, Ill., 1984-91; western regional sales mgr., midwest regional sales mgr. U.S. Pharmacist Mag. Jobson Pub. Co., N.Y.C., 1991-98; v.p. SK&A Info. Svcs., Irvine, Calif., 1998-99; assoc. pub. Health Mgmt. Technology Mag. Nelson Pub., Nokomis, Fla., 1999; pres., CEO Blossom Pub. Co., Wasco, Ill., 2000—. Author: (book) One Man's Life: A Poetic Review, 1995; co-author: (with Scott Mennie) The Original Parent and Family Logbook, 2002; singer (cassette tapes), designer (creative posters). With USN, 1970. Mem. VFW, Midwest Healthcare Mktg., Arlington Poetry Project. Republican. Roman Catholic. Avocations: writer, scuba, horsemanship, traveling, skydiving.

MCGUIRE, LUCY MIRIAM, editor, writer; b. Jackson, Miss., Sept. 26, 1948; d. Paul Timothy Whitsett and Miriam Mrytis Hilton; m. James Neville McGuire, Jan. 24, 1970; children: Jeremy, Paul, Jonathan. BS, Miss. State U., 1970. Cert. Montessori tchr., in Christian edn. With Deposit Guaranty, Jackson, 1970—71; reservationist Delta Airlines, 1971—77; tchr. Montessori Sch., 1977—80; photojournalist Clarion-Ledger Rankin County News, Brandon, 1986—89; neonatal photographer Woman's Hosp., Flowood, 1993—94; editor-in-chief EPC Reflections mag., Livonia, Mich., 1998—. Chmn. adv. bd. Connection Women's Newsletter, Northville, Mich., 1997—2001. Contbr. articles to newsletters, chpts. to books. Prayer ptnr. Presdl. Prayer Team, 2001—; bd. dirs. YMCA, Brandon, 1987—89. Named Writer of Yr., Am. Christian Writers, 1999; recipient photography awards, Kodak, 1970—80. Mem.: Evangelical Press Assn. (Most Improved Publ. award 1999), Humane Soc. Republican. Presbyterian. Home: 48028 Andover Dr Novi MI 48374

MCGUIRE, MATTHEW JUDD, writer, researcher; b. Waterbury, Conn., Oct. 26, 1964; s. Raymond George Jr. and Genevieve (Smith) McG. BA, Catholic U. Am., 1987; MA, King's Coll., London, 1990. Gen. staff Hopkins and Sutter, Attys. at Law, Washington, 1987-88; adj. instr. Middlesex C.C., Middletown, Conn., 1991-92; gen. staff reference divsn. Congl. Rsch. Svc. Libr. Congress, Washington, 1995-96. Adj. lectr. Teikyo Post U., Waterbury, Conn., 1997-98. Author: The Role of Women in the Novels of Charles Dickins, 1995. Benefactor Columbus Sch. Law Catholic U. Am., Washington. Mem. Am. Film Inst., Lib. of Congress Assocs., Nat. Mus. Women in Arts, Nat. Mus. Am. Indian, Nat. Holocaust Mus., English Speaking Union, Catholic U. Am. Alumni Assn., King's Coll. London Assn., U. London Convocation Trust, Young Dems. Am. (life), Cheshire Land Trust Inc. (life). Roman Catholic. Avocations: reading, travel, martial arts, golf. Home: PO Box 1144 Washington DC 20013-1144

MCGUIRE, MICHAEL JOHN, environmental engineer; b. San Antonio, June 29, 1947; s. James Brendan and Opal Mary (Brady) McG.; m. Deborah Marrow, June 19, 1971; children: David, Anna. BS in Civil Engring., U. Pa., 1969; MS in Environ. Engring., Drexel U., 1972, PhD in Environ. Engring., 1977. Diplomate Am. Acad. Environ. Engring.; registered profl. engr., Pa., N.J., Calif., Ariz. San. engr. Phila. Water Dept., 1969-73; rsch. assoc. Drexel U., Phila., 1976-77; prin. engr. Brown & Caldwell Cons. Engrs., Pasadena, Calif., 1977-79; water quality engr. Met. Water Dist. of So. Calif., L.A., 1979-84, water quality mgr., 1984-86, dir. water quality, 1986-90, asst. gen. mgr., 1990-92; pres. McGuire Environ. Cons., Inc., Santa Monica, Calif., 1992—. Cons. to subcom. on adsorbents, safe drinking water com. Nat. Acad. Scis., 1978-79, NRC, Drinking Water Contaminants (comm. mem.), 1998-99; cons. mem. Techs. Workgroup U.S. EPA, DBP Reg. Neg., 1992-93, 97, 98-2000. Editor: (with I.H. Suffet) Activated Carbon Adsorption of Organics from the Aqueous Phase, 2 vols., 1980, Treatment of Water by Granular Activated Carbon, 1983; contbr. articles to profl. jours. Mem. ASCE, Internat. Water Assn. (specialist group on taste and odor control 1982—, chmn. organizing com. 1991, off-flavor symposium 1987-91), Internat. Ozone Assn. (internat. bd. dirs. 1992-95), Am. Water Works Assn. (Calif.-Nev. sect. chmn. water quality and resources divsn. 1982-83, governing bd. 1984-87, 89-96, exec. com. 1989-96, chmn. 1991-92, nat. edn. divsn. chmn. 1982-83, dir. 1994-96, chair taste and odor com. 1993-98, exec. com. 1994-96, Acad. Achievement award 1978, Fuller award 1994, Publs. award 2000), Am. Chem. Soc., Sigma Xi, Sigma Nu, Sigma Tau. Office: McGuire Environ Cons Inc # 200 1919 Santa Monica Blvd Santa Monica CA 90404-1954

MCGUIRE, ROBERT C. retired federal bankruptcy judge; b. 1935; AB, Dartmouth Coll., 1957; JD, Boston Coll., 1960. Bar: Mass. 1960, Tex. 1961. Assoc. Turner, White, Dallas, 1961-64, Ungerman, Hill, Angrist & Dolginoff, 1965-78; probate judge Dallas County, 1979-80; ptnr. Skibell & McGuire, 1981-83; judge U.S. Bankruptcy Ct., Dallas, 1983—2002, chief judge, 1985—2002. Mem.: John C. Ford Am. Inn of Ct. (pres. 2000—01), Dallas Bar Assn., Tex. Bar Assn., Nat. Conf. Bankruptcy Judges. Office: US Bankruptcy Ct 1100 Commerce St Ste 1254 Dallas TX 75242-1496

MCGUIRE, ROGER ALAN, retired foreign service officer; b. Troy, Ohio, July 1, 1943; s. Charles M. and Mary L. (Coppock) McG.; m. Harriet H. Cooke, July 12, 1969; children: Sara, Casey. BA, Beloit Coll., 1965; MA, U. Wis., 1967. Country desk officer Dept. State, Washington, 1974-78; dep. chief of mission Am. Embassy, Maputo, Mozambique, 1978-80; congl. fellow Am. Polit. Sci. Assn., Washington, 1980-81; polit. officer Am. Embassy, Asuncion, Paraguay, 1981-83, Lusaka, Zambia, 1983-86; dep. dir. Office of West African Affairs Dept. of State, Washington, 1986-88; chief of mission Am. Embassy, Windhoek, Namibia, 1988-90; consul Am. Consulate, Porto Alegre, Brazil, 1990-92; U.S. amb. to Guinea-Bissau, 1992-95; counselor for polit. affairs Am. Embassy, Canberra, Australia, 1995-97; ret., 1997. Vol. Youth for Understanding. Recipient Superior Honor award U.S. Agy. for Internat. Devel., 1969. Mem. Rotary Internat., Phi Beta Kappa. Home: 3007 Russell Rd Alexandria VA 22305-1719

MCGUIRE, SANDRA LYNN, nursing educator; b. Jan. 28, 1947; d. Donald Armstrong and Mary Lue (Harvey) Johnson; m. Joseph L. McGuire, Mar. 6, 1976; children: Matthew, Kelly, Kerry. BSN, U. Mich., 1969, MPH, 1973, EdD, 1988, MSN, 1997. Staff nurse Univ. Hosp., Ann Arbor, Mich., 1969; pub. health nurse Wayne County Health Dept., Eloise, 1969-72; instr. Madonna Coll., Livonia, 1973; pub. health coord. Plymouth Ctr. for Human devel., Northville, 1974-75; asst. prof. cmty. health nursing U. Mich., Ann Arbor, 1975-83; asst. prof. U. Tenn., Knoxville, 1983-88, assoc. prof., 1990—, gerontol. nurse practitioners program coord., 1998—, chair MSN program Coll. Nursing. Dir. Kids Are Tomorrow's Srs. Program, 1988—; resource person Gov.'s Com. Unification of Mental Health Svcs. in Mich.; spkr. profl. assns. and workshops. Author (with S. Clemen-Stone and D. Eigsti)): Comprehensive Community Health Nursing, 1981, Comprehensive Community Health Nursing, 5th edit., 1998, Comprehensive Community Health Nursing, 6th edit., 2002. Bd. dirs. Ctr. Understanding Aging, 1987-93, v.p., 1995; bd. dirs. Mich. chpt. ARC, 1980-83, Knoxville chpt., 1984-85; founder Knoxville Intergenerational Network, 1989. USPHS fellow, 1972-73, Robert Woodruff fellow Emory U., 1996-97, Hewlett Innovative Tech. fellow U. Tenn., Knoxville, 1999-00, Profl. Devel. award U. Tenn. Knoxville, 1996-97, 99-2000. Mem. ANA, Tenn. Nurses Assn., Nat. Conf. Gerontol. Nurse Practitioners, Nat. Gerontol. Nursing Assn., Mich. Pub. Health Assn. (chmn. mental health sect. 1976, dir., co-chmn. residential svcs. com. 1976-79, chmn. health svcs. 1979-82), Nat. Assn. Retarded Citizens, Mich. Assn. Retarded Citizens, Nat. Coun. on Aging, Ctr. for Understanding Aging (v.p. 1994-95), Plymouth (chmn. residential svcs. com. 1975-77), Tenn. Assn. Retarded Citizens, So. Nursing Rsch. Soc., Sigma Theta Tau, Pi Lambda Theta, Phi Kappa Phi. Home: 11008 Crosswind Dr Knoxville TN 37922-4011 Office: 1200 Volunteer Blvd Knoxville TN 37996 E-mail: smcguire@utk.edu.

MCGUIRE, THOMAS PETER, show boat captain, secondary school educator; b. N.Y.C., Apr. 27, 1945; s. Thomas Edward and Susan Rose (Cafarelli) McG. BA, Calif. State U., 1979, postgrad., 1979-83, MA in English CUNY, 1993. co. mgr. Vaudeville Driftwood Floating Theatre, 1963-75; Tchr., St. Philip's Sch., Pasadena, Calif., 1981-83; prodr. Driftwood Floating Theatre, 1968-75; owner, capt. Driftwood ShowBoat, Kingston, N.Y., 1983-98; pres. Driftwood ShowBoat Co., 1983—; tchr. English John F. Kennedy H.S., N.Y.C., 1986—; guest lectr. Hayden Planetarium, N.Y.C., 1960-64. Contbr. articles to profl. jours. Activist in human rights and equal rights. Served with USN, 1966-68. Mem. Am. Guild Variety Artists, Soc. Am. Magicians, Lesbian and Gay Tchrs. Assn. N.Y.C. (pres. 1998—). Roman Catholic. Avocations: writing, ballooning, astronomy. Home and Office: Driftwood Showboat PO Box 1032 Kingston NY 12402-1032

MCGUIRE, TIM, editor; Editor, sr. v.p. Star Tribune, Mpls., 1993—2002. Juror Pulitzer Prize, 2002. Mem.: Amer. Soc. Newspaper Editors (pres. 2001—02). Roman Catholic. Office: Star Tribune 425 Portland Ave Minneapolis MN 55488-0002*

MCGUIRE, TIMOTHY JAMES, lawyer, editor; b. Mount Pleasant, Mich., Mar. 24, 1949; s. James Edward and Anita Matilda (Starr) McGuire; m. T. Jean Fannin, May 10, 1975; children: Tracy, Jason, Jeffrey. BA, Aquinas Coll., Grand Rapids, Mich., 1971; JD cum laude, William Mitchell Coll. Law, St. Paul, 1987. Bar: Minn. 1987. Mng. editor Ypsilanti Press, Mich., 1973—75, Corpus Christi Caller, Tex., 1975—77, Lakeland Ledger, Fla., 1977—79, Mpls. Star, 1979—82; mng. editor features and sports Mpls. Star and Tribune, 1982—84, mng. editor, 1984—91, exec. editor, 1991—93, editor, sr. v.p., 1993—2002. Pulitzer Prize juror, 1988—89, 1995—2002. Lay preacher at St. Joseph Roman Cath. Ch., Mpls., 1995—. Mem.: Minn. State Bar Assn., Am. Soc. Newspaper Editors (bd. dirs. 1992—, chmn. change com. 1994—95, chmn. program com. 1996—97, treas. 1998—99, sec. 1999—2000, v.p. 2000—01, pres. 2001—02). Roman Catholic. Home: 3645 Rosewood Ln N Minneapolis MN 55441-1127

MCGUIRE, TIMOTHY JAMES, operating engineer; b. Detroit, Dec. 13, 1948; s. James Thomas and Glenna Doreen (Elkins) McG. Student, Monroe County Cmty. Coll., Monroe, Mich., 1967; HVAC diploma, Nat. Inst. of Tech., Toledo, Ohio, 1983; student, Henry Ford Cmty. Coll., Dearborn, Mich., 1984. Cert. Refrigeration Engr. First Class, Mich. Refrigeration tech. McLouth Steel Products, Trenton, Mich., 1972-96; operating engr. Ritz Carlton Hotel, Dearborn, 1996—. Author: How to Collect Antique American Bottles (Inexpensively), 1990. Mem. Phi Theta Kappa. Democrat. Roman Catholic. Avocations: metal detecting, boating, camping, geology. Home: 24854 Strewing Rd Brownstown MI 48134-9507

MCGUIRE, TIMOTHY WILLIAM, economics and management educator, dean, management executive; b. Englewood, N.J., Nov. 30, 1938; s. Charles James and Marie (McCarthy) McG.; children: Timothy William Jr., Gretchen Elizabeth, Michael Joseph; m. Nancy Paule Melone, 1991. BS in Indsl. Mgmt., Carnegie Inst. Tech., 1960, MS in Econs., 1961; PhD in Econs., Stanford U., 1968. Staff mem. Coun. Econ. Advisors, 1963-64; rsch. assoc. in econs. Grad. Sch. Indsl. Adminstrn., Carnegie Mellon U., Pitts., 1964-66, asst. prof. econs., 1966-69, assoc. prof., 1969-75, prof., 1975-79, prof. mgmt. and econs., 1982—, dep. dean, 1983-90; prof. social scis. and econs. Dept. Social Scis. Carnegie Mellon U., 1981-82; prof. econs., chmn. dept. U. Iowa, Iowa City, 1979-80; dean, Harry B. Miller prof. bus. Charles H. Lundquist Coll. Bus., U. Oreg., Eugene, 1994-98; sr. exec. v.p., chief operating officer Mgmt. Sci. Assocs., Inc., Pitts., 1998—. Sr. visitor U. Cambridge, Eng., summer, 1970; bd. dirs. Mgmt. Sci. Assocs., Inc., Pitts.; bd. visitors Joseph M. Katz Grad. Sch. Bus., U. Pitts. Contbr. articles to profl. jours. Woodrow Wilson Nat. Hon. fellow Carnegie Inst. Tech., 1960-61; Stanford U. fellow, 1961-62; fellow Ford Found., 1962-63, 70-71. Mem.: Omicron Delta Kappa, Soc.

Judgment and Decision Making, Am. Mktg. Assn., Am. Econ. Assn., Internat. Soc. Bayesian Analysis, Tau Beta Pi. Home: 118 Lakeland Dr Mars PA 16046-2114 Office: Mgmt Sci Assocs Inc 6565 Penn Ave at 5th Pittsburgh PA 15206-4490 E-mail: tmcguire@msa.com.

MCGUIRE, WILLIAM, civil engineer, educator; b. S.I., N.Y., Dec. 17, 1920; s. Edward Joseph and Phoebe (Sellman) McG.; m. Barbara Weld, Feb. 5, 1944; children: Robert Weld, Thomas Rhodes. BSCE, Bucknell U., 1942; MSCE, Cornell U., 1947. Structural designer Jackson & Moreland (engrs.), Boston, 1947-49; faculty Cornell U., Ithaca, 1949—, prof. civil engring., 1960-90, prof. emeritus of civil engring., 1990—; dir. Cornell U. (Sch. Civil Engring.), 1966-68; vis. prof. civil engring. Asian Inst. Tech., Bangkok, Thailand, 1968-70. Vis. research engr. Nat. Bur. Standards, 1972; Gledden vis. sr. fellow U. Western Australia, 1973; cons. structural engr., 1951—; vis. prof. U. Tokyo, 1979, U. Strathclyde, 1986 Author: Steel Structures, 1967; author: (with R.H. Gallagher and R.D. Ziemian) Matrix Structural Analysis, 1979, 2d edit., 2000. Served to lt. USNR, 1942-45. Recipient Naval Letter of Commendation, award for Outstanding Achievement, Bucknell U., 1987, T.R. Higgins Lectureship award Am. Inst. Steel Constrn., 1992, G. Haaijer awrd Am. Inst. Steel Constrn., 2000. Fellow ASCE (pres. Ithaca 1964, Norman medal 1962, 94, Hardesty award 1992, honorary mem. 1994); mem. Internat. Assn. Bridge and Structural Engring., Nat. Acad. Engring., Sigma Xi, Chi Epsilon, Kappa Delta Rho. Congregationalist. Home: 121 Simsbury Dr Ithaca NY 14850-1728 E-mail: wm20@cornell.edu.

MCGUIRE, WILLIAM W. insurance company executive; b. Troy, N.Y., 1948; Grad., U. Tex., 1970, grad., 1974. Exec. v.p. United Healthcare Corp., Minnetonka, Minn., 1988—89, pres., 1989—98; chmn., CEO United Healthcare Corp. , 1991—98; pres., CEO, chmn., dir. UnitedHealth Group, 1991—2000, CEO, chmn., dir., 2000—. Bd. dirs. Minn. Bus. Partnership. Trustee Mpls. Inst. Arts; dir. Minn. Orch. Assn. Office: UnitedHealth Group PO Box 1459 Minnetonka MN 55343-9664*

MCGUIRE, WILLIAM DENNIS, health care consultant; b. Glen Ridge, N.J., Sept. 24, 1943; s. John William and Kathleen Mary (Sexton) McG.; m. Nancy Katherine Hoyne, Aug. 13, 1966; children: Kathleen Anne, Colleen Dempsey. BA, U. Notre Dame, 1965; M.H.A., U. Mich., 1968. Asst. adminstr. U. Wis. Hosps., Madison, 1971-74; adminstr. Children's Med. Ctr., Dayton, Ohio, 1974-79; COO Mercy Cath. Med. Ctr., Phila., 1979-80; CEO Wills Eye Hosp., 1980-85; pres., CEO Mercy Health Care Sys., Scranton, 1985-89, Mt. Carmel Health, Columbus, Ohio, 1989-92, Incarnate Word Health Svcs., San Antonio, 1992-95, Cath. Med. Ctrs. of Bklyn. and Queens, New York, 1996—2000; health care cons., 2000—02; pres., CEO Kaleida Health, Buffalo, 2002—. Adj. faculty dept. health care Trinity U., 1992-95; asst. prof. Ohio State U., 1990-92; asst. clin. prof. Wright State U. Sch. medicine, Dayton, Ohio, 1978-79; instr. U.Wis. Madison, 1972-73; mem. Wilkes Coll. Health Administrn. Adv. Com, 1988-89; bd. dirs. Coll. Misericordia Health Care Task Force, 1988-89; bd. govs. League Vol. Hosps., 1996-2000, sec., 1997-2000; mem. bd. govs. Fidelis Care N.Y., 1996-2000, Queensbrook Ins. Ltd., 1996-2000, vice chmn., 1996-97, chmn., 1997-2000; trustee Cmty. Blood Ctr., 1977-79; trustee Cath. Social Svcs., 1976-79, pres., 1978-79; bd. dirs. Coop. Purchasing Corp., 1974-79; mem. Dayton Pub. Schs. Lay Adv. Com. on Vocat. Edn., 1974-79; pres. Dayton Area Young Adminstrs. Group, 1977; pres. elect Greater Dayton Area Hosp. Assn., 1979; mem. allied health technologies adv. com. Sinclair Community Coll. 1974-79. Bd. dirs. Covenant Health Sys., 1992—, Fletcher Allen Health Care, 2002—, Consol. Cath. Risk Retention Group, 1992-95, Cath. Charities, 1996-2000, Primary Care Devel. Corp., 1997-2000; active Health Policy Forum, United Hosp. Fund, United Way, ARC. Mem. Am. Coll. Healthcare Execs., Acad. for Cath. Health Care Leadership, Mercy Leadership Group. Nat. Commn. Cath. Health Care Ministry-Resource Devel. Com. 1988-89), Maj. Cath. Health Alliance (sec. 1990-95, chmn. 1997-99), Health Care Fin. Mgmt. Assn., Am. Assn. Univ. Profs. Ophthalmology, Am. Soc. Law and Medicine, Am. Hosp. Assn., Am. Assn. Eye and Ear Hosps. (pres.-elect 1984-85), Health Mgmt. Edn. Assn. (pres. 1987-88), Hosp. Assn. N.Y. State (bd. dirs. 1998-2000), Greater N.Y. Hosp. Assn. (mem. bd govs. 1997-2000), Tex. Hosp.Assn., Ohio Hosp. Assn., Hosp. Assn. Pa., Cath. Health Assn., Am. Pub. Health Assn., Pa. Pub. Health Assn., Del. Valley Hosp. Council, Pa. Emergency Health Svcs. Coun., Del. County Emergency Health Svcs. Coun., Nat. Union Hosp. and Health Care Employees (plan trustee), Pa. Hosps. Ins. Co. Adv. Coun., 1988-89. C. of C., U. Notre Dame Alumni Assn., U. Mich. Alumni Assn., U. Wis. Med. Sch. Alumni Assn., Wills Eye Soc., Sorin Soc., Badin Guild, Notre Dame Club (pres. 1971, v.p. 1983-84), Plz. Club, Dominion Country Club. Home: 6 Abby Wood The Dominion San Antonio TX 78257-1253 Office: Kaleida Health 100 High St Buffalo NY 14203 E-mail: billmcg@together.net.

MCGUIRE, WILLIAM JAMES, social psychology educator; b. N.Y.C., Feb. 17, 1925; s. James William and Anne M. (Mitchell) McG.; m. Claire Vernick, Dec. 29, 1954; children— James William, Anne Maureen, Steven Thomas. BA, Fordham U., 1949, MA, 1950; PhD, Yale U., 1954; PhD (hon.), Eötvös U., Budapest, Hungary, 1990. Postdoctoral fellow U. Minn., 1954-55; assoc. prof. psychology U. Ill., 1958-61; prof. Columbia U., 1961-67, U. Calif., San Diego, 1967-70; vis. prof. London Sch. Econs., 1970-71; asst. prof. Yale U., New Haven, 1955-58, prof., 1970—, chmn. dept. psychology, 1971-73. Mem. adv. panel for sociology and social psychology NSF, 1963-65; mem. review panel for social scis. NIMH, 1968-72, cons., 1974-95. Author: Content and Processes in the Experience of Self, 1988, A Perspectivist Approach to Strategic Planning, 1989, Structure of Attitudes and Attitude Systems, 1989, The Content, Structure, and Operation of Thought Systems, 1991, Explorations in Political Psychology, 1993, Creative Hypothesis Generating in Psychology, 1997, Constructing Social Psychology: Creative and Critical Processes, 1999, After a Half Century of Election Studies: Whence, Where and Whither, 2001; contbr. to Ency. Brit.; editor Jour. Personality and Social Psychology, 1967-70; cons. editor European Jour. Social Psychology, 1978—, Jour. Applied Social Psychology, 1983—, Jour. Exptl. Social Psychology, 1994—, Comm. Rsch., 1988—, Human Comm. Rsch., 2001—, Jour. Commn., 2002—, Applied Psychology on Hungary; contbr. Ency. Psychology. With AUS, 1943-46. Recipient Ann. Social Psychology award AAAS, 1964, Gen. Electric Found. awards, 1963, 64, 66, Disting. Scientist award Soc. Exptl. Social Psychology, 1992, Disting. Sci. award Internat. Soc. Political Psychology, 1999; grantee NSF, 1960-79, NIH, 1979-99; Fulbright fellow Louvain (Belgium) U., 1950-51, Ctr. for Advanced Study in Behavioral Scis. fellow, 1965-66, Guggenheim fellow, 1970-71, William James fellow Am. Psychol. Soc., 1989—. Fellow APA (pres. divsn. personality and social psychology 1973-74, Disting. Sci. Contbn. award 1988), Am. Acad. Arts and Scis.; mem. Am. Sociol. Assn., Am. Assn. Pub. Opinion Rsch., Sigma Xi; Am. Acad. Arts Sci. Home: 225 St Ronan St New Haven CT 06511-2313 Office: Yale U Dept Psychology PO Box 208205 New Haven CT 06520-8205 E-mail: william.mcguire@yale.edu.

MCGUIRE, WILLIAM ROBERT, secondary education administrator, sports official; b. New Kensington, Pa., July 3, 1947; s. Lawrence Francis and Florence Gertrude (Jones) M.; m. Kathleen Ann Kasper, July 18, 1970. BS in Edn., Edinboro State U., 1969; MS in Edn., Duquesne U., 1971. Cert. secondary mathematics, program splst. in athletics, secondary principal. Secondary math tchr. Burrell Sch. Dist., Lower Burrell, Pa., 1969-85, secondary math tchr., athletic dir., 1986-93, athletic dir., coord. of discipline, 1993—. Bd. control Western Pa. Interscholastic Athletic League, Pitts., 1993-95; pres. We. Pa. Interscholastic Athletic League Athletic Dir.'s Assn., Pitts., 1996— (mem. softball com., 1989-91, football com., 1992—). Recipient Gift of Time Tribute award Pa. State Awards Com., 1993, Athletic Dir. Yr. award Eastern Assn. Interscholastic Football Officials, 1994, Pa. Boys Basketball Official of Yr. award Nat. Fedn. Interscholastic Officials Assn., 1995. Mem. NEA, Pa. Assn. Secondary Sch. Principals, Pa. State Edn. Assn., Burrell Edn. Assn. (v.p., chief negotiator, 1969—), Tri-State Intercollegiate Athletic Assn., Pa. Interscholastic Athletic Assn. (pres., v.p., 1969—), Basketball Officials Assn. Avocations: golf, gardening. Office: Burrell Sch Dist HS 1021 Puckety Church Rd Lower Burrell PA 15068-9706

MCGUIRE-RIGGS, SHEILA, chairman Democratic party; Chmn. Iowa Democrat Party, Iowa. Democrat. Mailing: 5661 Fleur Dr Des Moines IA 50321 Fax: 515-244-5051. E-mail: smriggs@iowademocrats.org.*

MCGUIRK, PAUL ROBERT, administrator, organic chemist; b. Jamaica, N.Y., June 8, 1951; s. John Thomas and Frances Marie (DeMarzo) McG.; m. Stephanie Ann Cantalupo, Aug. 19, 1979; children: Nicole Costa, Paul Sean. BS in Chemistry, SUNY, 1977; MS in Organic Chemistry, Cornell U., 1982, PhD in Organic Chemistry, 1983. Group dir. chem. technologies Pfizer Global Rsch. and Devel., Groton, Conn., 1982—. Presenter in field. Contbr. articles to profl. jours.; patentee in field. With U.S. Army, 1971-73. NIH Predoctoral fellow, 1980-82.

MCGUIRK, RONALD CHARLES, retired banker, economic advisor; b. Balt., Dec. 9, 1938; s. Charles F. and Grace E. (Delcher) McG.; m. Katherine Sauer, Oct. 1, 1960; children: Frank D., Ann E. Student, St. John's Coll., Annapolis, Md., 1956-59. Sr. data processing officer 1st Nat. Bank, Balt., 1966-72, v.p. data processing, 1972-76, v.p. mktg., 1976-80, sr. v.p. mktg., 1980-90, sr. v.p. corp. plan, chief of staff to CEO, 1990-94; sr. v.p., corp. sec. 1st Md. Bancorp, 1995-99; sr. econ. advisor Anne Arundel County, Md., 1999—. Bd. dirs., treas. North Arundel Hosp., Glen Burnie, Md., 1974—, Internet, Inc., 1990-95, Glen Burnie Town Ctr. Com., 1995—, Annapolis Symphony, 1991-92; trustee Mt. Washington Pediat. Hosp., 1997—; mem. adv. bd. Hist. Annapolis Found., 1982-85, dir., 1985-90; chmn. Annapolis Boundary Commn., 1983-84; mem. Anne Arundel County Coun., 1974-82, Anne Arundel County Libr. Bd., 1974-84; pres. Anne Arundel County Scholarship for Scholars/Bd. Edn., 1983-85, treas., 1985-88; mem. Anne Arundel County Charter Rev. Commn., 1986, Anne Arundel County Govt. Salary Commn., 1985, 89; chmn. Anne Arundel County Impact Fee Study Task Force, 1987; pres. Anne Arundel County YMCA, 1987-89, bd. dirs., 1982-87, 89-90; mem. Commn. for Ednl. Excellence, 1988-90; vice chmn. Ft. Meade Coordinating Coun., 1989-91; mem. Exec. Com. Md. Bus.-Industry PAC, 1991-99, Anne Arundel County Charter and Orgn. Transition Group, 1991; corp. ptnr. Sch. Bus. and Mgmt. Morgan State U., 1991-92; trustee Md. Hist. Soc., 1995-96; co-chair Anne Arundel County transition fin. com., 1998-99. Mem. Ctr. Club. Democrat. Roman Catholic. Office: Arundel Ctr Calvert St Annapolis MD 21401

MCGUIRK, TERRENCE, former broadcasting company executive; b. Bklyn., Apr. 2, 1925; s. William Edward and Loretta Beatrice (Lanigan) McG.; m. Gloria Helen Geoghan, June 17, 1950; children: Terence F., Sara McGuirk Duncan, Susan McGuirk Blank, Elizabeth McGuirk Magee, Melissa McGuirk Bowman, Bryan, Michelle McGuirk O'Connor. BS, Fordham U., 1950. Nat. sales mgr. St. WAGA-TV, Atlanta, 1966-68; mgr. Sta. WAGA-TV, 1970-75; eastern sales mgr. Storer TV Sales, N.Y.C., 1968-70; pres., gen. mgr. Sta. WTEN-TV, Albany, N.Y., 1976-82; pres. Knight-Ridder Broadcasting, Inc., 1982-85; ret. Assoc. trustee Siena Coll., Loudonville, N.Y., 1979-83; trustee Meml. Hosp. Found., 1980-83; dir. Albany chpt. ARC, 1987-91. Served with U.S. Army, 1943-46. Mem. Mariner Sands Country Club, Babylon Yacht Club (hon.).

MCGUIRL, MARLENE DANA CALLIS, law librarian, educator; b. Hammond, Ind., Mar. 22, 1938; d. Daniel David and Helen Elizabeth (Baludis) Callis; m. James Franklin McGuirl, Apr. 24, 1965. AB, Ind. U., 1959; JD, DePaul U., 1963; MALS, Rosary Coll., 1965; LLM, George Washington U., 1978; postgrad., Harvard U., 1985. Bar: Ill. 1963, Ind. 1964, D.C. 1972. Asst. DePaul Coll. of Law Libr., 1961-62, asst. law libr., 1962-65; ref. law librarian Boston Coll. Sch. Law, 1965-66; libr. dir. D.C. Bar Libr., 1966-70; asst. chief Am.-Brit. Law Divsn. Libr. of Congress, Washington, 1970, chief, 1970-90, environ. cons., 1990—; counsel Cooter & Gell, 1992-93; adminstr. Washington Met. Transit Authority, 1994—. Libr. cons. Nat. Clearinghouse on Poverty Law, OEO, Washington, 1967-69, Northwestern U. Nat. Inst. Edn. in Law and Poverty, 1969, D.C. Office of Corp. Counsel, 1969-70; instr. law librarianship Grad. Sch. of U.S. Dept. of Agr., 1968-72; lectr. legal lit. Cath. U., 1972; adj. asst. prof., 1973-91; lectr. environ. law George Washington U., 1979—; judge Nat. and Internat. Law Moot Ct. Competition, 1976-78, 90—; pres. Hamburger Haven, Inc., Palm Beach, Fla., 1981-91, L'Image de Marlene Ltd., 1986-92, Clinique de Beautè Inc., 1987-92, Heads & Hands Inc., 1987-92, Horizon Design & Mfg. Co., Inc., 1987—; dir. Stoneridge Farm Inc., Gt. Falls, Va., 1984—. Contbr. articles to profl. jours. Mem. Georgetown Citizens Assn.; trustee D.C. Law Students in Ct.; del. Ind. Democratic Conv., 1964. Recipient Meritorious Svc. award Libr. on Congress, 1974, letter of commendation Dirs. of Pers., 1976, cert. of appreciation, 1981-84. Mem. ABA (facilities law libr. Congress com. 1976-89), Fed. Bar Assn. (chpt. council 1972-76), Ill. Bar Assn., Women's Bar Assn. (pres. 1972-73, exec. bd. 1973-77, Outstanding Contbn. to Human Rights award 1975), D.C. Bar Assn., Am. Bar Found., Nat. Assn. Women Lawyers, Am. Assn. Law Libraries (exec. bd. 1973-77), Law Librarians Soc. of Washington (pres. 1971-73), Exec. Women in Govt. Home: 3416 P St NW Washington DC 20007-2705

MCGUIRL, ROBERT JOSEPH, lawyer; b. Jersey City, June 16, 1952; s. Joseph Francis and Edna Louise (Davis) McG.; m. Gloria Pauline Clemente, Oct. 10, 1981; children: Brian, Jennifer. BA cum laude, Coll. Holy Cross, Worcester, Mass., 1974; JD, Georgetown U., 1977. Bar: N.Y. 1978, U.S. dist. Ct. (so. and ea. dists.) N.Y. 1979, N.J. 1981, U.S. Dist. Ct. N.J. 1981, U.S. Supreme Ct. 1987, U.S. Ct. Appeals (3d cir.) 1988; cert. civil trial atty. Asst. dist. atty. Office of Dist. Atty. New York County, N.Y.C., 1977-81; ptnr. Priestley, McGuirl & Wachenfeld, Newark, 1981-92; pvt. practice law Westwood, N.J., 1992—. Mem. ABA (vice-chmn., com. profl. officers' and dir.'s liability 1987-89, contbg. editor self-insurers, risk mgrs. com. newsletter 1990), N.J. State Bar Assn. (chair products liability and toxic tort com. 1992—), Trial Attys. N.J., Bergen County Bar Assn. (vice-chmn. med. legal com. 1986-87), Def. Rsch. Inst. Roman Catholic. Office: 345 Kinderkamack Rd Ste B Westwood NJ 07675-1600 E-mail: rjmcguirl@att.net.

MCGULPIN, ELIZABETH JANE, nurse; b. Toledo, Oct. 18, 1932; d. James Orville and Leah Fayne (Helton) Welden; m. David Nelson Buster, Apr. 9, 1956 (div. Nov. 1960); children: David Hugh, James Ray, Mark Stephen; m. Fredrick Gordon McGulpin, Oct. 7, 1973. AA in Nursing, Pasadena City Coll., 1968. RN, Wash. Lic. nurse Las Encinas Hosp., Pasadena, Calif.; nurse Hopi Indian Reservation HEW, Keams Canyon, Ariz., 1969-70; nurse, enterostomal therapist Pasadena Vis. Nurse Assn., 1972-74; nurse Seattle King County Pub. Health, 1977-81; home care nurse Victorville, Calif., 1983-85; nurse Adult Family Home, Woodinville, Wash., 1986—. Vol. nurse, counselor Child Protective Svcs., Victorville, 1984; realtor Century 21, Lynden, Wash., 1993—. Vol. nurse Am. Cancer Soc., Pasadena, 1973-75, United Ostomy Assn., Los Angeles, Victorville, 1973-84; RN, ARC, 1996—. Am. Cancer Soc. grantee. Mem. Nat. Assn. Realtors, Wash. Assn. Realtors, Whatcom County Assn. Realtors, Vis. Nurse Assn. (Enterostomal Therpay grantee 1973). Avocations: reading, gardening, travel. Home: 18238 Deauville Dr Victorville CA 92392 *Personal philosophy: Life is very fragile; it goes so fast! We must all strive to be compassionate; supportive and yet strong enough to meet adversary with strength and positiveness. It isn't easy but it is possible with God's help.*

MCGUNIGLE, DOROTHY GREENE, interior designer, artist; b. Providence, Jan. 24, 1914; d. Dutee Thomas and Carrie May (Stewart) Greene; m. Douglas Campbell McGunigle, June 14, 1941 (dec. 1958); children: Jane Douglas (dec.), Bruce Campbell. Grad., R.I. Sch. Design, 1935, BFA (hon.), 1990. Interior designer Healy & Helgeson, Providence, 1935-36, Merriam Co., Providence, 1936-43; mgr. interior decorating dept. Shepard Co., 1960-70; owner Dorothy McGunigle Interiors, East Greenwich, R.I., 1970-95. Tchr. adult edn. Providence YMCA, 1958-59, Cranston High Sch., 1962, Warwick High Sch., 1964, East Greenwich High Sch., 1970-71; art shows include: Providence Art Club, 1972, 74, 76, 78, 80, 82; Indsl. Nat. Bank, Providence, 1974, 76; Warwick Pub. Library, 1980; cons. hist. restoration Varnum House Mus., 1963— . Paintings represented in permanent collection R.I. Hist. Soc. Bd. dirs. East Greenwich Preservation Soc., 1972-77, chmn. consultation com. hist. restoration; active Greenwich Civic Club. Recipient Hon. Mem. award Continental Ladies, Varnum House Mus., 1970; top 3% interior designers in Am., 1989, top 1% internat. designers, 1990. Mem. AID and ASID (visited fgn. designers in Greece, Spain, Portugal, Turkey, Austria, Italy, Switzerland, France, England, Sweden, Denmark, Finland, Norway, Russia to exchange ideas on projects), Providence Art (picture custodian 1974-85, chmn. ladies bd. 1978-79), Providence Pottery and Porcelain (pres. 1981-83), Colonial Dames, Mayflower Descendants, DAR, R.I. Sch. Design Alumni Assn.

MC GURK, JAMES HENRY, consultant company executive; b. Phila., July 24, 1936; s. James Henry and Ednah Mae (Kleinsmith) McG.; m. LaVerne M. Kraynek, 1960; children: Healther, Melanye. BS, Pa. State U., 1957; postgrad. in Econs., Temple U., 1960-62. Cons. mfg., various states, 1968-72; ops. chief mfg. cons. Manatech Internat., Westmont, N.J., 1970-72, A.T. Oxford Inc., N.Y.C., 1972-74; mem. corp. staff mfg. cons. Aspro Inc., Westport, Conn., 1974-77; cons. LHM, Inc., Rochester, Mich., 1977-79, also dir.; exec. v.p. Morse Hemco Inc., Holland, Mich., 1978-83; pres. Western Pegasus, Inc., 1983—, also bd. dirs. Dir. Pegasus Spline, Birmingham, Eng. Served with USAF, 1957-59. Mem. Am. Mgmt. Assn. Republican. Home: 326 Spyglass Dr Coppell TX 75019-5429 Office: 728 E 8th St Holland MI 49423-3080

MC GURN, BARRETT, communications executive, writer; b. N.Y.C., Aug. 6, 1914; s. William Barrett and Alice (Schneider) McG.; m. Mary Elizabeth Johnson, May 30, 1942 (dec. Feb. 1960); children: William Barrett III, Elizabeth (Mrs. Jerry Phelps), Andrew; m. Janice Ann McLaughlin, June 19, 1962; children: Summers, Martin Barrett, Mark Barrett. AB, Fordham U., 1935, LittD, 1958. Editor-in-chief Fordham Ram, 1934-35; with N.Y. Herald Tribune, 1935-66, asst. corr., 1939, bur. chief, 1946-52, 55-62, reporting staff, 1935-42, 62-66, bur. chief, 1952-55, acting chief bur. Moscow, 1958; with, assignments in Morocco, Algeria, Tunisia, Hungary (1956 revolution), Egypt, Greece, Yugoslavia, Poland, Cen. Africa, Gaza Strip.; press attache Am. Embassy, Rome, 1966-68, counselor for press affairs Vietnam, 1968-69; U.S. consular officer, sec. appointed by Pres., 1969; dir. U.S. Govt. Press Ctr., Vietnam, 1968-69; White House and Pentagon liaison for State Dept. spokesman Washington, 1969-72; World Affairs commentator USIA, 1972-73; dir. pub. info. U.S. Supreme Ct., Washington, 1973-82; dir. communications Cath. Archdiocese of Washington, 1984-87; pres. Carroll Pub. Co. pub. Cath. Standard and El Pregonero, 1987-91; dir. Our Sunday Visitor Pub. Co., 1988-98. Mem. Italian-Am. com. to select Italian fellowship winners for study in U.S., 1950-52; mem. U.S. Nat. Cath. Com. on Comm. Policy, 1970-74, White House Com. on Drug Control Info., 1970-72; mem. interdept. com. on U.S. govt. press info. policy, 1970, interdept. U.S. govt. task force to rescue 100 Ams. kidnapped in Jordan, 1970, one-man U.S. Presdl. mission to Cambodia on media news problems, 1970; archivist John Carroll Soc., Washington, 1990-97. Author: Decade in Europe, 1959, A Reporter Looks at the Vatican, 1962, A Reporter Looks at American Catholicism, 1967, America's Court, The Supreme Court and The People, 1997, The Pilgrim's Guide to Rome, 1999; contbg. author: The Best from Yank, 1945, Yank, the GI Story of the War, 1946, Combat, 1950, Highlights from Yank, 1953, Overseas Press Club Cook Book, 1962, I Can Tell it Now, 1964, U.S. Book of Facts, Statistics and Information, 1966, New Catholic Treasury of Wit and Humor, 1967, How I Got that Story, 1967, Heroes for Our Times, 1968, Newsbreak, 1975, Saints for all Seasons, 1978, Informing the People, 1981, The Courage to Grow Old, 1989, Am. Peoples Encyclopedia Yearbook, Close To Glory: Yank Correspondents Untold Stories of World War II, 1992; contbr. articles to profl. jours. Trustee Corrs. Fund, 1965-68; mem. bd. Anglo-Am. Charity Fund in Italy, 1967-68; v.p. Citizens Assn., Westmoreland Hills, Md., 1984-86. Sgt. AUS, 1942-45. Decorated Purple Heart; grand knight Italian Order of Merit; Vietnam Psychol. Warfare medal 1st class; recipient Polk award for outstanding fgn. reporting L.I. U., 1956; named best press corr. abroad Overseas Press Club, 1957; recipient N.Y.C. Fire Dept. Essay Silver Medal, 1924, N.Y. Times Oratorical Contest Bronze Medal, 1930; Christopher award for one of ten most inspiring books of year, 1959; named Man of Year Cath. Inst. Press, 1962, Fordham U. Alumnus of Year in communications, 1963; co-winner ann. Golden Typewriter award N.Y. Newspaper Reporters Assn., 1965, nominated by N.Y. Herald Tribune for Journalism Pulitzer Prize, 1965; outstanding pub. service award N.Y. chpt. Sigma Delta Chi, 1965; recipient Page One award N.Y. Newspaper Guild, 1966, Silurians award, 1966, award N.Y. Newspaper Reporters Assn., 1966, Citation for pub. service N.Y.C. Citizens Budget Commn., 1966, pres. commendation for Cambodia mission on news problems, Meritorious Honor award Dept. State, 1972; Ann. Achievement award Fordham U. Club, Washington, 1986 Mem. Fgn. Press Assn. Italy (v.p. 1951-52, pres. 1961-62), SHAPE Corrs. Assn. Paris (treas. 1955), Authors Guild, Am. Fgn. Svc. Assn., Pax Romana Soc. for Cath. Intellectuals, Overseas Press Club (pres. 1963-65), Nat. Press Club, Diplomats and Consular Officers, Ret., Kenwood Club, Cosmos Club, Fordham U. Club Washington (bd. govs. 1980—). Roman Catholic. Home: 5229 Duvall Dr Bethesda MD 20816-1875 E-mail: jmcgurn@erols.com. *Providing information to our democratic public has been the work of my life both as a foreign correspondent, as a government spokesman, and as a lecturer. The newsman and the person who speaks for government share the same objective of explaining government policy. The spokesman has an added responsibility— to help government policy succeed. The reporter and the spokesman sometimes are at war with one another, but it is a war in behalf of the same beneficiary: the people.*

MCGURN, WILLIAM BARRETT, III, lawyer; b. N.Y.C., Apr. 3, 1943; s. Barrett and Mary Elizabeth (Johnson) McG.; m. Catherine Roche, June 17, 1972; children Mary Anne, Edward Johnson. BA, Yale U., 1965; JD, Harvard U., 1972. Bar: D.C. 1973, Paris 1992. Assoc. Cleary, Gottlieb, Steen & Hamilton, Paris and Washington, 1972-80, Rome, 1981—. Chmn. Dem. Abroad, France, 1987-89; gov. Am. Hosp. Paris, 1991—. Lt. USNR, 1967-69. Mem. ABA, Am. Club Paris, Am. C. of C. France (bd. dirs. 1996—, v.p. 1998-2000, pres. 2000—02). Democrat. Home: vis del Piè di Marmo 166 00186 Rome Italy Office: Cleary Gottlieb Steen & Hamilton Piazza di Spogna 15 00187 Rome Italy Home: 75 Forest Ave Lebanon NH 03766

MCHAELEN, ROBIN PASSARIELLO, executive; b. Waterbury, Conn., Jan. 27, 1955; d. Rowland Anthony and Barbara Crane Passariello; m. Holly Lawrence McHaelen, Aug. 26, 1995; 1 child, Riley Crane. BA, U. Conn., 1976, MSW, 1994. Acct. exec. So. New England Telephone, 1986-89, product mgmt., 1989-90, sales support, 1991-95, tng. & devel., 1996-99; founder, exec. dir. True Colors, Inc., Sexual Minority Youth & Family Svcs. Conn, 1993—. Recipient Sexuality Educator of the Yr., 1998, Bayard Rustin award Conn. Coalition Lesbian, Gay Civil Rights, 1999. Office: True Colors Inc PO Box 1855 Manchester CT 06045 E-mail: robinmchaelen@ourtruecolors.org.

MCHALE, CATHERINE A. lawyer; b. Chgo., Aug. 20, 1964; d. Edward Michael and Nancy Ruth (Martin) McH. BA, Fordham U., 1992; MDiv, Harvard U., 1996; JD, Columbia U., 1999. Press attaché Karl Lagerfeld N.A., N.Y.C., 1988-90; tutor The Learning Ctr., 1990-92; curatorial asst. Peabody Mus., Cambridge, Mass., 1993-95; asst. to dir. Harvard Native Am. Program, 1995-96; cons. The Drawing Ctr., N.Y.C., 1996-97; with Sonnenschein Nath & Rosenthal, 1998—2000, Kay & Boose LLP, N.Y.C., 2000—. Author book chpt., poems, articles. Vol. The Repatriation Found., N.Y.C., 1997-99, Vol. Lawyers for the Arts, N.Y.C., 1997-99; mentor Mock Trial Program, N.Y.C., 1999; vol. N.Y. Cares, 2000—, N.Y. Hospice, 2001—. Charlotte Newcombe scholar, 1989, Vera Bellus scholar, 1994, Harland Fiske Stone scholar, 1999. Mem. Am. Acad. Religion, Soc. for Study of Native Am. Religious Traditions. Democrat. Avocations: reading, skiing, cooking. Office: Kay & Boose LLP 1 Dag Hammarskjold Plaza New York NY 10017

MCHALE, EDWARD ROBERTSON, retired lawyer; b. Chgo., Jan. 24, 1921; s. Edward F. and Martha (Robertson) McH.; m. Helen Louise Lindgren, Aug. 28, 1953; children: Nancy Ellen McHale Kaufman, Sally Jane McHale Cutler, John Robertson. BSS., Northwestern U., 1942; LL.B., Harvard U., 1948. Bar: Calif. 1949. Asst. U.S. atty. U.S. atty. So. Dist. Calif., 1949—61, chief tax div., 1954—61; assoc. Mitchell, Silberberg & Knupp, Los Angeles, 1961—64, ptnr., 1965—86, mgr. litigation dept, 1978—82; pres. Edward R. McHale, P.C., 1979—86; ret., 1986. Lectr. U. So. Calif. Law Center, 1958-61 Co-author: Handling Federal Tax Litigation, 1961. Served to lt. USNR, 1943-46. Mem. Fed. Bar Assn. (past pres. Los Angeles chpt., past nat. v.p. for 9th Circuit), Assn. Bus. Trial Lawyers (bd. govs. 1981-83), State Bar Calif., Delta Sigma Rho. Clubs: South Hills Country (West Covina) Clan Donnachaidh Soc. Lutheran. Home: 1116 S Serena Dr West Covina CA 91791-3754 E-mail: casu8@earthlink.net.

MC HALE, JOHN JOSEPH, baseball club executive; b. Detroit, Sept. 21, 1921; s. John Michael and Catherine M. (Kelly) McH.; m. Patricia Anne Cameron, Feb. 15, 1947; children: Patricia Cameron II, John Joseph, Jr., Kevin K., Anne F., Brian F., Mary M. AB cum laude, U. Notre Dame, 1947. Profl. baseball player, 1941-42, 45-47; asst. dir. minor league clubs Detroit Tigers Baseball Club, 1948, asst. farm dir., 1948-53, dir. minor league clubs, 1954-55, dir. player personnel, 1956-57, gen. mgr., 1957-58; v.p., gen. mgr.

Milw. Braves Baseball Club (became Atlanta Braves Baseball Club 1961), 1957-61, pres., gen. mgr., 1961-67; adminstrv. asst. to commr. baseball N.Y.C., 1967-68; pres. Montreal Expos Baseball Club, 1968-87, dep. chmn., CEO, 1987—; ret. Japan Sports Systems. Dir. Perini Corp. Ret. trustee, Intracoastal Hosp. Corp., West Palm Beach, Fla., 1986—, Schwartz Investment Trust. Mem. Nat. Monogram Club (U. Notre Dame), Assn. Profl. Ball Players Am. (pres.) Harbour Ridge Club. Address: Harbor Ridge 2014 NW Royal Fern Ct Palm City FL 34990-8025

MCHALE, MAUREEN BERNADETTE KENNY, controller; b. Scranton, Pa., July 2, 1955; d. John Theodore and Ann Marie (Slowey) McH. BFA cum laude, Wilkes Coll., 1977; postgrad., Wilkes Coll., Rome, 1977; MBA in Acctg. with honors, U. Notre Dame, 1984; MST with honors, Kings Coll., 1995. Internal auditor Cen. Tax Bur., Forty Fort, Pa., 1977-82; placement coord. U. Notre Dame, South Bend, Ind., 1983-84; sr. acct. Laventhol and Horwath, Wilkes Barre, Pa., 1984-88; contr. Greco Holdings, Inc., 1988-97; dir. fin. Mercy Health Care Ctr., Nanticoke, Pa., 1997—2000; CFO Little Flower Manor/St. Thérèse Residence, Wilkes-Barre, 2000—. Founder Entrepreneurship Lecture Series, U. Notre Dame, 1984. Leader Girl Scouts U.S., Forty Fort, 1977-82; chmn. County Children's Fingerprinting Program, Kingston, Pa., 1988; mem. exec. com., bd. dirs. Bishop O'Reilly H.S.; bd. dirs. Northeastern Pa. Choral Soc., 1996-2000, Mercy Ctr., Hoyt Libr., St. Michael's Sch. U. Notre Dame Scholar, 1984. Mem. Jaycees (bd. dirs. 1987-88), U. Notre Dame Scranton Alumni (bd. dirs.), Notre Dame Alumni Assn. N.E. Pa. (v.p.). Democrat. Roman Catholic. Avocations: walking, biking, Notre Dame football. E-mail: (office) (personal). Home: 31 Virginia Ter Forty Fort PA 18704-4929 Office: 200 S Meade St Wilkes Barre PA 18702-6221 E-mail: mmchale55@aol.com., MO7255@aol.com.

MCHALE, MICHAEL JOHN, lawyer; b. N.Y.C., Apr. 14, 1960; s. Michael Joseph and Mary Beatrice (Graddy) McH. BA, U. of the South, 1982; JD, Samford U., 1985. Bar: Ala. 1986, U.S. Dist. Ct. (no., mid. and so. dists.) Ala. 1986, U.S. Ct. Appeals (11th cir.) 1986, Fla. (cert. admiralty and maritime law) 1991, U.S. Dist. Ct. (mid. and so. dists.) Fla. 1991, U.S. Dist. Ct. (no. dist.) Fla. 1997, U.S. Supreme Ct. 1991; cert. admiralty and maritime lawyer Fla. Bar Bd. of Legal Specialization, mediator, arbitrator Fla. Supreme Ct. Assoc. Wagner, Nugent, Johnson, Roth, Romano, Eriksen & Kupfer, West Palm Beach, Fla., 1989-92; ptnr. Whalen & McHale, 1992-95, Daves, Whalen, McHale & Considine, West Palm Beach, 1995-98; sole practitioner Jensen Beach, 1998—; of counsel Deorchis, Corsa & Hillenbrand LLP, Miami, 1998—. Author: Strategic Use of Circumstantial Evidence, 2nd edit., 1991, Evaluating and Settling Personal Injury Claims, 1992, supplement through present, Making Trial Objections, 1993, supplement through present, Expert Witnesses: Direct and Cross Examination, 1993, supplement through present; editor, author: Litigating TMJ Cases, 1993 and yearly supplements. Named one of Outstanding Young Men of Am., 1988. Mem. ABA (mem. admiralty com.), ATLA, Am. Acad. Fla. Trial Lawyers, Maritime Law Assn. U.S. (procter), Southeastern Admiralty Law Inst., Fla. Bar (admiralty law com. editl. bd., admiralty and maritime cert. com.), Palm Beach Bar Assn., Martin County Bar Assn., Sigma Nu Phi. Avocation: vessel building. Home: 1905 NE River Ct Jensen Beach FL 34957-6423 Office: Deorchis Corsa & Hillenbrand LLP 2650 Biscayne Blvd Miami FL 33137-4531 Fax: 305-571-9250.

MCHALE, VINCENT EDWARD, political science educator; b. Jenkins Twp., Pa., Apr. 17, 1939; m. Ann Barbara Cotner, Nov. 8, 1963; 1 child, Patrick James. A.B., Wilkes Coll., 1964; M.A., Pa. State U., 1966, Ph.D. in Polit. Sci., 1969. Asst. prof. polit. sci. U. Pa., Phila., 1969-75, dir. grad. studies, 1971-73; assoc. prof. Case Western Res. U., Cleve., 1975-84, prof., 1984—, chmn. dept. polit. sci., 1978—; vis. lectr. John Carroll U., summer 1980, Beaver Coll., spring 1975. Author: (with A.P. Frognier and D. Paranzino) Vote, Clivages Socio-politiques et Developpement Regional en Belgique, 1974. Co-editor; contbr.: Evaluating Transnational Programs in Government and Business, 1980; Political Parties of Europe, 1983; edtl. adv. bd. Worldmark Ency. of Nations, 1994—. Contbr. chpts. to books, articles to profl. jours. Project cons. Council Econ Opportunity in Greater Cleve., 1978-81; mem. Morris Abrams Award Com., 1977—. Recipient Outstanding Prof. award Lux chpt. Mortar Bd., 1989, 90; named one of Most Interesting People of 1988, Cleve. Mag.; NSF grantee, 1971-72; HEW grantee, 1976-78; Woodrow Wilson fellow, 1968, Ruth Young Boucke fellow, 1967-68; All-Univ. fellow, 1967-68. Mem. Phi Kappa Phi. Home: 3070 Coleridge Rd Cleveland OH 44118-3556 Office: Case Western Res U Cleveland OH 44106

MC HARGUE, CARL JACK, research laboratory administrator; b. Jan. 30, 1926; s. John David and Virginia (Thomas) McH.; m. Edith Trovillion, Aug. 28, 1948; children: Anne Odell McHargue Diegel, Carol Virginia Hornberger, Margaret Katherine McHargue; m. Betty Ford, Sept. 30, 1960. BS in Metall. Engring., U. Ky., 1949, MS, 1951, PhD, 1953. Instr. U. Ky., Lexington, 1949-53; with Oak Ridge Nat. Lab., 1953-90, sect. head, 1960-80, program mgr. for materials scis., 1961-88, sr. rsch. staff, 1980-90; prof. metall. engring. U. Tenn., Knoxville, 1991—. Vis. prof. U. Newcastle upon Tyne, Eng., 1987; adj. prof. Vanderfilt U., 1988—; bd. dirs. Accreditation Bd. for Engring. and Tech., 1998—; bd. dirs. The Minerals, Metals and Materials Soc. Contbr. numerous articles in field to profl. jours. With AUS, 1944-46. Recipient Disting. Svc. award The Minerals, Metals and Materials Soc., 2001; named to Engring. Hall of Distinction, U. Ky., 1995. Fellow Metall. Soc. AIME, Am. Soc. for Metals; mem. Materials Rsch. Soc., Sigma Xi, Tau Beta Pi. Republican. Presbyterian. Home: 7201 Sheffield Dr Knoxville TN 37909-2414 Office: U Tenn 514 E Stadium Hill Knoxville TN 37996-0750 E-mail: crl@utk.edu.

MCHARGUE, MELISSA KAY, school counselor, speech pathologist; m. Jeff Ray McHargue. BS in Speech and Hearing Sci., U. South Ala., 1979; MS in Ednl. Psychology, Tex. A&M U., Corpus Christi, 1997. Cert. sch. counselor, speech pathologist, Tex.; lic. speech pathologist, Tex. Counselor Royalwood Elem. Sch., Houston, 2000—. Mem. ACA, Am. Sch. Counselor Assn., Tex. Counseling Assn., Tex. Sch. Counselors Assn. E-mail: mmchargue2000@yahoo.com.

MCHEDLISHVILI, GELA, physician; b. Telavi, Georgia, June 13, 1965; came to U.S., 1994; s. Givi and Venera (Kirvakidze) M. MD, Tbilisi Med. U., 1988. Diplomate Am. Bd. Internal Medicine; cert. electrocardiography Inst. for Clin. Evaluation. Surgeon, faculty, staff Inst. of Surgery, Tbilisi, Georgia, 1989-94; intern Emory U., Atlanta, 1994-95; resident Med. Coll. Pa./Hahnemann U., Phila., 1995-97; physician Family Practice of Monticello, Ga., 1997—; attending physician Citrus Meml. Hosp., Inverness, Fla., 1998—. Contbr. articles to profl. jours.; patentee heart valve prosthesis. Fellow ACP; mem. AMA, Am Soc. Internal Medicine, Fla. Med. Soc. Orthodox Christian. Avocations: travel, reading, history. Home: 816 Hemlock St Inverness FL 34452-5941 Office: Citrus Meml Hosp 508 N Lecanto Hwy Lecanto FL 34461-8547 Fax: (352) 527-2667. E-mail: gela5@mindspring.com.

MCHENRY, ANITA PETEI, historian, archaeologist; b. Coffeyville, Kans., Mar. 2, 1949; d. Woodrow Wilson Gordon and Erva Odile (Crevier) Hardy; m. Gray Richard McHenry, Dec. 12, 1981; children: Carrie Ann, Thomas Owen. BS in Anthropology, U. Calif., Riverside, 1992; MA in History, U. San Diego, 1997. Archaeologist, historian Gallegos & Assocs., Carlsbad, Calif., 1990-96; pub., owner GP Mktg., Escondido, 1996—. Vol. archivist Valley Ctr. (Calif.) Libr., 1996—; v.p. hist. com. Friends of Valley Ctr. Libr., 1996—. Author: History of Valley Center, 1997. Mem. Nat. Trust Historic Preservation, exec. dir. Valley Ctr. History Mus., 2001—. Recipient fellowship grant U. San Diego, 1995-96. Mem. Soc. Calif. Archaeology, San Diego Hist. Soc., Smithsonian Assn., San Diego County Archaeol. Soc., Phi Alpha Theta. Avocations: historical research, genealogy, archaeology, reading. Home and Office: GP Mktg 28338 Mountain Meadow Rd Escondido CA 92026-6907 E-mail: gpmch@att.net.

MCHENRY, HENRY MALCOLM, anthropologist, educator; b. Los Angeles, May 19, 1944; s. Dean Eugene and Emma Jane (Snyder) McH.; m. Linda Jean Conway, June 25, 1966; children: Lindsay Jean, Annalisa Jane. BA, U. Calif., Davis, 1966, MA, 1967; PhD, Harvard U., 1972. Asst. prof. anthropology U. Calif., Davis, 1971-76, assoc. prof. anthropology, 1976-81, prof. anthropology, 1981—, chmn. dept. anthropology, 1984-88. Fellow Am. Anthrop. Assn., Calif. Acad. Sci.; mem. Am. Assn. Phys. Anthropologists (exec. com. 1981-85), Soc. Study Evolution, Soc. Vertebrate Paleontology, Phi Beta Kappa, Phi Kappa Phi. Democrat. Buddhist. Avocation: winemaker. Home: 330 11th St Davis CA 95616-2010 Office: U of Calif Davis Dept Of Anthropology Davis CA 95616

MCHENRY, MARTIN CHRISTOPHER, physician, educator; b. Feb. 9, 1932; s. Merl and Marcella (Bricca) McH.; m. Patricia Grace Hughes, Apr. 27, 1957; children: Michael, Christopher, Timothy, Mary Ann, Jeffrey, Paul, Kevin, William, Monica, Martin Christopher. Student, U. Santa Clara, 1950-53; MD, U. Cin., 1957; MS in Medicine, U. Minn., 1966. Diplomate Am. Bd. Internal Medicine. Intern Highland Alameda County (Calif.) Hosp., Oakland, 1957-58; resident, internal medicine fellow Mayo Clinic, Rochester, Minn., 1958-61, spl. appointee in infectious diseases, 1963-64; staff physician Henry Ford Hosp., Detroit, 1964-67, Cleve. Clinic, 1967-72, chmn. dept. infectious diseases, 1972-92, sr. physician infectious diseases, 1992-98. Cons. infectious diseases, 1998—; asst. clin. prof. Case Western Res. U., 1970-77, assoc. clin. prof. medicine, 1977-91, clin. prof. medicine, 1991—; assoc. vis. physician Cleve. Met. Gen. Hosp., 1970-00; cons. VA Hosp., Cleve., 1973-74. Contbr. more than 100 articles to profl. jours., also chpts. to books. Chmn. manpower com. Swine Influenza Program, Cleve., 1976. With USNR, 1961-63. Named Disting. Tchr. in Medicine, Cleve. Clinic, 1972, 90; recipient 1st ann. Bruce Hubbard Stewart award Cleve. Clinic Found. for Humanities in Medicine, 1985, Nightingale Physician Collaboration award Cleve. Clinic Found. Divsn. Nursing, 1995, Clinician of Yr. award Acad. Medicine of Cleve./No. Ohio Med. Assn., 2002. Fellow ACP, Infectious Diseases Soc. Am. (Clinician award 2000), Am. Coll. Chest Physicians (chmn. com. cardiopulmonary infections 1975-77, 81-83), Royal Soc. Medicine of Gt. Britain; mem. Am. Soc. Clin. Pharmacology and Therapeutics (chmn. sect. infectious diseases and antimicrobial agts. 1970-77, 80-85, dir.), Am. Thoracic Soc., Am. Soc. Clin. Pathologists, Am. Fedn. Clin. Rsch., Am. Soc. Tropical Medicine and Hygiene, Am. Soc. Microbiology, N.Y. Acad. Scis., Assn. for Profls. in Infection Control and Epidemiology, So. Med. Assn. Home: 2779 Belgrave Rd Pepper Pike OH 44124-4601 Office: 9500 Euclid Ave Cleveland OH 44195-0001

MC HENRY, POWELL, lawyer; b. Cinn., May 14, 1926; s. L. Lee McHenry and Marguerite L. (Powell) Heinz; m. Venna Mae Guerrea, Aug. 27, 1948; children: Scott, Marshall, Jody Lee, Gale Lynn. AB, U. Cinn., 1949; LLB, Harvard U., 1951, JD, 1969. Bar: Ohio 1951, U.S. Ct. Appeals (6th cir.) 1964, U.S. Supreme Ct. 1966. Assoc. Dinsmore, Shohl, Sawyer & Dinsmore, Cinn., 1951-57; ptnr. Dinsmore, Shohl, Coates & Deupree (and predecessors), 1958-75; gen. counsel Federated Dept. Stores, Inc., 1971-75; assoc. gen. counsel Procter & Gamble Co., 1975-76, v.p., gen. counsel, 1976-83, sr. v.p., gen. counsel, 1983-91; counsel Dinsmore & Shohl, Cin., 1991—; bd. dirs. Eagle Picher Industries, Inc., 1991-97. Mem. com. Hamilton County Pub. Defender, Cin., chmn., 1996-2000. With USNR, 1944-46. Recipient award of merit Ohio Legal Center Inst., 1969. Mem. ABA, Ohio Bar Assn., Cin. Bar Assn. (pres. 1979-80, exec. com. 1975-81), Harvard U. Law Sch. Assn. Cin. (pres. 1960-61), Am. Law Inst., Assn. Gen. Counsel (pres. 1986-88), Harvard Club, Western Hill Country Club (bd. dirs. 1964-70, sec. 1966-69, 87-89, treas. 1969-70, 89-90), Queen City Club, Commonwealth Club (pres. 1996-97). Republican. Methodist. Office: Dimsmore & Shohl 1900 Chemed Ctr 255 E 5th St Cincinnati OH 45202-4700

MCHOES, ANN MCIVER, academic administrator, computer systems consultant; b. San Diego , June 17, 1950; d. Donald Anthony and Ann Mae McIver; children: A. Genevieve, Katherine Marie. BS in Math., U. Pitts., 1973, MS in Info. Sci., 1986. Tech. writer Westinghouse Electric Corp., Pitts., 1973—79; pres. McHoes & Assocs., 1981—; dir. enrollment svcs. Chatham Coll., 2002—. Mem. adj. faculty computer sci., Carlow Coll., Pitts., 1992— , Duquesne U., 1997-99; cons. Westinghouse Electric Corp., 1988-99, PNC Bank, Pitts., 1988—, CBS Corp., 1996-99, Intel, 1998—, McDonalds Corp., 1998-2001, commonwealth of Pa. Healthy Women Project, 1998—; vis. lectr. Pa. State U., State College, 1990-91; judge Pa. Jr. Acad. Sci., Pitts., 1993—; vol. tutor Greater Pitts. Literacy Coun., 1996-98; webmaster NVR Mortgage, 1998-2000; bd. dirs. Pitts. Playback Theatre, 2000-2001. Co-author: Understanding Operating Systems, 1991, 2d edit., 1997, 3d edit., 2000 (used in colleges and univs., North Am., Europe, Africa, Asia and Australia); assoc. editor: (4-vol. ency.) Computer Science for Students, 2002. Recipient 2001 Texty Excellence award Text and Academic Authors Assn., 2001. Mem. IEEE Computer Soc., Assn. Computing Machinery, Info. Sys. Security Assn. (chpt. sec. 1991-94, v.p. 1995-96, membership chair 1994—), Pa. Mid. Sch. Assn. (conf. exhibit chair 1996-97). Avocations: travel, tennis, golf. Office: Chatham Coll Braun Hall Woodland Rd Pittsburgh PA 15232

MCHOLD, SHARON LAWRENCE, lawyer, mediator; b. Albion, Mich., Mar. 26, 1941; d. Ted E. and Ruth M. (Whelan) McH.; m. Frank H. Lawrence, Apr. 4, 1964 (div. July 1987); children: Christopher, Brian, Kimberly. BS, U. Del., 1963; MS, Tufts U., 1965; JD, U. Maine, 1983. Researcher U. Ind. Med. Sch., Indpls., 1966-67; instr. Marian Coll., 1967-70, Westbrook Coll., Portland, Maine, 1973-79; assoc. Curtis Thaxter, 1985-91; pvt. practice Yarmouth, Maine, 1991-93; mediator Conflict Solutions, Portland, 1993—. Trustee Maine Audubon Soc., Falmouth, Maine, 1975-79; clk. Island Inst., Rockland, Maine, 1985-92; trustee Maine Island Trail Assn., Portland, 1993-94, Oceanside Conservation Trust, 1993-, Yarmouth Land Trust, 2001-. Nat. Def. fellow, 1963-65. Mem.: CRA, Maine Bar Assn. Home: 30 Riverbend Dr Yarmouth ME 04096-5337 Office: Conflict Solutions 75 Pearl St Portland ME 04101-1102

MCHUGH, BETSY BALDWIN, sociologist, educator, journalist, business owner; b. Concord, N.H., 1928; d. Walter Killenbeck and Eliza Alice (Hunt) Slater; m. Michael Joseph McHugh, Dec. 19, 1954; children: Betsy, Michael. MusB in Vocal Music, Syracuse (N.Y.) U., 1954; grad. student, Cornell U. Tchr. pub. schs., Juneau, Alaska, 1966-85. Owner, founder Cashè Pub. Co., Tampa, Fla., and Juneau, 1986—, Nikish Ki Lodges and Youth Camps subsidiaries Baldwin Enterprises. Named one of Alaska's Outstanding Educators, Gov. Alaska Woman's Commn., 1985, Uno of Yr., 1993, 94, Internat. Una of Yr., 1993, 94, one of 2000 Most Notable Women, 1994, Better Profl. WOmen, 1993, 94. Mem. Can. Nat. Libr., Nat. Press Club, Bus. Assn. N.Y. State, Libr. of Congress, Can. Bus., D.C. C. of C., Mex. C. of C., Sigma Delta Chi. Avocations: snorkeling, writing, sociology, dancing, music.

MCHUGH, CARIL EISENSTEIN DREYFUSS, art dealer, gallery director, consultant; b. New Haven; d. Irving and Gertrude (Lax) Eisenstein; m. Barney Dreyfuss II (div.); children: Caryn, Barney III (Terry), Andrew, Evan; m. James Marshall McHugh Jr., Dec. 31, 1976. BA, Smith Coll.; postgrad., Am. U., 1958-61. Libr. archivist, mem. staff art rental Washington Gallery of Modern Art, 1963-67; asst. to curator of prints and drawings Nat. Mus. Am. Art, Washington, 1967-69; dir. Studio Gallery, 1970-75; dir., ptnr. Parsons-Dreyfuss Gallery, N.Y.C., 1976-80; dir. Frank Marino Gallery, 1981, Humphrey Fine Art, N.Y.C., 1988-90, Gregory Gallery, N.Y.C., 1995-96; freelance curator, adv. bd. Hugo de Pagano Gallery, 1997—2000; rschr. Barnett Newman Found., N.Y.C., 2001—. Art cons., writer, N.Y.C., 1982—; arranger exhbns. Nat. Mus. Am. Art, Washington, 1968-69, USIA, Washington, 1976, Automation House, N.Y.C., 1983. Essays to catalogs, articles to profl. mags. Bd. dirs. Women's Nat. Dem. Club, Washington, 1972-76, Friends of the Corcoran, Washington, 1972-76, Smith Club of Washington, 1974-76; Sophia Smith Assoc. Smith Coll., Northampton, Mass., 1985, 90, 95, 2000, Women in the Arts, 1995—. Avocations: reading, hiking, swimming, designing accessories, writing poetry. Home: 241 Central Park W Apt 9C New York NY 10024-4545

MCHUGH, JAMES JOSEPH, retired naval officer, retired associate dean; b. Phila., Aug. 12, 1930; s. James Joseph and Patience Mary (McGowan) McH.; m. Rita Marie Huber, May 21, 1960; children: Margaret Marie, James Joseph IV. BA (with honors), U. Pa., 1951, LL.B., 1954; MS in Internat. Relations, George Washington U., 1972. Bar: Pa. 1955. Commd. ensign U.S. Navy, 1955, advanced through grades to rear adm., 1980; legal officer Naval Air Station, Point Mugu, Calif., 1955-58; staff officer Office Judge Adv. Gen., Washington, 1959-63; staff instr. U.S. Naval Justice Sch., Newport, R.I., 1963-65; counsel Bur. Naval Personnel, Washington, 1965-68; asst. fleet judge adv. to comdr. in chief U.S. Pacific Fleet, 1968-71; spl. counsel to chief naval ops. Washington, 1972-76; officer in charge Naval Legal Service Office, San Francisco, 1976-78; asst. judge adv. gen. Washington, 1978-80; dep. judge adv. gen. Alexandria, Va., 1980-82; judge adv. gen., 1982-84; asst. dean McGeorge Sch. Law, Sacramento, 1984-86, assoc. dean, 1987-93. Decorated D.S.M., Legion of Merit (2), Meritorious Svc. medal (2), Navy Commendation medal. Mem. ABA, Order of Coif (hon.), Phi Beta Kappa. Republican. Roman Catholic. Home: 4704 Olive Oak Way Carmichael CA 95608-5663

MCHUGH, JAMES JOSEPH, lawyer; b. Phila., Sept. 15, 1961; s. James Joseph and Helene Anne (Kiernan) McHugh; m. Colette Marie McHugh, May 20, 1989; children: Albert Taylor, James Joseph III, Cole Michael;1 child Sophia Kiernan. BSME, Drexel U., 1985; JD magna cum laude, Villanova (Pa.) Law Sch., 1992. Bar: Pa. 1992, N.J. 1992, U.S. Dist. Ct. (ea. dist.) Pa., U.S. Dist. Ct. N.J. Ptnr. McHugh Plumbing & Heating, Phila., 1984-89; project mgr. Fluidics Mech Contractors, 1989-92; assoc. Pepper, Hamilton & Scheetz, 1992-94, Beasley, Casey & Erbstein, Phila., 1994—. Author, editor case notes. Mem. adv. com. Penn Pub. Svc. Program, Sch. Law, U. Pa. Named to Order of the Coif, Villanova Law Sch., 1992. Mem. ATLA, Pa. Bar Assn., Phila. Bar Assn. Home: 65 Brooks Rd Moorestown NJ 08057-3855 Office: Beasley Casey & Erbstein 1125 Walnut St Philadelphia PA 19107-4918 E-mail: jjm@tortlaw.com.

MCHUGH, JAMES LENAHAN, JR. lawyer; b. Pitts., June 28, 1937; s. James Lenahan and Annette (Dalton) McH.; m. Mary-Ann Curto, Feb. 16, 1963 (div. 1988); children: Angela Dalton Sherrill, Hillary Lenahan Clagett; m. Rosa Lamoreaux, Sept. 8, 1991. BA, Duquesne U., 1959; LLB, Villanova U., 1962. Bar: D.C. 1963. Law clk. U.S. Dist. Ct. (ea. dist.) Pa., Phila., 1962-63; law clk. to Assoc. Justice Tom C. Clark, U.S. Supreme Ct., Washington, 1963-64; assoc. Steptoe & Johnson, 1967-70, ptnr., 1970-94; gen. counsel APA, 1994—2001, sr. counsel, 2001—. Mem. bd. consultors Law Sch., Villanova (Pa.) U., 1973—; dir. Higher Achievement Program, Washington, 1984-87; coord. Washington Lawyers' Project, Robert F. Kennedy Meml. Found., Washington, 1972-75. Editor-in-chief Villanova Law Rev., Vol. VII, 1961-62; chmn. editorial adv. bd. Fed. Comm. Law Jour., 1981-84. Bd. dirs. Columbia Hosp. for Women's Found., Washington, 1985-96, Children's Radio Theatre, Washington, 1983-86; chmn. exec. giving Archbishop's Appeal, Archdiocese of Washington, 1982-84; mem. bd. visitors Ctr. for Study of Orgns. and Mgmt., U. Md. Univ. Coll., 1987-92; bd. dirs. Human Resources Rsch. Orgn., Inc., 1978—; chmn. bd. dirs., 1991—; mem. advisors Inst. for Conflict Analysis and Resolution, George Mason U., 1990-94. Capt. U.S. Army, 1964-67. Mem. ABA (sect. on health law, tax, antitrust, intellectual property and legal edn.), D.C. Bar Assn., Choral Arts Soc., Order of Coif, Confrerie des Chevaliers du Tastevin. Home: 4112 Fessenden St NW Washington DC 20016-4227 Office: APA 750 1st St NE Washington DC 20002-4242 E-mail: jmchugh@apa.org.

MCHUGH, JOHN MICHAEL, congressman, former state senator; b. Watertown, N.Y., Sept. 29, 1948; s. Donald and Jane (O'Neill) McH. BA in Polit. Sci., Syracuse U., 1970; MPA, Nelson A. Rockefeller Grad. Sch. Pub. Affairs, 1977. Asst. city mngr. Watertown, 1968-73; confidential asst. Watertown City Mgrs. Office, 1971-76; chief of research, liaison with local govts. Office of N.Y. State Senator H.D. Barclay, 1976-84; U.S. senator from 46th N.Y. dist., 1984-93; chmn. joint legis. commn. on dairy industry devel., 1987-92; mem. U.S. Congress from 24th N.Y. dist., 1993—; mem. armed svcs. com., internat. rels. com., govt. reform com., chmn. subcom. on military pers. Mem. Legis. Commn. on Modernization of the Tax Code, Nat. Conf. State Legis., Commerce & Econ. Devel. Com., Commerce, Labor and Regulation Com. of the State Fed. Assembly, Coun. State Govt. Eastern Regional Conf. Com. on Fiscal Affairs. Recipient 40 Outstanding Alumni awards Syracuse U., Individual Achievement award N.Y. State Dept. Econ. Devel.; named to Hon. First Citizen, City of Watertown, 1976. Mem. Legis. on State Legislators (nat. conf. state legislators), Nat. Conf. State Legislators (vice chmn. agrl. and internat. trade com. State-Fed. Assembly), Am. Soc. Young Polit. Leaders. Republican. Roman Catholic. Avocations: boating, snow skiing, music. Office: US Ho of Reps 2441 Rayburn Ho Office Bldg Washington DC 20515*

MC HUGH, MARGARET ANN GLOE, retired psychologist; b. Salt Lake City, Nov. 8, 1920; d. Harold Henry and Olive (Warenski) Gloe; m. William T. McHugh, Oct. 1, 1943; children: Mary Margaret McHugh-Shuford, William Michael, Michelle McHugh Sprague. BA, U. Utah, 1942; MA in Counseling and Guidance, Idaho State U., 1964; PhD in Counseling Psychology, U. Oreg., 1970. Nat. cert. counselor. Tchr. kindergarten, Idaho Falls, Idaho, 1951-62; tchr. high sch. English, 1962-63; counselor Counseling Ctr., Idaho State U., Pocatello, 1964-67; instr. U. Oreg., Eugene, 1967-70; asst. prof. U. Victoria, B.C., Can., 1970-76; therapist Peninsula Counseling Ctr., Port Angeles, Wash., 1976-81, Sequim, 1976-81; psychologist McHugh & Assocs. Counseling Ctr., 1981-95; ret., 1995. Served with WAVES, 1943-44. Recipient Recogniton award for 25 yrs. vol. svc. to Hospice. Mem. APA, ACA, Am. Assn. Marriage and Family Therapy, Wash. Psychol. Assn. (rsch. women issues, depression and women, sexual abuse, adults with childhood and abuse trauma). Home: 1175 Cameron Rd Sequim WA 98382-7501 E-mail: whugh@olypen.com.

MCHUGH, PAUL R. psychiatrist, neurologist, educator; b. Lawrence, Mass., May 21, 1931; s. Francis Paul and Mary Dorothea (Herlihy) McH.; m. Jean Barlow, Dec. 27, 1959; children: Clare Mary, Patrick Daniel, Denis Timothy. AB, Harvard U., 1952, MD, 1956. Diplomate: Am. Bd. Psychiatry and Neurology. Intern Peter Bent Brigham Hosp., Boston, 1956-57; resident in neurology Mass. Gen. Hosp., 1957-60, fellow in neuropathology, 1958-59; teaching fellow in neurology and neuropathology Harvard, 1957-60; clin. asst. psychiatry Maudsley Hosp., London, Eng., 1960-61; mem. neuropsychiatry div. Walter Reed Army Inst. Research, Washington, 1961-64; asst. prof. psychiatry and neurology Cornell U., N.Y.C., 1964-68, assoc. prof., 1968-71, prof., 1971; dir. electroencephalography N.Y. Hosp., 1964-68; founder, dir. N.Y. Hosp. Bourne Behavioral Rsch. Lab., 1967-68, clin. dir., supr. psychiat. edn., founder, dir. Weschester divsn. dept. psychiatry, 1968-73; prof., chmn. dept. psychiatry U. Oreg. Health Sci. Center, Portland, 1973-75; Henry Phipps prof. psychiatry Johns Hopkins, Balt., 1975—, chmn. dept. psychiatry, 1975—, prof. dept. mental hygiene, 1976—; psychiatrist-in-chief Johns Hopkins Hosp., 1975—; dir. Blades Ctr. for Clin. Practice and Rsch. in Alcoholism Johns Hopkins Med. Inst., 1992—; chmn. med. staff Johns Hopkins Hosp., 1983-89, trustee, 1983—. Vis. prof. Guys Hosp., London, Eng., 1976; chmn. bio-psychology Study sect. NIH, 1986-89, mem. pres.'s coun. on bioethics, 2001—. Author: The Perspectives of Psychiatry, 1983; (with Phillip R. Slavney) Psychiatric Polarities, 1987, Genes, Brain and Behavior, 1990; contbg. author: Cecil-Loeb Textbook of Medicine; mem. editorial bd. Am. Jour. Physiology, Jour. Nervous and Mental Disease, Comprehensive Psychiatry, Medicine, Psychol. Medicine, 1976—, Am. Scholar; contbr. articles to profl. jours. Mem. Md. Gov.'s Adv. Com., 1977-80. Grantee NIH, 1964-68, 67-70, 70-74, 75—; recipient William C. Menninger award ACP, 1987. Fellow Royal Coll. Psychiatry, Am. Psychiat. Assn.; mem. Inst. Medicine-NAS, Am. Neurol. Assn., Am. Physiol. Soc., Harvey Soc., Am. Coll. Neuropsychopharmacology, Am. Psychopath. Assn., Pavlovian Soc., W Hamilton St. Club. Home: 3707 St Paul St Baltimore MD 21218-2403 Office: Johns Hopkins Med Insts Meyer 4-113 600 N Wolfe St Baltimore MD 21287-0005

MCHUGH, ROBERT ERNEST (BOB MCHUGH), pianist, composer; b. Kearny, N.J., July 20, 1946; s. Edward William and Marie (Spinello) McH.; m. Jane Regina Belli, June 27, 1970; children: Erik Bernard, Meredith Jane. BA, Jersey City State Coll., 1971. Cert. music tchr. N.J. Music tchr. gifted and talented Fairview (N.J.) Pub. Schs., 1986-91; pres. Jarob Pub., Pompton Lakes, N.J., 1989—; music tchr. Roseland, 1989—; rec. artist Alliance Records, 1993—. Lectr. in field; guest performer WNYC Around New York radio show. Performed as keyboardist with The Duprees, N.Y.C., 1978, The Chatterband, N.Y. and N.J., 1980-84; as pianist and keyboardist Perception Records, N.Y.C., 1979; as pianist Billy Battison Quartet, Long Branch, N.J., 1985; music dir. Bob McHugh Trios Pratos, Carlstadt, N.J., 1986-91; composer: Frank Chacksfield, Eros for BBC, London, 1989-91; composer, performer (jazz composition) Lincoln Center, 1975, (mus. composition) Am. Song Festival, 1978 (Cash prize), WNBC Hometown Album, 1979; rec. artist: Outstanding Records, Huntington Beach, Calif., Alliance Records, 1997, Lunge Music, 1999-00; composer film music Ed Hansen, Inc., Arcadia, Calif., Manduca Music Publs., Inc., Voice of Rockies; commd. composer N.J. Music Tchrs. Assn., 1998, 99; compositions included in Nat. Fedn. Music Clubs Festivals Bull., 2001; guest The Jazz Corner, Sta. WNTI, 2002. Performer Jazz Mass, Drew U., Upsala Coll., Riverside Ch., N.Y.C.; performer in documentary: The Art of Worship; tchr. Pequannock (N.J.) Twp. Sch. Music Programs; pianist Stony Hill Inn, Hackensack, N.J., Trumpets, Montclair, N.J., 1994, The Priory, Newark, 1997 concerts in N.Y. Pub. Libr. Mem. ASCAP (Popular award 1995-96, 96-97, 98, 99, 2000), NEA, Am. Fedn. Musicians, N.J. Edn. Assn., Music Tchrs. Nat. Assn. Avocations: bicycling, walking, swimming, collecting antique instruments. Home: 902 Lincoln Ave Pompton Lakes NJ 07442-1405 E-mail: jarobpub@aol.com.

MCHUGH, STUART LAWRENCE, materials engineer; b. San Francisco, Nov. 7, 1949; s. James and Ruth McHugh. BSc in Geophysics with high distinction, U. Nev., 1971, BSc in Geol. Engring. with high distinction, 1972; MS in Geophysics, Stanford U., 1974, MS in Materials Sci., 1976, PhD in Geophysics, 1977. Seismol. asst. U. Nev., Reno, 1971-72; intern, student geophysicist Humble Oil Co., New Orleans, summer 1972; geophysicist U.S. Geol. Survey, Menlo Park, Calif., 1973-77, SRI, Internat., Menlo Park, 1977-81; materials engr. Lockheed Martin Missiles & Space Co., Palo Alto, Calif., 1981—. Contbr. articles to profl. jours. Mem. Service League of San Mateo County (Calif.), Redwood City, 1982—. Recipient traineeship NSF, 1972-73; named MacKay Sch. Mines Outstanding Geologist, U. Nev., Reno, 1972. Mem. AAAS, AIAA, Am. Geophys. Union, Am. Phys. Soc. (human rights com. 1982—), Phi Kappa Phi. Avocations: fgn. lang. studies. Office: Lockheed Martin Space Systems Co Bldg 204 O/L9-21 3251 Hanover St Palo Alto CA 94304-1121

MCILRATH, THOMAS, physicist, educator; b. Dowagiac, Mich. s. William Frederick and Leora Lewis McIlrath; m. Valerie Hoy McIlrath, June 30, 1962; children: Christine, Laura. BS in Physics, Mich. State U., 1960; PhD in Physics, Princeton U., 1966. Rsch. assoc., instr. Harvard Coll. Obs., Cambridge, Mass., 1967-73; from assoc. prof. to prof. U. Md., College Park, 1973-98, assoc. dean for rsch. and grad. studies, 1995-96, prof. emeritus, 1998—; physicist Nat. Inst. Stds. and Tech., Gaithersburg, Md., 1974-97. Cons. AT&T Bell Labs., Holmdel, N.J., 1984-93, Princeton (N.J.) Plasma Physics Lab., 1984-90; program officer NSF, Washington, 1993-95; spkr. in field. Contbr. papers to profl. jours. Recipient Silver medal U.S. Dept. Commerce, 1980, IR-100 award Indsl. Rsch. Mag., 1981. Fellow Am. Phys. Soc. (treas. and pub. 1996—), Optical Soc. Am. (bd. dirs. 1993-95). Office: Am Phys Soc One Physics Ellipse College Park MD 20740 Fax: (301) 209-0844. E-mail: mcilrath@aps.org.

MCILRAY, JOHN FREDERICK, musician; b. Red Bank, N.J., Oct. 19, 1947; s. Elsie Eunice Brett-McIlray. B Music Edn, Westminster Choir Coll., 1970. Organist, choirmaster St. James Episcopal Ch., Eatontown, NJ, 1964—66; dir. music King of Kings Luth. Ch., Middletown, 1966—71; organist 1st United Meth. Ch., Asbury Park, 1971—77; organist, assoc. dir. John Calvin Presbyn. Ch., Apache Junction, Ariz., 1977—79; organist, assoc. dir. music Scottsdale United Meth. Ch., Scottsdale, 1979—96; organist, choirmaster St. Mark's Episcopal Ch., Mesa, 1996—; tchr. Middletown (N.J.) Twp. Pub. Schs. , 1970—77; tchr., intermediate chair Mesa (Ariz.) Pub. Schs., 1977—2001. Composer: (choral anthem) Lord, Who At Cana's Wedding Feast, 1999. V.p., bd. dirs. Ballet Ariz., Phoenix, 1982—85. Mem.: Am. Guild of Organists. Episcopalian. Avocations: travel, computers. Home: 5100 N. Miller Rd. Unit 8 Scottsdale AZ 85250 Office: St Mark's Episcopal Ch 322 N Horne St Mesa AZ 85203 Personal E-mail: JMcilray@aol.com.

MCILVAINE, BETSY, librarian; b. Lafayette, Ind., Jan. 26, 1945; d. J.L. and Mary Ann (Phillips) Owens; m. Paul M. McIlvaine, June 24, 1967. BA, U. Ill., 1967; MLS, U. R.I., 1973; MBA, U. Conn., 1983. Internat. documents libr. U. Conn. Libr., Storrs, 1973-79; head libr. Philips Rsch., Briarcliff Manor, N.Y., 1979—, project mgmt. coord., 1993-95, mgr. project coord., 1995-2000; mgr. U. Media Resources, 2000—. Author: Students Guide to Government Publications, 1982. Chmn., mem. Commn. on the Status of Women, Danbury, 1985-95; bd. dirs. Danbury Music Ctr., 1990—, Hispanic Ctr., Danbury, 1995—; mem. Project Mgmt. Inst. Mem. Spl. Librs. Assn., Project Mgmt. Inst. Office: Philips Rsch 345 Scarborough Rd Briarcliff Manor NY 10510-2027

MCILVAINE, PATRICIA MORROW, internist; b. Pitts., Feb. 4, 1947; d. James Morrow McIlvaine and Virginia Fuller Tucker. BS in Chemistry, Simmons Coll., 1969; MD, U. Utah, 1980. Rsch. technician Mass. Gen. Hosp., Boston, 1969-70, MIT, Cambridge, 1970-75, Utah State U., Logan, 1975-80; resident in internal medicine U. Mass. Hosp., Worcester, 1984-87; pvt. practice, Monson, Mass., 1987-2001; mem. pvt. group practice Walla Walla (Wash.) Clinic, 2002—. Staff physician Wing Meml. Hosp., Palmer, Mass., 1987-2001. Vol., trainer IRBIS Enterprises, Mongolia, 1998—. NFS summer scholar, 1968, Helena Rubinstein scholar Simmons Coll., 1968-69. Mem. ACP/Am. Soc. Internal Medicine, Sigma Xi. Avocations: fiber crafts, international travel, hiking, gardening, sailing. Home: 1249 Lancer Dr Walla Walla WA 99362

MCILVAINE, WILLIAM BROWN, JR. pediatric anesthesiologist; b. Lake Forest, Ill., Apr. 8, 1952; s. William Brown McIlvaine Sr. and Adele Ellis (Arrowsmith) Douglas; m. Stephan Barnes Parsons, Oct. 30, 1946; children: Julia Margaret Fenno, William Brown III. BA with honors, Stanford U., 1974; MD, CM, McGill U., Montreal, Can., 1978. Diplomate Am. Bd. Anesthesiology, Nat. Bd. Med. Examiners. Intern Queen Elizabeth Hosp., Montreal, 1978-79; resident in anaesthesia McGill U., 1979-82; fellow in pediat. anesthesia Children's Meml. Hosp. & Northwestern U., Chgo., 1982-83; asst. prof. anesthesiology Health Scis. Ctr. U. Colo., Denver, 1983-85, asst. clin. prof. anesthesiology, 1985—2002, dir. pediat. anesthesia Univ. Hosp., 1983-85, med. dir. operating rms. Univ. Hosp., 1983-85; mem. staff Children's Hosp., 1985—, Littleton (Colo.) Hosp., 1989—2002; assoc. chmn. for clin. anesthesiology svcs. Childrens Hosp., L.A., 2002—. Mem. courtesy staff Aurora (Colo.) Regional Med. Ctr., 1990-2002, Rose Med. Ctr., Denver, 1990-2002, Porter Meml. Hosp., Englewood, Colo., 1993-2002, Swedish Med. Ctr., Englewood, 1993-2002; mem. active staff Presbyn.-St. Luke's Med. Ctr., Denver, 1990-2002, St. Joseph's Hosp., Denver, 1990-2002; assoc. examiner Am. Bd. Anesthesiology, 1988-2002; vis. prof. pediat. anesthesia Richland Meml. Hosp. and U. S.C., Columbia, 1989; presenter Hosp. for Sick Children, Toronto, 1983, Children's Hosp., Denver, 1983; presenter numerous confs. Author: (with others) Ocular Therapeutics and Pharmacology, 1985, Textbook of Paediatric Anesthetic Practice, 1989, Clinical Practice of Regional Anesthesia, 1991, Acute Pain: Mechanisms and Management, 1992; contbr. articles to profl. jours. Fellow Royal Coll. Physicians and Surgeons (Can.), Am. Acad. Pediat.; mem. Am. Soc. Anesthesiologists, Can. Anesthetists' Soc., Internat. Anesthesia Rsch. Soc., Soc. for Pediat. Anesthesia. Home: Childrens Hosp of LA Dept Anesthesiology 4650 Sunset Blvd MS # 3 Los Angeles CA 90027

MCILWAIN, CARL EDWIN, physicist; b. Houston, Mar. 26, 1931; s. Glenn William and Alma Ora (Miller) McI.; m. Mary Louise Hocker, Dec. 30, 1952; children— Janet Louise, Craig Ian. BA, N. Tex. State Coll., Denton, 1953; MS, State U. Iowa, 1956, PhD, 1960. Asst. prof. State U. Iowa, 1960-62; assoc. prof. physics U. Calif.-, San Diego, 1962-66; prof. U. Calif., 1966—. Mem. space scis. steering com., fields and particles subcom. NASA, 1962-66; mem. anti-submarine warfare panel President's Sci. Adv. Com., 1964-67; mem. com. potential contamination and interference from space expts. Space Sci. Bd., Nat. Acad. Scis.-NRC, 1964-71; mem. advisory com. for radiation hazards in supersonic transports FAA, 1967-71; mem. Fachbeirat Inst. Extraterrestrial Physics, Max Planck Inst., Garching, Fed. Republic Germany, 1977-83, Space Sci. Bd., NRC, 1983-86. Author; patentee in field. Guggenheim fellow, 1968, 72; recipient Space Sci. award Am. Inst. Aeros. and Astronautics, 1970, Computer Art award U.S. Users Automatic Info. Display Equipment, 1971, Sr. U.S. Scientist award Alexander von Humboldt Found., Ger., 1976, Hannes Alfven medal European Geogphys. Soc., 2000. Fellow Am. Geophys. Union (John A. Fleming award 1975); mem. Am. Phys. Soc., Am. Astron. Soc. Home: 6662 Avenida Manana La Jolla CA 92037-6228 Office: U Calif San Diego Cass 0424 La Jolla CA 92093-0424 E-mail: cmcilwain@ucsd.edu.

MCILWAIN, CLARA EVANS, agricultural economist, consultant; b. Jacksonville, Fla., Apr. 5, 1919; d. Waymon and Jerusha Lee (Dickson) Evans; m. Ivy McIlwain, May 15, 1942 (dec. 1987); children: Ronald E., Carol A. McIlwain Edwards, Marilyn E. McIlwain Moody, Ivy J. McIlwain Lindsay. BS, U. D.C., 1939; M Agrl. Econs., U. Fla., 1972. Notary pub., Va.; lic. life and health ins. agt., Md., Va., D.C. Statis. asst. Hist. and Statis. Analysis Div., Washington, 1962-67; statistician Econ Devel. Div. USDA, 1967-70, 72, agrl. economist, 1972-74; program analyst Office Equal Opportunity, USDA, 1974-79; staff writer Sci. Weekly, Chevy Chase, Md., 1988-89; ins. agt. A.L. Williams, Primerica, Camp Springs, 1990-95; min. to sr. citizens New LIght Mission Ministries, Clincon, 1995—. Workshop coord. Author: Steps to Eloquence, 1989; co-author (Min. Carol M. Edwards): Blazing the Trail to the Kingdom of God, Old Testament and New Testament, 2001: contbr. to profl. publs. Dist. coord., instr. Youth Leadership and Speechcraft, Toastmasters Internat., Washington area, 1972-78; tchr., bd. dirs. Sat. Tutorial Enrichment Program, Arlington, Va., 1988-89; mem. network Christian women, mem. women's fellowship com. Love Internat. Ch.; min. sr. citizens New Light Mission Mins., Clinton, Md., 1999-2002; asst. in strategic bus. planning advanced environ. rsch., 1995-2002. Rockefeller Found. scholar, 1970-72. Mem. Toastmasters Internat. (past pres. Potomac Club, Gavel award 1976, Able Toastmaster award 1978), Am. Assn. Notaries, So. Assn. Agrl. Economists, Nat. Assn. Agrl. Econs., Internat. Platform Assn. Avocations: teaching public speaking, tutoring, attending conventions. Office: Evans Unlimited 6612 Denny Pl Mc Lean VA 22101-5505

MCILWAIN, JOHN KNOX, housing policy fellow; b. N.Y.C., Nov. 9, 1943; s. Knox and Emily Edey (Woods) McI.; m. Wende Lillian Sheffield, Oct. 28, 1972; 1 child, Knox. AB, Princeton U., 1966; JD, NYU, 1970. Bar: N.Y. 1970, D.C. 1979. Assoc. Dewey, Ballantine, Bushby, Palmer & Wood, N.Y.C., 1970-73; dep. dir. Maine State Housing Authority, Augusta, 1976-77; exec. asst. to asst. sec. for housing Fed. Housing Commn., HUD, Washington, 1977-79; ptnr. Cohen & Uretz, 1979-84; sr. v.p. Nordheimer Bros. Co., Arlington, Va., 1984-85; ptnr. Powell, Goldstein, Frazer & Murphy, Washington, 1985-96, mng. ptnr. Washington Office, 1988-92; mng. dir. Fannie Mae Am. Cmtys. Fund, 1996-97; pres., CEO Fannie Mae Found., Washington, 1997-98; sr. mng. dir. Fannie Mae Am. Cmtys. Fund, 1998—2002; sr. resident fellow, Ronald Terwilliger chair for housing Urban Land Inst., 2002—. Bd. dirs. NationsBank Cmty. Devel. Corp., 1995-97; bd. dirs., sec. Found. for Community Leadership, Inc., 1995—. Bd. dirs., exec. com. Ctr. for Housing Policy, 1992—, editl./policy rev. com., 2000—; bd. dirs., exec. com. Nat. Housing Conf., Washington, 1980-90, treas., 1985-90, vice chmn., 1990-93, pres., 1993-97; vestryman St. Mark's Episc. Ch., Washington, 1982-86; pres. Insight Mediation Comm. of Washington, 2001—, bd. dirs., v.p. Nat. Housing and Rehab. Assn., Washington, 1988-93, pres., 1993-95; bd. dirs. Cmty. Preservation and Devel. Corp., 2001—, bd. dirs., exec. com. Washington Area Housing Partnership, 1991-96, Coun. for Excellence in Govt., 1989-92; bd. dirs. Exec. Com. Children's Hosp. Found., 1997—, mem. Princeton U. Alumni Coun. Cmty. Svc. Com., 1995-96; bd. dirs. exec. com. Children's Hosp. Found., 1997—, D.C. Agenda, 1997-98. Mem. ABA, D.C. Bar Assn. (steering com. real estate sect. 1980-82), Cosmos Club (Washington). Democrat. Avocations: sailing, skiing, music. Home: 1737 New Hampshire Ave NW Apt 4 Washington DC 20009-2522 Office: Urban Land Inst 1025 Thomas Jefferson Se NW Ste 500W Washington DC 20007-5201 Office Fax: 202-624-7140.

MC ILWAIN, WILLIAM FRANKLIN, newspaper editor, writer; b. Lancaster, S.C., Dec. 15, 1925; s. William Franklin and Docia (Higgins) McI.; m. Anne Dalton, Nov. 28, 1952 (div. 1973); children: Dalton, Nancy, William Franklin III; m. K. L. Brelsford, June 5, 1978 (div. 1983). BA, Wake Forest Coll., 1949; postgrad., Harvard, 1957-58. Various positions with Wilmington (N.C.) Star, 1943, Charlotte (N.C.) Observer, 1945, Jacksonville (Fla.) Jour., 1945, Winston-Salem (N.C.) Jour.-Sentinel, 1949-52, Richmond (Va.) Times-Dispatch, 1952-54; chief copy editor Newsday, Garden City, N.Y., 1954-57, day news editor, 1957-60, city editor, 1960-64, mng. editor, 1964-66, editor, 1967-70; writer-in-residence Wake Forest U., 1970-71; dorm leader Alcoholic Rehab. Ctr., Butner, N.C., 1971; dep. mng. editor Toronto Star, 1971-73; mng. editor The Record, Hackensack, N.J., 1973-77; editor Boston Herald Am., 1977-79; dep. editor Washington Star, 1979-81, exec. mng. editor, 1981; editor Ark. Gazette, 1981-82; founding editor N.Y. Newsday, 1982-84; exec. editor Sarasota (Fla.) Herald-Tribune, 1984-90; sr. editor N.Y. Times Regional Newspaper Group, 1991-92; chmn. Bill Mc Ilwain, Inc., 1993—. Stone Ridge lectr., 1978 Author: The Glass Rooster, 1960, (with Walter Friedenberg) Legends of Baptist Hollow, 1949; collaborator: (with Newsday staff) Naked Came The Stranger, 1969, A Farewell to Alcohol, 1973; contbr. to: Reader's Digest, Harper's, Esquire, Atlantic Monthly; editor N.C. Writer's Workshop. Mem. Pres. Johnson's Commn. on Civil Rights. With USMC, 1944. Mem. Am. Soc. Newspaper Editors, Soc. Nieman Fellows. Home and Office: 305 N Channel Dr Wrightsville Beach NC 28480-2723 *As Fats Waller said, "One never knows, do one?".*

MCINDOE, CARRIE JANET, venture capital investment company executive; b. Pitts., Oct. 2, 1960; d. Eugene Preston and Janice Gay McIndoe. BS, Boston U., 1986; cert. in spl. studies, Harvard U., 1997. Pres., founder Strategic Capital Resources, Inc., Boston, 1992—, developer bus. plan boot camp. Bd. dirs. Boston U. Met. Coll.; founder Bus. Plan Boot Camp. Tour guide art and architecture Trinith Ch., Copley Sq., Boston; bd. advisors Skidmore Coll., Women Entrepreneurs in Sci. and Tech. West, Commonwealth Inst. Mem. Boston U. Alumni Assn. (vol. 1996—), Kappa Kappa Gamma. Office: Strategic Capital Resources Inc 535 Boylston St 2d Fl Boston MA 02116-3720

MC INDOE, DARRELL WINFRED, nuclear medicine physician, former air force officer; b. Wilkinsburg, Pa., Sept. 28, 1930; s. Clarence Wilbert and Dorothy Josephine (Morrow) McIndoe; m. Carole Jean McClain, Aug. 23, 1952; children: Sherri L. McIndoe, Wendy L. McIndoe, Darrell B. McIndoe, Ronald S. McIndoe, Holly B. McIndoe. BS, Allegheny Coll., 1952; MD, Temple U., 1956, MS, 1960. Commd. 2d lt. M.C. U.S. Air Force, 1956, advanced through grades to col., 1971; intern Brooke Army Med. Ctr., San Antonio, 1956-57; resident in medicine Temple U. Med. Ctr., Phila., 1957-60; chief internal medicine and hosp. svcs. Norton AFB, 1960-64; dir. divsn. nuc. medicine St. Joseph Hosp., Towson, Md., 1992-2000; chief internal medicine and hosp. services 7520 U.S. Air Force Hosp., U.K., 1964-68; vis. rsch. fellow Royal Post Grad. Med. Sch., London, 1968-69; chief endocrinology svcs., chmn. dept. nuc. medicine USAF Med. Center, Keesler AFB, Miss., 1969-75; dep. dir. Armed Forces Radiobiology Rsch. Inst., Def. Nuc. Agy., Bethesda, Md., 1975-77, dir., 1977-79; staff physician nuclear medicine br., dept. radiology Nat. Naval Med. Ctr., Bethesda, 1979-82; sr. lectr. mil. medicine Uniformed U. of Health Scis., 1975-80, asst. prof. radiology/nuc. medicine and rsch. program coord., 1980-82; assoc. divsn. nuc. medicine St. Joseph Hosp., Towson, Md., 1982-91; ret, 2000. Med. advisor Nev. ops. office Dept. Energy, Las Vegas; cons. in field. Fellow: Am. Coll. Nuc. Physicians (regent ea. USA), Fellow royal Soc. Medicine; mem.: AMA, Soc. Med. Cons.'s to Armed Forces, Assn. Mil. Surgeons U.S., Health Physics Soc. (dir. Balt., Washington chpt.), Md. Soc. Nuc. Medicine (past pres.), Soc. Nuc. Medicine (ho. of dels.), Uniformed Svcs. Nuc. Medicine Assn. (pres. 1975), Air Force Soc. Physicians (bd. govs. 1973—77), Alexander Graham Bell Soc. Home: 15510 Foxpaw Trl Woodbine MD 21797-8000 Office: St Joseph Hosp Towson MD 21204

MC INERNEY, DENIS, lawyer; b. N.Y.C., May 31, 1925; s. Denis and Anne (Keane) McI.; m. Mary Irene Murphy, Nov. 14, 1953; children: Kathleen Mc Inerney O'Hare, Denis J., Maura Mc Inerney Romano. BSS, Fordham U., 1948, JD cum laude, 1951, LLD (hon.), 1996. Bar: N.Y. 1951, D.C. 1961. Instr. philosophy Fordham U., 1948-51; assoc. Cahill Gordon & Reindel, N.Y.C., 1951-61, ptnr., 1961-90, sr. counsel, 1991—. Vice chmn. Com. Character and Fitness Admission State Bar N.Y., 1st Jud. Dept., 1979-97, chmn. Departmental Disciplinary Com., 1st Jud. Dept., 1997—; lectr. in field. Co-author: Practitioners Handbooks for Appeals to the Appellate Divisions of the State of New York, 1979, and to the Court of Appeals of the State of New York, 1981. Bd. dirs. Vols. of Legal Svc., Inc., 1985-2001, Cath. Youth Orgn., 1975—; mem. adv. bd. St. Vincent's Hosp., Westchester, N.Y., 1988—; chmn. bd. visitors Fordham Law Sch., 1989—; trustee Fordham U., 1988-94. Sgt. 82d Airborne Divsn. U.S. Army, 1943-46, ETO. Decorated Knight of Malta, Knight of the Holy Sepulcher; recipient Achievement in Law award Fordham U., 1977; St. Thomas More award Archdiocese NY Cardinal's Com. of Laity Lawyers' Divsn., 2001 Fellow Am. Coll. Trial Lawyers (state chmn. 1980-82); mem. ABA, N.Y. State Bar Assn., Bar Assn. City N.Y., New York County Lawyers Assn. (pres. 1982-84), N.Y. County Lawyers Assn. Inn of Ct. (pres. 1996-2002), Fordham U. Law Alumni Assn. (pres. 1968-72, medal of achievement 1975). Clubs: Westchester Country, Univ. Roman Catholic. Office: Cahill Gordon & Reindel 80 Pine St Fl 20 New York NY 10005-1790 E-mail: d.mcinerney@cahill.com.

MCINERNEY, JAMES EUGENE, JR. trade association executive; b. Springfield, Mass., Aug. 3, 1930; s. James Eugene and Rose Elizabeth (Adikes) McI.; m. Mary Catherine Hill, July 17, 1963; children: Anne Elizabeth, James Eugene, III. BS, U.S. Mil. Acad., 1952; MS in Engring., Princeton U., 1960; postgrad., Royal Air Force Staff Coll., 1964; MS in Internat. Affairs, George Washington U., 1970. Commd. 2d lt. USAF, 1952, advanced through grades to maj. gen., 1976; fighter pilot Korea, Japan and Ger.; comdr. tactical fighter squadron Thailand, 1967; tactical fighter wing Ger., 1971; sr. U.S. adviser Turkish Air Force, 1973; dir. mil. assistance and sales Hdqrs. USAF, 1975-78; comdt. Indsl. Coll. Armed Forces, 1978-79; dir. programs Hdqrs. USAF, 1979-80, asst. dep. chief of staff for programs and evaluation, 1980; dir. legis. liaison McDonnell Douglas Corp., Washington, 1980-83, dir. internat. affairs, 1983-86; from v.p. to exec. v.p. Am. League for Exports and Security Assistance, 1986-92, exec. v.p., 1989-92; v.p. Am. Def. Preparedness Assn., 1992-97, Nat. Def. Indsl. Assn., 1997—. Decorated Air Force Cross, D.S.M. (2), Silver Star (3), D.F.C. (7), Bronze Star, Air medal (18); Vietnamese Crosses of Gallantry with palm and star; Republic of Korea Cheongsu medal; comdr. Order of the Brit. Empire (CBE). Mem. Air Force Assn. (citation of honor 1968, Medal of Merit, 2002), Brit.-Am. Bus. Assn.-Washington (pres. 1982-94, chmn. 1994-96), Brit.-Am. Bus. Coun. (chmn. 1996-97), Am.-Air Mus. in Britain (exec. dir. 1984—), The Jefferson Islands Club, Capitol Hill Club, Congl. Country Club. Roman Catholic. Home: 1031 Delf Dr Mc Lean VA 22101-2009

MCINERNEY, JOSEPH ALOYSIUS, hotel executive; b. Oak Park, Ill., Sept. 2, 1939; s. Joseph Aloysius and Helene (Mustari) McI.; m. Ruth McClelland, Aug. 29, 1969; children— Joseph A., Susan B. Student, Loyola U., Chgo., 1959-61; BA cum laude, Boston Coll., 1974. With Sheraton-Chgo. Hotel, 1961-65, regional dir. franchise ops., 1966-67, dir. franchise devel., 1968-69; gen. mgr. Sheraton-Winston, Salem, 1969-70; v.p., asst. to pres. Sheraton Corp., 1970-73, sr. v.p., dir. franchise ops., 1973-79; sr. v.p. Sheraton Corp., pres. Sheraton Corp. (Franchise div.), 1979-86; pres. Hawthorn Suites, 1986-91; pres., chief exec. officer Travelodge Internat., 1991-92; pres., CEO, chmn. Forte Hotels, Inc., 1992-96; CEO Pacific Asia Travel Assn., 1997-2001; pres., CEO Am. Hotel & Lodging Assn., 2001—. Guest lectr. Cornell Hotel Sch., Boston U. Hotel Sch., U. N.H. Hotel Sch., Mich. State U., San Diego State U., Okla. State U. Former mem. industry sect. adv. com. U.S. Dept. Commerce, also U.S. trade rep.; mem. adv. bd. Master Sci. degree program in hospitality industry studies at NYU; mem. hospitality adv. bd. N.Mex. State, Calif. Poly. Hosp.; former trustee Boston U. Med. Ctr., Bethune-Cookman Coll.; bd. trustees St. Vincent de Paul Village; exec. com. CEO San Diego Roundtable. Mem. Am. Hotel & Motel Assn. (govtl. affairs com.), Am. Hotel & Motel Ednl. Inst. (former chmn.). Office: Am Hotel & Lodging Assn 1201 New York Ave NW Washington DC 20005-3931 Fax: 202-289-3106. E-mail: joe@ahla.com.

MCINERNY, RALPH MATTHEW, philosophy educator, writer; b. Mpls., Feb. 24, 1929; s. Austin Clifford and Vivian Gertrude (Rush) McI.; m. Constance Terrill Kunert, Jan. 3, 1953; children: Cathleen, Mary, Anne, David, Elizabeth, Daniel. BA, St. Paul Sem., 1951; MA, U. Minn., 1952; PhD summa cum laude, Laval U., 1954; LittD (hon.), St. Benedict Coll., 1978, U. Steubenville, 1984; DHL (hon.), St. Francis Coll., Joliet, Ill., 1986; DHL, St. John Fisher Coll., 1994, St. Anselm Coll., 1995; DHS (hon.) , Our Lady Holy Cross, New Orleans. Instr. Creighton U., 1954-55; prof. U. Notre Dame, Ind., 1955—, Michael P. Grace prof. medieval studies, 1988—, dir. dept., 1978-85. Vis. prof. Cornell U., 1988, Cath. U., 1971, Louvain, 1983, 95; founder Internat. Catholic Univ.; disting. vis. prof. Truman State U., Mo., 1999. Author: (philos. works) The Logic of Analogy, 1961, History of Western Philosophy, vol. 1, 1963, vol. 2, 1968, Thomism in an Age of Renewal, 1966, Studies in Analogy, 1967, New Themes in Christian Philosophy, 1967, St. Thomas Aquinas, 1976, Ethica Thomistica, 1982, History of the Ambrosiana, 1983, Being and Predication, 1986, Miracles, 1986, Art and Prudence, 1988, A First Glance at St. Thomas: Handbook for Peeping Thomists, 1989, Boethius and Aquinas, 1989, Aquinas on Human Action, 1991, The Question of Christian Ethics, 1993, Aquinas Against the Averroists, 1993, The God of Philosophers, 1994, Aquinas and Analogy, 1996, Ethica Thomistica, 1997, Vernunftgemässes Leben, 2000, Characters in Search of Their Authors, 2001, Conversion of Edith Stein, 2001, John of St. Thomas, Summa Theologiae, 2001; (novels) Jolly Rogerson, 1967, A Narrow Time, 1969, The Priest, 1973, Gate of Heaven, 1975, Rogerson at Bay, 1976, Her Death of Cold, 1977, The Seventh Station, 1977, Romanesque, 1977, Spinnaker, 1977, Quick as a Dodo, 1978, Bishop as Pawn, 1978, La Cavalcade Romaine, 1979, Lying Three, 1979, Abecedary, 1979, Second Vespers, 1980, Rhyme and Reason, 1981, Thicker than Water, 1981, A Loss of Patients, 1982, The Grass Widow, 1983, Connolly's Life, 1983, Getting Away with Murder, 1984, And Then There Were Nun, 1984, The Noonday Devil, 1985, Sine Qua Nun, 1986, Leave of Absence, 1986, Rest in Pieces, 1985, Cause and Effect, 1987, The Basket Case, 1987, Veil of Ignorance, 1988, Abracadaver, 1989, Body and Soil, 1989, Four on the Floor, 1989, Frigor Mortis, 1989, Savings and Loan, 1990, The Search Committee, 1991, The Nominative Case, 1991, Sister Hood, 1991, Judas Priest, 1991, Easeful Death, 1991, Infra Dig, 1992, Desert Sinner, 1992, Seed of Doubt, 1993, The Basket Case, 1993, Nun Plussed, 1993, Mom and Dead, 1994, The Cardinal Offense, Law and Ardor, 1995, Let's Read Latin, 1995, Aguinas and Analogy, 1996, The Tears of Things, 1995, Half Past Nun, 1997, On This Rockne, 1997, Penguin Classic Aquinas, 1997, The Red Hat, 1998, What Went Wrong With Vatican II, 1998, Lack of the Irish, 1998, Irish Tenure, 1999, Grave Undertakings, 1999, Student Guide to Philosophy, 1999, Heirs and Parents, 2000, Shakespearean Variations, 2000, Defamation of Pius XII, 2001, Book of Kills, 2001, Triple Pursuit, 2001, Still Life, 2001, Sub Rosa, 2001, Emerald Aisle, 2001; John of St. Thomas, Summa Theologiae, 2001, Conversion of Edith Stein, 2001, editor The New Scholasticism, 1967-89; editor, pub. Crisis, 1982-96; pub. Catholic Dossier, 1995—. Exec. dir. Wethersfield Inst., 1989-92; bd. govs. Thomas Aquinas Coll., Santa Paula, Calif., 1993-2001; bd. dirs. Southern Cross Found., 1999—. With USMCR, 1946-47. Fulbright rsch. fellow, Belgium, 1959-60, NEH fellow, 1977-78, NEA fellow, 1983, Catholic Scholars fellow; Fulbright scholar, Argentina, 1986, 87, Outstanding Philosophical scholar Delta Epsilon Sigma, 1990; recipient Thomas Aquinas medal U. Dallas, 1990, Thomas Aquinas Coll., 1991, Maritain medal Am. Maritain Assn., 1994, P.G. Wodehouse award CRISIS Mag., 1995; Gifford lectr. Glasgow U., Scotland, 1999-2000. Fellow Pontifical Roman Acad. St. Thomas Aquinas; mem. Am. Philos. Assn., Am. Cath. Philos. Assn. (past pres., St. Thomas Aquinas medal 1993), Cath. Acad. Scis., Am. Metaphys. Soc. (pres. 1992), Internat. Soc. for Study Medieval Philosophy, Medieval Acad., Mystery Writers Am. (Lifetime Achievement award 1993), Authors Guild, Fellowship Cath. Scholars (pres. 1992-95, Cardinal Wright award 1996). Home: 51236 Golfview Ct Granger IN 46530-6500 Office: U of Notre Dame Jacques Maritain Ctr 714 Hesburgh Notre Dame IN 46556-5677

MCINNES, DONALD GORDON, railroad executive; b. Buffalo, Nov. 6, 1940; s. Milton Gordon and Blanche Maae (Clunk) McI.; m. Betsy Campbell, Mar. 18, 1967 (dec. Feb. 1995); children: Campbell Gordon, Cody Milton; m. Carol Anne Haverty, Oct. 12, 1996; stepchildren: Molly Caroline, Lawrence Joseph. BA, Denison U., 1963; MS, Northwestern U., 1965; Cert. in Transp., Yale U., 1965. Budget mgr. operating AT&SF R.R. Co., Chgo., 1969-71; v.p., COO Burlington No. Santa Fe Corp., 1995—; asst. trainmaster AT&SF R.R. Co., San Bernardino, Calif., 1971-73, trainmaster TEmple, Tex., 1973-76, asst. supr. Carlsbad, N.Mex., 1976-77, supt. eastern divsn. Emporia, Kans., 1977-79, supr. L.A. divsn. San Bernardino, 1979-81, asst. to exec. v.p. Chgo., 1981-82, gen. supt. transp., 1983-87, gen. mgr. transp., 1987, gen. mgr. ea. region, 1988, v.p. adminstrn., 1989, v.p. intermodal, 1989-91, sr. v.p. intermodal, 1991-93, sr. v.p., COO, 1994-95. Bd. dirs. AT & SF Railway Co., TTX Corp., leader of group Intermodal Assn. N.Am., 1st chmn., 1991-93; bd. chmn. Intermodal Assn. N.Am. Found., Washington; bd. dirs. Thrall Car Mfg., Chgo. Trustee Vt. Acad., Saxtons River; chmn. bd. Found. for Intermodal Rsch. and Edn., Washington. Served to 2d lt. USAF, 1965-67; capt. U.S. Army, 1967-69. Decorated Bronze Star. Mem. Pass Club (Boca Grande, Fla.), Boca Grande Pass Yacht Club, Lemon Bay Golf Club (Englewood, Fla.), Ballymeade

Country Club (North Falmouth, Mass.), Coral Creek Club (Placida, Fla.), Falmouth Yacht Club. Home: PO Box 278 148 Carrick Bend Ln Boca Grande FL 33921 also: 75 Waterside Ave Falmouth MA 02540-3825 E-mail: dgmc@flash.net.

MC INNES, WILLIAM CHARLES, priest, academic administrator; b. Boston, Jan. 20, 1923; s. William Charles and Mary (Byrne) Mc Innes. BS, Boston Coll., 1946, AB, 1950, MA, 1951; STL, Weston Coll., 1958; PhD, N.Y. U., 1955. Joined Soc. of Jesus, 1946; ordained priest Roman Cath. Ch., 1957; prof. mktg. and bus. ethics Sch. Bus. Adminstrn. Boston Coll., 1959-63, assoc. dean Sch. Bus. Adminstrn., 1961-63, dir. honors program, 1963-64, mem. citizens seminar planning com., 1959-63, v.p. Nat. Jesuit Honor Soc., 1997—99; pres. Fairfield (Conn.) U., 1964-73, prof. urban problems, 1969-72; pres. U. San Francisco, 1972-77, Assn. Jesuit Colls. and Univs., 1977-89; campus min. U. Conn., Storrs, 1990-96. Vis. fellow Woodstock Theol. Ctr., 1990—91. Life mem. United Cerebral Palsy Assn. Fairfield County; mem. adv. com. Conn. Dept. Social Svcs., 1993—96; chaplain Boston Coll. Alumni Assn.; past chmn. bd. dirs. ABCD (cmty. action agys.); bd. dirs. Nat. Better Bus. Bur.; past pres. Conn. Assn. Cmty. Action Programs; founder Fairfield County Cmty. Forum Conn. Charter Oak Coll.; vice chmn. Nat. Better Bus. Bur. Found.; chmn. Calif. Coun. Humanities; dir. Support Our Aging Religious. Served to capt. USAAF, 1942—46, CBI. Mem.: Alpha Epsilon Delta, Phi Kappa Theta, Delta Sigma Pi, Alpha Sigma Nu, Beta Gamma Sigma. Home: Jesuit Cmty Boston Coll Chestnut Hill MA 02467 E-mail: MCINNEWI@bc.edu.

MCINNIS, SCOTT STEVE, congressman, lawyer; b. Glenwood Springs, Colo., May 9, 1953; s. Kohler McInnis and Carol Kreir; m. Lori McInnis; children: Daxon, Tessa, Andrea. BA, Ft. Lewis Coll., 1975; JD, St. Mary's Law Sch., 1980. Atty. Delaney & Balcomb P.C., Glenwood Springs, Colo., 1981—; mem. Colo. State Ho. of Reps., 1984-93, chmn. agrl. livestock and natural resources com., 1986-90, majority leader, 1990-92; mem. U.S. Ho. Reps. 103d-106th Congresses from 3d Colo. Dist., 1993—; mem. rules com. U.S. Ho. Reps., 1998, mem. house ways and means com., 2001—, chmn.resources subcom. on forests and forest health. Recipient Florence Sabin award, 1984, Guardian of Small Bus. award Nat. Fed. Ind. Bus., 1990, Lee Atwater Leadership award, 1991, and various awards from United Vets. Commn.; named Legislator of Decade and Legislator of Yr by Colo. Ski Country and Colo. Wildlife Found. Mem. Elks, Rotary, Phi Delta Phi. Republican. Roman Catholic. Office: US Ho Reps 320 Cannon Hob Washington DC 20515

MCINTIRE, LARRY VERN, chemical engineering educator; b. St. Paul, June 28, 1943; s. James Lawrence and Lenore Vineal (Converse) McI.; m. Suzanne G. Eskin, June 27, 1997. BChemE, MS, Cornell U., 1966; MA, Princeton U., 1968, PhD, 1970. Registered profl. engr., Tex. Asst. prof. Rice U., Houston, 1970-74, assoc. prof., 1974-78, prof. chem. engring., 1978—, E.D. Butcher prof., 1983—, chmn. dept., 1981-91, chmn. Bioscis. and Bioengring. Inst., 1991—, chmn. rsch. coun., 1988-91, dir. Biomed. Engring. Lab., 1980—, chmn. dept. biomed. engring., 1997—; spke faculty coun., 1994-95. Adj. prof. medicine Baylor Coll. Medicine, Houston, 1982—, U. Tex. Med. Sch., Houston, 1982—; chmn. blood/materials working group NIH, Bethesda, Md., 1982-85; mem. surgery and bioengring. study sect. NIH, 1984-88, 99—; mem. com. on bioprocessing NRC, 1991-94; chmn. rheology subcom. Internat. Coun. on Thrombosis and Hemostasis, 1985-89. Contbr. over 225 articles to profl. jours. Recipient Merit award NIH, 1989; NSF fellow Cornell U., Princeton U., 1965-69, NATO-NSF postdoctoral fellow Imperial Coll., London, 1976-77. Fellow Am. Inst. Med. Biol. Engring. (sec., treas. 1993-96, pres. 1997-98), AICHE (officer local sect. 1980-81, 86, Food Pharm. and Bioengring. divsn. award 1992, divsn. chair 1998), AAAS; mem. Biomed. Engring. Soc. (bd. dirs. 1992-97, pres. 1995-96, Disting. lectr. 1992), N.Am. Soc. Biorheology (v.p. 1992-94, pres. 1994-96), N.Y. Acad. Scis., Am. Heart Assn. (coun. on thrombosis, exec. com. 1994—), Faculty Club Rice U. (bd. dirs., chmn. 1982-84), Sigma Xi (nat. lectr. 1993-96), Nat. Acad. Engring. Presbyterian. Avocations: tennis, squash, classical music, hiking. Office: Rice U Inst Bioscis and Bioengring John W Cox Lab Biomed Engring Houston TX 77251-1892

MCINTIRE, MARY, university administrator; b. Chgo., Nov. 23, 1943; d. Philip Thomas and Helen Marie McEnery; m. Larry Vern McIntire, July 5, 1969 (div. May 1995); m. James Robert Pomerantz, May 23, 1998; stepsons: Andrew, William. BA, U. Fla., 1965, MA, 1968; PhD, Rice U., 1975. Instr. U. Houston, 1970-71, Rice U., Houston, 1977-78, program dir. Office Continuing Studies, 1977-81, dir., 1981-86, dean Sch. Continuing Studies, 1986—. Cons. Tex. Internat. Edn. Consrtium, Austin, 1998—; pres. adv. bd. Tex. Humanities Resource Ctr., Austin, 1992-93. Mem. Harris County Hist. Commn., Houston, 1978-81, 85-87; mem. exec. com. San Jacinto Girl Scouts, 1998—, bd. dirs., 2000—; mem. allocations com. Gulf Coast United Way, 1991-98, mem. adv. bd., 2001-; mem. adv. bd. Casa de Esperanza, 2000—; pres. Emerald Cir., 2000-02, bd. dirs., 1998—; mem. adv. bd. Yes Acad., 2001-. Recipient Meritorious Svc. award Rice U. Alumni Assn., 1998; named YWCA Woman of Yr. in Edn., Houston, 1994, Woman of Distinction, Greater Houston Women's Found., 1997, Woman on the Move, Tex. Exec. Women, 1999. Mem. Univ. Continuing Edn. Assn. (commr. 1998-2001), Rsch. Univ. Deans of Continuing Edn., Tex. Assn. Cmty. Svc. and Continuing Edn. (pres. 1986). Avocations: aerobics, swimming, hiking. Home: 1016 Barkdull St Houston TX 77006 Office: Rice U Sch Continuing Studies MS 550 PO Box 1892 Houston TX 77251-1892 E-mail: maryb@rice.edu.

MCINTIRE, WILLIAM TREDICK, II, municipal official, investment banker; b. Red Bank, N.J., Dec. 18, 1925; s. Frank and Elizabeth Bel (Ewing) McI.; m. Patricia Marie Mickleburgh, May 22, 1954; children: William Tredick III, Henry Dickson. AB, Harvard U., 1947; cert., U. Geneva, 1949. Salesman Dominick & Dominick, N.Y.C., 1949-57; asst. v.p. R.S. Dickson & Co., 1957-63; v.p. Shearson Hammill, 1963-66, White Weld & Co., N.Y.C., 1966-70; pres. Kleinwort Benson Inc., 1970-86; treas. Town of Darien, Conn., 1987—. Vol. exec. Internat. Exec. Svc. Corp., Stamford, Conn., 1987-93. Pres. Darien Red Cross, 1972-74, Darien Hist. Soc., 1976-80. Lt. USN, 1965-75. Recipient Congl. Cert. of Appreciation, U.S. Congress, 1993, Svc. award Gov. of Conn., 1997. Mem. Tokeneke Club, Harvard Club of N.Y.C., Rep. Club of Darien. Home: 9 Hickory Ln Darien CT 06820-3211 Office: Town of Darien 2 Renshaw Rd Darien CT 06820-5397

MCINTOSH, AMY BENNETT, publishing/internet company executive; b. Cin., Apr. 14, 1958; d. Robert Charles McIntosh and Nancy Allensworth Drysdale; m. Jeffrey Ross Toobin, May 31, 1986; children: Ellen Frances Toobin, Adam Jerome Toobin. AB, Harvard U., 1980, MBA, 1984. Various positions Am. Express, N.Y.C., 1984-99, v.p. mktg., 1991-93, sr. v.p. mktg., 1993-95; v.p. consumer mktg. Bell Atlantic (previously Nynex), 1995-98, pres., CEO, Network Data, Inc., 1998-2000; CEO Zagat Survey, 2000—. Rsch. analyst Bain & Co., Boston, 1980-82. Chmn. bd., Teach for Am.-N.Y., N.Y.C., 1997—. Mem. Internet Industry Assn. Am. (bd. mem. 1998-2000).

MCINTOSH, CAROLYN LEIGH, lawyer; b. Boulder, Colo., Dec. 10, 1955; d. Glen Elvis and Alice Joy McIntosh; m. Roger Alan bucholz, Oct. 4, 1980 (div. Dec. 1998); m. Leland Kioshi Marable, Dec. 11, 1998. BA cum laude, Middlebury Coll., 1978; JD, U. Colo., 1981. Bar: Colo. 1981, U.S. Dist. Ct. Colo. 1981, Mon. 1988 (specially admitted), U.S. Dist. Ct. Mont. 1989. Rsch. asst. Rocky Mountain Mineral Law Found., Boulder, 1979-80; assoc. Sisk, Foley, Hultin & Driver, Denver, 1981-83, Hultin, Driver & Spaanstra, Denver, 1983-85; asst. atty. gen. Colo. Dept. of Law, 1986-88; assoc. Cogswell & Wehrle, 1988-89, shareholder, 1989-90; spl. asst. atty. gen. State of Mont., 1988-90; sr. assoc. Patton, Boggs & Blow, Denver, 1990-92; ptnr. Patton Boggs, LLP, 1992—, mng. ptnr. Denver office, 1993—2002. Assoc. adj. prof. Colorado Sch. Mines, 1991-2000—; mem., atty. program to provide legal svcs. to indigent, Denver, 1982-86. Mem. procedural rules subcom. Colo. Air Quality Control Commn., 1983-84; mem. Lafayette Planning Commn., 1986-87, 95-99, Lafayette City Coun., 1987-99, mayor pro tem, 1989-91, mayor, 1995-99; mem. bd. Denver Regional Coun. Govts., 1990-99; mem. Regional Air Quality Coun., 1992-99, mem. exec. com., 1996-99; mem. Colo. Water Conservation Bd., 2001--. Mem. ABA (natural resources sect.), Colo. Bar Assn., Denver Bar Assn. (legal fees arbitration com. 1983-84, 86-87), Alliance Profl. Women (bd. dirs. 1986-90), Internat. Inst. Environ. Risk Mgmt. (bd. govs. 1996—). Office: Patton Boggs 1660 Lincoln St Ste 1900 Denver CO 80264-1901 E-mail: cmcintosh@pattonboggs.com. *Notable cases include: Environ. Def. Fund vs. Colo. Dept. Health, 1986, defending against unsuccessful challenge to the State of Colo.'s prevention of significant deterioration air quality regulations; State of Colo. vs. Idarado Mine Co., 1989, prosecution of superfund clean up claims against Idarado; Denver vs. Adolph Coons Co., et al, superfund cost recovery action.*

MCINTOSH, CAROLYN MEADE, retired educational administrator; b. Waynesburg, Ky., Oct. 21, 1928; d. Clarence Hobert and Sarah Letitia (Bentley) Meade; m. Edgar G. McIntosh, Aug. 21, 1948; children: Wayne, Jeanne, Penny, Jimmi, Carol. BS, Miami U., Oxford, Ohio, 1962; MEd, Xavier U., Cin., 1966. Elem. tchr., Ohio, 1961-79; prin. New Richmond (Ohio) Sch. Dist., 1980-91, ret., 1991. Tchr. Clermont County Adult Edn. Program, 1970-95, Clermont County dir.of Headstart 1971-72, Clearmont County Rep. to Ohio elem. adminstr., 1985-87, Pres. Clermont and Brown County adminstr., 1988-89; apptd. student achievement liaison team, New Richmond Bd. Edn. Editor Ret. Tchrs. Newsletter. Pres. New Richmond Bd. Edn.; v.p. U.S. Grant Vocat. Sch. Bd. Edn.; mem. Clermont County Excellence in Edn. Com.; mem. edn. adv. com. Clermont Coll., mem. long range planning com., 1999; ; mem. adv. bd. Bethany Children's Home; mem. Clermont 2001 Com.; mem. Rep. Ctrl. Com. of Clermont County; mem. New Richmond Continuous Improvement Com., 1999; mem. Clermont County Kids Voting Com.; mem. com. Renaissance New Richmond. Recipient New Richmond Adminstr. of the Yr. award City of New Richmond, 1989; named citizen of yr. Monroe Twp., 1996; selected for sr. leadership charter class, Clermont 2000—. Mem. AAUW, ASCD, NAESP, Nat. Sch. Bd. Assn., Ohio Sch. Bd. Assn., Ohio Assn. Elem. Sch. Adminstrs. (all county legis. liaison), Ohio County Ret. Tchrs. Assn., Clermont County Ret. Tchrs. Assn. (pres.), Order Eastern Star, Clermont County Comm. Svcs. Bd. (apptd. 1998), Phi Delta Kappa, Delta Kappa Gamma (pres. chpt.). Baptist.

MCINTOSH, CECILIA ANN, biochemist, educator; b. Dayton, Ohio, Apr. 30, 1956; d. Russell Edward McIntosh and Geraldine Rita (Cochran) Slemp; m. Kevin Smith Schweiker, May 28, 1978 (div. Mar. 1989); children: Katrina Lynn McIntosh Schweiker, Rebecca Sue McIntosh Schweiker. BA in Biology cum laude, U. South Fla., 1977, MA in Botany, 1981, PhD in Biology, 1990. Rsch. assoc. U. South Fla., Tampa, 1981-86; sci. mentor Ctr. for Excellence, U. So. Fla., 1984-90; tchg. and rsch. asst. dept. biology U. South Fla., 1986-90; postdoctoral fellow dept. biochemistry U. Idaho, Moscow, 1990-93; asst. prof. dept. biol. scis. East Tenn. State U., Johnson City, 1993-98, assoc. prof., 1998—, grad. student coord., 1997—; adj. assoc. prof. dept. biochemistry Quillen Coll. Medicine East Tenn. State U., 1995—. Sci. mentor U. So. Fla. Ctr. for Excellence, Tampa, 1984-90; rsch. forum judge Coll. Medicine Rsch. Forum, East Tenn. State U., Johnson City, 1994—. Contbr. articles to sci. jours. including Plant Sci., Plant Physiology, Archives Biochemistry and Biophysics. Sci. fair judge East Tenn. Regional Sci. Fair, Johnson City, 1994—. Strenghthening program grantee USDA, 1994-95, 97-98, Seed grantee, 1995-97, plant genetic mechanisms grantee, 1998-2001; rsch. devel. grantee East Tenn. State U. Rsch. Devel. Coun., 1994-96, 97-98, 2001-2002; grantee USDA NRI, 1998-2001; co-grantee Howard Hughes Med. Inst., 2000-. Mem. Am. Assn. Women in Sci., Am. Soc. Plant Physiologists, Phytochem. Soc. N.Am. (treas. 1998-2002), Sigma Xi (sci. fair workshop coord. Appalachian chpt. 1995, Dissertation award 1991). Achievements include characterization of new enzyme in plant flavonoid biosynthesis; biochemical characterization of plant mitochondrial membrane tricarboxylate and phosphate transporters and TCA cycle enzymes. Avocations: outdoor activities, sports, mysteries. Office: East Tenn State U Dept Biol Scis Box 70 703 Johnson City TN 37614-0703 E-mail: mcintosc@etsu.edu.

MCINTOSH, DAVID M. former congressman; b. June 8, 1958; m. Ruthie McIntosh. Grad., Yale Coll., 1980, U. Chgo., 1983. Bar: Ind., U.S. Supreme Ct. Spl. asst. domestic affairs to Pres. Reagan; spl. asst. to Atty. Gen. Meese; liaison Pres.'s Commn. on Privatization; spl. asst. to V.P. Quayle, dep. legal counsel to; exec. dir. Pres.'s Coun. on Competitiveness; sr. fellow Citizens for a Sound Economy; founder Federalist Soc. for Law & Pub. Policy, now co-chmn.; mem. U.S. Congress from Ind., Washington, 1995-2001; ptnr. Mayer, Brown, Rowe and Maw, 2002—; prof., dept of econ. Ball St. Univ. Sch. of Bus., 2002—. Mem. State Bar of Ind. Republican. Office: PO Box 3300 Muncie IN 47307 also: Mayer Brown Rowe nad Maw 1909 K St NW Washington DC 20006 E-mail: dmcintosh@mayerbrown.com.

MCINTOSH, DECOURCY EYRE, independent scholar and writer; b. Balt., Dec. 1, 1942; s. David Gregg and Grace (Wright) McI.; m. Susan Reed Bell, Nov. 11, 1967; children: Madeline Eyre, David Gregg. AB, Harvard U., 1965. Program officer Richard King Mellon Found., Pitts., 1969-74; exec. dir. Hist. Savannah (Ga.) Found., 1974-77; mng. dir. Minn. Landmarks, St. Paul, 1977-79; v.p. Mpls. Soc. Fine Arts, 1979-84; exec. dir. Helen Clay Frick Found., Pitts., 1984—, Frick Art and Hist. Ctr., Pitts., 1990—2001. Editor: (exhbn. catalogues) 19th Century French Drawings from Lyon, 1992, Renaissance & Baroque Bronzes in The Frick Art Museum, 1993, Florentine Drawings of the 17th & 18th Centuries from Lille, 1994; co-author: Collecting in the Gilded Age: Art Patronage in Pittsburgh, 1890-1910, 1997, Gérome and Goupil: Art and Enterprise, 2000, The Collector as Patron in the 20th Century, 2000; contbr. articles to profl. jours. Trustee Pitts. History & Landmarks, 1984—, Art Svcs. Internat., Alexandria, 1990-98; bd. dirs. Pitts. Parks & Playgrounds Fund, 1986—; exhbns. com. Am. Fedn. Arts., N.Y. Mem. Am. Assn. Mus., Century Assn., Pitts. Golf Club, Walpole Soc. Office: 19 E 70th St New York NY 10021

MCINTOSH, DENNIS KEITH, veterinarian, consultant; b. Newark, June 12, 1941; s. Sheldon Weeks and Enid Nicholson (Casey) McI.; children: Kevin, Jamie. BS in Animal Sci., Tex. A&M U., 1963, BS in Vet. Sci., 1967, DVM, 1968. Asst. county agrl. agt., Cleburne, Tex., 1963-65; owner, operator Park North Animal Hosp., San Antonio, 1970-75, El Dorado Animal Hosp., San Antonio, 1973—. Co-chmn. vet. tech. adv. coun. Palo Alto Coll. tchr. Animal Health Tech., San Antonio Coll., 1985-95; pres., mgr. Bexar County Emergency Animal Clinic, Inc., 1978-81; cons. vet. practice mgmt., mktg., client rels.; spkr. for vet. meetings, assns.; co-host Ask the Vet, Adopt a Pet, Sta. KENS-TV, 1980-93; vet. mem. Tex. Bd. Health, 1984-89, chmn. disease control com., pers. com.; mem. environ. health, hosps. com. Team capt. Alamo Roundup Club and Pres.' Club of San Antonio C. of C., 1970-75; mem. Guadalupe County Youth Fair Bd., 1978-80. Contbg. author: Mosby's Review Questions and Answers for Veterinary Boards, 1998, Chicken Soup for the Pet Lover's Soul, 1998; contbr. articles to profl. jours. With Vet. Corps, USAF, 1968-70. Recipient Alumnus award Guadalupe County 4-H Club, 1979, Outstanding Svc. award San Antonio Coll., 1986-87, Outstanding Bus. Ptnrs. award N.E. Ind. Sch. Dist., 1995-96. Mem. AMVA, Tex. Vet. Med. Assn. (pres., chmn. bd. dirs.), Tex. Acad. Vet. Practice (pres.), Am. Assn. Human-Animal Bond Vets., Vet. Hosp. Mgrs. Assn., San Antonio C. of C. (life), Tex. County Agrl. Agts. Assn. (4th v.p. 1964), Delta Soc. (pres. San Antonio chpt. 1989-90). Office: 13039 Nacogdoches Rd San Antonio TX 78217-1960 E-mail: dennis.mcintosh@att.net.

MC INTOSH, JAMES EUGENE, JR. interior designer; b. Dadeville, Ala., Nov. 13, 1938; s. James Eugene and Jessie (Latimer) McI. B.Interior Design, Auburn (Ala.) U., 1961. Designer contract div. Rich's Dept. Store, Atlanta, 1961-64; assoc. William Trapnell & Assocs., 1964-70; dir. Interior Concepts, Inc., 1970-72; dir. design comml. design div. Rich's Dept. Store, 1972-80; v.p. Comml. Interior Designs, Inc., 1980-82; exec. staff Rollins Inc., 1982—; pres. Gene Mc Intosh & Assocs., 1985—. Fellow Am. Soc. Interior Designers (Presdl. citation 1974); mem. Nat. Trust Hist. Preservation, Ala. Hist. Soc., High Mus. Art, Soc. Archtl. Historians. Office: Gene McIntosh & Assocs PO Box 81161 Conyers GA 30013-9161 E-mail: genem@starband.net.

MCINTOSH, JOHN OSBORN, engineering consultant; b. St. Petersburg, Fla., Apr. 4, 1955; s. Albert Parsons and Joan Lillian (Osborn) McI.; m. Marie-Louise Miller, Mar. 21, 1975 (div. Mar. 1983); 1 child, Heather Louise. BSEE, U. Cen. Fla., 1976, MSEE, 1979; MBA, Ea. Tenn. State U., 1984. Project mgr. Tex. Instruments, Johnson City, Tenn., 1977-82, Distributed Processing Tech., Maitland, Fla., 1982-83, GE, Plymouth, 1983-86; owner McIntosh & Assocs., Orlando, 1986-87; pres. McIntosh & Dwyer Securities Corp., Winter Park, 1988-89, Sunshine Securities, Oviedo, 1990—; engring. educator U. Cen. Fla., Orlando, 1989-98; cons. SLB Computer Tech. Inc., 1998—. Owner, operator Ancient Artifacts and Treasures. V.p., pres., bd. dirs. Camarata Inc.-Opera Chorus, Orlando, 1985-91; active Jaycees, Orlando, 1987-88. Mem. IEEE (STD 730 software quality assurance standard com.), IEEE Tenn. Coun. (treas. 1981-82), IEEE Computer Sci.-Tri City (co-founder 1980), Inst. Indsl. Engrs., Mensa, Tampa Bay Fossil Club, Fla. Fossil Hunters, Eta Kappa Nu, Tau Beta Pi, Alpha Pi Mu. Republican. Methodist. Achievements include patent for Intelligent Hysteresis for a Digital Setback Thermostat; research on digital architecture for a computer based imaging system. Avocations: paleontology, church solo singing. Office: Ciber Inc 2180 SR 434 West Ste 2150 Longwood FL 32779-5011 E-mail: john@mcintosh55.com.

MCINTOSH, JON CHARLES, illustrator, graphic designer; b. Alliance, Ohio, Aug. 8, 1947; s. John Cowles and Lucile Tipple (Ketcham) McI.; 1 child, Forgan Cowles; m. Jean Bogart Goodman, Apr. 24, 1993; stepchildren: Buffy Trott, Hays Spangler Trott. Student, Hobart Coll., 1965-67; BFA, R.I. Sch. of Design, 1974. Pres. McIntosh Ink, Inc., Vineyard Haven, Mass., 1971—. Bd. ov overseers New Eng. Conservatory of Music, Boston, 1989-95; bd. dirs. Sail Martha's Vineyard. Illustrator: (book) The Foolish Dinosaur Fiasco, 1978, The Mysterious Zetabet, 1980, The Doctor's Handbook, 1982, Witch Way to The Country, 1995, Witch Way to the Beach, 1997, The Longest Hair in the World, 1999; author, illustrator: Hooked On Golf, 1986. Artwork contbr. Ducks Unltd; art for advt. Bose, Wang, Digital, NASA. Recipient Silver medal V.I. Internat. Film Festival, 1976, Gold medal Soc. of Newspaper Designers, 1985, First place Francis Hatch Advt. Awards, 1987, First place New Eng. Newspaper Awards, 1998, Silver award Soc. Newspaper Designers, 2000. Mem. Soc. of Illustrators (Silver Funny Bone 1991), The Country Club, The West Chop Club. Republican. Episcopalian. Avocations: musician, ski racing, tennis, fishing, skeet shooting. Office: MacIntosh Ink Inc 620 Elizabeth St Key West FL 33040

MCINTOSH, LINDA CLAIR, special education program specialist; b. Dayton, Ohio, Sept. 5, 1948; d. Henry and Virginia (Harvey) Clair; m. Charles McIntosh, Oct. 19, 1985. BS in Edn., Wright State U., 1984. Cert. qualified mental retardation profl., spl. edn. and elem. tchr., program specialist, Ohio. Family care coord. Toward Independence, Xenia, Ohio, 1980-84; program specialist II Montgomery Bd. of Mental Retardation and Devel. Disabilities, Dayton, 1984—; co-owner Tri County Commercial McIntosh Comml. Refrigeration, 1990—. Recipient Erin Ritchey Meml. Challenge award Ohio Pub. Images Region I, 1991; Ky. Col., 1992. Roman Catholic. Office: 2122 Jergens Rd Dayton OH 45404-1228

MCINTOSH, L(ORNE) WILLIAM, marketing executive; b. Kingston, Ont., Can., May 1, 1945; s. Jack Lorne and Lillian (Oaks) McI.; m. Siobhan McAfee, May 18, 1998. BSBA, Lehigh U., 1967, MBA, 1968. Asst. prof. Union Coll., Cranford, N.J., 1968-72; sr. market rsch. analyst Merck, Sharp & Dohme, West Point, Pa., 1972-75, advt. copywriter, 1975-77, product mgr., 1977-80, assoc. dir. advt., 1980-82, dir. licensing and acquisitions, 1982, sr. dir. mktg., 1983-86; exec. v.p. mktg. Medco Containment Svcs., Inc., Fair Lawn, N.J., 1987-88; v.p. mktg. and bus. devel. Boehringer Mannheim Pharms., Rockville, Md., 1988-92; chmn. bd., chief exec. officer Target Mktg. Systems, Inc., Blue Bell, Pa., 1992-93; sr. v.p. bus. devel. and com. ops. Zynaxis, Inc., Malvern, 1993—95; sr. cons. SmithKline Beecham, Phila., 1995—97; sr. v.p. bus. devel. and fin., CFO VIMRx Pharms. Inc., 1995—97, Nexell Therapeutics, Irvine, Calif., 1997—98, pres., COO, 1998—2000; exec. v.p., CBO FASgen, Inc., 2001—. Mem. Am. Econ. Assn., Am. Mktg. Assn., Lic. Execs. Soc., Antique Automobile Club Am., Model A Ford Club Am., Vintage Chevrolet Club Am., Pontiac Oakland Owners Club, Beta Gamma Sigma. Avocations: antique automobiles, woodworking, antique furniture restoration, music. Home: 1711 Cannongate Rd Forest Hill MD 21050-2203 E-mail: Mcamci@msn.com.

MCINTOSH, MARTHA ANN, retired educator, religious education director; b. Columbus, Ohio, July 24, 1930; d. James H. and Bernadine (Siemer) Uhl; m. Richard H. McIntosh, June 13, 1953; children: Marie, Theresa, Mariam, Richard, Peter. BS in Edn., Ohio State U., 1952; MA in Edn., U. South Fla., 1977; BA in Religious Studies, St. Leo (Fla.) Coll., 1986. Tchr. elem. sch., Columbus Ohio, Crystal, Lake, Ill., Tampa, Fla., 1952-80; dir. religious edn. St. Patrick's Ch., Tampa, Fla., 1980-87, Christ the King Ch., Tampa, 1987-96. Mem. religious edn. handbook com., 1984-86, religious edn. advisory bd. Diocese St. Petersburg, Fla., 1986-89, spkr. catechist enrichment days, 1979-91. Contbr. articles to religious and secular mags. including Wordsmith. Recipient Religious Edn. Excellence Regional award Nat. Cath. Edn. Assn. and Nat. Parish Coords. and Dirs., Washington, 1994. Home: 4115 W Wyoming Ave Tampa FL 33616-1147 E-mail: martham@rapidsys.com.

MCINTOSH, MOLLY JEAN, interior designer; b. Spokane, Wash., Feb. 4, 1951; d. Keith L. and Dolores J. (Hensel) Yates; m. Forrest E. McIntosh, Dec. 18, 1971; children: Jennifer, Brandon. Student, N.W. Christian Coll., 1971. Archtl. signage salesperson Clarke & Assoc., Santa Ana, Calif., 1983-84; interior designer Precept Design, Worthington, Ohio, 1984-85, Gracious Living, Redmond, Wash., 1985—. Recipient Silver award Master Builder Assn., 1994. Mem. Am. Soc. Interior Designers (allied mem., showhouse com. 1998), N.W. Soc. Interior Designers (profl. mem., 2d pl. for residential design 1994). Mem. Christian Ch. (Disciples Of Christ). Avocation: traveling. Fax: (425) 836-0311.

MCINTOSH, ROBERTA EADS, retired social worker; b. Milw., Oct. 1, 1936; d. Robert Howard and Carlene (Rosboro) Eads; m. James Stuart Cameron McIntosh, Sept. 19, 1959; children: Ronald Stuart, Ian Robert, Peter Cameron. BA, Bucknell U., 1958; MS in Social Adminstrn., Case Western Reserve U., 1977. Lic. social worker, Ohio, Fla. Foster care caseworker Monroe County Child Welfare, Rochester, N.Y., 1958-63; group home counselor Betterway, Inc., Elyria, Ohio, 1974-75; group program coord. Elyria YWCA, 1975; caseworker, group home supr. Lorain County Children's Svcs., Elyria, 1977-83; treatment counselor Glenbeigh Adolescent Hosp., Cleve., 1984-86; youth dir. Washington Ave. Christian Ch., Elyria, 1984-85; outreach counselor Spouse Abuse Shelter Religious Community Svcs., Clearwater, Fla., 1986-93; pvt. practice Dunedin, 1993-97; ret., 1997; substitute tchr. Pinellas County Schs., 2000—. Bd. pres. Elyria YWCA, 1972—75; sec., pres. Cmty. Coordinated Child Care, Lorain County, 1970—72; del. to Russia Nat. Coalition Against Domestic Violence; vol. Religious Cmty. Svcs., Women's Peacepower Found.; vol. long term care ombudsman dist. 5B North Pinellas County, 2001—; bd. dirs. Religious Cmty. Svcs., 1998—2002, Women's Peacepower Found., 2001—. Named Friend of Guidance Guidance Counselors Assn., 1982, Woman of Interest Elyria YWCA and City of Elyria, 1985. Mem.: NASW, Emmanuel Cmty. Ch. (bd. dirs. 2000—), Ctrl. Christian Ch. Christian Womens Fellowship (pres. 1988—89), Victim Rights Coalition Pinellas County (v.p. bd. 1992—93), Deaf Svc. Ctr. (bd. dirs. 1991—94), Leadership Pinellas, Fla. Coalition Against Domestic Violence (v.p. bd. 1993—94), Acad. Cert. Social Workers, Delta Zeta (alumni pres. 1998—2001). Democrat. Avocations: walking, gardening, reading, grandchildren. Home: 1501 Pleasant Grove Dr Dunedin FL 34698-2341

MCINTOSH, TERRIE TUCKETT, lawyer; b. Ft. Lewis, Wash., July 20, 1944; d. Robert LeRoy and Elda (Perry) Tuckett; m. Clifton Dennis McIntosh, Oct. 13, 1969; children: Alison, John. BA, U. Utah, 1967; MA, U. Ill., 1970; JD, Harvard U., 1978. Bar: N.Y. 1979, Utah 1980. Assoc. Hughes, Hubbard & Reed, N.Y.C., 1978-79, Fabian & Clendenin, Salt Lake City, 1979-84, shareholder, 1984-86; staff atty. Questar Corp., 1986-88, sr. atty., 1988-92, sr. corp. counsel, 1992—. Instr. philosophy Douglass Coll. Rutgers U., New Brunswick, N.J., 1971-72; mem. adv. com. civil procedure Utah Supreme Ct., Salt Lake City, 1987—; mem. jud. nominating com. 5th Cir. Ct., Salt Lake City, 1986-88. Mem. Utah State Bar (ethics and discipline screening panel 1989-96, vice chair ethics and discipline com. 1996-99, co-chair law related edn. com. 1985-86), Women Lawyers of Utah (chair exec. com. 1986-87), Salt Lake Legal Aid Soc. (trustee 1999—), Harvard Alumni Assn. Utah (bd. dirs. 1987—), Phi Beta Kappa, Phi Kappa Phi. Office: Questar Corp PO Box 45433 180 E 1st S Salt Lake City UT 84111-1502

MCINTOSH, WILLIAM DAVID, mathematics educator; b. Pryor, Okla., Oct. 14, 1936; s. Marion Maynard and Willma Mary McIntosh; m. Elizabeth Jeanette McIntosh, June 16, 1974. Student, El Dorado Jr. Coll., 1954-56; BA, Southwestern Coll., 1958; MA, U. Kans., 1960, PhD, 1965. Asst. prof. math. U. Mo., Columbia, 1965-70; prof. math. Cen. Meth. Coll., Fayette, 1970—, chmn. dept. math., 1970-80. Mem. AAUP, Am. Math. Soc., Math. Assn. of

Am. United Methodist. Avocation: music. Home: 323 Green Acres Dr Fayette MO 65248 Office: Cen Meth Coll 411 Central Methodist Sq Fayette MO 65248 E-mail: wmcintos@cmc2.cmc.edu.

MCINTURFF, FLOYD M. retired state agency administrator; b. Greenback, Tenn., May 1, 1923; s. Samuel Floyd and Hazel Agnes (Vaden) M.; m. Merle Celeste Sosna, May 27, 1950; children: Judith Margaret, Laura Ellen, Melissa Ann. BS, U. Tenn., Knoxville, 1950. Asst. to the chief engr., missiles Rockwell Internat., Columbus, 1957-73; chief, targeted jobs tax credit program Ohio Bur. Employment Svcs., 1974-88; ret., 1988. Commd. officer U.S. Army Signal Corps., 1942-46, 51-52. Mem. Opera Columbus, Columbus Astron. Soc., Am. Atheists, Sons of Revolution, First Families of Tenn. Avocations: music, astronomy, photography, elderhostel. Home: 4985 Beatrice Dr Columbus OH 43227-2114

MCINTYRE, ANITA GRACE JORDAN, lawyer; b. Louisville, Jan. 29, 1947; d. Blakely Gordan and Shirley Evans (Grubbs) Jordan; m. Kenneth James McIntyre, Oct. 11, 1969; children: Abigail, Jordan Kenneth. BA, Smith Coll., 1969; JD, U. Detroit, 1975. Bar: Mich. 1975, U.S. Dist. Ct. (ea. dist.) Mich. 1975, U.S. Dist. Ct. (we. dist.) Mich. 1979, U.S. Ct. Appeals (6th cir.) 1979. Ptnr. Rollins White & Rollins, Detroit, 1975-79; vis. assoc. prof. Detroit Coll. Law, 1979-81; assoc. Tyler & Canham, Detroit, 1981-82; prin. Anita G. McIntyre, P.C., Grosse Pointe, Mich., 1982-87, 91—; of counsel Nederlander Dodge & Rollins, Detroit, 1987-90; assoc. Damm & Smith, P.C., 1990-91. Hearing panel chmn. Atty. Discipline Bd., 1985—. Editor, author (case notes) U. Detroit Jour. Urban Law, 1975; contrbr. articles to profl. jours. Sec. Berry Subdivsn. Assn., Detroit, 1975-77; pres. Smith Coll. Club Detroit, 1982-86; mem. parents bd. U. Liggett Sch., Grosse Pointe, Mich., 1991,95; vice chair state pub. affairs com. Mich. State Coun. Jr. Leagues, 1998-2000, chair, 2001-. Mem.: Wayne County Juvenile Trial Lawyers Assn., Wayne County (Mich.) Probate Bar Assn., State Bar Mich., Edgemont Park Assn. (sec.), Jr. League Detroit (chair pub.affairs com. 1998—2001, vice chair Mich. state pub. affairs com. 1999—2001, chair 2001—). Episcopalian. Avocations: skiing, swimming, needle point. Office: 15324 Mack Ave Ste 201 Grosse Pointe Park MI 48230 E-mail: agmcintyr@cs.com.

MCINTYRE, BERNICE KAY, lawyer, management consultant; b. Worcester, Mass., Aug. 9, 1950; d. William James and Theodora Grace (McCullough) M.; m. Michael Henry Pete, June 25, 1994. BA, Oberlin Coll., 1972; JD, Boston U., 1977. Bar: Mass. 1977. Asst. gen. counsel Dept. Pub. Welfare, Boston, 1977-78, Coastal Zone Mgmt., Boston, 1978-79, gen. counsel, 1979-81, Exec. Office Environ. Affairs, Boston, 1981-83, asst. sec., 1982-83; commr. Dept. Pub. Utilities, 1983—; appointed by gov. chmn. Pub. Utilities Commn., 1987-90. Active Clinton Gore Energy Transition Team, 1992-93; mgr., sr. cons. Arthur D. Little, Inc., 1991-95; prin., pres. B.K. McIntyre & Assocs., Inc., 1995—; assoc. prof. mgmt. dept. Southeastern U., Washington. Contbr. chpts. to books. Office: BK McIntyre & Assocs Inc 1250 24th St NW Ste 350 Washington DC 20037-1124

MCINTYRE, BRUCE HERBERT, media and marketing consultant; b. Takoma Park, Md., Jan. 24, 1930; s. Orrin Raymond and Leila Hazel (Olmsted) McI.; m. Natalie Ann Wolff, Oct. 10, 1953; children: Douglas A., Elizabeth W., Emily O., Catherine N., Jane A. Student, Gannon Coll., 1954-57, U. Akron, 1958-61. Reporter, city editor Erie (Pa.) Times and News, 1949-57; reporter, city editor, asst. to exec. editor Akron (Ohio) Beacon Jour., 1958-67; with Battle Creek (Mich.) Enquirer & News, 1967-71, asst. mng. editor, 1967-68, mng. editor, 1968-71; exec. v.p., editor Oakland Press, Pontiac, Mich., 1971-77, pub., 1977-95; v.p., pub. div. Capital Cities/ABC Inc., 1987-96; chmn. Great Lakes Media Inc., 1995-96; ptnr. McIntyre Media LLC, Farmington Hills, Mich., 1997—; sec., dir. Clarkston State Bank, Clarkston, 1998—; councilman City of Orchard Lake Village, 1998—2002, mayor, 2000—. Lectr. Am. Press Inst., 1968— ; journalism juror Pulitzer Prizes, 1972— Served with AUS, 1951-53; lt. col. Res. ret. Mem. Soc. Profl. Journalists. Clubs: Pine Lake Country (Bloomfield, Mich.). Episcopalian. E-mail: bhmcintyre@comcast.net.

MCINTYRE, CAROL CHRISMAN, social services administrator; b. Bloomington, Ill., Aug. 24, 1955; d. Robert L. and Norma J. (Garner) C.; m. Ronald P. McIntyre, Feb. 28, 1981; children: Brian, Valerie. BS, Ill. State U., 1976; MSW, Loyola U., Chgo., 1982; cert. in geriatrics, U. Ill., 1996. Lic. clin. social worker, Ill.; cert. care mgr. Nat. Acad. Cert. Care Mgrs.; registered guardian Nat. Guardianship Assn. Crisis worker Ravenswood Hosp. Mental Health Ctr., Chgo., 1978-82; social worker Leyden Family Svc. and Mental Health Ctr., Franklin Park, Ill., 1982-83, Lake County Health Dept., Zion, 1984-85, State of Ill., Elgin, 1985-89; exec. dir. Elderday Ctr., Geneva, 1991-97. Qualified examiner CPC Streamwood (Ill.) Hosp., 1991-95; field instr. sch. social work Aurora (Ill.) U., 1992-97; clin. social worker; owner The Caring Connection, P.C., St. Charles, Ill., 1997—; cons. in geriat. psychotherapy and social security disability representation; instr. Gerontology program Elgin C.C., 1999—. Bd. dirs. Women's Ctr. Delnor Cmty. Hosp., Geneva, 1993-94; founding bd. mem. Bobbi Burrow Children's Bereavement Ctr., St. Charles, Ill., 1992-95; bd. dirs. United Way of St. Charles, sec., 1999-2001, mem. allocations com., 1999-. Mem. NASW, Nat. Assn. Profl. Geriat. Care Mgrs. (advanced profl.), Zonta (bd. dirs. 1995-98—).

MCINTYRE, DOUGLAS CARMICHAEL, II, congressman; b. Lumberton, N.C., Aug. 6, 1956; s. Douglas Carmichael and Thelma Riley (Hedgpeth) McI.; m. Lola Denise Strickland, June 26, 1982; children: Joshua Carmichael, Stephen Christopher. BA, U. N.C., 1978, JD, 1981. Bar: N.C. 1981, U.S. Dist. Ct. (ea. dist.) N.C. 1984, U.S. Dist. Ct. (mid. dist.) N.C. 1985., U.S. Ct. Appeals (4th cir.) 1987, U.S. Supreme Ct., 1987. Assoc. Law Office Bruce Huggins, Lumberton, 1981-82, McLean, Stacy, Henry & McLean, Lumberton, 1982-86; ptnr. Price & McIntyre P.A., 1987-89; prin. McIntyre Law Firm, P.A., 1989-96; congressman U.S. Ho. of Reps., 1997—. Mem. law-focused edn. adv. com. N.C. Dept. Pub. Instrn., 1986-87; mem. U.S. Ho. Com. on Agr., 1997—, Nat. Security Com., 1997—; co-chmn. Coalition Task Force on Edn., 1997-98, Congrl. Task Force on Promotion of Fatherhood, Rural Health Care Coalition, 1999—, Democratic Task Force on Children, 1999-2000, Coalition Task Force on Bus. and Tech., Spl. Forces Caucus, 2002—; mem. President's Summit on Am.'s Future, 1997. Del. Dem. Nat. Conv., N.Y.C., 1980, N.C. Dems., Raleigh, 1974—; pres. Robeson County Young Dems., Lumberton, 1982; sec.-treas. 7th Congl. Dist. Young Dems., N.C., 1983, chmn., 1984; 2d vice chmn. 7th Congl. Dist. Dems. So. N.C., 1986-89, 1st vice chmn., 1989; mem. state adv. bd. North Carolinians Against Drug and Alcohol Abuse, Raleigh, 1984-85; chmn. Morehead Scholarship Selection Com., Robeson County, 1985-94; deacon, elder, clk. of session Presbyn. Ch.; active Boy Scouts Am., Lumberton, 1983; mem. N.C. Commn. on Children and Youth, 1987-89, N.C. Commn. on the Family, 1989-91; mem. Young Life Lumberton com., 1987-89; chmn. Robeson County U.S. Constn. Bicentennial com., 1986-87; mem. lawyers' adv. com. to N.C. Commn. on Bicentennial of U.S. Constn., 1986-89; bd. dirs. Robeson County Group Home, Lumberton, 1984-87, Lumberton Econ. Advancement for Downtown, Inc., 1987-90, pres., 1988-89, 89-90; chmn. legis. affairs com. C. of C., 1991, 92, 93, bd. dirs., 1992-94; mem. N.C. Mus. of History Assocs., 1987-89; mem. regional selection com. Gov.'s Award for Excellence in Teaching Social Studies, 1991. Morehead Found. scholar, 1974-78; named one of Outstanding Young Men in Am., 1981, 84, 85, 88; Outstanding Young Dem. Robeson County Young Dems., 1984-85; one of State's Outstanding Young Dems. Young Dems. N.C., 1984, 85; recipient Algernon Sydney Sullivan award U. N.C., 1978, Outstanding Young North Carolinian award N.C. Jaycees, 1988, Outstanding Young North Carolinians, Heart Robeson Jaycees, 1988, Nat. Bicentennial Leadership award for Individual Achievement Coun. for Advancement of Citizenship and Ctr. for Civic Edn., Washington, 1987, Gov.'s Outstanding Vol. Svc. award, 1989, Thomas Jefferson award Food Distbrs. Internat., 1998, 2002, Guardian of Small Bus. award, Nat. Fedn. Independent Bus., 1997-99, Nat. Rural Health Legislative award, 1999, Outstanding Health Svc. award Cmty. Ptnrs. Health Net, 2000, Spirit of Enterprise award, U.S. C. of C., 1997-98, Super Hero award Nat. Assn. Cmty. Health Ctrs., 2001, 2002, Internat. Pub. Policy award Internat. Assn. Personnel Employment, 2002, Law Enforcement award, N.C. NArcotics Officers Asn., 2002Quality Pub. Svc./Pub. Edn. and Health Care award Am. Fedn. Tchrs., 2001, Charles Dick Medal of Merit Nat. Guard Assn., 2000, Disting. Svc. to Agriculture award Robeson County Crop Promotion Assn., 2001. Mem. ABA (exec. com. citizenship edn. com. 1985-87, nat. cmty. law week com. 1982-83), Internat. Platform Assn., N.C. Bar Assn. (chmn. youth edn. and constn. bicentennial com. 1986-87, youth edn. com., exec. coun. young lawyers divsn. 1986-87), Robeson County Bar Assn. (founder, chmn. citizenship edn. com. 1982-94, law day com.), 16th Jud. Dist. Bar Assn., N.C. Acad. Trial Lawyers, N.C. Coll. Advocacy, Christian Legal Soc. (state adv. bd. 1986-90, state pres. 1987), Lumberton C. of C. (bd. dirs. 1992-94), The Ret. Officers' Assn. (hon. life), Order of Old Well, Lumberton Rotary Club (bd. dirs. 1995-96), Phi Beta Kappa, Phi Eta Sigma. Avocations: tennis, snow skiing, softball, dancing, Bible study. Home: 1701 N Chestnut St Lumberton NC 28358-3839 Office: 228 Cannon Washington DC 20515-3307 E-mail: congmcintyre@mail.house.gov.

MCINTYRE, JAMES OWEN, insurance executive; b. Cleve., July 21, 1958; s. Owen Eugene and Carole Diane (Saladin) McI.; m. Marina Zeccardi, Dec. 4, 1981 (div.); children: Antoinette, Owen, Helen, Robert; m. Enid Draviczky, Apr. 4, 1998. BS, Pa. State U., 1980, M of Mgmt., 1992. CLU. Sales rep. Liberty Mutual Ins. Co., Boston, 1982-89; sales mgr. Prudential Ins. Co., Blue Bell, Pa., 1989-94, adv. coun. agents Ft. Washington, 1989; mgr. Del. Valley Fin. Group (agy. of Provident Mutual), Radnor, 1994-96; sales support and competition cons. Provident Mut. Ins. Co., Valley Forge, 1996-97, dir. competition and sales support officer, 1997-99, regional v.p., 1999—. Author: Economic Effect of Banks Entering the Insurance and Financial Services Industry, 1992. Mgr. Hatfield Area Little League, Pa., 1991-97; den leader Boy Scouts of Am., Hatfield, Pa., 1994-96. Recipient Pa. Life Roundtable award Pa. Assn. Life Underwriters, 1991. Fellow Life Underwriting Tng. Coun.; mem. Nat. Assn. Life Underwriters, Am. Soc. CLU & ChFC, Gen. Agt. and Mgrs. Assn. Republican. Lutheran. Avocation: golf. Home: 354 Carlyn Ct Downingtown PA 19335-4207 Office: Provident Mut Ins Co 1000 Chesterbrook Blvd Berwyn PA 19312-2421 E-mail: JamesMcIntyre@providentmutual.com.

MCINTYRE, JANE LONDON, foundation executive; b. Charlotte, July 16, 1946; d. John Rutherford and Harriette (Iler) London; m. Dewitte Gray McIntyre, July 27, 1968; children: Chandler Murphy, Jane London, Sally Gray. BS, Columbia Coll., 1968; MBA, Queens Coll., 1996. Spl. edn. tchr. Laurel (Md.) Elem., 1968-70; sales assoc./mgr. Carolinas/Va. Trade Market, Charlotte, N.C., 1978-90; dir. mktg. RHNB Nat. Bank, 1990-92; corp. planner, dir. bus. devel. and corp. rels. Carolinas Health Care Sys., 1992-97; dir. spl. programs and svcs. Carolinas Healthcare Found., 1997-2000; exec. dir. YWCA Cen. Carolinas, 2000—. Mem. bd. edn. Charlotte Mecklenburg Schs., 1987—95, vice chair, 1992—95; mem. Charlotte Jr. League, 1978—86; mem. bd. visitors Columbia Coll., 1995—99, Kanuga Episcopal Conf. Ctr., 1990—; mem. Smart Start Bd. Coun. for Agy. Execs., United Way Ctrl. Carolinas; bd. dirs. YWCA of Ctrl. Carolinas, Charlotte, 1994—98, pres., 1998—2000. Home: 1901 Wandering Way Dr Charlotte NC 28226-5739 Office: YWCA Cen Carolinas 3420 Park Rd Charlotte NC 28209 E-mail: jane_ywca@yahoo.com.

MCINTYRE, JERILYN SUE, academic administrator; b. June 24, 1942; d. Frank Otto and Maxine (Ward) McIntyre; m. W. David Smith. Student, Stanford U., Italy, 1962; AB in History with distinction, Stanford U., 1964, MA in Journalism, cert. Summer Radio-TV Inst., Stanford U., 1965, tchrs. cert., 1968; PhD in Comms., U. Washington, 1973; postgrad. Inst. Ednl. Mgmt., Harvard U., 1993. Corr. World News Bureau McGraw-Hill Pub. Co., L.A., 1965-67; asst. prof. dept. mass comm. Chico (Calif.) State Coll., 1968-70; asst. prof. Sch. Journalism U. Iowa, Iowa City, 1973-77; assoc. prof., prof. dept. comm. U. Utah, Salt Lake City, 1977-2000, assoc. dean Coll. Humanities, 1984-88, assoc. v.p. acad. affairs, 1988-90, interim pres., 1997, v.p. acad. affairs, 1990-98; pres. Ctrl. Wash. U., Ellensburg, 2000—. Dir. Wall St. Jour. Publs. Workshop, Chico State Coll., 1968; mem. edn. adv. bd. NFL, 1996; mem. exec. com. coun. acad. affairs Nat. Assn. State Univs. and Land Grant Coll., 1995—98, chair, 1997; mem. steering com. Utah Edn. Network, 1995—98. Editl. asst. Chemical Week Mag., 1965-66, World News Bureau, 1966-67; mem. editl. bd. Journalism History; co-author: Symbols & Society; contbr. articles to profl. jours., chpts. to books. Mem. Utah Women's Forum. Named a David P. Gardner fellow, 1984; recipient Yesterday's Girl Scout Today's Successful Woman, Utah Girl Scout Coun., 1996. Mem.: Assn. Edn. in Journalism and Mass Comm., AAUW (Dist. Woman Utah Salt Lake City chpt. 1994). Office: 400 E 8th Ave Ellensburg WA 98926-7501

MCINTYRE, JERRY L. lawyer; b. Atlantic City, July 1, 1941; AB, Columbia U., 1963; JD, Fordham U., 1969. Bar: N.Y. 1969, R.I. 1970. Mem. McIntyre, Tate, Lynch & Holt, Providence. Com. mem. Family Ct. Bench/Bar Com., 1985—. Pres. town coun., Town of Jamestown, R.I., 1983-89. Fellow Am. Acad. Matrimonial Lawyers; mem. ABA (sect. family law), N.Y. State Bar Assn. (sect. trusts and estates law), R.I. Bar Assn., R.I. Bar Found. Office: McIntyre Tate Lynch & Holt 321 S Main St Providence RI 02903-7108

MCINTYRE, JOHN ANDREW, environmental and economic planner, geography educator; b. Chgo., Mar. 4, 1958; s. Donald Merrill McIntyre and Rosemary Martha (Windgassen) Peters; m. Nancy Lynn Curtis, Sept. 17, 1983. Ba in Geog. Studies, So. Ill. U., 1988, MS in Geography, 1993; diploma in econ. devel., U. Okla., 1993; grad. cert. in pub. adminstrn., Ind. State U. Cert econ. developer; cert. planner. Sales mgr. Bally Mfg. Inc., Chgo., 1981-87; dir. econ. devel. Riverbend Growth Assn., Godfrey, Ill., 1987-91; dir. Argonne Regional Consortium, Palos Hills, 1991-93; cmty. devel. dir. Homer Twp., Lockport, 1993—. Adj. faculty dept. natural scis. Joliet (Ill.) Jr. Coll., 1994—; mem. mktg. com. I&M Canal Nat. Heritage Corridor, Lockport, 1993—; bd. dirs. Applied Geography Conf., Denton, Tex., 1993—. Contbr. articles to profl. jours. Trustee Village Orland Hills, Ill., 1992-94; instr. Jr. Achievement, Orland Park, 1993; facilitator Riverbend in 90's, Alton, Ill., 1989-91. Sgt. USAF, 1977-81. Recipient Superior Lit. award Mid-Am. Econ. Devel. Coun., Deerfield, Ill., 1993. Mem. Assn. Am. Geographers (meteorology splty. group), Am. Econ. Devel. Coun. (Howard Roepke award 1994), Am. Planning Assn. (environ. splty. group), Am. Inst. Cert. Planners. Libertarian. Achievements include research on geographic information systems as applied to economic development, on economic impacts of federal research laboratories at local and regional levels; research on environmental and geological aspects of the Illinois and Michigan canal national heritage corridor. Home: 9212 Quail Ct Orland Hills IL 60477-5916 Office: Homer Twp 14350 W 151st St Lockport IL 60441-6776 E-mail: rogueplanner@chicago.usa.com.

MCINTYRE, JOHN ARMIN, physics educator; b. Seattle, June 2, 1920; s. Harry John and Florence (Armin) McI.; m. Madeleine Forsman, June 15, 1947; 1 son, John Forsman. BS, U. Wash., 1943; MA, Princeton U., 1948, PhD, 1950. Mem. faculty elec. engring. Carnegie Inst. Tech., Pitts., 1943; radio engr. Westinghouse Elec. Co., Balt., 1944; research assn. Stanford, 1950-57; mem. faculty Yale, 1957-63, assoc. prof., 1960-63; prof. physics Tex. A&M U., College Station, 1963-95, emeritus prof., 1995—; asso. dir. Cyclotron Inst., 1965-70. Mem. council Oak Ridge Asso. Univs., 1964-71 Fellow Am. Phys. Soc., Am. Sci. Affiliation (exec. council 1968-73); mem. AAAS. Presbyterian. Achievements include research and publs. on scintillation counters for gamma ray spectroscopy; determination of nuclear charge distbns. by electron scattering; study of nuclear structure by neutron transfer reactions; devel. variable energy gamma ray beams, gamma ray cameras. Home: 2316 Bristol St Bryan TX 77802-2405 Office: Tex A&M U Dept Physics College Station TX 77843-0001 E-mail: jmcintyre@physics.tamu.edu.

MCINTYRE, JOHN GEORGE WALLACE, real estate development and management consultant; b. Toronto, Ont., Can., July 26, 1920; s. George Crerar and Gwendolyn Alberta (Wallace) McI.; m. Ruth Elizabeth Wilson, July 26, 1945 (dec.); children: Angus, Heather, Robert, Anne. B of Commerce, U. Toronto, 1941; MBA, Harvard U., 1947. Budget acct. Abitibi Paper Co., Toronto, 1947-51; budget mgr., asst. gen. mgr. Ford of Can., Windsor, Ont., 1951-58, gen. mgr. mfg. ops., 1963-65; asst. mng. dir., mng. dir. Ford of Australia, Melbourne, 1958-63; exec. v.p., pres. Columbia Cellulose Ltd., Vancouver, B.C., Can., 1965-67; v.p. retail devel. and distbn. Hudson's Bay Co., Toronto, 1967-84; pres. Rupert's Land Tng. Co., Hudson's Bay Co. Devels. Ltd.; trustee Internat. Council of Shopping Ctrs., 1970-84; v.p., gen. mgr. Broadcast Ctr. Devel. Project Can. Broadcasting Corp., 1984-88; cons., 1988—. Chmn. Soldiers' Tower Com., U. Toronto, 1998. Served to capt. Royal Can. Ordnance Corps., 1942-45, ETO. Address: Ste 412 Richview Residence 105 Clement Rd Etobicoke ON Canada M9R 4C2

MCINTYRE, KAYE, non-profit organization executive, consultant; b. Hartford, Conn., Oct. 13, 1950; d. Richard Arthur and Helen Marie (von Richter) Tillotson; m. Daniel Brian McIntyre, Feb. 21, 1969 (div. Dec. 1979). AS in Human Svcs., N.W. Conn. Community Coll., 1983; BSBA, Charter Oak Coll., 1985; MA in Liberal Studies, Wesleyan U., 1990. Cert. hypnotherapist. Counselor McCall House, Torrington, Conn., 1979-80; freelance photographer, 1980—; exec. dir. Warner Theatre, Torrington, 1982-84, Elderly Health Screening Svc., Inc., Waterbury, Conn., 1982—. Cons. in field. Asst. coord. Conn. Earth Action Group, Litchfield, 1971; regional coord. Conn. Citizens Action Group, Litchfield County, Conn., 1971-72; pres. N.W. Conn. Assn. for the Arts, Inc., Torrington, 1981-84; bd. dirs. Torrington Trust for Hist. Preservation, Inc., 1981-85; 6th dist. coord. Office of Protection and Advocacy for the Handicapped and Developmentally Disabled, Litchfield County, 1982; chairperson adult programming com. YWCA of Waterbury, 1985-87; v.p. Thomaston Opera House Found., 1985-88. Recipient citation Conn. Soc. Prevention of Blindness, 1984, Conn. Gen. Assembly, 1984, 86, 92, Project Health award U.S. Dept. HHS Adminstrn. Aging, 1986, Secs. Excellence award U.S. Dept. HHS Community Health Promotion Program, 1986. Mem. NAFE, AAAS, Am. League Hist. Theatres, N.Y. Acad. Scis., Community Assocs. of Conn., Inc. (bd. dirs.), Am. Pub. Health Assn., Nat. Assn. Fundraising Execs., Am. Soc. on Aging, Gerontological Soc. Am., Nat. Coun. on Aging, N.Y. Acad. Scis., Conn. Assn. Hist. Theatres (pres. 1984—), Internat. Platform Assn., Nat. Trust for Hist. Preservation, Mensa (Litchfield County coord. 1979-84). Democrat. Taoist. Office: Elderly Health Screening Svc Inc 161 N Main St Waterbury CT 06702-1405

MCINTYRE, LISA JEAN, sociologist, educator; b. Sedro Woolley, Wash., Apr. 14, 1953; d. David Gillespie and Jean Francis McI. BA, Smith Coll., 1975; MA, U. Chgo., 1978, PhD, 1986. Asst. prof. sociology Wash. State U., Pullman, 1987-93, assoc. prof. sociology, 1993—. Author: The Public Defender, 1987, Law in the Sociological Enterprise, 1994, The Practical Skeptic: Core Concepts in Sociology, 1999; author, editor: Families & Law, 1993. Mem. Am. Sociol. Assn., Sociologists for Women in Soc., Law & Soc. Assn. Office: Wash State U Dept Sociology Pullman WA 99164-0001 E-mail: ljmcint@wsu.edu.

MCINTYRE, LOUISE S. income tax consultant; b. Cin., Jan. 29, 1924; d. George Washington and Bertha (McDaniels) Sullivan; m. Harry McIntyre Jr., Jan. 18, 1947; children: Carol L., Patricia A., Harriet L., Harry J., Brenda R. AA, Mira Costa Coll., Oceanside, Calif., 1972; grad. in auditing, Nat. Tax Practice Inst., 1989. Enrolled agt. Hydraulic testor Paterson Field, Fairfield, Ohio, 1942-45; control clk. Hickam Field, Honolulu, 1945-47; clk.-typist Patterson Field, Fairfield, 1947-49, Camp LeJeune, Jacksonville, N.C., 1951-56; sec., bookkeeper Mission Bowl, Oceanside, 1973-79; income tax cons., 1974—. Mem. Oceanside Human Rels. Commn., 1970; bd. dirs. Armed Forces YMCA, Oceanside, 1969-71, Oceanside Christian Women's Club, 1988-91, North County Concert Assn. Aux., 1993-96; active PTA, Girl Scout U.S. Mem. Inland Soc. Tax Cons. (bd. dirs. 1988—), Am. Soc. Women Accts. (v.p. 1989-90), Enrolled Agts. Palomar, Nat. Assn. Enrolled Agts., Nat. Soc. Pub. Accts., Calif. Assn. Ind. Accts., Palmquist PTA (hon. life). Avocations: bowling, dancing, crafts, interior decorating, cake decorating. Home: 328 Camelot Dr Oceanside CA 92054-4515

MCINTYRE, MARY MAUREEN, social services consultant; b. Decatur, Ill. d. Leo M. and Madge Eleanor (Daniels) McInroe; m. David McIntyre (dec. Sept. 1978); children: Laura, Kathy, Michael, Ellen, Paul. AA in Journalism/Comm., Cosumnes River Coll., 1994. Founder, dir. Sheltering Wings, Elk Grove, Calif., 1984-94, Washougal, Wash., 1996-97, Merimac Enterprises (a/k/a Sheltering Wings), Elk Grove, Calif., 1997—. Communicator, cons. on prevention of child abuse and homelessness; coord./conduct seminars/workshops on conflict resolutions, getting organized and successful living. Author: 8 Steps to Successful Living, 1987, (puppet prodn. script) Rochester Betsy, 1989, songs; contbr. articles to newspapers. Bd. dirs. Calvary Chapel, Camas, Wash., sec.-treas., 1996. Avocations: gardening, writing, music, travel. Home and Office: Merimac Enterprises 8698 Elk Grove Ste 3 #218 Elk Grove CA 95624 E-mail: merimac@cwo.com.

MCINTYRE, MIKE, congressman; b. Lumberton, N.C., Aug. 6, 1956; m. Dee Strickland; children: Joshua, Stephen. BA, U. N.C., 1978, JD, 1981. Atty., Lumberton; mem. U.S. Congress from 7th N.C. dist., 1997—; mem. agr. and armed svcs. coms. Pres. Lumberton Economic Advancement Downtown, Inc.; state chmn. citizenship edn. com. Young Lawyers divsn. N.C. Bar Assn.; mem. law-focused edn. adv. com. N.C. Law; mem. exec. com. citizen edn. com. Young Lawers divsn. ABA; co-chmn. Congl. Rural Health Care Coalition, 1999. Columnist For the Family. Vol. Lumberton Recreation Dept., coach; active PTA, Boy Scouts Am., Lumberton Youth Baseball Assn.; elder, deacon, Sunday sch. tchr., clerk of session, chmn. weekday sch. and day care com. First Presbyn. Ch.; chmn. legis. com. Lumberton C. of C., bd. dirs., mem. exec. com.; mem. Lumberton's All-Am. City Del.; vice-chmn. Lumberton Commn. Youth and Family; chmn. Robeson County's U.S. Constitution Com.; co-chmn. Congl. Task Force on Fatherhood, 1997—. Named one of state's Ten Most Outstanding Young Dems., 1984, 85, Outstanding Young North Carolinian N.C. Jaycees, 1987; recipient Nat. Bicentennial Leadership award, 1988, Gov.'s Award for Outstanding Vol. Svc., 1989; Legislative award, Nat. Rural Health Assn., 2000, Super Hero award, Nat. Assn. of Cmty. Health. Ctrs., 2001-02, Congrl. Ptnrship. award, Nat. Assn. of Devel. Orgns., 2002, Law Enforcement award, N.C. narcotics Officers Assn., 2002. Mem. Phi Beta Kappa. Democrat. Office: US House of Representatives 228 Cannon Ho Office Bldg Washington DC 20515

MCINTYRE, MILDRED JEAN, clinical psychologist, writer, neuroscientist; b. Boston; d. William James and Theodora Grace (Jackson-McCullough) McI. BA, Swarthmore Coll., 1965; MA, Clark U., 1972, PhD, 1975. Lic. psychologist, Mass., Alaska, Hawaii. Ford Found. fellow, 1972, 73. Mem. APA, Internat. Neuropsychol. Soc., Cognitive Neurosci. Soc. Avocations: art, music, travel. Office: PO Box 990124 Boston MA 02199-0124

MCINTYRE, NORMAN F. petroleum industry executive; b. Pangman, Sask., Can., Oct. 21, 1945; s. Donald and Jean (Cruickshank) McI.; m. Lana Jean, June 10, 1967; children: Jason Lee, Spencer James. BSc in Petroleum Engring., U. Wyo., 1971; MS in Mgmt., MIT, 1991. Various positions with Mobil Oil, U.S., Can., to 1982; group mgr. engring. offshore divsn. Petro-Can., 1982-83, gen. mgr. frontier devel. offshore divsn., 1983, v.p. frontier devel., 1983-86, v.p. prodn. devel., 1986-89; sr. v.p. western region Petro-Can. Products, 1989-90; pres. Petro-Can. Resources, Calgary, Canada, 1990-95, exec. v.p. Canada, 1995—2002, pres. Canada, 2002—. Past chmn., dir. Panarctic Oils Ltd. Campaign chair United Way of Calgary and Area. Mem. Can. Assn. of Petroleum Producers (chmn. 1998), Can. Assn. World Petroleum Congresses (chmn.), Assn. of Profl. Engineers, Geologists and Geophysists of Alberta, Assn. Profl. Engrs., Glencoe Golf and Country Club, Calgary Petroleum Club (bd. mem.). Office: Petro Canada Bowater House 114 Knightsbridge London SW1X7LD England

MCINTYRE, OSWALD ROSS, physician; b. Chgo., Feb. 13, 1932; m. Jean Geary, June 5, 1957; children— Margaret Jean, Archibald Ross, Elizabeth Geary. AB cum laude, Dartmouth Coll., 1953, postgrad, 1953-55; MD, Harvard U., 1957. Intern U. Pa. Hosp., 1957-58; resident in medicine Dartmouth Med. Sch. Affiliated Hosps., 1958-60; instr. medicine Dartmouth Coll., 1964-66, asst. prof. medicine, 1966-69, assoc. prof., 1969-75, prof., 1976—, James J. Carroll prof. oncology, 1980-95, dir. Norris Cotton Cancer Center, 1975-92, prof. emeritus, 1995—; attending physician VA Hosp., White River Junction, Vt., 1964. Cons. in hematology and oncology; acting chmn. dept. medicine Dartmouth-Hitchcock Med. Ctr., 1987-89; chmn. Cancer and Leukemia Group B.; 1990-95. Mem. Am. Soc. Hematology, Am. Assn. Cancer Rsch., Am. Soc. Clin. Oncology, Assn. Cancer Inst. (pres. 1988-89), New Eng. Cancer Soc. (pres. 1989-90). Home: 34 Lamphire Hill Ln Lyme NH 03768-3109

MCINTYRE, PETER MASTIN, physicist, educator; b. Clewiston, Fla., Sept. 26, 1947; s. Peter Mastin and Ruby Eugenia (Richaud) McI.; m. Rebecca Biek, June 29, 1968; children: Peter B., Colin H., Jana M., Robert J. AB with honors, U. Chgo., 1967, MS, 1968, PhD, 1973. Asst. prof. Harvard U., Cambridge, Mass., 1975-80; group leader Fermilab, Batavia, Ill., 1978-80; assoc. prof. Tex. A&M U., College Station, 1980-84, prof. physics, 1985—, assoc. dean Coll. of Sci., 1990-92; pres. Accelerator Tech. Corp., Bryan, Tex.,

1988—. Dir. Tex. Accelerator Ctr., The Woodlands, 1991—93. Recipient IR-100 award, Indsl. Rch. Mag., 1980; fellow, Sloan Found., 1976—78. Fellow: Am. Phys. Soc. (pres. Tex. sect. 1990—91); mem.: AAAS. Achievements include Proton-Antiproton Colliding Beams; patents for Continuous Unitized Tunneling System, Gigatron High Power Microwave Amplifier, Microstrip Chamber for Medical Imaging; Electronic Pasteurization Sys. for killing bacteria in food and removing organic contaminants in water; 16 Tesla Superconducting magnets for future hadron colliders; silicon microdevices for DNA sequencing; structured cable using high-temperature superconductors for practical coils, proton-driven thorium fission for electric power production; flux-coupled isochonous cyclotron driver for thorium-cycle nuclear fission power. Home: 611 Montclair Ave College Station TX 77840-2868 Office: Tex A&M U Dept Physics College Station TX 77843-0001

MCINTYRE, ROBERT WALTER, church official; b. Bethlehem, Pa., June 20, 1922; s. Simon Jesse and Ruth (Young) McI.; m. Edith Jones, Sept. 1, 1944 (dec. Jan. 1953); m. Elizabeth Norman, Nov. 6, 1953; children: Judith McIntyre Keilholtz, Joy McIntyre McCallum, John, James, June McIntyre Irvine. Student, Miltonvale Wesleyan Coll., 1939-43; B.Religion, Marion Coll., 1944, LittD (hon.), 1980, BA, 1959; postgrad., Ball State U., 1960-61; D.D. (hon.), Ea. Pilgrim Coll., 1969; LLD (hon.), Houghton Coll., 1976; DHL (hon.), Ctrl. Wesleyan Coll., 1988. Ordained to ministry The Wesleyan Ch., 1945. Pastor, Marengo, Ohio, 1944-47, Columbus, 1947-52, Coshocton, 1952-55; exec. sec. dept. youth The Wesleyan Ch., Marion, Ind., 1955-68; editor The Wesleyan Youth, 1955-68; gen. editor The Wesleyan Ch., editor The Wesleyan Adv., 1968-73; assoc. editor The Preacher's Mag., 1973-88; gen. supt. The Wesleyan Ch., 1973-88, mem. gen. bd. adminstrn., 1955-88, mem. Commn. Christian Edn., 1959-73, 76-80, chmn. Commn. Christian Edn., 1976-80, mem. exec. bd., 1968-88; chmn. Commn. on World Missions, 1973-76, Commn. on Publs., 1980-84, Commn. on Extension and Evangelism, 1984-88; spl. asst. to the pres. Ind. Wesleyan U., Marion, 1988-93; asst. pastor Spl. Adult Ministries, Lakeview Wesleyan Ch., 1998—2002. Denominational rep., bd. adminstrn. Nat. Assn. Evangelicals, 1973-83, exec. com., 1978-80, 81-87, 2d v.p., 1981-82, 1st v.p., 1982-84, pres., 1984-86, mem., 1973—; denominational rep. The Lord's Day Alliance, 1973-76; trustee Marion Coll., Asbury Theol. Sem., 1976—; bd. dirs. Wesleyan Investment Found., 1988-99. Author: Ten Commandments for Teen-Agers, 1965; editor: Program Pathways for Young Adults, 1964, Mandate for Mission, 1970; contbr. articles to religious jours. Mem. Christian Holiness Partnership (chmn. social action commn. 1971-73, sec. 1973-76), Wesleyan Theol. Soc., Best Yrs. Fellowship (gen. dir. 1992-98), Wesleyan Bible Conf. Assn. (bd. dirs. 1993—, v.p. 2001—). Home: 4613 S Star Dr Marion IN 46953-7303 E-mail: remacin@aol.com.

MCINTYRE, ROBERT WHEELER, conservation organization executive; b. Chgo., Aug. 26, 1936; s. Henry Langenberg and Winifred (Wheeler) McI.; m. Emily Beardsley Taylor, Oct. 12, 1961 (div. 1985); children: W. Burley, Nancy T., Oliver W., Shanna L., Amanda K.; m. Miriam de Jesus Zarate, June 23, 1990 (div. 1998); m. Myung Sook Son, Jan. 6, 2001. AB in Sociology, Stanford U., 1959; MBA, Harvard U., 1964. Loan analyst Wells Fargo Bank, San Francisco, 1964-65; supr. budget analysis Ford Aerospace, Palo Alto, Calif., 1965-69; controller Allied Life Scis., San Leandro, 1969-70; ptnr. Diplomat Mfg. Co., Palo Alto, 1970-71; staff cons. Opportunity Through Ownership, San Francisco, 1971-72; gen. mgr. Quality Metal Finishers, 1972-73; sr. v.p., chief fin. officer The Trust for Pub. Land, 1973—. Mem. adv. bd. Peninsula Open Space Trust, Menlo Park, 1978—; mem. Marin Headlands Adv. Com., 1978—81, Resource Renewal Inst., Sausalito, 1988—, Water Heritage Trust, Sausalito, 1988—, Dorothy Erskine Open Space Fund, San Francisco, 1978—; bd. dirs. Environ. Vols., Palo Alto, 1980—; bd. dirs., treas. Robert C. Wheeler Found., 1965—95; chair, bd. dirs. Families Adopting Interracially, San Jose, 1971—74; bd. dirs. Sempervirens Fund, Mountain View, 2002—. Recipient Presdl. Citation award, The Trust for Pub. Land, 1988, Spl. Svc. award, Environ. Vols., 1989. Mem. Harvard Club N.Y., Harvard Club Boston, San Francisco Tennis Club, USS Coral Sea Assn., Palo Alto Tennis Club. Avocations: hiking, backpacking, tennis, travel. Office: The Trust for Public Land 116 New Montgomery St Fl 4 San Francisco CA 94105-3680

MCINTYRE, VICKY JOYCE, business owner; b. Glasgow, Mont., Dec. 12, 1952; d. Frank Smith Jr. and Mary Helen (Smith) McIntyre; m. John Peter Oleksey, Jr., Aug. 7, 1976 (div. May 1984); 1 child, Kathryn Elizabeth. Student, U. Colo., 1973-76, U. Md., Fed. Republic Germany, 1977-81; BSBA, U. Phoenix, 1984; MBA, Boise State U., 1988. Cert. quality analyst, quality award examiner, Minn.; cert. Myers Briggs Personality Typing, Star Performance and ISO 9000 auditor. Keytape operator 1st Security Bank, Glasgow, 1968-71; programmer analyst Baldwin Data Svcs., Denver, 1973-76; acctg. technician dept. non-appropriated funds U.S. Govt., Ramstein, Fed. Republic Germany, 1977-79, systems operator dept. non-appropriated funds Fed. Republic Germany, 1979-80; programmer analyst II, United Banks Colo., Denver, 1982-85; programmer analyst Moore Fin. Group, Boise, Idaho, 1985-87, career developer, 1987-88; mgr. quality assurance West One Bancorp, 1988-90; mgr. quality assurance software products Bankers Systems, Inc., St. Cloud, Minn., 1991-93, sr. bus. analyst, 1993-95; owner Applied Bus. Strategies, 1995—; exec. dir., founder Ctrl. Minn. Quality Coun., 1996-99; prof. St. Cloud State U., 1997—2002; asst. prof. mgmt. Coll. St. Benedict, 2002—. Dir. bus. program St. Cloud State U., 2000—01. Mem. pers. com., leader single parents group 1st Presbyn. Ch., 1988-89; bd. dirs. St. Cloud All-City H.S. Marching Band, 1995-96, Forum of Exec. Women, 1996. Recipient Outstanding Project Chmn. award, Jaycee of Month award U.S. Jaycees-Idaho, 1989, Staff Officer of Yr., 1991, Project Chmn. of Yr. 1991, Ambassador, 1993; named Statesman Minn. Jaycees, 1993, Single Parent of the Yr., 1994. Mem. Am. Bus. Women's Assn. (v.p. Boise chpt. 1987-88, Woman of Yr. award 1987), Capitol Jaycees (v.p. for mgmt. devel. 1989), Sartell Jaycees (pres. 1992-93, state del. 1993-94). Republican. Episcopalian. Avocations: skiing, camping. Home: 2808 21st Ave S Saint Cloud MN 56301-9063 Office: 2808 21st Ave S Saint Cloud MN 56301-9063

MCINTYRE-IVY, JOAN CAROL, data processing executive; b. Port Chester, N.Y., Mar. 1, 1939; d. John Henry and Molly Elizabeth (Gates) Daugherty; m. Stanley Donald McIntyre, Aug. 24, 1857 (div. Jan. 1986); children: Michael Stanley McIntyre, David John McIntyre, Sharon Lynne McIntyre; m. James Morrow Ivy IV, June 1, 1988. Student, Northwestern U., 1956-57, U. Ill., 1957-58. Assoc. editor Writer's Digest, Cin., 1966-68; instr. creative writing U. Ala., Huntsville, 1974-75; editor Strode Pubs., 1974-75; paralegal Smith, Huckaby & Graves (now Bradley, Arant, Rose & White), 1976-82; exec. v.p. Micro Craft, Inc., 1982-85, pres., 1985-89, ceo, chmn. bd., 1989—; also bd. dirs., co-owner. Author: numerous computer operating manuals for law office software, 1978—; co-author: Alabama and Federal Complaint Forms, 1979; editor: Alabama Law for the Layman, 1975; contbr. Hon. scholar Medil Sch. Journalism Northwestern U., 1956. Mem. Huntsville Literary Soc. (bd. dirs. 1976-77). Republican. Methodist. Office: 123 Fairington Rd NW Huntsville AL 35806-2249 E-mail: verdictsos@aol.com.

MC ISAAC, GEORGE SCOTT, retired management consultant, government official; b. Auburn, N.Y., July 25, 1930; s. Robert Scott and Agnes Congalton (Aitchison) McI.; m. Betsy Clark, Sept. 11, 1954; children: Ian Scott, Christopher Clark (div. 2000); m. Mary Olds Post, Feb. 2001. BS, Yale U., 1952; MS, U. Rochester, 1961. In mfg. mgmt. Eastman Kodak Co., Rochester, N.Y., 1954-62; dir. McKinsey & Co. (Mgmt. Consultants), N.Y.C., Dusseldorf, Ger., Washington, 1962-78; asst. sec. of energy for resource applications U.S. Dept. Energy, Washington, 1978-80; sr. v.p. ops. Schlegel Corp., Rochester, 1980-85. AT&T resident mgmt. fellow; exec. prof. bus. and pub. policy William E. Simon Grad. Sch. Bus. Adminstrn., U. Rochester, 1985-97; cons. various govts., mfg. cos., fin. instns., non-profit enterprises. Contbr. articles to bus. jours. Bd. dirs. Rochester Hosp. Corp., 1987-94, vice chmn., 1991-93, Rochester Gen. Hosp., 1983-89, chmn., 1986-88; trustee emeritus Internat. Mus. Photography, George Eastman House, chmn. 1987-90. Lt. USMC, 1952-54. Mem.: Met. (Washington), Genesee Valley (Rochester), Owasco (Auburn).

MCIVOR, DONALD KENNETH, retired petroleum company executive; b. Winnipeg, Man., Can., Apr. 12, 1928; s. Kenneth MacIver and Nellie Beatrice (Rutherford) McI.; children: Gordon, Deborah, Duncan, Donald, Daniel. BS with honors in Geology, U. Man., 1950; postgrad., Nat. Def. Coll., 1973. Geophysical trainee seismic crew Imperial Oil Ltd., Alta., 1950, various operational and rsch. positions in exploration, 1950-58, held various positions including asst. to exploration mgr., suprv. exploration planning, mgr. exploration rsch., 1958-68, with Jersey Prodn. Rsch. Co. Angola, France and Tulsa, Okla.; asst. mgr., mgr. corp. planning Toronto HO, 1968-69, mgr. exploration, 1970-72, sr. v.p., dir., 1973, exec. v.p., 1975; v.p. oil and gas exploration and prodn. Exxon Corp., 1977-81; dep. chmn., dir. Imperial Oil Ltd., 1981, chmn., chief exec. officer, 1982-85; dir., sr. v.p. Exxon Corp., Dallas, 1985-92. Bd. dirs. Nat. Coun. on Econ. Edn., Internat. Exec. Svc. Corps., N.W. Oil Co. Mem. Can. Soc. Petroleum Geologists, Am. Petroleum Inst. Home: 79 Lukes Wood Rd New Canaan CT 06840-2202 E-mail: mcivordon@aol.com.

MCIVOR, MARCIA LYNN, law educator, program director, editor; b. Ann Arbor, Mich., Nov. 8, 1937; d. Edgar William and Roberta (Evans) McI.; m. Morton Gitelman, May 15, 1977; children: Neil Gitelman, Lynn Wood Ohl, Eliot Gitelman, Bruce Wood, Ronald Gitelman. BA, Mich. State U., 1958; JD, U. Ark., 1977. Staff atty. Ozark Legal Svcs., Fayetteville, Ark., 1977-85, dir. of litigation, 1985-90, dep. dir., 1990-92; supr. atty. Sch. of Law, U. Ark., 1992-93, assoc. prof., acting dir. local clinic, 1993, dir. clin. edn., 1993—. Editor M&M Press, Fayetteville, 1988—; spl. assoc. justice Ark. Supreme Ct.; del. Ark. Constnl. Conv. Co-author: (books) Arkansas Rules of Evidence, 1988; contbr. chpts. to books in field. Mem. exec. com. Ark. Juvenile Justice Commn., Little Rock, 1989; chair Washington County Juvenile Justice Adv. Bd., 1992-94. Recipient Clin. Legal Edn. award U.S. Dept. Edn., 1993, 94, 95, Law Sch. Legal Edn. award Legal Svcs. Corp., 1994. Mem. ABA, Am. Judicature Soc., Ark. Bar Assn., Ark. Bar Found. Democrat. Unitarian Universalist. Avocations: gardening, photography. Office: Sch of Law U Ark Fayetteville AR 72701

MCKAIN, JOSHUA VAN KIRK, library director; b. Stamford, Conn., Feb. 14, 1967; s. David Wilbur and Sharon Darleen (Daniels) McK.; m. Amy Elizabeth Westerman, June 25, 1994; children: Henry Van Kirk, Lucy Jane Hill. BA, Coll. Wooster, Ohio, 1990; MEd, Widener U., Chester, Pa., 1995; MLS, Simmons Coll., Boston, 1996. Assoc. tchr. Wilmington (Del.) Friends Sch., Del., 1990-92; legal asst. Richards, Layton & Finger, Wilmington, 1992-94; grad. asst. Widener U., Chester, 1994-95; reference libr. Bridgewater (Mass.) State Coll., 1996; libr. dir. Fisher Coll., Boston, 1996—. Peer tutor, copy editor Coll. Wooster, Ohio, 1989-90; editor Nat. Ind. Coll. Coun. Newsletter, 1999—; reviewer Electronic Resources Rev., 1999-2000. Active recreation commn., Scituate, Mass., 1997—; mem. Friends Scituate Pub. Libr.; mem. Cmty. Preservation Com., Scituate; mem. Field Study Com. Mem. ALA, Assn. Coll. Rsch. Librs., Libr. Adminstrn. Mgmt. Assn. Avocations: tennis, Scrabble, basketball, cooking, ping pong. Office: Fisher Coll 118 Beacon St Boston MA 02116-1546 E-mail: jmckain@fisher.edu.

MCKAIN, MARY MARGARET, musician; b. Spokane, Wash., June 11, 1940; d. Neil Dunn and Elinore (Bien) McK. BA in Music and Police Sci., Calif. State U., L.A., 1968; studied trumpet with Rafael Mendez, Jane Sager, Sidney Lazar, and others. Trumpet player Peter Meremblum Jr. Symphony, 1954-59, Jack Benny at Greek Theater, 1963, Highland Park Symphony, L.A., 1955-66, Beverly Hills (Calif.) Symphony, 1960-66, South East Symphony, Downey, Calif., 1957-70, Santa Monica (Calif.) Elks Club, 1965-70, The Foresters, 1965-69, Latin Am. Symphony, L.A., 1961-63, L.A. Concert Band, Mexican Tipica Orch. Symphony, West Covina (Calif.) Symphony, 1976-79, Monterey Park (Calif.) Band, 1970-81, Calif. Concert Band, 1978-81, L.A. Police Dept. Concert Band, 1956-65, San Fernando Valley (Calif.) Opera, 1955-61, Iturbi on Tour, 1961; leader, trumpet player Pieces of 8 Polka Band, L.A., 1961-96; band leader, dir. Elks 99 Concert Band, 1996—, Hollywood Showcase Orch., 1998—. 1st female dep. marshal, L.A. County, 1964-99; Sheriff, 1973; part time musician TV series Here Come The Brides, 1972; musician for film E.T., 1983, leader Elks 99 Concert Band; also numerous TV commls., recordings, 1980—. Mem. Quartz Hill Town Coun.; active Alads, Sheriff's Relief. Mem. Musicians Local 47 (life), Sons and Daughters Mont. Pioneers (life), Wild Life Fedn., U.S. Humane Soc., Marshals Assn. (sec., dir.), Internat. Police Assn. Avocations: fishing, bicycling, genealog. rsch. Home: 43212 45th St W Quartz Hill CA 93536-5523

MCKANE, DAVID BENNETT, business executive; b. Salem, Mass., July 10, 1945; s. Vernon Wilson and Barbara Inez (Bennett) McK.; m. Wilson Lineburgh Baldwin, Apr. 16, 1977; adopted daughters, Taylor A., Lee and Paige Baldwin. BA, Dartmouth Coll., 1967; MBA, Amos Tuck Sch., 1969. Product mgr. Church & Dwight Co. Inc. (Arm and Hammer Products), N.Y.C., 1969-72; v.p. NTA Inc. N.Y.C., Nanuet, N.Y., 1972-75; v.p., exec. asst. to chmn. Schick Inc., Westport, Conn., 1975-77, sr. v.p., 1977-79, COO, exec. v.p., 1979-84, treas., 1980-84; chmn., CEO A.I. Friedman, Inc., N.Y.C., 1985-87; chmn. McKane Robbins & Co. Inc., N.Y.C. and Westport, 1986-96; mng. gen. ptnr. Riverland and Indian Sun, L.C., Westport, 1996—. Bd. dirs. Oakhurst Dairy, Portland, Maine, Impax Corp., Westport. Bd. trustees Greens Farms (Conn.) Acad., 1991—. Mem. New Eng. Soc. in City N.Y., Mass. Mayflower Soc., Union Club (N.Y.C.), Country Club Fairfield, John's Island Club (Vero Beach, Fla.), RedStick Golf Club (Vero Beach, Fla.). Episcopalian. Home: 48 Owenoke Park Westport CT 06880-6833

MCKAUGHAN, HOWARD PAUL, linguistics educator; b. Canoga Park, Calif., July 5, 1922; s. Paul and Edith (Barton) McK.; m. Barbara Jean Budroe, Dec. 25, 1943; children: Edith Santoro, Charlotte Barnhart, Patricia (Mrs. Stephen B. Pike), Barbara (Mrs. Ronald Chester Bell), Judith Rudebusch. AB, UCLA, 1945; MTh, Dallas Theol. Sem., 1946; MA, Cornell U., 1952, PhD, 1957. Mem. linguistic rsch. team Summer Inst. Linguistics, Mexico, 1946-52, assoc. dir. Philippines; also assoc. dir. summers sessions U. N.D., 1952-57, dir. Philippine br., 1957-61; rsch. asst. prof. anthropology U. Wash., 1961-62, rsch. assoc. prof., 1962-63; assoc. prof. linguistics U. Hawaii, 1963-64, prof. linguistics, 1964-88, prof. emeritus, 1988—, chmn. dept., 1963-66, dir. Pacific and Asian Linguistics Inst., 1964, 66-69, assoc. dean grad. divsn., 1965-72, dean grad. divsn., dir. rsch., 1972-79, acting chancellor, 1979, interim vice chancellor acad. affairs, 1981-82, acting dir. rsch., 1982-84, acting dean grad. div., 1982-83, dean, 1984-87, dir. rsch. rels., 1987-88. Lectr. linguistics U. Philippines, summers, 1954, 60; Fulbright vis. prof. Philippine Normal Coll.-Ateneo-De La Salle Consortium, Philippines, 1977, De La Salle U., Philippines, 1992; vis. prof. linguistics Bukidnon State Coll., Malaybalay, Philippines, 1993, 94; linguistic cons. Summer Inst. Linguistics, Malaysia br., 1995—; prin. Wycliffe Sch. Linguistics, summers 1953, 61; vis. prof. Australian Nat. U., Canberra, 1970; adj. prof. linguistics U. Okla., summers 1984, 85, 86; vis. prof., head dept. linguistics Payap U., Chiang Mai, Thailand, 1989-90. Author: (with B. McKaughan) Chatino Dictionary, 1951; (with J. Forster) Ilocano: An Intensive Language Course, 1952; The Inflection and Syntax of Maranao Verbs, 1959, (with B. Macaraya) A Maranao Dictionary, 1967, rev. edit., 1996; editor: Pali Language Texts: Philippines, 21 vols., 1971; The Languages of the Eastern Family of the East New Guinea Highlands Stock, 1973, Maranao Stories, 1995; Stories from the Darangen, 1995; contbr. articles, chpts. to books, sci. jours. Sr. scholar East-West Ctr., Honolulu, 1964; NDEA Maranao-Philippines rsch. grantee, 1963-65; Office of Edn. Hawaii English grantee, 1965-66; NSF Jeh Language of South Vietnam grantee, 1969-70, Maranao Linguistic Studies, 1971-72, numerous other rsch. grants. Mem. Am. Linguistic Soc., Philippines Linguistic Soc., Western Assn. Grad. Schs. Linguistic Soc. (pres. 1978), Hawaii Linguistic Soc., Linguistic Circle N.Y., Philippine Assn. Lang. Tchrs., Hawaii Govt. Employees Assn., Phi Beta Kappa, Phi Kappa Phi. Home: 420 S Hill Rd Mcminnville OR 97128-9105 E-mail: howard_mckaughan@sil.org.

MCKAY, ALEXANDER GORDON, classics educator; b. Toronto, Dec. 24, 1924; s. Alexander Lynn and Marjory Maude Redfern (Nicoll) McKay; m. Helen Jean Zulauf, Dec. 24, 1964; stepchildren: Julie Anne Stephanie Brott, Danae Helen Fraser. BA, U. Toronto, 1946; MA, Yale U., 1947, Princeton U., 1948, PhD, 1950; LLD (hon.), U. Man., 1986, Brock U., 1990, Queen's U., 1991; DLitt (hon.), McMaster U., 1992, U. Waterloo, 1993. Mem. faculty classics Wells Coll., 1949-50, U. Pa., 1950-51, U. Man., 1951-52, 55-57, Mt. Allison U., 1952-53, Waterloo Coll., 1953-55; mem. faculty McMaster U., 1957-90, prof., chmn. dept. classics, 1962-68, 76-79, dean humanities, 1968-73, mem. faculty senate, 1968-73, 85-87, prof. emeritus, 1990—; Disting. vis. prof. classics U. Colo., 1978; prof. in charge Intercollegiate Center for Classical Studies, Rome, 1975; vis. mem. Inst. Advanced Study, Princeton, 1979, 81. Vis. scholar U. Tex., Austin, 1987, Hardt, Vandoevres, Geneva, 88; vis. fellow Trinity Coll., Cambridge, 1988; adj. prof. Miami U., Oxford, Ohio, 1989, Oxford, 1992—95; adj. prof. humanities York U., 1990—96; Disting. vis. lectr. Concordia U., Montreal, 1992—93, prof. emeritus, 2001—; vis. scholar Rockefeller Study and Conf. Ctr., Bellagio (Como), Italy, 1993. Author: Naples and Campania: Texts and Illustrations, 1962, Roman Lyric Poetry: Catullus and Horace, 2d edit., 1974, Vergil's Italy, 1970, Cumae and the Phlegraean Fields, 1972, Naples and Coastal Campania, 1972, Houses, Villas and Palaces in the Roman World, 1975, reprint, 1998, Roman Satire, 1976, Vitruvius, Architect and Engineer, 1978, 2d edit., 1985, Römische Häuser, Villen und Paläste, 1980, Roma Antiqua: Latium and Etruria, 1986; co-author: Selections from Vergil, Aeneid I, IV and VI (Dido and Aeneas), 1988, Festschrift, The Two Worlds of the Poet: New Perspectives on Vergil, 1992, Tragedy, Love, and Change: Roman Poetic Themes and Variations, 1994, Arma Virumque: Heroes at War (Aeneid 10 and 12), 2 vols., 1998, Classics at McMaster (1890-2000), 2000. Pres., bd. govs. Hamilton Philharm. Orch., 1967-96, Hamilton Chamber Music Soc., 1965-67, Hamilton br. Archtl. Conservancy Ont., 1965-67, Hamilton and Region Arts coun., 1971-72; bd. dirs. Can. Fedn. Humanities, 1980-82; v.p., dir. Internat. Acad. Union, 1978-90; v.p. U. Bristol, Inst. Hellenic & Roman Studies; trustee Hamilton Found., 1972-75; bd. govs. Art Gallery Hamilton; bd. govs., dir. Boris Brott Summer Music Festival, 1989-2001, Montreal Chamber Music Festival, 1997—; presdl. bd. trustees McMaster U. Art Gallery, 1985-91; pres. Sir Ernest MacMillan String Ensemble, 1988-90, Nat. Acad. Orch., 2001–; mem. adv. bd. Inst. for Classical Tradition, Boston U., 1987-88; v.p., dir. Bach-Elgar Choral Soc., Hamilton, 1992-95. Decorated knight comdr. Order St. John of Jerusalem; officer Order of Can.; recipient Silver Jubilee medal Queen Elizabeth II, 1977, 125th Anniversary medal Can. Confedn.; Woodrow Wilson fellow, 1947-48, Can. Coun. fellow, 1973-74, Killam rsch. fellow, 1979-80, fellow Vanier Coll., York U., 1991—, vis. scholar, 1996—. Fellow Royal Soc. Can. (hon. editor 1970-83, pres. 1984-87, past pres. 1987-89, Centennial medal 1982); mem. Vergilian Soc. (pres. 1972-74, Hon. Pres. for Life 1988—, chmn. Villa Vergiliana mgmt. com. 1993—), Classical Assn. Mid. West and South (award of merit com. 1989-91), Classical Assn. Can. (v.p. 1970-72, 76-78, pres. 1978-80), Ont. Classical Assn. (hon. pres. 1994—), Master Print and Drawing Soc. (Toronto) (v.p. 1998-2001, pres. 2001-—), Yale Club (N.Y.C.), Univ. Club (Pitts.), Tamahaac Club (Ancaster), Arts and Letters Club (Toronto), X Club (Toronto), Univ. Club (McMaster). Home: 1 Turner Ave Hamilton ON Canada L8P 3K4 Office: McMaster U Dept of Classics Hamilton ON Canada L8S 4M2 E-mail: ag.mckay@sympatico.ca.

MCKAY, DAN BOIES, JR. lawyer; b. Monroe, La., Aug. 31, 1948; s. Dan Boies and Joanna Irwin (McCoy) McK.; m. Adrienne Lee, Aug. 20, 1977; children: Holly, Managan, Dan B. III. BA, U. La., 1970; BS, U. Tex., 1975; JD, La. State U., 1980. Bar: La. 1980, U.S. Dist. Ct. (mid. dist.) La. 1981, U.S. Dist. Ct. (we. and ea. dists.) La. 1982, U.S. Ct. Appeals (5th cir.) 1982, U.S. Supreme Ct. 1993. Assoc. N.M. Lee & Assocs., Bunkie, La., 1980-83; sole practice, 1984—. Atty. City of Bunkie, 1982-90; magistrate, atty. Village of Hessmer, La., 1984—. Defender indigents Avoyelles Parish, Marksville, La., 1984-88, chief indigent defender, 1991—. Mem. ABA, La. State Bar Assn. (ho. of dels. 1984-87, 92—), La. Pub. DefendersAssn., Rotary (pres. Bunkie chpt. 1984-85), La. City Attys. Assn. (pres. 1988-89). Democrat. Southern Baptist. Avocation: bicycling. Home: 701 Lake St Bunkie LA 71322-1734 Office: PO Box 720 404 Walnut St Bunkie LA 71322-1765

MCKAY, DIANNE ADELE MILLS, humanities educator, educator; b. New Brunswick, N.J., Mar. 23, 1947; d. George M. and Dorothy Allen Mills; m. Thomas McKay III; children: Robert Allen, Heather Anne. BA in Am. Studies, Douglass Coll., 1969; MA, U. Pa., 1970, postgrad. Cert. substitute tchr., N.J. Mgr., trainer Fidelity Mut. Life Ins. Co., 1977-80; instr. humanities U. So. Colo., 1991—, Burlington County Coll., 1990—, Fairleigh Dickinson U., 2000—. Trustee New Covenant Presbyn. Ch., 1988—; mem. Hainesport Twp. Bd. Edn., 1983-90, 93-96, v.p., 1985-90; mem. Hainesport Twp. Zoning Bd. Adjustment, 1983-94, chair, 1985-89; bd. dirs. Burlington County Girl Scout Coun., 1993-95, Girl Scouts of the South Jersey Pines, 1995-96, Burlington County Red Cross, 1994—; Burlington County Com. on Women, 1993-98, chair, 1994; adv. com. mem. N.J. Coalition for Battered Women, 1993-97; gender equity task force N.J. State Employment and Tng. Commn., 1993-95; equity adv. com. N.J. Dept. Edn., 1993–, chair, 1998; chair N.J. Coun. on Gender Parity in Labor and Edn.; chair N.J. Adv. Commn. on the Status of Women, 1998–. Mem. LWV, AAUW (pres. N.J. 1995-98, bd. dirs., exec. com, v.p. N.J. membership 1989—, br. pres. 1985-87), Assoc. Alumnae of Douglass Coll. (bd. dirs. 1989—, alumnae class pres. 1985-89, 94—), Douglass Soc., Delta Kappa Gamma. Home: 12 Whittier Dr Hainesport NJ 08036-4812

MC KAY, EMILY GANTZ, civil rights professional; b. Columbus, Ohio, Mar. 13, 1945; d. Harry S. and Edwina (Bookwalter) Gantz; m. Jack Alexander McKay, July 3, 1965. BA, Stanford U., 1966, MA, 1967. From pub. info. specialist to rsch. assoc. Cmty. Action Pitts., 1967-70; freelance cons., 1969-70; pub. rels. & materials specialist Met. Cleve. JOBS Coun., 1971-72; rsch. & mgmt. cons. BLK Group, Inc., Washington, 1970-73; dir. tech. products Am. Tech. Assistance Corp., McLean, Va., 1973-74; rsch. and mgmt. cons. CONSAD Rsch. Corp., Pitts., 1974-76, v.p., 1976-78; spl. asst. to pres. for planning and eval. Nat. Coun. La Raza, Washington, 1978-82, v.p. rsch., advocacy & legislation, 1981-88, exec. v.p., 1983-88, cons. to pres., 1988-90, v.p. instl. devel., 1991-93, sr. v.p. instl. devel., 1993-94. Pres. Mosaica: Ctr. for Nonprofit Devel. and Pluralism, 1994—; cons. resource devel. New Israel Fund, 1989-91; cons. City of Cleve., Nat. Assn. Cmty. Devel., Nat. Coun. La Raza, 1975-78, Ford Found., 1989, Nat. AIDS Network, 1988-89, Am. Cultural Ctr., Israel, 1990, 2000, Nat. Hispana Leadership Inst., 1993; vol. orgnl. cons. SHATIL, Jerusalem and cmty. based groups in Israel, 1987—; guest faculty Union Inst. Grad. Sch.; adj. faculty Sch. Internat. Svc. Am. U., Washington, 1995—. Author devel. tng. materials and HIV/AIDS tech. assistance materials. Co-chmn. Citizens Adv. Com. to D.C. Bar, 1986-87; mem. Mayor's Commn. Coop. Econ. Devel., 1981-83; non-lawyer mem. bd. govs. D.C. Bar, 1982-85; exec. com., bd. dirs. Indochina Resource Action Ctr., 1982-92; bd. dirs. exec. com. Southeast Asia Resource Action Ctr., 1993-97; co-chmn. Citizens Commn. Adminstrn. Justice, 1982-84; exec. com. Coalition on Human Needs, 1981-88; mem. Washington area steering com. New Israel Fund, 1989-91; co-chmn. adv. com. to Washington dist. office dir. Immigration and Naturalization Svc., 1984-88; chair Refugee Women in Devel., 1987-90, vice-chair, 1990-94; nat. adv. bd. Project Blueprint United Way of Am., 1992-94, diversity com., 1994-96; vice-chair, treas. Fund for the Future of Our Children, 1994—; sec. bd. dirs. New Bosnia Fund, 1995-99, U.S. vice-chair, 1997-99; bd. advisors Internat. Ctr. for Residential Edn., 1994-96; bd. dirs. Mary's Ctr. Maternal and Child Care, 1995-2000, treas., 1996-2000; treas., bd. dirs. AVODAH: The Jewish Svc. Corps., 1996-99; bd. dirs. Nat. Hispana Leadership Inst., 1997—, treas., 1998—; mem. working group Memorandum of Understanding between HHS and Israeli Ministry of Labour and Social Welfare, 1990-94, chair subcom Youth at Risk, 1992-94; adv. merit sel. panel Superior Ct. D.C., 1987-90; mem. US-Israel Women to Women planning task force, 2000-2001. Recipient I. Pat Rios award Guadalupe Ctr., 1988; Ford Found. nat. honors fellow, 1966-67. Mem. NAACP, Nat. Coun. La Raza, Phi Beta Kappa. Democrat. Home: 3200 19th St NW Washington DC 20010-1006 Office: 1522 K St NW Ste 1130 Washington DC 20005-1225 E-mail: Emily@mosaica.org.

MCKAY, JOHN, lawyer; b. Seattle, June 19, 1956; s. John Larkin and Kathleen (Tierney) M. BA, U. Wash., 1978; JD, Creighton U., 1982. Bar: Wash. 1982, U.S. Dist. Ct. (we. dist.) Wash. 1982, U.S. Supreme Ct. 1990, U.S. Ct. Appeals (9th cir.) 1990, D.C. 1999. Ptnr. Lane Powell Spears Lubersky, Seattle, 1982-92, Cairncross & Hempelmann, Seattle, 1992-97; pres. Legal Svcs. Corp., Washington, 1997—2001; U.S. atty. We. dist. Wash. U.S. Dept. Justice, 2001—. White House fellow, Washington, 1989-90. Mem. ABA (bd. govs. 1991-94), Wash. State Bar Assn. (pres. young lawyers divsn. 1988-89). Republican. Roman Catholic. Avocations: soccer, golf. Office: US Atty 601 Union St Ste 5100 Seattle WA 98101-3903

MCKAY, JOHN DOUGLAS, lawyer; b. Wheeling, W.Va., Feb. 27, 1960; s. Douglas and Margaret Ann McK.; m. Jennifer Hall, June 13, 1987; children: John Wallace, Megan Diane, Hannah Nadine, Katherine Lorraine. BA with distinction, U. Va., 1982; JD, U. Maine, 1985. Bar: W.Va. 1985, Maine 1985, U.S. Dist. Ct. (so. dist.) W.Va. 1985, U.S. Dist. Ct. Maine 1985, U.S. Ct. Appeals (1st cir.) 1986, Va. 1988, U.S. Ct. Appeals (4th cir.) 1988, U.S. Dist. Ct. (we. dist.) Va. 1988, Colo. 1997, Fla. 1999, N.Y. 2002, Calif. 2002. Assoc. Petruccelli, Cohen, Erler & Cox, Portland, Maine, 1985-88, Taylor & Zunka,

Ltd., Charlottesville, Va., 1988-91; ptnr. McKay & Cattano PLC, 1991-97; prin. McKay Law Offices, 1997—. Founder, editor (legal newsletter) Equine Law & Bus. Letter, 1990-95; contbr. articles to profl. jours. Elder Presbyn. Ch. Recipient Best Adv. award U. Maine Sch. of Law, 1988. Mem. Va. State Bar (7th dist. disciplinary com. 1994-2000), W.Va. State Bar, Charlottesville-Albemarle Bar Assn. (bd. dirs. 1994-96), Thomas Jefferson Inn of Ct. (past pres). Office: McKay Law Offices 1 Boars Head Ln Charlottesville VA 22903-4610

MCKAY, JOHN JUDSON, JR. lawyer; b. Anderson, S.C., Aug. 13, 1939; s. John Judson and Polly (Plowden) McK.; m. Jill Hall Ryon, Aug. 3, 1961 (div. Dec. 1980); children: Julia Plowden, Katherine Henry, William Ryon, Elizabeth Hall; m. Jane Leahey, Feb. 18, 1982; children: Andrew Leahey, Jennifer McFaddin. AB in History, U. S.C., 1960, JD cum laude, 1966. Bar: S.C. 1966, U.S. Dist. Ct. S.C. 1966, U.S. Ct. Appeals (4th cir.) 1974, U.S. Supreme Ct. 1981, U.S. Dist. Ct. (so. dist.) Ga. 1988, U.S. Ct. Appeals (11th cist.) 1990. Assoc. Haynsworth, Perry, Bryant, Marion & Johnstone, Greenville, S.C., 1966-70; ptnr. Rainey, McKay, Britton, Gibbes & Clarkson, P.A. predecessor, 1970-78; sole practice Hilton Head Island, S.C., 1978-80; ptnr. McKay & Gertz, P.A., 1980-81, McKay & Mullen, P.A., Hilton Head Island, 1981-88, McKay & Taylor, Hilton Head Island, 1988-91; pvt. practice, 1991—. Editor-in-chief U. S.C. Law Rev., 1966; contbr. articles to legal jours. E-mail: jmckay@mckaylawfirm.com. Served to lt. (j.g.) USNR, 1961-64; lt. comdr. Res. (ret.). Mem. ABA, S.C. Bar Assn. (pres. young lawyers sect. 1970, exec. com. 1971-72, assoc. mem. grievance and disciplinary com. 1983-87), S.C. Bar, Beaufort County Bar Assn., Hilton Head Bar Assn., Assn. Trial Lawyers Am., S.C. Trial Lawyers Assn., S.C. Bar Found. (pres. 1977), Blue Key, Wig and Robe, Phi Delta Phi. Clubs: Poinsett (Greenville). Episcopalian. Home: 17 Foxbriar Ln Hilton Head Island SC 29926 Office: 203 Watersedge Hilton Head Island SC 29928-3541 E-mail: jmckay@mckaylawfirm.com.

MCKAY, JOHN M. state senator; b. Winter Haven, Fla., Sept. 23, 1948; m. Michelle Dodson; children: Mary Patricia, Sara Jane, Meredith. BS, Fla. State U., 1972. Real estate broker; mortgage broker; senator 26th dist. Fla. State Legislature, 1990—, pres., 2002—. Mem. agr. com., children, families and srs. com., natural resources com., rules and calendar com., ways and means com., human svcs. subcom., WAGES Targeted Econ. Devel. select com., joint legis. mgmt. com., chmn. cmty. affairs com. Fla. State Senate. Chmn. Bradenton (Fla.) Downtown Devel. Authority, 1989-90, Bradenton Cmty. Redevel. Agy., 1989-90; bd. dirs. Habitat for Humanity, 1989-90; elder 1st Presbyn. Ch., Bradenton, Fla. With U.S. Army N.G., U.S. Army Res., 1969-75. Recipient Cornerstone of Fla. Bus. award Fla. C. of C., 1993, 95, Legis. Svc. award Fla. Assn. C.C.s, 1993, Legis. Leadership award Fla. Med. Assn., 1993, Legislator of Yr. award Fla. Alcohol and Drug Abuse Assn., 1994, Fla. Assn. Realtors, 1995, Internat. Coun. Shopping Ctrs., 1995, Friends of Agr. award Fla. Farm Bur., 1994, Honors award Fla. Educators of Hearing Impaired, 1995, Legis. award Fla. Sheriffs Assn., 1995, Organized Fishermen of Fla., 1995, Svc. award Tampa Bay Regional Planning Coun., 1996, Appreciation award Port Authority of Manatee County, 1996, Cmty. Comm. award Tampa Ednl. Cable Consortium, 1996, County Champion award Fla. Assn. of Counties, 1996. Mem. Learning Disability Assn. of Fla. (bd. dirs.), Manatee and Sarasota C. of C., Kiwanis. Republican. Avocations: golf, sailing. Office: Fla Capitol 404 S Monroe St Tallahassee FL 32399-6526 also: 3653 Cortez Rd W # 90 Bradenton FL 34210-3106*

MCKAY, JOHN PATRICK, history educator; b. St. Louis, Aug. 27, 1938; s. John Price and Eleanor Jeffrey McKay; m. JoAnn Ott, Apr. 21, 1961; children: John Philip, Thomas Jeffrey. BA, Wesleyan U., Middletown, Conn., 1961; MA, Tufts U., 1962; PhD, U. Calif., Berkeley, 1968. From instr. to assoc. prof. history U. Ill., Urbana, 1966-76, prof., 1976-99, prof. emeritus, adj. tchg. prof., 1999—. Mem. author's adv. bd. Houghton Mifflin Co., Boston, 1992-94. Author: Pioneers for Profit: Foreign Entrepreneurship and Russian Industrialization, 1885-1913, 1970 (Herbert Baxter Adams prize Am. Hist. Assn. 1970), Tramways and Trolleys: The Rise of Urban Mass Transit in Europe, 1976; co-author: (with B. Hill and J. Buckler) A History of Western Society, 1979, 6th edit., 1999, (with B. Hill, J. Buckler and P. Ebrey) A History of World Societies, 1983, 5th edit., 2000; mem. editl. bd. Bus. History Rev., 1980—. Fellow for western Europe, Fgn. Area Program, 1964-66, John Simon Guggenheim fellow, 1970, Internat. Rsch. Exch. fellow, USSR, 1970, fellow NEH, 1984. Mem. Am. Hist. Assn., Econ. History Assn., Bus. History Conf., World History Assn., French Hist. Soc. Avocations: hiking, travel, gardening, pool. Office: U Ill Dept History 810 S Wright St Urbana IL 61801

MCKAY, JOHN ROBERT, music educator; b. Montreal, Que., Can., Nov. 11, 1938; arrived in U.S., 1974; s. Gordon Douglas and Denise Isabel (Lamontagne) McKay; m. Sara Hayden McKay, Sept. 9, 1964; children: Johanna Ethel, Edward Murray, Elizabeth Denise. MusB, McGill U., Montreal, 1961; MusM, Eastman Sch. Music, 1975, DMA, 1978. Tchr. piano U. Toronto, Canada, 1969—72; asst. prof. Dalhousie U., Halifax, Canada, 1972—74; prof. music Gustavus Adolphus Coll., St. Peter, Minn., 1976—. Home: 428 Wabasha St Saint Peter MN 56082 Office: Gustavus Adolphus Coll. 800 College Ave Saint Peter MN 56082

MCKAY, KENNETH GARDINER, physicist, electronics company executive; b. Montreal, Que., Can., Apr. 8, 1917; came to U.S., 1946, naturalized, 1954; s. James Gardiner and Margaret (Nicholas) McK.; m. Irene C. Smith, July 25, 1942; children— Margaret Craig, Kenneth Gardiner B.Sc., McGill U., 1938, M.Sc., 1939; Sc.D, MIT, 1941; D.Eng. (hon.), Stevens Inst. Tech., 1980. Research engr. Nat. Research Council Can., 1941-46; with Bell Telephone Labs., 1946-66, 73-80, dir. solid state device devel., 1957-59, v.p. systems engring., 1959-62, exec. v.p. systems engring., 1962-66, exec. v.p., 1973-80; v.p. engring AT&T, 1966-73; chmn. bd. Bellcomm Inc., 1966-73, Charles Stark Draper Lab., 1982-87. Advisor Min. of Transp. and Comms., Republic of China, 1982-95. Trustee Stevens Inst. Tech., 1974-87; bd. govs. McGill U., 1972-77, N.Y. Coll. Osteo. Medicine, 1980-89; mem. vis. com. for engring. Stanford U., 1974-87; mem. sci. and acad. adv. com. U. Calif., 1980-88; mem. Sci. and Tech. Adv. Group, Republic of China, 1982-96. Fellow IEEE, Am. Phys. Soc., N.Y. Acad. Scis.; mem. NAS, NAE (councillor 1970-73), Century Assn. Home and Office: 200 E 66th St Apt A1901 New York NY 10021-9179

MCKAY, LAURA L. banker, consultant; b. Watonga, Okla., Mar. 3, 1947; d. Frank Bradford and Elizabeth Jane (Smith) Drew; m. Cecil O. McKay, Sept. 20, 1969; 1 child, Leslie. BSBA, Oreg. State U., 1969. Cert. cash mgr., Treasury Mgmt. Assn. New br. research U.S. Bank, Portland, Oreg., 1969-80, cash mgmt. officer, 1980-82, asst. v.p., 1982-87, v.p., 1987-94; founder, cons. LLM Cons., Milw., 1994-97; co-founder, mng. ptnr. DMC & Assocs. LLC, Portland, 1997—; v.p. treasury mgmt., sales mgr. West Coast Bank, 2000—. Cert. trainer Achieve Global and Edge Learning. Chmn. Budget Com., North Clackamas Sch. Dist., 1982-84. Mem. ASTD, Assn. for Fin. Profls., Nat. Assn. Bank Women (chmn. Oreg. group 1979-80), Portland Cash Mgrs. Assn., Portland C. of C. Republican. Office: DMC & Assocs 5686 SE Viewcrest Dr Portland OR 97267-4146 E-mail: lauramckay@aol.com.

MCKAY, MICHAEL DENNIS, lawyer; b. Omaha, May 12, 1951; s. John Larkin and Kathleen (Tierney) McK.; m. Christy Ann Cordwin, Apr. 22, 1978; children: Kevin Tierney, Kathleen Lindsay, John Larkin. BA in Polit. Sci. with distinction, U. Wash., 1973; JD, Creighton U., 1976. Bar: Wash. 1976, U.S. Dist. Ct. (we. dist.) Wash. 1978, U.S. Dist. Ct. (ea. dist.) Wash. 1982, U.S. Ct. Appeals (9th cir.) 1982, U.S. Supreme Ct. 1993. Sr. dep. pros. atty. King County, Seattle, 1976-81; ptnr. McKay & Gaitan, 1981-89; U.S. atty. we. dist. Wash., 1989-93; ptnr. Lane Powell Spears Lubersky, 1993-95, McKay Chadwell PLLC, Seattle, 1995—. Bd. dirs. Mental Health North, Seattle, 1982-85, St. Joseph Sch. Bd., 1984-87, Our Lady of Fatima Sch. Commn., 1994-97, Creighton U., 1988-90; mem. stadium adv. bd. Seattle Kingdome, 1987-89; mem. U.S. Atty. Gen. Adv. Com., 1991-93, vice chmn., 1992; mem. Washington Citizens' Commn. on Salaries for Elected Officials, 1997—; vice chmn., 1999—; vice chmn. Seattle Expert Rev. Panel, 1999; co-chair Washington State George W. Bush Campaign, 2000. Mem. Creighton U. Alumni Assn. (pres. 1988-90, nat. alumni bd. 1988-92), Wash. Athletic Club, Columbia Tower Club. Republican. Roman Catholic. Avocations: swimming, golf. Office: McKay Chadwell PLLC 701 5th Ave Seattle WA 98104-7097 E-mail: mckay@mckay-chadwell.com.

MCKAY, MONROE GUNN, federal judge; b. Huntsville, Utah, May 30, 1928; s. James Gunn and Elizabeth (Peterson) McK.; m. Lucile A. Kinnison, Aug. 6, 1954; children: Michele, Valanne, Margaret, James, Melanie, Nathan, Bruce, Lisa, Monroe. BS, Brigham Young U., 1957; JD, U. Chgo., 1960. Bar: Ariz. 1961. Law clk. Ariz. Supreme Ct., 1960-61; assoc. firm Lewis & Roca, Phoenix, 1961-66, ptnr., 1968-74; assoc. prof. Brigham Young U., 1974-76, prof., 1976-77; judge U.S. Ct. Appeals for 10th Cir., Denver, 1977-91, chief judge, 1991-94, sr. judge, 1994—. Mem. Phoenix Community Council Juvenile Problems, 1968-74; pres. Ariz. Assn. for Health and Welfare, 1970-72; dir. Peace Corps, Malawi, Africa, 1966-68; bd. dirs., pres. Maricopa county Legal Aid Soc., 1972-74. Served with USMCR, 1946-48. Mem. Ariz. Bar Assn. Mem. Lds Ch. Office: US Ct Appeals 10th Cir Fed Bldg 125 S State St Ste 6012 Salt Lake City UT 84138-1181

MCKAY, NEIL, banker; b. East Tawas, Mich., Aug. 9, 1917; s. Lloyd G. and Rose (McDonald) McK.; m. Olive D. Baird, Nov. 11, 1950; children: Julia B., Lynn B., Hunter L. AB, U. Mich., 1939, JD with distinction, 1946. Bar: Mich. 1946, Ill. 1947. With firm Winston & Strawn, Chgo., 1946-63, partner, 1954-63, mem. mgmt. com., 1958-63; with First Nat. Bank of Chgo., 1963-83, from v.p. charge heavy industry lending div., gen. mgr. London br., to exec. v.p., cashier, 1970-75, vice chmn. bd., 1976-83, also dir. Exec. v.p., sec. First Chgo. Corp., 1970-75, vice chmn. bd., 1976-83; also bd. dirs.; bd. dirs. Baird & Warner, Inc., Chgo.; founding dir. Student Loan Mktg. Assn. Mem.: U. Mich. Law Rev; assoc. editor-in-chief: U. Mich. Law Rev., 1942, sr. editor, 1946. Trustee Morton Arboretum; former trustee Kalamazoo Coll. and Ill. Inst. Tech. Served with USNR, 1942-46. Mem. ABA, Ill. Bar Assn., Dunham Woods Riding Club, Chgo. Hort. Soc. (bd. dirs.), Chgo. Club, Mid-Day Club, Geneva Golf Club. Office: 21 S Clark St Ste 2590 Chicago IL 60603

MCKAY, RENEE, artist; b. Montreal, Que., Can. came to U.S., 1946, naturalized, 1954; d. Frederick Garvin and Mildred Gladys (Higgins) Smith; m. Kenneth Gardiner McKay, July 25, 1942; children: Margaret Craig, Kenneth Gardner. BA, McGill U., 1941. Tchr. art Peck Sch., Morristown, N.J., 1955-56. One woman shows include Pen and Brush Club, N.Y.C., 1957, Cosmopolitan Club, N.Y.C., 1958; group shows include Weyhe Gallery, N.Y.C., 1978, Newark Mus., 1955, 59, Montclair (N.J.) Mus., 1955-58, Nat. Assn. Women Artists, Nat. Acad. Galleries, 1954-78, N.Y. World's Fair, 1964-65, Audubon Artists, N.Y.C., 1955-62, 74-79, N.Y. Soc. Women Artists, 1979-80, Provincetown (Mass.) Art Assn. and Mus., 1975-79; traveling shows in France, Belgium, Italy, Scotland, Can., Japan; represented in permanent collections: Slater Meml. Mus., Norwich, Conn., Norfolk (Va.) Mus., Butler Inst. Am. Art, Youngstown, Ohio, Lydia Drake Libr., Pembroke, Mass., Nat. Arts Club, N.Y.C., Provinceton Mus.- Mass., Provincetown, many pvt. collections. Recipient Jane Peterson prize in oils Nat. Assn. Women Artists, 1954, Famous Artists Sch. prize in watercolor, 1959, Grumbacher Artists Watercolor award 1970, Solo award Pen and Brush, 1957, Sadie-Max Tesser award in watercolor Audubon Artists, 1975, Peterson prize in oils, 1980, Michael Engel prize Nat. Soc. Painters in Casein and Acrylic, 1983. Mem. Nat. Assn. Women Artists (2d v.p. 1969-70, adv. bd. 1974-76), Audubon Artists (pres. 1979, dir. oils 1986-88), Artist Equity (dir. 1977-79, v.p. 1979-81), N.Y. Soc. Women Artists, Pen and Brush, Nat. Soc. Painters in Casein and Acrylic M.J. Kaplan prize 1984, Nat. Arts Club, Provincetown Art Assn. and Mus., Key West Art Assn., Cosmopolitan Club.

MCKAY, RICHARD JAMES, lawyer; b. Eugene, Oreg., Mar. 16, 1959; s. John H. and Nancy Jean (Hunter) McK.; m. Terrin Lea Few, May 19, 1984; children: K. Hunter, John Crosby. BA, Princeton U., 1981; JD, Stetson Coll. Law, St. Petersburg, Fla., 1984. Bar: Fla. 1984, U.S. Dist. Ct. (mid. dist.) Fla. 1984. Law clk. Judge William Terrell Hodges U.S. Dist. Ct. (middle dist. Fla.), Tampa, 1984-86; ptnr. Hill, Ward & Henderson, Fla., 1986-92, Tampa Bay Bucaneers, 1992—, gen. mgr. Adj. prof. Stetson Coll. Law, St. Petersburg, 1989-92; co-chmn. NFL Competition Com., 1994—. Office: Tampa Bay Buccaneers One Buccaneer Pl Tampa FL 33607 E-mail: mckayr@buccaneers.nfl.com.

MCKAY, SUSAN BOGART, social worker, consultant, artist; b. Miami, Fla., Sept. 25, 1957; d. Frederic Stanley and Jeanette Sophie (Braka) B.; m. Mark G. McKay, Jan. 14, 1989. AAS, Westchester C.C., 1986; BS in Social Work magna cum laude, Mercy Coll., 1988. Child care counselor Oaklane Day Care, Chapagua, N.Y., Children's Village, Dobbs Ferry; swim instr. for blind and visually impaired teens and adults YMCA, White Plains; group leader spl. svcs. programs, supr. teens vol. programs YM and YWHA of Mid-Westchester, Scarsdale; healthcare and benefit cons. in pvt. practice, Mamaroneck. Cons. Midland Credit Corp., N.Y.C. Exhibited art works, Westchester, N.Y., 1997-99. Participant human rights commn. Nat. UN Model Conf., 1987. Mem. NASW, Mercy Coll. Alumni Assn., Alpha Chi.

MCKAY, THOMAS FREDERICK, retired radiologist; b. Seattle, Jan. 18, 1928; s. Thomas Alexander McKay and Annie Rosina (Cond) Parker; m. Mary Ann Cordes, May 22, 1954; children: Wendy, Michelle, Thomas, Daniel. BS, U. Wash., 1950, MD, 1953. Diplomate Am. Bd. Radiology. Intern Salt Lake Gen. Hosp., Salt Lake City, 1953-54; resident in pathology U. Chgo. Clinic, 1955; resident in radiology U. Calif., San Francisco, 1957-60; instr. radiology U. Wash., 1963-65. With U.S. Army, 1947—48, Korea. Mem. Am. Roentgen Ray Soc., Radiol. Soc. N.Am., Am. Heart Assn. Democrat. Episcopalian. Office: 1297 Stone Hearth Ln Lincoln CA 95648

MCKEACHIE, WILBERT JAMES, psychologist, educator; b. Clarkston, Mich., Aug. 24, 1921; s. Bert A. and Edith E. (Welberry) McK.; m. Virginia Mae Mack, Oct. 30, 1942; children: Linda, Karen. BA, Mich. State Normal Coll., 1942; MA, U. Mich., 1946, PhD, 1949; LLD, Ea. Mich. U., 1957, U. Cin.; ScD, Northwestern U., 1973, Denison U., 1975, Nat. Acad. Edn., 1977, Alma Coll., 1995; DLitt (hon.), Hope Coll., 1985; LHD (hon.), Shawnee State U., 1994. Faculty U. Mich., 1946—, chmn. dept., 1961-71, dir. Center for Research in Learning and Teaching, 1975-83. Mem. nat. adv. mental health council NIMH, 1976-80; mem. spl. med. adv. group VA, 1967-72 Author: (with J.E. Milholland) Undergraduate Curricula in Psychology, 1961, (with Charlotte Doyle and Mary Margaret Moffett) Psychology, 1966, 3d edit., 1977 (also Spanish edit. and instr.'s manual), Teaching Tips, 11th edit., 2002. Trustee Kalamazoo Coll., 1964-77; trustee-at-large Am. Psychol. Found., 1974-84, 92-96, pres., 1979-82. Officer USNR, 1943-45. Recipient Outstanding Tchr. award U. Mich. Alumni Assn., Am. Coll. Testing-Am. Ednl. Rsch. Assn. award for outstanding rsch. on coll. students, 1973, career contbns. award, 1990, award for disting. teaching in psychology Am. Psychol. Found., 1985, Gold medal award Am. Psychol. Found., others. Mem. APA (sec., dir., pres. 1976-77, Disting. Career Contbn. to Edn. and Tng. in Psychology award 1987, E.L. Thorndike award for outstanding rsch., 1988), Internat. Assn. Applied Psychology (pres. div. ednl. instrn. and sch. psychology 1982-86), Am. Assn. Higher Edn. (dir. 1974-80, pres. 1978), AAUP (pres. U. Mich. chpt. 1970-71), AAAS (chmn. sect. on psychology 1976-77), Sigma Xi. American Baptist. Home: 4660 Joy Rd Dexter MI 48130-9706 Office: U Mich Dept Psychology 525 E University Ave Ann Arbor MI 48109-1109 E-mail: billmck@umich.edu.

MCKEAGUE, DAVID WILLIAM, judge; b. Pitts., Nov. 5, 1946; s. Herbert William and Phyllis (Forsyth) McK.; m. Nancy L. Palmer, May 20, 1989; children: Mike, Melissa, Sarah, Laura, Elizabeth, Adam. BBA, U. Mich., 1968, JD, 1971. Bar: Mich. 1971, U.S. Dist. Ct. (we. dist.) Mich. 1972, U.S. Dist. Ct. (ea. dist.) 1978, U.S. Ct. Appeals (6th cir.) 1988. Assoc. Foster, Swift, Collins & Smith, Lansing, Mich., 1971-76, ptnr., 1976-92, sec.-treas., 1990-92; adj. prof. Thomas M. Colley Law Sch., 1995—96; judge U.S. Dist. Ct., Western Dist. Mich., Lansing, 1992—. Adj. prof. TDetroit Coll. of Law, Mich State U., 1998—. Nat. com. U. Mich. Law Sch. Fund, 1980-92; gen. counsel Mich. Rep. Com., 1989-92; adv. coun. Wharton Ctr., Mich. State U., 1996—; adv. bd. Corp. for Supportive Housing, 2002—. Mem. FBA (bd. dirs. Western Mich. chpt. 1991—), Mich. Bar Assn., Am. Inns of Ct. (pres. Mich. State U. Detroit Coll. of Law chpt. 1999-01), Country Club Lansing (bd. govs. 1988-92, 96—), The Federalist Soc. for Law and Pub. Studies (lawyers divsn. Mich. chpt. 1996—). Roman Catholic. Office: US Dist Ct 315 W Allegan St Lansing MI 48933-1500

MCKEAGUE, NANCY PALMER, trade association executive; b. Detroit, Apr. 12, 1955; d. Spencer Jay and Barbara Jeanne (Murray) Palmer; m. Ronald Martin Nowak, Oct. 23, 1971 (div. 1978); children: Michael M., Melissa J.; m. David William McKeague, May 20, 1989; stepchildren: Sarah E., Laura K., Elizabeth A., Adam D. AA, Oakland Community Coll., Bloomfield Hills, Mich., 1979; BA, Spring Arbor (Mich.) Coll., 1986; MS, Ctr. Mich. U., 1993. Cert. sr. profl. human resources. Reporter The Times Newspapers, Pontiac, Mich., 1979-81; legis. aide Ho. of Reps., Lansing, 1981-84, Mich. State Senate, Lansing, 1984-85, adminstrv. aide, 1985-86; exec. v.p. Mich. Ins. Fedn., Lansing, 1986-88, pres., 1988-91; dir. govt. rels. Mich. C. of C., 1991-95, v.p. human resources, 1995-2000, sr. v.p., 2000—. Apptd. by gov. as Chmn. Workers' Compensation Qualifications Adv. Com., 1991—. Contbr. articles to profl. jours. Commr. Meridian Twp. Parks Commn., Okemos, Mich., 1984-90; state com. mem. Mich. Rep. State com., Lansing, 1987-88; exec. com. Ingham County Rep. Party, 1984-90; devel. com. Lansing Symphony Orch., 1989, bd. dirs., 1990—, v.p. devel., 1991-92; bd. dirs. Accident Fund Co., 1995—, Sparrow Physicians Health Network, 1996—; trustee Ctrl. Mich. U., 2001—. Recipient Community Contbn. award, Ingham County Bd. Commrs., 1987. Mem. Mich. Soc. Assn. Execs., Soc. for Human Resource Mgmt. (legis. action com. 1997—). Republican. Lutheran. E-mial. Office: Mich C of C 600 S Walnut St Lansing MI 48933-2209 E-mail: nmckeague@michamber.com.

MC KEAN, JOHN ROSSEEL OVERTON, university dean; b. Cortland, N.Y., July 31, 1928; s. Norman Dodge and Janet (Passage) McK.; m. Ruth MacDonald, July 2, 1955; children: Janet, Annalise. BA, Coll. William and Mary, 1951; M.Ed., Cornell U., 1956, Ed.D., 1961. Tchr. Landon Sch. for Boys, Washington, 1952-53; tchr. Central Sch., Homer, N.Y., 1953-55; asst. prof. history, dean students Allegheny Coll., 1957-67; headmaster Kingswood Sch. for Girls, Cranbrook, Bloomfield Hills, Mich., 1967-68; dean Hobart Coll., 1968-73; v.p. Coll. Kenyon Coll., Gambier, Ohio, 1973-77; dean arts and scis. State U. N.Y. at Canton, 1977-92. Mem. SUNY Coun. Deans Arts and Scis., Nat. Assn. Student Personnnel Adminstrs. (pres. Pa. 1958-59), SUNY Coun. Two-Yr. Bus. Adminstrs., Nat. Assn. Student Personnel Adminstrs. (dir. 1959-61), Am. Assn. Higher Edn., C.C. Gen. Edn. Assn., Middle States Assn. Colls. and Secondary Schs., Direct Descs. Signers Declaration Independence (historian), St. Lawrence County Hist. Soc., Geneva Concerts Assn., (dir. 1969-72), Am. Hist. Assn., Round Table, English-Speaking Union, St. Andrews Soc., Chapel Hill Tennis Club, Rotary, Phi Delta Kappa, Kappa Sigma. Home: 25 Flemington Rd Chapel Hill NC 27517-5638

MCKEAN, KEVIN, editor-in-chief, editor, writer; b. Ann Arbor, Mich. BA in English cum laude, Yale U. Police reporter City New Bur. Chgo., 1974; gen. assigment writer, broadcast editor Denver, New Orleans, 1975; nat. sci. writer NY, 1978; staff writer, sr. editor Discover mag., 1981—87; sr. editor, founding new media editor Money mag., 1987—97; exec. editor Forbes.com; editl. dir., v.p. PC World mag., 2000—. Asst. mng. editor bus. and fin. Time Inc. New Media; spkr. in field. Sci. editor (3 hr. WGBH-produced pub. TV spl.) Living Against the Odds; contbr. chapters to books; appeared (TV programs) NBC'S Today show, CBS This Morning, CNN, CNBC, CNNfn. Office: PC World Mag 501 Second St San Francisco CA 94107 Office Fax: 415-442-1891.*

MCKEAN, ROBERT JACKSON, JR. retired lawyer; b. N.Y.C., Dec. 21, 1925; s. Robert Jackson and Isabel (Murphy) McK.; m. Sally H. Ament; children from previous marriage: Katherine, Douglas, Lauren, Andrew. BA, Amherst Coll., 1950; LL.B., Harvard U., 1953. Bar: N.Y. 1954. Assoc. Simpson Thacher & Bartlett, N.Y.C., 1953-62, ptnr., 1962-85. Trustee Amherst Coll., Mass., Folger Shakespeare Library, Washington. Served with U.S. Army, 1944-46, ETO. Recipient medal for eminent service Amherst Coll., 1968 Mem. Phi Beta Kappa. Democrat.

MCKEAN, THOMAS WAYNE, dentist, retired naval officer; b. Adams County, Ind., May 18, 1928; s. Gorman F. and Elmira B. (Staley) McK.; m. Marilyn Kimberlin, Aug. 9, 1952; children: Thomas Wayne, Randall K., Dana K. D.D.S., Ind. U., 1953; grad., Naval Dental Sch., 1963. Diplomate: Am. Bd. Oral Surgery. Commd. ensign Dental Corps USN, 1949, advanced through grades to rear adm., 1980; stationed at Naval Tng. Ctr., Great Lakes, Ill., 1953; dental officer U.S.S. Randall, 1953-56; head dental svc., asst. dental officer U.S. Naval Acad./Naval Hosp., Annapolis, Md., 1956-59; dental officer FASRON III; asst. dental officer U.S. Naval Sta., Bermuda, 1959-63; postgrad. student Naval Dental Sch., Bethesda, Md., 1963-64; resident oral and maxillofacial surgery Naval Hosp., Great Lakes, Ill., 1964-66; dental officer U.S.S. America, 1966-68; chief oral surgery Naval Hosp., Orlando, Fla., 1968-70; dir. oral surgery and gen. practice residency tng. programs Naval Regional Med. Ctr., Great Lakes, 1970-74, chmn. dept. dentistry, 1970-74; cons., lectr. U.S. Army, Fort Sheridan, Ill., 1970-74; dir. oral surgery and gen. practice residency tng. programs Naval Regional Med. Ctr., Oakland, Calif., 1974-78, chmn., dept. dentistry, 1974-78; lectr. oral surgery Letterman Army Med. Ctr., San Francisco, 1974-78; clin. lectr. dept. oral surgery U. of Pacific Sch. Dentistry, 1974-78; comdg. officer Naval Regional Dental Ctr., Pensacola, Fla., 1978-80; lectr. oral surgery Pensacola (Fla.) Jr. Coll., 1978-80; cons., lectr. Dwight D. Eisenhower Army Regional Med. Ctr., Augusta, Ga., 1978-80; insp. gen. dental Bur. Medicine and Surgery, Dept. of Navy, Washington, 1980-81; comdg. officer Naval Regional Dental Ctr., San Diego, 1981-82; insp. gen. Naval Med. Command, Washington, 1983-85; ret. USN, 1985. Contbr. articles to profl. jours. Chmn. bd. trustees UMC, Winter Park, 1992, mem. bd. adminstrs. 1995-98; bd. dirs. Circle of Friends Fla. Hosp. Found., 1989-91, Fla. Hosp. Found., 1991—, chmn. bd., 1995-96; bd. dirs. Fla. Hosp. Found., 1996—; chmn. Fla. Hosp. Shares, 1994—; mem. Fla. Hosp. Cmty. Benefits subcom., 1996—. Decorated Humanitarian Service medal, Legion of Merit with Gold Star, Meritorious Service medal, Nat. Def. Service medal with star, Vietnam Service medal, Republic of Vietnam Campaign medal with device, others; recipient Alumnus of Yr. award Ind. U. Sch.of Dentistry Alumnus Assn., 1988. Fellow Am. Dental Soc. of Anesthesiology, Internat. Coll. Dentists, Am. Coll. Dentists, Internat. Assn. Oral Surgeons; mem. Am. Assn. Oral and Maxillofacial Surgeons, ADA, Western Soc. Oral Surgeons, Assn. Mil. Surgeons U.S. (medal), Fla. Soc. Oral Surgeons, Delta Sigma Delta, Sigma Chi (Significant Sig award 1983). Home: 1309 Temple Grove Ct Winter Park FL 32789-2716

MCKEAND, PATRICK JOSEPH, newspaper publisher, educator; b. Anderson, Ind., June 10, 1941; s. William Dale and Iva Pearl (Shaw) McK. BA, Ind. U., 1963; MA, Ball State U., 1983. Staff writer The St. Petersburg (Fla.) Times, 1963; mng. editor The Anderson (Ind.) Herald, 1968-79; adminstr. analyst Ind. Medicaid Program, Indpls., 1980-81; assoc. prof. Defense Info. Sch., Ft. Ben Harrison, Ind., 1981-89; owner p.m. ink!, Indpls., 1989—. Pub. bd. dirs. Student Pub. at Ind. U., Purdue U. at Indpls., 1992—; bd. dirs. Miss Indpls. Scholarship Pageant, Indpls, 1994—. Capt. U.S. Army, 1964-68. Decorated Bronze Star, Army Commendation medal with 1 Oak leaf cluster. Mem. Soc. Profl. Journalists (bd. dirs.), Soc. Newspaper Design, Assn. Educators in Journalism and Mass Comm., Associated Press Mng. Editors Assn., Investigative Reporters and Editors, Ind. Collegiate Press Assn. (bd. dirs., exec. dir.), Coll. Media Advisors (Disting. Newspaper Adviser award 1998). Home: 4450 E 56th St Indianapolis IN 46220-5710 Office: Sch of Journalism 902 W New York St Indianapolis IN 46202-5197 E-mail: pmckeand@iupui.edu.

MCKECHNIE, JOHN CHARLES, gastroenterologist, educator; b. Louisville, Feb. 1, 1935; s. Albert Hay and Edna Scott (Johnson) M.; children: Steven Keith, Kevin Stuart. BA, U. Louisville, 1955; MD, Baylor Coll. Medicine, 1959. Diplomate Am. Bd. Internal Medicine, Am. Bd. Gastroenterology. Intern Jefferson Davis Hosp., Houston, 1959-60; resident in internal medicine Baylor Affiliated Program, Houston, 1960-61, 65-66; gen. practice medicine, Benham, Ky., 1964; practice medicine specializing in gastroenterology, Houston, 1966—; clin. instr. Baylor Coll. Medicine, Houston, 1966-69, asst. prof., 1969-72, assoc. prof., 1972-77, prof., 1977— ; mem. staff Methodist Hosp.; cons. Ben Taub Hosp., St. Luke's Episcopal Hosp. Served to capt. USMC, 1962-64. Fellow Am. Coll. Gastroenterology (gov. Tex. 1979-80, trustee 1981-84), ACP; mem. AMA, So. Med. Assn., Tex. Med. Assn., Am. Gastroent. Assn., Digestive Disease Found., Am. Soc. Gastrointestinal Endoscopy, Tex. Soc. Gastrointestinal Endoscopy, Houston Gastroent. Soc. (pres. 1983), Alpha Omega Alpha. Republican. Presbyterian. Contbr. numerous articles to profl. jours. Office: 6560 Fannin St Ste 1630 Houston TX 77030-2734

MCKEE, ADELE DIECKMANN, retired church music director, educator; b. Atlanta, Oct. 29, 1928; d. Christian William and Emma Pope (Moss) D.; m. Dean Greer McKee, Nov. 14, 1972 (dec. July 1987). BA summa cum laude,

Agnes Scott Coll., 1948; MA, Wellesley Coll., 1949; M in Sacred Music magna cum laude, Union Theol. Sem., N.Y.C., 1955. Tchr. Latin and music theory, chapel organist The Northfield Schs., East Northfield, Mass., 1949-53; tchr. Latin and English Westminster Schs., Atlanta, 1955-58; dir. music, organist Trinity Presbyn. Ch., 1955-83; asst. organist Cathedral St. Philip, 1984-85; organist, choir master St. Luke's Presbyn. Ch., 1985-89; ret., 1989. Dir. Montreat Conf. on Worship and Music, 1968; chmn. new music commns. Am. Guild of Organists Nat. Convention, Atlanta, 1992—. Choral reviewer The Am. Organist, 1967-71; contbr. articles to Reformed Liturgy mag., 1970—. Mem. City of Decatur Hist. Preservation Task Force, 1989-90. Fellow Am. Guild Organists (nat. councillor 1967-70, dean 1964-66, 76-78, program chmn. nat. conv. 1966, chmn. cert. work Atlanta chpt., mem. exec. com. 1999—); mem. Choristers Guild (nat. bd. dirs. 1976-79), Decatur Book Lovers' Club, Atlanta Young Singers, Young Singers Callanwolde (bd. dirs. 1993—, pres. bd. dirs. 1994-98.

MC KEE, ALLEN PAGE, investment company executive; b. L.A., July 26, 1941; s. Norman C. and Eleanor (Page) McK. BA in Econs., U. Mich., 1964; MBA, U. Calif., Berkeley, 1971. Area rels. officer internat. divsn. Bank of Am., San Francisco, 1967-70; investment officer BankAm. Internat. Fin. Corp., 1971-73; v.p., dir. internat. investments Union Bank, 1973-74; pres. bd. dirs. Montgomery Assocs., Inc., 1975—. Mng. dir. Fal N.V., 1979—87, Willhurst Co., 1980—96; dir., CFO Advanced Combustion Tech., Inc., 1995—98; v.p., CFO, dir. Procyon Power Sys., Inc., 1996—99, pres., CEO, 2000—. Served to lt. USN, 1964-67, Vietnam. Mem. World Affairs Coun. No. Calif., Soc. Calif. Pioneers, Calif. Bus. Alumni Assn., San Francisco Yacht Club, Commonwealth Club of Calif., Delta Kappa Epsilon. Republican. Office: PO Box 2230 Ste 200 425 California St San Francisco CA 94126 Home: 9 Sutter Ct Belvedere Tiburon CA 94920-1328

MCKEE, CATHERINE LYNCH, law educator, lawyer; b. Boston, June 7, 1962; d. Robert Emmett and Anne Gayle (Tanner) Lynch; m. Bert K. McKee Jr., Dec. 25, 1990; children: Timothy Kingston, Shannon Lancaster. BA in Biol. Sci., U. Calif. Berkeley, 1984; JD, U. San Diego, 1988. Bar: Calif. 1988, U.S. Dist. Ct. (cen., so. and ea. dists.) Calif. 1989, U.S. Ct. Appeals (9th cir.) 1989. Assoc. Parkinson, Wolf, Lazar & Leo, L.A., 1988-89, McCormick & Mitchell, San Diego, 1989-91; prof., mock trial coach, paralegal program dir. Mt. San Antonio Coll., Walnut, Calif., 1994—. Certification review hearing officer, Orange County, 1994—; legal counsel Imperial Valley Lumber Co., Valley Lumber and Truss Co., 1998—; coach nat. champion C.C. mock trial team, 2000. Contbr. weekly newspaper column, 1993-99; prodr., star videos An Attorney's Guide to Legal Research on the Internet, 1998, 99; co-author: Jeff and Catherine's World's Best List of Legal (and Law-related) Internet Sites. Chair scholarship com. U. Calif. Alumni Assn., Diamond Bar area, 1995—; capt. auction team SCATS Gymnastics, 2000-02. Named Cmty. Person of Yr. Diamond Bar C. of C., 1995. Mem. State Bar Calif. (probation monitor 1993—), Ea. Bar Assn. L.A. (trustee 2000—), Am. Inns of Ct., Calif. Assn. Lanterman-Petris-Short Hearing Officers. Avocations: weight lifting, photography, reading. Office: Mount San Antonio Coll 1100 N Grand Ave Walnut CA 91789-1341 E-mail: cmckee@mtsac.edu.

MCKEE, CHRISTOPHER FULTON, librarian, historian, educator; b. Bklyn., June 14, 1935; s. William Ralph and Frances McKee; m. Ann Adamczyk, 1993; children: Sharon, David. AB, U. St. Thomas, Houston, 1957; AMLS, U. Mich., 1960. Catalogue libr. Washington and Lee U., Lexington, Va., 1958-62; social sci. libr. So. Ill. U., Edwardsville, 1962-66, book selection officer, 1967-69, asst. dir., 1969-72; libr. of coll. Grinnell Coll., Iowa, 1972—, Samuel R. and Marie-Louise Rosenthal prof. Sec. of Navy rsch. chair naval history Naval Hist. Ctr., Washington, 1990—91; trustee Bibliog. Ctr. Rsch., Denver, 1984—88. Author: (book) Edward Preble, 1972, A Gentlemanly and Honorable Profession: The Creation of the U.S. Naval Officer Corps 1794-1815, 1991, Sober Men and True: Sailor Lives in the Royal Navy 1900-1945, 2002. Recipient U.S. Naval History prize, 1985, John Lyman Book award, N.Am. Soc. Oceanic History, 1991, Samuel Eliot Morison Disting. Svc. award, USS Constn. Mus., 1992; fellow NEH-Newberry Libr., 1978—79, Newberry Libr.-Brit. Acad., 1995—96. Mem.: U.S. Naval Inst., Soc. Historians Early Am. Republic, Orgn. Am. Historians, Soc. Mil. History, Navy Records Soc., Can. Nautical Rsch. Soc., Am. Hist. Assn. Home: 2382 Willowbrooke Ln Iowa City IA 52246-1834 Office: Grinnell Coll Burling Libr 1111 6th Ave Grinnell IA 50112-1690

MCKEE, CHRISTOPHER FULTON, physicist, educator, astronomer, educator; b. Washington, Sept. 6, 1942; m. Suzanne P. McKee; 3 children. AB in Physics summa cum laude, Harvard U., 1963; PhD in Physics, U. Calif., Berkeley, 1970. Physicist Lawrence Livermore (Calif.) Labs., 1969-70, cons., 1970—; rsch. fellow in astrophysics Calif. Inst. Tech., Pasadena, 1970-71; asst. prof. astronomy Harvard U., Cambridge, 1971-74; asst. prof. physics and astronomy U. Calif., Berkeley, 1974-77, assoc. prof., 1977-78, prof., 1978—, Miller Rsch. prof., 1984-85, 99; chair dept. physics, 2000—; assoc. dir. Space Scis. Lab., Berkeley, 1978-83, acting dir., 1983-84, dir., 1985-98, Theoretical Astrophysics Ctr., Berkeley, 1985. Co-chair Astronomy and Astrophysics Survey com., NRC, 1998—. Fannie and John Hertz Found. fellow, 1963-69, Guggenheim fellow, 1998; Sherman Fairchild Disting. scholar, 1981, Nat. Acad. Scis., 1992. Fellow AAAS, Am. Phys. Soc. (exec. com. astrophysics div. 1986-88); mem. Am. Astron. Soc. (councillor 1981-84), Internat. Astron. Union, Phi Beta Kappa. Office: U Calif Dept Physics Berkeley CA 94720-0001

MCKEE, DAVID CHARLES, physician, neurologist; b. May 19, 1961; m. Marie-Laure Mazquiain, Dec. 29, 1984; children: Tyvand, Camille, Charlotte, Alexanne. BA in Chemistry, Macalaster Coll., 1983; MD, U. Wis., 1987. Diplomate Am. Bd. Psychiatry and Neurology, Am. Bd. Electrodiagnostic Medicine. Resident in neurology Oreg. Health Scis. U., 1987—91; Jeanne Timmins fellow Montreal Neurol. Inst., 1991—92; clin. neurologist Northland Neurology and Myology, Duluth, Minn., 1992—; chief sect. neurology St. Lukes Hosp. and Regional Trauma Ctr., 1993—; clin. assoc. prof. neurology U. Minn.-Duluth Med. Sch., 1993—; pres. Northland Med. Assocs., 2000—02. Chmn. bd. dirs. Care North Health Sys., 2001—02. Comdr. USNR med. corp., 1998—. Fellow: Am. Assn. Electrodiagnostic Medicine; mem.: European Neurol. Soc., Am. Acad. Neurology, Alpha Omega Alpha, Phi Beta Kappa. Office: 1000 E 1st St Ste 202 Duluth MN 55805-2297 Home: 2215 E Superior St Duluth MN 55812

MCKEE, DAVID JOHN, government official; b. Detroit, Jan. 11, 1947; s. Russell Osborne and Marie Helen (Woodruff) McK.; m. Susan Adams, Sept. 4, 1965; children: Shawn Alysun, Carl Patrick Russell. BA, U. South Fla., 1968; MS, Fla. State U., 1971, PhD, 1976; MBA, Duke U., 1980. Lab. technician Oak Ridge (Tenn.) Nat. Lab., 1965-67; lectr. chemistry U. South Pacific, Suva, Fiji, 1973-74; lab. dir., chemist City of Tallahassee, 1975-79; project mgr. Environ. Criteria Assessment Office, EPA, Research Triangle Park, N.C., 1977-80, program mgr. Office Air Quality Planning and Standards, Durham, 1980—. Disting. lectr. AMA, Chgo., 1987. Editor 3 books; contbr. numerous articles to profl. jours., chpts. to books. Recipient bronze medal EPA, 1979, 94, spl. achievement award, 1979, 80, 84-91, sustained superior performance award, 1986, outstanding performance award, 1989. Mem. Soc. for Risk Analysis (treas. Research Triangle chpt. 1987-92), Air and Waste Mgmt. Assn., Am. Fed. Govt. Employees Assn. (local treas. 1984-90, v.p. 1990-92), Internat. Soc. Exptl. Analysis. Home: PO Box 71037 Durham NC 27722-1037

MCKEE, DAVID LANNEN, economics educator; b. St. John, N.B., Can., Apr. 18, 1936; came to U.S., 1961; s. Horace George and Mary K. (Lannen) McK.; m. Yosra A. Amara, Dec. 23, 1995. BA magna cum laude, St. Francis Xavier, 1958; MA, U. N.B., Fredericton, 1959; PhD, U. Notre Dame, 1966. Lectr. Ind. U., Ft. Wayne, 1965-66, asst. prof., 1966-67, Kent (Ohio) State U., 1967-69, assoc. prof., 1969-74, prof. econs., 1974—. Author: Growth, Development, and the Service Economy in the Third World, 1988, Schumpeter and the Political Economy of Change, 1991, Urban Environments in Emerging Economies, 1994; editor: Canadian American Economic Relations: Conflict and Cooperation on a Continental Scale, 1988, Hostile Takeovers: Issues in Public and Corporate Policy, 1989, Energy, the Environment and Public Policy, 1991, External Linkages and Growth in Small Economies, 1993; co-author: Developmental Issues in Small Island Economics, 1990, Accounting Services, the International Economy and Third World Development, 1992, Accounting Services, Growth, And Change in the Pacific Basin, 1996, Accounting Services and Growth in Small Economies, Evidence from the Caribbean Basin, 1998, Accounting Services, the Islamic Middle East and the Global Economy, 1999, Offshore Financial Centers, Accounting Serivces and the Global Economy, 2000, Crisis, Recovery, and the Role of Accounting Firms in the Pacific Basin, 2002, others; co-editor: Regional Economics: Theory and Practice, 1970, Spatial Economic Theory, 1970, Urban Economics: Theory Development and Planning, 1970, Structural Change in an Urban Industrial Region, 1987; contbr. articles to profl. jours. Mem. So. Econ. Assn., Internat. Acad. of Bus. Disciplines (pres.-elect 2002), Am. Soc. for Competitiveness (adv. bd.). Roman Catholic. Home: 616 Yacavona Dr Kent OH 44240-3318 Office: Kent State U Dept Econs Kent OH 44242-0001 Fax: 330-672-9808. E-mail: dmckee@bsw3-kent.edu.

MCKEE, ELLSWORTH R. food products executive; BA in Bus. and Econs., So. Adventist U., 1954; postgrad., Andrews U., 1987. Shipping/receiving clk. Jack's Cookie Co., Charlotte, N.C., 1949-50; various positions McKee Foods, Collegedale, 1951-54, v.p. prodn. and fin., 1954-62, exec. v.p., treas., 1962-71, pres., CEO, 1971-96, also bd. dirs., 1954—, chmn. bd. dirs., 1997—. Bd. dirs. So. Adventist U., Collegedale, 1971—, Andrews U., Berrien Springs, Mich., 1976-2000. Recipient Pvt. Sector Initiative Commendation Pres. Ronald Reagan, 1988. Office: McKee Foods PO Box 750 Collegedale TN 37315-0750

MCKEE, FRANCIS JOHN, medical association consultant, lawyer; b. Bklyn., Aug. 31, 1943; s. Francis Joseph and Catherine (Giles) McK.; m. Antoinette Mary Sancis; children: Lisa Ann, Francis Dominic, Michael Christopher, Thomas Joseph. AB, Stonehill Coll., 1965; JD, St. John's U., 1970. Bar: N.Y. 1971. Assoc. Samuel Weinberg, Esquire, Bklyn., 1970-71, Finch & Finch, Esquire, Long Island City, N.Y., 1971-72; staff atty. Med. Soc. of State of N.Y., Lake Success, 1972-77; prin. Francis J. McKee Assocs., Clinton, NY, 1984—2001; exec. dir. Suffolk Physicians Rev. Orgn., East Islip, N.Y., 1977-81, N.Y. State Soc. Surgeons, Inc., Clinton, 1981-2000, N.Y. State Soc. Orthopaedic Surgeons, Inc., Clinton, NY, 1981—2002, Upstate N.Y. chpt. ACS, Inc., Clinton, N.Y., 1981-2000, N.Y. State Ophthalmol. Soc., 1984-92, N.Y. State Soc. Obstetricians and Gynecologists, 1985-2001, Orthopac of N.Y., 1986-2000, Nat. Com. for the Preservation Orthopaedic Practice, New Hartford, N.Y., 1989-2000; L.I. Ophthalmological Soc., 1994-2000. Coun. Suffolk County Med. Soc., Hauppauge, N.Y., 1977-81. With U.S. Army, 1966-68. Mem. N.Y. State Bar Assn., Oneida County Bar Assn., Skenandoa Club, Am. Legion. Republican. Roman Catholic. Home and Office: 19 Mulberry St Clinton NY 13323-1532 Fax: (315) 859-1137. E-mail: Frank4Mets@aol.com.

MCKEE, GEORGE MOFFITT, JR. civil engineer, consultant; b. Valparaiso, Nebr., Mar. 27, 1924; s. George Moffitt and Iva (Santrock) McK.; m. Mary Lee Taylor, Aug. 11, 1945; children: Michael Craig, Thomas Lee, Mary Kathleen, Marsha Coleen, Charlotte Anne. Student, Kans. State Coll. Agr. and Applied Sci., 1942-43, Bowling Green State U., 1943; BSE in Civil Engring., U. Mich., 1947. Registered profl. civil engr., Kans., Okla., land surveyor, Kans. Draftsman Jackson Constrn. Co., Colby, Kans., 1945-46; asst. engr. Thomas County, 1946; engr. Sherman County, Goodland, Kans., 1947-51; salesman Oehlert Tractor & Equipment Co., Colby, 1951-52; owner, operator George M. McKee, Jr.; cons. engrs. Colby, 1952-72; sr. v.p. engring. Contract Surety Cons., Wichita, Kans., 1974-2000; engring. cons., 2000—. Adv. rep. Kans State U., Manhattan, 1957-62; mem. adv. com. N.W. Kans. Area Vocat. Tech. Sch., Goodland, 1967-71; chmn. ofcl. bd. Meth. Ch., 1966-67. With USMCR, 1942-45. Mem. Kans. Soc. Profl. Engrs. (pres. N.W. profl. engrs. chpt. 1962-63, treas. cons. engrs. sect. 1961-63), Kans. County Engr.'s Assn. (dist. v.p. 1950-51), N.W. Kans. Hwy. Ofcls. Assn. (sec. 1948-49), Nat. Soc. Profl. Engrs., Kans. State U. Alumni Assn. (life, pres. Thomas County 1956-57), Am. Legion (Goodland 1st vice comdr. 1948-49), The Alumni Assn. U. Mich. (life), Colby C. of C. (v.p. 1963-64), Goodland Jr. C. of C. (pres. 1951-52), Masons (32 degree, Shriner), Order of the Ea. Star. Home: 8930 Suncrest St Apt 502 Wichita KS 67212-4069

MCKEE, HARRY W. federal judge; b. 1940; PhB, U. N.D., 1963; LLB, George Washington U., 1966. Trial atty. U.S. Dept. Justice, 1966-79; spl. asst., 1979; asst. U.S. atty. U.S. Dept. Justice, 1979-82; apptd. magistrate judge ea. dist. U.S. Dist. Ct. Tex., 1982. Mem. ABA, State Bar Tex., Smith County Bar Assn. Office: 210 Federal Bldg 211 W Ferguson St Tyler TX 75702-7212 Fax: 903-590-1168.

MCKEE, JOHN MORRISON, management consultant; b. Winnipeg, Man., Can., Sept. 2, 1951; s. Gordon John Frederick and Lee Rae (Morrison) M.; m. Susan Leslie Lewis, Apr. 13, 1974; children: Sean Adam, Jessica Lee, Trevor James. BA, U. Winnipeg, Can., 1975. Retail store mgr. Eaton's of Can., 1975-79; gen. mktg. mgr. Hudson Bay Co., Can., 1979-90; v.p. sales and mktg. CUC Broadcasting Ltd., Can., 1990-92; v.p. gen. mgr. DIRECTV Can., 1992-95; sr. v.p. spl. markets DIRECTV, Inc., El Segundo, Calif., 1995-99, sr. v.p., gen. mgr., 1999—2002; pres., mgmt. cons. Four Windows No Walls Cons., LLC, 2002—. Home: 2456 S Oak Ridge Rd Sedalia CO 80135 E-mail: jmckee7307@aol.com.

MCKEE, KATHRYN DIAN GRANT, human resources consultant; b. L.A., Sept. 12, 1937; d. Clifford William and Amelia Rosalie (Shacher) G.; m. Paul Eugene McKee, June 17, 1961; children: Scott Alexander, Grant Christopher. BA, U. Calif., Santa Barbara, 1959; grad. Anderson Sch. Mgmt. Exec. Program, UCLA, 1979. Cert. compensation and benefits. Mgr. Mattel, Inc., Hawthorne, Calif., 1963-74; dir. Twentieth Century Fox Film Corp., L.A., 1975-80; sr. v.p. 1st Interstate Bank, Ltd., 1980-93; sr. v.p. and human resources dir. Am.'s Std. Chartered Bank, 1993-95; pres. Human Resources Consortia, Santa Barbara, Calif., 1995—. V.p. cons. Right Mgmt. Cons., 1997-98; dir. Accordia benefits of Southern Calif., 1991-96, mem. exec. com. H.R. div. of Am. Bankers Assn., 1991-93; bd. dirs. Bank Certification Inst. Am. Bankers Assn., 1992-94; treas. Pers. Accreditation Inst., 1983-86, pres., 1986. Contbr. articles to profl. jours. Pres. GEM Theatre Guild, Garden Grove, Calif., 1984-86; bd. dirs. Vis. Nurses Assn., L.A., 1984-88, SHRM, 1986-92, treas., 1989, vice-chmn., 1990, chmn., 1991, pres. SHRM Found., 1994, 95; bd. dirs. Laguna Playhouse, 1996-2000, pres., 1998-99; dir. Ensemble Theatre Co., 2002—; dir. Ctr. for Info. Tech. and Society, Old Spanish Days, 2001—; mem. U. Calif. Santa Barbara Found., 2001—, vice chmn. stewardship, 2001–; dir. Old Spanish Days. Recipient Sr. Honor Key award U. Calif., Santa Barbara, 1959, William Winter award Am. Compensation Assn., 1986, Excellence award L.A. Pers. Indsl. Rels. Assn., 1990, Profl. Excellence award SHRM, 1994; named Outstanding Sr. Woman, 1959. Mem. Internat. Assn. Pers. Women (various offices, past nat. pres., Mem. of Yr. 1986), U. Calif. Santa Barbara Alumni Assn. (bd. dirs. 1995-2001, pres.-elect 1999, pres. 1999-2000). Office: Human Resources Consortia 3730 Cedar Vis Santa Barbara CA 93110-1578 E-mail: kmckee3730@cox.net.

MCKEE, KEITH EARL, manufacturing technology executive; b. Chgo., Sept. 9, 1928; s. Charles Richard and Maude Alice (Hamlin) McK.; m. Lorraine Marie Celichowski, Oct. 26, 1951; children: Pamela Ann Houser, Paul Earl. BS, Ill. Inst. Tech., 1950, MS, 1956, PhD, 1962. Engr. Swift & Co., Chgo., 1953-54; rsch. engr. Armour Rsch. Found., 1954-62; dir. design and product assurance Andrew Corp., Orland Park, Ill., 1962-67; dir. engring. Rsch. Ctr. Ill. Inst. Tech., Chgo., 1967-80, dir. mfg. prodn. ctr., 1977—. Prof. Ill. Inst. Tech., Chgo., 1979—; coord. Nat. Conf. on Fluid Power, Chgo., 1983-88; mem. com. on materials and processing Dept. Def., Washington, 1986-92. Author: Productivity and Technology, 1988; editor: Automated Inspection and Process Control, 1987; co-editor: Manufacturing High Technology Handbook, 1987; mng. editor: Manufacturing Competitiveness Frontier, 1977-97. Capt. USMC, 1950-54. Recipient outstanding presentation award Am. Soc. of Quality Control, Milw., 1983. Fellow World Acad. Productivity Scis.; mem. ASCE, Am. Def. Preparedness Assn. (pres. Chgo. chpt. 1972-95), Am. Assn. Engring. Soc. (Washington) (coor. com. on productivity 1978-88), Inst. of Indsl. Engrs., Soc. Mfg. Engrs. (Gold medal 1991), Am. Assn. for Artificial Intelligence, Robotic Industry Assn. (bd. dir. 1978-81), Assn. for Mfg. Excellence, Soc. for Computer Simulation. Democrat. Roman Catholic. Home: Ste 504 3115 S Michigan Ave Chicago IL 60616 Office: Illinois Inst Tech Mfg Productivity Ctr 10 W 32d St Chicago IL 60616-3793 E-mail: mckee@iit.edu.

MCKEE, MARGARET JEAN, federal agency administrator; b. New Haven, June 20, 1929; d. Waldo McCutcheon and Elizabeth McKee. AB, Vassar Coll., 1951. Staff asst. United Rep. Fin. Com., N.Y.C., 1952, N.Y. Rep. State Com., N.Y.C., 1953—55, Crusade for Freedom (name later changed to Radio Free Europe Fund), N.Y.C., 1955—57; researcher Stricker & Henning Rsch. Assocs., Inc., 1957—59; exec. sec. New Yorkers for Nixon (name later changed to N.Y. State Ind. Citizens for Nixon Lodge), 1959—60; asst. to Raymond Moley, polit. columnist, 1961; asst. campaign com. Louis J. Lefkowitz for Mayor, 1961; rsch. programmer, treas. Consensus, Inc., 1962—67; spl. asst. to U. S. Senator Jacob K. Javits, 1967—73; adminstr. asst., 1973—75; dep. adminstr. Am. Revolution Bicentennial Adminstrn., 1976, acting adminstr., 1976—77; chief of staff Perry B. Duryea (minority leader) N.Y. State Assembly, 1978; pub. affairs cons., 1979—80; dir. govt. rels. Gen. Mills Restaurant Group, Inc., 1980—83; exec. dir. Fed. Mediation and Conciliation Svc., 1983—86; mem. Fed. Labor Rels. Authority, 1986—89, chmn., 1989—94; mem. Nat. Partnership Coun., 1993—94; chmn. adv. bd. Workplace Solutions, 1996—. Mem. U.S. Adv.Commn. on Pub. Diplomacy, 1972—82; dir. scheduling and spkrs.' bur. N.Y. Com. to Re-elect the Pres., 1972; mem. bd. govs. Women's Nat. Rep. Club, N.Y.C., 1963—66; mem. N.Y. State Bingo Control Commn., 1965—72; pres. Bklyn. Heights Slope Young Rep. Club, 1955—56; co-chmn. Bklyn. Citizens for Eisenhower-Nixon, 1956; chmn. 2nd Jud. Dist. Assn. N.Y. State Young Rep. Clubs, Inc., 1957—58, vice chmn., mem. bd. govs., 1958—60, v.p., 1960—62, pres., 1962—64; mem. exec. com. Fedn. Women's Rep. Clubs N.Y. State, Inc., 1960—64; asst. campaign mgr. Kenneth B. Keating for Judge Ct. Appeals, NY, 1965; dir. scheduling Gov. Rockefeller campaign, 1966, Sen. Charles E. Goodell campaign, 1970; dir. planning and strategy Conn. Reagan-Bush campaign, Hartford, 1980; mem annual fund adv. com. Vassar Coll., 1992—96, chmn. 50th Reunion, 2001. Mem.: New Eng. Historic Genealogical Soc. (mem. adv. coun. 2001—), Nat. Women's Edn. Fund. (mem. bd.), Exec. Women on Govt. (chmn. 1986), Nat. Soc. Colonial Dames, Vassar Club (past dir., Bklyn.), Am. Newspaper Women's Club, Jr. League of Bklyn. (past dir.). Episcopalian. Home: 532 S Brooksvale Rd Cheshire CT 06410-3515 also: 3001 Veazey Ter NW Apt 1225 Washington DC 20008-5407

MCKEE, ROGER CURTIS, retired federal judge; b. Waterloo, Iowa, Feb. 11, 1931; s. James A. and Leonace (Burrell) McK.; m. Roberta Jeanne Orvis, Sept. 3, 1954; children: Andrea Jane, Brian Curtis, Paul Robert. BA, State Coll. of Iowa, 1955; MA, U. Ill., 1960; JD, U. San Diego, 1968. Bar: Calif. 1970, U.S. Dist. Ct. (so. dist.) Calif. 1969, U.S. Ct. Appeals (9th cir.) 1971. Telegrapher, agt. Ill. Cen. R.R., 1950-55; tng. asst. No. Ill. Gas Co., Aurora, 1959-60; with indsl. rels. dept. Convair div. Gen. Dynamics Corp., San Diego, 1960-68; contract adminstr. and supr. Datagraphix div. Gen. Dynamics Corp., 1968-69, asst. counsel, 1969-70; ptnr. Powell & McKee, 1970-75, Millsberg, Dickstein & McKee, San Diego, 1975-83; magistrate judge U.S. Dist. Ct. for So. Dist. Calif., 1983-97; presiding magistrate judge, 1993-97. Bd. trustees So. Calif. Presbyn. Homes, L.A., 1979-81; moderator Presbytery of San Diego, 1980. Capt. USNR, 1949-85. Mem. Calif. Bar Assn., Fed. Magistrate Judges Assn., Navy League U.S., Naval Res. Officers Assn., Res. Officers Assn., Dixieland Jazz Soc. (bd. dirs. San Diego chpt. 1984—). Republican. Fax: (858) 277-0444. E-mail: rcmckee10@cs.com.

MCKEE, RONALD GENE, vocational education educator; b. Williamsville, Mo., May 5, 1947; s. Enos Elmer and Elsie Mae (Chiles) McK.; m. Sondra Mae Malone, Dec. 1, 1968; 1 child, David. Student, Pearl River C.C., 1992-94; BS in Geol. Engring., U. Miss., 1999. Cert. tchr., Miss. Enlisted man, electronics warfare repairman USAF, 1966-73; enlisted man USCG, 1973, advanced through grades to electronics technician 1st class, 1973-87; ret., 1987; tchr. electronics Picayune (Miss.) Vocat.-Tech. Ctr., 1988-95, Pascagoula (Miss.) P.S.D. Applied Tech. Ctr., 1995—. Mem. Vocat. Indsl. Clubs. Am. Avocations: radio-controlled airplanes, oil painting, informal target shooting, amateur radio. Home: 2205 Dolphin Rd Gautier MS 39553-7080 Office: Pascagoula Sch Dist Applied Tech Ctr 2602 Market St Pascagoula MS 39567-5158 E-mail: ronmckee@hotmail.com.

MCKEE, THEODORE A. federal judge; b. Rochester, NY, 1947; BA, SUNY, Cortland, 1969; JD magna cum laude, Syracuse U. Coll. of Law, 1975. Dir. of minority recruitment & admissions SUNY, Binghamton, 1969—72; atty. Wolf, Block, Schorr & Solis-Cohen, Phila., 1975—77; asst. U.S. atty., Eastern Dist., 1977—80; asst. U.S. atty., Eastern Dist. Gen. Crimes Unit, Narcotics and Firearms Unit, then Polit. Corruption Unit; lectr. Rutgers U. Coll. of Law, 1980—91; dep. city solicitor Law Dept., Phila., 1980—83; gen. counsel Phila. Parking Auth., 1983; judge Ct. of Common Pleas, 1st Jud. Dist, Pa., 1984—94, judge major felony program, 1986, judge orphans' ct. divsn., 1992; judge U.S. Ct. Appeals (3d cir.), Phila., 1994—. Bd. dirs. Diagnostic and Rehab. Ctr. of Phila. Trustee Edna McConnell Clark Found.; mem. adv. bd. City Yr. for Phila. Mem.: ABA, Temple Inn of Ct., Barristers' Assn. Phila., Am. Law Inst., Nat. Bar Assn., Crime Prevention Assn. (bd. dirs.). Office: 20614 US Courthouse 601 Market St Philadelphia PA 19106*

MCKEE, THOMAS J. association administrator; b. Fairfax Station, Va. m. Patricia Rizzuto; children: Michelle, Catherine, Thomas McKee Jr. BA in Polit. Sci., S.E. Mo. State U., 1970; grad. Emerging Exec. Program, Pa. State U., 1983. Customer requirements rep. Grumman Aerospace Corp., Bethpage, NY, dir. Air Force requirements, corp. v.p. Washington; exec. br. customer rels. Northrop Grumman Corp., 1994; nat. sec. Air Force Assn., under 40 nat. dir., nat. pres., nat. chmn. bd. Va., 2001—. Chmn. bd., past pres. Aerospace Edn. Found.; chmn. resolutions com. and indsl. assoc. task force, exec. com., comm. com. Air Force Assn.; chpt. v.p., pres., chmn. Nat. Air Force Salute Found.; bd. trustees Air Force Meml. Found., Falcon Found. With USAF. Recipient Presdl. citation; fellow, Doolittle. Office: c/o AFA Nat Hqrs 1501 Lee Hwy Arlington VA 22209-1198*

MCKEE, TIMOTHY CARLTON, taxation educator; b. South Bend, Ind., Mar. 9, 1944; s. Glenn Richard and Laura Louise (Niven) McK.; m. Linda Sykes Mizelle, Oct. 13, 1984; children: Brandon Richard. BS in Bus. Econs., Ind. U., 1970, MBA in Fin., 1973, JD, 1979; LLM in Taxation, DePaul U., 1980. Bar: Ill. 1980, U.S. Dist. Ct. (no. dist.) Ill. 1980; CPA, , Va.; cert. govt. fin. mgr. Procedures analyst Assocs. Corp., South Bend, Ind., 1969-71; asst. dir. fin. Ind. U., Bloomington, 1971-79; sr. tax mgr. Peat Marwick Mitchell & Co., Chgo., Norfolk, Va., 1979-84; corp. counsel K & K Toys, Norfolk, 1984; assoc. prof. acctg. Old Dominion U., 1985-98, chmn. dept., 1994-95, chmn. acctg., fin. and law dept., 1995, univ. prof. dept. acctg., 1998—. Computer coord. Peat, Marwick, Mitchell & Co., 1982-84; micro computer cons. Old Dominion U., 1985-91. Contbr. articles to profl. jours. Mem. Friends of Music, Bloomington, 1978, Art Inst., Chgo., 1981; loaned exec. United Way, Chgo., 1981; telethon chmn. Va. Orch. Group, Norfolk, 1983. Mem. Assn. Govt. Accts., Am. Acctg. Assn., Am. Assn. Atty. CPAs, Inc., Am. Tax Assn., Fin. Execs. Inst. (pres. 1995-96), Hampton Rds. Tax Forum, Inst. Internal Auditors, Beta Alpha Psi, Beta Gamma Sigma. Home: 412 Rio Dr Chesapeake VA 23322-7144 Office: Old Dominion U Constant Hall Rm 2153 Norfolk VA 23529

MCKEE, WILLIAM HERMAN, JR. accountant; b. Charleston, W.Va., Sept. 17, 1948; s. William H. and Anne K. (Carper) McK.; m. Martha Brooks, Oct. 6, 1985; children: William H. III, Martha C., Margaret M. BS in Bus. Adminstrn., Concord Coll., 1970. CPA, W.Va., Va.; personal fin. specialist; CFP. Computer ops. staff Columbia Gas, Inc., Charleston, 1970-72; external auditor W.Va. Dept. Hwys., 1972-73; mem. Arnett & Foster, PLLC, 1974-98, mem. exec. com., 1998—. Spkr. in field. Treas. Greenbrier Valley Theater, Inc., Lewisburg, W.Va., 1978-80; asst. sec. Lewisburg Rotary Club, 1979-80; pres. Lilliput Orch., Inc., Charleston, 1980-83; treas., campaign chair, pres. Fund for Arts, 1986-2002; bd. dirs. Charleston Estate Planning Coun., 2000—, Concord Coll. Found., 2002-. Mem. C. of C. (CEO Forum), Kanawha Bus. Club (v.p. 1994-96, pres. 1996-98), Kanawha Valley Bus. Forum (v.p. and pres. 1984-85), Charleston Rotary Club (treas. 1988-94), Charleston Tennis Club. Avocations: travel, community service, tennis. Office: Arnett & Foster PLLC 101 Washington St E Charleston WV 25301-1516 E-mail: bill_mckee@afnetwork.com.

MCKEE, WILLIAM LEE, economist, arbitrator, mediator; b. Springfield, Mo., Aug. 15, 1946; s. Thomas Lynn and Lynna Evelyn (Tracy) McK.; m. Cecilia Ann Newton, June 1, 1968; children: Angela, Amy, Lauren. BS in Econs., Math., Southwest Mo. U., 1968; MA in Econs., U. Mo., 1970, PhD in

Econs., 1975. Instr. U. Mo., Columbia, 1974-76; asst. prof. Ky. State U., Frankfort, 1976-77; staff assoc. Brookings Inst., Washington, 1977-78; prof. U. North Tex., Denton, 1978—. Cons. economist William L. McKee & Assocs., Denton, 1980—; pvt. practice labor arbitrator, mediator, Denton, 1986—, Brookings staff assoc. U.S. Dept. Labor, Wahsington, 1977-78. Co-author: Where the Jobs Are, 1985, Targeting Your Labor Market, 1989, others; contbr. articles to profl. jours. Chair bd. dirs. North Tex. Edn. & Tng. Corp., Denton, 1978—; bd. dirs. Hope, Inc., Denton, 1990-95; mem. blue ribbon com. Flow Hosp., Denton, 1985-86. Grantee Nat. Occupation Info. Coordinating Com., Washington; grantee U.S. Dept. Labor, 1978-84. Mem. Fed. MEdiation and Conciliation Svc. (panel mem. 1988—), Am. Arbitration Assn. (panel mem. 1985—), Nat. Mediation Bd. (panel mem. 1986-90), Indsl. Rels. Rsch. Assn. (pres. North Tex. chpt. 1985-87), Am. Econ. Assn. Avocations: jogging, reading, investments. Office: U North Tex PO Box 311143 Denton TX 76203-1143

MCKEE-DUDLEY, SANDRA IRENE, correctional health care professional; b. Nashua, N.H., June 9, 1949; d. Robert Henry Corliss and Elizabeth Juliette (Duffina) Knowles. Diploma in Nursing, Yoville Hosp., Cambridge, Mass., 1971; postgrad., Regents Coll., 1992—. LPN, Fla.; cert. BLS, corr. health profl., IV nurse, AIDS counselor, staff tng. officer. LPN staff nurse Yoville Hosp., Cambridge, Mass., 1972-73, Huntington Gen. Hosp., Brookline, 1973-76, Riverview Nursing Home, 1976-77, Cohassett Nursing Home, 1977-78, Rosary Hill, Hawthorne, N.Y., 1982-84, Humana Hosp. Pasco, Dade City, Fla., 1984-85, Pasco County Sheriff Office, Land-o-Lakes, 1985—. Cons. Sunrise of Pasco, Dade City, 1987—, sec. bd. dirs., 1990-92, pres. bd. dirs., 1992; cons. Oaks Royal Civic Assn., Zephyrhills, Fla., 1987—, social svcs. dir. subdivsn. III; bd. advisors Sunrise Domestic Violence Shelter, Dade City. Mem. Am. Jail Assn., Am. Correctional Health Svcs. Assn., Fla. Correctional Health Svcs. Assn., Nat. League of Nursing, Fla. Jail Assn., Cert. Correctional Health Profls. Republican. Roman Catholic. Avocations: educational activities, reading, classical music, computers, the sea. Home: 36440 Malibu Way Zephyrhills FL 33541-2060 Office: Pasco County Sheriff's Office 10200 Central Blvd Land O'Lakes FL 34639-7001 E-mail: ismd@juno.com.

MCKEEL, LILLIAN PHILLIPS, retired education educator; b. Rocky Mount, N.C., Aug. 23, 1932; d. Ellis Elma and Lillian Bonner (Archbell) Phillips; m. James Thomas McKeel Jr., July 23, 1955; children: Sarah Lillian McKeel Youngblood, Mary Kathleen McKeel Welch. BA, U. N.C., 1954; MEd, Pa. State U., 1977, DEd, 1993. Tchr. State Coll. (Pa.) Area Schs., 1964-90; instr. Pa. State U., University Park, 1990-93; asst. prof. Shippensburg (Pa.) U., 1993—2001; ret., 2001. Mem. of panel NSTA Book Rev. Panel/Outstanding Sci. Tradebooks for Children, Washington, 1992; faculty sponsor Shippensburg U. Sch. Study Coun., 1993-95. Contbr. articles to profl. jours. Recipient Presdl. award for Excellence in Sci. and Math. Tchng., NSF, Washington, 1990; finalist Tchr. of Yr. program Pa. Dept. Edn., Harrisburg, 1992, cert. Recognition, Hon. Robert Casey/Gov., Harrisburg, Pa., 1991; named Achieving Women of Penn State, Pa. State U., 1993. Mem. Nat. Sci. Tchrs. Assn., Soc. Presdl. Awardees, Assn. Edn. Tchrs. in Sci., Coun. Elem. Sci. Internat., Phi Delta Kappa (Disting. Svc. award 1992), Pi Lambda Theta, Phi Kappa Phi. Avocations: photography, collecting antique toys. Home: 637 Wiltshire Rd State College PA 16803 E-mail: lmcke637@aol.com.

MCKEEL, SHERYL WILSON, pharmacist; b. Nashville, Apr. 6, 1957; d. Robert Lewis and Norma Anne (Cox) Wilson; m. Vaughn Allen McKeel, Apr. 22, 2000. BS in Biology, David Lipscomb U., 1979; BS in Pharmacy, Auburn U., 1985. Lic. pharmacist, Tenn. Student extern/intern East Alabama Med. Ctr., Opelika, Ala., 1982-86; staff pharmacist Metro Nashville Gen. Hosp., 1987-95, PharmaThera, Inc., Nashville, 1995-99, Mid. Tenn. Mental Health Inst., Nashville, 1999-2000. Flutist Nashville Cmty. Concert Band, 1973-97; presch. tchr. Donelson Ch. of Christ, 1988—; active Lipscomb U. Cmty. Chorus, 1998—. Mem. Am. Pharm. Assn., Am. Soc. Health Sys. Pharmacists, Am. Soc. Parenteral and Enteral Nutrition, Tenn. Soc. Health Sys. Pharmacists, Nashville Area Pharmacists Assn. Democrat. Avocations: art, music, reading, cooking, sewing. Home: 1439 McGavock Pike Nashville TN 37216-3231 E-mail: mckeelsw@prodigy.net.

MCKEEN, ALEXANDER C. retired engineering executive, foundation administrator; b. Albion, Mich., Oct. 10, 1927; s. John Nisbet and Janet (Callander) McK.; m. Evelyn Mae Feldkamp, Aug. 18, 1951; Jeffrey, Brian, Andrew. BSME, U. Mich., 1950; MBA, Mich. State U., 1968. Registered profl. engr., Mich. From asst. supt. maintenance to supt. final assembly Cadillac Motor Car divsn. GM, Detroit, 1961-69; asst. dir. reliability cadillac motor car divsn. GM, 1969-72, exec. engr. product assurance Warren, 1972-75, from asst. dir. to dir engring. analysis, 1975-87; pres., owner Engring. Analysis Assocs., Inc., Bingham Farms, 1987-99; cons. Detroit Exec. Svc. Corps, 1999—; pres. McKeen Found., 2002—. Pres. Dells of Bloomfield Home Owners Assn., Bloomfield Hills, Mich., 1987-88; trustee Kirk in Hills, Bloomfield Hills, 1990-93, elder, 1995-97. Mem. Soc. Auto. Engrs., Am. Soc. Quality Control, Econ. Club Detroit, Detroit Athletic Club, Stonycroft Hills Golf Club, Pelican Nest Golf Club, Beta Gamma Sigma. Avocations: tennis, golf, photography, travel, gardening. Home: 5071 Champlain Cir West Bloomfield MI 48323-3530 Office: Detroit Executive Service Corps 16250 Northland Dr Southfield MI 48075

MC KEEN, CHESTER M., JR. business executive; b. Shelby, Ohio, Mar. 18, 1923; s. Chester Mancil and Nettie Augusta (Fox) McK.; m. Alma Virginia Pierce, Mar. 1946 (dec. Feb. 1998); children: David Richard, Karin, Thomas Kevin; m. Sally Ann Werst, Nov. 1999; 1 stepchild, Stephen Harry Werst. BS in Mil. Sci., U. Md., 1962; MBA, Babson Coll., Wellesley, Mass., 1962. Advanced through grades to maj. gen. U.S. Army, 1942-77; dir. logistics Bell Helicopter Internat., Tehran, Iran, 1977-79; v.p. procurement Bell Helicopter Textron, Ft. Worth, 1979-82, v.p. materiel, 1982-89; pres. Logistics Svcs. Internat., Arlington, Tex. Chmn. bd. dirs. ISES Inc. Adv. bd. Salvation Army, Cancer Care Svcs. Decorated D.S.M., Legion of Merit (3), Commendation medal (3); named to U.S. Ordnance Hall of Fame. Mem. Am. Mgmt. Assn., Nat. Def. Indsl. Assn., Assn. U.S. Army, Ridglea Country Club, Rotary, Masons (33 degree), Shriners, Sojourners, Sigma Pi. Home: 2310 Woodsong Trail Arlington TX 76016-1037 Office: ISES Inc 328 Pipeline Rd Hurst TX 76053 E-mail: cmmckeen@aol.com. *To live for oneself is to pursue emptiness. To live for others is to insure fulfillment.*

MCKEEN, ELISABETH ANNE, oncologist; b. New Castle, Pa., Oct. 13, 1950; d. Richard Douglas and Harriette Elisabeth McK; m. Barry Nixon Walker; children: Anne, Matthew. BS in Biology, Rensselaer Polytech. Inst., 1974; MD, Albany Med. Coll., 1974. Diplomate Nat. Bd. Med. Examiners, Am. Bd. Internal Medicine, Am. Bd. Med. Oncology, Am. Bd. Hospice and Palliative Medicine; cert. in familial cancer assessment and mgmt. Intern Emory U. Affiliated Hosps., Atlanta, 1974-75, resident, 1975-76; fellow cancer epidemiology Nat. Cancer Inst., Bethesda, Md., 1976-78; fellow med. oncology Georgetown U. Hosp., Washington, 1978-79; clin. instr. in medicine Georgetown U. Hosp., 1979-82; clin. asst. prof. U. Fla., Gainesville, 1987—; from assoc. to ptnr. Harris & McKeen MDs, P.A., W. Palm Beach, Fla., 1982-90; Palm Beach Oncology/Hematology Good Samaritan Med. Ctr., 1993—, Helen and Harry Gray Cancer Inst., 1997—. Clin. investigator Nat. Cancer Inst., Bethesda, Md. 1979-82; med. dir. Hospice Palm Beach County, 1985-93, faculty, 1990; chmn. med. edn. com. Palm Beach County chpt., 1983—; cons. assoc. dept. medicine Duke U., Durham, N.C., 1994—; med. dir. cancer genetics and counseling, Dr. Mary Tarzian Cancer Genetic Program, 1997—; med. dir. Norma E. and Miles M. Zisson Comprehensive Breast Ctr. Good Samaritan Med. Ctr., W. Palm Beach, 1997—; staff mem. St. Mary's Hosp., West Palm Beach, chair pharmacy and therapeutic com., 1992-93, transfusion com. 1989-90; mem. quality assurance, 1987-88, pharmacy and therapeutic 1991-92, continuing edn. com., 1992-93; cons. Palm Beach Gardens Med. Ctr., Palm Beach Gardens, Fla., 1982—; co-chmn. breast com. Duke Comprehensive Cancer Ctr., 1993—. Contbr. articles to profl. jours. including Am. Jour. Human Genetics, Am. Soc. Human Genetics, Proceedings Am. Soc. Clin. Oncology, Am. Assn. Cancer Rsch., Jour. Nat. Cancer Inst., Lancet, Annals Internal Medicine, Internat. Jour. Cancer; speaker to sci. groups and in ednl. insts. Fla. Chmn. med. edn. com. Am. Cancer Soc., Palm Beach County, 1983—, bd. dirs. 1984-88; mem. speaker's bur. VNA, 1984-88; bd. dir. S. Fla. chpt. Susan G. Komen Breast Cancer Found., Dallas, 1991—; peer reviewer cancer related pain guideline for health care providers Agy. for Health Care Policy and Rsch. and Pain Mgmt. Panel, 1992. Fellow ACP; mem. AMA, Am. Acad. Hospice Physicians (bd. dirs. 1988—, chmn. edn. and tng. com. 1988—), So. Assn. for Oncology, Fla. Soc. Clin. Oncology (bd. dirs. 1991-93, legis., legal and ethics com. 1992-93), Israel Cancer Assn. (regional sci. bd.), Am. Soc. Breast Disease, Am. Soc. Clin. Oncology, Palm Beach County Med. Soc., Am. Soc. Internal Medicine, Fla. Cancer Control and Rsch. Adv. Bd., Gilda's Club of S. Fla. (profl. adv. bd.). Office: Helen & Harry Cancer Inst Good Samaritan Med Ctr 1309 N Flagler Dr West Palm Beach FL 33401-3406 E-mail: rlixsbethmckeen@tenethealth.com.

MCKEEVER, BRIAN EDWARD, general contractor; b. Hartford, Conn., Feb. 24, 1957; s. John Edward and Mary Elizabeth (Quish) McK.; m. Lise Evan Engelbrecht, Apr. 4, 1992; children: Madison Coreigh, Seamus Edward, Connor Patrick. Student, Manchester C.C., 1975-77, U. Hartford, 1990-96. Cert. emergency med. technician. Pres. BMK Corp./The MAK Co., Manchester, Conn. Mem.-at-large Steel Structures Painting Coun. Northern New Eng. chpt. Mem. Manchester 8th Dist. Vol. Fire Dept., 1973; mem. Emergency Accident-Illness Simulation Team, Conn. Dept. Health, 1975; active Big Bros. Am. Mem. Constrn. Inst. U. Hartford (chairship of mem. com.), Painting and Decorating Contractors Am., Remodeling Contractors Assn., Water Jet Tech. Assn., Internat. Assn. Concrete Repair Specialists, Hartford Indsl. Mgmt. Clu, Better Bus. Bur., Manchester C. of C., Conn. Assn. Real Estate Investors, Civitan, Lions, Elks, Irish Am. Home, NRA, Rockville Fish and Game Club, K.C. Roman Catholic. Office: The MAK Co PO Box 882 Vernon Rockville CT 06066-0882

MCKEEVER, JEFFREY D. computer company executive; b. Marion, Ind., 1942; Grad., U. Ariz., Tucson, 1965; MBA, U. Ariz., 1973. V.p. First Interstate Bank of Arizona; chmn., CEO, co-founder MicroAge Inc., Tempe, Ariz., 1976—. Office: MicroAge Inc 1330 W Southern Ave Tempe AZ 85282-4545*

MCKEEVER, JOHN EUGENE, lawyer; b. Phila., Oct. 24, 1947; s. John James and Marie Julia (Supper) McK.; m. Kathleen Marie Wynne, Dec. 9, 1995; children: John Joseph, Jeannine Marie. BA magna cum laude with distinction, U. Pa., 1969, JD magna cum laude, 1972. Bar: Pa. 1972, U.S. Dist. Ct. (ea. dist.) Pa. 1972, U.S. Dist. Ct. (mid. dist.) Pa. 1977, U.S. Ct. Appeals (3rd cir.) 1979, U.S. Ct. Appeals (D.C. cir.) 1981, U.S. Supreme Ct. 1981. Assoc. Schnader, Harrison, Segal & Lewis, Phila., 1972-80, ptnr., 1980-98, Piper Marbury Rudnick & Wolfe, Phila., 1998—. Mem. Pres. Coun. Allentown Coll. St. Francis De Sales, Center Valley, Pa., 1980—, Bus. Leadership Organized for Cath. Schs., Phila., 1984—, adv. com. De Sales Sch. Theology, Washington, trustee, 1988-91; capt. spl. gifts com. Cath. Charities Appeal, Phila., 1986-91; bd. dirs. Jr. Achievement, Phila., 1986—; co-chair Oblates of St. Francis De Sales Capital Campaign, 1998-99. Mem. Pa. Bar Assn., Phila. Bar Assn., Pro-Life Lawyers' Guild (bd. dirs. 1983-84, chancellor 1984-86), St. Thomas More Soc. (gov. 1979-91, pres. 1981-82), Order of Coif, Phi Beta Kappa, Pi Gamma Mu. Republican. Roman Catholic. Office: Piper Marbury Rudnick & Wolfe 2400 Two Logan Sq 18th and Arch Sts Philadelphia PA 19103-2762 E-mail: john.mckeever@piperrudnick.com.

MCKEEVER, JOSEPH FRANCIS, III, lawyer; b. Weymouth, Mass., July 21, 1950; s. Joseph Francis Jr. and Virginia Agnes McK.; m. Janice Danielle Kearney, Oct. 17, 1970. BA, George Washington U., 1972, JD, 1978. Bar: D.C. 1978, U.S. Supreme Ct. 1989. Editor Congl. Rsch. Svc. Libr. Congress, Washington, 1974-78; law clk. Honorable Harry Wood U.S. Ct. Claims, 1978-79, Honorable Wilson Cowen U.S. Ct. Claims, Washington, 1979-80; atty. Sutherland, Asbill & Brennan, 1980-85; ptnr. Davis & Harman LLP, 1985—. Author, editor: Annuities Answer Book, 1999; contbr. articles to profl. jours. Mem. ABA (chair sect. on taxation com. on ins. cos. 2000-02). Avocations: gardening, bicycling. Home: 2812 34th Pl NW Washington DC 20007-1405 Office: Davis & Harman LLP Willard Office Bldg 1455 Pennsylvania Ave NW Washington DC 20004-1008

MCKEEVER, MICHAEL PIERCE, SR. economics and business educator; b. Glendale, Calif., Mar. 3, 1941; s. Samuel Pierce and Martha Frances (Darby) McK.; m. Jeanetta Ross, Oct. 20, 1964 (div. June 1970); 1 child, Nancy; m. Marjorie Alice McKean, Dec. 17, 1970; children: Michael P. Jr., Johnathan Brooks. BA with honors, Whittier (Calif.) Coll., 1963; MS in Econs., London Sch. Econs., 1966. Life credential bus., econs., social sci. Calif. C.C. Owner Counseling Brokerage Group, Santa Rosa, Calif., 1980-84, Bus. Plan Workshop, Santa Rosa, 1980-95; asst. prof. econs. and bus. Armstrong U., Berkeley, Calif., 1995-97; founder McKeever Inst. Econ. Policy Analysis, 1995—. Instr. Vista Coll., Berkeley, Calif., 1998—. Author: How to Write a Business Plan, 1981, Conceptual Economics, 1993, Moral Economics, 2001. Dir. Inst. Small Bus. Dept. Sonoma State U., 1981; pres. We Care, Santa Rosa, 1984; chmn. adv. com. Suppression of Drug Abuse in Schs. Sonoma County, Santa Rosa, 1985. Recipient award Role Recognition-Downtown Devel., Santa Rosa City Coun., 1983; named Vol. of Yr. Santa Rosa City Schs., 1984. Avocations: men's senior baseball league player and coach. Home and Office: 3060 Curran Ave Oakland CA 94602-3124 E-mail: mckeever@ccnet.com.

MCKEIGHEN, RONALD EUGENE, physicist; b. Marion, Ill., Oct. 17, 1942; s. George A. and Aileen (Reach) McK.; m. Loretta M. Ward, Sept. 3, 1966; children: Kevin, Christy. BS in Engring. Physics, U. Ill., 1964, MS in Nuclear Engring., 1965, PhD in Physics, 1971. Postdoctoral in cancer rsch. and nuclear medicine Oak Ridge Nat. Lab., 1972-73; sr. prin. rsch. scientist Searle/Siemens Ultrasound, Des Plaines, 1973-79; sr. R&D engr. KB-Aerotech, Lewistown, Pa., 1979-83; staff scientist Advanced Diagnostic Rsch., Tempe, Ariz., 1983-85; prin. staff engr. Motorola Space Elect, Scottsdale, 1985-86; mgr. advanced devel. Advanced Tech. Labs., Bothel, Wash., 1986-93; dir. advanced devel. Acoustic Imaging inc., Phoenix, 1993—2001; prin. rsch. engr. Lockheed-Martin, Litchfield Park, 2001—. Contbr. articles to profl. jours. and chpts. to books. Spl. fellow in nuclear engring. AEC. Mem. IEEE. Mem. Pentecostal Ch. Achievements include patent for concept of digital beamformer for ultrasonic phased array, developed ultrasonic transducer arrays and sensors. Home: 1432 E Desert Flower Ln Phoenix AZ 85048-5932 Office: Lockheed-Martin Litchfield Park AZ

MCKEITHEN, WALTER FOX, secretary of state; b. Columbia, La., Sept. 8, 1946; s. John Jesse and Marjorie (Funderburk) McK.; m. Yvonne May; children: Marjorie, Marianne, Rebecca, John Jesse. B in History and Social Studies, La. Tech. U., 1972. Owner, operator Apparel Mart Dept. Store, Columbia, 1974-83, McKeithen Chem. & Cementing, Columbia, 1979-88; mem. appropriation, natural resources and joint budged coms. La. Ho. of Reps., Baton Rouge, 1983-87; sec. of state State of La., 1987—. Tchr., coach Caldwell Parish High Sch., Grayson, La., 1975-78; past mem. La. Assn. Educators. Past v.p. Caldwell Parish Jaycees; trustee La. Sch. Employees' Retirement System; mem. La. Tourist Devel. Commn.; second injury bd. La. Workmen's Compensation; mem. State Bd. Election Supervisors and State Bond Commn., La. Farm Bur., Am. Petroleum Inst.; administrv. bd. Broadmoor Meth. Ch. Recipient Outstanding Legislator award La. Assn. Educators, 1985, Golden Apple award La. Fedn. Tchrs., 1986. Republican. Methodist. Office: Dept of State State Capitol 20th Fl PO Box 94125 Baton Rouge LA 70804-9125*

MCKELDIN, WILLIAM EVANS, management consultant; b. Richmond, Va., Aug. 14, 1927; s. Robert A.W. and Mary E. (Burk) McK.; children: William Evans, Roberts Evans; m. Phyllis Shellhase, Jan. 23, 1982. BSBA, Temple U., 1951, postgrad., 1951-53, U. Pitts., 1953-54. Various mgmt. positions Westinghouse Corp., Pitts., 1950-62, Farrel Corp., Rochester, N.Y., 1963-66, Gen. Signal Corp., Norwalk, Conn., and Watertown, N.Y., 1966-71, Copperweld Steel Co., Warren, Ohio, 1971-75, Tenn. Forging Steel, Knoxville, 1975-77, Val Bradley Assocs., West Chester, Pa., 1977-79; pres., owner McKeldin Assocs., 1979-95; founder, co-owner McKeldin Group, Bala Cynwyd, Pa., 1995—. Contbr. articles to profl. jours. Bd. dirs. United Fund, YMCA, ARC, Rochester Inst. Tech., Jefferson C.C., Kent State U. With USAAF, 1945-47. Mem. Inst. Mgmt. Cons., Am. Soc. Safety Engrs., Am. Soc. Personnel Adminstrn., C. of C. (bd. dirs.), Masons, Rotary. Republican. Presbyterian. Office: The McKeldin Group 24 Timber Ln Hilton Head Island SC 29926-1002 E-mail: mckeldin@webtv.net.

MCKELL, CYRUS M. retired college dean, plant physiologist; b. Payson, Utah, Mar. 19, 1926; s. Robert D. and Mary C. (Ellsworth) McK.; m. Betty Johnson; children: Meredith Sue, Brian Marcus, John Cyrus. BS, U. Utah, 1949, MS, 1950; PhD, Oreg. State U., 1956; postgrad., U. Calif., Davis, 1957. Instr. botany Oreg. State U., Corvallis, 1955-56; range rsch. plant physiologist U. Calif. USDA-Agrl. Research Service, Davis, 1956—61; prof., dept. chmn. U. Calif., Riverside, 1961—69; prof. dept. head., dir. Utah State U., Logan, 1969-80; v.p. research NPI, Salt Lake City, 1980-88; dean Coll. of Sci. Weber State U., Ogden, 1988-94; pres., prin. Applied Ecol. Svcs. Inc., Logan, 1995—. Cons. Ford Found. 1968-72, Rockefeller Found., 1964-70, 89, UN, 1978, 90, NAS, 1980, 89, 91, 92, 93, USAID, 1972, UN Devel. Program, 1989; mem. faculty of sci. adv. bd. UAR Nat. U., 2000-02. Editor: Grass Biology and Utilization, 1971, Useful Wildland Shrubs, 1972, Rehabilitation of Western Wildlife Habitat, 1978, Paradoxes of Western Energy Development, 1984, Resource Inventory and Baseline Study Methods for Developing Countries, 1983, Shrub Biology and Utilization, 1989, Wilderness Issues, Arid Lands of the Western United States, 1992; contbr. over 230 articles to profl. jours. Chmn. Cache County Planning Commn., Logan, 1974-79; mem. Utah Energy Conservation and Devel. Coun., 1976-79, Gov.'s Sci. Adv. Coun., 1988-97, chmn., 1990-91, 96-97; mem. Commn. of the Californiaas, Riverside, 1965-68. Recipient Utah Gov.'s Sci. and Tech. medal, 1990, Gardner Prize in Sci., awarded by Utah Acad. Scis., Arts and Letters, 1999; Fulbright scholar Spain, 1967-68; World Travel grantee Rockefeller Found., 1964. Fellow AAAS (com. chmn. 1979-89, sci. exchange to China grantee 1984-85, 89, sci. panel U.S.-Chile 1987); mem. Am. Soc. Agronomy, Soc. Range Mgmt. (pres. Calif. sect. 1965, pres. Utah sect. 1982). Mem. Lds Ch. Avocations: travel, photography. Home: 2248 E 4000 S Salt Lake City UT 84124-1864 Office: 550 N Main St Ste 302 Logan UT 84321-3957 E-mail: cmmckell@xmission.com.

MCKELLEN, IAN, actor; b. Burnley, England, May 25, 1939; s. Denis Murray and Margery (Sutcliffe) McK. Student, St. Catharine's Coll., Cambridge. Prof. Oxford U., 1990-91. First stage appearance as Roper in A Man for All Seasons, Belgrade Theatre, Coventry, Eng., 1961; numerous other parts include title roles in Henry V, Luther, Ipswich, 1962-63, Aufidius in Coriolanus, Arthur Seaton in Saturday Night and Sunday Morning, title role in Sir Thomas More, Nottingham Playhouse, 1963-64; London debut as Godfrey in A Scent of Flowers, 1964, Claudio in Much Ado About Nothing, Andrew Cobham in Their Very Own and Golden City, 1966; title part in O'Flaherty, V.C. and Bonapart in The Man of Destiny, 1966, (Broadway debut) Leonidik in the Promise, London, 1966-67, Richard II, Edward II, Hamlet, Prospect Theatre Co., 1968-71; Captain Plume in The Recruiting Officer; founder-mem. Actors' Co., Edinburgh Festival, 1972 and touring as Giovanni in Tis Pity She's a Whore, Page-Boy in Ruling the Roost, title role Wood Demon; debut with R.S.C. as Dr. Faustus, Edinburgh Festival, 1974; title role in The Marquis of Keith, Philip the Bastard in King John, 1974-75, Young Vic Colin in Ashes, 1975; Royal Shakespeare Co.: Burglar in Too True to be Good, Romeo, MacBeth, Leontes in the Winter's Tale, Face in the Alchemist, Bernick in Pillars of the Community, Langevin in Days of the Commune, 1976-78, Ivanov in Every Good Boy Deserves Favour, Toby Belch in Twelth Night, Andrei in The Three Sisters, Max in Bent, 1979, Amadeus, N.Y.C., 1980, Iago in Othello, The Other Place, Stratford, 1989; European tour of one-man show Acting Shakespeare, 1983, also L.A., N.Y.C., 1984, one-man show A Knight Out at the Lyceum (devised especially for Gay Games IV U.K. and South Africa tour), 1994; assoc. dir. Nat. Theatre, London, 1984-86, plays include: Venice Preserved, Wild Honey, Coriolanus, Duchess of Malfi, The Cherry Orchard, King Lear, Richard III, Napoli Milionaria, Uncle Vanya, An Enemy of The People, Peter Pan, others; dir. first prodn. The Prime of Miss Jean Brodie, Liverpool Playhouse, 1969, A Private Matter, 1973, The Clandestine Marriage, 1975; films include; Alfred the Great, 1969, The Promise, 1969, A Touch of Love, 1969, The Keep, 1982, Plenty, Zina, 1985, Scandal, 1988, The Ballad of Little Jo, 1992, I'll Do Anything, 1992, Last Action Hero, 1993, Six Degrees of Separation, 1993, The Shadow, 1994, Jack and Sarah, 1994, Restoration, 1994, Richard III, 1995, Cold Comfort Farm, 1995, Bent, 1996, Swept From the Sea, 1996, Apt Pupil, 1997, Gods and Monsters, 1997; TV appearances include: David Copperfield, 1965, Ross, 1969, Richard II, Edward II and Hamlet, 1970, Hedda Gabler, 1974, Macbeth, Every God Boy Deserves Favour, Dying Day, 1979, Acting Shakespeare, 1981, The Scarlet Pimpernel, 1982, And the Band Played On, 1993 (Emmy nomination, Supporting Actor, 1996), X-Men, 2000, Lord of the Rings: The Fellowship of the Ring, 2001 (Outstanding Performance by Male Actor in Supporting Role SAG award 2002, nominee Best Supporing Actor Acad. award 2002, Best Supporting Actor Saturn award 2002; nominee Best Performance by Actor BAFTA Film award, Empire award, Golden Satellite award, MTV Movie award, and OFCS award 2002), Lord of the Rings: Th Two Towers, 2002. Recipient Clarence Derwent award, 1964, Variety and Plays and Players awards, 1966; Actor of Year, Plays and Players, 1976, Soc. of West End Theatres for Best Actor in Revival award, 1977, for Best Comedy Performance, 1978, for Best Actor in a New Play, 1979, Tony Award for Best Actor, Drama Desk award, Outer Critics Circle award, N.Y. Drama League award, 1981, Performer of the Yr. award Royal TV Soc., 1983; decorated comdr. Order Brit. Empire, knight Bachelor. Mem. Brit. Actors' Equity (coun. 1970-71).*

MCKELLIPS, TERRAL LANE, mathematics educator, university administrator; b. Terlton, Okla., Dec. 2, 1938; s. Raymond Orlando and Patrice Lillian (Fuller) McK.; m. Karen Kay Sweeney, Sept. 7, 1958; children: Marty Suzanne, Kyle Bret. BS in Edn., S.W. Okla. State U., 1961; MS, Okla. State U., 1963, EdD, 1968. Asst. prof. S.W. Okla. State U., Weatherford, 1962-66; prof., dept. chmn. Cameron U., Lawton, Okla., 1968-72, 73-83, prof., dean Sch. Math. Applied Scis., 1983-89, provost, 1989—2001. Vis. prof. Okla. State U., Stillwater, 1972-73. Contbr. articles to profl. jours. State coord, Dept. Leadership Inst., Am. Coun. Edn., 1982-83; chair Okla. State Regents for Higher Edn. Coun. on Instrn., 1997-98. NSF Sci. Faculty fellow, 1966-68. Mem. Math. Assn. Am. (cons. bur. 1975—), Nat. Coun. Tchrs. Math., Lawton Country Club (dir. 1982-89, pres. 1986-89), Pi Mu Epsilon, Phi Kappa Phi. Democrat. Avocations: golf, genealogy. E-mail: terralm@cameron.edu.

MCKELVEY, GERALD, public relations executive; b. Waynesboro, Pa., June 27, 1943; s. Gerald Campbell and Mary Lou (Dunn) McK. BA, Wash. Coll., 1965. Reporter The Record Herald, Waynesboro, Pa., 1965-67; reporter, editor Phila. Inquirer, 1967-76; night city editor Newsday, Melville, 1976-81; dep. met. editor N.Y. Newsday, 1981-88; spl. asst. Manhattan Dist. Atty.'s Office, N.Y.C., 1988-96; sr. v.p. Rubenstein Assocs., Inc., 1996-00, exec. v.p., 2000—. Trustee Ch. of St. Mary Virgin, N.Y.C., 1996-00. Mem. SAR, The Inner Cir. Office: Rubenstein Assocs Inc 1345 Avenue Of The Americas New York NY 10105-0302

MCKELVEY, JAMES MORGAN, chemical engineering educator; b. St. Louis, Aug. 22, 1925; s. James Grey and Muriel (Morgan) McK.; m. Edith Rothbauer, Dec. 28, 1957; children: James, Robert; m. Judith Hood Forgotson, Sept. 4, 1992. BS, U. Mo.-Rolla, 1945; MS, Washington U., St. Louis, 1947, PhD, 1950. Research engr. E.I. DuPont de Nemours & Co., Inc., 1950-54; asst. prof. chem. engring. Johns Hopkins U., Balt., 1954-57; mem. faculty Washington U., St. Louis, 1957—, dean Sch. Engring. and Applied Sci., 1964-91, prof. chem. engring., 1991-98, sr. prof. chem. engring., 1998—. Recipient Disting. Educator award Soc. Plastics Engrs., 1979 Home: 9861 Copper Hill Rd Saint Louis MO 63124-1063

MCKELVEY, VIRGINIA MAUDE, educator; b. Pueblo, Colo., June 5, 1935; children: Daniel Helman, Nancy Schuessler BA in English/Edn., U. So. Colo., 1994; MLS in Lang. Comm., Regis U., 1998; PhD, Walden U., Mpls., 2002. Acctg. and bus. adminstr., 1964-92; collector and seller rare and new books; tchr. English, Sch. Dist. 60, Pueblo, 1994-2000, U.S. Peace Corps, Bangkok, 2001—. Mem. Am. Acad. Poets, Virginia Woolf Soc., Sierra Club, Humane Soc. Am., Phi Delta Kappa. Democrat. Avocation: travel. Office: US Peace Corp 1111 20th St NW Washington DC 20526

MCKELVY, MICHAEL JOHN, materials chemist, research scientist; b. Berkeley, Calif., Apr. 19, 1954; s. Andy Milton and Dagmar Marie (Johnson) McK.; m. Margaret Knight Riddall, Aug. 2, 1975; children: Robin, Adam, Evan. BS in Chemistry, U. Calif., Berkeley, 1975; MS in Chemistry, Ariz. State U., 1981, PhD in Chemistry, 1985. Engr. crystal growing lab., ctr. solid state sci. Ariz. State U., Tempe, 1976-82, materials sci. engr. II, 1982-84, rsch. specialist, 1984-90, mgr. materials facility, 1986-94, assoc. rsch. scientist, 1990-99, affiliate assoc. prof. sci. & engring. of materials PhD program, 1993-99, dir. materials facility, 1994—, dir. Goldwater materials sci. labs., 1995—, acting dir. ctr. solid state sci., 1997, sr. rsch. scientist, 1999—, affiliate prof. sci. and engring. materials grad. program, 1999—. Invited asst. prof. Inst. des Matériaux de Nantes, U. Nantes, France, 1993; proposal reviewer Petroleum Rsch. Fund, Washington, 1992-94, U.S. Dept. Energy, 2000—. Contbr. articles to profl. jours.; manuscript reviewer Chemistry of Materials, 1994—, Jour. Physics and Chemistry of Solids, 1995, Jour. Solid State Chemistry, 1996—, Molecular Crystals and Liquid Crystals, 1997-98, Jour. Am. Chem. Soc., 1998—. Coach Chandler (Ariz.) Youth Baseball, 1988-95, Chandler Am. Little League, 1996-97; com. chmn. cub scouts Boy Scouts Am., Mesa, Ariz., 1992, mem. Boy Scout com., Chandler, 1993-95. Rsch. grantee NSF, 1986—, Petroleum Rsch. Fund, 1992-95, Dept. Energy, 1995—; NRC sr. rsch. assoc., 2002. Mem. Am. Chem. Soc., Materials Rsch. Soc. Democrat. Presbyterian. Achievements include patents for method for detection of chemical components, chemical switch and method for detection of chemical compounds, and chemical switch for detection of chemical components; co-development of atomic-level imaging of lamellar intercalation reaction processes using dynamic high-resolution transmission electron microscopy and scanning tunneling microscopy/spectroscopy; research in new materials synthesis, materials reaction mechanisms, carbon dioxide mineral sequestration, intercalation chemistry, thermal chemistry and analysis, materials sci. edn. Office: Ariz State U Ctr for Solid State Science Tempe AZ 85287-1704 E-mail: mckelvy@asu.edu.

MCKELVY, NIKKI KAY, nurse; b. Honolulu, May 16, 1956; d. Donald and Virginia Katherine (Davis) McK.; m. David Stuart Murry, Dec. 9, 1978 (dec. 1992); children: Ryan Cobb, Caleb Murry. AA, Saddleback Coll., 1989; BSN, Dominican Coll., 1994. RN. Customer svc. clk. United Parcel Svc., Little Rock, 1974-78; resident/extern Vets. Hosp., Montrose, N.Y., 1993-94; staff nurse Harrison (Ark.) Nursing Ctr., 1995-96, 99; sub. tchr. Branson (Mo.) Sch. Dist., 2000—. Salesperson Nana's Fashions for Kids, 1999—2000. Fellow Sigma Theta Tau; mem. Nursing Assn. Dominican Coll. (v.p.). Democrat. Roman Catholic. Avocations: reading, swimming, travel. Home: 255 Bunker Rd Harrison AR 72601-7529

MCKELWAY, ALEXANDER JEFFREY, religion studies educator; b. Durham, N.C., Dec. 8, 1932; s. Alexander Jeffrey and Alice (Gibbon) McK.; m. Adelaide Bullard, Sept. 17, 1960; children: Alexander J., Daniel, Matthew Phillip. AB, Davidson Coll., 1954; BD, Princeton Theol. Sem., 1954-57; ThD, U. Basil, 1963. Ordained to ministry Presbyn. Ch., 1957. Min. Vienna (Austria) Cmty. Ch., 1958-60; asst. prof. Dartmouth Coll., Hanover, N.H., 1963-65; Paul B. Freeland prof. religion Davidson (N.C.) Coll., 1965-98, faculty chair, 1991-94. Vis. prof. Princeton (N.J.) Theol. Sem., 1973, 86, 87, Duke U. Div. Sch., Durham, N.C., 1999; mem. Fulbright Commn., Vienna, 1958-60. Author: The Systematic Theology of Paul Tillich, 1964, The Freedom of God and Human Liberation, 1991; editor: The Context of Contemporary Theology, 1974. Chair jud. com. Synod of N.C., 1975; moderator Charlotte (N.C.) Presbytery, 1985; active Kincaid for Congress Com., Charlotte, 1980, Exec. Com. Dem. Party, Davidson, 1975-77. Fellow in theology Princeton Sem., 1957, Younger Scholars fellow NEH, 1969, Ctr. for Theol. Inquiry fellow, 1997—. Mem. Am. Acad. Religion, Calvin Studies Soc., Duodecim Theol. Soc. (sec.), Am. Theol. Soc.

MCKENNA, ALVIN JAMES, lawyer; b. New Orleans, Aug. 17, 1943; s. Dixon N. Sr. and Mabel (Duplantier) McK.; m. Carol Jean Windheim, 1963; children: Sara, Alvin James Jr., Martha, Andrea, Erin, Rebecca. AB, Canisius Coll., 1963; JD, Notre Dame U., 1966. Bar: N.Y. 1966, Ohio 1967, U.S. Dist. Ct. (so. dist.) Ohio 1968, U.S. Dist. Ct. (no. dist.) Ohio 1978, U.S. Ct. Appeals (6th cir.) 1969, U.S. Supreme Ct. 1977. Law clk. to judge of U.S. Dist. Ct. (so. dist.), Columbus, Ohio, 1966-68; asst. U.S. atty., 1968-70; ptnr. Porter, Wright, Morris & Arthur, 1970—. Mem. Gahanna (Ohio) City Council, 1972-80, 82-84; chmn. Gahanna Charter Rev. Commn., 1981; pres. Community Urban Redevel. Corp., Gahanna, 1984—. Named one of Ten Outstanding Young Persons in Columbus, Jaycees, 1974. Mem. ABA, Ohio Bar Assn., Fed. Bar Assn. (pres. Columbus chpt. 1973-74), Columbus Bar Assn. (chair fed. cts. com. 1972-74). Home: 202 Academy Ct Columbus OH 43230-2104 Office: Porter Wright Morris & Arthur 41 S High St Ste 2800 Columbus OH 43215-6194 E-mail: amckenna@porterwright.com.

MCKENNA, ANDREW JAMES, paper distribution and printing company executive, baseball club executive; b. Chgo., Sept. 17, 1929; s. Andrew James and Anita (Frain) McK.; m. Mary Joan Pickett, June 20, 1953; children: Suzanne, Karen, Andrew, William, Joan, Kathleen, Margaret. BS, U. Notre Dame, 1951; JD, DePaul U., 1954. Bar: Ill. Chmn., CEO Schwarz Paper Co. (name now Schwarz), Morton Grove, Ill., 1964—; dir. Chgo. Nat. League Ball Club Inc., Chgo. Bears. Bd. dirs. Skyline Corp., AON Corp., Click Commerce, Inc., McDonald's Corp. Chmn. trustees, emeritus U. Notre Dame; trustee Mus. Sci. & Industry, Chgo.; bd. dirs. Catholic Charities of Chgo., Children's Meml. Med. Ctr. Chgo. Mem. Chgo. Athletic Assn., Econ. Club Chgo., Lyric Opera (bd. dirs.), Chgo. Club, Comml. Club Chgo. (chmn.), Execs. Club Chgo., Glenview Golf Club, Old Elm Club, Merit Club, Casino Club, The Island Club, Chgo. Metropolis 2020. Home: 60 Locust Rd Winnetka IL 60093-3751 Office: Schwarz 8338 Austin Ave Morton Grove IL 60053-3288

MCKENNA, FRANK JOSEPH, lawyer; b. Apohaqui, N.B., Can., Jan. 19, 1948; s. Durward and Olive (Moody) McK.; m. Julie Friel; children: Tobias John, Christine Alice, James Durward. BA with honors, St. Francis Xavier U., 1970; postgrad., Queen's U., 1970-71; LLB, U. N.B., 1974; DSc (hon.), Université de Moncton, Can., 1988; LLD (hon.), University of N.B., Can., 1988, Mt. Allison U., 1991. Spl. asst. to pres. Privy Council, 1971; rsch. asst. Constl. Law Unit, 1973-74; v.p. U. N.B. Faculty of Law Liberal Assn., Fredericton, 1974; ptnr. Martin, Lordon, McKenna & Bowes, Chatham, 1974-87; mem. N.B. Liberal Party, 1982, leader, 1985; premier Province of N.B., Fredericton, 1987-97; with McInnes Cooper, Moncton, NB, Can. Dir. Bank of Montreal, Noranda Inc., Zenon Environ., Acier LeRoux, various provincial, nat. and internat. cos. Recipient Vanier award, 1988, Distinction award Can. Advanced Tech. Assn., 1994; named Econ. Developer of Yr., Econ. Developers' Assn. Can., 1993, Chair, Can. Quality Month, 1994. Mem. Can. Bar Assn., N.B. Bar Assn. Liberal. Avocations: jogging, baseball, hockey. Office: McInnes Cooper PO Box 1368 Moncton NB Canada E1C 8T6

MCKENNA, GEORGE LAVERNE, art museum curator; b. Detroit, Dec. 7, 1924; s. John LaVerne and Carolyn Georgia (Schwab) McK.; m. Janice Ballinger, July 22, 1966. Student, U. Oreg., 1943-44, U. Calif., Berkeley, 1948-49, U. Chgo., 1950; AB, Wayne State U., 1948, MA, 1951. Curator prints, drawings and photographs Nelson-Atkins Mus. Art, Kansas City, Mo., 1952-96, cons, 1997—. Cons. Hallmark Cards, Inc., Kansas City, 1974-76. Curator, author exhbn. and coll. catalogues. With U.S. Army, 1943-46. Mem. Am. Assn. Mus., Print Coun. Am. Office: Nelson-Atkins Mus Art 4525 Oak St Kansas City MO 64111-1873

MCKENNA, GEORGE NORTON, government educator; b. Chgo. s. Robert Emmet and Helen Elizabeth McK.; m. Sylvia Rhea McKenna, Aug. 29, 1964; childre: Laura, Maria, Christopher. AB, U. Chgo., 1959; MA, U. Mass., 1962; PhD, Fordham U., 1967. Lectr. CCNY, N.Y.C., 1963-67, asst. prof., 1967-75, assoc. prof., 1975-84, prof., 1984—. Author: The Drama of Democracy, 1998; co-editor: Taking Sides: Controvesial Voices of Political Issues, 12th edit., 2001; contbr. articles to profl. jours. Candidate Clarkstown (N.Y.) Town Coun., 1975; pres. Save the Lake Assn., Clarkstown, 1970-73. Carnegie Found. fellow, 1963. Roman Catholic. Office: CCNY Dept Polit Sci 138th Convent Ave New York NY 10031

MCKENNA, JEANETTE ANN, archaeologist; b. N.Y.C., Aug. 6, 1953; d. Edward Patrick and Ann Jeanette (O'Brien) McKenna; children: Stephanie Jane, Daniel Glen Edward. AA in Phys. Edn., Mount San Antonio Jr. Coll., 1974; BA in Anthropology, Calif. State U., Fullerton, 1977, MA in Anthropology, 1982; postgrad., Ariz. State U., 1981-84, U. Calif., Riverside, 1991-92. Field archaeologist Archaeol. Rsch., Inc., Costa Mesa, Calif., 1976-79; rsch. asst. Calif. State U., 1979; lab dir. Environ. Rsch. Archaeologists, L.A., 1978-79; staff archaeologist Ariz. State U., Tempe, 1979-82; rsch. archaeologist Soil Systems, Inc., Phoenix, 1982-84, Sci. Resource Surveys, Huntington Beach, Calif., 1984-87; co-owner, prin. Hatheway & McKenna, Mission Viejo, 1987-89; owner, prin. McKenna et al., Whittier, 1989—; dir. Divsn. Cultural Resource Mgmt. Svcs. EIP Assocs., Chino, 1996-97. Contbr. numerous articles to profl. jours. and reports. Bd. dirs. Whittier Conservancy, 1987-98, interim treas., 1994, pres., 1994-95, bd. dirs. Residents' Voice, 1998—. Recipient Gov.'s award for Hist. Preservation/Calif., The Whittier Conservancy, 1995. Mem. Soc. Profl. Archaeologists (bd. dirs. 1993-97), Archaeol. Inst. Am., Am. Soc. Conservation Archaeology, Am. Mus. Natural History, Soc. Am. Anthropology, Ariz. Archaeol. Coun., Ariz. Hist. Found., Calif. Hist. Soc., Nat. Arbor Day Found., Nat. Parks and Conservation Assn., Nat. Trust for Historic Preservation, Soc. Calif. Archaeology, Soc. Hist. Archaeology, S.W. Mus. Assn., Wilderness Soc., Whittier Conservancy, Southwestern Anthrop. Assn., Gene Autry Western Heritage Mus. Assn., Nature Conservancy, Smithsonian Assocs., Sierra Club, otehrs. Democrat. Roman Catholic. Avocations: traveling, reading, hiking, camping, gardening. Office: McKenna et al 6008 Friends Ave Whittier CA 90601-3724

MCKENNA, JOHN DENNIS, environmental testing engineer; b. N.Y.C., Apr. 1, 1940; s. Hubert Guy and Elizabeth Ann (Record) McK.; m. Christel Klages, Dec. 26, 1964; children: Marc, Michelle. BSChemE, Manhattan Coll., 1961; MSChemE, Newark Coll. Engring., 1968; MBA, Rider Coll., 1974; PhD, Walden U., 1991. Tech. asst. to pres. Eldib Engring. & Rsch. Co., Newark, 1964-67; project mgr. Princeton (N.J.) Chem. Rsch., Inc., 1967-68; projects dir. Rsch. Cottrell Environ. Sys., Bound Brook, N.J., 1968-72; CEO Enviro-Sys. & Rsch., Inc., Roanoke, 1973-79, v.p., then pres. Va., 1979-91; chmn. bd. pres. ETS Internat. Inc., 1991-98; CEO ETS, Inc., 1998—. Chmn. air pollution adv. bd. State of Va., 1993; workshop lectr., sci. reviewer publs. EOA, 1978-79. Author chpts. in books; contbr. articles to profl. jours. Recipient Alumni Achievement Honor Roll award N.J. Inst. Tech., 1998; named Outstanding Engring. Grad., recipient Centennial award Manhattan Coll., 1992. Mem. AIChE (treas. chpt.), Air Pollution Control Assn., Air and Waste Mgmt. Assn. (divsn. chmn. tech. coun.), Tau Beta Pi (Eminent engr.). Roman Catholic. Home: 1884 Brick Church Rd Rocky Mount VA 24151-4008 Office: ETS Inc 1401 Municipal Rd NW Roanoke VA 24012-1309 E-mail: jmck@etsi-inc.com.

MCKENNA, JOHN FRANCIS, media executive; b. Bakersfield, Calif., Feb. 18, 1961; s. Frank Joseph and Linda Rae (Antongiovanni) McK.; m. Diana McKenna, May 31, 1997. Portuguese Lang., Curso Sao Joao Bosco, São Paulo, Brazil, 1979-80. Youth dir. Blue Army of Our Lady of Fatima, São Paulo, Brazil, 1981-87; mng. dir. Cath. Radio and TV Network, Brussels, 1988-97; mgr. Fedn. Field Sports Assns. of the European Cmty., 1998-99; network adminstr. Edgemail Techs., Bakersfield, Calif., 2000. Cons. Sts. Cyril and Methodius Ctr., Paris, 1990-98, Internationaler Hilfsfonds e.V., Frankfurt, Germany, 1990-97, Conservative Caucus Found., Washington, 1991; western Europe corr. Lithuanian Weekly, Vilnius, Lithuania, 1992-93. Producer documentary film A Hill Apart, 1995; contbr. articles to profl. jours. Recipient Diploma for Outstanding Orgn., Kaunas Tech. U., 1995. Mem. INITIO (dir. 1994-96), Cath. Radio and TV Network (pres. 1993-99), Internat. Lithuanian Ctr. (mng. dir. 1990-99), Serban Sound Systems. Roman Catholic. Avocations: judo, reading, learning langs., concerts, theater.

MCKENNA, KATHLEEN KWASNIK, artist; b. Detroit, Nov. 6, 1946; d. John J. and Eleanor H. (Ciosek) K.; m. Frank J. McKenna, Jr., Mar. 16, 1968. Cert., Cooper Sch. Art, Cleve., 1973; student, Art Students' League, N.Y.C., 1972, 74. Instr. portrait painting Baycrafters, Bay Village, Ohio, 1976-79; self-employed painter, 1972—; part-time mem. faculty fine arts dept. Lakeland C.C., Kirtland, Ohio, 1996—. One-person shows include Ctrl. Nat. Bank, Cleve., 1975, Women's City Club Gallery, Cleve., 1979, Kennedy Ctr. Art Gallery, Hiram, Ohio, 1980, Chime Art Gallery, Summit, N.J., 1985, Bolton Art Gallery, Cleve., 1986, 91, Lakeland C.C. Gallery, Kirtland, Ohio, 1996; group shows include Butler Inst. Am. Art, 1981, 89, 91, 93, Mansfield (Ohio) Art Ctr., 1990, 98, Circle Gallery, N.Y.C., 1978, Canton (Ohio) Art Inst., 1990, others. Recipient Pres.'s award Am. Artists Profl. League, 1993, other awards. Mem. New Orgn. for the Visual Arts, Catharine Lorillard Wolfe Art Club (Pastel Soc. plaque 1989, Mae Berlind Bach award 1983, Cert. of Merit 1981), Allied Artists Am. (assoc.; Gold medal of Honor 1989). Roman Catholic. Avocations: art-related travel, tennis, skiing. Studio: 15914 Chadbourne Rd Shaker Heights OH 44120

MCKENNA, MARGARET ANNE, college president; b. R.I., June 3, 1945; d. Joseph John and Mary (Burns) McK.; children: Michael Aaron McKenna Miller, David Christopher McKenna Miller. BA in Sociology, Emmanuel Coll., 1967; postgrad., Boston Coll. Law Sch., 1968; JD, So. Meth. U., 1971; LLD (hon.), U. Upsala, N.J., 1978, Fitchburg (Mass.) State Coll., 1979, Regis Coll., 1982; D Community Affairs, U. R.I., 1979; LLD (hon.) , Emmanuel Coll., 2000. Bar: Tex. 1971, D.C. 1973. Atty. Dept. Justice, Washington, 1971-73; exec. dir. Internat. Assn. Ofcl. Human Rights Agys., 1973-74; mgmt. cons. Dept. Treasury, 1975-76; dep. council to Pres. White House, 1976-79; dep. undersec. Dept. Edn., 1979-81; dir. Mary Ingraham Bunting Inst., Radcliffe Coll., Cambridge, Mass., 1981-85; v.p. program planning Radcliffe Coll., 1982-85; pres. Lesley Coll., 1985—. Bd. dirs. Dominion Resources, Inc., Cisco Learning Inst., The Jason Found. for Edn. Bd. dirs. Coun. Ind. Colls., Washington, Am. Assn. Coll. for Tchr. Edn.; chmn. higher edn. task force Clinton Transition, 1992-93; chmn. edn. task force Mayor Thomas Menino Transition Com., 1994; bd. overseers Peabody Essex Mus. Recipient Outstanding Contribution award Civil Rights Leadership Conf., 1978; named Woman of Yr. Women's Equity Action League, 1979, Outstanding Woman of Yr. Big Sister Assn., 1986, Pinnacle award for Lifetime Achievement, Lelia J. Robinson award Women's Bar Assn. Mass., 1996, Valeria Addams Knapp award, The Coll. CLub, 1995; named Margaret A. McKenna Day, Gov. DePrete, R.I. Mem. Boys Scouts Am., Big Sisters Ass. Boston, Y.W.C.A. Cambridge, Women's Equity Action League, Nat. Women's Polit. Conf., Nat. Assn. Official Human Rights Agencies. Democrat. Office: Lesley Coll Office of the President 29 Everett St Cambridge MA 02138-2702

MCKENNA, PATRICK JAMES, management consultant; b. Edson, Alta., Can., Oct. 31, 1951; s. James Edward and Madeline (Watson) McKenna; m. Monique, 1 Child, David. CIM, Can. Inst. Mgmt., Toronto, Ont., 1979, P. Mgr., 1977, MBA, 1982, ICIA, 1985. Asst. div. mgr. Hudsons Bay Co., Edmonton, Alta., 1973-75; gen. mgr. Alta. C. of C. Edmonton, 1975-78; mng. dir. QCTV Ltd., Edmonton, 1978-81; v.p. Achieve Enterprises Ltd., Edmonton, 1981-83; ptnr. Edge Intl., Edmonton, 1983—; dir. Can. Inst. Mgmt., 1981-85. Author: Building Business Abroad, 1985; co-author: Creating the Marketing Mindset, 1989; contbg. author: The Lawyer's Handbook, 3d edit., 1992; co-author, Herding Cats, 1995, Beyond Knowing, 2000, First Among Equals, 2002 contbr. articles to profl. jours.; mem. publ. adv. bd. Partner-to-Partner Advisory, The Marcus Letter on Profl. Svcs. Mktg. Mem. ABA, Strategic Leadership Forum. Conservative. Home: 11226 60th St Edmonton AB Canada T5W 3Y8

MCKENNA, PETER DENNIS, lawyer; b. Amityville, N.Y., Aug. 15, 1937; s. John Paul and Margaret (Foley) McK.; children: Michael A., Suzanne E. AB cum laude, Coll. of the Holy Cross, Worchester, Mass., 1959; JD cum laude, N.Y.U., 1968. Bar: N.Y. 1968, U.S. Dist. Ct. (so. dist.) N.Y. 1970, U.S. Supreme Ct. 1973, U.S. Ct. Appeals (4th cir.) 1977, U.S. Ct. Appeals (7th cir.) 1979, U.S. Ct. Appeals (2nd cir.) 1983. Assoc. Wachtell, Lipton, Rosen & Katz, N.Y.C., 1968-71, ptnr., 1972-91, of counsel, 1992—. Mem. pres.'s coun. NYU, Weinfeld assoc. NYU Law Sch.; regent mem. pres.'s coun. Coll. Holy Cross. Editor-in-chief N.Y.U. Law Review, 1967-68; contbr. articles to profl. jours. Mem. Cmty. Sch. Bd. Dist. 26, Queens, N.Y., 1973-77; adv. bd. St. Aloyisius Sch. for Cen. Harlem Inner-City Children, 1992—, mem. exec. com., 1994—; founding dir. Ctrl. Harlem Initiative for Learning and Devel., 1994—; bd. dirs. Mt. St. Michael Acad., 1994—, mem. exec. com., 1994-99. Lt. USN 1959-65. MEM. ABA, Fed. Bar Coun., Am. Arbitration Assn. (comml. and securities panels), Am. Judicature Soc., N.Y. State Bar Assn., Assn. of Bar of City of N.Y., Order of Coif. Democrat. Roman Catholic. Avocations: travel, history, public affairs, swimming, golf. Office: Wachtell Lipton Rosen & Katz 51 W 52nd St New York NY 10019-6150 Address: Apt 1403 3802 NE 207th St Miami FL 33180-3852

MCKENNA, ROBERT E., JR. medical science liaison manager, physician assistant; b. Honolulu, Mar. 4, 1954; s. Robert E. and Alice Jeanne (Stone) McK.; children: Devin S., Brandon S. BS, physician assoc., U. Okla., 1981; MPH, Portland (Oreg.) State U., 1996. Cert. Nat. Commn. Cert. Physician Assts., 1981. Physician asst. Plaza Med. Ctr., New Port Richey, Fla., 1981-84; profl. hosp. rep. Merck Human Health Divsn., Tampa, 1984-87, sr. coord. health sci. assoc., 1987-90, exec. health sci. assoc. Portland, Oreg., 1990-96, mgr. cardiovascular market devel. western U.S., 1996-97, mgr. acad. and profl. affairs, arthritis and analgesia, west and south ctrl. U.S., 1998—2000; mgr. arthritis, analgesia and metabolic bode disease Health Sci. Assocs. Western U.S., 2000—. Mem. tech. com. Oreg. Scorecard Consortium, Oreg. Health Policy Inst., Portland, 1995; invited participant Health Cmtys. 2000, Portland/Multnomah Progress Bd., 1995; adv. bd. cmty. health improvement program Providence Health Sys., Portland, 1995; strategic planner Oreg. Health Policy Inst., 1995, Heart Inst., Spokane, Wash., 1994-95; lectr. in field. To E-5 hosp. corpsman, USN, 1975-79. Mem. Am. Acad. Physician Assts., Am. Heart Assn. (coun. on clin. cardiology), Oreg. Pub. Health Assn. Avocations: sailing, skiing, gourmet cooking, computers, reading fiction. Home: 2035 SE Ellis St Portland OR 97202-5120

MCKENNA, SIDNEY F. retired technical company executive; b. Detroit, Nov. 27, 1922; s. Michael James and Elizabeth Josephine McK.; m. Helen Mary Spiroff, Sept. 20, 1944; children— Lynne Marie McKenna Hoss, Dennis Michael, Patrick Conlon, Mary Elizabeth McKenna Raimondi, Maureen T. McKenna Anderson, Christopher John. AB, U. Mich., Ann Arbor, 1947; MA, Wayne State U., 1948. With Ward Baking Co., Detroit, 1939-41; prodn. worker Cadillac Motor Co. (div. Gen. Motors Corp.), 1941-42; mem. indsl. relations staff Ford Motor Co., Dearborn, Mich., 1942-79, v.p., 1974-79; sr. v.p. United Techs. Corp., Hartford, Conn., 1980-90. Bd. dirs. Schwartz Value Fund. Adv. bd. Providence Hosp., Detroit, 1972-80; bd. dirs. Brighton (Mich.) Hosp., 1976-80, Mercy Coll., Detroit, 1976-80, United Found., 1976-80, St. Francis Hosp., Hartford, Conn., 1983-89, St. Joseph's Coll., 1988-89. Served with USN, 1942-46. Decorated knight St. Gregory. Mem. Labor Policy Assn. (chmn.), Bus. Roundtable, Orgn. Resources Counselors, Nat. Assn. Mfrs. (bd. dirs. 1988-89), Bloomfield Hills Country Club, Birmingham Athletic Club, Mariner Sands Golf Club, K.C. Roman Catholic. Home: 5680 SE Winged Foot Dr Stuart FL 34997-8642 E-mail: SFMcK@aol.com.

MCKENNA, TERENCE PATRICK, retired insurance company executive; b. Oldham, Lancashire, Eng., Sept. 3, 1928; came to U.S., 1929, naturalized, 1939; s. Patrick A. and Mary F. McK.; m. Patricia Buckley, Sept. 22, 1973. Student, St. Thomas Coll., Bloomfield, Conn., 1946-48. With John Hancock Mut. Life Ins. Co., 1951-87, gen. agt. N.J., 1963-67, field v.p. gen. agy. dept. Atlanta, 1967-69, field v.p. dist. agy. dept. Boston, 1969-73, 2d v.p. mktg. ops. dept., 1973-74, v.p. dept., 1974-76, sr. v.p. dept., 1976-83, sr. v.p. gen. agy. sales dept., 1983-87; ret., 1987. V.p., also bd. dirs. John Hancock Variable Life Ins. Co.; chmn. bd. mgrs. I.V.A.; bd. dirs. John Hancock Distbrs. Inc., John Hancock Property and Casualty Ins. Co. Served with USMC, 1952-54. Mem.: Am. Soc. CLUs, Am. Coll. Life Underwriters, Woods Hole Golf Club (Falmouth, Mass.), Palm Beach Gardens Club, Frenchman Creek Country Club. E-mail: tmcke1@aol.com.

MCKENNA, WILLIAM FRANCIS, lawyer; b. Meriden, Conn., May 14, 1910; s. Francis Joseph and Alice Nancy (Downes) McK.; m. Catherine Agnes Donahue, June 25, 1935 (dec.); children: William Francis (dec.), Daniel Joseph. PhB, Yale U., 1930, JD, 1932. Bar: Conn. 1932, Md. 1940, U.S. Dist. Ct. D.C. 1950, U.S. Ct. Appeals (D.C. cir.) 1951, U.S. Ct. Mil. Appeals 1953, U.S. Supreme Ct. 1938. Assoc. Buckley, Creedon & Danaher, Hartford, Conn., 1932-35; atty., counsel pub. loans sect. RFC, Washington, 1935-42; chief airports br. War Assets Adminstrn., 1945-47; counsel U.S. Senate Com. on Banking and Currency, 1947-57; assoc. Ford Motor Co., 1957-58; house counsel Nat. Assn. Mut. Savs. Banks, N.Y.C., 1958-59, dir.-counsel Washington, 1959-63; gen. counsel, v.p., sec. Nat. Savs. and Loan League, 1963-75; assoc. Housley, Goldberg & Kantarian PC, 1976-86; pvt. practice Silver Spring, Md., 1986—. Adminstr. asst. to U.S. Senator William Benton, Washington, 1950, counsel U.S. Congl. Joint Com. on Def. Prodn., 1950-51; commdg. officer USNR Law Co. 5-11, Washington, 1956-57, 64-65; chmn. exec. com. Knickerbocker Fed. Savs. and Loan Assn., N.Y.C., 1980. Editor: (periodical) Nat. League Legal Bull., 1973—75; co-author, editor: Frank J. McKenna 1884-1967, 1968. Pres. Conn. Dem. in D.C., 1939-40; lector, server St. Matthews Cathedral, Washington, 1986-86; extraordinary minister St. Michaels Roman Cath. Ch. Silver Spring, 1986, liturgy com., 1982-99. Capt. USNR, 1943-45, PTO. Mem. Inter-Am. Bar Assn., D.C. Bar Assn., Assn. Former Senate Aides, Holy Name Soc., Univ. Club, Exchequer Club (chancellor 1962-63), Phi Beta Kappa. Home and Office: 6516 Pilgrims Cv Derwood MD 20855-1533

MCKENNA, WILLIAM JOHN, textile products executive; b. N.Y.C., Oct. 11, 1926; s. William T. and Florence (Valis) McK.; m. Jean T. McNulty, Aug. 27, 1949 (dec. Nov. 1984); children: Kevin, Marybeth, Peter, Dawn; m. Karen Lynne Hilgert, Aug. 6, 1988; children: Katherine Lynne, William John IV. BBA, Iona Coll., 1949; MS (Univ. Store Service scholar), NYU, 1950. V.p. Hat Corp. Am., N.Y.C., 1961-63, v.p. mktg., 1961-63, exec. v.p., 1963-67; pres. Manhattan Shirt Co., 1967-74; pres., dir. Lee Co., Inc., Shawnee Mission, Kans., 1974-82, Kellwood Co., St. Louis, 1982—, chief exec. officer, 1984—, also bd. dirs., chmn., CEO, 1991-97, chmn., 1991-99, chmn. emeritus, 1999—. Dir. United Mo. Bancshares, Kansas City, Mo., United Mo. Bank of St. Louis. Trustee emeritus St. Louis U., Boys Hope, St. Louis U. H.S.; permanent deacon Archdiocese St. Louis. With USN, 1944-46, PTO. Mem. Sovereign Mil. Order Malta, St. Louis Club, Bellerive Country Club. Roman Catholic. Office: Kellwood Co PO Box 14374 Saint Louis MO 63178-4374 E-mail: william_mckenna@kellwood.com.

MCKENNA, WILLIAM MICHAEL, advertising executive; b. Washington, Apr. 4, 1951; s. William H. and Betty Ann (Cashin) McK.; m. Lynn Stevenson, Dec. 18, 1976; children: James Langdon, Lee Stevenson. BA, Wesleyan U., 1973; MS in Journalism, Boston U., 1978. V.p., creative dir. Ingalls Quinn & Johnson, Boston, 1981-88; sr. v.p., creative dir. Young & Rubicam, N.Y.C., 1988-94; chief creative officer, exec. v.p. AF GL Internat., 1994-95; mng. dir., chief creative officer Citigate Albert Frank, 1996-99; mng. dir., COO, Marsteller Advt., 1999-2000, pres., CEO, 2000—. Recipient CLIO, Hatch, N.Y. Film Soc. creative advt. awards, 1982-95. Home: 26 Wildwood Darien CT 06820-5231 Office: Burson Marsteller 230 Park Ave S New York NY 10003-1513 E-mail: michael_mckenna@bm.com.

MCKENNAN, JOHN T. lawyer; b. New Hartford, N.Y., Nov. 25, 1918; s. John Patrick and Rena C. (Dowd) McK.; m. Marguerite Gallagher, May 7, 1955; children: John, Timothy. BS, Utica Acad., 1938, Scarborough Sch., 1939; postgrad., Syracuse U., 1939-41; LLB, Union U., 1945. Bar: N.Y. 1945. Assoc. Hawkins, Delafield & Longfellow, N.Y.C., 1945; pvt. practice Utica, N.Y., 1946—. Judge N.Y. State Supreme Ct. for 5th Jud. Dist., 1982. Mem. N.Y. State Senate, 1949-51; mayor City of Utica, 1956-60; sec. N.Y. State Constl. Conv., Albany, 1967. Mem. Yahnundasis Golf Club. Democrat. Roman Catholic. Avocation: golf. Home: 15 Foxcroft Rd New Hartford NY 13413-2734

MCKENNEY, SCOTT ALAN, oncologist; b. Lakewood, Ohio, July 8, 1955; s. Richard Whitney and Margaret May (Collins) M. ; m. Joan White, June 6, 1977; children: Mark Aaron, Chad Andrew, Meredith Martha. BS with honors, Lamar U., 1977; MD with honors, Baylor U., 1980. Resident U. Utah Affiliated Hosps., Salt Lake City, 1980-83; fellow in med. oncology Baylor Coll. Medicine, Houston, 1983-85; oncologist McFaddin Ward Cancer Ctr., Beaumont, Tex., 1985—, med. dir., 1987-88. Coach Spindletop Youth Soccer, Beaumont, 1987. Fellow Am. Coll. Physicians; mem. Am. Soc. Clin. Oncology, Tex. Soc. Med. Oncology (founding), Alpha Omega Alpha (edn. com. 1986). Avocations: soccer, skiing. Office: Beaumont Oncology Assocs 690 N 14th St Beaumont TX 77702-1449

MC KENNEY, WALTER GIBBS, JR. lawyer, publishing company executive; b. Jacobsville, Md., Apr. 22, 1913; s. Walter Gibbs and Mary (Starkey) McK.; m. Florence Roberta Rea, July 17, 1939. Student, Dickinson Sem., 1935-37; Ph.B. Dickinson Coll., 1939; JD, U. Va., 1942; LL.D., Dickinson Sch. Law, 1964; LHD, Lycoming Coll., 1984. Bar: Md. 1942. Practiced in Balt., 1942—; partner McKenney, Thomsen & Burke; partner, gen. mgr., editor Taxes & Estates Pub. Co., Balt., 1946—. Chmn. trust com. Equitable Bank, N.A., Balt., 1970-84; dir. Equitable Bancorp., 1960-84; lectr. Southwestern Grad. Sch. Banking, 1966-76 Editor Taxes and Estates, 1946— , Minimizing Taxes, 1946-84, The Educator, 1965— , The Patron, 1968-84. Pres. Kelso Home for Girls; mem. bd. child care Balt. Conf. Meth. Ch., pres., 1961-64; pres. Balt. Estate Planning Council, 1963-64; trustee Goucher Coll., 1968-84, Dickinson Coll., Lycoming Coll., Wesley Theol. Sem., Loyola Coll. at Balt., 1975-83, Franklin Sq. Hosp., Franklin Square Found., Franklin

Square Health System, Helix Health System. Served to lt. USNR, 1942-45. Mem. ABA, Md., Balt. bar assns. Republican. Methodist. Home: 105 Brightwood Club Dr Lutherville MD 21093-3628

MCKENNON, KEITH ROBERT, chemical company executive; b. Condon, Oreg., Dec. 25, 1933; s. Russel M. and Lois E. (Edgerton) McK.; m. Patricia Dragon, Sept. 30, 1961; children: Brian, Marc, Kevin. BS, Oreg. State U., 1955. Rsch. chemist Dow Chem. Co., Pittsburg, Calif., 1955-67, sales mgr. Houston, 1967, research mgr. Midland, Mich., 1968-69, bus. mgr., 1969-80, v.p., 1980-83, group v.p., 1983-87, exec. v.p., 1987-92, also bd. dirs.; pres. Dow USA, 1987-90; chmn., chief exec. officer Dow Corning Corp., 1992-94, also bd. dirs.; chmn. PacifiCorp, Portland, Oreg., 1994-99, CEO, 1998-99. Patentee. Recipient Chemical Industry medal Soc. of Chemical Industry, 1994 Republican. Presbyterian. Home: 6079 N Paradise View Dr Paradise Valley AZ 85253-3828

MCKENZIE, CLIF ALLEN, Indian tribe official, accountant; b. Lawton, Okla., Sept. 29, 1942; s. Robert Allen and Rubie (Paukei) Williams; m. Michele Ann Martin, Aug. 4, 1972; children: Kasey Roberta, Kristen Marti. BS in Acctg., U. Okla., 1965; MBA, Pa. State U., 1976. Fin. analyst United Tribes of Okla., Shawnee, 1973-75; credit officer Bur. Indian Affairs, Dept. Interior, Horton, Kans., 1975-77; liaison officer Syracuse, N.Y., 1977-80; program analyst Denver, 1980-81; tribal administr. Kiowa Tribe of Okla., Carnegie, 1981-82; CEO tribal bus. mgr. Cheyenne and Arapaho Tribe of Okla., Concho, 1982-84; pres. Indian Devel. Corp., Oklahoma City, 1973—; prin. ptnr. McKenzie & Assocs., 2002—. Contracting officer Bur. Indian Affairs, Anadarko, Okla., 1984-89, agy. ops. officer, Concho, Okla.; contract specialist, Gen. Svc. Administr., Ft. Worth, 1989-92, Dept. Health Human Svc., Pub. Health Svc., supervisory contract specialist, Oklahoma City, 1992-94; asset mgr. HUD Loan Mgmt. Br., Oklahoma City, 1994-01. Police commr. City of Horton, 1976-77, city commr., 1976-77 dir. LECO, Inc., Tulsa. Capt. U.S. Amy, 1959-68. Recipient H.M. Hefner First Amendment award Playboy Found., 1985, Nat. Notary Pub. of the Yr. award Nat. Notary Assn., 1996. Mem. DAV (life), U. Olka. Alumni Assn.; mem. Kiowa Black Legging Soc., Nat. Assn. Accts., Am. Soc. Notaries (dir. govt. affairs 1975-80), Nat. Taxpayers Investigative Fund (Whistleblower award 1982), Elks, Moose Republican. Home: 3708 Epperly Dr Del City OK 73115-3610 Office: McKenzie & Assocs PO Box 15613 Oklahoma City OK 73155-5613 also: HUD 500 W Main St Oklahoma City OK 73102-2253 E-mail: clifmck@swbell.net.

MCKENZIE, CRAIG R. M. psychology educator; b. Whittier, Calif., July 29, 1962; s. Richard E. and Fern G. McKenzie; m. Asa C. Attlehed. BA in Psychology, U. Calif., Irvine, 1985, BA in Philosophy, 1987; PhD in Psychology, U. Chgo., 1994. Assoc. prof. psychology U. Calif.-San DiegoLa Jolla, 1994—. Recipient career award NSF, 1996-2001. Mem. Psychonomic Soc., Soc. for Judgment and Decision Making (Hillel Einhorn New Investigator award 1994). Office: U Calif San Diego 9500 Gilman Dr Dept 0109 La Jolla CA 92093-0109 E-mail: cmckenzie@ucsd.edu.

MCKENZIE, GWENDOLYN VERON, public relations, marketing and business development executive; b. Durham, N.C., Aug. 10; d. Lionel Wilfred and Blanche (Veron) McK. BS, U. Rochester, 1977; MEd, Harvard U., 1982. Adminstrv. asst. Kennedy Sch. Govt., Cambridge, Mass., 1981; mktg. coord. Payette Assocs., Boston, 1983-86; mktg. mgr. Profl. Designs Inc., 1986, Staats Internat., Boston, 1987-89; sen. assoc., dir. corp. mktg. for urban planning, arch. graphic and interior design Arrowstreet Inc., Somerville, Mass., 1990—. Mem. lobby group Nat. Breast Cancer Coalition; Mass. spokesperson Am. Cancer Soc. Mem. Urban Land Inst. (internat. coun. 2000-2001, Boston exec. com.), Internat. Assn. Corp. Real Estate Execs. (pres. New Eng. chpt. 1993-94), Am. Hotel and Motel Assn., New Eng. Women in Real Estate (mem. program com.), Boston Soc. Architects, Harvard Club Boston, Harvard Faculty Club. Avocations: travel with Architects on Tour, personal and spiritual development, social activism. Office: Arrowstreet Inc 212 Elm St Somerville MA 02144-2913 E-mail: mcKenzie@arrowstreet.com.

MCKENZIE, HARRY JAMES, cardiothoracic surgeon, surgical researcher; b. Meyersdale, Pa., Aug. 7, 1960; s. Henry Sadrus and Betty Elaine (Reiber) McK.; m. Judith Palmieri, July 6, 1985; children: Henry James, Anne Christine, Mark Angus. BS, Duquesne U., 1984; postgraduate, U. Pitts., 1986-87; MD, Hahnemann U., 1992. Surg. intern Temple U., Conemaugh Med. Ctr., Johnstown, Pa., 1992-93, surg. resident, 1993-97; cardiothoracic resident Med. Coll. Ga., Augusta, 1997-99. Mem. problem task force Conemaugh Med. Ctr., 1992-93. Contbr. articles to profl. jours.; presenter in field. Hosp. vol. Ctrl. Med. Pavilion, Pitts., 1981-84, Presbyn. Hosp., Pitts., 1986-87; med. exam. officer, Phila. Special Olympics, 1989-90; grad. banquet spkr. Salisbury (Pa.) H.S., 1993.. Recipient 3d place rsch. competition award, ACS Region III com. on trauma, Norfolk, Va., 1993; recipient 1st place rsch. competition award ACS-Pa. com. on trauma, Hershey, 1993. Mem. ACS, AMA, Am. Soc. Gen. Surgeons, Soc. Am. Gastrointestinal Endoscopic Surgeons, Soc. Thoracic Surgeons. Avocations: skiing, golfing, jogging, fishing, hiking. Home: 4130 N Tara Cir Wichita KS 67226-3367

MC KENZIE, JOHN MAXWELL, physician; b. Glasgow, Scotland, Nov. 13, 1927; came to U.S., 1980; s. Thomas Wilson and Isabell Connor (Spencer) McK.; m. Vieno Laine Kangas, June 29, 1957; children— Ann, Ian, Lesley, Gordon. M.B., Ch.B., U. St. Andrews, Scotland, 1950, MD, 1958. Intern U. St. Andrews, 1950-51, resident, 1953-55, fellow, 1955-56, 57-58; research trainee, fellow Tufts U., 1956-57, 58-59; clin. asst. medicine McGill U., Montreal, Que., Can., 1959-61, asst., then assoc. prof., 1961-68, prof., 1968-80, U. Miami, 1980—, chmn. dept. medicine, 1980-94. Contbr. numerous articles to profl. jours. Served with Royal Army Med. Corps, 1951-53. Recipient Killam award Can. Coun., 1980. Mem. Am. Thyroid Assn. (Parke-Davis disting. lectr. 1981, pres. 1983-84), Am. Soc. Clin. Investigation, Endocrine Soc. (Ayerst award 1961, Rorer Pharm. Clin. Investigator award 1990), Am. Physiol. Soc., Assn. Am. Physicians, Am. Fedn. Clin. Rsch., AAAS, Internat. Soc. Neuroendocrinology, European Thyroid Assn. (corr.) Home: 12505 SW 63rd Ave Miami FL 33156-5531 Office: U Miami Jackson Meml Med Ctr 1611 NW 12th Ave Miami FL 33136-1005 E-mail: jmmckenzie@med.miami.edu.

MCKENZIE, KATHLEEN JULIANNA, artist; b. Jan. 20, 1957; Artist, Torrington, Conn., 1987—. Paintings featured in 7th, 9th and 11th Encyclopedia of Living Artist. Work represented in 7th, 9th, 11th Ency. Living Artists. Address: 1655 Mountain Rd Torrington CT 06790-2750 E-mail: kj_mckenzie_studios@hotmail.com.

MCKENZIE, KEVIN PATRICK, artistic director; b. Burlington, Vt., Apr. 29, 1954; s. Raymond James and Ruth (Davison) McK. Grad. high sch., Washington. Mem. corps de ballet Nat. Ballet of Washington, 1972-74; prin. Joffrey Ballet, N.Y.C., 1974-78, Am. Ballet Theatre, N.Y.C., 1979-91; artistic assoc. Washington Ballet, 1991-92; artistic dir. Am. Ballet Theatre, N.Y.C., 1992—. Pres. bd. dirs. Am. Ballet Theatre Dancers Fund, Inc., 1982-89; assoc. dir. New Amsterdam Ballet, N.Y.C., 1984—; founding bd. mem. Keats Acon Internat. Dance Ctr., 1991—. Appeared in film Unicorn, Gorgon and Monticore, Sta. WETA-TV, Washington, 1971; guest dancer Houston Ballet, 1978, Spoleto Festival, 1980, 84, Theatre des Champs Elysees, Paris, 1981, Sadler's Wells Theatre, London, 1981, Asami Maki Ballet Co., Tokyo, 1983, Aspen Festival, 1982; producer, dir. The Party of the Year, 1982; choreographer Groupo Zambaria Ballet, 1984, Liszt Etudes, 1991, Lucy and the Count, 1992, The Nutcracker, 1993; created roles in Adrienne Dellos' The Blind Man's Daughter, Seoul, Korea, 1986, Amnon V'Tamar, S.P.E.B.S.Q.S.A.; appeared with Martine Van Hamel in Swan Lake, Nat. Ballet of Cuba, Havanna, 1986, Merrill Ashley in Tchaikovsky Pas de Deux, Bolshoi Theater, Moscow, 1986; repertoire as dancer includes La Bayadere, Carmen, Cinderella, Coppelia, Dim Lustre, Don Quixote, Giselle, The Garden of Villandry, Jardin aux lilas, The Leaves Are Fading, Pillar of Fire, Raymonda, Requiem, Rodeo, Romeo and Juliet, The Sleeping Beauty, Swan Lake, La Sylphide; other dances include Paquita, Sylvia Pas de Deux, Theme and Variations. Recipient Silver medal Varna (Bulgaria) Internat. Ballet Competitions, 1972, Artistic Achievement medal Dept. State, U.S. Govt., 1972, Artistic Achievement medal Mayor of Burlington, Vt., 1984, Performing Arts award, Am. Ireland Fund, 1994; Kevin McKenzie Day proclaimed by City of Burlington, 1985. Office: Am Ballet Theatre 890 Broadway New York NY 10003-1211

MC KENZIE, LIONEL WILFRED, economist, educator; b. Montezuma, Ga., Jan. 26, 1919; s. Lionel Wilfred and Lida (Rushin) McK.; m. Blanche Veron, Jan. 2, 1943 (dec. July 1999); children— Lionel Wilfred (dec.), Gwendolyn Veron, David Rushin. AB, Duke U., 1939; MA, Princeton U., 1946, PhD, 1956; BLitt, Oxford (Eng.) U., 1949; postgrad., U. Chgo., 1950-51, LLD (hon.), 1991; D of Econ. (hon.), Keio U., Japan, 1998. Asst. economist WPB, 1942; instr. Mass. Inst. Tech., 1946; from asst. prof. to assoc. prof. Duke, 1948-57; prof. econs. U. Rochester, 1957-64, John Munro prof. econs., 1964-67, Wilson prof. econs., 1967-89, Wilson prof. emeritus, 1989—, chmn. dept., 1957-66. Taussig research prof. Harvard U., 1980-81; Mem. math. divsn. NRC, 1960-63, mem. behavioral scis. divsn., 1964-70; mem. math., social scis. bd. Center Advanced Study in Behavioral Scis., Palo Alto, Calif., 1964-70, chmn., 1969-70 Author: Classical General Equilibrium Theory, 2002; assoc. editor Internat. Econs. Rev., 1964-96, Jour. Econ. Theory, 1970-73, Jour. Internat. Econs., 1970-84, Econ. Theory, 1991-95; contbr. articles to profl. jours. Lt. (s.g.) USNR, 1943-45. Recipient Rising Sun award Japan, 1995; Rhodes scholar Oriel Coll. Oxford U., 1939; Guggenheim fellow, 1973-74, fellow Center for Advanced Study in Behavioral Scis., 1973-74. Fellow Econometric Soc. (coun. 1973-78, pres. 1977), Am. Acad. Arts and Scis., Am. Econ. Assn.; mem. NAS, Royal Econ. Soc., Am. Math. Soc., Am. Econ. Assn. (Disting. Fellow 1993), Phi Beta Kappa (chpt. v.p. 1968-70, chpt. pres. 1972-73). Home: 225 Dorchester Rd Rochester NY 14610-1322 E-mail: mcke@troi.cc.rochester.edu.

MCKENZIE, MARY BETH, artist; b. Cleve. d. William Jennings and Mary Elizabeth (McCray) McK.; m. Tony Mysak, May 8, 1974; children: Zsuzsa McKenzie Mysak, Maria McKenzie Mysak. Student, Mus. Fine Arts, Boston, 1964-65, Cooper Sch. Art, Cleve., 1965-67; diploma, NAD, N.Y.C., 1974. Painting instr. NAD, 1981—, Art Students League, 1995—. Author: A Painterly Approach, 1987; contbr. articles;one-woman shows include Nat. Arts Club, N.Y.C., 1976, FAR Gallery, 1980, Perin and Pharpe Gallery, New Canaan, Conn., 1981, Frank Caro Gallery, N.Y.C., 1988—89, Joseph Keiffer Gallery, 1991, Union County Coll., 1998, exhibited in group shows at Sindin Gallery, N.Y.C., 1985—86, Ice Collection, 1995—96, Susan Conway Gallery, Washington, Galerie Yoramgil, Beverly Hills, Met. Mus. Art, 2001, Represented in permanent collections The Butler Mus. Am. Art, Met. Mus. Art, N.Y.C., Mus. City of N.Y., NAD, Art Students League of N.Y., Nat. Mus. Women in the Arts, Nat. Mus. Am. Art, Smithsonian Instn., Bklyn. Mus. Art, New Britain Mus. Am. Art, N.Y. Hist. Soc., David Findlay Gallery, Susan Conway Gallery, Galerie Yoramgil, Beverly Hills, Calif., self portrait. Recipient Nat. Scholastic award Mus. Fine Arts, Boston, numerous awards including Thomas B. Clark prize and the Isaac N. Maynard prize Nat. Acad. Design, Greenshields Found. grantee, Stacey Found. grantee. Mem. Nat. Acad. Design, Pastel Soc. Am. (Best In Show, Award of Exceptional Merit, Exhbn. Com. award), Allied Artists Am. (Gold medal, The Jane Peterson award, Grumbacher Cash award, Silver medal), Audubon Artists (Pastel Soc. Am. award). Home: 525 W 45th St New York NY 10036-3414

MCKENZIE, NORMA DEEANN, psychiatrist, educator; b. Reno, Nov. 4, 1943; d. James Norman and Miriam Isabelle (Perry) McK.; m. James Kenneth Schmitt, Aug. 17, 1973; children: James Eric, Brian Lawrence. BA, Stanford U., 1965; MS, U. Oreg., 1967; MD, U. Calif., San Francisco, 1971. Diplomate Am. Bd. Psychiatry and Neurology; lic. psychiatrist, Calif., Va. Dir. clinic B U. Calif., 1977-83; chief resident in psychiatry Med. Coll. of Va., Richmond, 1986-87, dir. med. svcs. district 19 cmty. mental health, asst. prof., 1987—. Contbr. articles to profl. jours. Mem. AMA, Am. Psychiat. Assn., Va. Psychiat. Assn., Richmond Psychiat. Assn. (bd. dirs. 1987-88).

MCKENZIE, ROBERT ERNEST, lawyer; b. Cheboygan, Mich., Dec. 7, 1947; s. Alexander Orlando and Edna Jean (Burt) McK.; m. Theresia Wolf, Apr. 26, 1975; 1 child, Robert A. BA in Personnel Adminstrn., Mich. State U., 1970; JD with high honors, Ill. Inst. Tech., 1979. Bar: Ill. 1979, U.S. Dist. Ct. (no. dist.) Ill. 1979, U.S. Tax Ct. 1979, U.S. Ct. Appeals (7th cir.) 1979, U.S. Supreme Ct. 1984; lic. pvt. pilot. Revenue officer IRS, Chgo., 1972-78; ptnr. McKenzie & McKenzie, 1979-2000, Arnstein & Lehr, 2000—. Lectr. Tax Seminars Inst., Chgo., 1984—. Author: Representation Before the Collection Divison of the IRS, 1989; co-author: Representing the Audited Taxpayer Before the IRS, 1990; contbr. articles to profl. jours. Mem. tax adv. com. Nat. Bankruptcy Rev. Commn., 1997; del. Rep. Nat. Conv., Detroit, 1980, Ill. State Rep. Conv., Peoria, 1980. Served with U.S. Army, 1970. Recipient scholarship Mich. State U., 1966-70, State of Mich., 1966-70, Silas Strawn scholarship ITT, 1977. Fellow Am. Bar Found., N.W. Suburban Bar Assn; mem. ABA (chmn. employment tax com. tax sect. 1992-94, co-chmn. bankruptcy task force 1997-98, coun. tax sect. 1998-2001), Chgo. Bar Assn. (chmn. com. devel. tax com. 1996-97), Fed. Bar Assn. (tax com.), Rotary (pres. Norridge club 1985-86). Office: Ste 1200 120 S Riverside Plz Chicago IL 60606 E-mail: remckenzie@arnstein.com.

MCKENZIE, STANLEY DON, academic administrator, English educator; b. Yakima, Wash., July 10, 1942; s. Don Guy and Jean Elizabeth McKenzie; m. Michal A. Koehler, Sept. 21, 1968 (div. Sept. 1974); 1 child, Thomas Charles. BS, MIT, 1964; MA, U. Rochester, 1967, PhD, 1971. Prof. lit. Rochester (N.Y.) Inst. Tech., 1967--, asst. to v.p. student affairs/judicial affairs, 1972-87, 92-94, acting dean, Coll. Liberal Arts, 1987-88, provost, v.p. acad. affairs, 1994--. Vice-chair bd. dirs. RIT Rsch. Corp., Rochester, 1994--; bd. dirs. CIMS Print, Rochester, Am. Coll. Mgmt. & Tech., Dubrovnik, Croatia. Author: Shakespeare Studies, 1987; (with others) The Practice of Theory, 1992, Other Voices, Other Views, 1999. Mem. ACLU, AAUP, MLA. Democrat. Avocations: hiking, reading. Office: Rochester Inst Tech 6 Lomb Memorial Dr Rochester NY 14623-5604 E-mail: SDMPRO@RIT.edu.

MCKENZIE-ANDERSON, RITA LYNN, psychologist; b. Boston, Nov. 25, 1952; d. Wallace Andrew and Angelina Rita (Bagnoli) McK; m. Brien Anderson, Oct. 22, 1994; 1 child, Liam Wallace. BA, Framingham State Coll., 1974; MEd, Northeastern U., 1975; PhD, Temple U., 1983. Lic. psychologist, Mass. Pvt. practice, Fairfield, Conn., 1984-86; psychologist Johnson Life Ctr., Springfield, Mass., 1986-87, dir. outpatient therapy, 1987-88; pvt. practice, 1988—; investigator Springfield Juvenile Ct., 1989—. Adj. faculty Holyoke (Mass.) Community Coll., 1989-90, Springfield Tech. Community Coll., 1989-90; dir. day treatment DuBois Day Treatment Ctr., Stamford, Conn., 1982-86; cons. psychologist Community Care Mental Health Ctr., Springfield, 1989-97, Spofford Hall Treatment Ctr., Ludlow, Mass., 1991-92. Trustee Northampton (Mass.) State Hosp., 1989-93; mem. organizing com. Week of Young Child, Springfield, 1988-93; bd. dirs. Stop Abuse Against Kids. Mem. Women Bus. Owners Alliance, Zonta Internat. Office: 380 Union St Ste 14 West Springfield MA 01089-4123

MCKEON, HOWARD P. (BUCK MCKEON), congressman, former mayor; b. L.A. m. Patricia; 6 children. BS, Brigham Young U. Mem. Coun. City of Santa Clarita, Calif., 1987-92, mayor, 1987-88; mem. edn. and workforce, armed svcs. and vet. affairs 103rd-106th Congresses from 25th Calif. dist., 1993—. Founding dir., chmn. Valencia Nat. Bank; co-owner Howard & Phil's Western Wear, Inc. Hon. chmn. Leukemia Soc. Celebrity program, 1990, Red Cross Community Support Campaign, 1992; active Dist. Com. Boy Scouts Am.; chmn., trustee William S. Hart Sch. dist., 1979-87; chmn., dir. Henry Mayo Newhall Meml. Hosp., 1983-88; mem. Calif. Rep. State Ctrl. Com., 1988-92; bd. dirs. Santa Clarita Valley Sml. Bus. Devel. Ctr., 1990-92, Canyon Country C. of C., 1988-92. Office: US Ho Reps 2242 Rayburn Ho Ofc Bldg Washington DC 20515 E-mail: tellbuck@mail.house.gov.*

MCKEON, JOHN ALOYSIUS (JACK MCKEON), former professional baseball manager; b. South Amboy, N.J., Nov. 23, 1930; m. Carol McKeon; children: Kelly, Kasey, Kristi, Kori. BA in Phys. Edn. and Sci., Elon Coll. Baseball mgr. in 13 maj. and minor league cities; mgr. Kansas City Royals, Am. League, 1973-75, Oakland A's, 1977-78; v.p. baseball ops. San Diego Padres, Nat. League, 1980-93, mgr., 1988-90, Cincinnati Reds, 1997—2002. Bd. dirs. San Diego Make-a-Wish Found. NL Mgr. of The Year, 1999. Office: Cincinnati Reds Cinergy Field 100 Cinergy Fld Cincinnati OH 45202-3543*

MCKEONE, CHARLES E. military officer; b. Syracuse, N.Y., Mar. 7, 1951; s. Charles J and Josephine B. McKeone, Josephine B McKeone; m. Anita V Coll; children: Christina, Elizabeth, Gregory. BS, US Naval Acad., Annapolis d., 1973; BSEE, US Naval Postgrad. Sch., Monterey Calif., 1980; MSEE, US Naval Postgrad.Sch., 1980. Commd. USMC, Washington, 1973—93; sr. analyst HQ USAF/TEP, 1993—. Mem.: Mil. Order of the Carabao (None). Roman Catholic. Home: 1530 Air Force Pentagon Washington DC 20330-1530 Office: HQ USAF/TEP 1530 Air Force Pentagon Washington DC 20330-1530 Home Fax: 703-614-6961; Office Fax: 703-614-6961. Personal E-mail: mckeonec@pentagon.af.mil. Business E-Mail: mckeonec@pentagon.af.mil.

MCKEOUGH, WILLIAM DARCY, investment company executive, director; b. Chatham, Ont., Can., Jan. 31, 1933; s. George Grant and Florence Sewell (Woodward) McK.; m. Margaret Joyce Walker, June 18, 1965; children: Walker Stewart, James Grant. BA, U. Western Ont., 1954; LLD (hon.), Wilfred Laurier U., 1980. Chmn. McKeough Supply Inc. D. dirs. C.P.L. Long Term Investment Trust, Can. Imperial Bank Commerce, Can. Gen. Tower Ltd., Intertan Inc., CableServ Inc. Former mem. exec. com. Anglican Diocese of Huron; former mem. Gen. Synod, Anglican Ch., Can.; mem. Chatham City Coun., 1960-63; also mem. Planning Bd. and Lower Thames Valley Conservation Authority; former mem. Chatham-Kent adv. bd. Can. Nat. Inst. of the Blind; former bd. dirs. Chatham YMCA, Chatham Little Theatre; former chmn. and pres. bd. govs. pres. Ridley Coll.; former bd. govs. Stratford Shakespearian Festival, Wilfrid Laurier U.; former mem. Can. group Trilateral Commn.; mem. Ont. Legislature, 1963-78, minister without portfolio, 1966, minister mcpl. affairs, 1967; treas. and minister of econs., also chmn. Treasury Bd., 1971-72, minister mcpl. affairs, 1972, treas. and minister of econs. and intergovtl. affairs, 1972, parliamentary asst. to premier Ont., 1973, minister of energy, 1973-75, treas. and minister econs. and intergovtl. affairs, 1975-78; chmn. Ridley Coll. Found.; chmn. Huron Coll. Found. Decorated officer of Order of Can. Home and Office: PO Box 940 Chatham ON Canada N7M 5L3

MCKEOWN, H. MARY, lawyer, educator; b. West Palm Beach, Fla., Sept. 17, 1952; d. Honore Stephen McKeown and Margaret Berg McKeown Growney; m. Jon Henry Barber, Sept. 18, 1981; children: Sean Patrick, Mary Kathleen. AA, St. Petersburg Jr. Coll., Fla., 1970; BA in Polit. Sci. and Sociology, U. South Fla., 1972; JD cum laude, Samford U., 1976. Bar: Fla. 1976, U.S. Dist. Ct. (mid. dist.) Fla. 1977, U.S. Ct. Appeals (5th and 11th cirs.) 1981, U.S. Supreme Ct. 1992. Asst. state atty. 6th Jud. Ct., Clearwater, Fla., 1976-90; ptnr. Growney, McKeown & Barber, St. Petersburg, 1976—. Adj. prof. Stetson Coll. of Law, St. Petersburg, 1990—. Chairperson Child Welfare Std. and Tng. Coun., 1995—98; mem. nominee qualifications rev. com. Health and Human Svcs. Bd. Dist. 5, 1992—2000; mem. Study Commn. Child Welfare, 1990—91; leader Girl Scouts U.S., 1991—2001. Recipient Victim Advocacy award Pinellas County Victims Rights Coalition, 1984, Law and Order award Elks, Pinellas County, 1991. Mem.: St. Petersburg Bar Assn., Fla. Bar Assn., Acad. Fla. Trial Lawyers, Phi Alpha Delta. Office: 7455 38th Ave N Saint Petersburg FL 33710-1228

MCKEOWN, JAMES CHARLES, accounting educator, consultant; b. Cleve., Nov. 3, 1945; s. Charles Joseph and Dara Ferrol (Prew) McK.; m. Mary Alinda Park, Jan. 2, 1965 (div. May 1980); children— Jeffrey Charles, Pamela Lynn; m. 2d, Nancy Ann Stratton, Jan. 3, 1981 BS in Math. with high honors, Mich. State U., 1966, PhD in Bus. Adminstrn., 1969. Asst. prof. accountancy U. Ill., Urbana-Champaign, 1968-73, assoc. prof., 1973-76, prof., 1976-80, Weldon Powell prof. accountancy, 1980-83, A.C. Littleton prof. accountancy, 1983-89; disting. prof. acctg. Pa. State U., University Park, 1989-92, Ernst & Young prof. acctg., 1992-99, Mary Jean and Frank P. Smeal chaired prof. acctg., 1999—. Cons. research, computers; expert witness Editor: Inflation and Current Value Accounting, 1979; author computer-delivered acctg. course PLATO for Elementary Accounting, 1978; contbr. numerous articles to acad. jours. Recipient Instructional award U. Ill., Urbana-Champaign, 1970, Weldon Powell award, 1973; Fred Roedgers Research award U. Ill., 1978; Ford Found. fellow, 1967-68 Mem. Am. Acctg. Assn. (Manuscript award 1970), Am. Statis. Assn., Decision Scis. Inst., Inst. Mgmt. Accts. Republican. Office: Pa State U 210 Beam Bus Adminstrn Bldg University Park PA 16802

MCKEOWN, LORRAINE LAREDO, travel company executive, writer; b. N.Y.C., Mar. 20, 1928; d. Frank A. and May (Collins) Laredo; m. William Taylor McKeown, July 9, 1964; children: Beth Ellison, Kate Taylor, Suzanne Harris. Talent agt. Carl Eastman, N.Y.C., 1960-65; cooking/travel columnist Camping Jour./Boating Jour., 1968-70; travel agt. Beecher Travel, 1968-70; founding ptnr. Computer Travel Info., 1984, v.p., pres., 1985-90, CEO, 1990—. Contbr. articles to various publs. Bd. dirs. Chapin-Brearley Exch., N.Y.C., 1980. Mem. Freelance Assocs., Beacon Conservation Coun. E-mail: mckeown@bestweb.net.

MCKEOWN, MARY MARGARET, federal judge; b. Casper, Wyo., May 11, 1951; d. Robert Mark and Evelyn Margaret (Lipsack) McKeown; m. Peter Francis Cowhey, June 29, 1985; 1 child Megan Margaret. BA in Internat. Affairs and Spanish, U. Wyo., 1972; JD, Georgetown U., 1975. Bar: Wash. 1975, D.C. 1982. Assoc. Perkins Coie, Seattle, 1975—79, Washington, 1979—80; White House fellow U.S. Dept. Interior and White House, 1980—81; ptnr., mem. exec. com. Perkins Coie, Seattle, 1981—98, mng. dir. strategic planning and client rels., 1990—95; judge U.S. Ct. Appeals for 9th Cir., 1998—2001, San Diego, 2001—. Trustee The Pub. Defender, Seattle, 1982—85; rep. 9th Cir. Judicial Conf., San Francisco, 1985—89; mem. gender bias task force, 1992—93; jud. conf. Com. on Codes of Conduct, 2001—; exec. com. 9th Cir., 2001—. Author: Girl Scout's Guide to New York, 1990; contbr. chpt. to book and articles to profl. jours. Nat. bd. dirs. Girl Scouts U.S., N.Y.C., 1976—87; mem. exec. com. Corp. Coun. for the Arts, Seattle, 1988—98; bd. gen. counsel Downtown Seattle Assn., 1986—89; mem. exec. com. Wash. Coun. Internat. Trade, 1994—; bd. mem. YMCA Greater Seattle, 1998—; bd. dirs. Family Svcs., 1982—84. Named one of 100 Young Women of Promise, Good Housekeeping, 1985, Washington's Winningest Trial Lawyers, Washington Jour., 1992, Top 50 Women Lawyers, Nat. Law Jour., 1998; recipient Rising Stars of the 80's award, Legal Times Washington, 1983; fellow Japan leadership, 1992—93. Fellow: ABA (ho. of dels. 1990—); mem.: Nat. Assn. Iolta Programs (bd. dirs. 1989—91), Wash. Women Lawyers (bd. dirs., pres. 1978—79), Legal Found. Wash. (trustee, pres. 1989—90), Seattle-King County Bar Assn. (trustee, sec. 1984—85, Outstanding Lawyer award 1992), Wash. Bar Assn. (chmn. jud. recommendations 1989—90), Fed. Bar Assn. (trustee western dist. Wash. 1980—90), White House Fellows Found. (bd. dirs. 1998—, pres. 2000—01). Avocations: travel, classical piano, hiking, gourmet cooking, tennis. Office: US Ct Appeals 401 West A St Ste 2000 San Diego CA 92101-7908 E-mail: Judge_McKeown@ca9.uscourts.gov.

MCKEOWN, MARY ELIZABETH, educational administrator; d. Raymond Edmund and Alice (Fitzgerald) McNamara; m. James Edward McKeown, Aug. 6, 1955. BS, U. Chgo., 1946; MS, DePaul U., 1953. Supr. h.s. dept. Am. Sch., 1948-68, prin., 1968-99, trustee, 1975—, v.p., 1979, ednl. dir., 1979—, exec. v.p., 1992—. Author study guides for algebra, geometry, and calculus. Mem.: Distance Edn. and Tng. Coun. (chair person rsch. and edn. com. 1988—93), N. Ctrl. Assn. Colls. and Schs. (exec. bd. 1990—93), NASSP, LWV. Office: 2200 E 170th St Lansing IL 60438-1002

MCKEOWN, MICHAEL EUGENE, psychologist, consultant; b. Clovis, N.Mex., May 10, 1947; s. Julian Perry and Jean (Young) Keown; m. Elisabeth Anna McKeown, Sept. 26, 1997; children: Andrew Michael, Kimberly Anne. BA in Psychology, Pomona Coll., Claremont, Calif., 1969; M of Mgmt., Vanderbilt U., 1974; PhD in Psychology, Peabody/Vanderbilt U., 1976. Lic. psychologist, Wis., Colo., Tenn., Calif.; Erickson cert. in conflict and divorce mediation. Clin. psychologist VA Med. Ctr., Murfreesboro, Tenn., 1976-79, Grand Junction, Colo., 1979-83, Tomah, Wis., 1984-88; clin. psychologist in pvt. practice Ten., Wis., Colo., Calif., 1978-95; clin. psychologist Wis. Dept. Corrections, Racine, 1994-95, Naval Hosp. and Tng. Ctr., Great Lakes, Ill., 1995-97; dir. family advocacy Naval Air Facility, El Centro, Calif., 1997-2000, Naval Med. Ctr., San Diego, 2000—. Adj. instr. U. Ill., Chgo. Med. Sch., 1995-97, Sch. Profl. Psychology, Chgo., 1995-97, Mesa Coll., Adams State Coll., Grand Junction, 1982-83. Author, editor, developer various programs. Mem. APA, Nat. Register Health Svc. Providers in Psychology. Episcopalian. Avocations: fly fishing, woodworking, welding. Office: Mental Health Svcs Navel Med Ctr San Diego CA 92134

MCKEOWN, PETER PHILIP, medical center administrator, medical educator, cardiothoracic surgeon; b. Newcastle, NSW, Australia, Feb. 1, 1951; came to U.S., 1977; s. Arthur Lindsay and Phyllis Joyce McKeown. MB BS, U. Queensland, NSW, Australia, 1975; BA, U. Queensland, Australia, 1976; MBA, U. South Fla., 1996; MPA, Harvard U., 1998, MPH, 1999. Asst. prof.

surgery U. Wash., Seattle, 1984-88; assoc. prof. surgery U. South Fla., Tampa, 1989-98; dir. surgery VA Med. Ctr., Asheville, N.C., 1998—; cons. prof. surgery Duke U., Durham, 1999—. Dir. cardiovascular and thoracic surgery U. South Fla., 1989-94, mem. faculty coun., 1991-94, UMSA bd. dirs., 1991-94, univ. senate, 1993-96; pres. QMEDA, Inc., Tampa, 1993—. Author: (software) QMEDA H&P, 1994. Bd. dirs. Fla. Am. Heart Assn., St. Petersburg, 1992-94, chair pub. liason, 1996. Commonwealth Univ. scholarship Australian Govt., 1968, Alley-Sheridan scholarship Thoracic Surgery Found. for Rsch. Edn., 1997. Fellow Royal Coll. Physician and Surgeons Can., Royal Australasian Coll. of Surgeons; mem. Am. Coll. of Chest Physicians (state gov. 1997-99), Phi Kappa Phi, Beta Gamma Sigma. Office: Dept Surgery VA Med Ctr 1100 Tunnel Rd Asheville NC 28805-2043

MCKEOWN, WILLIAM PHILIP, judge; b. Quebec City, Que., Can., Mar. 10, 1936; m. Elizabeth McKeown; 4 children. B Comm., McGill U., Montreal, Que., 1956; LLB, U. Toronto, 1959. Queen's counsel Ont. 1983. Counsel Dept. Health, Province Ont., Toronto, 1962-63, McMillan Binch, Toronto, 1963-64, Can. GE, Toronto, 1965-74; dep. dir. investigation and rsch. Bur. Competition Policy, Ottawa, Ont., 1974-77; ptnr. Stephens French McKeown, Toronto, 1977-86; judge Supreme Ct. Ont., 1986-90, Gen. Divsn., Ont. Ct. Justice, Toronto, 1990-93, Trial Divsn., Fed. Ct. Can., Ottawa, 1993—; judge, chmn. Competition Tribunal. Mem. Can. Bar Assn., Toronto Lawyers' Club. Office: Fed Ct Can Trial Divsn Ottawa ON Canada K1A 0H9

MC KEOWN, WILLIAM TAYLOR, magazine editor, author; b. Ft. Collins, Colo., July 4, 1921; s. Stuart Ellison and Eunice Harris (Akin) Mc K.; m. Lorraine Laredo; children: Elizabeth Ellison, Katherine, Suzanne. AB, Bowdoin Coll., 1942; student, Columbia U. Grad. Sch., 1948. Editor Fawcett Library Series, 1953-56; founding editor True's Boating Yearbook, 1955-56, Popular Boating mag., 1956, editor-in-chief, 1956-62; CEO The Mc Keown Co., N.Y.C., 1993—; editl. dir. Computer Travel Info., 1994—. Travel editor Davis Publs.; outdoor/boating/travel editor Popular Mechanics, 1971-82; sr. editor Outdoor Life, 1983-93. Author weekly NEA syndicated newspaper column American Afloat, 1959-65; contbr. fiction, non-fiction to nat. mags., 1947—; author: Boating Handbook, 1956, Boating in America, 1960. Pilot USAAF, WW II, ETO. Mem. Am. Power Boat Assn., U.S. Power Squadrons, 357 FIghter Group Assn., N.Y. Yacht Club, Overseas Press Club, Royal Danish Yacht Club (Copenhagen), Turtles Internat. Avocation: international competitor in power and sail racing events. Office: The Mc Keown Co 52 Monell Pl Beacon NY 12508-1424

MCKERNS, CHARLES JOSEPH, lawyer; b. Shenandoah, Pa., July 17, 1935; s. Charles Francis and Bridgett Ann (Barrett) McK.; m. Helen Patricia Nott, Feb. 13, 1960; children: Charles J. Jr., Michael H., Patricia B. BS, Georgetown U., 1957, JD, 1960. Bar: D.C. 1960, U.S. Ct. Appeals (D.C. cir.) 1961, U.S. Supreme Ct. 1971, Va. 1992. Law clk. to assoc. judge U.S. Ct. Appeals (D.C. cir), Washington, 1960-61; assoc. Dow, Lohnes & Albertson, 1961-65, ptnr., 1965-91, of counsel, 1991-95; ptnr. McKerns and McKerns, Heathsville, Va., 1991-96, of counsel, 1996-98. 1st lt. U.S. Army, 1957-59. Mem. ABA, University Club (Washington), Belle Haven Country Club (Alexandria, Va.), Indian Creek Yacht and Country Club (Kilmarnock, Va.). Republican. Roman Catholic. Avocations: hiking, reading, swimming. Home: Windy Blue PO Box 248 Ophelia VA 22530 Office: McKerns & McKerns PO Box 188 Heathsville VA 22473-0188 also: Dow Lohnes & Albertson 1200 New Hampshire Ave NW Washington DC 20036-6802

MCKERNS, KENNETH WILSHIRE, science educator, researcher; b. Hong-Kong, Mar. 5, 1919; s. Fredrich William McKerns and Daisy Peel; m. Dorothy Vivian McDuffy, Feb. 20, 1943; children: Maureen Kendra, Leslie Allison. BSc, U. of Alta., Edmonton, Alberta, 1942, MSc, 1946; PhD, McGill U., Montral, Quebec, 1949. Chief biochemist Can. Packers Ltd., Toronto, Canada, 1950—54; lectr. St. Andrews U., Saint Andrews, Scotland, 1954—55; group leader Laderle Labs, Pearl River, NY, 1955—60; assoc. prof. U. of Fla., Gainesville, Fla., 1960—63, prof., coll. medicine, 1960—63; grad. rsch. prof. Univerisity of Fla., 1963—79; pres. Internat. Found. Biochemical Endocrin, Trenton, Maine, 1979—. Capt. Royal Can. Artillary, 1942—45, Europe. Fellow Fellow, Nat. Res. Coun. Can., 1959, 1960, Nat. Inst. Health, 1969, 1970, Fellow - Lectr., Haryand Med. Sch., 1970, 1971. Achievements include patents for Inventor, Isolation & Purification ACTH; US Patent 4,193,915 18 Mar. 1980: Inhibitory & Antibody Generating Peptides for Contraception & Cancer Inhibition; Pre patent application, August , 1999, Inhibitory Prostate Cancer by Unique Synthetic Peptides. Avocations: professional artist, coastal sailing. Office: International Foundation Bio Endocrin 126 Fox Run Road Trenton ME 04605

MC KETTA, JOHN J., JR. chemical engineering educator; b. Wyano, Pa., Oct. 17, 1915; s. John J. and Mary (Gelet) McK.; m. Helen Elisabeth Smith, Oct. 17, 1943; children: Charles William, John J. III, Robert Andrew, Mary Anne. BS, Tri-State Coll., Angola, Ind., 1937; BSE., U. Mich., 1943, MS, 1944, PhD, 1946; D.Eng. (hon.), Tri-State Coll., 1965, Drexel U., 1977; Sc.D., U. Toledo, 1973. Diplomate: registered profl. engr., Tex., Mich. Group leader tech. dept. Wyandotte Chem. Corp., Mich., 1937-40, asst. supt. caustic soda div., 1940-41; teaching fellow U. Mich., 1942-44, instr. chem. engring., 1944-45; faculty U. Tex., Austin, 1946—, successively asst. prof. chem. engring., assoc. prof., then prof. chem. engring., 1951-52, 54—, E.P. Schoch prof. chem. engring., 1970-81, Joe C. Walter chair, 1981-94, prof. emeritus, 1994—. Asst. dir. Tex. petroleum research com., 1951-52, 54-56, chmn. chem. engring. dept., 1950-52, 55-63, dean Coll. Engring., 1963-69; exec. vice chancellor acad. affairs U. Tex. System, 1969-70; editorial dir. Petroleum Refiner, 1952-54; pres. Chemoil Cons., Inc., 1957-73; chmn. Tex. AEC, So. Interstate Nuclear Bd., 1963-70; mem. Tex. Radiation Adv. Bd., 1978-84; chmn. Nat. Energy Policy Com., 1970-72, Nat. Air Quality Control Com., 1972-85; mem. adv. bd. Carnegie-Mellon Inst. Research, 1978-84; pres. Reagans's rep. on U.S. Acid Precipitation Task Force, 1982-88; apptd. mem. Nuclear Waste Tech. Rev. Bd., 1992-97. Author: series Advances in Petroleum Chemistry and Refining (10 vols.); Chmn. editorial com.: series Petroleum Refiner; mem. adv. bd.: series Internat. Chem. Engring. mag; exec. editor: series Ency. of Chem. Processing and Design (68 vols.). Bd. regents Tri-State U., 1957—. Recipient Bronze plaque Am. Inst. Chem. Engrs., 1952, Charles Schwab award Am. Steel Inst., 1973, Lamme award as outstanding U.S. educator, 1976, Joe J. King Profl. Engring. Achievement award U. Tex., 1976, Gen. Dynamics Teaching Excellence award, 1979, Triple E award for contbns. to nat. issues on energy, environment and econs. Nat. Environ. Devel. Assn., 1976, Boris Pregal Sci. and Tech. award NAS, 1978, Internat. Chem. Engring. award, Italy, 1984, Pres. Herbert Hoover award for advancing well-being of humanity and developing richer and more enduring civilization Joint Engring. Socs., 1989, Centennial award exceptional contbn. Am. Soc. Engring. Edn., 1993; named Disting. Alumnus U. Mich Coll. Engring., 1953, Tri-State Coll., 1956; fellow Allied Chem. & Dye, 1945-46; named Disting. fellow Carnegie-Mellon U., 1978; Chem. Engring. Dept. at U. Tex. named The John J. McKetta Ctr. for Excellence in Chem. Engring. Edn. in his honor, 1995, Chem. Engring. Dept. at Tri State U. named The Dr. John J. McKetta Chem. Engring. Dept. in his honor, 1998. Mem. Am. Chem. Soc. (chmn. Central Tex. sect. 1950), Am. Inst. Chem. Engrs. (chmn. nat. membership com. 1955, regional exec. com., nat. dir., nat. v.p. 1961, pres. 1962, service to soc. award 1975), Am. Soc. Engring. Edn., Chem. Markets Research Assn., Am. Gas Assn. (adv. bd. chems. from gas 1954), Houston C. of C. (chmn. refining div. 1954, vice chmn. research and statistics com. 1954), Engrs. Joint Council (dir.), Engrs. Joint Countil Profl. Devel. (dir. 1963-85), Nat. Acad. Engring., Sigma Xi, Chi Epsilon, Alpha Psi Omega, Tau Omega, Phi Lambda Upsilon, Phi Kappa Phi, Iota Alpha, Omega Chi Epsilon, Tau Beta Pi, Omicron Delta Kappa. Home: 5227 Tortuga Trl Austin TX 78731-4501 E-mail: mcketta@mail.utexas.edu., mcketta@che.utexas.edu.

MCKEY, THOMAS J. lawyer; b. Detroit, Jan. 9, 1934; s. Thomas J. and Pauline H. (Feys) McK.; m. Lila W. Webber, Sept. 3, 1960; children: Tim, Christopher, Heather, Brenda. BS, USCG Acad., 1955; JD, U. Mich., 1962; MA in Psychology, Antioch U., 1995. Bar: Wash. 1962. With Bogle & Gates, Seattle, 1962-94, ptnr., 1970-94; arbitrator/mediator, pres., bd. dirs. North Pacific Dispute Resolution Svc., 1996—2001. Former chmn. N.W. Admiralty Law Inst., Seattle; mem. permanent adv. bd. Tulane Admiralty Law Inst., New Orleans, 1981—. Former bd. dirs. Bellvue (Wash.) Area Self-Improvement Coun., N.W. Seaport, Seattle, Coast Guard Mus. N.W., Seattle, Friends of Youth, Seattle, Resource Inst., Seattle. Comdr. USCGR. Mem. Maritime Law Assn. U.S. (exec. com. 1979-82), Seattle C. of C. (former chmn. maritime steering com.).

MCKEY, WINSTON JACKSON (JACK MCKEY), artist, boat designer, builder; b. Biloxi, Miss., Feb. 15, 1942; s. Winston Carlile and Dorothy Mae (Jackson) McK.; m. Betty Jean McKey, Dec. 3, 1973. Student, Gordon Mil. Coll., Barnesville, Ga., 1958-61, Valdosta State Coll., 1962. Owner, operator Wilderness Guide Svc., Valdosta, Ga., 1964-69; outdoor writer, photographer, 1964-73; asst. dr., dir. dept. recreation and tourism Coastal Plain Area Planning and Devel. Commn., 1968-73; boat designer, builder for recreation and comml. use Fla. and Alaska, 1973-82, 90-94; artisan, rsch. ancient tech. Blackfeet Reservation, Mont. Tlingit Villages, S.E. Alaska, Nez Perce Reservation, Idaho, 1982—. Cons. most phases of Native Am. lifeways, Ga., Fla., Mont., Alaska, Idaho, 1961—; lectr., presenter ancient tech. mus., hist.-ednl. groups, Ga., Fla., Mont. Alaska, Idaho, 1964—; writer Native Am. culture, 1964—; instr., mentor Native Am. tech., 1986-99; cons. PBS Lewis and Clark--The Journey of the Corps of Discovery, Orofino, Lewiston, Idaho, 1997; dug-out canoe expert Idaho PBS documentary Lewis and Clark in Idaho, Boise, 1997-98; acknowledged expert in Indian weapons and early Indian tech.; founder, bd. dirs. ZI.KI.A., Inc. Mem. Lewis and Clark Bicentennial Com., 1997—. Mem. Soc. Primitive Tech., Glacier County Hist. Soc. (life), J.W. Schultz Soc. (life). Avocations: hunting, fishing, canoeing, birdwatching, reading, Western horseman. Address: PO Box 337 Whitefish MT 59937 E-mail: bjmckey@3rivers.net.

MCKHANN, GUY MEAD, physician, educator; b. Boston, Mar. 20, 1932; s. Charles Fremont and Emily (Priest) McKhann; m. Katherine E. Henderson, Nov. 30, 1957 (div. 1983); children: Ian, James, Emily, Guy, Charles; m. Marilyn S. Albert, Sept. 27, 1997; children: Joshua, Katie. Student, Harvard U., 1948—51; MD, Yale U., 1955. Intern N.Y. Hosp., 1955—56; asst. resident pediat. Johns Hopkins Hosp., Balt., 1956—57; clin. assoc. NIH, Bethesda, 1957—60; resident neurology Mass. Gen. Hosp., Boston, 1960—63; asst. and assoc. prof. pediat. and neurology Stanford (Calif.) U., 1963—69; prof. neurology Johns Hopkins, Balt., 1969—, Kennedy prof. neurology, head neurology dept., 1969—88, prof. neurology, dir. Zanvyl Krieger Mind Brain Inst., 1988—2000; acting dir. for clin. activities Nat. Inst. Neurol. Diseases and Stroke NIH, 2000—01. Served with USPHS, 1957—60. Scholar, Markle, 1964—69, Joseph P. Kennedy Jr., 1963—69. Fellow: AAAS; mem.: Inst. Medicine, Soc. Neuroscis., Am. Neurochem. Soc., Am. Neurol. Assn., Alpha Omega Alpha. Achievements include research in on normal and abnormal human nervous system. Home: 6526 Montrose Ave Baltimore MD 21212-1023 Office: Zanvyl Krieger Mind/Brain Inst Johns Hopkins U 338 Krieger Hall Baltimore MD 21218 E-mail: guy.mckhann@jhu.edu.

MCKIBBEN, BILL, writer; b. Palo Alto, Calif., Dec. 8, 1960; s. Gordon Charles and Margaret Hayes McK.; m. Sue Halpern, Mar. 6, 1988; 1 child, Sophie Crane. BA, Harvard Coll., 1982; PhD (hon.) , Lebanon Valley Coll., 1992, Green Mountain Coll., 1995. Author: The End of Nature, 1989, The Age of Missing Information, 1992, Hope, Human and Wild, 1995, Maybe One, 1998, Hundred Dollar Holiday, 1998, Long Distance, 2000. Trustee Paul Smith's Coll., N.Y.C., 1997—, TV-Free Am., Washington, 1995-99, Future Generations, Franklin, W.Va., 1999—, Florence & John Schumann Found., N.Y.C., 1999—. Fellow, Lyndhurst Found., 1990, Guggenheim Found., 1994; scholar vis. scholar, Middleburg Coll., 2001—. Methodist. Home: 46 Garnet Lake Rd Johnsburg NY 12843-2501

MCKIBBEN, HOWARD D. federal judge; b. Apr. 1, 1940; s. James D. and Bernice McKibben; m. Mary Ann McKibben, July 2, 1966; children: Mark, Susan. BS, Bradley U., 1962; MPA, U. Pitts., 1964; JD, U. Mich., 1967. Assoc. George W. Abbott Law Office, 1967-71; dep. dist. atty. Douglas County, Nev., 1969-71, dist. atty., 1971-77; dist. ct. judge State of Nev., 1977-84; judge U.S. Dist. Ct. Nev., Reno, 1984—. Mem. Nev. Bar Assn., Am. Inns of Ct. (pres. Nev. chpt. 1986-88). Methodist. Avocations: tennis, golf, racquetball. Home: PO Box 588 Verdi NV 89439-0588 Office: US Dist Ct 400 S Virginia St Ste 804 Reno NV 89501-2197

MCKIBBEN, JAMES DENIS, marketing and sales executive; b. Pitts., Mar. 19, 1951; s. Charles Thomas and Selma Catherine (Wild) McK.; m. Barbara Joyce Ross (div.); 1 child, Erin Crystal; m. Sally Joanne Kolberg (div.). BS in Chemistry, U. Pitts., 1974; MBA, Rivier Coll., 1978. Mktg. mgr. J.T. Baker Chem. Co., Phillipsburg, N.J., 1974-83; major acct. mgr. GCA Corp., Sunnyvale, Calif., 1983-84; regional mgr. Wild Leitz USA, San Francisco, 1984-88; dir. sales and mktg. MRS Tech., Inc., Chelmsford, Mass., 1988-92; dir. sales and mktg. FPD divsn. Semiconductor Sys. Inc., Fremont, Calif., 1992-94; v.p. mktg. and sales MRS Tech. Inc., Chelmsford, 1994-96; v.p. worldwide sales and mktg. Tegal Corp., Petaluma, Calif., 1996—2001; pres. Tegal Japan, Inc., 2001—. Cons. high definition systems and flat panel displays, Sausalito, Calif., 1989—. Contbr. articles to profl. jours. Mem. Sausalito (Calif.) Art Festival com. Mem. IEEE, Soc. Photo-Optical and Instrumentation Engrs., Semicondr. Equipment and Materials Inst., Soc. for Info. Display, Am. Electronics Assn. (mem. advanced TV task force 1988—, trade and investment com. 1989—), Bay Area Microlithography Soc., Sausalito C. of C., Sausalito Yacht Club. Republican. Roman Catholic. Avocations: skiing, boating, golfing, playing saxophone. Office: Tegal Corp 2201 S Mcdowell Blvd Petaluma CA 94954-6903

MCKIBBON-TURNER, BAMBI, management firm executive; b. Columbus, Ohio, Apr. 12, 1947; d. Alfonso Jackson and Myra Josephine (Kelley) McKibbon; (div. 1971); children: John M. III, Linda Marie, Lisaj Denise Turner Chappelle. BS in Human Svcs., MS in Community Econ. Devel., N.H. Coll., 1989. Caseworker Office of Congressman Don J. Pease, Washington, 1977-79, fed. grant specialist, 1979-89, econ. devel. and fed. grant specialist, 1989-90, legis. asst. and econ. devel. specialist, 1990-91, econ. devel. dir., 1991-93; pres., CEO JCAA Enterprises, Inc., 1997—; deputy clerk Town of Lake Park, Fla., 2000—. Mem. No. Va. Dem. Club, Arlington, 1991. Named Outstanding Young Woman of Am., 1983. Mem. v.p., Kiwanis Club, Lake Park, 2000-. Avocations: classical violinist, philately, travel. Office: PO Box 530946 Lake Park FL 33403-0929

MCKIBLE, ADAM DAVID, educator; b. Newburgh, N.Y., Apr. 13, 1962; s. Joel Stephen and Rachel Atalia M. BA, State U. N.Y., 1984; MA, Univ. N.C., 1990, PhD, 1998. Asst. prof. English John Jay Coll. Criminal Justice, N.Y.C., 1998—. Mem. Modern Lang. Assn. Avocation: music. Office: English Dept John Jay Coll 445 West 59th St New York NY 10019

MC KIE, TODD STODDARD, artist; b. Boston, Apr. 25, 1944; s. Roy Albert and Lois E. (Barwood) McK.; m. Judy Anne Kensley, Apr. 10, 1967; 1 son, Jesse Simon. BFA, RISD, 1966. Vis. artist RISD, 1977, Mass. Coll. Art, 1977-78, Sch. Mus. Fine Arts, Boston, 1979; artist-in-residence Isabella Stewart Gardner Mus., Boston, 2000; lectr. schs. and museums. Exhibited in one-man shows Harcus Krakow Gallery, Boston, 1977, 79, 83, Aquavella Gallery, N.Y.C., 1978, 79, 81, Hokin-Kaufman Gallery, Chgo., 1983, Helander Gallery, N.Y.C., 1990, 92, Toale Gallery, Boston, 1994, Barbara Singer Gallery, Boston, 1996, Greenville (S.C.) Mus. of Art, 1997, Littlejohn Contemporary Art, 1999, Clark Gallery, Lincoln, Nebr., 2001; exhibited in group shows including, Whitney Museum Am. Art, N.Y.C., 1975, Harcus Krakow Gallery, 1975, 78, Mus. Fine Arts, Boston, 1975, 77, 81, Acquavella Gallery, 1976, 78, 79, 81, Inst. Contemporary Art, Boston, 1979, Addison Gallery Am. Art, 1981; represented in permanent collections including Fogg Art Mus., Cambridge, Mass., M.I.T., Cambridge, Brockton (Mass.) Mus., Mus. Fine Arts, Boston, DeCordova Mus., Lincoln, Mass., Rose Art Mus. Brandeis U., Mus. of Modern Art, Fidelity Investments, Microsoft; also numerous pvt. collections. Recipient Blanch E. Colman award Colman Found., 1974; Artists fellowship Villa Montalvo, 1995; Artists Found. fellow Boston, 1975, 89. Home and Office: 82 Holworthy St Cambridge MA 02138-4579

MCKILLIP, PATRICIA CLAIRE, operatic soloist; b. Milw., Apr. 28; d. Lester J. and Ruth J. (Lohneis) McK.; m. Mark Richard McKillip, June 16, 1990. BA in English-Drama, Creative Writing, Lit., Alverno Coll., 1980; MusB in Applied Music, Alverno Coll., Milw., 1981; postgrad., Wis. Conservatory of Mus., 1981-82, U. Wis., Milw., 1982, MS in Fine Arts Edn., 1996; postgrad., The Juilliard Sch., 1982-84, Am. Acad. Dramatic Arts, 1983-84, Adelphi U., 1984; MS in Fine Arts Edn., U. Wis., Milw., 1996, MA in English-Creative Writing and Lit., 1997. Soloist Amadeus Opera Co.; instr. vocal music seminars various high schs., N.Y. Co-founder, co-dir. The Masque Consort, N.Y.C., 1990-91, exec. v.p., 1991; v.p., co-founder Creative Learning Assocs.; instr. Cardinal Stritch Coll., Milw., 1994—. Performed with numerous opera cos. including The Florentine Opera Co., Music Under the Stars Prodns., Milw. Opera Co., Westchester Lyric Opera Co., Profl. Opera Workshop at Lincoln Ctr., Met. Opera Co., N.Y. Grand Opera Co., Monteverdi Opera Guild Prodns., Republic Opera Co., La Puma Opera Co., and other chamber, theater and folk groups; puppeteer, costumer, designer Puppet Art Troupe; performed in over 50 mus. shows and prodns., 6 solo recitals, also medieval concerts, choruses, orchestras, oratorio; 42 other recitals. Exec. v.p. Masque Consort, a multi-media theatrical orgn. Music dept. scholar Alverno U. Mem. AFTRA, SAG, Nat. Assn. Music Tchrs., Music Educators Nat. Conf. (treas.), Internat. Platform Assn., Wis. Fedn. Music Clubs, Music Clubs Am., Am. Guild Mus. Artists, Q'ahal-Liturgical Music Soc., Delta Omicron (v.p., chaplain, warden Gamma Gamma chpt., WMA State and Regional Vocal award 1978, Star of Delta Omicron award 1980, 40 music medals from state and dist. WSMA), Alpha Sigma Tau. Democrat. Roman Catholic. Avocations: dance, creative writing, art. Home: 4860 S 69th St Greenfield WI 53220-4452 E-mail: pattyandmark@owol.net.

MCKIM, PAUL ARTHUR, management consultant, retired petroleum executive; b. Milford, Conn., Feb. 1, 1923; s. Arthur Wheatley and Helen Agnes (Brennan) McK.; m. Daisy Flora Brown, June 18, 1945; 1 dau., Meredith Ann. Student, Lamar Inst. Tech., 1940-42; BS in Chem. Engring., La. State U., 1943, MS, 1947, PhD, 1949; grad. Advanced Mgmt. Program, Harvard, 1959; grad. Aspen Inst. Humanistic Studies Exec. Program, 1970. With Ethyl Corp., 1949-62, asst. gen. mgr. research and devel. operations, 1958-62; v.p., gen. mgr. rsch. and devel. Atlantic Refining Co., Phila., 1962-66; v.p. Atlantic Richfield Co., 1966-78; v.p. comml. devel. Arco Chem. Co., 1966-69, v.p. nuclear operations and comml. devel., 1969-73; exec. v.p. Sinclair Koppers Co., 1973; pres. Arco Polymers, Inc., 1974-78; asst. to pres. Tex. Eastern Corp., 1978-80, v.p., 1980-84, sr. v.p., 1985-88. Chmn. US Organizing com. for 12th World Petroleum Congress, Houston, 1987. Past bd. mgrs. Franklin Inst. Research Labs; past vice chmn. bd. mgrs. Spring Garden Coll., Phila. Coll. Art.; past vice chmn. World Affairs Council of Phila. Served to lt. (j.g.) USNR, 1944-46. Mem. AIChE, Am. Petroleum Inst., Merion (Pa.) Cricket Club, Merion Golf Club, Houston Club, Shreveport (La.) Country Club, Alpha Chi Sigma, Omicron Delta Kappa, Tau Beta Pi, Phi Lambda Upsilon, Phi Kappa Phi, Delta Kappa Epsilon. Home: 5405 Holly Springs Dr Houston TX 77056-2021

MCKIM, SAMUEL JOHN, III, lawyer; b. Pitts., Dec. 31, 1938; s. Samuel John and Harriet Frieda (Roehl) McK; children: David Hunt, Andrew John; m. Eugenia A. Leverich. AA cum laude, Port Huron Jr. Coll., 1959; BA cum laude, U. Mich., 1961, JD cum laude, 1964. Bar: Mich. 1965, U.S. Dist. Ct. (so. dist.) Mich. 1965, U.S. Ct. Appeals (6th cir.) 1969, U.S. Supreme Ct. 1994. Assoc. Miller, Canfield, Paddock and Stone, PLC, Detroit, Bloomfield Hills, 1964-71, sr. mem., 1971—, head state and local tax sect., 1985—, chmn. tax dept., 1989-94, mng. ptnr., 1979-85, chmn., mng. ptnr., 1984-85. Mem. tax coun. State Bar Mich., 1981-94, chmn. state and local tax com. real property sect., 1982-90; adj. prof. law sch. Wayne State U., 1993-99. Assoc. editor Mich. Law Rev. Bd. dirs., past chmn. Goodwill Industries of Greater Detroit, 1970-2000; dir. Goodwill Industries Found., 1982-95; tchg. elder Presbyn. Ch., Stevens min.; coun. mem. at large Detroit area coun. Boy Scouts Am., 1987—. Fellow: Am. Tax Counsel; mem.: ABA, Barrister's Soc., Detroit Bar Assn., Mich. Bar Assn., Mariner Sands Country Club, Port Huron Golf Club, Nomads Club, Order of Coif, Phi Delta Phi. Home: 32778 Friar Tuck Ln Beverly Hills MI 48025-2500 Office: Miller Canfield Paddock & Stone 150 W Jefferson Ave Ste 2500 Detroit MI 48226-4416

MCKINLEY, CAMILLE DOMBROWSKI, psychologist; b. Buffalo , May 6, 1922; d. Eugene Anthony and Anne Victoria (Sliwinska) Dombrowski; m. Thomas Leroy Smith, Dec. 30, 1944 (div. 1977); children: Thomas Dan, Cynthia Camille (dec.), Pamela Susan; m. William Frank McKinley, Oct. 7, 1984 (dec. Mar. 1985); m. Stuart Peebles Parker, Dec. 20, 1996. BA, Syracuse U., 1943, MA, Boston U., 1947; edn. specialist, Mich. State U., 1970, PhD, 1978. Acad. advisor Mich. State U., East Lansing, 1966-70, dir. Career Ctr., 1970-81, counseling psychologist Counseling Ctr., 1981-91; pres. Priam Pubs., 1978—. Mem. Career Planning and Placement Coun. Mich. State U., 1970-91. Editor: The Mich. State Univ. Referral Directory, 1970-91, The Gracious Reader, 1970-80; editor, publisher The CAM Report, 1978—. Founding pres. Greater Lansing chpt. Planned Parenthood, Mich., 1967; v.p. Opera Co. of Mid-Mich., 1983-85; mem. inner cir. Wharton Ctr. for Performing Arts, Mich. State U., mem. Platinum Cir. Mem. Mich. State U. Pres.'s Club and Beaumont Tower Soc., Zonta Internat., Zeta Tau Alpha. Home: PO Box 1862 East Lansing MI 48826-1862 Fax: 517-351-9054. E-mail: mckinl118@msu.edu.

MCKINLEY, DOUGLAS WEBSTER (WEBB MCKINLEY), consultant; b. Bay City, Mich., May 26, 1917; s. Frank and Amelia Ingraham (Webster) McK.; m. Martha Slade, July 12, 1945; children: Judith Anne, Martha Webster (Mrs. Duane Kissick), Mary Slade (Mrs. Joel Bingham), Jane Elizabeth; m. Roberta Baughman Burton, Nov. 25, 1994; m. Peggy Lighter. BA, Amherst Coll., 1939. Reporter Ann Arbor News, 1940-41, 46-47; staff AP, Detroit, 1947-53, Rome, 1953-57, chief of bur. Istanbul, 1957-60, chief Middle East services Beirut, 1960-65, news editor world services, 1965-82; cons. to agys. in developing nations Zimbabwe, Malaysia, Morocco, Tunisia, 1982—. Author: Trouble in the Middle East. Served to maj. AUS, 1941-45. Mem. Phi Kappa Psi. Home: 619 Old Plantation Rd Jekyll Island GA 31527-0723

MCKINLEY, ELLEN BACON, priest; b. Milw., June 9, 1929; d. Edward Alsted and Lorraine Goodrich (Graham) Bacon; m. Richard Smallbrook McKinley, III, June 16, 1951 (div. Oct. 1977); children: Richard, Ellen Graham, David Todd, Edward Bacon. BA cum laude, Bryn Mawr Coll., 1951; MDiv, Yale U., 1976; STM, Gen. Theol. Sem., N.Y.C., 1979; PhD, Union Theol. Sem., N.Y.C., 1988. As deacon Episcopal Ch., 1980, as priest Episcopal Ch., 1981. Intern St. Francis Ch., Stamford, Conn., 1976-77; pastoral asst. St. Paul's Ch., Riverside, 1979-80, curate, 1980-81; asst. St. Saviour's Ch., Old Greenwich, 1982-90; interim asst. Trinity Ch., Princeton, NJ, 1990—91; priest assoc. All Saints Ch., 1992—97, St. Christophers Ch., Chatham, Mass., 1997—. Bd. dirs. Chatham Old Village Assn.; mem. Episc. election com. Diocese of Conn., 1986—87, mem. com. on human sexuality, 1987—90, mem com. donations and bequests, 1987—90; mem. major chpt. Trinity Cathedral, Trenton, NJ, 1992—96; interim rector All Saints Ch., Princeton, NJ, 1993. Secy Greenwich Comt Drugs, 1970—71; bd dirs Greenwich YWCA, 1971—72; mem Jr League, Episcopal Women's Caucus. Mem.: Colonial Dames Am.

MCKINLEY, JAMES FRANK , JR. retired manufacturing executive; b. Chgo., Feb. 17, 1943; s. James F. Sr. and Annabell I. (Williams) McK.; m. Sharon M., Dec. 7, 1968; children: James P., Scott J., Rebecca L. BS, Monmouth Coll., 1964; MS, Ill. Inst. Tech., 1966; MBA, Stanford U., 1987. Salesman Joseph T. Ryerson & Son, Chgo., 1961-66, Scot Forge Co., Cicero, 1966-71, v.p. sales, 1971-76, exec. v.p., 1976-85, pres., COO, 1985-92, pres., CEO, COO, 1992—; pres., bd. dirs. Ringmasters (formerly Ovaco Ajax), Wayne, Mich., 1996—; ptnr. NAm. Forgemasters, 1997, vice-chmn., 2001; now ret. Dir. Fox Waterway Agy., state office, 1997—, chmn. 2000—. Capt. USCG Aux., Fox Lake, Ill., 1985—; dir. Allendale Sch., Lake Villa, Ill., 1983-96; regent Milw. Sch. Engring., 1995; McHenry County mem. Sheriff Merit Commn., 2000. Mem. Am. Soc. Metals, Forging Industry Rsch. Found., Forging Industry Assn. (bd. dirs. 1986—, gov. coun. 1990—, dir. 1998, v.p. 1999, pres. 2000—), Ill. St. Andrews Soc. (bd. govs., v.p. 1996-97), Profl. Capts. Assn., McHenry C. of C. (chmn. 1999). Republican. Avocations: boating, skiing, scuba diving, golf. Home: 16213 Captiva Dr Captiva FL 33924 E-mail: jmkinleyjr@msn.com.

MCKINLEY, JENEAL RUTH, computer company executive; b. Yuma, Colo., Nov. 19, 1951; d. Harry Ellsworth and JoAnna Ruth Jackson; m. Stephen McKinley; children: Jeffrey Coseo, Shantel Coseo, Eve, Erin, Caitlin, Chloe; m. Jeneal Jackson (div.). Office mgr. Weinland Constrn., Inc., Loveland, Colo., 1992—99; pres. Excel Computer Services, Inc., 1965—; owner Endless Memories, 2001—; tech. writer Goldco Industries, Inc.,

2001—02; dance instr. Aspen Lodge, Estes Park, 1993—, City of Loveland, 1992—99. Founding pres. Prevent Unwanted Pets, Loveland, 1976—78. Conservative. Avocation: travel, horseback riding, writing. Office: Excel Computer Svc Inc 5350 N Garfield Ave Loveland CO 80538

MCKINLEY, JIMMIE JOE, business executive; b. Bertram, Tex., July 23, 1934; s. Joseph Crofford and Velma Anne (Barnett) McK. AA, Kilgore Coll., 1953; BJ, U. Tex., 1955; MS, U. Ky., 1964. Asst. libr. Bethel Coll., McKenzie, Tenn., 1961-63, reference libr., 1966-70, acting head libr., 1970-71; owner, mgr. Longview (Tex.) Book Co., 1974—, Longview Dwellings and Workplaces, 1999—. Former mem., bd. dirs. Longview-Piney Woods chpt. ARC; trustee Bethel Coll., 1977-86. Mem. ALA, East Tex. Hist. Assn., Gregg County Hist. Soc., Burnet County Heritage Soc., History Club East Tex., East Tex. Oil Mus. Guild (pres. 1996-97), Celtic Heritage Soc. East Tex., Tex. Shakespeare Festival Guild, U.S. Lighthouse Soc., Longview Supper Club, Summit Club. Presbyterian. Home and Office: PO Box 2106 Longview TX 75606-2106

MCKINLEY, JOHN CLARK, lawyer; b. Lima, Peru, Nov. 5, 1960; came to U.S., 1961; s. Stuart M. and Barbara C. (Clark) McK.; m. Kathleen F. Jolovich, Nov. 2, 1985; children: Jesse F., Elizabeth C., Laura K. BS in Agrl. Bus., U. Wyo., 1983, MBA, 1984, JD, 1989. Bar: Utah 1989, Wyo. 1989; U.S. Dist. Ct. Utah 1989, U.S. Dist. Ct. Wyo. 1989. Gen. ptnr. J.M. Constrn., Torrington, Wyo., 1984-85; contract landman Marathon Oil Co., Casper, 1985-86; assoc. Richards, Brandt, Miller & Nelson, Salt Lake City, 1989-94; ptnr. Davis & Cannon, Cheyenne, Wyo., 1994—. Mng. editor Land and Water Law Rev., U. Wyo. 1989. Recipient Am. Jurisprudence award 1987. Mem. Utah Bar Assn., Wyo. Bar Assn., Order of the Coif, Phi Kappa Phi. Republican. Avocations: skiing, fly fishing. Office: Davis & Cannon 2710 Thomes Ave Cheyenne WY 82001-3029

MC KINLEY, JOHN KEY, retired oil company executive; b. Tuscaloosa, Ala., Mar. 24, 1920; s. Virgil Parks and Mary Emma (Key) McK.; m. Helen Grace Heare, July 19, 1946; children: John Key Jr., Mark Charles. BS in Chem. Engring, U. Ala., 1940, MS in Organic Chemistry, 1941, LL.D. (hon.), 1972; grad., Advanced Mgmt. Program, Harvard U., 1962; LL.D. (hon.), Troy State U., 1974. Registered profl. engr., Tex. With Texaco Inc., 1941-86, asst. dir. research N.Y., 1957-59, asst. to v.p., 1959-60, mgr. comml. devel., 1960, gen. mgr. petrochem. dept., 1960-67, v.p. petrochem. dept., v.p. in charge supply and distbn., 1967-71, sr. v.p. worldwide refining, petrochems., also supply and distbn., 1971, pres., dir., 1971-80, pres., chief operating officer, chmn. exec. com., 1980, chmn. bd., pres., chief exec. officer, 1980-83, chmn. bd., chief exec. officer, 1983-86, ret., 1986. Bd. dirs. emeritus Federated Dept. Stores, Inc. Patentee for chem. processing. Hon. bd. dirs. Met. Opera Assocs.; nat. chmn. Met. Opera Centennial Fund, 1980; bd. dirs. The Ams. Soc.; mem. Bus. Coun. Maj. AUS, 1941-45, ETO. Decorated Bronze Star; recipient George Washington Honor medal Freedoms Found., 1972; Andrew Wellington Cordier fellow Columbia U.; named to Ala. Bus. Hall of Fame, 1982, Ala. Acad. Honor, 1983, State of Ala. Engring. Hall of Fame, 1992. Fellow Am. Inst. Chem. Engrs.; mem. Am. Petroleum Inst. (hon. dir.), Wee Burn Country Club, Links Club, Brook Club, Augusta Nat. Golf Club, Blind Brook Country Club, North River Yacht, Sigma Xi, Tau Beta Pi, Gamma Sigma Epsilon, Kappa Sigma. Office: 1 Canterbury Grn Stamford CT 06901-2032

MCKINLEY, KEVIN L. neurologist; b. Joplin, Mo., Apr. 24, 1961; s. Galen Dean and Mary Alice (Hunt) McK.; m. Dawn Marie Sokol, May 7, 1988; children: Megan, Michael, Erin. BA, U. Mo., 1982, MD, 1985. Diplomate Am. Bd. Psychiatry & Neurology. Resident in neurology Baylor U., Houston, 1985-89, fellow in neuromuscular medicine, 1989-90; instr. Baylor Medicine, 1990-92; faculty Ochsner Clinic, New Orleans, 1992—, chmn. dept. neurology, 1992—; asst. prof. Tulane Medicine, 1992—. Mem. AMA, Am. Acad. Neurology. Avocations: painting, collecting music memorabilia. Office: Ochsner Clinic 1514 Jefferson Hwy New Orleans LA 70121-2483

MCKINLEY, LOREN DHUE, museum director; b. Tillamook, Oreg., Feb. 1, 1920; s. Henry Raymond and Flora (Phillips) McK.; m. Mary Eileen Sessions, May 22, 1942; children: Candace Eileen, Scott Dhu, Kevin Loren, Laurie Lee, Maris Colleen. Student, Oreg. State U., U. Oreg.; D.Sc., U. Portland, 1973. Advt. mgr. Headlight Herald, Tillamook, 1946; partner Kenwood Press, 1949; dir. Oreg. Mus. Sci. and Industry, Portland, 1960-78, chief exec. officer, 1978—. Bd. dirs. Fred Hutchinson Cancer Rsch. Ctr. Found., Oreg. Mus. Sci. and Industry; sr. devel. officer Office of Devel. Oreg. State U. Mayor of Tillamook, 1954-60; pres. Leukemia Assn. Oreg. Inc., 1983—; bd. dirs. St. Mary's Acad., 1993—; bd. trustees Oreg. Mus. Sci. and Industry; mem. Oreg. State U Found. Served with AUS, World War II, ETO, MTO. Decorated Bronze Star with oak leaf cluster; named 1st Citizen of Oreg., 1951; recipient award Oreg. Mus. Sci. and Industry, 1965, Elsie M.B. Naumberg award as outstanding sci. mus. dir., 1968, citation for outstanding svc. Oreg. Acad. Sci., 1971, Aubrey Watzek award Lewis and Clark Coll., 1973, Barbara Stallcup Miller Profl. Achievement award Willamette Valley Devel. Officers, 1999; named alumni of yr. Oreg. State U., 1999, recipient heart of gold award, 1999. Mem. Assn. Sci. and Tech. Ctrs. Am. (pres. 1973—), League Oreg. Cities (past pres.), Kappa Sigma. Republican. Home and Office: 11925 SW Belvidere Pl Portland OR 97225-5805

MCKINLEY, RHETA CHIPMAN, foundation administrator; b. Boston, Apr. 17, 1926; d. Willis Edward and Nellie (Thistle) Chipman; (div. Oct. 1975); children: Paul, Gail, Mark, Joan. Assoc. in Bus., Fisher Bus. Coll., Boston, 1945; cert. achievement, Bunker Hill Community Coll., Charlestown, Mass., 1979. Admin. asst. War Dept., Boston, 1945-47; dir. Reading (Mass.) Coun. on Aging, 1977-88. Dir. Mystic Valley Elder Svcs., Inc., Malden, Mass., 1986—, treas., 1987—. Mem. outreach com., oversight com. Episcopal Ch., Reading, 1987—. Recipient Cert. of Appreciation, Greater Lynn (Mass.) Mental Health and Retardation Soc., 1987. Mem. Mass. Coun. on Aging Dirs., Soc. of Craftsmen, Reading Garden Club. Republican. Episcopalian. Avocations: stained glass, stencilling, furniture refinishing, golf, gardening.

MCKINLEY-HAAS, MARY, artist; b. St. Louis; d. Lee Carrington and Florence (Dowden) McK.; m. Saul Haas; children: Christopher, Matthew. BA, Smith Coll.; student, Art Students League, 1973-74, Nat. Acad. Design, 1965-66, Studio and Forum Stage Design. Head costume design dept. ABC-TV, NYC, 1968-73. Solo exhbns. include Tarlowe Gallery, Westhampton Beach, N.Y., 1974, Fontbonne Gallery, St. Louis, 1977, Gallery Yssa, N.Y.C., 1979, Vered Gallery, East Hampton, N.Y., 1981, Netherlands Bank & Ludlow-Hyland Gallery, N.Y.C., 1981, U. Tex., Austin, 1988, RVS Fine Art, Southampton, N.Y., 1990, TSS Gallery, N.Y.C., 1992, U. Tex., Austin, 1992, TAI Gallery, N.Y.C., 1999; group exhbns. include Guild Hall, East Hampton, N.Y., 1974, 75, 76, 78, 81, 85, 96, Parrish Art Mus., Southampton, 1975, 76, 78, 81, Water Mill Mus., 1983, 92, Vared Gallery, East Hampton, N.Y., 1985, Queens Coll. Art Ctr., Flushing, N.Y., 1991, Stony Brook U. Art Gallery, N.Y., 1994, Women in Art and Culture, Beijing, 1995, Elite Gallery, Moscow, 1995, Nat. Mus. Women in Arts, Washington, 1996, Soho 20 Gallery, N.Y.C., 1998—, Canajoharie (N.Y.) Libr. and Art Ctr., 2000, Weill Cornell Med. Libr., N.Y.C., 2002, others; represented in permanent collections at Nat. Mus. of Women in the Arts, Washington, Tari Women's Cultural Ctr., Papua, New Guinea, Fontbonne Coll., St. Louis, No. Trust Naples (Fla.); also numerous pvt. collections; costume designer for Broadway and network TV shows, Harkness Ballet, Holiday on Ice, others. Mem. United Scenic Artists, Women in the Arts, N.Y. Artists Equity. Address: 280 Lafayette St Loft5B New York NY 10012-3303

MCKINNELL, HENRY A. pharmaceutical company executive; BA, U. B.C.; MBA, PhD, Stanford U. Joined Pfizer, Inc., Tokyo, 1971; pres. Pfizer Asia, Hong Kong; chief fin. officer, pres. med. technology group Pfizer, Inc., exec. v.p., 1992—99; pres. Pfizer Pharms., 1997—2001; pres., chief operating officer Pfizer, Inc., N.Y.C., 1999—2001, chmn., CEO, 2001—. Mem. Presidential Advisory Council on HIV/AIDS; mem. bd. of dir. Moody's Corp., John Wiley & Sons, Inc., and the Business Roundtable; chmn. emeritus Pharma. Research and Manuf. of Amer.; vice chmn. Com. Econ. Devel.; chmn. Food and Drug Law Inst. Trustee N.Y. Pub. Libr., N.Y.C. Police Found. Office: Pfizer Inc 235 E 42d St New York NY 10017-5755*

MCKINNELL, ROBERT GILMORE, zoology, genetics and cell biology educator; b. Springfield, Mo., Aug. 9, 1926; s. William Parks and Mary Catherine (Gilmore) McK.; m. Beverly Walton Kerr, Jan. 24, 1964; children: Nancy Elizabeth, Robert Gilmore, Susan Kerr. AB, U. Mo., 1948; BS, Drury Coll., 1949, DSc (hon.), 1993; PhD, U. Minn., 1959. Research assoc. Inst. Cancer Research, Phila., 1958-61; asst. prof. biology Tulane U., New Orleans, 1961-65, assoc. prof., 1965-69, prof., 1969-70; prof. zoology U. Minn., Mpls., 1970—, prof. genetics and cell biology St. Paul, 1976—, prof. emeritus, 1999—; NATO sr. sci. fellow St. Andrews U., Scotland. Vis. scientist Dow Chem. Co., Freeport, Tex., 1976; guest dept. zoology U. Calif., Berkeley, 1979; Royal Soc. guest rsch. fellow Nuffield dept. pathology John Radcliffe Hosp., Oxford U., 1981-82; NATO vis. scientist Akademisch Ziekenhuis, Ghent, Belgium, 1984; faculty rsch. assoc. Naval Med. Rsch. Inst., Bethesda, Md., 1988; secretariat Third Internat. Conf. Differentiation, 1978; organizer, secretariat 6th Internat. Conf. on Pathology of Reptiles and Amphibians, 2001; mem. amphibian com. Inst. Lab. Animal Resources, NRC, 1970-73, mem. adv. coun., 1974; mem. panel genetic and cellular resources program NIH, 1981-82, spl. study sect., Bethesda, 1990. Author: Cloning: Amphibian Nuclear Transplantation, 1978, Cloning, A Biologist Reports, 1979; sr. editor: Differentiation and Neoplasia, 1980, Cloning: Leben aus der Retorte, 1981, Cloning, of Frogs, Mice, and other Animals, 1985, (with others) The Biological Basis of Cancer, 1998; mem. editl. bd. Differentiation, 1973—; assoc. editor: Gamete Research, 1980-86; mem. bd. advisors Marquis Who's Who; contbr. articles to profl. jours. Served to lt. USNR, 1944-47, 51-53. Recipient Outstanding Teaching award Newcomb Coll., Tulane U., 1970; Disting. Alumni award Drury Coll., 1979, Morse Alumni Teaching award U. Minn., 1992; Research fellow Nat. Cancer Inst., 1957-58, Prince Hitachi award Japanese Found. Cancer Rsch., 1998; Sr. Sci. fellow NATO, 1974 Fellow AAAS, Linnean Soc. (London); mem. Am. Assn. Cancer Rsch. (emeritus), Am. Assn. Cancer Edn. (sr.), Am. Inst. Biol. Scis., Indian Soc. Devel. Biology (lifetime emeritus mem.), Internat. Soc. Differentiation (exec. com., sec.-treas. 1975-92, pres. elect 1992-94, pres. 1994-96), Gown-in-Town Club, Sigma Xi. Home: 2124 Hoyt Ave W Saint Paul MN 55108-1315 Office: U Minn Dept Genetics Cell Bio Saint Paul MN 55108-1095 E-mail: mckin002@tc.umn.edu.

MCKINNEY, ALEXANDER STUART, neurologist, retired; b. N.Y.C., Feb. 3, 1933; s. John McDowell and Katherine Elizabeth (Morse) McK.; m. Carolyn Clifton Braman, Aug. 15, 1958 (div. July 1985); children: James, David, Mark; m. Susan Lowe Childress, July 30, 1985; children: Josephine, Mary, Jennifer. AB, Princeton U., 1955; MD, Columbia U., 1959. Diplomate Am. Bd. Neurology. Intern St. Luke's Hosp., N.Y.C., 1959-60; resident N.Y. Neurological Inst., 1960-63; prof. neurology Emory U., Atlanta, 1965-85; pvt. practice Mountain Med. Assocs., Clyde, N.C., 1985-95; chief of staff Haywood County Hosp., 1989-90. Contbr. articles to profl. jours. Served to lt. comdr. USNR, 1963-65. Fellow Am. Acad. Neurology, Royal Soc. Medicine; mem. N.C. Med. Soc. (vice councillor 1991-94), N.C. Neurol. Soc. (pres. 1992). Avocations: travel, gardening. Home: 9 Charles Wesley Dr Waynesville NC 28786-3066 E-mail: ssmck@primeline.com.

MCKINNEY, CHARLES CECIL, investment company executive; b. Newdale, N.C., Nov. 30, 1931; s. Sherbert Day and Florence Van (Hall) McK.; children— Emry Lynn, Robin Ashley, Marc Jason; m. Suzanne Reeves, Apr. 3, 1988. Student, U. Tenn., 1950-52; BA, U. N.C., 1957. V.p., creative dir. J.T. Howard Advt., 1957-68; chmn. bd., chief exec. officer McKinney & Silver, Raleigh, N.C., 1968-90; chmn., pres., chief exec. officer Onyx Corp., 1991—. Trustee N.C. Symphony, Raleigh, 1983-87; bd. visitors U. N.C., Chapel Hill, 1989-91, Kenan Flagler Sch. Bus., 1985-94; mem. Nat. Trust for Historic Preservation Coun., 2002—. Recipient profl. awards Mem. N.C. Mus. Art, Sphinx Club, Carolina Country Club, Figure Eight Yacht Club. Republican. Home: 1006 Harvey St Raleigh NC 27608-2332

MCKINNEY, CYNTHIA ANN, congresswoman; b. Atlanta, Georgia, Mar. 17, 1955; d. Billy and Leola Mckinney. BA, U. So. Calif., 1978; postgrad., Ga. State U., U. Wis.; Tufts U. Former instr. Clark Atlanta U., Atlanta Met. Coll.; mem. Ga. Ho. of Reps., 1988-92, U.S. Congress from 4th and 11th Ga. dist., 1993—; mem. banking and fin. svcs. com., com. housing and cmty. devel. 103rd Congress from 11th Ga. dist.; mem. internat. rels. com. internat. ops. and human rights 103rd-106th Congress from 11th Ga. dist., mem. nat. security com.; mem. NAACP, congress. black caucus and prog. caucus. Instr. Agnes Scott Coll. Recipient Diplomatic fellow, Spellman Coll., 1984. Office: US Ho of Reps 124 Cannon Bldg Washington DC 20515-1004*

MCKINNEY, DENNIS KEITH, lawyer; b. Ottawa, Ill., May 12, 1952; s. Robert Keith and Delroy Louise (Clayton) McK.; m. Patricia Jean Boyle, Oct. 4, 1986; 1 child, Geoffrey Edward. BS, Ball State U., 1973; JD, Ill. Inst. Tech., 1976. Bar: Ind. 1977, U.S. Dist. Ct. (so. dist.) Ind. 1977, U.S. Supreme Ct. 1993. Appellate dep. Ind. Atty. Gen, Indpls., 1977-78, trial dep., 1978-79, sr. trial dep., 1979-81, chief real estate litigation sect., 1981-94; clk. to Hon. James S. Kirsch Ind. Ct. Appeals, 1994-95; staff atty. Ind. Supreme Ct. Disciplinary Commn., 1995—. Author: Eminent Domain, Practice and Procedure in Indiana, 1991, A Guide to Indiana Easement Law, 1995, A Railroad Ran Through It, 1996; contbg. author: Indiana Real Estate Transactions, 1996; contbr. articles to profl. jours. Active Indpls.-Scarborough Peace Games, 1983-84. Avocations: reading, volleyball, wargaming. Office: Ind Supreme Ct Disciplinary 115 W Washington St Indianapolis IN 46204-3420

MCKINNEY, DONALD LEE, magazine editor; b. Evanston, Ill., July 12, 1923; s. Guy Doane and Cora Redfield (Brenton) McK.; m. Mary Frances Joyce, Dec. 14, 1958; children— Jennifer Joyce, Douglas Guy. AB, U. N.C., 1948. Salesman textbooks John Wiley & Sons, N.Y.C., 1949-52; freelance writer mostly comic books with some short articles and fiction, 1952-54; asst. mng. editor True mag., N.Y.C., 1955-62; editor articles Saturday Evening Post, 1962-69; spl. features editor N.Y. Daily News, 1969-70; mng. editor McCalls mag., N.Y.C., 1969-86; Gonzales prof. journalism U. S.C., Beaufort, 1986-90, prof. emeritus, 1990—. Author: Magazine Writing That Sells, 1994; reporter, book reviewer. Served with USNR, 1943-46. Democrat. Home: 9 Spanish Moss Rd Hilton Head Island SC 29928-4412 *I learned early that it is important to speak up if you think you are being treated unfairly; sometimes it's true, and nobody else will complain if you don't. I also learned that in my business, and probably in most others, it is best to always say what you think. Truth is usually more helpful than any assortment of euphemisms, and it also saves a lot of worry over who you have lied to and just what you've said. Truth is not only the best policy— by all odds it's the easiest to keep track of.*

MCKINNEY, E. KIRK, JR. retired insurance company executive; b. Indpls., Mar. 27, 1923; s. E. Kirk and Irene M. (Hurley) McK.; m. Alice Hollenbeck Greene, June 18, 1949; children: Kirk Ashley, Alan Brooks, Nora Claire McKinney Hiatt, Margot Knight. AB, U. Mich., 1948. Asst. treas. Jefferson Nat. Life Ins. Co., Indpls., 1949-52, asst. to pres., asst. treas., 1952-53, treas., asst. to pres., 1953-55, v.p., treas., 1955-59, pres., 1959-90, chmn. bd., 1970-90, ret., 1990; vice chmn. bd. Somerset Group Inc., 1986-89, ret., 1990. Corp. relations com. U. Mich.; former pres., former chief exec. officer, bd. govs. , treas., bd. dirs., exec. com. Indpls. Mus. Art; past bd. dirs. (hon.) Greater Indpls. Progress Com.; former vice chmn. Indpls.-Marion County Bd. Ethics; former dir. Park Tudor Sch., Community Svc. Coun. Indpls., Hosp. Devel. Corp., Ind. Repertory Theater; past adv. com. Indpls. Retirement Home; former bd. dirs., and pres. Episcopal Community Services, Inc.; former vice chmn., life trustee Nature Conservancy; mem. adv. bd. Ind. U., Purdue U.; active Indpls. Symphony Orch.; former bd. dirs. Ind. Pub. Broadcasting Soc.; bd. dirs. Indpls. Civic Theater, 2001—. Mem. Life Office Mgmt. Assn. (bd. dirs. 1981-83), Am. Council Life Ins. (state v.p. 1973-75, dir., exec. com. 1976-79), Assn. Ind. Life Ins. Cos. (pres. 1969-71), Indpls. C. of C., Sigma Chi. Clubs: Economic of Indpls. (bd. dirs.). Democrat. Home: 250 W 77th St Indianapolis IN 46260-3608 Office: 1330 W 38th St #100 Indianapolis IN 46208-4103 E-mail: ekirkjr@aol.com.

MCKINNEY, FRANCES HATHAWAY, university program administrator; b. Edenton, N.C., Sept. 9, 1950; d. William Sr. and Martha Emma (Blount) H.; m. Luther McKinney Jr., Dec. 20, 1996; children: Terri Denise Wilson, Tyrone Wilbert Wilson. BS, Elizabeth City State U., 1973; EdS, MA, U. Mich., 1977, PhD, 1981. Rsch. assoc. Howard U., Washington, 1980-82; bus. edn. instr. U.S. Dept. Labor, 1982-83; freshman advisor U. Md. Eastern Shore, Princess Anne, 1988—, bus. edn. instr., 1995-96, rep. acting v.p. instnl. advancement, 1993—, Title III coord., 1983—. Mem. adv. team Nat. Title III Performance Staff U.S. Dept. Edn., 1996—; chair univ. needs assessment forum U. Md. Eastern Shore, 1994, mem. planning commn., 1994—. Co-author: (resource book) Regional Directory of Title III Funded Activities, 1987; co-editor (resource book) National Directory of Title III Funded Activities, 1989. Organist Met. United Meth. Ch., Princess Anne, 1989—. Recipient Advising/Mentoring Achievement award Md. Assn. Higher Edn., Annapolis, 1992. Mem. Nat. Assn. Title III Coords. Avocations: singing, playing musical instruments. Home: PO Box 388 Princess Anne MD 21853-0388 Office: U Md Eastern Shore College Backbone Rd Princess Anne MD 21853 E-mail: FHMcKinney@mail.umes.edu.

MCKINNEY, GEORGE HARRIS, JR. training systems analyst; b. Birmingham, Ala., Nov. 23, 1943; s. George Harris and Elizabeth Dickey (Fikes) McK.; m. Lynda Jeanne Ponder, June 26, 1965 (div. Aug. 18, 1992); children: Michael Thomas, Carol Elizabeth; m. Tambri Sue Hillis, Aug. 19, 1992. BS in Polit. Sci., U.S. Air Force Acad., 1965; MS in Psychology, Troy State U., 1977. Commd. 2d lt. U.S. Air Force, 1965, advanced through grades to lt. col., 1981, fighter pilot, 1965-85, ret., 1985; tng. sys. cons. in pvt. practice, Milton, Fla., 1985—. Author tech. reports. Decorated D.F.C. (5), Air medal (26), Purple Heart, Meritorious Svc. medal (3). Mem. Order of Daedalians, USAFA Assn. Grads., Air Force, Assn., Am. Def. Preparedness Assn. Avocations: whitetail deer hunting, fishing. Home: 3101 Chippewa Dr Milton FL 32571-9603

MCKINNEY, JAMES CLAYTON, electronics executive, electrical engineer; b. Charleston, W.Va., June 3, 1940; s. George Clayton and Leona (Adams) McK. BSE.E., W.Va. Inst. Tech., 1963. Mem. staff Sta. WMON, Montgomery, W.Va., 1961-63; stringer AP, Charleston, 1961-63; with FCC, Washington, 1963-87, chief ops. br., 1969-73, chief monitoring div., 1973, chief enforcement div., 1974, dep. chief Field Ops. Bur., 1974-80, chief Field Ops. Bur., 1980-81, chief Pvt. Radio Bur., 1981-83, chief Mass Media Bur., 1983-87; dep. asst. to Pres., dir. White House Mil. Office Washington, 1987-89; chmn. Advanced TV Systems Com., 1989-96; CEO Model HDTV Sta. Project, Inc., 1996-97. Chmn. U.S. del. UN Conf. on Radio, Geneva, 1986.; mem. U.S. Dels., Geneva, 1978-79, Can., 1984, Italy, 1985, Mexico, 1986, S.Am., 1986, Fed. Republic Germany, 1990; mem. presdl. dels., NATO, UN, Mexico, USSR, Can., Eng., Finland, Econ. Summit, 1987-88; U.S. Spokesman High Definition TV Conf., Geneva, 1989. Author: (with Eliot Maxwell) Future of Electronic Information Handling at the FCC— Blue Print for the 80's, 1980; (with G.A. Fehlner) Direct Broadcast Satellites in the United States, 1985; New Look at AM Radio, 1986, HDTV Approaches the End Game, 1991. Vice chmn. Montreux Medal Award Com., 1990-95; chmn. High Definition TV World Conf., 1990-93; chmn. strategic planning group for Internat. Consultative Com. for Radio, Dept. State, 1990-91; bd. dirs. Bowler Found., 1990-95, PICA Found., Inc., 1996-97, HDTV Sta. Project, Inc., 1996-97. Recipient Outstanding Fed. Exec. award FCC, 1979, 80, 82, 83, 85, 86; Presdl. Rank award for disting. exec. svc., 1985, Gold medal for disting. fed. svc., 1987, TV Engring. Achievement award, 1992, NAB award of honor, 1996, Broadcast Pioneers' Disting. Svc. award, 1996; W.Va. Broadcasters Disting. West Virginian, 1997. Fellow Radio Club Am., Soc. Broadcast Engrs. (sr.), Broadcast Pioneers, Soc. Motion Picture and TV Engrs. (presdl. proclamation 1991); mem. Fed. Exec. Assn., Cosmos Club of Washington. Episcopalian. Home: 10055 Heather Lake Ct W Jacksonville FL 32256-3595

MCKINNEY, JAMES DEVAINE, JR. lawyer; b. Muscatine, Iowa, Dec. 13, 1931; s. James D. and Jeffie Lillian (Eblen) McK.; m. Betty A. Guy, June 10, 1966; children: James D. III, Cynthia Dee, Jennifer Jean. BA, U. Iowa, 1956, LLB, 1958. Bar: Iowa 1958, D.C. 1960, U.S. Ct. Appeals (D.C. cir.) 1961, U.S. Supreme Ct. 1962. Trial atty. FPC, Washington, 1958-60; assoc. Law Offices Charles E. McGee, 1960-65, Ross, Marsh & Foster, Washington, 1965-68, ptnr., 1968—. Mem. ABA, D.C. Bar Assn., Energy Bar Assn. (exec. com. 1979-82), Met. Club, Washington Golf and Country Club. Home: 6105 Lee Hwy Arlington VA 22205-2110 Office: Ross Marsh & Foster 2001 L St NW Washington DC 20036-4910 E-mail: jmckinney@rossmarshfoster.com.

MCKINNEY, JANE-ALLEN, artist and educator; b. Owensboro, Ky., Jan. 8, 1952; d. William Holland and Jane Wilhoit (Moore) McK. BA, Scarritt Coll., Nashville, 1974; MA, Vanderbilt U., 1977; MFA, Memphis Coll. of Art, 1993. Grad. asst. dept. art Peabody Coll. for Tchrs., Vanderbilt U., Nashville, 1975-76; tchr. Smyrna (Tenn.) Comprehensive Vocat. Ctr., 1977-78; pres., bd. dirs. Jane Allen Flighton Artworks Inc., Nashville, 1978—; jeweler Wright's Jewelry Store, Clarksville, Tenn., 1982; tchr. art Belmont U., Nashville, 1984-88, Met. Centennial Park Art Ctr., Nashville, 1988-91, Cheekwood Mus. of Art, Nashville, 1990-94, Nossi Coll. of Art, Nashville, 1991-94, Western Ky. U., Bowling Green, 1991-94. Ednl. cons. fine art Nossi Coll. Art, Nashville, 1993—; artist for Women of Achievement awards, sculptures and jewelry YWCA, Nashville, 1992—; artist for Bus. Award Sculpture, C. of C., Nashville, 1990. One and two person shows include Cheekwood Mus. Art, 1981, 93, Owensboro Mus. Fine Art, 1992, Western Ky. U., 1992-94, Belmont U., 1984, others; exhibited in group shows, including Watkins Art Inst., Nashville, 1991, Western Ky. U., 1992, Parthenon, Nashville, 1992, Owensboro Mus. Art, 1993, Tenn. Performing Arts Ctr., 1995; invitational and juried exhibits include Sculptors of Mid. Tenn. Arts in the Airport, Nashville, 1996, Nat. Coun. on the Edn. of Ceramics Arts, Rochester, N.Y., 1996, Ceramic Exhibn. Tenn. State U., 1996, and numerous others; represented in permanent collections including Chattanooga's Visitors Ctr., IBM, Bapt. Hosp., Nations Bank of Tenn., Mass. Pub. Libr., First Am. Bank Corp., Andrew Jackson Hermitage Mus., Tenn. State U., also numerous pvt. collections. Adv. bd. Belmont U., Nashville, 1984—, Nossi Coll. Art, 1993—; mem edn. com. Nat. Mus. of Women in the Arts, Tenn., 1992—; artist for fundraising sculpture Arthritis Found., Nashville, 1989-90; vol. singer VA Hosp., Nashville, 1989—; bd. dirs. Visual Arts Alliance Nashville, 1996; vol. soloist Vet.'s Hosp., 1991-96; artist for ann. fundraiser YWCA, 1993-96; mem. So. Regional Honors Coun. Recipient Best Tchr. award Nossi Coll. Art, 1992-93; grantee City of Chattanooga Welcome Ctr., 1993, Memphis Arts Festival Spl. Projects, 1994, 96. Mem. AAUW, Assn. of Visual Artists, Soc. of N.Am. Goldsmiths, Visual Artists Alliance of Nashville, Nat. Art Edn. Assn., Internat. Sculpture Ctr., Nat. Coun. on Edn. of the Ceramic Arts, Tenn. Assn. of Craft Artists, Coll. Art Assn. Avocations: boating, running, singing, dancing, hiking. Home: PO Box 120454 Nashville TN 37212-0454

MCKINNEY, JANET KAY, law librarian; b. Kansas City, Mo., Feb. 15, 1959; d. Charles Durward and Helen Jean (Bost) Freeman; m. Larry Emmett McKinney, July 11, 1981. BA, Avila Coll., 1981; MA in Libr. Sci., U. Mo., 1989; MA in Religious Studies, Ctrl. Bapt. Theol. Sem., 1997. Circulation libr. Midwestern Bapt. Theol. Sem., Kansas City, 1981-84, acquisitions libr., 1984-85, reference libr., 1985-90; environ. divsn. libr. Black & Veatch, 1990-91; dir. collection resources U. Mo. Leon E. Bloch Law Libr., 1991-2000; computer svcs. libr. Shook, Hardy & Bacon, 2000—. Mem. ALA, Am. Assn. Law Librs. (com. on rels. with info. vendors 1994-96, editl bd. Tech. Svcs. Law Libr. 1994-96, tech. svcs. spl. interest sect. chair 1999-2000, treas pvt. law librs. spl. interest sect. 2001—, index to fgn. legal periodicals adv. com. 2001—), Mid-Am. Assn. Law Librs. (newsletter adv. mgr. 1993-94, treas. 1997-99), Southwestern Assn. Law Librs., N.Am. Serials Interest Group, Spl. Librs. Assn. (chpt. employment com. chmn. 1990-91, chpt. treas. 1991-94, chpt. pres. 1995-96), Kansas City Assn. Law Librs. (v.p., pres. 2000). Office: Shook Hardy & Bacon LLP 1200 Main St Kansas City MO 64105 E-mail: jmckinney@shb.com.

MCKINNEY, JERRY WAYNE, journalist; b. Esperanza, Tex., Sept. 17, 1937; s. Lee Parker McKinney and Elsie Margaret Haass; m. Violet Elizabeth Davenport, Oct. 1959 (div. Oct. 1969); m. Valda Kay Cooper, Feb. 12, 1972; children: Kathleen Low, Ellen. Announcer, comml. mgr. Sta. KVOU Radio, Uvalde, Tex., 1959-62; announcer Sta. K-SIX Radio, Corpus Christi, 1962-66; reporter, editor Corpus Christi Caller-Times, 1966-74; polit. editor Albuquerque Tribune, 1974-79; mgr. pub. rels. Mountain Bell Telephone, Albuquerque, 1979-80; press sec. Congressman Joe Skeen Washington, 1980-85; Tokyo bur. chief Voice of Am., 1993-95, corr., 1985-93, 95-99, mng. editor news divsn., 1999—2001, ret., 2001; press sec. Congressman Joe Skeen, 2001—02; polit. cons., 2002—. Mem. exec. com. Rep. Party N.Mex., Albuquerque, 1979-80; mem. exec. com. Chaparral chpt. Girl Scouts Am., Corpus Christi, 1972-74. With USN, 1955-59. Mem. Soc. Profl. Journalists (pres. N.Mex. profl. chpt., dep. regional dir. region 9), Corpus Christi Press Club (pres. 1971-72), Overseas Press Club Am., Fgn. Corr. Club Japan (hon. mem., fgn. corr.). Avocations: reading, travel.

MCKINNEY, JOHN ADAMS, JR. lawyer; b. Washington, Mar. 10, 1948; s. John A. and Cleo G. (Turner) McK.; m. Carol A. Cowen, Dec. 22, 1970; children: John III, Thomas. BA, Principia Coll., 1970; JD, Coll. William and Mary, 1973. Bar: N.J. 1973. Assoc. Mason, Griffin & Pierson, Princeton, N.J., 1973-77; gen. atty. Nabisco, Inc., East Hanover, 1977-79; asst. counsel Republic Steel Corp., Cleve., 1979-84; atty. and sr. atty. AT&T, Berkeley Heights, N.J., 1984-90; ptnr. McCarter & English LLP, Newark, 1990—. Adj. prof. Sch. of Law, Seton Hall U., 1997—. Co-editor: CERCLA Enforcement, 1996. Mem. ABA (vice-chair sect. natural resources energy and environ. law solid and hazardous waste com. 1990-98, chair, teleconf. programs 1994-97), N.J. Bar Assn. (dir. environ. law sect. 1992-96, chair 1996-97), bd. trustees Hackettstown, N.J. Free Public Library, 1998—. Office: McCarter & English 4 Gateway Ctr 100 Mulberry St Newark NJ 07102-4056

MCKINNEY, JOHN GAGE, purchasing agent, writer; b. Oceanside, Calif., Apr. 21, 1951; s. Verlon David and Jacqueline Yvonne (Hughes) McK.; m. Linda Christine Brown, Dec. 29, 1974 (div. June 1979); m. Ilka Maria Weber, Aug. 1, 1986. BA in English, U. Calif., Berkeley, 1973; MA in English, U. Calif., Irvine, 1975. Gen. mgr., v.p. MacBeth Hardwood Co., L.A., 1975-81; pres. McKinney Hardwood Co., Mountain View, Calif., 1981-83; purchasing agt. Lockheed Missiles and Space Co., Sunnyvale, 1983-95; purchasing mgr. Recognition Sys., Inc., Campbell, 1995—. Author: Hardwood People, 1981, A High and Holy Place: A Mining Camp Church at New Alamader, 1997, When Miners Sang, 2001; editor: Four Mining Engineers, 1996. Recipient Lit. Arts award Montalvo Found., Saratoga, Calif., 1987, Calif. Essay award Calif. Pioneers, San Jose, 1991. Mem. Phi Beta Kappa. Episcopalian. E-mail: gage_mckinney@irco.com.

MCKINNEY, JOSEPH ARTHUR, economist, educator; b. Marion, N.C., May 21, 1943; s. Henry Clay and Mary Effie (Greene) McK.; children: Laura Helen, David Johnmichael. BA in Econs., Berea Coll., 1965; MA in Econs., Mich. State U., 1967, PhD in Econs., 1970. Asst. prof. U. Va., Charlottesville, 1970-76; exchange prof. Seinan Gakuin U., Fukuoka, Japan, 1977-78; prof. Baylor U., Waco, Tex., 1976—. Co-dir., master Internat. Mgmt. Program, Baylor, U., Waco, 1978-89; dir. rsch. Region N. Am. Project, Baylor U., Waco, 1988—. Co-editor: (books) Readings in International Economic Relations, 1989, Region North America, 1990, Implications of North American Free Trade Region: Multidisciplinary Perspectives, 1992; contbr. articles to profl. jours. Recipient Woodrow Wilson Fellowship, Woodrow Wilson Found., Princeton, N.J., 1965. Mem. Am. Econs. Assn., Acad. Internat. Bus., Internat. Trade and Fin. Assn., Assn. of Christian Economists, Assn. for Canadian Studies in U.S., Assn. Japanese Bus. Studies, Japan-Am. Soc. of Dallas. Republican. Baptist. Avocations: reading, jogging. Home: 9515 Stony Point Dr Waco TX 76712-3249 Office: Baylor U PO Box 98003 Waco TX 76798-8003

MCKINNEY, JUDSON THAD, broadcast executive; b. Sacramento, Aug. 21, 1941; s. Judson Bartlet and Mildred Eoline (Taylor) McK. Student, Sacramento State U., 1959-61, Western Bapt. Bible Coll., 1961-62, Am. River Coll., 1962-63. Prodn. dir. Sta. KEBR, Sacramento, 1962-65; prodn. dir. Sta. KEAR, Merced, Calif., 1965-68; sta. mgr. Sta. KAMB, 1968-75, Sta. KEAR, San Francisco, 1975-78, 79-88, WFME, Newark, 1978; western regional mgr. Family Stas. Inc., 1988—. Pres. Abounding Love Ministries, 2000—. Chmn. 1st. Bapt. Ch. San Francisco, 1985—91; recording engr. 1st Bapt. Ch. Los Altos (Calif.). Mem. Nat. Religious Broadcasters., Nat. Assn. Evangs., Gideons. Republican. Baptist. Note, exact names of churches are not listed unless an office is held therein, per style. Office: Family Stations Inc 290 Hegenberger Rd Oakland CA 94621-1436

MCKINNEY, LARRY, religious organization administrator; m. Debra Ann Dillworth; 2 children. BS in Bible, Phila. Coll. Bible, Langhorne, Pa., 1972; MA in Ednl. Ministries, Wheaton (Ill.) Coll., 1974; EdD in Ednl. Adminstrn., Temple U., 1986. Ordained to ministry Evang. Free Ch., 1974. Former pastor local chs., N.J., Pa.; exec. dir. Fay-West Youth for Christ, Uniontown, Pa., 1972-73, 74-80; dean students, v.p. for student devel. Phila. Coll. Bible, 1980-93; pres. Providence Coll. and Sem., 1993—, Assn. Can. Bible Colls., 1994—. Former instr. numerous grad. and postgrad. ednl.-related fields; frequent spkr. for chs., confs., seminars; former mem. or chmn. 6 evaluation teams Accrediting Assn. Bible Colls.; mem. coun. Evang. Fellowship Can. Contbr. numerous articles to mags. and ednl. jours. Avocations: reading, history, running, weightlifting, watching sports. Office: Providence Coll & Sem Otterburne MB Canada R0D 1G0

MCKINNEY, LARRY J. federal judge; b. South Bend, Ind., July 4, 1944; s. Lawrence E. and Helen (Byers) McK.; m. Carole Jean Marie Lyon, Aug. 19, 1966; children: Joshua E., Andrew G. BA, MacMurray Coll., Jacksonville, Ill., 1966; JD, Ind. U., 1969. Bar: Ind. 1970, U.S. Dist. Ct. (so. dist.) Ind. 1970. Law clk. to atty. gen. State of Ind., Indpls., 1969-70, dep. atty. gen., 1970-71; ptnr. Rodgers and McKinney, Edinburgh, Ind., 1971-75, James F.T. Sargent, Greenwood, 1975-79; judge Johnson County Cir. Ct., Franklin, 1979-87, U.S. Dist. Ct. (so. dist.) Ind., Indpls., 1987—, chief judge, 2001—. Presbyterian. Avocations: reading, jogging. Office: US Dist Ct 204 US Courthouse 46 E Ohio St Indianapolis IN 46204-1903

MCKINNEY, LOUISE CHESTNUT, volunteer; b. Waterbury, Conn., Apr. 5, 1967; d. Thomas Lee and Alice Phoenix (McLean) McK. BFA, U. Conn., 1990; MS in Art History, Ctrl. Conn. State U., New Britain, 1995. Mail desk previewer Hartford Ins. Co., Southington, Conn., 1990-91; fashions customer svc. assoc. K-Mart, 1992-93; sales assoc. Express, Meriden, Conn., 1994-95; fashions customer svc. assoc. J.C. Penney, 1995-96; invoice processor Timex, Waterbury, Conn., 1996; file processor First Union, 1996—; ATM stager/processor Webster Bank, Bristol, Conn., 1998-99; fashion assoc. TJ Maxx, Southington, 2001—; owner Chessis Creations, 2001—. Graphics intern Ulsaker Studio, New Britain, 1989; grad. asst. Ctrl. Conn. State U., New Britain, 1992. Mus. vol. Mattatuck Mus., Waterbury, 1995, Barnes Mus., Southington, 1995-96. Mem. NAACP. Democrat. Methodist. Avocations: reading, writing, crafts, music, visiting museums.

MCKINNEY, MARK ALAN, independent businessman, musician; b. Memphis, July 1, 1972; s. Ronald Lee and Peggy Faye McKinney. B. English/Creative Writing, U. Memphis, 1995. Salesperson B&M Printing, Memphis, 1996—, CVRM Ent., Memphis, 2001—; ptnr., co-founder MAD-JACK Records, 1998—. Musician: (full length recording) Rest of Our Days, 1998, Dogsbody Factotum, 2000; prodr.: (full length recording) Day Late and a Dollar Short, 1999. Advisor Memphis & Shelby County Music Commn. Adv. Bd., Memphis, 2001. Mem.: NARAS (voting member).

MCKINNEY, MICHAEL EUGENE, broadcast technician; b. Waco, Tex., Jan. 9, 1958; s. Eugene Calvin and Treysa McK. BA, U. Tex., 1980, BS, 1981. Photographer Lackland Air Force Base, San Antonio, 1982-85; master control operator Sta. KRRT-TV, 1985-86, from film editor to film dir., 1986-93, master control supr., 1993-95; master control operator Sta. KTXA-TV, Dallas, 1995-96; master control supr. Sta. WUPA-TV, Atlanta, 1996—. Office: WUPA-TV 2700 NE Expressway Bldg A Atlanta GA 30345

MC KINNEY, MICHAEL WHITNEY, trade association executive; b. San Angelo, Tex., Aug. 23, 1946; s. Wallace Luster and Mitzi Randolph (Broome) McK.; m. Martha LaNan Hooker, Feb. 24, 1973; children: Wallace Blake, Lauren Brooke. BA in Govt., U. Tex., Austin, 1973. Adminstrv. asst. to lt. gov. State of Tex., Austin, 1968-69, adminstrv. asst. to gov., 1969-73; asst. to dir. Tex. Water Quality Bd., 1973-76; chief of staff Tex. Alcoholic Beverage Commn., 1976-83; v.p. for industry affairs Wholesale Beer Distbrs., Tex., 1984-88, exec. v.p., chief exec. officer, 1989—. Bd. govs. Keep Tex. Beautiful, 1997—98; mem. Travis County Zoo Task Force, 1986, Senate Com. on Fees and Grants, 1982—83; bd. dirs. Friends of Gov.'s Mansion, 1993—97, Bob Bullock Tex. State History Mus. Found., 2002—. Recipient Bert Ford award Tex. Alcholic Beverage Commn., 1996, Pres. award for legis. excellence Nat. Beer Wholesalers Assn., 1998. Mem.: Nat. Wholesale Beer Assn. Execs. (pres. 2001—02), Austin Assembly, Sam. Houston Soc., Knights of the Symphony, Austin Club (bd. dirs. 1989—, exec. com. 1994—, Mem. of Yr. 1994), Austin Country Club, Masons (32 deg., K.T.), Phi Kappa Psi. Home: 1708 Intervail Dr Austin TX 78746-7630 Office: 823 Congress Ave Ste 1313 Austin TX 78701-2434

MCKINNEY, MONICA LORRAINE, media/communications company executive; b. San Diego, June 22; d. Ricardo John and Jeannette Elizabeth (Mark) McK. BBA in Mgmt., U. Miami, 1984. Computer instr., operator ADIA, Inc., San Diego and Atlanta, 1985-90; internat. tng. and devel. coord. Coca-Cola Co., Atlanta, 1990-92; pres. film, video, print prodn., telecom. software devel. MLM Comms., Inc., Atlanta, Las Vegas, L.A., 1990—. Graphic designer promotional campaign material, 1984 (plaque 1985); writer, prodr., dir. Drug's In The Work Place, 1992 (various awards 1992); prodr., dir. nat. radio spl. Crack Down, 1994 (trophy 1995, The Communicator award 1997, The Videographer award 1998, Silver Telly award 1998, Outstanding People of the 20th Century medal 1999); creator, host, prodr. TV series CELEBS, 1995; actress various TV and film feature prodns.; contbg. author: Daydreams, 2000. Vol. drug prevention program Nat. Ctr. Tng. and Devel., Miami, 1985; prodr. AIDS fund concerts, Atlanta, 1993; internat. media liaison 25th Anniversary Martin Luther King Jr. Ctr., Atlanta, 1992. Mem. NAFE, Internat. TV Assn. (chair exec. com. 1990—, VidFest Bumper award 1991), Am. Women in Radio and TV (chair 1992-93), Small Bus. Adminstrn./NSET (dir. comms. 1996—, grant 1995), T.R.E.T.ment, Inc. (pub. rels. chair 1995—, bd. dirs., cert. 1997), Woman Inc. Democrat. Avocations: horseback riding, photography, print and runway modeling. Office: MLM Comms Inc 23052 Alicia Pkwy Ste H256 Mission Viejo CA 92692 E-mail: monica@mlmideas.com.

MCKINNEY, OWEN MICHAEL, security executive, consultant; b. Jeffersonville, Ind., Mar. 9, 1950; s. Owen Howard and Frances Marie (Hall) McK.; m. Janice Elaine Wilson, Sept. 2, 1972; 1 child, Sean Michael. BS in Police Adminstrn., U. Louisville, 1976; AA, SUNY, Albany, 1978; MS in Adminstrn. of Justice, U. Louisville, 1978; diploma in pastoral ministries, So. Bapt. Conv., 1980; MAT in Secondary Edn., U. Louisville, 1987; cert., Ctr. Ednl. Leadership, 1995, Leadership Ky., 1996; MEd in Instrnl. Tech., U. Louisville, 2002. Cert. 5-12 tchr., learning disabilities, behavior disorders, physically handicapped, community-based edn., learning strategies, social skills, history, geography, polit. sci., sociology, Ky. Probation and parole officer Commonwealth of Ky., Louisville, 1978; security mgr. First Nat. Tower John W. Galbreath & Co., 1981-82; v.p. Safety Arms Security & Police Equipment Co., Portsmouth, Va., 1980; area mgr. CPP Security Svc., Norfolk, 1979-80, Louisville, 1982-83; tchr. Jefferson County Pub. Schs., 1985-88, spl. edn. tchr., 1988—98; pres. Cambridge Cons Inc, 1995—. Owner Owen McKinney Detective Agency, Louisville, 1973-79, The McKinney Agency, Louisville, 1983-87; commr. City of Richlawn, Ky., 1990-92; presenter in field. Editor, writer, publisher The Renaissance Magazine, 1979-81; editor, publisher: Security Gazette, 1982, The Private Investigator, 1983-84, Private Security Report, 1983; editor, writer: (newspaper) Richlawn Gazette, 1990, 91; contbr. articles to profl. jours. Mem. George Bush for Pres., Jefferson County, 1988, Rebecca Jackson for Jefferson County Clerk, 1989, Owen M. McKinney for City Comsnr., Richlawn, 1989, Al Brown for U.S. Congress, 3d congl. dist., Louisville, 1990, Vote for the Library Tax campaign, Jefferson County, 1992; Rep. del. 3d congl. dist. meeting 32d Legis. Dist., 1990, del. Rep. State Conv. 32nd legis. dist. chmn. 1993-94; hon. amb. labor Sec. Labor, Ky. Staff sgt. U.S. Army, 1969-73, Vietnam, mem. USAR, 1977-85, hon. air assault soldier. Recipient Commendation medal U.S. Army, 1971, cert. of appreciation Pres. of U.S., 1973, Outstanding Staff award JCPS, 1991, 92, 93, 94, 95, 96, 97, 98, Minerva award U. Louisville, 1993, Disting. Citizen award Mayor City Louisville, Cold War Cert. of Recognition Sec. of Def., U.S., 2000; named to Hon. Order Ky. Cols., sr. fellow U. Louisville Soc., numerous others; named Duke of Paducah Mayor City of Paducah, Ky.; named hon. citizen and given key to City of Mayfield, Ky. Mem. VFW (life), Internat. Assn. Profl. Security Cons., Assn. U.S. Army (life), Am. Soc. Indsl. Security (cert. protection profl. 1985-, chmn. seminar com. Louisville chpt. 1983-84, cert. appreciation Louisville chpt. 1984, Quarter Century Club award 2001), Coun. Exceptional Children (chpt. gen. bd. 1988-89, v.p. 1989-90, pres. elect 1990-91, chpt. pres. 1991-92, 97-98, state gen. bd. 1991-92, chpt. past pres. 1992-93, 98—, state v.p. 1993-94, state pres.-elect 1994-95, state pres. 1995-96, 96-97, state past pres. 1997-98, Svc. award 1990, cert. merit Ky. Fedn. 1990, 98, cert. Outstanding Svc. 1991-92, outstanding mem. of yr. award 1993, 98, awarded profl. recognized spl. educator), Acad. Security Educators and Trainers, Nat. Crime Prevention Alumni Assn., Internat. Crime Prevention Through Environ. Design, Commonwealth Atty.'s Citizen Adv. Coun., DeMolay Alumni Assn. (life, Rep. DeMolay award 1976, 25 Yr. mem. award 1991), U. Louisville Alumni Assn. (exec. com. 1976—), Am. Mensa Soc., elected to chap. exec. com., 1998-99, Am. Legion, York Rite, Scottish Rite, USCG Aux., The Wild Geese (hon.), Masons (past master, grand lodge com.), Order of Eastern Star, Grotto, KP (chancellor comdr. 1994, Internat. Svc. award 1993), Rosicrucian Order, Royal Order Scotland (life), Societas Rosicruciana in Civitatibus Foederatis VII (life), Shrine, Golden Key Hon. Soc. (life), Internat. High 12 (Internat. Svc. award 1994, chpt. 1st v.p. 1996, chpt. pres. 1997), Alpha Phi Sigma (nat. criminal justice hon. soc. (life), Phi Delta Kappa (chpt. sec. 1992-93, v.p. 1993-94, Mem. Recognition Cert. 1995). Avocations: reading, tennis, weight lifting, photography, master scuba diver. Home: 7400 Moredale Rd Louisville KY 40222-4139 Office: Cambridge Cons Inc PO Box 22841 Louisville KY 40252 Business E-Mail: camconinc@yahoo.com.

MCKINNEY, RONALD W. lawyer; b. Greenville, S.C., Mar. 23, 1948; s. William R. and Doris (Chadwick) McK.; m. Kathleen Crum, Jan. 13, 1979; children: William, Kathleen. BA, Furman U., 1970; MA, U. N.C., 1973; JD, U. S.C., 1978. Bar: S.C. 1978. Atty. S.C. Consumer Advocate's Office, Columbia, 1978-81; ptnr. Duggan, Reese & McKinney, Greer, S.C., 1981-95; city atty. City of Greenville, 1995—, interim city mgr., 2000. Chair Greenville County Transportation Com., 1994-95. Mem. ABA, S.C. Bar Assn., Internat. Mcpl. Lawyers Assn., S.C. Mcpl. Attys. Assn. (pres. 1997). Methodist. Avocations: travel, reading. Office: City of Greenville PO Box 2207 Greenville SC 29602-2207 E-mail: mckinnr@greatergreenville.com.

MCKINNEY, ROSEMARY KASUL, social work educator; b. Chgo., Oct. 19, 1941; d. Vincent J. Therese (DeKreon) Kasul; m. Neal Edward McKinney, Nov. 11, 1962 (div. Jan. 1992); children: Michael, Kevin. B in Social Work, George Williams Coll., 1978, MSW, 1980. Lic. clin. social worker, Ill.; cert. sr. addiction counselor, eating disorders counselor, gerontol. counselor. Coord. inpatient program The Abbey, Winfield, Ill., 1980-82; counselor Parkside Med. Svcs., 1982-83, coord. tng. Park Ridge, Ill., 1983-86; clin. social worker Pape & Assocs., Wheaton, 1986-88; prof. Coll. of Du Page, Glen Ellyn, 1988—; counseling and cons. McKinney, Blair and Assocs., Wheaton, 1995—. Co-tchr. nat. symposium Internat. Assn. Eating Disorder Profls., 1994, 95, 96, 97; presenter Midwest NOHSE conf. 1995; presenter in field. Mem. NASW, Am. Soc. on Aging, Addiction Counselor Tng. Program Dirs. Home: 1240 Reading Ct Wheaton IL 60187-7710 Office: Coll of DuPage 22D And Lambert Glen Ellyn IL 60137

MCKINNEY, ROSS ERWIN, civil engineering educator; b. San Antonio, Aug. 2, 1926; s. Roy Earl and Beatrice (Saylor) McK.; m. Margaret McKinney Curtis, June 21, 1952; children: Ross Erwin, Margaret E., William S., Susanne C. BA, BSCE, So. Meth. U., 1948; SM, MIT, 1949, ScD, 1951. San. scientist S.W. Found. for Research and Edn., San Antonio, 1951-53; asst. prof. MIT, 1953-58, assoc. prof., 1958-60; prof. U. Kans., 1960-63, chmn. dept. civil engring., 1963-66, Parker prof. civil engring., 1966-76, N.T. Veatch prof. environ. engring., 1976-93, prof. emeritus, 1993—. Adj. prof. Tongji U., Shanghai, Peoples Rep. China, 1985; v.p. Rolf Eliassen Assocs., Winchester, Mass., 1954-60; pres. Environ. Pollution Control Services, Lawrence, Kans., 1969-73; adj. prof. environ. engring. Duke U., 1997—. Author: Microbiology for Sanitary Engineers, 1962; Editor: Nat. Conf. on Solid Waste Research, 1964, 2d Internat. Symposium for Waste Treatment Lagoons, 1970. Mem. Cambridge (Mass.) Water Bd., 1953-59, Lawrence-Douglas County Health Bd., 1969-76, Kans. Water Quality Adv. Council, 1965-76, Kans. Solid Waste Adv. Council, 1970-76, Kans. Environ. Adv. Bd., 1976-85. Served with USNR, 1943-46. Recipient Harrison P. Eddy award, 1962, Rudolph Hering award, Water Pollution Control Fedn., 1964, U.S. Presdl. Commendation 1971, Environ. Quality award, EPA Region VII, 1979, Chancellors Tchg. award, U. Kans., 1986, Lifetime Achievement award, Environmental-Water Resources Inst. Am. Soc. Civil Engrs., 2001. Mem.: AAAS, NAE, ASCE (hon. Lifetime Achievement award 2001), Am. Soc. Microbiologists, Am. Chem. Soc., Water Pollution Control Fedn. (Thomas R. Camp medal 1982), Am. Water Works Assn., Kans. Water Pollution Control Assn. (hon. Gordon M. Fair medal 1991), Tau Beta Pi, Chi Epsilon, Kappa Mu Epsilon, Sigma Tau, Sigma Xi. Achievements include patent for water treatment process. Home: 3100 Annandale Rd Durham NC 27705-5494 E-mail: remck@mindspring.com.

MCKINNEY, RUSSELL RAYMOND, lawyer; b. Visalia, Calif., Sept. 26, 1942; s. Russell R. and Alice (McKerral) McK.; m. Sharon K. McKinney, Aug. 22, 1964; children: Kristin, Russell L. BA, Stanford U., 1964; JD, U. Calif., 1967; postgrad., U.S. Naval War Coll., 1995. Pvt. practice, Visalia, Calif., 1968—. Capt. JAGC, USNR, 1981—. Paul Harris fellow Rotary Internat. Office: 220 S Mooney Blvd Visalia CA 93291-4512

MCKINNEY, SALLY VITKUS, state official; b. Muncie, Ind., Aug. 6, 1944; d. Robert Brookins and Mary (Mann) Gooden; m. Alan George Vitkus (div. Jan. 1979); m. James Larry McKinney, Feb. 1, 1986. AA, William Woods U., 1964; BS, U. Ariz., 1966; postgrad., U. Nev., Las Vegas, 1966-68. Tchr. Las Vegas Day Sch., 1972—76; salesperson Globe Realty, Las Vegas, 1976—79; owner, pres. Realty West, 1979—96; chief investigator State of Nev. Real Estate Divsn., 1996—2000; broker McKinney Realty, 2000—; corp. broker, dir. bus. and devel. Real Estate Temps. Rec. sec. Clark County Rep. Cen. Com., Las Vegas, 1982, 1st vice chmn., 1985; vice chmn. Nev. Rep. com., 1986, chmn., 1987-88; mem. Assistance League Las Vegas; state chmn. Nev. Rep. Party. Recipient award Nat. Assn. Home Builders, 1981, 82, 83. Mem. Nat. Assn. Realtors, Las Vegas Bd. Realtors, Greater Las Vegas C. of C., Gen. Fedn. Womens Clubs (nominee Outstanding Young Woman Am. 1979, exec. bd. 1980-82), Jr. League Las Vegas, Mesquite Club (chmn. pub. affairs com. 1986-87, past pres., secret witness exec. bd. 1994-96, vice chmn.). Presbyterian. Avocations: bridge, fly fishing. Home: 460 Golden State St Henderson NV 89012-2509

MCKINNEY, SHANNON J. retired secondary school educator; b. Huntingburg, Ind., Sept. 12, 1942; d. Lester Maxey and Clarice V. Corn; m. David E. McKinney, May 18, 1963; children: David E. Jr., Karla K. BS, Oakland City U., 1965; MA, U. Evansville, 1971. Tchr. Plaineville (Ind.) H.S., 1965—66, Barr-Reeve H.S., Montgomery, 1966—67, Dale (Ind.) H.S., 1968—69, East Gibson Sch. Corp., Oakland City, 1969—2001; ret., 2001. Author: (poetry) Apple Skins, 2001, (novels) Fences, 2002; contbr. articles, short story to profl. publs. Sec., bldg. rep., v.p. East Gibson Classroom Tchr.'s Assn., Oakland City. Recipient Hon. Mention, Rising Sun Fund Poetry Competition, 2002. Mem.: NEA, Ind. State Tchr.'s Assn. Avocations: gardening, writing, camping, travel, photography. Home: 1542 E Arthur Church Rd Winslow IN 47598

MCKINNEY, WILLIAM DOUTHITT, JR. sales and engineering company executive; b. Memphis, Sept. 2, 1955; s. William Douthitt Sr. and Virginia (Grisham) McK. BBA, U. Miss., 1978. CLU. Bus. fin. acct. exec. Met. Life Ins. Co., Memphis, 1978-79; def. back Dallas Cowboys Football, 1979-80, Carloss Well Supply Co., Memphis, 1980-82, San Francisco 49ers, 1981; pres. McKinney and Assocs., Collierville, Tenn., 1981—; sales and engring. mgr. Bryan Custom Plastics, 1991-92; sales mgr. Dresden Products, 1993-94, No. Techs., 1995-99, Menasha Packaging Corp., 2000—01. Mem. Statue of Liberty-Ellis Island Centennial Commn., Presdl. Innercir., 1991—. Recipient Outstanding Young Men of Am. award U.S. Jaycees and Disting. Ams. Bd. Advisors, 1985, A Thousand Points of Light Vol. award U.S. Pres. George Bush, 1989, Internat. Man of Yr. award Internat. Ctr. Bd. Advisors of Cambridge, Eng., 1991-92, Admired Man of Decade award Am. Inst. Humanity, Shield award of Valor, Twentieth Century award for Achievement Internat. Ctr., Cambridge, Eng.; named Man of Achievement Internat. Ctr., Cambridge. Mem. Mfrs. Agts. Nat. Assn., United Assn. Mfrs. Reps., Am. Mktg. Assn., Am. Inst. Chem. Engrs., Soc. Plastic Engrs., Am. Water Ski Assn., U. Miss. Alumni Assn., Presdl. Inner Circle, Dallas Cowboys Alumni Assn., Nat. Football Found. and Coll. Hall of Fame, Phi Kappa Psi, Delta Sigma Pi, Pi Sigma Epsilon. Republican. Presbyterian. Avocations: water skiing (U.S. team 1984-85), racquetball, football, collecting antiques. Home and Office: McKinney and Assocs 1735 John Ridge Dr Collierville TN 38017-7607

MCKINNEY, WILLIAM LYNN, education educator; b. Marshalltown, Iowa, Dec. 30, 1941; s. Otis G. and Helen Marie (Gethmann) McK.; children: Megan Brooke, Andrew Scott. BA, Cornell Coll., 1964; MA, U. Denver, 1968; PhD, U. Chgo., 1973; cert. in pub. adminstrn., Ind. U., 1982. Exec. dir. Indpls. Settlements, 1979-82; dir. R.I. Campus Compact, Kingston, 1992-94; prof. edn. U. R.I., 1993—, co-dir. PhD in edn., 1995-98. Mem. Gov.'s Adv. Com. on Human Svcs., Providence, 1988-90. Contbr. chpt. to book and articles to profl. jours. Bd. mem., sec. Srs. Helping Others, Kingston, 1984-88; bd. mem., pres. VIA The Vol. Ctr., Providence, 1984-96, R.I. Coalition Against Domestic Violence, Warwick, 1994—, pres. 1997—; bd. dirs. AIDS Care Ocean State, Providence, 1994—, sec., 1998—. Mem. Nat. Orgn. for Human Svc. Edn. (jour. editor 1986-90, v.p. for confs. 1989-93, Miriam Clubok award 1990, Lenore McNeer award 1993, pres. 1998—), New Eng. Orgn. Human Svc. Edn. (various offices 1984-90). Home: 200 Kingstown Rd Narragansett RI 02882-3235 Office: Univ RI 107 Quinn Hall Kingston RI 02881

MCKINNEY, WILLIAM MARK, retired geologist; b. Spring Valley, N.Y., Dec. 26, 1923; s. John and Mabel Genevieve (Munger) McKinney; m. Georgia Anna Coleman, June 2, 1951; 1 child Mark Warren (dec.). Student, U. N.C., Raleigh and Chapel Hill, 1940—42; BA, New Sch. Social Rsch., N.Y.C., 1948; MA, U. Fla., 1949, PhD, 1958. Cons. Ga. Dept. Pub. Health, Atlanta, 1953—58; asst. prof. So. Oreg. U., Ashland, 1958—63; asst. prof. to prof. U. Wis., Stevens Point, 1963—88; ret., 1988. Guest rschr. Lowell Obs., Flagstaff, Ariz., 1969—78. Contbr. Pres. Unitarian Soc., Medford, Oreg., 1959—62, Stevens Point, Wis., 1970—73. With USN, 1943. Mem.: Geol. Soc. Am. Unitarian Universalist. Avocations: comparative religion, astronomy, railroads. Home: 1540 NW Kings Blvd Corvallis OR 97330

MCKINNIS, LEE VERN, communications executive; b. Norman, Okla., May 6, 1948; s. Lee Vern Jr. and Edia Delma Bacon; m. Beverly Kay Hampton; children: Charles, Nathaniel. BS in Physics, Cen. State U., Edmond, Okla., 1973. Tchr. physics, chemistry Sand Springs (Okla.) Sch. System, 1973-74; electronic repair technician D & G Audio, Tulsa, 1974-78; equipment technician Southwestern Bell, 1978-82, network service supr. Oklahoma City, 1982-90, mgr. current planning, 1990—. Served as sgt. USAR, 1968-94. Mem.: Morse Telegraph. Avocation: amateur radio. Home: PO Box 19202 Oklahoma City OK 73144-0202

MCKINNIS, MICHAEL B. lawyer; b. St. Louis, May 31, 1945; s. Bayard O. and Doris (Lammert) McK.; m. Patricia Butow, Aug. 24, 1968; children: Scott, Christopher, Elizabeth. BS, Drake U., 1967; JD, U. Mo., 1970. Bar: Mo. 1970, U.S. Dist. Ct. (ea. dist.) Mo. Ptnr. Bryan Cave, St. Louis, leader firm litigation practice, mem. firm operating group. Editor U. Mo. Law Rev., 1969-70. Mem. ABA, Mo. Bar Assn., Order of Coif, Phi Delta Phi. Office: Bryan Cave 1 Met Sq 211 N Broadway Saint Louis MO 63102-2733

MCKINNON, ARNOLD BORDEN, retired transportation company executive; b. Goldsboro, N.C., Aug. 13, 1927; s. Henry Alexander and Margaret (Borden) McK.; m. Oriana McArthur, July 19, 1950; children: Arnold Borden Jr., Colin McArthur, Henry Alexander. AB, Duke U., 1950, LLB, 1951; grad. Advanced Mgmt. Program, Harvard U., 1972. Bar: D.C. 1951, N.C. 1966. With Norfolk So. Corp. (formerly So. Ry. System), Norfolk, Va., 1951-2000, from v.p. law to chmn., 1971-92, chmn. exec. com., 1992-2000, ret., 2000. Bd. trustees Chrysler Mus. Art; active Mil. Civilian Liaison Group; bd. dirs. Norfolk Forum, Inc. With U.S. Army, 1946—47. Mem.: ABA, Am. Soc. Corp. Execs., D.C. Bar Assn., N.C. Bar Assn., Rotary, Norfolk German Club, Bonita Bay Club, Cedar Point Club, Met. Club, Chevy Chase Club, Norfolk Yacht and Country Club. Presbyterian. Home: 552 Mowbray Arch Norfolk VA 23507-2130 Office: Norfolk So Corp 3 Commercial Pl Norfolk VA 23510-2108

MCKINNON, CAROLYN ANN, child care center director; b. Bangor, Maine; d. Joseph Russell and Muriel Ann (Capen) Johnston; m. James Coolidge McKinnon, July 24, 1967; step-children: Michael, Ronald, Shaun, Jeannine; children: William, John. RN, D.C. Gen. Hosp., Washington. RN, N.Y., Colo., Maine. Nurse D.C. Gen. Hosp., Washington, Onondago Gen. Hosp., Syracuse, N.Y., Colo. Gen. Hosp., Denver, Bangor (Maine) Mental Health Inst.; dir., adminstr. A Small World Day Care Ctr., Bangor; ad copy writer Interactive Mktg. Group. Spkr. TV and radio programs, 1997. Author: Insanity, Inc., 1996. Roman Catholic. Avocations: theater and musical organizations. Home: 287 Birch St Bangor ME 04401-4025 Office: A Small World Day Care Ctr 300 Forest Ave Bangor ME 04401-3947 also: Interactive Mktg Group 304 Hancock St Bangor ME 04401-5123

MC KINNON, CLINTON DAN, aerospace transportation executive; b. San Bernardino, Calif., Jan. 27, 1934; s. Clinton Dotson and Lucille V. (McVey) McK.; m. Janice Bernard; children: Holly Jean, Sherri Lynn, Clinton Scott, Lisa Caroline BA, U. Mo., 1956; honorary doctorate, Nat. U., 1987. Page U.S. Ho. of Reps., 1950-52; reporter, photographer, advt. salesman Sentinel Newspaper, San Diego, 1960-62; owner, pres. KSON Radio, 1962-85, KSON-FM, San Diego, 1964-85; pub. La Jolla (Calif.) Light Jour., 1969-73; owner House of Hits (book and music pub.), San Diego, 1972—; co-owner KIll-TV, Corpus Christi, Tex., 1964—, KBMT-TV, Beaumont, 1976—, KUSI-TV, San Diego, 1992—; chmn. CAB, Washington, 1981-84; with spl. projects CIA, 1985-86; chmn., pres. North Am. Airlines, Jamaica, N.Y., 1989—. Author: Bullseye--One Reactor (aka Bullseye Iraq), 1986, The Ten Second Message, 1994, Words of Honor, 1995, Rescue Pilot, 2002, Safe Air Travel Companion, 2002. Chmn. exec. com. Greater San Diego Billy Graham Crusade. Served as aviator USNR, 1956-60. Recipient Advt. Man of Year award San Diego Advt. and Sales Club, 1971; Radio Sta. Mgr. of Year award Billboard Mag., 1973; Internat. Pres.'s award Youth for Christ, 1975; Man of Distinction award Mexican-Am. Found., 1976; George Washington Honor medal Freedoms Found., 1976; Headliner of Yr. (govt.), San Diego Press Club, 1985 Mem. Country Music Assn. (pres. 1977, recipient pres. award 1980), C. of C. (dir.), Nat. Assn. Broadcasters (bd. dirs. 1970-74), Calif. Broadcasters Assn. (dir.), Navy League (Media Man of Yr. 1980), Wings Club (bd. govs. 1995-98, pres. 2002--). Clubs: Rotary (San Diego). Achievements include setting Navy helicopter peacetime rescue record of 62 air/sea rescues, 1958; 1st person to close down fed. govt. regulatory agy., CAB, 1984. Office: JFK International N Am Air Ste 250 Bldg 75 Jamaica NY 11430

MCKINNON, DANIEL WAYNE, JR. naval officer; b. St. Joseph, Mo., Apr. 26, 1934; s. Daniel Wayne and Amber Ruth McK.; m. Rae Lynne Hopper, Apr. 21, 1957; 1 child, Daniel W. III. BSBA, U. Mo., 1956; MBA with distinction, U. Mich., 1966; grad. (disting.), Indsl. Coll. Armed Forces, Washington, 1975. Commd. ensign USN, 1956, advanced through grades to rear adm., 1983; exec. asst. to comdr. Naval Supply Systems Command, Washington, 1970-74, dir. supply corps pers., 1982-83, dep. comdr. for inventory and systems integrity, 1983-84, vice comdr., 1984-86, comdr., 1988-91; ship supply readiness officer, supply systems ops. officer Naval Logistic Command, Pacific Fleet, Pearl Harbor, Hawaii, 1975-78; dir. shipbuilding contracts div. Naval Sea Systems Command, Washington, 1978-80; comdg. officer Naval Supply Depot, Subic Bay, The Philippines, 1980-82; dep. dir. for acquisition mgmt. Def. Logistics Agy., Cameron Station, Va., 1986-88; chief Navy supply corps, comdr. Naval Supply Systems, 1988-91; ret. USN, 1991—; pres., CEO NISH (formerly Nat. Industries for Severly Handicapped), Vienna, 1992—. Chmn. Annandale (Va.) Ctrl. Bus. Dist. Planning Com., 1986-91, Pres.'s Com. for Purchase from the Blind and Other Severely Handicapped, Washington, 1986-91; mem. strategic devel. bd. U. Mo.; bd. dirs. Va. Industries for Blind, 1991—, Project Handclasp, 1994—. Decorated D.S.M., Legion of Merit. Recipient Disting. Svc. award Nat. Industries for Severely Handicapped, 1991; Capstone fellow Nat. Def. U., 1986. Mem. Navy Supply Corps Assn. (pres. 1988-91), Nat. Contract Mgmt. Assn. (bd. advisors 1986—), Navy Fed. Credit Union (vice chmn. 1998—), Navy Mut. Aid Assn. (bd. dirs. 1982-91), Comprehensive Tech. Internat. (bd. dirs. 1992—), Army and Navy Club, Beta Theta Pi, Beta Gamma Sigma, Phi Kappa Phi.

MCKINNON, ELIZABETH LONGO, musician, educator; b. Springfield, Ohio, Apr. 24, 1943; d. Michael Jr. and Anne Virginia (James) Longo; m. Harmon Seals, Nov. 6, 1976 (dec. May 1981); m. John A. McKinnon, Dec. 24, 1992. MusB, Wittenberg U., 1965; MusM in Edn., Mich. State U., 1971. Tchr. instrumental music Fairborn (Ohio) City Scsh., 1966-69; dir. orch. Lakeview Pub. Schs., St. Clair Shores, Mich., 1970-76, elem. music tchr., 1976—. Founder, artistic dir. Macomb Chamber Music Soc., Fraser, Mich., 1982—; prin. cellist Grosse Pointe (Mich.) Symphony, 1984-89, Fine Arts Strings, Scottsdale, Ariz., 1995-2000; cellist Warren (Mich.) Symphony, 1984-89, Sun City Symphony, 1996-98; bus. ptnr. Allegro quartet, 1992—; cello studio instr., 1992—; cons. orch. Highland H.S., Gilbert, Ariz., 1999—. Contbr. (news mag.) Living in Fraser, 1982-84. Cons. Fraser Pub. Schs. Mem. Nat. Edn. Assn., Mich. Edn. Assn., Am. Fedn. Musicians, Am. String Tchrs. Assn. Lutheran. Avocations: bicycling, hiking, photography. Home: 1653 W Milagro Ave Mesa AZ 85202-7418

MCKINNON, FLOYD WINGFIELD, textile executive; b. Columbus, Ga., Dec. 1, 1942; s. Malcolm Angus and Sarah C. (Bullock) McK.; m. Barbara Evans Roles, June 18, 1966; children: James Wingfield, Sarah Elizabeth, Robert Kent. AB, Washington and Lee U., 1964. Lic. airplane pilot. Pres. Cotswold Industries, Inc., N.Y.C., 1966—, also bd. dirs.; v.p., corp. sec. Cen. Textiles, Inc., S.C., 1984—, also bd. dirs. Arbitrator Am. Arbitration Assn., 1983-2001; bd. dirs. Scarsdale Leasing Corp. Pres. Berkley-in-Scarsdale Assn., 1980; admissions rep. Washington and Lee U., 1979-89, 93-99. Mem. Aircraft Owner's and Pilot's Assn., St. Andrews Soc. N.Y., Union League Club (bd. govs. 1974-77, 88-91, 97—, sec. 1981-83, chmn. admissions com. 1996), (N.Y.C.); Scarsdale Golf Club (bd. govs. 1983-91, pres. 1990-91) (Hartsdale, N.Y.), Bras Coupe Club (exec. com. 1980—) (Maniwaki, Can.). Republican. Episcopalian. Home: 26 Taunton Rd Scarsdale NY 10583-5610 Office: Cotswold Industries 10 E 40th St Rm 3410 New York NY 10016-0367 E-mail: wink@cotswoldindustries.com.

MCKINNON, F(RANCIS) A(RTHUR) RICHARD, utility executive; b. Delburne, Alta., Can., Mar. 5, 1933; s. John Donald and Ruth Rebecca (Sundberg) McK.; m. Elma Lorraine Lebsack, June 1, 1957; children: Kenneth Richard, Stephen David, Karen Diane. B. Commerce, U. Alta., 1954; postgrad., Stanford Exec. Program, Stanford U., 1982. With Alta. Gas Trunk Line Co. Ltd., Calgary, 1960-75, treas., 1971-75; dir. fin. TransAlta Utilities Corp. (formerly Calgary Power Ltd.), 1975—, treas., 1976-81, v.p. fin., 1981—, Trans Alta Energy Corp., Trans Alta Corp.; pres. ELM FARMS CONS., INC., Calgary, 1996—. Bd. dirs. AEC Power Ltd. Past bd. dirs. Foothills Gen. Hosp., Calgary. Fellow Inst. Chartered Accts. of Alta.; mem. Can. Inst. Chartered Accts., Fin. Execs. Inst. Can. (past chmn., past pres., bd. dirs. Calgary chpt., v.p.), Fin. Execs. Inst. (bd. dirs.). Clubs: Calgary Petroleum, Canyon Meadows Golf and Country. Office: ELM FARM CONS INC 1412 Windsor St NW Calgary AB Canada T2N 3X3

MCKINNON, JAMES BUCKNER, real estate sales executive, writer, researcher; b. Tacoma, Dec. 5, 1916; s. James Mitchell and Rochelle Lenore (Buckner) McK.; m. Mary C. Corbitt, Dec. 1961 (div. June 1963); 1 child, James H.C.; m. Marylyn Adelle Coote, Mar. 12, 1967 (div. May 1977); 1 child, Michelyn; m. Martha Sackmann, June 12, 1977. BA in Internat. Studies, U. Wash., 1983, H.M. Jackson Sch. Police detective Los Angeles Police Dept., 1946-50; bn. security officer 1st med. bn. 1st Marine div. Fleet Marine Force, 1950-53; owner, operator, mgr., dir. promotional sales The Saucy Dog Drive-In, Venice, Calif., 1953-63; salesman new car sales and leasing Burien Mercury, Seattle, 1963-66; real estate salesman and appraiser various firms, 1966—; instr., lectr. U.S. Naval Support Activity, Sandpoint, Wash., 1964-74. Mem., lectr. NRC 11-8, Naval Postgrad. Sch., Monterey, Calif., 1975-76; Burien Mercury announcer KOMO TV. Author: (poetry) On the Threshold of a Dream, Vol. III, 1992, Best Poems of the 90's, 1992; contbr. to anthologies: Where Words Haven't Spoken, 1993, Fire From Within, 1994; contbr. articles to various newspapers and mil. jours. Mem. br. adv. com. Wash. State YMCA, Seattle, 1994—, treas., 1986-94, 95, mem. so. dist. fin. bd., 1989-93, 94, 95-96. With USN, 1939-53, PTO, Korea. Recipient Wilmer Culver Meml. award Culver Alumni Fictioneers, Seattle, 1979, Silver Poet award World of Poetry Press, 1986, Golden Poet award, 1987-92, Best Poet of the 90's Nat. Libr. of Poetry, 1992, First Place with Editor's Preference award Creative Arts and Scis. Enterprises, 1996; Occidental Coll. scholar, 1935; named to Honorable Order Ky. Cols., 1976; named One of Best New Poets, Am. Poetry Assn. Anthology, 1988; inducted into the Internat. Poetry Hall of Fame, 1996. Mem. Internat. Soc. Authors and Artists (1st place award for 1997 poem), Internat. Platform Assn., U.S. Naval Inst. (life), Internat. Soc. Poets (life), N.W. Writers Conf., Acad. Am. Poets, Ret. Officers Assn. (life), Mensa, Acad. Am. Poets, KP, Masons. Republican. Home: 2312 41st Ave SW Seattle WA 98116-2060 *Personal philosophy: To realize one's greatest potential pursue goals that hold the greatest meaning in life.*

MCKINNON, KATHLEEN ANN, software engineer; b. Berwyn, Ill., July 27, 1960; d. James Walter and Linda Lee (Belford) Turek; m. Donald Lee McKinnon, Jr., July 27, 1980; 1 child, Donald Lee III. AA in Computer Sci., Pensacola Jr. Coll., 1980; BS in Computer Sci. and Info. Systems, U. Md., 1986. SIGINT Morse interceptor U.S. Army, Ft. Meade, Md., 1982-86; computer scientist Dept. Def., 1986-90; software engr. Harris Corp., Melbourne, Fla., 1990—, group leader, 1994—. Mem. missions com. Pineda Presbyn. Ch., Melbourne, 1991—; moderator Pineda Presbyn. Women, 1995-96, group leader, 1994-98, treas., 1997-98. Recipient achievement medal U.S. Army, 1983, spl. achievement award Dept. Def., 1989. Republican. Avocations: photography, painting and drawing, aerobics.

MCKINNON, RUSSEL FRANCIS DANIEL, professional society administrator; b. Springfield, Mass., Feb. 11, 1944; s. John Phee Joseph McKinnon and Margret Louise Bates; m. Deborah Anne Oplinger, July 11, 1987; 1 child, John. AB in History, Coll. Holy Cross, 1966; M in Mgmt., George Washington U., 1988. Pres. The Mackinnon Co., Alexandria, Va., 1972—; exec. Nat. Rural Electric Coop. Assn., Arlington, 1994—; pres. Internat. Theos Found., Alexandria, 1998—. Photographer Parade Mag., 1989. Lt. USNR, 1966-72. Mem. Am. Soc. Assn. Execs. (cert.), Assn. Meeting Planners. Avocations: skiing, golf. Office: Nat Rural Electric Coop Assn 4301 Wilson Blvd Arlington VA 22203-1867

MCKINNON, WILLIAM MITCHELL PATRICK, surgeon; b. Houston, Mar. 17, 1924; s. William M. and Rosina Mary McKinnon; m. Elizabeth Jean Beall, Oct. 3, 1953; children: William, Stuart, Mary, John, Fraser, David (dec.). Student, St. Michael's Coll., Toronto, Can., 1942, Tex. A&M State U., 1943, U. Tex., 1947; BS maxima cum laude, St. Edward's U., Austin, Tex., 1948; MD, Baylor U., 1952. Diplomate Am. Bd. Surgery; lic. physician, La., N.Y., Tex. Intern Royal Victoria Hosp., Montreal, Can., 1953; resident in surgery 2d surg. divsn. Bellevue Hosp., 1954; asst. resident thoracic surgery Triboro Hosp. for Chest Disease, 1955; asst. resident in surgery Queens Hosp. Ctr., Jamaica, N.Y., 1955, asst. resident in pathology, 1956, assoc. resident, 1957, asst. surgeon, 1959-61; chief resident surgery, fellow in surg. rsch. Maimonides Hosp. of Bklyn., 1958; asst. attending surgeon Flower & Fifth Ave. Hosps., 1961-64, attending surgeon, 1965-67; staff surgeon Alton Ochsner Found. Hosp., 1968-96; staff, dept. surgery Ochsner Clinic, 1968-96, assoc. dir., dept. surgery, 1979-84, co-dir., breast screening, 1982-92; dir. Breast Ctr., Ochsner Clinic, 1992-96. Clin. asst. in surgery SUNY Med. Ctr. Coll. Medicine, 1957-59; asst. surgeon Kew Gardens (N.Y.) Gen. Hosp., 1959-61, Jamaica Hosp., 1960-61; vis. surgeon Met. Hosp. and Bird S. Coler Hosp., 1961-66, Tulane divsn. Charity Hosp., 1968—; dist. med. cons. N.Y. State Edn. Dept. Vocat. Rehab., 1960-67; surg. cons. VA Hosp., Lyons, N.J., 1963-67, E.A. Conway Meml. Hosp., Monroe, La., 1968-79; asst. prof. to assoc. prof. surgery N.Y. Med. Coll., 1961-67; clin. assoc. prof. surgery Tulane U., 1968-92, clinical prof. dept. surgery, 1992—, Tulane U. Hosp. and Clinic, 1997—, Univ. Hosp., 1997—; chief clin. breast disease program, med. dir. Breast Health Ctr., Tulane Cancer Ctr., 1997—; prin. investigator Nat. Surg. Adjuvant and Breast Project Protocols, 1999—, Nat. Surg. Adjuvant Breast and Bowel Project. Contbr. articles to med. jours. Bd. dirs. Am. Cancer Soc., New Orleans, 1953, Komen Found., New Orleans, 1953. Capt. USAF, 1948-52. Recipient 1st prize for med. writing Queensborough Med. Soc., 1957; USPHS rsch. fellow Nat. Heart Inst., 1958. Fellow ACS; mem. AMA, Soc. for Surgery of Alimentary Tract, So. Med. Assn., Am. Gastroenterol. Assn., Societe Internationale de Chirugie, Collegium Internationale Chirugie Digestivae, So. Surg. Assn., New Orleans Surg. Soc. (pres. 1988), Orleans Parish Med. Soc., Tulane Surg. Soc., Alton Ochsner Surg. Soc. (pres. 1985). Avocations: duplicate bridge, woodworking, computers. Home: 1529 Nashville Ave New Orleans LA 70115-4254 Office: Tulane U Med Ctr Dept Surgery SL22 1430 Tulane Ave New Orleans LA 70112-2699 also: Tulane Metairie Clinic 4770 S I 10 Service Rd W Metairie LA 70001-1215 also: Tulane Uptown Clinic 200 Broadway St Ste 230 New Orleans LA 70118-3544 E-mail: wmpm@bellsouth.net., wmckinn@tulane.edu.

MCKINSEY, DAVID STEPHEN, infectious diseases specialist; b. Dallas, Oct. 24, 1955; s. John Jerome and Jacqueline (Ronay) McK. BS cum laude, Tulane U., 1977; MD, U. Mo., 1981. Diplomate Am. Bd. Internal Medicine, Am. Bd. Infectious Diseases. Intern, then resident in internal medicine U. Iowa Hosps. and Clinics, Iowa City, 1981-84; fellow in infectious diseases U. Tenn., Memphis, 1984-86; co-dir. dept. infectious disease Rsch. Med. Ctr., Kansas City, Mo., 1986—; clin. asst. prof. medicine U. Mo., 1986-90; clin. assoc. prof. medicine U. Kans., 1991—2002, clin. prof. medicine, 2002—; med. dir. Health Midwest Pharmacy, 1999—. Recipient Outstanding Young Physician award U. Mo., Columbia, 1999. Fellow ACP, Infectious Diseases Soc. Am. (Clinician of Yr. award 1998); mem. AMA, Am. Soc. Microbiology, Soc. Hosp. Epidemiologists Am., Kansas City S.W. Clin. Soc. (pres. 1992). Office: Ste 392 6400 Prospect Ave Kansas City MO 64132-1199 E-mail: dsmckinsey@healthmidwest.org.

MCKINSEY, ELIZABETH, college dean; b. Columbia, Mo., Aug. 10, 1947; d. J. Wendell and A. Ruhamah (Peret) McK.; m. Thomas N. Clough, June 18, 1977; children: Emily, Peter. BA, Radcliffe Coll., 1970; PhD, Harvard U., 1976. From instr. to asst. prof. English Bryn Mawr (Pa.) Coll., 1975-77; from asst. to assoc. prof. English Harvard U., Cambridge, Mass., 1977-85; dir. Bunting Inst. Radcliffe Coll., 1985-89; dean Carleton Coll., Northfield, Minn., 1989—. Author: Niagara Falls: Icon of the American Sublime, 1985; contbr. articles and revs. to profl. jours. and lit. mags. NEH fellow, 1980. Mem. MLA, Am. Conf. Acad. Deans, Nat. Coun. for Rsch. on Women (assoc.), Am. Studies Assn., Nat. Assn. Women in Edn., Phi Beta Kappa (pres. Iota of Mass. chpt. 1986-89). Home: 815 2nd St E Northfield MN 55057-2308 Office: Carleton Coll 1 N College St Northfield MN 55057-4001 E-mail: emckinse@carleton.edu.

MCKINSTRY, DORIS VERON See BERG, DORIS VERON

MCKINSTRY, RONALD EUGENE, lawyer; b. Bakersfield, Calif., Aug. 11, 1926; s. Melville Jack and Lillian Agatha (Saner) McK.; m. Shirley Danner, June 19, 1948; children: Michael R., Jill I. McKinstry Epperson, Jeffrey A., Carol A. McKinstry Sundquist. BS, U. Wash., 1950, JD, 1951. Bar: Wash. 1951, U.S. Ct. Claims 1970, U.S. Ct. Appeals (D.C. cir.) 1981, U.S. Supreme Ct. 1982. Assoc. Evans, McLaren, Lane, Powell & Beeks, Seattle, 1951-55, Bogle, Bogle & Gates, Seattle, 1955-61; ptnr. Bogle & Gates, 1962-91, chmn. litigation dept., 1970-91; sr. trial ptnr. Ellis Li & McKinstry, 1992—. Apptd. spl. master by U.S. Dist. Ct. (we. dist.) Wash., 1976-81, apptd. settlement mediator, 1980— Editor-in-chief Washington Civil Procedure Before Trial Deskbook, 1981, Supplement to Deskbook, 1986; contbr. articles to profl. jours. Attends Christ Meml. Ch., Poulsbo, Wash. With USN, 1944-46, PTO. Recipient Svc. award Western Ctr. for Law and Religious Freedom, 1990. Fellow Am. Coll. Trial Lawyers (regent 1978-82); mem. ABA, Internat. Assn. Def. Counsel (mem. exec. com. 1974-78, voted Best Lawyers in Am., 1983—), CPR Panels of Disting. Legal Neutrals, AAA Club Wash. (mem. exec. com. 1983-98). Mem. Christ Meml. Ch. Avocations: golf, travel. Office: Ellis Li & McKinstry Two Union Square 601 Union St Ste 4900 Seattle WA 98101-3906 E-mail: rmckinstry@ellisi.com.

MCKINZIE, CARL WAYNE, lawyer; b. Lubbock, Tex., Dec. 3, 1939; s. J. Clyde and Flora (Cates) McK.; m. Rowena Ann Williams; children: Wayne, Clinton, Morgan (dec.). BBA, Tex. Tech U., 1962, MBA, 1963; JD, So. Meth. U., 1966. From assoc. to ptnr. Nossaman, Guthner, Knox & Elliott, L.A., 1966-80; prin. Riordan & McKinzie, 1980—. Bd. dirs., exec. com., Saint John's Health Ctr., Santa Monica, Calif., 2001-. Contbr. articles to law jours. Trustee Jaquish Found., Raymond Marshall Found.; bd. visitors Sch. Law So. Meth. U., Dallas, 1979-82, 90—, bd. dirs., 1970-73, 84-89, chmn. exec. com., 1996-98; bd. visitors Ariz State U. Coll. Law, 1990-98; bd. dirs. Riordan Found., Rx for Reading, Libr. Found. L.A., 2002-; pub. counsel, bd. dirs. Calif. Cmty. Found., 1994-98; bd. advisors Coll Law, U. Wyo., 1987-91, 2001—. Recipient disting. alumni award So. Meth. U., Dallas, 1994. Mem. ABA (chmn. current devel. subcom., com. tax problems 1978-80), Nat. Assn. Real Estate Investment Trusts (bd. govs. 1986-89), Calif. Bar Assn., Los Angeles County Bar Assn., Jonathan Club, City Club on Bunker Hill, L.A. Country Club. Republican. Home: 527 21st Pl Santa Monica CA 90402-3047 Office: Riordan & McKinzie 29th Fl 300 S Grand Ave Ste 29 Los Angeles CA 90071-3110

MCKINZIE, JAMES S. librarian; b. Sweetwater, Tex., Dec. 15, 1951; s. John O. and Laverne McKinzie; m. Anna B. Baker; children: Amy, Jane, Jonathan, William. BA in History, Tex. A&M U., 1975; MA in History, E. Carolina U., Greenville, NC, 1982; MLS, Vanderbilt U., 1988. Social sci. libr. Dickinson Coll., Carlisle, Pa., 1988—. Contbr. articles and book revs. to profl. jours. Presbyterian. Home: 1217 N West St Carlisle PA 17013 Office: Dickinson Coll Libr High St Carlisle PA 17013 Office Fax: 717-245-1439. E-mail: mckinzie@dickinson.edu.

MCKIRAHAN, RICHARD DUNCAN, classics and philosophy educator; b. Berkeley, Calif., July 27, 1945; s. Richard Duncan and Helen Marion (Hixson) McK.; m. Voula Tsouna, June 3, 1961; 1 child, Helen Hamilton. AB, U. Calif., Berkeley, 1966; BA, U. Oxford, Eng., 1969; MA, Oxford U., Eng., 1979; PhD, Harvard U., 1973. Teaching fellow, tutor Harvard U., Cambridge, Mass., 1971-73; asst. prof. classics and philosophy Pomona Coll., Claremont, Calif., 1973-79, assoc. prof., 1979-87, E.C. Norton prof. classics and philosophy, 1987—, chair dept. classics, 1992—. Author: Socrates and Plato, A Comprehensive Bibliography, 1958-1973, 1978, Plato's Meno, 1986, Principles and Proofs: Aristotle's Theory of Demonstrative Science, 1992, Philosophy Before Socrates, 1994, A Presocratics Reader, 1996, Cicero, De Natura Deorum I, 1997, Simplicius, On Aristotle's Physics, book 8, chpts. 6-10, 2001; contbr. articles on Greek philosophy, math. and scis. Marshall Aid Commemoration Commn. scholar, U. Oxford, 1966-69, Fulbright Sr. scholar, 1999, Overseas Vis. scholar St. John's Coll., Cambridge, 1999; Woodrow Wilson Found. fellow, 1966-67; NEH grantee, 1975, 85, 90, 98. Mem. Am. Philol. Assn., Soc. Ancient Greek Philosophy, Phi Beta Kappa. Office: Pomona Coll Dept Classics 140 W 6th St Claremont CA 91711-4301 E-mail: rmckirahan@pomona.edu.

MCKISSICK, MICHAEL LANDON, transportation consultant; b. Clearfield, Pa., June 12, 1950; s. Robert Charles and Ruby Delores (Landon) McK. AS in Mech. Design, Pitts. Tech. Inst., 1979, AS in Computer System Mgmt., 1985. Registered profl. engr., Pa. Inventory control coord. Aerotech, Inc., Pitts., 1974-75; owner, operator No. Photographic Svcs., Warren, Pa., 1975-77; drafter bearings div. TRW, Falconer, N.Y., 1979; proposal engr. Blaw Knox F&MM Co., Pitts., 1979-80; instr. Pitts. Tech. Inst., 1980-82, v.p., 1982-85; instr. Carnegie Mellon U., Pitts., 1981-82; cons. Pa. Dept. Transp., Trout Run, 1985—. Mem. Pitts. Tech. Inst. Bd. Advs., 1985—; speaker in field. Author: (book) Computer Aided Drafting and Design, 1987. Mem. Intergraph Users Group. Avocations: music, photography, scale modeling. Home and Office: 2566 Frenchtown Rd Trout Run PA 17771-9282

MCKISSICK-MELTON, S. CHARMAINE, mass communications educator; b. Durham, N.C., July 31, 1955; d. Floyd Bixler Sr. and Evelyn C. (Williams) McKissick; div. 1990; children: Maceo Christopher Kemp Jr., Daniel Ernest Kemp. BA, U. N.C., 1977; MA, No. Ill. U., 1978; postgrad., U. Ky., 1993-96. Sales mgr. WDUR-AM Radio, Durham, 1979-83; account exec. WTVD-TV 11, 1983, WKFT-TV 40, Fayetteville, N.C., 1984-85; office mgr. Atty. M. Christopher Kemp, Sr., Lumberton, 1985-88; learning disabled/extremely mentally handicapped tchr. Lumberton Jr. High Sch., 1988; account exec. WQOK-FM Radio, Raleigh, N.C., 1989; instr. Fayetteville State U., 1989, A&T State U., Greensboro, N.C., 1988-93; assoc. prof. Bennett Coll., 1989—, chair dept. mass comm., 1991-93. Vis. prof. U. Notre Dame, Ind., 1992. Bd. dirs. N.C. Ctr. for Study of Black History, Durham, 1989-96, Durham Bus. and Profl. Chain, 1990-91, Women's Shelter for hope, Durham, 1989-91, Southeastern Family Violence Ctr., Lumberton, 1985-89. Coca Cola Faculty fellow U. Notre Dame, 1992, Lyman T. Johnson Rsch./Tchg. fellow, 1993-96. Mem. AAUW, AAUP (Bennett Coll. chpt. founding mem.), Speech Comm. Assn., Bennett Coll. Faculty Senate (exec. com. 1991-93), Women in Comm. (faculty advisor 1989-93), Am. Women in Radio and TV (N.C. chpt. pres. 1985-86). Avocations: swimming, aerobics, reading, public speaking. Home: 705 Reynolds Ave Durham NC 27707-4641 Office: Bennett Coll PO Box 25 Greensboro NC 27402-0025

MCKISSOCK, DAVID LEE, retired manufacturing company executive; b. Boston, Mar. 27, 1933; s. Allan and Elizabeth (Lee) McK.; m. Diana Parish, Sept. 1, 1956; children: David Lee Jr., Christopher Lee. BA, Middlebury Coll., 1955. Salesman Am. Flange and Mfg. Co., N.Y.C., 1957-62, asst. to v.p. sales Linden, N.J., 1962-64, salesman rip cap closures, 1964-73, v.p. rip cap closures, 1973-89, also bd. dirs. With USNR, 1955-57. Mem. Rumson Country Club, Seabright Lawn Tennis and Cricket Club. Republican. Unitarian Universalist. Avocations: tennis, golf, platform tennis. Home: 20 Hance Rd Fair Haven NJ 07704-3210

MCKITTRICK, NEIL VINCENT, lawyer; b. Framingham, Mass., June 21, 1961; s. Harold Vincent and Dorothy Frances (Alexander) McK.; m. Karen Beth Hoffman, May 30, 1987; children: Kerry Alexandra, Brian Hoffman, Robert Hoffman. AB magna cum laude, Brown U., 1983; JD, U. Va., 1987. Bar: Mass. 1988, U.S. Dist. Ct. Mass. 1989, U.S. Ct. Appeals (1st cir.) 1989, U.S. Supreme Ct. 1999. Law clk. to Hon. Frank M. Johnson Jr. U.S. Ct. Appeals (11th cir.), Montgomery, Ala., 1987-88; assoc. Hill & Barlow, Boston, 1988-95, mem., 1995—; pub. defender Suffolk County (Mass.) Bar Advocate, 1990-91; asst. dir. White House sec. rev. U.S. Dept. Treasury, 1994-95; case conf./mediator Boston Mcpl. Ct. Alternative Dispute Resolution Program, 1997—. Mem. steering com. Lawyers' Com. Civil Rights Under Law, 1998—. Editor U. Va. Law Rev., 1985-87. Bd. trustees Lawyers' Com. for Civil Rights Under Law, 2001—. Recipient Assn. for Retarded Citizens Mass. Disting. Citizens award, 1996, Charles River Arc Gala Benefit award, 2001; fellow Dillard fellow, U. Va., 1985—86. Mem.: FBA (exec. com. 1997—, treas. 2000—01, sec. 2001—02, Mass. chpt.), ABA (Pro Bono Publico award 2001), Boston Bar Assn. (bd. dirs. lawyer's com. civil rights under law 1998—), Mass. Bar Assn. (coun. mem. Access to Justice Sect. Coun. 2001—02, Access to Justice Pro Bono Publico award 2001), Order of the Coif, Theta Delta Chi, Phi Beta Kappa. Office: Hill & Barlow One International Pl Boston MA 02110 E-mail: nmckittrick@hillbarlow.com.

MCKITTRICK, WILLIAM WOOD, lawyer; b. Mt. Carmel, Ill., July 11, 1915; s. Lafe E. and Mary Lynn (Wood) McK.; m. Carolyn Lenne Davis, Dec. 19, 1942; children: Lynn McKittrick Pond, Bruce W. AB, DePauw U., 1936; JD, Northwestern U., 1939. Bar: Ill. Assoc. Pope & Ballard, Chgo., 1939-48, ptnr., 1948-52; atty. Office Gen. Counsel, Panama C.Z., 1942; ptnr. Vedder, Price, Kaufman & Kammholz, Chgo., 1952-95; lectr. on labor law Northwestern U. Sch. Law, 1961-62. Case note editor, mem. editorial bd. Ill. Law Rev., 1938-39. Life trustee Orchestral Assn. of Chgo. Symphony Orch., 1980—, Chgo. Symphony Musicians Pension Trust, 1987-98; bd. dirs. Am. Symphony Orch. League, 1986-93, mem. exec. com., 1988-91; trustee Newberry Libr., Chgo., 1984-98, life trustee, 1998—, exec. com., 1989-98; vice chmn. exec. bd. Libr. Coun., Northwestern U., 1984-96; chmn. Friends of Ryerson & Burnham Librs., Art Inst. Chgo., 1988-90, mem. com. on librs., 1982—. Lt. USNR, 1943-45, PTO. Recipient Svc. award Northwestern U., 1968. Mem. ABA, Ill. Bar Assn., Chgo. Bar Assn. (lectr. various programs 1940-70, bd. mgrs. 1961-63), Lawyers Club of Chgo., Univ. Club (Chgo.), Michigan Shores Club, Skokie Country Club, Caxton Club of Chgo. (v.p. 1982-83, pres. 1983-85). Home: 232 Essex Rd Kenilworth IL 60043-1122

MCKNIGHT, JOSEPH WEBB, law educator, historian; b. San Angelo, Tex., Feb. 17, 1925; s. John Banning and Helen Katherine (Webb) McK.; m. Julia Ann Dyer, July 19, 1957 (dec. Jan. 1972); children— John Banton, Joseph Adair; m. Mildred Katherine Virginia Payne, Aug. 9, 1975 BA, U. Tex., 1947, Oxford U., Eng., 1949, B.C.L., 1950, MA, 1954; LL.M., Columbia U., 1959. Bar: Tex. 1951, U.S. Ct. Appeals (5th cir.) 1982. Assoc. Cravath, Swaine & Moore, N.Y.C., 1951-55; asst. prof. So. Meth. U., Dallas, 1955-57, assoc. prof., 1957-63, prof. law, 1963—, acad. dean, 1977-80, Larry and Jane Harlan faculty fellow, 1991—. Vis. prof. various univs. Gen. editor Creditors' Rights in Texas, 1963, History of the Texas Supreme Court Project, 1998—; author: (with William A. Reppy, Jr.) Texas Matrimonial Property Law, 1983, 3d edit. 2000; contbr. articles to profl. jours. Pres., Tex. Old Missions and Forts Restoration Assn., 1977-79, 99-2001; bd. dirs. San Jacinto Mus. History Assn., 1976-99; mem. exec. coun. Tex. State Hist. Assn., 1988-91. Served to lt. USNR, 1942-47 Rhodes scholar, 1947-50; James Kent fellow, 1958-59; Academico, Acad. Mexicana de Derecho Internat., 1988, Hall of Legends, State Bar of Texas Fam. Law Sec., 1997. Fellow, Soc. for Advanced Legal Studies (London), 1998; mem. ABA, State Bar Tex., Dallas Bar Assn., Tex. Bar Found. (v.p. 1959), Nat. Legal Aid and Defenders Assn. (bd. dirs.

1963-66), Selden Soc., Am. Soc. Legal History (v.p. 1967-68, bd. dirs. 1967-75), Inst. Texan Cultures (exec. bd. 1990-95), Sigma Chi. Democrat. Episcopalian. Office: So Meth U Law Sch 3315 Daniel Ave Dallas TX 75275-0116

MCKNIGHT, JOYCE SHELDON, adult educator, community organizer, mediator; b. Meadville, Pa., Oct. 12, 1949; d. Seth Carlyle and Juanita Bessie (Sheets) Sheldon; m. Hugh Frank McKnight, Aug. 22, 1970; children: Frank Nathan, Joanna Michelle. BA in Psychology and Sociology, Allegheny Coll., 1971; MEd in Counseling, Gannon Coll., 1977; EdD, Pa. State U., 1995. Cert. nat. counselor. Asst. met. dir. Ecumenical Inst., Chgo. and Tulsa, 1970-73; health planner East Okla. Devel. Dist., Muskogee, 1973; juvenile counselor Tulsa County Aftercare Program, 1973; program specialist psycho-social rehab. Counseling Svcs. Ctr., Corry, Pa., 1975-77; counselor Adult Diploma Program, 1974-79; dir. Anchor House Agy., 1977-78; community programs dir. Warren-Forest Counties Econ. Opportunity Coun., Warren, 1979-80; dir. Corry Ctr. Mercyhurst Coll., Corry, 1981-87; cons. Pulaski, 1987-89. Adj. faculty Mercyhurst, 1981-87, program devel. cons., 1987-89, program devel. cons. for new ch. Heritage Hills Ch., 1988-89; adj. faculty Allegheny Coll., 1984, Jamestown C.C., 1991-93; planner Pa. State U., Shenango Valley, 1989; mentor Empire State Coll. SUNY, 1989-93; coord. adult svcs. Alfred State Coll., 1992-95, adj. faculty mem., 1994-95, distance edn. team, 1994-95; dir. Inst. for Support of Cmty. Initiative, 1995-97; dir. McKnight Mediation, 1997—; mem. faculty Cambria County Area C.C., 1998—, adj. grad. faculty Pa. State U., 2000; cons. higher edn., cmty. svc., ch. growth. Contbr. articles to profl. jours; co-author: Doing Democracy. Pres., Corry Concerned for Youth, Inc., 1975-77; pres. Community Care Coun. of Agys., Corry, 1976-79, sec., 1975; mem. steering com. Vol. Action Ctr., Corry, 1977, bd. dirs. Erie County Citizens Coalition for Human Svcs., Erie, 1979-80, Horizon House for Women, 1981-87; mem. coordinating bd. Corry Reindustrialization Coun. 1983-87; mem. Allegany County N.Y Gateway Project, 1993-95; mem. mediation com. Allegheny Mennonite Conf. Mem. NAACP (Johnstown chpt., adv. com. family ctr.), Regional Coalition Cmty. Builders (bd. dirs.), Pa. Assn. Pub. Continuing Adult Edn. (dir. 1977-78), Pa. Assn. for Adult Continuing Edn. (bd. dirs. 1985-90) Cambria County Comty. Action (bd. dirs.), Coalition of the So. Alleghenies Mennonite. Home and Office: 632 Menoher Blvd Johnstown PA 15901-2711 E-mail: jmedcon@aol.com., jmckni@mail.ccacc.cc.pa.us.

MCKNIGHT, LENORE RAVIN, child psychiatrist, educator; b. Denver, May 15, 1943; d. Abe and Rose (Steed) Ravin; m. Robert lee McKNight, July 22, 1967; children: Richard Rex, Janet Rose. Student, Occidental Coll., 1961-63; BA, postgrad., U. Colo., 1965-67; MD, U. Calif., San Francisco, 111969. Diplomate in adult and child psychiatry Am. Bd. Psychiatry and Neurology. Intern in pediat. Children's Hosp., San Francisco, 1969-70; resident in gen. psychiatry Langley Porter Neuropsychiat. Inst., 1970-73, fellow in child psychiatry, 1972-74, asst. clin. prof., 1974—; pvt. practice child psychiatry, Walnut Creek, Calif., 1974-93; child psychiatrist Kaiser Permanente Med. Group, 1993—. Child psychiatrist Youth Guidance Center, San Francisco, 1974-74; asst. clin. prof. psychiatry U. Calif. San Francisco Med. Ctr. Internat.; med. dir. CPC Walnut Creek (Calif.) Hosp., 1990-93. Insts. Edn. fellow U. Edinburgh, 1964; grantee to study childhood nutrition NIH, 1966. Fellow Am. Acad. Child and Adolescent Psychiatry, Internat. Arabian Horse Assn. Office: Kaiser Martinez Inpat Psych 200 Muir Rd Martinez CA 94553-4672

MCKNIGHT, PATRICIA GAYLE, musician, artist, writer, educator; b. Rochester, Minn., Aug. 9, 1935; d. William Robert and Maxine Matilda (Hutchings) McK.; m. James Russell Grittner, Nov. 24, 1962; children: Leah Kristin, Rachel Anne. BS in Music, U. Wis., Superior, 1982, MA in Art, 1990, MA in Art History, 1993. Asst. MS editor Am. Acad. Ophthalmology and Otolaryngology, Rochester, Minn., 1958-63. Musician U. Iowa Symphony Orch., U. Iowa Opera Orch., U. of Iowa Small Ensembles, U. Wis. Superior Symphony Orch., Rochester Symphony Orch. Exhibited in group exhibitions including Kruk Gallery, Rochester Cmty. Coll., Duluth Art Inst. Biennial, 1988, 90, Port Wing (Wis.) Gallery; author: Zenith City Arts newspaper. Mem. historic preservation com. City of Superior, 1996—. Avocations: playing cello, viola da gamba. Home: 2325 Hughitt Ave Superior WI 54880-4920

MCKNIGHT, PATRICIA MARIE, elementary education educator; b. Jersey City, June 7, 1952; d. John M. and Reginia C. (Broderick) O'Connor; m. Reese J. McKnight, June 29, 1974; children: Jason, Gregory. BS, Madison Coll., Harrisonburg, Va., 1974. Tchr. 4th and 5th grades Prince William County Schs., Woodbridge, Va., 1974-80; tchr. 5th grade A.G. Wright Middle Sch., Stafford, 1980-88, Grafton Village Elem., Stafford, 1989—. Mem. NEA, Stafford County Edn. Assn.

MCKNIGHT, REGINALD, English educator; b. FürstenFeldbrück, Germany, Feb. 26, 1956; s. Frank and Pearl McKnight; m. Julie Scott, Nov. 29, 1999; children: Rachael, Moriah, Eve. AA in Anthropology, Pikes Peak C.C., Colorado Springs, Colo., 1978; BA in African Studies, Colo. Coll., 1981, doctorate, 1991; MA in English, U. Denver, 1987. Asst. prof. U. Pitts., 1988-91; assoc. prof. Carnegie Mellon U., Pitts., 1991-94; prof. U. Md., College Park, 1994-2000, U. Mich., Ann Arbor, 2000—02; Hamilton Holmes prof. English U. Ga., Athens, 2002—. Author: Moustapha's Eclipse, 1988 (Drue Heinz award 1988), I Get on the Bus, 1990, The Kind of Light That Shines on Texas, 1992, White Boys, 1998, He Sleeps, 2001; mem. editl. bd. African Am. Rev., 1994—, Kenyon Rev., 1998—. Cpl. USMC, 1975—77. Recipient NEA award, 1991, Pushcart prize, 1995, Whiting Writers award, 1998, Addison M. Metcalf award AAAL, 1999. Mem. PEN Am. Avocations: music, writing, performing, meditation. Office: U Ga Dept English Park Hall Athens GA 30602 E-mail: rmckn48194@aol.com.

MCKNIGHT, STEVEN LANIER, molecular biologist; b. El Paso, Tex., Aug. 27, 1949; s. Frank Gillespie and Sara Elise (Stevens) McK.; m. Jacquelynn Ann Zimmer, Sept. 16, 1978; children: Nell, Grace, Frances, John Stevens. BA summa cum laude, U. Tex., 1974; PhD, U.Va., 1977. Postdoctoral fellow Carnegie Instn. Washington, Balt., 1977-79, staff assoc., 1979-81, mem. staff, 1984-92; co-founder, dir., dir. rsch. Tularik Inc., 1991—. Prof., chmn. dept. biochemistry U. Tex. Southwestern Med. Ctr., 1995—; hon. prof. Johns Hopkins U., scientific rev. bd. Howard Hughes Med. Inst., 1997—; trustee Carnegie Inst., Washington, 2000—. Contbr. articles to jours. in field. With U.S. Army, 1969-71, Vietnam. Decorated ARCOM medal; recipient Eli Lilly prize Am. Soc. Microbiology, 1987, Newcomb-Cleveland prize Sci. mag., 1989, NAS Molecular Biology award Nat. Acad. Sci., 1991. Fellow Carnegie Inst. Washington (hon.), Am. Soc. Microbiology (hon.); mem. NAS, Am. Acad. Arts and Scis., Am. Soc. for Biochemistry and Molecular Biology, Am. Soc. for Cell Biology, Japanese Biochem. Soc. (hon.). Home: 3717 Euclid Ave Dallas TX 75205-3161 Office: U Tex Southwestern Med Ctr Dept Biochemistry 5323 Harry Hines Blvd Dallas TX 75390-7208 also: Tularik Inc Two Corp Dr South San Francisco CA 94080

MCKNIGHT, THERESA HADDEN, family nurse practitioner, nursing educator; b. Highland Park, Mich., Dec. 3, 1952; d. Raymond Arthur and Mary Elizabeth (Tebo) Cooks; m. Gary Jay Hadden, Oct. 2, 1970 (div. Oct. 1978); children: Timothy, Brian; m. Alton Henry McKnight, Aug. 5, 1983. ADN, St. Clair County C.C., Port Huron, Mich., 1975; BSN, No. Mich. U., 1980; MSN in Nursing, MSN in Edn., U. Wis., Oshkosh, 1985. Cert. BLS, ACLS. Emergency rm. head nurse Marquette (Mich.) Gen. Hosp., 1976-80; emergency rm. svcs. head nurse F.A. Bell Meml. Hosp., Ishpeming, Mich., 1980-82; nurse practitioner, asst. prof. No. Mich. U., Marquette, 1982-90, Dr. B. Lyons, Marquette, 1982-90, S.W. Med. Assocs., Las Vegas, Nev., 1990-94, Premiere Med. Ctr., Las Vegas, 1994—. Cons. McKnight & Summers, Skandia, Mich., 1982-90, U. Las Vegas, 1992—; instr. B ay de Noc C.C., Escanaba, Mich., 1988-90; nurse practitioner Dr. Al Walters, Henderson, Nev., 1991—, U.S. Olympic Luge Team, Marquette, 1985—; educator Kaplan Testing Svcs., Las Vegas, 1991—. Bd. dirs. Am. Heart Assn., 1980—. Lt. comdr. USN, 1985-94. Recipient Grad. Rsch. award Oshkosh, 1985, Spooner Rsch. award, 1985. Faculty Rsch. award N.M.U., 1986, Hulse Sensitivity award, 1991. Mem. ANA (cert. FNP, bd. dirs. 1975—), Am. Acad. Nurse Practitioners. Avocations: reading, camping, traveling, learning new things. Home: 7640 W Red Coach Ave Las Vegas NV 89129-5315 Office: Premiere Med Ctr 111 E Harmon Ave Las Vegas NV 89109-4500

MCKNIGHT, THOMAS FREDERICK, artist; b. Lawrence, Kans., Jan. 13, 1941; m. Renate Hödl. BA cum laude, Wesleyan U., Middletown, Conn., 1963; postgrad., Columbia U., 1963-64. One-man shows Basel (Switzerland) Art Fair, 1975-77, Tomic Galerie, Dusseldorf, Germany, 1976, Hartmann Gallery, Munich, 1977, Newport (R.I.) Art Assn., 1981, Kobe (Japan) Mcpl. Art Mus., 1993, R² Gallery, N.Y.C., 2002; exhibited in group shows Llubljana, Yugoslavia, 1981, Tokyo, 1989, Davison Art Ctr., Wesleyan U., 1988, 98, numerous others; represented in permanent collections Davison Art Ctr., N.Y. State Mus., Albany, Smithsonian Instn., Washington, Met. Mus. Art, N.Y.C.; represented in Art in Embassies program; commns. include poster and print U.S. Constn. Bicentennial, 1989, prints Am.'s Cup, 1992, paintings and prints Urban Fair, Kobe, Japan, 1991, White House Christmas card, 1994, 95, 96; author: Thomas McKnight: Voyage to Paradise, 1993. Recipient Disting. Alumni award Wesleyan U., 1998. E-mail: tmck@thomasmcknight.com.

MCKNIGHT, TOM, mechanical engineer, consultant; BS in Mech. Engring., U. Md., 1959, MS in Mech. Engring., 1964, PhD in Mech. Engring., 1970. Registered profl. engr., Md. Rsch. engr. Naval Surface Warfare Ctr., 1958—89; rsch. sci. Assoc. & Ferren, 1989—90; pres. Am. Startech Corp., 1986—; rsch. sci. Walt Disney Imagineering, 1990—; mfg. rschr. Nike, Inc., 1991—99. Lt. U.S. Army, 1952—55. Recipient Meritorious Civilian Svc. award, USN. Mem.: ASME, IEEE. Office: SAAL ASB 2511 Jefferson Davis Hwy Ste 11500 Arlington VA 22202-3911*

MCKNIGHT, WILLIAM BALDWIN, physics educator; b. Macon, Ga., July 4, 1923; s. Gilbert Franklin and Exie (Baldwin) McK.; m. Helen Mabel Bowling, Oct. 1, 1955; children: Tandy Ringoringo, Linda McKnight Gibson. BS, Purdue U., 1950; PhD, Oxford U., 1968. Physicist Underwater Sound Reference Lab., Orlando, Fla., 1952-53, U.S. Army Missile Command, Redstone Arsenal, Ala., 1953-61, supervisory rsch. physicist, 1961-74; cons. Ballistic Missile Def. Advanced Tech. Ctr., 1975; rsch. prof. physics U. Ala., Huntsville, 1974—; pres. Tech. Rsch. Assocs. Inc., 1984—. Contbr. articles to profl. jours. Vice pres. Cotaco Cmtys. League, Somerville, Ala., 1964-65; mem. Madison County Rep. Exec. Com.; mgr. Gordo Area C. of C., 1993-97; chmn. transp./infrastructure com. Pickens County Strategic Planning, 1994-96; mem. North-South Hwy. Corridor, West Ala. Coalition Task Force, 1995-96; chmn. Citizens for the Improvement of Pickens County, 1997—; chmn. adv. coun. Pickens County Commn.; bd. dirs. West Ctrl. Partnership of Ala.; chair Gordo Area Indsl. Devel. Authority; mem. Ala. Silver-Haired Legislature, 2001. Decorated D.F.C., Air medal with three oak leaf clusters; recipient Research and Devel. award U.S. Army, 1961, 64, Presdl. Unit Citation with oak leaf cluster; Sec. of Army fellow, 1966-67. Fellow Optical Soc. Am.; mem. IEEE (sr.), Am. Phys. Soc., Rotary (pres. Gordo club 1997-98), Oxford and Cambridge Club, Tuscaloosa Univ. Club, Sigma Xi, Sigma Pi Sigma. Mem. Ch. of Christ. Home: 770 Clear Creek Rd Gordo AL 35466-4446

MCKNIGHT, WILLIAM EDWIN, minister; b. Grenada, Miss., Mar. 21, 1938; s. Leslie Spurgeon and Lucy Jennings (Sistrunk) McK.; m Sue Belle Roberts, Aug. 5, 1960; children: Susan Michele, William Roberts. BA, Millsaps Coll., 1960; BD, Lexington (Ky.) Theol. Sem., 1963. Ordained to ministry, 1964. Chaplain intern Grady Hosp., Atlanta, 1963-64; pastor First Christian Ch., Cleveland, Miss., 1964-67, Inverness, 1964-67, assoc. pastor Jackson, 1967-70; regional minister Christian Ch. (Disciples of Christ) in Miss., 1971—. Bd. dirs. Nat. City Christian Ch., Washington, Christian Brotherhood Homes, Jackson, So. Christian Svcs., Macon, Ga.; mem. Gen. Bd. the Christian Ch., Indpls., 1969—, bd. dirs. fin. coun., 1979-82; mem. bd. higher edn., St. Louis, 1979-80. Named one of Outstanding Young Men Am. U.S. Jaycees, 1976. Mem. Miss. Religious Leadership Conf. (pres. 1984-85), Conf. Regional Ministers and Moderators (pres. 1985-86). Office: Christian Ch Disciples Christ in Miss PO Box 4832 Jackson MS 39296-4832 E-mail: ccdmsbill@aol.com.

MCKOIN, HAZEL MCKINNEY, social worker, instructor; b. Berryville, Ark., Sept. 15, 1942; d. Joe Nordley and Elsie Irene (Wilson) McKinney; m. John Allen McKoin II, Dec. 4, 1971; 1 child Rachel Anne. BA summa cum laude, U. Ark., 1964; MSW, Tulane U., 1968. Lic. clin. social worker. Child welfare worker Ark. Welfare Dept. (named changed to Ark. Dept. Human Svcs), Little Rock, 1964-68; social work supr. Ark. State Hosp., 1968-72; caseworker III Family Svc. Agy. Cen. Ark., North Little Rock, 1972-91; mem. staff profl. practice and pers. com. Family Svc. Agy. Ctrl. Ark., 1988-91; social worker pediatric rehab. unit Ark. Children's Hosp., 1991-94; ret., 1994. Cons. Parents Autism Network; v.p. Ctrl. Ark. Head Injury Network, 1991-94. Co-founder adult women's sexual abuser survivors Rape Crisis Ctr., 1992; vol. partial hospitalization program, group leaders resdl. facility programs Greater Little Rock Mental Health Ctr., 1994—; vol. Ark. chpt. Nat. Alliance for the Mentally Ill., 1997—; supt. Sunday sch. Trinity United Meth. Ch., 1987—97, vol. in child care, 1997—. MIMH grantee, 1982. Mem.: AARP, AAUW (rec. sec. 1970—71), NASW, Bus. and Profl. Women's Assn. (rec. sec. 1970—71), Nat. Acad. Cert. Social Workers, Brotherhood Locomotive Engrs., Pulaski County Humane Soc. Aux., Order Ea. Star (Adah 1970—71, Esther 1971—72). Democrat. Avocations: walking, reading, teddy bear collecting, senior fitness programs, outreach to support ill and grieving.

MCKOWEN, DOROTHY KEETON, librarian, educator, consultant; b. Bonne Terre, Mo., Oct. 5, 1948; d. John Richard and Dorothy (Spoonhour) Keeton; m. Paul Edwin McKowen, Dec. 19, 1970; children: Richard James, Mark David. BS, Pacific Christian Coll., 1970; MLS, U. So. Calif., 1973; MA in English, Purdue U., 1985, postgrad., 1991—. Libr.-specialist Doheny Libr., U. So. Calif., L.A., 1973-74; asst. libr. Pacific Christian Coll., 1974-78; serials cataloger Purdue U. Librs., 1978-88; head children's and young adult svcs. Kokomo-Howard County Pub. Libr., Ind., 1988-89, coord. children's and tech. svcs., 1989-91; cataloger, network libr. Ind. Coop. Libr. Svcs. Authority, 1991-2001; libr. cons. and contractor, 2001—. Mem. adj. faculty C.C. of Ind., 2001—. Mem. ALA, MLA, Soc. Early Americanists, Assn. for Libr. Collections and Tech. Svcs. (bd. dirs. 1986-90, 95-96, vice chair, chair-elect coun. of regional groups 1986-88, chair 1988-90, conf. program com. 1986-88, internat. rels. com. 1986-88, micropub. com. 1986-87, subject analysis com., membership com. 1988-90, planing and rsch. com. 1988-90, chair program initiatives com. 1991-93, orgn. and bylaws com. 1991-92, 99-2001), Network OCLC Svc. Mgrs. (MARC Task Force 2000-01), Ind. Coun. Libr. Automation (bibliog. stds. task force), Ind. Libr. Fedn. (chair tech. svcs. divsn. 1984-85), Ohio Valley Group Tech. Svcs. Libr. (chmn. 1985-86). Republican. Home: 7625 Summit Ln Lafayette IN 47905-9729 E-mail: mckowen@remconline.net.

MCKOWN, CHARLES HENRY, dean; b. Huntington, W.Va., Dec. 29, 1934; BS, W.Va. U., 1956; MD, Med. Coll. Va., 1960. Intern Med. Coll. Va., 1961; resident in radiology McGuire VA Hosp., 1961—62; fellow NIH, 1964—67; prof. radiology, chmn. dept. radiology Marshall U., Huntington, W.Va., 1975—88, v.p. health scis., dean Sch. Medicine, 1989—. Office: Marshall U Joan C Edwards Sch Medicine Ste 3400 1600 Medical Center Dr Huntington WV 25701-3655

MC KOY, BASIL VINCENT CHARLES, theoretical chemist, educator; b. Trinidad, W.I., Mar. 25, 1938; came to U.S., 1960, naturalized, 1973; s. Allan Cecil and Doris Augusta McK.; m. Anne Ellen Shannon, Mar. 18, 1967; 1 son, Christopher Allan. B.Chem. Eng., N.S. Tech. U., 1960; PhD in Chemistry (Univ. fellow), Yale U., 1964. Instr. chemistry Calif. Inst. Tech., 1964-66, asst. prof. chemistry, 1966-69, asso. prof., 1969-75, prof. theoretical chemistry, 1975—, chmn. of faculty, 1985-87. Cons. Lawrence Livermore Lab., U. Calif., Livermore, 1974— , Inst. Def. Analysis, 1984—; vis. prof. Max Planck Inst., Munich, Ger., 1976— , U. Paris, 1968— , U. Campinas, Brazil, 1976— ; lectr. Nobel Symposium, Goteborg, Sweden, 1979. Contbr. articles to Jour. Physics, London, chem. Physics Lettters, Phys. Rev., Jour. Chem. Physics; bd. editors; Chem. Physics Jour., 1977-79, mem. adv. editoral bd., 1992—; co-editor: Electron-Molecule and Photon-Molecule Collisions, 1979, 83, Swarm Studies and Inelastic Electron-Molecule Collisions, 1986; co-author: Electron-Molecule Collisions and Photoionization Processes, 1982. Recipient medal Gov.-Gen. Can., 1960; Alfred P. Sloan Found. fellow, 1969-73; Guggenheim fellow, 1973-74 Fellow Am. Phys. Soc. Home: 3855 Keswick Rd La Canada Flintridge CA 91011-3945 Office: Calif Inst Tech Divsn Chemistry Pasadena CA 91125-0001

MCKUEN, PAMELA DITTMER, journalist, educator; b. Glencoe, Minn., Aug. 4, 1951; d. Lowell Leo and Yvonne Esther (Kopischke) D. BA in Eng. Lit., Elmhurst (Ill.) Coll., 1974. Freelance journalist, 1978—; instr. journalism Columbia Coll., Chgo., 1995—. Mem. Nat. Assn. Real Estate Editors (2nd place for series of articles 1996), Fashion Group Internat. Office: 511 Timber Ridge Dr Carol Stream IL 60188-2822

MCKUSICK, JAMES CHASE, English educator; b. Wilmington, Del., Apr. 5, 1956; s. Blaine Chase and Marjorie Jane (Kirk) McK.; m. Paige Anne Willard, June 27, 1998 BA in English, Dartmouth Coll., 1979; MA in English, Yale U., 1980, MPhil in English, 1982, PhD in English, 1984. Asst. prof. English U. Md., Balt., 1984-89, assoc. prof. English, 1989—2002, prof. English, 2002—, chair English dept., 1998—. Author: Coleridge's Philosophy of Language, 1986, Green Writing: Romanticism and Ecology, 2000, Literature and Nature: Four Centuries of Nature Writing, 2001. Mem. Assn. for Study of Lit. and Environ., Wordsworth-Coleridge Assn. (pres. 1995—), Friends of Coleridge (N.Am. sec. 1992-98), John Clare Soc. N.Am. (exec. dir. 1997—), Keats-Shelley Assn., N.Am. Soc. for Study of Romanticism (exec. bd. 1995-98). Office: U Md Baltimore County English Dept 1000 Hilltop Cir Baltimore MD 21250-0001

MCKUSICK, VICTOR ALMON, geneticist, educator, physician; b. Parkman, Maine, Oct. 21, 1921; s. Carroll L. and Ethel M. (Buzzell) Mc K.; m. Anne Bishop, June 11, 1949; children: Carol Anne, Kenneth Andrew, Victor Wayne. Student, Tufts Coll., 1940-43; MD, Johns Hopkins U., 1946; DSc (hon.), N.Y. Med. Coll., 1974; MD (hon.), Liverpool U., 1976; DSc (hon.), U. Maine, 1978, Tufts U., 1978, U. Rochester, 1979, Meml. U., Nfld., 1979; DMCh (hon.), U. Helsinki, 1981; D Med. Sci. (hon.), Med. U. S.C., 1979; MD (hon.), Edinburgh U., 1984; DSc (hon.), Aberdeen U., 1988, Med. Coll. Ohio, 1988, Bates Coll., 1989; PhD (hon.), Tel Aviv U., 1989; MD (hon.), Zurich (Switzerland) U., 1990; DSc (hon.), Colby Coll., 1991, U. Chgo., 1991, Mt. Sinai Sch. Medicine, 1992. Diplomate Am. Bd. Internal Medicine. Tng. in clin. medicine, lab. rsch. Johns Hopkins U./USPHS, 1946-52; instr. medicine Johns Hopkins Sch. Medicine, 1951-54, asst. prof., 1954-57, assoc. prof., 1957-60, chief divsn. med. genetics, dept. medicine, 1957-73, prof. medicine, 1960-85, prof. epidemiology, biology, 1969-78, William Osler prof. medicine, 1978-85, chmn. dept. medicine, 1973-85; physician-in-chief Johns Hopkins Hosp., 1973-85, Univ. prof. medical genetics, 1985—, chief div. med. genetics, 1957-73, 85-89. Mem. rsch. adv. com. Nat. Found., 1959-78, med. adv. bd. Howard Hughes Med. Inst., 1967-83, com. mapping and sequencing of human genome Nat. Acad. Sci., 1986-88; pres. Internat. Med. Congress, Ltd., 1972-78; mem. Nat. Adv. Rsch. Resources Coun., 1970-74; mem. bd. sci. advisers Roche Inst. Molecular Biology, 1967-71; trustee Jackson Lab., 1979—; founding mem. Am. Bd. Med. Genetics, 1979-82; pres. 8th Internat. Congress of Human Genetics, 1991; mem. human genome adv. com. NIH, 1988-92, NIH/DOE work group on ethical, legal and societal implications of human genome project, 1990-95; co-chmn. Centennial of Johns Hopkins Hosp., 1989-90; co-founder, co-dir. ann. short course in med. and exptl. mammalian genetics, Bar Harbor, Maine, 1960—; co-founder, co-dir. European Sch. Med. Genetics Sestri Levante, 1988—; chmn. com. on DNA tech. in forensic sci. NRC/NAS, 1989-92, adv. update com., 1993-96; mem. sci. adv. bd. Celera Genomics, 1998—; founding fellow Am. Coll. Med. Genetics. Author: Heritable Disorders of Connective Tissue, 1956, 60, 66, 72, 93, Cardiovascular Sound in Health and Disease, 1958, Medical Genetics 1958-60, 1961, Human Genetics, 1964, 69, On the X Chromosome of Man, 1964, Mendelian Inheritance in Man, 1966, 68, 71, 75, 78, 83, 86, 88, 90, 92, 94, 98, Medical Genetics Self-Instruction Guide, 1993, (with others) Osler's Textbook Revisited, 1967, Genetics of Hand Malformations, 1978, Medical Genetic Studies of the Amish, 1978, A Model of its Kind, 1989, Osler's Legacy, 1990, A Century of Biomedical Science at Johns Hopkins, 1993; author, editor: Online Mendelian Inheritance in Man, 1985—; editor-in-chief Medicine jour., 1985—; founding co-editor-in-chief Genomics jour. 1987—; editor med. textbook. Recipient Disting. Achievement award Modern Medicine, 1965, John Phillips award ACP, 1972, Silver medal U. Helsinki, 1974, Gairdner Internat. award, 1977, Premio Internazionale Sanremo per le Ricerche Genetiche, 1983, Col. Saunders award March of Dimes, 1988, Disting. Alumnus award Johns Hopkins U., 1983, Alumnus Svc. award Johns Hopkins Med. Sch., 1989, Passano award, 1989, Disting. Svc. award Miami Biotech. Winter Symposium, 1991, Frank Bradway Rogers Info. Advancement award Med. Libr. Assn., 1991, Silver Columbus medal Comune di Genova, 1992, Maine prize (with twin), 1993, Mendel medal Villanova U., 1995, Big "M" award Maine State Soc. Washington, D.C., 1995, Coriell medal Coriell Inst., Camden, NJ, 1997, Lasker award for lifetime achievement in med. sci., 1997, City of Medicine award, Durham, NC, 1997; named to Internat. Pediatrics Hall of Fame, 1987, hon. citizen City of Genoa, 1997. Fellow AAAS (chair med. scis. sect. 1991), Am. Acad. Orthopedic Surgeons (hon.), Royal Coll. Physicians (London), Hastings Ctr., Am. Coll. Med. Genetics (hon.); mem. Nat. Acad. Sci. (James Murray Luck award 1982), Am. Philos. Soc. (v.p. 1996—, Benjamin Franklin medal for disting. achievement in scis. 1996), Am. Soc. Human Genetics (pres. 1975, Wm. A. Allan award 1977), Assn. Am. Physicians (Kober medal 1990), Am. Soc. Clin. Investigation (v.p. 1967), Human Genome Orgn. (founder pres. 1988-89), Am. Acad. Arts and Sci., Little People of Am. (hon. life), Acad. Nat. Médecine (France; corr.), Phi Beta Kappa, Alpha Omega Alpha, Johns Hopkins Club, West Hamilton St. Club, St. Andrew's Soc. Balt. Presbyterian (elder). Home: 221 Northway Baltimore MD 21218-1141 Office: Johns Hopkins Hosp Inst Genetic Medicine-Blalock 1007 600 N Wolfe St Baltimore MD 21287-4922

MCKUSICK, VINCENT LEE, former state supreme court chief justice, lawyer, arbitrator, mediator; b. Parkman, Maine, Oct. 21, 1921; s. Carroll Lee and Ethel (Buzzell) McK.; m. Nancy Elizabeth Green, June 23, 1951; children: Barbara Jane McKusick Liscord, James Emory, Katherine McKusick Ralston, Anne Elizabeth. AB, Bates Coll., 1943; SB, SM, MIT, 1947; LLB, Harvard U., 1950; LLD, Colby Coll., 1976, Nasson Coll., 1978, Bates Coll., 1979, Bowdoin Coll., 1979, Suffolk U., 1983; LHD, U. So. Maine, 1978, Thomas Coll., 1981. Bar: Maine 1952. Law clk. to Chief Judge Learned Hand, 1950-51; to Justice Felix Frankfurter, 1951-52; partner Pierce, Atwood, Scribner, Allen & McKusick and predecessors, Portland, Maine, 1953-77; chief justice Maine Supreme Jud. Ct., 1977-92; of counsel to Pierce Atwood (formerly Pierce, Atwood, Scribner, Allen, Smith, & Lancaster), Portland, Maine, 1992—. Mem. adv. com. rules civil procedure Maine Supreme Jud. Ct., 1957-59, chmn., 1966-75, commr. uniform state laws, 1968-76, sec. nat. conf., 1975-77; mem. Conf. Chief Justices, 1977-92, bd. dirs., 1980-82, 91-92, pres.-elect, 1989-90, pres., 1990-91; dir. Nat. Ctr. for State Ctrs., 1988-89, chmn.-elect, 1989-90, chmn., 1990-91; spl. master U.S. Supreme Ct. Conn. v. N.H., 1992-93, La. v. Miss., 1994-96, Kans. v. Nebr., 1999—; master Mass. S.J.C. Liquidation Am. Mutual Liability Ins. Co., 1995-96; leader Am. Judges Del. to China, 1983, USSR, 1988, U.S. State Dept. Rule of Law Del. to Republic of Ga., 1992; mem. permanent com. Oliver Wendell Holmes Devise, 1993-2001. Author: Patent Policy of Educational Institutions, 1947, (with Richard H. Field) Maine Civil Practice, 1959, supplements, 1962, 67, (with Richard H. Field and L. Kinvin Wroth) 2d edit., 1970, supplements, 1972, 74, 77; also articles in legal pubs. Trustee emeritus Bates Coll.; mem. adv. com. on pvt. internat. law U.S. State Dept., 1980-85, Fed.-State Jurisdiction com., Jud. Conf. of U.S., 1987-89. With AUS, 1943-46. Recipient The Maine prize U. Maine Sys., 1993, Benjamin E. Mays award Bates Coll., 1994, Big M award Maine State Soc. Washington, 1995, Paul C. Reardon award Nat. Ctr. for State Ctrs., 1999. Fellow Am. Bar Found. (bd. dirs. 1977-87), Am. Philos. Soc. (coun. 1990-96, 97—); mem. ABA (chmn. fed. rules com. 1966-71, bd. editors jour. 1971-80, chmn. 1976-77, mem. study group to China 1978, ho. dels. 1983-87, coun. sr. lawyers divsn. 1997—), Maine Bar Assn., Cumberland County Bar Assn., Am. Arbitration Assn. (bd. dirs. 1994—), Am. Judicature Soc. (dir. 1976-78, 92-98), Am. Law Inst. (coun. 1968—), Maine Jud. Coun. (chmn. 1977-92), Inst. Jud. Adminstrn., Supreme Ct. Hist. Soc. (trustee 1994—), Rotary Club (hon., past pres. Portland club), Phi Beta Kappa, Sigma Xi, Tau Beta Pi. Republican. Unitarian Universalist. Home: 1152 Shore Rd Cape Elizabeth ME 04107-2115 Office: 1 Monument Sq Portland ME 04101-1110 E-mail: judgemac@aol.com., vmckusick@pierceatwood.com.

MCLACHLAN, SARAH, composer, musician; b. Halifax, Nova Scotia, Jan. 28, 1968; Albums include Touch, 1989, Solace, 1991, Live EP, 1992, Fumbling Towards Ecstasy, 1994, Freedom Sessions, 1995, Rarities, B-Sides, and Other Stuff, 1996, Surfacing, 1997, Mirrorball (live), 1999; appearances include Gravity, 1991, Island of Circles: A Nettwork C, 1991, No Alternative, 1993, Christmas at Mountain Stage, 1994, Testimonial Dinner: the Songs of Xt, 1995, Memories of the Soul Shack Survivor, 1996, Heroine, 1996; worked with Delerium, Donovan; founder, performer Lilith Fair, 1997, 98, 99. Recipient Best Female Pop Vocal Performance award Grammy, 1998, Best Pop Instrumental Performance award, 1998. Office: c/o Arista Records 6 W 57th St New York NY 10019-3901*

MCLACHLIN, BEVERLEY, Canadian supreme court chief justice; b. Pincher Creek, Alta., Can., Sept. 7, 1943; m. Roderick McLachlin (dec. 1988); 1 child Angus ; m. Frank E. McArdle, 1992. BA, MA in Philosophy, LLB, U. Alta., LLD (hon.) , 1991, U. B.C., 1990, U. Toronto, 1995, York U., 1999, Law Soc. Upper Can., 2000, U. Ottawa, 2000, U. Calgary, 2000, Brock U., 2000, Simon Fraser U., 2000, U. Victoria, 2000, U. Alberta, 2000, U. Lethbridge, 2001, Bridgewater State Coll., 2001, Mt. St. Vincent U., 2002, U. PEI, 2002. Bar: Alta. 1969, B.C. 1971. Assoc. Wood, Moir, Hyde and Ross, Edmonton, Canada, 1969—71, Thomas, Herdy, Mitchell & Co., Fort St. John, Canada, 1971—72, Bull, Housser and Tupper, Vancouver, 1972—75; lectr., assoc. prof., prof. with tenure U. B.C., 1974—81; appointed to County Ct., Vancouver, 1981; justice Supreme Ct. of B.C., 1981—85, B.C. Ct. of Appeal, Canada, 1985—88; chief justice Supreme Ct. of B.C., Canada, 1988; justice Supreme Ct. Can., Ottawa, Canada, 1989—2000, chief justice Canada, 2000—. Co-author: B.C. Supreme Court Practice, B.C. Court Forms, Canadian Law of Arch. and Engring.; contbr. articles to profl. jours. Office: Supreme Ct Bldg 301 Wellington St Ottawa ON Canada K1A 0J1

MCLAFFERTY, FRED WARREN, chemist, educator; b. Evanston, Ill., May 11, 1923; s. Joel E. and Margaret E. (Keifer) McLafferty; m. Elizabeth E. Curley, Feb. 5, 1948; children: Sara L., Joel P., Martha A., Samuel A., Ann E. BS, U. Nebr., 1943, DSc (hon.), 1983, MS, 1947; PhD, Cornell U., 1950; DSc (hon.), U. Liege, Belgium, 1987, Purdue U., 1995. Fellow U. Iowa, 1949-50; rsch. chemist, divsn. leader Dow Chem. Co., 1950-56; dir. Eastern Rsch. Lab., 1956-64; prof. chemistry Purdue U., 1964-68, Cornell U., 1968-92, Peter J.W. Debye prof. chemistry emeritus, 1992—. Chem. sci. and tech. bd., numerical data adv. bd., bd. Army sci. tech., bd. radioactive waste mgmt. NRC; chem. co-chmn. World Bank's Chinese Univ. Devel. Project. Author: Mass Spectrometry of Organic Ions, 1963, Mass Spectral Correlations, 2d edit., 1981, Interpretation of Mass Spectra, 4th edit., 1993, Tandem Mass Spectrometry, 1983, Advances in Analytical Chemistry and Instrumentation; (with C.N. Reilley), Vols. 4-7, 1967-70, Index and Bibliography of Mass Spectrometry, (with J. Pinzelik), 1967, Atlas of Mass Spectral Data; (with E. Stenhagen and S. Abrahamsson), 1969, Registry of Mass Spectral Data, 1974; (with D.B. Stauffer) Wiley/NBS Registry of Mass Spectral Data, 1989, Important Peak Index of Mass Spectral Data, 1991; editor: Accounts of Chemical Research, 1986-94; co-editor: (with E. Stenhagen and S. Abrahamsson) Archives of Mass Spectral Data, 1969-72. With AUS, 1942-45, ETO. Decorated Purple Heart, Combat Inf. badge, Bronze Star with 4 oak leaf clusters, Presdl. Unit citation; recipient Pitts. Spectroscopy award Spectroscopy Soc. Pitts., 1975, Gold medal U. Naples, 1989, Robert Boyle Gold medal Royal Soc. Chemistry, 1992, Bijvoet medal U. Utrecht, 1997, W.L. Evans award Ohio State U., 1987, Jaroslav Heyrovsky Gold medal Czech Acad. Scis., 1999, Giulio Natta Gold medal Italian Chem. Soc., 2000, Torbern Bergman medal Swedish Chem. Soc., 2001; John Simon Guggenheim fellow, 1972, Overseas fellow Churchill Coll., Cambridge (Eng.) U., 1979. Fellow: AAAS, NAS, Am. Acad. Arts and Scis., N.Y. Acad. Scis.; mem.: Italian Nat. Acad. Scis. (fgn.), Am. Inst. Chemists (Chem. Pioneer award 1996), Am. Soc. Mass. Spectrometry (founder, sec. 1957—58), Assn. Analytical Chemists (Anachem award 1985), Internat. Spectrometry Orgn. (Sir J.J. Thompson gold medal 1985), Am. Chem. Soc. (chmn. analytical chem. divsn. 1969, chmn. Midland sect. 1956, Northeastern sect. 1964, award chem. instrumentation 1971, award analytical chemistry 1981, Nichols medal N.Y. sect. 1984, Oesper award Cin. sect. 1986, award mass spectrometry 1989), Soc. Analytical Chemists (Pitts. Analytical Chemist award 1987, Pioneer Analytical Instrumentation award 1994), Alpha Chi Sigma, Phi Lambda Upsilon, Sigma Xi. Home: 103 Needham Pl Ithaca NY 14850-2120 E-mail: Fredwmcl@aol.com.

MCLAIN, DAVID ANDREW, internist, rheumatologist; b. Chgo., Aug. 16, 1948; s. William Rex and Wilma Lucille (Raschka) McL.; m. Pamela Rose Fullmer, June 15, 1974; children: Edward, Richard. BA, Northwestern U., 1970; MD with Honors, Tulane U., 1974. Diplomate Am. Bd. Internal Medicine, Am. Bd. Rheumatology. Intern Oschner Clinic, New Orleans, 1974-75; resident Barnes Hosp., St. Louis, 1975-77; fellow in rheumatology Washington U., 1977-79, instr. dept. medicine, 1979-81; with VA Hosp., 1979-81; pvt. practice Birmingham, Ala., 1981—; chief rheumatology sect. dept. internal medicine Brookwood Med. Ctr., 1983-87, 89-90, 91-95, 1997—, med. dir. phys. therapy, 1986-96, mem. exec. com., chmn. med. edn. com., 1997—. Mem. staff St. Vincent's Hosp., Birmingham, 1981—, Shelby Med. Ctr., Alabaster, Ala., 1982—, Lakeshore Rehab. Hosp., Birmingham, 1983-97, HealthSouth Hosp., 1989—; dir. courses continuing med. edn., 1983—; mem., investigator musculoskeletal acad. clin. consortium U. Ala., Birmingham, 1997-2001. Editor: (jour. series) Internal Medicine; contbr. articles, abstracts to profl. jours. Mem. med. adv. com. Birmingham chpt. Lupus Found. Am., 1982—, co-originator Lupus Day, Brookwood Med. Ctr., 1983—; bd. dirs. north ctrl. br. Arthritis Found., 1982-96, organizer, originator Benefit Horse Show and Art Fair, Birmingham, 1985, del. nat. coun., 1987, chmn. med. and sci. com. Ala. chpt., 1988-89; active Nat. Arthritis Found.; med. advisor Sjogren's Syndrome Found., 1988—; mem. Coun. Healthcare Advisors, 1999—. Recipient award of Appreciation Ala. Podiatry Assn., 1984, Ala. Chpt. Arthritis Found., 1986, award for Decade of Leadership in Rheumatology, 1992, Excellence in Tchg. award Med. Assn. State of Ala., 1995, Significant Physician award Arthritis Found. Ala. Chpt., 1999. Fellow: ACP; mem.: AMA (Physicians Recognition 1979, 1982, 1985, 1988, 1991, 1991, 1997, 2000), Ala. Arthritis Prevention and Treatment Coalition, Brookwood Splty. Physicians Assn. (pres. 1990—97, founding incorporator, bd. dirs.), Jefferson County Med. Soc., Med. Assn. State Ala. (Excellence in Tchg. award 1995), Ala. Soc. Internal Medicine, Ala. Soc. Rheumatic Diseases (sec.-treas. 1996—97, v.p. 1997—98, rep. medicare carrier adv. com. 1997—2000, pres. 1998—99), Am. Med. Equestrian Assn. (bd. dirs. 1995—97, coord. ann. meeting 1997, treas. 2001—), Am. Soc. Internal Medicine, Am. Coll. Rheumatology (com. on rheumatol. care network 1997—, founding mem.), Nat. Equestrian Fedn. (safety com. 2001—), U.S. Combined Tng. Assn. (bd. govs. 1992—94, chmn. safety com. 1992—98, chmn. ad hoc coalition to promote equestrian helmet safety 1993—95, ann. meeting com. 1996—97, U.S. equestrian savety com. 2001—, area coun., editor newsletter, dult riders com.), U.S. Dressage Fedn. (founder aux. U.S. Test Callers Assn.), Alpha Omega Alpha. Avocation: equestrian combined training or eventing. Office: Birmingham Rheumatology 2022 Brookwood Med Ctr Dr Ste 509 Birmingham AL 35209-6807 E-mail: dmclain@pol.net.

MCLAIN, DONALD J. educational consultant; b. St. Louis, Sept. 15, 1935; s. Clyde and Genevieve Dwyer McLain; m. Geraldine Peach McLain, May 13, 1961; children: James P., Matthew J. BS, St. Louis U., 1958. Dir. United Fund, St. Louis, 1963-68; exec. dir. Am. Optometric Found., 1968-74; exec. v.p. Optometric Progress Fund, 1968-74; alumni dir. profl. schs. Washington U., 1974-77; v.p. instnl. advancement Maryville U., 1977-93, Logan Coll. Chiropractic, St. Louis, 1993—2002; campaign cons. Humane Soc. Mo., 2001—. Participant confs. in field. Mem. pub. rels. com. Christmas in St. Louis; mem. allocations com. United Way; past pres. Wedgewood Improvement Assn.; v.p. fair Pub. Rels. Com. Sgt. U.S. Army, 1957, USAR, 1957-62. Mem. Nat. Soc. Fund Raising Execs., Am. Soc. Assn. Execs., Nat. Coun. on Philanthropy, Chesterfield C. of C., Sales and Mktg. Club St. Louis, Advt. Club, St. Louis COUNTS, Deferred Giving Club of St. Louis, Kiwanis, Rotary (past pres. West County chpt.). Roman Catholic. Address: 2009 Long Gate Ct Chesterfield MO 63017

MCLAIN, JOHN LOWELL, resource specialist, consultant; b. Havre, Mont., Jan. 23, 1942; s. Woodrow B. and Ann Teresa (Bolta) McL.; m. Carolyn Louise Peterson, June 27, 1964; children: Nicole Rachelle, Tanya Lynn. BS in Range Mgmt., Mont. State U., 1969. Cert. range mgmt. cons.; cert. soil erosion & sediment control specialist. Soil conservationist USDA Soil Conservation Svc., Miles City, Mont., 1969-71, range conservationist Glendive, 1971-74, area range conservationist Minden, Nev., 1974-76, dist. conservationist, 1976-78; co-founder, prin. resource specialist Resource Concepts Inc., Carson City, 1978—. Bd. dirs. Range Mag., Carson City; keynote spkr. Desert Tech. IV Internat. Conf., 1997; mem. governing bd. Policy Analysis Ctr. for Western Pub. Lands. Mem. citizens adv. bd. U. Nev.-Reno, 1981—; Nev. del. Coun. for Agrl. Rsch. Ext. and Tchg., Washington, 1983-97, 99—. Recipient Outstanding Achievement award Carson Valley Conservation Dist., 1978; named Man of 1980s Nevada Appeal City newspaper, 1980. Fellow Soc. for Range Mgmt. (pres. Nev. sect. 1980, Rangeman of Yr. Nev. sect. 1987); mem. Soil and Water Conservation Soc. (pres. Nev. sect. 1982), Soc. Range Mgmt (dir. 1993-96), Soc. Range Mgmt. (pres. 2000), Resource Restoration Internat. (mem. adv. com. 1992), Range Edn. Inst. (dir. 1995—). Roman Catholic. Avocations: fishing, guitar/singing, horseback riding, skiing, hunting. Home: 2424 Manhattan Dr Carson City NV 89703-5416 Office: Resource Concepts Inc 340 N Minnesota St Carson City NV 89703-4152

MCLAIN, WILLIAM ALLEN, lawyer; b. Chgo., Oct. 19, 1942; s. William Rex and Wilma L. (Raschka) McL.; divorced; children: William A., David M., Heather A.; m. Kristine R. Zierk. BS, So. Ill. U., 1966; JD, Loyola U., Chgo., 1971. Bar: Ill. 1971, U.S. Dist. Ct. (no. dist). Ill. 1971, U.S. Ct. Appeals (7th cir.) 1971, Colo. 1975, U.S. Dist. Ct. Colo. 1975, U.S. Ct. Appeals (10th cir.) 1975. Law clk. U.S. Dist. Ct. (no. dist.) Ill., Chgo., 1971-72; assoc. Sidley & Austin, 1972-75; ptnr. Welborn, Dufford, Brown & Tooley, Denver, 1975-86; pres. William. A. McLain PC, 1986—; ptnr. McLain & Singer, Denver, 1990—. Mem. Dist. 10 Legis. Vacancy Commn., Denver, 1984-86. Served with U.S. Army, 1966-68. Recipient Leadership and Scholastic Achievement award Loyola U. Alumni Assn., 1971. Mem. Colo. Bar Assn. (lobbyist 1983-85), Denver Bar Assn., Colo. Assn. Commerce and Industry (legis. policy coun. 1983-88), Colo. Mining Assn. (state and local affairs com. 1978-88), Inst. Property Taxation, Mt. Vernon Country Club, Roundup Riders of the Rockies Club, Masons, Shriners, Scottish Rite, York Rite. Republican. Home and Office: 3962 S Olive St Denver CO 80237-2038

MCLAIN, WILLIAM TOME, principal, educator; b. Washington, July 10, 1935; s. Ronald Alpha and Dorothy Smithson (Tome) McL.; m. Meurial Claire Webb, Nov. 20, 1977; 1 child, Laura Louisa McLain. BA, U. Del., 1957, MEd, 1966. Secondary Prin. Cert., Del. Math. tchr. Newark Sch. Dist., 1957-69, high sch. adminstrv. asst., 1969-78; high sch. assoc. prin. New Castle County Sch. Dist., Newark, 1978-81; high sch. asst. prin. Christina Sch. Dist., 1981-84, middle sch. asst. prin., 1984-87, prin. adult edn. program, 1987—. Treas., past chmn. Del. Coalition for Literacy; past pres. Del. Assn. for Adult and Cmty. Edn. Recipient Tchrs. medal Freedoms Found., 1968, Silver Beaver award Boy Scouts Am., 1967, Walace Johnson Cmty. Svc. award New Castle County C. of C., 1979, Adult and Family Lit. Outstanding Svc. award State of Del., 1992, Pres.'s award Del. Assn. for Adult and Cmty. Edn., 2001. Mem. Interagency Coun. on Adult Lit. United Methodist. Avocations: travel, history. Home: 95 Dallas Ave Newark DE 19711-5123 Office: Christina School District 925 Bear Corbitt Rd Bear DE 19701-1323

MCLANAHAN, CHARLES SCOTT, neurosurgeon; b. Chgo., Sept. 23, 1946; s. Charles Jackson and Anna Martin (Findley) McL.; m. Mary Ivey, Aug. 23, 1975; children: George, Ward, Matt. BA, Yale U., 1969; MD, Columbia U., 1973. Diplomate Am. Bd. Neurol. Surgery, Am. Bd. Pediat. Neurol. Surgery. Resident in neurosurgery Emory U., Atlanta, 1973-78, instr. neurosurgery, 1979; asst. prof. neurosurgery La. State U. Med. Sch., New Orleans, 1979-80; neurosurgeon Carolina Neurosurgery & Spine Assocs., PA, Charlotte, 1980—. Mem.: N.C. Neurosurg. Soc. (sec.-treas. 1997—99, pres. 1999—2001). Republican. Avocation: golf. Office: Carolina Neurosurg & Spine Assocs PA 1010 Edgehill Rd N Charlotte NC 28207-1885

MCLANE, BOBBIE JONES, retired government executive, genealogist, publisher; b. Hot Springs, Ark., Feb. 19, 1927; d. Julian Everette and Eula (Deaton) Jones; m. Gerald Bert McLane, Aug. 14, 1954 (dec. 1994). Chief clk. Army and Navy Hosp., Hot Springs, 1950-52; adminstrv. asst. Wis. Mil. Dist., Milw., 1952-54; exec. sec. to postmaster U.S. Postal Svc., Hot Springs, 1954-70, supr. employment svcs., 1970-74, dir. employee and labor rels., 1974-80, acting postmaster Arkadelphia, Ark., 1978, dir. employee and labor rels. Ft. Smith, 1980-86; ret., 1986. Compiler, author pub. Ark. Ancestors, 120 titles, 1962; editor The Record, 1966—. Organizer, charter mem. Garland County Hist. Soc., Hot Springs, 1960—, exec. dir. archives, 2001—; bd. dirs., chmn. Ark. History Commn.-State Archives, 1966-80, 90—; charter mem., bd. dirs. Cmty. Players Hot Springs, 1949-55. Recipient award for contbns. to hist. and geneal. rsch. Am. Assn. State and Local History, 1967, Bicentennial award Postmaster Gen. U.S. Postal Svc., 1976; named One of 100 Ark. Women of Achievement, Ark. Press Women, 1980; Am. Assn. State and Local History fellow Vanderbilt U., 1967. Mem. Profl. Genealogists Ark. (bd. dirs. 1988—), Ark. Geneal. Soc. (charter, bd. dirs. 1960—, past pres.). Democrat. Episcopalian. Home and Office: 222 Mcmahan St Hot Springs National Park AR 71913-6243

MCLANE, DAVID GLENN, lawyer; b. Dallas, Jan. 17, 1943; s. Alfred Ervin and Dixie Marie (Martin) McL.; m. Sally Ruth Payne, Apr. 5, 1963; children: Cynthia Lynn, Kathleen Michelle, Michael Scott; m. Beverly Anne Bledsoe, Feb. 5, 1983; children: Morgan Elizabeth, Nicholas Martin, Elizabeth Clark. BA, So. Meth. U., 1963, LLB, 1966. Bar: Tex. 1966, U.S. Supreme Ct. 1971. Briefing atty. Supreme Ct. Tex., 1966-67; assoc., then ptnr. Gardere Wynne Sewell LLP (and predecessor firm), Dallas, 1967—. Lectr. in field. Author: Texas Corporations - Law and Practice, 1984; editor: Incorporation Planning in Texas, 1977. Bd. dirs. urban Svcs. br. YMCA, Dallas, 1977-84, Dallas Symphony assn., 1980-93; mem. Dallas County AIDS Planning Commn. Task Force, 1988; pres. Coun. Dallas Theol. Sem., 1994—; exec. bd. Law Sch. So. Meth. U., 1997—; mem. ministry coun. Josh McDowell Ministries, 1997—. Mem. ABA, Tex. Bar Assn., Dallas Bar Assn., S.W. Benefits Assn. (bd. dirs. 1975-80, prs. 1978-79), So. Meth. U. Law Alumni Assn. (sec., bd. dirs. 1981-85, Vol. of Yr. award 1984), So. Meth. U. Alumni Assn. (bd. dirs. 1972-77). Presbytrian. Office: 3000 Thanksgiving Tower Dallas TX 75201 E-mail: dmclane@gardere.com.

MCLANE, FREDERICK BERG, lawyer; b. Long Beach, Calif., July 24, 1941; s. Adrian B. and Arlie K. (Burrell) McL.; m. Lois C. Roberts, Jan. 28, 1967; children: Willard, Anita. BA, Stanford U., 1963; LLB, Yale U., 1966. Bar: Calif. 1967, U.S. Dist. Ct. (cen. dist.) Calif. 1967. Assoc. prof. law U. Miss., Oxford, 1966-68; assoc. O'Melveny & Myers LLP, L.A., 1968-74, ptnr., 1975—. Com. of counsel HUD, Los Angeles, 1979-84; lectr. in field. Pres., bd. dirs. Legal Aid Found., L.A., 1974-83; deacon Congl. Ch., Sherman Oaks, Calif., 1979-83; vice-chair L.A. Music Ctr., Unified Fund, 1992-94; bd. dirs. Calif. Sci. Ctr. Found., 1991-2000. Mem. ABA (banking com., fed. regulation of securities com.), Calif. Bar Assn. (fin. insts. com., uniform comml. codes), L.A. Bar Assn., Order of Coif, Calif. Club (L.A.), L.A. Country Club (bd. dirs.), Lakeside Golf Club (L.A.). Democrat. Avocations: golf, walking, reading. Office: O'Melveny & Myers 400 S Hope St Los Angeles CA 90071-2899 E-mail: fmclane@omm.com.

MCLANE, HENRY EARL, JR. philosophy educator; b. Statesboro, Ga., Aug. 18, 1932; s. Henry Earl and Lillie Ora (Beasley) McL.; m. Barbara Helen Gardner, Nov. 7, 1934; children— Debra Lynn, Shawn Creg BA, George Washington U., 1955; postgrad., Johns Hopkins U., 1955-56; MA, Yale U., 1958, PhD, 1961. Instr. philosophy Washburn U. of Topeka, Kans., 1960-61, asst. prof., 1961-64, assoc. prof., 1964-65; vis. assoc. prof. philosophy Coll. of William and Mary, Williamsburg, Va., 1965-66, assoc. prof., 1967-77, prof., 1978-96, prof. emeritus, 1996—. Diving coach Coll. of William and Mary, 1976-87. Contbr. articles to profl. publs. Danforth Found. fellow, 1955-60 Mem. Am. Philos. Assn. Democrat. Baptist. Avocations: playing violin; music. Home: 116 Dogwood Dr Williamsburg VA 23185-3743

MCLANE, WILLIAM DELANO, mechanical engineer; b. Ralls, Tex., Aug. 22, 1936; s. Clyde and Lillian Helen (Earp) McL.; m. Mary Ann Clark, Feb. 17, 1962; children: William Devin, Keri, Kristi, Mandy. BSME, Tex. Tech. U., 1961. Profl. engr. Tex. Engr. Texaco Inc., Tulsa, 1961-63; plant engring. mgr. Owens-Corning Fiberglas Corp., Toledo, 1963-72; pres., CEO Tucker-McLane Tire Corp., Waxahachie, Tex., 1972-89; commr. County of Ellis, 1989-93; engr. Morrison Knudsen Corp., Dallas, 1993-94, MK-Ferguson, Albuquerque, 1994-95, Parsons Brinckerhoff, Dallas, 1995-96; quality control mgr. Sedalco, Inc., Ft. Worth, 1996-97; engring. mgr. Fortra Fiber-Cement, LLC., Waxahachie, 1997-2001; constrn. mgr. FWTA commuter rail project Parsons Brinckerhoff Constrn. Svcs., Inc., Dallas, 2001—. Mem. adv. bd. Guaranty Fed. Bank, Waxahachie, 1993—, Citizens Nat. Bank, Waxahachie, 1991-92, City of Waxahachie, 1990-91, Tex. State Tech. Coll., Inc., Waco, 1998—, Navarro Coll., Corsicana, 1998—, Portland Cement Assn., Skokie, Ill., 1998—. Sec. bd. Waxahachie Sch. Dist., 1979-88; vice chmn. Ctrl. Tex. Econ. Devel. Dist., Waco, 1989-93; mem. adv. com. Tex. State Tech. Coll., Waco, 1998—. Mem. ASME, ASCE, NSPE, Tex. Soc. Profl. Engrs., So. Bldg. Code Congress Internat., Internat. Soc. Tribologists and Lubrication Engrs., Internat. Conf. Bldg. Officials, Waxahachie C. of C. (pres. 1977). Republican. Presbyterian. Avocations: civic and political volunteer work, golf, fishing, cooking. Home: 1612 Alexander Dr Waxahachie TX 75165-1902 Office: Parsons Brinckerhoff Constrn Svcs Ste 1333 2777 Stemmons Fwy Ste 1333 Dallas TX 75207 E-mail: delmclane@aol.com.

MCLAREN, ARCHIE CAMPBELL, JR. marketing executive; b. Atlanta, Sept. 25, 1942; s. Archie Campbell and Virginia Lynn (Sides) McLaren; m. Georgia Mae Blunt, 1969 (div. 1971); 1 child Leslie Michelle ; m. Yvette Rubio, June 17, 1995 (div. Dec. 2001). BA, Vanderbilt U., 1964; JD, Memphis State U., 1968. Clk. FBI, Memphis, 1965-66; tchr., tennis coach Memphis U. Sch., 1966-68; tchr. Hunt High Sch., Columbus, Miss., 1968-69; tennis coach Miss. State U., Starkville, 1968-69; concierge The Roosevelt Hotel, New Orleans, 1969-70; sales rep. West Pub. Co., St. Paul, 1970-84, adminstr. internat. mktg. The Orient, 1985-90; freelance wine cons., 1985—. Cons. Calif. Ctrl. Coast Wine Growers Assn., Santa MAria, 1987-91; lectr. advanced wine appreciation Calif. Poly. U. Extended Edn., San Luis Obispo, 1986-90; dir. KCBX Ctrl. Coast Wine Classic, San Luis Obispo, 1985—, KHPR Wine Classic, Honolulu, 1987-91, Winesong, Ft. Bragg, Calif., 1987-96, WETA Washington Wine Classic, 1989-90, KCRW Summerday, 1991, Santa Barbara Wine Auction, 1997-98, auction dir., 1992-94, 97, 98—; auction cons. Am. Inst. of Wine And Food, 1994—; chmn. Edna Valley Arroyo Grande Valley Vinters' Assn., 1999—. Host talk show Pub. Radio Sta. KCBX, San Luis Obispo, 1984—; columnist (newspaper) San Luis Obispo Telegram-Tribune, 1992-95, New Times San Luis Obispo, 1995-96; contbg. writer: Adventures in Dining, 1994-95, Santa Barbara Mag., 1998-2001. Dir. Internat. Festival Champagne and Sparkling Wine, 1992—98; mem. Avila Valley Adv. Coun., 1993—95, City of San Luis Obispo Tourism Coun., 2000—; founder Avila Drum Day; chmn. Avila Beach Cmty. Arts Com., 2000—; bd. dirs. Avila Beach County Water Dist., 1992—95, pres., 1992—94, San Luis Obispo (Calif.) Mozart Festival, 1988—92, 1991—92, mem. festival devel. com., 2000—01; bd. dirs. Am. Inst. Wine and Food, 2002—, Guild South County Ctr. for Performing Arts, 1993—94, San Luis Obispo County Arts Coun., 2000—, San Luis County Visitors and Confs. Bur. Decorated Commndeur d'Honneur, Commanderie du Bontemps de Medoc on des Graves de Sauternes on Barsac, France, 2001. Mem.: Austrian Wine Brotherhood, Internat. Food, Wine and Travel Writers' Assn., San Luis Obispo Vintners and Growers Assn. (chmn. 1999—), Marin County Food and Wine Soc., Ctrl. Coast Chaine des Rotisseurs (chpt. pres. 1987—89), Avila Bay Wine Soc., Vintners Club San Francisco, German Wine Soc. Honolulu, Am. Soc. Wine Educators, Calif. Ctrl. Coast Wine Soc. (pres. 1985), San Luis Yacht Club, Avila Bay Club. Avocations: racquetball, tennis, hiking, collecting wine, basketball. Office: PO Box 790 Avila Beach CA 93424-0790

MCLAREN, FELICIA DIBLE (IRIS MCLAREN), volunteer; b. Plum Boro, Pa., Dec. 22, 1924; d. George Featherston and Susan Louise (Koch) Dible; (widowed Mar. 1977). Student, U. Pitts. Check writer Nat. Union Fire Ins. Co., Pitts., 194-53, sec. San Francisco, 1953-55, Old First Presbyn. Ch., San Francisco, 1955-56; sec., audio visual supr. Cokesbury Book Store, 1956-59; sec. McIndoes (Vt.) Acad., 1967-68. Reporter, compiler State Grange Newspaper, 1979-83. Clk. of session Barnet Ctr. (Vt.) Presbyn. Ch., 1984-89; buyer, chmn. hosp. gift shop NVRH, St. Johnsbury, Vt., 1979-89; mem. com. on ministry Presbytery of No. New Eng., Haverhill, Mass., 1988-89, voting del. to gen. assembly Presbyn. Ch., 1988; chmn. Fall Foliage Festival, Town of Barnet, Vt., 1963—; chmn. Shepherd Pomona Food Booth, Caledonia County Fair, Lydonville, Vt. Mem. Barnet Hist. Soc. (pres. 1985-88), Lakeview Grange, Shepherd Pomona Grange (master 1983-88). Republican. Avocations: geneology, fall foilage. Home: RR 1 Box 32 East Ryegate VT 05042-9710

MCLAREN, JOHN EDWARD, economics educator; b. Wadsworth, Ohio, May 21, 1962; s. Edward and Marion (Rae) McL.; m. Alev Erisir, Nov. 14, 1997. BSc, McGill U., 1986; MA, U. Toronto, 1987; PhD, Princeton U., 1992. Asst. prof. Columbia U., N.Y.C., 1992-98, assoc. prof., 1998-2000; prof. U. Va., Charlottesville, 2000—. Vis. asst. prof. Yale U., New Haven, Conn., 1996, Princeton (N.J.) U., 1997. Contbr. articles to profl. jours.; mng. editor, co-editor Economics and Politics jour., 1999—. Rsch. grantee NSF, 1999; faculty rsch. fellow Nat. Bur. Econ. Rsch., Cambridge, Mass., 2000—. Mem. Am. Econ. Assn. Office: Dept Econs U Va Rouss Hall Charlottesville VA 22903 E-mail: jmclaren@virginia.edu.

MCLAREN, JOSEPH, Black literature educator; b. N.Y.C., Feb. 14, 1948; children: Natasha, Anikah. BA, Queens Coll., 1970; MA, CCNY, 1974; AM, Brown U., 1977, PhD, 1980. Prof. English Mercy Coll., Dobbs Ferry, N.Y., 1976-90; assoc. prof. English Hofstra U., Hempstead, 1990—. Author: Langston Hughes, 1997; co-editor: Migrating Words and Worlds, 1999, African Visions, 2000; editor: The Big Sea, by Langston Hughes; contbr. articles to African Am. Ency., Ency. of Multiculturalism, Harlem Renaissance: Revaluations. Recipient Duke Ellington Legacy award Black Am. Heritage Found., 1994; NEH grantee, 1994, Faculty Devel. grantee Hofstra U., 1994. Mem. African Lit. Assn., African Studies Assn., Popular Culture Assn., Duke Ellington Soc. Avocations: jazz improvisation, jogging, travel, photography. Office: Hofstra U Dept English Hempstead NY 11549-0001

MCLAREN, SUSAN SMITH, therapist, healing touch practitioner, instructor; b. Plymouth Meeting, Pa., Jan. 21, 1941; d. Robertson Fobes and Jane (Leiper) Smith; m. Michael Eric McLaren (div. 1993). BA, Mount Holyoke Coll., 1962; cert. orthoptic technician, Bellevue Hosp., N.Y.C., 1963; MS, Villanova U., 1994. Cert. counselor Nat. Bd. Cert. Counselors, Inc. Orthoptist Bascom Palmer Eye Inst., Miami, Fla., 1963-69; lab. technician Pvt. Pathology Practice, Sydney, N.S.W., Australia, 1970-78, Nambour, Queensland, 1981-87; asst. renal medicine Mater Hosp., Sydney, 1978-81; hospice vol. Hospice of Watauga County, Boone, N.C., 1988-91; cert. practitioner, instr. Healing Touch Internat., Inc., 1991—; Reiki, CranioSacral, Spirit Releasement Therapy, Kimberton, Pa., 1995—. Adv. Camphill Village, Kimberton, 1993—, Cmty. Supported Agr., Kimberton, 1994—. Mem. editl. bd.: Aspen Publ., Inc., 1994—; contbr. articles. Judge of elections East Vincent Twp. Mem. ACA, Nat. Hospice Orgn., Nat. Fedn. Spiritual Healers, Inst. Noetic Scis. Avocations: swimming, cross-stitching, cooking, pottery.

MCLARTY, COLIN SLATOR, philosophy educator; b. Lancaster, Pa., July 12, 1951; s. Colin Slator McLarty and Sarah Baldwin Suplee; m. Patricia Princehouse. BS in Math., Case Inst. Tech., 1972; PhD in Philosophy, Case Western Res. U., 1980. Machinist Bardons & Oliver Machine Tools, Cleve., 1980-84; assoc. prof. philosophy Case Western Res. U., 1986—, chair dept. philosophy, 1998—. Author: Elementary Categories, Elementary Toposes, 1991. Vis. scholar Harvard Math. Dept., Cambridge, Mass., 1995-97. Home: 9573 Mentor Rd Chardon OH 44024-8607 Office: Case Western Res U Dept Philosophy Cleveland OH 44106 E-mail: cxm7@po.cwru.edu.

MCLAUCHLAN, SYLVIA JUNE, charity organization executive; b. Hornchurch, Essex, Eng., June 8, 1935; d. Sydney George and Muriel May (Treweek) Smith; m. Derek John A. McLauchlan, Aug. 6, 1960. MB, ChB, U. Bristol, Eng., 1959; MSc, U. Manchester, Eng., 1979. Gen. practitioner, Bristol, 1960-66; med. officer Portsmouth (Eng.) City Coun., 1970-76; pub. health physician Univ.-Regional Health Authority, Manchester, 1976-85, S.W. Thames Regional Health Authority, London, 1985-91; dir. pub. health Ealing (Eng.) Health Authority, 1991-93; dir. gen. The Stroke Assn., London, 1993-97. Cons. in pub. health medicine; chmn. primary care Facilitation Trust; gov. Treloar Sch. for Physically Disabled Young People; trustee E. Thames Care. Fellow Faculty Pub. Health Medicine.

MCLAUGHLIN, BRUCE DUANE, materials scientist; b. Muncie, Ind., June 25, 1942; s. Earl McLaughlin and Imogene Joyce (Kelley) Patberg; m. Sandra Joyce Murray, June 6, 1980; children: Margo, Kelley, David. BMechE, Kettering U., 1966; MMetE, Rensselaer Polytech. Inst., 1966; D in Materials Sci., MIT, 1969. Lic. min. Wesleyan Ch. Rsch. engr. Sandia Labs., Albuquerque, 1969-74; researcher Los Alamos (N.Mex.) Sci. Lab., 1974-77, Savannah River Lab., Aiken, S.C., 1977-80; group leader Mobil R & D Corp., Paulsboro, N.J., 1980-95; pres. McLaughlin Consulting, Sewell, 1995-2001; adj. prof. So.

Wesleyan U., 2001—. Mem. tech. adv. com. Materials Tech. Inst., St. Louis, 1983-91; adj. prof. North Greenville Coll., 2002—. Author: (book) Science, Logic and the Thinking Christian, 1990; author chpt. to book; contbr. articles to Jour. Electroanalytical Chemistry, Water Rsch., Corrosion, Jour. Colloid and Interface Sci., Chem. Engring. Comm., others; patentee in field. State cabinet mem. Gideons Internat., N.J., 1989-90 Recipient GM fellowship, Rennselaer Polytech. Inst., 1965-66, NSF traineeship, MIT, 1966-69. Mem. AAAS, Am. Chem. Soc., N.Y. Acad. Scis., Electrochem. Soc., Nat. Assn. Corrosion Engring., Am. Sci. Affiliation, Assn. Consulting Chemists and Chem. Engrs., Math. Assn. Am., Sigma Xi. Republican. Achievements include devel. of first workable model for computer simulation of stress corrosion cracking; patents on hydrogen outgassing optimization, amine unit corrosion control and water injection for removal of ammonium salts from process streams. Home and Office: 103 Selwood Ct Easley SC 29642-3315 E-mail: bruce_mclaughlin@msn.com.

MCLAUGHLIN, CALVIN STURGIS, biochemistry educator; b. St. Joseph, Mo., May 29, 1936; s. Calvin Sturgis and Agnes Jane McLaughlin; m. Chin Helen Moy, Sept. 7, 1960; children: Heather Chin Chu, Christine Leng Oy, Andrew Calvin Moy BS, King Coll., 1958; postgrad., Yale U., 1958-59; PhD, MIT, 1964. Postdoctoral fellow Institut de Biologie Physico-Chimique, Paris, 1964-66; prof. biochemistry U. Calif., Irvine, 1966—, dir. Cancer Rsch. Inst., 1981-83; vis. prof. Sch. Botany Oxford U., Eng., 1976, 80. Mem. peer rev. panels Am. Cancer Soc., NSF, NIH, VA Contbr. numerous articles to profl. jours.; mem. editl. bds. Jour. Bacteriology, 1975-80, Exptl. Mycology, 1980-86; reviewer profl. jours. Bd. dirs. Am. Cancer Soc., Orange County, 1980-89; mem. Traffic Affairs Com., Newport Beach, Calif., 1972-78. Named Outstanding Tchr. U. Calif.-Irvine, 1978, Gabriel Lester Meml. Lectr. Reed Coll., 1979; fellow Rockefeller Found., 1958-59, Upjohn Found., 1959-60, Nutrition Found., 1960-61, NIH, 1961-64, Am. Cancer Soc., 1964-66 Mem. Genetics Soc. Am., Am. Soc. Biochemistry and Molecular Biology, Am. Soc. Microbiology, Am. Soc. Mycology, Am. Soc. for Cell Biology, Yeast Genetics and Molecular Biology Soc. Am. (co-chair 1986-88), Electrophoresis Soc. Presbyterian. Office: U Calif Irvine Dept Biol Chemistry Irvine CA 92697-0001 E-mail: cal@uci.edu.

MCLAUGHLIN, CAROLYN LUCILE, elementary school educator; b. Pensacola, Fla., June 16, 1947; d. John Franklin and Mamie Lou (Rayburn) Wells; m. Richard Allen McLaughlin, Sept. 5, 1969; children: Allen Wayne, Kristen Lynn. BA, U. West Fla., 1970. Cert. early childhood, elem. edn. tchr., ESOL. Elem. tchr. Santa Rosa Sch. Bd., Milton, Fla., 1970-95, reading specialist tchr., 2000-2001. Lobbyist for edn. State Fla. Legis. Com., 1999-2001. Youth ch. tng tchr, music and youth dir., Sunday sch. youth tchr. Billory Bapt. Ch., East Bay Bapt. Ch., Midway Bapt. Ch., 1970-95, Navarre Baptist Ch.; dir. Bible Sch. Holley Assembly God, 2001; mem. County Tchr. Edn. Coun., Santa Rosa, v.p., 1995-97, pres., 1998-2000, 2001. Grantee Jr. League 1986, 91-99, Chpt. II Fed. grantee Elem. and Secondary Edn. Act, 1992. Mem. Internat. Reading Assn. (v.p. Santa Rosa chpt. 1998-99, pres. elect 1999-2000, pres. 2001—), Fla. Reading Assn., Santa Rosa Profl. Educators (dist. VII rep., negotiations team com., county calendar com., sec. county restructuring steering com., county curriculum com., tchr. of yr. com.), Navarre C. of C. (edn. com. 1998-2001), Navare Kiwanis (children priority one com. 1998-2001). Home: 3586 Ginger Ln Navarre FL 32566-9616 E-mail: richcarol@cs.com., mclaughlincl@mail.santarosa.klz-fl.us.

MC LAUGHLIN, DAVID THOMAS, academic administrator, business executive; b. Grand Rapids, Mich., Mar. 16, 1932; s. Wilfred P. and Arlene (Sunderlin) McL.; m. Judith Ann Landauer, Mar. 26, 1955; children: William, Wendy, Susan, C. Jay. BA, Dartmouth Coll., 1954, MBA, 1955. With Champion Internat. Co., 1957-70; v.p., gen. mgr. Champion Internat. Co. (Champion packages div.), 1957-70; pres., chief exec. officer Toro Co., Bloomington, Minn., 1970-77, chmn., chief exec. officer Mpls., 1977-81; pres. Dartmouth Coll., Hanover, N.H., 1981-87; chmn. The Aspen (Colo.) Inst., Aspen and Queenstown, Md., 1987-88; pres., emeritus, 1988-97; chmn. Orion Safety Products (AKA Std. Fusee Corp.), 1988—. Bd. dirs., Viacom, Inc., N.Y.C.; chmn. bd. of govs. ARC. Served with USAF, 1955-57. Mem. Am. Bar Assn. (ethics com.). Office: The Gallery 46 Newport Rd Ste 205 New London NH 03257-4240

MCLAUGHLIN, DONA HOUGEN, library director; b. Berea, Ky., Aug. 6, 1943; d. Richard Torger and Mary (Groser) Hougen; m. Peter Jay Marshall, Sept. 1, 1964 (div. 1977); children: Christiana, Cary Hougen; m. Paul Victor McLaughlin, June 23, 1979. AB in Fine Arts, Coll. William & Mary, 1965. Libr. West Point (Va.) High Sch., 1965; tchr. art, English and French York Acad., Shackelfords, Va., 1966; tchr. English, French Eli Whitney Sch., Westboro, Mass., 1967; continuity dir. WBLG Radio, Lexington, Ky., 1968; owner Cookie People, Westboro, 1969-78; editor of publs. Thom McAn Shoe Co., Worcester, Mass., 1978-79; substitute libr. Starr Libr., Rhinebeck, N.Y., 1980-89, dir., 1989—. Bd. trustees, v.p., pres. Friends of Starr Libr. Mem. Mid-Hudson Libr. Sys. Dirs. Assn. (mem. interlibr. loan adv. com.), Dutchess County Pub. Libr. Dirs. Assn. Home: 20 South St Rhinebeck NY 12572-1602 Office: Starr Libr 66 W Market St Rhinebeck NY 12572-1419

MCLAUGHLIN, GARLAND EUTRÉÉ, librarian; b. Asheville, N.C., Nov. 1, 1948; s. Alice Elizabeth (McLaulin) Johnson; m. Gloria D. Hicks, June 26, 1973 (div. May, 1990); 1 child, Garland Laiotis; m. Imani Sheila Newsome, Sept. 26, 1992. BA, Livingstone Coll., 1971; MLS, Simmons Coll., 1976. Young adult libr. Mattapan (Mass.) Br.-Boston Pub. Libr., 1972-76, Boston Pub. Libr., 1978, Dudley Br.-Boston Pub. Libr., Roxbury, Mass., 1978-82; generalist Egleston Br.-Boston Pub. Libr., 1976-78; br. libr. South End (Mass.) Br.-Boston Pub. Libr., 1982-90, Parker Hill Br.-Boston Pub. Libr., Roxbury, 1990—. Pres. hist. materials Cultural Concepts, 1994. Author: African Americans on Postage Stamps, 1992. Historian New Eng. chpt. Tuskegee Airman, 1991—; adv. bd. mem. Harvard Sch. Pub. Health, Boston, 1995. Daniel Sharp Ford scholar Boston Pub. Libr., 1974, Alumni scholar Simmons Coll., 1975. Mem. ALA (black caucus 1990—, pub. librs. 1994—), Mass. Black Libr. Network (recording sec. 1994—), Mass. Livingstone Coll. Alumni Assn. (pres.) Methodist. Avocations: photography, stamp collecting, writing, rose gardening. Home: 147 Hamilton St Cambridge MA 02139-4526 Office: Parker Hill Br Libr 1497 Tremont St Roxbury MA 02120-2909

MCLAUGHLIN, GWENN ELIZABETH, pediatrician, educator; b. North Tonawanda, N.Y., June 17, 1959; d. Curtis Perry and Tanya (Meeker) McL.; m. Douglas Shure Feltman. BA in Biology, Swarthmore Coll., 1981; MD, U. N.C., 1985. Diplomate Am. Bd. Pediatrics. Intern. in pediat. N.Y. Hosp., N.Y.C., 1985-86, resident in pediat., 1986-88; fellow in pediatric critical care medicine Cornell U., 1988-90; asst. prof. U. Miami, Fla., 1990-98, assoc. prof., 1998—. Contbr. articles to profl. jours. Fellow Am. Acad. Pediat., Soc. Critical Care Medicine; mem. Am. Thoracic Soc., Fla. Critical Care Medicine Soc. (pres. 1999-2000). Office: U Miami 1611 NW 12th St, ET 6006 Miami FL 33101

MCLAUGHLIN, HARRY ROLL, architect; b. Indpls., Nov. 29, 1922; s. William T. and Ruth E. (Roll) McL.; m. Linda Hamilton, Oct. 23, 1954. Registered architect, Ind., Ohio, Ill., Nat. Coun. Archtl. Registration Bds. Past pres. James Assocs. Inc., Indpls. Specializing in restoration of historic bldgs. and domestic architecture. Restorations include Old State Bank State Meml, Vincennes, Ind., Andrew Wylie House, Bloomington, Ind., Old Opera House State Meml, New Harmony, Ind., Old Morris-Butler House, Indpls. (Merit award 1972), Market St. Restoration and Maria Creek Baptist Ch., Vincennes, Benjamin Harrison House, Old James Ball Residence, Lafayette, Ind. (1st Design award 1972), Lockerbie Sq. Master Plan Park Sch., Indpls., Knox County Ct. House, Vincennes, 1972, J.K. Lilly House, Indpls., 1972, Waiting Station and Chapel, Crown Hill Cemetery, Indpls., 1972, Blackford-Condit House Ind. State U., Terre Haute, several Indian houses Angel Mounds Archaeol. Site and Interpretative Ctr. near Evansville, Ind.; architect: Glenn A. Black Mus. Archaeology, Ind. U., Bloomington; Restoration Morgan County Ct. House, Indpls. City Market, Hist. Schofield House, Madison, Ind., Ernie Pyle Birthplace, Dana, Ind., Phi Kappa Psi Nat. Hdqrs, Indpls., 1980 (Design award), East Coll. Bldg, DePauw U., Greencastle, Ind., Pres.'s House Restoration, DePauw U., 1992; contbr. articles to profl. jours.; Illustrator: Harmonist Construction. Past chmn. bd., past pres., now chmn. emeritus Historic Landmarks Found., Ind.; bd. dirs., archtl. adviser, bd. advisers Historic Madison, Inc.; mem. adv. coun. Historic Am. Bldgs. Survey, Nat. Park Svc., 1967-73; past mem. Ind. profl. rev. com. for Nat. Register nominations, 1967-81; past adv. bd. Conner Prarie Mus., Patrick Henry Sullivan Found.; past adviser Indpls. Historic Preservation Commn.; past mem. preservation com. Ind. U.; architect mem. Meridian St. Preservation Commn., Indpls., 1971-2001; hon. mem. Ind. Bicentennial Commn.; bd. dirs. Park-Tudor Sch., 1972-85; past nat. bd. dirs. Preservation Action; bd. dirs. Historic New Harmony; trustee Masonic Heritage Found.; bd. dirs. Masonic Home, 1984-91, Inpls. Pub. Libr. Found., treas. 1988, 95—, v.p., 1989, pres. 1990-97; past trustee Eiteljorg Mus. Western Art, mem. adv. and planning com., 1999; past mem. Hamilton County Tourism Commn., 1989-91. Recipient numerous award including gov.'s citation State of Ind., 1967, Sagamore of Wabash award, 1967, 80, 82; Mayor's citation for svcs. in preservation archtl. heritage City of Indpls., sec.'s citation U.S. Dept. Interior, design and environ. citation for work in preservation, 1975. Fellow AIA (nat. com. historic bldgs., chmn. historic resources com. 1970); mem. Ind. Soc. Architects (state preservation coord. 1960—, Biennial award 1972, Design award 1978), Nat. Trust Historic Preservation (past trustee, bd. advisers), Soc. Archtl. Historians (Wilbur D. Peat award Ctrl. Ind. chpt. outstanding contbns. to understanding and appreciation of archtl. heritage 1993, past bd. dirs.), Ind. Com. for Preservation of Archtl. Records, Indpls. Mus. Art. (trustee, chmn. bldgs. com., bd. govs. 1986-95), Assn. Preservation Tech., Zionsville C. of C. (hon. bd. dirs.), U.S. Capitol (hon. trustee), Ind. Hist. Soc. (pres. 1999, trustee, bldg. com.), Marion County Hist. Soc. (past v.p., bd. dirs.), Zionsville Hist. Soc. (hon. life), Navy League U.S. (life), Ind. State Mus. Soc. (life), English Speaking Union (bd. dirs. Indpls.), Hamilton County Hist. Soc. (life), Woodstock Club (bd. dirs. 1982-86, pres. 1985, ex-officio 1986), Literary Club Found. (trustee), Amateur Movie Club, Skyline Club (life), Packard Club, Masons (33 deg.). Home and Office: 950 W 116th St Carmel IN 46032-8864

MC LAUGHLIN, JEROME MICHAEL, lawyer, shipping company executive; b. St. Louis, Jan. 11, 1929; s. John Thomas and Mary Adelaide (White) McL.; m. Delphine M. McClellan, June 15, 1957; children— Margaret D., Mary Martha, Elizabeth O., Jerome Michael, John T. AB, St. Louis U., 1950, JD, 1954. Bar: Mo. 1954, U.S. Supreme Ct. 1972. V.p. Internat. Indemnity, St. Louis, 1955-56; asst. circuit atty. City of St. Louis, 1957-58; partner firm Willson, Cunningham & McClellan, St. Louis, 1958-78; v.p., gen. counsel Alexander & Baldwin, Inc., Honolulu, 1978-79; sr. v.p. Philippines, Micronesia & Orient Navigation Co., San Francisco, 1979-87, chmn. bd. dirs., 1996—. Instr. philosophy St. Louis U., 1955-60 Served to capt. USMC, 1951-53, Korea. Mem. Mo. Bar Assn., Maritime Law Assn. U.S., Soc. Maritime Arbitrators San Francisco (past pres.). Republican. Roman Catholic. Home: 820 Smoketree Ct San Marcos CA 92078-4980 Office: 353 Sacramento St San Francisco CA 94111-3620

MCLAUGHLIN, JOHN E. federal agency administrator; BA, Wittenberg U., 1964; MA, Johns Hopkins U., 1966; postgrad., SAIS Ctr., Bologna, Italy, U. Pa. With CIA, 1972—, with State Dept., Bur. European and Can. Affairs, 1984—85, deputy dir. Office European Analysis, 1985—89, dir. European analysis, 1989, dir. Slavic and Eurasian analysis, 1989—95, numerous diplomatic delegations, 1995—2000, deputy dir., 2000—. With U.S. Army, 1966—69. Office: CIA Office of Dir Washington DC 20505*

MC LAUGHLIN, JOHN FRANCIS, civil engineer, educator; b. N.Y.C., Sept. 21, 1927; s. William Francis and Anna (Goodwin) McL.; m. Eleanor Thomas Trethewey, Nov. 22, 1950; children: Susan, Donald, Cynthia, Kevin. B.C.E., Syracuse U., 1950; MS in Civil Engring., Purdue U., 1953, PhD, 1957. Mem. faculty Purdue U., 1950-95, prof. civil engring., 1963-95, head Sch. Civil Engring., 1968-78, asst. dean engring. Sch. Civil Engring., 1977-80, assoc. dean engring., 1980-94, interim dean engring., 1994-95; ret. Sch. Civil Engring., 1995. Cons. in field. Served with USAAF, 1945-47. Fellow ASCE, Hwy. Rsch. Bd.; mem. ASTM (bd. dirs. 1984-86), Am. Concrete Inst. (hon. mem., bd. dirs., v.p. 1977-79, pres. 1979), Am. Nat. Stds. Inst. (bd. dirs. 1992-94), Sigma Xi, Tau Beta Pi, Chi Epsilon, Theta Tau. Home: 112 Sumac Dr West Lafayette IN 47906-2157 E-mail: JmackSumac@aol.com.

MCLAUGHLIN, JOHN J. broadcast executive, television producer, political commentator, journalist; b. Providence, Mar. 29, 1927; s. Augustus Hugh and Eva Philomena (Turcotte) McL.; m. Ann Lauenstein, Aug. 23, 1975 (div. 1992); m. Cristina Vidal, Jun. 22, 1997. AB, Boston Coll., 1951, MA in Philosophy, 1952, BDiv, 1959, MA in English, 1961; PhD, Columbia U., 1967. Ordained priest Roman Catholic Ch., 1960. Mem. Jesuit Order, N.E., N.Y. and Washington; resigned order and active ministry, 1975; tchr., dir. communications Fairfield (Conn.) Univ. and Preparatory Sch., 1960-64; assoc. editor America Mag., N.Y.C., 1967-70; dep. spl. asst. to Pres. Richard Nixon and Gerald Ford, Washington, 1971-74; pres. McLaughlin and Co. Pub. Policy Cons., 1975-79; radio talk-show host Sta. WRC-AM, 1979-82; pres., chmn. bd. dirs. Oliver Prodns., Inc, 1983—. Lectr. numerous univs., corps. and orgns. nationwide and abroad, 1963—; host various TV series, Sta. WJAR-TV, Providence, 1962-63, Sta. WNHC-TV, New Haven, 1963, Sta. WTIC-TV, Hartford, 1963, Sta. WOR-TV, N.Y.C., 1964; host, exec. producer Biafra Today report ABC-TV Network, 1969; radio commentator Sta. WSTC, Stamford, Conn., 1964, CBS Network Radio, N.Y.C., 1964, Nat. Pub. Radio All Things Considered, Washington, 1981-85; dir. film insts. Yale U., Holy Cross Coll., Manhattanville Coll.; juror Am. Film Festival, 1969; congressional testimony pub. broadcasting and TV license renewal, Washington, 1967, 69. Author: Love Before Marriage, 1970; editor National Review, Washington, 1981-89, columnist From Washington Straight, 1982-89; TV host and exec. producer The McLaughlin Group NBC and PBS TV stas., 1982—, John McLaughlin's One on One, 1984—, McLaughlin CNBC cable system, 1989-94; TV appearances (host spl. episode) Cheers, 1990, (cameo) Murphy Brown, 1995, Lateline, 1998; Motion picture appearances: Dave, 1993, Mission Impossible, 1996, Independence Day, 1996, Murder at 1600, 1997, Bulworth, 1998. Rep. candidate U.S. Senate, R.I., 1970. Recipient Excellence in Journalism award Cath. Press Assn., 1969, News Media award VFW, 1984; nominee Nat. Acad. Cable Programming ACE award, 1989, 90, 91, 94; The McLaughlin Group named Best Polit. Talk Show, Washingtonian mag., 1987-93, George Mag., 1998. Mem. NATAS (Emmy award 1984), Am. Fedn. TV and Radio Artists, Screen Actors Guild. Office: Oliver Prodns Inc 1211 Connecticut Ave NW Ste 810 Washington DC 20036-2703 E-mail: slucian@mclaughlin.com.

MCLAUGHLIN, JOHN J., JR. lawyer; b. Boston; s. John J. and Alyce McLaughlin; m. Anne Hayes. AB, Boston Coll., Chestnut Hill, Mass., 1981; MA, Havard U., Cambridge, Mass. , 1986; MPA, Havard U., 1988; JD, Suffolk Law Sch., Boston, 1992. Host radio talk show WMBR 88 FM, Cambridge, 1989—92; host Talk Am. Radio Network, Boston, 1992—99; host talk show WMEX , 2001, WRKO , Boston, 2001; chief investigator Dist. Atty.'s Office, Cambridge, 1985—90; dep. insp. gen. Commonwealth of Mass., Boston, 1992—97; dep. dir. State Bur. Spl. Investigations, 1997—99; pres. McLaughlin & Assocs. , Lynnfield , 1999—. Alumni counselor Boston Coll., Chestnut Hill, Mass., 1981—, Harvard U., Cambridge, 1986—, Suffolk U. Law Sch., Boston, 1992—. Fellow: John F. Kennedy Libr.; mem.: Sufolk U. Law Sch. Alumni Assn., Boston Coll. Alumni Assn., Harvard Univ. Alumni Assn., Harvard Club of Boston, Harvard Faculty Club. Home: 915 Main St Lynnfield MA 01940 Office: McLaughlin & Assocs 38 Summer St #3 Lynnfield MA 01940

MCLAUGHLIN, JOHN RICHARDSON, electric motor company executive; b. New Orleans, Sept. 8, 1929; s. Thomas Phillip and Louise (Fortier) McL.; m. Lorraine Bergstrom, Aug. 9, 1952; children: Elizabeth, Richard, Thomas. BSChemE, Tulane U., 1950, MBA in Mgmt., 1953. Gen. mgr. housewares mfg. dept. GE Co., Bridgeport, Conn., 1953-78; group v.p. Lear Siegler Co., Greenwich, 1978-85; pres. Electric Indicator Co. Inc., Norwalk, 1985—. Bd. dirs. Japanese Products Corp., Norwalk. Selectman Town of Easton (Conn.), 1997-99; chmn. ch. coun. Easton Congl. Ch., 2000—. Recipient Official Citation Gen. Assembly State of Conn., 1999. Mem. Easton Exch. Club. Republican. Congregationalist. Avocations: tennis, fishing, chess. Home: 105 Norton Rd Easton CT 06612-1550 Office: Elec Indicator Co Inc 120 Fiske St Fairfield CT 06432-6104

MCLAUGHLIN, JOHN SHERMAN, lawyer; b. Pitts., Apr. 1, 1932; s. John H. and Dorothy I. (Schrecongost) McL.; m. Suzanne Shaver, June 5, 1971; children— Dorothy, Sarah, Martha. AB, Harvard U., 1954, LLB, 1957. Bar: Pa. 1958, U.S. Supreme Ct. 1967. Assoc. Reed, Smith, Shaw & McClay, Pitts., 1957-71, ptnr., 1971—2002, of counsel, 2002—. Trustee Harmarville Rehab. Ctr., Inc., 1980-87; pres., trustee Western Pa. Sch. for the Deaf, 1985—; pres. Pa. NG Assn., 1976-78; justice of peace Borough of Edgewood, 1963-73; trustee Winchester Thurston Sch., 1987-94, emeritus trustee, 1994—; life trustee Carnegie Libr. of Pitts., Carnegie Inst., 1994—, Carnegie Mus. Art, 1997—; dir. Pitts. Symphony, 1985-95, adv. 1996-99. Lt. col. Air NG, 1957-79. Mem.: Allegheny County Bar Assn., Am. Law Inst., Rolling Rock Club (Ligonier, Pa.), Duquesne Club. Office: Reed Smith Shaw & McClay 435 6th Ave Ste 2 Pittsburgh PA 15219-1886 E-mail: jmclaughlin@reedsmith.com.

MCLAUGHLIN, JOSEPH, lawyer; b. Newark, Aug. 1, 1941; s. Joseph Nicholas and Genevieve Veronica (Lardiere) McL.; m. Elisabeth Lippold, July 31, 1965; children: Elisabeth, Jessica, Emilie. AB, Columbia U., 1962, LLB, 1965. With Sullivan & Cromwell, N.Y.C., 1968-76; v.p., gen. counsel Goldman, Sachs & Co., 1976-88, cons., 1988-90; ptnr. Sidley Austin Brown & Wood, N.Y.C., 1993—. Adj. prof. law NYU Sch. Law, 1988-92; spkr., presenter in field. Author: (with C.J. Johnson Jr.) Corporate Finance and the Securities Laws, 2d edit., 1997; contbr. articles to profl. jours. Trustee Greenwich (Conn.) Acad., 1988-2000; treas. Presbyn. Ch. Old Greenwich, 1988-91; bd. dirs. United Way, Greenwich, 1993-97; mem. Rep. Town com., Greenwich, 1993-96. Jervey fellow Parker Sch. Fgn. Comparative Law, Columbia Law Sch., U. Munich, 1966-68. Mem. ABA (sect. bus. law, fed. regulation securities com., subcom. broker-dealer matters 1985—, subcom. civil litigation and SEC enforcement matters 1989—, chair task force rule 10b-6 1995-97, co-chair task force sellers' due diligence and similar defenses under fed. securities laws 1989-92, chair task force on market manipulation 1997—), Am. Law Inst., Assn. of Bar of City of N.Y. (internat. law com. 1979-84, chair 1981-84, civil rights com. 1984-87, internat. arms control and security affairs com. 1988-90), N.Y. Stock Exch. (legal adv. com. to bd. govs. 1985-88, subcom. corp. governance, subcom. internat. issues 1988—), Securities Industry Assn. (fed. regulations com. 1978-88, chair 1982-84), Nat. Assn. Securities Dealers, Inc. (corp. financing com. 1983-86), Am. Arbitration Assn. (dir. 1986-90). Republican. Congregationalist. E-mail: jmclaughlin@sidley.com.

MCLAUGHLIN, JOSEPH MICHAEL, federal judge, law educator; b. Brooklyn, N.Y., Mar. 20, 1933; s. Joseph Michael and Mary Catherine (Flanagan) McLaughlin; m. Frances Elizabeth Lynch, Oct. 10, 1959; children: Joseph, Mary Jo, Matthew, Andrew. AB, Fordham Coll., 1954, LL.B., 1959; LL.M., NYU, 1964; LL.D., Mercy Coll., White Plains, N.Y., 1981; LLD, Fordham U., 1998. Bar: N.Y. 1959. Assoc. Cahill, Gordon, N.Y.C., 1959—61; prof. law Fordham U., 1961—71, dean Sch. of Law, 1971—81, adj. prof., 1981—; judge U.S. Dist. Ct. Eastern Dist. N.Y., Bklyn., 1981—90; judge U.S. Ct. Appeals (2nd Cir.), N.Y.C., 1990—98; sr. judge, 1998—. Adj. prof. St. John's Law Sch., N.Y.C., 1982—97; chmn. N.Y. Law Revision Commn., Albany, 1975—82. Author (with Peterfreund): New York Practice, 1964; author: Evidence, 1979, also articles. Capt. Corps of Engineers U.S. Army, 1955—57, Korea. Mem.: ABA, N.Y. State Bar Assn., Assn. of Bar of City of N.Y., Lotos Club. Roman Catholic. Office: US Courthouse US Ct Appeals 40 Foley Sq Rm 2402 New York NY 10007-1502*

MCLAUGHLIN, LEIGHTON BATES, II, journalism educator, former newspaperman; b. Evanston, Ill., Apr. 10, 1930; s. Leighton Bates and Gwendolyn I. (Markle) McL.; m. Beverly Jean Jeske, May 5, 1962; children: Leighton Bates III, Jeffrey, Steven, Patrick. Student English lit., Kenyon Coll., Gambier, Ohio, 1948-50, Northwestern U., 1951; BA in English lit., UCLA, 1983; MA in communications, Calif. State U., Fullerton, 1990. Copyboy, reporter, rewriteman City News Bur., Chgo., 1957-58; reporter, rewriteman Chgo. Sun-Times, 1958-62; rewriteman, asst. city editor Ariz. Jour., Phoenix, 1962; reporter Miami (Fla.) Herald, 1962-64; successively rewriteman, night city editor, 1st asst. city editor, telegraph editor Chgo. Sun-Times, 1964-74; dir. Chgo. Daily News/Sun-Times News Service, 1974-79; editorial coord. electronics newspaper div. Field Enterprises, 1975-79; adminstr. reference libr. and communications ctr. Field Newspapers, 1976-79; editor News Am. Syndicate, Irvine, Calif., 1979-85; mng. editor San Gabriel Valley Daily Tribune, 1986; assoc. prof. journalism Riverside (Calif.) C.C., 1987-96, chmn. performing arts and media dept., 1993-96, coll. publs. editor, ret., 1996-99; lectr. in journalism Calif. State U.-Fullerton, 1984-96; fill-in editor The Press-Enterprise, Riverside, Calif., 1988-95. Lectr., condr. seminars in field. Author articles in field. Served to 1st lt. USMC, 1951-54. Recipient Stick-o-Type award for best feature story Chgo. Newspaper Guild, 1961, Best News story award Ill. AP and UPI, 1967 Mem. Soc. Profl. Journalists, Verban Soc., Psi Upsilon. Office: Riverside CC 4800 Magnolia Ave Riverside CA 92506-1242 *Reporting the news is like any other intellectual activity in that it involves research, verification, organization, and clarity of presentation. But news reporting is unique in that all this is done on a dead run, in time for the day's editions.*

MCLAUGHLIN, LISA MARIE, educational administrator; b. Sioux City, Iowa, Dec. 27, 1957; d. Donald James and Shirley Jean (Bartlett) Warden; m. Steven A. McLaughlin, Apr. 22, 1978; children: Mark Alan, Catherine Lynn. BS, Ctrl. State U., Edmond, Okla., 1978, MEd, 1982; EdD, Okla. State U., 2000. Cert. tchr., Okla. Tchr. learning disabilities Putnam City Schs., Oklahoma City, 1979-80, tchr. visually impaired, 1980-81; devel. therapist Child Study Ctr., Okla. Teaching Hosps., 1981-83; ednl. cons., 1983-85; regional program specialist Okla. State Dept. Edn., 1985-87, spl. edn. data cons., 1987-90, tech. assistance officer, 1990-91, asst. state dir. spl. edn., 1991-92; ednl. cons., vision specialist, special edn. adminstr. Edmond, 1992-95; asst. elem. prin., 1995-96; elem. prin., 1996-98; dir. spl. svcs. Western Hts. Publ Schs., Oklahoma City, 1998-99, asst. supt., 1999—. Contbr. chpt. to book. Mem. coun. on adminstrn. Ione br. YWCA, Oklahoma City, 1985-88, 92-94; mem.-at-large bd. dirs. Met. br. YWCA, Oklahoma City, 1989-91; mem. adv. com. Okla. Sch. for Blind, 1992—; chmn. Parkview Sch. for Blind Ednl. Found., 1994-96; bd. dirs. Prevent Blindness Okla., 1993—. Mem. Coun. Exceptional Children (v.p. Oklahoma City chpt. 1988-89, Spl. Educator of Yr. 1991), Learning Disabilities Assn., Assn. for Edn. and Rehab. of Blind and Visually Impaired (state pres. Okla. chpt. 1989-90), Advocates and Parents of Okla. Sight Impaired (treas. 1984-87), Okla. Women in Edn. Adminstrn., Delta Kappa Gamma (2d v.p. 1990-92), Kappa Delta Pi. Avocations: handmade bobbin lacemaking, reading, piano, walking. Office: 8401 SW 44th St Oklahoma City OK 73179-4010

MCLAUGHLIN, MARCELLUS H. MARK, III, writer, historian, activist; b. Bryn Mawr, Pa., Aug. 4, 1951; s. Marcellus H. Jr. and Caroline (Rollins) McL. AA in History, Northeastern Christian Jr. Col, Villanova, Pa., 1974; BA in History, Ea. Coll., St. Davids, Pa., 1976; MA, Villanova U., 1978; MS, 1983. Appraiser Main Line Coin and Stamp, Ardmore, Pa., 1981; archivist Villanova U., 1981; researcher, interviewer Ch. of the Redeemer, Bryn Mawr, 1983; tour guide, lectr. Old Christ Ch., Phila., 1983-84; libr. shelver Lexington Pub. Libr., Bryn Mawr, 1985; journalist Daily Liberty Gazette, Drexel Hill, Pa., 1987; subst. tchr. Ocean City (N.J.) Bd. Edn., 1990-93; writer, activist Citizens Historic Preservation, Inc. (CHIPS), Ocean City, 1998—. Historian (picture history) Greetings from Ocean City, N.J., 1995, Ocean City in Postcards, 999. Mem. SAR, Pa. SAR. (bell com. 2002-), N.J. SAR, Soc. War of 1812 (asst. sec. color guard 1975—, sec. asst. 85-90), Scotch-Irish Soc. Democrat. Lutheran. Avocations: antiques, historical research, travel, photography, collecting newspaper mastheads. Office: CHIPS Inc 1119 Central Ave Ocean City NJ 08226

MCLAUGHLIN, MICHAEL ANGELO, mortgage consultant, author; b. Medford, Mass., Mar. 13, 1950; s. Bernard Thadeus and Rose Francis (DiStasio) McL.; m. Karen Jean Parker, Nov. 19, 1972 (div. 1985); m. Claudia Chuber, June 29, 1985; 1 child, Camila; 1 stepchild, Sebastian Ortega. BS with honors, Northeastern U., 1975, MPA, 1978. Asst. juvenile supr. Dept. Youth Svcs., Boston, 1972-73; correction officer Dept. Correction, Billerica, Mass., 1974, Dept. Correction-MCI Walpole, Boston, 1974-80; facility mgr. 1st Security Svc. Corp., 1980-82; from sales mgr. to owner Solar Resources Internat., Danvers, Mass., 1982-84; account exec. New Eng. Rare Coin Galleries, Boston, 1985, Progressive Consumers Fed. Credit Union, 1985, br. mgr., 1988-90; mortgage broker McLaughlin Fin., Inc., 1991—; br. mgr. CitiMortgage, Inc., 2000-01; mortgage broker McLaughlin Fin., Inc., 1991—. Lectr. Northeastern U., Boston, 1981; pres. local chpt. Am. Fedn. State, County and Mcpl. Employees, Mass., 1977-79. Author: Screw: The Truth about Walpole State Prison by the Guard Who Lived It, 1989. Candidate, mem. Com. to Elect Mike McLaughlin Sheriff, Middlesex County, Mass., 1980; mem. Spl. Legis. Conf. Com., Boston, 1979, Joint Labor Mgmt. Com., Boston, 1978. Mem. Am. Correctional Assn., Am. Jail Assn., MPA Assn. (activities com. 1982), Sigma Epsilon Rho. Roman Catholic. Avocations: golf, sailing, skiing, pocket billiards, tennis, racquetball. Home: 3 White St Salem MA 01970-5609 E-mail: mfiloans@mindspring.com.

MCLAUGHLIN, MICHAEL JOHN, retired insurance company executive; b. Cambridge, Mass., Feb. 14, 1944; s. Michael John and Evelyn Katherine (Quinn) McL. AB, Boston Coll., 1965; JD, N.Y. U., 1968. Bar: N.Y., Mass. With N.Y. Life Ins. Co., 1968—, sr. v.p. info. systems and services dept., 1982-88, sr. v.p., 1988-91, sr. v.p., dep. gen. counsel, 1991-95, sr. v.p., gen. counsel, 1995-2000. Mem. ABA, N.Y. State Bar Assn. E-mail: mmclau2260@aol.com.

MCLAUGHLIN, MICHAEL ROB, secondary school educator, coach; b. Springfield, Mo., Aug. 14, 1967; s. Thomas Judd and Marcia Ruth (Hopkins) McL.; m. Sarah L. Kirchoff, Dec. 29, 1990. BA in History, Edn., William Jewell Coll., 1989; MA in Am. History, Lincoln U., Mo., 1995. Cert. tchr. social studies 7-12, Mo. Tchr. 8th grade Am. history Jefferson City (Mo.) Sch. Dist., 1989-93, tchr. 7th grade world geography, 1993-98; tchr. history and geography Olathe (Kans.) Sch. Dist., 1998—. Asst. coach wrestling, Jefferson City H.S., 1989-98, football, 1999—; head wrestling coach Olathe South H.S., 1998—. Head coach Jays Kids Wrestling Club, Jefferson City, Mo., 1989-98; com. mem. Lord of Life Luth. Ch., 1999—. Nominee Tchr. of Yr., Jefferson City Sch. Dist., 1996, Finalist, 1997. Mem. NEA (parliamentarian, bldg. rep. Mo. chpt. 1992-94, Kans. chpt. 2001—), Nat. Coun. Social Scis., Mo. Geographic Alliance, Mo. MIddle Sch. Assn., Mo. Hist. Soc., Mo. Wrestling Coaches Assn., Kans. Wrestling Coaches Assn., Nat. Wrestling Coaches Assn., Eagles Internat., Phi Alpha Theta. Avocations: movies, reading, sports.

MCLAUGHLIN, MIKE, race car driver; b. Waterloo, N.Y., Oct. 6, 1956; m. Katie McLaughlin. Race car driver, Busch Series Joe Gibbs Racing. Achievements include Featherlite Modified Series, NASCAR Touring champion, 1988. Mailing: Joe Gibbs Racing 13415 Reese Blvd. West Huntersville NC 28078*

MCLAUGHLIN, PATRICIA ANN, writer; b. Apr. 17, 1933; AA, Mt. San Antonio Coll., Walnut, Calif., 1972. Presenter 95th ann. conv. Nat. Cath. Ednl. Assn., 1998. Author: The Jesus Walk: The Road to Healing Body and Soul, 1997, Rooted in Jesus: Healing Generational Defects, 2002; (with others) People's Almanac 2, 1978, (70 stories) The Reading Game, 1977-79; editor The Intraocular Lens Manual, 1975-77; pub., author Wholly Spirit Newsletter, 1985-87; staff writer Biomed. Safety and Standards, 1973, Biomed. Tech., 1974; stories adapted for radio broadcast Pat's Story, 1991, Parable of the Wise King, 1991, The Master's Garden, 1991. Active in pastoral ministry. Mem. Assn. Christian Therapists, Soc. Children's Book Writers and Illustrators, Charismatic Renewal of the Cath. Ch.

MCLAUGHLIN, PATRICK MICHAEL, lawyer; b. Monahans, Tex., July 23, 1946; s. Patrick John and Ann (Donnelly) M.; m. Christine Manos, Aug. 21, 1970; children— Brian Patrick, Christopher Michael, Conor Andrew B.Gen. Studies, Ohio U., 1972; JD, Case Western Res. U., 1976. Bar: Ohio 1976, U.S. Dist. Ct. (no. dist.) Ohio 1978, U.S. Ct. Appeals (6th cir.) 1979, U.S. Supreme Ct. 1980; U.S. Dist. Ct. (so. dist.) Ohio 1989, U.S. Ct. Appeals (5th cir.). Dir. vets. edn. project. Am. Assn. Community and Jr. Colls., Washington, 1972-73; law clk. Common Pleas Ct., Cleve., 1976-77; law clk. to judge 8th Jud. Dist. Ct. of Appeals, 1977-78; asst. U.S. atty. No. Dist. Ohio, 1978-82, chief civil div., 1982-84, U.S. atty., 1984-88; ptnr. Janik & McLaughlin, 1988-89, Mansour, Gavin, Gerlack & Manos Co., L.P.A., Cleve., 1989-97; apptd ind. spl. prosecutor Ohio Attorneys General, 1993-96; mng. ptnr. McLaughlin & McCaffrey, LLP, Cleve., 1997—. Cons. Nat. League of Cities, U.S. Conf. Mayors, 1971-72; co-creator Opportunity Fair for Veterans Concept, 1971 Editor-in-chief Case Western Res. Jour. Internat. Law, 1975-76 Chmn. North Ohio Drug Abuse Task Force, 1986-88; chmn. Law Enforcement Coordinating Commn., North Ohio, 1985-88; chmn. civil issues subcom. Atty. Gen.'s Adv. Com., 1986-88; exec. v.p. Greater Cleve. Vets. Meml., Inc., 1993, pres., 1994—. Decorated Silver Star, Bronze Star, Purple Heart, Army Commendation medal, Vietnamese Cross of Gallantry with Silver and Bronze Stars Mem. ABA, FBA, Ohio Bar Assn., Cleve. Bar Assn., Nat. Assn. Former U.S. Attys., Soc. 1st Divsn., 18th Inf. Regiment Assn., Order of Ahepa, Vietnam Vets. Am., Nat. Vietnam Vets. Network (Disting. Vietnam Vet. award 1985), Nat. Assn. Concerned Vets. (nat. v.p. external affairs 1971-72, exec. dir. 1972-73), Cuyahoga County Vets. (award 1985), Nat. Soc. SAR (law enforcement commendation medal 1989). Republican. Roman Catholic. Office: McLaughlin & McCaffrey LLP Eaton Ctr 1111 Superior Ave Ste 1350 Cleveland OH 44114-2500

MCLAUGHLIN, PHILIP T. state attorney general; b. Nashua, N.H., Jan. 23, 1945; s. Philip J. and Pauline (Reilly) McLaughlin; m. Janice Livingston, 1968; children: Matthew, Timothy, Emily, Katherine, Philip. AB in History, Holy Cross coll., 1967; MPA, U. R.I., 1971; JD, Boston Coll., 1974. Bar: N.H. 1974. Atty. Belknap County, NH, 1979—81; ptnr. McLaughlin, Hemeon & Lahey, P.A., Laconia, 1981—97; atty. gen. State of N.H., 1997—. Past pres. Lakes Region Mental Health Ctr., Laconia; mem. Laconia City Coun., 1976—80, Laconia Sch. Bd., 1985—94, also chair; mem. prof. conduct com. N.H. Supreme Ct., 1983—92, 1994—97; del. N.H. Constl. Conv., 1984. Lt. USN, 1969—71. Office: Atty Gen Office 33 Capitol St Concord NH 03301-6397

MCLAUGHLIN, PHILIP VANDOREN, JR. mechanical engineering educator, researcher, consultant; b. Elizabeth, N.J., Nov. 10, 1939; s. Philip VanDoren and Ruth Evans (Landis) McL.; m. Phoebe Ann Feeney, Aug. 19, 1961; children: Philip VanDoren III, Patrick Evans, Christi M. Barton. BSCE, U. Pa., 1961, MS in Engring. Mechanics, 1964, PhD in Engring. Mechanics, 1969. Assoc. engr. Boeing-Vertol, Morton, Pa., 1962-63, engr. II, 1963; rsch. engr. Scott Paper Co., Phila., 1963-65, rsch. project engr., 1965-69, sr. rsch. project engr., 1969; asst. prof. theoretical and applied mechanics U. Ill., Urbana, 1969-73, asst. dean engring., 1971-72; project mgr. Materials Scis. Corp., Blue Bell, Pa., 1973-76; assoc. prof. mech. engring. Villanova (Pa.) U., 1976-81, prof., 1981—. Judge Cons. Engrs. Coun. Ill. 1st Ann. Engring. Excellence Awards Competition, 1972; cons. Naval Air Engring. Ctr., Lakehurst, N.J., 1977-79, U.S. Steel Corp., Trenton, 1980-82, RCA Corp., Moorestown, N.J., 1986, Coal Tech Corp., Merion Station, Pa., Air Products and Chems., Inc., Allentown, Pa., 1988, Aircraft divsn. Naval Air Warfare Ctr., Patuxent River, Md., 1995-96, Christini Technologies, Phila., 1999—, Alpha Scientific Corp., Southeastern, Pa., 2000—; vis. prof. dept. engring. U. Cambridge, Eng., 1990-91. Reviewer Prentice Hall, 1980—, Jour. Engring. Mechanics, 1973-83, AIAA Jour., 1970-87, Materials Evaluation, 1988, Jour. Composite Materials, 1988—, Composites Sci. and Tech., 1990—, others; contbr. articles to Jour. Applied Mechanics, Internat. Jour. Solids and Structures, Jour. Engring. Materials and Tech., NDT Internat., others. Rsch. grantee NSF, 1970-72, Naval Air Engring. Ctr., 1978-84, Lawrence Livermore Nat. Lab., 1979-81, Naval Air Devel. Ctr., 1985-86, RCA Corp., 1986-87; sr. rsch. assoc. NRC, Washington, 1983-84; USN-Am. Soc. for Engring. Edn. sr. faculty fellow, 1995. Mem. ASCE (chmn. engring. mechanics divsn. com. on inelastic behavior 1977-79, assoc. editor Jour. Engring. Mechanics Divsn. 1977-79, mem. aerospace divsn. com. on structures and materials 1986-95), ASME (chmn. applied mechanics divsn. Phila. sect. 1981-83, mem. materials divsn. com. on composites 1992—), Am. Acad. Mechanics, Am. Soc. for Engring. Edn., Am. Soc. Composites, Sigma Xi. Achievements include research and consulting on composite materials and structures, structural analysis and design and inelastic behavior. Office: Villanova U Dept Mech Engring 800 Lancaster Ave Villanova PA 19085-1681 E-mail: philip.mclaughlin@villanova.edu.

MCLAUGHLIN, REX JAMES, aerospace marketing professional; b. L.A., Oct. 22, 1934; s. Rex James and Margaret Agnes (Mealey) McL.; m. Patricia Ann Egan, Aug. 27, 1955; children: Anne Theresa, Christopher Michael, Thomas Joseph, John Patrick, Joseph James, Patrick Dennis. MBA, Pepperdine U., 1980. Sales mgr. Dallons Instruments, El Segundo, Calif., 1971-73; bus. devel. mgr. Lockheed, Ontario, 1973-82; v.p. sales Lockheed Data Plan, Los Gatos, 1982-83; pres. Liaisonx, Irvine, 1983-88; business devel. mgr. Lockheed Martin Skunk Works, Palmdale, 1988-97, Gen. Dynamics, Burlington, Vt., 1997-99; v.p. DLB & Assocs., Inc., Washington, 1999—. Mem. Cabrillo Beach Yacht Club. Roman Catholic. Avocations: sailing, hunting. Home: 29331 Clear View Ln Highland CA 92346 Office: DLB & Assocs Inc West Coast Office 29331 Clear View Ln Highland CA 92346 E-mail: rexmclaughlin@earthlink.net.

MCLAUGHLIN, RICHARD WARREN, retired insurance company executive; b. Boston, Nov. 25, 1930; m. Marilyn Slye, 1956; children: Kathleen, Richard Warren Jr., Thomas, Judy. BS, Boston Coll., 1952; grad. Advanced Mgmt. Program, Harvard U., 1979. Trainee Travelers Ins. Co., Hartford, Conn., 1956, asst. sec., 1966-69, sec., 1969-70, 2d. v.p., 1970-73, v.p., 1973-81, sr. v.p., 1981-85; exec. v.p. Travelers Corp., 1985-91; pres. Travelers Ins. Co., 1991—; chmn. Travelers Indemnity Co., 1991—. Corporator St. Francis Hosp. Capt. USAF, 1952-56, Korea. Mem. Eastward Ho Club (Chatham, Mass.), the Moorings Club (Vero Beach, Fla.). Home: PO Box 947 Eastham MA 02642-0947

MCLAUGHLIN, SHERRY, association administrator; m. Art McLaughlin; 3 children. With Emil H. Dutler unit 177 Am. Legion Aux., 1956, unit pres., 3d dist. pres., Dept. of Iowa pres., 1985—86, nat. v.p., nat. pres., 2001—; counselor Iowa Girls State. Chmn. Aux. Emergency Fund; mem. numerous coms. Am. Legion Aux. Vol. Iowa Vets. Home, Iowa Braille, Vinton-Shellsburg Schs., Union Sch.; Ct. apptd. spl. advocate; confirmation tchr. Trinity Luth. Ch. Recipient Gov.'s Vol. of the Yr. award, 1999, 2000. Office: American Legion Auxiliary 777 N Meridian St 3rd Flr Indianapolis IN 46204*

MCLAUGHLIN, SYLVIA CRANMER, community volunteer, environmentalist; b. Denver, Dec. 24, 1916; d. George Ernest and Jean Louise (Chappell) Cranmer; m. Donald Hamilton McLaughlin, Dec. 29, 1948; children: Jean Katherine McLaughlin Shaterian, George Cranmer McLaughlin. AB, Vassar Coll., 1939. Co-founder Save San Francisco Bay Assn., Berkeley-Oakland, Calif., 1961-99, pres., 1993-95. Bd. dirs. Ptnrs. for Liveable Cmtys., Washington, 1975-78; mem. waterfront adv. com. City of Berkeley, Calif., 1964-68; sec., bd. dirs. Resource Renewal Inst., 1980—, Citizens for Eastshore State Park, 1980—; founder, bd. dirs. Pub. Trust Group, Oakland, Calif., 1997—; mem. awards com. Berkeley Cmty. Fund, 1998—; mem. adv. bd. Greenbelt Alliance, San Francisco, 1982—; mem. nat. adv. coun. Trust for Pub. Land, San Francisco, 1986—, Ecocity Builders, Berkeley, 1990—. Mem. Nat. Aubudon Soc. (bd. dirs. 1970-76), Nat. Recreation and Parks Assn. (bd. dirs. 1974-78), East Bay Conservation Corps (bd. dirs. 1985-97), Student Conservation Assn. (bd. dirs. 1979-84). Avocations: outdoor activities, adventure and travel, reading, children and grandchildren, working out. Home: 1450 Hawthorne Ter Berkeley CA 94708-1804

MCLAUGHLIN, T. MARK, lawyer; b. Salem, Mass., Apr. 20, 1953; s. Terrence E. and Mary E. (Donlon) McL.; m. Sandra L. Roman, Oct. 16, 1982; children: Daniel, Kathleen, Eileen. BA in Econs., U. Notre Dame, 1975, JD, 1978. Bar: Ill. 1978, U.S. Dist. Ct. (no. dist.) Ill. 1978, U.S. Dist. Ct. (cen. dist.) Ill. 1992, U.S. Dist. Ct. (ea. dist.) Wis. 1992, U.S. Ct. Appeals (7th cir.) 1982, U.S. Ct. Appeals (11th cir.) 1982, U.S. Ct. Appeals (8th cir.) 1998. Assoc. Mayer Brown Rowe & Maw, Chgo., 1978-84, ptnr., 1985—. Adj. faculty law Loyola U., Chgo., 1983, 86-90. Bd. dirs. no. Ill. affiliate Am. Diabetes Assn., Chgo., 1985-94. Mem. ABA (franchising forum com. antitrust law sect.), Phi Beta Kappa. Office: Mayer Brown Rowe & Maw 190 S La Salle Street Ste 3100 Chicago IL 60603-3441 E-mail: mmclaughlin@mayerbrownrowe.com.

MCLAUGHLIN, WILLIAM IRVING, space technical manager; b. Oak Park, Ill., Mar. 6, 1935; s. William Lahey and Eileen (Irving) McL.; m. Karen Bjorneby, Aug. 20, 1960; children: William, Margot, Walter, Eileen. BS with highest honors, U. Calif., Berkeley, 1963, MA, 1966, PhD, 1968. Mem. tech. staff Bellcomm, Inc., 1968-71, Jet Propulsion Lab., Pasadena, Calif., 1971-99. Supr. terrestrial planets mission design group, 1981-83, mission design mgr. for Infrared Astron. Satellite, 1976-83, mgr. flight engring. office for Voyager/Uranus project, 1983-86; mgr. mission profile and sequencing sect., 1986-92; dep. mgr. astrophysics and fundamental physics program office, 1992-96, mgr. mission and syss. architecture sect., 1996-99. Served with USMC, 1957-60. Recipient Apollo Achievement award, 1969, Exceptional Svc. medal NASA, 1984, Outstanding Leadership medal NASA, 1986; asteroid 4838 Billmclaughlin named in his honor. Fellow Brit. Interplanetary Soc. (L.J. Carter Meml. lectr. London 2002, Space Achievement Bronze medal 1993); mem. Internat. Acad. Astros., Phi Beta Kappa, Sigma Xi.

MCLAUGHLIN, WILLIAM LOWNDES, physicist, researcher; b. Stony Point, Tenn., Mar. 30, 1928; s. John Calvin Brown and Fanny Dargen (McCaa) M.; m. Nancy Elizabeth Shepherd, Mar. 27, 1951 (dec. 1996); m. Nancy Scott Anderson, June 13, 1999; children: Peter Shepherd, David Wallace. BS summa cum laude, Hampden-Sydney Coll., 1949; MS in Physics, George Washington U., 1963. Physicist Nat. Inst. Stds. and Tech., Washington, 1951-96, scientist emeritus, fellow Gaithersburg, Md., 1996—; cons. Internat. Atomic Energy Agy., Vienna, 1977-99. Editor: Trends in Radiation Dosimetry, 1982, Electron Spin Resonance Dosimetry and Applications, 1989, Physics, Radiation Physics and Chemistry, 1993—; editor-in-chief Applied Radiation and Isotopes, 1989-99; editl. bd. Radiation Physics and Chemistry, 1979-2001; author: Dosimetry for Food Irradiation, 1977, rev. edit., 2001, Dosimetry for Radiation Processing, 1989; patentee in field. With U.S. Army Signal Corps, 1954-56. Recipient Silver medal for rsch. U.S. Dept. Commerce, 1969, Gold medal, 1979, Radiation Sci. and Tech. award, Am. Nuclear Soc., 1987, Tech. Transfer award Fed. Lab. Consortium, 1984, Applied Rsch. award Nat. Bur. Stds., 1985, R&D 100 award 1988, 90, 2000, 9th Internat. Radiation Processing award, 1994, Applied Radiation and Isotopes medal, 1995, Hampden-Sydney Coll.; Faculty fellow for Natural Scis., 1997, Rotary Internat. fellow 1950-51; U. Tuebingen fellow. Mem. St. Andrews Soc., Optical Soc. Am., Am. Phys. Soc., Soc. Photographic Sci. and Engring. (dir. 1964-67), Radiation Rsch. Soc., Cosmos Club. Home: 625 Marshall St Lexington VA 24450-1921 Office: Nat Inst Standards and Tech Radiation Physics Lab Gaithersburg MD 20899-0001

MCLAURIN, HUGH MCFADDIN, III, military officer, historian consultant; b. Sumter, S.C., Jan. 30, 1936; s. Hugh McFaddin and Louise Mellette (Nettles) McL.; m. Virginia Anne Harvin, Aug. 22, 1958; children: Mary Louise, Virginia Harvin, Hugh IV. BS, Clemson U., 1959; hon. grad., Command & Gen. Staff Coll., Ft. Leavenworth, Kans., 1978. Commd. 2d lt. U.S. Army, 1958, advanced through grades to col., 1985; exec. officer 151st Field Artillery Brigade, Sumter, 1975-85; dir. pers. S.C. NG, Columbia, 1986-91, dir. logistics, 1991-95, rank of brig. gen., ret., 1996; owner McLaurin Farms, Wedgefield, S.C., 1999—. Cons. S.C. Ednl. TV, Columbia, 1992-93; moderator Nat. Def. Seminar, Washington, 1978. Author: History of South Carolina National Guard and Militia, 1989. Elder, Presbyn. Ch., Wedgefield, 1961, moderator Presbytery Coun., 2001—; v.p. Com. for Progress, Sumter, 1963; chmn. bd. dirs. S.C. NG Mus., Columbia, 1982-99. Fellow Co. Mil. Historians; mem. Field Artillery Soc. S.C. (pres. 1987), SAR (historian), Sumter County Hist. Soc. (dir. 1996-99, pres. 2000), The Sumter Assembly (pres. 1991), Soc. of High Hills of Santee (steward 2002), Hon. Order St. Barbara, Fortnightly Club. Avocation: American Revolution research. Home: Stirling Plantation 6380 Mclaurin Rd Wedgefield SC 29168-9393

MCLAWHON, RONALD WILLIAM, pathology educator, biochemist; b. Chgo., Sept. 10, 1957; s. William Columbus and Esther Shirley (Bukowski) McL. AB in Biol. Scis., U. Chgo., 1979, MS in Biochemistry, 1980, PhD in Biochemistry, 1982; MD, Rush Med. Coll., 1986. Diplomate Am. Bd. Pathology. Rsch. assoc. pediat. Joseph P. Kennedy Jr. Mental Retardation Rsch. Ctr., Chgo.; rsch. assoc. pediatrics U. Chgo. Pritzker Sch. Medicine, 1982-83; resident in pathology Rush-Presbyn.-St. Luke's Med. Ctr., Chgo., 1986-87, pathologist, 1987-88; instr. Rush Med. Coll., 1986-87, asst. prof., 1987-88; resident in pathology U. Chgo. Med. Ctr., 1988-90; asst. prof. U. Chgo. Pritzker Sch. Medicine, 1990-96, assoc. prof., 1996—; dir. clin. chemistry, attending physician U. Chgo. Med. Ctr., 1990—; dir. outreach and clin. support svcs. U. Chgo. Hosps. and Health Sys., 1997, dir. regional lab. svcs. and med. dir. of hosp. labs., 1998—. Contbr. articles to Jour. Biol. Chemistry, Molecular Pharmacology, Jour. Neurochemistry, Jour. Membrane Biology, Procs. of NAS, Am. Jour. Clin. Pathology, Clin. Chemistry. U.S. Pub. Health Predoctoral fellow NIH, 1981-82; James B. Herrick scholar Rush Med. Coll., 1986-87; recipient Young Investigator award Acad. Clin. Lab. Physicians and Scientists, 1990. Fellow Nat. Acad. Clin. Biochemistry, Coll. Am. Pathologists, Am. Soc. Clin. Pathologists,; mem. AAAS, Am. Assn. Clin. Chemistry, Am. Soc. Investigative Pathology, Am. Soc. for Biochemistry and Molecular Biology, Am. Soc. for Cell Biology, Sigma Xi. Achievements include research in biochemistry of cell membrane receptors and signal transduction in the nervous system, molecular pharmacology of opiates and opioid peptides, regulation of complex carbohydrate and lipid metabolism, clinical laboratory automaton and robotics. Office: U Chgo Pritzker Sch Medicine Dept Pathology 5841 S Maryland Ave MC0004 Chicago IL 60637-1470

MCLAWHORN, REBECCA LAWRENCE, mathematics educator; b. Newport News, Va., July 13, 1949; d. Marion Watson and Hazel Estelle (Babb) Lawrence; m. James Richard McLawhorn, June 23, 1973 (dec. 1980); 1 child, Susan Annette. BS, East Carolina U., 1971, MEd, 1974. Tchr., coach Greene Cen. H.S., Snow Hill, N.C., 1972-76, Ridgecroft Sch., Ahoskie, 1976-78, Gates County H.S., Gatesville, 1978-86; prof. Chowan Coll., Murfreesboro, 1986—. Pianist Gatesville Bapt. Ch., 1977—; active Athletic Boosters Club, Gatesville, 1984-91, 93—, Chowan Coll. Braves Club, 1993—, Chowan Coll. Friends of the Libr., 1993—. Mem. ASCD, Nat. Coun. Tchrs. of Math., N.C. Coun. Tchrs. of Math. Democrat. Avocations: piano, volleyball, softball, basketball, crocheting. Office: Chowan Coll Murfreesboro NC 27855

MCLAWHORN, WILLIAM BENJAMIN, audit administrator; b. Kinston, N.C., June 23, 1960; s. Bobby Laverne and Annie Lucille (Crawford) McL. BSBA, Appalachian State U., 1982; MBA, Campbell U., 1987; cert., Burroughs Wellcome Mgmt. Inst., U. N.C., 1991. Cert. info. systems auditor, fraud examiner. Internal auditor BB&T Fin. Corp., Wilson, N.C., 1982-85; asst. state auditor N.C. Dept of the State Auditor, Raleigh, 1985-89; sr. info. tech. audit specialist Burroughs Wellcome Co., Research Triangle Park, N.C., 1989-94, fin. analyst, 1994-95; internal audit mgr. N.C. Dept. State Contr., Raleigh, 1995—. Ptnr. Capital City Investors, 1990-93, Pinnacle Investment Group, 1997-99. Mem. alumni coun. Appalachian State U., Boone, N.C., 1988-91, mem. scholarship com., 1987—, mem. alumni corp. com., 1992-94, mem. health care mgmt. adv. com., 1999—; advisor Jr Achievement, 1990-92, campership drive Wake County Boys and Girls Clubs, 1993-2000. Named to N.C. Order of the Long Leaf Pine, 1992. Mem. EDP Auditors Assn. (2d v.p. 1990-91, dir. 1991-92, pres. 1992-94), Inst. Internal Auditors, Assn. Cert. Fraud Examiners. Home: 730-106 Washington St Raleigh NC 27605 Office: NC Dept State Contr 3512 Bush St Raleigh NC 27609

MCLEAN, ALLAN THOMAS, insurance executive; b. Boston, Apr. 9, 1939; s. Allan Sanford and Anne Regina (McGovern) McL.; m. Mary Ann Cole, June 15, 1963; children: James, Mark, Scott. BA in Econ., Boston Coll., 1960; MS in Fin. Svcs., Am. Coll., Bryn Mawr, Pa., 1972. CLU; ChFC. Field underwriter Home Life Ins. Co. N.Y., Newton, Mass., 1967-70, assoc. mgr., 1970-84; v.p. Alexander & Alexander, Boston, 1984-97, Lynch Assocs., Boston, 1998—. Bd. dirs. Ins. Inst., Boston. Trustee Berklee Coll. Music, Boston, 1972—, chmn. bd., 2001—; trustee Leonard Morse Hosp., Natick, 1985-91, chmn. bd., 1983-91, also treas.; trustee MetroWest Health, Inc., 1991—, chmn. bd., 1995—; pres. Natick Comets Youth Hockey Inc., 1981-85; chmn. Bd. MetroWest Med. Ctr., Framingham, Mass., 1991-95; bd. trustees Mary Ann Morse Healthcare Corp., Natick, 1988—, chmn. bd., 1988-92; bd. dirs. MetroWest Emergency Physicians Inc., 1991—. Capt. USMC, 1960-67. Mem. Soc. Fin. Svcs. Profls. (pres. Boston chpt. 1986-87), Blue Water Sailing Club (bd. dirs. 1991-95), Constn. Yacht Club, Natick Racquet Club. Roman Catholic. Avocations: yacht racing, ice hockey, tennis, skiing. Home: 5 Eliot Hill Rd Natick MA 01760-5514 Office: William J Lynch & Assocs 200 Clarendon St Boston MA 02116 E-mail: allan@wjlinc.com.

MCLEAN, ARTHUR FREDERICK, mechanical engineer; b. Bristol, Eng., Apr. 16, 1929; came to U.S., 1959; naturalized, 1966; s. Frederick Robert and Edith (Hawkings) McL.; m. Oriole R. Robinson, Aug. 30, 1952; children: Mark F., Peter A. Nat. and Higher Nat. degrees in Mech. Engring., Bristol Coll. Tech., 1952. Sr. engr. aircraft control sys. Bristol Aero.-Orenda Engines Can., 1954-59; sr. engr. power sys. rsch. Bendix Corp., Southfield, Mich., 1959-61; supr. turbine sys. sect. Ford Motor Co., Dearborn, 1961-66, mgr. turbine R & D, 1967-78, mgr. ceramic materials rsch., 1979-86, mgr. materials engring., 1987-88; pvt. practice Oceanside, Calif., 1988—. Patentee in field; contbr. articles to profl. jours. With RAF, 1951-54. Recipient Soichiro Honda medal. Fellow ASME (past chmn. vehicular com., ceramics com.), Am. Ceramic Soc.; mem. Soc. Automotive Engrs. (past turbine com.), Inst. Mech. Engrs. Home: 3764 Southridge Way Oceanside CA 92056-5428 E-mail: artmcl@prodigy.net.

MCLEAN, CRAIG ELLIOTT, retired non-commissioned officer; b. Muskegon, Mich., Dec. 12, 1950; s. Elliot Garber and Margaret Irene (Carlson) McL. Grad., Langley H.S., McLean, Va., 1969. Enlisted U.S. Army, 1971, advanced through ranks to sgt. first class; served in continental U.S., West Germany and West Berlin; ret., 1992. Contbr. short stories and poetry to profl. publs. Field rep. Law Enforcement Alliance Am., Falls Church, Va., 1998—; mem. Coun. Conservative Citizens, St. Louis, 1999—. Decorated French Commando Badge, French Army, 1981. Mem. DAV, Golden Key Nat. Honor Soc., U-Boot-Archiv (full friend), Model Warship Combat Club, Sigma Tau Delta. Avocations: study of World War II and U-boat history, writing. E-mail: craigm@ngks.com.

MCLEAN, DECKLE, journalism educator; b. Jersey City, Aug. 17, 1941; s. Lionel Deckle and Ella Nora (Ayres) M; m. Pamella Ruth Blake, June 19, 1965; children: Bradley, Matthew, Sarah. BA, Harvard U., 1963; LLB, Boston Coll., 1966. Reporter Providence Jour.-Bull., 1966-68; asst. editor Ebony, Chgo., 1968; mag. staff writer The Boston Globe, 1968-75; journalism prof. Syracuse (N.Y.) U., 1975-82, Western Ill. U., Macomb, 1982—, journalism dir., 1995—. Author: Privacy and Its Invasion, 1995, Essay on the First Amendment, 2000; editor: Eye of the Reporter, 1996; contbr. articles to profl. jours. Mem. Assn. for Edn. in Journalism and Mass Comm. Home: 135 S Yorktown Rd Macomb IL 61455-9404 Office: Dept English/Journalism Simpkins Hall Western Ill Univ Macomb IL 61455

MC LEAN, DONALD MILLIS, microbiology, pathology educator, physician; b. Melbourne, Australia, July 26, 1926; s. Donald and Nellie (Millis) McL.; married. BSc, U. Melbourne, 1947, MB, 1950, MD, 1954. Fellow Rockefeller Found., N.Y.C. and Hamilton, Mont., 1955; vis. instr. bacteriology U. Minn., Mpls., 1957; med. officer Commonwealth Serum Labs., Melbourne, 1957; virologist Research Inst., Hosp. for Sick Children, Toronto, Ont., Can., 1958-67; assoc. prof. microbiology, assoc. in pediatrics U. Toronto Med. Sch., 1962-67; prof. med. microbiology U. B.C. Med. Sch., Vancouver, Can., 1967-91, prof. emeritus Pathology Can., 1991—. Author: Virology in Health Care, 1980, Immunological Investigation of Human Virus Disease, 1982, Same-Day Virus Diagnosis, 1984, Virological Infections, 1988, Medical Microbiology Synopsis, 1991, Acute Viral Infections, 1991; contbr. articles to profl. jours. Fellow Royal Coll. Physicians (Can.), Royal Coll. Pathologists; mem. Am. Epidemiological Soc., Am. Soc. Tropical Medicine, Can. Med. Assn., Am. Soc. Virology, Soc. for Vector Ecology, Soc. for Gen. Microbiology. Home: 6-5885 Yew St Vancouver BC Canada V6M 3Y5

MCLEAN, DONNA, federal agency administrator; BS in Polit. Sci., M of Pub. Affairs, Ind. U. Mem. staff U.S. Ho. of Reps.; asst. adminstr. fin. svcs. FAA; asst. sec. Office Budget and Programs, CFO U.S. Dept. Transp., Washington, 2001—. Office: US Dept Transp Budget and Programs 400 7th St SW Washington DC 20590*

MCLEAN, HON. WALTER FRANKLIN, international consultant, pastor, legislator; b. Leamington, Ont., Can., Apr. 26, 1936; s. J.L.W. McL.; m. Barbara Muriel Scott, Aug. 19, 1961; children: Scott, Chima, Ian, Duncan BA, Victoria Coll., U. B.C., 1957; M.Div., Knox Coll., U. Toronto, 1960; LLD (hon.), Wilfrid Laurier U., 1995; DD (hon.) , 2002. Ordained to ministry, Presbyterian Ch. Min. Knox Presbyn. Ch., Waterloo, 1971-79; mem. House of Commons, Ottawa, Ont., Can., 1979-93, Sec. of State of Can. Can., 1984-85; sworn to Privy Coun., 1984; min. of immigration House of Commons, Ottawa, Ont., Can., 1985-86; min. responsible for status of women Govt. of Can., 1984-86. CUSO, Nigeria coord., 1962-67; chaplain U. Nigeria, 1962-67; dep. dir. Internat. Program Can. Centennial, 1967; exec. dir. Man. Assn. for World Devel., 1970; past chmn. World Concerns Commn. Canadian Coun. Chs.; Can. del. Gen. Assemblies UN, 1986-93; apptd. spl. rep. Commonwealth and South African affairs, 1989-93; Can. rep. So. Africa Devel. Coordination Conf., 1987-93; del. Commonwealth Fgn. Mins. Against Apartheid, 1987-93, African

Devel. Bank, 1990-91, Assn. West European Parliamentarians Against Apartheid, 1988-89; leader fact finding mission to Mozambique, 1987, Can. delegation UN Conf. on Women, Nairobi, 1985; led Parliamentary del. to observe the pre-election process and attended Namibian Indpedence, Mar. 21, 1990; chmn. paliamentary Com. on Devel. and Human Rights; Commonwealth observer South African and Sri Lanka elections 1994; pres. Franklin Cons. Ltd. Alderman City of Waterloo, Ont., 1976-79; co-founder UN based Parliamentarians Global Action; hon. consul of the Rep. of Namibia, 1994—; convenor Millenium Celebration Presbyn. Ch., 1998-2000; prin. The Osborne Group, 2000. Chaplain 404 wing RCAF; mem. Ont. Criminal Injuries Compensation Bd., 2000—. Recipient Can. U. Svcs. Overseas award, 1990, Can. Bur. Internat. Edn. award, 1994; Paul Harris fellow, 1984. Mem. UN Assn. Can. (chair human rights com.), Rotary. Progressive Conservative. E-mail: franklinltd@sympatico.ca.

MCLEAN, HUGH ANGUS, management consultant; b. Salt Lake City, Feb. 19, 1925; s. George Mark and Rose (Powell) McL.; m. Martha Lane Green, Nov. 23, 1949; children: Michael Hugh, Merrie Smithson. Student, U. Kans., 1943-44; BSME, Iowa State U., 1946; postgrad., U. Utah, 1946, 61-66. Registered profl. engr., Utah. With Utah Oil Refining Co., Boise, Idaho, Twin Falls, Idaho and Salt Lake City, 1953-61, Am. Oil Co., Salt Lake City and 11 western states, 1961-66; cons. Standard Oil (Ind.), Chgo., 1966-69; v.p. Mahler Assocs., Midland Park, N.J., 1969-76; pres. McLean Mgmt. Systems, Wyckoff, 1976-84, Heber City, Utah, 1984—. Author: There Is a Better Way to Manage, 1982, Developmental Dialogues, 1972, Career Planning Program, 1975; creator, host (TV) live shows and commls., 1956-57; creator stewardship mgmt. system, 1987. Rep. election judge, Salt Lake City, 1964, Operation Eagle Eye, Chgo., 1968; pub. communications dir. Ch. Jesus Christ Latter-Day Saints, N.Y. metro area, 1981-84; introduced SAFE HOMES in county and state, 1987; chmn. bd. dirs. Town Hall Playhouse, 1990-96; elected Daniel Twp. Planning Commn., 1996-2000; emergency preparedness coord. Daniels Canyon area of Wasatch County, Utah, 2000—. Served to lt. (j.g.) USNR, 1943-46. Recipient Silver award Am. Petroleum Inst., 1957. Mem. Am. Soc. Tng. Devel. (chmn. N.Y. metro chpt. field trips 1972-74). Office: McLean Mgmt Sys PO Box 251 Heber City UT 84032-0251 *Personal philosophy: How the critical decision-points are handled by the decision-makers in a business is the key to managing productivity, innovation, and leadership.*

MCLEAN, HULDA HOOVER, volunteer, conservationist, naturalist, artist; b. Palo Alto, Calif., Aug. 19, 1906; d. Theodore Jesse and Mildred (Brooke) Hoover; m. Charles Alexander McLean (dec. 1981); children: Charles Alexander, Allan Hoover, Robertson Brooke. BA, Stanford U., 1927. Rancher, Santa Cruz County, Calif., 1943-85; v.p. Waddell Creek Assn., Davenport, 1985—; vol. mgr. Waddell Creek Ranger Sta., 1993—. Author: Uncle Bert, 1975, Hulda's World, 1848-1884, 1989, Tidedrift Shells of Monterey Bay, 1995, The Herbert Hoover Family, 1996, Almost 100 Years, 2001. Pres. Calif. Coun. Youth, Sacramento, 1961-65; mem. Santa Cruz County Bd. Suprs., 1956-63, foreman County Grand Jury, 1980-81; vol. Calif. Dept. Parks and Recreation, 1975—; conservation chmn. Native Daus. of Golden West, 1990-96. Named Farmer of Yr., Santa Cruz County Farm Bur., 2002; named one of 25 Most Influential People in Santa Cruz County, 2000; recipient Superior Achievement award, Calif. Dept. Parks and Recreation, 1996. Mem. DAR (conservation chmn. 1985—, Conservation award 1990), LWV (pres. Calif . 1941-43), AAUW, Am. Pen Women, Soroptimists Internat. (Woman of Achievement, 1965, Woman of Distinction, 1998), Santa Cruz Bus. and Profl. Women (Woman of Yr. Santa Cruz County 1982), Santa Cruz Art League, Santa Cruz C. of C (Woman of Yr. 1998). Home: 512 Walnut Ave Santa Cruz CA 95060-3636

MCLEAN, IAN SMALL, astronomer, physics educator; b. Johnstone, Scotland, Aug. 21, 1949; s. Ian and Mary (Small) McL.; (div.); 1 child, Jennifer Ann; m. Janet Wheelans Yourston, Mar. 4, 1983; children: Joanna, David Richard, Graham Robert. BS with hons., U. Glasgow, Scotland, 1971, PhD, 1974. Rsch. fellow dept. astronomy U. Glasgow, 1974-78; rsch. assoc. Steward Obs. U. Ariz., Tucson, 1978-80; sr. rsch. fellow Royal Obs. U. Edinburgh, Scotland, 1980-81, sr. sci. officer Royal Obs. Scotland, 1981-86; prin. sci. officer Joint Astronomy Ctr., Hilo, Hawaii, 1986-89; prof. dept. physics and astronomy UCLA, 1989—, dir. Infrared Imaging Detector Lab., 1989—. Author: Electronic and Computer-Aided Astronomy: From Eyes To Electronic Sensors, 1989, Infrared Astronomy with Arrays: The Next Generation, 1994, Electronic Imaging in Astronomy: Detectors and Instrumentation, 1997; contbr. articles to profl. jours. Recipient Exceptional Merit award U.K. Serc, Edinburgh, 1989; NSF grantee, 1991, 93. Fellow Royal Astron. Soc.; mem. Internat. Astron. Union (pres. com. Paris chpt. 1988-91, v.p. 1985-88), Inst. Physics, Am. Astron. Soc. Achievements include discovery of relationship between polarization of light and orbital inclination of close binary stars; development of first CCD spectropolarimeter, first fully automated infrared camera for astronomy used to achieve images of faintest high redshift galaxies, first twin-channel infrared camera; first high resolution infrared spectrograph for studies of brown dwarfs, galactic center and high redshift galaxies; research in polarization measurements of radiation from astronomical sources, use of CCDs and infrared array detectors. Office: UCLA Dept Physics and Astronomy 405 Hilgard Ave Los Angeles CA 90095-9000

MCLEAN, IAN WILLIAM, ophthalmic pathologist, researcher; b. Durham, N.C., Sept. 21, 1943; s. I. William and Brita (Rosenqvist) McL.; m. Susan R. Gabler, June 14, 1987; children: Elenor Lee, Rebecca Ann, January D. BS, U. Mich., 1965, MD, 1969. Diplomate in anatomic pathology Am. Bd. Pathology. Pathology intern U. Colo. Med. Ctr., Denver, 1969-70, resident in pathology, 1970-73; staff pathologist, dept. ophthalmic pathology Armed Forces Inst. Pathology, Washington, 1973-83, acting chmn. dept. ophthalmic pathology, 1983-86, chmn. dept., 1986—. Contbr. more than 175 articles to sci. jours. Col. U.S. Army, 1973-94. Recipient Gold medal U. Sao Paulo, 1988. Mem. Assn. for Rsch. in Vision and Ophthalmology, Eastern Ophthalmic Pathology Soc., Am. Acad. Ophthalmology, Am. Assn. Ophthalmic Pathologists, Verhoeff Soc. Office: Armed Forces Inst Pathology Dept Ophthalmic Pathol Washington DC 20306-6000

MC LEAN, JACKIE, jazz saxophonist, educator, composer, community activist; b. N.Y.C., May 17, 1932; Mus D (hon), Trinity Coll., Hartford. Bandmaster, counselor N.Y. State Correction Dept.; chmn., prof. Hartt Sch. Music, Hartford, Conn., from 1968; founder Artist Collective, Inc., 1970; founder African Am. music program (jazz degree) Hartt sch. music U. Hartford. With Art Blakey's Jazz Messengers, performed with, Charles Mingus; actor: film The Connection; albums include Monuments, New York Calling, Antiquity, Live at Montmarte, Ode To Super, A Ghetto Lullaby, Lights Out, Dr. Jackle, The Meeting, Jack Knife, New and Old Gospel, Let Freedom Ring, Destination Out, One Step Beyond, Grachan Moncur III, (with Jackie McLean Quintet) Dynasty, 1990, Rites of Passage, 1991, Triloka: Rhythm of the Earth, 1992, Jackie MacAttack, 1993, Rhythm of the Earth, 1993, Jackie's Hat Trick, 1995, Swing, Swang, Swingin', 1997, Fire & Love, 1998, Nature Boy, 2000, Blue Note - Fire and Love; guest artist album by Jazz Messengers Midnight Session, 1993; led McLean Jazz Dynasty tour with son Rene in 6 countries in Southern Africa, 1993. Decorated officer of the Arts (France); recipient Bent award U. Hartford, State of Conn. Blue Book Registration Manual award, 1996, Master Award, Nat. Endowment for the Arts; named # 1 in Downbeat Mag. Critics Poll, 1993, 94, 95, # 1 in Jazz Times Mag. Readers' Poll, 1993, 94, 95; Jackie McLean Inst. of Jazz named in his honor Music Dept. Hartt Sch. Music. Univ. Hartford, 2000, Beacon award New Sch. Univ., N.Y.C., 2001. Office: Artists Collective 1200 Albany Ave Hartford CT 06112-2104

MCLEAN, JAMES ALBERT, artist, educator; b. Gibsland, La., Nov. 25, 1928; s. Charles Edward and Lucille (Bowdon) McL.; m. Ocelia Jo Perkins, Nov. 27, 1954; 1 child: Gregory Scott. BA, Southwestern La. Inst., 1950; BD, So. Meth. U., 1953; MFA, Tulane U., 1961. Meth. student dir. Centenary Coll., Shreveport, La., 1957-59; head art dept. LaGrange (Ga.) Coll., 1964-66; assoc. prof. art Ga. State U., Atlanta, 1967-68, prof. art, 1968-95; ret., 1995. Exhibited in numerous group shows including Brooklyn Mus., 1976-77, Positive/Negative Exhbn., 1988, Siggraph Exhbn. 1988, 89, Clemson U. Nat. Print and Drawing Exhbn., 1989, Purdue U. Small Print Exhbn., 1990. Mem. Siggraph. Avocations: animation, puppetry. Home: 1256 Dunwoody Knoll Dr Atlanta GA 30338-3219 E-mail: jmc545694@aol.com.

MCLEAN, JULIANNE DREW, concert pianist, educator; b. Stoneham, Mass., Sept. 12, 1928; d. Benjamin Drew and Elizabeth Anna McLean; m. Carmelo Addario, Oct. 18, 1958 (dec.); 1 child, Angela Elizabeth Addario. BMusic, Conservatory of Music, Kansas City, Mo., 1949, MMusic, 1950. Concert pianist NAC, U.S., Europe, Near and Far East, 1956—; tchr. pvt. classes, Kans., Hawaii, Va., 1956—; rec. artist Wichita State U., 1987—; lectr. in field. Musician: appearances on TV; musician: (invited pianist) Survivors of Andrea Doria Reunion; musician: live on Vatican Radio. Bd. dirs. Maud Powell Found., Falls Church, Va., 1995—. Recipient scholarships. Mem. Mu Phi Epsilon. Roman Catholic. Avocation: cooking.

MCLEAN, KATHLEEN, critical care nurse; b. Glasgow, Scotland, Jan. 21, 1954; came to U.S., 1981; d. Michael and Margaret (McDermott) McL. BS, Paisley (Scotland) Coll. Tech., 1976. ACE cert. clin. exercise specialist. Staff and charge nurse Stobhill Hosp., Glasgow, 1976-79; rsch. nurse Stobhill Hosp.-U. Glasgow, 1979-81; staff nurse, head nurse, nurse fellowship program Parkland Hosp., Dallas, 1981-83; staff and charge nurse Danbury (Conn.) Hosp., 1983-84, staff and charge nurse surg. ICU, 1984-85; staff and charge nurse med. ICU Parkland Hosp., 1985-92, assoc. unit mgr. med. ICU, 1992-95, med. exercise specialist, personal trainer, 1995-2000, staff nurse, med. ICU, 2000—; clin. exercise specialist, 2000—. Co-author: Research into Antihypertensives, 1984; contbr. articles to profl. jours. Mem. Am. Assn. Critical Care. Avocations: walking, weight training, running, swimming, classical music. Home: 2821 Carlisle St Apt 219 Dallas TX 75204-4049 E-mail: amscot54@aol.com.

MCLEAN, LYNNE MARIE, social worker; b. Sharon, Pa., Feb. 1, 1957; d. Merle Alfred and Grace Buckley Johnson; m. William Paul McLean, May 18, 1991. BSW, U. Tex., Arlington, 1979, MSW, 1981. Caseworker investigations Child Protective Svcs., Dallas, 1981-85, supr., 1985-90, cmty. coord., 1990-91, program dir., 1991-95; dir. family life edn. Child and Family Guidance Ctr., 1995-99; exec. dir. CPS Cmty. Ptnrs., 1999—2002, Greater Tex. Cmty. Ptnrs., Dallas, 2002—. Chmn. Sexual Abuse Intervention Network of Dallas, 1995-97; mem. Respite Care Coalition, Dallas, 1998—; mem. advocacy com. Child Abuse Prevention Ctr., 1999—, pub. awareness chmn., 1996; chmn. Sexual Abuse Group Treatment Bd., 1991-95; presenter tng. programs to numerous cmty. orgns. Chmn. social activities St. Thomas Episcopal Ch., Dallas, 1996-98, mem. team 50th anniversary celebration, 1999-2000. Democrat. Avocations: crochet, reading, gardening, genealogy. Office: CPS Cmty Ptnrs 2355 Stemmons Dallas TX 75207 E-mail: mcleanl2@tdprs.state.tx.

MCLEAN, R. BRUCE, lawyer; b. N.Y.C., Nov. 15, 1946; BS with honors, Ind. U., 1968, JD cum laude, 1971. Bar: Ind. 1971, DC 1974. Atty. appellate ct. br. Nat. Labor Rels. Bd., 1971—73; chmn. Akin, Gump, Strauss, Hauer & Feld L.L.P., Washington. Bd. visitors Ind. U. Sch. Law, 1989—, vice chair, 1998—. Mem.: ABA, DC Bar, Fed. Bar Assn., Order of Coif, Phi Alpha Delta. Office: Akin Gump Strauss Hauer & Feld LLP 1333 New Hampshire Ave NW Washington DC 20036-1564 E-mail: bmclean@akingump.com.

MCLEAN, RICHARD THORPE, artist; b. Hoquiam, Wash., Apr. 12, 1934; s. Alfred Henry McLean and Dorothy Agnes Thorpe; m. Darlene Helen Young, June 26, 1955; children: Ian Bruce, Caitlin Margarette. BFA, Calif. Coll. Arts and Crafts, 1958; MFA, Mills Coll., 1962. prof. art San Francisco State U., 1963-96. Exhibited in collections Whitney Mus. Am. Art, N.Y.C., Solomon R. Guggenheim Mus., N.Y.C., Smithsonian Instn., Washington, Va. Mus. Fine Arts, Richmond, San Francisco Mus. Modern Art, Milw. Art Ctr., Portland (Oreg.) Art Mus., Oakland (Calif.) Art Mus., Kunstmuseum Hanover, Germany, Utrecht (Netherlands) Mus. Contemporary Art, Mus. Boymans Van Beuningen, Rotterdam, The Netherlands, Galerie Ludwig, Aachen, Germany. Specialist 4th class U.S. Army, 1958-60. Home: 20530 Crow Creek Rd Castro Valley CA 94552-3730

MCLEAN, ROBERT, III, real estate company executive; b. Balt., May 23, 1928; s. Robert Jr. and Mary Somerville (Iglehart) McL.; m. Elizabeth Madison Lewis, May 21, 1960; children: Elizabeth, Alexander, Mary, John. BA, Yale U., 1950; MA, U. Pa., 1965. Mktg. exec. Owens-Ill., Toledo, 1957-65; mktg. cons. Old Phila. Devel. Corp., Phila., 1966-70; 2001vice chmn. Cushman & Wakefield, N.Y.C., 1970—2001; chmn. directorate Cambridge Inst. of Applied Rsch., McLean, Va., 2001—. Mem. real estate investment com. Yale U., New Haven, Conn., 1982-90; mem. bd. Cushman & Wakefield, N.Y.C., 1986-2000. Author: Countdown to Renaissance II, The New Way Corporate America Builds, 1984. Chmn. Nat. Bldg. Mus., Washington, 1992-95; mem. bd. Washington Nat. Cathedral, 1980-88. S/Sgt. USMC, 1953-56. Mem. Rolling Rock Club, Metropolitan Club, Center Club, Gibson Island Club. Republican. Episcopalian. Avocations: tennis, golf, skiing. E-mail: robert. Home: 631 Stillwater Rd Gibson Island MD 21056 Office: Cambridge Inst 7008 Capital View Dr Mc Lean VA 22101 Fax: 703-893-5124. E-mail: rmclean05@aol.com.

MCLEAN, ROBERT ALEXANDER, lawyer; b. Memphis, Oct. 24, 1943; s. Albert A and Harriet Spencer (Pond) McLean; m. Sydney Ross, July 16, 1977; children: Robert Alexander, Ross Andrew. BA with honors, Rhodes Coll., 1965; MA, Princeton U., 1968, PhD, 1974; JD, U. Memphis, 1978. Bar: Tenn 1979, US Dist Ct (we dist) Tenn 1979, US Dist Ct (ea dist) Wis 1985, US Ct Appeals (5th cir) 1986, US Dist Ct (ea and we dists) Ark 1990, US Ct Appeals (8th cir) 1990, US Ct Appeals (10th cir) 1991, US Ct Appeals (6th cir) 1998, US Supreme Ct 1998. Asst. prof. Russian lit. U. Calif., Santa Cruz, 1971-76; staff atty. FCA, Washington, 1979-81; assoc. Wildman, Harrold, Allen, Dixon & McDonnell, Memphis, 1981-88, ptnr., 1988-89, McDonnell Boyd, Memphis, 1989-94; mem. McDonnell Dyer, PLC, 1994-95; spl. counsel Wolff Ardis, P.C., 1995-96, shareholder, 1997; mem. Farris Mathews Branan Bobango & Hellen, PLC, 1997—; asst. city atty. Germantown, Tenn., 1981—. Adj asst prof Russian lang Rhodes Col, Memphis, 1982—86. Translator: (book) Mozart and Salieri, 1973; mem: journal Univ Memphis Law Rev, 1977—78. Mem session Germantown Presby Ch, Tenn, 1988—, chmn fin comt, 1989—94. Fellow Charlotte Elizabeth Procter, Princeton Univ, 1968, Fulbright, USSR, 1969, Regents, Univ Calif, Santa Cruz, 1975. Mem.: ABA, Memphis Bar Asn, Tenn Bar Asn. Republican. Avocations: golf, quail hunting, tennis. Home: 8820 Somerset Ln Germantown TN 38138-7375 Office: Farris Matthews et al Ste 2000 One Commerce Sq Memphis TN 38103 E-mail: envtlatty@aol.com.

MCLEAN, ROBERT JAMES CAMERON, microbiologist, educator; b. Toronto, Sept. 18, 1956; came to U.S., 1993; m. Martha Elaine Law, May 21, 1988; children: Malcolm Albert Campbell, Alistair Ian Law. BSc, U. Guelph, Ont., Can., 1978; PhD, U. Calgary, Alta., Can., 1986. Asst. prof. Queens U., Kingston, Ont., 1988-93; from asst. prof. to assoc. prof. S.W. Tex. State U., San Marcos, 1993—. Cons. Kingston Techs., Trenton, N.J., 1991, Q-Life Systems, Inc., Kingston, 1992-93, ICET, Inc., Norwood, Mass., 1995, Sulzer Carbomedics Inc., Austin, Tex., 1999-2001. Author: Immobilized Biosystems, 1994, (with A.W. Decho) Molecular Ecology of Biofilms, 2002; mem. editl. bd. Applied and Environ. Microbiology, 1999—, Bioresource Tech., 1997—, Geomicrobiology Jour., 1999—; contbr. articles to profl. jours. Recipient Pres. award Microscopical Soc. Can., 1986. Mem. Am. Soc. for Microbiology (pres.-elect Tex. br. 2001), Can. Soc. Microbiologists (chmn. morphology and structure sect. 1994-96) Sigma Xi. Presbyterian. Achievements include first experimental bacterial biofilm formation during space flight; co-discovery of quorum sensing signal molecules in naturally occurring biofilms; research on gene expression including slow growth, starvation survival and quorum sensing genes in biofilm growth. Office: SW Tex State Univ Dept Biology San Marcos TX 78666 E-mail: RM12@swt.edu.

MCLEAN, RYAN JOHN, sales professional; b. Ashland, Wis., Aug. 29, 1959; s. John Wallace and Dorothy Marie (Johnson) McL. AAS, Vermilion Coll., 1980; BS, Northland Coll., 1998. Refuge mgr.'s aid U.S. Fish & Wildlife Svc., Trempealeu, Wis., 1979; wildlife technician U.S. Forest Svc., Ely, Minn., 1980; forest inventory specialist Lake County Land & Timber, Two Harbors, 1980-82; hydrological field asst. U.S. Geol. Survey, Vancouver, Wash., 1982-83; forester Minn. Dept. Natural Resources, Grand Rapids, Minn., 1983-85; pvt. woodlands forester Carlton County Soil & Water Conservation, Barnum, 1985; tech. dir. La. Pacific Corp., Hayward, Wis., 1986-88; tech. svc. person Dynea Overlay's, Inc., 1988—, sales mgr. engineered wood products, 2001—.

MCLEAN, STEPHEN M. lawyer; b. Minot, N.D., May 19, 1948; s. Robert M. and Louise M. McLean; m. Susan J. Sheldon, May 29, 1971; 3 children. BA, N.D. State U., 1970; JD, U. N.D., 1973. Bar: N.D. Pvt. practice law, Oakes, N.D., 1974—; states atty. Dickey County, 1998—. City atty. City of Oakes, 1974—; Dickey County State's atty., Oakes-Ellendale, 1998—; indigent def. atty. barnes, Dickey and LaMoure Counties, N.C., 1989-98. Adv. bd. Oakes Good Samaritan Ctr., 1976-94; pres. ch. coun. Grace Luth. Ch., 1997-98. Capt. USAF, 1973. Mem. S.E. N.D. Bar Assn. (sec.-treas. 1998—, pres. elect), N.D. Mcpl. Attys. Assn. (pres. bd. dirs. 1995-97), N.D. State Bar Assn., Oakes C. of C. (sec.-treas. 1974-86), Lions (pres. 1992), Oakes Country Club (pres. 1975). Republican. Office: 606 Main Ave Oakes ND 58474-1639

MCLEAN, SUSAN RALSTON, lawyer; b. Fayetteville, Tenn., Feb. 28, 1948; d. Joseph Frederick and Clara (Robertson) Ralston; m. Arthur Edward McLean, Apr. 16, 1983. AB, Randolph-Macon Woman's Coll., 1970; MAT in English, Vanderbilt U., 1971; JD, U. Tenn., 1979; LLM in Taxation, So. Meth. U., 1984. Bar: Tenn. 1979, Tex. 1981, Ark. 1984. Assoc. Rose Law Firm, Little Rock, 1984-85, Brice & Mankoff, Dallas, 1986-87; counsel tax divsn. Dept. Justice, 1987-96. Contbr. articles to profl. jours. Advocate for treatment of reactive attachment disorder. Mem. ABA (tax sect., litigation sect.), Tex. Bar Assn. (tax and litigation sects.), Randolph-Macon Woman's Coll. Alumnae (pres. 1992-94). Presbyterian. Avocations: brain rehabilitation through various therapies, swimming, gardening, music, walking. Home: 4025 McFarlin Blvd Dallas TX 75205-1723

MCLEAN, VINCENT RONALD, former manufacturing company financial executive; b. Detroit, June 1, 1931; s. Frederick Ronald and Bernice Mary (Vincent) McL.; m. Joyce Adrienne Koch, July 23, 1960; children— Judith Adrienne, Bruce Ronald BBA, U. Mich., 1954, MBA, 1955. Fin. analyst Ford Motor Co., Detroit, 1954-55, Mobil Oil Corp., N.Y.C., 1958-69; treas. Mobil Chem. Co., 1966-69; v.p. fin., treas. NL Industries, 1969-76, exec. v.p. fin. and planning, dir., 1976-82; exec. v.p., chief fin. officer, dir. Sperry Corp., 1982-86; sr. advisor Wertheim Schroder & Co., 1988-89. Bd. dirs. Legal and Gen. Am., Inc., William Penn Life Ins. Co. NY, Banner Life Ins. Co., Md., Morgan Stanley nInstnl. Funds. Served with U.S. Army, 1955-57 Mem. N.Y. Soc. Security Analysts, Econ. Club N.Y. Home: 702 Shackamaxon Dr Westfield NJ 07090-3408

MCLEER, LAUREEN DOROTHY, drug development and pharmaceutical professional; b. N.Y.C., Feb. 5, 1955; d. William Myers and Una Lee (Massey) McL. BS, Columbia U., 1977; MBA, U. London, 1981. RN, N.Y., D.C.; state registered nurse Eng., Wales. Staff nurse NYU Med. Ctr., N.Y.C., 1977-78; charge nurse Scripps Clinic and Rsch. Found., La Jolla, Calif., 1979-80; clin. rschr. Ayerst Labs., N.Y.C., 1982; sales rep. Pfizer, Inc., 1983-87, Cahners Pub. Co., N.Y.C., 1988-89; dir. bus. devel. Pro Clinica, 1990-91; account supr. Salthouse Torre Norton, Inc., Rutherford, N.J., 1992-93; dir. bus. devel. Med. & Tech. Rsch. Assocs., Inc., Wellesley, Mass., 1993-94; sr. project dir. Quiltiles Inc., Arlington, Va., 1994-99; project mgr. product devel. and commercialization Aventis Pharms., Inc., Berwyn, Pa., 1999—2002; clin. trial mgmt. leader AstraZeneca, LP, Wilmington, Del., 2002—. Mem. com. for helathcare issues and legislation United Hosp. Fund., N.Y.C., 1992-94. Chmn. Help Our Neighbors Eat Yr. 'Round, N.Y.C., 1987-89; trustee Murray Hill Com., N.Y.C., 1988-90; bd. dirs. East Midtown Svcs. for Older People, 1987-94; vol. nurse Whitman Walker Clinic, 1995-99; bd. dirs. Cecil Land Inst., 2002. Mem. Regulatory Affairs Profl. Soc., Drug Info. Assn. Home: PO Box 681 Chesapeake City MD 21915 also: Mansion Farm Courthouse Point Rd Chesapeake City MD 21915 Office: AstraZeneca LP Bldg D2C 725 Chesterbrook Wayne PA 19087 E-mail: laureen.mcleer@astrazeneca.com.

MCLEES, AINSLIE ARMSTRONG, secondary education educator; b. Phila., Feb. 17, 1947; d. Maurice Whitman and Irene (Macdonald) Armstrong; m. John Hill McLees Jr., June 5, 1969; children: Angus Armstrong, Ainslie Heather Armstrong. Diplomes, McGill U. Fr. S.S., Montreal, Que., Can., 1966, 67, 68; BA, Ursinus Coll., Collegeville, Pa., 1968; MA, Bryn Mawr Coll., 1969; diplôme, U. Sorbonne Nouvelle, Paris, 1974; PhD, U. Va., 1980. Instr. French Mary Washington Coll., Fredericksburg, Va., 1969-70, Kapiolani C.C., Honolulu, 1970-73, No. Va. C.C., Sterling, 1979-85; teaching asst., instr. U. Va., Charlottesville, 1973-77; lang. cons. Fairfax, Va., 1977-79; adj. prof. U. Richmond, 1985-87; vis. assoc. prof. romance langs. Randolph-Macon Coll., Ashland, 1985-93; fgn. langs. curriculum specialist Regional Gov.'s Sch., Richmond, 1993-97, master French tchr., 1997—. Coord. Bryn Mawr Coll. Career Network, Washington, 1979; bd. dirs., editor bull. Fgn. Lang. Assn. Va., 1986-96, editor; project dir. Acad. Alliance in Fgn. Lang. and Lit., Richmond, 1990—. Author: Baudelaire's Argot Plastique, 1989. Sec. Guilford Coll. Parents Assn., Greensboro, N.C., 1989-91. Recipient Bull & Bear award, Va. Econ. Edn. Commn., 1997; grantee, U. Va. and Am. Coun. on Tchg. of Fgn. Langs., 1988, Va. Fund. Humanities, 1996, U. Va. Ctr. for Liberal Arts, 1997, Am. Assn. Tchrs. of French/Va. Commonwealth U. Film Festival, 1998, 2002, U. Va. Ctr. for Liberal Arts/NEH tchr.-scholar fellow, 1999. Mem. Am. Pen Women (sec. 1987-88), Fgn. Lang. Assn. Va. (bd. dirs. 1986-96), Am. Assn. Tchrs. of French, MLA, South Atlantic MLA (chair women's caucus disc group II 1992-93, bd. dirs. 1993-96), Va. Writers Club (treas. 1991-92). Home: 1628 Park Ave Richmond VA 23220-2909 Office: Regional Gov's Sch 1000 North Lombardy St Richmond VA 23220 Fax: 804-354-6939. E-mail: mcleesainslie@hotmail.com.

MCLEES, JOHN ALAN, lawyer; b. Mpls., Jan. 19, 1948; s. Alan L. and Marian G. (Melby) McL.; m. Bozena Nowicka, June 25, 1993; children: Alexandra, Thomas. BA, U. Chgo., 1970, MBA, 1973, JD, 1974; MS in Econs., London Sch. Econs., 1971. Bar: D.C. 1974, Ill. 1975. Assoc. Keck Mahin & Cate, Chgo., 1975-79; atty. advisor office of sec. U.S. Dept. Energy, Washington, 1979-81; mng. atty. Sidley & Austin, Muscat, Oman, 1981-83, assoc. Chgo., 1983-88, Morgan Lewis & Bockius, Washington, 1988-91; dir. Latin Am. tax svc. Coopers & Lybrand, Chgo., 1991-97; ptnr. Baker & McKenzie, 1997—. Organizer, chmn. confs. on Mex. and Latin Am. tax laws, 1992—. Editor (loose leaf treatise) CCH Latin Am. Tax Guide, 2000; contbr. articles to profl. jours. Adv. bd. Com. for Pub. Autonomous Schs., Washington, 1989—; chmn. of bd. dirs. Mid Am. Chpt., U.S. Mex. C. of C., 1993-97. Named Leading Tax Advisor, Euromoney Guide to Leading U.S. Tax Lawyers, 1997, Euromoney Guide to the World's Leading Tax Advisors, 1999, Leading Advisor on Latin Am. Tax, Internat. Tax. Review, 1996-2001. Mem. ACLU, ABA, Internat. Fiscal Assn. Episcopalian. Home: 1434 S Plymouth Ct Chicago IL 60605-2729 Office: Baker & McKenzie 130 E Randolph Dr Ste 3700 Chicago IL 60601-6342 E-mail: john.a.mclees@bakernet.com.

MCLELAND, KIM ALLEN, financial planner, accountant; b. Washington, May 5, 1949; s. Jeff Roger and June Alice (Pontlitz) McL.; m. Le-Nhung Tran, June 18, 1972; children: Ian Michael Minh, Claire Le-Anh. BA, George Mason U., 1971. CPA; cert. fin. cons. Staff acct. Westheimer, Fine, Berger & Co. CPA's, Washington, 1971-73, Homes, Lowry Horn & Johnson CPA's, Vienna, 1973-76; ptnr. McLeland & Pincock CPA's, 1976-77; v.p. Cooper, Jones & McLeland, Ltd., Fairfax, Va., 1977—. Mem. AICPA, Fin. Planning Assn. (pres.), Rotary. Christian Scientist. Office: Cooper Jones & McLeland Ltd 9679 Main St Ste C Fairfax VA 22031-3766

MCLELLAN, A. ANNE, Canadian government official; b. Hants County, N.S., Can., Aug. 31, 1950; d. Howard Gilmore and Joan Mary (Pullan) McL. BA, Dalhousie U., LLB, 1974; LLM, King's Coll., U. London, 1975. Bar: N.S., 1976. Asst. prof. law U. N.B., Can., 1976-80; assoc. prof. law U. Alta., Edmonton, Can., 1980-89, assoc. dean faculty of law Can., 1985-87, prof. law Can., 1989-93, acting dean Can., 1991-92; M.P. for Edmonton West Ho. of Commons, Can., 1993—; min. Natural Resources Can., Ottawa, Ont., Can., 1993-97, Justice and Atty. Gen. Can., Ottawa, Canada, 1997—2002; min. of health Ho. of Commons, Canada, 2002—. Commentator on Can. Charter of Rights and Freedoms and on human rights issues. Contbr. articles to profl. publs. Past bd. dirs. Can. Civil Liberties Assn., Alta. Legal Aid; past v.p. U. Alta. Faculty Assn. Office: 306 Justice Bldg House of Commons Ottawa ON Canada K1A 0A6 E-mail: McLellan.A@parloge.ca.

MCLELLAN, JOHN SIDNEY, III, judge; b. Kingsport, Tenn., Jan. 16, 1946; s. John Sidney Jr. and Opal Lee (Poe) McL.; M. Wanda Ruth (Gulley), June 5, 1966; children: John Richardson, Jason Ray. BS, U. Tenn., 1968, JD, 1970. Bar: Tenn. 1971, U.S. Dist. Ct. Tenn. 1971, U.S. Ct. Appeals (6th cir.) 1972. Atty. McLellan Law Offices, Kingsport, 1971-94; cir. ct. judge 2d Jud. Dist., 1994—. County atty. Sullivan County, Blountville, Tenn., 1978-1994.

Recipient Honor for Support award Tenn. Paralegal Assn. (Tri-cities chpt.), 1994. Mem. Am. Trial Lawyers Assn., Am. Judges Assn., Tenn. Jud. Conf. (exec. com. 1997—, sec. 1995-96), Tenn. Trial Judges Assn. (v.p. 1996-97), Kingsport Bar Assn., Ct. of the Judiciary. Democratic. Episcopal. Office: City Hall 225 W Center St Kingsport TN 37660-4265 E-mail: jmclellan@tscmail.state.tn.us.

MCLELLAN, ROBERT, gynecologist, oncologist, educator; b. Miami Beach, Fla., 1954; m. Krista E. McLellan, Sept. 1991; children: David John, James Robert. BS in Biology summa cum laude, Boston Coll., 1976; MD, U. Md., 1980. Diplomate Am. Bd. Ob-Gyn., Am. Bd. Gynecol. Oncology. Resident in ob-gyn. St. Agnes Hosp., Balt., 1980-84; fellow in ob-gyn. Johns Hopkins U. Hosp., 1987-89; sr. surgeon Lahey Clinic Med. Ctr., Burlington, Mass., 1989—, dir. sect. gynecol. oncology; clin. instr. Harvard U. Sch. Medicine, Boston. Adj. assoc. prof. ob-gyn. Dartmouth Med. Sch. Contbr. articles to sci. and profl. jours. Trustee Lahey Clinic, Burlington, 1994—, bd. govs., 1993-96. Lt. comdr. Med. Corps USNR. Mem. AMA, ACOG, Soc. Gynecol. Oncologists, New. Eng. Cancer Soc., Mass. Med. Soc., Obstetric Soc. Boston. Office: Lahey Clinic Med Ctr 41 Mall Rd Burlington MA 01805-0002

MCLELLON, RICHARD STEVEN, aerospace engineer, consultant; b. Lawton, Okla., May 28, 1952; s. Robert Nelson and Jane (Warriner) McL. BSME, Old Dominion U., 1979. Aerospace engr. Naval Engring. Support Office, Norfolk, Va., 1979-82, U.S. Army Aviation Systems Commd., Ft. Eustis, 1982-86; lead dynamicist Astronautics Space Launch Sys. Lockheed Martin Corp., Denver, 1986—. Cons. Aircraft Devel., Inc., Littleton, Colo., 1991—.

MCLEMORE, GARY, quality engineer; b. Peoria, Ill., Sept. 14, 1952; s. James Alford and Marie Agnes (Dinkins) McL.; m. Patricia Sullivan; children: Lina Nicole, Eric Sean. Student, Mesa Coll., San Diego, 1984-92, Orange Coast Coll., Costa Mesa, Calif., Ill. Ctrl. Coll., Peoria; BA in Mgmt., BSBA, U. Phoenix, 1994. Cert. mfg. engr. Machinist apprentice Caterpillar Inc., Peoria; sr. machinist MSI Data Corp., Costa Mesa, Calif.; sr. mfg. engr. Solar Turbines, Inc., San Diego, 1992-97, Kaizen continuous improvement engr., 1998—. Bd. dirs. Calif. Hist. Group; mem. Solar Turbines Employee Vol. Orgn.; vol. Rep. Nat. Conv. Mem. Soc. Mfg. Engrs. (sr.), Nat. Assn. Underwater Instrs., Mfg. Engring. Cert. Inst., Solar Profl. Mgmt. Assn., Solar Employees Recreation Assn., San Diego Aerospace Mus., MS-1 Airplane Restoration Club. Home: 11949 Avenida Sivrita San Diego CA 92128-4555

MCLEMORE, HARRY KIMBRELL, retired economic developer; b. Nashville, June 23, 1929; s. Richard Aubrey and Nannie (Pitts) McL.; m. Monita Prine, Mar. 9, 1952; children: Risa Lyn, Richard Alby. BS, U. So. Miss., 1950. Cert. indsl. developer. Rsch. economist N. Miss. Indsl. Devel. Assn., W. Point, 1953-57; exec. v.p. Indsl. Devel. Com., Shreveport, La., 1957-64; mgr. econ. devel. dept. Little Rock C. of C., 1964-74; mgr. Ctr. S., Jackson, Miss., 1974-80; exec. dir. Pensacola (Fla.) Escambia Devel. Commn., 1980-90; mgr. econ. devel. Jackson County Port Authority, Pascagoula, Miss., 1990-93; ret., 1993; spl. assignment IESC, Armenia, 1999. With U.S. Army, 1951—53. Fellow Am. Econ. Devel. Coun. (hon. life); mem. SAR (pres. Gulf Coast chpt.), SCV (v.p. 1699 hist. com.), So. Econ. Devel. Coun. (hon. life) (pres.), , Miss. Econ. Devel. Coun. (hon. life). Methodist. Avocations: travel, flying, amateur radio. Home: 110 Winchester Dr Ocean Springs MS 39564-5419

MCLEMORE, MATTHEW HUNTER, education educator; b. Deport, Tex., Dec. 17, 1933; s. Johnnie Elmo and Virginia Adele (Bailey) McL.; m. Janice Juanita Seay, Dec. 21, 1957; children: Kevin Hunter, Kirk Darren, Kara Jan. AA, Paris (Tex.) Jr. Coll., 1953; student, Trinity U., San Antonio, Tex., 1953-54; BS, Tex. A&M U., Commerce, 1955, MEd, 1958; EdD, U. North Tex., 1967. Cert. profl. supt., prin., h.s. and elem. sch. tchr., driver edn. supr., Tex. Coach, math. tchr. Pub. Schs. in Tex., Commerce, Amarillo, Tyler, 1957-61; athletic dir., coach Weatherford (Tex.) Coll., 1962-66; grad. asst. U. N.Tex., Denton, 1961-62, 66-67; asst. prof. Sam Houston State U., Huntsville, Tex., 1967-68; prof. Tex. A&M U./Commerce, 1968-89, 1989—. Adj. prof. Tex. Christian U., Ft. Worth, 1989-94. Sgt. U.S. Army, 1955-57. Mem. AAUP, AAHPERD, Tex. Assn. Health, Phys. Edn., Recreation and Dance, Assn. Tex. Profl. Educators. Baptist. Home: 2944 Knollwood Dr Plano TX 75075-6428 Office: Tex A&M Univ/Commerce Dept Health/Phys Edn Commerce TX 75429

MCLEMORE, MICHAEL KERR, lawyer, minister; b. Atlanta, May 19, 1949; s. Gilbert Carmichael Sr. and Jeannie (Gulley) M.; m. Colleen Owen, Aug. 19, 1972; children: Megan, Shannon. BA, Haverford Coll., 1971; JD, U. Ga., 1974; MDiv, Candler Sch. Theology, 1997. Bar: Fla. 1974, U.S. Dist. Ct. (mid. and so. dists.) Fla. 1974, U.S. Ct. Appeals (5th cir.) 1974, U.S. Ct. Appeals (11th cir.) 1981, U.S. Supreme Ct. 1984; ordained deacon Methodist Ch., 1997, elder, 1999. Shareholder Kimbrell & Hamann P.A., Miami, Fla., 1974-91. Pres. Haverford Soc. South Fla., Miami, 1978-91; Fla. Alumni admissions rep. coord. Haverford Coll., 1978-91, alumni coun., 1980-91; lay leader 1st United Meth. Ch., South Miami, 1986-90; lay del. Fla. Ann. Conf., 1986-90, chmn. adminstrv. bd., 1991—, property and compensation com., 1988-90; co-chmn. Miami dist. Work Area on Stewardship, 1987—; chair deferred gifts Epworth Village, 1990-91; pastor Bishop Circuit United Meth. Ch., 1995-97, New Pentecost United Meth. Ch., 1997—. 1st lt. USAR, 1976-78. Mem. ABA, Fla. Bar Assn. (aviation sect.), Dade County Def. Bar Assn. (bd. dirs. 1989—, treas. 1990—), Nat. Transp. Safety Bd. Assn., Lawyer-Pilot Bar Assn. Democrat. Home: 268 Moss Side Dr Athens GA 30607-2109 Office: New Pentecost United Meth Ch 385 Pleasant Hill Church Rd Winder GA 30680

MCLENDON, DOROTHY, school psychologist; b. Crawfordsville, Ind., Feb. 20, 1918; d. Joseph Newton and Dora (Ryall) Fullenwider; m. Hiram James McLendon, May 23, 1942; 1 child, Hiram James McLendon, Jr. AB, Olivet Coll., Kankakee, Ill., 1942; MA, Boston U., 1945, EdD, 1970. Diplomate Am. Bd. of Profl. Psychology. Spl. edn. tchr. Kingsley Schs., Belmont Jr. High, Boston, 1943-46, 56-57; tchr. Homerton Coll., Cambridge, Eng., 1946-47; sch. psychologist Alameda County Schs., Oakland, Calif., 1949-52, Paris Am. Army Dependent Sch., France, 1957-58, Brookline (Mass.) Pub. Schs., 1958-81; pvt. cons. Cambridge, Mass., 1981—; cons. Cocoa, Fla., 1981—. Address: 1660 Rosetine St Cocoa FL 32926-5502

MC LENDON, HEATH BRIAN, securities investment company executive; b. San Francisco, May 24, 1933; s. Jesse Heath and Clara Martha (Nelson) McL.; m. Judith Nelson Locke, May 30, 1959; children: Laurie, Eric, Brian and Michael (twins). BA, Stanford U., 1955; MBA, Harvard U., 1959. With Shearson Lehman Brothers, N.Y.C., 1960-93; mng. dir. Salomon Smith Barney, 1993—; chmn. Strategy Advisors, N.Y.C., 1971—. Chmn. The Italy Fund, Inc., 1986—, Zenix Income Fund. Pres. bd. trustees N.J. Shakespeare Festival, 1975-76; trustee Drew U., 1975—, chmn. bd., 1992-97. Served to 1st lt. AUS, 1955-57. Mem. N.Y. Soc. Security Analysts, Nat. Assn. Bus. Economists, Money Marketeers. Clubs: Baltusrol, Bay Head Yacht. Presbyterian.

MCLENDON, JESSE LAWRENCE, protective services official; b. Kansas City, Mo., Aug. 6, 1950; s. Jesse Lewis and Sara (Boyd) McL.; m. Jean Creason Wilhelm, Sept. 24, 1982. AAS Criminal Justice Adminstrn., Maple Wood C.C., 1984; BS summa cum laude, BS summa cum laude, Park Coll., 1988, M with honors, 1993; grad., FBI Nat. Acad., 1993, FBA Ctrl. State Law Enforcement Exec. Devel., 1995. Cert. police officer Mo. Dept. Pub. Safety, P.O.S.T. tng. instr. U. Mo.'s Law Enforcement Tng. Inst., 1991—. Chief communications officer Dept. Police, Riverside, Mo., 1969-70, patrolman Lake Waukomis, 1971-72, corporal Platte Woods, 1970-72, patrolman North Kansas City, 1972-76, detective, 1976-86, sgt., 1986-90; lt., comdr. support svcs. divsn., 1990-92; capt., comdr. investigation divsn. Dept. Police, North Kansas City, 1992-94, maj., asst. chief of police, comdr. patrol divsn., 1994-97, comdr. support svcs. divsn., 1997—. Instr. tng., outreach program Kansas City Regional Acad., 1985-86, North Kansas City Police Res. Unit, 1977-78, Ctrl. States Law Enforcement Exec. Devel. FBI, 1995; adj. instr. criminal justice adminstrn. and pub. adminstrn. Park Coll., 1988—; investigator Clay County Med. Examiner, Liberty, Mo., 1976-90, Kansas City Major Case Squad, 1976—, Clay County Prosecutor's Office, Liberty, 1976-87. Recipient Valor award Met. Chiefs and Sheriffs, 1978, 83, Profl. Svc. award North Kansas City Kiwanis, 1984; named Outstanding Law Enforcement Officer, So. Clay County Jaycees, 1977. Mem. ASPA, Am. Criminal Justice Assn., Internat. Assn. Chiefs of Police, Mo. Soc. for Pub. Adminstrn., FBI Nat. Acad. Assocs., Internat. Assn. Identification (Mo. divsn.), Ctrl. States Law Enforcement Exec. Devel. Assn., Mo. Peace Officers Assn., Am. Soc. Law Enforcement Trainers, Mo. Profl. Photographers Assn., Delta Tau Kappa. Democrat. Episcopalian. Avocations: skiing, golf, showing horses. Home: 3613 N Wabash Ave Kansas City MO 64116-2882 Office: North Kansas City Police Dept 2010 Howell St Kansas City MO 64116-3526

MCLENDON, MELBURNE DEKALB, lawyer, arbitrator; b. Atlanta, Apr. 21, 1921; s. Jesse Martin and Elizabeth Lee (Sartain) McL.; m. Loyce Jacqueline Kirkland, Dec. 31, 1949; children: James Kirkland, Loyce Eloise McLendon Snyder. LLB, U. Ga., 1948. Bar: Ga. 1949, U.S. Dist. Ct. (no. dist.) Ga. 1949, U.S. Ct. Appeals (5th cir.) 1965, U.S. Supreme Ct. 1973, U.S. Dist. Ct. (mid. dist.) Ga. 1985. Law clk. Fulton County Superior Ct., Atlanta, 1949-50; ptnr. Carter Ansley Smith & McLendon, 1950-86; dir. Amica Mutual Ins. Co., 1976-96; cons. U.S. VA Hosp., Decatur, Ga., 1996—; pro bono. Arbitrator N.Y. Stock Exch., 1980-88, U.S. Dist. Ct. (mid. dist.) Ga., Macon, 1988—. Scout master Boy Scouts Am., Atlanta, 1959-70; active pro bono work for war vets., 1998—. Staff sgt. USAAF, 1942-45. Recipient Disting. Svc. award U. Ga., 1996, Exceptional Performance citation def. Rsch. Inst., 1985. Mem. Ga. Def. Lawyers Assn. (pres. 1984), Atlanta Bar Assn., Lawyer's Club of Atlanta, Univ. Yacht Club, Buckhead Men's Garden Club, Masons (32 deg.). Republican. Methodist. Avocations: gardening, woodwork, travel, fishing, spectator sports. E-mail: melburnem@aol.com.

MCLENDON, RICHARD CHARLES, music educator; b. Troy, Ala., July 9, 1953; s. Charles Elie and Doris Dean McLendon; m. Michelle Rene Buck, June 25, 1988 (div. July 2, 1996); children: Zachary, Ryan. BS in Edn., Jacksonville State U., 1977; MusM, U. Southwestern La., 1979; Ednl. Specialist, Troy State U., 1997; postgrad., Argosy U., 2000. Cert. tchr. Ga. Grad. asst. U. Southwestern La., Lafayette, 1977; band dir. Murray (Ky.) Ind. Sch. Sys., 1979—80; program coord. Pride of Cin., Inc., 1980—82; instr. of percussion Murray (Ky.) State U., 1981—82; band dir. Colquitt County Jr. H.S., Moultrie, Ga., 1984—93; dir. of bands Colquitt County H.S., 1993. Assoc. condr. European tour US Collegiate Wind Band, 1998; creative & instrnl. staff tour of Ecuador and Colombia US All-Star Marching Band, 1978. Composer: Medigated Goo II, 1984 (3rd Pl., 11th Internat. Percussion Composition Contest, Percussive Arts Soc., 1984). Mem.: Music Educators Nat. Conf., Nat. Band Assn., Comparative and Internat. Edn. Soc., Am. Assn. for the Advancement of Slavic Studies, Ga. Music Educators Assn. (dist. chmn. 2002—), Kappa Delta Pi, Pi Kappa Lambda, Phi Mu Alpha Sinfonia. Avocations: swimming, bicycling, hiking, travel. Home: 1725 Gatewood Circle Moultrie GA 31768 Office: Colquitt County HS 1800 Park Ave Moultrie GA 31768 Office Fax: 229-890-6166. Personal E-mail: rmclendon@alltel.net. E-mail: rmclendo@colquitt.k12.ga.us.

MCLENDON, SUSAN MICHELLE, lawyer, nurse; b. N.Y.C., Mar. 5, 1964; d. James McLendon, Sr. BSN, SUNY, 1987; JD, Temple U. Sch. Law, 1990. Bar: N.J. 1991, D.C. 1998, N.Y. 2000; RN N.Y., 1986. Asst. regional counsel Social Security Adminstrn., Office Gen. Counsel, N.Y.C., 1990-98; pvt. practice, 2000—. Bus. entertainment strategies NBC, CNBC, MSNBC, other networks & cable sta. Editor-in-chief: Environ. Law Digest, 1989—90. Fundraiser Race for the Cure, March of Dimes, UNCF, United Negro Coll. Fund. Scholar, N.Y. State Regents, 1982—86, Academic scholarship, 1982—86, 1989—90. Avocations: singing, writing, running, tennis, skiing.

MCLENNAN, BARBARA NANCY, management consultant; b. N.Y.C., Mar. 25, 1940; d. Sol and Gertrude (Rochkind) Miller; m. Kenneth McLennan, Aug. 14, 1962; children: Gordon, Laura. BA magna cum laude, CCNY, 1961; MS, U. Wis., 1962, PhD, 1965; JD, Georgetown U., 1983. Bar: DC 1983, U.S. Ct. Internat. Trade 1988, U.S. Ct. Appeals (DC cir.) 1988, U.S. Supreme Ct. 1988, Va. 1991. From asst. prof. to assoc. prof. Temple U., Phila., 1965-78; budget analyst Com. Budget, U.S. Ho. of Reps., Washington, 1978-81; legis. asst. fin. and budget Sen. Dan Quayle, 1981-84; internat. tax specialist IRS, U.S. Dept. Treasury, 1984-89; dep. asst. sec. trade, info. and analysis U.S. Dept. Commerce, 1989-91; prin., atty.-at-law Bitonti and Wilhelm, PC., McLean, Va., 1991-93; staff v.p. govt.-legal affairs consumer electronics group Electronic Industries Assn., Washington, 1993-94, staff v.p. tech. policy, consumer electronics group, 1994-95; v.p. Van Scoyoc Assocs., 1995-96; cons. on tax related issues in U.S., former Soviet Union McLean, Va., 1996—. Sr. polit. scientist SRI-Internat., Arlington, Va., 1971—74; vis. prof. Am. Coll., Paris, 1975—76; cons. UNESCO, Paris, 1977—78. Author: (book) Comparative Political Systems, 1975; contbr. articles to profl. jours. Mem. parents adv. coun. Randolph-Macon Coll., Ashland, Va., 1989—92. Fellow NDEA, 1962—65. Mem.: ABA, Fed. Bar Assn., DC Bar Assn., Am. Soc. Assn. Execs., Phi Beta Kappa. Home: 1620 Harbor Rd Williamsburg VA 23185 E-mail: barb.mcl@cox.net.

MCLENNAN, BERNICE CLAIRE, human resources professional; b. Malden, Mass., Dec. 26, 1936; d. Ralph Cyril Worth and Alice Seaman (Hunter) Worth Barrett; m. Hubert Earle McLennan, Oct. 28, 1961; 1 child, Cynthia Alice. Student, Moody Bible Inst., 1958, Salem State Coll., 1988, Bentley Coll., 1989. Youth dir. Faith Evangelical Ch., Melrose, Mass., 1971-77; adminstrv. asst. Boston Redevel. Authority, 1977-85, adminstr. coord., 1985-87, asst. sec. to the authority, 1981—, dir. human resources, 1988-95, asst. dir., 1995-99, dep. dir. for human resources, 1999—. Moderator Faith Evangelical Ch., Melrose, 1985-88, Christian edn. chair, 1973-76. Sec. Melrose (Mass.) Sch. Com., 1983-85; vol. Boston (Mass.) Youth Campaign, 1989, 90; bd. dirs. Chime Time Children's Ctr., Melrose, 1998-99; mem. 1st Bapt. Ch. of Melrose, 1999-. Mem. Internat. Pers. Mgmt. Assn., Assn. Affirmative Action Profls., Christian Edn. Com. Avocations: Christian edn., women's issues, drug/alcohol edn. Home: 31 Botolph St Melrose MA 02176-1126 Office: Boston Redevel Authority City Hall One City Hall Sq Boston MA 02201 E-mail: bernice.mclennan.bra@ci.boston.ma.us.

MCLENNAN, ROBERT GORDON, asset management company executive; b. Chgo., Aug. 13, 1943; s. Robert G. and Grace (Anderson) McL.; m. Rebecca Ann Martin, Aug. 14, 1965; children: Robert Martin, Douglas Andrew. BA, Cornell Coll., 1965; JD, U. Ill., 1968. Bar: Ill. 1968. Atty. Amoco Oil Co., Chgo., 1968-70; ptnr. McLennan Co., Park Ridge, Ill., 1970-81; chmn. MTI Construction Svcs. LLC, 1982—; pres. Beacon Mgmt. Co., Wheeling, Ill., 1995—. Bd. dirs. Adv. Health Care, Oak Brook, Ill., 1988—; trustee Village of Glenview, Ill., 1995-99; chmn. caucus Glenview Elem. Sch., 1972-73. Mem. Chief Execs. Orgn., World Presidents Orgn., Chgo. Presidents Orgn., Econs. Club. Avocations: running, skiing, tennis, scuba. Fax: 847-541-8855.

MCLEOD, ALEXANDER CANADAY, physician; b. Fayetteville, N.C., Jan. 14, 1935; s. Walter Guy and Vida (Canaday) McLeod; m. Dorothy Venning Woods, Aug. 21, 1965; children: Alexander Woods, Dorothy Seward. Akat., Städische Akad. Tönkunst, 1955; AB, Princeton U., 1956; postgrad., Johns Hopkins U., 1959-60; MD, Duke U., 1960; MBA, Vanderbilt U., 1988. Diplomate Am. Bd. Internal Medicine, Nat. Bd. Med. Examiners. Intern, asst. resident N.Y. Hosp.-Cornell Med. Ctr., N.Y.C., 1960-62; resident in medicine and neurology, fellow Vanderbilt U. Hosp., Nashville, 1964-67; pvt. practice internal medicine, 1967-98; clin. prof. med. adminstrn. Vanderbilt U., 1999—, clin. prof. medicine, 1999—, adj. prof. mgmt. Owen Grad. Sch. Mgmt., 1995—, faculty coord. health care mgmt. Owen Grad. Sch. Mgmt., 1996-2000. Bd. dirs. Nat. Security Alliance, Inc., 1990—2000; cons. internal medicine student health svc. Vanderbilt U., Nashville, 1991—96, cons. health ins., 1997—99. Contbr. Trustee Friends of Heard Libr. Vanderbilt U., Nashville, 1998; past trustee, past chmn. Dunvegan Found.; bd. dirs. Nashville Symphony, 1988—91, Skye Terrier Found., 1998—2000; past music com. mem. Westminster Presbyn. Ch., 1989—91, liturgy com. mem.; past vestryman, jr. warden St. George's Epis. Ch. With USNR, 1962—64. Recipient Physicians Achievement award, AMA, 1971, 1974, 1977, 1981, 1984, 1987, 1990, 1993, 1996, 1999; fellow Summer fellow in neurology, USPHS, 1957—58, Mid. Tenn. Heart Assn., 1966—67. Fellow: ACP, Hugenot Soc. Gt. Britain and Ireland, Soc. Antiquaries of Scotland; mem.: Nashville Acad. Medicine, Tenn. Med. Assn., Am. Coll. Physician Execs., Coun. Scottish Clan Assns., Inc. (former trustee), Associated Clan MacLeod Socs. (assoc. past co-chmn. Alasdair Crotach com., past exec. v.p., pres. 1998—), St. Andrew's Soc. N.C., Scottish Soc. Mid. Tenn. (life), Clan MacLeod Soc. (life; past pres.), Heraldry Soc. Scotland, Sloane Club, Farmington Country Club, Tower Club Princeton, Princeton Club Nashville (past pres. and trustee), Princeton Club N.Y., Univ. Club Nashville, Skye Terrier Club Am., Grolier Club. Republican. Presbyterian. Avocations: reading, gardening, writing. Home: 203 Evelyn Ave Nashville TN 37205-3307 Office: PO Box 50451 Nashville TN 37205-0451

MCLEOD, ANDREW HARVEY, conservationist; b. N.Y.C., Mar. 23, 1960; s. Richard H. and Barbara McL. BA, George Washington U., 1983; MA, Georgetown U., 1987; MPA, Harvard U., 1991. Press sec. U.S. Sen. Lowell Weicker, Washington, 1984-86; spl. asst. U.S. Rep. Jim Leach, 1987; press sec. U.S. Sen. John Chafee, 1987-89; asst. sec. Calif. Resources Agy., Sacramento, 1991-95, deputy sec., 1995-97; dir. R.I. Dept. Environ. Mgmt., Providence, 1997-99; dir. nat. conservation fin. Trust for Pub. Land, Boston, 1999—. Office: Trust for Pub Land 33 Union St Boston MA 02108-2414

MCLEOD, E. DOUGLAS, real estate developer, lawyer; b. Galveston, Tex., Aug. 6, 1941; s. Vaughn Watkins McL. and Dorothy (Milroy) Burton; m. Sarah Jackson Helms, Mar. 20, 1965 (div. 1979); children: Chanse, Alexandra, Lindsey; m. Joan Margaret Williams, Dec. 26, 1979; 1 child, Joanie; stepchildren: Meg, Libbie. BBA, U. North Tex., 1965; postgrad., So. Meth. U., 1965-66; JD, South Tex. Coll. Law, 1990; LLM, U. Houston, 1993. Lic. real estate broker. Pres., owner McLeod Properties & co., Galveston, Tex., 1967—; tchr. Galveston Ind. Sch. Dist., 1967-69; banker W.L. Moody & Co., Galveston, 1969-72; developer, broker McLeod Properties/Builders, 1972-82; developer Moody Found., 1982—. Bd. dirs. Am. Nat. Ins. Co., Galveston, Nat. Western Life Ins. Co., Austin, Anrem Corp., Galveston, Moody Gardens Inc., Galveston, chmn., 1984—; bd. dirs. Colonel Inc., Galveston. Mem. editl. bd.: Currents Internat. Trade Law Jour., 1992—. Pres., trustee Galveston Ins. Sch. Dist., 1969—73; mayor pro-tem, mem. city coun. City of Galveston, 1973—76; state legislator Tex. Ho. Reps., Austin, 1976—83; bd. visitors So. Tex. Coll. Law, 1990—96; mem. adv. bd. U. Houston, 1986—95; bd. dirs. Ronald McDonald House, 1986—93, Trinity Episcopal Sch. , 1990—96, Galveston Econ. Devel. Partnership , 1998—. With USMC, 1961—67. Mem. Granaderos De Galvez, Marine Corps League. Episcopalian. Avocations: physical fitness advocate, legal history collector, family archivist. Home: 53 Cedar Lawn Cir Galveston TX 77551-4631 Office: The Moody Found 2302 Post Office St Ste 704 Galveston TX 77550-1994

MCLEOD, HARRY O'NEAL, JR. petroleum engineer, consultant; b. Shreveport, La., Feb. 26, 1932; s. Harry O'Neal Sr. and Odelle Nan (Crow) McL.; m. Sandra Lou Mahaffey, Feb. 6, 1959; children: Kathleen Odelle, Bryan O'Neal. Degree in engring., Colo. Sch. of Mines, 1953; MS in Petroleum Engring., U. Okla., 1963, PhD in Engring. Sci., 1965. Registered profl. engr., Okla. Prodn. engr. Phillips Petroleum Co., 1953-58; rsch. engr. Jersey Prodn. Rsch. Co., Tulsa, 1963-64; sr. rsch. engr. Dowell div. Dow Chem. Co., 1965-69; dir. info. svcs. dept. U. Tulsa, 1969-75; from sr. prodn. engr. to sr. staff engr. Conoco, Inc., Houston, 1975-86, engring. profl., 1986-91, sr. engring. profl., 1992-97; pvt. practice cons., 1998—. 1st lt. U.S. Army, 1954-56. Mem. Soc. Petroleum Engrs. (Prodn. Engring. award 1989, Disting. Mem. award 1995, disting. author, 1983, disting. lectr. 1987-88, 96-97), Sigma Xi. Republican. Methodist. Home: 2006 Southwick St Houston TX 77080-6315

MCLEOD, JOHN HUGH, JR. mechanical and electrical engineer; b. Hattiesburg, Miss., Feb. 27, 1911; s. John Hugh and Martha (Caldwell) McL.; m. Suzette Boutell, 1951; children: John Hugh III, Robert Boutell. BS, Tulane U., 1933. Registered profl. engr., Calif. Engr. various firms, 1933-39; field engr. Taylor Instrument Co., Rochester, N.Y., 1940-42; R&D engr. Leeds & Northrup, Co., Phila., 1943-47; sect. head guidance sys. and guided missiles U.S. Naval Air Missile Test Ctr., Point Mugu, Calif., 1947-56; design specialist Gen. Dynamics./Astronautics, San Diego, 1956-63; cons., 1963-64; pvt. practice mech. and elec. engring. cons. La Jolla, Calif., 1964—. Disting. vis. prof. Calif. State U., Chico, 1975; mem. exec. com. Fall Joint Computer Conf. Am. Fedn. Info. Processing Socs., 1965; co-founder San Diego Symposium Biomed. Engring., 1961. Author: Simulation: The Dynamic Modeling of Ideas and Systems with Computers, 1968; Computer Modeling and Simulation: Principles of Good Practice, 1982; editor, pub. Simulation Coun. Newsletter, 1952-55; editor: Simulation, 1963-74; assoc. editor Instruments & Control Systems, 1955-63, Behavioral Sci., 1973—; tech. editor Simulation in the Service of Soc., 1971—; co-author: Large-Scale Models for Policy Evaluation, 1977. With USN, 1942-43. Recipient Sr. Sci. Simulation award Electronic Assocs., Inc., 1965, TIMS award Inst. Mgmt. Scis., 1986; NEH, NSF grantee, 1983; McLeod Inst. Simulation Sci. named in his honor at 18 acad. instns. including Calif. State U., Chico, U. Calgary, Can., U. Ottawa, Can., U. Ghent, Belgium, Istituto per la Recerca, Naples, Italy, Polish Acad. Scis., Warsaw, U. Edinburgh, Scotland, Beijing U. Aeronautics and Astronautics, Riga Tech. U., Latvia, Hungarian Acad. Scis., Budapest. Mem. IEEE, AAAS, Soc. Computer Simulation (founder, chmn. com. on profl. ethics, publs. advisor, John McLeod award 1987). Home: 8484 La Jolla Shores Dr La Jolla CA 92037-3019 Office: Soc Computer Simulation PO Box 17900 San Diego CA 92177-7900 E-mail: mcleod@sdsc.edu.

MCLEOD, STEPHEN GLENN, education educator, language educator; b. Pensacola, Fla., Mar. 30, 1949; AA, Pensacola Jr. Coll., 1969; BA, U. West Fla., 1971; MA, Vanderbilt U., 1973; EdD, Nova Southeastern U., 1992. Commd. 2d lt. U.S. Army, 1978, advanced through grades to capt., 1981, resigned, 1984; sr. assoc. prof. mil. edn. program St. Leo Coll., Hurlburt Field, Fla., 1984-92; adj. instr. Pensacola Jr. Coll., 1984-86, 91—; West Fla. cluster adminstr. programs for higher edn. Nova Southeastern U., Pensacola/Ft. Lauderdale, Fla., 1994—. Contbr. articles to profl. publs. Capt. U.S. Army, 1975-84. Recipient Rsch. award Phi Delta Kappa, 1989. Mem. Internat. Fellowship of Christians and Jews, Two-Year Coll. English Assn. Southeast, Nat. Coun. Tchrs. English. Avocations: golf, travel. Home: 1313 Wisteria Ave Pensacola FL 32507-2250 E-mail: mcleods@bellsouth.net., mcleods@nova.edu.

MCLEOD, WALTON JAMES, lawyer, state legislator; b. Walterboro, S.C., June 30, 1937; s. Walton James Jr. and Rhoda Lane (Brown) McL.; m. Julie Edwina Hamiter, Feb. 15, 1969; 1 child, Walton James IV. BA, Yale U., 1959; LLB, U. S.C., 1964. Bar: S.C. 1964, U.S. Supreme Ct. 1974. Law clk. to Chief Judge Clement Haynsworth U.S. Ct. Appeals (4th cir.), Richmond, Va., 1964-65; assoc. Pope and Schumpert, Newberry, S.C., 1965-67; asst. U.S. Atty. Columbia, 1967-68; gen. counsel S.C. Dept. Health & Environ. Ctrl., 1968-94, spl. counsel, 1994-96; dep. S.C. atty. gen., 1987-88. Magistrate Newberry County, Little Mountain, S.C., 1973-81; mcpl. judge Town of Little Mountain, 1981-83, mayor, 1983-89, 93-96; mem. S.C. Ho. of Reps., Columbia, 1996—. Author: Legal Perspectives of Environmental Health, 1973; co-author: Environmental Quality Law, 1975, Hospital Franchising Law and Regulation, 1979. Pres. Newberry (S.C.) Jaycees, 1967; bd. dirs. S.C. Housing Fin. & Devel. Authority, Columbia, 1977-96; chair Ctrl. Midlands Coun. Govts., Columbia, 1981-82; trustee S.C. State Mus., Columbia, 1981-85. Lt. (j.g.) USN, 1959-61, served to Capt. USNR, 1961-92, ret. Recipient Outstanding Jaycee award Newberry Jaycees, 1967, Howell Excellence award Naval Res. Law Program, Washington, 1991; named Outstanding Freshman Rep. of Yr. Carolina Hist. Found. Soc., Inc., 1997. Fellow S.C. Bar Found.; mem. S.C. Magistrates Assn. (pres. 1976-77, Disting. Jud. Svc. award 1975, 77), Judge Advs. Assn. (nat. pres. 1991-92), S.C. Res. Officers Assn. (state pres. 1981-82, Res. Officer of Yr. 1998), S.C. Soc. (pres. 1990-93). Democrat. Luth. Avocations: jogging, reading. Home: 308 Pomaria St Little Mountain SC 29075-9003 Office: SC House of Reps PO Box 11867 Columbia SC 29211-1867 Fax: 803-345-0770.

MCLEOD, WILLIAM LASATER, JR. lawyer, former judge and state legislator; b. Marks, Miss., Feb. 27, 1931; s. William Lasater and Sara Louise (Macaulay) McL.; m. Marilyn Qualls, June 16, 1962; children: Sara Nelson Judson, Martha Ellen Livanec, Ruth Elizabeth Rohs. AB, Princeton U., 1953; JD, La. State U., 1958. Bar: La. 1958, U.S. Supreme Ct. 1980. Pvt. practice, Lake Charles, La., 1958—90, 1997—; ptnr. McLeod & Little, 1976—90; dist. judge Calcasieu Parish, 1991—96. Mem. La. Ho. of Reps., 1968-76; mem. La. Senate, 1976-90. Chmn. adv. bd. Lake Charles Salvation Army, 1965-66; pres. Calcasieu Area coun. Boy scouts Am., 1978; elder Presbyn. Ch. With U.S.

Army, 1953-55. Recipient Disting. Svc. award Lake Charles Jaycees, 1963, Civic Svc. award S.W. La. C. of C., 1986. Mem. La. Bar Assn., S.W. La Bar Assn. (pres. 1980), Masons. Democrat. Office: 120 W Pujo St Lake Charles LA 70601-4257

MCLEOD, WILLIS B. college president; m. Jacqueline Cumbo; 1 child, Jeffrey. BS in Math., MEd in Elem. Sch. Adminstrn., Fayetteville State U.; EdD in Sch. Adminstrn., U. Va. Pres. Fayetteville (N.C.) State U., 1995—.

MCLESKEY, CHARLES HAMILTON, anesthesiology educator, medical lab director; b. Phila., Nov. 8, 1946; s. W. Hamilton and Marion A. (Butts) McL.; m. Nanci S. Simmons, June 3, 1972; children: Travis, Heather. BA, Susquehanna U., 1968; MD, Wake Forest U., 1972. Diplomate Am. Bd. Anesthesiology. Intern Maine Med. Ctr., Portland, 1972-73; resident in anesthesiology U. Wash. Sch. Medicine, Seattle, 1973-76, NIH rsch. trainee, l974-75; clin. teaching assoc. dept. anesthesiology U. Calif., San Francisco, l976-78; asst. prof. anesthesiology Wake Forest U. Bowman Gray Sch. Medicine, Winston-Salem, N.C., l978-83, assoc. prof., l983-84, U. Tex. Med. Br., Galveston, 1985-87; assoc. prof. anesthesiology U. Colo. Health Sci. Ctr., Denver, 1987-91, prof., 1991-93, dir. acad. affairs, 1987-93; prof., chmn. dept. anesthesiology Tex. A&M U., 1993-2000; chmn. dept. anesthesiology, med. dir. perioperative svcs. Scott and White Clin. and Meml. Hosp., Temple, Tex., 1993-2000; assoc. med. dir. Scott and White Health Plan, 1995-2000; sr. dir. clin. devel. Abbott Labs., Abbott Park, Ill., 2000—. Cons., lectr. Janssen Pharmaceutica, Piscataway, N.J., 1980-98, Alza Corp., Palo Alto, Calif., 1986-99; cons. Glaxo-Wellcome Co., Research Triangle Park, N.C., Abbott Labs., Chgo., Hoechst, Marion, Roussel, Kansas City, Kans., Aspect Med., Natick, Mass., Baxter Labs., Chgo., Scott Labs., Lubbock, Tex.; lectr. to over 500 nat. and state med. orgns., 1982—; examiner Am. Bd. Anesthesiology; lectr. Ohmeda, Liberty Corner, N.J. Assoc. editor Anesthesiology Rev., Anesthesiology News, Pharmacy Practia News; editor Geriatric Anesthesiology, 1997; contbr. numerous articles to med. jours. Mem. choir Friendswood (Tex.) Meth. Ch., 1985-87; mem. Friendswood Fine Arts Commn., 1985-87; mem. Temple Chamber Arts Adv. Coun., 1997-99. Lt. comdr. M.C., USN, 1976-78. Woodruff-Fisher scholar, l964-68. Mem.: Temple C. of C., Evergreen Newcomers, Soc. Acad. Anesthesia Chairs (councilman 1996—99), Soc. for Ambulatory Anesthesia (program chair 1999), Internat. Anesthesia Rsch. Soc., Colo. Soc. Anesthesiologists (past pres.), Soc. for Edn. in Anesthesiology (past v.p., past pres.), Am. Soc. Anesthesiologists (del. 1983—85, 1988—90), Assn. U Anesthetists, Nat. Spkrs. Assn., Internat. Platform Assn., Mensa, Alpha Omega Alpha. Republican. Presbyterian. Avocations: running, fishing, racquetball, squash. Address: 21038 W Andover Dr Mundelein IL 60060 E-mail: charles.mcleskey@abbott.com.

MCLINN, ANNA RUTH, educator; b. Magnolia, Ark., May 11, 1941; d. Willie Mae Heard and Onzelow Reed; m. Cecil Edward McLinn; children: Tiffany, David. BA in Edn., George Pepperdine U., 1963, MS in Mgmt. and Adminstrn., 1973; D (hon.) , St. Sephens Coll. With L.A. Unified Sch. Dist.; prin. Marvin Ave. Sch.; prof. U. Phoenix, Calif. Adj. prof., student tchr. supr. Nat. U., Phoenix U.; spkr. in field. Numerous guest appearences on TV. Vol. House of Blues Found., 1996—, Kayne-Eras Found., fundraising com. Recipient Unsung Hero award Reliastar Life Ins. Co., L.A., 1997; Outstanding Tchr. of Yr. Theta Rho Delta Soc., 1963; Kellogg scholar, 1995. Mem. Calif. Coun. Quality and Svc. (Eureka award 1996), Associated Adminstrs. L.A., Phil-Art-Lit-Mor Club, Women on Target, Delta Sigma Theta. Democrat. Baptist. Avocations: singing, dancing, painting, antique collecting. Home: 6526 W 6th St Los Angeles CA 90048

MCLOONE, EUGENE P. education educator; b. Phila., Nov. 11, 1929; married. BA, LaSalle Coll., 1951; MS in Govt. Mgmt., U. Denver, 1952; PhD, U. Ill., 1961. Carnegie fellow U. Denver, 1951-52; staff Ark. Legis. Rsch. Coun. Study on Sch. of Fin., 1952; rsch. asst. Bur. of Ednl. Rsch. U. Ill., 1952-55; Fed. Exec. fellow The Brookings Instn., 1961; specialist Sch. of Fin. U.S. Office of Edn., 1958-65; postdoctoral rsch. fellow Stanford U., 1966-67; rsch. dir. Nat. Ctr. for Edn. Stats./U.S. Dept. Edn., Washington, 1979-81; assoc. prof. U. Md. Coll. Edn., College Park, 1967-75, prof. edn. dept. edn. policy, planning and adminstrn., 1975-96, assoc. prof. dept. econs., 1967-94; sr. staff scientist George Washington U., 1966-67; postdoct. fellow Stanford U., 1967-68; assoc. dir. rsch. divsn. NEA, Washington, 1968-69, staff contact, com. for sch. fin., 1968-70; atty. gen. State of N.J., 1981-83, State of W.Va., 1981; prof. emeritus U. Md., College Park, 1996—. Cons. Addison-Wesleyan Pubs., 1992-93, Bur. of Spl. Edn., Dept. Edn., 1992, Jour. Econs. and Edn., 1989-95, Jour. Edn. Fin., 1989—, Nat. Tax Assn., 1989, Office Edn. Rsch. and Improvement, 1989, others; lectr. in field; panel mem. Statis. for Supply and Demand of Pre-Collegiate Sci. and Math. Tchrs., Nat. Rsch. Coun., NAS, 1986-90; with Heald Commn. Higher Edn. N.Y., 1960; treas. Brightright of Johnstown, 2000. Author: Pre-College Science and Mathematics Teachers: Monitoring Supply, Demand, and Quality, 1990, Report of Panel, Toward Understanding Teacher Supply and Demand: Priorities for Research and Development Interim Report, Profiles in School Support, 1969-70; co-author: Public School Finance: Profiles of the State, 1979, Documentation and Analysis of Maryland Special Services Information System, 1977; contbr. articles to profl. jours.; editor books in field. Treas. Birthright of Johnstown, 2000-02. Grantee Ford Found., 1966-68, Bur. of the Handicapped, U.S.O.E., 1977, Nat. Ctr. for Edn. Stats., 1971, 73; recipient awards in field. Mem. NEA, Am. Econ. Assn., Am. Assn. Sch. Adminstrs., Am. Edn. Fin. Assn. (pres.-elect 1995-96, pres. 1996-97, immediate past pres. 1997-98, Outstanding Svc. awsard for Contbns. to Field 2000), Phi Delta Kappa.

MCLOONE, JAMES BRIAN, psychiatrist, educator; b. Phoenix, Mar. 21, 1950; s. John Joseph and Lorraine Suzette (Hughes) McL.; m. Cathy Ebel; children: Katherine Ann, Brian Bathe. BA, U. Ariz., 1972; MD, George Washington U., 1976. Diplomate Am. Bd. Psychiatry and Neurology. Inpatient med. dir. Maricopa Med. Ctr., Phoenix, 1980-81; dir. psychiatry residency Good Samaritan Regional Med. Ctr., 1981—, chmn. dept. psychiatry, 1992—. Prof. clin. psychiatry U. Ariz. Coll. Medicine, Tucson, 1982—, assoc. head dept. psychiatry for acad. and clin. affairs, Phoenix campus, 1997—; chair med. edn. com. Good Samaritan Regional Med. Ctr., Phoenix, 1990—, exec. com., 1992—. Mem. Men's Art Coun. Phoenix Art Mus., 1981-87; student advisor U. Ariz. Coll. Medicine, Tucson, 1982—, Brophy Coll. Prep., Phoenix, 1982. Fellow Am. Psychiatric Assn.; mem. Am. Assn. Dirs. Psychiat. Residency Tng., Assn. Geropsychiatrists, Paradise Valley C. C., Alpha Omega Alpha. Roman Catholic. Avocations: golf, gardening. Office: Good Samaritan Reg Med Ctr 925 E Mcdowell Rd Phoenix AZ 85006-2579

MCLOUD, THERESA CLAIRE, radiologist; b. Boston, Jan. 5, 1944; d. Malcolm and Veronica Beatrice McLoud. BS, Boston Coll., 1964; MD, McGill U., Montreal, Que., 1968; MA, Harvard U., 1993. Rotating intern Royal Victoria Hosp., Montreal, 1968-69, diagnostic radiology resident, 1969-73; Winchester fellow, chest radiology fellow Yale U. Sch. Medicine, New Haven, 1973-74; dir. thoracic radiology Mass. Gen. Hosp., Boston, 1982—2001, assoc. radiologist in chief, 1997—, dir. edn., 1997—. Author: The Requisites: Thoracic Radiology; contbr. articles to profl. jours. Bd. dirs. Notre Dame Acad., Hingham, Mass. Fellow Am. Coll. Radiology; mem. Am. Roentgen Ray Soc. (pres. 1999-2000), Radiol. Soc. N.Am. (dir. sci. program 1998-2000, Ann. Oration 1994, bd. dirs. 2000—), Soc. Thoracic Radiology (treas. 1986-88, pres. elect 1988-89, pres. 1989-90), Mass. Med. Soc. (councillor 1986-2002), Harvard Club Boston, Sigma Xi. E-mail: tmcloud@partners.org.

MCLOUGHLIN, LUCILLE C. physician; b. Jersey City, Aug. 25, 1952; d. Joseph W. and Luciana Victoria (Tavolara) McLoughlin. BS in Biology, St. Peter's Coll., Jersey City, 1974; MD, U. Autonoma de Guadalajara, Mex., 1979. Diplomate in pediatrics and pediatric gastroenterology Am. Bd. Pediatrics. Resident in pediat., then fellow U. Medicine and Dentistry N.J., Newark, 1980-86; dir. pediatric gastroenterology Children's Hosp. of N.J., 1994-96, assoc. dir. pediatric gastroenterology, 1991-94; attending pediatric gastroenterologist Newark Beth Israel Hosp., 1996-97; chief pediatric gastroenterology UMDNJ-N.J. Med. Sch., Newark, 1997-2001, med. dir. pediatric liver transplant, 1996-2000; chief pediatric gastroenterology Penn State Children's Hosp., Hershey, Pa., 2001—. Contbr. articles to profl. jours. Home: 653 Hillside Ave Hummelstown PA 17036 Office: Penn State Children's Hosp 500 Univ Dr PO Box 850 Hershey PA 17033-0850

MCLUCAS, JOHN C. language educator; b. Bellefonte, Pa., June 28, 1952; s. John Luther and Patricia (Knapp) McLucas. BA in Latin, Wesleyan U., Middletown, Conn., 1974; MA in Italian, Yale U., 1978, PhD in Italian, 1983. Asst. prof. Towson State U., Balt., 1984—92, assoc. prof., 1992—2000, prof. dept. lang., 2000—; instr., vocal coach Peabody Conservatory, 1985—. Lectr. on art and music history; concert and oratorio singer. Contbr. Elder 1st and Franklin St. Presbyn. Ch., Balt., 1990—; bd. dirs. Chase-Brexton Clinic, 1987—90. Democrat. Presbyterian. Home: 2826 Saint Paul St Baltimore MD 21218 Mailing: Towson Univ Dept Modern Lang Towson MD 21252

MC LUCAS, JOHN LUTHER, aerospace company executive; b. Fayetteville, N.C., Aug. 22, 1920; s. John Luther and Viola (Conley) McL.; m. Patricia Knapp, July 27, 1946 (div. 1981); children: Pamela McLucas Byers, Susan, John C., Roderick K.; m. Harriet D. Black, Sept. 25, 1981. BS, Davidson Coll., 1941; MS, Tulane U., 1943; PhD, Pa. State U., 1950, D.Sc., 1974. V.p., tech. dir. Haller, Raymond & Brown, Inc., State College, Pa., 1950-57; pres. HRB-Singer, Inc., 1958-62; dep. dir. rsch. and engring. Dept. Def., 1962-64; pres., chief exec. officer Mitre Corp., Bedford, Mass., 1966-69; undersec. of Air Force, 1969-73; sec. of Air Force, 1973-75; adminstr. FAA, 1975-77; pres. Comsat Gen. Corp., Washington, 1977-79; exec. v.p. COMSAT, 1979-80, pres. world systems div., 1980-83, exec. v.p., chief strategic officer, 1983-85. Bd. dirs. Orbital Scis. Corp.; mem. USAF Sci. Adv. Bd., 1967-69, 77-84, Def. Sci. Bd., 1968-69; chmn. USAF SDAG, 1979-83; chmn. bd. dirs. Internat. Space U., 1987-93, active, 1987—. Author: Space Commerce, 1991; contbr. articles to tech. lit.; patentee and author in field. Chmn. bd. Wolf Trap Found., 1986-88; chmn. bd. Arthur C. Clarke Found. of U.S.; chmn. bd. dirs. ISY Internat. Space Yr. Assn. U.S., 1987-93; chmn. NASA adv. council, 1988-91. Served with USNR, 1943-46. Recipient Disting. Service award Dept. Def., 1964, 1st bronze palm, 1973, silver palm, 1975 Fellow IEEE, AAAS, AIAA (hon., pres.); mem. NAE (coun. 1988-93), Nat. Rsch. Coun. (chmn. Air Force studies bd. 1987-91), Belle Haven Club, Sigma Xi, Sigma Pi Sigma. Home and Office: 1213 Villamay Blvd Alexandria VA 22307-2051

MC LURE, CHARLES E., JR. economist, consultant; b. Sierra Blanca, Tex., Apr. 14, 1940; s. Charles E. and Dessie (Evans) McL.; m. Patsy Nell Carroll, Sept. 17, 1962. BA, U. Kans., 1962; MA, Princeton U., 1964, PhD, 1966. Asst. prof. econs. Rice U., Houston, 1965-69, assoc. prof., 1969-72, prof., 1972-79, Allyn R. and Gladys M. Cline prof. econs., 1973-79; exec. dir. for research Nat. Bur. Econ. Research, Cambridge, Mass., 1977-78, v.p., 1978-81; sr. fellow Hoover Instn., Stanford U., 1981—; dep. asst. sec. Dept. Treasury, 1983-85. Sec. Dept. Treasury, 1983-85; sr. staff economist Coun. Econ. Advisers, Washington, 1969-70; vis. lectr. U. Wyo., 1972; vis. prof. Stanford U., 1973; cons. U.S. Treasury Dept., Labor Dept., World Bank, UN, OAS, Interam. Devel. Bank, Tax Found., Com. Econ. Devel., IMF, Internat. Tax and Investment Ctr., govts. Can., Colombia, Malaysia, Panama, Jamaica, Bolivia, Indonesia, New Zealand, Brazil, Trinidad and Tobago, Venezuela, Guatemala, Peoples Republic China, Egypt, Malawi, Mex., Bulgaria, Brazil, Russia, Ukraine, Romania, Kazakhstan, South Africa, Vietnam, Chile, Argentina. Author: Fiscal Failure: Lessons of the Sixties, 1972, (with N. Ture) Value Added Tax: Two Views, 1972, (with M. Gillis) La Reforma Tributaria Colombiana de 1974, 1977, Must Corporate Income Be Taxed Twice?, 1979, Economic Perperspectives on State Taxation of Multijurisdictional Corporations, 1986, The Value Added Tax: Key to Deficit Reduction, 1987; co-author: Taxation of Income from Business and Capital in Colombia, 1989; also numerous articles on econs. and public finance. Ford Found. faculty research fellow, 1967-68 Mem. Am. Econ. Assn., Nat. Tax Assn., Beta Theta Pi. Home: 250 Yerba Santa Ave Los Altos CA 94022-1609 Office: Stanford U Hoover Instn Stanford CA 94305-6010 E-mail: mclure@hoover.stanford.edu.

MCLURE, JOHN DOUGLAS, government relations; b. Melita, Man., Can., July 10, 1942; s. Malcolm Alexander and Rachel (Simpson) McL.; m. Nicole Lafrance, Aug. 26, 1967. BSc, U. Man., Winnipeg, 1963; Ammunition Tech. Officer, Royal Mil. Coll. Sci., Wiltshire, Eng., 1964. Program analyst Treasury Bd. Secretariat, Ottawa, Ont., Can., 1975-79, group chief industry and natural resources divsn. Can., 1979-80, dir. industry and natural resources divsn. Can., 1980-82, asst. sec. econ. devel. Can., 1982-84; asst. dep. min. small bus. and spl. projects Dept. Regional Indsl. Expansion, 1984-85, asst. dep. min. crown investments and spl. projects, 1985-86, asst. dep. min. native econ. devel., 1986-87; asst. dep. min. fin., pers., adminstrn. Dept Industry, Sci. & Tech., 1987-89; asst. dep. min. fin. Dept. Nat. Def., 1989-95, assoc. dep. min., 1995-96; dep. min. Dept. Western Econ. Diversification, 1996-97; sr. v.p. Hill and Knowlton Can. Ltd., 1997-2000; pres., CEO JDM Consulting Inc., 2000—; sr. assoc. Hill and Knowlton Can. Ltd., Ottawa, 2000—. Chmn. bd. Def. Constrn. Can., 2001—. Maj. Can. Land Forces, 1960-75. Recipient N.Am. Best Practice Recognition, Ctr. Creative Leadership, Greensboro, N.C., 1994. Mem. Assn. Profl. Execs. (Leadership award 1995), Hylands Golf Club. Avocations: golf, alpine skiing. Home: 35 Somerset St W Ottawa ON Canada K2P OH3 Office: Hill and Knowlton Can Ltd 55 Metcalfe St Ste 1300 Ottawa ON Canada K1P 6L5 E-mail: john.mclure@hillandknowlton.ca.

MCLURKIN, THOMAS CORNELIUS, JR. lawyer; b. L.A., July 28, 1954; s. Thomas Cornelius and Willie Mae (O'Connor) McL.; m. Charmaine Bobo. BA, U. So. Calif., 1976, MPA, 1980, postgrad., 1998; JD, U. LaVerne, 1982. Bar: Calif. 1984, U.S. Dist. Ct. (ctrl. dist.) Calif. 1984, U.S. Dist. Ct. Hawaii 1984, U.S. Ct. Appeals (9th cir.) 1984, U.S. Dist. Ct. (ea., no. and so. dists.) Calif. 1985, U.S. Tax Ct. 1988, U.S. Ct. Mil. Appeals 1989, U.S. Army Ct. Mil. Rev. 1993, U.S. Supreme Ct., 1995. Law clk. dept. water and power City of L.A., 1979-82; jud. clk. cen. dist. U.S. Dist. Ct., L.A., 1982-83; law clk. Office City Atty., 1983-84, dep. city atty., 1984—. Author (with others): Facts in American History, 1968, 2nd edit. 1989, Eagle Scout, 1970. Mem. L.A. World Affairs Coun., 1980—, Smithsonian Assocs.; bd. dirs. L.A. Area coun. Boy Scouts Am., Hillsides Homes for Children; provisional patron Tournament of Roses Assn., Pasadena, 1994—; mem. Verdugo Hills Area coun. Boy Scouts Am. Mem. ABA, ALA, ASPA, Los Angeles County Bar Assn., Assn. Trial Lawyers Am., Langston Law Assn. L.A., U. So. Calif. Gen. Alumni Assn. (bd. govs. exec. bd. 1986-90), U. So. Calif. Black Alumni Assn.-Ebonics (pres. 1988-89), U. So. Calif. Pres.'s Cir., Elks, Am. Legion, Phi Alpha Delta, Kappa Alpha Psi. Republican. United Methodist. Avocations: sailing, tennis, volunteer work, American and world history. Office: LA City Atty Office 200 N Main St Ste 1700 Los Angeles CA 90012-4110 E-mail: tmclurk@atty.lacity.org.

MCMAHAN, BARBARA JEAN, medical staff coordinator; b. Stephenville, Tex., Feb. 28, 1946; Student, Tarleton State U., 1964-65. Cert. med. transcriptionist, med. staff coord. Med. staff coord. Harris Meth. Erath County, Stephenville, Tex., 1968—, dir. vol. svcs., 1984—. Mem. Am. Assn. Med. Transcription, Nat. Assn. Med. Staff Svcs., Tex. Soc. Med. Staff Svcs., Dallad Chpt. Med. Transcription. Baptist. Avocations: antiques, quarter horse riding, crafts, fishing, travel. Office: Harris Methodist Erath County PO Box 1399 411 N Belknap St Stephenville TX 76401-3415

MCMAHAN, GALE ANN SCIVALLY, education educator; b. Anna, Ill., Oct. 19, 1946; d. George Oliver and Jessie Lee (Johnson) Scivally; m. Joe Henry McMahan, Dec. 14, 1963; children: Randy Scott, Joseph Paul. BS, So. Ill. U., 1971, MS, 1974, PhD, 1994. Cert. tchr., supr., adminstr., Ill. Resource tchr. Jonesboro (Ill.) Sch. Dist. 43, 1971-73, dir. early intervention, 1991-94; resource tchr. Anna Sch. Dist. 37, 1973-94; supt. Lick Creek Sch. Dist. 16, Buncombe, Ill., 1994-95, Vienna (Ill.) Pub. Sch. Dist. 55, 1995-97; asst. prof. S.E. Mo. State U., Cape Girardeau, 1997—. Lectr. Shawnee C.C., Ullin, Ill., 1986-88, So. Ill. U., Carbondale, 1990, 92, 93; reader U. Ill. Bd. Edn., Springfield, 1989, 92; mem. adv. bd. for early intervention Anna Interagy. Coun., 1991—, Ill. Interagy. Coun., Springfield, 1991—; mem. peer monitor spl. edn. dept. Ill. Bd. Edn., 1993—, mem. monitoring team for tchr. preparation programs; mem. content adv. com. Ill. Cert. Testing Sys., 1994—. Co-author: (video) Jenny...Our Child of Today!, 1991; editor: Churches in Clear Creek Association, 1988. Recipient Those Who Excel in Edn. award of recognition Ill. Bd. Edn., 1992, grantee, 1990—. Mem. Coun. Exceptional Children (presenter 1991), Ill. Supt. Assn., Ill. Prin. Assn., Ill. Women Adminstrs., Anna Elem. Edn. Assn. (pres. 1992-94), DAR, Delta Kappa Gamma (scholar 1989-90, co-contbr. article to Bull. 1993), Phi Kappa Phi, Kappa Delta Phi, Phi Delta Kappa. Baptist. Avocations: genealogy, reading, painting, walking, swimming. Home: 4890 State Route 146 E Anna IL 62906-3530 Office: 1 University Plz Cape Girardeau MO 63701-4710

MCMAHAN, RICHARD LAMAR, investment company executive, financial planner; b. Gastonia, N.C., Nov. 5, 1943; s. Hughlen LaFayette and Ruth May (Porter) McM.; m. Laura Elizabeth Shampert, Dec. 18, 1966 (div. Sept. 1980); children: Devin LeRobert, Deirdre Elizabeth; m. Gloria Ann Weiland, Sept. 3, 1982; 1 stepchild, Robert C. Raines. AB, Newberry (S.C.) Coll., 1966; MusM, East Carolina U., Greenville, 1973; EdD, U. S.C., 1977. CFP. Tchr. Darling County Schs., Lamar, S.C., 1966-67, Lexington (S.C.) County Schs., 1968-79; owner Comml. Music Prodns., Columbia, S.C., 1980-92; ptnr. G.E.M. Recs., 1984-92, G.E.M. Properties, Columbia, 1984-96; account exec. Dean Witter, 1992-96; assoc. v.p. Morgan Stanley Dean Witter, 1997—. Author: (fin. newsletter) The Retirement Planner, 1992—; contbr. articles to profl. jours.; composer, arranger music, 1962-92. Comdr. 246th Army Band, Columbia, 1985-91; bd. dirs. S.C. Arts Commn., Columbia, 1980-82, So. Arts Jazz Panel, Atlanta, 1981-84; sr. v.p. bd. dirs. Timberlake Property Owners Assn., Chapin, S.C., 1998—. With U.S. Army N.G., 1968-91. Named Outstanding Educator, Lexington C. of C., 1974; recipient Army Achievement medal, 1987. Mem. S.C. C. of C., Columbia C. of C. (grad. Leadership Columbia 1980), Internat. Assn. Fin. Planners, Investment Mgmt. Consultants Assn. Avocations: golf, boating, cooking, music. Home: 128 Water Links Dr Chapin SC 29036-7786

MCMAHON, ANTHONY HUGH, SR. computer program manager, systems integrator; b. Nesbitt, Miss., Nov. 16, 1960; s. Sam Ernest Batmon and Velma Louise (Brown) McMahon; m. Queen Esther Harris Taylor, Sept. 9, 1989 (div. June 1993); children: Anthony Hugh Jr. AS in Bus. Tech. and Acctg., State Tech. Inst., Memphis, 1979. Correspondence tax auditor IRS, Memphis, 1981-84, computer systems analyst Washington, 1984-88, program analyst, 1988-91, tech. support chief electronic filing sys. Memphis, 1990-94, program mgr., sys. integrator, 1994—. Recipient spl. achievement cash award IRS, 1986, 89, 91-95, mgr.'s award, 1992, Disting. Performance award, 1992, 93. Mem. Black Data Processing Assocs., Assn. for Improvement of Minorities, Info. Sys. Fed. Users Group. Democrat. Baptist. Avocations: pool, video movies, photography, music, football. Home: 5508 Edwin Forest Rd Memphis TN 38141-2411 Office: IRS 5333 Getwell Rd Memphis TN 38118-7703

MCMAHON, CRAIG ROGER, lawyer; b. Meriden, Conn., July 5, 1950; s. Roger and Marie (Couch) McM. BA, George Washington U., 1972; JD, New Eng. Sch. Law, 1976. Bar: Conn. 1976. Magistrate Alaska Ct. Sys., Aniak, 1977-84, Bethel, 1984—. Mem. Bethel Actor's Guild (pres. 1998—), Bethel Coun. on Arts (treas. 1988-98, sec. 2001—). Avocations: genealogy, photography, travel. Home: PO Box 1346 Bethel AK 99559-1346 Office: Alaska Court Sys PO Box 130 Bethel AK 99559-0130

MCMAHON, DEBRA BRYLAWSKI, management consultant; b. Washington, Jan. 1, 1956; d. E. Fulton Brylawski and Laura (Carizzoni) Brylawski Miller; m. Neil M. McMahon, Oct. 2, 1982; children: Alexa Lauren, Brendan Patrick, Morgan Lane. BA, Northwestern U., 1976; MBA, Kellogg Grad. Sch. Mgmt., 1977. Asst. brand mgr. Gen. Mills Inc., Mpls., 1977-80; mgr. new products and corp. devel. William Wrigley Jr. Co., Chgo., 1980-84; v.p., strategic capabilities practice Mercer Mgmt. Cons., Washington, 1984—. Contbr. articles to profl. jours. Mem. Beta Gamma Sigma. Republican. Roman Catholic. Avocations: recreational sports, travel, art. Office: Mercer Mgmt Cons 2300 N St NW Ste 800 Washington DC 20037-1194

MCMAHON, DENNIS C. lawyer, writer; b. Bklyn., Aug. 4, 1950; s. John Thomas and Ruth Mildred McMahon. BA summa cum laude, Fordham U., 1972; JD, Bklyn. Law Sch., 1977. Bar: N.Y. 1978, U.S. Dist. Ct. (so. and ea. dists.) N.Y. 1978, U.s. Dist. Ct. (no. dist.) N.Y. 1984, U.S. Ct. Appeals (3d cir.) 1992. Reporter, news editor Home Reporter and Sunset News, Bklyn., 1972-77; weekly press coord. Speaker's Office, N.Y. State Assembly, N.Y.C., 1977; atty. McHugh & O'Conor, 1978-87, Peter F. Broderick, N.Y.C., 1987-93; pvt. practice, 1993—. Arbitrator N.Y.C. Small Claims Ct., Bklyn., 1985—; cons. law firms in Republic of Ireland. Author column Bklyn. Spectator, 1983—. Bd. dirs. N.Y.C. Econ. Devel. Corp., 1987-97; mem. Sch. Bd. Dist. 20, Bklyn., 1977-93, pres., 1989-90. Recipient local civic awards. Mem. Am. Arbitration Assn. (arbitrator), KC, Commodore Barry Club, Ancient Order of Hibernians, Downtown Athletic Club (bd. dirs.). Democrat. Roman Catholic. Avocations: Ireland, music, travel, politics. Home and Office: 7032 4th Ave Brooklyn NY 11209-1666 E-mail: dennislaw@aol.com.

MCMAHON, DONALD AYLWARD, investor, corporate director; b. N.Y.C., Feb. 20, 1931; s. William F. and Anne (Aylward) McM.; m. Nancy Lantz, Apr. 12, 1953; children: Gail, Brian, Lisa, Glenn, Ann, Carol, William, Douglas. MBA, Emory U., 1982. With Dime Savs. Bank, Bklyn., 1952; salesman Monroe Calculating Machine Co., 1952-55, asst. br. mgr. Pitts., 1955-56, br. mgr. Phila., 1956-63, asst. gen. sales mgr. Orange, N.J., 1963-64, Eastern regional gen. sales mgr., 1964-65, v.p. mktg., 1965-66; pres. Monroe Calculator Co. div. Litton Industries, Inc., Orange, 1966-70; v.p. Litton Industries, 1967-70; pres., chief operating officer, dir. Baker Industries, Inc., Parsippany, N.J., 1970-74; pres., chief exec. officer, dir. Royal Crown Cos., Inc., Atlanta, 1975-85. Bd. dirs. Intelligent Systems Corp., Atlanta. Bd. dirs. Boys Clubs Metro Atlanta. Mem. Sovereign Order of Knights of Malta. Home: 1665 Winterthur Close NW Atlanta GA 30328-4688

MCMAHON, DONALD J. statistician, consultant; b. Evanston, Ill., July 24, 1950; s. Carol J. McMahon; m. Mary Jane Alexander, July 30, 1983; children: Caitlin Elizbeth, Mollie Margaret. BA, BS, MacMurray Coll., 1972; MS, Adelphi U., 1975, PhD, 1977. Instr. stats. Adelphi U., Garden City, NY, 1975—76; asst. dir. clin. rsch. sys. Nathan Kline Inst., Orangeburg, 1976—81, dir. clin. trial data mgmt., 1999—; dir. clin. rsch. info. sys. Columbia U., N.Y.C., 1981—99. Sr. lectr. Columbia Sch. Nursing, N.Y.C., 1995—99; stat., data mgr. various Nat. Inst. Health grants. Editor (stat. editor): (jours.) Neurology and Urodynamics, 1990—99, Jour. Clin. Endocrinology and Metabolism, 1999—; contbr. articles to profl. jours. Chmn. Village Peoples Party, South Nyack, NY, 1998—. Mem.: Soc. Clin. Data Mgmt., Endocrine Soc., Soc. Clin. Trials. Home: 98 Depot Pl Nyack NY 10960-4404 E-mail: depotpl@cs.com.

MCMAHON, EILEEN MARIE, artist agent; b. Jersey City, July 15, 1953; d. William John and Marie Rita (Stringer) M. BA in Art, Jersey City State Coll., 1974; postgrad., Rutgers U., 1974-76, New Sch. for Social Research, 1976-77, Sch. of Visual Arts, 1976. Asst. curator Jersey City Mus., 1975-77; curator Ian Woodner Family Collection, N.Y.C., 1977-78; assoc. rep. Artist's Assocs., Inc., 1978-81; sr. rep. Gerald and Cullen Rapp, Inc., 1981-86; mktg. dir. Corey Chaloner Millen, 1986-88; assoc. rep. John Locke Studios Inc., 1988-97; pres. Eileen McMahon & Co., Bayonne, N.J., 1997—. Co-author, designer: mus. catalog, August Will: Scenes of Old Jersey City, 1976. Named Jersey Jour. Woman of Achievement, 1977. Office: Eileen McMahon & Co PO Box 1062 Bayonne NJ 07002-1062 E-mail: eileenmcmahon@earthlink.net.

MCMAHON, JAMES CHARLES, lawyer; b. Bklyn., Dec. 4, 1951; s. James Charles and Rosemary Margaret (Gilroy) McM.; m. Nancy M. Neble, Oct. 30, 1984; children: Deirdre Kathleen Wright, Laura Elizabeth, Elizabeth Jane. BA, Boston Coll., 1973; JD, Fordham U., 1977. Bar: N.Y. 1978, Mass. 1996, U.S. Supreme Ct. 1996. Assoc. Winthrop Stimson Putnam & Roberts, N.Y.C., 1977-78, Brodsky, Linett, Altman, Schechter & Reicher, N.Y.C., 1978-82; ptnr. Brodsky, Altman & McMahon, LLP, 1982—, mng. ptnr., 1988—. Exec. sec., counsel N.Y. Movers Tariff Bur., Inc., N.Y.C., 1984-99; gen. counsel Mass. Movers Assn., Woburn, 1986—, Commonwealth Transp. Compensation Corp., Andover, Mass., 1992—, Transport Health Plan, Woburn, 1994—, N.Y. State Movers and Warehousemen's Assn., N.Y.C., 1984—, Nat. Moving and Storage Assn., Fairfax, Va., 1988-98, Am. Moving & Storage Tech. Found., Alexandria, Va., 1988--. Mem. editl. bd. Fordham Urban Law Jour., 1976. Recipient Disting. Svc. award Mass. Movers Assn., 1992. Mem. N.Y. State Bar Assn. (labor and employment law sect.), Assn. Bar City N.Y. (transp. com. 1997-99), Assn. Comml. Fin. Attys., Transp. Lawyers Assn., Assn. for Transp. Law, Logistics and Policy, N.Y. Athletic Club. Democrat. Roman Catholic. Home: 196 Pinesbridge Rd Ossining NY 10562-1428 Office: Brodsky Altman & McMahon LLP 60 E 42d St Ste 1540 New York NY 10165-1544 also: 10 State St Woburn MA 01801-6820 E-mail: jmcmahon@mcmahonlaw.com.

MCMAHON, JOCEYLYN PATTEN, elementary school educator; b. Phila., Mar. 7, 1966; d. Robert Lowery and Faith LaForge (Charles) Patten; m. Christopher John McMahon, Oct. 9, 1993; 1 child Aidan Christopher. BA ,

Bryn Mawr Coll., Phila., 1992; MEd in Art Edn., Univ. of the Arts, Phila., 1995. Cert. Art tchr (permanent) Pa. Art tchr. Strath Haven Middle Sch., Wallingford, 1996—. Home: 413 Green Ln Philadelphia PA 19128-3305

MCMAHON, JOHN ALEXANDER, law educator; b. Monongahela, Pa., July 31, 1921; s. John Hamilton and Jean (Alexander) McMahon; m. Betty Wagner, Sept. 14, 1947 (div. Mar. 1977); children: Alexander Talpey, Sarah Francis, Elizabeth Wagner, Ann Wallace; m. Anne Fountain Willets, May 1, 1977 (dec. June 1996); m. Anne Hall Davis, Apr. 18, 1999. AB magna cum laude, Duke U., 1942; student, Harvard U. Bus. Sch., 1942—43; JD, Law Sch., 1948; LLD, Wake Forest U., 1978; DSc (hon.) , Georgetown U. Sch. Medicine, 1985. Bar: N.C. 1950. Prof. pub. law and govt., asst. dir. Inst. Govt. U. N.C., 1948—59; gen. counsel, sec.-treas. N.C. Assn. County Commrs., Chapel Hill, 1959—65; v.p. spl. devel. Hosp. Saving Assn., NC, 1965—67; pres. N.C. Blue Cross and Blue Shield, Inc., 1968—72, Am. Hosp. Assn., Chgo., 1972—86; chmn. dept. health adminstrn. Duke U., Durham, NC, 1986—92, exec.-in-residence Fuqua Sch. Bus., 1992—. Mem. Chapel Hill bd. N.C. Nat. Bank, 1967—72; bd. govs. Blue Cross Assn., 1969—72; mem. Orange County Welfare Bd., 1956—63; chmn. N.C. Comprehensive Health Planning Coun., 1968—72, Health Planning Coun. of Ctrl. N.C., 1963—69; mem. Pres.'s Com. on Health Edn., 1971—72; mem. com. health svcs. industry and health industry adv. com. Econ. Stblzn. Program, 1971—74; mem. adv. coun. Kate Bitting Reynolds Health Care Trust, 1971—95, Northwestern U., 1973—86; mem. med. adv. com. VA, 1975—85; bd. dirs. The Forest at Duke, Durham, NC, 1994—2002, Exec. Svc. Corps of Greater Triangle, 1986—99, mem. adv. bd., 2000—. Author: North Carolina County Government, 1959, The North Carolina Local Government Commission, 1960; editor: N.C. County Yearbook, 1959—64, Proceedings of the Annual National Forum on Hospital and Health Affairs, 1993—2000. Chmn. bd. trustees Duke U., 1971—83, chmn. emeritus, 1983—; bd. mgrs., mem. exec. com. Internat. Hosp. Fedn., London, 1975—85, pres., 1981—83; mem. Orange County Dem. Exec. Com., also chmn. Kings Mill Precinct, 1964—68; bd. dirs. Rsch. Triangle Found., 1971—83, 1992—, Nat. Ctr. for Health Edn., 1974—86. With USAAF, 1942—46, col. Res., ret. Recipient Citation Disting. Svc. by Layman, AMA, 1978, Special award, Ill. Hosp. Assn., 1985, Dallas-Fort Worth Hosp. Coun., 1985, many others. Mem.: Inst. Medicine of NAS (Disting. Svc. award 1979), N.C. State Bar, Duke Alumni Assn. (pres. 1968—70), Dunes Golf and Beach Club (Myrtle Beach) (Silver Medal award 1986), Hope Valley Country Club (Durham). Democrat. Presbyterian. Home: 181 Montrose Dr Durham NC 27707-3929 Office: Duke U Fuqua Sch Bus Durham NC 27708-0120

MCMAHON, JOHN PATRICK, lawyer; b. Monroeville, Ohio, Feb. 8, 1919; s. George James and Eleanor Helene (Ruffing) McM.; m. Patricia Patterson McDanel, May 6, 1950 (dec. July 1983); children: Colleen, Kevin, Patricia, Brian, Barry, Michael; m. Mary Echard, Mar. 7, 1987. BA cum laude, Ohio State U., 1940, JD summa cum laude, 1942. Bar: Ohio 1942, U.S. Supreme Ct. 1949, U.S. Dist. Ct. Ohio 1949, U.S. Ct. Appeals (6th cir.) 1959, U.S. Ct. Appeals (D.C. cir.) 1975. Ptnr. George, Greek, King, McMahon, Columbus, Ohio, 1954-79, Baker & Hostetler, Columbus, 1979-85; with nat. coun. Ohio State U. Coll. Law, 1980—. Capt. USAAF, 1943-46, PTO. Mem. ABA, Ohio Bar Assn., Columbus Bar Assn., Transp. Lawyers Assn., Pres.' Club of Ohio State U. (Columbus), Athletic Club (Columbus), Home: 2880 Halstead Rd Columbus OH 43221-2916 Office: Baker & Hostetler 65 E State St Ste 2100 Columbus OH 43215-4260 E-mail: jmemahon@columbus.rr.com.

MCMAHON, JOSEPH EINAR, lawyer, consultant; b. Chgo., Aug. 26, 1940; s. Reynold Bernard and Dorothy Marie (Oftedahl) McM. BA cum laude, Denison U., 1962; JD, U. Mich., 1965. Bar: Mass. 1968, D.C. 1980. Asst. to Atty. Gen. and Senator Edward Brooke, Boston and Washington, 1965-67; exec. asst. Lt. Gov. Sargent of Mass., Boston, 1967-69; v.p. BedStuy D&S Corp. Restoration, Bklyn., 1969-74; dir. govt. regulations Westinghouse Electric Corp., Washington, 1974-78; v.p. corp. affairs Federated Dept. Stores, Cin., 1978-80; atty., cons. McMahon and Assocs., Washington, 1980—. Exec. dir. (part time), bd. dirs. The Get Ahead Found./USA, 1991-99. Trustee Denison U.; visitor U. Mich. Law Sch.; 1st v.p. Boston Rep. Com., 1968-69; presdl. appointee Nat. Coun. Econ. Opportunity, 1975-76; exec. dir. Nat. Bus. for Reagan-Bush Com., 1980; dir. Luther Inst., Washington, Rodale Inst., Emmaus, Pa.; dir. Luth. Lesbian and Gay Min., San Francisco; mem. outreach bd. Evang. Luth. Ch. in Am., 1995-2001. Mem. Phi Delta Phi, Pi Sigma Alpha, Omicron Delta Kappa. Clubs: Nat. Press, Capitol Hill (Washington). Lutheran. Office: McMahon & Assocs 1924 N St NW Washington DC 20036-1604

MCMAHON, JOYCE ARLENE, public relations professional; b. Beverly, Mass., Aug. 29, 1964; d. John J. and Constance A. (McNeil) McMahon. BS in Speech cum laude, Emerson Coll., 1986. Pub. rels. asst. S.D. Warren Co., Boston, 1986-88; conf. coord. New Medico Assn., Lynn, Mass., 1988-89; mktg. specialist Caravan for Commuters, Boston, 1989-90; exec. dir. Peabody (Mass.) Downtown Partnership, 1990-94; pub. info. officer Mass. Divsn. Energy Resources, Boston, 1995-98, dir. pub. info., 1998-2000; acct; supr. Mullen, Wenham, Mass., 2000—. City coun. City of Beverly, Mass., 1994—2001, v.p., 2000—01; coun. rep. Econ. Devel. Coun., 1994—2001; chmn. Com. on Fin. and Property, 1996—97, 2000—01, Com. on Legal Affairs and Accts., Beverly, 1998—99; bd. dirs. Spar & Spindle Girl Scout Coun., North Andover, 1993—99, Beverly Youth Collaborative, Beverly, 2002—. Mem. LWV. Avocations: reading, cycling, travel. Home: 15 1/2 Rowell Ave Beverly MA 01915-2921 E-mail: joycemccal@aol.com.

MCMAHON, MARGOT ANN, sculptor, art educator; b. Lake Forest, Ill., Apr. 15, 1957; d. William Franklin and Irene Mary (Leahy) McM.; m. Daniel Joseph Burke, June 25, 1988; children: Brendan McMahon Burke, Mary Irene McMahon Burke, Aubrey McMahon Burke. BA, Hamline U., 1979; MFA, Yale U., 1984. Sculpture asst. Hamline U., St. Paul, 1978; editl. artist World Book Ency., Chgo., 1979-82; tchg. asst. Yale U., New Haven, 1982-84; tchr. Yale Summer Sch., Norfolk, Conn., 1983; mem. sculpture faculty Sch. of Art Inst., Chgo., 1986-89; lectr. Art Inst. Assocs., 1989—, DePaul U., Chgo., 1998. Vis. artist Sch. of Art Inst., 1992, 96, St. Xavier Coll., Chgo, 1995; presenter in field. Prin. works include sculptures and mural at St. Patrick Ch., Lake Forest, Ill., John D. MacArthur State Park, North Palm Beach., Fla., DePaul U., One Northfield Plz., Northfield, Ill., Lake Bluff, Ill., St. Mary's Sch., Lake Forest, Robert Irwin Park, Homewood, Ill., Highwood (Ill.) Pub. Libr., St. Francis Retreat Ctr., Oak Brook, Ill., Chgo. Botanic Garden, Northfield Pub. Libr., Beye Sch., Oak Park, Ill.; represented in permanent collections Chgo. Hist. Soc., Chgo. Horticultural Mus., DePaul U., John D. and Catherine T. MacArthur Found., Lake Forest H.S., Mobil Oil Internat., Fairfax, Va., Mus. Contemporary Art, Chgo., Nat. Portrait Gallery, Smithsonian Instn., Washington, Sch. of St. Mary, Lake Forest, Silberline Co., Inc., Tamaqua, Pa., Tuthill Corp., Hinsdale, Ill., Yale U., and numerous pvt. collections; represented in DeBilzan Gallery, Santa Fe, N.Mex. Bd. dirs. Palette and Chisel, Chgo., 1989, Oak Park Area Arts Coun., 1999, Nat. Mus. of Women in the Arts, 1999—; mem., exhibitor Deerpath Art League, Lake Forest, 1990-00, Hyde Park Art Ctr., Chgo., 1992—, Oak Park Area Arts Coun., 1992—, Chgo. Arts Club. Recipient Fellowship award Barat Coll., 2000, Rose Phillipine Duchasne award, 2000; grantee Retirement Rsch. Found., Chgo., 1989, Ragdale Found., 1993, Steans Family Found., 1991. Mem. Internat. Sculpture Soc., Nat. Sculpture Soc. (Alex B. Hexter award 1991), Renaissance Soc., Ragdale Found., Mus. Contemporary Art, Arts Club of Chgo. Roman Catholic. Avocations: book clubs, sailing, music, softball. Home: 310 S Humphrey Ave Oak Park IL 60302-3528 E-mail: mmcmahom@mediaone.net.

MCMAHON, MARIA DRISCOLL, artist; b. Sayre, Pa., Jan. 8, 1959; d. Thomas James and Betty Jane (Taylor) Driscoll; m. Hugh Michael McMahon, May 27, 1978; children: Ian Thomas, Lea Shea. BS in Art Edn. summa cum laude, U. Pa. Kutztown, 1988; MA in Studio Art, Marywood Coll., 1993. Cert. art tchr., N.Y. Tchr. art Horseheads (N.Y.) Ctrl. Sch. Dist., 1989-94; artist Ithaca, N.Y., 1993—. Lectr. Allentown (Pa.) Art Mus., 1987; artist, speaker Victims rights Week Ceremony, Dryden, N.Y., 1997; artist Carantouan Greenway Restoration Project, Athens, Pa., 1997. One-person shows include Three River Reading Series, Corning, N.Y., 1996, Arcadian Winery, Watkins Glen, N.Y., 1997, 171 Cedar Arts Ctr., Corning, 1998, State of the Art Gallery, 1998; exhibited in group shows at Contemporary Gallery at Marywood Coll., Scranton, Pa., 1997, Bradford County Regional Exhbn., 1995, State of Art Gallery, Ithaca, 1993—, Susquehanna Regional Art Exhbn., 1994, Merit award, 1994, N.Y. State Fair, 1993, State of the Art Gallery, 1996, George Waters Gallery, Elmira Coll., N.Y., 1996, State of the Art Gallery, Ithaca, 1998, Cedar Arts Ctr., Corning, N.Y., 1998; author: (poem) Steele Meml. Libr. Poetry Festival, Elmira, N.Y., 1980, Merit award, 1980; featured poet Ten West Espresso, Mansfield, Pa., 1997. Vol. Schrader Creek Assn., Bradford County, Pa., 1993—. Mem. NYSUT, Cmty. Arts Partnership of Tompkins County. Democrat. Avocations: sailing, theatre, cross country skiing, making children's toys, poetry. Home and Office: 4 Main St Lockwood NY 14859-9766

MCMAHON, MARIBETH LOVETTE, physicist; b. Bradford, Pa., June 8, 1949; d. James Harry and Josephine Rose (Sylvester) Lovette; m. Frank Joseph MaMahon, Nov. 19, 1976 (div.). BS in Math., BS in Physics, Pa. State U., 1971, MS in Physics, 1974, PhD in Physics, 1976. Research asst. Pa. State U., 1971-76; advanced research and devel. engr. GTE Sylvania, Danvers, Mass., 1976-78; sr. physicist 3M Co., St. Paul, 1978-79, market devel. supr., 1979-83; market devel. mgr. Galileo Electro-Optics Corp., Sturbridge, Mass., 1983-84; product mgr. Varian Assocs., Lexington, 1984-85; mktg. dir. Bowmar, Acton, 1985-86; pres. Kilduff Inc., Peoria, Ariz., 1986—. Recipient Cert. in Appreciation of Service Pa. State U., 1971 Mem. Optical Soc. Am., Assn. Women in Sci., Assn. Physicists in Medicine, Sigma Pi Sigma, Sigma Chi Home and Office: 11327 N 82nd Dr Peoria AZ 85345-5895

MCMAHON, NEIL MICHAEL, real estate executive; b. N.Y.C., Oct. 12, 1953; s. Thomas Joseph and Catherine Margaret (Lane) M.; m. Debra Brylawski, Oct. 2, 1982; children: Alexa Lauren, Brendan Patrick, Morgan Lane. BA, Loyola Coll., Balt., 1975; MBA, U. Notre Dame, 1980. Sr. acct. Coopers & Lybrand, Balt., 1975-77; sr. assoc. Korn/Ferry Internat., Chgo., 1980-84; mgr. real estate fin. Prudential Ins. Co., Washington, 1984-87, gen. mgr. real estate devel., 1987-88; mng. dir. Capital Ptnrs. Inc., 1988—; pres. Madison Investment Assocs., Inc., 1993—, also bd. dirs. Bd. dirs. Lawrence Hall Sch. for Boys, Chgo., 1981-84. Named Senatorial Scholar State of Md., 1971-75. Mem. Nat. Assn. Indsl. and Office Parks, Real Estate Group Washington, Mortgage Bankers Assn., Notre Dame Club. Republican. Roman Catholic. Avocation: triathalons. Office: Capital Ptnrs Inc 1101 30th St NW Ste 500 Washington DC 20007-3708

MCMAHON, PAUL FRANCIS, finance company executive; b. Malone, N.Y., Apr. 28, 1945; s. Philip Francis and Shirley (Roy) M.; m. Sheila Ann Lester, Nov. 30, 1963; children: Michael, Marsha BS, Syracuse U., 1968. CPA, N.Y., Oreg.; cert. mgmt. acct., mgmt. cons. With Ernst & Young, Syracuse, N.Y., 1968-73, mgr., 1975-79, ptnr. in charge of mgmt. cons. in Europe Brussels, 1979-84, vice-chmn. Cleve., 1984-87; exec. ptnr. Ernst & Young Internat., N.Y., 1987-93; chmn. Ernst & Young Ea. Europe, 1990-93; regional dir. Asia/Pacific Ernst & Young Internat., Singapore, 1994-96; contr. Coop. Mktg. Agy., Syracuse, 1973-75; COO Amrop Internat., Brussels, 1997-2001; ptnr. Network Journey, 2002—. Steering com. Oreg. Emerging Bus. Initiative. Treas. Bus. Coun. for Internat. Understanding. Mem. AICPA, Oreg. Inst. CPA's, Oreg. Emerging Bus. Initiative, N.Y. Soc. CPA's, Inst. Mgmt. Acctg., Assn. Mgmt. Cons. Firms (bd. dirs.), Coun. Cons. Orgns. (past chmn.), Art Harvest (bd. dirs.). Democrat. Roman Catholic. Avocations: photography, sculpture, travel, gardening, biographies. Home: 35680 NE Wilsonville Rd Newberg OR 97132-7181 E-mail: pfmcmahon@msn.com.

MCMAHON, ROBERT M. physician, lawyer; b. Chambersburg, Pa., Sept. 6, 1949; s. Robert James and Bernice G. (Moore) McM.; 1 child, Natalie Ann. BA, U. Calif., San Diego, 1971; JD, U. Calif., San Francisco, 1974; MD, Washington U., St. Louis, 1989. Bar: Mo., Calif., U.S. Supreme Ct.; diplomate Am. Bd. Internal Medicine, Am. Bd. Gastroenterology. Staff counsel State Bar of Calif., L.A., 1975-80; sole practice law Beverly Hills, Calif., 1980-85; physician Jewish Hosp., St. Louis, 1989-92, St. Joseph's Hosp., St. Charles, Mo., 1992-93, U. Ark., Little Rock, 1993-95; pvt. practice in gastroenterology, 1995-97, St. Louis, 1997—. Judge pro tem Superior Ct., L.A., 1983-85. Author, contbr.: California Attorney Practice, 1985. Dir. South Ctrl. Bar Assn., Compton, Calif., 1983-85. Fellow Am. Coll. Legal Medicine; mem. Am. Soc. Gastrointestinal Endoscopy, St. Louis Met. Med. Soc. (councillor 2000—). Avocations: computer hobbyist, graphic arts, model aircraft, golf. Office: St Louis GE Cons PC Ste 35 13303 Tesson Ferry Rd Saint Louis MO 63128

MCMAHON, TERRENCE JOHN, retired foreign service officer; b. Rockford, Ill., Aug. 7, 1936; s. Hugh Raymond McMahon and Lucile Isabelle (Hayes) Driscoll; m. Phyllis Ruth Anderson, Dec. 2, 1967; children: Kevin, Michael, Kathleen, Marianne. BS in Accountancy, U. Ill., 1958; M Internat. Pub. Policy, Johns Hopkins U., 1983. CPA, Ill. Audit supr. Coopers and Lybrand, Rockford, Ill., 1958-68; fin. analyst U.S. AID, Washington, 1968-70, dep. contr. Rio de Janeiro, 1970-73, contr. Kabul, Afghanistan, 1973-77, Amman, Jordan, 1977-79, dep. contr. Washington, 1979-83, contr. Cairo, 1983-86, dir. Office of Procurement Washington, 1986-92, dir. Kiev, Ukraine, 1993-95. Recipient Presdl. Meritorious Svc. award for fgn. svc. Pres. of U.S., 1985, 92. Roman Catholic. Avocations: fishing, boating, travel. Home: 430 Marine Dr Sequim WA 98382-8037

MCMAHON, THOMAS FRANCIS, priest, educator; b. Chgo., Sept. 4, 1928; s. Robert and Estelle McM. AB in Philosophy, St. Ambrose Coll., 1950; STD in Moral Theology, U. St. Thomas, 1962; MBA in Mktg., George Washington U., 1970. Ordained priest Roman Cath. Ch., 1954. Prof. moral theology Viatorian Sem., 1957-67, Washington Theol. Coalition, 1968-71; from assoc. prof. bus. law to prof. emeritus Loyola U., Chgo., 1971-99, prof. emeritus, 1999—. Vis. lectr. Cath. U., Washington, 1968-71; vis. prof. St. Mary's of Calif., 1971; cons. Am. Pharmaceutical Assn., Washington, 1965-73, Nat. Conf. Christian Employers and Mgrs., Chgo., 1955-84; com. chmn. advt. review BBB, Chgo., 1985-2000; dir. Loyola Ctr. Values in Bus., Chgo., 1982-95. Author: Transforming Justice, 2000; editor Weekend on Socio-Ethical Values, 1982-93; contbr. articles to profl. jours. Bd. trustees St. Viator H.S., 2001—. Recipient Educator of Yr. award BBB, Chgo., 1980, Chgo. Mayoral Proclamation, 1999. Mem. Soc. Bus. Ethics, Beta Gamma Sigma. Home: 1212 E Euclid Arlington Heights IL 60004 Office: Loyola Univ Chgo 820 N Michigan Ave Chicago IL 60611-2147 E-mail: tomfmcmahon@aol.com.

MCMAHON, WILLIAM EDWARD, philosophy educator; b. Chgo., Sept. 25, 1937; s. Daniel Patrick McMahon and Mary Lois Hurley; m. Mary Louise Owens, Dec. 29, 1962; children: Elizabeth Maura, Coleman William. AB, U. Notre Dame, 1959, PhD, 1970; AM, Brown U., 1961. Instr. St. Vincent Coll., Latrobe, Pa., 1961-64; asst. prof. John Carroll U., Cleve., 1967-69, U. Akron, 1969-77, assoc. prof. to prof., 1977-99, dept. chair, 1985-96, prof. emeritus, 1999—. Fellow Pullman Found., 1955-59, Brown U., 1960-61; grantee for Inst. in Medieval Philosophy, NEH, 1980. Mem. Internat. Naval Rsch. Orgn., Soc. for Am. Baseball Rsch., N.Am. Assn. for History of Lang. Scis., Am. Philos. Assn., Soc. for Medieval and Renaissance Philosophy, Ohio Philos. Assn. (v.p. 1985-91), Henry Sweet Soc. Democrat. Roman Catholic. Avocations: baseball and naval history, stamp collecting. Home: 606 Nome Ave Akron OH 44320-1681 Office: U Akron Philosophy Dept 302 Olin Hl Akron OH 44325-0001 E-mail: mcmahon@uakron.edu.

MCMAHON MASTRODDI, MARCIA A. secondary education educator, artist; b. Akron, Ohio, Dec. 26, 1953; d. James R. and Marla June McMahon; m. Dennis W. Mastroddi, Aug. 22, 1987. BA in Art, Ursuline Coll., Cleve., 1978; MA in Art, Western Res. U., 1980. Cert. K-12 art tchr., Ill. Instr. art Cuyahoga C.C., Warrensville Heights, Ohio, 1978-87; lectr. art Spoon River Coll., Canton, Ill., 1989, Ill. Ctrl. Coll., Peoria, 1990; tchr. art CBS Alternative H.S., Beardstown, Ill., 1993-95, Ursuline Acad., Springfield, 1996-97, Dist. 186, Springfield, 1997-98; tchr. art, chmn. dept. Tower Hill (Ill) Consol. Unified Sch. Dist. 66, 1999—. Lectr. art for gifted Lincoln Land C.C., Springfield, part-time 1995-98, Author: (wiht Marcia Mcmahon) Diana Speaks to the World, 2002. Houseparent Am. Youth Hostels, 1988-89. Recipient svc. award for tchr. Cuyahoga C.C., 1989, Rosie Richmond award Springfield Area Arts Coun., 1998. Mem. Prairie State Orchid Soc., Ill. tate Mus. Soc., Washington Park Bot. Gardens, Tower Hill Art Club. Mem. Unity Ch. Avocations: designing jewelry, hiking, sketching, portraiture, collecting antiques.

MCMAKIN, JOSEPH HAMILTON, chemical industry executive; b. Wilmington, Del., Jan. 28, 1946; s. Joseph Purple and Bernadine Joan (Hamilton) McM.; m. Gail Lynn Pierce, Jan. 24, 1970 (div. Aug., 1982); children: Sean Joseph, Dana Lynn; m. Diane Rose Sidoti, Apr. 28, 1984; 1 step-child Ryan John Signarovitz, 1 child, Lauren Taylor. BS ChemE, U. Del., 1968. Tech. dir. plastics Air Products and Chems., Inc., Allentown, Pa., 1979-81, dir. mktg. indsl. chems., 1981-85, bus. mgr. amines, 1985-87, gen. mgr. bus. devel., 1987-90, gen. mgr. performance chems., 1990-93, v.p., gen. mgr. polyurethane and performance chems., 1993-96, chief info. officer, 1996—. Author: (with others) Encyclopedia of Chemical Technology, 1997. V.p. YMCA, Allentown, 1991; trustee Hillside Sch., Allentown, 1997; bd. dirs. Good Shepherd Home, Allentown, 1997. Mem. AIChE, Brookside Country Club. Roman Catholic. Office: Air Products and Chems Inc 7201 Hamilton Blvd Allentown PA 18195-1526 E-mail: mcmakijh@apci.com.

MCMANAMAN, KENNETH CHARLES, lawyer; b. Fairfield, Calif., Jan. 25, 1950; s. Charles James and Frances J. (Holys) McM.; m. Carol Ann Wilson, Apr. 15, 1972; children; Evan John, Kinsey Bridget, Klerin Rose. BA cum laude, S.E. Mo. State U., 1972; JD, U. Mo., Kansas City, 1974; grad., Naval Justice Sch., Newport, R.I., 1975; MS in Bus. Mgmt. summa cum laude, Troy State U., Montgomery, Ala., 1978; LLM in Advanced Litigation, Nottingham-Trent U., 2002. Bar: Mo. 1975, U.S. Dist. Ct. (we. dist.) Mo. 1975, Fla. 1976, U.S. Dist. Ct. (No. and mid. dists.) Fla. 1976, U.S. Dist. Ct. Mil. Appeals 1977, U.S. Ct. Appeals (5th and 8th cirs.) 1977, U.S. Dist. Ct. (ea. dist.) Mo. 1978, U.S. Supreme Ct. 1978, D.C. 1991; cert. mil. judge spl. and gen. ct. martials; diplomate Am. Bd. Forensic Examiners. Ptnr. O'Loughlin, O'Loughlin & McManaman, Cape Girardeau, Mo., 1978—; prof. bus. law Troy (Ala.) State U., 1976-78, S.E. Mo. State U., Cape Girardeau, 1978-84, prof. criminal justice, 1998—; prof. leadership Sch. Law William Woods U., 1998—; prof. bus. mgmt., Sch. Law, Cert. to Teach Trial Advocacy Nat. Inst. Trial Advocacy. Mem. Cape Girardeau County Coun. on Child Abuse, 1980—89; membership dir. S.E. Mo. scouting coun. Boy Scouts Am., 1980—82; mem. Cape Girardeau County Mental Health Assn., 1982—92; sponsor drug edn./prevention program in schs.; sec., pres. Jackson Area Soccer Assn., 1987—93; mem. Jackson R-2 Alt. Sch. ADv. Bd., 1999—; mem. dept. acctg. and fin. adv. bd. S.E. Mo. State U., 2001—; active local and state Dem. Party, del. Dem. Nat. Conv., San Francisco, 1984; chmn. County Dem. Com., 1984—96; mem. 8th Congl. Dist. Dem. Com. , 1984—86; mem. 27th State Dem. Senatorial Com., 1980—90; ward committeeman Dem. Party, 1984—94; bd. dirs. Area-wide Task Force on Drug and Alcohol Abuse , 1984—87, Cape County chpt. Nat. Kidney Found. , 1988—93. Capt. JAGC USNR, 1994—. Recipient Robert Chilton award City of Jackson for Leadership, Integrity and Responsibility, 1995-97; named One of Outstanding Young Men Am., 1981, 82, 84, 85, Outstanding Pub. Svc. award Cape Girardeau Police Dept. Mem. ABA (Mo. del. young lawyers divsn. 1982-83), Mo. Bar Assn. (chmn. trial advocacy task force 1983), Mo. Bar (young lawyers sect. coun. rep. dist. 13 1980-85), Fla. Bar Assn., Kansas City Bar Assn., Assn. Trial Lawyers Am., Fed. Bar Assn., Nat. Coll. Dist. Attys., Cape Girardeau County Bar Assn. (founder, pres. young lawyers sect. 1981-82), Cape County Bar Assn. (sec. 1999, treas. 2000, v.p. 2001), Naval Res. Assn. (v.p. Southeast Mo/So. Ill. chpt. 1980-85), S.E. Mo. State Alumni Coun., Sigma Chi (numerous awards), Sigma Tau Delta, Pi Delta Epsilon. Roman Catholic. Bus. Home: 1162 Trail Ridge Dr Jackson MO 63755-3507 Office: O'Loughlin O'Loughlin McManaman 1736 N Kingshighway St Cape Girardeau MO 63701-2190 E-mail: oomlc@midwest.net., kcmcm@prodigy.net.

MCMANIS, JAMES, lawyer; b. Haverhill, Mass., May 28, 1943; s. Charles and Yvonne (Zinn) McM.; m. Sara Wigh, Mar. 30, 1968. BA, Stanford U., Palo Alto, Calif., 1964; JD, U. Calif., Berkeley, 1967. Bar: Calif. 1967, U.S. Dist. Ct. (no. dist.) Calif. 1967, U.S. Ct. Appeals (9th cir.) 1967, U.S. Supreme Ct. 1971. Dep. dist. atty. Santa Clara County Dist. Atty., 1968-71; mem. McManis, Faulkner & Morgan, San Jose, Calif., 1971—. Spl. master tech. equities litigation, 1987—; spl. examiner State Bar Calif., 1995-98; prof. law Lincoln U. Law Sch., San Jose, 1972-82; lectr. Calif. Continuing Edn. of Bar, 1989-90; instr. U. Calif. Law Sch., 1992-96, Stanford U. Sch. Law, 1994-99. Pres. Santa Clara County Bar Assn. Law Found., 1996, dir., 1987—. Fellow Am. Coll. Trial Lawyers, Internat. Acad. Trial Lawyers; mem. ABA, State Bar Calif., Calif. Trial Lawyers Assn., Santa Clara County Bar Assn., Boalt Hall Alumni Assn. Avocations: history, books, travel, running. Office: McManis Faulkner & Morgan Inc 160 W Santa Clara St Fl 10 San Jose CA 95113-1701 Fax: 408-279-3244. E-mail: jmcmanis@mfmlaw.com.

MCMANIS, KENNETH LOUIS, civil engineer, educator; b. Lake Charles, La., Oct. 20, 1941; s. Louis Barber McManis; m. Josephine Agnes Agnew (div. 1975); 1 child, Patrick James; m. Julie Ann Sander, Aug. 5, 1978; 1 child, Kelly Lynn. BS, U. Southwestern La., 1963; MS, La. State U., 1966, PhD, 1975. Registered profl. engr., profl. land surveyor, La. Prodn. engr. Mobil Oil Co., Morgan City, La., 1963-64; with engring. design dept. W.S. Engrs. and Architects, Inc., New Orleans, 1966-68; prof., dean engring. tech. Delgado Jr. Coll., 1968-78; prof., dept. chmn. dept. civil engring. U. New Orleans, 1978—, contractor's ednl. trust fund professorship, 1995—, dir. urban waste mgmt. and rsch. ctr., 1990—. Adv. bd. Inst. for Recyclable Materials La. State U., Baton Rouge, La., 1991—, La. Transp. Rsch. Ctr., Baton Rouge, 1987-89; tech. com. Transp. Rsch. Bd., Washington, 1990—; mem. Licensure Bd. La. Profl. Engrs. and Land Surveyors, 2000—. Contbr. articles to ASTM Geotech. Testing Jour., Transp. Rsch. Record. Chmn. Landfill Siting Pub. Adv. Com., New Orleans, 1991-92; mem. Gov.'s Transition Com. on Solid Waste, La., 1992, Metrovision Subcom. on Solid Waste, New Orleans, 1992. Lt. cpl. USMCR, 1960-66. Named Michael Claus grad. La. State U., 1975; recipient Professionalism award La. Engring. Found., 1992. Mem. ASCE, La. Engring. Soc. (edn. com. 1980-83). Achievements include research in areas of soil sampling, soil stabilization, pile foundations, use of waste by-products in construction and waste management.

MCMANN, EDITH BROZAK, performance artist; b. Totowa, N.J., Mar. 26, 1929; d. Henry and Lena (Ulmer) Brozek; m. Frank Richard McMann, May 26, 1957; children: Robert, Stephen. Dance student, Sch. Am. Ballet, N.Y.C., 1945-57; art student, Westchester Art Workshop, Art Students League, N.Y.C., 1976-84; B in Profl. Studies in Dance and Visual Arts, SUNY, 1984; MS in Studio Art, Coll. of New Rochelle, 1989. Performing artist Alicia Alonso's Nat. Ballet Cuba tours, 1948-50, George Balanchine's N.Y.C. Ballet, 1950-57; visual artist, 1970—; intern Silvermine Coll. Art, 1989. (exhibitions) Depicting Dance in Art, Greenburgh Libr., White Plains, 1990, Xavier Gallery , New Rochelle, N.Y., 1989—94, Mamaroneck Artist Guild Gallery , Larchmont, N.Y. , 1990—, Beaux Arts Exhibits , 1991—94, Manhattanville Coll., Purchase, N.Y. , 1991, Town Ctr. Gallery , Mamaroneck , 1993—, N.Y.C. Ballet , Lincoln Ctr., N.Y., 1993—, Westbeth Gallery , N.Y.C., 1994, Hammond Mus. , Salem, N.Y., 1994, Town House Gallery , Stamford, Conn. , 2000—02, Tower Perrins , Stamford , 2000—02, (represented in archives) Libr. of Performing Arts, Lincoln Ctr., N.Y.C., N.Y.C. Ballet Archives, Nat. Mus. for Women in Arts , Washington , (also in pub. and pvt. collections), U.S. , abroad, performing artist (ballets) Alicia Alonso's Nat. Ballet Cuba, Mex. , Ctrl. Am., South Am., 1948—50, Apollo, Sleeping Beauty , Pas de Quatre, Ensayo Symphonica, George Balachine's N.Y.C. Ballet, 1950—57, U.S., Swan Lake, Symphony C , Con Amore, Nutcracker. Recipient numerous awards for sculpture, painting and graphics including Cert. of Merit U.S. Senator-N. Spano, 1989, U.S. State Assemblyman-R. Brodsky, 1989, Letter of Appreciation U.S. Senator Pat Moynihan, 1989, Letter of Congratulations U.S. Congressman -B. Gilman, 1989. Mem. Allied Artist of Am., Hudson River Contemporary Arists, Nat. Mus. for Women in Art, Silvermine Guild of Artists, Scarsdale Art Soc., Stamford Art Assn., Mamaroneck Artists Guild (bd. dirs. assoc. rep. 1990-91, receiving com. 1992). Home: 10 Burkewood Rd Hartsdale NY 10530-2933 E-mail: emcmann200@aol.com.

MCMANUS, CONSTANCE, lawyer; b. Savannah, Ga. d. Joseph John McManus and Lucy Youngquist; (div.); 1 child, Kristen Marie. BS in Edn., U. Ga., 1972; postgrad., Coll. of William & Mary, 1972; JD, Woodrow Wilson Coll. Law, 1980. Bar: Ga. 1980, U.S. Dist. Ct. (no. dist.) Ga. 1981, U.S. Supreme Ct. 1985. Tchr., West Point, Va., 1973; claims supr. Home Ins. Co., Atlanta, 1974-77; pvt. practice Marietta, Ga., 1980—. Editor Law Rev., Woodrow Wilson Coll. of Law, 1979-80. Former bd. dirs., officer Horseshoe Bend Civic Club, Marietta; bd. dirs., officer Anna L. Haas Humane Soc., Marietta, 1985-92; bd. dirs. Stingrays, Inc.,1989-93, Marietta Civitan Club, Ga. N.G. Youth Challenge Acad.; chmn. Ga. AAU, 1991-93; pres. bd. dirs. Oaks Homeowners Assn., Club Office Park; bd. dirs. Youth Challenge Acad., Ga. Nat. Guard. Mem. ATLA, Ga. Bar Assn. (juvenile com.), Cobb Bar Assn. (Law Day com. 1993-94, cir. defender panel 1993-99), Atlanta Bar Assn., Ga.

Criminal Def. Lawyers, Atlanta Track Club, Chattahoochee Road Runners Club (v.p. 1992-94, pres. 1994-95). Baptist. Avocations: running, tennis, aerobics. Office: 540 Powder Springs St SE Marietta GA 30064-3549

MCMANUS, DOUGLAS ALEXANDER, economist; b. Boston, May 29, 1957; s. Richard Owen and Eleanor Susan (Keenan) McM.; m. Susan Alberts; children: Heather, Emilia. BA, U. Mass., 1979; PhD in Econs., U. Pa., 1985. Asst. prof. econs. Va. Polytech. Inst., Blacsburg, Va., 1984-87, U. Iowa, Iowa City, 1987-88; economist Fed. Reserve Bd., Washington, 1988-94; prin. economist Freddie Mac, McLean, Va., 1994—. Vis. fellow Inst. for Math. Studies in the Social Scis., Palo Alto, Calif., summers 1987, 88; vis. scholar Indra Gandhi Inst. Devel. Rsch., Bombay, India, 1990-91. Contbr. articles to profl. jours. including Jour. Econometrics, Econometric Theory, Jour. of Banking and Fin., Proceedings of Am. Stats. Assn. Meetings. Office: Freddie Mac 8200 Jones Branch Dr Mc Lean VA 22102-3110

MC MANUS, EDWARD JOSEPH, federal judge; b. Keokuk, Iowa, Feb. 9, 1920; s. Edward W. and Kathleen (O'Connor) McM.; m. Sally A. Hassett, June 30, 1948 (dec.); children: David P., Edward W., John N., Thomas J., Dennis Q.; m. Esther Y. Kanealy, Sept. 15, 1987. Student, St. Ambrose Coll., 1936-38; BA, U. Iowa, 1940, JD, 1942. Bar: Iowa 1941. Gen. practice of law, Keokuk, 1946-62; city atty., 1946-55; mem. Iowa Senate, 1955-59; lt. gov. Iowa, 1959-61; chief U.S. judge No. Dist. Iowa, 1962-85, sr. U.S. judge, 1985—. Del Democratic Nat. Conv., 1956, 60. Served as lt. AC USNR, 1942-46. Office: US Dist Ct 329 US Courthouse 101 1st St SE Cedar Rapids IA 52401-1202

MCMANUS, F. SHIELDS, lawyer; b. Phila., 1947; s. Frank A. McManus, Jr. and Sara Ann Shields; m. Bertha M. McManus, Sept. 21, 1968; children: Barry, Justin. AA, St. John Vianney Coll., Miami, 1967; BA in Govt., Fla. State U., 1969, JD cum laude, 1972. Bar: Fla. 1972, U.S. Trial Bar (so. dist.) Fla. 1984, U.S. Supreme Ct. 1978, Ga. 2002, U.S. Dist. Ct. (no. dist.) Ga.; bd. cert. civil trial law, Fla. Local bills aide Martin/St. Lucie/Indian River/Brevard County Fla. Legislator, 1970; pvt. practice Stuart, Fla., 1972-75; mem. McManus, Stewart, Ferraro & Sewell PA and predecessor firms, 1976-89, Kohl, Bobko, McKey, McManus, Higgins PA, Stuart, 1990-93; ptnr. Gary, Williams, Parenti, Finney, Lewis, McManus, Watson & Sperando, 1993—. Bd. govs. young lawyers sect. Fla. Bar, 1977-81, chmn. legal forms com. young lawyers sect., 1980-81; pres. Martin County Bar Assn., 1982-83; chmn. 19th Cir. Jud. Nominating Commn., 1982-84; mem. 19th Cir. Grievance Com., 1983-85; chmn. fla. Bar Jud. Nominating Procedures Com., 1984-85; mem. Supreme Ct. Com. on Standards of conduct Governing Judges, 1987, others. Contbr. articles to profl. jours. Mem. adv. bd. Cath. Charities for Martin and St. Lucie Counties, 1988-96; active Martin County United Way Campaign, 1993; legal advisor Holy Redeemer Cath. Ch., Palm City, Fla., 1983-99, others. Capt. USAR, 1969-81. Mem. Fla. Bar Found. (dir. 1989-92), Stuart-Martin County C. of C. (pres. 1983-84). Home: 5910 SE Forest Glade Trl Hobe Sound FL 33455-7899 Office: Gary Williams Parenti Finney Lewis McManus Watson & Sperando Waterside Profl Bldg 221 SE Osceola St Ste 300 Stuart FL 34994-2289

MCMANUS, JAMES LAUGHLIN, writer, educator; b. N.Y.C., Mar. 22, 1951; s. Kevin Joseph McM. and Mary Agnes Madden; m. Susan Romanelli, Apr. 1, 1974 (div. Jan. 1990); childre: Bridget Madden, James Kevin; m. Jennifer Arra, July 9, 1992; children: Beatrice Mairead, Grace Malek. MA in Writing, U. Ill., 1977. Prof. Art Inst. Chgo., 1981—. Author: Ghost Waves, 1988, Going to the Sun, 1996, Positively Fifth Street, 2002; author of poems; contbr. articles to profl. jours. Recipient Carl Sandburg prize, 1996, Peter Lisagor award, 2001; Guggenheim Found. fellow, 1994, Rockefeller Found. fellow, 1997. Mem. PEN. Home: 605 Wayland Ave Kenilworth IL 60043-1050 Office: The Sch of the Art Inst of Chgo 112 S Michigan Chicago IL 60603-3002 E-mail: jarra@artic.edu.

MCMANUS, JAMES WILLIAM, lawyer; b. Kansas City, Mo., Aug. 1, 1945; s. Gerald B. and Mary M. (Hagan) McM.; m. Julie C. Waters, Feb. 17, 1973. BA, Rockhurst Coll., 1967; JD, St. Louis U., 1971. Bar: Mo. 1971, U.S. Dist. Ct. (we. dist.) Mo. 1972, U.S. Ct. Appeals (8th cir.) 1974, U.S. Supreme Ct. 1979, U.S. Ct. Appeals (10th cir.) 1984, U.S. Dist. Ct. Kans., 1995. Law clk. to presiding justice U.S. Dist. Ct. (we. dist.) Mo., 1971-73; assoc. Shughart, Thomson & Kilroy, P.C., Kansas City, 1973-76, dir., 1977-94; counsel Dysart, Taylor, Lay, Cotter & McMonigle, P.C., 1994—2002, DeWitt & Zeldin, L.L.C., Kansas City, 2002—. Course lectr. med. jurisprudence U. Health Scis., Coll. Osteo. Medicine, Kansas City, 1994. Mem. adv. coun. St. Joseph Health Ctr., 1989—. Mem. ABA, Mo. Bar Assn., Kansas City Lawyers Assn., Kansas City Met. Bar Assn. (chmn. alternate dispute resolution com. 1996-97, vice chmn. 1994-95, chmn. med. malpractice com. 1989), St. Louis Alumni Assn. (pres. 1984-92), St. Louis U. Law Sch. Alumni Assn. Home: 6824 Valley Rd Kansas City MO 64113-1929 Office: DeWitt & Zeldin LLC Harzfeld Bldg Ste 700 Town Pavilion 1111 Main St Kansas City MO 64105 E-mail: jamesmcmanus@justice.com.

MCMANUS, JAMES WILLIAM, chemist, researcher; b. Atlanta, Oct. 7, 1944; s. Claude William and Sara Louise (Cook) McM.; m. Ruth Krieger, Apr. 10, 1971; children: Angela Ruth, Meagan Joy. BS in Chemistry, Auburn U., 1971. Mgr. Cook's Grocery Co., Atlanta, 1970-73; analytical chemist North Chem. Co., 1973-74, Merck & Co., Inc., Albany, Ga., 1974-75, staff chemist, 1975-76, sr. staff chemist, 1976-78, sr. chemist, 1978-89, rsch. fellow, 1989-94. Bd. dirs. M. Taylor, Inc., Albany, 1988—, chmn. chemistry sect., 1994—, mgr. tech. ops., 2000—. Mem. editorial bd. Process Control and Quality, 1990-95; inventor, patentee in field. Mem. adv. bd. Sch. Chemistry, U. Tex., Dallas, 2000—. Mem. Am. Chem. Soc. (cert.). Republican. Baptist. Office: Merck and Co Inc 3517 Radium Springs Rd Albany GA 31705-9596

MCMANUS, JASON DONALD, editor, retired; b. Mission, Kans., Mar. 3, 1934; s. John Alan and Stella Frances (Gosney) McM.; m. Patricia Ann Paulson, Oct. 18, 1958 (div. Feb. 1966); 1 child, John Alan; m. Deborah Hall Murphy, Dec. 2, 1973; children: Sophie Eleanor, Mage Caroline. BA, Davidson Coll., 1956, LittD. (hon.), 1979; M.P.A., Princeton U., 1958; postgrad., Oxford U., 1958-59; LittD (hon.), Monmouth Coll., 1988, U. N.C., 1991, Loyola U., Balt., 1992. Common Market bur. chief Time Mag., Paris, 1962-64, assoc. editor N.Y.C., 1964-68, sr. editor, 1968-75, asst. mng. editor, 1975-78, exec. editor, 1978-83, mng. editor, 1985-87; corp. editor Time Inc., 1983-85; editor-in-chief Time Warner Inc., 1987-95; ret. Author: short stories Introduction, 1960. Mem. presdl. adv. commn. Internat. Edn. Exchange, 1982-83. Rhodes scholar, 1958-59 Mem.: Century Assn. (N.Y.C.).

MCMANUS, JOHN FRANCIS, III, advertising executive; b. Bklyn., Mar. 8, 1919; s. John Francis and Helen Jane (Cleary) McM.; m. Regina Delores Smith, Feb. 12, 1942 (div. June 1950); m. Sara Grace Scerra, Mar. 8, 1951 (dec. Aug. 1970); children: John Francis IV, Jane Frances, Stephan George, Kathleen Elizabeth; m. Jane Caroline Lewis, Apr. 25, 1974. Student, N.Y. Art Students League, 1933—37; BFA, Cooper Union Inst. Art, N.Y.C., 1941; student, Silvermine Guild Art Ctr., Norwalk, Conn., 1987, 88, 89; BA, NYU, 1947. Advt. dir. Thayer, Inc., Gardner, Mass., 1948-52; account supr. and copy chief Zimmer, Keller, Calvert, Detroit, 1952-57; account mgmt. McCann-Erickson, Inc., N.Y.C., 1957-58; v.p., mgmt. supr. Doyle Dane Bernbach Inc., 1958-69; sr. v.p., mgmt. Super-Smith/Greenland, Inc., 1969-70; pres., creative dir. The McManusCo., Westport, Conn., 1970—. Bd. dirs. Stamford Art Assn., Homes Conn., Holiday Cruise Lines; official artist USCG, 1988—. Writer series on Am. Way of Life, mag., 1949 (Freedom Found. gold medals 1949, 50); mgmt. supr. Avis, We Try Harder campaign, 1964, Mobil Detergent Campaign, 1968, Rheingold Would You Have the Guts? campaign, 1971 (Clio, Effie awards 1971). Capt. USAAF, 1942—46, Army Air Corp, WWII. Recipient Le Premier Prix Festival Internat., DU Film Publicitaire, Venice, France, 1960, Freedoms Found. Gold medals, Freedoms Found. Inc., Valley Forge, Pa., 1969-70, Effie, Am. Mktg. Assn., N.Y.C., 1972, Archie award, Nat. Assn. Indsl. Advts., N.Y.C., 1984. Mem. Am. Watercolor Soc., Am. Soc. Marine Artists, Westport Arts Council, Fairfield County Bus. Execs. Republican. Roman Catholic. Avocations: painting marine and seascapes, writing, photography, travel. Office: The McManus Co PO Box 446 Greens Farms CT 06436-0446

MCMANUS, JOSEPH WARN, urban planner, architect; b. Detroit, Mar. 24, 1931; s. Joseph Warn and Margaret Catherine (McNeil) McM.; m. Barbara Ann Luger, June 10, 1961; children: Margaret A. Ballas, Catherine M. McManus, Sarah T. Nielsen, Noel B., John L. BArch, U. Notre Dame, 1953; M in City Planning, U. Mich., 1963. Registered arch., Mich. Job capt. Haughey & Black, Archs., Battle Creek, Mich., 1954-56, Setter, Leach, Lindstrom, Archs., Mpls., 1956-59, Matson & Wegleitner, Archs., Mpls., 1959-61; prin. planner Barton-Aschman Assocs., Inc., Evanston, Ill., 1963-71; planning supr. Skidmore, Owings & Merrill, Archs., Chgo., 1971-73; planner III City of Miami (Fla.) Planning Dept., 1973-76; asst. dir. City of Miami Planning, Bldg. and Zoning Dept., 1976-92, dep. dir., 1993-95; adminstr. Coconut Grove NET, 1992; cons., 1995—2000. Zoning adv. Miami-Dade County Dept. Planning and Zoning, 2000—. U. Mich. fellow, 1962. Mem. Am. Inst. Cert. Planners, Am. Planning Assn. (Gold Coast chpt.), Fla. Planning and Zoning Assn. (George W. Simons Meml. award, 1997, v.p. So. Fla. chpt. 1983-85, pres. 1986, 95, 96, bd. dirs. 1987—), Emerald Soc. South Fla. (bd. dirs. 1995, v.p. 1996), Country Club of Coral Gables, K.C., Tau Sigma Delta.

MCMANUS, PATRICK FRANCIS, educator, writer; b. Sandpoint, Idaho, Aug. 25, 1933; s. Francis Edward McManus and Mabel Delana (Klaus) DeMers; m. Darlene Madge Keough, Feb. 3, 1954; children: Kelly C., Shannon M., Peggy F., Erin B. BA in English, Wash. State U., 1956, MA in English, 1962, postgrad., 1965-67. News reporter Daily Olympian, Olympia, Wash., 1956; editor Wash. State U., Pullman, 1956-59; with Ea. Wash. U., Cheney, 1959—; ret., 1983; news reporter Sta. KREM-TV, 1960-62; assoc. prof. Ea. Wash. U., Cheney, 1971-74, prof., 1974-83, prof. emeritus, 1983—. Author: A Fine and Pleasant Misery, 1978, Kid Camping form Aaaaiii! to Zip, 1979, They Shoot Canoes, Don't They?, 1981, Never Sniff a Gift Fish, 1983, The Grasshopper Trap, 1985, Rubber Legs & White Tail-Hairs, 1987, The Night The Bear Ate Goombaw, 1989, Whatchagot Stew, 1989, Real Ponies Don't Go Oink!, 1991, The Good Samaritan Strikes Again, 1992, How I Got This Way, 1994, Never Cry "Arp!" and Other Great Adventures, 1996, Into the Twilight, Endlessly Grousing, 1997, The Deer on a Bicycle, Excursions Into the Writing of Humor, 2000, The Bear in the Attic, 2002, (stage play) A Fine and Pleasant Misery: The Humor of Patrick F. McManus, 1994, Misery II: McManus In Love, 1995, Pat McManus, Endlessly Grousing, 1997, Pott's Luck, 1999; assoc. editor Field & Stream mag., 1977-81; editor-at-large Outdoor Life, 1981—. Recipient Booksellers award P.N.W. Booksellers, 1983, Trustees medal EWU, 1984, Gov.'s award Wash. State Libr., 1985, Excellence in Craft award OWAA, 1986, Disting. Achievement award WSU, 1994, Founder's Day award EWU, 1994; named to Idaho's Hall of Fame, 1995. Mem.: Outdoor Writers Am. (bd. dirs. 1981—84, Excellence award 1986), Authors Guild. Roman Catholic. Avocations: outdoor sports, woodworking, traveling. Office: PO Box 28216 Spokane WA 99228-8216

MCMANUS, PATRICK J. mayor, lawyer, accountant; b. Lynn, Mass., July 20, 1954; s. Robert A. and Kathryn M. (Gainey) McM. BA in Govt., Bowdoin Coll., 1976; MBA, Suffolk U., 1981; JD, Boston Coll., 1985. CPA, Mass.; cert. managerial acct., Mass. Tchr. Lynn Pub. H.S.; assoc. prof. bus. and fin. Salem (Mass.) State Coll.; lawyer pvt. practice Lynn; councillor at large City of Lynn, 1986-91, mayor, 1992—. Mem., trustee U.S. Conf. of Mayors, Washington, Brownsfield Task Force, Washington, Urban and Econ. Policy, Washington, Arts, Culture and Recreation, Washington; co-chair Urban Water Coun. Mem. KC, Ancient Order of Hibernians. Democrat. Roman Catholic. Office: Mayor's Office 3 City Hall Sq Lynn MA 01901-1093

MCMANUS, RICHARD GRISWOLD, JR. lawyer; b. Rockville Centre, N.Y., May 12, 1943; s. Richard Griswold and Ruth Mary (Frost) McM. BBA, U. Notre Dame, 1965; JD, U. Denver, 1970. Bar: Colo. 1970, U.S. Dist. Ct. Colo. 1970, U.S. Ct. Appeals (10th cir.) 1971, U.S. Supreme Ct. 1974. Law clk. Office Atty. Gen., State of Colo., Denver, 1969-70, asst. atty. gen., 1970-78; pvt. practice, 1978-80, 88—; ptnr. Miles & McManus, 1980-86, Miles, McManus & Epstein, Denver, 1986-88; mcpl. judge Aurora, 1993—, Federal Heights, 1996—, Thornton, 2002. Rep. candidate for Colo. Atty. Gen., 1990. 1st lt. U.S. Army, 1965-67. Fellow Colo. Bar Found.; mem. Colo. Bar Assn. (bd. govs. 1984-86, v.p. 1986-87), Denver Bar Assn., Catholic Lawyers Guild, Colo. Bd. of Examiners of Psychologists, Assn. State and Provincial Psychology Bds. (mobility com.). Home: 1521 Central St Unit 3F Denver CO 80211-3945 Office: Ste 1100 1801 Broadway Denver CO 80202-3839

MCMANUS, RICHARD PHILIP, lawyer, agricultural products company executive; b. Keokuk, Iowa, Oct. 20, 1929; s. Edward William and Kathleen (O'Connor) M.; m. Marjorie Theresa Mullaney, Nov. 5, 1955; children: Michael L., Mark J., Matthew A. BA, St. Ambrose U., Davenport, Iowa, 1949; JD, U. Mich., 1952; MBA, Roosevelt U., Chgo., 1965. Bar: Calif. 1982, Ill. 1958, Iowa 1952. Ptnr. McManus & McManus, Keokuk, 1953-63; div. counsel USN Facility Enging. Command, Great Lakes, Ill., 1963-66; v.p., dir. law Household Fin. Corp., Chgo., 1966-81; exec. v.p., sec. Security Pacific Fin. Svcs., Inc., San Diego, 1981-91; exec. v.p./sec. Bank Am. Fin. Svcs., 1991-92; pres., bd. dirs. Mosamac Co., Inc., 1992—. Mem. gen. com. Conf. Consumer Fin. Law, Chgo., 1975-92. Contbr. articles to profl. jours. Bd. dirs., treas., atty. Tijuana/San Diego Habitat for Humanity, Inc., 1992-95; trustee Village of Lake Bluff, Ill., 1974-78. Recipient of the San Diego Vol. Lawyer Disting. Svc. award, 1995-2001, Pres. Calif. Bar Pro Bono Svs., award, 1998. Mem. Calif. Bar Assn., San Diego Bar Assn., Calif. Fin. Svcs. Assn. (chmn. law com. 1981-92), Am. Fin. Svcs. Assn. (chmn. law forum 1980-81, Disting. Svc. award 1990), Lions, Elks, KC, Beta Gamma Sigma. Democrat. Roman Catholic. Avocations: golf, flying, sailing, woodworking. E-mail: mcman1000@cs.com.

MCMANUS, WALTER LEONARD, investment executive; b. N.Y.C., Apr. 27, 1918; s. Charles E. and Eva M. (Olt) McM.; m. Lillian Ziegler, June 6, 1941; children: Walter Leonard, Peter David, Susan. Student, Harvard Bus. Sch.; BS in Fin. Sci., Georgetown U., 1940. With Crown Cork & Seal Co., Inc., Balt., 1940-60, became sec., 1945, v.p., 1949, sec.-treas., 1958-60. Pres., dir. Cem Securities Corp.; assoc. Castlewood Realty Co.; dir. Hospice of Martin County, Fla. Mem. Halifax River Yacht Club, Lighthouse Point Yacht Club, Cocoanut Point Yacht Club, Internat. Order of Blue Gavel. Home: 1766 NW Harbor Pl North River Shores Stuart FL 34994 Office: 204 E Joppa Rd Towson MD 21286-3183 E-mail: wmcmanus@adelphia.net.

MCMANUS, WILLIAM RAYMOND, JR. transportation executive; b. Bklyn., June 14, 1967; s. William Raymond and Margaret Ann (Coady) McM. BBA, St. Johns U., Jamaica, N.Y. Crew coord. TWA, Jamaica, N.Y., 1987-88, mgr., 1988-89, ops. controller, 1989-90; mgr. ops., 1990—. Republican. Roman Catholic. Avocations: pilot, motocycle enthusiast. Office: TWA Hanger 12 JFK Airport Jamaica NY 11430 Address: 4700 Washington St Apt 302 Hollywood FL 33021-7660

MCMASTER, BELLE MILLER, religious organization administrator; b. Atlanta, May 24, 1932; d. Patrick Dwight and Lila (Bonner) Miller; m. George R. McMaster, June 19, 1953; children: Lisa McMaster Stork, George Neel, Patrick Miller. BA, Agnes Scott Coll., 1953; MA, U. Louisville, 1970, PhD, 1974. Assoc. corp. witness Presbyn. Ch. USA, Atlanta, 1974-77, dir. corp. witness, 1977-81, dir. div. corp. and social mission, 1981-87, dir. social justice and peacemaking unit Louisville, 1987-93; acting dir. program women in theology and ministry Candler Sch. Theology Emory U., 1993-96; dir. advanced studies Candler Sch. Theology Emory U., 1995—. Vice moderator chs. commn. internat. affairs World Coun. Chs., 1984-91, mem. Justice, Peace and Creation Commn., 1991-99; chair commn. internat. affairs Nat. Coun. Chs., N.Y.C., 1986-89, v.p., 1990-95, chair ch. world svc. and witness unit com., 1990-95, mem. exec. bd., 1990—; bd. dirs. Ecumenical Devel. Corp. U.S.A., 1992-99, Prison Ministries with Women, 1995-99, Christians Assoc. for Rels. with Eastern Europe, 1997-99; chair fin. com. Ch. World Svc. & Witness Unit Com., N.C., 1997-99, mem. ch. world svc. and witness, 1990—, bd. dirs. Author: Witnessing to the Kingdom, 1982, book columnist "What I Have Been Reading" in Church and Society Magazine, 1993-2001; contbr. articles to profl. jours. Pres. League of Women Voters, Greenville, S.C., 1963-64; bd. dirs. Interfaith Housing, Atlanta, 1975-81. Danforth fellow, 1969-74. Mem.: MLA, Soc. for Values in Higher Edn., Acad. Am. Religion, Phi Beta Kappa. Office: Emory U Candler Sch Theology Atlanta GA 30322-0001 E-mail: lmcmast@emory.edu.

MCMASTER, BRIAN JOHN, artistic director; b. May 9, 1943; With internat. artists dept. EMI, 1968-73; contr. opera planning English Nat. Opera, 1973-76; mng. dir. Welsh Nat. Opera, Cardiff, 1976-91; dir. Edinburgh (Scotland) Internat. Festival, 1991—; artistic dir. Vancouver (B.C.) Opera, Can., 1983-89. Office: Edinburgh Internat Festival The Hub Castlehill Edinburgh EH1 2NE Scotland

MCMASTER, HENRY DARGAN, lawyer; b. Columbia, S.C., May 27, 1947; s. John Gregg and Ida Bacot (Dargan) McM.; m. Peggy Jean McAbee, Mar. 18, 1978 BA, U. S.C., 1969, JD, 1973. Bar: S.C., U.S. Dist. Ct. S.C., U.S. Ct. Claims, U.S. Ct. Appeals (4th cir.), U.S. Supreme Ct. Atty., legis. asst. U.S. Senator Strom Thurmond, Washington, 1973-74; ptnr. Tompkins, McMaster and Thomas, Columbia, S.C., 1974-81, 98; U.S. atty. Dist. S.C., 1981-85. Mem. U.S. Atty. Gen.'s adv. com. of U.S. Attys., Washington, 1981-83; chmn. Com. on Ct. Rules and Legislation, Washington, 1983-85. Contbr. articles to legal publs. Mem. region IV youth adv. bd. EPA, Atlanta, 1972; mem. S.C. Commn. on Higher Edcn., 1991-94; chmn. S.C. Rep. Party, 1993-2002; bd. dirs. S.C. Policy Coun., 1991—. Mem. Richland County Bar Assn. (program com. 1978), S.C. Bar, ABA, Nat. Assn. R.R. Trial Counsel, Def. Rsch. Inst., Forest Lake Club, Centurian Soc., Caroliniana Ball Club, St. Andrew's Soc. (Columbia), Phi Delta Phi, Blue Key, Kappa Alpha (dep. province comdr. 1974-75, province comdr. 1975-91). Presbyterian. Office: Tompkins & McMaster 1400 Main St Ste 4 Columbia SC 29201-2832 also: PO Box 7337 Columbia SC 29202-7337*

MCMASTER, JULIET SYLVIA, English language educator; b. Kisumu, Kenya, Aug. 2, 1937; emigrated to Can., 1961, naturalized, 1976; d. Sydney Herbert and Sylvia (Hook) Fazan; m. Rowland McMaster, May 10, 1968; children: Rawdon, Lindsey. BA with honors, Oxford U., 1959; MA, U. Alta., 1963, PhD, 1965. Asst. prof. English U. Alta., Edmonton, Can., 1965-70, assoc. prof., 1970-76, prof. English, 1976-86, Univ. prof., 1986—2000, prof. emeritus, 2000—. Author: Thackeray: The Major Novels, 1971, Jane Austen on Love, 1978, Trollope's Palliser Novels, 1978, (with R.D. McMaster) The Novel from Sterne to James, 1981, Dickens the Designer, 1987, Jane Austen the Novelist, 1995; co-editor: Jane Austen's Business, 1996, Cambridge Companion to Jane Austen, 1997; gen. editor Juvenilia Press, 1993—; illustrator/editor children's picture book: (by Jane Austen) The Beautifull Cassandra, 1993; contbr. articles to profl. jours. Fellow Can. Coun., 1969-70, Guggenheim Found., 1976-77, Killam Found., 1987-89; recipient Molson prize in Humanities for Outstanding Contbn. to Canadian Culture, 1994. Fellow Royal Soc. Can.; mem. Victorian Studies Assn. Western Can. (founding pres. 1972), Assn. Can. Univ. Tchrs. English (pres. 1976-78), MLA, Jane Austen Soc. N.Am. (dir. 1980-91). Office: U Alta Dept English Edmonton AB Canada T6G 2E5 E-mail: juliet.mcmaster@ualberta.ca.

MCMASTER, MARY RICE, civic worker; b. Winnsboro, S.C., May 16, 1930; d. Hugh Buchanan and Nancy Elizabeth (Moore) McM. Student, Lander U., 1947-48, Columbia Coll., 1948-51, Columbia Comml. Coll., 1967. Mem. DAR (historian Thomas Woodward chpt. 1990-2002), UDC (pres. John Bratton chpt. 1985—), Friends of Fairfield County Libr. (life), S.C. Soc. (life), Montreal Hist. Soc. (life), Clan Buchanan Am. (life), Fairfield County Genealogy Soc. (pres. 1995—), Am. Legion Aux. (poppy chmn. 1990-2002). Home: 418 Evans Street Ext Winnsboro SC 29180-6310

MCMASTER, MICHELE, communications educator; b. Chgo. d. Robert B. and Dorothy McM. BA, Knox Coll., 1971; MA in Counseling, Governors State U., 1975, MA in Comm., 1989; PhD in Comm. and Consciousness, Union Inst., 1999. Nat. cert. counselor. Educator Tinley Park (Ill.) Mental Health Ctr., 1971-78; coord. out-patient psychiat. svcs. Olympia Fields (Ill.) Osteo. Med. Ctr., 1979-80; pvt. practice Park Forest, Ill., 1980-96; coord. women's svcs. South Suburban YWCA, 1982-84; prof. Governors State U., University Park, 1992—. Bd. mgrs. South Suburban YWCA, Park Forest, 1978-81. Office: Governors State U Coll Arts and Scis University Park IL 60466-0975

MCMEEKIN, DOROTHY, botany, plant pathology educator; b. Boston, Feb. 24, 1932; d. Thomas LeRoy and Vera (Crockatt) McM. BA, Wilson Coll., 1953; MA, Wellesley Coll., 1955; PhD, Cornell U., 1959. Asst. prof. Upsala Coll., East Orange, N.J., 1959-64, Bowling Green State U., Ohio, 1964-66; prof. natural sci. Mich. State U., East Lansing, 1966-89, prof. botany, plant pathology, 1989—. Author: Diego Rivera: Science and Creativity, 1985; contbr. articles to profl. jours. Mem. Am. Phytopath. Soc., Mycol. Soc. Am., Soc. Econ. Bot., Mich. Bot. Soc. (former bd. dirs.), Mich. Women's Studies Assn., Sigma Xi, Phi Kappa Phi. Avocations: gardening, sewing, travel, drawing. Home: 1055 Marigold Ave East Lansing MI 48823-5128 Office: Mich State U Dept Botany-Plant Pathology 221 N Kedzie Hall East Lansing MI 48824-1031 E-mail: mcmeekin@msu.edu.

MCMEEKIN, THOMAS OWEN, dermatologist; b. Shelby, Nebr., Apr. 17, 1945; s. Wallace Walton and Evajane (Taber) McM.; m. Dale Goodwin, 1999; children: Michele, Sean. BA with distinction, Stanford U., 1967; MD with honors, U. Rochester, 1971. Intern Beth Israel Hosp., Boston, 1971-72; resident U. Rochester (N.Y.), 1974-76, Mass. Gen. Hosp., Boston, 1976-78; clin. prof. depts. medicine, pediatrics, dermatology U. Rochester Sch. Medicine, 1978—; dermatologist pvt. practice, Rochester, 1978—; clin. asst. prof. SUNY, Buffalo, 1997—. Pres. Geneese Valley Laser Ctr., Rochester, 1990—. Capt. USPHS, 1972-74. Kohn fellow U. Rochester, 1980-81; recipient Doren J. Stephens Alumni award U. Rochester, 1971, Brian Flanagan Teaching Svc. award, 1995. Fellow Am. Acad. Dermatology (Svc. award 1993), Am. Bd. Internal Medicine, Am. Soc. LAser MEdicine (co-chmn. 1993-94), Am. Soc. Dermatologic Surgery (edn. com. 1983—); mem. N.Y. State Dermatological Soc. (v.p. 1993, treas. 1992), Buffalo Rochester Dermatological Soc. (pres. 1990), Rochester Dermatological Soc. (pres. 1980-89), Alpha Omega Alpha. Avocations: golf, tennis, computers. office e-mail: gvlasercentre.com. Office: 300 White Spruce Blvd Rochester NY 14623-1606 E-mail: 041745@msn-.com.

MC MEEL, JOHN PAUL, newspaper syndicate and publishing executive; b. South Bend, Ind., Jan. 26, 1936; s. James E. and Naomi R. (Reilly) McM.; m. Susan S. Sykes, Apr. 16, 1966; children: Maureen, Suzanne, Bridget. BS, U. Notre Dame, 1957. Sales dir. Hall Syndicate, 1960-67; asst. gen. mgr., sales dir. Publishers-Hall Syndicate, 1968-70; co-founder Universal Press Syndicate, Kansas City, Mo., 1970; pres. Andrews McMeel Universal, 1970—. Bd. dirs. Newspaper Features Coun.; chmn. bd. Andrews McMeel Pub., 1973—; mem. arts and letters U. Notre Dame. Co-founder Christmas in October, Kansas City, 1984—, James F. Andrews fellowship program, U. Notre Dame, 1981, adv. com. program in journalism; trustee Nelson-Atkins Mus. Art, The Civic Coun. Greater Kansas City. Mem. Fed. Assn. USA, Sovereign Mil. Order Malta, Internat. Press Inst. (chmn. Am. com., mem. internat. bd. dirs.). Home: Three Sunset Pl 5300 Sunset Dr Kansas City MO 64112-2358 Office: Andrews McMeel Universal 4520 Main St Kansas City MO 64111-1816

MCMEEN, ELMER ELLSWORTH, III, retired lawyer, guitarist; b. Lewistown, Pa., June 3, 1947; s. Elmer Ellsworth II and Frances Josephine McM.; m. Sheila Ann Taenzler, July 31, 1971; children: Jonathan Ellsworth, Daniel Biddle, James Cunningham and Mary Josephine (twins). BA cum laude, Harvard U., 1969; JD cum laude, U. Pa., 1972. Bar: 1973, U.S. Ct. Appeals (2nd cir.) 1973, U.S. Dist. Ct. (so.and ea. dists.) NY 1975. Assoc. Cravath, Swaine & Moore, N.Y.C., 1972-75, LeBoeuf, Lamb, Greene & MacRae, LLP, N.Y.C., 1975-78, ptnr., 1979-99, of counsel, 2000, retired, 2001. Lectr. Editor U. Pa. Law Rev., 1970-72. Author: numerous guitar books; contbr. articles to legal jours.; , musician numerous solo guitar recordings , (solo instrnl. audio and video lessons and performance videos) Stefan Grossman's Guitar Workshop and Rounder Records. Chmn. N.Y.C. regional com. U. Pa. Law Sch., 1984-86; class sec. Northfield Mt. Hermon Sch. Class of 1965, Mass., 1984-91. Mem.: Rockaway River Country Club. Office: 30 Oak Ln Mountain Lakes NJ 07046-1343 E-mail: elmcmeen@yahoo.com.

MCMENAMIN, HELEN MARIE FORAN, home health care, pediatric, and maternal nurse; b. Buffalo, May 21, 1943; d. John Michael and Helen Marie (McCarty) Foran; m. John Patrick McMenamin, Aug. 21, 1965; children: Maureen Regina, Kathleen Noelle, Terence Michael, Amy Colleen, Shannon Rosemary, Barry Patrick. BSN, Niagara U., 1965; cert. instr. natural family planning, St. Margaret's Hosp., Boston, 1983. RN N.Y., N.H., Maine, D.C., Va., Md., Pa.; cert. childbirth educator; cert. Motherwell instr./trainer. Instr.

perinatal, neonatal nursing Mercy Hosp. Sch. Nursing, Portland, Maine, 1981-83; staff/charge nurse neonatal intensive care unit Georgetown U. Hosp., Washington, 1984-93, 99; staff nurse neonatal ICU, renal unit, home care case mgr. Children's Hosp. Nat. Med. Ctr., 1986-93; educator infant APNEA/CPR, Fairfax Hosp. Infant APNEA Program, Fairfax, Va., 1988-89; pediatric and maternal-child case mgr. Vis. Nurse Assn. No. Va., Arlington, 1992; staff nurse pediatric emergency room Mercy Hosp., Balt., 1992-93; case mgr. maternal-child health pediatrics, high-risk neonatal home care Bay Area Health Care, 1993-95; mgr. maternal-child/neonatal and pediatric program 1st Am. Home Care, Hanover, Pa., 1994-95; coord. high risk maternal-child and pediatric program Future Health Corp., Timonium, Md., 1995-97; mgr. sch.-based clinic U. Md. Sch. Nursing, Balt., 1998; maternity staff nurse Hanover (Pa.) Hosp., 1998; pvt. duty home care, in-hosp. staff Mt. Washington Pediat. Hosp., Balt., 1995-99; case mgr. for high-risk neonates Sierra Mil. Health Svcs., 1999; NICU, nursery and maternity staff nurse Adventist Preferred Nursing Svcs., Silver Spring, 1999-2000; RN II, maternity nurse St. Agnes Health Care, Balt., 2000; NICU/ped. case mgr. Franklin Sq. Hosp. Ctr. Recruitment Specialists, Inc., Balto, 2000-2001; NICU/high-risk maternity case mgr./reviewer Georgetown U. Med. Ctr., Washington, 2001; physician chart reviewer, maternal/child NICU and pediatric utilization mgr. utilization Johns Hopkins Health Care/Intrastaff, Balt., 2001—. Organizer, co-dir. health clin. Cathedral Elem. Sch., Portland, Maine, 1981—83; breastfeeding instr. tng. St. Margaret's Hosp., Boston, 1982. Block capt. Am. Cancer Assn., Springfield, Va., 1986—90; mem. Healthy Mothers/Healthy Babies and Teen Pregnancy Coalition York County; leader 4-H Club, Limerick, Maine, 1977—84; active pro-life and outreach coms. Annunciation of BVM Ch., McSherrystown, Pa., 1997—, Eucharistic min., 2000—, right-to-life com., core liturgy com. Mem. Nat. Assn. Pro-Life Nurses (bd. dirs. of Pa.), Nat. Assn. Pediatric Nurses. Roman Catholic. Avocations: art, gardening, knitting, piano, baking. Home: 1075 Hobart Rd Brodbecks PA 17329-9757

MCMENAMIN, JOAN STITT, headmistress; b. May 7, 1925; d. William Britton and Josephene Lloyd (White) Stitt; m. Edward B. McMenamin, Jan. 24, 1953. BA in Econs., Smith Coll., 1946. With Econ. Cooperation Adminstrn., Paris, 1949-50; office mgr. Ford Found., N.Y.C., 1951-52; history tchr. Nightingale-Bramford Sch., 1962-63, asst. to headmistress, 1963-65, asst. headmistress, 1965-71, headmistress, 1971-92, headmistress emerita, 1992—; interim head San Francisco U. H.S., 1996-97. Mem. adv. council for nonpub. schs. N.Y. State Commr. of Edn., 1985-87; pres. Guild Ind. Schs. N.Y., 1983-85; mem. admissions com. Nat. Assn. Ind. Schs., 1977-79. Vice chmn. English-Speaking Union Exch. Scholarship Program, 1977-79; spl. advisor Parents League N.Y.; bd. dirs. Coun. for Religion in Ind. Schs., 1976-79, Ind. Sch. Orchs., Inc., 1980-84; trustee A Better Chance, Inc., 1977-83, The Town Sch., 1975-77, Ind. Ednl. Svcs., 1985-89, Coun. for Basic Edn., Washington, 1978-96, Clark Found., 1979—, Robert Coll. of Istanbul, Turkey, 1979—, Axe-Hought Found., 1985—; trustee Buckley Sch., 1977-92, trustee emerita, 1998—; trustee Waterford Inst., 1976—, The Masters Sch., 2000—; trustee Lawrenceville Sch., 1989-2000, trustee emerita, 2000—. Mem. Nat. Assn. Prins. of Girls' Schs. (pres. 1983-85), N.Y. State Assn. Ind. Schs. (bd. dirs. 1980-82, chmn. 1985-87), Headmasters Assn., Educators' Collaborative (ptnr.), Country Day Sch. Headmasters Assn. (v.p. 1987-90, exec. com. 1987-90), Headmistresses Assn. of East, Cosmopolitan Club, Bridgehampton Club. Democrat. Episcopalian. Avocation: reading. Home: PO Box 768 172 Church Ln Bridgehampton NY 11932

MC MENIMEN, KATHLEEN BRENNAN, secondary education educator; b. June 15, 1944; d. John Joseph and Catherine (Healy) Brennan; m. Joseph Paul McMenimen, Aug. 22, 1970; children: Meghan, Joseph Paul. BS in Edn., Boston Coll., 1966, MEd, 1974. Tchr. Boston pub. schs., 1966—2002; pvt. ednl. cons. McMenimen Assocs., 2002—. Tchr. Operation Head Start, Charlestown, Mass., summers 1966-68; ednl. dir. John F. Kennedy Family Service Center, Charlestown, 1969; seminar leader Worcester (Mass.) State Coll., 1974. Author: A Curriculum Guide for Operation Head Start, 1970; prodr.: (cable) Tick-Talk. Bd. dirs. John F. Kennedy Family Svc. Ctr., 1970-71; mem. Waltham Dem. City Com., 1975—; commr. Waltham Housing Authority, 1982-86; mem. Waltham City Coun., 1986—; elected to Waltham City Coun., 1986-87, re-elected, 1988—, v.p., 1988, chair fin. com., 1990; ward councillor City of Waltham, 1976-78, councillor-at-large, 1986-99; candidate for mayor City of Waltham, Mass., 1999. Recipient Commendation for cmty. svc. Waltham City Coun., 1978, Disting. Svc. award Waltham Jaycees, 1978, Disting. Dem. award, 1996. Mem. Boston Coll. Alumni Assn. (bd. dirs. 1972-74, sec. 1987, treas. 1988, v.p. 1989, pres. 1990), Boston Tchrs. Union. Democrat. Home: 147 Trapelo Rd Waltham MA 02452-6305

MC MENNAMIN, GEORGE BARRY, advertising agency executive; b. N.Y.C., May 23, 1922; s. Harold G. and Hazel F. (Stanbridge) McM.; m. Marilynn L. Simon, Sept. 9, 1946; children: Marilynn Breeze, Karen Foster. BS, Harvard U., 1945. With Doremus & Co., N.Y.C., 1946-88, exec. v.p., 1967-73, pres., 1973-84, vice chmn., 1984-88, also mem. exec. com.; pub. Worldpaper, Boston, 1988. Served to lt. (j.g.) USNR, 1944-46. Mem. Fin. Advt. and Mktg. Assn. Met. N.Y. (pres. 1967), Down Town Assn., Hasty Pudding Inst. 1770, Harvard Coll. Speakers Club, Harvard Club, New Canaan Country Club, Pilgrims Club of U.S. Republican. Episcopalian. Home: 28 Cross Ridge Rd New Canaan CT 06840-0523

MCMENNAMY, ROGER NEAL, automobile dealership executive; b. Amarillo, Tex., Oct. 9, 1942; s. Wilson Foch and Mildred Evelyn (Freudiger) McM.; m. Marilyn Kay Gibbons, Jan. 1, 1967; children: Timothy Neal, Traci Nicole. Student, Abilene Christian U., 1961-62; BBA in Mgmt. cum laude, U. Tex., Arlington, 1970; MBA in Fin., U. Tex., Austin, 1971. CPA, Tex. Contr., treas. E.N. Wolcott Corp., Houston, 1971-73; mem. corp. staff ELPAC, Inc., 1973-74; gen. mgr. BS&B Mfg., 1974-75; gen. mgr. adminstrn. Gulf Interstate Co., 1975-77; exec. v.p., CFO NWS Supply Group, 1977-83; v.p., CFO Newpark Resources, Inc., Metairie, La., 1983-86; sr. v.p., chief fin. officer Gemcraft, Inc., 1986-88; exec. v.p., chief fin. officer Cooper Communities, Inc., Bella Vista, Ark., 1988-90, pres., CEO, 1990-97; pres., CEO, gen. mgr. Daryl Hickman Chevrolet, Inc., Siloam Springs, 1998—. Bd. dirs., exec. v.p. Guaranteed Auto Fin., Inc., Starr-Hickman Acceptance Corp. Bd. dirs. Walton Arts Ctr., Fayetteville, 1994—. With USMC, 1962-66, Viet Nam. Mem. AICPA. Avocations: travel, golf, waterfowl hunting. Office: Daryl Hickman Chevrolet Inc PO Box 399 Siloam Springs AR 72761-0399

MCMICHAEL, DONALD EARL, lawyer; b. Denver, Aug. 8, 1931; s. Earl L. and Charlotte F. McM.; m. Zeta Hammond, July 6, 1955; children: Lauren A. McMichael Burnett, Thomas D., Susan E. McMichael Markle. AB, Dartmouth Coll., 1953; LLB, U. Colo., 1956. Bar: Colo. 1956, U.S. Dist. Ct. Colo. 1956, U.S. Ct. Appeals (10th cir.) 1956. Assoc. Holme Roberts & Owen, 1956-58; pres. Corp. Ins. Assocs., 1958-70; dir. trust devel. Ctrl. Bank Denver, 1970-72; ptnr. Brenman, Sobol & Baum, Denver, 1972-74, McMichael, Sell & Agresti (formerly McMichael, Multz & Lipton), Denver, 1974-99; pvt. practice, 1999-2000; of counsel Schmidt & Horen, 2000—. Chmn. Denver Ctrl. YMCA, 1971-73. Capt. USAR, 1956-64. Named Layman of Yr. Denver Ctrl. YMCA, 1973, named to Denver Metro YMCA Hall of Fame, 1989. Mem. Colo. Bar Assn., Denver Bar Assn., Denver Estate Planning Coun. (sec. 1971-73). Republican. Methodist. Office: 6325 W Mansfield Ave Unit 234 Denver CO 80235-3015 E-mail: dmcmic@aol.com.

MCMICHAEL, GUY H., III, federal official; b. South Bend, Ind., Dec. 26, 1939; m. Nancy Moore. AB, Harvard U., 1962; JD, U. Mich., 1967. Pvt. practice, 1967—71; dept. prosecuting atty. State of Ind., 1967—71; gen. counsel com. vet. affairs U.S. Senate, Washington, 1971—77; gen. coun. Dept. Vet. Affairs (formerly VA), 1977—81; adminstrv. judge bd. contract appeals Dept. Vet. Affairs, 1981—90, chmn., chief adminstrv. judge, 1990—, acting chief staff, 2000—01, acting chief info. officer, 2001, acting under sec. benefits, 2000—02. With U.S. Army, 1962-64. Mem. ABA, Bds. Contract Appeals Judges Assn. (pres. 1989-90), Ind. Bar Assn., D.C. Bar Assn. Office: Dept Vet Affairs Bd Contract Appeals 810 Vermont Ave NW # 09 Washington DC 20420-0001

MCMICHAEL, J(ACK) RICHARD, real estate developer; b. Berkeley, Calif., Mar. 9, 1943; s. Jack R. and Dorothy (Dwyer) McM.; m. Karen Lois Moore, Nov. 15, 1964; children: J. Richard IV, Erik C. BA, U. Calif., Berkeley, 1964, JD, 1969. Bar: Calif.; lic. real estate broker, Calif. Assoc. Pettit and Martin, San Francisco, 1969-71; pres. Sutter Hill Ltd., Palo Alto, 1971-78; exec. v.p. Genstar Pacific Corp., San Francisco, 1978-79; gen. mgr. investment property div. Citation Builders, San Leandro, 1979-84; prin. JRM Properties, Palo Alto, 1984-88; pres. The Fairway Land Co., Laguna Niguel, Calif., 1988-90; v.p., gen. mgr. Quadrant Corp., San Ramon, 1990-92; v.p. Weyerhauser Real Estate Co., Federal Way, Wash., 1992—. Bd. dirs., Western Real Estate Fund, Inc., Menlo Park, Calif. Chmn., Scholar Opera, Palo Alto, 1982-85; bd. mgrs., Palo Alto YMCA, 1987-91; chmn. troop com., Palo Alto area Boy Scouts Am., 1987-88. Comdr. USN, 1964-66, Vietnam. Mem. Internat. Coun. Shopping Ctrs. Republican. Presbyterian. Avocations: running, golf. Office: Weyerhaeuser Real Estate Co EC3-3B9 PO Box 9777 Federal Way WA 98063 E-mail: rick.mcmichael@wreco1.com.

MCMILLAN, ADELL, retired educational administrator; b. Portland, Oreg., June 22, 1933; d. John and Eunice A. (Hoyt) McM. AB in Social Sci., Whitman Coll., 1955; MS in Recreation Mgmt., U. Oreg., 1963. Program dir. Erb Meml. Union, U. Oreg., Eugen, 1955-68; program cons. Willard Straight Hall, Cornell U., Ithaca, N.Y., 1966-67; assoc. dir. Erb Meml. Union, U. Oreg., Eugene, 1968-75, dir., 1975-91, dir. emeritus, 1992—. Editor, co-author: College Unions: Seventy-Five Years, 1989; interviewer, editor oral history interviews, 1978, 92-94, 96. Bd. dirs. United Way, Lane County, Oreg., 1976-83, 87-97, 98—,pres., 1982-83, 88-90; commr. Eugene City Planning Commn., 1992—; mem. Hist. Rev. Bd., 1992—; mem. Tree Commn., 1992-93; bd. dirs., treas., 1994-95, Eugene Opera Co., 1992-2000; bd. dirs. Eugene Pub. Libr. Found., 2002—. Named Woman of Yr. Lane County Coun. Orgns., Eugene, Oreg., 1985; re-named Erb Meml. Union Art Gallery, U. Oreg. as Adell McMillan Art Gallery, 1998. Mem. Assn. Coll. Unions-Internat. (v.p. 1977-80, pres. 1981-82, Butts-Whiting award 1987, hon. 1992, editor Vets. newsletter, 1993-2000), Zonta Club of Eugene, Zonta Internat. (pres. 1984-86, dist. treas. 1990-92, 92-94), Emerald Valley Women's Golf Club (pres. 1995). Democrat. Episcopalian. Avocations: golf, reading. Office: 55 W 39th Ave Eugene OR 97405-3344 E-mail: adellmcm@oregon.uoregon.edu.

MCMILLAN, BARTLENE FAYE, b. Algood, Tenn., July 15, 1926; d. Luther Bartlett McCormich and Amelia Merredith (Sussner) McMillan; m. James Keith, July 3, 1947; children: James Keith, Luther Tate Keith, Amelia Meredith Keith. BA, U. S.C., Columbia, 1947. Organist First Baptist Ch., Mullins, S.C., 1983-99; assoc. editor Mullins Enterprise, 1965-93. Author: (book) History of Mullins, 2001. Recipient Citizen of Yr., Mullins C. of C., 1976. Home: 1400 Sandy Bluff Rd Mullins SC 29574-4222

MCMILLAN, BETTIE BARNEY, English language educator; b. Fayetteville, N.C., Mar. 14, 1941; d. Booker T. and Sarah Estelle (Barney) McM.; children: Gregory L., Kenneth A., Ronald D., Pamela M., Deirdre Y., Michael A. BA in Psychology/Sociology, Meth. Coll., 1978. Program supr. Adminstrv. Office of the Cts.-Guardian Ad Litem Program, Raleigh, N.C.; English instr. Cmty. Coll., Fayetteville; info. specialist, case mgr. Big Bros./Big Sisters. Author: A Plea For Love, 1995, The Language of Love (award of merit 2002).. Leader, nat. officer United Order of Tents, Norfolk, Va., 1982-92; vol. N.C. Guardian Ad Litem, Raleigh, 1992—; mem. Atlanta Com. for Olympic Games, 1996. Recipient Copyright award plaque Copyright award, 1996, Poet Merit award Nat. Libr. Congress, 1995, Shakespeare Trophy of Excellence, 2002, Poet of Yr. Medallion, 2002. Mem. Internat. Soc. of Poets (Disting. mem., 1995-96, Poets Choice award 1995), Sigma Omega Chi. Baptist. Avocations: reading, writing, literary works, community volunteer, gardening, travel. Home: 5509 Ramshorn Dr Fayetteville NC 28303-2736

MCMILLAN, C. STEVEN, consumer packaged goods company executive; b. Tyler, Tex., Dec. 10, 1945; s. Charles and Faye (Mills) McM.; children: Mandy, Megan BS, Auburn U., 1968; MBA, Harvard U., 1973. Mgmt. cons. McKinsey & Co., Chgo., 1973-76; pres., CEO Aqualux Water Processing Co., Ft. Lauderdale, Fla., 1976—79; pres. Electrolux Corp., Toronto, Ont., Can., 1979-82, CEO Canada, 1982—86; sr. v.p. strategy devel. Sara Lee Corp., Chgo., 1986-90; sr. v.p., CEO Sara Lee Bakery-Worldwide, 1990-97; pres., COO Sara Lee Corp., 1997-2000, chmn., pres., CEO, 2001—. Bd. dirs. Sara Lee/DE, Pharmacia, Monsanto, Bank of Am. Active Joffrey Ballet, Chgo., Chgo. Symphony Orch., Chgo.; mem. adv. bd. Stedman Nutrition Ctr. Duke U. Med. Sch., J.L. Kellogg Grad. Sch. Mgmt. Mem. Grocery Mfrs. Assn., Harvard Bus. Sch. Club of Chgo. (v.p.) Office: Sara Lee Corp 3 First National Plz Chicago IL 60602

MCMILLAN, CAMPBELL WHITE, pediatric hematologist; b. Soochow, China, Jan. 10, 1927; s. Henry Hudson and Leila McNeill (Memory) McM.; m. Florence Jean MacKenzie, June 11, 1955; children: Ian Johnson, Sally Hudson, Donna Jean, Andrew Duncan, Bridget White, Wendy McNeill. BS summa cum laude, Wake Forest Coll., 1948; MD, Bowman Gray Sch. Medicine, 1952. Diplomate Am. Bd. Pediatrics, Pediatric Hematology-Oncology. Intern Harvard Med. Service, Boston City Hosp., 1952-53; resident in pediatrics Children's Hosp. Med. Center, Boston, 1953-55; registrar in pediatrics St. Mary's Hosp., London, 1955; pediatrician Nemazee Hosp., Shiraz, Iran, 1956-58; fellow in pediatric hematology Harvard U., 1958-60; instr. pediatrics, 1960-61; gen. practice pediatrics Laurinburg, N.C., 1961-63; asst. prof. pediatrics U. N.C., Chapel Hill, 1963-68, asso. prof., 1968-72, prof., 1972-92, chief div. pediatric hematology, 1963-83, prof. emeritus, 1992—. Asso. dir. Clin. Research Center, U. N.C., 1966-78 Assoc. editor: Blood Diseases of Infancy and Childhood, 1978, 84; contbr. articles profl. jours., chpts. in books. Served with USNR, 1945-46. Recipient Lederle Med. Faculty award, 1964, Disting. Alumnus award Bowman Gray Sch. Medicine, 1972, Outstanding Career Achievement award Nat. Hemophilia Found., 1998. Fellow Am. Acad. Pediatrics; mem. Soc. Pediatric Rsch., Am. Pediatric Soc., Phi Beta Kappa, Alpha Omega Alpha. Democrat. Episcopalian. Home: 408 Ridgecrest Dr Chapel Hill NC 27514-2103 E-mail: mempim@mindspring.com. *It was my extremely good fortune to live and to work in a time of the most explosive growth medical knowledge had ever undergone.*

MCMILLAN, CHARLES WILLIAM, consulting company executive; b. Ft. Collins, Colo., Feb. 9, 1926; s. Charles and Margaret (Jennings) McM.; m. Jardell Hollier, Feb. 12, 1951; children: Brett W., Kurt C., Scott P. BS, Colo. State U., 1948. Asst. 4-H agt., Denver, 1948; county agrl. agt. LaJara, Colo., 1949-50, Julesburg, 1950-53; faculty Colo. State U., 1954; div. head, agrl. research dept. Swift & Co., Chgo., 1954-59; exec. v.p. Am. Nat. Cattlemen's Assn., 1959-77; v.p. Nat. Cattlemen's Assn., 1977-81; asst. sec. for mktg. and inspection services USDA, Washington, 1981-85; pres. McMillan and Farrell Assocs., Inc., 1985-94, C.W. McMillan Co., Alexandria, Va., 1994—. Served to lt. (j.g.) USNR, World War II. Mem. Sigma Alpha Epsilon. Home: 4003 Pine Brook Rd Alexandria VA 22310-2144 Office: PO Box 10009 Alexandria VA 22310-0009

MCMILLAN, CYNTHIA ANNE, computer systems analyst; b. Omaha, Aug. 13, 1943; d. William Harry and Grace Leora (Gillette) McM. BA in History and Math., U. Nebr., Omaha, 1965; MA in History, U. Va., 1967, PhD in History, 1970. Asst. prof. history Huron (S.D.) Coll., 1970-72, Tufts U., Medford, Mass., 1972-77; programmer/analyst No. Natural Gas, Omaha, 1977-86; staff analyst Enron, 1986-88; advanced systems engr. Electronic Data Systems, 1989-93; application architect First Data Corp., 1994—. Fellow Woodrow Wilson Found., 1965-66, AAUP, 1966-68; fellow, grantee Am. Assn. Learned Socs., 1973. Mem. Friends of the Omaha Pub. Libr., Phi Beta Kappa. Avocations: collecting ethnographic art, book collecting, antiques. Office: 6855 Pacific St Omaha NE 68106-1052

MCMILLAN, DONALD EDGAR, pharmacologist; b. Butler, Pa., Sept. 23, 1937; s. Chandler Burdell and Ruth Elizabeth (Beach) McM.; m. Marjorie Ann Leavitt, Feb. 4, 1963; children: David Craig, Pamela Jean. BS, Grove City Coll., 1959; MS, U. Pitts., 1962, PhD, 1965. Postdoctoral fellow Harvard U. Med. Sch., 1965-66; instr. in pharmacology SUNY Downstate Med. Ctr., N.Y.C., 1967-68, asst. prof., 1968-69; asst. prof. pharmacology U. N.C., 1969-72, asso. prof., 1972-76, prof., 1976-78; prof., chmn. dept. pharmacology U. Ark. for Med. Scis., 1978-80, prof., chmn. dept. pharmacology and toxicology, 1980—, prof. psychiatry, 1985—, Wilbur D. Mills prof. alcoholism and drug abuse prevention, 1991—; dir. Substance Abuse Treatment Clinic. Vis. lectr. U. Ctrl. Caracas, Venezuela, 1974; IRG mem. neurobiology rev. panel NSF, 1979-80; IRG mem. Nat. Inst. Drug Abuse, 1982-88, 92-95, chair 1994-95, SRC mem., 1988-95; mem. scientist award com. Historically Black Colls. and Univs., 1998, mem. minority instns. drug abuse rsch. devel. program com., 1998; bd. dirs. Chapel Hill (N.C.) Drug Action Com., 1977-78; cons. Health Effects Inst., 1985-87; cons. sci. adv. bd., children/sensitive subpopulations for rev. com. EPA, 1985-89; spl. merit rev. bd. Armed Forces Radiobiology Rsch. Inst., 1982; mem. com. toxicity data elements NRC, 1980-83. Author: Central Nervous System Pharmacology— A Self Instruction Text, 1974, 2d, rev. edit., 1979; rsch., numerous publs. in behavioral pharmacology and drug abuse; bd. editors Jour. Exptl. Anal. Behavior, 1967-70, 71-74, Jour. Pharmacology and Exptl. Therapeutics, 1972—, Psychopharmacology, 1973-81, Neurotoxicology, 1979-82, Toxicology and Applied Pharmacology, 1982-89, Neurobehavioral/Toxicology and Teratology, 1982-90, Behavioral Pharmacology, 1989—. Recipient Dole-Nyswander award Am. Methodone Treatment Assn., 2000; grantee NIMH, 1971-74, Nat. Inst. Environ. Health Scis., 1976-80, N.C. Alcoholism Rsch. Authority, 1975-77, EPA, 1982-85, Kellogg Found., 1987-92, U.S. Dept. Edn., 1989-91, Nat. Inst. Drug Abuse, 1976—. Mem. AAAS, Behavioral Pharmacology Soc. (pres. 1982-84), Behavioral Toxicology Soc. (pres. 1988-90), Am. Soc. Pharmacology and Exptl. Therapeutics, Am. Psychol. Soc., European Behavioral Pharmacology Soc., Soc. Toxicologists (pres. So. Cen. chpt. 1985-86), Coll. on Problems of Drug Dependence, Fedn. Am. Socs. for Exptl. Biology (chair publs. and comm. com. 2000—). Home: 100 Longway Dr Little Rock AR 72223-9531 Office: U Ark Med Scis Sch Medicine Dept Pharmacology & Toxicol 4301 W Markham St Little Rock AR 72205-7101 E-mail: mcmillandonalde@uams.edu.

MCMILLAN, GEORGE ALFRED MONTCLAIR, obstetrician, gynecologist; b. Kingston, Jamaica, Dec. 12, 1941; came to U.S., 1970; s. Alfred and Anita (Dunkley) McM.; m. Cynthia Rose Walters, June 28, 1969 (div. 1979); children: Gary, Patrice, Jason; m. Margaret Elizabeth Hospedales, Sept. 4, 1982; children: Marisa, Meika. BS, MB, U. W.I., 1969; MD, U. W.I., Jamaica, 1969. Diplomate Am. Bd. Ob-Gyn. Intern U. Hosp. West Indies, Kingston, 1969-70; resident in ob-gyn. Harlem Hosp., N.Y.C., 1970-74; obstetrician Brookdale Hosp., Bklyn., 1975—. Mem. attending staff N.Y. Meth. Hosp., 1996—; dir. ob-gyn. Ambulatory Surgery, Bklyn., 1997—; mem. med. bd. Brookdale Univ. Med. Ctr., Bklyn., 1997—. Fellow Am. Fertility Soc., Am. Coll. Ob-Gyn.; mem. AMA, Kings County Med. Soc. Office: 614 Eastern Pkwy Brooklyn NY 11225-1604 E-mail: gmcmillan2@hotmail.com.

MC MILLAN, GEORGE DUNCAN HASTIE, JR. lawyer, former state official; b. Greenville, Ala., Oct. 11, 1943; s. George Duncan Hastie and Jean (Autrey) McM.; m. Ann Louise Dial, Nov. 20, 1971; children: George Duncan Hastie, III, Ann Dial. BA magna cum laude, Auburn U., 1966; LL.B. (Southeastern Regional scholar), U. Va., 1969. Bar: Ala. bar 1969. Research asst. dept. agronomy Auburn U., summers 1963-65; law clk. firm Lange, Simpson, Robinson & Somerville, Birmingham, Ala., summers 1967-68; law clk. to judge U.S. Dist. Ct. No. Dist. Ala., 1969-70; instr. U. Ala. Law Sch., 1969-70; individual practice law Birmingham, 1970-71; ptnr. firm McMillan & Spratling, 1971-86; of counsel Haskell, Slaughter, Young and Lewis, 1986; ptnr. McMillan, Jones and Assocs., 1987-90; pres. McMillan Assocs., 1990—; mem. Ala. Ho. of Reps., 1973, Ala. Senate, 1974-78; lt. gov. Ala., 1979-83. Vice-chmn. Nat. Conf. Lt. Govs., 1980-82; mem. Permanent Study Commn. on Ala.'s Jud. System, 1975-79 Chmn. Ala. Film Commn., 1976-83; mem. Arts Task Force, Nat. Conf. State Legislatures, 1978-80, Multi-State Transp. Adv. Bd., 1974-79; mem. exec. com. So. Growth Policies Bd., 1974-83, vice chmn., 1981-83; bd. dirs. Campfire, Inc., 1975-82, Met. YMCA, Birmingham, Boys and Girls Ranches, Ala., Positive Maturity, 1987—; chmn. bd., pres. Birmingham Cultural and Heritage Found., 1988—; pres., bd. dirs. Birmingham Repertory Theatre, 1989—; exec. producer City Stages; Served to lt. USAR, 1969. Recipient award Ala. Nurses Assn., 1975; named Legislator of Yr. Ala. Forestry Assn., 1978; Hardest Working Senator Capitol Press Corps, 1976; 1 of 4 Outstanding Young Men Ala. Jaycees, 1977; 1 of 10 Most Outstanding State Legislators Assn. Govtl. Employees, 1978; award Birmingham Emancipation Assn., 1977; award Ala. Hist. Commn., 1978; James Tingle award, 1979, Citizen of Yr. award City of Birmingham, 1990. Mem. Birmingham Bar Assn., Ala. Bar Assn., Am. Bar Assn., Birmingham Jaycees, Ala. Jaycees (dir. 1970-72), Birmingham Urban League, United Negro Coll. Fund. Democrat. Mem. Ch. of Christ. Club: Rotary (Birmingham). Office: Mc Millan Assocs PO Box 11311 Birmingham AL 35202-1311

MCMILLAN, JULIA A. pediatrician; b. Pinehurst, N.C., July 10, 1946; MD, SUNY, Syracuse, 1976. Intern SUNY Upstate Med. Ctr., Syracuse, 1976-77, resident in pediatrics, 1977-78, 79-80, fellow in infectious diseases, 1979-81; mem. staff Johns Hopkins U. Hosp., Balt.; assoc. prof. Johns Hopkins U.; chair. Am. Bd. of Pediatrics, Chapel Hill. Mem. ASM, IDSA, Am. Acad. Pediatrics. Office: Johns Hopkins Hosp Dept Pediatrics 600 N Wolfe St Dept Baltimore MD 21287-0005*

MCMILLAN, LARRY DONALD, engineering executive; b. Trout Lake, Mich., June 10, 1936; s. Ira Duncan and Lilly Bell (Reed) McM.; m. Theresa Ann Mayer, June 25, 1955 (div. July 1975); children: Aaron, Keith, Curt, Adam, Kent, Craig, Andrea; m. Victoria Jeanne Cronin, Nov. 5, 1977. BSEE, Aquinas Coll., Grand Rapids, Mich., 1965; MSEE, Ariz. State U., 1972; postgrad., U. Colo., Colorado Springs, 1990-97. Elec. engring. mgr. Motorola, Inc., Phoenix, 1966-76; mgr. process engring. Am. Microsys., Inc., Santa Clara, Calif., 1976-77; dir. engring. Nat. Cash Register Corp., Colorado Springs, 1977-79; v.p., gen. mgr. microtech. ops. Storage Tech. Corp., Louisville, 1979-80; v.p. Stephenson Western, Inc., Aurora, 1980-82; engring. mgr. Honeywell, Inc., Colorado Springs, 1982-84; v.p. rsch. and devel., corp. founder Ramtron Corp., 1984-88; CEO, pres., corp. founder Symetrix Corp., 1988—. Adj. prof. Mich. Technol. U., Houghton, 1986-88. Co-author: (chpt.) Ferroelectric Ceramics, 1993; contbr. articles to Integrated Ferroelectrics, Nature, Jour. Integrated Ferroelectrics, Condensed Matter News, Nikkei Electronics, Ferroelectrics, Jour. Applied Physics, Applied Physics Letters. Achievements include patents for Method of Making Barium Strontium Titanate, Integrated Circuit Capacitors and Process for Making the Same, Process for Making Metal Oxides, Metal Polyoxyalkylated Precursor Solutions in an Octane Solvent and Method of Making the Same, Ferroelectric Integrated Circuit, Precursors and Processes for Making Metal Oxides, Memory with Ferroellectric Capacitor Connectable to Transistor Gate, Ferroelectric Memory and Non-Volatile Memory Cell for Same, Misted Deposition Apparatus for Fabrication an Integrated Circuit, Non-Volatile Memory, Ferroelectric Dielectric Memory Cell can Switch at Least GIG Cycles and has Low Fatigue, ABO3 Structured Solid Solutions Mixed and Average Perovskites for High Dielectric Constant DRAMs and Capacitors, Precursors and Processes for Making Metal Oxides, Low Temperature Process for Fabricationg Layered Superlattice Materials and Making Electronic Devices Including Same, others. Home: 3005 Blodgett Dr Colorado Springs CO 80919-4510 Office: Symetrix Corp 5055 Mark Dabling Blvd Colorado Springs CO 80918-3834

MCMILLAN, LEE RICHARDS, II, lawyer; b. New Orleans, Aug. 26, 1947; s. John H. and Phoebe (Skillman) McM.; m. Lynne Clark Pottharst, June 27, 1970; children: Leslie Clark, Hillary Anne, Lee Richards III. BS in Commerce, Washington and Lee U., 1969; JD, Tulane U., 1972; LLM in Taxation, NYU, 1976. Bar: La. 1972. Assoc. Jones, Walker, Waechter, Poitevent, Carrere & Denegre, New Orleans, 1976-79, ptnr., 1979—, sect. head, corp. and securities sect., 1987-90, 94—, exec. com., 1990-94, 96-99, 2001—, chmn. exec. com., 1991-94, 96-98, 2001—. Vice-chmn. Mech. Equipment Co., Inc., New Orleans, 1980-86, chmn. bd., 1986—, pres. 1989-99; mem. The Bus. Coun. Greater New Orleans, 1998—, exec. com., 1999—; bd. dirs. The Chamber/New Orleans and the River Region, 1996-98; bd. trustees Alton Ochsner Med. Found., 1995—. Trustee New Orleans Mus. Art., 1989-95; bd. dirs. Bur. Govt. Rsch. New Orleans, 1987-93, Louise S. McGehee Sch., New Orleans, 1982-88, co-chmn. capital fund dr., 1984-86, pres. bd. dirs., 1986-88; bd. govs. Isidore Newman Sch., New Orleans, 1991-95. Lt. JACG USNR, 1972-75. Mem. ABA (com. on negotiated acquisitions 1986-94), La. State Bar Assn. (chmn. corp. and bus. law sect. 1985-86, mem. com. on bar admissions 1986-87), Young Pres. Orgn., Washington and Lee U. Alumni Assn. (bd. dirs. 1995-99). Republican. Episcopalian. Avocation: sailing. Office: Jones Walker Waechter Poitevent Carrere & Denegre 201 Saint Charles Ave Ste 5100 New Orleans LA 70170-5101

MCMILLAN, M. SEAN, lawyer; Diploma, U. Munich, 1963; cert., Internat. Sch., Copenhagen, Denmark, 1962; SB, U. So. Calif., 1967; JD, Harvard U., 1970. Bar: Calif. 1971. Spl. projects dir. Mass. Gen. Hosp., Boston, 1967-70; ptnr. Keatinge, Libbott, Bates & Loo, Los Angeles, 1970-74, Loo, Merideth &

McMillan, Los Angeles, 1974-85, Bryan Cave LLP, Los Angeles/Santa Monica, 1986—2001, Greenberg Traurig LLP, L.A., 2001—. Editor: Harvard Internat. Law Jour., 1968-70.. Mem. Assn. Computing Machinery, ABA, Am. Soc. Internat. Law, Phi Beta Kappa, Phi Kappa Phi. Office: Greenberg Traurig LLP 2450 Colorado Ave Ste 400E Santa Monica CA 90404 E-mail: mcmillan@gtlaw.com.

MCMILLAN, MARILYN AYRES, information systems scientist, university official; b. Jersey City, Aug. 20, 1946; d. Joseph John and Ruth Carolyn (Sayre) Ayres; m. David R. McMillan, June 18, 1967 (dec. June 1987); children: Courtenay Ruth, Dwight Joseph. BA in Polit. Sci., Rutgers U., 1967. Computer programmer Naval Ships Systems Command, Boston, 1967-69; sys. analyst Computer Applications Inc., Reading, 1969-70; rsch. assoc. No. Va. Planning Dist. Commn., Falls Church, 1976-77; sr. sys. analyst, project mgr. MIT, Cambridge, 1977-81, area mgr. fin. sys., 1981-82, mgr. application svcs., 1982-84, dir. adminstrv. sys., 1984-87, dir. architecture and strategic tech., 1987-89, dir. info. sys. planning, 1989-96; dir. application assembly and integration Stanford (Calif.) U., 1996—98; chief info. tech. officer NYU, 1998—2002, assoc. provost and CITO, 2002—. Bd. dirs. Cause; mem. EDUCOM; presenter on methodology and tech. at profl. meetings. Contbr. articles to profl. jours. Chair Winchester Housing Partnership Bd., 1992-94; bd. dirs. Counseling Resource Ctr., Winchester, Mass., 1987-90. Mem. Soc. for Info. Mgmt., Phi Beta Kappa. Mem. United Ch. of Christ. Avocations: refurbishing Victorian home, choral music, sailing. Office: NYU 251 Mercer St Rm 302 New York NY 10012-

MCMILLAN, MARY BIGELOW, retired minister, volunteer; b. St. Paul, July 30, 1919; d. Charles Henry and Allison (McKibbin) Bigelow; m. Richard McMillan, June 26, 1943; children: Richard Jr., Charles B., Douglas D., M. Allison, Anne E. BA, Vassar Coll., 1941; MDiv, United Theol. Sem. Twin Cities, 1978, DDiv (hon.), 1989. Ordained to ministry Presbyn. Ch., 1978. Asst. min. House of Hope Presbyn. Ch., St. Paul, 1978-82; interim pres. United Theol. Sem. Twin Cities, New Brighton, Minn., 1982-83, ret., 1987. Contb. author: The Good Steward, 1983. Trustee Minn. Ch. Found., Mpls., 1984-99, United Theol. Sem. Twin Cities, 1977-89, also chmn. bd. trustees; bd. dirs. Inst. for Ecumenical and Cultural Rsch., Collegeville, Minn., 1982—; regional dir. Assn. Jr. Leagues, N.Y.C., 1959-61, pres. St. Paul chpt., 1957-59; vice chair Ramsey County Welfare Bd., St. Paul, 1962-66, St. Paul Health and Welfare Planning Coun., 1964-70, F.R. Bigelow Found., St. Paul, 1988-95, also 1st vice chair; 1st vice chair, trustee Wilder Found., 1973-89; active Presbyn. Homes Found., 1996—. Recipient award for community planning United Way, 1965, also for yr. round leadership, 1973, Leadership in Community Svc. award YWCA, 1980, Sisterhood award NCCJ, Mpls., 1989; named Disting Alumna award St. Paul Acad. and Summit Sch., 1988 Mem.: Univ. Club, New Century Club. Avocations: golf, knitting, reading. Home: 2925 Lincoln Dr #713 Roseville MN 55113

MC MILLAN, R(OBERT) BRUCE, museum executive, anthropologist; b. Springfield, Mo., Dec. 3, 1937; s. George Glassey and Winnie Mae (Booth) McM.; m. Virginia Kay Moore, Sept. 30, 1961; children: Robert Gregory, Michael David, Lynn Kathryn. BS in Edn, S.W. Mo. State U., 1960; MA in Anthropology, U. Mo., Columbia, 1963; PhD in Anthropology (NSF fellow), U. Colo., Boulder, 1971. Rsch. assoc. in archaeology U. Mo., 1963-65, 68-69; assoc. curator anthropology Ill. State Mus., Springfield, 1969-72, curator anthropology, 1972-73, asst. mus. dir., 1973-76, mus. dir., 1977—; exec. sec. Ill. State Mus. Soc., 1977—. Lectr. anthropology Northwestern U., 1973. Editor: (with W. Raymond Wood) Prehistoric Man and His Environments, 1976. Mem. Ill. Spl. Events Commn., 1977-79, program chmn., 1977-78; commr. Ill. and Mich. Canal Nat. Heritage Corridor Commn., 1988—; bd. dirs. Found. Ill. Archaeology, 1978-83. Grantee NSF, 1971-72, 80, Nat. Endowment for Humanities, 1978. Fellow AAAS, Am. Anthrop. Assn.; mem. Am. Assn. Mus. (council 1982-86), Midwest Mus. Conf. (pres.), Soc. Am. Archaeology, Current Anthropology (asso.), Am. Quaternary Assn., Sigma Xi. Office: Ill State Mus Spring And Edwards Sts Springfield IL 62706-0001 also: Dickson Mounds Museum Lewistown IL 61542 E-mail: rbm@museum.state.il.ul.

MCMILLAN, ROBERT RALPH, lawyer; b. N.Y.C., May 21, 1932; s. Harry and Vivian (Beatty) McM.; m. Phoebe Parker Bunn, Nov. 2, 1996; children: Robin, Karen, Kenneth. Student, Adelphi U., 1951-52, 55-56; JD, Bklyn. Law Sch., 1960. Bar: N.Y. 1960. Spl. asst. staff of Richard M. Nixon, N.Y., Washington, 1960, 64-65; counsel Senator Kenneth B. Keating, Washington, 1960-62; govt. rels. advisor Mobil Oil Co., N.Y.C., 1962-63, 65-68; v.p. Avon Products, 1973-78, 79-85; sr. v.p. A&S Dept. Stores, 1978-79; counsel Rivkin, Radler, Bayh, Hart & Kremer, Uniondale, N.Y., 1986-91; ptnr. McMillan, Rather, Bennett & Rigano, P.C., Melville, 1991—. Bd. dirs. Empire Blue Cross Blue Shield, Panama Canal Comm., 1989-94, chmn., 1993-94; bd. dirs. Interboro Mut. Indemnity Ins. Co.; mem. nat. adv. coun. FannieMae, 1998-2000. News commentator Sta. WLIW-TV, 1993—. Trustee Adelphi U., 1984-89; bd. dirs. L.I. (N.Y.) Assn.; chmn. L.I. Housing Parntership, 1988-2002. 1st lt. U.S. Army, 1952-54. Decorated Bronze Star. Mem. Nassau County Bar Assn., Suffolk County Bar Assn. Republican. Avocations: golf, fishing. Office: McMillan Rather Bennett & Rigano 48 S Service Rd Melville NY 11747-2335 E-mail: mcmillan@aol.com.

MCMILLAN, STEPHEN WALKER, artist; b. Berkeley, Calif., Dec. 21, 1949; s. Edwin Mattison and Elsie Walford (Blumer) McM.; m. Susan Irene Sanford, Mar. 25, 1989. BA in Art, U. Calif., Santa Cruz, 1972, BFA in Art, 1975. Artist Graphic Arts Workshop, San Francisco, 1975-79, Kala Inst., Berkeley, Calif., 1989-84, 87-92, Petaluma, 1993—. Instr. aquatint etching Kala Inst., 1980-92. Artist, printmaker; creator over 225 aquatint etchings and 25 lithographs; exhibited work in over 25 galleries across the U.S. Recipient James D. Phelan Art Award in Printmaking, The San Francisco Found., 1995, 4th prize 3d Kochi (Japan) Internat. Triennial Exhbn. of Prints, 1996. Mem. Calif. Soc. Printmakers. Avocations: bicycling, backpacking, bicycle touring, photography. E-mail: aquatint@sonic.net.

MCMILLAN, TERRY L. writer, educator; b. Port Huron, Mich., Oct. 18, 1951; d. Edward McMillan and Madeline Washington Tillman; 1 child, Solomon Welch. BA in Journalism, U. Calif., Berkeley, 1979; postgrad., Columbia Univ., N.Y.C., 1979. Instr. U. Wyoming, Laramie, 1987-88; prof. U. Ariz., Tucson, 1988-91. Author: Mama, 1987, Disappearing Acts, 1989, Waiting to Exhale, 1992, How Stella Got Her Groove Back, 1996, A Day Late & A Dollar Short, 2001; editor: Breaking Ice: An Anthropology of Contemporary African-American Fiction, 1990; screenwriter (with Ron Bass) (movies) Waiting to Exhale, 1995, How Stella Got Her Groove Back, 1998. Recipient National Endowment for the Arts fellowship, 1988.

MCMILLAN, WENDELL MARLIN, agricultural economist; b. Dallastown, Pa., June 14, 1923; s. John Walter and Alice Mary (McCormick) McM.; m. Eleanor Unser, July 14, 1946; children: Susan, Barbara, Douglas. Grad., York (Pa.) Jr. Coll., 1943; BS, Juniata Coll., 1948; MS, Pa. State U., 1950, PhD, 1954. Rsch. & extension asst. Pa. State U., 1950-54; agrl. economist, asst. dir. U.S. Dept. Agriculture, Washington, 1955-64; project mgr., mktg. advisor Food and Agriculture Orgn. of UN, Jordan, Saudi Arabia and Afghanistan, 1964-72; agrl. economist The World Bank, Caribbean, Sudan, 1972-76; agrl. and policy economist U.S. Dept. Agr./USAID, Syria, Indonesia, Lesotho, Liberia, 1977-80; agrl. economist Africa Bur. USAID, Washington, 1980-89. Mem. mktg. subcom. Nat. Commn. on Cooperative Devel., Washington, 1964; adj. prof. York (Pa.) Coll., 1990. Author tech./policy publs. on agr. Dist. chmn. Campfire Girls, No. Va., 1959-61; chmn. bd. dirs. Am. Cmty. Sch., Amman, Jordan, 1966-67, UN Staff Assn., Kabul, Afghanistan, 1969-70; bd. dirs. Hist. York, Inc., 1987-97, pres., 1995-97; mem. Hist. Soc. York County, 1987—, mem. libr. com., 1990—; trustee York County Acad., 1991—. Recipient Fulbright award U.S. Dept. State, U. Copenhagen, Denmark, 1954-55, Merit certificates USDA, 1960, 84, Hall of Fame award William Penn Sr. H.S. Mem. Am. Agrl. Econs. Assn., Soc. for Internat. Devel., Alumni Assn. York Coll. (bd. dirs. 1986-91, Svc. award 1991, Disting. Alumnus 1982, Dir. Emeritus award 1997), Alumni Assn. Juniata Coll. (Nat. Alumni Achievement award 1984, William Penn Sr. H.S. Hall of Fame 1999), Pi Gamma Mu. Democrat. Avocations: stamp collecting, nature study, opera. Home and Office: 1775 Powder Mill Rd #209 York PA 17403-4955

MCMILLEN, ABBIE, environmental manager; b. N.Y.C., Oct. 10, 1942; d. Albert Edward and Beatrice Cuthbert (Collingwood) Miller; m. David S. Page, Sept. 30, 1964; children: David C., Vivian W.; m. Michael A. McMillen, Feb. 14, 1980. BS in Chemistry, Brown U., 1964; MS, Purdue U., 1969. Registered Maine guide, 1997—. Mem. Maine gov.'s cabinet, dir. Maine Office Energy Resources, Augusta, 1975-77; project dir. Roy F. Weston, Inc., Burlington, Mass., 1981-92; pres. McMillen Environ. Inc., 1992-93. Exec. dir. Island Heritage Trust, 1993-95. founder, organizer Lafayette (Ind.) Environ. Action Fedn., 1969; mem., chmn. Poland (Maine) Planning Bd., 1971-73; mem. exec. com., chmn. solid waste com., Poland rep. Androscoggin Valley Regional Planning Commn., 1971-73; chmn. New Eng. steering com. for ERDA pub. meeting, 1975; mem. New Eng. Congl. Caucus Energy Congress, 1979, New Eng. Power Plant siting task force, 1980. Contbr. articles to profl. jours. Treas., Concord Art Assn., 1987-89; through-hiker Long Trail, 1989; bd. dirs. Solid Waste Composing Coun., 1991-93; pres., Castine Conservation Trust, 1994-97. David Ross fellow Purdue U., 1965. Mem. ASME (tech. papers chmn. solid waste divsn. 1991-93), Maine Organic Farmers and Gardeners Assn. (organizer, v.p. 1970-72), Friends of Brooksville Libr. (v.p. 1997—), Brooksville Hist. Soc. (treas. 2000—), Mensa. Avocations: swing dancer, website manager.

MCMILLEN, ELIZABETH CASHIN, artist; b. Chgo. d. James Blaine and Hortense (Fears) Cashin; m. John Stephen Jerabek; 1 child, Michael N. Student, Western Coll. for Women, 1961-63; BA, Bard Coll., 1965. Coord. com. and juror Spectra I, sponsor state exhbn. women artists Westbrook Coll., Portland, Maine, 1979; dir. Hancock County Auditorium Art Gallery, Ellsworth, Maine, 1984, 85. Exhibited at Frick Gallery, Belfast, Maine, 1993, 94, Maine Coast Artists Juried Show, Rockport, 1994, Portland Children's Mus., 1995, Lakes Gallery, Sebago, Maine, 1995—, Maine Coast Artists, Rockport, 1998, Portland Mus. Art, 1998, 2001, American Embassy Santiago Chili, 1998—, Maine Art Gallery, Wiscasset, 2001, Payson Gallery, Portland, 2002; one-person shows include Area Gallery, Portland, 1994, Frick Gallery, Belfast, Maine, 1995, Lakes Gallery, Sebago, Maine, 1997, June Fitzpatrick Alternative, Portland, 1999, 2001, June Fitzpatrick Gallery, Portland, 2001; two persons show Maine Coast Artists, Rockport, 1996. Dem. chair Town of Lamoine, Maine, 1984-85, 86-87, 88-89; legislation coord. Amnesty Internat., Ellsworth, 1991-97. Democrat. Episcopalian. Avocations: writing, politics, teaching, African-Am. history.

MCMILLEN, IRMA FEICHTINGER, retired librarian, association administrator; b. Grafenschachen, Austria, July 16, 1920; came to U.S., 1922; d. Frank and Mary (Tunkl) Feichtinger; m. Donald McMillen, June 20, 1948; children: Joseph, Phyllis, Denise, Matthew. BS in English and German, Mich. State U., 1950; MLS, Wayne State U., 1965. Librarian Pontiac (Mich.) Schs., 1950-84; dir. YWCA, Pontiac, 1984-91; ret., 1991. Vol. Oakland County Health Dept. Childrens Eyes, 1995, Oakland County Mich. Dept. Drug Abuse Control, 1989, Pontiac Bicentenial com., 1976; hon. life mem. YWCA; mem. study com. Pontiac Hist. Dist., 1977; sec. Tuesday Musical, 1995-96; bd. dirs. Pontiac Symphony Orch., 1980-95; judge student art projects, 1994-97. Recipient Heart of Gold award Pontiac City Coun., 1989, Honor award cert. Archaeol. Project, Pontiac, 1983, 125th Anniversary Celebration award City of Pontiac, 25 Yr. award Austrian Soc., 1972-97. Mem. AAUW (pres.), Pontiac Area Ret. Tchrs. Assn. (pres. 1997), Oakland County Pioneer Soc. (bd. mem. 1992-98), Farm and Garden Club, Lioness Club (dist. gov., 1994-95, pres. 1994-97, plaque 1997, Melvin Jones award 1996), Pontiac Edn. Assn., Alpha Delta Kappa. Avocations: world travel, music, photography, archaeology, philately. Home: 496 W Iroquois Rd Pontiac MI 48341-2019

MCMILLEN, JULIE LYNN, educator; b. Olney, Ill., Dec. 19, 1954; d. Glenn Everett and Carol Marie (Blood) Bowen; m. Robert Nelson McMillen, June 5, 1976. BA, Ea. Ill. U., 1976, MA, 1980. Tchr. English, speech Cmty. Unit Sch. Dist. # 10, Bridgeport, Ill., 1976—. Recipient Isabella Coleman award, 1976. Mem. DAR (regent 1984-86, treas. 1990—), Order Ea. Star (Worthy Matron 1982, 85, 89, 92, 97, 2002, grand rep. N.D. 1986-88, grand lectr. 1986—, grand rep. R.I. 1997-98, grand martha 2001), Delta Kappa Gamma (pres. 1996-98, v.p. 1994-96, state music com. 1995-97, 99—). Republican. Avocations: reading, singing, piano, collecting dolls and music boxes. Home: 1106 Willow Dr Lawrenceville IL 62450-2481 Office: Red Hill High Sch 908 Church St Bridgeport IL 62417-1845

MCMILLEN, ROBERT PAUL, agricultural engineer; b. Mansfield, Tex., Nov. 20, 1952; s. Charles William and Janie Lee (Dixon) McM. BS in Agrl. Engring., Tex. Tech. U., 1978. Reg. profl. engr., Tex. Agrl. engr. U.S. Dept. Agr.-Soil Conservation Svc., Lubbock, Vernon, Tex., 1978-82; design engr. Parkhill, Smith & Cooper, Inc., Lubbock, 1982-88, project mgr., 1988-96, corp. assoc., 1996—. Mem. adv. bd., tech. subcom. Reese Air Force Base Restoration, Lubbock, 1995—. Mem. NSPE, ASCE, Am. Soc. Agrl. Engrs., Nat. Ground Water Assn., Tex. Soc. Profl. Engrs. (chpt. dir. 1995-99), Water Environ. Assn. Tex. (chpt. sec. 1995-99, chpt. pres. 1999-2001). Avocations: piloting. Home: 5502 56th St Apt 214 Lubbock TX 79414-2039 Office: Parkhill Smith & Cooper Inc 4222 85th St Lubbock TX 79423-1930

MCMILLEN, ROBERT STEWART, lawyer; b. Yonkers, N.Y., Feb. 25, 1943; s. David Harry and Blodwyn Elizabeth (Evans) McM; m. Dorothea Anne Murray, July 2, 1966; children: Elissa London, Tara Evans. BS, U. Rochester, 1964; JD cum laude, Albany Law Sch. Union U., 1969. Bar: N.Y. 1969, U.S. Dist. Ct. (no. dist.) N.Y. 1969. Assoc. Clark, Bartlett & Caffry, Glens Falls, N.Y., 1969-73; ptnr. Caffry, Pontiff, Stewart, Rhodes & Judge, 1974-80; prin. Bartlett, Pontiff, Stewart & Rhodes, P.C., 1981—. Sr. law examiner N.Y. State Bd. Law Examiners, Albany, 1986-2001, bd. mem. 2001—; bd. dirs. Cmty. Title Agy., Inc., Glens Falls, 1984—, pres., 1984-99, v.p., sec., 1999—. Editor-in-chief Albany Law Rev., 1968-69. Bd. dirs., officer Voluntary Action Ctr. of Glens Falls Area, Inc., 1970-97; bd. dirs., treas. Arts and Crafts Ctr. of Warren County, Inc., Glens Falls, 1984-94; mem. Warren County Rep. Com., Queensbury, N.Y., 1979-2001; alt. or del. Rep. Jud. Nomination Com. 4th Jud. Dist. N.Y., 1977—. Recipient Disting. Svc. award Voluntary Action Ctr. of Glens Falls Area, Inc., 1990. Mem. ABA, N.Y. State Bar Assn. (mem. com. profl. ethics 1990-99, 2000—), Warren County Bar Assn. (bd. dirs. 1979-82, treas. 2001—), Adirondack Regional C. of C. (bd. dirs. 1997-2000, vice chmn. 1999-2000, counsel 2000—), Rotary. Avocations: travel, downhill skiing, boating. Home: 147 Assembly Point Rd Lake George NY 12845-5201 Office: 1 Washington St Glens Falls NY 12801-2963

MCMILLEN, SALLY GREGORY, history educator; b. Pasadena, Calif., Mar. 9, 1944; d. Theodore Roy and Elizabeth Shambaugh Gregory; m. Bruce Charles McMillen, June 11, 1966 (div. May 1988), remarried, Apr. 27, 1991; children: Blair, Carrie. BA, Wellesley Coll., 1966; MLS, Pratt U., 1968; PhD, Duke U., 1985. Asst. prof. history Mid. Tenn. State U., Murfeesboro, 1985-88, Davidson (N.C.) Coll., 1988-91, assoc. prof. history, 1991-98, prof. history, 1998—. Author: Motherhood in the Old South, 1990, Southern Women: Black and White in the Old South, 1991, 2d edit., 2002, To Raise Up the South: Black and White Sunday Schools in the New South, 1865-1915, 2002; co-editor: Major Problems in the History of the American South , 1999; mem. editl. bd.: N.C. Hist. Rev., 1990—93. NEH fellow, 1991-92; recipient Hunter-Hamilton Love of Tchg. award, 2000. Mem. Orgn. Am. Historians, So. Hist. assn., So. Assn. Women Historians (exec. bd. 1998—). Democrat. Avocations: running, hiking, biking, reading, cooking. Office: Davidson Coll Dept History Davidson NC 28035-6994

MCMILLEN, TIMOTHY JAMES, music educator; b. Sulphur, La., Nov. 16, 1964; s. Charles Lee and Cora Faith McMillen; m. Rebecca Marie Soileau, Oct. 24, 1967; children: Mathew, Gabrielle. MusB, McNeese State U., Lake Charles, La., 1988; MusM, U. North Tex., Denton, 1990. Network cons. Superior Office Sys., Lake Charles, La., 1997—99; music tchr. W.W. Lewis Mid. Sch., Sulphur, 1999—. Composer, arranger, trombonist McMillen Music Svcs., Sulphur, 1997—. Composer: The Nth Degree, 1989, First Words, 1989, Continuation, 1998, Space Age Polymer, 1998, Morning, 2001. With USAF, 1990—96. Mem.: Internat. Trombone Assn. (mem. 1982—90), Internat. Assn. Jazz Educators (mem. 2001—02), Am. Fedn. Musicians (mem. 2002—02), Phi Mu Alpha Sinfonia Music (mem. 1983—2002). Republican. Baptist. Avocations: fishing, basketball. Office: McMillen Music Svcs 208 N Marauder St Sulphur LA 70663 Home Fax: 928-244-2973; Office Fax: 928-244-2973. E-mail: mcmillen@cox-internet.com.

MCMILLIAN, THEODORE, federal judge; b. St. Louis, Jan. 28, 1919; m. Minnie E. Foster, Dec. 8, 1941. BS, Lincoln U., 1941, HHD (hon.), 1981; LLD, St. Louis U., 1949; HHD (hon.), U. Mo., St. Louis, 1978. Mem. firm Lynch & McMillian, St. Louis, 1949-53; asst. circuit atty. City of St. Louis, 1953-56; judge U.S. Ct. Appeals (8th cir.), 1978—. Judge Circuit Ct. for City St. Louis, 1956-72, Mo. Ct. Appeals eastern div., 1972-78; asso. prof. adminstrn. justice U. Mo., St. Louis, 1970— ; asso. prof. Webster Coll. Grad. Program, 1977; mem. faculty Nat. Coll. Juvenile Justice, U. Nev., 1972—. Served to 1st lt. Signal Corps U.S. Army, 1942-46. Recipient Alumni Merit award St. Louis U., 1965, ACLU Civil Liberties award, 1995, Disting. Lawyer award Bar Assn. Met. St. Louis, 1996, Salute to Excellence Civil Rights award St. Louis Am., 1997; named Disting. Non-Alumnus U. Mo.-Columbia Law Sch., 1999. Mem. Am. Judicature Soc., Am. Bd. Trial Advs. (hon. diplomate), Lawyers Assn. Mo., Mound City Bar Assn., Phi Beta Kappa, Alpha Sigma Nu. Office: Thomas F Eagleton Court House Ste 25 162 111 S 10th St Saint Louis MO 63102

MCMILLIN, BARBARA ANN, English educator, university dean; b. Ripley, Miss., Sept. 8, 1959; d. Walter Clarence and Mary Sue (Coombs) Childers; m. Larry McMillin, July 2, 1983. AA, N.E. Miss. C.C., Booneville, 1979; BA in English, Union U., Jackson, Tenn., 1981; MA in English, U. Miss., 1982, DA in English, 1987. Instr. English, N.E. Miss. C.C., Booneville, 1987-92; assoc. prof. English, Union U., Jackson, Tenn., 1992-99, chair dept., 1993-99, dean Coll. Arts and Scis., 1999—. Dir. self-study Union U., 1993-96. Mem.: MLA, Tenn. Philol. Assn., Coll. English Assn. Baptist. Office: Union U 1050 Union University Dr Jackson TN 38305-3697 E-mail: bmcmilli@uu.edu.

MCMILLIN, DAVID ROBERT, chemistry educator; b. East St. Louis, Ill., Jan. 1, 1948; s. Robert Cecil and Clara Rose McMillin; m. Nicole Wilson, Nov. 3, 1974; children: Robert Stephen, Andrew Wilson. BA, Knox Coll., 1969; PhD, U. Ill., 1973. Postdoctoral fellow Calif. Inst. Tech., Pasadena, 1974; asst. prof. chemistry Purdue U., West Lafayette, Ind., 1975-80, assoc. prof., 1980-85, prof., 1985—. Contbr. articles to profl. jours. Recipient F.D. Martin Teaching award Purdue U., 1975. Mem. Am. Chem. Soc., Inter-Am. Photochem. Soc. (sec. 1986-90, v.p. 1994-96, pres. 1996-98), Phi Beta Kappa, Sigma Xi. Presbyterian. Avocations: sports, reading. Office: Purdue U Dept Chemistry West Lafayette IN 47907-1393 E-mail: mcmillin@purdue.edu.

MCMILLIN, JOAN AUSTIN, social worker; b. Hartford, Conn., July 4, 1941; d. John Francis and Charlotte (Kilmer) Austin; m. J. Michael McMillin, May 9, 1970; children: John Andrew, Christy. BA, U. Conn., 1963; MSW, Boston Coll., 1966. Cert. social worker, Ill., S.D. Social worker, student suor. Hamm Psychiat. Clinic, St. Paul, 1970-74; social worker Mass. Gen. Hosp., Boston, 1966-70, VA Hosp., Sioux Falls, S.D., 1980—; clin. social worker Charter Counseling Ctr., 1991-96, dir. social svcs., 1996—. Parent trainer S.D. Parent Connection, Sioux Falls, 1986-88; bd. dirs. Community Disabilities, 1990—. Bd. dirs. Coun. for Disability Rights, Chgo., 1988-89; del. United Cerebral Palsy Assn., N.Y.C., 1987, bd. dirs., pres. S.D. chpt., Sioux Falls, 1980-87; sec., bd. dirs. Vis. Nurses Assn., Sioux Falls, 1984-88. U.S. Dept. Vocat. Rehab. grantee, 1964-66; recipient T. Brown Community Svc. award Sioux Falls Masons, 1986. Mem. Nat. Assn. Social Workers (S.D. chpt.), Am. Bd. Examiners in Clin. Social Work, Phi Beta Kappa, Phi Kappa Phi. Home: 4409 Yellowstone Ln Sioux Falls SD 57105-6756

MCMILLION, JOHN MACON, retired newspaper publisher; b. Coffeyville, Kans., Dec. 25, 1929; s. John Dibrell and Mattie Anna (Macon) McM.; m. Melanie Ann McMillion; children: John Thomas, Johanna, Jennifer, Amanda Student, Vanderbilt U., 1947-49; BS in Journalism, U. Kans., 1956. Police reporter Amarillo (Tex.) Globe-News, 1956; sports editor, telegraph editor Grand Junction (Colo.) Daily Sentinel, 1956-58; mng. editor Alliance (Nebr.) Times-Herald, 1958-59, Clovis (N.Mex.) Jour., 1959-62; gen. mgr. Pasadena (Tex.) Citizen, 1962; bur. mgr. UPI, 1962-66; exec. editor Albuquerque Jour., 1966-69; bus. mgr. Albuquerque Pub. Co., 1971-75; pub. Herald and News-Tribune, Duluth, Minn., 1975-86, Akron (Ohio) Beacon Jour., 1986-90, ret. Campaign mgr. gubernatorial campaign, 1969-71 Served with USN, 1950-54. Address: 302 Knife Island Rd Two Harbors MN 55616-4030

MCMINDES, ROY JAMES, aggregate company executive; b. Essex, Md., July 12, 1923; s. Roy Preston and Edith S. (Sh) McMindes; m. Prudence Atsinger, June 8, 1946; children: Gail Karen, Joan Susan, James Lee. BS, U. Md., 1948. Pres. Sheridan Corp., Lebanon, Pa., 1951—, Grays Ferry Brick Co., Lebanon, 1971—2001, Waylite Co., Lebanon, 1976-88. Chmn. bd. Peoples Nat. Bank, Lebanon, 1984—92, dir., 1965—92. Bd. dirs. Lebanon YMCA, 1968—86, Good Samaritan Hosp., Lebanon, 1970—93. With A.C. USN, 1943—46, with USNR, 1946—52. Recipient Founders Day award, Lebanon Valley Coll., 1987. Mem.: Lebanon Valley C. of C. (pres. 1973), Lebanon Country Club, Jesters, Shriners. Republican. Presbyterian. Office: 1212 W Maple St Lebanon PA 17046-2701

MCMINN, JOHN ALHANE, musician, educator; b. Miami, Fla., Apr. 6, 1952; MusB, Manhattan Sch. Music, 1974, MusM, 1975. Instrumentalist Valerie Caiers Orch., N.Y.C., 1972-74, Guys and Dolls, N.Y.C., 1973, Bubbling Brown Sugar, N.Y.C., 1976-77; music dir. Ain't Misbehavin', internat. tour, 1980-83; mus. dir. various clubs, Miami and Wichita, 1984—. Arranger, instrumentalist Spl. Forces Band, Miami, 1985—; writer Decision Band, Miami, 1985—. Recipient award for work performed Thespians, 1981, Kozah Temple, 1985. Mem. Am. Fedn. Musicians. Home: 900 NW 75th St Miami FL 33150-3355

MCMINN, VIRGINIA ANN, human resources consulting company executive; b. Champaign, Ill., Apr. 7, 1948; d. Richard Henry and Esther Lucille (Ellis) Taylor; m. Michael Lee McMinn, Dec. 29, 1973. BA in Teaching of English, U. Ill., 1969; MS in Indsl. Rels., Loyola U., Chgo., 1985. Pers. sec. Solo Cup Co., Urbana, Ill., 1972-74; pers. asst. Rust-Oleum Corp., Evanston, 1974-75, asst. pers. mgr., 1974-80, mgr. employee rels. Vernon Hills, 1980-81, mgr. human resources, 1981-84; dir. human resources Field Container Corp., Elk Grove Village, 1984-87; regional mgr. human resources Hartford Ins. Corp., Chgo., 1987-90; owner, pres. McMinn & Assocs., Ltd., Palatine, Ill., 1988—; founder S.W. Human Resources Group, Chandler, Ariz., 1995. Instr. bus. and mgmt. divsn. Trinity Coll., Deerfield, Ill., 1984-85; instr. bus. and social scis. Harper Coll., Palatine, Ill., 1990-93; bd. dirs. Nierman's Hard-To-Find Sizes Shoes, Chgo.; ptnr. ManagersAdvantage.com, 2002; spkr. in field. Bd. dirs. Ill. Crossroads coun. Girls Scouts USA, Elk Grove, 1988-92; mem. Ill. Com. to Implement Clean Indoor Air Act, Chgo., 1990-91; past mem. adv. bd. Coll. of Lake County, 1982-84. Mem. Soc. for Human Resource Mgmt., Nat. Network Sales Profls. (program chmn. 1990-93), Women in Mgmt. (chpt. Leadership award corp. category, past pres.), Ariz. Employers' Coun., Ariz. Small Bus. Assn. Avocations: reading, golf, crafts. E-mail: ginny@mcminnhr.com.

MCMINN, WILLIAM LOWELL, JR. engineer; b. Wilmington, N.C., Apr. 1, 1943; s. William Lowell McMinn Sr. and Elma Dell (Jordan) Higgins; m. Dorothy Ellen Kochert, Apr. 26, 1967; children: Jeffery Allan, Lori Ellen. Grad. high sch., Peru, Ind. Registered profl. engr., 1966. Locomotive engr. C.S.X. Transp., Riverdale, Ill., 1963—. Mem. Main St. United Meth. Ch., Peru. Mem. Brotherhood Locomotive Engrs. (sec. Peru chpt. 1977—, treas. 1991—), Peru Male Chorus, Elks, Moose. Avocations: camping, golf, traveling, walking, farming. Home: 1728 S Riverview Rd Peru IN 46970-7263

MCMONAGLE, DONALD R. retired astronaut, retired military officer; b. Flint, Mich., May 14, 1952; m. Janyce Morton; 2 children. BS in Astro. Engring, Air Force Acad., Colo. Springs, Colo. , 1974; MS in Mech. Engring., Calif. State U., Fresno, 1983. Commd. 2d lt. USAF, 1974, advanced through grades to col., retired; Fighter pilot trainee USAF , Columbus AFB, Miss., 1974—75; F-4 fighter pilot USAF, Kinsan Air Base, Republic of Korea, 1975—76, Holloman (N. Mex.) AFB, 1977—79; F-15 instr. pilot USAF, Luke (Ariz.) AFB, 1979—81, student test pilot Edwards (Calif.) AFB, 1971—72; ops. officer, project test pilot USAF Advanced Fighter Tech. Integration F-10 Aircraft, 1982—85; ops. officer 6513th Test Squadron , Edwards AFB, Calif., 1985—87; astronaut NASA Johnson Space Ctr., Houston, 1987—99; mgr. launch integration space shuttle program NASA Kennedy Space Ctr, Fla., 2000—. Decorated Disting. Flying Cross USAF; recipient Liethen-Tittle award, USAF Test Pilot Sch., 3 NASA Space medals. Mem.: Assn. Space

Explorers, Soc. Exptl. Test Pilots, Assn. Grads. Air Force Acasd. Achievements include over 5000 hours of flying experience in a variety of aircraft plus 3 space flights, thousands of hours in space. Office: Astronaut Office Johnson Space Ctr Houston TX 77059

MCMORROW, MARGARET MARY (PEG MCMORROW), retired educator; b. N.Y.C., Dec. 18, 1924; d. Patrick Joseph and Ellen Veronica (Quinn) McIntyre; m. Joseph Patrick McMorrow, Oct. 12, 1948; children: Linda Karen, Robert Michael (dec.), Patrice Ann, Jane Ellen. BS, Queens Coll., 1946; MS in Edn., Hofstra U., 1959. Space controller Am. Airlines Co., N.Y.C., 1946-48; bus. rep. N.Y. Telephone Co., 1948-52; tchr. Elwood Sch. Dist, Huntington, N.Y., 1965-89, ret., 1989. Fellow Elwood Tchrs. Assn., L.I. Scribes, N.Y. State United Tchrs., Mensa; mem. Elwood Ret. Tchrs. Assn., Alpha Lambda Omicron. Roman Catholic. Avocation: calligraphy.

MCMULKIN, FRANCIS JOHN, retired steel company executive; b. Sault Ste. Marie, Ont., Can., Dec. 7, 1915; s. George Alexander and Leanor Augusta (Zryd) McM.; m. Margaret Lilian Winch, Sept. 21, 1946; children: John Bruce, Mary Diane. BS in Metallurgy, Mich. Coll. Mining and Tech., 1937; ME, Mich. Tech. U., 1945, DEngring (hon.), 1972. Formerly metallurgist Algoma Steel Corp., Sault Ste. Marie, 1937-42; rsch. fellow Ont. Rsch. Found., Mississauga, 1942-47; R&D engr. Dominion Foundries & Steel Ltd., Hamilton, Ont., Can., 1947—, dir. rsch., until 1964, v.p. rsch., 1964-85; ret. Contbr. articles to profl. publs. Recipient Disting. Alumnus award Mich. Tech. U., 1976 Fellow Am. Soc. Metals (life, William Hunt Eisenman award 1968), Engring. Inst. Can.(life, John Galbraith prize 1945, elected fellow 1981); mem. Can. Inst. Mining and Metallurgy (H.T. Airey Meml. Ann. Conf. lectr. award), AIME (Basic Oxygen Steel award 1963), Iron and Steel Soc. (charter, Disting. mem.), Metall. Soc. (elected 1997, Howe Meml. lectr. 1973), Mich. Tech. U. Metall. and Materials Acad. (charter mem. 1996), Iron and Steel Inst. (U.K.), Royal Over-Seas League (London), Hamilton Club, Hamilton Golf and Country Club, Mid Ocean Club (Bermuda). Mem. United Ch. of Canada. Home: 270 Roseland Crescent Burlington ON Canada L7N 1S3

MCMULLAN, ALEXANDER JOSEPH, municipal official; b. Bklyn., Nov. 27, 1941; s. Alexander J. McMullan; m. Christine J., Oct. 10, 1962; children: Tim, Jennifer. AAS in Mech. Tech., N.Y.C. C.C., 1968; BA, Queens Coll., 1982; cert. in plumbing, Mechanics Inst., 1987. Lic. plumbing insp., N.Y.; lic. cross connecting tester, N.Y.; lic. system operator, N.Y. Pipe laying insp. City of N.Y. Dept. Environ. Protection, 1972, plumbing insp. tapping, area chief tapping, five borough tapping chief. With U.S. Navy, 1962-65. Mem. Am. Water Works Assn. N.J., Internat. Assn. Plumbing and Mech. Ofcls., Plumbing Insps. Assn. Office: City of NY DEP 40 Worth St Rm 338 New York NY 10013-2904

MCMULLAN, JAMES FRANKLIN, retired financial planner; b. Atlanta, Feb. 24, 1928; s. Jesse James and Ruth Guinn (Thomason) McM.; m. Gladis Jo Anne Lovern, Sept. 13, 1951 (dec. May 1998); children: Anne, Martha Jane (dec.), Lynn, Robert Lovern, Beth; m. Patricia Leary Warren, Aug. 20, 1999. BBA, Emory U., 1949; MS, Am. Coll., 1986. CLU, chartered fin. cons.; cert. fin. planner. Emeritus gen. agt. Allmerica Fin., Atlanta, 1955—; pres., founder Strategic Asset Adv. Corp., 1968-99; pres., cons. McMullan Fin. Planning Svcs., East Point, Ga., 1999—. Elder, pastor World of Life Fellowship, East Point, Ga., 1984—. Home and Office: 70 Ashland Grove Ct Sharpsburg GA 30277-3448 Fax: 770-253-6758. E-mail: jamesfmac@earthlink.net.

MCMULLAN, KATHRYN OATMAN, watercolor painter, promotion specialist; b. Bridgeport, Conn., June 16, 1943; d. Kenneth Webb and Kathryn (Mahlstedt) Oatman; m. John Brockett McMullan, Aug. 31, 1979; 1 child, Kenneth Roger. Grad., Riverview H.S., Sarasota, Fla., 1962; student, Ringling Sch. Art, 1982-88. Mgr. gift shop Sarasota Visual Art Ctr., 1985-88; retail salesperson Sarasota, 1988-93; pub. rels. specialist Art League Manatee County, Bradenton, Fla., 1994-95; event promotion specialist Manatee County Cultural Alliance, 1993-98. Mem. spl. events subcom. Downtown Devel. Authority, City of Bradenton, 1998; mem. Crosley Estate Found., bd. dirs., 1998, holiday dir., chmn., 2000-; festival dir. arts and crafts booths Hernando De Soto Hist. Soc., Desoto Celebration Fla. Heritage Festival at Bradenton Seafood Fest, 1996—; bd. dirs. Artarget, 1998-99, Sarasota Visual Art Ctr., 1999; bd. dirs. Performing Arts Downtown, Inc., 2001—. Mem. Soc. Nat. Preservation, Fla. Suncoast Watercolor Soc. (pres. 1990-92, publicist 1993-98), Art League Manatee County (sec. 1995-96, bd. dirs. 1994—, v.p. 1998, pres. 1999-2001, hon. 2001-), Manatee County Cultural Alliance (event dir. 1993, sec. 1995-96, publicist 1995-97, city revitalization com. 1995), Manatee C.C. (redevel. com.), Asoto Theater Guild (pres. 2001-), Women's Caucus for Art (v.p. 1994-95, publicist 1993-98, pres. 1995-98. Democrat. Avocations: collecting elephants, gardening, traveler, animal preservation, watercolor painting. Home: 220 25th St W Bradenton FL 34205-4916

MCMULLAN, WILLIAM PATRICK, III, investment banker; b. Newton, Miss., Dec. 29, 1952; s. William Patrick Jr. and Rosemary (Lyons) McM.; m. Rachel Smiley McPherson, Oct. 16, 1982. BA, Vanderbilt U., 1974; MBA, U. Pa., 1976. V.p. Lehman Bros. Kuhn Loeb, N.Y.C., 1976-82; assoc. dir. Prudential-Bache Securities, 1982-85; mng. dir. Donaldson, Lufkin & Jenrette Securities Corp., 1985-2000; mng. dir., chmn. global health care Credit Suisse First Boston, 2000—. Bd. dirs. Lar Lubovitch Dance Co., Project Reach Youth, The Consolidated Corp. Fund, Lincoln Ctr. Mem. Met. Club, Mashomack Fish and Game Club, Confrerie des Chevaliers du Tastevin. Home: 607 6th St Brooklyn NY 11215-3701 Office: Credit Suisse First Boston 11 Madison Ave New York NY 10010

MCMULLEN, DAVID WAYNE, education educator; b. Canton, Ill., Apr. 6, 1957; s. Earl Eugene and Juanita Elaine (Estep) McM.; m. Faye Anne Whitaker, Mar. 28, 1981; 1 child, James Earl. BS, Bradley U., 1980, MS, 1984; PhD, U. Ill., 1989. Cert. sec. tchr., Ill. Tchr. 7th and 8th grade sci. Bartonville (Ill.) Grade Sch., 1980-83; grad. asst., instr. U. Ill., Urbana, 1985-89; instr. Bradley U., Peoria, Ill., 1987-89, assoc. prof. edn., 1989—, dir. Ctr. Rsch. and Svc. Coll. Edn. and Health Scis., 1995-98. Instr. gifted program Bradley U. Inst. for Gifted and Talented Youth, Peoria, summers 1984-85, 88—; computer cons. MicroComputer Cons., Morton, Ill., 1984-85; instr. Computer Terminal, Peoria, 1984; system operator Free Ednl. Electronic Mail, Peoria, 1991-96. Author: (software) Science Fair Success, 1984. Sec. bd. Common Place, Peoria, 1992. Mem. ASCD, Assn. Computing Machinery, Assn. Advancement Computing Edn., Internat. Soc. for Tech. in Edn., Phi Delta Kappa, Phi Kappa Phi, Phi Alpha Theta. Mem. Christian Ch. (Disciples Of Christ). Avocations: computers, amateur radio, woodworking. Office: Bradley Univ 208 W Lake Ave Peoria IL 61614

MC MULLEN, EDWIN WALLACE, JR. English language educator; b. Quincy, Fla., Dec. 8, 1915; s. Edwin Wallace and Sara Della (Moore) McM.; m. Marian Elizabeth Hoper, June 9, 1946; children: William Wallace, Charles Edwin. BA, U. Fla., 1936; MA, Columbia U., 1939, PhD, 1950. Instr. English Pa. State U., 1946-48, State U. Iowa, 1950-52; spl. instr. in report writing U.S. Dept. Def., Washington, 1953, sr. reporter, 1952-57; asst. editor Merriam Webster Dictionary Co., 1957; asst. prof. English Lehigh U., 1957-61, Fairleigh Dickinson U., Madison, N.J., 1961-62, assoc. prof., 1962-72, prof., 1973-82, chmn. dept. lang. and lit., 1962-65, emeritus, 1982; founder, dir. Names Inst., 1962-86. Chmn. publs. subcom. Morris County Tercentenary Com., N.J., 1962-63 Author: English Topographic Terms in Florida, 1563-1874, 1953; contbr. articles to profl. publs.; editor: Names, 1962-65; editor, contbr.: Pubs, Place-Names and Patronymics: Selected Papers of the Names Institute, 1980; editor, contbr. Names New and Old: Papers of the Names Inst., 1993, 2d edit., 2002. Served with Signal Corps, U.S. Army, 1942-46. Mem. MLA, Am. Name Soc. (pres. 1976), Internat. Congress on Onomastic Scis., Internat. Linguistic Assn., Am. Dialect Soc., English Place-Name Soc., Morris County Hist. Soc., Old Guard of Summit (N.J.), Nat. Coun. Tchrs. English, Meth. Friendship Club (past co-pres.). Democrat. Methodist. Home: 15 Rosewood Dr Madison NJ 07940-1120 Office: Fairleigh Dickinson U Dept English Madison NJ 07940 *Chaucer sums up my philosophy in his description of the Clerk: "And gladly wolde he lerne and gladly teche.".*

MCMULLEN, G. ARTHUR, physician, cardiologist; b. Greeneville, Tenn., May 28, 1954; s. Raymon Wesley and Zora Jean (Spear) McM.; m. Shelley Speelman; children: Geremy, Heather, Dustin, Phillip, David. BS, Pacific Union Coll., Angwin, Calif., 1976; MD, Loma Linda U., 1979. Diplomate in internal medicine and cardiovascular diseases Am. Bd. Internal Medicine. Intern Kettering Meml. Hosp., Dayton, Ohio, 1980-81, resident, fellow, 1981-83, 84-87; cons. and practicing cardiologist and internal medicine specialist, Pt. Charlotte/Punta Gorda, Fla., 1987—. Fellow ACP, Am. Coll. Cardiology; mem. AMA, Alpha Omega Alpha. Avocations: tennis, skiing, boating, travel, computers, golf. Office: Cardiology Cons Charlotte 1655 Tamiami Trl Port Charlotte FL 33948-1042

MCMULLEN, JOHN ALFRED, management consultant; b. Dec. 10, 1941; AB with honors, Columbia U., 1963, BS with honors, 1964; MBA with high distinction, Harvard U., 1972, JD with honors, 1973. Bar: Mass. 1974, N.Y. 1974, D.C. 1979. Faculty assoc., univ. officer Harvard U. Sch. Bus., 1972-73; cons. Boston Cons. Group, 1975-78; v.p., dir. Resource Planning Assocs., Cambridge, Mass., 1978-84; mng. prin. Cambridge Meridian Group, 1984—. Also dir. Mem. Gov.'s Adv. Task Force for Dept. Revenue, 1983; mem. faculty law sch. Harvard U., 1986-90; bd. dirs. PSDI, Ezenia! Dir. Cambridge Ctr. for Adult Edn., 1990—; Rep. candidate for U.S. Senate from Vt., 1998. Lt. USN, 1964-69. Baker scholar, Harvard U.; Sheldon Traveling fellow, Harvard U., 1972. Mem. ABA, Mass. Bar Assn., D.C Bar Assn., N.Y. Bar Assn., Harvard U. Bus. Sch. Assn., Harvard U. Law Sch. Assn., Columbia Coll. Alumni Assn., Boston Com. Fgn. Rels., Harvard Club (N.Y.C.), Harvard Faculty Club, Phi Beta Kappa. Republican. Address: 193 Howard St Burlington VT 05401-4032

MCMULLEN, JOHN HENRY, JR. manufacturing company executive, educator; b. Phila., Sept. 9, 1944; s. John Henry and Clara (Johnson) McM.; m. Evelyn Corrine Lawson, July 19, 1964; children: Yolanda, John III, Yvette, Yvonne. BS, Tuskegee U., Ala., 1969; MBA, Anna Maria Coll., 1984; postgrad., New Enb. Sch. Law. Cert. purchasing mgr. Asst. program planner Ingall's Shipbldg., Pascagoula, Miss., 1969-71; indsl. engr. supr. Luken's, Coatesville, Pa., 1971-76; mgr. mfg. engring. Newport News (Va.) Shipbldg., 1976-78; gen. supr. Polaroid Corp., Cambridge, Mass., 1978-85; mfg. mgr. Keene Corp., East Providence, 1985-86; master scheduler Prime Computer, Natick, 1987-89; small bus. and small disadvantaged bus. liaison officer GTE Govt. Systems Corp. (now Gen. Dynamics), Needham Heights, 1989—; mng. small bus. programs Gen. Dynamics, CA Sys., Taunton, 1999—. Instr. Anna Maria Coll., Paxton, Mass., 1983-86; adv. bd. Purchasing Ctr. Ct.-apptd. spl. advocate Suffolk County Juvenile Ct., Boston, 1983; bd. dirs. Mattapan (Mass.) Cmty. Health Ctr., 1983-93, treas. 1984-86, pres. 1987-91; treas. ADAPT, Inc., Roxbury, Mass., 1986-88, v.p., 1988-89; active Urban League Ea. Mass., 1987-91; pres., founder Alpha Phi Alpha Edn. Found, 1983-87; bd. dirs. Dr. William Price unit Am. Cancer Soc. Mem. Nat. Assn. Purchasing Mgmt. (minority bus. devel. group 1991—, contbr. Purchasing Today mag., Charles J. McDonald Minority Bus. Advocacy of Yr. award 1997), Purchasing Mgmt. Assn. Boston (treas. 1996-97), Inst. Indsl. Engrs., Exec. MBA Assn. Anna Maria Coll. (bd. dirs. 1983-86), Nat. Black MBA Assn. (co-founder, treas. Boston chpt. 1985-87), Afro-Am. Cultural Assn. Sharon (founder), Polaroid Found., Tuskegee Alumni Club (chpt. fin. sec. 1985-96, pres. 1992-93, asst. regional fin. sec. 1988-90, asst. regional dir. 1985-91, regional dir. 1993-97, Outstanding Alumni award 1988), Tuskegee Nat. Alumni Assn. (bd. dirs.), Elks, Shriners, Alpha Phi Alpha (chpt. pres. 1981-86, Alpha Man of Yr. 1986). Avocations: bowling, racquetball, jogging, chess, motorcycling. Home: 8 Pine St Sharon MA 02067-1616 Office: 400 John Quincy Adams Rd Taunton MA 02780-1069 E-mail: tuskegee@alumnidirector.com., john.mcmullen@gdcas.com.

MCMULLEN, JOHN J. former professional hockey team executive, management consultant; m. Jacqueline McMullen; children: Peter, Catherine, John Jr. BSEE, U.S. Naval Acad., 1940; DMechE, Swiss Fed. Tech. Inst.; M in Naval Architecture and Marine Engring., MIT. Commd. ensign USN, 1940, advanced through grades to comdr., resigned, 1954; chief ship constrn. and repair U.S. Maritime Adminstrn. Office, Washington, 1954-57; chmn. John J. McMullen Assocs., Inc., 1957—98; ltd. ptnr. N.Y. Yankees Baseball Team, 1974; chmn. Houston Astros Baseball Team, 1979-92, N.J. Devils Hockey Team, East Rutherford, NJ, 1982—2000; with McMullen Cons., Secaucus. Office: 200 Plaza Dr Secaucus NJ 07094-3607

MCMULLEN, MARY M. secondary school educator; b. Milford, Conn., June 17, 1961; d. William Joseph and Gloria Maria (Catania) McM.; m. Wendell C. Jones, Aug. 6, 1999. AS in Gen. Edn., South Ctrl. C.C., 1983; student, U. Salamanca, Spain, 1990; BA in English, So. Conn. State U., 1993, postgrad., 2000—; MA in Liberal Studies, Wesleyan U., 1996. Libr. rschr. New Haven Register, 1993-98; tchr. creative writing dept. Coop. Arts and Humanities Magnet H.S., 1995-2000, lead tchr. creative writing, 2000—02; coord. sr. rsch. project Coop. H.S., 2002—. Writing instr. S.A.Y.!/ARTSPACE, New Haven, Conn., summers 1996, 97; writer Conn. Life Mag., 1995-96. Scholar Daus. Women Vets., 1983, So. Conn. State U. Women's Alumni Assn., 1983, H.W. Wilson scholar So. Conn. State U., 2000, 02, scholar Conn. Libr. Assn., 2001, 02. Mem. ALA, (New Mems. Roundtable), Tchrs. and Writers Collaborative. Avocations: gardening, writing, reading, walking, cooking. Office: Coop Arts and Humanities Magnet HS 444 Orange St New Haven CT 06511 E-mail: marymcmullen@yahoo.com.

MCMULLEN, PAMELA R. TEMPLES, small business owner, interior designer; b. Columbia, S.C., Mar. 27, 1949; d. Marvin C. and Margaret (Berry) Reames; m. Samuel E. Temples, Feb. 6, 1971 (div. Dec. 1980); children: Stephanie Dawn, Melissa Gayle; m. Edwin H. McMullen, June 10, 1989. BFA, U. S.C., 1971. Designer S. Sjoberg Interiors, 1970-73; designer sales dept. R.L. Bryan Co., 1973-75; instr. in interior design U. S.C., Columbia, 1975-79; designer sales dept. Archtl. Interiors, 1976-78; pres. PTI Assocs., Columbia, 1979-88, Pamela Temples Interiors, Lakeland, Fla., 1989—; v.p. McMullen & Elliott, Lakeland and Chgo., 1991—. Speaker Am. Land Devel. Assn. Conf., Atlanta, 1984, New Orleans and Orlando, Fla., 1985, Nashville, 1986, Am. Resort and Residential Devel. Assn. Conf., Las Vegas, Nev., 1987, New Orleans, 1988, South African Resort Property Devel. Assn., Durbin, 1988, Australian Timeshare Conf., Gold Coast, Australia, 1988, Resort Condominiums Internat. European Conf., Nice, France, 1990. Contbr. articles to profl. jours. Member Nat. Historic Preservation Soc.; co-chmn. fundraising com. Polk County Mus.; mem. Columbia C. of C., 1982-89, Leadership Columbia, 1984. Winner 1st Pl., Am. Land Devel. Assn., 1984, Am. Soc. Interior Designers, 1987; recipient Bronze and Gold awards, 1989, Silver award Illuminating Engring. Soc., 1989. Mem. Am. Soc. Interior Designers (1st Pl. award 1987), Internat. Found. Timesharing (bd. dirs.), Am. Resort and Residential Devel. Assn. (past bd. dirs., Gold (2) and Silver (4) awards, 1988, 89, Gold award 1990, 91, Silver award 1990), Vacation Ownership Coun. (bd. dirs.), Am. Resort Devel. Assn. (Gold (4) and Silver 2 awards). Republican. Methodist. Avocations: reading, snow skiing, family. Home: 9154 Great Heron Cir Orlando FL 32836-5487 Office: 7652 Ashley Park Ct Ste 306 Orlando FL 32835-6199

MCMULLEN, PATRICK REGIS, finance educator, researcher; b. Louisville, July 16, 1964; s. Thomas Edward McMullen, Nancy Jane McMullen; m. Sandra Kay Lisle; children: Kirby, Abby. PhD, U. Oreg. Prof. Harvard U., Cambridge, Mass., 1997—2000, Auburn (Ala.) U., 1999—2002. Contbr. articles to profl. jours. Mem.: Decision Scis. Inst. Office: Auburn Univ Coll Bus Auburn AL 36849 Office Fax: 334-844-6511. Personal E-mail: pmcmullen@business.auburn.edu. Business E-Mail: pmcmullen@business.auburn.edu.

MCMULLEN, RALPH EDGAR, convention center administrator; b. Abilene, Tex., Aug. 18, 1944; s. Ralph and Laurette McMullen; m. Vicky Jo McMullen, Sept. 18, 1971. AA, Valley Coll., 1966; BA, Boise State U., 1986; MPA, U. Ctrl. fla., 1990. Exec. dir. Jackson Hole C. of C., Jackson, Wyo., 1977-84, Elko (Wyo.) Convention and Visitors Authority, 1998—; dir. Idaho Travel Coun., Boise, 1984-87, Brevard County TDC, Merritt Island, Fla., 1987-90, Mammoth Lakes (Calif.) Visitors Bur., 1990-98. Chmn. Coun. Area and Regional Travel Orgn., Washington, 1989—90; vice chmn. Cowboy Country, Nev., 1999—; chmn. Mono County Rep. Party, Mammoth Lakes, 1996—98; Calif. rep. state cen. com. Nev. Rep. State Ctrl. Com., Carson City, 2001—. Recipient Big Wyo. award Wyo. Travel Coun., 1983, Named Citizen of the Yr. award Jackson Hole C. of C., 1978. Mem. Nev. Civic Club (pres.), Navy League (pres.), Rotary, Lions. Avocations: hunting, fishing.

MCMULLEN, SHARON JOY ABEL, marriage and family therapist; b. Peoria, Ill., June 21, 1933; d. Richard Glen Abel and Harriet Bernice Copland; m. David Winston McMullen, Dec. 27, 1956; children: David Paul, Jeniffer Joy. BA, UCLA, 1955; MA in Marriage and Family Therapy, St. Joseph Coll., 1996. Lic. marriage and family therapist; life cert. tchr. Calif. Counselor First Ch. of Christ, Wethersfield, Conn., 1996—, Stafford Family Svcs., Stafford Springs, 1996—. Vol. staff asst. Master Therapists Workshop Series, U. Conn. Health Ctr., 1996—. Chair counseling task force 1st Ch. of Christ, Wethersfield, 1997-98, co-founder, team tchr. couples ministry, co-facilitator premarital workshops, 1997—. Mem. Am. Assn. of Marriage and Family Therapists (advocacy com. 1997-98), Conn. Assn. of Marriage and Family Therapists, Am. Assn. of Pastoral Counselors, Am. Assn. of Christian Counselors. Democrat. Avocations: reading, genealogy, gardening, walking. Home: 44 Auburn Rd West Hartford CT 06119-1303 Office: Stafford Family Svcs 21 Hyde Park Rd Stafford Springs CT 06076-1507 E-mail: sm@dmcma.com.

MC MULLEN, THOMAS HENRY, retired air force officer; b. Dayton, Ohio, July 4, 1929; s. Clements and Adelaide Palmer (Lewis) McM.; m. Clara Faye Kirkwood, Mar. 28, 1956; children— Susan Marie, Thomas Clements, John Kirkwood. Student, St. Mary's U. Tex., 1945-47; BS in Mil. Engring, U.S. Mil. Acad., 1951; MS in Astronautics, Air Force Inst. Tech., 1964; MS in Adminstrn, George Washington U., 1971; student, Indsl. Coll. Armed Forces, Ft. McNair, Washington, 1970-71. Commd. 2d lt. U.S. Air Force, 1951, advanced through grades to lt. gen., 1980; flight trainee Hondo AB, Tex., Bryan AFB, Tex. and Nellis AFB, Nev., 1951-52; fighter pilot/flight comdr. (K-13 AB), Suwon, Korea, 1952-53; flight test maintenance officer Kelly AFB, Tex., 1953-59; Air Force flight acceptance test pilot at (Gen. Dynamics Inc.), Ft. Worth, 1959-62; project officer, Gemini Launch Vehicle Program, officer (Space Systems Div.), Los Angeles, 1964-66; air liaison officer 25th Inf. Div. Cu Chi, South Vietnam, 1967-68; asst. mission dir. Apollo Program Hdqrs. NASA Washington, 1968-70; B-1 dep. system program dir. Wright Patterson AFB, Ohio, 1971-73; A-10 System program dir., 1973-74; vice comdr. Tactical Air Warfare Center Eglin AFB, Fla., 1974-75; comdr. (Tactical Air Warfare Center), 1975-76; dep. chief of staff/requirements Hdqrs. Tactical Air Command Langley AFB, Va., 1976-79; dep. chief of staff/systems Hdqrs. Air Force Systems Command Andrews AFB, Md., 1979-80; vice comdr. Tactical Air Command, 1980-82; comdr. Aero. Systems Div. Wright-Patterson AFB, Ohio, 1982-86; ret. USAF, 1986; cons. in aerospace Washington, 1986—. Decorated D.S.M. with two oak leaf clusters, Silver Star, Legion of Merit, D.F.C. with oak leaf cluster, Bronze Star, Meritorious Service medal with oak leaf cluster, Air Force Commendation medal with oak leaf cluster, Air medal with 18 oak leaf clusters, Purple Heart; Cross of Gallantry with palm Vietnam; recipient Exceptional Service medal NASA, 1969, Group Achievement award, 1969, 71. Fellow AIAA (asso.); mem. Air Force Assn., Order Daedalians, Tau Beta Pi. Presbyterian. Home and Office: 6301 Chaucer View Cir Alexandria VA 22304-3548 *The key to success is a combination of fortunate circumstance, hard work, and a willingness to accept responsibility. Few people get ahead without some combination of all three.*

MCMULLIN, ERNAN VINCENT, philosophy educator; b. Donegal, Ireland, Oct. 13, 1924; came to U.S., 1954; s. Vincent Paul and Carmel (Farrell) McM. BSc, Maynooth (Ireland) Coll., 1945, BD, 1948; postgrad. theoretical physics, Dublin Inst. Advanced Studies, 1949-50; BPh, U. Louvain, Belgium, 1951, LPh, 1953, PhD, 1954; DLitt (hon.) , Loyola U., Chgo., 1969, Nat. U. Ireland, 1990; PhD (hon.) , Maynooth Coll., Ireland, 1995; D Lang. Arts (hon.) , Stonehill Coll., 2000; DLaws (hon.) , U. Notre Dame, 2002. Ordained priest Roman Catholic Ch., 1949; faculty U. Notre Dame, 1954-57, 59—, assoc. prof. philosophy, 1964, prof. philosophy, 1966-94, prof. emeritus, 1994—, chmn. dept., 1965-72, O'Hara prof. philosophy, 1984-94. Postdoctoral fellow Yale U., 1957-59; vis. prof. U. Minn., 1964-65, U. Cape Town, summers 1972-73, UCLA, 1977, Princeton U., 1991, Yale U., 1992; Cardinal Mercier lectr. U. Louvain, Belgium, 1995, U. Oslo, 1997; mem. exec. bd. Coun. Philos. Studies, 1970-75; chmn. philosophy of sci. div. Internat. Congress Philosophy, 1968, 73; chmn. U.S. Nat. Com. for History and Philosophy of Sci., 1982-84, 86-87. Author: Newton on Matter and Activity, 1978, The Inference That Makes Science, 1992; editor: The Concept of Matter, 1963, Galileo, Man of Science, 1967, The Concept of Matter in Modern Philosophy, 1978, Death and Decision, 1978, Issues in Computer Diagnosis, 1983, Evolution and Creation, 1985, Construction and Constraint: The Shaping of Scientific Rationality; co-editor: (with J.T. Cushing) The Philosophical Consequences of Quantum Theory, 1989, The Social Dimensions of Science, 1992; cons. editor Studies History and Philosophy of Science, 1970-75, 1983—, Brit. Jour. Philos. Sci., 1988—, Perspectives on Science, 1992—, Ency. of the Scientific Revolution, 1994—, Oxford Companion to the History of Science and its Uses, 1998—. Romanell-Phi Beta Kappa Prof. of Philosophy, 1993-94; NSF rsch. grantee Yale U., 1957-59, Cambridge U., 1968-69; vis. rsch. fellow Cambridge U., 1973-74, 83, 87, U. Pitts., 1979. Fellow AAAS (chmn. sect. L 1977-78), Am. Acad. Arts and Scis., Internat. Acad. History Sci.; mem. Am. Cath. Philos. Assn. (pres. 1966-67, Aquinas medal 1981), Philosophy of Sci. Assn. (governing bd. 1969-73, pres. 1980-82), Metaphys. Assn. Am. (exec. coun. 1968-72, pres. 1973-74, Founder's medal 1997), Am. Philos. Assn. (exec. coun. 1977-81, pres. western divsn. 1983-84), History of Sci. Soc. (exec. coun. 1988-92). Address: PO Box 1066 Notre Dame IN 46556-1066

MCMULLIN, RUTH RONEY, publishing executive, trustee, management fellow; b. N.Y.C., Feb. 9, 1942; d. Richard Thomas and Virginia (Goodwin) Roney; m. Thomas Ryan McMullin, Apr. 27, 1968; 1 child, David Patrick. BA, Conn. Coll., 1963; M Pub. and Pvt. Mgmt., Yale U., 1979. Market rschr. Aviation Week Mag., McGraw-Hill Co., N.Y.C., 1962-64; assoc. editor, bus. mgr. Doubleday & Co., 1964-66; mgr. Natural History Press, 1967-70; v.p., treas. Weston (Conn.) Woods, Inc., 1970-71; staff assoc. GE, Fairfield, Conn., 1979-82; mng. fin. analyst, credit analyst corp. GECC Transp., Stamford, 1982-85; credit analyst corp. fin. dept. GECC, 1984-85; sr. v.p. GECC Capital Markets Group, Inc., N.Y.C., 1985-87; exec. v.p., COO John Wiley & Sons, 1987-89, pres., CEO, 1989-90, Harvard Bus. Sch. Pub. Corp., Boston, 1991-94; mem. chmn.'s com., acting CEO UNR Industries Inc., Chgo., 1991-92, also bd. dirs.; mgmt. fellow, vis. prof. Sch. Mgmt. Yale U., New Haven, 1994-95; chairperson trustees Eagle-Picher Personal Injury Settlement Trust, 1996—; chairperson Claims Procesing Facility, Inc., 1998—. Bd. dirs. Bausch & Lomb, Rochester, N.Y.; vis. prof. Sch. Mgmt., Yale U., New Haven, 1994-95; chair bd. trustees Eagle Picher Personal Injury Settlement Trust, 1996—. Mem. dean's adv. bd. Sch. Mgmt. Yale U., 1985—92; bd. dirs. Yale U. Alumni fund, 1986—92, Yale U. Press, 1988—99, Math. Scis. Edn. Bd., 1990—93; bd. dirs., treas. Mighty Eighth Air Force Heritage Mus., 2000—; bd. dirs. Savanna Symphony, 1999—, The Landings Club, 2002—. Mem. N.Y. Yacht Club, Stamford Yacht Club. Avocations: sailing, skiing, golf, tennis. Home: 8 Breckenridge Ln Savannah GA 31411-1701 Office: Eagle Picher Trust P O box 206 652 Main St Cincinnati OH 45202-2542 E-mail: RRmcmullin@att.net., rrmcmullin@aya.yale.edu.

MCMURPHY, MICHAEL ALLEN, energy company executive, lawyer; b. Dothan, Ala., Oct. 1, 1947; s. Allen L. and Mary Emily (Jacobs) McM.; m. Maureen Daly, Aug. 8, 1970; children: Matthew, Kevin, Patrick. BS, USAF Acad., 1969; MA, St. Mary's U., San Antonio, 1972; JD, U. Tex., 1975. Bar: Tex. 1975, U.S. Supreme Ct. 1977, U.S. Ct. Mil. Appeals, D.C. 1978, U.S. Ct. Appeals (fed. cir.) 1982. Commd. 2d lt. USAF, 1969, advanced through grades to capt.; instr. Air U., Ala., 1975-79; resigned USAF, 1979; atty., advisor Oak Ridge (Tenn.) ops. U.S. Dept. Energy, 1979-83; gen. counsel COGEMA, Inc., Washington, 1983-87, v.p., 1987-88, pres., chief exec. officer Bethesda, Md., 1988—. Pres., CEO Va. Fuels, Inc., Lynchburg, 1987-92; co-CEO AREVA Enterprises, Inc., Washington, DC, 2002—, bd. dirs. Nuclear Energy Inst., Washington, Soc. Gen. Techs. Nouvelles, S.A., St. Quentin, France, U.G./USA, Atlanta, Transnuclear, Inc., Hawthorne, N.Y., Canberra Industries, Meriden, Conn., Cogema Resources, Inc, Casper, Wyo., Cogema Engring. Co., Richland, Wash., Numatec Hanford Co., Wash., FANP, INc., Lynchburg, Va. and Richland, Wash.; bd. govs. Duke Cogema Stone & Webster, LLC, Charlotte, N.C., 1998—; pres. Uranium Producers Am., 1991-92. Mem. editorial bd. Air Force Law Rev., 1977-79. Decorated chevalier Nat. Order of Merit (France). Avocation: skiing. Office: COGEMA Inc 7401 Wisconsin Ave Bethesda MD 20814-3400 E-mail: mcmurphy@cogema-inc.com.

MCMURRAY, EARL WILLIAM, psychotherapist, poet; b. Balt., July 15, 1951; s. Earl William and Suzanne Marie McMurray. BA, MacMurray Coll., 1973; MFA, U. Ark., 1985; MSW, Barry U., 1994. Tchg. asst. U. Ark., Fayetteville, 1981—84, instr., 1984—85; vis. creative writer Miss. State U., Starkville, 1985—86; instr. Office Instrnl. Resources U. Fla., Gainesville, 1990; pvt. practice Palm Beach Gardens, 1997—. Active Poets in the Schs.

program Ark. Arts Coun., 1981—84. Author: (chapbook) Perfect Stranger, 1997; contbr. numerous poems to publs. Named winner Ann. Poetry Chapbook Contest, Ledge Press, 1997; recipient prize, Acad. Am. Poets, 1985. Mem.: NASW.

MCMURRAY, JAMIE, race car driver; Race car driver Brewco Motorsports, Central, Ky. Named Champion, Lebanon I-44 Speedway, 1997. Office: c/o Brewco Motorsports PO Box 37 106 Brewer Dr Central City KY 42330*

MCMURRAY, STEPHEN D. nephrologist; b. Bloomington, Ind., July 20, 1947; s. R.D. and Barbara McMurray; m. Linda C. Shands (div.); 1 child, Jeffrey; m. Barbara McMurray; stepchildren: Jon Gladieux, Angie Gladieux. BS in Zoology, Ind. U., 1968; MD, Ind. U., Indpls., 1972. Diplomate Am. Bd. Internal Medicine, Am. Bd. Nephrology; cert. continuous ambulatory peritoneal dialysis; lic. physician Ind., Ohio. Intern Ind. U. Med. Ctr., Indpls., 1972-73, resident in internal medicine, 1973-74, fellow in nephrology, 1974-75, rsch. fellow in nephrology, 1975-77; nephrologist Ft. Wayne (Ind.) Nephrology, 1977-89, Ind. Regional Med. Consultants, P.C., Ft. Wayne, 1989-98, Ind. Med. Assocs., Ft. Wayne, 1998—. Mem. exec. com. N.E. Ind. Kidney Ctr., Ft. Wayne; pres. DMN Dialysis Mgmt. Consulting, Ft. Wayne, 1986-97, med. staff Luth. Hosp., Ft. Wayne, 1995; founder Renal Care Group, Nashville, Tenn., 1996; mem. staff Luth. Hosp., Ft. Wayne, 1977—, Parkview Meml. Hosp., Ft. Wayne, 1977—; mem. courtesy staff St. Joseph Med. Ctr., Ft. Wayne, 1977—, Rehab. Hosp., Ft. Wayne, 1995—, Select Splty. Hosp., Ft. Wayne, 1997—, Marion (Ind.) Gen. Hosp., 1986—, Wabash (Ind.) County Hosp., 1997—. Contbr. articles to profl. jours. Ind. Kidney Found. fellow Nat. Kidney Found., 1975-76. Fellow ACP; mem. Am. Soc. Nephrology, Renal Physicians Assn., Ind. State Med. Assn., Kidney Found. of Ind., Nat. Kidney Found. of Ind., Tri-State Renal Disease Netowrk (v.p. 1993-95), The Renal Network (med. adv. bd. 1994—), Internat. Soc. Nephrology. Office: Ind Med Assocs LLC 7900 W Jefferson Blvd Ste 201 Fort Wayne IN 46804-4128

MCMURRY, IDANELLE SAM, educational consultant; b. Morganfield, Ky., Dec. 6, 1924; d. Sam Anderson and Aurelia Marie (Robertson) McM. BA, Vanderbilt U., 1945, MA, 1946. Tchr. English Abbot Acad., Andover, Mass., 1946-50, Hockaday Sch., Dallas, 1951-54, San Jacinto High Sch., Houston, 1954-55; dean of girls Kinkaid Sch., 1955-63; headmistress Harpeth Hall Sch., Nashville, 1963-79, Hockaday Sch., Dallas, 1979-89; ret.; now pvt. sch. cons. The Edn. Group, Dallas. Bd. dirs. Ednl. Records Bur., 1979-85, trustee, 1980-85. Bd. dirs. Tex. council Girl Scouts U.S., 1980-82, Town North YMCA; trustee Winston Sch., 1979-85, Spl. Care Sch., 1979-81, Asheville Sch., Manzano Day Sch. Mem. Nat. Study Sch. Evaluation (bd. dirs. 1979-83), Headmasters Assn., Nat. Assn. Ind. Schs. (bd. dirs. 1974-84, acad. com. 1974-79, sec. 1978-80, chmn. 1980-84), So. Assn. Ind. Schs. (pres. 1974-75), Tenn. Assn. Ind. Schs. (pres. 1967-68), Mid-South Assn. Ind. Schs. (pres. 1972-73), Ind. Schs. Assn. S.W. (v.p. 1967—), Nat. Assn. Prins. Schs. for Girls (sec. 1970-72, pres. 1975-77, coun. 1970-79), Nat. Assn. Secondary Sch. Prins., Country Day Sch. Headmasters Assn. (exe. com. 1984-87, v.p. 1988-89), So. Assn. Colls. and Schs. (adminstrv. coun. 1974-77, ctrl. reviewing com. 1972-77, vice chmn. secondary commn. 1975-76, chmn. 1976-77, bd. dirs. 1976-81), Ladies Hermitage Assn., Vanderilt Aid Soc. (sec. 1971-73, pres. 1994-96), Ind. Edn. Svcs. (trustee 1980-88, chmn. 1986-88), Susan Komen Found. (adv. bd.), Belle Meade Club, Centennial Club, Phi Beta Kappa, Pi Beta Phi. Republican. Presbyterian. Office: 5 Strawberry Hill Nashville TN 37215-4118

MCMURRY, JOHN EDWARD, chemistry educator; b. N.Y.C., July 27, 1942; s. Edward and Marguerite Ann McMurry; m. Susan Elizabeth Sobuta, Sept. 4, 1964; children: Peter Michael, David Andrew, Paul Matthew. BA, Harvard U., 1964; MA, Columbia U., 1965, PhD, 1967. Prof. chemistry U. Calif., Santa Cruz, 1967-80, Cornell U., Ithaca, N.Y., 1980—. Author: Organic Chemistry, 2000, Chemistry, 2001, other textbooks; assoc. editor: Accounts of Chem. Rsch., 1975—95. Recipient Humboldt Sr. Sci. award, 1987; Sloan Found. fellow, 1969-71; Career awardee NIH, 1975-80. Fellow AAAS; mem. Am. Chem. Soc. Home: 625 Highland Rd Ithaca NY 14850-1411 Office: Cornell Univ Dept Chemistry Baker Lab Ithaca NY 14853 E-mail: jem24@cornell.edu.

MCMURRY, WILLIAM MORTIMER, retired sales executive; b. Miami, Dec. 30, 1926; s. Charles Taylor and Elizabeth Lucille (Lemmon) McM.; m. Vivian Smolorski, Dec. 2, 1950 (div. Nov. 1979); children: Charles Michael, Nancy Jane, William Patrick. BS in Chemistry, U. Fla., 1950. Lic. pvt. pilot. Pharm. sales rep. Charles Pfizer & Co., N.Y.C., 1950-57; pharm. sales rep. Hoffman-LaRoche Labs., Nutley, N.J., 1958-65; med. electronics sales IVAC, Jacksonville, Fla., 1966-67; stock broker Hayden-Stone, Inc., 1967-70; store mgr. Rhodes Furniture Co., 1971-78; pres. McMurry & Company (import/export), 1980-89. Libr., mem. ch. coun., mem. choir West Normandy Bapt. Ch., Jacksonville. With U.S. Navy, 1944-46. Mem. Mensa (co-founder chpt. 1952), Phi Gamma Delta. Baptist. Avocations: astronomy, particle physics, Actinides/Lanthanides rsch., gardening, computering. Home: 1624 Brier Way E Jacksonville FL 32221-1433

MC MURTRY, JAMES GILMER, III, neurosurgeon; b. Houston, June 11, 1932; s. James Gilmer and Alberta Elizabeth (Matteson) McMurtry. Student, Rice U., Houston, 1950—53; MD cum laude, Baylor U., Houston, 1957. Intern Hosp. U. Pa., Phila., 1957—58; resident gen. surgery Baylor U. Affiliated Hosps., Houston, 1958—59; asst. neurol. surgery Coll. Physicians and Surgeons, Columbia U., N.Y.C., 1959—60; asst. resident neurol. surgery and neurology Neurol. Inst. N.Y., Columbia Presbyn. Med. Ctr., 1960—62, chief resident neurol. surgery, 1963—65, assoc., 1965—68, asst. prof. clin. neurol. surgery, 1968—73, assoc. prof., 1973—89, prof., 1989—. Asst. attending neurol. surgeon Neurol. Inst. N.Y., N.Y.C., 1964—73, assoc. attending neurol. surgeon, 1973—89, attending neurol. surgeon, 1989—; chief neurol. surgery clinic Vanderbilt Clinic, Columbia Presbyn. Med. Ctr., N.Y.C., 1964—68; attending-in-charge neurosurgery Lenox Hill Hosp., N.Y.C., 1970—91; assoc. cons. neurol. surgery Englewood (N.J.) Hosp., 1964—; asst. cons. neurol. surgery Harlem Hosp., N.Y.C., 1964—; cons. neurol. surgery Bronx (N.Y.) VA Hosp., 1964—65; mem. NIH Parkinson Rsch. Group, Columbia U., 1965—; mem. med. adv. bd. N.Y. State Athletic Commn. Author: Medical Examination Review Book-Neurological Surgery, 1970, rev. edit., 1975, Neurological Surgery Case Histories, 1975; contbr. articles. Trustee Glimmerglass Opera, Morris-Jumel, Opera Manhattan. Fellow Allen fellow dept. neurol. surgery, Columbia U., 1964—65; scholar Jesse H. Jones scholar, Baylor U. Coll. Medicine, 1953—57. Fellow: ACS, Linnean Soc. (London); mem.: AMA, AAAS, AAUP, The Med. Soc. of London, Med. Strollers, Baylor U. Coll. Medicine Alumni Assn., Osler Soc., N.Y. County Med. Soc., Med. Soc. State N.Y., N.Y. Neurosurg. Soc., N.Y. Acad. Sci., N.Y. State Neurosurgery Soc., N.Y. State Soc. Surgeons, Pan Am. Med. Assn., Am. Soc. Stereotaxic Surgeons, European Congress Pediatric Neurosurgery, Am. Assn. Neurol. Surgeons, The Harveian Soc., Norfolk Yacht and Country, Met. Opera (N.Y.C., dir. and v.p. 2002), The Garrick Club (London), The Union Club, The Atheneum (London), Alpha Omega Alpha. Home: 1 Cobb Ln Tarrytown NY 10591-3003 Office: 710 W 168th St New York NY 10032-2603

MCMURTRY, R. ROY, chief justice; b. Toronto, Ont., Can., May 31, 1932; s. Roland Roy and Doris Elizabeth (Belcher) McM.; m. Ria Jean Macrae, Apr. 18, 1957; children: Janet, James, Harry, Jeannie, Erin, Michael. BA with honors, U. Toronto, 1954; LLB, Osgoode Hall Law Sch., 1958; LLD (hon.), U. Ottawa, 1983, Leeds U., U.K., 1988, York U., 1991, U. Toronto, 1998. Bar: Called to bar 1958, created Queen's counsel 1970. Partner firm Benson, McMurtry, Percival and Brown; mem. Provincial Parliament for Eglinton, 1975-85; atty. gen. for Ont., 1975-85; solicitor gen. for Ont., 1978-82; high commnr. for Can. to Gt. Brit. and No. Ireland, 1985-88; ptnr. Blaney, McMurtry Stapells, Toronto, 1988-91; chmn. Can. Football League, 1989-91; assoc. chief justice Ont. Ct. Justice, Toronto, 1991-94, chief justice, 1994-96; chief justice of Ont. Ont. Ct. of Appeal, 1996—. Freeman of City of London, 1986. Mem. United Ch. of Can. Office: Ont Ct of Appeal 130 Queen St W Toronto ON Canada M5H 2N5

MCMURTRY, ROBERT Y. academic dean; b. Toronto, Mar. 6, 1941; s. Roland Roy and Elizabeth McMurtry; m. Jane Macdougall, May 6, 1979; children: Angus, Abbey, Sean, Meghan. MD, U. Toronto, 1965, FRCSC, 1972. FRCSC. Fellow Hosp. Sick Children, Toronto, Can., 1972-74; orthopedic surgeon, head dept. emergency svcs., founder and dir. regional trauma unit Sunnybrook Med. Ctr., 1975-87; asst. to assoc. prof. U. Toronto, 1976-87; head dept. surgery Foothills Hosp., Calgary, Can., 1988-92; dean faculty medicine U. Western (Can.) Ont., 1992-99, dean faculty medicine and dentistry, 1997-99; Cameron chair Health Can., 1999-2001, vis. asst. dep. min. Population and Pub. Health br., 2000—01, asst. dep. min., 2001—02; spl. advisor to commr. Royal Commn. of Health Care in Can., 2002—. Worker Mission Hosp./Can. Internat. Devel. Agy., Africa, 1965-70; chmn. dept. surgery, prof. surgery U. Calgary, 1988-92; vis. prof., Can and internationally; chmn. provincial com. on role, function and financing acad. health ctrs., 1994-95; reviewer Provincial Cancer Network, 1994-95. Editor: Management of Blunt Trauma, 1990; contbr. articles to profl. jours. and chpts. to books. Am., Brit. Can. Travelling fellow, 1981. Fellow ACS, Royal Coll. Surgeons (Can.); mem. Med. Rsch. Coun. Can., Assn. Can. Med. Colls., Can. Orthopedic Assn., Coll. Physicians and Surgeons Ont., Can. Med. Protective Assn., Ont. Med. Assn. Address: 83 Mackay St Ottawa ON Canada K1M 2E4

MCNAB, SUSAN ELIZABETH, human resources executive; b. Nov. 4, 1949; d. James Orville and Betty Edith (Westlake) McN. BA, Purdue U., 1971; MA, U. Md., 1977; MBA, U. Puget Sound, 1984; postgrad., Fielding Inst., 1998—. SPHR lic. Assoc. buyer Procter & Gamble, Cin., 1971-72; counselor U. Md., College Park, 1972-73; pers. cons. Girl Scouts U.S., Burlingame, Calif., 1973-76; pers. and safety supt. Monsanto Corp., Seattle, 1976-80; mgr. pers. St. Louis, 1980-82; dir. pers. Lanoga Corp., Seattle, 1982-85, v.p., 1986-87; sr. v.p. human resources Ernst Home and Nursery, 1987-90; mgr. human resources Komo TV, 1996; v.p. human resources and adminstrn. Wizards of the Coast, 1997—. Lectr. in field. Contbg. author: Strike Preparation Manual, 1982; contbr. articles to profl. jours. Pres. Totem coun. Girl Scouts U.S., Seattle, 1986-90; bd. dirs. Seattle Seafair Orgn., 1980, Gov.'s Com. for Handicapped, St. Louis, 1980-82, Intiman Theater, 1998—; pres. Chinook Learning Ctr. and Capital Campaign Com., 1986-90, Grace Found., 1996—; bd. dirs. Ethnic Heritage Coun., 1997—, pres., 1998—; mem. U. Wash. Vis. Com., Sch. Social Work, 1999—. Named Time Mag. Newsmaker of Tomorrow, 1978, Outstanding Sr. Woman, Purdue U., 1971; recipient Cmty. Action award Girl Scouts U.S., 1980. Mem. Soc. for Human Resources Mgmt. (nat. com. employee and labor rels.), Internat. Tng. in Comm. (v.p. chpt. 1986-87, winner Internat. Speech Contest 1986, Toastmistress), Pacific N.W. Pers. Mgmt. Assn. (pres. 1998-99), Rotary (chair cmty. svc. com. Seattle club 1988-90, 97—, bd. dirs. 1999—), Jr. League Seattle, Wash. Athletic Club, Seattle Yacht Club. Roman Catholic. Home: 252 Lake Dell Ave Seattle WA 98122-6311 Office: Wizards of the Coast 1801 Lind Ave SW Renton WA 98055-4068

MCNABB, CORRINE RADTKE, librarian; b. Detroit, Dec. 18, 1956; d. Eugene R. and Dorothy A. (Dorosz) Radtke; m. Daniel M. McNabb, Oct. 6, 1978; children: Brynne Catherine, Kalen Daniel. BA, Aquinas Coll., 1978; MS, Drexel U., 1982, cert. advanced study, 1997. Cert. tchr., Pa., 1997. Assoc. Nat. Libr. Medicine, Bethesda, Md., 1982-83; dir. libr. svcs. Carbondale (Pa.) Gen. Hosp., 1983-85; libr. dir. Interboro Libr., Peckville, Pa., 1985-86; reference libr. U. Scranton, 1986-87; libr. Cmty. Med. Ctr., Scranton, 1987-95; elem. libr. Carbondale Area Sch. Dist., 1995-96, Mountain View Sch. Dist., Kingsley, Pa., 1996—. Bd. dirs. Carbondale Pub. Libr., 1993—. Mem. ASCD, ALA, Pa. Sch. Librs. Assn. Roman Catholic. Avocations: reading, travel, walking. Home: RR 1 Box 1104 Carbondale PA 18407-9015 Office: Mountain View Elem Libr RR 1 Box 339A Kingsley PA 18826-9778 E-mail: mcnabber@icontech.com.

MCNABB, DIANNE LEIGH, investment banker, accountant; b. Huntsville, Ala., Sept. 7, 1956; d. Walter David and Mary Josephine (Hawkins) McN.; m. William Roland Lantz, July 1, 1983; 1 child, Sarah Elizabeth. BS in Acctg., U. Ala., Tuscaloosa, 1976. CPA, Ga., Ala. Acct. Lilly Flagg Assocs. & Subsidiaries, Huntsville, 1977-78; mgr. Johnston, Joyce & Wigginton, CPA's, 1978-84; sr. mgr. KPMG Peat Marwick, CPA's, Atlanta, 1984-91; mng. dir. A.G. Edwards & Sons, Inc., 1991—. Mem. ways and means com. Atlanta Jr. League, 1991-98; instr., advisor Jr. Achievement, Atlanta, 1985-88; mem. hospitality com. Dem. Nat. Conv., Atlanta, 1988; vol. Ga. Spl. Olympics, Atlanta, 1989-91. Mem. AICPA, Govt. Fin. Officers Assn. (spl. rev. com. 1991-95), Ga. Soc. CPA (govtl. acctg. and auditing com. 1992), Assn. of Govt. Accts. (bd. dirs. Atlanta chpt. 1990-92), Ala. Soc. CPA (sec.-treas. 1984), Am. Soc. Women Accts. (pres. Huntsville chpt. 1983-84), U. Ala. Alumni Assn. (treas. 1983-84), Zeta Tau Alpha (advisor 1988-93, v.p. 1983, treas. 1987-89, pres. 1984, 89-91, panhellenic del. 1988-91, dist. pres. 1993-95, Cert. of Merit 1992, Zeta Lady award 1991, Alum Chum award 1991). Avocations: tennis, scuba. Home: 2530 Alpine Way Duluth GA 30096-4440 Office: A G Edwards 3399 Peachtree Rd NE Ste 1100 Atlanta GA 30326-1150

MCNABB, DONOVAN, football player; b. Chgo., Nov. 25, 1976; s. Samuel and Wilma McNabb. Degree in speech comm., Syracuse U., 1998. Backup guard Syracuse's basketball teams, 1995—96, 1996—97; profl. football player Phila. Eagles, 1999—. Co-host with Beasley Reece The Donovan McNabb Show. Established own scholarship found.; serve Life as a Rookie panel rookie symposium, 2000. Office: Phila Eagles NovaCare Way Philadelphia PA 19145*

MCNABB, KEVIN LAVERNE, physician assistant, military officer; b. Keosauqua, Iowa, Apr. 24, 1960; s. Kenneth LaVerne and Pearl Pauline (Randolph) McN.; m. Charlotte Ann Burkett, June 28, 1981; children: Megan Ann, Travis Richard, Rachel Elaine, Kelly LaVerne (dec.), Celine Aimalee, Hunter Esmond. BS, U. Nebr. Med. Ctr., Omaha, 1993, M Physician Asst., 1997. Cert. physician asst., Nat. Commn. of Physician Assts. Commd. 2d lt. USAF, 1993, advanced through grades to capt., 1997; primary care physician asst. 89th Med. Ops., Andrews AFB, Md., 1993-94, mucosal exposure protocol officer, 1994; family practice physician asst. 55th Med. Ops., Offutt AFB, Nebr., 1994—2001; asst. course supr. Phase II physician asst. program Offutt AFB, 1997-99; mem. pharmacy and therapeutics com. 55th Med. Group, Offutt AFB, 1995—2001; med. cons. 341 Med. Ops., Malmstrom AFB, Mont., 2001—. Mem. Soc. Air Force Physician Assts., 1991—. Democrat. Methodist. Avocations: hunting, fishing, camping, reading, travel. Home: 1222 Locust St Great Falls MT 59405-7978 Office: 341 Med Ops/SGO PRP 7300 N Perimeter Rd Great Falls MT 59402 E-mail: KCMTR1@juno.com., kevin.mcnabb@malmstrom.af.mil.

MCNABB, LEONARD MATTHEW, clinical social worker, administrator; b. Hornell, N.Y., Nov. 24, 1948; s. John Wallace and Loretta Catherine (Leonard) McN.; m. Marla Sue Krakowsky, Dec. 19, 1970; 1 child, Alissa Marie. BS, Shippensburg U., 1970; MSW, Marywood Coll., 1973; postgrad., U. Scranton. Coord. St. Michael's Sch. for Boys, Hoban Heights, Pa., 1973-74; human svc. planner Wyo. County Children and Youth, Tunkhannock, 1974-76, supr., 1976-78; social svcs. mgr. United Svcs. Agy., Wilkes-Barre, 1978-81; clinician Advanced Psychol. Svcs., Tunkannock, 1990—; mgr. Community Counseling Svcs., 1981—. Bd. dirs. Victims Resources Policy Bd., Tunkhannock, 1986—. Asst. patrol dir. Montage Nat. Ski Patrol, 1988. Grantee Bur. of Corrections, 1971. Mem. NASW, Acad. Cert. Social Workers (diplomate in clin. social wk.), Alpha Delta Mu. Avocations: skiing, running, golf, mustangs. Home: 1017 Sleepy Hollow Rd Clarks Summit PA 18411-2709 Office: Community Counseling Svcs 99 Bridge St Tunkhannock PA 18657-1303

MCNABB, TALMADGE FORD, religious organization administrator, retired military chaplain; b. Johnson City, Tenn., Mar. 22, 1924; s. Robert Pierce and Dora Isabelle (Bailey) McN.; m. Nesbia Orlene Boswell, Dec. 3, 1950 (dec.); children: Darlene Roberta, Marla Dawn; m. Pirkko Marjotta Pelttari, Nov. 11, 1962; children: Valerie Anne, Lisa Rhea, Marcus Duane. Student, East Tenn. State U., 1941-43, 46; BA, Southwestern U. Assemblies of God, Waxahachie, Tex., 1947, BTh, 1949; BS, Birmingham Southern Coll., 1952; MA, U. Ala., 1957; HHD (hon.), S.E. Univ., Greenville, S.C., 1978. Ordained to ministry Assemblies of God, 1959. Evangelist Assemblies of God, 1948-49; pastor 1st Assembly of God, Warrior, Ala., 1949-53, Tuscaloosa, 1955-56; commd. 1st lt. U.S. Army, 1955, advanced through grades to lt. col., 1966, chaplain Ala., 1953-54, Korea, 1954-55, Ft. Benning, Ga., 1957-59, France, 1959-61, Ft. Knox, Ky., 1961-66, Ft. Dix, N.J., 1967-69, chaplain William Beaumont Hosp. El Paso, Tex., 1971-72, ret., 1972; writer, evangelist, speaker, 1973—; founder, pres. Worldwide Christian Ministries, Browns Mills, N.J., 1981—. Ministered in Ecuador, India, Russia, China, France, Belgium, The Netherlands. Contbr. articles on religious and ethnic topics to newspapers and mags. Mem. DAV (life), Mil. Ret. Officers Assn. (life), Mil. Chaplains Assn. (life, del.). Republican. Home and Office: Worldwide Christian Ministries 1 Springfield Rd Browns Mills NJ 08015-6709 *I believe every person born into this world is gifted by God the Creator with special talents and gifts, and has a niche to fill no other person can fill; to fulfill God's purpose for us is our greatest accomplishment.*

MCNAIR, CARL HERBERT, JR. army officer, aeronautical engineer; b. Pensacola, Fla., Sept. 22, 1933; s. Carl Herbert and Hallie Rebecca (Edwards) McN.; m. Jo Ann Wilson, Oct. 26, 1957; children: Cynthia Leigh, Carl Herbert III, Courtney Ann. BS, U.S. Mil. Acad., 1955; B.Aero. Engring., MS in Aero. Engring., Ga. Inst. Tech., 1963; MS in Pub. Adminstrn., Shippensburg State Coll., 1971. Commd. 2d lt. U.S. Army, 1955, advanced through grades to maj. gen., 1987; comdr. troop brigade U.S. Army Aviation Ctr., Fort Rucker, Ala., 1974-75; dep. for aviation to asst. sec. of Army Office Sec. of Army, U.S. Army, Washington, 1975-77, exec. to dep. chief of staff for research, devel. and acquisition, 1977-78; dep. dir. requirements and aviation officer Office of Dep. Chief of Staff for Ops. and Plans, 1978-79; dep. comdg. gen. U.S. Army Aviation Ctr., Fort Rucker, Ala., 1979-80, comdg. gen., 1980-83; dep. chief of staff combat devels. U.S. Army Tng. and Doctrine Command, Fort Monroe, Va., 1983-84, chief of staff, 1985-87; ret. U.S. Army, 1987; v.p. Burdeshaw Assocs., Ltd., Bethesda, Md., 1988-90; pres. Dyncorp Support Svcs. Div., Reston, Va., 1990-94, Dyncorp Enterprise Mgmt., Reston, 1994-99; corp. v.p. Dyncorp, 1994-99. Spl. asst. to CEO, Dyncorp, 1999—; bd. dirs., chmn. audit com. Air Methods Corp., Englewood, Colo., 1995—; mem. strategic adv. bd. A&T Systems, Inc., Silver Spring, Md., 2002--; chmn. bd. Dynport Vaccine Co., Frederick, Md., 1997--. Contbr. articles to profl. jours. Pres. Uniformed Svcs. Benefit Assn., Kansas City, Mo., 1980-82, (life) Assn. of U.S. Army, Washington, 1988-92, Washington chpt., exec. v.p. 2 region 1992-96, pres. 2 region 1996-98, coun. of trustees, chmn. fin. com., audit com., 1997—; v.p. Ala.-Fla. coun. Boy Scouts Am., Dothan, Ala., 1979-83; mem. nat. bd. dirs. Mil. Cmty. Youth Ministries, 1988-93; pres. West Point Soc., Washington, 1992-95; mem. bd. dirs. Army Aviation Mus. Found.; mem. West Point Fund Com.; trustee U.S. Mil. Acad., 1992-2002, U.S. Mil. Acad. Assn. Grads.; lay leader Aldersgate United Meth. Ch., 2001—; bd. dirs. Army Hist. Found., 1999—. Decorated D.S.M. with oak leaf cluster, Legion of Merit with two leaf clusters, D.F.C. with three oak leaf clusters, Bronze Star medal with V devices with oak leaf cluster, Air medal with V devices and 51 oak leaf clusters, Disting. Service medal State of Ala.; named Disting. Grad. Sch. Aerospace Engring. Ga. Inst. Tech., Sigma Gamma Tau, 1963; recipient Silver Beaver Achievement Boy Scouts Am., 1981; recipient Crosses of Military Svc., Korean Conflict, Vietnam, Jeff Davis award United Daus. of the Confederacy, 1987, 88; numerous fgn. awards Korea, Vietnam, France, Republic of China. Mem. Assn. U.S. Army (mil. advisor 1979-87), Army Aviation Assn. Am. (life, v.p. 1979-83, 85-87, 90-93, sec.-treas. 1993-97, sr. v.p. 1997-99, pres. 1999-2001), Am. Def. Preparedness Assn. (bd. dirs. Washington chpt. 1993-97, sec. 1994-95, 2nd v.p. 1995-97, 1st v.p. 1997-98), Nat. Def. Indsl. Assn. (pres. Wash. chpt. 1998, bd. dirs. Wash. chpt.), Order of Daedalians (life), Am. Helicopter Soc., Air Force Assn., Navy League, Ret. Officers Assn. (life), Masons, Fairfax County C. of C. (bd. dirs.), Easter Seal Soc. (dir., child devel. ctr. of No. Va. adv. bd. 1996—, sec. bd. 1999--). Methodist. Home: 7821 Friars Ct Alexandria VA 22306-2717 Fax: 703-261-5050. E-mail: carl.mcnair@dyncorp.com. *The military service, perhaps more than any other profession, provides us with a unique opportunity to serve both our fellow man and our God -in preserving the Peace and the Freedom cherished by mankind. It is within such a framework that I have charted the course of my life, remembering always Duty-Honor-Country.*

MCNAIR, JOHN FRANKLIN, III, banker; b. Laurinburg, N.C., Apr. 12, 1927; s. John Franklin and Martha (Fairley) McN.; m. Martha Fowler, June 16, 1951; children: John Franklin IV, Elizabeth Fowler. BS, Davidson Coll., 1949; postgrad., U. N.C., 1954-56. Pres. McNair Automotive Co., Inc., Laurinburg, 1949-66, The State Bank, Laurinburg, 1966-68; sr. v.p. Wachovia Bank & Trust, 1968-70, Raleigh, N.C., 1970-72, exec. v.p. Winston-Salem, 1972-77, vice chmn., 1977-85, The Wachovia Corp., Winston-Salem, 1977-87, pres., chief exec. officer, 1987-90, Wachovia Bank & Trust Co, 1987-90, also dir.; exec. v.p. First Wachovia Corp., 1986-90. Bd. dirs., pres. N.C. R.R. Co., 1993-97. Mem. N.C. State Hwy. Commn., Raleigh, 1965-69, Commn. on future N.C., Raleigh, 1981-83; chmn. N.C. Bd. Econ. Devel., 1979-85, N.C. Coun. Econ. Edn., Greensboro, 1980-82, Ind. Coll. Fund N.C., 1989-91, N.C. Citizens for Bus. and Industry, 1988-89; trustee Peace Coll., Raleigh, 1980-89, Davidson Coll., 1985-93, St. Andrews Presbyn. Coll., Laurinburg, N.C., 1968-75; trustee Old Salem, Inc., 1985-98, 99—, treas., 1990-97, chmn., 1997-98; trustee Winston-Salem Found., 1983-91, chmn., 1989-91; co-chmn. gov.'s adv. com. Superconducting Supercollider Project, 1988; trustee, mem. exec. com. Rsch. Triangle Found., 1986-99, vice chmn., 1990-93, chmn., 1992-2000; trustee exec. com. Winston-Salem Bus., Inc., 1986-02, chmn., 1990-95, mem. adv. coun., 2002--; mem. govt. performance com. State of N.C., 1991-93; bd. dirs. N.C. Enterprise Corp., 1988-93, Sr. Svcs., Inc., 1994—, exec. com., 1998—, chmn., 1999-2000; chmn. Qual Choice N.C. Inc., 1994-99, bd. dirs., 1994-2002; bd. mem. N.C. Stroke Assn., 1998—, Save Our State, 1998—. With USN, 1945-46. Recipient Young Man of Yr. award Laurinburg Jaycees, 1962, Silver Beaver award Boy Scouts Am., 1967, Disting. Alumni award Davidson Coll., 1994. Mem. Am. Bankers Assn. (state v.p. 1980-81), Res. City Bankers Assn., N.C. Bankers Assn. (pres. 1976-77), Old Town Club, Piedmont Club, St. Andrews Soc., Rotary. Democrat. Presbyterian. Home: 1244 Arbor Rd # 236 Winston Salem NC 27104 Office: Wachovia Bank NC 420 W 4th St Ste 100 Winston Salem NC 27101-2837 E-mail: jfmiii@bellsouth.net.

MCNAIR, JOHN WILLIAM, JR. civil engineer; b. Asheville, N.C., June 17, 1926; s. John William and Annie (Woody) McN.; m. June Clemens Kratz; childrn: Jeffry, Marsha, Cathy. BS in Forestry, Pa. State U., 1950; BSCE, Va. Poly Inst. State U., 1955; postgrad. in engring., U. Va., 1957-58. Registered profl. engr., Va. and other states. Forester U.S. Forest Svc., Flagstaff, Ariz., 1950, U.S. Gypsum Co., Altavista, Va., 1951; mem. engring. faculty U. Va., Charlottesville, 1955-58; prin. John McNair & Assocs., Waynesboro, Va., 1958—; owner Brucheum Group, 1983—; chmn., CEO Info. Systems Support, Inc., 1998—. With Va. Bd. Architects, Profl. Engrs. and Land Surveyors, 1969-79, v.p., 1977-78, pres., 1978-79. Author numerous engring. and land mgmt. study reports. Mem. Waynesboro City Coun., 1968-72, vice mayor, 1970-72; chmn. Waynesboro Indsl. Devel. Authority, 1984-2000. Capt. AUS, 1944-46, 51-53, France, Okinawa. Recipient Disting. Svc. cert. Va. Soc. Profl. Engrs., 1971. Fellow ASCE; mem. Acad. Environ. Engrs. (diplomate), Rotary, Rappahannock River Yacht Club (founding mem.). Republican. Presbyterian. E-mail: jmcnair@brucheum.com.

MCNAIR, NIMROD, JR. foundation executive, consultant; b. Tuscaloosa, Ala., Nov. 2, 1923; s. Nimrod and Salemma (Flowers) McN.; m. Amy Ernestine Phillips, Apr. 27, 1943; children: Janice Lee McNair Bradd, John Rodney. BSChemE, U. Ala., 1949; MS in Aerospace Engring., Air Force Inst. Tech., 1961. Cert. mgmt. cons. Sales engr. Hunt Oil Co., Tuscaloosa, 1949-51; commd. officer USAF, 1950, advanced through grades to lt. col., 1966; prof. N.C. State U., Raleigh, 1951-55; command pilot SAC, 1955-59; grad. student USAF Inst. Tech.; dir. space planning Space Div., L.A., 1961-65; dir. mgmt. rsch. and devel. USAF, Dayton, 1969-72, staff officer, Pentagon Washington, 1965-68, reconnaissance pilot Vietnam, 1968-69; ret., 1972; pres. Exec. Leadership, Inc., Chgo., 1973-80, Exec. Ministries, Inc., Atlanta, 1981-86; chmn., chief exec. officer, bd. dirs. Environ. Control Atlanta, Inc., 1973—, McNair Assocs., Inc., Atlanta, 1980—, Exec. Leadership Found., Inc., Atlanta, 1986—. Bd. dirs. ADA Metals, Inc., Lincolnwood, Ill.; developer, instr. bus. ethics program, U.S., Can., South Am., West Europe, East Europe, U.S.S.R. Author; Mega Values--Ten Principles for Business Success, Ten Principles for a Successful Marriage. Trustee Rep. Presl. Task Force; Rep. cand. for Gov., Ga., 1994. Decorated DFC, medal (Vietnam); recipient Gov.'s award State of Ky., State of Ark., Commendation award for bus. ethics program U.S. Pres., Chief Exec. Officer of Fortune 500 Corps., numerous awards for speaking. Mem. Am. Mgmt. Assn. President's Assn., Ret. Officers Assn., Christian Businessmen's Com. U.S.A., Inst. for Absolute Ethics (assoc., bd. dirs.), Air Force Assn., Internat. Platform Assn., Nat. Speakers Assn., Nat. Honor Soc., Tau Beta Pi, Phi Eta Sigma. Anglican. Avocations: flying, travel, reading. Office: Exec Leadership Found 4090 Northlake Creek Cv Tucker GA 30084-3416 Fax: 770-491-9039. E-mail: nimrodmcnair@aol.com.

MCNAIR, NORMA DIANNE, nurse; b. Berkeley, Calif., July 1, 1953; d. Norman David and Shirley Claire (Grady) McNair. BSN, Calif. State U., 1976; MSN, Yale U., 1985; nurse practitioner cert., Calif. State U., Long Beach, 1997. Staff nurse Sutter Gen. Hosp., Sacramento, 1976-79, U. Calif., Sacramento, 1979-80, The Nat. Hosp., London, 1980-81, Sutter Gen. Hosp., Sacramento, 1982-83, Hosp. St. Raphael, New Haven, 1984; clin. nurse specialist, trainee Veteran's Adminstrn., West Haven, 1984-85; clin. nurse specialist Hermann Hosp., U. Tex. Med. Sch., Houston, 1986-89, Mercy Gen. Hosp., Sacramento, 1989-91, UCLA Med. Ctr., 1991—. Cultural Affairs, Am. Red Cross, Houston, 1987-88. Mem. ANA, AACN, Am. Assn. Neuroscience Nurses (bd. dirs. 1988-90). Democrat. Presbyterian. Avocations: water skiing, snow skiing, snorkeling. E-mail: nmcnair@mednet.ucla.edu.

MCNAIR, RUSSELL ARTHUR, JR. lawyer; b. Detroit, Dec. 2, 1934; s. Russell Arthur and Virla (Standish) McN.; m. Rosemary M. Chesbrough, Apr. 6, 1957; children: Julie McNair Schwerin, Russell Arthur III, Douglas S. AB in Econs. cum laude, Princeton U., 1956; JD with distinction, U. Mich., 1960. Bar: Mich. 1960, Fla. 2001. Assoc. Dickinson, Wright, Moon, Van Dusen & Freeman (now Dickinson Wright, PLLC), Detroit, 1960-67, ptnr., 1968-98, chmn., 1994-98. Cons. Evans & Luystale, Boca Raton, 2000-; adj. prof. U. Detroit Sch. Law, 1968-72; mem. adv. bd. Fin. Transactions Inst., 1984-94; adj. prof. Wayne State U. Law Sch., 1994-96; spkr. in field. Trustee Children's Home, Detroit, 1975-95, pres. 1986-87, hon. trustee 1995—; mem. community leaders coun., United Way, 1994-98; dir. Mich. Jobs Commn., 1995-98. Mem. Mich. Bar Assn., Detroit Bar Assn., Am. Law Inst., Am. Coll. Real Estate Lawyers. Republican. Presbyterian. Avocations: golf, tennis, platform tennis. Home: 4383 Gleneagles Dr Boynton Beach FL 33436-4802 Office: Evans & Lyptak 4th Fl 4700 NW Boca Raton Blvd Boca Raton FL 33431 E-mail: ramcnair@aol.com., ramcnair@bellsouth.net.

MCNAIR, STEVE LATREAL, professional football player; b. Mount Olive, Miss., Feb. 14, 1973; m. Mechelle McNair; 1 child, Tyler. Student, Mt. Olive H.S. Quarterback Tenn. Oilers (now called Tenn. Titans), 1995—. Became youngest (25) and only fourth quarterback in franchise history to post 3000 yard passing seasons, 1999, joining Warren Moon, George Blanda and Ken Stabler; 1997 total was 3d highest rushing total by a quarterback in NFL history behind Randall Cunningham (942 yards in 1990) and Bobby Douglas (968 yards in 1972); has started 33 consecutive games entering 1999 season. Office: Tennessee Titans 460 Great Circle Rd Nashville TN 37228-1404*

MCNAIR, TIMOTHY DEAN, lawyer; b. Richfield, Ohio, Aug. 21, 1954; s. Fred Denman and Marjorie Faye (Grady) McN.; m. Karin P. Sarner Loucy, Oct. 22, 1988; 1 child, Peter Michael; stepchildren: James Sarner Loucy, Gregory Sarner Loucy, Brianne Patrice Loucy. BA, Allegheny Coll., 1977; JD, U. Pitts., 1981. Bar: Pa. 1981. Jud. clk. to Hon. Jess S. Jiuliante Ct. Common Pleas, Erie, Pa., 1982-84; assoc. Schroeck & Segel, 1984-87, Bifulco, Scarpitti et al, Erie, 1987-90; ptnr. Vendetti Talarico & McNair, 1990-94, Talarico & McNair, Erie, 1994-97; pvt. practice, 1997—. Mem. exec. com. Erie County Dem. Party, 2000—, parliamentarian, 2001—. Owens fellow U. Pitts., 1979-81. Mem. ATLA, Pa. Trial Lawyers Assn. (bd. govs. 1996—), Erie County Bar Assn. Presbyterian. Avocations: computer technology, boating. Office: 821 State St Erie PA 16501-1316 E-mail: tmcnair@velocity.net.

MCNAIRN, PEGGI JEAN, speech pathologist, educator; b. Dallas, Sept. 22, 1954; d. Glenn Alton Harmon and Anna Eugenia (McVay) Hicks; m. Kerry Glen McNairn, Jan. 27, 1979; children: Micah Jay, Nathan Corey. BS in Speech Pathology, Tex. Christian U., 1977, MS in Communications Pathology, 1978; PhD in Edn., Kennedy Western U., 1991. Cert. speech pathologist, mid mgmt., asst. tech. practitioner. Staff speech pathologist, asst. dir. infant program Easter Seal Soc. for Crippled Children and Adults Tarrant County, Ft. Worth, 1978-80; staff speech pathologist, spl. edn. lead tchr. Sherrod Elem. Sch. Arlington (Tex.) Ind. Sch. Dist., 1981-84, secondary speech/lang. specialist, early childhood assessment staff, 1984-89, mem. state forms com., 1985-86, chairperson assessment com., 1986-87; owner, dir. Speech Assocs., 1989—92; cons. augmentative communication Prentke Romich Co., 1992-97; distance learning coord. Edn. Svc. Ctr., Tex. Womens U., 1998—2001; with Edn. Svc. Ctr., Ft. Worth, 2001—. Adj. prof., clin. supr. Tex. Christian U., Ft. Worth, 1978-79; clin. speech pathologist North Tex. Home Health Assn., Ft. Worth, 1980-92; adj. prof. Tex. Women's Univ., 1997—. Author: Quick Tech Activities for Literacy, 1993, Readable, Repeatable Stories and Activities, 1994, Quick Tech Magic: Music-Based Literacy Activities, 1996, AAC Feature Match Software, 1996, A First Course in Dysphagia, 2001. Chair United Cerebral Palsy Toy Lending Libr., 1989-90; dir. comms. & tech. Easter Seal Soc. for Children & Adults; sunday sch. tchr. 1st United Meth. Ch., Arlington, 1982-87; active South Arlington Homeowners Assn., Arlington, 1985-87; 3rd v.p. Bebensee Elem. PTA. Recipient Outstanding Svc. to Handicapped Am. Biog. Inst., 1989; Cert. of Achievement John Hopkins U. for computing to assist persons with disabilities, 1991. Mem. Internat. U.S. Tex. Socs. for Augmentative and Alternate Comm. (sec. Tex. branch, exec. bd. mem. 1996—), Neurodevelopmental Assn., Assn. for Curriculum and Supervision, Am. Speech and Hearing Assn., Tex. Speech-Lang.-Hearing Assn., Tex. Speech and Hearing Assn. (task force mem for augmentative comm.) Teaching Tex. Tots Consortium, Tex. Christian U. Speech and Hearing Alumni Assn., Kappa Delta Pi, Alpha Lambda Delta. Democrat. Avocations: doll making, sewing. Home: 4924 Brazoswood Cir Arlington TX 76017-1094 Office: Edn Svc Ctr 3001 North Fwy Fort Worth TX 76106

MCNALL, SCOTT GRANT, sociology educator; b. New Ulm, Minn., Jan. 16, 1941; s. Everett Herman and Dorothy Grant (Brown) McN.; m. Sally Anne Allen, Oct. 31, 1960; children— Miles Allen, Amy Ellen BA, Portland State U., 1962; PhD, U. Oreg., 1965. Instr. sociology U. Oreg., Eugene, 1964-65; asst. prof. U. Minn., Mpls., 1965-70; from assoc. prof. to prof. Ariz. State U., Tempe, 1970-76; prof., chmn. dept. sociology U. Kans., Lawrence, 1976-89, prof, chmn. dept. Am. studies, 1989-90; dean coll. arts and scis. U. Toledo, 1990-94; provost, v.p. acad. affairs Calif. State U., Chico, 1994—. Author: The Sociological Experience, 1969, 3d edit., 1974, The Greek Peasant, 1974, Social Problems Today, 1975, Career of a Radical Rightist, 1975, (with Sally A. McNall) Plains Families: Exploring Sociology Through Social History, 1983, The Road to Rebellion, 1988; editor: The Sociological Perspective, 1968, 4th edit., 1977, Theoretical Perspectives in Sociology, 1979, Current Perspectives in Social Theory, 1980, 6th edit., 1985, Political Economy: A Critique of American Society, 1981, (jour.) Current Perspectives in Social Theory, 1980-87, (with others) Studies in Historical Social Change, 1986—, The Road to Rebellion: Class Formation and Kansas Populism, 1865-1900, 1988, (with Rhonda Levine) Bringing Class Back In, 1991, (with Sally A. McNall) Sociology, 1992; assoc. editor: The Am. Sociologist, 1975-78, Jour. Polit. and Mil. Sociology, 1982—; adv. editor: Sociol. Quar., 1969-72; contbr. articles to profl. jours. Fulbright lectr., Greece, 1968-69; East-West Center vis. fellow, 1978; Mid-Am. State U. Assn. vis. lectr., 1982-83; Fulbright grantee, 1983 Mem. Midwest Sociol. Soc. (pres. 1982-83), Am. Sociol. Assn. (chair Marxist sect. 1989-90), Pacific Sociol. Soc. Democrat. Congregationalist. Home: 520 Crestwood Dr Paradise CA 95969-3825 Office: Calif State U VPAA Office Chico CA 95929

MCNALLY, ANDREW, IV, publishing executive, director; b. Chgo., Nov. 11, 1939; s. Andrew and Margaret C. (MacMillin) McN.; m. Jeanine Sanchez, July 3, 1966; children: Andrew, Carrie, Ward. BA, U. N.C., 1963; MBA, U. Chgo., 1969. Bus. mgr. edn. divsn. Rand McNally & Co., Chgo., 1967-70, exec. v.p., sec., 1970-74, pres., 1974-97, CEO, 1978-97, also chmn. bd. dirs., 1993-97; prin. Hammond Kennedy Whitney, 1998—; chmn. River Rd. Ptnrs., 1998—. Bd. dir. Hubbell Inc., Reinhold Industries, Seneca Inc. Trustee Newberry Libr.; bd. dirs. Children's Meml. Hosp.; active vis. com. of libr. U. Chgo. With Air Force N.G., 1963-69. Mem. Chgo. Club, Saddle and Cycle Club, Commonwealth Club, Glen View Golf Club, Racquet Club, Links (N.Y.C.). Office: Hammond Kennedy Whitney 333 N Michigan Ave Ste 501 Chicago IL 60601-3903

MCNALLY, CONNIE BENSON, magazine editor, publisher, antiques dealer; b. Chgo. d. Peter D. and Joanna Agriostathes; m. Dick Benson, Nov. 19, 1955 (div. mar. 1961); 1 child, Douglas; m. William C. McNally, July 27, 1975. Student, Univ. Wis., 1954-55; BA, Baylor, 1962. Midwest supr. Slenderella Internat., Chgo., 1955-59; dir. John Roberts Powers Sch., Dallas, 1960-62; backgammon tchr., profl. Racquet Club, Palm Springs, Calif., 1969-75, La Costa (Calif.) Resort, 1973-75; antique dealer Palm Springs, 1975—; ptnr. Carriage Trade Antiques, 1975-78; owner, mgr. McNally Co. Antiques, 1978—; editor, pub. Silver Mag., Inc., Rancho Santa Fe, Calif, 1993—. Mem. Am. Assn. Antique Dealers, Antique Dealers Assn. Calif., Country Firends (vol. chair 1985-87, area dir. 1988-89, publicity chair 1990-91, program chair 1992-93, corr. sec. 1994-95, bd. dirs.), Social Svc. League La Jolla, Soc. Am. Silversmiths, Rancho Santa Fe Rep. Women's Club. Avocations: equestrian, gourmet cook. Office: Silver Mag Inc PO Box 9690 Rancho Santa Fe CA 92067-4690

MCNALLY, JAMES HENRY, physicist, defense consultant; b. Orange, N.J., Dec. 18, 1936; s. James Osborne and Edith Maude (Jones) McN.; m. Nancy Lee Eudaley, July 4, 1976. B. in Engring. Physics, Cornell U., 1959; PhD in Physics, Calif. Inst. Tech., 1966. Staff mem. program mgr. Los Alamos (N.Mex.) Nat. Lab., 1965-74; asst. dir for laser and isotope separation tech. AEC/ERDA, Washington, 1974-75; assoc. div. leader, dep. for inertial fusion, asst. for nat. sec. issues Los Alamos Nat. Lab., 1975-86; dep. asst. dir. Arms Control and Disarmament Agy., Washington, 1986-88; dir. office staff Los Alamos Nat. Lab., 1988-90, Washington Inst., 1990-94; cons., 1990—. U.S. del. Geneva Conf. on Disarmament, 1969, 73, 74, Threshold Test Ban Treaty, Moscow, 1974, Nuclear Testing Talks, Geneva, 1986-88. Bd. dirs. Wilson Mesa Met. Water Dist., 1976-88; mem., v.p., pres. Mountain Canine Corps, 1994-98. Recipient Meritorious Honor award Arms Control and Disarmament Agy., 1988. Mem. AAAS, Am. Phys. Soc., Internat. Inst. Strategic Studies. Home and Office: 41 Bowen Rd Kittery ME 03904-1355

MCNALLY, JOHN JOSEPH, retired lawyer; b. N.Y.C., July 1, 1927; s. Edward E. and Virginia L. (O'Brien) McNally; m. Sally Vose Greeley, Jan. 25, 1958; children: Martha, Sarah, Elizabeth, Julie, Thomas. AB, Coll. Holy Cross, 1950; LLB, Harvard U., 1953. Bar: N.Y. 1953. Assoc. White & Case, N.Y.C., 1953-63, ptnr., 1964-94; ret., 1994. Bd. dirs. Mohawk Paper Mills, Inc. Pres. Lavelle Fund for the Blind, 1999—; bd. govs. Lawrence Hosp., Bronxville, NY, 1990—95; trustee Caedmon Sch., N.Y.C., 1968—, Lavelle Sch. for Blind, N.Y.C., 1997—99, All Hallows Found., 2000—, All Hallows H.S., N.Y.C., 2001. Fellow: Am. Bar Found.; mem.: Assn. Bar of City of N.Y., N.Y. County Lawyers Assn., N.Y. State Bar Assn. Home: 58 Avon Rd Bronxville NY 10708-1723 Office: White & Case 1155 Ave of Americas New York NY 10036-2711

MCNALLY, MICHAEL JAMES, priest; b. Waterloo, N.Y., July 30, 1947; s. James Arthur and Francesca (Ilacqua) McN. BA, St. Vincent DePaul Sem., Boynton Beach, Fla., 1969, MDiv, 1972, MTh, 1973; MA in History, U. Notre Dame, 1980, PhD in History, 1983. Ordained priest Roman Cath. Ch., 1973. Asst. pastor St. John Bosco Parish, Miami, Fla., 1973-74, Visitation Parish, Miami, 1974-75; dean of students, instr. religion St. John Vianney Coll. Sem., 1975-79; archivist Archdiocese of Miami, 1983-84; dir. permanent diaconate Diocese of Palm Beach, Palm Beach Gardens, Fla., 1985-86; archivist St. Vincent DePaul Sem., Boynton Beach, 1986-93, head spiritual dir., 1989-90; vis. prof. ch. history St. Charles Borroneo Sem., Wynnewood, Pa., 1993-95, prof. ch. history, homiletics, 1995—; full-time faculty mem. Pontifical Theol. Inst. St. Charles Borromeo Sem., 2000—. Prof. ch. history St. Vincent de Paul Sem., Boynton Beach, 1982-93; sec. to presbyterial coun. Diocese of Palm Beach, 1984-89; confessor Poor Clare Nuns, Delray Beach, 1984-93; adv. com. for study of Hispanics Cushman Ctr. for Study of Am. Catholicism, Notre Dame, Ind., 1990-92; chmn. libr. com. for reaccreditation St. Charles Borroneo Sem., 1997-98. Author: Catholicism in South Florida 1868-1968, 1984, Catholic Parish Life on Florida's West Coast, 1996; mem. com. on publ. Am. Cath. Hist. Soc. Jour. Am. Cath. Studies, 2001-02; contbr. articles to profl. jours. Mem. supt.'s adv. com. on tchg. religion Palm Beach County Pub. Schs., 1987; mem. com. on publ. Am. Cath. Hist. Soc. jour. Am. Cath. Studies, 2001—; mem. theol. commn. Phila. Archdiocese, 2001—02. Cushwa fellow, 1982, St. Vincent de Paul Sem. Sabbatical grantee, 1990, Curé d'Ars award St. John Vianney Sem., Miami, Fla., 1999. Mem.: Am. Cath. Hist. Soc., Fla. Hist. Soc., So. Hist. Assn., Am. Soc. Ch. History, Am. Hist. Assn. Office: St Charles Borromeo Sem 100 E Wynnewood Rd Wynnewood PA 19096-3001

MCNALLY, RICHARD PATRICK, priest; b. Fall River, MA, Mar. 2, 1950; s. Michael Jerome and Anna Catherine (Wall) McN. BA, St. Mary's Coll., Winona, Minn., 1972; MA, Washington Theol. Union, Silver Spring, Md., 1978; Licentiate in Sacred Theology, Gregorian U., Rome, 1982. Joined Congregation Sacred Hearts, Roman Cath. Ch., ordained priest. Assoc. pastor St. Mary's and St. Francis chs., Fairhaven, Mass., 1975-80; retreat dir. Sacred Hearts Retreat House, Wareham, 1982-83; pastor Sts. Peter and Paul's Ch., Rochester, N.Y., 1983-86; dir. initial formation Congregation of Sacred Hearts, Cheverly, Md., 1986-88, provincial superior Fairhaven, 1988-91, provincial councillor, 1982-88; assoc. pastor St. Ann's Ch., Kaneohe, Hawaii, 1991—. Chpt. del. Congregation of Sacred Hearts, El Escorial, Spain, 1988, gen. councilor, 1994-2000; dir. Sacred Heart Retreat Ctr. Trustee Washington Theol. Union, 1988-91. Home and Office: 226 Great Neck Rd Wareham MA 02571

MCNALLY, THOMAS CHARLES, III, lawyer; b. San Francisco, Dec. 5, 1938; s. Thomas Charles and Claire Marie (Egan) McN.; m. Paula Ann Berger, Sept. 3, 1960; children: Megan, Martin, J. Tevis. BS, U. San Francisco, 1960; JD, U. Calif., San Francisco, 1963. Bar: Calif. 1964. Dep. atty. gen., State Calif., 1964; assoc. firm Bohnert, Flowers & McCarthy, San Francisco, 1965-68; asst. sec., counsel DiGiorgio Corp., 1968-73, sec., counsel, 1974-75; sec., gen. counsel Consol. Fibres, Inc., San Francisco, 1975-88, v.p., 1981-88, also bd. dirs.; of counsel McInerney & Dillon, P.C., Oakland, Calif., 1989-91; pvt. practice San Francisco, 1991—. Lectr. McGeorge Bar Rev., 1964-65, Continuing Edn. of Bar, U. Calif., 1975-76; judge moot ct. U. San Francisco, 1974-84; arbitrator Am. Arbitration Assn., NASD, 1988—. Co-chmn. Mill Valley Citizens Adv. Com., 1974-76; mem. pub. affairs com. San Francisco Assn. Mental Health, 1965-69; commr. Mill Valley Park and Recreation Commn., 1988-93, chmn., 1990; lector Roman Cath. ch. Mem. ABA, State Bar Calif., San Francisco Bar Assn., Olympic Club (bd. dirs. 1999—, v.p. 2001), Scott Valley Tennis Club (founder, bd. dirs. 1971-76, 80-82, pres. 1980-82), World Trade Club. Republican. Home: 108 Hawthorne Ave Larkspur CA 94939 Office: 455 Market St Ste 1900 San Francisco CA 94105-2448 E-mail: tmcnally@lmi.net.

MCNALLY, THOMAS WILLIAM, entrepreneur; b. Rockville Centre, N.Y., June 25, 1948; s. Robert John and Alice Elizabeth (Proulx) McN.; m. Margaret Caroline Rogers, May 6, 1972 (div. Feb. 1980); children: James Patrick, Katharine Valiant; m. Virginia May Harpley, Aug. 1990; 1 child, Keegan Proulx. Student, Hamilton Coll., 1966-69; BSBA in Econs., Old Dominion U., l977; postgrad., Am. Grad. Sch. Internat. Mgmt., Glendale, Ariz., 1979. Asst. v.p. lst Union Nat. Bank, Charlotte, N.C., 1977-8l, Merc. Trust Co., St. Louis, l98l-84; v.p. Citizens & So. Nat. Bank, Atlanta, l984-87; exec. v.p., prin. fin. officer Summit Bank Corp., 1987-91; exec. v.p. Summit Nat. Bank, 1988-91, also bd. dirs.; prin. JKK Cons. Corp., 1991—. Bd. dirs. Microbial Aquatic Treatment Systems. Bd. dirs. Candler Road Redevel. Corp., Atlanta, VP/GM Chemfree Corp. Mem. Japan-Am. Soc. Ga. Lutheran. Home: 5860 Wilbanks Dr Norcross GA 30092-1409 Office: 8 Meca Way Norcross GA 30093-2919 E-mail: tmcnally@chemfree.com.

MCNALLY, VINCENT JOSEPH, educator, researcher; b. Philadelphia, PA, Feb. 6, 1943; s. Joseph Edward McNally, Dorothy Elizabeth McNally nee Connor. PhD, Univ. of Dublin, Trinity College, Dublin, Ireland, 1971—77. Professor of Church History Sacred Heart School of Theology, Hales Corners, WI, 1992—2002; Assistant Professor of History Simon Fraser University, Burnaby, Canada, 1987—92. Author: (Book) The Lord's Distant Vineyard: A History of the Oblates and the Catholic Community in British Columbia, 2000, Reform, Revolution and Reaction: Archbishop John Thomas Troy and the Catholic Church in Ireland, 1787-1817, 1995, "Hope for the Future: the Church's Challenges of the New Millennium" , 2000, (Journal: Historical Studies) Challenging the Status Quo: An Examination of the History of Catholic Education in British Columbia, 1999, (Journal: Western Oblate Studies) "Fighting for a Foundation: Oblate Beginnings in Far Western Canada, 1847-1864, 1996, (Journal: Canadian Church Historical Soci) "Fighting City Hall: The Church Tax Exemption Battle Between the City and Roman Catholic Diocese of Victoria" , 1992, (Journal of Church and State) "Church-State Relations and American Influence in British Columbia before Confederation" , 1992, (Catholic Historical Review) "Archbishop John Thomas Troy and the Establishment of St. Patrick's, Maynooth, 1791-1795", 1981, (Book) Education Facsimiles 241-260: Catholic Emancipation, 1793-1829, 1976, (Research Project) Practicing What We Preach: Testing and Publishing a Guide for Implementing a Pastoral Theology of Acceptance and Reconciliation in Northern Ireland", 2001 (Assoc. of Theological Schools in US and Canada: Lilly Research Award, 2001), (Research Project:) "Challenging Prejudice: Creating a Theology of Acceptance and Reconciliation in the Schools of Northern Ireland, 2000 (Pew Charitable Trusts, 2000), (Research Award) Researching, Writing and Publishing of a survey history: Irish Catholics: The Catholic Church in Ireland from the Reformation to the Present, 1999 (Eli Lilly Fellowship, 1999), Developing Healthy Theological Imaginations, 1998 (Lilly Endowment Fellowship for Teaching and Learning in Theology and Religion, 1998). : American Catholic Historical Society (Peter Guilday Prize 1981). Avocation: travel and playing harpsichord. Office: Sacred Heart School of Theology P.O. Box 429 Hales Corners WI 53130 Office Fax: 414-529-6999. Personal E-mail: vmcnally@shst.edu. Business E-Mail: vmcnally@shst.edu.

MCNAMARA, AIDA SHAHID, insurance executive; b. Tehran, Iran, May 25, 1959; came to U.S., 1981; d. Labib and Esmat (Meshkat) S.; m. Cyrus Meshki, Oct. 24, 1977 (div. 1985); 1 child, Hamed; m. Bernard T. McNamara, Aug. 31, 1991; children: Hamed Meshki, Brendan McNamara, Dylan McNamara.[ ]M Econs., Farah Pahavi U., Tehran, 1981. CLU. Office mgr. Barnes Ins. Svc., Santa Monica, Calif., 1981-82; asst. to life specialist E.F. Hutton, 1982-84; salesperson Mut. Omaha, Burbank, Calif., 1984-86; ins. agt. Met. Life Ins. Co., Woodland Hills, 1986-88; ind. ins. agt., security rep., 1988—; dist. sales mgr. Mut. Omaha, L.A., 1991-98, Encino, Calif., 1998—. Mem. Nat. Assn. Life Underwriters (Nat. Quality Award), Nat. Assn. Securities Dealers, Am. Soc. CLUs and ChFCs, Million Dollar Round Table (chmn. coun.). Office: Mut Omaha 11845 W Olympic Blvd # 800 Los Angeles CA 90064 Fax: 310-268-0776. E-mail: aidaminla@aol.com.

MCNAMARA, ANN DOWD, medical technologist; b. Detroit, Oct. 17, 1924; d. Frank Raymond and Frances Mae (Ayling) Sullivan; m. Thomas Stephen Dowd, Apr. 23, 1949 (dec. 1980); children: Cynthia Dowd Restuccia, Kevin Thomas Dowd; m. Robert A. McNamara, June 15, 1985. BS, Wayne State U., 1947. Med. technologist Woman's Hosp. (now Hutzel Hosp.), Detroit, 1946-52, St. James Clin. Lab., Detroit, 1960-62; supr. histo-pathology lab. Hutzel Hosp., 1962-72, Mt. Carmel Mercy Hosp., 1972-87, ret., 1987. Docent Domino's Ctr. Architecture & Design, Ann Arbor, Mich. 1988. Mem. Am. Soc. Clin. Pathologists, Am. Soc. Med. Technology, Mich. Soc. Med. Technology, Nat. Soc. Histotechnology, Mich. Soc. Histotechnologists, Wayne State U. Alumni Assn., Smithsonian Assocs., Detroit Inst. Arts Founders Soc. Home: 2488 Signature Dr Pinckney MI 48169

MCNAMARA, BRENDA NORMA, secondary education educator; b. Blackpool, Lancashire, Eng., Aug. 8, 1945; came to U.S., 1946; d. Milford Hampson and Nola (Welsby) Jones; m. Michael James McNamara, July 19, 1969. BA in History, Calif. State U., Long Beach, 1967; postgrad., Calif. State U., various campuses, 1967—. Cert. secondary tchr. and lang. devel. specialist, Calif. Tchr. history West High Sch., Torrance, Calif., 1968—, dept. chair, 1989-99, 2000—. Cons. Calif. State Dept. Edn. Golden State Examination in History, 1998; state del. NEA Annual Meeting, 2000; cons. in field. Co-author: World History, 1988. Western Internat. Studies Consortium grantee, 1988. Mem. Calif. Tchrs. Assn., Calif. Coun. for Social Studies, Torrance Tchrs. Assn. (bd. dirs. 1992—), So. Calif. Coun. for Social Studies, Nat. Tchrs. Assn., Nat. Coun. for Social Studies, Am. Hist. Assn. Avocations: travel, theater, mystery reading, gourmet cooking. Office: West H S 20401 Victor St Torrance CA 90503-2255

MCNAMARA, DAVID JOSEPH, financial and tax planning executive; b. Osceola, Iowa, Feb. 6, 1951; s. Loras Emmett and Nadine Evelyn (DeLancey) McN.; m. Ruth Ellen Hanken, Oct. 4,1974; children: Benjamin, Shawna, Heather. BGS, U. Iowa, 1974. Cert. fin. planner Coll. Fin. Planning, 1985; registered prin. Nat. Assn. Securities Dealers. Pres. The Planners, 1985; ptnr. VF Realty Ptnrs., West Desmoines, Iowa, 1987—. Mem. Fin. Planning Assn. (bd. dirs. Iowa chpt. 1984-850. Republican. Office: Integrated Tax/Fin Planning Svc 1012 Grand Ave West Des Moines IA 50265-3255

MCNAMARA, DENNIS LOUIS, sociology educator; b. Portage, Wis., Mar. 11, 1945; s. Louis Vincent and Lucille Mary (O'Connell) McN. BA, St. Louis U., 1969; MA, Fordham U., 1974; MDiv, Jesuit Sch. Theology, Berkeley, 1976; PhD, Harvard U., 1983. Lectr. Sogang U., Seoul, Korea, 1969-72; instr. sociology Marquette U., 1976-77; fellow Inst. East Asian Studies, U. Calif., Berkeley, 1983-84; prof. sociology Georgetown U., Washington, 1984—, Park prof. sociology and Korean studies. Cons. Fgn. Svc. Inst., Washington, 1986—, Bus. Coun. for Internat. Understanding, Washington, 1987—, Coun. Fgn. Rels., 1999—; chmn. sociology dept. Georgetown U., 1995—. Author: Colonial Origins of Korean Enterprise, 1990, Textiles and Industrial Transition in Japan, 1995, Trade and Transformation in Korea, 1876-1945, 1996, Corporatism and Korean Capitalism, 1999, Market and Society in Korea, 2002; contbr. articles to profl. jours. Fulbright fellow Coun. for Internat. Exchange of Scholars, 1987, U. Calif. fellow, 1983, NSF fellow, 1991, Fulbright-Hayes fellow, Korea, 1992, Fulbright fellow, Japan, 1998. Mem. Am. Sociol. Assn. Assn. for Asian Studies, Internat. Sociol. Assn., Coun. on Fgn. Rels., Fulbright Alumni Assn. Roman Catholic. Avocations: golf, swimming. Office: Georgetown U Dept Sociology Washington DC 20057-0001 E-mail: mcnamara@georgetown.edu.

MCNAMARA, EMMA JULIA, information scientist; b. Havana, Cuba, Apr. 12, 1943; d. German E. and Emma H. (Sanchez) Fonseca; m. Thomas Edmund McNamara, June 11, 1966; children: David F., Michelle A. BA, U. Md., 1979, MLS, 1985. Libr. dir. Am. Sch., Kinshasa, Zaire, 1980-83; EPA libr. program dir. Labat Anderson Inc., Washington, 1986-88; cons. U.S. AID, Colombia, S.Am., 1989-91; program mgr. Infoterra NFP EPA, Washington, 1992—96, leader info. access team, 1996—98, dir. divsn., 1998—. Contbr. articles to profl. jours. Bd. dirs. Humanities Coun. of Washington, 1994-99; vol. Boy Scouts Am., Kinshasa, 1980-83, Brownie troop Girl Scouts USA, Kinshasa, 1980-83, Girl Scouts USA, Washington, 1984-88. Recipient Gold Rose award Govt. of Colombia, 1991. Mem. ALA, Spl. Libr. Assn., Am. Assn. of Fgn. Svc. Women, Army Navy Club, Beta Phi Mu. Avocations: reading, sailing, crafts, cooking, ikebana. Office: US EPA MC 2843 401 M St SW Washington DC 20460-0001

MCNAMARA, FRANCIS JOSEPH, JR. retired foundation executive, lawyer; b. Boston, Nov. 30, 1927; s. Francis Joseph and Louise (English) McN.; m. Noreen E. O'Connor, June 18, 1953 (dec. Feb. 1984); children: Francis Joseph III, Moira Patricia (Mrs. Lance F. James), John Allen, Kathleen Louise (Mrs. Robert J. Hugin), Martha Jeanne (Mrs. James R. Bordewick), Mark Jeffrey; m. Lois L. Magner, Jan. 17, 1986. AB, Georgetown U., 1949, LLB, 1951; LLD, Fairfield U., 1983. Bar: Conn. 1952. Assoc. firm Pullman, Comley, Bradley & Reeves, 1953; asst. U.S. Atty., dist. Conn., 1953-57; assoc. firm Cummings & Lockwood, Stamford, Conn., 1957-59, ptnr., 1959-91. Guest lectr. Salzburg (Austria) Seminar, 1981; chmn. grievance com. U.S. Dist. Ct. Conn., 1983-89; mem. panel comml. arbitrators Am. Arbitration Assn., Ctr. Dispute Resolution. Trustee Fairfield (Conn.) U., 1968-80, trustee emeritus, 1980—; trustee Charles E. Culpeper Trust, 1968-2001; chmn. bd. Charles E. Culpeper Found., 1968-99, pres., 1991-99. With USNR, 1946, 51-53. Fellow Am. Bar Found., Am. Coll. Trial Lawyers (state com. 1985-91, state chmn. 1989-90); mem. U.S. Supreme Ct. Hist. Soc. (Conn. state chmn. 1989-91, trustee 1992-2000), Navy League U.S., Knight of Holy Sepulchre, Knight of Malta, Knight of St. Gregory the Great, Wee Burn Country Club (Darien, Conn.), Orchid Island Golf and Beach Club (Vero Beach, Fla.). Republican. Roman Catholic. Home: 75 Bank St New Canaan CT 06840-6203 also: 10 Lost Beach Ln Vero Beach FL 32963-5000 Office: 11 Burtis Ave New Canaan CT 06840

MCNAMARA, JAMES M. priest; b. Queens, N.Y., Jan. 21, 1945; s. Joseph Michael and May Catherine McNamara. BA in Philosophy, Immaculate Conception Sem., Huntington, N.Y., 1967; MDiv in Theology, Immaculate Conception Sem., 1971; MS in Ednl. Counseling, Iona Coll., New Rochelle, N.Y., 1981. Assoc. pastor St. Martin of Tours Ch., Amityville, NY, 1971—78; spiritual dir. faculty Immaculate Conception Sem., Huntington, 1978—82; dir. of advising faculty N.Am. Coll., Rome, 1982—87; dir. ministry to priests Diocese of Rockville Center, NY, 1987—90, dir. priest pers., 1990—94, pastoral care of the sick, 1994—95; pastor Our Lady of Grace Ch., West

Babylon, 1995—. Vice chmn. bd. trustees Christa House, West Babylon, 1997—. Author: The Power of Compassion, 1983, In the Presence of the Wise/Gentle Christ, 1993; columnist (newspaper) The Long Island Cath., 1999—; contbr. Home and Office: Our Lady of Grace Church 666 Albin Ave West Babylon NY 11704

MCNAMARA, J(OHN) DONALD, retired lawyer, business executive; b. Bridgeport, Conn., Feb. 28, 1924; s. John T. and Agnes (Keating) McN.; m. Shirley Addison Holdridge, Nov. 5, 1960. BA, Dartmouth Coll., 1945; MA in Govt., Harvard U., 1947, LLB, 1950. Bar: N.Y. 1951, Conn. 1951. Assoc. Hall, Haywood, Patterson & Taylor, N.Y.C., 1951-53, 55-56; asst. U.S. Atty. U.S. Dist. Ct. (so. dist.) N.Y., 1953-55; assoc. Wickes, Riddell, Bloomer, Jacobi & McGuire, N.Y.C., 1956-57; assoc., then ptnr. Nottingham & McEniry (and successor), 1957-59; sec., gen. counsel Interpub. Group of Cos., Inc., 1960-79, dir., 1965-85, sr. v.p., 1966-73, exec. v.p., 1973-79, pres., 1980-85, mem. exec. com., 1967-85, mem. fin. com., 1980-85. Chmn. U.S. Nat. Tennis Championships, 1965. Served to lt. (j.g.) USNR, 1943-46. Mem. River Club, Univ. Club, Met. Opera Club (bd. dirs. 1999—), Ekwanok Country Club (bd. govs. Manchester, Vt. 1991-95), Dorset (Vt.) Field Club (bd. govs. 1996-99, pres. 1997-98), West Side Tennis Club (pres. Forest Hills, N.Y. 1964-66, 79-80). Home: 350 E 57th St New York NY 10022-2953 also: River Rd Manchester VT 05254

MCNAMARA, JOHN J(OSEPH), advertising executive, writer; b. Yonkers, N.Y., Mar. 7, 1934; m. Patricia A. Widmann, Sept. 14, 1963; children: Mary, John. BS, Yale U., 1956; MBA, NYU, 1963. Exec. v.p., eastern regional dir. Young & Rubicam, N.Y.C., 1979; pres. Young & Rubicam Inc., from 1982; later pres. McCann Erickson Worldwide, ret., 1988. Writer, cons., bd. dirs. in field. Author: Advertising Agency Management, 1989; columnist: Gulf Stream mags. Pres. Pelham United Way, NY; chmn. Pelham Manor Planning Bd.; trustee City of Pelham Manor, mayor, 1989—90; pres. Boys and Girls Club, Indian River County, Fla., John's Island Property Island Assn. Mem.: John's Island Club (bd. dirs., pres.), Winged Foot Club, Pelham Country Club (pres.). Office: PO Box 8204 Vero Beach FL 32963-8204

MCNAMARA, JOHN STEPHEN, artist, educator; b. Cambridge, Mass., Feb. 16, 1950; s. John Stephen and Mary (Adams) McN. BFA in Painting, Mass. Coll. Art, Boston, 1971, MFA in Painting, 1977. Tchr. Mus. Fine Arts Sch., Boston, 1983, 90-92; undergrad. and grad. painting tchr. Mass. Coll. Art, 1988; undergrad. painting tchr. Boston Archtl. Ctr.; color fundamentals tchr. Mass. Coll. Art, 1987, undergrad. drawing and painting, 1975-88. Vis. lectr. San Francisco Art Inst., 1992, 93, U. Calif., Berkeley, 1993—. One-man shows include The Exhbn. Space at 112 Greene St., N.Y.C., 1982, Stavaridis Gallery, Boston, 1983-85, 86-89, Bess Cutler Gallery, N.Y.C., 1984, 85, 86, 88, Mass. Coll. Art, 1986, Honolulu Acad. Fine Art, 1987, Nielsen Gallery, 1990, 92, Miller Block Gallery, Boston, 1995, Ebert Gallery, San Francisco, Clark Gallery, Lincoln, Mass., others; exhibited in group shows at Boston Collects, Mus. Fine Arts, Stavaridis Gallery, 1986, Bess Cutler Gallery, N.Y.C., 1987, Am. Painters and Sculptors, Met. Mus. Art, N.Y.C., 1988, Resonant Abstraciton, Fuller Mus. Art, Brockton, Mass., 1989-90, Tucson Mus. Fine Art, 1996, DeCordova Mus., Lincoln, Mass., 2002, Painting in Boston, 1950-2000. Mass. Art and Humanities grantee, 1980, 83, 86, 89, Award in the Visual Arts grantee, 1982, Nat. Endowment Arts grantee, 1981, Outstanding Alumnus award Mass. Coll. Art, 1986; McDowell Colony fellow, 1985. Home: 2127 California St Berkeley CA 94703-1472 E-mail: namara@uclink4.berkeley.edu.

MC NAMARA, JOSEPH DONALD, researcher, retired police chief, novelist; b. N.Y.C., Dec. 16, 1934; s. Michael and Eleanor (Shepherd) McN.; divorced; children: Donald, Laura, Karen. BS, John Jay Coll., 1968; fellow, Harvard Law Sch., 1970; DPA (Littauer fellow), Harvard U., 1973. Served to dep. insp. Police Dept., N.Y.C., 1956-73; police chief Kansas City, Mo., 1973-76, San Jose, Calif., 1976-91; rsch. fellow Hoover Instn., Stanford U., 1991—. Adj. instr. Northeastern U., 1972, John Jay Coll., 1973, Rockhurst Coll., 1975-76, San Jose State U., 1980; cons. U.S. Civil Rights Commn., 1978; lectr., appearances on nat. TV; apptd. nat. adv. bd. U.S. Bur. Justice Stats., 1980, U.S. Drug Control Policy Office, 1993; commentator Pub. Broadcasting Radio. Author: (non-fiction) Safe and Sane, 1984, (novel) The First Directive Crown, 1985, Fatal Command, 1987, The Blue Mirage, 1990, Code 211 Blue, 1996; contbr. articles to profl. publs. Bd. dirs. Drug Policy Found., Washington; active NCCJ. Served with U.S. Army, 1958-60. Named one of 200 Young Am. Leaders Time mag., 1975; recipient disting. alumni award John Jay Coll., 1979, Pres.'s award Western Soc. Criminology1979, Morrison Gitchoff award Western Soc. Criminology, 1992, H.B. Spear award Drug Policy Found., 1992; Kansas City police named Best in Country by Nat. Newspaper Enterprises, 1974, San Jose Police Dept. named Nat. Model U.S. Civil Rights Commn., 1980; named Law Enforcement Officer of Yr., Calif. Trial Lawyers Assn., 1991. Mem. Internat. Assn. Chiefs of Police, Calif. Police Chiefs Assn., Calif. Peace Officers Assn., Major Cities Police Chiefs Assn., Police Exec. Research Forum (dir.) Office: Hoover Instn Stanford CA 94305 *In our country, social mobility is possible for people from even the most humble backgrounds. Despite problems, our nation has provided more liberty and dignity for the common individual than any other civilization in history. Continuation of our free society depends upon how successful we are in teaching each new generation an appreciation of our precious freedoms and the patience to achieve progress within our democratic process.*

MCNAMARA, KEVIN JOHN, academic administrator; b. Abington, Pa., Oct. 6, 1957; s. John Kerwin and Dolores Ann (Auchinleck) McN; m. Juliane Cary Roebuck, July 17, 1982; children: Hilary Megan, Whitney Morgan. BA, Temple U., 1989; cert., U. Pa., 1994; MA, Temple U., 1995; cert., U. Va., 2000. Journalist Calkins Newspapers Inc., Doylestown, Pa., 1981-85; congl. aide U.S. Rep. R. Lawrence Coughlin, Washington, 1985-88; asst. dir. Fgn. Policy Rsch. Inst., Phila., 1988-93, rapporteur, 1990-93, adj. scholar, 1994—; dir. devel. Intercollegiate Studies Inst., 1994-98; assoc. v.p. Drexel U., 1998—. Author: The Presidency, 2000; contbg. editor Directors and Boards, 1989-90, Orbis: A Jour. of World Affairs, 1990-93; contbr. articles to profl. jours. Vol. Sam Katz for Gov., 1994, Craig Snyder for Congress, 1992, George Bush for Pres. Com., 1987-88, Snyder for State Ho. Com., 1990; cons. Coughlin for Congress Com., 1986; bd. dirs. Abington Free Libr., 1992-93. Mem. Am. Polit. Sci. Assn., Phila. Com. Fgn. Rels., Acad. Polit. Sci., Assn. of Fundraising Profls. Republican. Avocations: reading, writing, gardening. Office: 3141 Chestnut St Ste 310 Philadelphia PA 19104-2816 E-mail: kevinjmcnamara@aol.com.

MCNAMARA, KEVIN MICHAEL, floorcovering company executive; b. Webster, Mass., June 28, 1957; s. Bernard Francis and Genevieve Anastasia (Ostrokolowicz) McN. AD in Bus. Adminstrn., Quinsigamond C.C., Worcester, Mass., 1982; BS/BA cum laude, Clark U., Worcester, 1985. Personalized svc. rep. Norton Co., Worcester, 1976-83; sys. sales engr. Wells Fargo Alarm Svcs., Chelsea, Mass., 1983-84; dist. sales mgr. Sherwin-Williams Co., San Diego, 1984-96; sr. account exec. Solar Contract Carpet, 1996—2001, Criterion Custom Floors, 2001—. Named Salesman of Yr., Painting and Decorating Contractors Am., State of Conn., 1985, 86. Mem. San Diego C. of C., San Diego Apt. Assn., Friendly Sons of St. Patrick, Elks, Sons of the Am. Legion, Hon. Deputy Sheriff's Assn. Democrat. Roman Catholic. Avocations: golf, skiing, tennis, water sports, travel, food. Home: 4905 Refugio Ave Carlsbad CA 92008-3730

MC NAMARA, LAWRENCE J. bishop; b. Chgo., Aug. 5, 1928; s. Lawrence and Margaret (Knusman) McN. BA, St. Paul Sem., 1949; S.T.L., Catholic U. Am., 1953. Ordained priest Roman Catholic Ch., 1953; parish priest, tchr. Kansas City-St. Joseph Diocese, 1953-57; dir. diocesan Refugee Resettlement, 1957-60; chaplain Jackson County Jail, 1957-64; exec. dir. Campaign for Human Devel., 1973-77; bishop of Grand Island Nebr., 1978—. Office: Chancery Office PO Box 1531 Grand Island NE 68802-1531

MCNAMARA, MARY E. nonprofit executive, asset manager, minister; b. Mpls., Dec. 18, 1943; d. Edward Emmanuel and Gladys Theresa (Mattson) Bjorklund; m. Peter Alexander McNamara II; children: Peter Alexander III, Nathaniel Paul. BA, Carleton Coll., 1965; MDiv, Harvard U., 1968. Cert. fin. planner. Program dir. St. Peter's Ch., N.Y.C., 1968-72, program dir., dep. exec., 1977-80; program dir. Ctr. Ch. on-the-Green, 1972-74; program developer Westminster Presbyn. Ch., Springfield, Ill., 1974-77; assoc. Gen. Assembly Coun. Presbyn. Ch., N.Y.C., 1980-87; dir. not-for-profit sector City of N.Y., 1987-90; pres., exec. dir. Interchurch Ctr., N.Y.C., 1990-99; exec. v.p. Union Theol. Sem., 1999—. V.p. Pathways for Youth, Bronx, NY, 1987—96; pres. Morningside Area Alliance, N.Y.C., 1991—98; parish assoc. Fifth Ave. Presbyn. Ch., 1998—. Moderator Presbyn. N.Y.C., 1995—96, chair com. on ministry, 1992—95, chair implementation task force, 1996—98; chmn. bd. dirs. exec. com. Presbyn. Conf. Ctr., Stony Point, 1996—; bd. dirs. Union Theol. Sem., 1996—99, Blanton/Peale Inst. on Religion and Health, 1994—, Wartburg Adult Care Cmty., 1999—, chair elect, 2001—, chmn. pers. com., exec. com., 2001—. Home: 99 Claremont Ave Apt 321 New York NY 10027-5711 Office: Union Theol Sem 3041 Broadway New York NY 10027-5710

MCNAMARA, PATRICK ROBERT, lawyer; b. Conneaut, Ohio, Dec. 16, 1950; s. Robert John and Retagene (Bailey) McN.; m. Sue Brozina, July 12, 1975; children: Brian, Meghan, Erin, Robert. BS in Edn., Northwestern U., 1973; JD, U. Ariz., 1976. Bar: Ariz. 1976, U.S. Dist. Ct. Ariz. 1976, U.S. Ct. Appeals (9th cir.) 1981; cert. specialist workers' compensation law Ariz. Bd. Legal Specialization. Assoc. Davis, Eppstein & Tretschok, Tucson, 1976-79; adminstrv. law judge Indsl. Commn. Ariz., 1979-81; ptnr. Tretschok & McNamara, P.C., 1981—. Mem. Pima County Bar Assn., Assn. Trial Lawyers Am., Ariz. Trial Lawyers Assn., Ariz. State Bar (past pres. worker's compensation law sect.), So. Ariz. Workers Compensation Claims Assn., Nat. Orgn. Social Security Claimants Reps. Democrat. Roman Catholic. Office: Tretschok & McNamara PC PO Box 42887 Tucson AZ 85733-2887 Fax: 520 792 2417. E-mail: mcnamara@tmpllaw.com.

MCNAMARA, ROBERT JAMES, English language educator, poet; b. N.Y.C., Mar. 28, 1950; s. James Joseph and Doris Agnes (Maier) McN.; m. Bridget Culligan (div. 1985); 1 child, Catlin; m. Judith Lightfoot. BA, Amherst Coll., 1972; MA, Colo. State U., 1975; PhD, U. Wash., 1985. Lectr. English U. Wash., Seattle, 1985—. Author: Second Messengers, 1990; editor L'Epervier Press, Ft. Collins, Colo., Seattle, 1977—; contbr. articles and poems to profl. jours. Fellow Nat. Endowment for the Arts, 1987-88, Fullbright, 1993. Mem. Acad. of Am. Poets, PEN. Office: Dept English GN-30 U Wash Seattle WA 98195-0001

MCNAMARA, ROBERT M., JR. federal agency administrator, lawyer; b. Ohio; m. Patti Devenney; children: Brendan, Caitlin. BA, Mt. Carmel Coll., 1967; AB, John Carroll U., 1968; JD, Georgetown U., 1973. Law clk. to Hon. George C. Edwards, Jr. U.S. Ct. Appeals (6th cir.), Cin.; dep. dir. enforcement Commodity Futures Trading Commn.; gen. counsel Peace Corps.; legis. counsel U.S. Senate Judiciary com.; asst. U.S. atty. U.S. Senate Watergate Com., asst. majority counsel; asst. gen. counsel enforcement Dept. Treasury; gen. counsel CIA, Washington, 1997—. Adj. prof. law Georgetown U. Law Ctr. Symposium editor: Am. Criminal Law Rev. Office: CIA Office of Gen Counsel Washington DC 20505-0001 Office Fax: 703-482-1739.*

MCNAMARA, ROBERT STRANGE, former banking executive, cabinet member; b. San Francisco, June 9, 1916; s. Robert James and Clara Nell (Strange) McN.; m. Margaret Craig, Aug. 13, 1940 (dec.); children: Margaret Elizabeth, Kathleen, Robert Craig. AB, U. Calif., 1937; MBA, Harvard U., 1939; LLD (hon.), U. Calif., U. Mich., Columbia U., Harvard U., George Washington U., Princeton U., Amherst Coll., Williams Coll., U. Ala., Ohio State U., NYU, U. Notre Dame, U. Pa., U. St. Andrews, U. Philippines, Aberdeen U., Oxford U., U. S.C. Asst. prof. bus. adminstrn. Harvard U., 1940-43; exec. Ford Motor Co., 1946-61, pres. co., 1960-61, co. dir., 1957-61; sec. U.S. Dept. Def., 1961-68; pres. World Bank, 1968-81. Mem. , trustee pub. and pvt. instns. including Overseas Devel. Coun., Urban Inst., Enterprise Found., Brookings Inst.; spl. cons. War Dept., 1942. Author: The Essence of Security, 1968, One Hundred Countries-Two Billion People, 1973, The McNamara Years at the World Bank, 1981, Blundering Into Disaster, 1986, Out of the Cold, 1989, In Retrospect, 1995, Argument Without End, 1999, Wilson's Ghost, 2001. Served as lt. col. USAAF, 1943-46. Decorated Legion of Merit, D.S.M.; recipient Presdl. Medal of Freedom with distinction, 1968, Christian A. Herter Meml. award, Albert Pick Jr. award U. Chgo., 1979, Franklin D. Roosevelt Freedom from Want medal, 1983, Onassis Athinai prize, 1988. Mem. Phi Beta Kappa. Office: 1350 I St NW Washington DC 20005-3305

MCNAMARA, STEPHEN, newspaper executive; b. Chgo., July 9, 1934; s. Robert Charles McNamara Jr. and Susan (Deuel) Shattuck; m. Hanne Mogensen Petterson, Feb. 21, 1960 (div. Aug. 1970); children: Lise, Natalie, Kevin; m. Kay Copeland, June 10, 1978; children: Christopher, Morgan. AB in Am. History, Princeton U., 1955. Reporter Winston-Salem (N.C.) Jour., 1955-57; sports writer Miami Herald, 1957-59; contbg. European editor Car & Driver, N.Y.C., 1960; asst. news editor, exec. sports editor, Sunday editor San Francisco Examiner, 1961—66; CEO, editor, pub. Pacific Sun, Mill Valley, Calif., 1966—; co-pub. The Ark, Tiburon, 1987-99; pres. Marin Sun Printing Co., Mill Valley, 1967-93; mng. gen. ptnr. Sunlight Investment Co., 1980—. Vis. lectr. San Francisco State U., 1967; mem. innovation and planning commn. Calif. Dept. Edn., Sacramento, 1980; co-founder, pres. Marin Solar Village Corp., Mill Valley, 1976—, Marin Cmty. Video, Mill Valley, 1973-78. Mem. Soc. Profl. Journalists, Nat. Assn. Alternative Newsweeklies (pres. 1978-81), Calif. Assn. Alternative Newsweeklies (pres. 1990-92), Calif. Soc. Newspaper Editors (pres. 1985-86, bd. dirs. 1983-93), Calif. Newspaper Pubs. Assn. (bd. dirs. 1989-93), San Francisco Press Club (1st place newspaper writing award 1967, 3-2d place awards), Cap and Gown Club (Princeton U.). Democrat. Home: 2 Bradford Way Mill Valley CA 94941-1111 Office: Pacific Sun Pub 21 Corte Madera Ave Mill Valley CA 94941-1800 E-mail: smcnamara@aol.com., steve.mcnamara@pacificsun.com.

MCNAMARA, TIMOTHY JAMES, mathematics educator; b. Buffalo, June 24, 1952; s. Vincent Michael and Peggy Jo (Matthews) McN.; m. Julie Ann McCready, Aug. 25, 1979; children: James Vincent, Lucille Ann. BA in Math., Niagara U., 1975; EdM, SUNY, Buffalo, 1979, MBA, 1984; cert., Sch. Adminstrv. & Supr., 1997; PhD in Math., Pacific Western U., 1998. Tchr. Williamsville East High Sch., East Amherst, N.Y., 1975-84, Maryvale Sr. High Sch., Cheektowaga, 1984-86; tchr. gifted math. program SUNY, 1987-90; coord. math. The Nichols Sch ., Buffalo, 1991-93; K-12 math. supr. West Irondequoit Schs., Rochester, 1993-2000; asst. prof. math. Monroe C.C., 2000—. Lectr. in field. Author: Italics, 1997; faculty editor student math. jour. The Nth Degree; contbr. articles to profl. jours. Recipient N.Y. State Presdl. award for Excellence in Secondary Math. Teaching, 1993, finalist, 1990, 91. Mem. Nat. Coun. Tchrs. Math., Assn. Math. Tchrs. N.Y. State (exec. bd. dirs. 1992-94), N.Y. State Assn. Math. Suprs., Assn. Math Tchrs. Rochester Area (exec. bd. dirs. 1993—, v.p. 1998-99, pres. 1999-2001), Phi Delta Kappa. Avocations: gardening, travel, bicycling. Home: 1093 Marigold Dr Webster NY 14580-8765 Office: Monroe CC 1000 E Henrietta Rd Rochester NY 14623 E-mail: tmcnamara@monroecc.edu.

MCNAMARA, TOM, scientific consulting corporation executive; b. Battle Creek, Mich., May 23, 1944; s. George P. (stepfather) and Mildred E. Lunt. Grad. in Chemistry, Boston U., 1966; M.B.A., Northeastern U., 1970; m. Ellen K. LaRue, Sept. 24, 1977; 1 child, George Lunt. With corp. planning dept. Reynolds Aluminum, Richmond, Va., 1970-72; sr. cons. Technomic Cons., Chgo., 1972-74; founder, pres. NUVENTURES Cons., Inc., Chgo. and San Diego, 1975—; speaker trade convs. and confs. worldwide; frequent guest TV and radio talk shows; on water advisor Am.'s Cup, 1988, 91, 94. Author: Henry Lunt and The Ranger, 1991, Henry Lunt and The Spymaster, 1994, Skull and Crossbones, 1997; co-author: America's Changing Workforce, 1990; editor: George and The Pitching Machine, 1994; contbr. articles to profl. publs. Rep. nominee Ill. Gen. Assembly, 1974, 76; mem. various coms. United Fund and Chgo. Assn. Commerce and Industry, 1975-79; Spokesman 200th Anniversary U.S. Bill of Rights tour, 1991. 1st lt. Ordnance Corps, U.S. Army, 1966-69. Recipient Presdl. Commendation for heroism, 1974, Commendation award Chgo. Police Dept., 1974, Pulitzer Prize nominee, 1991. Mem. Acacia, Bahia Corinthian Yacht Club, San Diego Tennis and Racquet Club. Contbr. articles to profl. publs. Office: PO Box 2489 La Jolla CA 92038-2489

MCNAMARA-RINGEWALD, MARY ANN THÉRÈSE, artist, educator; b. Hempstead, N.Y., Apr. 11, 1935; d. William George Schlichtig and Alice Agnes Rakeman; m. Raymond Anthony McNamara, Apr. 22, 1957 (div. Sept. 1975); children: Thomas William, Raymond Gerard, William Daniel, Peter Joseph, James Francis Jude; m. John Drew Ringewald, Feb. 17, 1984. BS, Fordham U., 1957, Barbizon Sch., NYC, 1953; M in Studio Arts, Adelphi U., 1972; postgrad., Parsons Sch. Design, 1973-75; student, Art Students League, N.Y.C., 1973-74; postgrad., Goddard Coll., Calif., 1986-87; student, Progoff Intensive Jour. Program, N.Y.C., 1999—, Cape Cod Sch., 1993. Cert. elem. edn. and art N.Y. Elem. sch. art tchr. Dept. Edn., Freeport, N.Y., 1957-58, Farmingdale, NY, 1967; jr. and h.s. art tchr. Massapequa (N.Y.) Sch. Dist., 1970-90; owner, pres. South Shore Creative Arts Ctr., Massapequa, 1975; pvt. art tchr. various locations, 1970-90. Illustrator Doubleday, Inc., N.Y.C.; art advisory bd. Chesapeake Coll. Wye Mills, Md., 1995— (lectr., 1998, 99, 2000), Snow Princess, Fordham U., 1954; symposium coord. Hofstra U., N.Y.; lectr. Naples Philharm., 1992; judge, lectr. in field; architectural designer, M.E. 1977, M.D., 1988-, F.L., 1990. One-woman shows include Fordham U., 1954, Andonia Gallery, Massepequa, N.Y., 1974, Isis Gallery, Islip, N.Y., 1974, For the Birds, Salisbury, Conn., 1978, Harguen Gallery, Pt. Jefferson, N.Y., 1979, Adelphi U., Garden City, N.Y., 1992, Wohlfarth Gallery, Washington, 1994-95, SpanBauer Gallery Naples, Fla., 1996, Naples Philharmonic, Naples, Fla., 1992, Gallery 44, Millbrook, N.Y., 1997-98; groups shows: Acad. of Arts, Easton, Md., 1993. works exhibited at Kennedy Gallery, Key West, Fla., 1997-99, Chesapeake Coll., Md., 1998-99; represented in pvt. collections General Motors, The Benedictines, Prudential Life, St. Michael's Maritime Mus., Yupo Corp., Japan; illustrator: From a Lighthouse Window, Chesapeake Bay Maritime Mus., 1992 (Best of Balt. Book award 1993, Book award Tabasco N.Y.C. 1994); original poetry published. Pres. AAUW, L.I., 1969-71; bd. dirs. L.I. (N.Y.) Art Tchrs. Assn., 1973-76; docent U.S. Fish and Wildlife Svc., Washington, 1994-95; mem. Am. Farmland Trust; vol. Delmarva Chpt., ARC, 2001-. Recipient Nat. Middle Sch. Art Tchrs. award, Nassau County Middle Sch. Art Tchrs. Assn., 1988, Very Spl. Arts Festival for Handicapped, 1977, Festival of Creation, Diocese of RVC, 1975, Catalyst, 1975; named to Outstanding Young Women of Am., 1969; works featured in Nat. Anthology of Poetry, 1953. Mem. Internat. Welcome Fla. Assn. Series (lectr. 1994—), Nat. League Am. Pen Women (founder, pres. Naples, Fla. br. 1995—), Nat. Gallery Art (copyist 1993—), Order of the Benedictines (oblate 1990—), Working Artists Forum (Easton, Md.), NY State Art Tchrs. Assn. (bd. mem. 1972-80). Roman Catholic. Avocations: horticulture, travel, illuminations, music, poetry. Address: Marafour 5493 Anderby Dr Royal Oak MD 21662 Office: Marafour Studio 27098 Del Ln Bonita Springs FL 34135-4409

MCNAMEE, SISTER CATHERINE, educator; b. Troy, N.Y., Nov. 13, 1931; d. Thomas Ignatius McNamee and Kathryn McNamee Marois. BA, Coll. of St. Rose, 1953, DHL (hon.), 1975; MEd, Boston Coll., 1955, MA, 1958; PhD, U. Madrid, 1967. Grad. asst. Boston Coll., 1954-55; asst. registrar Boston Coll. (Grad. Sch.), 1955-57; mem. faculty Coll. St. Rose, Albany, N.Y., 1960-65, acad. v.p., 1968-75; dir. liberal arts Thomas Edison Coll., Trenton, 1975-76; pres. Trinity Coll., Burlington, Vt., 1976-79, Coll. St. Catherine, St. Paul, 1979-84; dean Dexter Hanley Coll., U. Scranton, Pa., 1984-86; pres. Nat. Cath. Ednl. Assn., Washington, 1986-96; sr. scholar Ctr. for Cath. Studies, U. St. Thomas, St. Paul, 1996-2000; prof. U. Catolica, Talca, Chile, 2000—. Bd. dirs. Am. Forum for Global Edn. Trustee assoc. Boston Coll. Spanish Govt. grantee, 1965-67; OAS grantee, 1967-68; Fulbright grantee, 1972-73 Mem. Inter-Am. Confedn. Cath. Edn., Internat. Orgn. Cath. Edn., Nat. Cath. Ednl. Assn., Internat. Fedn. Cath. Univs., Delta Epsilon Sigma. Roman Catholic. Home: Casilla 712 Talca Chile E-mail: cmncsj@chilesat.net.

MC NAMEE, MAURICE BASIL, English language educator; b. Montello, Wis., June 5, 1909; s. James Patrick and Ida (Griffith) McN. AB, St. Louis U., 1933, A.M., 1934, S.T.L., 1941, PhD, 1945. Joined S.J., 1927, ordained priest Roman Cath. Ch., 1940. Tchr. Creighton U. H.S., 1936-37; mem. faculty St. Louis U., 1944—, prof. English, 1960—, dir. dept., 1956-70, dir. honors program, 1950-61. Lectr. fgn. workshops, 1957-60 Author: Literary Decorum in Francis Bacon, 1950, Reading for Understanding, 1958, 68, Honor and the Epic Hero, 1960, (with J. Cronin, J. Rogers) Literary Types and Themes, 1960, 70, Essays by the Masters, 1968, Essays in Exposition, 1969, Bacon's Inductive Method and Humanistic Grammar, 1971, The Origin of the Vested Angel as a Eucharistic Symbol in Flemish Painting, 1972, The Structure of the Ignatian Meditation Pattern in Some of the Poetry of Gerard Manley Hopkins, 1990, Vested Angels: A Study of the Eucharistic Symbolism in Early Netherlandish Painting, 1999, Recollections in Tranquility, 2002. Mem. Cath. Commn. Intellectual and Cultural Affairs, 1971— ; exec. dir. Samuel Cupples House Found., 1974; mem. Mayor's Council Cultural Affairs, 1979; mem. Commn. Art Archdiocese of St. Louis. Recipient Nancy McNeir Ring Outstanding Faculty award, 1973; Fleur de Lis medal St. Louis U.; Research grantee St. Louis U., 1955; Ford Found. Jesuit Faculty Fund St. Louis U., 1966; Fulbright research follow Belgium, 1966; research grantee in humanities Am. Philos. Soc., 1966, 78, Research Grant from the Beaumont Fund, St. Louis University, 1983; Research Grant from the Mellon Fund, St. Louis University and from the National Arts and Educational Foundation, 1985, Mellon Fund of St. Louis U. research grant, 1985, 87, 90, NEH research grant, 1985. Mem. Modern Lang. Assn., Soc. Art Historians (pres. 1962-64), Coll. Art Assn., Phi Beta Kappa. Democrat. Home and Office: 3601 Lindell Blvd Saint Louis MO 63108-3301

MCNAUGHTON, ALEXANDER BRYANT, lawyer; b. Atlanta, Apr. 2, 1948; s. William James and June Florence (Gibson) McN.; m. Susan Mary Knox, Mar. 7, 1981; children: Alexis Loren, Elizabeth Adelyn. BS, Ga. State U., 1974; postgrad., Oxford (England) U., 1980; JD, U. Okla., 1981. Bar: Okla. 1981, U.S. Dist. Ct. (we. dist.) Okla. 1981, U.S. Ct. Appeals (10th cir.) 1982, U.S. Ct. Mil. Appeals 1984, U.S. Supreme Ct. 1985. Social worker State of Ga. Dept. Human Svcs., Bainbridge, 1974-75; farmer MC Farms, Cole, Okla., 1975-81; trial lawyer Mattoon Law Offices, Norman, 1981-82, Jones, Gungoll, Jackson et al, Enid, 1982-83, Jones, McNaughton & Blakley, Enid, 1983-85, McNaughton & McNaughton, Enid, 1985-94; ptnr. Norman, Edem, McNaughton & Wallace, 1994-2001, McNaughton & Bonner, Enid, 2001—. Expert cons. in field. Contbr. to book chpt. Scoutmaster Boy Scouts Am., Norman. With U.S. Army, 1966-68. Mem. ABA (litigation med. negligence, tort and ins. sects.), ATLA (pres.' club), Okla. Trial Lawyers Assn. (bd. dirs. 1993—), Okla. Bar Assn. (rules of profl. conduct com., 1997—, chnmn. med.l-legal code subcom., 1997—, civil procedure com. 1998—, evidence com. 1999—). Avocations: camping, bicycling, sports car racing, swimming. Home: 2567 Homestead Rd Enid OK 73703-1647 Office: McNaughton & Bonner 110 N Independence St Enid OK 73701-4001

MCNAUGHTON, KENNETH JOHN, publisher; b. Melbourne, Australia, July 22, 1940; arrived in U.S., 1970; s. Charles Dudley and Lilian May (Besant) McN.; m. Victoria Ann Yocum, Oct. 28, 1972 (div. Oct. 1982); children: Aurelius John, Candace Ann. B chem. engr., Univ. Melbourne, 1961; M in engr. sci., Monash Univ., Clayton, Australia, 1964. Dir. communications network Found. Faith, N.Y., 1966-77; asst. editor Chemical Engring., 1978-81, assoc. editor, 1981-86; editor-in-chief Industrial Chemist, 1986-89; dir. new publs. divsn. sci. and tech. Warren Gorham & Lamont, 1989-90; mng. editor Physics Today, 1991-94; assoc. pub. The Industrial Physicist, College Park, Md., 1995—. Pres. McNaughton Communications, N.Y., 1978—. Contbr. over 100 articles to profl. jours. Mem. Friends of Benjamin Banneker Hist. Park, Oella, Md., 1996—; founder Campaign to Save the Trees, Roosevelt Island, N.Y., 1991; pres. PTA H.S. for the Humanities, N.Y., 1990-91; pres. bd. dirs. Greystone Condominiums, 2002—; mem. Romnet Newsgroup, 1997-99; mem. Patapsco Valley and Heritage Greenway, 2002--. Recipient Broadcast awards Coun. of Chs., 1976, 78, 79, Golden Mike awards Am. Legion, 1978, 79. Mem. Port Philip Pioneers Group, Univ. Melbourne Alumni Assn. (founding pres. 1988-90, northeastern br. pres. 1992-94), Australia Soc. Phila. Avocations: music, dance, film, swimming, walking, traveling. Home: 3778 College Ave Ellicott City MD 21043-4662 Office: Am Inst Physics One Physics Ellipse College Park MD 20740-3842 E-mail: kmcnaugh@aip.org.

MCNAUGHTON, WILLIAM FRANK, translator, educator; b. Westboro, Mo., May 21, 1933; s. Frank McNaughton and Ruth Ellen (Flanders) Francis; m. Margaret Orminski, Apr. 4, 1956 (div. 1971); children: John Ferenc, Dorothy Ellen; m. Li Ying, Apr. 8, 1990; 1 child, Andrea. Student, U. Mo., 1951-53; studied poetry and translation with Ezra Pound, 1953-56; student, Georgetown U., 1953-54; BA, Bklyn. Coll., 1961; PhD, Yale U., 1965. Asst. prof. Oberlin (Ohio) Coll., 1965-70; lectr. Exptl. Coll., Oberlin, 1970-71; vis. lectr. Bowling Green (Ohio) State U., 1972-74, Denison U., Granville, Ohio, 1972-78; prof. Program for Afloat Coll. Edn. (PACE) USN, Norfolk, Va., 1978-84; vis. prof. King Saud U., Abha, Saudi Arabia, 1984-85; sr. lectr. English, translation City Poly. Hong Kong, 1986-89, prin. lectr. translation, 1989-94; univ. sr. lectr. City U., Hong Kong, 1994-95, assoc. prof., 1995-98;

retired, 1998. Guest lectr., U. degli Studii, Venice, Italy, 1975; coord. Tri-Coll. Chinese program, Gt. Lakes Colls. Assn., Ann Arbor, 1965-68; cons., Asian Lit. program, Asia Soc., N.Y.C., 1967-80, Nat. Translation Ctr., Austin, Tex., 1965-68, Ballantine Books, N.Y.C., 1985, Princeton U. Press, 1965; presenter papers at lit. confs. Author: Reading and Writing Chinese, 1979, rev. edit., 1999, Pound's Usura and the Islamic Concept of Riba, 1996; co-translator: Poem Without a Hero and Selected Poems of Anna Akhmatova, 1989, As Though Dreaming: The Tz'u...of Li Ch'ing-chao, 1977, A Gold Orchid: The Love Poems of Tzu Yeh, 1972; editor, translator: Light from the East, 1978, The Confucian Vision, 1974, The Book of Songs, 1971, The Taoist Vision, 1971, Guerilla War, 1971; contbr. articles to profl. publs., translations to various lit. mags.; editor-in-chief: City Univ. Bull., 1995-98; mem. editl. bd. City Univ. Press, 1996-98. Woodrow Wilson Found. fellow, 1961-62; modern fgn. lang. fellow, NDEA, 1962-65; grantee, Nat. Translation Ctr., Austin, 1967, Gt. Lakes Colls. Assn., Ann Arbor, 1965, 67-68, Asia Soc., N.Y.C., 1971-72, 74; Fulbright fellow, 1968-69. Avocations: sailing, music, Venetian culture and history. Home and Office: Flat 20C Block 26 Baguio Villa 555 Victoria Pokfulam Hong Kong

MCNAUGHTON, WILLIAM JOHN, retired bishop; b. Lawrence, Mass., Dec. 7, 1926; s. William John Sr. and Ruth Irene (Howe) McN. BA, U. of State of N.Y., Ossining, 1948, B of Sacred Theology, 1953; M in Religious Edn., Maryknoll Sem., Ossining, 1953. Ordained Maryknoll priest, 1953; cert. in Korean Lang. Studies, Yale U., 1954. Pastor Pouk Moun Ro Cath. Ch., Chong Ju Diocese, Korea, 1955-57, Nae Duk Dong Cath. Ch., Chong Ju Diocese, Korea, 1957-60; consultor Chong Ju Diocese, 1958-59, vicar gen., 1959-60; consecrated bishop Inchon (Korea) Diocese, 1961—2002, ret., 2002. Address: 39 Woodburn Dr Methuen MA 01844-2812

MCNEAL, DALE WILLIAM, JR. biological sciences educator; b. Kansas City, Kans., Nov. 23, 1939; s. Dale William and Geraldine Estelle (Reed) McNeal; m. Arlene Joyce Purvis, Feb. 26, 1966. BA, Colo. Coll., 1962; MS, SUNY Coll. Environ. Sci. and Forestry, Syracuse, 1964; PhD, Wash. State U., 1969. Asst. prof. dept. biol. scis. U. Pacific, Stockton, Calif., 1969-74, assoc. prof., 1974-79, prof., 1979—2002, chmn. dept., 1978-84. Contbr. articles to profl. jours. Served with U.S. Army, 1964—66. Mem.: Calif. Acad. Scis., Internat. Soc. Plant Taxonomy, Am. Soc. Plant Taxonomists, Calif. Bot. Soc. (pres. 1987—88), Am. Bot. Soc., Sigma Xi. Republican. Episcopalian. Office: U Pacific Dept Biol Scis Stockton CA 95211-0001

MCNEAL, JEANNETTE JOHNSON, social worker; b. Ft. Bragg, N.C., Feb. 16, 1955; d. Thomas C. and Dorothy Alease Johnson; m. Thomas Michael McNeal, July 21, 1990. BSW summa cum laude, N.C. Agrl./Tech. State U., 1977; MSW, U. N.C., Chapel Hill, 1979. Maternal and child health social worker Cleveland County Health Dept., Shelby, N.C., 1979-81; social worker Gaston-Lincoln Area Mental Health, Gastonia, 1981-85; clin. social worker, supr. Mecklenburg Mental Health Ctr., Charlotte, 1985-88; counselor/social worker Charlotte Mecklenburg Schs., 1988—. Awards sec. Friendship Missionary Bapt. Ch., 1994, awards chair, 1996—98. Mem. Nat. Assn. Black Social Workers (v.p. met. chpt. 1988-90), N.C. Assn. Black Social Workers (corr. sec. 1988-90), N.C. Agrl. and Tech. State U. Alumni Assn. (past chpt. treas. Queen City chpt.), N.C. Sch. Social Workers Assn. Alumnae Assn. (Charlotte chpt.), Delta Sigma Theta (cotillion com. co-chair, 1994-96, asst. treas. 1996-98, treas. 1998-2000, 1st v.p. 2000—), Friendship Missionary Bapt. Ch. (MEG sec. 1994). Avocations: reading, cross-stitch, latch hook work, white water rafting, sports spectator. Home: PO Box 31124 9743 Dauphine Dr Charlotte NC 28231-1124 Office: East Mecklenburg High Sch 6800 Monroe Rd Charlotte NC 28212-6821

MCNEAL, THOMAS ROY, computer software company executive; b. Indpls., May 2, 1949; s. Robert Paul and Mary Margaret (Girard) McN.; m. Sandra Jean Gruver; stepchildren: Guy Falsetti, Christine Falsetti, Ed Falsetti, Rachel Falsetti. BS in Physics, U. Tex., 1973, BS in Math., 1976; MS in Computer Sci., U. Iowa, 1978. Software devel. engr. Hewlett-Packard, Corvallis, Oreg., 1979-80, Cupertino, Calif., 1980-98, software devel. project mgr., 1998—2000; dir. ops. West Coast office Mission Critical Linux, Inc., Santa Clara, 2000—02. Contbr. articles to mags. Avocations: gardening, horticulture, viniculture, music. E-mail: mcneal@mclinux.com.

MCNEALEY, J. JEFFREY, lawyer, corporate executive; b. Cin., Feb. 8, 1944; s. J. Lawrence and Louise McNealey; m. Sara Wilson, Sept. 24, 1988; children: Anne Elizabeth, John Alexander. BA, Cornell U., 1966; JD, Ohio State U., 1969. Ptnr. Porter, Wright, Morris & Arthur, Columbus, Ohio, 1969—. Bd. dirs. TRC Cos., Windsor, Conn., 1985—; sec., bd. dirs. The Smoot Corp., Columbus, 1972—. Trustee Columbus Cancer Clinic, 1972—, past pres.; trustee German Village Soc., Columbus, 1986—, past pres.; bd. dirs. Columbus chpt. ARC, 1983-86, Columbus Urban League, 1984-90; active Union League Chgo., 1981—, Columbus/Dresden Sister City, Inc., 1996—; mem. vestry Trinity Episcopal Ch., 2000—. Mem. ABA, Ohio State Bar Assn. (past chmn. environ. com. 1978-84), Columbus Bar Assn., Columbus Country Club, Capital Club of Columbus, Cornell Club of Ctrl. Ohio (trustee 1978—, past pres.). Episcopalian. Avocations: flying, racquet sports, wood working, flyfishing. Office: Porter Wright Morris & Arthur 41 S High St Ste 30 Columbus OH 43215-6101

MCNEALY, SCOTT G. computer company executive; b. 1954; BA, Harvard U., 1976; MBA, Stanford U., 1980. With Rockwell Internat. Corp., Troy, Mich., 1976-78, sales engr.; staff engr. FMC Corp., Chgo., 1980-81; dir. ops. Onyx Systems, San Jose, Calif., 1981-82; chmn. bd., pres., CEO, Sun Microsystems Inc., Palo Alto, 1982—, also bd. dirs., 1985. Office: Sun Microsystems Inc 901 San Antonio Rd Palo Alto CA 94303-4900*

MCNEAR, BARBARA BAXTER, retired financial communications executive, consultant; b. Chgo., Oct. 9, 1939; d. Carl Henden and Alice Gertrude (Parrish) Baxter; m. Robert Erskine McNear, Apr. 13, 1968 (div. 1981); 1 child, Amanda Baxter; m. Glenn Philip Eisen, June 7, 1987. BS in Journalism, Northwestern U., 1961. Editorial asst. Scott Foresman & Co., Chgo., 1961; pub. rels. dir. Market Facts Inc., 1961-63; account supr. Philip Lesly Co., 1963-68, 69; account exec. Burson-Marsteller, 1968; dir. communications CNA Fin. Corp., 1969-74; dir. pub. rels. Gould Inc., 1974; v.p. Harris Bank, 1974-80, Fireman's Fund Ins. Co., San Francisco, 1980-83; sr. v.p. First Chgo. Corp., 1983-86; v.p. communications Xerox Fin. Svcs., Inc., Stamford, Conn., 1987-93; mgr. shareholder comm. Xerox Corp., 1993-99; ret. Mem. Pub. Rels. Soc. Am., Fairfield County Pub. Rels. Assn., Nat. Investor Rels. Inst. (pres. Chgo. chpt. 1974-75, bd. dirs. Chgo. chpt.), Cliffdwellers, Princeton Club. Episcopalian. Home: 23 Telva Rd Wilton CT 06897-3733 E-mail: bbmcnear@aol.com.

MCNEELY, CAROL J. dentist; b. Chgo., July 17, 1954; d. Lewis W. and Jessie O. (Woodfin) McN.; divorced; 1 child, Matthew. Student, U. Chgo., 1972-74; DDS, U. Ill., Chgo., 1979; cert. in cosmetic dentistry, Case Western Res. U.; M of Mgmt., Northwestern U., 1995. Cert. cosmetic dentistry, 1993. Pvt. practice, Chgo., 1979—; pres. HealthS.M.A.R.T. Strategies, 1995—. Ptnr. Provident Dental Assocs., Chgo., 1983-85; owner Soulful Expressions, Chgo., 1987—; dental cons. Dental Network Am., Oakbrook Terrace, Ill., 1988-92. Mem. assoc. bd. dirs. Chgo. Child Care Soc., 1982-85; mem. scholarship fund com. Chgo. Urban League, 1989. Recipient Ptnrs. in Community award Nat. Bar Assn., 1985. Mem. ADA (task force on women and minorities 1992-93), Acad. Cosmetic Dentistry, Am. Assn. Dental Cons., Nat. Dental Assn., Chgo. Assn. Black Women Dentists (pres. 1992-94), U. Chgo. Alumni Assn. (minority mentor program). Office: 7931 S King Dr Chicago IL 60619-3701 E-mail: there4Vcoach@aol.com.

MCNEELY, DAVID JOHN, computer programmer; b. Ft. Bragg, N.C., Sept. 24, 1958; s. James William and Eleanor Marie (Kmiecik) McN.; m. Amy Michelle McNeely, Nov. 5, 1994; children: Hannah Marie, Connor David. BA in Math., U. Fla., 1980. Programmer Utility Ptnrs., Tampa, Fla., 1998-99, Eagle Asset Mgmt., St. Petersburg, 1999—. Mem. Mensa, U.S. Chess Fedn. Democrat. Home: 1530 McCrea Dr Lutz FL 33549 E-mail: dmcneely@eagle.rjf.com.

MCNEELY, MARK, marketing professional, journalist; Grad. in journalism, U. Tenn., 1970. Reporter The Knoxville Jour., The Commerical Appeal, The Knoxville Jour., Knoxille News-Sentinel; pvt. practice as sr. ptnr., 1987—. Served in key staff and and campaign roles U.S. Senator Al Gore, Jr., former U.S. Senator Jim Sasser, and former Nashville Mayor Richard Fulton, Tenn. Supreme Ct. Office: 611 Commerce St Ste 2800 Nashville TN 37203 Business E-Mail: mmcneely@mpf.com.*

MCNEELY, ROBERT A. lawyer; b. Dallas, Apr. 24, 1959; s. W. Eugene McNeely and Joan M. (McCampbell) Schmedemann; m. Cynthia A. Myers, May 26, 1990; children: R. Andrew II, John R., Jade E., Jazlyn A. BS in Journalism, U. Kans., 1981; JD, Fla. State U., 1993. Morning news anchor, editor Kans. Info. Network, Wichita, 1982-83, statehouse bur. chief Topeka, 1983-84; spl. assignment reporter Sta. KANU-FM, Lawrence, Kans., 1984-85; news dir. Sta. WFSU-FM, Tallahassee, 1985-88; statehouse bur. chief Kans. Pub. Radio, Topeka, 1989-90; rsch. analyst Fla. Taxwatch, Tallahassee, 1990-91; law clerk Steel, Hector & Davis, 1991-93, assoc. Miami, Fla., 1993-95, McFarlain & Cassedy, Tallahassee, 1995-2000, shareholder, 2000—. Immediate past pres. Nat. Congress for Fathers and Children (Fla. chpt.), Tallahassee, 1995-98. Mem. Fla. Commn. on Responsible Fatherhood, 1996—; sec., treas. With Arms Wide Open Found., 2000—. Recipient 1st place award Kans. Assn. Broadcasters, 1981-83, UPI, 1982-88, Assn. of News Broadcasters of Kans., 1986, Fla. Tchg. Profession-NEA, 1988. Mem. ABA (family law sect., sports and entertainment forum), Fla. Bar (family law sect., entertainment and sports law sect.). Democrat. Presbyterian. Office: McFarlain & Cassedy PA 215 S Monroe St Ste 600 Tallahassee FL 32301-1804 E-mail: rmcneely@mcfarlain.com.

MCNEELY, THOMAS HOLMES, writer, educator; b. Mpls., Nov. 29, 1967; s. Robert Holmes McNeely, Joan Cochran Terrell; m. Cheryl Elaine McGrath, Sept. 14, 2001. MFA, Emerson Coll., 1997. Investigator Tex. Appellate Practice and Ednl. Resource Ctr., Austin, 1991—94; adj. instr. Emerson Coll., Boston, 1997—2001. Author: (short stories) Sheep, 1999 (reprinted in New Stories from the South: The Year's Best and The Best American Mystery Stories, 2000), Tickle Torture, 2001, Snow, Houston, 1974, Pictures of the Shark, Elvis, 2002. Fellow, The MacDowell Colony, 1999, J. Frank Dobie Meml., Tex. Inst. Letters, 2000, Wallace Stegner, Stanford U., 2001—, Helene Wurlitzer Found., 2002. Personal E-mail: thmcneely@hotmail.com.

MC NEESE, WILMA WALLACE, social worker; b. Chgo., Apr. 30, 1946; d. Nettie Fletcher Wallace; m. Mose D. Mc Neese, Dec. 27, 1969; children: Derrick, Christina. Student, Wilson City Coll., 1964-66; BA, So. Ill. U., 1969; MSW, Loyola U., Chgo., 1976. Program coord. Intensive Tng. and Employment Program, East St. Louis, Ill., 1970-71; methods and procedures advisor Ill. Dept. Pub. Aid., Chgo., 1972-73; social work intern Robbins (Ill.) Presch. Ctr., 1974; with U.S. Probation Office, Chgo., 1975; officer U.S. Pretrial Svcs. Agy., 1976-87; chief U.S. pretrial svcs. officer for western dist. Pa., 1987—. Fieldwork instr. Aurora Coll., 1981, Chgo. State U., 1981-82; grad. fieldwork instr. U. Ill. Sch. of Social Work, 1986; mem. bd. trustees The Wesley Inst. Inc., 1993—, chmn. bd. trustees, 1999—. Recipient Cmty. Svc. award Village of Robbins, 1975; advanced tng. cert. Fed. Jud. Ctr. Mem. Nat. Assn. Social Workers, Acad. Cert. Social Workers, Nat. Assn. Pretrial Svcs. Agencies, Greater Pitts. Commn. for Women. Baptist. Home: 833 Chalmers Pl Pittsburgh PA 15243-1967 Office: 1000 Liberty Ave Ste 822 Pittsburgh PA 15222-4003

MCNEIL, DAVID JAMES, communications executive, marketing consultant; b. Torrance, Calif., Jan. 20, 1958; s. James Eugene and Nancy Anne (Williams) McN.; m. Sheryl Lillian Stark, Aug. 31, 1980. BA in Bus. Adminstrn. and Mktg., Calif. State U., Northridge, 1982. Pres. McNeil Glass Co., Westlake, Calif., 1978-81; coordinator mktg., pay-per-view devel. Group W Cable, Torrance, 1982-86; mgr. mktg., programming Daniels Cablevision, Arcadia, Calif., 1986, bus. mgr. pay-per-view, 1986; mgr. prodn. and devel. pay-per-view United Artists Entertainment, Inc., Glendora, 1986-89; asst. v.p. Calif. Casualty Mgmt. Co., Orange, 1989—. Mktg. cons. Cornucopia Mktg. Co., Torrance, 1986-88, Golden Rule Mktg. Co., Torrance, 1986-88. Mem. Am. Mktg. Assn. (life), So. Calif. Mktg. Coun., Mensa, Torrance C. of C., Simi Valley Jaycees, Torrance Sister City Assn., Delta Sigma Pi (life). Avocations: collecting classic automobiles, motorcycle racing, video production. Home: 28879 Modjeska Canyon Rd Silverado CA 92676-9748 Office: Calif Casualty Mgmt Co 600 City Pkwy W Ste 500 Orange CA 92868-2946

MCNEIL, EDWARD WARREN, real estate company executive; b. Alhambra, Calif., Jan. 5, 1942; s. Murray Charles and Helen Katherine (Curtis) McN.; m. Jutta Bocking, Apr. 1, 1941; children: Anja Britt, Bradley Stuart. Student, U. Calif., Berkeley, 1960-63. Structures engr. Peter Kiewit Sons Co., various cities, Calif., 1961-63; project engr. Huntington Harbour, Sunset Beach, 1963-64; project supt. Coordinated Realty, Inc., Anaheim, 1964-65; field ops. mgr. Lear Siegler, Saigon, Vietnam, 1965-67; project engr. Constructora Emkay, Rio Blanco, Chile, 1968-69; ptnr. The Pyramid Cos., Syracuse, N.Y., 1969-75, The Pioneer Group, Syracuse, 1975-95, ret., 1995. Past chmn., bd. dirs. Crouse Irving Meml. Hosp. Found., Syracuse, 1986—; trustee, past vice-chmn. Everson Mus. of Art, Syracuse, 1981-94; bd. dirs. Syracuse Stage, 1981-93, past chmn., vice-chmn.; chmn. Adirondack chpt. Nature Conservancy, 1994-2001, trustee N.Y. state bd., 1998-; trustee Adirondack Land Trust, 1990-2002, chmn., 1994-2001; trustee Manlius Pebble Hill Sch., 1984-86, 1994-99, emeritus, 1999—; vol. pilot Nature Conservancy, No. Wings.. Recipient award for svc. to the arts, Cultural Resource Coun., Syracuse, 1987. Mem. Seaplane Pilots Assn., Slocum Soc., Century Club, Lake Amphibian Flyers Club, Warbirds of Am., No. Lake Pilots Club. Avocations: ocean sailing, canoeing, fly fishing, seaplane flying, aerobatics.

MCNEIL, HELEN JO CONNOLLY, nursing educator, public health administrator; b. Olympia, Wash., June 15, 1925; d. James Ambrose and Corinne Marie (Bordeaux) Connolly; m. Robert Phillip McNeil, Aug. 16, 1947; children: Sheryl Ann Andrews, Robert John, Maureen Connolly McNeil, Kevin Charles. BSN, Seattle Coll., 1947; MSN, U. Wash., 1961, postgrad., 1974-80. RN Wash., S.C., Tex., Va., cert. pub. health nurse, 1962. Clinic nurse Schutt Clinic, Bremerton, Wash., 1947-49; staff nurse Providence Hosp., Seattle, 1950-60, Overlake Hosp., Bellevue, Wash., 1961-62; pub. health nurse Seattle King County Health Dept. and Vis. Nurse Svc., 1962-64, pub. health nurse supr., 1964-65, assoc. dir. pub. health nursing and vis. nurse svc., 1965-70, health planning and evaluation specialist, 1970-73, adminstr. S.E. dist., 1973-78, adminstr. Ctrl. dist., 1979-81, adminstr. N. dist., 1981-84, dir. nursing rsch., 1984-85; lectr. Sch. Nursing U. Wash., Seattle, 1985-87; mem. faculty S. Puget Sound C.C., Olympia, 1987-88; vis. faculty Sch. Nursing Clemson (S.C.) U., 1988; instr. coll. nursing allied health U. Tex., El Paso, 1988-90; dir. pub. health nursing Commonwealth Va., Richmond, 1990-93; lectr. Sch. Nursing Seattle U., 1995; cons. Seattle, Seaview, Wash., 1995—. Mem. panel in nursing edn. Am. Assn. Colls. of Nursing, 1985—87; adj. assoc. prof. Sch. Pub. Health U. N.C., Chapel Hill, 1980—92; adj. asst. prof. U. Wash. Sch. Nursing, 1965—85; rev. com. nursing census USPHS, 1970—72; health care cons. , 1976; lectr. Congress on Nutrition, Rio de Janeiro, 1978. Author: Reaching Out, 1998; contbr. articles to profl. jours., chpts. to books. Mem. task force Seattle Health Policy, 1981, Seattle 2000 Commn., 1973; lectr. Internat. Congress Social Psychiatry, Athens, 1974; with Project Hope Internat. Approaches in Health Care of Elderly, Milwood, Va., 1983, 84; co-project dir. occupl. health con. edn. for cmty. nurses divsn. nursing U. Wash., 1983-86; mem. ARC Disater Team, Seattle, 1995-97, Parent and Home Health Bd., Richmond, Va., 1990-93. With U.S. cadet nursing corps USPHS, 1943-47. Stress Rsch. grantee Heath Resources Adminstrn., 1974; W. K. Kellog Found. grantee U. Tex., El Paso, 1990, grantee U. Wash., 1983-86; recipient Nursing Adminstrn. recognition award Jour. Nursing Adminstrn., 1993. Fellow: APHA (nursing sect. pres. 1992—93, Ruth B. Freeman Disting. Career award 1998); mem.: Seattle Mgmt. Assn. (pres. 1976, Disting. Adminstrv. Svc. award City of Seattle 1976), Wash. State Pub. Health Assn. (pres. 1976—77, Adminstrv. Svc. award 1975), Assn. Cmty. Health Nurse Educators (founder, pres. 1985), Seattle U. Alumni (mem. nursing adv. bd. 1993—96, Cmty. Svc. Alumni award 1992), Alpha Tau Delta, Sigma Theta Tau (internat. rsch. conf. Seoul, South Korea 1984). Avocations: gardening, travel, writing, cooking, paddocks for six hourses. Home and Office: PO Box 173 Seaview WA 98644-0173

MCNEIL, MARK SANFORD, lawyer; b. Shawnee, Okla., Feb. 4, 1950; s. Irving Jr. and Sylvia Louise (Sanford) McN.; m. Cathy Marleen Yandell, Sept. 7, 1974; children: Elizabeth, Laura. Assoc. Lillick McHose & Charles, San Francisco, 1974-76; rsch. asst. Kyoto (Japan) U., 1976-77; internat. law cons. Amita & Hirokawa, Osaka, Japan, 1976-77, Ono Law Office, Osaka, 1976-77; internat. counsel Medtronic, Inc., Mpls., 1978-84; mgr. contract adminstrn. Cray Rsch., Inc., 1985, internat. counsel, 1986-88, dir. internat. contracts, 1988-91, dir. corp. contacts, 1991; assoc. Briggs and Morgan, P.A., 1995-97. Adj. prof. William Mitchell Coll. Law, St. Paul, 1989-91. Bd. dirs. Midwest China Ctr. Mem. ABA, Minn. Bar Assn. (chmn. internat. bus. law sect. 1986-87), Hennepin County Bar Assn., Corp. Counsel Assn., Minn. World Trade Assn. (bd. dirs. 1996—, pres. 1998-99). Avocations: photography, music, fiction writing, rafting. Home: 514 5th St E Northfield MN 55057-2220 Office: Lindquist and Vennum PLLP 4200 IDS Ctr Minneapolis MN 55402 E-mail: mmcneil@lindquist.com.

MCNEIL, PAUL JOSEPH, JR. employment security interviewer; b. Winthrop, Mass., Oct. 11, 1941; s. Paul Joseph Sr. and Helen Margaret (Carr) McN. Cert. in ins., U. R.I., 1965; cert. in travel agts., Travel Sch. of Am., 1968; cert., Labor Sch. of Boston, 1976, Labor Studies Inst., 1989. Field investigator R.I. Food Stamp Unit, Providence, 1965-68; cmty. rels. Coordinator Ecology Action for Rhode Island, 1970-71; sec. and rsch. asst. R.I. Worker Assn., 1973-74; enumerator R.I. Polk & Co., Providence, 1970-83; sr. employment security interviewer R.I. Dept. Employment Tng., 1984-96; sr. employment & tng. interviewer R.I. Dept. Labor & Tng., 1996—. Rec. sec. Local 189 New Eng. chpt., Boston, 1973-76, treas., 1989—; mem. bd. dirs. of R.I. Workers Assn., 1973-74, 75-76, census enumerator U.S. Census Bur., Providence, 1990; mail handler U.S. Post Office, Providence, 1980; claims interviewer R.I. Dept. Employment Security, Providence, 1979-84; rec. sec. R.I. Employment Security Alliance, Providence, 1980-90; v.p. Community Econs. Edn. Ctr., Providence, 1988-91. Exec. com. R.I. State Employees Assn., 1966-68, Community Labor Organizing Com., Providence, 1983-89, Sane Freeze, Washington, 1989-90; shop steward Local 401 SEIU, Providence, 1990-92, 1st v.p., 1992-96; rec. sec. R.I. Sane Freeze, Providence, 1988-94; mem. Nat. Com. Peace Action, 1993—; v.p. Peace Action R.I., 1994-95, pres., 1995—; coord. R.I. Nation Readers Group, 1995—; state committeeman Amvets Dept. R.I., 1965-69, 96—, adj. posts, 1965-68, trustee post 6, 1995-96; v.p. Labor Party R.I., 1994-97, treas., 1997—, pres., 1999, chmn., 1999; exec. bd. R.I. Coalition for Consumer Justice, 1997—; bd. dirs. Injured Workers R.I., 1996—, Warwick Cmty. Action, 1967-69, R.I. Legal Svcs., 1967-69; founder East Greenwich Dem. Youth Club, 1959; co-chmn. Human Rights Action Coun., Warwick, 1968-70; del. R.I. Dem. State Conv., 1976, 78; mem. R.I. Dem. State Com., 1980-86, bd. dirs., 1985-87; mem. Dem. Study Group R.I., 1986-88; organizer United Farm Workers, 1968-71; mem. Fox Point Neighborhood Housing Corp. Dirs., 1980-87, pres., 1981-83, sec., 1983-87. With U.S. Army, 1960-63, ETO. Mem. Internat. Assn. Pers. in Employment Security (R.I. chpt. bd. dirs. 1989-93, sec. 1991-93), Greater R.I. Indsl. Rels. Rsch. Assn., R.I. ACLU (bd. dirs. 1974-80, bd. sec. 1975-77, exec. com. 1979-80), Union of Peace Profls. (exec. bd. 1988-90), Nat. Writers Union, R.I. Cen. Am. Network, Cath. Peace Fellowship, Pax ChristiAncient Order, Order of Hibernians (rec. sec. Providence chpt. 1990-91, 97-98, v.p., 1998—, pres. 1991-92, state sec. 1993-96, pres. 1996—), K. of C., Sierra Club, Newport Mus. Irish History, Am. Irish Hist. Soc., R.I. Hist. Soc., R.I. Labor History Soc., Gaspee Days Com., Americans for Dem. Action, Debs Found., Edward Bellamy Meml. Assn., R.I. Irish Famine Meml. Com., Am. Legion, Indsl. Rels. Rsch. Assn., Assn. Can.-Am., Am. French Geneal. Soc., Irish Nat. Caucus, Am. Irish Polit. Edn. Com., Friendly Sons of St. Patrick (East Greenwich, R.I.). Democrat. Avocation: writing. Home: PO Box 945 Providence RI 02901-0945

MCNEIL, RAMSEY ENGLISH, religious studies educator; b. Franklin County, Va., Sept. 28, 1937; d. George Wilson and Eva Woody English; m. Carl Nixon McNeil, June 2, 1967; 1 child Carl Nixon. BS in Edn., Radford Coll., Va., 1958; MS in Edn., Radford U., Va., 1968. Sch. tchr. Franklin County Pub. Sch., Rocky Mount, NC, 1958—59, Danville City Pub. Sch., Danville, Va., 1959—63, Roanoke (Va.) City Sch., 1963—67, Mongomery County Sch., Christiansburg, Va., 1967—70; tchr. adult Sunday sch. local chs., 1966—2001, tchr. Bible quiz, 1978—89. Den mother Boy Scouts Am., Christiansburg, 1978—80; sec. bd. dis. Montgomery Mus., Va., 1995—2001; sch. vol. Mongomery County, 1976—91. Mem.: United Daus. Confederacy (pres. 1974—99, v.p. 1999—2001), Ea. Star (pianist 1989—96, chaplain 1998—2001). Republican. Baptist. Avocations: reading, antiques, flowers, travel. Home: 5234 Old Pagelyn Rd Radford VA 24141-6518

MCNEIL, RODNEY MALCOLM, poet, writer; b. Jersey City, Sept. 13, 1966; s. Wilbur James and Betty Louise McNeil; 1 child, Zakee Dawu Al-Kabeer Boyd. Student, Hampton (Va.) U., 1984, Rutgers U., Newark, 1985-87, 95-98. Acctg. clk. Roy Greene Assocs., Newark, 1988; appointment clk. VA Hosp., East Orange, N.J., 1989; file clk. Newark Beth Israel Hosp., 1997—. Author: Mirrors, 1996; contbg. author: In the Tradition, 1992, contbg. author: New Rain, Vol. 9, 1999, contbg. author: Jour. N.J. Poets, 1997, contbg. author: Sons of Lovers, 2000. Rschr., author Weequahic Pk. Assn., Newark, 1999-2000. Democrat. Baptist. Avocations: exercising, jazz, writing historical and philosophical data, watching TV sports. Home: 821 S 10th St Newark NJ 07108

MCNEILL, DANIEL RICHARD, writer; b. San Francisco, June 1, 1947; s. Daniel Harry and Maureen Evangeline (Sherriff) McN.; m. Rosalind Deborah Gold, Dec. 20, 1984. AB, U. Calif., Berkeley, 1975; JD, Harvard U., 1982. Author: Fuzzy Logic, 1993 (L.A. Times Book prize in sci. and tech. 1993), The Face, 1998. Mem. Authors Guild. Avocations: photography, bodybuilding. Home and Office: 8110 Redlands St #306 Playa Del Rey CA 90293

MCNEILL, G. DAVID, psycholinguist, educator; b. Santa Rosa, Calif., Dec. 21, 1931; s. Glenn H. and Ethel G. (Little) McN.; m. Nobuko Baba, Dec. 17, 1957; children: Cheryl, Randall L.B.. AB, U. Calif. at Berkeley, 1953, PhD, 1962. Research fellow Harvard U., 1962-65; asst. prof. psychology U. Mich., 1965-66, assoc. prof., 1966-68; prof. psychology and linguistics U. Chgo., 1969—2001, chmn. dept. psychology, 1991-97, prof. emeritus, 2001—. Vis. fellow Ctr. for Humanities, Wesleyan U., Middletown, Conn., 1970; mem. Inst. Advanced Study, Princeton, 1973-75; fellow Netherlands Inst. for Advanced Studies, 1983-84; visitor Max Planck Inst. for Psycholinguistics, Nijmegen, Germany, 1998-99. Author: The Acquisition of Language, 1970, The Conceptual Basis of Language, 1979, Psycholinguistics: A New Approach, 1987, Gengo Shinrigaku, 1991, Hand and Mind: What Gestures Reveal about Thought, 1992; editor: Language and Gesture. Recipient Faculty Achievement award, 1991, Ann. Excellence in Pub. award Assn. Am. Pubs., Gordon G. Laing prize U. Chgo. Press, 1995; Guggenheim fellow, 1973-74; grantee NSF, 1983-89, 97—, Spencer Found., 1979-82, 89-92, 95-99, NIDCD, 1992-96. Fellow AAAS, Am. Psychol. Soc.; mem. Internat. Soc. Gesture Studies (v.p. 2002—), Cognitive Sci. Soc., Linguistic Soc. Am., Violoncello Soc., Phi Beta Kappa, Sigma Xi. Office: U Chgo Dept Psychology 5848 S University Ave Chicago IL 60637-1515 E-mail: dmcn@ccp.uchicago.edu.

MCNEILL, JEANETTE N. executive secretary, writer; b. Hartsville, S.C., June 16, 1925; d. Samuel Bartow and Effie Thel (Howle) Norwood; m. Cameron McNeill, Oct. 29, 1956; 1 child Rose Cameron McNeill Gandy. Grad. h.s., Hartsville. Exec. sec. Aetna Ins. Co., Charlotte, NC, 1946—53; sec. coleman & Adams Ins., Asheville, 1953—54, Carolina Power & Light Co., Florence, SC, 1954—64; ret., 1964. Author: Legacy of the Northwoodes, 1997, The Memory of the Heart, 1999, (plays) 150 Year History of First Baptist Church, 2000 (History award S.C. Bapt. Hist. Soc., 2001). Membership chair, v.p. Cmty. Concert Assn., Hartsville, 1980—99. Recipient 15 Yr. Svc. award, Hartsville Cmty. Concert Assn., 1995. Mem.: Darlington County Hist. Soc. (recording sec. 1995—2002, sec. 1995—2002), Pilot Club Hartsville (pres. 1983—85). Democrat. Baptist. Avocations: reading, writing, travel, sewing. Home: 153 W Home Ave Hartsville SC 29550

MCNEILL, JOAN REAGIN, volunteer consultant; b. Atlanta, July 8, 1936; d. Arthur Edward and Annie May (Busby) Reagin; children: Thomas Pinckney, Clyde Reagin. Student, U. Louisville, 1955-57; BA, U. Tenn., Chattanooga, 1976. Founding pres. Family and Children's Svcs. Assocs., Chattanooga, 1987-88, bd. dirs., 1996—; bd. dirs. Chattanooga Symphony and Opera Assn., 1984-88, 99—, pres., 1984-87; pres. Chattanooga Ballet Assn., 1986-88; bd. dirs. U. Chattanooga Found., 1986-89, A.I.M. Ctr. of Chattanooga, 1997—, Eos Orch., N.Y.C., 1998—; v.p. devel. Chattanooga Cares, 1997—; chair Spl. needs and Svcs. for the Elderly of Chattanooga, 1997—; mem. bd. dirs. Hosanna House, 2001—; mem. vol. coun. bd. dirs. Am. Symphony Orch.

League, Washington, 1986-96; pres.-elect, 1992-93, pres., 1993-95; bd. dirs. Hosanna House of Chattanooga, pres., 2002-; juror Inst. Conducting Competition, Kharkov, Ukraine, 2002. Recipient Outstanding Svc. award U. Tenn., Chattanooga, 1988; named Chattanooga's Disting. Woman, 1999. Mem. U. Tenn. Chattanooga Alumni Assn. (pres. 1985-86), Golden Key, Order of Omega, Sigma Kappa Found. (trustee 1992-98, sec. 1993-94, pres. 1994-98, Colby award for volunteerism 1990). Republican. Episcopalian. Office: 7457 Preston Cir Chattanooga TN 37421-1839 E-mail: clownjoni@aol.com.

MCNEILL, JOHN HUGH, pharmaceutical sciences educator; b. Chgo., July 5, 1938; s. John and Agnes Margaret (McLean) McN.; m. Sharon Keneffy, July 27, 1963; children: Sandra, Laurie. BS, U. Alta., Can., 1960, MS, 1962; PhD, U. Mich., 1967. Lectr. pharmacy Dalhousie U., 1962-63, U. Alta., 1963; research assoc. U. Mich., Ann Arbor, 1963-65, teaching fellow, 1965-66; asst. instr. Mich. State U., East Lansing, 1966-67, asst. prof., 1967-71; assoc. prof. U. B.C., 1971-72, assoc. prof., chmn. div. pharmacology and toxicology, 1972-75, dir. research and grad. studies Faculty Pharm. Scis., 1977-78; prof. Faculty Pharm. Scis., 1975—; asst. dean U. B.C., 1978-81, research prof. Med. Research Council, 1981-82, prof., assoc. dean research and grad. studies, 1982-84, dean Faculty Pharm. Scis., 1985-96. Contbr. over 400 tech. articles to profl. jours. Fellow Royal Soc. Can.; mem. Pharm. Soc. Can. (various coms. 1974-88, coun. 1977-83, v.p. 1979, pres. 1980-81), Am. Soc. for Pharm. and Therapeutics (J.J. Abel award com. 1981, Upjohn award com., 1978-80, chmn. mem. com. 1983-86), Western Pharm. Soc. (coun. 1977-81, pres. 1979-80, past pres. 1980-81), N.Y. Acad. Scis., Internat. Soc. for Heart Rsch. (coun. 1986-95), AAAS, B.C. Coll. Pharms. (coun. 1985-96), Internat. Union Pharmacologists (Can. rep. 1982-88), Am. Pharm. Assn. Office: Univ BC Fac Pharm Scis 2146 East Mall Vancouver BC Canada V6T 1Z3 E-mail: jmcneill@interchange.ubc.ca.

MCNEILL, MARY KATHRYN MORGAN, librarian; b. Greenville, S.C., Feb. 22, 1958; d. Harvey Eugene and Mary Anna (Walser) Morgan; m. George Terrence McNeill, May 17, 1980; 1 child, Terrence Morgan. BS, Winthrop Coll., 1980; MLS, Emory U., 1985. Media specialist Thurston Elem. Sch., Thomaston, Ga., 1980-85; asst. libr. Oxford (Ga.) Coll. Libr. Emory U., 1985-88, dir., 1988—. Sunday Sch. tchr. Thomaston United Methodist Ch., 1981. Mem. ALA, Assn. Coll. and Rsch. Librs., Libr. Adminstrn. and Mgmt. Assn., Southeastern Libr. Assn., Ga. Libr. Assn., Delta Kappa Gamma (sec. chpt. 1992-96, pres. chpt. 1996-98). Home: 6012 Lakemont Trl Monroe GA 30656-3366 Office: Emory U Oxford Coll Libr PO Box 1448 Oxford GA 30054-1448

MCNEILL, SUSAN, real estate marketing and sales professional; b. Prescott, Ariz., Feb. 26, 1936; d. Glenn S. and Alma Johnson Hunter; m. Richard G. Bryant, Dec. 19,1 956 (div. Apr. 1971); children: Robert (dec.), Kathleen; m. Kenneth I. McNeill, Nov. 23, 1972; 1 child, John. BA, U. Ariz., 1957. Real estate owner Seaview Properties, Palos Verdes, Calif., 1978-82; real estate mktg. staff Coldwell Banker, 1982-99, Summit Group, Palos Verdes, 1999-2000, ReMax, Palos Verdes, 2001—. Art tchr., dir. Arts Unlimited Chadwick Sch., Palos Verdes, 1982-90; owner Bright Ideas, Palos Verdes, 1982—; founder Art At Your Fingertips, Palos Verdes. Bd. dirs. Norris Theater, Palos Verdes C. of C. Recipient Cmty. Svc. award City of L.A., 1993; named Palos Verdes Citizen of Yr., 2000. Mem. Palos Verdes Arts Ctr. (bd. dirs., exhbn. curator). Home: 32735 Seagate Dr Palos Verdes Peninsula CA 90275-5886 also: PO Box 2370 Palos Verdes Peninsula CA 90274-8370 Office: 63 Malaga Cove Plz Palos Verdes Estates CA 90274

MCNEILL, THOMAS B. retired lawyer; b. Chgo., Oct. 28, 1934; s. Donald T. and Katherine M. (Bennett) McN.; m. Ingrid Sieder, May 11, 1963; children: Christine, Thomas, Stephanie. BA, U. Notre Dame, 1956, JD, 1958. Ptnr. Mayer, Brown, Rowe & Maw, Chgo., 1962—99. Dir. Deltona Corp., Ocala, Fla. Served to capt. JAGC USAF, 1959-62. Fellow Am. Coll. Trial Lawyers; mem. Chgo. Bar Assn., Chgo. Council Lawyers, The Lawyers Club (Chgo. chpt.). Clubs: Indian Hill (Winnetka, Ill.). Home: 2418 Iroquois Rd Wilmette IL 60091-1335 E-mail: tomingrid@aol.com.

MCNEILL, THOMAS RAY, lawyer; b. Pitts., June 2, 1952; s. Thomas William McNeill and Mary (Shiveley) Hiss; m. Patsy Lynch, June 25, 1977; children: Elizabeth, Kathleen, Thomas. BSBA, U. Fla., 1974; JD, Emory U., 1977. Bar: Ga. 1977, U.S. Dist. Ct. (no. dist.) Ga. 1977. Assoc. Powell, Goldstein, Frazer & Murphy, LLP, Atlanta, 1977-84, ptnr., 1984—, mgr. corp. dept., 1993-95, bd. ptnrs., 1998—. Mem. Ga. Bar Assn., Emory U. Alumni Assn. (pres. exec. com. Atlanta chpt. 1988-89, Law Sch. coun. 1990-2000), Soc. of Internat. Bus. Fellows, Beta Gamma Sigma. Office: Powell Goldstein Frazer & Murphy 191 Peachtree St NE Ste 1600 Atlanta GA 30303-1700 E-mail: tmcneill@pgfm.com.

MCNEILL, WILLIAM, environmental scientist; b. Evanston, Ill., Jan. 1, 1930; s. John and Ebba Katrina (Hansen) McN.; m. Caryl Mook, June 15, 1951 (dec. 1969); children: Elizabeth Marie, Charles Craig, Margaret Ruth; m. Caecilia Cinquanto, Oct. 10, 1970. BA, Colgate U., 1951; MA, Temple U., 1955, PhD, 1961. Chief phys. chemistry br. Frankford Arsenal U.S. Army, Phila., 1959-70, dir. applied sci., 1970-75, chief scientist, environ. mgr. Rocky Mountain Arsenal Denver, 1975-80, dir. tech. ops., 1980-85; gen. mgr. Battelle Denver Ops., 1985-88; sr. tech. adviser Sci. Applications Internat. Corp., Golden, Colo., 1989-92, dir. tech. devel. Oak Ridge, Tenn., 1992-93. Mem. materials adv. bd. ceramics NAS/Nat. Rsch. Coun., Washington, 1966; mem. Gov.'s Task Group on Rocky Mountain Arsenal, 1976, Colo. Pollution Prevention Adv. Bd., Denver, 1991-99. Contbr. articles to Jour. Chem. Physics, Applied Physics Letters, other profl. publs. Mem. Am. Chem. Soc., Hazardous Material Control Rsch. Inst., Air and Waste Mgmt. Assn. Achievements include 10 patents for electrochemical processes, inorganic materials synthesis, electro-optical devices; demonstration and use of narrow-band optical absorbers for laser protection; leader in development of Army environmental programs; preparation of reports of expert testimony in cases involving solvent usage and disposal on military installations. Home: 319 Cliffrose Ct Lafayette CO 80026-9391 E-mail: wzmcn@indra.com.

MCNEILL, WILLIAM HARDY, retired history educator, writer; b. Vancouver, B.C., Can., Oct. 31, 1917; s. John Thomas and Netta (Hardy) McN.; m. Elizabeth Darbishire, Sept. 7, 1946; children: Ruth Netta, Deborah Joan, John Robert, Andrew Duncan. BA, U. Chgo., 1938, MA, 1939; PhD, Cornell U., 1947; 20 hon. degrees. Faculty U. Chgo., 1947-87, prof. history, 1957-87, Robert A. Millikan Disting. Svc. prof., 1969-87, prof. emeritus, 1987—, chmn. dept., 1961-67; pres. Demos Fund, 1968-80; chmn. bd. Demos Found., 1980-86. George Eastman vis. prof. Oxford (Eng.) U., 1980-81 Author: Greek Dilemma, War and Aftermath, 1947, Report on the Greeks, 1948, History Handbook of Western Civilization, 1948, rev. and enlarged 6th edit., 1986, America, Britain and Russia, Their Cooperation and Conflict, 1941-46, 1953, Past and Future, 1954, Greece: American Aid in Action, 1947-56, 1957, Rise of the West: A History of the Human Community, 1963, 9th edit., 1991 (Nat. Book award, Gordon J. Laing prize), Europe's Steppe Frontier, 1500-1800, 1964, A World History, 1967, 4th edit., 1998, The Contemporary World, 1967, 2d edit., 1975, The Ecumene: Story of Humanity, 1973, Venice, the Hinge of Europe, 1081-1797, 1974, The Shape of European History, 1974, Plagues and Peoples, 1976, revised edit., 1998, Metamorphosis of Greece since World War II, 1978, The Human Condition, An Ecological and Historical View, 1980, Pursuit of Power, 1982, The Great Frontier, 1983, Mythistory and other Essays, 1986, A History of the Human Community, 1986, 6th edit., 1998, Polyethnicity and National Unity in World History, 1987, Arnold J. Toynbee: A Life, 1989, Population and Politics Since 1750, 1990, Hutchins' University: A Memoir of the University of Chicago 1929-50, 1991, The Global Tradition: Conquerors, Catastrophes and Community, 1992, Keeping Together in Time: Dance & Drill in Human History, 1995, Colebrook: An Historical Sketch, 1996, De excentriciteit van het wiel en audere wereld-historische essays, 1996, The Disruption of Traditional Forms of Nurture, 1998; editor: Lord Acton, Essays in the Liberal Interpretation of History, 1967, (with others) Readings in World History, Vols. I-X, 1968-73, Human Migration, 1978, Jour. Modern History, 1971-79, Jour. Modern Greek Studies, 1983-85; bd. editors Ency. Brit., 1981-98; contbr. numerous articles and reviews to profl. jours., chpts. to books. Trustee Athens Coll., 1970-88; vice chmn. Christopher Columbus Quincentenary Jubilee Commn., 1985-93; co-chair curriculum task force Nat. Commn. on Social Studies, 1987-89; mem. Bradley Commn. on the Teaching of History, 1986-89; vice chmn. Nat. Coun. for History Edn., 1990-94, Nat. Coun. for History Standards, 1992-94. Recipient Erasmus prize, 1996; Fulbright Research scholar Royal Inst. Internat. Affairs, Eng., 1950-51; Rockefeller grantee, 1951-52; Ford Faculty fellow, 1954-55; Carnegie grantee, 1957-62, 63-64; Guggenheim fellow, 1971-72, 86-87; Josiah H. Macy grantee, 1973-74; Rockefeller grantee, 1976 Fellow Am. Philos. Soc., Am. Acad. Arts and Scis., Brit. Acad. Arts and Scis. (corr.), Royal Hist. Soc. (corr.); mem. Am. Hist. Assn. (council, del. Am. Council Learned Socs., pres. 1985) Office: PO Box 45 Colebrook CT 06021-0045

MCNEIL STAUDENMAIER, HEIDI LORETTA, lawyer; b. Preston, Iowa, Apr. 7, 1959; d. Archie Hugo and Heidi (Waltert) McN.; m. L. William Staudenmaier III; children: Kathleen Louise McNeil Staudenmaier, Jacob William Staudenmaier. BA in Journalism and Broadcasting with distinction, U. Iowa, 1981, JD with distinction, 1985. Bar: Ariz. 1985, U.S. Dist. Ct. Ariz. 1985, U.S. Ct. Appeals (9th cir.) 1985, U.S. Ct. Appeals (10th cir.) 1990. Sports journalist The Daily Iowan, Iowa City, 1977-81, Quad City Times, Davenport, Iowa, 1981-82; ptnr. Snell & Wilmer, Phoenix, 1985—. Judge pro tem, Maricopa County, Phoenix, 1992—, Ariz. Ct. Appeals, 1998—. Mem. ABA (mem. domestic violence commn. 1995-98, Ho. of Dels. 1995-98, 2001—, chair young lawyers career issues com. 1992-93, mem. affiliate assistance program com. 1992-93, dir. 1993-94, spl. projects coord. 1994-95, bus. law sect., editor-in-chief Bus. Law Today, co-chair fellows program), Internat. Assn. Gaming Attys., Ariz. Bar Assn. (Indian law sect. exec. coun. and chair, 1995-99, young lawyers exec. coun. 1991-94), Maricopa County Bar Assn. (bd. dirs. 1991—, young lawyers divsn. 1987-93, pres. 1991-92, 99-2000), Ariz. Women Lawyers, Phoenix Assn. Def. Counsel, Native Am. Bar Assocs., Phi Beta Kappa, Phi Eta Sigma. Lutheran. Avocations: running, golf, skiing, hiking, bicycling.

MCNELIS, EDWARD JOSEPH, chemistry educator; b. Phila., Aug. 17, 1930; s. Edward Joseph and Ellen Frances McNelis; m. Katerina Toumpopoulou, Sept. 8, 1956; children: John, Joseph. BS, Villanova Coll., 1953; PhD, Columbia U., 1960. Rsch. chemist Sun Oil Co., Marcus Hook, Pa., 1960-66; vis. prof. Haverford (Pa.) Coll., 1966-67; prof. chemistry NYU, N.Y.C., 1967—, chmn. dept., 1977-87. Lt. (j.g.) USN, 1953-56. Fellow AAAS, Am. Inst. Chemists; mem. Am. Chem. Soc. Office: NYU 100 Washington Sq E New York NY 10003 E-mail: em2@is.nyu.edu.

MCNELLEY, JUDY ANNE, small business owner; b. Commerce, Ga., Oct. 19, 1956; d. Marvin Ellis and Florence Evelyn Duncan; m. Harold Michael McNelley, Aug. 14, 1977; children: Jeremy Michael, James Todd, Joshua Duncan. Student, Young Harris Coll., 1976-77. Co-owner M & J Vending, Tunnel Hill, Ga., 1988—. Columnist Banks County News, 1992. Chmn. Whitfield County Rep. Party, 1995—, precinct capt., 1991-93, 1st vice chmn. 1993-95, conv. del., 1988—; cons. Dalton State Coll. Reps., 1998—; exec. com. 9th Congl. Dist. Ga. Rep. Party, 1995—, conv. del., 1989—; 2d v.p. Rep. Women N.W. Ga., 1993-97; mem. sex. edn. adv. com. Whitfield County Schs., Dalton, Ga., 1991-98, mem. sys. level media adv. bd., 1995-96; Sunday sch. tchr. Tunnel Hill United Meth. Ch., 1986-97; charter mem. Coun. Women Advisors to Congress, Washington, 1995. Named Hon. Life Mem. Ga. PTA, 1991, Rep. Woman of Yr., Rep. Women N.W. Ga., 1995, Cmty. Hero Torchbearer, Atlanta Com. Olympic Games, 1996; recipient Ronald Reagan award 9th Congl. Dist. Ga. Rep. Party, 1997, Vol. of Yr. award Tunnel Hill Elem. Sch., 1991. Republican. Christian. Avocations: volunteer work, collecting autographed memorabilia, reading, concerts. Home: 306 Scenic Dr Tunnel Hill GA 30755-9712

MC NELLY, FREDERICK WRIGHT, JR. psychologist; b. Bangor, Maine, Apr. 14, 1947; s. Frederick Wright and E. Frances (Cutter) McNelly; 1 adopted child Roger McNelly foster children: Joseph, Ronald, Michael, Jeffrey. BA magna cum laude, U. Minn., 1969; MA, U. Mich., 1971, PhD, 1973. Registered clin. psychologist Ill., cert. profl. qualification, state and provincial bds. of psychology, early intervention program provider Ill. Rsch. coord. NSF project U. Minn., Morris, 1968-69, lab. instr., 1969, trainee USPHS, 1969-70, 72; teaching fellow psychology U. Mich., Ann Arbor, 1970-72; edn1. examiner Ann Arbor Pub. Schs., 1971; dir. psychol. svcs. Children Devel. Ctr., Rockford, Ill., 1972-82, program dir., 1982-86; cons. psychologist, 1986—. Lectr. Rock Valley Coll., Rockford, 1974—75; part-time pvt. practice psychology, Rockford and Belvidere, Ill., 1980—86, Beloit, Wis., 1985—86; full time, 1986—; mental health cons. Rockford Head Start, 1982—, United Cerebral Palsy, Blackhawk Region, 1986—, Access Svcs., Mendota, Ill., 1992—; mem. health svcs. adv. com. human resources dept. City of Rockford, 1985—; presenter state and regional workshops and confs. Contbr. articles to profl. jours. Active Boy Scouts Am., 1978—83; chmn. spl. edn. regional adv. com. Bi-County Office Edn., Rockford, 1976—78; mem. Nat. and Ill. Com. Child Abuse, 1975—85; co-chmn. Winnebago County Child Protection Assn., 1980; elder Willow Creek United Presbyn. Ch., Rockford, 1980—83; mem. stronghold renovation session com. Presbytery Blackhawk, Oregon, Ill., 1985. Named U.S. Jaycees Outstanding Young Man of 1977. Mem.: Ill. Assn. Infant Mental Health, No. Ill. Alliance Mentally Ill, Nat. Assn. Mentally Ill, Nat. Assn. Disability Examiners, State Provincial Bds. Psychology, Nat. Register Health Svc. Providers Psychology, Coun. Exception Children, No. Ill. Pvt. Practice Metnal Health Assn., Wis. Psychol. Assn. (v.p. 1993, pres. 1994—95), No. Ill. Psychol. Assn., Ill. Psychol. Assn. Home: 11591 Beverly Ln Belvidere IL 61008-8708 Office: Childrens Devel Ctr 650 N Main St Rockford IL 61103-6994 also: 972 N Main St Rockford IL 61103-9652

MCNELLY, JOHN TAYLOR, journalist, educator; b. Lancaster, Wis., Oct. 2, 1923; s. Stephen Sumner and Caroline Hurd (Taylor) McN.; m. Pamela Edith Thompson, Dec. 20, 1952; children: Barbara, Duncan. BA, U. Wis., 1946, MA, 1957; PhD, Mich. State U., 1961. Reporter AP, Milw., 1948-52, Reuters, London, 1952-53; news editor U. Wis. News Service, Madison, 1957; instr., then assoc. prof. Mich. State U., East Lansing, 1957-66; assoc. prof., then prof. U. Wis., Madison, 1966-82, Evjue-Bascom prof., 1982-88, prof. emeritus, 1988—. Asst. dir. Inter-Am. Mass Communications Program, San Jose, Costa Rica, 1961-62; vis. prof. Berlin Inst. Mass. Communication in Developing Nations, W.Ger., 1965, Agrarian U., Lima, Peru, 1968-69; communication cons. UNESCO, Latin Am., 1970-75; lectr. USIA, Latin Am., 1968, 74, 80 Co-author: Communication and Social Change in Latin America, 1968; assoc. editor: Journalism Quar., 1975-77; contbr. monographs and articles to communication publs. Served with USAF, 1942-43. Fulbright-Hays Faculty fellow Lima, Peru, 1968-69 Home: 134 Larkin St Madison WI 53705-5116

MCNERNEY, KATHLEEN, literature educator; b. Albuquerque, Oct. 11, 1945; d. John and Rosemary McNerney. PhD, U. N.Mex., 1977; lang. cert., Girona Lang. Sch., 1983. Prof. lit. W.Va. Univ., Morgantown, 1980—. Author: Undestanding Garcia Marquez, 1988; translator: Blue Roses for a Dead-...Lady, 1998; editor: Voices & Visions, 1999. Mem. MLA, N.Am. Catalan Soc. (pres. 1998-01). Office: Fgn Langs PO Box 6298 W Va Univ Morgantown WV 26506

MCNERNEY, W. JAMES, manufacturing executive; BA, Yale U.; MBA, Harvard U. Pres. GE Info. Svcs.; exec. v.p. GE Capital; pres., CEO GE Elec. Distribution and Control; pres. GE Asia-Pacific; pres., CEO GE Aircraft Engines; chmn., CEO 3M Co, St. Paul, 2001—. Office: 3M Co 3M Ctr Saint Paul MN 55144*

MCNEW, BENNIE BANKS, economics and finance educator; b. Greenbrier, Ark., Nov. 12, 1931; s. Roland H. and Stella (Avery) McN.; m. Bonnie Lou Stone, Mar. 31, 1956; children— Bonnie Banks, Mary Kathleen, William Michael. BS, Ark. State Tchrs. Coll., 1953; MBA, U. Ark., 1954; PhD, U. Tex., 1961. Asst. nat. bank examiner, 1954-56; indsl. specialist U. Ark. Indsl. Research and Extension Center, 1956-59; lectr. finance U. Tex., 1959-61; prof. banking U. Miss., University, 1961-65; dean U. Miss. (Sch. Bus. Adminstrn.), 1965-79, Sch. Bus., Middle Tenn. State U., Murfreesboro, 1980-88; prof. econs. and fin. U. Cen. Ark., Conway, 1988-98; ret. Asst. dir., v.p. Grad. Sch. Banking of South, La. State U., 1966-97. Author: (with Charles L. Prather) Fraud Control for Commercial Banks, 1962; contbg. author: Money and Banking Casebook, 1966, The Bankers Handbook, 1966, A History of Mississippi, 1973. Served with AUS, 1950-51. Mem.: Lions (pres. Oxford, Miss. 1964—65). Home: 12 Bainbridge Dr Conway AR 72034-7217 E-mail: benm@ipa.net.

MCNICHOLAS, EDWARD, lawyer; b. St. Louis, Jan. 27, 1969; s. Robert and Helen McNicholas; m. Andrea, Aug. 10, 1996. AB, Princeton U., 1991; JD, Harvard U., 1996. Bar: D.C. 1996, Md. 1996. Law clk. to Hon. P. Niemeyer U.S. Ct. Appeal (4th Cir.), Balt., 1996—97; assoc. counsel to Pres. The White Ho., Washington, 2000—01. Author several law rev. pieces Harvard Law Rev., 1995; editor Harvard Law Rev., Cambridge, Mass., 1994-96. Roman Catholic. Office: Sidley Austin Brown and Wood 1501 K St NW Washington DC 20005 E-mail: emcnicho@sidley.com.

MCNICHOLS, GERALD ROBERT, consulting company executive; b. Cleve., Nov. 21, 1943; s. Charles Wellington and June Beatrice (Kalal) McN.; m. Paula Kay Austin, Dec. 26, 1964; children: G. Robert Jr., Katherine Lynn Loftis, Melissa Sue Cardon. BS with honors, Case-Western Res. U., 1965; MS, U. Pa., 1966; ScD, George Washington U., 1976. Cert. cost estimator/analyst. Sr. ops. analyst Office of Sec., Dept. of Def., Washington, 1970-76; v.p. GenTech, Inc., Bethesda, Md., 1976-77, J. Watson Noah, Inc., Falls Church, Va., 1977-78; pres., chief exec. officer Mgmt. Cons. and Rsch., Inc., McLean, 1978-99; sr. v.p. GRC Internat. (acquired Mgmt. Cons. and Rsch., Inc.), 1999-2000, also bd. dirs.; CEO McNichols & McNichols, Inc., Middleburg, Va., 2000—. Pres. McNichols Family Found., 2000—; chmn. bd. Metier, Ltd.; bd. dirs. Hadron, Inc., several pvt. small bus. Co-author: Operations Research for Decision Making, 1975; contbg. author: Software Reliability, 1986, Software System Design Methods, 1986, Electronic Systems Effectiveness and Life Cycle Costing, 1983; editor Cost Analysis, 1984; contbr. articles to profl. jours. Pres. Rondelay Civic Assn., Fairfax Sta., Va., 1985-87; bd. dirs. Kennedy Ctr. Cir., 1995-2000. Capt. USAF, 1966-70. Recipient Meritorious Achievement award, Case Western Res U., 1995, Engr. Alumni Achievement award, George Washington U., 1989. Mem. Inst. Cost Analysis (pres. 1985-88), Internat. Soc. Parametric Analysts (bd. dirs. 1982-84, Frieman Lifetime Achievement award 1990), Ops. Rsch. Soc. Am. (chmn. mil. applications sect.), Assn. for Small Rsch., Engring., and Tech. Svcs. Cos. (pres.), Mil. Ops. Rsch. Soc. (sec., treas. 1986-87, v.p. adminstrn. 1987-88, bd. dirs. 1985-88, 92-96), Soc. Cost Estimating and Analysis (bd. dirs. 1990-93, Lifetime Achievement award 2000), Century Club George Mason Univ. (bd. dirs. 1997-2000). Home: 23349 Parsons Rd Middleburg VA 20117-2817 Office: McNichols & McNichols Inc PO Box 2226 Middleburg VA 20118-2226 E-mail: drmcnichols@mcnichols.org.

MCNICOL, DAVID LEON, federal official; b. South Gate, Calif., May 18, 1944; s. Charles D. and Mary W. (Heisel) McN.; m. Lore Anne Long, Mar. 25, 1967; children: Katharine Anne, Elizabeth Mary. BA magna cum laude, Harvard U., 1966; MS, MIT, 1968, PhD, 1973. Asst. prof. econs. U. Pa., Phila., 1971-75; sr. staff economist Pres.'s Coun. of Econ. Advisors, Washington, 1976; vis. assoc. prof. econs. Calif. Inst. Tech., Pasadena, 1976-77; sr. economist Office of the Sec., U.S. Dept. of Treasury, Washington, 1977-79; dir. Office of Econ. Analysis U.S. Dept. Energy, 1980-81, dep. asst. adminstr. Office of Applied Analysis, 1981-82; dir. Econ. Analysis and Resource Planning Divsn. Office of Sec. of Def., Office of Program Analysis and Evaluation, 1982-88, dep. asst. sec., dep. dir., 1988—, chmn. cost analysis improvement group, 1988—. Author over 20 publs. on commodity markets, regulatory econs., energy issues and econ. aspects of the U.S. def. program. Recipient Spl. Svc. award Dept. Energy, 1981, Presdl. Rank award U.S. Govt., 1988, 93, 96, Disting./Meritorious Civilian Svc. medal Dept. Def., 1988, 91, 93, 96, 97, 2001. Home: 6901 Pineway University Park MD 20782-1163 Office: Dept Def OSD: PA&E The Pentagon Washington DC 20301-0001 E-mail: dave.mcnicol@osd.pentagon.mil.

MCNIDER, JAMES SMALL, III, lawyer; b. Richmond, Va., Aug. 23, 1956; s. James Small Jr. and Phoebe Warwick (Johnston) McNider; m. Anna Mary Van Buren, Apr. 30, 1983; children: Anna Lee, Mary Tyler, James S. IV, Ellen Page. BS, Washington & Lee U., 1978, JD, 1981. Bar: Va. 1981, U.S. Tax Ct. 1981, U.S. Dist. Ct. (ea. dist.) Va. 1986. Assoc. Kaufman & Canoles, Norfolk, Va., 1981-85, Willcox & Savage, Norfolk, 1985-87, ptnr., 1987-95, James S. McNider, III P.L.C., Hampton, 1995—. Author (with others): (book) ABA Sales and Use Tax handbook, 1988. Mem.: ABA, Va. BAr Assn. (chmn. tax sect. 1993—94), Princess Anne Country Club, Omicron Delta Kappa. Episcopalian. Avocations: private pilot, tennis, golf. Home: 808 Park Pl Hampton VA 23669-4152 Office: PO Box I Hampton VA 23669-0256 E-mail: jmcnider@valaw.com.

MCNIEL, ELIZABETH ANN, veterinarian, educator; b. Dallas, Feb. 3, 1965; d. James Samuel McNiel Jr. and Marie H. McNiel. BS, U. Tex., 1988; DVM, Tex.A&M U., College Station, TX, 1992; MS, Colo. State U., 1996, PhD, 2000. Diplomate oncology Am. Coll. Vet. Internal Medicine. Intern in gen. medicine and surgery Angell Meml. Animal Hosp., Boston, 1992—93; resident in med. oncology Colo. State U. Vet. Tchg. Hosp., Ft. Collins, 1993—96; rsch. assoc. Colo. State U., 2000—01; asst. prof. U. Minn., St. Paul, 2001—02. Recipient Mentored Clin Scientist award, Nat. Cancer Inst., 2001—06. Mem.: AAAS, Vet. Cancer Soc. (Robert S. Brodey award for excellence in clin. rsch. 1995), Am. Assn. for Cancer Rsch. (Travel award 1998), Am. Vet. Med. Assn., Am. Coll. Vet. Internal Medicine, Radiation Rsch. Soc. (Travel award 1998, 1999). Office: U Minn 1352 Boyd Ave Saint Paul MN 55108 Office Fax: 970-491-0623. Business E-Mail: mcnie001@umn.edu.

MCNIERNEY, LISA MARIE, critical care nurse; b. Lackawanna, N.Y., Dec. 22, 1958; d. Gerald Francis and Marie Frances (Carlin) Buck; divorced; children: Melissa, William, Brooke, Corey, Cameron, Brittany. ADN, Trocaire Coll., 1979. Nurse Sheehan Meml. Hosp., Buffalo, 1979-80, Erie County Med. Ctr., Buffalo, 1980-81, 94—, charge nurse night shift, cardio thoracic unit; nurse St. Francis Hosp., Evanston, Ill., 1981-93; asst. head nurse cardiothoracic unit Erie County Med. Ctr., 1996—. Mem. AACN, N.Y. State Nurses Assn. Home: 202 Fairfax Park Hamburg NY 14075-3566

MCNIESH, LAWRENCE MELVIN, radiologist; b. Appleton, Wis., Oct. 30, 1949; s. Vaughn Arley and Gladys Marie (Junion) McN.; m. Susan Irene White, July 14, 1972; children: Michael, Matthew, Carrie, Casey, Nicholas. BS, U. Calif., Davis, 1971; MD, Georgetown U., 1975. Diplomate Am. Bd. Med. Examiners, Am. Bd. Radiology. Intern and resident in radiology Letterman Army Med. Ctr., San Francisco, 1975-79; chief skeletal radiology Walter Reed Army Med Ctr., Washington, 1979-82, 84-87; asst. prof. Uniformed Svcs. U. Health Scis., Bethesda, Md., 1981-82, 84-87, clin. assoc. prof., 1988—; asst. prof. Health Sci. Ctr. U. Tex., San Antonio, 1982-84; chief radiology Audie Murphy VA Hosp., 1983-84; pvt. practice Olney, Md., 1987-91, Johnstown, Pa., 1991—; chief of radiology Windber (Pa.) Hosp., 1992—. Pres. med. staff Windber (Pa.) Hosp., 1996; cons. in field. Contbr. articles to profl. jours. Bd. dirs. Meml. Med. Ctr., Johnstown, 1998—; vol. Girl Scouts U.S., 1979-95, Montgomery County Coalition for Homeless, 1987-88, Little League Baseball, 1992-98. Lt. col. U.S. Army, 1975-82. Mem. Calif. Scholastic Fedn. (life), Radiol. Soc. N.Am., Am. Coll. Radiology. Republican. Lutheran. Avocations: golf, running, alpine skiing. Home: 208 Mayluth Rd Johnstown PA 15904-2635 Office: Cambria-Somerset Radiology 1086 Franklin St Johnstown PA 15905-4305

MCNIFF, CHRISTINE MARIE, psychotherapist; b. Concord, Mass., July 13, 1946; d. John Nicholas and Anna Elizabeth (Casey) D'Errico; m. John Thomas McNiff, June 20, 1970; children: Lisa Ann, Sean Patrick. BS in Human Resource Mgmt., Boston U., 1990; MA in Counseling, Antioch U., 1994. Lic. psychotherapist. Designer, trainer Digital Mgmt. Edn., Bedford, Mass., 1978-84; sr. pers. cons. Digital Equipment Corp., Nashua, N.H., 1984-86, tng. mgr., 1986-87, human resource mgr. Maynard, Mass., 1987-88, pers. mgr., 1988—93; psychotherapist Christine McNiff Counseling Svcs., Concord, 1993—. Vol. Concord Family Svcs. Young Parent Program; tchr. Confraternity of Christian Doctrine. Mem.: ACA, Mass. Mental Health Counselors Assn. Avocation: volunteering. Office: Christine McNiff Counseling Svcs 191 Sudbury Rd Concord MA 01742

MCNINCH, MICHEL COTTINGHAM, artist, educator; b. Charleston, S.C., Dec. 12, 1961; d. David Ellis and Sophie Ellen (Blanchard) Cottingham; m. Robert Lide McNinch, May 28, 1983. AA, Midlands Coll., Columbia, S.C., 1980; BA, U. S.C., 1992. Legal sec. Nexsen Pruet Jacobs and Pollard, 1988-98; pvt. practice artist Chapin, S.C., 1991—; art instr. Midlands Tech. Coll., Columbia, 1997—; artist in residence Alternative Acad., Chapin, 1997—; artist in residence with learning disabled Irmo Mid. Sch., 1999—. Grants reveiwer Pee Dee Ednl. Found., Florence, S.C., 1998. Recipient 2d pl. Chapin Celebrates Arts, 1995, 96, Grand prize Culture in Agr., S.C. Watermelon Bd./S.C. State Fair, 1997, 2d pl. Aiken Ctr. Arts, 1998, 1st pl. Chapin Celebrates the Arts, 1999, 1st pl. Old Santee Canal, 1999, Best in Show Partanburg County Mus., 2002, Best in Show Stanpipe Ann., Belton, S.C., 2002 Mem. S.C. Watercolor Soc., About Face, (sec. 1997-98), Crooked Creek Art League (pres. 1997-98), S.C. approved artists roster. Roman Catholic. Avocations: nature, travelling, museum tours, working with at-risk kids. Office: McNinch Art Studios PO Box 641 Chapin SC 29036-0641 E-mail: mcmofsc@sc.rr.com.

MC NITT, WILLARD CHARLES, business executive; b. Chgo., June 6, 1920; s. Willard C. and Louise (Richardson) McN.; m. Charlotte D. Boyd, Sept. 14, 1946; children: Willard Charles, James D., Peter B. McNitt. BA, Amherst Coll., 1942; A.M., Harvard Grad. Sch. Bus. Adminstrn., 1942; student, Northwestern Grad. Sch. Bus. Adminstrn., U. Chgo. Sch. Bus. Adminstrn., 1947. Asst. market planning and research Foote, Cone & Belding Co., Chgo., 1946-47; asst. sales promotion and advt. Bell & Gosset Co., Morton Grove, Ill., 1947-48; v.p. sales and mktg. Bowes Industries, Inc., Chgo., 1948-54; gen. mgr. sales and mktg. Clayton Mark & Co., Evanston, Ill., 1954-58; pres., dir. Bowey's, Inc., Chgo., 1958-62; pres., dir., mem. exec. com. H.M. Byllesby Co., 1962-63; group v.p., dir. Consol. Foods Corp., 1963-67; exec. v.p. consumer products group W.R. Grace & Co., N.Y.C., 1967-72; exec. v.p., dir., mem. exec. com. Ward Foods, Inc., Wilmette, Ill., 1972-73, chief operating officer, pres., dir., mem. exec. com., 1973-76; pres., chief exec. officer, dir. Westgate-Calif. Corp., and Sun Harbor Industries, San Diego, 1977-80; pres., chief exec. officer Nalley's Fine Foods, Tacoma, 1980-83; chmn., dir. Joseph Magnin Inc., 1982-85; chmn. Blue Moon Cheese Co., Thorpe, Wis., 1983—; operating ptnr. Wallner & Co., La Jolla, Calif.; vice chmn., pres., chief exec. officer, dir., mem. exec. com. Foremost Dairies, Inc., San Francisco, 1983-85. Chmn. Epcom; bd. dirs. ATI, NCIC, Blue Moon Cheese, Del. Lightweight. Troop head local Boy Scouts Am., 1957-67. Served to lt. (s.g.) USNR, 1942-46. Mem. Executives Club (Chgo.), Amherst Club, Harvard Bus. Sch. Club (Chgo., N.Y.C.), Indian Hill Country Club (Winnetka), Dairymen's Club (Boulder Junction, Wis.), Rancho Santa Fe Country Club, Fairbanks Ranch Country Club (Rancho Santa Fe), Rio Mar Country Club (Vero Beach, Fla.), Chi Psi. Republican. Congregationalist. Address: 1630 Sheridan Rd Apt 3A Wilmette IL 60091-1889

MC NIVEN, HUGH DONALD, engineering science educator, earthquake engineering researcher; b. Toronto, Ont., Can., Aug. 6, 1922; came to U.S., 1953; s. James and Pearl Mary (Jackson) Mc N.; m. Marion Fitzhugh, Sept. 12, 1959; 1 dau., Carolyn Fitzhugh. BASc., U. Toronto, 1944; M.C.E., Cornell U., 1948; PhD, Columbia U., 1957. Prof. engring. sci. U. Calif.-Berkeley, 1957—, dir. Earthquake Engring. Research Ctr., 1980-85. Contbr. articles to profl. jours. Pres. Univ. Art Mus. U. Calif.-Berkeley, 1970-72. Served to capt. Can. Army, 1944-46. Fellow Acoust. Soc. Am.; mem. ASCE, ASME, Earthquake Engring. Research Inst., Seismology Soc. Am. Clubs: Bohemian (San Francisco); Mira Vista Golf (El Cerrito, Calif.); Fox House, American (London). Home: 1440 Hawthorne Ter Berkeley CA 94708-1804 Office: Earthquake Engring Research Ctr U Calif 1301 S 46th St Richmond CA 94804-4600

MCNOWN, CADE, professional football player; b. Oreg., Jan. 12, 1977; Student, UCLA. Football player Chgo. Bears, 1999—2000, Miami Dolphins, 2001, San Francisco 49ers, 2002. Office: San Francisco 49ers 4949 Centennial Blvd Santa Clara CA 95054*

MCNULTY, CARRELL STEWART, JR. retired manufacturing company executive, architect; b. Newark, Dec. 4, 1924; s. Carrell Stewart and Marjorie (Yaegerlehner) McN.; m. Barbara Brokaw, June 21, 1952; children: Peter Carrell, Susan Abigail. Student, Emory U., 1941-43, U. N.C., 1943-44; BArch, Columbia U., 1950, MS in Urban Planning, 1963. Registered architect, Conn. Assoc. SMS Architects, Stamford, Conn., 1950-58, gen. ptnr., 1958-73; pvt. practice architecture Weston, 1973-76; pres. CMW Co., 1975-77, NB Products, Inc., Horsham, Pa., 1976-94, NB Instruments, Inc., Horsham, 1979-93, Environ. Svcs. and Products, Inc., Horsham, 1994-96; ret. Mem. Conn. Soc. Architects, 1963-73, sec., 1964-67, pres., 1969-70. Chair S.W. Regional Planning Agy., Norwalk, Conn., 1967-71; mem. Gov.'s Com. on Environment, New Haven, 1970, chair Gov.'s Task Force on Housing, Norwalk, 1972; bd. dirs., sec. Habitat for Humanity of Greater Bucks, Doylestown, Pa., 1990-97; pres. Ctrl. Bucks Crossroads, 1995-96. Lt. (j.g.) USNR, 1943-46; PTO. Recipient citation Am. Assn. Sch. Adminstrs., 1960, 6th Biennial Design award HUD, 1973; grantee HUD, Housing Rsch., 1970. Fellow AIA (mem. urban design com. 1963-73, chmn. 1971); mem. Bucks County Choral Soc., Sigma Nu. Democrat. Mem. United Ch. of Christ (deacon 1965-71, elder 1989-92). Avocations: computers, watercoloring, choral music. Home: 14179 SE 88th Ct Summerfield FL 34491 E-mail: llerracm@aol.com.

MCNULTY, DIANE ROSE, library director; b. Belleville, Ill., Mar. 1, 1956; d. Kenneth Edgar and Ethel Mae (Boettcher) Poll; m. Richard J. McNulty, Jr., Nov. 26, 1988; children: Deirdre Claire, Connor Kenneth. BS, Ill. State U., 1978; MLS, No. Ill. U., 1982. Children's libr. Broadview (Ill.) Pub. Libr., 1979-80, Barrington (Ill.) Area Pub. Libr. Dist., 1980-82, head tech. svcs., 1982-94; libr. dir. Cary (Ill.) Area Pub. Libr. Dist., 1994—. Mem. ALA, Ill. Libr. Assn., Pub. Libr. Assn. Office: Cary Area Pub Libr Dist 1606 3 Oaks Rd Cary IL 60013-1637

MCNULTY, JOHN KENT, lawyer, educator; b. Buffalo, Oct. 13, 1934; s. Robert William and Margaret Ellen (Duthie) McN.; m. Linda Conner, Aug. 20, 1955 (div. Feb. 1977); children: Martha Jane, Jennifer, John K. Jr.; m. Babette B. Barton, Mar. 23, 1978 (div. May 1988). AB with high honors, Swarthmore Coll., 1956; LL.B., Yale U., 1959. Bar: Ohio 1961, U.S. Supreme Ct. 1964. Law clk. Justice Hugo L. Black, U.S. Supreme Ct., Washington, 1959-60; vis. prof. Sch. Law U. Tex., summer 1960; assoc. Jones, Day, Cockley & Reavis, Cleve., 1960-64; prof. law U. Calif., Berkeley, 1964-91, Roger J. Traynor prof. law, 1991—. Of counsel Baker and McKenzie, San Francisco, 1974-75; acad. visitor London Sch. Econs., 1985, Cambridge U., 1994, U. Edinburgh, 1994; vis. fellow Wolfson Coll., Cambridge, 1994, U. Innsbruck, 1996, Trinity Coll., Dublin, 1997; vis. prof. Yale U., U. Tex., U. Leiden, U. Tilburg, U. Tokyo, U. San Diego, others; lectr. univs. Cologne, Hamburg, Hitotsubashi, Kansei, Kyoto, London, Munich, Seoul, Tokyo, Tilburg, Amsterdam, Rotterdam, Vienna Econ., Tohoku, Tübingen, others; mem. adv. bd. Tax Mgmt. Author: Federal Income Taxation of Individuals, 6th edit., 1999, Federal Estate and Gift Taxation, 5th edit., 1994, Federal Income Taxation of S Corporations, 1992; (with Westin & Beck) Federal Income Taxation of Business Enterprises, 1995, 2d edit., 1999; mem. bd. overseers Berkeley Jour. Internat. Law. Guggenheim fellow, 1977 Mem. ABA, Am. Law Inst. (life), Internat. Fiscal Assn. (coun. U.S. br.), Order of Coif, Phi Beta Kappa. Home: 1176 Grizzly Peak Blvd Berkeley CA 94708-1741 Office: U Calif Sch Law 422 Boalt Hl Berkeley CA 94720-7200 E-mail: mcnultyj@law.berkeley.edu.

MCNULTY, JOHN WILLIAM, retired public relations executive, automobile company executive; b. N.Y.C., June 29, 1927; s. Christopher and Margaret (Kennedy) McN.; m. Margaret Rose Cooney, Nov. 11, 1950 (dec. Aug. 1978); children: Suellen McNulty Kinna, Jean McNulty Crocker, John, Peter, Jodi Wyatt Phelan, Russell Wyatt; m. Jean Fayette Winslow, Sept. 6, 1980. BS, Fordham U., 1949. Dir. pub. relations Lincoln Ctr., N.Y.C., 1958-63; assoc. John D. Rockefeller 3rd, 1963-66; asst. to Pres. Lyndon B. Johnson, Washington, 1966-68; exec. asst. to exec. v.p. fin., pub./industry-govt. rels. GM, Detroit, 1968-74, exec. asst. to vice chmn., 1974-76, pub. affairs coord., 1976-77, dir. corp. comm., 1977-79, v.p. pub. rels., 1979-90, ret., 1990. Trustee Nat. Racing Mus., Saratoga. Served with USN, 1945-46, PTO. Recipient Communications Achievement award Fordham U., 1977 Democrat. Home: 1071 Celestial St Cincinnati OH 45202-1689

MCNULTY, KATHLEEN ANNE, clinical social worker, psychotherapist, business consultant; b. Hackensack, N.J., Oct. 6, 1958; d. Alfred Edward and Gertrude Natalie (Currie) McN.; m. Henry Stanislaw Kowal, Sept. 16, 1988. BA, Rutgers U., 1980; MSW, Smith Coll., 1984; postgrad. , Fielding Grad. Inst., 2001—. Lic. marriage and family therapist. Mental health aide Belleville (N.J.) Mental Health Clinic, 1980-82; clin. social worker Albert Einstein Coll. Medicine, Bronx, N.Y., 1984-86, Family Guidance Bergen, Hackensack, 1986-87, Cliffwood Mental Health Ctr., Englewood, N.J., 1986-87; pvt. practice Rutherford, 1987-99, Ridgewood, 1999—. Cons. Meadowlands Weight Control, Rutherford, 1988—, St. Lukes-Roosevelt Hosp. Ctr., N.Y.C., 1988. Contbr. articles to profl. jours. Mem. Am. Orthopsychiat. Assn., Acad. Cert. Social Workers (cert.), Nat. Assn. Social Workers. Avocations: painting, singing, sports, poetry.

MCNULTY, MICHAEL ROBERT, congressman; b. Troy, N.Y., Sept. 16, 1947; s. John J. and Madelon McN; m. Nancy Ann Lazzaro; children: Michele, Angela, Nancy, Maria. Grad., St. Joseph's Inst., Barrytown, N.Y., 1965, Loyola U. Rome Ctr., 1968, Hill Sch. Ins., N.Y.C., 1970; BA in Polit. Sci., Coll. Holy Cross, 1969; LHD honoris causa, Coll. St. Rose, 1991; LLD honoris causa, Siena Coll., 1993, Rensselaer Polytech. Inst., 1995, Excelsior Coll., 2000. Town supr. Town of Green Island, N.Y., 1969-77, mayor, 1977-81; mem. N.Y. State Assembly, 1982-88, chmn. subcom. on town and village elections, mem. legis. commn. on rural resources, 1983-88, asst. dir. adminstrv. regulations rev. commn., 1977-82, mem. adminstrv. regulations rev. com., 1983-88; past chmn. planning com. Capital Dist. Transp. Com.; mem. 101st-102d Congresses from 23rd N.Y. dist., 1989-92, 103d-107th Congresses from 21st N.Y. dist., 1993—; mem. ways and means com.; ranking mem. subcom. on select revenue measures. Past chmn. task force for constrn. Troy-Green Island Bridge; chmn. United Way campaign, 1982 Mem. staff com. on edn. N.Y. State Constl. Conv., 1967; campaign mgr. John J. McNulty Jr. for Sheriff of Albany County, N.Y., 1973; participant 1974 polit. campaign mgmt. inst. Kent State U., Ohio; past mem. Albany County Dem. Com.; past chmn. Green Island Dem. Com.; past mem. N.Y. State Dem. Com. Office: US Ho of Reps 2161 Rayburn Hob Washington DC 20515-0001

MCNULTY, ROBERT HOLMES, non-profit executive; b. Oakland, Calif., June 20, 1940; s. Frederick James and Ruth (Holmes) McN.; m. Penelope Cuff, Dec. 27, 1964; children: Maria, Abigail. BS in Bus. Adminstrn., U. Calif., Berkeley, 1962, JD, 1965. Bar: Calif. 1965. Property acquisition planner Safeway Stores, Internat., Oakland, 1962; archeol. asst. Colonial Williamsburg, Va., 1968; rsch. asst. Nat. Mus. of History and Tech. The Smithsonian Instn., Washington, 1968-69, asst. to the dir., 1969-70; environ. advisor GSA, 1970-71; asst. dir. architecture and environ. arts program NEA, 1971-78; acting dir. grad. program in hist. preservation Sch. Architecture Columbia U., N.Y.C., 1978-79; pres. Ptnrs. for Livable Communities, Washington, 1979—. Cons. Task Force on Land Use and Urban Growth, 1972, Task Force on Neighborhood Economic Development, 1976, German Marshall Fund, Washington, 1978; bd. visitors U. Ind. Sch. Pub. Adminstrn., 1991—; mem. NY St. Council of the Arts, Architecture & Enviromental Arts Prgm (panelist 1973-74, advisor 1974-75), Taskforce under President Reagan on Private Sector Initiatives, 1981, Urban Land Inst. Cultural Fac. (co-chair adv. comm.) 1984, The Micronesian Inst. (adv. council) 1985—, Oversight Comm. of L'Axe Majeur de Cergy-Pontoise, Paris, 1988, Internat. Prgm. Adv. Comm. to the Natl. Endowment for the Arts, 1990-92, Internat. Ecotourism Soc., 1992-99, City Innovation Natl. Adv. (bd. mem.) 1993—, President's Natl. Preparatory Comm. for the Human Settlements Conference, Istanbul, 1996, Inst. for the Regl. Community (bd. trustees) 1997-98, Am. Assembly on Improving the Economic Hlth. of Am. Distressed Communities, 1997; lect. in field. Author: Neighborhood Conservation: A Handbook of Methods and Techniques, 1976, Economics of Amenity, 1985, Entrepreneurial American City, 1985, Return of the Livable City, 1986; editor: (book) Better Cities Book, 1989, (report) State of the American Community, 1994; contrib. articles to profl. journals. Pres. Brookmont and Vicinity Civ. League, 1976-77, bd. mem., 1975-76, 77-78, 91-92; served to capt. U.S. Army, 1966-68. Smithsonian Inst. grantee, 1972, 73, Graham Found. grantee 1978; Loeb fellow Harvard U., 1973-74, Pierson Coll. guest fellow, Yale U., 1985, adj. sr. fellow Hudson Inst., 1989—; recipient AIA Gold Medal to the Architecture, Planning & Design Prgm. of NEA, 1979. Mem. Calif. Bar Assn., Nat. Press Club., Royal Soc. for the Arts in the U.S. (fell. 1992—), Inst. of Current World Affairs, Lambda Alpha Internat. Office: Ptnrs for Livable Community 1429 21st St NW Washington DC 20036-5902 Fax: 202-466-4845. E-mail: bmcnulty@livable.com.

MCNULTY, THOMAS L. sociology educator; b. Potsdam, N.Y., Oct. 12, 1959; s. John Riley and Suzanne McNulty; m. Janet Lynn McNulty, Oct. 12, 1985; children: Nicholas John, Jessica Mary. BA summa cum laude, SUNY, Albany, 1988, MA, 1990, PhD, 1996. Rsch. scientist N.Y. State Office of Mental Health, Albany, 1990-96; prof. U. Ga., Athens, 1996—. Contbr. articles to profl. jours. Mem. Am. Sociol. Assn., Am. Soc. Criminology, Phi Beta Kappa. Office: Sociology Dept U Ga Baldwin Hall Athens GA 30602-1611 E-mail: tmcnulty@arches.uga.edu.

MCNULTY-MAJORS, SUSAN ROSE, special education administrator; b. Fargo, N.D., Oct. 5, 1944; d. Leo G. McNulty and Jane Lyon (McDonald) McNulty-Schmallen; d. Herbert G. Schmallen (stepfather); m. B. Joseph Majors II, Aug. 23, 1975. BS, N.D. State U., 1966; MA, U. Mich., 1969. Lic. tchr., Mass., Minn.; lic. ind. clin. social worker; cert. chem. dependency practitioner. Tchr. sci. Incarnation Sch., Mpls., 1966-67; tchr. English George Daly Jr. High Sch., Flint, Mich., 1967-68; tchr. New Boston (Mich.) Elem. Sch., 1969-70; tchr. home econs. Newton (Mass.) Jr. High Sch., 1970-73; program adminstr. Bell Hill Recovery Ctr., Wadena, Minn., 1973-80, exec. dir., 1980-85; coord. emotionally and behavior disordered edn. Wadena Pub. Schs. TOW Spl. Edn. Coop., 1985-94; dir. spl. edn. PAWN Spl. Edn. Coop., Park Rapids, Minn., 1994-95; educator, cons. emotional/behavioral disorders Northland High, Remer, 1995—; therapist Neighborhood Counseling, Wadena, 1995—; emotional/behavioral disorders educator, dir. spl. edn. Remer-Longville Dist. 118, Remer, 1996—. Mem. Wadena Tech. Adv. Bd., 1978—. Mem. adv. bd. Todd-Wadena Community Corrections, Long Prairie, Minn., 1975—, chairperson 1997); mem. Woodview adv. bd., 1990—; mem. fund adminstrn. bd. Ctrl. Minn. Initiative, 1996—. Fresh Air Camp fellow U. Mich., 1968; recipient Ashland Oil Golden Apple Achievement award. Roman Catholic. Avocations: sailing, biking, reading. Home: 843 7th St SW Wadena MN 56482-1934 Office: Northland High Remer MN 56672

MCNUTT, GWYN BELLAMY, archivist; b. Memphis, Jan. 23, 1935; d. Thomas Robert and Mattie Kate (Dennis) Bellamy; m. Bobby Gene McNutt, Aug. 21, 1955; children: Valeria, Walter. Tchr. Memphis/Shelby County Bd. Edn., 1956-58, Paris (Tenn.) Spl. Edn. Dist., 1958-68, Henry County (Tenn.) Bd. Edn., 1968-80. Dir. genealogy Henry County, 1982—; columnist Paris Post-Intelligencer, 1994— Author, pub.: Wills Index of Henry County, Tenn., 1822-1988, Census Index for Henry County, Tenn., for 1820, 1830, 1840, 1880 and 1900, Marriage Records of Henry County, Tenn., 1901-1907, Tax Lists of Henry County, Tenn. for 1927, 1845, 1890; co-compiler, pub. Index of Ridgeway Funeral home Records 1945-1995, Index McEvoy Funeral Home Records 1901-1988. Co-dir. Preservation/Conservation of Henry County Archival Records, 1990-97. Mem. DAR, Order Ea. Star, United Daughters Confederacy, Henry County Geneal. Soc., Henry County Hist. Soc. Baptist. Avocation: genealogy. Home: 210 Fairview St Paris TN 38242-5408

MCNUTT, RICHARD HUNT, manufacturing company executive; b. Princeton, N.J., Mar. 11, 1943; s. John and Dorothy Elizabeth (Hunt) McN. Student, Delaware Vly. Coll. Sci./Agr., 1965-68, Temple U., 1978-81; BS in Indsl. Engring., Shelbourn U., 1986. Cert. in vocat. edn.; cert. mfg. engr. Diemaker Custom Tool Co., 1964-67; toolmaker Penn Engring., 1967-69; machine shop mgr., R&D engr. Inertial Motors Corp., 1969-73; machinery design engr. Phila. Rivet Co., Doylestown, Pa., 1973-76; R&D mgr. PHL, Inc., 1976-82; asst. chief engr. PHL Inc./Levv/Air Inc., Prefco Products Inc., 1982-85; chief engr. PHL Inc./Levv/Air Inc., Prefro Products Inc., 1985-86, v.p. ops., 1986-89, dir. engring., 1993—; owner Sunrise Solar Heat Co.; cons. Pipersville, Pa.; ptnr. Mediation Assocs., 1990—. Exec. v.p. Del. Water Study Citizens Group for Sound Resource Mgmt.; councillor Probational Vol. Svcs.; founding bd. dirs. Del-Aware Unltd., Inc., Del-Art Inc., Ctr. for Performing Arts, Bucks County, Pa., Del. River Greenway Partnership, Inc.; mem. Environ. Polit. Action Com.; founder AWARE, Montgomery County, 1985—, STAND, Bucks County, 1986—, Holicong CSA; mem. exec. bd. Earth Day, 1990, Earth Days Alliance, Bucks County Conservation Dist., 1993—, Del. River Greenway, 1994-96, vice chmn., 1995-96, chmn., 1996-98; v.p. Del. River Greenway Partnership Inc., 1998-99, pres., 1999-; mem. econ. devel. com. Del. River Wild and Scenic Study Commn., Dept. Interior Nat. Park Svc., 1994-96; founder Solebury Forum, Bucks County, Environ. Party Com.; mem. Plumstead Twp. Parks and Recreation Commn., sec., 1992-97, vice chmn., 1997-98, chmn., 1998—; vice chmn. Plumstead Twp. Shade Tree Commn., 1992—; planning commn. tech. adv. com. Cape May County, 2001—; founding ptnr. Rising Nation, Native Am. Cultural Heritage Project, 2000-. Served with USMC, 1960-64. Mem. ASHRAE, NRA (life), VFW, Soc Mfg. Engrs., Bucks County Assn. Corrections and Rehab., Am. Legion (life), Vietnam Vets. Am. (life), Ctrl. Bucks County C. of C. (environ. and govt. com. 1986—), Internat. Air Movement and Control Assn. (mem. code rev. com., fire-smoke engring. com.), Nat. Fire Protection Assn., Underwriters Lab. (standards com.). Republican. Zen Buddhist. Home: 5556 Stump Rd Pipersville PA 18947-1090 Office: Prefco Products Inc 3853 Old Easton Rd Doylestown PA 18901-1195 E-mail: mcnuttrh@yahoo.com.

MCPARTLAND, JAMES MICHAEL, university official; b. N.Y.C., Sept. 26, 1939; s. James J. and Helen M. (Leddy) McP. BS, Cornell U., 1961, MS, 1963; PhD, Johns Hopkins U., 1968. Rschr. U.S. Office Edn., Washington, 1965-67, U.S. Commn. Civil Rights, Washington, 1967-68; asst. dir. Ctr. Social Orgn. Schs., Johns Hopkins U., Balt., 1968-75, co-dir., 1976-94; dir., 1994—. Co-author: Equality of Educational Opportunity, 1966, Encyclopedia of Educational Research, 1992, Review of Research in Education, 1993; co-editor: Violence in Schools, 1977, Comprehensive Urban School Reform, 2002. Mem. Am. Ednl. Rsch. Assn., Am. Sociol. Assn., Am. Statis. Assn. Democrat. Roman Catholic. Avocation: music. Home: 1102 S Streeper St Baltimore MD 21224-4873 Office: Johns Hopkins U CSOS 3003 N Charles St Ste 200 Baltimore MD 21218-3888 E-mail: jmcpartland@csos.jhu.edu.

MCPARTLAND, PATRICIA ANN, health educator and administrator; b. Passaic, N.J. d. Daniel and Josephine McP. BA, U. Mo., 1971; MCRP, MS in Preventive Medicine, Ohio State U., 1975; EdD in Higher and Adult Edn., Columbia U., 1988; cert. distance edn., Tex. A&M U., 2000, cert. distance edn. web pub. cert., 2001. Cert. health edn. specialist, distance edn. web pub., grants specialist. Sr. health planner Merrimack Valley HSA, Lawrence, Mass., 1977-79; planning cons./adminstr. Children's Hosp., Boston, 1979-80; exec. dir. Southeastern Mass. Area Health Edn. Ctr., Marion, Mass., 1980—. V.p., cons. New Bedford (Mass.) Cmty. Health Ctr, 1993—94; chmn. edn. and tng. com. Health and Human Svc. Coalition, 1988—89; mem. project expert panel Office of Minority Health, 1997—; mem. New Eng. Regional Minority Health Conf. Com., 1997—99; vis. lectr. Bridgewater State Coll.; lectr. in field ; project expert panel Office Minority Health's Culturally and Linguistically Appropriate Svcs. ; mem. New Eng. Regional Minority Health Conf. Com., 2001—. *Executive Director with over fifteen years experience in administration, marketing, development and management. Dr. McPartland is an administrator, educator, researcher, analyst, and event planner. She is the author of a book entitled Promoting Health in the Workplace, along with numerous publications, and is the editor of a quarterly publication. Patricia founded a regional educational program. She designed, implemented, administered and marketed over 800 programs and products which generated several million dollars for her service area. She presents lectures and provides consultation for national and international programs throughout the world. Patricia conducts seminars on health, marketing, life enhancement, communication and leadership skills.* Mem. editl. bd. Jour. Healthcare Edn. and Tng., 1989-93; author: Promoting Health in the Workplace, 1991; reviewer Qualitative Health Rsch. Jour.; contbr. articles to profl. jours. Vol. speaker March of Dimes Found., Wareham, Mass., 1992-93; coll.-wide vocat. Cape Cod C.C., Hyannis, Mass., 1989—; planning adv. 2nd Internat. Symposium, Pasco, Wash., 1992; v.p New Bedford chpt. Am. Cancer Soc., 1985-90. Recipient award Excellence in Continuing Edn. Nat. AHEC Ctr. Dirs. Assn., 1994, 95, 96, 97, Sec.'s awards for Outstanding Progam in Community Health, Nat. Cancer Inst., Washington, 1990. Mem.: APHA, Nat. Assn. Workforce Devel. Profls. (bd. dirs.), Nat. Planning Conf. (mem. com. 1984—87), Southeastern Mass. Health Planning (bd. dirs., sec. 1982—87), Inst. for Disease Prevention (steering com. 1982—). Avocations: writing, acting, dance, theatre, travel, hiking. Home: PO Box 1116 Marion MA 02738-0020 Office: Southeastern Mass AHEC PO Box 69 2 Spring St Marion MA 02738-1519 E-mail: pmcpartland@attbi.com., smahec@tiac.net.

MCPEAK, ALLAN, career services director, educator, lawyer, consultant; b. Hot Springs, Ark., Oct. 1, 1938; s. Kenneth L. and Dorothy (Whiteman) McP.; m. Judith L. Mathison, Oct. 26, 1973. BA, U. Fla., 1960, JD, 1965; MS, Nova U., 1984; PhD, Fla. State U., 1987; MS Instructional Systems Fla. State U., 1994. Bar: Fla. 1965, U.S. Supreme Ct. 1980. Sole practice, Naples, Fla., 1965-85; asst. dir. the career ctr. Fla. State U., 1987, assoc. dir., 1989; dir. Career Svcs. U. South Ala., Mobile, 1994—. cons. in human relations, organizational devel. and career devel., Tallahassee, 1984-94, Mobile, 1994—; pres. Lawyers Abstract Sevc., Naples, Fla., 1978-80; organizer Marine Savs. & Loan, Naples, 1980-81; Contbr. articles to profl. jours. Served with U.S. Army, 1960-63. Mem. Nat. Assn. Colls. and Employers, So. Assn. Colls. and Employers, Ala. Assn. Colls. and Employers, Fla. Bar Assn., Blue Key, Pi Sigma Alpha.

MCPEAK, MERRILL ANTHONY, business executive, consultant, retired officer; b. Santa Rosa, Calif., Jan. 9, 1936; s. Merrill Addison McPeak and Winifred Alice (Stewart) McPeak Bendall; m. Elynor Fay Moskowitz, Nov. 10, 1956; children— Mark Allen, Brian David AB, San Diego State Coll., Calif., 1957; MS, George Washington U., Washington, 1974. Commd. 2d lt. USAF, 1957, advanced through grades to gen., 1988; pilot USAF Thunderbirds, Nellis AFB, Nev., 1966-68; comdr. Misty Forward Air Controllers, Phu Cat, Republic of Vietnam, 1969, 20th Tactical Fighter Wing, RAF, Upper Heyford, Eng., 1980-81, 12th Air Force, Bergstrom AFB, Tex., 1987-88; comdr.-in-chief Pacific Air Forces, Hickam AFB, Hawaii, 1988-90; chief of staff USAF, Washington, 1990-94; co. dir., cons., 1994—. Chmn. ECC Internat., 1997—. Officer USAF, retired. Decorated DSM, Silver Star, Legion of Merit, DFC. Mem. Air Force Assn., Coun. Fgn. Rels., Daedalians, Sigma Chi. Home: 17360 Grandview Ct Lake Oswego OR 97034-6362 E-mail: tmcpeak@earthlink.net.

MCPETERS, SHARON JENISE, artist, writer; b. San Bernardino, Calif., Oct. 17, 1951; d. Cecil L. and Mary I. (Tanner) McP.; 1 child, Angela M. Benders. BA in Journalism and English, U. So. Calif., 1981. Proofreader Ventura (Calif.) Coll., 1979. Prin. works include My Professors, 1993, Interpretations, 1994, The Thoughts of Socrates, 1995, Self Portrait, 1995, Happiness, 1996, My True Self, 1998, Czechoslovakia 1923, 1999, Liszt, 1999, Portrait of Ten Artists, 2000; author: (autobiography) A Human Mind, 1997, (novels) Domestic Symphonies, 1986, The Broken Heart of the World , 1999, An Illuminated Manuscript, 1994, The Library of Heaven, 2000, A Girl Without A Name, 2001, short stories. Avocation: philosophical reading.

MCPHAIL, CARLTON EARL, SR. organization executive; b. Roanoke Rapids, N.C., Dec. 30, 1947; s. Roosevelt Boose McPhail and Harriett Lee Winfield-McPhail; m. Mary Louise Nixon-McPhail, Sept. 15, 1972; children: Shanta Revita, Carlton Earl Jr., Howard Lee. BA, MS in Mass. Comm., Shaw Coll., 1980. Quality steel inspector United Steel Workers, Detroit, 1970—84; occpl. safety insp. State of Mich., Lansing, 1987—99; occpl. job coach Jewish Vocational Svc., Southfield, 2001—. Pres. & founder Concerned Citizens for Youth, Detroit, 1992—; coach Cath. Youth Orgn., 1983—; organizer Dem. Party, 1980—. Specialist U.S. Army, 1967—70, Germany. Recipient Semi Pro Football Coach of Yr. award, Mich. Football League, 1997, Cath. Youth Coach of Yr. award, Cath. Youth Orgn., 2000. Mem.: Amateur Athletic Union (organizer 1983—2002), Detroit Affiliation Basketball (pres. 1986—2002). Democrat. Roman Catholic. Achievements include invention of The Flying Dutchman Bicycle. Avocations: woodworking, collecting old books, reading, writing, fishing. Home: 15433 Archdale Detroit MI 48227

MCPHAIL, JOANN WINSTEAD, writer, publisher, art dealer; b. Trenton, Fla., Feb. 17, 1941; d. William Emerson and Donna Mae (Crawford) Winstead; m. James Michael McPhail, June 15, 1963; children: Angela C. McPhail Morris, Dana Denise McPhail Gaizutis, Whitney Gold McPhail Casso. Student, Fla. So. Coll., 1959-60, St. John's River Jr. Coll., Palatka, Fla., 1960-61, Houston (Tex.) C.C. With Jim Walter Corp., Houston, 1961-62; receptionist, land lease sec. Oil and Gas Property Mgmt. Inc., 1962-63; sec. to mng. atty. State Farm Ins. Co., 1963-64; saleswoman, decorator Oneil-Anderson, 1973; sec. Law Offices of Ed Christensen, 1980-82; advt. mgr. Egalitarian Houston (Tex.) C.C. Systems, 1981; fashion display artist, 1985-86; entrepreneur, writer, art agt. Golden Galleries and Antiques, Houston, 1990-95; owner, property mgr. APT Investments, 1994-98; lyricist, publisher Anna Gold Classics, 1995—, writer song lyrics, 1996—. Freelance writer, photographer: Elegance of Needlepoint, 1970, S.W. Art Mag., A Touch of

Greatness, 1973, Sweet 70's Anthology, The Budding of Tomorrow, 1974 (award); columnist, photographer: Egalitarian: Names Can be Symbols, Design Your Wall Covering, Student Profile, 1981, National Library of Poetry, Fireworks (award), 1995; contbr. poetry various publs.; playwright, 1993—; screenwriter, 1996—; writer, pub. The Missing Crown, religious drama World Wide Christian Radio, Sta. KCBI-FM, KYND-AM, and other radio stas., 1996—, baby publ. Hello...World...Hello, 1997; author: (poetry) The Budding of Tomorrow, 1997; music pub., 1999—. Vol. PTO bd. Sharptown Middle Sch. Mem. ASCAP, Manuscriptors Guild. Methodist. Home: 361 N Post Oak Ln Apt 333 Houston TX 77024-5950

MCPHAIL, PATRICIA DYER, real estate broker; b. Andver, Mass., Apr. 23, 1932; d. E. Dewey and Rose A. (Desjardins) Dyer; m. James H. McPhail, July 23, 1955; children— Barry, Brian, Steven, Kent. B.S., U. Lowell, 1954. Broker, owner Colonial Realty, Hattiesburg, Miss., 1976— ; pres. Pat McPhail Inc., Hattiesburg, 1978— ; v.p. McPhail Resorts Inc., Hattiesburg, 1985— ; pres. Realtors Multiple Listing Service, Hattiesburg, 1983-84. Vice pres. N.E. Lamar Devel. Found., Hattiesburg, 1984; nat. scholarship chmn. Nat. Assn. Jr. Auxs., 1985— . Mem. Nat. Assn. Realtors, Miss. Assn. Realtors, Hattiesburg Bd. Realtors (bd. dirs. 1983-85, treas. 1984-85, sec. 1985—). Democrat. Roman Catholic. Home: Lake Serene 1 Shady Ln Hattiesburg MS 39402-9578

MCPHAIL-GEIST, KARIN RUTH, secondary education educator, realtor, musician; b. Urbana, Ill., Nov. 23, 1938; d. Wilber Harold and Bertha Amanda Sofia (Helander) Tammeus; m. David Pendleton McPhail, Sept. 7, 1958 (div. 1972); children: Julia Elizabeth, Mark Andrew; m. John Charles Geist, June 4, 1989 (div. 1995). BS, Juilliard Sch. Music, 1962; postgrad., Stanford U., 1983-84, L'Academia, Florence and Pistoia, Italy, 1984-85, Calif. State U., 1986-87, U. Calif., Berkeley, 1991, 92. Cert. tchr., Calif.; lic. real estate agt., Calif. Tchr. Woodstock Sch., Musoorie, India, 1957, Canadian, Tex., 1962-66, Head Royce Sch., Oakland, Calif., 1975-79, 87—, Sleepy Hollow Sch., Orinda, 1985-2001; realtor Freeholders, Berkeley, 1971-85, Northbrae, Berkeley, 1985-92, Templeton Co., Berkeley, 1992—. Organist Kellogg Meml., Musoorie, 1956-57, Mills Coll. Chapel, Oakland, 1972—; cashier Trinity U., San Antonio, 1957-58; cen. records sec. Riverside Ch., N.Y.C., 1958-60; sec. Dr. Rollo May, N.Y.C., 1959-62, United Presbyn. Nat. Missions, N.Y.C., 1960, United Presbyn. Ecumenical Mission, N.Y.C., 1961, Nat. Coun. Chs., N.Y.C., 1962; choral dir. First Presbyn. Ch., Canadian, Tex., 1962-66; assoc. in music Montclair Presbyn. Ch., Oakland, 1972-88; site coord., artist, collaborator Calif. Arts Coun. Artist; cons. music edn. videos and CD Roms Clearvue EAV, Chgo., 1993—. Artist: produced and performed major choral and orchestral works, 1972-88; prodr. Paradiso, Kronos Quartet, 1985, Magdalena, 1991, 92, Children's Quest, 1993—. Grantee Orinda Union Sch. Dist., 1988. Mem. Berkeley Bd. Realtors, East Bay Regional Multiple Listing Svc., Calif. Tchrs. Assn., Commonwealth Club (San Francisco). Democrat. Home: 7360 Claremont Ave Berkeley CA 94705-1429 E-mail: kmcphailge@aol.com.

MCPHEARSON, GERALDINE JUNE, medical and surgical nurse; b. Red Bud, Ill., June 3, 1938; d. Arthur and Viola (Liefer) Althoff; children: Deborah, Michael, Belinda, Sabrina. Diploma, Evang. Deaconess Hosp. Sch. Nursing, St. Louis, 1959. RN. Sch. nurse San Antonio Ind. Sch. Dist.; head nurse Bethesda Gen. Hosp., St. Louis; supr. Am. Blood Components, Inc.; nurse mgr. Meml. Hosp., Belleville, Ill. Coord. arthritis svc. staff Meml. Hosp. Mem. Nat. Assn. Orthopaedic Nurses (1st pres., sec., v.p., organizer Ill. chpt.).

MCPHEE, ALEXANDER HECTOR, consulting engineer; b. Bklyn., Nov. 26, 1911; s. Alexander Hendry and Charlotte Elizabeth (Kraus) McP.; m. Cynthia Rose Agar, July 26, 1947; 1 child, Alexander Hector. Student, Pratt Inst., 1928-34, Bklyn. Poly. Inst., 1935-41. Registered profl. engr., N.Y., N.J., Pa., Conn., D.C., P.R., W.Va., also nat. engrng. cert. Nat. Coun. Engrng. Examiners. Asst. chief engr. Peter Clark Inc., 1934-37; engr. U.S.S. Yorktown & Enterprise Airplane Elevators, 1934-37; ptnr. Howard V. Harding & Co., 1937-38; asst. chief engr. Lukenweld div. Lukens Steel Co., 1938-44; ptnr. McPhee & Johnston, 1945-48; pvt. practice cons. engr., 1948—; v.p. Hepworth Machine Co., Inc., Port Washington, N.Y., 1953-57, pres., 1957-80, chmn. bd., 1962-80, also dir.; v.p. Olaf Soot Assocs., P.C., 1979-81; cons. Midlantic Engrng., P.C., 1985-88, Charles Birnstiel, PC., 1979—. Designer 90-foot turntable for Aircraft Nuclear Propulsion Project, Idaho Falls, Idaho, 1953, 76-foot turntable for Jones Beach Marine Amphitheatre; engrng. cons. mfr. movable auditorium ceiling Juilliard Sch. Music, 1967-69; mech. stage equipment John F. Kennedy Center for Performing Arts, 1968-71; gondola hoists and controls Nassau County Vets. Meml. Coliseum, 1972; mech. and elec. cons. Bronx Zoo Skyride, 1972-73; approved welding inspection agy. N.Y.C. Dept. Bldgs. Patentee flashwelding machine control, vertical conveyor, centrifugal machines, dry cask handling system, alert hangar door, others. Troop com. mem., Scoutmaster Boy Scouts Am.; mem. bd. appeals Village of Plandome Heights, N.Y. Mem. ASME (life), ASTM, NSPE, Am. Def. Preparedness Assn., Nassau County Grand Jurors Assn., Mac Fie Clan Soc. N.Am. (life), Pi Tau Sigma (hon.). Home and Office: 11941 Snider Rd Cincinnati OH 45249-1226

MC PHEE, HENRY ROEMER, lawyer; b. Ames, Iowa, Jan. 11, 1925; s. Harry Roemer and Mary (Ziegler) McP.; m. Joanne Lambert, May 19, 1956 (div. Dec. 1991); children: Henry Roemer III, Joanne, Larkin, Charles; m. Selby Fleming, Jan. 27, 1999. AB cum laude, Princeton U., 1947; LLB, Harvard U., 1950. Bar: N.J. 1951, Ill. 1961, D.C. 1966. Exec. asst. to gov. State of N.J., Trenton, 1950-52; assoc. R.E. & A.D. Watson, New Brunswick, N.J., 1952-54; asst. to gen. counsel FTC, Washington, 1954; exec. asst. White House, 1954-57; asst. spl. counsel Pres. U.S., 1957-58, assoc. spl. counsel, pres., 1958-61; ptnr. Hamel & Park, 1961-88, mem. mgmt. com., 1975-85, mng. ptnr., 1980-83; ptnr. Hopkins & Sutter, 1988-93, of counsel, 1994—. Sec. N.J. Commn. on Interstate Cooperation, 1952-54; gen. counsel Rep. Nat. Fin. Com., 1968-73, Rep. Nat. Com., Washington, 1968. Chmn. bldg. com. Potomac (Md.) Presbyn. Ch., 1965-67; v.p. Rep. Club, Princeton, 1952-54; bd. dirs. Eisenhower World Affairs Inst., 1983—, treas., 1991-93, mem. exec. com., 1991—. Mem. ABA, D.C. Bar Assn., N.J. Bar Assn., Lincoln's Inn Soc. Harvard Law Sch. Clubs: Tower (Princeton U.); Princeton (Washington) (pres. 1970-72), Metropolitan (Washington), Capitol Hill (Washington). Republican. Presbyterian. Avocation: tennis. Address: C/O Eisenhower Inst 1620 Eye St NW Ste 703 Washington DC 20006-4005 Office: Hopkins & Sutter 888 16th St NW Ste 600 Washington DC 20006-4105

MCPHEE, JOHN ANGUS, writer; b. Princeton, N.J., Mar. 8, 1931; s. Harry Roemer and Mary (Ziegler) McP.; m. Pryde Brown, Mar. 16, 1957; children: Laura, Sarah, Jenny, Martha; m. Yolanda Whitman, Mar. 8, 1972; stepchildren: Cole Harrop, Andrew Harrop, Katherine Ryan, Vanessa Speir. AB, Princeton U., 1953; postgrad., Magdalene Coll., Cambridge (Eng.) U., 1953-54; LittD (hon.), Bates Coll., 1978, Colby Coll., 1978, Williams Coll., 1979, U. Alaska, 1980, Coll. William and Mary, 1988, Rutgers U., 1988; ScD, Maine Maritime Acad., 1992. TV playwright for Robert Montgomery Presents, N.Y.C., 1955-56; contbg. editor, assoc. editor Time mag., 1957-64; staff writer The New Yorker mag., 1965—; Ferris prof. journalism Princeton U., 1975—. Author: A Sense of Where You Are, 1965, The Headmaster, 1966, Oranges, 1967, The Pine Barrens, 1968, A Roomful of Hovings, 1968, Levels of the Game, 1969, The Crofter and the Laird, 1970, Encounters with the Archdruid, 1971, The Deltoid Pumpkin Seed, 1973, The Curve of Binding Energy, 1974, Pieces of the Frame, 1975, The Survival of the Bark Canoe, 1975, The John McPhee Reader, 1976, Coming into the Country, 1977, Giving Good Weight, 1979, Basin and Range, 1981, In Suspect Terrain, 1983, La Place de la Concorde Suisse, 1984, Table of Contents, 1985, Rising from the Plains, 1986, The Control of Nature, 1989, Looking for a Ship, 1990, Assembling California, 1993, The Ransom of Russian Art, 1994, The Second John McPhee Reader, 1996, Irons in the Fire, 1997, Annals of the Former World, 1998, The Founding Fish, 2002. Recipient award in lit., Am. Acad. and Inst. Arts and Letters, 1977, Woodrow Wilson award, Princeton U., 1982, Journalism award, Am. Assn. of Petroleum Geologists, 1982, 1987, John Wesley Powell award, U.S. Geol. Survey, 1988, John Burroughs medal, 1990, Walter Sullivan award, Am. Geophys. Union, 1993, James H. Shea award, Nat. Assn. Geology Tchrs., 1995, Award for Outstanding Achievement, Am. Inst. Petroleum Geologists, 1997, award of merit, Field Mus. Natural History, 1998, Pulitzer Prize in Gen. Non-Fiction, Annals of the Former World, 1999, Public Service award, Geological Society of America, 2002. Fellow Geol. Soc. Am.; mem. Am. Acad. Arts and Letters.

MCPHEE, MARK STEVEN, medical educator, physician, gastroenterologist; b. Kansas City, Mo., Nov. 8, 1951; s. William Robert and Mary Kay (Paige) McP.; m. Christina Marie Luebke, July 14, 1974; children: Molly Amanda, Ian Andrew. BA magna cum laude, Pomona Coll., Claremont, Calif., 1973; MD summa cum laude, U. Kans., Kansas City, 1976. Diplomate Nat. Bd. Med. Examiners; diplomate in internal medicine and gastroenterology Am. Bd. Internal Medicine. Intern, resident, fellow Harvard U. Med. Sch., Boston, 1976-80; dir. gastrointestinal endoscopy unit Kans. U. Med. Ctr., Kansas City, 1980-85; chief sect. gastroenterology St. Luke's Hosp., Mo., 1988-93, chair dept. medicine, 1992-97, assoc. dir. med. edn., 1995-97, dir. med. edn., 1997—; assoc. dean U. Mo.-Kansas City Med. Sch., 1997—. Asst. prof. medicine U. Kans., KansasCity, 1980-85, assoc. prof., 1985; clin. prof. medicine U. Mo., Kansas City, 1970-97, prof. medicine, 1997—. Author: Annotated Key References in Gastroenterology, 1982; contbr. chpts. to textbook, articles to profl. jours. Bd. dirs. St. Luke's Hosp., Kansas City,Mo., 1993—, Am. Digestive Health Found., Bethesda, Md., 1996—. Fellow ACP, Am. Coll. Gastroenterology; mem. Am. Gastroent. Assn. (mem. governing bd., treas.), St. Lukes Hosp. Physicians Assn. (bd. dirs.), HealthNet Physician Ptnrs. (bd. dirs.), Alpha Omega Alpha. Episcopalian. Avocations: poetry, hiking/camping, golf, tennis, sporting clay target shooting. Office: St Lukes Hosp Dept Med Edn 44th and Wornall Rd Kansas City MO 64111

MCPHEE, PENELOPE L. ORTNER, foundation executive, television producer, writer; b. Louisville, Nov. 24, 1947; d. Alvin B. and Loyce L. Ortner; m. Raymond Hunter McPhee, Aug. 25, 1973; 1 child, Cameron Brook. BA with honors, Wellesley Coll., 1969; MS in Journalism, Columbia U., 1970. Dir. pub. rels. Am. Sch. in Switzerland, Lugano, 1970-71; writer, rschr. Sta. WTVJ-TV, Miami, Fla., 1972-73; prof. journalism and film Fleming Coll., Florence, Italy, 1972-73; freelance writer, prodr. Miami, 1973-80; exec. prodr. for cultural programming Sta. WPBT-TV, 1980-88; instr. documentary filmmaking Fla. Internat. U., 1987-88; ind. TV prodr., cons., 1988-90; program officer arts and culture Knight Found., Miami, 1990-96, v.p., chief program officer, 1996—. Author: Martin Luther King, Jr.: A Documentary, Montgomery to Memphis, 1976 (Best of Books award ALA 1983), Beauty Ency., 1978, King Remembered, 1986, Your Future in Space, 1986; contbg. author: Underwater Photography for Everyone, 1978. Trustee Dade County Art in Pub. Places Trust, 1985, vice chmn., 1988-89, chmn., 1989-90; trustee Grantmakers in the Arts, 1992-98, chmn. 1995-96, Southeastern Coun. on Foundations, 1999—, Coun. on Founds., 2001—; adviser Indep. Sector Comm. com., 1999—. Recipient Iris award Nat. Assn. TV Program Execs., 1983, Children's Programming award Corp. for Pub. Broadcasting, 1982, local program award Corp. Pub. Broadcasting, 1984, 90, Emmy award, 1984, 88, N.Y. State Martin Luther King, Jr. Medal of Freedom, 1986; Sackett scholar Columbia U., 1970. Mem. Miami Wellesley (v.p. 1976-80, admissions rep. 1980-85, 1989-90). Office: 2 S Biscayne Blvd Ste 3800 Miami FL 33131-1808 E-mail: Mcphee@knightfdn.org.

MCPHEE, SCOTT DOUGLAS, occupational therapist, academic administrator; b. Tacoma, May 2, 1950; s. William Archibald and Georgia Mae (Lynch) McP.; m. Tana Arlene Wright, June 25, 1983; children: Sarah, Jennifer, Carter, Anthony. MS, Va. Commonwealth U., 1983; diploma, Command and Gen. Staff Coll., 1987; MPA, Western Ky. U., 1987; DPH, U. Tex., 1990. Registered occupl. therapist, Tenn. Enlisted U.S. Army, 1973, advanced through grades to lt. col., 1986, ret., 1994; occupl. therapist Walter Reed Army Med. Ctr., Washington, 1978-81; dir. occupl. therapy Ireland Army Cmty. Hosp., Fort Knox, Ky., 1983-86; dir. sch. occupl. therapy specialist Acad. Health Scis., Fort Sam Houston, Tex., 1990-94; chmn. dept. occupl. therapy Coll. Misericordia, Dallas, 1994-96; chmn. dept. occupl. therapy, assoc. dean Belmont U., Nashville, 1996—. Cons. WHO, Washington, 1987-92, Nat. Inst. Health Stats., Washington, 1994-96; v.p., bd. dirs. Tech. Access Ctr. Middle Tenn., Nashville, 1996—; chmn.-elect Tenn. Edn. Coun. for Health Sci. Professions, 2000—; chmn. occupl. therapy stds com. Internat. Commn. on Health Professions, 2000—. Mem. editl. bd. Mil. Medicine, 1990-94, Am. Jour. Occupl. Therapy, 1990-92, Occupl. Therapy in Health Care, 1994—, Innovations in Occupl. Therapy Edn., 1998-2000; contbr. over 20 articles to profl. jours. Decorated Legion of Merit, Order of Mil. Med. Merit; recipient Myra McDaniels writer's award, 1992, 94. Fellow Am. Occupl. Therapy Assn. (mem. roster of accreditation evaluators, 1997, Svc. award 1992-93, 95-96, 2001); mem. Tenn. Occupl. Therapy Assn. (ethics chmn. 1997—, award of excellence in rsch. 2000). Methodist. Avocations: golf, soccer. Office: Belmont U 1900 Belmont Blvd Nashville TN 37212-3757 Fax: 615-460-6475. E-mail: mcphees@mail.belmont.edu.

MC PHEETERS, EDWIN KEITH, architect, educator; b. Stillwater, Okla., Mar. 26, 1924; s. William Henry and Eva Winona (Mitchell) McP.; m. Patricia Ann Foster, Jan. 29, 1950 (div. 1981); children: Marc Foster, Kevin Mitchell, Michael Hunter; m. Mary Louise Marvin, July 21, 1984. B.Arch., Okla. State U., 1949; M.F.A., Princeton U., 1956. Instr. architecture U. Fla., 1949-51; asst. prof. Ala. Poly. Inst., Auburn U., 1951-54; fellow Princeton U., 1955, 81; from asst. prof. to prof. U. Ark., 1956-66; prof. Rensselaer Poly. Inst., 1966-69, dean, 1966-69; prof. Auburn (Ala.) U., 1969-89, dean Sch. Architecture and Fine Arts, 1969-88, dean, prof. emeritus, 1989—; adj. prof. Frank Lloyd Wright Sch. of Architecture, 1992—. Mem. Ala. Bd. Registration for Architects, 1978-87; profl. adviser South Ctrl. Bell Telephone Co., 1977-79, So. Co., 1979-81, Ala. Power Co., 1979-81, Okla. State U., 1983, Ala. Sch. Fine Arts, 1985-86; cons. Taliesin Architects, 1988-92. Served to 2d lt. USAAC, 1943-45; capt. USAFR 1945-57. Recipient Disting. Architect award Ala. Archtl. Found., 2001. Fellow AIA (pres. Ala. coun. 1978, Merit award 1976, East Ala. Design awards 1986, 87, 90, 92); mem. Assn. Collegiate Schs. Arch. (bd. dirs. 1970-77, Disting. Prof. 1989), Blue Key, Kappa Sigma, Omicron Delta Kappa, Kappa Kappa Psi, Tau Sigma Delta, Rotary, Watercolor Soc. Ala. (pres. 2000—). Episcopalian.

MCPHERON, BRUCE ALAN, entomologist; b. Port Deposit, Md., Dec. 26, 1954; m. Marilyn Beth Turner, May 1, 1976; children: Neale, Brenna. BS, Ohio State U., 1976; MS, U. Ill., 1980, PhD, 1987. County extension agt. Ohio Cooperative Extension Svc., Batavia, Ohio, 1980-83; asst. prof. Pa. State U., 1988-94, assoc. prof., 1994-2000, prof. Pa., 2000—, assoc. dean, 2002—. Editor: Fruit Fly Pests, 1996, Evolution of Insect Pests, 1993. Mem. Entomological Soc. of Am., Soc. for the Study of Evolution, Soc. for Molecular Biology and Evolution, Soc. of Systematic Biologists. Office: Pa State U 217 Ag Admin Bldg University Park PA 16802

MCPHERON, JOANN MARIE, music educator, poet; b. Racine, Wis., Feb. 19, 1938; d. Joseph Eugene-Reath and Ann Bernadette (Mostek) Stetka; m. Lamont Preston McPheron II, Oct. 14, 1961; children Dawn Marie and Lamont P. III (twins). Student, U. Wis., Parkside, 1958-60. Adminstrv. asst. Racine County Social Svc. Dept., Wis., 1958-63; pvt. piano, music theory tchr. Racine, 1970—. Contbr. poems to anthologies and mags.; performer Racine Summer Theater, 1957. Asst. programs Children's Theatre, Racine, 1975; chmn. Minority Scholarship Program, 1970; active Roosevelt Sch. PTA, 1968—74; vol. All Saints Hosp., 2002—, Performing Arts Ctr., Milw., 1994—97; mem. Milw. Zoo, Art Inst. Chgo., United Performing Arts, Milw., Milw. Art Mus.; vol. fundraiser Miller Ride for the Arts, 1994—2000, AIDS March, Milw.; contbr. Racine Arts Coun.; bd. dirs. St. Luke's Hosp. Aux., Racine, Wis., 1992—98. Recipient award for poetry Racine Art Coun., 1990; nominated Graduates of Distinction William Horlick H.S., Racine, 1992. Fellow Wis. Fellowship of Poets; mem. Racine Music Tchrs. Assn., Wis. Music Tchrs. Assn., Music Tchrs. Nat. Assn., Root River Poets. Mem. Unitarian Universalist Ch. Avocations: grandchildren, poetry, walking, gardening, painting. Home: 516 Augusta St Racine WI 53402-4408

MCPHERSON, ALICE RUTH, ophthalmologist, educator; b. Regina, Sask., Can., June 30, 1926; came to U.S., 1938, naturalized, 1958; d. Gordon and Viola (Hoover) McP. BS, U. Wis., 1948, MD, 1951; DSc, 1997. Diplomate Am. Bd. Ophthalmology. Intern Santa Barbara (Calif.) Cottage Hosp., 1951-52; resident anesthesiology Hartford (Conn.) Hosp., 1952; resident ophthalmology Chgo. Eye, Ear, Nose and Throat Hosp., 1953, U. Wis. Hosps., 1953-55; ophthalmologist Davis and Duehr Eye Clinic, Madison, Wis., 1956-57; clin. instr. U. Wis., 1956-57; fellow retina service Mass. Eye and Ear Infirmary, 1957-58; ophthalmologist Scott and White Clinic, Temple, Tex., 1958-60; practice medicine specializing in ophthalmology and retinal diseases Houston, 1960—. Staff Meth., St. Luke's, Tex. Children's Hosps., Houston; clin. asst. prof. Baylor Coll. Medicine, Houston, 1959-61, asst. prof. ophthalmology, 1961-69, clin. assoc. prof., 1969-75, clin. prof., 1975-98, prof., 1998—; cons. retinal diseases VA Hosp., Houston, 1960—, Ben Taub Hosp., Houston, 1960—; mem. adv. com. for active staff appt. sect. ophthalmology Meth. Hosp., 1986-91, mem equipment com., 1993-95, mem. grievance panel, 1997; vol. clin. faculty appts. and promotions com., 1993—; bd. dirs. Highlights of Ophthalmology; v.p. N.Am. Highlights of Ophthalmology Internat. Editor: New and Controversial Aspects of Retinal Detachment, 1968, New and Controversial Aspects of Vitreoretinal Surgery, 1977, Retinopathy of Prematurity: Current Concepts and Controversies, 1986. Amb. Houston Ballet, mem. Houston Ballet Found.; mem. pres.'s council Houston Grand Opera; conductors circle Houston Symphony, mem. Houston Symphony Soc.; mem. campaign for 80s Baylor Coll. Medicine; mem. Assn. for Community TV, Better Bus. Bur., Physicians' Benevolent Fund, South Tex. Diabetes Assn. Inc., Jr. League Houston; bd. dirs. U. Wis. Found., Madison. Recipient Award of appreciation KT Eye Found., 1978, Woodlands Medal for Outstanding Contbn. to the Econ. Devel. of Community, 1988, spl. recognition award Assn. for Rsch. in Vision in Ophthalmology, Crystal award Recognizing Generous Support-Ptnrs. with an Eye for Vision Found. Am. Acad. Ophthalmology, 2000, Banjamin Boyd Humanitarian award Pan Am. Assn. Ophthalmology, 2001, Philip Corboy Meml. award Disting. Svc. Ophthalmology, 2002, Women of Vision Houston Delta Gamma Found., 2002; Alice R. Mc Pherson Lab for Retina Rsch. dedicated Baylor Ctr. for Biotech., 1988, Philip Corboy Meml. award for dist. svc., 2002, Women of Vision Delta Gamma Found., 2002; Alice R. Mc Pherson Day proclaimed in her honor Mayor of City of Houston, Mar. 12, 1988. Fellow: ACS (credentials and Tex. credentials com., com. on applications), Am. Acad. Ophthalmology (2nd v.p. 1979, vice chmn. program devel. found. bd. trustees 1993—, com. for pub. and profl. rels., bd. dirs. opthalmology ednl. trust fund found., honor award 1956, sr. honor award 1986, guest of honor 1998 meeting); mem.: N.Am. Highlights Ophthal. Internat. (v.p.), Schepens Internat. Soc. (sec. 1986—93, v.p. 1993—95, pres. 1995—97), Internat. Med. Assembly S.W. Tex., French Ophthal Soc., U. Wis. Ophthal. Alumni Assn. (founding pres. 1990—93, founded Alice R. McPherson lectureship 1994), Assn. Rsch. Surgeons, Pan Am. Assn. Ophthalmology Found., Soc. Eye Surgeons, Tex. Ophthalmol. Assn., So. Med. Soc., Rsch. to Prevent Blindness, Pan Am. Assn. Opthalmology (v.p. 1991—92, pres. elect 1992—95, AJO lectr. 1993, pres. 1995—97, pres. found. 1997—, bd. dirs., membership com., Benjamin Boye Humanitarian award 2001), 9th Dist. Med. Soc., Macula Soc. (credentialing com. 1992—), Internat. Soc. Eye Rsch. (credentials com. 1992—), Houston Ophthalmol. Soc. (pres. 1990—91, credentials com.), Harris County Med. Soc., Am. Bd. Laser Surgery, Am. Soc. Contemporary Ophthalmology (Charles Schepens Hon. award), Internat. Coll. Ocular Surgeons (vice regent 1991), Retina Soc. (v.p. 1976—77, pres. 1978—79, credentials com.), Am. Med. Women's Assn., Internat. Coll. Surgeons (vice regent 1991—), Tex. Med. Assn., AMA, Vitreous Soc., Jules Gonin Club (assoc.). Achievements include research in vision and ophthalmology. Office: Tex Med Ctr 6560 Fannin St Ste 2200 Houston TX 77030-2715

MCPHERSON, DONALD SCOTT, employment relations educator, arbitrator/mediator; b. Sharon, Pa., June 11, 1947; s. Donald McMillan and Lily (Smith) McP.; m. Linda Jo Leighty, Aug. 16, 1969; 1 child, Kimra Leigh. BA, Indiana U. of Pa., 1969, MA, 1971; PhD, U. Pitts., 1977. Dir. residence life Indiana U. of Pa., 1969-77, prof. employment rels., 1977-93, chmn. dept., 1977-87, disting. univ. prof., 1993—. Pres. Assn. Pa. State Coll. and Univ. Faculty, Indiana U. Pa. chpt., 1980. Author: Resolving Grievances, 1983; contbr. articles to profl. jours. Elder Calvary Presbyn. Ch., 1983—; sec. St. Andrew's Soc. of Indiana, 1991-94. Recipient disting. faculty award for svc., Commonwealth of Pa., 1983, Outstanding Alumni award, Indiana U. of Pa., 1983. Mem. Nat. Acad. Arbitrators, Am. Arbitration Assn., Assn. for Conflict Resolution, Indsl. Rels. Rsch. Assn. (exec. dir. Western Pa. chpt. 1982-89), Found. for Indiana U. of Pa. (bd. dir. 1977-82), Indiana Coun. on the Arts, Indiana U. of Pa. Alumni Assn. (pres. 1975-79), Clan MacPherson Assn. (life), Phi Kappa Phi. Democrat. Presbyterian. Home: 240 Oriole Ave Indiana PA 15701-1419 Office: Indiana U of Pa Dept Indsl Rels Indiana PA 15705-0001

MCPHERSON, DONALD PAXTON, III, lawyer; b. Balt., Aug. 9, 1941; s. Donald Paxton Jr. and Janet Lewis Russell McPherson; m. Anna Mary Teaff; children: David Russell, Cynthia Quandt. AB, Princeton U., 1963; LLB, Columbia U., 1966. Bar: Md. 1966, U.S. Dist. Ct. Md. 1967, U.S. Ct. Appeals (4th cir.) 1967. Assoc. Piper & Marbury, Balt., 1966-74, ptnr., 1974-98, head real estate dept., 1980-94, of counsel, 1998—. Mem. ABA, Md. Bar Assn. Democrat. Presbyterian. Avocations: swimming, bicycling, hiking. Office: Piper Marbury Rudnick & Wolfe LLP 6225 Smith Ave Baltimore MD 21209-3600

MCPHERSON, EDWARD RUSSELL, federal agency administrator; b. Balt., Sept. 18, 1945; s. Donald Payton and Janet (Russell) McP.; m. Sally Thompson, May 12, 1969; children: Beth, Edward. BA, Williams Coll., Williamstown, Mass., 1967; MS, George Washington U., 1971. Mgmt. cons. Klein & Saks Inc., Washington, 1968, Booz Allen & Hamilton, Washington, 1971-73; v.p. corp. planning and investor relations Republic Bank Dallas, 1973-76; sr. v.p. corp. planning and investor relations RepublicBank Corp., Dallas, 1978-83, sr. v.p., chief fin. officer, 1983-84, exec. v.p., chief fin. officer, 1984-87, First RepublicBank Corp., Dallas, 1987—2001; chief fin. officer USDA, Washington, 2001—. Bd. dirs. Republic Venture Group, Dallas. Trustee Hockaday Sch., Dallas, 1987, Dallas Fiscal Affairs Com., 1983-87. Served to lt. USN, 1968-71. Office: USDA 1400 Independence Ave. SW Washington DC 20250*

MC PHERSON, HARRY CUMMINGS, JR. lawyer; b. Tyler, Tex., Aug. 22, 1929; s. Harry Cummings and Nan (Hight) McP.; m. Clayton Read, Aug. 30, 1952 (div.); children: Courtenay, Peter B.; m. Mary Patricia DeGroot, Oct. 17, 1981; 1 child, Sam B. BA, U. South, 1949, DCL, 1965; student, Columbia U., 1949-50; LLB, U. Tex., 1956. Bar: Tex. 1955, D.C. 1969. Asst. gen. counsel Democratic policy com. U.S. Senate, 1956-59, assoc. counsel, 1959-61, gen. counsel, 1961-63; dep. under sec. internat. affairs Dept. Army, 1963-64; asst. sec. ednl. and cultural affairs Dept. State, 1964-65; spl. asst. and counsel to Pres. Johnson, 1965-66, spl. counsel, 1966-69; pvt. practice law Washington, 1969—. Chmn. task force on domestic policy Dem. Adv. Coun. Elected Ofcls., 1974-76; mem. Pres.'s Commn. on Accident at Three Mile Island, 1979; vice chmn. John F. Kennedy Ctr. for Performing Arts, 1969-76, gen. counsel, 1977-91; bd. dirs. Woodrow Wilson Internat. Ctr. for Scholars, 1969-74; pres. Fed. City Coun., 1983-88; apptd. vice chmn. U.S. Internat. Cultural and Trade Ctr. Commn., 1988-93. Author: A Political Education, 1972, 88, 95. Mem. U.S. Base Closure and Realignment Commn., 1993. 2d lt. USAF, 1950-53. Recipient Disting. Civilian Svc. award Dept. Army, 1964, Arthur S. Flemming award, 1968, Judge Learned Hand Human Rels. award Am. Jewish Com., 1994. Mem. D.C. Bar Assn., N.Y. Council on Fgn. Relations (dir. 1974-77), Econ. Club. of Washington (pres. 1992-99). Democrat. Episcopalian. Home: 10213 Montgomery Ave Kensington MD 20895-3325 Office: 901 15th St NW Washington DC 20005-2327 E-mail: hcmcpherson@verner.com.

MCPHERSON, JAMES ALAN, writer, educator; b. Savannah, Ga., Sept. 16, 1943; s. James and Mable (Smalls) McP.; 1 dau., Rachel Alice. BA, Morris Brown Coll., 1965; LLB, Harvard, 1968; MFA, U. Iowa, 1971. Asst. prof. lit. U. Calif., Santa Cruz, 1969-71, Morgan State U., 1975-76; assoc. prof. English U. Va., Charlottesville, 1976-81; prof. English U. Iowa, 1981—. Mem. lit. panel Nat. Endowment for Arts, 1977-80; lectr., Japan, 1989-90; vis. scholar Yale Law Sch., 1978-79. Author: Hue and Cry, 1969, Railroad, 1976, Elbow Room, 1977 (Pultizer prize 1978), A World Unsuspected, 1987, The Prevailing South, 1988, Confronting Racial Differences, 1990, Lure and Loathing, 1993, Crossings, 1993, Crab Cakes, 1998, Fathering Daughters, 1998, The View From Exile, 2000; editor Double Take Mag., 1995—; contbr. editor Atlantic Monthly, Boston, 1969. Atlantic grantee, 1968; Guggenheim fellow, 1972-73, Ctr. Behavioral Studies fellow, Stanford, Calif., 1997-98; Recipient award in lit. Nat. Inst. Arts and Letters, 1970, MacArthur Found. award, 1981, Excellence in Tchg. award U. Iowa, 1991, Green Eyeshades award Soc. So. Journalists, 1994; stories selected for O'Henry Collection and Best American Short Stories, 1969, 73, Best Am. Short Stories of the 20th Century, Best Am. Essays various Norton Anthologies, 1990, 93, 94, 95, Pushcart prize, 1995, 96. Mem. ACLU, NAACP, P.E.N., Am. Acad. Arts and Scis. (elected mem. 1995), Authors League.

MCPHERSON, JAMES LOWELL, writer; b. Cin., Jan. 25, 1921; s. Clarence Lowell and Carolyn Marie (Mohorter) McP.; m. Gertrude Huntington Wright, July 25, 1947 (div. May 1973); children: Karen Sue, Christopher Wright; m. Phyllis Wright King, Aug. 25, 1978. Student, Middlebury Coll., 1938-40; BA, W.Va. U., 1942; postgrad., Columbia U., N.Y.C., 1946-48. Instr. sociology Boston U., 1949-52, Smith Coll., Northampton, Mass., 1952-55; freelance writer, editor Conn., 1955-59; postmaster U.S. Post Office, Marble Dale, Conn., 1960-68; freelance writer N.Y.C., 1970—. Part-time asst. Ideal Book Store, N.Y.C., 1975-98. Author: (novel) Goodbye Rosie, 1965. Poet Laureate, W.Va., 1943-46. With inf., U.S. Army, 1942-45, ETO. Mem. Authors Guild, Acad. Am. Poets, Poets Ho. Home: 33 Riverside Dr Apt 13fa New York NY 10023-8021

MC PHERSON, JAMES MUNRO, history educator; b. Valley City, N.D., Oct. 11, 1936; s. James Munro and Miriam (Osborn) McP.; m. Patricia Rasche, Dec. 28, 1957; 1 dau., Joanna Erika. BA, Gustavus Adolphus Coll., 1958; PhD, Johns Hopkins U., 1963. Mem. faculty Princeton U., 1962—, prof. history, 1972—, Edwards prof. Am. history, 1982, George Henry Davis '86 prof. Am. history, 1991. Jefferson lectr., 2000. Author: Struggle for Equality, 1964 (Ainsfield-Wolf award race rels. 1965), The Negro's Civil War, 1965, Marching Toward Freedom: The Negro in the Civil War, 1968, Blacks in America: Bibliographical Essays, 1971, The Abolitionist Legacy: From Reconstruction to the NAACP, 1975, Ordeal by Dire: The Civil War and Reconstruction, 1981, 2d edit., 1992, Battle Cry of Freedom: The Civil War Era, 1988 (Pulitzer prize for history 1989), Abraham Lincoln and the Second American Revolution, 1991, Images of the Civil War, 1992, Gettysburg, 1993, What They Fought For, 1861-1865, 1994, The Atlas of the Civil War, 1994, Drawn With the Sword: Reflections on the American Civil War, 1996, For Cause and Comrades: Why Men Fought in the Civil War, 1997 (Lincoln prize 1998), Lamson of the Gettysburg: The Civil War Letters of Lt. Roswell H. Lamson, U.S. Navy, 1997 (Theodore and Franklin D. Roosevelt prize in naval history 1998), Is Blood Thicker than Water? Crises of Nationalism in the Modern World, 1998, Writing the Civil War: The Quest to Understand, 1998, To the Best of My Ability, 2000, The American Presidents, 2000, Days of Destiny, 2001. Danforth fellow, 1958-62, Guggenheim fellow, 1967-68, Huntington-Nat. Endowment for Humanities fellow, 1977-78, fellow Behavioral Scis. Ctr., Stanford U., 1982-83, Huntington-Seaver Inst. fellow, 1987-88. Mem.: Orgn. Am. Historians, So. Hist. Assn., Am. Hist. Assn. (pres.-elect 2002—), Am. Philos. Soc., Phi Beta Kappa (Jefferson lectr. 2000). Home: 15 Randall Rd Princeton NJ 08540-3609

MCPHERSON, JOANNE FRANCES, art educator, artist, special education educator; b. St. Paul, Apr. 26, 1946; d. Tony J. and Frances L. (Stephani) Kushlan; m. Robert Waite McPherson Sr.; children: Robert Waite McPherson, Jr., Melanie Anne McPherson. BS, St. Cloud State U., 1969; MEd, U. Minn., 1986. Licensed art tchr. grades K-12, Minn.; licensed spl. edn. tchr. Art educator Rocori H.S., Cold Spring, Minn., 1969-70; fed. title 1 tchr. Juvenile Correctional Facility, Lino Lakes, 1970-72; art educator Ind. Sch. Dist. 622, Maplewood, 1972-89, chairperson curriculum coordination coun., 1986-89, 95—; spl. edn. educator Tartan H.S., Oakdale, 1989-95; art, spl. edn. educator North St. Paul (Minn.) Sr. H.S., 1995—. Instr. Creative Learning Ctr., Roseville, Minn., 1986-89; vol. artist Ind. Sch. Dist. #622, North St. Paul and Maplewood, Minn., 1989—. Mem. Coon Rapids Fine Arts Commn., 1979-83. Profl. opportunity program grantee Minn. Coun. Arts Edn. State of Minn., 1994, found. grantee Dist. 622, 1997, 99; recipient certification of appreciation Coon Rapids Fine Arts Commn., 1990. Mem. Minn. Edn. Assn., Mpls. Woman's Club, St. Andrew's Soc. Minn. (pres. 1997-99), Phi Delta Kappa. Avocations: watercolor painting, gourmet cooking, biking, photography, travel. Home: 4629 Wild Canyon Trl Woodbury MN 55129-9606 Office: North St Paul Sr H S 2416 11th Ave E North Saint Paul MN 55109-2200

MCPHERSON, JOHN DOUGLAS, molecular biologist, educator; b. Edmonton, Alta., Can., Mar. 15, 1960; s. Victor Allon and June Maitland McPherson. PhD, Queen's U., Kingston, Ont., Can., 1988. Asst. prof. U. Calif., Irvine, 1993—95; assoc. prof. Washington U. Sch. Medicine, St. Louis, 1995—. Co-dir. Genome Sequencing Ctr., St. Louis, 1997—. Author: (human genome sequencing) Initial sequencing and analysis of the human genome, 2001. Office: Genome Sequencing Ctr 4444 Forest Park Ave Saint Louis MO 63108

MCPHERSON, LARRY E(UGENE), photographer, educator; b. Newark, May 1, 1943; s. Eugene Edward and Ethel Grace (Lehman) McP. BA, Columbia Coll., Chgo., 1976; MA, No. Ill. U., 1978. Instr. Columbia Coll., 1971-76; assoc. prof. photography U. Memphis, 1978—. Instr. Sch. of Art Inst. Chgo., spring 1972; workshop instr. Ohio State U., Columbus, summer 1980, VSW Summer Inst., Rochester, N.Y., summer 1988. One-man shows include Art Inst. Chgo., 1969, 78, 81, Dayton Art Inst., 1992; exhibited in group shows at Mus. Modern Art, N.Y.C., 1978, Corcoran Gallery Art, Washington, 1982, George Eastman House, Rochester, N.Y., 1982, New Orleans Mus. Art, 1992, Milw. Art Mus., 1996, Birmingham Mus. Art, 1996, Art Inst. Chgo., 1997; represented in permanent collections Mus. Modern Art, Art Inst. Chgo., George Eastman House, New Orleans Mus. Art, Mus. Fine Arts, Houston, Memphis Brooks Mus. Art, The Dayton Art Inst., Birmingham Mus. Art, Milw. Mus. Art, Ogden Mus. So. art. Faculty Devel. grantee U. Memphis, 1983, 92, 99; grantee-fellow Nat. Endowment for Arts, 1975, 79; Guggenheim fellow, 1980. Mem. Soc. Photog. Edn. Home: 7725 Shadow Bend Ln Arlington TN 38002-8051 Office: U Memphis Dept Art Memphis TN 38152-0001 E-mail: lmcphersn@memphis.edu.

MCPHERSON, LUZ MARIA, fashion, beauty and health products company owner; b. Mexico City, Mar. 9, 1938; came to U.S., 1956; d. Vicente Maciel and Josefina (Lopez) Maciel; m. Frank S. McPherson, Mar. 8, 1958; children: Patrick, Mary Evelyn, Jorge Luis, Linda Frances. Student, Fashion Acad., Calif.; degree in pub. rels., Colegio Progreso, Mex.; studies with Suzanne Caygill, San Francisco; studies with Ben and Marcella Benda, Can. Owner Rose Petals Assn. of Color and Image Cons., Vienna. Cons. World Bank, Orgn. Am. State, Inter-Am. Devel. Bank, others; lectr. Image Reflections, Charlottesville, Va.; radio talk show presenter Health and Beauty, Washington; pvt. cons. to First Lady of Mex., Senora de la Madrid; guest speaker radio and talk shows. Founder, facilitator Hermanita Project Youth Leadership, Va.; pres. Mex.-Am. Nat. Org., 1989; dir. Latin Am. Festival Beauty Pageant, Washington, 1991. Named Hispanic of Week, Pregonero Newspaper, Washington, 1987. Mem. Ibero-Am. Assn. (hon.), Color Assn. USA, Exec. Women's Club, Mex. Am. Women's Nat. Assn., Reston C. of C. Office: Rose Petals PO Box 2711 Bonita Springs FL 34133-2711

MCPHERSON, MELVILLE PETER, academic administrator, former government official; b. Grand Rapids, Mich., Oct. 27, 1940; s. Donald and Ellura E. (Frost) McP.; m. Joanne McPherson; 4 children. JD, Am. U., 1969; MBA, Western Mich. U., 1967; BA, Mich. State U., 1963. Peace Corps vol., Peru, 1965-66; with IRS, Washington, 1969-75; spl. asst. to pres. and dep. dir. Presdl. Pers. White Ho., 1975-77; mng. ptnr. Washington office Vorys, Sater, Seymour & Pease, 1977-81; administr. AID, Washington, 1981-87; dep. sec. Dept. Treasury, 1987-89; group exec. v.p. Bank of Am., San Francisco, 1989-93; pres. Mich. State U., East Lansing, 1993—. Mem. D.C. Bar Assn., Mich. Bar Assn. Republican. Methodist. Office: Office of the Pres Mich State U 450 Administration East Lansing MI 48824-1046

MCPHERSON, MICHAEL ROBERT, information scientist, university director; b. Fayette, Mo., June 14, 1956; s. Robert Ernest and Doris La Verne McP.; m. Carolyn Owens, Sept. 5, 1992; stepchildren: Michael, Daniel, Stephen, Elizabeth. BA, Mich. State U., 1989. Programmer Mich. State U., East Lansing, 1978-81, sys. analyst, 1981-85, mgr. opers., 1985-91, project mgr., 1991-95; dir. info. tech. U. Mich., Ann Arbor, 1995—. Contbr. articles to profl. jours. Mem. AAAS, Assn. Computing Machinery, U. Mich. Flyers (bd. dirs. 1998-99). Avocations: private pilot, curling. Office: U Mich 1007 E Huron St Ann Arbor MI 48104-1628

MCPHERSON, MICHAEL STEVEN, academic administrator, economics educator; b. June 6, 1947; married; two children. BA in Math., U. Chgo., 1967, MA in Econs., 1970, PhD in Econs., 1974. Instr. econs. dept. U. Ill., Chgo., 1971-74; asst. prof. econs. Williams Coll., 1974-81, assoc. prof. econs., 1981-84, prof. econs., 1984-96, chmn. econs. dept., then dean of faculty, 1986-91; pres. Macalester Coll., St. Paul, 1996—. Cons. Data Resources, Inc., 1979, Nat. Research Coun. Commn. Human Resources, 1979, Modern Lang. Assn., 1980, Nat. Acad. of Edn., 1980, Smith Coll., 1982, The Coll. Bd., 1983, Rand Corp., 1985-86, U.S. Dept. Edn. Ctr. for Statistics, 1986. Author: (with M.O. Shapiro) Keeping College Affordable: Government and Educational Opportunity, 1991, The Student Aid Game: Meeting Need and Rewarding Talent in American Higher Education, 1998, (with D. Hausman) Economic Analysis and Moral Philosophy, 1996; editor: The Demand for New Faculty in Science and Engineering, 1980, Democracy, Development, and the Art of Trespassing: Essays in Honor of Albert O. Hirschman, 1986; contbr. articles to profl. jours. Trustee Coll. Bd., 1997—. Ford Found. grantee 1981-83, Mellon Found grantee 1984-86; Am. Coun. Learned Socs. Study fellow, 1977-78, vis. fellow Princeton U., 1977-78, sr. fellow Brookings Instn., 1984-86. Home: 1750 Summit Ave Saint Paul MN 55105-1834 Office: Macalester Coll 1600 Grand Ave Saint Paul MN 55105-1801

MCPHERSON, MILTON MONROE, history educator; b. Beatrice, Ala., Oct. 19, 1928; s. Laurence Milton and Annie Mae (Bell) McP.; m. Carolyn Elizabeth Coley, Dec. 16, 1955; children: Milton Jr., Herbert L., Gretchen M. BA, U. Ala., 1950, MA, 1959, PhD in Am. History, 1970. Asst. prof. history Miss. Coll., Clinton, 1959-60, Mercer U., Macon, Ga., 1960-61, Ala. Coll., Montevallo, 1961-62, Pensacola (Fla.) Jr. Coll., 1962-68; assoc. prof. history Troy (Ala.) State U., 1968-87, prof. history, 1987-89; prof. history emeritus, 1989—. Author: The Ninety-Day Wonders: OCS and the Modern American Army, 2001; editor: Memories That Lingered: The Life and Times of Laurence Milton McPherson, 1993, Timeless Moments: Essays in American History, 1995. 1st lt. U.S. Army, 1950-53. Mem. NEA, Ala. Hist. Assn., So. Hist. Assn. Avocations: writing, reading, photography, walking, traveling. Home: 206 Sherwood Ave Troy AL 36081-4534

MC PHERSON, PAUL FRANCIS, publishing and investment banking executive; b. Boston, Apr. 30, 1931; s. William Andrew and Margaret Frances (Rice) McP.; m. Mary Loretta Sanders, June 10, 1953; children: Paul, Kevin, Gary, Scott. BSBA, Boston Coll., 1952; MBA, Babson Coll., 1955. With McGraw Hill, Inc., N.Y.C., 1955-89; advt. sales mgr. McGraw-Hill Pub. Co., 1963-66, group v.p., 1973-76, exec. v.p., 1976-79; pres. McGraw-Hill Info. Systems Co., 1979-80, McGraw-Hill Pub. Co., 1980-83, exec. v.p., 1983-89; pres., chief exec. officer FM Bus. Publs. Inc., N.Y.C., 1988-92; sr. advisor AdMedia Corp. Advisors, 1992-93, mng. dir., 1993—. Served with U.S. Army, 1952-54. Mem. Am. Bus. Press (bd. dirs., past chmn.), Mag. Pubs. Am. (bd. dirs., past chmn.), Advt. Coun. (dir., past vice chmn.), Audit Bur. Circulations (dir., past vice chmn.), Woodway Country Club. Home: 10 Drum Hill Ln Stamford CT 06902-1406 Office: AdMedia Ptnrs 444 Madison Ave New York NY 10022-6903

MC PHERSON, PETER, university president; BA in Polit. Sci., Mich. State U., 1963; MBA, Western Mich. U., 1967; JD, Am. U., 1969; LHD (hon.), Va. State U., 1984, Mt. St. Mary;s Coll., 1986; LLD (hon.), Mich. State U., 1984. Tax law specialist IRS, 1969-75; spl. asst. to Pres. Ford, deputy dir. presdl. personnel The White House, Washington, 1975-77; ptnr. Vorys, Sater, Seymour & Pease, 1977-80; adminstr. Agy. for Internat. Devel., 1981-87; deputy sec. Treasury Dept., Washington, 1987-89; group exec. v.p. Bank Am., 1989-93; pres. Mich. State U., East Lansing, 1993—. Chmn. bd. Overseas Pvt. Investment Corp., 1981-87. Gen. counsel Reagan-Bush Transition, 1980-81; vol. Peace Corps, Peru, 1964-65. Recipient Humanitarian of Yr. award Am. Lebanese League, 1983, UNICEF award.

MCPHERSON, RICHARD CLARK, surgeon; b. Lisbon, Ohio, Aug. 15, 1926; s. Hugh and Helen Agnes (Clark) McP.; m. Dorothy Jean Werstler, June 10, 1951; children: Gregg Alan, Kimberly Sue McPherson Vratil. BS, Mt. Union Coll., Alliance, Ohio, 1950; MS, Ohio State U., 1953, 60, MD, 1954. Diplomate Am. Bd. Surgery. Intern Akron (Ohio) City Hosp., 1954-55; resident in surgery Ohio State U. Hosp., Columbus, 1955—56, 1956—57, 1960—61; instr., asst. prof. surgery U. Louisville, 1961-63; pvt. practice Lafayette, Ind., 1963—. Capt. USAF, 1959—60. Fellow ACS (pres. Ind. chpt. 1978); mem. AMA, Ctrl. Surgery Assn., Soc. for Physicians in Adminstrn., Med. Group Mgmt. Assn. (pres. 1996-97). Office: Arnett Clinic PO Box 5545 Lafayette IN 47903-5545

MC PHERSON, ROLF KENNEDY, clergyman, religious organization administrator; b. Providence, Mar. 23, 1913; s. Harold S. and Aimee (Semple) McP.; m. Lorna De Smith, July 21, 1931 (dec.); children— Marlene (dec.), Kay; m. Evangeline Carmichael, Jan. 31, 1997. Grad., So. Cal. Radio Inst., 1933; D.D. (hon.), L.I.F.E. Bible Coll., 1944; LLD (hon.), L.I.F.E. Bible Coll., Los Angeles, 1988. Ordained to ministry Internat. Ch. Foursquare Gospel, 1940. Pres. Internat. Ch. Foursquare Gospel, L.A., 1944-88, dir., 1944-92; pres. emeritus, 1988—; pres., dir. L.I.F.E. Bible Coll., Inc., L.A., 1944-88. Mem. Echo Park Evangelistic Assn. (pres. 1944—). Office: Internat Ch Foursquare Gospel 1910 W Sunset Blvd Ste 200 Los Angeles CA 90026-3295 E-mail: drrolfe@pacbell.net.

MC QUADE, LAWRENCE CARROLL, lawyer, corporate executive; b. Yonkers, N.Y., Aug. 12, 1927; s. Edward A. and Thelma (Keefe) McQ.; m. de Rosset Parker Morrissey, Aug. 3, 1968 (dec. Oct. 1978); 1 child, Andrew Parker; m. Margaret Osmer, Mar. 15, 1980. BA with distinction, Yale U., 1950; BA, Oxford (Eng.) U., 1952, MA, 1956; LLB cum laude, Harvard U., 1954; MA (hon.), Colby Coll., 1981. Bar: N.Y. 1955, D.C. 1968. Assoc. Sullivan & Cromwell, N.Y.C., 1954-60; spl. asst. to asst. sec. for internat. security affairs U.S. Dept. Def., Washington, 1961-63; dep. asst. sec. U.S. Dept. Commerce, 1963-64, asst. to sec., 1965-67, asst. sec., 1967-69; pres. Procon Inc., Des Plaines, Ill., 1969-75, CEO, dir., 1969-75; v.p. Universal Oil Products Co., 1972-75, W.R. Grace & Co., N.Y.C., 1975-78, sr. v.p., 1978-83, exec. v.p., 1983-87, also bd. dirs.; vice chmn. Prudential Mut. Fund Mgmt., 1988-95; mng. dir. Prudential Securities Inc., 1988-92; chmn. Qualitas Internat., 1994—. Chmn., CEO Universal Money Ctrs., 1987—88; co-chmn. River Capital Internat., 1997—; expert advisor commn. on transnat. corps. UN, 1989—93; bd. dirs. BUNZL, Quixote Corp., Oxford Analytica, Solar Outdoor Lighting, Laredo Nat. Bancshares. Author: (with others) The Ghana Report, 1959; contbr. (with others) articles to profl. jours. Bd. dirs. Fgn. Bondholders Protective Coun., N.Y.C., 1978—, The Am. Forum, 1985-96, Am. Coun. on Germany, 1985-94; trustee Colby Coll., 1981-89, trustee emeritus, 1989—; dir. Czech and Slovak Am. Enterprise Funds, 1994-96; chmn. Czech and Slovak AE Fund, 1995-96; dir. Paul and Daisy Soros Fellowships for New Ams., 1998—. Rhodes scholar Oxford U., 1952. Mem. Coun. Fgn. Rels. N.Y., Chgo. Coun. Fgn. Rels. (bd. dirs. 1969-75), Nat. Fgn. Trade Coun. (bd. dirs. 1979-87), Atlantic Coun. U.S. (bd. dirs. 1969-99), Mgmt. and Devel. Inst. (bd. dirs. 1970-99), Overseas Devel. Coun. (bd. dirs. 1974-87), Pres.'s Cir. of NAS, Harvard Club, Century Club, Met. Club (Washington), Phi Beta Kappa. E-mail: lmcquade@rivercapital.com.

MCQUAID, ROBERT A., JR. federal judge; Apptd. magistrate judge U.S. Dist. Ct. Nev., 1996. Office: US Courthouse 400 S Virginia St Rm 405 Reno NV 89501-2193 Fax: 775-686-5865.

MCQUAID, RONALD WILLIAM, economic development educator, consultant, researcher; b. Ont., Can., 1955; BA with honors, Lancaster (U.K.) U., 1977; MS in Econs. with distinction, London Sch. Econs., 1979; PhD, Harvard U., 1984. Head dept. econs. Coun., Stirling, Scotland, 1985-87, Strathkelvin, Scotland, 1987-90; sr. lectr. Napier U., Edinburgh, U.K., 1990—; acting dir. Employment Rsch. Inst. Treas. Scout Group, Stirling. Mem. Regional Sci. Assn. Internat. (Brit. and Irish br. treas. 1997—), Chair Region Studies (Scottish br.). Office: Napier U South Craig Criaghouse Rd Edinburgh EH10 5LG Scotland

MCQUAIN, JEFFREY HUNTER, writer, editor, word historian; b. Frederick, Md., Nov. 23, 1955; s. Robert Hunter and Genetta (Dolly) McQ. AA in Gen. Edn., Montgomery Coll., Rockville, Md., 1974; BA in English, U. Md., 1976, MA in English, 1977; PhD in Lit. Studies, Am. U., Washington, 1983. Rschr. to William Safire The N.Y. Times, Washington, 1983—; writer, columnist United Media, N.Y.C., 1988-94; editor, writer Copy Editor newsletter, 2000—01. Author: Power Language, 1996 (Best Lang. Book award Words from Home, Phoenix 1997), Never Enough Words, 1999, Honegrown English, 2002; co-author: The Elements of English, 1986, Coined by Shakespeare, 1998. Sec. Doing Things for Animals, Sun City, Ariz., 1992-99. Mem. MLA, Am. Dialect Soc. Democrat. Methodist. Avocations: drama, word collecting, travel. Office: The Word Doctor PO Box 4008 Rockville MD 20849-4008

MCQUARRIE, DONALD GRAY, surgeon, educator; b. Richfield, Utah, Apr. 17, 1931; s. John Gray and LaRetta (Smith) McQ.; m. Dolores Jean Dietrich, July 16, 1956; children— William Gray, Michelle Dolores Colton. BS, U. Utah, 1952, MD, 1956; PhD, U. Minn., 1964. Diplomate Am. Bd. Surgery, Am. Bd. Thoracic and Cardiovascular Surgery. Intern U. Minn. Hosps., 1956—57; resident in surgery U. Minn., Mpls., 1957—59, resident, 1961—65, asst. prof. surgery, 1964—68, assoc. prof. surgery, 1968—72, prof. surgery, 1972—2001, prof. emeritus, 2002—, vice chmn. dept. surgery, 1993—99; mem. surg. staff Mpls. VA Hosp., 1964—99, chief surg. svc., 1993—99, resident in thoracic surgery, 1965—66, dir. surg. rsch. lab., 1964—78. Vis. prof. U. Tex.-San Antonio, 1974, U. Ind. and Indpls. VA, 1977, affiliated program U. Ariz., Phoenix, 1982, Case Western Res. U., 1986. Editor, contbg. author: Head and Neck Cancer, 1986, Reoperations in General Surgery, 1991, 2d edit., 1996; contbr. articles on surg. and basic med. scis. to profl. publs., 1955— Served to lt. M.C., USN, 1959-61 USPHS postdoctoral fellow, 1962-65 Fellow ACS (commn. on cancer 1980-89, exec. council commn. on operating room environ. 1985-91, pres. Minn. chpt. 1983-84, liaison to Assn. Oper. Rm. Nurses 1985-97, gov. 1990-96); mem. Minn. Surg. Soc. (pres. 1980-81), Assn. Acad. Surgery, Mpls. Surg. Soc. (pres. 1978-79), Soc. Head and Neck Surgeons, Central Surg. Assn., Western Surg. Soc., Soc. Univ. Surgeons, Société Internationale de Chirurgie, Am. Surg. Assn., Royal Soc. Medicine, Assn. VA Surgeons (pres. 1987), Soc. Surg. Oncology, Hennepin County Med. Soc., Minn. Med. Assn., Am. Soc. Clin. Oncology, Phi Beta Kappa, Phi Kappa Phi Clubs: Minneapolis, Interlachen Country (Mpls.). Avocations: computer applications to medicine, jewelry design, lapidary work. Home: 6625 Mohawk Trl Minneapolis MN 55439-1029

MCQUARRIE, IRVINE GRAY, neurosurgeon, educator, consultant; b. Ogden, Utah, June 27, 1939; s. Irwin Bruce and Ruby Loretta (Epperson) McQ.; m. Katharine Gamble Rogers, Mar. 11, 1967 (div.); children: Michael Gray, Mollie; m. Maryann Kaminski, Aug. 14, 1980; children: Morgan Elizabeth, Gray. BS in Biology, U. Utah, 1961; MD, Cornell U., 1965, PhD, 1977. Diplomate Am. Bd. Neurol. Surgery. Intern, asst. surgeon, surgeon N.Y. Hosp., N.Y.C., 1965-71, 72-73; research fellow dept. physiology Cornell U. Med. Coll., N.Y.C., 1971-72, 74-76, asst. prof. depts. physiology and surgery, 1976-81; vis. asst. prof. dept. anatomy Case Western Res. U., Cleve., 1979-81, asst. prof. neurosurgery, 1981-85, assoc. prof., 1985—, tenure prof. 1987—; asst. prof. devel. genetics and anatomy, 1981-85, assoc. prof., 1985-88, assoc. prof. neurosci., 1988—; clin. investigator VA Med. Center, Cleve., 1981-84, med. investigator in neurosurgery, 1984—; asst. neurosurgeon Univ. Hosps. Cleve., 1981—; mem. adv. bd. VA office Regeneration Rsch. Programs, 1986-88, chmn. 1988-89. Contbr. articles to sci. jours. Comdr., M.C. USNR, 1973-74. Recipient Andrew W. Mellon Tchr.-Scientist award, 1977-79; NIH fellow, 1971-72, 74-76; VA individual research grantee, 1981—; Paralyzed Vets. Am. grantee, 1979-82; NIH grantee, 1982-89, Spinal Cord Soc. grantee, 1986-88, Elizabeth Crosby lectr. U. Mich., 1989. Mem. AAAS, Soc. for Neurosci., Am. Soc. for Cell Biology, Congress Neurol. Surgeons, Am. Assn. Neurol. Surgeons. Democrat. Research on mechanism of axonal regeneration in central nervous system; biochem. investigations on maintenance and replacement of nerve cell processes (called axons and dendrites) by complex intraneuronal transport mechanisms. Home: 13805 Shaker Blvd Cleveland OH 44120-1509 Office: 2119 Abington Rd Cleveland OH 44106-2333

MCQUARRIE, TERRY SCOTT, technical director; b. Springville, Utah, Dec. 27, 1942; s. Evan Dain and Fay (Torkeldsen) McQ.; m. Judith Lynn Lewellen, June 20, 1970; children: Devin Daniel, Melanie Fay. BA, U. Oreg., 1966; MA, San Jose State U., 1977; PhD, Hamilton U., 2000. Prodn. mgr. Lunastran Co., San Jose, Calif., 1974-76; group leader Koppers Co., Inc., Pitts., 1978-79, industry mgr., 1980-87; v.p., tech. dir. Glasforms, Inc., San Jose, Calif., 1987—. Bd. dirs. Glasforms, Inc. Contbr. articles to profl. jours. Recipient award for excellence in leadership Composites Fabricators Assn., 2000. Mem. ASTM, Soc. Plastics Industry (chmn. Composites Inst. 1998, chmn. pultrusion industry coun. 1988-90, Excellence award 1998, Man of Yr. award 1999). Republican. Mem. Lds Ch. Achievements include patent for pultrusion polyester resins and process. E-mail: terrym@glasforms.com.

MCQUARY, VAUGHN, management company executive; BA, U. Ark., 1978. Asst. mgr. Little Rock Airport, 1996-98; v.p. Rector Phillips Morse Mgmt. Co., Little Rock, 1980—. Chmn. Ark. State Dem. Party. Mem. Assn. State Dem. Chairs (chmn. 1997—).*

MCQUEEN, JUSTICE ELLIS (L. Q. JONES), actor, director; b. Beaumont, Tex., Aug. 19, 1927; s. Justice Ellis and Pat (Stephens) McQ.; m. Sue Helen Lewis, Oct. 10, 1950 (dec.); children: Marlin Randolph, Marilyn Helen, Steven Lewis. Student, Lamar Jr. Coll., 1944, Lon Morris Coll., 1949, U. Tex., 1950-51. Actor, writer, dir.: motion picture films including A Boy and His Dog, 1975 (recipient Hugo award, Sci. Fiction achievement award for dramatic presentation); actor White Line Fever, 1975, Mother, Jugs & Speed, 1976, Winterhawk, 1976, Fast Charlie, The Moonbeam Rider, 1979, Timerider: The Adventures of Lyle Swann, 1982, The Beast Within, 1982, Sacred Ground, 1983, Lone Wolf McQuade, 1983, Bulletproof, 1988, River of Death, 1989, The Legend of Grizzly Adams, 1990, Lightning Jack, 1994, The Friends of Harry, 1995, Casino, 1995, Ben Johnson: Third Cowboy on the Right, 1996, The Edge, 1997, The Patriot, 1998, The Mask of Zorro, 1998, numerous others; tv movies include The Sacketts, 1979, Tornado!, 1996, In Cold Blood, 1996, The Jack Bull, 1999, numerous others; appeared in tv series including Gunsmoke, 1955, Alias Smith and Jones, 1971, Cannon, 1971, Cade's County, 1971, Kung Fu, 1972, Matt Helm, 1975, Charlie's Angels, 1976, Columbo: The Conspirators, 1978, The Dukes of Hazzard, 1979, The Fall Guy, 1981, The Yellow Rose, 1983, The A-Team, 1983, Walker, Texas Ranger, 1993, numerous others; producer The Big Thickett, Come In, Children, The Witchmaker; author, prodr.: The Brotherhood of Satan, 1971; dir., prodr. The Devil's Bedroom, 1964, (tv series) The Incredible Hulk, 1978. Served with USNR, 1945-46. Nominee 4 Emmy awards. Mem. Screen Actors Guild. Republican. Methodist. Home and Office: 2144 1/2 N Cahuenga Blvd Los Angeles CA 90068-2708 *Contribute to a space that no one can or will fill.*

MCQUEEN, MARJORIE MARIE WYNKOOP, retired archivist, writer; b. Mexico City, Mar. 31, 1927; d. George Melvin Wynkoop and Marie Chabert; m. Halton Stephen McQueen, Mar. 8, 1952 (dec. 1982); children: Kathleen Marie Edwards, Michael Patrick(dec.), Stephen Halton, Patricia Ann. AA, San Antonio Coll., Tex., 1951; AA in Bus. Mgmt., Coll. of Desert, Palm Desert, Calif., 1981; BA in Polit. Sci., U. Calif., Riverside, 1983; AA, Riverside City Coll., 1990. Archivist Def, Visual Info. Ctr.; ret., 1996. Contbr. numerous articles to newspapers and mags. Vol. Danforth Mus., Framingham; publicity dir. Rancho Mirage C. of C., 1976—80, Rancho Mirage Cmty. Assn. Recipient 1st place black and white picture sect., L.A. County Fair, 3d place, Hemet Fair, 1st place, Indio Date Festival, Nat. awards, Photographic Soc. Am. Mem.: Nat. Assn. Ret. Fed. Employees, Nat. League Am. Pen Women (Calif. state historian 1980—82, pres. Palm Springs br. 1976—80, 3d place photography award), Callahan Sr. Ctr. Genealogy Group.

MCQUEEN, REGENIA, writer; b. Summerville, S.C., Oct. 29, 1945; d. William McQueen and Mary Stoutamire-McQueen; m. John Ray Sanders Teasley, Oct. 11, 1961; children: John Ray Sanders Teasley, Tonya Teasley, Ieishia Teasley, Nairobi Teasley, Rhodesia Teasley, Donnish Lindsey-Teasley. A, Cin. Tech. Coll., 1985; cert., Blackstone Sch. of Law, Dallas, 2000. Clk. Western-So. Life Ins., Cin., 1967-72, IRS, Covington, Ky., 1985-87. Author: Regenia McQueen: Born to Search, 2000, Nairobi Teasley: 1-1/2 Hourse Defenseless Lamb , 2000, Witnesses to the Impossible Dreams, 2002, Regenia McQueen Life Stolen, 2002. V.p. 13th St Tenant Assn., 1979-85; trustee Owning the Realty, 1983-85. Recipient Achievement award Ho. of Reps., Ohio, 2000. Avocations: researching, writing. Home: PO Box 15311 118A Promontory Dr Covington KY 41015

MC QUEEN, ROBERT CHARLES, retired insurance executive; b. Santiago, Chile, Jan. 23, 1921; s. Charles Alfred and Grace Juanita (Abrecht) McQ.; m. Donna Marie Ikeler, Oct. 6, 1945; children: Scott, Jerry, Monte, Donald. AB, Dartmouth Coll., 1942. Mathematician, Equitable Life Assurance Soc., N.Y.C., 1945-49; group actuary Union Central Life Ins. Co., Cin., 1949-57; with Mut. Benefit Life Ins. Co., Newark, 1957-85, exec. v.p., 1969-71, sr. exec. v.p., chief adminstrv. officer, 1971-85, dir., 1978-85. Bd. dirs. St. Barnabas Corp. (formerly Trimark Corp.). Pres. Millburn Twp. (N.J.) Bd. Edn., 1969-71, Naples (Fla.) Bridge Ctr., 1994-96; chmn. BBB Met. N.Y.,

1978-80; chmn. bd. trustees St. Barnabas Hosp., Livingston, N.J., 1983-91, trustee, 1991—. With OSS, 1943-45. Fellow Soc. Actuaries; mem. Am. Acad. Actuaries, Internat. Actuarial Assn., Canoe Brook Country Club, Quail Creek Club. Republican. Episcopalian. Home: 11408 Oakmont Ct Fort Myers FL 33908

MCQUEEN, SANDRA MARILYN, educator, consultant; b. Greenville, S.C., Nov. 30, 1948; d. Clement Edgar and Sarah Elizabeth (Gentry) McQ. BA, Presbyn. Coll., 1970; MA, Presbyn. Sch. Christian Edn., 1972; PhD, Ga. State U., 1987. Cert. early childhood, spl. edn., ESL gifted tchr., spl. edn. supr., Ga. Dir. christian edn. com. Rock Spring Presbyn. Ch., Atlanta, 1972-74; early childhood educator Atlanta Bd. of Edn., 1974-80, educator gifted children, 1980—. Curriculum developer, in-svc. educator Atlanta Bd. Edn., 1989—; tchr., cons. Ga. Geographic Alliance. Mem. Justice for Women, Atlanta, 1980—, chair, 1985-86, co-chair, 1989-91; mem. Rock Spring Chancel Choir, Atlanta, 1978—, sec., 1987-89; mem. Rock Spring Presbyn. Ch., Atlanta, 1972—, elder, 1986-88, 91-93; mem. Refugee Resettlement, Greater Atlanta Presbytery, 1989—; mem. Crossties Network, 1989, coun., 1991—; mem. suburban art com. High Mus. Young Careers; mem. Alliance Theatre Angel, Metro Atlanta Gifted Consortium, Suburban Arts Com.; troop com. chairperson Boy Scouts Am., 1992—; del. leader People to People Friendship Caravan, 1992, 93, 95; assoc. envoy for Latvia, 1996 Olympics; del. Saxony Exch., 2001; mem. Atlanta Interfaith Sisterhood, 1995—, mem. coord. coun., 1996—; mem. Cobb County Blue Ribbon Edn. Com., 1999—; mem. Buckhead Bus. Assn. Leadership Class 2000, Six Star Refugee Partnership, 2000—. Named Tchr. of Yr. Sutton Middle Sch., 1985; Apple Corp. grantee, 1986; recipient Fulbright Scholarship, 1990. Mem. NEA, ASCD, Ga. Edn. Assn., Ga. Assn. for Gifted Children, Atlanta Assn. Educators, Metro Consortium Gifted Educators, Ga. Supporters of Gifted, Nat. Assn. for Gifted Edn., Coun. Evang. Chs. in Nicaragua, Crossties Network of Foxfire, Kappa Delta PI. Office: 4360 Powers Ferry Rd NW Atlanta GA 30327-3417 E-mail: challenge@mindspring.com.

MCQUEEN, SCOTT ROBERT, broadcasting company executive; b. Peekskill, N.Y., June 30, 1946; s. Robert Charles and Donna Marie (Ikeler) McQ.; m. Loretta A. Dybala, May 17, 1980; children: Geoffrey Scott, Mallory Morgan, Brian Daniel; 1 child, by previous marriage, Tasha Lea. BA, Dartmouth Coll., 1968. Founder Sconnix Radio Ent., Inc., Laconia, N.H., 1968, Sconnix Radio Ent., Inc. (became Sconnix Group Broadcasting, Inc.), 1971, pres., 1971—. Pres. Charisma Ventures, Ltd., 1995—. Vice-chmn. bd. dirs. Pinecrest Sch., Ft. Lauderdale, Fla.; chmn. bd. advisors Pinecrest Sch., Boca Raton, Fla. With N.H.N.G., 1968-69. Mem. Nat. Assn. Broadcasters, Nat. Radio Broadcsters Assn., Lakes Region C. of C. (dir. 1977-81), Rotary, Royal Palm Yacht and Country Club. Home: 431 E Coconut Palm Rd Boca Raton FL 33432-7915

MCQUEEN, THERESA BETH, medical transcription service executive; b. Smyrna, Tenn., Feb. 6, 1956; d. Everett Lee and Reba A. Henson; m. Don E. McQueen, May 21, 1977; 1 child Ryan. Cert. med. transcriptionist. Med. transcriptionist Mercy Health Ctr., Oklahoma City, 1977—81; owner, operator Terri's Med. Transcription, 1981—. Author: Medical Transcription in the Real Word, 2001. Office: Terri's Med Transcription PO Box 720698 Oklahoma City OK 73172-0698 Fax: 405-722-4868.

MCQUEENEY, HENRY MARTIN, SR. publisher; b. N.Y.C., Oct. 29, 1938; s. John Henry and Catherine Mary (Quigg) McQ.; m. Elizabeth Bernino, May 14, 1960; children: Mary E., Henry M. Jr., John P., Matthew S. BBA, St. Johns U., 1961; postgrad., U. Rochester, 1965-67. Advt. sales Curtis Circulation div. Curtis Pub. Co., 1960-62, asst. mgr., 1962-63, field mgr. Rochester, N.Y., 1964-67, dept. mgr., account exec. Phila., 1968-74; v.p. sales, exec. v.p. mktg. Manor Books, Inc., N.Y.C., 1974-79; pres. Wood Hill Press, Inc., 1979-89, Scott Mag. Dist. Corp., N.Y.C., 1989-93, Kearny Pub., Inc., N.Y.C., 1993-96, Princeton Pub., Inc., N.Y.C., 1996-98; CEO, DMI Worldwide, 1998—; pres. Tribeca Pub., Inc., 1999—; v.p. Irish Connections Mag., 2000—, Iron Cross, Ltd., 1999—. Rep. Western N.Y. Pubs.; cons. Bipad Ednl. Program. Pres. parish bd. Roman Catholic Ch., 1965, editor newspaper, Spencerport, N.Y., 1965, diocesan leader, mem. lay bd., Rochester, 1964-67; certified as tchr. Confraternity Christian Doctrine, Diocese of Rochester, 1964. Served with USAFR, 1956-64. Mem. Am. Legion, Ancient Order of Hiberninas. Home: 12 Blenheim Ln Centerport NY 11721-1704 Office: DMI Worldwide PO Box 603 Centerport NY 11721-0603 Fax: (631) 261-6532. E-mail: dmi33@aol.com.

MCQUEENEY, ROBERT J. physicist; b. Bronx, N.Y., Dec. 12, 1968; s. Charles J. and Maria A. McQueeney; m. Shelly Lynn Kagel, Feb. 11, 1996. BS, U. Conn., 1991; PhD, U. Pa., 1996. With Los Alamos Nat. Lab., Los Alamos, N.Mex. Mem.: AAAS, Am. Physical Soc., Phi Beta Kappa. Office: Los Alamos Nat Lab Mail Stop H805 Los Alamos NM 87545 also: Los Alamos Nat Lab PO Box 1663 Los Alamos NM 87545-0001 Office Fax: 505-665-2676. Business E-Mail: mcqueeney@lanl.gov.

MCQUEEN-GIBSON, ETHLYN, clinical nurse specialist; b. Cleve., Oct. 28, 1959; d. Joshua and Mary (Johnson) McQueen; m. Carl A. Gibson, Apr. 20, 1988; children: Faith Alysia, Carla Renee. BSN, Ursuline Coll., 1983; MSN, Med. Coll. of Ga., 1997. RN, Ga.; cert. med.-surg. nurse, ANA. Clin. adult med./surg. nurse specialist Tacoma Gen. Hosp., 2001—. 1st lt. U.S. Army, 1984-88. Office: Tacoma Gen Hosp 315 ML King Way Tacoma WA 98415 E-mail: ethlyngibson@aol.com.

MCQUERN, MARCIA ALICE, newspaper publishing executive; b. Riverside, Calif., Sept. 3, 1942; d. Arthur Carlyle and Dorothy Louise (Krupke) Knopf; m. Lynn Morris McQuern, June 7, 1969. BA in Polit. Sci., U. Calif., Santa Barbara, 1964; MS in Journalism, Northwestern U., 1966. Reporter The Press-Enterprise, Riverside, 1966-72, city editor, 1972-74, capitol corrs., 1975-78, dep. mng. editor news, 1984-85, mng. editor news, 1985-87, exec. editor, 1988-94, pres., 1992—; editor, publisher, 1994—; asst. metro editor The Sacramento Bee, 1974-75; editor state and polit. news The San Diego Union, 1978-79, city editor, 1979-84. Juror Pulitzer Prize in Journalism, 1982, 83, 92, 93. Bd. advisors U. Calif.-Berkeley Grad. Sch. Journalism, 1991—96, U. Calif.-Riverside Grad. Sch. Mgmt., 1994—2000, U. Calif.-Riverside Coll. of Humanities, Arts and Social Sciences, 2000; mem. Riverside C.C. Found., 1993—, pres., 1996—98; mem. Mount San Jacinto C.C. Found., 2001—; trustee U. Calif.-Riverside Found., 1996—. Recipient Athena award, YWCA, 1994, Disting. Alumni award, U. Calif., Santa Barbara, 2002. Mem.: Soc. Profl. Journalists, Calif. Press Assn. (bd. dirs. 1996—99, named Newspaper Exec. of Yr. 2000), Calif. Newspaper Pubs. Assn. (bd. dirs. 1992—, pres 2001—02), Calif. Soc. Newspaper Editors (bd. dirs. 1988—95), Am. Soc. Newspaper Editors (bd. dirs. 1992—98), U. Calif.-Santa Barbara Alumni Assn. (bd. dirs. 1983—89). Home: 5717 Bedford Dr Riverside CA 92506-3404 Office: Press-Enterprise Co 3512 14th St Riverside CA 92501-3878

MCQUIGG, JOHN DOLPH, retired lawyer; b. Abilene, Tex., Oct. 19, 1931; s. John Lyman and Dorothy Elinor (King) McQ.; m. Sandra Elainea Duke, Oct. 18, 1969 (div. 1989); 1 child, John Revel. BA, Denison U., 1953; LLB, U. Tex., 1962. Bar: Fla. 1962, U.S. Supreme Ct. 1971. Account exec. San Antonio Light, 1957-59; assoc. Shackleford, Farrior, Stallings & Evans, 1962-66, ptnr. Fla., 1966-73; pres. John McQuigg, P.A., 1973-80; shareholder Fowler, White, Gillen, Boggs, Villareal & Banker, P.A., 1980-92; of counsel Stephen Rosen, P.A., 1993; pvt. practice, 1994-2000; ret., 2000. Arbitrator U.S. Dist. Ct., 1990—. Judge Compensation Claims pro hac vice, 1993; bd. dirs. Fla. Gulf Coast R.R. Mus., Inc., Am. Assn. Pvt. Railroad Car Owners; pres. Fla. Coalition R.R. Passengers, 1990-99. 1st lt. USAF, 1953-57. Mem. ABA, Fla. Bar, Tampa Club. Episcopalian.

MCQUIGGAN, MARK C. urologist; b. Detroit, May 15, 1933; s. Mark Ronald and Catherine Charlotte (Corbeille) McQ.; m. Carolyn Ann Brunk, Mar. 25, 1961. BS, U. Mich., 1954, MD, 1958. Diplomate Am. Bd. Urology. Resident in surgery and urology U. Mich., 1959-64; group practice Urology Assocs., Detroit, 1964-67; dir. med. edn. Providence Hosp., Southfield, Mich., 1967-69; clin. instr. urology U. Mich., 1969-70; pvt. practice Southfield and Farmington Hills, 1969—. Pres. med. staff North Detroit Gen. Hosp., 1983-84, pres. Providence med. staff, 1995, 96; chmn. credentialling com. Providence Hosp., 1997, 98. Named Providence Physician of Yr., 2001. Fellow ACS; mem. AMA, Am. Urological Assn., Mich. Urological Assn. (exec. com. 1987-94, pres. 1992-93). Republican. Methodist. Home: 29653 Club House Ln Farmington Hills MI 48334-2015 Office: 30055 Northwestern Hwy Ste 210 Farmington Hills MI 48334-3234

MCQUILKIN, JOHN ROBERTSON, religion educator, academic administrator, writer; b. Columbia, S.C., Sept. 7, 1927; s. Robert C. and Marguerite (Lambie) McQ.; m. Muriel Elaine Webendorfer, Aug. 24, 1948; children: Helen Marguerite, Robert Paul (dec.), David John, Virginia Anne, Amy Lambie, Douglas Kent. BA, Columbia Internat. U., 1947; M.Div., Fuller Theol. Sem., 1950; postgrad., No. Bapt. Theol. Sem., 1947-48. Prof. Greek, religious edn. and theology Columbia (S.C.) Internat. U., 1950-52; pres. Internat. U., 1968-90. Headmaster Ben Lippen Sch., Asheville, N.C., 1952-55; missionary The Evang. Alliance Mission, Japan, 1956-68; acting pres. Tokyo Christian U., 1963-65. Author: Measuring the Church Growth Movement, 1974, Understanding and Applying the Bible, 1992, The Great Omission, 1984, An Introduction to Biblical Ethics, 1995, Life in the Spirit, 1997, A Promise Kept, 1998, Living the Life, 2000; contbr. articles to religious jours. Mem. Evangel. Missiological Soc. (gen. dir. 1994-97). E-mail: mcquilkin@aol.com.

MCQUILLAN, BARBARA GLATZ, paralegal; b. Buffalo, June 11, 1945; d. Edward D. and Lauretta (May) Glatz; m. David C. McQuillan, Nov. 10, 1979. BA, SUNY, Buffalo, 1967. Asst. concert mgr. SUNY, 1963-67; editl. asst., proofreader Christian Sci. Monitor, Boston, 1967-74; proofreader Christian Sci. Pub. Soc., 1974-79; paralegal McNair Law Firm, Columbia, S.C., 1979—. Pres. Elmwood Pk. Neighborhood Assn., Columbia, 1990; mem. Columbia Coun. of Neighborhoods19, 1990; dir. Sterling Chamber Players, Columbia, 1997—; chmn. exec. bd. First Ch. of Christ Scientist, 1992—93, treas., 1995—99, organist, 1995—99, 1st reader, 1999—2002; bd. dirs. Carolina Haven Found., Inc., 2000—, chmn., 2002—; organist First Ch. of Christ Scientist, 2002—. Mem. Palmetto Paralegal Assn. (2nd v.p., treas., pres., bd. dirs.). Home: 32 Gibbes Ct Columbia SC 29201-3924 Office: McNair Law Firm 1301 Gervais St Ste 17 Columbia SC 29201-3326

MCQUILLAN, FRANCES CARROLL, artist; b. Chgo.; d. Thomas William and Jane Ellen (Connors) Carroll; m. Edward J. McQuillan, Apr. 23, 1941; children: Thomas, Kathleen. BA, Caldwell Coll., 1975; postgrad., Parsons Sch. Design, 1932. Fashion artist, N.Y. and Chgo. papers, 1933-35; freelance window display, N.Y. and N.J., 1936-38; instr. art Yard Art Sch., 1967-69, 83-84, Montclair Art Mus. Sch. Art (N.J.), 1950-89; instr. art home studio; one person shows Argent Galleries, N.Y.C., Seton Hall U., Newark, Caldwell (N.J.) Coll.; exhibited in group shows Nat. Arts Club, N.Y.C., Dayton Art Inst., Conn. Acad. Fine Arts, Seton Hall U., Paris, Exposition Continental, Monaco and Dieppe, France, Mus. Fine Arts, Springfield, Mass. Mem. Am. Artists Profl. League, N.J. Watercolor Soc., Montclair Art Mus., Art Centre N.J. Home and Office: 106 SW Terry Ct Port Saint Lucie FL 34953-3554

MCQUILLEN, DANIEL PAUL, infectious diseases physician, medical educator; b. Feb. 28, 1959; s. Michael P. and Louise (Devlin) McQ. BS in Biology magna cum laude, Georgetown U., 1981; MD, Med. Coll. Wis., 1985. Diplomate Nat. Bd. Med. Examiners, Am. Bd. Internal Medicine; bd. cert. internal medicine & infectious diseases. Intern and resident dept. medicine Med. Coll. Wis. Affiliated Hosps. Inc., Milw., 1985-88; clin. fellow in infectious diseases Boston U. Sch. Medicine, 1988-89, instr. in medicine, 1991, asst. prof. medicine, 1992-99; rsch. fellow in infectious diseases Maxwell Finland Lab. Infectious Diseases, Boston City Hosp., 1988-92; staff physician Dept. Veterans Affairs Med. Ctr., Boston, 1990-2001, Deaconess Glover Hosp., 1990—, Beth Israel Deaconess Med. Ctr., 1999—. Staff physician Boston Medical Ctr., 1992—; instr. medicine Harvard Med. Sch., 1999—. Contbr. articles to profl. jours. Recipient Physician Scientist award NIH/Nat. Inst. Allergy & Infectious Diseases, 1991, Trainee Investigator award Am. Fedn. Clin. Rsch., 1992, Maxwell Finland Young Investigator award Mass. Infectious Diseases Soc.; Dr. Henry R. Viets Med. Student Rsch. fellow Myasthenia Gravis Found., 1980, 81, Eli Lilly Co. fellow in infectious diseases Nat. Found. Infectious Diseases, 1990. Mem. Am. Coll. Physicians, Am. Soc. Microbiology, Infectious Diseases Soc. Am., Mass. Med. Soc., Mass. Infectious Diseases Soc. Office: 100 West St Ste 1 Needham MA 02494-1319

MCQUILLEN, JAMES FRANCIS, industrial executive; b. Beijing, Apr. 4, 1940; came to U.S., 1940; s. Francis J. and Alice D. (McWilliams) McQ.; m. Jeanne T. Perrin, Sept. 12, 1964; children: David, Michael. BS in Gen. Engring., U.S. Mil. Acad., 1962. Sales engr. BMC Industries, San Jose, Calif., 1973-74, internat. devel. mgr. St. Paul, 1974-76, gen. mgr. Elk Grove Village, Ill., 1976-80; product mgr. Nat. Semiconductor, Santa Clara, Calif., 1980—82; gen. mgr. BMC Industries, 1982-83, group gen. mgr., 1982—86; v.p. Jade Corp. subs. Hanson Industries Inc.; gen. mgr. Jade Techs., Inc., Elk Grove Village, 1986—92; gen. mgr. connector products Methode Electronics, Chgo., 1993—95, v.p., gen. mgr., 1995—2000, pres., exec. v.p. interconnect products group, 2001—. Vice chmn. Cupertino (Calif.) Pks. Dept., 1972. Served to maj. U.S. Army, 1962-69, including Vietnam. Decorated Bronze Star with oak leaf cluster, Air Medal, Combat Infantryman's badge. Republican. Roman Catholic. Office: 7401 W Wilson Ave Chicago IL 60706-4548

MCQUILLEN, JEREMIAH JOSEPH, distribution executive; b. Buffalo, Jan. 7, 1941; s. Joseph Bernard and Marca Rita (Ammerman) McQ.; m. Maureen Elaine Brett; children: Michael, Karen, Kathleen. BS, Canisius Coll., 1962. Nat. sales mgr. Birge Wallcoverings, Buffalo, 1973-74, v.p., gen. mgr., 1976-79; v.p. mktg. Reed Decorative Products, Toronto, 1974-76; exec. v.p. Atlanta, 1979-81, Northeastern Wallcoverings, Boston, 1981-88, pres., 1989-91; pres. comml. wallcoverings Forbo Wallcoverings Inc., 1991-92; exec. v.p. Hytex Industries, Randolph, Mass., 1992-98, pres., CEO, 1998—. Served to 1st lt., U.S. Army, 1962-64. Mem. Wallcovering Distbrs. Assn. (sec., treas. 1987—, v.p. 1988, pres. 1989-90), Wallcovering Info. Bur. (pres. 1980), Wallcovering Mfg. Assn. (v.p. 1980). Republican. Roman Catholic. Avocations: tennis, racquetball. Home: 3 Nauset St Medfield MA 02052-3006

MCQUILLEN, MICHAEL PAUL, neurologist, educator, clinical ethicist; b. N.Y.C., Sept. 9, 1932; s. Paul and Dorothy Marian (Moore) McQ.; m. Louise Devlin; children: Daniel, Thomas, Patrick, Kathleen. BA cum laude, Georgetown U., 1953, MD, 1957; MA, U. Va., 1994. Diplomate Am. Bd. Psychiatry and Neurology (bd. dirs. 1991-95, exec. com. 1995), added qualification in clin. neurophysiology. Rotating intern Royal Victoria Hosp., Montreal, Que., Can., 1957-58; resident in neurology Georgetown U. Med. Center, 1958-60; fellow in physiology Johns Hopkins U. Med. Sch. and Hosp., 1960-62, instr. medicine, 1962-65; mem. faculty U. Ky. Med. Center, 1965-74, prof. neurology, 1972-74, prof., chmn. neurology, 1987-93; prof. neurology, chmn. dept. Med. Coll. Wis., Milw., 1974-87; clin. faculty mem. dept. neurology U. Va. Health Sci. Ctr., Charlottesville, 1993-94; prof. neurology U. Rochester, N.Y., 1995—. Vis. sci. Inst. Neurophysiology U. Copenhagen, 1971-72; vis. prof. U. Ky. Med. Ctr., 1978, Royal Coll. Surgeons, Ireland, 1983. Author articles, papers in field. Mem. Cath. Commn. on Intellectual Affairs. Recipient Neurology medal Georgetown U. Med. Sch., 1957; Clin. Teaching award Med. Coll. Wis., 1976; Disting. Service award N.Y. Med. Coll., 1983; named to Johns Hopkins Soc. Scholars, 1981 Fellow Am. Acad. Neurology; mem. AMA, Royal Acad. Medicine Ireland, Nat. Myasthenia Gravis Found. (chmn. 1981-83), Am. Neurol. Assn., Am. Assn. Electromyography and Electrodiagnosis, Wis. Neurol. Assn. (pres. 81-82), Rochester Acad. Medicine, Alpha Omega Alpha. Home: 4 Bragdon Dr Rochester NY 14618-3755 Office: 911 Westfall Rd Bldg C Rochester NY 14618-2633 E-mail: michael_mcquillen@urmc.rochester.edu.

MCQUILLIN, RICHARD ROSS, management consultant; b. Elyria, Ohio, Oct. 15, 1956; s. Wayne Rupp and Frana Rose (Romp) McQ.; m. Riko Koga; children: Richard K., Sean K. BS, Ohio State U., 1979; MS, U. So. Calif., L.A., 1983; MBA, UCLA, 1990. Sr. staff mem. TRW Inc., Redondo Beach, Calif., 1979-88; sr. cons. Deloitte & Touche, L.A., 1990-91; cons. mgr. NetBase Computing, El Segundo, Calif., 1993-2000; chief tech. officer When2Click.com, 2000—. Treas., controller Patio Creek Homeowners Assn., Torrance, Calif., 1986-91, pres. 1991—; pres. TRW Investment Club, Redondo Beach, 1984-87. UCLA fellow, 1989. Mem. IEEE, Beta Gamma Sigma. Home: 1281 Tennyson St Manhattan Beach CA 90266-6956 Office: NetBase Computing Inc 2101 Rosecrans Ave Ste 5250 El Segundo CA 90245-4771

MCQUISTON, ROBERT EARL, lawyer; b. Pitts., Feb. 4, 1936; s. Theodore O. and Bertha L. (Kegley) McQ.; m. Mary Hope Missimer, June 30, 1962; children: Mary Hope, Elizabeth Ann. BA magna cum laude, Yale U., 1958; JD cum laude, Harvard U., 1961. Bar: Pa. 1962. Assoc. Ballard, Spahr, Andrews & Ingersoll, Phila., Balt., Denver, Washington, Salt Lake City, 1962-69, ptnr., 1969—2001, sr. counsel, 2001—. Mem. nat. adv. group to Commr. IRS, Washington, 1985-87; lectr. in law Temple U., 1968-69, also various tax insts.; bd. dirs. Macromedia Inc., Hackensack, N.J., Gateway Communications, Inc., Binghamton, N.Y. Contbr. articles to profl. jours. Mem. Rep. Fin. Com., Harrisburg, Pa., 1983-86; trustee Am. Soc. Hypertension, 1992-98. Mem. ABA (active numerous coms. sect. taxation 1969—, including coun. mem. 1979-85, vice chmn., sec. 1982-85), Phila. Bar Assn. (bd. govs. 1978-80, mem. coun. 1969-84, sec. treas sect. on taxation 1973-75, vice chmn. 1976-78, chmn. 1978-80), Am. Coll. Tax Counsel (charter, regent 1990-98, vice chmn. 1993-94, chmn. 1994-96), Am. Tax Policy Inst. (trustee 1996—, pres. 2001—), Nat. Conf. Lawyers and CPAs, Pyramid Club. Episcopalian. Home: 111 Ridgewood Rd Wayne PA 19087-2810 Office: Ballard Spahr Andrews et al 1735 Market St Ste 5100 Philadelphia PA 19103-7599 E-mail: mcquiston@ballardspahr.com.

MCQUOWN, ELOISE, librarian; b. Santa Monica, Calif. d. Franklyn King and Paula (Rogers) McQ. BA, U. Utah, Salt Lake City, 1965; MLS, Rutgers U., New Brunswick, N.J., 1968; MS, U. Utah, Salt Lake City, 1976. Libr. U. Utah Librs., Salt Lake City, 1969-80, head access svcs., 1980-84; asst. dir.adminstrv. svcs. San Francisco State U., 1984-89, libr. instrnl. and rsch. svcs., 1989—. Conf. workshop leader Calif. Libr. Assn., Oakland, 1993; conf. spkr. Utah Libr. Assn., St. George, 1989, Am. Libr. Assn., Chgo., 1984, libr. cons. Children's Ctr., Salt lake City, 1970-73. Author: Business Information, 1974; contbg. editor: Network, 1978-84; contbr. articles to profl. jours. Del. Dem. Nat. Conv., N.Y.C., 1976, 80; candidate Utah State Legis., Salt Lake City, 1980. Recipient Susa Young Gates award Utah Women's Polit. Caucus, 1975; named Disting. Woman of Yr. in Utah., Salt Lake City, 1979. Mem. Am. Libr. Assn., Assn. Coll. and Rsch. Librs., Calif. Faculty Assn. (chair polit. action, legis. com. 1995—, dir. voter registration project. 1996, chair statewide legis. polit. action com. 1999—). Democrat. Avocations: travel, tennis, human rights. Office: San Francisco State U Library 1630 Holloway Ave San Francisco CA 94132-1722

MCQUOWN, JUDITH HERSHKOWITZ, author, financial advisor; b. N.Y.C., Apr. 8, 1941; d. Frederick Ephraim and Pearl (Rosenberg) H.; m. Michael L. McQuown, Jan. 13, 1969 (div. 1980); m. Harrison Roth, Dec. 8, 1985 (dec. 1997). AB, Hunter Coll., 1963; postgrad., N.Y. Inst. Fin., N.Y.C., 1965-67. Chief underwriting div. mcpl. securities City of N.Y., 1972-73; CEO Judith H. McQuown & Co., Inc., N.Y.C., 1973—. Author: Inc. Yourself: How to Profit by Setting Up Your Own Corporation, 10th edit. , 2002, Tax Shelters That Work for Everyone, 1979, The Fashion Survival Manual, 1981, Playing the Takeover Market, 1982, How to Profit After You Inc. Yourself, 1985, Keep One Suitcase Empty: The Bargain Shopper's Guide to the Finest Factory Outlets in the British Isles, 1987, Keep One Suitcase Empty: The Bargain Shopper's Guide to the Finest Factory Outlets in Europe, 1988, Use Your Own Corporation to Get Rich, 1991; contbg. editor: Boardroom Reports, contbg. editor: Physician's Fin. News, contbg. editor: Physician's Guide to Money Mgmt.; contbr. seminars, . Mem. Am. Soc. Journalists and Authors. Home and Office: One Gracie Ter Apt 9C New York NY 10028

MCRAE, CHARLES R. (CHUCK MCCRAE), state supreme court presiding justice; BA, Marietta Coll., 1962; JD cum laude, Miss. Coll. Sch. Law, 1970. Trial atty., Pascagoula, Miss., 1970—90; spl. chancellor, cir. ct. judge Jackson, Forrest and Lincoln Counties, 1990; justice Miss. Supreme Ct, Jackson, 1991—. Mem.: ABA, Magnolia Bar Assn., Fed. Bar Assn., Am. Judicature Soc., ATLA, Miss. Trial Lawyer's Assn. (life). Office: Supreme Court Gartin Bldg PO Box 249 Jackson MS 39205*

MCRAE, HAMILTON EUGENE, III, lawyer; b. Midland, Tex., Oct. 29, 1937; s. Hamilton Eugene and Adrian (Hagaman) McR.; m. Betty Hawkins, Aug. 27, 1960; children: Elizabeth Ann, Stephanie Adrian, Scott Hawkins BSEE, U. Ariz., 1961; student, USAF Electronics Sch., 1961-62; postgrad., U. Redlands, Calif., 1962-63; JD with honors and distinction, U. Ariz., 1967; LHD (hon.), Sterling Coll., 1992; vis. fellow, Darwin Coll. and Martin Ctr., Cambridge (Eng.) U., 1996-97. Bar: Ariz. 1967, U.S. Supreme Ct. 1979; cert. real estate specialist, Ariz. Elec. engr. Salt River Project, Phoenix, 1961; assoc. Jennings, Strouss & Salmon, 1967-71, ptnr., 1971-85, chmn. real estate dept., 1980-85, mem. policy com., 1982-85, mem. fin. com., 1981-85, chmn. bus. devel. com., 1982-85; ptnr. and co-founder Stuckey & McRae, 1985—; co-founder, chmn. bd. Republic Cos., 1985—. Magistrate Paradise Valley, Ariz., 1983-85; juvenile referee Superior Ct., 1983-85; pres., dir. Phoenix Realty & Trust Co., 1970—; officer Indsl. Devel. Corp. Maricopa County, 1972-86; instr. and lectr. in real estate; officer, bd. dirs. other corps.; adj. prof. Frank Lloyd Wright Sch. Architecture, Scottsdale, Ariz., 1989—; instr. Ariz. State U. Coll. Architecture and Environ. Design; lead instr. ten-state-bar seminar on Advanced Real Estate Transactions, 1992; evaluation com. for cert. real estate specialist Ariz. Bar, 1994-96; mem. real estate adv. commn. Ariz. Bar, 1996—. Author: Development in Third World Countries, 2002; exec. prodr. film documentary on relief and devel. in Africa, 1990; contbr. articles to profl. jours. Elder Valley Presbyn. Ch., Scottsdale, Ariz., 1973-75, 82-85, 96-98, chair evangelism com. 1973-74, corp. pres., 1974-75, 84-85, trustee, 1973-75, 82-85, chmn. exec. com., 1984, mem. mission com. 1993—, chmn. 1998; trustee Upward Found., Phoenix, 1977-80, trustee, Valley Presbyn. Found., 1982-83, Ariz. Acad., 1971—; trustee, mem. exec. com. Phi Gamma Delta Ednl. Found., Washington, 1974-84; trustee Phi Gamma Delta Internat., 1984-86; bd. dirs. Archon, 1986-87, Hall of Fame Ariz., 1999; founder, trustee, pres. McRae Found., 1980—; bd. dirs. Food for Hungry Inc. (Internat. Relief), 1985-95, exec. com., 1986-95, chmn. bd. dirs., 1987-92; chmn. bd. dirs. Food for Hungry Internat., 1993-95, pres. adv. coun., 1995—, mem. building com., 1999—; trustee, mem. exec. com. Ariz. Mus. Sci. and Tech., 1984—, 1st v.p., 1985-86, pres., 1986-88, chmn. bd. dirs., 1988-90, exec. com. 1984-90, exhibits com. 1990—, strategic planning com., 1999—, svc. recognition 1999; Lambda Alpha Internat. Hon. Land Econs. Soc, 1988-98; sec.-treas. Ariz. State U. Coun. for Design Excellence, 1989-90, bd. dirs. 1988-99, pres. 1990-91, trustee 1999—; mem. Crisis Nursery Office of the Chair, 1988-89, Maricopa Community Colls. Found., 1988—, sec. 1990-91, 2d v.p. 1993-94, 1st v.p. and pres. elect 1994-95, pres. 1995-96, mem. Elsner scholarship com., 1999—, web site com., 1999, capital campaign cabinet, 1995-96, 98-99, mem. of chair, 1998-99, mem. nominating com., 1997—, deferred gifts com., 1999—, strategic planning com., 2000—, mem. adv. bd., 2002—; mem. Phoenix Cmty. Alliance, 1988-90, Interchurch Ctr. Corp., 1987-90, Western Art Assocs., bd. dirs., 1989-91, Phoenix Com. on Fgn. Rels., 1988-99, U. Ariz. Pres.'s Club, 1984—, chmn., 1991-92; bd. dirs. Econ. Club of Phoenix, 1987— , sec.-treas., 1991-92, v.p., 1992-93, pres. 1993-94; bd. dirs. Ctrl. Ariz. Shelter Svcs., 1995—, bd. dir., Ariz. Community Found., 1996—, invest. com., 1996—, chair, 2000, exec. com. 1997—, treas. 1997—, chair nominating com. 1997-98, vice chair bd. dirs., 1999—, chair devel. com., 1999—, advancement com., 1999—, chair, 1999—, fin. and adminstrn. com. 1999—; founding mem. Alliance linking poverty and homelessness, 1996-98, bd. dirs., 1996-98, mem. exec. com., 1996-98, co-chair long range planning com., 1997-98; mem. adv. bd. Help Wanted USA, 1990-92; vol. fund raiser YMCA, Salvation Army, others; bd. dirs. Frank Lloyd Wright Found., 1992—, chair fin. com. 1997-98, chmn. bd. dirs., 1998—; mem. Taliesin Coun., 1985—; bd. dirs. Taliesin Arch., 1992-98, Taliesin Conservation Com. (Wis.), 1992—; founding mem. Frank Lloyd Wright Soc., 1993—; mem. fin. com. Kyl for Congress, 1985-92, bd. dir. campaign bd. Kyl for U.S. Senate, 1993-94, 99—; Senator Kyl Council, 1995—; campaign com. Symington for Gov. '90, 1989-90, mem. gubernatorial adv. bd., 1990-91; mem. Gov.'s Selection Com. for State Revenue Dir., 1993; mem. bond com. City of Phoenix, 1987-88; mem. Ariz. State U. Coun. of 100, 1985-89, investment com., 1985-89; bd. govs. Twelve Who Care Hon Kachina, 1991; mem. adv. coun. Maricopa County Sports Authority, 1989-93; mem. Ariz. Coalition for Tomorrow, 1990-92; founding mem., bd. dirs. Waste Not Inc., 1990-94, pres., 1990-92, chmn., 1992-94, adv. bd. 1996—; bd. dirs. Garden Homes at Teton Pines Home Owners Assn., 1996—; selected as bearer for the Olympic Torch Relay Team, 1996; adv. bd. KAET TV PBS (Channel 8). 1st lt. USAF, 1961-64. Recipient various mil. awards; 1st place award Ariz. Bar exam, 1967; named to Ariz. Hall of Fame, 1999. Mem. ABA, AIEE, AIME, Ariz. Bar Assn.,

Maricopa County Bar Assn., U. Ariz. Alumni Assn., Nat. Soc. Fund Raising Execs. (Philanthropy award Ariz. chpt. 1991, 97), Clan McRae Soc. N.Am. Phoenix Exec. Club, Internat. Platform Assn., Am. Friends of the U. Cambridge (Eng.), Jackson Hole Racquet Club, Teton Pines Country Club, Tau Beta Pi. Republican. Address: Republic Cos 11811 N Tatum Blvd Ste 1005 Phoenix AZ 85028-1617 E-mail: repcos@aol.com.

MCRAE, JOHN LEONIDAS, civil engineer, consultant; b. Sept. 16, 1917; s. James Wright and Lota (O'Bryant) McR.; m. Thelma Lucile Nabors, Mar. 23, 1940; children: John Malcolm, Virginia Margaret McRae Pugh. BSCE and Geotech. Engring., Northwestern U., 1948. Chief bituminous and chemistry lab. U.S. Army Engring. Waterways Exptl. Sta., Vicksburg, Miss., 1950-61, rsch. engr. mobility and environ. divsn., 1961-72; CEO Engring. Devel. Co. Inc., 1960—. Cons. on soil mechanics and bituminous pavements. Contbr. numerous tech. papers to profl. lit.; patentee in field. Fellow ASCE; mem. NSPE, ASTM, Assn. Asphalt Paving Technologists, Nat. Asphalt Paving Assn., Am. Road and Transp. Builders Assn. Baptist (deacon). Home: 416 Groome Dr Vicksburg MS 39180-5108 Office: PO Box 1109 Vicksburg MS 39181-1109 E-mail: jlmcrae@edco-gtm.com.

MCRAE, MARION ELEANOR, critical care nurse; b. Kingston, Ont., Can., Sept. 19, 1960; d. James Malcolm and Madeline Eleanor (MacNamara) McR. BSN, Queen's U., Kingston, 1982; MSN, U. Toronto, 1989, ACNP diploma, 2001. RN, Calif., CCRN; cert. BCLS, ACLS, PALS. Staff nurse thoracic surgery Toronto (Can.) Gen. Hosp., 1982-83, staff nurse cardiovascular ICU, 1983-85; nurse clinician critical care Michael's Hosp., Toronto, 1985-87; external critical care clin. tchr. Ryerson Poly. Inst., 1986-87; staff nurse cardiovascular ICU The Toronto Hosp.-Toronto Gen. Divsn., 1987-89; clin. nurse specialist cardiac surgery The Toronto Hosp., 1989-90; clin. nurse II cardiothoracic ICU UCLA Med. Ctr., 1990-92, clin. nurse III cardiothoracic ICU, 1992-2000; nurse practitioner cardiovasc. surgery Toronto Gen. Hosp., 2000—. Mem. critical care nursing adv. bd. George Brown Coll., Toronto, 1987-88. Contbr. articles to profl. nursing jours. Recipient Open Master's fellowship U. Toronto, 1987-88, M. Keyes bursary Toronto Gen. Hosp., 1988-89, Nursing fellowship Heart and Stroke Found. Ont., 1988-89, Outstanding Svc. award UCLA Med. Ctr., 1994, Cardiothoracic ICU Nurse of Yr. award UCLA, 1995. Mem. AACN, Am. Heart Assn. Coun. on Cardiovascular Nursing. Office: Toronto Gen Hosp 6NU-146 200 Elizabeth St Toronto ON Canada M5G 2C4 E-mail: marion.mcrae@uhn.on.ca.

MCRAE, ROBERT MALCOLM, JR. federal judge; b. Memphis, Dec. 31, 1921; s. Robert Malcolm and Irene (Pontius) McR.; m. Louise Howry, July 31, 1943; children: Susan Campbell, Robert Malcolm III, Duncan Farquhar, Thomas Alexander Todd. BA, Vanderbilt U., 1943; LLB, U. Va., 1948. Bar: Tenn. 1948. Practice in. Memphis, 1948-64; judge Tenn. Circuit Ct., 1964-66, U.S. Dist. Ct. (we. dist.) Tenn., Memphis, 1966-94, chief judge, 1979-86, sr. judge, 1987-94, inactive sr. judge, 1995—; mem. Jud. Council 6th Cir., 1982-85, Jud. Conf. Commn. Adminstrn. Criminal Law, 1979-86, Jud. Conf. U.S., 1984-87; ret. (sr. status), 2001—. Pub.: Oral History of the Desegregation of the Memphis City Schools (1954-74), 1997. Pres. Episcopal Ch. men of Tenn., 1964-65. Mem. Dist. Judges Assn. 6th Circuit (pres.). Home: 1914 Poplar Ave Apt 902 Memphis TN 38104

MCRAE, THOMAS KENNETH, retired investment company executive; b. Richmond, Va., July 7, 1906; s. Christopher Duncan and Sarah Alice (Lawrence) McR.; m. Marion Lanier White, Sept. 11, 1937; children: Thomas Kenneth Jr., John Daniel. B.A., U. Richmond, 1927; postgrad. Sch. Banking, Rutgers U., 1936-38. Asst. cashier First Mchts. Nat. Bank, Richmond, 1940-46, asst. v.p., 1946-49, v.p., 1949-63, sr. v.p., 1963-71; v.p. Davenport and Co., Richmond, 1971-85, sr. investment officer, 1985-90. Trustee Va. Supplemental Retirement System, 1964-71; active Va. Mus. Fine Arts. Mem. Richmond Soc. Fin. Analysts. Republican. Baptist. Clubs: Country of Va. Lodges: Masons, Rotary. Avocations: golf; stamp collecting.

MCRAITH, JOHN JEREMIAH, bishop; b. Hutchinson, Minn., Dec. 6, 1934; s. Arthur Luke and Marie (Hanley) McR. BA, Loras Coll., Dubuque, Iowa, 1956. Ordained priest, Roman Cath. Ch., 1960. Assoc. pastor St. Mary's Ch., Sleepy Eye, Minn., 1960-64, assoc. pastor, 1968-71; pastor St. Michael's Ch., Milroy, 1964-67, St. Leo's Ch., St. Leo, 1967-68; dir. Nat. Cath. Rural Life, Des Moines, 1971-78; vicar gen. Diocese of New Ulm, Minn., 1978-82; bishop Owensboro, Ky., 1982—. Home: 501 W 5th St Owensboro KY 42301-0765 Office: 600 Locust St Owensboro KY 42301-2130

MCRANEY, JOAN KATHERINE, artist; b. Magee, Miss., Mar. 21, 1936; d. Harold Bryce and Ruth Katherine (Graves) McRaney; m. William Cummings Hollis, Mar. 14, 1966 (div. June 1970); m. Richard Felder, 1997. BFA, Inst. Allende, San Miguel de Allende, Mex., 1975; postgrad., U. So. Miss., 1990—; pvt. study, Miss. sculptor Dan Askew, 1999-2000. Profl. portrait artist and contemporary sculptor, McComb, Hattiesburg, Miss., 1979—. Lectr. Lauren Rogers Mus. Art, Laurel, Miss., 1996; artist-in-residence Gethsemane Project, Hattiesburg, Miss., 2002. Exhibitions include Inst. Allende Gallery, 1973, Bellas Artes Gallery, San Miguel de Allende, 1974, Gulf South Gallery, McComb, 1982—84, Images '84, Mass Pavilion, New Orleans World Fair, 1984, Cottonlandia Mus., Greenwood, Miss., 1985—86, Woods Gallery So. Artists Invitational, U. So. Miss., 1990, Saenger Gallery, Hattiesburg, 1990, Woods and Locke Gallery, U. So. Miss., 1992—96, Lucille Parker Gallery, William Carey Coll., 1993, Miss. Collegiate Art Competition, Lauren Rogers Mus. Art, Laurel, Miss., 1996, Meridian (Miss.) Mus. Arts, 1997, USM Mus. Art, 1998, Lauren Rogers Mus., 1999, Exit Gallery, Hattiesburg Downtown Gallery Walk, 1999, 2000, Impressions Gallery, 2000, 2001, McComb Pub. Libr., 2000, Southwest C.C., 2002. Recipient Louie B. Holmes Meml. award, McComb, 1980, 81, hon. mention Nat. Portrait Seminar, Houston, 1981, 1st pl. Pastel award South Miss. Art Assn. Cloverleaf Show, 1992, 1st pl. Drawing award, 1992, Dean's Outstanding Creativity award, 1993, 94, 1st pl. Painting award Umpteenth Ann. Student Show, Woods Gallery, 1995, Fred A. Waits Endowment, 1995, 1st pl. Drawing award, 1995, Best of Show award (mixed media sculpture), Miss. Collegiate Art Competition, 1997, Best of Sculpture award Best of Show (mixed media sculpture) Dept. Art Annual Student Exhbn., 1998, honored by Hattiesburg Arts Coun., 1998; winner juried competition Laurel Arts League, 1999, Meridian Mus. Art, 1999. Mem.: Golden Key Soc., Kappa Delta. Avocations: canoeing, photography, yoga, meditation, cooking. Home: PO Box 94 Hattiesburg MS 39403 E-mail: refelder@netdoor.com.

MCREE, CELIA, composer, singer, actress, writer, producer; b. Memphis; d. John Louis and Leta Gwendolyn (Phillips) McR. Student, Phila. Coll. Art (U. of Arts), 1976-77, Herbert Berghof Studio, 1989, Playwrights Horizon Theater, 1989; cert. with distinction, Nat. Acad. Paralegal Studies, Christian Bros. U., 1992. Pres. Mother Records, Memphis, 1984—, You Should Meet My Mother (Publishing), Memphis, 1984—, Wild Thing Music, Memphis, 1987-99, Mother Prodns., Memphis, 1986—; producer, host Indian Talk, WEVL-FM90, 1992-95; ptnr. The Cinema Group, N.Y.C., 1997—. Artist, group and solo exhbns. including Eads Gallery, Grover Cleveland Arts Inst., Phila. Mus. Natural History; screenwriter, film scoring; singer, writer (nat. album) including Celia McRee/Back From Under, 1985 (ASCAP Spl. Pop award 1985-86, 86-87), Archives of Modern Music NY., Celia McRee/Passion, 1994; composer, arranger, producer, pub. background and feature music ABC Network, Cable TV and Radio; signature model for KeTukla, 1st Native Am. fashion designer; co-writer Circle of Love, 1999. Entertainer Vets. Bedside Network, N.Y.C., 1981. Recipient cert. of scholarly distinction Nat. Acad. for Paralegal Studies, 1992, cert. of appreciation United Music Heritage, 1990, spl. pop award ASCAP, 1982-84, 87-93, 95-96, 96-97, 97-98, 98-99, 99-2000, 2000-01, Henrietta Hickman Morgan writing award DAR; named Female Pop Songwriter and Female Pop Vocalist of Yr., Entertainer Indi-Assn., 1994, Female Vocalist and Female Entertainer of Yr., 1995; named Most Popular Female Entertainer, Entertainer Indi-Assn., 1996, Female/Artist/Entertainer, 1996, 97, Eia's Female Entertainer/Writer, 1997. Mem. AFTRA, ASCAP, NARAS, Nat. Mus. of the Am. Indian (charter), Animal Legal Def. Fund, N.Y. Acad. Sci., Humane Soc. U.S., Mensa, Memphis Kennel Club. Office: Mother Prodns 5159 Wheelis Dr # 110 Memphis TN 38117-4519

MCREE, JOHN BROWNING, JR. physician; b. Anderson, S.C., Dec. 9, 1950; s. John Browning and Melinda Bratton (Beaty) McR.; m. Melody Lynnn Jennings, May 29, 1976; children: Ansley, Sarabeth. BS, Presbyn. Coll., Clinton, S.C., 1973; MD, Med. U. of S.C., 1977. Diplomate Am. Bd. Family Physicians. Resident Anderson (S.C.) Meml. Hosp., 1977-80; physician Family Practice Assocs., North Augusta, S.C., 1980—. Asst. clin. prof. family medicine Med. Coll. Ga., 1982—. Fellow Am. Acad. Family Physicians. Presbyterian. Home: 201 Oakhurst Dr North Augusta SC 29860-9719 Office: Family Practice Assocs 509 W Martintown Rd North Augusta SC 29841-3108

MCREYNOLDS, ALLEN, JR. retired investment company executive; b. Carthage, Mo., Dec. 25, 1909; s. Allen and Maude (Clark) McR.; m. Virginia Madeliene Hensley, Jan. 17, 1946; children: Sharron Anne, Amy Elizabeth, Mary Armilda, Allen IV. Student, N.Mex. Mil. Inst., 1926-29, U. Mo., 1929-31. Pres. Joplin (Mo.) Stockyards, Inc., 1945-83; v.p., dir. First Nat. Bank, Monett, Mo., 1943-80, v.p., cashier Golden City, 1950-56; dir. First Nat. Bancorp, Joplin, 1982-87; asst. adminstr. Mo. State Coun. Civil Defence, 1941-44. Pres. Jasper County Assn. for Soc. Services, 1976-78, Mo. State Southern Coll. Found., Joplin, 1984-85. Mem. Sigma Nu. Democrat. Episcopalian. Avocation: farming. Home: 1202 Mississippi Ave Joplin MO 64801-5344 Office: Lower Level LLS Bancorp Bldg Rm 021 Joplin MO 64801

MCREYNOLDS, CHARLES BERTRAM, architect; b. Texas City, Ill., Sept. 26, 1916; s. Samuel Elvis and Mabel L. (Harris) McR.; m. Virginia M. Merriman, Mar. 25, 1971; children: Linda Louise McReynolds Little, Kimberly Marie. BArch cum laude, U. So. Calif., 1952. With Van Dyke and Barnes, 1953; dir. N.Y.C. office Welton Becket Assocs., 1962-70; sr. v.p., dir. L.A. office Becket Internat., 1970-75, pres., 1975-81, also bd. dirs.; owner, operator jewelry store Newport News, Va., 1986—. Bd. dirs. Welton Becket Assocs., ESPDC Corp. Prin. landscape works include pk. design for City of Monterey Park, Calif. (Excellence in Pk. Design award So. Calif. Producers Coun. 1950, 51); prin. archtl. works include Nile Hilton, Cairo, Manila Hilton, Auckland (New Zealand) IHC Hotel, Juffali Bros. Hdqrs., Jeddah, Saudi Arabia, Nassau (N.Y.) Coliseum, Xerox Sq., Rochester, N.Y., Great Wall Hotel, Beijing. With USNR, 1942-46. Fellow AIA; mem. U. So. Calif. Alumni Assn. (life), Scarab, Skull and Dagger, Union League, James River Country Club, Tau Sigma Delta. Republican. Address: 694 Todd Trl Newport News VA 23602-9037

MCREYNOLDS, DAVID HOBERT, hospital administrator; b. Bristol, Tenn., Dec. 28, 1953; s. Hobart Evans and Lena Mae (Brewer) McR.; m. Cynthia Carole Yambert, Sept. 6, 1974; children: Amy, Joseph, John, Rachel. MS, U. S.C., 1983. Diplomate Am. Bd. Forensic Acctg.; CPA, Tenn; cert. mng. care profl. Corp. acct. Gen. Care Corp., Nashville, 1975-80; controller Athens-Limestone Hosp., Athens, Ala., 1980-82; dir. fin. St. Mary's Med. ctr., Knoxville, Tenn., 1982-85; v.p. Archbishop Bergan Mercy Hosp., Omaha, 1985-87, Regional Healthcare, Inc., Brooksville, Fla., 1987-91; exec. dir. Hernando Healthcare, Inc. dba Brooksville Regional Hosp. (formerly Lykes Meml. Hosp.), 1987-91; v.p., corp. controller Peninsula Healthcare System, Knoxville, 1991-93; v.p., adminstr. Peninsula Village, Louisville, 1993-96; coo Covenant Behavioral Health (formerly Peninsula Healthcare), 1996-99; v.p., CFO Peninsula Behavioral Health, 1999—. Pres. United Meth. Men., Brooksville, 1988-89; mem. Hernando County Health Adv. Bd., Brooksville, 1988-90; bd. dirs. United Way Hernando County, 1987-90, Hernando Cmty. Blood Bank, 1987-91; treas. Hernando Assn. for Retarded Citizens, 1990-91; mem. Knox County Com. on Spl. Edn., 1993-94. Fellow Healthcare Fin. Mgmt. Assn.; mem. Am. Coll. Healthcare Execs., Inst. Mgmt. Accts., Tenn. Assn. Child Care (bd. dirs. 1996—), East Tenn. Assn. Child Care (pres. 1996-98), Rotary (bd. dirs. Brooksville chpt. 1988-89). Presbyterian. Home: 4323 Near Shore Dr Louisville TN 37777-5231

MCREYNOLDS, LARRY AUSTIN, molecular biologist; b. Eugene, Oreg., May 27, 1946; s. Austin D. and Ellen Gwenn (Ellis) McR.; m. Sara Murphy, Nov. 27, 1977; children: Elizabeth, Andrew. BS in Chemistry with honors, Oreg. State U., 1968; PhD in Cell Biology, Mass. Inst. Tech., 1974. Fellow Baylor Coll. Medicine, Houston, 1974-78; asst. prof. biochemistry U. Ariz. Coll. Medicine, Tucson, 1978-82; sr. scientist New England Biolabs, Beverly, Mass., 1983—, dir. eukaryotic rsch., 1999—. Vis. scientist Med. Rsch. Coun. Lab. Molecular Biology, Cambridge, England, 1977—78; grant reviewer Rsch. Strenghtening Grants for TDR Fillariasis at WHO, NSF; spl. rev. com. Tropical Med. Rsch. Ctrs., NIH, 1990, 94; WHO steering com. Sci. Group om Fillariasis , Geneva, 1987—93; hon. prof. Hunan Med. U., Changsha, China, 1998; mem. bd. assocs. Whitehead Inst., 2002—. Mem. editl. bd. Molecular and Biochemical Parasitology, 1990—; reviewer: Am. Jour. Tropical Medicine and Hygiene, Internat. Collaborations in Infectious Disease Rsch.; contbr. articles to profl. jours. Grantee NIH, 1979-82, 85-87, Instnl. Cancer Rsch., 1978-79, WHO, 1987-88, 95-2000, Edna McConnell Clark Found., 1992-94. Mem. AAAS, Am. Soc. Tropical Medicine and Hygiene, N.Y. Acad. Scis., Am. Heartworm Soc., Phi Lambda Upsilon. Office: New England Biolabs 32 Tozer Rd Beverly MA 01915-5599 E-mail: mcreynolds@neb.com.

MCREYNOLDS, MARY ARMILDA, lawyer; b. Carthage, Mo., Sept. 2, 1946; d. Allen and Virginia Madeliene (Hensley) McR. BA, Mt. Holyoke Coll., 1968; JD, Georgetown U., 1971; LLM, Harvard U., 1973. Bar: D.C. 1971, U.S. Ct. Appeals (D.C. cir.) 1971, U.S. Ct. Appeals (2d cir.) 1975, U.S. Ct. Appeals (4th cir.) 1979, U.S. Ct. Appeals (1st, 5th, 6th, 9th 10th cirs.) 1980, U.S. Supreme Ct. 1980, U.S. Ct. Appeals (11th cir.) 1981, U.S. Ct. Appeals (3rd, 7th, 8th cirs.) 1983, U.S. Ct. Appeals (fed. cir.) 1988. Law clk. U.S. Ct. Appeals for D.C. cir., 1971-72; assoc. Wilmer, Cutler & Pickering, Washington, 1973-77; sr. trial atty. civil divsn. fed. program br. U.S. Dept. Justice, 1977-79, mem. appellate staff, 1979-81; ptnr. McReynolds & Mutterperl, Washington, 1981-83, Wilner & Scheiner, Washington, 1983-89, Haley, Bader & Potts, 1989-92; prin. Law Offices of Mary A. McReynolds, P.C., 1992—. Bd. dirs., gen. counsel Washington Bach Consort, 1977-81, 1985-92, pres. 1981-82, 89-90; pres. Calla, 1993—. Contbr. articles to profl. jours. Bd. dirs., gen. counsel Washington Bach Consort, 1977-81, 85-92, pres. 1981-82, 89-90; pres. Calla, 1993—. Mem. ABA, Fed. Comms. Bar Assn., Kenwood Club, City Tavern Club. Episcopalian. Home: 2101 Connecticut Ave NW Apt 26 Washington DC 20008-1754 Office: Ste 300 1701 Pennsylvania Ave NW Washington DC 20006 E-mail: marymcreynolds@aol.com.

MCREYNOLDS, MARY MAUREEN, municipal environmental administrator, consultant; b. Tacoma, July 15, 1940; d. Andrew Harley and Mary Leone (McGuire) Sims; m. Gerald Aaron McReynolds, Dec. 10, 1964. BA, U. Oreg., 1961; PhD, U. Chgo., 1966; postgrad., San Diego State U., 1973-75. NIH postdoct. fellow U. Tex., Austin, 1966-68, mem. adj. faculty, 1980-82, mem. biohazards com., 1981—; rsch. assoc. Stanford U., Calif., 1968-71; chemist assoc. Syva Co., Palo Alto, 1972; environ. splst. County of San Diego, 1973-75; dept. head City of Austin, 1976-84; chief environ. officer, 1984-85; utility environ. mgr., 1985-92; mgr. environ. and regulatory svcs., 1992—. Dir. Ctr. Environ. Rsch., 1992—; part-time mem. faculty Austin C.C., 1993-98; cons. enologist Mirassou Vineyards, San Jose, Calif., 1969-72; lectr. Wright Inst., Berkeley, Calif., 1971-72; instr. San Diego State U., 1974-75; co-owner McReynolds Winery, 1998—. Editor: Dist. 56 newsletter, 1989-90; contbr. articles to profl. jours. Mem. Austin-Saltillo Sister City Assn., 1980-99; U.S.-Mex. Sister Cities del., 1983-85; sponsor, chaperone Tex.-SouthAustralia Youth Exch., 1986; active Leadership Austin, 1987-88; mem. Austin-Adelaide Sister City Com., 1986—, chmn., 1989-91, sec., 1992-96; bd. dirs. Internat. Hospitality Coun. Austin, 1989-96; mem. steering com. Colo. River Clean Rivers; mem. adv. panel Lake Austin. USPHS tng. grantee U. Chgo., 1961-66. Mem.: Tex. Assn. Met. Sewage Agys. (sec. 1994, v.p. 1995, pres. 1996), Am. Inst. Cert. Planners (cert.), Am. Planning Assn., Water Environment Fedn. (v.p. local chpt. 1988—89, pres. 1990—91, sect. rep. 1991—94), Sweet Adelines (bd. dirs. Tex. Star chpt. 1998—2001), Toastmasters Internat. (club pres. 1981, area gov. 1981—82, div. lt. gov. 1982—83, club pres. 1988, 2000—01, Able Toastmaster 1983, Dist. 56 Table Topics award 1986, Disting. Toastmaster award 1987, Outstanding Toastmaster Dist. 56, Able Toastmaster Bronze award 1990, Able Toastmaster Silver award 1993, Competent Leader award 2001), Soroptimists (dir. Soroptimist Manor 1978—80, 1983—85, pres. chpt. 1985—87, rep. youth citizenship award com. 1986—88, chpt. dir. 1987—88, chmn. south central region UN com. 1988—90, rep. youth forum com. 1990—92, chpt. corr. sec. 1999—2001), Zeta Tau Alpha. Avocations: gourmet food and wine, barbershop singing. Office: City of Austin PO Box 1088 Austin TX 78767-8865

MCREYNOLDS, NEIL LAWRENCE, management consultant; b. Seattle, July 27, 1934; s. Dorr E. and Margaret (Gillies) McR.; m. Nancy Joyce Drew, June 21, 1957; children: Christopher, Bonnie. BA in Journalism, U. Wash., 1956, postgrad. bus. and fin., 1973-76. Assoc. editor Bellevue (Wash.) Am., 1956-60, editor, 1960-67; press sec. to Gov. Dan Evans State of Wash., Olympia, 1967-73; N.W. regional mgr. for pub. rels. and pub. affairs ITT Corp., Seattle, 1973-80; v.p. corp. rels. Puget Sound Power & Light, Bellevue, 1980-87, sr. v.p., 1987-95; prin. McReynolds & Assocs., Seattle, 1995-97; v.p. external affairs Kaiser/Group Health, 1997-99; pres. Donworth-McReynolds Co., 1999—. Bd. dirs. HomeStreet Bank, Seattle, Wash. Dental Svcs., Seattle, Adinfonitum, Inc., Seattle, Eastern Wash. U., Cheney; chmn. exec. adv. com. Edison Electric Inst., 1984-85; mem. rsch. adv. coun. Electric Power Rsch. Inst., 1989-90. Bd. dirs. Seattle Symphony, 1980-89, Ind. Colls. of Wash., 1984-95, Mus. of History and Industry, 1995—, Corp. Coun. for Arts, 1985-94, Wash. Nat. Parks Fund, 1995-2000, Seattle Repertory Theatre, 1996—; chmn. bd. dirs. Fred Hutchinson Cancer Rsch. Ctr., 1993-95, Leadership Tomorrow, Seattle, 1987, Seattle-King County Econ. Devel. Coun., 1994; pres. Seattle Ctr. Found., 1979-80; chair U. Wash. Bus. and Econ. Devel. Program, 1996-98; nat. pres. Electric Info. Coun., 1988; chmn. bd. trustees Bellevue C.C., 1976-77; state chmn. Nature Conservancy, 1988-90; mem. Wash. State Commn. on Trial Cts., 1990; chmn. King County 2000, 1988-90; mem. campaign cabinet United Way of King County, 1998-2001. Named Citizen of Yr., Bellevue, One of Wash. State's Three Outstanding Young Men; recipient Pres. medal Pacific Luth. U. Mem. Pub. Rels. Soc. Am. (accredited), N.W. Elec. Light and Power Assn. (pres. 1982-83), Greater Seattle C. of C. (officer 1979-81), Soc. Profl. Journalists, Rainier Club (trustee 1995-01, v.p. 1997-98, pres. 1999-2000), Overlake Golf and Country Club (trustee 1993-96), Rotary (pres. Downtown Seattle Club 1991-92). Republican. Episcopalian. Avocations: golf, hiking, skiing, photography, mountain climbing. Home: 14315 SE 45th St Bellevue WA 98006 Office: McReynolds Assocs Inc 2033 Sixth Ave Ste 1001 Seattle WA 98121 E-mail: nmcreyolds@seanet.com.

MCREYNOLDS, STEPHEN PAUL, lawyer; b. Sacramento, Oct. 16, 1938; s. Leslie N. and Mary C. McR.; m. Chodi D. Greene, Sept. 29, 1970. AB, U. Calif., Davis, 1969; JD, U. Calif., 1972. Bar: Calif. 1972. Sole practice, Sunnyvale, Calif., 1972—. Served with U.S. Navy, 1956-62. Mem. Mensa Internat. Office: 1111 W El Camino Real # 329 Sunnyvale CA 94087-1056

MCROBBIE, MICHAEL ALEXANDER, computer scientist, researcher, academic administrator; b. Melbourne, Australia, Oct. 11, 1950; s. Alexander Hewitt and Joyce Victoria (Gair) McRobbie; m. Andrea Shirley Gibson, Dec. 22, 1973; children: Josephine Elizabeth Joyce, Lucien Richard Vernon, Arabella Diana Grace. BA with honors I, U. Queensland, 1974; PhD, Australian Nat. U., 1979. Rsch. fellow La Trobe U., Melbourne, 1979-81, U. Melbourne, 1981-83, Australian Nat. U., Canberra, 1983-87; head Automated Reasoning Project, 1985-91; reader, exec. dir. Ctr. for Info. Sci. Rsch., 1987-90; prof., exec. dir. Ctr. for Info. sci. Rsch., 1990-96; CEO CRC for Advanced Computational Systems, 1992-96; v.p. info. tech., chief info. officer Ind. U., Bloomington, 1997—, prof. computer sci., prof. philosophy, prof. computer tch., 1997—. Vis. prof. U. Kaiserlautern, Germany, 1987; Fulbright sr. fellow Argonne Nat. Lab., 1988. Co-author: (book) Automated Theorem Proving in Non-Classical Logics, 1986; author, co-author, editor: over 100 papers, articles, reports and books. Mem.: IEEE, Assn. Computer Machinery, Assn. Automated Reasoning, Columiba Club (Indpls.), Commonwealth Club (Canberra), Univ. Ho. (Australian Nat. U.). Avocations: art, book collecting, weightlifting, cricket. Office: Ind U 601 E Kirkwood Ave Franklin Hall 116 Bloomington IN 47405 E-mail: vpit@indiana.edu.

MCROBERTS, JUNE HATTIE, interior designer; b. Grosse Pointe, Mich., Mar. 26, 1931; d. Willard Winfield and Cleo Velma (Holloway) Bishop; m. Nelson Leon McRoberts, June 6, 1953; children: Ann McRoberts Johnson, Eric, Sara McRoberts Mascetti. AA, Coll. DuPage, 1972; postgrad., Chgo. Acad. Fine Arts, 1974-75; BA, No. Ill. U., 1981. Owner, designer June McRoberts Interiors, Batavia, Ill., 1971—; pres. Flutes & Swags Ltd., 1988—. Contbr. pub. newsletter The Designing Eye, 1980-82. Mem. adv. com. interior design program Coll. DuPage, Glen Ellyn, Ill., 1973-80. Mem. Interior Design Soc. (copywriter newsletter 1983-85, pres. Chgo. chpt. 1985-87). Baptist. Avocations: travel, canoeing. Home: 1255 Woodland Ave Batavia IL 60510-3051

MCRORIE, WILLIAM EDWARD, lawyer, retired life insurance company executive; b. Rutherfordton, N.C., Apr. 8, 1940; s. Cyrus Brown and Rosalie (Thompson) McR.; m. Hope Evangeline Foster, Sept. 9, 1962; children: Mark Edward, Jennifer Lynn. LLB, U. N.C., 1964. CLU; Bar: N.C., Va. State mgr. Sturdivant Life Ins. Co., Lynchburg, Va., 1965-68; sr. v.p., gen. counsel First Colony, 1969-2000. Sec. Jamestown Life Ins. Co., Lynchburg, 1981-2000. Councilman City of Lynchburg. Mem. N.C. Bar Assn., Va. Bar Assn., Assn. Life Ins. Counsel, John Lynch Soc. (sec. 1970—). Home: 2600 Link Rd Lynchburg VA 24503-3012

MC ROSTIE, CLAIR NEIL, economics educator; b. Owatonna, Minn., Dec. 16, 1930; s. Neil Hale and Myrtle Julia (Peterson) McR.; m. Ursula Anne Schwieger, Aug. 29, 1968. BSBA cum laude, Gustavus Adolphus Coll., 1952; MA in Mktg., Mich. State U., 1953; PhD in Fin., U. Wis., 1963; postgrad., U. Minn., 1971-72, Am. Grad. Sch. Internat. Mgmt., 1980-81; cert., Coll. for Fin. Planning, 1990. Cert. fin. planner. Faculty Gustavus Adolphus Coll., St. Peter, Minn., 1958-96; emeritus prof., 1996—; chmn. dept. econs. and bus. Gustavus Adolphus Coll., 1967-83, chmn., mem. various coms., 1971-96; teaching asst. Sch. Commerce, U. Wis., 1960-62. Lectr. European div. U. Md., 1966-67; vis. prof. Am. Grad. Sch. Internat. Mgmt., 1980-81; pres. Minn. World Trade Week, Inc., 1987; bd. arbitrators NASD Regulations Inc. Editor: Global Resources: Perspectives and Alternatives, 1978, The Future of the Market Economy, 1979. Congregation pres. First Luth. Ch., St. Peter, Minn., 1972-73, 93, chmn. pastoral call com., 1968-69, chmn. staffing com., 1975, mem. ch. council, 1968-74, 89-93; chmn. social ministry com. Minn. Synod, Luth. Ch. Am., 1975, mem. long range planning com. Southwestern Minn. Synod; chmn. Rep. council arts professions, scis., Minn., 1968-70, co-chmn. state task force on Vietnam, 1968; mem. adv. commn. Minn. Dept. Manpower Services, 1967-71; mem. North Central Regional Manpower Adv. Com.; bd. dirs. Midwest China Resource Study Center; del. White House Conf. Aging, 1971. Served with U.S. Army, 1954-56. Recipient Leavey Found. award Freedoms Found., Valley Forge, Pa.; Research fellow Fed. Res. Bank of Chgo., 1962-63 Mem. Nat. Assn. Securities Dealers (bd. arbitration), Fin. Execs. Inst., Inst. Cert. Fin. Planners, Minn. Econs. Assn. (bd. dirs. 1974-75, 79-80), Sierra Club (exec. com. North Star chpt., Midwest regional conservation com., 4th officer nat. coun. 1972-78), Masons (master, Royal Arch chpt., Zuhrah Shrine Temple, Scottish Rite), Alpha Kappa Psi, Iota Delta Gamma, Sigma Epsilon. Republican. Lutheran. Avocations: bird watching, backpacking, fitness and health. Home: 1208 Pine Pointe Curv Saint Peter MN 56082-1344

MCSHAN, CLYDE GRIFFIN, II, financial executive; b. New Orleans, Feb. 8, 1945; s. Clyde G. and Ursula C. (Mumme) McS.; m. Deborah A. Lark, Oct. 16, 1971; children: Madylin, Kristy, Suzanne. BA, Southeastern La. U., 1966. Cert. internal auditor, cert. govt. fin. mgr., cert. office automation profl. Auditor Office of the Inspector Gen., New Orleans, 1965-72; audit br. chief Cen. Voucher Payment Ctr., 1972-73; evaluation staff chief Nat. Fin. Ctr., 1973-74, processing br. chief, 1974, ops. div. chief, 1974-78, acctg. div. chief, 1978-79, ops. div. chief, 1979-80, dep. dir., 1980-81, dir., 1981-93; dep. chief fin. officer, dir. fin. mgmt. U.S. Dept. Commerce, 1993-97; v.p. Affiliated Computer Svcs., Inc., New Orleans, 1997-2001, sr. v.p. affiliated computer svcs., 2001—. Contbr. articles to profl. jours. Chmn. CASU Tenant Bd. Dirs., New Orleans, 1989-93, policy com. Fed. Exec. Bd., New Orleans, 1990-93, chmn., 1989-90, 92-93; chmn. unit I United Way of Greater New Orleans, 1989-90, chair mktg. and comm., 1991, vice chmn. community resources divsn. 1991, chair 1992-93, trustee, 1990-94, 98—, chmn. unit VII, 1990, chmn. CFC, 1989, chair cmty.-wide campaign, 2001-2002; mem. Tulane U. pub. adv. com. for computer info. sys., 1987--; acctg. dept. advt. bd. U. New Orleans, 1991-93; pres. acctg. bd. U. New Orleans, 1992-93, bd. dirs. Ctr. for Non-profit Resources, 1997-2002; bd. dirs. YMCA Greater New Orleans, 1990-93, 1997--, chmn. bd., 2002--. With U.S. Army, 1965-71. Recipient Leadership award United Way, 1989, Communication and Leadership award Toastmasters, 1991, award New Orleans chpt. Federally Employed Women,

1990, 91, Presdl. Meritorious Rank award, 1988, 95, New Orleans Fed. Exec. Bd. award for outstanding leadership, 1989, Spl. award Office of the Comptroller Gen., 1989, Disting. Exec. Svc. award Sr. Exec. Assn. USDA, 1989, Elmer Staats Disting. Leadership award, 1993, Donald L. Scantlebury Meml. award for Disting. Leadership in Fin. Mgmt., 1995, Robert W. King Meml. award for disting. career accomplishments, 1997; named one of Outstanding 1990 Campaign Vols. of Yr., United Way, 1991, Fed. 100 Info. Systems Mgrs., Fed. Computer Wk., 1990, 96, to Info. Tech. Hall of Fame, 1997. Mem. Assn. Govt. Accts. (New Orleans chpt. pres. 1972-73, dir. 1970-71, 73-74, 74-75, 76-77, S.W. region v.p. 1975-76, South Ctrl. region v.p. 1981-82, mem. nat. exec. com. 1983-84, 93-96, chmn. fin. mgmt. enhancement bd. 1988-89, chmn. emerging issues 1990-91, chmn. tech. program com. 1991-93, nat. pres.-elect 1993-94, nat. pres. 1994-95), Inst. Internal Auditors, Sr. Exec. Assn., Fed. Exec. Inst. Alumni Assn. Republican. Roman Catholic. Avocation: gardening. Home: V50 5624 Camphor St Metairie LA 70003-2210 E-mail: clyde.mcshan@acs-gsg.com.

MCSHANE, FRANKLIN JOHN, III, nurse anesthetist; b. Columbia, S.C., July 25, 1962; s. Franklin John Jr. and Helga Rita (Fischer) McS.; m. Leesa Ann West, Sept. 24, 1988; children: Amanda Nicole, Hannah Ryan. BSN, U. Mass., 1985; MSN, U. Tex., Houston, 1995. RN, Wis.; cert. RN anesthetist ANCC.; cert. ACLS instr., CPR, PALS provider Am. Heart Assn. Commd. 2d lt. U.S. Army, 1985, advanced through grades to maj., 1995; clin. staff nurse oncology unit Letterman Army Med. Ctr., San Francisco, 1985-86, clin. staff nurse surg. ICU and post anesthesia care unit, 1987-90; head nurse emergency room 67th Evacuation Hosp., Würzburg, Germany, 1990-92, infection control nurse Germany, 1992-93; staff nurse anesthetist Walter Reed Army Med. Ctr., Washington, 1996-98, asst. program dir. US Army grad. program anesthesia nursing, 1998-2000; staff nurse anesthetist 2290th Gen. Hosp. (Reserves), 2000—; CHN Anesthesia Svcs., Berlin. Adj. lectr. emergency med. svcs. tract City Colls. Chgo. Europe, 1991-93; adj. clin. faculty U. Tex. Grad. Program in Anesthesia Nursing, Walter Reed Army Med. Ctr., 1996-98, asst. prof. clin. nursing U. Tex. Houston Health Sci. Ctr., 1998-2000, Uniformed Svcs. U. Health Scis., 1998-2000; mem. CHN Anesthesia Svcs. Group, 2000—; presenter in field. Contbr. articles to nursing jours. Mem. ANA, Am. Assn. Nurse Anesthetists, Sigma Theta Tau. Avocations: reading, cooking, triathlon. Office: CHN Anesthesia Svcs 225 Memorial Dr Berlin WI 54923-1243 E-mail: skytrane@powercom.net., fmcshane@partnershealth.org.

MCSHANE, JOSEPH MICHAEL, priest, theology studies educator; b. N.Y.C., June 19, 1949; s. Owen Patrick and Catherine Veronica (Shelley) McS. AB, AM, Boston Coll., 1972; MDiv, STM, Jesuit Sch. Theology, Berkeley, Calif., 1977; PhD, U. Chgo., 1981. Ordained priest Roman Cath. Ch., 1977. English tchr. Canisius H.S., Buffalo, 1972-74; asst. prof. religious studies LeMoyne Coll., Syracuse, N.Y., 1982-87, assoc. prof. religious studies, 1987-91, prof., 1991-92, chairperson, 1991-92; dean Fordham Coll., Bronx, 1992-98, prof. theology, 1992-98; pres., prof. theology U. Scranton, 1998—. Vis. prof. history Loyola House, Berkley, Mich., 1986—87. Author: Sufficiently Radical: Catholicism, Progressivism and the Bishops' Program of 1919, 1986; author chpt. to book; creator video: The Pilgrimage of the People of God: An Introduction to the Study of Church History, 1991; contbr. articles to profl. jours. Bd. dirs. U. Scranton, Pa., Scranton Prep. Sch., Fordham U., N.Y.C., Fordham Prep. Sch., Bronx, NY, Regis H.S., N.Y.C., Canisius Coll., Buffalo, St. Joseph's Prep. Sch., Phila. Recipient First prize Cath. Press Assn., 1992. Mem. Am. Cath. Hist. Assn., Am. Soc. Ch. History, Phi Beta Kappa. Democrat. Office: Office of Pres Scranton Univ Scranton PA 18510

MCSHANE, MICHAEL JOHN, lobbyist; b. N.Y.C., Jan. 8, 1944; s. James Joseph Patrick and Theresa Elizabeth (Curtis) McS. BS, East Carolina U., 1966; cert. bus. adminstrn., Georgetown U., 1986. Pres. sec., legis asst. Congressman John J. Rooney, 1973-75; fgn svc. officer, mem. Sec. of State Henry Kissinger's staff U.S. Fgn. Svc., Jerusalem, 1975-76; v.p. Nat. Energy Rsch. Orgn., 1979-82; chmn. govt. rels. com. Am. Electronics Assn., 1982-86; sr. adv., polit. strategist Am. Embassy and Govt. of Taiwan, Taipei, 1986—; lobbyist, dir. govt. rels. TRW, Inc., Arlington, Va., 1991—. Guest lectr. Am. politics Am. U. Ctr. Congl. and Presdl. Studies, Grad. Sch. Pub. Policy Georgetown U., Notre Dame U., Randolph-Macon Coll., Univ. prof.'s lecture series Boston U., East Carolina U.; mem., team capt. 1996 local elections Official US Delegation to Albania, 1996; mem. advance team, traveling party Pres. Carter's State Visit to France, 1978, v.p. Mondale's Official Visit to The Philippines and New Zealand, 1978; founder, chair Coalition to Preserve Health Benefits, 1994; chair Dem. Leadership Coun. domestic cluster 1996 Clinton/Gore transition team, chair Chgo. Convention Com., 1996, inaugural com., 1997, bd. dirs.; adv., polit. strategist Clinton/Gore Reelection Campaign, to Sandy Thurman asst. to President for AIDS rsch., to Lanny Davis spl. counsel to President, the White House. Author: Lobbying: An Academic vs. Practical Comparison, 1997; commentator C-SPAN. Mem. staff Carter-Mondale Campaign, 1976-79; vice chair to former astronaut Sally Ride 1992 Clinton-Gore Transition Sci., Space and Tech. Cluster; mem. faculty Bryce Harlow Found. Capt. USAF, 1966-72, Vietnam. Recipient People to People Internat. award 1990, named Diplomat of Yr., 1996; recipient Torch of Birmingham Internat. Acad. for Leadership in Bus. and Adminstrn., 1995, Alumni of Yr. award East Carolina U., 1998. Mem. Am. Electronics Assn. (Outstanding Lobbyist of Yr. award 1986, chair govt. rels. com.), Coun. Fgn. Affairs. Episcopalian. Avocations: travel, teaching. Home: 104 Gibbon St Alexandria VA 22314-3836 Office: TRW 1001 19th St N Ste 800 Arlington VA 22209-1749

MCSHANE, ROSEMARY, lawyer; b. Tucson, May 4, 1950; d. John B. and Jean Ann Jacobson McShane; m. James Allen Dator, Sept. 4, 1981; 1 child, McShane Allen Dator. BA, U. Hawaii, 1973; JD, William S. Richardson Sch. Law, 1981. Pvt. practice, Honolulu, 1981-82; lawyer corp. counsel, family support divsn. City and County of Honolulu, 1983-89; lawyer dept. atty. gen., social svcs. divsn. State of Hawaii, Honolulu, 1989-93; adminstr., head hearings officer dept. atty. gen. Office Child Support Hearings, State of Hawaii, 1993-95; atty., divsn. head dept. corp. counsel, family support div. City and County of Honolulu, 1995—. Contbg. author: (book) Our Rights, Our Lives, 3d edit., 1996, (manual) Hawaii Divorce Manual, 3d edit., 1996. Mem. Hawaii Women Lawyers (bd. dirs. 1995-97, 99—, v.p. 1997-98, pres. 1998-99), Hawaii State Bar Assn., William S. Richardson Sch. Law Alumni Assn. Office: Dept Corp Counsel Family Support Divsn # 703 204 Makee Rd Honolulu HI 96815-3978

MCSHEFFERTY, JOHN, retired research company executive, consultant; b. Akron, Ohio, Mar. 14, 1929; s. John and Jean (Conway) McS.; m. Glenna Gloria Childs, Apr. 18, 1959; children: John III, Amy Childs. BSc, U. Glasgow, 1953, PhD, 1957. Various rsch. positions Sterling Winthrop Rsch. Inst., Rensselaer, N.Y., 1957-62; dir. pharm. devel. Ortho Pharm. Corp. div. Johnson and Johnson, Raritan, N.J., 1962-75; dir. rsch. Janssen R & D, Inc., Piscataway, 1975-77; v.p. R & D family products Internat. Playtex, Paramus, 1977-79; pres. Gillette Rsch. Inst., Gaithersburg, Md., 1979-97; retired, 1997; cons. Darnestown, Md., 1997—. Cons. NSF. Fellow Royal Pharm. Soc. of Gt. Britain; mem. Indsl. Rsch. Inst. (bd. dirs. 1988-92, emeritt com. 1998—), Am. Acad. Dermatology, Am. Mgmt. Assn. (bd. dirs. 1994-97), Am. Chem. Soc., Am. Pharm. Assn., N.Y. Acad. Scis., Soc. Cosmetic Chemists, Dirs. Indsl. Rsch., Assn. Rsch. Dirs., Rotary, Sigma Xi.

MCSHERRY, WILLIAM JOHN, JR. lawyer, consultant; b. N.Y.C., Oct. 28, 1947; s. William John Sr. and Mary Elizabeth (Dunphy) McS.; m. Elizabeth Ann Crosby, June 8, 1974; children: Brendan, Sean, Rory. AB cum laude, Fordham U., 1969; JD cum laude, Harvard U., 1973. Bar: N.Y. 1974, U.S. Dist. Ct. (so. dist.) N.Y. 1975, U.S. Ct. Appeals (2d cir.) 1977. Assoc. Spengler, Carlson, Gubar, Brodsky & Frischling, N.Y.C., 1973-78, ptnr., 1979-88, Bryan, Cave, McPheeters & McRoberts, N.Y.C., 1989-91, Battle Fowler LLP, N.Y.C., 1991—. Exec. dir. U.S. Football League, N.Y.C., 1985-86; chmn. litigation dept. Battle Fowler, 1992-96; pres., bd. dirs. Playtex Mktg. Corp.; bd. dirs. Questron Tech., Inc. Author: (with others) Tender Offer Regulation: The Federal SEC's Challenge and New York State's Response. Derivatives Risk and Responsibility, 1996, Attorney Client Privilege in tge Second Circuit, 1998. Mem. Zoning Bd. Appeals, Village of Larchmont, N.Y., 1988-91, dep. mayor, 1992-98, bd. trustees, 1991-98. Served with USAR, 1970-75. Mem. ABA (litigation, antitrust, entertainment and sports, corp. banking and bus. law sects., subcom. litigation 1940 Act; vice-chair com. alt. dispute resolution), Assn. of Bar of City of N.Y. (mem. 1979-82 com. state cts. superior jurisdiction, 1987-90, com. arbitration and alternative dispute resolution, mem. sports law com. 1998—), Fed. Bar Council, Council N.Y. Law Assocs. (bd. dirs., treas. 1975), Phi Beta Kappa. Roman Catholic. Avocations: community involvement, sports, writing. Home: 2 Summit Ave Larchmont NY 10538-2930 Address: 75 E 55th St New York NY 10022-3205

MCSLARROW, KYLE E. federal agency administrator; b. Va. m. Allison McSlarrow. Bachelor's, Cornell U.; law degree, U. Va. Asst. to gen. counsel of U.S. Army office sec. U.S. Army, 1985; assoc. Hunton & Williams, Washington; dep. chief of staff, chief counsel to sen. majority leaders Bob Dole and Trent Lott, 1995—97; chief of staff to late U.S. Sen. Paul Coverdell; nat. chmn. Quayle 2000 Presdl. Campaign, 1998—2000; v.p. polit. and govt. affairs, lead Washington office Grassroots.com; chief of staff to energy sec. Spencer Abraham Dept. Energy, 2001—02, dep. sec., 2002—. Mem. Arlington County, Va. Planning Commn. Office: Dept Energy Office of Sec 1000 Independence Ave SW Washington DC 20585-0001*

MCSLOY, STEVEN PAUL, lawyer; b. Syosset, N.Y., June 12, 1964; s. Paul Thomas and Emilie Helen (Winter) McS.; m. Alison Jane Rooney, Oct. 26, 1991. BA magna cum laude, NYU, 1985; JD cum laude, Harvard U., 1988. Bar: N.Y. 1989. Atty. Cravath, Swaine & Moore, N.Y.C., 1988-91, 98—; prof. St. John's Law Sch., Queens, N.Y., 1991-95; gen. counsel Oneida Indian Nation, Oneida, 1995-98. Lectr. BAR/BRI Bar Rev., N.Y.C., 1991-97; adj. prof. law Syracuse (N.Y.) Law Sch., 1995-98, NYU Law Sch., 1993-95, Cardozo Law Sch., N.Y.C., 1990, 93-95. Contbr. articles to law revs. Office: Cravath Swaine & Moore Worldwide Plz 825 8th Ave New York NY 10019-7475

MCSORLEY, DANNY EUGENE, sales executive; b. Huntington, W.Va., Nov. 26, 1960; s. Bernard Eugene and Doris M. (Newman) McS. BBA, Marshall U., Huntington, W.Va., 1983. Mgmt. trainee Lavalette (W.Va.) State Bank, 1980-83; with Profl. Bank Svc., Louisville, 1983-84; territory mgr. Bunzl Paducah (Ky.), 1984-91; sales mgr. Con-Jel Sales, Huntington, W.Va., 1991—. Mem. Marshall Quarterback Club, Marshall Tipoff Club, Big Green Scholarship Club. Democrat. Baptist. Avocations: boating, sports, athletics. Home: 5229 Mays Branch Rd Lavalette WV 25535-9741 Office: Con-Jel Sales 511 28th St Huntington WV 25702-1355

MCSPADDEN, DEREK, financial and accounting consultant and analyst; b. Dallas, Aug. 25, 1970; s. Larry E. and Cherry (Gill) McS.; m. Terese Collura, Aug. 4, 1990; children: Andrew, Christopher, Patrick. BS in Acctg., MS in Acctg., U. North Tex., 1993. Cert. mgmt. acct. Divsn. contr. Arrow Industries divsn. ConAgra, Carrollton, Tex., 1995-97; dir. pricing and profitability Daisytek Internat., Plano, 1997—. Home: 7101 Cinnabar Dr Frisco TX 75035-6175

MCSPADDEN, KATHERINE FRANCES, English language educator; b. Niagara Falls, N.Y., Nov. 13, 1941; d. John Hehir and Mildred Lorraine (Allen) M. BA, Niagara U., 1963; MA, Loyola U., Chgo., 1967, PhD, 1985. Tchr. Madonna H.S., Niagara Falls, 1962-63; tchg. asst. Loyola U., 1964-68; English educator Truman Coll., Chgo., 1968—, asst. chair dept. comm., 1992-2000, pres. faculty coun., 1991-92, 98-99, interim asst. dean arts and humanities, 2001—02; mem. design team U.S. Dept. Edn. Title II Tchr. Quality Enhancement Grant, Ill. Mid. Level Tchr. Cert., 2002—; Truman Coll. coord. U.S. Dept. Edn. Title II Tchr. Quality Enhancement Grant, Ill. Profl. Learners Partnership, 2002—. Bd. dirs. Chgo. Area Women's Studies Assn., 1977-79; mem. exec. com. Midwest Women's Caucus for Modern Langs., 1982-83; mem. alumni adv. bd. grad. sch. Loyola U., Chgo., 1996-98; mem. nat. screening coms. for Fulbright U.S. Grad. Student Program, 1997-99. Contbr. articles to profl. jours. Leader Girl Scouts Am., Chgo., 1982-83; bd. dirs. Friends of Northtown Libr. br. of Chgo. Pub. Libr. Fulbright Tchr. Exch. Program scholar, United Kingdom, 1986-87. Mem. Nat. Coun. Tchrs. English, Conf. on Coll. Composition and Communication, Two-Yr. Coll. English Assn., Tchrs. English Spkrs. Other Langs., Am. Assn. Women in Cmty. Colls. (pres. Truman Coll. chpt. 1995-96, chosen for Nat. Inst. Leadership Devel. 1997, Ruth Burgos-Sasscer Leadership award Truman chpt. 1998, sec. Truman Coll. chpt., 2001-02), Fulbright Assn., Ill. TESOL/Bilingual Educators. Avocations: traveling, outdoor activities, photography, folk music and dancing. E-mail: kmcspadden@ccc.edu.

MCSPADDEN, PETER FORD, retired advertising agency executive; b. Montclair, N.J., Oct. 2, 1930; s. Chester F. and Janet (Chase) McS.; m. Barbara Dodds, June 30, 1956; children— Douglas Dodds, David Ford, Peter Chase. AB, Dartmouth, 1952. Account exec. McCann-Erickson, Inc., N.Y.C., 1956-59; with Dancer-Fitzgerald-Sample, Inc., from 1959, v.p., account supr., 1965-68, sr. v.p., mgmt. supr., 1968-72, exec. v.p., 1972-74, pres., chief operating officer, from 1974; chmn. bd., chief operating officer Saatchi & Saatchi DFS Inc., 1986-88, also bd. dirs., ret., 1988. Pres., bd. dirs. DFS/Dorland Worldwide; bd. dirs. Am. Advt. Fedn., Am. Assn. Advt. Agys., TriState U.; mem. Nat. Advt. Rev. Bd.; bd. trustees Bradford Coll; vice chmn. Broadstreet TV Inc, 1989—. Chmn. bd. visitors Rockefeller Ctr., Dartmouth Coll., 1989-97; pres. Greenwich (Conn.) Young Republican Club, 1966-67; bd. dirs. United Way of Tri-State, 1995 Spl. Olympic Games; campaign mgr. Congressman Lowell P. Weicker, 1968, Senator Weicker, 1970, 76, 82, 88; mem. Rep. Town Com., Greenwich, 1965-68; trustee, mem. exec. com. Greenwich Hosp.; trustee Farnsworth Mus., Rockland, Maine. Served to lt. (j.g.) USNR, 1952-55. Mem. Am. Assn. Advt. Agys. (dir.) Clubs: Riverside (Conn.) Yacht, Greenwich Country, Meguniticook Golf. Home: 46 Carriglea Dr Riverside CT 06878-2402

MCSWAIN, BYRDIE ENGLE, laboratory scientist, immunohemotologist; b. Ethel, Ark., Oct. 13, 1939; d. James Marvin and Katherine Engle (Martin) McSwain. BS, U. Ark., 1968; BS in Med. Tech., U. Ark. Sch. Medicine, 1969; MS, U. Ctrl. Ark., 1973; Specialist in Blood Banking, U. Ark. Med. Scis., 1976. Cert. in regulatory affairs (RAPS). Supr. blood bank Univ. Ark. Med. Scis., Little Rock, clin. instr.; dir. tech. svcs., dir. product mgmt. ARC Blood Svcs., dir. transplantation svcs., dir. regulatory affairs, South Ctrl. area dir. tech. and regulatory svcs., acting area dir. quality assurance. Contbr. 13 articles to profl. jours. Grad. scholar Am. Soc. Med. Tech.; recipient Omicron Sigma award, Am. Soc. for Med. Tech., Outstanding Svc. award, Disting. Alumni award U. Ark. for Med. Scis. Mem. Ark. Soc. Clin. Lab. Scientists (Med. Technologist of Yr.), Am. Assn. Blood Banks, South Ctrl. Assn. Blood Banks (pres., author, editor), Am. Soc. Clin. Lab. Scientists, Clin. Lab. Mgmt. Assn. (pres. Ark. chpt.), Am. Soc. Clin. Pathologists, Regulatory Affairs Profl. Soc., Am. Soc. Quality Assurance, Phi Beta Kappa. Address: 2619 Fair Park Blvd Little Rock AR 72204-5149

MCSWAIN, LARRY LEE, retired academic administrator, religion educator; b. Pond Creek, Okla., Nov. 10, 1940; s. Joseph Kelly McSwain and Glorene May Brown Kirk; m. Rebecca Sue Stidham, Aug. 26, 1963; children: Laura Suzanne, Michael Lee. BA, Okla. State U., 1963; BD, Southwestern Bapt. Theol. Sem., 1966; STD, So. Bapt. Theol. Sem., 1970. Ordained to ministry So. Bapt. Conv., 1962. Pastor Morrison (Okla.) Bapt. Ch., 1961-63, Vernon (Ind.) Bapt. Ch., 1967-69; sr. rsch. asst. urban studies ctr. U. Louisville, 1968-70; asst. to prof. ch. and community So. Bapt. Theol. Sem., Louisville, 1970-88, dean sch. theology, 1988-91, provost, 1991-93; pres. Shorter Coll., Rome, 1993-2000. Bd. dirs. Acts, Nashville, 1988-91. Co-author: Conflict Ministry in Church, 1981, Church Organization Alive, 1987; contbg. author numerous books; contbr. articles, book reviews to religious jours. Pres. Rome and Floyd County United Way. Curriculum grantee Assn. Theol. Schs., 1976-77; named Cons. of Yr. So. Bapt. Conv., 1987, also Recognition award, 1988. Mem. Rotary Internat. (bd. dirs.), Assn. of So. Bapt. Colls. and Schs., Ga. Found. for Ind. Colls. Democrat.

MCSWAIN, MICHAEL, race car driver; b. Mount Holly, N.C., Jan. 17, 1967; m. Deanna McSwain. Grad., Nashville Auto Diesel Coll., 1986. Owner Race Car Bldg. Co., 1986—92; fabricator Lake Speed's Team, 1992; car chief Harry Hyde Melling Racing -drivers Bickle and Parsons, 1993—95; shop foremen Richard Jackson Precision Products, 1996—97, crew chief for Morgan Shepard, 1997—99; crew chief Rudd Performance Motorsports, 1999; crew mem. Robert Yates Racing, 1999—2001, crew chief, 2001—. Office: Robert Yates Racing 292 Rolling Hill Rd Mooresville NC 28115

MC SWAIN, ROSS FRANCIS, JR. columnist; b. Longview, Tex., Nov. 18, 1929; s. Ross Francis and Elizabeth (Griffin) McS.; m. Lou Ella Murrah, 1949 (div. 1957); children: Thomas, Elizabeth, Robert (dec.), Angela; m. Jean Timmons, Nov. 23, 1963. Student, Tarleton State U., 1947-48. Mgr. Feed Store, LLano, Tex., 1949-51, Stock Farm, Brady, 1951-57; reporter, editor San Angelo (Tex.) Standard Times, 1959-68; asst. exec. dir. Mohair Coun. Am., San Angelo, 1968-78; bus. editor regional, columnist Standard-Times, 1978—. Author: Out Yonder Revisited, 1988, Another Look Out Yonder, Vol. II, 1991, Tales for Out Yonder, 2001. Pres. Tom Green County Hist. Commn., San Angelo, 1987-88, pres. Tom Green County Hist. Preservation League Inc., 1988-89; pres. Tom Green County Hist. Soc., 1989-2000; pres. Permian Hist. Soc., 2002—. Named Booster of Yr. Tex. Hereford Assn., 1968, Newsman of Yr. Tex. Sheep & Goat Raisers Assn., 1968; recipient Mark Francis Excellence award Tex. Vets. Med. Assn., 1980. Mem. San Angelo Press Club (v.p. 1982-83). Baptist. Avocations: camping, hunting, photography. Office: San Angelo Standard-Times PO Box 5111 San Angelo TX 76902-5111 E-mail: yonder1@juno.com.

MCSWEENEY, FRANCES KAYE, psychology educator; b. Rochester, N.Y., Feb. 6, 1948; d. Edward William and Elsie Winifred (Kingston) McS. BA, Smith Coll., 1969; MA, Harvard U., 1972, PhD, 1974. Lectr. McMaster U., Hamilton, Ont., Can., 1973-74; asst. prof. Wash. State U., Pullman, 1974-79, assoc. prof., 1979-83, prof. psychology, 1983—, chmn. dept. psychology, 1986-94. Cons. in field. Contbr. articles to profl. jours. Woodrow Wilson fellow, Sloan Fellow, 1968-69; NSF fellow, 1970-72; NIMH fellow, 1973. Fellow APA, Am. Psychol. Soc.; mem. Psychonomic Soc., Assn. Behavior Analysis, Phi Beta Kappa, Sigma Xi, Phi Kappa Phi. Home: 860 SW Alcora Dr Pullman WA 99163-2053 Office: Wash State U Dept Psychology Pullman WA 99164-4820

MCSWEENEY, MAURICE J. (MARC MCSWEENEY), lawyer; b. Chgo., July 3, 1938; s. Thomas J. and Margaret F. (Ahern) McS.; m. Sandra A. Panosh, Sept. 30, 1967; children: Erin, Sean. BS, DePaul U., 1960; JD, U. Chgo., 1963. Ptnr. Foley and Lardner, Milw., 1963—. Bd. dirs. Harambee Elem. Sch., Internat. Clown Hall of Fame. Bd. dirs. Milw. Pub. Schs., 1973-79, Milw. chpt. ARC, 1979-85, Alverno Coll., Milw., 1984—, Health Edn. Ctr. of Wis., 1987-96. Fellow Am. Coll. Trial Lawyers; mem. ABA, Wis. Bar Assn., Milw. Bar Assn., Am. Judicature Soc. (bd. dirs. 1988-93), Milw. Area Tech. Coll. Found., Rotary (bd. dirs. Milw. 1986-88). Avocations: skiing, tennis, karate. Office: Foley & Lardner 777 E Wisconsin Ave Ste 3800 Milwaukee WI 53202-5367

MCSWEENEY, WILLIAM LINCOLN, JR. retired publishing executive; b. Nov. 9, 1930; s. William Lincoln and Ruth Patricia (Desmond) McS.; m. Anne Cornelia Bulman, Aug. 18, 1956; children: Anne C., William L., Siobhan White, Arthur J., Sean B. BS, Boston Coll., 1953; MLA, So. Meth. U., 1980; LHD, Rockhurst Coll., 1997. Tchr. English Killingly (Conn.) H.S., 1956-57; with Hallmark Cards, Inc., Kansas City, Mo., 1957-86, area pers. mgr., 1968, sales tng. mgr., 1969-86, dir. corp. tng. and devel., 1970-86; pub. Nat. Cath. Reporter Co., 1986-96. Bd. dirs. Cath. Social Svcs., Kansas City Archdiocese, 1975-88, pres., 1980-84; bd. dirs. United Cmty. Svcs. Kansas City , 1978-84, mem. exec. com., 1978-84; bd. dirs. Kansas City Amigos De Las Americas, 1977-80, pres., 1979; bd. dirs. Johnson City YMCA, 1978-79, Jesuit Vol. Corps, Midwest, 1989-95, Mex. Am. Cultural Ctr., San Antonio, 1990—, Minority Mus., 1994-2000; bd. dirs. Pan Ednl. Inst., 1979-83, pres., 1980-81; mem. Boston Coll. Alumni Admissions Coun., 1976-96; mem. chancellor's adv. bd. Met. Cmty. Colls., 1979-80; mem. Dem. Com., Johnson County, Kans., 1980-86; bd. advisors Sch. Social Welfare U. Kans., 1983-2000, chair, 1983-91, 93-94, Avila Col., 1991-2000; chair Mayor's UN Day Dinner, Kansas City, Mo., 1990, Mayor's Breakfast, 1994—; trustee NCCJ, 1991-95, co-chmn., 1995—. With U.S. Army, 1953-56. Recipient Kansas City World Citizen of Yr. award, 1995, William V. McKenney award Boston Coll., 2000. Mem. Internat. Rels. Coun. of Kansas City (bd. dirs. 1989-2000), Cath. Press Assn., Assoc. Ch. Press, Internat. Press Inst. (bd. dirs. Am. Com. 1999—), UN Assn., Boston Coll. Alumni Assn. (past bd. dirs.), Boston Coll. Club (Kansas City), Knights of Malta. Roman Catholic. Office: 115 E Armour Blvd PO Box 419281 Kansas City MO 64141-6281

MCSWEENY, WILLIAM FRANCIS, petroleum company executive, author; b. Haverhill, Mass., Mar. 31, 1929; s. William Francis and Mary Florence (Doyle) McS.; m. Dorothy Pierce, Jan. 20, 1969; children: William Francis III, Cathy Ann, Ethan Madden Maverick, Terrell Pierce. Reporter, columnist, fgn. corr. Hearst Newspapers, 1943-67; dep. chmn., dir. pub. affairs Democratic Nat. Com., 1967-68; spl. asst. to White House Chief of Staff, 1968-69; sr. exec. v.p., bd. dirs. Occidental Internat. Corp., Washington, 1969-76, pres., 1976-91; exec. v.p. Occidental Petroleum Corp., 1984-91, cons. to chmn., 1991-95; dir. Fin. Gen. Bankshares Co., 1978-82, Chevy Chase FSB, 1985—. Mem. Lloyd's of London; pres.'s rep. to USSR, 1979; mem. Pres.'s Inaugural Com., 1980, 84, 92; Presdl. spl. rep. to Oman, 1980, Bolivia, 1982; Pres.'s com. Korean War Meml., 1987; Pres.'s commr. Exec. Exch., 1976-81; Pres.'s trustee The Kennedy Ctr., 1995—, Pres.'s rep. to Korea, 2000; mem. N.E. White Ho. Fellows Bd.; mem. U.S. Com. UNESCO; spl. counsel speaker of Ho. of Reps., 1971-72; chmn. Maverick-McSweeny Cattle Co. Author: Go Up for Glory, 1965, Violence Every Sunday, 1966, The Impossible Dream, 1967; contbr. articles to profl. jours. Bd. overseers Fletcher Sch. Law and Diplomacy, Tufts U.; bd. advisors Karl F. Landegger Program Internat. Bus. Diplomacy, Sch. Fgn. Svc., Georgetown U.; trustee, pres. Holton Arms; chmn. Washington Episc. Sch.; chmn. Meridian House Internat., life trustee; mem. World Affairs Coun.; bd. dirs. The Atlantic Coun., Overseer Exec. Coun. Fgn. Diplomats, Dept. of State, The Brookings Instn. Coun., 1991-98; vice chmn. Sec. of State Fine Arts Commn.; chmn. Ford's Theatre, 1988-95, life trustee; bd. dirs. Very Spl. Arts, Arena State, Corcoran Gallery Art, Africare, Fed. City Coun., Washington Opera, Folger Shakespeare Theater, Cities in Schs. Nat. Learning Ctr., USO, Arms Control Assn., Nat. Assn. So. Poor, Duke Ellington Sch., Washington Ednl. TV, 1989-95; v.p. Ct. of Mary Rose, Portsmouth, Eng.; pres. Commn. to Preserve U.S. Cultural Heritage Abroad; co-chmn. State Dept. diplomatic rooms endowment; chmn. Lombardi Cancer Ctr. Coun., Georgetown U. Med. Ctr.; pres. Ams. Internat. Insts. for Advanced Studies; vice-chmn. Kennedy Ctr. Cmty. Bd., 1991-92; trustee V.P. Residence Found., Lyndon Baines Johnson Sch. Pub. Affairs, U. Tex.; juror The Heinz Found., 1995-2000; chmn. Chevy Chase for Cmty. Com., Coun. Ct. Excellence, 1996-99. Maj. inf. U.S. Army, 1950-53. Decorated Combat Inf. badge; recipient Outstanding Young Man award, Boston Jaycees, 1961, U.S. Disting. Svc. award, 1969, Outstanding Svc. spl. awrd, 1969, DC Disting. Citizen award, 1981, Paul Hill award, Kennedy Ctr., 1983, DC Cultural award, 1983, Armenian Earthquake Hero medal, 1989, Lincoln medal, 1991, Helen Hayes awrd, 1991, Washingtonian of Yr. award, 1995, Golden Plate award, Am. Acd. Achievement, 1999, Cultural Alliance award, 2000, Torch of Liberty award, Anti Defamation League, 2001, awards for domestic reports and reporting from Vietnam and Mid. East, including Best U.S. Reporting award, 1964. Mem. Smithsonian Instn. (nat. adv. com. Kellogg Project), Alfalfa Club, Cosmos Club, 1925 F St. Club (trustee), Internat. Club (trustee).

MCSWINEY, CHARLES RONALD, lawyer; b. Nashville, Apr. 23, 1943; s. James W. and Jewell (Bellar) Mc.; m. Jane Detrick McSwiney, Jan. 2, 1970. BA, Kenyon Coll., Gambier, Ohio, 1965; JD, U. Cin., 1968. Assoc. Smith & Schnacke, Dayton, Ohio, 1968-72, ptnr., 1972-89, pres. and mng. ptnr., 1984-89; sr. v.p., gen. counsel The Danis Cos., 1989-92, 99-2000; vice chmn. Carillon Capital, Inc., 1992-99. Chmn., CEO Crysteco, Inc., Wilmington, Ohio, 1995-99; pres. interchange exec. Presdl. Commn. on Pers. Interchange, Washington, 1972-73. Chmn., pres. bd. trustees Dayton Ballet Assn., 1985-88; trustee Columbus (Ohio) Symphony Orch., 1981-84; chmn. Dayton Performing Arts Fund, 1989-92, Dayton Devel. Coun., 1987-90, Wright State U. Found., Dayton, 1988-94, Miami Valley Sch., Dayton, 1988-94, Arts Ctr. Found., 1986—; mem. bd. advisors Wright State U. Coll. Bus. Adminstrn., 1988-98; bd. vis. U. Cin. Coll. Law, 1987-89. Recipient Bronze Medal for Performance U.S. EPA, 1973. Mem. ABA, Ohio Bar Assn., Dayton Bar Assn., Dayton Area C. of C. (trustee 1987-90). Republican. Presbyterian. Home: 5916 C Rayton Rd Naples FL 34103 Office: McSwiney & Co Ltd 2 River Pl Ste 400 Dayton OH 45405-4936 E-mail: ron.mcswiney@worldnet.att.net.

MC SWINEY, JAMES WILMER, retired pulp and paper manufacturing company executive; b. McEwen, Tenn., Nov. 13, 1915; s. James S. and Delia (Conroy) McS.; m. Jewel Bellar, 1940; children: Charles Ronald, Margaret

Ann. Grad., Harvard Advanced Mgmt. Program, 1954. Lab. technician, shipping clk. Nashville div. The Mead Corp., 1934-39; asst. office mgr. Harriman div., 1939; plant mgr. Rockport, Ind., 1940; asst. office mgr. Kingsport (Tenn.) div.), 1941-44; exec. asst. to pres. Dayton, Ohio, 1954-57; v.p. devel., 1957-59; adminstrv v.p. Harriman div. (Kingsport (Tenn.) div.), 1959; group v.p., gen. mgr. Mead Bd. div., 1961-63, exec. v.p. corp., 1963-67, pres., chief exec. officer, 1968-71, chmn. bd., chief exec. officer, 1971-78, chmn. bd., 1978-82; ret., 1982. Acct., office mgr., asst. sec.-treas. Brunswick Pulp & Paper Co., Ga., 1944-45; bd. dirs. Ultra-Met, Gosinger, Inc., Sea Island Co. Trustee Com. for Econ. Devel. Aviation cadet USAAF, 1942-44. Home: PO Box 30604 401 Ocean Rd Sea Island GA 31561 E-mail: mcswiney@adelphia.net.

MCTAGGART, TIMOTHY ROBERT, state agency administrator, lawyer; b. Phila., May 6, 1960; s. James Francis and Patricia Ann (Berry) McT. AB cum laude, Harvard U., 1982, JD, 1985. Bar: Mass. 1985, D.C. 1987. Atty. gen. counsel's office Bd. Govs. FRS, Washington, 1985-87; assoc. Morrison & Foerster, 1987-89, Fried, Frank, Harris, Shriver & Jacobson, Washington, 1989-91; counsel U.S. Senate Com., 1991-94, Del. Bank Commr., 1994-98; ptnr. Nixon Peabody LLP and predecessor firm, Washington, 1999—. Mem. ABA, Mass. Bar Assn., D.C. Bar Assn. Avocations: reading, basketball, softball, squash, movies. Office: Nixon Peabody LLP 401 9th St NW Ste 900 Washington DC 20004-2134 E-mail: tmctaggart@nixonpeabody.com.

MCTAGGART, TIMOTHY THOMAS, secondary education educator; b. Danville, Pa., Dec. 8, 1949; s. Thomas Francis and Mary Elizabeth (Russial) McT. BS, Bloomsburg (Pa.) U., 1971; MDiv, St. Vincent Coll., Latrobe, Pa., 1974; MEd, Millersville (Pa.) U., 1980; EdD, Pacific Western U., Honolulu, 1991. Cert. in secondary edn., Pa. Math. tchr. Lancaster (Pa.) Cath. High Sch., 1978-85; math. and computer sci. tchr. Columbia (Pa.) Sr. High Sch., 1985—. Head track coach Columbia High Sch., 1986—. Mem. Pa. Athletic Assn. (football ofcl.), K.C. (knight 4th deg.). Home: 728 Sharon Dr Mount Joy PA 17552-9711 Office: Columbia H S 901 Ironville Pike Columbia PA 17512-9513

MCTAGUE, JOHN PAUL, materials scientist, educator, chemist, researcher; b. Jersey City, Nov. 28, 1938; s. James Aloysius and Teresa Eugenia (Hanley) McT.; m. Carole Frances Reilly, Dec. 30, 1961; children: Kevin W., Catherine E., Margaret A., Maureen E. BS in Chemistry, Georgetown U., 1960; PhD, Brown U., 1965, DSc (hon.), 1997. Mem. tech. staff N.Am. Rockwell Sci. Ctr., Thousand Oaks, Calif., 1964—70; prof. chemistry, mem. Inst. Geophysics and Planetary Physics UCLA, 1970—82; dep. dir. Office Sci. and Tech. Policy, Exec. Office of Pres., Washington, 1983—86, acting sci. advisor to Pres. Reagan, 1986; v.p. rsch. Ford Motor Co., Dearborn, Mich., 1986—90, v.p. tech. affairs, 1990—99; v.p. lab. mgmt., Office of Pres. U. Calif., Oakland, 2001, prof. materials Santa Barbara, 2001—. Adj. prof. chemistry Columbia, U., 1982-83. Mem. Pres.'s Coun. Advisors on Sci. and Tech., 1990-93; mem. adv. bd. Sec. Energy, 1990—; chmn. bd. overseers Fermilab, 1994-99. Alfred P. Sloan Research fellow, 1971-73; NATO sr. fellow, 1973; John Simon Guggenheim Meml. fellow, 1975-76. Fellow AAAS, Am. Phys. Soc. (George E. Pake prize 1998); mem. Am. Chem. Soc. (Calif. sect. award 1975), Nat. Acad. Engring., Sigma Xi. E-mail: john.mctague@ucop.edu.

MCTAGUE, LAWRENCE JOHN, III, financial accountant; b. Bronx, N.Y., Oct. 25, 1960; s. Lawrence John Jr. and Lois (Lavelle) McT. BA in Bus. Mgmt., Franklin and Marshall Coll., 1982; MBA in Corp. Fin., Pace U., 1986, APC in Pub. Acctng., 1990. CMA. Tax acct. Merrill Lynch, N.Y.C., 1982-84; acct. mgr., corp. trust Chase Manhattan Bank, 1984-86; cons. Leaton Fin. Group, 1986-87; asst. controller, N.E. ops. URS Cons., Paramus, N.J., 1987-89, John Brown, Stamford, Conn., 1989-92, mgr. fin. reporting, planning and analysis Houston, 1992—. Avocations: tennis, skiing, weight tng. Office: John Brown 7909 Parkwood Circle Dr Houston TX 77036-6565 Address: 12419 Shadowmist Dr Houston TX 77082-2368

MCTEE, CINDY, classical musician, educator; b. 1953; BM, Pacific Luth. U., 1976, studied with David Robbins; MM, Yale U., 1978, studied with Krzysztof Pendereckl, Jacob Druckman, and Bruce MacCombe; PhD, U. Iowa, 1981, studied with Richard Hervig; studied with Penderecki, Marek Stachowski, and Krystyna Moszumanska-Nazar, Higher Sch. Music, Cracow, Poland. Tchr. Pacific Luth. U., Tacoma, 1981-84; assoc. to full prof. music composition U. North Tex., Denton, 1985—. Fulbright-Hayes Sr. Lectr. fellow in computer music Acad. Music, Cracow, 1990. Recipient comms. from Nat. Symphony Orch., Big Eight Band Dirs. Assn., Voices of Change, Barlow Endowment for Music Composition, Am. Guild Organists, Coll. Band Dirs. Nat. Assn., Phi Kappa Lambda Bd. Regents; works performed by Am. Symphony Orch., Nat. Repertory Orch., St. Louis Symphony, Memphis Symphony, Honolulu Symphony, Pitts. New Music Ensemble, Nat. Symphony Orch., Nippon Housou Kyoukai (NHK) Symphony Orch., Philharm. Orch., London. Recipient BMI award, Guggenheim Fellowship, 2001; grantee Wash. State Arts Commn.; Composers fellow NEA, Goddard Lieberson fellow AAAL; Acad. award in Music, AAAL, 2002. Home: 1217 Piping Rock St Denton TX 76205-8126 Office: U of North Tex Coll of Music Denton TX 76203

MCTEER, ROBERT D., JR. banker; Pres., CEO, Fed. Res. Bank Dallas, Tex. Office: Fed Res Bank Dallas 2200 N Pearl St Dallas TX 75201-2272 E-mail: info@dallasfed.org.

MCTERNAN, ANN CIBUZAR, adult nurse practitioner; b. Brainerd, Minn., Nov. 26, 1950; BS in Family Social Sci., U. Minn., 1973; BSN, U. N.C., Greensboro, 1976; MSN-N.P., George Mason U., Fairfax, Va., 1990. RN, Va., Md., Calif., Minn.; cert. adult nurse practitioner. Mem. nursing staff U.S. Naval Hosp., Beaufort, S.C., 1976-77, Eskaton Monterey Hosp., Monterey, Calif., 1977-78; staff Drug Enforcement Adminstrn., Bangkok, 1978-80; mem. nursing staff US Naval Hosp., Okinawa, Japan, 1981-82; mem. nursing staff. St. Joseph's Med. Ctr., Brainerd, 1986-87, Potomac Hosp., Woodbridge, Va., 1980-81, 87-90, Marymount U., Arlington, 1989-90; low impact/expectant mothers aerobic instr. Saratoga Dance Ctr., Springfield, 1990-94; adult nurse practitioner Prime Care, Annandale, 1991-95; nurse practitioner cons. AW Rsch. Lab. and Image Engring., Brainerd, Minn., 1995—. Aerobic fitness instr. Am. Coun. on Exercise, San Diego, 1990—. Mem. AAUW, Am. Coll. Sports Medicine, Am. Acad. Nurse Practitioners. Home: care Cibuzar 4222 Cottage Grove Dr Baxter MN 56425 Office: AW Rsch Lab Image Engring 2403 Airport Rd NE Brainerd MN 56401-9733

MCTIER, CHARLES HARVEY, foundation administrator; b. Columbus, Ga., Jan. 28, 1939; s. Roy and Julia (Harvey) McT.; m. Margaret Lucy Ruyl, Aug. 23, 1962; children: Margaret Marie, Charles Harvey Jr. BBA, Emory U., 1961. Administrv. asst. hosp. Emory U., Atlanta, 1961-63, bus. mgr. dept. psychiat. Sch. Med., 1963-66, assoc. dir. personnel, 1966-69, asst. to pres., bd. trustees, 1969-71; sec. Robert W. Woodruff Found., Joseph B. Whitehead Found., Lettie Pate Evans Found., Inc., Lettie Pate Whitehead Found., Inc., 1971-77, sec., treas., 1977-87, v.p., sec., treas., 1987-88, pres., 1988—. Chmn. Atlanta Founds. Forum, 1985-86; trustee Southeastern Coun. Founds., Atlanta, 1985-92, chmn. membership com., 1986-89, chmn. program com., 1989, chmn. bd. trustees, 1989-90; vice chmn. Coun. on Founds., Washington, 1995-97, program com., 1985-87, nominating com., 1987-88, chmn. audit and fin. com., 1990-95, chmn. mgmt. com., 1996-97; chmn. bd. trustees Found. Ctr. N.Y.C., 1994-2000, fin. and audit com., 1991-2000, exec. com., 1992-93, chmn. nominating com.; pub. mem. Joint Commn. on Accreditation of Health Care Orgns., 1994—; dir. SunTrust Bank of Ga., SunTrust Bank Atlanta, 1995—, Coca-Cola FEMSA. Trustee, Meth. Ch. Ga. United Meth. Found., 1985—; trustee, treas. Meth. Found. Ret. Mins., 1980; chmn. new ch. devel. com. North Ga. United Meth. Conf., 1980-85; mem. bd. vis. Emory U., 1985-87. Mem. Assn. Emory Alumni (bd. govs. 1987-91), Pres.'s Cir. of NAS/Inst. of Medicine, Commerce Club (bd. dirs.), Peachtree Golf Club, Piedmont Driving Club. Avocations: golf, travel. Office: Robert W Woodruff Found Inc 50 Hurt Plz SE Ste 1200 Atlanta GA 30303-2951

MCTURNAN, LEE BOWES, lawyer; b. N.Y.C., Sept. 13, 1937; s. Lee M. and Alice (Light) McT.; m. Susan Cassady, Aug. 2, 1969; children: John M., Sarah D. AB magna cum laude, Harvard U., 1959; diploma in law, Oxford (Eng.) U., 1961; JD, U. Chgo., 1963. Bar: Ill. 1965, U.S. Dist. Ct. (no. dist.) Ill. 1965, U.S. Ct. Appeals (7th cir.) 1966, U.S. Supreme Ct. 1969, Ind. 1978, U.S. Dist. Ct. (so. dist.) Ind. 1978, U.S. Dist. Ct. (no. dist.) Ind. 1987. Law clk. to hon. justice U.S. Supreme Ct., Washington, 1963-64; assoc. Sidley & Austin, Chgo., 1964-69, ptnr., 1970-78, Hackman, McClarnon & McTurnan, Indpls., 1978-88, McTurnan & Turner, Indpls., 1989—. Assoc. spl. counsel procs. on chief justice R.I. Commn. Jud. Tenure and Discipline, Providence, 1985; mem. Local Rules Adv. Com. for So. Dist. Ind., 1995-2000. Adminstrv. bd. Meridian St. United Meth. Ch., 1987-90. Mem. ABA, Ind. Bar Assn., Ill. Bar Assn., Indpls. Bar Assn., 7th Cir. Bar Assn., Law Club of Indpls. (pres. 1988-90), Legal Club of Chgo., Columbia Club, Woodstock Club, Lit. Club, Rotary. Republican. Avocations: running, reading, gardening. Home: 9907 Summerlakes Dr Carmel IN 46032 Office: McTurnan & Turner 2400 Market Tower 10 W Market St Indianapolis IN 46204-2954

MCTYEIRE, ROBERT ADAMS, sound company executive; b. Birmingham, Ala., July 21, 1949; s. William Walter Jr. and Katherine Elizabeth (Meadow) McT.; m. Pamela Ann Huffstutler, Apr. 18, 1978. BS in Commerce and Bus. Adminstrn., U. Ala., 1972. Ind. sound engr., Tuscaloosa, 1972-73; owner, chief engr. Ram Sound, 1973-89, Mary Esther, Fla., 1989—. Charter mem. nominating com. Ala. Music Hall of Fame, Muscle Shoals; cons. Klipsch and Assocs., Inc., Hope, Ark., 1984—. Sound engr. for numerous entertainers including Tony Bennett, Dave Brubeck, Ray Charles, Ry Cooder, Fats Domino, Roy Orbison, Bob Hope, Tom Jones, B.B. King, Wynton Marsalis, Dolly Parton, Bonnie Raitt, Ray Stevens, Ramsey Lewis, George Jones, B.J. Thomas. Mem. Tuscaloosa Arts Coun. With U.S. Air N.G., 1969-71. Mem. Muscle Shoals Music Assn. Republican. Avocations: boating, cruising, fishing, music. Home and Office: Ram Sound 369 W Miracle Strip Pky Mary Esther FL 32569-1833

MCTYER-CLARKE, WANDA KATHLEEN, interior designer; b. St. Louis, Apr. 06; d. Wiley and Lorain (Perkins) Howard. BSBA, St. Louis U., 1982; MS in Econs., So. Ill. U., Edwardsville, 1989; postgrad., Sheffield Sch. Interior Design, N.Y.C.; MBA in Organizational Behavior, Heriot-Watt U. Sch. Bus. Edinburgh Sch., Scotland, 1997; cert., N.Y. Sch. of Interior Design, 1995. Cert. nutritionist, aerobic dance instr., folk art paint technique instr.; decorative painters cert. Plaid Co. OSCI. Sec. clk. St. Louis U.; substitute tchr., aerobic dance instr. St. Louis Bd. Edn.; caseworker Mo. Div. Family Social Svcs., St. Louis; interior designer; with McTyer-Clarke Designs, 1992-96. Block capt. Operation Brightside (cert. of appreciation); Ms. Mahogany Social Clubs 2d Runner Up, 1981-82, Miss Galaxy 1st Runner-Up, 1984. Alpha Kappa Alpha scholar, Sigma Ghamma Rho scholar, Washington Tabernacle Ch. scholar, Cotillion de Leon's Alternate scholar. Address: PO Box 142673 Saint Louis MO 63114-0673

MCVAY, BARBARA CHAVES, secondary education mathematics educator; b. Dallas, July 6, 1950; d. Joe M. and Dorothy May (Nock) Chaves; m. David Clyde McVay, Dec. 23, 1968; 1 child, Kathryn McVay Hearn. BS in Math., U. Tex., Arlington, 1971, MS in Math., 1999. Cert. secondary tchr. math., English, Tex. Tchr. math. C.W. Nimitz High Sch. Irving (Tex.) Ind. Sch. Dist., 1972—. Bldg. rep. Dallas Tchrs. Credit Union, 1982—; part time lab. instr. North Lake/Dallas County Community Coll., Irving, 1988—. Tchr. Sunday sch. North Dallas Bapt. Ch., 1971-80; ch. tng. leader 1st Bapt. Ch., Irving, 1981-85. Mem. NEA, Tex. State Tchrs. Assn., Irving Edn. Assn. (rep. 1980—), Nat. Coun. Tchrs. Math., Tex. Coun. Tchrs. Math., Greater Dallas Coun. Tchrs. Math., Math. Assn. Am., Delta Kappa Gamma. Republican. Avocations: crafts, sewing, needlework. Office: CW Nimitz High Sch 100 W Oakdale Rd Irving TX 75060-6833 E-mail: bjcmcvay@yahoo.com.

MCVEIGH-PETTIGREW, SHARON CHRISTINE, communications consultant; b. San Francisco, Feb. 6, 1949; d. Martin Allen and Frances (Roddy) McVeigh; m. John Wallace Pettigrew, Mar. 27, 1971; children: Benjamin Thomas Pettigrew, Margaret Mary Pettigrew. BA with honors, U. Calif.-Berkeley, 1971; diploma of edn., Monash U., Australia, 1975; MBA, Golden Gate U., 1985. Tchr., adminstr. Victorian Edn. Dept., Victoria, Australia, 1972—79; supr. Network Control Ctr. GTE Sprint Comms., Burlingame, Calif., 1979—81, mgr. customer assistance, 1981—84, mgr. state legis. ops., 1984—85, dir. revenue programs, 1986—87; comm. cons. Flores, Pettigrew & Co., San Mateo, 1987—89; telemktg. Apple Computer Inc., Cupertino, 1989—94; prin. The Call Ctr. Group, San Mateo, 1995—. Telecomm. cons. PPG Svcs., 1994—; telecomm. spkr. Dept. Consumer Affairs, Sacramento, 1984. Panelist Wash. Gov.'s Citizens Coun., 1984; founding mem. Maroondah Women's Shelter, Victoria, 1978; organizer nat. conf. Bus. Women and the Polit. Process, New Orleans, 1986; mem. sch. bd. Boronia Tech. Sch., Victoria, 1979. Recipient Tchr. Spl. Responsibilities award, Victoria Edn. Dept., 1979. Mem.: Women's Econ. Action League, Am. Telemktg. Assn. (bd. dirs. 1992), Peninsula Profl. Women's Network, Am. Mgmt. Assn., Women in Telecom. (panel moderator Sann Francisco 1984). Democrat. Roman Catholic.

MCVEY, ALICE LLOYD, social worker; b. N.Y.C., Mar. 21, 1935; d. George John and Alice Wood (Lloyd) Mc Vey. MS, Syracuse U., 1970; M of Profl. Svc., N.Y. Theol. Sem., 1977; cert. pastoral counseling, Postgrad. Ctr. Mental Health, 1977; cert. in gerontology, Adelphi U., 1983; MSW, Fordham U., 1991. Tchr. elem. Schs. in Diocese of Bklyn., 1955-66; tchr. biology Holy Family High Sch., Huntington, N.Y., 1966-75; regional superior Sisters of St. Joseph, Brentwood, 1975-82; pastoral minister to older adults Our Lady of Grace Ch., West Babylon, 1982-96, dir. parish social min. office, 1996—. Mem. Acad. Cert. Social Workers. Avocations: gardening, birding, hiking.

MCVEY, DIANE ELAINE, accountant; b. Wilmington, Del., Apr. 20, 1953; d. C. Granville and Margaret M. (Lindell) McV. AA in Acctg., Goldey Beacom Coll. (Del.), 1973, BS in Acctg., 1980; MBA in Mgmt., Fairleigh Dickinson U., 1985. Acct. Audio Visual Arts, Wilmington, 1973; cost acct. FMC Corp., Kennett Sq., Pa., 1973-75; asst. acct. NVF Corp., 1978-80; staff analyst GPU Nuclear, Parsippany, N.J., 1980-93; staff acct., 1993-95, GPU Svc., Morristown, 1995-2000, Reading, Pa., 2000—. Owner, Demac Cons., Dover, N.J., 1988-2000, Reading, 2000—. Elder First Presbyn. Ch., Rockaway, N.J., 1986—, session mem., 1988-91; commr. to bd. adjustment, Dover, N.J., 1994-2000. With U.S. Army, 1975-78. Mem. Assn. MBA Execs. Republican. Presbyterian. Avocations: reading mystery books, writing and performing music, needlework. E-mail: d.mcvey@gpu.com., d.e.mcvey@worldnet.att.net.

MCVEY, FRANCIS DANIEL, mechanical engineer, software developer, educator; b. St. Louis, Jan. 19, 1929; s. Martin Patrick and Marguy Josephine (Boeckler) McV.; m. Anna Elizabeth Moss, Nov. 26, 1958 (dec. Dec. 1990); children: Mark Andrew, Marguy Denise, Michael Sean. BS in Mech. Engring., Washington U., St. Louis, 1952, MS, 1954. Inst. mech. engring. Washington U., St. Louis, 1954-55; group project engr., missiles engring. divsn. McDonnell Aircraft Co., 1955-58, assoc. scientist rsch. divsn., 1961-64, br. mgr. engring. tech. divsn., 1964-74, prin. staff engr., 1974-83; chief aerodynamicist Cleve. Pneumatic Co., Washington, 1959-61; engring. fellow McDonnell Douglas, 1983-86, sr. fellow, 1986-97, dir. CAD/CAM, 1986-97; sr. tech. fellow Boeing Co., 1997—, staff engring. dir., 1997-99; retired, 1999. Lectr. St. Louis U., 1964—70, 2000—, U. Mo.-Rolla extension, 1971; adj. prof. aero. and mech. engring. dept. St. Louis U., 2000—; engring. and automotive cons. Mem. exec. adv. com. on engring. St. Louis U., 1998-2001. Served with AUS, 1946-48. Recipient Lloyd R. Koenig prize in engring. Washington U., 1952. Fellow: AIAA (assoc.; chmn. St. Louis sect. 1963—66, mem. mgmt. com. 1998—2002); mem.: Am. Rocket Soc. (chmn. St. Louis sect.), Sigma Xi. Roman Catholic. Avocation: reading. Home: 7030 Delmar Blvd University City MO 63130-4301 E-mail: fmcveyd@aol.com.

MCVEY, HENRY HANNA, III, retired lawyer; b. Richmond, Va., Aug. 12, 1935; s. Henry Hanna Jr. and Eva Lawson (Jennings) McVey; m. Reba Jean Robinson, Dec. 12, 1964; children: Margaret Anne McVey Singleton, Lewis Lawson, Ian Douglas. BS, BA magna cum laude, Hampden-Sydney Coll., 1957; LLB, U. Va., 1960. Bar: Va. 1960, U.S. Dist. Ct. (ea. dist.) Va. 1960, U.S. Ct. Appeals (4th cir.) 1965, U.S. Supreme Ct. 1970. Assoc. Battle, Neal, Harris, Minor & Williams, Richmond, 1960-66; ptnr. McGuireWoods LLP and predecessor firms, 1966-99; ret., 1999. Mem. adv. group under Civil Justice Reform Act of 1990 U.S. Dist. Ct. (ea. dist.) Va. Trustee Hampden-Sydney Coll., 1989—94, 1995—2000, 2001—; mem. Commn. on Archtl. Rev. City of Richmond, 1985—95; mem. Planning Commn. Gloucester County, 2001—; vice-chair Hampden-Sydney, 2001—02; bd. dirs. Richmond Symphony, 1977—78, 1987—99, v.p., 1979—81, exec. v.p., 1981—83, pres., 1983—85, chmn. bd. dirs., 1985—87, pres. Symphony Coun., 1999—; bd. dirs. Carpenter Ctr. for Performing Arts, 1982—89, Rosewell Found., 1999—, pres., 2001—02. Recipient Algernon Sydney Sullivan medallion for svc. to coll., Hampden Sydney Coll., 2001. Fellow: Am. Bar Found., Am. Coll. Trial Lawyers; mem.: ABA, Va. Bar Assn., Bar Assn. City of Richmond, Fedn. Defense and Corp. Counsel, Def. Rsch. and Trial Lawyers Assn. (past state chmn., regional v.p. 1985—87, bd. dirs. 1987—90), Va. Assn. Def. Attys. (v.p. 1981—83, treas. 1983—84, pres.-elect 1984—85, pres. 1985—86), Ware River Yacht Club (bd. dirs. 2000—). Presbyterian. Home: PO Box 43 Schley VA 23154-0043 E-mail: mcvey@rivnet.net.

MCVEY, WALTER LEWIS, lawyer, educator; b. Independence, Kans., Feb. 19, 1922; s. Walter Lewis and Nona (Inge) McV.; m. Rose Mary Ayers, Oct. 28, 1944 (div. Oct. 1962); children: Walter Lewis III (dec.), David Ayers; m. Velma Graham Hulett, Apr. 3, 1964 (dec. Aug. 7, 1998). BA, U. Kans., 1947, JD, 1948; MA, Ga. State U., 1976. Bar: Ga. 1965. Lawyer McVey, McVey & McVey, Independence, 1948-61; rep. U.S. Congress, Washington, 1961-63; sole practice law Atlanta, 1965-95. State rep. Kans. State Legislature, Topeka, 1949-52; judge Ct. Independence, 1952-56; state senator Kans. Legislature, Topeka, 1957-61; adj. prof. Ga. State U., 1968-73, Mercer U., Atlanta, 1971-74, DeKalb Coll., Ga., 1968-93; trustee IRS, Montgomery County, Kans., 1954-55; mgm. cons., 1968-98; evening dean DeKalb Coll. North, Dunwoody, Ga., 1996-98, Ga. Perimeter Coll., Dunwoody, 1998-2001; writer, 2001—. Republican. Methodist. Home: 712 E Paces Ferry Rd NE Atlanta GA 30305-2717

MCVICKER, JESSE JAY, artist, educator; b. Vici, Okla., Oct. 18, 1911; s. Jesse Allen and Clara Mae (Hendrick) McV.; m. Laura Beth Paul, Aug. 20, 1938. BA, Okla. State U., 1940, MA, 1941. Faculty Okla. State U., Stillwater, 1941—, prof. art, 1959-77, prof. emeritus, 1977—, head dept., 1959-77. Exhbns. include Med. Mus. Art, Mus. Non-Objective Painting, Chgo, Art Inst., N.A.D., Library of Congress, San Francisco Mus. Art, Denver Art Mus., Pa. Acad. Fine Arts, Carnegie Inst., Print Club Phila., Salon Des Realities Nouvelles, Paris, France, Dallas, Mus. Fine Arts, Galleria Origine, Rome, Italy, Whitney Mus. Am. Art; represented in permanent collections Library of Congress, Seattle Art Mus., Dallas Mus. Fine Arts, Met. Mus. Art, Joslyn Meml. Art Mus.; bibliography Graphic Works by J. Jay McVicker, 1986. Served with USNR, 1943-46. Mem. Soc. Am. Graphic Artists, Audubon Artists (John Taylor Arms award 1990), Print Club Phila., Pi Kappa Alpha.

MCVISK, WILLIAM KILBURN, lawyer; b. Chgo., Oct. 8, 1953; s. Felix Kilburn and June (DePear) Visk; m. Marlaine Joyce McDonough, June 20, 1975. BA, U. Ill, 1974; JD, Northwestern U., 1977. Bar: Ill. 1977, Ind. 1999, U.S. Dist. Ct. (no. dist.) Ill. 1977, U.S. Ct. Appeals (7th cir.) 1978, U.S. Dist. Ct. (no. and so. dists.) Ind. 1999. Assoc. Jerome H. Torshen, Ltd., Chgo., 1977-80, Silets & Martin, Chgo., 1980-81, Peterson & Ross, Chgo., 1981-85, ptnr., 1985-95, Johnson & Bell Ltd., Chgo., 1995—. Contbr. articles to profl. jours. Mem.: ABA, Ill. Assn. Def. Trial Lawyers (chmn. ins. coverage com.), Ill. Assn. Hosp. Attys. (pres., bd. dirs.), Am. Health Lawyers Assn., Def. Rsch. Inst., Chgo. Bar Assn. Office: Johnson & Bell 55 E Monroe St Fl 41 Chicago IL 60603-5713 E-mail: mcviskw@jbltd.com.

MCWADE, JESSICA CHRISTY, communications executive; b. Malden, Mass., May 10, 1956; d. Stanley Bernard and Doris Marie McWade; children from previous marriage: Zachary, Jackson. BS, Boston U., 1978; MBA, NYU, 1980; MPA, Harvard U., 1987; cert. econs., Stockholm Sch. Econs., 1980. Photographer Gov.'s Office, Boston, 1976—78; dep. press sec. Mayor's Office, City of Boston, 1982—84; dir. corp. rels. BankBoston, 1987—94, internat. loan officer, 1984—87; dir. corp. comms. Textron, Providence, 1994—95; v.p. corp. affairs Raytheon Co., Lexington, Mass., 1996—98; CEO Lexington Comms. Group, 1998—. Pres. World Affairs Coun. Boston, 1992—96. Active The Coun. Fgn. Rels., N.Y.C., 1993—; allocations committeewoman United Way of Mass Bay, Boston, 1989—94; treas. Whittier St. Neighborhood Health Ctr., 1990—93. Comdr. USNR, 1980—. Decorated Navy Commendation medal, Navy Achievement medals; named Ten Outstanding Young Leaders, Boston Jaycees, 1987; recipient Twice a Citizen award, USNR Assn., 1985; fellow fellow, The Salzburg Seminar, 1998, The British-Am. Fellowship, 1994. Roman Catholic. Office: Lexington Comms Group 24 Muzzey St Lexington MA 02421

MCWANE, JOYCE HOBBS, title company executive; b. Lynchburg, Va., May 4, 1947; d. Earle Benjamin Sr. and Marie (Goode) Hobbs; m. Hudson, Nov. 26, 1966 (div. 1978); m. Lawrence Henry McWane, Jr., April 5, 1986; children: Kevin, Rodney, Meghan. Student, Radford U., 1965-66; grad. in mortgage banking, Northwestern U., 1986; mgmt. cert., U. Va., 1990. V.p. Ctrl. Fidelity Bank/Wachovia Bank, Lynchburg, 1973-98; pres. Home Buyer Solutions, Inc., Nellysford, Va., 1998—. Adv. bd. GreenPoint Credit, LLC, Roanoke, Va., 1999; cons. Yates Home Sales, Blairs, Va., 1998-99. Frequent contbr. Manufactured Housing Mag. Treas. Area 8 Spl. Olympics, Roanoke, 1988-90; chair, coord. Ptnrshp. Habitat for Humanity and Va. Manufactured Housing, Lynchburg, 1997. Paul Harris fellow Rotary Internat., Hardy, 1991. Mem. Fin. Women Internat. (sec. 1997-98, membership chair 1998-99), Va. Manufactured Housing Assn. (treas. 1996-98, sec. 1998-2000, bd. mem. of yr. 1998, chmn. 2000—), Rotary (charter pres. Hardy, Va. 1990-92, Paul Harris fellow 1991). Avocations: golf, reading. Home: RR 1 Box 814 Roseland VA 22967-9215 Office: Home Buyer Solutions Inc PO Box 586 12 Rockfish Valley Hwy Nellysford VA 22958-3001 Fax: 434-361-2227. E-mail: jmcwane@aol.com.

MCWETHY, JOHN FLEETWOOD, journalist; b. Aurora, Ill., Feb. 28, 1947; s. John Adams and Mary Helen (Bell) McW.; m. Laurie Duncan, June 25, 1971; children: Adam Duncan, James Ian. BA, DePauw U., 1969; MS, Columbia U., 1970; Doctorate in Journalism (hon.) , DePauw U., 2002. Def. writer Congl. Quar., Washington, 1970-72; sci. editor U.S. News & World Report, 1972-77, chief White House corr., 1977-79; chief Pentagon corr. ABC News, 1979-84; chief corr. ABC News Nat. Security and Sr. State Dept., 1984—. Contbg. author: Power of the Pentagon, 1972. Recipient DuPont award Columbia U. Sch. Journalism, 1984; 4 Emmy awards, 1984, 91, 92, 99, Overseas Press Club award for Inside the Other Side, 1987, Peabody award for coverage of Sept. 11, 2001. Home: 5028 30th St N Arlington VA 22207-2717

MCWETHY, PATRICIA JOAN, educational association administrator; b. Chgo., Feb. 27, 1946; d. Frank E. and Emma (Kuehne) McW.; m. H. Frank Eden; children: Kristin Beth, Justin Nicholas. BA, Northwestern U., 1968; MA, U. Minn., 1970; MBA, George Washington U., 1981. Geog. analyst CIA, McLean, Va., 1970-71; rsch. asst. NSF, Washington, 1972-74, spl. asst. to dir., 1975, assoc. program dir. human geography and regional sci. program, 1976-79; exec. dir. Assn. Am. Geographers, Washington., 1979-84, Nat. Assn. Biology Tchrs., Reston, Va., 1984-95, Nat. Sci. Edn. Leadership Assn., Arlington, 1995-97; edn. dir. Nat. Alliance for Mentally Ill, 1998-99. Prin. investigator grant on biotech. equipment ednl. resource partnership NSF, 1989-93, NSF funder internat. symposium on Basic Biol. Concepts: What Should the World's Children Know?, 1992-94; co-prin. investigator NSF grant, 1995-97; mem. chmn.'s adv. com. Nat. Com. Sci. Stds. and Assessment, 1992-95; mem. Commn. for Biology Edn., Internat. Union Biol.. Sci., 1988-97; mem. exec. com. Alliance for Environ. Edn., 1987-90, chmn. program com., 1990; condr. seminars in field; lectr. in field. Author monograph and papers in field; editor handbook. NSF grantee, 1989-93, 95-97; NSF fellow, 1968-69; recipient Outstanding Performance award, NSF, 1973. Mem. Phi Beta Kappa.

MCWHARTER, DIANE, writer; b. Birmingham, Ala. Grad., Wellesley Coll. Writer, N.Y.C. Contbr. Home: 258 Riverside Dr Apt 10A New York NY 10001*

MCWHINEY, GRADY, history educator; b. Sherveport, La., July 15, 1928; s. Henry Grady and Mayme (Holland) McW.; m. Sue B. Baca, Nov. 20, 1947. BS, Centenary Coll. of La., 1950; MA, La. State U., 1951; PhD, Columbia U., 1960. Asst. prof. Troy State U., Ala., 1952-54, Millsaps Coll., Jackson, Miss., 1956-59, Northwestern U., Evanston, Ill., 1960-65; assoc. prof. to prof. U.B. C., Vancouver, Can., 1965-70; vis. prof. U. Calif. - Berkeley, 1959-60, 67-68; prof. Wayne State U., Detroit, 1970-75; vis. prof. Tulane U., New Orleans, summer 1970, U. Mich., Ann Arbor, 1972-73; prof. history, dir. and disting. sr. fellow ctr. for study of so. history and culture U. Ala. University, 1975-83; Lyndon Baines Johnson prof. Am. history Tex. Christian U., Ft. Worth, 1983-96, emeritus, 1996—; disting. historian in residence U. So. Miss., Hattiesburg, 1996-97. Mem. NEH Selection Com., 1973, Jefferson Davis Award Com., 1970-72, 75-77; James Murfin Meml. lectr., 1990, Marian

Alexander Blake lectr., 1991; Conf. Meml. speaker, 1991; vis. disting. prof. McMurry U., Abilene, Tex., 1997-98; pres. McWhiney Rsch. Found., 1997—. Author: Braxton Bragg and Confederate Defeat, Vol. 1, 1969, Southerners and Other Americans, 1973; (with Perry D. Jamieson) Attack and Die: Civil War Military Tactics and the Southern Heritage, 1982, Cracker Culture: Celtic Ways in the Old South, 1988, An American Civil War Primer, 1992, Battle in the Wilderness: Grant Meets Lee, 1994, 2d edit., 1998; editor: (with Sue McWhiney) To Mexico with Taylor and Scott, 1845-1847, 1969, Grant, Lee, Lincoln and the Radicals, 1964; (with Robert Weibe) Historical Vistas, 2 vols., 1963-64, Reconstruction and the Freedmen, 1963, (with Douglas Southall Freeman) Robert E. Lee's Dispatches to Jefferson Davis, 1957, 2d edit., 1994, Confederate Crackers and Cavaliers, 2001. With USMC, 1945—47. Recipient Earl A. Davis award, 1996, Frank E. Vandiver award Houston Civil War Round Table, 1993, Charles L. "Pie" Dufour award New Orleans Civil War Round Table, 1994, Outstanding Scholar award U. Ala., 1980, Gallant Service award Chgo. Civil War Round Table, 1979, Harry S. Truman award, 1970, Pacific Br. award Am. Hist. Assn., 1969; Huntington Library fellow, 1984; recipient Jefferson Davis medal United Daughters of the Confederacy, 1992, Honor award Sons Confederate Vets Tex. Divsn., 1993; rsch. fellow Mosher Inst. Defense Studies, 1988—, 1st recipient Grady McWhiney award, 1998. Fellow St. George Tucker Soc.; mem. Ala. Hist. Assn. (pres. 1978-79), So. Hist. Assn. (exec. council 1976-79), Civil War Round Table U.K. (hon.), Phi Beta Kappa (Disting. Scholar). Home: 3566 Winston Rd Fort Worth TX 76109-2822

MCWHINNEY, EDWARD WATSON, Canadian government legislator; b. Sydney, Australia, May 19, 1924; s. Matthew and Evelyn Annie (Watson) McW.; m. Emily Ingalore Sabatzky, June 27, 1951. LLB, U. Sydney, 1949; LLM, Yale U., 1951, D Juridical Sci., 1953; diploma, Acad. de Droit Internat., The Hague, 1950; LLD, U. Thessaloniki, Greece, 1998. Bar: called to Australian bar 1949, apptd. Queen's counsel, Can 1967. Crown prosecutor, Sydney, 1949-50; lectr., then asst. prof. Law Sch. and Grad. Sch., Yale U., 1951-55; prof. law, mem. Centre Russian Studies, U. Toronto, Ont., Can., 1955-66; prof. law, dir. Inst. Air and Space Law, McGill U., Montreal, Que., Can., 1966-71; prof. law, dir. internat. and comparative legal studies U. Ind., Indpls., 1971-74; disting. prof. Simon Fraser U., Burnaby, B.C., 1974-93; mem. Permanent Ct. Arbitration, The Hague, 1985-91; Paul Martin prof. U. Windsor, Can., 1986; prof. emeritus, 1992; M.P. Ho. of Commons, Ottawa, Ont., Can., 1993-2000; co-chmn. joint standing com. Senate and Ho. of Commons, Can., 1993-95, parliamentary sec. (fisheries and oceans) Can., 1996-97, parliamentary sec. (fgn. affairs), 1997-2000; fed. govt. rep. nat. unity commn. Govt. of B.C., 1997-98. Vis. prof. Ecole Libre des Hautes Etudes, 1952, Heidelberg and Max-Planck-Inst., 1960-61, 90, NYU, 1954, Faculté Internat. de Droit Comparé, Luxembourg, 1959-60, U. San Antonio, 1963, U. Laval, Que., 1967, U. Paris, 1968, U. Madrid, 1968, U. Aix-Marseille, 1969, U. Nacional Autónoma de México, 1965, Inst. Univ. Luxembourg, 1972, 74, 76, Acad. Internat. Law, The Hague, 1973, 90, 2002, Aristotelian U., Thessaloniki, Greece, 1974, 78, 85, 96, U. Nice, 1976-77, Jagellonian U., Cracow, Poland, 1976, U. Paris I (Sorbonne), 1982, 85, Coll. de France, Paris, 1983, Meiji U., Tokyo, 1987, Inst. Internat. Relations, Bejing, 1987, 92; legal cons. UN, 1953-54; cons. Japanese Commn. Constn., mem. prime minister Ont. Adv. Com. Confedn., 1964-71; cons. U.S. Naval War Coll., 1961-68; legal cons. Ministère de la Justice, Que., 1969-70; 74-75; constl. adviser to prime minister of Que., 1974-75; royal commr. Commn. Lang. Rights. Que., 1968-72; cons. U.S. Senate select com. presdl. campaign activities, 1973; spl. commr. inquiry Legislature B.C., 1974-75; chief adv. Fed. Govt.'s Task Force on Nat. Unity, 1978; commr. of enquiry, City of Vancouver, 1979; constl. adv. Fedn. Can. Municipalities, 1978-82; spl. advisor Can. del. UN Gen. Assembly, ann. sessions, 1981, 82, 83, 96; constl. adviser Indian Nations (Treaties 6-9), Can., 1980-82; mem. Assoc. de l'Inst. de Droit Internat., 1967, membre titulaire, 1975, pres. 1999-2001; mem. Assoc. de l'Acad. Internat. de Droit Comparé, Paris, 1986, mem. titulaire, 2002--; mem. Deutsche Gesellschaft für Völkerrecht, 1992. Author: Judical Review, 4th edit, 1969, Canadian Jurisprudence, 1958, Föderalismus und Bundesverfassungsrecht, 1961, Constitutionalism in Germany, 1962, Comparative Federalism, 2d edit, 1965, Peaceful Coexistence and Soviet-Western International Law, 1964, Law Foreign Policy and the East-West Détente, 1964, Federal Constitution- Making for a Multi-National World, 1966, International Law and World Revolution, 1967, Conflit idéologique et ordre public mondial, 1970, (with M.A. Bradley) The Freedom of the Air, 1968, New Frontiers in Space Law, 1969, The International Law of Communications, 1970, Aerial Piracy and International Law, 1971, (with Pierre Pescatore) Federalism and Supreme Courts and the Integration of Legal Systems, 1973, Parliament and Parliamentary Power Today, 1976, The Executive and Executive Power Today, 1977, (with J-D Gendron and others) La situation de la lanque française au Québec (3 vols.), 1973, The Illegal Diversion of Aircraft and International Law, 1974, Parliamentary Privilege and the Broadcasting of Parliamentary Debates, 1975, The International Law of Detente, 1978, The World Court and the Contemporary International Law-making Process, 1979, Quebec and the Constitution, 1979, Municipal Government in a New Canadian Federal System, 1980, Conflict and Compromise: International Law and World Order in a Revolutionary Age, 1981, Constitution-Making: Principles, Process, Practice, 1981, Canada and the Constitution, 1982, United Nations Law Making, 1984, Supreme Courts and Judicial Law-Making, 1986, Les Nations-Unies et la Formation du Droit, 1986, Aerial Piracy and International Terorism, 1987, The International Court of Justice and the Western Tradition of International Law, 1987, (with Nagendra Singh) Nuclear Weapons and Contemporary International Law, 1988, Judicial Settlement of International Disputes, 1990, (with G.I. Tunkin and V.S. Vereshchetin) From Coexistence to Cooperation: International Law and Organisation in the Post-Cold War Era, 1991, (with J. Zaslove and W. Wolf) Federalism-in-the-Making, Contemporary Canadian and German Constitutionalism, National and Trans-national, 1992, Judge Shigeru Oda and the Progressive Development of International Law, 1992, Judge Manfred Lachs and Judicial Law-Making, 1994, The United Nations and a New World Order for a New Millennium, 2000, (with N. Ando and R. Wolfrum) Liber Amicorum Judge Shigeru Oda, 2002; bd. editors Australian Quar., 1949-50, Can. Yearbook of Internat. Law, 1963—, Jour. Media Law and Practice, 1980-85, Annuaire International de Justice Constitutionnelle, 1987—; editl. adv. com. Ency. Brit., 1985—; mem. bd. advisors Chinese Jour. Internat. Law, 2002—; contbr. to Ency. Brit. Served as officer Australian Air Force, 1943-45. Fellow Carnegie Endowment, 1951; Fulbright fellow, 1950-51; Sterling fellow Yale, 1950-51; Rockefeller fellow, 1960-61, 66-68; Can. Council fellow, 1960-61; fellow Am. Soc. Internat. Law, 1962-63. Mem. Australian Inst. Polit. Sci. (dir.), Internat. Law Assn. (pres. Toronto br. 1964-66, pres. Montreal br. 1970-71, chmn. exec. com. Canadian br. 1972-75), Canadian Bar Assn. (council Ont. 1956-58), Yale Law Sch. Assn. (pres. Can. 1964-69), Canadian Civil Liberties Assn. (v.p. 1965-67), Am. Soc. Internat. Law (council 1965-68), Am. Fgn. Law Assn., Inst. interamericano de Estudios Juridicos Internacionales (dir. 1965—), Inst. Grand-Ducal de Luxembourg, Internat. Commn. Jurists (mem. coun. Can. br. 1988—), Deutsche Gesellschaft für Völkerrecht (hon. mem.), Knights of Mark Twain (U.S.) (hon., Aristotle Medal 1997). Home: 1949 Beach Ave Ste 402 Vancouver BC Canada V6G 1Z2

MCWHINNEY, IAN RENWICK, physician, medical educator; b. Burnley, Eng., Oct. 11, 1926; arrived in Can., 1968, naturalized, 1981; s. Archibald Renwick and Mary (Freeland) McWhinney; m. Betty Heap, Aug. 30; children: Heather, Julie. MB, BChir, Cambridge (Eng.) U., 1949, MD; MD (hon.), U. Oslo, 1991; DSc (hon.), U. Western Ont., 2000. Intern St. Bartholomews Hosp., London, 1949—50; resident Warwick (Eng.) Hosp., 1953—54; pvt. practice medicine Stratford-on-Avon, England, 1954—68; prof. family medicine U. Western Ont., London, Canada, 1968—92, prof. emeritus Canada, 1992—; med. dir. palliative care unit Parkwood Hosp., Canada, 1986—91. Author: The Early Signs of Illness, 1964, Introduction to Family Medicine, 1981, A Textbook of Family Medicine, 1989, 1997. Capt. M.C. Royal Army, 1951—53. Recipient Excellence cert., Soc. Tchrs. Family Medicine, 1979, Curtis G. Hames Rsch. award, 1989, Hippocrates medal, Euro World Orgn. Nat. Colls. and Acads. of Gen. Practice, 2000. Fellow: Royal Coll. Physicians, Royal Coll. Gen. Practitioners, Coll. Family Physicians (Victor Johnston orator 1980); mem.: Inst. Medicine-NAS (fgn. assoc.), Order of Can. (officer 1998—). Office: U Western Ont Dept Family Medicine London ON Canada N6A 5C1 E-mail: irmcwhin@uwo.ca.

MCWHINNEY, MADELINE H. (MRS. JOHN DENNY DALE), economist, director; b. Mar. 11, 1922; d. Leroy and Alice (Houston) McW.; m. John D. Dale, June 23, 1961; 1 child, Thomas Denny. BA, Smith Coll., 1943; MBA, NYU, 1947. Economist Fed. Res. Bank, N.Y.C., 1943-73, chief fin. and trade statis. divsn., 1955-59, mgr. market stats. dept., 1960-65, asst. v.p., 1965-73; pres. First Women's Bank, 1974-76, Dale, Elliott & Co., Inc., Red Bank, N.J., 1977-97. Trustee Retirement System Fed. Res. Bank, 1955-58; vis. lectr. N.Y.U. Grad. Sch. Bus., 1976-77; mem. N.J. Casino Control Commn., 1980-82, Women's Econ. Round Table, 1978-89, chmn. 1987-88; bd. govs. Am. Stock Exch., 1977-81. Trustee Monmouth Mus., 1995—, Vis. Nurse Assn. Ctrl. Jersey, 1995—, Planned Parenthood Ctrl. Jersey, 1995—; Carnegie Corp. N.Y., 1974-82, Central Savs. Bank of N.Y., 1980-82, Charles F. Kettering Found., 1975-93, chmn. 1987-91, Inst. Internat. Edn., 1975--, Investor Responsibility Rsch. Ctr., Inc., 1974-81; asst. dir. Whitney Mus. Am. Art, 1983-86; dir. Atlantic Energy Co., 1983-93; trustee The Mgrs. Funds, 1983—; mem. adv. com. prof. ethics N.J. Supreme Ct., 1983-98. Recipient Smith Coll. medal, 1971, Alumni Achievement award NYU Grad. Sch. Bus. Adminstrn. Alumni Assn., 1971, NYU Crystal award, 1982. Mem. Am. Fin. Assn. (past dir.), Money Marketeers (v.p. 1960, pres. 1961-62), Alumni Assn. Grad. Sch. Bus. Adminstrn. NYU (dir. 1951-63, pres. 1957-59), Soc. Meml. Ctr., N.J. Com. for Humanities, Phi Beta Kappa Fellows (v.p. 1979-87). Home: 24 Blossom Cove Rd Red Bank NJ 07701-6302 Office: PO Box 458 Red Bank NJ 07701-0458 : 192 Heritage Court Little Silver NJ 07739 E-mail: mdale38569@aol.com.

MCWHIRTER, BRUCE J. lawyer; b. Chgo., Sept. 11, 1931; s. Sydney and Martha McWhirter; m. Judith Hallett, Apr. 14, 1960; children: Cameron, Andrew. BS, Northwestern U., 1952; LLB, Harvard U., 1955. Bar: DC 1955, Ill 1955, US Ct Appeals (7th cir) 1963, US Supreme Ct. Assoc. Lord, Bissell & Brook, Chgo., 1958-62; from assoc. to sr. ptnr. Ross & Hardies, 1962-95, of counsel, 1996—. Editor: Donnelley SEC Handbook, 1972—87; contbr. articles to profl jours. With U.S. Army, 1955—57. Mem.: ABA, Harvard Law Soc Ill., Chgo. Bar Assn., Harvard Club (N.Y.C.), Lawyers Club Chgo., Phi Beta Kappa. Democrat. Home: 111 Sheridan Rd Winnetka IL 60093-4223 Office: Ross & Hardies 150 N Michigan Ave Ste 2500 Chicago IL 60601-7567 E-mail: jbmcw@aol.com.

MCWHIRTER, GLENNA SUZANNE (NICKIE MCWHIRTER), retired newspaper columnist; b. Peoria, Ill., June 28, 1929; d. Alfred Leon and Garnet Lorene (Short) Sotier; m. Edward Ford McWhirter (div.); children: Suzanne McWhirter Orlicki, Charles Edward, James Richard. BS in English Lang. and Lit., U. Mich., postgrad., 1960-63. Editl. asst. McGraw-Hill Pub. Co., Detroit, 1951-54; staff writer Detroit Free Press, Inc., 1963-70, asst. city editor, 1971-77, columnist, 1977-88, Detroit News Inc., Detroit, 1988-97; advt. copy writer Campbell-Ewald Co., 1967-68; ret., 1997. Author: Pea Soup, 1984 Winner 1st Place Commentary award UPI, Mich., 1979; 1st Place Columns AP, Mich., 1978, 81; 1st Place Columns Detroit Press Club Found., Mich., 1978; Disting. Service award State of Mich., 1985 Mem. Women in Comm. (Headliner award 1978), Alpha Gamma Delta. Avocations: flower gardening, interior design. Home: 498 Saint Clair St Grosse Pointe MI 48230-1504

MCWHIRTER, JAMES HERMAN, consulting engineering business executive, financial planner; b. Mercer, Pa., July 4, 1924; s. John Herman and Blanche Rebecca (Anderson) McW.; m. Suzanne Kibler, July 5, 1952; children: Kathleen, Meg Allyn, John Richard, Thomas Charles, Robert Brian. BS, Columbia U., 1945; MS, Carnegie Inst. Tech., 1947. Registered profl. engr., Pa; cert. fin. planner. Devel. engr. Westinghouse Electric Corp., Sharon, Pa., 1948-65; rsch. engr. Westinghouse Rsch. Labs., Pitts., 1965-89; registered rep. Allegheny Investments, Ltd., 1987—; pres. Optimization, Ltd., Murrysville, Pa., 1989—. Contbr. articles on engring. and fin. planning to profl. jours.; spkr. on fin. planning. Lt. (j.g.) USNR, 1945-58. Mem.: IEEE, Third Friday Poetry, Chowder & Marching Soc. Republican. Presbyterian. Avocation: "Big Band" musician. Home and Office: 3660 Forbes Trail Dr Murrysville PA 15668-1054

MCWHIRTER, JOHN RUBEN, chemical engineering educator; b. East St. Louis, Ill., Dec. 29, 1937; s. Walter and Mildred (Johnson) McW.; m. Gail Balthrope, June 28, 1958 (div. Aug. 1978); children: John Winfield, Andrew James, Mark Steven, Brian Michael; m. Anne Burlingham, Mar. 31, 1979 (div. Dec. 1990); m. Jeanette D. Heiser, Mar. 21, 1992. BS in Chem. Engring., U. Ill., 1959; MS in Chem. Engring., Pa. State U., 1961, PhD in Chem. Engring., 1962; postgrad. exec. program, Stanford U., 1971. Research engr. E.I. Du Pont de Nemours & Co., Wilmington, Del., 1962-63; mgr. research and devel. Mixing Equipment Co., Rochester, N.Y., 1963-66; section engr. engring. devel. lab. Linde div. Union Carbide Corp., Tonawanda, 1966-67, div. engr. engring. devel. lab., 1967-68, mgr. chem. engring. div. and special projects, 1968-69, product mgr., 1969-70, mgr. wastewater treatment systems N.Y.C., 1970-72, gen. mgr. environ. systems dept., 1973-76, v.p., gen. mgr. environ. systems dept., 1977-78; v.p., gen. mgr. insecticides and intermediates agrl. products div. Union Carbide, 1978-83, v.p., gen. mgr. agrl. chems., 1983-86; prof. chem. engring. Pa. State U., State College, Pa., 1986-99; gen. ptnr. Copper Beech Townhome Cmtys., LLP, 1999—. Pres., CEO McWhirter Property Mgmt., Inc., 1996—, Mixer and Mass Tranter Techs. LLC, 2001—. Author: The Use of High Purity Oxygen in the Activated Sludge Process, 1978; contbr. articles to profl. jours.; presented numerous papers at profl. confs.; patentee in field. Recipient Best Paper Presentation award Nat. Am. Inst. Chem. Engrs., 1963, Outstanding Personal Achievement award Chem. Engring. Mag., 1970, Kirkpatrick award, 1971, Outstanding Engring. Alumnus award Pa. State U., 1984, Arthur Dehan Little award Am. Inst. Chem. Engrs., 1991. Mem. AICE, AAAS, Am. Mgmt. Assn., Am. Chem. Soc. (Jacob F. Schoellkopf medal 1976), N.Y. Acad. Scis., Water Pollution Control Fedn., Tau Beta Pi, Phi Lambda Upsilon, Sigma Tau, Alpha Chi Sigma, Delta Tau Delta. Republican. Home: 101 Aspen Dr Boalsburg PA 16827-1737

MCWHORTER, ALAN LOUIS, retired electronics researcher, electrical engineering educator; b. Crowley, La., Aug. 25, 1930; s. Arthur Walton and Andree (Genet) McW. Student, Tulane U., 1947-48; BEE, U. Ill., 1951; ScD, MIT, 1955. Staff mem. Lincoln Lab., MIT, Lexington, 1955-59, asst. head. solid state div., 1962-63, assoc. head, 1963-65, head, 1965-94, fellow, 1994—; from asst. to assoc. prof. elec. engring. MIT, Cambridge, 1959-66, prof. elec. engring., 1966-96. Mem. elec. engring. adv. coun. U. Pa., 1987-93; cons. mem. adv. group on electron devices Office of the Under Sec. of Def., Acquisition and Tech., 1991—. Contbr. articles to profl. jours. Fellow IEEE (assoc. editor Transaction on Electron Devices 1961-64, editl. bd. Proc. 1966-68, 74-76, David Sarnoff award 1971), Am. Phys. Soc. (exec. com. divsn. solid state physics 1968-70); mem. Nat. Acad. Engring. Home: 215 Massachusetts Ave Arlington MA 02474-8607

MCWHORTER, HOBART AMORY, JR. lawyer; b. Birmingham, Ala., Dec. 24, 1931; s. Hobart Amory and Marjorie (Westgate) McW.; remarried Feb. 1, 1997; children: Margaret G., Marjorie W. BA, Yale U., 1953; LLB, U. Va., 1958. Bar: Ala. 1958. Ptnr. Bradley Arant Rose & White, Birmingham, 1958—. 1st lt. U.S. Army, 1953-55. Fellow Am. Coll. Trial Lawyers; mem. Internat. Assn. Ins. Counsel, Nat. Assn. r.R. Counsel. Republican. Presbyterian. Office: Bradley Arant Rose & White One Federal Pl 1819 Fifth Ave N Birmingham AL 35203-2104

MCWHORTER, KATHLEEN, orthodontist; b. Houston, May 29, 1953; d. Archer and Lucile (Taft) McW. BA summa cum laude, U. Houston, 1986; DDS with honors, Baylor Coll., 1990. Mgr. Am. Internat. Rent-A-Car, Houston, 1974-79; mktg. researcher Concoco Oil Co., 1979-83; orthodontist Baylor Coll. Dentistry, Dallas, 1990—. Presenter Am. Assn. Dental Rsch., Montreal, Que., Can., 1988, Cin., 1990; rsch. fellow Baylor Coll. Dentistry, Dallas, 1987, 88, 89. Contbr. articles to profl. jours. Mem. ADA, Am. Assn. Orthodontists, Am. Assn. Women Dentists, Am. Assn. Dentistry for Children, Internat. Assn. Dental Rsch., Am. Assn. Dental Rsch., Tex. Dental Assn., Dallas County Dental Soc., The Crescent Club. Avocations: tennis, walking, music, water skiing. Office: Baylor U Coll Dentistry Dept Orthodontics 3302 Gaston Ave Dallas TX 75246-2027

MCWHORTER, RUTH ALICE, counselor, marriage and family therapist; b. Norfolk, Va., May 14, 1946; d. Lester Arthur and Mabel Winifred (Hopwood) Gorman; m. Dean Gundersen, Dec. 27, 1967 (div. Oct. 1971); m. R. Dale Lawhorn, Jan. 6, 1972 (div. Nov. 1979); m. Brent Wilson McWhorter, Aug. 16, 1986; stepchildren: Daniel Chastin, Kenley Reid, Scott Jason. BA in Edn., Ariz. State U., 1970, M of Counseling Psychology, 1979. Cert. profl. counselor, Ariz., cert. marriage and family therapist, Ariz. Tchr. lang. arts Globe (Ariz.) Mid. Sch., 1969-72; tchr. English Isaac Jr. High Sch., Phoenix, 1973-74; real estate salesperson Ben Brooks & Assocs., 1975-76, Century 21 Metro, Phoenix, 1976-77; overnight counselor The New Found., 1978-80; family therapist Youth Svc. Bur., 1980-81; owner, corp. officer, profl. counselor/marriage & family Family Devel. Resources (now Family Psychology Assocs.), 1981—. Cons., vol. counselor Deseret Industries, Phoenix, 1992-96. Bd. dirs. Westside Mental Health Svcs., Phoenix, 1982-87; vol. facilitator Ariz. Multiple Sclerosis Soc., Phoenix, 1988; vol. disaster mental health team ARC-Ctrl. Divsn., Phoenix, 1996—. Mem.: ACA, Assn. Mormon Counselors and Psychotherapists (sec.-treas. 1990—2000), Am. Assn. Christian Counselors, Ariz. Mental Health Counselors Assn. (sec.-treas. ctrl. chpt. 1982, sec. ctrl. chpt. 1995), Ariz. Counselors Assn., Am. Mental Health Counselors Assn., Am. Assn. Marriage and Family Therapists. Avocations: antiques and collectibles, movies, reading, golf. Office: Family Devel Resources PC PO Box 55291 Phoenix AZ 85078-5291

MCWHORTER, SHARON LOUISE, business executive, inventor, consultant; b. Feb. 22, 1951; d. Leroy Byron Harris Jr. and Josiebell (Richards) Harris Aaron; m. Abner McWhorter II, Mar. 15, 1969 (div. Aug. 1974); 1 child, Abner III. BA, Wayne State U., 1988; cert., SBA, Detroit, 1978; cert. in sound engring., Detroit Rec. Inst., Warren, Mich., 1982. Directory asst. Mich. Bell Telephone Co., Detroit, 1969; quality control clk. Chevrolet Gear & Axle, 1971-74; circulation clk. Wayne County C.C., 1977-85, mem. libr. standing com. and open house com., 1983-84; pres. Galactic Concepts & Designs, 1977-88, cons., 1983—. Gen. ptnr., mgr. S.M.J. Corridor Devel., Detroit, 1982—, hist. rschr., 1982; del. Small Bus. Conf., 1981; ad hoc mem. Minority Tech. Coun., 1981-82; elected alt. Mich. del. White House Conf. on Small Bus., Washington, 1985-86; lectr., cons. Author, editor: Creative Dilemma newsletter, 1985—; co-patentee cup holding apparatus. Vol. counselor Barat House/March of Dimes, Detroit, 1977; active Concerned Citizens Cass Corridor, Detroit, 1982-87, Cass Corridor Citizen's Patrol, Detroit, 1983-84, Empowerment Zone Devel. Corp., Detroit, 1996—, bd. dirs., corp. chair, 1997—; pres. Wayne County chpt. MADD, Mich., 1987-88; apptd. citizen rev. com, 1988—; mem. adv. bd. Neighborhood Family Initiative, Southeastern Cmty. Found.; pres. Am. Res. Tng. Sys., Inc., 1990—. Recipient Hist. Landmark award Dept. Interior, 1983, cert. appreciation Tri-County Substance Abuse Awareness Com., 1984. Mem. Inventors Coun. Mich. (bd. dirs. 1985-88), Black Women in Bus. (sec. 1984-85), Greater Detroit C. of C., South Cass Bus. Assn. (v.p. 1987-88, pres. 1988-89), Detroit Econ. Club. Democrat. Methodist. Avocations: inventing, photography, video production. Office: SMJ Corridor Devel Co 453 Myrtle St Ste 102 Detroit MI 48201-2311

MCWHORTER, STANLEY BRUCE, English educator, researcher; b. Osco, Ky., June 17, 1930; s. Stanley Vergil and Myrtie Alice (Stearns) M. BA, Transylvania Univ., Lexington, 1954; MA, U. Ky., 1961, PhD, 1963. Life Cert. Edn. Ky., 1950. Instr. English Southwestern Coll., Winfield, Kans., 1959-60, Morehead State Univ., Ky., 1960-61, Ea. Ky. State Univ., Richmond, 1961-63; asst. prof. English W. Va. Wesleyan Coll., Buckhannon, 1963-67; assoc. prof. English Univ. S. C., Florence, 1967-70; prof. English Xavier Univ., Cincinnati, 1972-75, Univ. Dayton, Ohio, 1975-95; ret., 1995—. Ednl. coord. Natl. Folk Festival Assoc. Am., Wash. D.C., 1963-67. Author: Annotated Bibilography of William Wordsworth's Writings and Ana from 1935-1941, 1961, The Annual Anthology of College Poetry and Literature, 1965, The Idea of Religious Struggle in Four Seventeenth Century English Poets, 1967, The Use of the Folk Ballad in the English Class, 1971, Superstitions of Appalachia, 1975. Dir. civic activities Lions Clubs, Jamestown, Ky., 1953-55. Grantee continued study in chosen field, 1965; recipient Southwestern grant for Tchg. Excellence, 1959-60, Cmty. Leadership award, Lions Club Am., 1961-63, Wesleyan plaque Internat. Rels., 1963-67 Wesleyan grant for study Brit. Am. Balladry, 1963-67. Life mem. MLA Am. (editl. supervisor, 1963-67, scholarship advanced studies, 1963), Nat. Coun. Tchrs. English, Nat. Edn. Assn. Am., Coll. Assn. English Tchrs., Am. Assn. Univ. Profs. D-Conservative. United Methodist. Avocations: running, swimming, travel. Office: Univ Dayton 300 Coll Park Ave Dayton OH 45469 Home: P O Box 3455 Dayton OH 45401 E-mail: mcwhrca@aol.com.

MCWHORTER, SUSAN CAROL, English language educator; b. Elkhart, Ind., Apr. 24, 1947; d. Benjamin E. and Anna M. (Pontious) Kirts; m. John R. McWhorter, June 20, 1970 (div. 1984); 1 child, Carole. BA in Speech, Drama and English, Butler U., 1969; MS in English Edn., Troy State U., 1974; EdS in English Edn., Fla. State U., 1985. Tchr. speech and drama Elkhart (Ind.) H.S., 1969-70; tchr. English Ben Davis H.S., Indpls., 1970-72; GED instr. Ala. Tech. Inst., Ft. Rucker, 1972-74; adminstr., coord. Vincennes U., Ft. Benjamin Harrison, Ind., 1974-75; tchr. English Jinks Jr. High, Panama City, Fla., 1975-76; adj. instr. English Gulf Coast C.C., 1977—; tchr. Bay High School, 1982-98; resource tchr. Bay Dist. Schs., 1998—. Mem. Bay Arts Alliance, Panama City, 1985—, Friends of the Libr., Panama City, 1980-90; mem., mentor Orch. of St. Andrew Bay, 1997—. Recipient Golden Apple award News Channel 13, 1989. Mem. Nat. Coun. Tchrs. English, Fla. Coun. Tchrs. of English (cons. 1983—), Bay Lang. Arts Coun. (pres. 1982—), Bay County Reading Coun., Assn. Bay City Educators, Bay Edn. Found. Avocations: playing flute, ballet dancing, swimming. Home: 1880 W 24th Ct Panama City FL 32405-2228 Office: Bay Dist Schs 1311 Balboa Ave Panama City FL 32401-2080 Fax: (850) 873-7128.

MCWILLIAM, JOANNE ELIZABETH, retired religion educator; b. Toronto, Ont., Can., Dec. 10, 1928; d. Cecil Edward and Edna Viola (Archer) McW.; children, Leslie Mary Giroday, Elizabeth McEwen, Sean Dewart, Colin Dewart; m. C. Peter Slater, June 6, 1987. BA, U. Toronto, 1951, MA, 1953, U. St. Michael's, Toronto, 1966, PhD, 1968. Asst. prof. religious studies U. Toronto, 1968-74, assoc. prof., 1974-87, prof., 1987, chairperson dept. religious studies, 1990-92, 93-94; Mary Crooke Hoffman prof. of Dogmatic Theology The Gen. Theol. Sem., N.Y.C, 1994-99; ret., 1999. Author: The Theology of Grace of Theodore of Mopsuestia, 1971, Death and Resurrection in the Fathers, 1986; editor: Augustine: Rhetor to Theologian, 1991, Toronto Jour. Theology. Mem. Can. Soc. for Patristic Studies (pres. 1987-90), Conf. Anglican Theologians (pres. 1990-91), Can. Soc. for the Study of Religion, Can. Theol. Soc., Am. Theol. Soc., Am. Acad. Religion. Anglican. Home: 59 Duggan Ave Toronto ON Canada M4V 1Y1 E-mail: joanne.mcwilliam@utoronto.ca.

MCWILLIAMS, BEATRIZ DURAN, communications educator; b. Chula Vista, Calif., Nov. 15, 1969; d. Donald Albert and Maria (Duran) McW. BA in Comms., San Diego State U., 1992; MS in Comms., So. Ill. U., 1993. Instr. Southwestern Coll., Chula Vista, 1993-95, Palomar coll., San Marcos, Calif., 1993-95; prof. Miracosta Coll., Oceanside, 1995—. Acad. advisor Latina Leadership Network, Mira Costa Coll., Oceanside, 1996—. Mem. Speech Comms. Assn., Western States Comms. Assn., Internat. Comms. Assn., Am. Comm. Assn.

MCWILLIAMS, BETTY CARROL, state official; b. Princeton, Ind., July 11, 1934; d. Herbert C. and Helen Elizabeth (Short) Miller; m. Charles Edward McWilliams, Feb. 18, 1956; children— David Kevin, Theresa Lynn, Michael Edward. Grad. high sch., Spurgeon, Ind. Installment loan clk. Old Nat. Bank, Evansville, Ind., 1953-56; installment loan teller Mercantile Bank, Hammond, Ind., 1956-61; data processor Calumet Nat. Bank, Hammond, 1969-70, Kuhn, Olson & West, Munster, Ind., 1970-76; pvt. practice acctg., 1976-83; procurement outreach specialist Pvt. Industry Council, Hammond, 1983-84; pres. Ptnrs. in Contracting, Hammond, 1984-85; asst. dir. fed. mktg. devel. div. Ind. Dept. Commerce, 1985—. Editor Robur Editor news booklet, 1979, 80. Mem. Nat. Contract Mgmt. Assn., VANI (bd. dirs.), The Inventor and Entrepreneurs Soc. Ind., Inc., Sigma Alpha (nat. pres. 1982-83). Home: 7858 Hunters Path Indianapolis IN 46214-1533

MCWILLIAMS, BETTY JANE, science administrator, communication disorders educator, researcher; b. Martins Ferry, Ohio; d. Harry J. and Martha (McClure) McW. BS, Ohio State U., 1949; MS, U. Pitts., 1950, PhD, 1953. Prof. emeritus U. Pitts., 1991—, dir. Cleft Palate-Craniofacial Ctr., 1969-91, dir. emeritus, 1993—. Recipient Herbert Cooper Meml. award Cooper Clinic, 1979, award of recognition Pa. Acad. Dentistry for Children, 1989, award of recognition Pa. Dental Soc., 1991; named Disting. Alumna, U. Pitts., 2000. Fellow Am. Speech, Lang. and Hearing Assn. (cert. clin. competence, Frank R.

Kleffner Career award 1995), Am. Coll. Dentists; mem. APA, Am. Cleft Palate-Craniofacial Assn. (pres. 1965, asst. sec. gen. 1st internat. congress 1969, editor 1975-81, pres. Cleft Palate Found. 1982-83, svc. award 1975, Honors of Assn. 1987), Pa. Fedn. Cleft Palate Clinics (pres. 1980-82, 89-90). Home and Office: 512 Bigham Rd Pittsburgh PA 15211-1412 Fax: 412-481-3597. E-mail: chathambee@aol.com.

MCWILLIAMS, C. PAUL, JR. engineering executive; b. Louisville, June 4, 1931; s. Cleo Paul and Audrey Dora (Hale) McW.; m. Barbara Ann Sparks, Feb. 22, 1950 (div. 1962); children: Bruce Kevin, Craig Tinsley; m. Barbara Ann Heintz, Apr. 25, 1980; 1 stepchild, Kimberly Jean Moorhouse Swigert. B Chem. Engring., U. Louisville, 1954, M Engring., 1972. Lic. profl. engr., N.Y., N.C., Pa. Sr. process devel. engr. Olin Mathieson Chem. Corp., Brandenburg, Ky., 1958-66, Rochester, N.Y., 1958-66; sr. chem. engr. GTE Sylvania, Seneca Falls, 1966-74, Eastman Kodak Co., Rochester, 1974-81; prin., treas. Flint & Sherburne Assocs., P.C., 1981-89; project engr. Roy F. Weston, Inc., 1989-92; engring. mgr. ECCO, Inc. (Environ. Cons. Co., Inc.), Buffalo, 1992-94; pres. ECCO Engring., 1993-94; staff engr. Environ. Products & Svcs., Inc., Rochester, N.Y., 1994-96; pvt. cons. engr. Webster, 1996—. Cons. water tech. Water Tech. Corp., Tonawanda, N.Y., 1973-76; product rsch. panel Chem. Engring. Mag., 1982-83. Author: Waste Disposal Manual, 1976. Life mem. Rep. Presdl. Task Force, Webster, N.Y., 1986—; mem. Rep. Nat. Com., Webster, 1991-92. 1st lt. USAF, 1954-58, ret. lt. col. USAF Res., 1982. Decorated Meritorious Svc. medal. Mem. NSPE, AIChE, Soc. Am. Mil. Engrs., Res. Officers Assn. (life), Monroe Profl. Engrs. Soc. (environ. com. 1972-75, chmn. 1973-75, bd. dirs. 1982-84, program chmn. 1984), Cons. Engrs. Coun. N.Y. State (program chmn. Rochester chpt. 1986-87, sec. 1987-88, treas. 1989). Episcopalian. Achievements include replacing boiler feedwater regulators, related instrumentation and control systems and blow-down at a N.Y. State U. facility; system design for dry fabric dust collectors to remove fly ash from coal-fired boilers' flue gas. Home: 1132 Woodbridge Ln Webster NY 14580-8709 Office: C Paul McWilliams PE Cons Engr 1132 Woodbridge Ln Webster NY 14580-8709

MCWILLIAMS, CHRIS PATER ELISSA, elementary school educator; b. Cin., Oct. 23, 1937; d. Ray C. and Mary Loretta (Collins) Pater; m. Nabeel David Elissa, Aug. 15, 1964 (dec. Aug. 1975); children: Sue Renee Caplan, Ramsey Nabeel; m. Jim Bill McWilliams, Apr. 14, 1977 (dec. Sept. 1993). BA, Our Lady of Cin. Coll., 1959; MEd, Xavier U., 1965. Cert. tchr. elem., social studies, environ. edn., Tex. Elem. tchr. Cin. Parochial Schs., 1960-64, Champaign County Schs., Urbana, Ohio, 1968; tchr. social studies St. Mary's Elem. Sch., 1968-73; tchr. Granbury (Tex.) Ind. Sch. Dist., 1981—. Instr. Tarleton State U., Stephenville, Tex., 1989-90. Contbr. (text) Texas: Yesterday, Today and Tomorrow, 1988; music editor (newspaper) Jerusalem Star, 1966. Me. Hood Gen. Hosp. Aux., 1978—; chmn. Hood County Blood Drive, Granbury, 1978-82. Recipient scholarship Our Lady of Cin. Coll., 1955, Betty Crocker Homemaker award, Gen. Mills, 1955. Mem. Tex. Alliance for Geog. Edn., Phi Delta Kappa, Delta Kappa Gamma (pres. Lambda Pi chpt. 1988-90, 96-98). Roman Catholic. Avocations: piano, reading, needlework, cooking, walking. Home: 3801 E 14th St #204 Granbury TX 75074

MCWILLIAMS, EDWIN JOSEPH, banker; b. Spokane, Washington, Aug. 11, 1919; s. Frank S. and Alice (Conlan) McW.; m. Betty J. Galbreath, Aug. 15, 1944; children: Lawrence, Barbara Anne, Marijoan, Peter. Student, U. Notre Dame, 1937-38, Marquette U., 1938-40; BS in Bus. Adminstrn, Gonzaga U., 1943. With Fidelity Mutual Savings Bank, Spokane, 1940-82, exec. v.p., 1955-58, pres., 1958-82, Fidelity Service Corp., 1983-87. Mem. adv. council Wash. State Dept. Commerce and Econ. Devel., 1977-80; U.S. del. Internat. Savs. Bank Inst., 1975, 76, 79; vice chair, dir. NW Edn. Loan Assn; pres., dir. Heritage Funeral Home. Pres. United Crusade Spokane County, 1966; past pres., mem. exec. bd. Inland Empire coun., region 11 exec. com. Boy Scouts Am.; past pres. Spokane Unltd.; mem. adv. coun. Sch. Bus., Gonzaga U.; bd. dirs., mem. exec. com. Expo '74 World's Fair; past mem. bd. regents Ft. Wright Coll., Spokane; past bd. dirs. Sacred Heart Med. Ctr.; past bd. regents Wash. State U.; bd. dirs. Fairmont Meml. Assn. Served to lt. (j.g.) USNR, 1943-45. Mem. Nat. Assn. Mut. Savs. Banks (chmn. 1976-77), Mut. Savs. Banks Assn. State of Wash. (pres. 1980), Am. Savs. and Loan Inst. (past gov. dist. XI), Spokane C. of C. (pres. 1974-75) Clubs: Rotary of Spokane, K.C. Roman Catholic. Home: 2804 E Deerwood Ct Spokane WA 99223

MCWILLIAMS, JOHN LAWRENCE, III, lawyer; b. Phila., Dec. 21, 1943; s. John Lawrence Jr. and Elizabeth Dolores (Chevalier) McW.; m. Paula Ann Root, July 19, 1969 (dec.); children: John Lawrence, IV, Robert Root, Anne Elizabeth, David Stanford, Peter Farrell; m. Kathleen Nolan Pradella, Apr./ 3, 1993. BS, St. Joseph's U., 1965; JD, Seton Hall U., 1969. Bar: N.J. 1969, N.Y. 1975, U.S. Supreme Ct. 1975, Fla. 1977. Trial atty., regional office SEC, N.Y.C., 1969-72; assoc. Mudge Rose Guthrie & Alexander, 1972-77; mem. Freeman, Richardson, Watson & Kelly, P.A., Jacksonville, Fla., 1977-89, chmn., pres., 1984-89; ptnr. Squire, Sanders & Dempsey, 1989-98, Livermore, Freeman & McWilliams, P.A., Jacksonville, 1998—. Trustee Mcpl. Svc. Dist. Ponte Vedra Beach, 1981-85, chmn. bd. trustees, 1984-85; treas. Ponte Vedra Cmty. Assn., 1980-82; mem. Leadership Jacksonville, 1981, mem. steering com., 1982; dir. Jacksonville Country Day Sch., 1985-87; pres. Jacksonville Beaches Ponte Vedra Unit Am. Cancer Soc., 1988-90; bd. dirs. Sawgrass Property Owners Assn., Inc., 2000-2002. Mem. Nat. Assn. Bond Lawyers, The Fla. Bar, Jacksonville C. of C. Clubs: Ponte Vedra, Sawgrass, River. Republican. Roman Catholic. Home: 3040 Timberlake Pt Ponte Vedra Beach FL 32082-3726 Office: Livermore Freeman & McWilliams PA 1301 Riverplace Blvd Ste 1825 Jacksonville FL 32207-9029

MCWILLIAMS, JOHN MICHAEL, lawyer; b. Annapolis, Md., Aug. 17, 1939; s. William J. and Helen (Disharon) McW.; m. Frances Edelen McCabe, May 30, 1970; children: M. Edelen, J. Michael Jr., James McC. BS, Georgetown U., 1964; LL.B., U. Md., 1967; LLD (hon.), U. Balt., 1993. Bar: Md. 1967, U.S. Supreme Ct. 1970, U.S. Ct. Internat. Trade 1991, U.S. Ct. Mil. Appeals 1992; cert. mediator NASD. Law clk. Chief Judge Roszel C. Thomsen, U.S. Dist. Ct. Md., 1967-68; assoc. Piper and Marbury, Balt., 1968-69; asst. atty. gen. State of Md., 1969-76; gen. counsel Md. Dept. Transp., 1971-76; sr. ptnr. Tydings and Rosenberg, Balt., 1977-97; pres. McWilliams Dispute Resolution, 1997—. Permanent mem. 4th Cir. Jud. Conf.; mem. panel of disting. neutrals CPR Inst. for Dispute Resolution, 1994—; mem. Md. Alt. Dispute Resolution Commn. Asst. editor Law Rev., U. Md., 1967; mem. nat. bd. advisors Ohio State Jour. Dispute Resolution. Chmn. Md. adv. coun. to Nat. Legal Svcs. Corp., 1975-78; mem. Gov.'s Commn. to Revise Annotated Code of Md., 1973-78; transition dir. Md. Gov.-Elect Harry Hughes, 1978-79; mem. Md. Indsl. Devel. Financing Authority, 1980; mem. Greater Balt. Com., 1979-94; mem. exec. com. Econ. Devel. Coun. Greater Balt., 1979-83; vice chmn. bd. Washington/Balt. Regional Assn., 1980-83; mem. Md. Econ. and Cmty. Devel. Adv. Commn., 1983-87; chmn. bd. Md. Econ. Devel. Corp., 1984-89. Served to 1st lt. U.S. Army, 1958-60. Fellow Am. Bar Found. (bd. dirs. 1986-88, 91-93), Internat. Acad. Mediators (v.p. 1998—), Coll. Comml. Arbitrators (sec. 2000—), Md. Bar Found. (dir. 1980-82); mem. ABA (pres. 1992-93, mem. ho. of dels. 1976—, chmn. 1986-88, chmn. Md. del. 1976-86, bd. editors jour. 1986-88, 91-93) Md. Bar Assn. (pres. 1981-82), Nat. Conf. Bar Pres. (exec. council 1982-85), Bar Assn. Balt. City, Am. Law Inst., Am. Judicature Soc. (dir. 1974-81, exec. com. 1975-77), Am. Acad. Judicature Edn. (dir. 1977), Md. Law Rev. (trustee 1980-83), Md. Inst. Continuing Edn. Lawyers (trustee 1980-83), Inst. Internat. Bus. Law and Practice (corr.), Md. Club, Rule Day Club. Democrat. Roman Catholic. Home: 3 Merryman Ct Baltimore MD 21210-2815 Office: 1106 N Charles St Ste 300 Baltimore MD 21201 E-mail: mcw@triallaw.com.

MCWILLIAMS, MICHAEL G. writer; b. Detroit, Aug. 28, 1952; s. Henry and Mary (Toarmina) McW. BA, Wayne State U., 1975; MFA, Columbia U., 1978. Free-lance writer Monthly Detroit mag., 1979-82, Village Voice, Rolling Stone, TV Guide, Advt. Age, N.Y. Daily News, L.A. Herald Examiner, N.Y.C., 1982-87; TV critic, 1988—. Author: TV Sirens, 1987, (with others) The Premiere Guide to Movies on Video, 1991. Recipient Assn. of Sunday and Feature Editors award, 1st pl. Arts Criticism, 1992. Mem. Phi Beta Kappa. Avocations: TV, movies, theater, music.

MCWILLIAMS, MIKE C. lawyer; b. Dallas, Nov. 10, 1948; s. Earl Dewitt and Mary Louise (Campbell) McW.; m. Sally Swatzell, Sept. 1, 1973; children: Michael, Matthew. BBA in Fin., U. Tex., 1969, JD, 1973. Bar: Tex. 1973. Assoc. Elliott, Meer, Vetter, Denton & Bates, Dallas, 1973-78; ptnr. Denton & Generis, 1978-80, Moore & Peterson, P.C., Dallas, 1980-89, Winstead, Sechrest & Minick, Dallas, 1989—. Editor: Texas International Law Journal, 1972-73. Mem. Tex. State Bar Assn., Dallas Bar Assn., Phi Delta Phi, Beta Gamma Sigma. Office: Winstead Sechrest & Minick 5400 Renaissance Tower 1201 Elm St Ste 5400 Dallas TX 75270-2199

MCWILLIAMS, ROBERT HUGH, federal judge; b. Salina, Kans., Apr. 27, 1916; s. Robert Hugh and Laura (Nicholson) McW.; m. Catherine Ann Cooper, Nov. 4, 1942 (dec.); 1 son, Edward Cooper; m. Joan Harcourt, Mar. 8, 1986. AB, U. Denver, 1938, LL.B., 1941. Bar: Colo. bar 1941. Colo. dist. judge, Denver, 1952-60; justice Colo. Supreme Ct., 1961-68, chief justice, 1969-70; judge U.S. Ct. Appeals (10th cir.). Denver, 1970—, now sr. judge. Served with AUS, World War II. Mem. Phi Beta Kappa, Omicron Delta Kappa, Phi Delta Phi, Kappa Sigma. Republican. Episcopalian. Home: 137 Jersey St Denver CO 80220-5918 Office: Byron White US Courthouse 1823 Stout St Rm 216 Denver CO 80257-1823

MCWILLIAMS, ROBERT LINDSAY, music educator, musician, conductor; b. Melbourne, Vic., Australia, July 31, 1957; came to U.S., 1991; s. Lindsay Frank and Peggy Irene (Cox) McW. BME, U. Melbourne, 1980; MMus, Fla. State U., 1993; PhD, U. Minn., 1996. Music tchr. Eltham Coll., Australia, 1980-86; prof. U. Melbourne, 1986-91; asst. prof. U. Wis., Oshkosh, 1996—. Keynote spkr. Australian Soc. of Music Educators, Brisbane, 1997, Queensland Band and Orch. Clinic, Brisbane, 1999; conductor Australian Wind Orch., 1991—, Musically Oustanding Students Wind Ensemble, Queensland, 1997, 99. Contbr. articles to profl. jours. Mem. Music Educators Nat. Conf., Coll. Band Dirs. Assn., Australian Band and Orch. Dirs. Assn., Wis. Music Educators Assn. Office: U Wis Oshkosh Music Dept 800 Algoma Blvd Oshkosh WI 54901-3551

MCWILLIAMS, SAMUEL ROBERT, secondary education educator; b. Wilkensburg, Pa., May 4, 1948; s. Paul Wigle and Elizabeth (Witman) McW.; m. Rita Mary Nock, July 31, 1983; 1 chld, Karla Marie. BA in Edn./Sci., W.Va. Wesleyan U., 1971; MA in Edn./Curriculum, Pa. State U., 1974; Ms in Microcomputers, U. Pitts., 1984. Cert. tchr., Pa.; cert. computer instr., Pa. Tchr. sci. and math. Penn-Trafford Schs., Harrison City, Pa., 1971—. Self-employed master of ceremonies and disc jockey, Level Green, Pa., 1967—. Mem. NEA (life), Alpha Psi Omega Nat. Dramatics Honorary (life), Penn-Trafford Edn. Assn., Pa. Edn. Assn., Pa. Sci. Tchrs. Assn., Bushy Run Lions Club, Psi Omega. Democrat. Presbyterian. Avocations: classic/antique autos, environmental issues, botany/gardening, discography. Home: 348 Meadowbrook Rd Level Green PA 15085-9712 Office: Penn-Trafford Sch Dist Mill St Harrison City PA 15636

MCWILLIAMS MORSE, ANNE WASHBURN, retired journalist, writer; b. Camp Hill, Ala., Mar. 22, 1929; d. Thomas Emmett and Johnnie Lou (Allen) Washburn; m. William David McWilliams, Sept. 25, 1955; m. Jerry Morse, Feb. 17, 2001. BA, Judson Coll., 1950; M in Religious Edn., Southwestern Bapt. Theol. Sem., Ft. Worth, 1954; MA, Miss. Coll., 1970. 4th grade tchr. Fairfax (Ala.) Pub. Sch., 1950-52; from editl. assoc. to assoc. editor The Bapt. Record, Jackson, Miss., 1953-92. Author: South of the Sahara, 1971, Beside the Point, 1967, rev. edit., 1989, Sent to Love, 1988, When Faith Triumphs, 1981. Chaplain Pilot Club, Jackson, Miss., 1968. Named Outstanding Alumna Judson Coll., 1984. Mem. Nat. Fedn. of Press Women, Miss. Media Profls. (historian 1996-99, State Communicator of Achievement award 1997). Avocations: travel, reading, walking. Home: 121 Waycross Court Jackson MS 39206 E-mail: annewmcw@aol.com.

MEACHAM, CHARLES HARDING, government official; b. Newman, Calif., Sept. 21, 1925; s. Vernon A. and Sara (Paulsen) M.; m. June Lorraine Yunker, June 22, 1946; children— Charles Paulsen, Bruce Herbert. BS, Utah State U., 1950. Biologist Calif. Dept. Fish and Game, 1950-56, Alaska Dept. Fisheries, 1956-59; regional supr. regions II and III Alaska Dept. Fish and Game, 1959-68; dir. internat. fisheries Office Gov. Alaska, 1968-69; commr. U.S. Fish and Wildlife Service, Dept. Interior, 1969-70, dep. asst. sec. for fish and wildlife, pks. and marine resources, commr. Internat. North Pacific Fisheries Commn. and Gt. Lakes Fishery Commn., 1969-70, commr. Internat. Pacific Salmon Fisheries Commn., 1969-70, commr. Great Lakes Fishery Commn., 1969-70, spl. asst. to area dir. Alaska, 1971-74; dir. internat. affairs Office of Gov., Juneau, 1975-80; pres. Meacham & Assocs., Anchorage, 1980—. Dep. commr. U.S. North Pacific Fur Seal Commn.; mem. Pacific and North Pacific Fisheries Mgmt. Councils, 1976-81; chmn. nat. park system adv. bd. U.S. Dept. Interior. Bd. dir. Resource Devel. Coun. for Alaska. With USMCR, 1943-46. Mem. Am. Fisheries Soc., Wildlife Soc., Pacific Fisheries Biologists, Internat. Assn. Game, Fish and Conservation Commrs., Ducks Unlimited, Alaska Miners Assn., Am. Legion. Clubs: Elks. Address: PO Box 428 Sequim WA 98382-0428 E-mail: cmeacham@olypen.com.

MEACHAM, CHARLES P. president, capital consulting; b. Susanville, Calif., Apr. 29, 1947; m. Charlene D. Heriot, 1969; 3 children. BS, Humboldt State U., 1969, MS in Fisheries, 1971. Comml. fisherman, Bristol Bay, Alaska, 1963-66; with Bumble Bee Seafoods, Bristol Bay, S.E. Alaska, 1967-69; fisheries cons. Winzler & Kelly Engring., Eureka, Calif., 1970; seafood insp. U.S. Army, Ft. Richardson, Alaska, 1971-74; staff biologist Alaska Dept. of Fish and Game, Juneau, 1974-75, rsch. biologist Artic Char investigations Dillingham, 1975-77, Bristol Bay rsch. project leader Anchorage, 1978-81, regional rsch. supr., 1981-89, mgr. fisher program Exxon Valdez oil spill impact assessment, 1990-91, dep. commr. Juneau, 1991-95; pres. Capital Consulting, 1995—. Affiliate faculty U. Alaska, 1983-87; mem. Bering Sea/Aleutians plan team N. Pacific Fisheries Mgmt. Coun., 1989, Alaska Regional Marine Rsch. Bd., 1992—, Pacific Fisheries Mgmt. Coun., 1991-95; commr. Pacific States Marine Fisheries Commn., 1991-95; presdl. appt. as commr. Pacific Salmon Commn., 1991-95. Mem. Mayor's Task Force on Fisheries, Anchorage, 1988-89, Alaska Tourism Coordinating Commn., 1992-95; mem. rev. team Alaska Sci. & Tech. Found., 1989; alt. mem. Exxon Valdez Oil Spill Trustee Coun., 1992-95; mem. adv. bd. Exxon Valdez Trustee Coun., 1997—, chmn. 2001—; bd. dirs. Prince William Sound Sci. Ctr., 1997—. Mem. NAS, OSB (fisheries com., 1992-95), Am. Fisheries Soc. (life, v.p. Alaska chpt. 1975, pres. elect 1977, pres. 1978, chair past pres. com. 1995-98), Am. Inst. of Fishery Rsch. Biologists. Home: 533 Main St Juneau AK 99801-1153 E-mail: ffcpm1@aurora.alaska.edu.

MEACHIN, DAVID JAMES PERCY, investment banker; b. Teignmouth, Devon, Eng., Jan. 1, 1941; came to U.S., 1969; s. James Alfred and Ena Annie Meachin; m. Barbara Marshall Maxwell, Sept. 25, 1971; children: Jonathan J.M., Philip D.M. BS in Phys. Sci., U. Natal, Republic of South Africa, 1960; BSChemE, U. Cape Town, Republic of South Africa, 1963; MS in Petroleum Engring., French Petroleum Inst., Paris, 1965; diploma in Indsl. Mgmt., Cambridge (Eng.) U., 1966; MBA with distinction, Harvard U., 1971. Project engr. Humphreys and Glasgow Ltd., London, 1966-69; 2nd v.p. investment banking Smith Barney and Co. Inc., N.Y.C. and Tokyo, 1971-75; v.p., gen. mgr. internat. corp. fin. Salomon Bros., N.Y.C. and London, 1975-81; mng. dir. investment banking divsn. Merrill Lynch Capital Markets, N.Y.C., 1981-91; chmn., CEO, Cross Border Enterprises L.L.C., 1991—; dir. Millennium Chemicals Inc. Bd. dirs. Millenium Chems. Inc. Past chmn. Brit. Am. Ednl. Found.; elder Brick Presbyn. Ch., N.Y.C., 1988—; bd. dirs., vice-chmn. U. Cape Town Fund, N.Y.C., 1985—. Mem. Misquamicut Club (bd. govs.), Hurlingham Club (U.K.), United Oxford and Cambridge Club (U.K.), Harvard Club, Union Club, Sky Club, Kelvin Grove Club (South Africa). Avocations: sailing, golf, tennis, squash. Home: 351 E 84th St New York NY 10028 Office: Cross Border Enterprises LLC 441 Lexington Ave New York NY 10017-3910

MEAD, CARL DAVID, retired educator; b. Cadiz, Ohio, May 4, 1913; s. Carl David and Neva Eloine (Walker) M.; m. Lillian Martha Felton, Apr. 15, 1938; children: Susan, Nancy. Student, Washington and Jefferson Coll., 1932-34; BS, Ohio State U., 1936, MA, 1938, PhD, 1947. Instr. English Denison U., 1938-39, Ohio State U., 1946-47; faculty Mich. State U., 1948-81, prof. English, 1957-81, head dept., 1959-66; Fulbright lectr. Philippines, 1964. Cons., chief univ. adv. group to U. Ryukyus, Okinawa, 1955-57 Author: Yankee Eloquence in the Middle West, 1951, (with others) Prentice-Hall Handbook for Writers, 1951, The American Scholar Today, 1970; Adv. editor: Dodd, Mead & Co, 1963-75; editor: Centennial Review, 1966-82. Served with AUS, 1943-46. Decorated Legion of Merit. Mem. MLA, Am. Studies Assn. Home: 1229 Glenmeadow Ln East Lansing MI 48823-2223 E-mail: mead2@pilot.msu.edu.

MEAD, CHRISTINA DYKSTRA, church administrator; BA, U. Wis., Madison; MS in Pub. Adminstrn., NYU. Exec. asst. to chief exec. for fin. N.Y.C. Health and Hosps. Corp.; exec. McKinsey & Co. Internat. Cons.; v.p. , CFO Reading is Fundamental; CFO Washington Nat. Cathedral, 2000—. Trustee Shipley Sch., Bryn Mawr, Pa., Campaign for Wis.; House of Ruth Washington, DC. Office: Washington Nat Cathedral Massachusetts & Wisconsin Aves NW Washington DC 20016-5098

MEAD, FRANK WALDRETH, taxonomic entomologist; b. Columbus, Ohio, June 11, 1922; s. Arlington Alfred and Edith May (Harrison) M.; widowed; children: David Harrison, Gregory Scott. BS, Ohio State U., 1947, MS, 1949; PhD, N.C. State U., 1968. Rsch. asst. dept. physiology Ohio State U., Woods Hole, Mass., summer 1941, rsch. asst. dept. entomology Columbus, 1948-50; Japanese beetle scout bur. entomology and plant quar. USDA, summer 1948, biol. aid bur. entomology and plant quar., 1950-53; entomologist div. plant industry Fla. Dept. Agr., Gainesville, 1953-58, 60, biologist IV, 1983-95, emeritus, 1995—; rsch. asst. N.C. State U., Raleigh, 1958-60; state survey entomologist Fed.-State Coop. Survey, Gainesville, 1969-80. Courtesy assoc. prof. dept. entomology U. Fla., Gainesville, 1973-95, emeritus, 1995—, Fla. A&M U., Tallahassee, 1977-95, emeritus, 1995—. Co-editor Tri-ology Technical Report; contbr. articles to profl. jours. Bd. dirs., treas. Alachua Audubon Soc., Gainesville, 1968-75, 77-82; bd. dirs. Alachua County Hist. Soc. (hon. lifetime mem. 1998), Gainesville, 1980-82; former mem. steering com. Civitan Regional Blood Bank, Gainesville, 1977-79; vol. photographer P.K. Yonge Devel. Rsch. Sch. U. Fla., Gainesville, 1978—; vol. Project Graduation, U. Fla., 1994—. Nominee Cmty. Svc. award, Gainesville Sun, 2002; named to Registry of Remembrances, Nat. World War II Meml.; recipient award, P.K. Yonge Devel. Rsch. Sch., 2001; fellow, Ohio Acad. Sci., 1966. Mem. VFW, Internat. Order of Merit, Cambridge, Entomol. Soc. Am. (bd. dirs. S.E. br. 1978-79), Ga. Entomol. Soc., Fla. Entomol. Soc. (hon., sec. 1968-82, Cert. of Appreciation 1975, 82, 91, Cert. of Merit 1986), Fla. Mosquito Control Assn., Entomol. Soc. Washington, Soc. Systematic Biologists, SAR (Benjamin Franklin chpt. Columbus, Ohio), The Am. Legion (life), Sierra Club, Fla. Track Club, Military Book Club. Avocations: photography, history, birding. Home: 2035 NE 6th Ter Gainesville FL 32609-3758 Office: Fla Dept Agr and Cons Svcs Divsn Plant Industry PO Box 147100 Gainesville FL 32614-7100

MEAD, JAMES MATTHEW, insurance company executive; b. Erie, Pa., June 10, 1945; s. James Leonard and Olga (Richter) M.; m. Rhoda Ginsburg, Sept. 2, 1967 (div. 1971); m. Elaine Margaret Lytle, Mar. 8, 1975. BS, Pa. State U., 1967, MA, 1970. Instr. bus. Pa. State U., Middletown, 1968-71; asst. to ins. commr. Commonwealth of Pa., Harrisburg, 1971-74; asst. to pres. Capital Blue Cross, 1974-78, sr. v.p., 1978-84, pres., CEO, 1984—. Bd. dirs. Blue Cross & Blue Shield Assn., Chgo., BCS Fin., Chgo., Greater Harrisburg Found.; bd. dirs. Fed. Res. Bank Phila., chmn. 1994-95; trustee Plan Investment Fund Contbr. articles on health care to profl. publs. Mem. bd. advisors Pa. State U., 1985-93; chmn. savs. bond campaign for Ctrl. Pa., U.S. Treasury Dept., Harrisburg, 1986-87; bd. dirs. United Way Capital Region, 1994-98, campaign chair, 1994; bd. dirs. Harrisburg Symphony Soc., 2000—. Paul Harris fellow Rotary Internat., 1988, Alumni fellow Pa. State U., 1986. Mem. Capital Region C. of C. (bd. dirs., treas. 1987-90), Country Club of Harrisburg, Blue Ridge Country Club. Home: 1752 Conway Heath Camp Hill PA 17011 E-mail: j.mead@capbluecross.com.

MEAD, JOHN MILTON, banker; b. Schenectady, Oct. 26, 1924; s. Milton Samuel and Jane (Drake) M.; m. Marguerite Ann Stone, Jan. 3, 1948; children: Ann Elizabeth, Jane Stone, Mary Ames. BS, U. Mo., 1950; postgrad., U. Wis., 1963-65. Auditor Schenectady Trust Co., 1950-51; v.p., auditor First Trust & Deposit Co., Syracuse, N.Y., 1955-77; v.p., compliance officer Key Corp., Albany, 1977-86, ret., 1986. Served with USAAF, 1943-46; Served with USAF, 1951-55. Mem. Inst. Internal Auditors (past pres. Central N.Y. chpt.), Am. Legion (past post comdr.) Clubs: Marcellus Optimist (past pres.), Glens Falls Country. Republican. Presbyterian. Home: 27 Yorkshire Dr Queensbury NY 12804-8620

MEAD, JOHN STANLEY, university administrator; b. Indpls., Dec. 9, 1953; s. Judson and Jane Mead; m. Virginia Potter, Aug. 11, 1979; children: Christopher, Carolyn. BA, Ind. U., 1976; JD, U. Ill., 1979. Bar: Ill. Staff atty. Ill. Energy Resources Commn., Springfield, 1979-82, staff dir., 1982-85; mgr. coal rsch. Ill. Dept. Energy Natural Resources, 1985-87, dir. office of coal devel. and mktg., 1987-89; dir. coal rsch. ctr. So. Ill. U., Carbondale, 1989—, assoc. dean Grad. Sch., 1996—. Bd. dirs. Mid-West Univ. Energy Consortium Inc., Chgo.; mem., past chair Ill. Clean Coal Inst., 1986—. Mem. Ill. Bd. Natural Resources and Conservation, 1997—, sec., 2000—; mem. dist. com., scoutmaster Boy Scouts Am. Recipient gold medal Tech. Univ. Ostrava, Czech Republic, 1992, Georgius Agricola medal, 1994. Mem. Am. Radio Relay League, Ill. State Bar Assn., Carbondale Rotary Breakfast (pres. 2000-2001). Lutheran. Home: 78 Magnolia Ln Carbondale IL 62901-7665 Office: So Ill U Coal Rsch Ctr Mail Code 4623 Carbondale IL 62901 E-mail: jmead@siu.edu.

MEAD, KATHRYN NADIA, astrophysicist, educator; b. Jacksonville, Fla., Aug. 6, 1959; d. Charles A. Mead and Nadia L. Mead. BS in Physics, Rensselaer Poly. Inst., 1981, MS in Physics, 1983, PhD in Physics, 1986. Cooperative rsch. assoc. Naval Rsch. Lab., Washington, 1986-88; adj. asst. prof. Union Coll., Schenectady, N.Y., 1988-90, vis. asst. prof., 1990-93. Vis. sci. Nat. Radio Astronomy Obs., 1994-975 Mem. bd. visitors Bolles Sch., Jacksonville Fla. Recipient Career Devel. award Dudley Observatory, 1990, Faculty Rsch. Fund award Union Coll., 1990, 92, award Fund for Astrophysical Rsch., 1992. Mem. AAUW, Am. Astron. Soc. (editor Status 1995-98, Gaposchkins Rsch. Fund award 1991), Assn. for Women in Sci. (pres. So. Ariz. chpt. 1997), Sigma Xi, Sigma Pi Sigma. Achievements include discovery of the existence of molecular clouds and star formation much farther from the center of the Milky Way than previously known; research on molecular clouds and star formations outside the solar circle in our Galaxy, broad CO line wings near T-Tauri stars, the origin and structure of isolated dark globules, high resolution studies of the HII region/molecular cloud interface in NGC1977.

MEAD, KENNETH MINOR, federal agency administrator; b. May 14, 1947; m. Elizabeth Guerry; children: Jennifer, Hillary. Baccalaurette Degree, So. Conn. U., 1970; JD, U. S.C., 1975; John F. Kennedy Sch. Sr. Mgrs. in Govt., Harvard U., 1991. Sr. atty. Office Gen. Counsel U.S. Gen. Acctg. Office, Washington, 1975-82, asst. dir. Office Quality Assurance, 1982-86, assoc., asst. dir. transp., dir. transp. & telecom. issues, 1986-96, dep. asst. comptr. gen. for policy, 1996-97; inspector gen. U.S. Dept. Transp., 1997—. Mem. Pres. Coun. on Integrity and Efficiency, 1997—, Comptr. Gen.'s U.S. Domestic Accountability Bd., 2001—. With USN, 1970-72. Mem. Am. Numismatic Assn., D.C. Bar Assn. Office: Dept Transp 400 7th St SW Washington DC 20590-0003*

MEAD, LAWRENCE MYERS, JR. retired aerospace executive; b. Plainfield, N.J., May 11, 1918; s. Lawrence Myers and Eleanor Whitman (Machado) M.; m. Janet Chase, Feb. 21, 1942; children— Lawrence Myers, Kirtland Chase, Jonathan Taylor, Bradford Machado. BSE., Princeton U., 1940, C.E., 1941; postgrad. mgmt., Harvard Bus. Sch., 1964. With Grumman Corp., Bethpage, N.Y., 1941-93; v.p. tech. ops. Grumman Aerospace Corp., 1972-75, sr. v.p. dept. ops., 1975-81, sr. v.p. tech. ops., 1981-83; sr. mgmt. cons., 1983-93. Patentee in field. Trustee, police commr., dep. mayor Village of Huntington Bay, N.Y., 1975-80; trustee N.Y.C. Hall of Sci. Fellow Poly. U., 1981. Fellow AIAA; mem. NAE, L.I. Forum on Tech. (bd. dirs., past chmn. bd.), Soc. Logistic Engrs., Soc. Advancement Materials and Process Engring., Princeton U. Alumni Assn. Democrat. Achievements include designing A6A Intruder Navy All Weather Bomber, Gulfstream III Exec. Jet Transport. Home: 88 Notch Hill Rd Apt 253 North Branford CT 06471-1851 E-mail: lmmead@aol.com.

MEAD, LAWRENCE MYERS, III, political science educator; b. Huntington, N.Y., June 9, 1943; s. Lawrence Myers Jr. and Janet (Chase) M.; m. Robin Elizabeth Brady, May 11, 1996. BA, Amherst Coll., 1966; MA, Harvard U., 1968, PhD, 1973. Mgmt. intern HEW, Washington, 1973-75; rsch. assoc.

Urban Inst., 1975-78; dep. rsch. dir. Rep. Nat. Com., 1978-79; prof. politics NYU, 1979—. Vis. prof. U. Wis., Madison, spring 1987, Harvard U., Cambridge, Mass., 1993-94, Princeton (N.J.) U., 1994-95; vis. scholar Hoover Instn., Stanford, Calif., 1988; vis. fellow Princeton (N.J.) U., 1995-96. Author: Beyond Entitlement, 1986, The New Politics of Poverty, 1992; author, editor: The New Paternalism, 1997; co-author: From Welfare to Work, 199. Adviser on welfare policy Rudolph Giuliani Mayoral Campaigns, N.Y.C., 1993, 97, Reagan Adminstrn., Washington, 1986-87, State of Wis., Madison, 1996—, Human Resources Adminstrn., N.Y.C., 1997—. Fulbright scholar, 1970. Mem. Am. Polit. Sci. Assn. (coun. pub. policy sect. 2000—), Assn. for Pub. Policy Analysis and Mgmt. (conf. com. 1987, 96, 98), Policy Studies Orgn., Am. Soc. for Polit. and Legal Philosophy. Republican. Avocations: sailing, crossword puzzles. E-mail: llm1&nyu.edu. Office: NYU Dept Politics 715 Broadway New York NY 10003 E-mail: LLM1@nyu.edu.

MEAD, LINDA MCCULLOUGH, secondary education educator, adult education specialist; b. Lubbock, Tex., May 15, 1946; d. Hugh Davenport and Maxine (Fry) McCullough; children: Richards Mead III, Erin Kate Mead. BS, U. Tex., 1968; MEd, No. Ariz. U., 1998. Cert. secondary tchr., Tex., Calif., Ariz.; cert. trainer Nat. Ctr. Family Literacy. Torchbearer U.S. Olympics, Phoenix, 1996. Mem. ASCD, TESOL, Ariz. Assn. Lifelong Learning, Kappa Kappa Gamma. Democrat. Methodist. Avocations: swimming, reading, movies. Office: Mesa Pub Schs 549 N Stapley Dr Mesa AZ 85203-7203 E-mail: lmead@mpsaz.org.

MEAD, MILLARD WILMER, retired minister; b. Cherry Valley, Ohio, May 27, 1930; s. Myrlen Lomas and Winifred Irene (Mills) M.; m. Janet Wilma Hummell, Aug. 7, 1948 (dec. Sept. 1994); children: Jacqueline Mead Doyle, David, Susan Mead Dyer; m. Marilyn Mae Kiess, July 8, 1995. BS, Kent State U., 1970; MDiv, Meth. Sch. Theology, 1973. Ordained to ministry United Meth. Ch., 1974. Pastor Johnston Federated United Meth. Ch., Cortland, Ohio, 1963-75, Grace United Meth. Ch., Bucyrus, 1975-84, St. Mark Ch., Galion, 1984-92; ret., 1992. Dist. sec. United Meth. Ch., 1974-75, mem. conf. coun. on ministry, 1973-76, 80-84, dist. coun. ministry, 1974; mem. East Ohio Conf. Archives and History, 1976-2001, sec. commn., 1976-84; mem. East Ohio Conf. Historian, 1984-88; East Ohio del. United Meth. Conf., Hawaii, 1981, World Meth. Camp Meeting, Ocean Grove, N.J., 1984; pres. North Cen. Jurisdiction Archives and History, 1984-88. Mem. adv. coun. agr. Trumbull County, Ohio, 1968-75, Commn. on Aging, 1973-75; chmn. svc. unit Salvation Army, Cortland, 1973-75; trustee Flat Rock Children's Home, 1975-93, pres. bd. trustees, 1989-93; trustee, pres. bd. trustees North Shore Retirement Home, 1992—. Recipient Young Farmers award Dairyman's Coop. Sales Assn., 1962, Nat. Hwy. Safety award, 1975, Trustee of Yr. award U. Meth. Assn. Health and Welfare Ministries, 1996. Mem. Coun. on Ministries, Gen. Conf. Archives and History, East Ohio Conf. Town and Country Fellowship, United Meth. Hist. Soc. (charter, treas. 1997—), United Meth. Hist. Soc. Ohio (life, past v.p., pres., treas.-sec.), Grange Club (master 1955-65), Masons (coun.). Address: 212 Erie Beach Rd Lakeside OH 43440-1305

MEAD, NANCY ROSE, software engineer; b. Englewood, N.J., Jan. 16, 1942; d. Stephen Robert and Lucy Adelaide (Pastor) Gardiner; m. John L. Hall, Apr. 23, 1966 (div. 1971); m. Elwood Howard Mead, June 6, 1987. BA, NYU, 1963, MS, 1967; PhD, Poly. Inst. N.Y., 1983. Programmer Chase Manhattan Bank, N.Y.C., 1965-66; sr. mem. tech. staff IBM, Boulder, Colo., 1966-90, Software Engring. Inst., Pitts., 1990—. Adv. bd. MSE program Monmouth U., 1997-2000, Embry-Riddle Aero. U., 1997-2000. Software category editor: ACM Computing Revs., 1992-98; mem. editl. bd. Annals Software Engring., 1997—. Mem. Edn. Com. Software Patent Inst., Steering Com. Eire Ctr. Tchg. Computing, 1994-99, Internat. Conf. Requirements Engring., 1996—, chair, 2000—. NSF grantee, N.Y.C., 1971. Mem. IEEE (sr., mem. editl. bd. 1995—), Assn. Computing Machinery. Avocations: dancing, cooking, golfing. Office: Software Engring Inst 5000 Forbes Ave Pittsburgh PA 15213-3815

MEAD, PHILIP BARTLETT, healthcare administrator, obstetrician, educator; b. Poughkeepsie, N.Y., June 23, 1937; s. Ralph Allen and Altina (Gervin) Mead; m. Ann Elaine Smith, June 27, 1964; children: Ralph Allen II, David Smith. BA, Hamilton Coll., 1959; MD, Cornell U., 1963. Diplomate Nat. Bd. Med. Examiners, Am. Bd. Ob-gyn. Intern in medicine Bellevue Hosp., N.Y.C., 1963-64; resident in ob-gyn. N.Y. Hosp./Cornell Med. Ctr., 1964-69; asst. prof. U. Vt. Coll. Medicine, Burlington, 1971-76, assoc. prof., 1976-81, prof., 1981—2001, prof. emeritus, 2001—; hosp. epidemiologist Med. Ctr. Hosp. of Vt., 1984-93; dir. clin. sys. Vt. Acad. Med. Ctr., 1993-95; sr. v.p., med. dir. Fletcher Allen Health Care, 1995-97; prof., chmn. ob-gyn. U. Vt. Coll. Medicine, 1997—2001, prof. and chmn. emeritus, 2001—; physician leader women's health care svcs. Fletcher Allen Health Care, Burlington, 1997—2001. Lt. comdr. M.C. USN, 1969—71. Fellow: ACOG, Infectious Disease Soc. Am.; mem.: Soc. Hosp. Epidemiologists, Infectious Disease Soc. Ob-Gyn. (pres. 1987—88), Phi Beta Kappa, Alpha Omega Alpha. Home: 203 Pinehurst Dr Shelburne VT 05482-6882 Office: Fletcher Allen Health Care 111 Colchester Ave Burlington VT 05401-1416 E-mail: PBMeadMD@aol.com.

MEAD, PHILOMENA, mental health nurse; b. Yonkers, N.Y., June 23, 1934; d. Alfonso F. and Jennie (Saltarelli) D'Amato; m. Kenneth Mead, Nov. 10, 1956; children: Scott Kenneth, Jeanne Bette. RN, St. Vincents Hosp., Bridgeport, Conn., 1955; BS in Psychology, Sacred Heart U., 1980; cert. in nursing mgmt., Fairfield U., 1988. Cert. psychiat. mental health nurse, nursing specialist, nat. chem. dependency nurse, CPR. Day supr.-relief, night supr. Hall Brooke Hosp., Westport, Conn., 1956-58, day supr., asst. dir. nurses, 1958-66, evening supr.-relief, 1967-68, team nurse, 1974-83, coord. nursing care, 1983-86, adminstrv. coord., 1986-87, nursing care coord. substance abuse treatment unit, 1987-91; charge evening nurse Carolton Hosp., Fairfield, 1971-73; nurse psychiat. emergency rm. and brief treatment unit West Haven (Conn.) VA, 1991—, mem. staff psychiat. emergency rm., 1995-97, ret., 1997. Roman Catholic. Avocation: genealogy. Home: 67 Adams Rd Fairfield CT 06430-3018

MEAD, WALTER RUSSELL, editor, foreign policy organization fellow; b. June 12, 1959; s. Loren Benjamin and Polly Ayers Mead. BA in English, Yale U., 1976. Chief writer Cuomo Commn. on Competetiveness and Trade, N.Y.C., 1987-88; contbg. editor L.A. Times, 1991—, Worth Mag., N.Y.C., 1993-96, sr. contbg. editor, 1996—; pres.'s fellow World Policy Inst., New Sch. U., 1994-97; sr. fellow U.S. fgn. policy Coun. on Fgn. Rels., 1997—. Author: Mortal Splendor, 1987, Special Providence, 2001; chief staff writer: U.S.-Cuban Relations in the 21st Century: Report of an Independent Task Force Council on Foreign Relations, 1999; contbr. articles to profl. jours. Bd. dirs. New Am. Found., Washington, Arca Found., Washington. Finalist L.A. Times Book award, 1986, finalist for essays and commentary Nat. Mag. awards, 1998; fellow Breadloaf Writers' Conf., 1987; recipient NYU Olive Br. award, 1993. Fellow Fgn. Policy Assn. (hon.); mem. Author's Guild, Coun. Fgn. Rels. Office: Coun on Fgn Rels 58 E 68th St New York NY 10021-5953

MEAD, WILLIAM CHARLES, physicist; b. Hazleton, Pa., Dec. 6, 1946; s. Norman Joseph and Ruth Crawford Mead; m. Carol Edna Jerome, May 24, 1969; children: Bennett R. BS, Syracuse U., Syracuse, NY, 1968; MA, Princeton U., Princeton, NJ, 1970, PhD, 1974. Physicist Lawrence Livermore Nat. Lab., 1973—83; physicist, mgr. Los Alamos Nat. Lab., 1983—94; pres., chief scientist Adaptive Network Solutions Rsch. Inc., 1995—. Cons. Lawrence Livermore Nat. Laboratories, Livermore, Calif., 1995—99, Impulse Devices Inc., Grass Valley, Calif., 1999—, Complexica Inc., Sant Fe, N.Mex., 1999—. Contbr. articles to profl. jours. Second lt. USAF, 1973—73. Fellow: Am. Phys. Soc. (fellowship 1987); mem.: Internat. Neural Network Soc. Achievements include first to Lead designer for Cairn 50X Intermediate density target, the first laser-driven target to achieve compression of DT to 10 g/cc and a major milestone of the Inertial Confinement Fusion Program; research in Tested and extended the understanding of ICF physics, providing ideas, simulations and guidance for many important and successful laser-plasma coupling experiments; Performed numerical simulations extending knowledge in areas such as the behavior of fluid instabilities in high-grain ICF pellets and the scaling of laser-driven ablation; first to Developed teh Connectionist Hyperprism Classification network to perform task of automated ion mobility spectrum analysis; development of Adaptive Teaching and Learning Laboratory and an Adaptive Tutor for teaching basic arithmetic facts; research in Assisted LLNL in testing and validating ICF3D and KULL, 3D hydrocodes under development; design of C+ engine for Agent-Based Crisis Simulator; research in Principal Investigator for theoretical and computational effort to explore feasibility of Sonic-Cavitation-Driven Fusion. Avocations: classical music, classical music. Office: Adaptive Network Solutions Research 10 Bonito Pl Los Alamos NM 87544 E-mail: wcm@ansr.com.

MEADE, ANGELA KAYE, special education educator; b. Bryon, Ohio, Mar. 14, 1969; d. Douglas MacAuther and Thelma Judy (Williams) Smith; m. Steven Andrew Meade, June 1, 1991; 1 child, Alexander Jefferson. AA in Edn. summa cum laude, AA in Gen. Studies, S.W. Va. C.C., 1989; BA in English with distinction, M Tchg. in Spl. Edn., U. Va., 1992. Cert. K-12 tchr. learning disabilities and mental retardation, Va. Tchr. spl. edn. Newport News (Va.) Pub. Schs., 1992—. Yearbook sponsor Newport News (Va.) Pub. Schs., 1992—, implemented collaborative tchg. program, 1994—, writing lead tchr., 1998—; counselor Summer Youth Program, Lebanon and Richmond, Va., 1993-94. Organizer Spl. Olympics Va., Newport News, 1993-94. Mem. ASCD, Internat. Reading Coun., Newport News Reading Coun. (co-chmn. banquet 1993-95).. Avocations: reading, writing. Office: Woodside HS 13456 Woodside Ln Newport News VA 23608-1809 E-mail: akm69@aol.com.

MEADE, CARL J. b. Chanute AFB, Ill., Nov. 16, 1950;

MEADE, DALE MICHAEL, experimental physicist; b. Lodi, Wis., Aug. 7, 1939; children: Loretta, Carla Fleming. BS with high honors in Elec. Engring., U. Wis., 1961, MS in Physics, 1962, PhD in Physics, 1965. Asst. prof. physics U. Wis., Madison, 1967-69, assoc. prof., 1969-72, prof., 1972-74; head FM-1 Princeton (N.J.) Plasma Physics Lab., 1973, head PDX Ops., 1975-80, head exptl. divsn. rsch. dept., head TFTR rsch. program, 1980-82, head exptl. divsn., head TFTR rsch. ops. divsn., 1982-86, head exptl. physics rsch. dept., head TFTR project, 1986-91, dep. dir., 1991-97, head advanced fusion concepts, 1997—. Recipient Disting. Svc. Citation U. Wis. Coll. Engring., Madison, 1990, Disting. Assoc. award U.S. Dept. Energy, Washington, 1994, Leadership award Fusion Power Assocs., 1999; Disting. Alumni fellow physics dept. U. Wis., 2002. Fellow Am. Phys. Soc.; mem. AAAS. Office: Princeton U Plasma Physics Lab PO Box 451 US Rt 1 N Princeton NJ 08543 E-mail: dmeade@pppl.gov.

MEADE, DOROTHY WINIFRED, retired educational administrator; b. N.Y.C., Jan. 26, 1935; d. Percival and Fraulien Franklin; m. Gerald H. Meade (div. 1987); 1 child, Myrla E. BA in Am. History, Queens Coll., Flushing, N.Y., 1970; MA in Corrective Reading, Bklyn. Coll., 1975; BA in Religious Edn., United Christian Coll., Bklyn., 1980; postgrad., Bklyn. Coll., 1984. Tchr. social studies cluster Pub. Sch. 137, Bklyn., 1979-83, curriculum coord. Follow Through Program, 1984-88, adminstrv. intern, 1983-84; staff developer social studies Cen. Sch. Dist. 23, 1988-89, dist. coord. Project Child, 1989-91. Mem. faculty Coll. of New Rochelle, Bklyn., 1994-97; mem. coop. bd. dirs. 1053 E 13th St., Bklyn. Participant Crossroads Africa, 1958; active Agape Tabernack Internat. Fellowship, 2000; former mem. Ch. of the Master; theol. intern Mt. Lebanon Bapt. Ch., 2001. Mem. African Christian Tchrs., N.Y. Pub. Sch. Early Childhood Edn., N.Y. Geography Inst., Women Organizing, Mobilizing, Bldg. Pentecostal. Avocations: bicycling, swimming, roller skating, singing, traveling. Home: 538 E 86th St Brooklyn NY 11236

MEADE, KENNETH ALBERT, retired minister; b. Sweet Valley, Pa., June 14, 1935; s. Delbert H. and Dorothea I. (Myers) M.; m. Jeanette H. Quigley, Dec. 18, 1954 ; children: Jane M. Meade Ulm, Mark K. Ministerial cert., Ea. Christian Inst., East Orange, N.J., 1955; DD (hon.), Milligan Coll., Tenn., 1986, Ea. Christian Coll., Bel Air, Md., 1986. Ordained to ministry Ch. of Christ, 1955. Student min. Ch. of Christ, Bklyn. and Greenpoint, N.Y., 1952-53; mem. Meade-Bennett Evangelistic Team, East Orange, 1953-55; sr. min. Ch. of Christ at Manor Woods, Rockville, Md., 1956—2001; amb. for Christ, Ch. of Christ at Mann Woods, 2001—. Pres. N.Am. Christian Conv., Cin., 1986, Ea. Christian Conv., Rockville, 1969, 74, 82; mem. Chaplaincy Endorsement Commn.; sec. Polish Christian Ministries, Bel Air, Md. Contbr. numerous articles to religion mags. Recipient Award of Honor, Am. Legion, 1952, Highest Comml. award Lehman High Sch. Alumni Assn., 1952.

MEADE, KENNETH JOHN, realty company owner, broker; b. N.Y.C., Nov. 25, 1925; s. John Joseph and Blanche (Woodworth) M.; m. Alice Elizabeth (Steinmann), Nov. 8, 1952; children: Steven, Janet, Patricia. Student, N.Y. Inst. Fin., 1960-62. Cert. real estate residential broker. Sales broker Del Webb Devel., Sun City, Ariz., 1974-82; mgr. Mull Realty Inc., 1982-83; broker, owner 6 offices Ken Meade Realty Inc., 1983—. Dir., treas. Sun City Bd. Realtors, 1988—. Bd. dirs., v.p. Sun City Ambs., 1988—. With USN, 1942-45. Mem. Nat. Assn. Realtors, Ariz. Assn. Realtors, Dale Carnegie Club (past instr. sales course, Outstanding Achievment 1964). Republican. Lutheran. Avocations: stock market technics, charts, sales psychology. Home: 13306 W Meeker Blvd Sun City West AZ 85375-3815 Office: Ken Meade Realty Inc 16991 N Boswell Blvd Sun City AZ 85351-1281

MEADE, MARION, author; b. Pitts., Jan. 7, 1934; d. Surain S. and Mary Elizabeth (Homoney) Sidhu; m. Charles F. Meade, 1952 (div. 1956); m. Forbes Linkhorn, 1960 (div. 1971); 1 child, Alison Linkhorn Sprague. BS, Northwestern U., 1955; MS in Journalism, Columbia U., 1956. Author: Bitching, 1973, Free Woman: The Life and Times of Victoria Woodhull, 1976, Eleanor of Aquitaine: A Biography, 1977, Stealing Heaven: The Love Story of Heloise and Abelard, 1979, Madame Blavatsky: The Woman Behind the Myth, 1980, Sybille, 1983, Dorothy Parker: What Fresh Hell Is This?, 1988, Buster Keaton: Cut to the Chase, 1995, The Unruly Life of Woody Allen: A Biography, 2000, TimeOut Book of New York Walks, 2000; contbr. N.Y. Times, New Republic, Nation, McCall's, Ms. Mag., Village Voice, Aphra, off our backs, Balt. Sun, Brill's Content, others. Mem. Authors Guild, Nat. Arts Club, Biography Seminar of NYU. Home and Office: 801 West End Ave New York NY 10025-5368 E-mail: mmeade@mindspring.com.

MEADE, PATRICIA SUE, marketing professional; b. Columbus, Ohio, Mar. 14, 1960; d. Harold Eugene and Glenna Rhae (Croaff) M. BS in Communications, Ohio U., 1982, M in Sports Administrn., 1984, MS in Communications, 1986. Dir. advt. The Pensacola (Fla.) Civic Ctr., 1984-85; asst. dir. mktg. Ohio Ctr. Co., Columbus, 1985-86; asst. v.p. mktg. Doctors Hosp., 1986-88; regional mgr. mktg. Jacobs, Visconsi & Jacobs Co., Cleve., 1988-89; dir. bus. devel. and pub. affairs Deaconess Hosp., 1989-91; div. head mktg. and pub. affairs Lake Metroparks, Concord Township, Ohio, 1991-93; sr. health care cons. Cohen & Co., Cleve., 1993-95; pres. Creative Works, Inc., 1995—. Trustee Cleve. Mus. Art, Cleve. Bot. Garden. Mem. Am. Mktg. Assn., New Orgn. Visual Artists, Ctr. for Contemporary Art, Cleve. Mus. Art, Edison Biotech. Ctr. Avocations: traveling, fitness, cartooning. Office: Creative Works Inc 12195 Coit Rd Cleveland OH 44108-1101 E-mail: cre8vewrk@aol.com.

MEADE, THOMAS CHARLES, employee benefits executive; b. Detroit, Jan. 23, 1963; s. George Charles and Cynthia Dawn (Styles) M.; m. Becky Sue Smith, Oct. 15, 1988; children: Christopher Charles, Corinne Marie. BS, Oakland U., 1986. CFP. Agt., registered rep. The Equitable of N.Y., Troy, Mich., 1987-89; field rep., registered rep. The Guardian, Southfield, 1989-92; ptnr. Fin. Network Svcs., Sterling Heights, 1991—; v.p. employee benefits Simplified Employment Svc., 1991—, v.p. customer satisfaction, 1995—. Pres.'s adv. coun. Am. Med. Security, Farmington Hills, 1993—. Author (newsletter) Bits N Pieces, 1993. Del. Rep. Party, Warren, Mich., 1988; sustaining mem. Rep. Nat. Com., Macomb, Mich., 1992—; active mem. Hands That Help, Farmington Hills, 1993—. Named one of Top Ten Producer, Am. Med. Security, 1991, 92, 93, 94; recipient Assoc. Silver key Am. Family Life, 1992, Eagle award #1 Sales in Territory, Am. Family Life, 1992, Fireball Triple Crown award Am. Family Life, 1993. Mem. Nat. Assn. Health Underwriters, Mich. Food and Beverage Assn., Mich. Bus. and Profl. Assn. Republican. Avocations: softball, sports memorabilia, biking, fishing, Sunday sch. tchr. Home: 46175 Windsor Ct Macomb MI 48044-3523

MEADER, JOHN DANIEL, judge; b. Ballston Spa, N.Y., Oct. 22, 1931; s. Jerome Clement and Doris Luella (Conner) M.; m. Joyce Margaret Cowin, Mar. 2, 1963; children: John Daniel Jr., Julia Rae, Keith Alan. BA, Yale U., 1954; JD, Cornell U., 1962. Bar: N.Y. 1963, U.S. Dist. Ct. (no. dist.) N.Y. 1963, U.S. Ct. Appeals (2d cir.) 1966, U.S. Supreme Ct. 1967, U.S. Ct. Mil. Appeals 1973, Ohio 1978, U.S. Dist. Ct. (no. dist.) Ohio 1979, Fla. 1983, U.S. Ct. Appeals (4th cir.) 1992, U.S. Ct. Appeals (fed. cir.) 1993. Sales engr. Albany (N.Y.) Internat. Corp., 1954-59; asst. track coach Cornell U., 1959-62; asst. sec., asst. to pres. Albany Internat. Corp., 1962-65; asst. atty. gen. State of N.Y., Albany, 1965-68; ops. counsel, attesting sec. GE, Schenectady, 1968-77; gen. counsel, asst. sec. Glidden div. SCM Corp., Cleve., 1977-81; chmn. bd., pres. Applied Power Tech. Co., Fernandina Beach, Fla., 1981-84; pres. Applied Energy, Inc., Ballston Spa, 1984-88; judge N.Y. State Workers Compensation Bd., Albany, 1988—. Dir. Saratoga Mut. Fire Ins. Co. Author: Labor Law Manual, 1972, Contract Law Manual, 1974, Patent Law Manual, 1978. Candidate U.S. Ho. of Reps., 29th Dist. N.Y., 1964, N.Y. Supreme Ct., 1975, 87, 93. Col. JAGC, USAR, 1968—, dep. staff judge adv. 3d U.S. Army & Cen. Command, 1984. Nat. AAU High Sch. 1000 Yard Indoor Track Champion, 1949, Nat. AAU Prep. Sch. 440 and 880 Yard Indoor Track Champion, 1950, Nat. AAU Outstanding Performer award, Melrose Games Assn., 1950, Heptagonal Track 880-Yard Champion 1954. Mem. ABA, N.Y. State Bar Assn., Fla. Bar, Amelia Island Plantation Club, Cyprus Temple Club, Yale Club Jacksonville (pres.), Masons. Republican. Presbyterian. Home: 271 Round Lake Rd Ballston Lake NY 12019-1714 Office: NY State Workers Compensation Bd 100 Broadway Albany NY 12241-0001 E-mail: john.meader@wcb.state.ny.us.

MEADOR, CHARLES LAWRENCE, management and systems consultant, educator; b. Dallas, Oct. 7, 1946; s. Charles Leon and Dorothy Margaret (Brown), m. Diane E. Collins, May 18, 1985. BSME with honors, U. Tex., 1970; MSME, MS in Mgmt., MIT, 1972. Engring. staff Union Carbide Corp., Houston, 1967-68; instr. Alfred P. Sloan Sch. Mgmt. MIT, Cambridge, 1972-75, asst. dir. Ctr. Info. Systems Rsch., 1976-78, lectr. Sch. Engring., co-dir. Macro-Engring. Rsch. Group, 1978-99. Founder, pres. Decision Support Tech., Inc., 1974-92; co-founder, vice-chmn., dir. Software Productivity Rsch., Inc., 1985-87; pres., dir. The Softbridge Group, 1989-92; founder, CEO, Mgmt. Support Tech. Corp., 1992-99; sr. v.p., chief info. officer CIGNA Property and Casualty, 1995-98; vice-chmn., dir. Condor Tech. Solutions, Inc., 1998—; co-founder, chmn., dir. Clinician Support Tech., Inc., 1999—; commr. Nat. Imagery and Mapping Agy., 2000-2001; mem. Def. Sci. Bd. Task Force, 2001. Editor: How Big and Still Beautiful? Macro-Engineering Revisited, 1980, Macro-Engineering: The Rich Potential, 1981, Macro-Engineering and the Future: A Management Perspective, 1982, Macro-Engineering: Global Infrastructure Solutions, 1992, Macro-Engineering: MIT Brunel Lectures on Global Infrastructure, 1997; mem. editorial bd. Computer Comm., 1979-91; contbr. articles to profl. jours. NSF trainee, 1970; MIT Wilfred Lewis fellow, 1971, Draper Lab. fellow, 1974. Mem. Computer Soc. IEEE (vice-chmn. Ea. Hemisphere and Latin Am. area com. 1977-83), Am. Soc. for Macro-Engring. (bd. dirs. 1992-96), Cosmos Club, St. Botolph's Club, Sigma Xi, Tau Beta Pi, Pi Tau Sigma. Home: 3 Windy Hill Ln Wayland MA 01778-2612 Office: Clinician Support Tech Inc 3 Speen St Framingham MA 01701-4679

MEADOR, DANIEL JOHN, law educator; b. Selma, Ala., Dec. 7, 1926; s. Daniel John and Mabel (Kirkpatrick) M.; m. Janet Caroline Heilmann, Nov. 19, 1955; children: Janet Barrie, Anna Kirkpatrick, Daniel John. BS, Auburn U., 1949; JD, U. Ala., 1951; LLM, Harvard U., 1954; LLD (hon.), U. S.C., 1998. Bar: Ala. 1951, Va. 1961. Law clk. to Justice Hugo L. Black U.S. Supreme Ct., 1954-55; assoc. firm Lange, Simpson, Robinson & Somerville, Birmingham, Ala., 1955-57; faculty U. Va. Law Sch., Charlottesville, 1957-66, prof. law, 1961-66; prof., dean U. Ala. Law Sch., 1966-70; James Monroe prof. law U. Va., Charlottesville, 1970-94, prof. emeritus, 1994—; asst. atty. gen. U.S., 1977-79; dir. grad. program for judges, 1979-95. Fulbright lectr., U.K., 1965-66; vis. prof. U.S. Mil. Acad., 1984; chmn. Southeastern Conf. Assn. Am. Law Schs., 1964-65; chmn. Cts. Task Force Nat. Adv. Commn. on Criminal Justice, 1971-72; dir. appellate justice project Nat. Ctr. for State Cts., 1972-74; mem. Adv. Coun. on Appellate Justice, 1971-75, Coun. on Role of Cts., 1978-84; bd. dirs. State Justice Inst., 1986-92; exec. dir. commn. on structural alternatives Fed. Ct. Appeals, 1998-99. Author: Preludes to Gideon, 1967, Criminal Appeals-English Practices and American Reforms, 1973, Mr. Justice Black and His Books, 1974, Appellate Courts: Staff and Process in the Crisis of Volume, 1974, (with Carrington and Rosenberg) Justice on Appeal, 1976, Impressions of Law in East Germany, 1986, American Courts, 1991, 2000 (with J. Bernstein) Appellate Courts in the United States, 1994, His Father's House, 1994, Unforgotten, 1999, (with Rosenberg and Carrington) Appellate Courts: Structures, Functions, Processes, and Personnel, 1994; editor: Hardy Cross Dillard: Writings and Speeches, 1995; editor Va. Bar News, 1962-65; contbr. articles to profl. jours. 1st lt. U.S. Army, 1951-53; col. JAGC, USAR ret. Decorated Bronze Star.; IREX fellow German Dem. Republic, 1983 Mem. ABA (chmn. standing com. on fed. jud. improvements 1987-90), Ala. Bar Assn., Va. Bar Assn. (exec. com. 1983-86), Am. Law Inst., Am. Judicature Soc. (bd. dirs. 1975-77, 80-83), Soc. Pub. Tchrs. Law, Am. Soc. Legal History (bd. dirs. 1968-71), Order of Coif, Raven Soc., Phi Delta Phi, Omicron Delta Kappa, Kappa Alpha. Presbyterian. Office: U Va Sch Law 580 Massie Rd Charlottesville VA 22903-1738

MEADOR, JOHN MILWARD, JR. university dean; b. Louisville, Nov. 4, 1946; s. John Milward and Ruth Inez (Miller) M.; m. Judith Ann Hay, Dec. 22, 1969; children: John Milward III, Elise Kathleen. BA, U. Louisville, 1968; MA, U. Tex., 1972, MLS, 1973; cert. in pub. adminstrn., U. Utah, 1982. Cert. tchr., Ky., Tex. Stacks supr. U. Louisville Librs., 1965-68; English bibliographer M.D. Anderson Libr. U. Houston, 1973-74, head reference dept. social scis. and humanities, 1974-77, head gen. reference dept., 1977-80; asst. dir. pub. svcs. Marriott Libr. U. Utah, Salt Lake City, 1980-84; dean libr. svcs. S.W. Mo. State U., Springfield, 1984-93; dean librs. U. Miss., University, 1993—. Bd. dirs. Mo. Libr. Network Corp., 1984-90, St. Louis, S.W. Mo. Libr. Network, Springfield; cons. Dayco Corp., Springfield, 1984-86; chmn. Mo. Northwestern Online Total Integrated Systems (NOTIS) Users Group, 1988-89. Co-author: The Robinson Jeffers Collection at the University of Houston, 1975; contbr. articles to profl. jours. Sponsor Community Alternative Svc. Program, Springfield and St. Louis, 1985-93; mem. governing bd. Mo. Rsch. and Edn. Network, MOREnet, 1991-93; With U.S. Army, 1969-71, Vietnam. Recipient Nat. Essay award Propeller Club of U.S., 1964; named to Honorable Order of Ky. Colonels, Gov. Ky., 1978; summer scholar English-Speaking Union, Edinburgh, Scotland, 1968; Apple Computer's Higher Edn. Acad. Devel. Donation Program grantee, 1990. Mem. ALA, Am. Assn. for Higher Edn., Assn. Coll. Rsch. Librs., Bibliog. Soc. Am., Libr. Adminstrn. and Mgmt. Assn., other profl. orgns., English-Speaking Union Club, Rotary (chmn. students guests com. Springfield chpt. 1986-89, chmn. scholarships com. 1989-90, bd. dirs. 1990-91, bd. dirs. Oxford chpt. 1995-96), Phi Kappa Phi. Avocations: raising pure bred airedale terriers, fishing, book collecting. Home: PO Box 787 University MS 38677-0787 Office: U Miss J D Williams Libr University MS 38677 E-mail: jmm@olemiss.edu.

MEADOR, RON, newspaper editor, writer; b. Buffalo, Nov. 24, 1952; s. Meril E. and Evelyn (Lyons) M.; divorced; 1 child, Benjamin Brian. BA, Ind. U., 1975. Copy editor The Courier-Journal, Louisville, 1975-78, The New York Times, 1978-80; reporter, state editor, city editor, asst. mng. editor Star Tribune, Mpls., 1980-96, mem. editl. bd., editl. writer, 1996—. Mem. Investigative Reporters and Editors, Inc., Nat. Conf. Editl. Writers, Soc. Environ. Journalists. Office: Star Tribune 425 Portland Ave Minneapolis MN 55488-0002

MEADOR, VALERIE LANE, clinical dietitian; b. Huntington, W.Va., June 17, 1957; d. Phillip Jarrell and Anna Lee (Law) Meador; m. Edward Lee McCallum, May 13, 1978 (div. 1990); children: Shaun Jeffrey, Briana Marie; m. Miles W. Cheatham III, Oct. 26, 1990 (div. 2000). BS in Biology, James Madison U., 1979; MS in Nutrition, Clemson U., 1986. Registered dietitian, 1987. Cytotechnologist Roanoke (Va.) Meml. Hosp., 1979-80; greenhouse mgr. Greenwood Nurseries, Princeton, W.Va., 1980-81; vet. technician Lewisburg (W.Va.) Animal Hosp., 1981-82; rsch. asst. Clemson (S.C.) U., 1984-86; clin. dietician Anderson (S.C.) Meml. Hosp., 1986-87, asst. food svc. dir., 1987-91, nutritionist III dept. health and environ. control, 1991-93; program mgr. woman, infant and child health-prenatal svcs. Anderson County Health Dept., 1994-97; dist. dir. nutrition Anderson County Appalachia I Health Dist., 1997—. Mem. Am. Dietetic Assn., Piedmont Dist. Dietetics Assn. (sec.), S.C. Dietetics Assn., S.C. Pub. Health Assn. Avocations: practical pistol shooting, Isshinryu karate, sewing, reading. Home: 110 Bob White Ln Anderson SC 29625-5717 Office: Dept Health Environ Control 220 McGee Rd Anderson SC 29625-2104 E-mail: meadorvl@andrsn62.dhec.state.sc.us.

MEADORS, ALLEN COATS, health administrator, educator; b. Van Buren, Ark., May 17, 1947; s. Hal Barron and Allene Coats (Means) M. AA, Saddleback Coll., 1981; BBA, U. Ctrl. Arki., 1969; MBA, U. No. Colo., 1974; MPA, U. Kans., 1975; MA in Psychology, Webster U., 1979, MA in Health Svcs. Mgmt., 1980; PhD in Adminstrn., So. Ill. U., 1981. Assoc. adminstr. Forbes Hosp., Topeka, 1971-73; asst. dir. health svcs. devel. Blue Cross Blue Shield of Kans., 1973-76; asst. dir. Kansas City Health Dept. (Mo.), 1976-77; program dir., asst. prof. So. Ill. U., Carbondale, 1978-82, Webster U., St. Louis, 1978-82; assoc. prof., dir. divsn. health adminstrn. U. Tex., Galveston, 1982-84; exec. dir. N.W. Ark. Radiation Therapy Inst., Springdale, Ark., 1984-87; prof., chmn. dept. health adminstrn. U. Okla., Oklahoma City, 1989-90, dean Coll. Pub. Health, 1989-90; mem. faculty Calif. State U., Long Beach, 1977-81; mem. grad. faculty Sch. Bus. Adminstrn. U. Ark., Fayetteville, 1984-87; prof., chmn. dept. health adminstrn. U. Okla., 1987-90; dean Coll. Health, Social and Pub. Svcs. Ea. Wash. U., Cheney, 1990-94; CEO, dean Pa. State U., Altoona, 1994-99; chancellor U. N.C., Pembroke, 1999—. Cons. Surgeon Gen. Office and Air Force Sys. Contbr. articles to profl. jours. Command bd. dirs. Blair County Hall of Fame, Blair County Hist. Soc., Martin Luther King Hosp., Health Care Svcs. Adv. Bd.; bd. dirs., mem. exec. com. Altoona Symphony Orch.; bd. dirs. Southwestern Regional Med. Ctr., Home Health Agy. With Med. Svc. Corps, USAF, 1969-73. Fellow Am. Coll. Healthcare Execs.; mem. Am. Hosp. Assn., C. of C. (v.p.). Home: Chancellors Residence Pembroke NC 28372 Office: U NC at Pembroke Chancellors Office PO Box 1510 Pembroke NC 28372-1510 E-mail: acm@uncp.edu.

MEADORS, HOWARD CLARENCE, JR. electrical engineer; b. Chgo., July 31, 1938; s. Howard Clarence and Eileen May (Baker) M.; m. Phyllis Anne Rennebaum, July 18, 1964; children: Henry Charles, William Howard, Laura Phyllis, Pamela Susan. SB, MIT, 1960, SM, 1962, Profl. Degree in Elec. Engring., 1964; PhD, Poly. Inst. NY, 1976. Mem. tech. staff Bell Tel. Labs., Inc., Holmdel, NJ, 1966—82; disting. mem. tech. staff AT&T Info. Systems Labs., 1983—85, supr. product devel., 1985—86; supr. adv. data communications AT&T Bell Labs., Middletown, NJ, 1986—91; Disting. mem. tech. staff AT&T Bus. Communications Systems, Holmdel, 1991—91; disting. mem. tech. staff AT&T Network Systems, 1994—96, Lucent Technologies, Holmdel, 1996—2001. Ednl. counselor MIT, 1973—, regional vice chmn., 1983-96, ctrl. N.J. chmn., 1996—. Inventor in field. With Signal Corps, U.S. Army, 1964-66. Mem. IEEE (sr. mem. 1987), Sigma Xi, Eta Kappa Nu. Office: Lucent Techs Crawfords Corner Rd Holmdel NJ 07733

MEADOW, CHARLES, information scientist, consultant; b. Paterson, N.J., Dec. 16, 1929; s. Abraham and Florence (Troub) M.; m. Harriet Reiss, Sept. 9, 1956 (div.); children: Debra Lynne, Sandra Lee; m. Mary Louise Shinskey, June 24, 1972; children: Alison Maria, Benjamin Niland. BA, U. Rochester, 1951; MS, Rutgers U., 1954. Mathematician David Taylor Model Basin USN, Washington, 1954-55; asst. mathematician RAND Corp., Lexington, Mass., 1955-56; unit mgr. GE Co., Bethesda, Md., 1956-60; sr. sys. analyst IBM Corp., Gaithersburg, 1960-68; chief sys. devel. divsn. U.S. Nat. Bur. Stds., 1968-71; tech. asst. Office of Sci. and Tech. Exec. Office of the Pres., Washington, 1970-71; asst. dir. divsn. mgmt. info. and telecom. sys. U.S. AEC, 1971-74; prof. Drexel U., Phila., 1974-82; project mgr. Dialog Info. Svcs., Inc., Palo Alto, Calif., 1982-84; prof. faculty info. studies U. Toronto, Ont., Can., 1984-94, assoc. dean Can., 1990-94, prof. emeritus Can., 1994—; cons. Meadow Info. Sys. Ltd., 1994—. Vis. prof. U. Sheffield, 1980-81, U. West Indies, 1990-91, U. Washington, 1993, U. N.C., 1995. Author: The Analysis of Information Systems, 1967, 2nd edit., 1973, Man-Machine Communication, 1970, The Story of Computers, 1970, Sounds and Signals: How We Communicate, 1975, Applied Data Management, 1976, Text Information Retrieval Systems, 1992, 2nd. edit, 1999; co-author: (with Pauline A. Cochrane) Basics of Online Searching, 1981, (with Albert S. Tedesco) Telecommunications for Management, 1985, (with Bert R. Boyce and Donald H. Kraft) Measurement in Information Science, 1994, Ink Into Bits: A Web of Converging Media, 1998; editor Jour. Am. Soc. for Info. Sci., 1976-84, Can. Jour. Info. Sci., 1986-87. 1st Lt. USMC, 1951-53. Mem. Assn. Computing Machinery, Am. Soc. Info. Sci. and Tech. (disting. lectr. award N.J. chpt. 1986, ann. rsch. award 1995, info. sci. book of yr. award 2000), Can. Assn. Info. Sci. (pres. 1994), N.Y. Acad. Sci. (honorable mention children's sci. book awards 1975), Ret. Academics and Librs. U. Toronto (exec. com. 2000—, coms. dir. 2001—), Sigma Xi. Avocation: photography. Home: 160 Frederick St # 205 Toronto ON Canada M5A 4H9 Office: U Toronto Faculty Info Studies 140 St George St Toronto ON Canada M5S 3G6 E-mail: meadow@fis.utoronto.can.

MEADOW, LYNNE (CAROLYN MEADOW), theatrical producer and director; b. New Haven, Nov. 12, 1946; d. Frank and Virginia R. Meadow BA cum laude, Bryn Mawr Coll., 1968; postgrad., Yale U., 1968-70. Dir. Theatre Communications Group, 1978-80. Adj. prof. SUNY, Stony Brook, 1975-76, Yale U., Circle in the Sq., 1977-78, 89-91, NYU, 1977-80; theatre and music/theatre panelist Nat. Endowment for Arts, 1977-88; artistic advisor Fund for New Am. Plays, 1988-90. Artistic dir. Manhattan Theatre Club, N.Y.C., 1972—; guest dir. Nat. Playwrights Conf., Eugene O'Neill Theatre Ctr., 1975-77, Phoenix Theatre, 1976; dir. Ashes for Manhattan Theatre Club and N.Y. Shakespeare Festival, 1977; prodr. off-Broadway shows Ain't Misbehavin', 1978, Crimes of the Heart, 1981, Miss Firecracker Contest, 1984, Frankie and Johnny, 1987, Eastern Standard, 1988, Lisbon Traviata, 1989, Lips Together, Teeth Apart, 1991, Four Dogs and a Bone, 1993, Love! Valour! Compassion!, 1994; dir. Principia Scritoriae, 1986, Woman in Mind, 1988 (Drama Desk award), Eleemosynary, 1989, Absent Friends, 1991; dir. Broadway prodn. A Small Family Business, 1992, The Loman Family Picnic, 1993, Nine Armenians, 1996(Drama Desk nominee), Captains Courageous: The Musical, 1999, The Tale of the Allertist's Wife, 2000; (dir. Broadway prodn. and nat. tour) The Tale of the Allergist's Wife, 2000; co-prodr. off-Broadway and Broadway show Mass Appeal, 1981. Recipient Citation of Merit Nat. Coun. Women, 1976, Outer Circle Critics award 1977, Drama Desk award, 1977, Obie award for Ashes, 1977, Margo Jones award for Continued Encouragement New Playwrights, 1981, Critics Circle award Outstanding Revival on or off Broadway for Loot, 1986, Lucille Lortel award for Outstanding Achievement, 1987, Spl. Drama Desk award, 1989, N.Y. Drama Critics Circle award Best Fgn. Play for Aristocrats, 1989, Torch of Hope award, 1989, Manhattan Mag. award, 1994, Lee Reynolds award League Profl. Theatre Women, 1994; named Northwood Inst. Disting. Woman of Yr., 1990, Person of Yr., Nat. Theatre Conf., 1992. Office: Manhattan Theatre Club 311 W 43rd St Fl 8 New York NY 10036-6413

MEADOWS, JUDITH ADAMS, law librarian, educator; b. Spartanburg, S.C., June 5, 1945; d. Thomas Taylor and Virginia (Dayton) Adams; m. Bruce R. Meadows; children: Beth Ann Blackwood, Ted Adams Meadows. BA, Am. U., 1967; MLS, U. Md., 1979. Law libr. Aspen Sys. Corp., Gaithersburg, Md., 1979-81; dir. Fairfax (Va.) Law Libr., 1981-84, State Law Libr., Helena, Mont., 1984—. Vis. prof. U. Wash., Seattle, 1994; adj. prof. U. Great Falls, Mont., 1989-96; presiding ofcl. Gov.'s Conf. on Libr. Info. Svc., Helena, Mont., 1991. Author: (book chpts.) From Yellow Pads to Computers, 1991, Law Librarianship, 1994; contbr. articles to profl. jours. Bd. dirs. Helena Presents, 1986-92, Holter Mus. Art, 1995—. Recipient Disting. Svc. award State Bar of Mont., 1991. Mem. Am. Assn. Law Librs. (treas. 1992-95, v.p., v.p. 1996—, pres. 1997-98, past pres. 1998—), N.W. Consortium of Law Librs. (pres.), Mont. Libr. Assn. (sec. 1986-88). Avocations: gourmet cooking, cross-country skiing, reading, gardening. Office: State Law Libr PO Box 203004 Helena MT 59620-3004 E-mail: jmeadows@state.mt.us.

MEADOWS, LOIS ANNETTE, elementary education educator; b. Harrisville, W.Va., Jan. 12, 1948; d. Orvle Adam and Una Pauline (Slocum) Ingram; m. David Alan Meadows, June 15, 1969; children: Lynecia Ann, Eric Justin. BA, Glenville State Coll., 1969; MA, W.Va. U., 1980. Cert. music, elem. edn., reading, computer tech. edn., W.Va.; nat. cert. elem. tchr. Tchr. grade six Acad. Park-Portsmouth (Va.) City Schs., 1969-73; elem. substitute Wood County Schs., Parkersburg, W.Va., 1973-77; real estate agt. Nestor Realty, 1974-77; tchr. grade five/music Emerson Elem. Wood County Schs., W.Va., 1977-78, tchr. grade three, 1978—; edn. cons. World Book, 1986—. Mentor tchr.-trainer Wood County Schs., parkersburg, 1990—; W.Va. S.T.E.P. Test com./trainer W.Va. Dept. Edn., Charleston, 1994—, mem. pool of talented educators, presenter sessions goals and objectives Ctr. Profl. Devel. Gov.'s Inst.; grant writer and spkr. in field; mem. W.Va. Dept. Edn. State Writing Manual Com., 1996-2001; coord. W.Va.-Ohio-Ky. Nat. Read-In.; presenter Gov's Summer Insts. for Ctr. for Profl. Devel., 1994—; mem. standards com. 4th grade writing assessment W.Va. Dept. Edn., 1994—. Author: (reading projects) Operation Blackout, 1986-94 (grant 1994), The Reading Room, 1988 (grant 1990), Storytime at the Mall, 1986— (grant 1994, 95); contbg. author W.V. Math Workbook, 1998, 99. Life mem. Emerson PTA, Parkersburg, 1977—; Sunday Sch. tchr. North Parkersburg Bapt. Ch., 1976-98, children's choir dir., 1976-88; fund raiser local charities, Parkersburg. Women of Excellence and Leadership Timely Honored award, W. Va. State Reading Tchr. of Yr., 1988, Finalist W. Va. State Tchr. of Yr., W.Va. Dept. Edn., 1993, Wood County Tchr. of Yr., 1993, Ashland Oil Golden Apple Achiever award, 1995, Ashland Oil Tchr. Achievement Award Winner (1 0f 10 for WV), 1998, Wood Co. PTA Outstanding Educator of Yr. award, 1995-96, award for ann. contbrs. and project work Emerson PTA, Wealth award Women of Excellence and Leadership Timely Honored, 1993, 2001; Nat. writing fellow W.Va. Writing Project, 1999. Mem. W.Va. Reading Assn. (pres. 1993-94, mem. chmn. 1994—, Spl. Svc. award 1997), Internat. Reading Assn., Wood County Reading Coun. (past pres. 1986-88, 90-92), Am. Fedn. Tchrs., Delta Kappa Gamma. Republican. Avocations: children's literature, collecting autographed books, bridge, basket weaving, family times. Home: 142 Jomar Dr Parkersburg WV 26104-9169 Office: Wood County Schs Emerson Elem 1605 36th St Parkersburg WV 26104-1939

MEADOWS, PATRICIA BLACHLY, art curator, civic worker; b. Amarillo, Tex., Nov. 12, 1938; d. William Douglas and Irene Bond Blachly; m. Curtis Washington Meadows, Jr., June 10, 1961; children: Michael Lee, John Morgan. BA in English and History, U. Tex., 1960. Program dir. Ex-Students Assn., Austin, Tex., 1960-61; co-founder, dir. Dallas Visual Art Ctr., 1981-86, curator, 1987-98, bd. dirs., 1981-99, pres. bd. dirs., 1982-85, founder The Collectors, 1988; founder, prin. cons. Art Connections, Dallas, 1996—; sr. v.p. Hall Fin. Group Ltd., 1999—. Exhbn. dir. Tex. bd. Nat. Mus. Women in Arts, Washington, 1986-91; mem. acquisition com. Dallas Mus. Art, 1988-92; chmn. adv. bd. Oaks Bank and Trust, 1993-96; juror numerous exhibits, Dallas and Tex.; spkr. on arts subjects; cons. city, state and nat. project concerning arts; chmn. bd. dirs. State-Thomas TIF Zone #1, 1994-99, bd. dirs. 1989-99. Author: (art catalogues) Critic's Choice, 1983-97, Texas Women, 1989-90, Texas: reflections, rituals, 1991; organizer many exhbns. including Presenting Nine, D-Art Visual Art Ctr., 1984, Mosaics, 1991-97, Senses Beyond Sight, 1992-93. Bd. dirs. Mid-Am. Arts Alliance, Kansas City, Mo., 1989-93, Tex. Bd. Commerce, Austin, 1991-93, Women's Issues Network, Dallas, 1994-96; bd. dirs. Dallas Summit, 1989-95, pres., 1993-94, mem. 1988—; mem. Charter 100, 1993—, Dallas Assembly , 1993—, Leadership Tex., 1987; co-founder, mem. steering com. Emergency Artists Support League, Dallas, 1992-99; mem. originating task force Dallas Coalition for Arts, 1984; also others. Recipient Dedication to Arts award Tex. Fine Arts Assn., 1984, Assn. Artists and Craftsmen, 1984, Southwestern Watercolor Soc., 1985, Flora award Dallas Civic Garden Ctr., 1987, James K. Wilson award TACA, 1988, Maura award Women's Ctr. Dallas, 1991, Disting. Woman award Northwood U., 1993, Excellence in the Arts award Dallas Hist. Soc., 1993, Legend award Dallas Visual Art Ctr., 1996. Mem. Tex. Assn. Mus., Arts Dist. Mgmt. Assn. (bd. dirs., exec. com. 1984-92, Artists and Craftsmen Assn. (pres. bd. dirs. 1982-83), Dallas Art Dealer's Assn. (pres. 1997-99). Presbyterian. Office: Hall Financial Group 6801 Gaylord Pkwy Ste 100 Frisco TX 75034-8545

MEADOWS, ROD G. lawyer; b. Manchester, Ga., Aug. 2, 1949; s. Earl F. and Sara R. (Moncus) M.; m. Betty Foster, Jan. 29, 1972; children: Mandy J., Monica E. BS Edn cum laude, Ga. So. U., Statesboro, 1971; JD, U. Ga., 1976. Bar: Ga. 1976, U.S. Dist. Ct. (no. and mid. dists.) Ga. 1977, U.S. Ct. Appeals (5th cir.) 1977, U.S. Ct. Appeals (11th cir.) 1981. Ptnr. Smith, Welch & Meadows, McDonough, Ga., 1976-85; ptnr., pres. Meadows & Futch P.C., 1985—2002, Meadows & Lewis PC, 2002—. Founder, chair Long-Term Health Care Law in Ga. conf., Athens, 1992—; counsel Hosp. Authority of Henry Country and Henry County Devel. Authority, 1985—; mem. exec. com., health law sect. State Bar Ga., 1999—; adj. prof. healthcare law U. St. Francis. Bd. mem., vice chair Ga. So. U. Found., Statesboro, 1995—; past-pres., bd. mem. Henry Med. Ctr. Found.,, Stockbridge, Ga., 1984—; elder, deacon, fin chair McDonough Presbyn. Ch. Lt. USCG, 1971-74. Mem. Ga. Acad. Hosp. Attys. (bd. mem. 1985-95, pres. 1992-93), Am. Health Lawyers Assn., Am. Counsel Assn., Ga. Hosp. Assn. (coun. on trustee devel. 1985—), McDonough Kiwanis Club (pres., bd. mem. 1978-92). Avocations: travel, musical theater, music, church activities. Home: PO Box 730 Mcdonough GA 30253-0730

MEADOWS, VICKERS B. federal agency administrator; Grad., Green Mountain Coll. Procuremen, dir. presdl. gifts White House, Washington, 1989—89, spl. asst. to the vice for adminstrn., 1985—89; dep. dir., dir. exec. svc. Dept. Transp., 1989—93; dir. adminstrn. Gov. Bush, 1995—2000; spl. asst., dir. White House Mgmt. White House, Washington, dir. adminstrn. Bush-Cheney Transition; asst. sec. for adminstrn. office Dept. HUD, 2002—. Office: Dept HUD Adminstrn Office 451 7th St SW Washington DC 20410-1047*

MEADOWS-ROGERS, ROBERT DENTON, art history educator; b. St. Louis, Oct. 16, 1949; s. Robert Franklin and Emma Pearl Meadows; m. Arabella Thomas, Aug. 12, 1972; children: Matthew, Sarah. PhD U.N.C., 1997; MA, U.N.C., 1989; MDiv, Union Theological Seminary, N.Y.C., 1974; BA, Duke U., 1971. Parish pastor United Methodist Ch., NY, 1974—77, 1980—85; devel., spl. events Mus. Modern Art, 1977—80; adj. tchr., 1985—92; asst. prof. art history Concordia Coll., Moorhead , Minn., 1992—. Exhibitions include Plains Art Mus. , Fargo, N.D., 2002; contbr. articles to jour. Mem.: Coll. Art Assn. Roman Catholic. Home: 1800 CentreSq Moorhead MN 56560 Office: Concordia Coll 901 S 8th St Moorhead MN 56562 E-mail: rogers@cord.edu.

MEADS, WALTER FREDERICK, executive recruitment consultant; b. Ft. Wayne, Ind., Mar. 11, 1923; s. Frederick C. and Minnie E. (Stephenson) M.; m. Mary E. Smith, Mar. 21, 1975; children by previous marriage: Kenneth W., Catherine L. BS, Kent State U., 1948; MA, Fairfield U. With Norman Malone & Assos., Akron, Ohio, 1946-48, Griswold-Eshleman Co., Cleve., 1949-53, Fuller, Smith & Ross, Cleve., 1953-55; sr. v.p., head of creative svc., mem. mgmt. com., vice chmn. plans and rev. bds. J. Walter Thompson Co., N.Y.C., 1955-72; pres. Meads & Assocs., 1972—. With USAAF, 1943-45. Recipient numerous nat. and local advt. industry awards. Home: 4420 Orangewood Loop E Lakeland FL 33813-1844 Office: 4420 Orangewood Loop E Lakeland FL 33813 *Creative freedom is probably the core concept at the heart of my life— not only for myself but for others. Life is never static; it either deteriorates or grows. All growth, to me, springs from the creative doers of the world. The rest of humanity goes along for the ride. And creative growth, in any field or endeavor, demands an attitude of freedom to shake off the shackles of habit and find new and better ways of doing things.*

MEAGHER, GEORGE VINCENT, mechanical engineer; b. Halifax, N.S., Can., Apr. 23, 1919; s. John Nicholas and Blanche Margaret (Seals) M.; m. Evelyn Margaret Hamm, June 2, 1945; children: Maureen, Lindsey, Lise, Shelagh. BSc, Dalhousie U., Halifax, 1940; B of Engring., McGill U., 1942. Engring. and mgmt. positions in industry, 1942-56; with Dilworth, Secord, Meagher & Assocs. Ltd., Toronto, 1957-92, chmn., 1988-92; pres. Tatacan Ltd., 1985-96; vice chmn. Tata-DSMA, Bombay, 1970-93; dir. State Bank India, Can. Ltd., Toronto, 1984-94; founding dir., past chmn. Can.-India Bus. Coun.; pres. George V. Meagher Inc. Fellow Engring. Inst. Can.; mem. Profl. Engrs. Ont. Home: 500 Avenue Rd Apt 1402 Toronto ON Canada M4V 2J6 E-mail: meaghergv@aol.com.

MEAGHER, JAMES PROCTOR, editor; b. Rock Island, Ill., June 2, 1935; s. Edmund Joseph and Pauline Marie (Proctor) M.; m. Marie Therese Lyman, Sept. 12, 1959; children: Kathleen Ann Raffa, Christopher James. BA, U. Notre Dame, 1957. Copy editor Chgo. Tribune Co., 1959-61; staff writer Nat. Observer, Washington, 1961-62, news editor Silver Spring, Md., 1962-65, sr. editor, 1965-76, asst. mng. editor, 1976-77; assoc. editor Barron's Bus. and Fin. Weekly, N.Y.C., 1977-78, news editor, 1978-82, asst. mng. editor, 1982-86, dep. editor, 1986-92, mng. editor, 1992-93, editor, 1993-95; exec. editor Dow Jones Mag. Group, 1995—. Served to 1st lt. U.S. Army, 1957-59. Mem. Soc. Profl. Journalists, Sigma Delta Chi. Roman Catholic. Home: 25 Hedges Ave Chatham NJ 07928-2503 Office: Barron's Fin Weekly 200 Liberty St New York NY 10281-1003

MEAGHER, ROBERT FRANCIS, international economic law consultant; b. Bklyn., May 13, 1927; s. Frances Xavier and Marie Janet (Tallent) M.; m. Donna Marie Dowsett, May 21, 1973 (div. Mar. 1974). B Social Sci., CCNY, 1949; JD, Yale U., 1952. Bar: N.Y. Assoc. Winthrop Stimson Putnam & Roberts, N.Y.C., 1954-58; lawyer UN Relief & Works Agy., Beirut, Lebanon, 1958-60; vis. and adj. prof., assoc. dir. internat. legal rsch. Columbia U. Law Sch., N.Y.C., 1961-73; internat. econ. law cons. Somerville, Mass., 1964—. Prof. internat. law Fletcher Sch. Law and Diplomacy Tufts U., Medford, Mass., 1967-92, prof. emeritus, 1992—; prof. Tufts Inst. for Learning in Retirement, 2002; legal advisor India Interest Group, 1993—; vis. sr. fellow Overseas Devel. Coun., Washington, 1975-76; vis. prof. Law Harvard Law Sch., Cambridge, Mass., 1984, 89, Melbourne (Australia) U., Monash U., Australia, 1981, Indian Law Inst., New Delhi, 1987-88; lectr. on fgn. policy, fgn. aid, fgn. investment; mem. study groups Coun. Fgn. Rels.; coord. Peace Corps tng. program for lawyers going to Somalia, 1967; coord. workshops in field; lectr. on various fgn. policy issues Asia, Africa, Mid. East and U.S., 1952—; adj. prof. law Columbia Law Sch., N.Y.C., 1964-71. Editor, contbr. chpt.: Law and Social Change, 1988; co-author: International Financial Aid: A Comparative Study of Policies, Institutions and Methods, 1966; author: An International Redistribution of Wealth and Power: A Study of the Charter of Economic Rights and Duties of States, 1979, Proposed Options for the Future Activities of the U.S. Office of International Activities of the Environmental Protection Agency, 1979, Popular Participation and Development in the Least Developed Countries: Case Studies of Tanzania, Nepal and Bangladesh for UNCTAD, 1991; contbr. articles, revs. to profl. publs. Chmn. fgn. policy com. N.Y. Young Dems., N.Y.C., 1956-58; exec. dir. Citizens for Johnson & Humphrey, N.Y.C., 1964; fgn. policy cons. Michael Dukakis, Boston, 1988. With U.S. Army, 1945-46, ETO. Fulbright scholar Bombay (India) Sch. Econs., 1952-53, Indian Law Inst., 1987-88; Ford Found. grantee, 1961, Rockefeller grantee, 1975. Mem. ABA (African law subcom., Mid. Eastern law subcom.), African Studies Assn., Am. Fgn. Law Assn., Am. Soc. Internat. Law (bd. rev. and devel. 1980-85, panel on pvt. investment in less developed countries), Asia Soc. (India coun., program com. 1967-69), Assn. Asian Studies, Assn. Bar City of N.Y. (fgn. law com. 1956-58, 65-68, internat. commn. jurist com. 1965-67, lawyers' role in search for peace com. 1976-78, 80-82), Inter-Am. Affairs (program com. 1977-79), Coun. African-Am. Inst., Coun. Fgn. Rels., Internat. Law Assn. (com. fgn. investment), Soc. Internat. Devel., Trade Policy Rsch. Ctr., UN Assn. (bd. dirs. greater Boston/Mass. 1978—), World Peace Through Law Ctr (com. fgn. investments 1967-74). Avocation: wine tasting. Home and Office: 108 Curtis St Somerville MA 02144-1242 E-mail: rfm2@erols.com., rfm28@hotmail.com.

MEAGHER, ROBERT MICHAEL, software engineer; b. Stoneham, Mass., Aug. 14, 1952; s. Thomas Edward and Mildred Edna (Roberts) M.; m. Elizabeth Norton Tannebring, June 8, 1974 (div. Feb. 1985); children: R. Michael Jr., Jeffrey Stephen; m. Linda Jean Thomas, June 23, 1990. BSEE, MIT, 1973; MBA, U. N.H., 1982. Data processing dir. Cambridge (Mass.) Sch. Dept., 1973-74; software engr. Educomp Corp., Hartford, Conn., 1974-76, Digital Equipment Corp., Merrimack, N.H., 1976-83, software engring. mgr., 1983-86, software cons., 1987-90, prin. software engr. Nashua, N.H., 1990-94; sr. engr. Computer Methods Corp., Marlton, N.J., 1986-87; prin. software engr. Datamedia Corp., Nashua, 1994-95, Digital Equipment Corp., Nashua, N.H., 1995-96, Sun Microsystems, Chemlsford, Mass., 1996-97, PictureTel Corp., Andover, 1997-98, Compuware Numega Lab, Nashua, N.H., 1998—. Contbr. articles to profl. jours. Mem.: Assn. Computing Machinery, Sigma Xi, Eta Kappa Nu. Avocations: creative computing, gourmet cooking, running, gardening. Home: 14 Hillsboro Cir Milford NH 03055-3236 Office: Compuware Numega Lab 9 Townsend W Nashua NH 03063-1217 E-mail: meagher@alum.mit.edu.

MEAKEM, CAROLYN SOLIDAY, investment executive, financial planner, money manager, consultant; b. Columbus, Ohio, Jan. 11, 1936; d. Junius Dean and Mary Elizabeth (Thomas) Soliday: m. Thomas James Meakem, Aug. 26, 1956; children: Thomas James III, Timothy Dean, Traci Lynn. BS, West Liberty Coll., 1959; MEd., U. Md., 1970. cert. fin. planner. Tchr. Westchester Elem. Sch., Ellicott City, Md., 1956-59, Riverdale (Md.) Elem. Sch., 1959-60, Buckingham Elem. Sch., Willingboro, N.J., 1962-64, Beacon Heights Elem Sch., Riverdale, 1964-68; dir. Christian edn. Forest Lake Presbyn. Ch., Columbia, S.C., 1961-62; supr. student tchrs U. Md., College Park, 1968-69; tchr. Norwood Sch., Bethesda, Md., 1975-77; with Ferris and Co. Inc., 1978-88, v.p., 1984-86, sr. v.p., mem. pres.'s coun., chrmn.'s coun., 1986-88, also bd. dirs.; sr. v.p. Legg Mason, Inc., 1988—. Guest lectr. George Washington U., 1982-83; trustee, tchr. Wharton Sch. Security Industry Inst., Phila., 1986-95, tchr., speaker Bus. Inst. for Educators, Bethesda, 1987-95. Author: Teachers Activity Guide for Dental Health Education, 1973. Trustee, bd. dirs. Holton-Arms Sch., Bethesda, 1985-94; trustee Nat. Econ. Edn. Found., Security Industry Assn., continuing edn. com., chair ethics edn. sub-com.; founding bd. dirs., treas. Leadership Montgomery, Montgomery County, Md.; hon. bd. dirs. Found. for Boys and Girls Homes Md.; bd. dirs. Child Care Connection; trustee, governing bd. Coun. on Econ. Edn. Md. Mem. LWV (corp. bd. Montgomery County), Nat. Adv. Coun., Security Industry Assn. (regional coord. econ. edn., Best Dist. award 1992), Internat. Assn. Fin. Planners. Presbyterian. Avocations: snow and water skiing, sailing, reading, rose gardening. Home: 10215 Gainsborough Rd Potomac MD 20854-4039 Office: Legg Mason Wood Walker 6701 Democracy Blvd Ste 100 Bethesda MD 20817-1573

MEAKER, MARIJANE AGNES, author; b. Auburn, N.Y., May 27, 1927; d. Ellis R. and Ida T. M. BA, U. Mo., 1949; PhD (hon.), Southampton Coll., 1996. Author: novels (under own name) Sudden Endings, 1965, Hometown, 1967, Game of Survival, 1969, Don't Rely on Gemini, 1971, Shockproof Sydney Skate, 1972, 2d edit., 1990; (under pseudonym M.E. Kerr), Dinky Hocker Shoots Smack, 1972, Gentlehands, 1978, If I Love You, Am I Trapped Forever, 1973, I'll Love You When You're More Like Me, 1977, Is That You, Miss Blue?, 1975, Love is a Missing Person, 1975, The Son of Someone Famous, 1975, Little Little, 1981 (Soc. Children's Books Writers award 1982), What I Really Think of You, 1982, Me Me Me Me Me: Not a Novel (Best Books for Young Adults ALA), 1983, Him She Loves?, 1984, I Stay Near You (Best Books for Young Adults ALA), 1985, Night Kites, 1986, Fell, 1987, Fell Back, 1989, Fell Down, 1990; (under pseudonym Mary James) Shoebag, 1990, The Shuteyes, 1993, Frankenlouse, 1994, Shoebag Returns, 1996, (M.E. Kerr) Linger, 1993, Deliver Us from Evie, 1994, Hello, I Lied, 1997, Blood on the Forehead, 1998, What Became of Her, 2000, Slap Your Sides, 2001. Recipient Notable Children's Book award ALA, 1972, Book of Yr. award Sch. Library Jour., 1972, 77, 78, Christopher award, 1978, Night Kites award ALA, 1986, Margaret A. Edwards award ALA, 1993, Lifetime Achievement award, The Publishing Triangle, 1998, Lifetime Achievement award The Knickerbocker, 1999, Lifetime Achievement award ALAN, 2000. E-mail: mekerr13@aol.com.

MEAL, LARIE, chemistry educator, researcher, consultant; b. Cin., June 15, 1939; d. George Lawrence Meal and Dorothy Louise (Heileman) Fitzpatrick. BS in Chemistry, U. Cin., 1961, PhD in Chemistry, 1966. Rsch. chemist U.S. Indsl. Chems., Cin., 1966-67; instr. chemistry U. Cin., 1968-69, asst. prof., 1969-75, assoc. prof., 1975-90, prof., 1990—, rschr., 1980—. Cons. in field. Contbr. articles to profl. jours. Mem. AAAS, N.Y. Acad. Scis., Am. Chem. Soc., NOW, Planned Parenthood, Iota Sigma Pi. Democrat. Avocations: gardening, yard work. Home: 2231 Slane Ave Norwood OH 45212-3615 Office: U Cin 2220 Victory Pky Cincinnati OH 45206-2822

MEALIE, CARL A. physician, educator; b. Astoria, N.Y., Jan. 26, 1948; s. Patrick and Natalie (Previti) M.; m. Maureen Frances Maybury, Apr. 24, 1993; children: David, Ian, Daniel. BA, NYU, 1969; MD, N.Y. Med. Coll., 1974. CCRN. Chmn. Dept. Emergency Medicine St. Mary's Hosp., Roswell, N.Mex., 1975-83; emergency dept. attending physician Guadalupe Med. Ctr., Carlsbad, 1979-83, L.I. Jewish Med. Ctr., New Hyde Park, N.Y., 1993—, chmn. disaster preparation com., 1991—, asst. chief emergency dept., 1989-95, chief clin. ops., 1995; asst. prof. emergency medicine Albert Einstein Coll. Medicine, N.Y.C., 1995. Mem. ambulance adv. bd. Chavez County Med. Soc., Roswell, 1980-83, ambulance bd., 1981-87. Mem. City Roswell EMS Bd., 1981-93. Fellow Am. Coll. Emergency Physicians (key contact 1987—), N.Y. Acad. Medicine; me,. AMA, Am. Acad. Emergency Medicine, N.Y. State

Med. Soc., Soc. Acad. Emergency Medicine. Roman Catholic. Avocations: skiing, sailing, hunting, golf. Home: 33 Heights Rd Northport NY 11768-2629 Office: LI Jewish Med Ctr Lakeville New Hyde Park NY 11040

MEALMAN, GLENN, corporate marketing executive; b. Prescott, Kans., June 10, 1934; s. Edgar R. and Mary E. (Holstein) M.; m. Gloria Gail Proch, June 12, 1955; children: Michael Edward, Cathy Gail. BS in Bus., Kans. State Coll., Emporia, 1957; postgrad., Harvard U., 1970. With Fleming Cos., Topeka, 1957—, sr. v.p. mktg., 1981-82, exec. v.p. mktg., 1982-86, exec. v.p. Mid-Am. region, 1986-93, exec. v.p. nat. accts., 1994-96. Dir. PBI-Gordon Co., Furrs Supermarkets. Pres. bd. Topeka YMCA, 1981; trustee Ottawa U., Kans., 1980. Served with USNR, 1954-56. Mem. Kans. State C. of C. and Industry (bd. dirs. 1991—), Blue Hills Country Club, Gainey Ranch Country Club, Keystone Ranch Country Club, Rotary, Sigma Phi Epsilon (Kans. chpt.). Presbyterian. Office: PO Box 7448 Shawnee Mission KS 66207-0448

MEANA, SUSAN DEAN, literature educator; b. Washington, Sept. 18, 1956; d. Teymour Ehtesham-Zadeh, Sarah Dean Kale; m. Jesus Meana, July 5, 1985; children: Asia, Elias. BA in Philosophy, Stanford U., 1978; MAT, Agnes Scott Coll., 1996. Tchr. English and Philosophy Iranzamin Internat. Sch., Tehran, Iran, 1979—81; tchr. English Colegio San Patricio, Madrid, 1981—82; adj. prof. English Coll. Fgn. Lang. and Lit., Tehran, 1983—85; tchr. English Internat. Coll. Spain, Madrid, 1985—88; chair English dept. Atlanta Internat. Sch., Ga., 1989—96; tchr. English The Lovett Sch., Atlanta, 1997—2000; chair English dept. Costa Blanca Internat. Sch., Lliber, Spain, 2000—01; tchr. English Pace Acad., Atlanta, 2001—. Freelance writer, rschr. Ravenscroft Sch., Raleigh, NC, 1997—98; curriculum writer bigchalk.com, 2000—01. Author (sch. history): Ravenscroft: Story of a Southern School, 1998; author: (textbook) Basic Texts for Comprehension, 1983; translator (poetry): e.e. cummings: 30 poems, 1985; contbr. Mem.: European Coun. Internat. Schs. Avocation: Avocations: swimming, travel, writing. Home: 713 Neese Rd Woodstock GA 30188

MEANS, CATHERINE ELIZABETH, nurse; b. Logansport, Ind., Dec. 4, 1954; d. Elmer Clyde and Margaret (Stewart) M. BS, Tuskegee U., 1977. Staff nurse Meml. Hosp., Logansport, Ind., 1977; staff nurse neonatal unit Home Hosp., Lafayette, 1978-80; charge nurse Americanna Health Care, 1980; asst. head nurse St. Elizabeth Med. Ctr., 1980-95; staff nurse George Davis Manor, West Lafayette, Ind., 1999—. Mem. Apostolic Ch. Avocations: stitchery, camping, cooking. Office: George Davis Manor 1051 Cumberland Ave West Lafayette IN 47906-1447

MEANS, DAVID HAMMOND, retired advertising executive; b. Lebanon, Pa., Dec. 15, 1928; s. W. Horace and June (Zimmerman) M.; m. Nancy N. Downes, June 21, 1952; children: Elizabeth N., Susan Z., Emily M., David H. BA, Amherst Coll., 1950. With CIA, 1950-53, N.W. Ayer Inc., 1953-89, exec. v.p., 1976-89; ret., also bd. dirs. Mng. dir. Ayer U.S.A. and Ayer Enterprises, Inc. Bd. dirs. Waveny Care Ctr., New Canaan Nature Ctr., Schoolhouse Apts., Get About Inc. 1st lt. USAF, 1953. Mem. Bus. Profl. Advt. Assn., Merion (Pa.) Golf Club, Amherst Club (N.Y.C.), Country Club New Canaan (Conn.), Gridiron Club (New Canaan), Sr. Men's Club (New Canaan, bd. dirs.), Psi Upsilon. Episcopalian. Home: Wahackme Ln New Canaan CT 06840 E-mail: davenan28@aol.com.

MEANS, DWIGHT BARDEEN, JR. financial consultant, educator; b. Pitts., July 21, 1943; s. Dwight B. Sr. and Betty (Feick) M.; div.; children: Melissa Means Morris, Blake Elizabeth. BSEE, Carnegie-Mellon U., 1965; MBA, U. Pitts., 1969, PhD, 1984. Various positions Bell Telephone Co. Pa., Pitts., 1965-70; asst. prof., dept. chair C.C. Allegheny County, 1970-78; from asst. to assoc. prof. Saginaw (Mich.) Valley State U., 1978-86; prof., dept. chair Clarion (Pa.) U. Pa., 1986-88; asst. prof. U. Memphis, 1988-95; adj. prof. numerous univs., 1996—; cons. Pitts., 1995—. Presenter in field. Reviewer Fin. Practice and Edn., Jour. Econs. and Fin., Jour. Real Estate Rsch., Jour. Applied Bus. Rsch; contbr. articles to profl. jours. Mem. Acad. Fin. Svcs. (program com. 1990-95), Am. Econ. Assn., Midsouth Acad. Econs. and Fin. (dir. 1993-95), Fin. Mgmt. Assn. (program com. 1989), Midwest Fin. Assn. (program com. 1995-96), S.W. Fin. Assn. (program com. 1994-95), So. Fin. Assn. (program com. 1992-95). Avocations: hunting, fishing, camping, reading. Home: 138 Owendale Ave Pittsburgh PA 15227-1951 E-mail: meansdb@aol.com.

MEANS, ELIZABETH ROSE THAYER, financial consultant, writer, lawyer; b. N.Y.C., Aug. 29, 1960; d. Cyril Chesnut and Rosaline (Limtiuco y Sy) M. Student, Sch. of Am. Ballet-Lincoln Ctr, N.Y.C., 1970-75, Harvard Coll., 1980, Tufts U., 1981, Fletcher Sch. Law/Diplomacy, 1983-84; BS, Chatham Coll., 1983; cert. in comparative law, Heidelberg U., 1988; JD, Samford U., 1989; LLM in Internat. Banking Law, Boston U., 1990. Bar: Mass. 1991, Pa. 1991; cert. for piloting, seamanship and small boat handling USCG Aux. Dancer The N.Y.C. Ballet Co., 1971, Balanchine Cast for PBS The Nutcracker Suite, N.Y.C., 1971; docent The Hammond Castle Mus., Gloucester, Mass., 1982-85; asst. mgr. The Gallery, Rockport, 1977-83; cons. The Galleries, Ltd., Wellesley, 1988; legal intern U. Ala. Health Svcs. Found., Birmingham, 1988-89; loan officer UN/UNFCU, N.Y.C., 1984-86; overnight counselor Germaine Lawrence Sch., Arlington, Mass, 1989-90; contracts mgr. for Eastern Region Unisys Corp., Berkeley Heights, N.J., 1990-92; fin. cons. Innovatech, Lexington, Mass., 1992-93, 94-95; contract analyst Guy Carpenter & Co., Inc., N.Y.C., 1994; gen. counsel Mojo Working Prodns., 1996. Chair Cordell Hull Speakers' Forum, Birmingham, 1988-89; alumnae class sec. Chatham Coll. Class of 1980s, Pitts., 1983-87, 97—. Clk. of vestry The Ch. of the Resurrection, N.Y.C., 1993-95, mem. vestry, 1995-97; overnight counselor The Germaine Lawrence Sch., Arlington, Mass., 1989-90. Recipient Cert. of Appreciation 1990 Alumni award Cumberland Sch. Law, 1990; named to Nat. Dean's List, 1989-90. Mem. DAR (Cape Ann chpt. const. week chair 1993-94, Mass. const. week chair 1995-97, N.Y.C. chpt. jr. com. mem. Sons and Daus. Gala Ball 1996), The Federalist Soc. (Cumberland chpt. treas. 1988-89, adv. bd. 1983, sec. 1987-88), Clan Menzies Soc. N.Am., Clan Menzies Soc. Scotland, Princeton Club, Thayer Families Assn., Daus. Union Vets. of Civil War 1861-65: Hudson Valley-N.Y. Metro Tent, Mass. Soc. Mayflower Descs., Baronial Order Magna Charta, Dames of Ct. of Honor, Nat. Soc. Magna Charta Dames and Barons, Nat. Soc. Col. Daus. Seventeenth Century (Rensselaerswyck chpt.), Nat. Soc. First Families of Minn., Soc. of the Friends of St. George's and Descs. of Knights of the Garter, Soc. of Desc. of Knights of the Most Noble Order of the Garter, Hugnenot Soc. Am., Order of Wash., N.Y. State Continental Soc. Daus. of Indian Wars 1607-1900, St. Georges Soc. N.Y., First Families Ohio, Colonial Order the Crown, The Sovereign Colonial Soc. Ams. of Royal Descent, The Plantagenet Soc., Nat. Soc. Descs. of Early Quakers, Nat. Soc. Colonial Daus. of the 17th Century. Republican. Episcopalian. Avocations: lobstering, sailing, fishing, swimming, bicycling. Address: Brier Neck 13 Salt Island Rd Gloucester MA 01930-1972 Fax: 516-498-1729. E-mail: meansert@email.msn.com.

MEANS, JAMES ANDREW, engineer; b. Heavener, Okla., Oct. 11, 1937; s. Edward Andrew and Lorena (Nobles) M.; Therese Louise Zimmermann, Feb. 21, 1959; children: James A. Jr., William R., Charles E., Vicky M. Locken. BSEE, U. Ariz., 1962, MSEE, 1966; PhD, U. Calif., Santa Barbara, 1972; MS in Computer Sci., Chapman U., Orange, Calif., 1988. Engr. Pacific Missile Test Ctr., Pt Mugu, Calif., 1962-72, engr. mgr., 1972-79; tech. dir. Space and Missile Test Orgn., Vandenberg AFB, Calif., 1979-89; sr. tech. advisor SRI Internat., Menlo Park, 1990—. Cons. Agri-Craft, Camarillo, Calif., 1968-70, Astro-Geo-Marine, Ventura, Calif., 1972-74. Patentee in field. Mem. Internat. Found. for Telemetering (pres. 1989-95), Internat. Test and Evaluation Assn. (Allen R. Mattews Award, 1991). Democrat. Baptist. Avocations: water skiing, fishing, hunting, old cars. Home and Office: 284 St Andrews Way Lompoc CA 93436-1355 E-mail: jim.means@sri.com.

MEANS, JOHN BARKLEY, foreign language educator, association executive; b. Cin., Jan. 2, 1939; s. Walker Wilson and Rosetta M. Miller (Barkley) M. BA, U. Ill., 1960, MA, 1963, PhD, 1968. U.S. govt. intelligence rsch. analyst on Brazil CIA, Washington, 1962-64; assoc. prof. Spanish and Portugese Temple U., Phila., 1972-82, prof. Portuguese and critical langs., 1982—, co-chmn. dept. Spanish and Portuguese, 1971-75, dir. Center for Critical Langs., 1975—, dir. Inst. for Langs. and Internat. Studies, 1987—, chmn. dept. Germanic and Slavic Langs. and lit., 1992-94, chair univ. core programs, 1995-97. Cons. on Brazilian-Portuguese and second lang. acquisition and self instrnl. programs for less commonly taught langs. , 1968—; cons. editor for langs. Norton Pubs., 1979—95; cons. in field. Editor: Essays on Brazilian Literature, 1971; author: (with others) Language in Education: Theory and Practice, 1988—, (CD-ROM) Critical Language Series; contbr. articles to profl. jours. Trustee Bristol (Pa.) Riverside Theatre, 1990-2002; mng. trustee Means Charitable Trust, 1993—. 1st lt. U.S. Army, 1960-62. NDEA fellow, 1962, 64; grantee U.S. Dept. Edn., 1979-83, Japan Found., 1980, 82, 89-91, ARCO Chem. Found., 1991, 93. Mem. MLA, S.E., S.R., Nat. Coun. on Langs. and Internat. Studies (bd. dirs.), Joint Nat. Com. for Langs. (bd. dirs.), Nat. Assn. Self-Instrnl. Lang. Programs (exec. dir. 1977-98, editor jour. 1978-94, exec. dir. emeritus 1999—), Am. Coun. on Teaching Fgn. Lang., Nat. Coun. Orgns. Less Commonly Taught Langs. (exec. sec.-treas. 1990-2001), Nat. Assn. State Univs. and Land Grant Colls. (commn. on internat. affairs), Pi Kappa Phi, Phi Lambda Beta, Sigma Delta Pi. Home: PO Box 829 Washington Crossing PA 18977-0829 Office: Temple U Ctr for Critical Langs Anderson Hall 1114 W Berks St Philadelphia PA 19122-6090 E-mail: means@temple.edu.

MEANS, LANE LEWIS, entertainer; b. Livermore, Calif., Jan. 8, 1951; d. Richard Leroy and Norma Lillian (Ghiozzi) Lewis; m. David Albert Means, Apr. 30, 1984. BA in Phys. Edn., Calif. State U., Chico, 1973; BA in Dance, U. Calif., Irvine, 1975, MFA, 1977. Dancer Penrod-Plastino Movement Theater, Irvine, 1977-80, America by Nite, Bangkok, Manila and Japan, 1980, Penthouse Pet Revue, Reno, 1981, Bal du Moulin Rouge, Reno, 1981-82, Hello Hollywood, Ito, Japan, 1982-83; ice skater Razzle Dazzle, Reno, 1984-85, Las Vegas on Ice, Acapulco, Mex., 1986—. Choreographer, dance instr. Directions in Dance, Torrance, Calif., 1977—78, Irvine Acad. Performing Arts, 1978; choreographer Kenai Alaska Jr. Miss Fashion Show, 1991—95; guest artist Kenai Peninsula Coll. Dancers, 1990; adj. faculty, dance instr. Kenai Peninsula Coll., 1991—2002, choreographer, 1991; vol. advisor Kenaitze-Dena'ing Jabila'ina Dancers, vol. asst. dance leader; dir., choreographer Skyview H.S. Skylight Dancers, 1998—2001; dir. Kenai Swinging Golden Girls, 1998—2002; mem. Fireweed Dancers, 1998. Treatment specialist Kenai Peninsula Community Care Ctr., 1988-90. Home and Office: PO Box 1363 Kenai AK 99611-1363 E-mail: lmeans@gci.net.

MEANS, NATRONE JERMAINE, professional football player; b. Apr. 26, 1972; Student, U. N.C. Running back San Diego Chargers, 1991-96, 98—, Jacksonville Jaguars, 1996-97, San Diego Chargers, 1998-99, Carolina Panthers, 2000—. Selected to Pro Bowl, 1994. Achievements include being a mem. San Diego Chargers AFC Champions, 1994. Office: Carolina Panthers Ericsson Stadium 800 S Mint St Ste 2 Charlotte NC 28202-1502*

MEANS, ROBERT TAYLOR, JR. hematologist, educator; b. Midland, Tex., July 14, 1957; s. Robert Taylor and Anna Therese (Cassidy) M.; m. Stacey W. McKenzie, May 23, 1992; children: Anna, Robert III, Patrick. BA in Biochemistry, Rice U., 1979; MD, Vanderbilt U., 1983. Diplomate Am. Bd. Internal Medicine; cert. in hematology. Resident Baylor Coll. Medicine, Houston, 1983-86; fellow in hematology Vanderbilt U., Nashville, 1986-88, instr. medicine, 1988-90, asst. prof. medicine, 1990-92; assoc. investigator VA Med. Ctr., 1988-91, asst. chief hematology/oncology Cin., 1992-98; assoc. prof. med. U. Cin., 1992-98; prof. med., head hematology, assoc. divsn. chief Med. U. S.C., 1998-2000, dir. divsn. hematology-oncology, 2000—; chief hematology/oncology VA Med. Ctr., Charleston, S.C., 1998—. Contbr. chpts. to books, articles to profl. jours. Recipient Career Devel. award Dept. Veterans Affairs., 1988, Henry Christian award Am. Fedn. Clin. Rsch., 1991. Mem. Am. Soc. Hematology, Internat. Soc. Exptl. Hematology, Soc. Exptl. Biology and Medicine, Phi Beta Kappa. Achievements include being first to report response of anemia of chronic disease to erythropoietin; first description of erythropoietin receptor in polycythemia. Home: 2575 Marsh Creek Dr Charleston SC 29414-6578 Office: Hematology Oncology Ste 903 96 Jonathan Lucas St Charleston SC 29425 E-mail: meansr@musc.edu.

MEANS, ROSALINE, business executive, business educator; b. Manila, The Philippines; came to U.S., 1952; d. Cheng Peng and Lu Chong (Siy) Limtiuco; m. Cyril Chestnut Means, Jr., Nov. 8, 1958 (dec Oct., 1992); children: Elizabeth Rose Thayer Means, Annette Thayer Means, Cyril III. AA in Pre-law, U. Santo Tomas, Manila, The Philippines, 1949; BS in Comm. Edn., U. East, Manila, 1951; MA in Edn., U. Iowa, 1953; postgrad., CUNY, 1956-58. Tchr. Chinese Rep. Sch., Manila, 1947-52; corp. dir. and officer various cos. and corps., 1950-70; edn. specialist U. Hosp. Sch., Iowa City, 1952-53; lectr. SUNY Urban Ctr., Bklyn., 1967-73; adj. lectr. cmty. coll. CUNY, 1969-72, various positions, 1973-84; adj. prof. L.I. U., Bklyn., 1978; lectr. Ednl. Opportunity Ctr., 1973-95. Author: First Steps in Conversation, 1954; stage performances include Two for the Seesaw, The Defender, Stage Door. Mem. Legis Adv. Com. N.Y. State Senate, 11th. Dist., 1990; treas. PSC/CUNY. Recipient Cmty. Leaders and Noteworthy Ams. award, 1975-76, formal recognition Bus. and Profl. Women of Cape Ann, 1996; named Goddess of Arts-Beauty Queen, 1954, Miss Fashion Model of Yr., 1954. Mem. Liedenkranz of City of N.Y. (music libr. and treas.). Avocations: classical music, fishing, boating; candidate Mrs. N.Y. Am. Beauty Pageant, 1990. Home: 44 Fairview Ave Great Neck NY 11023-1224

MEANS, THOMAS CORNELL, lawyer; b. Charleston, S.C., Oct. 3, 1947; s. Thomas Lucas and Dean (Cornell) M.; m. Judith Faye Perlmutter, Sept. 10, 1977; children: Benjamin, Samuel. AB, Dartmouth Coll., 1969; postgrad., Princeton Theol. Sem., 1970-71; M of Pub. Adminstrn., U. Colo., 1975; JD, George Washington U., 1978. Bar: D.C. 1978, U.S. dist. Ct. (D.C. dist.), U.S. Ct. Appeals (4th and D.C. cirs.) 1979, U.S. Ct. Appeals (10th cir.) 1983, U.S. Ct. Appeals (6th and 11th cirs.) 1989, U.S. Ct. Appeals (9th cir.) 1992, U.S. Ct. Appeals (8th cir.) 1993, U.S. Ct. Appeals (5th cir.) 1996. Social worker Vinyard Childcare, Ann Arbor, Mich., 1969-70; rsch. analyst, registered lobbyist Colo. Counties, Inc., Denver, 1972-75; assoc. Jones, Day, Reavis and Pogue, Washington, 1978-79; assoc. then ptnr. Crowell & Moring LLP, 1979—. Mem. state adv. coun. on pub. Pers. Mgmt., Colo. State Govt., Denver, 1974-75; lectr. mining law; chmn. coal com. Ea. Mineral Law Found., 1988-89, chmn. spl. insts., ass. sec., 1989-91, sec., 1991-92, v.p., 1992-93, pres., 1993-94, exec. com., 1989-96, trustee, 1989—, mem. bd. editors, 1994—; bd. advisors Nat. Law Ctr., 1993-94. Contbr. articles to profl. jours. Mem. George Washington Law Alumni Assn. (bd. dirs. 1986-96, exec. com. 1987-96, treas. 1987-88, sec. 1988-90, pres. 1992-94), Order of Coif, Cosmos Club (Washington), Phi Beta Kappa. Home: 6411 Dahlonega Rd Bethesda MD 20816-2101 Office: Crowell & Moring LLP 1001 Pennsylvania Ave NW Fl 10 Washington DC 20004-2595

MEANS, TINA, police officer, consultant; b. L.A., June 9, 1961; d. Melvin Julian and Theresa Alberta Means; m. Marvin Alton Hatchett, July 7, 1995; children: Ciyani, Taliya, Naleya. AA in Liberal Arts, Santa Monica Coll., 1982; BSBA, Calif. State U.-Dominguez Hill, Carson, 1984; MPA, City U., Bellevue, Wash., 1996; postgrad., Capella U. Basic, intermediate and advance certs., Calif. Commn. on Peace Officers and Tng.; cert. cons. Police officer trainee, police officer City of Pasadena, Calif., 1990-91; police officer sch. police dept. Pasadena Unified Sch. Dist., 1991—. Cons. Pasadena Prep. Sch., 1999—, Internat. Outreach Ministry, Inc., Pasadena, 1999—. Bd. dirs. Pasadena Family Ctr. Mem. ASPA, ASTD, Justice Rsch. and Stats. Assn. Avocations: reading, cooking, singing, planning training seminars. Office: Pasadena Unified Sch Dist Sch Police Dept 351 S Hudson Ave Pasadena CA 91101-3599 Home: 1291 N Vallejo Way Upland CA 91786-3052 E-mail: tlm.fifthdegree@verizon.net.

MEANS COLEMAN, ROBIN RENEE, communications educator; b. Pitts., Feb. 26, 1969; d. Marcel Theodore Sr. and Patricia (Lloyd) M.; m. Randy Tyrone Coleman, July 28, 1996. BA in Comm., Chatham Coll., 1991; MA in Comm., U. Mo., Columbia, 1993; PhD in Mass Comm., Bowling Green State U., 1996; postgrad., U. Pitts., 1996-98. Adminstrv. asst. Bethesda Adult Literacy Program, Pitts., 1990; tchg. fellow U. Mo., 1991-93; tchg.-adminstrv. fellow Bowling Green State U., 1993-96; rsch. assoc. U. Pitts., 1996-98; asst. prof. media ecology NYU, 1998—. Project cons. Ctr. Family Excellence, Pitts., 1996—. Author: African American Viewers and the Black Situation Comedy: Situating Racial Humor, 1998; contbr. profl. articles to The Bulletin, 1996. Ballot counter Boone County, Columbia, 1992; vol. voter registration Urban League, Pitts., 1988. Postdoctoral fellow U. Pitts., 1996. Mem. Internat. Comm. Assn., Speech Comm. Assn. Democrat. Baptist. Avocations: cinema, African-Am. literature, travel, 5K walk races, concerts. Home: 15 Washington Pl Apt 4J New York NY 10003-6645 Office: NYU Dept Culture and Comm 239 Greene St # 735 New York NY 10003-6674

MEANY, PHILIP AUGUSTUS, library director; b. Oakland, Calif., Oct. 20, 1938; s. John Philip and Mary Gertrude (Deasy) M. BA, St. Mary's Coll., Moraga, Calif., 1960; M Librarianship, U. Wash., 1963. Asst. libr. Centralia (Wash.) Coll., 1963-68, media svcs. and tech. processes libr., 1969-88, libr. dir., 1988—. Mem. Wash. State Bicycling Adv. Com., Olympia, 1990-99; pres. Destination Centralia Mktg. Assn., 1999-2001. Recipient Platinum Pedal, N.W. Bicycle Fedn., 1997. Mem. Coll. Librs. and Media Specialists Wash. State (pres. 1987-88), N.W. Mgmt. Ednl. Tech. Assn. Avocation: bicycling. Office: Centralia Coll Libr 600 W Locust St Centralia WA 98531

MEARA, ANNE, actress, playwright, writer; b. Bklyn., Sept. 20; d. Edward Joseph and Mary (Dempsey) M.; m. Gerald Stiller, Sept. 14, 1954; children: Amy, Benjamin. Student, Herbert Berghoff Studio, 1953-54. Apprentice in summer stock, Southold, L.I. and Woodstock, N.Y., 1950-53; off-Broadway appearances include A Month in the Country, 1954, Maedchen in Uniform, 1955 (Show Bus. off-Broadway award), Ulysses in Nightown, 1958, The House of Blue Leaves, 1970, Bosoms and Neglect, 1986, After-Play, 1996; Shakespeare Co., Two Gentlemen of Verona, Ctrl. Park, N.Y.C., 1957, Romeo and Juliet, 1988; Broadway plays: Spookhouse, 1982, Eastern Standard, 1989, Anna Christie, 1993 (Tony nomination Best Supporting Actress); film appearances include The Out-of-Towners, 1968, Lovers and Other Strangers, 1969, The Boys From Brazil, 1978, Fame, 1979, Nasty Habits (with husband Jerry Stiller), 1976, An Open Window, 1990, Mia, 1990, Awakenings, 1991, Reality Bites, 1994, Daytrippers, 1997, The Fish in the Bathtub, 1998, Southie, 1999, The Independent, 2001, Like Mike, 2002, comedy act, 1963—; appearances Happy Medium and Medium Rare, Chgo., 1960-61, Village Gate, Phase Two and Blue Angel, N.Y.C., 1963, The Establishment, London, 1963, QE II, 1990; syndicated TV series Take Five with Stiller and Meara, 1977-78; numerous appearances on TV game and talk shows, also spls. and variety shows; rec. numerous commls. for TV and radio (co-recipient Voice of Imagery award Advt. Bur. N.Y.); star TV series Kate McShane, 1975, Archie Bunker's Place, 1979, Alf, 1986-88; other TV appearances The Sunset Gang, The Detective, 1990, Avenue Z Afternoon, 1991, Murphy Brown, 1994, Homicide, 1996 (Emmy nomination), Will and Grace, 2002, Sex in the City, 2002, (TV movie) Jitters, 1997, All My Children, 1994-99, (TV movie) What Makes a Family, 2001; writer, actress TV movie The Other Woman, 1983 (co-recipient Writer's Guild Outstanding Achievement award 1983), Alf, To Make Up to Break Up, The Stiller and Meara pilot; author, actor (play) After-Play, 1996; author (play) Down the Garden Paths, 2000; video host (with Jerry Stiller) So You Want to Be an Actor? Recipient Outer Critic's Cir. Playwriting award for After-Play, 1995.

MEARDY, WILLIAM HERMAN, association executive; b. Peoria, Ill., Feb. 28, 1925; s. Herman and Madeleine (McReynolds) M.; m. Joyce Dorothy Horn, Mar. 28, 1946; children: William Wesley, Karen Lynn. Student, Bradley U., 1948-51; BA, Calif. State U., L.A., 1952, MA, 1958; postgrad., UCLA, 1964. Tchr. La Puente (Calif.) Union H.S., 1953-56; acad., personal and job placement counselor Mt. San Antonio Coll., Walnut, Calif., 1956-63; dean student pers. svcs. Rio Hondo Coll., Whittier, 1963-67; dean student services and activities Shasta Coll., Redding, 1967-70; exec. sec. Coun. Cmty. Coll. Bds., Evanston, Ill., 1970-72; founding exec. dir. Assn. Cmty. Coll. Trustees, Washington, 1972-88. Contbr. articles to profl. jours. Bd. dirs. Nat. Coun. for Responsible Pub. Interest Groups; chmn. West Covina (Calif.) coun. Boy Scouts Am., 1960-61. With USN, 1943-46, 1st lt. USAFR, 1952. Mem. Masons, Shriners (sec.). Home and Office: 13675 Sycamore Dr Whittier CA 90601-3848 E-mail: wmeardy2001@yahoo.com., w.h.meardy@att.net. *As I have made my way along life's road, I am often reminded of those who cared enough to help me over the rough spots. They gave me encouragement, support and love during those times I was in most need. My wife, my parents, my children, my teachers and my friends were my support team. From them I drew the strength that made me what I am today. Without them there would have been no bright tomorrow.*

MEARS, LINDA SHAW, artist; b. L.A., Apr. 23, 1949; d. Richard Frank and Lorae Veda (Lenhart) Shaw; m. Barney Edward Jensen, Aug. 18, 1983 (div. Aug. 1988); 1 child, Amy Rae Jensen Mears; m. Charles Everts Mears, July 22, 1989; 1 child, Elizabeth Ann Mears. AA, Sacramento (Calif.) City Coll., 1986. RN; lic. vocat. nurse. Nurse various, Sacramento, L.A., 1970-89; artist, 1987—. Works exhibited at Celebrity Centre Internat., Hollywood, 1993, Galerie Je Revins, Westport, Conn., 1996—, Yvon Daigle Galerie Art Naif, Quebec, 1996—, Galerie Pro Arte Kasper, Switzerland, 1992, 98, Uruguary Exhbn. of Am. Art, 1998-2001, toad Hall Galleries, Cooperstown, N.Y., N.Y.C., 1987—, Jay Johnson Am.'s Folk Heritage Gallery, N.Y.C., 1987-92, Frank J. Miele Gallery, N.Y.C., 1992—; oil paintings in permanent collection of Le Musee d'Art Internat. Yvon-M. Daigle, Quebec; oil paintings in the permanent collection of Musee d'Art Internat. Pyrenees, Rousillon, France; oil paintings in pvt. collections of Hollywood celebrities; group of oil paintings featured in "The Education of a Speculator" by Victor Niederhoffer, 1997; art on Christmas cards by Hallmark Cards, Inc., 1993—, calendars by Golden Turtle Press, 1991—, calendars at Japanese banks, Mega Press Agy., 1988—; art included in books "Naive Art Celebrates Mother Nature," 1999, "Naive Art Gallery," 1991. Mem. L.A. County Art Mus. Mem. Folk Art Mus. N.Y.C., Folk Art Soc. Home and Studio: 3309 Carse Dr Los Angeles CA 90029- Office: Linda Mears Studio 3309 Carse Dr Los Angeles CA 90029- E-mail: mearstudio@earthlink.net.

MEARS, PATRICK EDWARD, lawyer; b. Oct. 3, 1951; s. Edward Patrick and Estelle Veronica (Mislik) M.; m. Geraldine O'Connor, July 18, 1981. BA, U. Mich., 1973, JD, 1976. Bar: N.Y. 1977, Ill. 1996, Ind. 1997, U.S. Dist Ct. (so. and ea. dists) N.Y. 1977, Mich. 1980, U.S. Dist. Ct. (we. and ea. dists.) Mich. 1980, U.S. Ct. Appeals (6th cir.) 1983, Ill. 1996, Ind. 1997, U.S. Dist. Ct. (no. dist.) Ill. 1998, U.S. Dist. Ct. (no. dist.) Ind. 1998. Assoc. Milbank, Tweed, Hadley & McCloy, N.Y.C., 1976-79; ptnr. Warner, Norcross & Judd, Grand Rapids, Mich., 1980-91; sr. mem. Dykema Gossett PLLC, memnd Rapids, 1991—2002; with Dickinson Wright, PLLC, Grand Rapids, 2002—. Adj. prof. Grand Valley State U., Allendale, Mich., 1981-84; dir. Children's Law Ctr., 1994, Grand Rapids Ballet, 1994-99, East Grand Rapids Pub. Sch. Found., 1994-98. Author: Michigan Collection Law, 1981, 2d edit., 1983, Basic Bankruptcy Law, 1986, Bankruptcy Law and Practice in Michigan, 1987, 95, Revised Article 9 of the UCC in Michigan, 2001; contbg. author Collier Bankruptcy Practice Guide; contbr. articles to profl. jours. Chmn. legis. com. East Grand Rapids PTA, 1992-94. Fellow: Mich. State Bar Found. (sec. coun. real property sect. 1993—97, chair Uniform Comml. Code com. bus. law sect. 2000—), Am. Coll. Bankruptcy; mem.: ABA (chmn. com. real property sect. 1997—, chmn. workouts, bankruptcy and foreclosures), Fed. Bar Assn. (chmn. bankruptcy sect. We. Mich. chpt. 1992—94, newsletter editor 1998—, pres. 2001—02), Am. Law Inst., Am. Bankruptcy Inst., Mich. State Bar Assn., East Hills Athletic Club. Office: Dickinson Wright PLLC 200 Ottawa Ave NW Ste 900 Grand Rapids MI 49503 E-mail: pmears@dickinsonwright.com.

MEARS, WALTER ROBERT, journalist; b. Lynn, Mass., Jan. 11, 1935; s. Edward Lewis and Edythe Emily (Campbell) M.; m. Sally Danton, Dec. 28, 1956 (dec. Dec. 1962); children: Pamela (dec.), Walter Robert Jr. (dec.); m. Joyce Marie Lund, Aug. 4, 1963 (div. 1983); children: Stephanie Joy, Susan Marie; m. Carroll Ann Rambo, Mar. 1, 1986 (div. 1995); m. Frances R. Richarson, July 5, 1997. BA, Middlebury Coll., 1956, Litt.D. (hon.), 1977. Newsman AP, Boston, 1956, corr. Montpelier, Vt., 1956-60, state house corr. Boston, 1960-61, newsman Washington, 1961-69, chief polit. writer, 1969-72, asst. chief Washington bur., 1973-74, spl. corr., 1975, chief, 1977-83, v.p., 1978-2001, exec. editor, 1984-88, v.p., columnist, 1989-2001. Author: (with John Chancellor) The News Business, 1983, The New News Business, 1995. Trustee Middlebury Coll., 1980-84. Recipient ann. award AP Mng. Editors Assn., 1973; Pulitzer prize for Nat. Reporting, 1977 Mem. Phi Beta Kappa, Delta Kappa Epsilon. Clubs: Gridiron, Burning Tree. Address: 3831 N Tazewell St Arlington VA 22207

MEATS, STEPHEN EARL, English educator, editor, writer; b. LeRoy, Kans., Mar. 16, 1944; s. Cecil Eugene and Ruby Irene Meats; m. Mary Beth Williams, May 29, 1964 (div. Apr. 1983); m. Deborah Ann Leins, Aug. 20,

1983; children: John Isaac, Laura Elizabeth, Owen Williams, Edward Kane. BA in English, U. S.C., 1966, MA in English, 1968, PhD in English, 1972. Prof. English USAF Acad., Colorado Springs, Colo., 1968-72, U. Tampa, Fla., 1972-79, Pittsburg (Kans.) State U., 1979—. Chairperson humanities divsn. U. Tampa, 1974-79, dept. English, Pittsburg State U., 1979-85, 90—. Author: (poems) Looking for the Pale Eagle, 1993; editor: Revolutionary War Novels of William Gilmore Simms, 8 vols., 1976, Writings of Benjamin Franklin Perry, 3 vols, 1980; poetry editor The Midwest Quar., 1985—; author poetry, short stories; contbr. articles to profl. jours. Capt. USAF, 1968-72. Home: 2310 E Eighth St Pittsburg KS 66762 Office: Pittsburg State Univ 1701 S Broadway Pittsburg KS 66762 Fax: 620-235-4686. E-mail: smeats@pittstate.edu.

MEAUX, ALAN DOUGLAS, retired facilities technician, sculptor; b. Joliet, Ill., Sept. 10, 1951; s. Berry Lee and Luella Ann (Ferguson) M.; m. Letta Sue Nygaard, Sept. 15, 1984; children: Ashley Nicole, Lacey Marie. Student, Joliet Jr. Coll., 1969-71, Bradley U., 1971-72, U.S. Dept. Agr. Grad. Sch., 1972, Skagit Valley Coll., 1983-85. Photographer J.J.C. Blazer, Joliet Herald News, Joliet, 1969-71; auto mechanic Pohanka Olds and Fiat, Hillcrest Heights, Md., 1972-74, Hoffman Olds and Rolls Royce, Hartford, Conn., 1974-75; carpenter Klappenbach Constrn. Co., Moscow, 1975-79; property mgr. Olympic Builders, Oak Harbor, Wash., 1979-86; maintenance technician Troubleshooters Inc., 1986-87; facilities technician Island County Govt., Coupeville, Wash., 1987—. Chmn. safety com. Island County Govt., 1997, 98, 99, 2000; bronze sculptor Ronin Art Prodns., Oak Harbor, 1979—; appraiser class A Mid-Am. Appraisers Assn., Springfield, Mo., 1986—; bd. dirs. North West Token Kai, U. Wash., Seattle, 1989—, lectr., 1985; contbr. Nanka Token Kai, L.A., 1985—. Author: Japanese Samurai Weapons, 1989; prin. works exhibited at Mini Guild Children's Orthopedic Show, Ballard, Wash., 1986, Worldfest/Ethnic Heritage Coun., Seattle, 1988, 89, 90, Stanwood (Wash.) Invitational Art Show, 1988. Asst. coach Whidbey Islanders Soccer League, 1997-99; safety com. chmn. Island County Govt., 1998-2000. Mem. NRA (life), Law Enforcement Alliance Am. (life), Japanese Sword Soc. U.S. (life), N.W. Token Kai (charter, bd. dirs. 1989-91), Western Mus. Conf., Wash. Mus. Assn., Ethnic Heritage Coun., Nanka Token Kai, Japan Soc., Wash. Arms Collectors Assn., North Whidbey Sportmen's Assn. (chmn. range com., trustee), Leisure Acres Water Assn. (pres. 1998-2000), Internat. Defensive Pistol Assn., Ctrl. Whidbey Sportmen's Club, Whidbey Islanders Futbol Club (asst. coach for girls under 12, 1997-99). Avocations: hunting, fishing, woodworking, reading, collecting Japanese antiques. Office: Ronin Art Prodns 1287 E Hideaway Ln Oak Harbor WA 98277

MEBANE, BARBARA MARGOT, artistic director, choreographer; b. Sylacauga, Ala., July 21, 1947; d. Audrey Dixon and Mary Ellen (Yaikow) Baxley; m. James Lewis Mebane, Dec. 31, 1971; 1 child, Cieson Brooke. Grad., Brookhaven Coll., Dallas. Line performer J. Taylor Dance Co., Miami, Fla., 1964-65; sales mgr. Dixie Readers Svc., Jackson, Miss., 1965-67; regional sales mgr. Robertson Products Co., Texarkana, Tex., 1967-75; owner, pres. Telco Sales, Svc. and Supply, Dallas, 1976-90; dir. The Dance Factory performing co., Lewisville, Tex.; owner, artistic dir. Dancers Workshop Studios, Inc. Mem. Dance Masters, Miami, 1975—; mgr., choreographer music videos for pay/cable TV, 1985—; prodr. theatrical/musical shows to profl. theatre, coll. dists. and high schs; pub. speaker in field of positive thinking for women. Author: Paper on Positive Thinking, 1983. Sponsor Cancer Rsch. Ctr., Dallas, Flower Mound Bus. Womens Group. Named Bus. Woman of the Yr., Gov. Anne Richards, Tex., 1994. Mem. Nat. Fedn. Ind. Businesses, Internat. Register of Profiles Cambridge, Eng., Female and Minority Owned Bus. League, PDTA (Dallas Dance Coun.), TITAS. Avocations: working with children, teaching dance, writing. Office: Dancers Workshop 705 S Mill Lewisville TX 75057

MEBANE, FELICIA EUGENIA, healthcare educator; b. Greensboro, N.C., Mar. 23, 1967; d. William E. Mebane, Joyce G. Mebane. BSPH, U. N.C., 1989, MSPH, 1994; PhD, Harvard U., 1998. Fin. mgmt. trainee GE, Hickory, NC, 1989—92; post-doctoral fellow Harvard U., Cambridge, Mass., 1998—2001; asst. prof. health policy, politics and comms. U. N.C., Chapel Hill, 2001—. . Avocations: travel, reading, running, dancing. Business E-Mail: fmebane@unc.edu.

MEBANE, WILLIAM BLACK, controller, financial consultant; b. Vernon, Tex., Dec. 15, 1927; s. David Mitchell and Ida Virginia (Black) M.; m. Joan Hebbard Dumper, Nov. 24, 1956; children— David Alexander, Virginia Ann. BBA, Tex. A&M U., 1952; MBA, Harvard U., 1954. Mem. treas.'s office staff Gen. Motors Corp., N.Y.C., 1954-70; sec.-treas. Alfred P. Sloan Found., 1971-78; dir. fin. and adminstrn. Am. Diabetes Assn., 1979-80, dir. planning, 1981; v.p., comptroller NCCJ, Inc., N.Y.C., 1981-86, v.p. for fiscal affairs, 1987-88; fin. cons. Internat. House, 1989-90; ind. fin. cons., 1990-91; contr. Better Bus. Bur., N.Y.C., 1991-99. Vol. Essex Council Boy Scouts Am., 1967— . Served with USAAF, 1946-49. Recipient Silver Beaver award Boy Scouts Am., 1982 Mem.: Harvard Bus. Sch. (N.Y.C.); Short Hills (N.J.). Republican. Episcopalian. Home: 36 Haddonfield Rd Short Hills NJ 07078-3402

MEBUST, WINSTON KEITH, surgeon, educator; b. Malta, Mont., July 2, 1933; s. Hans G. and Anna C. (Leiseth) M.; m. Lora June Peterson, Sept. 15, 1955; children— Leanne, Kevin, Kreg, Kari. Student, U. Wash., 1951-54, MD, 1958. Diplomate: Am. Bd. Urology (trustee 1983-89, pres. 1988-89). Intern King County Hosp., Seattle, 1958-59; resident Virginia Mason Hosp., 1959-63, Kans. U. Med. Center, 1963-66; practice medicine, specializing in urology, 1966—; instr. surgery and urology U. Kans. Med. Center, Kansas City, 1966-69, asst. prof., 1969-72, asso. prof., 1972-76, chmn. urology sect., 1974—, prof., 1977—; chief urology service VA Hosp., Kansas City, Mo., 1966-75. Contbr. articles, chpts. to med. jours. and texts. Served with U.S. Army, 1961-63. Mem. ACS, Am. Cancer Soc., Am. Bd. Surgery, Kansas City Urol. Assn., Assn. for Acad. Surgery, Am. Urol. Assn. (pres. S. Ctrl. sect. 1983, exec. com. 1992—, treas. 1996—, pres. elect 2001-02, pres., 2002—), Wyandotte Med. Soc., Kans. Med. Assn., Soc. Univ. Urologists, Am. Assn. Genitourinary Surgeons, Sigma Xi, Alpha Omega Alpha. Republican. Home: 422 Lansbrook Dr Venice FL 34292-4620 Office: 39th and Rainbow Blvd Kansas City MO 66103 E-mail: wmebust@comcast.net.

MECABE, EDWIN JOSEPH, brokerage clearing company executive; b. Bklyn., Dec. 24, 1956; s. Catherine and Edwin Mecabe. Registered securities rep. With reorgn. dept. Drexel Burnham Lambert Inc., 1977-81; reorgn. mgr., ops. officer Becker Paribas Inc., 1981-84; reorgn. supr. Prudential-Bache Securities Inc., 1984; reorgn. account coord. The Depository Trust Co., 1984-85; v.p., reorgn./proxy dept. John Hancock Clearing Corp., 1985-93; mgr. securities ops. dept. N.Y. Stock Exch., N.Y.C., 1993—. Author book on reorgn. and corp. actions. Mem. Securities Industry Assn. (reorgn. div. officer, bd. dirs. 1988-90, chmn. reorgns. CNS com. 1988-90), CAM Group of L.I., Inc. (pres.). Home: 2088 Decker Ave North Merrick NY 11566-2125 Office: New York Stock Exchange One World Fin Ctr 20 Broad St New York NY 10005-2601

MECARTNEY, MARTHA L. engineering educator, researcher; b. Prairie du Chien, Wis., Sept. 8, 1955; d. John M. and Nancy (Wells) Mecartney; m. Lyle K. Norton; children: Iris. BA in Classics, BS in Metallurgical Engring. and Materials Sci., Case Western Res. U., 1979; PhD in Materials Sci. and Engring., Stanford U., 1984. Vis. scientist Max-Planck-Inst. fur Metalforschung, Stuttgart, Germany, 1984—85; faculty chem. engring. and materials sci. U. Minn., Mpls., 1985—90; prof. chem. engring. and materials sci. U. Calif., Irvine, 1990—, assoc. dean grad. studies, 1998—2000. Contbr. articles to profl. jours. Recipient Crystal award, MANA of Orange County, 2001; fellow Packard in sci. and engring., Packard Found., 1988. Mem.: Microscopy Soc. Am., Materials Rsch. Soc., Am. Ceramics Soc. Avocation: social justice. Office: Univ Calif Irvine Dept Chem Engring & Materials Sci Irvine CA 92697-2575 Office Fax: 949-824-2541. Business E-Mail: martham@uci.edu.

MECH, TERRENCE FRANCIS, library director; b. Birdorup Park, Wiltshire, Eng., Feb. 24, 1953; s. Emil Paul and Madelyn (Tremmel) M. BS, U. Wis., Stevens Point, 1975; MS, Ill. State U., 1978; MLS, Clarion U., 1979; EdD, Pa. State U., 1994. Pub. svcs. libr. Tusculum Coll., Greensville, Tenn., 1979-80; libr. dir. Coll. of the Ozarks, Clarksville, Ark., 1980-82, King's Coll., Wilkes-Barre, Pa., 1982—, dir. libr., 1982—, v.p. for info. and instrnl. techs., 1994—2001. Bd. dirs. Northeastern Pa. Bibliographic Ctr., 1982—; mem., officer Coun. Pa. Libr. Networks, 1984-89, chair, 1987-89. Contbr. chpts. to books and articles to profl. jours. Mem. ALA, Pa. Libr. Assn. (bd. dirs. 1986-87, various coms. 1985—). Office: Kings Coll 14 W Jackson St Wilkes Barre PA 18701-2010

MECHAM, GLENN JEFFERSON, lawyer, mayor; b. Logan, Utah, Dec. 11, 1935; s. Everett H. and Lillian (Dunford) M.; m. Mae Parson, June 5, 1957; children: Jeff B., Scott R., Marcia, Suzanne. BS, Utah State U., 1957; JD, U. Utah, 1961; grad., Air Command and Staff Coll., 1984, Air War Coll., 1984. Bar: Utah 1961, Supreme Ct. U.S., U.S. Ct. Appeals (10th cir.), U.S. Dist. Ct. Utah, U.S. Ct. Claims. Gen. practice law, 1961-65; atty. Duchesne County, Utah, 1962, City of Duchesne, 1962; city judge Roy City, Utah, 1963-66; judge City of Ogden, 1966-69, mayor, 1992-2000. Lectr. law and govt. Stevens-Henager Coll., Ogden, 1963-75; asst. U.S. atty., 1969-72; ptnr. Mecham & Richards, Ogden, Utah, 1972-82; pres. Penn Mountain Mining Co., South Pacific Internat. Bank, Ltd.; mem. Bur. Justice Stats. Adv. Bd., U.S. Dept. Justice, U.S. Conf. Mayors; chmn. Marina Capital Inc. Chmn. Ogden City Housing Authority, Marine Capital, Inc.; chmn. bd. trustees Utah State U., Space Dynamics Lab; mem. adv. coun. Fed. Home Loan Bank; pres. Utah League Cities and Towns, 1981—82; vice chmn. Wasatch Front Reg. Coun. Col. USAF, 1957; chmn. Marina Capital, Inc.; No. Utah liaison U.S. Sen. Robert F. Bennett. Recipient Disting. Svcs. award Utah State U., Weber State U. Mem ABA, Weber County Bar Assn. (pres. 1966-68), Utah Bar Assn., Am. Judicature Soc., Weber County Bar Legal Svcs. (chmn. bd. trustees 1966-69), Utah Assn. Mcpl. Judges (sec.), Ogden-Weber C. of C. (Order of the Big Hat), Sigma Chi, Phi Alpha Delta. Home: 1715 Darling St Ogden UT 84403-0556

MECHAM, STEVEN RAY, school system administrator; b. Salt Lake City, Oct. 10, 1938; s. Milton Claudius and Marjorie (White) M.; m. Donna Jean Johnson, Jan. 22, 1943; children: Brian Paul, Allan LeRoy. AS, Weber State Coll., 1958; BS, U. Utah, 1963; MA, Tchrs. Coll., Columbia U., 1965; postgrad., McGill U.; PhD, U. Calif., Santa Barbara, 1981. Prin. Montreal Oral Sch., 1966-70; state dir. hearing impaired Conn. Dept. Edn., 1970-71; dir. guidance Lexington Sch. for Deaf, N.Y.C., 1971-72; supt. Exton Elem., Ana Frank Jr. and sr. H.S., Mexico City, 1972-77; coord. spl. edn. Weber Sch. Dist., Ogden, Utah, 1977-78; prin. Roosevelt Elem. Sch., 1978-82; asst. supt. Weber County Schs., 1982-87; assoc. supt. Utah Schs., 1990-93; supt. Weber Sch. Dist., 1993-98, dir. Odyssey, 1998—. Instr. U. Utah, 1965-66, St. Joseph Coll., Hartford, Conn., 1970-71; pres. Finnish Mission-LDS Russia and Baltic States, 1987-90; adj. prof. McGill U.; instr. Tchrs. Coll., Columbia U., 1968-70; aching chmn. dept. edn. U. Americas, Mexico City, 1976-77; cons. Far West Labs., San Francisco. Contbr. articles to profl. jours. Bd. dirs. Instituto Mexicano Norte Americano de Relaciones Culturales, Mexico City, 1975-76; bishop, stake pres. Ch. Jesus Christ of Latter-day Saints, pres. Finnish Mission; bd. dirs. Am. Cancer Soc. Weber County. Mem. Am. Orgn. Educators Hearing Impaired (pres.), Can. Hearing Soc. (dir.), Utah Assn. Elem. Sch. Prins., Nat. Assn. Elem. Sch. Prins., Internat. Reading Assn., Am. Assn. Sch. Adminstrs., Alexander Graham Bell Assn., PTA, Rotary. Home: 518 Padre Lakes Dr Ivins UT 84738

MECHANIC, DAVID, social sciences educator; b. N.Y.C., Feb. 21, 1936; s. Louis and Tillie (Penn) Mechanic; m. Kathleen Mars Wiltshire; children: Robert Edmund, Michael Alexander. BA, CCNY, 1956; MA, Stanford U., 1957, PhD, 1959. Faculty U. Wis., Madison, 1960—79, prof. sociology, 1965—73, John Bascom prof., 1973—79; dir. U. Wis. (Center for Med. Sociology and Health Services Research), 1971—79, chmn. dept. sociology, 1968—70; prof. social work and sociology Rutgers U., New Brunswick, NJ, 1979—, acting dean faculty arts and scis., 1980—81, Univ. prof., dean faculty arts and scis., 1981—84, Univ. prof. and Rene Dubos prof. behavioral scis., 1984—, dir. Inst. for Health, Health Care Policy and Aging Research, 1985—. Nat. dir. Robert Wood Johnson Found. Investigators awards in Health Policy Rsch. Program, 2000—; mem. panel on health svcs. rsch. Pres.'s Sci. Adv. Com., 1971—72; mem. treatment com. on reduction of cancer mortality Nat. Cancer Inst., 1984; vice-chmn. com. pain, disability and chronic illness behavior Inst. Medicine-NAS, 1985—86, mem. panel on prevention of disability, 1989—90, mem. panel on new data for an aging world, 1999—2000; mem. com. on capitalizing on social sci. and behavioral rsch. to improve the pubs. health Inst. Medicine, 1999; mem. Com. on Prevention of Mental Disorder, 1992—94; coord. panel Pres.'s Commn. Mental Health, 1977—78; mem. Nat. Adv. Coun. Aging, NIH, 1982—86; expert adv. panel on mental health WHO, 1984—89; mem. health adv. bd. GAO, 1987—95; mem. panel on tech., ins. and health care sys. Office of Tech. U.S. Congress, 1992—95; mem. nat. com. on vital and health stats. HHS, 1988—92; mem. commn. on behavioral and social scis. and edn. NRC, 1992—95; mem-.commn. on med. edn. Robert Wood Johnson Found., 1990—92; mem. adv. com. Picker/Commonwealth Scholar's Program, 1992—99; nat. adv. com. Robert Wood Johnson Scholars in Heatlh Policy Rsch. Program, 1992—99, mem. tech. adv. com., 2001—; mem. panel on Rethinking Disability Policy Nat. Acad. Social Ins., 1993—96; vis. scholar Kings Fund Inst., London, 1994—95. Author: Students Under Stress, 1962, Students Under Stress, 2d edit., 1978, Medical Sociology, 1968, Medical Sociology, rev. edit., 1978, Mental Health and Social Policy, 1969, Mental Health and Social Policy, rev. edit., 1980, 1989, 1999, Public Expectations and Health Care, 1972, Politics, Medicine and Social Science, 1974; author: (with Charles E. Lewis and Rashi Fein) A Right to Health, 1976; author: Growth of Bureaucratic Medicine, 1976, Future Problems in Health Care, 1979, From Advocacy to Allocation: The Evolving American Health Care System, 1986, Painful Choices: Research and Essays on Health Care, 1989, Inescapable Decisions: The Imperatives of Health Reform, 1994; author, editor: Symptoms, Illness Behavior and Help-Seeking, 1982; editor: Handbook of Health, Health Care and the Health Professions, 1983, Improving Mental Health Services: What the Social Sciences Can Tell Us, 1987, General Hospital Impatient Psychiatry, 1997, Managed Behavioral Health Care: Current Realities and Future Potential, 1998; co-editor (with Robert Hauser, Archibald Haller and Tess Hauser): Social Structure and Personality, 1982; co-editor: (with Linda Aiken) Applications of Social Science to Clinical Medicine and Social Policy, 1986; co-editor: Paying for Services: Promises and Pitfalls of Capitation, 1989; co-editor: (with Marian Osterweis and Arthur Kleinman) Pain and Disability: Clinical Behavior and Public Policy Perspectives, 1987; co-editor: (with Carl Taube and Ann Hohmann) The Future of Mental Health Services Research, 1989. Recipient Ward medal, CCNY, 1956, Med. Sociologists award, Am. Sociol. Assn., 1983, Carl Taube award, APHA, 1990, Disting. Investigator award, Assn. for Health Svcs. Rsch., 1991, Disting. Contbn. award mental health sect., Soc. for Study of Social Problems, 1991, Emily Mumford medal, Columbia U., 1991, Investigator award in health policy rsch., Robert Wood Johnson Found., 1995—99, Health Svcs. Rsch. prize, Assn. of U. Programs in Health Adminstrn. and the Baxter Allegiance Found., 1997; fellow Ford Behavioral Sci. fellow, 1956—57, NIMH rsch. fellow, 1965—66, Ctr. for Advanced Study in Behavioral Scis., 1974—75, Guggenheim fellow, 1977—78, Disting. fellow, Assn. Health Svcs. Rsch., 1996. Fellow: AAAS (chmn. sect. social, econ. and polit. scis. 1985), Assn. Health Svcs. Rsch. (disting. 1996); mem.: NAS, Hogg Found. Mental Health (nat. adv. coun. 1987), Nat. Acad. Social Ins. (founding), Am. Acad. Arts and Scis., Inst. Medicine-NAS (governing coun. 1972—74), Sociol. Rsch. Assn. (pres. 1991—92), Am. Sociol. Assn. (chmn. med. sociol. sect. 1969—70, governing coun. 1977—78, chmn. publs. com. 1989—91, chmn. mental health sect. 1992—93, Lifetime Achievement award mental health sect. 1994, Disting. Career award 2001), Phi Beta Kappa. Office: Rutgers U Inst Health Policy Aging Rsch 30 College Ave New Brunswick NJ 08901-1283 Home: 5 Overbrook Dr Princeton NJ 08540-3924 E-mail: mechanic@rci.rutgers.edu.

MECHEM, CHARLES STANLEY, JR. former broadcasting executive, former golf association executive; b. Nelsonville, Ohio, Sept. 12, 1930; s. Charles Stanley and Helen (Hall) Mechem; m. Marilyn Brown, Aug. 31, 1952; children: Melissa, Daniel, Allison. AB, Miami U., Oxford, Ohio, 1952; LL.B., Yale U., 1955. Bar: Ohio 1955. Practice in, Cin., 1955-67; partner Taft, Stettinius & Hollister, 1965-67; chmn. bd. Taft Broadcasting Co., Cin., 1967-90; commr. LPGA, Daytona Beach, Fla., 1990-95, commr. emeritus, 1995—; chmn. U.S. Shoe, 1993-95; chmn. Cin. Bell, Inc., 1996-98, Convergys Corp., 1998-2000; cons. Arnold Palmer Enterprises, Cin., 1996—. Bd. dir. Myers Y. Cooper Co., J.M. Smucker Co., Royal Precision, Inc., Molecular Circuitry, Inc., Messer Constrn., Inc. Capt. JAGC U.S. Army, 1956—59. Mem.: Cin. C. of C. (pres. 1977), Comml. Club. Office: Taft Stettinius & Hollister LLP 425 Walnut St Ste 1800 Cincinnati OH 45202-4122

MECHLIN, GEORGE FRANCIS, electrical manufacturing company executive; b. Pitts., July 23, 1923; s. George Francis and Ruth (Butler) M.; m. Mary Louise Megaffin, June 25, 1949; children— Thomas Walker, Ann Louise. BS in Physics, U. Pitts., 1944, MS in Physics, 1949, PhD in Physics, 1951. With Westinghouse Electric Corp., 1949-87, gen. mgr. astronuclear/oceanic div., 1971-72, v.p. astronuclear lab., oceanic and marine divs., 1972-73, v.p. R & D Pitts., 1973-87; pub. svc. cons., 1990—. Past bd. dirs. Buhl Planatarium. Recipient Meritorious Public Service award U.S. Navy, 1961, John J. Montgomery award Nat. Soc. Aerospace Profls. and San Diego Aerospace Mus., 1961; Order of Merit award Westinghouse Electric Corp., 1961 Mem. Am. Phys. Soc., AIAA, Nat. Acad. Engring., Sigma Xi. Home: 960 Via Malibu Aptos CA 95003-5617 E-mail: gfmi@pacbell.net.

MECIK, Z. RICHARD, communications executive; b. Poland; came to U.S., 1980. MS, Pace U., 1986; BBA, Maritime Acad., Gdynia, Poland, 1976. Chief adminstrn. officer Polish Ocean Lines, Gdansk, Poland, 1976-81; investment acct. Columbia U., N.Y.C., 1981-84; tax cons. Mecik & Co., 1984-86; sr. auditor Leshkowitz & Co., 1986-89; fin. contr. Goodrich & Sherwood, 1989-90; CFO Fada Industries, 1990-92; COO Basic Am. Foods, San Francisco, 1992-95; dir. fin. Sprint Internat./Global One, Reston, Va., 1995—.

MECIMORE, CHARLES DOUGLAS, retired accounting educator; b. Belmont, N.C., Aug. 20, 1934; s. John Edgar and Hattie (Bolick) M.; m. Barbara Jean Chiddie, June 7, 1959; children: Laura Jean, Charles D. Jr., John Amos. BS, Pfeiffer Coll., 1958; MS, U. N.C., 1962; PhD, U. Ala., 1966. CPA, N.C.; CMA. Asst. prof. U. Ala., Tuscaloosa, 1966-67; assoc. prof. U. Ga., Athens, 1967-71; prof. U. Cin., 1971-79; prof. acctg. Sch. Bus. and Econs., U. N.C., Greensboro, 1980-98; ret., 1998. Head dept. U. N.C. Sch. Bus. and Econs., 1980-89, 96-98. Served with USAF, 1951-55. Univ. scholar, 1963-66; Haskins and Sells fellow, 1962-64; Beyer bronze medal, 1974. Mem. AICPAs, N.C. Assn. CPAs (Outstanding Educator 1985), Am. Acctg. Assn., Inst. Mgmt. Acctg. Home: 430 Marshall View Ct Winston Salem NC 27101-5285 E-mail: MecimoreC@CS.com.

MECKE, WILLIAM MOYN, public affairs consultant; b. Detroit, May 7, 1957; s. Theodore Hart McCalla Jr. and Mary Eleanor (Flaherty) M. BA, Georgetown U., 1979; MA, Am. U., 1982; postgrad., Oxford U., 1982, U. N.C., 1982-85. Asst. dir. Found. Study Presdl. and Congrl. Terms, Washington, 1979-82; acct. exec. Hill and Knowlton, Inc., Chgo., 1985-86; tchr. The Bolles Sch., Jacksonville, Fla., 1986-88, St. Andrew's Sch., Savannah, 1988-91, Joseph Walker Sch., Marietta, Ga., 1991-92; polit. cons. various Democratic candidates, 1992-95; tech. writer Total Sys. Svcs. Inc., Columbus, Ga., 1995; dir. mktg. Habitat for Humanity Internat., Americus, 1995-2000, media svcs. mgr., 2000-2001; mgr. comms. Ga. Regional Transp. Authority, 2001—. Co-author, editor: Presidential and Congressional Term Limitation: The Issue That Stays Alive, 1981. Asst. dir. Found. Study Presd. and Congl. Terms, Washington, 1979-82. Mem. Pub. Rels. Soc. Am. Office: Ga Regional Transp Authority Ste 900 245 Peachtree Ctr Ave NE Atlanta GA 30303 E-mail: wmecke@grta.org.

MECKEL, PETER TIMOTHY, arts administrator, educator; b. Yankton, S.D., Nov. 28, 1941; s. Myron Eugene and Cynthia Ann (Turnblom) Meckel; m. Louise Gloria Mudge, Sept. 8, 1962; children: Christina Louise, Christopher Mark; m. Adrienne Dawn Maravich, Dec. 30, 1972; children: Moya Ann, Jon-Peter. Ed., Rockford Coll., Occidental Coll. Founder, gen. dir. Hidden Valley Music Seminars, Carmel Valley, Calif., 1963—; dir. Hidden Valley Opera Ensemble, Masters Festival of Chamber Music, Master Class Series. Cons. in field. Mem. Music Educators Nat. Conf. Congregationalist. Office: Hidden Valley Opera Ensemble PO Box 116 Carmel Valley CA 93924-0116 E-mail: hvms@aol.com.

MECKLENBURG, GARY ALAN, hospital executive; m. Lynn Kraemer; children: John, Sarah. BA, Northwestern U., 1968; MBA, U. Chgo., 1970. Adminstrv. resident Presbyn.-St. Luke's Hosp., Chgo., 1969-70, adminstrv. asst., 1970-71, asst. supt., 1971-76, assoc. supt., 1976-77, U. Wis. Hosps., Madison, 1977-80; adminstr. Stanford U. Hosp. Clinics, Calif.; pres., CEO St. Joseph's Hosp., Milw., 1980-85; pres., dir. Franciscan Health Care Inc., 1985; pres., CEO Northwestern Meml. HealthCare, Chgo., 1985—. Preceptor, guest lectr., mem. adv. bd. Kellogg Sch. Mgmt., chgo., 1986—; pres., chief exec. officer, dir. Northwestern Healthcare Network, 1990-92. Recipient Todd Scout award Boy Scouts Am., 1998, Chgo. Bus. Hall of Fame award Jr. Achievement, 2000, GSB Disting. Pub. Svc./Pub. Sector Alumnus award U. Chgo., 2000. Mem. Am. Hosp. Assn. (sect. met. hosps., governing coun. 1984-92, chmn. 1991, 2001, trustee 1996—, exec. com. 1997—, mem. regional policy bd., #5 1984, 87-89, 91-93, 95-99, chmn. 1996-99, 2001, mem. ho. dels. 1984, 87-89, 91—, mem. com. on med. edn. 1976-80), Ill. Hosp. Assn. (bd. dirs. 1988-95, chmn. 1994, mem. adv. panel coun. tchg. hosps. 1997—), U. Chgo. Hosp. Adminstrn. Alumni Assn. (pres. 1985-86), Econ. Club Chgo., Comml. Club Chgo. Office: Northwestern Meml Hosp 251 E Huron St Ste 3-708 Chicago IL 60611-2908

MECKSEPER, FRIEDRICH, painter, printermaker; b. Bremen, Germany, June 8, 1936; s. Gustav and Lily (Debatin) M.; m. Barbara Muller, Jan. 5, 1962; children: Julia, Josephine, Cornelius. Student, Acad. Fine Arts, Stuttgart, Germany, 1955-57, Acad. Fine Arts, Berlin, Germany, 1957-59. Prof. art Summer Acad., Salzburg, Austria, 1977-79. 200 one-man shows include Tokyo Galerie, 1972, Galerie Cramer Genf, 1973, Fischer Fine Art, London, 1976, Gimpel & Weitzenhoffer, N.Y.C., 1976, Mus. Boymans van Beuningen, Rotterdam, 1977, Worthington Gallery, Chgo., 1980; exhibited in roup shows, internat print biennales; represented in permanent collections at Staatsgalerie Stuttgart, Victoria and Albert Mys., London, Mus. Modern Art, N.Y.C., Nat. Gallery of Victoria, Melbourne, Mus. Boymans van Beuningen. Recipient German Rome prize Villa Massimo, 1964; prize Internat. Print-Biennale, Tokyo, 1970, Norwegian Internat. Print-Biennale, 1982. Address: Landhausstrasse 13 10717 Berlin Germany

MEDAGLIA, MARY-ELIZABETH, lawyer; b. Suffern, N.Y., Oct. 13, 1947; d. Joseph Mario and Edith Elizabeth (Price) M. BA, Sweet Briar Coll., 1969; JD, U. Va., 1972. Bar: Va. 1972, D.C. 1974, U.S. Ct. Appeals (D.C. cir.) 1974, U.S. Supreme Ct. 1980, U.S. Ct. Appeals (4th, 5th, 9th and 11th cirs.) 1981, U.S. Ct. Appeals (10th cir.) 1982, Md. 1990, U.S. Ct. Appeals (2d cir.) 1998. Law clk. to judge D.C. Ct. Appeals, Washington, 1972-74; asst. atty. U.S. Atty.'s Office, 1974-79; deputy solicitor Fed. Labor Relations Authority, 1979-82, acting solicitor, 1982; assoc. Jackson & Campbell P.C., 1982-84, ptnr., 1984—. Sec. D.C. Bar, 1983-84, bd. govs. 1984-87. Fellow Am. Bar Found.; mem. ABA (chmn. TIPS com. on ins. coverage litigation 1989-91, ho. of dels. 1981-83), D.C. Bar Assn. (bd. dirs. 1980-83, chmn. young lawyers sect. 1980-81), Women's Bar Assn. D.C. (pres. 1982-83), Charles Fahy Am. Inn of Ct. (pres. 1990-92), Fedn. Def. and Corp. Counsel, Am. Soc. Writers on Legal Subjects, Phi Beta Kappa. Office: Jackson & Campbell PC South Tower 1120 20th St NW Ste 300S Washington DC 20036-3437 E-mail: LMedaglia@jackscamp.com.

MEDAK, PETER, film director; b. Budapest, Hungary; arrived in Eng., 1956; came to U.S., 1979; s. Gyula and Elisabeth (Diamonstein) M.; m. Julia Migenes, July 31, 1989; children: Christopher, Karen, Joshua, Cornelia, Martina, Jessica. Dir. (films) Negatives, 1968, A Day in the Death of Joe Egg, 1970, The Ruling Class, 1971, Ghost in a Nonnday's Sun, 1973, The Odd Job, 1977, The Changling, 1979, Zorro the Gay Blade, 1980, The Men's Club, 1986, The Krays, 1989, La Voix Humane, 1990, Let Him Have It, 1991, Romeo is Bleeding, 1992, Pontiac Moon, 1994, Hunchback of Notre Dame, 1996, Species 2, 1997, David Copperfield, 1998-99, Feast of All Saints, 2000, (stage) Miss Julie, 1977 (opera) Salome, 1988, La Voix Humane, and others. Mem. Dir.'s Guild of Am., Dir.'s Guild of U.K., Assn. of Cinematographers, Allied Technicians, Dir.'s Guild of Can. Jewish. Office: Scott J Feinstein 16255 Ventura Blvd Ste 625 Encino CA 91436-2307 also: Armstrong and Hirsch 1888 Century Park E Ste 1888 Century City CA 90067-1702

MEDAK, WALTER HANS, lawyer; b. Vienna, Austria, May 10, 1915; came to U.S., 1938; s. Hugo and Grete (Figdor) M.; m. Edith Rhodes, 1944 (div. 1957); 1 child, Ronald Harvard; m. Renée Rasens, 1996. Grad., Acad. of

Commerce, Vienna, 1934, U. Vienna, 1938; postgrad., U. Ga., 1939-40; MA in Econs., U. Calif., Berkeley, 1949; JD, Harvard U., 1948. Prodn. mgr. Mabs, Inc., L.A., 1942-43; prodn. engr. Kaiser Co., Richmond, Calif., 1943-45; atty. Belli & Medak, Walnut Creek, 1957-59; pvt. practice law Walnut Creek and Moraga, Calif., 1950—. Bd. dirs. Snyder/Newell, Inc., San Francisco; bd. dirs. Carnelian Woods, Carnelian Bay, Calif., pres., 1974-80. Mem. ABA, Calif. County Bar Assn., Assn. Trial Lawyers Am., Calif. Trial Lawyers Assn., Harvard Club (chmn. admissions and scholarship com. San Francisco chpt. 1973-74). Avocations: skiing, swimming, music, travel, French and German. Home: 2833 Ptarmigan Dr Apt 3 Walnut Creek CA 94595-3135 E-mail: walterhmedak@aol.com.

MEDALIE, JACK HARVEY, physician; b. Buhl, Minn., Jan. 8, 1922; married; 3 children. BSc, Witwatersrand U., Johannesburg, 1941, MD, BChir, 1945; MPH cum laude, Harvard U., 1958. Instr. dept. anatomy U. Witwatersrand, 1942—43; resident Johannesburg, 1945—47; rural family physician, 1948—53; sr. lectr. dept. social medicine Hebrew U., Hadassah, Jerusalem, 1962—66; from assoc. prof. to prof., chmn. dept. family medicine Tel Aviv U., 1966—74; chmn. dept. family medicine Case Western Res. U., 1975—87, prof. cmty. health, 1976—87, prof. family medicine, 1976—, prof. med. and pediat., 1978—87, prof. emeritus, 1992—; med. dir. Family and Cmty. Health Ctr., Jerusalem, 1953—62. Prin. investigator Israel Ischemic Heart Disease Study, 1962—75; co-prin. investigator congenital abnormality study NIH, 1972—74; Robert Wood Johnson Found. fellowship program Case Western Res. U., 1978—88; vis. prof. family medicine and epidemiology U. N.C., Chapel Hill, 1973—74; vis. sr. rsch. scientist Nat. Heart, Blood and Lung Inst., Bethesda, Md., 1974, Bethesda, 1990—91; med. coun. U. Hosps., Cleve., 1975—87; com. impaired physicians U. Hosps. , Cleve., 1980—87; med. edn. com. Case Western Res. U., 1980—85, chmn. ambulatory and primary care clerkship com., 1981—83; task force health consequences bereavement NAS, 1982—85, membership com., 1984—88; dir. dept. family practice U. Hosps., Cleve., 1982—87; rsch. cons. Mt. Sinai Med. Ctr., Cleve., 1991—99. Contbr. articles. With U.S. Army, 1942—45, active Israel Def. Force, 1948—49. Recipient Lifetime Achievement award in medicine, Golden Age Ctrs., 1997. Fellow: Royal Soc. Med. Found., Am. Heart Assn., Am. Acad. Family Physicians; mem.: Soc. Behavioral Medicine, Soc. Tchrs. Family Medicine (chmn. task force 1985—87, Curtis Hames Career Rsch. award 1988, Cert. Excellence 1988, Maurice Saltzman award 1988), Inst. Medicine-NAS. Office: Case Western Res Univ Dept of Family Medicine 10900 Euclid Ave Cleveland OH 44106-4901

MEDALIE, RICHARD JAMES, lawyer; b. Duluth, Minn., July 21, 1929; s. William Louis and Mona (Kolad) M.; m. Susan Diane Abrams, June 5, 1960; children: Samuel David, Daniel Alexander. BA summa cum laude, U. Minn., 1952; cert., U. London, 1953; A.M., Harvard U., 1955, JD cum laude, 1958. Bar: D.C. 1958, N.Y. 1963. Law clk. to Hon. George T. Washington U.S. Ct. Appeals, Washington, 1958-59; asst. solicitor gen. U.S., 1960-62; assoc. Kaye, Scholer, Fierman, Hays & Handler, N.Y.C., 1962-65; dep. dir. Ford Found. Inst. Criminal Law and Procedure, Georgetown U. Law Ctr., 1965-68; ptnr. Friedman & Medalie and predecessors, Washington, 1968-98; pres. Pegasus Internat., 1970—; exec. dir. The Appleseed Found., 1993-94, chmn. bd., 1993—2002, pres., 1995-98; of counsel Brock Ptnrs. LLC, N.Y.C., 1995—; pvt. practice Washington, 1998—. Adj. prof. adminstrv. and criminal law Georgetown U. Law Center, 1967-70; Mem. D.C. Law Revision Commn., 1975-87, chmn. Criminal Law Task Force, mem. exec. com., 1978-82; panel comml. arbitrators Am. Arbitration Assn., 1964— ; vice chmn. Harvard Law Sch. Fund, 1981-84, chmn. nat. maj. gifts, 1984-86, dep. chmn., 1986-87, chmn. 1987-89; v.p., bd. dirs. Trial Lawyers for Pub. Justice, Washington, 1998—. Author: From Escobedo to Miranda: The Anatomy of a Supreme Court Decision, 1966; co-author: Federal Consumer Safety Legislation, 1970; co-author, editor: Commercial Arbitration for the 1990s, 1991; co-editor: Crime: A Community Responds, 1967; staff: Harvard Law Rev., 1956-58; case editor, 1957-58; contbr. articles to legal jours. Bd. dirs. alumni assn. Expt. in Internat. Living, Brattleboro, Vt., 1961-64, pres., 1962-63. Fulbright scholar, 1952-53; Ford fellow, 1954-55. Mem. ABA (program chair 1984, 90, chair legis. subcom. 1986-89, ADR/arbitration com., rep. on adv. com. nat. conf. Emerging ADR Issues in State and Fed. Cts. 1991, vice chair 1991-94, arbitration com. litigation sect., co-chair nat. conf. Critical Issues in Arbitration 1993), D.C. Unified Bar, Assn. Bar City of N.Y., Am. Law Inst., D.C. Estate Planning Coun.; fellow Am. Bar Found., Harvard Law Sch. Assn. D.C. (pres. 1976-77, nat. v.p. 1977-78), Harvard Alumni Assn. (law sch. dir. 1991-95), Cosmos Club, Harvard Club of Washington, Phi Beta Kappa, Phi Alpha Theta. Home: 3113 Macomb St NW Washington DC 20008-3325 Office: 1750 K St NW Ste 1200 Washington DC 20006-2303 E-mail: rmedalie@worldnet.att.net.

MEDALIE, SUSAN DIANE, lawyer, management consultant; b. Boston, Oct. 7, 1941; d. Samuel and Matilda (Bortman) Abrams; m. Richard James Medalie, June 5, 1960; children: Samuel David, Daniel Alexander. BA, Sarah Lawrence Coll., 1960; MA, George Washington U., 1962, cert. pubs. spec., 1977; JD, Am. U., 1986. Bar: Pa. 1987, DC 1987. Pres. Medalie Cons., Washington, 1980—; dep. dir. U.S. Holocaust Meml. Coun., 1980-82; assoc. pub. Campaigns & Elections, 1983-84; legis. analyst Subcom./House Energy and Commerce, 1985; ea. regional dir. Josephson Found. for Adv. Ethics, L.A., 1986-88; asst. dean for external affairs George Washington U. Nat. Law Ctr., Washington, 1988-90; exec. dir. Internat. Soc. Global Health Policy, Washington and Paris, 1990-93; pvt. practice Washington, 1993-2000; exec. dir. Women's Campaign Fund, 2000—. Corp. liaison First Hosp. Corp., Norfolk, Va., 1986—88. Editor, pub.: Getting There mag., 1977—80, sr. editor: Am. U. Law Rev., 1984—86; assoc. prodr., cons. (TV series) Prof. Arthur Miller's "Headlines on Trial", 1987—91. Mem. exec. bd., DC Bar rep. Coalition Against Drugs and Violence, 1997—2000; nat. dep. fin. dir. Edward M. Kennedy for Pres. Com., Washington, 1979—80; del. DC Ward 3 Dem. Ctrl. Com.; bd. dirs., mem. exec. com. Women's Campaign Fund, 1999—2000. Mem.: ABA, DC Bar Assn. Office: 734 15th St NW Washington DC 20005 E-mail: susanmedalie@wcfonline.org.

MEDAVOY, MIKE, motion picture company executive; b. Shanghai, China, Jan. 21, 1941; arrived in U.S., 1957, naturalized, 1962; s. Michael and Dora Medavoy; m. Irena Medavoy; children: Nicholas, Brian. BA, UCLA, 1963. With Casting dept. Universal Studios, 1963; agt. Bill Robinson Assos., Los Angeles, 1963-64; v.p. motion picture dept. GAC/CMA Co., 1965-71, IFA Co., 1971-74; sr. v.p. United Artists Corp., 1974-78; one of founders, exec. v.p. Orion Pictures Co., Burbank, Calif., 1978-82; exec. v.p. Orion Pictures Corp. (formerly Orion Pictures Co.), Century City, 1982-90; chmn. Tri-Star Pictures, Inc., Culver City, 1990—, Phoenix Picture Corp., 1995—. Jury chmn. Tokyo Film Festival 1994; hon. co-chair St. Petersburg (Russia) Film Festival, 1992; adv. bd. Shanghai Film Conf.; co-chmn. Am. Cinematheque, 1997—. Author: You're Only as Good as Your Next One, 2002. Chmn. Ctr. Internat. Rels.; co-founder Sundance Film Inst.; bd. govs. Sundance Inst., 1980-86; bd. dirs. Calif. Mus. Sci. and Industry Studio, 1984-87; commr. L.A. Bd. Parks and Recreation, 2001; exec. adv. bd. Calif. Anti-Terrorism Info. Ctr., 2002; bd. dirs. U. Tel-Aviv. Recipient Academy Award (mem. of team that produced), One Flew Over the Cuckoo's Nest, Rocky, Annie Hall, Amadeus, Platoon, Dances with Wolves, Silence of the Lambs, Motion Picture Pioneer award, 1992, Career Achievement award, UCLA Alumni, 1997, Prodrs. award, Cannes Film Festival, 1998, Neil H. Jacoby award, 1999, Fred Zinnoman award, Anti-Defamation League, 2001. Mem. Acad. Motion Picture Arts and Scis. (gov. 1977-81), UCLA Found., UCLA Chancellors Assocs.

MEDCALF DAVENPORT, NEVA ANN, education educator; b. Las Cruces, N.Mex., Sept. 26, 1941; d. Morris G. and Bernice (Baxter) May; children: Morrisa Ann Booker, William Eric Medcalf. BS in Edn., Baldwin Wallace Coll., 1963; MA in Edn., Ariz. State U., 1969; EdD, U. N.Mex., 1991. Cert. elem. sch. tchr., adminstr., reading specialist. Pvt. reading tutor, Rochester, Mich., 1969-80; 1st grade tchr. Hope Christian Sch., Albuquerque, 1982-83, prin., 1983-90; reading supr. U. N.Mex., 1989; dir. Calvary Christian Sch., Pacific Palisades, Calif., 1990-91; prof. dept. edn. St. Mary's U., San Antonio, 1991—. Researcher early childhood and lang. devel., tech. in edn. Vol. ministry to former drug addicts and convicts Barrios for Jesus, 1988-90; mem. ministry to homeless Venice (Calif.) Bible Tabernacle, 1990-91; active children's music programs University United Meth. Ch., San Antonio, 1997-. Bible Study fellow City of Albuquerque, 1981-82. Mem. ASCD, Internat. Reading Assn., Tex. State Reading Assn., Alamo Rading Coun. (past pres.), Pi Lambda Theta. Avocations: music, painting, sewing, crafts. Home: 5601 Bandera Rd # 347 San Antonio TX 78238-1979

MEDD, MARJORIE MURRAY, volunteer, educator, consultant; b. Pitts., June 23, 1942; d. Joseph Francis Murray and Florence Juliet Domergue; m. William Lowell Medd, July 13, 1942; children: Catherine, Donald, Michael. BS in Edn., Tufts U., 1964; cert. in phys. edn., Bouvé Boston Sch., 1964; MPA, Harvard U., 1999. Co-chair phys. edn. dept. Mt. Ida Jr. Coll., Newton, Mass., 1964-65; instr. U. Rochester, Rochester, NY, 1965—69. Vice-chair tchr. study group Nat. Assn. of State Bds. of Edn., 1991, mem. higher edn. study group, 1994; co-chair task force on alt. sch. calendar Dept. of Edn., 1993-94; chair Initial Tchr. Cert. Pilot Project, 1993-94; vice-chair Results-Based Initial Tchr. Cert. Exec. Com., 1994; mem. Bowdoin Coll. Program Approval Visitation Team, 1994, 96, Westbrook Coll. Program Approval Visitation Team, 1991; mem. exec. com. Coalition for Excellence in Edn., 1995—; mem. Maine LEADership Consortium, 1994-97; spkr., presenter numerous ednl. panels. Chmn. task force learning results Goals 2000 Panel, 1993—96; corporator Stephens Meml. Hosp., 1987—2000; mem. Gov.'s Coun. on Phys. Fitness and Sports, 1993—94, Gov.'s Task Force on Sch. Funding, 1993—94; pres. Maine Children's Alliance, 1999—2002; mem., chair sch. bd. Oxford Hills Sch. Dist., South Paris, 1977—87; mem. Maine State Bd. Edn., Augusta, 1987—99, chair, 1992—94, 1995—96; bd. dirs. New Eng. Assn. Schs. and Colls, 1995—99; mem. Jobs for Maine's Grads. Exec. Bd., 1988—, sec., 2001—; vice chair exec. bd. N.E. and Islands Regional Ednl. Lab. at Brown U., 1996—2002; mem. Maine Health Care Sys. and Health Care Security Bd., 2001—; chair Growth Coun. Oxford Hills, 2001—; chair growth coun. commn. Western Maine U. and Tech. Coll. Ctr., 2000—; mem. Tufts Alumni Admissions Program, 1992—. Recipient Maine Coalition for Excellence in Edn. Recognition award, 1994, Layperson award Maine Assn. Phys. Health, Edn., Recreation and Dance, 1993, Nat. Svc. award Jobs for Am.'s Grads., 1998; selected as one of 25 Nat. State Bd. Edn. mems. to participate in March for Remembrance in Poland, 1994. Mem. AAUW, Oxford Hills C. of C. (chair edn. com. 1990-96). Roman Catholic. Office: PO Box 126 Norway ME 04268-0126

MEDDING, WALTER SHERMAN, retired environmental engineer; b. St. Louis, Mar. 4, 1922; s. Walter Lyman and Elizabeth Steele (Sherman) M.; m. Mary Agnes Patty Johnson, Apr. 22, 1944; children: Jean, Walter, Mauri. BSCE, Va. Poly. Inst., 1947, MS in Sanitary Engring., 1970. Registered profl. engr., Va., N.C., Kans. Various positions U.S. Army, 1942-64; student officer advanced course The Engr. Sch., Ft. Belvoir, Va., 1952—54, head fixed bridges sect., 1954—55; asst. engr. Asmara Eritrea, chief design br. Mediterranean Divsn., Gulf Dist., Tehran, Iran, 1955-57; asst. divsn. engr. 9th Infantry Divsn., Ft. Carson, Colo., 1957-59; resident engr. USACAG, chief constrn. ops. U.S. Army Engring. Command Europe, Frankfurt, Germany, 1959-72; chief contract adminstrn. U.S. Army Engring. Divsn. Europe, Germany, 1972-75; chief environ. engring. Office, Chief of Engrs., U.S. Army, Washington, 1975-86; sr. engr. Romem Aqua Sys. Co., Woodbridge, Va., 1986-97. Cons. U.S. army Ctr. for Pub. Works, Ft. Belvoir, Va., 1997-98; music tchr. Co-author: (textbook) Non-standard Military Fixed Bridges, 1954, (with E. Farago) Which Musical Instrument Shall I Play?, 1985; editor, pub. Letter to Lyman, 1978; contbr. articles to profl. jours. Mem. ASCE, Am. Waterworks Assn., Water Environ. Fedn., Conf. of Fed. Environ. Engrs. Republican. Episcopalian. Achievements include development of mil. bridge classification procedures for load carrying and rapid field design. Home: 204 Brooke Dr Fredericksburg VA 22408-2004 E-mail: wsmedding@aol.com.

MEDDLES, SHARON DIANE GUNSTREAM, school counselor; b. Pasadena, Calif., Feb. 9, 1947; d. Jarrell William and Vivian Irene (Heffner) Gunstream; m. Larry Wayne Meddles, June 16, 1973; children: Brittany Dawn, Brooke Reneé. BA in English, Pasadena Coll., 1968; MEd in Counseling, U. Phoenix, 1996. Cert. tchr., Ariz. English and music tchr. Coronado Hills Jr. H.S. Adams County Dist. 12, Thornton, Colo., 1969-72; 8th grade lang. arts tchr. Ocotillo Sch. Washington Elem. Sch. Dist. 6, Phoenix, 1972-76, homebound tchr., 1985-86, 88-90; sr. high tchr. N.W. Christian Acad., Glendale, Ariz., 1986-87; 7th and 8th grade English and reading tchr. Cholla Mid. Sch. Washington Sch. Dist., Phoenix, 1990-96, sch. counselor Lakeview and Sunburst Elem. Schs., 1996-2000; adminstrv. asst. Sunburst Elem. Sch., Glendale, 2000—. Adj. faculty mem. Southwestern Coll., 2000—. Core group leader Cmty. Bible Study, Phoenix, 1988-90; bd. dirs. Orangewood Ch. of the Nazarene, Phoenix, 1982-84, 93; local pres. Nazarene World Missionary Soc., 1982-84; dist. dir. Point Loma Alumni Bd., San Diego, 1990-93, sec., 1993-96; mem. Orangewood Ch. of the Nazarene. Republican. Avocation: singing. Home: 1115 W Le Marche Ave Phoenix AZ 85023-4429

MEDEARIS, KENNETH ROBERT, medical products manufacturing company executive. b. Woodside, N.Y., Apr. 30, 1939; s. Kenneth Calvin and Elizabeth Marie (Stacy) M.; BSBA, Fairleigh Dickinson U., 1973; m. Ida Jane Hunter, Apr. 4, 1964. Mgr. quality assurance engring. Lockheed Electronics Co., Plainfield, N.J., 1971-74; dir. quality assurance/regulatory affairs instrument div. Baxter-Travenol, Silver Spring, Md., 1974-76, dir. mfg. ops., 1976-78; v.p. ops. Corometrics Med. Systems, Inc., Wallingford, Conn., 1978-89; pres., chief exec. officer Kontron Instruments, Inc., Everett, Mass., 1989-90, pres., CEO prin., Pinnacle Mmgt. Ltd., Madison, Conn., 1990-94, v.p., gen. mgr. Monaghan Med. Corp., Plattsburgh, N.Y., 1994—. Served with USN, 1957-61. Mem. Assn. Advancement Med. Instrumentation, Am. Mgmt. Assn., Am Soc. Quality Control, Barnes Indsl. Park Assn. Republican. Home: PO Box 8255 Essex VT 05451-8255 Office: 5 Latour Ave Plattsburgh NY 12901-7207

MEDEARIS, MILLER, lawyer; b. Liberty, Mo., Jan. 19, 1921; s. Thomas Whittier and Mara (Miller) M.; children: Christy Crochet, Kellee Reed. LLB, Cumberland U., 1948; JD, Stamford U., 1969. Bar: Okla. 1948, Calif. 1957. Claims adjustor Transit Casualty Co., L.A., 1950-56, atty., trial counsel, 1956-58; ptnr. Hagenbaugh, Murphy & Medearis, 1958-69, Medearis and Grimm, L.A., 1969—. Sec., Bd. Med. Quality Assurance, Sacramento, 1979-84, v.p., 1984-86; bd. dirs. Pico Rivera Cmty. Hosp., 1975-85; mem. Dem. Bus. Council, L.A., 1980; commr. L.A. Bd. Transp., 1986-92. With USN, 1945-46. Mem. ABA, State Bar Calif., Calif. Trial Lawyers Assn., Okla. Bar Assn., Lawyers Club L.A. Democrat. Baptist. Avocations: boating, water skiing, downhill skiing. Home: 2175 Ridge Dr Los Angeles CA 90049-1153 Office: Medearis and Grimm 1331 W Sunset Blvd Los Angeles CA 90026-4499

MEDEIROS, M. JOYCE, community health educator; b. Boston, Feb. 17, 1954; d. Raymond A. and D. Jean (Russell) Harrington; m. Joseph A. Medeiros, July 26, 1977; children: Jessica A., Jo Ellen. Grad., Youville Hosp. Sch. Practical Nursing, 1973; BS in Cmty. Health Edn., U. Maine, Farmington, 1992. Lic. social worker. Staff nurse Goddard Meml. Hosp., Stoughton, Mass., 1973-87; dist. dir. Somerset Family YMCA, 1988-90; ITV aide Skowhegan (Maine) H.S., 1990-91; intern Somerset Residential Care Ctr., 1991-92, WARNACO, 1992; dir. edn. Sebasticook Valley Hosp., 1992-96; spl. needs edn. tech. transition III MSAD # 59 Madison (Maine) H.S., 1996-99; children's case mgr. Youth & Family Svcs., 1999—. Camp nurse, dir. 4-H Camp Farley, 1982-87, Camp at Eastward Starks, Maine, 1990. Selectman Town of Starks, 1995. Completed 2000 Honolulu Marathon, Leukemia, Lymphoma Soc. Mem.: Phi Sigma Pi, Eta Sigma Gamma. Avocations: camping, bowling, photography, ceramics, collecting music boxes. Home: 241 Dill Rd Starks ME 04911

MEDEIROS, MATTHEW FRANCIS, lawyer; b. Little Compton, R.I., Apr. 30, 1945; s. Manuel S. and Marie F. (Goulart) M.; m. Sarah Judith Medjuck, July 26, 1970. AB, Brown U., 1967; JD, NYU, 1970. Bar: R.I. 1970, Mass. 1985, U.S. Dist. Ct. R.I. 1971, D.C. 1971, U.S. Dist. Ct. D.C. 1971, U.S. Ct. Appeals (1st cir.) 1972, U.S. Ct. Appeals (D.C. cir.) 1972, U.S. Supreme Ct. 1974. Summer assoc. Lewis & Roca, Phoenix, 1969; law clk. to chief judge U.S. Dist. Ct. R.I., 1970-71; assoc. Covington & Burling, Washington, 1971-76; on leave with Neighborhood Legal Svcs. Program, 1973; ptnr. Edwards & Angell, Providence, 1977-87, Flanders & Medeiros Inc., Providence, 1987-2000, Little, Bulman, Medeiros & Whitney, P.C., 2000—. Chmn. planning com. 1st Cir. Jud. Conf., 1980-81; mem. jud. screening coms. U.S. Bankruptcy Judge and U.S. Magistrate, 1981-82; mem. adv. com. for U.S. Ct. Appeals (1st cir.), 1983-88; adj. prof. fed. trial practice So. New Eng. Sch. Law, 1986-88; editor: NYU Law Rev., 1969-70; bd. dirs. Associated Alumni Brown U., 1969-71; bd. dirs. R.I. br. ACLU, 1977-79. Mem. ABA, Am. Bd. Trial Advocates, Fed. Bar Assn. (pres. R.I. chpt. 1978-80), R.I. Bar Assn. Office: Little Bulman Medeiros & Whitney 72 Pine St Providence RI 02903

MEDEIROS, PRISCA BICOY DANIEL, former religious educator, poet; b. Mar. 29, 1928; d. Petronilo Bicoy and Paula Daniel; m. Joseph Patro Medeiros; children: Nathalie R. Wilson, Edwin V., Paul N. Anderson, Jacqueline M. Moran, Theresa T. Washington, Jolynn A. Kaiama. Cert., Atkinson Bus. Coll., 1958, Vlautin Coll. Beauty, 1968; lic. cosmetologist, Palo Alto Beauty Coll., 1968; cert. physician asst., Bryman Med. Sch., 1974; cert., Inst. Childrens Lit., 1988; student, Acad. Police, 1994—. Religion tchr. St. Anthony Cath. Ch. Sch. Religion, Menlo Park, Calif., 1962-89, ret. Impressionistic artist for 30 yrs. Author of poetry; song composer. Mem. St. Anthony Cath. Ch. Choir; leader Girls Scouts Am., 1946-48; pres. PTA Kilohana Sch., 1948; past mem. Hawaii Home Demonstration Coun., 1952-56; mem. Am. Legion Aux., 1958-69, Com. of Art of Stanford, 1963-77, Am. Heart Assn., 1970-77, VA Hosp. Chaplain Svc., Palo Alto and Menlo Park; field rep. ARC, 1979-81; vol. St. Anthony's Dining Room; mem. Dem. Congl. Com., Washington, 1994-98. Recipient cert. of merit Outstanding Lyrical Writing, Gospel Recording Co., Mass., 1985, Best Song of the Month award The Cross of Jesus, Chapel Recording, Mass., 1985, J. Edgar Hoover gold medal for Disting. Pub. Svc., 1991, Best Citizen award for Fgn. Affairs, Australia, 1995, Royal Proclamation, Queensland, Hutt River, Australia, 1996. Mem. Song Writer's Club Am. (life), Song Bank, Nat. Acad. Songwriters, World Peace Movement (sect. pres. 1994), mem. Am. Fedn. Police (1990-1999). Address: PO Box 2074 Kaunakakai HI 96748-2074

MEDEL, REBECCA ROSALIE, artist; b. Denver, Mar. 26, 1947; d. Natividad and Josefa (Apodaca) M. BFA, Ariz. State U., 1970; MFA, UCLA, 1982. Asst. prof. fibers dept. head Tenn. Technol. U., Smithville, 1983-88; lectr. Dept. of Design, UCLA, 1989-91; studio artist, 1991—; assoc. prof. Tyler Sch. Art Temple U., 1995—. Lectr. N.C. State U., Raleigh, San Diego State U., SUNY, Purchase, 1992, Penland Sch. Asheville, N.C., Textile Study Group, N.Y.C., Calif. Coll. of Arts & Crafts, Oakland, Calif., San Jose State U., Am. Ctr., Kyoto, Japan, City Ctr., Sapporo, Japan, 1986; vis. artist U. N.D., 1985. One-woman shows include Brown Grotta Gallery, Wilton, Conn., 1996, Neuberger Mus. of Art, Purchase, N.Y., 1992-93, Bellas Artes Gallery, N.Y.C., 1991, N.D. Mus. Art, Grand Forks, 1985, Maya Behn Galerie, Zurich, 1984, UCLA, 1982; two-person exhbns. include Heath Gallery, Atlanta, 1987, Maya Behn Gallerie, 1986; group shows include Bellas Artes Gallery, Santa Fe, N.Mex., 1992, N.C. State U. Gallery, 1992, Portland Art Mus., 1995, Madison (Wis.) Art Ctr., 1995, Santa Monica (Calif.) Art Gallery, 1995, Maya Behn Gallerie, 1991, Mus. Van Bommel-Van Dam, Venlo, Netherlands, 1990, Palo Alto Cultural Ctr., 1990, Barbican Ctr. Concourse Gallery, London, 1998, Montclair (N.J.) State U. Gallery, 1998, Art Inst. Chgo., 1999, Yokohama (Japan) Mus. Art, 1999, Biennial 2000, Del. Art Mus., Wilmington, L.A. Mus. Art, many others. Recipient bronze medal Triennial of Tapestry, 1985; visual artist fellow Nat. Endowment for Arts, 1986, 88, fellow for emerging visual artists So. Arts Fedn. NEA, 1985; Pew fellow in the arts, 1999, fellow Pa. Coun. on Arts, 2001; scholar to Arcosanti, Nat. Endowment for Arts, 1986, 88. Home: 2920 Meyer Ave Glenside PA 19038-1920

MEDEN, ROBERT PAUL, interior design educator; b. Cleve., Jan. 24, 1950; s. Paul Joseph and Irene Theresa (Chuey) M.; m. Maryellen Hudak, June 22, 1979; children: Christina Rose, Patrick Michael. BArch, Kent State U., 1973, MArch, 1975; DArch, Cath. U. Am., 1989. Registered architect, Ohio, Md., Va., Ind. Planner, draftsman John Roush, Architects, Cleve., 1975; hist. sites restoration coord. hist. preservation div. N.Y. State, Office of Parks and Recreation, Albany, 1976-77; designer, draftsman Robert C. Gaede, Cleve., 1977; interior design instr. Sch. Family and Consumer Studies Kent (Ohio) State U., 1977-79; asst. prof. interior design Mt. Vernon Coll., Washington, 1979-82; asst. prof. architecture Ball State U., Muncie, Ind., 1982-85; dir. preservation programs The Am. Inst. Architects, Washington, 1985; assoc. prof. interior design Marymount. U. Sch. Arts and Scis., Arlington, Va., 1986-90; prof. Marymount U. Sch. Arts and Scis., 1990—, program chair, 1989—. Hist. architect U.S. Dept. Interior Tech. Preservation Svcs., Washington, 1980; architect Turner Renovations, Inc., Washington, 1979-82, Suburban Contractors, Inc., Vienna,Va., 1986-87; architect, preservation specialist Browning, Day, Mullins, Dierdorf, Inc., Indpls., 1984-85; condr. numerous seminars and presentations. Author: Architectural Character Study of the Buckeye Road District, 1975; co-author and illustrator: History of Housing and Furnishings Handbook, 1977; editor and illustrator: Access to Historic Buildings for the Disabled, 1981. Asst. to dir. Mayfield (Ohio) Recreation Com., 1968-73; basketball coach St. Mary's Ch., Cath. Youth Orgn., Albany, 1976-77, basketball coach St. Lawrence Ch., Cath. Youth Orgn., Muncie, 1982-83, woman's varsity soccer coach Marymount U., 1986-88. Recipient ASID Scalamandre Hist. Preservation award, 1978, Dora Brahms award, 1980, 83, Nat. Endowment for Arts, Design Arts Program, Entering Profl. award, 1981; grantee The Cleve. Found., 1979, The Nat. Endowment for the Arts Design Arts Program, 1981. Mem. AIA, Am. Soc. Interior Designers, Interior Design Educators Coun., Internat. Assoc. Lighting Designers. Roman Catholic. Home: 6013 27th St N Arlington VA 22207-1232 Office: Marymount U 2807 N Glebe Rd Arlington VA 22207-4299

MEDEROS, CAROLINA LUISA, transportation policy consultant; b. Rochester, Minn., July 1, 1947; d. Luis O. and Carolina (del Valle) M. BA, Vanderbilt U., 1969; MA, U. Chgo., 1971. Adminstrv. asst. Lt. Gov. of Ill., Chgo., 1972; sr. research assoc. U. Chgo., 1972; project mgr., cons. Urban Dynamics, Inner City Fund and Community Programs Inc., Chgo., 1972-73; legis. asst. to Senate pres. Ill. State Senate, Chgo. and Springfield, 1973-76; program analyst Dept. Transp., Washington, 1976-79, chief, trans. assistance programs div., 1979-81, dir. programs and evaluation, 1981-88, chairwoman, sec.'s safety rev. task force, 1985-88, deputy asst. sec. for safety, 1988-89; cons. Patton Boggs LLP, Washington, 1990—. Recipient award for Meritorious Achievement, Sec. Transp. 1980, Superior Achievement award U.S. Dept. Transp., 1981, Sec.'s Gold Medal Award for Outstanding Achievement, 1986, Presdl. Rank award, 1987. Home: 2723 O St NW Washington DC 20007-3128 Office: Patton Boggs LLP 2550 M St NW Washington DC 20037-1350 E-mail: cmederos@pattonboggs.com.

MEDIAVILLA, ANTONIO FELIPE, surgeon; b. Santurce, P.R., Sept. 13, 1935; m. Carolyn R. Benz, Oct. 29, 1960; children: Laurie M., Kathleen D., Anthony S., David A., Eric P. BS, U. P.R., 1956, MD, 1959. Diplomate Am. Bd. Surgery, Nat. Bd. Med. Examiners. Intern Mercy Hosp., Buffalo, 1960-61; resident in surgery VA Hosp., San Juan, P.R., 1960-61, 65-68; commd. USAF, 1961-91, advanced through grades to col.; chief surg. svcs. 2973d USAF Hosp., Seville, Spain, 1961-65, March AFB Regional Hosp., Riverside, Calif., 1968-71, Torrejon AFB Hosp., Madrid, 1971-75, Homestead (Fla.) AFB Hosp., 1975-80, USAF Acad. Hosp., Colorado Springs, Colo., 1980-85, 86-91; chmn. dept. surgery Carswel Regional Hosp., Ft. Worth, 1985-86; pvt. practice Colorado Springs, 1991—. Staff surgeon Meml. Hosp., Colorado Springs, 1991—, Penrose Hosp., Colorado Springs, 1991—, St. Francis Health Sys., Colorado Springs, 1991—; cons. gen. surgery USAF Surgeon Gen., 1982—91; clin. preceptor PA Phase II program Uniformed Svcs. U. Health Scis., Bethesda, Md., clin. asst. prof. surgery, 1984—. Decorated Legion of Merit. Fellow ACS; mem. Colo. Med. Soc., Colorado Springs Surg. Soc., El Paso County Med. Soc., KC. Roman Catholic. Avocations: music, painting, gardening, travel, reading. Office: 325 Parkside Dr Colorado Springs CO 80910-3134

MEDICI, ROCHELLE, psychologist, brain researcher; b. Morris, Minn., Dec. 31, 1933; d. Albert and Johanna (Ulvestad) Johnson; m. Michael A. Medici, July 4, 1970 (div. 1995); 1 child, Bianca Cristina. BA magna cum laude, U. Minn., 1954, PhD, 1962. Lic. psychologist, Calif. USPHS postdoctoral fellow U. Minn., Mpls., 1965-67; asst. biologist Calif. Inst. Tech., Pasadena, 1967-68; assoc. prof. anatomy Brain Rsch. Inst., UCLA, 1968-79; pvt. practice neuropsychology, San Marino, Calif., 1980—. Cons. AEC, Washington, 1976, WHO, Washington, 1976, Neurosci. Rsch. Program, Boston, 1977. Rschr. numerous publs.; contbr. articles to profl. jours (Nature, Brain Research, et al) Mem. APA, AAAS, Explorers Club, Phi Beta Kappa. Democrat. Avocations: music, art, travel, politics, literature. Home: 2220 El Molino Pl San Marino CA 91108-2317

MEDICUS, HEINRICH ADOLF, physicist, educator; b. Zurich, Switzerland, Dec. 24, 1918; came to U.S., 1950; s. Friedrich Georg and Clara Anna (Frey) M.; m. Hildegard Julie Schmelz, June 15, 1961. Diploma, Swiss Fed. Inst. Tech., Zurich, 1943, DSc, 1949. Rsch. assoc. Swiss Fed. Inst. Tech., Zurich, 1943-50; visitor Lawrence Berkeley (Calif.) Lab., 1950-51, MIT, Cambridge, Mass., 1951-52, instr., vis. asst. prof., 1952-55; from assoc. prof. to prof. Rensselaer Poly. Inst., Troy, N.Y., 1955-87, prof. emeritus, 1987—. Vis. scientist Atomic Energy Research Establishment Harwell, Eng., 1967-68, Swiss Inst. Nuclear Research, Villigen, 1974-75. Co-author: Fields and Particles, 1973; contbr. articles to profl. jours. With Swiss Army, 1937-50. Fellow Swiss Found., 1950-52 Mem. Am. Phys. Soc., Swiss Phys. Soc., Hist. of Sci. Soc., Swiss Am. Hist. Soc., Soc. Wine Educators, Hudson-Mohawk Swiss Soc. (pres. 1974—), Soc. Vignerons, Delta Tau Delta (pres. house corp. of Upsilon chpt. 1984-91, faculty adv. 1991-95), Swiss Alpine Club. Presbyterian. Avocations: wine education, internat. student exchange programs. Home: 1 The Knoll East Acres Troy NY 12180 Office: Rensselaer Poly Inst Dept Physics Troy NY 12180 E-mail: medich@rpi.edu.

MEDIN, A. LOUIS, computer company executive; b. Balt., Oct. 2, 1925; s. Nathan and Bessie (Zell) M.; m. Julia A. Levin, Dec. 24, 1950; children: Douglas, David, Thomas, Linda. BSChemE, Johns Hopkins U., 1948; PhD-ChemE, Ohio State U., 1951. Registered profl. engr., Md. Chmn. engr. AEC, Wilmington, Del., 1951-53; rsch. engr. Ford Motor Co., Dearborn, Mich., 1953-55; chief chem. nuclear reactor tech. ALCO Products, Schenectady, 1955-58; head nuclear rsch. engr. U.S. Steel, Monroeville, Pa., 1958-63; project mgr. missile design AVCO Corp., Wilmington, Mass., 1963-65; mgr. sci. applications IBM, Manassas, Va., 1965-72, mgr. advanced applications, 1975-87; exec. dir. Inst. for Simulation and Tng., Orlando, Fla., 1987-2000; sr. assoc. Mgmt. and Ednl. Tech. Assocs., 2000—. Chmn. symposia on def. research and devel.; asst. dir. environment and life scis. Dept. Def., 1972-74; lectr. in field. Contbr. articles to profl. and tech. jours. Mem. Monroeville Parks and Recreation Commn., 1960; chmn. Monroeville Mental Health Assn., 1961; mem. Monroeville Zoning and Planning Commn., 1961; dep. precinct chmn. Montgomery County Rep. Com., 1982; chmn. sci. and engring. tech. divsn. Nat. Def. Indsl. Assn., 1999--. With USN, 1944-46, PTO. Recipient award Am. Chem. Soc., 1957. Fellow Am. Inst. Chemists; mem. Nat. Security Indsl. Assn., Am. Inst. Chem. Engrs., Am. Def. Preparedness Assn. (chmn. sci. and engring. tech. divsn. 1981-90, ednl. advisor Def. Jour., Am. Def. award 1984, Gold medal 1990), Am. Metall. Soc., John's Hopkins U. Alumni Assn., Ohio State U. Alumni Assn. Home: 11401 Ridge Mist Ter Potomac MD 20854-7002 E-mail: lmedin@comcast.net.

MEDIN, JULIA ADELE, mathematics educator, researcher; b. Dayton, Ohio, Jan. 16, 1929; d. Caroline (Feinberg) Levitt; m. A. Louis Medin, Dec. 24, 1950; children: Douglas, David, Thomas, Linda. BS in Maths. Edn., Ohio State U., 1951; MA in Higher Edn., George Washington U., 1977; PhD in Counseling and Edn., Am. U., 1985. Cert. tchr., Fla., Md. Rsch. engr. Sun Oil Co., Marcus Hook, Pa., 1951-53; tchr. maths. Montgomery County Pub. Schs., Rockville, Md., 1973-88; asst. prof. maths. U. Ctrl. Fla., Orlando, 1988-90, sr. ednl. technologist Inst. for Simulation and Tng., 1990-99; sr. assoc. Mgmt. and Ednl. Tech. Assocs., 1999—. Adv. steering com. U.S. Dept. Edn. Title II, Washington, 1985-89; sr. math. educator, rschr. Inst. for Simulation and Tng., Orlando, 1988-90; judge, co-chair GII Nar. Awards; co-acad. advisor I/ITSEC Conf.; condr. nationwide rsch. project on effective use of technology in the classroom; spkr. in field. Author: Loc. of Cont. and Test Anxiety of Mar. Math. Studies, 1985; contbg. author: Math for 14 & 17 Yr. Olds, 1987; editor: Simulation and Computer-Based Technology for Education; contbr. articles to profl. jours. Dem. committeewoman Town of Monroeville, Pa., 1962; religious sch. dir. Beth Tikva Religious Sch., Rockville, 1971; cons. Monroeville Mental Health, 1960. Mem. Nat. Coun. Tchrs. Math., Math. Assn. Am. (task force on minorities in math.), Women in Math. in Edn., Nat. Coalition for Tech. in Edn. and Tng., Phi Delta Kappa, Kappa Delta Pi. Home and Office: 11401 Ridge Mist Ter Potomac MD 20854-7002 E-mail: jmedin@comcast.net.

MEDIN, LOWELL ANSGARD, management executive; b. Shafer Twp., Minn., Aug. 28, 1932; s. Ansgaard Phillip Magnus and Adelaide Marie Christine (Grandstrand) M.; m. Frances Irene Knutson, Sept. 13, 1958; children: Kimberly June, James Lowell. AS in Liberal Arts, U. Minn., 1957, BBA, 1959. Dairy farmer Medin Farm, Franconia Twp., 1951-53; silo builder Lindstrom Silo, 1956-58; employment mgr. John Wood Co., St. Paul, 1959; salesperson Diversey Co., LaCrosse, Wis., 1959-60; rebuyer, inventory mgr. Montgomery Ward, St. Paul, 1960-67, rebuyer, rebuyer mgr. Chgo., 1967-85; with sales dept. J.T. Gen. Store, Palatine, Ill., 1986; rebuying mgr. Sportsmen's Guide, Golden Valley, Minn., 1987; inventory mgr. Donald Bruce and Co., Chgo., 1988-91; supr. Pinkerton Security Ops., 1992-96. Pics coord. Hickory Farms, Itasca, Ill., 1995-98. Author: (with others) Shafer Swamp to Village, 1978, The Pioneers of Chicago County 1838-1870, 1992, The Knutson/Stavenau Family Roots, 1994. Candidate for polit. office, Mpls., 1967; del. Minn. State Dem.-Farm Labor Conv., 1956, 58; chmn. cancer drive Village of Palatine, 1968, mem. dist. 6 adv. coun., 1989-97; mem. Homeowners Coun., Palatine, 1976-77; mem. coun. Christ Luth. Ch., Palatine, 1981-86; officer Chicago County DFL Party, 1956-60; del. Chicago County DFL Conv., 1956, 58; pres. Palonis Park Homeowners Assn., Palatine, 1976-82. Cpl. U.S. Army, 1953-55, ETO. Mem. No. Ill. Civil War Roundtable (chartered officer 1983-86, trustee, sec., 2d v.p.), VFW (life, post 981, Arlington Hts.), Am. Legion (life, post 690, Palatine), Alpha Phi Omega. Republican. Lutheran. Avocations: genealogy, gardening, Am. history, Civil War period. Home: 121 S Linden Ave Palatine IL 60074-6342

MEDIN, MYRON JAMES, JR. city manager; b. Ladysmith, Wis., July 8, 1931; s. Myron James and Mildred Clara (Johnson) M.; m. Alice Louise Moholt, May 14, 1955; children: John, Karen, Anne. BA, St. Olaf Coll., 1954; MPA, U. Mich., 1959. Adminstrv. asst. to city mgr. City of Fond du Lac, Wis., 1959-64, city mgr., 1967-83, City of New Ulm, Minn., 1964-67; city adminstr. City of Kansas City, Kans., 1983-85; pres., gen. mgr. Bella Vista Village Property Owners Assn., Ark., 1986-92. Mem. com. human devel. Nat. League of Cities, Washington, 1974-80, com. on govtl. relations, 1971-73; chmn. City Plan Commn., Fond du Lac, Wis., 1967-83 Bd. dirs. United Way, Kansas City, Kans., 1984-85, YMCA, 1984-85, Kansas City C.C. Found., 1984-85; mem. Gov.'s Regionalism Task Force Adv. Com., Madison, Wis., 1968-70; trustee Phillips Pro-Celebrity Golf Tennis Charity Classic, 1991-92; vol. historic house mus. and gardens. Lt. USAF, 1955-57. Recipient Community Service award Fond du Lac Assn. of Commerce, 1978 Mem. Internat. City Mgmt. Assn., Wis. City Mgmt. Assn. (pres. 1975-76), Wis. League of Municipalities (bd. dirs. 1978-80), Wis. Alliance of Cities (v.p. 1972-73), Am. Soc. Pub. Adminstrn. (bd. dirs. 1984-85, Pub. Adminstr. of Yr. award 1985), Bella Vista-Bentonville C. of C. (bd. dirs. 1987-91), Nat. Trust for Hist. Preservation, Benton County Hist. Soc. Lutheran. Avocations: swimming, reading, tennis, gardening, genealogy. Home: 1 Audley Cir Bella Vista AR 72714-5645

MEDINA, HAROLD RAYMOND, III, marketing executive; b. N.Y.C., May 25, 1938; s. Harold Raymond, Jr. and Janet Brevoort (Williams) M.; m. Pamela Carter Huck, Feb. 20, 1965; 1 child: Scott Arthur. AB, Princeton U., 1960. Various direct mktg. positions Time-Life Books, N.Y.C., 1962-69; mng. dir. Time-Life Books U.K., London, 1969-73; pres. Wine of Month, Redwood City, Calif., 1973-75; direct mktg. positions Franklin Mint, Franklin Center, Pa., 1975-83, gen. mgr. catalog group, 1983-84; sr. v.p. Nat. Liberty Ins. Corp., Valley Forge, Pa., 1984-92; pres. Medina Assocs., 1992—. Dir. mktg. cons. Medina Assocs., 1974-75, assoc. dir. mktg. cons., 1992—; guest lectr. direct mkgt. NYU, 1983. Membership chmn. Rose Valley Folk Pa.; chmn., bd. dirs. Hedgerow Theatre, Rose Valley; regional fund raising chmn. Exeter Acad., N.H., 1977-78; mem. fund raising com. Children's Aid Soc., N.Y.C., 1967-69. Served to 1st lt. U.S. Army, 1960-62. Mem. Am. Soc. Aging (exec. com., bus. forum on aging), Nat. Assn. Sr. Living Industries (bd. dirs. 1987-87), Direct Mktg. Assn. (chmn. ethics com. 1998—, seminar faculty 1994—), Direct Mktg. Idea Exch., Westhampton Country Club (N.Y., bd. dirs. 1967-69). Republican. Presbyterian. Home and Office: 12 Hilltop Rd Wallingford PA 19086-6243 E-mail: kurtmedina@aol.com.

MEDINA, JESSE JAMES, protective services official, educator; b. Roma, Tex., May 18, 1956; s. Benigno and Celia Gonzalez M.; m. Dina Pena, May 25, 1979; children: Gerardo J., Rebecca A. AAS, Laredo (Tex.) Jr. Coll., 1977; BS, St. John's U., Springfield, Mo., 2000. Dep. sheriff Starr County, Rio Grande City, Tex., 1975-78; police officer City of Pharr, 1978-79, detective sgt., 1984-99, lt., 1984-90, capt., 1990-92, asst. chief police, 1992-96, chief police, 1996—. Sgt.-at-arms Rio Grande Valley Chief Assn., 1998. Editor State Mag. Chmn., 1983. V.p. Self Sufficiency Counsel, 1999; sec. treas. team plan com. Traffic Problem, 2000; mem. Internat. Bridge Traffic Adv. Coun., 2002–. Recipient Leadership award, Mexican Govt., 1999. Fellow Tex. Atty. Gens. Office (Excellence award 1989). Republican. Menonite. Avocations: hunting, fishing, camping. Home: 810 Tarrant Cir Pharr TX 78577-3942 Office: Pharr Police Dept 202 E Clark Ave Pharr TX 78577-3942 E-mail: jmedina@pharrpd.net.

MEDINA, KATHRYN BACH, book editor; b. Plainfield, N.J. d. F. Earl and Elizabeth E. Bach; 1 child. BA, Smith Coll.; MA, NYU. With Doubleday Pub. Co., Inc., N.Y.C., 1965-85; exec. editor, sr. v.p. Random House, 1985—. Assoc. fellow Jonathan Edwards Coll., Yale U., New Haven, 1982—; fellow Bunting Inst., 1994—95; cons., 1995—96, Coun. Fgn. Rels. Editor books by James Atlas, Peter Benchley, Amy Bloom, Tom Brokaw, Anita Brookner, Ethan Canin, Michael Chabon, Robert Coles, Agnes deMille, Jane Fonda, Max Frankel, Henry Louis Gates, Jr., Mary Gordon, David Halberstam, Kathryn Harrison, John Irving, Tracy Kidder, Wynton Marsalis, Bobbie Ann Mason, James A. Michener, Sandra Day O'Connor, Anna Quindlen, Nancy Reagan, James Reston, William Safire, Maggie Scarf, Christopher Tilghman, Alice Walker, Daniel Yergin, Wynton Marsalis, others.

MEDINA, MARISA CLAUDETTE, physician; b. N.Y.C., July 2, 1959; MD, U. of East, Philippines, 1986. Intern New Rochelle (N.Y.) Hosp., 1989-90, resident, 1990-92, chief resident, 1992-93. Office: 2110 E Flamingo Ste 208 Las Vegas NV 89119

MEDINA, SANDRA, social worker, educator; b. Tulsa, Oct. 4, 1947; d. James and Erleen (Austin) Meeks; m. Michael Sellman, 1966 (div. 1979); children: Rhainnie, Morgan; m. Ernest Medina, Aug. 21, 1985; 1 child, Brendyn. Cert., Community Coll. of Denver, 1975; BS summa cum laude, Met. State Coll., Denver, 1981; MSW, U. Denver, 1983, postgrad. Lic. clin. social worker, Colo. Dir. Lafayette (Colo.) Presch./Playtime, 1973-75, Bennett (Colo.) Non-Denominational Presch., 1975-76; intern. in clin. social work Brighton (Colo.) Schs., 1981-82; adminstrv. social work intern Jefferson County (Colo.) Schs., 1982-83; med. social worker Las Animas County Health Dept., Trinidad, Colo., 1985-85; psychiat. social worker Colo. State Hosp., Pueblo, 1985-89; clin. social worker PsychCare, Greeley, 1990-92; counselor high sch. U. Northern Colo. Lab. Sch. Instr. Trinidad State Jr. Coll., 1984-85; field instr. N.Mex. Highlands U., Las Vegas, 1986-87, U. So. Colo., Pueblo, 1988-89; adj. prof. social work U. Denver, 1996-97; asst. prof. social work, practicum coord. Chadron State Coll., 1997-99. Mem. exec. com. Gov.'s Task Force on Child Abuse, Denver, 1985; bd. dirs. Adams County Rep. Advs. for Children Today, Denver, 1978-79; chairperson membership com. Met. Child Protection Coun., Denver, 1982-83. Mem. NASW. Democrat. Presbyterian.

MEDINA, SUE O'NEAL, librarian; b. Knoxville, Nov. 18, 1945; d. Floyd and Violet Bloomer; m. Albert Medina. BA in History, Fla. State U., 1966, MS in Libr. Sci., 1971, PhD, 1983. Base libr. Ft. Bruckner Spl. Svcs., Ryukyu Islands, 1969; head libr. Kubasaki H.S., Ryukyu Islands, 1970; asst. humanities ref. libr. U. Ga. Librs., Athens, 1971-72; head Cottage Hill br. Mobile (Ala.) Pub. Libr., 1972-74; dir. Ala.-Tombigbee Libr. Sys., Camden, 1975-76; cataloger Fla. State U., 1977; cons. for planning and rsch. Ala. Pub. Libr. Svc., Montgomery, 1977-85; dir. Network of Ala. Acad. Librs., 1985—. Reader for preliminary rev. of manuscripts Coll. and Undergrad. Librs., Haworth Press, 1993-2000, Jour. Interlibr. Loan, Document Delivery and Info. Supply, 1995—; lectr. in field; cons. in field. Contbr. articles to profl. jours.; editor The Golden Nugget, 1992-93, 1995-2000. Mem. Ala. Adv. Coun. on Librs., 1985-86; mem. Ala. Union List of Serials Adv. Com., 1989-2000. Named to Outstanding Young Women of Am., 1978, 81, Ala. Libr. Yr., 1990, Ala. Eminent Libr. of the Yr., 1996, Ala. Libr. Roll of Honor, 1999; recipient Award of Excellence for best article about use of microforms in librs. for "Major Microform Sets: The Alabama Experience", UMI, Inc., 1994; grantee ALA/NEW, 1979-80, Humanities Alliance, 1982-83, NEH, 1983-85, 87-89, U.S. Office of Edn., 1989, Ala. State Coun. on Arts and Humanities, 1990, U.S. Dept. Edn., 1990, 93-94, Inst. Mus. and Libr. Svcs., 2001-2003. Mem. ALA, Assn. Specialized and Coop. Libr. Agencies (ex-officio bd. dirs., editor Interface 1983-86), Assn. for Libr. Collections and Tech. Svcs., Southeastern Libr. Assn. (mem. ad hoc com. on SELA/SOLINET coop. 1993), Ala. Libr. Assn. (exec. coun. 1987-88, chair bibliographic com. 1996, legis. devel. com. 1988—, Eminent Libr. of Yr. 1996), Southeastern Libr. Network, Rsch. and Acad. Librs. of Ga., Montgomery Gem and Mineral soc. (editor chpt. newsletter), Beta Phi Mu (Libr. of Yr. 1990, Disting. Mem. medal 1998). Office: Network of Alabama Academic Libraries PO Box 302000 100 N Union St Montgomery AL 36104-3719

MEDINA-PUERTA, ANTONIO, scientist; b. Almeria, Spain, Jan. 20, 1956; s. Antonio and Maria Mar (Puerta) Medina. MS, U. Politecnica, Madrid, 1979, MIT, 1982; OD, U. Complutense, Madrid, 1979; diploma in elec. engring., MIT, 1983; PhD, U. Politecnica, Madrid, 1987. Optometrist Centro de Vision Luz, Almeria, 1978-79; engr. Philips, Eindhoven, The Netherlands, 1979-80; rsch. asst. MIT, Cambridge, 1981-83; sci. assoc. Harvard Med. Sch., Boston, 1983-88; task mgr. Calif. Inst. Tech., Pasadena, 1988-91. Adviser NASA, Washington, 1988—, USN, 1989—; dir. rsch. Delta Optics, Covina, 1992—; prof. U. Madrid. Contbr. articles to profl. publs.; patentee in field. Fellow Christ's Coll., Cambridge Univ., Eng. Fellow Acad. Applied Sci.; mem. IEEE, Optical Soc. Am. Roman Catholic. Achievements include invention of pneumatic keratology medical procedure. Avocations: scuba diving, sailing. Home and Office: PO Box 2355 Costa Mesa CA 92628-2355

MEDINGER, C. WYNN, design and branding consultant; b. Chestnut Hill, Pa., June 30, 1950; s. Charles W. and Margaret (Wynn) M.; m. Betsy S. Medinger; children: Christopher Wynn, Jill Barbara. BFA, Univ. of the Arts, 1972. Designer Gottschalk & Ash, Montreal, Que., Can., 1972-76; sr. designer Anspach, Grossman, Portugal, N.Y.C., 1977-98; pres. JMK Corp., Ridgefield, Conn., 1977-2000; CEO BrandLogic Corp. (merger), Wilton, 2000—, JMK, Context and Navistream Corps. Involved n corp. identity programs for GE, Texaco, IBM, Wyeth, others. Recipient numerous awards in field, including Am. Inst. of Graphic Arts, Art Dirs. Club of Chgo., Art Dirs. Club of N.Y., Can. Pub. Rels. Soc., Gold Ink awards, IBM design awards, others.

MEDINS, GUNARS, surgeon; b. Riga, Latvia, Sept. 21, 1924; came to U.S., 1950; s. Janis and Olga Medins; m. Jacqueline Burright, Nov. 28, 1953 (div. May 1959); 1 child, Peter; m. Carol Jean Benson, Nov. 7, 1959; children: Lisa, Juliette, Gunars, John, Christian, Maria. MD, Philipps U., Marburg, Germany, 1950; MS in Surgery, Northwestern U., 1957; postgrad. surgery tng., Loyola U., 1954-56, 57-58, Northwestern U., 1956-57, 58-60, U. Tenn., 1960-61. Diplomate Am. Bd. Surgery, Am. Bd. Thoracic Surgery. Resident, Chgo., 1957-58, 58-59, Memphis, 1960-61; pvt. practice Ill., 1952-54, 63-65; staff surgeon Canal Zone, 1961-63; chief surgery Samoa, 1965-67; pvt. practice Hawaii, 1967-88, Ga., 1988—. Vol. surgeon Palau, Micronesia, 1977-78, Kinshasa, Zaire, 1974-76, Pago Pago, Samoa, 1985-86, St. Lucia, 1989, Peshawar, Pakistan, 1991. Rsch. fellow, Chgo., 1956-57, clin. fellow, 1959-60. Fellow ACS, Am. Coll. Chest. Physicians; mem. Sigma Xi. Republican. Lutheran. Avocations: history, linguistics. Home: 4750 Cove Cir Apt 603 Madeira Beach FL 33708-4801 E-mail: gmedins@tampabay.rr.com.

MEDITZ, WALTER JOSEPH, engineering consultant; b. Bklyn., June 4, 1917; s. Joseph and Marie (Gaspar) M.; m. Elizabeth M. Cagney, Jan. 9, 1944; children— Jeannette Jordan, Mary Beth Banks. BCE, Bklyn Poly. Inst., 1939, MME, 1941; M in Indsl. Engring., Ga. Inst. Tech., 1951. Research engr., lab. instr. Bklyn. Poly. Inst., 1939-40; civil engr., supt. Spencer, White & Prentice, 1940-41; asst. to design and prodn. mgr. Frederick R. Harris, 1941-43; chief indsl. engr. Naval Aircraft, Norfolk, Va., 1943-46; asst. chief engr. Boyle-Midway, N.Y.C., 1946-47, plant mgr. Atlanta, 1947-51, asst. to pres. N.Y.C., 1951-55, Standard Packaging Corp., N.Y.C., 1955-57, v.p. for mfg., 1957-67; mgr. facilities to divisional v.p. Doubleday & Co., Inc., Garden City, N.Y., 1967-83; pres. Meditz Engring. Assocs., 1984—. Served from ensign to lt. (s.g.) USNR, 1943-46. J. Waldo Smith fellow ASCE, 1939; Bklyn. Poly. Inst. fellow, 1939 Mem. Soc. for Adcancement Mgmt., Alpha Pi Mu. Home: 1371 S Ocean Blvd Pompano Beach FL 33062-7130

MEDLAND, MAURICE BLUE, writer; b. Centerville, Iowa, Sept. 29, 1936; s. William C. and Avis N. (Blue) M.; m. Karen A. McFarland, Aug. 7, 1965; children: Melissa A., Steven W. BS, Truman State U., 1961; MBA, Pepperdine U., 1977. Mgmt. sys. analyst Rockwell Internat. Corp., Downey, Calif., 1961-70; dir. Fluor Corp., Irvine, 1970-85; v.p. PacifiCare Health Sys., Cypress, 1985-87; novelist, 1987—; instr. U. Calif., Irvine, 1998—. Adv. Calif. State U. Fullerton Writer's Program, 1998—. Author: Point of Honor, 1997. With USN, 1954-57. Recipient Apollo Achievement award NASA, 1969. Mem. The Authors Guild. Home: 19842 Villager Cir Yorba Linda CA 92886-4454 Fax: 714 779-9831. E-mail: mauricemedland@msn.com.

MEDLAND, WILLIAM JAMES, college president; b. Logansport, Ind., Jan. 1, 1944; s. Thomas Gallagher and Mary Elizabeth (Hassett) M.; m. Donna Lee Bahnaman, Mar. 12, 1977; children: Bridget Marie, Mark David, Jeanne Nicole. BA, U. Notre Dame, 1966; student, St. Louis U., 1972-74; MA in History, Ball State U., 1967, MA in Edn., 1979, PhD in History, 1980; postgrad., Inst. for Mgmt. Lifelong Edn., Harvard U., 1985, Ctr. Internat. Cooperation and Security Studies, U. Wis., 1988, Ctr. Internat. Studies, MIT, 1989, Freie Universitat, Berlin, 1991. Instr. history and philosophy Donnelly coll., Kansas City, Kans., 1967-70; curricular advisor Ball State U., Muncie, Ind., 1970-71, teaching fellow, 1977-80; asst. dean St. Louis (Mo.) U., 1971-75; employee supr. Wilson, Inc., Logansport, 1975-76; ops. mgr. Watson-Jenkins, Inc., Indpls., 1976-77; dean of coll., asst. prof. history Springfield (Ill.) Coll., 1980-81; acad. dean, assoc. prof. history and edn. Marymount Coll., Salina, Kans., 1981-86; exec. v.p., provost, prof. history St. Mary's U., Winona, Minn., 1986-91; pres., prof. history Viterbo U., LaCrosse, Wis., 1991—. also bd. dirs., CEO, 1991—. Edn. cons. Am. Inst. Banking, Springfield, 1980-81; advisor Adv. Com. to Sch. Bd., Salina, 1984, Salina Diocesan Bd. Edn., 1981-83; evaluator North Ctrl. Assn., Chgo., 1987-2000. Author: Cuban Missile Crisis of 1962-Needless or Necessary?, 1988, reprint, 1990, A Guide to Writing College Research Papers, 1989, The Catholic School: A Bibliographical Resource Guide, 1990; editor: Ind. Acad. Social Scis. jour., 1979, Perspectives: A Liberal Arts Exchange (faculty jour.), 1988. Coll. solicitor United Way, St. Louis, 1973; coord. Coll./Cmty. Artist Series, Salina, 1981—84; mem. Franciscan-Skemp Healthcare Cmty. Bd., 2002—; bd. dirs. Immaculate Heart of Mary Sem., Winona, 1987—91, La Crosse Med. Health Sci. Consortium, 1993—, Wis. Found. for Ind. Colls., 1994—98, Assn. Franciscan Colls. and Univs., 1999—; chair La Crosse Diocesan Edn. Commn., 1994—2001. Fellow Ctr. Internat. Studies, MIT/Harvard U., 1989. Mem.: KC, Wis. Assn. Ind. Colls. and Univs. (bd. dirs. 1991—), Am. Assn. Ind. Coll. Pres., Am. Assn. Coll. Pres., Am. Assn. Higher Edn., La Crosse C. of C. (bd. dirs. 2000—, exec. com. 2001—), Rotary, Phi Delta Kappa, Phi Alpha Theta (rsch. award Ball State U. 1979). Roman Catholic. Avocations: reading, research. Home: 119 Calla Ct Onalaska WI 54650-8317 Office: Viterbo Univ Office of Pres 815 9th St S La Crosse WI 54601-4777 E-mail: wjmedland@viterbo.edu.

MEDLER, MARY ANN L. federal judge; JD, St. Louis U., 1983. Atty. Thompson Coburn, St. Louis, 1983-85; asst. cir. atty. Office of Cir. Atty. of City of St. Louis, 1985-92; atty. Union Pacific R.R., St. Louis, 1992-93; magistrate judge U.S. Dist. Ct. (ea. dist.) Mo. Office: 111 S 10th St Rm 13S Saint Louis MO 63102 E-mail: Mary_Ann_Medler@MOED.USCOURTS.gov.

MEDLEY, ALEX ROY, executive minister; b. Columbus, Ga., Aug. 4, 1948; s. Howard and Clois Mildred (Chumney) M.; m. Patricia Stauffer, May 10, 1975; children: James Ethan, Christopher Jordan. BA magna cum laude, U. Chattanooga, 1970; cert., Grad. Sch. Ecumenical Studies, Celigny, Switzerland, 1973; MDiv, Princeton Sem., 1974. Ordained to ministry Bapt. Ch., 1975. Assoc. pastor First Bapt. Ch. Trenton, N.J., 1974-77; adminstrv. intern Nat. Ministries Am. Bapt. Chs. U.S.A., Valley Forge, Pa., 1977, nat. dir. Christian ctr., 1978-85; min. of world mission support, area min. Am. Bapt. Chs. N.J., East Orange, 1986-92, exec. min., 1992—. Intern World Coun. Chs., Geneva, Switzerland, 1973; rep. N.Am. Bapt. Fellowship, Washington, 1975-77; mem. domestic hunger/poverty working group Nat. Coun. Chs. of Christ, 1978-85, mem. gen. assembly; conf. speaker Am. Bapt. Chs., 1979; Am. Bapt. Ch. U.S.A. del. to Nat. Coun. Chs. of Christ. Editor (newsletter) Social Edn. for Action Newsletter, 1978-79. Bd. dirs. Ch. World Svc./CROP, N.J., 1975-77, Occupational Tng. Ctr., Burlington, N.J., 1992-99; sec. Key Inmate Edn. Project, Trenton, 1986; participant Nat. Religious Leadership Program, 1997-99, Bapt. World Alliance Commn. on Freedom and Justice, 2000—. Mem. Am. Bapt. Regional Exec. Mins. Coun. Avocations: reading, fishing, hiking. Home: 22 Story Ct Freehold NJ 07728-5322 Office: Am Bapt Chs NJ 3752 Nottingham Way Ste 101 Trenton NJ 08690-3802

MEDLEY, DONALD MATTHIAS, education educator, consultant; b. Faulkton, S.D., Feb. 18, 1917; s. Thomas Arnot and Cecilia Agnes (Kellen) M.; m. Betty Ann Robertsen, Aug. 23, 1948; 1 child, Timothy Laurence. BS, Coll. of St. Thomas, St. Paul, 1938; MA, U. Minn., 1950, PhD, 1954. Tchr. Am. Sch. Guadalajara, Mex., 1941-42, Floodwood (Minn.) Pub. Schs., 1946-48; instr. English, Coll. of St. Thomas, 1948-50; asst. prof. CUNY, 1954-59, assoc. prof., 1959-64, prof., 1964-65; sr. rsch. psychologist Ednl. Testing Svc., Princeton, N.J., 1965-70; disting. prof. U. Va., Charlottesville, 1970-87, prof. emeritus, 1987—. Mem. exec. bd. Consortium for the Improvement of Tchr. Evaluation, Atlanta, 1985-87. Author: (with others) Measurement-Based Evaluation of Teacher Performance, 1984, Handbook of Research on Teaching, 1963, The Teather's Handbook, 1971, Research on Teaching, Concepts, Findings, and Implications, 1979, Ency. of Educational Research, 5th edit., 1982, 6th edit., 1992, Developing Skills for Instructional Supervision, 1984, Measurement-Based Evaluation of Teacher Performance, 1984, Advances in Teacher Education, 1984, International Ency. of Education: Research and Studies, 1984, 2d edit., 1994, Assessment of Teaching: Purposes, Practices, and Implications for the Profession, 1999; contbr. articles to profl. jours. Staff Sgt. U.S. Army, 1942-46. Fellow APA; mem. Am. Ednl. Rsch. Assn. (divsn. sec. 1962), Nat. Coun. on Measurement in Edn., Assn. Tchr. Educators. Democrat. Roman Catholic. Avocations: conjuring, travel. E-mail: dm4c@aol.com.

MEDLEY, NANCY MAY, nurse; b. Oct. 8, 1948; d. Donald Raymond and Josephine Ruth (Blakley) M. AA, Riverside City Coll., 1970. RN, Calif. Staff nurse in medicine Riverside Gen. Hosp., Calif., 1970-71; staff nurse neonatal unit Kaiser Permanente Hosp., Hollywood, 1971-72; critical care nurse neurosurg./ICU unit Harbor-UCLA Hosp., Torrance, 1972-78, nurse mgr. cardiac care unit, 1978—2001, temp. nurse mgr. neurosurg. ICU, 1988-90, nurse mgr. surg. ICU and cardiothoracic units, 1992-94, nurse mgr. cardiology svcs. med-surg. telemetry unit, progressive care unit, cardac rehab., and chest pain unit, 1997—2001, nurse mgr. employee health svcs., 2001—. Mem. AACN, Am. Heart Assn. Republican. Presbyterian. Home: 636 Manhattan Ave Apt C Hermosa Beach CA 90254-4529 Office: Harbor-UCLA Hosp 1000 W Carson St Torrance CA 90502-2004

MEDLIN, JOHN GRIMES, JR. banker; b. Benson, N.C., Nov. 23, 1933; s. John Grimes and Mabel (Stephenson) M. BS in Bus. Adminstrn., U. N.C., 1956; grad., The Exec. Program, U. Va., 1965. With Wachovia Bank & Trust Co., Winston-Salem, N.C., 1959-93, pres., 1974; pres., CEO Wachovia Bank and Wachovia Corp., 1977-93; chmn. bd. Wachovia Corp., 1987-98, chmn. emeritus, 1998—. Bd. dirs. U.S. Airways Group, Inc., Burlington Industries Inc., Media Gen. Inc. Trustee Nat. Humanities Ctr., Wake Forest U., The Duke Endowment, The Rsch. Triangle Found., Kenan Inst. for Ethics; mem. State Jud. Coun. N.C., 2000—; active numerous civic and svc. orgns. With USNR, 1956-59. Mem. Phi Delta Theta. Office: Wachovia Corp PO Box 3099 100 N Main St Winston Salem NC 27101-4047

MEDLOCK, DONALD LARSON, lawyer; b. Port Chester, N.Y., Mar. 8, 1927; s. J. Harold and Emma Adelaide (MacLennan) M.; m. Katharine Smedes Nicholson, May 21, 1955; children: Katharine Baird, Margaret MacLennan, William Nicholson. BA with honors, Yale U., 1947, LLB, 1950. Bar: N.Y. 1950, U.S. Dist. Ct. (so. dist.) N.Y. 1951, U.S. Dist. Ct. (ea. dist.) N.Y. 1952, U.S. Tax Ct. 1952, U.S. Ct. Custom and Patent Appeals, U.S. Ct. Appeals (2d cir.) 1951. Assoc. Putnam & Roberts, N.Y.C., 1950-56, ptnr., 1957-94, sr. counsel, 1995—. Bd. dirs. Bancard Sys. of N.Y. Inc., Port Washington. Editor Yale Law Jour., New Haven, 1948-50. Sec., bd. dirs. Port Washington Community Chest, 1959-61; bd. dirs. Port Washington Estates Assn., 1958-61; mem. ann. fund parents com. Taft Sch., 1979-81; bd. mgrs., exec. com.

William Sloane Ho. YMCA of Greater N.Y., 1979-84; chmn. univ. coun. com. on Law Sch. Yale U., 1979-86; chmn. Yale Alumni Fund, 1984-86, bd. dirs., 1955—, exec. com., 1980-88; chmn. Yale Law Sch. Fund, 1974-76; mem. devel. bd. Yale U., 1984-88, exec. com., 1984-86; exec. com. Yale Law Sch., 1975-79, hon., 1979—; bd. dirs. Assn. Yale Alumni, 1984-86, rep.-at-large, 1979-82, com. on undergrad. admisssions, 1979-82, com. on Yale medal, 1981; exec. com. Assn. Families U. Denver, 1982-84. Recipient citation Yale Law Sch., 1977, Yale Alumni Fund Chmn.'s award, 1979, 87, Yale medal, 1994. Mem. Fed. Power Bar Assn., Assn. of Bar of City of N.Y. (com. on profl. ethics 1958-61), Corbey Ct. Yale Law Sch., Tuscarora Club (Margaretville, N.Y., bd. dirs. 1963-95, sec. 1970-86, v.p. 1984-86), Country Club of Landfall, Manhasset Bay Yacht Club, Mory's Assn., India House, Scroll and Key Soc., Yale Club N.Y.C., Phi Beta Kappa, Phi Delta Phi. Avocations: trout fishing, tennis, reading, crossword puzzles, golf. Home: Landfall 800 Oyster Lndg Wilmington NC 28405-5292

MEDLOCK, ERIC PRESTON, computer scientist; b. Oklahoma City, Feb. 6, 1977; s. Gary P. Medlock and Constance L. Young; m. Jennifer Schulz Schulz, Apr. 17, 1999; children: Racheal Schulz. Cert. BrainBench Java 1, BrainBench Java 2. Cons. ComSys Inc., Charlotte, NC, 1997; sys. engr. First Union Nat. Bank, 1997—98; sr. analyst lead VF Inc., Greensboro, 1998—2001; cons. Pepsi Bottling Group, Winston-Salem, 2001—. Tech. advisor Mecklenburg County Bar Assn., Charlotte, 1997. Contbr. articles to profl. jours. Activist/database coord. Guilford County Libertarian Party, Greensboro, 2000—02. Libertarian. Avocations: Tae Kwon Do, creative writing. Personal E-mail: eric.medlock@yahoo.com.

MEDNEY, TANIA LEVY, advertising agency executive; b. Rio de Janeiro, June 19, 1955; d. Samuel and Paulette (Schinazi) L.; children: Matthew Levy, Samantha Jennifer. BA cum laude, SUNY, Albany, 1977. Sec. Benton & Bowles, Inc., N.Y.C., 1977-78, network coord., 1978-79, sr. media planner, 1979-81, Young & Rubicam, Inc., N.Y.C., 1981-82, media supr., 1982-87; media dir. Young & Rubicam Bravo, 1987-88; sr. media supr. Young & Rubicam, 1987-89, tng. specialist, 1983-89, mktg. and media cons., tng. specialist, 1989—; media supr. Foote, Cone & Belding, 1998-99; assoc. media dir. Bates USA, 1999—2001; media and mktg. cons., 2001—. Song specialist, dance and guitar instr. Author: Supervisory Skills Manual, 1984. Democrat. Avocations: dancing, playing guitar, travel, photography, skiing. E-mail: tlmrio@aol.com.

MEDNICK, ROBERT, accountant; b. Chgo., Apr. 1, 1940; s. Harry and Nettie (Brenner) M.; m. Susan Lee Levinson, Oct. 28, 1962; children: Michael Jon, Julie Eden, Adam Charles. BSBA, Roosevelt U., Chgo., 1962. CPA Ill. Staff asst. Arthur Andersen, Chgo., 1962-63, sr. acct., 1963-66, mgr., 1966-71, ptnr., 1971-98, mng. dir. SEC policies, 1973-76, mng. dir. auditing procedures, 1976-79. Vice chmn. com. on profl. stds. Andersen Worldwide, 1979-82, chmn. com., 1982-98, mng. ptnr. profl. and regulatory matters, 1993-98; mem. faculty Northwestern U. Kellogg Grad. Sch. Mgmt., 1999. Contbr. articles to profl. jours. Bd. dirs. Roosevelt U., Chgo., 1977—, vice chmn., 1986-94, sr. vice chmn., 1994—, life trustee, 1999—; bd. dirs. Auditorium Theatre Coun., 1990-96, Lake Shore Drive Synagogue, 1992—; co-chmn. adv. coun. Chgo. Action for Soviet Jewry, Highland Park, Ill., 1983-87; bd. dirs., mem. exec. com. Am. Judicature Soc., 1990-95, vice chmn., 1993-95; bd. overseers Rand Corp. Inst. Civil Justice, 1994-98; bd. dirs. Nat. Bur. of Econ. Rsch., 1998—, treas., 1999—. Sgt. USAFR, 1965-69. Recipient Silver medal Ill. CPA Soc., 1962; named One of Ten Outstanding Young Men in Chgo., Chgo. Jr. C. of C., 1973-74; recipient Rolf A. Weil Disting. Service award, Roosevelt U., Chgo., 1983; Max Block award N.Y. State C.P.A. Soc., 1984; Ann. Literary award Jour. Accountancy, 1986, 88; Andrew D. Bradin award for distinctive contbns. to discipline of accountancy Case Western Res. U., Cleve., 1996; Disting. Alumni award Roosevelt U. Walter E. Heller Coll. Bus. Adminstrn., 1997; Disting. Vis. scholar Hebrew U., Jerusalem, 1999, 2000. Mem. AICPA (bd. dirs. 1986-87, 92-94, 95-98, vice chmn. 1995-96, chmn. 1996-97, numerous coms., Elijah Watt Sells award 1962, Gold Medal for Disting. Svc. 1998), Ill. CPA Soc. (acctg. prins. com. 1973, legal liability com. 1986-89, mgmt. of acctg. practice com. 1991-94, regulation and legis. com. 1998—). Jewish. Avocations: collecting art, travel. E-mail: robert.mednick@awo.com.

MEDNICOFF, DAVID MICHAEL, lawyer, educator; b. Bangor, Maine, Oct. 25, 1959; s. Irma Mednicoff; m. Joya Misra, Mar. 24, 1996; 1 child Amina Mednicoff-Misra. AB, Princeton (N.J.) U., 1982; JD, Harvard U., 1989, AM, 1988, postgrad. Cons. Amnesty Internat., Washington, 1994-98; asst. prof. U. Mass., Amherst, 1999—. Pres., bd. dirs. U. Georgia Hillel Found., Athens, 1996-99; exec. com., bd. dirs. Atlanta Jewish Young Adult Agy., 1996-99; cons., advisor Nat. Conf. of Christians and Jews, Boston, 1987-88; mem. Congregation B'nai Israel. Fulbright scholar Coun. for Internat. Exch. of Scholars, 1990, 92-93. Democrat. Avocations: choral performance, piano, travel, cooking. Office: U Mass 221 Hampshire House 131 County Cir Amherst MA 01003-9257 Fax: 413-545-1640. E-mail: mednic@legal.umass.edu.

MEDOFF, MARK HOWARD, playwright, screenwriter, novelist; b. Mt. Carmel, Ill., Mar. 18, 1940; s. Lawrence Ray and Thelma Irene (Butt) M.; m. Stephanie Thorne, June 24, 1972; children: Debra, Rachel, Jessica. BA, U. Miami, Fla., 1962; MA, Stanford U., 1966; D.H.L., Gallaudet Coll., 1981. Instr. English and drama N.Mex. State U., 1966-79, dramatist in residence, 1974—, head dept. drama, 1978-87, prof. drama, 1979-93, artistic dir., 1982-87, Am. S.W. Theatre Co., 1984-87. Author: (plays) When You Comin' Back, Red Ryder?, 1974, The Wager, 1975, The Kramer, 1975, The Halloween Bandit, 1978, The Conversion of Aaron Weiss, 1978, Firekeeper, 1978, The Last Chance Saloon, 1979, Children of a Lesser God, 1980 (Soc. West Theatres best play award 1982), The Majestic Kid, 1981, The Hands of Its Enemy, 1984, Kringle's Window, 1985, The Heart Outright, 1986, Road to a Revolution, 2001, (novel) Dreams of Long Lasting: (films) When You Comin' Back, Red Ryder?, 1979, Off Beat, 1986, Apology, 1986, Children of a Lesser God, 1986, Good Guys Wear Black, 1978, Clara's Heart, 1988, The Majestic Kid, 1988, City of Joy, 1992, Homage, 1995, Santa Fe, 1997, Who Fly On Angel's Wings, 2000; works appear in Best Plays, 1973-74, 75-75, 79-80, Best Short Plays, 1975, The Homage that Follows, 1987; plays Stumps, 1989, Stefanie Hero, 1990, Showdown On Rio Road, 1995, Gila, 1995, A Christmas Carousel, 1996, Crunch Time, 1996, Gunfighters, A Gulf War Chronicle, 1997, A Christmas Carousel, 1998, Tommy J and Sally, 2000; dir. (film) Children on Their Birthdays. Guggenheim fellow, 1974-75; recipient Obie award, Drama Desk award, Outer Critics Circle award, Media award Pres.'s Com. Employment Handicapped, Tony award; Oscar award nominee for Best Screenplay for Children of A Lesser God, 1987. Mem. SAG, Coll. Fellows Am. Theater, Dramatists Guild, Writers Guild Am., Actors Equity Assn., Pen, Coll. Fellows of the Am. Theatre. Office: PO Box 3072 Las Cruces NM 88003-3072

MEDREK, JOSEPH, computer operator; b. Springfield, Mass., Dec. 30, 1953; s. Joseph and Eileen Patricia Medrek; m. Emily Sui-Ling Lam; 1 child Samantha. Cert. network adminstr. Author: (book) New Creation, 1998, Napkin Talk, 1998, The Adventures In The Life of Charlie Onion, 1997, America At The Millenium "The Best Poems and Poets of the 20th Century, 2000 (Disting. Poet, 2000). Pres. Taxpayers Action Network, Bridgeport, 1991—93. Sgt. USAF, 1972—76.

MEDVECKY, ROBERT STEPHEN, lawyer; b. Bridgeport, Conn., Feb. 12, 1931; s. Stephen and Elizabeth (Petro) M.; m. Ellen R. Munt, Nov. 11, 1966; children— Allison L., Beth A., Craig R. AB, Dartmouth, 1952; JD, Harvard, 1955. Bar: Ill. bar 1955, Conn. bar 1958, D.C. bar 1972, Fla. bar 1989. Asso. firm Lord, Bissell & Brook, Chgo., 1955-57; gen. atty. So. New Eng. Telephone Co., New Haven, 1957-71; v.p., gen. counsel, sec. Amtrak, Washington, 1971-75; partner firm Lord, Bissell & Brook, 1975-78, Reid & Priest, N.Y.C., 1978-87. Clubs: Harvard (N.Y.C.), Fiddlesticks Country (Ft. Meyers, Fla.), Saphire Valley Country (Cashlers, N.C.). Home: 15491 Kilbirnie Dr Fort Myers FL 33912-2424 also: 457 Round Hill Rd Sapphire NC 28774-7608 E-mail: bmedvecky@yahoo.com.

MEDVECKY, THOMAS EDWARD, lawyer; b. Bridgeport, Conn., Apr. 22, 1937; s. Stephen and Elizabeth P. Medvecky; m. Patricia Conneally, Aug. 25, 1967; 1 son, Thomas Edward, II. A.B., Bowdoin Coll., 1959; LL.B., St. John's U., 1962. Bar: Conn. 1962. Assoc., Louis Katz, Danbury, Conn., 1963-68; sole practice, Bethel, Conn., 1968—; asst. town counsel Town of Bethel, 1963-67; assoc. dir. State Nat. Bank Conn. Mem. budget com. Danbury (Conn.) Community Chest, 1966-68. Served with USAR, 1962-68. Recipient Am. Jurisprudence award 1962. Mem. ABA, Conn. Bar Assn., Danbury Bar Assn. Democrat. Lutheran. Office: 99 Greenwood Ave PO Box 272 Bethel CT 06801-0272

MEDVED, MICHAEL, film critic, author, talk show host; b. Phila., Oct. 3, 1948; s. David Bernard and Renate Rosa (Hirsch) M.; m. Nancy Harris Herman, Aug. 5, 1972 (div. 1983); m. Diane Elvenstar, Jan. 27, 1985; children: Sarah Julia, Shayna Elana, Daniel Joshua. BA, Yale U., 1969, student in law, 1969—70; MFA, Calif. State U., San Francisco, 1974. Speech writer, polit. cons. various campaigns and politicians, Conn., Calif., D.C., 1970-73; advt. creative dir. Anrick Inc., Oakland, Calif., 1973-74; freelance writer L.A., 1974—; on-air film critic People Now, Cable News Network, 1980-83; on-air film critic, co-host Sneak Previews PBS, 1985-96; chief film critic N.Y. Post, 1993-98; Hollywood corr. The Sunday Times of London; nationally syndicated radio talk show host Salem Radio Network, Seattle, 1998—. Radio talk show host KVI AM, Seattle, 1996—98; critic The Worst of Hollywood Channel 4, England, 1982. Author: What Really Happened to the Class of '65?, 1976, The Shadow Presidents, 1979, Hospital, 1983, Hollywood vs. America, 1992; co-author: (with Harry Medved) The 50 Worst Films of All Time, 1978, The Golden Turkey Awards, 1980, The Hollywood Hall of Shame, 1984, Son of Golden Turkey Awards, 1986, (with Diane Medved) Saving Childhood, 1998. Co-founder, pres. Pacific Jewish Ctr., Venice, Calif., 1977-94; pres. Emanuel Streisand Sch., Venice, 1980-85. Mem. Writers Guild Am., AFTRA. Avocation: classical music. Office: 1809 7th Ave Ste 200 Seattle WA 98101-1327

MEDVED, PAUL STANLEY, lawyer; b. Milw., May 6, 1956; s. Frank F. and Evelyn F. (Poplawski) M.; m. Danita C. Cole, Aug. 27, 1988. BA with honors, Marquette U., 1978; JD, Columbia U., 1981. Bar: Wis. 1981, U.S. Dist. Ct. (ea. dist.) Wis. 1981, U.S. Dist. Ct. (we. dist.) Wis. 1984, U.S. Ct. Appeals (7th cir.) 1984. Assoc. Michael, Best & Friedrich, Milw., 1981-88, ptnr., 1988-97; shareholder Mallery & Zimmerman, S.C., 1997—. Office: Mallery & Zimmerman SC 731 N Jackson St Ste 900 Milwaukee WI 53202-4697 E-mail: pmedved@mzmilw.com.

MEDVED, SANDRA LOUISE, elementary education educator; b. Moscow, May 26, 1953; d. Donald James and Pearl Helen (Brown) Jensen; m. Jeffrey Alan Medved, Aug. 6, 1977. BS in Edn., U. Idaho, 1975; postgrad., Boise State U., 1976, U. Idaho, 1977—. Tchr. St. Mary's Elem. Sch., Boise, Idaho, 1975-78, Coeur d'Alene (Idaho) Sch. Dist., 1978—. Tchr. edn. U. Idaho, 1987-88; instr. Lewis and Clark State Coll., 1994-98; lead tchr. Coeur d'Alene Sch. Dist., 1997-2000, assessment literacy facilitator, 2001—, decade of change com., 1997—, supervision and evaluation com., 1998—, puppeteer, 1985-91, tchr. edn. instr., 1986-88, 92-94, lang. arts com., 1988—, dist. coord. handicap awareness program, 1989-91, staff devel. curriculum adv. com., 1990-95, mentor tchr., 1990-93, 99-2000, mem. phonics spelling com., 1996-98, mem. Educator of the Yr. com., 1997—, mem. staff devel. com., 1997—; active Idaho State Sch. Reform Com., 1994-95; rep. Goals 2000 Tchr. Forum, 1995. Vol. Kootenai County Diversion Program, Coeur d'Alene, 1980's. Recipient grants EXCEL, Coeur d'Alene, 1991-92. Mem. ASCD, NEA, Idaho Edn. Assn., Coeur d'Alene Edn. Assn., Internat. Reading Assn., Panhandle Reading Assn., Phi Delta Kappa. Avocations: reading, swimming, walking. Office: Sorensen Elem Coeur D Alene Sch Dist 9th and Coeur d'Alene Ave Coeur D Alene ID 83814

MEDVEI, VICTOR CORNELIUS, endocrinology consultant; b. Budapest, June 6, 1905; arrived in Eng., 1937; s. Maurice William Cornelius and Frederica (Ladany) M.; m. Sheila Mary Wiggins, May 9, 1946 (dec. 1989); children: Riccarda Maria, Victoria Maria, Cornelius Malcolm. MD, U. Vienna, 1930. Chief asst. Med. Policlinic, Vienna, 1932-37; sr. registrar endocrine dept. Bart's Hosp., London, 1948-82; prin. med. officer Fgn. Svc., 1958-70. Author: The Mental and Physical Effects of Pain, 1949 (Buxton Browne prize 1948), The History of Clinical Endocrinology, 1993; author, editor: The Royal Hospital of St. Bartholomew, 1973, A History of Endocrinology, 1984; contbr. numerous articles to profl. jours. Decorated Order of Merit (France); comdr. Order Brit. Empire. Fellow Royal Soc. Medicine, Royal Soc. Physicians (London), Royal Coll. Physicians; mem. Garrick Club, Pen Club; mem. of Fellow of Royal College of Physicians of London, (FRCP). Roman Catholic. Avocations: reading, travel, music.

MEDWEDEFF, FRED M(ARSHALL), dentist; b. Flint, Mich., Nov. 20, 1926; s. Marshall Herbert and Elsie Ella (Miller) M.; m. Joan Lenore Kampmeier, June 17, 1950 (div. 1973); children: Carol Medwedeff Grosvenor, Linda Medwedeff Mello, John Davis; m. Carolyn Adams Payne Gothard, Dec. 30, 1977; 1 child, Carol Lynn Gothard. BS, U. Mich., 1949; DDS, Emory U., 1954. Diplomate Am. Bd. Oral and Maxillo-Facial Radiology. Gen. practice dentistry, Nashville, 1955—; instr., then asst. prof. Vanderbilt U. Sch. Medicine, 1955-83; staff mem. Vanderbilt U. Hosp., 1955-83; asst. prof. Meharry Med. Coll., 1970. Founder, pres. Precision X-Ray Co., Nashville, 1964-74; lectr. tour on x-rays to dentists, Japan, 1973. Contbr. articles to profl. jours.; patentee in field. Served with USAAF, 1945. Mem. ADA, Tenn. Dental Assn., Nashville Dental Soc., Am. Acad. Oral and Maxillo Facial Radiology, Mid. Tenn. Acad. Implant Dentistry (founding), Pierre Fauchard Acad. (life), Psi Omega. Home: 9646 New Hwy 96 W Franklin TN 37064-4782 Office: 21st Plaza Bldg 121 21st Ave N Nashville TN 37203-5213

MEECH, SONJA ROSEMARY, interior design studio owner; b. Mpls., Jan. 16, 1950; d. Frank Mike and Elvira Gertrude (Stolzman) Schumm; m. Frank Otis, Feb. 17, 1968 (div. 1975); 1 child, Christopher; m. James W. Bretall, Oct. 16, 1992. Student pub. schs., Robbinsdale, Minn. Non-foods mgr. Red Owl, Mpls., 1968-71; real estate agt. Century 21, Mpls., 1976-79; teller Valley Nat. Bank, Tucson, 1981-85; owner Sonja's, Tucson, 1981—. Telephone solicitor Rep. Party, Tucson, 1982. Mem. Assn. Gen. Contractors (spl. events Tucson 1985-86).

MEECHAM, WILLIAM CORYELL, engineering educator; b. Detroit; s. William Edward and Mabel Catherine (Wilcox) M.; m. Barbara Jane Brown, Sept. 4, 1948 (dec.); children: Janice Lynn, William James; m. Della Fern Carson BS, MS, U. Mich., 1948; PhD in Physics, U. Mich. and Brown U., 1954. Head acoustics lab. Willow Run Labs., Ann Arbor, Mich., 1959-60; asst. prof. U. Mich., 1958-60; prof. U. Minn., Mpls., 1960-67; prof. fluid mechanics and acoustics UCLA, 1967—, chmn. dept. mechanics and structures, 1972-73. Cons. Aerospace Corp., El Segundo, Calif., 1975-80, Rand Corp., Santa Monica, Calif., 1964-74, Bolt, Beranek and Newman, Cambridge, Mass., 1968-73, Arete Assocs., Encino, Calif., 1976— , CRT Corp., Chatsworth, Calif., 1985—; expert witness numerous cmty. noise ct. cases, L.A., Las Vegas, 1986—. Author: (with R. Lutomirski) Lasar Systems, 1973; author 140 papers on fluid mechanics and acoustics. Treas. Unitarian Ch., Ann Arbor, Mich., 1958-60; advisor U.S. Congress Com. on Pub. Works, Congl. Record Report N.J., 1972; mem. Calif. Space and Def. Council, U.S. Congress, 1982— . Served with U.S. Army, 1944-46. Mich. Alumni scholar 1942-44, Donovan scholar U. Mich., 1944-45; UCLA senate rsch. grantee, 1968—, NASA rsch. grantee, 1971—, Office Naval Rsch. grantee, 1977-85; recipient Disting. Svc. award U.S. Army. Fellow Acoustical Soc. Am. (gen. chmn. meeting 1973), AIAA (assoc. fellow); mem. Internat. Inst. Acoustics and Vibration, Am. Phys. Soc. (fluid dynamics div.), Inst. Noise Control Engrng., Sigma Xi, Tau Beta Pi Home: 927 Glenhaven Dr Pacific Palisades CA 90272-2202 Office: UCLA Sch Engring & Applied Sci Los Angeles CA 90024

MEEGAN, WILLIAM JOHN, b. Jersey City, June 17, 1948; Author: Conquest of Genesis! A Study in Universal Creation Mathematics, 1998. Mem.: Dante Soc. Am. (life). Avocations: mythology, symbolism, esoterism, metaphysics, ancient cultures. Home: Harrison House # 1803 80 Presidential Plz Syracuse NY 13202

MEEHAN, JEAN MARIE ROSS, human resources, occupational health and safety management consultant; b. Chgo., Mar. 16, 1954; d. A. Ronald Gonzalez and Barbara Marx Shipley; m. John J. Meehan, 1993; 1 child, Jenna A.; 1 child from previous marriage, Justin L. Ross. Diploma in Nursing, St. Mary of Nazareth Hosp., Chgo., 1974; BS in Health Arts with high honors, U. St. Francis, 1988; MPA with honors, Roosevelt U., 2000. Cert. occupl. health nurse specialist, pharmacy technician. Staff nurse St. Mary of Nazareth Hosp., Chgo., 1973-75; head nurse ambulatory care Edgebrook Med. Diagnostic Ctr., 1975-76; occupl. health nurse Williams Electronics, Inc., 1976-84; adminstr. safety and benefits Reliable Power Products, Franklin Park, Ill., 1984-90; corp. dir. human resources and risk MacLean-Fogg Co., Mundelein, 1990—; pres., cons. Auriel Mgmt. Sys., Island Lake, 1992—; pres. Claim Masters LLC, 1998-99. Gov., apptd. mem. Ill. Pollution Prevention Adv. Coun., Springfield, Ill., 1993-98, mem. coun., 1993-98; adv. bd. dirs. Gt. Lakes Health Care Alliance, 1996-97; spkr. in workshops. Poetry included in Visions of Beauty, 1999 (Editor's Choice award 1999), Tides of Memory, 2000, America at the Millennium—The Best Poems and Poets of the 20th Century, 2000. Guest speaker local schs. and environ. groups, also I.E.P.A. and U.S. E.P.A. workshops; corp. campaign chmn. Charitable Preference Drives, Mundelein, Ill., 1991-; mem. Lake County Employer Coun. Bus./Govt. Partnership, 1996-99. Recipient Leadership Civic citation United Way Charities of Lake County, 1993, 94. Mem. Am. Assn. Occupl. Health Nurses, Ill. Assn. Occupl. Health Nurses, Suburban Chgo. Occupl. Health Nurses, Soc. for Human Resources Mgmt., Lake County Violence Intervention and Prevention, Lake County Employer Coun. Avocations: parenting, interior design, reading, entertaining. Office: MacLean-Fogg Co 1000 Allanson Rd Mundelein IL 60060-3804 E-mail: j.rossmeehan@worldnet.att.net.

MEEHAN, JOHN JUSTIN, lawyer; b. N.Y.C., Feb. 14, 1947; m. Daizy Rice; children: John, Jason. Student, Javeriana U., Colombia, 1967; BA cum laude, St. Louis U., 1969, JD, 1975. Bar: Mo. 1976, U.S. Dist. Ct. (we. dist.) Mo. 1976, U.S. Dist. Ct. (ea. dist.) Mo. 1977, U.S. Ct. Appeals (8th cir.) 1978. Tchr. St. Francis Xavier Grad Sch., St. Louis, 1970-72; pvt. practice, 1978—. Tchr. tai chi and qigong St. Louis U., Mo. Bot. Gardens; tchr. tai chi I and II, St. Louis C.C.-Meramec, 1994-98; lectr. in field. Mo. bd. dirs. Chinese Cultural Assn., 1976-80; pres. Chinese Internal Arts Ctr., 1991—; v.p. Lafayette Towne Neighborhood Assn., 1994; bd. dirs. Better Family Life, 1995—, Nigerian Cultural Assn., 1994—, Laclede Towne Cmty., 1976-80; active Big Bro. program Pruitt Igoe, 1965-69; mem. John Burroughs Diversity Com., 1998, St. Louis African Chorus, 2000—; pro bono legal counsel Eiretrean Assn., Brazilian Assn., Vietnamese Buddhist Assn. Recipient Human Rights award St. Louis Coalition for Human Rights, 1997, Human Dignity award YMCA, 2001. Mem. Mo. Bar Assn., Met. Bar Assn. St. Louis, Mound City Bar Assn. (mem.-at-large 1991-92, 98-99, Legal Svc. award 1998), NAACP (life). Roman Cath. Avocation: foreign travel, Taiji, Qigong. Office: Lafayette Towne Profl Bldg 2734 Lafayette Ave Ste 1 Saint Louis MO 63104-2040 Fax: 314-772-3604.

MEEHAN, MARTIN THOMAS, congressman, lawyer; b. Dec. 30, 1956; s. Martin T. and Alice (Britton) M.; m. Ellen T. Murphy. BA in Polit. Sci., Edn. cum laude, U. Mass., Lowell, 1978; MPA, Suffolk U., 1981, JD, 1986; student, Harvard U., 1987-88. Adminstrv. asst. to mayor City of Lowell, Mass., 1978-79; press asst. Congressman James M. Shannon, 1979-81; del. Dem. Nat. Conv., 1980, 84, 88; head rsch. analyst Joint Com. on Elec. Laws Mass. State Senate, 1981-84; dir. pub. affairs Govt. of Mass., 1985-86, dep. sec. state, 1986-90; 1st asst. dist. atty. Middlesex County, Mass., 1991-92; mem. U.S. Congress from 5th Mass. dist., 1993—, mem. armed svcs. com., judiciary com. Former teacher, adj. instr. U. Lowell, Mass.; lawyer 1986—. Named Student of Yr. Lowell Exchange Club, 1975. Mem. ABA, Mass. Bar Assn., U. Lowell Alumni Assn., The Newspaper Guild, Internat. Fedn. Journalists. Democrat. Roman Catholic. Office: US Ho of Reps 2447 Rayburn House Office Bldg Washington DC 20515-0001*

MEEHAN, MICHAEL JOSEPH, lawyer; b. St. Louis, Aug. 28, 1942; s. Joseph Michael and Frances (Taylor) M.; m. Sharon Kay McHenry (div. 1988); m. Patricia Ann Shive, July 8, 1989 (dec. 1999); m. Shelly Fujiho Lee, 2002. BS in Engring., U.S. Coast Guard Acad., 1964; JD with high distinction, U. Ariz., 1971. Bar: Ariz. 1971, U.S. Ct. Appeals (6th, 8th, 9th and 10th cirs.), U.S. Supreme Ct. 1975. Law clk. Assoc. Justice William H. Rehnquist, U.S. Supreme Ct., 1972; assoc. Molloy, Jones & Donahue, P.C., Tucson, 1971-75, shareholder, 1975-93; chmn. exec. com., head trial dept., 1986-93; founder Meehan & Assocs., Tucson, 1993-2001; ptnr. Quarles & Brady/Striech Long, 2001—. Mem. fed. appellate rules adv. com. Jud. Conf. U.S., 1994-99. Author chpt. on appellate advocacy: State Bar of Arizona Appellate Practice Handbook. Fellow Am. Acad. Appellate Lawyers (treas.); mem. Ariz. Bar Assn. (past chair appellate practice sect. 1995-99). Republican. Lutheran. Avocation: golf. Office: Quarles & Brady 1 S Church Ave Ste 1700 Tucson AZ 85701-1621 E-mail: mmeehan@quarles.com.

MEEHAN, RICHARD ANDREW, investment banker; b. Rockville Centre, N.Y., Apr. 22, 1964; s. William Campbell and Therese Marie (Copin); m. Linda Dmytriw, July 27, 1996. BS in Computer Sci., St. John's U., Jamaica, N.Y., 1988. Cert. in child and adult CPR and first aid. Computer operator asst. Nassau County Dept. Gen. Svcs., Mineola, N.Y., 1988-89; jr. govt. specialist Morgan Stanley & Co., Inc., N.Y.C., 1989-90, sr. govt. specialist, 1990-96; lector Our Lady of the Miraculous Medal Ch., Ridgewood, N.Y., 1998-2000; child life technician Beth Israel Med. Ctr., 1999—. Computer lab. asst. St. John's U., 1985-88. Vol. coord. Mary Brennan Inn, Hempstead, N.Y., 1992-93. L.I. Academic Caddie scholar, 1982; named one of Outstanding Young Men of Am., 1987. Avocations: camping, bicycling, boating, swimming. Home: 1919 Palmetto St Ridgewood NY 11385-2932 E-mail: rlmee@aol.com.

MEEHAN, ROBERT HENRY, human resources executive, electronics company executive, business educator; b. Hackensack, N.J., June 19, 1946; s. Horace Miles and Pauline Jeannette (Pente) M.; m. Ruth Ann Auletta, Sept. 28, 1969; children: Robert Michael, Brian John. BA, Montclair State U., 1968; MA magna cum laude, Fairleigh Dickinson U., 1972; D in Profl. Studies, Pace U., 1997. Cert. secondary sch. tchr. of social studies, N.J., compensation and benefits profl. Job analyst Citicorp, N.Y.C., 1969-70, sr. job analyst, 1970-72, ofcl. asst., 1972, project specialist human resources practices/policy rev., 1973, project specialist attitude surveys, 1973-75, human resources officer nat. banking group, 1975-76; asst. dir. human resources N.Y. Power Authority, White Plains, 1976-84, dir. compensation, 1984-93, dir. compensation and human resources info. sys., 1993-94, dir. compensation and benefits strategy and devel., 1994-95, dir. compensation and benefits, 1995-98; dir. compensation Philips Electronics N.Am., 1998-2000; mng. dir. R.H. Meehan Assocs., Human Capital Cons., Maywood, NJ, 2000—01; dir. compensation, benefits and HRIS, ASML, Tempe, Ariz., 2001—. Instr. Am. Compensation Assn., Scottsdale, Ariz., 1986—, course coord., 1992-94; adj. assoc. prof. Lubin Grad. Sch. Bus., Pace U., 1995-2001; mem. N.Y. Power Pool Salary com., 1990-98, chair, 1998; speaker at profl. confs. Sr. author: Managing a Direct Pay Program, Cert. Course 4A, 1991, Determining Compensation Costs: An Approach to Estimating and Analyzing Expense, 1991; editor books; mem. exec. adv. panel Acad. Mgmt. Exec., 1993—; contbr. articles to profl. jours. Scoutmaster, Boy Scouts Am., Ridgefield Park, N.J., 1968; also scouting coordinator, Maywood, N.J., 1982-83; vestryman, sr. warden St. Martin's Episcopal Ch., Maywood, 1977-84. Mem. Am. Compensation Assn. (cert. instr. 1986—, course coord. 1992-94, mem. cert. and currency com. 1988-89, direct compensation com. 1990-91, chmn. 1992-93, bd. dirs. 1993), Soc. for Human Resource Mgmt. (mem. compensation and benefits com. 1998-2001), Human Resources Assn. N.Y. (compensation com. 1998-2001), Acad. Mgmt. (exec. adv. panel jour. The Exec.), N.Y. Compensation Assn., Order DeMolay (master councilor 1963, 65, scribe, adv. bd. 1965-68, Meritorious Svcs. award 196), Psi Chi, Delta Mu Delta, Beta Gamma Sigma. Episcopalian. Avocations: golf, sailing, furniture making. Office: ASML 8555 S River Pkwy Tempe AZ 85284 Business E-Mail: Robert.Meehan@asml.com.

MEEHAN, TAMIYE MARCIA, library director; b. Chgo., Oct. 14, 1942; d. Thomas and Virginia Fujibayashi; m. Rudolph J. Trejo, Jr., Sept. 1, 1962 (div. 1980); m. James E. Meehan, Jr., Oct. 4, 1981; children: Terrence, Theodore, Timothy, Rosalind. MALS, Rosary Coll., 1974; MBA, De Paul U., 1980. Librarian Chgo. Pub. Libr., 1974-75, br. libr. head, 1975-77, dist. chief, 1977-96, staff devel., 1996-97; dir. Indian Trails Pub. Libr. Dist., Wheeling, Ill., 1997—. Mem. ALA (chmn. ethnic multicultural and info. roundtable 1998-99), Ill. Libr. Assn. (bd. dirs. 1999—, treas. 2000-02). Office: Indian Trails Pub Libr Dist 355 S Schoenbeck Rd Wheeling IL 60090-4467 E-mail: TMeehan@iTpld.lib.il.us.

MEEHAN, TERENCE A. minister; b. Cincinnati, Ohio, Jan. 30, 1941; s. Thomas Joseph Meehan and Maxine Elizabeth Underwood. AB, Mt. St. Mary's Sem., Cincinnati, OH, 1962, MA, 1964; MSW, St. Louis U., St. Louis, MO, 1970. H.s. tchr. Cath. Ctrl. H.S., Springfield, Ohio, 1968—69; assoc. pastor St. Paul Ch., Cincinnati, 1970—71; asst. dir. Cath. Social Services,

Dayton, 1971—75, dir., 1975—78; pastor St. Joseph Ch., Cincinnati, 1978—84, St. Columbkille Ch., Wilmington, 1984—90, Holy Name Ch., Cincinnati, 1990—, St. Andrew Ch., Cincinnati, 1994—; chaplain Hamilton County Justice Ctr., 1990—; pastor Our Lady of Sorrows Ch., Monroe, 2002—. Roman Catholic. Home: 30 Guido St Cincinnati OH 45202

MEEHL, PAUL EVERETT, psychologist, educator; b. Mpls., Jan. 3, 1920; s. Otto John and Blanche Edna (Duncan) Swedal; m. Alyce M. Roworth, Sept. 6, 1941 (dec. 1972); children: Karen, Erik; m. Leslie Jane Yonce, Nov. 17, 1973. AB, U. Minn., 1941, PhD, 1945; Sc.D., Adelphi U., 1984. Diplomate Am. Bd. Profl. Psychology (clin. psychology, bd. dirs.1957-62, Disting. Svc. and Outstanding Contbns. award 1989). Instr., asst., assoc. prof., chmn. dept. psychology U. Minn., 1951-57, prof., 1952—, prof. dept. psychiatry Med. Sch., 1952-90, regents' prof. psychology, 1968-89, Hathaway-Meehl prof. psychology, 1990-93, regent's prof. psychology emeritus, 1993—; prof. Minn. Ctr. for Philosophy of Sci., 1953-56, 69—, prof. philosophy, 1971—; acting chief clin. psychology VA Hosp., Mpls., 1947-49; participant Dartmouth Conf. on Behavior Theory, 1950; mem. panel on criminal deterrence Nat. Acad. Sci., 1975-77; practice psychotherapy, 1951-94; staff Nicollet Clinic, 1970-80. Author: (with S.R. Hathaway) Atlas for Clinical Use of MMPI, 1951, (with others) Modern Learning Theory, 1954, Clinical Versus Statistical Prediction, 1954, What, Then, Is Man?, 1958, Psychodiagnosis, 1973, Selected Philosophical and Methodological Papers, 1991, (with N. Waller) Multivariate Taxometric Procedures, 1998; contbr. articles to profl., legal and philos. jours. Recipient Ednl. Testing Svc. award for contbns. to measurement, 1994, Clin. Psychology Centennial prize for lifetime achievement APA, Bruno Klopfer disting. contbn. award, 1979, Gold medal for life achievement application of psychology Am. Psychol. Found., 1989, Disting. Svc. award Am. Bd. Profl. Psychologists, 1989, Joseph Zubin prize lifetime contbns. to psychopathology, 1993; William James fellow Am. Psychol. Soc., 1989. Fellow Am. Psychol. Soc. (James McKeen Cattell fellow 1998), Inst. for Advanced Study in Rational Psychotherapy; mem. APA (pres. 1961-62, Disting. Contbr. award clin. divsn. 1967, Disting. Sci. Contbr. award 1958, Disting. Scientist award 1976, Disting. Contbn. to Knowledge award 1993, award for Outstanding Lifetime Contbn. to Psychology 1996), Am. Acad. Arts and Scis., Nat. Acad. Sci., Philosophy of Sci. Assn., Phi Beta Kappa, Sigma Xi, Psi Chi. Home: 1544 E River Ter Minneapolis MN 55414-3646 Office: U Minn N218 Elliott Hall 75 E River Rd Minneapolis MN 55455-0280 E-mail: pemeehl@umn.edu.

MEEK, AMY GERTRUDE, retired elementary education educator; b. Frostburg, Md., Jan. 3, 1928; d. Arthur Stewart and Amy Laura (Brain) M. BS, Frostburg State U., 1950; MEd, U. Md., 1956; postgrad., Columbia U., 1964, Am. U., 1968-70. Cert. tchr., Md. Tchr. elem. sch. Prince Georges County Schs., Bradbury Heights, Md., 1950-51, Allegany County Schs., Cumberland, 1951-60, Frostburg, 1960-84; now ret. Author: (with others) Stir Into Flame, 1991; contbr. articles to hist. publs. Mem. Frostburg Hosp. Aux., 1987-91; bd. dirs. Frostburg Hist. Mus., 1989—, Coun. of Alleghenies, 1991, sec., 1991—; sec. Braddock Estates Civic Assn., Frostburg, 1988; mem. com. Frostburg Libr., 1989; tchr. Ch. Conf. Schs. Missions, 1970; vol. tutor, 1986-92; pres. Ch. Women United, Frostburg, 1989-95; trustee Frostburg United Meth. Ch., 1992—; mem. endowment fund com. Balt. Conf. United Meth. Ch., 1992—; pres. Cumberland-Hagerstown dist. United Meth. Women, 1985-89, chmn. fin. interpretation Balt. Conf., 1990-94; lay spkr. United Meth. Ch., 1975—; pres. bd. dirs. Frostburg Museum, 2000. Mem. AAUW (pres. 1993-95, treas. Md. divsn. 1974, Woman of Yr. award Frostburg br. 1980, New Frostburg Libr. Bldg. Com. 1994-98, chair pub. policy com. Frostburg br. 2001—, bd. ordained ministry Cumberland-Hagerstown Dist. United Meth. Ch., 2000—. Republican. Avocations: travel, reading, gardening, genealogy, historical research.

MEEK, BARBARA SUSAN, elementary education educator; b. Monaca, Pa., Feb. 8, 1951; d. Michael Frederick and Sarah Ellen (Hall) Fronko; m. Joseph William Meek Jr., Nov. 25, 1977. BS in Edn., Ohio U., 1973; MA in Edn., Marietta Coll., 1999. Cert. elem. tchr., Ohio. 3d grade tchr. Warren Local Schs., Vincent, Ohio. Martha Holden Jennings scholar, 1976-77. Mem. NEA, Ohio coun. Tchrs. Math., Ohio Coun. Internat. Reading Assn., Ohio Edn. Assn., Warren Local Edn. Assn. Home: 5371 Veto Road Vincent OH 45784-5118

MEEK, CARRIE P. congresswoman; b. Tallahassee, Apr. 29, 1926; 3 children. BS, Fla. A&M U., 1946; MS, U. Mich., 1948. Mem. Fla. Ho. of Reps., Tallahassee, 1979-82, Fla. Senate, Tallahassee, 1982—93, U.S. Congress from 17th Fla. dist., 1993—; mem. appropriations com.; mem. subcommittee on Treasury, Postal Svc. and Gen. Gov., subcommittee on VA, HUD, and Ind. Agencies. Democrat. Office: US Ho of Reps 2433 Rayburn Ho Office Bldg Washington DC 20515-0917

MEEK, FORREST BURNS, retired trading company executive; b. Tustin, Mich., June 11, 1928; s. Robert B. and Electa I. (Gallup) M.; m. Jean R. Grimes, June 26, 1953; children: Sally, Thomas, Nancy, Charles. AA, Spring Arbor Coll., 1950; AB, Mich. State U., 1953; postgrad., U. Ga., 1965; MA, Cen. Mich. U., 1967. Exec. sec., chmn. bd. Edgewood Press, Clare, 1971—; gen. mgr. Blue Water Imports, 1985; dir. Ctr. for Chinese-Am. Scholarly Exchs., Inc., 1989-97; gen. mgr. Blue-Water Internat. Trading Co., Inc.; retired, 1998. Vis. prof. Wuhan U., China, 1986—87; dist. office mgr. Fed. Decennial Census, 1990; instr. phys. geology and astronomy Mid Mich. C.C., 2002; mem., chmn. Red team East Ctrl. Mich. Planning and Devel. Regional Commn. Author: Michigan Timber Battleground, 1976, Michigan Heartland, 1979, One Year in China, 1988, Michigan Logging Railroad Era, 1850-1963, 1989, Railways and Tramways, 1990, Lumbering in Eastern Canada, 1991, Pearl Harbor Remembered, 1991, Heroes of The Twentieth Century, 2000. Coordinator Clare County Bicentennial Com., 1975-76; Rep. fin. chmn., Clare County, 1966-71, asst. treas. 10th dist. Mich, 1967-69; trustee local sch. bd., 1992-96; chmn. local county jury bd., 1991-98; mem. bd. commrs. Clare County (Mich.) Dist. 4 Commn., 1998-2000. Mem. Am. Entrepreneur Assn., Mich. Sci. Tchrs. Assn., Mich. Hist. Soc., Heartland Mich. Geneal. Soc., White Pine Hist. Soc. (exec. sec.). Republican. Avocations: astronomy, silviculture. Fax: 989-386-4511.

MEEK, HARRIET WILSON, social worker; b. Ft. Wayne, Ind., Dec. 29, 1941; d. Ben Wilson and Anna Margaret (Newell) M. BS, N. Tex. State U., 1964; MSW, Smith Coll., 1967, PhD, 1986; postdoctoral, Tavistock Clinic, London, 1985-87. Lic. clin. social worker, Ill., Mass.; cert. social worker, Eng. Clin. social worker U. N.Mex., Albuquerque, 1967-68, Albuquerque Child Guidance Ctr., 1969-73, 75-78; child psychotherapist The Counseling Ctr., East Machias, Maine, 1973-75; clin. social worker U. N.Mex. Hosps., Albuquerque, 1978-80; clin. supr. Valley Counseling Ctr., Holyoke, Mass., 1980-85; clin. and rsch. assoc. Tavistock Clinic, London, 1985-87; pvt. practice Chgo., 1987—; lectr. U. Chgo., 1990—. Mem. editorial bd., corr. editor Jour. Social Work Practice, 1987—; guest editor, 1989. Mem. Nat. Assn. Social Workers. Office: 180 N Michigan Ave Ste 350 Chicago IL 60601-7401

MEEK, MARK ALAN, investment executive; b. Wichita, Kans., Sept. 16, 1949; s. Elmo L. and Margaret Dorothy (Craig) M.; 1 child: Holly Marie. BS in Economics, U. Ctrl. Fla., Orlando, 1996; MA in Applied Economics, U. Ctrl. Fla., 1998. Dir. asset mgmt. Sweetser Cos., Oklahoma City, 1981-83; divsn. mgr. C.B.S. Property Svcs., Inc., Albuquerque, 1983-85; dist. mktg. mgr. Turner Devel. Corp., Tampa, Fla., 1985-87; pres. Turner Real Estate Mgmt., Inc., 1987-89; gen. mgr. Collier Enterprises, Orlando, 1989-93; principal Litigation Cons., 1993-98; asst. v.p. AmTrust Bank, Tampa, 1998-99; v.p. Colonial Bank, 1999—. Author: (book) Currency Valuation & Structural Models: Lessons from the Asian Experience, 1998. Lay leader, Hyde Park United Meth. Ch., Tampa, 1999. Mem. Nat. Assn. Bus. Economists, Real Estate Investment Coun., Nat. Assn. Home Builders, Golden Key Nat. Honor Soc. Republican. Meth. Avocations: sailing, skiing, travel. Office: Colonial Bank 400 N Tampa St Ste 2500 Tampa FL 33602-4708 Home: Apt 2212 1000 S Harbour Island Blvd Tampa FL 33602-5717 E-mail: mameek@gte.net.

MEEK, MARY VIRGELIA CLEVELAND, special education administrator, psychologist; b. Frankfort, Ky., Sept. 16, 1937; d. James T. and Agnes (Redden) Cleveland; m. Willoughby F. Meek, Dec. 14, 1957; children: Elizabeth, J.B. AB, Transylvania U., Lexington, Ky., 1958; MA, U. Ark., 1969; EdS, Ga. State U., 1988. Cert. assoc. sch. psychologist Svc. 6, Ga. Coord. presch. Child and Adolescent Psychoednl. Ctr., Dalton, Ga., 1975-90, Whitfield County Schs., Dalton, 1990—; ret. instr. North Ga. Regional Edn. Svcs. Agy. Com. mem. Presch. Adv. Task Force, Ga. Dept. Edn., Atlanta, 1991; mem. adj. faculty West Ga. Coll., Carrollton, 1991; mem. continuing edn. faculty Dalton Coll., 1989—. Deacon 1st Presbyn. Ch., Dalton, 1986-89, mem. child care com., 1976—. Mem. Coun. for Exceptional Children, Nat. Assn. Sch. Psychologists, Ga. Assn. Sch. Psychologists, LWV, Lesche Women's Club (officer 1976-94). Avocation: swimming.

MEEK, SUSAN BIEBER, lawyer, physician, mediator, consultant; b. Chgo., Nov. 15, 1951; d. Martin S. and Anita (Felsenthal) Bieber; m. Charles Capps Meek, Jan. 16, 1977; children: Ryan, Kevin, Katy, Ann. BS, U. Ill., 1973; JD, No. Ill. U., 1976; MD, Chgo. Med. Sch., 1980. Bar: Ill. 1984, U.S. Dist. Ct. (no. dist.) Ill. 1984, Tex. 1988, U.S. Dist. Ct. (so. dist.) Tex. 1988. Intern Mayo Clinic, Rochester, Minn., 1980-81; resident in ophthalmology U. Ariz.; Corneal Rsch. fellow La. State U.; ptnr. M. Bieber and Assocs., Chgo. Med. legal cons. to numerous firms, Houston; cons. Dept HHS Office of Hearings and Appeals. Contbr. articles to profl. jours. Mem. Gov.'s Task Force on Aging. Mem. AMA, ABA (litigation, corp., health law and adminstrv. law sects.), Tex. Bar Assn. (med. malpractice com. 1991), Houston Bar Assn., Ill. Bar Assn., Chgo. Bar Assn., Health Care Lawyers Group, Am. Soc. Law and Medicine, Assn. Am. Trial Lawyers, Tex. Trial Lawyers Assn., Women Trial Lawyers Assn., Am. Judicature Soc., Am. Acad. Ophthalmology, Am. Coll. Eye Surgeons, Pan Am. Ophthalmology Soc., Contact Lens Assn., Tex. Med. Assn., Harris County Med. Soc., Sigma Xi, others. Home: 2929 Buffalo Speedway Houston TX 77098-1707

MEEKER, ARLENE DOROTHY HALLIN (MRS. WILLIAM MAURICE MEEKER), manufacturing company executive; b. June 13, 1935; d. Haddon Eric and Martha (Randow) Hallin; m. William Maurice Meeker, Aug. 1966; 1 child, William Michael. Grad., John Muir Jr. Coll., 1953; student, L.A. Valley Coll., 1956-58; BA, Whittier Coll., 1973, MBA, 1980. Statewide sec. pub. rels. United Reps. Calif., L.A., 1964; pers. specialist Sanford Mgmt. Svcs., Inc., 1964-66; v.p. pers. Grover Mfg. Corp., Montebello, Calif., 1966-75, pres., 1975—, bd. dirs., 1969—. chmn. bd. dirs., 1975—. Bd. dir. Brit. Marine Industries, Montebello, 1969-86, chair bd. 1986—, Grover Ltd., Clonakilty, County Cork, Ireland, 1986—, Grover Internat., 1969—. Author: Stress Differences Between Male and Female Executives, 1980. Mem. City of Whittier Transp. and Parking Commn., 1976-84; mem. L.A. County Art Mus., 1969-80; chair fine arts bd. Hillcrest Congl. Ch., ch. coun., 1977-79; trustee Oxford Prep. Sch., Whittier, 1983-89; press chmn. Whittier Rep. Women Federated, 1977-78, 1st v.p., 1981-83; Rep. precinct capt., 1964; active L.A. World Affairs Coun.; pres. Friendly Hills Property Owners Assn., 1982-84. Mem. AAUW, Docian Soc. (pub. rels. chair 1967-68), Conglist., Ocean Club Homeowners Assn. (treas., pres. 1996-98), Newport Harbor Yacht Club, Friendly Hills Country Club, Whittier Lincoln Club (pres. 1982-84). Office: 620 S Vail Ave Montebello CA 90640-4952

MEEKER, DAVID ANTHONY, public relations executive; b. Akron, Ohio, June 1, 1939; s. Charles Anthony and Lucia Pauline (Schweikert) M.; m. Anita Marie De Jacimo, June 24, 1961; children: Christine Marie, Elizabeth Ann, Eileen Louise, David Edgerton. BS in Indsl. Journalism, Kent State U., 1961, postgrad., 1963-64; MS in Comms. Mgmt., Syracuse U., 1998. Editor Recordak Record, Eastman Kodak Co., N.Y.C., 1961-62; journalist Akron Beacon Jour., 1962-66, St. Louis Post-Dispatch, 1966-69; exec. sec. to mayor City of St. Louis, 1969-71; asst. dir. Ohio Dept. Natural Resources, Columbus, 1971-73; exec. dir. Ohio Dem. Party, 1973-74; pres. Urbanistics, Inc., 1974-76; ptnr. Meeker-Mayer Pub. Rels., 1976-84; pres. David A. Meeker & Assocs., Inc., Akron, 1984-89; sr. counselor Edward Howard & Co., 1989—; also bd. dirs. Bd. dirs. Akron Regional Devel.; Dem. candidate for mayor City of Akron, 1987; mem. regional environ. priorities project pub. com. Kent State U. Sch. Journalism, 1996-97, mem. adv. bd.; chmn. Summit County Charter Commn., 1995; chmn. bd. dirs. Uilbje St. Edward. Recipient Con Lee Kelliher award Kent State U., 1966, Disting. Alumnus award Sch. Journalism, 1983, Lighthouse award Cleve. Pub. Rels. Soc. Am., 2001. Fellow Pub. Rels. Soc. Am. (nat. honors and awards com. 1981-83, chmn. 1983, nat. membership com. 1980-81, chmn. 1984, past del.-at-large nat. assembly, chmn. Counselors Acad. spring conf. 1987, pres. Akron chpt. 1982, immediate past chmn. and dir. environ. sects., past chmn. Coll. of Fellows); mem. SAR, Internat. Pub. Rels. Assn., Soc. Profl. Journalists (past pres. Buckeye chpt., John S. Knight award 1999), N.E. Ohio Regional Alliance (pres.). Roman Catholic. Avocations: tennis, fishing, antiques. Home: 269 S Rose Blvd Akron OH 44313-7843 Office: One Cascade Pla 19th Fl Akron OH 44308

MEEKER, DELBERT BRENT, engineer; b. Lampassas, Tex., July 30, 1939; s. Riley Morris and Lillian Mae (Hart) M.; m. Mary Louise Haake, Aug. 17, 1963 (div. 1977); children: Kirsten Rene, Gennifer Collette; m. Marsha Ellen Remington, Jan. 27, 1979; children: Barrett Russell, Lara Robin. BS in Physics, U. Tex., 1962; MS in Computer Sci., U. Calif., Santa Barbara, 1991. Physicist Naval Missile Ctr., Point Mugu, Calif., 1962-76; elec. engr. Pacific Missile Test Ctr., 1976-88, sr. technologist, 1988—. Author: Test and Evaluation of the Tactical Missile, 1989; contbr. articles to profl. jours. Mem. Am. Phys. Soc., Inst. Environ. Sci. (reliability testing com. 1985). Achievements include development of flight test simulation method of reliability testing for air-launched missiles. Office: Naval Air Warfare Ctr Code P035 Pt Mugu Nawc CA 93042-0001

MEEKER, GUY BENTLEY, banker; b. Calcutta, India, Nov. 4, 1945; (parents Am. citizens); s. Lincoln Voght and Fortune Helen (Bentley) M.; m. Lavenia Yale Nelson, Apr. 27, 1967 (div. 1979); children: G. Bentley Jr., Melissa Anne ; m. Marcia Lee Zink, Nov. 4, 1984 (div. 1993). BSBA, Georgetown U., 1967; MBA, George Washington U., 1970. Cons. OAS, Washington, 1971-73; v.p. The Deltec Banking Corp., Nassau, Bahamas & N.Y.C., 1973-78, Comml. Credit Internat. Banking Corp., Balt., 1978-82; sr. v.p., gen. mgr. Union Planters Internat. Bank, N.Y.C., 1982-84; exec. v.p., gen. mgr. Worthen Bank Internat., 1984-86; exec. v.p. and chief exec. officer N.Am. Bank Cen. Asia, 1984-95; supervisory dir. BCA Bank Europe N.V., Amsterdam, The Netherlands, 1993-95; pres. G.B. Meeker & Co., N.Y.C., 1996—. Author articles and monographs in field. Mem. Bankers Assn. Fgn. Trade (internat. adv. coun. 1992-95, vice chmn. IAC 1994-95), Inst. Internat. Bankers (legis. and regulatory com. 1992-94, bd. trustees 1994-95), Asia Soc. (corp. coun. 1987-95), River Club, Dutch Treat Club. Roman Catholic.

MEEKER, MILTON SHY, manufacturing company executive; b. Nov. 9, 1933; s. David and Helen Elizabeth (Kendrick) M.; m. Nancy Orbison, Nov. 27, 1976 (dec.); 1 child, Sherwin Kendrick. BA, U. Calif., Berkeley, 1955, BS, 1959; MBA, U. Mich., 1963. With Ford Motor Co., 1959-68; dir. purchasing, mtg., rsch. mgr. Paccar, Inc., Seattle and Newark, Calif., 1968-71; commr. fed. supply svc., commr. automated data & telecomms., assoc. dep. adminstr. GSA, Washington, 1972-75; dir. purchasing chem. group FMC Corp., Phila., 1975-77, dir. purchasing planning and adminstrn. Chgo., 1977-79; gen. sales mgr. Peterbilt Motors Co. divsn. Paccar, Newark, 1979-80; mktg. mgr. Petergilg Motors Co., 1980—89; dir. dealer devel. Paccar, Inc., Bellevue, Wash., 1989-91, exec. asst. to vice chmn., 1991-99. Chmn. Pres.'s Com. for Purchase of Products from Blind, 1973-74; bd. dirs. Nat. Industries for the Blind, 1976-86. With U.S. Army, 1957-58. Republican. Home: 7900 NE 32nd St Medina WA 98039-1030

MEEKER, ROBERT ELDON, retired manufacturing company executive; b. Moline, Ill., Sept. 6, 1930; s. Paul Edwin and Esther (Carlson) M.; m. Dorothy Elaine Nelson, Dec. 23, 1951; children: Julie Lynn Meeker Gratton, Laurie Allison Meeker Gamel, Bradford Nelson (dec.). BS in Chemistry, Ill. Wesleyan U., 1952; PhD in Phys. Chemistry, Northwestern U., 1955. Chemist, supr. Shell Devel. Co., Emeryville, Calif., 1955-64; mgr.-dir. synthetic rubber tech. ctr. Shell Chem. Co., Torrance, 1964-66, mgr. new projects N.Y.C., 1966-69; dir. exploratory sci., exploration and prodn. rsch. ctr. Shell Devel. Co., Houston, 1969-71; gen. mgr., head new enterprises divsn. Royal Dutch-Shell Co., London, 1971-72; v.p. comml., gen. mgr. Billiton Aluminum B.V. Billiton Internat. Metals subs. Shell Co., The Hague, The Netherlands, 1972-74; pres. Roxana Shale Oil Co. subs. Shell Co., Houston, 1974-76; v.p., gen. mgr. energy systems mgmt. div. TRW, Inc., Redondo Beach, Calif., 1976-80, v.p., gen. mgr. maj. programs, 1980-86; pvt. practice cons., real estate developer Tucson, 1986-94. Patentee in field Trustee Ill. Wesleyan U., Bloomington, 1982-94, trustee emeritus, 1994—; v.p., bd. dirs. Cobblestone Homeowners Assn., 1991-92, pres., bd. dirs., 1992-94, security chmn., 1994-97. Recipient Disting. Alumnus award Ill. Wesleyan U., 1981 Mem. Am. Parkinson Disease Assn. Inc. (pres. Ariz. chpt. 1996-2000, nat. bd. dirs. 1996—), Mercedes Benz Club Am. (pres. Chaparral sect. 1992-94). Republican. Lutheran. Avocations: photography; swimming; travel. Home and Office: 7240 N Star Fury Pl Tucson AZ 85718-1345 E-mail: remeeker@theriver.com.

MEEKER, ROBERT GARDNER, English language educator; b. Lackawanna, N.Y., Mar. 22, 1927; s. David Magie and Helen Amelia (Kilburn) M.; m. Kathryn Mary Bryan, Sept. 30, 1950 (dec. Apr. 1981); children: David John, Robert Bryan, John Townley; m. Beverly Jane Smith, Mar. 17, 1984. BA in English, Lafayette Coll., 1950; MA in English, U. Scranton, 1962; PhD in English, Lehigh U., 1989. Editl. asst., house organ United Fruit Co., N.Y.C., 1950-52; analyst, report writer Dun and Bradstreet, Newark, 1952-55, Scranton, Pa., 1955-58; English instr. Wyoming Seminary Preparatory Sch., Kingston, 1958-59; English tchr. Dallas (Pa.) Area H.S., 1959-60; prof. English Bloomsburg (Pa.) State Coll. (now Bloomsburg Univ.), 1962-91; adj. prof. English Wilkes U., Wilkes-Barre, Pa., 1994—, Keystone Coll., La Plume, 1996—, Pa. State U., Wilkes-Barre, 1998—. Cons. textbooks McGraw Hill Book Co., N.Y.C., 1987. Author: A Descriptive Analysis of the Kinds of Essays in Johnson's Rambler, 1990. Seaman 2d class USN, 1945-46. Mem. AAUP, Am. Soc. for Eighteenth Century Studies, Assn. Pa. State Coll. and Univ. Ret. Faculties. Avocations: classic jazz, bird watching, shelling. Home: 128 Yeager Ave Forty Fort PA 18704-4032

MEEKERS, DOMINIQUE ARMAND, health and demographics researcher; b. Diepenbeek, Belgium, June 23, 1962; came to U.S., 1987; BA magna cum laude, Free U. Brussels, 1985; MA, U. Pa., 1988, PhD, 1990. Rschr. Free U. Brussels, 1985-87; rsch. assoc. NAS, Washington, 1990-91; asst. prof., rsch. assoc. Pa. State U., University Park, 1992-96; assoc. Johns Hopkins U., Balt., 1996-2001; rsch. dir. Population Svcs. Internat., Washington, 1996—2001; prof. dept. internat. health and devel. Tulane U., New Orleans, 2001—. Cons. John Snow, Arlington, Va., 1992—93, Demographic and Health Surveys, Macro Internat., Calverton, Md., 1993—97, Population Svcs. Internat., 2001—; invited mem. Com. Reproductive Health, 2000—, Internat. Union Sci. Study Population; adj. assoc. prof. dept. internat. health and devel. Tulane U., New Orleans, 2000—01. Contbr. articles to profl. publs. Rsch. grantee Spencer Found., 1995, U. Md., 1996, UNICEF, Bucharest, Romania, 1997, UNAIDS, 1997, Deloitte Touche Tohmatsu, 2002, UNICEF, 2002. Mem. APHA, Population Assn. Am., Internat. Union for Sci. Study of Population. Office: Tulane U Dept Internat Health and Devel 1440 Canal St Ste 2200 New Orleans LA 70112 Home: 5633 Durham Dr New Orleans LA 70131 E-mail: dmeekers@tulane.edu.

MEEKINS, AUSTIN VALIANT, retired missionary pastor; b. Balt., Nov. 25, 1921; s. Austin and Edna Earle Meekins; m. Mae Elizabeth Gordon, Mar. 29, 1942; children: Gordon, Sharon, David, Esther (dec.). Student, Balt. Sch. of Bible, 1940-42, Moody Bible Coll., 1946, Md. Inst. Art. Ordained, Ill., 1950. Missionary Alaska Mission to the Ams., Wheaton, Ill., 1950-89, missionary Utah, 1967-89; v.p., instr. Mont. Bible Coll., Bozeman, 1997-2000. Pres. Evangel. Mins. Assn., Salt Lake City, 1971-84; mem., Salt Lake police chaplain Salt Lake Police Dept., 1978-83; new ch. coord. Mission to the Ams.-Western States, 1983-87, N.W. rep., Portland, 1987-89; graphic artist, art dir. Richardson, Sherman, Olson Assocs., Chgo., 1946-50, Walter Luedke Assocs., Rockford, Ill., 1965-67. Baptist. Avocations: interior design, cabinet woodworking, hunting.

MEEKINS, FREDERICK BOYD, librarian; b. Takoma Park, Md., Feb. 1, 1974; s. Jewell LeRoy Meekins, Bonnie Jo Meekins. AA in Gen. Studies, Prince George's CC, 1994; BS in Govt., Politics and History, U. Md., 1996; postgrad., Trinity Theol. Sem., 1997—. Libr. technician U. Md., College Park , 1997—. Editor, webmaster Am. World View Dispatch. Personal E-mail: fm70@umail.umd.edu.

MEEKISON, MARYFRAN, writer, photographer; b. Napoleon, Ohio, Apr. 9, 1919; d. Frank J. and Elizabeth (Keyes) Shaff; m. David Meekison, June 17, 1939; children: Maureen Meekison Houppert, David Francis, Beth Ann. Student, St. Mary's Coll., Notre Dame, Ind., 1936-39. Hist. writer, photographer, Napoleon, 1963—, St. Augustine Ch., 1983—. Author: (photographer) Canal Days to Modern Ways Revisited, 1984; (brochure) Canal Days to Modern Ways, 1963; mem. editorial adv. bd. Courier mag., 1989-91; contbr. articles to numerous mags. Steering com. Napoleon Susquicentennial, 1984; trustee Napoleon Pub. Lib., 1976-01. Recipient Spl. citation Courier Alumnae mag., also numerous photography and writing awards, Pres.'s medal, St. Mary's Coll., Notre Dame, Ind., 1991; named Citizen of Yr., Napoleain Area C. of C., 1990; named to St. Mary's Coll. Athletic Hall of Fame Notre Dame, 2001. Mem. Alumnae Assn. St. Mary's Coll. (bd. dirs. 1985-91), Literary Club. Democrat. Roman Catholic. Avocations: tennis, sailing. Home: PO Box 253 Napoleon OH 43545-0253

MEEKS, CAROL JEAN, educator; b. Columbus, Ohio, Mar. 9, 1946; d. Clarence Eugene and Clara Johanna (Schwartz) B.; m. Joseph Meeks, Aug. 17, 1968 (div. 1981); children: Catherine Rachael, Tiffany Johannah. BS, Ohio State U., Mex., 1968; MS, Ohio State U., 1969, PhD, 1972. Rsch. asst., assoc. Ohio State U., Columbus, 1968-71; internship Columbus Area C. of C., Ohio, 1970; lectr. Ohio State U., Columbus, 1970, 72; asst. prof. U. Mass., Amherst, 1972-74, Cornell U., Ithaca, N.Y., 1974-78, assoc. prof., 1978-80; legis. fellow Senate Com. Banking, 1984; supr. economist, head housing section USDA, Washington, 1980-85; assoc. prof. housing and consumer econs. U. Ga., Athens, 1985-90, prof., 1990-97, head housing and consumer econs., 1992-97; dean Coll. Family and Consumer Scis. Iowa State U., Ames, 1997—. Rsch. fellow Nat. Inst. for Consumer Rsch., Oslo, Norway, 1992; cons. Yale U., 1976-77, HUD, Cambridge, Mass., 1978, MIT Ctr. for Real Estate Devel. Ford Found. Project on Housing Policy; del. N.E. Ctr. for Rural Devel. Housing Policy Conf. Reviewer Home Econ. Rsch. Jour., 1987—, ACCI conf., 1987—; contbr. articles to profl. mags. Mem. panel town of Amherst Landlord Tenant Bd.; bd. dirs. Am. Coun. Consumer Interests; mem. adv. coun. HUD Nat. Mfg. Housing, 1978-80, 91-93; chair Housing Mfg. Inst. Consensus Commn. on Fed. Standards. Recipient Leader award AAFCS, 1996, Disting. Alumni award Ohio State U., 1999; named one of Outstanding Young Women of Am., 1979; Columbus Womens Chpt. Nat. Assn. Real Estate Bds. scholar, Gen. Foods fellow, 1971-72, HEW grantee, 1978, travel grantee NSF bldg. rsch. bd., AID grantee, USDA Challenge grant, 1995-98. Mem. Am. Assn. Housing Educators (pres. 1983-84), Nat. Inst. Bldg. Sci. (bd. sec. 1984, 85, 89-92, bd. dirs. 1981-83, 85, 87-93), Internat. Assn. Housing Sci., Com. on Status on Women in Econs., Nat. Assn. Home Builders (Smart House contract 1989, treas. bd. human sci. 2001-), Epsilon Sigma Phi, Phi Upsilon Omicron, Gamma Sigma Delta, Phi Beta Delta, Kappa Omicron Nu (v.p. of programs 1995-96), Phi Kappa Phi, others. Office: Iowa State U 122 Mackay Hl Ames IA 50011-0001

MEEKS, GREGORY WELDON, congressman; b. N.Y.C., Sept. 25, 1953; s. James Weldon and Mary (McNeal) M.; m. Simone-Marie Meeks; children: Ebony Renee, Aja J., Nia-Aiyana. BA, Adelphi U., 1975; JD, Howard U., 1978. Asst. dist. atty. Queens Dist. Atty.'s Office, 1978-81; asst. spl. narcotics prosecutor Office of Spl. Narcotics Prosecutor, 1981-83; asst. counsel State Commn. of Investigation, 1983-84; hearing officer N.Y. Family Ct., 1984-85; judge N.Y. Workers' Compensation Bd., 1985-87, supervising judge, 1987-93; mem. N.Y. State Assembly, 1993-98, 106th Congress from NY 6th dist., 1998—; mem. com. on banking and fin.svcs., 1999—; mem. com. on internat. rels., 1999—. Bd. dirs. Peninsula Gen. Hosp.; chmn. bd. Joseph P. Addabbo Family Health Care Ctr., 1990-92. Recipient Outstanding Vol. Mentor award N.Y. Mentoring, 1990, Cmty. Leader award Boy Scouts Am., 1992. Mem. Macon B. Allen Black Bar Assn. (v.p.), Queens County Bar Assn., Far Rockaway NAACP (Polit. Leadership award 1989). Address: 660 Grassmere Ter Far Rockaway NY 11691-2556 Office: Ho of Reps 1710 Longworth Hob Washington DC 20515-0001 E-mail: congmeeks@mail.house.gov.*

MEEKS, HERBERT LESSIG, III, pastor, former school system administrator; b. National City, Calif., May 12, 1946; s. Herbert Lessig Jr. and Hazel Evelyn (Howard) M.; m. Ardena Lorraine Bice, June 30, 1971; children: Herbert Lessig IV, Laura Dawn, Misty Danae. Grad. in Theology, Bapt. Bible Coll., 1972; BS in Interdisciplinary Studies, Liberty U., Lynchburg, Va., 1989; MS in Edn., Tenn. Temple U., 1989; MA in Religion, Liberty U., 1990. Tchr. Mt. Vernon Christian Sch., Stockbridge, Ga., 1975-82; prin. Mt. Zion Christian Acad., Jonesboro, 1982-90; elem. prin. Des Moines Christian Sch., 1990-93; prin. N.W. Acad., Houston, 1993-94; sr. pastor 1st Bapt. Ch. Genoa,

1994—. Instr. ARC, Atlanta; candidate Ga. Ho. of Reps., Atlanta, 1980; bd. dirs. Concerned Christian for Good Govt., Atlanta, 1980-82; notary pub., Clayton County, Ga., 1983-90. Served to sgt. USAF, 1966-69. Mem. Assn. Christian Schs. Internat. (conv. planning com. 1985-90, accreditation/cons. chmn., Behind the Scenes award 1986), Nat. Rifle Assn. (life), Am. Pistol and Rifle Assn. Republican. Avocations: flying, hunting, politics, econs. Home: 12102 Palmcroft St Houston TX 77034-3721 Office: 1st Bapt Ch Genoa 12717 Almeda Genoa Rd Houston TX 77034-4639

MEEKS, MARK ANTHONY, minister; b. Dallas, Sept. 24, 1946; s. Frederick Earl and Lillie Mae (Chaddick) M.; m. Debra Ann Yeager, Oct. 30, 1985; children: Jessica, Lillian, Sonya. AA, Dallas Bapt. Coll., 1967; BA, U. Tex. at Arlington, 1969; postgrad., Southwestern Bapt. Sem., 1969-72; MDiv, So. Bapt. Sem., 1973. Ordained to ministry Bapt. Ch., 1973. Pastor Grace Bapt. Ch., Heidelberg, Germany, 1973-76; co-dir. Karis Community, Denver, 1978-80; spiritual leader Capitol Heights Presbyn. Ch., 1979—. Mem. ecumenical ministry team Capitol Heights Presbyn and Ten-Thirty Cath. Community, Denver, 1982-92. Regional coord. Amnesty Internat., Denver; mem. Colo. Jud. Performance Commn. for Dist. II, 2002--. Mem.: Dietrich Bonhoeffer Soc., Assets Based Cmty. Devel. Religious Network, Colo. Environ. Coalition, Families and Allies Working Together, Nat. Alliance for the Mentally Ill, Capitol Hill United Ministries (pres. 1986—91, 1998—2001, chaplain 1991—94), Sierra Club. Home: 399 Blackbird Dr Bailey CO 80421-2077 Office: Capitol Heights Presbyn Ch 1100 Fillmore St Denver CO 80206-3334 E-mail: chpc@denpres.org. *The primary sacrament is the sacrament of presence. God's first and most enduring question is "Where are you?" Our life long task is to become present to God in and through all the stuff of our existence.*

MEEKS, WAYNE A. religious studies educator; b. Aliceville, Ala., Jan. 8, 1932; s. Benjamin L. and Winnie (Gavin) M.; m. Martha Evelina Fowler, June 10, 1954 (dec. May 29, 1996); children: Suzanne, Edith, Ellen; m. Judith Colton, Mar. 18, 2000. BS, U. Ala.-Tuscaloosa, 1953; BD, Austin Presbyn. Theol. Sem., 1956; MA, Yale U., 1964, PhD, 1965; Doctor Theologiae honoris causa, U. Uppsala, Sweden, 1990. Instr. religion Dartmouth Coll., Hanover, N.H., 1964-65; asst. prof. religious studies Ind. U., Bloomington, 1966-68, assoc. prof., 1968-69; assoc. prof. religious studies Yale U., New Haven, 1969-73, prof. religious studies, 1973-84, Woolsey prof. Bibl. studies, 1984—, emeritus, 1999—, dir. divsn. Humanities, 1988-91. Author: Go From Your Father's House, 1964, The Prophet-King, 1967, Moral World of the First Christians, 1986, First Urban Christians, 1983, Origins of Christian Morality, 1993, In Search of the Early Christians, 2002; contbr. articles to profl. jours. Fulbright fellow, 1956-57; Kent fellow, 1962-64; NEH fellow, 1975-76; Guggenheim fellow, 1979-80. Fellow Brit. Acad.; mem. Soc. Bibl. Lit. (pres. 1985), Am. Acad. Religion (bd. dirs. 1974-77), Studiorum Novi Testamenti Societas (editl. bd. 1979-82). Democrat. Presbyterian. Avocations: cabinet-making, hiking. Office: Yale U Dept Religious Studies PO Box 208287 New Haven CT 06520-8287 E-mail: wayne.meeks@yale.edu.

MEEKS, WILLIAM HERMAN, III, lawyer; b. Ft. Lauderdale, Fla., Dec. 30, 1939; s. Walter Herman Jr. and Elise Walker (McGuire) M.; m. Patricia Ann Rayburn, July 30, 1965; 1 son, William Herman IV; m. 2d, Miriam Andrea Bedsole, Dec. 28, 1971; 1 child, Julie Marie. AB, Princeton U., 1961; LLB, U. Fla., 1964; LLM in Tax, NYU, 1965. Bar: Fla 1964, U.S. Dist. Ct. (so. dist.) Fla. 1965, U.S. Tax Ct. 1966, U.S. Ct. Appeals (11th cir.) 1981, U.S. Supreme Ct. 1985. Ptnr. McCune, Hiaasen, Crum, Ferris & Gardner, Ft. Lauderdale, 1964-89, Fleming, O'Bryan & Fleming, Ft. Lauderdale, 1990-95, Niles, Dobbins, Meeks, Raleigh & Dover, Ft. Lauderdale, 1995—. Dir. Attys. Title Svcs., Inc., 1978-79, Attys. Title Svcs. of Broward County, Inc., 1971—, chmn., 1976-77; mem. Attys. Real Estate Coun. Broward County. Mem. ABA, Fla. Bar Assn., Broward County Bar Assn., Attys. Title Ins. Fund, Ft. Lauderdale Hist. Soc., Ft. Lauderdale Mus., Kiwanis, Lauderdale Yacht Club, Tower Club (Ft. Lauderdale), Phi Delta Phi. Democrat. Presbyterian. Office: Niles Dobbins Meeks Raleigh & Dover 4th Fl 2601 E Oakland Park Blvd Fl 4 Fort Lauderdale FL 33306-1606 E-mail: whmeeks@ndmrd.com.

MEELDIJK, VICTOR ANTHONY, engineering professional; b. N.Y.C., May 17, 1953; s. Anthony and Freda M. BEE, CCNY, 1975. Safety and design engr. Ward Leonard Electric Co., Inc., Mt. Vernon, N.Y., 1975-77, New Brunswick Sci. Co., Inc., Edison, N.J., 1977-78; mgr. reliability and maintainability engrng. DRS Technologies (formerly Diagnostic/Retrieval Sys.), Oakland, 1978-98; mgr. components engr. Dialogic Corp. (Divsn. of Intel), 1998—. Author: Electronic Components: Selection and Application Guidelines, 1994, update, 1996, Component Identifier and Sourcebook, 1996, rev. 1998; cons. editor mag. Electronic Servicing and Tech., 1986; contbr. The Electronics Handbook, 1996, Semiconductor Devices And Circuits, 1999, MicroElectronics Handbook, 1999, Electronic Packaging Handbook, 2000, REA FE/EIT PM Electrical Exam, 2000; contbr. articles to profl. jours. Mem. IEEE, Inst. Environ. Scis., Electrostatic Overstress/Electrostatic Discharge Assn., The Authors Guild. Home: 1343 Valley Rd Apt E Wayne NJ 07470-8011 E-mail: v.meeldijk@dialogic.com.

MEEM, JAMES LAWRENCE, JR. nuclear scientist; b. N.Y., Dec. 24, 1915; s. James Lawrence and Phyllis (Deaderick) M.; m. Buena Vista Speake, Sept. 5, 1940; children: James, John. BS, Va. Mil. Inst., 1939; MS, Ind. U., 1947, PhD, 1949. Aero. research sci. NACA, 1940-46; dir. bulk shielding reactor Oak Ridge Nat. Lab., 1950-53, in charge nuclear operation aircraft reactor expt., 1954-55; chief reactor sci. Alco Products, Inc., 1955-57; in charge startup and initial testing Army Package Power Reactor, 1957; prof. nuclear engrng. U. Va., Charlottesville, 1957-81, dept. chmn., dir. reactor facility, 1957-77, prof. emeritus, 1981—; cons. U.S. Army Fgn. Sci. and Tech. Ctr., 1981-90. Vis. cons. nuclear fuel cycle programs Sandia Labs., Albuquerque, 1977-78; vis. staff mem. Los Alamos Sci. Lab., 1967-68; mem. U.S.-Japan Seminar Optimization of Nuclear Engring. Edn., Tokai-mura, 1973 Author: Two Group Reactor Theory, 1964. Fellow Am. Nuclear Soc. (sec. reactor ops. div. 1966-68, vice chmn. 1968-70, chmn. 1970-71, Exceptional Service award 1980); mem. Am. Phys. Soc., Am. Soc. Engring. Edn., SAR Home: University Village # 1201 500 Crestwood Dr Charlottesville VA 22903-4890 E-mail: lmeem@aol.com.

MEENAN, ROBERT FRANCIS, rheumatologist, researcher, academician; b. Cambridge, Mass., Apr. 5, 1947; s. Paul Leo and Anna Bernadine (Curtin) M.; m. Lynda Jane Fortman, Apr. 29, 1972(div. April 1999); children: Molly, Mark. BA, Harvard U., 1968; MD, Boston U., 1972; MPH, U. Calif., Berkeley, 1977; MBA, Boston U., 1989. Diplomate Am. Bd. Internal Medicine and Rheumatology. Asst. prof. Sch. of Medicine Boston U., 1977-82, assoc. prof. Sch. of Medicine, 1982-88, prof. Sch. of Medicine, 1988—, assoc. dir. Arthritis Ctr., 1977-88, chief arthritis sect. Sch. of Medicine, 1988-92, dir. Arthritis Ctr., 1988-92, dean and prof. Sch. Pub. Health, 1992—. Mem. nat. arthritis adv. bd. NIH, Washington, 1988-92; Svartz Meml. lectr. Swedish Med. Soc., 1989; mem. nat. adv. coun. AHRQ, Washington, 2000—. Contbr. Jour. Arthritis Impact Measurement Scales, Jour. Social Security Disability, Jour. Dictionary of Rheumatic Disease, Outcome Assessmentation Clin. Moles; contbr. over 75 articles to profl. jours. Trustee Arthritis Found., 1989—, sec., 1999-2000. Internat. League Against Rheumatism fellow, 1981; recipient Nat. Svc. award Arthritis Found., 1989. Fellow ACP, Am. Coll. Rheumatology (pres. 1990-91); mem. Am. Soc. for Clin. Investigation. Achievements include development of arthritis impact measurement scales. Office: Boston U Sch Pub Health 715 Albany St Boston MA 02118-2526

MEENDSEN, FRED CHARLES, retired food company executive; b. Garden City, N.Y., Oct. 28, 1933; s. Frederick Herman and Charlotte Mabel (Reiss) M.; m. Nancy Lou Gross, Nov. 16, 1957; children: Fred Charles, Martha Anne. BA, Colgate U., 1954; MBA, Harvard U., 1956. Mem. mktg. and sales mgmt. dept. Velsicol Chem. Corp., Chgo., 1957-63; with Bestfoods Internat., Englewood Cliffs, N.J., 1963-96; pres. subs. Peterson/Puritan, Inc., Danville, Ill., 1977-83, Can. Starch Co., 1983-84, v.p. parent co., 1983-96, pres. N.Am. region corn wet milling divsn., 1984-88, v.p. corp. affairs, 1988-93, v.p. govt. affairs, 1994-96. Dir. Can. Starch Co., 1983-88; chmn. Casco Co., 1983-85; mem. U.S. C. of C. Can. Rels. Com., 1986-96, Food and Agr. Com., 1988-96; sec. Agr. Adv. Comm. on Trade, 1987-92. Author: Atomic Energy and Business Strategy, 1956. Pres. Colgate U. Alumni Corp., 1991-93, bd. dirs., 1988—; trustee Colgate U., 1993-99, trustee emeritus, 1999—; gov. Chesapeake Bay Maritime Mus., 1997—; dir. Meml. Hosp., Easton, Md., 1997—. 1st lt. U.S. Army, 1956-59. Recipient Disting. Alumnus award Colgate U., 1999. Home: 24472 Trice Field Ct Saint Michaels MD 21663-2618

MEERSON, FELIX ZALMANOVICH, cardiologist; b. Moscow, Aug. 5, 1926; came to U.S., 1993; s. Zalman Moshevich and Minna Iyruhemonna (Ezra) M.; m. Lia Victorovna Shohova, 1953 (div. 1973); children: Nataly, Elena; m. Elena Vorontsova, Oct. 16, 1982; 1 child, Dmitry. MD, Moscow Med. Inst., 1949, PhD, 1952; DSc, Ctrl. Inst. Improving, Moscow, 1958. Sr. rsch. assoc. Inst. Phys. Methods Therapy, Yalta, 1954-55; sr. rsch. assoc. Inst. High Nervous Functioning USSR Acad. Sci., Moscow, 1955-56; assoc. prof. clin. physiology Ctrl. Inst. Improving Physician's Qualifications, 1956-57, prof., 1957-59; prof., head Lab. Exptl. Cardiology Inst. Gen. Pathophysiology Russian Acad. Med. Scis., Moscow, 1960-89, prof., dir. Ctr. Adaptive Medicine, 1990-93, mem. doctorate bd., 1960-93, mem. sci. coun., 1960-93. Sci. cons. Hypoxia Med., Ltd., Moscow, 1990-93, med. insts., Orenburg, Omsk, Irkutsk, Chelyabinsk, Russia, 1970-93; sci. head high mountain expdns. Russian Acad. Med. Scis., Caucasus, Tien Shan, 1980-93. Author: The Myocardium in Hyperfunction, Hypertrophy and Heart Failure, 1969, General Mechanisms of Adaption and Prophylactics, 1973, The Failing Heart: Adaption and Deadaptation, 1983, Adaption, Stress and Prophlaxis, 1984, Physiology of Adaptive Processes, 1986, Adaption to Stressful Situation and Physical Loads, 1988, Adaption to Hypoxia in Therapy and Prophylactics, 1989, Adaptive Protection of the Heart: Protecting Against Stress and Ischemic Damage, 1990, Protective Effects of Adaptation and Prospects of the Development of Adaptive Medicine, 1990, Protective Cross-Effects of Adaptation, 1993, Essentials of Adaptive Medicine: Protective Effects of Adaptation: A Manual, 1994; mem. editl. bd. CV World Report, 1985—, Clin. Cardiology, 1985—, Kardiology, 1985—; contbr. articles to profl. jours. Recipient medal Budapest U., Hungary, 1979, Jan Purkinie medal Prague U., Czechoslavakia, 1970, Laureate of State award USSR Govt., 1978, Hon. Scientist of Russia, Russian Govt., 1988, Gold medal USSR State Exbhn., 1989. Me. Internat. Soc. Adaptive Medicine (pres. 1990-95, founder, life pres. 1995—). Achievements include research in adaption to repeated moderate action of any environmental factor may protect animals and humans from damages impacts of other factors (cross-protective effect of adaptation); develpment of theory of long-term adaptation, a selective increase in expression of certain genes and accumulation of certain structures is the material basis of adaptation; formulation of new discipline Adaptive Medicine which is directed to study fundamental mechanisms of adaptation and use of adaptation for the treatment of diseases. Address: 2875 Cowley Way Apt 510 San Diego CA 92110-1010

MEESE, CELIA EDWARDS, pharmaceutical company executive; b. San Diego, May 10; d. Roy Clifford Edwards and Bessie Lucille (Lang) Hill; m. Jed D. Meese; 1 child, Scott Edwards. BA, U. Wis.; BA (hon.), U. Taiwan. Pres. Vitaline Corp., Ashland, Oreg., 1972—; v.p. RenalChem, Inc., San Jose, Calif., 1982-90, Formulations Tech., Inc., Oakdale, Calif., 1982—; dir. trustee Oreg. Shakespeare Festival Endowment, Pacific Retirement Svcs., Medford, Oreg. Mem. Pharm. Mfrs. Assn., Mensa. Home: 88 Granite St Ashland OR 97520-2711

MEESE, ROBERT ALLEN, architect; b. St. Paul, Mar. 16, 1956; s. Lloyd George and Drusilla (Deis) M.; m. Nancy Ann Jensen, July 16, 1988. BArch, U. Minn., 1981. Registered architect, Minn. Job capt., draftsman James Cooperman & Assoc., Mpls., 1979-80; assoc. architect Ellerbe Assoc., 1981-86; project architect Boarman Assoc., 1986-87; project mgr. Heise, Reinen, MacRae & Assocs. Inc., 1987-88; project architect Opus Corp., 1988-89; project mgr., assoc. v.p. Hammel Green & Abrahamson, Inc., 1989—. Prin. works include St. Paul Winter Carnival Ice Palace (Progressive Architecture award 1986), U. Minn. Hosps. Unit J., ConAgra Product Devel. Facility, Brian Coyle Cmty. Ctr., Target Corp. Bd. dirs. Westbrooke West Condominium Assn., 1990-95, treas. Mem. AIA (Minn. Honor award 1986). Mem. United Church of Christ. Club: Afton (Minn.) Alps Ski Patrol (advisor 1985). Home: 6150 Concord Hill Ln Hopkins MN 55345-6092 Office: Hammel Green & Abrahamson Inc 1201 Harmon Pl Minneapolis MN 55403-1920 E-mail: rmeese@hga.com.

MEEZAN, ELIAS, pharmacologist, educator; b. N.Y.C., Mar. 5, 1942; s. Maurice and Rachel (Epstein) M.; m. Elisabeth Gascard, May 14, 1967; children: David, Nathan, Joshua. BS in Chemistry, CCNY, 1962; PhD in Biochemistry, Duke U., 1966. Asst. prof. physiology and pharmacology Duke U., Durham, N.C., 1969-70; asst. prof. pharmacology U. Ariz., Tucson, 1970-75, assoc. prof., 1975-79; prof., chmn. dept. pharmacology U. Ala., Birmingham, 1979-89, prof., dir. Metabolic Diseases Rsch. Lab., 1989-93, prof. dept. pharmacology, 1993—. Asso. editor: Life Sci, 1973-79. Helen Hay Whitney postdoctoral fellow, 1966-69; recipient NIH Research Career Devel. award, 1977-79 Mem. Am. Soc. Pharmacology and Exptl. Therapeutics, Am. Soc. Biol. Chemistry, AAUP, AAAS, N.Y. Acad. Sci., Assn. Med. Sch.Pharmacology. Democrat. Jewish. Achievements include isolation of retinal microvasculature; development of method for isolating ultrastructurally and chemically intact basement membranes. Home: 1202 Cheval Ln Birmingham AL 35216-2037 Office: U Ala Dept Pharmacology Birmingham AL 35294-0001 E-mail: Elias.Meezan@ccc.uab.edu.

MEEZAN, WILLIAM ALAN, social work educator, consultant; b. N.Y.C., Mar. 10, 1947; s. Joseph and Beatrice (Rauch) M. BA in Psychology, U. Vt., 1967; MSW, Fla. State U., 1969; cert. in advanced social welfare, Columbia U., 1973, DSW, 1978. Social worker The Children's Village, Dobbs Ferry, N.Y., 1969-70; rsch. asst. child welfare rsch. program Sch. of Social Work Columbia U., N.Y.C., 1970-72, part-time rsch. asst. child welfare rsch. program, 1972-73; rsch. assoc. Ctr. for N.Y.C. Affairs New Sch. for Social Rsch., 1973-75; study dir. Child Welfare League of Am., 1975-77; cons. Children's Bur., Adminstrn. for Children, Youth and Families, Office Human Devel. Svcs. HEW, Washington, 1978; asst. prof. Jane Addams Coll. of Social Work U. Ill., Chgo., 1978-81, assoc. prof. Jane Addams Coll. of Social Work, 1981-86, chair PhD program, prof. Jane Addams Coll. of Social Work, 1986-88; John Milner prof. child welfare Sch. Social Wk., U. So. Calif., L.A., 1988—, chair PhD program, 1989—. Part-time instr. Ctr. of Social Work and Social Rsch., Fairleigh Dickinson U., Teneck, N.J., 1974-75, Adelphi U. Grad. Sch. of Social Work, Garden City, N.Y., 1978; adj. asst. prof. NYU Sch. of Social Work, N.Y.C., 1975-78; spl. asst. to exec. dir. Jewish Children's Bur., Chgo., 1986-88. Author: Adoption Without Angencies: A Study of Independent Adoptions, 1978, Care and Commitment: Foster Parent Adoption Decisions, 1985, Evaluating Family Based Services, 1995, Family Preservation and Family Functioning, 1997, (monographs) The Impact of Welfare on Family Stability, 1975, Foster Care Needs and Alternatives to Placement: A Projection for 1975-85, 1975, Adoptions Services in the States, 1980; editor: Child Welfare: Current Dilemas-Future Decisions, 1983; mem. editl. bd. Social Work Rsch., Child Welfare, Children and Youth Svcs. Rev., Social Work, others; contbr. chpts. to books, articles to jour HEW fellow, 1967-68, NIMH fellow, 1972-73, AAAS Congl. Sci. fellow, 1984-85; HEW scholar, 1975-77, U.S. Dept. Health and Human Svcs. scholar, 1980-83, 2000—; Stuart Found. scholar, 1989-95, Fulbright scholar, 1994-95, State of Calif., 1996-99. Mem. NASW, Am. Orthopsychiat. Assn., Acad. of Polit. Sci., Acad. Cert. Social Workers, Nat. Ctr. for Infant Programs, Coun. on Social Work Edn., Group for the Advancement of Doctoral Edn., L.A. Roundtable for Children. Home: 3132 Birchwood Dr Ann Arbor MI 48105-9266 Office: Univ Mich 1080 S University Ann Arbor MI 48109

MEFFERT, ROLAND MATTHEW, periodontist, educator; b. Cross Plains, Wis., June 30, 1932; s. John Michael and Lorraine Catherine (Garfoot) Meffert; m. Marcella Ann Czarnecki, June 12, 1954; children: Jeffrey, Lisa, Sarah, Gregory, Douglas. DDS, Marquette U., 1955; cert. in periodontics, U. Tex., Houston, 1961; cert. in periodontics, Wilford Hall USAF Med. Ctr., 1962. Commd. 1st lt. USAF, 1954, advanced through grades to col., 1970, ret., 1974; prof. dept. periodontics U. Tex. Health Sci. Ctr., San Antonio, 1974—84, 1992—, La. State Med. Ctr., New Orleans, 1984—92. Contbr. chapters to books, articles to profl. jours.; co-editor: Implant Dentistry; editor emeritus: Practical Periodontics and Aesthetic Dentistry. Recipient Spl. Citation award, Am. Acad. Periodontology, 1993, 1997, Meffert-Mutlu Implant Inst. named in honor, Ankara, Turkey, 1997. Master: Am. Acad. Implant Prosthodontics; fellow: Internat. Colll. Dentists, Am. Coll. Dentists; mem.: Am. Soc. Osseointegration (diplomate, pres. 1992, Oral Implantologist of Yr. 1988), Internat. Congress Oral Implantology (diplomate, pres. 1990, Internat. Edn. award 1992, 1994), Am. Bd. Periodontology (diplomate, dir., chmn. 1990—96).

MEGAHED, MOHAMED SALAH, neurologist, educator; b. Aug. 18, 1928; MB, BChir, Cairo U., 1951, MD, 1960. Diplomate Am. Bd. Psychiatry and Neurology. Physician Royal Palace of King Saud, 1954-60; clin. clk. Inst. Nervous Diseases Nat. Hosp. Queen Square, London, 1961-64; resident in neurology SUNY, Buffalo, 1964-67, fellow in neurology, cons. attending neurologist, 1967-69; pvt. practice North Tonawanda, N.Y., 1973; chief EEG and neurology depts. Niagara Falls (N.Y.) Meml. Med. Ctr., Mt. St. Mary's Hosp., Lewiston, N.Y. Clin. assoc. prof. U. Rochester (N.Y.)-Strong Meml. Hosp., until 1996, clin. prof., 1996—. Fellow ACP, Royal Coll. Physicians (Edinburgh), Am. Acad. Neurology; mem. AMA, N.Y. State Med. Soc. Office: 1089 Kinkead Ave North Tonawanda NY 14120-2840

MEGAHY, DIANE ALAIRE, physician; b. Des Moines, Oct. 12, 1943; d. Edwin Dare and Georgiana Lee (Butcher) Raygor; m. Mohamed H. Saleh Megahy, Sept. 20, 1969; children: Hassan, Hamed, Hala, Heba. MD, U. Alexandria, Egypt, 1981. Diplomate Am. Bd. Family Practice. Intern Univ. Hosps., Alexandria, Egypt, 1982-83; resident Siu Family Practice, Belleville, Ill., 1987—2001; physician St. Joseph's Hosp., Highland, 1988—2001. Mem. steering com. on domestic violence 3d Jud. Cir. Ct., co-chmn. health care subcom. Mem.: AAUW, AMA, Assn. Emergency Rm. Physicians, Ill. State Med. Soc. (com. for CME accreditation, del. internat. med. grad. com.), So. Ill. Med. Assn. (pres.), Am. Coll. Forensic Examiners. Avocations: student education in local schools, domestic violence education. Home: 2 Bay Meadow Pl Belleville IL 62223 Office: 7300 Twin Pyramid Pkwy Belleville IL 62223 Fax: (618) 234-1793. E-mail: dialmeg@msn.com.

MEGAN, THOMAS IGNATIUS, retired judge; b. Chgo., Dec. 24, 1913; s. Charles P. and May M. (Magan) M.; m. Lucyanne Flaherty, Apr. 17, 1948; children: Anne, Thomas, Jane, Sarah, William, Molly. AB, U. Ill., 1935; JD, U. Chgo., 1938. Bar: Ill. 1939, N.Y. 1941. Mem. firm Pruitt & Grealis, Chgo., 1939-40, Pruitt, Hale & MacIntyre, N.Y.C., 1941; atty. U.S. Ordnance Dept., Chgo., 1941-42, Chgo., Rock Island and Pacific R.R. Co., Chgo., 1945-70, v.p., gen. counsel, 1970-74, v.p. law, 1974-75; adminstrv. law judge ICC, Washington, 1975-81, HHS, Washington, 1981, FERC, Washington, 1981-96; ret., 1996. Served to maj. AUS, 1942-45. Mem. ABA, Soc. Trial Lawyers Chgo., Chgo. Law Club, Phi Kappa Tau, Phi Delta Phi. Clubs: Union League (Chgo.). Home: 11108 Waycroft Way Rockville MD 20852-3217

MEGARGEL, ESTHER L. music educator; b. Oakland, Jan. 5, 1942; d. Charles Bernard Strong and Winifred Loraine Woodcock; m. Monty Wardell Megargel, June 5, 1965; children: Alan, April, Forrest. BS with honors, Western Oreg. U., 1975. Violin tchr. V.I.P. Sch. for Strings, Monmouth, 1975-76; elementary music specialist Oreg. Pub. Schs., Turner, 1975-78; piano tchr., 1975—; dir. Yamaha Music Sch., Eugene, Oreg., 1990-94. Composer choral music Rejoice Ye Daughters of Zion, 1982 (3rd prize Relief Soc. Song Contest), for string trio Cast Thy Burden, 1998 (Spl. Recognition, Ch. Music Contest). Mem. Music Tchrs. Nat. Orgn. (nat. cert.), Oreg. Music Tchrs. (state composition chair, state sec.). Mem. Lds Ch. Avocations: travel, classic literature, American history. E-mail: argele@cs.com.

MEGAY-NESPOLI, KAREN PATRICIA, elementary school educator; b. N.Y.C., May 4, 1954; d. Charles A. and Audrey J. (Duddy) Megay; m. Michael A. Nespoli, Oct. 13, 1979; children: Lauren Brynn, Caitlin Bree. BA, CUNY, 1976, MS, 1978; profl. diploma in adminstrn. & supr., St. John's U., 1981; EdD, Columbia U., 1998. Tchr. 3d grade Our Lady of the Miraculous Medal Sch., Queens, N.Y., 1977-84, adminstrv. asst. to prin., 1980-84, primary coord., 1981-84; tchr. 4th grade P.S. 87, 1984-89. Adj. asst. prof. CW Post campus L.I. U. Author: The First Year of Elementary School Teachers, 1983; contbr. articles to profl. jours. Mem. AAUW, ASCD, Internat. Reading Coun., Nat. Assn. Gifted Children, Nat. Coun. Math. Tchrs., Nassau Reading Coun., Phi Delta Kappa, Kappa Delta Pi. Office: LI U CW Post Campus Dept Curriculum and Instrn 720 Northern Blvd Greenvale NY 11548

MEGEE, GERALDINE HESS, social worker; b. Newark, June 9, 1924; d. A.P. Hess and Ethel Stoyle Luther; children: John Megee, Sarah Martens, Thomas Megee. BS, Northwestern U., 1944; MSEd, Ind. U., 1976, MSW, 1978; PhD candidate, Fielding Inst. Cert. social worker, Ill., Fla.; cert. addictions profl., Fla., criminal justice specialist; diplomate in social work; diplomate Am. Bd. Sexology; nat. cert. psychologist. Dir. Foster Care Prog., Webster-Cantrel Hall, Decatur, Ill., 1978-81; owner, dir. Family Systems Ctr., 1981-98; pvt. practice clinic and employee assistance, 1981-98; dir. Charter Counseling Ctr., Charter Glade Hosp., Naples, Fla., 1985-87; owner Family-Works, 1991—. Mem. NASW, Am. Assn. Marriage and Family Therapists, Am. Acad. Sexologists, Sigma Pi Lambda. Home and Office: 9856 Tonya Ct Bonita Springs FL 34135-4717

MEGGERS, BETTY J(ANE), anthropologist, researcher; b. Washington, Dec. 5, 1921; d. William Frederick and Edith (Raddant) M.; m. Clifford Evans, Sept. 13, 1946. AB, U. Pa., 1943; MA, U. Mich., 1944; PhD, Columbia U., 1952; D (hon.), U. de Guayaquil, Ecuador, 1987, U. Fed. Rio de Janeiro, Brazil, 1994, U. Nat. La Plata, Argentina, 1997, U. Católica de Goiás, Brazil, 1999. Instr. anthropology Am. U., Washington, 1950-51; rsch. assoc. Smithsonian Instn., 1954—, expert, 1981—; founder, pres. Taraxacum Inc., 1977—. Hon. prof. U. de Azuay, Ecuador, 1991. Author: Environmental Limitation on the Development of Culture, 1954, Ecuador, 1966, Amazonia, 1971, 2d edit., 1996, Prehistoric America, 1972, Evolucion y Difusion Cultural, 1998, Ecologia y Biogeografia de la Amazonia, 1999, (with Clifford Evans) Archeological Investigations at the Mouth of the Amazon, 1957, Archeological Investigations in British Guiana, 1960, (with Clifford Evans and Emilio Estrada) Early Formative Period of Coastal Ecuador, 1965, (with Clifford Evans) Archeological Investigations on the Rio Napo, Eastern Ecuador, 1968; editor: Prehistoria Sudamericana, 1992. Recipient award for sci. achievement Washington Acad. Sci., 1956; gold medal 37th Internat. Congress of Americanists, 1966; Order Al Merito Govt. Ecuador, 1966; Order Bernardo O'Higgins Govt. Chile, 1985; Sec.'s Gold medal for exceptional service Smithsonian Instn., 1986; Order Andres Bello Govt. Venezuela, 1988; Order Al Mérito por Servicios Distinguidos Govt. Peru, 1989. Fellow: AAAS, Assn. Tropical Biology (hon.; councilor 1976—78, pres.-elect 1982, pres. 1983); mem.: Academia Nacional Historia Ecuador (corr.), Anthrop. Soc. Wash. (treas. 1955—60, v.p. 1965—66, pres. 1966—68), Am. Anthrop. Assn. (exec. sec. 1959—61), Museo Antropológico de la Cultura Andina (hon.), Soc. Am. Archeology (exec. bd. 1962—64), Am. Ethnol. Soc., Phi Beta Kappa, Sigma Xi. Home: 1227 30th St NW Washington DC 20007-3410 Office: Smithsonian Instn Washington DC 20560-0001

MEGGINSON, ROBERT EUGENE, mathematics educator; b. Washington, Feb. 23, 1948; s. Robert Cecil and Katherine Mae (Harding) M.; m. Kathleen Ann Schroeder, Jan. 7, 1978. BS in Physics, U. Ill., 1969, AM in Stats., 1983, PhD in Math., 1984. Computer sys. software specialist Roper Corp., Kankakee, Ill., 1969-77; asst. prof. math. Ea. Ill. U., Charleston, 1983-86, assoc. prof. math., 1986-92, U. Mich., Ann Arbor, 1992—. Mem. human resources adv. com. Math. Scis. Rsch. Inst., Berkeley, Calif., 1994—. Mem. Am. Math. Soc., Math. Assn. Am. (life, chair com. on minority participation in math. 1995—, mem. coordinating coun. human resources 1995—), Soc. Advancement Chicanos and Native Ams., Am. Indian Sci. and Engring. Soc. (life, Sequoyah fellow 1991), Astro. Soc. the Pacific. Avocations: astronomy, music, bicycling, travel. Home: 5231 Bradford Cir Brighton MI 48114-9065 Office: U Mich Dept Math 3220 Angell Hall Ann Arbor MI 48109-1003

MEGGS, WILLIAM JOEL, toxicologist, internist, emergency physician, educator; b. Newberry, S.C., May 30, 1942; s. Wallace Nat and Elizabeth (Pruitt) M.; m. Susan Nancy Spring, June 11, 1966 (div. June 1998); m. Susan Krause Martin, Apr. 21, 2001; children: Jason Nathaniel, Benjamin Maffey, Thomas Clute. BS, Clemson U., 1964; PhD, Syracuse U., 1969; MD, U. Miami, 1979. Diplomate Am. Bd. Internal Medicine; diplomate Am. Bd. Allergy and Immunology; diplomate Am. Bd. Emergency Medicine, Am. Bd. Med. Toxicology. Resident in internal medicine Rochester (N.Y.) Gen. Hosp., 1979-82; staff fellow in allergy and clin. immunology Nat. Inst. Allergy and Infectious Diseases, Bethesda, Md., 1982-85; asst. dir. med. edn. emergency dept. Washington Hosp. Ctr., 1985-88; asst. prof. allergy, immunology E.

Carolina U. Sch. of Medicine, Greenville, N.C., 1988-91, asst. prof. clin. toxicology dept. emergency medicine, 1991-95; assoc. prof. clin. toxicology E. Carolina U. Sch. Medicine, 1995-98; prof. emergency medicine, vice chmn. for clin. affairs E. Carolina U. Sch. of Medicine, 1999—; chmn., dir. emergency dept. Lenoir Meml. Hosp., Kinston, 1990-91. Mem. Emergency Svcs. Com., Lenoir Meml. Hosp., Kinston, N.C., 1988-92; mem workshop on immune testing, Agy. for Toxic Substances and Diseases Registry, 1992, workshop on equity in environ. health, U.S. EPA, 1992, workshop on multiple chem. sensitivity syndrome, Nat. Rsch. Coun., 1991. Contbr. numerous articles and abstracts to profl. jours. Vol. physician Indigent Clinic East Carolina U., Pitt County Med.Soc., 1988—, Pitt County Shelter, 1989—; advanced cardiac life support instr. East Carolina U. Sch. of Medicine, 1988-2000, advanced trauma life support instr., 1991-2002; mem. Pitt County Traffic Injury Prevention Program, 1989-92; bd. dirs. Rachael Carson Coun., 1988—; mem. adv. bd. Pamplico Tar River Found., 1990—. Named Woodrow Wilson Hon. Fellow, 1964, NSF post-doctoral fellow, 1969; grantee:N.C. United Way, 1988-89, Greer Labs., 1989-90, Am. Lung Assn. N.C., 1992-93. Fellow Am. Coll. Emergency Physicians; mem. AMA, Am. Acad. Allergy and Immuniology,, Am. Acad. Clin. Toxicology, Pitt County Med. So, N.C. State Med. Soc., Soc. for Acad. Emergency Medicine, N.C. Thoracic Soc. (physicians' sect.). Office: E Carolina U Sch Medicine Dept Emergency Medicine Brody Bldg 4-W54 600 Moye Blvd Greenville NC 27858-4300 E-mail: meggsw@mail.ecu.edu.

MEGHABGHAB, GEORGE VICTOR, computer scientist, educator; b. Ein Zehalta, Lebanon, July 8, 1957; came to U.S., 1984; s. Victor George and Souad Mary (Layoun) M. MS in Engring., Inst. Superieur d'Electronique, Lille, France, 1980; PhD in Computer Sci., U. Pierre et Marie Curie, Paris, 1983, Fla. State U., 1988. Asst. prof. U. Nantes, France, 1983-84, Valdosta (Ga.) State U., 1988-93; assoc. prof. Valdosta (Ga.) U., 1993-97, prof., 1998—. Researcher Fla. State U., Tallahassee, 1986-88, Electricite de France, Paris, 1980-83. Author: An Introduction to Unix, 1996; contbr. articles to profl. jours. Grantee Ctr. Nat. de Recherche Sci., Nantes, 1984. Mem. IEEE, Am. Soc. for Info. Sci. (officer 1990—), Am. Assn. for Artificial Intelligence, Assn. Computing Machinery. Roman Catholic. Avocations: tennis, walking, reading. Office: Valdosta State U Dept Math Computer Sci Valdosta GA 31698-0001 Home: Apt 13D 1635 E Park Ave Valdosta GA 31602-3435

MEGHREBLIAN, ROBERT VARTAN, manufacturing executive, physicist; b. Cairo, Sept. 6, 1922; came to U.S., 1923, naturalized, 1946; s. Vahan V. and Mary (Kurkjian) M.; m. Margaret M. Gordon, 1987; children: David V., Susan M. B.Engring. (Gotshall-Powell scholar), Rensselaer Poly. Inst., 1943; MS (Guggenheim fellow), Calif. Inst. Tech., 1950, PhD (Guggenheim fellow), 1953. Lectr. Oak Ridge Nat. Lab., 1952-55, assoc. project mgr., 1955-58; chief sect. Physics Jet Propulsion Lab., Calif. Inst. Tech., 1958-60, mgr. space scis. div., 1960-68, dep. asst. lab dir., 1968-71, assoc. prof. applied mechanics, 1960-61; v.p. research and engring. Cabot Corp., Boston, 1971-79, v.p., 1971-87; pres. Distrigas Corp., 1979-85; gen. mgr. Cabot Crystals Bus. Unit, 1985-86, dir. corp. planning and devel., 1986-87. Author: Reactor Analysis, 1960. Served to lt. (j.g.) USN, 1941-46, PTO, ATO. Fellow AIAA (assoc.), Am. Nuclear Soc.; mem. Tennis Club Santa Barbara, Santa Barbara Club, Montecito Assn. (bd. dirs. 1992-98, v.p. 1994, pres. 1995, 96, chair archtl. rev. com. 1993-95), Sigma Xi. Home: 440 Woodley Rd Montecito CA 93108-2006

MEGILL, ALLAN D. historian; b. Regina, Sask., Can., Apr. 20, 1947; came to U.S., 1980; s. Ralph Peter and Jean Tudhope (Dickson) M.; divorced; children: Jason Robert, Jessica Susan, Jonathan David; life ptnr. Rita Felski; 1 child, Maria Megill Felski. BA, U. Sask., 1969; MA, U. Toronto, 1970; PhD, Columbia U., 1975. From instr. to prof. history U. Iowa, Iowa City, 1974-90; prof. history U. Va., Charlottesville, 1990—. Rsch. fellow in history of ideas Australian Nat. U., Canberra, ACT, 1977—79, temp. lectr. modern European studies, ACT, 1979; dir. d'études invité École des Hautes Études en Scis. Sociales, Paris, 1997. Author: Prophets of Extremity, 1985, Karl Marx: The Burden of Reason, 2002; editor: Rethinking Objectivity, 1994; co-editor: The Rhetoric of the Human Sciences, 1987; cons. editor: Jour. of History of Ideas, 1986—89, mem. editl. bd.: , 1990—, mem. editl. bd.: Rethinking History, 1996—, mem. editl. bd.: U. Press of Va., 1991—94; contbr. articles to profl. jours. Chmn. Page-Barbour and Richard Lectures com. U. Va., 1994-96. Mem. Am. Hist. Assn. Office: University of Virginia Corcoran Dept of History PO Box 400180 Charlottesville VA 22904 E-mail: megill@virginia.edu.

MEGNA, STEVE ALLAN, middle school education educator; Elem. tchr. Glen Meadow Sch., Vernon, N.J. Recipient Tech. Excellence award Internat. Tech. Edn. Assn. and Tech. Edn. Assn. N.J., 1992, Tech. Program of Yr. award Tech. Edn. Assn. N.J., 1989. Office: Glen Meadow School PO Box 516 Vernon NJ 07462-0516

MEHAFFEY, JOHN ALLEN, marketing, newspaper management and advertising executive; b. Brainerd, Minn. m. Mary Jean Mehaffey; children: Mark, Scott, Chris. Student, Minn. Sch. Bus. With Mehaffey Internat., Naples, Fla., 1954—. Bd. govs. Verified Audit Circulations. Ga . Nat. Newspaper Assn., Newspaper Assn. Am., Nat. Press Club (Washington), Ill. Press Assn., Assn. Free Cmty. Papers, Ind. Free Papers Assn., Fla. Free Papers Assn., Am. Mktg. Assn., Inland Press Assn., Fla. Press Assn., Soc. Profl. Journalists, Chgo. Headline Club, Internat. Platform Assn., Am. Telemktg. Assn., Naples Area C. of C., Suburban Newspaper Assn., Ctrl. States Circulating Mgrs. Assn., Inland Press Assn., Southeastern Advt. Pubs. Assn., Brainerd Lakes Area C. of C., St. Joseph's Med. Ctr. Found. (charter), Nat. Alliance for Mentally Ill., Greater Chgo. and AIll. Alliance for Mentally Ill, Motion Picture and TV Assn., Marine Habitat Found. (founding), Naples Aquarium (founding), Founding One Thousand, Naples Philharm. Ctr. for Performing Arts, Naples Conservancy, Northland Arboretum, Paul Bunyan Nature Learning Ctr. (life), Nat. Rails-to-Trails Conservancy, Internat. Press Club (Chgo.), Naples Press Club, Elks, Moose, Sigma Delta Chi. Avocation: boating. Home and Office: Mehaffey Internat PO Box 2956 Naples FL 34106-2956

MEHAFFEY, SCOTT ALAN, landscape architect; b. Princeton, Ill., Mar. 1, 1965; s. John Paul and Barbara Jean (Schaefer) M. B Landscape Architecture, U. Ill., 1987. Registered landscape architect, Ill. Landscape architect Scott Byron & Co., Inc., Lake Bluff, Ill., 1988-89, Jacobs/Ryan Assocs., Chgo., 1989-93, Morton Arboretum, Lisle, Ill., 1993—. Coun. mem. Garfield Park Conservatory Alliance, 1996-98. Contbr. articles to profl. jours. Mem. Preservation Fund com. Landmarks Preservation Coun. of Ill., 2000-02. Recipient Yamagami-Hope fellowship Landscape Architecture Found., 1991, student rsch. grant U. Ill. Bd. Trustees, Champaign-Urbana, 1988, award of merit Am. Hort. Soc., Chgo. Flower and Garden Show, 1996, 97. Mem. Am. Soc. Landscape Architects (continuing edn. chmn. Ill. chpt. 1991-93, pres.-elect Ill. chpt. 1997-98, pres. Ill. chpt. 1998-99, chmn. historic preservation open com. 1995-96, ann. meeting com. 1995-99), Am. Assn. Bot. Gardens and Arboreta, Am. Assn. Museums (mus. mgmt. com. 2002--), Am. Assn. for State and Local History. Avocations: gardening, bicycling, travel, writing, community service. Office: The Morton Arboretum 4100 Illinois Route 53 Lisle IL 60532-1293 E-mail: mehaffey@mortonarb.org.

MEHALCHIN, JOHN JOSEPH, entrepreneur, finance executive; b. Hazleton, Pa., Aug. 8, 1937; s. Charles and Susan (Korba) M.; divorced; 1 child, Martin. BS with honors (1st in class), Temple U., 1964; MBA, U. Calif., Berkeley, 1965; postgrad., U. Chgo., 1964. Supr. costs Winchester-Western, New Haven, 1965-67; mgmt. cons. Booz-Allen & Hamilton, N.Y.C., 1967-68; mgr. planning TWA, 1968-69; officer Smith Barney, N.Y.C. and Paris, 1970-74; CFO, pres. Storage Tech. Corp., Louisville, 1974-79; sr. v.p. Heizer Corp., 1979; pres., founder Highline Fin. Svcs., Inc. and fgn. subs., Boulder, Colo., 1979—; also London, Paris and Frankfurt, Germany. Mem. strategic planning com. Coll. and Grad. Sch. Bus., U. Colo., Denver; bd. advisors U. Colo. Ctr. Entrepreneurship, U. Colo. Bus. Sch., Wolf Ventures. With AUS, 1958—61. Recipient Mack Easton award for Excellence, 1998, U. medal, U. Colo., 2002; fellow, U. Calif., Berkeley, 1964, 1965. Mem. Fin. Execs. Inst., Equipment Leasing Assn., Beta Gamma Sigma, Omicron Delta Epsilon. Home and Office: Highline Fin Svcs Inc 2930 Center Green Ct Ste 200 Boulder CO 80301-5419

MEHAN, GEORGE TRACEY, III, federal agency administrator; Grad., St. Louis U. Dir. Mo. Dept. Natural Resources, 1989—91; assoc. deputy adminstr. EPA, 1992—93; dir. Office of Great Lakes, Mich. Dept. Environ. Quality; asst. adminstr. water EPA, Washington, 2001—. Office: EPA 1200 Pennsylvania Ae NW MC 4101 Washington DC 20460*

MEHDI, YUSUF, information technology executive; married; 2 children. BA in Econs., Princeton U.; MBA, U. Wash. Product mgr. Reuters Group PLC; dir. mktg. Microsoft Windows op. sys. Microsoft, Redmond, Wash., corp. v.p. MSN Personal Svcs. and Bus. Office: One Microsoft Way Redmond WA 98052-6399*

MEHDIZADEH, MOSTAFA, economics educator; b. Yazd, Iran, Jan. 4, 1949; came to U.S., 1974; s. Abbas and Zivar (Sadrieh) M.; m. Khadijeh Abdol-Hamidzadeh, Apr. 8, 1982; children: Yalda-April, Meetra-Hope. BS in Econs., U. Tehran, Iran, 1971; MBA, Cen. State U., Edmond, Okla., 1975; PhD in Econs., U. Okla., 1980, MS in Environ. Sci., 1982. Project analyst Plan and Budget Orgn. of Iran, Tehran, 1970-72; econ. and mktg. analyst Army Factories of Iran, 1972-74; assoc. prof. econs. Morris Coll., Sumter, S.C., 1981-82; asst. prof. Miami U.-Middletown, Ohio, 1982-88, assoc. prof., 1989—. Referee for publ. of articles Am. Economist, N.Y.C., 1985, 87, Am. Jour. Econs. Sociology, Babson Park, Md., 1996. Contbr. articles to profl. jours., 1985—. Mem. Midwest Econs. Assn., Southwestern Econs. Assn. Friends of Iranian Culture, Omicron Delta Kappa, Omicron Delta Epsilon. Islamic. Avocations: reading, family activities. Office: Miami U 4200 N University Blvd Middletown OH 45042-3497

MEHDIZADEH, PARVIZ, insurance company executive; b. Tehran, Iran, Sept. 15, 1934; came to U.S., 1981; s. Alexander and Sedigheh (Siavooshy) M.; m. Manijeh Sadri, Sept. 12, 1961; children: Sheida, Peyman, Pejman. BS, Forestry Sch., Tehran, 1958; MS, N.C. State U., 1963, PhD, 1966. Pres. Rsch. Inst. Natural Resources, Tehran, 1968-73; assoc. prof. U. Tehran, 1973-74; prof. environ. sci. U. Tabriz, Iran, 1974-76; chmn. resolution com. FAO, Rome, 1976-77; chmn. natural resources Ctrl. Treaty Orgn., Ankars, Turkey, 1977-78; spl. adviser to sec. Ministry of Agr., Tehran, 1978-79; dist. mgr. Am. Family Life Assurance Co., Beverly Hills, Calif., 1981—; v.p. Point Internat. Corp. Inc., Los Angeles, 1986—; pres. ZMS Fin. Network Corp. Inc., Beverly Hills, Calif., 1995-98, Active Universal Corp., 1998—. Cons. Ministry of Sci., Tehran, 1972-75, UN U., Tokyo, 1975-76; gen. agt. AFLAC, 1995. Author: Flowering Plants of Semi-Arid Regions, 1976, Economizing of Water Use in Agriculture, 1977; editor Khandamhayeh Hafteh, 1979. Mem. U.S. Senatorial Club, Washington, 1984; charter mem. Rep. Presdl. Task Force, Washington, 1984. Mem. Life Underwriters Assn. (L.A. chpt., Health Ins. Quality award 1985, 88, 89), Rotary (chmn. dist. 5280 1992, Paul Harris Fellow award 1989). Avocations: tennis, golf. *Personal philosophy: The future belongs to those with vision and understanding of their environment. Nature conservancy and the wise use of renewable natural resources are the keys to a prosperous future for man kind.*

MEHELAS, THOMAS JAMES, neuro-ophthalmologist, educator; b. Detroit, June 9, 1953; s. E. James and Mary Louise Mehelas; m. Ann Marie Mehelas, Feb. 6, 1993; 1 child, Michelle. BS, U. Toledo, Ohio, 1975; MD, Med. Coll. Ohio, Toledo, 1978. Diplomate Am. Bd. Ophthalmology. Resident internal medicine Mich. State U., Lansing, 1979; resident ophthalmology Med. Coll. Ohio, Toledo, 1982; resident neuro-ophthalmology Harvard - Mass. Gen. Hosp., Boston, 1983; resident orbital disease Harvard - Mass. Eye & Ear Infirmary, 1984; ophthalmologist Regency Park Eye Assocs., Toledo, 1984-92; assoc. prof. surgery ophthalmology divsn. Med. Coll. Ohio, 1992—. Mem. profl. adv. coun. Nat. Multiple Sclerosis Soc., N.W. Ohio chpt., Toledo, 1988-99, mem. med. adv. com., N.Y.C., 1993-95.; councillor Acad. of Medicine of Toldo, 1992-95. Reviewer Jour. Neuro-Ophthalmology; contbr. articles to profl. jours., chpt. in book. Named Outstanding Profl., Nat. Multiple Sclerosis Soc., N.W. Ohio chpt., Toledo, 1991. Mem. AMA, Am. Acad. Ophthalmology, N.Am. Neuro-Ophthalmology Soc., Great Lakes Neuro-Ophthalmology Club, Ohio State Med. Soc. Avocations: golf, tennis, skiing, jazz. Office: Med Coll Ohio Ruppert Health Ctr # 6 3120 Glendale Ave Toledo OH 43614-5811

MEHL, DONALD EDWARD, retired marketing professional; b. Omaha, Jan. 28, 1923; s. Arthur Julius and Cecilia Mehl; m. Alice Mae Toland, Apr. 15, 1950 (dec. 1977); children: David, Kathleen Chadwick, Janice Rossi, Arthur, Therese Sellers. Student, U. Omaha, 1942, U. Minn., 1943—44; BS, Creighton U., 1949. Engring. mgr. Inland Broadcasting Co., 1942—52; telecomm. mktg. mgr. Graybar Electric, Kansas City, Mo., 1952—59; editor, pub. Tech. Publs. , Inc., 1959—61; advt. and mktg. prof. Collins Radio, Richardson, Tex., 1961—73; mktg. dir. Rockwell Internat., Kansas City, Mo., 1973—87. Author, pub.: Top Secret Communications of World War II-Sigsaly, 1997, author, pub.: Top Secret Communications of World War II-Sigtot, 2002, founder, editor, pub.: Broadcast Engring. Jour. 1st lt. signal corps U.S. Army, 1943—46. Mem.: Am. Radio Relay League. Avocation: amateur radio. Home: 11605 Minor Dr Kansas City MO 64114

MEHLENBACHER, DOHN HARLOW, civil engineer, consultant; b. Huntington Park, Calif., Nov. 18, 1931; s. Virgil Claude and Helga (Sigfridson) M.; m. Nancy Moss; children: Dohn Scott, Kimberly Ruth, Mark James, Matthew Lincoln. BSCE, U. Ill., 1953; MS in City and Regional Planning, Ill. Inst. Tech., 1961; MBA, U. Chgo., 1972. Registered profl. engr., Ill.; lic. structural engr., Ill. Structural engr., draftsman Swift & Co., Chgo., 1953-54, 56-57, DeLeuw-Cather Co., Chgo., 1957-59; project engr. Quaker Oats Co., 1959-61, mgr. constrn., 1964-70, mgr. real property, 1970-71, mgr. engring. and maintenance L.A., 1961-64; chief facilities engr. Bell & Howell Co., Chgo., 1972-73; v.p. design Globe Engring. Co., 1973-76; project mgr. I.C. Harbour Constrn. Co., Oak Brook, Ill., 1976-78; dir. estimating George A. Fuller Co., 1978; pres. Food-Tech. Co., Willowbrook, Ill., 1979-80; dir. phys. resources Ill. Inst. Tech., Chgo., 1980-92; cons. Exec. Svc. Corp., 1994—. Arbitrator Am. Arbitration Assn. With USAF, 1954-56. Fellow ASCE. Home and Office: 436 Leitch Ave La Grange IL 60525-6126

MEHLER, BARRY ALAN, humanities educator, journalist, consultant; b. Bklyn., Mar. 18, 1947; s. Harry and Esther Mehler; m. Jennifer Sue Leghorn, June 2, 1982; 1 child, Isaac Alan. BA, Yeshiva U., 1970; MA, CCNY, 1972; PhD, U. Ill., 1988. Rsch. assoc. Washington U., St. Louis, 1976-80, instr. history, 1977; NIMH trainee racism program U. Ill., Champaign, 1981-85, rsch. asst. IBM EXCEL project, 1986-88; asst. prof. humanities Ferris State U., Big Rapids, Mich., 1988-93, assoc. prof., 1993-99, prof., 1999—. Media cons. Scientist's Inst. for Pub. Info., N.Y.C., 1980-98; cons. Calif. Humanities Coun., 1995, ZDF/arte (Zweite Deutsches Fernshen--German pub. TV), 1995, House Subcom. on Consumer Protection, 1994, McIntosh Commn. for Fair Play in Student-Athlete Admissions, 1994, Can. Broadcast Svc., Toronto, Ont., 1985-92; judge Women's Caucus Awards for Excellence, St. Louis, 1989-91, 93; dir. Inst. for Study of Acad. Racism, 1993—; mem. Pres.'s Initiative on Race, 1998, One Am. initiative, named Promising Practices; presenter Performance Art in the Classroom, Minority Equity Conf. XI, 2001. Contbg. editor: Encyclopedia of Genocide, 1997; contbr. more than 100 articles and revs. to profl. jours. Mem. vol. com. parents A Different Look at DARE, 1995; mem. adv. bd. Homes for the Homeless, Austin, Tex., 2000-01, Internat. Inst. for Study of Psychiatry and Psychology Washington, 1999—; founder, sec.-treas. Internat. Com. to Free Russell Smith, 1977-79; co-founder Gay Peoples Alliance, St. Louis, 1978; mem. adv. bd. Stop Prison Rape, 2001. Recipient cert. of recognition Ferris State Bd. of Control, 1994, Hesburgh award for excellence in undergrad. edn., TIAA-CREFF and Am. Coun. on Edn., 2000; NSF rsch. fellow, 1976-80, Babcock fellow U. Ill., 1985-86; grantee Rockefeller Found., 1977; structured learning assistance program grantee Office of Minority Affairs, Lansing, Mich., 1994-97. Mem. Am. Hist. Soc., Behavior-Genetics Assn., NAACP, Ctr. for Dem. Renewal, History of Sci. Soc., Internat. Behavioral and Neural Geneteics Soc., Orgn. Am. Historians, B'nai B'rith (Anti-Defamation League), Coalition for Human Dignity, Facing History. Jewish. Avocations: hiking, camping. Home: 216 Rust Ave Big Rapids MI 49307-1726 Office: Ferris State U 901 S State St Big Rapids MI 49307-2295 E-mail: bmehler@netonecom.net.

MEHLINGER, HOWARD DEAN, education educator; b. Hillsboro, Kans., Aug. 22, 1931; s. Alex and Alice Hilda (Skibbee) M.; m. Carolee Ann Case, Dec. 28, 1952; children: Bradley Case, Barbara Ann, Susan Kay. BA, McPherson (Kans.) Coll., 1953; MS in Edn, U. Kans., 1959, PhD, 1964. Co-dir. social studies project Pitts. pub. schs., 1963-64; asst. dir. fgn. relations project North Central Assn. Schs. and Colls., Chgo., 1964-65; mem. faculty Ind. U., Bloomington, 1965-97, prof. history and edn., 1974-97, dean Sch. Edn., 1981-90, dir. Ctr. for Excellence in Edn., 1990-99. Social studies adviser Houghton Mifflin Pub. Co.; cons. U.S. Office Edn. Co-author: American Political Behavior, 2d edit., 1977, Count Witte and the Tsarist Government in the 1905 Revolution, 1972, Toward Effective Instruction in the Social Studies, 1974, School Reform in the Information Age, 1995, Technology and Teacher Education: A Guide for Educators and Policymakers, 2002; editl. bd. Education and Society, history tchr.; editor: UNESCO Handbook on the Teaching of Social Studies, 1981; co-editor: Yearbook on the Social Studies, 1981. STAG grantee Dept. State, 1975 Mem. NEA, Nat. Council Social Studies, Am. Edn. Research Assn., Am. Hist. Assn., Am. Assn. for Advancement Slavic Studies, Phi Beta Kappa, Phi Alpha Theta, Pi Sigma Alpha, Phi Delta Kappa. Home: 3271 N Ramble Rd E Bloomington IN 47408-1094

MEHLIS, DAVID LEE, publishing executive; m. Marjie Bauman; children: Michelle, Stephen. BA in History, Wheaton Coll., 1965; postgrad., Trinity Evang. Sem., 1965-67. Various positions in mktg., then v.p. and gen. mgr. David C. Cook Pub. Co., Elgin, Ill., 1967—; now pres., CEO Cook Comm. Ministries., Colorado Springs, Colo. Trustee Judson Coll., Elgin, 1991. Bd. mem. Scripture Press Ministries, Colorado Springs Symphony, Kids Around the World, Kingsway Publ. Ltd. Mem. Christian Booksellers Assn., Evang. Christian Pub. Assn. (bd. dirs.). Office: Cook Comm Ministries 4050 Lee Vance Vw Colorado Springs CO 80918-7102

MEHLMAN, BRUCE P. federal agency administrator; Grad., Princeton U., U. Va. Gen. counsel Nat. Rep. Congl. Com., 1996—99; gen. counsel, policy dir. House Rep. Conf.; telecom. policy counsel Cisco Sys., 1999—2001; asst. sec. for tech. policy Dept. Commerce, Washington, 2001—. Office: Dept Commerce Tech Policy 14th & Constitution Ave NW Washington DC 20230*

MEHLMAN, DAVID JOEL, physician, cardiologist, medical educator; b. Chgo., 1948; AB, Princeton U., 1969; MD, Johns Hopkins U., 1973. Diplomate Am. Bd. Internal Medicine, Am. Bd. Cariology, Nat. Bd. Ecocardiography with subspecialty in adult comprehensive echocardiography. Intern Johns Hopkins Hosp., Balt., 1973-74, resident in medicine, 1974-76; fellow cardiology U. Chgo. Hosps., 1976-78; asst. prof. medicine U. Chgo. Med. Sch., 1978-80, Northwestern U. Med. Sch., Chgo., 1980-86, assoc. prof. medicine, 1986—; dir. adult cardiovasc. disease tng. program McGaw Med. Ctr. Northwestern U., 1988-95, assoc. dir., 1995—. Assoc. dir. echocardiography lab. Northwestern Meml. Hosp., Chgo., 1980-95, co-dir. echocardiography lab., 1995— Fellow Am. Coll. Cardiology, ACP; mem. AHA, Am. Soc. Echocardiography. Office: Northwestern U Med Sch Galter 8-203A 251 E Huron Chicago IL 60611-2914

MEHLMAN, EDWIN STEPHEN, endodontist; b. Hartford, Conn., Nov. 30, 1935; s. Sol Abraham and Rose (Slitt) M.; m. Lesley Judith Lunin, June 13, 1959; children: Jeffrey Cole, Brian Scott, Erik Van. BA, Wesleyan U., 1957; DDS, U. Pa., 1961; cert. endodontics, Boston U., 1965. Diplomate Am. Bd. Endodontists. Instr. oral medicine Sch. Dental Medicine Harvard U., Boston, 1965-67; clin. instr. endodontics Sch. Dental Medicine Tufts U., 1968-70; lectr. endodontics Sch. Dental Medicine, Harvard U., 1970-72, asst. clin. prof. endodontics, 1972—; staff assoc. Forsyth Dental Ctr., 1965—; asst. prof. endodontics Boston U. Sch. Dental Medicine, 1995—; pvt. practice Providence, 1965—. Vis. lectr. dental hygiene U. R.I., Kingston, 1965-71, Community Coll. R.I., Lincoln, 1990—; cons. com. on accreditation of Dentists and Dental Aux. Edn. Programs, 1974-78. Contbr. articles to profl. jours. Pres. Temple Habonim, Barrington, R.I., 1968-70, Bur. Jewish Edn. of R.I., 1980-84; area v.p. Jewish Fedn. R.I., 1975-78; mem. R.I. Legis. Commn. to Study Malpractice Crisis, 1985-86; chmn. R.I. Dental Polit. Action Com., 1987-90. Capt. USAF, 1961-63. Recipient Etherington award Six N.E. Dental Assns. for Outstanding Contbns. to Dentistry. Fellow Am. Coll. Dentists, Internat. Coll. Dentists (dep. regent 1994-98), Pierre Fauchard Acad. (Award of Merit); mem. ADA (coun. on govt. affairs and fed. dental svcs. 1988-92, vice chmn. 1991-92, 1st v.p. 1994-95, 1st dist. trustee 1999—), Am. Assn. Endodontists (dir. 1988-91), R.I. Dental Assn. (pres. 1986-87), N.E. Dental Assns. (Outstanding N.E. Dentist 1995, Disting. Practitioner 2000). Jewish. Avocations: tennis, reading, civic activities. Home: 3 Hanley Farm Rd Warren RI 02885-4376 Office: 130 Waterman St Providence RI 02906-2010 also: 1090 New London Ave Cranston RI 02920-3035

MEHLMAN, LON DOUGLAS, information systems specialist; b. Los Angeles, Apr. 29, 1959; s. Anton and Diane Mehlman. BA, UCLA, 1981; MBA, Pepperdine U., 1983. Systems programmer Ticom Systems Inc., Century City, Calif., 1978-81; systems analyst NCR Corp., 1981-83; sr. systems analyst Tandem Computers Inc., L.A., 1983-91; sr. computer scientist Computer Scis. Corp., El Segundo, Calif., 1991-97; dir. info. tech., CIO Globe Cast Comms. N.Am., Culver City, 1997-2000; chief technology officer MediaConnex.com, Hollywood, 2000-01; v.p. software devel. Micro Gen. Corp., Santa Ana, 2001—. Author: Establishing an Enterprise Information Systems Infrastructure, 1995, Implementing TQM, 1995, Lessons Learned from the Navstar GPS Engineering Management System Project, 1997. Mem. Am. Mgmt. Assn., Assn. for Info. and Image Mgmt., Armed Forces Communications and Electronics Assn., Sierra Club, Phi Delta Theta. Avocations: golf, tennis, sailing, skiing, world travel. Office: Micro Gen 2510 Red Hill Ave Santa Ana CA 92705 E-mail: lonmx@worldnet.att.net.

MEHLMAN, MARK FRANKLIN, lawyer; b. L.A., Dec. 18, 1947; s. Jack and Elaine Pearl (Lopater) M.; m. Barbara Ann Novak, Aug. 20, 1972; children: David, Jennifer, Ilyse. BA, U. Ill., 1969; LLB, U. Mich., 1973. Bar: Ill. 1973; U.S. Dist. Ct. (no. dist.) Ill. 1973. Assoc. Sonnenschein, Nath & Rosenthal, Chgo., 1973-80, mem. policy and planning com., 1989—. Trustee Groveland Health Svcs., Highland Park (Ill.) Hosp., 1991-97; trustee, treas., exec. com. Spertus Inst. Jewish Studies, Chgo., 1992-97, vice chmn. bd. trustees, 1996—; vice-chmn. regional bd. Anti-Defamation League, 1987-89, hon. life mem. nat. comm., 1993—. Fellow Am. Bar Found.; mem. ABA (chmn. mortgages and other debt financing subcom. 1991-95, supervisory coun. 1997—), Am. Coll. Real Estate Lawyers (bd. govs. 2000—, chmn. MDP com. 2000—, chmn. mem. selection com. 2000-01), Nat. Conf. Lawyers and CPAs, Ango-Am. Real Property Inst., Legal Club of Chgo., Lake Shore Country Club, Standard Club, Exec. Club of Chgo. Office: Sonnenschein Nath & Rosenthal 233 S Wacker Dr Ste 8000 Chicago IL 60606-6491

MEHLMAN, MAXWELL JONATHAN, law educator; b. Washington, Nov. 4, 1948; s. Jacob and Betty (Hoffman) M.; m. Cheryl A. Stone, Sept. 15, 1979; children: Aurora, Gabriel. BA, Reed Coll., 1970, Oxford U., England, 1972; JD, Yale U., 1975. Bar: D.C. 1976, Ohio 1988. Assoc. Arnold & Porter, Washington, 1975-84; asst. prof. Case Western Res. U., Cleve., 1984-87, assoc. prof., 1987-90, prof. law, 1990-96, Arthur E. Petersilge prof., 1996—, prof. biomed. ethics, 1998—. Spl. counsel N.Y. State Bar, N.Y.C., 1988-94, Nat. Kidney Found., 1991; cons. Am. Assn. Ret. Persons, Washington, 1992. Editor: High Tech Home Care, 1991, (with T. Murray) Encyclopedia of Ethical, Legal and Policy Issues in Biotechnology; author: (with J. Botkin) Access to the Genome: The Challenge to Equality, 1998, (with Andrews and Rothstein) Genetics: Ethics, Law and Policy, 2002; contbr. articles to profl. jours. Active steering com. AIDS Commn. Greater Cleve., 1986-90. Rhodes scholar, 1970; Rsch. grantee NIH, 1992-94, 97—. Mem. Am. Assn. Law Schs. (chmn. sect. on law, medicine and health care 1990), Phi Beta Kappa. Avocations: skiing, choral music, sea kayaking. Office: Case Western Reserve U Sch Law-Law Medicine Ctr Gund Hall 11075 E Blvd Cleveland OH 44106

MEHNE, PAUL RANDOLPH, associate dean, medical educator; b. Wilmington, Del., May 27, 1948; s. Paul Herbert and Doris Ruth (Longfritz) M.; m. Carol Ann Starner, June 12, 1971; children: Meredith Lynn, Amy Elizabeth. BS in Environ. Sci., SUNY, Syracuse, 1970; PhD, SUNY, 1976, Syracuse U., 1976. Asst. prof. Sch. Allied Health East Carolina U., Greenville, N.C., 1975-76, assoc. dir. Ctr. Edn. Devel. and Evaluation Sch. Medicine, 1976-79, coord. of curriculum Sch. Medicine, 1979-81, asst. dean, 1981-85, assoc. dean, 1985-89, assoc. prof., 1988-89, dir. Ctr. Health Scis. Edn. and Info., 1988-89; assoc. dean U. Pa., Phila., 1989—91; assoc. dean acad. and student affairs, assoc. prof. environ. and community medicine, family medicine Robert Wood Johnson Med. Sch., Piscataway, N.J., 1992—; chair u.-wide telemedicine videocom distance learning com. U. Medicine and Dentistry N.J., 1995-2000, chmn. acad. info. tech. adv. com., 1996-98. Chmn. exec. bd. dirs.

MEDCOMP Supercomputer Consortium, Athens, Ga., 1986—89; vis. prof. U. N.C., Chapel Hill, 1986, Tulane U., New Orleans, 1988; mem. steering com. Assn. Am. Med. Colls. Clin. Campus Deans, 2000—; sec.-treas. Assn. Am. Med. Colls. Orgn. of Regional Med. Campuses, 2001—. Contbr. articles to profl. jours. Chmn. Cmty. Appearance Commn., Greenville, 1980—85; ex officio trustee Cooper Hosp. Univ. Med. Ctr., 2001—. Recipient Interactive Video Instrn. award Digital Equipment Corp., 1985, Med. Edn. Cost Containment award Kate B. Reynolds Health Care Trust, 1985-88, Telemedicine and Med. Informatics award, 1996-99, U.S. Dept. Commerce NTIA/TIIAP award for telemedicine, 1996-98. Mem. IEEE, Am. Pub. Health Assn., Am. Med. Informatics Assn., Am. Edn. Rsch. Assn., Assn. Am. Med. Colls. (chair consortium on student and profl. well-being 1993-94), Soc. for Med. Decision Making, Am. Telemedicine Assn., Soc. of Tchrs. of Family Medicine. E-mail: mehne@umdnj.edu.

MEHO, LOKMAN I. library and information scientist, educator; b. Beirut, Lebanon, Oct. 17, 1968; arrived in US, 1996; s. Ibrahim M. Meho and Leyla S. Hussain. BA in Polit. Sci., Am. U. Beirut, 1991, MA in Polit. Sci., 1996; MS in Libr. Sci., N.C. Ctrl. U., Durham, 1996; MS. in Info. and Libr. Sci., U. N.C., Chapel Hill, 2001. Libr. asst. Am. U. Beirut, 1986—95; freelance bibliographer Beirut and U.S., 1991—; lectr. Sch. Libr. and Info. Scis. N.C. Ctrl. U., Durham, 1997—98; tchg. fellow Sch. Info. and Libr. Sci. U. N.C., Chapel Hill, 1999—2001; asst. prof. SUNY, Albany, 2001—. Compiler: Libraries and Information in the Arab World, 1999, compiler: Kurdish Culture and Society, 2001. Sec. Lebanese Kurdish Charity Assn., Beirut, 1992—95; youth mem. Lebanese Red Cross, 1989—95. Mem.: Assn. Libr. and Info. Sci. Edn., Assn. Coll. and Rsch. Librs., ALA, Am. Soc. Info. Sci. and Tech. Avocations: soccer, reading, painting. Office: SUNY Albany Draper 113 135 Western Ave Albany NY 12222 E-mail: meho@albany.edu.

MEHRA, JAGDISH, economics educator; b. Amritsar, Punjab, India, Nov. 12, 1934; came to U.S., 1962; s. Manmohan and Savitri (Devi) M.; m. Sneh L. Mehra, May 19, 1949; children: Reena, Benu. BA, Birla Inst. Tech., Pilani, Rajasthan, 1955, MA, 1957; PhD, SUNY, Buffalo, 1970. Asst. prof. econs. Banasthali U., Rajasthan, 1959-60; rschr. Nat. Coun. Applied Econ. Rsch., New Delhi, 1960-61; asst. prof. Econs. Birla Inst. Tech., Pilani, 1961-62; grad. asst., econs. instr. SUNY, Buffalo, 1962-65; asst. prof. econs. Youngstown (Ohio) U., 1965-71, assoc. prof. econs., 1971-81, prof. econs., 1981—; sr. rsch. fellow Am. Inst. Econ. Rsch., Great Barrington, Mass., 1982-83. Contbr. articles to profl. jours. Avocations: reading, tennis. Home: 4892 Westchester Dr Apt 2 Youngstown OH 44515-6515 Office: Youngstown State U Dept Econs Youngstown OH 44555 E-mail: JCmehra@cc.ysu.edu.

MEHRA, MAN MOHAN, medical products executive, small business owner; b. Delhi, Nov. 21, 1941; came to U.S., 1968; s. Prakash C. and Ramkumari Mehra; m. Asha Kapur, Dec. 3, 1967; children: Anmol, Ridhi. MS, U. Vikram, India, 1963; PhD, U. Poona, India, 1967. Rsch. assoc. U. Chgo., 1968-73; group leader Becton-Dickinson, Orangeburg, N.Y., 1974-76, E.R. Squibb & Sons, Princeton, N.J., 1977-83; pres. Biotecx Labs., Houston, 1984—. Contbr. over 25 articles to profl. jours. Mem. Am. Chem. Soc., Am. Assn. Clin. Chemistry, Sigma Xi. Achievements include discovery of commerical products developed in clinical diagnostics and molecular biology; research in prostaglandins, steroids and terpenes. Home: 702 Pine Needle Dr Friendswood TX 77546-5265 Office: Biotecx Labs 6023 South Loop E Houston TX 77033-1041

MEHRA, RAMAN KUMAR, data processing executive, automation and control engineering researcher; b. Lahore, Punjab, India, Feb. 10, 1943; came to U.S., 1964; s. Madan Mohan and Vidya Vati (Khanna) M.; m. Anjoo Talwar; children: Archana, Mandira, Kunal. BEE, Punjab Engring. Coll., 1964; MS in Engring., Harvard U., 1965, PhD, 1968. Assoc. prof. Harvard U., Cambridge, Mass., 1972-76; pres., chief exec. officer Sci. Systems, Co., Inc., Woburn, 1976—. Author: System Identification, 1976; also tech. papers on model algorithmic control (Best Paper award Internat. Fedn. Automatic Control, 1983). Recipient Eckman award Am. Automatic Control Coun., St. Louis, 1971. Fellow IEEE. Avocations: hiking, golf, tennis. Home: 5 Angier Rd Lexington MA 02420-1608 Office: Sci Systems Co Inc 500 W Cummings Park Woburn MA 01801-6503 E-mail: rkm@ssci.com.

MEHRABIAN, ALBERT, psychology educator, author, researcher; b. Tabriz, Iran, Nov. 17, 1939; came to U.S., 1957; s. Vartan and Victoria M.; m. Linda Sanfilippo, Jan. 14, 1986. BS, MS, MIT, 1961; PhD, Clark U., Worcester, Mass., 1964. Asst. prof. psychology UCLA, 1964-70, assoc. prof., 1970-76, prof., 1976—. Researcher in field. Cons. editor Jour. Personality and Social Psychology, 1973-76, Sociometry, 1974-77; mem. editorial bd. Jour. Nonverbal Behavior, 1975-86, Jour. Psycholinguistic Rsch., 1971—; author: An Analysis of Personality Theories, 1968, Tactics of Social Influence, 1970, Silent Messages, 1971, Nonverbal Communication, 1972, A Theory of Affiliation, 1974, An Approach to Environmental Psychology, 1974, Public Places and Private Spaces: The Psychology of Work, Play, and Living Environments, 1976, Basic Dimensions for a General Psychological Theory: Implications for Personality, Social, Environmental, and Developmental Studies, 1980, Eating Characteristics and temperament: General Measures and Interrelationships, 1987, The Name Game: The Decision That Lasts a Lifetime, 1990, Your Inner Path to Investment Success, 1991, numerous others. Libertarian. Avocation: running. Home: 1130 Alta Mesa Rd Monterey CA 93940-4603

MEHRING, NANCY, medical and surgical nurse, administrator; b. Lorain, Ohio, June 13, 1943; d. d. Stacy C. and Mary B. (Sascik) Jezewski; m. Frank Mehring, July 16, 1966; children: Gregory M., Stacey M. Diploma, M.B. Johnson Sch. Nursing, Elyria, Ohio, 1964; BSN, U. Akron, 1984. Staff nurse, asst. head nurse, head nurse Elyria Meml. Hosp., 1964-84, admission coord., mgr., 1984-2000; nurse mgr. P.A.T. and Ambulatory Care Ctr.; onsite mgr. Amherst (Ohio) Hosp., 2000—. Mem. adv. com. U Akron Outreach Program. Mem. ANA, Ohio Nurses Assn., M.B. Johnson Sch. Nursing Alumni Assn., Lorain County Dist. Nurses Assn., Sigma Theta Tau.

MEHRING, TERESA ANN, dean, education educator; b. Helena, Mont., Apr. 30, 1952; d. Donald V. and Patricia M. BS, BME, BM, St. Mary Coll., 1974; MS, Southwest Mo. State U., 1975; MSEd, U. Kans., 1979, PhD, 1981. Psychologist Mont. Spl. Edn. Regional Svcs., Glendive, 1975-78; core rschr. U. Kans, Inst. Learning Disabilites, Lawrence, 1978-81; dean, faculty mem. Emporia State U., Kans., 1981—. Bd. dirs. Nat. Tchr. Hall of Fame, Emporia, 1995—; cons. Nat. Coun. Accreditation Tchr. Edn., 1995—, United Arab Emirates U., 2001; adv. bd. Olathe Dist. Schs., Kans, 1995—. Author: (novels) Crisis Intervention for General and Special Education, 1997, Project AIM: Assessment Activities and Rubrics for Mathematics, 1993; contbr. articles. Mem. Guardian Angels Ch., Kansas City, 1978—. Named Adminstr. of Yr. Assn. Health Phys. Edn., Recreation and Dance Profls., 2000-2001, Kans. Educator of Yr. U. Kans. Alumni Assn., 1995, Dist. Profl. of Yr. Internat. Coun. Learning Disabilities, 1994. Mem. Am. Assn. Coll. Tchr. Edn. (nat. bd. dirs. 1998-2001), Tchr. Edn. Coun. State Coll. and Univs. (exec. com., pres. 2001—), Renaissance Group (bd. dirs. 1997-2001, exec. com.), Emporia C. of C. Roman Catholic. Avocations: reading, hiking, traveling, music performance. Office: The Tchrs Coll Emporia State Univ 1200 Commercial Emporia KS 66801-5087 E-mail: mehringt@emporia.edu.

MEHRINGER, CHARLES MARK, medical educator, educator; b. Dickinson, N.D., Nov. 21, 1945; m. Ruth Herrman; 1 child, Sydney. BS in Biology, Lamar U., 1966; MD, U. Tex., 1970. Diplomate Am. Bd. Radiology, Am. Bd. Neuroradiology. Intern UCLA Hosp., 1970-71; resident in diagnostic radiology Harbor-UCLA Med. Ctr., Torrance, Calif., 1971-74, fellow in neuroradiology, 1976-77; asst. prof. dept. radiology UCLA Sch. Medicine, 1977-80, dir. spl. procedures, 1980-94, assoc. prof. dept. radiology, 1986-96, prof. dept. radiology, 1996—, acting chmn. radiology, 1996—. Vice-chmn. dept. radiological scis. UCLA Sch. Medicine, Torrance, 1992—, acting chmn. dept. radiology, 1992—, chief diagnostic radiology, 1983-92; chief radiological svcs., cons. U.S. Air Force for Japan and Korea, 1974-76; cons. U. Calif./Irvine (Calif.) Med. Ctr., 1988—, St. Marys Med. Ctr., Long Beach, Calif., 1986—, Long Beach VA Hosp., 1979—, L.A. County Dept. Chief Med. Examiner-Coroner, 1977—; bd. dirs. Rsch. and Ednl. Inst.; presenter in field. Co-author: (with others) Neurological Surgery of the Ear and Skull Base, 1982, Vascular Surgery, 1984, 2d edit., 1994, Youman's Neurological Surgery, 1990, Common Problems in Infertility and Impotence, 1990, Intraluminal Imaging of Vascular and Tubular Organs: Diagnostic and Therapeutic Applications, 1993, Neuroradiology, A Study Guide, 1995; contbr. articles to profl. jours. Bd. dirs., exec. com. Med. Found. Harbor-UCLA Med. Ctr., 1992—. Recipient numerous grants for rsch., 1977—. Mem. Am. Coll. Radiology, Am. Soc. Neuroradiology (sr. mem.), Western Neuroradiologic Soc., L.A. Radiologic Soc. Office: Harbor UCLA Med Ctr Box 27 1000 W Carson St Torrance CA 90502-2004

MEHRMANN, CRAIGANN, nurse practitioner; b. Hershey, Pa., Jan. 6, 1953; d. Charles Craig and Martha Alene (Shepler) M. BS, Bloomsburg State Coll., 1974; AA in Nursing, Harrisburg Area C.C., 1979; BSN, Pa. State U., 1985; MSN in Nursing, U. Pa., 1986. RN, Pa. Substitute tchr. Derry Twp., Ctrl. Dauphin, and Middletown Area Sch. Dists., 1974-77; nursing asst. Milton Hershey Med. Ctr., 1978; staff nurse Holy Spirit Hosp.; Camp Hill, Pa., 1979, Milton Hershey Med. Ctr., 1979-80; clin. coord. Hillcrest Women's Med. Ctr., Harrisburg, Pa., 1980-85; nurse practitioner Tri County Planned Parenthood, 1986-89, Orndorf, Raschid and Assocs., 1989-2001, Women's Health Profls. Chambersburg, 2001—. Nurse lectr. Pa. State U., 1986, Messiah Coll., 1987-89, U. Pa., 1990—. Vol. Am. Cancer Soc., ARC. Mem. AAUW, Assn. Women's Health, Obstetric and Neonatal Nurses, Am. Acad. Nurse Practitioners, Natl. Assn. Nurse Practitioners Women's Health, Harrisburg Area C.C. Alumni Assn., U. Pa. Sch. Nursing Alumni Assn., Bloomsburg State Coll. Alumni Assn., Messiah Coll. Nursing Honor Soc., Sigma Theta Tau. Methodist. Office: 757 Norland Ave Ste 210 Chambersburg PA 17201

MEHRTENS, SUSAN EMILY, research company executive; b. Elmhurst, N.Y., Sept. 27, 1945; d. William Frederic, and Pauline (Kaufmann) M.; m. Edwin M. Davis, May 31, 1981 (div. Apr. 1984). BA, Queens Coll., 1967; MPhil, Yale U., 1969, PhD, 1973. Asst. prof. Queens Coll., Flushing, N.Y., 1971-77; assoc. prof. Coll. of Atlantic, Bar Harbor, Maine, 1977-87; pres., chief exec. officer Potlatch Group Inc., Mineola, N.Y., 1987—. Cons. Family Care Am., Phoenix, 1991, F.C. Nahser Advt. Inc.; instr. Mt. Desert (Maine) Island Adult Edn., 1977-87, U.S. Power Squadron-Sewanaka, Freeport, N.Y., 1975-77. Author: Earthkeeping, 1974, Being Human in the West, 1991, Ecoguide, 1991, Revisioning Science, 1991, Dreaming to Wake to Life, 1997, Wake Up, South Africa, 2000; co-author: The Fourth Wave, 1993. Intuitive Imagery: A Resource at Work, 1997, The Leap Frog Option, 1999; contbr. articles to profl. jours. Grantee Am. Philos. Soc., 1974, 86, Am. Coun. Learned Socs., 1974; Yale U. fellow, 1967-69. Mem. Phi Beta Kappa. Avocations: spiritual studies, psychic healing, sailing, harpsichord. Home and Office: PO Box 21 Waterbury VT 05676-0021

MEHTA, ASHOK VALLAVDAS, pediatric cardiologist; b. Bakor, India, Jan. 16, 1951; arrived in U.S., 1975; s. Vallavdas H. and Sushila V. (Doshi) M.; m. Pragna Sheth, Apr. 2, 1978; 1 child. B of Surgery, B of Medicine, Baroda (India) Med. Coll., 1974. Diplomate Am. Bd. Pediatrics, Am. Bd. Pediatric Cardiology. Intern dept. of pediatrics Baroda Med. Coll., 1975; resident dept. of pediatrics Misericordia-Lincoln-Fordham Hosp., Bronx, N.Y., 1976-78; postdoctoral fellowship divsn. of pediatric cardiology U. Miami Sch. Medicine, 1978-80, spl. rsch. fellowship in cardiac electrophysiology, 1980-81; asst. prof. pediatrics Temple U. Sch. of Medicine, Phila., 1981-86, St. Christopher's Hosp. for Children, Phila., 1981-86; chief divsn. of pediatric cardiology James H. Quillen COM, East Tenn. State U., Johnson City, 1986-97, assoc. prof. pediatrics, 1986-93, prof. pediatrics, 1993; pvt. practice, 1997—. Vis. prof. divsn. pediatric cardiology U. W.Va. Sch. Medicine, 1985; lectr. in field; dir. pediatric preceptor program, family practice resident, Kingsport, 1986-90; dir. pediatric CME program Holston Valley Hosp. Med. Ctr., Kingsport, 1987-91; dir. Tri-Cities Children's heart Ctr., Kingsport, 1986—; cons. pediatric cardiology Holston Valley Hosp. and Med. Ctr., Johnson City Hosp. and Med. Ctr., Bristol (Tenn.) Meml. Hosp., Indian Path Hosp., Kingsport, Crippled Children's Svc. State of Tenn., Sycamore Shoals Hosp., Elizabethton, Tenn.; dir. pediatric cardiac electro-physiology and pacing fellowship, assoc. pediatric cardiologist St. Christopher's Hosp. Children, Phila., 1981-86; cons. pediatric cardiology Med. Coll. Pa., Phila., 1981-86. Referee reviewer Pediatric Cardiology, Am. Jour. of Diseases of Children; contbr. numerous articles to profl. jours. Fellow Am. Coll. Cardiology, Am. Acad. Pediatrics; mem. AMA (Physician's recognition award 1979—), Am. Heart Assn. (Southeastern Pa. chpt. 1981-86, coun. cardiovascular disease in the young 1992—, bd. dirs. Greater Kingsport chpt. 1990-92, Washington County chpt. 1992—, Young Investigator award Pa. chpt. 1982-84), Cardiac Electrophysiology Soc., Pediatric Cardiac Electrophysiology Soc., S.E. Pediatric Cardiology Soc., Tenn. Pediatric Cardiology Assn., Tenn. Pediatric Soc. (Tenn. chpt. AAP). Republican. Hindu. Avocations: stamp and coin collecting, travel, tennis. Home: 1903 Round Tree Dr Johnson City TN 37604-4104 Office: Tri-City Pediat Cardiology 4540 W Stone Dr Ste E Kingsport TN 37660-8494

MEHTA, EILEEN ROSE, lawyer; b. Colver, Pa., Apr. 1, 1953; d. Richard Glenn and Helen (Wahna) Ball; m. Abdul Rashid Mehta, Aug. 31, 1973. Student, Miami U., 1971-73; BA with distinction, Fla. Internat. U., 1974; JD cum laude, U. Miami, 1977. Bar: Fla. 1977, U.S. Dist. Ct. (so. dist.) Fla. 1977, U.S. Ct. Appeals (11th cir.) 1981. Law clk. to presiding judge U.S. Dist. Ct. (so. dist.) Fla., Miami, 1977-79; asst. atty. County of Dade, 1979-89; shareholder Fine Jacobson Schwartz Nash Block & England, Fla., 1989-94; ptnr. Eckert Seamans Cherin & Mellott, 1994-98, Bilzin Sumberg Dunn Baena Price & Axelrod, Miami, 1998—. Lectr. in field; v.p., bd. dirs. Mehtatron Enterprises, Inc., Miami, Shalimar Homes Inc., Anderson, S.C. Miami U. scholar, 1971-73. Mem. Fla. Bar Assn., Dade County Bar Assn. Office: Sumberg Dunn Baena Price & Axelrod 2500 First Union Fin Ctr Miami FL 33131

MEHTA, HARSHAD R. cardiologist; b. Paddhari, Gujrat, India, Aug. 19, 1949; came to U.S., 1974; s. Ratiical O. and Sharda R. M.; m. Rekha H. Mehta, Feb. 24, 1976; children: Viraj, Nisha. Degree in Inter Sci., Jaihind Coll., Bombay, 1967; MBBS, T.N.M. Coll., Bombay, 1972. Diplomate Am. Bd. Internal Medicine, Am. Bd. Cardiovascular. Intern, resident Franklin Sq. Hosp., Balt., 1974-77; fellow Albert Einstein Med. Ctr., Phila., 1977-79; chief cardiology St. Clair Hosp., Pitts., 1979—. Fellow Am. Coll. Cardiology, Am. Coll. Chest Physicians. Avocations: tennis, golf, jogging, bowling. Home: 124 Marshall Dr Pittsburgh PA 15228-1728 Office: South Hills Cardiology Assocs 1050 Bower Hill Rd Ste 308 Pittsburgh PA 15243-1870 E-mail: mehtahr@hotmail.com.

MEHTA, HETAL R. pediatrician; d. Vinodray C. and Jyoti V. Sanghavi; m. Ravindra M. Mehta, Apr. 10, 1997. MBBS, Grant Med. Coll., Mumbai, India, 1992. Resident dept. pediat. Brookdale U. Hosp. and Med. Ctr., Bklyn., 1998—2000; Fellow, Pediatric cardiology North shore-long Island Jewish Medical Center, Manhasset, 2001—; Chief Resident, Department of Pediatrics Brookdale University Hospital and Medical Center, Brooklyn, 2000—01. Fellow: Am. Acad. Pediat.; mem.: Am. Coll. Cardiology. Home: 215 Grant Ave Mineola NY 11501 Office: North Shore U Hosp Manhasset NY

MEHTA, JATIN VINODRAI, biomedical engineer; b. Bombay, June 7, 1966; s. Vinodrai Purushottamdas and Ramaben Vinodrai Mehta; m. Parul Manharlal Timbadia, Apr. 16, 1994; 1 child, Sarth. BE, TKIET, Kolhapur, India, 1987; PhD, Indian Inst. Tech., 1993. Trainee engr. Godrej and Boyce, Bombay, 1987-88; chief biomed. engr. Jaslok Hosp., 1993-96; dep. chief biomed. engr. Bahrain (India) Internat. Group WLL, 1996; asst. prof. dept. biomed. engring. DJ Sanghui Coll. Engring., U. Mumbai (India), 1997-98; lead software developer Software Internat. Inc., N.J., 1998-99; sr. cons. Mgmt. Info. Consulting, Va., 1999—. Dir. tech. Jesica Securities Ltd., Bombay, 1995—96, Insight Meditronics, Bombay, 1995—; CEO MetaSense Inc., 1999. Editor Modern Medicine Internat., 1995-96; contbr. articles to profl. jours. With Indian Army, 1977-81. Ministry Human Resource Devel. fellow; Coun. for Sci. and Indsl. Rsch. fellow. Mem. IEEE, Nat. Soc. Fluid Mechanics and Fluid Powers, Inst. Elec. and Telecomm. Engrs., Inst. for Pub. Health Engrs., Indian Soc. Tech. Edn., Indian Assn. Biomed. Scientists, Nat. Biomed. Engrs. Soc. Avocations: basketball, cricket, acting, mime. Home and Office: 2807 Charter Dr # 104 Troy MI 48083 E-mail: mehtajatin@hotmail.com.

MEHTA, JAWAHAR LAL, cardiologist; b. India, Aug. 10, 1946; s. Mohan L. and Ishwar D. (Valecha) M.; m. Paulette Smedresman, Oct. 20, 1977; children: Asha, Jason. MD, GN Med. Coll. U. Amritsar, 1968; PhD, U. Uppsala (Sweden). Diplomate Am. Bd. Internal Medicine, Am. Bd. Cardiovascular Diseases. Intern N.Y. Med. Coll., Valhalla, 1970, resident in pediats. N.Y., 1971; resident Mt. Sinai-Beth Israel Hosp., N.Y.C., 1971-73; fellow in cardiology L.I. Jewish Med. Ctr., New Hyde Park, N.Y., 1973-75; from asst. prof. to prof. medicine & physiology U. Fla. Coll. Medicine, Gainesville, 1976-2000; dir. cardiovascular medicine, Stebbins chair in cardiology U. Ark. for Med. Sci., Little Rock, 2000—. Rsch. fellow, instr. in medicine U. Minn., Mpls., 1975-76; U. Ark. Med. Scis. Hosp., VA Hosp., Little Rock. Fellow ACP, Am. Coll. Cardiology; mem. Am. Heart Assn., Am. Soc. Clin. Investigation, Assn. Am. Physicians, Assn. Univ. Cardiologists. Office: U Ark for Med Scis Slot 532 Little Rock AR 72205-7199 E-mail: MehtaJL@uams.edu.

MEHTA, JAY, financial executive; b. Varanasi, India, Aug. 16, 1943; came to U.S., 1970; m. Vineeta Mehta, Feb. 20, 1969; children: Nina, Vineet. MBA in Fin., Rutgers U., 1974; MBA in Taxation, Fairleigh Dickenson U., 1983. CPA, N.J.; cert. mgmt. acct. Contract estimator NE region Otis Elevator Co. Subs. United Techs. Inc., Montvale, N.J., 1970-73, sr. contract estimator NE region, 1974-75, corp. staff acct. N.Y.C., 1976-77, sr. corp. acct., 1978; div. contr. OKI Electric Overseas Corp., Hackensack, N.J., 1979-84; corp. contr. OKI Am. Inc., 1984—, sr. dir. fin., treas., 1990, v.p. fin., treas., 1994-99; personal fin. advisor Am. Express, 2000—. Trustee OKI Am. Savs. Plan, 1981-99; ofcl. grader Inst. Mgmt. Acctg., Montvale, N.J., 1986—. Mem. AICPA, Am. Mgmt. Assn., N.J. Soc. CPAs. Republican. Avocations: reading, golf, computers. Office: OKI Am Inc Mack-Cali Ctr IV 3 University Plz Ste 612 Hackensack NJ 07601-6232 also: Am Express Mack Cali Ctr IV Paramus Rd Paramus NJ 07052

MEHTA, KISHOR CHANDULAL, civil engineering educator; b. Ahmedabad, Gujarat, India, Feb. 19, 1936; came to the U.S., 1954; s. Chandulal Harilal and Vimala Chhaganlal (Shah) Mehta; m. Mary Ann Gaffney, Dec. 27, 1960; children: David, Jatin, Anna, Raajan. BS in Civil Engring., U. Mich., 1957, MS in Civil Engring., 1958; PhD in Structural Engring., U. Tex., 1965. Design engr. Merritt-Chapman & Scott Corp., N.Y.C. and Page, Ariz., 1958-61; rsch.-tchg. asst. U. Tex., Austin, 1961-64; from asst. to Horn prof. civil engring. Tex. Tech. U., Lubbock, 1964—, dir. Wind Engring. Rsch. Ctr., 1988—. Prin. McDonald-Mehta Engrs., Lubbock, 1970—; chmn. Nat. Rsch. Coun.-Com. NaturalDisasters, Washington, 1983-87; pres. Am. Assn. for Wind Engring., Buffalo, N.Y., 1985-89. Author/editor Minimum Design Loads for Building, 1995 (Nat. Hurricane Conf. Svc. awards, 1997, 2000). Pres. Christ The King Sch. Bd., Lubbock, 1973-75. Recipient Svc. award Am. Assn. for Wind Engring., L.A., 1989. Fellow ASCE (local chpt. pres. 1971-72, chmn. wind load com. 1978-95); mem. NSPE (local chpt. pres. 1975-76), Am. Meteorol. Soc., Internat. Assn. for Wind Engring. (pres. 1999—). Achievements include establishment of one of a kind wind engineering research field laboratory under the sponsorship of the National Science Foundation to investigate wind effects on buildings, a multidisciplinary program to conduct research in mitigation of windstorm effects; chaired the development of the national standards in 1982, 1988 and 1995 for wind loads on buildings; direction of TTV/NIST Cooperative Agreement for Windstorm Mitigation. Avocations: travel, presentations and lectures, reading. Home: 3808 55th St Lubbock TX 79413-4620 Office: Tex Tech Univ PO Box 41023 Lubbock TX 79409-1023 E-mail: kishor.meht@wind.ttu.edu.

MEHTA, NARINDER KUMAR, marketing executive; b. Lahore, Punjab, India, Feb. 18, 1938; came to U.S., 1959; s. Puran Chand and Raj Rani Mehta; m. Narayanaswamy Sampath; children: Kiren, Ravi. B of Commerce, U. Delhi, India, 1958; MA, U. Minn., 1961. Program dir. All India Mgmt. Assn., New Delhi, India, 1963-67; with Am. Express Co., Chgo., 1968-82, nat. sales dir. N.Y.C., 1975-80, v.p. sales, 1980-82; sr. v.p. Shearson Lehman/Am. Express, Boston, 1982-85; sr. v.p. mktg. & sales Capital Credit Corp., Fairfield, N.J., 1985-94; sr. v.p. internat. mktg. Outsourcing Solutions, Inc., 1994-97; pres. Mehta Cons. Group, Dover, Mass., 1997—. Sr. v.p. Temporary Investment Funds, 1982-85, Trust for Short Term Fed. Securities, 1982-85, Mcpl. Fund for Calif. Investors, 1983-85; conducted seminars for profl. assns., colls. and univs. Contbr. articles to profl. jours. Nat. v.p. Muscular Dystrophy Assn., N.Y.C., 1984-86; student body pres. U. Delhi, India, 1958-59. Recipient 1st prize inter-coll. debate, 1958. Mem. Am. Mgmt. Assn., Tau Kappa Epsilon. Avocations: running, swimming, traveling, reading. Office: Mehta Cons Group PO Box 547 4 Bryant Ln Dover MA 02030-2401 E-mail: nkmehta@aol.com.

MEHTA, NIKHIL KIRTIKAR, surgeon, researcher; b. Ahmedabad, India, Apr. 3, 1964; came to U.S., 1991; s. Kirtikar and Teresa Mehta; m. Preeti Shroff; 1 child, Naomi Shroff-Mehta. MD, St. Johns Med. Coll., Bangalore, India, 1987. Diplomate Am. Bd. Surgery. Project mgr., med. officer St. Xavier's Non Formal Edn. Soc., Ahmedabad, 1988-90; cons. surg. pathologist Harisiddha Pathology Labs., 1991; rsch. fellow Meml. Sloan Kettering Cancer Ctr., N.Y.C., 1991-92; rsch. fellow, primary investigator SUNY, Buffalo, 1994-96; assoc. chief surgery Peninsula Health Care, Dr. G.B. Cross Meml. Hosp., Nfld., Can., 1999-2000; thoracic surgery fellow dept. cardiothoracic surgery Allegheny Gen. Hosp., Pitts., 2000—. Cons. U. Argentina Exptl. Genetics, 1996, Misereor Found., Germany, 1998-90, Gujarat (India) Vol. Health Assn., 1988-90. Inventor in field; contbr. articles to profl. jours. Mem. ACS, Am. Assn. for Cancer Rsch. (del. 1996, 97), Soc. Univ. Surgeons (del. 1996), Assn. for Acad. Surgery. Avocation: mountaineering. Home: 1309 Alamogordo St Deming NM 88030 Office: 122 S Gold St Ste 1 Deming NM 88030

MEHTA, RAVI RAVINDER SINGH, international trade finance consultant, banking trainer and researcher, trade specialist; b. Rawalpindi, Punjab, Pakistan, May 20, 1945; s. Harbans Singh and Swinder Kaur (Duggal) M.; m. Davinder Kaur Kohli, Nov. 7, 1977; 1 child, Gurpreet. BSc, Delhi U., 1967, MSc, 1970; MLitt, Punjabi U., Patiala, India, 1976; PhD, Panjab U., Chandigarh, India, 1991. Cert. trade specialist. Rsch. scholar Panjabi U., Patiala, 1971-74; officer operational banking Punjaband Sind Bank, Bombay, 1977-80, officer trainer Chandigarh, 1980-96, mgr. internat. banking tng., 1996-2000; retail mktg. rsch. assoc. Wal-Mart Stores, Inc., 1999—. Fac. mem. Internat. Trade and Banking Inst. (Canada), online teaching internat. trade fin., 2000—, correspondent, Documentary Credits Insight Mag., Internat. C. of C., France; export fin. cons. Internat. Trade Ctr. UNCTAD/WTO, Geneva, Switzerland, 2001—. Author: Sociology of Banking, 1976, Autobiography of a Cheque, 1982, Fundamentals of Banking, 1984, Signature Verification, 1990, Journey Through British Banking, 1991, Banking on Lombard Street, 1993, Bank Training in the U.K., 1994, Pictorial Biography of a Bank Training Centre in Switzerland, 1994, Early Banking in England, 1994, Expertly Handling of Export Letters of Credit: A Handbook For The Exporter and His Banker and Freight Forwarder, 2000; mem. editorial bd. LC Monitor Mag. (Ontario, Canada); contbr. articles to profl. and trade jours. Recipient several awards. Mem. Indian Inst. Bankers (life), Internat. Trade Assn., Internat. Trade and Banking Inst. (bd. dirs.). Sikh. Avocations: travel, gardening, philately. Address: 1025 S Beach St Apt 141 Daytona Beach FL 32114-6278 Office: Wal-Mart Supercenter 1590 Dunlawton Ave Port Orange FL 32127-4752 E-mail: aea16@hotmail.com.

MEHTABDIN, KHALID RAUF, economist, educator; b. Sialkot, Pakistan, Nov. 6, 1944; s. Haji and Atiiya Mehtabdin; m. Durdana Ansarie, Jan. 26, 1951; children: Mehvish, Khurram. MA, U. Punjab, 1968; MPA, U. Pitts., 1974, M in Pub. and Internat. Affairs, 1977, PhD, 1979. Asst. prof. econs. Niagara U., Niagara Falls, N.Y., 1980-84, assoc. prof., 1985-86, St. Rose Coll., Albany, 1986—. Mem. bus. adv. coun. Niagara U., 1980-86; cons. M.H. Bros., Karachi, Pakistan, 1980-82. Author: Comparative Management, 1986, Reagonomics, 1986, Macro Eco, 1987. Recipient Outstanding Cmty. award Pakistani Cmty. Albany, N.Y., 1995. Mem. Am. Econs. Assn., Ea. Econs. Assn. (bd. dirs. 1986-90), Islamic Ctr. of Capital Dist. Home: 312 Torquay Blvd Albany NY 12203-4927

MEHURON, WILLIAM OTTO, government official; b. Hammond, Ind., Nov. 20, 1937; s. Arthur and Margaret Irene (Soroka) M.; m. Charlotte Anne Nyheim, Aug. 26, 1982; children: Kimberly Anne, Kristine Lynn, Susan, Geoffrey. BSEE, Purdue U., 1959; MSEE, U. Pa., 1962, PhD, 1966. Tech. dir. naval intelligence Dept. Navy, Washington, 1974-81; dir. rsch. and engring. Nat. Security Agy., Ft. Meade, Md., 1981-85; v.p., gen. mgr. data systems div. Ampex Corp. subs. Allied-Signal Co., Redwood City, Calif., 1985-86; sr. v.p. product ops. Daisy Systems Corp., Mountain View, 1986-88; v.p., gen. mgr. Networks and Info. Security div. Security div. Unisys Def. Systems, McLean, Va., 1988-91; pres. Mehuron Assocs. Inc., 1991-95; dir. sys. acquisition office

NOAA, USG, Washington, 1995-99; dir. Info. Tech. Lab., Nat. Inst. Stds. and Tech., Gaithersburg, Md., 1999—. Avocations: amateur radio (W4XM), running, cooking, antiques. Home: 6667 Madison Mclean Dr Mc Lean VA 22101-2902

MEI, CHIANG CHUNG, civil engineer, educator; b. Wuhan, China, Apr. 4, 1935; m. Caroline J. Schmitt, 1965; 1 child. BS, Nat. Taiwan U., 1955; MS, Stanford U., 1958; PhD, Calif. Inst. Tech., 1963. Rsch. fellow engring. sci. Calif. Inst. Tech., 1963-65; mem. tech. staff Nat. Engring. Sci. Co., Calif., 1965; from asst. prof. to prof. MIT, Cambridge, 1965-93, Edmund K. Turner prof. civil engring., 1993—. Hon. prof. U. Hong Kong, 1992—; instr. mechanics Chinese Acad. Sci., Beijing, 1994. Recipient J.T. Hsieh award, 1984, Rosenstiel award, 1988, Moffatt & Nichol award, 1992. Fellow Acad. Sinica; mem. ASCE, Nat. Acad. Engring., Am. Phys. Soc., Am. Geophys. Union, Soc. Indsl. and Applied Math. Office: Dept Civil Environ & Engr MIT Cambridge MA 02139 E-mail: ccmei@mit.edu.

MEI, DOLORES MARIE, research administrator; b. Ludlow, Mass., Sept. 3, 1955; d. Paul John and Pauline Lavoie M.; m. Jack Irwin, June 28, 1981 (div. Feb. 1988); 1 child, Robert Aaron. AB in Psychology cum laude with honors, Smith Coll., 1977; MA, Columbia U., 1979, M of Philosophy, 1980, PhD, 1981. Rsch. assoc. Columbia U., Henry Krumb Sch. Mines, N.Y.C., 1981-82; mem. staff Office Ednl. Rsch., Bklyn., 1982-83, evaluation mgr., 1983-96; dep. exec. dir. Divsn. of Assessment and Accountability, 1997—2001, dir., 2001—. Ind. cons. N.Y. Zool. Soc., Bronx, 1980-82, 86—. Recipient Nat. Rsch. Svc. award Nat. Inst. Mental Health, 1979-80. Democrat. Roman Catholic. Avocation: biking. Home: 138 71st St Apt 1F Brooklyn NY 11209-1141 Office: Divsn of Assessment and Accountability 110 Livingston St Rm 728 Brooklyn NY 11201-5004

MEIBAUER, AMERY FILIPPONE, special education educator; b. Newark, Mar. 4, 1955; d. Frederick J. and Gloria J. (Ricciardi) Filippone; m. Karl D. Meibauer, Sept. 4, 1981; children: Karlee Constance, Lea Agnes, Madeline Kelly. BA, Marymount Coll., 1973; MS in Spl. Edn., Monmouth Coll., West Long Branch, N.J., 1985. Cert. elem. tchr., tchr. of handicapped, N.J. Counselor Rehab. Ctr. Monmouth Ctr. for Vocat. Rehab., Tinton Falls, N.J.; tchr. neurologically impaired Harbor Sch., Eatontown, Oceanport (N.J.) Bd. Edn.; basic skills instr. Red Bank (N.J.) Bd. Edn. Supplemental instr. West Long Branch (N.J.) Bd. Edn.; transitional neurologically impaired tchr. Lenna Conrow Sch., Long Branch, N.J.; spl. edn. tchr. Long Branch Middle Sch., Long Br. Bd. Edn.; resource specialist Audrey W. Clark Elem. Sch. Named one of Outstanding Young Women of Am. Gen. Fedn. Women's Clubs, 1987. Mem. NEA, ASCD, N.J. Edn. Assn. Home: 67 Werah Pl Oceanport NJ 07757-1538 E-mail: harborshuttle@comcast.net.

MEIBEYER, CHARLES WILLIAM, JR. lawyer, mediator; b. Saginaw, Mich., Nov. 12, 1951; s. Charles William Sr. and Shirley Ann (Coty) M.; children: Coty Walker, Leland Mathew, Melissa Campbell. BA (with distinction), U. Mich., 1975; JD, U. Calif., Berkeley, 1982; postgrad., U. Calif., San Francisco, 1979-80. Bar: Calif. 1982. Assoc. Morrison & Foerster, San Francisco, 1982-83, Dickenson, Peatman & Fogarty, Napa, Calif., 1983-88, ptnr., 1988-89; pvt. practice, 1989—. Profl. mediator, 1992—. Assoc. editor Indsl. Rels. Law Jour., 1980-81. Pres. Mental Health Assn., Napa, 1987-89; bd. dirs. Calif. Mental Health Assn., 1987-89, Napa Valley Unified Edn. Found., 1989-93, pres., 1992-93; trustee Napa Valley Unified Sch. Dist., 1992-96, pres., 1996; bd. dirs. St. Helena C. of C., 2001—. Milton D. Green scholar, 1979-80. Mem. ABA (bus. law, law practice mgmt., real property, probate and trust law sects.), Sonoma County Bar Assn., Napa County Bar Assn., State Bar Calif. (real property and bus. sects.). Office: 1236 Spring St Saint Helena CA 94574 also: 1001 2nd St Ste 333 Napa CA 94559-3030 Fax: 707-963-4897. E-mail: meibeyerlaw@aol.com.

MEIBURG, CHARLES OWEN, business administration educator; b. Seneca, S.C., Dec. 17, 1931; s. Albert and Gladys Katherine (Burley) M.; m. Elizabeth Rhodes Glenn, June 11, 1955; children: Charles O. Jr., Howard Glenn, Elizabeth Rhodes. BS in Arts and Scis., Clemson U., 1953; MA in Econs., U. Va., 1958, PhD in Econs., 1960. Assoc. prof. U. Va., Charlottesville, 1964-69, prof., 1969-82, J. Harvie Wilkinson, Jr. prof. bus. adminstrn., 1982-99, prof. emeritus, 1999—. Dir. Taylor Murphy Inst. U. Va., 1967-83; assoc. dean Darden Sch. U. Va., 1983-89. Co-author: Cases on Financial Institutions, 1979, Cases in Bank Management, 1986; editor (with others) Loan Officers Handbook, 1986. 1st lt. U.S. Army, 1953-55. Mem. Am. Econ. Assn., Fin. Mgmt. Assn., Assn. for U. Bus. and Econ. Rsch. (pres. 1971). Home: 3345 Kirkwood Ct Keswick VA 22947-9138 Office: U Va Darden Sch PO Box 6550 Charlottesville VA 22906-6550 E-mail: com@virginia.edu.

MEIDL, KEVIN, secondary education educator; b. Manitowoc, Wis., Dec. 10, 1960; s. Kenneth John LeRoy and Bernita Ann (Pritzl) M. MusB, Lawrence U., 1983; MusM in Music Edn. summa cum laude, Northwestern U., 1991; PhD in Edn. summa cum laude, LaSalle U., 1995. Tchr. music Einstein Jr. H.S., Appleton, Wis., 1983-85, Appleton (Wis.) H.S. West, 1985—. Conductor, Fox Valley Symphony Chorus, Appleton, 1983-88, St. Edward's Ch. Choir, Mackville, Wis., 1983-88, Appleton Boy Choir, 1983—; bd. dirs. A Better Chance, Appleton, 1985-91. Named Secondary Educator of Yr., Mielke Found., 1994-95. Mem. Am. Choral Dirs. Assn. (mem. state bd. 1980—), Internat. Fedn. Choral Music, Music Educators Nat. Conf., Soc. Acad. Achievement, Wis. Choral Dir. Assn. (pres.-elect 1992, pres. 1995-97), Mortar Bd., Pi Kappa Lambda, Phi Mu Alpha (pres. 1982-83). Roman Catholic. Home: 916 S Park Ave Neenah WI 54956-4259 Office: Appleton High Sch West 610 N Badger Ave Appleton WI 54914-3448 E-mail: kevinmeidl@myexcel.com.

MEIER, DIANE JONES, non-profit organization administrator; b. Huron, S.D., Jan. 20, 1951; d. Daryl D. and Delila D. (Waldner) Jones; m. Kenneth J. Meier, Dec. 31, 1972. AB, U. S.D., 1972; JD, Syracuse U., 1976. Bar: Tex. 1976, Okla. 1978, Wis. 1986. Assoc. Williams & Meier, Houston, 1976-77; pvt. practice, 1977; title ins. underwriter, abstractor Southwest Title & Trust Co., Oklahoma City, 1978-81; assoc. Linn & Helms, 1981-85; staff atty. Wis. Ct. of Appeals, Milw., 1986-98; vol. coord. Habitat for Humanity, Bryan, Tex., 1999—2002. Local officer Women's Equity Action League, Houston, 1976-77; bd. dirs., pres. Women's Resource Ctr., Norman, Okla., 1979-83 Mem.: Bryan-College Station Bus. and Profl. Women's Club, Tex. Fedn. Bus. and Profl. Women's Clubs, Wis. Fedn. Bus. and Profl. Women's Clubs (chair com. 1993—95), Bus. and Profl. Women Milw. (bd. dirs., pres. 1990—92), Assn. for Women Lawyers (treas. 1996—97), College Station Lions Club. Home: 3200 Westchester Ave College Station TX 77845-7910

MEIER, ELEANOR TYNDALL, artist, retired art educator; b. N.Y.C., May 26, 1935; d. Henry Francis and Mary Agnes (Callan) Tyndall.; m. William Joseph Meier, July 11, 1959; children: Mary Meier Bahr, Nancy Meier Kempner. BS in Edu., Nazareth Coll., 1957; MALS, SUNY, Stony Brook, 1973. Permanent cert. tchr., sch. adminstr., supr., N.Y.; permanent cert. tchr. art, N.Y. Art tchr. Valley Stream (N.Y.) Cen. H.S. Dist., 1957-60, Comsewogue Sch. Dist., Port Jefferson Station, N.Y., 1960-90, dept. head. Co-chairperson juried show Huntington Twp. Art League, Elwood, N.Y. 1994-95,96; chairperson juried show Art League of L.I., 1997; juror of awards ann. open juried show Alliance of Queens Artists, Fed. Hall, N.Y.C. Exhibited in galleries including Strathmore Hall Arts Ctr., North Bethesda, Md., Banana Factory, Bethlehem, Pa., Arts Ctr., Old Forge, N.Y., Heritage Hall Mus., Talladega, Ala., Shoestring Gallery, Rochester, N.Y., Chamot Gallery, Jersey City, Ramscale Art Assocs.-Danette Koke Fine Art, N.Y.C., Nat. Acad. Design, N.Y.C., Cultural Ctr. Hellenic Exhbn., Athens, Greece, Perry Galleries, Alexander, Va., Water Mill (N.Y.) Mus., Heckscher Mus., Huntington, N.Y., Mills Pond House, Smithtown Arts Coun., St. James, N.Y., Nassau Mus., Rosyln, N.Y., Christopher Gallery, Stony Brook, N.Y., Gallery North, Setauket, N.Y., Saginaw (Mich.) Art Mus., Vincent Louis Gallery, N.Y.C., Elaine Benson Gallery, Bridgehampton, N.Y.; represented in permanent collections at Jane Voorhees Zimmerli Art Mus., Rutgers U., New Brunswick, U.S. Ambassador Residence, Port Moresby, Papua, New Guinea. Mem. Nat. Assn. Women Artists, Catherine Lorillard Wolfe Art Club (bd. dirs. 1996—, 2d v.p. 1999, pres. 2000—). Democrat. Roman Catholic. Avocations: golf, swimming. Home: PO Box 2134 11 Conscience Bay Rd Setauket NY 11733-2201 E-mail: el.Meier@worldnet.att.net.

MEIER, ENGE, preschool educator; b. N.Y.C., Jan. 17; d. Rudolf and Kate (Furstenow) Pietschyck; children: Kenneth Randolph, Philip Alan. BBA, Western States U., 1987, MBA, 1989. Tchr. nursery sch., Neu Ulm, Fed. Republic Germany, 1963-64; sec. Brewster (N.Y.) Mid. Sch., 1969-72; teaching asst. Brewster Elem. Sch., 1972-73; office asst. Bd. Coop. Edn., Yorktown Heights, N.Y., 1973-76; sec. Am. Can. Co., Greenwich, Conn., 1976-77, adminstrv. sec., 1977-79, exec. sec., 1979-84; adminstrv. asst. U. Tex., Austin, 1984-85, 88-90, adminstrv. assoc., 1985-86, sr. adminstrv. assoc., 1986-88; exec. asst. DTM Corp., 1990; funds asst. mgr. Tex. Assn. Sch. Bds., 1991-92; nursery sch. tchr. Westlake Presbyn. Sch., 1992-95; tchr. Grace Covenant Christian Sch., 1995-96; office mgr. Dr. G. Roebuck, Austin, 1996—. Docent LBJ Libr. and Mus., Austin, 1984—; mem. Women's Polit. Caucus, 1988—; bd. dirs. Leadership, Edn. and Devel., 1991. Mem. Women in Mgmt., Bus. and Profl. Women (pres. 1989, bd. dirs. Austin chpt. 1987—), Women's C. of C. Presbyterian. Avocations: golf, swimming. E-mail: enge@earthlink.net.

MEIER, GERALD MARVIN, economics educator; b. Tacoma, Feb. 9, 1923; s. Max and Bessie (Nagel) M.; m. Gilda Slote, Oct. 23, 1954; children: David, Daniel, Jeremy, Andrew. BA in Econs., Reed Coll., 1947; BLitt in Econs., Oxford (Eng.) U., 1952; PhD, Harvard U., 1953; MA (hon.), Wesleyan U., Middletown, Conn., 1959. Instr. Williams Coll., Williamstown, Mass., 1952-54; asst. prof. Wesleyan U., 1954-59, prof. econs., 1959-63, Stanford (Calif.) U., 1963—. Research assoc. Oxford U., 1957-58; vis. lectr. Yale U., New Haven, 1955-56, vis. assoc. prof., 1956-59, vis. prof., 1959-61; vis. prof. Stanford U., 1962; cons. Asia Soc., Bank Am., East-West Ctr., Food and Agrl. Orgn., Goodyear Internat., NSF, others; internat. lectr. in field. Author: International Trade and Development, 1963, Leading Issues in Development Economics, 1964, The International Economics of Development, 1968, 2d edit., 1978, Leading Issues in Economic Development: Studies in International Poverty, 7th edit., 2000; (with R.E. Baldwin) Economic Development, 1957; gen. editor: Econ. Devel. Series, Econ. Theory and the Underdevel. Countries, Human Resources as the Wealth of Nations, 1973, Fin. Deepening in Econ. Devel., 1975, Agrl. and Structural Transformation, 1975, Gen. X-Efficiency Theory of Econ. Devel., 1978; editor: International Economic Reform: Collected Papers of Emile Despres, 1973, Problems of Trade Policy, 1973, Problems of a World Monetary Order, 1982, Problems of Cooperation for Development, 1977, Toward a New International Development, 1982, La Nueva Era de Desarollo, 1978, Internat. Econs. of Development, International Economics: Theory of Policy, 1982, New International Development Policy, 1982, Pricing Policy for Development Management, 1983, Pioneers in Development, 1985, Emerging from Poverty: The Economics that Really Matters, 1984, Financing Asian Development, 1986, Pioneers in Development, 1987, Asian Development: Economic Success and Policy Lessons, The International Environment of Business, 1998, (with Joseph Stiglitz) Frontiers of Development Economics, 2001; author numerous chpts. to books and articles to profl. jours. Rhodes scholar, 1948-52, Rockefeller Found. Study Ctr. resident scholar, 1981; Guggenheim fellow, 1957-58, Brookings Nat. Research fellow, 1961-62, Russel Sage Found. resident fellow, 1976-77; Social Sci. Research Council Faculty research grantee, 1968, Internat. Legal Ctr. research grantee, 1970, Rockefeller Found. research grantee, 1974-75 Mem. Am. Assn. Rhodes Scholars, Am. Econ. Assn., Royal Econ. Soc., Am. Soc. Internat. Law, Phi Beta Kappa. Home: 774 Santa Ynez St Stanford CA 94305-8441 Office: Stanford U Grad Sch Bus Stanford CA 94305-5015 E-mail: meier_gerald@gsb.stanford.edu.

MEIER, HENRY GEORGE, architect; b. Indpls., July 14, 1929; s. Virgil and Elizabeth (Whiteside) M.; m. Peggy Nelson, June 28, 1953; children: Scott J., Bruce W., Paul T., Thomas A. BArch, U. Cin., 1953. Lic. architect Ind.; lic. landscape architect Ind. Pvt. practice architecture, Indpls., 1964-90; sr. architect Ball State U., Muncie, Ind., 1990-97; now cons. in field, 1997—. Contbr. Indiana Architect mag. Bd. dirs. Am. Bapt. Chs./U.S.A., Valley Forge, Pa., 1970-77, Bd. Bldg. Appeals, Indpls., 1979-85. Served to 1st lt. USMC, 1953-55. Fellow AIA (bd. dirs. 1981-85); mem. Ind. Soc. Architects (pres. 1975, Edward D. Pierre award 1979), Constrn. Specifications Inst., Interfaith Forum on Religion Art and Architecture (v.p. 1981), Masons, Scottish Rite. Republican.

MEIER, KENNETH JOHN, political scientist; b. Aberdeen, S.D., Mar. 3, 1950; s. John and Elizabeth (Malsam) M.; m. Diane Jones Meier, Dec. 31, 1972. BA, U. S.D., 1972; PhD, Syracuse U., 1975. Prof. polit. sci. Rice U., Houston, 1975-78, U. Okla., 1978-85, U. Wis., Madison, 1985-89, Milw., 1989-97; Charles Puryear prof. liberal arts Tex. A&M U., College Station, 1998—, Sara Lindsey prof. govt., 2001—. Fellow com. for hispanic pub. policy issues Inter Univ. Program Social Sci. Rsch. Coun., 1991-92; dir. Ctr. for Presdl. Studies, Policy and Governance, 2001-02. Author: Race, Class and Education, 1989, The Politics of Hispanic Education, 1991, Politics and the Bureaucracy, 1993, The Politics of Sin, 1994, The Case Against School Choice, 1995, Regulation and Consumer Protection, 1995, Applied Statistics for Public Administration, 1997, What Works: A New Approach to Program and Policy Analysis, 2000, Reinventing the Presidency, 2000; editor Am. Jour. Polit. Sci., 1994-98; assoc. editor Jour. Pub. Adminstrn. Rsch. and Theory. Recipient Clarence A. Kulp award, 1990, Gustavus Myers award, 1991, 93, Herbert Kaufman award, 1992, 2002, Herbert A. Simon award, 1999, award Acad. Mgmt., 2000. Mem. APHA, ASPA, Am. Polit. Sci. Assn., S.W. Polit. sci. Assn. (pres.-elect 1998-99, pres. 1999-2000). Office: Tex A&M U Dept Polit Sci TAMUS 4384 College Station TX 77843-0001 E-mail: kmeier@polisci.tamu.edu.

MEIER, LOUIS LEONARD, JR. lawyer; b. Hawthorne, Calif., Oct. 12, 1918; s. Louis Leonard and Celestine Helen (Gabriel) M.; m. Donna Eleonora Tomacelli-Filomarino, June 5, 1954; children: Renée, Sharon Clark, Catherine Gallo, Marina. BS, U.S. Naval Acad., 1942; LL.B., Georgetown U., 1951; grad., U.S. Naval War Coll., 1963. Bar: Va. 1951, U.S. Supreme Ct. 1970, D.C. 1973. Legal and legis. asst. to Chmn. Joint Chiefs of Staff, Washington, 1965-67; comdr. Guided Missile Destroyer Squadron 18, Atlantic Fleet, U.S. Navy, 1967-69; mem policy planning staff Office Sec. State, Washington, 1969-72; Washington counsel ASCE, 1972-82, exec. dir., 1982-83; sole practice Washington, 1983—. Served to capt. USN, 1941-72. Decorated Legion Merit; recipient U.S.S. Gherardi Battle Efficiency award, 1951, U.S.S. John S. McCain Battle Efficiency award, 1954, Pres. award for svc. to country ASCE, 1996. Mem. ABA, Nat. Inst. Bldg. Scis., Conf. Fedn. Environ. Engrs., Met. Club, Chevy Chase Country Club, N.Y. Yacht Club, Spouting Rock Beach Assn. Republican. Roman Catholic. Home and Office: 5132 Baltan Rd Bethesda MD 20816-2350

MEIER, MARGARET DIANNE, advanced practice nurse practitioner; b. Stevens Point, Wis., Jan. 23, 1953; d. Lester James and Cecelia Jessica (Wiza) Searl; m. John Mathew Meier, Oct. 19, 1996; 1 child, Todd Joseph. AD in Respiratory Therapy, Midstate Tech. Coll., 1983; BSN, U. Wis., Oshkosh, 1987; MS in Nursing Adminstrn., U. Ill., Chgo., 1990; grad., Marquette U., 1996; NP in Geriatrics. Cert. respiratory therapist. Respiratory therapist Wausau (Wis.) Hosp. Ctr., 1983-84, ICU staff nurse, 1988; oncology staff nurse U. Wis. Hosp., Madison, 1987-88; float nurse U. Ill. Hosp., Chgo., 1989-90; med. staff, charge nurse Northwestern Meml. Hosp., 1988-90; per diem float nurse U. Wis. Hosp., Madison, 1990-94; nursing instr. North Ctrl. Tech. Coll., Wausau, 1991; 3d level lead nursing instr. Midstate Tech. Coll., Wisconsin Rapids, Wis., 1992-94; nursing instr. Milw. Area Tech., 1994; asst. prof. nursing Carroll-Columbia Coll., 1995; nurse, on-call nurse sexual assault svcs. Sinai-Samaritan Med. Ctr., Milw., 1994-98; advanced practice nurse practitioner Racine Correctional Instn., State of Wis. Dept. Corrections, Sturtevant, 1996—2000; ind. home ventilator nurse, 2001; patient care coord. Heartland Home Care and Hospice, 2002—. Mem. ANA, Wis. Nurse Assn., Milw. Metro Nurse Practitioners. Home: 8393 S Wadsworth Ct Littleton CO 80128

MEIER, MARIANNE MARLYN, hospital chaplain; b. Milw., Jan. 19, 1939; f. Helmuth Diederich and Gertrude Rose (Elschner) M.; m. Wayne V. Dittrich, Feb. 8, 1964 (div. June 1980); children: Victor W. Dittrich, Elizabeth Dittrich Acharya, Wayne W. H. Dittrich. BS, Washington U., St. Louis, 1965; MA, U. Mich., 1976, EdD, 1986; MDiv, Wesley Theol. Sem., 1995. Pub. rels. adminstrv. asst. Concordia Sem., St. Louis, 1959—62; English tchr. N.E. Sr. H.S., Kansas City, 1965—69; fashion merchandising tchr. Baker Coll., Flint, Mich., 1976—79, Cleary Coll., Ypsilanti, 1980—83; acad. advisor, mem. faculty Coll. Lifelong Learning Concordia Coll., Ann Arbor, 1988—91; 1st resident chaplain William Beaumont Hosp., Royal Oak, 1992—93; student asst. min. Good Shepherd United Meth. Ch., Silver Spring, Md., 1993—95; assoc. min. pastoral care and visitation First United Meth. Ch., Birmingham, Mich., 1995—97, Immanuel United Meth. Ch., Eastpoint, 1995—97; pastor Grace United Meth. Ch., Britton, 1997—98; chaplain William Beaumont Hosp., Royal Oak, 1998—. Lectr. in ednl. founds. and philosophy Oakland U., Rochester, Mich., 1998—99. Author: Understanding the School Prayer Issue and the Related Character Education and Charter School Movements, 2002. V.p. bd. dirs. Chandler Park Acad., Detroit, 1996-99; parent vol. Ann Arbor Schs. Open Classroom Program, 1980-86; pres., v.p., program chair, chaplain Lapeer County (Mich.) Gen. Hosp. Aux., 1972-76; bd. dirs. Lapeer County Day Care Ctr., 1974. Mem.: S.E. Mich. Healthcare Chaplains Assn., Mich. Acad. Sci., Arts and Letters. Avocations: reading, writing, travel. Home: 100 W Hickory Grove Rd # F3 Bloomfield Hills MI 48304

MEIER, MARK FREDERICK, research scientist, glaciologist, educator; b. Iowa City, Dec. 19, 1925; s. Norman C. and Clea (Grimes) M.; m. Barbara McKinley, Sept. 16, 1955; children: Lauren G., Mark S., Gretchen A. BSEE, U. Iowa, 1949, MS in Geology, 1951; PhD in Geology and Applied Mechanics, Calif. Inst. Tech., 1957. Instr. Occidental Coll., L.A., 1952-55; chief glaciology project office U.S. Geol. Survey, Tacoma, 1956-85; dir. Inst. Arctic and Alpine Rsch. U. Colo., Boulder, 1985-94. Vis. prof. Dartmouth Coll., Hanover, N.H., 1964; rsch. prof. U. Wash., Seattle, 1964-86; prof. geol. scis. U. Colo., 1985-96, prof. emeritus, 1997—; pres. Internat. Comn. on Snow and Ice, 1967-71; pres. Internat. Assn. Hydrol. Scis., 1979-83; Mendenhall lectr. U.S. Geol. Survey, 1982, Walter Orr Roberts Disting. lectr. Aspen Global Change Inst., 1992. Contbr. articles to profl. jours. With USN, 1945-46. Recipient 3 medals Acad. Scis., Moscow, 1970-85, Disting. Svc. award (Gold medal) U.S. Dept. Interior, 1968, Internat. Hydrology prize Internat. Assn. Hydrol. Scis./World Meteor. Orgn./UNESCO, 1999; Meier Valley, Antarctica named in his honor U.S. and U.K. Bd. Geog. Names. Fellow AAAS (John Wesley Powell Meml. lectr. 1994), Am. Geophys. Union (com. chmn., Robert E. Horton medal 1996), Geol. Soc. Am., (com. mem.), Internat. Glaciological Soc. (v.p., coun., Seligman Crystal 1985), Arctic Inst. N.Am. (gov. 1987-93). Office: U Colo Inst Arctic Alpine Rsch 1560 30th St Boulder CO 80309-0450 E-mail: mark.meier@colorado.edu.

MEIER, MATTHIAS S(EBASTIAN), historian; b. Covington, Ky., June 4, 1917; s. Matthias J. and Mary (Berberich) M.; married; 5 children. BA, U. Miami, 1948; MA, Mexico City Coll., 1949; PhD in Latin Am. History, U. Calif.-Berkeley, 1954. Lectr. U.S. history San Francisco State Coll., summers 1953-55; lectr. U.S. and Latin Am. history Bakersfield Coll., 1955-63; asst. prof. Fresno State Coll., summer 1956, fall 1962; asst. prof. Latin Am. history Santa Clara U., 1963-66, assoc. prof., 1966-72, prof., 1972-89, Patrick A. Donohoe prof. history, 1983-89, emeritus. Fulbright lectr. Nat. U. Tucuman and Inst. Nacional de Profesorado Secundario, Buenos Aires, Argentina, 1958-59; lect. U. Ibero-Am., summer 1965; vis. prof. San Jose State Coll., spring 1968 Author: (with Feliciano Rivera) The Chicanos: A History of Mexican Americans, 1972, A Bibliography for Chicano History, 1972; editor: (with Feliciano Rivera) Readings on La Raza: Twentieth Century, 1973, Dictionary of Mexican American History, 1981, Bibliography of Mexican American History, 1984, Mexican American Biographies, 1988, update of Carey McWilliams's North From Mexico (publ. 1949), 1990, revision, update The Chicanos (new title Mexican Americans/American Mexicans), 1993, Notable Latino Americans, 1997, Encyclopedia of the Mexican American Civil Rights Movement, 2000. Served with Signal Corps U.S. Army, 1942-46. Mem. Pacific Coast Council Latin Am. Studies (pres. 1964-65, 76-77), Latin Am. Studies Assn., Conf. Latin Am. Historians, Assn. Borderlands Scholars, Nat. Assn. for Chicano Studies. Office: Santa Clara U Dept History Santa Clara CA 95053-0001 E-mail: mmeier@scu.edu.

MEIER, PAUL FREDERICK, chemist, chemical engineer; b. St. Louis, Dec. 30, 1952; s. Mildred Louise M.; m. Theresa Ann Sutherland; children: Allison, Tim. BS in Chemistry with high honors, U. Ark., 1975; MA in Phys. Chemistry, Rice U., 1977; PhD in Phys. Chemistry, 1979. Registered profl. engr., Okla. Rsch. chemist Phillips Petroleum Co., Bartlesville, Okla., 1978-85; sr. rsch. chemist, 1985-91; rsch. assoc., 1991—. Presenter in field. Contbr. articles to profl. jours.; patentee in field. Coach MathCounts St. John Sch., Bartlesville, 1995-98; basketball coach YMCA, Bartlesville, 1991-98, leader Y-Indian Guides, 1991-98; organist Redeemer Luth. Ch., Bartlesville, 1978-2002; mem. Boy Scout com. troop 23, Boy Scouts Am., Bartlesville, 1998-2002. Pre-doct. fellow Welch Found., 1975-78; recipient Cmty. Svc. award C. of C., 1982. Mem. ACS, Nat. Soc. Profl. Engrs., Okla. Soc. Profl. Engrs., Ednl. Career Devel., Sigma Xi, Alpha Chi Sigma. Lutheran. Avocations: tennis, golf, piano, backpacking, sailboarding. Home: 1100 Cherokee Ave Bartlesville OK 74003 Office: Phillips Petroleum Co 365-A PL/PRC Bartlesville OK 74004 Fax: (918) 662-1097. E-mail: pfmeier@ppco.com.

MEIER, RICHARD LOUIS, futurist, planner, behavioral scientist; b. Kendallville, Ind., May 16, 1920; s. Walter A. and Mary (Lottman) M.; m. Gitta Unger, May 20, 1944 (dec.); children: Karen Reeds, Andrea Meier Whitmore, Alan; m. Robin Standish, Apr. 21, 1992. Student, No. Ill. State Tchrs. Coll., 1936-39; BS, U. Ill., 1940; MA, UCLA, 1942, PhD, 1944. With Calif. Research Corp., 1943-47; exec. sec. Fedn. Am. Scis., 1947-48; with Petrocarbon, Ltd., 1949-50; Fulbright scholar Manchester U., Eng., 1949-50; asst. prof. program of edn. and research in planning U. Chgo., 1950-56; research social scientist Mental Health Research Inst., U. Mich., Ann Arbor, 1957—, asso. prof. conservation, 1960-65, prof., 1965-67; prof. environ. design U. Calif., Berkeley, 1967-90, prof. emeritus, 1990—. Vis. lectr. Harvard U., 1959-60; vis. prof. Grad. Sch. Ekistics, Athens, 1962, U. Calif., Berkeley, 1966; cons. on social planning and resources planning Joint Ctr. for Urban Studies, MIT and Harvard U., in Venezuela, 1963-65. Author: Science and Economic Development, 1956, Modern Science and the Human Fertility Problem, 1959, A Communications Theory of Urban Growth, 1962, Developmental Planning, 1965, Resource-Conserving Urbanism for South Asia, 1968, Planning for an Urban World, 1974, Urban Futures Observed: In the Asian Third World, 1980; contbr. numerous articles to profl. jours. Mem. AAAS, Am. Planning Assn., Am. Chem. Soc., Soc. for Gen. Sys. Rsch., Fedn. Am. Scis., Holis-Soc. for Sustainable Future. Home: 636 Colusa Ave Berkeley CA 94707-1518

MEIER, STEPHEN CHARLES, foundation executive; b. L.A., Apr. 22, 1950; s. Erwin William Henry and Betsy R. Meier; m. Carol Williams Meier, Apr. 20, 1974; children: Charles, Marilyn. BA, Occidental Coll., 1972; MBA, Harvard U., 1977. Budget analyst Calif. Legis., Sacramento, 1973—75; various exec. positions Times Mirror, L.A., 1977—89, v.p. adminstrn. and cmty. affairs, 1989—96, v.p. pub. and govt. affairs, corp. sec., 1996—2000; bd. dirs. Pfaffinger Found., L.A., 1993—, chmn., CEO, 1997—. Liaison Calif. Bus. Roundtable, Sacramento, 1996-2000, L.A. Bus. Advisors, 1996-2000. Bd. dirs. L.A. Visitors and Conv. Bur., 1999-2000, L.A. Econ. Devel. Corp., 1998-2000, YMCA of Met. L.A., 1995—, Tomas Rivera Policy Inst., Claremont, Calif., 1994—, Constl. Rights Found., L.A., 1993—. Fellow Thomas Watson Found., 1972-73. Mem. The Calif. Club. Congregationalist. Avocations: teaching with BSF Internat. Office: Pfaffinger Found 316 W 2d St Ste PH-C Los Angeles CA 90012

MEIER, THOMAS JOSEPH, museum director, author; b. Denver, June 23, 1939; s. Henry Joseph and Helen Miriam (Croke) M.; m. Beverly Joyce Loeffler, June 8, 1963; children: Thomas, John. BS in Edn., U. Colo., 1964. Cert. tchr., Colo. Space mgmt. dir. U. Colo., Boulder, 1966-69; owner Sturtz & Copeland, 1969-77; historian and writer Mesa Press, 1977-90; dir. Boulder Mus. History, 1990—. Author: The Pictureman, 1994, (booklet) The Early History of Boulder 1993, contbr. articles to profl. jours. Mem. mass transit com. City of Boulder, 1973; mem. City Planning Bd., Boulder, 1974-75, City Landmark Bd., Boulder, 1974-75. Served with USMC, 1957-60. Mem. Boulder Hist. Soc. (pres. 1985), Colo. Hist. Soc. Home: 2850 Vassar Dr Boulder CO 80305-5737 Office: Boulder Mus of History 1206 Euclid Ave Boulder CO 80302-7224

MEIER, THOMAS KEITH, college president, English educator; b. Houston, Apr. 12, 1940; s. Herbert H. and Madeleine (Keith) M.; m. Mila Hillard, June 30, 1962; children: John Hillard, Keith Reilly. BA, U. Tex., 1962; AM, Columbia U., 1963; MBA, Harvard U., 1967; PhD, Columbia U., 1969. Fin.

mgr., employee rels. mgr. Exxon Co., U.S.A. and Exxon Rsch. Engring. Co., Houston, Florham Park, N.J., 1969-79; pres. Castleton (Vt.) State Coll., 1979-87; pres., Simeon Benjamin prof. English lit. Elmira (N.Y.) Coll., 1987—. Regent Lee Coll., Baytown, Tex., 1972-73; pres. Vt. Higher Edn. Coun., 1981-82; mem. Johnson Found. (Troutbeck) Leadership Seminar, 1991—; mem. adv. coun. The Pres.'s Found. for Support of Higher Edn.; bd. dirs. Chemung Canal Trust Co., Coll. Consortium Finger Lakes, N.Y., Ind. Coll. Fund of N.Y., Coun. Ind. Colls. and Univs., Christopher Isnerwood Found. Author: Defoe and the Defense of Commerce, 1987; contbr. articles to profl. jours. Bd. dirs. Union County Urban League, Elizabeth, N.J., 1973-76, Rutland Region C. of C., 1982-86, Arnot Art Mus., 1987-99, So. Tier Econ. Growth, 1987—, N.E.-Midwest Congl. Leadership Coun., 1988—; bd. dirs. Chemung County United Way, 1990-93, chmn. 1992-93; corp. bd. dirs. Rutland Hosp., 1980-87; bd. dirs. Ind. Coll. Fund, 1995-97. Lt. U.S. Army, 1963-65. Recipient Outstanding Periodical Essay award Tex. Books Rev., 1979, medal of merit Elmira Coll. Alumni Assn., 1991; Weaver fellow, 1968. Mem. Pico Ski Club (Va.), Elmira Country Club, Elmira City Club, Univ. Club of N.Y.C., Harvard Club of N.Y.C., Phi Beta Kappa, Phi Eta Sigma, Phi Alpha Theta, Omciron Delta Kappa, Theta Xi, Alpha Sigma Lambda, Sigma Beta Delta. Episcopalian. Home: The President's Home 855 College Ave Elmira NY 14901-2001 Office: Elmira Coll Office of Pres Elmira NY 14901

MEIER, WILBUR LEROY, JR. industrial engineer, educator, former university chancellor; b. Elgin, Tex., Jan. 3, 1939; s. Wilbur Leroy and Ruby (Hall) M.; m. Judy Lee Longbotham, Aug. 30, 1958; children: Melynn, Marla, Melissa. BS, U. Tex., 1962, MS, 1964, PhD, 1967. Planning engr. Tex. Water Devel. Bd., Austin, 1962-66, cons., 1967-72; research engr. U. Tex., 1966; asst. prof. indsl. engring. Tex. A&M U., College Station, 1967-68, assoc prof., 1968-70, prof., 1970-73, asst. head dept. indsl. engring., 1972-73; prof., chmn. dept. indsl. engring. Iowa State U., Ames, 1973-74; prof., head sch. of indsl. engring. Purdue U., West Lafayette, Ind., 1974-81; dean Coll. Engring., Pa. State U., University Park, 1981-87; chancellor U. Houston System, 1987-89; prof. indsl. engring. Pa. State U., University Park, 1989-91; dir. div. engring. infrastructure devel. NSF, Washington, 1989-91; dean Coll. Engring. N.C. State U., 1991-93, prof. indsl. engring., 1991—; program mgr. ABB Electric Systems Tech. Inst., Raleigh, N.C., 2000—. Mem. bd. visitors Air Force Inst. Technology; cons. Ohio Bd. Regents, 1990, U. Arizona, 1989, Indsl. Rsch. Inst., St. Louis, 1979, Environments for Tomorrow, Inc., Washington, 1970-81, Water Resources Engrs., Inc., Walnut Creek, Calif., 1969-70, Computer Graphics, Inc., Bryan, Tex., 1969-70, Kaiser Engrs., Oakland, Calif., 1971, Tracor, Inc., Austin, 1966-68, div. planning coordination Tex. Gov.'s Office, 1969, Office of Tech. Assessment, 1982-86, Southeast Ctr. for Elec. Engring. Edn., 1978— ; mem. rev. team Naval Rsch. Adv. Com. Editor: Marcel Dekker Pub. Co., 1978—; Contbr. articles to profl. jours. Recipient Bliss medal Soc. Am. Mil. Engrs., 1986, Am. Spirit award USAF, 1984; named Outstanding Young Engr. of Yr. Tex. Soc. Profl. Engrs., 1966, Disting. Grad. Coll. Engring., U. Tex. at Austin, 1987; USPHS fellow, 1966. Fellow AAAS, Am. Soc. Engring. Edn. (chmn. indsl. engring. divsn. 1978-83), Inst. Indsl. Engrs. (dir. ops. rsch. div. 1975, pres. Ind. chpt. 1976, program chmn. 1973-75, editorial bd. Trans., publ. chmn., newsletter editor engring. economy div. 1972-73, v.p. region VIII 1977-79, exec. v.p. chpt. ops. 1981-83, pres. 1985-86), Soc. Mfg. Engrs. (Internat. Edn. award 2000), World Acad. Productivity Sci.; mem. ASCE (sec.-treas. Austin br. 1965-66, chmn. rsch. com., tech. coun. water resources planning and mgmt. 1972-74), Am. Assn. Engring. Socs. (bd. govs. 1984-86), Nat. Assn. State Univ. and Land Grant Colls. (mem. engring. legis. task force 1983-87), Assn. Engring. Colls. Pa. (pres. 1985-86, treas. 1981-87), Air Force Assn. (advisor sci. and tech. com. 1984-87), Nat. Soc. Profl. Engrs., Profl. Engrs. in Edn. (vice chmn. N.E. region 1985-87, bd. govs. 1983-85), Sigma Xi, Tau Beta Pi, Alpha Pi Mu (asso. editor Cogwheel 1970-75, regional dir. 1976-77, exec. v.p. 1977-80, pres. 1980-82), Phi Kappa Phi, Chi Epsilon. Lodges: Rotary. Home: 7504 Grist Mill Rd Raleigh NC 27615-5411

MEIGHAN, STUART SPENCE, hospital consultant, internist, writer; b. Glasgow, Scotland, Jan. 30, 1923; came to U.S., 1962; s. Stuart Spence and Annie Louise (Brown) M; m. Anne Stewart Henderson, Nov. 4, 1952 (div. 1968); children: Jane Spence, Stuart Spence; m. Louise Rhys McGregor, July 7, 1985. MB, U. Glasgow, 1945. Registrar, sr. registrar Nat. Health Svc., U.K., 1948-57; sr. staff mem. Allan Blair Meml. Clinic, Regina, Sask., Can., 1957-62; internist Cleland Clinic, Oregon City, Oreg., 1962-64; dir. med. affairs Good Samaritan Hosp., Portland, 1964-78; pres. Spence Meighan and Assocs., 1978—. Cons. several hosps. and orgns. Contbr. over 100 articles to profl. jours. Lt. Royal Navy, 1946-48. Recipient Disting. Svc. award Am. Soc. Internal Medicine. Fellow Am. Coll. Physicians, Royal Coll. Physicians. Avocations: sailing, tennis, theater, rugby football, music. Home and Office: 408 NW Rainier Ter Portland OR 97210-3347

MEIGHER, S. CHRISTOPHER, III, communications and media executive, publisher; b. N.Y.C., Sept. 23, 1946; s. Stephen Christopher and Denise (Connor) Todd; m. Grace Tebbutt, Aug. 8, 1970; children: Elizabeth, Amanda Powers. BA, Dartmouth Coll., 1968; grad. program mgmt. devel., Harvard U., 1974. Dir. circulation Fortune mag., N.Y.C., 1972-74, Sports Illustrated mag., N.Y.C., 1974-76, Time mag., N.Y.C., 1976-79; v.p. circulation Time, Inc., 1981-83; pres. Time Distbn. Svc., 1979-81; pub. People mag., 1983-85, exec. v.p., group pub., 1985-90; pres. Time Inc. Mags. N.Y., 1990-92; gen. ptnr., CEO, chmn. Meigher Comm., L.P., 1993—; CEO Questmedia LLC, 2000—. Bd. dirs. Individual Investor Group, 1998—; bd. vis. Rockefeller Ctr. at Dartmouth Coll., 1997—; delegate U.S. State Dept. USA-USSR, 1988; mem. Bilateral Info. Talks, Moscow. Pub. Saveur mag., Garden Design mag., Quest mag., Smarth Health mag., Friends mag., 1992-2000. Trustee Boys Club N.Y.C., 1979—, Internat. House, 1985-92, Am. Ballet Theatre, 1993—, South St. Seaport, 1987-97, St. Paul's Sch., 1997—; mem. dream team Meml. Sloan Kettering, 1990—; mem. comm. com. St. James Episcopal Ch., 1989-95. Recipient Disting. Service award Brandeis U., 1983 Mem. Am. Pubs. Assn. (bd. dirs. 1988-92), Mag. Publs. Assn. (bd. dirs. 1988-92, 97—), River Club, Bath & Tennis Club (Palm Beach), Brook Club, Racquet & Tennis Club (N.Y.), N.Y. Yacht Club (trustee 1987-92), Lake George Club (trustee 1995—), Clove Valley Rod and Gun Club, Saratoga Reading Room. Office: Meigher Comm LP 920 First Ave New York NY 10022 E-mail: scmiii@aol.com.

MEIGS, JOHN FORSYTH, lawyer; b. Boston, Dec. 4, 1941; s. Charles H. Meigs and Florence S. Truitt; m. Carolyn J. Adams, Aug. 11, 2002; children: Amy, Perry, John. BA, Yale U., 1964; LLB, U. Pa., 1969. Bar: Pa. 1969, U.S. Supreme Ct. 1977. Assoc. Saul, Ewing, Remick & Saul (now Saul Ewing LLP), Phila., 1969-76, ptnr., 1976—. Co-chair estates and trusts Saul Ewing LLP, 1997—; chair personal wealth svcs. Group Saul Ewing LLP , 2000—. Contbr. articles to profl. jours. Trustee Independence Seaport Mus., 1978—, Woodmere Art Mus., 1987—; mem. Com. of 70, 1976—. Mem. ABA, Pa. Bar Assn., Phila. Bar Assn. Episcopalian. Home: 6 Norman Ln Philadelphia PA 19118-3617 Office: Saul Ewing LLP 3800 Centre Sq W Philadelphia PA 19102 E-mail: jmeigs@saul.com.

MEIGS, JOHN LIGGET, artist; b. Chgo., May 10, 1916; s. James L. and Mary Margaret (Cookly) M.; 1 adopted son, Clinton Taylor (dec.). Student, U. Redlands, 1933-34, Gand Chaumier Acad., Paris. 50 one-man shows in U.S., France; author: Peter Hurd The Lithographs, Peter Hurd Sketch Book, Cowboy in American Graphics; contbr. numerous articles to profl. jours. With USN, 1951, PTO. Avocations: book collector, original art collector. Home and Office: PO Box 107 San Patricio NM 88348-0107

MEIGS, JOSEPH CARL, JR. retired English language educator; b. New London, N.C., Aug. 29, 1930; s. Joseph Carl and Lola Vann (Eddins) M.; m. Elizabeth Eleanor Stevenson, Sept. 12, 1953; children: Geoffrey Montgomery, Jonathan Hervey, Edward Stevenson. BA, Wake Forest U., 1952; MA, Tulane U., 1957. English and French tchr. Aquadale (N.C.) High Sch., 1952-53; tchr. Metairie (La.) Park Country Day Sch., 1954-55; instr. in English Salem Coll., Winston-Salem, N.C., 1957-62, Tulane U., New Orleans, 1962-64, Marquette U., Milw., 1964-67; from asst. prof. to assoc. prof. English Ea. Conn. State U., Willimantic, 1967-93, chmn. dept. English, 1972-74, 87-88, 1990-93; ret., 1993. Vis. prof. U. Hawaii, Hilo, 1988-89, 94-95. Grantee Carnegie Inst., 1953, Danforth Found., 1960. Mem. Linguistic Soc. Am., Soc. for Pidgin and Creole Studies, Phi Beta Kappa, Omicron Delta Kappa. Democrat. Avocations: photography, gardening, cooking, hiking, ceramic arts. Home: PO Box 852 Brooklyn CT 06234-0852 E-mail: meigs@neca.com.

MEIGS, MONTGOMERY CUNNINGHAM, JR. military officer; b. Annapolis, Md., Jan. 11, 1945; s. Montgomery Cunningham and Elizabeth Shoemaker (Griggs) M.; m. Mary Ann Mellenbruch, July 6, 1968; children: William Bradford, Matthew Montgomery. BS, U.S. Mil. Acad., West Point, N.Y., 1967; MA in History, U. Wis., 1977, PhD in History, 1982. Commd. 2d lt. U.S. Army, 1967, advanced through grades to gen.; internat. affairs fellow Coun. Fgn. Rels., N.Y.C., 1981-82; exec. officer 2d Armored Cavalry Regiment, Nurnberg, Germany, 1982-84; comdr. 1st Squadron, 1st Cavalry, 1st AD, Schwabach, Germany, 1984-86; rsch. fellow Nat. Def. U., Washington, 1986-87; chief strategic applications br. J-5 Joint Staff, 1987-90; comdr. 2d Bde 1st Armored Divsn., Erlangen, Germany, 1990-91; comdg. gen. 7th Army Tng. Command, Grafenwoehr, Germany, 1991-93; chief of staff V U.S. Corps, Frankfurt, Germany, 1993-94; dep. chief of staff Ops. HQ USAREUR & 7th Army, Heidelberg, Germany, 1994; comdg. gen. 3d Infantry Divsn., 1995-96, 1st infantry Divsn., Wurzburg, Germany, 1996-97, COMEAGLE, Bosnia-Herzegovina, 1996-97, Combined Arms Ctr., Ft. Leavenworth, Kans., 1997-98; commdg. gen. U.S. Army, COMSFOR, Herzegovina, Bosnia, 1998-99; comdg. gen. U.S. Army Europe and 7th Army, 1998—. Author: Slide Rules and Submarines, 1990; contbr. articles to profl. jours. Decorated Def. Disting. Svc. medal, Def. Superior Svc. medal, Army Disting. Svc. medal, Legion of Merit with oak leaf cluster, Bronze Star medal with V device and 2 oak leaf clusters, Purple Heart. Avocations: history, hunting. Home: CG USAREUR Cmr 420 Box 1 APO AE 09063-0001

MEIJER, PAUL HERMAN ERNST, educator, physicist; b. The Hague, Netherlands, Nov. 14, 1921; came to U.S., 1953, naturalized, 1959; s. Herman Willem and Elisabet (Kossmann) M.; m. Marianne Schwarz, Feb. 17, 1949; children: Onko Frans (dec.), Miriam, Daniel, Mark, Corinne. PhD, U. Leiden, Netherlands, 1951. Research assoc. U. Leiden, 1952-53, Duke U., 1954-55; vis. lectr. Case Inst. Tech., 1953-54; asst. prof. U. Del., 1955-56; asso. prof. Cath. U., Washington, 1956-60, prof. physics, 1960-92, prof. emeritus, 1992—, chmn. dept., 1980-83. Vis. prof. U. Paris, 1964-65, 72, 78, U. Nancy, 1984, 88; part-time appointment Nat. Bur. Standards; short time appointments at Naval Ordnance Lab., Livermore Radiation Lab., Naval Research Lab., Night Vision Lab., Ft. Belvoir. Author: (with E. Bauer) Group Theory, 1962, (with P. Papon, J. Leblond) The Physics of Phase Transition, 2002; editor: Group Theory and Solid State Physics, 1964. Fulbright grantee, 1953-55, 77-78; Guggenheim grantee, 1964-65; Fulbright sr. fellow, 1978 Fellow Am. Phys. Socs.; mem. European Phys. Soc., Phys. Soc. Netherlands, Fedn. Am. Scientists, Fulbright Alumni Assn., Sigma Xi. Research, publs. statis. mechanics solids and liquids, group theory and other fields. Home: 1438 Geranium St NW Washington DC 20012-1518 Office: Cath U Am Dept Physics Hannan Hall Washington DC 20064 also: Phys and Chem Properties Div Nat Inst Stds And Tech Gaithersburg MD 20899-0001 E-mail: meijer@cua.edu.

MEIKLE, PHILIP G. engineer, retired government agency executive; b. Glendale, W.Va., Dec. 5, 1937; s. Philip and Caroline Elizabeth (Stephens) M.; m. Linda Kay Price, July 14, 1961 (div. Aug. 1976); children: Philip Kevin, Melissa Kay BS in Mining Engring., W.Va. U., 1961, MS in Mining Engring., 1965; M.Engring. Adminstrn., George Washington U., 1980. Registered profl. engr. Mining engr. Duquesne Light Co., Pitts., 1961-63; research engr. W.Va. U., Morgantown, 1963-66; materials engr. Mobay Chem. Co., New Martinsville, W.Va., 1966-68; asst. dir. Nat. Ash Assn., Washington, 1968-72; staff mining engr. U.S. Bur. Mines, 1972-82, divsn. chief, 1982-95; ret., 1995. Mem. U.S. Nat. Com. for Tunneling Tech., Nat. Acad. Scis., Washington, 1985-90, chmn., 1988-89; adj. prof. George Washington U., 1985—; pres. Clan Lamont Soc. N.Am., 1998—. Contbr. articles to profl. jours., chpts. to books Recipient Superior Svc. award Dept. Interior, 1980, Meritorious Svc. award, 1986, Disting. Svc. award, 1991, Presdl. Rank award, 1991. Mem. Nat. Assn. Ret. Fed. Employees (life), Fed. Exec. Inst. Alumni Assn., Sr. Execs. Assn. (life), Sigma Xi (life), Tau Beta Pi (life), Masons, Shriners. Republican. Baptist. Home: 6819 Brian Michael Ct Springfield VA 22153-1004

MEIKLEJOHN, ALVIN J., JR. state legislator, lawyer, accountant; b. Omaha, June 18, 1923; m. Lorraine J. Meiklejohn; children: Pamela Ann, Shelley Lou, Bruce Ian, Scott Alvin. BS, U. Denver, JD, 1951; LLD (hon.), U. No. Colo., 2000. Mem. Colo. state Senate from 19th Dist., 1976-96, chmn. com. edn.; mem. Edn. Commn. of States, 1981-96; chmn. Colo. Commn. on Ach. in Edn., 1995, mem., 1993-96, Jefferson Sch. Dist. No. R-1 Bd. Edn., 1971-77, pres., 1973-77; commr. Commn. on Uniform State Laws, 1988-96. Dir. Red Rocks C.C. Found., Aviation and Space Ctr. of the Rockies. Capt. U.S. Army, 1940—46, maj. USAF, 1947—51. Mem. Colo. Soc. CPA's, Arvada C. of C., Masons, Shriners, Transp. Lawyers Assn. (pres. 1972-73). Republican. Home: 7540 Kline Dr Arvada CO 80005-3732 Office: Jones & Keller PC 1625 Broadway Ste 1600 Denver CO 80202-4727 E-mail: ajmeiklejohn@joneskeller.com.

MEIKLEJOHN, MINDY JUNE (LORRAINE MEIKLEJOHN), political organizer, realtor; b. Staunton, Colo., June 9, 1929; d. Edward H. and Erna E. (Schwabe) Mindrup; m. Alvin J. Meiklejohn, Apr. 25, 1953; children: Pamela, Shelley, Bruce, Scott. Student, Ill. Bus. Coll., 1948, Red Rocks C.C., 1980-81. Pvt. sec. Ill. Liquor Commn., 1948-51, David M. Wilson, Ill. Sec. of State's Office, 1951-52; flight attendant Continental Airlines, 1952-53, pvt. sec. to mgr. flight svcs. office, 1953-54; orgnl. dir. Colo. Rep. Party, Denver, 1981-85, mem. Ctrl. Com., 1987—. Campaign coord. Hank Brown's Exploratory Campaign for Gov., 1985, mgr. Hank Brown for Congress, 1985-86; dep. campaign dir. Steve Schuck for Gov., 1985-86; vice chmn. 2d Congl. Ctrl. Com. Colo.; active campaigns; del., alt. to various county, state, dist. and nat. assemblies and convs.; Colo. chmn. Citizens for Am., 1987-96; realtor, sales assoc. Metro Brokers, Inc.; mem. polit. action com. Jefferson County Bd. Realtors; bd. dirs. Humphrey Meml. Park and Mus., 1996—, Sci. and Cultural Facilities Dist., 1989-94, Jefferson County chpt. Am. Cancer Soc., 1987-91, Jefferson Found., 1991-97; apptd. trustee Harry S. Truman scholarship Found., 1991; mem. Jefferson County Hist. Commn., Colo., 1974-82, pres., 1979; vol. Jefferson County Legal Aid Soc., 1970-74; vice chmn. Jefferson County Rep. Party, 1977-81, exec. com., 1987; vice chmn. Colo. State Rep. Party, 1981-85; chmn. Rep. Nat. Pilot Project on Volunteerism, 1981; mem. adv. coun. Peace Corps, 1982-84; sect. chmn. Jefferson County United Way Fund Drive; mem. exec. bd. Colo. Fedn. Rep. Women; pres. Operation Shelter, Inc., 1983-99; chair bd. dirs. Rocky Mountain Butterfly Consortium, 1996—; state chair Citizens for Am., 1987-96. Mem. Jefferson County Women's Rep. (edn. chmn. 1987-91). Home: 7540 Kline Dr Arvada CO 80005-3732

MEIKSIN, ZVI H. electrical engineering educator; b. 1926; BSEE, Israel Inst. Tech., Haifa, 1950, Dipl. Ing., 1951; MSEE, Carnegie Mellon U., 1953; PhDEE, U. Pitts., 1959. Registered profl. engr., Pa. Design engr. McGraw Edison, Cannonsburg, Pa., 1953-54; sr. project engr. Westinghouse Electric Corp., Pitts., 1956-59; prof. dept. elec. engring. U. Pitts., 1959-91; prof. emeritus, 1991—; pres. Transtek, Inc. (formerly Transcom. Co.), Pitts., 1989—. Cons. entr. 33 orgns. in U.S., Europe, 1959—. Author: Thin & Thick Films, 1976, Active Filter Design, 1990; co-author: Electronic Design, 1980, 84, Microprocessor Based Design, 1986; jour. referee profl. publs., 1970—; contbr. articles to profl. jours.; inventor, holder 6 patents in field. Fellow IEEE (award coms.); mem. Eta Kappa Nu, Sigma Xi. Office: Transtek Inc 35 Wilson St Ste 103 Pittsburgh PA 15223-1719 E-mail: meiksin@transtekcorp.com.

MEILAN, CELIA, food products executive; b. Bklyn., Jan. 21, 1920; d. Ventura Lorenzo and Susana (Prego) Meilan. Student, CCNY, 1943-46. Codes and ciphers translator security divsn. U.S. Censorship Office, N.Y.C., 1942-46; sec., treas. Albumina Supply Co., 1946-55; co-founder, co-owner, sec., treas., fin. officer Internat. Proteins Corp. (now AnimalFeeds Internat. Corp.), Clark, N.J., 1955-86, exec. v.p., 1986-92, pres., 1992-94, chair emeritus, bd. dirs., 1994—, v.p., co-owner, 1998—. Bd. dirs. Pesquera Taboquilla, Panama City, Panama, Inversiones Pesqueras S.A., British Virgin Islands; v.p., bd. dirs. Atlantic Shipers of Tex. Inc., Port Arthur, 1989; bd. dirs. Atlantic Shippers Inc., Morehead City, NC, Empacadora Nacional S.A., Panama City; exec. v.p., bd. dirs. AnimalFeeds Internat. Peru S.A., Lima; v.p., dir. AnimalFeeds, Internat., Santiago, Chile. Named One of Top 50 Women Bus. Owners, Working Woman Mag./Nat. Found. Women Bus. Owners, 1994; recipient, 1995. Mem.: Nat. Found. Women Bus. Owners, Spanish Benevolent Soc. (bd. dirs. 1955—62). Avocation: Avocations: travel, hand crafts, backgammon, puzzles. Office: AnimalFeeds Internat Corp 77 Brant Ave Ste 305 Clark NJ 07066-1540 Fax: 732-827-0325.

MEILMAN, EDWARD, physician; b. Boston, Apr. 6, 1915; s. Harry and Jennie (Sholofsky) M.; m. Rhoda Berman, Mar. 6, 1946. AB, Harvard U., 1936, MD, 1940. Intern Mt. Sinai Hosp., N.Y.C., 1940-42; resident Beth Israel Hosp., Boston, 1946-48, assoc. in med. and med. research, 1948-53; chmn. dept. medicine L.I. Jewish-Hillside Med. Center, New Hyde Park, N.Y., 1953-82, chmn. emeritus dept. medicine, 1982—. Prof. medicine SUNY, Stony Brook, 1971— Contbr. articles to profl. jours. Served with USAAF, 1942-46. Fellow N.Y. Acad. Medicine, N.Y. Acad. Scis.; mem. Am. Heart Assn. (fellow council clin. cardiology, council arteriosclerosis), Am. Fedn. Clin. Research, Harvey Soc., Am. Rheumatism Assn., Phi Beta Kappa, Alpha Omega Alpha. Clubs: Harvard (N.Y.C.); Harvard (L.I.). Democrat. Jewish. E-mail: emeilman@mindspring.com.

MEIMA, RALPH CHESTER, JR. retired diplomat, corporate executive; b. Chgo., Mar. 29, 1927; s. Ralph Chester and Grace Georgine (Larson) M.; children: Ralph Chester III, Stephen H.; m. Elizabeth B. Frazier, 1994. BA, U. Ams., Mexico City, 1952; MBA, Am. U., 1964. With Carborundum Co., Perth Amboy, 1952-53, Johns-Manville Corp., N.Y.C., 1953-58, Security Storage Co., Washington, 1958-61, Dept. of Commerce, 1961-68; joined U.S. Fgn. Svc., 1968; consul gen. Marseille, France, 1977-80; on loan export devel. cons. State of Md., 1980-82; pres. Atlantic Eastern Corp., 1982-87, Phoenix Internat. Mktg. Corp., 1987-89; pres., chief exec. officer FTI Inc., Annapolis, Md., 1989-95; pres. DERCO, Inc., Balt., 1995—2002. Govt. rels. iJET Travel Intelligence, Inc. Served with USN, 1945-46. With USN, 1945—46. Office: 900 Bestgate Rd Annapolis MD 21403 E-mail: rmeima@earthlink.net.

MEINCKE, DAVID LEE, obstetrician; b. Roanoke, Va., 1946; BS in Chemistry, Roanoke Coll., 1969; MD, Med. Coll. Va., 1973. Diplomate Am. Bd. Obstetrics & Gynecology. Resident in ob/gyn Med. Coll. Va., Richmond, 1973-76; pvt. practice, 1976—. Mem. Am. Coll. Obstetrics & Gynecology, Med. Soc. Va., Va. Obstetrics & Gynecology Soc. Office: Med Arts Bldg 3708 S Main St Ste B Blacksburg VA 24060-7007

MEINDERS, HILDRED MCCANTS, lawyer; b. Guthrie, Okla., Jan. 27, 1908; d. James Franklin and Maude Alberta (Putman) McCants; m. Wesley H.meinders,May 22, 1937 (dec.); children: Janet Ruth Charalampous, Don Wesley, Ann Hildred Heaton, Mary Joan Johnson. BS, U. Okla., 1932; JD, John B. Ogden Law Sch., Ardmore, Okla., 1941. Bar: Okla. 1942. Tchr. Carter County (Okla.) Schs., 1927-32; sec. County Agt./Carter County, 1932-36, U.S. Govt., 1936-60; pvt. law practice Garvin County, Okla., 1960—. County atty. Garvin County. Mem. AAUW, Order Eastern Star. Democrat. Methodist. Home: 405 N Chickasaw St Pauls Valley OK 73075-2405

MEINDL, JAMES DONALD, electrical engineering educator, administrator; b. Pitts., Apr. 20, 1933; s. Louis M. and Elizabeth F. (Steinhauser) M.; m. Frederica Ziegler, May 21, 1961; children: Peter James, Candace Ann. BS, Carnegie Mellon U., 1955, MS, 1956, PhD, 1958. Engr. Autonetics Co., Downey, Calif., 1957, Westinghouse Co., Pitts., 1958-59; head sect. microelectronics U.S. Army Electronics Command, Ft. Monmouth, N.J., 1959-62, chief br. semicondr. and microelectronics, 1962-65, dir. div. integrated electronics, 1965-67; assoc. prof. elec. engring. Stanford U., 1967-70, prof., 1970-84, John M. Fluke prof. elec. engring., 1984-86, assoc. dean research, 1984-86, dir. integrated circuits lab., 1969-84; co-founder Telesensory Systems Inc., 1971-84; dir. Electronics Labs., Stanford U., 1972-86, dir. Ctr. Integrated Systems, 1981-86; v.p. acad. affairs, provost Rensselaer Poly. Inst., Troy, N.Y., 1986-88, prof. sci. and engring., 1986-93, sr. v.p. acad. affairs, provost, 1988-93; Joseph M. Pettit Chair prof. microelectronics Ga. Inst. Tech., Atlanta, 1993—, dir. Microelectronics Rsch. Ctr., 1997—. Cons. to govt., industry. Author: Micropower Circuits, 1969; editor: Brief Lessons in High Technology, 1989; patentee integrated cir. field; contbr. numerous articles to profl. publs. Served to 1st lt. AUS, 1959-61. Recipient Arthur S. Flemming Commn. award Washington Jr. C. of C., 1967; J.J. Ebers award IEEE Electron Devices Soc., 1980, Univ. Rsch. award Semiconductor Industries Assn., 1999. Fellow IEEE (Solid State Circuits Coun. editor jour. 1966-71, Internat. Outstanding Paper ann. awards 1970, 75-78, Beatrice K. Winner award Internat. conf. 1988, solid State Circuits medal, 1989, Edn. medal 1990, Third Millenium medal 2000), AAAS, Am. Acad. Arts and Scis.; mem. AAUP, NAE, Am. Soc. Engr. Edn. (Benjamin Garver Lamme edal 1991), Electrochem. Soc., Biomed. Engring. Soc. (co-editor Annals of Biomed. Engring. 1976-80), Sigma Xi, Tau Beta Pi, Eta Kappa Nu, Phi Kappa Phi. Office: Ga Inst Tech Microelectronics Rsch Ctr 791 Atlantic Dr Atlanta GA 30332-0001

MEINDL, ROBERT JAMES, English language educator; b. Wausau, Wis., Sept. 17, 1936; s. George Martin and Adeline Emilie (Goetsch) M.; m. Victoria Lynn Chavez; children: Karin Rose, George Andrew, Damian Kurt, Erika Wittmer, Christopher Smith, Gabrielle Remelia. BS, U. Wis., 1958; MA, U. Conn., 1960; PhD, Tulane U., 1965; postdoctoral studies, U. Calif., Berkeley, 1967—68, Goethe Inst., Liblar, Germany, 1979, U. Cologne, Germany, 1970. Teaching asst. U. Conn., Storrs, 1958-60; teaching fellow Tulane U., 1960-62; lectr. U. Wis., Green Bay, 1963-65; from asst. to full prof. English Calif. State U., Sacramento, 1965—. Translator: Studies in John Gower, 1981; book rev. editor Studia Mystica Jour., 1984-89; contbr. numerous articles to profl. jours. With USNR, 1953-61. 79-96. Nat. Endowment for the Humanities fellow Stanford U., 1982. Mem. MLA, Medieval Acad. Am., Medieval Assn. of Pacific, Early English Text Soc., John Gower Soc., New Chaucer Soc. Home: 2301 Pennland Dr Sacramento CA 95825-0329 Office: Calif State U 6000 J St Sacramento CA 95819-2605

MEINE, ANDREA LYNN, artist, poet, writer; b. Defiance, Ohio, July 3, 1968; d. Frederick George Meine and Florence Sylvia Brown. Author: (poem) Fires of Sunset. Animal rights activist PETA, 1992. Avocations: drawing, drawing, drawing, drawing, drawing. Home: PO Box 427 Arivaca AZ 85601 Personal E-mail: andreameine@yahoo.com.

MEINEL, ADEN BAKER, optics scientist; b. Pasadena, Calif., Nov. 25, 1922; s. John G. and Gertrude (Baker) M.; m. Marjorie Steele Pettit, Sept. 5, 1944; children: Carolyn, Walter, Barbara, Elaine, Edward, Mary, David. AB, U. Calif., Berkeley, 1947, PhD, 1949; DSc (hon.), U. Ariz., 1990. Assoc. prof. Yerkes Obs., U. Chgo., Williams Bay, Wis., 1950-58; dir. Kitt Peak Nat. Obs., Tucson, 1958-61; prof. U. Ariz., 1961-85; dir. Steward Obs., 1962-66, Optical Scis. Ctr., Tucson, 1966-73; Disting. scientist Jet Propulsion Lab., Pasadena, 1985-92; ret., 1993. Regent Calif. Luth. Coll., 1961-71; cons. USAF Spl. Projects Office, 1965-80. Co-author: Applied Solar Energy, 1976, Sunsets, Twilights and Evening Skies, 1983. Recipient Warner prize Am. Astron. Soc., 1954, Van Blesbroeck award Astron. Soc. Pacific, 1990, NASA Exceptional Scientific Achievement medal, 1993; Aden B. Meinel bldg. U. Ariz., dedicated 1993 Fellow Am. Acad Arts and Scis., Optical Soc. Am. (pres. 1972-73, Adolph Lomb medal 1952, Ives medal 1980), Internat. Optical Engring. Soc. (Goddard award 1984, Kingslake medal and prize, 1993, Gold medal 1997). Home: 1600 Shoreline Dr Santa Barbara CA 93109-2024 E-mail: ameinel@earthlink.net.

MEINER, SUE ELLEN THOMPSON, gerontologist, nurse practitioner, nursing educator and researcher; b. Ironton, Mo., Oct. 24, 1943; d. Louis Raymond and Verna Mae Thompson; m. Robert Edward Meiner, Mar. 5, 1971; children: Diane Romeril, Suzanne Russell. AAS, Meramec C.C., 1970; BSN, St. Louis U., 1978, MSN, 1983; EdD, So. Ill. U., Edwardsville, 1991. RN, Mo.; cert. gerontol. nurse practitioner; cert. clin. specialist in gerontol. nursing. Staff RN St. Joseph's Hosp., St. Charles, Mo., 1976-78; nursing supr. Bethesda Gen. Hosp., St. Louis, 1975-76, 71-74; adult med. dir. Family Care Ctr.-Carondelet, 1978-79; program dir., lectr. Webster Coll./Bethesda Hosp., Webster Groves, 1979-82; diabetes clin. specialist Washington U. Sch. Medicine, St. Louis, 1982; chmn. dept. nursing, asst. prof. St. Louis C.C., 1983-88; vis. nurse assoc. St. Louis, 1970—71; chmn. dept. nursing, asst. prof. Barnes Hosp. Sch. Nursing, 1988-89; instr. U. Mo., St. Louis, 1989; assoc. prof. St. Charles County C.C., St. Peters, 1990-92, Deaconess Coll. of Nursing, 1991-93; patient care mgr. Deaconess Hosp., St. Louis, 1993-94; assoc. prof. Jewish Hosp. Coll. of Nursing and Allied Health, 1994-99; gerontol. nurse, rschr. Wash. U. Sch. Med., St. Louis, 1996-2000; asst. prof. nursing U. Nev., Coll. of Health Scis., Las Vegas, 2000—. Nat. dir. edn. Nat. Assn. Practical Nurse Edn. and Svc., Inc., St. Louis, 1984-86; mem. task force St. Louis Met. Hosp. Assn., 1987-88; mem. adv. com. Bd. Edn. Sch. Nursing, St. Louis, 1986-90; grant coord. Kellogg Found. Gerontology and Nursing, 1991-92; project dir. NIH Grant Washington U., St. Louis, 1996—2000; mem.

editorial bd. geriatric Nursing Journ., 1999-2002; legal nurse cons. Author and editor profl. books; contbr. articles to profl. jours. Chmn. bd. dirs. Creve Coeur Fire Protection Dist. Mo., 1984-89; vice chmn. Bd. Cen. St. Louis County Emergency Dispatch Svc., 1985-87; asst. leader Girl Scouts U.S., St. Louis, 1975; treas. Older Women's League, St. Louis, 1992-93. Recipient Woman of Worth award Gateway chpt. Older Women's League, 1993. Mem.: ANA, Mid.-Am. Congress on Aging, Am. Soc. of Aging, Nat. League for Nursing, Am. Nurses Found., Am. Coll. Nurse Practitioners, Am. Acad. Nurse Practitioners, Job's Daus. (guardian 1979—80), Order Ea. Star (chaplain 1970), Creve Coeur C. of C., Sigma Theta Tau (fin. chmn. 1984, archivist 1985—87, v.p.Zeta Kappa chpt., v.p. 2001—), Kappa Delta Pi, Sigma Phi Omega. Avocations: travel, reading. Home and Office: 3722 Violet Rose Ct Las Vegas NV 89147-7400 E-mail: sueellen.meiner@ccmail.nevada.edu., agingwell2002@msn.com. *Personal philosophy: From my earliest memories, I have established goals that were obtainable only through very hard work and perseverance. I always sought support and assistance from significant others as each goal was reached before setting another one. My life has been enriched by family and very dear friends. An important belief and practice has been to return the benefits of my education to my community and to be an advocate for those persons needing assistance. I hold a special place for support of all older adults.*

MEINERS, PHYLLIS BLOOM, publisher, training consultant, author; b. Boston, Nov. 8, 1940; d. Samuel Henry and Edith (Salvin) Bloom; m. William F. Meiners Jr.; 1 child, Hilary Cynthia Henri. BA, U. Calif., Berkeley, 1962; postgrad., MIT, 1971-72, Rockhurst Coll., 1980-83. Cert. fund raising exec. Dir. rsch. Harbridge House, Boston, 1964-70; rsch. assoc. MIT, Cambridge, 1970-71; advocate planner Urban Planning Aid, 1972-73; program adminstr. U. Hawaii, Honolulu, 1974-79, Mo. div. Community Devel., Kansas City, 1980—97; founder, pres. Corp. Resource Cons., Mo., 1982-95. Founder libr. corp. philanthropy Corp. Resource Ctr., 1988; founder, pres. CRC Publ. Co., 1994—. Mem. Nat. Com. of Responsive Philanthropy, Friends of Art, Kansas City; staff coord. Mayor Charles B. Wheeler Campaign; mem. Temple B'nai Jehudah; mem. steering com. Nat. Ctr. for Am. Indigenous Cultures at Line Creek; mem. Women's Pub. Svc. Network , Kansas City. Mem. Nat. Soc. Fundraising Execs., Greater Kansas City C. of C. (entrepreneurs coun.), Nat. Ctr. Black Philanthropy, Greater Kansas City Coun. Philanthropy, Native Ams. in Philanthropy, Native Am. Libr. Assn., Nat. Coun. Jewish Women, Pubs. Mktg. Assn. Democrat. Jewish. Avocations: fine arts, music. Office: PO Box 22583 Kansas City MO 64113-0583 E-mail: books@crcpub.com.

MEINERT, JOHN RAYMOND, investment banker, clothing manufacturing and retailing executive; b. White Cloud, Mich., Aug. 11, 1927; m. Joyce Macdonell, Nov. 5, 1955; children: Elizabeth Tinsman, Pamela Martin. Student, U. Mich., 1944-45; BS, Northwestern U., 1949. C.P.A., Ill., 1952. With Hart Schaffner & Marx/Hartmarx Corp., Chgo., 1950-90, exec. v.p., 1975-80, vice chmn., 1981-85, sr. vice chmn., 1985-86, chmn., 1987-90, chmn. emeritus, 1990—, also bd. dirs.; prin. investment banking J.H. Chapman Group, LLC, Rosemont, Ill., 1990—, chmn., 1995—. Bd. dirs. County Seat Stores, Inc., N.Y.C., 1998-99, The John Evans Club, BBB, Chgo. C.of C.; trustee Amalgamated Ins. Fund, 1980-90, Rotary Internat. Retirement Fund, 2000—; dir. Evanston Hosp., 1988-94, Clothing Mfrs. Assn., pres., 1982-87, chmn. 1987-90; instr. acctg. Northwestern U., 1949; faculty Lake Forest Grad. Sch. Mgmt., 1994-95; arbitrator Am. Arbitration Assn., 1993—. Chmn. bus. adv. coun. U. Ill., 1989-90; mem. Fin. Acctg. Stds. Adv. Coun., 1989-92, Chgo. Coun. Fgn. Rels., Sisters City Com.; mem. adv. coun. Northwestern U. Kellogg Grad. Sch. Recipient Alumni Merit award Northwestern U. Kellogg Grad. Sch., 1989; named Humanitarian of Yr., Five Hosp. Found., 1995. Mem. AICPA (v.p. 1985-86, bd. dirs. 1975-78, coun. 1971-93, trustee benevolent fund 1992-95, gold medal 1987), Ill. CPA Soc. (pub. svc. award 1996, pres. 1982-83, bd. dirs. 1966-68, 81-84, hon. award), Chicago-land C. of C. (bd. dirs.), Rotary (pres. Chgo. 1989-90, trustee found. 1991-95, asst. dist. gov. 1997-2000), Univ. Club, Execs. Club, Rolling Green Country Club. Presbyterian (elder). Home: 634 N Ironwood Dr Arlington Heights IL 60004-5818 Office: J H Chapman Group LLC 9700 W Higgins Rd Rosemont IL 60018-4796

MEINERT, WALTER, retired chemical company executive, consultant; b. Walcott, Iowa, May 18, 1922; s. Minnie and Theodore F. Meinert; m. Delores C. Mengel, Oct. 24, 1946; children: Susan Diane, Lawrence David, Walter T. Meinert Jr. BS, St. Ambrose U., Davenport, IA, 1943—47; MS, Inst. of Textile Tech., Charlottesville, VA, 1947—49. V.p. Emery Industries, Cincinnati, Ohio, 1949—80. Mem. Hamilton County Hosp. Commn., 1982—85, Bd. Trustees St. Francis-St. George Hosp., 1980—85. Lt. U.S. Navy, 1942—46, Wwii. Mem.: The Hidden Valley Golf Club. Home: 2885 Country Woods Lane Cincinnati OH 45248

MEINHARDT, VICKI R. communications executive, consultant; b. Topeka, Dec. 12, 1959; d. Sidney M. Meinhardt and Mary V. Moyer; m. Dylan W. Johnson, Sept. 20, 1986; children: Cameron, Connor, Callie. BA in Journalism and Mass Comm., BA in Polit. Sci. and Pub. Adminstrn., Kans. State U., 1984. Assoc. news dir. Sta. KMAN, Manhattan, Kans., 1984-86; reporter Sta. KFAB, Omaha, 1987-89; sr. staff aid Mayor City of Omaha, 1989-94; v.p. First Data Corp., Atlanta, 1994-99; owner Meinhardt Comms., Omaha, 1999—. Session mem. Presbyn. Ch. of the Master, Omaha, 1998-2001 bd. dirs. Planned Parenthood, Omaha, 1991. Recipient Silver Platter award Kans. chpt. Nat. Edn. Assn., 1985, 86, Spot News award AP, 1985, Crystal award The Communicator, 1997. Mem. Internat. Assn. Bus. Communicators (silver quill award 1996). Republican. Avocations: my family, church, scrapbooking.

MEINHOLD, CHARLES BOYD, health physicist; b. Boston, Nov. 1, 1934; s. Russell and Jane (Boyd) M.; m. Anne Elizabeth DuVally, Oct. 20, 1956; children: Anne Frances, Patricia Marie, Michael John, Peter Russell, Catherine Louise. BS in Physics, Providence Coll., 1956; postgrad., U. Rochester, 1956-57. Staff scientist health physics div. Brookhaven Nat. Lab., Upton, N.Y., 1957-72, head, sr. health physicist safety and environ. div., 1972-88, sr.scientist, div. head, 1988-91; sr. scientist radiol. sci. divsn. Dept. Advanced Tech., 1991-2001; pres. Nat. Coun. on Radiation Protection and Measurement, Bethesda, Md., 1991—2002; govt. scientist dept. of nat. security, 2001—; pres. emeritus Nat. Coun. on Radiation, 2002—. Mem. Internat. Commn. on Radiol. Protection, 1978-2001, vice chmn., 1992-2001; mem. Nat. Commn. on Radiol. Protection, 1977—. Pres. South Haven Bd. Edn., Brookhaven, N.Y., 1965-87. Named Hon. Prof., China Inst. Atomic Energy, 1995, China Inst. Radiation Protection, 1997. Fellow Health Physics Soc. (pres. 1980-81); mem. Internat. Radiation Protection Assn. (v.p. 1988-92, pres. 1992-96). Roman Catholic. Avocations: woodworking, sailing. Home: 41 Old South Country Rd Brookhaven NY 11719-9526 Office: Brookhaven Nat Lab Bldg 197D Upton NY 11973-5000 E-mail: cbmeinhold@aol.com.

MEINIG, DONALD WILLIAM, geography educator; b. Palouse, Wash., Nov. 1, 1924; s William August and Annie (Malsed) M.; m. Lee McAuliffe, June 29, 1946; children: Laurel, Kristin, Lee. BS, Georgetown U., 1948; MA, U. Wash., 1950, PhD, 1953; DHL (hon.), Syracuse U., 1994. From asst. prof. to assoc. prof. U. Utah, Salt Lake City, 1950-59; assoc. prof. geography Syracuse U., N.Y., 1959-73, Maxwell prof. geography, 1973-89, Maxwell rsch. prof., 1990—. Lectr. St. Andrews U., Scotland, 1973, Charles Homer Haskins lectr. ACLS, 1992; vis. prof. Hebrew U., Jerusalem, 1974; adv. editor Wadsworth Pub. Co., 1957-61, Harper & Row, N.Y.C., 1965-83; chief editl. cons. Nat. Geog. Soc., Washington, 1982-88; councilor Am. Geog. Soc., 1993-96. Author: On the Margins of the Good Earth, 1962, The Great Columbia Plain, 1968, Imperial Texas, 1969, Southwest, 1971, The Shaping of America, Vol. 1: Atlantic America 1492-1800, 1986, Vol. 2: Continental America 1800-1867, 1993, Vol. 3: Transcontinental America 1850-1915, 1998; editor: The Interpretation of Ordinary Landscapes, 1979. Mem. N.Y. Council for Humanities, 1979-86. Served to 2d lt. U.S. Army, 1943-46. Recipient Emil and Kathleen Sick award in Western History, 1968, award of Merit Seattle Hist. Soc., 1968, award of Merit Am. Assn. State and Local History, 1969, Summerfield G. Roberts award Sons Republic of Tex., 1969, Faculty Enrichment award Can Embassy, 1980, Master Tchr. award Nat. Coun. for Geog. Edn., 1986, Charles P. Daly medal Am. Geog. Soc., 1986; Fulbright rsch. scholar U. Adelaide, 1958; Guggenheim fellow, 1966-67, NEH fellow, 1987-88. Fellow Brit. Acad. (corr.); mem. Assn. Am. Geographers (councilor 1965-67, Meritorious Contbn. award), Am. Antiquarian Soc. Office: Syracuse U Dept Geography Syracuse NY 13244-0001

MEININGER, ERIC THOMAS, pediatrician, internist; b. Dearborn, Mich., Sept. 8, 1970; s. Thomas Alexander and Nancy Katherine (Grace) M. BS, U. Mich., 1992, MD, 1995. Diplomate Am. Bd. Pediats. Resident U. Minn., Mpls., 1995-99, fellow in adolescent medicine, 1999—. Mem. Am. Acad. Pediat., AMA, Soc. Adolescent Medicine, Gay and Lesbian Med. Assn. Home: 1718 Clinton Ave Apt 6 Minneapolis MN 55404-1856 Office: University Gateway 200 Oak St SE Ste 260 Minneapolis MN 55455-2016 E-mail: meininger@iname.com.

MEINKE, ALAN KURT, surgeon; b. Eaton Rapids, Mich., May 25, 1952; s. Richard Keydel and Kaarina Elli (Ranta) M.; m. Lori Anne Alley, Sept., 1985; children: Christopher Richard, Mary Elizabeth, William Alan. BA, Albion (Mich.) Coll., 1974; MD, Wayne State U., 1978. Intern Mayo Clinic, Rochester, Minn., 1978, resident gen. surgery, 1978-82, chief resident, 1982-83; sr. attending physician, dir. surg. edn. Norwalk (Conn.) Hosp., 1983—; faculty surg. residency program Norwalk Hosp.-Yale U. Sch. Medicine, 1983—; ptnr. Surg. Assocs., Westport, Conn., 1985—. Med. dir. Wilton Vol. Ambulance Corp., 1983-93; mem. med. adv. com. Fairfield-Westchester Crohn's and Colitis Found., 1992—. Contbr. articles to profl. jours. Active med. sect. United Way of Westport and Weston, 1989-94; bd. dirs. Interfaith Housing Assn., Westport, 1994—. Fellow ACS (credentials com. Conn. chpt. 1991—), Priestly Soc., Soc. Internat. de Chirurgie; mem. AMA, Internat. Microsurg. Soc., Soc. Am. Gastrointestinal Endoscopic Surgeons, Soc. Surgery of Alementry Tract, Am. Coll. Sports Medicine, Conn. Med. Soc., Norwalk Med. Soc., Fairfield County Med. Soc., Phi Beta Kappa. Office: Surg Assocs PC Kings Hwy N Westport CT 06880

MEINKE, PETER THOMAS, scientist; b. Boonton, N.J., Apr. 7, 1960; s. James Peter and Jeanne M.; m. Rosemary Vittoria Sampogna, Aug. 8, 1988. BS, Eckerd Coll., 1982; PhD, Syracuse U., 1987. Dir. Merck Rsch. Labs., Rahway, N.J., 1989—. Postdoctoral fellow Columbia U., N.Y.C., 1987-89. Office: Merck Rsch Labs PO Box 2000 R800-B101 Rahway NJ 07065-0900 Fax: 732-594-9556. E-mail: peter_meinke@merck.com.

MEINTSMA, PETER EVANS, history and political science educator; b. Maple Lake, Minn., Apr. 1, 1928; s. Peter and Hazel Irene (Davis) M.; m. Senora LaRea Strouse, Dec. 10, 1955; children: Kevin Jon, Kurt Robert. MA, U. Minn., 1964. Instr. Northwestern Coll., Mpls., 1958-62, 64-66, U. Wis., Superior, 1963-64; prof. Anoka Ramsey C.C., Coon Rapids, Minn., 1966—2001. Mayor City of Crystal, Minn., 1974-84, 91—; chmn. Met. Waste Control Commn., St. Paul, 1984-88; bd. mem. Assn. Met. Municipalities, 1999—; mem. steering com. cmty. and econ. devel. Nat. League of Cities. Recipient Cert. for Reflective Leadership Humphrey Inst., 1980; named Outstanding Educator of Am., 1971. Avocations: gardening, biking, music.

MEINWALD, JERROLD, chemist, educator; b. Bklyn., Jan. 16, 1927; s. Herman and Sophie (Baskind) M.; m. Yvonne Chu, June 25, 1955 (div. 1979); children: Constance Chu, Pamela Joan; m. Charlotte Greenspan, Sept. 7, 1980; 1 child, Julia Eve. PhB, U. Chgo., 1947, BS, 1948; MA, Harvard, 1950, PhD, 1952, U. Göteborg, 1989. Mem. faculty Cornell U., 1952-72, 73—, Goldwin Smith prof. chemistry, 1980—, mem. sci. directing group Inst. Rsch. Chem. Ecology, 1992—; rsch. dir. Internat. Centre Insect Physiology and Ecology, Nairobi, 1970-77; A. Mellon Term prof., 1992-95; prof. chemistry U. Calif. at San Diego, 1972-73. Chem. cons. Schering-Plough Rsch. Inst., 1957-99, Procter & Gamble Pharms., 1958-95, Cambridge Neurosci. Rsch., 1988-92; vis. prof. Rockefeller U., 1970, Harvard Med. Sch., 1997; Camille and Henry Dreyfus Disting. scholar Mt. Holyoke Coll., 1981, Bryn Mawr Coll., 1983, Dartmouth Coll., 1996; Kolthoff lectr. U. Minn., 1985; Beckman lectr. Calif. Inst. Tech., 1986; Swiss "Troisième Cycle" Lectr., 1986; Russell Marker lectr. Pa. State U., 1987; mem. vis. com. chemistry Brookhaven Nat. Lab., 1969-72, chmn., 1972; mem. med. A chemistry study sect. NIH, 1963-67, chmn., 1965-67; mem. adv. bd. Petroleum Rsch. Found., 1971-73; mem. adv. coun. chemistry dept. Princeton U., 1978-83 ; mem. adv. bd. Rsch. Corp., 1978-83; mem. adv. bd. chemistry div. NSF, 1979-83; organizing chmn. Sino-Am. Symposium on Chemistry of Natural Products, Shanghai, 1980; mem. adv. bd. A.P. Sloan Found., 1985-91; Frontiers of Rsch. lectr. Coun. Chem. Rsch., 1987; mem. sci. adv. bd. Agridyne Corp., 1989-93; adv. com. chem. ecology Max-Planck Soc., 1994-96, Nat. Inst. Sericulture and Entomological Scis., Tsukuba, Japan, 1997-2001; adv. bd. Xerces Soc., 1995—; adv. com. Biosphere 2, 1999—; Carlton Coll. Convocation, 1993; Mary Aldridge lectr., American U., 1993; K. Pfister lectr. MIT, 1992, Hilldale lectr. U. Wis., 1991, Nat. Undergrad. Rsch. Symposium, Plenary lectr., Mpls., 1992; UNOCAL lectr. Calif. State U., Long Beach, 1992; Max T. Rogers lectr. Mich. State U., 1994; Jean Day lectr. Rutgers U., 1994, Max T. Rogers lectr., Mich. State U., 1994, Disting. Grad. Sch. lectr. U. Md., 1994. Merck lectr. Lafayette Coll.; plenary lectr. 3d Pan Am. Chem. Congress; Inaugural Paul G. Gassman lectr. Canisius Coll., 1996, Disting. Sci. Lectr. Bard Coll., 1996, hon. visiting sci., Taiwan, 1997, Gassman lectr. U. Minn., 1999, Partners in Sci. lectr., Rsch Corp., 2000, Iscol award lectr., Cornell U., 2000, Chemistry as a life sci. X Symposium, 2000, IUPAC plenary lectr., Brazil, 2000, W.S. Johnson Symposium, Stanford, 2000, Berzelius Days plenary lectr., Stockholm, 2001, Nat. ACS Organic Symposium lectr., 2001, others; mem. internat. sci. com. Programa Brasileiro de Ecologia Molecular/Amazonia, 1997—; Grandpierre lectr. Columbia U., 1998; sci. adv. bd. Inst. Chemistry & Biochemistry, Czechoslovak Acad. Sci., 1999—. Mem. bd. editors Jour. Organic Chemistry, 1962-66, Organic Reactions, 1968-78, Organic Synthesis, 1968-72, Jour. Chem. Ecology, 1974—, Insect Sci., 1979-90, Current Organic Chemistry, 1999—; contbr. articles to profl. jours. Recipient Tyler Environ. Achievement prize U. So. Calif., 1990, Gustavus J. Esselen award for Chemistry in the Pub. Interest, 1991, Heyrovsky medal Acad. Scis. of the Czech Rep., 1996, Pioneer's award Am. Inst. Chemists, 1997; Sloan fellow, 1958-62, Guggenheim fellow,, 1960-61,76-77, spl. postdoctoral fellow NIH, 1967-68, fellow Japan Soc. Promotion of Sci., 1983, Ctr. for Advanced Study in Behavioral Sci., 1990-91; Fogarty internat. scholar NIH, 1983-85; Bert L. and Natalie K. Vallee Found., Inc. fellow, 1997. Mem. NAS (exch. scholar 1987), AAAS, Am. Acad. Arts and Scis. (coun. 1999—), Am. Philos. Soc., Am. Chem. Soc. (chmn. organic divsn. 1969, E Guenther award 1985, Disting. Scientist award Kalamazoo sect. 1985, A.C. Cope Scholar award 1989), Internat. Soc. Chem. Ecology (pres. 1988, Silver medal 1991), Phi Beta Kappa, Sigma Xi (nat. lectr. 1965, 75, 92-94). Office: Cornell U Dept Chemistry/Chem Biology Baker Lab Ithaca NY 14853-1301 E-mail: circe@cornell.edu.

MEIRELLES, RICARDO MARTINS DA ROCHA, endocrinologist; b. Sao Paolo, Brazil, Dec. 17, 1946; s. Walter and Lobelia (Martins de Rocha) M.; m. Lucia Maria de Castro Noronha, Apr. 28, 1973; 1 child, Tatiana Noronha de Meirelles. Degree in medicine, Fed. U. Rio de Janeiro, 1971. Coord. dept. nutrition and dietetics Brazilian Beneficient Rehab. Assn., Rio de Janeiro, 1972-73; staff endocrinologist Nat. Inst. Med. Care of Social Welfare, 1976-89, State Inst. Diabetes and Endocrinology, Rio de Janeiro, 1976-90, dir., 1990—; assoc. prof. endocrinology Cath. U., 1981—. Dir. 18th Brazilian Congress of Endocrinology, Rio de Janeiro, 1986-88; cons. endocrinology Financier of Studies and Projects, Brazil, 1993—. Editor: Clinical Endocrinology, 1988; co-editor Brazilian Archives of Endocrinology and Metabolism, 1991—. Cultural attache Carlos Chagas Acad. Ctr., Rio de Janeiro, 1967-68; mem. ethical commn. Regional Coun. Medicine, Rio de Janeiro, 1985-87; del. 2nd Mcpl. Health Conf., Rio de Janeiro, 1993. Recipient Citation, Gov. of State of Rio de Janeiro, 1982. Mem. Brazilian Soc. Endocrinology and Metabolism (regional pres. 1984-86, nat. v.p. 1988-90), Brazilian Soc. for Study of Obesity (v.p. 1990-92), Endocrine Soc. (educator). Avocations: theater, music, reading, movies, computers. E-mail: rmeirelles@openlink.com.br.

MEIRING, LINDA JEAN, communications executive; b. Mpls., Mar. 16, 1963; d. Philip William Kirchner and Margaret Ann Vnuk; m. Michael Wayne Meiring, Sept. 10, 1994. BA in Journalism, U. Minn., 1994. Ops. supr. United Parcel Svc., Mpls., 1984-88, employee comm. supr., 1988-91, employee comm. mgr. Atlanta, 1991-93, Toronto, Ont., Can., 1993-94, BellSouth Corp., Atlanta, 1994-95, employee comms. dir., 1995—. Mem. adv. bd. comms. dept. Kennesaw (Ga.) State U., 1999—. Mem. Internat. Assn. Bus. Communicators. Avocations: step aerobics, holiday crafts, waterskiing, travel. Office: BellSouth Corp 1155 Peachtree St NE Rm 19g03 Atlanta GA 30309-7629

MEIROWITZ, CLAIRE CECILE, publishing executive; b. Frankfurt, Fed. Republic Germany, Jan. 14, 1934; came to U.S., 1939; d. Karl and Margot (Herrmann) Bier; m. Richard Meirowitz, Sept. 12, 1954 (div., July, 1969); children: Diane, Laura, Linda; m. Joseph Spiegel, Apr. 20, 1975. AA, Nassau C.C., 1971; BA magna cum laude, Hofstra U., 1976; postgrad., N.Y. Inst. Tech., 1987-90. Pres., owner, editor, writer, pub. rels. and mktg. cons. Profl. Editing Svcs., Babylon, N.Y., 1972-76, 92—; editl. asst. United Tech. Publs., Garden City, 1976-77; publs. assoc. N.Y. Inst. Tech., Old Westbury, 1977-79; asst. dir. coll. rels., dir. publs. SUNY, 1979-87, dir. cmty. rels. and publs., 1987-92. Pres. SUNY Coun. for Univ. Affairs and Devel., 1987-89; cons. Guarino Graphics, Greenville, N.Y., 1985-92, editor, copywriter, 1986-92. Manuscript editor Jour. of Collective Negotiations in Pub. Sector, 1972-91, editr., 1991—. Jour. of Individual Employment Rights, 1992—; editor art catalog South Africa/South Bronx, 1981 (art excellence award 1982); author: New Student Prospectus, The College at Old Westbury, 1979, Labor-Management Relations Among Government Workers, 1983; co-editor: Strategies for Impasse Resolution, 1992; editor Alzheimer's Assn. L.I. chpt. newsletter; contbr. articles to profl. jours. V.p., treas., sec., Taxpayers Edn. Assn., Hicksville, N.Y., 1962-68; mem. The Nature Conservancy, Cold Spring Harbor, N.Y., 1980-91; tutor Lit. Vols. Am. Suffolk County Chpt., 1996-99; newsletter editor Babylon Breast Cancer Coalition, 1997—, The Active Retiree, United Univ. Professions, 1999-2002. Recipient Excellence in Profl. Svc. award SUNY, Albany, 1987, Disting. Svc. award SUNY Coun. Univ. Affairs, 1989, award for excellence in communications SUNY Westbury Alumni Assn., 1992, award for disting. leadership L.I. Women's Coun. for Equal Edn., Employment and Tng., 1992, award for newsletter excellence N.Y. State United Tchrs., 2001. Mem. L.I. Communicators Assn., Internat. Assn. of Bus. Communicators (steering com., sec. L.I. Women's Coun. 1990-99), Babylon Village Womens Club, Babylon Bus. and Profl. Women's Assn. Democrat. Jewish. Avocation: computers. Home: 167 Cadman Ave Babylon NY 11702-1607 E-mail: clair-m@worldnet.att.net.

MEISBURG, JOHN MARSHALL, JR. lawyer; b. Louisville, Sept. 14, 1946; s. Jack M. and Marion (Lucas) M.; m. Denise Beth Eanett, Aug. 16, 1980; children: Rachel Michelle, John III, Micah Gabriel. AB, U. Ky., 1968, JD, 1971. Bar: Ky. 1971, Va. 1978, D.C. 1978. Law clk. U.S. Dist. Ct., Louisville, 1971-73; trial atty. U.S. EEOC, Atlanta, 1973-75, sr. trial atty. Miami, Fla., 1979-82; atty. U.S. Dept. Justice, Washington, 1975-77; subcom. counsel, legis. aide U.S. Congressman John B. Breckinridge, 1977-78; pvt. practice, 1978-79; gen. atty. U.S. Office of Spl. Counsel, 1983-91; sr. atty. FDIC, Orlando, Fla., 1991—. Producer The Electric Ch., 1988-90. Pres. Seneca Chase Homeowner's Assn., 1987; bd. dirs. Christian Conciliation Svc., 1984-85; chmn. Virginians United for Quality Edn. 1990—. Mem. ABA, Fed. Bar Assn. (bd. dirs.), Lake Braddock Community Assn. (bd. dirs. 1985-86). Office: US Office of Spl Counsel 1120 Vermont Ave NW Ste 1100 Washington DC 20005-3523

MEISCH, LYNN ANN, anthropologist, educator; b. Mpls., Feb. 17, 1945; d. Francis Roman Meisch and Elaine Agnes Hanson. BA in History, Reed Coll., 1968; MA in Humanities, San Francisco State Coll., 1973; MA in Anthropology, Stanford U., 1990, PhD in Anthropology, 1997. Freelance photographer, 1973—; tour and trekking guide South Am., 1978—; textile cons. U.S. Agy. for Internat. Devel., Ecuador, 1985-86; assoc. prof. anthropology St. Mary's Coll., Moraga, Calif., 1997—. Cons. The Textile Mus., Washington, 1988—; mem. textile arts coun. de Young Mus., San Francisco, 1996—; cons., on-camera narrator Pub. TV, 1997, Andean Entrepreneurs: Otavalo Merchants in the Global Arena, 2002. Author: A Traveler's Guide to El Dorado and the Inca Empire, 1977, Otavalo: Weaving, Costume and the Market, 1987, Costume and Identity in Highland Ecuador, 1998; editor (mus. catalog) Traditional Textiles of the Andes: Life and Cloth in the Highland, 1997. Mem. Friends of Ethnic Art, San Francisco, 1987—, bd. dirs., 1987-93; pres., founder Fundacion Jatari: Andean Edn. and Rsch. Found., San Francisco, 1980—. Fulbright fellow, 1977-79, 96; grantee NSF, 1992-95, Wenner-Gren Found. for Anthropol. Rsch., 1992-93; Stanford Ctr. on Conflict and Negotiation fellow, 1997. Mem. Soc. L.Am. Anthropology (co-chmn. human rights com. 1998—), Am. Anthropol. Assn., L.Am. Studies Assn. Avocations: Andean textiles, bead collecting, music. Home: 428 Westcliffe Circle Walnut Creek CA 94597 Office: 428 Westcliffe Cir Walnut Creek CA 94597-3211 E-mail: lmeisch@stmarys-ca.edu., lynnmeis@aol.com.

MEISEL, ALAN, law educator; b. Newark, Dec. 24, 1946; s. Stanley and Beatrice (Katz) M.; m. Linda S. Serody, Mar. 6, 1982; children: Matthew, Julia. BA, Yale U., 1968, JD, 1972. Bar: Conn. 1972, Pa. 1973, U.S. Dist. Ct. Conn. 1972, U.S. Dist. Ct. (we. dist.) Pa. 1973, U.S. Ct. Appeals (3d cir.) 1985. Assoc. Goldstein & Peck, P.C., Bridgeport, Conn., 1972-73; prof. psychiatry U. Pitts., 1973—, prof. law, 1976—, Dickie, McCamey Chilcote prof. bioethics/law and psychiatry, 1995—, dir. Ctr. for Med. Ethics, 1986—. Asst. dir. for legal studies Pres.'s Commn. for Study of Ethical Problems in Medicine and Biomed. and Behaviorial Rsch., Washington, 1982; mem. ethics working group Presdl. Task Force on Healthcare Reform, 1993; mem. adv. coun. Nat. Heart, Lung and Blood Instit., 1998—. Author: The Right to Die, 1989, 2d edit., 1995; co-author: Informed Consent: A Study of Decision Making in Psychiatry, 1984, Informed Consent: Legal Theory and Clinical Practice, 1987; contbr. articles to legal and med. jours. Grantee NIMH, grantee Pres.'s Commn. for Study of Ethical Problems in Medicine and Biomed. and Behavioral Research, 1981-82, Founds. Fund for Research in Psychiatry grantee, 1979-82, Legal Services Corp. grantee, 1985-87; fellow Hastings Ctr.; award for The Right to Die Am. Assn. Publs., 1989. Office: U Pitts Sch Law Pittsburgh PA 15260

MEISEL, DAN, chemist; b. Tel Aviv, July 4, 1943; s. Arie and Mariasha Miriam (Ribak) M.; m. Osnat Meisel, Dec. 30, 1965; children: Einat, Omer. BSc, Hebrew U., 1967, MSc, 1969, PhD, 1974. Dir. radiation lab., prof. chemistry U. Notre Dame, Ind., 1998—. Adv. bd.: Jour. Phys. Chem., 1993—2002; editor: Photochem. Energy Conversion, 1989, Semiconductors Nanoclusters, 1997. Mem. AAAS, Am. Chem. Soc., Am. Nuclear Soc. Office: U Notre Dame Radiation Lab Notre Dame IN 46556-0579 E-mail: dani@nd.edu.

MEISEL, GEORGE VINCENT, lawyer; b. St. Louis, Sept. 24, 1933; s. Leo Otto and Margaret (Duggan) M.; m. Joy C. Cassin, May 18, 1963 BS summa cum laude, St. Louis U., 1956, JD cum laude, 1958. Bar: Mo. 1958. Assoc. Grand Peper & Martin, St. Louis, 1961-64, ptnr., 1965; jr. ptnr. Bryan Cave McPheeters & McRoberts, St. Louis, 1966-69; ptnr. Bryan Cave, LLP, 1970-2000, of counsel, 2000—. Served to 1st lt. USAF, 1958-61 Mem. ABA, Bar Assn. Met. St. Louis, Mo. Bar Assn. Clubs: Saint Louis, Mo. Athletic (St. Louis). Roman Catholic. Home: 2029 S Warson Rd Saint Louis MO 63124-1151 E-mail: gvmeisel@bryancavellp.com.

MEISEL, JOHN, political scientist; b. Vienna, Austria, Oct. 23, 1923; s. Fryda and Ann M. BA, U. Toronto, 1948, MA, 1950; PhD in Polit. Sci., London Sch. Econs., 1959; LLD, Brock U., 1983, U. Guelph, 1985, Carleton U., 1990, U. Toronto, 1993, Queen's U., 1996, U. Regina, 1999, U. Calgary, 2000; DU (hon.), U. Ottawa, 1983; D of Social Scis. (hon.), Laval U., 1988; LittD (hon.), U. Waterloo, 1998. Head dept. polit. studies Queen's U., Kingston, Ont., Can., 1963-67, Hardy prof. polit. sci. Can., 1963-80, Sir Edward Peacock prof. polit. sci. Can., 1983-93, prof. emeritus Can. Former chmn. Can. Radio-TV and Telecomms. Commn.; moderator symposia on finding common grounds for polit. issues confronting Yugoslavia, UN, Vienna, 1995. Author: The Canadian General Election of 1957, 1962, Papers on the 1962 Election, 1964, Ethnic Relations in Canadian Voluntary Associations, 1972, Working Papers on Canadian Politics, 1975; editor: Internat. Polit. Sci. Rev., 1979-95, (with Jean Laponce) Debating the Constitution/Débat sur la constitution, 1994. Decorated companion Order of Can.; recipient Killam award Can Coun., 1968-73; sr. rsch. fellow Ctr. for the Study of Democracy Queens U. Fellow Royal Soc. Can. (pres. 1992-95); mem. Rideau Club (Ottawa), Univ. Club (Toronto). Home: Colimaison Tichborne ON Canada K0H 2V0 Office: Queen's U Kingston ON Canada K7L 3N6

MEISEL, MARTIN, English and comparative literature educator; b. N.Y.C., Mar. 22, 1931; s. Joseph and Sally (Rössler) Mörsel; m. Martha Sarah Winkley, Dec. 22, 1957; children— Maude Frances, Andrew Avram, Joseph Stoddard AB, Queens Coll., 1952; MA, Princeton U., 1957, PhD, 1960; postgrad., U. Rome, 1959. Instr. English Rutgers U., New Brunswick, N.J.,

1957-58; instr., asst. prof., assoc. prof. Dartmouth Coll., Hanover, N.H., 1959-65; prof. English U. Wis., Madison, 1965-68; prof. English and comparative lit. Columbia U., N.Y.C., 1968—, Brander Matthews prof. dramatic lit., 1987—, chmn. dept., 1980-83, 99-01, acting v.p. arts and scis., 1986-87, v.p. arts and scis., 1989-93. Trustee Columbia U. Press, 1990-94. Author: Shaw and the 19th Century Theater, 1963, Realizations: Narrative, Pictorial, and Theatrical Arts in 19th Century England (George Freedley Meml. award Theater Libr. Assn. 1984, Barnard Hewitt award Am. Theatre Assn. 1984), 1983; mem. editorial and adv. bds. Jour. Victorian Studies, PMLA, Jour. Contemporary Lit., Bull. Rsch. in the Humanities, 19th Century Contexts. Served with U.S. Army, 1954-56 Fellow Guggenheim Found., 1963-64, 1987-88, Am. Council of Learned Socs., 1970-71, Inst. for Advanced Studies in the Humanities, Edinburgh, 1977, Huntington Library and Art Gallery, 1978, 80, 83, Nat. Humanities Ctr., 1983-84, Wilson Ctr., Smithsonian Instn., 1987-88. Mem. MLA, Acad. Lit. Studies, Am. Soc. Theatre Rsch., Century Assn. Home: 18 Bacon Hill Rd Pleasantville NY 10570-3502 Office: Columbia U 611 Philosophy Hall New York NY 10027 E-mail: mm28@columbia.edu.

MEISEL, PERRY, English educator; b. Shreveport, La., Jan. 26, 1949; s. I.S. and Rebecca (Abramson) M. BA, Yale U., 1970, MPhil, 1973, PhD, 1975. Asst. prof. English NYU, N.Y.C., 1975-81, assoc. prof. English, 1981-87, prof. English, 1987—. Author: Thomas Hardy, 1972, The Absent Father, 1980, The Myth of the Modern, 1987, The Cowboy and the Dandy, 1998; co-editor: Bloomsbury/Freud, 1985; editor: Freud, 1981. Mem. MLA, AAUP, PEN. Office: NYU Dept English 19 University Pl New York NY 10003-4556

MEISELAS, SUSAN CLAY, photographer; b. Balt., June 21, 1948; d. Leonard and Murrayl (Groh) M. BA, Sarah Lawrence Coll., 1970; EdM, Harvard U., 1971; DFA (hon.), Parsons Sch./New Sch., N.Y.C., 1988, Art Inst. of Boston, 1996, Trinity Coll., Hartford, 1999. Photographic cons. Community Resources Inst., N.Y.C., 1972-74; artist-in-residence S.C. Arts Commn., 1974-75; photography tchr. New Sch., N.Y.C., 1975; free-lance photographer Magnum Photos, 1976—, v.p., 1986-91. Author: Carnival Strippers, 1976, Nicaragua, 1981, Kurdistan: I the Shadow of History, 1997, Pandora's Box, 2001; co-editor: El Salvador, 1983; editor: Chile from Within, 1991; editor Learn to See, 1974; co-dir.: (film) Living at Risk, 1985, Pictures from a Revolution, 1991. Recipient Robert Capa gold medal Overseas Press Club, 1979, Leica award of excellence New Sch., 1981, Photojournalist of Yr. award Am. Soc. Mag. Photographers, 1981, award Nat Endowment for Arts, 1987, Hasselblad Found., 1994, Maria Moors Cabot prize Columbia U., 1994; MacArthur fellow, 1992. Office: Magnum Photos Inc 151 W 25th St New York NY 10001-7204 E-mail: susan@magnumphotos.com.

MEISELMAN, ALYSON, lawyer, mediator/arbitrator; b. Washington, Jan. 24, 1951; BA, U. Md., 1973; JD, Potomac Sch. Law, Washington, 1979. Bar: U.S. Dist. Ct. Md. 1981, Md. 1981, U.S. Supreme Ct. 1993, U.S. Ct. Appeals (4th cir.) 1994. Pvt. practice, Frederick, Md., 1981-84, Rockville, 1986-87, 92—; assoc. Alan D. Massengill, PA, Gaithersburg, 1984-86; prin. Haspel & Meiselman, Chartered, Rockville, 1987-92. Mem. ABA, ATLA, Md. Bar Assn., Bar Assn. Montgomery County, Nat. Assn. Women Lawyers, Harry Benjamin Internat. Gender Dysphoria Assn., Nat. Lesbian and Gay Law Assn., Women's Bar Assn., Harry Benjamin Internat. Gender Dysphoria Assn., Inc. Office: 14400 Lake Winds Way North Potomac MD 20878-4309 E-mail: famlaw@his.com.

MEISELMAN, DAVID ISRAEL, economics educator; b. Boston, May 21, 1924; s. Samuel and Sarah (Bovarnick) M.; m. Winifred Charm, Jan. 24, 1966; children: Ellen, Nina, Samuel Adam. AB, Boston U., 1947; MA, U. Chgo., 1951, PhD, 1961. Instr. Ill. Inst. Tech., Chgo., 1952-55; lectr. econs. CCNY, 1957-58; asst. prof. econs. U. Chgo., 1958-62; economist Office Sec. Treasury, Washington, 1962-63; sr. economist com. on banking and currency U.S. Ho. of Reps., 1963; lectr. polit. economy Johns Hopkins U., 1963-64; sr. economist OAS Inter-Am. Devel. Bank Fiscal Mission to Peru, 1964; sr. economist, asso. editor Nat. Banking Rev., Office Comptroller Currency, U.S. Treasury Dept., Washington, 1964-66; Frederick R. Bigelow prof. econs., dir. bur. econ. studies Macalester Coll., St. Paul, 1966-71, acting chmn. dept. econs., 1968-69; prof. econs., dir. No. Va. grad. econs. program Va. Poly. Inst. and State U., 1971—, assoc. dir. Ctr. for Study Futures and Options, 1989—. Adj. scholar Am. Enterprise Inst. for Pub. Policy Rsch., 1976— , Heritage Fedn., Cato Inst.; bd. dirs. Visa Money Fund; fin. acctg. Standards Adv. Coun., 1983-86, Commodities Futures Trading Commn., Fin. Products Adv. Com., 1985—; sr. cons. IBRD, 1966; econ. cons. Sec. Treasury, 1969-77, Rep. Senatorial Campaign Com., 1974, Planning Rsch. Corp., 1970, ICC, 1972, Commodity Futures Trading Commn., 1975, Labor Dept., 1976; cons. U.S. Treasury, 1981-82, Coopers & Lybrand, 1976, Bache Halsey Stuart, Inc., 1976-77, Wainwright Securities, Inc., 1977-78, Law and Econs. Ctr., U. Miami Sch. Law, 1977-81, Fed. Home Loan Bank Bd., 1980-81, N.Y. Stock Exch., 1979, City of St. Louis, 1983, Oppenheimer & Co., Inc., 1980-81, Taubman Co., 1982, Wachtell Lipton, Rosen & Katz, 1984, Coffee, Sugar, Cocoa Exch., 1983-85, Smathers & Thompson, 1984, Steel, Hector & Davis, 1985, Cadwalader, Wickersham & Taft, 1986, Sidley & Austin, Hall, McNichol, 1986, Hall, Dickler, 1987-88, Klenda, Mitchell, 1988, Townley and Updike, 1988; chmn. Presdl. Task Force on Inflation, 1968-69 Author: The Term Structure of Interest Rates, 1962, (with Eli Shapiro) The Measurement of Corporate Sources and Uses of Funds, 1964; editor: Varieties of Monetary Experience, 1970; co-editor: (with Arthur Laffer) The Phenomenon of Worldwide Inflation, 1975, Welfare Reform and The Carter Public Service Employment Program: A Critique; mem. adv. bd.: Jour. Money, Credit and Banking, 1968-71; chmn. editorial bd.: Policy Rev., 1977— ; contbr. articles to profl. jours. Bd. dirs., sec.-treas. Manhattan Inst., 1977-86. Served with AUS, 1942-46. Winner Ford Found. Doctoral Dissertation competition, 1960; named Miles B. Lane lectr. Ga. Inst. Tech., 1968; named to Collegium Disting. Alumni Boston U., 1974 Mem. Am. Econ. Assn., Royal Econs. Soc.; mem. So. Econ. Assn. (v.p. 1981-82); Mem. Phila. Soc. (pres. 1973-75), Mont Pelerin Soc. Jewish. Home: 2346 Centreville Rd Herndon VA 20171-3016

MEISELS, GERHARD GEORGE, academic administrator, chemist, educator; b. Vienna, May 11, 1931; came to U.S., 1951, naturalized, 1961; s. Leo and Adele Josefa Maria (Seehofer) M.; m. Sylvia Claire Knopsnider, June 28, 1958; 1 dau., Laura Germaine. Student, U. Vienna, 1949-51, 52-53; MS, U. Notre Dame, Ind., 1952, PhD, 1956. Postdoctoral rsch. assoc. U. Notre Dame, 1955-56; chemist Gulf Oil Corp., Pitts., 1956-59; part-time instr. Carnegie Inst. Tech., 1956-58; chemist nuclear divsn. Union Carbide Corp., Tuxedo, N.Y., 1959-63, asst. group leader, 1964-65; assoc. prof. U. Houston, 1965-70, prof., 1970-75, dept. chmn., 1973-75; prof., chmn. dept. chemistry U. Nebr., Lincoln, 1975-81, dean Coll. Arts and Scis., 1981-88; provost, COO U. South Fla., Tampa, 1988-94; dir. Coalition Sci. Literacy, 1994—, Suncoast Area Ctr. for Ednl. Enhancement (SACEE), 1996-99. Cons. Union Carbide Corp., Gearhart-Owen Industries. Editor (spl. issue) Jour. Radiation Physics and Chemistry, 1980; contbr. writings in field to profl. publs. Sec., pres. Ramsey (N.J.) Jr. C. of C., 1959-64; active rsch. bd. All Children's Hosp.; chmn. Fla. Coalition for Improving Math. and Sci. Edn., 1998—, chmn. interim exec. dir. Fulbright fellow, Smith-Mundt fellow, 1951-52; sr. fellow Sci. Rsch. Coun., Eng., 1976. Mem. Am. Chem. Soc. (com. chmn.), Am. Soc. for Mass Spectrometry (charter, com. chmn., v.p. 1984-86, pres. 1986-88, bd. dirs. 1988-90), Fla. Acad. Scis., AAAS, Am. Phys. Soc., Coun. Sci. Soc. Pres. (exec. bd. 1989-92, chmn. elect 1990, chmn. 1991, chmn. com. on sci. priorities), Nat. Alliance State Sci. and Math. Coalitions (bd. dirs. 1999—), Coun. for Chem. Rsch. (bd. dirs. 1982-85), Conformation Judges Assn. Fla. (pres. 1996—), Fla. Higher Edn. Consortium Math. and Sci. (ctrl. steering com. 1995—, chmn. 1998-2000), Houston Kennel Club (bd. dirs. 1968-70), Cornhusker Kennel Club (pres., bd. dirs., del. to Am. Kennel Club 1976-81), St. Petersburg Dog Fanciers Assn. (sec. 1996-98, 2000—, del. to Am. Kennel Club 1998—), Sigma Xi. Home: PO Box 1347 Thonotosassa FL 33592-1347 Office: U South Fla 4202 E Fowler Ave/HMS 456 Tampa FL 33620 E-mail: meisels@csl.usf.edu.

MEISELS, JUDITH A. piano instructor, pianist; b. Budapest, Hungary, July 23, 1938; came to U.S., 1957; d. Stephan and Margaret Benjamin; m. Irving M. Meisels, May 30, 1964; children: Jason D. Meisels, Adrienne C. Meisels. Matura diploma, Veres Palne Women's Gymnazium & Coll., Budapest, Hungary, 1956; Diploma in piano performance, Buda Acad. Music and Budapest Conservatory of Music, Budapest, Hungary, 1950-54; student, Franz Liszt Acad. Music, Budapest, Hungary, 1954-56, Bklyn. Coll., 1958-61; Piano pedagogy cert., New Sch. Music Studies, Princeton, NJ, 1977; postgrad., Westminster Choir Coll., Princeton, NJ, 1984—90. Cert. profl. tchr. music, N.J. Music Tchrs. Assn., nat. cert. profl. tchr. music Music Tchrs. Nat. Assn. Exec. bd. rsch., planning and selecting internat. artists series, Spectrum com., Monmouth County Arts Coun., 1980-85; cultural com., exec. bd. internat. concert and lecture series Monmouth County "Y", 1971-93; spkr., lectr. in field; panelist, conductor master classes Piano Tchrs.' Groups, N.Y.C., 1976-99; adjudicator high level prestigious piano auditions and competitions. Piano performances: classical solo and ensemble Radio Budapest, Hungary, Ministerium of Fgn. Affairs, 1948-49, Franz Liszt Acad., Budapest, 1948-56, solo performances Hungary, Austria, U.S.A., 1954-56, 73-80. Grantee Franz Liszt Acad., 1956-57. Mem. Music Tchrs. Nat. Assn., N.J. Music Tchrs. Assn., Leschetizky Assn. N.Y., Piano Tchrs. Cong. N.Y., Nat. Guild Piano Tchrs., Shore Music Educators Assn.(exec. bd., publicity chair 1976-80, recording sec. 1987-93), Cecilian Music Club of Freehold, N.J.. Avocations: power walking, swimming, reading, music, arts, gardening.

MEISEN, AXEL, chemical engineering educator, university dean; b. Hamburg, Germany, Oct. 17, 1943; came to Can., 1966; s. Paul and Emmi (Schaaf) M.; children: Nadine Ramona, Kai Noel. B.Sc., Imperial Coll., 1965; M.Sc., Calif. Inst. Tech., 1966; PhD, McGill U., 1970. Registered profl. engr., B.C. Asst. prof. chem. engring. U. B.C., Vancouver, 1969-74, assoc. prof., 1975-79, assoc. dean, 1976-85, prof., 1979-99, dean, 1985-97; environ. engr. Imperial Oil Enterprise Ltd., Sarnia, Ont., 1974-75; pres., vice chancellor Meml. U. Newfoundland, St. John's, 1999—. Environ. engr. Imperial Oil Enterprise, Ltd., Sarnia, Ont,, 1974-75. Contbr. articles to profl. jours. Chmn. Can. Engring. Accreditation Bd., 1989-90. Fellow Chem. Inst. Can., Instn. Engrs. Ireland, Can. Acad. Engring.; mem. Can. Soc. Chem. Engrs. (pres. 1994), Assn. Profl. Engrs. B.C., Vancouver Club. Office: Meml Univ Press Off Saint John's NF Canada A1C 5S7 E-mail: president@mun.ca.

MEISNER, GARY WAYNE, landscape architect; b. Terre Haute, Ind., Oct. 19, 1949; s. Ervin Gustav and Mary Lou (Marett) M.; children: Christopher Wayne, Kira Valora. BS in Landscape Architecture, Mich. State U., 1972. Lic. landscape architect, Ohio, Mich., Ind., Ill., Ky., W.Va. Designer Huron Clinton Metro Parks, Detroit, 1969, City of East Lansing, Mich., 1970, Fairfax County Park Authority, Annandale, Va., 1971; city design adminstr. Akron (Ohio) Dept. Planning and Urban Devel., 1972-79; prin. Bentley Meisner Assocs., Inc, Cin., 1979-94, Myers, Schmalenberger, Meisner Inc., Cin. and Columbus, Ohio, 1994-99, Meisner & Assocs., Cincinnati, 1999—. Designer Akron Downtown Plan, 1978, King Sch. Plan, 1980 (honor award 1982), master plan Toyota Regional Office, 1983 (honor award 1987), Falls at Cumberland Hill, 1987 (honor award 1989), Cin. Mus. Ctr., 1990 (honor award 1990), Walk Across Am. Garden, 1990 (honor award 1991), Dayton Nat. Cemetery, 1993 (honor award 1994), Piatt Park on Garfield Place, 1990 (honor award OPWA grand award 1992), Dayton Plaza of Flight (honor award 1995), Taylor Park Historic Riverwalk, 1995 (Ky. Gov.'s award 1996), Walnut Hills H.S. Master Plan (honor award 1999), Ea. Corridor Land Use Vision Plan (AIA award 2000). Trustee Cin. Hillside Trust, 1987—, Capitol Square Renovation Found., Columbus, Ohio, 1987—93, cin. Sculpture Coun., 1989—94, Hubbard Ednl. Trust, 1988—, Ohio Gov.'s Residence Commn., 2000—. Recipient gov.'s commendation State of Ohio, 1985, Ohio Arts Coun. fellow, 1992-93, Apple award Architecture Found. of Cin., 1995. Fellow Am. Soc. Landscape Architects (nat. trustee 1982-89, chmn. nat. cmty. assistance team program 1983-86, chmn. editorial bd. Garden Design mag. 1986-90, mem. nat. publs. bd. 1988-92, 96-98, Nat. Com. Assistance Team commendation 1986, Trustee commendation 1989); mem. Am. Soc. Botanic Garden and Arboretum, Urban Land Inst., Am. Underground Space Assn, Scenic Ohio (treas. 1985—). Mem. Unity Ch. Home: 4137 Jora Ln Cincinnati OH 45209-1406 Office: Meisner & Assocs 2043 Madison Rd Cincinnati OH 45208-3218

MEISSINGER, ELLEN MURRAY, artist, educator; b. Raleigh, N.C., June 19, 1947; d. William Don and Sarah (Elliott) Murray; m. Lonnie Dean Meissinger, Jan. 10, 1975; children: Logan Don, Jordan Daniel. BFA, U. N.C., Greensboro, 1969, MFA, 1971. Prof. Okla. State U., Stillwater, 1971-86, Ariz. State U. Sch. of Art, Tempe, 1986—. Juror Rocky Mountain Nat. Water Media Exhibit, Foothills Art Ctr., Golden, Colo., 1997; mem. painting and print commn. Ariz. State U., Tempe, 1997. Invitational exhbns. include Am. Still Life Painting, 1998, Watercolor Now V/Springfield Art Mus., 1997; featured in books: Best of Watercolor Painting Composition, 1997, Best of Watercolor Painting Texture, 1997. Mem. Nat. Watercolor Soc., Watercolor USA Honor Soc. (pres. 1993-95, bd. dirs. 1995-97), Coll. Art Assn. Avocation: gardening. Office: Ariz State U Sch of Art PO Box 871505 Tempe AZ 85287-1505

MEISSNER, DOROTHY THERESA, reading specialist; b. Jersey City, Apr. 20, 1932; d. John and Mary (Garofalo) Biondo; m. Carl Frederick Meissner; children: Kathleen Ann, Mary Gertl. BA summa cum laude, Jersey City State Coll., 1970, MA summa cum laude, 1974. Cert. tchr. of reading, reading specialist, supr. and adminstr.; cert. guidance counselor. Metallographer Engelhard Industries, Newark, 1953-61; 2nd grade tchr. Rutherford (N.J.) Bd. Edn., 1970-74, 4th grade tchr., 1974, reading specialist, 1974-94, 94—; instr. Fairleigh Dickinson U., Rutherford, 1977. Spl. edn. steering com. Kearny (N.J.) Pub. Schs., 1968-69; G&T adv. coun. Rutherford Pub. Schs., 1978-79; v.p. Union Fin. Chain, Rutherford, 1985-89, pres., 1989-92; adj. prof. reading dept. Jersey City State Coll. Contbr. articles to profl. jours.; designer sculpture; artist charcoal drawing (hon. mention 1987). Lector Roman Cath. Ch., Kearny, 1988—; coord. William Carlos Williams Project, Rutherford, 1984. Recipient Gov.'s Tchr.'s Recognition State of N.J., 1987, Mary G. Filosa reading tchr. of yr. award N.J. Reading Tchrs. Assn., 1996-97; seminar grantee N.J. Coun. for Humanities, 1995. Mem. Internat. Reading Assn. (program chair 1992-93, v.p. 1994-95, pres. 1995—, rec. sec. North Jersey coun. 1996—, svc. project chair 2000-2002, Celebrate Literacy award 2002), N.J. Reading Assn. (tchr. of yr. 1996-97, hospitality chair for conf., bd. dirs., awards com. chairperson 2000-2002), Women's Coll. Club, Phi Delta Kappa, Kappa Delta Pi. Avocations: reading, tennis, gardening, art, music. Home: PO Box 355 Kearny NJ 07032-0355

MEISSNER, EDWIN BENJAMIN, JR. retired real estate broker; b. St. Louis, Dec. 27, 1918; s. Edwin B. and Edna (Rice) Meissner; m. Nina Renard, Dec. 17, 1946; children: Edwin Benjamin III, Wallace, Robert;1 child Donald. BS, U. Pa., 1940. Joined St. Louis Car Co., 1934, asst. to pres., v.p., exec. v.p., 1950-56, pres., gen. mgr., 1956-61; pres. St. Louis Car div. Gen. Steel Industries, Inc., 1961-67; sr. v.p., dir. Gen. Steel Industries, Inc., 1968-74; v.p. Bakewell Corp., 1974-85; real estate broker, v.p. Hilliker Corp., St. Louis, 1985-96. Mem. pres.' coun. St. Louis U.; bd. dirs. Washington U. Med. Ctr. Redevel. Corp., Barnard Free Skin and Cancer Hosp.; past bd. dirs. James S. McDonnell USO; outreach com. St. Louis Symphony Soc.; hon. dir. Humane Soc. Mo.; v.p. Gateway Ctr. Met. St. Louis; chmn. Ladue (Mo.) Police and Fire Commn.; mem. Jefferson Nat. Expansion Meml. Commn.; mil. affairs com. Regional Commerce. Mem. Am. Ordnance Assn. (life), Internat. Assn. Chiefs of Police (assoc.), Mo. Athletics Club, Westwood Country Club, Bridlespur Hunt Club, St. Louis Club, Beta Gamma Sigma. Office: 509 Olive St Ste 608 Saint Louis MO 63101-1855 Home: Ste 608 509 Olive St Saint Louis MO 63101-1855

MEISSNER, KATHERINE GONG, city official; b. Stockton, Calif., 1955; BA, U. Phoenix, Stockton, Calif., 1999. Mem. comty. planning dept. staff City of Stockton, Calif., 1982-85, exec. asst. city clk., 1985-96, city clk., 1996—. Office: City Stockton Office City Clk 425 N El Dorado St Stockton CA 95202-1997

MEISSNER, SUZANNE BANKS, pastoral associate; b. Flint, Mich., July 12, 1943; d. Leon J. and Eunice Alberta (Conners) Banks; m. Edward J. Meissner, Aug. 20, 1966 (div. Sept. 1975). BA, North Park Coll., 1965; MA, Ea. Mich. U., 1979; M in Pastoral Studies, Loyola U., New Orleans, 1991. Cert. secondary educator, spiritual dir., Hypnotist, Mich.; commd. min. Diocese of Lansing, 1997. Tchr. Flint (Mich.) Cmty. Schs., 1965-94; pastoral assoc. St. Michael Ch., Flint, 1985—2002, Holy Redeemer Ch., Burton, Mich., 2002—. Mem. adv. bd. New Covenant Initiative, Diocese of Lansing, Mich., 1994—98; co-chmn. Profl. Pastoral Mins. Assn., 1994—98, mem. adv. bd., 2002—, chmn. diocesan pastoral coun., 1986—88, mem. docesan strategic pastoral planning commn.; mem. pastoral planning adv. com. Hurley Med. Ctr.; adj. faculty Siena Heights U., Adrian, Mich. Mem. presdl. search com. Mott C.C.; spiritual dir. Gerholz Christian Counseling Ctr. Mem. Internat. Assn. Counselors and Therapists, Rotary Internat., Phi Kappa Phi, Phi Delta Kappa. Democrat. Avocations: theatre, Audi owners, opera, travel. Home: 7217 N Mckinley Rd Flushing MI 48433-9046 Office: Holy Redeemer Ch 1227 E Bristol Rd Burton MI 48529 E-mail: suzmeis@aol.com., meissnersuzanne@hotmail.com.

MEISTAS, MARY THERESE, endocrinologist, diabetes researcher; b. Grand Rapids, Mich., July 22, 1949; d. Frank Peter and Anne Therese (Karsokas) M. MD, U. Mich., 1975. Diplomate Am. Bd. Internal Medicine, Am. Bd. Endocrinology. Intern, then resident in internal medicine Cleve. Clinic Hosp., 1975-78, endocrinology fellow, 1978-79; fellow in pediatric endocrinology Johns Hopkins Hosp., Balt., 1979-81; diabetes researcher Joslin Diabetes Ctr., Boston, 1981-86; assoc. in medicine Brigham and Women's Hosp., 1981-86; asst. in medicine, diabetes researcher Mass. Gen. Hosp., 1986-92; staff endocrinologist Emerson Hosp., Concord, Mass., 1989-2000; pvt. practice Boston, 2000—. Mem. ACP, Am. Diabetes Assn., Am. Fedn. Clin. Research, Endocrine Soc. Office: Emerson Hosp 747 Main St Ste 111 Concord MA 01742-3325

MEISTER, ALICE MARIE, librarian; b. Dec. 15, 1944; BA, MacMurray Coll., 1966; MA in Libr. Sci., U. Wis., Milw., 1971; Cert. Advanced Studies, U. Denver, 1980; MPA, U. Wyo., 1994. Tchr. English Bloom Twp. H.S., Chicago Heights, Ill., 1966-68, Whitefish Bay H.S., Milw., 1968-70; ref. libr. East Baton Rouge Parish Libr., 1972-73; libr. dir. Summit County Libr., Frisco, Colo., 1973-79; placement dir. Grad. Sch. Librarianship and Info. Mgmt., U. Denver, 1979-80; libr. dir. Sheridan County (Wyo.) Fulmer Pub. Libr., 1981-97; sch. libr. Vela H.S., Umtata, South Africa, 1995-96; libr. dir. Bozeman (Mont.) Pub. Libr., 1997—. Chair Wyo. State Libr. Stds. Com., 1983, 88. Sec., program chair Bighorn Audubon Soc., 1985-88; mem. Fine Arts Club, 1987-97; arts and crafts coord. Miss Indian Am. Bd., 1982-84; program chair Wyo Theater, 1989-92, Sheridan Arts Coun., 1988-91; sec. Cloud Peak chpt. Am. Bus. Women Assn., 1987-92; vol. Play Therapy, 1982-88; grantsperson Sheridan Civic Theatre Guild Bd., 1984-88; treas. Sheridan County Wine Tasting Club, 1985-89. Recipient Outstanding Woman award Sheridan chpt. Bus. and Profl. Women, 1988, Libr. of Yr. award Wyo. Libr. Assn., 1995. Mem. NEA, ALA, Wyo. Libr. Assn. (sec. 1986-87, pub. libr. sec. sec. 1984-85, pres. 1994-95, chair legis. com. 1992-94, Libr. of Yr. 1995), Wyo. Coun. for Humanities (sec. 1992-93), Colo. Libr. Assn. (chmn. intellectual com., vice-chmn. and sec. legis. com.), Mountain Plains Libr. Assn. (awards com. 1985-87), Mont. Libr. Assn. (sec.-treas., 1998—). Office: Bozeman Pub Libr 220 E Lamme St Bozeman MT 59715-3630 E-mail: ameister@mtlib.org.

MEISTER, BERNARD JOHN, chemical engineer; b. Maynard, Mass., Feb. 27, 1941; s. Benjamin C. and Gertrude M. (Meister); m. Janet M. White, Dec. 31, 1971; children: Mark, Martin, Kay Ellen. BSChemE, Worcester Poly. Inst., 1962; PhD in Chem. Engring., Cornell U., 1966. Engring. rschr. Dow Chem. Co., Midland, Mich., 1966—, sr. rsch. specialist, 1978-81, assoc. scientist, 1981-85, sr. assoc. scientist, 1985-92, rsch. scientist, 1992—. Contbr. articles to profl. jours. Mem. United Meth. Ch. Mem. Am. Inst. Chem. Engrs., Am. Chem. Soc., Soc. Plastics Engrs., Soc. Rheology, Sigma Xi. Methodist. Home: 2925 Chippewa Ln Midland MI 48640-4181 Office: Dow Chem Co 438 Bldg Midland MI 48667-0001 *Free the mind of things you can't change, and let it focus on things you can accomplish.*

MEISTER, HARTMUT, research engineer; b. Siegen, Germany, Oct. 28, 1963; s. Artur and Helga (Kohl) M. Diploma, U. Siegen, 1987, U. Wuppertal, Germany, 1991; PhD, U. Cologne, 1999. Lectr. HDT-Essen, Germany, 1991-92, educator Germany, 1992—; rschr. ENT-Clinic, Cologne, Germany, 1992—. Inventor complete middle ear prosthesis, 1997; contbr. articles to profl. jours. Mem. German Soc. Acoustics, German Audiolog. Soc. Office: ENT Clinic U Cologne JOS Stelzmann Str 9 50931 Cologne Germany

MEISTER, JOHN EDWARD, JR. technical educator, systems administrator; b. Elgin, Ill., Nov. 17, 1956; s. John Edward and Marilyn Barbara (Futter) M.; m. Rebecca Marie Buehner, Nov. 15, 1975; children: Christine Marie, Mark Christopher. AA, Cen. Tex. Coll., 1979, U. Md., 1980, BS cum laude, 1981; postgrad., Western Conservative Baptist Sem., 1982-83. Enlisted U.S. Army, 1974, advance through grades to staff sgt., 1980; electronics technician Frankfurt, Fed. Republic of Germany, 1974-77; maintenance supr. Darmstadt, Fed. Republic of Germany, 1978-81; transferred from 232d Signal Co. Telecommunications, 1981; instr. U.S. Army Signal Sch., Ft. Gordon, Ga., 1981-82; resigned U.S. Army, 1982; sr. electronics instr. ITT Tech. Inst., Portland, Oreg., 1982-83; equipment engring. and engring. svcs. technician Intel Corp., Aloha, 1983-85; ind. lifetime AMSOIL Dealer, Snohomish, Wash., 1983—; electronic designer Boeing Electronics Co., Everett, 1985-89; systems analyst Boeing Comml. Airplanes, 1989-95; telecomm. designer UNIX Network Boeing Info. and Support Svcs., 1995; UNIX instr. Boeing Info. & Support Svcs., Delivery Sys. Cert. and Tng., Bellevue, Wash., 1995-96; cons. Clearview Cons., Snohomish, 1996—; sr. engring. CAD Sys. adminstr. Intermec Corp., Everett, 1997—. Instr. computing Boeing Off-Hour Tng., 1994-96; electronics engr. Innovative Designs and Electronic Sys. Techs., Portland, 1982-85; UNIX specialist. Bd. dirs. Machias Ridge East Homeowner's Assn., 1988-91; fin. advisor Jr. Achievement, Everett High Sch., 1988-89. Mem. NRA, Pacific N.W. 4-Wheel Dr. Assn. Republican. Baptist. Avocations: photography, writing books on Jeeps and Unix, automotive mechanics, full-size Jeeps. web server: wagoneers.com. Home and Office: 14809 State Route 9 SE Snohomish WA 98296-8784 E-mail: john@wagoneers.com. *Personal philosophy: I always try to see the big picture while keeping an eye on the bottom line, I believe the Bible teaches such a balance. My primary objective is to be a good steward and to get the job done, success comes from knowing I did the best I could with what I had.*

MEISTER, MARK JAY, museum director, professional society administrator; b. Balt., June 26, 1953; s. Michael Aaron and Yetta (Haransky) M.; m. Carla Steiger, Aug. 7, 1977; children: Rachel, Kaitlin. AB, Washington U., St. Louis, 1974; MA, U. Minn., 1976; cert. mus. mgmt., U. Calif., Berkeley, 1983. Asst. lectr. St. Louis Art Mus., 1974; asst. coord. young people's program Mpls. Inst. Arts, 1975-76, coord. mobile program, 1976, coord. tchrs. resource svcs., 1976-77; dir. Mus. Art and History, Port Huron, Mich., 1978-79, Midwest Mus. Am. Art, Elkhart, Ind., 1979-81; exec. dir. Children's Mus., St. Paul, 1981-86; dir. Mus. Art, Sci. and Industry, Bridgeport, Conn., 1986-89; exec. dir. Archaeol. Inst. of Am., Boston, 1989-99; exec. dir. Archl. Inst. Am. Inst. Archeologique d'Amerique, Boston and Toronto, 1994-99; exec. dir. Dayton Soc. Natural History, 2000—. Adj. lectr. museology Kenyon Coll., Gambier, Ohio, 1977; adj. lectr. art history Ind. U., South Bend, 1980—81; regional reviewer Inst. Mus. Svcs., Washington, 1985—86, Washington, 1989; treas., vice chmn. Minn. Assn. Mus., St. Paul, 1983—86; ex-officio trustee U.S. com. Internat. Coun. on Monuments and Sites, 1995—99. Bd. dirs. Seaway Arts Coun., St. Clair County, Mich., 1978-79, Dayton Sister Cities Com., 2000—, Dayton Peace Accords Project, 2000—; mem. Mayor's Arts Adv. Com., Elkhart, 1981; mem. projects with industry bus. adv. coun. Goodwill Industries of Southwestern Conn., 1988-89; mem. exec. com., Conf. Adminstrv. Officers, Am. Coun. Learned Socs., 1994-97; pres. Asian Arts Ctr., Dayton, 2002. NEH museology fellow, Mpls. Inst. Arts, 1976-77, Kress fellow U. Minn. 1977-78, Bush leadership summer fellow, Bush Found., St. Paul, 1983; named One of Outstanding Young Men Am., 1981. Mem.: Assn. Children's Mus., Ohio Mus. Assn., Assn. Sci. and Tech. Ctrs., Am. Zoo and Aquarium Assn., Assn. Sci. Mus. Dirs., Archeol. Inst. Am., Soc. for Am. Archaeology, Am. Coun. Learned Socs. (chair nominating com. 1997, mem. exec. com. conf. of adminstrv. officers 1994—97), Am. Assn. Mus. Office: Dayton Soc Natural History 2600 Deweese Pkwy Dayton OH 45414-5400

MEISTER, ROBERT ALLEN, lawyer; b. N.Y.C., July 17, 1936; s. Milton and Sheba M.; m. Margaret A. Lewiston Goodman, July 15, 1962 (div. Oct. 15, 1969); 1 child, Deborah A.; m. Jeanne C. Cioffi, June 15, 1986; 1 child, Danielle M. AB, N.Y.U., 1959; LLB, Columbia U., 1962. Bar: N.Y. 1963, U.S. Dist. Ct. (so. dist.) N.Y., U.S. Dist. Ct. (no. dist.) N.Y., U.S. Dist. Ct. (ea. dist.) N.Y., U.S. Dist. Ct. (we. dist.) N.Y., U.S. Ct. Appeals (2d, 3rd, 5th, 9th, 11th, D.C. and fed. cirs.), U.S. Ct. Claims, U.S. Supreme Ct. Assoc. Dewey, Ballantine, Bushby, Palmer & Wood, N.Y.C., 1962-72; mem. Varet & Fink, P.C., A/K/A/ Milgrim, Thomajan & Lee, P.C., 1972-95; ptnr. Piper Marbury Rudnick & Wolfe, L.L.P., 1995—. Adj. prof. law Cardozo Sch. Law, N.Y.C.,

1999—; arbitrator civil ct. City of N.Y., 1971—. Inspector Office of Equal Opportunity, Washington, 1966; coord. rules and credentials McCarthy for Pres., 1968; coord. Kennedy for Pres. com., N.Y.C., 1972. Joseph P. Chamberlain fellow Columbia U. Sch. Law, 1961-62. Mem. ABA, N.Y. State Bar Assn., Assn. of the Bar of the City of N.Y. (mem. fed. cts. com. 1970-73). Democrat. Avocations: classical music, skiing, tennis. Office: Piper Marbury Rudnick & Wolfe LLP 1251 Avenue Of The Americas New York NY 10020-1104

MEISTER, RONALD WILLIAM, lawyer; b. Bklyn., Mar. 19, 1947; s. Marvin and Helen Selma (Schwartz) M.; m. Jane M. Sovern; children: Beth Rose, Sarah Miriam, David Henry. BA summa cum laude, Yale U., 1967, JD, 1970. Bar: (D.C.) 1970, (U.S. Ct. Appeals Armed Forces) 1971, (U.S. Ct. Appeals (1st cir.)) 1972, N.Y. 1975, U.S. Dist. Ct. (so. and ea. dists.) N.Y. 1975, U.S. Ct. Appeals (2d cir.) 1975, U.S. Ct. Claims 1977, U.S. Supreme Ct. 1977, U.S. Ct. Internat. Trade 1994. Assoc. Paul, Weiss, Rifkind, Wharton & Garrison, N.Y.C., 1974-80; ptnr. Kornstein, Meister & Veisz, 1980-84, Meister Leventhal & Slade, N.Y.C., 1984-93, Eaton & Van Winkle, N.Y.C., 1993—95, Cowan, Liebowitz & Latman, N.Y.C., 1995—. Contbr. articles to profl. jours. Served to lt. JAGC, USNR, 1970-74. Mem. Fed. Bar Coun., Am. Law Inst. Office: Cowan Liebowitz & Latman 1133 Ave of Americas New York NY 10036-6710 E-mail: rwm@cll.com.

MEITES, SAMUEL, clinical chemist, educator; b. St. Joseph, Mo., Jan. 3, 1921; s. Benjamin and Frieda (Kaminsky) M.; m. Lois Pauline Maranville, Mar. 11, 1945; 1 child, David Russell. AS, St. Joseph Jr. Coll., 1940; AB, U. Mo., 1942; PhD, Ohio State U., 1950. Diplomate Am. Bd. Clin. Chemistry. Clin. biochemist VA Hosp., Poplar Bluff, Mo., 1950-52, Toledo Hosp., 1953-54; Children's Hosp. Columbus, Ohio, 1954-91; prof. dept pediatrics Coll. Medicine Ohio State U., Columbus, 1972-91, prof. dept. pathology, 1974-91, prof. emeritus, 1991—. Prof. dept. pediats. Ohio State U. Coll. Medicine, Columbus, 1972-91, prof. emeritus, 1991—, prof. dept. pathology, 1974-91; cons. Brown Labs., Columbus, 1968-83, VA, Chillicothe, Ohio, 1980-84. Co-author: Manual of Practical Micro and General Procedures in Clinical Chemistry, 1962; editor: Standard Methods of Clinical Chemistry, Vol. 5, 1965, Pediatric Clinical Chemistry, 1st edit., 1977, 3d edit., 1989; co-editor: Selected Methods for the Small Clinical Chemistry Laboratory, 1982, Biography of Otto Folin, 1989; assoc. editor Geriatric Clin. Chemistry, 1994; contbr. articles to profl. jours. 1st lt. U.S. Army, 1942-46. Fellow AAAS; mem. Am. Chem. Soc., Am. Assn. Clin. Chemistry (Bernard Katchman award Ohio Valley sect. 1971, Fisher award 1981, Miles-Ames award 1990, sec. 1975-77, chmn. com. on archives, 1982-86, history divsn., 1992-99), Nat. Acad. Clin. Biochemists (hon., Johnson & Johnson award 1996), Midwest Assn. Toxicology (hon., award 1998). Democrat. Jewish. Avocations: gardening, history of clinical chemistry. Office: Childrens Hosp Dept Clin Biochemistry 700 Childrens Dr Columbus OH 43205-2696

MEITNER, PAMELA, lawyer, educator; b. Phila., Aug. 23, 1950; d. Alfred Victor Meitner and Claire Jane (Carroll) Harmer; m. William Bruce Larson, Sept. 13, 1980; 1 child, William Bruce, Jr. BS in chem. engring., Drexel U., 1973; JD, Del. Law Sch., 1977. Bar: Del. 1977, U.S. Dist. Ct. Del. 1977, U.S. Patent and Trademark Office 1977. Engr. DuPont Co., Deepwater, N.J., 1973-77, lawyer Wilmington, Del., 1977. Prof. Del. Law Sch., Wilmington, 1985-89. Commr. State Emergency Response Com., Dover, Del., 1986-90, 97—. Mem. Del. Bar Assn. Clubs: DuPont Country (Wilmington) (bd. govs. 1984-85). Home: 211 Welwyn Rd Wilmington DE 19803-2951 Office: DuPont Co Legal Dept 1007 S Market St Wilmington DE 19801-5227

MEITZLER, ALLEN HENRY, electrical engineering educator, automotive scientist; b. Allentown, Pa., Dec. 16, 1928; s. Herbert Henry and Estella Irene (Wagner) M.; m. Joan Catherine Egan, June 13, 1953; children: Thomas Joseph, Peter Michael, David Christopher. BS, Muhlenberg Coll., Allentown, Pa., 1951; MS, Lehigh U., 1953, PhD, 1955. Mem. tech. staff Bell Labs., Whippany and Murray Hill, N.J., 1955-72; prin. research scientist, research staff Ford Motor Co., Dearborn, Mich., 1972-96, elec. engring. educator, 1996—. Adj. prof. U. Mich.-Dearborn. Patentee ultrasonic and ferroelectric devices, automotive electronic devices and systems. Prof. Wackernagel scholar, 1947-51; Hood grad. fellow, 1954-55 Fellow IEEE, Acoustical Soc. Am.; mem. Am. Phys. Soc. Republican. Home: 3055 Foxcroft St Ann Arbor MI 48104-2827

MEITZLER, LELAND KEITH, executive editor; b. Enumclaw, Wash., Apr. 13, 1950; s. Theodore Canfield and Virginia Francis Cornett-Feller; m. Patty Sue Daffern, Sept. 1, 1968; children: Leland Neal, Dale Ralph. AA with honors, Green River C.C., Auburn, Wash., 1983. Mgr. Meitzler's Greenhouse & Nursery, Puyallup, Wash., 1970-72; sales mgr. Meitzler's Wholesale Greenhouses, Orting, 1972-75; terminal mgr. Green Thumb Products Corp., Apopka, Fla., 1975-76; owner, mgr. Northwest Tropicals, South Prairie, Wash., 1976-82; pres. Meico Assocs., 1982-84; co-founder, pres. Heritage Quest Mag., Orting, 1985-92, mng. editor Bountiful, Utah, 1992-95, exec. editor, 1996—, touring editor, 1993-2000; v.p., print publs. and acquisitions Heritage Quest, North Salt Lake, 2000—. Mem. Assn. Profl. Genealogists, Tacoma-Pierce County Geneal. Soc. (corr. sec. 1982-83, pres. 1983-85), South Prairie Hist. Soc. (pres. 1982-85). Republican. Avocations: country music, genealogy, collecting political and national recovery act memorabilia. Office: Heritage Quest 669 West 900 North North Salt Lake UT 84054 Address: PO Box 540193 North Salt Lake UT 84054-0193 E-mail: leland@heritagequest.com.

MEJIA, ELVIRA, medical assistant; b. Zacatecas, Mexico, May 14, 1948; came to U.S., 1968; d. Ramiro and Rosa Maria (Gutierrez) M. BS, Benito Juarez Coll., Fresnilio, Mexico, 1967; grad., Laural Sch., Phoenix, 1983. Lab. tech. Scott & White Meml. Hosp., Temple, Tex.; office mgr. Raul & Alicia Lopez-Guerra M.D., P.A., Corpus Christi. Mem. NAFE, Am. Inst. for Cancer Rsch. Home: 3545 Ocean Dr Corpus Christi TX 78411-1340

MEKA, GAIL JEAN, chemist, consultant; b. New Haven, Oct. 2, 1950; d. John Augusta Stponaitis and Lillian Catherine Langer; m. Dennis Michael Meka, Aug. 20, 1952; 1 child, Daniel Michael. BS in Chemistry, Merrimack Coll., 1972; MS in Organic Chemistry, So. Conn. State U., 1979. Cardiopulmonary technician St. Raphael's Hosp., New Haven, 1973-75; chief technician Faulkner Hosp., Boston, 1975-77; synthetic organic chemistry Pfizer, Inc., Groton, Conn., 1978-84; rsch. chemist DuPont Pharms., Wilmington, Del., 1984-86, prof. sales rep. Boston, 1986-91, mgr. worldwide chem. mfg. Wilmington, 1991-92, gen. mgr., sales & mktg. Puerto Rico, 1992-94, dir. worldwide bus. devel., 1994-97; global healthcare cons. Boston, 1997—. Project leader new pub. garden, Beverly, Mass., 1998-99. Mem. Guild Beverly Artists, Wenham Lake Watershed Assn. (bd. dirs. 2000-01). Republican. Avocations: adventure travel, oil painting. Home and Office: PO Box 2 East Stoneham ME 04231 E-mail: meka@pivot.net.

MEKEEL, ROBERT K. lawyer; b. Ossining, N.Y., Mar. 21, 1950; s. Ira III and Carmen E. (Munson) M.; m. Martha J. Keller, Sept. 29, 1979; 1 child, Meryl Fox. BA, Wesleyan U., Middletown, Conn., 1972; JD, U. Puget Sound, 1978. Bar: N.H. 1978, N.Y. 1979, U.S. Dist. Ct. (so. dist.) N.Y. 1980, U.S. Ct. Appeals (2d cir.) 1981, U.S. Dist. Ct. N.H. 1983, U.S. Ct. Appeals (1st cir.) 1983. Asst. dist. atty. Westchester County N.Y. Dist. Atty., White Plains, N.Y., 1979-82; assoc. Craig Wenners & McDowell, Manchester, N.H., 1983-84; clk. ct. Coos County Superior Ct., Lancaster, 1985; ptnr. McKible & Mekeel, P.A., Concord, 1986-89, Cullity Kelley & McDowell, Manchester, 1989-93, McDowell & Mekeel P.A., Manchester, 1994-96; prin. Robert K. Mekeel, P.A., Concord, 1996—. Mem. mentor program Franklin Pierce Law Sch., Concord, 1992; lectr. Nat. Bus. Inst., Eau Claire, Wis., 1993-95; mem. Million Dollar Advocates forum; mediator N.H. Superior Cts.; pvt. mediator, arbitrator disputes involving personal injury claims, pvt. mediation svcs. Fellow N.H. Bar Found.; mem. ATLA (N.H. rep.), N.H. Trial Lawyers Assn. (amicus com. 1994-96), N.H. Bar Assn. (com. on cooperation with cts., lectr. evidence seminar 1994). Democrat. Avocations: running, biking, swimming, drawing, wood working. Home and Office: 73 Main St Contoocook NH 03229-2628

MEKEEL, STEVEN LEYON, lawyer; b. Davenport, Iowa, Aug. 15, 1945; s. Herman Temple and Maxine Elizabeth (Hughett) M.; m. Susan J. Crume, June 22, 1967 (div. Sept. 1981); children: Kristin L., David S.; m. Diane L. Mathieus, June 15, 1982. BA, Knox Coll., Galesburg, Ill., 1967; JD, Washington U., St. Louis, 1970; postgrad., Johnson Mgmt. Inst., Racine, Wis., 1981. Bar: Wis., Ind. Atty. Barnes, Hickam, Pantzer & Boyd, Indpls., 1970-72; with S.C. Johnson & Son, Inc., Racine, 1972—, now corp. counsel. Bd. dirs. Racine Comml. Airport Corp., 1996—; officer, bd. dirs. numerous subs. of S.C. Johnson & Son, Inc., 1972—. Mem. bd. editors Washington U. Law Rev., 1967-70, Bd.dirs., chmn. Racine Redevel. Authority, 1976-80; bd. dirs., officer Racine Montessori Sch., Coop. Nursery Sch., Ch. of the Covenant, Racine Area Soccer Assn., others. Mem. ABA, Wis. Bar Assn., Racine County Bar Assn., Friar's Honor Frat. of Knox Cl., Order of Coif. Avocations: reading, cooking, boating, gardening. Home: 4527 Bluebird Ln Racine WI 53406 Office: SC Johnson & Son Inc 1525 Howe St Racine WI 53403-2237

MEKENNEY, C. ROBERT, management analyst, tax accountant; b. Chester, Pa., Nov. 30, 1944; s. William Hatred and Alfreda Frances (Laskoski) M.; m. Susan Mary Szollosi, Sept. 2, 1977; children: Jonathan, Christopher. BS in Bus. Mgmt., Pa. State U., 1966. Cert. tax specialist. Pers. mgmt. specialist Drug Enforcement Adminstrn., Phila., 1972-74, regional pers. officer Kansas City, Mo., 1974-76, pers. mgmt. specialist Washington, 1976-78; employee benefits specialist U.S. Customs Svc., 1978-80, employee benefits officer, 1980-90, mgmt. analyst, 1990—, inst. orgnl. mgmt., 1978—. Participant Citizen Amb. Program teaching acctg. to Russian businessmen. Exec. treas. Boy Scouts Am., Falls Church, Va., 1993—. Served with USN, 1967-71. Mem. Nat. Assn. Tax Practitioners, Nat. Soc. Pub. Accts., Internat. Assn. for Fin. Planning, Nat. Soc. Tax Profls. Roman Catholic. Avocations: cooking.

MEKLER, ARLEN B. lawyer, chemist; b. N.Y.C., May 4, 1943; s. Lev A. and Ethel (Fox) M.; children from previous marriage: Jeffrey Arlen, Rebecca Ann, Ann-Marie Laura, Victoria Arlene, Lamar Adam, Lars Arlen; m. Molly L. Malone, Feb. 3, 1995. BS in Chemistry, Reed Coll.-San Jose State U., 1953; MS in Organic Chemistry, Iowa State U., 1955; PhD, Ohio State U., 1958; JD, Temple U., 1972. Bar: Del. 1972, Pa. 1972, U.S. Supreme Ct. 1976. Sr. rsch. chemist E.I. du Pont de Nemours & Co., Wilmington, Del., 1958-69; ptnr. Mekler and Maurer, 1972—. Chief appellate div. Office Pub. Defender, State of Del., 1973-77; pres. Del. Law Ctr., Wilmington, 1973— ; instr. constl. law Wilmington Coll., 1976-80; dir. Bar Rev. Del., 1972— ; mem. 3d Circuit Ct. Appeal Jud. Nominating Commn., 1977-81, 3d Circuit Ct. Appeals Jud. Conf. Contbr. monographs to legal publs. Pres. Mental Health Aux. for Gov. Bacon Health Ctr., 1964-66; mem. Citizens Conf. for Modernization of State Legislatures, 1964-68; state chmn., Reform Commn. for Modernization Polit. Party Rules, 1965-68; pres. Del. Citizens for Fair Housing, 1965-69; state commr. Nat. Conf. on Uniform State Laws, 1972— ; pres. Democratic Forum Del., 1966-70; mem. Del. Dem. Platform Com., 1966, 68, 72, 76; research dir. Del. Citizens for Humphrey-Muskie, 1968, Citizens for Biden, 1972, 78, 84, Citizens for McDowell, 1986—, Biden for Pres., 1986—; del. Dem. Nat. Conv., 1980; mem. social action com. Unitarian Ch., Wilmington, 1962-68. Recipient Keyman award, 1964, 65; State Govtl. Affairs award, 1964, 65 Mem. ABA, Del. Bar Assn. (com. on rules of criminal procedure 1973-74, supreme ct. com. on revision of criminal law 1973— , supreme ct. com. on rules of evidence 1976— , com. on revised rules of evidence 1976— , com. on revised rules of Del. Supreme Ct. 1974— , family law com. 1979— , continuing legal edn. com. 1981—), Pa. Bar Assn., Am. Chem. Soc., N.Y. Acad. Scis., Chem. Soc. (London), AAAS, Catalyst Club Phila., Wilmington Organic Chemists Club, ACLU (bd. dirs.), Sigma Xi, Phi Alpha Delta Home: Brandywine Hills 714 W Matson Run Pky Wilmington DE 19802-1912 Office: PO Box 2285 Wilmington DE 19899-2285 E-mail: drlaw@mac.com.

MELADY, THOMAS PATRICK, academic administrator, ambassador, author, public policy expert, educator; b. Norwich, Conn., Mar. 4, 1927; m. Margaret Judith Badum; children: Christina, Monica. BA, Duquesne U., 1950; MA, Cath. U. Am., 1952, PhD, 1954. Former mem. faculties Fordham and St. John's Univs.; founder Inst. African Affairs Duquesne U., 1957; cons. to founds., govts., corps., 1959-67; hon. doctorates from 28 univs. Africa Service Inst.; prof. Afro-Asian affairs, chmn. dept. Asian studies and NonWestern civilization Seton Hall U., South Orange, N.J., 1967-69, regent, 1987-90; prof. Afro-Asian affairs, dir. Office of Internat. Studies, 1973-74; exec. v.p., prof. politics St. Joseph's U., Phila., 1974-76; pres. Sacred Heart U., Fairfield, Conn., 1976-86, prof. polit. sci., 1976-86, pres. emeritus, 1986—; asst. sec. for postsecondary edn. U.S. Dept. Edn., Washington, 1981-82; amb. to Burundi, 1969-72; amb. to Uganda, 1972-73; sr. adviser to U.S. del. to 25 UN Gen. Assembly, 1970; chmn. Conn. Conf. Ind. Colls., 1979-81; pres., chief exec. officer Conn. Pub. Expenditures Coun., 1986-89; U.S. amb. to The Holy See, Vatican City, 1989-93, 94-95; exec. dir. Cath. Network of Vol. Svc., 1993-94; v.p. Capital Formation Counselors, 1993—. Disting. vis. prof. George Washington U. and St. John's U., 1993—94; vis. prof. Rome Grad. Ctr., 1998—99, Pontifical Gregorian U., 2001; chmn. nat. com. Cath. Campaign for Am., 1994—99; counsel to govts. and bus.; sr. diplomat in residence Inst. of World Politics, 2001—. Author: Ambassadors Story: The United States and The Vatican in World Affairs, 1994, and 14 other books. Knighted by Pope Paul VI, 1968 and by Pope John Paul II, 1983, 91; honored by 6 countries; recipient Native Son award, Grand Cross, Order of Malta, 1993. Mem.: The Cincinnati Soc., The Sacred Mil. Constantinian Order of St. George, Order of Malta. E-mail: ambmelady@aol.com.

MELAMED, ARTHUR DOUGLAS, lawyer; b. Mpls., Dec. 3, 1945; s. Arthur Charles and Helen Beatrix (Rosenberg) M.: m. Carol Drescher Weisman, May 26, 1983; children: Kathryn Henrie, Elizabeth Allyn. BA, Yale U., 1967; JD, Harvard U., 1970. Bar: D.C. 1970, U.S. Ct. Internat. Trade 1985, U.S. Ct. Appeals (9th cir.) 1971, U.S. Ct. Appeals (2d cir.) 1975, U.S. Ct. Appeals (D.C. cir.) 1978, U.S. Ct. Appeals (8th cir.) 1981, U.S. Ct. Appeals (fed. cir.) 1985, U.S. Ct. Appeals (4th cir.) 1989, U.S. Ct. Appeals (10th cir.) 1993, U.S. Supreme Ct. 1981. Law clk. U.S. Ct. Appeals for 9th Circuit, 1970-71; assoc. Wilmer, Cutler & Pickering, Washington, 1971-77, ptnr., 1978-96, 2001—; prin. dep. asst. atty. gen. U.S. Dept. Justice, 1996-2000, acting asst. atty. gen. antitrust divsn., 2000-2001. Vis. prof. Georgetown U. Law Ctr., 1992-93, adj. prof., 1993-94. Contbr. articles to profl. jours. Class agt. Alumni Fund Yale U.; D.C. area chair Yale campaign, 1993-97; mem. social scis. coun. com. Yale U., 1989-94; trustee Nat. Child Rsch. Ctr., 1990-93, Sidwell Friends Sch., 2000—. Mem. ABA, Am. Law Inst., Yale Club (N.Y.C.), Kenwood Country Club. Home: 6405 Shadow Rd Bethesda MD 20815-6613 Office: Wilmer Cutler & Pickering 2445 M St NW Washington DC 20037 Business E-Mail: dmelamed@wilmer.com.

MELAMED, CAROL DRESCHER, lawyer; b. N.Y.C., July 12, 1946; d. Raymond A. and Ruth W. (Schwartz) Drescher; m. Arthur Douglas Melamed, May 26, 1983; children: Kathryn, Elizabeth;children from previous marriage: Stephanie Weisman, D. Wynne Brown. AB, Brown U., 1967; MAT, Harvard U., 1969; JD, Cath. U. Am., 1974. Bar: Md. 1974, D.C. 1975, U.S. Ct. Appeals (D.C. cir.) 1975, U.S. Dist. Ct. D.C. 1981, U.S. Supreme Ct. 1982. Tchr. English Wellesley (Mass.) H.S., 1968-69; law clk. U.S. Ct. Appeals (D.C. cir.), Washington, 1974-75; assoc. Wilmer, Cutler & Pickering, 1975-79; assoc. counsel The Washington Post, 1979-95, v.p. govt. affairs, 1995—. Mem. Phi Beta Kappa. Office: The Washington Post 1150 15th St NW Washington DC 20071-0002

MELAMED, LEO, global consulting firm executive; b. Bialystok, Poland, Mar. 20, 1932; came to U.S., 1941, naturalized, 1950. s. Isaac M. and Fayga (Barakin) M.; m. Betty Sattler, Dec. 26, 1953; children: Idelle Sharon, Jordan Norman, David Jeffrey. Student, U. Ill., 1950-52; JD, John Marshall Law Sch., Chgo., 1955. Bar: Ill. 1955. Sr. ptnr. Melamed, Kravitz & Verson, Chgo., 1956-66; chmn., CEO Sakura Dellsher, Inc., 1965—2000, Melamed & Assoc., Inc., Chgo., 1993—. Mem. Chgo. Merc. Exch., 1953—, mem. bd. govs., 1967—91, chmn. emeritus, 1991—, chmn. bd., 1969—71, 1975—77, chmn. exec. com., 1985—91, also spl. counsel, apptd. sr. policy advisor, 1997—; chmn. bd. Internat. Monetary Market, 1972—75, spl. counsel, 1976—91; mem. Chgo. Bd. Trade, 1969—; mem. corp. adv. bd. U. Ill., Chgo., 1991—; mayor Chgo. Coun. Manpower and Econ. Advisors, 1972; adv. coun. mem. Grad. Sch. Bus. U. Chgo., 1980—. Author: (sci. fiction novel) The Tenth Planet, 1987, Leo Melamed on the Markets, 1993, Escape to the Futures, 1996; editor: The Merits of Flexible Exchange Rates, 1989. Trustee Trustee John Marshall Law Sch., 1991—; coun. mem. U.S. Holocaust Meml. Mus., 1992—, dir. Named Man of Yr., Israel Bonds, 1975; recipient Am. Jewish Com. Human Rights medallion, 1991. Fellow: Internat. Assn. Fin. Engrs. (sr.); mem.: ABA, Nat. Bur. Econ. Rsch. (bd. dirs.), Chgo. Bar Assn., Ill. Bar Assn., Am. Judicature Soc., Nat. Futures Assn. (chmn. 1982—89, spl. advisor 1989—), Am. Contract Bridge League (life master), Standard Club, Chgo. Club, Union League Club, Econs. Club Chgo. Avocations: writing, jogging. Office: Melamed & Assocs Inc 10 S Wacker Dr Ste 3275 Chicago IL 60606-7442

MELANÇON, JOSEPH HERMAN, artist, educator; b. Baton Rouge, Dec. 16, 1938; s. Joseph Herman and Margaret (Trista) M.; m. Wanda Sharon Sanchez, Aug. 19, 1961 (div. Oct., 1983); children: Jill, Janet, Mark, Michelle; m. Belle Gordon Heneberger, Apr. 14, 1987; children: Josh, Jake. BA, La. State U., 1962; MFA in Painting, Tex. Women's U., 2000. Curator of exhibits Charlotte (N.C.) Children's Mus., 1962-63, Fort Worth Mus. Sci. and Industry, Fort Worth, Tex., 1963-68; designer, photographer Peter Wolf Assocs., Dallas, 1968-77; artist, owner Joseph Melançon Studios, 1977—. Instr. drawing and taxidermy Eastfield C.C., Dallas, 1972-90. Painter: exhbns. include Western Fedn. Watercolor Socs., 1993 (Best of Show), Nat. Watercolor Soc. (Georgio award), Am. Watercolor Soc. 125th Ann. (CFS medal), 1998, Nat. Arts for the Parks Top 100, 22d Ann. Watercolor Exhbn., Panama City, Fla. (Best of Show), others; contbr. (book): Splash 3: America's Best Contemporary Watercolorists, 1994. Mem. Southwestern Watercolor Soc. (pres. 1997-98, Appreciation award 1998), Western Fedn. Watercolor Socs. (signature mem.), Nat. Watercolor Soc. (signature mem.), Phi Kappa Phi. Achievements include creation of World's largest functional mousetrap, 1998 Guiness Book of World Records. Avocations: model building, toy collecting, sailing, reading, travel. Home: 3350 Pine Valley Dr Sarasota FL 34239

MELAND, N. BRADLY, plastic surgeon; b. Northwood, N.D., May 19, 1953; s. Noren M. and Audrey M. Meland; m. Sue Jean Revier, Aug. 19, 1978; children: Angela, Shaina, Jessica, Tessa. BS in Natural Scis., U. N.D., 1975, MS in Medicine, 1977, MD, 1979; postgrad., U. Minn., 1977-78. Diplomate Am. Bd. Surgery, Am. Bd. Plastic Surgery. Gen. surgery resident Mich. State U., Saginaw (Mich.) Coop. Hosp., 1979-84; plastic surgery fellow Mayo Grad. Sch., Rochester, Mich., 1984-86, ortho micro surg. fellow, 1986; hand fellow U. Fla., Tampa, 1987; cons. plastic surgery, cons. orthopedic hand surgery Mayo Clinic, Rochester, 1987-93, cons. plastic surgery Scottsdale, Ariz., 1993-98, chief sect. hand surgery, 1994-98; med. dir. S.W. Plastic Surgeons, Paradise Valley, Ariz., 1998—. Staff St. Mary's Hosp., Rochester, 1987-98, Meth. Hosp., Rochester, 1987-98, Maricopa County Hosp., Phoenix, 1993—, St. Lukes Hosp., Jacksonville, Fla., 1993—, Scottsdale Healthcare Shea, 1993—, Scottsdale Healthcare Osborn, 1998—; co-dir. microsurg. tchg. lab. Med. Scis. Bldg., Rochester, 1987-93; annual faculty flap dissection workshop East Va. Med. Sch., Norfolk, 1988—; co-dir., annual faculty European Flap Workshop, Hanover, Germany, 1989, 93; residency program dir. plastic surgery program Mayo Grad. Sch., Rochester, 1989-93; edn. chmn., fellowship preceptor divsn. plastic surgery Mayo Clinic Scottsdale, 1993-98; asst. prof. plastic surgery, orthopedic surgery Mayo Grad. Sch. Medicine, Rochester, 1987-90, assoc. prof. plastic surgery, orthopedic surgery, 1990-98; oral examiner Am. Bd. Plastic Surgeons, 1997—; vis. prof., lectr., presenter in field. Assoc. editor Plastic Surgery Outlook Quarterly, 1994-96, Jour. Plastic Surg. Techniques, 1994-96, European Jour. Plastic Surgery, 1994-98; assoc. contbg. editor Yearbook of Hand Surgery, 1987-98; ad-hoc reviewer Plastic Reconstructive Surgery, 1994—, Annals Plastic Surgery, 1995—; contbr. chpts. to books and articles to profl. jours. 8th grade Sunday sch. tchr. Christ Ch. Luth., 1995-97, chmn. sch. bd., 1995-97. Fellow ACS; mem. AMA, Internat. Soc. Reconstructive Microsurgery, Internat. Coll. Surgeons, Am. Assn. Plastic Surgeons (program com. 1998), Am. Soc. Plastic and Reconstructive Surgery (socioeconomic com. 1994-97, coding com. 1994-96, practice and devel. com. 1998, chmn. sci. meeting evaluation com. 1998, program chmn. annual meeting 1999, others), Am. Assn. Hand Surgery (bylaws com. 1990, program com. 1993, tech. exhibits chair 1993-96, bd. dirs. 1995-97, membership chair 1998—, others), Am. Soc. Surgery of the Hand, Am. Soc. Reconstructive Microsurgery (audit fin. com. 1989-91, tech. exhibits com. 1989-91, program com. 1991, edn. com. 1992), Am. Assn. Clin. Anatomists, Assn. Acad. Chmn. Plastic Surgery, Midwestern Assn. Plastic Surgeons (bd. dirs. 1991-92, program chmn. 1992), Maricopa County Med. Soc., Maricopa County Plastic Surg. Soc., Rocky Mountain Assn. Plastic and Reconstructive Surgeons, Priestley Surg. Soc., Sigma Xi. Avocations: skiing, golfing, fishing, camping, sailing. Home: 10301 N 70th St Unit 230 Paradise Valley AZ 85253-1460 Office: Meland Plastic Surgery Clinic 7032 Cochise St Ste A200 Scottsdale AZ 86351

MELANSON, RICHARD ALLEN, political science educator; b. Perth Amboy, N.J., Nov. 4, 1944; s. Melvin Joseph and Helen (Hurley) Ml; m. Jane Louise Maxim, Feb. 14, 1983. BA, Rutgers U., 1966; postgrad., Harvard U., 1966-67; PhD, Johns Hopkins U., 1974. Lectr. polit. sci. UCLA, 1972-74; prof. polit. sci. Kenyon Coll., Gambier, Ohio, 1974-90; dir. internat. studies Brown U., Providence, 1990-92; prof. nat. security policy Nat. War Coll., Washington, 1992—. Author: Writing History and Making Policy, 1983, Reconstructing Consensus, 1991, U.S. Foreign Policy Since Vietnam, 2000; co-editor: Reevaluating Eisenhower, 1987 (Choice award 1987); mem. bd. revs. Mershon Rev. Internat. Studies. NEH fellow, 1981. Mem. Am. Polit. Assn., Soc. Historians of Am. Fgn. Rels., Internat. Studies Assn. Avocations: crossword puzzles, lieder, cycling. Office: Nat War Coll 4th St SW Washington DC 20319-0001 E-mail: melansonr@ndu.edu.

MELANSON, SUSAN C. herbalist; b. Boston, May 6, 1946; d. Arthur Wood and Marion (Saunders) Chapman; m. Arthur S. Melanson. AA, Colby-Sawyer Coll., 1966; BA, Hiram Coll., 1970. Founder, pres. Gem Island Software, Reading, Mass., 1985-90, dir. Carlisle, 1990-93; property mgr. Finard & Co., Burlington, 1993-98; founder, herbalist Oak Hill Farm, South Hiram, Maine, 1998—. Co-owner Washington Kennel; breeder, trainer, racer Siberian and Alaskan huskies. Author: Wentworth-By-The-Sea, 1969: A Novel. Class historian Wellesley High Class, 1964. Mem. Omicron Beta. Avocations: genealogy, growing medicinal herbs, collecting Inuit art, Native American studies.

MELARO, CONSTANCE LORAINE, pianist, organist, instructor; b. Oakmont, Pa., Nov. 15, 1929; d. John Baptist and Rose Eileen (Toia) M. BA in French, St. Mary's Coll., 1951; postgrad., U. Pitts., 1954-57; MA in French, Middlebury Summer Lang. Schs., 1956; postgrad., U. Md., 1964-72. Cert. tchr., Pa., Md. Tchr. English and spelling Ford City (Pa.) Jr. High Sch., 1951-52; tchr. French and English West Deer Twp. High Sch., Cheswick, Pa., 1952-54; tchr. French Oakmont (Pa.) High Sch. and Elem. Sch., 1954-61; tchr. French and English Glenelg High Sch., Howard County, Md., 1963-64; lectr. French Am. U., Washington, summer 1964; tenured asst. prof. French Dunbarton Coll. Holy Cross, 1964-73; tchr. French and Social Studies La Reine High Sch., Forestville, Md., 1973-75; pianist, organist, instr., 1976—. Acting chmn. modern lang. dept. Dunbarton Coll., Washington, 1972-73; organist, pianist St. John the Baptist. Ch., Silver Spring, Md., 1963-99; organist Hines/Rinaldi Funeral Home, Silver Spring, 1975-99. Author: Bitter Harvest, 1965; columnist Greensburg Tribune Rev., 1975-77; contbr. articles to profl. jours. Democrat. Roman Catholic. Avocations: music, writing. Home: 9242 Spring Valley Rd Ellicott City MD 21043-6432

MELBOURNE, ROBERT ERNEST, civil engineer; b. Oceanside, Calif., July 17, 1929; s. Thomas Powell and Helen Millicent (Plausse) M.; m. Jeanne Edith Kuhn, Apr. 8, 1961; children: Ann Teresa Farley, Maria Helen, Steven Thomas, Louise Clare Vance. BSCE, U. So. Calif., 1951, PhD in History, 1996; MSCE, Stanford U., 1955; MA in History, U. San Diego, 1990. Registered civil engr., Calif. Engr. Morrison-Knudsen Co., Boise, Noxon, Mont., 1955-57, J.E. Haddock Ltd., Pasadena, Calif., 1957-58; pres. R.E. Melbourne Co. Inc., San Luis Rey, 1958-66; designer, chief engr. San Diego County Water Authority, San Diego, 1966-90; mil. historian in pvt. practice, 1990—. Mem. adv. bd. Colorado River Bd., L.A., 1967-83. Commr. Oceanside Historic Preservation, 1997—. Lt. USN, 1951-54, PTO. Fellow ASCE; mem. U.S. Naval Inst., Soc. Am. Mil. Engrs. Soc. Mil. History, Navy League of U.S., Marine Corps Heritage Found. Republican. Roman Catholic. Home: PO Box 9 San Luis Rey CA 92068-0009

MELBY, EDWARD CARLOS, JR. veterinarian; b. Burlington, Vt., Aug. 10, 1929; s. Edward C. and Dorothy H. (Folsom) M.; m. Jean Day File, Aug. 15, 1953; children: Scott E., Susan J., Jeffrey T., Richard A. Student, U. Pa., 1948-50; D.V.M., Cornell U., 1954. Diplomate: Am. Coll. Lab. Animal Medicine. Practice veterinary medicine, Middlebury, Vt., 1954-62; instr. lab. animal medicine Johns Hopkins U. Sch. Medicine, Balt., 1962-64, asst. prof.,

1964-66, assoc. prof., 1966-71, prof., dir. div. comparative medicine, 1971-74; prof. medicine, dean Coll. Vet. Medicine, Cornell U., Ithaca, N.Y., 1974-84; v.p. R & D SmithKline Beecham Animal Health, 1985-90, v.p. sci. and tech. assessment, 1990-91; ind. cons., 1992—. Cons. VA, Nat. Research Council, NIH. Author: Handbook of Laboratory Animal Science, Vols. I, II, III, 1974-76. Served with USMC, 1946-48. Mem. Am., N.Y. State, Md., Pa. Veterinary Med. Assns., Am. Assn. Lab. Animal Sci., Am. Coll. Lab. Animal Medicine, AAAS, Phi Zeta. Home: PO Box 248 Charlotte VT 05445-0248 Office: 736 Lime Kiln Rd Charlotte VT 05445-9141 E-mail: ecmelby@aol.com.

MELBY, JOHN B. composer, educator; b. Whitehall, Wis., Oct. 3, 1941; s. John B. Sr. and Margaret (Edmundson) M.; m. Carol A. Wurtz, July 7, 1961 (div. 1977); 1 child, John; m. Jane H. Thompson, June 15, 1978; children: Kirsten, Charles. MusB, Curtis Inst., 1966; MA, U. Pa., 1967; MFA, Princeton U., 1971, PhD, 1972. Assoc. prof. West Chester (Pa.) U., 1971-73; prof. music U. Ill., Urbana, 1973-97, prof. emeritus, 1997—. Assoc. U. Ill. Ctr. for Advanced Studies, 1989-90. Composer numerous mus. works for live performers, computer-synthesized tape, vocal, chamber, choral and orchestral music, works pub. by Associated Music Pubs., Merion Music, Inc.; recs. on Composers Recs., Inc., New World Records, Advance Records, Centaur Records, Zuma Records. Recipient 1st prize 7th Internat. Electroacoustic Music Awards, Bourges, France, 1979, Am. Acad./Inst. Arts and Letters award, 1984; Guggenheim fellow, 1983. Mem. BMI. Democrat. Avocations: railroading, cooking, herpetology. Home: 501 N Willis Ave Champaign IL 61821-2709 E-mail: jbmelby@johnmelby.com.

MELBY, ORVILLE ERLING, retired banker; b. Butte, Mont., Oct. 9, 1921; s. Ole and Esther (Jacobsen) M.; m. Arvilla L. Underland, Nov. 24, 1956; children— Steve E., James E., Ann-Margaret. BA magna cum laude, U. Wash., 1949. C.P.A., Wash., Oreg. Treas. Boeing Co., 1956-66; sr. v.p. fin. Continental Airlines, Los Angeles, 1966; v.p. Bank of Am., San Francisco, 1967; treas. Bendix Corp., Detroit, 1968; v.p., treas. Vought Aeronautics, Dallas, 1969-70, Bonanza Internat., Dallas, 1971-74; vice chmn. Rainier Nat. Bank, Seattle, 1974-87. Bd. dirs. Health Care Property Investors, Los Angeles. Served with USAAF, 1942-46. Mem. Fin. Execs. Inst., Phi Beta Kappa. Clubs: Mason. Presbyterian. Home: 510 Lake St S Apt 101 Kirkland WA 98033-6486

MELBY, PAUL ELLIOTT, electrical engineer; b. Fergus Falls, Minn., Sept. 23, 1949; s. Jerry Ambrose and Geraldine Elizabeth (Elliott) M.; m. Susan Diane Duenow, Dec. 5, 1970; children: Jason Paul, Staci Nicole. AA, Fergus Falls Jr. Coll., 1970; BS, N.D. State U., 1973. Elec. engr. North Ctrl. Electric Coop., Bottineau, N.D., 1973-75; cons. engr. Dunham Assocs., Edina, Minn., 1975-76; elec. engr. Wright-Hennepin Electric, Buffalo, 1976-80; applications engr. Border States Electric, Plymouth, Minn., 1980-86; elec. engr. People's Coop. Power, Rochester, 1986—2001, Brookings (S.D.) Mcpl. Utilities, 2001—. Coach youth basketball Am. Athletic Union, Rochester, 1987—. Lutheran. Avocation: sports. Home: 228 Pine Ridge Rd Brookings SD 57006 Office: Brookings Mcpl Utilities 525 Western Ave Brookings SD 57006 E-mail: susamel1@hotmail.com.

MELCHER, ARLYN JOHN, management educator; b. Monroe, Nebr., Sept. 5, 1931; s. Raymond John and Violet Louise (Mark) M.; m. Debbie Bateman, July 3, 1993; children: Teresa, Michael, Jocelyn, Nyla, Hollie. BS, UCLA, 1953, MBA, 1954, U. Chgo., 1961, PhD, 1964. Staff asst. So. Calif. Gas Co., L.A., 1956-58; prof. Kent (Ohio) State U., 1962-95; prof., chair dept. mgmt. So. Ill. U., Carbondale, 1989—. Cons. Gen Corp., Akron, Ohio, 1986-88, P.R. Cement Co., San Juan, 1980-86. Author: Structure of Process and Organizations, 1976. With U.S. Army, 1954-56. Mem. AAUP (pres. 1970), Acad. Mgmt., TIMS. Avocations: running, travel, art. Home: 20 Pinewood Dr Carbondale IL 62901-5200 Office: So Ill U Dept Mgmt Carbondale IL 62901

MELCHER, DAVID F. military officer; b. Allentown, Pa., May 20, 1954; s. Donald Frederick and Gloria Melcher. BSc, U.S. Military Acad., 1976; MBA, Harvard U., 1983; MPA, Shippensburg U., 1996. Registered profl. engr., N.H. Commd. 2d. lt. U.S. Army, 1976, advanced through grades to brig. gen., various staff positions, 1976—92; battalion commdr. Fort Wainwright, Ark., 1992—94; regimental tactical officer U.S. Mil. Acad., West Point, NY, 1994—95; brigade commdr. 1st Cavalry Divsn., Fort Hood, Tex., 1996—98; dep. chief staff The Pentagon, Washington, 1998—99, dep. dir., 1999—2000; comdg. gen. S.W. divsn. Army Corps. Engrs., Dallas, 2000—. Contbr. articles to profl. jours. Mem. sch. bd. Fairbanks North Star Burough, Fairbanks, Alaska, 1993—94. Fellow, Commn. White House Fellowships, 1987—88. Mem.: Army Engr. Assn., Assn. U.S. Army, Soc. Am. Military Engrs. Office: Southwestern Division US Army Corp Engrs 1100 Commerce Street Dallas TX 75242

MELCHER, JAMES P. political scientist, educator; b. Madison, Wis., Feb. 3, 1963; s. John William and Beatrice Hagensick Melcher; m. Nancy Patricia Finnegan, Jan. 2, 1999. BA, U. Wis., 1985; PhD, U. Minn., 1995. Asst. dept. rsch. Minn. Ho. of Reps., St. Paul, 1989—; vis. asst. prof. St. John's U., Collegeville, 1995, Coll. St. Benedict, St. Joseph, 1995, U. Wis., Eau Claire, 1996; vis. term prof. Cleve. State U., 1996—99; asst. prof. U. Maine, Farmington, 1999—. Contbr. articles to profl. jours.; assoc. editor: website Electnet, 1996—2001. Del. Maine Dem. Conv., 2000, 2002; vestry mem. St. Mark's Episc. Ch., Augusta, 2000—. Recipient Disting. Faculty award, Cleve. State U. Alumni Assn., 1999. Mem.: Am. Polit. Sci. Assn. Episcopalian. Avocations: collecting postcards, bicycling, fantasy football, fantasy baseball. Home: 11 Meadow Rd #204 Augusta ME 04330 Office: U Maine Farmington Dept Social Scis and Bus Farmington ME 04938 Business E-Mail: jim.melcher@maine.edu.

MELCHER, THORSTEN, biotechnology company executive; b. Marne, Germany, June 14, 1968; s. Thomas Melcher, Ellen Melcher. PhD, University of Heidelberg, Heidelberg, Germany, 1993—96. Founder and Chief Scientific Officer EnVivo Pharmaceuticals, Inc., Redwood City, CA, 2001—02; Founder and Vice President AGY Therapeutics, Inc., South San Francisco, 1998—2001. Scientific Advisor Xantos Biomedicine AG, Martinsried, Germany, 2001—02. Author: (Scientific articles) Nature, Science, Neuron and others, 1996 (PCR Award for young scientists, 1996), (Technology patents) USPTO, 2001. Mem.: Society for Neuroscience. Office: EnVivo Pharmaceuticals, Inc 3696 Haven Ave, Suite B Redwood City CA 94063

MELCHER, TRINI URTUZUASTEGUI, accounting educator; b. Somerton, Ariz., Dec. 1, 1931; d. Francisco Juan and Dolores (Barraza) Urtuzuastegui; m. Arlyn Melcher, Aug. 3, 1957 (div. Feb. 1972); children: Teresa Dolores, Michael Francis, Jocelyn Marie. BS, Ariz. State U., 1954; MBA, Kent State U., 1964; PhD, Ariz. State U., 1977. Acct. CPA firm, L.A., 1954-56; instr. L.A. Sch. Dist., 1956-58, Dolton (Ill.) Sch. Dist., 1958-61; asst. prof. Kent (Ohio) State U., 1962-72; prof. Calif. State U., Fullerton, 1976-89, founding faculty mem. San Marcos, 1990—. Author: Intermediate Accounting Study Guide, 1984; co-author: International Accounting: A Global Perspective, 1997. Treas. Community Devel. Coun., Santa Ana, 1985-88, chmn. bd., 1989; mem. com. U.S. Dept. Labor, 1989—. Named Outstanding Educator, League of United Latin Am. Citizens, Stanton, Calif., 1987, Mex. Am. Women's Nat. Assn., Irvine, Calif., 1987, One of Ten Women of Merit, N. County Times, 1999, One of 80 Elite Hispanic Women, Hispanic Bus., 2002; recipient Outstanding Faculty award Calif. State U. Sch. Bus., 1983, Pub. Svc. award Am. Soc. Women CPAs, San Antonio, 1996; Affirmative Action grantee, 1990. Mem. AICPA (editorial bd. The Woman CPA), Am. Acctg. Assn., Calif. Soc. CPAs (Merit award 1991), Hispanic CPAs. Avocations: music, travel. Home: 2024 Sequoia St San Marcos CA 92069-5454 Office: Calif State U San Marcos CA 92096-0001

MELCHERT, ELIZABETH CHRISTINE, optometrist; b. Appleton, Wis., Nov. 27, 1960; d. Henry William and Adela Fern (Peters) M.; children: Kathryn, Kelsey; m. Thomas Lee La Violette, Mar. 9, 1996. BA, Ripon Coll., 1982; BS, Ill. Coll. Optometry, 1983, OD, 1985. Optometrist Broadway Optical, Waupaca, Wis., 1985-86, Pearle Vision, Oshkosh, 1986-87, Ophthalmology Northwest, Chgo., 1987-92, Wesley-Jessen Contact Lens Co., Chgo., 1992-93, Dougal, McClellan & Sullivan Eye Assocs., Chgo., 1992-93, Pearle Vision, Sheboygan, Wis., 1993-95, Dr. Davison & Assocs., Appleton, Oshkosh, 1995-98, The Eye Clinic, Neenah, 1998—. Mem. ch. choir United Ch. of Christ Physician's Network. Recipient scholarship Wis. Optometric Assn., 1982. Mem. Fox Valley Optometric Assn., Wis. Optometric Assn., Am. Optometric Assn., Beta Sigma Kappa. Avocation: music. Office: The Eye Clinic 240 1st St Neenah WI 54956-2719

MELCHERT, JAMES FREDERICK, artist, educator; b. New Bremen, Ohio, Dec. 2, 1930; s. John Charles and Hulda Lydia (Egli) M.; m. Mary Ann Hostetler, June 18, 1954; children: Christopher, David, Renee. AB, Princeton U., 1952; MFA, U. Chgo., 1957; MA, U. Calif., Berkeley, 1961. Prof. art U. Calif., Berkeley, 1965-76, 81-84, 88-92, prof. emeritus, 1992—; dir. Am. Acad. in Rome, 1984-88. Dir. Visual Arts Program, Nat. Endowment for Arts, Washington, 1977-81 Exhibited in one man shows at San Francisco Art Inst., 1970, San Francisco Mus. Modern Art, 1975, Holly Solomon Gallery, N.Y.C., 1991; group shows at Biennale de Paris, 1963, Whitney Mus., N.Y.C., 1966, 68, 70, Documenta 5, Kassel, Germany, 1972, World Ceramic Exposition, Korea, 2001; commd. for Artwork (new Biology Bldg.) at MIT, 1993-94, Biomed. Rsch. Bldg. at Case Western Res. U., 1994. Recipient Adaline Kent award San Francisco Art Inst., 1970; Nat. Endowment for Arts artist fellow, 1973; hon. DFA, San Francisco Art Inst., 1984, Md. Inst. Coll. Arts, 1993. Home: 6077 Ocean View Dr Oakland CA 94618-1844 E-mail: jfmelchert@earthlink.net.

MELCHERT, SANDRA ANN, science educator, researcher; b. Chgo., July 7, 1954; d. Clifford Colburn and Germania Erna (Muenzer) De La Monte Heverly de Heverly; m. David J. Holmes, Jan. 15, 1995; children: Yolanda, Heather, Amethyst, Erika. BSBA, Ea. Wash. U., 1986; MA, MS, Ea. Washington U., 1990; PhD, U. Idaho, 1993. Cert. elem. and secondary tchr., Wash. Tchr. Wilson Creek (Wash.) Pub. Schs., 1986; tchr. 6th grade Moses Lake (Wash.) Sch., 1986-89; teaching asst. Ea. Wash. U., Cheney, 1989-90; sci. and maths. tchr. Spokane (Wash.) Pub. Schs., 1990; project coord., inst. sci. U. Idaho, Moscow, 1990-93; asst. prof. sci. edn. U. S.D., Vermillion, 1993-96, Messiah Coll., Grantham, Pa., 1996—. Reviewer sch. sci. and math. U. Mo., 1993—; reviewer nat. sci. stds. Fund for Improvement and Rsch. Sci. Tng., U.S. Dept. Edn., 1992-96; grant reviewer NSF, 1996. Author and editor: Topically Relevant Approaches for Increasing Learning in Science-Biological/Physical/Earth Sciences, series 1992-94; author and editor video tape series; contbr. articles to profl. jours. Mem. steering com. Vermillion Water Festival, 1993-96, rep. Civic Coun., Vermillion, 1994-6, promoter, supporter cultural arts First Nighter, Vermillon, 1994-96; vol. Vermillion Beautification Com., 1993-96. Recipient ASCD Outstanding Dissertation award, 1994; CHEM Nat. fellow, 1994—; Porject N.O.V.A. (NASA Opportunities for Visionary Acads.) grantee, 1998. Fellow Am. Meterol. Soc. (reviewer nat. sci. stds. 1991—); mem. AAAS, AAUW, NSTA (publs. com. 1998—, periodicals subcom. 1998—, reviewer tchr. resource material 1998—), Nat. Assn. Rsch. in Sci. Tchg., Nat. Mid. Schs. Assn., Nat. Com. for Study Options for Rural Sci. Edn., Assn. for Edn. Tchrs. in Sci., Sch. Sci. and Math. Assn. (membership com. 1994-97, manuscript reviewer 1995—), Kappa Delta Pi, Phi Delta Kappa (sec. Wilkes chpt. 1996—). Avocations: needle work, gardening, bread making, preserving foods, sewing. Home: 418 Clemens Dr Dillsburg PA 17019-1321 Office: Messiah Coll Ste 308 College of Edn Grantham PA 17027

MELCHIOR, IB JORGEN, author, television and motion picture writer, director; b. Copenhagen, Sept. 17, 1917; arrived in U.S., 1938; s. Lauritz Lebrecht Hommel and Inger Thora (Nathansen) M.; m. Harriet Hathaway Kale, Mar. 15, 1942 (div. 1960); 1 child, Leif; m. Cleo Baldon-Chute, Jan. 18, 1964; stepchild, Dirk Arin. Postgrad., U. Copenhagen, 1937. Actor, stage mgr., co-dir. The English Players, Paris, 1937-39; stage mgr. Radio City Music Hall, Ctr. Theater, N.Y.C., 1941-42; actor, writer, 1946-49; assoc. dir. CBS-TV, 1949-50, dir., 1951-56; assoc. prodr. G-L Enterprises, 1952-53; screenwriter, dir., novelist, 1957—. Author: (novels) Order of Battle, 1973, Sleeper Agent, 1975, The Haigerloch Project, 1977, The Watchdogs of Abaddon, 1979, The Marcus Device, 1980, The Tombstone Cipher, 1983, Eva, 1984, V-3, 1985, Code Name: Grand Guignol, 1987, (biography) Quest, 1990, Order of Battle: Hitler's Werewolves, 1991, (autobiography) Case by Case, 1993; author: (with Cleo Baldon) Steps & Stairways, 1989, Reflections on the Pool, 1997; screenwriter Live Fast, Die Young, 1957, The Angry Red Planet, 1959, Reptilicus, 1962, Journey to the 7th Planet, 1962, Ambush Bay, 1965, Robinson Crusoe on Mars, 1964, The Time Travelers, 1964, others; dir. Angry Red Planet, The Time Travelers; translator, narrator (tapes) Hans Christian Andersen Fairy Tales, 1986; creator Space Family Robinson (spl. advisor Lost in Space, 1997-98); subject of biography: (by Robert Skotak) Ib Melchior: Man of Imagination, 2000. Mem. adv. bd. Mayor's Narcotics Info. Clinic, L.A., 1972-73; adv. coun. Danish Immigrant Mus., Elk Horn, Iowa, 1985—. With U.S. Army Mil. Intelligence, 1943-46. Decorated Bronze Star, Knight Commander Cross, Militant Order of St. Brigitte of Sweden, 1965; recipient King Christian X Erindringsmedalje, 1948, Medal of Merit Old Guard, 1965, Golden Scroll award Best Writing Acad. Sci. Fiction, 1976, Hamlet award Best Legitimate Play Shakespeare Soc. Am., 1982; named Scandinavian of Yr. Am. Scandanavian Found. L.A., 1995, Mem. Writers Guild Am. West, Dirs. Guild Am., Acad. Sci. Fiction (hon.), Manuscript Soc., Authors Guild Inc., Royal Danish Guard Assn., Danish Lucheon Club (L.A.), Adventures Club (L.A.). Home and Office: 8228 Marmont Ln Hollywood CA 90069-1624 E-mail: ijmelchior@aol.com.

MELCONIAN, JERRY OHANES, engineering executive; b. Cairo, Egypt, Jan. 22, 1934; came to U.S., 1967; s. Melik Melconian and Zarouca Papazian; m. Veronique Kocifay, June 12, 1998; 1 child, Terran Kirk. BSc, U. London, 1957. Section leader Otis Elevator Co., London, Eng., 1957-61, Rolls Royce Ltd., Derby, Eng., 1961-66; program coord. Textron Lycoming, Stratford, Conn., 1967-74; mgr., TF34 Design to Cost Gen. Electric Co., Lynn, Mass., 1974-77; mgr. mktg. No. Rsch. and Engring. Co., Woburn, 1977-82; pres. SOL-3 Resources Inc., Reading, 1982—. Editor: Design and Development of Gas Turbine Combustors, 1980; patentee in field. Mem. Am. Inst. Aeronautics and Astronautics. Office: SOL-3 Resources Inc 76 Beaver Rd Reading MA 01867-1310

MELCZEK, DALE J. bishop; b. Nov. 9, 1938; AB, St. Mary Coll., Orchard Lake, Mich.; MDiv, St. John Sem., Plymouth, Mich.; MA in Edn., U. Detroit; postgrad., U. Notre Dame. Ordained priest Roman Cath. Ch., 1964, appointed aux. bishop, 1982. Assoc. pastor St. Sylvester Ch., Warren, Mich., 1964-70, co-pastor, 1970-72; pastor St. Christine Ch., Detroit, 1972-75; vicar West Detroit Vicariate, 1973-75; asst. vicar for parishes Archdiocese of Detroit, 1975-77, sec. to archbishop and vicar gen., 1977-82, archdiocesan consultor, 1972-83, aux. bishop, titular bishop of Trau, 1982-95; regional bishop Detroit N.W. Region, 1983-92; apostolic adminstr. Diocese of Gary, Ind., 1992-95; coadjutor Bishop of Gary Diocese of Gary, Ind., 1995-96; bishop of Gary Diocese of Gary, Ind., 1996—.

MELDMAN, CLIFFORD KAY, lawyer; b. Milw., July 27, 1931; s. Edward H. and Rose (Bortin) M.; children: Mindy, David, Linda, James, Noah. JD, Marquette U., 1956. Bar: Wis. 1956. Ptnr. Meldman & Meldman, Milw., 1956-73; pres. Meldman & Meldman S.C., 1973-98; pvt. practice, 1956—. Contbr. articles to profl. jours., also editor. Mem.: Wis. Bar Assn. (chmn. family law sect.), Milw. Bar Assn. (bd. dirs. 1984—86, pres. 1986—87, chmn. family law sect.), Am. Acad. Matrimonial Lawyers (Wis. chpt., pres. 1982). Home and Office: 170 W Cherokee Cir Milwaukee WI 53217-2716

MELDMAN, ROBERT EDWARD, lawyer; b. Milw., Aug. 5, 1937; s. Louis Leo and Lillian (Gollusch) M.; m. Sandra Jane Setlick, July 24, 1960; children: Saree Beth, Richard Samuel. BS, U. Wis., 1959; LL.B., Marquette U., 1962; LL.M. in Taxation, NYU, 1963. Bar: Wis. 1962, Fla. 1987, Colo. 1990, U.S. Ct. Fed. Claims, U.S. Tax Ct. 1963, U.S. Supreme Ct. 1970. Practice tax law, Milw., 1963—; pres. Meldman, Case & Weine, Ltd., 1975-85; dir. tax div. Mulcahy & Wherry, S.C., 1985-90; shareholder Reinhart, Boerner, Van Deuren, S.C., 1991—. Adj. prof. taxation U. Wis., Milw., 1970—2000, mem. tax adv. coun., 1978—2000; adj. prof. Marquette U. Sch. Law, Milw., 2001—, The U. of Queensland T.C. Beirne Sch. Law, 2002; mem. Internat. Revenue Svc. Taxpayer Adv. Panel, 2001—; sec. Profl. Inst. Tax Study, Inc., 1978—; bd. dirs. Wis. Bar Found., 1988—94; exec. in residence Deloitte & Touche Ctr. for Multistate Taxation, U. Wis., Milw., 1996—2000. Co-author: Federal Taxation Practice and Procedure, 1983, 1986, 1988, 1992, 1998, Practical Tactics for Dealing with the IRS, 1994, A Practical Guide to U.S. Taxation of International Transactions, 1996, 1997, 2000, Federal Taxation Practice and Procedure Study Guide/Quizzes, 1998; editor: Jour. Property Taxation, 1996—2002; mem. editl. bd.: Tax Litigation Alert, 1995—2000; contbr. articles to legal jours. Recipient Adj. Taxation Faculty award UWM Tax Assn., 1987; named Outstanding Tax Profl. 1992 Corp. Reports Wis. Mag. and UWM Tax Assn. Fellow Am. Coll. Tax Coun.; mem. ABA, Fed. Bar Assn. (pres. Milw. chpt. 1966-67), Milw. Bar Assn. (chmn. tax sect. 1970-71), Wis. Bar Assn. (bd. dirs. tax sect. 1964-78, chmn. 1973-74), Internat. Bar Assn., The Law Assn. for Asia and the Pacific (chair tax sect. 2000—, dep. chair bus. law sect.), Marquette U. Law Alumni Assn. (bd. dirs. 1972-77), Milw. Athletic Club, Wis. Club, B'nai B'rith (trustee, Ralph Harris Meml. award Century Lodge 1969-70), Phi Delta Phi, Tau Epsilon Rho (chancellor Milw. chpt. 1969-71, supreme nat. chancellor 1975-76, v.p. Wis. chpt., tech. 1992-2000). Jewish (trustee congregation 1972-77). Home: 7455 N Skyline Ln Milwaukee WI 53217-3327 Office: 1000 N Water St Ste 2100 Milwaukee WI 53202-3197 E-mail: rmeldman@reinhartlaw.com.

MELDRUM, PETER DURKEE, venture capital/biotechnology company executive; b. Salt Lake City, June 26, 1947; s. Benjamin Nibley and Grace Natalie (Durkee) M.; m. Catherine Roper, June 16, 1970; children: Christopher Shawn. BSChemE, U. Utah, 1970, MBA, 1974. Asst. to pres. Terra Tek, Inc., Salt Lake City, 1974-78; pres., CEO Resource Enterprises, Inc., 1978-81, AgriDyne Techs., Salt Lake City, 1981-91, Founder's Fund Inc., 1991—95, Myriad Genetics Inc., Salt Lake City, 1992—. Bd. dirs. Dairy Equipment Co. Utah, Salt Lake City, Paradigm Bioscis. Inc., Alaxis, Inc., Manticore Pharms. Vice-chmn. fundraising Salt Lake Boy's Club, 1978-79; bd. dirs., vice chmn. ARC Golden Spike, Salt Lake City, 1980-90; mem. State of Utah Council Sci. and Tech., 1984-89; adv. bd. High Tech Mktg. Rev., Austin, Tex., 1986-88; mem. Gov.'s Task Force on Entrepreneurship; mem. rev. panel Utah Tech. Fin. Corp., Gov.'s Com. on Biomed. Industry, 1988-91; mem. bioengring. adv. bd. U. Utah, bus. adv. bd. Coll. Bus. Weber State U.; bd. arbitrators NASD, 1991-98; mem. adv. bd. U. Utah Coll. Sci.; bd. dirs. Ballet West. 1st lt. USAR, 1970-72. Named Entrepreneur of Yr., 2001. Mem. Utah Life Scis. Assn. (bd. dirs. 1995—), Tau Beta Pi, Phi Kappa Phi, Beta Gamma Sigma. Republican. Presbyterian. Avocations: skiing, backpacking, basketball, racquetball. Home: 1808 Mohawk Way Salt Lake City UT 84108-3363 Office: Myriad Genetics 320 Wakara Way Salt Lake City UT 84108-1214

MELDRUM, RICHARD JAMES, electrical engineer; b. Mt. Clemens, Mich., July 2, 1969; s. James Richard and Susan Kathleen (Harris) M. BSEE, Mich. Technol. U., 1991, MS in Ops. Mgmt., 1994. From quality technician to quality engr. Fisher Dynamics, St. Clair Shores, Mich., 1994-98; launch quality engr. Jabil Circuit, Inc., Auburn Hills, 1998—. Mem. IEEE. Home: 2346 London Bridge Dr Unit 62 Rochester Hills MI 48307-4267 E-mail: rmeldrum@earthlink.com.

MELE, ALFRED R. philosophy educator; b. Detroit, May 22, 1951; s. Alfred Emil and Rosemary (Pardo) M.; children: Al, Nick, Angela. BA, Wayne State U., 1973; PhD, U. Mich., 1979. Asst. prof. Philosophy Davidson (N.C.) Coll., 1979-85, assoc. prof., 1985-91, prof., 1991-95, Vail prof., 1995-2000; William H. and Lucyle T. Werkmeister prof. Fla. state U., Tallahassee, 2000—. Author: Irrationality, 1987, Springs of Action, 1992, Autonomous Agents, 1995, Self-Deception Unmasked, 2000; contbr. articles to profl. jours. Fellow NEH, 1985-86, 92-93, 99-00, Nat. Humanities Ctr., Rsch. Triangle Park, N.C., 1992-93, Australian Nat. U., 1999. Mem. Am. Philos. Assn., So. Assn. Philosophy and Psychology, Internat. Soc. for Rsch. on Emotion. Avocations: racquetball, tennis. Office: Dept Philosophy Fla State Univ Tallahassee FL 32306-1500

MELE, GREGG CHARLES, management information systems director, attorney; b. Hackensack, N.J., May 4, 1965; s. Charles Archangelo and Jennie (Johobowska) M. BS cum laude, Montclair State Coll., 1986; MS, Steven Inst. Tech., 1988; MBA, Baruch Coll., 1998; JD cum laude, N.Y. Law Sch., 1998; LLM, NYU, 2000. Bar: N.J. 1998, N.Y. 1999. Lab. asst. Montclair (N.J.) State Coll., 1984-86; computer programmer Bac Data Med. Info. Systems, Wayne, N.J., 1985-86; computer programmer/analyst corp. hdqrs. AT&T, Somerset, 1986-90; computer systems analyst, project leader The Bank of N.Y., N.Y.C., 1990-94; project leader Andersen Consulting, 1994-96; project mgr. Mutual Benefit Life, Newark, 1996; acct. mgt. IMI Systems, N.Y.C., 1996-97; asst. treas. Bankers Trust Co., 1997-98; asst. v.p. Merrill Lynch, 1998-2000; v.p., MIS dir. Deutsche Bank, 2000—. Author: The Best in the Business, 1983, Baker's Dozen, 1987. Garden State scholar Montclair State Coll., 1984, 85; finisher in N.Y.C. Marathon, 1991. Roman Catholic. Home: 40 Sulfrian Rd New Providence NJ 07974-1227 Office: Deutsche Bank Fl 6 Rm 678 31 W 52d St New York NY 10019

MELE, JOANNE THERESA, dentist; b. Chgo., Dec. 5, 1943; d. Andrew and Josephine Jeanette (Calabrese). Diploma, St. Elozabeth's Sch. Nursing, Chgo., 1964; diploma in dental hygiene, Northwestern U., 1977; AS, Triton Coll., 1979; DDS, Loyola U., 1983. RN, dental hygienist. Staff nurse medicine/surgery St. Elizabeth's Hosp., Chgo., 1964-66, oper. room nurse, 1966-67; head nurse oper. room Cook County Hosp., 1967-76, head nurse ICU, 1976-77; dental hybienist Mele Dental Assocs., Ltd., Oakbrook, Ill., 1977-79, practice dentistry, 1983—. Clinical asst. prof. Loyola U., Chgo., 1988. Recipient Northwestern U. Dental Hygiene Clinic award, 1977; Dr. Duxler Humanitarian award scholar Loyola U., 1982. Mem. Chgo. Dental Soc., Ill. State Dental Soc., Acad. Gen. Dentistry, Am. Assn. Women Dentists, Acad. operative Dentistry, Am. Prosthodontic Soc., Psu Omege (Kappa chpt.). Roman Catholic. Avocations: reading, music, golfing, jogging, skiing. Home: 3 N Tower Rd Oak Brook IL 60523

MELE, JOSEPH ANTHONY, III, plastic surgeon; b. Oceanside, N.Y., Sept. 21, 1962; s. Joseph Anthony Jr. and Josephine Elizabeth (Mirabile) M. BS in Elec. and Computer Engring., U. Calif., Davis, 1985, MD, 1989. Diplomate Am. Bd. Surgery, Am. Bd. Plastic Surgery. Intern U. Calif. Davis Med. Ctr., Sacramento, 1989-90; resident San Joaquin Gen. Hosp., Stockton, Calif., 1990-94; fellow in plastic surgery Saint Francis Meml. Hosp., San Francisco, 1994-97; pres., plastic surgeon Joseph A. Mele III, MD, Inc., Walnut Creek, Calif., 1997—. Fellow ACS (No. Calif. chpt.); mem. AMA, Am. Soc. Plastic Surgeons,Am. Soc. Aesthetic Plastic Surgeons, Calif. Med. Assn., Calif. Soc. Plastic Surgeons, Alameda/Contra Costa County Med. Assn. Avocations: computer graphics, broomball, running, fishing, golf. Office: Joseph A Mele III MD Inc 1515 Ygnacio Valley Rd Ste B Walnut Creek CA 94598-3005 E-mail: dmele@aol.com.

MELEIS, AFAF IBRAHIM, nurse sociologist, educator, clinician, researcher; b. Alexandria, Egypt, Mar. 19, 1942; d. Abdel Baki Ibrahim and Soad Hussein Hassan; m. Mahmoud Meleis, Aug. 21, 1964; children: Waleed, Sherief. BS magna cum laude, U. Alexandria, 1961; MS, UCLA, 1964, MA, 1966, PhD, 1968; D of Pub. Svc. (hon.), U. Portland, 1989. Instr. U. Alexandria, 1961-62; acting instr. UCLA, 1966-68, asst. prof. nursing, then assoc. prof., 1968-75; assoc. prof., dean Health Inst., Kuwait, 1975-77; prof. nursing U. Calif., San Francisco, 1977—2001, also dir. Study Immigrant Health and Adjustment; dean Univ. of Penn. Sch. of Nursing, 2002—. Vis. prof. colls. in Sweden, Brazil, Japan, Saudi Arabia, Kuwait, Egypt; 1st Centennial prof. Columbia U., N.Y.C., 1992-94; cons., speaker in field. Author: theoretical Nursing: Development & Progress, 1985 (Book of Yr., am. Jour. Nursing, 1985), 2d edit., 1991, 3d edit., 1997; contbr. articles to rsch. and profl. jours. Recipient Helen Hahm award U. Calif. Sch. Nursing, San Francisco, 1981, Teaching awards U. Calif., San Francisco, 1981, 85, Pres. Hosni Mubarak medal of Excellence, 1990; Kellogg Internat. fellow, 1986-89. Fellow Am. Acad. Nursing; mem. Coun. Nurse Researchers, Western Soc. Research in Nursing, Am. Nurses Assn. Avocations: jogging, symphony, reading, international affairs, women's issues. Office: Univ of Penn Sch of Nursing 420 Guardian Dr, Rm 465 NEB Philadelphia PA 19104-6096*

MELENDEZ, JOAQUIN, retired orthopedic assistant; b. San Gabriel, Calif., Aug. 16, 1929; s. Guadalupe and Gudelia (Maldonado) M.; m. Lola Hester Harris, Sept. 3, 1954. BS, Instituto del Estado, Chihuahua, Mex., 1949; AA, Foothill Coll., Los Altos Hill, Calif., 1973. Enlisted U.S. Army, 1950, advanced through grades to sgt. 1st class, ret., 1971; orthopedic asst. St. Vrain Valley Orthopedics (name now Longmont Orthopedics and Sports Medicine Clinic), Longmont, Colo., 1973-93; ret., 1973; translator Mcpl. Ct., Police Dept. and City of Longmont. Tchr. pub. spkg. and Spanish for med. office use. Author: (poems) Saturday Night, 1990, Reflections, 1991, Freedom, 1992, Season of Life, 1998, Letter to Stephen-The Unmarried Vows, 2000; translator: Video Parliamentary Procedure, 1999-2001. Bd. dirs. Hospice of Boulder

County, Boulder County Corrections Bd. With U.S. Army, 1950-71. Decorated Bronze Star with V, Meritorious Svc. medal with V; recipient marathon awards. Mem. Colo. Acad. Physician Assts., Nat. Assn. Parlimentarians, Colo. Assn. Parliamentarians (2d v.p. 1998-99), Toastmasters (named Outstanding Divsn. Gov. 1988-89, Divsn. Gov. of Yr. 1995-96, Silver Level of Recognition 1995, recipient speech awards), Internat. Soc. Poets. Republican. Roman Catholic. Avocations: pub. speaking, writing, photography, running, hist. rsch. Home: 3331 Mountain View Ave Longmont CO 80503-2155 E-mail: jlpokey@hotmail.com.

MELENDEZ ALVIRA, DANIEL J. meteorologist, researcher; b. P.R. s. Jose Melendez Contreras. PhD, U. Mich., 1989. Research physicist Naval Rsch. Lab., Washington, 1993—99; meteorologist NOAA/NWS Office of Sci. and Tech., Silver Spring, Md., 1999—. Author techn. monographs. Recipient Sci. and Engrng. Achievement award, U. Ala. Huntsville, 1993. Mem.: AGU. Achievements include research in incoherent scatter radar, EUV remote sensing, airglow, plasmasphere, and theory. Office: NOAA W/OST12 1325 East West Hwy Silver Spring MD 20910

MELENDY, DAVID RUSSELL, broadcast journalist; b. Corpus Christi, Tex., Oct. 19, 1948; s. Harold Orville and Marguerite Doris (Waller) M.; m. Lorna Sandra Katz, Mar. 19, 1972; children: Seth Howard, Andrew Scott. Student, George Washington U., 1966-70; BA magna cum laude, U. Hartford, 1972. News dir. Sta. WINY, Putnam, Conn., 1971-77; news anchor, reporter Sta. WPOP, Hartford, 1977-80; news dir. Sta. WNVR, Waterbury, 1980-81; news anchor, reporter St. WDRC, Hartford, 1980—81; news anchor Sta. WCBS-FM, N.Y.C., 1981; prodr., assignment editor, anchor, reporter AP Broadcast Svcs., Washington, 1981—. Instr. journalism Briarwood Coll., Southington, Conn., 1977-81; mem. broadcast adv. com. Briarwood Coll., Southington, 1978-81. Prodr., writer, reporter (audio spl. report series) Star Wars: Strategic Defense Initiative, 1985, (daily audio feature) Flashback, 1986—. Publicity chmn. Woodstock (Conn.) Players Cmty. Theater, 1972—77, Quinebaug Valley C.C. Found., Danielson, Conn., 1973—75, fundraising chmn., 1976; neighborhood coord. Am. Heart Assn., Washington, 1994, 1999, 2001; troop com. mem. Boy Scout Troop 500, 1998—99; pack com. chmn. Cub Scout Pack 230, 2000—01. Mem. House and Senate Radio-TV Corr. Assn., Radio and TV News Dirs. Assn., Newspaper Guild/Comms. Workers of Am., Com. Concerned Journalists, Nat. Press Club, Elks. Avocations: personal computers, photography, hiking, swimming. Office: AP Broadcast Svcs 1825 K St NW Washington DC 20006-1202 E-mail: david@melendy.com., dmelendy@ap.org.

MELEY, ROBERT WAYNE, structural and storage tank engineer; b. Warren, Pa., June 10, 1952; s. Nathan Arnold and Audrey Elizabeth (Dunn) M.; m. Kathy Dorien McDonald, Oct. 20, 1973; children: Kathy Dorien, Helen Renee, January Lynn. B of Archtl. Engrng., M of Engrng., Pa. State U., 1979; PhD, Columbia Pacific U., 1989. Registered engr. Scientist Douglas Aircraft Co., Long Beach, Calif., 1979-80; sr. devel. engr. Rexnord, Inc., Warren, 1980-85; pres. Meley Engrng. Enterprises, Cooksburg, Pa., 1979-96; lectr. Pa. State U., Beaver, 1986-87; chief engr. Brown Boiler and Tank Works, Ltd., Franklin, Pa., 1987-90; pres. Meley Engrng. Corp., 1996—. Mem. adv. bd. Pa. Dept. Environ. Resources, Harrisburg, Pa., 1989—. Author: Inspecting Above Ground Storage Tanks, 1990, Probabilistic Analysis of Storage Tanks, 1992, Evaluating Storage Tanks, 1992. Mem. ASCE, Am. Soc. Nondestructive Testing, Nat. Assn. Corrosion Engrs., Nat. Soc. Archtl. Engrs. Achievements include a new design of leak detection system for storage tanks. Office: Meley Engrng Corp HC 1 Box 10 Cooksburg PA 16217-9704

MELHADO, L. LEE, social worker, chemist; b. Bryn Mawr, Pa., July 9, 1945; d. Louis H. Jr. and Mary Eugenia (Coleman) Roddis; m. Evan M. Melhado, Dec. 30, 1971; children: Asa D., Raif S. BA in English, Carnegie Mellon U., 1968; MA in Chemistry, Washington U., 1972, PhD, 1976; MSW, U. Ill., 1991. Lic. clin. social worker, Ill.; cert. Acad. Cert. Social Workers. Rsch. assoc. U. Ill., Champaign-Urbana, 1976-82, vis. asst. prof., 1982-84, dir. Radioisotope Lab., 1984-91; crisis clinician Mental Health Ctr., Champaign, 1991-93, coord. intensive svcs., 1993-94, mgr. crisis triage svcs., 1994-95; dir. psychiat. svcs. The Pavilion, 1995-98; exec. dir. Champaign-Urban Jewish Fedn., 1998—. Bd. dirs. Tng. Edn. Coord. Com., Champaign, 1995—, Human Svcs. Tech. Program, Parkland Coll., 1998—. Contbr. articles to profl. jours. Bd. dirs., v.p. Hillel Found., Champaign, 1990-94; chair human svcs. com., bd. dirs. Champaign-Urbana Jewish Fedn., 1990-96. Mem. Am. Chem. Soc., NASW, Sigma Xi, Alpha Chi Sigma, Phi Kappa Phi, Alpha Mu Delta. Achievements include 2 U.S. patents.

MELHEM, ELIAS R. radiologist; b. Beirut, Lebanon, Apr. 12, 1964; s. Rafic E. and Muna T. Melhem; m. Lina Y Namek; children: Rafic, Randa. MD, U. S. Ala., 1988. Chief neuroradiology U. Pa., Phila., 2001—. Mem. study sect. NIHLB, 2002. Author: Diffusion Tensor MR Imaging of the CNS, 2002.

MELI, SALVATORE ANDREW, lawyer; b. N.Y.C., Sept. 18, 1947; s. Andrew and Marie (Ruggiero) M.; m. Barbara Ann Chiesa, Aug. 16, 1970. BA, St. John's U., Jamaica, N.Y., 1969, JD, 1975. Bar: N.Y. 1976, Fla. 1976, U.S. Dist. Ct. (ea. and so. dist.) N.Y. 1976. Sole practice, Flushing, N.Y., 1976-78; ptnr. Muratori & Meli, Flushing and Lake Worth, Fla., 1978-97; sole practice, 1997—. Lectr. Lawyers in the Classroom program, N.Y.C., 1977-81; mem. adv. bd. Title Ins. Co., Queens, N.Y., 1985—. Recipient Regents Scholarship, N.Y. State Bd. Regents, 1965. Mem. ABA, N.Y. State Bar Assn., Fla. Bar Assn., Queens County Bar Assn.

MELICH, DORIS S. public service worker; b. Salt Lake City, Apr. 8, 1913; d. Edward Harrison and Marie Cushing Snyder; m. Mitchell Melich, June 3, 1935; children: Tanya Marie Melich Silverman, Michael E., Nancy Lynne, Robert Allen. BA in Western History, U. Utah, 1934. Mem. Nat. Commn. Arthritis and Related Musculoskeltal Diseases, 1974-76, Nat. Arthritis Adv. Bd., 1977-84, 86-90; Utah del. Nat. Ho. of Dels. Arthritis Found., 1982-87; pres. Utah Arthritis Found. Bd., 1975-78, v.p., 1968-69, 73-74; Utah rep. Arthritis Found. Govt. Affairs, 1983—. Leader, founder 1st Girl Scouts Lone Troop U.S., Moab, Utah, 1947, regional selections com., 1958-67; active Utah Ballet Guild, Salt Lake Art Ctr., Utah Arts Coun., 1988—, Utah State Rep. Women, YWCA; trustee emeritus Arthritus Found. Recipient Pyramid award Nat. Arthritis Found., 1986, Utah Girl Scouts Regional award, 1987, Thanks Badge, 1963, Merit Honor award U. Utah Emeritus Club, 1978, Minute Man award Utah N.G., 1985; named to Nat. Women's Wall of Fame, Seneca Falls, N.Y., 1993. Mem. AAUW, Nat. Assistance League of Salt Lake City (charter mem.), Utah Women's Forum, Order Ea. Star, Alpha Delta Pi, Beta Sigma Phi (sponsor). Home: 900 Donner Way Apt 708 Salt Lake City UT 84108-2112

MELICHER, RONALD WILLIAM, finance educator; b. St. Louis, July 4, 1941; s. William and Lorraine Norma (Mohart) M.; m. Sharon Ann Schlarmann, Aug. 19, 1967; children: Michelle Joy, Thor William, Sean Richard. BSBA, Washington U., St. Louis, 1963, MBA, 1965, DBA, 1968. Asst. prof. fin. U. Colo., Boulder, 1969-71, assoc. prof., 1971-76, prof. fin., 1976—, chmn. fin. div., 1978-86, 90; chmn. fin. and econ. div., 1993-2000; MBA/MS programs dir. U. Colo., Boulder, 1990-93. Assoc. dir. space law bus. and policy ctr. U. Colo., 1986-87; rsch. cons. FPC, Washington, 1975-76, GAO, Washington, 1981, RCG/Hagler, Bailly, Inc., 1985—, Ariz. Corp. Commn., 1986-87, Conn. Dept. Pub. Utility Control, 1989, U.S. SEC, 1992-95; cons. tech. edn. IBM Corp., 1985-91; dir. ann. Exch. Program for Gas Industry, 1975-94; instr. ann. program Nat. Assn. Regulatory Utility Commrs., Mich. State U., 1981-94. Co-author: Real Estate Finance, 1978, 2d edit. 1984, 3d edit. 1989, 5th edit., 1982; Finance: Introduction to Markets, Institutions and Management, 1980, 84, 88, 92, Finance: Introduction to Institutions, Investments, and Management, 9th edit., 1997, 10th edit., 2000; assoc. editor Fin. Mgmt. Jour., 1975-80, The Fin. Rev., 1988-91. Recipient News Ctr. 4 TV Teaching award, 1987, MBA/MS Assn. Teaching award, 1988, Boulder Faculty Assembly Teaching award, 1988, Grad. Bus. Students Teaching award, 1995, 98; grantee NSF, 1974, NASA, 1986, 87; scholar W.H. Baughn Disting., 1989-2000, U. Colo. Pres.'s Teaching, 1989—. Mem. Fin. Mgmt. Assn. (mem. com. 1974-76, regional dir. 1975-77, v.p. ann. mtg. 1985, v.p. program 1987, pres. 1991-92, exec. com. 1991-93, bd. trustees 1992-99, chmn. 25th Anniversary com. 1994-95, mem. search. com. for editor of Financial Mgmt. Jour., 1995-96, chmn. search com. editor of Fin. Practice and Edn. Jour. 1996, mem. search com. for sec./treas. 1999, 2001), Am. Fin. Assn. Western Fin. Assn. (bd. dirs. 1974-76), Fin. Execs. Inst. (acad. mem. 1975—), Ea. Fin. Assn., Southwestern Fin. Assn., Midwest Fin. Assn. (bd. dirs. 1978-80), Alpha Kappa Psi, Beta Gamma Sigma. Presbyterian. Home: 6348 Swallow Ln Boulder CO 80303-1456 Office: U Colo Coll Bus PO Box 419 Boulder CO 80303 E-mail: Ronald.Melicher@colorado.edu.

MELICK, CLIFFORD FRANCIS, sociologist, researcher; b. Albany, N.Y., Sept. 6, 1947; s. Francis Joseph Melick, Marion Dorothy Campbell; life ptnr. Evelyn Louise Mazo. BA, Siena Coll., Loudonville, N.Y., 1971; MA, SUNY, Albany, 1973, PhD, 1979. Rsch. scientist N.Y. State Divsn.1 for Youth, Albany, 1980—83, dir. revenue and reporting svcs., 1983—86, chief program analysis and rsch., 1986—90; dir. rsch. Greater Balt. Med. Ctr., 1990—. Mem. editol adv. bd. Rsch. in Healthcare Fin. Mgmt., Balt., 2000—; prin. advisor NEMA Rsch., Inc., N.Y.C., 1997—; mem. Greater Balt. Med. Ctr. Instnl. Rev. Bd., Balt., 1990—; bd. dirs. Analytica, Ltd., Albany, NY. Contbr. book Chronic Wound Care, 2nd edit., 1997 , Chronic Wound Care, 3d edit., 2001, Current Surgical Therapy, 4th edit., 1992, Current Surgical Therapy, 5th edit., 1995, articles to profl. jours. Mem.: Acad. for Health Svcs. Rsch. and Health Policy, Soc. for the Art and Sci. of Wound Management, Internat. Soc. for Rschs. in Healthcare Fin. Mgmt., The Free State Corvette Club. Avocation: sports cars. Home: 8207 Spring Bottom Way Baltimore MD 21208 Office: Greater Baltimore Medical Center 6569 N Charles St Se 701 Baltimore MD 21204 Office Fax: 410-828-3435. Personal E-mail: cmelick@comcast.net . Business E-Mail: cmelick@gbmc.org.

MELICK, GEORGE FLEURY, mechanical engineer, educator; b. Morristown, N.J., Sept. 7, 1924; s. George Fleury and Esther Purdy (Udall) M.; m. Florence Miriam Bevins, Dec. 28, 1946; children: Robert A., Linda S., Judith E., Karen L. BSE, Princeton U., 1944; MS, Stevens Inst. Tech., 1955; ME, Columbia U., 1963; MA, NYU, 1970. Registered profl. engr., N.J. Asst. chief engr. Worthington Corp., Harrison, N.J., 1946-55; asst. prof. Stevens Inst. Tech., Hoboken, 1955-58; assoc. in mech. engring. Columbia U., N.Y.C., 1958-61; assoc. prof. mech. engring., dean Rutgers U., New Brunswick, N.J., 1961-77; cons. engr. Stone & Webster Engring. Corp., Cherry Hill, 1977-87; dir. engring. mgmt. program Drexel U., Phila., 1987-91; chmn. bd. Anastasio & Melick Assocs., Cherry Hill, N.J., 1987—. Cons. Worthington Corp., Harrison, 1956-65, Pub. Svc. Elec. & Gas, Newark, 1966-76. Author: John Mark and the Origin of the Gospels, 1979. Mem. countycom. Dem. Party, Franklin Twp., N.J., 1976. 1st lt. U.S. Army, 1945-52. Decorated Bronze Star medal. Mem. ASME (life), Am. Soc. Engring. Mgmt. (life), Am. Soc. Engring. Edn. (life), Soc. Bibl. Lit., Am. Acad. Religion (charter), Sigma Xi, Pi Tau Sigma, Tau Beta Pi. Presbyterian. Home: 9 Attleboro Ct Red Bank NJ 07701-5410 Office: Anastasio & Melick Assocs 30 Crofton Commons Cherry Hill NJ 08034-1142 E-mail: geomelick@aol.com.

MELIGNANO, CARMINE (EMANUEL MELIGNANO), video engineer; b. N.Y.C., Dec. 19, 1936; s. Salvatore and Lita (Poggialli) M.; m. Eileen Kinzie; children: Lori Ann, Robert, Michael. BS in Elec. Engring., Stevens Inst. Tech., Hoboken, N.J., 1959; postgrad., William Paterson Coll., 1978, Pace U., 1979. Registered profl. engr., N.J. Quality contr. Isomet Corp., Palisades Park, N.J., 1959-63; sales engr. RCA Service Corp., Camden, 1963-73; video engr. N.J. Sports and Expn. Authority, East Rutherford, 1974-77; chief engr. Price Waterhouse, N.Y.C., 1978—. Engring. cons. Passaic County Vocat. Edn. High Sch., Wayne, N.J., 1971-77, Meadowlands Racetrack, East Rutherford, 1973-77, Royal Sound, Eatontown, N.J., 1984-86. Bd. trustees N.Y.C. chpt. Leukemia Soc., 1981-86, pres., 1987-90, nat. bd. trustees, 1990—. Recipient Emmy award NATAS, 1985, Outstanding Svc. award Leukemia Soc. Nat. Bd., 1986, Vincent T. Lombardi Humanitarian award, 1990, Pres.' award Leukemia Soc. Am., 1991, People's award, 1991, Outstanding Svc. award in New Orleans, 1994, Disting. Am. award Nat. Football Found. and Coll. Hall of Fame, 1999. Mem. Soc. Motion Picture and TV Engrs. (sec., treas. elect N.Y.C. chpt. 1984-86), Nat. Sports Com., Nat. Performing Arts Com. (vice chmn. 1985—), Friar's Club Internat. (N.Y.C., profl. mem., mem.-elect). Lodges: KC. Republican. Roman Catholic. Avocations: sports, chess, organ and piano. Office: CarMel Prodns 10 Dell Glen Ave Lodi NJ 07644-1758 Home: 421 Farnham Ave Lodi NJ 07644-1204

MELILLO, JOSEPH VINCENT, producer, performing arts; b. New Haven, Nov. 15, 1946; s. Vincent and Viola (Fucci) M. BA, Sacred Heart U., 1968; MFA, Cath. U. Am., 1972. Adminstr. City Ctr. Music and Drama, N.Y.C., 1972-75; mktg. dir. The Walnut St. Theatre, Phila., 1975-76; dir. FEDAPT, N.Y.C., 1976-80; gen. mgr. New World Festival of Arts, Miami, Fla., 1982; dir. Next Wave Festival, N.Y.C., 1983-89; artistic dir. N.Y. Internat. Festival, 1990-91, exec. prodr., 1999—; producing dir. Bklyn. Acad. Music, 1991—, exec. prodr., 1999—. Trustee EnGarde Arts, N.Y.C., 1991-96; v.p., bd. dirs. Assn. Performing Arts Presenters, Washington, 1991-93; cons.-specialist Opera Am. Washington, 1991-93; cons. The Japan Found. "Performing Arts Japan", The Bush Found., St. Paul, Arts Internat., N.Y.C.; adj. prof. Theater Dept. Bklyn. Coll.; co-chair Internat. Presenters Forum; mem. cultural challenge panel N.Y.C. Dept. Cultural Affairs; bd. advisors Etantdonnes, 2000, 2001, 2002. Editor: Market the Arts, 1980. Mem. adv. bd. materials for the arts, Africa Exchange: 651 program com. N.J. Performing Arts Ctr., Newark, 1997—; mem. New Haven Festival of the Arts and Ideas. Decorated chevalier Order of Arts and Letters. Democrat. Avocations: reading, travel. E-mail: programming@bam.org.

MELILLO, ROBIN MARIE BOHACS, secretary; b. Charleston, S.C., June 29, 1961; d. Richard James and Rosemarie (Balint) B.; m. Kenneth Melillo, May 19, 1990; children: Nicole Ashley, Fallon Lindsey. Grad. high sch., Metuchen, N.J. Credit investigator Gen. Electric Credit Corp., Rahway, N.J., 1979-80; adminstrv. asst. Young Adult Conservation Corps, Highland Park, 1980; receptionist Futurecraft, Inc., Colonia, 1980-81; with Amerada Hess Corp., Woodbridge, 1981-82, Westward Ho Hotel & Casino, Las Vegas, Nev., 1982-83; sec. Pharmacia LKB Biotechnology, Inc., Piscataway, N.J., 1983-97, Amersham Pharmacia Biotech, Inc., Piscataway, 1998—. Sec. ladies guild John Calvin Ch., Perth Amboy, N.J., 1984-86; cheer coach, bd. dirs. Metuchen Popwarner. Fellow PS for Profl. Secs. (Cert. 1989), NAFE. Avocations: reading, music, piano. Office: Amersham Pharmacia Biotech Inc 800 Centennial Ave Piscataway NJ 08854-3911

MELIN, ROBERT ARTHUR, lawyer; b. Milw., Sept. 13, 1940; s. Arthur John and Frances Madgalena (Lanser) M.; m. Mary Magdalen Melin, July 8, 1967; children: Arthur Walden, Robert Dismas, Nicholas O'Brien, Madalyn Mary. BA summa cum laude, Marquette U., 1962, JD, 1967. Bar: Wis. 1966, U.S. Dist. Ct. (ea. dist.) Wis. 1966, U.S. Ct. Appeals (7th cir.) 1966, U.S. Ct. Mil. Appeals 1967, U.S. Surpeme Ct. 1975. Law clk. U.S. Dist. Ct. Eastern Dist., Wis., 1966; instr. bus. law U. Ga., Hinesville, 1968; lectr. bus. law U. Md., Asmara, 1970; lectr. law Halle Salassie I. U. Law Faculty, Addis Ababa, Ethiopia, 1971-72; with Walther & Halling, Milw., 1973-74, Schroeder, Gedlen, Riester & Moerke, Milw., 1974-82; ptnr. Schroeder, Gedlen, Riester & Melin, 1982-84, Schroeder, Riester, Melin & Smith, Milw., 1984—. Author: Evidence in Ethiopia, 1972; contbg. author Ann. Survey African Law, 1974; contbr. numerous articles to legal jours. Rep. Class of 2000, West Point Parent Assn. Wis., 1996-99, 99—, exec. bd., 1997-98, 98—; lectr. charitable solicitations and contracts Philanthropy Monthly 9th Ann. Policy Conf., N.Y.C., 1985; chmn. Milw. Young Dems., 1963-64. Capt. JAGC, AUS, 1967-70. Mem. ABA, Wis. Acad. Trial Lawyers, Wis. Bar Assn., Milw. Bar Assn., Am. Legion, Friends Ethiopia, Delta Theta Phi, Phi Alpha Theta, Pi Gamma Mu. Roman Catholic. Home: 8108 N Whitney Rd Milwaukee WI 53217-2752 Office: 135 W Wells St Milwaukee WI 53203-1807

MELITO, CARL FRANK, lawyer, information scientist, consultant; b. Pueblo, Colo., Jan. 22, 1961; s. James Vincent and Mary Marie Melito. BS in Computer Sci., MBA in Fin., U. Denver, 1983; JD, U. Iowa, 1993. Bar: Tex. 1994, U.S. Patent and Trademark Office 1995; cert. EDS Systems Programmer, Oracle DBA. Tech. rep. Software AG Systems, Lakewood, Colo., 1981—83, account rep., 1984—85; customer svc. rep. Applied Data Rsch., Dallas, 1983—84; systems programmer Electronic Data Systems, Plano, 1985—89; sr. database adminstr. GTE Directories Corp., Dallas-Ft. Worth Airport, 1989—91; patent atty. pvt. practice Dallas, 1995—; pres. Advanced Resources, Inc., 1995—. Cons. Computer Assoc. Rels. Program, L.I., NY, 1999—2000. Author: Comprehensive Guide to U.S. & International Trademarks, 1994; contbr. articles to profl. jours. Mem.: IEEE, ABA, Toastmasters Internat. Avocations: hiking, running, weightlifting, skiing. Office: Advanced Resources Inc 12225 Greenville Ave Ste 800 Dallas TX 75243 Fax: 972-479-8809. E-mail: carl@melito.com.

MELLBERG, JAMES RICHARD, dental research chemist; b. Manitowac, Wis., June 3, 1932; s. Millard Filmore Mellberg and Marion Eleanor (Elmer) Zimmerman; m. Gail Maureen Loehning, Sept. 26, 1956; children: Eric, Diane, Laura. BS, Wis. State U., Oshkosh, 1955; MS, Loyola U., Chgo., 1960. Head dental rsch. dept. Kendall Co., Barrington, Ill., 1958-75; assoc. dir. dental rsch. Colgate-Palmolive Co., Piscataway, N.J., 1975-94. Cons. Naval Dental Rsch. Inst., Great Lakes, Ill., 1972-94. Author: Fluoride in Preventive Dentistry, 1983; patentee in field; contbr. over 100 articles in field to sci. publs. Recipient 20 sci. exhibit awards ADA, 1964-87. Mem. Internat. Assn. Dental Rsch. (Disting. Scientist award). Avocations: cycling, woodworking. Home: 675 Ridge Top Rd Tryon NC 28782

MELLBERG, LEONARD EVERT, physicist; b. Springfield, Mass., Dec. 18, 1935; s. Evert and Dorothy (Baker) M.; m. Pamela Narbeth. BS in Physics, U. Mass., 1961; MS in Physics, Trinity Coll., Hartford, Conn., 1968. Rsch. physicist Navy Underwater Sound Lab., New London, Conn., 1961-68, SACLANT Undersea Rsch. Ctr., LaSpezia, Italy, 1968-72, Office of Naval Rsch., London, 1968-72, Naval Underwater Systems Ctr., Newport, R.I., 1972-91; sr. scientist Marine Acoustics Inc., 1991-94; chief scientist Sci. Applications Internat. Corp., R.I., 1994-2000, Ocean Physics Assocs., South Dartmouth, Mass., 2000—. Govt. and profl. tech. adv. bds. and coms. Contbr. over 70 articles to profl. jours. Pres. Verdandi Swedish Cultural Found., Providence, 1992-97; bd. dirs. Verdandi Chorus Am. Union Swedish Singers, Providence, 1992—. Recipient Naval Underwater Sys. Ctr. Excellence in Sci. award, 1977, 84, Civilian Navy Meritorious Svc. medal Dept. of Navy, 1991. Fellow Acoustical Soc. Am.; mem. IEEE (sr.), AIAA (Svc. award 1977), Am. Geophys. Union, Oceanic Soc. of IEEE. Achievements include research in ocean physics, ocean acoustic propagation, anti-submarine warfare acoustics, Arctic sea-ice ridges and lighter than air vehicles. Home and Office: 41 Hidden Bay Dr South Dartmouth MA 02748-3021 E-mail: lenmellberg@ieee.org.

MELLEMA, DONALD EUGENE, retired radio news reporter and anchor; b. Chgo., Mar. 30, 1937; s. Raymond Cornelius and Dorothy Sofia (Miller) M.; m. Freda Dieterlen Mellema, Sept. 23, 1961; children: Darryl Emerson, Duane Edward. BA in Speech, Beloit (Wis.) Coll., 1959. News dir. WGEZ Radio, Beloit, 1959; evening host, newsman WOSH Radio, Oshkosh, Wis., 1959-63; morning host, newsman WANE Radio, Ft. Wayne, Ind., 1963-65; news dir. WATI Radio, Indpls., 1965-67; news writer WGN Radio, Chgo., 1967-69; news reporter, anchor WBBM Radio, 1969-96; ret., 1996. Mem. publs. adv. bd., pres's adv. coun., cons. Beloit Coll., 1996-2000, also profl.-in-residence. Speaker, motivator Chgo. Pub. Sch. Youth Motivation Program, 1993-96; advisor, cons. media rels. to various police and civic orgns.; commr., unit leader Boy Scouts Am., 1971-81; ch. deacon Park Ridge (Ill.) Presbyn. Ch., 1980-83. Recipient regional award Radio TV News Dirs. Assn., 1994, Newsfinder award AP, 1995, career recognition award Chgo. Police Dept., 1997, Mark Twain award Ill. AP, 1997; named to Taft H.S. Hall of Fame, 1995. Mem. Ill. News Broadcasters Assn. (Silver Dome 1st Place award 1994), Soc. Profl. Journalists (Peter Lisagor award 1991, 96), Am. Legion. Republican. Avocations: woodworking, reading, photography, birding, travel. E-mail: DONMELLEMA@NETSCAPE.NET.

MELLEN, FRANCIS JOSEPH, JR. lawyer; b. Williamsport, Pa., Dec. 19, 1945; s. Francis Joseph and Mary Emma (Oberst) M.; m. Mary Wilder Davison, Aug. 2, 1975 (div. 1987); m. Beverly Joan Glascock, Sept. 2, 2000; children: Elizabeth, Catherine, Robert, Christine. BA, U. Ky., 1967, MA, 1971; JD, Harvard U., 1973. Bar: N.Y. 1974, Ky. 1975, U.S. Dist. Ct. (so. dist.) N.Y. 1974, U.S. Dist. Ct. (ea. dist.) Ky. 1977, U.S. Dist. Ct. (we. dist.) Ky. 1978, U.S. Ct. Appeals (2d cir.) 1975, U.S. Ct. Appeals (6th cir.) 1982. Assoc. atty. Rogers & Wells, N.Y.C., 1973-75, Wyatt, Grafton & Sloss, Louisville, 1975-80; ptnr. Wyatt, Tarrant & Combs, 1980—. Co-author: Kentucky Mineral Law, 1986, Kentucky Forms and Transactions, 1991. Contbr. articles to profl. jours. Mem. spl. study com. for Uniform Commercial Code, Ky. Legis. Rsch. Comsn., Frankfort, 1984-91; bd. dirs. Leadership Louisville Found., 1995-2002, counsel, 1996-98, 2000-02; bd. dirs. Stage One: The Louisville Children's Theatre, 1995-2001, v.p., 1997-98, pres., 1998-2000; bd. dirs. Louisville-Jefferson County A.W.A.R.E. Coalition, 1994-98. Mem. ABA, Am. Arbitration Assn. (panel), Ky. Bar Assn. (ho. dels. 1986-92), Louisville Bar Assn. (chmn. com. profl. responsibility 1992-94), Jefferson Club, Filson Club, Am. Mensa. Republican. Home: 2944 Lexington Rd Louisville KY 40206-2934 Office: Wyatt Tarrant & Combs 2800 Citizens Plz Louisville KY 40202 E-mail: fmellen@wyattfirm.com.

MELLENDORF, PATRICIA JEAN, retired personnel professional; b. Terre Haute, Ind., Mar. 12, 1948; d. LeRoy Benjamin and Sue Jean (Nickerson) Patterson; m. Loren D. Mellendorf; 1 child, Peggy Marie. BA, U. Iowa, 1971, MA in English, EdS, U. Iowa, 1973. Cert. sr. profl. human resources. Related edn. chair Ivy Tech Coll., Richmond, Ind., 1974-84; sec. Am. Water Sys., 1984-86, cmty./employee rels. mgr., 1986-88, asst. dir. pers. devel., 1988-96, dir. pers. svcs., 1996-98; ret., 1998. Lectr. EEOC, N.Y.C., Phil. Health Maintenance, 1991-95. Editor mag. Am. Water, 1994-96. Mem. econ. edn. adv. coun. Ind. U. East, Richmond, 1988. Mem. Soc. Human Resource Mgmt., ASTD (dir. utilities industry group 1992-95), Am. Water Works Assn., Phi Beta Kappa. Presbyterian.

MELLER, ROBERT LOUIS, JR. lawyer; b. Mpls., Apr. 24, 1950; s. Robert Louis and June Louise (Grenacher) M. BA, Carleton Coll., 1972; JD, Cornell U., 1975. Bar: Minn., 1975, U.S. Dist. Ct. (no. dist.), 1975. Atty. Best & Flanagan, Mpls., 1977—, ptnr., 1982—. Mem. ABA, Minn. State Bar Assn., Mpls. Club, Phi Beta Kappa, Sigma Xi. Republican. Episcopalian. Home: 1800 Major Dr N Minneapolis MN 55422-4153 Office: Best and Flanagan 4000 US Bank Pl 601 2nd Ave S # D Minneapolis MN 55402-4303

MELLEY, STEVEN MICHAEL, lawyer; b. Rhinebeck, N.Y., Jan. 3, 1950; s. James Christopher and Virginia (Madonna) M.; children: Aliza, Steven Jonathan, Olivia, Bennett; m. Phoebe Kirwood. BA in Russian Studies with honors, Colgate U., 1972; JD, Tulane U., 1975. Bar: N.Y. 1976, U.S. Dist. Ct. 1976, U.S. Supreme Ct. 1980. Law clk. to hon. Matthew Braniff Criminal Dist. Judge, Orleans Parish, New Orleans; assoc. Woody N. Klose Law Offices, Red Hook, N.Y., 1975-78; ptnr. Klose & Melley, Rhinebeck, 1978-83; pvt. practice, 1983—. Atty. Village of Tivoli, N.Y., 1977-78. Contbg. editor: New York Motor Vehicle Accidents, 1999; assoc. editor Tulane Forum, 1974-75. Mem. ABA, ATLA (sustaining), N.Y. State Bar Assn. (past com. mem. on specialization), Dutchess County Bar Assn. (sustaining), N.Y. State Trial Lawyers Assn., Million Dollar Advocates Forum, Phi Alpha Delta, Kappa Delta Rho. Office: 24 Closs Dr Rhinebeck NY 12572 Fax: (914) 876-5745. E-mail: melleyinjurylaw@aol.com.

MELLI, MARYGOLD SHIRE, law educator; b. Rhinelander, Wis., Feb. 8, 1926; d. Osborne and May (Bonnie) Shire; m. Joseph Alexander Melli, Apr. 8, 1950; children: Joseph, Sarah Bonnie, Sylvia Anne, James Alexander. BA, U. Wis., 1947, LLB, 1950. Bar: Wis. 1950. Dir. children's code revision Wis. Legis. Coun., Madison, 1950-53; exec. dir. Wis. Jud. Coun., 1955-59; asst. prof. law U. Wis., 1959-66, assoc. prof., 1966-67, prof., 1967-84, Voss-Bascom prof., 1985-93, emerita, 1993—. Assoc. dean U. Wis., 1970-72, rsch. affiliate Inst. for Rsch. on Poverty, 1980—; mem. spl. rev. bd. Dept. Health and Social Svcs., State of Wis., Madison, 1973—. Author: (pamphlet) The Legal Status of Women in Wisconsin, 1977, (book) Wisconsin Juvenile Court Practice, 1978, rev. edit., 1983, (with others) Child Support & Alimony, 1988, The Case for Transracial Adoption, 1994; co-editor: Child Support: The Next Frontier, 1999; contbr. articles to profl. jours. Bd. dirs. Am. Humane Assn., 1985-95; chair A Fund for Women, Madison, Wis., 2002. Named one of five Outstanding Young Women in Wis., Jaycees, 1961; rsch. grantee NSF, 1983; recipient Belle Case LaFollette award for outstanding svc. to the profession, 1994, award for Outstanding Contbn. to Advancement of Women in Higher Edn., 1991, award for Lifelong Contbn. to Advancement of Women in the Legal Prof., 1994, Rotary Sr. Svc. award, Madison, Wis., 2002. Fellow Am. Acad. Matrimonial Lawyers (exec. editor jour. 1985-90); mem. Am. Law Inst. (cons. project on law of family dissolution), Internat. Soc. Family Law (v.p. 1994-2000, 02—), Wis. State Bar Assn. (reporter family law sect.), Nat. Conf. Bar Examiners (chmn. bd. mgrs. 1989, editl. adv. com.). Democrat. Roman Catholic. Avocations: jogging, swimming, collecting art. Home: 2904 Waunona Way Madison WI 53713-2238 Office: U Wis Law Sch Madison WI 53706 E-mail: msmelli@facstaff.wisc.edu.

MELLING, JACK, biotechnologist, director; b. Aspull, Lancashire, Eng., Feb. 8, 1940; s. John and Mary (Marsden) M.; m. Susan Melling, May 27, 1967. BSc, Manchester U., Eng., 1963, MSc, 1965; PhD, Bath U., Eng., 1968. Rsch. asst. Bath U., Eng., 1965-68; lectr. Heriot-Watt U., Scotland, 1968-69; sr. sci. officer Ministry of Def., Eng., 1969-73, prin. sci. officer Eng., 1973-79; dir. vaccine rsch. and product lab. Pub. Health Lab. Svc., Eng., 1979-87; head biologics divsn. and dep. dir. Ctr. for Applied Microbiology & Rsch., Porton Down, Salisbury, England, 1987-92, dir. Porton Down, Salisbury, Eng., 1992-96, Salk Inst., Swiftwater, Pa., 1996-2000, Karl Landsteiner Inst., Vienna, 2000—. Vis. prof. Rutgers U. 1979-84, Aston U., 1981-96, Westminster U., 1995—, Zurich U., 1999—; mem. MRC Vaccine Com., 1979-96; sec. Brit. Coord. Com. for Biotech., London, 1981-85; mem. Com. Safety of Medicines, Biologic, London, 1982-99, Ministry of Agr. Toxicants in Foods com., London, 1982-94; mem. rsch. adv. com. on Gulf War vets. illnesses U.S. Dept. Vets. Affairs, 2002--; counsellor, tutor Open U., Salisbury, 1971-74; sr. sci. advisor Internat. AIDS Initiative, N.Y.C., 1999—. Editor: Microbial Adhesion, 1980; editor Chem. Tech. and Biotech. Jour., 1985—; contbr. over 100 articles to profl. jours. Active Swiss Diasaster Relief Orgn. Fellow Royal Pharm. Soc. G.B., Inst. of Biology. Fellow Royal Soc. Medicine, Royal Coll. Pathologists; mem. Soc. Chem. Industry (coun. mem. 1975-83, 98—, sec. 1975-81, chmn. biotech. group 1981-83, chmn. publs. com. 1999—). Avocations: skiing, walking. Office: Karl Landsteiner Inst Rennweg 95B A1030 Vienna Austria E-mail: jmelling@ptdprolog.net.

MELLING, JOHN KENNEDY, accountant; b. Westcliff-on-sea, Essex, Eng., Jan. 11, 1927; s. John Robert and Ivy Edith May (Woolmer) M. Chartered acct.; chartered tax cons. Audit clk. Younghusband, Taft & Co., Derby, Eng., 1942-43; articled clk., chartered acct. Jones, Shinner & Co., London and Southend, Eng., 1943-53; sr. asst. Howard, Howes & Co., London, 1953-59; pvt. practice London & Westcliff, Eng., 1959—. Dramatic critic The Stage, Eng., 1957-90, Fur Weekly News, Eng., 1968-73; lectr., radio and TV broadcaster in field; columnist Crime Time, Eng., 1996—2002. Author: Southend Playhouses Since 1793, 1969, Discovering Lost Theatres, 1969, Discovering London's Guilds and Liveries, 1973, 5th edit., 1995, Discovering Theatre Ephemera, 1974, She Shall Have Murder, 1987, Alchemy of Murder, 1993, Gwendoline Butler-Inventor of the Women's Police Procedural, 1993, Murder Done to Death, 1996, (plays) George-From Caroline, Murder at St. Dunstan's, The Toast Is series, also filmscripts, audio books; co-author: Scaling the High C's, 1996; editor: The Farrier & His Craft, 1981, Crime Writers' Practical Handbook, 1989 (CWA Spl. award); editor The Liveryman Mag., 1970-75, Black Dagger Series, 1986-91, Murder in the Library, 1986; contbr. articles to profl. jours. Gov. Corp. of the Sons of the Clergy, Eng., 1981—; hon. life internat. v.p. Am. Fedn. Police, 1985—; com. mem. Crime Writers' Assn., Eng., 1985-88; spl. agt., hon. chief police Nat. Drugs Task Force, 1989—. Decorated knight Order St. Basil the Great (Russia); knight comdr. Order Knights of Justice, knight grand cross Order St. Michael the Archangel, 1980-81; master Worshipful Co. of Poulters; liveryman Farriers and Bakers Cos.; freeman Constructors Co.; recipient Award Police medal of Honor 1984. Fellow Faculty of Bldg., Royal Soc. Arts; mem. Brit. Acad. Film and TV Arts, City Livery Club (editor and coun. mem. 1970-75), Cookery and Food Assn., Marylebone Rifle & Pistol Club, Westcliff Film and Video Club (founder, pres. 1962, first hon. life mem. 1999), Edinburgh Press Club. Conservative. Anglican. Avocations: reading, shooting, collecting crime fiction. Home: 44A Tranquil Vale Blackheath London SE3 0BD England also: 85 Chalkwell Ave Westcliff-on-sea Essex SS0 8NL England

MELLINGER, BARRY LEE, community college president, vocational educator; b. Colorado Springs, Colo., Dec. 19, 1939; s. Paul Diffenbach and Edna R. (Detwiller) M.; m. Dorothy Bugg, June 20, 1964; children: Mim Hatten, Debbie (dec.), Sharon Sanders, Jay, Christa. AS, Perkinston (Miss.) Jr. Coll., 1960; BS, Miss. State U., 1962, MEd, 1963; PhD, Purdue U., 1973. Asst. dir. vocat.-tech. edn. Miss. Gulf Coast C.C., Perkinston, 1963-65, dir. vocat-tech. edn., 1965-67; instr. Purdue U., West Lafayette, Ind., 1967-68; asst. exec. sec. Commn. on Colls., So. Assn. Colls. and Schs., Atlanta, 1968-72, assoc. exec. sec., 1972-77; dir. vocat-tech. sch., dean occupl. edn. Dekalb C.C., Clarkston, Ga., 1977-79; v.p. instnl. affairs Miss. Gulf Coast C.C., 1979-85, pres., 1986-98; ret., 1998. Cons. Nunez C.C., Chalmette, La., 1993, Northwestern State U., Natchitoches, La., 1993. Mem. Miss. Higher Edn. Assistance Corp., Jackson, 1984-97; bd. dirs. Kids Voting Miss., 1996, 97; mem. exec. bd. Miss. Pub. Edn. Forum, 1993—; mem. Harrison County Devel. Commn., Econ. Devel. Network, 1988-89; mem. info. resource coun., Miss. Dept. Info. Tech. Svcs., 1996, 97. Recipient CEO award Assn. C.C. Trustees, 1994. Mem. Am. Assn. Cmty. and Jr. Colls. (bd. dirs. 1987-90), Nat. Alliance Cmty. and Tech. Colls. (pres. 1985-86), So. Assn. Colls. and Schs. (mem. exec. coun. 1994-96, commn. on colls. 1994-96, criteria rev. com. 1994, chmn.'s corps; chmn. reaffirmation com. to Patrick Henry C.C., Martinsville, Va. 1997, Delgado C.C., New Orleans 1996, Tex. State Tech. Coll., Amarillo 1995, Daytona Beach C.C. 1993, Santa Fe C.C., Gainesville, Fla. 1993), Miss. Assn. Colls. (mem. audit com. 1992, pres. 1990), Miss. C.C. and Jr. Coll. Assn. (chmn. 1996—), So. Assn. Cmty., Jr., and Tech. Colls. (v.p. 1988), Rotary Club (Wiggins, Miss.), Phi Delta Kappa, Iota Lambda Sigma. Avocations: woodworking, antique cars. Home: 66 Bluff Creek Rd Wiggins MS 39577-9714 Office: Miss Gulf Coast Cmty Coll PO Box 67 Perkinston MS 39573-0002

MELLINK, MACHTELD JOHANNA, archaeologist, educator; b. Amsterdam, Holland, Oct. 26, 1917; came to U.S., 1949; d. Johan and Machteld (Kruyff) M. BA, U. Amsterdam, 1938, MA, 1941; PhD, Utrecht (Netherlands) U., 1943; LLD (hon.), U. Pa., 1987, Anatolian U., Turkey, 1990. Faculty Bryn Mawr Coll., 1949-88, prof. classical and Near Eastern archaeology, 1962-88, chmn. dept., 1955-83; staff mem. excavations Tarsus, Turkey, 1947-49, Gordion, Turkey, 1950-74; field dir. excavations Karatas-Semayuk, Lycia, Turkey, 1963—; staff mem. Troy, 1988—. Rsch. assoc. U. Mus., U. Pa., 1955-82, cons. scholar, 1982—. Author: A Hittite Cemetery at Gordion, 1956; author: (with Jan Filip) Frühe Stufen der Kunst-Propyläen Kunstgeschichte XIII, 1974; editor: Dark Ages and Nomads c. 1000 B.C., 1964, Troy and the Trojan War, 1986, Elmali-Karatas I, 1992, II, 1994; author: Kizilbel, An Archaic Painted Tomb Chamber in Northern Lycia, 1998; contbr. articles to profl. jours. Recipient Lucy Wharton Drexel medal U. Pa. Mus., 1994—. Fellow Am. Acad. Arts and Scis.; mem. Archaeol. Inst. Am. (pres. 1981-84, gold medal 1991), German Archaeol. Inst., Am. Oriental Soc., Am. Philos. Soc.; corr. mem. Royal Netherlands Acad. Scis., Austrian Archaeol. Inst. (corr.), Türk Tarih Kurumu (hon.), Am. Research Inst. Turkey (v.p. 1977-87, pres. 1988-92). Home: 264 Montgomery Ave Haverford PA 19041-1531

MELLINKOFF, SHERMAN MUSSOFF, medical educator; b. McKeesport, Pa., Mar. 23, 1920; s. Albert and Helen Mussoff Mellinkoff; m. June Bernice O'Connell, Nov. 18, 1944; children: Sherrill, Albert. BA, Stanford U., 1941, MD, 1944; LHD (hon.), Wake Forest U., 1984, Hebrew Union Coll., L.A., 1988. Diplomate Am. Bd. Internal Medicine, Am. Bd. Gastroenterology, Am. Bd. Nutrition. Intern asst. resident Stanford U. Hosp., San Francisco, 1944—45; asst. resident Johns Hopkins Hosp., Balt., 1947—49, chief resident, 1950—51, instr. in medicine, 1951—53; fellow in gastroenterology Hosp. of U. Pa., Phila., 1949—50; from asst. prof. to prof. medicine UCLA Sch. of Medicine, L.A., 1962—86; dean UCLA Sch. Medicine, 1962—86, emeritus prof. of medicine, 1990—; disting. physician of VA Wadsworth VA Medical Ctr., 1990-93. Mem. sci. adv. panel Rsch. to Prevent Blindness, Inc., N.Y.C., 1975—93; mem. program devel. com. Nat. Med. Fellowships, Inc., N.Y.C., 1984—. Editl. bd.: The Pharos, 1986; contbr. articles to profl. jours. Apptd. by Gov. of Calif. to McCone Com., 1965. Capt. U.S. Army, 1945—57. Recipient Abraham Flexner award, Assn. Am. Med. Colls., 1981, J.E. Wallace Sterling Disting. Alumnus award, Stanford U. Sch. of Medicine, 1987. Master: ACP; fellow: Royal Coll. of Physicians; mem.: The Johns Hopkins Soc. of Scholars, Am. Acad. of Arts and Scis., Inst. of Medicine of NAS, Assn. Am. Physicians, Am. Gastroenterol. Assn. Assn. Avocations: reading, hiking. Office: UCLA Dept Medicine 44 138 Chs Los Angeles CA 90095-0001

MELLINS, HARRY ZACHARY, radiologist, educator; b. N.Y.C., May 23, 1921; s. David J. and Ray (Hoffman) M.; m. Judith Alice Weiss, Dec. 26, 1950; children— Elizabeth, William, Thomas. AB, Columbia Coll., 1941; MD, L.I. Coll. Medicine, 1944; MS in Radiology, U. Minn., 1951; AM (hon.), Harvard U., 1970. Intern Jewish Hosp., Bklyn., 1944-45, asst. resident in radiology, 1945-46; resident in radiology U. Minn., Mpls., 1948-50, instr. radiology, 1950-52, asst. prof., 1952-53; clin. asst. prof. radiology Wayne State U., Detroit, 1953-56; dir. radiology Sinai Hosp., 1953-56; prof., chmn. dept. radiology SUNY, Coll. Medicine, N.Y.C., 1956-69; chief radiology Kings County Hosp. Center, Bklyn., 1956-69; radiologist-in-chief State Univ. Hosp., 1966-69; prof. radiology Harvard Med. Sch., Boston, 1969-91, prof. radiology emeritus, 1991—; dir. diagnostic radiology Peter Bent Brigham Hosp., 1969-79, Brigham and Women's Hosp., 1980-87, dir. edn. and tng., dept. radiology, 1987-94; co-dir. edn. and tng. dept. radiology, 1994-97; chief of radiology Harvard U. Health Svc., 1988-97; radiologist Brigham and Women's Hosp., 1998-99. Nat. cons. in radiology to surgeon gen. U.S. Air Force, 1968-79; mem. radiation study sect. NIH, 1967-71; mem. subcom. for written exam. in diagnostic radiology Am. Bd. Radiology, 1970-75; mem. radiology tng. com. research tng. grants br. Nat. Inst. Gen. Med. Scis.; mem. diagnostic research adv. group div. cancer biology and diagnosis Nat. Cancer Inst., 1975-79; guest examiner Am. Bd. Radiology. Served to capt. M.C. USAAF, 1946-48. Mem. Bklyn. Radiol. Soc. (pres. 1965-66), N.Y. Roentgen Soc. (pres 1966-67), Assn. Univ. Radiologists (pres. 1969-70, Gold medal 1986), Soc. Uroradiology (pres. 1975-76, Gold medal 2000), Am. Roentgen Ray Soc. (pres. 1977-79, Gold medal 1989), Radiol. Soc. N.Am., New Eng. Roentgen Ray Soc. (pres. 1986-87), Soc. Gastrointestinal Radiology, Alpha Omega Alpha (alumnus). E-mail: judymellins@aol.com.

MELLINS, ROBERT B. pediatrician, educator; b. N.Y.C., Mar. 6, 1928; s. David J. and Ray H. (Hoffman) M.; m. Sue Mendelsohn, Apr. 19, 1959; children: Claude Ann, David Rustin. AB, Columbia U., 1948; MD, Johns Hopkins U., 1952. Intern Johns Hopkins Hosp., 1952-53; mem. epidemic intelligence svc, founder poison control program Ctr. Disease Control, Chgo., 1953-55; resident in pediatrics N.Y. Hosp., 1955-56, Presbyn. Hosp., N.Y.C., 1956-57, dir. pediatric ICU, 1970-75; assoc. prof. pediatrics Columbia U., 1970-75, prof. pediatrics, 1975—, dir. Cystic Fibrosis Ctr., 1978-91, dir. pediatric pulmonary div., 1972-97. Christmas Seal prof. Can. Lung Assn., 1979-80; 1st Deans Disting. lectr. in clin. scis. Columbia U. Coll. P&S, 1982; mem. Am. Bd. Pediatrics, founding mem. sub-bd. on pediatric pulmonology; bd. dirs. A.P. Gold Fedn. to promote humanisim in medicine. Mem. editl. bd. Am. Rev. Respiratory Diseases, 1974-81, assoc. editor, 1984-90; contbr. articles to med. jours. V.p. Am. Lung Assn., 1987—89; chmn. steering com. mulitctr. study heart & lung complications of HIV infection in children NIH, 1989—92; bd. dir. Am. Lung Assn., 1981—83, LA Jonas Found., 1970—78, 1990—, Symphony of UN, 1990—. Recipient Career Devel. award NIH, 1966-71, Career Scientist award Health Rsch. Coun. N.Y.C. Health Rsch. Coun., 1975, Stevens Triennial award for rsch. Columbia U., 1980, Health Edn. Rsch. award Nat. Asthma Edn. Program, 1992, Will Ross medal Am. Lung Assn., 1996, 2001 Life & Breath award Am. Lung Assn. N.Y. Mem.: Am. Acad. Allergy & Immunology, Soc. Critical Care Medicine, Am. Thoracic Soc. (bd. dir. 1975, 1981—84, nat. pres. 1982—83, v.p., disting. achievement award 1996), Am. Acad. Pediat. (med. edn. lay edn. award 1995), Am. Soc. Pharmacology & Exptl. Therapeutics, Am. Physiol. Soc., Soc. Pediatric Rsch., Am. Pediatric Soc., Fleischner Soc. (pres. 1995—), Alpha Omega Alpha. Home: 2 W 67th St New York NY 10023-6241 Office: Childrens Hosp of NY-Presbyn 3959 Broadway CHS 746 New York NY 10032 E-mail: rbm3@columbia.edu.

MELLINS, THOMAS HARRISON, architectural historian; b. Bklyn., Apr. 6, 1957; s. Harry Zachary and Judith (Weiss) M.; m. Judith Weinstein, Jan. 13, 1996; 1 child, Samuel Soren. BA in History, Columbia Coll., N.Y.C., 1979; MA in Creative Art, CUNY, 1981. Editor Inst. Architecture Urban Studies, N.Y.C., 1981-82; assoc. Robert A.M. Stern Archs., 1983-2000. Scriptwriter (with others)(documentary TV script) Pride of Place, 1986; author: (with others) New York 1930, 1987 (nat. book award nomination, 1987), New York 1960, 1995, (with others) Changing Paris, 2000, Restoring Gotham, 2002. Recipient citation AIA, 1994, Book of Yr. award, 1995, 1st prize for pub. Quito Bienial, 1998, N.Y.C. Centennial Historian, 1999, Book Yr. award N.Y. Soc. Libr., 1999. Office: 50 W 96th St Ste 15B New York NY 10025-6545 E-mail: thmellins@aol.com.

MELLION, MORRIS BERNARD, physician, educator; b. Providence, Dec. 24, 1939; s. Frank and Yvette Gladys (Shaset) M.; m. Irene Mabel Conner, June 6, 1970; children: Rose Conner, Frank Bruce. BA with honors, Cornell U., 1961; postgrad., Tulane U., 1964-66; MD, Yale U., 1970. Diplomate Am. Bd. Family Practice (relevancy com. 1988-89, cons. sports medicine com. 1988). Intern, resident U. Vt. Sch. Medicine, Burlington, 1970—74; pvt. practice, Moran and Teton Village, Wyo., 1971-72, Jackson, 1974-82; asst. and assoc. prof. Sch. Health, Phys. Edn.-Recreation, U. Nebr., Omaha, 1986-90, supr. practicum worksite, 1986—, adj. assoc. prof., 1990—; coord., dir. family practice fellowship in sports medicine U. Nebr. Med. Ctr., 1988-90, clin. assoc. prof. family practice and orthopaedic surgery, 1990—; med. dir. Sports Medicine Ctr., 1990-96, HMO Nebr. Inc. (Blue Cross Blue Shield managed care subs.), 1996; sr. v.p. health care policy, chief med. officer Blue Cross Blue Shield of Nebr., 1996—. Mem. nat. coun. med. mgmt. Blue Cross Blue Shield Assn. (vice chmn. 1998, 2000, chmn. managed care com., 1999, mem. innovations com., chmn. Blue Cross Blue Shield Assn. Policy com., 2000, mem. pharmacy adv. group, 1999—, chmn. Nat. Coun. Physician Execs., 2001; clin. asst. prof. preventive and family medicine U. Colo. Sch. Medicine, Denver, 1980-92; del. Coun. Med. Splty. Socs., Lake Forest, Ill., 1991-92; mem. rev. panel Am. Family Physician, 1988—, Physician and Sportsmedicine, 1988—, Medicine and Sci. in Sports and Exercise, 1990-96, Jour. Musculoskeletal Medicine and Exercise, 1990-95; mem. exec. bd. Midwest Youth Coaches Assn., Omaha, 1991, cons., 1992-94; tournament physician NCAA, Omaha, 1988; med. advisor Dept. Vocat. Rehab., Teton County, 1976-82; med. dir. Cornhusker Winter Games, 1995-96. Editor, author: Office Management of Sports Injuries and Athletic Problems, 1988, The Team Physician's Handbook, 1990, 3d edit., 2001, Sports Medicine Secrets, 1994, 3d edit., 2002, Office Sports Medicine, 1996; mem. editl. bd.: Family Practice Bull., 1988—90, assoc. editor: Heart Disease and Stroke, 1991—94; contbr. articles to profl. jours. Bd. dirs. Athletes Fighting Substance Abuse, Omaha, 1990; med. cons. Teton Community Mental Health Ctr., Jackson, 1975, bd. dirs., 1976-79, pres. bd., 1977-78; med. advisor Teton County chpt. Am. Cancer Soc., Jackson, 1974-76; mem. Nat. Ski Patrol, Grand Targhee Ski Area, Alta, Wyo., 1977-81; mem. adv. bd. Jackson Hole Arts Ctr., 1982, Dignity, Inc., Jackson, 1981-82; mem. bd. Community Children's Project, Jackson, 1976-78; also others. Lt. (j.g.) USN, 1961-65. Recipient Cornell Aero. Lab. award Cornell U., 1965, Spl. Recognition award U. Nebr., 1988-89; scholar Naval ROTC, 1961-65; Woodrow Wilson fellow, 1965. Fellow Am. Acad. Family Physicians (vice speaker Congress of Dels. 1984-88, speaker Congress of Dels. 1988-90, pres.-elect 1990-91, pres. 1991-92, exec. com. 1990-93, chair Com. on Health Edn. 1984-87, chair Task Force on Sports Medicine 1988-89, parliamentarian congress of dels. 1995-96); mem. AMA, Soc. Tchrs. Family Medicine, Nebr. Acad. Family Physicians, Nebr. Med. Assn., Metro Omaha Med. Soc., Am. Acad. Allergy, Am. Coll. Sports Medicine), Am. Heart Assn. (coun. on arteriosclerosis), Nat. Strengt and Conditioning Assn., Nat. Athletic Trainers Assn. (adv.), Cycling Rsch. Assn., Am. Med. Soc. for Sports Medicine (charter), Phi Beta Kapa, Pi Sigma Alpha. Jewish. Avocations: bicycling, skiing, mountain climbing, nature photography. Home: 12209 Leavenworth Rd Omaha NE 68154-3048 Office: Blue Cross Blue Shield of Nebr 7261 Mercy Rd Omaha NE 68124-2349 E-mail: mellion@home.com.

MELLITZ, NELSON LEONARD, government official; b. Phila., July 31, 1948; s. Martin and Rose Ruth (Rockstein) M.; m. Debra Meryl Mellitz, Mar. 25, 1979; children: Diana Susan, Cynthia Alexis. BS in Acctg., Point Park Coll., 1981; BBA, Temple U., 1976; MS in Acquisitions, Am. Grad. U., 1989. Staff analyst Westinghouse Corp., Pitts., 1981-84; sr. contracts rep. RCA/GE Corp., Moorestown, N.J., 1984-90; procurement staff officer Dept. Def., Phila., 1990-94; regional contracts specialist Dept. Labor, 1994-98; N.E. area chief procurement officer Dept. Treas. IRS, N.Y.C., 1998—. Author: How to Sell to the Federal Government, 1991. Bd. dirs. Congregation Beth El, 1997-2001; dep. acad. liaison officer USAF Acad., Colorado Springs, 1994—. Col. USAFR, 1997—. Fellow Nat. Contract Mgmt. Assn. (v.p. 1986-87, coun. 1984—, cert. contract profl. mgr.), South Jersey Men's Club (bd. dirs. 1984—). Avocation: numismatics. Home: 5 Green Vale Rd Cherry Hill NJ 08034-1703 Office: NE Area Field Procurement 290 Broadway Fl 3D New York NY 10007-1823 E-mail: nmellitz@cs.com.

MELLMAN, LEONARD, real estate investor and advisor; b. Mar. 23, 1924; s. Morris and Luba (Levin) M. BA, Temple U., 1949. Prin., owner L. Mellman Co., Phila., 1949-84, retired, 1984; prin., owner Mellman Investments, 1960—; ptnr. Mellman, Blume Co., 1979—, Cunniff, Mellman Co., Phila., 1982—. Gen. ptnr. Diamond Acres, Phila., 1981-86, Van Pelt Ct. Ltd. pres., 1985-91; pres. MLC Bd. Settlement Music Sch., Phila., 1985-91, sec. ctrl. bd., 1985-91, v.p. ctrl. bd., 1997—. Pres. arts and sci. alumni bd. Temple U., Phila., 1976-78; bd. dirs. Art Growth 2000, 1998—. With U.S. Army, 1943-46. Mem. Credit Mchts. Assn. (pres. 1970-72, man of yr. award 1970), Phila. Bd. Realtors, Temple U. Gen. Alumni Assn. (pres. 1992-94, disting. alumni award 1985), Singing City Choir (bd. dirs., pres. 1988-90), Phila. Opera Guild (bd. dirs. 1995—, pres. 1997-99, chmn. of bd. 1999—), Opera Vols. Internat. (treas. 1999—), Union League Phila. (chair, bd. trustees Scholarship Found.), Opera Vols. Internat. Democrat. Jewish. Home and Office: 220 W Rittenhouse Sq Apt 22C Philadelphia PA 19103 E-mail: oprabuf@aol.com.

MELLO, MICHAEL WILLIAM, educational administrator; b. Waterbury, Conn., Apr. 8, 1941; s. Manuel Sousa and Mary Doris (Araujo) M.; m. Elizabeth Ann Ambaragocy, Feb. 11, 1973; children— William Michael, David Michael. B.Ed., R.I. Coll., 1962, M.Ed., 1965. With Portsmouth Sch. Dept. (R.I.), 1962—, dir. instructional tech., 1968-81, dir. grant programs, 1975-81, dir. instrn., 1981-89, asst. supt., 1989—; instr. R.I. Coll. Pres. Citizens Scholarship Found. of Bristol, R.I., Inc., 1963-66; bd. trustees Portsmouth Free Library, 1981—, v.p. 1981-82, pres., 1982-84, 85—, treas., 1984-85. Served with U.S. Army, 1966-68. Mem. NEA, Assn. Ednl. Communication and Tech., R.I. Audiovisual Edn. Assn. (pres. 1969-71), Assn. Supervision and Curriculum Devel., R.I. Ednl. Media Assn. (pres. 1984-85, bd. dirs. 1980—, recipient Man of the Yr. award 1974, Linda Aldrich Leadership award 1992), R.I. Assn. Sch. Supts. (position paper chairperson, 1987-88), Portsmouth Sch. Adminstrs. Assn. (pres. 1978-80). Home: 486 Water St Portsmouth RI 02871-4229 Office: 29 Middle Rd Portsmouth RI 02871-1250

MELLOAN, GEORGE RICHARD, editor, columnist, writer; b. Greenwood, Ind., Nov. 10, 1927; s. James and Sara ollie (Merideth) M.; m. Joan Minner, July 1, 1951; children: James, Melissa, Maryanne. BS, Butler U., 1950. Reporter Logansport (Ind.) Press, 1950, Muncie (Ind.) Press, 1951, Wall Street Jour., Chgo. and Detroit, 1952-59, bur. mgr. Cleve. and Atlanta, 1959-61, page one writer N.Y.C., 1961-66, fgn. correspondent London, 1966-70, edit. writer N.Y.C., 1970—, dep. editor, edit. page, 1974—, op-ed columnist, 1987—. Co-author: The Carter Economy, 1978. Sgt. U.S. Army, 1946-47. Recipient Gerald Loeb award G&R Loeb Found., 1981, Daily Gleaner awards Inter-Am. Press Assn., 1983, 87. Mem. Coun. on Fgn. Rels., Dutch Treat Club, Echo Lake Country Club. Avocations: traveling, golf, hiking, photography. Office: Wall Street Jour 200 Liberty St New York NY 10281-1003

MELLON, BRADLEY FLOYD, pastor, religion educator; b. Suffern, N.Y., Sept. 20, 1949; s. Floyd and Ethel Dorothea (Hastings) M.; m. Marilyn Estelle Rapp, Aug. 7, 1976; children: Melissa Joy, Kimberly Hope. BA, Houghton Coll., 1971; MDiv with high honors, Bibl. Sem., Hatfield, Pa., 1980, STM, 1985; postgrad., Dropsie Coll., 1986—; PhD in Hermeneutics and Bibl. Interpretation, Westminster Sem., 1996. Ordained to ministry Ind. Bapt. Ch., 1980. Youth min. H.S. Evangelism, Tenafly, N.J., 1971-75; assoc. pastor Trinity Ch., Clifton, 1975-77; sr. pastor Grace Ind. Ch., Molino Village, Pa., 1981-88, Kimmels Ch. of God, Orwigsburg, 1988-91; adj. prof. N.T., Bibl. Theol. Sem., Hatfield, pa., 1993—, Bethel Sem. of East, Dresher, Pa., 1993-97, 2001—; dir. chaplain svcs. Frederick (Pa.) Mennonite Cmty., 1996—. Lectr. New Testament Westminster Sem., Phila., 1988—. Mem. adv. bd. Salvation Army, Montclair, N.J., 1977; chaplain svcs. Town Coun., Hatfield, Pa., 1979-80. Mem. Am. Acad. Religion (assoc.), Soc. Bibl. Lit. (assoc.), Interdisciplinary Bibl. Rsch. Inst. (assoc.), Bibl. Sem. Student Assn. (pres. 1979-80), Bibl. Sem. Alumni Assn. (v.p. 1989-90, pres. 1990-91), Ctr. for Bioethics and Human Dignity. Home: 7 Valley Dr Telford PA 18969-2253 Office: Frederick Mennonite Cmty PO Box 498 Frederick PA 19435-0498 E-mail: bmellon@frederick-mennonite.org., bfmellon@hotmail.com.

MELLON, SEWARD PROSSER, investment executive; b. Chgo., July 28, 1942; s. Richard King and Constance Mary (Prosser) Mellon Burrell; m. Karen Leigh Boyd, Sept. 10, 1966 (div. 1974); children— Catharine Leigh, Constance Elizabeth; m. Sandra Springer Stout, 1975. Grad., Choate Sch., 1960; BA, Susquehanna U., 1965, DH, 1993. With Mellon Nat. Corp., Pitts., 1965-69; with T. Mellon & Sons, 1969-71; pres. Richard K. Mellon & Sons, Ligonier, 1971—. Bd. dirs. Mellon Bank N.A., Mellon Fin. Corp. Trustee Richard King Mellon Family Found.; trustee, pres. Richard King Mellon Found.; chmn. real estate com., chmn. bd. mem. fin. and exec. com. Valley Sch. Ligonier. Mem. Western Pa. Conservancy (life), LoyalHanna Assn. (pres.), Vintage Club (Palm Springs, Calif.), Duquesne Club (Pitts.), Laurel Valley Golf Club (Ligonier), Rolling Rock Club, Rolling Rock Hunt, Phi Mu Delta. Republican. Home: Huntland Downs Box K Ligonier PA 15658 Office: PO Box Rkm Ligonier PA 15658-0780

MELLOR, JOHN WILLIAMS, economist, policy consultant firm executive; b. Paris, Dec. 28, 1928; came to U.S., 1929; s. Desmond W. and Katherine (Beardsley) M.; m. Arlene Patton, June 15, 1950 (div. Sept. 1972); children: Michael, Brian, Mark (dec.); m. Uma Lele, Feb. 17, 1973 (div. Apr. 1992); m. Zarmina Said, Oct. 16, 1997. BS, Cornell U., 1950, MS, 1951, PhD, 1954; Diploma, Oxford (Eng.) U., 1952. Prof. Cornell U., Ithaca, N.Y., 1953-75; chief economist USAID, Washington, 1975-77; dir. Internat. Food Policy Rsch. Inst., 1977-91; pres. John W. Mellor Assocs., Inc., 1991-98; v.p. Abt Assocs., Inc., 1998—. Mem. bd. on agrl. NAS, 1989-92; mem. Agrl. Credit Commn., Res. Bank India, 1986-88. Author: Economics of Agricultural Development, 1966 (Am. Agrl. Econs. Assn. award 1978), Accelerating Food Production Growth in Sub-Saharan Africa, 1987, Agricultural Price Policy for Developing Countries, 1988 (hon. mention Am. Agrl. Econs. Assn. 1989), Agriculture on the Road to Industrialization, 1992. Mem. Internat. Commn. on Food and Peace, 1988—. Recipient Wihuri Internat. prize Wihuri Found., Helsinki, 1985, Presdl. End Hunger award The White House, 1987, Outstanding Alumni award Cornell U., 1987. Fellow AAAS, Am. Acad. Arts and Scis., Am. Agrl. Econs. Assn. (Best Pub. Rsch. award 1967). Avocations: sailing, skiing. Office: John Mellor Assocs Inc Ste PH18 801 Pennsylvania Ave NW Washington DC 20004-2668 E-mail: john_mellor@abtassoc.com.

MELLOR, RONALD JOHN, history educator; b. Bklyn., Sept. 30, 1940; s. Ronald Green and Eleanor Teresa (Walsh) M.; m. Anne Tidaback Kostelanetz, June 7, 1969; 1 child, Ronald Blake. AB, Fordham Coll., 1962; cert., U. Louvain, Belgium, 1961; AM, Princeton U., 1964, PhD in Classics, 1968. Asst. prof. Classics Stanford (Calif.) U., 1965-75; assoc. prof. history UCLA, 1976-82, prof. history, 1982—. Vice-chmn. history UCLA, 1985-86, 1991-92, 1998-99, chmn. history, 1992-97; visitor Princeton Inst. Advanced Studies, 1997-98. Author: Thea Rhome, 1975, Tacitus, 1993, Tacitus and the Classical Tradition, 1995, The Roman Historians, 1999; editor: From Augustus to Nero: The First Dynasty of Imperial Rome, 1990, The Historians of Ancient Rome, 1997, Text and Tradition: Studies in Greek History and Historiography in Honor of Mortimer Chambers, 1999. Fellow NEH, 1969, Am. Coun. Learned Socs., 1972, Humanities Rsch. Ctr. Australian Nat. U., Canberra, Australia, 1990; hon. fellow U. Coll. London, Eng., 1969, 72, 83-85. Mem. Am. Hist. Assn., Am. Philol. Assn., Am. Inst. Archaeology, Assn. Ancient Historians, Soc. for the Promotion of Roman Studies. Democrat. Avocations: opera, travel, theater , tennis. Home: 2620 Mandeville Canyon Rd Los Angeles CA 90049-1004 Office: UCLA Dept History 405 Hilgard Ave Los Angeles CA 90095-1473 E-mail: mellor@history.ucla.edu.

MELLORS, ROBERT CHARLES, physician, scientist, educator; b. Dayton, Ohio, 1916; s. Bert S. and Clementine (Steinmetz) M.; m. Jane K. Winternitz, Mar. 25, 1944; children: Alice J., Robert C., William K., John W. PhD, Western Res. U., 1940; MD, Johns Hopkins, 1944. Diplomate Am. Bd. Pathology. Intern Nat. Naval Med. Ctr., Bethesda, Md., 1944-45; rsch. fellow medicine Meml. Center Cancer and Allied Diseases, N.Y.C., 1946-50; rsch. fellow pathology Meml. Ctr. Cancer and Allied Diseases, 1950-53, asst. attending pathologist, 1953-57, assoc. attending pathologist, 1957-58. Sr. fellow Am. Cancer Soc., 1947-50; sr. clin. rsch. fellow Damon Runyon Meml. Fund, 1950-53; asst. attending pathologist Meml. Hosp., N.Y.C., 1953-57, assoc. attending pathologist, 1957-58; asst. attending pathologist Ewing

Hosp., N.Y.C., 1953-57, assoc. attending pathologist, 1957-58; instr. biochemistry Western Res. U., 1940-42; rsch. assoc. Poliomyelitis Rsch. Ctr. and Dept. Epidemiology Johns Hopkins U. Sch. Hygiene, 1942-44; asst. prof. biology Meml. Ctr. Cancer and Allied Diseases, N.Y.C., 1952-53; asst. prof. pathology Sloan Kettering div. Cornell U., 1953-57, assoc. prof., 1957-58; prof. pathology Cornell U. Med. Coll., 1961-90, prof. emeritus, 1990—; adj. prof. pathology N.Y. Med. Coll., 1997—; assoc. attending pathologist N.Y. Hosp., 1961-72, attending pathologist, 1972-86; pathologist-in-chief, dir. labs., 1958-84, emeritus, 1984-85, hon. staff, 1986—; assoc. dir. rsch. Hosp. for Spl. Surgery, N.Y.C., 1958-69, dir. rsch., 1969-84, emeritus, 1984-85, scientist emeritus, 1986—; mem. rsch. adv. com. NIH, 1962-66; adv. com. Nat. Inst. Environ. Health Sci., 1966-69; com. nomenclature and classification of disease Coll. Am. Pathologists, 1960-64. Author: Analytical Cytology, 1955, 2d edit., 1959, Analytical Pathology, 1957. Served as lt. (j.g.), M.C. USNR, 1944-46. Recipient Kappa Delta award Am. Acad. of Orthopedic Surgeons, 1962 Fellow Royal Coll. Pathologists, Molecular Medicine Soc., Am. Soc. Clin. Pathology; mem. Internat. Soc. for Optical Engring., Am. Assn. Pathologists, Am. Assn. Immunologists, Am. Soc. Biochemistry and Molecular Biology, Am. Coll. Rheumatology, Am. Orthopedic Assn. (hon.). Home: 3 Hardscrabble Cir Armonk NY 10504-2222

MELLOTT, ROBERT VERNON, retired advertising executive; b. Dixon, Ill., Jan. 1, 1928; s. Edwin Vernon and Frances Rhoda (Miller) M.; m. Sarah Carolyn Frink, June 11, 1960; children: Lynn Mellott Finzer, Susan Mellott Dodge, David Robert. BA, DePauw U., 1950; postgrad., Ind. U., 1950-51, 59-61, MA, 1983. TV prodr., dir. Jefferson Std. Broadcasting Co., Charlotte, N.C., 1951-59; asst. dist. mgr. GM, Chgo., Flint, Mich., 1961-62; TV and radio comml. supr. NW Ayer & Son, Chgo., 1962-65; TV and radio prodr. Foote, Cone & Belding Advt. Inc., 1965-67, mgr. midwest prodn., 1967-69, mgr. comml. coordination, 1969-74, v.p., mgr. comml. svcs., 1974-93; ret. Cons. speech and broadcasting comm. mem. media adv. com. Coll. of Dupage, Glen Ellyn, Ill., 1971-82; chmn. Cub Scout Com., Wheaton, Ill., 1978-79; bd. dirs. Chgo. Unltd., 1969-71. Trustee Evang. Christian Ch. Mem.: World Comm. Assn., Am. Assn. Advt. Agys. (broadcast adminstrn. policy com., broadcast talent union rels. ANA-AAAA joint policy com. 1984—93), Ind. U. Alumni Assn., DePauw U. Alumni Assn., Alpha Tau Omega, Phi Delta Phi. Republican. Mem. Evang. Christian Ch. Home: 26w130 Tomahawk Dr Wheaton IL 60187-7823

MELLOY, MICHAEL J. federal judge; b. Dubuque, IA, 1948; m. Jane Anne Melloy; children: Jennifer, Katherine, Bridget. BA, Loras Coll., 1970; JD, U. Iowa, 1974. With O'Conner & Thomas P.C. (formerly O'Conner, Thomas, Wright, Hammer, Bertsch & Norby, Dubuque, Iowa, 1974-86; judge U.S. Bankruptcy Ct. (no. dist.) Iowa, 1986-92, U.S. Dist. Ct. (no. dist.) Iowa, Cedar Rapids, 1992—2002; chief judge, 1992—99; judge U.S. Ct. Appeals (8th Cir.), 2002—. With U.S. Army, 1970-72, USAR, 1972-76. Mem. ABA, Comml. Law League Am., Nat. Conf. Bankruptcy Judges, Eighth Cir. Judicial Coun. (bankruptcy judge rep., bankruptcy com.), Iowa State Bar Assn. (coun. mem. bankruptcy and comml. law sect.), Ill. State Bar Assn., Dubuque County Bar Assn., Linn County Bar Assn., Mason L. Ladd Inn of Ct., Rotary. Office: US Ct Appeals 8th Cir 111 S 10th St Rm 24.32 St Louis MO 63102*

MELLUM, GALE ROBERT, lawyer; b. Duluth, Minn., July 5, 1942; s. Lester Andrew and Doris Esther (Smith) M.; m. Julie Murdoch Swanstrom, July 23, 1966; children: Eric Scott, Wendy Jane. BA summa cum laude, U. Minn., 1964, JD magna cum laude, 1968. Bar: Minn. 1968. Assoc. Faegre & Benson, Mpls., 1968-75, ptnr., 1976—, mem. mgmt. com., 1986-98. Planning com. Garret Corp. and Securities Law Inst., Northwestern U. Law Sch., 1984—; adv. bd. Quali Tech Inc., Chaska, Minn., 1985-98, bd. dirs.; bd. dirs. The Tesseract Group, Inc., Mpls.; corp. sec. Excelsior-Henderson Motorcycle Mfg. Co., Belle Plaine, Minn., 1997-2000. Hockey chmn. LARC Bd., Mpls., 1980—85. Mem. ABA (fed. securities regulation com.), Minn. Bar Assn., Hennepin County Bar Assn. (securities regulation com.). Republican. Lutheran. Avocations: tennis, golf, snow and water skiing, handball, boating. Home: 3833 Thomas Ave S Minneapolis MN 55410 Office: Faegre & Benson 2200 Wells Fargo Ctr 90 S 7th St Ste 2200 Minneapolis MN 55402-3901 E-mail: gmellum@faegre.com.

MELMAN, CYNTHIA SUE, special education educator; b. Pottsville, Pa., Nov. 13, 1946; d. Earl J. and Lillian (Zubroff) M. BA in English, Lebanon Valley Coll., 1969; MEd, Western Md. Coll., 1978. Advanced profl. cert. Md. State Dept. Edn. English tchr. Susquehanna Twp. Sch. Dist., Harrisburg, Pa., 1969-70; tchr. of the deaf Am. Sch. for the Deaf, West Hartford, Conn., 1978-80; sign lang. interpreter for the deaf Montgomery County Pub. Schs., Rockville, Md., 1980-81, tchr. of the deaf/hard of hearing, 1981—. In-svc. program masters plus 30, Montgomery County Pub. Schs., Rockville, 1982-96, base sch. rep. for energy saving and recycling program, 1994-95. Co-author: (one workbook in a series) Writing Sentences, 1981. Mem.: NEA, Montgomery County Assn. for Hearing Impaired Children. Avocations: theater , movies, music, reading, walking.

MELMAN, JOY, civic volunteer; b. St. Louis, Jan. 15, 1927; d. Simon Monroe and Esther Marion (Friedman) Werner; m. Albert Morris Melman, June 5, 1949; children: Robin Melman Feder, Kenneth, Mark. Student, Washington U., St. Louis, 1943; BS in Speech and Hearing, Emerson Coll., 1948. Cert. tchr., Mo. Tchr. Cen. Inst. for Deaf, St. Louis, 1948-50. Bd. dirs. Temple Israel, St. Louis, 1974-80, Dance St. Louis Adv. Coun., 1996-1998, Arts and Edn. Coun., St. Louis, 1977-79, Nat. Coun. Jewish Women, St. Louis, 1980-91, Gifted Resource Coun., St. Louis, 1983-88, KWMU Pub. Radio, St. Louis, 1980-84, Jewish Community Ctrs. Assn., St. Louis, 1980-90, treas., 1986-88; v.p. St. Louis Symphony Women's Assn., 1975; adv. coun. KETC-TV pub. broadcasting, St. Louis, 1978—; adv. coun. Dance St. Louis, 1998-2002, lifetime bd. dirs., 2001—. Chmn. Camelot fund raiser Arts and Edn. Coun., St. Louis, 1972, 77; dir. fund raising auction PBS, 1978; adminstrv. chmn. St. Louis Bicentennial, 1974-76; Mo. chmn. Nat. Advs. for Arts, Washington, 1975-77; dir. fund raising auction PBS, 1978; chmn. Jewish Book Festival, Jewish Community Ctrs. Assn., St. Louis, 1980; Couturier sale chmn. Nat. Coun. Jewish Women, St. Louis, 1982, v.p. fund raising, 1984-86; chmn. 3,000 vols. Nat. Sr. Olympics, 1987, 89; vol. chmn. vols. Jewish Hosp. Assocs., 1991; chmn. Phantom of Opera fund raiser Nat. Coun. Jewish Women, 1993; chmn. fundraiser featuring Thomas Keneally, Nat. Coun. Jewish Women, 1994; co-chair Street of Dreams Fundraiser Jewish Hosp., 1995; bd. dirs. Women of Achievement, 1998—, treas., 1999, 2000. Named Woman of Achievement for Cmty. Svcs., St. Louis Globe-Democrat, 1984. Home: 10933 Rondelay Dr Saint Louis MO 63141-7757

MELNER, SINCLAIR LEWIS, insurance company executive, retired; b. Reno, Apr. 6, 1928; s. Abraham H. and Carol Rachel (Myers) M.; m. Roma F. Garner, Dec. 26, 1949; children: Catherine, Michael, Joan. BS, U. Nev., 1949; MS in Internat. Affairs, George Washington U., 1969. Commd. 2d lt. U.S. Army, 1949, advanced through grades to lt. gen. Ind., formerly comdg. gen.; later dep. chmn. NATO Mil. Command, Brussels; ret., 1984; v.p., corp. sec. Hudson Inst., 1984-88; sr. advisor Am. Amicable Life Ins. Co. Tex., 1989-95; ret., 1995. Decorated Silver Star with oak leaf cluster, Def. Superior Service medal, Def. D.S.M., Army D.S.M., Legion of Merit with oak leaf cluster. Home: 301 E Braeburn Dr Phoenix AZ 85022-3621 E-mail: RMelner@aol.com.

MELNGAILIS, IVARS, solid state researcher; b. Riga, Latvia, Nov. 13, 1933; came to U.S., 1949; s. Janis and Jakobine (Zile) M.; m. Valda Dreimanis, June 6, 1964; children: Nils, Zinta. BS, Carnegie-Mellon U., 1956, MS, 1957, PhD, 1961. Mem. staff. Lincoln Lab., MIT, Lexington, 1961-67, asst. group leader, 1967-71, group leader, 1971-75, assoc. divsn. head, 1975-96; cons., 1996—. Fellow IEEE; mem. Am. Phys. Soc., Am. Optical Soc. Office: MIT Lincoln Lab Solid State Div 244 Wood St Lexington MA 02421-6426

MELNICK, ALICE JEAN (AJ MELNICK), counselor; b. St. Louis, Dec. 25, 1931; d. Nathan and Henrietta (Hausfater) Fisher; m. Harold Melnick, May 24, 1953; children: Susan, Vikki, Patrice. BJ, U. Tex., Austin, 1952; MEd, U. North Tex., 1974. Lic. profl. counselor. Reporter San Antonio Light, 1952-53; instr. journalism project Upward Bound So. Meth. U., Dallas, 1967-71. Instr. writing El Centro Dallas County C.C., Dallas, part time 1972-74; instr. human devel. Richland C.C., Dallas, part-time 1974-79; tchr. English, journalism and psychology Dallas Ind. Sch. Dist., 1969-81; counselor Ursuline Acad., 1981-94; part-time instr. human devel. Sante Fe C.C.; freelance documentary photographer. Mem. Dallas Sports Car Club, N.Mex. Jewish Hist. Soc., Temple Beth Shalom. Jewish. Home: 101 Monte Alto Rd Santa Fe NM 87508-8865 E-mail: aj@melnick.net.

MELNICK, BRUCE E. retired astronaut; b. N.Y.C., Dec. 5, 1949; m. Kaye Aughtman; 2 children. BS in Engring., 1972; MS in Aero. Systems, U. W. Fla., 1975. Commd. ensign USCG , 1972; advanced through grades to cmmdr. USCG; deck watch officer USCG Cutter Steadfast, 1972—74; student pilot Naval Flight Tng., Pensacola, Fla., 1974; coast guard rescue pilot USCG, Cape Cod, Mass., 1975—78, Sitka , Alaska, 1978—81; tester. trainer Aircraft Program Office, Grand Prix, Tex., 1982—86; ops. officer CGAS, Traverse City, Mich., 1986—87; astronaut NASA Johnson Space Ctr., Houston, 1987—92; ret. NASA, 1992; v.p., dir. shuttle engring. Lockheed Space Ops. Co. Kennedy Space Ctr., Fla., 2002—. Named to NCAA Acad. All Am. Football Team, 1971; recipient Navy Heliocopter Search and Rescue Aircrew award, USN, 1983, Heroism award, Sec. Transportation, 1983, Disting. Alumni award, U.S. Coast Guard Acad., 1992, 2 Disting. Flying Crosses, USN, 2 NASA Space Flight medals, David G. Schilling award, Air Force Assn., 1992, Flight Achievement award, Am. Astron. Soc., 1993. Mem.: Nat. Mgmt. Assn., USCG Pierodactyl Soc., USCG Acad. Alumni Assn., Naval Aviation Mus. Found., N.Am. Hunters Club, Early and Pioneer Naval Aviators, Elks. Achievements include 2 space flights, over 900 hours in space. Avocations: fishing, golf, hunting, tennis. Office: Astronaut Office/CB Johnson Space Ctr Houston TX 77058

MELNICK, JODI, dancer; Mem. Twyla Tharp Dance Co., 1991—; tchr. dance, choreographer, collaborator. Performer with Sara Rudner, with Dennis O'Connor, with Vicky Shick, with Yoshiko Chuma, with Susan Rethorst.*

MELNICK, MICHAEL, geneticist, educator; b. N.Y.C., Sept. 24, 1944; s. Lester and Evelyn (Rosenberg) M.; m. Anita Goldberger, June 19, 1966; children: Cliff, Lynn. BA in Biology, NYU, 1966, DDS, 1970; PhD in Genetics, Ind. U., 1978. Instr. oral medicine Ind. U., Indpls., 1973-74, fellow in med. genetics, 1974-77, asst. prof. med. genetics, 1977-78; rsch. assoc. prof. U. So. Calif., L.A., 1978-85, assoc. prof., 1985-89, prof. genetics, 1989—. Cons. in human genetics NIH, Bethesda, Md., 1977-88, grant reviewer, 1978—; manuscript referee Am. Jour. Human Genetics, Chgo., 1980—, Am. Jour. Med. Genetics, Helena, Mont., 1980—; MRC vis. prof. McGill U., Montreal, que., 1990. Author, editor 5 books on human genetics; editor-in-chief Jour. Craniofacial Genetics, 1980—; contbr. more than 100 articles to profl. jours. Mem. nat. bd. Com. of Concerned Scientists, N.Y.C., 1983—; vice chmn. Youth Towns of Israel, L.A., 1986—. Capt. M.C. U.S. Army, 1970-73. Recipient Ind. U. Disting. Alumnus award, 1984; Warwick James fellow U. London/Guy's Hosp., 1992. Fellow AAAS; mem. Soc. Craniofacial Genetics (pres. 1978-79), Soc. for Developmental Biology, Am. Soc. Human Genetics, Sigma Xi. Achievements include research in delineated major gene causation of cleft lip and palate; delineated insulin-like growth factor, type 2, receptor control of fetal lung, salvary gland and palate development; application of probability neural networks to multi-gene analysis. Avocations: art, philosophy, chess. Office: Univ of Southern California Den 4266 Mc 0641 Los Angeles CA 90089-0641 E-mail: mmelnick@usc.edu.

MELNICK, RALPH, library director, secondary school educator; b. N.Y.C., Sept. 14, 1946; s. Lester and Evelyn Melnick; m. Rachel Shana Levy, June 1, 1969; children: Joshua Jacob, Ross David. BA, NYU, 1968; MS in LS, Columbia U., 1970, MA, 1974, MPhil, 1975, PhD, 1977. Libr., archivist Am. Jewish Hist. Soc., Waltham, Mass., 1971-72, freelance archivist, 1985-89; libr., archivist Zionist Archives and Libr., N.Y.C., 1975-77; head spl. collections Coll. of Charleston, S.C., 1977-84; libr., dir. tchr. religion Williston Northampton Sch., Easthampton, Mass., 1984—. Author: From Polemics to Apologetics, 1981, The Stolen Legacy of Anne Frank, 1997, Life and Work of Ludwig Lewisohn, Vol. I, 1998, Vol. II, 1998, Justice Betrayed, 2002. Founding mem., archivist Avery Inst. for Afro-Am. History and Culture, Charleston, 1980-84. Rsch. fellow Am. Philos. Soc., 1980, Loewenstein fellow Am. Jewish Archives, 1981, fellow NEH, 1984. Mem. ALA, Assn. for Jewish Studies, Authors Guild, Phi Beta Kappa. Jewish. Avocations: book collecting, antiques, travel. Office: Williston Northampton Sch Libr 19 Payson Ave Easthampton MA 01027-2246 E-mail: rmelnick@williston.com.

MELNICOFF, JOEL NIESEN, lawyer, sports agent; b. Syracuse, N.Y., Mar. 30, 1939; s. Morris Gerson and Anne (Weiner) M.; m. Judith Ellen Lebwohl, July 6, 1969; children: Marlena Carol, Matthew Ryan. BA in Polit. Sci., Syracuse U., 1961, LLB (now JD), 1964. Bar: N.Y., 1965. Assoc. Eric S. Rose, Atty., Syracuse, 1965-66; sole practitioner, 1966—. Spkr. on collection law and trade law, 1985—. Exec. vice chmn., then chmn. N.Y. State Conservative Party, Onandaga County, Syracuse, 1975-76. Staff sgt. USAR, 1964-70. Mem. Nat. Assn. Retail Collection Attys. (v.p. 1996, candidate for nat. treas. 1997), Comml. Law League of Am. Republican. Jewish. Avocations: sports, spectator sports, travel. Home: 4756 Edgeworth Dr Manlius NY 13104 Office: 622 University Bldg Syracuse NY 13202

MELNIK, SELINDA A. lawyer; b. Ft. Worth, Aug. 22, 1951; d. Mitchell Mandel Melnik and Sylvia (Hoffman) Goldberg. BA, Temple U., 1972; M of City and Regional Planning, Rutgers U., 1974; JD summa cum laude, N.Y. Law Sch., 1984. Bar: N.Y. 1985, Del 2001, U.S. Dist. Ct. (so. and ea. dists.) N.Y. 1985, U.S. Dist. Ct. Del. 2001, U.S. Ct. Appeals (D.C. cir.) 1993, Ct. Internat. Trade 1993. Program assoc. to John D. Rockefeller III, 1974-78; cons. to various orgns. U.S., internat., 1975—; sr. policy analyst Planned Parenthood, 1978-79; dir. Ms. and Free to Be Founds., 1979-81; assoc. Milbank, Tweed, Hadley & McCloy, N.Y.C., 1984-87, LeBoeuf, Lamb, Leiby, MacRae, N.Y.C., 1987-90; ptnr. Dechert, Price & Rhoads, 1991-93; internat. counsel Rogers & Wells, 1993-96; pres. Internat. Counsel, NYC, 1996-2000; ptnr. Smith, Katzenstein & Furlow LLP, Wilmington, Del., 2000—02; shareholder Buchanan Ingersoll P.C., 2002—. Founder, 1st pres. Internat. Women's Insolvency and Restructring Confederation, cons. internat. law, trade Cross Border Insolvency and Bankruptcy Prevention Planning, 1987—; cons. fgn. govts. internat. trade and insolvency law; writer, lectr. internat. trade and insolvency law. Mem. ABA, Internat. Bar Assn. (chair membership, chair com. on creditors rights and insolvency 2000--, rep. to UN Commn. on Status of Women), Internat. Lawyers Club, N.Y. State Bar Assn., Order of Coif. Office: Buchanan Ingersoll PC 1201 N Market St Ste 1501 Wilmington DE 19801 E-mail: samelnik@aol.com.

MELNIKOV, YURI AFANASIEVICH, applied mathematician, educator, researcher; b. Onor, Russia, Mar. 3, 1942; s. Afanasy Mikhailovich and Antonina Iosifovna (Zhebrovskaya) M.; m. Alexandra Pavlovna Tyomnaya, June 6, 1964; children: Maxim, Mikhael. MSc, Dnepropetrovsk State U., Ukraine, 1964, PhD, 1971; DSc, Civil Engring. Inst., Moscow, 1982. Project engr. aircraft engines plant, Zaporozhye, Ukraine, 1965-68; rsch. asst. Dnepropetrovsk State U., 1968-71, assoc. prof. applied math., 1971-82, prof., chair applied math., 1982-92; vis. prof. applied mechanics Vanderbilt U., Nashville, 1992; prof. math. Mid. Tenn. State U., Murfreesboro, 1992—. Mem. doctoral qualification com., Dnepropetrovsk U., 1981-92. Author: Green's Functions for Equations of Elliptic Type, 1991, Green's Functions in Applied Mechanics, 1995; reviewer Internat. Jour. Engring. Sci., Quarterly of Applied Mechanics, 1993—; contbr. over 140 articles to profl. publs. Mem. Soc. Engring. Soc. Avocations: reading, travel. Office: Mid Tenn State U 1500 Greenland Dr Murfreesboro TN 37132-3100

MELNYCZUK, ASKOLD, writer; b. Irvington, N.J., Dec. 12, 1954; s. Edward and Olena (Zahajkewycz) M.; m. Alexandra Diane Marie Johnson, Nov. 11, 1949. BA, Rutgers U.; MA, Boston U., 1978. Editl. asst. Antioch Rev., Yellow Spring, Ohio, 1972-73; preceptor Harvard U., Cambridge, Mass., 1990-92; editor, preceptor Boston U., 1982—; lectr. Bennington Grad. Writing Seminars, Vt., 1995—. Author: What is Told, 1994 (N.Y. Times Notable book), Ambassador of the Dead, 2001; co-editor: From Three Worlds, 1996; contbr. articles. Fellowship Lila Wallace Reader's Digest Writers award 1996, Fiction fellowship Mass. Arts Coun., 1996; recipient McGinnis Fiction prize S.W. Rev., 1993. Mem. PEN (vice chair 1997-99, treas., 1999—), New England Poetry Club. Office: Boston U 236 Bay State Rd Boston MA 02215-1403

MELNYK, EUGENE N. private investigator; Founder, pres., CEO Trimel, 1983—91; chmn. bd. dirs. BCI, 1991—94; chmn., CEO Biovail Corp., Mississauga, Canada, 1994—. Office: Biovail Corp 2488 Dunwin Dr Mississauga ON Canada L5L 1J9

MELO, STELLA MARIS LUDOVICO, physicist; b. Goiania, Goias, Brazil, Feb. 2, 1961; d. Ivo P. and Suzete L. Melo; m. Marden Herbert Silva Souza; children: Gustavo S., Camille S. Undergrad. degree in Physics, U. Fed. de Goiás, Brazil, 1986; MSc in Phys. Chemistry, U. Fed. de Santa Catarina, Brazil, 1989; PhD in Space Sci., Inst. Pesquisas Espaciais, Brazil, 1994. Vis. rschr. INPE, Sjcampos, Brazil, 1994-96; postdoctoral fellow York U., North York, Ont., Can., 1996-97, U. Western Ont., London, 1997-2000, U. Toronto, 2000—. Contbr. articles to profl. jours. Recipient Sci. Project grantee Fundação Amparo Pesquisa, Brazil, Inpe, 1995-96, CRESTech, Can., 1999. Mem. Am. Geophys. Union. Avocations: literature, plastic arts. Office: U Toronto Dept Physics 60 St George St Toronto ON Canada M5S 1A7 E-mail: stella@atmosp.physics.utoronto.ca.

MELOAN, TAYLOR WELLS, marketing educator; b. St. Louis, July 31, 1919; s. Taylor Wells and Edith (Graham) M.; m. Anna Geraldine Leukering, Dec. 17, 1944 (div. 1974); children: Michael David, Steven Lee; m. Jane Innes Bierlich, Jan. 30, 1975. BS cum laude, St. Louis U., 1949; MBA, Washington U., St. Louis, 1950; D of Bus. Admin., Ind. U., 1953. Advt. mgr. Herz Corp., St. Louis, 1941-42; sales promotion supr. Liggett & Myers Tobacco Co., 1942-43; asst. prof. mktg. U. Okla., Norman, 1953; asst., then assoc. prof. mktg. Ind. U., Bloomington, 1953-59; prof., chmn. dept. mktg. U. So. Calif., Los Angeles, 1959-69, prof. mktg., 1969-92, Robert E. Brooker prof. mktg., 1970-79, disting. prof. mktg. emeritus, 1997—, dean Sch. Bus. Adminstrn. L.A., 1969-71, assoc. v.p. acad. adminstrn. and research, 1971-81. Prof. bus. adminstrn. U. Karachi, Pakistan, 1962; vis. prof. mktg. Istituto Post U. Per Lo Studio Dell Organizzazione Aziendale, Turin, Italy, 1964, U. Hawaii, 1993, Madrid Bus. Sch., 1993; disting. vis. prof. U. Witwatersrand, Johannesburg, 1978, U. Hawaii, 1993; editl. advisor bus. adminstrn. Houghton Mifflin Co., Boston, 1959-73; cons. to industry and govt., 1953; bd. dirs Inst. Shipboard Edn. Author: New Career Opportunities, 1978, Innovation Strategy and Management, 1979, Direct Marketing: Vehicle for Department Store Expansion, 1984, Preparing the Exporting Entrepreneur, 1986, The New Competition: Dilemma of Department Stores in the 1980's, 1987, Franchise Marketing: A Retrospective and Prospective View of a Contractual Vertical Marketing System, 1988; co-author: Managerial Marketing, 1970, Internationalizing the Business Curriculum, 1968, Handbook of Modern Marketing, contbg. author, 1986; co-author, co-editor: International and Global Marketing: Concepts and Cases, 1994, International and Global Marketing Concepts and Cases, Vol. 2, 1997; bd. editors Jour. Mktg., 1965-72. Trustee World Affairs Coun. Orange County, 1994—. Lt. (j.g.) U.S. Maritime Svc., 1943-46. Mem. Am. Mktg. Assn. (pres. L.A. chpt. 1963-64), Order of Artus, Beta Gamma Sigma, Delta Pi Epsilon, Calif. Yacht Club, Univ. Club, Rotary. Home: 23442 El Toro Rd #W321 Lake Forest CA 92630 Office: U So Calif Dept Mktg Los Angeles CA 90089-0001 E-mail: meloan@aimnet.com.

MELODY, MICHAEL EDWARD, publishing company executive; b. Streator, Ill., Dec. 22, 1943; s. Giles Lambert and Rose Mary (Moreschi) M.; m. Carol Ann Weir, June 8, 1968 (div.); 1 dau., Alison Anne; m. Bonnie Kaye Binkert, Mar. 26, 1983. BA, Ala. Coll., 1966. Exec. editor, asst. v.p. Prentice-Hall, Inc., Englewood Cliff, N.J., 1974-79; v.p., editor-in-chief coll. div. Macmillan Pub. Co., N.Y.C., 1979-80, sr. v.p., pres. coll. div., 1980-87, pres. sch. div., 1987-88; v.p. higher edn. group Simon & Schuster, 1988-90; sr. v.p. Houghton Mifflin Co., Boston, 1990-91, exec. v.p., 1991-95; prin. Michael E. Melody Cons., 1995-96; v.p., gen. mgr. info. prod. Inso Corp., 1996-99; pres, CEO Sage Pubs., Inc., Thousand Oaks, Calif., 1999—, also bd. dirs. Chmn. bd. dirs. Appleton & Lange, N.Y.C., 1989-90; bd. dirs. Sage Publs., Ltd., London. Bd. overseers Huntington Theatre Co., Boston, 1993-96; bd. advisors Boston U. Sch. for the Arts, 1997-2000; bd. dirs. Judge Baker Ctr. for Children, Harvard U. Med Sch., 1997-99, mem. exec. com.; pres. avd. coun. Calif. Luth. U., 2001—. Mem. Assn. Am. Pubs. (vice chmn. coll. divsn. 1981-83, chmn. coll. divsn. 1983-86, exec. com. sch. divsn. 1987-88, exec. com. higher edn. divsn. 1990—), Nat. Assn. Coll. Stores (trustee 1986-87, 94-95).

MELONE, ALBERT P. political science educator, writer, researcher, consultant; b. Chgo., Apr. 25, 1942; s. Dominic A. and Katherine Ann Melone; m. Peggy Jo Harles, Aug. 26, 1971; children: Dominic, Ann, Peter. AA, Mt. San Antonio Coll., Walnut, Calif., 1962; BA, Calif. State U., 1964, MA, 1967; PhD, U. Iowa, 1972. Lectr., instr. Idaho State U., Pocatello, 1966-67; instr. Calif. State U., L.A., 1968; asst. prof. N.D. State U., Fargo, 1970-75, assoc. prof. polit. sci., 1975-80, So. Ill. U., Carbondale, 1980-85, prof., 1985—. Chair dept. polit. sci. N.D. State U., 1973-76; vis. assoc. prof. So. Ill. U., Carbondale, 1979-80, faculty pres., 1996-97. Author: Lawyers, Public Policy and Interest Group Politics, 1977, Primer on Constitutional Law, 1982, Research Essentials of Administrative Law, 1983, Bridges to Knowledge in Political Science, 1984, Judicial Review and American Democracy, 1988, Researching Constitutional Law, 1990, 2d edit., 2000, Creating Parliamentary Government: The Transition to Democracy in Bulgaria, 1998, The American Legal System Foundations, Processes, and Norms, 2003; editor: The Legal System and American Constitutional Democracy, 1993; contbr. articles to profl. jours. Mem. NEA, AAUP (N.D. State U. chpt. v.p. 1975-76, pres. 1977-78), Am. Polit. Sci. Assn., Am. Judicature Soc., Midwest Polit. Sci. Assn., Western Polit. Sci. Assn., Ill. Edn. Assn., N.D. Edn. Assn., Internat. Polit. Sci. Assn. Green Party. Roman Catholic. Avocation: golf. Home: 109 N Rod Ln Carbondale IL 62901 Office: So Ill U Carbondale Dept Polit Sci Carbondale IL 62901-4501 Fax: (618) 453-3163. E-mail: melone@siu.edu.

MELONE, JOSEPH JAMES, retired insurance company executive; b. Pittston, Pa., July 27, 1931; s. Dominick William and Beatrice Marie (Pignone) M.; m. Marie Jane DeGeorge, Jan. 23, 1960; children— Lisa, Carol. BS, U. Pa., 1953, MBA, 1954, PhD in Econs, 1961. C.P.C.U., 1964, ChFC, 1984. Assoc. prof. ins. U. Pa., 1959-66, mem. pension rsch. coun., 1961-66; rsch. dir. Am. Coll. Life Underwriters, 1966-68; v.p. Prudential Ins. Co., Boston, 1969-76, sr. v.p. Newark, 1976-81, exec. v.p., 1981-84, pres., 1984-90; pres., COO, bd. dirs. The Equitable Life Assurance Soc. U.S., 1990-94; pres., COO The Equitable Life Assurance Soc. of U.S., 1990-94, also bd. dirs.; pres., COO The Equitable Cos., Inc., 1992-96, now bd. dirs., pres., CEO, 1996-98; chmn. The Equitable Life Assurance Soc. U.S., 1994-98. Chmn., CEO Equitable Variable Life Ins. Co.; bd. dirs. Foster Wheeler Corp., bd. dirs. BISYS, Inc., chmn. Horace-Mann Educators Corp.; chmn. emeritus The Equitable Cos. Author: Collectively Bargained Multi-Employer Pension Plans, 1961; co-author: Risk and Insurance, 1963, Pension Planning, 1966. Trustee Newark Mus.; chmn. ins. divsn. Cardinal's Commn. Laity N.Y. Archdiocese; bd. overseers Wharton Sch. U. Pa.; bd. dirs. Greater N.Y. couns. Boy Scouts Am. Mem. Am. Risk and Ins. Assn., Am. Soc. CLUs, Am. Coll. (trustee), Internat. Ins. Soc., Internat. Acad. Mgmt., Morris County Country Club, Baltusrol Golf Club, Alpha Tau Omega. Home: Gen Delivery New Vernon NJ 07976-9999 Office: Equitable Cos Inc 1290 Ave of Americas New York NY 10104

MELOY, SYBIL PISKUR, retired lawyer; b. Chgo., Dec. 1, 1939; d. Michael M. and Laura (Stevenson) Piskur; children: William S., Bradley M. BS with honors, U. Ill., 1961; JD, Chgo. Kent Coll. Law, 1965. Bar: Ill. 1965, Fla. 1985, D.C. 1995, U.S. Dist. Ct. (no. dist.) Ill. 1965, U.S. Supreme Ct. 1972, U.S. Ct. Appeals (fed. cir.) 1983, U.S. Dist. Ct. (so. dist.) Fla. 1985, D.C. 1995. Patent chemist, patent atty., sr. atty., internat. counsel G.D. Searle & Co., Skokie, Ill., 1961-72; regional counsel Abbott Labs., North Chicago, 1972-78; pvt. practice Arlington Heights, 1978-79; asst. gen. counsel Alberto Culver Co., Melrose Park, 1979-83; corp. counsel Key Pharms., Inc., Miami, Fla., 1983-86; assoc. Ruden, Barnett, McCloskey, Smith, Schuster and Russell, Pa., 1987-89, ptnr., 1990-91, Foley & Lardner, Miami, Washington, 1991—2001. Adj. prof. Univ. of Miami Sch. of Law, 1986-92. Contbr. article on fertility control and abortion laws, book rev. on arbitration to law revs. Recipient Abbott Presdl. award, 1977; Bur. Nat. Affairs prize, 1965; Law Rev. prize for best article. Mem. ABA, Chgo. Bar Assn. (chmn.-elect and vice chmn. internat. and fgn. law com.), Am. Patent Law Assn., Am. Chem. Soc., Licencing Execs. Soc., Phi Beta Kappa, Phi Kappa Phi. Patentee oral contraceptive, 1965. Home: 2850 NE 9th Ct Pompano Beach FL 33062-4211 also: 1676 32d St NW Washington DC 20007-2960 E-mail: smeloy@aol.com.

MELSHEIMER, HAROLD, obstetrician, gynecologist; b. Legenfeld, Germany, June 11, 1927; came to U.S., 1955; naturalized, 1960; s. Louis and Hella Leonie (Schwehr) Peterman; m. Norma Sykes Sabrina, Nov. 27, 1967; children: Laura, Linda. BS, Marburg U., West Germany, 1951, MD, 1954. Diplomate Am. Bd. Ob-Gyn. Intern Baden County Hosp., West Germany, 1954-55, St. Mary's Hosp. Med. Ctr., Long Beach, Calif., 1955-56; resident Queens Hosp. Med. Ctr., Honolulu, 1956-57, Calif. Hosp. Med. Ctr., L.A., 1957-59; pvt. practice ob-gyn. Encino, Calif., 1959-87; ret. Former dept. chief, now hon. staff mem. Am. Med. Internat. Med. Ctr., Tarzana, Calif., Encino Hosp.; founder Technion Inst. of Tech. Contbr. articles to profl. jours. Operational mem. USCG Aux., 1971. Recipient cert. of honor Wisdom Soc.; named Hon. Citizen, Rep. of Korea, 1966. Fellow ACS (life), Am. Coll. Ob-Gyn., Internat. Coll. Surgeons; mem. AMA, Calif. Med. Assn., L.A. County Med. Assn., Am. Physicians Fellowship for Israel Med. Assn., N.Y. Acad. Scis., Braemar Country Club. Avocations: travel, art, history, sailing. Home: 25660 Deertrail Dr Tehachapi CA 93561-9140 E-mail: hm4611@aol.com.

MELSHEIMER, MEL P(OWELL), venture capital and consumer products executive; b. Los Angeles, July 9, 1939; s. Oscar Merrill M.; m. Sara Sturdevant, Sept. 1, 1962; children: Heidi, Erich, Douglas. AB in Econs., Occidental Coll., 1961; MBA, U. So. Calif., 1965. With United Calif. Bank, Los Angeles, 1962-66; sr. fin. analyst Ford Motor Co., Newport Beach, Calif., 1966-67; v.p., chief fin. officer Pepsi Cola Co. Pepsico, Inc., Purchase, N.Y., 1968-75; exec. v.p., chief operating officer AZL Resources, Inc., 1975-84; chmn. bd., chief exec. officer PHX Pacific, Inc., 1984-89; pres., chief exec. officer MPM Capital Corp., 1987-89; exec. v.p. Finevest Foods, Inc., Greenwich, Conn., 1989-92; pres., CEO Land-O-Sun Dairies Inc., 1991-92, Atlanta Dairies, Inc., 1991-92; exec. v.p., sec., chief oper. officer Dairy Holdings, Inc., Johnson City, Tenn., 1992-94; exec. v.p., COO, CFO Sonex Internat. Corp., Brewster, N.Y., 1994; pres., CEO M.P. Melsheimer & Co., Ridgefield, Conn., 1994-97; pres. NFX, 1995-96; pres., COO/CFO Harris & Harris Group, Inc., N.Y.C., 1997—. Served with U.S. Army, 1961-62.

MELSON, GORDON ANTHONY, chemistry educator; b. Sheffield, Yorkshire, Eng., July 6, 1937; came to U.S., 1969, naturalized, 1977; s. John Albert and Dorothy Whiley (Nelson) M.; married; children— Michael Iain, Sharon Jane. B.S. with honors, Sheffield U., Eng., 1959, Ph.D., 1962. Research assoc. Ohio State U., 1962-64; lectr. chemistry Strathclyde U., 1964-69; asst. prof. Mich. State U., 1969-75; assoc. prof. Va. Commonwealth U., 1975-80, prof., 1980— , chmn. dept. chemistry, 1983— . Editor: Coordination Chemistry of Macrocyclic Compounds, 1979, Transition Metal Chemistry #8, 1983, Transition Metal Chemistry #9, 1985. Mem. Am. Chem. Soc.

MELSOP, JAMES WILLIAM, architect; b. Columbus, Ohio, June 2, 1939; s. James Brendan and Juanita Kathryn (Van Scoy) M.; m. Sandra Lee Minnich, Sept. 21, 1957; children: Deborah Lee, Susan Elizabeth, Kathryn Anne. BArch, Ohio State U., 1964; MArch, Harvard U., 1965; MBA, U. Chgo., 1975. Reg. architect, profl. engr. Architect The Austin Co., Chgo., 1967-69, mgr. bus. devel., 1969-74, asst. dist. mgr., 1974-75; pres., mng. dir. Austin Brasil, Sao Paulo, 1975-78; asst. dist. mgr. The Austin Co., Roselle, N.J., 1978-80, dist. mgr. Detroit, 1980-81, v.p., dist. mgr. Cleve., 1986, group v.p., dir., 1986—, exec. v.p. chief oper. officer, 1992, pres., CEO, 1992—, also chmn., bd. dirs.; founder, prin. owner Austin Holdings, Inc., 1997—. Named E&Y Entrepreneur of Yr., 1999. Mem. Am. Inst. Architects., Harvard Club N.Y.C., Presidents' Club, Ohio State U. (Disting. Alumnus award 1989). Home: 3165 Trillium Trail Cleveland OH 44124-5205 Office: Austin Co 3650 Mayfield Rd Cleveland OH 44121-1791

MELSTED, MARCELLA H. retired administrative assistant, civic worker; b. Mayville, N.D., Mar. 3, 1922; d. Hans Morris and Betsy (Stenerson) Hanson; m. Alvin K. Melsted, June 6, 1965 (dec. June 1994). BS in Commerce, U. N.D., 1946, postgrad. Sec. Off. Sci. R&D, Washington, 1943-45; adminstrv. asst. Am. Embassy (Marshall Plan), Oslo, 1948-50, Paris, 1950-52, N.D. Geol. Survey, Grand Forks, 1953-65. Co-editor: Memories of Homemakers, 1988. Pres. Borg Home Auxiliary, 1984—; apptd. cons. rep. State Plumbing Bd.; chmn. needlepointing dining room chairs N.D. Gov.'s mansion; parliamentarian N.D. Extension Homemakers, Women of Evang. Luth. Ch. Am., v.p., bd. dirs., 1985-91; mem. N.D. Humanities Coun., 1985-91; bd. dirs. Friends of N.D. Mus., Alpha Beta Ednl. found., 1996—; mem. Red River Valley Comty. Action Bd., 1995—. Recipient Sioux award U. of N.D., 1995. Mem. AAUW (parliamentarian N.D. State divsn., 2 fellowships, author br. history, state pres. 1962-64, nat. membership com. 1964-66), N.D. State Fedn. Garden Clubs (state pres., life, tree chmn. nat. bd., state treas. 1991-97), Four Seasons Garden Club (sec.-treas. 1987—), Homemakers Clubs (various coms.), China Painters Guild (various coms.), Am. Legion Aux. (sec. Edinburg chpt. 1999-), Gardar Ladies Aid (treas. 1998-), Gamma Phi Beta. Democrat. Avocations: antiques, china painting, stamp collecting. Home: 7862 127th Ave NE Edinburg ND 58227-9604

MELTEBEKE, RENETTE, career counselor; b. Portland, Oreg., Apr. 20, 1948; d. Rene and Gretchen (Hartwig) M. BS in Sociology, Portland State U., 1970; MA in Counseling Psychology, Lewis and Clark Coll., 1985. Lic. profl. counselor, Oreg.; nat. cert. counselor. Secondary tchr. Portland Pub. Schs., 1970-80; project coord. Multi-Wash CETA, Hillsboro, Oreg., 1980-81; coop. edn. specialist Portland C.C., 1981-91; pvt. practice career counseling, owner Career Guidance Specialists, Lake Oswego, Oreg., 1988—. Mem. adj. faculty Marylhurst (Oreg.) Coll., 1989-93, Portland State U., 1994—, Lewis and Clark Coll., 2001—; assoc. Drake Beam Morin Inc., Portland, 1993-96; career cons. Managed Health Network, 1994—, Career Devel. Svcs., 1990—, Life Dimensions, Inc., 1994; presenter Internat. Conf., St. Petersburg, Russia, 1995. Rotating columnist Lake Oswego Rev., 1995-99; creator video presentation on work in Am. in 5 langs., 1981. Pres. Citizens for Quality Living, Sherwood, Oreg., 1989; mem. Leadership Roundtable on Sustainability for Sherwood, 1994-95; bd. dirs. Bus. for Social Responsibility for Oreg. and Southwestern Wash., 1999, 2000. Recipient Esther Matthews award for outstanding contbn. to field of career devel., 1998. Mem. Assn. for Psychol. Type, Nat. Career Devel. Assn., Oreg. Career Devel. Assn. (pres. 1990), Assn. for Humanistic Psychology (presenter nat. conf. Tacoma 1996), Willamette Writers. Avocations: walking, swimming, bicycling, cross-country skiing, photography. Home: 890 SE Merryman St Sherwood OR 97140-9746 Office: Career Guidance Specialists 15800 Boones Ferry Rd Ste C104 Lake Oswego OR 97035-3492

MELTER, ROBERT ALAN, mathematics educator, researcher; b. N.Y.C., Mar. 20, 1935; s. George I. and Hattie (Eisenstein) M.; m. Therese Balavoine, Oct. 10, 1965; 1 child, Vanessa. AB, Cornell U., 1956; AM, U. Mo., 1960, PhD, 1962. Asst. prof. math. U. R.I., Kingston, 1962-64, U. Mass., Amherst, 1964-67; assoc. prof. math. U. S.C., Columbia, 1967-71; dir. sci. div. L.I. U., Southampton, N.Y., 1986-88, prof. math., 1971-97, prof. emeritus, 1997—. Assoc. editor: Math. Revs., 1973-74, Pattern Recognition, 1994—; translator Problems in Combinatorics, 1985, Combinatorial Configurations, 1988; chmn. (hon.) Vision Geometry, 1999—; contbr. articles to profl. jours. NAS Exch. fellow, 1981; Fulbright prof., 1985. Mem. Am. Math. Soc. Office: LI U Dept Math Southampton NY 11968 E-mail: rmelter@aol.com.

MELTON, AUGUSTUS ALLEN, III, technologist; b. Washington, May 11, 1963; s. Augustus Allen Melton Jr. and Carole Hawkins Melton, La' Rhett Melton (Stepmother); m. Dawn Michelle Graves, Apr. 27, 2001; children: Bret Michael Arrington, Augustus Allen IV, Carolyn Olivia. BA in Music Performance, Jacksonville State U., 1986, BS in Music Edn., 1989. Cert. K-12 instrumental music edn. Asst. band dir. Simpson Mid. Sch., Marietta, Ga., 1990—93; band dir. East Cobb Mid. Sch., 1993—2001; tech. support JMJ Techs., 2001—. Mem.: Ga. Music Educator's Assn., Phi Mu Alpha. Avocations: music, outdoor sports, family. Personal E-mail: me0644@aol.com.

MELTON, BARRY, lawyer, musician; b. N.Y.C., June 14, 1947; s. James Gerald and Terry Melton; m. Barbara Joy Langer; children: Kingsley, Kyle. Bar: Calif. 1982, U.S. Dist. Ct. (no. dist.) Calif. 1982, U.S. Dist. Ct. (cen. dist.) Calif. 1983, U.S. Ct. Appeals (9th cir.) 1983, U.S. Dist. Ct. (ea. dist.) Calif. 1985, U.S. Supreme Ct. 1988. Pvt. practice, San Francisco, 1982-94; pub. defender Yolo County, 2000—. Musician, pub. Seafood Music, San Francisco, 1965—; pro-tem judge San Francisco Mcpl. Ct., 1987-94. Musician, composer various mus. recs., 1965—. Mem. State Bar Calif. (cert. criminal law specialist 1993—, vol. legal svc. awards 1983-87), Calif. Attys. Criminal Justice, Calif. Pub. Defenders Assn. (bd. dirs. 1999—). Office: Yolo County Pub Defender 814 North St Woodland CA 95695-3538 E-mail: melton@counterculture.net., thefish@counterculture.net.

MELTON, CAROL A(NNE), corporate executive; b. St. Augustine, Fla., 1954; m. Joseph M. Hassett; children: Matthew, Meredith. BA with honors, Wake Forest U., 1976; MA in Journalism and Comms., U. Fla., 1977; JD with honors, Am. U., 1981. Assoc. in comms. group Hogan and Hartson, Washington, 1981-82; asst. gen. counsel Nat. Cable TV Assn., 1983-86; legal advisor Fed. Comms. Commn. Chmn. Mark Fowler, 1986-87; Washington counsel Warner Comms., 1987-91; v.p. law and pub. policy Time Warner Inc., Washington, 1992-97; sr. v.p. govt. affairs, exec. officer Viacom, Inc., 1997—. Trustee The Media Inst., Washington, 1997—, Washington Performing Arts Soc., 1997-99, The Potomac Sch., McLean, Va., 1999-2000; mem. Fed. City Coun., 1997—. Mem. Nat. Assn. Broadcasters (bd. dirs. 2000-2001). Office: Viacom Inc 1501 M St NW Ste 1100 Washington DC 20005-1729

MELTON, CHARLES ESTEL, retired physicist, educator; b. Fancy Gap, Va., May 18, 1924; s. Charlie Glenn and Ella (Ayers) M.; m. Una Faye Hull, Dec. 7, 1946; children— Sharon (Mrs. Lawrence Husch), Wayne, Sandra (Mrs. Glenn Allen). BA, Emory and Henry Coll., 1952, D.Sc., 1967; MS, Vanderbilt U., 1954; PhD, U. Notre Dame, 1964. Physicist Oak Ridge Nat. Lab., 1954-67; prof. chemistry U. Ga., Athens, 1967-97, head dept., 1972-77; now ret. Author: Principles of Mass Spectrometry and Negative Ions, 1970, Ancient Diamond Time Capsules, Secrets of Life and the World, 1985, Primordial Petroleum, 1989; contbr. articles to profl. jours. Served with USNR, 1943-46. Recipient DeFriece medal Emory and Henry Coll., 1959, numerous research grants. Fellow AAAS; mem. Am. Phys. Soc., Am. Chem. Soc., Ga. Acad. Sci. Presbyterian. Home: 817 Glenn Carrie Rd Hull GA 30646-4265

MELTON, DAVID REUBEN, lawyer; b. Milw., Apr. 4, 1952; s. Howard and Evelyn Frances (Cohen) M.; m. Nancy Hillary Segal, May 22, 1981; children: Michelle, Hannah. BA, U. Wis., 1974; JD, U. Chgo., 1977. Bar: Ill. 1977, U.S. Dist. Ct. (no. dist.) Ill. 1977, U.S. Ct. Appeals (7th cir.) 1981, U.S. Supreme Ct. 1982, U.S. Fed. Cir. Ct. Appeals, 1991. Assoc. Karon, Morrison & Savikas, Ltd., Chgo., 1977-83; ptnr. Karon, Morrison & Saviskas, Ltd., 1983-87, Karon, Savikas & Horn, Ltd., Chgo., 1987-88, Keck, Mahin & Cate, Chgo., 1988-96; counsel Mayer, Brown & Platt, 1996-99, ptnr., 2000—. Office: Mayer Brown & Platt 190 S Lasalle St Ste 3900 Chicago IL 60603-3410 E-mail: dmelton@mayerbrown.com.

MELTON, DOUGLAS A. molecular and cell biology educator; BS Honors Biology, U. Illinois, Champaign-Urbana, 1971—75; BA History, Phil. of Sci., Cambridge U., 1975—77; PhD Molecular Biology, Trinity Coll. & MRC Lab. Molecular Biology, Cambridge U., Eng., 1980. Asst. prof. dept. bio chem. and molecular biology Harvard U., 1981—84, assoc. prof., 1984—87, J.L. Loeb assoc. prof. nat. sci., 1987, prof. dept. molecular and cellular biology Mass., 1988—; biologist (med.) Mass. Gen. Hosp., Boston; assoc. mem. Children's Hosp. , 1994—; investigator Howard Hughes Med. Inst., 1994—; Thomas Dudley Cabot prof. Natural Sci. Harvard U., Cambridge, Mass., 1999—. Recipient Richard Lounsbery award NAS, 1995. Mem.: Inst. Medicine. Office: Harvard Univ Dept Molecular & Cellular Bio 7 Divinity Ave Cambridge MA 02138*

MELTON, GARY BENTLEY, psychology and law educator; b. Salisbury, N.C., June 4, 1952; s. Harold Sumner Jr. and Marion Adair (Reeves) M.; m. Robin Jo Kimbrough, Aug. 7, 1999; children by previous marriage: Jennifer Lynn, Stephany Beth. BA, U. Va., 1973; MA, Boston U., 1975, PhD, 1978. Asst. prof. psychology Morehead (Ky.) State U., 1978-79, U. Va., Charlottesville, 1979-81; from asst. prof. to full prof. psychology and law U. Nebr., Lincoln, 1981-87, Carl A. Happold prof. psychology and law, 1987-94; dir. Consortium on Children, Families and the Law, 1987—; prof. neuropsychiatry U. S.C., Columbia, 1994-99, adj. prof. law, pediat. and psychology, 1994-99, dir. Inst. Families in Soc., 1994-99; prof. psychology Clemson U., 1999—. Dir. Inst. Family and Neighborhood Life, Clemson U., 1999—. Author: Child Advocacy: Psychological Issues and Interventions, 1993; co-author: Community Mental Health Centers and the Courts: An Evaluation of Community-Based Forensic Services, 1985, Psychological Evaluations for the Courts: A Handbook for Mental Health Professionals and Lawyers, 1987, 2d edit., 1997, Pediatric and Adolescent AIDS: Research Findings from the Social Sciences, 1992, Ethical and Legal Issues in AIDS Research, 1995, No Place to Go: Civil Commitment of Minors, 1998; editor numerous books. Mem. U.S. Adv. Bd. on Child Abuse and Neglect, 1989-93, vice-chair, 1991-93. Recipient Frederick Howell Lewis award Psi Chi, 1993, Lynn Stuart Weiss award Am. Psychol. Found., 2000. Fellow APA (chmn. various coms., Cert. of Recognition for Psychology in Pub. Interest 1981, Disting. Contbn. to Psychology in Pub. Interest award 1985, Nicholas Hobbs award 1992, Harold Hildreth award 1992, Disting. Contbn. to Pub. Svc. award 1999); mem. Am. Psychology-Law Soc. (pres. 1990-91), Prevent Child Abuse in Am. (Donna Stone award 1992). Democrat. Mem. Unitarian Ch. Office: Clemson U Inst Family and Neighborhood Life 158 Poole Agrl Ctr Clemson SC 29634-0132 E-mail: gmelton@clemson.edu.

MELTON, HOWELL WEBSTER, SR. federal judge; b. Atlanta, Dec. 15, 1923; s. Holmes and Alma (Combee) M.; m. Margaret Catherine Wolfe, Mar. 4, 1950; children— Howell Webster, Carol Anne. JD, U. Fla., 1948. Bar: Fla. 1948. With Upchurch, Melton & Upchurch, St. Augustine, 1948-61; judge 7th Jud. Circuit of Fla., 1961-77, U.S. Dist. Ct. (mid. dist.) Fla., Jacksonville, 1977-91, sr. judge, 1991—. Past chmn. Fla. Conf. Cir. Judges, 1974; past chmn. coun. bar pres.'s Fla. Bar. Trustee Flagler Coll., St. Augustine. Served with U.S. Army, 1943-46. Recipient Disting. Service award St. Augustine Jaycees, 1953 Mem. ABA, St. Johns County Bar Assn., Jacksonville Bar Assn., Fed. Bar Assn., Fla. Blue Key, Ponce de Leon Country Club, St. Augustine Fla. Officers Club, Masons, Phi Delta Theta, Phi Delta Phi. Methodist. Office: US Dist Ct PO Box 52957 Jacksonville FL 32201-2957

MELTON, JUNE MARIE, nursing educator; b. St. Louis, Oct. 16, 1927; d. Thomas Jasper and Alice Marie (Sloas) Hayes; m. Malcolm Adrian Essen, July 12, 1947 (dec. July 1978); children: Alison, William, Terrence, Mark, Cathleen, Melodie; m. Denver A. Melton, Sept. 6, 1989 (dec.). Grad., Jewish Hosp. Sch. Nursing, 1948; student, U. Mo., Lincoln U., U. Colo., Stephens Coll., U. S.W. RN, Mo.; nurse ARC. Instr. home nursing U. Mo., Columbia, 1948-49; acting dir. nurses, 1957-68; supr. instr., obstet. supr. Charles E. Still Hosp., Jefferson City, Mo.; supr. nurse ICU, primary nurse St. Mary's Health Ctr.; health dir. Algoa Correctional Instn., 1979-83; home health vis. nurse A&M Home Health, 1983-96, parish nurse, 1998—. Mem. adv. bd. A&M Home Nursing, Jefferson City; instr. GED Lincoln U., Jefferson City; participant study of premature baby nursing U. Colo., 1964. Vol. ARC, Belle-Rolla, Mo., instr. home nursing; missionary to Togo, West Africa Mo. Synod. Luth. Ch., 1996—97, parish nurse, 1998—, harvester for Christ, 1999—; parish nurse TsletaLuth. Mission, 2002. Mem. U.S. Nurse Corps. Democrat. Lutheran. Avocations: fishing, sewing, reading, traveling. Home: Winterwood Estates 15 B St Holts Summit MO 65043

MELTON, MICHAEL ERIC, lawyer, engineer; b. Dallas, Sept. 14, 1958; BSEE, U. Mo., 1981, JD, 1984. Bar: Mo. 1984, Tex. 1992, U.S. Dist Ct. (ea. dist.) Mo. 1984, U.S. Ct. Appeals (fed. and 8th cirs.) 1984, U.S. Dist. Ct. (no. dist.) Tex. 1991, U.S. Patent and Trademark Office 1986, U.S. Supreme Ct. 2000. Patent advisor Office of Naval Rsch. U.S. Dept. Navy, Washington, 1984-86; assoc. Haverstock, Garrett and Roberts, St. Louis, 1986-87, Spensley, Horn, Jubas and Lubitz, Washington, 1987-88; license counsel Tex. Instruments, Inc., Dallas, 1988-92, European counsel Nice, France, 1993-95; corp. sec. Texas Instruments Info. Engring. Internat., Inc., 1993-96; corp. patent counsel mgr. legis. affairs intellectual property, 1995-96; assoc. tech. counsel, chief patent counsel MCI Comms. Corp., Washington, 1996-99; ptnr. Hickman Stephens and Coleman, 1999; vice pres., deputy gen. coun. Pitney Bowes, Inc., Shelton, Conn., 1999—2002; pres., mng. ptnr. TME Enterprises, Atlanta. Mem. U.S. Naval Rsch. Lab., EEOC, 1985-86; lectr. continuing legal edn. Mound City Bar Assn., St. Louis, 1986-87. Editl. assoc. Insight into Cts. newsletter, 1989-92, Jour. Cts., Health Sci. and the Law, 1989-92. Statewide officer Mo. Young Dems., 1986-87; vol. lectr. Mo. and Tex. Pub. Sch. Dists., 1986-96, others; bd. govs. Dallas Symphony Assn., 1991-94, mem. mktg. com., 1992, cmty. affairs com., 1992. Fellow Dallas Bar Found.; mem. ABA, Am. Intellectual Property Lawyers Assn. (vice chmn. minority issues com. 1997-98, vice-chair licensing com. 1998-99, chair licensing com. 1999—, nominating com. 2000-2001, mem. bd. govs. Intellectual property owners, 2000-2002, Assn. Corp. Patent Coun., 2000—), Am. Intellectual Property Law Edn. Found. (vice-chair scholarship com. 2001-2002), Nat. Bar Assn., J.L. Turner Legal Assn. (v.p. 1991, bd. dirs. 1992, co-chair polit. action com. 1996), Dallas Bar Assn., Fed. Bar Assn., Nat. Soc. Black Engrs. (Region V adv. bd. 1991-92), Am. Inn of Ct., Coll. State Bar of Tex. Roman Catholic. Home: PO Box 320 Dunn Loring VA 22027-0320

MELTON, WAYNE CHARLES, real estate executive; b. Oak Ridge, Aug. 30, 1954; s. Charles Estel and Una Faye (Hull) M.; m. Maria Tobar-Condi; children: Bonnie Elizabeth, Ingrid Tatiana. AB in European Intellectual History, U. Ga., 1975. Br. rep. Household Internat. Consumer Fin. Co., Athens, Ga., 1975-76; asst. mgr. Athens and Hickory, N.C., Doraville, 1976-77; pres., ceo Impact Realty-Melton & Assocs. Inc., Athens, 1987—. Cons. Ga. Furniture, Charlotte (N.C.) Realty, 1987—. Trustee Mu Inc., Page, Ga. Ho. of Reps., 1968; chmn. Madison County Reps., 1973-74; mem. Congl. Bus. Coun., 2002. Mem. Zeta Beta Tau. Office: 855 Sunset Dr Bldg Ste 11 Athens GA 30606-7718

MELTSER, THOMAS AVRUM, corporate executive; b. Phila., June 26, 1935; s. Harry K. and Ethel (Howell) M.; m. Hope Sandra Rudolph, Dec. 13, 1959 (dec. Mar. 1968); children: Sharon Gail, Mark Stephen. BA in Arts and Letters, Pa. State U., 1956. Intelligence officer, Washington, 1963-75; dir. recruitment Lawrence Personnel, Phila., 1966-75; owner, prin. Acad. Career Tng., 1975-82; with Wyeth Labs., Radnor, Pa., 1986-89; exec. dir. Patriot Assocs., Wayne, 1989—. Mem. sch. bd. Whitemarsh Twp., Lafayette Hill, Pa., 1966-68. 1st lt. USAF, 1957-63. Mem. AAUS, U.S. Naval Acad. Info. (officer 1987—), Am. Legion, VFW, Drug Info. Assn. Republican. Avocations: mil. history, jazz, sports, stamp and coin collecting. Office: Patriot Assocs 125 Strafford Ave Wayne PA 19087-3318 E-mail: tompatriot@aol.com.

MELTZ, DAVID BARRY, law educator; b. Bklyn., Mar. 12, 1945; s. Joseph and Claire Meltz; m. Sandra Jacqueline Rosenberg, July 3, 1968; children: Anne Robin, Robert Alan, Rachel. BA cum laude, Bklyn. Coll., 1965; PhD in Polit. Sci., U. Rochester, 1970; JD, Woodrow Wilson Law Sch., 1977. Asst. prof. polit. sci. Mich. State U., Lansing, 1969-73; assoc. prof. econs. and pub. policy Ga. Inst. Tech., Atlanta, 1973-78; atty. Levine & Meltz, PC, 1977-91; acad. dean, prof. law John Marshall Law Sch., 1991-98, Disting. prof. law, 1999—. Jewish. Home: 2764 Cosmos Dr NE Atlanta GA 30345-1353 Office: John Marshall Law Sch 1422 W Peachtree St NW Atlanta GA 30309-2947 E-mail: conprof@aol.com.

MELTZER, ALLAN H. economist, educator; b. Boston, Feb. 6, 1928; s. George B. and Minerva I. (Simons) M.; m. Marilyn Ginsburg, Aug. 27, 1950; children: Bruce Michael, Eric Charles, Beth Denise. AB, Duke U., 1948; MA, UCLA, 1955, PhD, 1958. Lectr. econs. U. Pa., Phila., 1956-57; faculty Carnegie Mellon U. Grad. Sch. Indsl. Adminstrn., Pitts., 1957-64, prof. econs., 1964—, Maurice Falk prof. econs. and social sci., 1970-80, John M. Olin univ. prof. polit. economy and pub. policy, 1980-91; univ. prof. polit. economy and pub. policy Carnegie Mellon U. Grad. Sch. Indsl. Adminstrn., 1991-97, Allan H. Meltzer univ. prof. polit. economy, 1997—. Vis. prof. U. Chgo., 1964-65, Fundacao Getulio Vargas, Rio de Janeiro, 1976-79, City U., London, 1979—; vis. fellow Hoover Instn., 1977-78; vis. scholar Am. Enterprise Inst., Washington, 1989—; co-chmn. Shadow Open Market Com., 1974-89, chmn., 1989-2000; cons. U.S. Treasury, joint econ. com. U.S. Congress, 1960; com. on banking and currency U.S. Ho. of Reps., 1963-64; mem. Pres.'s Econ. Policy Adv. Bd., 1988-90; acting mem. Coun. Econ. Advisors, 1988-89; panel econ. advisors Congl. Budget Office, 1995—; cons., bd. govs. FRS, FDIC; dir. Cooper Tire & Rubber Co., 1983-98, chmn. audit and compensation com., 1996-98; hon. advisor Inst. Monetary and Econ. Studies Bank of Japan, 1987—; bd. dirs. Sarah Scaife Found., Commonwealth Found.; dir. Stillhalter Vision AG, Zurich, 1994-2002, Advanced Materials Group, 1994-2001; chmn. Internat. Fin. Instn. adv. com. to U.S. Congress, 1999-2000. Author: Monetary Economics, 1989, Keynes's Monetary Theory: A Different Interpretation, 1988; (with Karl Brunner) Money and the Economy: Issues in Monetary Analysis, 1993; (with Alex Cukierman and Scott Richard) Political Economy, 1991, Report of the International Financial Institution Advisory Commission, 2000, A History of the Federal Reserve, vol. 1, 2002; editor: (with Karl Brunner) Carnegie-Rochester Conf. Series, 1976-89; (with Charles Plosser), 1989-97; contbr. articles to profl. jours. Recipient Outstanding Achievement award UCLA, 1983, Money Marketeers, 1997; Social Sci. Rsch. Coun. fellow, 1955-56, Ford Found. fellow, 1962-63; named Man of Yr in Fin., Pitts., 1995-96. Fellow: Nat. Assn. Bus. Economists; mem.: Am. Fin. Assn., Western Econ. Assn. (pres. 1985—86), Internat. Atlantic Econ. Assn. (pres. 1999—2000), Am. Econ. Assn. (v.p. 1990, Disting. fellow 2002), Phila. Soc. (v.p. 1981—83), Cosmos Club. Avocations: research in macroeconomics, money, political economy, monetary history. Office: Carnegie Mellon U Dept Econs Pittsburgh PA 15213 E-mail: am05@andrew.cmu.edu.

MELTZER, BERNARD DAVID, law educator; b. Phila., Nov. 21, 1914; s. Julius and Rose (Welkov) M.; m. Jean Sulzberger, Jan. 17, 1947; children: Joan, Daniel, Susan. AB, U. Chgo., 1935, JD, 1937; LL.M., Harvard U., 1938. Bar: Ill. 1938. Atty., spl. asst. to chmn. SEC, 1938-40; assoc. firm Mayer, Meyer, Austrian & Platt, Chgo., 1940; spl. asst. to asst. sec. state, also acting chief fgn. funds control div. State, 1941—43; asst. trial counsel U.S. prosecution Internat. Nuremberg War Trials, 1945-46; from professorial lectr. to disting. svc. prof. law emeritus U. Chgo. Law Sch., 1946—; counsel Vedder, Price, Kaufman & Kamnholz, Chgo., 1954-55, Sidley and Austin, Chgo., 1987-89. Hearing commr. NPA, 1952-53; labor arbitrator; spl. master U.S. Ct. Appeals for D.C., 1963-64; bd. publs. U. Chgo., 1965-67, chmn., 1967-68; mem. Gov. Ill. Adv. Commn. Labor-Mgmt. Policy for Pub. Employees in Ill., 1966-67, Ill. Civil Service Commn., 1968-69; cons. U.S. Dept. Labor, 1969-70 Author: Supplementary Materials on International Organizations, 1948, (with W.G. Katz) Cases and Materials on Business Corporations, 1949, Labor Law Cases, Materials and Problems, 1970, supplement, 1972, 75, 2d edit., 1977, supplements, 1980, 82 (with S. Henderson), 3d edit. (with S. Henderson), 1985, supplement, 1988; also articles. Bd. dirs. Hyde Park Community Conf., 1954-56, S.E. Chgo. Commn., 1956-57. Served to lt. (j.g.) USNR, 1943-46. Mem. ABA (co-chmn. com. devel. law under NLRA 1959-60, mem. spl. com. transp. strikes), Ill. Bar Assn., Chgo. Bar Assn. (bd. mgrs. 1972-73), Am. Law Inst., Coll. Labor and Employment Lawyers, Am. Acad. Arts and Scis., Order of Coif, Phi Beta Kappa Home: 1219 E 50th St Chicago IL 60615-2908 Office: U Chgo Law Sch 1111 E 60th St Chicago IL 60637-2776

MELTZER, DANIEL B. playwright, educator; b. New York City, N.Y., Oct. 24, 1940; s. Jacob Gordon Meltzer and Kitty Talber-Meltzer; m. Laurie Lisle, June 1986 (div. 1993). BA in Film and English Lit., City Coll. N.Y., 1965; MA in Theatre, Hunter Coll., 1979; postgrad., City U. N.Y., 1980—82. Lectr. theatre Hunter Coll., N.Y.C., NY, 1979—80; dir. creative writing programs Sharon Creative Arts Found., 1989—90; adj. prof. journalism N.Y. U., N.Y.C., NY, 1990—. Mgr. studio ops. Am. Broadcasting Co., 1968—69; prodn. mgr. Group W Prodns., 1969—70; unit mgr. ABC News and Spl. Events, 1970—75; workshop leader Henry St. Settlement, N.Y.C., NY, 1992—96; instr. comm. Pa. State U., Hazleton, 1995—98; guest lectr. writing workshop Chautaugua Instn., 1995, 96, 98; dir. urban journalism workshop N.Y. U., 1997—; asst. prof. comm. St. Johns U., N.Y.C., NY, 1998—2000; adj. prof. theatre, critical thinking Marymount Manhattan Coll., N.Y.C., NY, 1999—; lectr. and reader in field. Columnist/reporter Westsider, 1990—98, Chelsea Clinton News, 1990—98; editor: Chelsea Clinton News, 1994—95, Westsider, 1994—95; (script writer): (plays) Waiting for to Go, 1978; The Battling Brinkmires, 1978; A Good Time for a Change, 1978; The Square Root of Love, 1978; Movie of the Month, 1982; Intermission, 1989; La Radice Quadrata Dell'Amore, 1995; contbr. articles and short stories; prodr.: (plays) Actors Theatre of Louisville, Circle Repertory, Hunter Playwrights, Raft Theatre, Syracuse Stage, Shadowbox Cabaret, numerous others; drama critic WBAI Radio, 1977, writer, editor, prodr. WPIX-TV News, 1975—78, writer, editor CBS News, 1980—88, columnist Newsday, Balt. Sun, Albany Times Union, NY Post, 2001—. Recipient John Golden Playwriting award, 1980, O. Henry prize for fiction, 1992, Creative Non-Fiction award, N.Y. Press Assn., 1993, Pushcart prize for fiction, 1997. Mem.: Chautauqua Writers Ctr. (bd. advisors), PEN, N.Y. Dramatists Guild. Office: NY Univ 10 Washington Pl New York NY 10003 E-mail: dm22@nyu.edu.

MELTZER, DAVID, author, musician, educator; b. Rochester, N.Y., Feb. 17, 1937; s. Louis and Roseamunde (Lovelace) M.; m. Christina Meyer, Apr. 1, 1958; children— Jennifer, Margaret, Amanda, Adam Benjamin ben David. Student, Los Angeles City Coll., 1955-56, U. Calif. at Los Angeles, 1956-57. Mem. cons. bd. Coordinating Coun. of Lit. Mags.; instr. M.A. program in poetics New Coll., San Francisco, 1980—, coord. writing and lit. program in undergrad. humanites program, 1987—. Author: (numerous books of poetry including) Tens, Selected Poems, 1973, Six, 1976, Two-way Mirror: Notebook on Poetry, 1977, The Art, The Veil, 1981, The Name, Selected Poetry, 1973-1983, 1983; editor: The San Francisco Poets, 1971, Birth, 1973, The Secret Garden: Anthology of the Classic Kabbalah, 1977, 1998, Birth: An Anthology of Ancient Texts, Songs, Prayers and Stories, 1981, Death: An Anthology of Ancient Texts, Songs, Prayers and Stories, 1983, The Book Within the Book: Approaching the Kabbalah, 1990, Arrows: Selected Poetry: 1952-92, 1994, Reading Jazz, 1993, Writing Jazz, 1999, No Eyes: Lester Young, 2000, San Francisco Beat: Talking with the Poets, 2001, Tree; editor, pub. The Agency, 1968, The Agency Trilogy, 1994, Under, 1995, also Tree Books, songwriter, musician, vocalist Serpent Power, 1968, Poet Song, 1970, Green Morning, 1999, soundtrack Chance, 1978. Bd. dirs. Before Columbus Found., 1977—. Coordinating Coun. of Lit. Mags. grantee, 1973-74, 81, Nat. Endowment of Arts grantee for creative writing, 1974, for pub., 1975, Calif. Arts Coun. grantee, 1979; recipient Tombstone award for poetry John Ryan Morris Meml. Found., 1992. Office: PO Box 9005 Berkeley CA 94709-0005 E-mail: dmelt@earthlink.net.

MELTZER, DAVID OWEN, internist, educator, economist; b. N.Y.C., N.Y., Apr. 17, 1964; s. Herbert Yale and Sharon Bittenson Meltzer. BS, Yale U., 1986; PhD, U. of Chgo., 1992, MD, 1993. Diplomate Am. Bd. Internal Medicine, 1996. From lectr. to assoc. prof. U. of Chgo., Chgo., 1991—2001; resident in internal medicine Brigham & Women's Hosp. Harvard Med. Sch., Boston, 1993—96; assoc. prof. U. of Chgo., 2001—. Rsch. assoc. Nat. Bur. Econ. Rsch., Cambridge, 1992. Recipient Lee Lusted prize, NIH, 1996, Outstanding Paper award, 1998. Mem.: Phi Beta Kappa, Alpha Omega Alpha. Office: University of Chicago 5841 S Maryland Chicago IL 60637 Office Fax: 773-834-2238. Business E-Mail: dmeltzer@medicine.bsd.uchicago.edu.

MELTZER, DONALD RICHARD, treasurer; b. Boston, Sept. 1, 1932; s. Leo N. and Betty (Flesher) M.; m. Mary Douglas Seelye, Dec. 7, 1963; children: Kimberly, Christopher. AB, Dartmouth Coll., 1954, MBA, 1955. Mgr. Peat, Marwick, Mitchell & Co., Boston, 1955-67; asst. controller United Fruit Corp., 1968-69, controller, 1969-70, v.p., controller, 1970-73; v.p., chief acctg. office United Brands Co., N.Y.C., 1973-74, v.p. fin. and adminstrn., 1974-76; v.p. fin., treas. Instron Corp., Canton, Mass., 1976-88; v.p. fin. and adminstrn., treas., chief fin. officer Dialogue, Inc., Braintree, 1988-90. Corp. fin. cons., Sudbury, Mass., 1988-96. Overseer Children's Hosp. Med. Ctr., Boston, 1980-94; fin. com. Town of Sudbury, Mass., 1967; chmn. bd. trustees First Parish Ch., Sudbury, 1970-71, treas., 1991-93; pres. Mass. Parents Assn. for Deaf and Hard of Hearing, Boston, 1976-77, bd. dirs., 1973-86. Mem. AICPA, Mass. Soc. CPAs, Fin. Execs. Inst., Am. Assn. Indsl. Mgmt. (bd. dirs. 1980-85), Walk 'N Mass Volkssport Club (co-pres. 1993-95). Avocation: postal history, stamp collecting. Home: 341 Old Lancaster Rd Sudbury MA 01776-2035 E-mail: meltzwalk@aol.com.

MELTZER, E. ALYNE, educator, social worker, volunteer; b. Jersey City, May 16, 1934; d. Abraham Samuel and Fannie Ruth (Nydick) M. BA, Mich. State U., 1956. Acctg. clerk Louis Marx Co. Inc., N.Y.C., 1957-60; tchr. social studies Haverstraw H.S., N.Y., 1960-61; tchr. Sachem Ctrl. Sch. Dist., Farmingville, 1961-63, East Paterson Sch. Dist., N.J., 1964-65; case worker dept. social svc. Human Resource Adminstrn., N.Y.C., 1966-89. Mem. Yorkville Civic Coun., 1988—93; policy advisor Senator Roy Goodman Adv. Com., Albany, 1987—90; mem. Temple Shaaray Tefila. Recipient Sabra Soc. Plaque award State of Israel New Leadership Divsn., N.Y.C., 1979, Prime Min. Club Plaque award State of Israel Bonds, 1986-87, 96, Pin award, 1986-87, 90, 94-96, others. Mem.: AAUW, Jewish Genealogy Soc., Assn. Ref. Zionists Am., Am. Jewish Com., Internat. Coun. Jewish Women (participant Jerusalem seminar 1991), Nat. Coun. Jewish Women (participant nat. conv. 1987, Albany Inst. 1987, Washington Inst. 1987, N.E. dist. conv. 1988, Albany Inst. 1988, Israel Summit V 1988, Washington Inst. 1989, sec. sect. pub. affairs com. 1990—93, mem. state and sec. pub. affairs com. 1990—, Albany Inst. 1991, Washington Mission 1991, co-chair Hunger Program Sunday Family Soup Kitchen 1991—93, nat. Israel affairs com. 1991—96, bd. dirs. N.Y. sect. 1991—, Jewish/Israel affairs com. sect. 1991—, Washington Inst. 1992, participant nat. conv. 1993, Albany Inst. 1993, chair Roosevelt Island Svcs. 1993—, participant nat. conv. 1996, Israel Roundtable 1996—99, co-chair fundraising jour. 1998—2000, co-chair sec. Yad B'Yad (Hand in Hand with Israel) cmty. svc. project 1999—, co-chair sec. Jewish/Israel Affairs com. 2001—, film festival com. The Eleanor Leff Jewish Women's Resource Ctr. 2001—, life N.Y. and Rockland County sects., Outstanding Vol. award 1973—74, 1990—91, Donor award 1987—93, 1996), Jewish Hist. Soc. N.Y., Mich. State U. Alumni Orgn. (life; sec. N.Y. chpt. 1959—60), Women's League for Israel (life), Mothers and Others, Rockland County Jewish Home for the Aged (life), Hadassah (life), Rockland County Jewish Home for the Aged (life), Sierra Club.

MELTZER, JAY H. lawyer, retail company executive; b. Bklyn., Mar. 30, 1944; s. Solomon G. and Ethel L. (Kraft) M.; m. Bonnie R. Rosenberg, June 27, 1965; children: Wendy, Elizabeth, Jonathan. AB, Dartmouth Coll., 1964; JD, Harvard U., 1967. Bar: N.Y. 1968, Mass. 1978, U.S. Dist. Ct. Mass. 1979. Law clk. to U.S. dist. judge, 1967-68; assoc. firm Shearman & Sterling, N.Y.C., 1968-72; with Damon Corp., Needham Heights, Mass., 1972-84, gen. counsel, sec., 1973-84, v.p., 1979-84; v.p., corp. counsel The TJX Cos., Inc., Framingham, Mass., 1984-87, v.p., gen. counsel, sec., 1987-89, sr. v.p., gen. counsel, sec., 1989—. Dir. coun. Better Bus. Bur., 1990-93. Mem. ABA, Am. Soc. Corp. Secs., Am. Corp. Counsel Assn. (bd. dirs. N.E. chpt. 1991-2000), Retailers Assn. Mass. (bd. dirs., exec. com., sec.), New Eng. Corp. Counsel Assn. (bd. dirs.). Office: TJX Cos Inc 770 Cochituate Rd Framingham MA 01701-4672 E-mail: jay_meltzer@tjx.com.

MELTZER, MILTON, author; b. Worcester, Mass., May 8, 1915; s. Benjamin and Mary (Richter) M.; m. Hilda Balinky, June 22, 1941; children: Jane, Amy. Student, Columbia, 1932-36. Adj. prof. history U. Mass., Amherst, 1977-80. Author: of more than 100 books including Mark Twain Himself, 1960; (with Walter Harding) A Thoreau Profile, 1962, Langston Hughes: A Biography, 1968, Bread and Roses, 1967, Brother, Can You Spare a Dime, 1968, Never to Forget: The Jews of the Holocaust, 1976, Dorothea Lange: A Photographer's Life, 1978; co-editor: Lydia Maria Child: Selected Letters, 1817-1880, 1982, The Terrorists, 1983, A Book About Names, 1984, The Black Americans, 1984, Ain't Gonna Study War No More, 1985, Mark Twain: A Writer's Life, 1985, Poverty in America, 1986, George Washington and the Birth of Our Nation, 1986, The Landscape of Memory, 1987, The American Revolutionaries, 1987, Benjamin Franklin: The New American, 1988, Rescue: The Story of How Gentiles Saved Jews in the Holocaust, 1988, Starting From Home: A Writer's Beginnings, 1988, Voices From the Civil War, 1989, Columbus and the World Around Him, 1990, The Bill of Rights: How We Got It and What It Means, 1990, Crime in America, 1990, Thomas Jefferson: Revolutionary Aristocrat, 1991, The Amazing Potato, 1992, Slavery: A World History, 1993, Lincoln: In His Own Words, 1993, Andrew Jackson and His America, 1993, Gold, 1993; (with Langston Hughes, C. Eric Lincoln, and Jon Michael Spencer) A Pictorial History of African-Americans, 1994, Cheap Raw Material: How Our Youngest Workers Are Exploited and Abused, 1994, Theodore Roosevelt, 1994, Who Cares? Millions Do: A Book About Altruism, 1994, Frederick Douglass: In His Own Words, 1995, Weapons and Warfare, 1996, Tom Paine, 1996, The Many Lives of Andrew Carnegie, 1997, Ten Queens: Portraits of Women of Power, 1998, Food, 1998, Carl Sanburg, 1999, Witches and Witch Hunts, 1999, Driven from the Land, 2000, They Came in Chains, 2000, Ten Kings, 2001, The Day the Shy Tell, 2002, Walt Whitman, 2002. Served with USAAF, 1942-46. Recipient Laura Ingalls Wilder award, Am. Libr. Assn., 2001. Mem. Orgn. Am. Historians, Authors Guild, P.E.N. Address: 263 W End Ave New York NY 10023-2612

MELTZER, RAE, social worker; b. Russia, Jan. 7, 1922; d. Ely and Ida (Belatzkin) Libin; m. Jack Meltzer, June 26, 1944; children: Richard, Marc, Ellen. BA, U. Chgo., 1943, MA, 1959. Cert. social worker, Tex., Ill. Pvt. practice clin. social worker, Dallas, Chgo.; vis. assoc. prof. U. Tex., Dallas; field wk. assoc. prof. U. Chgo.; translator, transliterator U.S. Holocaust Meml. Mus., Washington, 1995—. Author: Under the Canopy: Yiddish Marriage Wisdom, 2001, Yiddish Wisdom for Parents, 2001; contbr. articles to profl. jours. Founder, chmn. bd. dirs. Park Forest Family Counseling Svc.; bd. dirs. Virginia Frank Child Devel. Ctr. Mem. Am. Coun. Social Wk., Nat. Assn. Social Workers, Am. Group Psychotherapy Assn., Register of Clin. Social Workers, Acad. Cert. Social Workers. Home: 4550 N Park Ave Apt 803 Chevy Chase MD 20815-7237 E-mail: raejack@earthlink.net.

MELTZER, RICHARD STUART, cardiologist; b. N.Y.C., Sept. 6, 1948; s. Ezra and Hilda M.; m. Colette Haesaerts, Aug. 8, 1971; children: Michelle, Sara. BA magna cum laude, Harvard Coll., 1970; MD, Harvard Md. Sch., Boston, 1974. Diplomate Am. Bd. Med. Examiners; diplomate in internal medicine, cardiovascular disease Am. Bd. Internal Medicine; cert. in echocardiography. Intern, resident N.Y. Hosp.-Cornell Med. Ctr., 1974-77; fellow in cardiology Stanford (Calif.) U., 1977-79; staff cardiologist Erasmus U., Rotterdam, The Netherlands, 1979-82; from asst. prof. to assoc. prof. cardiology Mt. Sinai Med. Sch., N.Y.C., 1983-86; from assoc. prof. to prof., dir. echocardiography U. Rochester, N.Y., 1986-97; pvt. practice, Las Cruces, N.Mex., 1997—. Vis. assoc. prof. Heart Inst., Chaim Sheba Med. Ctr., Tel Hashomer, Israel, 1982, 92-93. Fellow Am. Coll. Cardiology, European Soc. Cardiology, Am. Heart Assn. (coun. clin. cardiology); mem. Am. Soc. Echocardiography, Am. Inst. Ultrasound in Medicine, Internat. Soc. Cardiovasc. Ultrasound. Home: 5313 Redman Rd Las Cruces NM 88011-7557 Office: Assoc Cardiology Cons NMex 2405 S Telshor Blvd Las Cruces NM 88011-5049 E-mail: meltzer@zianet.com.

MELTZER, ROBERT CRAIG, lawyer, educator; b. Chgo., July 31, 1958; s. Franklyn Richard and Zelma (Cohen) M. BA, U. Colo., 1980; cert., Inst. de Internat., Strasbourg, France, 1984; JD, No. Ill. U., DeKalb, 1985; postgrad., U. Salzburg, Austria, 1985. Bar: Ill. 1985, U.S. Dist. Ct. (no. dist.) Ill. 1985, U.S. Ct. Appeals (7th cir.) 1988, U.S. Supreme Ct. 1989. Law clk. Hurwitz & Abramson, Washington, 1980, Mayer, Brown & Platt, Chgo., 1983; lawyer UN WHO, Geneva, Switzerland, 1985; assoc. Robert C. Meltzer & Assocs., Chgo., 1986-91, Katz, Randall & Weinberg, Chgo., 1991-93, Arnstein & Lehr, Chgo., 1993-98, Grotefeld & Denenberg, Chgo., 1998-99; pres. Visanow.com, Inc., 1999—. Creator online immigration processing. Contbr. articles to profl. jours.; editor The Globe, Springfield, Ill., 1984-99. Pro bono lawyer Fed. Bar Assn., Chgo., 1985-98. Recipient Medal of Appreciation, Ministry of Justice, Beijing, 1996. Mem. Ill. State Bar Assn. (internat. and immigration law sect. 1985—, pres. internat. law sect. 1990-91, Editor's award 1989, 94), Am. Immigration Law Assn. Avocations: history, racquet sports, golf, arts, music. Home: 71 E Division St Chicago IL 60610 Office: Visanow.com Inc 33 N La Salle St # 300 Chicago IL 60602-2603 E-mail: meltzer@visanow.com.

MELTZER, SHARON BITTENSON, English language and humanities educator; b. Bklyn., Feb. 22, 1940; d. Abraham and Lena Yetta (Bienstock) Bittenson; m. Herbert Yale Meltzer, June 12, 1960; children: David Owen Meltzer, Danielle Beth Meltzer Cassel. AB, Barnard Coll., 1961; AM, Yale U., 1962, PhD, 1970. Lectr. CUNY, 1963; instr. Tufts U., Medford, Mass., 1965-66; lectr. U. Chgo., 1970-71, asst. prof., 1971-76, asst. dean of students, social scis., 1977-80; assoc. prof. Chgo. City-Wide Coll., 1981-85, prof., 1985-91; prof. English Richard J. Daley Coll., Chgo., 1991—. Recipient Woodrow Wilson fellowship Yale U., 1961, 64, Jr. Sterling fellowship Yale U., 1962, U. Chgo. Outstanding Tchr. award, 1989, 90, 95, 98. Mem. Modern Lang. Assn., Nat. Coun. Tchrs. English, Midwest Modern Lang. Assn., C.C. Humanities Assn., Assn. Literary Scholars and Critics, Phi Beta Kappa. Avocations: travel, fine arts, dancing, gardening. Home: 83 Altentann Nashville TN 37215-5816 Office: Richard J Daley Coll 7500 S Pulaski Rd Chicago IL 60652-1242 E-mail: sharonmel@aol.com.

MELTZER, YALE LEON, economist, educator; b. N.Y.C., Nov. 3, 1931; s. Benjamin and Ada (Luria) M.; m. Annette Schoenberg, Aug. 7, 1960; children: Benjamin Robert, Philippe David. BA, Columbia U., 1954, postgrad. Sch. Law, 1954-55; MBA, NYU, 1966. Asst. to chief patent atty., prodn. mgr. Beaunit Mills, Inc., Elizabethton, Tenn., 1955—58, prodn. mgr., 1956—58; rsch. chemist N.Y. Med. Coll., N.Y.C., 1958-59, H. Kohnstamm & Co., Inc., N.Y.C., 1959-66, mgr. comml. devel., market rsch., patents and trademarks, 1966-68; sr. security analyst Harris, Upham & Co., Inc., 1968-70; instr. dept. econs. NYU, N.Y.C., 1972-79; adj. prof. dept. acctg., fin. and mgmt. Pace U., 1974-80, adj. assoc. prof., 1980-84; lectr. dept. polit. sci., econs. and philosophy Coll. S.I., CUNY, 1977-82, asst. prof. dept. polit. sci., econs. and philosophy, 1983—. Lectr. bus., fin., econs., sci. and tech.; presenter papers confs. Author: Soviet Chemical Industry, 1966; Chemical Trade with the Soviet Union and Eastern European Countries, 1967; Chemical Guide to GATT, The Kennedy Round and International Trade, 1968; Phthalocyanine Technology, 1970; Hormonal and Attractant Pesticide Technology, 1971; Urethane Foams: Technology and Applications, 1971; Water-Soluble Polymers: Technology and Applications, 1972; Encyclopedia of Enzyme Technology, 1973; Economics, 1974; Foamed Plastics: Recent Developments, 1976; Water-Soluble Resins and Polymers: Technology and Applications, 1976; Putting Money to Work: An Investment Primer, 1976; (with W.C.F. Hartley) Cash Management: Planning, Forecasting, and Control, 1979; Water-Soluble Polymers: Recent Developments, 1979; Putting Money to Work: An Investment Primer for the '80s, 1981, updated edit., 1984; Water-Soluble Polymers: Developments since 1978, 1981; Expanded Plastics and Related Products: Developments Since 1978, 1983; contbr. articles to profl. publs.; translator Russian, French and German tech. lit. Mem. AAAS, Am. Econ. Assn. Home: 14110 82nd Dr Apt 537 Jamaica NY 11435-1106 Office: Coll Staten Island 2800 Victory Blvd Staten Island NY 10314-6609 E-mail: meltzer@postbox.csi.cuny.edu.

MELUCCI, RICHARD CHARLES, research institute administrator; b. Oceanside, N.Y., July 17, 1946; s. Richard Joseph and Marcia Jane (Lockwood) M.; m. Rosanne Alice Kessel, Dec. 15, 1968; children: Christine Ann, Donna Marie, Richard Paul, Robert Joseph, John Charles. BS, Adelphi U., 1968, MBA, 1971. Planning engr. Sperry Gyroscope Co., Great Neck, NY, 1967-70; planning adminstr. PRD Elecs., Inc., Syosset, 1970-73, program adminstr., 1973-74; sr. staff asst. dept. physics Brookhaven Nat. Lab., Union, 1974-79, adminstr. dept. applied sci., 1979-95, lab. budget officer, 1995—. Adj. assoc. prof. computer info. systems Dowling Coll., Oakdale, N.Y., 1978—; vis. prof. SUNY at Oswego, 1982—. Recipient Cert. Inst. Certification of Computer Profls. Office: Brookhaven Nat Lab Bldg 460 Upton NY 11973 E-mail: melucci@bnl.gov.

MELUSKY, JOSEPH ANTHONY, political science educator; b. Pottsville, Pa., June 2, 1952; s. George John and Eleanor Elizabeth (Parulis) M.; m. Marie Ann Belecanech, Mar. 28, 1976; children: Michael Joseph, Jessica Marie. BA, West Chester State Coll., 1974; MA, U. Del., 1978, PhD, 1983. Lectr. U. Del., Newark, 1979-80; prof. polit. sci., chmn. dept. St. Francis U., Loretto, Pa., 1980—. Dean gen. edn. Saint Francis Coll., 1993-94, pres. faculty senate, 1985-87, v.p. faculty senate, 1984-85, 90-92. Author: The Constitution: Our Written Legacy, 1991; co-author: To Perserve These Rights: The Bill of Rights 1791-1991, 1991, Bill of Rights: Our Written Legacy, 1993, The American Political System: An Owner's Manual, 2000. Judge Am. Legion H.S. oratorical contests on U.S. Constn., 1991-92, 95, 97, 2000; judge We the People: The Citizen and the Constitution, Pa. State Finals, 2001, 02; mem. Blair County Dem. Com., 1985-90; election judge Blair Twp., East Hollidaysburg 9 Dist., 1997—. Mem.: Northeastern Polit. Sci. Assn. (exec. dir. 1993—97, dir. employment svcs. 1985—), Pa. Polit. Sci. Assn. (v.p. 1994—96, 2002—, pres. 1997—99). Office: St Francis U Dept History and Polit Sci Loretto PA 15940 E-mail: jmelusky@francis.edu.

MELUSKY, RAYMOND GABRIEL, electrical engineer; b. Pottsville, PA, Sept. 12, 1961; Master of Science in Electrical Engineering, University of Central Florida, Orlando, Florida, 1995—96. Electrical Engineer ONI, Washington, 1998—2002, Naval Undersea Warfare Center, Newport, RI, 1992—98. Senior Member Institute for Electronic & Electrical Engineers, New York, NY, 1999—2002. Author: (Journal of Underwater Acoustics) Multiplicative Array Processing Topics, 2001. Sergeant USMCR, 1979—83, USA. Mem.: Mensa (IQ at or above 98th percentile 1988). Roman Catholic. Avocation: exercise. Home: 18 West Glebe Road Alexandria VA 22305 Office: ONI 4251 Suitland Road Washington DC 20395-5720 Office Fax: 301-669-3671. Personal E-mail: raymel@bellatlantic.net. Business E-Mail: rmelusky@nmic.navy.mil.

MELVILLE, RICHARD ALLEN, investment company executive; b. Springfield, Mass., Sept. 15, 1932; s. Charles Raymond and Vera Alice (Brooks) M.; m. Maria-Angela Garcia-Martinez, June 15, 1963; children: Thomas Alexander, Andrew Michael, Charles Peter. BA, Bates Coll., Lewiston, Maine, 1954; MA, Johns Hopkins U., 1959. Counsel U.S. State Dept., Phnom Penh, Cambodia, 1959-63; v.p. Irving Trust Co., N.Y.C., 1963-70; pres., CEO Allied Bank Group, 1970-83; dir. Fiduciary Trust Internat., 1984-87; chmn. bd. Alexander, Andrews & Peters, Hong Kong, 1988—. Chief internat. advisor State Commn. for Reform of the Economy, Govt. of People's Republic of China, Beijing, 1993—; cons. Govt. of State of Cambodia, 1991-93. Author: Cambodia: HRAF, 1963, A Northeast Forest, 2000, Pseudonovibos spiralis, 2001; editor: Second Chance, 1989; contbr. articles to profl. jours. Trustee Johns Hopkins U., Balt., 1979-85, Bates Coll., 1976-90; adv. coun. Hopkins-Nanjing Ctr., China, 1981-90, Nitze Sch. of Advanced Internat. Studies, Washington, 1978-90. With Mil. Dist. of Washington, 1955-56. Mem. Coun. on Fgn. Rels. Republican. Episcopalian. Avocations: cycling, tennis, writing. Home: PO Box 125 Bristol ME 04539-0125 Office: China Internat Centre 18 Bei San Huan Beijing 100011 China E-mail: melville@tidewater.net.

MELVILLE, ROBERT SEAMAN, chemist; b. Worcester, Mass., Nov. 20, 1913; s. Carey Eyster and Maud Tesmer (Seaman) M.; m. Eleanor Elisabeth Vogel, Mar. 6, 1942; children: Robert Andrew, John Frederick, Margaret Ellen, Emily Jean, Martin Carroll. AB in Chemistry, Clark U., 1937; PhD in Biochemistry, State U. Iowa, 1950. Chief chemist St. Luke's Hosp., Chgo., 1950-54; chief biochemist VA Hosp., Iowa City, 1954-63; chief biochemist, lab. requirement specialist VA Cen. Office, Washington, 1963-65; health sci. adminstr. Nat. Inst. Gen. Med. Scis., NIH, Bethesda, Md., 1965-67, chief automated clin. lab. program, 1967-77, spl. asst. to dir. of biomed. engring., 1977-81; dir. In Vitro Diagnostic Device Standards div. Bur. Med. Devices, FDA, Silver Spring, 1981-82; cons. in clin. scis., 1983—. Clin. prof. pathology George Washington U. Med. Ctr., Washington, 1977—; pres. Trans-Tech. Biomed., 1983—. Contbr. articles on clin. lab. automation to profl. publs. With U.S. Army, 1942-46. Fellow AAAS, Am. Chem. Soc., Am.. Assn. Clin. Chemistry (Joseph H. Rowe award 1972, Nat. Fisher award 1976, pres. 1969-70), Instrument Soc. Am., Assn. for Advancement of Med. Instrumentation; mem. Am. Bd. Clin. Chemists (pres. bd. dirs. 1978-81), Am. Inst. Chemists (chmn. cert. commn. in chem. engring. and chemistry 1981-84, 87-91, cert. chemist 1989—), Alpha Chi Sigma (Profl. Chemist award 1990), Lambda Chi Alpha. Clubs: Cosmos. Lodges: Masons. Unitarian Universalist. Home and Office: 11112 Kenilworth Ave PO Box 56 Garrett Park MD 20896-0056 E-mail: rsmel@starpower.net.

MELVILLE, SANDRA BAUER, nurse practitioner; b. Lynn, Mass., Mar. 15, 1952; d. Paul Sherman and Ann (Parker) Bauer; m. Daniel F. Melville, Oct. 6, 1984. BSN cum laude, Alderson-Broaddus Coll., Philippi, W.Va., 1974; MSN, W.Va. U., 1985. Cert. adult nurse practitioner. Staff nurse, head nurse, staff.-charge nurse Charleston (W.Va.) Area Med. Ctr., Meml. div., 1974-85; clin. nurse specialist Lakes Region Gen. Hosp., Laconia, N.H., 1986-93; nurse practitioner Rohrer Assoc., Brighton, Mass., 1994-97. Nurse practitioner Meredith (N.H.) Family Practice, 1986-95; provider Lakes Region Gen. Hosp., 1993-95; adj. clin. faculty U. N.H., 1986; vol. nurse coord., facilitator W.Va. Health Right, 1983-85. Contbr. articles to profl. jours. and publs. Mem. Sigma Theta Tau. Home: 42 Hoy Ter Milton MA 02186-4736

MELVIN, BEN WATSON, JR. petroleum and chemical manufacturing executive; b. Nashville, Mar. 27, 1926; s. Ben Watson and Virginia (Darden) M.; m. Elizabeth Cooper Hershey, May 10, 1952; children— Ben W., Landis Anne, Thomas C., Mark C. B.Chem. Engring., U. Del., 1950. With E. I. duPont de Nemours & Co., Inc., Wilmington, Del., 1950-91, ret., 1991. Served with USAAF, 1944-46. Mem. AICE, Soc. Plastics Engrs., So. Chem. Industry, Wilmington Country Club.

MELVIN, BILLY ALFRED, clergyman; b. Macon, Ga., Nov. 25, 1929; s. Daniel Henry and Leola Dale (Seidell) M.; m. Marcia Darlene Eby, Oct. 26, 1952; children: Deborah Ruth, Daniel Henry II. Student, Free Will Baptist Bible Coll., Nashville, 1947-49; BA, Taylor U., Upland, Ind., 1951; postgrad., Asbury Theol. Sem., Wilmore, Ky., 1951-53; B.D., Union Theol. Sem., Richmond, Va., 1956; D.D., Azusa (Calif.) Coll., 1968; LL.D. (hon.), Taylor U., 1984; DD, Huntington Coll., 1995. Ordained to ministry Free Will Baptist Ch., 1951; pastor First Free Will Baptist Chs., Newport, Tenn., 1951-53, Richmond, 1953-57, Bethany Ch., Norfolk, Va., 1957-59. Exec. sec. Nat. Assn. Free Will Baptists, 1959-67; exec. dir. Nat. Assn. Evangelicals, 1967-95.

MELVIN, CHARLES ALFRED, III, superintendent of schools; b. Milw., May 19, 1950; s. Charles A. Jr. and Audry M. (Dart) M.; m. Almira M. Tiedke, Aug. 1985; children: Sean Charles, Katherin Almira. Ba, U. Wis., 1972, MA, 1975, PhD, 1979. Supr. U. Wis., Madison, 1975; prin. Sch. Dist. Beloit (Wis.) Turner, 1980, dir. instr., 1982, supt., 1986—. Recipient sch. improvement grant, Carnegie Found., Beloit Found.; named one of Top 100 Exec. Educators, NSBA. Mem. ASCD, Am. Assn. Sch. Adminstrs., Nat. Assn. Secondary Sch. Prins. Home: 1911 Vail Ter Beloit WI 53511-3148

MELVIN, CHARLES EDWARD, JR. lawyer; b. Greensboro, N.C., July 13, 1929; s. Charles Edward and Mary Ruth (Plunkett) M.; m. Jacklyn McDaniel, Mar. 1, 1958; 1 child, Dana W. BS, U. N.C., 1951, JD with honors, 1956. Bar: N.C. 1956. Of counsel Smoth Moore LLP, Greensboro, 1958—. Capt. U.S. Army, 1952-54. Mem. N.C. Bar Assn. (chmn. real property sect. 1981), Am. Coll. Real Estate Lawyers, Greensboro C. of C. (pres. 1978). Office: Smith Moore LLP PO Box 21927 Greensboro NC 27420-1927 E-mail: charlie.melvin@smithmoorelaw.com.

MELVIN, HIRAM JOSEPH, religious organization administrator, minister; b. Milton, Fla., July 26, 1956; s. Hiram Mack Melvin, Emma Gray Barnhill; m. Cecilia Diana Hathaway; children: Dana Careen, Rachel Tiara Greenhill, Lucy Elaine Carter, Gabrial Joseph, Lydia Janeen. Grad., Pensacola Jr. Coll., 1996, Pensacola Bible Inst., 1992. Ordianed minister 1994; lic. airframe and powerplants FAA. Missionary to Scotland Bible Bapt. Mission, Inc., Pensacola, Fla., 1992—2000; pres., founder Indep. Arctic Mission, Inc., Milton, Greenland, 1999—. Pres., founder, dir. Gabriel's Vending, Inc., Milton, 2001—. Pipe major, founder The Fourth Watch Pipe Band, Pensacola, 1990—93; piper Linwood Caledonian Pipe Band, Linwood, Scotland, 1995—96; pastor, founder Larkfield Bapt. Ch., Greenock, Scotland, 1995—97, King James Bible Bapt. Ch., Ayr, Scotland, 1997—2000. Pvt. U.S. Army, 1974—74, Ft. Jackson, S.C. Baptist. Avocations: bagpipes, fiddle. Home: 6178 Swainson St Milton FL Office: Indep Arctic Mission Inc 6178 Swainson St Milton FL 32570 Business E-Mail: arcticmission@netzero.net.

MELVIN, JAY WAYNE, computer programmer; b. Oak Park, Ill., Feb. 3, 1946; s. Kendred Wayne and Margarita Alice (Pérez) M.; m. Linda Hansen, Dec. 10, 1980. MA in Urban Studies, Claremont (Calif.) Grad. Sch., 1975, postgrad., 1977. Hot line/prodn. mgr. Forth, Inc., Hermosa Beach, Calif., 1981-85; sr. software engr. Maxtor Corp., San Jose, 1986-88; computer programmer Tracor-Ultron Labs., 1988-90, Comtech Labs., Palo Alto, Calif., 1990-92; programmer, team leader, mgr. software devel. lab. Omnipoint Corp., Colorado Springs, Colo., 1992-96; mgr. applications integration lab. Pacific Bell Mobile Svcs., Pleasanton, Calif., 1996-98, network contr., network ops. ctr., 1998; contract employee VoiceStream Wireless Corp. Mem. T1 del. to 3d Generation Partnership Project, 2000; cons. phenomenoLOGIC, La Honda, Calif., 1985-92, infoPATH, La Honda, 1990—, Cingular Wireless, 2001—. Contbr. articles to profl. jours. Peace Corps vol. U.S. State Dept., Bengal, India, 1966-68; fire dept. vol. Calif. Dept. Forestry, Kings Mountain, 1986-88; fire dept. lt. Vol. Fire Brigade, La Honda, San Mateo, 1988-94; radio operator Mil. Affiliate Radio Svc., Jackson, Miss., 1962-64. Recipient Beyond War award, 1987; grad. fellowship Law Enforcement Adminstrn. Assn., 1975-77. Mem. Amateur Radio Relay League (life), Amateur Satellite Corp. (life), Forth Interest Group, San Mateo Masonic Lodge #226, Pi Sigma Alpha. Avocation: amateur radio astronomy, visiting the WWW site infopath.com E-mail. Home and Office: 80 N Cabrillo Hwy Ste Q-419 Half Moon Bay CA 94019 E-mail: jmelvin@infopath.com.

MELVIN, LELAND D. astronaut; b. Lynchburg, Va., Feb. 15, 1964; s. Deems and Grace Melvin. BS in Chemistry, U. Richmond, 1986; MS in Materials Sci. Engring., U. Va., 1991. Rschr. fiber optic sensors group, nondestructive evaluation scis. br. Langley Rsch. Ctr., NASA, Va., 1989—94, head vehicle health monitoring team, 1994—98; astronaut, mission specialist candidate Johnson Space Ctr. NASA, Houston, 1998—. Named Acad. All Am., NCAA Divsn. I; named to U. Richmond Athletic Hall of Fame; recipient Key to City of Lynchburg, Va. Achievements include being chosen by the Detroit Lions in the 11th round of the 1986 NFL college draft; participation in Toronto Argonauts and Dallas Cowboys football training camps. Avocations: piano, reading, music, cycling, tennis. Office: Astronaut Office/CB NASA Johnson Space Ctr Houston TX 77058*

MELVIN, NORMAN CECIL, lawyer; b. Balt., Aug. 21, 1916; s. Norman Cecil and Anna H. (Holzworth) M.; m. Louise A. Gillen, Feb. 10, 1945 (dec. Oct. 1958); children: Leigh G., Norman Cecil III; m. Virginia Brown Lester, Nov. 2, 1959; 1 dau., Susan A. AB, Johns Hopkins U., 1939; LL.B., Harvard U., 1942. Bar: Md. 1942. Practice law, Balt., 1946—; mem. firm Brown & Brune, 1946-52; gen. atty. Western Md. Ry. Co., Balt., 1952-66, gen. solicitor, 1966-68, v.p., gen. counsel, 1968-75, dir., 1970-75. Asst. peoples counsel Pub. Service Commn. Md., 1951-52; instr. U. Balt., 1957-66 Served to capt. AUS, 1942-46. Recipient Erskine M. Ross essay award ABA, 1950 Mem. ABA, Md. Bar Assn., Balt. Bar Assn., Soc. Colonial Wars (coun. 1966-69), SAR, Johns Hopkins Alumni Assn. (pres. 1968-70, Disting. Alumni award 1970, Heritage award 1980), Harvard Club, Johns Hopkins Club. Home: 4202 Wickford Rd Baltimore MD 21210-2930

MELVIN, PAMELA LEE, artist; b. Port Lyanty, Morocco, Nov. 26, 1956; d. Gene Norman and Mary Elizabeth (Doyle) M.; 1 child Leah Germaine. Student, U. South Fla., Tampa, 1975-76, Corcoran Sch. of Art, Washington, 1977, Art Students League, 1979-84, NAD, Sch. Visual Arts. Exhibited in group shows at Gallery 345, N.Y., 1982, Norton Mus., West Palm Beach, 1983, Earth Art Gallery, West Palm Beach, Fla., 1987, Corbino Galleries, Sarasota, Fla., 1987, 1988, 1989, 1990—93, Artifacts Art Gallery, Miami Beach, Fla., 1987, Gallery Gemini, Palm Beach, Fla., 1988, 1989, H.B. Starr Gallery, Palm Beach, 1993, Flamingo Pk. Art Studio, West Palm Beach, 1998, Coral Springs (Fla.) Art Guild, 2001 (Merit award), DeGraaf Fine Art Gallery, West Palm Beach, 2002, Gallery of Am. Fine Arts, N.Y., Now Gallery NYC, Ann Jacob Gallery, Atlanta and Highlands, N.C. Home: 922 North O St Lake Worth FL 33460-2746

MELVIN, PETER JOSEPH, astrophysicist, educator; b. Seattle, Mar. 12, 1944; s. William Leopold and Virginia (Stevens) M.; m. Alice Sue Pfiester, May 25, 1975 (dec. 1994); children: Robert Dennis, Chloe Anne. BA, Western Wash. State Coll., 1965; MS, U. Ill., 1966, PhD, 1970. NASA trainee U. Ill., Urbana, 1966-68, instr. phys. sci., 1970-72, asst. prof., 1972-77; sr. engr. Martin-Marietta Aerospace Co., Denver, 1977-80, staff engr., 1980-83; sr. specialist engr. engring. tech. applications divsn. Boeing Computer Svcs., Seattle, 1983-86; astrophysicist U.S. Naval Rsch. Lab., Washington, 1986-99, ret., 1999; pres. B-Gravity, Inc., Waldorf, Md., 1999—. Vis. faculty applied math. divsn. Nat. Bur. Stds. Boulder (Colo.) Labs., 1977. Contbr. articles to sci. jours.; patentee in field. Mem. AIAA, Am. Math. Soc., Soc. Indsl. and Applied Math., Am. Geophys. Uion, Am. Astronautical Soc. E-mail: melvin@nrl.navy.mil., melvin@radix.net.

MELVIN, RONALD MCKNIGHT, retired museum director; b. Regina, Sask., Can., Oct. 25, 1927; came to U.S., 1953; s. M. Gordon and Mary Gillespie (McKnight) M.; m. Gwen Ellis, Apr. 30, 1955; children: Mary Fleming, Catharine Carley. Student, U. B.C., 1945-49. Various positions Powell River Co. Ltd., Vancouver, B.C., Can., 1947-56; asst. to pres. Trans Union Corp., Chgo., 1956-58; mng. dir. Procor Ltd. subs. Trans Union Corp., Toronto, Ont., Can., 1958-64; ptnr. Blunt Ellis & Simmons, Chgo., 1964-71, pres., 1971-78; vice chmn. Blunt Ellis & Loew, 1978-80; founding dir. Terra Mus. Am. Art, Evanston, Ill., 1980-84. Dir. Chef Pierre, Traverse City, Mich., 1972-77, Lawter Internat., Chgo., 1977-84. Author, organizer: (art exhbns.) Important Western Art from Chicago Collections, 1980 Five American Masters of Watercolor, 1981, American Naive Paintings From National Gallery of Art, 1982, Solitude--Inner Visions in American Art, 1982, Woman, 1984. Avocation: collecting Worcester porcelain. Home: 585 Norfolk Rd PO Box 278 Southfield MA 01259-0278 E-mail: birch@bcn.net.

MELVIN, RUSSELL JOHNSTON, magazine publishing consultant; b. New Castle, Pa., Nov. 16, 1925; s. Russell Conwell and Anna Katharine (Johnston) M.; m. Helen Margaret Connery, Aug. 6, 1949; children: Thomas Kirk, Meredith. BA, U. Pa., 1949. Reporter Phila. Inquirer, 1949; copywriter, then asst. to circulation mgr. Time mag., 1949-53; with Newsweek mag., 1953-86, dir. Pacific edits., 1960-64, mng. dir. internat. edits., 1964-68, mng. editor internat. editorial service, 1969-86; cons. internat. affairs and profl. edn. Mag. Pubs. Am. (formerly Mag. Pubs. Assn.), N.Y.C., 1986—. V.p. Newsweek, Inc., 1965-85; founding editor The Journal, Tokyo, 1963; founding dir. Newsweek Feature Service, 1968; mem. UN Communications Adv. Coun. Served with USNR, 1942-46. Mem. Internat. Advt. Assn. (chmn., CEO 1980-85, exec. dir. Chgps. Corp. 1985-86, bd. dirs. 1988-91, mem. world coun. 1990), Internat. Fedn. Periodical Press (mem. exec. and mgmt. bd.), Univ. Club, Chappaqua Tennis Club, The Century Assn. Home: 153 Douglas Rd Chappaqua NY 10514-3104 Office: Mag Pubs Am 919 3rd Ave New York NY 10022-3902

MELZACK, RONALD, psychology educator; b. Montreal, Que., Can., July 19, 1929; s. Joseph and Annie (Mandel) M.; m. Lucy Birch, Aug. 7, 1960; children: Lauren, Joel. BSc, McGill U., Montreal, 1950, MSc, 1951, PhD, 1954; DLitt (hon.), U. Waterloo, 1992. Lectr. Univ. Coll., London, 1957-58; assoc. prof. MIT, 1959-63; lectr. psychology McGill U., 1953-54, prof., 1963—, E.P. Taylor prof., 1986. Author: The Day Tuk Became a Hunter, and Other Eskimo Stories, 1967, Raven, Creator of the World, 1970, The Puzzle of Pain, 1973, Why the Man in the Moon is Happy, and Other Eskimo Creation Stories, 1977, (with P.D. Wall) The Challenge of Pain, 1982, 2nd edit., 1988, Pain Measurement and Assessment, 1983, (with P.D. Wall) Textbook of Pain, 1984, 4th edit., 1999 (with D.C. Turk) Handbook of Pain Assessment, 1992. Decorated Officer, Order of Can., 1995, Order of Quebec, 2000; recipient Molson prize Can. Coun., 1985, Gaston Labat award Am. Soc. Regional Anesthesia, 1989, J.J. Bonica award VI World Congress on Pain, 1990, Prix du Que. Marie-Victorin, 1994; recipient Disting. Contbn. award Can. Pain Soc., 1995, Rsch. Recognition award Canadian Anesthesiology Soc., 1997, Janet Travell award Am. Acad. Pain Mgmt., 1997, Killam prize, 2001. Fellow APA, AAAS, Royal Soc. Can., Can. Psychol. Assn. (Disting. Contbns. to Psychol. Sci. award 1986, hon. pres. 1988-89, gold medal award 2002); mem. Internat. Assn. Study of Pain (hon., past pres.). Home: 51 Banstead Rd Montreal QC Canada H4X 1P1

MELZER, BARBARA EVELYN, minister; b. Queens, N.Y., July 1, 1946; d. Anthony A. Jr. and Irene C. (Lane) M. BS in Elem. Edn., SUNY, Geneseo, 1967; AA in Acting, Am. Acad. Dramatic Arts, 1971; MA in Edn., Adelphi U., 1971; diploma in adminstrn. and supervision, L.I. U., 1977, MA in Theater, 1981; MDiv, N.Y. Theol. Sem., 1992. Cert. minister of youth; ordained to ministry United Methodist Ch., 1997, ordained elder, 2000. Tchr. Unified Sch. Dist. #30, Valley Stream, N.Y., 1967-96; pastor Beach and East Quogue United Meth. Chs., 1996-2000, Woodbury (N.Y.) United Meth. Ch., 2000—. Cons. workshops in Christian edn., youth and children's ministries. Formerly active Christian edn. and youth ministry Grace United Meth. Ch., Valley Stream; mem. Syosset-Woodbury Interfaith Clergy Group; active Bishop's Task Force on Children and Poverty, N.Y. Annual Conf. Mem. Internat. Assn. Women Mins., PEO. E-mail: WUMC11797@aol.com.

MELZER, JOHN T. S. translator, editor; b. Sept. 9, 1938; s. John Henry and Dorothy (Garrett) M. AB, Auburn U., 1961; MA, U. Va., 1964; PhD, Tulane U., 1978; hon. diploma, U. Villareal, Lima, Peru, 1990. Prof. Georgetown (Ky.) Coll., 1964, Columbus (Ga.) State U., 1964-67, U. West Ala., 1977; dir. hist. rsch. St. Augustine (Fla.) Restoration Commn., 1968; drilling fluids cons., 1979—; scholar-in-residence, prof. English, Translex Inst., Miraflores, Lima, 1985-92; editor-in-chief Oakbowery Books, Auburn, Ala., 1994—. Investigator ad honorem Nat. Inst. Culture, Peru, 1989—. Author: Field Spanish, 1985, Bastion of Commerce in the City of Kings, 1991, Oilfield Spanish, 1997; contbr. articles to jours., mags. Address: 74 Curtis St Camp Hill AL 36850-3362

MEMEL, SHERWIN LEONARD, lawyer; b. Buffalo, Mar. 28, 1930; s. Maurice and Nellie (Munshen) M.; m. Iris C. Gittleman, Aug. 17, 1952; children: Jana Sue, Steven Keith, David Scott, Mara Jean. BA, UCLA, 1951, JD with honors, 1954. Bar: Calif. 1955, U.S. Ct. Appeals (9th cir.) 1955, U.S. Dist. Ct. (cen. dist.) Calif. 1959, U.S. Supreme Ct. 1963, D.C. 1979. Sr. ptnr. health law practice group Manatt, Phelps & Phillips, LA, 1987—. Bd. dirs., former chmn. bd. Pac. Pub. Radio Sta. KLON; past instr. health law USC Sch. Pub. Adminstrn.; past instr. health UCLA; cons. and lectr. in field. Co-author: (with R. Barak) Real Estate Issues in the Health Care Industry, 1996; contbr. articles to profl. jours. Chmn. LA Arts Council, 1986-87, Jazz Bakery non-profit pub. performance space; vice-chmn. Dem. Bus. Council, Washington, 1985-86; past pres. Calif. Bd. Med. Quality Assurance. Recipient Disting. Service award Fedn. Am. Hosps., 1970. Mem. ABA (com. health law), Am. Hosp. Assn. (life, Award of Honor 1971), Am. Soc. Law and Medicine, Am. Health Lawyers Assn., Calif. Soc. for Healthcare Attys. (life, pres. 1983), Calif. Bar Assn., D.C. Bar Assn., L.A. County Bar Assn. Office: Manatt Phelps & Phillips 11355 W Olympic Blvd Los Angeles CA 90064-1614

MEMMI, ALBERT, sociologist, educator; b. Tunis, Tunisia, Dec. 15, 1920; arrived in France, 1956; s. François and Marguerite (Sarfati) M.; m. Marie-Germaine Dubach; children: Daniel, Dominique, Nicolas. PhD(hon.) , U. de Beer Schéba. Prof. Lycee Carnot a Tunis, 1953; dir. Ctr. de Psycho-Pedagogie de Tunis, 1953—57; conf. head Ecole Pratique des hautes Etudes, 1958; prof. Ecole des Hautes Etudes Commerciales, 1958—64; maitre de conf. U. Nanterre, 1970. Author: La Statue de Sel, 1953, Agar, 1955, Le Scorpion, 1969, Le Désert, 1977, Le Pharaon. Decorated Officier de la Légion d'Honneur, Officier des Palmes Acads., Officier des Arts et des Lettres, Officier de l'Ordre de la République Tunisienne. Mem. du Comité de Patronage de la maison des Ecrivains, du Comité de Patronage de la LICRA, du Comité de Patronage du MRAP, French Soc. Sociology. Address: 5 rue Saint Merri, 75004 Paris France

MEMORY, JASPER DURHAM, academic administrator, physics educator; b. Raleigh, N.C., Dec. 10, 1936; s. Jasper Livingston and Margaret Moore (Durham) M.; m. Carolyn Hofler, June 4, 1961; children— Margaret Carolyn, Jasper William BS summa cum laude, Wake Forest U., 1956; PhD, U. N.C., 1960. Successively asst. prof., assoc. prof. physics U. S.C., Columbia, 1960-64; assoc. prof. N.C. State U., Raleigh, 1964-67, assoc. dean, physics and math. scis., 1973-82, prof. physics, 1967—98, vice-provost, grad. dean, 1982—86, dir. corp. and govtl. affairs, 1998-99; v.p. for research U. N.C. System, 1986—98, prof. emeritus, 1998—. Bd. govs. Research Triangle Inst., Research Triangle Park, N.C., 1983-84, Triangle Area rsch. dir., 1981-98; cons. NASA Langley, Hampton, Va., 1970-74, Ohio Bd. Regents, 1993-95, Ark. Bd. Regents, 1987, Mass. Bd. Regents, 1998; N.C. State U. rep. Oak Ridge Associated Univs., 1982-85, Grad. Record Exam. Bd., 1985-90, chair, 1989, Policy Coun., Test of English as a Fgn. Lang., 1987-88, chair, 1988. Author: Quantum Theory of Magnetic Resonance Parameters, 1968; (with others) NMR of Aromatic Compounds, 1982, High Resolution NMR in the Solid State: Fundamentals of CP/MAS, 1994. Recipient Outstanding Tchr. award N.C. State U., 1967, Disting. Alumni Service award Wake Forest U., 1981 Fellow Am. Phys. Soc.; mem. Am. Assn. Physics Tchrs., Phi Beta Kappa, Sigma Xi. Democrat. Presbyterian. Home: 124 Talon Dr Cary NC 27511-8604 E-mail: jmemory@nc.rr.com.

MENAKER, RONALD HERBERT, retired bank executive; b. N.Y.C., Dec. 17, 1944; s. Harold L. Menaker and Gladys (Bleiberg) Ross; m. Kathleen Sager Thomas, Sept. 11, 1966; children: Meredith E., Kyri D. Student, Queen's Coll., 1965-66. Mng. dir. J.P. Morgan & Co., Inc., N.Y.C., 1966-2000. Trustee Sinai/NYU Med. Ctr. and Health Sys., N.Y.C., 1991, The Am. Kennel Club Mus. of the Dog, St. Louis, 1989—; bd. dirs., chmn., Am. Kennel Club, N.Y.C.; trustee, past chmn. NYU Downtown Hosp., 1991—; dir. ATALanta Sosnoff Capital Corp., N.Y.C., 1999—, Reckson Assocs. Realty Corp., 2002-; bd. overseers U. Pa. Vet. Sch., 2000—. Mem. Westminster Kennel Club (gov.). Avocations: sporting art, judging dogs.

MENAND, LOUIS, literature educator; Disting. prof. English Grad. Ctr. CUNY; prof. English Princeton U., Columbia U., U. Va. Sch. Law. Contbg. editor: N.Y. Rev. of Books, 1994—; author: Discovering Modernism: T.S. Eliot and His Context, 1987—; editor: The Metaphysical Club, 2001—; editor: (with A.W. Litz and L. Rainey) The Cambridge History of Literary Criticism, Vol. 7: Modernism and the New Criticism, 2000—; editor: The Future of Academic Freedom, 1998—, Pragmatism: A Reader, 1997—; editor: (with L. Berlowitz and D. Donoghue) America in Theory, 1988—. Office: CUNY Grad Ctr 365 Fifth Ave New York NY 10016-4309*

MENARD, JOAN M. state legislator; BS, Bridgewater State Coll., 1967; MEd, Boston U., 1971; postgrad., Boston Coll., 1997—. Mem. Mass. Senate, Boston, 1979—; majority whip Mass. Ho. of Reps., 1984, 92-96, asst. majority whip, 1991, mem. house rules and joint rules comns., house vice chairperson election laws; elem. tchr. Somerset (Mass.) Pub. Schs., 1966-70, spl. edn. tchr., 1970-74, adminstr. spl. needs, 1974-78. Bd. dirs. Fall River Five Cents Savs. Bank, Steppinstone. Mem. adv. bd. Southeastern Mass. Labor Ctr.; chair Dem. State Com., 1993-95, del., 1980; chairwoman Mass. Dem. Party, 1997—2001, State Senator, Mass. Rep. Party, Somerset, Mass., 2000-. Mem. LWV, NOW, Women's Polit. Caucus, Somerset Cath. Womens Club, Bus. and Profl. Women's Club. Office: 27 Water St., Ste. 309 Wakefield MA 01880*

MENCARELLI, VICTOR ARISTIDE, microbiologist; b. College Point, N.Y., Jan. 13, 1971; s. Edward and Madalene M.; m. Kristine Ann Iannaccone, May 16, 1998; 1 child, Johnathan. BS in Biology, D'Youville Coll., 1993. Quality control microbiologist Del Labs., Inc., Farmingdale, N.Y., 1995—. Author: Death and Dying: Attitudes of Adolescents, 1993. Dir. Long Island Youth Bowling Tour, North Babylon, N.Y., 1994-98; vol. Muscular Dystrophy Assn., Hauppauge, N.Y., 1998-2001. Mem. Am. Soc. Microbiology, AAAS, Long Island Bowlers Assn. (dir. 1994-2001), Ea. Long Island Jr. Bowlers Assn. (assoc. dir. 1998-2001), N.Y. State Youth Leader Alumni, N.Y. Acad. Sci. Avocations: sports, reading, music, history. Home: 22 Heathcote Rd Lindenhurst NY 11757 Office: Del Labs Inc 565 Broad Hollow Rd Farmingdale NY 11735 Fax: (516) 844-2019. E-mail: qcsientist@aol.com., vic_mencarelli@dellabs.com.

MENCER, GLENN EVERELL, federal judge; b. Smethport, Pa., May 18, 1925; s. Glenn Hezekiah and Ruth Leona (Rice) M.; m. Hannah Jane Freyer, June 24, 1950; children— Ruth Ann, Cora Jane, Glenn John BBA, U. Mich., 1949, JD, 1952. Bar: Pa. 1953, U.S. Dist. Ct. (we. dist.) Pa. 1953, U.S. Supreme Ct. 1958. Sole practice, Eldred, Pa., 1953-64; dist. atty. McKean County, 1956-64; judge 48th Jud. Dist. Ct., Smethport, 1964-70, Commonwealth Ct. of Pa., Harrisburg, 1970-82, U.S. Dist. Ct., Erie, Pa., 1982—. Served with U.S. Army, 1943-45, ETO Mem. Fed. Judges Assn., Pa. Bar Assn., McKean County Bar Assn. Lodges: Masons (33 degree). Republican. Methodist. Home: 30 W Willow St Smethport PA 16749-1524 Office: US Dist Ct Fed Courthouse PO Box 1820 Erie PA 16507-0820

MENCEY, HELEN VERONICA LOUISE, educator; b. Anahuac, Tex., Oct. 19, 1960; d. Milton M. and Narvis C. (Malone) M. BFA, Sam Houston State U., 1983; tchr. cert., Lamar U., 1985; MEd, Prairie View Coll., 1989; postgrad., Tex. Woman's U., 1990, U. Houston, 1990. Dyslexia spec. Service. ctr., 1995. Tutor in field. Mem. NEA, ACLD, Tex. State Tchrs. Assn., NAFE, Tex. Reading Assn., Internat. Reading Assn., Platform Soc., Pi Lambda Theta. National Education Assn., 1998-. Natural Assoc. Female EXC Assoc. Children Learning Disabilites. Avocations: writing poetry, weight lifting.

MENCH, FRED CHARLES, classics educator; b. Phila., Dec. 22, 1937; s. Fred Charles and Violet M.; m. Martha Duvall, June 2, 1962 (dec. Feb. 1996); childre: Edward Harold, Sarah Elizabeth; m. Mary Jo Swindle, Mar. 13, 1999. BA, Kenyon Coll., 1959; MA, Yale U., 1960, PhD, 1968. Asst. prof. classics U. Tex., Austin, 1964-71; assoc. prof. classics Stockton Coll., Pomona, N.J., 1971-85, prof. classics, 1985—. Bd. dirs. Fictional Rome website. Contbr. articles to profl. jours. Woodrow Wilson fellow, 1959-62, Fulbright fellow, 1962-63. Mem. Am. Philological Assn., Classical Assn. Atlantic States (pres. 1980-81), Classical Humanities Soc. South Jersey (pres. 1972-98, 2000--). Home: 104 Iona Ave Linwood NJ 08221-2116 Office: Richard Stockton Coll NJ Jimmie Leeds Rd Pomona NJ 08240

MENCH, JOHN WILLIAM, retail store executive, electrical engineer; b. N.Y.C., Feb. 27, 1943; s. John William and Edna (Ilgen) M.; m. Rose Irene Miller, Aug. 12, 1962 (dec. Jan. 1997); 1 child, William Ilgen; m. Ann Ward Frentress, Mar. 7, 1998. BSEE, U. S.C., 1969; MBA, Ohio U., 1983; PhD, Calif. Coast U., 1994; cert. in heating, ventilating, and air conditioning, State Tenn. U., 1974. Registered profl. engr., Ohio, Ga. Elec. engr. Uniroyal, Shelbyville, Tenn., 1969-74; facility engr. Kroger, Nashville, 1974-77, asst. mgr. facility engring. Atlanta, 1977-79, Kroger mktg. area mgr. facility engring. Columbus, Ohio, 1979-85; divsn. mgr. facility engring., v.p. Safeway Stores, Inc., Oakland, Calif., 1985-86; v.p. constrn., engring. Big V Supermarkets, Inc., Florida, N.Y., 1986-95; pres. Mench & Assocs. Inc., 1994-98. Assoc. prof. Pa. Coll. Tech., 1996-99; faculty So. Poly. State U., 1999—; prof. Am. Contr. Exch., 1999. Author (tech. manuals) Comments on Commercial Refrigeration, 1998, Comments on Commercial Air Conditioning, 1998, Plan Review, 1995, others. Trustee Meth. Ch., 1987-93; bd. dirs. Goshen Day Care Ctr., 1988-95; past v.p. Tri State V.W. Assn.; exec. adv. bd. Ohio U. Coll. Bus. Adminstrn., 1992-97, life mem.; bd. dirs. Elec. Distbn. Systems, 1993-94. Mem. ASHRAE, IEEE (sr.), Assn. Energy Engrs. (sr.). Republican. Methodist. Avocation: Volkswagens. E-mail: johnmench@aol.com.

MENCHACA, FRANK, editorial director; b. Huntington Station, N.Y., Aug. 5, 1961; s. Antonio and Anna (Lopez) M.; m. Deirdre Sullivan, Sept. 16, 1988; children: Gabriel, Aidan, William. BA, NYU, 1983; MA, Yale U., 1986. Jr. editor John Wiley & Sons, N.Y.C., 1983-85; assoc. editor Chelsea Hare Pubs., 1985-88; lit. editor George Braziller, 1988-90; assoc. editor Weekly Reader Corp., Middletown, Conn., 1990-92; acquisitions editor Millbrook Press, Brookfield, 1992-94; editl. dir. Gale Group, Woodbridge, 1994—. Book reviewer Pubs. Weekly, N.Y.C., 1990-93, participant seminar for acquisition of Latin Am. Libr. materials. Author: (books) Nicolo G and the Days of November, 1991 (VLS award 1991), AL, 1998. Instr. World Prison Poetry Ctr., New Haven, Conn., 1985-88. Mem. MLA, Am. Soc. for 18th Century Studies, Phi Beta Kappa. Democrat. Avocations: writing, publishing. Office: Primary Source Media 12 Lunar Dr Woodbridge CT 06525-2322 Home: 14 Sterling St Fairfield CT 06432-7437

MENCHE, DAVID SOLOMON, orthopaedic surgeon; b. Chgo., Mar. 4, 1954; s. Herman and Ann Menche; m. Paula P. Menche, July 3, 1978; children: Livia, Alexa, Julia. BA, Yeshiva U., 1975; MD, NYU, 1979. Diplomate Am. Bd. Orthop. Surgery. Gen. surg. intern Beth Israel Hosp., 1979-80; orthop. surg. resident Hosp. Joint Diseases Orthop. Inst., N.Y.C., 1980-84, attending orthop. surgeon, 1985—, Meth. Hosp., 1995—; asst. prof. clin. orthop. surgery Med. Ctr. NYU, 1990; assoc. dir. sports medicine Hosp. Joint Diseases Orthop. Inst., N.Y.C., 1988-98, med. dir. phys./occupl. therapy, 1992-98. A-O Internat. Trauma fellow, Switzerland, 1983; Henry W. Frauenthal Sports Medicine travelling fellow, 1984; chief orthop. surgeon U.S. Open Tennis Championships, 1992—, Physician Olympic Festival, USA Basketball, 1995. Reviewer CLin. Orthopaedics & Related Rsch. Mem. Am. Acad. Orthopaedic Surgery, Acad. Orthopedic Soc., Am. Orthopedic Soc. for Sports Medicine, Ea. Orthopedic Assn., Internat. Soc. Arthroscopy Knee Surgery and Orthopedic Sports Medicine, Olympic Sports Medicine Soc., Orthopedic Rehab. Assn. Office: 800A 5th Ave Ste 101 New York NY 10021-7215

MENCHER, BRUCE STEPHAN, judge; b. Washington, May 21, 1935; s. Emanuel and Bertha Miriam (Robbin) M.; m. Janet Patricia Whitfield, Nov. 24, 1974; children by previous marriage: Sean Robbin, Marc Nadzo. BA, George Washington U., 1957, JD with honors, 1960. Bar: D.C. 1960, U.S. Supreme Ct. 1964. Gen. atty. Office Gen. Counsel, Dept. Agr., 1960-61; asst. corp. counsel for D.C., 1961-67; atty.-adviser Office Gen. Counsel, Bur. for Africa, AID, 1967-69; ptnr. Wilkes & Artis, Washington, 1969-75; assoc. judge Superior Ct. D.C., 1975-91; sr. judge, 1991—; presiding judge Family div. Superior Ct. D.C., 1988-90. Professorial lectr. law George Washington U. Nat. Law Ctr., 1982-83; lectr. criminal justice Nat. Cathedral Sch./St. Albans Sch., 1985; faculty advisor Nat. Jud. Coll., 1995. Asst. rsch. editor George Washington Law Rev., 1959-60; contbr. articles to law revs. Mem. gen. alumni gov. bd. George Washington U., 1972-80; bd. dirs. Nat. Child Support Enforcement Assn., 1994-97, The Washington Savoyards Ltd., 1991-96, Trinity Chamber Orch., 2001--. Recipient Alumni Svc. award, 1975, Judge of Yr. award Assn. Plaintiffs Trial Attys., 1983, Samuel Green award for disting. svc. to Washington legal comty. and Phi Delta Phi, 1985, Disting. Alumni Achievement award George Washington U., 1987, also various appreciation and recognition awards local bar assns., D.C. and fed. govts. for work in area of family law and child support enforcement. Mem. ABA, Bar Assn. D.C., D.C. Bar, George Washington Law Assn. (exec. com. 1972-77), The Barristers (exec. com. 1981), George Washington Am. Inn of Ct. (pres. 1999—2000, Phi Delta Phi (pres. Barrister Inn 1974-75) Office: Superior Ct DC 500 Indiana Ave NW Rm 5520 Washington DC 20001-2131 *While it may sound old-fashioned, I attribute my appointment to the bench, in large part, to hard work, dedication, a love of the law and respect for my fellow man. One should maintain his sense of balance, always try to understand the other person's position and, at all costs, maintain a sense of humor throughout.*

MENCHER, MELVIN, journalist, retired educator; b. Bklyn., Jan. 25, 1927; s. Peter and Theresa (Sherman) M.; m. Helen Chamberlain, Aug. 27, 1947; children: Thomas, Marianne, Nicholas. Student, U. N.Mex., 1943-44; BA, U. Colo., 1947; postgrad. (Nieman fellow), Harvard, 1952-53. Reporter UP, 1947-50; state polit. corr. Albuquerque Jour., 1951-54; reporter Fresno (Calif.) Bee, 1954-58; asst. prof. journalism U. Kans., Lawrence, 1958-62; asst. prof. Columbia U., N.Y.C., 1962-65, assoc. prof., 1965-75, prof., 1975-90, assoc. dir. summer program for journalism edn. of minorities, 1971, prof. emeritus, 1990—. Contbg. author: Evaluating the Press, 1973; author: News Reporting and Writing, 1977, Basic Media Writing, 1983; editor: The FNMA Guide to Buying, Financing and Selling Your Home, 1973; contbr. articles to profl. jours. Mem. Soc. Profl. Journalists, Nat. Council Coll. Pubs. Advisers, Kappa Tau Alpha. Home: 450 Riverside Dr New York NY 10027-6801

MENCHER, STUART ALAN, sales and marketing executive; b. N.Y.C., Apr. 25, 1939; s. Meyer H. and Mildred B. (Finger) M.; m. Judith Leslie Schneider; children: Jane Lizabeth, Tracy Ellen. B in Mgmt. Engring., Rensselaer Poly. Inst., 1960; MBA, NYU, 1965. Sales rep. Sperry Rand Univac, Albany, N.Y., 1960-62; various sales and mktg. mgmt. positions IBM Corp., White Plains, 1965-78, br. mgr. data processing div. Harrison, 1978-81; dr. mktg. ops. planning, bus. mktg. dept. AT&T, Basking Ridge, N.J., 1981-83; dir. market planning, sales and mktg. div. AT&T Info. Systems, Morristown, 1983, dir. data systems mktg., 1983-84, v.p. mktg., large bus. systems div., 1985-87; sr. v.p. sales and mktg. MCI Communications Corp., Washington, 1987-90; sr. v.p., gen. mgr. U.S. distbn. div. Motorola/Codex Corp., Mansfield, Mass., 1990-91; sr. v.p., gen. mgr. Teleport Communications, N.Y.C., 1992-93, sr. v.p. nat. sales and mktg., 1994-98; v.p. strategic planning AT&T Bus. Svcs., Bridgewater, N.J., 1998-99; mng. ptnr. The Mencher Group, East Hampton, NJ, 1999—. Bd. dirs. Broadview Networks, N.Y.C. Pres. Westfield Men's Coll. Scholarship Club, NJ, 1977; coach Westfield Young Soccer Assn., 1976—81; mem. budget rev. com. United Fund, Westfield, 1983—85; mem. adv. bd. N.Y.C. Tech. Coll., 1993; mem. Mayor's Telecomms. Mutual Aid and Restoration Com., N.Y.C., 1992—93; v.p., bd. dirs. Ctr. Children and Families/Safespace, 1999—; chmn. mktg. adv. com. YMCA Greater N.Y., 1999—. Lt. USCGR, 1962—65. Avocations: golf, travel, theater, arts. Office: PO Box 5134 East Hampton NY 11937-6165

MENCHIK, PAUL LEONARD, economist, educator; b. N.Y.C., Sept. 16, 1947; s. Irving and Elinor (Swedlow) M.; m. Bettie Ann Landauer, May 28, 1972; children: Daniel Aron, Jeremy Matthew. BA, SUNY, Binghamton, 1969; AM, U. Pa., 1971, PhD, 1976. Lectr. Rutgers Coll., New Brunswick, N.J., 1974-76; rsch. assoc. Inst. for Rsch. on Poverty, U. Wis., Madison, 1976-79; prof. dept. econs. Mich. State U., East Lansing, 1979—, chairperson dept. econs., 1992-96; sr. economist, econ. policy Office Mgmt. & Budget, Washington, 1990-91. Acad. visitor Stanford (Calif.) U., 1980, London Sch. Econs., 1987-88; vis. assoc. prof. U. Pa., Phila., 1982-83; vis. scholar Congrl. Budget Office, 1997-98; cons., advisor in field. Mem. editl. bd. Jour. Income Distbn., Amsterdam, 1992—; contbr. articles to profl. jours. Grantee NSF, Social Security Adminstrn., U.S. Dept. Health and Human Svcs.; recipient Best Article of Yr. award Econ. Inquiry, 1987. Mem. Am. Econ. Assn., Nat. Tax Assn., Nat. Bur. Econ. Rsch. Conf. on Income & Wealth. Avocations: bowling, racquetball, golf, travel, camping. Office: Mich State U 101 Marshall Hall E Circle Dr East Lansing MI 48824

MENDE, HOWARD SHIGEHARU, mechanical engineer; b. Hilo, Hawaii, Nov. 19, 1947; s. Tsutomu and Harue (Kubomitsu) M. BSME, U. Hawaii, 1969; MSME, U. So. Calif., 1975. Registered profl. engr., Calif. Mem. tech. staff I Rockwell Internat., Anaheim, Calif., 1970-71, L.A., 1971-73, mem.

tech. staff II, 1973-77, mem. tech. staff IV, 1984-86; devel. engr. AiRsch. Mfg. Co., Torrance, Calif., 1977-83; mech. engr. Def. Contracts Mgmt. Dist. West, Santa Ana, 1987-94, electronics engr., 1994—. Lectr. Pacific States U., L.A., 1974-75. Mem. ASME. Democrat. Buddhist. Home: 1946 W 180th Pl Torrance CA 90504-4417 Office: Def Contracts Mgmt 2525 W 190th St Torrance CA 90504-6002 E-mail: hmende@dcmdw.dcma.mil.

MENDE, ROBERT GRAHAM, retired engineering association executive; b. Newark, Dec. 4, 1926; s. Herman Ernest and Etta (Hillenbrand) M.; m. Joan B. Tamlyn, Apr. 12, 1958; children: Lisa Anne, Robert Graham Jr. Student, Mass. Inst. Tech., 1944-45; degree, N.Y. State Maritime Acad., 1947; BS, Webb Inst. Naval Architecture, 1951. Project engr. Foster Wheeler Corp., N.Y.C., 1953-56; dist. mgr., naval architect Bird-Johnson Co., 1956-62; sr. naval architect J.J. Henry Co., Inc., 1962-69; exec. dir. Soc. Naval Architects and Marine Engrs., 1969-91. Mem. marine engring. coun. Underwriters Labs., Inc., 1969-91; ad hoc vis. com. Engrs. Coun. for Profl. Devel., 1970-72. Bd. dirs. Friends of World Maritime U., 1987-91; trustee Webb Inst. Naval Architecture, 1987-91. Lt. USNR, 1951-53. Fellow Royal Inst. Naval Architects, Soc. Naval Architect and Marine Engrs. (hon. life v.p., chmn. N.Y. sect. 1968-69, Vice Admiral E.S. Jerry Land medal 1991, Robert G. Mende Bldg. hdqrs. bldg. named in his honor); mem. ASME, Am. Soc. Naval Engrs., Am. Soc. Assn. Execs., Coun. Engring. and Sci. Soc. Execs. (bd. dirs. 1988-91), Maritime Coll. Assn., N.E. Coast Inst. Engrs. and Shipbuilders, Webb Alumni Assn. (pres. 1970-72). *Hard work, perseverance, humility and a dash of deprivation almost always insure success. It also doesn't hurt to be in the right place at the right time.*

MENDEL, JERRY MARC, electrical engineering educator; b. N.Y.C., May 14, 1938; s. Alfred and Eleanor (Deutch) M.; m. Letty Susan Grossman, June 26, 1960; children: Jonathan, Aileen. BMechE cum laude, Poly. U., 1959, MEE, 1960, PhD in Elec. Engring., 1963. Registered profl. engr., Calif. Instr. elec. engring. Poly. Inst. Bklyn., 1960-63; engring. scientist and sect. chief McDonnell-Douglas Astronautics Co., Huntington Beach, Calif., 1963-74; prof. dept. elec. engring. systems U. So. Calif., L.A., 1974—, chmn. dept., 1984-91, dir. Signal and Image Processing Inst., 1991-94, assoc. dir. edn. Integrated Media Sys. Ctr., 1996—. Pres., founder MENTECH, Culver City, Calif., 1983—; pres. United Signals and Systems, Inc., 1989-2001. Author: Discrete Techniques of Parameter Estimation: The Equation Error Formulation, 1973, Optimal Seismic Deconvolution: An Estimation Based Approach, 1983 (Phi Kappa Phi award 1984), Lessons in Digital Estimation Theory, 1987, Maximum-Likelihood Deconvolution, 1990, Lessons in Estimation Theory for Signal Processing, Communications and Control, 1995; editor: Prelude to Neural Networks: Adaptive and Learning Systems, 1994, Uncertain Rule-Based Fuzzy Logic Systems: Introduction and New Directions, 2001; co-editor: Adaptive Learning and Pattern Recognition Systems, 1970. Fellow IEEE (Centennial medal 1984Third Millennium medal 2000); mem. IEEE Control Systems Soc. (Disting. mem.; pres. 1986). Office: U So Calif Dept Elec Engring Sys Eeb 400 Los Angeles CA 90089-2564 E-mail: mendel@sipi.usc.edu.

MENDEL, MAURICE, audiologist, educator; b. Colorado Springs, Colo., Oct. 6, 1942; married; 3 children. BA, U. Colo., 1965; MS, Washington U., 1967; PhD in Audiology, U. Wis., 1970. Asst. prof. audiology U. Iowa Hosp., 1970-74, assoc. rsch. scientist, 1975-76; assoc. prof. U. Calif., Santa Barbara, 1976-84, prof. audiology, 1984-88; chmn. dept. audiology and speech pathology Memphis State U., 1988-92; dean Sch. Audiology and Speech-Lang. Pathology U. Memphis, 1993—. Program dir. speech and hearing sci. U. Calif., Santa Barbara, 1980-82. Fellow Am. Speech-Lang.-Hearing Assn., Soc. Ear Nose and Throat Advance in Children; mem. Am. Acad. Audiology, Internat. Elec. Response Audiology Study Group, Internat. Soc. Audiology, Tenn. Assn. Audiology and Speech-Lang. Pathologists, Sigma Xi. Achievements include research in middle components of the auditory evoked potentials and their subsequent clinical applications to hearing testing. Office: U Memphis CRISCI 807 Jefferson Ave Memphis TN 38105-5042

MENDEL, ROBERTA, editor, publisher, writer; b. Cleve., Apr. 30, 1935; d. Jack and Gertrude Nadine Bailus; m. Leonard Mendel; children: Valerie Anne Mendel Knight, Stuart Craig, Todd Rhys. BA in History-Philosophy magna cum laude, John Carroll U., 1971, MA in Am. History, 1973. Tchr. Beachwood (Ohio) Schs., 1971-75; instr. Cuyahoga C.C., Cleve., 1974; editor, pub. The Pin Prick Press, Shaker Heights, Ohio, 1977—; realtor various cos., 1981-95. Reviewer ABC/CLIO Press, 1973-80. Author: The Human Condition, 2001; contbr. poetry to lit. jours., including Reflections from the Western Res., Mushroom Dreams, Treasured Poems of Am. Anthology, Fishing for a Story. Mem. Authors Guild, Authors League, Acad. Am. Poets, Lit. Network. Avocations: travel, reading, investments. Home and Office: 23511 Chagrin Blvd #519 Beachwood OH 44122-5539

MENDELL, OLIVER M. banking executive; b. N.Y.C., Apr. 4, 1925; s. M. Lester and Malvina Mendell; m. Shelley R. Disick, Sept. 24, 1962; children: Steven, David. Grad., Washington and Lee U., 1950; postgrad., Columbia U. Asst. treas. Bankers Trust Co., N.Y.C., 1950-56; v.p., dir. Queens Nat. Bank, 1956-58; sr. v.p. Chem. Bank (now Chase Manhatten Bank), 1958—; ret. Dir. Cartier, Inc., 1967-69. Pres. Fifth Ave. Assn., 1978-82, chmn., 1982-87; trustee Washington and Lee U. Alumni Assn., vice chmn. alumni fund campaign; bd. dirs. Citizens Budget Commn. N.Y., SSS, 1962-76, JFK Internat. Synagogue, Park 86th Apt. Corp., 1966-71, Joint Distbn. Com.; gov. USOI World Bd. Govs.; chmn. USO of Met. N.Y.; co-treas., bd. dirs. United Jewish Appeal Greater N.Y., Inc.; mem. adv. bd. Regional Emer. Med. Svcs. Coun. N.Y.C.; bd. dirs., 1040 Park Ave. Corp., mem. exec. com. Am. Jewish Com.; trustee Bernard J. Moncharsh Found., Inc., Temple Shaaray Tefila, 1971-74, Fedn. Jewish Philanthropies, B;nai B'rith Banking Lodge; mem. com. legacies and bequests ARC; trustee NYU Real Estate Inst.; vice chmn. steering com., treas. N.Y. Bus. Coun. Clean Air, 1966-71. With USAF, 1943-46. Recipient numerous civic awards; Brandeis U. fellow. Mem. Assn. Better N.Y. (mem. exec. com.), Harmonie Club (N.Y.C.), Rockrimmon Country Club (Stamford, Conn.), Admiral's Cove Club (Jupiter, Fla.), Phi Epsilon Pi (nat. budget com.), Omicron Delta Kappa. Home: 1040 Park Ave New York NY 10028-1032

MENDELOW, GARY N. physician, emergency consultant; b. Buffalo, Sept. 4, 1940; s. Martin and Katherine (Rosenthal) M.; m. Elaine Susan Barron, Mar. 31, 1973; children: Ronald, Raquel. Attended, U. Buffalo, 1958-60; natural science cert., U. Basel, Switzerland, 1962, MD, 1970. Diplomate Am. Bd. Emergency Medicine, 1991. Intern Charity Hosp., New Orleans, 1970-71; resident Erie County Med. Ctr., Buffalo, 1972-74; emergency physician Am. Coll. Emergency Physicians, Dallas, 1974—, VA Med. Ctr., West Palm Beach, Fla. Fellow Am. Coll. Emergency Physicians. Jewish. Avocations: traveling, history, swimming. Home: 22221 Morning Glory Ter Boca Raton FL 33433-4811 Office: VA Med Ctr 7305 N Military Trl West Palm Beach FL 33410-6415 E-mail: GMen56789@aol.com.

MENDELOWITZ, ALLAN IRWIN, federal agency administrator; b. Middletown, Conn., May 1, 1943; s. Madeline Sylvia (Shlien) M.; m. Shereen Lee Lawall, June 18, 1967; children: Eitan G., Rina Y. AB, Columbia U., 1966; MA, Northwestern U., 1969, PhD, 1971. Asst. prof. econs. Rutgers U., New Brunswick, N.J., 1970-75; econ. policy fellow Brookings Inst., Washington, 1975-76; asst. dir. U.S. GAO, 1976-80, assoc. dir., 1980-88, dir., 1988-93, mng.dir., 1993-95; exec. v.p. Export-Import Bank of the U.S., 1996—98; dir. Fed. Housing Finance Bd., 2001—. Contbr. articles to profl. jours. Mem. Am. Econ. Assn. Jewish. Avocations: swimming, skiing. Office: Fed Housing Finance Bd Off of the Chmn 1777 F St NW Washington DC 20006 Office Fax: 202-408-1435.*

MENDELS, JOSEPH, psychiatrist, educator; b. Cape Town, South Africa, Oct. 29, 1937; came to U.S., 1964; s. Max and Lily (Turecki) M.; m. Ora Kark, Jan. 22, 1960; children: Gilla Avril, Charles Alan, David Ralph. MB, BChir, U. Cape Town, 1960; MD, U. Witwatersrand, Johannesburg, South Africa, 1965. Asst. prof., assoc. prof. psychiatry and pharmacology U. Pa., Phila., 1967-73; prof. U. Pa. and VA Hosp., 1973-80; med. dir. Fairmount Inst., 1980-81; hon. prof. psychiatry and human behavior Thomas Jefferson Med. Ctr., 1985—; med. dir. Med. Inst., Phila., 1981-95, Therapeutics PC, Phila., 1981-98. Cons. NIMH, NIH, numerous pharm. cos., 1968—; lectr. to univs. and hosps. worldwide, 1968—. Author, editor: Concepts of Depression, 1971, Biological Psychiatry, 1973, Psychobiology of Affective Disorders, 1981; contbr. over 200 articles to med. jours. Fellow Internat. Coll. Neuropsychopharmacology, Am. Coll. Neuropsychopharmacology. E-mail: jos@DCA.net.

MENDELSOHN, HAROLD, sociologist, educator; b. Jersey City, Oct. 30, 1923; s. Louis and Bessie (Yulinsky) M.; m. Irene Sylvia Gordon, Apr. 10, 1949; 1 dau., Susan Lynn. BS, CCNY, 1945; MA, Columbia U., 1946; PhD, New Sch. Social Research, 1956. Sr. survey analyst U.S. Dept. State, Washington, 1951-52; research assoc. Bur. Social Sci. Research, Am. U., 1952-56; assoc. mgr. mktg. communications McCann-Erickson Advt., N.Y.C., 1956-58; assoc. dir. Psychol. Corp., 1958-62; prof. dept. mass communications U. Denver, 1962-89, prof. emeritus, 1989—, chmn., 1970-78, dean faculty social scis., 1984-86, spl. asst. to chancellor, 1986-88. Morton vis. disting. prof. Ohio U., spring 1981; cons. FTC, Denver Rsch. Inst., U.S. Consumer Product Safety Commn., The Gallup Orgn., Ford Found., Fedn. Rocky Mountain States, CBS, ABC, Children's TV Workshop; vis. prof. London Sch. Econs., 1973, Hebrew U., 1973. (Emmy award Nat. Acad. TV Arts Scis. 1968, Gold Camera award U.S. Indsl. Film Festival 1972); Author: Mass Entertainment, 1966, (with David H. Bayley) Minorities and the Police: Confrontation in America, 1969, (with Irving Crespi) Polls, Television and the New Politics, 1970, (with others) Television and Growing Up: The Impact of Televised Violence, 1972, (with Garrett O'Keefe) The People Choose a President, 1976; editor: Mass Communications series, 1967-69; contbr. articles to profl. jours. Mem. Denver Coun. Pub. TV, 1970-78; mem. U.S. Surgeon Gen.'s Sci. Adv. Com. on TV and Social Behavior, 1969-71; bd. dirs. Nat. Safety Coun., 1963-69; mem. pub. affairs adv. bd. Air Force Acad. Found., 1972-76; mem. cancer control and rehab. adv. com. Nat. Cancer Inst., 1976-81; mem. adv. coun., prevention div. Nat. Inst. Alcoholism and Alcohol Abuse, 1977-82; trustee Colo. Med. Svc., Inc., 1973-78. Recipient award TV Bur. Advt., 1962, Met. Life award Nat. Safety Council, 1967; Gold Eagle award, 1973; Silver award Internat. Festival Film and TV, 1974 Fellow Am. Psychol. Assn., Am. Sociol. Assn.; mem. Am. Assn. Pub. Opinion Research (pres. 1973-74), AAAS, N.Y. Acad. Scis., Sigma Delta Chi, Omicron Delta Kappa. Clubs: Chicago Press. Home: 1451 E Cornell Pl Englewood CO 80110-3013 Office: U Denver Dept Mass Comm Denver CO 80208-0001

MENDELSOHN, JOHN, oncologist, hematologist, educator; b. Cin., Aug. 31, 1936; s. Joe and Sarah (Feibel) M.; m. Anne Charles, June 23, 1962; children: John Andrew, Jeffrey Charles, Eric Robert. BA, Harvard U., 1958, MD, 1963. Diplomate Am. Bd. Internal Medicine, Am. Bd. Hematology, Am. Bd. Med. Oncology. Intern, resident Peter Bent Brigham Hosp., Boston, 1963-65, 67-68; fellow in hematology Washington U. Sch. Medicine, St. Louis, 1968-70; asst. prof. to prof. medicine U. Calif., San Diego, 1970-85, Am. Cancer Soc. prof. clin. oncology La Jolla, 1982-85, dir. Cancer Ctr., 1977-85; prof. medicine Cornell U. Med. Coll., N.Y.C., 1985-96; chmn. dept. medicine Meml. Sloan Kettering Cancer Ctr., 1985-96; pres., prof. medicine U. Tex. M.D. Anderson Cancer Ctr., Houston, 1996—. Bd. sci. counselors Nat. Cancer Inst., 1986-90, 96-2001; bd. dirs. ImClone; cons. Bristol-Myers, Thyreos, Progenics Pharms., Selective Genetics; founder, 1st dir. U. Calif. San Diego Cancer Ctr.; mem. Nat. Dialogue on Cancer, 1999; mem. TEam on Cancer Rsch., 2001; mem. U. Calif. San Diego External Adv. Com., 2000. Editor-in-chief: (textbook) The Molecular Basis of Cancer; mem. editl. bd. Growth Factors, Jour. Biol. Response Modifiers, Expert Rev. Anticancer Therapy; editor-in-chief Clin. Cancer Rsch.; contbr. articles to profl. jours. Mem. Gov.'s Cancer Adv. Coun., Calif., 1979-85; bd. dirs. Am. Cancer Soc., San Diego, 1981-85; active Greater Houston Partnership, 1997-2001, Houston Tech. Ctr., 1998—, nat. cancer policy bd., 1999—. Officer USPHS, 1965-67. Fulbright scholar U. Glasgow, Scotland, 1958-59; recipient Bourgine award for Excellence in Cancer Rsch. Service d'Oncologie Medicale Pitie-Saltpetriere, 1997, Breast Cancer Rsch. Found. Jill Rose award for outstanding breast cancer rsch., 1999, Medal City of Paris, 1997, Cancer Rsch. award Bristol-Myers Squibb, 1997; named Headliner of Yr. in Medicine, San Diego, 1985. Mem.: AAAS (electorate nominating com. sect. on med. scis. 2001), Harvard Overseers' Com., Royal Netherlands Acad. Arts and Scis., Inst. Medicine U.S. NAS, Century Assn. (Harvard Overseers com.), Am. Soc. Hematology, Am. Assn. Cancer Rsch. (4th Joseph H. Burchenal award 1999), Am. Soc. Clin. Oncology (lectr., David A. Karnofsky award 2002), Am. Soc. Clin. Investigation, Assn. Am. Physicians, Alpha Omega Alpha, Phi Beta Kappa. Achievements include rsch. in establishing inhibition of tumor growth by antibodies against growth factor receptors. Avocations: tennis, music, history, hiking. Office: U Tex MD Anderson Cancer Ctr 1515 Holcombe Blvd # 91 Houston TX 77030-4009 E-mail: jmendelsohn@manderson.org.

MENDELSOHN, LINDA JOY, physician; b. Wellsville, N.Y., Apr. 24, 1951; d. Ralph Duncan and Eleanor Josephine (Marsh) Taggart; m. Marc Raphael Mendelsohn, July 30, 1977. BS, Houghton (N.Y.) Coll., 1972; MD, Albany Med. Coll., 1976. Diplomate Am. Bd. Family Practice; cert. family practice Am. assn. Physician Splsts. Intern USPHS Hosp., Boston, 1976-77; assoc. attending physician Fillmore (Utah) Hosp., 1977-78; attending physician Douglas County Meml. Hosp., Armor, S.D., 1978-81, Cutskill Regional. Med. Ctr., Harris, 1982—; chmn. dept. family practice Cmty. Gen. Hosp. of Sullivan County, N.Y., 1992—. Resident in geriatrics Mt. Sinai Hosp., N.Y.C., 1991; mem. Cmty. Svcs. Bd., Sullivan County, 1983-94, mem. Health Adv. Coun., 1983-90, mem. Pub. Health Nursing Coun., 1986-89. Served with USPHS, 1977-81. Recipient Disting. Med. Svc. award USPHS, 1979, AMA Physicians Recogninition award, 1996,99,2002. Fellow Am. Acad. Family Practice; mem. AMA, Sullivan County Med. Soc., Alpha Omega Alpha. Reformed Presbyterian. Avocations: baking, skiing, embroidery, church choir, teaching Sunday school. Home: 91 Perry Rd Cochecton NY 12726-5800 Office: Bethel Med Rte 17B White Lake NY 12786

MENDELSOHN, LOUIS BENJAMIN, financial analyst; b. Providence, Mar. 26, 1948; s. Alvin Harold and Frances (Leitner) M.; m. Illyce Deborah Greenspan, Aug. 29, 1976; children: Lane Jeffrey, Ean Graham, Forrest Lee. BS, Carnegie Mellon U., 1969; MSW, SUNY, Buffalo, 1973; MBA with hons., Boston U., 1977. Rsch. asst. Mass. Gen. Hosp., Boston, 1969-71; regional health planner Comprehensive Health Planning Coun., Buffalo, 1973-74; adminstv. resident New Eng. Hosp., Boston, 1976; mgmt. specialist Humana Hosp. Bennett, Ft. Lauderdale, Fla., 1977-78; asst. exec. dir. Humana Women's Hosp., Tampa, 1978-80; pres., CEO Market Technologies Corp., Wesley Chapel, 1979—. Author: Trend Forecasting with Techinal Analysis: Unleashing the Hidden Power of Intermarket Analysis to Beat the Market, 2000; contbg. rschr.: The Encyclopedia of Technical Market Indicators, 1988; contbg. author: High Performance Futures Trading, 1990, Virtual Trading, 1995, Artificial Intelligence in the Capital Markets, 1995, Trade Your Way to Financial Freedom, 1999, Trading Chicago Style, 1999; contbg. writer Tech. Analysis of Stocks and Commodities Mag.; editor newsletter Neural-Financial News, 1991; developer investment software ProfitTaker, 1979—, Vantage-Point, 1988—. USPHS fellow, 1975-77. Mem. Market Technicians Assn., Colleague Internat. Fedn. of Tech. Analysts, Beta Gamma Sigma. Achievements include pioneering strategy back-testing and optimization in technical analysis software for microcomputers, 1983; introduction of first commercial strategy testing trading software in financial industry for microcomputers and first intermarket analysis software in fin. industry for microcomputers. Avocations: raising horses, antique collecting. Office: Mkt Techs Corp 25941 Apple Blossom Ln Wesley Chapel FL 33544-5108

MENDELSOHN, MARTIN, lawyer; b. Bkyln., Sept. 6, 1942; s. Syman and Gertrude M.; m. Syma Barbara Rossman, Aug. 15, 1964; children: Alice S., James D. BA, Bklyn. Coll., 1963; LLB, George Washington U., 1966. Bar D.C. 1967, U.S. Ct. Appeals (D.C. cir.) 1967, U.S. Supreme Ct. 1970, U.S. Ct. Appeals (3d cir.) 1971, U.S. Ct. Appeals (7th cir.) 1973, Ill. 1973, U.S. Ct. Appeals (9th cir.) 1987, U.S. Tax Ct. 1988, U.S. Ct. Appeals (2d cir.) 1988, U.S. Ct. of Appeals (5th cir.) 2000. With Gen. Counsel's Office, HEW, Washington, 1966—67; legal svcs., 1967—70, Pa., 1971—72, Ill., 1973—75; counsel Legal Svcs. Corp., Washington, 1976; adminstrv. asst. U.S. Congress, 1977; chief spl. litigation U.S. Dept. Justice, 1977—79, dep. dir. office spl. investigations, 1979—80; counsel House Judiciary Com., 1980; pvt. practice Washington, 1980—88; ptnr. Dilworth, Paxon, Kalish & Kauffman, 1989—91, Verner, Liipfeert, Bernhard, McPherson & Hand, 1991—2002, Schnader, Harrison, Segal and Lewis, Washington, 2002—. Author: (with Aaron Freiwald) The Last Nazi, 1994. Named officer, Order of Merit; recipient High Honor, Austria. Mem.: ABA, D.C. Bar Assn. Jewish. Home: 5705 Mckinley St Bethesda MD 20817-3638 Office: 901 15th St NW Ste 700 Washington DC 20005-2327

MENDELSOHN, NAOMI, biomedical pharmaceutical consultant; b. N.Y. BA, NYU; MA, Boston U.; PhD, CUNY, 1975. Fellow Meml. Sloan-Kettering Cancer Ctr., N.Y.C., 1975-78; asst. prof. Mt. Sinai Med. Ctr., 1978-82; assoc. sci. dir. Sterling Drug, Inc. Internat., 1982-91; dir. product devel. Innapharma, Inc., 1992-96; med. dir. Genecom, N.Y.C., 1998—. Adjunct asst. prof. Mt. Sinai Med. Ctr., 1982—. NSF fellow, 1969, NIH fellow 1975-78. Mem. AAAS, Am. Chem. Soc., Am. Med. Writer's Assn., Am. Soc. Hematology, Fedn. Am. Socs. Exptl. Biology (ednl. affairs com. 1989—), Am. Heart Assn., N.Y. Acad. Scis. (women sci. com., planning com. 1983-85), Drug Info. Assn., Fgn. Policy Assn., Licensing Exec. Soc. Avocation: piano. Office: 322 W 57th St New York NY 10019-3701

MENDELSOHN, ROBERT, clinical psychologist, psychoanalyst; b. Bklyn., Feb. 9, 1943; s. Ben and Ruth (Rubenstein) M.; m. Robin Wendy Yarmark, Oct. 10, 1981; children: Elise Ellen, Chelsey Jane, Tyler Kate. BA, Hofstra U., 1964; MS in Psychology, U. Mass., 1968, PhD in Clin. Psychology, 1969; cert. psychoanalysis, Adelphi U., 1975, cert. group psychotherapy, 1983. Diplomate Am. Bd. Profl. Psychology. Intern clin. psychology VA Hosp., Northampton, Mass., 1967; staff psychologist Northampton State Hosp., 1968; asst. prof. Hobart and William Smith Colls., Geneva, 1969; supervising clin. psychologist Nassau County Med. Ctr., East Meadow, 1970-74; prof. Inst. Advanced Psychol. Studies Adelphi U., Garden City, 1974—, dean, 1992-2000; pvt. practice psychotherapy and psychoanalysis Port Washington, 1970—. Cons. clin. psychologist Baldwin (N.Y.) Cmty. House; del. Nat. Coun. Schs. and Programs in Profl. Psychology, Coun. Univ. Dirs. Clin. Psychology. Contbr. chpts. to publs. and articles to profl. jours. Mem. APA (chair edn. and tng. divsn. psychoanalysis), Adelphi Soc. Psychoanalysis and Psychotherapy (pres. 1975-76), Ea. Psychol. Assn., Nassau County Psychol. Assn., N.Y. Soc. Clin. Psychologists, N.Y. State Psychol. Assn., Am. Group Psychotherapy Assn., Ea. Group Psychotherapy Soc. Jewish. Office: Adelphi Univ Inst Advanced Psychol Garden City NY 11530 E-mail: mendelso@adelphi.edu.

MENDELSOHN, ROBERT VICTOR, insurance company executive; b. July 18, 1946; s. Harold Victor and Mary Ellen (Muldoon) M. AB, Georgetown U., 1968; JD, Havard U., 1971. Bar: N.Y. 1971. Atty. Wilkie Farr & Gallagher, N.Y.C., 1971-74; pres., dir. W.R. Berkley Corp., Greenwich, Conn., 1974-93; group chief exec. Royal & Sun Alliance Group PLC, London, 1997—. Trustee Jose Limon Dance Found., 1979-95, trustee emeritus, 1997—; bd. regents Georgetown U. Mem. Internat. Ins. Soc, UK-China Forum, Liberalization of Trade in Svcs. Group, Fin. Leaders Group. Office: PO Box 1000 9300 Arrow Point Blvd Charlotte NC 28273-8136 also: Royal & Sun Alliance 30 Berkeley Square London W1J 6EW England

MENDELSOHN, STUART, lawyer, elected official; b. Jersey City, Aug. 8, 1952; s. Norman and Florence M.; m. Laura Dick, May 30, 1987; children: Michelle, Sarah. BS in Ocean Engring., Fla. Inst. Tech., 1974, MS in Environ. Engring., 1975; JD, George Mason U., 1984. Bar: Va. 1986, D.C. 1988. Project mgr. Naval Facilities Engring. Command, Washington, 1975-80; divsn. mgr. Analysis & Tech., Inc., Arlington, Va., 1980-87; mng. prin. Mendelsohn & Ishee, P.C., Fairfax, 1987-99; supr. Fairfax County Bd. Suprs., Mclean, 1996—; of counsel Piper Marbury Rudnick & Wolfe, Reston, 1999—. Bd. suprs. Fairfax County, 1996—; No. Va. Planning Dist. commn., 1996—; coord. coun. Transportation, 1997—; task force Fairfax county Tree Preservation, 1997—; active Boy Scouts Am., Patowomack Dist., 1996, 97; vice chair, sch. bd. mem. Fairfax County, 1993-95; sunday sch. tchr. Andrew Chapel United Meth. Ch., 1994—, adminstrv. bd. 1997-2000, staff-parish resl. com. 1995-97; cmty. roundtable on edn. WJLA-TV, 1992-93. Recipient Gold Medal award Spl. Olympics, Va., 1985, Spirit of Spl. Olympics award, 1987, Mem. Fairfax County C. of C. (bd. dirs. 1991—, exec. com. 1992-95, dir. 1994-95, com. co-chair 1991-93, edn. com. 1987—, legis. affairs com. 1988—, edn. subcom. 1991—, congressional affairs com. 1998—), Herndon C. of C., McLean C. of C., Elem. Sch. PTA (gov. Louise Archer Elem. Sch. 1991-92), Fairfax Bar Assn., Kiwanis (lt. gov. 1983-84, gov. 1991-92, charter pres. Fair Oaks club 1988, pres. McLean Club 1980-81). Republican. Methodist. Avocation: tennis. Office: Piper Marbury Rudnick & Wolfe, LLP 1775 Wiehle Ave S 400 Reston VA 20190 E-mail: stuart.mendelsohn@piperrudnick.com.

MENDELSOHN, WILLIAM ROLLER, lawyer; b. Boston, May 10, 1968; s. George E. and Stephany R. Mendelsohn; m. Lorie Debra Kram, Nov. 25, 1995; children: Nicholas Kram Mendelsohn, Augustus Kram Mendelsohn. AB magna cum laude, Harvard Coll., 1990; M in Theol. Studies, Harvard U., 1992; JD, Boston Coll., 1996. Bar: Mass. 1996. Law clk. Mass. Land Ct., Boston, 1997-98; assoc. Cohen & Fierman, LLP, 1998-99; ptnr. Kram & Mendelsohn, LLP, Littleton, Mass., 2000—. Mem. Mass. Bar Assn. Office: Kram & Mendelsohn LLP Ste 1A 256 Great Rd Littleton MA 01460 E-mail: wrm@kmlawgroup.com.

MENDELSOHN, ZEHAVAH WHITNEY, data processing executive; b. Houston, Nov. 22, 1956; d. Alfred Peter and Sarah (Carsey) Whitney. AA, College of DuPage, 1988; BA, Nat. Louis U., 1989. Cert. quality analyst, cert. software test engr. Mgmt. analyst U. Ill., Abraham Lincoln Sch. Medicine, Chgo., 1976-83; sr. analyst quality assurance Ofcl. Airline Guides, Oak Brook, Ill., 1983-95; dir. application quality mgmt. U.S. Cellular, 1995—. Mem. Quality Assurance Inst., Am. Soc. for Quality Control, Chgo. Quality Assurance Assn., Chicagoland Handicapped Skiers (pres. 1986-87, 89-91), Profl. Ski Instrs. Am. Avocations: skiing, roses, golf, birdwatching. Office: US Cellular 1101 Tower Ln Bensenville IL 60106

MENDELSON, ALAN CHARLES, lawyer; b. San Francisco, Mar. 27, 1948; s. Samuel Mendelson and Rita Rosalie (Spindel) Brown; children: Jonathan Daniel, David Gary; m. Agnès Marie Barbariol. BA with great distinction, U. Calif., Berkeley, 1969; JD cum laude, Harvard U., 1973. Bar: Calif. 1973. Assoc. Cooley Godward LLP, San Francisco, 1973-80, ptnr. Palo Alto, 1980-2000, mng. ptnr. Palo Alto office, 1990-95, 96-97; sec. acting gen. counsel Amgen Inc., Thousand Oaks, Calif., 1990-91; acting gen. counsel Cadence Design Sys., Inc., San Jose, 1995-96; sr. ptnr. Latham & Watkins, Menlo Park, 2000—. Bd. dirs. Valentis Inc., QLT Inc., USSearch.com, Inc., Connectix Corp.; co-chair venture & tech. group Latham & Watkins. Chmn. Piedmont (Calif.) Civil Svc. Commn., 1978-80; den leader Boy Scouts Am., Menlo Park, Calif.; fundraiser Crystal Springs Upland Sch., Hillsborough, Calif., Harvard Law Sch. Fund, U. Calif. Berkeley Health Svcs. Initiative, Lucille Packard Children's Hosp.; coach Menlo Park Little League, 1982-86; pres., mem. exec. com., bd. dirs. No. Calif. chpt. Nat. Kidney Found., 1986-98. With USAR, 1969-75. Recipient Disting. Svc. award Nat. Kidney Found., 1992; named U. Calif. Berkeley Alumni scholar, 1966, Scaife Found. scholar, 1966, One of 100 Most Influential Attys. in U.S. Nat. Law Jour., 1994, 97, 2000 (Best Lawyers in Am., 1993-2000). Mem. Bohemian Club, Phi Beta Kappa. Jewish. Home: 76 De Bell Dr Atherton CA 94027-2253 Office: Latham & Watkins 135 Commonwealth Dr Menlo Park CA 94025 E-mail: alan.mendelson@lw.com.

MENDELSON, DAVID FREY, retired neurology educator; b. St. Louis, Feb. 25, 1925; s. Harry and Lorine Esther (Korngold) M.; m. Mary Ann Lavis, June 21, 1956 (div. Mar. 1978); children: Lorine Ann, David Frey, Helen Elizabeth, Jonathan Joseph. BA, U. Calif., Berkeley, 1946; MD, Ind. U., Indpls., 1948. Diplomate Am. Bd. Psychiatry and Neurology. Intern Ind. U., Indpls., 1948-49; resident Barnes Hosp., St. Louis, 1950-51; fellow neurology U. Minn., Mpls., 1953-58, instr. neurology, 1956-58; practice medicine specializing in neurology St. Louis, 1958-70; ret., 1970; clin. asst. prof. St. Louis U., 1958-83; clin. asst. prof. emeritus Washington U., St. Louis, 1983—. Bd. dirs. Mo. Blue Shield, St. Louis, 1964-72, trustee, 1972-85, corp. bd. 1985-90. Served to capt. USAF, 1951-53. Fellow Am. Acad. Neurology; mem. St. Louis Met. Med. Soc., St. Louis Soc. Neurol. Scis., Rocky Mountain Traumatologic Soc. Clubs: St. Louis Racquet. Jewish. Home: 7906 Kingsbury Blvd Saint Louis MO 63105-3824

MENDELSON, ELLIOTT, mathematician, educator; b. N.Y.C., May 24, 1931; s. Joseph and Helen (Bienstock) M.; m. Arlene Zimmerman, Jan. 25, 1959; children— Julia, Hilary, Peter. AB, Columbia U., 1952; MA, Cornell U.,

1954, PhD, 1955. Instr. U. Chgo., 1955-56; jr. fellow Soc. Fellows, Harvard U., 1956-58; Ritt instr. Columbia U., 1958-61; mem. faculty Queens Coll., CUNY, 1961—, prof. math., 1965—. Dir., instr. NSF math. program for high sch. students, 1964-71; researcher axiomatic set theory and math. logic, especially ind. various important propositions of axiomatic set theory, axiom of choice, axiom of restriction; participant NSF Time 2000 Project for future secondary sch. math. tchrs., 1998—. Author: Introduction to Mathematical Logic, 1997, Boolean Algebra and Switching Circuits, 1970, Number Systems, 1973, Beginning Calculus, 1997, 3000 Solved Problems in Calculus, 1988, Differential and Integral Calculus, 1997, Quick Calculus, 1999; contbr. articles to profl. jours. Mem. Am. Math. Soc., Math. Assn. Am., Assn. for Symbolic Logic, Phi Beta Kappa. Home: 10 Pinewood Rd Roslyn NY 11576-2420 Office: Queens Coll Dept Math Flushing NY 11367

MENDELSON, HAIM, artist, educator, art gallery director; b. Siemiatycze, Bielsk, Poland, Oct. 15, 1923; s. David Cemach and Frieda (Konopiati) M.; m. Lita Joan Gordon, Mar. 30, 1955 (div. June 1966); children: Paul, Jan. Student, Am. Artists Sch., 1938-41, Saul Baizerman Sch. Art, 1940-43, Ednl. Alliance Art Sch., 1946. Tchr. Ednl. Alliance, N.Y.C., 1956-61; instr. CCNY, 1961-64; tchr. Columbia Grammar Sch., 1963-64, City and Country Sch., N.Y.C., 1964-91. Dir. Hudson Guild Art Gallery, N.Y.C., 1971-94. One-man shows include Creative Galleries, N.Y.C., 1954, Caravan Gallery, N.Y.C., 1957, Chase Gallery, N.Y.C., 1960, Hudson Guild Art Gallery, N.Y.C., 1961, 76, 79, 82, 94, Yellow Poui Art Gallery, Grenada, W.I., 1973, 76, 79, 82, Ednl. Alliance, N.Y.C., 1976, Berkshire Artisans Gallery, Pittsfield, Mass., 1987, Hudson Guild, 1994; group shows include Mus. Modern Art, N.Y.C., 1940-41, Pa. Acad. Fine Arts, 1965, Butler Inst. Am. Art, Ohio, 1965, 67, St. Paul Art Ctr., 1961, 66, NAD, N.Y.C., 1965, 68, 75, 77, 90, Bronx Mus. Arts, 1976, Prints U.S.A., 1982, Gallery Assn. N.Y. State, 1975-78, Internat. Art Biennale, Malta, 1995, Glass Gallery, N.Y.C., 1995, 96, Susan Teller Gallery, 1999, 2000, 2002; represented in permanent collections N.Y. Pub. Libr., Minn. Mus. Art, Edward Ulrich Mus., Wichita, Kans., St. Vincent Coll., Latrobe, Pa., Griffiths Art Ctr., Canton, N.Y., Manhattan Coll., Riverdale, N.Y., Flint (Mich.) Inst. Fine Arts, The Joe and Emily Lowe Found.; portfolio drypoint engravings Grass, 1963, The Artist and His Dead, 1975. Recipient numerous awards including Spl. Distinction award Graphics Internat. Art Biennial Malta, 1995, N.Y. Ctrl. graphics award Audubon Artists, 1996; Florsheim Art Fund grantee, 1999. Mem. Fedn. Modern Painters and Sculptors, Audubon Artists, Print Consortium, Am. Soc. Contemporary Artists. Home: 234 W 21st St # 63 New York NY 10011-3451 *Art is the avenue in which I express the significant experiences of my life. Out of feelings of expressive need, new forms and techniques spontaneously arise. The forms of the future are in life itself.*

MENDELSON, LAURANS ADAM, accountant; b. N.Y.C., July 7, 1938; s. Samuel and Blanche (Lederer) M.; m. Arlene Hope Lobel, Sept. 18, 1962; children: Eric Arthur, Victor Howard. BA, Columbia Coll., 1960; MBA, Columbia U., 1961. CPA, N.Y., Fla. Chmn., pres., CEO HEICO Corp., Hollywood, Fla. Bd. dirs., chmn. audit com. Hawker Pacific Aerospace; co-chmn., prin. dir. HEICO Corp.; panelist ethics in Am. seminar Columbia U. Bd. dirs. Greater Miami Opera Assn., Miami; mem. bd. vis. Columbia Col., N.Y.C.; bd. govs. Philharm. Orch. Fla., Standard Club; alumni adv. bd. to bd. trustees Columbia U.; mem. citizens bd. U. Miami. Recipient Ernst & Young Entrepreneur of Yr. award, 1999. Mem. AICPA, Fla. Inst. CPAs, Greater Miami C. of C. (trustee), Aerospace Industries Assn. (bd. govs.). Jewish. Office: HEICO Corp 3000 Taft St Hollywood FL 33021-4441

MENDELSON, LEE M. film company executive, writer, producer, director; b. San Francisco, Mar. 24, 1933; s. Palmer C. and Jeanette D. (Wise) M.; children: Glenn, Linda, Jason, Sean. BA, Stanford U., 1954. With Sta. KPIX-TV, 1961-63; chmn. bd., pres. Lee Mendelson Film Prodns. Inc., Los Angeles and Burlingame, Calif., 1963—. Guest instr. in communications Stanford U. Exec. producer, co-writer (miniseries) This Is America, Charlie Brown; producer: Charlie Brown, Cathy, Betty Boop, (TV spls.) John Steinbeck's Travels with Charley, American and Americans, The Fantastic Funnies, You Asked for It, Here Comes Garfield, (animated films) A Boy Named Charlie Brown, Snoopy Come Home, Race for Your Life Charlie Brown, Peanuts, Bon Voyage Charlie Brown (And Don't Come Back), Garfield and Friends, Mother Goose and Grim. Served to 1st lt. USAF, 1954-57. Recipient 7 Emmy awards, 3 Peabody awards. Mem. Writers Guild Am., Dirs. Guild Am. Office: Lee Mendelson Film Prodn Inc 330 Primrose Rd Ste 310 Burlingame CA 94010-4028

MENDELSON, RICHARD DONALD, former communications company executive; b. N.Y.C., Dec. 2, 1933; s. George and Martha (Goodman) M.; m. Marilyn Miller, July 28, 1956; children: Sandra, Kenneth. BS, Wharton Sch. U. Pa., 1955; JD, NYU, 1959. Bar: N.Y., 1960; CPA, N.Y. Asst. atty. gen. N.Y. State Dept. Law, N.Y.C., 1959-70; v.p., treas. Petry TV, 1971-75; v.p., dir. corp. devel. Katz Communications, Inc., 1975-77, sr. v.p. ops., 1977-79, sr. v.p., chief fin. officer, 1979-81, exec. v.p., chief operating officer, 1981-82, pres., chief oper. officer, 1982-89; free-lance writer, 1989—. Mem. Employee Stock Ownership Assn. Am. (pres. 1987-88, bd. dirs.). Home and Office: 71 Saint George Pl Palm Beach Gardens FL 33418-4024

MENDELSON, ROBERT ALLEN, polymer scientist, rheologist; b. Cleve., 1930; s. Julius and Theodora Anne (Bloch) M.; m. Lura Lauzon, 1971 (dec. 1999); children: John A. Blackstone, Marie L. Taylor. BS in Indsl. Chemistry, Case Inst. Tech., 1952, PhD in Phys. Chemistry, 1956. From sr. rsch. chemist to sci. fellow rsch. dept. Monsanto Co., Texas City, Tex., 1956-71, sci. fellow Springfield, Mass., 1972-89, sr. sci. fellow, 1989-91; rheology focus area leader Baytown (Tex.) Polymers Ctr. Exxon Chem., 1991-94, rheology prin. investigator, 1995-99; ret., 1999. Mem. com. for pub. policy Am. Inst. Physics, 1985-89; collaborator Univ. Rsch. Programs, Cornell U., 1989-91. Mem. editorial bd. Journal of Rheology, 1986-99; contbr. articles to profl. jours.; patentee in field. Mem. Soc. Rheology (pres. 1989-91, v.p. 1987-89, sec. 1974-78), Am. Chem. Soc. (Arthur Doolittle award div. organic coatings and plastics 1982), Soc. Plastics Engrs., AAAS. Home: 16503 Scenic Peaks Ct Houston TX 77059-5554 E-mail: robertamendelson@aol.com.

MENDELSON, SOL, physical science educator, consultant; b. Checonovska, Poland, Oct. 10, 1926; came to U.S., 1927; s. David C. and Frieda (Cohen) M. BME, CCNY, 1955; MS, Columbia U., 1957, PhD, 1961. Prof. engrng. CCNY, 1955-58; sr. scientist Sprague Electric Co., North Adams, Mass., 1962-64, Airborne Instruments Lab., Melville, N.Y., 1964-65; phys. metallurgist Bendix Rsch. Lab., Southfield, Mich., 1966-67; cons., rschr., writer, N.Y.C. and Troy, 1968-72; adj. prof. phys. sci. CUNY, 1972-87. Contbr. numerous articles to sci. jours. Mem. Am. Phys. Soc., Fedn. Am. Scientists, Sigma Xi, Tau Beta Pi, Pi Tau Sigma. Achievements include research on theory and mechanisms of Martensitic transformations. *We have to keep reminding ourselves that data proclaims theory, but theory does not proclaim anything if it does not address crucial data. Exaggerating ambiguous data or unrealistic models has brought prominence to theories by some scientists, but those who succeed in solving a problem are able to develop a theory which accounts for crucial experimental data.*

MENDENHALL, HARLAN VINCENT, research veterinary surgeon; b. Gulfport, Miss., Oct. 21, 1944; s. Harlan Harry Mendenhall and Catherine Rose (Cunningham) Cowell; m. Toni (Meglitsch) Winch, July 29, 1979 (div. May 1988); m. Diann Marie Frederick, Aug. 15, 1992; children: Tai Justin, Tiffany. DVM, Colo. State U., 1968, PhD, 1981. Staff surgeon Rangitaiki Plains Dairy Co., Edgecume, New Zealand, 1968-71; grad. student exptl. surgery Colo. State U., Fort Collins, 1971-75; surg. rsch. specialist 3M, St. Paul, 1975-91; owner/operator Veterinary Surg. Specialists, Stillwater, 1977-93; sr. rsch. surgeon Primedica Corp., Worcester, Mass., 1993—. Cons. biomed. surg. rsch., Stillwater, 1992-93; lectr. surg. anatomy Colo. State U., 1973; animal care cons. St. Paul Ramsey Hosp., 1980-85; working group mem. Health Industry Mfrs. Assn./Orthopedic Surg. Mfrs. Assn. FDA panel, 1987. Author: Anterior Cruciate, 1987; author, editor: Handbook Biomaterials, 1986, 2d edit., 1998; contbr. articles to Jour. Am. Vet. Med. Assn., Clin. Orthopedic Related Rsch. Mem. Soc. for Biomaterials (PhD students award 1982), Acad. Surg. Rsch. (mem. bd. 1996-97). Achievements in orthopedics include development of the concept of isometricity in ACL replacement surgery; achievements in ophthalmics include development of the importance of posteriorly convex lenses and haptics; achievements in microsurgery include development of the microvascular anastomotic system for small vessel anastomosis; leading research in chronic laboratory animal access. Home: 26 Grover Rd Ashland MA 01721-2510 Office: Primedica Corp 57 Union St Worcester MA 01608-1182 E-mail: vince.mendenhall@primedica.com.

MENDENHALL, JOHN RYAN, retired lawyer, transportation executive; b. Des Moines, Jan. 17, 1928; s. Merritt Blake and Elizabeth M. (Ryan) M.; m. Joan Lois Schafer, June 20, 1953; children: Thomas, James, Jane, Julie, Robert, Jennifer. BS, U. Notre Dame, 1950; JD, Harvard U., 1953. Bar: Iowa 1953, U.S. Tax Ct. 1954, D.C. 1975, U.S. Ct. Claims 1975. Mem. tax staff Arthur Andersen & Co., Cleve., 1953-63, ptnr., 1963-66, dir. taxes Chgo., 1966-70, ptnr. Washington, 1970-74, Williams, Connolly & Califano, Washington, 1974-76; gen. tax counsel Union Pacific Corp., N.Y.C., 1977-80, v.p. taxes, 1980-93. Bd. dirs. Empire Steel Castings, Reading, Pa. Co-author: Reforming the Tax Structure, 1973; contbr. articles on taxes to various jours. Bd. dirs. Cook County Hosp., Chgo., 1968-71, Inst. Rsch. on Econs. of Taxation, Washington, 1977-93, Burnside Plantation Inc., Bethlehem, Pa., 1989-93; trustee Convent of Sacred Heart, Greenwich, Conn., 1976-80; bd. govs. Bethlehem Area Found., 1989-93, chmn. 1991-92; pres. Greenwich Br. of English Spkg. Union, 1994-2000. With U.S. Army, 1946-47, Japan. Mem. ABA (tax sect., chmn. indexing com. 1985-86), Am. Coun. Capital Formation (bd. dirs. 1972-88), Bus. Roundtable (tax adv. group 1977-92), C. of C. U.S. (mem. tax com. 1972-92), Am. Law Inst. (tax adv. group 1974-88), Nat. Tax Assn. (pres. 1981-82), Nat. Chamber Found. (chmn. tax com. 1984-93), Chevy Chase (Md.) Club, Harvard Club (N.Y.C.), Belle Haven Club. Republican. Roman Catholic. Home: 47 Lafayette Pl Apt 6H Greenwich CT 06830-5402 E-mail: mendyjm@yahoo.com.

MENDER, MONA SIEGLER, writer, music educator; b. May 24, 1926; d. George and Freda (Steierman) Siegler; m. Irving M. Mender, Aug. 25, 1946; children: Donald Matthew, Judith Jill. BA, Mt. Holyoke Coll., 1947. Instr. piano and music theory, Fair Lawn, N.J., 1947-75. State edn. chmn. N.J. Symphony Orch., Newark, 1980-82, state chmn. bd. regents, 1983-84, bd. dirs., 1983-91. Author: Music Manuscript Preparation: A Concise Guide, 1991, Extraordinary Women in Support of Music, 1997, The Cock Crows No More, 2000. Recipient Women's Network commendation Sen. Bill Bradley, 1984. Mem. Mountain Ridge Country Club (West Caldwell, N.J.), Plantation Golf and Country Club (Venice, Fla.).

MENDES, SAM (SAMUEL ALEXANDER MENDES), film director, theater director; b. Reading, Eng., Aug. 1, 1965; s. James Peter and Valerie Helene (Barnett) M. Student, U. Cambridge, Eng. Dir. film American Beauty, 1999 (Outstanding Directorial Achievement in Feature Film Dirs. Guild Am. 1999, Golden Globe for best dir. 1999, Best Dir. award Dallas-Ft. Worth Film Critics Assn. 1999, Best Dir. award Online Film Critics Soc. 1999, Best Dir. award Broadcast Film Critics Assn. 1999, Best Dir. award L.A. Film Critics Assn. 1999, Oscar for best dir. 2000, Dir. of the Yr. London Film Critics Cir. 2000, Hamburg Shakespeare prize 2000), dir. prodr. Road to Perdition, 2002; artistic dir. The Rise and Fal of Little Voice (RNT, Aldwych, Olivier and Evening Standard awards), 1992, Cabaret (Tony award), 1998, The Blue Room, 1998; dir. plays London Assurance, 1989, Cherry Orchard, 1989, Kean, 1990, Plough & the Stars, 1991, Troillis & Cressida, 1991, The Alchemist, 1991, The Sea, 1991, Richard III, 1992, The Tempest, 1993, The Birthday Party, 1994, Othello, 1997, Assasins, Translations, Glengarry Glen Ross, Glass Managerie, Company, Habelis Corpus, Front Page, To the Green Fields Beyond, Call at Donmar Warehouse. Office: c/o Donmar Warehouse 41 Earlham St London WC2M 9LD England*

MENDES DE LEON, CARLOS F. epidemiologist, researcher; b. Maastricht, The Netherlands, May 9, 1958; s. Diego Edouard Mendes de Leon, Emilie P.C. Mendes de Leon; m. Mary Gordon Conner; 1 child Emilie 1 child Mary Margaret 1 child Andrew 1 child Julian. PhD, U.Tex.Med.Branch, 1988. Asst. prof. Yale U. Sch. Pub. Health, New Haven, 1992—96; assoc. prof. Rush-Presbyn.-St. Luke's Med. Ctr., Chgo., 1996—. Recipient Ewald W. Busse Rsch. award, Internat. Assn. of Gerotology, 2001. Fellow: Am. Coll. Epidemiology, Gerontological Soc. Am.; mem.: Am. Pub. Health Assn. Office: Rush-Presbyterian-St. Luke's Medical Cnt 1645 W. Jackson Blvd, Suite 675 Chicago IL 60612 Business E-mail: cmendes@rush.edu.

MENDEZ, ALBERT ORLANDO, industrialist, financier; b. Bogota, Colombia, Sept. 7, 1935; came to U.S., 1960; naturalized, 1968; s. Angelino Benjamin and Ana Isabel (Gutierre de Cetina) M.; children: Nicole C., Eric A. BS in Nuclear Physics, N.C. State U., 1961, MS in Nuclear Engrng., 1963; MBA, U. Hartford, 1970. Physicist, mgr. mfg. Combustion Engrng. Co., Windsor, Conn., 1963-67; mgr. corp. devel. and planning Gulf Oil Corp., Pitts., 1967-71; v.p. mktg., controller for Latin Am. Xerox Corp., Stamford, Conn., 1971-76; exec. v.p., COO, chmn. ops. com., bd. dirs. Ogden Corp., N.Y.C., 1976-84; chmn., chief exec. officer, prin. shareholder Am. Indstl. Corp., Stamford, 1984—, Argo-Tech Corp., Aerospace, Cleve., 1986-89. Bd. dirs. Catalyst Energy Co., N.Y.C., 1st Prin. Corp., N.Y.C., Demag, AG, Hamburg, Germany; gen. ptnr. Agnem Holdings Ltd. Partnership, New Canaan, Conn., 1984—; pres., CEO, bd. dirs., prin. shareholder Agnem Investment Co., New Canaan, 1983—; pres., CEO, prin. shareholder AM World Trade Corp., West Palm Beach, Fla.; chmn., CEO, prin. shareholder Arden Petroleum Corp., Palm Beach, Fla., 2000--; mem. Pres.'s Adv. Com. on Def. Preparedness and Intelligence, 1986-92. Contbr. articles to profl. jours. Mem. Internat. Platform Assn., Am. mgmt. Assn., Assn. of Corp. Dirs., The Conf. Bd., Am. Nuclear Soc., Palm Beach (Fla.) Polo Club, Mar-A-Lago Club (Palm Beach).

MENDEZ, ALEJANDRO, neurosurgeon; b. Santiago, Chile, Sept. 2, 1962; came to U.S., 1991; s. Jorge Mendez and Emilia Susaeta; m. Kristine Hildebrandt, May 2, 1998; 2 children: Jose Tomas, Emma Kristine. MD cum laude, Cath. U. of Chile, Santiago, 1988. Diplomate Am. Bd. Neurosurgery. Resident in surgery Cath. U. of Chile, Santiago, 1988-91, gen. surgery specialist, 1991; postgrad. rsch. assoc. U. Minn., Mpls., 1991-93, resident in neurosurgery, 1993—. Contbr. articles to profl. jours., chpts. to books. Mem. Am. Assn. Neurol. Surgery, Congress Neurol. Surgeons. Republican. Roman Catholic. Avocations: skiing, mountain biking, classical music. Office: Dept Neurosurgery U Minn 420 Delaware St SE Minneapolis MN 55455-0374 Home: 3304 Nathaniel Ct Saint Paul MN 55127-7139

MENDEZ, ANGELA M. director; b. Elmhurst, N.Y., Apr. 27, 1972; d. Paulina Magdalena Mendez, Rodolfo Alfonso Mendez; life ptnr. Marlene T. Monday. BA, So. Conn. State U., 1999. Co-author: Essential Love: poems about mothers and fathers, daughters and sons, 1999; contbr. articles to poetry jours. Mem.: Conn. Poetry Soc. (v.p. 1998—99, Joseph Brodine Nat. Poetry award 1997). Roman Catholic. Avocations: reading, interior decorating, sculpting, painting. Home: PO Box 26401 West Haven CT 06516 Personal E-mail: poetryang@hotmail.com. Business E-mail: poemlovr@yahoo.com.

MENDEZ, CARLOS, JR. music educator; b. Bronx, NY, July 7, 1969; s. Carlos and Sylvia Mendez. MusB in Music Edn., Ithaca Coll., 1991; MusM in Viola Performance, Binghamton U., 1996. Cert. tchr. NY. Orch. tchr. Cortland (NY) Enlarged City Sch. Dist., 1991—99, Fayetteville-Manlius Ctrl. Schools, Fayetteville, 1999—. Guest orchestral condr. various all-county/area, all-state orgns., NY, 1995—; dir./condr. Cortland Youth Orch., 1995—96; violinist, violist Ovation String Quartet, Syracuse, NY, 1999—. Author: (instructional booklet) Wonderful World of the Violin, 2002; editor: (publication) The Bridge, 2000. Named Concerto Competition winner, Binghamton U., 1995. Mem.: Fayetteville-Manlius Teachers Assn., Music Educators Nat. Conf., NY State Sch. Music Assn., NY Am. String Tchr. Assn. with Nat. Sch. Orch. Assn. (editor 1998—2000, president-elect 2000—02, pres. 2002—, sec. 1996—98). Democrat. Roman Catholic. Avocations: tennis, travel, music. Office: Wellwood Middle Sch 700 S Manlius St Fayetteville NY 13066 Personal E-mail: cmendez1@twcny.rr.com. E-mail: cmendez@fm.cnyric.org.

MENDEZ, CELESTINO GALO, mathematics educator; b. Havana, Cuba, Oct. 16, 1944; came to the U.S., 1962; naturalized, 1970. s. Celestino Andres and Georgina (Fernandez) M.; m. Mary Ann Koplau, Aug. 21, 1971; children: Mark Michael, Matthew Maximilian. BA, Benedictine Coll., 1965; MA, U. Colo., 1968, PhD, 1974, MBA, 1979. Asst. prof. maths. scis. Met. State Coll., Denver, 1971-77, assoc. prof., 1977-82, prof., 1982—2002, chmn. dept. math. scis., 1980-82, adminstrv. intern office v.p. for acad. affairs, 1989-90; vis. assoc. prof. of math. U. Mich., Ann Arbor, 2002—. Assoc. editor Denver Met. Jour. Math. and Computer Sci., 1993—; contbr. articles to profl. jours. including Am. Math. Monthly, Procs. Am. Math. Soc., Jour. Personalized Instrn., Denver Met. Jour. Math. and Computer Sci. and newspapers. Mem. advt. rev. bd. Met. Denver, 1973-79; parish outreach rep. S.E. deanery, Denver Cath. Cmty. Svcs., 1976-78; mem. social ministries com. St. Thomas More Cath. Ch., Denver, 1976-78, vice-chmn., 1977-78, mem. parish coun., 1977-78; del. Adams County Rep. Conv., 1972, 74, 94, Colo. 4th Congl. Dist. Conv., 1974, Colo. Rep. Conv., 1982, 88, 90, 92, 96, 98, 2000, Douglas County Rep. Conv., 1980, 82, 84, 88, 90, 92, 94, 96, 98, 2000; alt. del. Colo. Rep. Conv., 1974, 76, 84, 2000, 5th Congl. dist. conv., 1976, mem. rules com., 1978, 80, precinct committeeman Douglas County Rep. Com., 1976-78, 89-92, mem. ctrl. com., 1976-78, 89-92; dist. 29 Rep. party candidate Colo. State Senate, 1990; mem. Colo. Rep. Leadership Program, 1989-90, bd. dirs., 1990-98; Douglas county chmn. Rep. Nat. Hispanic Assembly, 1989—; bd. dirs. Rocky Mountain Better Bus. Bur., 1975-79, Rowley Downs Homeowners Assn., 1976-78; trustee Hispanic U. Am., 1975-78; councilman Town of Parker, Colo., 1981-84, chmn. budget and fin. com., 1981-84; chmn. joint budget com. Town of Parker-Parker Water and Sanitation Dist. Bds., 1982-84; commr. Douglas County Planning Commn., 1993-97; dir. Mile High Young Scholars Program, 1995-98. Recipient Excellence in Tchg. award U. Colo. Grad. Sch., 1965-67; grantee Benedictine Coll., 1964-65, Math. Assn. Am. SUMMA grantee Carnegie Found. N.Y., 1994; program dir., grantee NSF, 1995-98; nominated candidate for first v.p Math. Assn. Am., 1999, for 2d v.p., 2001. Mem. Math. Assn. Am. (referee rsch. notes sect. Am. Math. Monthly 1981-82, gov. Rocky Mountain sect. 1993-96, investment com. 1996-02, devel. com. 1995-01, task force on reps. 1994-96, sci. policy com. 2000—, bd. govs. 1993-96, 2002—), Am. Math. Soc., Nat. Coun. Tchrs. Math., Colo. Coun. Tchrs. Math. (bd. dirs. 1994-96), Colo. Internat. Edn. Assn., Assoc. Faculties of State Insts. Higher Edn. in Colo. (v.p. 1971-73). Republican. Roman Catholic. Home: 39 Hummingbird Dr Castle Rock CO 80104-9047 Office: PO Box 173362 Denver CO 80217-3362

MENDEZ, HERMANN ARMANDO, pediatrician, educator; b. Guatemala, Apr. 26, 1949; came to U.S., 1980; citizen of El Salvador; s. Hermann and Martha (Abularach) Mendez Fortun; m. Maria Elena Ortiz, Feb. 23, 1971; children: Natalia, Amalia. MD, U. El Salvador, 1977. Diplomate Am. Bd. Pediatrics, Am. Bd. Pediatric Infectious Diseases. Asst. prof. pediats. Health Sci. Ctr. SUNY, Bklyn., 1988-91, assoc. prof. pediat. medicine, 1991—2001, assoc. prof. medicine, 1999—2001; chief dept. pediat. Lincoln Hosp., South Bronx, 2000—; prof. clin. pediat. Weill Coll. Medicine, Cornell U., 2001—. Recipient Asst. Sec. for Health award USPHS, 1990, United U. Professions Excellence award Health Sci. Ctr., Bklyn., 1991, recognition award Bklyn. AIDS Task Force, 1997-98, Humanism in Medicine award Newark Beth Israel Healthcare Found., 1998, Attending of the Yr. award Children's Med. Ctr. of Bklyn., 1998, Gifts for Spl. Children award N.Y.C. Tech. Coll., 1998, N.Y. State Dept. Health Outstanding Svc. award, 1999. Fellow Am. Acad. Pediatrics, Infectious Disease Soc. Am. Achievements include clinical research in perinatal transmission of HIV, AIDS in children, adolescents and their families; development of systems of care for these populations and children in general, training of medical students and physicians. Office: Lincoln Med & Mental Health Ctr Dept Pediatrics 234 E 149th Bronx NY 10451-5504 Fax: 718-579-4700. E-mail: HAMENDEZ@aol.com.

MENDEZ, RUBEN POLICARPIO, diplomat, educator; b. Manila, Philippines, June 28, 1933; came to U.S., 1948; s. Mauro and Paz Policarpio M.; m. Matilda Currier McEwen, Apr. 8, 1961; children: Katherine McEwen, Tomas Currier. BA cum laude, Harvard U., 1953; MA, Columbia U., 1959; PhD, NYU, 1984. Economist Merrill Lynch, Pierce, Fenner & Smith, N.Y.C., 1959-63; econ. adviser to chmn. Nat. Econ. Coun., Manila, 1964-66; project officer UN Spl. Fund, N.Y.C., 1963-65; various positions UN Devel. Program, Africa, Asia, 1966-93; chief econ. advisor UN Environ. Program, Nairobi, Kenya, 1977-81; prin. officer, historian UN Devel. Program, N.Y.C., 1993—. Adj. prof., fellow, vis. lectr. NYU, 1991—, Columbia U., 1992, Yale U., 1994—; cons. Oxford U. Press, N.Y., 1999—. Author: International Public Finance: A New Perspective on Global Relations, 1992; contbr. articles to profl. jours., chpts. to books. Yale rep. Acad. Coun. on UN Sys. Grantee Carnegie Corp., N.Y.C., 1995-98, Internat. Devel. Rsch. Ctr., Ottawa, Can., 1994-97. Mem. Am. Econ. Assn., N.Y. Acad. Scis., Soc. Internat. Devel., Harvard Club (N.Y.C.), Harvard Faculty Club, Riverdale Yacht Club, United Kenya Club (Nairobi). Avocations: history, philosophy, classical music, sailing, personal computers. Home: 313 W 263d St Riverdale NY 10471 Office: UN Devel Programme 304 E 45th St New York NY 10017-3425 E-mail: rpmendez@post.harvard.edu.

MENDEZ, WILLIAM HUMBERT, family medicine physician; b. Mancos, Ancash, Peru, May 15, 1929; came to U.S., 1958; s. Humberto and Livia (De Los Angeles) M.; m. Ella Patricia Woltering, June 22, 1968; children: Bill, John, Michael, Angela. MD, U. San Marcos, Lima, Peru, 1958. Rotating intern Mercy Hosp., Oshkosh, Wis., 1958-59; resident in pathology St. Joseph Hosp., Marshfield, 1959-60; resident in surgery and pathology St. Joseph's Hosp., Milw., 1960-64; resident in surgery St. Luke's Hosp., Denver, 1964-66; pvt. practice Highland Med. Ctr., 1971—; asst. clin. prof. U. Colo. Med. Sch., 1995. Mem. prevention task force against drugs and violence Jeffco Bldg. Generation, Lakewood, Colo., 1985—; mem. Denver Met. YMCA, 1978—, St. Anthony Ctrs. and Luth. Med. Ctr. Fellow: Am. Acad. Family Practice; mem.: AMA (life), Am. Acad. Antiaging Medicine, Colo. Med. Soc., Am. Acad. Family Physicians (life), Peruvian Am. Med. Soc., Interam. Coll. Physicians and Surgeons. Republican. Roman Catholic. Avocation: music. Office: Highland Med Ctr 3120 W 29th Ave Denver CO 80211-3704 E-mail: WHM-Highland@juno.com.

MENDIETA, RAQUELIN MARIA DE LA CONCEPCIÓN, artist; b. Havana, Cuba, Aug. 4, 1946; came to the U.S., 1961; d. Ignacio Alberto and Raquel de San José (Oti) M.; m. Donald Raymond Holmes, Aug. 26, 1967 (div. Dec. 1973); m. James William Auman, Aug. 9, 1975 (div. July 1977); m. Thomas Joseph Harrington, May 17, 1978 (div. 2002); children: Raquel Cecilia, Paulette Ana, Shambhavi Elvira, Neel Miguel, Vitthal Pablo. Student, Mt. Mercy Coll., 1963-65; BA in Studio Art, U. Iowa, 1970, postgrad., 1970-72, MA in Edn., 1977. Pvt. practice exhbns. cons., 1987—. Cons. The Mus. Contemporary Art, N.Y.C., 1987, Galerie Lelong, N.Y.C., 1991—, Arts Alliance of Haverstraw, N.Y., 1992, Carla Stellweg Fine Arts, N.Y.C., 1993; humanities adv. bd. Fondo del Sol Visual Arts Ctr., Washington, 1990-93, co-chair exhbns., 1993-97; ednl. coord. Fondo del Sol, Washington, 1991; adj. prof. L.Am. studies Jersey City State Coll., 1991; trustee Arts Alliance Haverstraw, 1992-94; ednl. program specialist The Bronx (N.Y.) Mus. Arts, 1995-96; art dir., music cons. Corazon Prodns., Inc., Miami, Fla., 1996-98; lectr. in field. One woman shows include Rockland C.C., 1990, 96, Café Teatro Julia de Burgos, N.Y.C., 1993, Visceglia Arts Ctr., Caldwell, N.J., 1993, Ludwig Found. Galleries, Ltd., Havana, 2000; permanent collections Bronx Mus. Arts, Mus. of the Art Inst., Chgo. Trustee, liaison to univ. adminstrn., rep. to daycare coalition U. Parents Care Collective, Iowa City, 1971-75; vocat. advisor, arts supr. Bedford Hills (N.Y.) Correctional Facility for Women, 1985; mem. Hispanic Heritage Com., Rockland C.C., 1990-93, Hispanic Coalition Rockland County, N.Y., 1991-94. Recipient Cert. of Merit, Town of Ramapo, County of Rockland, 1992, Cert. of Recognition for developing arts programs Hispanic Coun. Rockland County, Haverstraw, 1992, Cert. of Merit, The Assembly of N.Y. State, 1993, award for contbns. to Am. art in sculpture Fondo del Sol Visual Arts Ctr., Washington, 1993. Mem. Arts Alliance of Haverstraw (hon., bd. dirs. 1993-94, trustee 1995—), Coast to Coast Nat. Women Artists of Color. Democrat. Siddha Yoga. Avocations: writing, music, personal computing, meditation, chanting. Home: 11615 SW 135th Pl Miami FL 33186-4429

MENDINI, DOUGLAS A. publishing company executive, writer; b. New Brunswick, N.J., June 13, 1953; s. T.F. Mendini and Helen Victoria Jones Mendini Renninger. BA, Seton Hall U., 1975. Sr. sales mgr. Kensington Pub. Corp., N.Y.C., 1990—. Author: What Was Hot, 1994, others; contbr. articles to numerous mags. Founder Block Assn., Manhattan, NY, 1990; bd. dirs. Cmty. Bd., Manhattan, 1990-93, bd. sec., 1993. Recipient Young Writers award Coordinating Coun. Lit. Mags., 1988. Democrat. Roman Catholic. Avocations: presidential history, furniture refinishing, American film history. Home: 403 W 54th St Apt 1D New York NY 10019-4469

MENDIOLA, ANNA MARIA G. mathematics educator; b. Laredo, Tex., Dec. 21, 1948; d. Alberto and Aurora (Benavides) Gonzalez; m. Alfonso Mendiola Jr., Aug. 11, 1973; children: Alfonso, Alberto. AA, Laredo C.C., Tex., 1967; BA, Tex. Woman's U., 1969, MS, 1974. Tchr. math. Laredo Ind. Sch. Dist., 1969-81; instr. math. Laredo C.C., 1981—, organizer Jaime Escalante program, 1991-92; tech. prep. com. mem., 1991-92; ednl. coun., sec. Christen Mid. Campus, 1992-94; mem. site based campus com. Martin H.S., 1994-2000. Vis. instr. St. Augustine Sch., Laredo. 1987-88; evaluator So. Assn., Corpus Christi, 1981, So. Assn. Colls. and Schs., United H.S., 1991; mem. quality improvement coun. Laredo C.C., 1993-94; mem. instrn. coun. Laredo C.C., 1995-96; participant SC3 Calculus Reform Inst., NSF, 1996; mem. adv. com. on core curriculum Tex. Higher Edn. Coord. Bd., 1997-99, mem. adv. com. on transfer issues and field of study, 2000—; mem. Laredo C.C. self-study steering com. So. Assn. Colls. and Schs. Reaffirmation, 1997-99, coord. honors program, 1999—; faculty assoc. NSF-LCC Rio Grande River Project, 1998-2000. V.p., bd. dirs. Our Lady of Guadalupe Sch., Laredo, 1988-91; sec. Laredo C.C. Faculty Senate, 1986-87, v.p., 1995-96, pres., 1996-97; rep. Laredo Ind. Sch. Dist. Parent Adv. Coun., 1997-98. Recipient Teaching Excellence award NISOD, 1993; named LCC Innovator of the Month, 1998. Mem. AAUW (pres. 1979-81, v.p. 1987-89, scholarship chair 1993-94, membership chair 1994-95, bylaws chair 1996-97, pub. policy chair 1997-99), Am. Math. Assn. Two-Yr. Colls., Tex. State Tchrs. Assn., Tex. C.C. Tchrs. Assn. (campus rep., sec. math. sect. 1997-98, vice chair math. sect. 1998-99, chair math. sect. 1999-2000, chair audit com. 1999-2000, co-chair membership com. 2001-02), Tex. Woman's U. Alumnae Assn., Blessed Sacrament Altar Soc., Delta Kappa Gamma (membership chair 1993-96, v.p. 2000-02). Democrat. Roman Catholic. E-mal. Office: Laredo CC West End Washington St Laredo TX 78040 E-mail: amendiola@laredo.edu.

MENDIS, PATRICK, economist, geographer, educator; b. Polonnaruwa, Sri Lanka, Apr. 7, 1960; came to U.S., 1983; s. B.W. Kamilus and Kusumawati M.; m. Cheryl Lynn Pattison, Oct. 8, 1988; children: Gamini, Samantha. BS in Bus. Admstrn. and Econs., U. Sri Lanka, 1983; MA in Internat. Devel., Fgn. Affairs, Hubert H. Humphrey Inst. Pub. Affairs, 1986; PhD in Geography/Applid Econs., U. Minn., 1989. Vis. scholar in applied econs. U. Minn., 1990—97, lectr. in internat. rels., 1990—97; grad. prof. govt. and econs. U. Md. U. Coll./U.S. Dept. Def., Heidelburg, Germany, 1997—99, Tokyo, 1999—2000; fgn. affairs officer for sci. and tech. U.S. State Dept., Washington, 2000—01, spl. asst. to Asst. Secy. State and Ednl. and Cult. Affairs, 2001—, Secretariat Dir., 2001—. Del. UN, Govt. Sri Lanka, N.Y.C., 1985; cons. World Bank, Washington, 1988, 89 summers, U.S. State Dept., Washington, 1991; Senate Fgn. Rels. Com., Washington; chmn. UN Youth Leadership Summit, N.Y.C., 1995; sr. policy fellow Inst. Agr. and Trade Policy, Mpls., 1996-97; vis. faculty Yale U. Ctr. for Internat. and Area Studies, 1996, 97 summers; spl. asst. former NATO amb. Harlan Cleveland, UN Univ.'s Leadership Acad., 1997, Asian Tour World Acad. Art and Sci., 1995; adj. prof. mgmt. and econs. U. Md., 2000-; vice chmn. Secretary of State's Open Forum, U.S. State Dept, 2001-2002; advisor U.S. Del. to the UN Commn. on Sustainable Devel., 2001-. Author: (book) Human Environment and Spatial Relations, 1992; contbg. editor Asian Am. Press, 1990-94; advisor Internat. Policy Rev. (jour.), 1991—; editor Global Issues and Economic Perspectives, two electronic journals of the U.S. State Dept., 2002; editl. bd. mem. Energy & Environment, 2001-. Pres. Soc. for Internat. Devel., Minn., 1993-95; v.p. 1995-97; sec. UN Assn., Minn., 1995-96, v.p. 1996-97; founding chmn. Asian-Pacific Endowment for Cmty. Devel. at St. Paul Found., 1993-95, v.p., 1995-97; bd. dirs. Ctr. for Victims of Torture, Minn., 1997—; trustee Humphrey Inst. Alumni Bd.; endowed two ann. scholarships in Mgmt. Studies and Leadership for Sri Lanka U. students, 1993-, Harlan Cleveland Leadership award for Sri Lanka U. students, 2002; mem. NASA Exec. Leadership Prog., U.S. Fed. Exec. Inst., 2001, Global Environment Change Prog., Harvard Med. Sch. Ctr. Health and Global Environment, 2002, Georgetown U. Prog. for Exec. in Legis. Operations, 2002. Recipient UN medal, 1985, Alumni award for outstanding leadership, 1986, Hubert Humphrey Inst., 1986, Gov.'s Asian-Pacific Heritage award, 1994, Aspen Inst. Global Leadership fellowship, 1995, Salzburg Seminar scholarship, 1995, Kennedy Sch, Leadership scholarship Harvard U., 1996, Sasakawa award Sasakawa Found., 1996, Harold Stassen award for UN Affairs, 1997, UN Univ. scholarship Internat. Leadership Acad., Jordan, 1997, Coolidge fellowship Columbia U., 1997, 21st. Century Trust fellow, Oxford, 2000, Diplomacy fellow AAAS, 2000, Socrates fellow Aspen Inst., 2001, Meritorious Honor award, U.S. State Dept., 2001. Fellow World Acad. Arts and Sci.; mem. Am. Com. on Fgn. Rels., U. Minn. Alumni Assn. (bd. dirs.), Internat. Inst. for Strategic Studies (assoc.), Soc. Internat. Devel. Avocations: running, reading, travel, hiking, swimming. Home: 11628 Newbridge Ct Reston VA 20191 Office: US State Dept 301 4th St SW Ste 800 Washington DC 20547 E-mail: pmendis@umuc.edu.

MENDIUS, PATRICIA DODD WINTER, editor, educator, writer; b. Davenport, Iowa, July 9, 1924; d. Otho Edward and Helen Rose (Dodd) Winter; m. John Richard Mendius, June 19, 1947; children: Richard, Catherine M. Graber, Louise, Karen M. Chooljian. BA cum laude, UCLA, 1946; MA cum laude, U. N.Mex., 1966. Cert. secondary edn. tchr., Calif., N.Mex. English teaching asst. UCLA, 1946-47; English tchr. Marlborough Sch. for Girls, L.A., 1947-50, Aztec (N.Mex.) High Sch., 1953-55, Farmington (N.Mex.) High Sch., 1955-63; chair English dept. Los Alamos (N.Mex.) High Sch., 1963-86; sr. technical writer, editor Los Alamos Nat. Lab., 1987—. Adj. prof. English, U. N.Mex., Los Alamos, 1970-72, Albuquerque, 1982-85; English cons. S.W. Regional Coll. Bd., Austin, Tex., 1975—; writer, editor, cons. advanced placement English test devel. com. Nat. Coll. Bd., 1982-86, reader, 1982-86, project equality cons., 1985-88; book selection cons. Scholastic mag., 1980-82. Author: Preparing for the Advanced Placement English Exams, 1975; editor Los Alamos Arts Coun. bull., 1986-91. Chair Los Alamos Art in Pub. Places Bd., 1987-92; chair adv. bd. trustees U. N.Mex., Los Alamos, 1987-93; pres. Los Alamos Concert Assn., 1972-73, 95-98; chair Los Alamos Mesa Pub. Libr. Bd., 1990-94, chair endowment com., 1995-99. Mem. Soc. Tech. Communicators, AAUW (pres. 1961-63, state bd. dirs. 1959-63, Los Alamos coordinating coun. 1992-93, pres. 1993-94), DAR, Order Ea. Star, Mortar Bd., Phi Beta Kappa (pres. Los Alamos chpt. 1969-72, 99, v.p. 1996-99, pres. 2000-01), Phi Kappa Phi, Delta Kappa Gamma, Gamma Phi Beta. Avocations: swimming, reading, hiking, astronomy, singing. Home: 124 Rover Blvd Los Alamos NM 87544-3634 Office: Los Alamos Nat Lab Diamond Dr Los Alamos NM 87544 E-mail: mendius@qwest.net., pmendius@lanl.gov.

MENDLIN, RONALD C. employment specialist, writer; b. San Francisco, Jan. 8, 1936; s. Joseph and Freda Mendlin; m. Lorraine F. Mendlin, Feb. 15, 1964; children: Andrew Scott, Susan Debra. Student, U. San Francisco, San Francisco State U.; degree, San Francisco Coll., 1958. Vocat. edn. tchg. credential, Calif. With City and County of San Francisco, 1962-92, ret.; employment specialist No. Calif. Svc. League, San Francisco, from 1993; part-time employment specialist, San Mateo. Job developer San Mateo Employment and Tng. Ctr., Advanced Career Tech., Peninsula Placement Agy.; placement counselor Scofield Employment Agy., San Francisco; lectr. in field. Co-author: (with Marc Polonsky) Putting the Bars Behind You series, 5 vols.: The Double You, Being Job-Ready, Job Search Tools, Networking and Interviewing for Jobs, Keeping Your Job, 2000. Vice pres. Fiesta Gardens Home Owners' Assn., San Mateo, Calif., 1976-79. With USAR N.G., 1954-63. Recipient numerous accolades Mayor's Office. Achievements include placing over 700 ex-felons from state prisons into jobs.

MENDLOWSKI, BRONISLAW, retired pathologist; b. Tarnopol, Poland, June 28, 1914; came to U.S., 1948; s. Eugeniusz and Kazimiera (Zielinski) M.; m. Zita Pawlowski, Apr. 16, 1926 (dec. 1988); children: Jerry, Michael, Anna. DVM, U. Lwow, Poland, 1944; MRCVS, U. Edinburgh, Scotland, 1947; MS (hon.), U. Ill., Urbana, 1963. Pathologist W. Scotland Agr. Coll., 1945-46, Wis. State Diagnostic Lab., 1951-60, U. Ill., Urbana, 1960-63; sr. rsch. fellow in pathology Merck Inst. for Therapeutic Rsch., West Point, Pa., 1963-84; ret., 1984. Contbr. articles to profl. jours. Mem. N.Y. Acad. Sci. Roman Catholic. Home: 1460 Lanes End Villanova PA 19085-2000

MENDOLA, LOUIS ANDRÉ MANTEGNA, business consultant marketing and advertising, historian; b. Rochester, N.Y., Apr. 1, 1961; arrived in Italy, 1991; s. Giuseppe Mendola and Giuseppina La Paglia. BA, SUNY, Albany, 1986. Dir. Italian Geneal. and Heraldic Inst., Palermo, Italy, 1990-96; pres. Mendola Design, 1996—. Guest lectr. NYU, 1990. Contbr. articles to profl. jours. Vol. Am. Cancer Soc., N.Y., 1985-88, Ethiopia-Europe Found., Geneva, 2000—. Named Knight, Constantian Order of St. George, Royal House of the Two Sicilies, Naples, 1988, Knight, Order of Civil Merit of Savoy, Royal House of Savoy, Italy, 1990, Knight, Order of Sts. Maurice and Lazarus, Royal House of Savoy, Italy, 1991, Knight Comdr., Order of Menelik II, Ethiopia, 1998, Knight, Order of Merit of Sovereign Mil. Order Malta, 2000. Avocations: martial arts, mountain climbing, weightlifting, painting. Home: Via Massimo DAzeglio 9-B 90143 Palermo Italy E-mail: louis@mendola.com.

MENDONSA, BOB, management consultant; b. Redwood City, Calif., Dec. 27, 1952; s. LeRoy John and Coeta Maxine Mendonsa; m. Theresa Carol Robberson; children: Jeremy, Timothy. MPA, Calif. State U., 1986. V.p. human resources Neopost, Hayward, Calif., 1985—96; cons. Bob Mendonsa & Assocs., Bellevue, Wash., 1996—. Author: (book) Working Choices, 2000, poetry. Patron Oreg. Shakespeare Festival, Ashland, 1990—2002. Recipient Phelan Lit. award, San Jose State U., 1977. Democrat. Avocations: music, theater , travel. Home and Office: 11109 NE 38th Pl Bellevue WA 98004 Fax: 425-827-6202. E-mail: bob@trainingplus.com.

MENDOZA, GEORGE, poet, author; b. N.Y.C., June 2, 1934; s. George and Elizabeth Mendoza; m. Ruth Sekora, 1967; children: Ashley, Ryan. BA, State Maritime Coll., 1953; postgrad., Columbia U., 1954-56. Author over 100 books for children and adults published worldwide; many included in Boston U.'s George Mendoza Collection, established 1984; children's books on display at the Centre Nat. d'Art et de Culture Georges Pompidou. Works include: And Amedeo Asked, How Does One Become a Man?, (illustrated by Ati Forberg), 1959, The Puma and the Pearl, 1962, The Hawk Is Humming: A Novel, 1964, A Piece of String, Astor-Honor, 1965, Gwot! Horribly Funny Hairticklers (illustrated by Steven Kellog), 1967, The Crack in the Wall and Other Terribly Weird Tales (illustrated by Mercer Mayer), 1968, Flowers and Grasses and Weeds (illustrated by Joseph Low), 1968, The Practical Man (illustrated by Imero Gobbato), 1968, Hunting Sketches (illustrated by Ronald Stein), 1968, A Beastly Alphabet (illustrated by J. Low), 1969, The Digger Wasp (illustrated by Jean Zallinger), 1969, Herman's Hat (illustrated by Frank Bozzo), 1969, The Starfish Trilogy (illustrated by Ati Forberg), 1969, (compiler) The World From My Window: Poems and Drawings (children's writings), 1969, Are You My Friend? (illustrated by F. Bozzo), 1970, The Marcel Marceau Alphabet Book, 1970, The Thumbtown Toad (illustrated by Monika Beisner), 1970, The Inspector, 1970, The Good Luck Spider & other bad luck stories, 1970, The Fearsome Brat (illustrated by F. Bozzo), 1971, Fish in the Sky (illustrated by Milton Glaser), 1971, Moonfish and owl scratchings, 1971, Moonstring, 1971, The Hunter, the Tick and the Gumberoo, 1971, The Marcel Marceau Counting Book, 1971, The Scarecrow Clock (illustrated by Eric Carle), 1971, Big Frog, Little Pond, 1971, The Scribbler, 1971, The Christmas Tree Alphabet Book, 1971, Shadowplay, 1974, Lord, Suffer me to Catch a Fish, 1974, Fishing the Morning Lonely, 1974, (with Carol Burnett) What I Want to Be When I Grow Up, 1975, (with Zero Mostel) The Sesame Street Book of Opposites, 1975, Norman Rockwell's Americana ABC (illustrated by N. Rockwell), 1975, Doug Henning's Magic Book, 1975, Lost Pony, 1976, Norman Rockwell's Boys and Girls at Play, 1976, Secret Places of a Trout Fisherman, 1977, Norman Rockwell's Diary for a Young Girl (illustrated by N. Rockwell), 1978, Magic Tricks, 1978, Mon livre de magie (French edit. of My Book of Magic), Norman Rockwell's Scrapbook for a Young Boy (illustrated by N. Rockwell), 1979, (with Andres Segovia) Segovia, My Book of the Guitar, 1979, Need a House? Call Ms. Mouse! (illustrated by Doris Susan Smith), 1981, Alphabet Sheep (illustrated by K. Reidy), 1982, The Sheepish Book of Opposites, 1982, Silly Sheep and other sheepish rhymes, 1982, Norman Rockwell's Four Seasons, 1982, Norman Rockwell's Happy Holidays, 1983, Henri Mouse (illustrated by Joelle Boucher), 1985, Henri La Souris, 1987, Norman Rockwell's Patriotic Times, 1986, (with Ivan Lendl) Hitting Hot, 1986, (with Sam Snead) Slammin' Sam, 1986, Norman Rockwell's Love and Remembrance, 1986, Top Tennis, 1987, L'Album des Noeuds, 1988, Norman Rockwell's Old Fashioned American Cookbook, 1988, Hairticklers (illustrated by Gahan Wilson), 1989, The Hunter I Might Have Been, reprint 1989, Were You a Wild Duck, Where Would You Go? (illustrated by Jane Osborn-Smith), 1990, Traffic Jam (illustrated by David Stoltz), 1990; also author screenplays for Petals from a Poem Flower, You Show Me Yours and I'll Show You Mine and scripts for Sesame Street; numerous others; over 15 books of poetry including The Hunter I Might Have Been (Lewis Carroll Shelf award 1968), The Mist Men, Goodbye, River, Goodbye; also dozens of articles in The N.Y. Times, Herald Tribune, Stern, Vogue, Harper's Bazaar, Ms., Esquire, Town & Country, Sports Afield, Men's Journal, Philadelphia Inquirer; special travel corr. Toronto Globe & Mail, 1991-94. Cited by Pres. Reagan for Norman Rockwell's Patriotic Times. Avocation: trout and salmon fishing. Worldwide fishing expeditions recorded for TV spls. *I believe we are living in a world where people no longer see each other as individuals. We have become invisible. It is necessary to save our souls. Go out to a field and pick up a fallen leaf. Look at the veins that river the leaf. Follow them until nothing else matters except for the leaf in your hand. Then you will become visible. You will see others and others will see you.*

MENDOZA, LYDIA, vocalist; Mem. El Cuarteto Carta Blanca. Recordings include: Mal Hombre, 1934; performances include Smithsonian Bicentennial Festival of Am. Folklife, Carter Presdl. Inauguration; author (compiled by Chris Strachwitz and James Nicolopulos): Lydia Mendoza: A Family Autobiography, 1993; author: (with Y. Broyles-Gonzales) Lydia Mendoza: My Life and Music, 2001. Recipient Nat. Medal of Arts, Am. Heritage award, Nat. Assn. for Chicana and Chicano Studies Lifetime Achievement Cmty. award, 1999; named a Nat. Treasure, Smithsonian Instn.; inductee Tex. Hall of Fame; Nat. Heritage fellow Nat. Endowment for the Arts, 1982. Office: c/o Arhoolie Records 10341 San Pablo Ave El Cerrito CA 94530-3123 E-mail: chris@arhoolie.com.

MENDOZA, MICHAEL C. engineer; b. Washington, Apr. 29, 1976; s. Michael Hermilo and Elaine Gerlak Mendoza; m. Krista Anne Soderstrom, Aug. 15, 1998. BS, U. Ill., 1998, MS, 2000. Engr. Caterpillar, Decatur and Champaign, Ill., 1998—2000, Cummins, Whitakers, NC, 2000—. Author: (novels) Spring Hope Canyon, 2001. Avocations: building/construction, writing, weightlifting. Home: 3593 Old Nash Rd Middlesex NC 27557-8082

MENDOZA, RYAN, artist; b. N.Y.C., Oct. 29, 1971; s. George and Ruth (Sekora) M. Student, Yale U., 1989, Washington U., St. Louis, Mo., 1990-91, Ind. U., 1991-92, Parsons Sch. Art and Design, Paris, 1992-94. One-person shows include Galleria Studio Legale, Caserta, 1997, Galleria In Arco, Torino, 1997, Studio Cannaviello, Milan, 1998, Galerie Bernd Klüser, Munich, 1999, 2000, Museum Modern and Contemporary Art, Trento, 2000, Massimo Minini, Brescia, 2000, Overbeck-Gesellschaft, Lübeck, 2001, White Cube, London, 2002; subject of art books: Cadaver Dog (Cristiana Perrella), 1997, Oh, Big Fishy (Sergio Bertaccini), 1997, Ryan Mendoza (Tullio Pironti and Alberto Fiz), 1998, Ryan Mendoza: A Cake for the Dead (Hubertus Gaßner), 1999, Ryan Mendoza (Skira), 2000, Ryan Mendoza (Overbeck-Gesellschaft and Simona Vendrame), 2001, Join Now for Instant Access (Ryan Mendoza and Irvine Welsh), 2002. Office: C/O The White Cube Gallery 44 Duke St- St James's London SW1Y 6DD England

MENDOZA, STANLEY ATRAN, pediatric nephrologist, educator; b. Pitts., May 7, 1940; s. Joseph William and Marian Ruth (Atran) M.; m. Carole Ann Klein, June 23, 1963; children: Daniel, Joseph. Student, Harvard U., 1957-59; BA, Johns Hopkins U., 1961, MD, 1964. Diplomate: Am. Bd. Pediatrics. Intern Johns Hopkins Hosp., Balt., 1964-65; jr. asst. resident dept. medicine Children's Hosp. Med. Ctr., Boston, 1965-66; asst. attending physician, dir. renal rsch. labs Children's Meml. Hosp., Chgo., 1969-71; asst. prof. pediatrics U. Calif. Sch. Medicine, San Diego, 1971—73, assoc. prof., 1973—79, prof. pediatrics dept. pediatrics divsn. pediatric nephrology, 1979—97, vice chmn. dept. pediatrics, 1986—87, chmn. dept. pediatrics, 1992—2000. Contbr. article in field to profl. publ. Served With USPHS, 1966-69. Fogarty Sr. Internat. fellow, 1978-79; Alan J. Wurtzburger research scholar, 1964; recipient Johns Hopkins Med. Soc. award, 1964, hon. mention Borden Undergrad. research award in medicine, 1964; Eleanor Roosevelt internat. fellow Internat. Union Against Cancer, 1984-85 Mem. Am. Fedn. Clin. Research, Am. Pediatric Soc., Am. Physiol. Soc., Am. Soc. Nephrology, Am. Soc. Pediatric Nephrology, Internat. Soc. Nephrology. Office: U Calif San Diego Dept Pediat 9500 Gilman Dr # 0696 La Jolla CA 92093-5004 E-mail: samendoza@ucsd.edu.

MENDOZA-DOMINGUEZ, ALBERTO, chemical engineering educator, researcher, consultant; b. Leon, Guanajuato, Mexico, Jan. 2, 1971; s. Alberto Mendoza-Lasso and Hortensia Dominguez-Olalde; m. Maria Gabriela Ortiz-Martinez, June 12, 1999. BS in Chem. Engring., Itesm, Monterrey, Mex., 1992, MS in Environ. Engring., 1996; PhD in Environ. Engring., Ga. Inst. Tech., 2001. Cert. engr., Mex. Environ. leader Prolec-Gen. Electric, Apodaca, Mexico, 1996; asst. prof. ITESM Campus Monterrey, Mexico, 2001—. Head air quality lab. ITESM Campus Monterrey, 2001—. Contbr. articles to profl. and sci. jours. Named Repatriated Scientist, Nat. Coun. Sci. and Tech., 2001. Mem.: Air and Waste Mgmt. Assn., Mexican Inst. Chem. Engineers (dir. 2002—), Ga. Tech. Assn. of Environ. Engrs. and Scientists (life). Office: ITESM Campus Monterrey Av Eugenio Garza Sada 2501 Sur 64849 Monterrey Nuevo Leon Mexico Office Fax: (81) 8328-4250. Business E-Mail: almendoz@campus.mty.itesm.mx.

MENE, MATTHEW PUGLIESE, urologist, surgeon; b. Queens, N.Y., Feb. 19, 1965; s. Albert J. and Patrician P. (Pugliese) M.; m. Susan E. Zunitch, July 21, 1989; children: Elizabeth, Ashley. BS, N.Y. Inst. Tech., 1987; DO, N.Y. Coll. Osteo. Medicine, 1990; MSc, Phila. Coll. Osteo. Medicine, 1996. Intern Massaequa Gen. Hosp., Seaford, N.Y., 1990-91; resident Phila. Coll. Osteo. Med., 1991-96; urologist Defiance (Ohio) Clinic, 1996—. Contbr. articles to profl. jours. Mem. Am. Coll. Osteo. Surgeons (resident achievement award 1994), Am. Osteo. Assn. (grantee 1994), Phila. Osteo. Medicine Assn. Republican. Roman Catholic. Avocations: weight training, swimming, reading. Home: 10 Suttonwood Dr Commack NY 11725-5614 Office: Defiance Clinic 1400 E 2nd St Ste 2 Defiance OH 43512-2494

MENEBROKER, ANN, special education educator, writer; b. Washington, Mar. 30, 1936; d. Harold Godfrey Reynolds Jr. and Edith Louise (Ellis) Reynolds; children: Audrey St Violet, Lauri Solari, Sue McElligot. Dir.'s asst. Artists' Contemporary Gallery, Sacramento, 1990—2000; instrnl. asst. in spl. edn. Natomas Sch. Dist., 2000—. Co-editor: (anthology) Landing Signals, 1985, Watching from the Sky, 1990; author: (poetry collection) Trying for the Ten Ring, 2000. Avocations: art, rare book collecting, music, walking. Home: 10 Azorean Ct Sacramento CA 95833-1142

MENEELEY, EDWARD STERLING, artist; b. Wilkes-Barre, Pa., Dec. 18, 1927; s. Edward Sterling and Louina Halter M. Student, Murray Art Sch., Wilkes-Barre, 1947-50, Sch. Visual Arts, N.Y.C., 1952-53. Vis. lectr. Belleville Coll., St. Louis, Art Students League, N.Y.C.; lectr. Lehigh Valley Sch. System, 1987, Rogers College, Istanbul, Turkey, 1991, Lafayette Coll., 1998; pres. ESM Documentations, N.Y.C.; fine arts cons. Arts Initiatives, Inc., N.Y.C.; founder Portable Gallery Press, 1957-67. One-man exhbs. include, Donovan Gallery, Phila., 1952, Parma Gallery, N.Y.C., 1962, Teuscher Gallery, N.Y.C., 1966, 68, Inst. Contemporary Arts, London, 1971, Victoria and Albert Mus., London, 1972, U. Sussex, Eng., 1972, Whitechapel Art Gallery, London, 1973, Demos Gallery, Athens, Greece, 1976, Frank Marino Gallery, N.Y.C., 1978, 79, 80, 81, 82, Sordoni Gallery, Wilkes (Pa.) Coll., 1981, Ericson Gallery, N.Y.C., 1980, Portfolio Gallery, Atlanta, 1983, Angela Flowers Gallery, London, 1985, J.T. Gallery, Jim Thorpe, Pa, 1987, 55 Mercer St., N.Y.C., 1987, Anita Shapolsky Gallery, N.Y.C., 1988, Bucknell U. Gallery Art, Lewisburg, 1988, Recent Painting & Sculptute, Coll. Misericordia, Dallas, Pa., 1989, Mixed Media, Craft Alliance Gallery, St. Louis, 1990, Provincetown (Mass.) Art Mus., 1993, De Arte Magick Gallery, Easton, Pa., 1997, New Works, N.Y.C., 1998, 181 Hudson St. N.Y.C., 1998, 70th St Gallery Collages, 2001. Served with USNR, 1945-47, 50-52. Nat. Endowment Arts grantee; Pollock-Krasner Found. grantee, 1986, 90, 2002. Mem. Artist Club N.Y.C., Inst. Contemporary Arts London, Josiah White Soc., Weissport, Pa.

MENEES, JOHN ROBERT, mechanical engineer; b. Chgo., Mar. 15, 1928; s. Thomas Orville and Elda Ruth (Johnston) M.; s. Patricia June Kyle, July 28, 1950; children: Gillian Sue, John Robert. BS in Mech. Engring., U. Ill., 1952. Corp. mgr. heavy industry sales Sinclair Refining Co., N.Y.C., 1953-67; sales Rogers (Conn.) Corp., 1967-92; prin. J.R. Menees Assocs., Olympia Fields, Ill., 1992—. Mem. Soc. Plastics Engrs. Republican. Presbyterian. Avocations: golf, travel, family genealogy, alumni activities. Home and Office: 3617 Ionia Ave Olympia Fields IL 60461-1316

MENEFEE, FREDERICK LEWIS, advertising executive; b. Arkansas City, Kans., Oct. 22, 1932; s. Arthur LeRoy and Vera Mae (Rather) M.; m. Margot Leuze, Sept. 16, 1955; children: Gregory S., Christina Menefee-Anderson. AA, Arkansas City Jr. Coll., 1952; BA, U. Wichita, 1958. Sports editor, bus. mgr. Ark. Light and Tiger Tales, 1949-52; sports reporter Arkansas City Daily Traveler, 1950-52; advt. mgr. Derby Star, Haysville Herald and Sedgwick County News, 1956-57; v.p., account exec. Associated Advt. Agy., 1958-64; with McCormick-Armstrong Adv. Agy. (now Menefee and Ptnrs., Inc.), Wichita, 1964—, agy. mgr., 1964—, account. supr., 1965—, gen. mgr., 1972—, pres., CEO, 1979—, chmn. bd., 1989-96. Vol. Wichita River Festival, 1974-98; pub. rels. chmn. Wichita Centennial Nat. Art Show and Exhibit, 1969-70. With AUS, 1953-55. Named Advt. Man of Yr., Advt. Club of Wichita, 1964, Advt. Man of Yr., 9th Dist. Am. Advt. Fedn. Colo., Nebr., Iowa, Mo., Kans., 1965, Adm. Windwagon Smith III Wichita Festivals Inc., 1976. Mem. Am. Advt. Fedn. (nat. bd. dirs. 1969-70, dist. gov. 1968-69, chmn. nat. coun. govs. 1969-70), Wichita Wagonmasters (founding mem., capt. 1974-75, dir., charter, founder, commodore 1999), Wichita Advt. Club (bd. dirs. 1958-68), v.p. awards 1961-62, v.p. membership 1962, v.p. programs 1963, pres. 1964-65), PAWS Inc. (founder, 1st pres. 1978-86), Alpha Delta Sigma (pres. 1957-58, Outstanding Svc. award 1958), Quill & Scroll. Home: 2235 Red Bud Ln Wichita KS 67204-5346 Office: Menefee & Ptnrs Inc 1065 N Topeka St Wichita KS 67214-2913

MENEFEE, JOHN WILLIAM, III, cinematographer, producer; b. Washington, Dec. 19, 1944; s. John William Menefee Jr. and Mary Claudia (Tudor) Upchurch. *John Menefee's ancestor, George Menefie (original spelling) arrived in 1623 on the ship "Samuel" and brought the first peach tree to Jamestown Colony. His great, great, grandparents Edwin and Emily (Farish) Holt founded Alamance Plaid Mill in 1837. Today, their home is the Alamance County Museum, but was once known as Locust Grove. He introduced dyed plaids and founded the Southern Textile industry in North Carolina.* Student, U. Va., 1964-66, Columbia Sch. for Motion Pictures and TV, L.A., 1992. Tour guide Universal Studios, Universal City, Calif., 1970-75, studio transp. driver, 1976; camera asst., trainee Dino d'Laurentis Orgn., Beverly Hills, 1976, Panavision (formerly Gen. Camera), N.Y.C., 1978; camera person Paramount Pictures, L.A., 1980, 20th Century Fox Film Corp., L.A., 1987, 96, Sony Pictures Corp., Culver City, Calif., 1992, 97, Paramount Pictures, L.A., 2000. Mem. film and TV action com. Bring Hollywood Home, L.A., 1999—; contbr., supporter World Wildlife Fund, Washington, Lambda Legal Def. Fund, N.Y.C., Cato Inst., Washington. Mem. Internat. Cinematographers Guild (cert.), Jamestown Soc. Episcopalian. Avocations: genealogy, Vedic astrology, tennis, acting. Home: The Talmadge 3278 Wilshire Blvd Apt 803 Los Angeles CA 90010. E-mail: mflea3@aol.com.

MENEFEE, LINNEA-NORMA, antique dealer; b. Mpls., Mar. 5, 1924; d. Arthur Wesley and Elsie Ida Buck; m. Edward Curial Menefee, June 15, 1946 (dec. 1980); children: Edward, Joan, Barbara, Judith. Student, U. Minn., Mpls., U. Minn., Duluth, McPhail Sch. Music, Mpls. Founder Albert Lea (Minn.) Art Ctr., 1959; county chairwoman Goldwater for Pres., Albert Lea. Mem. AAUW, Am. Med. Assn. Alliance, Nat. Fedn. Rep. Women, Nat. Women of the Arts, Nat. Am. Legion Aux., Nat. VFW Aux., Nat. Assn. Family and Cmty. Edn., Order of Ea. Star, Gillette Blue Blades, Kiwanis Internat., Zeta Phi Eta, Omega Upsilon, Zeta Beta Chi. Episcopalian. Avocations: writing, reading, painting, walking.

MENEFEE, SAMUEL PYEATT, lawyer, anthropologist; b. Denver, June 8, 1950; s. George Hardiman and Martha Elizabeth (Pyeatt) M. BA in Anthropology and Scholar of Ho. summa cum laude, Yale U., 1972; diploma in Social Anthropology, Oxford (Eng.) U., 1973, BLitt, 1975; JD, Harvard U., 1981; LLM in Oceans, U. Va., 1982, SJD, 1993; MPhil in Internat. Rels., U. Cambridge, Eng., 1995. Bar: Ga. 1981, U.S. Ct. Appeals (11th cir.) 1982, Va.

1983, La. 1983, U.S. Ct. Mil. Appeals 1983, U.S. Ct. Internat. Trade 1983, U.S. Ct. Claims 1983, U.S. Ct. Appeals (10th cir.) 1983, U.S. Ct. Appeals (fed., 1st, 3d, 4th, 5th, 6th, 7th, 8th and 9th cirs.) 1984, D.C. 1985, Nebr. 1985, Fla. 1985, U.S. Supreme Ct. 1985, U.S. Ct. Appeals (D.C. cir.) 1986, Maine 1986, Pa. 1986. Assoc. Phelps, Dunbar, Marks, Claverie & Sims, New Orleans, 1983-85; of counsel Barham & Churchill PC, 1985-88; sr. assoc. Ctr. for Nat. Security Law U. Va. Sch. Law, 1985—, fellow Ctr. for Oceans Law and Policy, 1982-83, sr. fellow, 1985-89, Maury fellow, 1989—, adv. bd., 1997—. Vis. lectr. U. Cape Town, 1987; vis. asst. prof. U. Mo.-Kansas City, 1990; law clk. Hon. Pasco M. Bowman, U.S. Ct. Appeals (8th cir.), 1994-95; vis. prof. Regent U., 1996-97, scholar-at-large, 1997—, prof., 1998—; adv. The Am. Maritime Forum/The Mariners' Mus., 1997-98; lectr. various nat. and internat. orgns.; mem. ICC Consultative Task Force on Comml. Crime, 1996—. Author: Wives for Sale: An Ethnographic Study of British Popular Divorce, 1981, Contemporary Piracy and International Law, 1995, Trends in Maritime Violence, 1996; co-editor: Materials on Ocean Law, 1982; contbr. numerous articles to profl. jours. Recipient Katharine Briggs prize Folklore Soc., 1992; Bates traveling fellow Yale U., 1971, Rhodes scholar, 1972; Cosmos fellow Sch. Scottish Studies U. Edinburgh, 1991-92, IMB fellow, ICC Internat. Maritime Bur., 1991—, Piracy Reporting Ctr. fellow, Kuala Lampur, 1993—, Huntington fellow The Mariners Mus., 1997. Fellow Royal Anthrop. Inst., Am. Anthrop. Assn., Royal Asiatic Soc., Royal Soc. Antiquaries of Ireland, Soc. Antiquaries (Scotland), Royal Geog. Soc., Soc. Antiquaries; mem. ABA (vice-chmn. marine resources com. 1987-90, chmn. law of the sea com. subcom. naval warfare, maritime terrorism and piracy 1989—, mem. law of the sea com. steering com. 1996—, mem. working group on terrorism), Southeastern Admiralty Law Inst. (com. mem.), Maritime Law Assn. (proctor, com. mem., chmn. subcom. law of the sea 1988-91, vice chmn. com. internat. law of the sea 1991— , chair working group piracy 1992—, UNESCO study group, 1998—), Marine Tech. Soc. (co-chmn. marine security com. 1991—), Selden Soc., Am. Soc. Internat. Law, Internat. Law Assn. (com. mem., rapporteur Am. br. com. EEZ 1988-90, rapporteur Am. br. com. Maritime Neutrality 1992, observer UN conv. on Law of the Sea meeting of States Parties 1996, chmn. Am. br. com. on Law of the Sea 1996—), rapporteur joint internat. working group on uniformity of the law of piracy 1998—, (Com. Maritime Internat.), Am. Soc. Indsl. Security (com. mem.), U.S. Naval Inst., USN League, Folklore Soc., Royal Celtic Soc., Internat. Studies Assn., Royal Scottish Geog. Soc., Royal African Soc., Egypt Exploration Soc., Arctic Inst. N.Am., Internat. Studies Assn., Am. Hist. Soc., Internat. Assn. Rsch. on Peasant Diaries (nat. editor 1996—), Nat. Eagle Scout Assn., Raven Soc., Jefferson Soc., Fence Club, Mory's Assn., Elizabethan Club, Yale Polit. Union, Leander Club, Cambridge Union, United Oxford and Cambridge Univ. Club, Yale Club (N.Y.C.), Paul Morphy Chess Club, Pendennis Club, Round Table Club (New Orleans), Phi Beta Kappa, Omicron Delta Kappa. Republican. Episcopalian. Avocations: anthropology, archaeology, social history, crew, hill walking. Office: U Va Ctr Nat Sec Law 580 Massie Rd Charlottesville VA 22903-1738

MENEFEE-GREENE, LAURA S. psychiatric nurse; b. Owensboro, Ky., June 4, 1953; d. Robert Gordon and Maxine Menefee. BSN, Berea Coll., 1976; MSN, U. Tenn., 1986. RN, Ky., Tenn.; Cert. Case Mgr. (CCM). Clinic nurse Mountain Maternal Health League, Berea, Ky., 1976-79; instr. Job Corps, Knoxville, Tenn., 1980-84; staff nurse Upjohn Health Care, 1980-86; leader, supr. hospice team St. Mary's Med. Ctr., 1990-92, gero-psychiat. clin. case mgr., 1992-93, clin. case mgr., 1993-94, adult psychiat. nurse, 1994-95, psychiat. case mgr., 1995—2002, HSL team leader behavioral svcs., 2002—. Cons. in field. Author: Hospice: History, Philosophy and Care Service, 1990; creator Life Cards. Instr., vol. ARC, Knoxville, 1980-92. Mem. NAFE, APHA, CCM, ACCM, Nat. Hospice Assn., Hospice Nurses Assn., Berea Coll. Alumni Country Dancers (pres. 1984-91), Sigma Theta Tau. Office: St Mary's Med Ctr Oak Hill Ave Knoxville TN 37917

MENENDEZ, ADOLFO, engineering company executive; m. Silvia Perez; children: José Adolfo, Mercedes Silvia. BSME, Manhattan Coll.; postgrad., Golden Gate U. Registered profl. engr. D.C., Va., Miss. Project mgr. internat. ops. Bechtel Power Corp.; pres., COO K & M Engring. & Cons, Corp., Washington, 1999; chmn., CEO Global Mgmt. Ptnrs., LLC, 1999—. Bd. dirs. KMR Power Corp.; cons. Wold Bank, Internat. Fin. Corp., European Bank for Reconstruction and Devel., USAID, others. Mem. Georgetown Club, U. Club, Lakewood Country Club. Office: Global Mgmt Ptnrs LLC Ste 535 1700 Rockville Pike Rockville MD 20852 Fax: 301-881-6997. E-mail: GMPLLC@worldnet.att.net.

MENENDEZ, MARCELINO EULOGIO (MARC MENENDEZ), marketing professional; b. Mexico City, Mex., June 1974; s. Marcelino and Sharon M. Menendez; m. Susan P. Gildo. BA, Columbia U., N.Y.C., 1996. Analyst Bayerish Vereinsbank, N.Y.C., 1993—95; mng. analyst Forest Labs., 1996—97, assoc. product mgr., 1997—98; dir. of pharms. SMG Mktg. Group, Inc., 1998—99; nat. sales dir. health svcs. SMG Mktg. Group, Inc./Quintiles Transnat. Corp, Chgo., 1999—2001; v.p. sales and mktg. Affiliated Network Services, LLC, 2001—. Dir. Roshamar, Inc., Mexico City, 1999—; prin. Guilmen Cons., Naperville, Ill., 1999—. Vol. Rep. Party, Chgo., 1997—2001. Recipient Fgn. Langs. award, Bank of Am., 1992. Mem.: Acad. of Managed Care Pharmacy, Nat. Assn. of Dental Plans, Nat. Dental EDI Coun. Orgn., Columbia U. Alumni Assn., Am. Mgmt. Assn., Med. Mktg. Assn. Avocations: exercise, technology/computers, culinary arts. Home: 3703 Mistflower Ln Naperville IL 60564 Office: Affiliated Network Svcs LLC 211 W Wacker Dr Ste 1100 Chicago IL 60606 Home Fax: 208-246-6762; Office Fax: 312-236-6623. Personal E-mail: MEM@Elative.com.

MENENDEZ, ROBERT, congressman, lawyer; b. N.Y.C., Jan. 1, 1954; s. Mario and Evangelina (Lopez) M.; m. Jane Jacobsen, June 5; children: Alicia, Robert. BA, St. Peter's Coll., 1976; JD, Rutgers U., 1979. Bar: N.J. 1980. Pvt. practice, Union City, N.J., 1980-92; mem. U.S. Congress from 13th N.J. dist., 1993—; mem. transp & infrastructure com., internat. rels. com; Dem. whip at large. Mem. Congl. Arts Caucus; mem. western hemisphere ranking Dem., Africa subcom; surface transp., water resources & environment coms.; chief dep. whip 105th Congress. Mayor of Union City, 1986-92; sec. Union City Bd. Edn., 1978-82, trustee, 1974-78; pres. Alliance civic Orgn., 1982-92; mem. Gov.'s Hispanic Adv. Com., Trenton, N.J., 1984—; mem. Gov.'s Ethnic Adv. Com., Washignton, 1985—. Recipient Cmty. Svc. award Gran Logia del Norte, 1981, Outstanding Svc. award Hispanic Law Enforcement, 1981, Outstanding Cmty. Svc. Revista Actualidades, 1982, Disting. Citizen award U. Medicine and Dentistry N.J., 1994, Man of Yr. award Kiwanis, 1994. Mem. N.J. Hispanic Elected and Apptd Ofcls. (chair), Hoboken Elks Club. Democrat. Roman Catholic. Avocations: chess, racquetball. Office: Ho of Reps 2238 RayburnHo Office Bldg Washington DC 20515 also: 911 Bergen Ave Jersey City NJ 07306-4301*

MENES, PAULINE H. state legislator; b. N.Y.C., July 16, 1924; d. Arthur B. and Hannah H. Herskowitz; m. Melvin Menes, Sept. 1, 1946; children: Sandra Jill Menes Ashe, Robin Joy Menes Elvord, Bambi Lynn Menes Gavin. BA in Bus. Econs. and Geography, Hunter Coll., N.Y.C., 1945. Economist Quartermaster Gen. Office, Washington, 1945-47; geographer Army Map Svc., 1949-50; chief clk. Prince George's County Election Bd., Upper Marlboro, Md., 1963; substitute tchr. Prince George's County H.S., 1965-66; mem. Md. Ho. of Dels., Annapolis, 1966—, mem. judiciary com., 1979—, parliamentarian, 1995—. Com. on rules and exec. nominations, Md. Ho. of Dels., Annapolis, 1979-94, 95—, chmn. spl. com. on drug and alcohol abuse, 1986—, chmn. Prince George's County del., 1993-95. Mem. Md. Arts Coun., Balt., 1968-95, Md. Commn. on Aging, Balt., 1975-95; bd. dirs. Prisoner's Aid Assn., Balt., 1971-94. Recipient Internat. Task Force award Women's Yr., 1977, Ann London Scott Meml. Excellence award NOW, 1976; named to Hall of Fame Hunter Coll. Alumni Assn., 1986, Women's Hall of Fame Prince George County, 1989. Mem. NOW, Nat. Conf. State Legislators (com. on drugs and alcohol 1987), Nat. Order Women Legislators (pres. 1979-80), Women's Polit. Caucus, Bus. and Profl. Women. Avocations: theater, music, dance show attending, stamp collector. Home: 3517 Marlbrough Way College Park MD 20740-3925 Office: Md Ho of Reps Rm 210 Lowe State Office Bldg Annapolis MD 21401

MENG, WEN JIN JIN, materials scientist, researcher; b. Beijing, China, June 24, 1962; s. Xian Chao Meng, Qi Hui Wen; m. Yuen Wun Lau; children: Andrew. BS, Calif. Inst. Tech., 1982, PhD, 1988. Postdoctoral rsch. fellow Argonne (Ill.) Nat. Lab., 1988-89; sr. rsch. scientist GM Rsch. Labs., Warren, Mich., 1989-92, staff rsch. scientist, 1992-98; scientist Delphi Automotive Systems R & D, 1999—. Author articles in Physical Review Letters, articles in Applied Physics Letters, articles in Physical Review, articles in Journal of Applied Physics, articles in Thin Solid Films, articles in Surface&Coatings Technology. Mem. Material Rsch. Soc. (grad. rsch. award 1987), Sigma Xi., Tau Beta Pi. Achievements include first rsch. findings of kinetic limitations on non-equilibrium crystal to glass transformations, structure and properties of crystals and superlattices formed by epitaxial growth, plasma assisted vapor phase synthesis and characterization of surface coatings.

MENG, XIANMIN, dermatologist, researcher; b. Benxi, Liaoning, China, Jan. 31, 1967; s. Zhaojun Meng and Sufan Wang; m. Yuhong Xiao; 1 child, Qingyu. MD, Dalian (China) Med. U., 1989, M Medicine, 1994; PhD in Med. Sci., Hirosaki (Japan) U., 1999. Physician dept. dermatology Dailan Med. U., 1989-91; rsch. fellow dept. dermatology Hirosaki U. Sch. Medicine, 1994-95; postdoctoral fellow dept. dermatology Thomas Jefferson U., Phila., 1999—. Contbr. numerous articles to profl. jours. Mem. Am. Soc. Gene Therapy, Soc. for Investigative Dermatology (diploma of dermatol. sci. 1998). Avocations: sports, auto camps, music, movies. Office: Thomas Jefferson U Dept Dermatology 233 S 10th St Rm 450 Philadelphia PA 19107-5541 Home: Apt D419 525 Newton Lake Dr Oaklyn NJ 08107 E-mail: mengderm@yahoo.com.

MENG, XIAOGUANG, engineering educator; s. XianXin Meng and Fuyun Wang; m. Wei Wang, 1985; children: Shuang. PhD, Syracuse U., 1992. Postdoctoral rsch. assoc. Stevens Inst. Tech., Hoboken, NJ, rsch. assoc. prof., 1997—98, assoc. prof., 1999—. Inventor, patentee in field. Finalist awards competition, The Tech Mus. of Innovation, 2001. Mem.: Am. Water Works Assn., Am. Chem. Soc. Office: Stevens Inst Tech Ctr for Environ Engring Hoboken NJ 08904 Office Fax: 201-216-8303. Business E-Mail: xmeng@stevens-tech.edu.

MENG, XIAO-LI, mathematician; b. Shanghai, China, Jan. 24, 1963; PhD, Harvard U., 1990. From asst. to assoc. to prof. stats. U. Chgo., Chicago, 1991—2001; prof. stats. Harvard U., Cambridge, Maine, 2001—. Assoc. editor: Annals of Stats., 1997—, assoc. editor: Jour. Am. Statis. Assn., 1996, assoc. editor: Biometrika, 2002—, assoc. editor: Statistica Sinica, 1992—97. Recipient 2001 COPSS award for outstanding statistician under age of 40, Com. of Pres. of Statis. Assn., 2001. Fellow: Royal Statis. Soc. (U.K.), Inst. Math. Stats. (program chair 1999—99); mem.: Internat. Soc. for Bayesian Analysis, Bernoulli Soc. for Math. Stats. and Probability, Internat. Chinese Statis. Assn. (life; bd. dirs. 1996—99), Biometric Soc. (regional adv. bd. 1995—97), Am. Statis. Assn. (program chair 2004 joint statis. meetings 2002—04). Office: Harvard U Dept Stats Sci Ctr Oxford St Cambridge MA 02138 Office Fax: 617-496-8057. Business E-Mail: meng@stat.harvard.edu.

MENGDEN, JOSEPH MICHAEL, retired investment banker; b. Houston, Sept. 28, 1924; s. Hippolyt Frederick and Amalia (Dittlinger) M.; m. Suzanne Miner, Sept. 30, 1950 (dec. July 1990); children: Anne Elise Mengden Giliberto, Amanda Mary, Michael Joseph, Charles Louis, Melissa Mary Mengden Bunker, Mary Miner Mengden Fitch; m. Dorothy Dugan, July 27, 1991. Ph.B., U. Notre Dame, 1949. V.p. Nat. Bank of Detroit, 1950-67; exec. v.p. First of Mich. Capital Corp., Detroit, 1967-90, sr. cons., 1990-95. Chmn. bd. dirs., CEO Saginaw (Mich.) Bay Broadcasting Corp. Served to 1st lt. USAAF, World War II. Decorated Air medal with 2 oak leaf clusters. Home: 321 Rivard Blvd Grosse Pointe MI 48230-1625 E-mail: men@comcast.net.

MENGEDOTH, DONALD ROY, commercial banker; b. Naperville, Ill., Aug. 10, 1944; s. Orville Gustav and Bernice Lydia (Fries) M.; m. Stacy K. Halverson; children: Paul Bernard, Daniel Lawrence, Mary Bernice. BS, Marquette U., 1968, MBA, 1973. Ops. officer 1st Bank, N.A.-Milw., 1968-69, asst. v.p., 1969-71, v.p., 1971-73, sr. v.p., 1973-79; v.p. 1st Bank System, Inc., Mpls., 1979-82, sr. v.p., 1983-87, pres., CEO, 1987—2000; chmn. Cmty. First Bankshares Inc., Fargo, ND, 1987—. Bd. dirs. Treasure Enterprises, Inc., Vail Banks Inc. Adv. bd. United Way Cass-Clay Campaign, Fargo, 1988-89; chmn. Cmty. 1st Polit. Action Com., Fargo, 1988-89; bd. dirs. Fargo Cath. Schs. Network Found., 1989-92; bd. dirs., vice chmn. Red River Zool. Soc., 1993-96; chmn. Diocesan God's Gift Appeals, Fargo, 1989. Mem. Am. Bankers Assn. (govt. rels. coun., pres. 2000-2001), Am. Mgmt. Assn., N.D. Bankers Assn., S.D. Bankers Assn., Greater N.D. Assn., Fargo Country Club. Avocations: tennis, golf, hunting, reading. Office: Cmty 1st Bankshares 520 Main Ave Fargo ND 58124-0001 E-mail: don_mengedoth@cfbx.com.

MENGEL, CHARLES EDMUND, physician, medical educator; b. Balt., Nov. 29, 1931; s. Charles LeRoy and Anna (Apgar) M.; m. Paula Padgett, June 5, 1978; children: Cheryl Lynn, Charles Edmund, Gregory John, Scott Alan, Carol Ann, Michael Daniel. AB in Chemistry, Lafayette Coll., 1953; MD, Johns Hopkins U., 1957. Intern Johns Hopkins Hosp., 1957-58; resident Duke Hosp., 1958-59, 61-62; clin. assoc. NIH, 1959-61; mem. faculty Duke U. Med. Sch., 1961-65; Doan prof., dir. hematology and oncology Ohio State U., 1965-69; prof. medicine U. Mo., Columbia, 1969-82, chmn. dept., 1969-81; pvt. practive gen. medicine Moberly, Mo., 1982-88; prof. medicine Kans. U. Med. Ctr., Kansas City, 1988-98; CEO MEC Enterprises, 1999—. Author textbook; contbr. articles to med. publs. With USPHS, 1959-61. Markle scholar acad. medicine, 1963 Mem. ACP, Am. Fedn. Clin. Rsch., Am. Soc. Hematology, Am. Soc. Clin. Investigation

MENGEL, CHRISTOPHER EMILE, lawyer, educator; b. Holyoke, Mass., Sept. 11, 1952; s. Emile Oscar and Rose Ann (O'Donnell) M.; m. Ellen Christine Creager, Dec. 6, 1991; children: Meredith Anne, Celia Claire; step-children: Cara Elizabeth Creager, Kristen Michele Creager. Student, U. Notre Dame, 1970-71; BA, Holy Cross Coll., 1974; JD, Detroit Coll. Law, 1979. Bar: Mich. 1979, U.S. Dist. Ct. (ea. dist.) Mich. 1989, U.S. Ct. Appeals (6th cir.) 1990. Tchr. Holyoke Pub. Schs., 1974-76; assoc. Fried & Sniokaitis P.C., Detroit, 1980-82; prof. Detroit Coll. Law, 1982-85; pvt. practice Detroit, 1982-91; mng. ptnr. Berkley, Mengel & Vining, PC, 1992—. Mem. coun. St. Ambrose Parish, Grosse Pointe Park, Mich., 1985-88, pres. 1986-87. Matthew J. Ryan scholar, 1970; recipient Disting. Brief award Thomas M. Cooley Law Rev., 1996. Mem. ABA, Mich. Bar Assn., Detroit Bar Assn. Democrat. Roman Catholic. Avocations: baseball, sailing, photography. Home: 1281 N Oxford Rd Grosse Pointe MI 48236-1857 Office: Berkley Mengel & Vining PC 3100 Penobscot Bldg Detroit MI 48226 E-mail: cmengel@flash.net.

MENGEL, DAVID BRUCE, agronomy and soil science educator; b. East Chicago, Ind., May 1, 1948; s. Bill M. and Thelma Lee (Miller) M.; m. Susan Kay Haverstock, Aug. 30, 1968; children: David, Erin. BS in Agricultural Edn., Purdue U., 1970, MS in Agronomy, 1972; PhD in Soil Sci., N.C. State U., 1975. Cert. profl. agronomist, soil scientist. Asst. prof. agronomy La. State U., Crowley, 1975-79, Purdue U., West Lafayette, Ind., 1979-82, assoc. prof., 1982-86, prof. agronomy, 1986-98; prof., head agronomy Kans. State U., Manhattan, Kans., 1998—. Mem. Am Soc. Agronomy, Soil Sci. Soc. Am., Internat. Soil Sci. Soc., Sigma Xi, Gamma Sigma Delta, Epsilon Sigma Phi, Delta Tau Delta. Avocations: fishing, woodworking. Office: Plant Sci Ctr Dept Agronomy Kans State U 2004 Throckmorton Manhattan KS 66506-5501 E-mail: dmengel@ksu.edu.

MENGELING, WILLIAM LLOYD, retired veterinarian, virologist; b. Elgin, Ill., Apr. 1, 1933; s. William Paul and Blanche Joyce (Wormwood) M.; m. Barbara Ann Ketchart, Aug. 23, 1958; children: Michelle, Michael. BS, Kans. State U., 1958, DVM, 1960; MS, Iowa State U., 1966, PhD, 1969. Diplomate M. Coll. Vet. Microbiologists (chmn. 1977-78, bd. dirs. 1975-77). Vet. clinician St. Francis Animal Hosp., Albuquerque, 1960-61; vet. med. officer Nat. Animal Disease Ctr., Ames, Iowa, 1961-69, rsch. leader, 1969—2001, U.S. Sr. Exec. Svc., 1991—; ret., 2001. Cons. numerous state, fed., pvt. U.S. and fgn. agys.; collaborative prof., mem. grad. faculty Iowa State U. Co-editor: Diseases of Swine, 5th, 6th, 7th, 8th editions; contbr. articles to jours., chpts. to books. With U.S. Army, 1953-55. Recipient cert. appreciation USDA, 1978, George Fleming award Brit. Vet. Jour., 1978, Disting. Svc. award USDA, 1984, Gov.'s medal sci. State of Iowa, 1985, Vet. Med. Rsch. award Am. Feed Industry Assn., 1989, Leadership Merit awards USDA, 1989, 90, 91, 93, Alumnus award Kans. State U. Coll. Vet. Medicine and Vet. Med. Alumni Assn., 1999, William P. Switzer award Iowa State U. Coll. Met. Medicine, 2000, Howard Dunne Meml. award, Am. Assn. Swine Vets., 2001; elected to Agrl. Rsch. Svc. Hall of Fame, 2001. Mem. AVMA (Vet. Med. Rsch. award 1989), U.S. Animal Health Assn., Conf. Rsch. Workers in Animal Disease (pres. 1987-88, coun. 1981-86), Kiwanis (pres. 1975-76). Methodist. Avocations: wilderness survival, canoeing, camping, fishing. Home: 4220 Phoenix St Ames IA 50014-3922 E-mail: bbmengeling@aol.com.

MENGLE, TOBI DARA, mechanical engineer, consultant; b. Pottsville, Pa., Dec. 17, 1960; s. Richard H. and Joyce Pauline (Shuey) M.; m. Barbara A. Brickey, 1992; children: Chase Tucker, Tanner Richard. BS, Pa. State U., 1982. Registered profl. engr., Pa. Assoc. engr. IBM Corp., East Fishkill, N.Y., 1982-84; devel. engr. AT&T Microelectronics, Reading, Pa., 1984-90; sr. mfg. engr. Lutron Electronics, Coopersburg, 1990-91; cons. AT&T Microelectronics, Reading, 1991-92, AT&T Bell Labs., Breinigsville, Pa., 1991-93, Associated Bio-Engrs. and Cons., 1993-95, Dana Spicer Systems Div., 1995-96; prin. engr., ptnr. Bio-Process Cons., 1996, pvt. practice, Birdsboro, Pa., 1997—. Mem. Union of Concerned Scientists, Cambridge, Mass., 1991. Named Lehigh Valley Young Engr. of Yr., 1993. Mem. ASME (sec. chmn. 1991-93), Internat. Soc. Pharm. Engring. Avocations: flying (instrument rated pilot), scuba diving, bicycling. Home and Office: 931 Lincoln Rd Birdsboro PA 19508-8831 E-mail: tobimengle@aol.com.

MENIHAN, CYDNEY AFRIAT, nurse midwife, medical sonographer; b. Newark, May 3, 1951; d. Donald S. and B. Patricia Afriat; m. Jack Menihan; stepchildren: Courtney, Christopher. BSN, U. Pitts., 1973; CNM, U. So. Calif., 1981; MSN, Calif. State U., L.A., 1986. Registered diagnostic med. sonographer. Staff nurse, perinatal rsch. assoc. Cedars-Sinai Med. Ctr., L.A., 1973-77; perinatal nurse specialist Corometrics Med. Systems, Inc., Newport Beach, Calif., 1977-79; perinatal cons. Perinatal Prodns., 1980-90, R.I., 1990—; nurse midwife L.A. County, U. So. Calif. Med. Ctr., Kaiser Permanente, 1982-83; pvt. practice Monterey, Calif., 1983-89; nurse midwife Women and Infants' Hosp., Providence, 1990—. Asst. clin. prof. U. R.I. Sch. Nursing; clin. tchg. assoc. Brown U. Sch. Medicine. Author: Electronic Fetal Monitoring: Concepts and Applications, 2001, Electronic Fetal Monitoring, 1989, Limted Sonography in Ob-Gyn. Triage, 1998; mem. editl. rev. bd. Jour. Perinatal/Neonatal Nursing and Jour. Obstetric, Gynecologic, and Neonatal Nursing, 1992-98; contbr. articles to profl. jours. Active Humane Soc. U.S. Mem. Assn. Women's Health, Obstetric and Neonatal Nursing, Soc. Diagnostic Med. Sonographers, Am. Inst. Ultrasound in Medicine, Am. Coll. Nurse Midwives. Jewish. Avocations: travel, swimming. Home: 240 Foddering Farm Rd Narragansett RI 02882-4306 Office: Women and Infants Hosp 101 Dudley St Providence RI 02905-2499

MENIL, VIOLETA CRUZ, mathematician, educator, consultant, researcher; d. Emilia Cruz Menil. BSE. maj. in Math., U. of San Carlos, Cebu, Philippines, 1961—65; MS in Applied Math & Stats., SUNY, Stony Brook, Long Island, New York, 1981—83; M. A. in Math. Edn., De la Salle U., Manila, Philippines, 1974—76; PhD(Mathematics & Stats.), NYU, New York City, 1983—88. Lectr. (math.) Baruch Coll. of the CUNY, New York, NY, 1983—88, instr. (stats.), 1988—89. Assoc. prof. De la Salle U., Manila, 1989—94; instr. Hostos CC of the CUNY, Bronx, NY, 1994—95; audit statistician NYC Comptroller's Office, New York City, NY, 1995—98; instr. Hostos CC of the CUNY, Bronx, NY, 1999—2000, asst. prof., NY, 2000—; rsch. dir. De la Salle U., Manila, 1990—93. Author: (multivariate behavioral research journal) Linear and Ordinal Data: INDSCAL vs. ALSCAL, 1993, (journal) Factor Analysis: An Analysis of Variable Interdependence, 1992, A Monte Carlo Evaluation of Two Multidimensional Methods for Fitting the Weighted Euclidean Distance Model: INDSCAL vs. ALSCAL, 1991, (participant) Manual on Statistical Sampling(Unpublished), 1998, (research paper) Statistics, 1991. Treas. Corner View Assn., Inc., Brooklyn, NY, 2000—01. Mem.: Asian Am. Higher Eduation Coun. (nyc 2001—02), Am. Statis. Assn. (va., alexandria 1989—2002). Home: 4407 4th Avenue Apt B4 Brooklyn NY 11220 Personal E-mail: menilv2@aol.com.

MENINGALL, EVELYN L. educational media specialist; b. Dothan, July 22, 1935; d. Earl and Luella Koonce; m. A. Richard Meningall, Jan. 17, 1958; children: Dawn, Tracy, Richard. BS in Edn., Wayne State U., 1975; MLS, Rutgers U., 1979. Cert. ednl. media specialist Dept. Edn. State N.J., elem. sch. dept. Dept. Edn. State N.J., profl. librs. cert. Dept. Edn. State N.J. Tchr. Detroit Bd. Edn., 1975—76; libr. East Brunswick (N.J.) Pub. Libr., 1978—80; ednl. media specialist Piscataway (N.J.) Bd. Edn., 1980—98. Author poetry. Active New Detroit, Inc., Delta Sigma Theta Sorority Ctrl. Jersey; vol. tutor/reader pub. schs.; vol. to holisitic score English tests Plainfield (N.J.) H.S.; recording sec. Scholarship Fund of St. Paul AME Ch. Mem.: ALA, Ednl. Media Assn., Nat. Sorority Phi Delta Kappa, Inc. (life; basileus 1987—89, exec. advisor 1989—91). Ame Church. Avocations: writing poetry, reading, fishing. Home: 23 Vauxhall Rd East Brunswick NJ 08816-1719

MENINO, THOMAS M. mayor; b. Dec. 27, 1942; m. Angela Faletra; children: Susan, Thomas Michael, Jr. Degree in Community Planning, U. Mass., 1988; cert. in State and Local Govt. Program, Harvard U. Mem. City Coun., Boston, 1985—, pres., 1993; mayor City of Boston, 1993—. Sr. rsch. asst. Joint Com. Urban Affairs, 1978-83. Contbr. articles to historic preservation jours. Regional chmn. Nat. Trust Historic Preservation; bd. dirs. Nat. League Cities, 1985—, mem. various coms. Office: Office of Mayor 1 City Hall Plz Fl 5 Boston MA 02201-1001*

MENIT, DEBORAH LEE, interior designer, appraiser, educator, journalist, modern dancer; b. Bklyn. d. Gustave and Edna (Schneider) M. BA cum laude, Adelphi U., 1954; MA, NYU, 1956. cert. interior designer, antique appraiser; adult edn. instr., N.Y.C. Tchr. Erasmus Hall High Sch., N.Y.C., 1956-60; interior designer Deborah Menit, Interiors, 1962—; instr. adult edn. Kingsborough Coll., Bklyn., 1966-76. Lectr. on antiques N.Y.C. Adult Ctrs., 1974—98, Craft Students League, N.Y.C., 1975—80; cons. in field, 1978—. Dancer with New Dance Alliance, 1999, NYC, Twyla Tharps Hundreds, 1999, Hunter Coll. Dance Dept. Benefit, 1999, Merle Lister's Urban Entanglements, 2000; contbr. dance articles to profl. pubs. Johnson Girl, mem. pub. com. Young Citizens for Johnson, 1964; past pres. 15th St. Tenants' Assn., N.Y.C.; hon. usher svcs. for students Hebrew Union Coll., 1981—; alt. del. Dem. Conv., 1964; mem. pub. com. Abe Beame Campaign for Mayor, N.Y.C., 1966. Recipient nomination for best writer Telent in Motion mag., 1999. Mem. (past) Mensa City Womens Club, Artists' Equity; mem. Victorian Soc. of Am., Metropolitan Chpt. Art Deco Soc. of NY. Jewish. Avocations: art history, antiquing, writing poetry, traveling, swimming.

MENIUS, ESPIE FLYNN, JR. electrical engineer; b. New Bern, N.C., Mar. 5, 1923; s. Espie Flynn and Sudie Grey (Lyerly) M.; adopted children: James Benfield, Ruben Hughes, James Sechler, Steve Walden. *In addition to adopting four older children, Flynn Menius has been a foster father to fifteen other children who lived in his home from several months to several years. He is currently revising and updating his book "Adoption of Older Children."* BEE, N.C. State U., 1947; MBA, U. S.C., 1973. Registered profl. engr., N.C., S.C., Tenn., Ga., Fla. With Carolina Power & Light Co., 1947-63, asst. to dist. mgr. N.C., 1947-50, Sumter, S.C., 1947-50; elec. engr. Asheville, Southern Pines, Dunn, N.C., 1950-52; dist. engr. Hartsville, S.C., 1952-63; sr. elec. engr. Sonoco Products Co., 1963-74; engring. group leader, 1974-89; sr. profl. engr., 1989-91; profl. cons., elec. engr., 1991—. Instr. Florence-Darlington Tech. Ednl. Ctr. *During World War II, 1st Lt. Espie Flynn Menius Jr. served as Adjutant of the 3160th Signal Service Battalion, the largest separate Battalion in the European Theater of Operation. This Battalion, attached to General Eisenhower's Headquarters Command, had small detachments all over Europe and was responsible for long distance telephone communications. This unit had the responsibility of rehabilitating and converting Allied military use, the French PTT, the Belgium RTT and the German Reichpost telephone systems. The 3160th received the distinguished unit award and Lt. Menius received combat medals for participation in the Rhineland and central Europe campaigns.* Author: Adoption of Older Children; contbr. articles to profl. jours. Active Hartsville Vol. Fire Dept., 1958-94; Fire dept. and Law Enforcement Chaplain 1985—; Eagle Scout Boy Scouts Am., 1938, scout troop leader New Bern, 1940-41, Raleigh, 1941-47, Henderson, 1948-49, Sumter, 1949-50, Asheville, N.C., 1950, Southern Pines, N.C., 1951-52, Hartsville, 1952-64; bd. mgrs. Nazareth Children's Home, Rockville, N.C., 1980—; chmn. bd. examiners City of Hartsville, 1980-90; advocate Thornwell Children's Home, Clinton, S.C., 1990—; bd. dirs. Darlington (S.C.) County Youth Home, 1992—; active Hartsville Leadership Coun., 1993—; deacon, elder, trustee, tchr. men's Bible class First Presbyn. Ch., Hartsville. Served with AUS,

1943-46. Recipient Citzenship award S.C. State Firemen's Assn., 1993; named Hartsville Citizen of Yr., Rotary, 1960; named to S.C. Fire Fighters Hall of Fame, 1995. Mem. IEEE, AAAS, VFW, Nat. Assn. Engrs., Am. Legion, Knight of St. Patrick, Scabbard and Blade, Eta Kappa Nu, Pine Burr, Phi Eta Sigma, Theta Tau, Beta Gamma Sigma. Presbyterian. Home and Office: 423 W Richardson Cir Hartsville SC 29550-5437

MENK, CARL WILLIAM, executive search company executive; b. Newark, Oct. 19, 1921; s. Carl William and Catherine Regina (Murray) M.; m. Elizabeth Cullum, May 31, 1947; children: Carl, Elizabeth (dec.), Mary, Paul. BSBA, Seton Hall U., 1943; MA, Columbia U., 1950. Sr. v.p. P. Ballantine & Sons, Newark, 1946-69; pres. Boyden Assocs., Inc., N.Y.C., 1969-84; chmn. Canny, Bowen, Inc., 1984-98, chmn. emeritus, 1998—. 2d Lt., pilot USAAF, 1943-46. Mem. Union League N.Y., Spring Lake Golf Club, Bent Pine Golf Club, John's Island Club, Internat. Exec. Svc. Corps, Svc. Corps Ret. Execs. Assn. Republican. Roman Catholic. Home: 950 Beach Rd Apt 193 Johns Island Vero Beach FL 32963

MENKE, ALLEN CARL, industrial corporation executive; b. Huntingburg, Ind., Feb. 16, 1922; s. William Ernest and Clara (Moenkhaus) M.; m. Virginia Lee MacDonald, Apr. 14, 1944; children: Janet, William, Sarah. BS in Mech. Engring, Purdue U., 1943, MS, 1948. Instr. Purdue U., 1946-48; with Trane Co., 1948-68, v.p. sales, 1963-64, exec. v.p. sales, mfg. and engring., 1964-68; v.p. Borg-Warner Corp., Chgo., 1969-76; chmn., pres., CEO Artesian Industries, Northbrook, 1976-88. Bd. dirs. Trane Co., SPS Techs., Hoover Co., Consolidated Papers Corp., York Corp., Am. Air Filter. Pres. Met. Housing Devel. Corp.; founder, pres. Winnetka Interch. Coun.; bd. dirs., past chmn. Presbyn. Home; past chmn. dean's adv. coun. Krannert Sch. Mgmt. Purdue U.; bd. dirs. McCormick Sem., U. Chgo.; trustee Kenilworth Union Ch. Served to 1st lt. AUS, 1944-46. Named Disting. Alumnus, Purdue U., 1965, Outstanding Engr. Grad., 1991, mem. Purdue Hall of Fame, Ind. Basketball Hall of Fame, 1999. Mem. Sigma Chi (Significant Order Constantine awards). Presbyterian (elder). Lodge: Mason. Home: 2 Arbor Ln #208 Evanston IL 60201

MENKE, CATHERINE CHRISTINE HUDSON, critical care, oncological nurse, cardiology information specialist; b. Indpls., Sept. 29, 1961; d. Charles Raymond and Nancy Jane (Sweetman) H. BSN, Ind. U., Indpls., 1988, postgrad. Microbiologist asst. Ind. Bd. Health, Indpls., 1980; med. sec. immunohematology, 1986-87; staff and charge nurse bone marrow transplant unit Ind. U. Hosp. and Med. Ctr., 1988-93; chmn. unit staff coun., pain monitor, mem. specialized practice group for mgmt. adult pain Ind. U. Hosp. and Med. ctr. Chmn. orientation com., bone marrow transplant rsch. nurse, Ind. U. Hosp. and Med. Ctr., Indpls., 1993-98; cardiology clin. info. specialist; mem. interventional Q.I. ICD-9 coding and case mgmt. Ind. Heart Inst., 1998—. Mem. AACN.

MENKE, WILLIAM CHARLES, lawyer; b. Cin., Aug. 30, 1939; s. William Garhardt and Margaret Philomena (Mercurio) M.; m. Mary Lou Lapan, Jan. 7, 1967; children: William Leo II, Lorelei Louise. BS, U. Detroit, 1961; MBA, Ind. No. U., 1972; JD, U. Detroit, 1976. Bar: Ohio 1977, U.S. Ct. Appeals (6th cir.) 1977; Masters Lic., USCG. Sr. engr. GE Co., Cin., 1964-67; v.p., gen. mgr. Preventicare Systems, Inc., Dearborn, Mich., 1967-71; dir. Comshare, Inc., Ann Arbor, 1971-76; CEO William C. Menke & Assocs., Inc., New Richmond, Ohio, 1976—. Chmn. Strategic Eight Cons. Group, 1996—, Luerum, Inc.; adj. prof. U. Cin., 1994—; bd. dirs. New Richmond Nat. Bank, Geocel Corp., Lucrum, Inc.; city atty. City of New Richmond, 1979-81; monthly columnist Cin. Bus. Record, 1994—. Lt. (j.g.) USN, 1961-64. Fellow Lawyers in Mensa; mem. ABA, Assn. Trial Lawyers Am., Ohio State Bar, Pres.'s Forum (chmn.), Mensa, KC. Republican. Roman Catholic. Office: 1612 S Fountainhead Rd Fort Myers FL 33919-6809 E-mail: wcmenke@aol.com.

MENKEL-MEADOW, CARRIE JOAN, law educator; b. N.Y.C., Dec. 24, 1949; d. Gary G. and Margot (Sinn) Menkel; m. Robert Gary Meadow, Aug. 22, 1971. AB magna cum laude, Columbia U., 1971; JD cum laude, U. Pa., 1974; LLD (hon.), Quinnipiac Coll. Law, 1995. Bar: Pa. 1974, U.S. Ct. Appeals (3d cir.) 1975, Calif. 1979, D.C., 1997. Dir. legal writing U. Pa. Law Sch., Phila., 1974-75, clin. supt., lectr., 1976-79; staff atty. Cmty. Legal Svcs., Phila., 1975-77; prof. UCLA, 1979—, prof. law, 1979-99, Georgetown Law Ctr., Washington, 1996—; holder Phyllis Beck chair Temple U. Law Sch., Phila., 1999. Vis. prof. law Harvard Law Sch., 2001; panel mem. NAS, Washington, 1986—87, NSF, Washington, 1987—90; cons. ABA, Chgo., 1979—84; dir. UCLA Ctr. for Conflict Resolution, 1994—99, Georgetown-Hewlett Program on Conflict Resolution and Problem Solving , 2001—. Author: Mediation: Theory, Practice and Policy; contbr. articles to profl. jours. Chairperson Ctr. for Study of Women, UCLA; bd. dirs. Western Ctr. on Law and Poverty, L.A., 1980-86; chair CPR Commn. on Ethics and ADR. Recipient William Rutter Found. for Tchg. award, 1992, 1st prize for Acad. Scholarship on Alternative Dispute Resolution Ctr. for Pub. Resources, 1983, 91, 98. Mem. Soc. Am. Law Tchrs. (trustee), Assn. Am. Law Schs. (alt. dispute resolution sect., law and social sci. sect., women in law sect., accreditation com. 1987-90), Ctr. for Law and Human Values (bd. dirs.), Law and Soc. Assn. (trustee), Am. Bar Found. (bd. dirs., sec., exec. com. 1994—), Am. Law Inst., Acad. Civil Trial Mediators, Phi Beta Kappa. Democrat. Office: Georgetown Law Ctr 600 New Jersey Ave NW Washington DC 20001-2075 E-mail: meadow@law.georgetown.edu.

MENKEN, JANE AVA, demographer, educator; b. Phila., Nov. 29, 1939; d. Isaac Nathan and Rose Ida (Sarvetnick) Golubitsky; m. Matthew Menken, 1960 (div. 1985); children: Kenneth Lloyd, Kathryn Lee; m. Richard Jessor, Nov. 13, 1992. AB, U. Pa., 1960; MS, Harvard U., 1962; PhD, Princeton U., 1975. Asst. in biostats. Harvard U. Sch. Pub. Health, Boston, 1962-64; math. statistician NIMH, Bethesda, Md., 1964-66; research assoc. dept. biostats., Columbia U., N.Y.C., 1966-69; mem. research staff Office of Population Research Princeton U., N.J., 1969-71, 75-87, asst. dir., 1978-86, assoc. dir., 1986-87, prof. sociology, 1980-82, prof. sociology and pub. affairs, 1982-87; prof. sociology and demography U. Pa., Phila., 1987-97, UPS Found. prof. social scis., 1987-97, dir. Population Studies Ctr., 1989-95; prof. sociology U. Colo., Boulder, 1997—, fac. assoc. Population Program, Inst. Behavioral Sci., 1997. Mem. social scis. and population study sect., NIH, Bethesda, Md., 1978-82, chmn., 1980-82, population adv. com. Rockefeller Found., N.Y.C., 1981-93, com. on population and demography, NAS, Washington, 1978-83, com. on population, 1983-85, com. nat. stats., 1983-89, com. on AIDS research, 1987-94, co-chair panel data and rsch. priorities for arresting AIDS in sub-Saharan Africa, 1994—, Commn. on Behavioral and Social Scis. and Edn., 1991—, sci. adv. com., Demographic and Health Surveys, Columbia, Md., 1985-90, Nat. Adv. Child Health and Human Devel. Council, 1988-91; cons. Internat. Centre for Diarrhoeal Disease Research, Bangladesh, Dhaka, 1984—. Author: (with Mindel C. Sheps) Mathematical Models of Conception and Birth, 1973; editor: (with Henri Leridon) Natural Fertility, 1979, (with Frank Furstenberg, Jr. and Richard Lincoln) Teenage Sexuality, Pregnancy and Childbearing, 1981, World Population and U.S. Policy: The Choices Ahead, 1986; contbr. articles to profl. jours. Bd. dirs. Alan Guttmacher Inst., N.Y.C., 1981-90, 93—. Nat. Merit scholar, 1957; John Simon Guggenheim Found. fellow, 1992-93, Ctr. for Advanced Study in Behavioral Scis. fellow, 1995-96. Fellow AAAS, Am. Statis. Assn.; mem. NAS, Am. Acad. Arts and Scis., Population Assn. Am. (Mindel Sheps award 1982, pres. 1985), Am. Pub. Health Assn. (Mortimer Spiegelman award 1975, program devel. bd. 1984-87), Am. Sociol. Assn., Soc. for Study of Social Biology, Internat. Union for Sci. Study of Population (coun. 1989—), Sociol. Research Assn. (exec. com. 1991—). Office: U Colo IBS-3 Campus Box 484 Boulder CO 80309-0484

MENKES, JOHN HANS, pediatric neurologist; b. Vienna, Austria, Dec. 20, 1928; came to U.S., 1940; s. Karl and Valerie (Tupler) M.; m. Miriam Trief, Apr. 14, 1957 (div. Feb. 1978); m. Joan Simon Feld, Sept. 28, 1980 (dec. Nov. 2000); children: Simon, Tamara, Rafael C. AB, U. So. Calif., 1947, MS, 1951; MD, Johns Hopkins U., 1952. Diplomate Am. Bd. Pediatrics, Am. Bd. Psychiatry and Neurology. Intern, jr. asst. resident Children's Med. Ctr., Boston, 1952-54; asst. resident pediatrics Bellevue Hosp., N.Y.C., 1956-57; resident neurology, trainee pediatric neurology Columbia-Presbyn. Med. Ctr., Neurological Inst. N.Y., 1957-60; asst. prof. pediatrics Johns Hopkins U., Balt., 1960-63, assoc. prof., 1963-66, asst. prof. neurology, 1964-66, chief pediatric neurology div., 1964-66; prof. pediatrics and neurology UCLA, 1966-74, chief pediatric neurology div., 1966-70, prof. psychiatry, 1970-74; chief Neurology-Neurochem. Lab. Brentwood (Calif.) VA Hosp., 1970-74; clin. prof. psychiatry, neurology and pediatrics UCLA, 1974-77, clin. prof. pediatrics and neurology, 1977-84, prof. pediatrics and neurology, 1985-89, prof. emeritus pediatrics and neurology, 1989—. Dir. pediatric neurology Cedars-Sinai Med. Ctr., 1997-99, dir. emeritus pediat. neurology, 1999—; mem. metabolism study sect. NIH, 1968-70, project com., 1969-70; mem. adv. com. Nat. Inst. Child Health and Human Devel., 1985-87; mem. Dept. Health Svcs., Calif., 1980-87; mem. vaccine safety commn. Nat. Inst. Medicine, 1995—; mem. Coun. Child Neurology Soc., Dysautonomia Found., med. adv. bd. Nat. Orgn. Rare Diseases, Nat. Wilson's Disease Found.; trustee Dystonia Med. Rsch. Found., Vancouver, Can., 1985—. Author: Textbook of Child Neurology, 6th edit., 2000; (play) The Last Inquisitor, 1985 (Drama-Logue Critics award 1985), The Salvation of Miguel Toruna, 1987; (screen play) Miguel, Open Ward, 1989, The Countess of Sligo, 1992, The White Darkness, 1996, Lady Macbeth Gets a Divorce, 2001; (novel) The Secret Diary of Alice in Wonderland, 1998, The Angry Puppet Syndrome, 1999, After the Tempest, 1999, The Waiting Game, 2000, A View of Fuji, 2000; contbr. numerous articles to profl. jours. Served with USAF, 1954-56. Mem. Am. Acad. Neurology, Am. Acad. Pediatrics, Am. Chem. Soc., Soc. for Pediatric Rsch., Sociedad Peruana de Neuro-Psiquiatria (hon.), Am. Neurochem. Soc., Am. Neurol. Assn., Am. Pediatric Soc., Child Neurology Soc. (Hower award 1980), Dramatist Guild, PEN. Jewish. Home: 1201 Park Way Beverly Hills CA 90210-3334 Office: 9320 Wilshire Blvd Beverly Hills CA 90212-3216 E-mail: jmenkes@ucla.edu.

MENKIN, EVA L. marriage and family therapist; b. Berlin, June 26, 1923; came to the U.S., 1934; d. Henry O. and Tamara G. Fuchs; m. Fred Landecker, Sept. 10, 1942 (div. 1972); children: Judy Hoffman, David, Anita, Peter; m. David B. Menkin, Feb. 17, 1974. BA in Psychology, Goddard Coll., 1971, MA in Marriage and Family Counseling, 1973. Lic. marriage and family therapist. Intern Beverly Manor Convalescent House, L.A., 1972, Winsor Manor Retirement Home, Glendale, Calif., 1972; intern, counselor So. Calif. Counseling Ctr., L.A., 1973-76; pvt. practice Westchester Ctr. for Counseling and Psychotherapy, 1975-76; pvt. practice psychotherapy Santa Barbara, Calif., 1976—. Coord. daytime programs for older adults Rutgers U., 1968-70; instr. UCLA Ext., 1974, Felicia Mahood Ctr., L.A., 1975, U. Calif., Santa Barbara, 1977-78; field faculty Goddard and Antioch Colls., 1976-81; cons., therapist Arthritis Found., Santa Barbara, 1976-80; cons. Sanctuary House, 1976-80, Santa Barbara City Coll., 1981, Casa Dorinda Residential Retirement Home, Santa Barbara, 1983-84. Co-authro: (with B. Weininger) Aging is a Lifelong Affair, 1978; contbr. articles to profl. jours. Mem. Am. Assn. Marriage and Family Therapy, Calif. Assn. Marriage and Family Therapists, Gerontol. Soc. Am. Home: 1011 Mission Ridge Rd Santa Barbara CA 93103-1618 E-mail: dmenkin@aol.com.

MENN, JULIUS JOEL, scientist; b. Danzig, Free City (now Poland), Feb. 20, 1929; came to the U.S., 1950, naturalized, 1959; s. David Gregory and Regina (Ajzenstadt) M.; m. Alma R. Zito, Aug. 31, 1952 (div. 1981); children: Leslie, David (dec.), Diana (dec.); m. Dianne R. Sagner, Apr. 17, 1992. BS, U. Calif., Berkeley, 1953, MS, 1954, PhD, 1958. Dir. biochem. and insecticide rsch. Stauffer Chem. Co., Mountain View, Calif., 1957-79; dir. agrichem. rsch. Zoecon Corp., Palo Alto, 1979-85; nat. program leader crop protection Agrl. Rsch. Svc., USDA, Beltsville, Md., 1985-88; assoc. dep. area dir. Beltsville Agrl. Rsch. Ctr., 1988-94; ret., 1994; sr. agrl. policy adviser USDA/FAS, 1999—. Internat. cons. crop protection and agr. biotechnology, 1994—; chmn. Gordon Rsch. Conf., 1989; adj. prof. environ. toxicology San Jose State U., Calif., 1979-84; adj. prof. entomology U. Md., College Park, 1986-95; vis. prof. Pa. State U., 1999-2002; mem. U.S./USSR Team on Environ. Pollution, 1974-85; tech. expert UNIDO, 1995—, The World Bank, 1998; vis. prof. Pa. State U., 1999—. Editor: Insect Juvenile Hormones, 1972, Insect Neuropeptides, 1991, 12 other tech. books; contbr. over 125 articles to profl. jours. Recipient Bussart Meml. award Ea. Br. Entomol. Soc. Am., 1990, Ciba-Geigy Recognition award Ea. Br. Entomol. Soc. Am., 1991, 92. Mem. Am. Chem. Soc. (fellow pesticide chem. divsn. 1973, chmn. 1976, councilor 1981-89, adv. bd. books dept. 1991-94, Agrochem. Divsn. Internat. award for rsch.in pesticide chem. 1979), Internat. Soc. Study Xenobiotics (councilor 1983-86). Achievements include pioneered pesticide metabolism studies and research on selective insect control agents including juvenile hormones and neuropeptides; patentee in field. Fax: (301) 854-0460. E-mail: jjmenn@erols.com.

MENN, LISE, linguistics educator; b. Phila., Dec. 28, 1941; d. David K. and Olga (Cohen) Waldman; m. Michael D. Menn, Dec. 8, 1962 (div. Mar. 1974); children: Stephen Philip, Daniel Joseph; m. William Oliver Bright, Nov. 28, 1986. BA, Swarthmore Coll., 1962; MA, Brandeis U., 1964, U. Ill., 1974, PhD, 1975. Rsch. asst. Boston U. Sch. Medicine, 1977-82, rsch. asst. prof. dept. neurology, 1982-86; assoc. prof. U. Colo., Boulder, 1986-94, prof., 1994—, chair dept. linguistics, 1991-95, 96-99. Mem. linguistics panel NSF, 1983-86; mem. comm. disorders rev. group NIH, 1992-95; adj. prof. Hunan U., 2001-2005. Co-author: Nonfluent Aphasia in a Multilingual World, 1995; co-editor: Exceptional Language Linguistics, 1982, Agrammatic Aphasia, 1990, Phonological Development, 1992, Methods for Study of Language Production, 2000; assoc. editor Aphasiology. Mem. Linguistic Soc. Am. (exec. com. 1994-97), Acad. Aphasia (sec. bd. govs. 1989-92, bd. govs. 2000—, mem. AAAS (sect. linguistics). Office: U Colo Linguistics Dept PO Box 295 Boulder CO 80309-0295 E-mail: lise.menn@colorado.edu.

MENNEMEYER, STEPHEN THOMAS, economist, public health educator; BA, St. John Fisher Coll., 1970; MA in Econs., SUNY, Buffalo, 1975, PhD in Econs., 1977. Asst. prof. Sch. Pharmacy SUNY, Buffalo, 1975-77; economist Health Sys. Agy. of Western N.Y., 1977-79; sr. economist Abt Assocs., Inc., Cambridge, Mass., 1979-89; assoc. prof. Sch. Pub. Health U. Ala., Birmingham, 1989—. Advisor U.S. Congress Office Tech. Assessment, Washington, 1994—; mem. adv. bd. on cost analysis U.S. Agy. for Health Care Policy and Rsch., Washington, 1993—. Contbr. articles to profl. publs. Grantee U.S. Health Care Financing Adminstrn., 1984-89, U.S. Ctrs. for Disease Control, 1993—. Mem. APHA, Internat. Health Econ. Assn., Inst. Medicine (mem. Medicare Lab. payment policy com. 2000), Am. Econ. Assn., So. Econ. Assn. Roman Catholic. Achievements include design of competitive bidding system for clinical laboratory tests. Office: U Ala at Birmingham Sch Pub Health Dept Health Care Orgn Birmingham AL 35294-0001

MENNIN, GERALD STANLEY, ophthalmologist; b. N.Y.C., Mar. 20, 1932; s. Daniel and Sadie (Krieger) M.; children: Danielle, Douglas. BA, NYU, 1954; MD, SUNY, N.Y.C. Intern Beth Israel Hosp., N.Y.C., 1958-59; resident Bronx Mcpl. Hosp. Ctr./Einstein Coll. Medicine, 1050-62; pvt. practice Yonkers; chief ophthalmology Yonkers Gen. Hosp., 1986—. Attending ophthalmologist Montefiore Hosp., Bronx, 1962—, Bronx Mcpl. Hosp., 1962—, St. John's Hosp., Yonkers, 1981—, Yonkers Gen. Hosp., 1962—, Manhattan Eye and Ear Hosp., N.Y.C., 1990—. Fellow ACS, Am. Acad. Ophthalmologists, Nat. Arts Club. Avocation: art. Office: 45 Ludlow St Yonkers NY 10705-1947 also: 710 Park Ave New York NY 10021-4944

MENNINGER, ROSEMARY JEANETTA, art educator, writer; b. N.Y.C., Feb. 2, 1948; d. Karl Augustus and Jeanetta (Lyle) M. BA, Washburn U., 1983, BFA, 1984. Cert. tchr., Kans. Rsch. specialist, grant writer Navajo Tribe Navajo Community Coll., Many Farms, Ariz., 1969, 71; adminstrv. asst., counselor San Francisco Drug Treatment Program, 1972-73; exec. dir. Inst. Applied Ecology, San Francisco, 1973-80; coord. Calif. Community Gardening program Gov.'s Office State of Calif., Sacramento, 1976-80; editor Whole Earth Catalogs and CoEvolution Quar., Sausilito, Calif., 1973-80; editor, rsch. specialist Dept. Agr. Scis. Colo. State U., Ft. Collins, 1981-82; instr. Mulvane Art Ctr., Topeka, 1982-86, 90—; art tchr. Topeka Pub. Schs., 1985—. Author: Community Gardening in California, 1977; editor: (newspaper) California Green, 1977-80; contbr. articles to profl. jours. Mem. San Francisco Parks and Recreation Open Space Commn., 1975-78; mem. master plan task force Calif. State Fair, Sacramento, 1978-80; commr. Gov.'s Commn. on Children and Families, Topeka, 1988-89; bd. dirs. The Villages, Inc., 1989—. Democrat. Presbyterian. Avocations: painting, gardening, swimming. Home: 4152 SW 6th Ave Apt 115 Topeka KS 66606-2157 E-mail: rmenning@networksplus.net.

MENNINGER, WILLIAM WALTER, psychiatrist; b. Topeka, Oct. 23, 1931; s. William Claire and Catharine Louisa (Wright) M.; m. Constance Arnold Libbey, June 15, 1953; children: Frederick Prince, John Alexander, Eliza Wright, Marian Stuart, William Libbey, David Henry. AB, Stanford U., 1953; MD, Cornell U., 1957; LittD (hon.), Middlebury Coll., 1982; DSc (hon.), Washburn U., 1982; LHD (hon.), Ottawa U., 1986; LLD (hon.), Heidelberg Coll., 1993. Diplomate Am. Bd. Psychiatry and Neurology, Am. Bd. Forensic Psychiatry. Intern Harvard Med. Service, Boston City Hosp., 1957-58; resident in psychiatry Menninger Sch. Psychiatry, 1958-61; chief med. officer, psychiatrist Fed. Reformatory, El Reno, Okla., 1961-63; assoc. psychiatrist Peace Corps, 1963-64; staff psychiatrist Menninger Found., Topeka, 1965—, coordinator for devel., 1967-69, dir. law and psychiatry, 1981-85, dir. dept. edn., dean Karl Menninger Sch. Psychiatry and Mental Health Scis., 1984-90, exec. v.p., chief of staff, 1984-93, CEO, 1993—2001, pres., 1993—96, 1999—2001, chmn. trustees, 2001—; clin. supr. Topeka State Hosp., 1969-70, sect. dir., 1970-72, asst. supt., clin., dir. residency tng., 1972-81; pres. Menninger Clinic, Topeka, 1991-96; staff Stormont-Vail Hosp., 1984-94, assoc., 1994—. Clin. prof. Kans. U. Med. Coll.; adj. prof. Washburn U.; mem. adv. bd. Nat. Inst. Corrections, 1975-88 , chmn., 1980-84; cons. U.S. Bur. Prisons; mem. Fed. Prison Facilities Planning Council, 1970-73; mem. adv. bd. FirstStar Bank, Topeka, 1999—. : syndicated columnist In-Sights, 1975—83; author: Happiness Without Sex an dOther Things Too Good to Miss, 1976, Caution: Living May Be Hazardous, 1978, Behavioral Science and the Secret Service, 1981, Chronic Mental Patient II, 1987; editor: Psychiatry Digest, 1971—74, Bull. of Menninger Clinic, 2001—; contbr. articles to profl. jours., chpts. to books. Mem. nat. adv. coun. Boy Scouts Am., 1970—, chmn., 1980—85, mem. nat. exec. bd., 1980—90, mem. nat. adv. coun., 1990—; bd. dirs. Nat. Com. Prevention Child Abuse, 1975—83; mem. nat. adv. health coun. HEW, 1967—71; mem. Nat. Commn. Causes and Prevention Violence, 1968—69; rsch. adv. com. U.S. Secret Svc., 1990—; pres. Jayhawk coun. Boy Scouts Am., 1998—2001; mem. Kans. Gov.'s Adv. Commn. Mental Health, Mental Retardation an dCmty. Mental Health Svcs., 1983—90, Kans. Gov.'s Penal Planning Coun., 1970; chmn. Kans. Gov.'s Criminal Justice Coun., 1970; trustee Kenworthy-Swift Found., 1980—; active Kans. Gov.'s Commn. on Crime Reduction and Prevention/Koch Commn., 1994—98; dir. Police Found., Washington, 1996—, Koch Crime Inst., 1998—2000; trustee Midwest Rsch. Inst., Kansas City, Mo., 1996—; ruling elder 1st Presbyn. Ch., Topeka, 1992—95. With USPHS, 1959—64. Fellow ACP, Am. Psychiat. Assn. (chmn. com. on chronically mentally ill 1984-86, chmn. Guttmacher award bd. 1990-96), Am. Coll. Psychiatrists; mem. AAAS, AMA, Group for Advancement of Psychiatry (chmn. com. mental health svcs. 1974-77, 91—), Inst. Medicine NAS, Am. Psychoanalytic Assn. (chmn. com. on psychoanalysis, community and society 1984-93), Am. Acad. Psychiatry and Law, Stanford (Univ.) Assocs. Office: Menninger Found PO Box 829 Topeka KS 66601-0829

MENNIS, EDMUND ADDI, investment management consultant; b. Allentown, Pa., Aug. 12, 1919; s. William Henry and Grace (Addi) M.; m. Selma Adinoff, Sept. 25, 1945; children: Ardith Grace, Daniel Liam. BA, CCNY, 1941; MA, Columbia U., 1946; PhD, NYU, 1961. Security analyst Eastman, Dillon & Co., N.Y.C., 1945-46; sr. rsch. asst. Am. Inst. Econ. Rsch., Great Barrington, Mass., 1946-50; security analyst Wellington Mgmt. Co., Phila., 1950-61, dir. rsch., 1958-61, v.p., mem. investment com., 1958-66, economist, 1953-66; sr. v.p., chmn. trust investment com. Republic Nat. Bank, Dallas, 1966-72; sr. v.p., chmn. investment policy com. Security Pacific Nat. Bank, L.A., 1973-81; pres., dir. Bunker Hill Income Securities, Inc., 1973-81; chmn. bd. Security Pacific Investment Mgrs., Inc., 1977-81; ind. cons. to investment mgmt. orgns., 1982—. Tech. cons. Bus. Coun., Washington, 1962-66, 72-77, 79-81; econ. adviser sec. commerce, 1967-68; mem. investment adv. panel Pension Benefit Guaranty Corp., 1981-83 Author: How the Economy Works, 1991, 2d edit., 1999; assoc. editor Fin. Analysts Jour., 1960-88; editor: C.F.A. Digest, 1971-86, Bus. Econs., 1985-99, editor emeritus, 2000—; editor: Banker's Econ. & Investment Alert, 1993—; author or editor books, chpts., numerous articles in field of econs. and investments. Trustee Fin. Analysts Rsch. Found., 1981-86. 1st lt. USAAF, 1942-45; capt. USAF, 1951-53. Fellow Nat. Assn. Bus. Economists (coun. 1967-69, David L. Williams Lifetime Achievement award 1996); mem. Fin. Analysts Fedn. (dir. 1970-72, Graham and Dodd award 1972, Molodovsky award 1972), Am. Econ. Assn., Am. Fin. Assn., L.A. Soc. Fin. Analysts, Conf. Bus. Economists (vice chmn. 1977, chmn. 1978), Inst. CFAs (pres. 1970-72, trustee 1968-74, C. Stewart Sheppard award 1978) Home: 721 Paseo Del Mar Palos Verdes Estates CA 90274-1222 Office: PO Box 1146 Palos Verdes Estates CA 90274-7946 E-mail: eamennis@cox.net.

MENO, JOHN PETER, chorepiscopus; b. Carlinville, Ill., Aug. 22, 1942; s. John Victor and Margaret Mary (Cena) M.; m. Rolanda A. Abyad, Sept. 14, 1968; 1 child, Peter James. MA, Am. U. Beirut, 1969; STM, Union Theol. Sem., 1972. Ordained priest Syrian Orthodox Ch. of Antioch, 1972, elevated to chorepiscopus, 1983. Gen. sec. Archdiocese of Syrian Orthodox Ch. in the U.S. and Can., Lodi, NJ, 1972—95; cathedral dean St. Mark's Syrian Orthodox Cathedral, Teaneck, N.J., 1975—; gen. sec. Archdiocese of the Syrian Orthodox Ch. for the Ea. U.S., 1996—. Co-sec. Standing Conf. of Oriental Orthodox Chs. in Am., N.Y.C., 1973—; co-chmn. U.S. Roman Cath.-Oriental Orthodox Cons., 1989—. Editor: Hymns of the Syrian Orthodox Church of Antioch, 1976; contbr. The Oriental Orthodox Chs. in the U.S., 1986, Dictionary of Christianity in America, 1990, Oriental Orthodox-Roman Catholic Interchurch Marriages and Other Pastoral Relationships, 1995, Nelson's New Christian Dictionary, 2001. Recipient Golden Cross of the Archdiocese of the Syrian Orthodox Ch. in U.S., and Can., 1992. Home: 263 Elm Ave Teaneck NJ 07666-2323 Office: St Marks Syrian Orth Cathedral 260 Elm Ave Teaneck NJ 07666-2318

MENON, GOPINATHAN KUNNARIATH, scientist, researcher; b. Cochin, Kerala, India, Dec. 23, 1948; came to the U.S., 1988; s. Jaishri S. Kothari, Apr. 28, 1973; children: Chirag, Priyanka. BS, Kerala U., 1967; MS, U. Baroda, Gujrat, India, 1969, PhD, 1974. Asst. prof. zoology U. Baroda, Gujrat, 1974-83, assoc. prof., 1983-88; rsch. assoc. dermatology U. Calif., San Francisco, 1988-93; prin. scientist R&D Avon Products, Suffern, N.Y., 1993-98; sr. prin. scientist Avon Products, Inc., 1998-99, rsch. fellow, 1999-2000, sr. rsch. fellow and head, skin biology rsch., 2000—. Vis. prof. Mich. State U., East Lansing, 1979. Contbr. chpts. to books and articles to profl. jours. Environ. activist Indian Soc. Naturalists, Baroda, 1980-88. Homi Bhabha fellow, Bombay, 1979-80. Fellow Calif. Acad. Scis.; mem. Soc. for Investigative Dermatology, Controlled Release Soc. Hindu. Achievements include two patents for cosmetic products. Avocations: bird watching, hiking, philately, coins, gardening. E-mail: gopi.menon.avon.com. Office: Avon Products Inc Avon Pl Suffern NY 10901

MENOUTIS, JAMES VASSILLIOS, research scientist; b. Hollis, N.Y., Oct. 3, 1954; s. Vassillios Dimitrios and Evangelia Eliadis M.; m. Angela Irene Parisi, July 3, 1976; children: William, Mary, Stephen, Jonathan. BS in Chemistry, N.J. City U., 1977; MA in Chemistry, Upsala Coll., 1979; PhD in Chemistry, Am. Western U., 1981. Cert. profl. chemist. Toxicology technician U.S. Testing Co., Hoboken, N.J., 1974-75; lab. supr. MetPath/Quest Clin. Labs., Teterboro, 1981-82; sr. scientist Givaudan Corp., Clifton, 1983-85; dir. R&D Intech BioLabs., East Brunswick, 1985-86; founder, CEO Analab, Inc., Edison, 1987-92; mng. dir. Lab. Tech. Venture Ptnrs. LLC, Princeton, 1992-95; CEO, sr. prin. scientist Quantex Labs., Edison, 1995—. Tech. cons. Witco Chem. Co., Perth Amboy, N.J., 1980-82; dir. CCS LLC, Cooper City, Fla., 2000—. Author: Dioxin: A Current Overview of the Occurance, Toxicity and Disposal of 2,3,7,8-Tetrachlorodibenzo-p-dioxin, 1984; editor: Cons. Guide Tech. Rev. Series Jour., 1990; contbr. articles to profl. jours. Fellow Am. Inst. Chemists; mem. Am. Chem. Soc., Nat. Assn. Rocketry. Office: Quantex Labs 22 Distribution Blvd Edison NJ 08817

MENQ, CHIA-HSIANG, engineering educator, consultant; b. Chia-Yi, Taiwan, July 29, 1956; m. Sissy Jhiang; 1 child Eric. PhD, Carnegie-Mellon U., 1985. Prof. mech. engring. Ohio State U., Columbus, 1985—. Contbr. Named Presdl. Young Investigator, NSF, 1989. Fellow: ASME. Office: Ohio State U 206 W 18th Ave Columbus OH 43210 Office Fax: 614-292-3163. Business E-mail: menq.1@osu.edu.

MENSCH, ALAN R. physician, educator; b. N.Y.C., Apr. 10, 1946; s. Edward and Natalie (Bernstein) M.; m. Monique Kleinman, Aug. 24, 1969; children: Amy, Deborah, Lisa. BA, Queens Coll., 1967; MD, Chgo. Med. Sch., 1973. Med. resident Nassau County Med. Ctr., East Meadow, N.Y., 1973-78; pvt. practice internal medicine, pulmonary diseases Island Pulmonary Internists, Plainview, 1978—; chief pulmonary medicine North Shore U. Hosp., 1990—, med. dir., 1995—, pres. med. staff, 1994, v.p. med. affairs, 2002—; asst. prof. clin. medicine SUNY, Stony Brook, 1993—. Pres.-elect Am. Lung Assn. Nassau-Suffolk. Fellow ACP, Am. Coll. Chest Physicians. Avocation: jogging. Office: Island Pulmonary Internists 453 S Oyster Bay Rd Plainview NY 11803-3311 E-mail: amensch@nshs.edu.

MENSCHEL, RICHARD LEE, investment banker; b. N.Y.C., Jan. 6, 1934; s. Benjamin and Helen (Goldsmith) M.; m. Ronay Arlt, Aug. 21, 1974; children: Charis, Sabina, Celene. BS, Syracuse U., 1955; MBA, Harvard U., 1959. Assoc. securities sales adminstr. Goldman, Sachs & Co., N.Y.C., 1959-67; v.p. Goldman. Sachs & Co., 1967-69; ptnr. securities sales Goldman, Sachs & Co., 1969-88, mgmt. com., 1980-88, ltd. ptnr., sr. dir., 1988—. Bd. dirs. T. Rowe Price Co-chmn. City of N.Y. Transitional Gov. Search Panel, 1977; pres., bd. dirs. Joffrey Ballet Found., 1977-79; bd. dirs. Nat. Corp. Fund for Dance, 1977-79; trustee Fed. Protestant Welfare Agys., 1978-81, The Hastings Ctr., 1995-97, Nightingale Bamford Sch., 1989-96, The Jewish Mus., 1987-2000, Nantucket Conservation Found., Storm King Art Ctr., Conn. Coll., 2001—; mng. dir. Horace W. Goldsmith Found., 1980—; bd. dirs. Mcpl. Art Soc., 1980-92; trustee, mem. exec. com. George Eastman House, Rochester, N.Y., 1980-94, Vera Inst. Justice, 1989—, Pierpont Morgan Libr., 1994—; trustee, treas., mem. exec. com. N.Y. Acad. Medicine, 1992-99; mem. vis. com. Harvard Grad. Sch. Bus. Adminstrn., 1985-91; dean's coun. Harvard Sch. Pub. Health; mem. exec. com. on univ. resources, co-chair Harvard U. campaign; mem. adv. bd. Mus. Modern Art, Oxford, 1987—; chmn., trustee Hosp. for Spl. Surgery, 1990—. 2d lt. USAF, 1955-56. Mem.: India House, Harvard. Home: 660 Park Ave New York NY 10021-5963 Office: Goldman Sachs & Co 85 Broad St New York NY 10004-2456

MENSCHEL, ROBERT BENJAMIN, investment banker; b. N.Y.C., July 2, 1929; s. Benjamin and Helen (Goldsmith) M.; m. Joyce Virginia Frank, Dec. 5, 1968; children: David F., Lauren E. BS, Syracuse U., 1951, LLD (hon.), 1991; postgrad., NYU, 1951-53. Mem. N.Y. Stock Exchange, N.Y.C., 1950-51; specialist HW Goldsmith and Co., 1951-54; with Goldman, Sachs & Co., 1954-66, gen. ptnr. instl. sales, 1966-78, ltd. ptnr., 1979-2000, sr. dir., 2000—. V.p. bd. trustees, mem. fin. and exec. com. Temple Emanu-El, N.Y.; pres., trustee, exec. and fin. com. Mus. Modern Art, mem. investment com., co-chmn. photography com.; trustee Inst. Advanced Study Princeton, Chess in the Schs., N.Y.C. ; trustee, exec. com. Syracuse U., Montefiore Hosp., N.Y., Guild Hall, East Hampton, past chmn. bd.; pres. bd. trustees, exec. com. Dalton Sch., N.Y.C.; past bd. advs. Grad. Sch. Inst. Internat. Bus. Pace U.; mem. exec. bd. N.Y. chpt. Am. Jewish Com.; bd. dirs., mem. fin., exec. and budget com. N.Y. Pub. Library, N.Y.C.; bd. dirs. Parks Council; bd. dirs., v.p. Emanu-El Midtown YMHA, mem. bd. trustees Human Rights Watch; mng. dir. Horace W. Goldsmith Found.; bd. dirs. associated YM-YWHA; mem. Pres. Clinton's com. on the arts and the humanities. Recipient George Arents medal Syracuse U., 1984. Mem. Investment Assn. N.Y. Clubs: India House, City Athletic (N.Y.C.); Dunes Racquet (East Hampton, N.Y.). Home: 920 5th Ave New York NY 10021-4160 also: Further East Ln Amagansett NY 11930 Office: Goldman Sachs & Co 85 Broad St New York NY 10004-2456 E-mail: robert.menschel@gs.com.

MENSCHER, BARNET GARY, steel company executive; b. Laurelton, N.Y., Sept. 5, 1940; s. Samuel and Louise (Zaimont) M.; m. Diane Elaine Gachman, June 12, 1966; children: Melissa Denise, Corey Lane, Scott Jay. Student, Centenary Coll., 1958-59; BBA, U. Tex., 1963. Vice pres. mktg. Ella Gant Mfg., Shreveport, La., 1964-66; warehouse mgr., dir. material control Gachman Steel Co., Fort Worth, 1966-68, gen. mgr. Houston, 1968-70; v.p. sales Gachman Metal Co., 1971-76; pres. Menko Steel Service, Inc., 1979—; CEO NEXTLEVEL, 1998—. Investment cons. D & L Enterprises, 1966—. Mem. solicitation com. United Fund, 1969-76; mem. Nat. Alliance of Businessmen Jobs Program, 1969—. Served with AUS, 1963-65. Mem. Tex. Assn. Steel Importers, Purchasing Agts. Assn. Houston, Credit Assn. Houston, Am. Mgmt. Assn., Assn. Steel Distbrs., Nat. Assn. Elevator Contractors, Phi Sigma Delta, Alpha Phi Omega. Home: 314 Tealwood Dr Houston TX 77024-6113 Office: PO Box 40296 Houston TX 77240-0296

MENSE, ALLAN TATE, research and development engineering executive; b. Kansas City, Mo., Nov. 29, 1945; s. Martin Conrad Mense and Nancy (Tate) Johnson; children from previous marriage: Melanie Georgia, Eileen Madelaine. BS, U. Ariz., 1968, MS, 1970; PhD, U. Wis., 1976; MS in Indsl. Engring., Ariz. State U., 1999. Registered profl. indsl. engr., ASQ cert. reliability engring. Scientist Oak Ridge (Tenn.) Nat. Lab, 1976-79; sr. staff sci. and tech. comm. U.S. Ho. Reps., Washington, 1979-81; sr. scientist McDonnell Douglas Astro. Co., St. Louis, 1981-85; from dep. chief scientist to chief scientist Dept. Def. Strategic Def. Initiative Orgn., Washington, 1985-88; v.p. rsch. Fla. Inst. Tech., Melbourne, 1988-92; pres. Advanced Tech. Mgmt., Inc., Tempe, Ariz., 1992-97; program mgr. Motorola Space Sys. Tech. Group, Chandler, 1998—2001; chief engr., engring. fellow Raytheon Missile Sys., 2002—. Vis. scholar Sloan Sch., MIT, 1995-96. Contbr. over 60 articles to profl. jours. Ariz. State U. scholar, 1996-97. Mem. AIAA (sr. mem.), IEEE (chmn. energy com. 1985—, sr. mem.), Nat. Def. Industries Assn., Am. Phys. Soc., Am. Nuclear Soc., Inst. Indsl. Engrs., Fla. Com. Nat. Space Club (charter), Sigma Xi, Theta Tau, Pi Mu Alpha. Episcopalian. Office: 1151 E Hermans Rd B840/MS8 Tucson AZ 85706 Home: 1052 E Baldy Spring Pl Green Valley AZ 85614

MENSES, JAN, artist, draftsman, etcher, lithographer, muralist; b. Rotterdam, Netherlands, Apr. 28, 1933; emigrated to Can., 1960, naturalized, 1965; s. Jan and Elisabeth Wilhelmina (Schwarz) M.; m. Rachel Régine Kadoch, Dec. 7, 1958; children: Salomon, Hnina Sarah, Nechamah Elisabeth Halo. Student, Acad. Fine Arts, Rotterdam, Officers Acad. Royal Dutch Air Force, 1953-55. Cert. Royal Can. Academician, Academician of Nations, Academician of Europe, Academician of Italy. Lectr. in fine arts Concordia U., Montreal, 1973-76, others. One-man shows include Montreal Mus. Fine Arts, 1961, 65, 76, Isaacs Gallery, Toronto, Ont., Can., 1964, Delta Gallery, Rotterdam, 1965, Galerie Godard Lefort, Montreal, 1966, Gallery Moos, Toronto, 1967, Rotterdam Art Found., 1974, Galerie Mira Godard, Toronto, 1977, Montreal, 1978, Seasons Galleries, The Hague, 1980, U. B.C. Fine Arts Gallery, Vancouver, 1981, Galerie Don Stewart, Montreal, 1981, Mead Art Mus., Amherst, Mass., 1983, Agnes Etherington Art Mus., 1984, Blom and Dorn Gallery, N.Y.C., 1985, 86-93, Maywood Coll. Mus., Scranton, Pa., 1985, Saraya-Wolfson Ctr., Safed, Israel, 1987, Mayanot Gallery, Jerusalem, 1987-88, Esperanza Gallery, Montreal, 1988, 89, Gallery Hamaayan Haradum, Safed, Israel, 1989-2000, Blom and Dorn Gallery, Hartford, Conn., 1995, Nora Gallery, Jerusalem, 1995, 96, 97, Artist's Colony, Safed, Israel; over 300 group shows include Montreal World Exhbn., 1967, Salon Internat. Art, Basel, Switzerland, 1972, 74, Can. Nat. Exhbn., 1972, Centennial Exhbn., Royal Can. Acad., Toronto, 1980, Que. Biennale I, II, III, Montreal, 1977, 79, 81, Foire Internat. D'Art Contemporain Paris and Internat. Fair Koln Germany, 1986, Migdal Ha-Emek, Israel, 1988, Group of 8 Israel, Toronto, 1990, Royal Can. Acad. Show, Toronto, 1991; represented in permanent exhbn. Gallery Hamaayan Haradum, Safed, Profl. Artists' Assn., Artists Colony, Safed; represented in permanent collections U. Coll. Cape Breton Art Gallery, Sydney, N.S., Canada, Museo Ciani di Villa Caccia, Lugano, Switzerland, The Art Gallery of Hamilton, Ont.,Can., David Giles Carter Collection, New Haven, Gallery of Nova Scotia-Halifax, Can, Jewish Public Libr. Collection, Montreal, Can., Cadillac Fairview Collection, Toronto, Can, Museum Modern Art, N.Y.C., Phila. Mus. Art, Solomon R. Guggenheim Mus., N.Y.C., Yivo Inst., N.Y.C., Bklyn. Mus., Art Inst. Chgo., Cleve. Mus. Art, Detroit Inst. Arts, Yale U., U. Montreal, Queens U., Kingston, Mead Art Mus., Amherst Coll., Jonathan Edwards Coll., New Haven, Victoria & Albert Mus., London, Vatican Mus., Rome, Quebec Art Bank, Concordia U., Montreal, Haifa Mus. Modern Art, Hebrew U., Jerusalem, Govt. of Que., Yad Vashem Holocaust Meml., Jerusalem, Mus. Boymans-van Beuningen, Rotterdam, Stedelijk Mus., Amsterdam, Rijksmuseum, Amsterdam, Nat. Gallery Can., Ottawa, Gallery Stratford, Montreal Mus. Fine Arts, Musée d'Art Contemporain, Montreal, Que. Provincial Mus., Que. Art Bank, Art Bank of the Can. Coun., Ottawa, Ariz. State Mus., Tucson, Hebrew U., Jerusalem, City of Safed-Israel, Holocaust Mus., Majdeanek, Poland, Holocaust Meml. Ctr., Toronto, Lavalin Mus. Coll, Montreal, Oshawa Mus., Ont., Dept. External Affairs Govt. Can., Ottawa, Can. Jewish Congress Mus., Montreal, Israel Mus., Jerusalem, Holocaust Mus., Majdanek, Poland, McGill U., Montreal, Olympia & York Collection, Toronto, CBC Collection, Montreal, Kingston (Ont.) U. Mus. Collection, N.Y. Pub. Libr., Worcester (Mass.) Art Mus., Currier Gallery Art, Manchester, N.H., Art Gallery of U. N.H., Durham, Mus. Art. RISD, Providence, Olympia & York Collection, Toronto, Collection Rishon Le'Zion, Jerusalem, Rose Art Mus., Brandeis U., Waltham, Mass., C.I.L. Collection Montreal, Tel Aviv U., McGill U. Coll., Montreal, Can. Jewish Congress Mus., Montreal, Young Israel of Montreal (Coll.), Can., Confedn. Art Ctr., Charlottetown-Prince Edward Island, Can., Thomas More Inst., Montreal; paintings include Klippoth Series, 1963-78, Kaddish Series, 1964-80, Hechaloth Series, 1973—, Tikkun Series, 1978—; mural for, Montreal Holocaust Meml. Center. Mem. Pres.'s Coun. of U. N.H. Served with Royal Dutch Air Force Res., 1953-55. Recipient 5 1st prizes Nat. Art Exhbn., Quebec, Que., 1960-65; Grand prize Concours Artistiques de la Province de Que., 1965; prize X and XI Winnipeg (Man., Can.) Shows, 1966, 68; prize IX Internat. Exhbn. Drawings and Prints, Lugano, 1966; prize Ofcl. Centennial Art Competition, Toronto; 1st prize Hadassah, 1969, 71, 82; Recipient Imago award U. Montreal, 1971; award Reeves of Can., 1969; Tigert award Ont. Soc. Arts, 1970; Loomis and Toles award, 1972; J. I. Segal award J. I. Segal Fund Jewish Culture, 1975; Gold medal Accademia Italia Delle Arte, Italy, 1980; Gold medal Internat. Parliament U.S.A., 1982; Gran Premio delle Nazioni, Italy, 1983, European Banner of Arts with Gold medal, 1984, Oscar d' Italia, 1985, 1st prize III Que. Biennale, 1981, OSA award of merit, Toronto, 1981, 82; World Culture prize Italy, 1984; Golden Flame of World Parliament (U.S.A.) award, 1986; Ish Shalom award Jerusalem, 1993; numerous others; Can. Council sr. arts fellow, 1969-70, 71-72, 81-82; grantee, 1966-67, 67-68; travel grantee, 1968, 73 Mem. Royal Can. Acad. Arts, Acad. Italia Arte e del Lavoro, Acad. Nazioni, Maestro Accademico-Accademia Bedriacense (Italy), Jewish Am. Acad. Arts and Scis., Israeli Art Assn. (Telaviv), Israel Assn. Profl. Artists Safed, Acad. Europa, Academician Italy, Israel Assn. Visual Art (Jerusalem). Jewish. Address: PO Box 43150 HAR NOF Jerusalem 91400 Israel *My works have dealt with death, the eclipse of faith, exile, the Galut. They are shaped by my childhood experiences, real and imagined, in Nazi-occupied Europe; influenced by and rooted in my principles and standards of conduct as an Orthodox Jew in the post-holocaust/pre-Messianic era. They are an attempt to translate these experiences into visual contemporary terms (imagery conflicts and reconciliations of conflicts) in order to ascend from the personal/specific to the universal/general. They are a lament, an elegy, a denial and confirmation, an expression of the attitude of the soul in its debasement and dignity towards its Creator; a striving towards serenity in anticipation of the Redemption: a form of prayer.*

MENSINGER NUNEZ, LINDA IRENE, engineer; b. Elizabeth, N.J., Sept. 28, 1960; d. Wardell Morris Jr. and Joan Mildred (Bley) Mensinger; m. Raymond Martin Nunez, June 19, 1982; children: David Matthew Nunez, Cara Mae Nunez, Rebecca Rose Nunez, Maria Patricia Nunez. BA in Math./Computer Sci./Stats., Rutgers U., 1982; MS in Computer Sci., Brown U., 1989. Software engr. Raytheon, Portsmouth, R.I., 1982-84; sr. modeling engr. Nestor, Inc., Providence, 1984—. Mem. Meadowbrook Farms Parent Tchr. Group, East Greenwich, R.I., 1996—, coord. Math Night, Ea. Greenwich, RI, 1998—. Recipient Book award Pi Mu Epsilon, 1981; named Citizen of Yr., Town of Carteret, N.J., 1978; Brown U. Math. Dept. fellow, 1982. Mem. Am. Assn. for Artificial Intelligence. Lutheran. Achievements include patent for method and apparatus for adaptive classification. Avocations: quilting, needlecrafts, children's activities. Home: 117 Tanglewood Dr East Greenwich RI 02818-2228 Office: Nestor Inc One Richmond Sq Providence RI 02906

MENTEER, DAVID HILTON, producer, production manager; b. L.A., Apr. 7, 1939; s. Hilton Greene and Virginia Rose (Kershner) Menteer; m. JoAnne Letty Bagwell, Dec. 30, 1960 (div. June 1986); children: Jon-David, Kevin James; m. Kathryn Jan Severson, May 30, 1987. BS, U. Miami, 1964. Tv cameraman WTVJ, Miami, Fla., 1962-65; tv engr. ABC Network, L.A., 1965-66, stage mgr., assoc. dir., 1966-68; freelance stage mgr., assoc. dir., 1968-73; asst. dir., second unit dir., prodn. mgr. Universal Studios, 1973-79; freelance producer, prodn. mgr., 1979—. With USN, 1957-61, PTO. Mem. Dirs. Guild Am. Avocations: profl. diver, comml. pilot. Office: Dolphin Cay Prodns 4515 Park Serena Calabasas CA 91302-1775

MENTER, MARTIN, retired lawyer; b. Syracuse, N.Y., July 1, 1915; s. Benjamin and Sarah (Kasmovitch) M.; m. Irene Rothschild, Nov. 10, 1940; children: Toby M. Berger, Joshua Lewis Menter. AB, Syracuse U., 1937, JD, 1939; LLM, George Wash. U., 1949. Bar: N.Y. 1939, U.S. Supreme Ct. 1948, U.S. Dist. Ct. (we. dist.) N.Y. 1939, U.S. Ct. Appeals D.C. 1962, Supreme Ct. Japan 1953. Pvt. practice, Rochester, N.Y., 1939-40, Washington, 1971-88; commd. 2d lt. U.S. Army, 1940-48, USAF, 1948-70, advanced through grades to brig. gen., ret., 1970; writer, speaker, 1950—. Atty., assoc. gen. counsel FAA, Washington, 1959-65; staff judge advocate USAF Far East Air Forces and UN Air Command, Tokyo, 1951-53, USAF Aerospace Def. Command and N.Am. Def. Command, Colorado Springs, 1965-70; speaker in field. Author: Astronautical Law, 1959; contbr. numerous articles to profl. jours., 1955-85. Bd. govs. World Hdqrs. USO, Washington, 1976-88, chair pers. com., mem. exec. com., 1974-78, chair by-laws com., 1983-86; life mem. bd. visitors Coll. of Law, Syracuse U., 1967—; bd. dirs. Nat. Jewish Welfare Bd., N.Y.C., 1970-78; v.p. Internat. Inst. Space Law, 1979-85, hon. dir., 1985—. Decorated D.S.M., Legion of Merit with Oak Leaf Cluster, Bronze Star; recipient Recognition Cert., Air Force Assn., 1969; Disting. Contbn. Internat. Inst. of Space Law, 1990, Lawyers Lawyer award N.Y.C. Assn. of USAFR Judge Advocates, 1964, Inter-Am. Bar Found. Space Law award, 1990. Mem. ABA, Am. Soc. Internat. Law, Am. Astronautical Soc., Fed. Bar Assn., Internat. Acad. Astronautics. Avocations: swimming, walking, reading, writing. Home: 4701 Willard Ave Apt 1726 Chevy Chase MD 20815-4632

MENTER, M(ARTIN) ALAN, dermatologist; b. Doncaster, Eng., Oct. 30, 1941; came to U.S., 1975; s. Harry Menter and Esme (Green) Behr; m. Pamela Mary Williams, Dec. 4, 1966; children: Keith, Colin, Kerith. MB, BChir, U. Witwatersrand, 1966; MMed in Dermatology, U. Pretoria, 1971. Diplomate Am. Bd. Dermatology. Intern Johannesburg (South Africa) Gen. Hosp., 1967, sr. intern, 1968; resident in dermatology U. Pretoria and Pretoria Gen. Hosp., 1968-71; sr. resident in dermatology Guy's Hosp., London, 1972; sr. resident, tutor in dermatology St. John's Hosp. for Disease of Skin, 1972-73; cons. dermatologist Pretoria Gen. Hosp., 1973-75; dermatologist Baylor U. Med. Ctr., Dallas, 1975—, chmn. divsn. dermatology, 1992—; med. dir. Nat. Psoriasis Found. Tissue Bank, Dallas, 1993—; clin. prof. dermatology U. Tex. Southwestern Med. Sch., 1996—. Fellow dept. dermatology U. Tex. Southwestern Med. Sch., Dallas, 1977-79, assoc. clin. prof. dermatology, 1977-95; med. dir. Psoriasis Ctr., Baylor U. Med. Ctr., Dallas, 1979—; clin. assoc. prof. dept. periodontics Baylor Coll. Dentistry, Dallas, 1985—; presenter in field. Mem. editl. bd. Jour. Am. Acad. Dermatology, 1993—; contbr. numerous articles to profl. jours., chpts. to books. Tex. state chmn. Dermatology Found.; rsch. chmn. Nat. Psoriasis Found., med. adv. bd. exec. com.; coach Rugby football team U. Pretoria, 1974; represented S. Africa Nat. Rugby football team, 1968; coach, commr. Boys Under 12 Classic League Soccer, Dallas, 1978-82; active various local civic organizations and coms. Recipient Clin. Rsch. award Imperial Chem. Industries, 1972-73. Mem. AMA, Acad. Dermatology (mem. com. on psoriasis 1988-93, chmn. 1990-93, mem. com. on stds. care for psoriasis 1988-92, chmn. 1989-92, dir. Psoriasis Symposium 1990-93, bd. dirs. 1995-97), Am. Acad. Dermatol. Surgery, Brit. Assn. Dermatology, Dallas County Med. Soc. (mem. med. student rels. com. 1989-94), Dallas Dermatol. Soc. (sec.-treas. 1979, pres. 1980, rep. to adv. coun. Am. Acad. Dermatology 1987-89), Dermatol. Therapy Assn. (pres. 1985), Tex. Dermatol. Soc. (program coord. 1987-93, pres. 1995-96), Tex. Med. Assn. (mem. subcom. on joint sponsorship 1992-95). Home: 5230 Royal Ln Dallas TX 75229-5525 Office: Tex Dermatology Assocs Tollhill Office Park W 5310 Harvest Hill Rd Ste 260 Dallas TX 75230-5805 E-mail: amenter@direcpc.com., amresearch@texasderm.com.

MENTZ, BARBARA ANTONELLO, lawyer; b. Kansas City, Mo., July 4, 1944; d. John Francis and Eleanor Barbara (Vagnino) Antonello; m. Lawrence Mentz, Nov. 10, 1973; children: Kathleen Elizabeth, Lawrence Goodwin. BA in Econs., U. Kans., 1965; JD magna cum laude, U. Notre Dame, 1973. Bar: N.Y. 1974, U.S. Dist. Ct. (so. and ea. dists.) N.Y. 1974, U.S. Ct. Appeals (2d cir.) 1974, U.S. Supreme Ct. 1977, U.S. Ct. Appeals (9th cir.) 1981, U.S. Ct. Appeals (3d cir.) 1983, N.J. 1985, U.S. Dist. Ct. N.J. 1986. Various positions with ins. cos., Chgo., 1965-68, Kansas City, Mo., 1968-70; assoc. Sullivan & Cromwell, N.Y.C., 1973-77, Forsyth, Decker, Murray and Hubbard, N.Y.C., 1977-79; ptnr. Hall, McNicol, Hamilton & Clark, 1979-86; sr. litig. counsel CBS, 1986-88; assoc. gen. counsel, prin. Deloitte & Touche USA LLP, N.Y.C., 1988—. Contbr. articles to profl. jours., chpt. to supplements, publs. Mem. ABA (antitrust sect. 1979-90), Nat. Futures Assn. (panel of arbitrators 1985—), Assn. Bar City of N.Y. (prof. discipline com. 1983-86, antitrust and trade regulation com. 1988-91). Home: 140 W 86th St Apt 2B New York NY 10024-4067 Office: Deloitte & Touche USA LLP 1633 Broadway New York NY 10019-6708 E-mail: bmentz@deloitte.com.

MENTZ, LAWRENCE, lawyer; b. N.Y.C., Nov. 5, 1946; s. Joseph Walter and Audrey Cecilia (Armstrong) M.; m. Barbara Antonello, Nov. 10, 1973; children: Kathleen Elizabeth, Lawrence Goodwin. BS in Physics, Rensselaer Poly. Inst., 1968; JD, U. Notre Dame, 1973. Bar: N.Y. 1973; Washington 1974. Assoc. Condon & Forsyth, N.Y.C., 1973-80, ptnr., 1981-89, Biedermann, Hoenig, Massamillo & Ruff, N.Y.C., 1990—; counsellor at law. Speaker Worldwide Airlines Customer Rels. Assn. Conf., Singapore, 1983, 2d Cir. Speakers Bur., Com. on BiCentennial of U.S. Constn., 1987; arbitrator U.S. Dist. Ct. (ea. dist.) Bklyn., 1986—; bd. dirs. Black Mountain Mgmt. Inc. With USNR, 1969-70. Mem. ABA, Fed. Bar Coun., N.Y. State Bar Assn. (exec. com. sect. on comml. and fed. litigation, fed. judiciary com., 1993, com. Supreme Cts.), Assn. of Bar of City of N.Y. (com. on aeronautics law, task force on N.Y. Constl. Conv., com. on state legis.), Wings Club. Roman Catholic. Avocations: swimming, running, philately. Office: Biedermann Hoenig Massamillo & Ruff 90 Park Ave New York NY 10016-1301 E-mail: lmentz@bhmr.com.

MENTZER, JOHN RAYMOND, electrical engineer, educator; b. Arch Spring, Pa., June 16, 1916; s. Walter Ray and Katheryn Henderson (Barr) M.; m. Bernice Roslyn Simon, Feb. 17, 1945; children— Jacqueline Ferne, Richard Alan. BS, Pa. State U., 1942, MS, 1948; PhD, Ohio State U., 1952. Engr. Westinghouse Electric Corp., Balt., 1942-46, Ordnance Research Lab., 1946-48; research asso. Ohio State U., 1948-52; mem. staff Lincoln Lab., M.I.T., 1952-54; mem. faculty Pa. State U., 1954—, prof. engring. scis., 1956—, head dept. engring. sci. and mechanics, 1974-81, prof. emeritus engring. scis., 1981—. Author: Scattering and Diffraction of Radio Waves, 1955. Recipient Service award Pa. State U., 1979 Sr. mem. IEEE; mem. Am. Soc. Engring. Edn., AAAS, Sigma Xi. Home: 557 Clarence Ave State College PA 16803-3456 Office: 227 Hammond Bldg University Park PA 16802-1401

MENTZER, RAYMOND ALBERT, religious history educator; b. Pitts., Sept. 20, 1945; s. Raymond A. and Anna M. (Snyder) M.; m. Elizabeth J. Palmer, Sept. 14, 1968; children: Sarah, John. BA, Fordham U., 1967; MA, U. Wis., 1970, PhD, 1973. Prof. history Mont. State U., Bozeman, 1973-2001; Krumm Family Prof. in Reformation Studies U. Iowa, Iowa City, 2001—. Author: Heresy Proceedings, 1984, Blood and Belief, 1994, La construction de l'identité Réformée, 2003; editor: Sin and the Calvinists, 1994; co-editor: Society and Culture in the Huguenot World, 2002; gen. editor Sixteenth Century Essays and Studies. Mem. Sixteenth Century Studies (pres. 1996-97), Phi Beta Kappa. Office: U of Iowa 314 Gilmore Hall Iowa City IA 52242 E-mail: raymond-mentzer@uiowa.edu.

MENTZER, ROBERT MELVIN, JR. surgeon; b. Omaha, Jan. 30, 1945; m. Monika Mentzer, Nov. 29, 1968; children: Markus, Stefan. BS, Coll. William & Mary, 1967; MD, U. Md., 1971. Resident U. Va. Med. Ctr., Charlottesville, 1980; thoracic surgeon Frankfurt Army Regional Med. Ctr., Frankfurt, Germany, 1980—82; asst. prof. physiology, dir. carotid-peripheral vascular U. Va. Med. Ctr., Charlottesville, 1982—86, assoc. prof. surgery, 1982—85, assoc. prof. surgery divsn. thoracic and cardiovasc. surgery, 1985—86; prof. dept. surgery and dept. physiology SUNY, Buffalo, 1987—91, vice chmn. dept. surgery, chief divsn. cardiothoracic surgery, 1987—91, head dept. surgery, dir. 2d heart transplant program in N.Y., 1987—91, interim chmn. dept. surgery, pres. u. surg. assn. dept. surg, 1990—91; prof., chmn. divsn. cardiothoracic surgery U. Wis. Sch. Medicine, Madison, 1991—97, dir. cardiopulmonary transplant program, 1991—97; Frank C. Spencer prof., chmn. surgery, prof. physiology U. Ky. Coll. Medicine, Lexington, 1997—, dir. UK transplant ctrl., 1997—2000. Pres., chmn., bd. dirs. Ky. Med. Svcs. Found., Lexington, 1998—; cons. surg. care VA Med. Ctr., Lexington, 1997—. Grantee NIH, 1994—. Mem. Soc. Thoracic Surgery (v.p. CCCETS), Assn. for Acad. Surgery, Am. Surg. Assn., Am. Soc. Transplant Surgeons. Office: U Ky Dept Surgery 800 Rose St Mn 264 Lexington KY 40536-0001 Fax: 606-323-1045. E-mail: mentzer@pop.uky.edu.

MENUTIS, JAMIE, training services executive, writer; b. Houston, June 4, 1964; d. James P. Menutis and Ruth Ann Pellerin-Menutis; 1 child Ana Sofia Rosales. BA, cert. refugee studies program, Webster U., Vienna, Austria, 1988; MA, Georgetown U., 1990. Cert. French lang. proficiency, Spanish lang. proficiency. Campaign asst. Campaign Calif., L.A., 1986—87; rsch. asst. refugee status adv. com. Govt. Can., Ottawa, Canada, 1986—87; rsch. asst. UN Ctr. for Social Devel. and Humanitarian Affairs, Vienna, 1988, U.S. Cath. Conf.-Migration and Refugee Services, Washington, 1989—90; resettlement program officer Internat. Rescue Com., Freetown, Sierra Leone, 1991—92, liaison officer Nairobi, Kenya, 1992; edn. program mgr.-emergency ops. Trocaire, Somalia, 1993; tng. dir. NEU, Inc., New Orleans, 1993—2001; dir. R & M R&D, 1993—. Cons. Ctr. for Effective Non-Profit Mgmt., New Orleans, 1993; fast track trainer U. New Orleans-Small Bus. Devel. Ctr., 1996; staff writer www.Gal.net, 2002—. Author: (book) Where the Natives Feast in New Orleans...A Secret Guide to Local Restaurants, 2002, (government reference) Ten Year Country Profile Reports on Chile, El Salvador and Nicaragua, 1987, (reference) United Nations Center for Social Development and Humanitarian Affairs Bulletin, 1988, (testimonial address for Congress) United States Policy towards Central American and Eastern Europeans Refugees, 1989; contbr. political newsletter; photographic exhbn.; author: (tng. manual) Customer Service Training "Understanding the Customer", 2001, Cultural Orientation Training-International Rescue Committee, Sierra Leone, 1992; contbr. curriculum, articles to profl. jours. Mem. Ladies Philoptochos Soc., New Orleans, 2002; supporter March of Dimes, 1999, Habitat for Humanity, New Orleans, 1998, Amnesty Internat., Washington, 1984. Recipient Medal of Honor for Svc., Internat. Rescue Com., 1992. Mem.: Fgn. Rels. Assn. New Orleans, Georgetown U. Alumni Assn., Pi Sigma. Avocations: photography, travel, yoga, gourmet cooking. Office: Ste 200 108 Royal St New Orleans LA 70130 Personal E-mail: jmenutis@mindspring.com. Business E-Mail: jamie@nativesfeast.com.

MENZA, CLAUDIA MARCELLA, literary agent; b. N.Y.C., June 11, 1947; d. John Gaetano and Antonina (di Lorenzo) M.; m. James R. Forker, May 29, 1971 (div. 1980); m. Charles Anthony Frye, Dec. 16, 1989 (dec. Oct. 1994). BA, Oberlin Coll., 1969. Asst. editor Evergreen Rev., N.Y.C., 1969-73; gen. editor, prodn. mgr. Grove Press, Inc., 1973-83; sr. editor Art Dir. News, 1983-85; pres. Claudia Menza Lit. Agy., 1983—. Cons. Riverrun Press, N.Y.C., 1983-96; guest lectr. Tex. A&M U., Prairie View, Tex., 1986, NYU, N.Y.C., 1986-87; cons., panelist Nat. Civil Rights Mus. Conf. The Power of the Word, Memphis, 1995; panelist NYU, 1998, The New Sch., N.Y.C., 2000, The Lost State Writers Conf., Greeneville, Tenn., 2000, Harlem Book Fair, Jully 2001. Author: Cage of Wild Cries, 1990, The Lunatics Ball, 1994, (plays) , 2002; co-author: The Dream Book: An Anthology of Writing by Italian-American Women, 1985 (Am. Book award, 1985); actor: Damned Pub. Riverside Studios, 1999. Working mem. Congress of Racial Equality, Hempstead, N.Y., 1961, Student Nonviolent Coord. Com., Oberlin, Ohio, 1965, Students for Dem. Soc., Oberlin, 1965, The West Village Com., N.Y.C., 1980. Mem. PEN, Internat. Platform Assn., Acad. Am. Poets, Italian-Am. Writers Assn., Assn. Authors Reps. Avocations: reading, music, theater. Office: Claudia Menza Lit Agy 1170 Broadway Ste 807 New York NY 10001-7507

MENZA, MATTHEW A. psychiatrist; b. Sept. 11, 1950; BA, U. Va., 1973; MD, Temple U., 1980; postgrad., Harvard U., 1985. Intern, resident NYU Med. Sch. Bellvue Hosp., 1980-84; chief divsn. clin. psychopharmacology Robert Wood Johnson Med. Sch., Piscataway, N.J., 1996—, assoc. chmn. dept. psychiatry, 1996—. Contbr. over 50 articles to profl. jours. Bd. govs. Univ. Med. Group, New Brunswick, N.J., 1999—. Office: Robert Wood Johnson Med Sch Dept Psychiatry 675 Hoes Ln Piscataway NJ 08854-5627 E-mail: menza@umdnj.edu.

MENZA, VINCENT LOUIS, engineer, architectural designer; b. Bloomfield, N.J., Oct. 8, 1951; s. Frank Peter and Assunta (Galileo) M. AAS in Arch., Essex County Coll., Newark, 1971. Lic. real estate sales agt., N.J. Owner, photographer Menza Photographics, Bloomfield, 1972-78; plant engr. ITT

Avionics Divsn., Clifton, N.J., 1978-88; constrn. supr. Egghead Software Inc., Issaquah, Wash., 1988-89, Merit Oil Corp., Haverford, Pa., 1989-2000; constrn. mgr. Trammell Crow Co., 2000—. Contbr. photographs to various publs. Bldg. chmn. Yankee Air Force Mus., 1986—; active Belleville (N.J.) Bldg. Devel. Coun., 1991—, Congl. Transp. Com. N.J., Patterson, 1993; docent USS Intrepid Mus., 1992—. Mem. USN League, Elks, Tailhook Assn., N.J. Aviation Hall of Fame, USS Intrepid Assn. Avocations: photography, military history, collecting aircraft ejection seats. Home and Office: PO Box 267 Belleville NJ 07109-0267 E-mail: mk75D@netscape.net.

MENZEL, WILLIAM CLARENCE, JR. nuclear quality engineer; b. Chgo., July 12, 1942; s. William Clarence and Iris Johnston M.; m. Margaret Ann Lagle, Apr. 3, 1964 (div. June 1977); children: Kimberly Menzel Bramlett, William Edward, Timothy Ian; m. Constance Ellen Carter, Mar. 27, 1992. BS in Math., U. Montevallo, 1965. Sr. field engr. reliability & quality assurance Bendix Launch Support Divsn., Kennedy Space Ctr., Fla., 1967-77; engr. quality assurance Rockwell Internat., 1977; mgr. supplier evaluation program Tenn. Valley Authority, Knoxville, TN, 1977-80, Chattanooga, 1981-94; supr. vendor audits Brown & Root, Houston, 1980-81; cons. nuclear engr., 1994—. Vol. fireman Bellwood (Fla.) Vol. Fire Dept., 1972-73, vol. fire chief, 1973-74; coach Shirley Temple Softball, Titusville, Fla., 1975. With U.S. Army Rserve, 1961-67. Baptist. Avocations: reading, water sports. Home and Office: 2613 Hills Chapel Rd Dandridge TN 37725-6809

MENZER, ROBERT EVERETT, toxicologist, educator; b. Washington, Dec. 21, 1938; s. Russell Ernest and Ora Taylor (Oates) M.; m. Sara Lee Gribbon, Dec. 29, 1962; children: R. Eric, Paul D., Joan Coleraine. BS in Chemistry, U. Pa., 1960; MS, U. Md., 1962; PhD, U. Wis., 1964. Instr. U. Wis. , Madison, 1964; mem. faculty U. Md., 1964-89, asst. prof. entomology, 1964-69, assoc. prof., 1969-73, prof., 1973-89, assoc. dean grad. studies and research, 1974-77, acting dean, 1977-80. chmn. grad. program marine-estuarine-environ. scis., 1978-89, dir. Water Resources Research Ctr., 1981-89; dir. environ. rsch. lab. EPA, Gulf Breeze, Fla., 1989-95, sr. sci. advisor Washington, 1995-2001. Prof. emeritus U. Md., 1990—; chmn. hazardous substances data bank rev. panel Nat. Library Medicine, 1973-97. Contbr. articles to profl. jours. Recipient U. Md. Alumni award, 1974 Fellow Washington Acad. Scis.; mem. AAAS, Am. Chem. Soc., Soc. Toxicology, Soc. for Environ. Toxicology and Chemistry, Estuarine Rsch. Fedn., Sigma Xi, Phi Kappa Phi. Clubs: Cosmos (Washington). Republican. Episcopalian. Home: 90 Highpoint Dr Gulf Breeze FL 32561-4014 E-mail: remenzer@att.net.

MENZIE, WILLIAM DAVID, II, geologist, educator; b. Berkley, W.Va., Feb. 28, 1949; s. William David and Ethel Fawcett Menzie; m. Carolyn Kruse, Sept. 5, 1970; children: William David III, Elizabeth Mary. Diploma, Culver Mil. Acad., 1967; BS in Geology, Dickinson Coll.; MS in Geology, Pa. State U., 1974, MA in Stats., PhD in Geology, Pa. State U., 1977. Rsch. geologist U.S. Geol. Survey, Menlo Park, Calif., 1977-87, supervisory geologist Reston, Va., 1987-92, rsch. geologist, 1992-98, supervisory geologist, 1998—. Adj. prof. grad. program in earth and environ. sci. and pub. policy Johns Hopkins U., Balt., 1995—. Contbr. articles to profl. jours. Youth baseball coach Chantilly (Va.) Youth Assn., 1988-96, Reston/Herndon Youth Baseball, 1996—. MMFC fellow, 1976-77, Centennial fellow Earth and Mineral Sci. Coll., Pa. State U., 1996; Metzgar Conway fellow Dickinson Coll., 1998. Fellow: Soc. Econ. Geology; mem.: Soc. Mining Engrs. (program chair DC sect.), Am. Statis. Assn., Sigma Xi, Omicron Delta Kappa. Methodist. Avocations: hiking, scuba diving, coaching. Home: 3202 Wildmere Pl Oak Hill VA 20171-3920 Office: US Geol Survey 991 National Center Reston VA 20192 E-mail: dmenzie@usgs.gov.

MENZIES, HENRY HARDINGE, architect; b. Hickory, N.C., Apr. 20, 1928; s. Henry Hardinge and Hallie (Lloyd) M. AB in Lit., U. N.C., 1948; postgrad., U. So. Calif., 1948-49; BArch, N.C. State U., 1958. Founder, ptnr. The Architects Group, Boston, 1962-63; individual practice architecture, 1964-78; ptnr. Menzies and LeMieux, N.Y.C., 1978-82; pvt. practice architecture New Rochelle, N.Y., 1983—. Lectr. in field. Works include coll. and seminary, Natick, Mass., 1964, Heights Sch., Washington, 1965, St. Marie's Ch., Lowell, Mass., 1966, Central Cath. H.S., Lawrence, Mass., 1971, Walker Sch., Needham, Mass., 1972, Baird Residence, Sherborn, Mass., 1972, Layton Cultural Ctr., Brookfield, Wis., 1974, Shellbourne Conf. Ctr., Valparaiso, Ind., 1974, Wespine Study Ctr., Pembroke, Mass, 1982, alterations to residences in Greenwich, Conn., 1984, Garwood Bldg. at Arnold Hall, 1986, Midtown Ctr., Chgo., 1986, Student Ctr., Houston, 1986, Windmoor Ctr., South Bend, Ind., 1986, alterations to student residences in Milw. and Providence, 1989-91, renovation of interior St. Aloysius Ch., New Canaan, Conn., 1993-96, chapel at Warwick House, Pitts., 1993, chapel at Westfield Residence, L.A., 1994, chapel at Allview Ctr., Columbia, Md., 1994, chapel at St. John Fisher Residence, Stamford, Conn., 1994, master plan, crypt chapel St. Mary of the Angels Ch., Chgo., 1996—, Shrine at Conf. Ctr., Schulenberg, Tex., chapel Lincoln Green student residence, Urbana, Ill., 1997—, new facade of St. Aloysius Ch., New Canaan, 1997—, Willows Acad., Chgo., 1997—, St. Eugene's Ch., Yonkers, 1998—, renovation St. John's Ch., Stamford, 1999—, Cath. Info. Ctr. Washington, 1999-2000, St. Michael's Ch., Gastonia, N.C., 2000—, Cathedral St. Augustine, Bridgeport, Conn., 2001, St. Mary's Ch., Ridgefield, Conn., 2001; contbr. articles to profl. jours. Served to 1st lt. USNR, 1951-55. Mem. AIA (N.Y. chpt. 1978-84, Westchester/Mid-Hudson chpt. 1985—). Roman Catholic. Office: 99 Overlook Cir New Rochelle NY 10804-4501 E-mail: hmenzies@aol.com.

MENZIES, IAN STUART, newspaper editor; b. Glasgow, Scotland, Mar. 11, 1920; came to U.S., 1944, naturalized, 1948; s. John S. and Gertrude (Mephius) M.; m. Barbara Edith Newton, June 16, 1945; children: Marla Ann, Gillian Jean, Alexa Stuart, Deborah Newton. Student, Royal Tech. Coll., 1937-39; Nieman fellow, Harvard U., 1961-62; L.H.D., Salem State Coll., 1978. Reporter Boston Globe, 1948-57, sci. editor, 1957-63, fin. editor, 1963-65, mng. editor, 1965-70, assoc. editor, 1970-85; sr. fellow John McCormack Inst. Pub. Affairs, U. Mass., Boston, 1985—. Vis. assoc. Joint Ctr. for Urban Studies, Mass. Inst. Tech.-Harvard, 1970-71. Mem. Hingham (Mass.) Sch. Com., 1962-68. Served to lt. Royal Naval Vol. Res., 1939-46. Decorated D.S.C.; recipient Pub. Service award Nat. Edn. Writers, 1961, Pub. Service award AAAS, 1963, Heywood Broun award, 1961, Sevellon Brown award, 1959, Rudolph Elie award, 1959, A.P. Big City award, 1958, U.P.I. award, 1959. Mem. Harvard Club, Hingham Yacht Club, Brit. Officers Club New Eng. Home and Office: 479 Main St Hingham MA 02043-4705 Office: U Mass McCormack Inst Boston MA 02125

MEO, ANTHONY, investment banker, financial planner; b. N.Y.C. BS in Hydrogeology and Pedology, SUNY, Buffalo, 1989; MBA in Fin. Mgmt., City U. Wash., 1995. Appraiser Green Point Bank, Flushing, N.Y., 1989-92; asset mgr. 1st Fed. Bank, 1992-93; asst. v.p. real estate CFS Bank, Woodhaven, 1993-97; asst. v.p. real estate fin. The Sakura Bank, Ltd., N.Y.C., 1997-98; v.p. Bank of Tokyo-Mitsubishi, 1998—. Mem. Real Estate Lenders Assn., Young Mortgage Bankers Assn., The Urban Land Inst., Am. Inst. of Banking. Office: 1251 Avenue Of The Americas New York NY 10020-1104

MEO, ROXANNE MARIE, critical care nurse; b. Saginaw, Mich., Oct. 10, 1959; d. Joseph S. and Margaret V. (Gillam) M. BSN, Saginaw Valley State U., University Center, Mich., 1982; student, Delta Coll., 1987-90; overseas studies, Mich. State U., 1983, MSN, 1998. Cert. neuro RN.; CNRN, Am. Bd. Neurosci. Nurses; cert. family nurse practitioner Am. Nurses Credentialing Ctr. Nurse extern St. Luke's Hosp., Saginaw, 1982, staff nurse, 1983-88; Nurse in Washington intern Nat. Fedn. Specialty Nursing Orngs., 1987; resource nurse Ask-A-Nurse, Saginaw, 1988-91, Seton Health Care Corp. East Cen. Mich.; staff nurse St. Mary's Hosp., Saginaw, 1983, 91—, The Nurse Corps, Inc., 1999—. Adj. faculty Delta. Coll., 1999—. Mem.: ANA, Emergency Nurses Cancel Alcohol Related Emergencies, Soc. Gastrointestinal Assts., Saginaw Nurses Assn., Mich. Nurses Assn., Am. Acad. Nurse Practitioners, Am. Assn. Neurosci. Nurses, Phi Kappa Phi, Sigma Theta Tau.

MEOLA, JANICE GRACE, lawyer; b. Newark, Jan. 10, 1966; d. William Frank and Rose Marie Meola. BS in Fin., Pa. State U., 1988; JD, U. N.C., Chapel Hill, 1991. Bar: N.J., U.S. Dist. Ct. N.J. Jud. clk. Superior Ct. of N.J., Jersey City, 1991-92; litigation assoc. Bumgardner, Hardin & Ellis, Springfield, N.J., 1992-94; environ. counsel CNA Ins. Cos., Cranbury, 1994-96; assoc. counsel Suburban Propane, L.P., Whippany, 1996-98, counsel, 1998-99, gen. counsel, sec., 1999—. Mem. ABA, Am. Corp. Counsel Assn., Am. Soc. of Corp. Secs., Propane Gas Def. Assn. Office: Suburban Propane LP PO Box 206 240 Route 10 Whippany NJ 07981-0206

MERANUS, LEONARD STANLEY, lawyer; b. Newark, Jan. 7, 1928; s. Norman and Ada (Binstock) M.; m. Jane B. Holzman, Sept. 20, 1989; children: Norman, James M., David. LittB, Rutgers U., 1948; LLB, Harvard U., 1954. Bar: Ohio 1954. Assoc. Paxton & Seasongood, cin., 1954-59, ptnr., 1959-85, pres., 1985-89; ptnr. Thompson, Hine and Flory, 1989-96, ptnr.-in-charge Cin. office, 1989-91, mem. firm mgmt. com., 1991-93, of counsel, 1998—; adj. prof. law U. Cin. Coll. Law, 1998-2000. Chmn. bd. dirs. Jewish Hosp., 1982-86; trustee Andrew Jergens Found., 1962-97. Mem. ABA, Ohio Bar Assn., Cin. Bar Assn., Am. Arbitration Assn. (chmn. comml. arbitration adv. com., Ohio panel large, complex arbitration cases). Office: Thompson Hine LLP 312 Walnut St Ste 14 Cincinnati OH 45202-4089

MERAT, FRANCIS LAWRENCE, engineering educator; b. Frenchville, Pa., Aug. 22, 1949; s. Lawrence Clarence and Lucille Magdalen (DeMange) M. BSEE, Case Western Res. U., 1972, MSEE, 1975, PhD, 1978. Rsch. engr. Case Western Res. U., Cleve., 1978-79, asst. prof. engring., 1979-85, assoc. prof., 1985—, exec. officer dept. elec. engring. and applied physics, 1994-98, with elec. engring. and computer sci., 1998-99, interim chair dept. elec. engring. and computer sci., 1999-2000, assoc. chair dept. elec. engring. and computer sci., 2001—; co-founder, sec./treas. PGM Diversified Industries, Inc., Parma Heights, Ohio, 1986—. Fellow summer faculty program USAF, Griffiss AFB, N.Y., 1980, U.S. Army, Ft. Belvoir, Va., 1987; cons. various law firms (expert forensic engr., patent infringement), NASA Glenn Rsch. Ctr. Contbr. articles to tech. jours. Named Disting. Advisor, Nat. Assn. Acad. Counseling and Advising, 1985. Mem. IEEE (sect. chmn. 1983-84, reviewer IEEE Robotics and Automation), Soc. Mfg. Engrs., Assn. Computing Machinery, Soc. Photo-optical Instrumentation Engrs., Sigma Xi. Roman Catholic. Avocations: photography, science fiction, movies. Home: 4398 Groveland Rd University Ht OH 44118-3958 Office: Case Western Res Univ 10900 Euclid Ave Cleveland OH 44106-7071 E-mail: flm@po.cwru.edu.

MERCADANTE, ANTHONY JOSEPH, special education educator; b. Newark, Mar. 10, 1951; s. Anthony Joseph Jr. and Anna Rose (Cocuzzo) M.; m. Barbara Ferrari, May 27, 1979; children: Anthony, Lisa, David. BS in Edn., Seton Hall U., 1973; MA in Audiology and Communication Sci., Kean Coll., 1978; cert. in adminstrn. and supervision, U. S. Fla., 1987. Cert. audiologist, adminstr./supr., tchr. bus. edn., tchr. hearing impaired. Acctg. clerk supply div. U.S. Steel Corp., Newark, 1973-75; acctg. and bookkeeping instr. Sch. Data Programming, Union, N.J., 1976-78; bus. adminstrn. instr., curriculum coord. Roberts-Walsh Bus. Sch., 1978-83; clin. audiologist Ea. Speech, Lang. and Hearing Ctr., Woodbridge, N.J., 1980-83; ednl. audiologist exceptional student edn. dept. Polk County Pub. Schs., Bartow, Fla., 1983—. Advisor Fla. Audiologists in Edn., Orlando, 1987—; mem. multidisciplinary team Polk County Pub. Schs., 1983—; mem. planning com. Project Healthy Start, Polk County Pub. Schs., Bartow, 1994—. Baseball coach S. Lakeland Babe Ruth Baseball League, Lakeland, Fla., 1993, 95, baseball mgr., 1994. Mem. AARP, Am. Speech, Lang. and Hearing Assn., Nat. Youth Sports Coaches Assn., Fla. Speech, Lang. and Hearing Assn. Avocations: tennis, golf, bowling, swimming, coaching. Home: 6122 Donegal E Lakeland FL 33813-3713 Office: Polk Life and Learning Ctr 1310 S Floral Ave Bartow FL 33830-6399

MERCADO, MARY GONZALES, cardiologist; b. Houston, July 9, 1959; d. Frank Reyes and Joyce (Byrd) Gonzales; m. Antonio Gonzalez Mercado, May 25, 1985. BS magna cum laude, U. Tex., San Antonio, 1987; MD with honors, Baylor Coll. of Medicine, 1992. Diplomate Am. Bd. Internal Medicine, Am. Bd. Cardiovasc. Diseases, Am. Bd. Nuclear Cardiology. Intern U. Tex. Affiliated Hosps., San Antonio, 1992-93, resident, 1993-95, chief resident, 1995-96, fellow in cardiology, 1996-99; pvt. practice, Ozark, Ala. Presenter confs. and symposiums. Contbr. articles to med. publs. Mem. AMA, Am. Soc. Echocardiography, Am. Coll. Cardiology, Am. Soc. Nuc. Cardiology, Tex. Med. Assn., Ala. Med. Assn., Bexar County Med. Soc., Dale County Med. Soc. Office: 203 Stonebridge Ln Ozark AL 36360-9290 E-mail: mgmercado@charter.net.

MERCADO-RAMOS, FERDINAND, secretary of state; b. Lares, P.R., June 18, 1957; m. Michelle Waters Munoz; children: Ferdinand Giovanni, Andres Fernando. BS in Psychology, U. P.R., 1978; JD, Inter-Am. U. P.R., 1981. Sec. of state, San Juan, PR, 2000—. Author: Grito a la Intimidad, 1976, Un Pensamiento en Viaje, 1990. Office: Apartado 9023271 San Juan PR 00902-3271*

MERCALDO, DAVID, elementary school educator, writer; b. Bklyn., Nov. 12, 1946; s. Isaac and Rose Mercaldo; m. Linda Ann Ciaravino, Dec. 16, 1995. BA in Edn., Ctrl. Bible Coll., 1967; MS in Edn., Richmond Coll., 1970; PhD in Humanities, Columbia U., 1996. Cert. learning disabilities tchr. N.Y., elem. tchr. N.Y. Tchr. N.Y. Pub. Sch., Staten Island, NY, 1968—73, Boces, L.I., 1973—78, asst. prin., 1978—81; prin. City of Tulsa , Tulsa, Okla., 1981—88; assoc. dir. The Summit Sch., Forest Hills, NY, 1988—89; tchr. City of N.Y., Staten Island, 1989—. Prof. Columbia Commonwealth U., Missoula, Mont., 2001; pres. Skyline Theater, Staten Island, 1992—. Author: (plays) Apartment to Let, 1979, FERRY, 2002. Mem.: United Fedn. Tchr., Beaux Arts Soc., Sons of Italy. Conservative. Moravian. Avocations: writing, composing, keyboard, model building, architecture. Home: 414 Pendale St Staten Island NY 10306

MERCANT, JON JEFFRY, lawyer, educator, musician; b. San Jose, Calif., Dec. 17, 1950; s. Anthony J. and Margie Vivian (Diaz) M. BA, U. Calif., Berkeley, 1972; JD, U. Calif., L.A., 1975. Bar: Calif. 1975. Atty., Redondo Beach, Calif., 1975—; prof. El Camino Coll., Torrance. Mem. exec. bd. Calif. Dem. Party, 1986—; mem. exec. bd., COPE chmn. El Camino Coll. Fedn. Tchrs., Torrance, 1991—; Dem. nominee for State Assembly, 1986, Los Angeles County Ctrl. Co., 1986-90; dir. Peninsula Symphony Assn., Consumer Coalition Calif., Enrichment Through Employment; dir., sec., founder South Bay Concern, Coastal Environ. Coalition; vice chmn., legal counsel Ret. Sr. Vol. Program. Named one of Outstanding Young Men of Am., 1984; named Redondo Beach Man of Yr., 2000-01. Mem. Rotary (bd. dirs., pres. North Redondo, Calif.), Redondo Beach C. of C. (pres., bd. dirs. 1990—), Phi Beta Kappa. Avocations: music performance, theatre, wine collecting, jogging, travel. Office: 707 Torrance Blvd Ste 220 Redondo Beach CA 90277-3492

MERCER, DANNY THOMAS, sales representative; b. Wilson, N.C., May 12, 1954; s. Roney Thomas and Peggy Ann (Walston) M.; m. Barbara Jean Denton, June 20, 1982. AAS, Nash C.C., 1974; student, Atlantic Christian Coll., 1978-79. Lic. gen. contractor, N.C. Pres., co-owner Rodan Devel., Inc., Wilson, N.C., 1993—; rep. Hughes Corp., Rocky Mount, 1998—. Owner Homeplace Storage. Mem. Wilson County Bd. Commrs., 1994-98, 98—; mem. Wilson County Dept. Social Svcs., Wilson County Bd. Health; mem. Tar River Basin Com.; former mem. Wilson-Greene Mental Health Bd.; mem. Wilson County Tourism Authority; mem., chmn. Wilson County Water and Sewer Com., Wilson County Facilities Com.; bd. dirs. Diversified Opportunities, Inc., Upper Coastal Plains Coun. of Govts. U.S. Jaycees scholar, Wilson, 1994, Wilson Jaycees scholar, 1995. Mem. Nat. Assn. Security Dealers. Republican. Free Will Baptist. Avocations: golf, landscaping, gardening. Home: 4546 Lamm Rd SW Wilson NC 27893-7762 E-mail: commish@geeksnet.com.

MERCER, EDWIN WAYNE, lawyer; b. Kingsport, Tenn., July 19, 1940; s. Ernest LaFayette and Geneva (Frye) M. BBA, Tex. Tech U., 1963; JD, S. Tex. Coll. Law, 1971. Bar: Tex. 1971, U.S. Dist. Ct. (no. dist.) Tex 1975, U.S. Supreme Ct. 1976, U.S. Ct. Appeals (5th Cir.) 1979. Pvt. practice, Houston, 1971-73; gen. counsel, corp. sec. Alcon Labs., Inc., Ft. Worth, 1973-81; ptnr. Gandy Michener Swindle Whitaker Pratt & Mercer, 1981-84; v.p., gen. counsel, corp. sec. Pengo Industries, Inc., 1984-90, also bd. dirs.; pvt. law practice, 1990—. Bd. dirs. Soc. for Prevention Blindness, 1979—. Mem. ABA, State Bar Tex., Houston Bar Assn., Coll. State Bar Tex., South Tex. Coll. Law Alumni Assn., Tex. Tech U. Ex-Assn., Ft. Worth Club, Delta Theta Phi, Phi Delta Theta. Methodist.

MERCER, FRANCES DECOURCY, artist, educator; b. Centreville, Miss., June 14, 1944; d. John Homer Jr. and Patricia Powers (Given) Mercer. BA in English Lit., U. Miami, 1969, MA in History of Art, 1971; MFA in Painting, San Francisco Art Inst., 1974. Cert. tchr. Fla. Instr. South Fla. Art Inst., Hollywood, Fla., 1979—81; tchg. asst. San Francisco Art Inst., 1974; instr. Broward C.C., Ft. Lauderdale, Fla., 1979—83; owner 17th St. Galleries, 1984—91; tchr. Broward County Sch. Bd., 1980—82; adj. prof. Fla. Atlantic U., 1979—80. Exhibited in group shows at Grove Art Gallery, Coconut Grove, Fla., 1973, Emanuel Walter Gallery, San Francisco, 1975, The Lucian LaBandt Gallery, 1976, The Both Up Gallery, Berkeley, Calif., 1976, Discover Ctr., Ft. Lauderdale, 1980, Nova U. Artoberfest, Art and Culture Ctr. Hollywood, 1981, Indian Hammock Hunt and Riding Club, Okeechobee, Fla., 1998, A.E. Backus Gallery and Mus., Ft. Pierce, Fla., 2000, pvt. collections. Scholar Tuition scholar, San Francisco Art Inst., 1972, 1973, 1974. Avocations: photography, trail hiking, kayaking, golf, sailing. Home: #200 Blue Heron Ln 32801 Hwy 441 Okeechobee FL 34972 E-mail: fmercer@floridawatercolors.com.

MERCER, JAMES LEE, management consultant; b. Sayre, Okla., Nov. 7, 1936; s. Fred Elmo and Ora Lee (Davidson) M.; m. Karolyn Lois Prince, Nov. 16, 1962; children: Tara Lee, James Lee. BS, U. Nev., 1964, MBA, 1966; postgrad. exec. devel. program, Cornell U., 1979. Cert. in mcpl. adminstrn. U. N.C., 1971; cert. mgmt. cons. Methods and results supr. Pacific Tel. & Tel., Sacramento, 1965-66; prodn. control supr. Gen. Dynamics, Pomona, Calif., 1966-67; nuclear submarine project mgr. Litton Industries, Pascagoula, Miss., 1967-70; asst. city mgr. City of Raleigh, N.C., 1970-73; nat. program dir. Pub. Tech., Inc., Washington, 1973-76; gen. mgr. Battelle So. Ops., Atlanta, 1976-79; v.p. Korn/Ferry Internat., 1979-81; pres. James Mercer & Assocs. Inc.; mgmt. cons. Atlanta, 1981-86; chief Indsl. Ext. Divsn., Ga. Inst. of Tech., 1981-83; dir. govtl. cons. svc. Coopers & Lybrand, 1983-84; regional v.p. Wolfe & Assocs., Inc., 1984-86; pres., CEO, chmn. Mercer, Slavin & Nevins, Inc., 1986-90, The Mercer Group, Inc., 1990—. Ad hoc prof. N.C. State U., 1972-73; bd. dirs. Taratec Corp., Columbus. Author: Public Management Systems, 1978, Public Technology, 1981, Managing Urban Government Services, 1981, Strategic Planning for Public Managers, 1990, Public Management in Lean Years, 1992; contbr. numerous articles to profl. jours. Chmn. Raleigh Mayor's Civic Ctr. Authority Study Commn., 1971; founding bd. dirs. Mordecai Sq. Hist. Soc., Nat. Civic League; founding mem. U. S.C. Master of Pub. Adminstrn. adv. bd., 1987-97; founding mem. Calif. Poly. State U., adv. coun. Coll. of Bus. Adminstrn., San Luis Obispo, 1980-95; lectr., pub. spkr.; founding mem., bd. trustees U. Nev. Found., Reno, 1985-91. With USN, 1955-59. Mem. Internat. City-County Mgmt. Assn., Am. Soc. Pub. Adminstrn., Am. Inst. Indsl. Engrs. (past pres.'s award 1970, pres. chpt. 1969-70), Tech. Transfer Soc. (dir. 1978-87, treas. 1985-86), Ga. Indsl. Devel. Assn., U. Nev. Alumni Assn. (exec. com. 1969-79), Atlanta C. of C., Rotary, Masons, Shriners, Contract Svcs. Assocs. of Am. (bd. dirs. 1994—). Home: 28 Sierra Del Sol Santa Fe NM 87508-2136 Office: 551 W Cordova Rd Ste 726 Santa Fe NM 87505-1825 E-mail: mercer@mindspring.com.

MERCER, JOHN A. former state legislator; b. Missoula, Mont., Jan. 21, 1957; m. Tine Mercer; children: Thomas, Michael. BA in Bus., U. Mont., 1979; JD, Northwestern U., 1982. Pvt. practice, Polson, Mont., 1982; mem. Mont. Ho. of Reps., 1984—, minority whip, 1989-90, minority leader, 1991-92, house spkr., 1993—2000, mem. rules com., mem. legis. administrv. com.; gov. bd. mem. Mont. St. U. Office: Montana St U MT Higher Education Complex 2500 Broadway Helena MT 59620 E-mail: john@polsonlaw.com.*

MERCER, KERMIT RAY, biophysicist; b. Brockport, N.Y., June 1, 1933; s. Harold R. and Elma H. (Case) M.; m. Janet L. Hollinger, 1988 (div.); children: Deborah L. Ross, Susan R. Morreall; m. Pamela C. Wade, Apr. 29, 1989. BS in Geology and Math., SUNY, Brockport, 1971. Rsch. assoc. GD Electronics, Rochester, N.Y., 1957-68; rsch. assoc. biochemistry dept. Eastman Dental, 1968-69; assoc. in biophysics U. Rochester, 1972—. Owner Electroscience, Brockport, 1971—. Mem. zoning bd. appeals Town of Clarkson, 1963-83; lt. Brockport Fire Dept., 1965—. With USAF, 1953-57. Mem. U.S. Power Squadron (comdr. 1991-92), IEEE, AAPT, Oak Orchard Yacht Club, VFW, Am. Legion. Avocations: sailing, flying, geology, amateur radio. Office: U Rochester Dept Biophysics Rochester NY 14642-0001 E-mail: kmercer1@rochester.rr.com., kermit-mercer@urmc.rochester.edu.

MERCER, MELVIN RAY, electrical engineer, educator; b. Lubbock, Tex., Sept. 5, 1946; s. Dixie Melvin and Ollie Faye (Sheppard) M.; m. Sharry Billene Cannon, Sept. 9, 1967; children: Rebecca Raylene, Elizabeth Anne. BSEE, Tex. Tech U., 1968; MSEE, Stanford U., 1971; PhD in Elec. Engring., U. Tex., 1980. Registered profl. engr., Tex. Rsch. and devel. engr. GTE Sylvania, Mountain View, Calif., 1968-73; mem. tech. staff Hewlett-Packard Labs., Palo Alto, 1973-77; lectr. U. Tex., San Antonio, 1977-80; mem. tech. staff Bell Labs., Murray Hill, N.J., 1980-83; asst. prof. elec. and computer engring. U. Tex., Austin, 1983-87, assoc. prof., 1987-91, prof., 1991-95; prof. computer engring. dept. elec. engring. Tex. A&M U., College Station, 1995—, computer engring. chair elec. engring., 1995—. Lectr. Kilgore (Tex.) Jr. Coll., 1977; cons. Rothe Devel. Co., San Antonio, 1979, Lockheed Missiles and Space Co., Austin, 1983, IBM, Austin, 1984, 88-90, Harris Semicondr., Dallas, 1983-86, 99-2000, State of Tex., Austin, 1984-85, CBS, N.Y.C., 1985-86, Teltech Resource Network, Mpls., 1986-93, Motorola Semicondr., Austin, 1987-88, 91, 99, TSSI, Beaverton, Oreg., 1988-94, MCC, Austin, 1989, Cimflex Teknowledge, Pitts., 1989-90, Rockwell, Newport Bch., Calif., 1991, 95, Integra-Test, L.I., N.Y., 1993, Teradyne, 1993-94, Sematech, 1994, AT&T, Oklahoma City, 1995-97, Sanke & Luck, Houston, 1997-98, Taylor & Dunham, 1995, 97, 99-2000, Fulbright & Jaworski, 1997, 99-2001, Hale & Dorr, 2001, Akin, Gump, Strauss, Haner & Feld, 2000, Harris Corp, Melbourne, Fla., 1999-2001, Sigma Tel, Austin, 1999-2000, others; advisor NSF, Washington, 1987-88, mem. engring. initiation awards evaluation panel, 1987, 1993; mem. program com. 1st MCC-Univ. Rsch. Symposium, 1987; lectr. in field. Contbr. articles to profl. jours.; patentee in field. Recipient Presdl. Young Investigator award NSF, 1986, rsch. award Office Naval Rsch., 1986-95, Advanced Projects Rsch. Adminstrn., 1992-95; Werner W. Dornberger Centennial tchg. fellow U. Tex., 1984-90, Engring. Found. endowed faculty fellow, 1990-91, Temple Found. endowed prof. engring., 1991-95; grantee Univ. Rsch. Inst., 1983, Bur. Engring. Rsch., 1984, AT&T Info. Sys., 1985-88, Microelectronics and Computer Tech. Corp., 1985-90, Internat. Test Found., 1986-89, Semicondr. Rsch. Corp., 1989-95, 2000—, IBM, 1989-92, Tex. Advanced Tech. Program, 1990-92, 98-2000, Motorola, 1991-98. Fellow IEEE (editor Design and Test of Computers mag. 1985-88, mem. program com. design for testability workshop Vail, Colo. 1989-95); mem. Computer Soc. of IEEE (vice chmn. Ctrl. Tex. chpt. 1983-85, chmn. 1985-86), Internat. Test Conf. (program com. 1986-89, program vice chmn. 1988, program chmn. 1989, steering com. 1988-93, mktg. vice chmn. 1990, planning chmn. 1992-93, best paper award 1982, hon. mention 1988), Internat. Conf. on CAD (program com. 1987), Design Automation Conf. (best paper award 1991, best paper award Very Large Scale Integrated Cir. Test Symposium 1999), Austin C. of C. (recruitment resource 1983-87), Tau Beta Pi, Eta Kappa Nu, Phi Kappa Phi, Phi Eta Sigma. Avocations: racquetball, swimming, scuba. Office: Tex A&M U Dept Elec Engring 214 Zachry Bldg College Station TX 77843-3259 E-mail: ray@rmercer.com.

MERCER, REBEKAH M. editor, writer; b. Ft. Worth, Sept. 26, 1952; d. Gilbert Royce McCullough and Mary Helen Kilman; m. John T. Ross, Feb. 1972; 1 child Matthew Eli Ross ; m. James R. Mercer III, May 30, 1980; children: James R. Mercer IV, Michael Colin. BA in English, U. Tex. at Arlington, 1997; MA in English, U. North Tex., 1999. Editor Harcourt Coll. Publishers, Ft. Worth; therapeutic writing instr. Pathways Consulting, 2002—; staff writer, editor McKinley Comm., Dallas, 2002—. Author: Past Lives; editor: McCullough Family Letters, 2002; author: Theories of Relativity, 2002.

MERCER, RICHARD JOSEPH, retired advertising executive, freelance writer; b. Elizabeth, N.J., Mar. 29, 1924; s. George Washington and Margaret Elizabeth (Walsh) M.; m. Muriel Davis, June 24, 1945 (dec. Mar. 1999); children: Richard George, Karen, James Davis, Lesley Ann; m. Joan Youmans Cozens, Apr. 2, 2001. L.B. in Journalism, Rutgers U., 1949. Announcer, copywriter, news reporter Sta. WCTC, New Brunswick, N.J., 1946-49; asso. creative dir., then v.p., dir. BBDO, Inc., N.Y.C., 1949-76; sr. v.p., creative exec. SSC&B, Inc., 1977-83, exec. v.p. creative, 1983-85; sr. v.p., assoc. creative dir. McCann-Erickson, Inc., 1985-87. Part-time lectr. Rutgers U. Sch. Bus., New Brunswick, N.J., 1988-89; speaker in field. Chmn. Roselle (N.J.) Police Raise Referendum Com., 1958; promotion chmn. Cranford (N.J.) United Fund, 1960; publicity dir. Friends of Mendham (N.J.) Libr., 1974-75; bd. dirs. Friends of Nantucket Atheneum, 1991-2000, pres., 1996-98; trustee Atheneum, 1993-98; mem. Nantucket Airport Commn., 1999-2002. With A.C.

USNR, 1943-45. Decorated Air medal.; Recipient 10 Clio awards, 2 Effie awards, also Silver Key award Advt. Writers Assn. N.Y.C. Mem. NATAS, Air Force Assn. (life), Col. Henry Rutgers Soc., Broadcasters Found. Roman Catholic. Home: 24 Pleasant St Nantucket MA 02554-3374

MERCER, RON, professional basketball player; b. May 18, 1976; Student, U. Ky. Guard Boston Celtics, 1997-99, Denver Nuggets, 1999-00, Orlando Magic, 2000, Chgo. Bulls, 2000—. Named SEC Player of the Yr., 1997. Office: c/o Chgo Bulls United Ctr 1901 W Madison St Chicago IL 60612-2459*

MERCER, WALT NEILSON, psychologist, researcher; b. Houston, Jan. 17, 1958; s. Neal Wilbur and Ophelia Devota (Smith) M.; m. Helen Warren Childs, May 18, 1991; children: Margaret Childs Mercer, Neilson Childs Mercer. BS in Home Econs., Tex. Tech. U., 1980; M in Religious Edn., So. Bapt. Theol. Sem., 1983; PhD, U. North Tex., 1994. Lic. psychologist, Tex. Tchg. asst. U. North Tex., Denton, 1987, tchg. fellow, 1987-92; psychotherapist Family Svcs., Inc., Bedford, Tex., 1987-93; psychology intern Henry Ford Hosp., Detroit, 1993-94, neuropsychology fellow, 1994-96; lic. psychologist, dir. rsch. Brownschools Rehab Ctr., Austin, Tex., 1986—. Contbr. articles to profl. jours. Named Outstanding Young Men of Am., Jaycees, 1984. Mem. APA (divsn. 40), Internat. Neuropsychol. Soc., Nat. Acad. Neuropsychology. Home: 5432 Moon Shadow Dr Austin TX 78735-6017 Office: Healthcare Rehab Ctr 1106 W Dittmar Rd Austin TX 78745-6328 Fax: 512-462-6636. E-mail: wmercer@brownschools.com.

MERCHANT, CAROLYN, environmental history educator; b. Rochester, N.Y., July 12, 1936; d. George Eugene and Elizabeth Merchant; m. Hugh Iltis, Aug. 5, 1961 (div.); children: David Iltis, John Iltis; m. Charles Grier Sellers, Sept. 5, 1993. AB, Vassar Coll., 1958; MA, U. Wis., 1962, PhD, 1967; D (hon.), Umeå (Sweden) U., 1995. From asst. to assoc. prof. U. San Francisco, 1969-78; from asst. prof. to prof. U. Calif., Berkeley, 1979—. Chancellor's prof. environ. history, philosophy and ethics, former chair dept. conservation and resource studies U. Calif., Berkeley; vis. prof. Ecole Normale Superieure, Paris, 1986; vis. fellow Sch. Social Scis., Murdoch U., Perth, Australia, 1991; lectr., cons. in field. Author: The Death of Nature: Women, Ecology and the Scientific Revolution, 1980, 2d edit., 1990 (also Japanese, German, Italian, Swedish and Chinese edits.), Ecological Revolutions: Nature, Gender and Science in New England, 1989, Radical Ecology: The Search for a Livable World, 1992 (also Japanese edit.), Earthcare: Women and the Environment, 1996, Columbia Guide to American Environmental History, 2002; editor, contbg. author: Major Problems in American Environmental History: Documents and Essays, 1993, Key Concepts in Critical Theory: Ecology, 1994, Green Versus Gold: Sources in California's Environmental History, 1998; contbr. numerous articles to profl. jours. Fellow Am. Coun. Learned Socs., 1978, Ctr. for Advanced Study in the Behavioral Scis., 1978, John Simon Guggenheim fellow, 1995, Nat. Humanities Ctr. fellow, 2001; Fulbright sr. scholar, 1984; grantee NEH, 1977, 1981-83, NSF, 1976-78, Nathan Cummings Found., 1992, Calif. Coun. for the Humanities, 1997-98. Office: Dept Environ Sci Policy and Mgmt U Calif 135 Giannini Hall Berkeley CA 94720-3312

MERCHANT, DONALD JOSEPH, retired microbiologist and educator; b. Biltmore, N.C., Sept. 7, 1921; s. Oscar Lowell and Bess Lee (Clark) M.; m. Marian Adelaide Yeager, May 31, 1943; children— Nancy Adele, Barry Scott, Karen Ruth. AB, Berea Coll., 1942; MS, U. Mich., 1947, PhD, 1950; Diploma of Merit, Gen. Assembly/Presbyn. Ch. of, Kinshasa, Rep. of the Congo, 2000. Instr. U. Mich., 1948-51, asst. prof., 1951-58, asso. prof., 1958-64, prof., 1964-69; dir., scientist W. Alton Jones Cell Sci. Center, Tissue Culture Assn., Lake Placid, N.Y., 1969-72; prof. U. Vt., 1969-72; prof., chmn. dept. microbiology and immunology Eastern Va. Med. Sch., Norfolk, 1973-86, prof. emeritus, from 1986. Dir. Tidewater Regional Cancer Network, 1974-88; cons. U.S. Army Biol. Lab., 1966-68; mem. sci. adv. bd. Found. for Research on the Nervous System, Boston, 1965-69, Masonic Med. Research Lab., Utica, N.Y., 1970-75; mem. Nat. Prostatic Cancer Task Force, Nat. Cancer Inst., 1972-79, 83-86. Author: (with others) Handbook of Cell and Organ Culture, 1960, 2d edit., 1964; Editor: (with J.V. Neel) Approaches to the Genetic Analysis of Mammalian Cells, 1962, Cell Cultures for Virus Vaccine Production, 1968, (with others) Biology of Connective Tissue Cells, 1962; contbr. articles to profl. jours., chpts. to books. Served with U.S. Army, 1944-46. Mem. Am. Acad. Microbiology, Am. Soc. Microbiology (past pres. Mich. br.), Soc. Exptl. Biology and Medicine, Am. Soc. Cell Biology, Tissue Culture Assn. (pres. 1964-68), Va. Acad. Sci., N.Y. Acad. Scis., Assn. Community Cancer Centers, Brit. Soc. Cell Biology, Royal Soc. Medicine. Presbyterian. Home: Virginia Beach, Va. Died Aug. 9, 2002.

MERCHANT, ISMAIL NOORMOHAMED, film producer, film director; b. Bombay, Dec. 25, 1936; arrived in U.S., 1958; s. Noormohamed and Hazrabi (Memon) Rehman. BA, St. Xavier's Coll., Bombay, 1958; MBA, NYU, 1960. V.p. Merchant Ivory Prodns. Inc., N.Y.C., 1962—. Prodr.: (films) The Householder, 1963, Shakespeare Wallah, 1965, The Guru, 1969, Bombay Talkie, 1970, Adventures of a Brown Man in Search of Civilization, 1971, 1972, Helen, Queen of the Nautch Girls, 1973, Autobiography of a Princess, 1975, The Wild Party, 1975, Sweet Sounds, 1976; prodr., prodr.: (films) Roseland, 1977, Hullabaloo Over Georgie and Bonnie's Pictures, 1978, The Europeans, 1979, The Five-Forty-Eight, 1979, Jane Austen in Manhattan, 1980, Quartet, 1981, Heat and Dust, 1983, The Bostonians, 1984, A Room With a View, 1986, The Deceivers, 1988, Slaves of New York, 1988, Mr. and Mrs. Bridge, 1990, Howards End, 1992, The Remains of the Day, 1993, Jefferson in Paris, 1995, Surviving Picasso, 1996, A Soldier's Daughter Never Cries, 1998, The Golden Bowl, 2000; dir.: Creation of Woman, 1960, Mahatma and the Mad Boy, 1973; prodr.: Feast of July, 1995; dir.: The Courtesans of Bombay, 1982, In Custody, 1993, The Proprietor, 1996, Cotton Mary, 1999, The Mystic Masseur, 2001; author: Ismail Merchant's Indian Cuisine, 1986, The Making of the Deceivers, 1988, Ismail Merchant's Vegetarian Cuisine, 1991, Ismail Merchant's Florence, 1994, Ismail Merchant's Passionate Meals: The New Indian Cuisine for Fearless Cooks and Adventurous Eaters, 2d edit., 2001, Once Upon a Time...The Proprietor, 1996, Ismail Merchant's Paris: Filming and Feasting in France, 1999; prodr.: (films) The Perfect Murder, 1988, The Ballad of the Sad Cafe, 1991; author: (autobiography) My Passage from India - A Film Makers Journey from Bombay to Hollywood and Beyond. Decorated comdr. des Arts and Lettres France, Padma Bhushan India. Fellow: Brit. Acad. Film and TV Arts (hon.). Home: 400 E 52nd St New York NY 10022-6404 Office: 250 W 57th St Ste 1825 New York NY 10107-1899 E-mail: imerchant@merchantivory.com.

MERCHANT, MYLON EUGENE, physicist, engineer; b. Springfield, Mass., May 6, 1913; s. Mylon Dickinson and Rebecca Chase (Currier) M.; m. Helen Silver Bennett, Aug. 4, 1937; children: Mylon David (dec.), Leslie Ann Merchant Alexander, Frances Sue Merchant Jacobson. BS magna cum laude, U. Vt., 1936, DSc (hon.), 1973; DSc, U. Cinn., 1941; DSc (hon.), U. Salford, Eng., 1980; D of Engring (hon.), Kettering U., 1994. Research physicist Milacron, Inc., 1940-48, sr. research physicist, 1948-51, asst. dir. research, 1951-57, dir. phys. research, 1957-63, dir. sci. research, 1963-69, dir. research planning, 1969-81, prin. scientist, mfg. research, 1981-83; dir. advanced mfg. research Metcut Research Assocs., Inc., 1983-90; sr. cons. TechSolve, Cinn., 1990—. Adj. prof. mech. engring. U. Cin., 1964-69, mfg. engring., 2001-; vis. prof. mech. engring. U. Salford, Eng., 1973—; hon. prof. U. Hong Kong, 1995—. Bd. dirs. Dan Beard council Boy Scouts Am., 1967-80, pres.'s council, 1980— . Recipient Georg Schlesinger prize City of Berlin, 1980; Otto Benedikt prize Hungarian Acad. Scis., 1981, 1st Japan Soc. Precision Engring. prize, 1997; named to Automation Hall of Fame, 1995. Fellow Soc. Tribologists and Lubrication Engrs. (pres. 1952-53), Am. Soc. Metals Internat., Ohio Acad. Sci., Soc. Mfg. Engrs. (hon. mem., pres. 1976-77); mem. NAE, ASME (hon., mfg. medal 1988), Internat. Instn. Prodn. Engring. Rsch. (hon., pres. 1968-69), Engrs. and Scientists of Cin. (pres. 1961-62), Fedn. Materials Socs. (pres. 1974), Phi Beta Kappa, Sigma Xi, Tau Beta Pi. Achievements include research on machining process and systems approach to manufacturing. Home: 3939 Erie Ave Apt 105 Cincinnati OH 45208-1913 Office: TechSolve 1111 Edison Dr Cincinnati OH 45216-2265 E-mail: merchant@techsolve.org., gmerchant@fuse.net.

MERCHANT, ROLAND SAMUEL, SR. hospital administrator, educator; b. N.Y.C., Apr. 18, 1929; s. Samuel and Eleta (McLymont) M.; m. Audrey Bartley, June 6, 1970; children: Orelia Eleta, Roland Samuel, Huey Bartley. BA, NYU, 1957, MA, 1960; MS, Columbia U., 1963, MSHA, 1974. Asst. statistician N.Y.C. Dept. Health, 1957-60, statistician, 1960-63, N.Y. Tb and Health Assn., N.Y.C., 1963-65; biostatistician, adminstrv. coord. Inst. Surg. Studies, Montefiore Hosp., Bronx, N.Y., 1965-72; resident in adminstrn. Roosevelt Hosp., N.Y.C., 1973-74; dir. health and hosp. mgmt. Dept. Health, City of N.Y., 1974-76; from asst. adminstr. to adminstr. West Adams Cmty. Hosp., L.A., 1976; spl. asst. to assoc. v.p. for med. affairs Stanford U. Hosp., Calif., 1977-82, dir. office mgmt. and strategic planning, 1982-85, dir. mgmt. planning, 1986-90; v.p. strategic planning Cedars-Sinai Med. Ctr., L.A., 1990-94; cons. Roland Merchant & Assocs., 1994—. Clin. assoc. prof. dept. family, community and preventive medicine Stanford U., 1986-88, dept. health rsch. and policy Stanford U. Med. Sch., 1988-90. With U.S. Army. 1951-53. USPHS fellow. Fellow APHA, Am. Coll. Healthcare Execs.; mem. N.Y. Acad. Scis. Home: 27335 Park Vista Rd Agoura Hills CA 91301-3639

MERCHENTHALER, ISTVAN JOZSEF, anatomist, neuroscientist; b. Baja, Hungary, Apr. 29, 1949; came to U.S., 1988; s. Istvan and Maria (Gomori) M.; m. Agnes Katalin Major, Nov. 6, 1969; children: Istvan, Boglarka, Nora. MD, U. Med. Sch., Pecs, Hungary, 1974; PhD, Hungarian Acad. Sci., Budapest, 1986; DsC, Hungarian Acad. Sci., 1992; DHabil, Albert Szent-Gyorgyi Med. Sch., Szeged, Hungary, 1997. Asst. prof. dept. anatomy Univ. Med. Sch., Pecs, Hungary, 1974-86, assoc. prof., 1986-92; vis. asst. prof. dept. anatomy U. N.C., Chapel Hill, 1981-83; vis. asst. prof. Hebert Rsch. Ctr. Tulane U., New Orleans, 1984; vis. scientist, head functional morphology sect. NIEHS/NIH, Research Triangle Park, N.C., 1988-94; dir. functional morphology Women's Health Rsch. Inst. Wyeth-Ayerst Rsch., Radnor, Pa., 1994—. Adj. assoc. prof. dept. cell biology and anatomy U. N.C., 1991-94. Contbr. more than 150 articles on hypothalamic hormones and estrogen receptors to profl. jours. and books. Recipient Lenhossek award Hungarian Assn. of Anatomists, 1984, Outstanding Young Scientist award Hungarian Acad. Scis., 1986. Achievements include research in estrogen action in brain; alzheimer's disease and ischemia.que. Office: Wyeth Rsch WHRI 500 Arcola Rd Collegeville PA 19426 E-mail: merchei@wyeth.com., istvanmerchenthaler@msn.com.

MERCIER, EILEEN ANN, management consultant; b. Toronto, Ont., Can., July 7, 1947; d. Thomas Sidley and Frances Katherine (Boone) Falconer; m. Ernest Cochrane Mercier, Feb. 8, 1980; children: Jenny, Sheelagh, Peter, Michael, Stuart. BA with honors, Waterloo Luth. U., 1968; MA, U. Alta., Can., 1969; fellow, Instn. Can. Bankers, 1975; MBA, York U., 1977. Mgr. corp. fin. Toronto-Dominion Bank, 1972-78, portfolio mgr. TD capital; dir., U.S. comm. ops. Canwest Capital Corp., Toronto, 1978-81; mgr. fin. strategy & planning Gulf Can. Ltd., 1981-86, mgr. corp. fin.; v.p. The Pagurian Corp., 1986-87; v.p., treas. Abitibi-Price, Inc., 1987-88, v.p. corp. devel., 1989-90, sr. v.p., CFO, 1990-95. Bd. dirs. Covington Fund, Inc., TeeKay Shipping Corp., The CGI Group Inc., Winpak Ltd., ING Bank Can., Quebecor World, Inc. Past chmn., mem. bd. govs. Wilfrid Laurier U., Waterloo, Ont.; vice chair Workplace Safety and Ins. Bd. Ont., York U., U. Health Network. Recipient Outstanding Bus. Leader award Sch. Bus. and Econs., Wilfrid Laurier U., 1991, Award for Outstanding Contbn. Schulich Sch. of Bus. York U., 1997. Office: Finvoy Mgmt Inc 199 Cranbrooke Ave Toronto ON Canada M5N 1M6

MERCKER, MARY ALICE, aviation school administrator; b. Kansas City, Mo., June 29, 1932; d. Kenneth Foster Rhees and Catherine Mary (Tellman) Henel; m. Reid Martin, Nov. 23, 1950 (div. Nov. 1969); children: Reid J., Kenneth C., Mark T., Mary M., Theodore H., Sylvia R., Ben X., Teresa I. Student, Phoenix Coll., 1949-50; AA, Pima Coll., 1990-93; student, U. Ariz., 1994. Fed. aviation adminstr.; comml. pilot; cert. flight instr. Instr. Ariz. Sch. Aviation, Tucson, 1979, Tucson Cmdr., 1980, AVRA Flt. Ctr., Marana, Ariz., 1976-78; pres., founder Alpha Air, Inc., Tucson, 1980—; sec., treas. Manasco Inc., 1987—. Aviation cons., Tucson, 1987—; adj. profl aviation Pima C.C., Tucson, 1988-94, curriculum cons., 1988-93. Author: Northumberland Dreaming, 1998, also numerous poems. Recipient 2nd Place Sparrowgrass Poetry Forum, 1996, 1st Place Sparrowgrass Chapbook award, 2001. Mem. Ariz. Pilots Assn., Aircraft Owners and Pilots Assn., 99's (life). Home: 6220 W Belmont Rd Tucson AZ 85743-9212 Office: Alpha Air Inc HC 2 Box 282 Tucson AZ 85735-9709 E-mail: alphair@msn.com.

MERCOLA, DANIEL A. medical researcher; BA in Psychology, UCLA, 1963, MS in Biophysics, 1967, PhD in Biophysics, 1969; MA, Oxford U., 1974; BM, U. Southampton, England, 1981. Diplomate Am. Bd. Pathology, lic. physician Calif. Postdoctoral fellow U. Oxford, England, 1969-74, mem. faculty agrl. and biol. scis. England, 1974-79; mem. faculty Wolfson Coll., Oxford, England, 1974-79; resident in pathology U. Calif., San Diego, 1981-85, asst. clin. prof. pathology dept., 1985-95; staff physician DVAMC, 1985-97; mem. staff Sidney Kimmel Cancer Ctr., 1993—, prof., 1998. Mem. grants review subcom. for oncology U.S. Dept. Vet. Affairs, 1994-98. Mem. editl. bd. Antisense and Nucleic Acid Drug Devel., Cancer Gene Therapy, 1992—; contbr. articles to profl. jours. Assoc. cancer ctr. U. Calif., San Diego, 1999—. Fellow Coll. Am. Pathologists, Royal Soc. Medicine; mem. Am. Assn. Clin. Chem. (mem. organizing com. ann. San Diego conf. 1992-97). Office: Sidney Kimmel Cancer Ctr 10835 Altman Row San Diego CA 92121-1131 Fax: 858-450-3251.

MERCORELLA, ANTHONY J. lawyer, former state supreme court justice; b. N.Y.C., Mar. 6, 1927; s. Sante and Josephine (Bozzuti) M.; m. Maria G. Delucia, June 16, 1956; children: Anne Mercorella Flynn, Susan Mercorella Creavin, Robert, Carole Crinieri. BA, L.I. U., 1949; LLD, Fordham U., 1952. Bar: N.Y. Law asst. City Ct., City of N.Y., 1955-62; chief law asst. Civil Ct., City of N.Y., 1962-65; mem. N.Y. State Assembly, 1965-72; councilman City Coun., City of N.Y., 1973-75; judge Civil Ct., City of N.Y., 1975-79; justice Supreme Ct., N.Y.C., 1980-84; ptnr. Wilson, Elser, Moskowitz, Edelman & Dicker, 1984—. Currently arbitrator and mediator in various dispute resolution systems. With USN, 1945-46, Europe, Pacific. Mem. ABA (del. N.Y. State Bar Assn.), N.Y. State Bar Assn., Assn. of Bar of City of N.Y., Bronx County Bar Assn. (pres. 1971), Columbian Lawyers Westchester County (pres. 1984). Office: Wilson Elser Moskowitz Edelman & Dicker 150 E 42nd St New York NY 10017-5612 E-mail: mercorellaa@wemed.com., ajmmediate@aol.com.

MERCOUN, DAWN DENISE, human resources executive; b. Passaic, N.J., June 1, 1950; d. William S. and Irene F. (Micci) M. BS in Bus. Mgmt., Fairleigh Dickinson U., 1978. Personnel payroll coordinator Bentex Mills, Inc., East Rutherford, N.J., 1969-72; employment mgr. Inwood Knitting Mills, Clifton, N.J., 1972-75; gen. mgr. Consol. Advance, Inc., Passaic, 1975-76; v.p. human resources Gemini Industries, Inc., Clifton, 1976-96; CEO, sr. human resource cons. DDM Cons. L.L.C., Bloomingdale, N.J., 1996—; v.p., bd. dirs. Contact Morris-Passaic. Mem. Soc. for Human Resource Mgmt., Am. Compensation Assn., Internat. Found. Employee Benefits, Earthwatch Rsch. Team, IMA Mgmt. Assn. (bd. dirs., trustee 1996-97), Daus. of the Nile (Maalas Temple No. 20, elective officer 1993-96, queen 1996-97). Republican.

MERCURI, JOAN B. foundation executive; b. N.Y.C. BA, Va. Commonwealth U., 1984. Mgmt. positions various corps., Ill., 1986-96; exec. dir. Frank Lloyd Wright Home and Studio Found., Oak Park, 1996—; pres., CEO Frank Lloyd Wright Preservation Trust, 2000—. Mem. Am. Assn. Museums, Nat. Trust for Hist. Preservation, Frank Lloyd Wright Bldg. Conservatory, Am. Soc. Assn. Execs., Assn. Fundraising Profls., Board Source.

MERCURIO, EDWARD PETER, natural science educator; b. Orange, Calif., Dec. 28, 1944; s. Peter Amadeo and Jeanne (Monteleone) M.; m. Jeanne Roussel Gable, Oct. 18, 1980 (div. Dec. 1984); 1 child, Katherine Roussel; m. Patricia Ann Kahler, Apr. 12, 1987; children: Peter Edward, Rose Sierra. BA, UCLA, 1967, MA, 1970, CPhil, 1978. Research asst. UCLA, 1971, teaching asst., 1968-71; instructional assoc. Golden West Coll., Huntington Beach, Calif., 1972-73; cons. Monterey County Planning Dept., Salinas, 1980; prof. Hartnell Coll., 1973—. Photographer in field, Calif., 1961—; lectr. in field, Calif., 1970—; cons. in field, 1980—; rschr. in field, 1994—. Fellow Woodrow Wilson Nat. Fellowship Found., 1967. Mem. AAAS, Sierra Club. Democrat. Avocations: writing and performing original songs, hiking, backpacking, plant and animal breeding, mountain bicycle riding. Home: 647 Wilson St Salinas CA 93901-1346 Office: Hartnell Coll 156 Homestead Ave Salinas CA 93901-1628 E-mail: mercurio@jafar.hartnell.cc.ca.us. *Personal philosophy: My personal philosophy can be summarized by five words beginning with the letter H: Hedonism, Holism, Hyperopia, Harmony and Health.*

MERCURIO, LAURA DEUBLER, textile design company executive; b. Akron, Ohio, Feb. 14, 1953; d. Lawrence Philip and Ruth Dale (Winders) Deubler; m. Joseph Michael Mercurio Jr., Sept. 23, 1979. Student, U. Ga., 1971-73; BS, Ga. Inst. Tech., 1976. Textile designer Maharam Fabric Corp., Hauppauge, NY, 1976-83; dir. product design J.M. Lynnd, Inc. div. Adam James Textiles, Smithtown, 1984-87; pres. Deubler Mercurio Color Design Cons., St. James, 1987—; bd. dirs. Color Mktg. Group, 1991—94; pres. Internat. Assn. Color Cons./Designers N.Am., Denver; vice chmn. Contract Color Directions, 2000—02. Vice chmn. edn. com. Color Mktg. Group, Richmond, Va., 1984-86; chmn. edn. com., 1987-89. Recipient IBD Gold award Inst. Bus. Designers, 1979, Roscoe award Resources Council, 1985, Product Design award Corp. Design Mag., 1987. Mem. NAFE, Color Assn. U.S., Assn. Contract Textiles, Am. Soc. Textiles and Materials. Avocations: perennial flower gardening, photography, birdwatching.

MERCURIO, PHILIP JOSEPH, computer programmer/analyst; b. Chgo., Nov. 2, 1958; Student, Calif. Inst. Tech., 1975-78; BA in Exptl. Psychology, U. Calif., San Diego, 1980. Programmer cognitive sci. lab. U. Calif., San Diego, 1979-83, programmer quantitative morphology lab., 1980-86; graphics cons. GTI Graphics Div., 1983-86; games programmer/designer FTL Games, 1987-89; staff programmer/analyst San Diego Supercomputer Ctr., 1989—. Graphics cons. Rsch. Inst. at Scripps Clinic, San Diego, 1988-89, Angel Studios, San Diego, 1986-88, Rockwell, Boeing, Hughes, L.A., 1985-88. Graphics specialist: (videotape) QMLab Demo reel, 1983, Cephalic Symbols (Dolphin Head Anatomy), 1986, Stokesian Dynamics Simulation of Fluid Flow, 1989; programmer: (computer game) Dungeon Master/Amiga, 1988. Mem. Assn. for Computing Machinery, IEEE Computer Soc. Office: San Diego Supercomputer Ctr PO Box 85608 San Diego CA 92186-5608

MERCURIO, RENARD MICHAEL, real estate corporation executive; b. N.Y.C., June 22, 1947; s. Pasquale J. and Ann F. Mercurio; m. Abbie Gonzalez, June 29, 1968; children— Kristin, Allison. BA, Queens Coll., N.Y.C., 1968; MBA, U. Rochester, 1969. CPA, N.Y.; lic. real estate broker, Calif. Sr. accountant Peat, Marwick & Mitchell, N.Y.C., 1969-73; mgr. Gulf & Western Industries, Inc., 1973-78; v.p., treas. Famous Players Ltd., Toronto, Ont., Can., 1978-81; exec. v.p. Famous Players Realty Ltd., 1981-84; pres. Design Twenty-Seven Ltd., 1984—, Renric Holdings, Ltd., 1987—; CFO Schickedanz Real Estate, Palm Beach Gardens, Fla., 1999—. Mem. AICPA, N.Y. State Soc. CPAs, Calif. Assn. Mortgage Brokers, Calif. Assn. Realtors.

MERDEK, ANDREW AUSTIN, publishing/media executive, lawyer; b. Portland, Maine, Oct. 11, 1950; s. Philip and Eleanor (Weiss) M.; m. Jeanne Mullen, July 22, 1983; children: David, Jonathan. AB, Middlebury Coll., 1972; JD, U. Va., 1978. Bar: D.C. 1978, U.S. Dist. Ct. D.C. 1979, U.S. Ct. Appeals (D.C. cir.) 1979, U.S. Supreme Ct. 1982. Reporter, editor Portland Press Herald, 1973-75; assoc. Dow, Lohnes & Albertson, Washington, 1978-86, ptnr., 1986-87; v.p., gen. mgr. Atlanta Constitution and Journal, 1987-92; v.p. legal affairs, corp. sec. Cox Enterprises, Inc., Atlanta, 1993—. Mem. Newspaper Assn. of Am. (chmn. legal affairs com.), Order of Coif, Phi Beta Kappa. Home: 445 Mount Vernon Hwy NW Atlanta GA 30327-4313 Office: Cox Enterprises Inc 6205 Peachtree Dunwoody Rd Atlanta GA 30328- E-mail: andy.merdek@cox.com.

MERDINGER, CHARLES JOHN, civil engineer, naval officer, academic administrator; b. Chgo., Apr. 20, 1918; s. Walter F. and Catherine (Phelan) M.; m. Mary McKelleget, Oct. 21, 1944; children: Anne, Joan, Susan, Jane. Student, Marquette U., 1935-37; BS, U.S. Naval Acad., 1941; BCE, Rensselaer Poly. Inst., 1945, MCE, 1946; DPhil (Rhodes scholar), Brasenose Coll., Oxford U., Eng., 1949; LHD (hon.), Sierra Nev. Coll., 1987; DLitt (hon.), U. Nev., Reno, 1994. Registered profl. engr., Wis. Commd. ensign USN, 1941, advanced through grades to capt. Civil Engr. Corps, 1959; served aboard USS Nevada, USS Alabama Atlantic and Pacific, 1941-44; design, constrn. pub. works Panama, 1946-47, Washington, Bremerton, Wash., Adak, Alaska and Miramar, Calif., 1949-56; comdg. officer, dir. U.S. Naval Civil Engring. Lab., Port Hueneme, 1956-59; pub. works officer U.S. Fleet activities, Yokosuka, Japan, 1959-62; head English, history and govt. dept. U.S. Naval Acad., Annapolis, Md., 1962-65; asst. comdr. ops. & maintenance Naval Facilities Engring. Command, Navy Dept., 1965-67; pub. works officer Seabees (NSA), DaNang, Vietnam, 1967-68; comdg. officer Western div. Naval Facilities Engring. Command, San Bruno, Calif., 1968-70; pres. Washington Coll., Chestertown, Md., 1970-73; v.p. Aspen (Colo.) Inst. Humanistic Studies, 1973-74; dep. dir. Scripps Instn. Oceanography, La Jolla, Calif., 1974-80; dir. Avco, 1978—. Author: Civil Engineering Through the Ages, 1963; contbr.: articles to Ency. Britannica; others. Mem. Md., Calif., Oreg. and Nev. Selection Coms. for Rhodes Scholars, sec. Nev. Com., 1982-89; exec. vol. Boy Scouts Am.; sec., mem. exec. com. Md. Ind. Coll. and Univ. Assn., 1971-72; mem. So. Regional Edn. Bd, 1971-73, Nat. Com. History and Heritage of Am. Civil Engring., 1965-72; Alumni trustee U.S. Naval Acad., 1971-74; mem. coun. Rensselaer Poly. Inst., 1972—; trustee Found. for Ocean Rsch., 1976-80, Desert Rsch. Inst. Found., Nev., 1983-92, U. Nev. Reno Found., 1986-93; chmn. bd. trustees Sierra Nev. Coll., 1980-87, chmn. bd. emeritus, 1987; commr. N.W. Assn. Commn. on Colls., 1988-93. Pfc Wis. Nat. Guard, 1935—37. Decorated Legion of Merit with combat V; named All-Am. in lacrosse, 1945, Papal Knight Grand Cross Equestrian Order of Holy Sepulchre of Jerusalem, 1992; inducted into Rensselaer Athletic Hall of Fame, 1983; recipient Disting. Eagle Scout award, 1984. Fellow ASCE (Nat. History and Heritage award 1972), Explorers Club, Soc. Am. Mil. Engrs. (Toulmin medal 1952, 57, 61); mem. NSPE, Soc. History Tech., Am. Soc. Engring. Edn., Brasenose Soc., Pearl Harbor Survivors Assn., Nat. Eagle Scout Assn. (regent), Phalanx, Sigma Xi, Tau Beta Pi, Chi Epsilon. Clubs: Vincent's, Oxford. Roman Catholic. Home: 726 Tyner Way PO Box 7249 Incline Village NV 89452-7249 also: 5538 Caminito Consuelo La Jolla CA 92037-7217

MEREDITH, BRADFORD L. musician, educator; b. Hays, Kans., Mar. 15, 1954; s. Lyle H. and Patricia L. Meredith; m. Debbie R. Brown, Sept. 3, 1988; children: Mitch, Monte. MusB in Edn., St. Mary Plains Coll., Dodge City, Kans., 1984. Cert. tchr. Fla. Music tchr. Pinellas County Schs., Largo, Fla., 1999—. Choral soloist, sect. leader Chapel by the Sea. Mem.: MENC-FMEA. Republican. Avocation: travel. Home: 9676 Lake Seminole Dr E Largo FL 33773 Office: Osceola HS 8751 98th St N Largo FL 33777 Home Fax: 727-319-0524; Office Fax: 727-545-6412. Personal E-mail: brad_m_33770@yahoo.com.

MEREDITH, DALE DEAN, civil engineering educator; b. Centralia, Ill., Mar. 24, 1940; s. Leslie Edward Meredith and Beulah Marie (McClelland) Nattier; m. Linda Jean Hutson, July 3, 1965; children: Sarah Elizabeth, Laura Jane. AA, Centralia Twp. Jr. Coll., 1961; BS, U. Ill., 1963, MS, 1964, PhD, 1968. Registered profl. engr., N.Y., Ill. Asst. prof. U. Ill., Urbana, 1968-73; assoc. prof. civil engring. SUNY, Buffalo, 1973-79, prof., 1979-2000, chmn. dept. civil engring., 1987-96, prof. emeritus, 2000—. Co-author: Design and Planning Engineering Systems, 1973, 2d edit., 1985; also over 50 articles. Vice pres. Baptist Conv. N.Y., Syracuse, 1982-84, 94-95, chmn. exec. bd., 1987. Grantee U.S. Office Water Research and Tech., 1966-73, 75-78, U.S. Dept. Interior, 1968-79, U.S. Dept. Commerce, 1976-79, various pvt. cos., 1979—, N.Y. State Agys., 1980-2000. Fellow ASCE (chmn. exec. com. Water Resources Planning and Mgmt. div., 1988, editor jour. Water Resources Planning and Mgmt. 1982-84); mem. Am. Geophys. Union, Am. Soc. Engring. Edn., Am. Water Resources Assn. (editor Water Resources Bull. 1990-91). Office: SUNY Dept Civil Engring Buffalo NY 14260-4300 E-mail: ciedale@eng.buffalo.edu.

MEREDITH, DONALD LLOYD, librarian; b. Batesville, Miss., Sept. 11, 1941; s. Duward Lee and Julia Mae (Ferguson) M.; m. Evelyn Charlene Rickett, Aug. 15, 1964; Christopher Todd, Tracey Hope. BA, Harding U., 1964; MTh, Harding Grad. Sch., 1967; MS in Libr. Sci., U. N.C., 1968. Asst. libr. Harding Grad. Sch. Religion, Memphis, 1968-70, assoc. libr., 1970-83, libr., 1983—. Mem.: Memphis Libr. Coun. (chmn. 1982—83, treas. 1994—96, 2000—), Tenn. Theol. Libr. Assn. (pres. 1981—82), Am. Theol. Libr. Assn. Home: 4897 Welchshire Ave Memphis TN 38117-5646 Office: Harding Grad Sch Libr 1000 Cherry Rd Memphis TN 38117-5424

MEREDITH, DONALD R. counselor; b. Eunice, La., Sept. 30, 1940; s. Roy and Esther Ruth M.; m. Sally Hill Meredith, Sept. 30, 1967; children: Todd, Carmen, Kathryn, Tiffany. Student, U. Tex. Stockbroker Bernett Hickman, Dallas, 1963-64; staff mem. Campus Crusade for Christ, Fayetteville, Ark.,

Dallas, 1964-71; pres., founder Christian Family Life, Dallas, Charlotte, N.C., 1971—. Founder Family Life Ministry, Little Rock, 1976-79, Fellowship Bible Ch., Dallas, 1972-75, Little Rock, 1975-79, Potomac Chapel, McLean, Va., 1979-87, Woodbridge (Va.) Fellowship, 1987-89; co-founder, v.p. Joe Gibbs Racing, 1989-2000. Author: Two Becoming One, 1999, Becoming One, 1979. Republican. Office: 5301 W WT Harris Blvd Charlotte NC 28269 E-mail: xnfamily@aol.com.

MEREDITH, GARY S. physician; b. N.Y.C., Apr. 13, 1954; s. Sidney and Ann M.; m. Michelle Rose Pantirer, Jan. 8, 1984; children: Joshua, David. BA, Boston U., 1976; MD, N.Y. U., 1981. Diplomate Am. Bd. Internal Medicine, Am. Bd. Rheumatology. Intern Bellevue Hosp., N.Y.C., 1981-82, resident, 1982-84; fellow NYU Med. Ctr., 1984-86, chief fellow rheumatology, 1985-86; chief divsn. rheumatology dept. internal medicine Franklin Hosp. Med. Ctr., Valley Stream, N.Y., 1990—; pvt. practice, Rockville Centre, 1986—. Physician NYU Med. Ctr., Franklin Hosp. Med. Ctr., Mercy Med. Ctr., South Nassau Cmtys. Hosp. Contbr. articles to profl. jours. Fellow ACP, Am. Coll. Rheumatology. Office: 242 Merrick Rd Rockville Centre NY 11570-5254

MEREDITH, HOWARD LYNN, American Indian studies educator; b. Galveston, Tex., May 25, 1938; s. Howard and Lillian (Pitts) M.; m. Mary Ellen Meredith; m. Lynn, Lee. BS, U. Tex., 1961; MA, Stephen F. Austin State U., 1963; PhD, U. Okla., 1970. Asst. prof. history Ky. Wesleyan Coll., Owensboro, 1967-71; exec. Indian work Exec. Coun. Episcopal Ch., N.Y.C., 1971-75; dir., hist. pres. Okla. Hist. Soc., Oklahoma City, 1975-79; adminstr., editor Eco. Co., Ginn, C. Merrill & Bacone, 1979-85; regents prof. interdisciplinary studies U. Sci. and Arts of Okla., Chickasha, 1985—. Author: Bartley Milam: Principal Chief, 1985, Hasinai, 1988 (award 1989), Modern American Indian Tribal Government, 1993-94, Dancing on Common Ground, 1995, Elohi, 1997 (award 1998), Short History of Native Americans in the United States, 2001. Bd. mem., sec. Red Earth, Oklahoma City, 1988-94; bd. mem. Nat. Indian Hall of Fame, Anadarko, 1990—; bd. dirs., chmn. Pan-Am. Indian Humanities Ctr., Chickasha. Recipient Muriel Wright award Okla. Hist. Soc., Oklahoma City, 1980, Co-Founders Book award Westerners Internat., Tucson, 1989, McCasland award Okla. Heritage Assn., Oklahoma City, 1994, Coke Wood award for Best Monograph, 1998. Episcopalian. Avocation: water colors. Office: Pan Am Indian Humanities Ctr U Sci and Arts of Okla Chickasha OK 73108-0001 E-mail: facmeredithhl@usao.edu.

MEREDITH, JOHN, non-profit executive; b. Oct. 1962; s. James and Sylvia Meredith; m. Shirley Shelton. BBA, North Ga. Coll. and State U., 1984; MSM, Ga. Tech., 1985; JD, Baylor U., 1988; MPA, Harvard U., 1997. Assoc. Woodard, Hall & Primm, Houston, 1988-96; pres., gen. counsel Aspiring Youth of Am., 1997—. Contbr. articles to profl. jours. Bd. dirs. Leadership Houston, 1999-2000; pres. Frostwood Homeowners Assn., Houston, 1994-96. Named one of 5 Outstanding Young Texans, Tex. Jr. C. of C., 2000, one of 5 Outstanding Young Houstonians, Houston Jr. C. of C., 2000; recipient Lewis Hine award for children and youth Nat. Child Labor Com., 1998 Mem. Tex. Young Lawyers Assn. (bd. dirs. 1994-96, 98-2000, Outstanding Young Lawyer of Tex. 1998), Houston Vol. Lawyers Assn. (bd. dirs. 1994-96, Outstanding Young Lawyer of Houston 1998). Office: Aspiring Youth of Am Ste 217 6250 Westpark Dr Houston TX 77057

MEREDITH, KAREN ANN, accountant, financial executive; b. San Antonio, Sept. 30, 1954; d. Carroll J. and Doris J. Keller; m. William F. Meredith, July 6, 1974; children: Brian, Matthew. BBA in Acctg., U. North Tex., 1979. CPA, Tex.; CFP. Sr. acct. Deloitte Haskins & Sells, Dallas, 1979-82; CFO, sr. v.p. Commerce Savs. Assn., 1982-86; exec. dir., chmn. bd. Am. Assn. Boomers, Irving, Tex., 1989-95; mng. ptnr. Meredith & Assocs., 1986—. Author various ednl. programs, 1991. Bd. dirs. Generations Found., N.Y.C., 1992. Recipient Fin. Edn. and Awareness award H.D. Vest Fin. Svcs., 1990. Mem. AICPA, Tex. Soc. CPAs (mem. Dallas chpt.), Internat. Assn. CFPs. Office: Meredith & Assocs 2621 W Airport Fwy Ste 101 Irving TX 75062-6069

MEREDITH, LYNNETTE ANN LOGAN, accountant; b. Carthage, Ill., Sept. 23, 1966; d. Ralph Kenneth and Eileen May (Redenius) Logan; m. Richard LaMont Meredith, Dec. 18, 1993. BA, Augustana Coll., Rock Island, Ill., 1988. Internal auditor Deere & Co., Moline, Ill., 1988—89, acct., 1989—93, 1996—2000, internal auditor, 1993—94; acct. John Deere Harvester Works, 1994—96; project mgr. Deere & Co., 2000—. Mem. panel United Way, Moline/Rock Island, 1990-93; advisor Jr. Achievement, Moline, 1990-94; treas. Cedars at Woodfield Condo Assn., 1992-94, pres., 1995, John Deere Mixed Softball League, 1992—, John Deere Mixed Volleyball League, 1992-98. Named Advisor of Yr. Jr. Achievement, 1993. Lutheran. Office: Deere & Co One John Deere Rd Moline IL 61265-1356

MEREDITH, MERI HILL, reference librarian, educator; b. Riverside, Calif., May 30, 1943; d. William Beans and Marie Louise (Zantzinger) Hill; m. William Rinehardt Meredith, Mar. 17, 1970 (div.); children William Rinehardt III, Sarah Daingerfield Meredith. AB in French, George Washington U., Washington, 1967; MLS, Ind. U., 1980. Cataloger Ind. U., Bloomington, 1980-81; bus. libr. Cummins Engine Co., Columbus, Ind., 1981-88; pres. Info. and Comm. Rsch., Inc., 1989-92; reference libr. Ohio State U. Bus. Libr., 1992—. Bd. dirs. Sch. of Libr. and Info. Sci., Ind. U., Bloomington; pres., co-founder Ind. On-Line Users Group, Indpls. Mem. AAUP, Spl. Librs. Assn., Acad. Libr. Assn. of Ohio. Republican. Roman Catholic. Home: 1800 Lafayette Pl Apt A1 Columbus OH 43212-1609 Office: Ohio State U Bus Libr Raymond E Mason Hall 250 W Woodruff Ave Columbus OH 43210-1133 E-mail: meredith.18@osu.edu.

MEREDITH, OWEN NICHOLS, public relations executive, genealogist; b. Etowah, Tenn., Mar. 27, 1924; s. Owen Habner and Ora (Nichols) M.; m. Mary Virginia Wright, July 19, 1980. BA, U. Va., 1946; MA, Syracuse U., 1952. Sub-features editor Together mag.-Meth. Pub. House, Nashville and Chgo., 1953-57; pub. info. dir. Nashville-Davidson County ARC, 1957-70; exec. dir. Tenn. State Mus., Nashville, 1970-72; owner, mgr. Gazetteer Typesetters, 1973-74; pub. relations dir. Tenn. ARC, 1974-89; pvt. practice, 1989—. Author: The Parish Activities Handbook, 1996, (with R. McBride) The Hedden Family of North Georgia, 1957, The Nichols Family of North Georgia, 1960, (with Lee Seitz) A History of the American Red Cross in Nashville, Tennessee, 1982, (with Mary Virginia Meredith and Susan Wright Lyons) One Cup Love and a Pinch of Catnip, 1998; editor: (with McBride and M. Rothrock) Eastin Morris' 1834 Tennessee Gazetteer, 2d edit., 1971; contbr. articles, photographs and book revs. to hist. jours. Mem. ARC Disaster Res., 1989—; vol. archivist Diocese of Nashville, 1992—. Mem. Pub. Rels. Soc. Am. (cert.), Tenn. Soc. Health Care Pub. Rels., Internat. Assn. Bus. Communicators, Confederate Meml. Lit. Soc. (Tenn regent 1972-80), Tenn. Exec. Residence Preservation Found., 1971—), Conf. for Pastoral Planning and Coun. Devel. Office: 410 Lancaster Ave Nashville TN 37212-4013 E-mail: meredithm@k12tn.net.

MEREDITH, RUBY FRANCES, radiation oncologist, researcher, educator; b. Sedalia, Mo., Feb. 6, 1948; d. Russell R. and Eunice (Curry) M.; m. Michael Pfaff. BA, U. Mo., 1969; MA, Ind. U., 1971, PhD, 1974; MD, Ohio State U., 1983. Diplomate in therapeutic radiology Am. Bd. Radiology. Intern, resident Med. Coll. Va., 1983-87; asst. scientist Allegheny-Singer Rsch. Corp., Pitts., 1978; asst. prof. U. Ala. Sch. Medicine, Birmingham, 1987-92, assoc. prof., 1992—. Audio reviewer Ednl. Revs., Inc., Birmingham, 1992—. Mem. edn. com. Cancer Supporters, Birmingham, 1990; bd. dirs. Leukemia Soc. Am., Pitts., 1979. Recipient Harold C. Bold rsch. award Am. Inst. Biol. Scientists, 1974, Circle of Excellence award Health Svc. Found., 1997, HSF Health Rsch. award United Way/Health Svcs., Pitts. Office: U Ala Birmingham Dept Radiation Oncology 619 19th St S Birmingham AL 35233-0001

MEREDITH, THOMAS BRIAN, healthcare consultant; b. Grand Rapids, Mich., Dec. 31, 1957; s. George William and Lucille Francis (Calandrino) M.; m. Colleen Masterson, Oct. 10, 1987; children: Mark Thomas, Brian Christopher. BS in Bus. Adminstrn. Acctg., Ohio State U., 1980. CPA. Acct. Shaker Med. Ctr., Cleve., 1980—83; asst. acctg./budget mgr. Luth. Med. Ctr., 1983—85; sr. mgr. KPMG Peat Marwick, 1985—95; ptnr. Advantage Consulting, Inc., Independence, 1995—. Mem. AICPAs, Healthcare Fin. Mgmt. Assn. (Follmer Bronze Merit award 1995, advanced mem., Reeves Silver award 1999), Healthcare Fin. Mgmt. Assn. Northeast Ohio (bd. dirs. 1996-98). Avocations: reading, music, golf. Office: Advantage Consulting Inc 4600 Rockside Rd Ste 105 Independence OH 44131-2132

MEREDITH, THOMAS C. academic administrator; Vice chancellor exec. affairs U. Miss., until 1988; pres. Western Ky. U., Bowling Green, 1988-97; chancellor U. Ala. Sys., Tuscaloosa, 1997—. Office: Univ Sys Ga 270 Washington St SW Atlanta GA 30334-9007 E-mail: chancellor@usg.edu.

MEREDITH, WILLIAM ROBERT, SR. physician, educator; b. Wright City, Okla., 1923; BS in Medicine, U. Ark., 1946, MD, 1947. Diplomate Am. Bd. Surgery. Intern Norfolk Gen. Hosp., 1947-48; resident Lloyd Nolan Hosp., Fairfield, 1953-57; with Jefferson Regional Med. Ctr., Pine Bluff, 1957-99; clin. prof. emeritus U. Ark. Sch. Med. Scis., 1978—. Mem. AMA, Am. Coll. Surgeons. Home: Apt 1310 3310 Washington Ave Pascagoula MS 39581

MERENBLOOM, ROBERT BARRY, hospital and medical school administrator; b. Balt., July 13, 1947; Philip William and Florence Ruth (Surosky) M. BA, U. Md., 1969; MS, Morgan State U., 1973; MBA, U. Balt., 1980. Mem. staff Mayor Balt. Office Manpower Resources, 1972-73; assoc. staff mem. Office Dean, U. Md. Med. Sch., 1976-80; adminstrv. officer rsch. and devel. Balt. VA Med. Ctr., 1974-80; assoc. adminstr. dept. medicine Sch. Medicine Johns Hopkins U., Balt., 1980-84, adminstr. dept. medicine Johns Hopkins Hosp., 1984-88, assoc. Sch. Hygiene and Pub. Health, 1984-88; lectr. dept. medicine Bowman Gray Sch. Medicine Wake Forest U., 1988-93, asst. chmn. dept. medicine, 1988-91, assoc. chmn. dept. medicine, 1991-93; vice chmn., asst. prof. medicine, clin. asst. prof. health adminstrn. & policy, asst. dean clin. ops. Med. U. S.C., Charleston, 1993—, asst. dean for clin. ops., 1993—. Instr. sociology U. Balt., 1973-76; adj. faculty Weekend Coll., Coll. Notre Dame, Balt., 1980—; assoc. mgmt. Babcock Grad. Sch. Bus. Wake Forest U. Exec. dir. J. Paul Sticht Ctr. on Aging. Recipient Hon. Corpsmen Leader award Office Mayor Balt., 1973; Outstanding Performance award Balt. VA Med. Ctr., 1975, Superior Performance award, 1980. Mem. Am. Gerontology Soc., So. Gerontology Soc., Soc. Rsch. Adminstrs., Nat. Coun. Univ. Rsch. Adminstrs., Adminstrs. Internal Medicine, Assn. Am. Med. Colls. (group on bus. affairs), Am. Hosp. Assn., Am. Pub. Health Assn., Am. Coll. Healthcare Adminstrs., Soc. Gen. Internal Medicine, Johns Hopkins Club, Piedmont Club, Harbour Club.

MERENDA, SAM JOHN, retired radiologist; b. Scammon, Kans., 1915; s. Frank and Domenica (Molinar) M.; married; children: Francis John, Laura Kay, Robert Michael, Mary Ann, Sam J. Jr., James Thomas, Joseph Charles. BS in Medicine, St. Louis U., 1937, MD, 1939. Cert. in radiology. Intern St. Louis City Hosp., 1939-40; resident in radiology St. Louis County Hosp., 1947-50. Fellow Am. Coll. Radiology; mem. AMA, Radiol. Soc. N.Am., Am. Roentgen Ray Soc., Am. Soc. Nuclear Medicine. Roman Catholic.

MERENDINO, K. ALVIN, surgical educator; b. Clarksburg, W.Va., Dec. 3, 1914; s. Biagio and Cira (Bivona) M.; m. Shirley Emma Jane Hill, July 6, 1943; children: Cira Anne Watts, Nancy Jane Napuunoa, Susan Hill Mitchell, Nina Merendino-Sarich, Maria King Merendino-Stillwell. BA, Ohio U., 1936, LLD (hon.), 1967; MD, Yale U., 1940; PhD, U. Minn., 1946. Diplomate Am. Bd. Surgery, Am. Bd. Thoracic Surgery. Intern Cin. Gen. Hosp., 1940-41; resident U. Minn. Hosp., Mpls., 1941-45; rsch. asst. Dr. Owen H. Wangensteen, 1942-43; trainee Nat. Cancer Inst., 1943-45; dir. program in postgrad. med. edn. in surgery Ancker Hosp., St. Paul, 1946-48; instr. dept. surgery U. Minn., Mpls., 1944-45, asst. prof. dept. surgery, 1945-48; assoc. prof. dept. surgery U. Wash., Seattle, 1949-55, dir. exptl. surgery labs., dept. surgery, 1950-72, prof. dept. surgery, 1955-81, prof. emeritus, 1981—, prof. and adminstrv. officer dept. surgery, 1957-64, prof., chmn., 1964-72; chmn. dept. surgery King Faisal Specialist and Rsch. Ctr., Riyadh, Saudi Arabia, 1976, dir. med. affairs Saudi Arabia, 1976-79, dir. Cancer Therapy Inst., spl. cons. to Coun., supr. for exec. mgmt., assoc. dir. med. affairs Saudi Arabia, 1981-82; dir. ops. King Faisal Med. City, 1981-85. Mem. adv. com. for med. rsch., Boeing Airplane Co., 1959-67, chmn., 1962l cons. Children's Orthopedic Hosp., Seattle, 1972-82; mem. adv. com. on heart disease and surgery for crippled children's svc., Wash. State Dept. Health and Div. Vocational Rehab., 1961; mem. surgery study sect. NIH, 1958-62, subcom. on prosthetic valves for cardiac surgery, chm. 1st Nat. Conf., 1960, mem. adv. com. 2d Nat. Conf. on Prosthetic Heart Valves, 1969, Surgery A study sect. chmn., 1970-72, Nat. Heart and Lung Inst. Tng. Com., 1965-69; cons. VA, Seattle, 1949-59, 65-81; mem. adv. com. on hosps. and clinics, USPHS, 1963-66; mem. surgery test com. Nat. Bd. Med. Examiners, 1963-67; mem. surgery resident rev. com., Conf. Com. on Grad. Edn. in Surgery, 1963-73, vice-chmn., 1972-73; chmn. 2d Saudi Arabian Med. Conf., Riyadh, 1978; mem. com. on postgrad. med. edn., Kingdom of Saudi Arabia Ministry of Health, 1978-79. Editor in chief: Prosthetic Valves for Cardiac Surgery, 1961; assoc. editor: Prosthetic Heart Valves, 1969; mem. editorial bd. Am. Jour. Surgery,. 1958-83, Jour. Surg. Rsch., 1961-69, Pacific Medicine and Surgery, 1964-68, King Faisal Hosp. Medicine Jour. (renamed Annals of Saudi Medicine), 1981-85; contbr. articles to profl. jours., chpts. to books; producer movies on surgery. Recipient cert. of merit Ohio U. Alumni Assn., 1957, Outstanding W.Va. Italian-Am. award W.Va. Italian Heritage Festival Inc., Clarksburg, W.Va., 1984, Spirit of Freedom award A. James Mancin, Sec. State W.Va., 1984, Disting. W. Virginian award State of W.Va., 1984, John Baird Thomas Meml. award Ohio U.; named Surgery Alumnus of Yr., U. Minn., 1981, Disting. Citizen Wash. State, Lt. Gov. John Cherberg, 1981; NIH grantee, 1951-76; Verdi scholar Yale U. Fellow ACS (numerous coms., bds.), Soc. of Univ. Surgeons (councilman at large 3 yrs.), Internat. Soc. Surgery; mem. Am. Surg. Assn. (adv. mem. com. 1959-64, v.p. 1972-73), Am. Assn. for Thoracic Surgery, Halsted Soc., Henry N. Harkins Surg. Soc., N. Pacific Coast Surg. Assn., Seattle Surg. Soc. (honored special tribute annual meeting 1997), So. Surg. Soc. (Arthur H. Shipley award 1972), Am. Bd. Surgery 1958-64 (vice chmn. 1962-63, chmn. 1963-64, emeritus 1964—); University Club, Seattle Golf Club, Phi Beta Kappa, Sigma Xi, Beta Theta Pi (sec., pres.), Phi Beta Pi (hon.). Republican. Episcopalian. Avocations: golf, fly fishing, bird hunting, gardening. Home: The Highlands Seattle WA 98177 Office: U Wash Sch Med Dept Surgery Seattle WA 98195-0001

MERESCHAK, VOLMAR A. retired obstetrician-gynecologist; b. Ansonia, Conn., 1921; MD, U. Pa., 1945. Diplomate Am. Bd. Ob-Gyn. Intern Grace-New Haven Cmty. Hosp., 1945-46; resident in ob-gyn. Kings County Hosp., Bklyn., 1948-49, Lincoln Hosp., N.Y.C., 1950-51; staff Warren Hosp., Phillipsburg, N.J.; ret. Fellow ACS; mem. ACOG, AMA, Am. Soc. Colposcopy and Cervical Pathology.

MERFELD, GERALD LYDON, artist; b. Des Moines, Feb. 19, 1936; m. Carol L. Fiser; 1 child, Elizabeth Ann. Studied with William Mosby, Chgo. Studio asst. Dean Cornwell; combat artist USN. Group exhbns. include Mass. Mus. of Fine Arts, Springfield, Smithsonian Inst., Audubon Artists, N.Y.C., Nat. Acad. of Western Art, others; represented in permanent collections Marietta Coll., USN Archives, John J. McDonough Collection of Am. Art, John Deere & Co. Bd. dirs. Frontier Pathway Scenic Byway, Colo., 1995-98. Recipient Gold Medal of Honor, Am. Artist Profl. League, 1989, Am. Artists Mag. award Knickerbocker Artists, 1989, 2 Gold medals Washington Sq. Exhibit, N.Y.S., Painting award Okal. Mus. of Art, 1975, Mainstreams Juror's award of Merit, Marietta Coll., 1976, Mainstreams award of Distinction, 1977, First prize Hope Show, 1980, First prize Butler Inst. of Am. Art. Office: Brookwood Gallery 2302 Muddy Rd Westcliffe CO 81252 E-mail: merfeld@ris.net.

MERGENOVICH, SHIRLEY ANN, educator; b. Clinchco, Va., July 13, 1938; d. Floyd Fuller and Cara Mae (Deel) Fuller; m. Carl Mullins (div. 1963); children: Roger Dean, Rex Dale; m. Peter Mergenovich, May 1, 1971 (dec.). AA, C.C. St. Louis, 1973, cert. in small bus. mgmt., 1989; BA in History summa cum laude, Maryville Coll., St. Louis, 1975; MEd in Adminstrn., U. Mo., 1980. Cert. lifetime secondary prin. and tchr. Retail sales rep. Libson Shops, St. Louis, 1960-61; inventory control and customer svc. Precision Auto Components Co., 1961-64; exec.sec. Precision Auto/TRW, 1964-65; city clk. City of Ballwin, Mo., 1965-66; exec. dir. Charter Rev. Commn., St. Louis County, 1966-67; asst. to planning dir. St. Louis County, 1968-69; asst. econ. rschr. Reg. Ind. Devel. Co., Clayton, Mo., 1969-70; tchr. Ea. history and culture N.W. R-1 Sch. Dist., House Springs, 1975-90; founder/dir. adult and continuing edn. prog. Jefferson Coll. R-1 Schs., 1985-86. Entrepreneurial grad., founder, prin. mgmt. cons. and exec. coach. Performance Builders, St. Louis, 1986; mem. adj. faculty C.C. St. Louis, Webster U., Maryville U., St. Louis; dir. adult continuing edn. Jefferson Coll., 1985-86; part-time mgmt. cons., 1970-79; writer, facilitator strategic planning and performance-based tng. programs; writer, implementor pilot study for tchrs. on tchg. and learning styles in pub. schs.; spearheaded and coordinated Korean-Am. cultural exch.; econ. rsch. Danforth Found. Grant Project. Author: A Statistical Summary of Vocational Technical Programs in St. Louis Metro Area, 1970; co-author: Analysis and Projection of Manpower Requirements in St. Louis Metro Area, 1970, Discipline Handbook, 1978; contbr. articles to profl. jours. Active Mentoring Women in Transition; exec. recruiter and coach Coaching and Placement of Downsized Execs. and Mgrs. Named Woman Entrepreneur, Small Bus. Adminstrn., 1989, others; Fulbright scholar to Korea on history, culture and quality, 1982. Mem. ASTD (bd. dirs., v.p. St. Louis chpt. 1984-88, editor/pub. Torch newsletter 1984-88), Am. Soc. for Quality, Mo. Cmty. Edn. Assn. (bd. dirs. 1979-81), St. Louis Woman's Commerce Assn. (mem. gov.'s adv. coun. on vocat. tech. edn. and regional indsl. growth 1968-70), N.W. St. Louis Hons. Assn., Woman Entrepreneurial Alumnae Assn., Employee Involvement Assn. (Heartland chpt.). Avocations: travel, reading, keeping fit, family, writing.

MERGENTHALER, MARY ELIZABETH, artist; b. Louisville, Oct. 23, 1934; d. Lively Burgess and Ann-Eliza Hall (Smith) Willoughby; m. Dean Dana Mergenthaler, Dec. 27, 1958; children: Sally Jo Mergenthaler Blanchat, Christopher Dean. BA, Stetson U., 1956; ASCP cert., 1957. Cytology technician U.S. Govt., Hagerstown, Md., 1957-58. One-woman shows include North Palm Beach C. of C., 1988, Barnett Bank Ctr., West Palm Beach, 1990, Palm Beach Gardens Cmty. Ctr., 1996; contbr. articles to profl. jours. Mem. Am. Watercolor Soc. (assoc.), Palm Beach Watercolor Soc., Artist Guild Norton Gallery (membership chmn. 1987-89, hon. mention 1988, Hallsey Griffith award 1988), Norton Gallery Art, Profl. Artist Assn., Palm Beach Coun. Arts, No. Palm Beaches C. of C., Women in Arts, Profl. Artists Registry. Republican. Episcopalian. Avocations: reading, swimming, piano. Studio: 1169 Old Dixie Hwy Lake Park FL 33403-2311

MERGLER, H. KENT, investment counselor; b. Cin., July 1, 1940; s. Wilton Henry and Mildred Amelia (Pulliam) M.; m. Judith Anne Metgzer, Aug. 17, 1963; children: Stephen Kent, Timothy Alan, Kristin Lee. BBA with honors, U. Cin., 1963, MBA, 1964. CFA, C.I.C. Portfolio mgr. Scudder, Stevens & Clark, Cin., 1964-68, exec. v.p. Chgo., 1970-73; v.p. Gibralter Rsch. & Mgmt., Ft. Lauderdale, Fla., 1968-70; ptnr. Stein Roe & Farnham, 1973-84; ptnr., pres., dir., prin. Stein Roe & Farnham, Inc., Chgo., 1984-91, also mem. exec. com.; pres. Stein Roe Investment Trust; mng. ptnr., chief investment officer Loomis, Sayles & Co., L.P., Palm Beach Gardens, Fla., 1992-2000; chmn., pres., CEO Northstar Capital Mgmt., Inc., 2000—. Arbitrator Nat. Assn. Security Dealers, Inc., 1976-82. Chmn. adminstrv. bd. Christ United Meth. Ch., Ft. Lauderdale, 1981-83; mem. fin. com. Kenilworth Union Ch., 1989-92, 1994-99, bd. dirs., 1994-99; chmn. investment com. Broward Cmty. Found., 1992-2001; mem. Martin County Econ. Coun., 1992-2000; bd. dirs. Pine Crest Prep. Sch., 1982-84, bd. advisors, 1984-87; corp. adv. bd. U. Cin. Coll. Bus. Adminstrn., 1991-94, 2001-; bd. dirs. Hibiscus House Children's Found., 1993-99, 2001—, chmn. investment com., 1994-99, 2001—; bd. dirs. Coral Ridge Little League, 1976-84, pres., 1980-81; elder, chmn. fin. com., mem. stewardship com. First Presbyn. Ch., Stuart, 2002--. Mem. Fin. Analysts Soc. So. Fla. (bd. dirs. 1974-78, pres. 1975), Bond Club Ft. Lauderdale (bd. dirs. 1978-82), Willoughby Golf Club, Cullasaja Club (Highlands, N.C.), City Club Palm Beach, Beta Gamma Sigma, Beta Theta Pi. Republican. Home: 3980 SE Old Saint Lucie Blvd Stuart FL 34996-5119 Office: 4400 PGA Blvd Ste 600 Palm Beach Gardens FL 33410-6559

MERGLER, HARRY WINSTON, engineering educator; b. Chillicothe, Ohio, June 1, 1924; s. Harry Franklin and Letitia (Walburn) M.; m. Irmgard Erna Steudel, June 22, 1948; children— Myra A. L., Marcia B. E., Harry F. BS, MIT, 1948; MS, Case Inst. Tech., 1950, PhD, 1956. Aero. research scientist NACA, 1948-56; mem. faculty Case Inst. Tech., 1957—, prof. engring., 1962—, Leonard Case prof. elec. engring. emeritus, 1988—; dir. Digital Systems Lab., 1959—. Vis. scientist, USSR, 1958; vis. prof. Norwegian Tech. U., 1962; cons. to industry, 1957— ; editor Control Engring. mag., 1956— ; pres. Digital/Gen. Corp., 1968-72; cons. Exploratory Research div. NSF. Author: Digital Systems Engineering, 1961, also articles, chpts. in books. Served with AUS, 1942-45. Recipient Case gold medal for sci. achievement Case Inst. Tech., 1980. Fellow IEEE (bd. dirs. 1987-89, v.p. 1989, Lamme medal 1978, Centennial medal 1984, 3d Millennium medal 2000); mem. NAE, Indsl. Electronic Soc. (pres. 1977-79), Cleve. Engring. Soc., N.Y. Acad. Scis., Blue Key, Sigma Xi, Tau Beta Pi, Theta Tau, Pi Delta Epsilon, Zeta Psi. Home: 9658 Halyards Ct Fort Myers FL 33919-4492 E-mail: hwmergler@aol.com.

MERGUERIAN, ARSHAG, architect; b. Gaza, Sept. 25, 1926; came to U.S., 1956; s. Merguer and Coharig (Hagopian) M.; m. Barbara-Joyce Nahigian, Aug. 13, 1961; children: Gayané-Karen, Tamara-Elaine. BA, Am. U. Beirut, 1950, BSc in Civil Engring., 1952; MArch, Harvard U., 1960. Registered architect, Mass. Civil engr. Motherwell Bridge, Qatar, 1952-55, British Somaliland, 1955-56; self-employed arch. Cambridge and Wellesley, Mass., 1966—. Author book revs. and articles on arch.; commd. projects, Saudi Arabia, 1977-80. Vice chair Wellesley Design Rev. Bd., 1980-90, mem., 1990—; chair Am. Gen. Benevolent Union Am., Watertown, Mass., 1962-64; mem. Wellesley Hist. Dist. Commn., 1980—. Mem. AIA. Armenian Apostolic. Avocations: skiing, tennis, swimming. Home: 21 Pine Tree Rd Wellesley MA 02482-4711

MERHIGE, ROBERT REYNOLD, JR. lawyer; b. N.Y.C., Feb. 5, 1919; s. Robert Reynold and Eleanor (Donovan) Merhige; m. Shirley Galleher, Apr. 24, 1957; children: Robert Reynold III, Mark Reynold. LLB, U. Richmond, 1942, LLD (hon.), 1976; LLM, U. Va., 1982; LLD (hon.), Washington and Lee U., 1990, Wake Forest U., 1994. Bar: Va. 1942. Ptnr. Bremner Merhige Montgomery & Baber, Richmond, 1945-67; judge U.S. Dist. Ct., 1967—; resigned, 1998; counsel Hunton & Williams, Richmond, 1998—. Guest lectr. trial tactics Law Sch. U. Va., Edwald Disting. prof. law, 1987—88; adj. prof. Law Sch. U. Richmond, 1973—87; appeal agt. Henrico County Draft Bd., 1954—67; mem. NCAA spl. com. discipline rules; profl.-in-residence, Zambia, 1994. Co-author: Virginia Jury Instructions. Mem. Richmond Citizens Assn. With USAAF, World War II. Decorated Air medal with four oak leaf clusters; named Citizen of the Yr., 3d Dist. Omega Psi Phi, 1972, Richmond Urban League, 1977, Richmonder of the Yr., Style Mag., 1984, 1987, Citizen of the Yr., 1986; named one of 100 Most Influential Richmonders of Last Century, Style Mag. and Valentine Mus., 2000; recipient Amara Civic Club award, 1968, Spl. award, City of Richmond, 1967, Disting. Alumni award, U. Richmond, 1979, Disting. Svc. award, Nat. Alumni Coun. U. Richmond, 1979, Herbert T. Harley award, Am. Judicature Soc., 1982, Athenian Citizen medal, 1979, Torch of Liberty award, Anti-Defamation League of B'nai B'rith, 1982, T.C. Williams Sch. of Law Disting. Svc. award, 1983, Pres.'s award, Old Dominion Bar Assn., 1986, William J. Brennan award, 1986, Merit Citation award, NCCJ, 1987, William B. Green award for professionalism, U. Richmond, 1989, Marshal-Wythe medallion (William & Mary Faculty award), 1989, Lewis F. Powell, Jr. award for professionalism and ethics, Am. Inss of Ct., 1999. Fellow: Va. Law Found.; mem.: Nat. Arbitration Forum (arbitrator), Nat. Patents Bd. (cert. panelist), FedNet (dispute resolution), John Marshall Inns of Ct. (founding mem.), Jud. Conf. U.S., Va. Trial Lawyers Assn. (chmn. membership com. 1964—65, Disting. Svc. award 1977), Am. Law Inst. (faculty), Richmond Bar Assn. (pres. 1963—64, multi-dist. lit. panel 1990—, Hill-Tucker award 1991), Va. Bar Assn., Omicron Delta Kappa (Hunter W. Martin Profl. award 1998). Office: Hunton & Williams Riverfront Plz East Tower 951 E Byrd St Richmond VA 23219-4074 E-mail: MerhigeR@Hunton.com.

MERIANOS, JOHN JAMES, medicinal chemist; b. Krokeai Sparta Laconia, Greece, Feb. 12, 1937; came to the U.S., 1957; s. Demetrios Nicholaos and Eleni (Patrianakos) M.; m. Stavroula P. Doumas, Apr. 21, 1974; children: Laura, Helen, Demetri. BS in Pharmacy magna cum laude, New Eng. Coll. Pharmacy, 1961; MS in Pharm. Chemistry, U. Wis., 1963, PhD in Medicinal Chemistry, 1966. Registered pharmacist, N.J. Rsch. chemist FMC Corp., Princeton, N.J., 1966-68; rsch. scientist, sr. rsch. scientist Millmaster Onyx Corp., Jersey City, 1968-87; sr. rsch. scientist GAF Corp., Wayne, 1987-92; rsch. fellow ISP Corp., 1992-95; dir. R & D Sutton Labs., Chatham, N.J., 1992-98; sr. sci. fellow preservative tech. ISP Internat. Specialty Products,

1999-00. Exec. dir. MerPan Chem. Cons. Diagnostic Reagents, Pharmaceutics, Middletown, N.J., 1974-00. Contbr. chpt. to book: Disinfection, Sterilization and Preservation, 5th edit., 2000. Pres. Krokeai Soc., U.S. and Can., 1990-95. Recipient Kappa Psi gold key Kappa Psi Fraternity, Boston, 1961, Microbiologist of Yr. award Soc. Indsl. Microbiologists, 1997. Mem. Am. Chem. Soc., Am. Assn. Pharm. Scientist, Soc. Cosmetic Chemists, Soc. Indsl. Microbiology, N.J. Pharm. Assn. Greek Orthodox. Achievements include 99 patents in indsl. biocides and synergisms in cosmetic preservatives; inventor of Onamer M, Polyquaternium-1 Polyquad TM a preservative system for contact lens cleaners. Avocations: volleyball, soccer, bowling. Home: 32 Doherty Dr Middletown NJ 07748-3303 Office: ISP Corp 1361 Alps Rd Wayne NJ 07470

MERIC, RENE PIERRE, JR. shipbuilding marine construction executive; b. Ama, La., Sept. 21, 1925; s. Rene Pierre and Frances Elizabeth (Sellers) M.; m. Ruth Elizabeth Rasch Meric, Nov. 24, 1945 (dec. Dec. 3, 1991); children: Nancy, Ruth, Robin, R. Pierre III, Philip; m. Millicent Clesi Meric, May 22, 1993 (dec. Feb. 2002). BEE, Tulane U., New Orleans, 1947; student, LSUNO Grad. Sch., New Orleans, 1967. Profl. engr., La. Tech. asst. to price negotiator to ship supv. Todd Johnson Drydocks, Inc., New Orleans, 1947-51; floor broker Loop-Weaver & Co., 1951-55; project engr. Avondale Industries, Inc., New Orleans, 1955, chief engr., 1968, asst. v.p., 1969, v.p. contract adminstrn, 1972, group v.p. contract adminstrn., 1978, group v.p. indsl. divsn., 1985, group v.p. indsl. group, 1987, corp. v.p. indsl. group, 1990, corp. v.p. indsl./comml. group, 1992-98; ret., 1998. Cons. Avondale Industries, Inc., New Orleans, 1998-99. Avondale rep. Jr. Achievement, New Orleans, 1950. With USN, 1943-45. Mem. Soc. Naval Architects and Marine Engrs., Am. Bur. Shipping (Engring. Com. 1978-82), The Propeller Club, Navy League of the U.S., Sigma Alpha Epsilon. Republican. Roman Catholic. Avocations: real estate, home improvement, secondary residence, genealogy. Home: 5863 Marcia Ave New Orleans LA 70124-1121

MERICLE, SUZANNE ELEANOR, retired secondary school educator; b. Columbus, Ohio, May 26, 1926; d. Idwal and Eleanor (Marker) Jones; m. Merlin Edward Stewart, July 26, 1945 (div. July 22, 1957); m. Donald Pershing Mericle, June 19, 1959; children: Sandy Sue Klinko, David Stewart. B, U. Toledo, 1954; M, Johns Hopkins U., 1968. Cert. tchr. Ohio, Md. Secondary tchr. Toledo (Ohio) Bd. Edn., 1954—61, Bd. Edn., Towson, Md., 1961—62, Harford County, 1962—86. Drama coach Libby H.S., Toledo, 1958—60; writer curriculum guide Bd. Edn., Harford County, 1970—72, Harford County, 1980—82, dept. chair, 1970—86. Author: Poetic Perceptions, 1997, Tripping Along with Mabel & Margaret, 1998. Vol. tchr. Fine Arts Coun., Brooksville, Fla., 1998, 1999; chair Just Poets, Hernando County, 1995—2002; chair charity Forest Green, Timber Pines, Spring Hill, 2000, 2001; asst. to pastor Trinity Luth. Ch., Joppa, Md., Holy Cross Luth Ch., Spring Hill. Recipient hon. mention award, Poet's Rev., 1996—2000. Mem.: Fla. State Poets Assn., Inc., Nat. Fedn. State Poetry Socs., Delta Kappa Gamma (program chair). Lutheran. Avocations: oil painting, porcelain dolls, poetry, travel, swimming. Home: 7426 Sugarbush Dr Spring Hill FL 34606 E-mail: suzanne-mericle@webtv.net.

MERIDAN, PAULA M. interior design executive; b. Boston, Sept. 9, 1955; d. Stuart Theodore and D. Elaine (Fuller) M. AA, Colby Sawyer Coll., 1975; BA, Wheaton Coll., Norton, Mass., 1977. Pres., chief exec. officer The Lily Pad, Westwood, Mass., 1977-87; broker Millward Assocs., Wellesley, 1987-90; pres., chief exec. officer pvt. interior design firm, 1990—. Bd. dirs. Brigham Women's Hosp. Aux., Boston, 1993—. Mem. Jr. League of Boston (bd. dirs. 1994—). Home: 42 Woodlawn St Dedham MA 02026-6918

MERIDEN, TERRY, physician; b. Damascus, Syria, Oct. 12, 1946; came to U.S., 1975; s. Izzat and Omayma (Aidi) M.; m. Lena Kahal, Nov. 17, 1975; children: Zina, Lana. BS, Sch. Sci., Damascus, 1968; MD, Sch. Medicine, Damascus, 1972, doctorate cum laude, 1973. Diplomate Am. Bd. Internal Medicine. Resident in infectious diseases Rush Green Hosp., Romford, Eng., 1973; house officer in internal medicine and cardiology Ashford (Eng.) Group Univ. Hosps., 1973-74; sr. house officer in internal medicine and neurology Grimsby (Eng.) Group Univ. Hosps., 1974; registrar in internal medicine and rheumatology St. Annes Hosp., London, 1974-75; jr. resident in internal medicine Shadyside Hosp., Pitts., 1975-76, sr. resident in internal medicine, 1976-77; fellow in endocrinology and metabolism Shadyside Hosp. and Grad. Inst., 1976-77; clin. asst. prof. U. Ill., Peoria, 1979; pres. Am. Diabetes Assn., 1982-84; dir. Proctor Diabetes Unit, 1984—, 1984—. Adviser to the Gov. of Ill. on Diabetes. Mem. editorial bd. Diabetes Forecast mag., Clin. Diabetes, 1990; contbr. articles to profl. jours. Fellow ACP, FACE, Am. Coll. Endocrinology; mem. AMA (Recognition award 1985, ADA (chmn. profl. edn. and rsch. 1980—, mem. editl. bd. and Spanish lit. bd. nat. bd. dirs. 1986—, vice chmn. nat. com. on diabetes edn. and affiliate svcs. 1986—, Outstanding Svc. award 1984, Outstanding Diabetes Educator award 1986), Am. Cancer Soc. (Life Line award 1983), Am. Assn. Clin. Endocrinology (founding), Am. Coll. Endocrinology, The Obesity Found. (Century award 1984, Recognition award 1985). Home: 115 E Coventry Ln Peoria IL 61614-2103 Office: 900 Main St Ste 300 Peoria IL 61602-1049

MERIDITH, DENISE PATRICIA, business consultant; b. N.Y.C., Apr. 14, 1952; d. Glenarva C. and Dorothy (Sawyer) M. BS, Cornell U., 1973; MPA, U. So. Calif., 1993. Various positions Bur. Land Mgmt., various locations, 1973-79, chief divsn. resources Alexandria, Va., 1980-83, dep. state dir., 1983-86, Sante Fe, 1986-89, assoc. state dir. Calif., 1989-91, state dir. Ea. states, 1991-93; dep. dir. BLM, Washington, 1993-95; state dir. Ariz., 1995—2002. Pres. Greater Phoenix Black C. of C., 1998-99; bd. dirs. Phoenix Black, Girl Scouts; mem. bd. trustees Cornell U. Recipient Meritorious Svc. award Dept. Interior, 1987, SBA Minority Bus. Vision 2000 award, 1999, Disting. Woman award, 2000, BLM Legend award, 2002; named Individual Minority Advocate of Yr., 1999, Entrepreneur of Yr. Phoenix, YWCA, 2001. Mem. NAFE, Wildlife Soc. (cert.), Soc. Am. Foresters, Soc. Range Mgmt., Federally Employed Women. Avocations: photography, writing, art, movies, public speaking. Home: PO Box 7305 Phoenix AZ 85011-7305 Office: Bur Land Mgmt 222 N Central Ave Phoenix AZ 85004-2203 E-mail: denise_meridith@blm.gov.

MERIGAN, THOMAS CHARLES, JR. internist, medical researcher, educator; b. San Francisco, Jan. 18, 1934; s. Thomas C. and Helen M. (Greeley) Merigan; m. Joan Mary Freeborn, Oct. 3, 1959; 1 child Thomas Charles III. BA with honors, U. Calif., Berkeley, 1955; MD, U. Calif., San Francisco, 1958. Diplomate Am. Bd. Internal Medicine. Intern 2d and 4th Harvard med. services Boston City Hosp., 1958—59, asst. resident medicine, 1959—60; clin. assoc. Nat. Heart Inst., NIH, Bethesda, Md., 1960—62; assoc. Lab. Molecular Biology, Nat. Inst. Arthritis and Metabolic Diseases, NIH, 1962—63; practice medicine specializing in internal medicine and infectious diseases Stanford, Calif., 1963—; asst. prof. medicine Stanford U. Sch. Medicine, 1963—67, assoc. prof. medicine, 1967—72, head div. infectious diseases, 1966—92, prof. medicine, 1972—, George E. and Lucy Becker prof. medicine, 1980—. Dir. Diagnostic Microbiology Lab. Univ. Hosp., 1966—72, dir. Diagnostic Virology Lab., 1969—99; dir. Ctr. AIDS Rsch. Stanford U., 1988—; hosp. epidemiologist, 1966—88; mem. microbiology rsch. tng. grants com. NIH, 1969—73, virology study sect., 1974—78; cons. antiviral substances program Nat. Inst. Allergy and Infectious Diseases, 1970—94, mem. AIDS clin. drug devel. commn., 1986—94; mem. Virology Task Force, 1976—78, bd. sci. counselors, 1980—85; mem. U.S. Hepatitis panel U.S. and Japan Coop. Med. Sci. Program, 1979—90; mem. AIDS subcom. Nat. Adv. Allergy and Infectious Diseases Coun., 1988—89; co-chmn. interferon evaluation group Am. Cancer Soc., 1978—81; vaccines and related biol. products adv. com. Ctr. for Drugs and Biols., FDA, 1984—88; internat. adv. com. on biol. sci. Sci. Coun., Singapore, 1985—88; adv. com. J.A. Hartford Found., 1979—84; mem. Albert Lasker awards jury, 1981—84; peer rev. panel U.S. Army Med. R&D Com., 1986—88; nat. com. to rev. current procedures for approval New Drugs for Cancer and AIDS, 1989—90; mem. Com. to Study Use of Coms. within FDA, 1991—92. Contbr. articles on infectious diseases, virology and immunology to jours.; editor: Antivirals with Clinical Potential, 1976, Antivirals and Virus Diseases of Man, 1979, Antivirals and Virus Diseases of Man, 4th edit., 1997, Regulatory Functions of Interferon, 1980, Interferons, 1982, Interferons as Cell Growth Inhibitors, 1986; assoc. editor: Virology, 1975—78, assoc. editor: Cancer Rsch., 1987—91; co-editor: (monograph series) Current Topics in Infectious Diseases, 1975—92, Cytomegalovirus Infect and Ganciclovir, 1988, Focus on Didanosine (ddI), 1990, Practical Diagnosis of Viral Infection, Textbook of AIDS Medicine, 1994, Practical Diagnosis of Viral Infection, Textbook of AIDS Medicine, 2d edit., 1999, Surrogate Markers for HIV Infection, 1995, Antimicrobial Therapy in Vaccines, 1999; mem. editl. bd.: Archives Internal Medicine, 1971—81, mem. editl. bd.: Jour. Gen. Virology, 1972—77, mem. editl. bd.: Infection and Immunity, 1978—81, mem. editl. bd.: Intervirology, 1973—85, mem. editl. bd.: Proc. Soc. Exptl. Biology and Medicine, 1978—87, mem. editl. bd.: Revs. of Infectious Diseases, 1979—89, mem. editl. bd.: Jour. Interferon Rsch., 1980—89, mem. editl. bd.: Antiviral Rsch., 1980—86, mem. editl. bd.: Jour. Antimicrobial Chemotherapy, 1981—91, mem. editl. bd.: Molecular and Cellular Biochemistry, 1982—89, mem. editl. bd.: AIDS Rsch. and Human Retroviruses, 1983—, mem. editl. bd.: Jour. Virology, 1984—89, mem. editl. bd.: Biotechnology Therapeutics, 1988—98, mem. editl. bd.: Jour. Infectious Diseases, 1989—94, mem. editl. bd.: Clin. Drug Investigation, 1989—, mem. editl. bd.: HIV: Advances in Rsch. and Therapy, 1999—2000, mem. editl. bd.: Internat. Jour. Antimicrobial Agts., 1990—99, mem. editl. bd.: The AIDS Reader, 1991—, mem. editl. bd.: AIDS, 1993—, mem. editl. bd.: Clin. Immunotherapeutics, 1994—, mem. editl. bd.: Antiviral Therapy, 1996—99. Recipient Borden award for Outstanding Rsch., Am. Assn. Med. Colls., 1973, Merit award, Nat. Inst. Allergy and Infectious Diseases, 1988, Maxwell Finland Lectureship award, Infectious Diseases Soc. Am., 1988; fellow Guggenheim Meml. fellow, 1972. Fellow: AAAS (counsilor); mem.: AMA, Royal Soc. Medicine, Calif. Acad. Medicine, Santa Clara County Med. Soc., Calif. Med. Assn., Internat. Soc. Interferon Rsch. (coun. 1983—89), Pan Am. Group for Rapid Viral Diagnosis, Inst. Medicine, Am. Soc. Virology, Infectious Diseases Soc. Am., Soc. Exptl. Biology and Medicine (publ. com. 1985—89), Western Soc. Clin. Rsch., Am. Fedn. Clin. Rsch., Am. Assn. Immunologists, Am. Soc. Clin. Investigation (coun. 1977—80), Am. Soc. Microbiology, Western Assn. Physicians, Assn. Am. Physicians, Alpha Omega Alpha. Home: 148 Goya Rd Portola Valley CA 94028-7307 Office: Stanford U Sch Medicine Divsn Infectious Diseases Stanford CA 94305

MERILAN, MICHAEL PRESTON, astrophysicist, educator, dean; b. Columbia, Mo., Jan. 5, 1956; s. Charles Preston and Phyllis Pauline (Laughlin) M.; m. Karene Anne Yanuklis, Sept. 2, 1995. BS summa cum laude in Physics, U. Mo., Columbia, 1978, MS, 1980; PhD in Astronomy, Ohio State U., 1985. Grad. tchg. asst. U. Mo., Columbia, 1978-80; grad. tchg. assoc., instr. dept. astronomy Ohio State U., Columbus, 1980-85; asst. prof. dept. physics and astronomy SUNY, Oneonta, 1985-91, assoc. prof., 1991—, chmn. dept. physics and astronomy, 1990-93, acting dean divsn. sci. and social sci., 1993-96, dean, 1996—. Astron. cons. Ohio Dept. Natural Resources, 1982-83; Oneonta smart node advisor Cornell Nat. Supercomputer Facility, Oneonta, 1987-92. Contbr. articles to profl. jours. O.M. Stewart fellow U. Mo., 1979; U. Mo. Curators scholar, 1974-78; Mahan Writing award U. Mo., 1975. Mem. AAAS, Am. Astron. Soc., Astron. Soc. Pacific, Internat. Amateur Profl. Photoelectric Photometry Assn., Sigma Xi, Phi Eta Sigma, Phi Kappa Phi, Phi Beta Kappa, Pi Mu Epsilon, Sigma Pi Sigma, Omicron Delta Kappa. Achievements include analytic and numeric investigation of protostellar hydrodynamics; determination of the properties of static and slowly rotating partially degenerate semirelativistic stellar structures. Office: Dean Sci and Social Sci SUNY-Oneonta 336 Netzer Bldg Oneonta NY 13820 E-mail: merilamp@oneonta.edu.

MERINGOLO, ROBERT DOUGLAS, internist, cardiologist, educator; b. N.Y.C., 1944; MD, Jefferson Med. Coll., 1969. Diplomate Am. Bd. Internal Medicine, Am. Bd. Cardiovasc. Disease. Intern Met. Hosp.-N.Y. Med. Coll., N.Y.C., 1969-70; resident in internal medicine St. Luke's Hosp., 1972-74, fellow in cardiovasc. disease, 1974-76; pvt. practice, Providence, 1976—. Clin. asst. prof. medicine Brown U., Providence. Fellow Am. Coll. Cardiology. Office: 1076 N Main St Providence RI 02904

MERINI, RAFIKA, foreign language, cultures and literatures educator; b. Fès, Morocco; came to U.S., 1972; d. Mohamed M. and Fatima Chraibi-Merini. BA in English cum laude, U. Utah, 1978, MA in Romance Langs. and Lits., 1981; postgrad., U. Wash., 1980-82; cert. in translation, SUNY, Binghamton, 1988, PhD in Comparative Lit., 1992. Tchg. asst. U. Utah, Salt Lake City, 1978-80, U. Wash., Seattle, 1980-82; adminstrv. asst., tchr. French, interpreter The Lang. Sch., 1982-83; lectr. Pacific Luth. U., Tacoma, spring 1983; instr. Ft. Steilacoom C.C. (now Pierce C.C.), 1983-85; tchg. asst. dept. romance langs. SUNY, Binghamton, 1985-87, tchg. asst. women's studies dept., summer 1988, tchg. asst. comparative lit. dept., 1986-88; vis. instr. Union Coll., Schenectady, N.Y., 1988-89; vis. instr. dept. fgn. langs. and lits. Skidmore Coll., Saratoga Springs, 1989-90; asst. prof. dept. modern and classical langs. State Univ. Coll. at Buffalo (SUCB), 1990-96, assoc. prof. dept. modern and classical langs., 1996—. Coord. BSC women's studies interdisciplinary unit State Univ. Coll. at Buffalo, 1993-99, adviser French Club, 1990-93; presenter and guest spkr. at seminars, workshops, confs. Author: Two Major Francophone Women Writers, Assia Djébar and Leïla Sebbar: A Thematic Study of Their Works, 1999, 2d printing, 2001; mem. editl. bd. Jour. MIddle Eastern and North African Intellectual and Cultural Studies; contbr. articles to profl. pubs. Grantee Nat. Defense Student award U. Utah, 1974; also numerous other grants and awards. Mem. MLA, AAUW, Am. Assn. Tchrs. French, Women in French, Conseil Internat. d'Etudes Francophones, Pi Delta Phi, Soc. Hon. Française, Kappa Theta (hon.). Home: PO Box 1063 Buffalo NY 14213-1063 Office: State Univ Coll-Buffalo Modern & Classical Langs 1300 Elmwood Ave Buffalo NY 14222-1095

MERINO, FERNANDO, economist, researcher, educator; b. Alicante, Spain, Nov. 7, 1966; s. Cipriano and Esperanza (De Lucas) M. B in Econs., U. de Alicante, 1989; MSc in Econs., Ctr. Monetary and Fin. Study, Madrid, 1991. Econs. rschr. Fundacion Empresa Publica, Madrid, 1992—; assoc. prof. U. de Alcala, 1995—. Co-author: Las Empresas Industriales Espanolas, 1992, rev. edit., 1995::::; contbr. articles to profl. jours. including Strategic Mgmt. Jour., Barcelona Mgmt. Rev., The Econ. Jour. Office: Fundacion Empresa Publica Quintana 2 3rd E-28008 Madrid Spain Fax: 34 91-5488359.

MERINO, PAMELA, medical administrator; b. Santo Domingo, Dominican Republic, Mar. 22, 1968; arrived in U.S., 1992; m. Angel A. Betancourt, Oct. 1991; 1 child, Alexandra. MD cum laude, U. Nacional Pedro Henriquez Ureta, Santo Domingo, 1991. Intern Danbury (Conn.) Hosp., Yale U., 1997; faculty residency program internal medicine Danbury Hosp.; med. dir. Adult Health Ctr., Danbury; asst. clin. prof. NYU Sch. Medicine, Yale New Haven Sch. Medicine and Nursing. Med. dir. Adult Health Ctr., Danbury Hosp.; outpatient faculty residency adviser Danbury Hosp. Contbr. rsch. articles to profl. jours. Mem. AMA, ACP, Am. Bd. Internal Medicine (diplomate), Conn. State Med. Soc. Avocations: reading, horseback riding. Office: 70 Main St Danbury CT 06810 Office Fax: 203-791-5055. E-mail: pamela.merino@danhosp.org.

MERIWETHER, HEATH J. newspaper publisher; b. Columbia, Mo., Jan. 20, 1944; s. Nelson Heath and Mary Agnes (Immele) M.; m. Patricia Hughes, May 4, 1979; children: Graham, Elizabeth. BA in History, BJ, U. Mo., 1966; MA in Teaching, Harvard U., 1967. Reporter Miami (Fla.) Herald, 1970-72, editor Broward and Palm Beach burs., 1972-77, exec. city editor, 1977-79, asst. mgr. editor news, 1979-80, mng. editor, 1981-83, exec. editor, 1983-87, Detroit Free Press, 1987-95, publisher, 1996—. Trustee Greenhills Sch., 1995—; bd. dirs. Detroit Symphony Orch., 1996—. Served to lt. USNR, 1967-70. Journalism fellow Stanford U., 1980. Roman Catholic. Avocation: tennis. Office: Detroit Free Press 600 W Fort St Detroit MI 48226-2706*

MERIWETHER, JAMES BABCOCK, retired English language educator; b. Columbia, S.C., May 8, 1928; s. Robert Lee and Margaret (Babcock) M.; m. Nancy Anderson Callcott, July 29, 1955 (div. May 1992); children: Rebecca, Robert, George, Nicholas, Margaret; m. Anne M. Blythe, Nov. 14, 1992. BA, U. S.C., 1949; MA, Princeton U., 1952, PhD, 1958. Asst. prof. English U. Tex., Austin, 1958-59, U. N.C., Chapel Hill, 1959-62, assoc. prof., 1962-64; prof. U. S.C., Columbia, 1964-70, McClintock prof. So. letters, 1970-90, dir. So. studies program, 1974-80, disting. prof. emeritus, 1990—, William Gilmore Simms rsch. prof., 1999, 2000. Appointed Bd. Fgn. Scholarships, Washington, 1982, 86, vice chmn., 1984, chmn. 1984-87; Fulbright prof. U. Paris, 1970-71, U. Bonn, 1980, Chinese U. Hong Kong, 1993. Author: The Literary Career of William Faulkner, 1961, others; editor: Essays, Speeches and Public Letters of William Faulkner, others; contbr. articles to profl. jours. Served with U.S. Army, 1953-56. Fellow Am. Coun. Learned Socs., 1960-61, Guggenheim Found., 1963-64, Earhart Found., 1989-90. Mem. MLA, Bibliographical Soc. Am., Am. Studies Assn., South Atlantic Modern Lang. Assn., Phi Beta Kappa. Home: 2526 Monroe St Columbia SC 29205-3154 E-mail: abmjbm@bellsouth.net.

MERJAN, STANLEY, civil engineer, inventor; b. N.Y.C., Jan. 10, 1928; s. Morris and Rose (Katz) M.; m. Florence Louise Malone, June 5, 1954; children: Barbara, David, Alice. BCE, CCNY, 1948. Registered profl. engr., N.Y., Fla., Mass. Constrn. engr. N.Y.C. Bd. Water Supply, Downsville, N.Y., 1948-50, Gull Contracting Co., N.Y.C., 1950-51; structural designer Gen. Dynamics Corp., New London, Conn., 1951-53; exec. v.p. Underpinning and Found. Constructors, Inc., N.Y.C., 1955—. Pres. Port Washington Comty. Synagogue Brotherhood, 1978-80; mem. Port Washington Cmty. Chest, 1984-90; chmn. United Jewish Appeal, Port Washington, 1986-92. With U.S. Army, 1953-55. Recipient Sci. and Tech. award Am. ORT Fedn., N.Y.C., 1991. Mem. ASCE (life), Am. Concrete Inst., N.Y. State Soc. Profl. Engrs., Deep Founds. Inst. (treas. 1992-94), The Moles. Democrat. Achievements include U.S. and foreign patents for TPT PILES (registered trademark) (composite piles with pre-cast concrete bases) and pile driving appurtenances. Home: 96 Barkers Point Rd Sands Point NY 11050-1328 Office: Underpinning & Found Contrs 46-36 54th Rd Maspeth NY 11378-1020

MERK, ELIZABETH THOLE, investment company executive; b. Salt Lake City, July 29, 1950; d. John Bernard and Emily Josephine (Knotek) Thole; m. J. Eliot Merk, July 26, 1996 (div.); 1 child from previous marriage William Lance Ulich. BA, U. Hawaii, Hilo, 1984, paralegal cert. cum laude, 1989; postgrad.in bus. administrn., U. Hawaii, Manoa, 1985-86. Lic. gen. agt. Hawaii, Tex.; registered investment advisor, stock broker Hawaii, Tex., Calif., Utah. Regional archtl. rep. Lightolier, Inc., Salt Lake City, 1978-80; group sales rep. FHP/Utah, 1980-81; health net rep. Blue Cross Corp., L.A., 1981-82; v.p. fin. Bus. Support Systems, Hilo, 1983-89; rep. Prudential Ins. and Fin. Svcs., Honolulu, 1989-97; registered rep. Pruco Securities Corp. subs. Prudential Ins. & Fin. Svcs., 1989-97; acct. exec. Dean Witter Reynolds, 1997-98; adv. assoc., registered prin. Mutual Svc. Corp., 1998—2001; adv. assoc. Centaurus Fin. Inc., 2001—. Docent Lyman House, 1984-85, L.A. County Mus. of Art, 1980-81, S.L.C. Art Mus., 1970-80; bd. dirs. YWCA, Hawaii Island, 1980-91, 1st v.p., 1988. Named YWCA Vol. of Yr., 1991, Top 25 Women owned Bus. in Hawaii, Pacific Bus. News, 2001; recipient Nat. Quality award 1991, 92, 93, 94, Nat. Sales Achievement award 1992, 93; Paul Harris fellow Rotary Internat., 1997. Fellow: Life Underwriters Tng. Coun.; mem.: AAUW (bd. dirs. Hilo chpt. 1987—89, fundraiser chmn. Kona chpt. 1992, Steven Bufton grantee 1985), Securities Industry Assn., Million Dollar Round Table (mem. ct. of the table 2000, mem. top of the table 2001—02), Nat. Assn. Ins. and Fin. Advisors, Nat. Assn. Life Underwriters (legis. rep. West Hawaii chpt. 1995—97, charter mem.), Am. Bus. Women's Assn. (pres. Nani O Hilo chpt. 1995—96, membership chmn. 1996—97, inner circle 1997—), Outdoor Circle, Soroptimists. Roman Catholic. Office: 118 Kamehameha Ave Hilo HI 96720 Office Fax: 808-883-8399. E-mail: emerk@emerk.com.

MERK, FREDERICK BANNISTER, biomedical educator, medical researcher; b. Cambridge, Mass., Feb. 21, 1936; s. Frederick and Lois Alberta (Bannister) M.; m. Linda Jean Poole, Oct. 22, 1966 (dec. Dec. 1994); children: John F., R. Daniel; m. Laura Ann Bradford, July 11, 1998; 1 stepchild, Letty A. Bradford. AB, Harvard Coll., 1958; PhD, Boston U., 1971. Asst. prof. pathology Boston U. Sch. Medicine, 1972-73; assoc. prof. dept. pathology Tufts U. Sch. Medicine, Boston, 1973—, assoc. prof. dept. anatomy, 1973—, also dir. electron microscopy facility, 1975-85. Cons. electron microscopy Mass. Gen. Hosp., Boston, 1964-85; cons. toxicol. testing Transgenic Scis., Worcester, Mass., 1988-91, U.S. Army, 1998-2001. Contbr. more than 60 articles to profl. jours. Trustee Broadway United Meth. Ch., Lynn, Mass., chmn. 1994-2000; lay rep. of Ch. to ann. New Eng. Conf., 2000—. Named Outstanding Tchr. in Basic Scis., Tufts U. Sch. Medicine, 1989, 91-93; NIH grantee, 1994-98. Mem. Am. Soc. Cell Biology, Fedn. Am. Soc. Exptl. Biology, Am. Assn. Anatomists, Microscopy Soc. Am., Boston Cancer Rsch. Assn., Sigma Xi. Achievements include research on biology of cells in target organs responding to hormones with emphasis on benign prostatic hypertrophy (enlargement) and prostate cancer. Avocations: photography, indoor gardening, swimming. Home: 17 Jefferson Rd Winchester MA 01890-3116 Office: Tufts Univ Sch Medicine Dept Pathology 136 Harrison Ave Boston MA 02111-1800 E-mail: fmerk@hotmail.com.

MERKEL, DANIEL A. dental products company executive; b. Marshfield, Wis., May 12, 1929; s. Anthony Arthur Merkel and Helen Ligman; m. Betty M. Dieringer, May 20, 1952; children: Douglas, Diane, Carol, Sandra. BS, Marquette U., 1951. CPA, Wis. Sr. acct. Ernst & Young, Milw., 1951-57; v.p., sec., treas. Hayssen Mfg., Sheboygan, Wis., 1957-66; CEO, chmn., founder Am. Orthodontics Corp., 1967—. Pres., bd. dirs. Hayssen Found., Sheboygan, 1966—. Patentee in field. Past mem. Sheboygan Sch. Bd., mem. bd. dirs. Firstar Bank, 1981-94. Named Wis. Sm. Business Man of Yr., 1984. Mem. Pine Hills Country Club. Avocations: golf, travel. Office: Am Orthodontics Corp 1714 Cambridge Ave Sheboygan WI 53081-2337

MERKEL, PATRICIA MAE, retired school system administrator; b. Spokane, Wash., June 18, 1935; d. Hugo Oscar and Mary Jane (Blackwelder) Koenig; m. Gordon Henry, Nov. 10, 1956 (div. 1973); children: Katherine Marie Merkel Fisk, Karol Ann Merkel Korte, John Henry. BA cum laude, Ea. Washington U., 1989. Cert. ednl. office employee. Acctg. clk. Pacific N.W. Bell, Spokane, 1954-56; book-keeper Edwall (Wash.) Sch. Dist., 1969-75, Reardan (Wash.)-Edwall Sch. Dist., 1975-78, bus. mgr., 1978-82; asst. to supr. fin. Dayton (Wash.) Sch. Dist., 1982-99. Mem. Town of Reardan Planning Commn., 1977-82, sec., 1978-82; treas. Citizens for Edn. Com., Dayton, 1983-91, Columbia County Courthouse Restoration Project, Dayton, 1988-99; mem. fin. adv. com. Dayton Gen. Hosp., 1986-90, Dayton City Coun., 1986-87; mem. vocat. bus. adv. com. Dayton High Sch., 1990-96. Recipient Mary Shields Wilson Medallion award. Mem. AAUW, Wash. Assn. Ednl. Office Profls. (treas. 1984-86, pres.-elect 1986-87, pres. 1987-88, Ednl. Office Profl. of Yr. award 1990), Nat. Assn. Ednl. Office Profls. (Ednl. Office Profl. of Yr. award 1990), Assn. Assn. Sch. Bus. Ofcls. (chmn. com. 1978-81), S.C. Assn. Ednl. Office Profls. (pres. 1991-92), Blue Mountain Assn. Ednl. Office Profls., Assn. Sch. Bus. Ofcls. Internat. (com. 1984-86, scholar 1987), Order of Eagles, Kiwanis (sec. 1991-99, Kiwaniain of Yr. award 1993, 99). Democrat. Methodist. Avocations: reading, quilting, needle work, doll and bear making. Home: 3324 W 19th Ave Trlr 102 Kennewick WA 99338-2292

MERKEL-HESS, MARY LYNNE, artist; b. Waterloo, Iowa, Apr. 6, 1949; d. Lee John and Margaret (Delagardelle) Hess; m. Stephen Paul Merkel, May 5, 1973; children: Kathryn, Matthias. BA, Marquette U., 1971; BFA, U. Wis., Milw., 1976; MA, U. Iowa, 1981, MFA, 1983. Adj. instr. Kirkwood C.C., 1998-99; guest curator Waterloo Mus. Art, 1993. Contbr. essays to book: Basketmaker's Art, 1986, photos to book: Papermaking for Basketry, 1988; represented in permanent collections at Met. Mus., Am. Craft Mus., Phila. Mus. Art, Wustum Mus. Art, Racine, Wis. Mem. Am. Craft Coun., Iowa City Arts Coun. (bd. dirs. 1988), Iowa Designer Crafts Assn. (v.p. 1987). Home: 2609 Friendship St Iowa City IA 52245-5006 E-mail: merkelhess@aol.com.

MERKER, STEVEN JOSEPH, lawyer; b. Cleve., Feb. 21, 1947; s. Steven Joseph and Laverne (Zamenik) M.; m. Janet L. Whyatt; children: Steven, Rena, Ashley, Matthew. BS, Case Inst. Tech., 1968; MS, U. Fla., 1973; JD, George Washington U., 1976. Bar: Ohio 1976, U.S. Dist. Ct. (no. dist.) Ohio, 1976, U.S. Dist. Ct. Colo. 1979, U.S. Ct. Appeals (10th cir.) 1979, U.S. Supreme Ct. 1989. Assoc. Jones, Day, Reavis & Pogue, Cleve., 1976-78, Davis, Graham & Stubbs, Denver, 1978-82, ptnr., 1983-96, chmn. labor and employment group, 1989-96; chmn. litigation and labor and employment groups Merrick, Calvin & Merker, LLP, 1996-97; ptnr. Dorsey & Whitney LLP, Denver, 1997—, mng. ptnr. Denver office, 2000—. Mem. Tenth Cir. Adv. Com., 1997-2000. Legal counsel Coloradans for Lamm-Dick campaign, Denver, 1982, Nancy Dick for U.S. Senate Com., Denver, 1984, Cantrell for Dist. Atty., Jefferson County, Colo., 1984; bd. dirs. Very Spl. Arts, Colo., 1994—. Capt. USAF, 1969-72. Mem. ABA, Colo. Bar Assn., Denver Bar Assn. Office: Dorsey & Whitney LLP 370 17th St Ste 4700 Denver CO 80202-5644 E-mail: werker.steve@dorseylaw.com.

MERKIN, ALBERT CHARLES, pediatrician, allergist; b. Chgo., Sept. 4, 1924; s. Harry A. and Goldie (Lamasky) M.; m. Eunice Aprill, Aug. 22, 1948; children: Audrey, Ellen, Joseph. Student, U. Ill., 1942-44; MD, U. Ill., Chgo., 1949. Diplomate Am. Bd. Allergy and Immunology, Am. Bd. Pediatrics. Intern, resident Cook County Hosp., Chgo.; resident Children's Meml. Hosp.; with Valley Pediatric and Allergy Clinic, Las Vegas, Nev. Capt. USAF, 1950-53. Fellow Am. Acad. Pediatrics (state chmn. Nev. 1961-64, sect. allergy and immunology), Am. Coll. Allergy; mem. Am. Acad. Allergy, Allergy Subsplty. Group of Acad. Pediatrics (cert. pediatric allergist). Avocations: reading, travel. Office: Valley Pediat & Allergy Clinic 222 S Rainbow Blvd Ste 119 Las Vegas NV 89145-5343

MERKIN, DONALD H. internist; b. Bronx, N.Y., Nov. 12, 1945; s. Eugene and Hortense Ruth (Erdrich) M.; children: Daniel Hansen, Andrew David. BA, Parsons Coll., 1968; MS, Colo. State U., 1972; PhD, Cornell U., 1974; MD, U. Autonoma de Ciudad, Juarez, Mexico, 1978. Asst. prof. U. So. Colo., Pueblo, 1973-74, Bethel Sch. of Nursing, Colorado Springs, 1973-74, U. Colo., Colorado Springs, 1973-74, So. Ill. U. Sch. Medicine, Springfield, Ill., 1975-76; internist Westside Med. Assocs., Bradenton, Fla., 1982-84, pvt. practice, Sarasota, 1984-88, Superior (Wis.) Clinic, Ltd., 1989-91, Gulf Coast Ortho. Ctr.- Inst. for Spl. Surgery, Hudson, Fla., 1991-94, dir. orthopedic medicine, 1992-94; pvt. practice Internal Medicine Assocs. of Pasco County, 1995-96; internist St. Luke's Cataract & Laser Inst., Tarpon Springs, 1998—, MD to You, Largo, 2001—. Med. dir. Physicians Injury and Wellness Ctr., Inc., New Port Richey, Fla., 1999-2001, Suncoast Spinal Med. and Rehab. Ctrs., Clearwater, Fla., 1999-2001, Suncoast Clin. Rsch., Inc., New Port Richey, Fla., 1999—; mem. elder affairs advisor com. to Fla. state rep. Heather Fiorentino, 1999-2000. Author: Pregnancy as a Disease, 1976. Officer candidate USMC, 1969. Nat. Inst. Child Health and Human Devel. fellow Cornell U., 1970-73; Fulbright fellow Nat. Assn. Colls. for Tchr. Edn., India, 1974. Lutheran. Avocations: tennis, snorkeling, travel, photography.

MERKIN, WILLIAM LESLIE, retired lawyer; b. N.Y.C., Apr. 30, 1929; s. Jules Leo Merkin and Rae (Levine) Lesser; children: Monica Jo, Lance Jeffrey, Tiffany Dawn. BA, U. Tex., Austin, 1950; JD, St. Mary's U., San Antonio, 1953. Bar: Tex. 1953, U.S. Ct. Mil. Appeals 1954, U.S. Dist. Ct. (we. dist.) Tex. 1957, U.S. Ct. Appeals (5th cir.) 1969, U.S. Supreme Ct. 1970. Pvt. practice, El Paso, Tex., 1956-71; sr. ptnr. Merkin & Gibson, 1972-78, Merkin, Hines & Pasqualone, El Paso, 1978-90; ret. Lectr. U. Tex.-El Paso, 1978—; cons. in field. Served to capt. JAGC, U.S. Army, 1953-56. Mem. Tex. State Bar Assn., Soc. Profls. in Dispute Resolution, Am. Trial Lawyers Assn., Tex. Trial Lawyers Assn., Common Cause, Internat. Wine and Food Soc. (pres. 1979-80), Am. Arbitration Assn. (part-time arbitrator), Nat. Assn. Securities Dealers (part-time arbitrator), Del Norte Club (El Paso), B'nai B'rith (pres. 1961-62), Phi Delta Phi. Home: 1442 Seacoast Dr Imperial Beach CA 91932-3183

MERLE, H. ETIENNE, restauranteur; b. N.Y.C., July 8, 1944; s. Pierre and Josephine Merle. BS, Cornell U., 1969. Mgr. food and beverage DiviDivi Beach Hotel, Aruba, 1969-70; restaurant mgr., chmn. food dept. Tng. Resources for Youth, N.Y.C., 1971; gen. mgr. L'Auberge du Cochon Rouge, Ithaca, N.Y., 1971-92; v.p. Pascale Wine Bar and Restaurant, Syracuse, 1982-94; splty. foods broker, pres. Etienne, Ithaca, 1999—. Ops. cons. Merle & Roy Assocs., N.Y.C., 1975—; chef, operator Atelier Etienne Corp., Valentine Café, Ithaca, N.Y., 1999. Mem. Cornell Hotel Soc., Chefs de Cuisine Assn. Am., Soc. Culinaire Philanthropique, L'Union Francaise (pres. 1975, 76, 86, 91—). Home: 1152 Danby Rd Ithaca NY 14850-9406 Office: PO Box 6769 Ithaca NY 14851-6769

MERLENO, TONI AUTUMN, personnel executive; b. Garfield Heights, Ohio, Jan. 16, 1954; d. Anthony and Joyce Irene (Price) M. BA in English, King's Coll., Briarcliff Manor, N.Y., 1976. Cert. secondary tchr., Ohio. Tchr. English, Heritage Christian Sch., Cleve., 1976-77, 1st Bapt. Christian Sch., Elyria, Ohio, 1977-84; pers. asst. May Dept. Stores Co., Cleve., 1984-85; coord. human resources cen. credit dept. May Co., Parma, Ohio, 1985-86, mgr. human resources Parmatown br., 1986-89; pers. mgr. Green Cir. Growers, Inc., Oberlin, 1989—. Soloist Weymouth Community Ch., Medina, Ohio, 1985—. Home: 268 Morgan St Oberlin OH 44074-1516 Office: Green Circle Growers Inc 15650 State Route 511 Oberlin OH 44074-9699

MERLINI, SANDRA ANN, librarian, writer; b. Marlboro, Mass., Dec. 30, 1944; d. Angelo John and Theresa Mary (Aglio) M. BA in History, Assumption Coll., 1983; MLS, Simmons Coll., 1997. Libr. aide Marlborough Pub. Libr., Marlboro, 1979-88; libr. Milstar Libr., 1988-93; clerical positions TAC Staffing, Marlboro area, 1993-96, 97—; mag. coord. Shrewsbury (Mass.) Vol. Pub. Libr., 1996-97; libr. asst St. Anne Convent, Marlboro, 1998; with Office Max, 1998—. Publicity Marlboro Enterprise, Longfellow Poetry Soc., Sudbury, Mass., 1993—; freelance writer Marlboro Enterprise, 1997—, Polo Mag., West Palm Beach, Fla., 1996—, Sidelines, West Palm Beach, 1997—. Author: JBK: The White House Floral Arrangements, 1988; contbr. poetry to jours. Republican. Roman Catholic. Avocations: polo, reading, sewing, crafts, sports. Office: Office Max Shoppers World Framingham MA

MERLIN KEARFOTT, DUVAL, health consultant; b. Montclair, N.J., Oct. 12, 1922; married 1944, 84; 3 children. AB, Dartmouth Coll., 1943; MD, Cornell U., 1946; DSc, NJ Coll. Medicine & Dentistry, Dartmouth Coll., Med. Coll. Wis., Coll. Osteopathic Medicine; LHD, Ohio Coll. Podiatric Medicine. Founding dean coll. medicine U. Ariz., 1964-79; asst. sec. for health Dept. Health, Edn. & Welfare, Washington, 1971-73; pres., CEO Nat. Ctr. for Health Edn., 1979-82, Am. Healthcare Inst., 1982-88; health cons., 1990—. Mem. AMA, Am. Coll. Surgeons, Am. Surg. Assn., Soc. Med. Adminstrs. Home: 3026 E Marlette Ave Phoenix AZ 85016-2239

MERLINO, ANTHONY FRANK, orthopedic surgeon; b. Providence, Jan. 21, 1930; s. Anthony Frank and C. Mildred (Campagna) M.; m. Dolores Mary Aucello, Nov. 22, 1956; children: Christa Marianne, Paula Nicole. BS, Providence Coll., 1951; MS, U. Conn., 1952; MD, Jefferson Med. Coll., 1956. Diplomate Am. Bd. Orthopedic Surgery. Intern St. Joseph Hosp., Providence, 1956-57; resident orthopedic surgery VA Hosp., Phila., 1959-63; pvt. practice medicine specializing in orthopedic surgery, Phila., 1963-68, Providence, 1968—; attending orthopedic surgeon St. Joseph Hosp., Providence, pres. med. staff, 1974-75, trustee, 1973-76, med. staff/trustee joint conf. com. 1982; attending orthopedic surgeon Our Lady of Fatima Hosp., North Providence, R.I.; vis. orthopedic surgeon R.I. State Hosp., Howard, 1968-75; asst. orthopedic surgery Hahnemann Med. Coll., Phila., 1965-69; pediatric orthopedic surg. cons. Crippled Children's Program of R.I., 1968-86; cons. orthopedic surgeon Roger Williams Gen. Hosp., Providence, 1969-89; v.p. R.I. Orthopedic Group, Inc., Providence, 1969-83; pres., 1983—; team physician hockey and basketball teams Providence Coll., 1968-87; mem. R.I. Gov.'s Med. Malpractice Commn., 1975-77, R.I. Bd. Examiners in Chiropractic, 1977-80; mem. study commn. R.I. Med. Rev. Bd., 1977-85; mem. corp. Blue Cross/Shield R.I., 1976-87; physician-adv. R.I. Assn. Med. Assts., 1979-84; mem. R.I. Workers' Compensation Adv. Panel, 1978-88; mem. adv. bd. Cath. Social Svcs., 1981-84; police surgeon Am. Law Enforcement Officers' Assn., 1980; cons. orthopedic surgery Am. Assn. Medicolegal Cons., 1980-90; pres. Hindle Bldg. Assocs., 1983—. Contbr. articles to profl. jours. Mem. med. splty. adv. bd. Medical Malpractice Prevention, 1985-90. Capt., M.C., USAF, 1957-59. Recipient Dr. William McDonnell award Providence Coll. Alumni Assn., 1981. Fellow Am. Acad. Orthopedic Surgeons, ACS, (pres. R.I. chpt. 1982-84), Internat. Coll. Surgeons, Latin Am. Soc. Orthopedics and Traumatology; mem. AMA, Orthopaedic Rsch. and Edn. Found. (life), Am. Coll. Legal Medicine, Am. Fracture Assn., Pan-Pacific Surg. Assn., New Eng., R.I. (sec.-treas. 1978-80, v.p. 1980-82, pres. 1982-84), Ea. Orthopedic Socs., Jefferson Orthopaedic Soc., R.I. Med. Soc. (commr. profl. rels. 1976, ho. of dels. 1976-82, commr. internal affairs 1982), Providence Med. Assn., Am. Profl. Practice Assn., Am. Acad. Compensation Medicine, Am. Coll. Sports Medicine, Am. Orthopedic Soc. for Sports Medicine, Am. Med. Photography Assn., Internat. Soc. Orthopedics and Traumatology, Internat. Soc. Rsch. in Orthopedics and Trauma, Am. Soc. Law and Medicine, Thomistic Inst. Drs. Guild, R.I. Hist. Soc., Boston Orthopedic Club, Mal Brown Club, The 100 of R.I. Club. Roman Catholic. Home: 2 Countryside Dr North Providence RI 02904-3419 Office: 655 Broad St Providence RI 02907-1444

MERLIS, GEORGE, television producer; b. Bklyn., Feb. 7, 1940; s. Martin Richard and Ethel (Pollack) M.; m. Susan Haviland Crane, Nov. 21, 1963; children: James Duncan, Andrew Richard. BA, U. Pa., 1960, MA, 1961. Sports editor Rome (Italy) Daily Am., 1961; reporter N.Y. World-Telegram and Sun, N.Y.C., 1962-65, asst. city editor, 1965-67; day city editor World Jour. Tribune, N.Y.C., 1967; supr. editorial tng. program N.Y. News, 1967-68; dir. pub. relations ABC News, 1967-72; field producer Reasoner Report, 1972-75; exec. producer Good Morning America, 1975-81, CBS Morning News, 1981-83, Entertainment Tonight, 1983-84, Dick Cavett, USA, 1985, Great Weekend, 1987-88; supervising producer ABC-TV's Home Show, 1988-91; exec. producer Willard Scott's Home and Garden Almanac, 1994—, Kitty Bartholomew You're Home, 1994-98, The Urban Gardener with Mesach Taylor, 1996; exec. producer, writer, dir. Harlem Hellfighters, 1997, Better Homes and Gardens, 1998-99. Dir. Closer to Truth, 1999; prodr., writer, dir. Secrets of San Simeon with Patricia Hearst, 2000; exec. prodr., dir. Flea Market Finds with the Kovels, 1999-2000. Author: V.P. a Novel of Vice Presidential Politics, 1971, (with Al Ubell) Al Ubell's Energy-Saving Guide for Homeowners, 1980, (with Al Ubell) Save Energy, Save Money, 2001; contbr. articles to TV Guide. Recipient Emmy award as exec. prodr. Better Homes and Gardens, 1999. Mem. Nat. TV Acad. Arts and Scis. Office: # Me22 4801 Wilshire Blvd Los Angeles CA 90010-3811

MERMELSTEIN, JULES JOSHUA, lawyer, township commissioner; b. Phila., Apr. 25, 1955; s. Harry and Ellen Jane (Greenberg) M.; m. Ruth Susan Applebaum, Aug. 18, 1974; children: Hannah Leona, Benjamin Isaac. BA, Temple U., 1977; JD, Am. U., 1979; MEd, Beaver Coll., 1994. Bar: Pa. 1980, U.S. Dist. Ct. (ea. dist.) Pa. 1980, U.S. Ct. Appeals (3d cir.) 1982, U.S. Supreme Ct. 1983. Ptnr. Mermelstein & Light, Norristown and Hatboro, Pa., 1980-83; v.p., gen. counsel Am. Ins. Cons., Feasterville, 1983; staff atty. Hyatt Legal Svcs., Phila., 1983-84, mng. atty., 1984-85; pvt. practice Phila./Montgomery County, 1985-93; tchr., social studies coord. The Bridge, 1997-99; ednl. cons. Interim House, 1998-2000. Prof. law, St. Matthew Sch. Law, Phila., 1985-87; adj. prof. criminal justice Glassboro State U., N.J., 1988; faculty polit. sci. dept. Temple U., 1989; atty. Levin & Assocs., Wyncote, Pa., 1998-2001; mng. atty. Levin & Assocs., Wyncote, Pa., 2002—. Editor: The Montco Democrat, 1990-92. Vol. atty. ACLU, Phila., 1980-93; chmn. Tikkun Olam (Repair the World) Com., 1989-92, 98-2000; area rep. Montgomery County Dem. Exec. Com., 1982-85, 88-94; treas., 1994-98, candidate coord., 1982, nominee for dist. atty., 1983, committeeman, 1973-77, 82-85, 88-92, campaign mgr. Talbot for state legis., 1988; Upper Dublin chmn. Dukakis-Bentsen, 1988, chair Upper Dublin Dem. Com., 1990-91, commr. Upper Dublin Twp., 1992—; Dem. candidate Pa. State Legis., 2000; bd. dirs. Reconstructionist Congregation Or Hadash, Ft. Washington, Pa., 1988-92, 96-2000, 2001—, confirmation tchr., 1994—. Jewish. Home: 18 Northview Dr Glenside PA 19038-1318 E-mail: JulesMermelstein@hotmail.com.

MERMIN, N. DAVID, physicist, educator, writer; b. New Haven, Mar. 30, 1935; s. John and Eva (Gordon) M.; m. Dorothy E. Milman, June 9, 1957; children: Jonathan George, Elizabeth Ruth AB summa cum laude, Harvard U, 1956, A.M., 1957, PhD, 1961. NSF postdoctral fellow U. Birmingham, Eng., 1961-63; postdoctoral fellow U. Calif., San Diego, 1963-64; asst. prof. physics Cornell U., Ithaca, N.Y., 1964-67, assoc. prof. physics, 1967-72, prof. physics, 1972-90, Horace White prof. physics, 1990—, dir. Lab. Atomic and Solid State Physics, 1984-90. Loeb lectr. Harvard U., Cambridge, 1980, Emil Warburg prof. U. Bayreuth, Germany, 1981, Walker Ames prof. U. Washington, Seattle, 1984; Wunsch lectr. Technion, Haifa, Israel, 1992; Japan Soc. for Promotion of Sci. fellow Nagoya U., 1982; Lorentz prof. U. Leiden, 1995. Author: Space and Time in Special Relativity, 1968, Solid State Physics, 1976, Boojums All the Way Through, 1990; contbr. articles to profl. jours. Sloan Found. fellow, 1966-68; Guggenheim Found. fellow, 1970-71 Fellow AAAS, Am. Acad. Arts and Scis., Am. Phys. Soc. (Julius Edgar Lilienfeld prize 1989); mem. NAS. Avocation: piano. Home: 75 Hickory Rd Ithaca NY 14850-9606 Office: Cornell U Lab Atomic and Solid State Phys 109 Clark Hall Ithaca NY 14853-2501

MERNA, GERALD FRANCIS, advertising executive, retired marine officer, retired postal executive; b. N.Y.C., Apr. 1, 1930; s. George F. Merna and Geraldine (Byers) Kraus; m. Dorothy May Sedlack, Feb. 10, 1951; children: Linda Carol Figura, Gerald Thomas. BS, George Washington U., 1973, MS, 1977; postgrad., U. So. Calif., 1975, U. Va., 1983. Enlisted USMC, 1947, advanced through grades to master gunnery sgt., 1966, commd. 2d lt., 1966, promoted to 1st lt. in Vietnam, 1967, with Korea, 1952-53, Vietnam, 1966-67; ret. USMC, 1968; various positions U.S. Postal Svc., Washington, 1968-82, exec. asst. to Postmaster Gen., 1978-82, sectional ctr. mgr. No. Va., 1982-87, ret., 1987; advt. dir. Signal mag.-Jour. Armed Forces Communications and Electronics Assn., Fairfax, Va., 1987-93; assoc. pub. Nat. Def. Mag., Arlington, 1993-98; v.p. Nat. Def. Indsl., 1993-98; ret., 1998. Publs. cons. Nat. Def. Indsl. Assn., 1998—. V.p. ops. Va. Hills Civic Assn., Alexandria, 1971-72; mem. covenants com. Cascades Comm. Assn., 1998-00, chair 2000—. Mem. The Ret. Officers Assn. (life), Marine Corps League, Marine Corps Res. Officers Assn. (life), 1st Marine Divsn. Assn. (life), 3rd Marine Divsn. Assn. (life), Nat. Def. Indsl. Assn. (life), Am. Legion, USMC Mustang Assn., VFW, Armed Forces Communications and Electronics Assn., Nat. League Postmasters U.S. (v.p. 1989-92). Home and Office: The Cascades 46386 Bluestem Ct Potomac Falls VA 20165-6461 E-mail: gmerna@erols.com.

MERO, MARJORIE ANNE, retired compensation specialist; b. Oregon City, Jan. 17, 1940; d. Richard Nyquist and Julia Annetta (Loy) Schopp; m. Gordon Duane Mero, Feb. 4, 1958; children: Sheryl Ann Mero Burns, Duane Morris. Student, Kinman Bus. U., 1972, Spokane Falls Community Coll., 1974-79. Cert. compensation profl. Dir. M. Smith Childcare Ctr., Kalispell, Mont., 1966-70; clk. Power Co., Spokane, Wash., 1970-71, engr. technician, 1972-75, job analyst, 1975-80; compensation supr. Wash. Water Power Co., 1980-89, compensation administr., 1989-91, compensation mgr., 1991-96, human resources strategist, 1996-98; ret. Mem. survey steering com. N.W. Electric and Light, 1984-96; mem. ops. com. Consumer Credit Counseling Svc., 1993-98, bd. dirs., 1994-96, chair pers. com., 1997-98. Artist watercolor paintings, 1967—. Panel chmn. United Way, Spokane, 1975-79; mem. Spokane Affirmative Action Group, 1996-98, chair, 1997-98; mem. Kootenai County Task Force on Human Rels., 1997—. Mem. Am. Compensation Assn. (western regional rep. for Wash., Oreg. and Alaska compensation groups 1991-94), Pacific Coast Gas Assn., N.W. Compensation Forum, Spokane C. of C. (workforce diversity com. 1996-98), Scripts and Scribes, Spokane Calligraphic Art Soc., Write On Calligraphers. Republican. Methodist. Avocations: art, reading, photography.

MEROLLA, MICHAEL B. secondary school music educator; b. Roslyn, N.Y., Mar. 26, 1954; s. Louis Bernard and Doris Barbara Merolla; m. Doris Barbara Merolla. BA summa cum laude, CUNY, 1977; MA summa cum laude, CNY, 1980. Cert. tchr., N.Y. H.S. music tchr. William Floyd Sch. Dist., Mastic Beach, N.Y., 1977—. Presenter in field. Recipient L.I. U. Tchr. of Yr. award, 1995. Mem. N.Y. State Music Tchrs. Assn. (pres. 1990-92, treas. 1992—), Music Tchrs. Nat. Assn. (divsn. rep. to nat. bd.). Avocation: gardening. Office: William Floyd Sch Dist 240 Mastic Beach Rd Mastic Beach NY 11951-1028

MEROLLA, MICHELE EDWARD, chiropractor, broadcaster; b. Providence, Feb. 20, 1940; s. Joseph and Viola (Horne) M.; m. Ednamarie H.; children: Michele Edward II, Matthew Joseph, Samantha Joan, Alexandra Marie. BS, Bryant Coll., 1961; DC, Chiropractic Inst. N.Y., 1965; LHD, Logan Chiropractic Coll., St. Louis, 1973. Owner chiropractic clinics chiropractic clinics, New Bedford, Taunton, Somerset, Seekonk, Attleboro, others, Mass., 1965—. Daily Network radio talk show hoset Holistic Hotline; owner radio sta. WJYT-AM, Attleboro, Mass. Editor: New Eng. Jour. Chiropractic. Mem. New Bedford City Coun., 1969-73, Airport Commn., 1972-75, Sch. Com., 1978-83, Recreation Commn., 1983-89, New Bedford Sch. Com., Fairhaven (Mass.) Sch. Com., 2000—; pres. New Bedford Aid Ctr., 1977; bd. dirs. Your Theatre Inc. Recipient Svc. award New Eng. Chiropractic Coun., 1973. Mem. Am. Chiropractic Assn., Nat. Assn. Broadcasters, Mass. Assn. Broadcasters, Southeastern Mass. Chiropractic Soc. (bd. dirs.), Mass. Chiropractic Soc., N.Y. Acad. Scis., Fla. Chiropractic Soc., New Bedford Preservation Soc. (bd. dirs.). Home: 62 Manhattan Ave Fairhaven MA 02719-1825 also: 62 Manhattan Ave Fairhaven MA 02719-1825 Office: 100 Bedford St New Bedford MA 02740-4839 E-mail: DRMEROLLA@AOL.COM.

MERON, THEODOR, law educator, researcher; b. Kalisz, Poland, Apr. 28, 1930; came to U.S., 1978, naturalized, 1984; s. Yhiel and Bluma (Lipschitz) Znamirowski; m. Monique Jonquet, Mar. 13, 1981; children: Daniel, Amos. M.J., Hebrew U., 1954; LL.M., Harvard U., 1955, S.JD, 1957; diploma in Pub. Internat. Law, Cambridge U., Eng., 1957. Bar: Israel 1971, N.Y. 1984. Legal advisor to Fgn. Ministry of Israel, 1967-71; Israeli ambassador to Can., 1971-75; permanent rep. Geneva, 1977; prof. law Sch. Law, NYU, N.Y.C., 1978—. Carnegie lectr. Hague Acad. Internat. Law, 1980; Sir Hersch Lauterpacht Meml. lectr.; vis. fellow All Souls Coll., Oxford U., England, Max-Planck Inst., Heidelberg, Germany; vis. prof. Grad. Inst. Internat. Studies, Geneva, prof. law, 1991—95; pub. mem. U.S. Del. Conf. on Human Dimension Conf. on Security and Coop. in Europe, Copenhagen, 1998; mem. U.S. del. Rome Diplomatic Conf. on the Establishment of an Internat. Criminal Ct.; vis. prof. law Harvard U., Berkeley Law Sch.; counselor on internat. law U.S. Dept. State, 2000—01; judge appeals chamber Internat. Criminal Tribunal for former Yugoslavia, 2001—. Author: Investment Insurance in International Law, 1976, The United Nations Secretariat, 1977, Human Rights Law-Making in the United Nations, 1986, Human Rights in Internal Strife: Their International Protection, 1987, Human Rights and Humanitarian Norms as Customary Law, 1989, Henry's Wars and Shakespeare's Laws, 1993, Bloody Constraint: War and Chivalry in Shakespeare, 1998; editor: Human Rights in International Law, 1984; editor in chief: Am. Jour. Internat. Law, 1983-88; contbr. articles to profl. publs. Rockefeller Found. fellow, 1975-76; Humanitarian Trust student Cambridge U., 1956-57. Mem.: Inst. of Internat. Law, Internat. Law Assn., Coun. on Fgn. Rels., Inst. of Internat. Humanitarian Law, French Inst. Internat. Law, Am. Soc. Internat. Law (Cert. Merit 1987), UN Assn. of U.S. (hon.). Office: NYU Law Sch 40 Washington Sq S New York NY 10012-1099

MEROW, JAMES F. federal judge; b. Salamanca, N.Y., Mar. 16, 1932; s. Walter and Helen (Smith) M. AB, George Washington U., 1953, JD, 1956. Bar: Va., 1956, D.C., 1958. Trial atty. U.S. Dept. Justice, Washington, 1959-78; trial judge U.S. Ct. Claims, 1978-82; judge U.S. Ct. Fed. Claims, 1982—. With JAGC, U.S. Army, 1956-59. Mem. ABA, Fed. Bar Assn., Va. State Bar. Office: US Ct Fed Claims 717 Madison Pl NW Washington DC 20005

MEROW, JOHN, lawyer; b. Little Valley, N.Y., Dec. 20, 1929; s. Luin George and Mildred Elizabeth (Stoll) M.; m. Mary Alyce Smith, June 19, 1957; 1 child, Alison. Student, UCLA, 1947-48; BS in Engring., U. Mich., 1952; JD, Harvard U., 1958. Bar: N.Y. 1958, U.S. Supreme Ct. 1971. Assoc. Sullivan & Cromwell, N.Y.C., 1958-64, ptnr., 1965-96, vice chmn., 1986-87, chmn., sr. ptnr., 1987-94, sr. counsel, 1997—. Bd. dirs. Seligman Group Investment Cos., Commonwealth Industries, Inc.; trustee, vice chmn. N.Y. Presbyn. Healthcare Sys., Inc.; trustee N.Y. Presbyn. Hosp.; trustee Friends of the Archbishop of Canterbury's Anglican Communion Fund. Chmn. bd. dirs. Am.-Australian Assn., 1986-99; vice chmn. bd. dirs. U.S.-New Zealand Coun.; bd. dirs. Mcpl. Art Soc. N.Y.; trustee Am. Friends of Nat. Gallery of Australia; trustee, mem. exec. com., sec. U.S. Coun. Internat. Bus.; bd. dirs., sec. Met. Opera Club, 1986-94; trustee Anglican Investment Agy. Trust. Named hon. officer Order of Australia. Mem. Am. Law Inst. (advisor corp. governance project 1978-92), Coun. on Fgn. Rels., Fgn. Policy Assn. (bd. dirs., treas.), Soc. Mayflower Desc., Links Club, Pilgrims, Piping Rock Club, Down Town Assn., Union Club, Griffis Faculty Club, River Club. Home: 435 E 52d St New York NY 10022 also: 51 Fruitledge Rd Glen Head NY 11545-3316 Office: Sullivan & Cromwell 125 Broad St New York NY 10004-2498 E-mail: merowj@sullcrom.com.

MEROWITZ, MORTON J. writer, translator; b. Phila., Nov. 15, 1936; s. Samuel L and Esther S (Linett) Merowitz; m. Arlene G Sherman, July 4, 1966. BA, Yeshiva Coll., 1960; MA, Dropsie Coll., 1964, SUNY, Buffalo, 1974; MLS, SUNY, Geneseo, 1975. Prin. H.S. of Jewish Studies, Bur. Jewish Edn., Buffalo, 1971-72; tchr. Kadimah Sch., 1972-74; mem. univ. facilities staff SUNY, 1976-99; ret, 1999. Contbr. articles to profl jours. Lectr. Wisdom Jewish Buffalo-Temple Beth-El, 1990, 1995. Mem.: Nat. Coalition Ind. Scholars, Assn. Jewish Librs., Am. Hist. Assn. Home: 71 N Maplemere Rd Buffalo NY 14221-3121 E-mail: merowitz@adelphia.net.

MERRELL, JAMES LEE, religious editor, clergyman; b. Indpls., Oct. 24, 1930; s. Mark W. and Pauline F. (Tucker) M.; m. Barbara Jean Burch, Dec. 23, 1951; children: Deborah Lea Merrell Griffin, Cynthia Lynn Archer, Stuart Allen. AB, Ind. U., 1952; MDiv, Christian Theol. Sem., 1956; LittD, Culver-Stockton Coll., 1972. Ordained to ministry Christian Ch., 1955; asso. editor World Call, Indpls., 1956-66, editor, 1971-73; pastor Crestview Christian Ch., Indpls., 1966-71; editor The Disciple, St. Louis, 1974-89; sr. v.p. Christian Bd. Publ., 1976-89; sr. minister Affton Christian Ch., St. Louis, 1989-94; interim chaplain Culver-Stockton Coll., Canton, 1995; interim sr. pastor Friedens United Ch. of Christ, Warrenton, 1995-98, St. Johns United Ch. of Christ, Mehlville, 1998—2002, Hamilton Christian Ch., Creve Coeur, 2002—. Bd. dirs. Horizons mag., 1995-98. Author: They Live Their Faith, 1965, The Power of One, 1976, Discover the Word in Print, 1979, Finding Faith in the Headlines, 1985, We Claim Our Heritage, 1992. Chmn. bd. Kennedy Meml. Christian Home, Martinsville, Ind., 1971-73; trustee Christian Theol. Sem., 1978-81. Recipient Faith and Freedom award Religious Heritage of Am., 1983; lifetime achievement award Mo. State Sen., 2000. Mem. Associated Ch. Press (award 1973, 79, 80, 81, 82, dir. 1974-75, 78-81, 1st v.p. 1983-85), Christian Theol. Sem. Alumni Assn. (pres. 1966-68), Religious Pub. Rels. Coun. (awards 1979, 80, 84, 87, 90, pres. St. Louis chpt. 1985-86), Sigma Delta Chi (award 1952), Theta Phi. Home: 6175 Clifton Oaks Pl Saint Louis MO 63129-4845 E-mail: JLeeMer@aol.com. *As a religious communicator and as a pastor, I have always believed in applying the same standards in the sacred realm as in the secular. I have tried to pursue the truth, to keep my constituency informed, to celebrate the noble in life, to fight against those who would lie, distort and hide God's truth in the name of some supposed good.*

MERRELL, JESSE HOWARD, writer; b. Shelby, Ala., Dec. 9, 1938; s. James Walton and Emma Thelma (Davis) M.; m. Betsy Lee Davis, Jan. 11, 1964 (div. 1979); children: Sandra, Mark, Brad, Carolyn, Gwen. Grad., Shelby High Sch., Columbiana, Ala., 1957. Pitcher Cin. Redlegs, 1958-62; reporter, news dir. WHAP Radio, Hopewell, Va., 1963; writer/editor Hopewell News, 1963-65; state editor Daily Progress, Charlottesville, Va., 1965-68; assoc. editor Transport Topics, Washington, 1968-75; spl. asst. to pres. Am. Trucking Assn., 1975-76; editor Transport Topics, 1976-77; pres. Merrell Ent., 1977—. Pub. rels. com. Am. Movers Conf., Washington, 1969-72; instr. Dale Carnegie courses, Washington, 1974-81, 1st pres., 1980-81; cons. Mid. Atlantic Conf., Riverdale, Md., 1981-82, Contract Carrier Conf., 1977-82; speechwriter ICC, Washington, 1982. Author: (novel) A Christmas Gift, 1979; syndicated columnist Religion and the Times, Washington Welter, (genealogy) The Merrells of Alabama, 1995, My Name is America! I Was Born at Jamestown!, 2002. Mem. Nat. Trust for Hist. Preservation, Assn. Preservation Va. Antiquities. With U.S. Army, 1960-62. Recipient Liberty award Congress of Freedom, Jackson, Miss., 1970, 71, Honor Cert., Freedoms Found., 1972, 1st place editorial writing Va. Press Assn., 1965, 1st place news writing, 1966. Mem. Nat. Press Club, Assn. Preservation Va. Antiquities, Gen. Washington's Coun. of the 1607 Soc. (charter mem.), Jamestown 2007 Spkrs. Bur., Jamestown-Yorktown Found., Colonial Williamsburg Raleigh Tavern Soc. Avocation: photography. Office: Merrell Ent 2610 Garfield St NW Washington DC 20008-4104

MERRELL, RONALD CLIFTON, surgeon, educator; b. Birmingham, Ala., June 18, 1946; s. Greene Lawrence and Florence (Jones) M.; m. Marsha Karen Cox, Dec. 24, 1966; children: Alexandria, Alison, R. Clifton. BS in Chemistry, U. Ala., 1967, MD, 1970. Diplomate Am. Bd. Surgery. Resident and fellow in surgery Wash. U., St. Louis, 1970-77; asst. prof. surgery Stanford (Calif.) U., 1979-84; assoc. prof. surgery U. Tex. Med. Sch., Houston, 1984-88, prof. surgery, 1988-94, M.D. Anderson Cancer Ctr., Houston, 1988-94; assoc. dean clin. affairs U. Tex. Med. Sch., 1988-92, vice dean, 1992-93; prof. surgery, chmn. dept. surgery Yale U., 1993-99; Stuart McGuire prof. surgery, chmn. dept. surgery Va. Commonwealth U., Richmond, 1999—. Author 3 books; contbr. over 95 articles to profl jours., 30 chpts. to books. Maj. U.S. Army, 1977-79. Recipient Basil O'Connor award March of Dimes, 1979, Rsch. Career Devel. award NIH, 1979-84, Henry J. Kaiser award Stanford U., 1982, 83, John P. McGovern Outstanding Tchr. award U. Tex. Med. Sch., 1988, Dean's Teaching Excellence award, 1983-89, Pub. Svc. award NASA, 1998, Disting. medal as Friend of Democritus, U. Greece, 1998; grantee NASA. Fellow ACS, Soc. Univ. Surgeons; mem. Am. Assn. Endocrine Surgery, Am.

Surg. Assn., Alpha Omega Alpha. Democrat. Episcopalian. Achievements include research in the transplantation of islets of Langerhans and telemedicine. Office: PO Box 980645 Richmond VA 23298-0645 E-mail: ronald.merrell@vcu.edu.

MERRELL, W. M. advertising executive; Grad., Fla. State U. Copywriter Liller, Neal, Battle & Lindsey; with Howard, McKinney & Silver, Raleigh, N.C.; pres., CEO Howard, Merrell & Ptnrs., 1976—. Office: Howard Merrell & Ptrns Ste 500 8521 Six Forks Rd Raleigh NC 27615*

MERRIAM, ALLEN HAYES, speech communication educator; b. Orange, N.J., July 28, 1942; s. Rutherford Douglas and Virginia (Johnson) M.; m. Sharan Ballard, Sept. 5, 1964 (div. 1981); children: Paul, Laura; m. Linda Kay Thompson, May 25, 1992. BA, Drew U., 1964; MA, Ohio U., 1970, PhD, 1972. Asst. prof. speech comm. Coll. N.J., 1972-77; asst. prof. U. Va., Charlottesville, 1977-78, Va. Tech. U., Blacksburg, 1978-82; assoc. prof. Mo. So. State Coll., Joplin, 1982-88, prof., 1988—. Author: Gandhi vs. Jinnah, 1980, People of the Millennium, 2000, America in Person, 2001; contbr. articles to profl. jours. Vol. Peace Corps, Kabul, Afghanistan, 1965-67. Mem. NAACP, SAR, Nat. Comms. Assn. Home: 1419 Marzelle Ct Joplin MO 64801-8263 Office: Mo So State Coll Dept Communication Joplin MO 64801 E-mail: merriam-A@mail.mssc.edu.

MERRIAM, DANIEL F(RANCIS), geologist; b. Omaha, Feb. 9, 1927; s. Faye Mills and Amanda Frances (Wood) M. m. Annie Laura Young, Feb. 12, 1946; children: Beth Ann, John Francis, Anita Pauline, James Daniel, Judith Diane. BS in Geology, U. Kans., 1949, MS, 1953, PhD, 1961; MSc in Geology, Leicester U., England, 1969; DSc, Leicester U., 1975. Geologist Union Oil Co. Calif., 1949-51, 52; asst. instr. U. Kans., 1951-53, instr., 1954, rsch. assoc., 1963-71; geologist Kans. Geol. Survey, 1953-58, head divsn. basic geology, 1958-63, chief geol. rsch., 1963-71; Jessie Page Heroy prof. geology dept. geology Syracuse U., 1971-81, chmn. dept. geology, 1971-80; Endowment Assn. Disting. prof. natural scis. dept. geology Wichita State U., 1981-93, chmn. dept. geology, 1981-87; sr. rsch. scientist Kans. Geol. Survey, U. Kans., 1993-97, emeritus, 1997—. Vis. rsch. scientist Stanford U., 1963; dir. Internat. Field Inst. to Japan, Am. Geol. Inst., 1967; vis. prof. geology Wichita State U., 1968-70; vis. geol. scientist Am. Geol. Inst., 1969; cons. nat. gas survey Fed. Power Commn., 1972-75, 78, chmn. supply tech. adv. com., 1975-77; ad hoc panel earth resources survey NAS/NRC, 1972-73, chmn. U.S. Nat. Com. for Internat. Geol. Correlation program, 1976-79, ex-officio, 1979-80, 81-83, U.S. Nat. Com. on History of Geology, 1989—; Esso Disting. lectr. U. Sydney, Australia, 1979; mem. U.S. Nat. Commn. for UNESCO, U.S. Dept. State, 1979-85; vis. prof. Centre d'Informatique Geologique, Ecole des Mines de Paris, Fontainebleau, 1980; vis. sr. scientist Kans. Geol. Survey, 1990-93; vis. scientist GeoForschungsZentrum, Potsdam, Germany, 1992; adj. prof. Emporia State U., Kans., 1993—. Author: The Geologic History of Kansas: Kansas Geological Survey , 1963, (with J.W. Harbaugh) Computer Applications in Stratigraphic Analysis, 1968, Computer Fundamentals for Geologists: COMPUTe, 1975, Bibliography of Computer Applications in the Earth Sciences, 1988; founder, editor-in-chief Jour. Math. Geology, 1968-76, 94-97, Computers & Geosciences, 1975-95; founder, editor Kansas Geological Survey, Computer Contributions, 1966-71, Syracuse University Geological Contributions, 1973-81; editor (series) Computer Applications in the Earth Sciences, 1969—, Computers and Geology, 1976-90, Computer Methods in the Geosciences, 1982—, (books and vols.) Mathematical Models of Sedimentary Processes, 1972, The Impact of Quantification on Geology, 1974, Random Processes in Geology, 1976, Geomathematics: Past, Present, and Prospects, 1978, Down-to-Earth Statistics: Solutions Looking for Geological Problems, 1981, Current Trends in Geomathematics, 1988, (colloquium) Geostatistics, 1970; translation editor Statistics for Geoscientists, 1987; co-editor Pacific Geology, 1971-83; editl. cons. Geosystems, 1971-83; mem. editl. rev. bd. Colo. Sch. Mines Quarterly, 1974-90; mem. editl. adv. bd. Geophysical Computer Programs, 1975-76, Applied Geochemistry, 1985-93; mem. editl. bd. History of Earth Science Soc., 1982-2000; reviewer for nat. and internat. jours.; contbr. notes, articles to numerous jours. Bd. dirs. Kans Geol. Found., 1989-92. Fullbright-Hayes Sr. Rsch. fellow, U.K., 1964-65. Fellow AAAS (sr., electorate nomination com. 1977-80, chairperson sect. E 1983-84, Sci. software adv. panel 1986-91, SWARM 64th local arrangement com. chmn. 1988), Geol. Soc. Am. (sr., com. on publs. 1973-76, chmn. com. geology dept. 1975-78), Geol. Soc. London (William Smith medal 1992), Sigma Xi (sec. Kansas chpt. 1994-96, pres. 1997-98); mem. Am. Assn. Petroleum Geologists (hon., chmn. 1954, 57, ednl. exhibits com., rsch. com., 1964-67, assoc. editor bulletin 1969-75, Geobyte 1985-92, computer applications in geology com. 1971-81, 86—, N.Y. Dist. rep. 1974-76, Kans. Dist. rep. 1956-57, 1985-91, chmn. 1989-91, Kans. rep. Midcontinent sect. 1988-92, Disting. Svc. award 1987, Cert. of Merit 1987, 93), Soc. Econ. Paleontologists and Mineralogists (hon., chmn. organizer rsch. group in computer tech. 1970-75, 82-82, 89-90, publs. com. 1980-83, chmn. publs. 1981-82, chmn. Pa. Stratigraphy working group Midcontinent sect. 1986—, ad. hoc. com. databases 1985-88, chmn databases 1986-88, organizer computer applications com. 1988—, chmn. computer applications 1988-92, procedures com. 1989-2001, chmn. 1993-94, spl. advisor headquarters and bus. com. 1988-91, chmn. 1991-98), Nat. Assn. Geology Tchrs. (v.p. Kans.-Okla. sect. 1986, pres. 1987-89, sec. 1994—), Geosci. Info. Soc. (program com 1980-81), Internat. Union Geol. Scis., Internat. Geol. Correlations Program (U.S. del. 1969, sci. com. 1975-79, 76-77, chmn. ad hoc com. publs. 1980, adv. bd. publs. 1980-89, chmn. 1980-84), Internat. Geol. Congress (alternate U.S. del. VII ordinary sessions coun. 1984, U.S. del. VIII ordinary sessions coun. 1989), Internat. Assn. Math. Geology (mem. coun. 1968—, sec.-gen. 1972-76, pres. 1976-80, interim archivist 1989-92, archivist 1992—, William Christian Krumbein medal 1981, pubs. com. 1997—, organizing com. 8th ann. meeting 2001), Leicester Geol. Soc. (hon. life 1965), Sylvester-Bradley Geol. Soc. (hon. v.p. 1978-79), Classification Soc. (chmn. mem. com., bd. dirs. 1968-71), N.Y. State Geol. Assn. (exec. sec. 1972-77, pres. 1977-78, bd. dirs. 1987-83), Kans. Geol. Soc. (hon., bd. dirs., dir. many confs., presdl. citation 1989), Kans. Acad. Sci. (mem. coun. at large 1983-86, v.p. 1987, pres.-elect 1988, pres. 1989, chmn. com. for 2001, 1989-92, assoc. editor Transactions 1990-92, editor, 1992—, strategic planning com. 2000—, gen. chmn. 119th Ann. Meeting 1987, 131st Ann. Meeting 2001), History of Earth Sci. Soc. (Earth Science History editorial bd. 1982—), Sigma Gamma Epsilon (pres. Alpha chpt. 1952-53, nat. coun. 1983-95, nat. pres. 1990-95, nat. editor The Compass, 1983-92, hon.), Phi Kappa Phi, Sigma Xi (Kans. chpt. 1994-96, pres. 1997-98). Office: Kans Geol Survey U Kans Lawrence KS 66047

MERRIAM, DWIGHT HAINES, lawyer, land use planner; b. Norwood, Mass., Apr. 20, 1946; s. Austin Luther and Lillian Diana (Olsen) M.; m. Cynthia Ann Hayes, May 21, 1966 (div. June 1992); children: Sarah Ann Leilani, Jonathan Hayes; m. Susan Manning Standish, May 6, 1995; children: Alexander Harlan, Lucy Caroline. BA cum laude, U. Mass., 1968; M in Regional Planning, U. N.C., 1974; JD, Yale U., 1978. Bar: Conn. 1978, Mass. 1980, U.S. Dist. Ct. Conn. 1981, U.S. Dist. Ct. Hawaii 1984, U.S. Supreme Ct. 1990, U.S. Ct. Appeals (4th cir.) 1993. Land use planner Charles E. Downe, Newton, Mass., 1968; assoc. Byrne, Buck & Steiner, Farmington, Conn., 1978, Robinson, Robinson & Cole, Hartford, 1979-83; ptnr. Robinson & Cole LLP, 1984—. Adj. prof. law Western New Eng. Coll., 1978-86, U. Conn., 1982, 84-87, Vt. Law Sch., 1994—; instr. planning U. Bridgeport, 1981-83, U. Conn., 1986-92; mem. faculty Nat. Coll. Dist. Attys., 1983-87, Nat. Jud. Coll., 1994; mem. faculty Am. Law Inst.-ABA Land Use Inst., 1988—; instr. city and regional planning Memphis State U., 1989, 94; speaker in field. Co-author: The Takings Issue, 1999; co-editor: Inclusionary Zoning Moves Downtown, 1985; contbr. Bd. dirs. Conn. chpt. Appleseed Found., 1997-2000, Am. Boat Builders and Repairers Assn., 1995—, Growth Mgmt. Inst., Washington, 1992—, Housing Edn. Resource Ctr., 1984-88, Housing Coalition for Capitol Region, Inc., 1984-86; bd. dirs. Conn. Fund for Environment, 1981-85, legal adv. com., 1985-88, legal adv. bd., 1978-81; mem. Environment 2000 environ. plan adv. bd. Conn. Dept. Environ. Protection, 1987-91; assoc. Environ. Law Inst., 1987—; mem. housing task force Conn. Dept. on Aging, 1981; mem. Gov.'s Housing Task Force, Conn., 1980-81. With USN, 1968-75, Vietnam; capt. USNR, 1975-99. Fellow: Am. Inst. Cert. Planners (pres. 1988—90); mem.: ABA, Am. Coll. Real Estate Lawyers, Assn. State Floodplain Mgrs., Internat. Mcpl. Law Assn. (chmn. sect. on zoning, planning and land devel. 1988—89), Am. Planning Assn. (bd. dirs. 1988—90, chmn. planning and law divsn. 1984—86, exec. com. planning and law divsn. 1978—88, chmn. legis. com. Conn. chpt. 1978—80, editl. adv. bd. 1984—92), Conn. Bar Assn. (exec. com. zoning and planning sect. 1985—87, 1991—). Democrat. Unitarian Universalist. Avocations: sailing, skiing. Home: 80 Latimer Ln Weatogue CT 06089 Office: Robinson & Cole LLP 280 Trumbull St 27th Fl Hartford CT 06103-3597

MERRIAM, JANET PAMELA, special education educator; b. L.A., Jan. 11, 1958; d. Allen Hugo and Linda (Teagle) Warren; m. Marshal Lockhart Merriam, Aug. 4, 1984 (div. June 1991); 1 child, Jennifer Elizabeth. BA, San Jose State U., 1981. Cert. tchr. learning handicapped, lang. devel. specialist, Calif. Asst. youth edn. dir. Christ Ch. Unity, San Jose, 1988-90; substitute tchr. Santa Clara (Calif.) Unified Sch. Dist., 1990; spl. day class tchr. Oak Grove Sch. Dist., San Jose, 1990—. Sunday sch. tchr. Christ Ch. Unity, San Jose, 1980-92. Mem. Coun. for Exceptional Children, Learning Disabilities Assn. Calif., Calif. Assn. Resource Specialists Plus. Republican. Avocations: reading, Star Trek, old movies. Home: 1657 Glenville Dr San Jose CA 95124-3808 Office: 530 Gettysburg Dr San Jose CA 95123-3234

MERRIAM, JOHN GOODWIN, political scientist, educator; b. Lausanne, Switzerland, Mar. 27, 1933; parents U.S. citizens; s. Gordon Phelps and Eunice Wilbur (Brandt) M.; m. Kathleen Howard, June 20, 1961 (div. 1989); children: Heather S., Christopher H., Jennifer S. Truax; m. Nancy J. Fox, Nov. 27, 1993. BA, Hamilton Coll., 1955; postgrad., Harvard U., 1961; MA, Boston U., 1962; PhD, Ind. U., 1970. Instr. Ricker Coll., Houlton, Maine, 1960-61, 64; teaching fellow Am. U. in Cairo, Egypt, 1964-66, asst. prof. Egypt, 1966-67; instr., asst. prof., assoc. prof. polit. sci. Bowling Green (Ohio) State U., 1967-93, assoc. prof. emeritus, 1993—. Part-time prof. Lourdes Coll., 1993—; bd. dirs. Alliance Francaise de Toledo, 1986-93, Ohio Middle East Policy Coun., 1987—. With U.S. Army, 1955-58. Grantee Ind. U., Bloomington, 1961-62; Ford Found fellow, 1962-64. Mem. Middle East Inst., Middle East Policy Coun., Pi Sigma Alpha, Delta Tau Kappa. Democrat. Episcopalian. Avocation: walking. Home: 3033 Hopewell Pl Toledo OH 43606-3105 Office: Bowling Green State U Dept Polit Sci Bowling Green OH 43403-0001

MERRIAM, OLIVER STEVEN, city manager; b. Chgo., Apr. 27, 1943; s. Robert Edward and Marguerite Elizabeth (De Ternova) M.; m. Joan Carol Wawrzyniak, Aug. 22, 1970; 1 child, Blake. BA, Beloit Coll., 1965; M Govt. Adminstrn., U. Pa., 1967. Adminstrv. asst. City of Salem, Oreg., 1966-69; asst. city mgr. City of Saginaw, Mich., 1969-74; city mgr. City of North Miami Beach, Fla., 1974-76, City of Oak Park, Mich., 1979-80; asst. to county mgr. Arlington County, Va., 1976-79; program dir. Am. Pub. Works Assn., Chgo., 1980-94; city mgr. City of Hiawatha, Iowa, 1995-99; adminstr. Village of Plover, Wis., 2000—. Editor: Public Works Today, 1990. With USAR, 1967-73. Fels scholar U. Pa., 1966. Mem. Am. Pub. Works Assn., Internat. City and County Mgmt. Assn., Inst. for Adminstrv. Mgmt. (sec. 1980-94). E-mail: eplover.com. Office: Village of Plover 2400 Post Rd Plover WI 54467

MERRIAM, ROBERT W. engineering executive, educator; b. Providence, July 18, 1923; s. Paul Adams and Marian Lewis M.; m. Nancy Ann Allen, Dec. 21, 1954; children: Susan Allen Jones, Paul Adams, II. BS in Engring. Sci. and Applied Physics, Harvard Coll., 1949; MS in Engring. Sci. and Applied Physics, Harvard Engring. Sch., 1950. Reg. profl. engr., R.I. Instr. elec. engring. Swarthmore (Pa.) Coll., 1950-52; engr. Metals & Controls Corp., Attleboro, Mass., 1953-55; pres. Merriam Instruments, East Greenwich, R.I., 1955-99. Assoc. prof. U. R.I., Kingston, 1969-79. Editor: History of Wireless Communication in the U.S., 1989; patentee in field; contbr. articles to popular publications. Pres., dir. N.E. Wireless and Steam Mus., East Greenwich, 1964—; chmn. Planning Bd., East Greenwich, 1970s; hon. trustee Heritage Trust of R.I. With U.S. Army Signal Corp., 1942-46, ETO. Recipient Antoinette Downing award State of R.I., 1998; named Engr. of Yr., Nat. Assn. of Power Engrs., 1998, award Soc. Indsl. Archeology Gen. Tools, 2001. Fellow Radio Club Am. (Batcher award 1979); mem. IEEE (life), Am. Radio Relay League (life), Nat. Marine Electronic Assn. (hon., dir. 1957), Nat. Assn. Power Engrs. (hon.), Vet. Wireless Assn. (Marconi Gold medal 1995), 20:00 Club (Meritorious Amateur Seamanship award 1955), Rhode Soc. Profl. Engrs. (Engr. of Yr. 1999), Hope Club, Harvard Club (Boston). E-mail: newsm.@ids.net.

MERRICK, BEVERLY GEORGIANNE, journalism, communications educator; b. Troy, Kans., Nov. 20, 1944; d. Horace Buchanan Merrick and Vola Yolantha (Clausen) Maul; m. John Douglas Childers, July 10, 1963 (div. 1998); children: John Kevin, Pamela Christine, Jessica Faye. BA in Journalism with honors, BA in English with honors, Marshall U., 1980, M Journalism, 1982; M Creative Writing, Ohio U., 1986, cert. in Women's Studies, 1984, PhD in Mass Comm. with honors, 1989. Reporter, photographer Ashland (Ky.) Daily Ind., 1981; tchr., instr. Albuquerque Pub. Schs., 1986-89; gen. assignment reporter, photographer Rio Rancho (N.Mex.) Observer, 1986; editor, rsch. cons. Ins. Pub. Law, Sch. of Law U. N.Mex., Albuquerque, 1990; asst. prof. Ga. So. U., Statesboro, 1991-94; assoc. prof. dept. mass comm. U. S.D., Vermillion, 1994-95; from asst. to assoc. prof. dept. journalism and mass comm. N. Mex. State U., Las Cruces, 1995—; faculty, photographer the Washington Ctr., 1999. Part-time tchr., tchg. assoc. Ohio U., Athens, 1981-84; part-time copy editor Albuquerque Tribune, 1991; vis. prof. East Carolina U., Greenville, N.C., 1989-90; adj. prof. Embry-Riddle U., Kirtland AFB, N.Mex., 1989, 91; organizer diversity conf., 1st amendment conf. Ga. So. U.; mem. session MIT, 1989; chair campus com. N.Mex. State U.; faculty Washington Ctr. Nat. Women in Leadership Interns Program, 1999; leadership trainer, N.Mex. No. U., Abiquiu, 1999; presenter in field Author: (poetry) Navigating the Platte, 1986, Pearls for the Casting, 1987, Closing the Gate, 1993, (monograph) Jane Grant, The New Yorker and Ross, 1999; contbr. poems to profl. publs., jours. and chpts. to books. Pub. rels. liaison Nat. Convention Bus. and Profl. Women, Albuquerque, 1988; pres. Albuquerque Bus. and Profl. Women, 1986-87, Rio Rancho Civic Assn., 1987-89, So. Ohio Improvement League, 1973-76; pres. bd. dirs. Pine Creek Conservancy Dist., 1976-83; chair Ted Turner and Jane Fonda Com., 1996, Sam Donaldson Native Sun Benefit Com., 1999; gov., girls State counselor, N.M., 2000; chair poster contest on media literacy Las Cruces Pub. Schs., So. N.Mex. Literacy Coun. Named Truly Fine Citizen of Ohio, Ohio Gen. Assembly, 1973, Outstanding Homemaker of Ohio, Gov. of Ohio, 1974, Outstanding Citizen, N.Mex. Legislature, 1988; grantee Reader's Digest, 1980, 83; John Houk Meml. grantee W.Va. Women's Conf., 1982; fellow Nat. Women's Studies Inst., Lilly Found., 1983, Freedom Forum Ethics, 1995, Am. Newspaper Inst., 1995; Newsday fellow Am. Soc. Newspaper Editors, 1998; E.W. Scripps scholar, 1984; recipient Silver Clover award 4-H, Writing award Aviation/Space Writers Assn., 1981, 1st place open rsch competition Nat. Assn. Women's Deans, Adminstrs. and Counselors, 1990 award 16th Ann. Gov.'s Awards for Outstanding N.Mex. Women, 2001; rsch. grantee N.Mex. State U., 1996. Mem. Soc. Profl. Journalists, Assn. for Edn. in Journalism and Mass Comm. (mem. nat. conv. com. 1993-94, vice head mag. divsn. 1995-96, head mag. divsn., 1996-97, chair southwest colloquium 1998), S.W. Edn. Coun. for Journalism and Mass Comm. (conf. chair 1998, bd. dirs. 1999—), Western Journalism Historians Assn. (conf. chair Berkeley Sch. Journalism 1999), N.Mex. State Poetry Soc. (pres. 1987-89), Sigma Tau Delta. Home: 985 Ivydale Dr Las Cruces NM 88005-0927

MERRICK, BRUCE ALEX, research scientist; b. Sacramento, Aug. 13, 1952; BS in Biology, U. Calif., Davis, 1974; BS in Pharmacy, U. N.Mex., 1978; MS, U. Nebr., 1980, PhD, 1984. Lic. pharmacist, Nebr., N.C. Group lead hepatotoxicology U.S. EPA, Cin., 1985-88; phys. scientist cancer rsch. and proteomics Nat. Inst. Environ. Health Scis., Research Triangle Park, N.C., 1988—. Contbr. articles to profl. jours.; patentee in field. Mem. Am. Assn. Cancer Rsch., Soc. Toxicology. Office: NIEHS/LMC PO Box 12233 Durham NC 27709-2233 E-mail: merrick@niehs.nih.gov.

MERRICK, DOROTHY SUSAN, interior designer; b. N.Y.C. BA, Skidmore Coll.; MA, Adelphi U. Owner, pres. Dorothy Merrick Interiors Ltd., Sands Point, N.Y., 1968—. Project published in Newsday, N.Y. Times, House Mag. Recipient Gold Archi award Nassau/Suffolk AIA, 1986. Mem. Internat. Interior Designers Assn., Am. Soc. Interior Designers, Allied Bd. of Trade, Knickerbocker Yacht Club, Village Club Sands Point. Avocations: sailing, reading, opera, golf.

MERRICK, GEORGE BOESCH, aerospace company executive; b. Burlington, Iowa, Mar. 9, 1928; s. Dale McKeen and Marjorie May (Boesch) M.; m. Eleanor Gamble Moore, Sept. 1, 1951; children: Charles, Ellen, Elizabeth. BS, U. Minn., 1949. With N.Am. Aviation (name changed to Rockwell Internat.), 1949; dir. Apollo Command and Service Module, Space div., 1966-72; v.p., program mgr. Apollo Program, 1972-74, v.p., program mgr. Space Shuttle Orbiter Program, 1974-76; pres. space div. Rockwell Internat., Downey, Calif., 1976-78, pres. space systems group, 1978-80, corp. v.p., 1980-91, ret., 1991. Recipient Pub. Service award NASA. Fellow Am. Astron. Soc., AIAA.

MERRICK, PATRICIA ANN, radiological nurse; b. Hartford, Conn., Mar. 17, 1955; d. John Leo Jr. and Joan Virginia (Lynch) M. Diploma, Meriden-Wallingford Hosp. Sch. Nursing, 1976; AS, Manchester Community Coll., 1982; BSN, Cen. Conn. State U., 1987; postgrad., U. Conn., U. Hartford; MSN, St. Joseph Coll., 2002. Cert. radiol. nurse. Supr. Am. Nursing Resources Inc., Farmington, Conn.; faculty E.C. Goodwin Tech., New Britain; supr. Meloria's Childrens Nursery, Prospect; staff nurse, charge nurse Newington VA Med. Ctr.; radiology nurse care coord. U. Conn. Health Ctr., Farmington. Contbr. articles to profl. jours. Mem. ANA, Conn. Nurses Assn., Am. Radiol. Nurses Assn. (past nat. pres., past pres. New Eng. chpt., past nat. sec., past chair, past chair cert. exam devel. com., contbg. author core curriculum), Sigma Theta Tau. E-mail: pmer317@aol.com.

MERRICK, ROSWELL DAVENPORT, educational association administrator; b. Kings County, N.Y., July 20, 1922; s. George Roswell and Marguerite Regina M.; m. Gladys K. Kinley, June 26, 1948; children— Gregory, Susan, Peter. BS, Springfield Coll., 1944; MA, N.Y. U., 1947; Ed.D., Boston U., 1953. Assoc. prof., head basketball coach Central Conn. U., New Britain, 1946-53; asst. dean (Coll. Edn.); dir. div. health, phys. edn., recreation and athletics So. Ill. U., Carbondale, 1953-58; exec. dir. Nat. Assn. Sport and Phys. Edn., Reston, Va., 1958-91, U.S. Fitness and Sport Coun., 1991—. Contbr. articles to profl. jours. Mem. U.S. Olympic Com. Served with USAAF, 1944-46. Mem. AAHPERD, Mt. Vernon Yacht Club. Methodist. Address: 4739 Neptune Dr Alexandria VA 22309-3132

MERRIER, HELEN, actress, writer; b. Chgo., Mar. 10, 1932; d. Miner Thompson and Helen (Hembree) Coburn; m. Tim Meier, Dec. 23, 1954; 1 child, William Frank. BA, Mills Coll., 1954; BS, Northwestern U., 1955. Radio roles include Ma Perkins, One Man's Family, Standard School House of the Air, 1934-52; stage roles include Finian's Rainbow, 1952, The Happy Time, 1952, The Night of January 16th, 1952, No Exit, 1953, Tiger at the Gates, 1953, Caeser and Cleopatra, 1953, The Cocktail Party, 1953, Streetcar Named Desire, 1953, Misalliance, 1956, Cry the Beloved Country, 1956, Cat in a Tin Roof, 1963, Take Me Along, 1966, Caucasian Chalk Circle, 1967, The Devils, 1968, Electra, 1969, Jean Harlow and Billy the Kid, 1969, Three-Penny Opera, 1969, A Shot in the Dark, 1970, Private Lives, 1970, The Importance of Being Earnest, 1971, Forty Carats, 1972, Paris is Out!, 1972, A Christmas Carol, 1973, The Sea Gull, 1975, Something more than Ordinary, 1976, Three Dollar Bill, 1976, Maid to Marry, 1977, Scrooge, the musical, 1984, Prisoner of Second Avenue, 1985, Tom Sawyer, 1986, Comedy of Errors, 1987, Juno and the Paycock, 1987, Woman of the Year, 1989, Time and the Conways, 1991, Cinderella, 1991, Sweney Todd, 1991, The Birds, 1993, Dreams of Defiance (rev.), 1994, Lady Lucinda's Scrapbook (solo play), 1996-98, As You Like It hike, 1998-99, A Midsummer Night's Dream hike, 1999, 2001, Vieux Carre, 1999, Woman Talk (cabaret), 1999, Healthy- Minded Little Old Lady Songs (solo cabaret), 2000—, Stephen Foster's Songs (solo cabaret), 2001—, William Inge Festival, 2000, Robin Hood hike, 2000-01, Rip van Winkle hike, 2001, (solo cabaret) Stephen Foster in Song and Story (solo cabaret), 2001. Recipient The Spirit of Theater award, 2000, Disting. Svc. award The Salvation Army, 2000. Mem. Victory Svcs. Club (London), Arts Club Chgo. Home: 915 Linden Ave Wilmette IL 60091-2712 E-mail: hmerrier@AmericanaProductions.com .

MERRIFIELD, DONALD PAUL, university chancellor; b. Los Angeles, Nov. 14, 1928; s. Arthur S. and Elizabeth (Baker) M. BS in Physics, Calif. Inst. Tech., 1950; MS, U. Notre Dame, 1951; A.M., Ph.L. in Philosophy, St. Louis U., 1957; PhD, MIT, 1962; S.T.M., U. Santa Clara, Calif., 1966; S.T.D. (hon.), U. So. Calif., 1969; D.H.L. (hon.), U. Judaism, 1984, Hebrew Union Coll.-Jewish Inst. Religion, 1986. Joined Soc. of Jesus, 1951; ordained priest Roman Cath. Ch., 1965; instr. physics Loyola U., Los Angeles, 1961-62; lectr. Engring. Sch., Santa Clara, 1965; cons. theoretical chemistry Jet Propulsion Lab., Calif. Inst. Tech., 1962-69; asst. prof. physics U. San Francisco, 1967-69; pres. Loyola Marymount U., Los Angeles, 1969-84, chancellor, 1984—2002; pastoral ministry, 2002—. Mem. Sigma Xi. Office: 2727 Pamoa Rd Honolulu HI 96822-1838 E-mail: dmerrifield@calprov.org. *In today's world, we all stand in need of that pragmatic hope which allows us to see the possibilities for building a more just society and meeting the challenges before us. Without such hope we are paralyzed before our difficulties. With a less realistic hope, too idealistic, we are continually overwhelmed by failures. But with an openness to possibilities, we can move ahead with determination.*

MERRIFIELD, DUDLEY BRUCE, business educator, former government official; b. Chgo., June 13, 1921; s. Fred and Anna (Marshall) M.; m. Paula Sorensen, June 8, 1949; children: Bruce, Robert, Marshall. AB in Chemistry, Princeton U., 1942; MS in Chemistry, U. Chgo., 1948, PhD in Chemistry, 1950. Disting. vis. prof. Georgetown U. Bus. Sch., Washington. Sr. rsch. chemist Monsanto, St. Louis, 1950-56; mgr. polymer rsch. Tex.-U.S. Chem. Co., Parsippany, N.J., 1956-63; dir. R & D Petrolite Corp., St. Louis, 1963-68; v.p. tech. and ventures Occidental Petroleum Co., Houston, 1968-77; v.p. tech. and venture mgmt. Continental Group, Stamford, Conn., 1977-82; asst. sec. for productivity, tech. and innovation Dept. Commerce, Washington, 1982-89; undersec. econ. affairs, 1986-87; Walter Bladstrom prof., emeritus Wharton Bus. Sch., U Pa., Phila., 1989-94; pres., CEO Pinnacle Rsch. Inst. Devel. Co., 1991—. Adv. bd. Binat R & D Found., U.S., Israel, France, India, 1979—; disting. vis. prof. mgmt., Georgetown U., Washington. Contbr. articles to profl. jours.; patentee in field. Exec. coun. Episcopal Ch., 1973-79; chmn. Princeton Alumni Coun., 1968-72. With USMC, 1943-46. Fellow AAAS, Inst. for Chemists; mem. Am. Chem. Soc., Indsl. Rsch. Inst. (dir., pres.-elect 1977-82 M. Holland award), Am. Mgmt. Assn. Hall of Fame (trustee, chmn. rsch. coun.), Dirs. Rsch., Sigma Xi Republican. Episcopalian. Office: Pridco Mgmt Corp Ste 604 1316 New Hampshire NW Washington DC 20036 E-mail: dr.bmerrifield@erols.com.

MERRIFIELD, LEROY SORENSON, law educator; b. Mpls., Nov. 18, 1917; s. Edgar Eugene and Alice Sorenson M.; m. Marian Grace Hansen, Apr. 25, 1943; children: Lois, Eric, Randall, Karen. BA, U. Minn., 1938, JD, 1941; MBA, Harvard U., 1943, SJD, 1956. Bar: Minn. 1941, D.C. 1979, U.S. Supreme Ct. 1957. Atty. U.S. Office Price Adminstrn., Boston, 1942, U.S. Dept. Justice, Washington, 1946; prof. law George Washington U., 1947-87; prof. emeritus, 1987—. Lt. USN, 1943-45. Mem. ABA, Am. Arbitration Assn., Internat. Indsl. Rels. Assn., Order of Coif, Phi Beta Kappa. Democrat. Unitarian Universalist. Avocations: singing, tennis, golf.

MERRIFIELD, ROBERT BRUCE, biochemist, educator; b. Ft. Worth, July 15, 1921; s. George E. and Lorene (Lucas) Merrifield; m. Elizabeth Furling, June 20, 1949; children: Nancy, James, Betsy, Cathy, Laurie, Sally. BA, UCLA, 1943, PhD, 1949; PhD (hon.) (hon.) , U. Colo., 1969, Uppsala U., 1970, Yale U., 1971, Newark Coll. Engring., 1972, Med. Coll. Ohio, 1977, Boston Coll., 1984, Fairleigh Dickinson U., 1985, N.J. U. Medicine & Dentistry, 1985, U. Barcelona, 1986, Adelphi U., 1987, U. Montpellier, 1988, Delaware Valley Coll., 1991, Scripps Rsch. Inst., 1998, Rockefeller U., 1998. Chemist Park Research Found., 1943—44; research asst. Med. Sch., UCLA, 1948—49; asst. Rockefeller Inst. for Med. Research, 1949—53, assoc., 1953—57; asst. prof. Rockefeller U., 1957—58, assoc. prof., 1958—66, prof., 1966—92, John D. Rockefeller prof., 1984—92, emeritus prof., 1992—. Assoc. editor: Internat. Jour. Peptide and Protein Research; contbr. Named one of Top 75 Contbrs. to Chem. Enterprise during past 75 yrs., Chem. & Engring. News, 1998; recipient Lasker award biomed. rsch., 1969, Gairdner award, 1970, Intra-Sci. award, 1970, Nichols medal, 1973, Alan E. Pierce award, Am. Peptide Symposium, 1979, Nobel prize in chemistry, 1984, UCLA Disting. Svc. medal, 1986, Royal Soc. Chemistry medal, 1987, Rudinger award, European Peptide Soc., 1990, Chem. Pioneer award, Am. Inst. Chemists, 1993, Glenn T. Seaborg medal, 1993, UCLA Alumnus of Yr. award, 1997, award, Assn. Biomolecular Resource Facilities, 1998. Mem.: NAS USA, Am. Soc. Biol. Chemists, Am. Chem. Soc. (award creative work synthetic organic chemistry 1972, Hirschmann award in peptide chemistry 1990, Glenn T.

Seaborg award 1993), Alpha Chi Sigma, Phi Lambda Upsilon, Sigma Xi. Achievements include discovery of solid phase peptide synthesis; completed (with B. Gutte) 1st total synthesis of an enzyme, 69. Office: Rockefeller Univ Dept Chemistry 1230 York Ave New York NY 10021-6307*

MERRILL, ARTHUR ALEXANDER, financial analyst; b. Honolulu, June 17, 1906; s. Arthur Merton and Grace Graydon (Dickey) M.; m. Elsie Louise Breed, Aug. 17, 1929; 1 child, Anne Louise Merrill Breiling. BS in Elec. Engring, U. Calif., 1927; MBA, Harvard U., 1929. Mem. engring., statistics, and mgmt. depts. Gen. Electric Co., Schenectady, also N.Y.C., 1927-61; fin. writer and analyst, pres. Merrill Analysis Inc., Haverford, Pa., 1961—. Author: How Do You Use a Slide Rule, 1961, Chess Openings Simplified, 1974, Behavior of Prices on Wall Street, 1985, Battle of White Plains, 1975, Seasonal Tendencies in Stock Prices, 1975, Filtered Waves, Basic Theory, 1977, Bias in Hourly, Daily and Weekly Wave Patterns, 1979, Remembering Names, 1985; editor: Tech. Trends, 1961-88. Mem. Market Technicians Assn. (chartered, Ann. award 1977), Fin. Analysts Fedn., N.Y. Soc. Security Analysts, Mensa, Intertel, Soc. Preservation and Encouragement Barber Shop Quartet Singing Am., Sigma Xi, Theta Chi, Tau Beta Pi, Eta Kappa Nu. Republican. Congregationalist. Home and Office: 3300 Darby Rd Apt 3325 Haverford PA 19041-1071

MERRILL, CHARLES EUGENE, lawyer; b. San Antonio, Aug. 26, 1952; s. Charles Perry and Florence Elizabeth Merrill; m. Carol Ann Rutter, Apr. 28, 1984; children: Elizabeth C., Charles C. AB, Stanford U., 1974; JD, U. Calif., Berkeley, 1977. Bar: Mo. 1977, Calif. 1983, Ill. 1993. Mem. Husch & Eppenberger, LLC, St. Louis, 1977—. Mem. ABA, Bar Assn. of Met. St. Louis. Office: Husch & Eppenberger LLC 190 Carondelet Plz Ste 600 Saint Louis MO 63105-3441 E-mail: charlie.merrill@husch.com.

MERRILL, DALE MARIE, lawyer; b. Melrose, Mass., Feb. 21, 1954; d. Richard Paul and Rosemarie Reine (Porelle) M. BA in English, U. of Lowell, Mass., 1976; MA in Am. Studies, Boston Coll., 1983; CSS in Mgmt., Harvard U., 1989; MBA, Boston Coll., 1992; JD, Suffolk U., 1997. Regional sales mgr. CompuServe Data Techs. (formerly Software House), Cambridge, Mass., 1983-89; internat. sales mgr. Hypersoft Corp., 1989-93; Praxis Internat., 1992-93; sales mgr. Dataware Technologies, 1993-98; atty. GTE Internetworking, Inc., Mass., 1998-00; atty. priv. prac., 2000—. Bd. dirs. U. Mass., Lowell Alumni Assn., 1993—, Reading Substance Abuse Prevention Coun. Author: How to Buy Software: Avoiding the Traps Salespeople Set, 1989; author, editor: Seeds mag. (Poetry award 1972), 1971-72; contbr. poetry to mags. Organizer 18x72 project, Stoneham, Mass., 1970-71; bd. dirs. Stoneham Hist. Commn., 1976-77, Reading Substance Abuse Prevention Com., 1997—. Recipient Top Sales award A-Copy Inc., 1976-77, Interviewer award Decision Rsch. Co., 1981, Triple Crown Sales award, 1985, 86, 87, Million Dollar Sales Club award, 1987, 88. Mem. ABA, Digital Equipment Co. User Soc., Mass. Bar Assn., Phi Delta Phi. Republican. Avocations: skiing, photography, painting, sculpturing, karate. Home: PO Box 2586 Woburn MA 01888-1186 Office: Law Office Dale Marie Merrill 875 Mass Ave Ste 31 Cambridge MA 02139

MERRILL, EARLENE BROWN, nurse educator; b. Montgomery Ala., Nov. 11, 1947; d. Sidney and Willie Ella (Richardson) Brown; m. Samuel Merrill, Jr.; children: Paula, Veronika, Ryan. BSN, Calif. State U., L.A., 1967; MSN, UCLA, 1973; EdD in Higher Edn., George Washington U., 1992. RN, Calif., Colo. Pub. health nurse Los Angeles County Health Dept., L.A., 1970-73; nursing supr. East Side Health Dist., Denver, 1973-74; instr. U. Colo., 1974-77; asst. prof. Howard U. Sch. Nursing, Washington, 1977-81; assoc. prof. Coppin State Coll., Balt., 1981-93, assoc. dean undergrad. program, 1993-97, prof. nursing, 1997-99. Mem. cmty. planning Md. AIDS Adminstrn., Balt., 1993-99, mem. exec. com., 1993-99. Contbr. articles and book revs. to profl. jours. Mem. D.C. Teen Pregnancy Task Force, Washington, 1980. Grantee USPHS, 1970-73, Fla. A&M. U., 1994-96. Mem. ANA (minority fellow 1990-92), APHA, Nat. League for Nursing (program evaluator 1993—), Md. Nurses Assn. (2d v.p. dist. 5 1992-94, bd. dirs. 1994-96, 1st v.p. 1994-96, chmn. task force on nursing practice and edn. 1994-96, bd. dirs. 1999—), Md. League for Nursing, Assn. Black Nursing Faculty, Chi Eta Phi. Avocations: travel, reading, collecting quotations and poems. Home: 18624 Hedgegrove Ter Olney MD 20832-1812 Office: Coppin State Coll 2500 W North Ave Baltimore MD 21216-3633 E-mail: vrmerrill@msn.com.

MERRILL, EDWARD WILSON, chemical engineering educator; b. New Bedford, Mass., Aug. 31, 1923; s. Edward Clifton and Gertrude (Wilson) M.; m. Genevieve de Bidart, Aug. 19, 1948; children: Anne de Bidart, Francis de Bidart. AB, Harvard U., 1945; DSc, MIT, 1947. Research engr. Dewey & Almy div. W.R. Grace & Co., 1947-50; mem. faculty MIT, 1950-98, prof. chem. engring., 1964-98, Carbon P. Dubbs prof., 1973-96, emeritus, 1998—. Cons. in field, 1950—; cons. in biochem. engring. Harvard U. Health Services, 1982-94. Author articles on polymers, rheology, med. engring.; patentee chem. and rheological instruments. Pres. bd. trustees Buckingham Sch., Cambridge, 1969-74; trustee Browne and Nichols Sch., Cambridge, 1972-74, hon. trustee, 1974—. Fellow Am. Inst. for Med. and Biol. Engring., Am. Acad. Arts and Scis.; mem. AIChE (Alpha Chi Sigma award 1984, Charles M.A. Stine award 1993, Founders award 2000), Am. Chem. Soc., Soc. for Biomaterials (Clemson U. Award 1990). Home: 90 Somerset St Belmont MA 02478-2010 Fax: 617-489-2165. E-mail: emerrill@mit.edu.

MERRILL, GEORGE VANDERNETH, lawyer, investment executive; b. N.Y.C., July 2, 1947; s. James Edward and Claire (Leness) M.; m. Janice Anne Humes, May 11, 1985; children: Claire Georgina, Anne Stewart. Student, Phillips Exeter Acad., 1960-64; AB magna cum laude, Harvard U., 1968, JD, 1972; MBA, Columbia U., 1973. Bar: N.Y. 1973, U.S. Dist. Ct. (so. and ea. dists.) N.Y. 1974, U.S. Ct. Appeals (2d cir.) 1974. Assoc. Cleary, Gottlieb, Steen & Hamilton, N.Y.C., 1974-77, Hawkins, Delafield & Wood, N.Y.C., 1977-79; v.p. Irving Trust Co., 1980-82, Listowel, Inc., N.Y.C., 1982-84, bd. dirs., exec. v.p., 1984-93; v.p. instl. portfolio mgmt. Shawmut Investment Advisors, 1993-95; also co-mgr. Shawmut Growth & Income Equity Mut. Fund; v.p. instl. portfolio mgmt. Fleet Investment Advisors, 1995-96, also co-mgr. Galaxy Growth & Income Equity Mut. Fund.; v.p. trust and instl. portfolio mgmt., mem. Fla. equity com. No. Trust Corp., Chgo., 1996-2000; v.p., sr. personal investment officer, sector head Bank of N.Y., N.Y.C., 2000—. Bd. dirs. Pres. Arell Found., N.Y.C., 1985-93, also bd. dirs., pres. Northfield Charitable Corp., N.Y.C., 1986-93; v.p., sec. Brougham Prodn. Co., N.Y.C., 1986-89, bd. dirs., sr. v.p., sec., 1990-93; v.p., sec. Marinetics Inc., N.Y.C., 1988-90, sr. v.p., sec., 1991-93, also bd. dirs., 1989-93; v.p. Sci. Design and Engring. Co., Inc., N.Y.C., 1987-88, bd. dirs., exec. v.p., 1989-93. John Harvard scholar; recipient Detur award Harvard U., 1968. Mem. ABA, Am. Mgmt. Assn., Nat. Cum Laude Soc., The Brook, Union Club (N.Y.C.), Down Town Assn., Racquet and Tennis Club, Somerset Club (Boston), Signet Soc. (Cambridge), Pilgrims of U.S. Home: 2 Pierce Rd Riverside CT 06878 Office: The Bank of NY 5th Fl 1290 Ave of the Americas New York NY 10104 E-mail: gmerrill@bankofny.com.

MERRILL, HARVIE MARTIN, manufacturing executive, director; b. Detroit, Apr. 26, 1921; s. Harvie and Helen (Nelson) M.; m. Mardelle Merrill; children— Susan, Linda. BS in Chem. Engring, Purdue U., 1942. Devel. engr. Sinclair Refining Co., 1946-47; research and gen. mgr. 3M Co., St. Paul, 1947-65; v.p. fabricated products Plastics div. Stauffer Chem. Co., N.Y.C., 1965-69; with Hexcel Corp., San Francisco, 1969-86, pres., chief exec. officer, 1969-86, chmn. bd., 1976-88. With USAF, 1942-46. Mem. Pacific-Union Club, Bohemian Club San Francisco, Villa Taverna (San Francisco), Burlingame Country Club. Home: 1170 Sacramento St San Francisco CA 94108-1943

MERRILL, JEAN FAIRBANKS, writer; b. Rochester, N.Y., Jan. 27, 1923; d. Earl Dwight and Elsie (Fairbanks) M. BA, Allegheny Coll., 1944; MA, Wellesley Coll., 1945. Feature editor Scholastic Mags., 1947-50; editor Lit. Cavalcade, 1956-57; publs. div. Bank St. Coll. Edn., 1964-65. Children's books include Henry, the Hand-Painted Mouse, 1951, The Woover, 1952, Boxes, 1953, The Tree House of Jimmy Domino, 1955, The Travels of Marco, 1956, A Song for Gar, 1957, The Very Nice Things, 1959, Blue's Broken Heart, 1960, Shan's Lucky Knife (Jr. Lit. Guild selection), Emily Emerson's Moon, 1960 (Jr. Lit. Guild selection), The Superlative Horse (Jr. Lit. Guild selection), 1961 (Lewis Carroll Shelf award 1963), Tell About the Cowbarn, Daddy, 1963, The Pushcart War (Lewis Carroll Shelf award), 1964 (Boys Club Am. Jr. Book award), High, Wide & Handsome, 1964 (Jr. Lit. Guild selection), The Elephant Who Liked to Smash Small Cars, 1967, Red Riding, 1968, The Black Sheep, 1969, Here I Come— Ready or Not!, 1970, Mary, Come Running, 1970, How Many Kids are Hiding on My Block?, 1970, Please, Don't Eat My Cabin, 1971, The Toothpaste Millionaire (Dorothy Canfield Fisher Meml. award 1975-76), 1972 (Sequoyah award 1977), The Second Greatest Clown in the World, 1972, The Jackpot, 1972, The Bumper Sticker Book, 1973, Maria's House, 1974, The Girl Who Loved Caterpillars, 1992; poetry books edited include A Few Flies and I, 1969; libretto for chamber opera Mary Come Running, 1983. Fulbright fellow India, 1952-53 Mem. Authors League, Vt. Arts. Coun., Vt. Inst. Natural Sci., Vt. Nat. Resources Coun., Fulbright Assn., Sierra Club, Audobon Soc., Phi Beta Kappa. *My interest in writing children's books may have derived from the impact certain books had on me as a child, and a wish to recreate the quality of that experience. As to my general motivation as a writer, I would say that it is to celebrate those aspects of the human experience that affirm the creative and life-reverencing instinct in man. I always hope that my stories may be essentially liberating, opening the reader to emotional, as well as intellectual experience, and that they may be entertaining, encouraging the capacity for joy by evoking the free play of a reader's curiosity, humor and inventiveness.*

MERRILL, JOSEPH MELTON, medical educator; b. Andalusia, Ala., Dec. 8, 1923; s. Walter C. and Mary T. (McLaney) M.; m. Gudrun Wallgren, Sept. 15, 1960; children: Maria, Caroline. MD, Harvard Med. Sch., 1948. Diplomate Am. Bd. Internal Medicine. With VA Med. Ctr., Nashville, 1960-64; chief Gen. Clin. Rsch. Ctrs. NIH, Bethesda, 1964-67; dean sci. affairs Baylor Coll. Medicine, Houston, 1967-77, prof., 1967—. Capt. USAF, 1951-53. Office: Baylor Coll Medicine One Baylor Plz Scurlock Ste 1406 Houston TX 77030

MERRILL, KENNETH COLEMAN, retired automobile company executive; b. South Bend, Ind., Feb. 20, 1930; s. Kenneth Griggs and Helen Shapley (Coleman) M.; m. Helen Jean Tagtmeyer, June 10, 1956; children: Barry, Diane, John. BA, Cornell U., 1953; MBA, Ind. U., 1956. With Ford Motor Co., Dearborn, Mich., 1956-91, asst. controller, 1967-71, gen. asst. controller, 1971-73, controller N.Am. automotive ops., 1973-79, exec. dir. parts ops., 1979-80, exec. dir. bus. planning and trust mgmt., 1980-87; pres. Ford Motor Credit Co., 1987-91, ret., 1991. Bd. dirs. Am. Dental Techs., 1990-96; v.p. Wadsworth (Ohio) Ford, 1992-99; adv. bd. Thompson-McCully Co., 1996-99. Pres. Plymouth (Mich.) Symphony Soc., 1969-70; vice chmn. bd. dirs. Detroit Inner City Bus. Improvement Forum, 1977-79; bldg. fund treas. St. John's Episcopal Ch., Plymouth, Mich., 1978-98; bd. dirs. Schoolcraft Coll. Found., 1982-94, pres., 1984-86, fin. com., 1982—; bd. dirs. Crossroads, 1992-94, 96-98, 99-2002, treas., 1994, 98-2002, counselor, 1993—; trustee Episcopal Diocese of Mich., 1998-2000, Thompson-McCully Found., 1999-2002, treas., 1999-2002. Mem. Greater Detroit C. of C. (bd. dirs. 1988-91, exec. com. 1990-91), Barton Hills Country Club (Ann Arbor, Mich.), Oaks Club (Sarasota, Fla.), Beta Gamma Sigma, Psi Upsilon. Episcopalian. Home: 1450 Maple St Plymouth MI 48170-1516 also: 8779 Midnight Pass Rd Sarasota FL 34242-2811 E-mail: kehe56@earthlink.net.

MERRILL, LELAND GILBERT, JR. retired environmental science educator; b. Danville, Ill., Oct. 4, 1920; s. Leland Gilbert and May (Babcock) M.; m. Virginia Gilhooley, Sept. 14, 1949; children: Susan Jane, Alison Lee. BS, Mich. State U., 1942; MS, Rutgers U., 1948, PhD, 1949. Research asst. entomology Rutgers U., 1946-49; asst. prof. entomology Mich. State U., 1949-53; mem. faculty Rutgers U., 1953-82, research specialist entomology, 1960-61, dean agr., 1961-71, dir. Inst. Environ. Studies, 1971-76, prof. center coastal and environ. studies, 1976-82; exec. sec. N.J. Acad. Sci., 1984-92. Served to maj. AUS, 1942-46. Medallist, Wrestling XIV Olympiad, 1948. Mem.: Entomol. Soc. Am., AAAS, Epsilon Sigma Phi, Alpha Zeta, Phi Kappa Phi, Alpha Gamma Rho, Sigma Xi. Home: 49 Gulick Rd Princeton NJ 08540-4111

MERRILL, LYNN BARTLETT, public relations executive, marketing and advertising company executive; b. Southampton, N.Y., Mar. 17, 1953; d. William Stuart and Marilyn (Bake) Bartlett; m. John A. Merrill, June 1, 1974; 1 child, Michael Bartlett. BS, Boston U., 1975. Intern U.S. Congress, N.H., 1974; account exec. Creative Promotions, Dover, 1974-75; pres., owner Merrill Assocs., Inc., Kingston, 1975—; dir. pub. rels. Daniel Webster Coll., Nashua, 1990-92; sr. counsel Jackson, Jackson & Wagner, 1997-99; v.p. pub. affairs, mktg. and resource devel. Elliot Hosp., 1999-2000; dir. mktg. Cath. Med. Ctr., 2000—02; pub. rels. exec. Merrill Assocs., Inc., Kingston, NH, 2002—. Chmn. Graniteer Awards Com., N.Y., 1983-86. Past chmn. save-the-ch. com. Kingston Hist. Soc., Kingston Recycling Com.; chmn. Kingston's 300th Anniversary Com., 1990-94. Recipient numerous Laurel awards for best radio commls. Cadillac Motor Car Divsn., 1985, 89, best radio spot, 1985, best TV comml., 1987, Telly award for best TV comml. Ins. Divsn., 1988, Graniteer awards, 1984, 86, 88, 89. Mem. ARC (vice chair Seacoast chpt. 2000—, bd. dirs.), Pub. Rels. Soc. Am. (bd. dirs. Yankee chpt., chmn. accreditation com., chmn. bylaws com. 1992-93, edn. com. 2000—), Kingston Bus. and Profl. Women's Club (past officer), Haverhill (Mass.) C. of C. (past chmn. bd. dirs., v.p. 1985—, Outstanding Businessperson award 1989), Am. Heart Assn. Republican. Congregationalist. Avocations: boating, swimming, reading, gardening. Office: Merrill Assocs Inc 89 Ball Rd Kingston NH 03848-3611

MERRILL, M. DAVID, education educator; b. Ogden, Utah, Mar. 27, 1937; s. David M. and Leola D. Merrill; m. Dixie R. Rogers; children: Roger David, Mardi Reber, Mondi Taylor, Misti Atkinson, MiKelle Andersen, Marriner Shaw. BA, Brigham Young U., 1961; MA, PhD, U. Ill., 1964. Asst. prof. George Peabody Coll. for Tchrs., Nashville, 1964—66; assoc. prof. Brigham Young U., Provo, Utah, 1966—79; vis. asst. prof. Stanford U., Palo Alto, Calif., 1967—68; prof. U. So. Calif., L.A., 1979—87, Utah State U., Logan, 1987—. Founder, dir. dept. instrnl. sci., divsn. instrnl. rsch., devel. and evaluation Brigham Young U., Provo, 1968—79; founder, dir., v.p. rsch. Courseware Inc., San Diego, 1971—81; founder, pres. Microtchr. Inc., San Diego, 1981—85; founder, gen. mgr. River Pk. Instrnl. Tech. LLC, Logan, Utah, 1996—97; dir. ID2 rsch. group Utah State U., Logan, 1987—98. Author: books; contbr. articles to profl. jours. Recipient Outstanding Jour. Article award, Jour. Instrnl. Devel., 1991, Ronald H. Anderson Meml. award, Am. Soc. Tng. and Devel., 1992. Fellow: APA, Assn. Devel. Computer-Based Instrnl. Sys. (Al Avner award 1992); mem.: Am. Ednl. Rsch. Assn., Assn. Ednl. Comms. and Tech. (Disting Svc. award 2001, Divsn. Instrl. Devel. Spl. award 1995). Avocation: model railroads. Home: 65 River Pk Dr Logan UT 84321 Office: Utah State U Dept Instrn Tech Logan UT 84322 Office Fax: 435-797-3851. E-mail: merrill@cc.usu.edu.

MERRILL, MARTHA, library media educator; b. Anniston, Ala., Apr. 21, 1946; d. Walter James and Polly (McCarty) M. BA, Birmingham-So. Coll., 1968; MS, Jacksonville (Ala.) State U., 1974; PhD, U. Pitts., 1979. Social worker Tuscaloosa (Ala.) County Dept. Human Resources, 1968-71, Calhoun County Dept. Human Resources, Anniston, Ala., 1971-73; social scis./bus. libr. Jacksonville State U., 1974-86, prof. instrnl. media, 1987—. Editor: Reference Services and Media, 1999; co-author: Dictionary for School Library Media Specialists, 2001. Mem. Friends of Libr. bd. Anniston-Calhoun County Pub. Libr., 1984—. Recipient Ala./SIRS Intellectual Freedom award, Intellectual Freedom Com., Ala. Libr. Assn., 1992, Ala. Beta Phi Mu chpt. Libr. of Yr. award, 1997. Mem. ALA (exec. bd., Intellectual Freedom Round Table 1987-93), Ala. Libr. Assn. (pres. 1990-91, Disting. Svc. award 1995), Ala. Assn. Coll. and Rsch. Librs. (pres. 1989-90), Southeastern Libr. Assn. (chair intellectual freedom com. 1986-88, chair resolutions com. 1990-92). Office: Jacksonville State U Coll Edn Dept Ednl Resources Jacksonville AL 36265

MERRILL, MARY LEE, professional society administrator; b. Wilmington, Del., Dec. 6, 1925; d. Claude William and Sue Athelia (Savage) Sutton; m. Alan Douglas Merrill, Sept. 1, 1962; 1 child, Stephen Andrew. Grad. high sch., Wilmington, 1944. Exec. sec. E.I. du Pont de Nemours, Wilmington, 1950-65; founder, gov. Pilgrim Edward Doty, 1982-87, The Fuller Soc., Friendship, Maine, 1992—99. Pres. United Meth. Women, Waldoboro, Maine, 1992-99, gov., 1992-00, gov. ex-officio, 2000—; vol. Farnsworth Mus., Rockland, Maine, 1995; docent Olson House, Cushing, Maine, 1995; gov. Fuller Soc., 1992-99; chmn. publicity Maine Fedn. Women's Clubs, 2000—, pub. rels. chmn., 2000—02. Mem. Nat. Mayflower Soc. (historic sites com. 1995—), Del. Mayflower Soc. (councillor 1986-88), Daus., Founders, Patriots (treas. 1992—), Daus. of 1812 (registrar 1991-92), Maine Mayflower Soc. (chmn. pub. rels. 1992-95), Waldoboro Woman's Club (chmn. pub. rels. 1993—), Fuller soc. (gov. 1992-99, founder), Maine Fedn. Women's Clubs (publicity chmn. 2000-02). Republican. Avocations: genealogy, travel, reading, civic work. Home: 514 Martin Point Rd Friendship ME 04547-4343 E-mail: merily@prefer.net.

MERRILL, RAY MARTELL, medical educator, consultant; b. Salt Lake City, Dec. 15, 1961; s. Non Moody and Barbara Hodson Merrill; m. Amy Valette Bryson; children: James, Grant, Phillip, Dallin. BA, Brigham Young U., 1986, MS, 1989; PhD, Arizona State U., 1994; MPH, Harvard U., 1995. Math. statistician Nat. Cancer Inst., Bethesda, Md., 1995—98; prof. Brigham Young U., Provo, Utah, 1998—. Cons. Nat. Cancer Inst., Bethesda, Md., 2001. Contbr. articles to profl. jours. Active Utah Comprehensive Cancer Control Inititative., 2000—02. Grantee, Nat.l Cancer Inst., 1997—98, Robert Wood Johnson Found., 2001—, Vis. Scientist grant, Internat. Agy. for Rsch. on Cancer, 2001—02. Mem.: Am. Pub.Health Assn., The Am. Coll. Epidemiology, Internat. Epidl. Assn., Soc. Epidl. Rsch., Am. Statis. Assn. (v.p. Utah chpt. 2001—02). Mem. Lds Ch. Avocation: running. Office: Brigham Young University 213 Richards Building Provo UT 84602 Fax: 801-422-0273. Business E-Mail: Ray_Merrill@byu.edu.

MERRILL, RICHARD JAMES, educational director; b. Milw., Apr. 15, 1931; s. Henry Baldwin and Doris (Lucas) M.; m. Kathleen Emden Keely, June 14, 1953 (dec. Jan. 1974); children— Wendy Ann, Vicki Louise, Robin Kay, Christina Suzanne; m. Terry Bradley Alt, Aug. 10, 1974 (div. 1976); m. Shannon Ann Lynch, June 19, 1977. BS, U. Mich., 1953; MA, Columbia U., 1957, Ed.D., 1960. Tchr. sci. Ramona High Sch., Riverside, Calif., 1958-62; secondary sci. coordinator Riverside city schs., 1960-62; exec. dir. chem. edn. material study Harvey Mudd Coll. and U. Calif. at Berkeley, 1962-65; curriculum specialist Mt. Diablo Unified Sch. Dist., Concord, Calif., 1965-91, dir. curriculum, 1980-81; assoc. dir. Inst. for Chem. Edn. and Project Phys. Sci., U. Calif., Berkeley, 1990-94. Bd. dirs. San Francisco Bay Area Sci. Fair; mem. sci. adv. com. Calif. Assessment Program, 1983-89, also mem. assessment adv. com. to state supt., pub. instrn., 1984-86; dir. N. Calif. W. Nev. Jr. Sci. and Humanities Symposium, 1993—; lectr. Calif. State U., Hayward, 1996-99. Author: (with David W. Ridgway) The CHEM Study Story, 1969; co-author: National Science Teachers Association Guidelines for Self-Assessment of Secondary Science Programs, 1975, Science Framework for California Public Schools, 1978, 84; co-author, editor: The Physical Science of Living in California, 1993. Bd. dirs. Ctr. for New Ams., Concord, Calif., 1984-91. Served from ensign to lt. (j.g.) USN, 1953-56. Mem. Nat. Sci. Tchrs. Assn. (past pres., past mem. exec. com.), Nat. Sci. Suprs. Assn., Elem. Sch. Sci. Assn. (coun. 1975-82, pres. 1983), Calif. Sci. Tchrs. Assn. (Disting. Svc. award 1990), Assn. Calif. Sch. Adminstrs., Acacia, Phi Delta Kappa. Home: 1862 2nd Ave Walnut Creek CA 94596-2553 Office: U Calif Lawrence Hall Of Sci Berkeley CA 94720-0001

MERRILL, ROBERT, baritone; b. Bklyn., June 4, 1919; s. Abraham and Lillian (Balaban) Miller; m. Marion Machno, May 30, 1954; children: David Robert, Lizanne. MusD(hon.) , Gustavus Adolphus Coll., 1970; MusD (hon.) , CUNY, 1996. Ind. baritone , N.Y.C. and on tour, 1945—. Baritone in concert, opera and on radio and TV: ; singer: (Operas) debut, 1945, Escamillo in Carmen, Germont in La Traviata, Valentine in Faust, Amonasro in Alda, Marcello in La Boheme, Don Carlo in La Forza del Destino, Sir Henry Ashton in Lucia de Lammermoor, sang in La Traviata condr. Arturo Toscanini over NBC network, with NBC, 1946—, opened Met. Opera season Rodrigo in Don Carlo, 1950, appeared in Toscanini's final opera performance and rec. as Renato in Un Ballo in Maschera, opened Met. season as Valentine in Faust, 1953, as Figaro in Barber of Seville, 1954, Rigoletto in Rigoletto, Barnaba in Giocanda, Scarpia in Tosca, Renato in Un Ballo in Maschera, Iago in Otello, Count di Luna in Il Trovatore, Tonio in Pagliacci , Gerard in Andrea Chenier, 1962, Sir Henry in Lucia, 1964, Valentine in Faust, 1965, Germont in La Traviata, 1967, Amonasro in Aida, 1969, also opened Met. Opera season, 1971, opened Royal Opera House-Covent Garden season as Germont in La Traviata, 1967, Met. Opera visit to Japan, Tokyo, 1975, appeared in concerts, 1975, (rec. artist) RCA-Victor, Angel, London, Columbia labels; author: (novels) The Divas, 1978, (autobiography) Once More From the Beginning, 1965, Between Acts, 1976. Mem. Nat. Coun. of the Arts, 1968—74. Named winner, Met. Auditions of the Air, 1945, Father of Yr. in Music, 1980; recipient Music Ann. award for rec. Ah, QDite Alla Giovine, 1946, Harriet Cohen Internat. Music award, 1961, best opera rec. award, NARAS, 1962, 1964, Handel medal, City of N.Y., 1970, medal, Westchester C.C. Found., 1981, Nat. Medal of Arts, 1993, Internat. Dor L'Dor award, B'nai B'rith, 1994, Lawrence Tibbett award, Am. Guild Mus. Artists Relief Fund, 1996, medal of honor for music, Nat. Arts Club, 1998, medal of honor, Ellis Island, 1999. Mem.: SAG, AGVA, AFTRA, Am. Guild Mus. Artists, Actors Equity Assn., Opera Guild, Friars Club (monk 1968—). Achievements include 1st American opera singer to give 500 performances at Metropolitan Opera, N.Y.C., 1973; official singer New York Yankees, 1967; performer for Pres. Roosevelt, Truman, Eisenhower, Kennedy, Johnson, Nixon, Ford, Carter, Reagan; only singer to perform for both houses of Congress at Roosevelt Meml. Avocations: golf, baseball, fine art. *If you honestly feel that you are doing your best, it makes good criticism even sweeter and bad criticism less painful.*

MERRILL, STEPHEN ALAN, psychiatrist; b. July 22, 1941; s. Michael H. and Nanette Merrill; m. Frances Linda Merrill, July 5, 1965; children: Andrew, Beth. AB, U. Rochester, 1963; MD, SUNY, Bklyn., 1967. Diplomate Am. Bd. Psychiatry and Neurology. Med. intern L.I.C.H., Bklyn., 1967-68; resident in psychiatry SUNY-Upstate Med. Ctr., Syracuse, 1968-71; pvt. practice N.Y., 1973—; clin. asst. prof. dept. psychiatry SUNY, 1973—. Maj. USAF, 1971-73. Mem. AMA, APA, Onon County Med. Soc., Med. Soc. State N.Y. Jewish. Office: 1400 State Tower Bldg Syracuse NY 13202

MERRILL, STEVEN WILLIAM, research and development executive; b. Oakland, Calif., Aug. 6, 1944; s. David Howard and Etha Nadine (Wright) M. BA in Chemistry, Calif. State U., 1986. Lic. pyrotechnic, Calif. Apprentice Borgman Sales Co., San Leandro, Calif., 1960-64; assembler Calif. Fireworks Display, Rialto, 1970; pyrotechnician Hand Chem. Industries, Milton, Ont., Can., 1972-74; dir. R&D Pyrospectaculars, Rialto, 1988-92; pyrotechnic cons., 1993—; owner, dir. Merrill Prodns. Ordnance, Crestline. Experimenter in field, 1958—; chief chemist Baron Blakesly Solvents, Newark, Calif., 1987-88; court expert San Francisco Superior Ct., 1971, Victorville (Calif.) Superior Ct. Counselor Xanthos, Inc., Alameda, Calif., 1970. Mem. AAAS, Am. Chem. Soc., Am. Stats. Assn., Am. Bd. Forensic Examiners, Internat. Platform Assn. Avocations: wood carving, sculpture, photography, electronics. Home and Office: Merrill Prodns Ordnance PO Box 676 Crestline CA 92325-0676

MERRILL, THOMAS WENDELL, lawyer, law educator; b. Bartlesville, Okla., May 3, 1949; s. William McGill and Dorothy (Glasener) M.; m. Kimberly Ann Evans, Sept. 8, 1973; children: Jessica, Margaret, Elizabeth. BA, Grinnell Coll., 1971, Oxford U., 1973; JD, U. Chgo., 1977. Bar: Ill. 1980, U.S. Dist Ct. (no. dist.) Ill. 1980, U.S. Ct. Appeals (5th cir.) 1982, U.S. Ct. Appeals (7th cir.) 1983, U.S. Ct. Appeals (9th and D.C. cirs.) 1984, U.S. Supreme Ct. 1985. Clk. U.S. Ct. Appeals (D.C. cir.), Washington, 1977-78, U.S. Supreme Ct., Washington, 1978-79; assoc. Sidley & Austin, Chgo., 1979-81, counsel, 1981-87, 90—; dep. solicitor gen. U.S. Dept. Justice, 1987-90; prof. law Northwestern U., Chgo., 1981—, John Paul Stevens prof., 1993—. Contbr. articles to profl. jours. Rhodes scholar Oxford U., 1971; Danforth fellow, 1971. Home: 939 Maple Ave Evanston IL 60202-1717 Office: Northwestern U Sch Law 357 E Chicago Ave Chicago IL 60611-3059

MERRILL, VINCENT NICHOLS, retired landscape architect; b. Reading, Mass., Apr. 28, 1912; s. Charles Clarkson and Bessie Louise (Nichols) M.; m. Anna Victoria Swanson, Jan. 20, 1943 (dec. Feb. 1996); m. Natalie Ames Prentice, Aug. 16, 1997. AB, Dartmouth Coll., 1933; M in Landscape Architecture, Harvard U., 1937. Office asst. Shurcliff & Shurcliff, Boston, 1937-42, 47-54, ptnr., 1954-58, Shurcliff & Merrill and predecessors Shurcliff, Shurcliff & Merrill, Boston, 1958-81; prin. Shurcliff & Merrill, Cambridge, 1981-89; retired, 1998. Founder, bd. dirs., pres. Charles River Watershed Assn., Auburndale, Mass., 1963-75; bd. dirs. Charles Basin Adv. Com., Boston, 1979-82; pres. Hubbard Ednl. Trust, Cambridge, 1981-89, bd. dirs., 1989-95. Capt. U.S. Army, 1942-46, ETO. Recipient Gold medal Mass. Hort.

Soc., 1988. Fellow Am. Soc. Landscape Architects; mem. Boston Soc. Landscape Architects (pres. 1961-63), Hort. Club of Boston (hon. mem., pres. 1992-94). Avocation: home landscaping. Home and Office: 860 SE Central Pkwy Stuart FL 34994

MERRILL, WILLIAM DEAN, retired architect, medical facility planning consultant; b. Portland, Oreg., June 1, 1915; s. Charles O. and Grace (Ruhl) M.; m. Bernice E. Wickham, Apr. 19, 1943 (dec. Sept. 1996); 1 child, Sue Ann Merrill Boardman; m. Irene Moe, July 30, 2001. Student in Fine Arts and Forestry, Oreg. State U., 1936-38; student in Architecture, U. Oreg., 1939-42. Registered architect, Oreg., Calif., NCARB Prin. W.D. Merrill, Architect, Portland, 1956-64; architect, ptnr. Bissell & Merrill, Architects, Stockton, Calif., 1964-68; architect, Kaiser Engrs., Kaiser Found. Hosps. design and constrn., 1968-81; pvt. practice hosp. design and constrn., residential design and constrn., Bay Area, 1981-91; hosp. and sch. constrn. insp. Office of State Health Planning and Devel., State of Calif., 1984-93; ret. 1996. Served as lt. (j.g.) USNR, 1942-44, PTO. Mem. AIA (emeritus). Republican. Home: 25411 E Cedar Glen Loop Welches OR 97067

MERRILL-NACH, SUZANNE MARIE, obstetrician, gynecologist; b. Oakland, Calif., 1954; MD, U. Calif., Davis, 1980. Diplomate Am. Bd. Ob-gyn. From intern to resident in ob-gyn. U.S. Naval Hosp., San Diego, 1980-81, 82-85, staff physician, 1985-87; physician U.S. Naval Airstation, North Island, 1981-82; med. staff Alvarado Hosp., San Diego; pvt. practice, 1988—. Mem. ACOG, Calif. Med. Assn., S.W. Obstet.-Gynecol. Soc. (coun. mem.), San Diego Co. Med. Soc. Office: 6719 Alvarado Rd Ste 302 San Diego CA 92120-5263

MERRIM, LOUISE MEYEROWITZ, artist, actress; b. N.Y.C. d. Leo and Jeanette (Harris) Meyerowitz; m. Lewis Jay Merrim, June 27, 1948; children: Stephanie, Andrea Merrim Goff (dec.). BFA, Pratt Inst., 1947; MFA, Columbia U., 1951; postgrad., Post Coll., 1971-72, New Sch., 1977-78. Art tchr. pub. schs., N.Y.C., 1947-51, Port Washington, N.Y., 1970-83. One-woman shows include Plandome Gallery, L.I., Isis Gallery, N.Y., San Diego art Inst., Pan Pacific Hotel, San Diego; exhibited in group shows at Nassau County Fine Arts Mus. (Bronze award), Heckscher Mus. (Nora Mirmont award), Nat. Acad., Nat. Assn. Women Artists (Medal of Honor, Charlotte Whinston award), Audubon Artists (Stephen Hirsch Meml. award), Cork Gallery, Warner Comm. Gallery, L.I. Art Tchrs. (two awards of excellence), L.I. Art Tchrs. Award Winners Show, Pt. Washington Libr. Invitational, Glen Cove (2nd prize), Manhasset Art Assn. (best in show, five 1st prizes), San Diego Art Inst., San Diego Mus. Art (Gold award), Oceanside Mus. Art, Hank Baum Gallery, San Francisco, Tarbox Gallery, Clark Gallery, Knowles Gallery, San Diego, Golden Pacific Arts Gallery, San Diego, Henry Chastain Gallery, Scottsdale; included in permanent collection of San Diego Mus. Art; appeared in numerous theatrical prodns. including Fiddler on the Roof, Barefoot in the Park, N.Y., Anything Goes, The Musical Comedy Murders of 1940, Anastasia (Drama award), Fiddler on the Roof, The Music Man, What's Wrong With this Picture?, Marvin's Room, San Diego, The Foreigner; dir. Under Milkwood; dir., appeared in Spoon River Anthology. Mem. Nat. Assn. Women Artists, N.Y. Soc. of Women Artists, Contemporary Artists Guild of N.Y., Audubon Artist (N.Y.), San Diego Art Inst., Artists Guild of San Diego Art Mus. (pres. 1993), Artists Equity, Actors Alliance. Avocations: tennis, poetry, travel. Home: 3330 Caminito Vasto La Jolla CA 92037-2929 E-mail: louisemer@hotmail.com.

MERRIMAN, WILLIAM RICHARD, JR. academic administrator; b. Lawrence, Kans., Dec. 8, 1954; s. William Richard and Neva Jane Merriman; m. Margot Elisabeth Kelman; children: Benjamin George, Aaron Richard. BS, Emporia State U., 1976, MS, 1978; PhD, Ind. U., 1986. Instr. Berea (Ky.) Coll., 1983-85; exec. dir. Jefferson Found., Washington, 1985-88; program officer NEH, 1988-89; devel. officer Le Moyne Coll., Syracuse, N.Y., 1989-94, dir. devel., 1994-96, v.p. for instnl. advancement, 1996-98; pres. Southwestern Coll., Winfield, Kans., 1998—. Editor: Rediscovering the Constitution, 1997. Bd. dirs. Cowley County Econ. Devel. Agy., Winfield, Kans., 2001. Mem. Kans. Ind. Coll. Assn. (exec. com. 1999—), Winfield C. of C. (edn. com. 1998-2001), Rotary (Winfield chpt.). Methodist. Avocations: running, Civil War history. Office: Southwestern Coll 100 College St Winfield KS 67156 E-mail: merriman@sckans.edu.

MERRIN, SEYMOUR, computer marketing company executive; b. Bklyn., Aug. 13, 1931; s. Joseph and Esther Bella (Manelis) M.; m. Elaine Cohen, Sept. 4, 1960 (dec. May 1962); m. Elizabeth Jenifer Slack, Oct. 12, 1963 (dec. Mar. 1995); children: Charles Seymour, Marianne Jenifer Weights; m. Helene Claire Singer, Sept. 1, 2001. BS, Tufts Coll., 1952; MS, U. Ariz., 1954; PhD, Pa. State U., 1962. Geologist Magma Copper Co., Superior, Ariz., 1954; geologist U.S. Geol. Survey, 1956-58; chemist IBM, Poughkeepsie, N.Y., 1962-64; mgr. package devel., mgr. reliability and failure analysis Sperry Semicondr. div. Sperry Rand, Norwalk, Conn., 1965-68; cons. materials tech. Fairfield, 1967-69; v.p., dir. Innotech Corp., Norwalk, 1969-74; div. mgr. Emdex div. Exxon Enterprises, Milford, Conn., 1974-78; chmn., dir. Computerworks, Westport, 1978-85; v.p., dir. personal computing service Gartner Group, Inc., Stamford, 1984-87; pres. Merrin Resources, Southport, 1987-89, Merrin Info. Svcs., Inc., Santa Fe, 1987—. Bd. dirs. Micrografx Corp., Allen, Tex.; mem. adv. panel Apple Computer Co., Cupertino, Calif., 1982-83; mem. adv. bd. Compaq Computer Corp., Houston, 1984-85, Computer and Software News, N.Y.C., 1984-89; mem. program adv. bd. Comdex, Boston, 1985—; lectr. in field. Contbr. numerous articles to profl. publs.; patentee in field Served with U.S. Army, 1954-56 Fellow Geol. Soc. Am., Am. Inst. Chemists; Computing Tech. Industry Assn. (founder, pres. 1981-83, bd. dirs. 1981-84). Home and Office: 560 Los Nidos Dr Santa Fe NM 87501-8356 E-mail: smerrin@aol.com.

MERRING, ROBERT ALAN, lawyer, arbitrator, mediator; b. Middletown, N.Y., Oct. 5, 1951; s. Merton Joseph and Mabel Ruth M.; m. Lynn S. Connor, Mar. 16, 1996. Student, Ohio Wesleyan U., 1969—70; AB, Stanford U., 1973; JD in Internat. and Fgn. Law with honors, Columbia U., 1977; cert. Pepperdine Sch. Law, Inst. for Dispute Resolution, 1996. Bar: Calif. 1977, U.S. Dist. Ct. (cen. dist.) Calif. 1978, U.S. Dist. Ct. (so. and ea. dists.) Calif. 1980, U.S. Ct. Appeals (9th cir.) 1980, U.S. Dist. Ct. (no. dist.) Calif. 1983, U.S. Supreme Ct. 1987, Colo. 1989. Assoc. Pacht, Ross, Warne, Bernhard & Sears, Inc., L.A., 1977-79, Donovan Leisure Newton & Irvine, L.A., 1979-81, Cutler and Cutler, L.A., 1983-88, Friedemann & Hart, Irvine, 1988-89; pvt. practice Newport Beach and Irvine, Calif., 1989—. Mem. San Diego-Orange County Am. Arbitration Assn. panel comml. arbitrators, 1993—; civil arbitrator, judge pro tem Orange County Superior Ct., 1993—; mediator U.S. Bankruptcy Ct. (ctrl. dist.) Calif., 1996—; mediator Orange County Superior Ct., 1998-2002; clin. prof. Loyola U. Law Sch., Los Angeles, 1981-82. Editor Columbia Jour. Transnat. Law, 1976-77. Columbia U. Internat. fellow, 1975-76. Mem. ABA, Orange County Bar Assn. (chair intellectual property and tech. law sect. 2000-01), Assn. Bus. Trial Lawyers, Am. Arbitration Assn., State Bar of Calif. (del. 1998—). E-mail: clawyer@attglobal.net.

MERRINGTON, OLIVER J. information scientist; b. London, Dec. 13, 1951; s. William and Maxine (Venables) M. BSc, U. London, 1973, MSc, 1974. Head libr. scis. Schering Agrochems. Ltd., Saffron Walden, England, 1977-94; mgr. ICSU World Data Ctr. Glaciology, Cambridge, England, 1995-98. Mgr. NERC Arctic Environ. Metadata Ctr., Cambridge, 1997-99; website mgr. Scott Polar Rsch. Inst., 1998—. Mem. Inst. Biology, Inst. Info. Scis. Office: U Cambridge Scott Polar Rsch Inst Lensfield Rd Cambridge CB2 1ER England

MERRION, ARTHUR BENJAMIN, mathematics educator, tree farmer; b. Williamstown, N.J., Oct. 25, 1938; s. Anthony Robert and Eva May Merrion; m. Martha Jane Banse, Dec. 26, 1965 (div. May 1977); children: Benjamin Thomas, Elizabeth Jane. AB in Math., Pfeiffer Coll. (now Univ.), 1965; MS in Numerical Sci., Johns Hopkins U., 1976. Navigations scientist Def. Mapping Agy. Hydrographic Ctr., Suitland, Md., 1966-78; fellow ops. rsch. analysis Sec. Army Pentagon, Washington, 1978-80; ops. rsch. analyst Asst. Sec. Army, 1980-86; tree farmer Huntingtown, Md., 1986-98. Instr. math. and stats. Embry-Riddle Aeronautical U., 1993-94; math. instr. Charles County C.C., 1990-91; tutor Literary Coun. Author: A Short Story By Edgar Allen Pooh. With U.S. Army, 1957-58. Mem. Md. Soc. SAR. Avocations: chess, violin, judo, wrestling, ice skating. Achievements include successful experimentation in applying mathematical chaos theory to weather modification. Home: PO Box 1639 West Jefferson NC 28694-1639 *The Bible says many different things to many different people. To Thomas Alva Edison it was a "Chemist's Handbook". To me it is the source of all man's creativity, directly from the greatest Creator of all. It is a source of inspiration, a solace for periods of depression, and a prescription when I'm in error.*

MERRIS, DONNA ROSE, lawyer; b. Bluffs, Ill., Nov. 25, 1939; d. Donald Doyle and Helen Louise (Frohwitter) M.; children: Laura Katherine Merris Huffman, Kristen Rose Merris Huffman. BS in Edn., Ill. State U., 1961; MMus, Northwestern U., 1965; JD, Bklyn. Law Sch., 1987. Bar: N.Y. 1989, N.J. 1989. Dir. instrumental music Lanark (Ill.) Pub. Schs., 1961-64, Winchester (Ill.) H.S., 1965-66; dir. music edn. Malden (Mass.) Pub. Schs., 1966-74; instr. music Mannes Coll. Music, N.Y.C., 1974-80; exec. dir. Bklyn. Music Sch., 1977-85; spl. asst. U.S. Atty. U.S. Dist. Ct. (so. dist.) N.Y., N.Y.C., 1988-90; asst. gen. counsel Office of the Comptroller, 1990-94; gen. counsel Mayor's Office of Contracts, 1994-99; adminstrv. law judge Office of Adminstrv. Trials and Hearings, 1999—. Adv. bd. Bklyn. Music Sch., 1986—; trustee Nat. Guild Cmty. Schs. of the Arts, N.Y.C., 1993-99. Mem. Assn. Bar City of N.Y. Home: 255 W End Ave Apt 13A New York NY 10023-3607 Office: 40 Rector St Fl 6 New York NY 10006-1705 E-mail: DMerris@oath.nyc.gov.

MERRISS, PHILIP RAMSAY, JR. banker; b. N.Y.C., June 7, 1948; s. Philip Ramsay and Elisabeth (Paine) M.; m. Janet Henry Hylan, Oct. 27, 1973. AB in Econs. magna cum laude, Lafayette Coll., 1970; MBA with high distinction, Dartmouth Coll., 1972. Assoc. corp. fin. dept. A.G. Becker and Co. Inc., N.Y.C., 1972-73; fin. analyst corp. banking dept. Chase Manhattan Bank, 1973, asst. treas. N.Y.C. dist., 1974-75, 2d v.p. mining and metals div., 1976-78, 2d v.p. petroleum div., 1979-86, client exec., v.p. pub. utilities component, 1987-89, client supv. officer, div. exec., v.p. U.S. pvt. banking, 1989-94; credit exec. J.P. Morgan Pvt. Bank, N.Y.C., 1994-97, mng. dir. and credit exec., 1997—. Served to capt. U.S. Army, 1978. Tuck scholar Dartmouth Coll., 1972. Mem. Am. Econ. Assn., Aircraft Owners and Pilots Assn., Weston Gun Club, Yale Club, Fairfield County Hunt Club, Fairfield County Fish and Game Club, Phi Beta Kappa. Republican. Episcopalian. Home: 100 Hills Point Rd Westport CT 06880-5111 Office: JP Morgan Chase & Co 345 Park Ave New York NY 10154-1002

MERRITT, BRUCE GORDON, lawyer; b. Iowa City, Oct. 4, 1946; s. William Olney and Gretchen Louise (Kuever) M.; m. Valerie Sue Jorgensen, Dec. 28, 1969; children: Benjamin Carlyle, Alicia Marie. AB magna cum laude, Occidental Coll., 1968; JD magna cum laude, Harvard U., 1972. Bar: Calif. 1973, D.C., 1996, N.Y. 1996. Assoc. Markbys, London, 1972-73, Nossman, Krueger & Marsh, L.A., 1973-79, ptnr., 1979-81; asst. U.S. Atty., L.A., 1981-85; ptnr. Hennigan & Mercer, 1986-88, Debevoise & Plimpton, L.A., 1989-95, N.Y., 1996—2001. Lay reader St. James Ch. Fellow Am. Coll. Trial Lawyers; mem. Calif. State Bar Assn. (exec. com. litigation sect. 1992-95), L.A. County Bar Assn. (del. state bar conf. 1984-86), Phi Beta Kappa, Harvard Club (N.Y.C.). Episcopalian (lay reader St. James Ch.). E-mail: BruceGMerritt@aol.com.

MERRITT, ELEANOR LYNETTE, artist, educator; b. N.Y.C., Aug. 17, 1933; d. Wilbert Alexander and Lynette Hyacinth Lipsett; m. Lorenzo Merritt, June 26, 1954 (div. Oct. 1975); m. W.H. Chris Darlington, July 26, 1980; children: Lori Ellen, Lisa Ann. BA, Bklyn. Coll., 1955, MA, 1958. Cert. secondary art tchr. N.Y.C. Art tchr. N.Y.C. Sch. Sys., 1955-59; secondary sch. art tchr. Westbury Schs., L.I., N.Y., 1960-70, dist. chairperson, 1971-82. Lectr. C.W. Post Coll., N.Y., 1978-82, Nassau C.C., N.Y., 1978-82, Art League Manatee County, Bradenton, Fla., 1997—; lectr., docent Ringling Mus. Art, Sarasota, Fla., 1989—. One-woman shows include Nassau County Cultural Mus., Hempstead, N.Y., 1974, Am. Internat. Coll., Springfield, Mass., 1975, 81, The Craftery Gallery, Hartford, Conn., 1976, Women's Resource Ctr., Sarasota, 1987, 92, Shrine of the Black Madonna, Cultural Ctr., Houston, 1988, U. Fla., St. Petersburg, 1988, Manatee C.C., Venice, 1988, Ctrl. Nat. Bank, Sarasota, 1991, Zora Neale Hurston Mus., Eatonville, Fla., 1993, Fine Arts Gallery Ctrl. Libr., Tampa, 1994, Barrier Island Group for the Arts, Sanibel, Fla., 1995, Unit Gallery, Sarasota, 1995, Hillsborough C.C., Tampa, 1997, Palm Harbor, Sarasota, 1998; exhibited in group shows at Salt Creek Art Works, St. Petersburg, Carver Cultural Ctr., San Antonio, Fla. State Capital Gallery, Tallahassee, Hillsborough C.C. Libr., Tampa, Artists Unlimited: The Channel Dist., Tampa, Women's Caucus for Art, Miami, Michael Gold Gallery, N.Y.C., Daytona (Fla.) Beach C.C., City U., Shimonoseki, Japan, 1996, Steinbaum Gallery, N.Y.C., 1997, Self Gallery, Hilton Head, S.C., 1998, Jacksonville Mus. Contemporary Art, 1998, Diverse Origins, Colo., 1998, African Am. Mus., Tampa, 1997, Venice Biennel, 1999, many others; exhibited in corp. exhbns. Atlanta Life Ins. Co., Isphording, Payne, Korp., Inc., Venice, Holiday Inn Crown Plaza, Tampa, Fla., Automatic Data Processing Corp., Roseland, N.J. V.p. Sarasota Arts Coun. Bd., 1996—; chairperson Sarasota County Commn. Art in Pub. Places, 1997—; pres. Venice (Fla.) Art Ctr. Bd., 1998—. Recipient Woman of Impact award County Commn. on the Status of Women, Sarasota, 1997; named Sarasota Artist of the Yr., Sarasota Visual Arts Ctr., 1994. Mem. Women's Mus. Art (charter), Women's Caucus for Art (pres. Sarasota chpt. 1988-93, v.p. nat. orgn. 1990-96, Nat. Pres. award 1996), Pen Women Am. (Sarasota chpt.), Fla. Artist Group (area III), Petticoat Painters. Avocations: gardening, traveling, lecturing.

MERRITT, GILBERT STROUD, federal judge; b. Nashville, Jan. 17, 1936; s. Gilbert Stroud and Angie Fields (Cantrell) M.; m. Louise Clark Fort, July 10, 1964 (dec.); children: Stroud, Louise Clark, Eli. BA, Yale U., 1957; LLB, Vanderbilt U., 1960; LLM, Harvard U., 1962. Bar: Tenn. 1960. Asst. dean Vanderbilt U. Law Sch., 1960-61, lectr., 1963-69, 71-75, assoc. prof. law, 1969-70; assoc. Boult Hunt Cummings & Conners, Nashville, 1962-63; asst. metro. atty. City of Nashville, 1963-66; U.S. Dist. atty. for (mid. dist.) Tenn., 1966-69; ptnr. Gullett, Steele, Sanford, Robinson & Merritt, Nashville, 1970-77; judge U.S. Ct. Appeals (6th cir.), 1977-2001, chief judge, 1989—96, sr. judge, 2001—. Exec. sec. Tenn. Code Commn., 1977. Mng. editor: Vanderbilt Law Rev, 1959-60; contbr. articles to law jours. Del. Tenn. Constl. Conv., 1965; chmn. bd. trustees Vanderbilt Inst. Pub. Policy Studies. Mem. ABA, Fed. Bar Assn., Tenn. Bar Assn., Nashville Bar Assn., Vanderbilt Law Alumni Assn. (pres. 1979-80), Am. Law Inst., Order of Coif. Episcopalian. Office: US Ct Appeals Customs Ho 701 Broadway Ste 303 Nashville TN 37203-3967 also: 532 Potter Stewart US Courthouse 100 E Fifth St Cincinnati OH 45202-3988*

MERRITT, HELEN HENRY, retired art educator, ceramic sculptor, art historian; b. Norfolk, Va., June 15, 1920; d. John Crockett and Mabel Deborah (Richards) Henry; m. James Willis Merritt, Jan. 22, 1946; 1 child, Deborah Branan Merritt Aldrich. BA, Colby Coll., 1942; MA, Rockford Coll., 1956; MFA, No. Ill. U., 1962; postgrad., Tokyo U. Fine Arts, Cambridge (Eng.) U. Sec. U.S. Naval Hosp., Norfolk, 1942-46; art tchr. DeKalb (Ill.) Schs., 1956-57; instr. art history No. Ill. U., DeKalb, 1964, asst. prof., 1965-71, assoc. prof., 1972-79, prof., 1980-90. Ceramic sculptor, DeKalb, 1952—. Author: Guiding Free Expression in Children's Art, 1964, Modern Japanese Woodblock Prints, 1990, Guide to Modern Japanese Woodblock Prints, 1992, Woodblock Kuchi-E Prints—Reflections of Meiji Culture, 2000; contbr. articles to profl. jours. Founding mem. Gurler Heritage Assn., DeKalb, 1978-97; cmty. activist DeKalb Pond, Fisk Block Group, 1989—. Home: 419 Garden Rd Dekalb IL 60115-6206 E-mail: hmerritt@niu.edu.

MERRITT, HOWARD SUTERMEISTER, retired art educator; b. Ithaca, N.Y., June 12, 1915; s. Ernest and Bertha (Sutermeister) M.; m. Florence Sederquest Hill, June 27, 1941; children— Jessica, Stephen, Jonathan, James. BA, Oberlin Coll., 1936; M.F.A., Princeton U., 1942, PhD, 1958. Mem. faculty U. Rochester, N.Y., 1946-80, prof. emeritus, 1980—. Cons. 19th Century Am. Painting, 1960— Contbr. exhbn. catalogues and articles to various publs. Served with AUS, 1942-45. Decorated Bronze Star; Nat. Endowment for Humanities summer grantee, 1966-68 Mem. Coll. Art Assn. Home: Rochester, NY. Died May 23, 2001.

MERRITT, JEAN, consulting firm executive; b. N.Y.C., Oct. 29, 1952; d. Harry and Ruth (Happel) Packman; m. Richard L. Kashinsky, Aug. 2, 1976 (div.); m. Richard L. Merritt, May 5, 1985 (div. June 2002); children: Courtney Morgan, Melissa Morgan Grad. high sch., Bayside, N.Y. Contr. Kaswol Corp., Richmond Hill, N.Y., 1973, jr. v.p., 1974-75, v.p., sec., treas., 1975-85; Corp. exec. Federated Cons. Svc., Inc., Bayside, CFO Jupiter, Fla., 1985—2002, sr. v.p., 1985—. Coach Queens Spl. Olympics, 1985. Mem. Nat. Trust for Hist. Preservation, Nat. Fedn. Wildlife, Ctr. for Environ. Edn., Defenders of Wildlife, Nat. Resource Def. Coun., Humane Soc. of U.S., Sierra Club, Amnesty Internat. Presbyterian. Avocations: flying, art collecting, painting, interior design, gourmet cooking. Home: 20 E 76th St New York NY 10021-2643 also: 120 Cypress Cove Jupiter FL 33458-8156 E-mail: jeanie22m@aol.com.

MERRITT, JOE FRANK, industrial supply executive; b. Paris, Dec. 9, 1947; s. Henry Grady and Margaret Leon (Murrell) M.; m. Barbara Jean Sands (div. May 1973); 1 child, Daniel Joe; m. Bonnie Louise McLure, Feb. 1, 1975; 1 stepchild, David Wright Dwyer. BA in Govt., U. Tex., Arlington, 1970; attending, All-Inclusive Sch., 1999. Cert. contractor Dept. Def. USA and Can. With purchasing A.F. Holman Boiler Works Inc., Dallas, 1970-77; supply salesman Stanco Indsl. Supply, 1977-79, Tool Specialty Indsl. Supply, Dallas, 1979-80, Briggs-Weaver Indsl. Supply, Dallas, 1980-81; owner, pres. Joe F. Merritt & Co., Inc., Carrollton, Tex., 1981; v.p., gen. mgr. Abrasives & Buffs Co., Dallas, 1981-83; owner, pres. Buff, Polish & Grind Indsl. Supply Co., Inc., Argyle, Tex., 1984—. Cons. The Broadway Collection, OLathe Kans., 1990, Offenhauser Co., Houston, 1993, 94, 98, Innovation Industries, Russellville, Ark., 1994; instr. buff, polish and grind methods quality control dept. Rsch. Facility, Peterbilt Motors Co., 1994; trainer Peterbilt Madison-Tenn. plant, 1997, DBC Indsl., Garland, Tex., 1999, Am. Ironhorse Motorcycle Co., Ft. Worth, Tex., 2000, Chgo. Iron and Bridge, Tex., 2000. Creator State of the Art Rsch. and Tchg. Facility, 1984, 100% Virgin Lambswool Buffing Belt, 1987, spl. extra wide spindle buffers to be manufactured by Baldor Electric, Ft. Smith, Ark., 1995, 97, 98; contbr. article to profl. jour. Recipient Cert. of Appreciation, City of Carrollton, Tex., 1981. Republican. Methodist. Avocations: travel, animals, Landrover-4 wheel drive vehicle. Office: Buff Polish & Grind Indsl Supply 1907 E FM407 Argyle TX 76226-9447 Fax: (940) 455-7385.

MERRITT, JOHN AUGUSTUS, geriatrician, educator; b. Greenwich, Conn., Nov. 1, 1931; AB, Dartmouth Coll., 1954; MD, Yale U., 1958. Diplomate Am. Bd. Internal Medicine, Am. Bd. Hematology, Am. Bd. Geriatric Medicine. Intern Upstate Med. Ctr., Syracuse, N.Y., 1958-59; resident in internal medicine Boostoon City Hosp., 1959-61, clin. fellow in hematology, 1961-62, rsch. fellow in hematology, 1962-63, assoc. vis. physician I and II med. svcs., 1966-70; asst. prof. medicine U. Md. Sch. Medicine, Balt., 1970-72; asst. prof., assoc. prof., prof. medicine U. Mass. Med. Sch., Worcester, 1972-88; chief geriatric medicine Hosp. of St. Raphael, New Haven, 1988—. Asst. prof. dept. medicine Tufts U. Sch. Medicine, Boston, 1967-70; lectr. medicine Harvard U. Sch. Medicine, Boston, 1969-70; attending physician Boston VA Hosp., 1966-70; chief div. hematology York (Pa.) Hosp., 1970-72; chief div. medicine and geriatric medicine Worcester City Hosp., 1985-88; tng. Geriatric Edn. Ctr., Harvard U., 1986-87; asst. clin. prof. medicine Yale U. Sch. Medicine, New Haven, 1989—. Author textbooks; contbr. articles to med. jours. Fellow ACP; mem. Am. Geriatric Soc. (co-founder, bd. dirs. Mass. com.), Gerontol. Soc. Am., Nat. Coun. on Aging, Conn. Med. Soc. (ho. of dels., bd. govs.), New Haven County Med. Assn. Office: Hosp of St Raphael 1450 Chapel St New Haven CT 06511-4440

MERRITT, JOHN HOWARD, secondary school educator; b. Salisbury, Md., May 19, 1948; s. Robert Wilson and Iris Amy (Horsey) M.; m. Carole A. Tramontana; children: Robert W. II, John H. Jr.; 1 stepchild, Stephen A. Capelli Jr. BS, Salisbury State Coll., 1971; MEd, Salisbury State U., 1990. Cert. secondary tchr., Md. Propr. constrn. bus., Salisbury, 1977-86; high sch. math. tchr. Wicomico Count Schs., 1986—. Instr. math. NROTC Prep Sch., San Diego, 1988-91. Capt. USNR, 1970—. Mem.: Kappa Delta Pi. Republican. Methodist. Avocations: swimming, gardening, residential real estate investments, commodity futures trading, ocean and river kayaking.

MERRITT, KEITH MCLEAN, photographer; b. Jacksonville, Tex., Feb. 19, 1960; s. Malcom Robert Merritt and Nancy Lovenia McLean; m. Casey Marie Samson, June 10, 1980 (dec. June 1982); m. Alyssa Jane Milano, Feb. 14, 1990; children: Leah Elaine, Lisa Milano, Gayla Lauren. BA, Austin (Tex.) C.C., 1982; student, U. Tex., 1984—85; MA, U. Calif., Santa Barbara, 1988; ThD, So. Career Inst., Boca Raton, Fla., 1992; D in Metaphysics, 2001. Cert. Internat. Freelance Photographers Orgn. Photo journalist IFPO Glamour Mag., Houston, 1983—85; graphics designer asst. IBM, Austin, 1985—86; effects asst. Warner Bros. Studio, Hollywood, 1986—90; mgr., owner Theurgical Invocations, Inc., Orlando, Fla., 1991—98; tech. cons. TDC Enterprises, Inc., Tennessee Colony, Tex., 1999—. Co-chmn. Hall. Euph. Awar. Dev. Soc., Austin, 1982—85; advisor Advanced Sys. Redesign Co., Dallas, 2001. Author: The Felon's Creed, 1987, A Basilisk's Book of Banes, 1999; photographer: Reflections of Kronus, 1986. Mem., activist The New Weatherman, Santa Avocado, Calif., 1988; pastor, lobby leader Our Lady of the Night Assembly, Tennessee Colony, 2002. Sgt. USAF, 1981—85. Mem.: The New Covenant Christian League (assoc. pastor, treas. 1999—2002). Libertarian. Avocations: stamp collecting, fishing, hunting, painting, skiing. Home: 461016 Coffield U Tennessee Colony TX 75884

MERRITT, LARAMIE DEE, lawyer; b. Montpelier, Idaho, June 5, 1967; s. Leon T. and Laurel Merritt; m. Gretchen Merritt; 3 children. BA, Brigham Young U., 1992, JD, 1995. Bar: Utah 1995, U.S. Dist. Ct. Utah 1996. Law clk. to hon. Steven L. Hansen, Utah 4th Dist. Ct., Provo, 1995-96; assoc. Duval Hansen Witt & Morley, Pleasant Grove, Utah, 1996-2000; solo practice Bluffdale, 2000—. Part-time faculty J. Reuben Clark Law Sch., Provo, 1997-98 Editor Brigham Young U. Jour. Pub. Law, 1994-95, note and comment editor, 1995. Mem. Mendelssohn Men's Chorus. Republican. Mem. Lds Ch. Avocations: vocal performance, hiking, writing, accordian. Office: 14850 S Concorde Park Dr Bluffdale UT 84065 E-mail: lawquest@juno.com.

MERRITT, LAVERE BARRUS, engineering educator, civil engineer; b. Afton, Wyo., Mar. 11, 1936; s. Joseph M. and Lera (Barrus) M.; m. Jackie Call, Jan. 5, 1956 (dec. Sept. 1999); m. Diane Mainord, July 14, 2001; children: Teri F., Lynn T., Rachel R., Shaun S. BSCE, U. Utah, 1963, MSCE, 1966; PhD, U. Wash., 1970. Registered profl. engr., Utah, Ariz. Prof. civil and environ. engring. Brigham Young U., Provo, Utah, 1970—, chmn. dept. civil engring., 1986-92; co-chmn. faculty senate, 1996-97. Spl. cons. Utah Div. Health, Salt Lake City, 1973-74; cons. engring. firms, 1970— Chmn. Provo Met. Water Bd., Utah, 1978-87. Named Utah Engring. Educator of the Yr. Utah Joint Enring. Coun., 1987. Mem. ASCE (nat. dir. 1982-85), Am. Acad. Environ. Engrs., Water Environment Fedn. (nat. dir. 1981-84, Bedell award), Am. Water Works Assn., Am. Soc. Engring. Edn., Sigma Xi. Republican. Mem. Lds Ch. Home: 562 E 3050 N Provo UT 84604-4264 Office: Brigham Young U 370 CB Provo UT 84602-4067 E-mail: merrittl@byu.edu.

MERRITT, MARTIN DAVID, counselor, tennis professional, educator, musician; b. Tallahassee, May 26, 1963; s. Charles Wesley and Nelda Virginia (Martin) M.; m. Wendee Michelle Wall, Apr. 11, 1992; children: Leslie Michelle, Julie Danelle. AA in Humanities, Andrew Coll., 1983; BA in Religion, LaGrange U., 1986; AA in Edn., Chattahoochee Valley C.C., 1999; postgrad., Troy State U., 1999—. Youth counselor Epworth by the Sea, St. Simons Island, Ga., 1982; dir. of youth Wesley United Meth. Ch./Trinity United Meth. Ch., Macon, Ga., Phenix City, Ala., 1983-86; tchr. Muscogee County Sch. Dist., Columbus, Ga., 1986-90; athletic dir. Boys Clubs of Am., 1991; adolescent counselor The Bradley Ctr., 1992-93; minister of programs Pinson U. Meth. Ch., Sylvester, Ga., 1994-95; profl. singer, songwriter, 1981—; tennis profl., instr. Chattahoochee Valley, Phenix City, 1996—. Supr. after-sch. program Parks and Recreation, Columbus, 1993-94. Author: Animals That God Planted, 1986, The Scarlet Leaves of May, 1986, The Creator's Hand, 1986, The Sparrow's Wing, 1986, For The King, 1986, The Knight's Quest, 1995; songwriter: Because I Love You, 1986, I Just Can't Wait, 1986, Jesus is Everything, 1986, Puppy Dogs and Teddy Bears, 1986, Rolling on a Rainbow, 1986, Is It Our Tomorrow?, 1993, I Think Of You, 1993, Life On The Run, 1994, On That Georgia Road, 1997, If Love Does Not Lead Me Here, 1998. Asst. scoutmaster Boy Scouts of Am., Waverly Hall, Ga., 1992-93; church/social work fund coord., vol. various orgns., 1982—; youth rep. City Coun., Waverly Hall, 1978-80; county newspaper columnist Harris County Jour., 1979-81; coord./vol. Salvation Army, Valley Rescue Mission, Goodwill, Columbus area, 1983—, Muscular Dystrophy Assn., St. Judes, Open Door, others. Columbus, 1983—; pres. Andrew Coll. Choralaires, 1982-83. Troy State U. presdl. scholar, 1999; recipient presdl. sports award, other sports awards. Mem. Alpha Omega (pres. 1982-83), Phi Theta Kappa (v.p. 1982-83), Chi Epsilon (v.p. 1985-86), Model United Nations (team leader 1991). Avocations: family, sports, games, acting, singing. Home: PO Box 844 Waverly Hall GA 31831-0844

MERRITT, MARY JANE, community volunteer; b. Milford, Mass., Feb. 6, 1942; d. Theodore and Rosemary Edith (Box) Bothfeld; m. Thomas Butler Merritt, July 23, 1966; children: Thomas Butler Jr., Haidee Soule, Theodore Bothfeld. AB, Boston U., 1964. Tchr. Perceptual Edn. Rsch. Ctr., Inc., Sherborn, Mass., 1964-66, Tenacre Country Day Sch., Wellesley, 1966-67, Head Start, Nashua, N.H., 1995-96; with ARC Bloodmobile, 1997-2001. Pres. Colonial Garden Club, Hollis, N. H., 1987-90; chmn. Governing Com. of Charles J. Nichols Fund, Hollis, N.H., 1989-95; mem. Master Plan Study com., Hollis, N.H., 1989-91; pres. Amherst Villagers Chpt. of The Questers, Inc., Amherst, N.H., 1995-97; pres. Hollis Woman's Club, 1999-2001. Recipient Community Svc. award Town of Hollis, N.H., 1993. Mem. Alpha Phi. Home: PO Box 344 Hollis NH 03049-0344

MERRITT, NANCY-JO, lawyer; b. Phoenix, Sept. 24, 1942; d. Robert Nelson Meeker and Violet Adele Gibson; children: Sidney Kathryn, Kurt, Douglas. BA, Ariz. State U., 1964, MA, 1974, JD, 1978. Bar: Ariz. 1978, U.S. Dist. Ct. Ariz. 1978, U.S. Ct. Appeals (9th cir.) 1984. Assoc. Erlichman, Fagerberg & Margrave, Phoenix, 1978-79, Pearlstein & Margrave, Phoenix, 1979-81, Corwin & Merritt, P.C., Phoenix, 1982-87; with Nancy-Jo Merritt & Assocs., P.C., 1987-88; ptnr. Bryan Cave, 1988-97, Bacon and Merritt, Phoenix, 1997-98; of counsel, mng. atty. Fragomen, Del Rey, Bernsen & Loewy, 1998—2001; shareholder Littler Mendelson, P.C., 2001—. Author: Understanding Immigration Law, 1993; sr. editor: Immigration and National Law Handbook, 1993—; contbr. articles to profl. jours. Chair bd. dirs. TERROS, 1995-97. Fellow Ariz. Bar Found.; mem. ABA, Am. Immigration Lawyers Assn. (chairperson Ariz. chpt. 1985-87, several coms., Pro Bono award), Am. Immigration Law Found. (trustee), Ariz. Bar Assn. (immigration sect.), Nucleus Club. Democrat. Avocations: modern literature, South American literature, hiking, gardening. Office: Littler Mendelson 2425 E Camelback Rd Ste 900 Phoenix AZ 85016 E-mail: njmerritt@littler.com.

MERRITT, SUSAN MARY, computer science educator, university dean; b. New London, Conn., July 28, 1946; d. Nelson Alfred and Mary (Cory) M. BA summa cum laude, Cath. U. Am., 1968; MS, NYU, 1969, PhD, 1982; Cert., Inst. for Edn. Mgmt., Harvard U., 1985. Joined Sisters of Divine Compassion, 1975; permanent cert. tchr., N.Y. Systems programmer Digital Equipment Corp., Maynard, Mass., 1969-70; tchr. Good Counsel Acad. High Sch., White Plains, N.Y., 1970-75; adj. instr. computer sci. Pace U., 1972-78, asst. prof., 1978-82, assoc. prof., 1982-85, prof., 1985—, chmn. dept., 1981-83, dean Sch. Computer Sci., 1983—. Mem. gen. coun. Sisters Divine Compassion, 1988-92. Contbr. articles to profl. jours. Recipient Cert. of Appreciation IEEE, 1990. Mem. Assn. for Computing Machinery (edn. bd. 1988—), Phi Beta Kappa, Sigma Xi. Roman Catholic. Office: Pace U 1 Martine Ave White Plains NY 10606-1932

MERRITT, THOMAS BUTLER, lawyer; b. Toledo, Apr. 3, 1939; s. George Robert and Bernice (Gerwin) M.; m. Mary Jane Bothfeld, July 23, 1966; children— Thomas Butler, Haidee Soule, Theodore Bothfeld AB magna cum laude, Harvard U., 1961, LLB cum laude, 1966. Bar: Mass. 1966, U.S. Supreme Ct. 1974, N.H. 1994. With N.Y. State Dept. Civil Svc., Albany, 1961-62; intern Office of Legal Advisr U.S. Dept. State, Washington, 1965; law clk. to assoc. justice Arthur E. Whittemore Supreme Jud. Ct. Mass., Boston, 1966-67; assoc. Nutter, McClennen & Fish, 1967-69, Palmer & Dodge, Boston, 1969-73; asst. counsel to Gov. Mass., 1973; reporter of decisions Supreme Jud. Ct. Mass., Boston, 1974-94; pvt. practice Hollis, N.H., 1994—. Contbr. articles to profl. jours. Mem. Conservation Commn. Town of Sherborn, Mass., 1969-74, chmn., 1972-74; mem. corp. Tenacre Country Day Sch., Wellesley, Mass., 1972-84, trustee, 1973-78; planning bd. Town of Hollis, N.H., 1995-98. 1st lt. U.S. Army, 1962-63, capt. USAR, 1963-69. Mem. Mass. Bar Assn., N.H. Bar Assn., Fed. Bar Assn., Am. Law Inst., Am. Soc. Internat. Law, Internat. Law Assn. (Am. br.), Nat. Assn. Reporters of Jud. Decisions (pres. 1983-84), Union Club, Harvard Club of Boston, Harvard Faculty Club (Cambridge). Episcopalian. Office: 5 Hutchings Dr PO Box 1646 Hollis NH 03049-1646

MERRITT, WILLIAM ALFRED, JR. lawyer, telecommunications company executive; b. N.Y.C., Aug. 7, 1936; s. William Alfred and Florence Anne (O'Connor) M.; m. Christine Marie Cartnick, Sept. 27, 1969; children— William Tyler, Brian Edward, Elizabeth Cody BA in Econs., Holy Cross Coll., Worcester, Mass., 1958; LLB, Harvard U., 1964. Bar: N.Y. 1965. Assoc. Olwine, Connelly, Chase, O'Donnell & Weyher, N.Y.C., 1964-68; atty., v.p. ops. and controls Bunge Corp., 1968-81; exec. v.p. TIE/Communications Inc., Seymour, Conn., 1981-90; pres. Wiltel Communications Systems Inc, Rolling Meadows, Ill., 1991-92; gen. counsel Carolina Barnes Capital Inc., Stamford, Conn., 1992—; ptnr. Seaboard Equities Inc., 1992—, KM Group, Stamford. Served to capt. USNR, 1958-80. Mem. Wee Burn Club, Harvard Club (N.Y.). Avocations: skiing, boating, golf. Home: 83 Brookside Rd Darien CT 06820-3505 Office: Ste 602 One Dock St Stamford CT 06902 E-mail: w59merr@aol.com.

MERROW, DOUGLAS ALAN, lawyer; b. Detroit, Dec. 12, 1958; s. Alvin Martin and Ella Lillian (Lada) Merrow; m. Debrah Jean Walton, Sept. 23, 1983; children: Kylie Elizabeth, Briana Kristine, Genevieve Elizabeth. BA, Wayne State U., 1980, JD, 1983. Bar: Mich. 1983, U.S. Dist. Ct. (we. dist.) Mich. 1983. Pvt. practice Law Office of Douglas A. Merrow P.L.L.C., Portage, Mich., 1983—. Contbr. to Wayne State U. Law Rev., 1982. Mem. Am. Trial Lawyers Assn., Mich. Trial Lawyers Assn., Mich. State Bar (negligence law, workers compensation sects.), Kalamazoo County Bar Assn., West Hills Tennis Club, Beacon Club, YMCA. Democrat. Avocations: sports, reading. Home: 1405 Long Rd Kalamazoo MI 49008-1319 Office: Law Office DA Merrow PLLC 700 Mall Dr Portage MI 49024-2812

MERROW, JOHN, broadcast journalist; b. Newark, June 14, 1941; s. John Griswold and Margaret (Lord) M.; m. Elise Kelsey, Dec. 21, 1968 (div. Sept. 1981); children: Joshua, Elise, Kelsey. AB, Dartmouth Coll., 1964; MA, Ind. U., 1968; EdD, Harvard U., 1973; LHD (hon.), Stockton State U., 1992. English tchr. P.O. Schreiber H.S., Port Washington, N.Y., 1965-66, Va. State Coll., Petersburg, 1969-70; prodr., host Options in Edn., Washington, 1974-82, Your Children, Our Children, PBS, Washington, 1983-84; corr. MacNeil/Lehrer News Hour, PBS, N.Y.C. and Washington, 1985-90; prodr., host Learning Matters, PBS, N.Y.C., 1991-92; exec. editor, host The Merrow Report, PBS, 1993—; exec. prodr., host The Merrow Report, Nat. Pub. Radio, N.Y.C., 1997—2001. Spkr. on edn. and family issues. Author: Choosing Excellence, 2001; columnist Children: A Mag. for Parents, 1986-88. Former chmn. alumni coun. Harvard Grad. Sch. Edn., Cambridge, 1994-97; bd. dirs. Hechinger Inst., Columbia U., 1996—, trustee Tchr.'s Coll., 2001—. Recipient Edn. Writers award, Edn. Writers Assn., 1975—82, 1994—2001, George Polk award, 1982, James L. Fisher award for disting. contbn. to edn., 2000, George Foster Peabody award, 2001. Mem. Edn. Writers Assn. (bd. dirs. 1978-84). Avocations: rollerblading, bicycling, collecting Pogo, crossword puzzles, kayaking. Office: Learning Matters Inc 6 E 32nd St Fl 8 New York NY 10016-5422 E-mail: jmerrow@merrow.org.

MERRY, ROBERT WILLIAM, publishing executive; b. Tacoma, Mar. 5, 1946; s. Robert Ellsworth and Carol Beatrice (Rasmussen) M.; m. Susan Diane Pennington, Sept. 20, 1969; children: Robert Ellsworth II, Johanna Lynn, Stephanie Ann. BA in Comms., U. Wash., 1968; MS in Journalism, Columbia U., 1972. Legis. reporter, gen. assignment reporter, copy editor Denver Post, 1972-74; reporter Nat. Observer Dow Jones & Co., Inc., 1974-77, reporter Wall St. Jour., 1977-86; exec. editor Roll Call, Newspaper of Capitol Hill, 1986-87; mng. editor Congl. Quar., Inc., Washington, 1987-89, exec. editor, 1990-97; also bd. dirs. Congl. Quar., Inc. and Times Publishing Co.; pres., publisher Congl. Quar., Inc., 1997—. Bd. dirs. Times Publ. Co., St. Petersburg, Fla.; appeared on CBS Face the Nation, NBC Meet the Press, ABC Good Morning Am., CNN Newsmakers, and Take Two, C-SPAN, numerous other local and Can. programs. Author: Taking On the World: Joseph and Stewart Alsop-Guardians of the American Century, 1996; contbr. chpts. to books. With U.S. Army, 1968-71. Avocations: jogging, biking, hiking, biography, movies. Office: Congl Quarterly Inc 1414 22nd St NW Washington DC 20037-1001 E-mail: rmerry@cq.com.

MERRYFIELD, DAVID W. pharmacist; b. Wichita Falls, Tex., July 30, 1953; s. Laddie E. and Lola Mae (Rasmussen) M.; m. Susan R. Pohl, May 18, 1974; children: Jessica L., Alexander J. BS in Pharmacy, U. Kans., Lawrence, 1976. Registered pharmacist. Pharmacist Trinity Luth. Hosp., Kansas City, Mo., 1976-84, coord. clin. svcs., 1984-92, co-interim dir., 1992; dir. pharmacy Cmty. Hosp., Anderson, Ind., 1992-97; clin. pharmacy coord. Cmty. Hosps., Indpls., 1997—. Adj. clin. instr. U. Mo., Kansas City, 1978-86, 89-92, lectr., 1983-92; lectr., instr. U. Kasn., Lawrence and Kansas City, 1980-87, 90-92; adj. instr. pharmacy practice Butler U., Indpls., 1992—. Contbr. articles to profl. jours. Mem. Am. Soc. Health-Sys. Pharmacists, Ind. Pharmacists Alliance, Rho Chi (pres. chpt. 1975-76).

MERSEL, LARRY, architect; b. N.Y.C., Mar. 22, 1933; s. David and Malvina (Guttman) M.; m. Irmgard Wirtgen; children: Andrew Marten, Alexis Judith. BArch, Carnegie Mellon U., 1956. Registered architect, N.Y. Project arch., assoc. Haines Lundberg Waehler, NYC, 1981—. Vis. prof. architecture Pratt Inst., Bklyn., 1974-99; instr. photography Clinton Hill Community, Bklyn, Bklyn. Mus. and Acad. Music, 1979, N.Y. Sch. Interior Design, 1995—. Archl. illustrator N.Y. Archtl. League, 1965, Mus. Modern Art., 1966; graphic designer Pratt Inst. Catalogue, 1978-79 (award 1979). Served with USAR, 1957-63. Democrat. Jewish. Home: 38 Park St Florham Park NJ 07932-1794 Office: HLW 115 Fifth Ave New York NY 10003 E-mail: lmersel@hlw.com.

MERSEREAU, HIRAM STIPE, wood products company consultant; b. Portland, Oreg., Aug. 4, 1917; s. E.W. and Ruth (Stipe) M.; m. Margaret Daggett, Dec. 25, 1937; children: Hiram Stipe, John Bradford, Timothy Daggett. Student, George Washington U., 1936-37, Harvard U., 1959. With Weyerhauser Timber Co., Klamath Falls, Oreg., 1937-38, Alexander-Yawkey Lumber Co., Prineville, 1938-52; gen. mgr. lumber div. Crossett Co., Ark., 1954-62; corp. sr. v.p., gen. mgr. So. div. Ga.-Pacific Corp., 1963-82, cons., 1982—. Past dir. Citizens & So. Nat. Bank, Augusta, Appalachian Hardwood Mfrs. Inc., Merry Cos., Inc., Augusta. Past bd. dirs. Young Life, Ga. Conservancy, Jr. Achievement Augusta; bd. dirs. Augusta br. Boys Clubs Am., Augusta Cancer Fund; trustee Paine Coll., Augusta. Mem. Nat. Forest Products Assn. (exec. com., dir.) Republican. Presbyterian (elder). Home: 6 Turnberry Ln Sea Pines Plantation Hilton Head Island SC 29928

MERSEREAU, JOHN, JR. Slavic languages and literatures educator; b. San Jose, Calif., Apr. 16, 1925; s. John Joshua and Winona Beth (Roberts) M.; m. Nanine Landell, July 11, 1953; children: Daryl Landell, John Coates. AB, U. Calif., 1945, MA, 1950, PhD, 1957. Teaching fellow, Slavic dept. U. Calif., Berkeley, 1950-52, research asst., 1953-54; instr. Slavic dept. U. Mich., Ann Arbor, 1956-59, asst. prof., 1959-61, assoc. prof., 1961-63, prof., 1963—, chmn. dept., 1961-71, 85-89, prof. emeritus, 1990—, dir. Residential Coll., 1977-85. Mem. Joint Com. Eastern Europe of Am. Council Learned Socs./Social Sci. Research Council, 1971-74, chmn., 1973-74. Author: Mikhail Lermontov, 1962, Baron Delvig's Literary Almanac: Northern Flowers, 1967, Translating Russian, 1968, Russian Romantic Fiction, 1983, Orest Somov, 1989, How to Grill a Gourmet, 2000; assoc. editor Mich. Slavic Publs., 1962—; contbr. articles to profl. jours. Served to lt. (j.g.) USNR, 1943-46, PTO. Calmerton Slavic scholar U. Calif., Berkeley, 1954-55; Ford Found. fellow, London and Paris, 1955-56, Guggenheim fellow, 1972-73; recipient Disting. Service award U. Mich., Ann Arbor, 1961. Mem. Am. Assn. Advancement Slavic Studies, U. Mich. Research Club. Clubs: Waterloo Hunt (Grass Lake, Mich., sec. 1970-80); Commanderie de Bordeaux (Detroit). Avocations: flying, gourmet cuisine, raising horses. Office: U of Mich Slavic Dept Ann Arbor MI 48109 E-mail: merserea@umich.edu.

MERSEREAU, STEPHEN CROCKER, electronic commerce executive; b. Miami, Fla., Sept. 18, 1950; s. Holland Crocker and Joanne (Stoptaugh) M.; m. Karen Marie Hosbein (div. 1990); children: Gage, Catherine; m. Lauren Melinda Tyler, May 3, 1992; children: Anson, Lena. BS with highest distinction, Ind. U., 1977; MBA, Harvard U., 1988. CPA, N.Y. Mgr. Price Waterhouse, N.Y.C., 1977-85; exec. v.p. ops. and fin. Am. Natural Beverage Corp., 1985-89; pres. Centerline Rehab Group, 1989-92; CEO INFINICOM, 1992-99, Connecity.Com, 1999-2000, Motoworld Network, 2000—. Bd. dirs. Best Practices Benchmarking & Cons., Inc. Mem. exec. com., treas. N.Y. Vietnam Vets. Memorial Comm. Office of the Mayor, 1983-*; spl. advisor N.Y. Cmty. Trust. Ssgt. USAF, 1971-75. Recipient Pres. Citation Campaign medal USAF, 1973; named Outstanding Young Man of Am., Jaycees, 1979. Mem. AICPA, DAV, N.Y. New Media Assn., Electronic Retailing Assn., Harvard Club N.Y.C., Ind. U. Alumni Assn., Beta Gamma Sigma, Beta Alpha Psi. Avocations: traveling, skiing, flying. Home: 914 Rock Rimmon Rd Stamford CT 06903-1220

MERSEREAU, SUSAN S. clinical psychologist; b. Atlanta, Apr. 9, 1947; d. John Andy Jr. and Dorothy Grace (Smith) Smith; m. Peter Roland Mersereau, May 30, 1970; children: Barrett, Travis, Courtney. AB, Vassar Coll., 1969; MSEd, Elmira Coll., 1973; D in Psychology, Pacific U., 1989. Lic. psychologist, Oreg.; diplomate Am. Coll. Forensic Medicine, Nat. Registry of Cert. Group Psychotherapists. Psychology intern Pacific Gateway Hosp., Portland, Oreg., 1987-88, Psychol. Svcs. Ctr., Hillsboro, 1988-89; psychology resident Lee Doppelt, Beaverton, 1990-91; staff Pac. Gateway Hosp., 1990—99; pvt. practice psychologist Beaverton, 1991-93; dir. Pacific Ctr. for Attention and Learning, 1993—. Mem. Neuropsychology Delegation to South Africa, 1996. Tchr. Incentive grantee Guam Dept. Edn., 1979. Mem. APA, Oreg. Psychol. Assn., Nat. Register Health Svc. Providers, Am. Coll. Forensic Examiners (diplomate), Nat. Registry Group Psychotherapist (cert. group psychotherapist), Vassar Club Oreg. (admissions com. 1984—, pres. 1984-88). Avocations: gardening, orchid growing. Office: Pacific Ctr Attention & Learning Lincoln Ctr 10300 SW Greenburg Rd Ste 430 Portland OR 97223-5453

MERSHON, CHARLES RICHARD, family physician; b. Bel Air, Md., Mar. 11, 1959; s. Millard Marsden and Joyce (Turner) M.; m. Sarah Jean Strickland, July 19, 1980; children: Peter Daniel, Ruth Anna. BS in Biology, Lebanon Valley Coll., 1980; MD, Oral Roberts U., 1984. Diplomate Am. Bd. Family Practice. Intern, resident in family practice Lancaster (Pa.) Gen. Hosp., 1984-87; mng. ptnr. Cornerstone Family Health Assocs., Lititz, Pa., 1987—; v.p. Physicians Alliance Ltd., Lancaster, 1996—. Assoc. med. dir. Hospice Lancaster County, 1994-96. Mem. adv. bd. House of His Creation, Lititz, 1987—; bd. dirs. Water St. Rescue Mission, Lancaster, 1991—; chmn. bd. dirs. Water St. Rescue Mission Clinic, 1995—; chmn. elder bd. Lancaster Evang. Free Ch., Lititz, 1990-2002. Fellow Am. Acad. Family Physicians; mem. AMA, Pa. Med. Soc. (Vol. Physician of Yr. 1996), Christian Med. and Dental Soc. Republican. Office: Cornerstone Family Health Assocs 6 W Newport Rd Lititz PA 17543-9491

MERSHON, JOHN LEE, reproductive endocrinologist; b. Martinsville, Ind., Aug. 10, 1960; s. Jack Belle and Janet Maebelle (Graves) M.; m. Ann Roberta Cutler, Sept. 9, 1988; children: Erin Elizabeth, John Patrick, Jack Sebastian. BS in Biology and Chemistry, Purdue U., 1981; MD, Ind. U., Indpls., 1985. Intern and resident in ob-gyn. Ohio State Med. Ctr., Columbus, 1985-89; fellow in reproductive endocrinology and infertility U. Cin. Med. Ctr., 1989-91, asst. prof. dept. ob-gyn., 1991—. Mem. Alpha Omega Alpha. Home: 1620 White Ash Dr Carmel IN 46033-9737

MERSKEY-ZEGER, MARIE GERTRUDE FINE, retired librarian; b. Kimberley, South Africa, Oct. 10, 1914; came to U.S., 1960, naturalized, 1965; d. Herman and Annie Myra (Wigoder) Fine; m. Clarence Merskey, Oct. 8, 1939 (dec. 1982); children: Hilary Pamela Merskey Nathe, Susan Heather Merskey Sinistore, Joan Margaret Merskey Schneiderman; m. Jack I. Zeger, July 15, 1984 (dec. Jan. 1997). Grad., Underwood Bus. Sch., Cape Town, South Africa, 1934; BA, U. Cape Town, 1958, Diploma in Librarianship, 1960. Sec. to Chief Rabbi Israel Abrahams, South Africa, 1945-49; sec. Jewish Sheltered Employment Coun., 1954-56; reference libr. New Rochelle (N.Y.) Pub. Libr., 1960-63; rsch. libr. Consumers Union, Mt. Vernon, N.Y., 1963-66; asst. readers svcs., head union catalog Westchester Libr. Sys., 1966-69, trustee, 1989-93, v.p., 1991; dir. Harrison (N.Y.) Pub. Libr. and West Harrison Br., 1969-84; acting dir. Mamaroneck (N.Y.) Free Libr., 1987-88, also trustee, 1988-93. Author: History of the Harrison Libraries, 1980; contbg. author: Celebration, Village of Mamaroneck Centennial, 1895-1995, History of Town/Village of Harrison Tricennial, 1696-1996; editor: Harrison Highlights and Anecdotes, 1989, (cookbook) On Harrison's Table, 1976; author articles. Pub. edn. officer USCG Aux Flotilla 63; bd. dirs Shore Acres Point Corp., Mamaroneck, 1985-89; program dir. Friends of the Mamaroneck Libr., 1993—. Recipient Brotherhood award B'nai B'rith, 1974; named Woman of Yr., Harrison, 1984. Mem. ALA, N.Y. Libr. Assn. (adult edn. com. for continuing edn. 1971-75, adult svcs. com. 1973-75, vice chmn. 1975, exec. bd. 1981-82), Westchester Libr. Assn., Pub. Libr. Dirs. Assn. (tech. svcs. com. chmn. Westchester County 1971, exec. bd. 1974-75, vice chmn. 1975), Charles Dawson History Ctr. (co-founder 1980, bd. dirs. 1980—), Mamaroneck Hist. Soc. Home: 316 S Barry Ave Mamaroneck NY 10543-4201

MERSKY, ROY MARTIN, law educator, librarian; b. N.Y.C., Sept. 1, 1925; s. Irving and Rose (Mendelson) Mirsky; m. Rosemary Bunnage; children: Deborah, Lisa, Ruth. BS, U. Wis., 1948, JD, 1952, MALS, 1953. Bar: Wis. 1952, U.S. Supreme Ct. 1970, Tex. 1972, U.S. Ct. Appeals (5th cir.) 1981, N.Y. 1983. U.S. govt. documents cataloger U. Wis. Law Libr., 1951-52; reference asst. Madison (Wis.) Free Libr., 1952; pvt. practice law Wis., 1952-54; readers adv., reference and catalog libr., mcpl. reference libr. at City Hall, Milw. Pub. Libr., 1953-54; chief readers and reference svc. Yale Law Libr., 1954-59; dir. Wash. State Law Libr., 1959-63; exec. sec. Jud. Coun. Commn. Wash. Court Report, State of Wash., 1959-63; prof. law, law libr. U. Colo., Boulder, 1963-65; prof. law, dir. rsch. U. Tex., Austin, 1965-84, William Stamps Farish Centennial prof. law, 1984—2000, Harry M. Reasoner Regents chair in law, 2000—; adj. prof. Grad. Sch. Libr. and Info. Sci. U. Tex. , 1976—. Vis. prof. law, dir. law libr. N.Y. Law Sch., N.Y.C., 1982-84; M.D. Anderson Found. vis. prof. law Queen Mary and Westfield Coll., U. London, 1994; interim dir. Jewish Nat. and Univ. Libr., Hebrew U., 1972-73; vis. fellow Australian Nat. U. Fac. of Law, Canberra, 1999; cons. to legal pubs. and law schs.; panelist various confs.; lectr. in field. Author: A Treasure in Jerusalem, 1974, (with J. Myron Dunn) Fundamentals of Legal Research, 7th edit., 1998, 8th, edit., (with Jacobstein Dunn) Legal Research Illustrated, An Abridgement of Fundamentals of Legal Research, 8th edit., 2002, (with Jacobstein Dunn) 8th edit., (with Albert P. Blaustein) The First One Hundred Justices: Statistical Studies on the Supreme Court of the United States, 1978, (with Gary R. Hartman and Suzanne F. Young) A Documentary History of the Legal Aspects of Abortion in the United States, 1990, 96 (with Jacobstein Dunn and Bonnie Koneski-White) Reports on Successful and Unsuccessful Nominations, 1992, 94, 96; contbr. articles to profl. jours., chpts. to books; editor numerous books in field. Bd. dirs. Ctrl. Tex. chpt. ACLU, pres., 1969; bd. dirs. Human Rights Documentation Exch., 1998-2001; mem. bd. advisors Anti-Defamation League, Austin, 1974-78; bd. dirs. Hillel Found., 1980-83; bd. dirs. Tex. Com. for Humanities, 1978-80, chair, 1980-82, conf. facilitator, 1982. With U.S. Army, 1944-46, ETO. Decorated Bronze Star. Fellow Am. Bar Found. (life), Coll. Law Practice Mgmt., Tex. Bar Found.; mem. ABA (various coms.), AAUP (chmn. nominating com. 1979-80), Am. Law Inst., Assn. Am. Law Schs. (various coms.), Internat. Assn. Lawyers and Jurists (bd. govs. Am. sect. 1980-95), Nat. Bar Assn., Am. Assn. Law Librs. (chair various coms.), Am. Soc. Info. Sci. (pres. Tex./Okla. chpt. 1992-93), Scribes (bd. dirs. 1974-95, book awards com. 1978-95, pres. 1991-93, chair Scribes Law Review Competition award com. 1993—), Soc. Am. Law Tchrs. (bd. govs. 1979-88, nominations com. 1984), ALA (rsch. librs. group 1987, libr. edn. divsn.), Am. Soc. Indexers, Internat. Assn. Law Librs. (U.S. adv. coun.), Internat. Fedn. Libr. Assns., Nat. Librs. Assn. (pres. 1980-81), Spl. Libr. Assn., State Bar Tex. (com. Tex. Bar Jour. 1983-90), State Bar Wis. (bd. mem. nonresident lawyers divsn. 1992-98), Nat. Assn. Coll. and Univ. Attys., Tex. Assn. Coll. Tchrs., Tex. Humanities Alliance (bd. dirs. 1986-88), Tex. Supreme Ct. Hist. Soc. (bd. trustees 1988—), Order of Coif (mem. triennial book award com.). Home: 6412 Cascada Dr Austin TX 78750-8157 Office: U Tex Sch Law Tarlton Law Libr 727 E Dean Kelton St Austin TX 78705-3224

MERTENS, DIANE K. secondary education educator; b. Sheboygan, Wis., Mar. 27, 1950; d. Robert E. and Winifred M. (Neumann) M.; m. W. Lawrence Neuman, June 16, 1984. BS, U. Wis., Oshkosh, 1972; MS, U. Wis., Madison, 1976. English tchr. Chilton (Wis.) H.S., 1972-75; tchg. asst. U. Wis., Madison, 1976; reading instr. Madison Area Tech. Coll., 1976; tchr., chair English dept. Edgewood H.S., Madison, 1976—. Curriculum reviewer Wis. Sch. Evaluation Consortium, 1984-94; supr. student/tchrs. practicum U. Wis., Madison, Edgewood Coll., 1985—; lit. mag. advisor, founder and chair fine arts festival Edgewood H.S., 1988—, coord. arts/history trip to France and Eng., 1998, 2000; lectr. of English Tohoku U., Sendai, Japan, 1995-96, Miyagi Gakuin Women's Coll., Sendai, 1996; faculty cons., advanced placement reader Ednl. Testing Svc., 1995, 97—; participant various workshops and seminars. Contbr. to Hamlet curriculum unit Shakespeare Set Free, 1994. Recipient NEH award Rutgers U., 1982, U. Md., 1986, Folger Libr., Washington, 1988, 89, Outstanding Madison Area H.S. Tchr. award Bassett Found., 1985, Wis. Writing Project scholar U. Wis., Madison, 1988-89, Outstanding Wis. Tchg. award Sen. Herbert Kohl, 1990, U. Chgo., 1991, Fulbright-Hays award Seminar in Japan on Japanese Culture, 1998, Nat. Coun. Tchrs. English and Ind. U. East Asian Studies Ctr. award, 2000. Mem. Nat. Coun. Tchrs. of English, Wis. Coun. Tchrs. of English (exec. bd. dirs., dist. dir. 1988-95), Japan Assn. Lang. Tchg., Wis. Alliance Arts Edn. Avocations: traveling, attending theater productions, reading, cooking. Home: 2935 Forest Down Madison WI 53711-5294 Office: Edgewood HS 2219 Monroe St Madison WI 53711-1901

MERTENS, JOAN R. museum curator, art historian; b. N.Y.C., Oct. 10, 1946; d. Otto R. and Helen H. M. BA, Radcliffe Coll., 1967; PhD, Harvard U., 1972. Curatorial asst. Met. Mus. Art, N.Y.C., 1972-73, asst. curator, 1973-76, assoc. curator, 1976-81, curator Greek and Roman dept., 1981—, curator, adminstr., 1983-90, mem. editorial bd. Mus. Jour., 1976—; adj. prof. NYU, Inst. Fine Arts, 1992—. Author: Attic White-Ground*Its Development, 1977, Greek Bronzes in the Metropolitan Museum of Art, 1985, (with others) Ancient Art from Cyprus: The Cesnola Collection in the Metropolitan Museum of Art, 2000. Mem. Archaeol. Inst. Am., German Archael. Inst. (corr. mem.) Home: 124 E 84th St New York NY 10028-0915 Office: Met Mus Art Fifth Ave at 82nd St New York NY 10028

MERTENS, THOMAS ROBERT, biology educator; b. Fort Wayne, Ind., May 22, 1930; s. Herbert F. and Hulda (Burg) M.; m. Beatrice Janet Abair, Apr. 1, 1953; children: Julia Ann, David Gerhard BS, Ball State U., 1952; MS, Purdue U., 1954, PhD, 1956. Research assoc. dept. genetics U. Wis.-Madison, 1956-57; asst. prof. biology Ball State U., Muncie, Ind., 1957-62, assoc. prof., 1962-66, prof., 1966-93, dir. doctoral programs in biology, 1974-93, disting. prof. biology edn., 1988-93, prof. emeritus, 1993—. Author: (with A. M. Winchester) Human Genetics, 1983 (with R.L. Hammersmith) Genetics Laboratory Investigations, 9th edit., 1991, 12th edit., 2001 (co-recipient William Holmes McGuffey Longevity award Text and Acad. Authors Assn. 1998); contbr. numerous articles to profl. jours. Co-recipient Gustav Ohaus award for innovative coll. sci. tchg. NSTA, 1986, recipient Disting. Svc. to Sci. Edn. citation, 1987; fellow NSF, 1963-64, Ind. Acad. Scis., 1969. Fellow AAAS; mem. Nat. Assn. Biology Tchrs. (pres. 1985, hon. mem. 1988), Am. Genetic Assn., Genetics Soc. Am. Episcopalian. Home: 4501 N Wheeling 9B-4 Muncie IN 47304-1277 Office: Ball State U Dept Biology Muncie IN 47306-0001

MERTINS, JAMES WALTER, entomologist; b. Milw., Feb. 18, 1943; s. Walter Edwin and Harriet Ellen (Sockett) M.; m. Marilee Eloise Joeckel, Dec. 8, 1979. BS in Zoology, U. Wis., Milw., 1965; MS in Entomology, U. Wis., 1967, PhD in Entomology, 1971. Project assoc. dept. entomology U. Wis., Madison, 1971-75, rsch. assoc. dept. entomology, 1975-77; asst. prof. dept. entomology Iowa State U., Ames, 1977-84; entomol. cons., 1984-89; entomologist Nat. Vet. Svcs. Labs. USDA Animal and Plant Health Inspection Svc., 1989—. Co-author: (textbook) Biological Insect Pest Suppression, 1977, Russian edit., 1980, Chinese edit., 1988; contbr. articles to profl. jours. NSF Grad. fellow, 1970. Mem. Entomol. Soc. Am. (Insect Photography award 1984, 86), Entomol. Soc. Can., Mich. Entomol. Soc., Wis. Entomol. Soc. (pres., sec., treas., bd. dirs.), Cyclone Corvettes, Inc. (co-founder, pres. 1978, 79, sec., treas., bd. dirs., Mem. of Yr. 1982), Am. Mensa. Avocations: insect photography, Corvette automobile activities, gardening, movies, insect collecting. Office: USDA Animal and Plant Health Inspection Svc PO Box 844 Ames IA 50010-0844 E-mail: James.W.Mertins@aphis.usda.gov.

MERTON, ROBERT C. economist, educator; b. N.Y.C., July 31, 1944; s. Robert K. and Suzanne (Carhart) M. BS in Engring. Math., Columbia U., 1966; MS in Applied Math., Calif. Inst. Tech., 1967; PhD in Econs., MIT, 1970; MA (hon.), Harvard U., 1989; LLD (hon.), U. Chgo., 1991; Prof. honoris causa degree, HEC Sch. Mgmt., Paris, 1995; D Econ. Sci. (hon.), U.

Lausanne, Switzerland, 1996; Dr honoris causa, U. Paris Dauphine, 1997; D of Mgmt. Sci. (hon.), Nat. Sun Yat-sen U., Kaoshiung, Taiwan, 1998; DS honoris causa, Athens U. Econs. & Bus., Greece, 2002. Instr. econs. MIT, Cambridge, 1969-70; asst. prof. fin. Alfred P. Sloan Sch. Mgmt., 1970-73, assoc. prof., 1973-74, prof., 1974-80, J.C. Penney prof. mgmt., 1980-88; vis. prof. fin. Harvard U., Boston, 1987-88, George Fisher Baker prof. bus. adminstrn., 1988-98, John and Natty McArthur University prof., 1998—. Rsch. assoc. Nat. Bur. Econ. Rsch., 1979—; mem. internat. bd. sci. advisors Tinbergen Inst.; co-founder Long-Term Capital Mgmt., L.P., Greenwich, Conn., 1993—99, Hancock, Mendoza, Dechille & Merton, Ltd., 2001—; mem. adv. bd. nuServe, 2001—, AlphaSimplex Group, 2001—, eCredit.com, 2000—; acad. adv. bd. Real Option Group, 1999—; bd. dirs. Vical Inc., MF Risk, Inc.; co-founder Integrated Fin. Ltd., LLC, 2002—. Author: Continuous-Time Finance, 1990, rev. edit., 1992; co-author: Casebook in Financial Engineering: Applied Studies of Financial Innovation, 1995, The Global Financial System: A Functional Perspective, 1995, Finance, 2000; editor: The Collected Scientific Papers of Paul A. Samuelson, vol. III, 1972; mem. editl. bd. Internat. Econ. Rev., 1972-77, Jour. Fin., 1973-77, Jour. Money, Credit and Banking, 1974-79, Jour. Fin. Econs., 1974-83, Jour. Banking and Fin., 1977-79, 92—, Fin. India, 1988—, Geneva Papers on Risk and Ins., 1989-96, Jour. Fixed Income, 1991—, Fin. Rev., 1992-97, Jour. Fin. Edn., 1995—, European Fin. Rev., 1997—; mem. adv. bd. The New Palgrave Dictionary of Money and Finance, Math. Fin., Rev. Derivatives Rsch., Nihon Finance Gakkai, The Brookings-Wharton Papers on Financial Policy, Internat. Jour. Theoretical & Applied Finance; contbr. articles to profl. jours. Recipient Leo Melamed prize U. Chgo. Sch. Bus., 1983, Roger Murray prize Inst. for Quantitative Rsch. in Fin., 1985, 86, Disting. Scholar award Ea. Fin. Assn., 1989, Internat. INA-Nat. Acad. Lincei prize Nat. Acad. Lincei, Rome, 1993, FORCE award for fin. innovation Fuqua Sch. Bus., Duke U., 1993, Fin. Engr. of Yr. award Internat. Assn. Fin. Engrs., 1993, Alfred Nobel Meml. Prize in Econ. Scis., 1997, Heroes Among Us award Boston Celtics, 1997, Michael Pupin medal Columbia U., 1998, Disting. Alumni award Calif. Inst. of Tech., 1999, MFD Lifetime Achievement award Boston U., 1999; inducted Derivatives Hall of Fame, 1998. Fellow Internat. Assn. Fin. Engrs. (sr.), Econometric Soc., Am. Acad. Arts and Scis., Inst. Quantitative Rsch., Fin. Mgmt. Assn., Am. Fin. Assn. (dir. 1982-84, pres. 1986, fellow 2000—); mem. NAS, Bachelier Fin. Soc., Soc. for Fin. Studies (v.p. 1993), Hon. Order Ky. Cols., Tau Beta Pi, Sigma Xi. Office: Harvard U Grad Sch Bus Adminstrn Morgan 397 Soldiers Field Rd Boston MA 02163 E-mail: rmerton@hbs.edu.

MERTON, ROBERT K. sociologist, educator; b. Phila., July 4, 1910; s. Harry David and Ida (Rosoff) Schkolnick; m. Suzanne Carhart, 1934 (sep. 1968, dec. 1992); children: Stephanie, Robert C., Vanessa; companion Harriet Zuckerman, 1968-92, m. June, 1993. AB, Temple U., 1931, LLD (hon.), 1956; MA, Harvard U., 1932, PhD, 1936, LLD (hon.), 1980; LHD (hon.), Emory U., 1965, Loyola U., Chgo., 1970, Kalamazoo Coll., 1970, Cleve. State U., 1977, U. Pa., 1979, Brandeis U., 1983, SUNY-Albany, 1986, New Sch. Social Rsch., 1995, Long Island U., 1996; Dr. honoris causa, U. Leyden, 1965, Jagiellonian U., Cracow, Poland, 1989; LLD (hon.), Western Res. U., 1966, U. Chgo., 1968, Tulane U., 1971, U. Md., 1982; LittD (hon.), Colgate U., 1967, SUNY, 1984, Columbia U., 1985, SUNY, Albany, 1986, Oxford U., 1986; Dr. Social Sci. (hon.), Yale U., 1968; DSC in Econ. (hon.), U. Wales, 1968; PhD (hon.), Hebrew U. of Jerusalem, 1980, U. Oslo, Norway, 1991; D of Polit. Sci. (hon.), U. Bologna, 1996; D honoris causa, U. Madrid, 1999, U. Athens, 1999, U. Rome, 2001. Tutor, instr. sociology Harvard U., 1936-39; prof., chmn. dept. Tulane U., 1939-41; from asst. prof. to prof. Columbia U., 1941-63, Giddings prof., 1963-74, univ. prof., 1974-79, spl. svc. prof., 1979-84, Univ. prof. emeritus, 1979—. Assoc. dir. Bur. Applied Social Rsch., 1942-71; adj. faculty Rockefeller U., 1979—; George Sarton prof. hist. sci. U. Ghent, Belgium, 1986-88; adv. editor sociology Harcourt Brace 1947-98; ednl. adv. bd. Guggenheim Found., 1963-79, chmn., 1971-79. Author: Science Technology and Society in 17th Century England, 3rd edit., 2001, Mass Persuasion, 3d edit., 2002, Social Theory and Social Structure, rev. edit., 1968, On the Shoulders of Giants, 1965, bicennial edit., 1985, post-Italianate edit., 1993, On Theoretical Sociology, 1967, The Sociology of Science, 1973, Sociological Ambivalence, 1976, Sociology of Science: An Episodic Memoir, 1979, Social Research and the Practicing Professions, 1982, Opportunity Structure, 1995, On Social Structure and Science, 1996; co-author: the Focused Interview, rev. edit., 1956, 3d edit., 1990, Freedom to Read, 1957, I Viaggi e le Avventura della "Serendipity", 2002; co-editor, co-author: Continuities in Social Research, 1951, Social Policy and Social Research in Housing, 1951, Reader in Bureaucracy, 1952, The Student-Physician, 1957, Sociology Today, 1959, Contemporary Social Problems, 4th edit., 1976, The Sociology of Science in Europe, 1977, Toward a Metric of Science, 1978, Qualitative and Quantitative Social Research: Papers in Honor of Paul F. Lazarsfeld, 1979, Sociological Traditions from Generation to Generation, 1980, Continuities in Structural Inquiry, 1981; co-editor Social Sci. Quotations, 2000. Trustee Ctr. Advanced Study Behavioral Scis., 1952-75, Temple U., 1964-68, Inst. Sci. Info., 1968—; mem. bd. guarantors Italian Acad. for Advanced Studies in Am., 1992-2000. Recipient MacArthur Prize fellow, 1983-88, Nat. Medal of Sci., 1994, Common Wealth award for Disting. Svc. to Sociology, 1979, award Meml. Sloan-Kettering Cancer Ctr., 1981, Derek Price award Scientometrics, 1995, Sutherland award Am. Soc. Criminology, 1996, Dinerman prize World Assn. Pub. Opinion Rsch., 2000; Disting. scholar in humanities Am. Coun. Learned Socs., 1962, Russell Sage Found. scholar, 1979-99, emeritus, 1999—, Haskins lectr., 1994; NIH lectr. in recognition of outstanding sci. achievement, 1964; Guggenheim fellow, 1962. Fellow Am. Acad. Arts and Scis. (Talcott Parsons prize 1979), Brit. Acad. (fgn.); mem. NAS, Am. Philos. Soc., Sociol. Rsch. Assn. (pres. 1968), Nat. Acad. Edn., Nat. Inst. Medicine, Am. Sociol. Assn. (pres. 1957, Disting. Scholarship award 1980, Cooley-Mead Award in social psychology 1997), Ea. Sociol. Soc. (pres. 1969), History of Sci. Soc., World Acad. Arts and Scis., Soc. Social Studies of Sci. (pres. 1975, Bernal prize), Royal Swedish Acad. Scis. (fgn.), Academia Europaea (fgn.), Polish Acad. Scis. (fgn.), N.Y. Acad. Scis. (hon. life mem.). Home: 71 Hither Ln East Hampton NY 11937-2634 E-mail: rm241@columbia.edu.

MERTZ, FRANCIS JAMES, university president; b. Newark, Sept. 24, 1937; s. Frank E. and Marian E. (Brady) M.; m. Gail Williams, Apr. 11, 1964; children: Lynn, Christopher, Suzanne, David, Amy, Jonathan. BA, St. Peter's Coll., 1958; JD, NYU, 1961; LLD (hon.), Felician Coll., 1984, Stevens Inst. Tech., Hoboken, N.J., 1988, Fairleigh Dickinson U., 1999, Kunghnam Univ., 1999, Coll. St. Elizabeth, 2002. Bar: N.J. 1967. Exec. v.p. St. Peter's Coll., Jersey City, 1972-78; v.p., CFO N.Y. Med. Coll., Valhalla, 1978-79; dir. adminstrn. Sage Gray Todd and Sims, N.Y.C., 1979-81; pres. Ind. Coll. Fund N.J., Summit, 1981-90, Assn. Ind. Colls. and Univs. N.J., Summit, 1982-90, Fairleigh Dickinson U., Teaneck, N.J., 1990-99, pres. emeritus. Mem. adv. bd. Fleet Bank, N.J. Bd. dirs. Ready Found., Tri County Scholarship Fund, Paterson, N.J., St. Joseph's Home for the Blind, 1998—, Ready Fund, also chmn. Home: 167 Stanie Brae Dr Watchung NJ 07069-6233 Office: Fairleigh Dickinson U 285 Madison Ave Madison NJ 07940-1099 E-mail: mertz@fdu.edu.

MERTZ, JANET ELAINE, molecular biology researcher, educator, consultant; b. N.Y.C., Aug. 9, 1949; d. Harry and Pauline (Schwartz) M.; m. Jonathan Michael Kane, Mar. 16, 1980; children: Daniel Morris Mertz Kane, Jeremy Solomon Mertz Kane. BS in Life Scis. and Elec. Engring., MIT, 1970; PhD in Biochemistry, Stanford (Calif.) U., 1975. Teaching asst. dept. biochemistry Stanford U., 1970-73; postdoctoral fellow Med. Rsch. Coun. Lab. Molecular Biology, Cambridge, Eng., 1975-76; asst. prof. oncology McArdle Lab. for Cancer Rsch. U. Wis., Madison, 1976-83, assoc. prof. oncology, 1983-92; prof. oncology McArdle Lab. for Cancer Rsch. U. Wis., Masison, 1992—. Ad hoc mem. study sects. NIH, Bethesda, Md., 1981—; panel mem. NSF, 1993-97; cons. Agrigenetics Corp., Madison, Wis., 1983-84. Mem. editorial bd. Molecular and Cellular Biology Jour., 1985-90, Virology Jour., 1988—, Jour. Virology, 1999—; contbr. numerous articles to profl. jours. Recipient Kallman award Stanford U., 1973; Jane Coffin Childs Meml. Fund fellow, 1975-76; numerous rsch. grants. Mem. AAAS, Am. Assn. for Cancer Rsch., Am. Soc. for Biochemistry and Molecular Biology, Am. Soc. for Microbiology, Am. Soc. for Virology, Assn. for Women in Sci. Office: U Wis McArdle Lab 1400 University Ave Madison WI 53706-1599 E-mail: mertz@oncology.wisc.edu.

MERTZ, JONATHAN FREDERICK, film producer, film director; b. Washington, May 23, 1978; s. Walter Day Mertz Jr. and Carol Mackay Mertz. Student, NC Sch. of the Arts, 1996—98. Pres. and founder JFM Entertainment LLC, Fort Valley, Va., 1998—; prodr. FilmFAN Pictures Inc., Asheville, NC, 2000—01. Executive producer (short film) The Boy Who Drew Cats, 2002; dir.: (short film) The Comic Book Kid, 1998. Democrat. Unitarian Universalist. Office Fax: 540-933-6761. E-mail: jfm_entertainment@hotmail.com.

MERTZ, WALTER, retired government research executive; b. Mainz, Germany, May 4, 1923; s. Oskar and Anne (Gabelmann) M.; m. Marianne C. Maret, Aug. 8, 1953. MD, U. Mainz, 1951. Intern County Hosp., Hersfeld, Germany, 1952-53; resident Univ. Hosp., Frankfurt, Germany, 1953; vis. scientist NIH, Bethesda, Md., 1953-61; chief dept. biol. chemistry Walter Reed Army Inst. Research, Washington, 1961-69; mem. staff Nutrition Inst., Agrl. Research Service, Dept. Agrl., Beltsville, Md., 1969-72, chmn. inst., 1972-92; ret. Dir. Human Nutrition Research Ctr.; lectr. George Washington U. Med. Sch., 1963-73 Served with German Army, 1941-46. Recipient Osborne and Mendel award Am. Inst. Nutrition, 1971, Superior Performance award Dept. Agr., 1972, Lederle award in Human Nutrition, 1982, Internat. prize for Modern Nutrition, 1987, award for Disting. Svc., Dept. Agr., 1988. Mem. Am. Inst. Nutrition, Am. Soc. Biol. Chemists, Am. Soc. Clin. Nutrition Home: 12401 Saint James Rd Rockville MD 20850-3744 E-mail: wmcmertz@aol.com.

MERULLO-BOAZ, LISA HELEN, marketing and fundraising executive; b. N.Y.C., Oct. 25, 1953; d. Irving and Hazel (Jacob) Siegel; m. Edward J. Merullo, Oct. 4, 1975 (div.); children: Aaron E., Jenny L.; m. Jeffrey A. Boaz, July 4, 1993. BA, Northeastern U., 1975. Prodn. and adminstrv. asst. Gennard Andreozzi Inc., N.Y.C., 1978; adminstrv. asst. WNET/13, 1978-79; prodn. sec. MacNeil/Lehrer Report, 1979-81, prodn. asst., 1981-82; membership, mktg. and fundraising adminstr. Leventhal-Sidman Jewish Cmty. Ctr., Newton, Mass., 1988-97; devel. assoc. Ben-Gurion U., Newton office, 1997-98; devel. mgr. AIDS Action Com., Boston, 1998—. Exec. prodr. (cable TV show) JCC-TV, 1994-97. Jewish. Avocations: cooking, camping, physical fitness. Office: AIDS Action Com 131 Claredon St Boston MA 02116-1443

MERVILDE, MICHAEL JOHN, clinical social worker; b. Mishawaka, Ind., Mar. 7, 1947; s. Armond Emil and Amelia (Canarecci) M.; m. Karen Sue Selig, Aug. 3, 1974; children: Lisa Marie, Michael John Jr. AB, St. Edwards U., Austin, Tex., 1969; MSW, Washington U., St. Louis, 1975. Cert. ind. clin. social worker Wis., bd. cert. diplomate in clin. social work. Acting exec. dir. Hotline, South Bend, Ind., 1973; clin. assoc. Drug Info. Ctr., St. Louis, 1973-74, Social Health Assn., St. Louis, 1975; mental health coord. Kewaunee County Unified Bd., Algoma, Wis., 1975-78; clin. social worker Bay Psychiat. Clinic, Green Bay, 1978-86; ptnr., clin. social worker Green Bay Wellness & Behavioral Health Clinic, 1985-97, owner, 1997—. Mem. NASW (bd. dirs. Wis. chpt. 1981-85), Acad. Cert. Social Workers, Acad. Family Mediators (assoc.), Optimists (charter, sec. Green Bay). Roman Catholic. Office: Green Bay Wellness/Behavioral Hlth Clinic 125 S Jefferson St Green Bay WI 54301-4500

MERVILLE, LAWRENCE JOSEPH, finance educator; b. Nashville, Apr. 7, 1943; s. Lawrence Augustus Merville and Emma June (Collier) Park; m. Sheryl Wolff, Aug. 9, 1968; 1 child, Lauren Anne. BA, Vanderbilt U., 1965; MBA, U. Tex., 1968, PhD, 1971. Fin. analyst Tex. Instruments, Dallas, 1968-70; asst. prof. fin. Ind. U., Bloomington, 1971-73; prof. fin. U. Tex., Dallas, 1973—. Pres. Merville & Assocs., Dallas; cons. Tex. Pub. Utility Com., Austin, 1983-85. Author: Economics and Finance, 1990; contbr. articles to profl. jours. Dir. Pub. Utility Programs, Dallas, 1978-82, Pub. Utility Ctr., Dallas, 1981-87. NSF fellow U. Tex., Austin, 1965. Mem. Am. Fin. Assn., Fin. Mgmt. Assn. (program com.), Western Fin. Assn. (program com.), Soc. for China Studies, Dallas Economist Club (membership com.), Phi Beta Kappa. Republican. Avocations: travel, jogging, fishing, theatre. Office: Univ Tex Dallas 2601 N Floyd Rd Richardson TX 75080-1407

MERVIS, BONNIE AARON, social worker; b. Chgo., Apr. 2, 1945; d. Herman Leonard Aaron and Rosalie (Zakroff) Ovson; m. Charles L. Mervis, May 25, 1975; children: Aaron, Jessica. BS, Cornell U., 1967; MA, U. Chgo., 1974; PhD, Inst. Clin. Social Work, Chgo., 1997. Lic. clin. social worker; cert. sch. social worker, Ill., bd. cert. diplomate. Tchr. Head Start, Elmira, N.Y., 1967-68; elem. sch. tchr. various cities, 1968-70; team leader Forest Hosp., Des Plaines, Ill., 1970-72; instr. dept. med. social work U. Ill. Hosp., Chgo., 1974-76; social worker Spl. Edn. Dist. North Lake County, Gurnee, Ill., 1979-82, Sch. Dist. 107 (now Sch. Dist. 112), Highland Park, 1982—. Pvt. practice, Highland Park, Ill., 1982—; assoc. faculty Chgo. Ctr. for Family Health; field instr., guest lectr. U. Chgo. Sch. Social Svc. Adminstrn.; presenter at profl. confs. Contbr. articles to profl. jours. Mem. Ill. Assn. Sch. Social Workers, NASW, NEA, Omicron Nu. Avocation: fiction book reviewing. Office: Sch Dist 112 2075 Saint Johns Ave Highland Park IL 60035-2416 E-mail: bmervis@d112.lake.k12.il.us.

MERWIN, DAVIS UNDERWOOD, newspaper executive; b. Chgo., June 22, 1928; s. Davis and Josephine (Underwood) M.; m. Nancy Snowden Smith Tailer, Nov. 14, 1958 (dec. Feb. 1995); children: Davis Fell, Laura Howell; m. Sharon Adkins Todd, May 12, 1998. AB, Harvard U., 1950; LLD (hon.), Ill. Wesleyan U., 1991. Pres. Evergreen Comm., Inc., Bloomington, Ill., 1969-80; pub. Daily Pantagraph, 1968-80; pres. Wood Canyon Corp., Tucson, 1989-93; vice-chmn. Bloomington Broadcasting Corp., 1993-99. Dir. State Farm Growth, Balanced Mcpl. Bond and Interim Funds, State Farm Variable Products Funds. Trustee emeritus Ill. Wesleyan U.; trustee Ill. Nature Conservancy. Recipient Disting. Svc. award U.S. Jaycees, 1959 Mem. Am. Newspaper Pubs. Assn., Inland Daily Press Assn. (pres. 1977, chmn. bd. dirs. 1978), Harvard Club (Chgo.), Phoenix-SK Club, Hasty Pudding Club, Bloomington Country Club, Ristigouche Salmon Club. Republican. Unitarian Universalist. Office: 2422 E Washington St Bloomington IL 61704-4478 Mailing: PO Box 1665 Bloomington IL 61702-1665 E-mail: DUMerwin@aol.com.

MERWIN, EDWIN PRESTON, health care consultant, educator; b. Revere, Mass., Oct. 13, 1927; s. George Preston and Edith Charlotte (Miller) M.; m. Marylynn Joy Bicknell, Nov. 3, 1979; 1 child by previous marriage, Ralph Edwin; stepchildren: Charles John Burns, Patrick Edward Burns, Stephen Allen Burns, John David Light, Robert Allen Light, Frederick John Light. BS, U. So. Calif., 1955, postgrad. Law Sch., 1957—57; postgrad., San Fernando Valley State Coll, 1965—66; MPH (USPHS fellow), U. Calif., Berkeley, 1970; PhD, Brantridge Forest, Eng., 1971. Tng. office Camarillo (Calif.) State Hosp., 1961—66; asst. coord. mental retardation programs State of Calif., Sacramento, 1966—67; project dir. Calif. Coun. Retarded Children, 1967—69; asst. dir. Golden Empire Comprehensive Health Coun., 1970—76, health care cons., 1976—77; gen. ptnr. EDRA Assocs., 1976—. Cons. Calif. Dept. Health, 1977-78, Calif. Office Statewide Health Planning and Devel., 1978-79; chief health professions career opportunity program State of Calif., Sacramento, 1979-81; chief health pers. info. and analysis sect. Office of Statewide Health Planning and Devel., 1981-82, asst. chief divsn. health professions devel., 1981-884, asst. dep. dir., 1984-85; project dir. Alzheimers Disease Insts., Calif., 1986-87; chief demonstration project sect. divsn. Health Projects and Analysis, 1987-89, chief Policy Analysis and Professions Devel. SEct., 1989-93; tchr. Ventura (Calif.) Coll., 1962-66, Merritt Coll., Oakland, Calif., 1969; sr. adj. prof. Golden Gate U., 1976; lectr. continuing edn. program U. Calif., Berkeley; inst. Los Rios C.C. Dist., 1982—; mem. Task Force for New Health Care Sys. in Macedonia; mem. adv. com. to health faculty Golden Gate U., 1995—; cons. NIMH, HEW, Calif. Assn. Health Facilities; founder, cons. Internat. U. Am., 1995—. Author: (with Dr. Fred Heck) Written Case Analysis, 1982; editor: T. Patrick Heck Meml. Case Series, 1982; contbr. articles to profl. jours. Mem. health adv. coun. San Juan Sch. Dist., 1972-73; treas. Calif. Camping and Recreation Coun., 1972-73; bd. dirs. Sacramento Rehab. Facility, 1970-86, v.p., 1973-76; bd. dirs. Sacramento Vocat. Svcs., 1986-93; founder, life mem. S.O.T.S., 1989—. Recipient Pres.'s award Golden Gate U., 1982. Mem. Am. Assn. Mental Deficiency, Calif. Pub. Health Assn., Sacramento Mental Health Assn., Sacramento Assn. Retarded (life; dir., Svc. award 1984), Nat. Assn. for Retarded Children, DAV (life), Am. Legion, Marines Meml. Assn. (life), AAAS, SCAPA Praetors U. So. Calif., Miles Merwin Assn., Phi Kappa Tau. Home: 8008 Archer Ave Fair Oaks CA 95628-5907 Office: Golden Gate U 3620 Northgate Blvd Ste 100 Sacramento CA 95834-1619

MERWIN, JOHN DAVID, retired lawyer, former governor; b. Frederiksted, St. Croix, V.I., Sept. 26, 1921; s. Miles and Marguerite Louise (Fleming) M.; m. Marjorie Davis Spaulding, Feb. 18, 1993. Student, U. Lausanne, Switzerland, 1938-39, U. P.R., 1939-40; BSc, Yale U., 1943; JD, George Washington U., 1948. Bar: Conn., V.I. 1949. Practice law, St. Croix, V.I., 1949-50, 1953-57, 67-85; gen. counsel, v.p. Rob't L. Merwin & Co., Inc., 1953-57; senator-at-large V.I. Legislature, 1955-57; govt. sec. for V.I., 1957-58; gov. V.I., 1958-61; rep. Chase Manhattan Bank, Nassau, Bahamas, 1961-65; exec. v.p. Equity Pub. Corp. Orford, N.H., 1965-67. Chmn. V.I. Port Authority, 1972-75; Rep. candidate for Pres. N.H. Primary Election, 1992; pres. The Nason Found., Cleve., 1981—. Served from 2d lt. to capt. F.A. AUS, 1942-46, 50-53. Decorated Bronze Star; Croix de Guerre with silver star. Mem. Conn., N.H., V.I. bar assns., Phi Delta Phi. Clubs: Tennis of St. Croix (V.I.), Yale (N.Y.C.)., Cosmos (Washington). Episcopalian. Home and Office: PO Box 2213 New London NH 03257-2213 E-mail: jdmerwin@hotmail.com.

MERWIN, PETER MATTHEW, teacher, writer; b. Chgo., June 20, 1944; s. Walter John and Agatha Agnes (Daugirdas) M. BA in English, Philosophy, De Paul U., 1967, MA, 1969, PhD, 1992. Cert. tchr. secondary schs., English, Ill. Tchr. of English Chgo. Bd. Edn., 1971—. Travel rschr. and writer Merwin Libr., Orland Hills, Ill.; instr. in philosophy De Paul U., Chgo., 1978-81; rschr. Newberry Libr., Chgo., 1982—; instr.The Sacred Pipe of the Lakotas, Field Mus. Nat. History, Chgo., 1984 Author: The Symbolic Forms of Ernst Cassirer and the Lakotas, 1992; also articles and presentations; editor Brand Book, Westerners Internat., 1997, investigative reporter, 1997—. Presenter of exhibit on Lakota Symbols and Culture, Orland Park (Ill.) Pub. Libr., 1993; Interviewee Chgo. Tribune, Southtown Daily on Subject, 1993. Recipient Arthur J. Schmitt fellowships De Paul U., Chgo., 1978-79, 79-80; Made Hon. Mem. Sicangu Nation, Rosebud (S.D.) Lakota Sioux, 1995—, Orland Park Authors, 1993. Mem. Timber Wolf Alliance, Lithuanian Golf Assn., Am. Philos. Assn., Soc. for Phenomological and Existential Philosophy, Internat. Assn. Philosophy and Lit. Avocations: swimming, hiking, woodworking, environ. action, bicycling. Home: 8821 Obrien Dr Orland Hills IL 60477-7462 Office: Benito Juarez HS 2150 S Laflin St Chicago IL 60608-4409

MERYHEW, VERN ARTHUR, engineering executive, retired; b. Agra, Kans., May 28, 1933; s. Nivas Lavern Meryhew and Ethel (Burton) Whitish; m. Sharie Karen Wallen, July 12, 1957 (dec.); children: Brad Allen, Pamela Ann Hudgins; m. Joan C. Bermes, Sept. 26, 1970; children: Sheryl Lynn, Sarah Kay; stepchildren: Michelle M. Nicholas, Kathy R. Fincher. Student, Highline Coll., Seattle, 1966-69. Drafting mgr. The Boeing Co., Seattle, 1966-70, adminstr., 1971-80, engring. mgr., 1980-90. Real estate developer, Seattle, 1969—. Leader Boy Scouts Am., Seattle, 1968-72; commr. Tukwila (Wash.) Civil Svc., 1990-92, comdr. Tukwila Planning com. and bd. of archtl. review, 1992—. Mem. Boeing Mgmt. Assn. Avocations: swimming, canoeing, woodworking, aviary enthusiast.

MERZ, JON FREDERICK, lawyer, educator; b. Bayshore, N.Y., Mar. 1956; s. Frederick Robert Merz; m. Marcie L. H. Merz. BS, Rensselaer Poly. Inst., 1978; MBA, U. North Fla., 1983; JD, Duquesne U., 1987; PhD, Carnegie Mellon U., 1991. Bar: Pa. 1987, U.S. Patent and Trademark Office 1988. Engr. EDS Nuclear/Impell Corp., Melville, NY, 1979—81; engr. contracts Westinghouse Electric Corp., Pitts., 1981—87, atty., 1987—88; postdoctoral rsch. fellow Carnegie Mellon U., 1991—92; assoc. policy analyst The RAND Corp., Santa Monica, Calif., 1992—95; asst. prof. bioethics U. Pa., Phila., 1995—. Home: 249 S Van Pelt St Philadelphia PA 19103 Office: U Pa Ste 320 3401 Market St Philadelphia PA 19104-3308 Office Fax: 215-573-4931. Business E-Mail: merz@mail.med.upenn.edu.

MERZ, MICHAEL, federal judge; b. Dayton, Ohio, Mar. 29, 1945; s. Robert Louis and Hazel (Appleton) M.; m. Marguerite Logan LeBreton, Sept. 7, 1968; children: Peter Henry, Nicholas George. AB cum laude, Harvard U., 1967, JD, 1970. Bar: Ohio 1970, U.S. Dist. Ct. (so. dist.) Ohio 1971, U.S Supreme Ct. 1974, U.S. Ct. Appeals (6th cir.) 1975. Assoc. Smith & Schnacke, Dayton, Ohio, 1970-75, ptnr., 1976-77; judge Dayton Mcpl. Ct., 1977-84; magistrate U.S. Dist. Ct. (so. dist.) Ohio, 1984—. Adj. prof. U. Dayton Law Sch., 1979—; mem. rules adv. com. Ohio Supreme Ct., 1989-96. Bd. dirs. United Way, Dayton, 1981-95; trustee Dayton and Montgomery County Pub. Libr., 1991—, Montgomery County Hist. Soc., 1995—, Ohio Libr. Coun., 1997-2000. Fellow Am. Bar Found.; mem. ABA, Fed. Bar Assn., Am. Judicature Soc., Fed. Magistrate Judges Assn. (trustee 1997-2000), Ohio State Bar Assn., Dayton Bar Assn. Republican. Roman Catholic. Office: US Dist Ct 902 Federal Bldg 200 W 2nd St Dayton OH 45402-1430

MERZBACHER, EUGEN, physicist, educator; b. Berlin, Germany, Apr. 9, 1921; came to U.S., 1947, naturalized, 1953; s. Siegfried and Lilli (Wilmersdoerffer) M.; m. Ann Townsend Reid, July 11, 1952; children: Celia, Charles, Matthew, Mary. Licentiate, U. Istanbul, 1943; AM, Harvard U., 1948, PhD, 1950; DSc (hon.), U. N.C., Chapel Hill, 1993. High sch. tchr., Ankara, Turkey, 1943—47; mem. Inst. Advanced Study, Princeton, NJ, 1950—51; vis. asst. prof. Duke U., Chapel Hill, NC, 1951—52; from mem. faculty to prof. physics U. N.C., 1952—91, prof. physics, 1991—. Vis. prof. U. Wash., 1967-68, U. Edinburgh, Scotland, 1986; Arnold Bernhard vis. prof. physics Williams Coll., 1993; vis. rsch. fellow Sci. and Engring. Rsch. Coun., U. Stirling, 1986; chair Internat. Conf. on Physics of Electronic and Atomic Collisions, 1987-89; sr. advisor APS, 1998-99. Author: Quantum Mechanics, 3d edit., 1998; also articles. NSF Sci. Faculty fellow U. Copenhagen, Denmark, 1959-60; recipient Thomas Jefferson award U. N.C., 1972; Humboldt sr. scientist award U. Frankfurt, Germany, 1976-77. Fellow AAAS, Am. Phys. Soc. (pres. 1990); mem. Am. Assn. Physics Tchrs. (Oersted medal 1992), Sigma Xi. Achievements include research on applications of quantum mechanics to study atoms and nuclei. Home: 1396 Halifax Rd Chapel Hill NC 27514-2724 E-mail: merzbach@physics.unc.edu.

MESA-LAGO, CARMELO, economist, educator; b. Havana, Cuba, Aug. 11, 1934; s. Rogelio M. and Ana Maria (Lago); m. Elena Mesa-Gross, Sept. 3, 1966; children: Elizabeth, Ingrid, Helena. LLB, U. Havana, 1956; LLD, U. Madrid, 1958; MA in Econs., U. Miami, 1965; PhD, Cornell U., 1968. Asst. prof. Cath U. Villanueva, Havana, Cuba, 1956-57, 59-61; rsch. assoc. U. Miami, Fla., 1962-65; asst. prof. U. Pitts., 1968-71, assoc. prof., 1971-76, prof., 1976-81, disting. prof. econs. and L.Am. affairs, 1981-99, disting. prof. emeritus, 1999—; dir. Ctr. L.Am. Studies, 1974-86; prof. Fla. Internat. U., 1999—. Vis. prof. Oxford U., 1977, Mellon vis. prof. Fla. Internat. U., 1995, vis. prof. Inst. Univ. Ortega y Gasset, 1990-91; Bacardi chair U. Miami, 1994; regional advisor Econ. Commn. Latin Am., Santiago, Chile, 1983-84; rsch. assoc. Max-Planck-Inst., Munich, 1991-92, 2002, Free U. Berlin, 1997; cons. in field. Author: Cuba in the 1970's, 1974, 2nd edit. 1978, Social Security in Latin America, 1978, The Economy of Socialist Cuba, 1981 (A.P. Whitaker 1982), The Crisis of Social Security and Health Care: Latin American Experiences and Lessons, 1985, Ascent to Bankruptcy: Financing Social Security in Latin America, 1989, Health Care for the Poor in Latin America and the Caribbean, 1992, Cuba After the Cold War, 1993, Changing Social Security in Latin America, 1994 (Outstanding Book Choice award 1995), Are Economic Reforms Propelling Cuba To the Market?, 1994, Do Options Exist? The Reform of Pensions and Health Care in Latin America, 1999, Market, Socialist and Mixed Economies: Comparative Policy and Performance, 2000; former editor: Yearbook Cuban Studies. Recipient numerous rsch. grants, 1986—, Alexander von Humboldt sr. rsch. prize, 1990-91, 96-97, 2001. Mem. Latin Am. Studies Assn. (pres. 1980), Caribbean Studies Assn. (eec. coun. 1973-74), Am. Econ. Assn., Assn. Comparative Econs., Internat. Assn. Labor Law and Social Security, Coun. on Fgn. Rels. and the Nat. Acad. of Social Ins. Democrat. Roman Catholic.

MESANA, THIERRY G. cardiologist, surgeon; b. Sidi Belabbes, Algeria; parents French citizens; s. Rene and Odile M.; m. Marie-Christine Casoni, Oct. 17, 1980; children: Virginie, Patrick, Laura, Terence. MD, Marseille, France, 1985, D of Med. Physics, 1991. Resident in surgery U. Hosp. Marseille, 1979-85; surgeon Hosp. Latimone, Marseille, 1985-88, assoc. prof. surgery, 1988-91, prof. thoracic and cardiovascular surgery, 1991-99; prof., chief cardiac surgery Hosp. Timone, 1999-2001; prof., chmn. divsn. cardiac surgery U. Ottawa Heart Inst., Ont., Can., 2001—. Dir. rsch. for circulatory assistance Hosp. Timone, Marseille, 1991—, dir. cardiovascular rsch., 1999—; vis. prof. surgery Harvard Med. Sch., Boston, 1996-97; sci. bd. various cos. Contbr. articles to profl. jours. Mem. AAAS, Am. Soc. for Internal Artificial Organs, European Assn. for Cardiothoracic Surgery, French Soc. Cardiothoracic Surgery. Office: U Ottawa Heart Inst 8 Cedar Rd 13385 Ottawa ON Canada U1J6L4 Fax: 33-4-91854140. E-mail: tmesana@ap-hm.fr.

MESAVAGE, RUTH MATILDE, language educator; BS Dance, Juilliard Sch.; MA, Hunter Coll., 1972; MPhil French, Yale U., 1975, PhD French, 1979; cert., Inst. Michelangelo, Florence, Italy, 1980; postgrad., U. Laval, Quebec, Canada, 1985. Tchg. asst. Yale U., 1973—74, 1975—76, instr., 1974, 1975—76; asst. prof. SUNY, Plattsburgh, 1977—79; asst. prof. French Wake Forest U., 1979—81; asst. prof. French and dance Rollins Coll., Winter Park, Fla., 1981—84, assoc. prof. French and dance, 1984—90, prof. French, 1990—, prof. French and dance, 1990—94, dir. Quebec studies, 1986, 1989, 1991, 1993, 1996; assoc. prof. U. Stendhal-Grenoble III, 1993—95. Instr., dir. intermediate French Yale Summer Lang. Inst., 1974, 75; vis. instr. Middlebury Coll., 1976—77, Ecole Francaise d'Ete Middlebury Coll., 1977. Contbr. articles to profl. jours. Fellow fellowship, Yale U., 1971—76; grantee Jack B. Critchfield grant, 1983, Summer grant, Rollins Coll., 1984, Govt. Canada, 1985, Jack B. Critchfield grant, 1986, 1991, 1992, Individual Devel. grant for rsch. on Quebec French, 1992; scholar scholarship, Svcs. Culturels Francais de l'Ambassade de France and Ctrs. Internat. Bus. Edn. and Rsch. San Diego State U. and U. Ill. Mem.: MLA, Southeast Coun. on Canadian Studies (founding mem.), Soc. des Profs. francais en Amerique, Am. Soc. 18th Century Studies, Soc. Internat. d'Etude du Dix-Huitieme Siecle, Assn. for Canadian Studies in the U.S., L'Assn. des litteratures Canadiennes et Quebecoise, Am. Coun. for Quebec Studies, Am. Assn. Tchrs. French, Conseil Internat. d'Etudes Francophones, Soc. Profs. Francais et Francophones d'Amerique. Home: 1620 Temple Dr Winter Park FL 32789-2052 Office: Rollins Coll Fgn Langs Winter Park FL 32789

MESCHER, ROBERT J. technology executive; b. Jan. 14, 1963; AS in Bus. Mgmt., El Camino Coll., Lawndale, Calif., 1993; BS in Acctg., Calif. State U., Dominguez Hills, 1996, MBA, 1998. Sr. acct. Hilton at Walt Disney World, Lake Buena Vista, Fla., 1983—87; asst. controller L.A. Airport Hilton, 1987—89; contr. Pasadena (Calif.) Hilton, 1989—90; CFL and COO Imperial Tech., El Segundo, Calif., 1990—. Treas. region 92 Am. Youth Soccer Orgn., El Segundo, 1996-2000. Office: Imperial Tech 2305 Utah Ave El Segundo CA 90245-4803

MESCHKE, DEBRA JOANN, polymer chemist; b. Elyria, Ohio, Oct. 22, 1952; d. Loren Willis and JoAnne Elizabeth (Meyer) M. BS, U. Cin., 1974; MS, Case Western Res. U., 1976, PhD, 1979. Sr. chemist Union Carbide Corp., South Charleston, W.Va., 1979-82, project scientist, 1982-85, chair research and devel. Exempt Women's Group, 1980-81, chair research and devel. Ctr. Safety Team, 1981-82, coordinator Polymer Methods Course, 1982-83, project scientist Tarrytown, N.Y., 1985-86; sr. prin. research chemist Air Products and Chems. Inc., Allentown, Pa., 1986-88, chmn. waste disposal com., 1986-88; rsch. scientist Union Carbide Corp., South Charleston, W.Va., 1988-95, sr. rsch. scientist, 1995—. Author chpts. in textbooks; patentee in field. Bd. dirs. Overbrook Home Owners Assn., Macungie, Pa., 1987. Case Western Res. U. grad. fellow, 1974-79. Mem. AAAS, Am. Chem. Soc. (Polymer div.), Iota Sigma Pi. Avocations: gardening, reading, automobiles, water sports, skiing. Home: 2022 Parkwood Rd Charleston WV 25314-2244

MESCHKOW, JORDAN M. lawyer; b. Bklyn., Mar. 25, 1957; s. Gerald Meschkow and Florence Y. (Katz) Silverman; m. Susan G. Scher, Aug. 10, 1980; children: Sasha Hayley, Alisha Sadie. BS in Biology, SUNY, Stony Brook, 1979; JD, Chgo. Kent Coll. Law, 1982. Bar: Ariz. 1982, Fla. 1983; registered U.S. Patent and Trademark Office 1983. Assoc. James F. Duffy, Patent Atty., Phoenix, 1982; ptnr. Duffy & Meschkow, 1983-84; sole practice, 1984-92; sr. ptnr. Meschkow & Gresham, P.L.C., 1992—. Frequent talk radio guest and spkr. at seminars on patent, trademark and copyright law. Contbr. article series to profl. jours.; patentee in field. Exec. bd. City of Phoenix Fire Pub. Awareness League, 1996—. Mem. Am. Intellectual Property Law Assn., State Bar Ariz. (intellectual property sect. 1982—), State Bar Fla. Avocations: gardening, motorcycling, bicycling, skating, swimming. Office: 5727 N 7th St Ste 409 Phoenix AZ 85014-5818 E-mail: MG@patentmg.com.

MESCHUTT, DAVID RANDOLPH, historian, curator; b. N.Y.C., May 29, 1955; s. Philip Frederick and Mary Evelyn (Mahanes) M.; m. Sarah Caroline Bevan, July 14, 1990. BA in Journalism, Washington and Lee U., 1977; MA in History Mus. Studies, SUNY, Cooperstown, 1988; postgrad., Attingham Summer Sch., Gt. Britain, 1988, 98, Royal Collection Studies Programme, 2000. Rschr. Thomas Jefferson Meml. Found., Charlottesville, Va., 1977-78, Frick Art Reference Libr., N.Y.C., 1980-86; curator art West Point (N.Y.) Mus./U.S. Mil. Acad., 1988-98; consulting curator N.Y. State Office of Pks., Recreation and Hist. Preservation, Waterford, N.Y., 1999—. Guest curator N.Y. State Hist. Assn., Cooperstown, 1986-87, Brandywine River Mus., Chadds Ford, Pa., 1992, Va. Hist. Soc., Richmond, 1999; cons. Curatorial Office, U.S. Dept. Treasury, Washington, 1988, Albany (N.Y.) Inst. History and Art, 1988. Author: A Bold Experiment: John Henri Isaac Browere's Life Masks of Prominent Americans, 1988; co-author: The Portraits and History Paintings of Alonzo Chappel, 1992; assoc. editor and contbr. Am. Nat. Biography, Oxford U. Press, 1994-99; contbr. articles to profl. jours. Nourse Found. fellow, 1986-87, Nat. Endowment for Arts fellow, 1987, Soc. Colonial Wars fellow, 1988, Andrew W. Mellon fellow Va. Hist. Soc., 1992, Anne S.K. Brown fellow Brown U., 1993, Mayers fellow Huntington Libr. and Art Gallery, 1997. Mem.: Walpole Soc., N.Y. State Hist. Assn., Va. Hist. Soc., Ralph Vaughan Williams Soc., Herbert Howells Soc., Historians Brit. Art, Assn. Historians Am. Art. Methodist. Avocation: music. Office: c/o Glass-Glen Burnie Found 530 Amherst St Winchester VA 22601-3802

MESERVE, JOHN SHACKFORD, II, retirement housing executive; b. Newark, Oct. 5, 1940; s. Julien Hill and Jane (Brydges) M.; m. Mary Ellen Meserve, Mar. 11, 1964; children: Michele Avella, John, Elizabeth. BS in Nautical Sci., Merchant Marine Acad., 1963; MS in Computer Sci., U.S. Naval Postgrad. Sch., 1975. Cert. retirement housing profl. Commd. USN, 1964, advanced through grades to capt.; commanding officer Naval Air Sta., Mayport, Fla., 1987-90; ret.; exec. dir. Beaches C. of C., Jacksonville, Fla., 1990-93, Fleet Landing, Atlantic Beach, 1993—. Mayor/commr. City of Atlantic Beach, 1995—; chmn. bd. Dean's Coun., Coll. of Health, Jacksonville, 1995—; chmn. Mayport (Fla.) Waterfront Partnership, 1996—. Decorated DFC. Mem. Beaches C. of C. (chmn. bd. 1993—), Meninak Club. Republican. Roman Catholic. Avocations: computers, woodworking, jogging. Home: 2126 Beach Ave Atlantic Beach FL 32233-5933 Office: Fleet Landing Retirement Cmty One Fleet Landing Blvd Atlantic Beach FL 32233

MESERVE, MOLLIE ANN, publisher; b. Dallas, Dec. 9, 1944; d. Ralph and Emly (Stewart) Lacey; m. Walter Joseph Meserve, June 18, 1981. BA, U. Tex., Dallas, 1976; MFA, Ind. U., 1981. Pres. Feedback Theatrebooks, 1983—, Prospero Press, Maine, 1992—. Dir. FS Drama award, 1985-87. Co-author, designer, illustrator A Chronological Outline of World Theatre, 1992, The Theatre Lover's Cookbook, 1992, The Musical Theatre Cookbook, 1993, Prospero's Almanac, Vol. I, 1997, co-editor, designer When Conscience Trod the Stage: American Plays of Social Awareness, 1998; co-editor, designer: Fateful Lightning: America's Civil War Plays, 2000, co-editor, designer: Americana Series, Pre-World War I American Plays : The Poor of New York, 2001, co-editor, designer: Nick of the Woods, 2001, co-editor, designer: The Great Divide, 2001, co-editor, designer: The Girl with the Green Eyes, 2001, co-editor, designer: Three Short Plays by William Dean Howells: The Garroters, The Moustrap, The Unexpected Guests, 2001, co-editor, designer, illustrator: Witchcraft, 2001, co-editor, designer, illustrator: Superstition, 2001, co-editor, designer, illustrator: The Octoroon , 2002, co-editor, designer, illustrator: The Mulligan Guard Ball, 2002, co-editor, designer, illustrator: The Easiest Way, 2002, co-editor, designer, illustrator: A Texas Steer, 2002, co-editor, designer, illustrator: The Ocotoroon, 2002; editor: The Playwright's Companion, 1985—99; co-editor, illustrator: Americana Series edit.: The Contrast , 1996, co-editor, illustrator: He and She, 2001; co-author: Aspirations, Challenges, and Accomplishments: America's Literary Dramatists of the 1850s , The Journal of American Drama and Theatre, 2001. Recipient Open Cir. Playwright award Goucher Coll., 1977, Biennial Promising Playwright award Colonial Players, 1977, Playwright Contest award Country Playhouse, 1984, Winning Work-in-Progress award Nat. Playwrights Showcase, 1988. Avocations: reading, writing, gardening, cooking, home design. Office: Feedback Theatrebooks PO Box 220 Brooklin ME 04616

MESERVE, WALTER JOSEPH, drama studies writer, publisher; b. Portland, Maine, Mar. 10, 1923; s. Walter Joseph and Bessie Adelia (Bailey) M.; m. Mollie Ann Lacey, June 18, 1981; children by previous marriage— Gayle Ellen, Peter Haynes, Jo Alison, David Bryan Student, Portland Jr. Coll., 1941-42; AB, Bates Coll., Lewiston, Maine, 1947; MA, Boston U., 1948; PhD, U. Wash., 1952. From instr. to prof. U. Kans., Lawrence, 1951-68; prof. dramatic lit. and theory Ind. U., Bloomington, 1968-88, assoc. dean rsch. and grad. devel., 1980-83, dir. Inst. for Am. Theatre Studies, 1983-88; disting. prof. grad. ctr. CUNY, N.Y.C., 1988-93, disting. prof. emeritus, 1993—. V.p. Feedback Svcs., N.Y.C., 1983— Author: An Outline History of American Drama, 1965, rev. edit., 1994, Robert Sherwood, 1970, An Emerging Entertainment, 1977, Heralds of Promise, 1986, A Chronological Outline of World Theatre, 1992; co-author: The Revels History of Drama in English, Vol. VIII, 1977; editor: Plays of WD Howells, 1960, On Stage, America! A Selection of Distinctly American Plays, 1996; co-editor: The Poet of New York, 2001, Nick of the Woods, 2001, Three Short Plays by William Dean Howells, 2001, He and She, 2001, The Girls with the Gren Eyes, 2002, A Texas Steer, 2002, The Octovoon, 2002; editor-in-chief Feedback Theatrebooks, 1985—; co-editor: Modern Literature from China, 1974, Modern Drama from Communist China, 1970, American Sateric Comedies, 1969, When Conscience Trod the Stage, 1998, Fateful Lightning, 2000, Americana Series--Pre World War I American Plays, 1995—; founder, co-editor: Jour. Am. Drama and Theatre, 1989-93; compiler: Studies in Death of a Salesman, 1972, American Drama to 1900, 1980; co-compiler: Who's Where in the American Theatre, 1990, 3d edit., 1992; co-author: Musical Theatre Cookbook, 1993, Playhouse America!, 1991, The Theatre Lover's Cookbook, 1992, Prospero's Almanac, Vol. I, 1994; adv. bd. College Literature, 1990-95. Reader Guggenheim Found., 1988-2000. With AC, U.S. Army, 1943-46 Fellow NEH, 1974-75, 83-84, 88-89, Rockefeller Found., 1979, Guggenheim Found., 1984-85 Mem. Cosmos Club (Washington), Algonquin Club (Boston).

MESERVE, WILLIAM GEORGE, lawyer; b. Medford, Mass., June 14, 1940; s. Robert William and Gladys Evangeline (Swenson) M.; m. Susan Mary Rycroft, Oct. 21, 1967; children: Daniel Scott, Susan Elizabeth, Jonathan Robert. BA, Tufts U., 1962; LLB, Harvard U., 1965; MSc, London Sch. Econs., 1966. Bar: Mass. 1966, U.S. Dist Ct. Mass. 1970, U.S. Ct. Appeals (1st cir.) 1973. Legal asst. to commr. FTC, Washington, 1966-67; staff counsel com. on commerce U.S. Senate, 1967-69; assoc. Ropes & Gray, Boston, 1970-76, ptnr., 1976—. Geology field asst. McMurdo Sound, Antarctica, 1959-60, Inglefield Land, Greenland, summer 1965. Bd. visitors Fletcher Sch. Law and Diplomacy, Tufts U., Medford, 1971—; trustee Tufts U., 1979-97, AFS Intercultural Programs Inc., N.Y.C., 1979-92, 93-96, New Eng. Med. Ctr., Inc., Boston, 1988-97, Lifespan of Mass., Inc., 1997—; bd. dirs. United South End Settlements, Boston, 1979—, Earthwatch Expdns., Inc., The Ctr. for Field Rsch., Maynard, 1996—; bd. govs. New Eng. Med. Ctr. Hosps., Boston, 1982-94, 95-97. Fellow Am. Coll. Trial Lawyers; mem. ABA, Boston Bar Assn., Phi Beta Kappa. Clubs: Appalachian Mountain (Boston) (rec. sec. 1977-78). Democrat. Office: Ropes & Gray 1 International Pl Fl 41 Boston MA 02110-2624

MESHACH, JOSEPH ROBERT, music educator; b. Newton, N.J., Oct. 28, 1962; s. Robert Frankin and Ruth Gertrude Meshach; m. Cathy Smith; children: Jennifer Grace. B in Music Edn., Newberry Coll., 1985. Band dir. Barnwell (S.C.) HS, 1985—92, Walterboro (S.C.) HS, 1992—. Choir dir. Bethel Presbyn. Ch., Walterboro, United States, 1994—. Named to All-Am. Hall of Fame Band Honors, Purdue U., 1980; recipient Dist. Achievement award, Am. Legion, 1981. Mem.: S.C. Band Dir.'s Assn. (All-State band chmn. 2001—, so. region band chmn. 1994—98, Outstanding Performance award 1992—2001, Lower State Marching Band Champions 1992—2001, State 4A Marching Band champions 1992, 1993, 1995, 1997), S.C. Music Educators Assn., Music Educators Nat. Conf., Phi Beta Mu, Phi Mu Alpha Sinfonia (Acad. Achievement award 1984). Home: 301 Canal St Walterboro SC 29488 Office: Walterboro High Sch 1379 Bulldog Ave Walterboro SC 29488 Office Fax: 843-538-8151. Personal E-mail: joejoe@lowcountry.com.

MESHBESHER, RONALD I. lawyer; b. Mpls., May 18, 1933; s. Nathan J. and Esther J. (Balman) M.; m. Sandra F. Siegel, June 17, 1956 (div. 1978); children: Betsy F., Wendy S., Stacy J.; m. Kimberly L. Garnaas, May 23, 1988; 1 child, Jolie M. BS in Law, U. Minn., 1955, JD, 1957. Bar: Minn. 1957, U.S. Supreme Ct. 1966. Prosecuting atty. Hennepin County, Mpls., 1958-61; pres. Meshbesher and Spence Ltd., 1961—. Lectr. numerous legal and profl. orgns.; mem. adv. com. on rules of criminal procedure Minn. Supreme Ct., 1971-91; cons. on recodification of criminal procedure code Czech Republic Ministry of Justice, 1994. Author: Trial Handbook for Minnesota Lawyers, 1992; mem. bd. editors Criminal Law Advocacy Reporter; mem. adv. bd. Bur. Nat. Affairs Criminal Practice Manual; contbr. numerous articles to profl. jours. Mem.: ABA, ATLA (bd. govs. 1968—71), Attys. for Criminal Justice, Trial Lawyers for Pub. Justice, Minn. Assn. Criminal Def. Lawyers (pres. 1991—92, Disting. Svc. award 2001), Minn. Trial Lawyers Assn. (pres. 1973—74, Lifetime Achievement award 2001), Nat. Assn. Criminal Def. Lawyers (pres. 1984—85), Am. Acad. Forensic Scis., Am. Bd. Criminal Lawyers (v.p. 1983), Am. Bd. Trial Advs., Am. Coll. Trial Lawyers, Internat. Acad. Trial Lawyers, Minn. Bar Assn. Avocations: biking, photography, travel, flying. Home: 2010 Sugarwood Dr Orono MN 55356-9339 Office: Meshbesher & Spence 1616 Park Ave Minneapolis MN 55404-1695 E-mail: rmeshbesher@meshbesher.com.

MESHEL, HARRY, state senator, political party official; b. Youngstown, Ohio, June 13, 1924; s. Angelo and Rubena (Markakis) Michelakis; children: Barry, Melanie. BSBA, Youngstown Coll., 1949; MS, Columbia U., 1950; LLD (hon.), Ohio U., Youngstown State U., Ohio Coll. Podiatric Medicine; LHD (hon.), Youngstown State U. Exec. asst. to mayor City of Youngstown, Ohio, 1964-68, urban renewal dir. Ohio, 1969; mem. 33d district Ohio Senate, Columbus, 1971-93, Dem. minority leader, 1981-82, 85-90, pres. and majority leader, 1983-84, com. mem. econ. develop., sci. & tech., state & local govt., ways & means, commerce & labor, controlling bd., state employment compensation bd., fin. chmn., 1974-81, rules chmn., 1983-84, com. mem. rules, reference & oversight, 1985-90; state chair Ohio Dem. Party, 1993-95. Real estate broker; adj. prof. polit. sci. Ohio U.; faculty mem. (limited svc.) Youngstown State U.; div. mgr. investment firm; Ohio Senate special com. mem. Task Force on Drug Strategies, Ohio Acad. Sci. Centennial Celebration Commn., Motor Vehicle Inspection & Maintenance Program, Legis. Oversight Com., Ohio Boxing Commn., Correctional Inst. Inspection Com., Ohio Small Bus. & Entrepreneurship Coun., Gov.'s Adv. Coun. Travel & Tourism, Legis. Svc. Commn., Capital Sq. Rev. & Adv. Bd., others. Past pres., past lt. gov. Am. Hellenic Ednl. Prog. Assn. (AHEPA); precinct committeeman Mahoning County Dem. Party, ward captain, mem. exec. com.; campaign mgr. local candidates, county campaign mgr. presdl. candidates; del. Dem. Mid-Term Conv., 1981; founder Great Lakes/N.E. Legis. Coalition; chmn., founder Nat. Dem. State Legis. Leaders Assn.; dir. State Legis. Leaders Found.; state/fed. assembly, mem. communications com. Nat. Conf. State Legis., legis. mgmt. com., govt. opers. com.; chair fiscal affairs com. Midwest Conf. Coun. State Govts., task force on econs. & fiscal affairs; del., exec. com. Dem. Nat. Com.; mem. Dem. Leadership Coun., State Dem. Exec. Com.; exec. com. Assn. State Dem. Chairs; bd. trustees Nat. Hall of Fame for Persons with Disabilities; mem. St. Nicholas Greek Orthodox Ch.; mem. Mill Creek Metro Park Bd. Commrs. With USN, 1943-46. Decorated two Bronze Battle Stars; recipient Dist. Svc. award Office of Pres., Top Legislator award Ohio Union Patrolmen Assn., Dist. Citizen award Med. Coll. Ohio, City of Hope Leadership award, 1993, Legis. Leadership award Ohio Coalition for Edn. of Handicapped Children, Phillips Medal of Pub. Svc., Ohio U., John E. Fogarty award Gov.'s Com. of Employment of Handicapped, Gov.'s award, 1992, U. Cin. Award for Excellence, Lamp of Learning award Ohio Edn. Assn., Black Cultural Soc. award East Liverpool, Mahoning Valley Man of Yr. award, Mahoning Valley Econ. Devel. Corp., Office Holder of Yr. award Truman-Johnson Dem. Women, Best Interest of Children award Fathers of Equal Rights, Founders Day award Circle of Friends Found., Helping Hand award Easter Seal Soc., Honorary Riverboat Captain award Mahoning County Dem. Party, Community Svc. and Special Svcs. awards Eastern Orthodox Men's Soc., Periclean award AHEPA, Academy of Achievement award Nat. AHEPA Ednl. Found., Nat. Svc. Dem. award AHEPA, 1994, Disting. Citizen award Youngstown State U. Alumni Assn., numerous appreciation and recognition awards; recipient Outstanding Legislator awards Ohio Acad. Trial Lawyers, Ohio Assn. Pub. Sch. Employees, Ohio Rehab. Assn., League Ohio Sportsmen; recipient Dist. Svc. awards Youngstown State U., Ohio Edn. Assn., Ohio Union Patrolmen Assn., Ohio Disabled Vets., AFL-CIO Ohio Barbers Union, AFL-CIO Nat. Assn. of Theatre Owners of Ohio; named Guardian of the Menorah, Youngstown B'nai B'rith, Outstanding Dem., Fairfield Dem. Club, 1993; named to Ohio Vets. Hall of Fame. Mem. (life) NAACP, ACLU, AMVETS (Legislator of Yr. 1993), VFW, Am. Legion, Cath. War Vets (Dist. Legislator award), Vet. Boxers Assn. Mercer County, Pa., Trumbull County Boxers' Legends of Leather (Man of Yr. award Hall of Fame), William Holmes McGuffey Hist. Soc., Buckeye Elks Lodge (hon.); mem. Kiwanis Internat., Urban League, Alliance C. of C., Southern Community Jaycees (hon.), Soc. for Preservation of Greek Heritage, Greek Am. Progressive Assn., Pan Cretan Assn., Arms Hist. Mus. Soc., Eagles, Moose, The Stambaugh Pillars.

MESHII, MASAHIRO, materials science educator; b. Amagasaki, Japan, Oct. 6, 1931; came to U.S., 1956; s. Masataro and Kazuyo M.; m. Eiko Kumagai, May 21, 1959; children: Alisa, Erica. BS, Osaka (Japan) U., 1954, MS, 1956; PhD, Northwestern U., 1959. Lectr., rsch. assoc. dept. materials sci. and engring. Northwestern U., Evanston, Ill., 1959-60, asst. prof., assoc. prof., then prof., 1960-88, chmn. dept. materials sci. and engring., 1978-82, John Evans prof., 1988—. Vis. scientist Nat. Rsch. Inst. Metals, Tokyo, 1970-71; NSF summer faculty rsch. participant Argonne (Ill.) Nat. Lab., 1975; guest prof. Osaka U., 1985; Acta/Scripta Metallurgica lectr., 1993-95. Co-editor: Lattice Defects in Quenched Metals, 1965, Martensitic Transformation, 1978, Science of Advanced Materials, 1990; editor: Fatigue and Microstructures, 1979, Mechanical Properties of BCC Metals, 1982; contbr. over 245 articles to tech. publs. and internat. jours. Recipient Founders award Midwest Soc. Electron Microscopists, 1987, Meritorious award for best paper Iron and Steel Soc., 1993; Fulbright grantee, 1956; Japan fellow, 1957. Fellow ASM (Henry Marion Howe medal 1968, Best Acad. Paper award 1994), Japan Soc. Promotion of Sci.; mem. AIME, Metallurgical Soc., Japan Inst. Metals (Achievement award 1972, hon. mem. 2000). Home: 3051 Centennial Ln Highland Park IL 60035-1017 Office: Northwestern U Dept Materials Sci Eng Evanston IL 60208-3108 E-mail: m-meshii@northwestern.edu.

MESHKE, GEORGE LEWIS, drama and humanities educator; b. Yakima, Wash., Oct. 7, 1930; s. George Joseph and Marye Elizabeth (Lopas) M. BA, U. Wash., 1953, MA, 1959, PhD in Drama, 1972. Cert. tchr., Wash. Tchr. English and drama Zillah High Sch., Wash., 1955-58, high sch., Bellevue, 1958-60, Federal Way, 1960-70; dir., actor Old Brewery Theatre, Helena, Mont., 1962-66; prof. drama Yakima Valley C.C., Yakima, 1970-2000, part-time instr., 2001—. Casting dir., dir. summer seminar Laughing Horse Summer Theatre, Ellensburg, Wash., 1989-96, Children's Lit. Inst., 2000; adj. prof. grad. studies Ctrl. Wash. U., Tchr. Exch., London, 1995, People-to People Exch., China, 2000, Mongolia, Manchuria, 2001; lectr. Inquiring Mind series Wash. State Humanities, 1989-91; regional dir. Am. Coll. Theatre Festival, Washington, 1980-86; arts dialogue J.F. Kennedy Ctr., Washington, 1987—; casting dir., actor Hollywood Ind. Prodns.; mem. adv. coun. Kennedy Ctr. Author, producer Towers of Tomorrow, 1985, The Halls of Yesterday-Yakima Hist. drama; appeared in Yakima, Washington, 1998. Regional bd. dirs. Common Cause, Yakima, 1971-73; active Nat. Hist. Soc., Nat. Wilderness Soc., Roosevelt Meml. Found., Wash. State Commn. Humanities, Drama League. With U.S. Army, 1953-55, Austria. Recipient Gold medallion Kennedy Ctr., 1985, Wash. State Humanities medal, 1983, NISAD medallion, 1989, Wash. State Drama award, 1999. Mem. ACLU, Wash. Edn. Assn., N.W. Drama Assn., Am. Edn. Theatre Assn., Am. Fedn. Tchrs., Kennedy Libr., Libr. Congress (assoc.), Phi Delta Kappa. Democrat. Avocations: travel, mountain climbing, skiing, reading. Home: 5 N 42nd Ave Yakima WA 98908-3214 Office: Yakima Valley CC 16th And Nob Hill Blvd Yakima WA 98907

MESHKINPOUR, HOOSHANG, gastroenterologist, educator; b. Tehran, Oct. 10, 1940; came to U.S., 1968; s. Habibolah Meshkinpour and Aghdas Yafa; m. Farzan Naeim, Sept. 23, 1967; children: Marjohn, Azin. MD, Tehran U., 1965. Bd. cert. Am. Bd. Internal Medicine, Am. Bd. Gastroenterology. With U. Calif.-Irvine, Orange, 1979—, prof. medicine, 1989—, assoc. chief for acad. affairs divsn. gastroenterology, 1996—. Author: Mankind Races, 1966, Know Your Child, 1967, From Jerusalem to Jerusalem, 1999; contbr. 71 articles to med. jours., 8 chpts. to books. Office: U Calif Irvine Med Ctr Divsn Gastroenterology 101 The City Dr S Orange CA 92868-3201 E-mail: hmeshkin@uci.edu.

MESHOWSKI, FRANK ROBERT, business consultant; b. Milw., Sept. 10, 1930; s. Frank Louis and Constance (Mockus) M.; m. Olga Skirka, Jan. 26, 1952; children: David, Laurie, Elaine. B. in Marine Engring., N.Y. State Maritime Acad., 1951; BSME, Newark Coll. Engring., 1954. Project mgr. Curtiss Wright, Woodridge, N.J., 1952-59; v.p. sales/mktg. Gulton Industries, Metuchen, 1959-68; sr. v.p. Nytronics, Inc., Alpha, 1968-72; v.p. mktg. Gulf & Western Industries, N.Y.C., 1972-79; pres., chief exec. officer Unicord div. Gulf & Western Industries, Westbury, N.Y., 1979-87; exec. v.p., chief operating officer, dir. OPT Industries, Phillipsburg, N.J., 1987-89. Bus. cons. strategic planning, mktg. and distbn., 1989—. Home and Office: 17 Turnberry Dr Jamesburg NJ 08831 Fax: 732-656-3169.

MESIA, AUGUSTO FAJARDO, pathologist; b. Naga City, Philippines, June 6, 1956; MD, U. of the East, Philippines, 1981. Diplomate Am. Bd. Pathology, Philippine Bd. Pathology. Internist Armed Forces of the Philippines, Philippines, 1981-82; res. to chief res. anatomic and clin. pathology U. Philippines Gen. Hosp., 1983-87; res. anatomic and clin. pathology SUNY Bklyn., 1991-95; fellowship NYU Med. Ctr., 1995-96; attending pathologist Bellevue Hosp. NYU Med. Ctr., N.Y.C., 1996—. Mem. AMA, Internat. Soc. Gynecologic Pathologists, Internat. Acad. Pathologists, Coll. Am. Pathologists. Office: NYU MC 560 1st Ave New York NY 10016-6402

MESKILL, THOMAS J. federal judge; b. New Britain, Conn., Jan. 30, 1928; s. Thomas J. M.; m. Mary T. Grady; children— Maureen Meskill Heneghan, John, Peter, Eileen, Thomas. BS, Trinity Coll., Hartford, Conn., 1950, LL.D., 1972; JD, U. Conn., 1956; postgrad., Sch. Law, NYU; LL.D., U. Bridgeport, 1971, U. New Haven, 1974. Bar: Conn. 1956, Fla. 1957, D.C. 1957, U.S. Ct. Appeals (2d cir.) 1975, U.S. Supreme Ct. 1971. Former mem. firm Meskill, Dorsey, Sledzik and Walsh, New Britain; mem. 90th-91st Congresses 6th Conn. Dist.; gov. Conn., 1971-75; judge U.S. Ct. Appeals (2d cir.), New Britain, Conn., 1975—, chief judge, 1992-93, now sr. judge. Pres. New Britain Council Social Agys.; asst. corp. council City of New Britain, 1960-62, mayor, 1962-64, corp. counsel, 1965-67; mem. Constl. Conv., Hartford, 1965. Served to 1st lt. USAF, 1950-53. Recipient Disting. Svc. award Jr. C. of C., 1964, Jud. Achievement award ATLA, 1983, Learned Hand medal for Excellence in Fed. Juridprudence, Fed. Bar Coun., 1994. Mem. Fla. Bar Assn., Con. Bar Assn. (Henry J. Naruk Jud. award 1994), Hartford County Bar Assn., New Britain Bar Assn., KC. Republican. Office: US Ct Appeals 114 W Main St New Britain CT 06051-4223

MESKILL, VICTOR P. college president, educator; b. Albertson, N.Y., May 9, 1935; s. James Joseph and Ida May (Pfalzer) M.; m. Gail King Heidinger, 1986; children by previous marriage— Susan Ann, Janet Louise, Gary James, Glenn Thomas, Kenneth John, Matthew Adam. BA, Hofstra U., 1961, MA (grad. scholar), 1962; PhD, St. John's U., 1967; postgrad. insts., Ohio State U., 1968; postgrad., Harvard U., 1972, NYU, 1973; DSc (hon.), Samara State Aerospace U., Russia, 1993; LHD (hon.), St. John's U., 1995; DCL (hon.), Moscow Internat. U., Russia, 1996; DCL (hon.), D Ecology/Biosphere (hon.), Coll. Puschino State U., Moscow, 1996; D of Pedagogy (PdD) (hon.), Dowling Coll., 1997; D of Econs. (hon.), U. Istanbul, Turkey, 1997; D of Sci., Yanshan U., Peoples' Republic of China, 1998. Lab. asst., instr. biology Hofstra U., 1960-62; N.Y. State teaching fellow St. John's U., 1962-63; instr. biology Nassau (N.Y.) C.C., 1963-64; tchr. sci. Central H.S. Dist. 2, Floral Park, N.Y., 1963-64; lectr. biology C.W. Post Coll., Greenvale, 1963-64, instr. biology, 1964-67, asst. prof., 1967-68, assoc. prof., 1968-74, assoc. dir. Inst. for Student Problems, supr. student tchrs., 1967-68, asst. dean Coll., dean summer sch., coordinator Admissions Office, coordinator adult and continuing edn. programs, 1968-69; dean adminstrn. C.W. Post Ctr. of L.I. U., 1969-70, v.p.

adminstrn., 1970-77, prof. biology, 1975-77; pres. Dowling Coll., Oakdale, L.I., 1977-2000, pres. emeritus, 2000—. Cons. in edn. and biology; chem. technician, detective Tech. Rsch. Bur., Nassau County Police Dept., 1958-63, mem. sci. adv. com., 1970; mem. adv. coun. Aerospace Edn. Coun. Inc., 1968; trustee, mem. state legis. com. Commn. Ind. Colls. and Univs.; mem. evaluation teams Mid. States Assn., 1971—; mem. higher edn. adv. com. N.Y. State Senate; mem. Nassau-Suffolk Comprehensive Health Planning Coun.; chmn. Internat. and Mediterranean Studies Group Conf. Author book; contbr. articles to profl. jours. Founding mem., vice-chmn. bd. trustees Nassau Higher Edn. Consortium; bd. dirs. Suffolk County coun. Boy Scouts Am.; mem. N.Y. State Energy Rsch. and Devel. Authority, Town of Islip Devel. Commn.; chmn. bd. trustees L.I. Regional Adv. Coun. Higher Edn.; chmn. L.I. Mid Suffolk Bus. Action; bd. dirs. Southside Hosp., N.Y.; v.p. L.I. Forum for Tech.; former commr. Suffolk County Vanderbilt Mus.; mem. Bus. Coun. N.Y.; hon. mem. U. Pau and Pays de l'Adour, Pau, France, 1994; hon. prof. Minjiang U., Fuzhou, Peoples Republic of China, 1994; active mem. Universal Life Keeping Problems Acad., Dept. Justice Russian Fedn., Moscow. Decorated commendatore dell'Ordine al Merito (Italy); NSF rsch. grantee, 1967-69; Named Tchr. of Year, Aesculapius Med. Arts Soc., C.W. Post Coll. of L.I. U., 1967; Disting. Faculty Mem. of Year, C.W. Post Ctr. L.I. U., 1977, Educator of Yr. WLIW Channel 21, 1996, Officier dans l'ordre des Palmes Académiques, 2001; recipient George M. Estabrook award Hofstra U., 1978, Higher Edn. Leadership award Corning Glass Works, 1987, Disting. Leadership award L.I., 1989, Diploma Merito, Garibaldi Inst., Rome, Diploma of Honor, Rsch. Ctr. for Islamic History, Art and Culture, Istanbul, Turkey, Advancement for Commerce and Industry Disting. Svc. award in field of edn., 1997. Mem. AAAS, Coun. Advancement and Support of Edn., Am. Assn. Collegiate Registrars and Admissions Officers, Am. Assn. Higher Edn., Am. Inst. Biol. Scis., Am. Soc. Zoologists, Am. Assn. U. Adminstrs., Commn. on Ind. Colls. and Univs. (trustee), Nat. Assn. Biology Tchrs., Nat. Sci. Tchrs. Assn., Soc. Protozoologists, N.Y. Acad. Scis., Camilo Josè Cela Found. (hon.), Met. Assn. Coll. and Univ. Biologists (founder, mem. steering com.), Bus. Coun. N.Y., Oakdale C. of C. (founding mem., dir.), Russian Soc. Plant Physiologists (corr.), Universal Life Keeping Problems Acad. Moscow, Tsiolkovski Space Acad. Moscow (fgn.), Univ. Club (N.Y.C.), Wings Club (N.Y.C.), Nat. Arts Club (N.Y.C.), L.I. Coun. Fgn. Rels., L.I. Assn. Commerce and Industry (v.p. edn., dir.), Alpha Chi, Kappa Delta Pi, Phi Delta Kappa, Sigma Xi, Beta Beta Beta, Alpha Eta Rho, Delta Mu Delta, Kappa Delta Rho. E-mail: vpmphd@aol.com.

MESLANG, SUSAN WALKER, educational administrator; b. Norfolk, Va., Sept. 15, 1947; d. Stanley Clay and Sybil Bruce (Moore) Walker. BS in Edn., Old Dominion U., 1973, MS in Spl. Edn., 1986. Cert. tchr., Va. Child devel. specialist Norfolk Pub. Sch., 1973-77, tchr. spl. edn., 1979-82, San Diego Pub. Schs., 1977-79; ednl. evaluator Va. Ctr. Psychiatry, Portsmouth, 1983-84; instr. child study, spl. edn. Norfolk, 1990—; dir. CHANCE Program, 1983—; dir. rsch. & grants devel. Darden Coll. Edn. Old Dominion U., 1989—. Cons. Eastern Va. Ctr. Children & Youths, Norfolk, 1993—, Cmty. Mental Health Ctr., Portsmouth, Va., 1993—. Bd. dirs. Va. Zool. Soc., Norfolk, 1990—, Va. Opera Assn., Norfolk, 1995—; mem. Norfolk Democratic com., 1995—, Children's Hosp. King's Downtown Cir., 1994—; dir. Va. Assistive Tech. Southeast Va. Dept. Rhabilitative Svcs., Norfolk, 1992—. Recipient Honor award Norfolk Commn. Persons with Disabilities, 1993, Commendation Va. House, 1994. Mem. Assn. Persons Supported Employment, Regional Grants Collaboration Group, Norfolk Pub. Schs. Spl. Edn. Adv. Com., Hampton Rds. Coalition Persons with Phys. & Sensory Disabilities. Democrat. Methodist. Avocations: tennis, sailing, walking. Office: Old Dominion U Coll Edn 4607 Hampton Blvd Norfolk VA 23508

MESLOH, WARREN HENRY, civil and environmental engineer; b. Deshler, Nebr., Mar. 17, 1949; s. Herbert Frederick and Elna Florence (Petersen) M.; m. Barbara Jane Anderson, Sept. 7, 1969; children: Christopher Troy, Courtney James. BS, U. Kans., 1975; postgrad., Kans. State U., 1976-77. Registered profl. engr. Colo., Kans., Nebr.; cert. expert witness Am. Consulting Engrs. Coun. Project mgr. Wilson & Co. Engrs., Salina, Kans., 1975-80, process design dir., 1980-82; engring. dir. Taranto, Stanton & Tagge, Fort Collins, Colo., 1982-85; pres. The Engring. Co., 1985—. Mem. civil engring. adv. bd. Kans. U., Lawrence, 1982—. Contbg. author (book) Pumping Station Design, 1989, (water pollution control manual) Manual of Practice No. OM-2, 1991, ACEC Certified Exper Witness, 1996; contbr. articles to profl. jours. Cub master Boy Scouts Am., Salina, 1980-81; active Luth. Ch., 1982—; vol. Paralyzed Vets. Orgn., Fort Collins, 1985—; pres. Foothills Green Pool Assn., Fort Collins, 1987-88. Sgt. U.S. Army, 1971-73, Germany. Named Outstanding Engr.-In-Tng. NSPE, 1978. Mem. Am. Pub. Works Assn., Am. Water Works Assn., Water Pollution Control Fedn., Fort Collins Country Club. Republican. Avocations: golf, boating, snow skiing. Office: The Engring Co 2310 E Prospect Rd Fort Collins CO 80525-9770 E-mail: wmesloh@tec-engrs.com.

MESNIAEFF, GREGORY, economist, securities analyst; b. N.Y.C., Jan. 13, 1958; s. Peter G. and Maria A. (Voropajeff) M.; m. Elizabeth Burke, June 18, 1989. BBA Baruch Sch. Bus., CUNY, N.Y.C., 1986; MA in Econs., Trinity Coll., Hartford, 1989. Market rschr. Blair TV, N.Y.C., 1989-90; industry analyst telecomms. Northern Bus. Info./McGraw Hill, 1990-94; assoc. v.p. equity rsch. Wheat First Butcher & Singer, Richmond, Va., 1994-96; sr. v.p. equity rsch. Robinson-Humphrey Co., Atlanta, 1996—2002; mng. dir. PT Capital LLC, N.Y.C., 2002—. Fellow Trinity Coll. Bd. Fellows, Hartford, 1994-96. Recipient All-Star Analyst Telecom. Equipment Wall St. Jour., 1998. Mem. Nat. Assn. Bus. Econs., Comms. Tech. Analysts Assn., Algonquin Club (Boston), N.Y. Athletic Club, Russian Nobility Assn. Am., Nat. Trust for Hist. Preservation, English-Speaking Union, Harlem Yacht Club. Republican. Russian Orthodox. Avocations: skiing, sailing, cycling, historic preservation. Home: PO Box 1021 Sharon CT 06069 Office: PT Capital LLC PO Box 7495 Greenwich CT 06830

MESNIKOFF, ALVIN MURRAY, psychiatry educator; b. Asbury Park, N.J., Dec. 25, 1925; s. Nathan and Rachel (Feinberg) M.; m. Wendy Savin, June 15, 1952; children: Nathaniel, Rachel, Joel, Ann. AB, Rutgers U., 1948; postgrad., Yale U., 1948-49, Stanford U., 1949-50; MD, U. Chgo., 1954; cert. Psychoanalytic medicine, Columbia U., 1962. Diplomate: Am. Bd. Psychiatry and Neurology. Pvt. practice, 1958—; collaborating psychoanalyst Columbia U. Psychoanalytic Ctr. for Tng. and Rsch., N.Y.C., 1962—; dir. Washington Heights Community, N.Y. State Psychiat. Inst., 1965-68; assoc. clin. prof. psychiatry Columbia U. Coll. Physicians and Surgeons, 1958-68; prof. psychiatry SUNY, Bklyn., 1968-81; dir. South Beach Psychiat. Ctr., S.I., N.Y., 1968-75; regional dir. N.Y. State Dept. Mental Health, N.Y.C., 1975-78, dep. commr. research, 1978-81; Marion E. Kenworthy prof. Psychiatry Columbia U. Sch. Social Work, 1981-89; lectr. Union Theol. Sem., N.Y.C., 1989-90. Cons. St. Vincent's Hosp., S.I., 1970-76; attending psychiatrist S.I. Hosp., 1972-76; sr. attending psychiatrist St. Luke's/Roosevelt Hosp. Ctr., N.Y., 1987—; cons. Ford Found., N.Y.C., 1980-81 Contbr. chpts. to books, articles to profl. jours. Bd. dirs. Reality House, 1967-74; mem. task force med. sch. enrollment and physician manpower N.Y. State Bd. Regents, 1973-75; mem. task force on gen. and splty. hosp. care N.Y. State Health Planning Commn., 1973-74. Served with U.S. Army, 1943-45. Grantee Ford Found., 1982 Fellow Am. Psychiat. Assn. (life); mem. Am. Psychoanalytic Assn., Assn. Psychoanalytic Medicine, Am. Friends Tel Aviv U. (chmn. 1974-75), Phi Beta Kappa. Jewish. Office: 360 Central Park W New York NY 10025-6541

MESROBIAN, ARPENA SACHAKLIAN, publisher, editor, consultant; b. Boston; d. Aaron H. and Eliza Sachaklian; m. William J. Mesrobian, June 22, 1940; children: William S.(dec.), Marian Elizabeth (Mrs. Bruce MacCurdy). Student, Armenian Coll. of Beirut, Lebanon, 1937-38; AA, Univ. Coll., Syracuse (N.Y.) U., 1959, BA magna cum laude, 1971; MSsc, Syracuse U., 1993. Editor Syracuse U. Press, 1955-58, exec. editor, 1958-61, asst. dir., 1961-65, acting dir., 1965-66, editor, 1968-85, assoc. dir., 1968-75, dir., 1975-85, 87-88, dir. emeritus, 1985. Dir. workshop on univ. press. pub. U. Malaysia, Kuala Lumpur, 1985; cons. Empire State Coll. Book rev. editor: Armenian Rev., 1967-75; author: (book) Like One Family: The Armenians of Syracuse, 2000; mem. publs. bd. Courier, 1970-94; mem. adv. bd. Armenian Rev., 1981-83; contbr. numerous articles, revs. to profl. jours. Pres. Syracuse chpt. Armenian Relief Soc., 1972-74; sponsor Armenian Assembly, Washington, 1975; mem. mktg. task force Office of Spl. Edn., Dept. Edn., 1979-84, Adminstrn. of Developmental Disabilities, HHS; mem. publs. panel Nat. Endowment for Humanities, Washington; bd. dirs. Syracuse Girls Club, 1982-87; pres. trustees St. John the Bapt. Armenian Apostolic Ch. and Cmty. Ctr., 1991-95. Named Post-Standard Woman of Achievement, 1980; recipient Chancellor's award for disting. service Syracuse U., 1985; Nat. award U.S. sect. World Edn. Fellowship, 1986; N.Y. State Humanities scholar. Mem. Women in Communications, Soc. Armenian Studies (adminstrv. council 1976-78, 85-87, sec. 1978, 85-87), Syracuse U. Library Assocs. (v.p. 1983-88), Am. Univ. Press Services (dir. 1976-77), Armenian Lit. Soc., Armenian Community Center, Assn. Am. Univ. Presses (v.p. 1976-77), UN Assn. (bd. dirs. 1983-88, v.p. 1985), Phi Kappa Phi, Alpha Sigma Lambda. Mem. Armenian Apostolic Ch. (past trustee). Club: Zonta of Syracuse (pres. 1979-80, 1st v.p. 1985-86, dist. historian Dist. 2 Zonta Internat. 1993-96).

MESSA, JOSEPH LOUIS, JR. lawyer; b. Phila., Mar. 24, 1962; s. Joseph Louis and Virginia (Ciaffoni) M. BS, Tulane U., 1984; JD, Temple U., 1988. Bar: Pa. 1988, N.J. 1988, U.S. Dist. Ct. N.J. 1988, U.S. Dist. Ct. (eastern dist.) Pa. 1998, U.S. Ct. Appeals (3d cir.) 1996. Assoc. Duane Morris & Heckscher, Phila., 1988-90; ptnr. Ominsky & Messa, 1990-2000, Messa & Assocs., P.C., Phila., 2001—. Ward leader Rep. Party, Phila. 1985—, city com., 1985—, exec. com., 1985—. Mem. ATLA, ABA, Pa. Trial Lawyers (cons., seminar presenter, liability com.), Phila. Trial Lawyers, N.J. Trial Lawyers, Pa. Bar Assn., N.J. Bar Assn., Phila. Bar Assn., Burlington County Bar Assn., Camden County Bar Assn., Million Dollar Advocates Forum. Roman Catholic. Avocations: physical fitness, bodybuilding, waterskiing, boating, traveling. Office: Messa & Assoc PC 123 S 22nd St Philadelphia PA 19103 E-mail: jlmessajr@aol.com.

MESSAC, ACHILLE, mechanical engineer, aerospace engineer; b. Haiti, Hawaii; m. Paula Messac. BS, MS, PhD in Aerospace Eng., Mass. Inst. Tech., 1986. Assoc. prof. Rensselaer Polytechnic Inst., Troy, NY, 2000—02, Northeastern U., Boston, 1994—2000. Assoc. editor AIAA Jour., Wash., DC, 1999—2002. Assoc. editor AIAA Jour., 1999—2002. Recipient CAREER award, NSF, 1997-2002. Office: Rensselaer Polytechnic Inst 110 8th St -- Mech Eng Dept Troy NY 12180

MESSAM, LEROY ANTHONY, accountant; b. Kingston, Jamaica, West Indies, July 24, 1923; came to U.S., 1951; s. David A. and Irene Beatrice (Patterson) M.; m. Ruby Patricia Jackson, July 25, 1964; children: LeRoy Jr., Andrea, Conrad, Mahalia. BA in Bus. Adminstr., Bryant & Stratton, Boston, 1958; MEd, Cambridge Coll., 1983; DD, Free Anglican Ch. in Am., 1979; DBA, Southland (Lassell) U., Pasadena, Calif., 1986; grad., Harvard U., 1980. CPA; accredited Accreditation Coun. for Accountancy. Prin. Leroy A. Messam, Pub. Acct., Boston, 1962—; bishop St. John's Episcopal Ch., Mattapan, Mass., 1986—. Author: Resource Handbook for Black & Minority Entrepreneurs, 1983; co-author Pub. Adminstrn. of Our Nat. Economy, 1983. Treas. NAACP, Boston, 1962; coord. Boy Scouts Am., Boston, 1984—; del. White House Conf. on Small Bus., Washington, 1986; bd. dirs. Mass. Dept. Social Svcs., Boston, 1987; chmn. Jamaican Hurricane Relief, 1988—. Recipient Community Svcs. award Boston Soc. Vulcans Inc., Black Profl. Fire Fighters, 1989. Fellow Reg. Pub. Accts. of Jamaica (v.p. 1975-76); mem. Nat. Soc. Pub. Accts., Mass. Assn. Pub. Accts., Jamaican Culture Soc. (pres. 1962-73), The Friends of BOAF (sec. 1989—). Republican. Episcopalian. Office: 96 Greenfield Rd Mattapan MA 02126-3203

MESSENGER, GEORGE CLEMENT, engineering executive, consultant; b. Bellows Falls, Vt., July 20, 1930; s. Clement George and Ethel Mildred (Farrar) M.; m. Priscilla Betty Norris, June 19, 1954; children: Michael Todd, Steven Barry, Bonnie Lynn. BS in Physics, Worcester Poly U., 1951; MSEE, U. Pa., 1957; PhD in Engring., Calif. Coast U., 1986. Rsch. scientist Philco Corp., Phila., 1951-59; engring. mgr. Hughes Semicondr., Newport Beach, Calif., 1959-61; divsn. mgr. Transitron Corp., Wakefield, Mass., 1961-63; staff scientist Northrop Corp., Hawthorne, Calif., 1963-68; cons. engr. Las Vegas, Nev., 1968—. Lectr. UCLA, 1969-75; v.p., dir. Am. Inst. Fin., Grafton, Mass., 1970-78; gen. ptnr. Dargon Fund, Anaheim, Calif., 1983—; v.p., tech. dir. Messenger and Assoc., 1987—, registered investment adviser, 1989—. Co-author: The Effects of Radiation on Electronic Systems, 1986, Single Event Phenomena, 1997; contbg. author: Fundamentals of Nuclear Hardening, 1972, Nonvolatile Semiconductor Memory Technology, 1998; contbr. articles to profl. jours.; patentee microwave diode, hardened semicondrs. Recipient Naval Rsch. Lab. Alan Berman award, 1982, Best Paper award HEART Conf., 1983, Spl. Merit award, 1983, Pete Haas award, 1992, Goddard award for outstanding profl. achievement Worcester Poly. Inst., 1996. Fellow IEEE (Merit award 1986); mem. Rsch. Soc. Am., Am. Phys. Soc. Congregationalist. Home and Office: 3111 Bel Air Dr Apt 7F Las Vegas NV 89109-1510 E-mail: gpmessenger@prodigy.net.

MESSENGER, JON CARLETON, government project manager; b. York, Pa., Oct. 20, 1960; s. Charles Henry and Nancy Gross (Hawkins) M.; m. Laura Christine LeGay, Jan. 7, 1984. BS in Pub. Svc., Pa. State U., 1982; MPA, Pa. State U., Middletown, 1985. Mgmt. intern Commonwealth of Pa., Harrisburg, 1984-85; presidential mgmt. intern U.S. Dept. Labor, Washington, 1985-87, project mgr. employment and tng. R&D, 1987-97, team leader employment and tng. R&D, 1998-2000; sr. rschr. Internat. Labor Orgn., Geneva, 2000—. Co-author: (rsch. monographs) Measuring Structural Unemployment, 1987, Self-Employment Programs for Unemployed Workers, 1992; co-editor: Self Employment as a Reemployment Option: Demonstration Results and National Legislation, 1994, Worker Profiling and Reemployment Services Policy Work Group: Final Report and Recommendations, 1999, The Quality of Self-Employment Jobs in the United States, 2000; contbr. chpt. to book. Task force mem. Pub. Svc. Acad., Washington, 1992—. Mem. Am. Soc. Pub. Adminstrn. (bd. dirs. nat. capital chpt. 1991-95, 97-99, chpt. treas. 1998-99, Spl. Recognition award 1991, Presdl. Citation of Merit award 1992, treas. 1998-99), Nat. Young Profls. Forum (nat. chair 1991-92), Presdl. Mgmt. Alumni Group. Presbyterian. Avocations: skiing, skin diving, travel. Home: Rue de Bâle 19 1201 Geneva Switzerland Office: Internat Labor Orgn Route des Morillons 4 1211 Geneva 22 Switzerland Business E-Mail: messenger@ilo.org.

MESSENKOPF, EUGENE JOHN, real estate developer and hotel executive; b. N.Y.C., Jan. 26, 1928; s. John Philip and Helen Bessie (Holden) M.; m. Martha Ann Crane, Jan. 29, 1955; children: Diane, Nancy, Eugene John, Susan. BBA, Iona Coll., 1950; MBA, NYU, 1956. CPA, N.Y. Sec.-treas. KLM Process Co., N.Y.C., 1952-54; acct. Am. Tobacco Co., 1954-56; staff acct. Peat, Marwick & Mitchell, 1956-60; exec. v.p. Donaldson, Lufkin & Jenrette, Inc., 1960-84, pres., chief exec. officer real estate div., 1977-84; pres., chief exec. officer Meridian Investing and Devel. Corp., 1977-84; pvt. practice cons., 1984—. Mem. adv. bd. NYU Real Estate Inst., 1981-85; mem. exec. coun. small scale devel. Urban Land Inst., 1983-90; chmn. Wall St. Tax Com., N.Y.C., 1965-68; bd. dirs. SIA Acctg. Div., N.Y.C., 1965-79. Trustee, chmn. fin. com. Mt. Vernon Hosp., 1982-87. Served as sgt. AUS, 1950-52, Korea. Recipient Brother Loftus award Iona Coll., 1976. Mem. AICPA, N.Y. State Soc. CPAs, Fin. Execs. Inst. Republican. Roman Catholic. Achievements include walking 2000 mile Appalachian Trail, 1987.

MESSENS, MARK RICHARD, entrepreneur; b. Detroit, Jan. 2, 1952; s. Paul Henry and Elizabeth Richard (Sam) M.; m. Lynn Elizabeth Deloney, July 16, 1977; children: Joseph Anthony, Paul Henry II. B in Bus., Southwestern U., 1974, M in Bus., 1976. Credit mgr. Prime Commercial Vendor, Detroit, 1977-79; bus. mgr. Finish Trade Sub-Contractor, 1979-82; corporate mgr. Prime Commercial Contractor, 1982-87; nat. sales mgr. Nuclear Materials Vendor, 1987; sales mgr. Energy Steel & Supply, 1988, nat. sales mgr., 1990; ind. bus. cons. Warren, Mich., 1990—. Chmn. UniMessens Corp., Detroit, 1979—; pres. Lynn Constrn. Mgmt., Detroit, Contractors Assistance Corp., Detroit; dir. John Paul & Assocs., Detroit; mem. U.S. Coun. for Energy Awareness; founder Willow Ln. Svcs. Co., 1991; regional dir. field ops. Ctrl. Intelligence Bur., Langley, Va. Sustaining mem. Nat. Rep. Com., 1986—; crime commr. City of Waren, dir. Warren Police dept. cert. program. Mem. Constrn. P.A.C., Gov.'s Comm. on Bus., C. of C., Constrn. Assn. Mich., Associated Gen. Contractors, Am. Nuclear Soc., Engring. Soc. of Detroit, Intelligence Operatives N.Am., Former Spl. Ops. Group, NATO Intelligence Operatives Group, Savoyard Club of Detroit, Univ. Club Detroit. Avocation: pleasure flying.

MESSER, ANDREA ELYSE, anthropologist, archaeologist, science writer; b. Freeport, N.Y., Apr. 4, 1952; d. Julius and Gloria Rhoda (Epstein) M. BA in Sci. and Culture, Purdue U., 1973; MA in Journalism and Sci. Comm., Boston U., 1976; MS in Anthropology, Pa. State U., 1995, postgrad., 1995—. Reporter Attleboro (Mass.) Sun Chronicle, 1975; tech. editor, writer Bell Labs., Whippany, N.J., 1976-79; editor Freund Pub. Co., Tel Aviv, 1980; pub. info. officer ASME, N.Y.C., 1981-88; sci. and rsch. comm. officer Pa. State U., State College, 1988—. Ad hoc mem. WISE Network, State College, 1994—. Contbr. articles to profl. jours. Mem. AAAS, Nat. Assn. Sci. Writers, Soc. of Am. Archaeology, Am. Geophys. Union, Am. Anthropological Assn. Office: Sci and Rsch Comm 201 Rider House University Park PA 16802 E-mail: aem1@psu.edu.

MESSER, DONALD EDWARD, theological school president, theology educator; b. Kimball, S.D., Mar. 5, 1941; s. George Marcus and Grace E. (Foltz) M.; m. Bonnie Jeanne Nagel, Aug. 30, 1964; children: Christine Marie, Kent Donald. BA cum laude, Dakota Wesleyan U., 1963; M. Divinity magna cum laude, Boston U., 1966, PhD, 1969; LHD (hon.), Dakota Wesleyan U., 1977. Asst. to commr. Mass. Commn. Against Discrimination, Boston, 1968-69; asst. prof. Augustana Coll., Sioux Falls, S.D., 1969-71; assoc. pastor 1st United Meth. Ch., 1969-71; pres. Dakota Wesleyan U., Mitchell, S.D., 1971-81, Iliff Sch. Theology, Denver, 1981-2000, pres. emeritus and prof. practical theology, 2000—. Author: Christian Ethics and Political Action, 1984, Contemporary Images of Christian Ministry, 1989, Send Me? The Intineracy in Crisis, 1991, The Conspiracy of Goodness, 1992, Caught in the Crossfire: Helping Christians Debate Homosexuality, 1994, Calling Church and Seminary Into the 21st Century, 1995, Unity, Liberty, and Charity: Building Bridges Under Icy Waters, 1996, How Shall We Die? Helping Christians Debate Assisted Suicide, 1997, The Befuddled Stork: Helping Persons of Faith Debate Beginning of life Issues, 2000; contbr. articles to Face to Face, The Christian Century, The Christian Ministry. Active Edn. Commn. of U.S., 1973-79; co-chmn. Citizens Commn. Corrections, 1975-76; vice chmn. S.D. Commn. on Humanities, 1979-81. Dempster fellow, 1967-68; Rockefeller fellow, 1968-69. Mem. Soc. Christian Ethics, Am. Acad. Religion, Assn. United Meth. Theol. Schs. (v.p. 1986-91, pres. 1991-92). Democrat. Office: Iliff Sch Theology 2201 S University Blvd Denver CO 80210-4798

MESSER, THOMAS MARIA, museum director; b. Bratislava, Czechoslovakia, Feb. 9, 1920; came to U.S., 1939, naturalized, 1944; s. Richard and Agatha (Albrecht) M.; m. Remedios García Villa, Jan. 10, 1948. Exch. student, Inst. Internat. Edn., 1939; student, Thiel Coll., Greenville, Pa., 1939-41; BA, Boston U., 1942; degree, U. Sorbonne, Paris, 1947; MA, Harvard U., 1951; DFA (hon.), U. Mass., 1962, U. of Arts, Phila., 1988. Dir. Roswell (N.Mex.) Mus., 1949-52, Am. Fedn. Arts, N.Y.C., 1952-56, trustee, 1972—75; prof. Johann Wolfgang Goethe U., Frankfurt, 1997—, hon. prof. Germany, 1998. Dir. Inst. Contemporary Art, Boston, 1957-61, Solomon R. Guggenheim Mus., N.Y.C., 1961-88, Peggy Guggenheim Collection, Venice, Italy, 1980-88, Solomon R. Guggenheim Found., N.Y.C., trustee, 1980-90, dir. emeritus, 1990—; chief curator Schirn Kunsthalle, Frankfurt, 1994-99; adj. prof. Harvard U., 1960, Barnard Coll., 1966, 71; prof. Hochschule für Angewandte Kunst, Vienna, Austria, 1984; pres. Assn. Art Mus. Dirs., 1974-75, hon. mem., 1988—; pres. internat. com. Modern Art Mus., 1976-80, hon. mem., 2000—; trustee Inst. Internat. Edn., 1990-98, hon. mem., 1998—; founding mem. Am. Arts Alliance, Washington, 1978-81; pres. The MacDowell Colony Inc., 1977-78; mem. adv. bd. Palazzo Grassi, Venice, 1986-97; trustee Fontana Found., Milan, 1996—, The Isamu Noguchi Found., N.Y.C. & Tokyo, 1988—; sr. cultural advisor, trustee Am.'s Soc., 1988-96; sr. advisor visual arts Caixa Found., 1991-96; mem. coun. Nat. Gallery, Czech Republic, 1994-99. Author: Edvard Munch, 1973, Vasily Kandinsky, 1997; contbr. to mus. catalogues, art jours. Decorated chevalier Legion d'Honneur, France, 1980, Officier Legion d'Honneur, France, 1989; recipient Goethe medal Fed. Republic Germany; spl. fellow for study in Brussels Belgian-Am. Ednl. Found., 1953; sr. fellow Ctr. Advanced Studies, Wesleyan U., 1966. Mem. Internat. com. for Mus. and Collections Modern Art, Met. Opera (N.Y.C.), Century Assn. (N.Y.C.). Home: 35 Sutton Pl New York NY 10022-2464 Office: 205 E 77th St New York NY 10021-2061 E-mail: tmmesser@aol.com.

MESSERE, FRANK, communications educator; b. Syracuse, N.Y., Oct. 7, 1948; s. Domenic Joseph and Santa (DiBello) M.; m. Nola Jane Heidlebaugh, Mar. 20, 1982; 1 child, Kathryn. BA in English, SUNY, Oswego, 1971, MA, 1976. Gen. mgr. WDWN-FM, Auburn, N.Y., 1973-76; internat. program supervisor Internat. Programs Exch., London, 1976-77; prof. Oswego State U., 1977-85; asst. to Commr. Mimi Dawson FCC, Washington, 1985-86; assoc. prof., chair comm. studies dept. Oswego State U., 1987-90, coord. broadcasting, 1990—. Sr. fellow, cons. Annenberg Washington Program in Comm. Policy, 1992-96; expert panelist Rural Policy Rsch. Inst., Columbia, Mo., 1998—. Co-author: Introduction to the Internet for Electronic Media, 1996, Broadcasting, Cable, The Internet and Beyond, 1999, Pro/con Media, 2002, Modern Radio Production, 2003; dir. (video) How to Prepare Your First Speech, 1987; prodr. (radio) The Plot to Overthrow Christmas, 1977. Bd. dirs. Friends of Pub. Radio, Syracuse, 1987-94. Grantee GTE Found., 1990. Mem. Broadcast Edn. Assn., Nat. Comm. Assn., Phi Delta Kappa. Roman Catholic. Avocations: playing mysteries, music, chess. Home: 285 Cemetery Rd Oswego NY 13126-6045 Office: Oswego State U 2 Lanigan Hall Oswego NY 13126

MESSERI, PETER ALAN, sociologist, educator; b. N.Y.C., Mar. 7, 1950; s. Sidney and Suzanne Messeri; m. Ellen Ruth Musikant, May 7, 1978; children: Jason, Lisa. BS, MIT, 1972; PhD, Columbia U., 1985. City planner Parsons, Brinckerhoff, Quade & Douglas, N.Y.C., 1972-74; staff assoc. Columbia U., 1981-85, asst. prof., 1985-91, assoc. clin. prof., 1991—. Acting dir. evaluation Am. Legacy Found., Washington, 1999—. Mem. APHA, Am. Sociol. Assn. Home: 8 Clonavor Rd West Orange NJ 07052 Office: Columbia U Mailman Sch Pub Health 722 W 168th St New York NY 10032

MESSERLE, JUDITH ROSE, medical librarian, public relations director; b. Litchfield, Ill., Jan. 16, 1943; d. Richard Douglas and Nelrose B. Wilcox; m. Darrell Wayne Messerle, Apr. 26, 1968; children: Kurt Norman, Katherine Lynn. BA in Zoology, So. Ill. U., 1966; MLS, U. Ill., 1967. Cert. med. libr. Libr. St. Joseph's Sch. Nursing, Alton, Ill., 1967-71, dir. med. info. ctr., 1971-76, dir. info. svcs., 1976-79; dir. ednl. resources and cmty. rels. St. Joseph's Hosp., 1979-84; dir. Med. Ctr. Libr. St. Louis U., 1985-88; libr. Francis A. Countway Libr. Harvard Med. Sch. and Boston Med. Libr., 1989—. Cons., 1973—; instr. Lewis and Clark Coll., 1975, Med. Libr. Assn. Bd. dirs. Family Svcs. and Vis. Nurses Assn., Alton, 1976-79. Fellow AAAS, Med. Libr. Assn. (search com. for exec. dir. 1979, dir. 1981-84, pres. 1986-87, legis. task force 1986-90, task force for knowledge and skills 1988-92, nominating com. 1996); mem. OCLC (spl. libr. adv. com. 1994-98), AMA (com. on allied health edn. and accreditation 1991-94), Assn. Acad. Health Sci. Libr. Dirs. (editl. bd. for ann. stats. 1989-94, Region 8 adv. bd. 1992-93, joint legis. task force 1992—, pres. 1993), Am. Med. Informatics Assn. (planning com. 1990, publs. com. 1994-96, ann. mtg. com. 1996-98), Ill. State Libr. Adv. Com., Midwest Health Sci. Libr. Network (div. health sci. coun.), St. Louis Med. Librs., Hosp. Pub. Rels. Soc. St. Louis, Nat. Libr. Medicine (biomed. libr. rev. com. 1988-92). Office: Countway Libr of Medicine 10 Shattuck St Boston MA 02115-6011

MESSERLI, DOUGLAS, writer, publisher; b. Waterloo, Iowa, May 30, 1947; s. John H. and Lorna (Caspers) M.; companion Howard N. Fox. BA in English, U. Md., 1972, MA in English, 1974, PhD in English, 1979. Admissions coord. U. Wis., Madison, 1967-69; asst. head protocol Columbia U., N.Y.C., 1969-70; grad. asst., tchr., coord. interns U. Md., 1973-77; pub. Sun & Moon Press, L.A., 1976—; prof. dept. English Temple U., Phila., 1979-84; dir. The Contemporary Arts Ednl. Project, Inc., 1983—; pub. Green Integer, 1998—. Part-time faculty mem. Calif. Inst. Tech., Pasadena, 1987-89, Otis-Parsons Sch. Arts, L.A., 1989; pub. Green Integer, 1998—. Author: (poetry) Dinner on the Lawn, 1979, Some Distance, 1982, River to Rivet: A Manifesto, 1985, River to Rivet: A Poetic Trilogy, 1985, Maxims from My Mother's Milk/Hymns to Him: A Dialogue, 1988, An Apple, A Day, 1993, After, 1998, primerias palavras, 1999, (drama) Silence All Round Marked: An Historical Play in Hysteria Writ, 1992, (as Kier Peters) The Confirmation, 1993, (fiction/film/poetry) Along Without: A Fiction in Film for Poetry, 1993, The Walls Come True: An Opera for Spoken Voices, 1996, (fiction as Joshua Haigh) Letters from Hanusse, 2000, (poetry) Primeiras palavras, 1999, Bow

Down, 2002; editor: From the Other Side of the Century: A New American Poetry 1960-1990, 1994, The Sun & Moon Guide to Eating Through Literature and Art, 1994, 50: A Celebration of Sun & Moon Classics, 1995, From the Other Side of the Century II: A New American Drama 1960-95, 1998, The PIP Anthology of World Poetry of the 20th Century. Recipient Carey-Thomas award Pubs. Weekly, 1987, Harry Ford Editor's award, 1994, Am. Book award, 1998. Mem. MLA, Am. Booksellers Assn. Office: Sun & Moon Press 6026 Wilshire Blvd Los Angeles CA 90036-3607 E-mail: djmess@greeninyeger.com.

MESSERSCHMIDT, GERALD LEIGH, pharmaceutical industry executive, physician; b. Vancouver, B.C., Can., Feb. 2, 1950; s. George Gus and Joan May (Chapman) M.; children: Jacqueline Diane, Victoria Leigh, Jonathan Leigh. BS, Portland State U., 1972; MD, U. Oreg., Portland, 1976. Diplomate Am. Bd. Internal Medicine, Am. Bd. Med. Oncology, Am. Bd. Hematology. Resident in internal medicine Letterman Army Med. Ctr., San Francisco, 1976-79; fellow in oncology and hematology NIH, Bethesda, Md., 1979-82; head exptl. hematology Nat. Cancer Inst., NIH, 1981-82; dir. bone marrow transplants for Dept. of Def. Wilford Hall Med. Ctr., San Antonio, 1982-88; dir. bone marrow transplants U. Mich. Med. Ctr., Ann Arbor, 1988-90; dir. med. affairs Ciba-Geigy Pharm., Summit, N.J., 1990-92, exec. dir. med. affairs, 1992-93; v.p. med. and regulatory affairs DNX Corp., Princeton, 1993-94; corp. v.p. C.R. Bard Inc., Murray Hill, 1994-95, sr. v.p., 1995-96; CEO, pres. Kimeragen, Inc., Newtown, Pa., 1996-2000; exec. chmn. Wild-Type Enterprises Worldwide, 2000—. Maj. USAF, 1982-88. Fellow ACP; mem. Am. Soc. Med. Oncology, Am. Soc. Hematology. Office: Wild-Type Worldwide LLC 270 Curwen Rd Bryn Mawr PA 19010-1617 Fax: (610) 527-4857. E-mail: gmesserschmidt@wild-type.net.

MESSERSMITH, LANNY DEE, lawyer; b. Laverne, Okla., Oct. 3, 1942; s. Harry D. and Vivian D. (Bowers) M.; m. Christine Diane Smith, Sept. 28, 1974; 1 child, Nicholas Ryan. BA, U. N.Mex., 1966, JD, 1969; DCL (hon.), Holy Cath. Apostolic Ch., 1975. Bar: N.Mex. 1969, U.S. Ct. Claims 1978, U.S. Supreme Ct. 1981. Asst. dist. atty. 1st Dist. State of N.Mex., Santa Fe, 1969-70, asst. atty. gen., 1974-76; assoc. Rhodes & McCallister, Albuquerque, 1970-72; ptnr. McCallister, Messersmith & Wiseman, 1972-74, Lanny D. Messersmith, PA, Albuquerque, 1974-85, Messersmith, Eaton & Keenan, Albuquerque, 1985-89, Schuler, Messersmith, Daley & Lansdowne, Albuquerque, 1989—. Cons., hon. consul Govt. of Fed. Republic of Germany, 1981—. Mem. Albuquerque Com. on Fgn. Rels., 1988—, Sister Cities, 1988—. Mem. N.Mex. Bar Assn. (bd. dirs. internat. com.), Albuquerque Bar Assn., N.Mex. Retail Assn. (pres. 1987), Albuquerque UN Assn. (bd. dirs. 1985), Albuquerque Country Club, Masons (scholarship chmn. Albuquerque chpt. 1984-87), Shriners, Rotary Internat. Avocations: sailing, reading. Home: 7904 Woodridge Dr NE Albuquerque NM 87109-5258 Office: Schuler Messersmith Daly & Lansdowne 4300 San Mateo Blvd NE Ste B380 Albuquerque NM 87110-8401 E-mail: mesersmith@aol.com .

MESSICS, MARK CRAIG, civil engineer; b. Allentown, Pa., June 8, 1960; BSCE, Lehigh U., 1982, MBA, 1987. Profl. engr., Pa. Civil engr. Pa. Dept. Transp., St. Davids, 1982-89; sr. project mgr. Waste Mgmt., Bensalem, Pa., 1989-98; dir. waste mgmt. LFG Energy, 1998—. Mem. ASCE, NSPE. Libertarian. Home: 1117 Grove Dr Orefield PA 18069-9065 Office: Waste Mgmt-Allentown Golden Key Rd Kutztown PA 19530

MESSIER, MARK DOUGLAS, professional hockey player; b. Edmonton, Alta., Can., Jan. 18, 1961; With Indpls. Racers, 1978, Cin. Stingers, 1979, Edmonton Oilers, 1979-91, team capt., 1988-91; with N.Y. Rangers, 1991-1997; center Vancouver Canucks, Vancouver, 1997—2000; with NY Rangers, 2000—. Player NHL All-Star Game, 1982-84, 86, 88-92, 94, Stanley Cup Championship Game, 1984, 85, 87, 88, 90, 94. Recipient Conn Smythe trophy, 1984, Lester B. Pearson award, 1989-90, 91-92, Hart trophy, 1990, 92; named NHL Player of Yr., 1989-90, 91-92; named to Sporting News All-Star Team, 1981-82, 82-83, 89-90, 91-92. Office: New York Rangers 2 Penn Plaza New York NY 10121*

MESSIER, PIERRE, lawyer, manufacturing company executive; b. Montreal, Que., Can., Mar. 3, 1945; s. Lionel and Anita (Caron) M.; m. Ginette Piche, July 11, 1970; 1 child, Mathieu. BA, Coll. St. Viateur, Outremont, Que., 1964; Lic. in Law, U. Montreal, 1968; diploma in adminstrv. scis., Ecole Hautes Etudes Commerciales, Montreal, 1973. Bar: Que. 1969. Assoc. Lemay & Messier, Montreal, 1969-75; v.p., sec. gen. counsel Can. Cement Lafarge, Ltd., 1975-84; v.p., sec. Lafarge Corp., 1983-84; v.p. bus. devel., legal affairs Norsk Hydro Can. Inc., Montreal, 1989-98; lawyer Leduc LeBlanc, 1998-2000; pvt. practice, cons., 2000—. V.p. Que. Bar Svc. Corp.; bd. dirs. Suralform Inc., Que. Bar Found. Pres. Centre Pedagogique Lucien-Guilbault Inc.; v.p. Coll. Jean de Brebeuf, 1991-97; pres. Greenfield Park Bd. Revision, 1973-74; bd. dirs. Societe Progres Rive Sud, Longueuil, Que., 1974-75. Mem. Can. Bar Assn. (pres. young lawyers sect. 1976, nat. exec. 1977-78), Montreal Jr. Bar (treas. 1972), Que. Mfrs. and Exporters Alliance (bd. dirs. 1996-98), St. Denis Club (Montreal), Que. Secs. and Gen. Counsel Assn. (sec. 1998). E-mail: pichemessier@sympatico.ca., pierre.messier@defence.bombardier.com.

MESSINA, JOANN L. court administrator; b. Port Chester, N.Y., Dec. 18, 1956; d. John L. and Marie (Federici) M.; m. Serle Ian Mosoff, 1991; 1 child, Jonna. BA, Union Coll., 1978; MS in Jud. Adminstrn., U. Denver, 1979. Rsch. asst. U.S. Ct. Appeals (2nd cir.), N.Y.C., 1979-80; asst. to clk. appellate divsn. N.J. Superior Ct., Trenton, 1980-83; trial ct. pers. coord. Adminstrv. Office of Cts., 1983-84; asst. trial ct. adminstr. N.J. Superior Ct. Counties of Somerset, Hunterdon and Warren, 1984-90; mng. dir. Sound Shore Indoor Tennis, Port Chester, 1990—. Editor Justice System Jour., 1980. Fellow Inst. Ct. Mgmt.; mem. ABA, NOW, LWV (mem., pres. Greenwich chpt., mem. state chpt.), Am. Judicature Soc., Inst. Jud. Adminstrn. Office: 303 Boston Post Rd Port Chester NY 10573-4701

MESSINA, LORRAINE, comedian, writer; b. Abington, Pa. children: Brian. AAS, Dutchess C.C., Poughkeepsie, N.Y., 1977. Author: (tv show) Tip of the Tongue, 2000, (play) WWW DOT, 2001, (book) Humor is the Best Medicine when you Follow the Instructions on the Label, 2001. Mem. YMCA.

MESSINA, PAUL FRANCIS, education consultant; b. Newport, R.I., Aug. 31, 1962; s. Nunzio Francis and Ilse Ingeborg (Maibaum) M. BS, SUNY, Albany, 1988; MS, Tex. A&M, Texarkana, 1992. Cert. tchr., Tex., La. Instr. math and physics St. Mary's High Sch., Natcitoches, La., 1989-91, Liberty-Eylau High Sch., Texarkana, Tex., 1991-93, chm. dept. sci., 1992-93; preventive medicine officer U.S. Army, 1993-98; edn. cons. Hewlett-Packard Co., Irving, Tex., 1998—. Adj. instr. physics Northwestern State U., Natchitoches, 1989-91; adj. instr. math. Texarkana Coll., 1991-93; mem. Merrill Pub. Physics Adv. Coun., 1990-93; adj. instr. physics Ga. Mil. Coll., 1993-95. With U.S. Army, 1988-89, USAR. Tandy Tech. scholar Tandy Corp., 1992; grantee Eisenhower mini-grant, Liberty-Eylau Ind. Sch. Dist., Texarkana, 1992. Mem. NEA, Tex. State Tchrs. Assn. (bldg. rep.), Am. Assn. Physics Tchrs., Tex. Acad. Sci., Sci. Tchrs. Assn. Tex., Cen. La. Astronomy Soc., U.S. Profl. Tennis Registry, Nat. Tennis Acad. Roman Catholic. Avocations: tennis, computing, music. Office: Hewlett-Packard Co 3301 W Royal Ln Irving TX 75063-6042 Home: 117 1st St Boerne TX 78006-2910

MESSING, ARNOLD PHILIP, lawyer; b. N.Y.C., Sept. 2, 1941; s. Louis Messing and Ruth Aaron; m. Esther S. Buchman, Oct. 1, 1967; 1 child, Noah. BA magna cum laude, NYU, 1962; JD, Yale U., 1965. Bar: N.Y. 1966, Mass. 1976, Pa. 1985, U.S. Dist. Ct. (so. and ea. dists.) N.Y., U.S. Dist. Ct. Mass. 1976, U.S. Ct. Internat. Trade 1977, U.S. Ct. Appeals (1st, 2d, 6th, D.C. and fed. cirs.), U.S. Supreme Ct. 1977, U.S. Tax Ct. 1984. Assoc. Cravath, Swaine & Moore, N.Y.C., 1967-76; ptnr. Gaston & Snow and predecessor firm, Boston, 1976-91, Choate, Hall & Stewart, Boston, 1991—. Bd. dirs. law alumni mentoring program NYU. Bd. dirs. Union Am. Hebrew Congregations; trustee nat. bd. N.E. Coun.; Boston adv. coun. Internat. Refugee Com. Served to sgt. USAFR, 1965-71. Mem. ABA, Boston Bar Assn., Yale Law Sch. Assn. (exec. com.), NYU Alumni Assn. (bd. dirs.) Home: 271 Mill St Newton MA 02460-2438 E-mail: apm@choate.com.

MESSING, CAROL SUE, communications educator; b. Bronx, N.Y. d. Isidore and Esther Florence (Burtoff) Weinberg; m. Sheldon H. Messing; children: Lauren, Robyn. BA, Bklyn. Coll., 1967, MA, 1970. Tchr. N.Y.C. Bd. Edn., 1967-72; prof. lang. arts Northwood U., Midland, Mich., 1973-93, prof., 1993—. Owner Job Match, Midland, 1983-85; cons. Mich. Credit Union League, Saginaw, 1984-87, Nat. Hotel & Restaurant, Midland, 1985-89, Univ. Coll. program, Continuing Edn. program, Northwood U., 1986—, Dow Chem. Employee's Credit Union, 1988—. Author: (anthology) Symbiosis, 1985, rev. edit., 1987, Controlling Communication, 1987, rev. edit., 1993, Creating Effective Team Presentations, 1995; co-author: PRIMIS, 1993. Mem. LWV, Nat Coun. Tchrs. English, Kappa Delta Pi, Delta Mu Delta (advisor). Avocations: reading, sewing. Office: Northwood U 3225 Cook Rd Midland MI 48640-2311

MESSING, DEBRA, actress; b. Bklyn., Aug. 15, 1968; Actor: (films) Walk in the Clouds, 1995, McHale's Navy, 1997, Prey, 1997, Celebrity, 1998, Mothman Prophecies, 2002, Hollywood Ending, 2002; (TV series) Ned and Stacey, 1995, Prey, 1998, Will & Grace, 1998—, numerous TV guest appearances, including Seinfeild, Partners, NYPD Blue, —. Office: c/o Gersh Agy 232 N Canon Dr Beverly Hills CA 90210

MESSING, KAREN, occupational health researcher; b. Springfield, Mass., Feb. 2, 1943; BA, Harvard U., 1963; MSc, McGill U., 1970, PhD in Biology, 1975. Rsch. asst. biochemistry Jewish Gen. Hosp., Montreal, Can., 1970-71; NIH fellow genetics Boyce Thompson Inst. Plant Rsch., 1975-76; prof. ergonomics U. Quebec, Montreal, 1976—, dir. Ctr. Study Biol. Interactions & Environ. Health, 1990-95, 2000—, dir. grad. ergonomics program, 1999-2000. Disting. fellow Que. Coun. for Social Rsch., 1995-97, Can. Inst. Health Rsch., 2001—; invited rschr. Inst. Cancer Montreal, 1983-95, Sweden Nat. Inst. Working Life, 1997-98; mem. bd. dirs. Quebec Sci. & Tech. Mus., 1984-86, Quebec Coun. Social Affairs, 1984-90. Author: One-Eyed Science: Occupational Health and Working Women, 1998, Integrating Gender in Ergonomic Analysis, 1999; editor: Internat. Jour. Health Svcs., Recherches Feministes Salud y Trabajo; co-editor: Women's Health at Work, 1998. Mem. Am. Pub. Health Assn., Assn. Can. Ergonomists. Office: Univ Que at Montreal CP 8888 succursale Centre-ville Montreal QC Canada H3C 3P8 E-mail: messing.karen@uqam.ca.

MESSINGER, BARRY NILES, orthopedist; b. Bridgeport, Conn., Mar. 5, 1952; s. Henry Juda and Beatrice Messinger; m. Geri Lynn Messinger, June 17, 1993; 1 child, Heidi. BS in Biology, Yale U., 1974; MD, U. Conn., 1979, degree orthopedic surgery, 1984. Diplomate Am. Bd. Orthopedic Surgery. Orthopedic surgeon Sports Medicine and Orthopedic Surgery of Manchester, Conn., 1985-95; pvt. practice Manchester, 1996—. Cons. U. Conn. divsn. athletics, Storrs, 1985—, Manchester Road Race, 1993—, World Games Spl. Olympics, New Haven, Conn., 1995; preceptor U. Conn. dept. family practice, Hartford, 1989—; clin. assoc. U. Conn. dept. orthopedic surgery, Farmington, 1985—. Fellow sports medicine Brookline Sports Medicine, 1984-85. Fellow Am. Acad. Orthopedic Surgery; mem. AMA, Conn. State Med. Soc. (med. aspects of sports com. 1989—), Hartford County Med. Assn. Office: 360 Tolland Tpke Ste 3C Manchester CT 06040-1759

MESSINGER, DONALD HATHAWAY, lawyer; b. Lyons, N.Y., July 1, 1943; s. Donald H. and Thelma (Hubbard) M.; m. Sara L. Stock, June 3, 1967; children— Michael David, Robert Stephen, Daniel Mark BA, Colgate U., 1965; JD, Duke U., 1968. Bar: Ohio 1968. Assoc. Thompson Hine LLP, Cleve., 1968-76, ptnr., 1976—, vice chair corp. practice group, 1989-92, ptnr.-in-charge Cleve. office, 1991-96, mem. exec. com., 1996-2000. Sec., bd. dirs. Am. Steel and Wire Corp., 1986-93; bd. dirs. Cedar Fair Mgmt. Co., 1993—. Trustee Community Info.-Vol. Action Ctr., 1981-88, pres. 1981-84; trustee Free Med. Clinic Greater Cleve., 1970—, sec., 1970-82, v.p. 1982-86, 96—; trustee Cleve. Hearing and Speech Ctr., 1980—, v.p. 1984-86, 92-93, pres., 1986-88, 98-2000; trustee U. for Young Ams., 1982-95, sec., 1982-86, pres., 1986-88, chmn. 1991-95; mem. exec. bd. Boy Scouts Am., 1983-88; Leadership Cleve., 1984—; trustee, sec. Bus. Vols. Unltd., 1992—; sec. Buckeye Area Devel. Corp., 1970-90; mem. adv. bd. Greater Cleve. New Stadium. Recipient Community Svc. award Fedn. for Community Planning, 1981-82; named one of Outstanding Young Citizens of Greater Cleve., 1971-75. Mem. ABA, Ohio Bar Assn., Cleve. Bar Assn. (trustee 1975-79, chmn. securities law inst. 1983), Nat. Assn. Bond Lawyers Home: 21550 Shelburne Rd Shaker Heights OH 44122

MESSINGER, MARINA TRABANINO, real estate investor; b. Guatemala, Central America, July 3, 1923; came to U.S., 1953; d. Jose Mariano and Romelita (Barrios) Trabanino; m. Max Oral Messinger, May 31, 1958 (Mar. 1978); children: Katherina, Alex. Student, U. San Carlos, 1948-51, Fac. Economia, 1956. Clk. sec. Ministerio de Economia, Guatemala, 1946-47; acctg. sec. Afiansadora Guatemalteca, 1948-49; with acctg. dept. De Sola Co. Coffee Exp., 1950-53; CPA Watson CPA, San Francisco, 1953-55; with acctg. dept. Arthur J. Fritz Co., 1956, Wilbur Ellis Co., San Francisco, 1957-58; Spanish tchr. Mercy H.S., Bulingame, Calif., 1961-64; real estate investor, 1978—. Pres. Cath. Charities Aux., San Mateo, 1969; active Exch. Students, Guatemala, 1961, San Mateo County, Calif., 1969; sec. Las Cadetes de Cristo, Guatemala, 1944-46. Home: 101 Barroilhet Ave San Mateo CA 94401-3704

MESSINGER, SHELDON L(EOPOLD), law educator; b. Chgo., Aug. 26, 1925; s. Leopold J. and Cornelia (Eichel) M.; m. Mildred Handler, June 30, 1947; children— Adam J., Eli B. PhD in Sociology, UCLA, 1969. Assoc. rsch. sociologist Ctr. Study Law and Soc. U. Calif., Berkeley, 1961-69, rsch. sociologist, 1969-70, prof. criminology, 1970-77, prof. law jurisprudence and social policy program, 1977-88, Elizabeth J. Boalt prof. law, 1988-91, prof. law emeritus, 1991—, prof. grad. sch., 1995-97, vice chmn., 1961-69, acting dean criminology, 1970-71, dean criminology, 1971-75, chmn. program, 1983-87. Author, co-author numerous books, articles. Mem. Coun. U. Calif. Emeriti Assns. (chair-elect 1999-2000, chair 2000-01). Home: 860 Indian Rock Ave Berkeley CA 94707-2051 Office: U Calif Sch Law Boalt Hall Berkeley CA 94720 E-mail: slm@uclink.berkeley.edu.

MESSINGER-RAPPORT, BARBARA J. physician; b. Bronx, N.Y., Oct. 6, 1959; d. Monroe and Esther Messinger; m. Kenneth H. Rapport, Aug. 7, 1983; children: Nathan, Jacob. BS, MIT, 1981; PhD, Case Western Res. U., 1988, MD, 1989. Bd. cert. internal medicine. Internal medicine resident Wilford Hall USAF Med. Ctr., 1989-92; physician Mt. Sinai Med. Ctr., Cleve., 1995-98; physician geriatrics sect. Cleve. Clin. Found., 1998—. Contbr. articles to med. jours., including Mil. Medicine, Jour. Gen. Internal Medicine, Cleve. Clinic Jour. Medicine, Geriatrics, others. Advisor SEGULA, Cleve., 1999—; founder Mended Hearts Club, Dover, Del., 1994. Maj. USAF, 1989-95. Recipient med. vol. award Cleve. Free Clin., 1999. Fellow Am. Coll. Physicians; mem. Biomed. Engring. Soc. Avocations: bicycling, cross-country skiing, tennis. Office: Cleve Clin Found Desk A91 9500 Euclid Ave Cleveland OH 44195-0001

MESSITER, ARTHUR FREDERIC, JR. aerospace engineering educator, researcher; b. Bklyn., Feb. 8, 1930; s. Arthur Frederic and Gertrude (Hunt) M.; m. Elizabeth Belle Rust, June 10, 1961; children: Susan Elizabeth, Stephen James, Paul Joseph, Patricia Anne, John Arthur. B of Engring. Physics, Cornell U., 1952, M of Aerospace Engring., 1953; PhD, Calif. Inst. Tech., 1957. Rsch. engr. Grumman Aircraft Corp., Bethpage, N.Y., 1953-54, Hughes Aircraft Co., Culver City, Calif., 1957-59; rsch. fellow Calif. Inst. Tech., Pasadena, 1959-62; assoc. prof. dept. aerospace engring. U. Mich., Ann Arbor, 1962-69, prof., 1969-97, François-Xavier Bagnoud prof., 1997-98, François-Xavier Bagnoud prof. emeritus, 1998—. Vis. faculty Fed. Inst. Tech., Zurich, 1976, Univ. Coll., London, 1991, Tech. U. Vienna, 1991; cons. NASA, 1990-94. Assoc. editor SIAM Jour. Applied Math., 1970-75; co-editor English translation: Asymptotic Theory of Separated Flows, 1998; contbr. articles to profl. jours. Fellow Am. Phys. Soc., AIAA (assoc.); mem. Am. Helicopter Soc. Roman Catholic. Home: 4671 Sawgrass Dr E Ann Arbor MI 48108-8617 Office: U Mich Dept Aerospace Engring Ann Arbor MI 48109

MESSITTE, PETER JO, judge; b. Washington, July 17, 1941; s. Jesse B. and Edith (Wechsler) M.; m. Susan P. Messitte, Sept. 5, 1965: children: Zachariah, Abigail. BA cum laude, Amherst Coll., 1963; JD, U. Chgo., 1966. Bar: Md. 1969, D.C. 1969, U.S. Ct. Appeals (4th cir.) 1977, U.S. Supreme Ct. 1973, U.S. Ct. Appeals (DC cir.) 1982, U.S. Ct. Appeals (5th cir.) 1983. Assoc. Zuckert, Scoutt & Rasenberger, Washington, 1968-71; solo practice Chevy Chase, Md., 1971-75; mem. Messitte & Rosenberg, P.A., 1975-81; prin. Peter J. Messitte, P.A., 1981-85; assoc. judge Cir. Ct. for Montgomery County Rockville, Md., 1985-93; judge U.S. Dist. Ct. Md., Greenbelt, 1993—. Mem. internat. jud. rels. com. Jud. Conf. U.S. Bd. dirs. Cmty. Psychiat. Clinic, Montgomery County, Md., 1974-85, v.p. 1980-85; Peace Corps vol., Sao Paulo, Brazil, 1966-68; Md. del. Dem. Nat. Conv., N.Y.C., 1980. Recipient teaching citations Fed. Deposit Ins. Corp. Bank Exam. Sch., 1975, 79, Am. Inst. Banking, 1978, Elizabeth Scull award for Outstanding Svc. to Montgomery County, Md., 1993, Spl. citation Divorce Roundtable Montgomery County, 1993, Gran Cruz de Ordem de São José Operário-Brazilian Labor Tribunal, Mato Grosso, 2001, Medalha de Mérito Académico, Academia Paulista de Magistrados, 2002, Contbr. Mental Health Cmty. Psychiat. Clinic, 1986. Fellow: Md. Bar Found. (H. Vernon Eney award for contbn. to adminstrn. of justice 2001); mem.: Jud. Inst. Md. (bd. dirs. 1989—93), Montgomery County Inn of Ct. (pres. 1988—90), Charles Fahy Inn of Ct. (master 1987—88), Fed. Judges Assn. (4th jud. cir.), Am. Law Inst., Montgomery County Bar Assn. (Century of Svc. award 1999), Instituto Paulista de Advogados (hon.), Md. Bar Assn., D.C. Bar Assn., Inter-Am. Bar Assn., FBA, ABA. Jewish. Office: US Courthouse 6500 Cherrywood Ln Greenbelt MD 20770-1249

MESSMER, DONALD JOSEPH, business management educator, marketing consultant; b. St. Louis, July 30, 1936; s. Edgar Louis and Lucille Louise (Straub) Messmer; m. Charlotte Jean Fox; 1 child Angeline Charlotte. BSBA with honors, Washington U., St. Louis, 1969, PhD, 1974. Asst. mgr. M.A. Bell Co., St. Louis, 1956-61; dist. sales exec. U. S. Gypsum Co., 1962-65; br. sales exec. Victor Comptometer Corp., 1965-68; asst. prof. Coll. William and Mary, Williamsburg, Va., 1973-76, assoc. prof., 1976-81, prof., 1981—, J.S. Mack prof., 1982—, dir. exec. MBA program, 1988-91, coord. MBA field studies program, 1998—; pres. The Wessex Group, Ltd., 1979—. Bd dirs Williamsburg Winery, Ltd, Chateau Hotels Ltd; co-founder Sr Execs Resource Corps. Editor (assoc ed): Decision Scis Jour, 1985—88; contbr. articles to profl jours. Bd dirs, treas Community Action Agency, Williamsburg, 1984—91, United Way Greater Williamsburg, 1985—91, pres, 1989. Mem.: Southeastern Decision Scis Inst (pres 1985—86), Am Mkt Asn (Dissertation Award 1974), Decision Scis Inst (mkt coord 1985—86), Rotary (bd dirs 1990—92, 2000—, Pres's Community Serv Award 1999), Beta Gamma Sigma, Alpha Mu Alpha. Republican. Avocations: fishing, golf. Office: Coll William and Mary Grad Sch Bus Williamsburg VA 23185-8795 Personal E-mail: don_messmer@wessexgroup.com. Business E-Mail: don.messmer@business.wm.edu.

MESSMORE, DAVID WILLIAM, construction executive, former psychologist; b. Indpls. s. Max J. and Betty G. (Miller) M.; m. Sondra Renée Bastian, Aug. 22, 1981; children: Kristen Nicole, Eric Christian William David. AB in Social Sci., Calif. State Coll., Long Beach, 1968; PhD in Student Devel., Counseling and Clin. Psychology, Mich. State U., 1972. Lic. class A gen. contractor, Tex., Va.; lic. psychologist, Calif., Mich.; lic. sch. psychologist, Calif.; cert. mediator Supreme Ct. Va. Counselor Okemas (Mich.) Pub. Sch., 1970-72; psychologist Frederick Ctr. Day Hosp., Grand Rapids, Mich., 1972-73, Newport-Mesa Schs., Newport Beach, Calif., 1973-80; commr. Bd. Med. Quality Assurance, State of Calif. Psychol. com., Sacramento, 1980-82; pres. and CEO Bridgewater Constrn., Inc., Chesapeake, Va., 1987-2001. Psychol. counselor Camp Highfields Residential Sch., Onondago, Mich., 1971; cons. The Open Door, Lansing, Mich., 1971-72, Juv. and Domestic Rels. Ct. the Family Ct., State of Va., Chesapeake, 1989-91; pres. Bridgewater Consultation Svcs., Chesapeake, 1989-91; intern Counseling Ctr., Calif. State U., Long Beach, asst. prof. ednl. psychology, 1981; instr. Golden West Coll., Huntington Beach, Calif., 1977-78; advisor, counselor dean of students Mich. State U., 1969-71; pres., CEO Hampton Rds. Multimedia, 1996-98; founding mem., pres. Va. Challenge Inc. (wrestling), 1999—. Author: (manual) The Impact of Divorce on Families, 1989; designer sch. crest Long Beach City Coll., 1965. Active Gt. Bridge Conf. Com., Chesapeake, 1987-91; treas. Paint Your Heart Out, Chesapeake, 1993, Hampton Rds. Rep. Alliance, 1996-97; coach parks and recreation, commr. transp. and safety City of Chesapeake, 1994-96, vice-chmn., 1995-96; fin. com. city com. Rep. Party of Chesapeake, vice-chmn., 1996-97, acting chmn., 1997; treas. Citizens for a Better Chesapeake, 1996-97; v.p. Virginia Challenge. Recipient Cert. of Appreciation Chesapeake Vols. in Youth Svcs., Inc., 1989, Outstanding Svc. award, 1990, Gov.'s award State of Va., 1990. Mem. Nat. Mid. Sch. Sch. Wrestling Champaionship (founding mem., v.p. 2001—), Rotary Internat. (bd. dirs. Chesapeake club 1990-94, Disting. Svc. award 1990) 1988-98, Nat. Youth Sports Coaches Assn., Delta Tau Delta. Avocations: tennis, reading, investments.

MESSNER, HOWARD MYRON, professional association executive; b. Newark, June 10, 1937; s. Elias and Freda (Trachtenberg) M.; m. Aletha Bragg, 1960 (div. 1980); children: Jennifer, Linda, David; m. Melba June Meador, June 22, 1986. BA, Antioch Coll., 1960; MA, U. Mass., 1962. Mgmt. analyst Office Gov., Mass., 1960-61; staff asst. to adminstr. NASA, Washington, 1962-65; mgmt. analyst Bur. Budget, 1965-71; dir. adminstrn. EPA, 1971-75, asst. adminstr. for adminstrn., 1983-87; asst. dir. Congl. Budget Office, 1975-77, Office Mgmt. and Budget, Washington, 1977-83; controller Dept. Energy, 1983; sr. advisor Am. Cons. Engrs. Council, 1987—. Recipient William A. Jump Meml. award, 1971, Presdl. Disting. Exec. award, 1986, Outstanding Pub. Service award Nat. Capital chpt. Am. Soc. Pub. Adminstrn., 1986, Chancellor's medal U. Mass., 1988. Mem. Nat. Acad. Pub. Adminstrn. (trustee), Cosmos Club. Democrat. Jewish. Home: 1683 Justin Dr Gambrills MD 21054-2012

MESSNER, LEONARD VINCENT, optometrist, educator; b. Johnstown, Pa., May 17, 1957; s. Leonard Francis and Julia (Pirich) M.; m. Stephanie Ann Saylor, July 25, 1981; 1 child, Jordan Anastasia. BS, U. Pitts., 1979; OD, Pa. Coll. Optometry, Phila., 1984. Diplomate Neuro-ophthalmic Disorders. Resident in optometry, advanced tng. vitreoretinal and neuro-ophthalmic disorders Eye Inst. Pa. Coll. Optometry, 1985; assoc. prof. optometry Ill. Coll. Optometry, Chgo., 1985—. Mem. ocular disease-trauma com., mem. clin. exam. coun. Nat. Bd. Examiners in Optometry, Bethesda, Md., 1994—; chief of staff Ill. Eye Inst., 1996-97, v.p. patient care svcs., 1998—. Contbr. articles to profl. jours., referee. Fellow Am. Acad. Optometry (neuro-ophthalmic disorders diplomate com.); mem. Am. Optometric Assn., Ill. Optometric Assn., Prentice Soc. Avocations: distance running, golf, baseball. Office: 3241 S Michigan Ave Chicago IL 60616-3849

MESSNER, ROBERT THOMAS, lawyer, banking executive; b. McKeesport, Pa., Mar. 27, 1938; s. Thomas M. and Cecilia Mary (McElhinny) M.; m. Anne Margaret Lux, Dec. 3, 1966; children: Megan Anne, Michael Thomas. AB, Dartmouth Coll., 1960; LL.B., U. Pa., 1963. Bar: Pa. 1965. With firm Rose, Schmidt & Dixon, Pitts., 1965-68; with G.C. Murphy Co., McKeesport, 1968-86, corp. sec., 1974—, gen. counsel, 1975-86, v.p., 1976-86; v.p., gen. counsel, corp. sec. Dollar Bank, Pitts., 1986—. Dir. G.C. Murphy Found. Mem. Point State Park planning com. City of Pitts.; Rep. candidate Pa. Legis., 1966; mem. Mayor's Com. on Fort Duquesne, Pitts.; bd. dirs. McKeesport YMCA, Downtown Pitts. YMCA, Mon-Yough Heritage Found., 1981—83, Braddock's Field Hist. Soc., 1994—; mem. adv. bd. Pa. Human Rels. Commn., 1968—69; mem. fin. adv. bd. Wilkinsburg, Pa., 1988—. 1st lt. U.S. Army, 1963—65. Decorated Commendation medal. Mem. ABA, Pa. Bar Assn. (chmn. corp. law dept. com.), Allegheny County Bar Assn. (coun. on corp., banking and bus. law), Am. Soc. Corp. Secs. (pres. Pitts. regional group, dir.), Am. Mgmt. Assn., Pa. Assn. Savs. Instns. (chmn. legal com. 1989—), Am. Corp. Counsel Assn., Theta Delta Chi. Clubs: Dartmouth Western Pa., Rivers. Home: 1061 Blackridge Rd Pittsburgh PA 15235-2719 Office: Dollar Bank Three Gateway Ctr Pittsburgh PA 15222

MESSNER, THOMAS G. advertising executive, copywriter; b. N.Y.C., Jan. 26, 1944; s. Malcolm V. Messner and Virginia M. Burkard; m. Terry Carol Bonaccolta, Nov. 28, 1971; 1 child, Zachary. Letter carrier U.S. Post Office, N.Y.C., 1965-67; copywriter Occidental Life Calif., L.A., 1967-68; mail boy D'Arcy Advt., N.Y.C., 1968; copywriter BBDO, 1968-69, Doyle Dane Bernbach, N.Y.C., 1969-72; creative dir. Ally and Gargano, 1972-86; founder, ptnr. Messner Vetere Berger Carey Schmetterer, 1986-92; ptnr. Messner Vetere Berger McNamee Schmetterer Euro RSCG, 1992—; founder Grand Old Website Co., 1999. Former prof. Sch. Visual Arts, N.Y.C.; copywriter MCI; bd. dirs., US. bd., internat. bd. Eurol RSCG; founder, pres. The Grand Old Website Co., Rep. Advt. Inc. Copywriter Ronald Reagan 1984 Presdl. campaign Repub. Nat. Com., NY, 1984; copywriter George Bush 1988 presdl. campaign, 1988, Bob Franks Senatorial Campaign, 2000, Andrew O'Rourke for Gov., NY, 1986. Named CLIO Hall of Fame. Mem. Mortons Group,

E-Media Investment Group, Fenway Club. Roman Catholic. Office: Messner Vetere Berger McNamee Schmetterer Euro RSCG 350 Hudson St Fl 7 New York NY 10014-4509 E-mail: tom.messner@mvbms.com.

MESTECHKIN, MIKHAIL MARKOVICH, math physicist; b. Kiev, Russia, June 2, 1932; s. Mark Mikhailovich and Bella Grigorjevna (Greben') M.; m. Liya Semenovna Gutyrya, Apr. 23, 1955; 1 child, Tanya. MS, Odessa State U., 1955; PhD in Math./Physics, Leningrad State U., 1961, ScD in Math./Physics, 1970. Tchr. high and mid. sch. Railway Sta., Yasinovataja, Ukraine, 1955-57; asst. prof. Mordovian State U., Saransk, 1960-65; head theoretical chemistry dept., prof. Inst. Phys. Organic and Coal Chemistry, Donetsk, Ukraine, 1965-96; ret. Author: Density Matrix Method in theory of Molecules, 1977, Spin-Extended Hartree-Fock Method, 1983 (Bronze medal of Soviet Ind. Exhbn. 1990), Hartree-Fock Instability Theory and Molecular Stability, 1986; contbg. author: Density Matrices and density Functionals, 1987, Fullerene Science and Technology, 1997; contbr. 200 articles to profl. jours., including Jour. Phys. Chemistry Ref. Data, others. Mem. World Assn. Theoretical Organic Chemists (diploma Soviet Union br.). Home: Unit 33 12773 Seabreeze Farms Dr San Diego CA 92130-3752 E-mail: mmm3ls@ixpres.com.

MESTEL, MARK DAVID, lawyer; b. May 15, 1951; s. Oscar L. and Katherine (Waldner) M.; m. Linda Antonik, Jan. 6, 1984; children: Brenton V., Spenser Andrew. BA, Northwestern U., 1973; JD, U. Mich., 1976. Bar: Mich. 1976, D.C. 1977, Wash. 1978, U.S. Dist. Ct. (we. dist.) Wash. 1979, U.S. Ct. Appeals (9th cir.) 1984, U.S. Dist. Ct. (ea. dist.) Wash. 1986, U.S. Supreme Ct. 1991; cert. criminal trial specialist Nat. Bd. Trial Advocacy, 1982, 86, 91. Atty. EPA, Washington, 1976-77; pvt. practice, 1977-78, Everett, Wash., 1981-84; staff atty. Snohomish County Pub. Defender, 1978-80, dir., atty., 1980-81; ptnr. Mestel & Muenster, 1984-94; pvt. practice, 1994—. Mem. ATLA, Nat. Assn. Criminal Def. Lawyers, Wash. Trial Lawyers Assn., Wash. Assn. Criminal Def. Lawyers. Office: Mark D Mestel Inc PS 3221 Oakes Ave Everett WA 98201-4407 E-mail: markmestel@bigfoot.com.

MESTER, LORETTA JEAN, economist, educator; b. Balt., Oct. 24, 1958; d. John Clark and Ann (Rugieri) M.; m. George Joseph Mailath, June 2, 1984. BA, Barnard Coll., 1980; MA, Princeton U., 1983, PhD, 1985. Economist Fed. Res. Bank, Phila., 1985-87, sr. economist, 1987-89, sr. economist, rsch. adviser, 1989-91, rsch. officer, economist, 1991-94; asst. v.p., economist Fed. Res. Bank., 1994—. Lectr. fin. U. Pa. Wharton Sch., Phila., 1988-92, adj. asst. prof., 1992—. Assoc. editor Jour. Banking and Fin., 1993—, Jour. Money, Credit and Banking, 1995—, Jour. Fin. Intermediation, 1995—, Jour. Fin. Svcs. Rsch., 1996—; editor Jour. Productivity Analysis, 1995—; contbr. articles to profl. jours. NSF fellowship, 1980-83, Princeton U. fellowship, 1983-84. Mem. Am. Econ. Assn., Am. Fin. Assn., Econometric Soc.

MESTRALLET, GÉRARD, professional society administrator; b. Paris, Apr. 1, 1949; arrived in Belgium, 1991; s. Georges Julien Marie and Paule Andrée Augustine (Besnard) M.; m. Joëlle Emilienne Renée Arcens, Sept. 7, 1974; children: Stephanie, Caroline, Bastien. Grad., Ecole Polytech., Paris, 1968, Ecole Aviation Civile, 1971, Inst. for Study of Politics, Toulouse, France, 1973; postgrad., Ecole Nat. d'Adminstrn., Paris, 1978. Counsellor Minister Transp., Econs., Fins., & Budget, Paris, 1973-84; chargé de mission Suez, 1984-86, dél. adjoint indsl. affairs, 1986-91, dir. gen. adjoint, 1991—; CEO Soc. Gen. de Belgique, Brussels, 1991; chmn., CEO Compagnie de Suez, Paris, 1995-97; CEO, pres. exec. bd. Suez Lyonnaise des Eaux, 1997—. Chmn. bd. Tractebel; mem. chief exec. Hong Kong's Coun. Advisors; mem. European Round Table of Industrialists. Dir. bd. Saint-Gobain, Ecole Polytechnique; mem. supr. bd. AXA, Casino, Crédit Agricole Indosuez, Soc. du Louvre; advisor to Mayor of Shanghai, China. Office: Suez 16 rue de la Ville lEveque 75008 Paris France

MESTRE, OSCAR LUIS, financial consultant; b. Havana, Cuba, Nov. 26, 1959; came to U.S., 1960; s. Oscar Luis and Ana Victoria (Arango) M.; m. Margaret M. Bozak, May 17, 1986; children: Melissa Anne, Victoria Elizabeth, Jessica Margaret. BS and BA, U. Del., 1982; cert. CLU, cert. ChFC, Am. Coll., Bryn Mawr, Pa., 1988. Account exec. Keystone Fin. Group, Bryn Mawr, 1982-87, New Eng. Fin. Group, Radnor, Pa., 1987—; ptnr. in charge of mktg. internat. ins., liason for Latin Am., internat. banking and securities AG Transnat., Ltd., Radnor and Huntington, N.Y., 1991—. Founding mem. Tech. Resource Alliance, 1998. Chmn. U. Del. golf fundraising com., Newark, 1986-92; bd. dirs. Haverford (Pa.) Sch. Alumni Assn., 1988-98, chmn. annual giving campaign, 1993-94, planned giving coun. 1998—; mem. profl. adv. coun. Cedars Med. Ctr., Miami, Fla., 1990-93; vol. St. Monica's Ch., Berwyn, Pa., Am. Heart Assn., Pa. chpt.; U.S. amateur golf contestant, 1999, British amateur golf contestant, 2000, U.S. Mid-amateur golf contestant, 2000. Named to U. Del. Athletic Hall of Fame, 2001; recipient Hon. Mention All Am. award, NCAA Div. I Golf, 1980—81, Top Club award, Penn Mut. Life Ins. Co., Phila., 1982, Ins. Prodn. Recognition award, Clerical Med. Internat., 1992. Mem. Am. Soc. CLUs and ChFCs (cert.), Tech. Resource Alliance (founding), Leaders Assn. New Eng. Fin., Overbrook Golf Club (bd. dirs. 1999—). Avocations: golf, travel, theater, music, family activities. Office: New Eng Fin Group 1255 Drummers Ln Ste 300 Wayne PA 19087-1565

MESTRES, JEAN L. See SULC, JEAN LUENA

MESTRES, RICARDO A., III, motion picture company executive; b. N.Y.C., Jan. 23, 1958; s. Ricardo Angelo Jr. and Ann (Farnsworth) M.; m. Tracy Stewart; children: Alexander Carson, Carrie Ann. AB, Harvard U., 1980. Creative exec. Paramount Pictures, L.A., 1981-82, exec. dir. prodn., 1982-84, v.p. prodn., 1984-85, Walt Disney Pictures, Burbank, Calif., 1985-86, sr. v.p. prodn., 1986-88; pres. prodn. Touchstone Pictures, 1988-89; pres. Hollywood Pictures, 1989-94; co-founder Great Oaks Entertainment, 1995-97; prin. Ricardo Mestres Prodns., Disney Studios, 1997—. Prodr: Jack, 101 Dalmations, Flubber, Home Alone 3, The Visitors, The Hunted. Mem. Acad. Motion Picture Arts and Scis. Office: Ricardo Mestres Prodns 500 S Buena Vista St Burbank CA 91521-0001

MESTRES, RICARDO ANGELO, JR. lawyer; b. N.Y.C., Aug. 12, 1933; s. Ricardo Angelo and Anita (Gwynne) M.; m. Ann Farnsworth, June 18, 1955; children: Laura, Ricardo III, Lynn, Anthony. AB, Princeton U., 1955; LLB, Harvard U., 1961. Bar: N.Y. 1962, U.S. Supreme Ct. 1970. Assoc. Sullivan & Cromwell, N.Y.C., 1961-67, ptnr., 1968-2000, chmn., sr. ptnr., 1995-2000, sr. counsel, 2001—. Trustee Unitarian Ch. All Souls, N.Y.C., 1973-79, 84-87; trustee Phillips Exeter Acad., 1989-99, pres. bd. trustees, 1993-99. Served to lt. USN, 1955-58. Mem.: ABA, Coun. Fgn. Rels., Am. Law Inst., Assn. Bar City N.Y. (corp. law, securities regulation law and state legis. coms.), N.Y. State Bar Assn., Mill Reef Club (Antigua), Links Club, Phi Beta Kappa. Office: Sullivan & Cromwell 125 Broad St Fl 32 New York NY 10004-2498

MESZNIK, JOEL R. investment banker; b. Beirut, Oct. 3, 1945; m. Lynne Gladstein, Mar. 25, 1979; children: Daniel, Jared, Kara. BS, CCNY, 1967; MBA, Columbia U., 1970. Engr. Ebasco Svcs., N.Y.C., 1967-70; banker Citibank, 1970-71, Newhouse Capital, N.Y.C., 1971-72, Matthews & Wright, N.Y.C., 1972-76; mng. dir. Drexel Burnham Lambert, 1976-89; pres. Meseo Ltd., 1990—. Office: 470 Main St Ste 315 Ridgefield CT 06877-4516

METALLO, THOMAS JOSEPH, international studies and political science educator; b. Balt., Sept. 27, 1951; s. Dominick Francis and Betty Jean Metallo; m. Joyce Katherine Metallo, Sept. 18, 1983. AB, Ind. Wesleyan U., 1986; MA in Pub. Policy, Regent U., 1990; PhD in Internat. Studies, U. Miami, 1998. Cons. Microleague Sports Assn., Newark, 1987-88; rsch. asst. Regent U., Virginia Beach, 1989-90; tchr. Virginia Beach Pub. Schs., 1990-91; rsch. analyst N./S. Ctr. U. Miami, Coral Gables, Fla., 1991-95; asst. prof. Oral Roberts U., Tulsa, Okla., 1996-2000, Ind. Wesleyan U., Marion, Ind., 2000—02, coord. fgn. lang. and lit. dept., 2000—02; asst. prof. Lee. U., Cleveland, Tenn., 2002—. Rsch. analyst U.S. News and World Report, 1994; adj. prof. Fla. Internat. U., Miami, 1996; faculty advisor Oral Roberts U., Tulsa, 1996—. Tchr., asst. dir. Youth With A Mission, 1980-86. Bowman Divisional scholar Ind. Wesleyan U., 1987-88, Acad. Merit scholar Regent U., 1988-90, N.S. Ctr. scholar U. Miami, 1991-95. Mem. Am. Polit. Sci. Assn., Latin Am. Studies Assn., Internat. Alliance Christian Polit. Parties and Movements. Presbyterian. Avocations: bird-watching, international travel, calligraphy, running. Home: 190 Shady Hollow Cir SE Cleveland TN 37323 Office: Lee U Cleveland TN 37320

METCALF, AUBREY WADE, psychiatrist; b. L.A., Sept. 3, 1931; s. Irwin Wade and Audrey Lucille (Aubrey) M.; m. Beverly June Meyer; children: Franz Aubrey, Heidi Jan. BA, U. Calif., Berkeley, 1955; MD, U. Calif., San Francisco, 1958. Am. Bd. Psychiatry and Neurology, Am. Bd. Child and Adolescent Psychiatry. Clin. prof. psychiatry U. Calif., San Francisco, 1979. Sr. supervising child and adolescent psychiatrist, U. Calif. San Francisco Med. Sch., 1967—; clin. prof. health and med. scis. U. Calif. Berkeley, 1979-86. Contbr. chpts to books dealing with adolescent devel. and hysteria in children. 1st lt. U.S. Army, 1951-53, Korea. Recipient clin. faculty ann. award, U. Calif. San Francisco Med. Sch., 1991. Fellow (life) Am. Psychiat. Assn., Am. Acad. Child Adolescent Psychiatry (pres. regional orgn. 1999). Home and Office: 1401 Monterey Blvd San Francisco CA 94127-2043 E-mail: aubmet@aol.com.

METCALF, CINDY W. political organization administrator; Former chair Vt. Dem. Party, Montpelier; chief of staff Office of the Lt. Gov., Vt., 2001—. Office: 115 State St., Drawer 33 Montpelier VT 05633*

METCALF, DONALD, biomedical researcher; BSc, U Sydney, Sydney, Australia; MB, BS, U Sydney; MD, U. Sydney. Carden fellow, cancer rsch. Walter & Eliza Hall Inst. Med. Rsch., Victoria, Australia, 1954—, head, cancer rsch. unit, asst. dir., 1965-96; rsch. prof., cancer biology U. Melbourne, Australia, 1986-96; emeritus prof. Walter & Eliza Hall Inst. Med. Rsch., Royal Melbourne Hosp., 1996—. Visiting prof., Australia, Britain, Canada, France, the Netherlands, New Zealand, Switzerland, and U.S. Author of over 600 articles in acad. journals. Recipient Armand Hammer Prize for Cancer Rsch., 1988, Sloan Prize, General Motors Cancer Rsch. Foundation, Albert Lasker Clinical Rsch. Award, 1993, Louisa Gross Horwitz Prize, Columbia U., 1993, Jessie Stevenson Kovalenko Medal Nat. Acad. of Sciences 1994, Gairdner Foundation Internat. Award, 1994. Mem., Royal Soc., 1983— (Wellcome Prize, 1986); foreign assoc. mem., Nat. Acad. Sciences, 1987—; hon. foreign mem., Assn. Amer. Physicians, 1988—. Achievements include being an important contributor to the clinical use of molecules called colony-simulating factors (CSFs), which control the growth and development of blood cells. Office: Royal Melbourne Hosp Hall Inst Med Rsch Melbourne Victoria 3050 Australia E-mail: Metcalf@wehi.edu.au.

METCALF, HOWARD, military officer; b. New Orleans; Student, U. Md. Enlisted U.S. Army, 1969—71, infrantryman 90th Replacement Bn. and 321st Transp. Co. Vietnam, 1970—71, enlisted as legal specialist, 1977, bn. legal NCO 1st Bn., 44th Air Def. Artillery Republic of Korea, NCOIC of claims Ky.; lawyer's asst., NCOIC of adminstrn. sect. and pre-trial sect. 21st Support Command, Germany, instr./developer Co. C, 1st Bn., Troop Brigade Ind.; sr. legal NCO Combined Field Army Korea; 71 D br. mgr. U.S. Army, Falls Church, Va., 1st sgr. Co. A, 369th AG Bn. Ft. Jackson, SC; chief legal NCO 8th US Army, Republic of Korea; sgt. mgr. Judge Advocate Gen.'s Corps, U.S. , Washington, 1998—. Decorated Def. Meritorious Svc. medal, Meritorious Svc. medal with 4 oak leaf clusters, Army Commendation medal with 1 oak leaf cluster, Army Achievement medal with 1 oak leaf cluster, Vietnam Svc. medal, Republic of Vietnam Campaign medal. Office: Office of Judge Advocate General US Army Pentagon Washington DC 20310-1500*

METCALF, JACK, former congressman, retired state senator; b. Marysville, Wash., Nov. 30, 1927; s. John Read and Eunice (Grannis) M.; m. Norma Jean Grant, Oct. 3, 1948; children: Marta Jean, Gayle Marie, Lea Lynn, Beverlee Ann. Student, U. Wash., 1944-45; BA, BEd, Pacific Luth. U., 1951. Tchr. Elma (Wash.) pub. schs., 1951-52, Everett (Wash.) pub. schs., 1952-81; mem. Wash. Ho. of Reps., 1960-64, Wash. Senate, 1966-75, 80-92, U.S. Ho. of Reps. from 2d Wash. dist., 1995-2001. Chmn. environment and natural resources com., 1988-92; mem. domestic & internat. monetary policy, fin. instns. & consumer credit, aviation, surface transp. coms. Hon. chmn. Innocent Property Owners Protection Initiative. Mem. Coun. State Govts., Wash. Edn. Assn. (bd. dirs.), Wash. Assn. Profl. Educators (state v.p. 1979-81, state pres. 1977-79), Nat. Conf. State Legislatures, Western States Recycling Coalition, South Whidbey Kiwanis, Deer Lagoon Grange. Republican. Home: 4693 E Saratoga Rd Langley WA 98260-9694 Office: IPOPI PO Box 3903 Lacey WA 98509*

METCALF, KAREN, foundation executive; b. Reading, Mass., Dec. 12, 1936; d. Albion Edmund and Natalie Viola (Ives) M. AB, Vassar Coll., 1958; MBA, Harvard U., 1968. CFA. Sec. Radio Liberty Com., N.Y.C., 1958-60; rsch. asst. Air Inc., Cambridge, Mass., 1960-64; sys. analyst Keydata Corp., Watertown, 1964-66; customer edn. cons. Interactive Data Corp., N.Y.C., 1968; portfolio mgr. Scudder, Stevens & Clark, 1969-81; v.p. fin. and adminstrn. N.Y. Cmty. Trust, 1981—2002. Episcopalian. Avocations: travel, opera.

METCALF, PAULINE CABOT, architectural historian; b. Providence, Mar. 31, 1939; d. George Pierce Metcalf and Pauline Pumpelly (Cabot) Metcalf Wykeham-Fiennes. BA, Sarah Lawrence Coll., 1960; MS in Hist. Preservation, Columbia U., 1978. Interior decorator Thedlow, Inc., N.Y.C., 1962-65; assoc. ptnr. Richard A. Nelson, Inc., 1966-75; pvt. practice PCM Interiors, 1975—. Cons. for interior restorations and renovations for hist. bldgs.; lectr. in field. Author, editor: Ogden Codman and the Decoration of Houses, 1988. Trustee RISD, Providence, 1989—, Preservation Soc. Newport Co., 1998—; bd. dirs. Victorian Soc. Am., 1984-94, adv. bd., 1995—; bd. dirs. Edith Wharton Restoration, Lenox, Mass., 1984—. Winterthur fellow, 1995-96. Mem. Canterbury Choral Soc., Nat. Soc. Colonial Dames, Decorator's Club, Art Club Providence, Cosmopolitan Club. Avocations: choral singing, gardening, skiing, tennis.

METCALF, ROBERT JOHN ELMER, industrial consultant; b. Glen Ellyn, Ill., June 27, 1919; s. Elmer Simpson and Vida Marie Metcalf; B.S.M.E., U. Pitts., 1947; m. Rosemarie Rusch, Sept. 11, 1947; children: Kathleen, Karen, Patti, Pamela. Asst. staff supr. Westinghouse Electric Co., Buffalo, 1949-52, assoc. engr., 1952-54; assoc. Gemar Assocs., Inc., Greenwich, Conn., 1954-66. v.p., 1966-83; cons., 1983-92 . Served with U.S. Army, 1943-46. Mem. Inst. Mgmt. Cons. (founding). Roman Catholic. Home and Office: 300 Woodette Dr Apt 201 Dunedin FL 34698-1762

METCALF, VIRGIL ALONZO, economics educator; b. Branch, Ark., Jan. 4, 1936; s. Wallace Lance and Luella J. (Yancey) M.; m. Janice Ann Maples, July 2, 1958; children: Deborah Ann, Robert Alan. BS in Gen. Agr., U. Ark., 1958, MS in Agrl. Econs., 1960; Diploma in Econs., U. Copenhagen, 1960; PhD in Agrl. Econs., U. Mo., 1964. Asst. prof. U. Mo., Columbia, 1964-65, asst. to chancellor, 1964-69, assoc. prof., 1965-69, prof., exec. asst. to the chancellor, 1969-71; prof. econs., v.p. adminstrn. Ariz. State U., Tempe, 1971-81, prof. Sch. Agribus. and Natural Resources, 1981-88, prof. internat. bus. Coll. of Bus., 1988—99, prof. emeritus, 2000—. Asst. to the chancellor U. Mo., 1964-69, coord. internat. programs and studies, 1965-69, mem. budget com., 1965-71, chmn., co-chmn. several task forces; cons. Ford Found., Bogota, Colombia, 1966-67; mem. negotiating team U.S. Agy. for Internat. Devel., Mauritania, 1982, cons., Cameroon, 1983, agrl. rsch. specialist, India, 1984, agribus. cons., Guatemala, 1987, 88, asst. dir. Reform Coops. Credit Project, El Salvador, 1987-90; co-dir. USIA univ. linkage grant Cath. U., Bolivia, 1984-89; cons. World Vision Internat., Mozambique, 1989. Contbr. numerous articles to profl. jours. Mem. City of Tempe U. Hayden Butte Project Area Com., 1979; bd. commrs. Columbia Redevel. Authority; mem. workable project com. City of Columbia Housing Authority. Econs. officer USAR, 1963, econ. analyst, 1964-66. Fulbright grantee U. Copenhagen, 1959-60, U. Kiril Metodij, Yugoslavia, 1973. Mem. Am. Assn. Agrl. Economists, Soc. for Internat. Devel., Samaritans (chmn. 1976, bd. dirs. 1976, mem. task force of health svc. bd. trustees 1974, health svc. 1974-78, chmn. program subcom. 1975), Kiwanis, Blue Key, Gamma Sigma Delta, Alpha Zeta, Alpha Tau Alpha. Democrat. Home: 1357 W Crystal Springs Dr Gilbert AZ 85233-6606 E-mail: vametcalf@hotmail.com.

METCALF, WILLIAM EDWARDS, museum curator; b. East Grand Rapids, Mich., Dec. 16, 1947; s. George Ellington and Ruthanne (Schnitzler) M.; m. Margaret Mary Finn, May 21, 1972 (annulled 1984); 1 son, Daniel F.; m. Jane Salinger, Oct. 26, 1991; 1 child, Lydia Qiao Salinger. BA, U. Mich., 1969, MA, 1970, PhD in Classical Studies (Horace H. Rackham prize fellow), 1973. Asst. curator Roman and Byzantine coins Am. Numismatic Soc., N.Y.C., 1973-75, assoc. curator, 1975-78, curator, dep. chief curator, 1978-79, chief curator, 1979-2000, hon. curator, 2000—. Adj. prof. art history and archaeology Columbia U., 1978—, adj. prof. classics, 1998; adj. prof. history, 1993; adj. prof. classics NYU, 1996, 2000-01, Princeton U., 1999, Bryn Mawr U., 2000, Yale U.; curator coins and medals Yale U. Art Gallery, 2002—; vis. prof. classics, NYU, 2001-02. Author: The Cistophori of Hadrian, 1980, The Silver Coinage of Cappadocia, Vespasian-Commodus, 1995; editor: Studies in Early Byzantine Gold Coinage, 1988, America's Gold Coinage, 1990, Mnemata: Papers in Memory of Nancy M. Waggoner, 1991; mem. adv. com. Lexicon Iconographicum Mythologiae Classicae, 1979—; mem. adv. bd. Am. Jour. Archaeology, 1980-97; editor book revs. Am. Jour. Numismatics, 1989-2000; contbr. articles on Roman and Byzantine coinage and revs. to profl. jours. NEA fellow for mus. profls., 1978; mem. Inst. for Advanced Study, 1988-89 Mem. Am. Numismatic Soc. (corr.), Royal Numismatic Soc., Am. Philol. Assn. (subcom. on classical bibliography 1979-89), Archaeol. Inst. Am. (exec. com. N.Y. 1976-80, chmn. numismatics com. 2000--), Columbia U. Seminar on Classical Civilization, Internat. Numismatic Commn. (1st v.p. 1997—). E-mail: william.metcalf@yale.edu.

METCALFE, DARREL SEYMOUR, agronomist, educator; b. Arkansaw, Wis., Aug. 28, 1913; s. Howard Lee and Mabel (De Marce) M.; m. Ellen Lucille Moore, May 16, 1942; children: Dean Darrel, Alan Moore. Tchr. cert., U. Wis. at River Falls, 1931; BS in Agronomy, U. Wis., 1941; MS, Kans. State U., 1942; PhD, Iowa State U., 1950. From instr. to prof. agronomy Iowa State U., 1946-56, asst. dir. student affairs, 1956-58; assoc. dean, dir. resident instrn., asst. dir. agrl. expt. sta., agronomist U. Ariz., Tucson, 1958—, dean, 1978-82, dean emeritus, 1982—. Chmn. resident instrn. sect., div. agr. Nat. Assn. State Univs. and Land Grant Colls., 1958-59; mem. com. edn. agr. and natural resources Nat. Acad. Sci., 1966-70, mem. rev. panel for Egypt, 1980-83, mem. Inst. Internat. Edn. Com., Somalia and Kenya, 1980-82; U.S. rep. OECD Conf. Higher Edn. in Agr., Paris, 1963-65; trustee Consortium for Internat. Devel., 1978-82; mem. AID missions to Brazil, 1962, 64, 66, 69, 71, 72, 73, Sultan Qaboos U. Com., Oman, 1982-86. Co-author: Forages, 4th edit., 1985, Crop Production, rev. edits, 1957, 72, 80. Served with AUS, 1942-46, PTO Named Hon. Alumnus U. Ariz., 1985. Fellow Am. Soc. Agronomy (Agronomic edn. award 1958, Agronomic Svc. award 1980, chmn. student activities sect. 1950-53, edn. div. 1956, editorial bd., tech. editor jour. 1961-65), Nat. Assn. Colls. and Tchrs. Agr. (E.B. Knight award 1967, pres. 1970-71, Disting. Educator award 1980, U. Ariz. Lifetime award), Kiwanis, Sigma Xi, Phi Kappa Phi, Phi Eta Sigma, Gamma Sigma Delta, Alpha Tau Alpha, Delta Theta Sigma, Acacia (medallion of merit 1966). Home: Tucson, Ariz. Died June 19, 2001.

METCALFE, DEAN DARREL, medical research physician; b. Medford, Oreg., June 27, 1944; s. Darrell S. and Lucille E. (Moore) Metcalfe; m. Joan I. Peterson, Dec. 21, 1977; children: Justin, Jonathan, Elisabet. BS, No. Ariz. U., 1966; MS in Microbiology, U. Mich., 1968; MD, U. Tenn., 1972. Medicine residency Univ. Mich. Hosps., Ann Arbor, 1972—74; clin. assoc. NIH, Bethesda, Md., 1974—77; Rheum fellow Harvard Med. Sch. and Hosp., Boston, 1977—79; clin. investigator NIH, Bethesda, 1979—85; head mast cell physiology sect. lab. of clin. investigation Nat. Inst. of Allergy and Infectious Diseases, 1985—93, head allergic diseases sect., 1994—95; chief lab. allergic diseases Nat. Inst. of Allergy and Infectious Diseases NIH, 1995—. Co-dir. Allergy-Immunology Tng. Program NIAID/NIH, Bethesda, 1979—; dir. Am. Bd. Allergy-Immunology, Phila., 1990—. Capt. USPHS, 1979—. Recipient Commendation medal, USPHS, 1985, Outstanding Svc. medal, 1991. Fellow: Am. Rheumatism Assn., Am. Acad. Allergy and Immunology (bd. dirs.); mem.: Assn. Am. Physicians, Am. Soc. for Clin. Investigation, Am. Fedn. Clin. Rsch. Office: NIH NI AID Dir 10 Center Dr Msc 1881 Bldg 10 Bethesda MD 20892-0001*

METCALFE, MURRAY ROBERT, venture capitalist; b. Toronto, Feb. 3, 1954; s. Marvin Earl and Joan Evelyne (Pepper) M.; m. Nancy Therese Lukitsh, Oct. 12, 1985. B Applied Sci., U. Toronto, 1977; MS, Stanford U., 1979, PhD, 1983. Mgmt. cons. McKinsey & Co., N.Y.C., 1983-87; v.p., gen. ptnr. The Sprout Group, Donaldson, Lufkin & Jenrette, Boston, 1987-94; pres. Chandos Tech. Mgmt., 1994-2000; mng. dir. Lee Munder Capital Group, Boston, 2001—. Episcopalian. Home: 52 Robin Rd Weston MA 02493-2437 Office: Lee Munder Capital Group 200 Clarendon St 28th Fl Boston MA 02116

METCALFE, ROBERT DAVIS, III, lawyer; b. Bridgeport, Conn., July 2, 1956; s. Robert Davis Jr. and Barbara Ann (Peaslee) M. BA summa cum laude, U. Conn., 1978, JD, 1981; MA, Trinity Coll., 1982, Am. Mil. U., 1997. Bar: Conn. 1981, U.S. Supreme Ct. 1986, D.C. 1990, Md. 1991. Judge adv. USN, Norfolk, Va., 1982-85; spl. asst. U.S. atty. U.S. Dept. Justice, 1985, trial atty. Washington, 1985—. Instr. ARC, Hartford, Conn., 1976-80; legis. asst. Conn. Gen. Assembly, Hartford, 1977. Served to lt. USN, 1982-85. Mem. Fed. Bar Assn., Conn. Bar Assn., Judge Adv. Assn., Mensa, Phi Beta Kappa. Republican. Roman Catholic. Avocations: martial arts, reading, sailing, trap and skeet shooting, philately.

METCALFE, WALTER LEE, JR. lawyer; b. St. Louis, Dec. 19, 1938; s. Walter Lee and Carol (Crowe) Metcalfe; m. Cynthia Williamson, Aug. 26, 1965; children: Carol, Edward. AB, Washington U., St. Louis, 1960; JD, U. Va., 1964. Bar: Mo. 1964. Ptnr. Armstrong, Teasdale, Kramer & Vaughan, St. Louis, 1964—81; sr. ptnr. Bryan Cave LLP, 1982—, now chmn. Dep. chmn. Fed. Res. Bd. St. Louis; bd. dirs. Washington U., Danforth Found., St. Louis RCGA, Pulitzer Found. for Arts. Mem.: ABA, St. Louis Bar Assn., Mo. Bar Assn., Noonday Club, Bogey Club (pres.). Episcopalian. Home: 26 Upper Ladue Rd Saint Louis MO 63124-1675 Office: Bryan Cave 211 N Broadway 1 Metropolitan Sq Ste 3600 Saint Louis MO 63102-2750

METCHIK, MORTIMER J. retired lawyer; b. N.Y.C. s. Joshua and Jenny Metchik; m. Evelyn Metchik, Aug. 6, 1950; children: Eric Wendell, Judith R. BA, Queens Coll., 1946; LLB, Columbia U., 1948, JD, 1958. Bar: N.Y. 1949. Assoc. Sherman, Citron & Karasik, N.Y.C., 1964-90. Pres. Dem. Club, Oceanside, N.Y., 1963-64. Sgt. USAF, 1943-45, ETO. Mem. Jewish War Vets. Home: 650 Shore Rd Apt 3T Long Beach NY 11561-4673 also: Apt C-2 3205 Portofino Pt Coconut Creek FL 33066

METIVIER, ROBERT EMMETT, retired mayor; b. Panama Canal Zone, Nov. 5, 1934; came to the U.S., 1956; s. William Henry and Loretta Jane (Rooney) M.; m. Carol Ann O'Brien, Aug. 16, 1958; 1 child, Michael E. (dec.). AA, Canal Zone Jr. Coll., 1954; student, U. Md., 1957-58; BS in Bus. Adminstrn., Bryant Coll., 1960. Bd. dirs. Pawtucket (R.I.) Credit Union, 1976-91, treas., mgr., 1977-87, pres., CEO, 1987-91; chmn. R.I. Credit Union League, Providence, 1991; mayor City of Pawtucket, R.I., 1992-98. Past pres. credit Exec. Assn. SNE; bd. mem. Meml. Hosp. Pawtucket, Pawtucket Local Devel. Corp.; rep. of 911 Uniform Emergency Telephone Sys. Adv. Commn. With U.S. Army, 1954-56. Recipient Len Tune award for best managed credit union in U.S., Nat. Credit Union Mgmt. Assn.; inductee Pawtucket Hall of Fame, 1999. Mem. NRI C. of C., To Kalon Club, Panama Canal Soc. Fla., R.I. League of Cities and Towns (pres.). Democrat. Roman Catholic. Home: 300 Parkview Dr Apt 24 Pawtucket RI 02861

METLTZOFF, NANCY JEAN, education educator; b. N.Y.C., Mar. 26, 1952; d. Julian and Judith (Novikoff) M.; children: Kimberly, Adam, Jesse Buckingham. PhD, U. Oreg. Coord. Super Summer Program, Eugene, Oreg., 1989; dir. Starts Program, 1990-91; asst. prof. of edn. Willamette U., Salem, Oreg., 1991-93; coord. grad. program, asst. prof. edn. Pacific U., Eugene, 1994—. Author: (novel) A Sense of Balance, 1978. Mem. Am. Edn. Rsch. Assn., Educators for Social Responsibility. Avocation: dance. Office: Pacific U 40 E Broadway Eugene OR 97401-3135

METRESS, SEAMUS P. anthropology educator, Irish studies researcher; b. Southampton, N.Y., Sept. 25, 1933; s. James Francis and Hilda Irene Metress; m. Eileen Katherine Ryan, Oct. 1974. BS, U. Notre Dame, 1955; MS, Columbia U., 1957; PhD with honors, Ind. U., 1971. Tchr. various schs., N.Y., Mich., 1955-64; prof. anthropology Clarion (Pa.) State Coll., 1966-69, U. Toledo, 1969-71, master tchr., 1991-93, Doermann Presdl. lectr., 1997. Participant profl. meetings. Author: (with C. Kart) Nutrition and Aging: A Review of the Literature, 1979, Nutrition, the Aged, and Society, 1984, (with S. Rogers) Guide to the Use of Library Information Sources in Anthropology, Sociology and the Applied Health Scis., 1979; Listen Irish People, 1979, The Irish-American Experience: A Guide to the Literature, 1981, The Hunger Strike and the Final Struggle, 1983, A Regional Guide to Informational Sources on the Irish in the United States and Canada, 1986, Human Osteology for the Archaeologist, 1989, Dying Colonialism and Irish Nationalism in Conflict, 1992, Outlines in Irish History, 1995, The American Irish and Irish Nationalism: Sociohistorical Introduction, 1995, The Irish in Canada, 1998, The American Irish and the Growth of Development of the Catholic Church, 1998, (with Kart and E. Metress) Aging, Health and Society, 1986, Human Aging and Chronic Disease, 1992, (with K. Annable) The Irish in the Great Lakes Region: A Bibliographic Survey, 1990, (with R. Rajner) The Great Starvation: An Irish Holocaust, 1996, (with D. Johnston) The Irish in America: A Regional Bibliography, 1999; contbr. articles to profl. jours., including Am. Gael, Linkages, Ohio Jour. Chiropractry, Internat. Affairs, Internat. Jour. Health Svcs., Sociol. Abstracts, Quar. Rev. Ideology, Jour. Am. Ethnic History, Nat. Jour. Sociology, Irish People. Pres. Clan Na Gael, Toledo, 1979—. Recipient Irish Freedom award Irish No. Aid. Mem. Am. Anthrop. Assn., Am. Cath. Hist. Soc., Am. Conf. on Irish Studies, Celtic League Internat., Can. Assn. for Irish Studies, Ctr. for Study Am. Catholicism, Cath. Hist. Soc., Immigration History Soc., Cath. Hist. Soc. Phila. Mem. Green Party. Latin Rite Catholic. Avocations: hiking, nature study. Office: U Toledo Bancroft St Toledo OH 43606

METREY, GEORGE DAVID, social work educator, academic administrator; b. Milw., July 23, 1939; s. Richard Joseph and Catherine (Evans) M.; m. Cheryl Ann Mosca, June 21, 1969 (dec. May 2000); 1 child, Mary Beth. AB, Marquette U., 1961; MSW, Fordham U., 1963; PhD, NYU, 1970. Lic. ind. clin. social worker, R.I., N.J. Social worker N.J. Diagnostic Ctr., Edison, 1963-64, asst. social work supr., 1964-66, dir. psychiat. social work, 1966-70; coordinator undergrad. social work program Kean Coll., N.J., 1970-73, assoc. prof. social work, 1970-74, prof., 1974-79, chmn. dept. sociology, anthropology and social work, 1973-77, dir. social work program, acting assoc. dean Sch. Arts and Sci., 1977-79; dean Sch. Social Work, prof. R.I. Coll., Providence, 1979—, ast. v.p. acad. affairs, 2000—02. Field instr. Fordham U. Sch. Social Service, 1966-70, adj. prof., 1969-77; adj. assoc. prof. Rutgers U. Grad. Sch. Social Work, 1972-73 Mem. program com. R.I. affiliate Am. Heart Assn., 1980-90, bd. dirs., 1983-89, chmn. program com., 1985-87, exec. com., 1985-87; sec. bd. dirs. Adoption R.I., 1987-89, pres. bd. dirs., 1989-92. Recipient Fordham U. Grad. Sch. Social Svc. Outstanding Alumni, 1984, Spl. Disting. Svc. award R.I. Coll. Alumni Assn., 1996. Mem. NASW (N.J. Social Worker of Yr. 1977, pres. 1978-80, parliamentarian R.I. 1981—, treas. R.I. chpt. 1986-87, mem. nat. competence cert. commn. 1989-91, nat. 2d v.p. 1978-80, chair nat. program com. 1981-83), Coun. on Social Work Edn. (bd. dirs. 1979-82, mem. commn. on accreditation 1996—), Acad. Cert. Social Workers, Nat. Assn. Deans and Dirs. Schs. Social Work (nominating com. 1993-96, program com. 1993-96), Alpha Phi Omega, Gamma Pi Mu, Alpha Delta Mu (regional v.p.). Roman Catholic. Home: PO Box 206 Wyckoff NJ 07481-0206 Office: RI Coll Sch Social Work Providence RI 02908 E-mail: gmctrey@ric.edu.

METROPOL, HARRY JACK, general and thoracic surgeon; b. Manning, S.C., Nov. 20, 1929; AB, Duke U., 1953, MD, 1956. Diplomate Am. Bd. Surgery, Am. Bd. Thoracic Surgery. Intern Albany Med. Ctr. Hosp., 1956-57; resident N.C. Bapt. Hosp., 1959-64, gen. and thoracic surgeon, 1964—, Richland Meml. Hosp., 1964—, Providence Hosp., 1964—, Lexington Med. Ctr., 1972—; assoc. med. dir. PHP S.C., 1994—; assoc. prof. surgery U. S.C. Mem. Am. Coll. Surgeons, S.C. Med. Assn., S.C. Soc. Surgeons, So. Med. Assn., Columbia Med. Soc. Office: 1333 Taylor St Ste 3 Columbia SC 29201-2947

METROPULOS, MITCHELL JAMES, lawyer; b. Crystal Lake, Ill., Aug. 5, 1960; s. James Peter and Phyllis Ann M.; m. Teri Gail Dahlby, Oct. 29, 1994; children: Sarah, Nicholas, Maxwell. BSc, Bradley U., 1982; JD, MA in Pub. Policy and Adminstrn., U. Wis., 1986. Bar: Wis. 1987, U.S. Dist. Ct. (western dist.) Wis. 1987. Asst. dist. attorney Chippewa County, Chippewa Falls, Wis., 1987-88, Outagamie County, Appleton, 1988—. Big Brother Pals Program Appleton, Wis., 1988-97; mem. Domestic Intervention Program Appleton, 1998, Chippewa Cmty. Restorative Justice Project, Sharon Baby Alliance. Avocations: golf, softball, volleyball. Office: District Attorneys Office 320 S Walnut St Appleton WI 54911-5918

METROS, MARY TERESA, librarian; b. Denver, Nov. 10, 1951; d. James and Wilma Frances (Hanson) M. BA in English, Colo. Women's Coll., 1973; MA in Librarianship, U. Denver, 1974. Adult svcs. libr. Englewood (Colo.) Pub. Libr., 1975-81, adult svcs. mgr., 1983-84; systems cons. Dataphase Systems, Kansas City, Mo., 1981-82; circulation libr. Westminster (Colo.) Pub. Libr., 1983; pub. svcs. supr. Tempe (Ariz.) Pub. Libr., 1984-90, libr. dir., 1990—. Librarian; b. Denver, Nov. 10, 1951; d. James and Wilma Frances (Hanson) M. BA in English, Colo. Women's Coll., 1973; MA in Librarianship, U. Denver, 1974. Adult svcs. libr. Englewood (Colo.) Pub. Libr., 1975-81, adult svcs. mgr., 1983-84; libr. systems cons. Dataphase Systems, Kansas City, Mo., 1981-82; circulation libra. Westminster (Colo.) Pub. Libr. 1983. Mem. ALA, Pub. Libr. Assn., Ariz. Libr. Assn., Libr. Adminstrn. and Mgmt. Assn. Democrat. Office: Tempe Pub Libr 3500 S Rural Rd Tempe AZ 85282-5405

METS, LISA ANN, academic administrator; b. Lapeer, Mich., Feb. 24, 1954; d. Harald and Meeta Alexandra (Linnas) M. BA, U. Mich., 1976, postgrad., 1984-87, 90-97; MA, Ind. U., 1978. Asst. prof. Vincennes (Ind.) U., 1979-83, dept. chair, 1981-85, assoc. prof., 1983-85; sr. asst. to v.p. adminstrn. and planning Northwestern U., Evanston, Ill., 1987-90; assoc. dir. Ctr. for Rsch. on Learning and Tchg., U. Mich., 1995—. Co-editor: Key Resources on Higher Education Governance, Management, and Leadership, 1987, (monograph) Improving Teaching and Learning through Research, 1988, (monograph) Using Academic Program Review, 1995, Planning and Management for a Changing Environment, 1997; editor News from SCUP, 1988-91; contbr. chpt. to book. Mem. Am. Assn. for Higher Edn., Assn. for the Study Higher Edn., Assn. for Instnl. Rsch., Soc. for Coll. and Univ. Planning, Profl. Orgnl. Devel. Network, Phi Delta Kappa. Lutheran.

METTEE, STEPHEN BLAKE, publishing executive; b. L.A., Oct. 29, 1947; s. Eugene Blake and Mary Helen (Hustead) M.; m. Suzanne Crawford, Mar. 31, 1969 (div. June 1977); 1 child, Joshua Blake; m. Donna Parker, July 25, 1987. AA, Fresno (Calif.) C.C., 1967; BA, Calif. STate Univ., Fresno, 1984. Pres. Calif. Wholesale Wines, Inc., Fresno, 1970-77; pres., CEO Apple Eddies, Inc., 1978-82; owner Calif. Color, The Printing Co., 1982-94; pub. Quill Driver Books/Word Dancer Press, Inc., 1993—. Author: The Fast-Track Course on How to Write a Nonfiction Book Proposal; editor: The Portable Writers Conference, 1996. Mem. bd. dirs. Fresno Downtown Assn., 1979-82. With U.S. Army, 1969-75. Mem. Writers Internat. Network (bd. dirs.), bd. dirs., Fresno Cty. Friends of Library. Republican. Avocations: reading, writing, family activities, travel, scuba diving. Office: Quill Driver Books Word Dancer Press 950 N Van Ness Ave Fresno CA 93728-3428

METTEE-MCCUTCHON, ILA, municipal official, retired career officer; b. Mobile, Ala., May 1, 1945; d. John Martin and Anna Ruth (Cleveland) Mettee; m. John Robert McCutchon, Oct. 13, 1974; 1 child, Erin Tempest. BS, Auburn (Ala.) U., 1967, MS, 1969; grad., various army schs. Rsch. psychologist VA Hosp., Tuskegee, Ala., 1967-69; clin. psychologist U. Ala. Med. Ctr., Birmingham, 1969-71; commd. 1st lt. U.S. Army, 1971, advanced through grades to col., 1992. Officer in charge Alcohol and Drug Abuse Rehab. Ctr., Presidio, San Francisco, 1971-73; strategic intelligence officer 8th Psychol. Bn., 1973-75; tactical intelligence officer, ops. officer, co. comdr. 525th MI Brigade (Airborne), Ft. Bragg, N.C., 1976-79; project officer Command, Control, Comms. and Intelligence Directorate, Combined Arms Combat Devel. Activity, Ft. Leavenworth, Kans., 1979-82; student Command and Gen. Staff Coll., 1982-83; ops. officer Army Spl. Security Group, Washington, 1983-86; Def. Lang. Inst. Presidio of Monterey, 1986-87; chief U.S. So. command Joint Intelligence Ctr., Republic of Panama, 1987-89; comdr. 741st M.I. Bn., Ft. Meade, Md., 1989-91; U.S. Army War Coll., 1991-92; strategic intelligence officer Internat. Military Staff NATO, Brussels, Belgium, 1992-94; comdr. Presidio of Monterey and Ft. Ord, Calif., 1994-96, chief base realignment and closure/environ. mgmt., 1996-97, ret. with honors, 1997. Elected to Marina City Coun., 1998, Rep. cen. com. Monterey County, 2000; trustee World Affairs Coun.; apptd. City Svcs. and Improvement Commn. City of Marina; apptd. housing cmty. and econ. devel. policy com. League Calif. Cities', 1999—. Decorated Army Commendation medal (3), Meritorious Svc. medal (4), Def. Meritorious Svc. medal (1), Army Achievement award (2), Legion of Merit (2), Def. Superior Svc. medal (1); named Woman of Yr. Marina, 2001, Philanthropist of Yr., 2001. Mem. NAFE, Nat. Assn. Univ. Women, Nat. Women's Polit. Caucus, VFW, Assn. U.S. Army, Alumni Assn. U.S. Army War Coll., WAC Found., Women in NATO, Am. Legion (post 694), Ft. Ord Alumni Assn. (adv. bd.), Girl Scouts of Monterey Bay (bd. dirs.), Cmty. Human Svcs. (chair, bd. dirs.), Coalition of Homeless Svc. Providers (cmty. adv.), Rotary Internat. (local chpt.), Monterey Rep. Women, Marina C. of C., Marina Bus. Assn., Marina Larger Libr. Com. Home: 3181 DeForest Rd Marina CA 93933 Office: City Hall City of Marina 211 Hillcrest Ave Marina CA 93933-3534

METTER, RONALD ELLIOT, lawyer; b. Phila., June 27, 1945; s. Harry H. and Ann (Shapiro) Metter; m. Helene Rochelle Gross, June 22, 1968 (div. June 1974); children: Jodi, Jamie; m. Angela Marie Carricato, Sept. 26, 1981 (div. 2001); children: Jonathan, David. BS, Temple U., 1968, JD, 1971. Bar: Pa. 1971, U.S. Dist. Ct. (ea. dist.) Pa. 1971. Assoc. Samuel C. Katz Ltd., Phila., 1971-74; ptnr. Metter & Simon, 1974-85; prt. practive, 1985-88; counsel Semanoff & Hendler, 1988-92; ptnr. Metter & Gusoff, 1992-2000, Metter Elliot, Huntingdon Valley, 2000—. Panelist Law Jour. WXYZ TV; bd. dirs. Awbury Sch., Phila. (adv. bd.); judge pro tem Phila. Ct. Comm. Pleas. Editor Temple Law Quarterly. Commnr. Pa. Valley Sports Assn., Narberth, 1980-84. Recipient Jacob Kossman award, Hon. Chas. Weiner award. Mem. ATLA (judge student trial advocacy competition), Pa. Bar Assn., Pa. Trial Lawyers Assn., Phila. Bar Assn. (legal rights persons with disabilities com., spkrs. bur., medico-legal com., bar news media com.), Phila. Trial Lawyers Assn. Avocations: sports, antique automobiles, travel, tropical fish, music. Home: 300 Heathcliff Rd Huntingdon Valley PA 19006

METTERS, SAMUEL, engineering executive; b. Tex., Nov. 12, 1934; Grad., U.S. Army Comd. Gen. Staff Coll., U.S. Army Air Def. Missile Ctr., Indsl. Coll. Armed Forces; BS in Arch. Engring., A&M U.; BA in Arch., Urban Planning, U. Calif., Berkeley; MS in Sys. Mgmt., MS in Pub. Adminstrn., D in Pub. Adminstrn., U. So. Calif.; grad. owner/pres. mgmt. program, Harvard U. Lic. profl. engr. Commd. U.S. Army, 1958, various assignments, 1962-65, stationed at, 1968, Fort Bliss, Tex., 1969-72, various assignments Vietnam, 1972-74, stationed at Washington, 1977-79, ret., 1979; program mgr., mgmt. info. sys. coord. HBH Co., Rosslyn, Va. Bd. dirs. U.S. Black Engrs. Pubs., Inc.; bd. advisors Riggs Nat. Bank, Va. Commerce Bank. Bd. dirs. Granville Acad., United Black Coll. Fund, U.S. Black Engr. of Yr. Awards Program, No. Va. Urban League, A&M U. Found., Univ. Louisville; trustee Fairfax Bus. Partnership; mem. dean's adv. com. coun. George Mason U.; treas., pres. Nat. Capital Coun. Boy Scouts Am. Mem. Nat. Purple Heart Assn., Nat. Aeronautics Space Adminstrn. Adv. Coun., Armed Forces Comm. Electronic Assn., Profl. Svc. Coun., U. So. Calif. Alumni Assn. (life), A&M Nat. Alumni Assn. (pres.). Office: Metters Industries Inc 8200 Greensboro Dr Mc Lean VA 22102-3803

METTERS, THOMAS WADDELL, sports writer; b. Columbus, Ohio, Apr. 17, 1939; s. Thomas Hammond and Charlotte Ann (Waddell) M. BS in Journalism, Ohio U., 1965. Sports editor The Traveller, Ft. Lee, Va., 1960-62; sports writer The Athens (Ohio) Messenger, 1965—. Asst. to officials Legion Baseball, Athens, 1962—. Contbr.: Ohio Interscholastic Athletic Media Guide, 1985. Bd. dirs. Athens H.S. Booster Club, 1975—, Athens H.S. Athletic Hall of Fame, 2000; ofcl. scorekeeper Am. Legion World Series, Millington, Tenn., 1989. With U.S. Army, 1959-62. Named to Ohio H.S. Basketball Coaches Assn. Hall of Fame, 1993; recipient Contributor award Ohio H.S. Track & Field Coaches Assn., 1995, Ohio H.S. Athletic Assn. Media Svc. award, 1998. Mem. Soc. Profl. Journalists (Recognition plaque 1973), Ohio Associated Press Sports Writers Assn. (pres. 1984), Green & White Club (sec. 1983—, Jonesy Sams award 1987), Ohio Prep Sports Writers Assn. (Hall of Fame 1990), Ky. Colonels, Am. Legion. Republican. Avocation: bowling. Home: 71 Sunnyside Dr Athens OH 45701-1921 Office: The Athens Messenger 9300 Johnson Rd Athens OH 45701

METTINGER, KARL LENNART, pharmaceutical executive; b. Helsingborg, Sweden, Nov. 1, 1943; came to the U.S., 1989; s. Nils Allan and Anna Katarina (Hallberg) M.; m. Chesne Maree Ryman, 1979; m. Miki Ilaw, 1998. MD, U. Lund, 1973; PhD, Karolinska Inst., 1982. Intern Stockholm Hosps., 1973-74; resident Karolinska Hosp., Stockholm, 1974-77, clin. neurologist, 1977-85; med. dir. Kabi Hematology, 1985-87; dep. gen. mgr. Kabi Cardiovascular, 1987-89; med. dir. Ivax/Baker Norton Pharms., Miami, Fla., 1989-93, sr. clin. rsch. dir., 1993-98, exec. dir., clin. rschr., 1998-2000; sr. v.p. chief med. officer SuperGen, San Ramon, 2000—. Assoc. prof. Karolinska Inst., Stockholm, 1983-91; cons. neurologist Odenplan Med. Ctr., Stockholm, 1984-89. Author: Cerebral Thromboembolism, 1982, Refaat--Myths and Billions in Biotech, 1987; editor: Coronary Thrombolysis: Current Answers to Critical Questions, 1988, Controversies in Coronary Thrombolysis, 1989. Bd. dirs. Bass Mus. Arts, 1999-2001; v.p. Friends of Music, U. Miami, 2000-2001. Lt. Swedish Army, 1979. Recipient Silver award Spanish Health Ministry, 1989, Classical Langs. award King Gustav V Found., 1963. Mem. Swedish Stroke Soc. (bd. dirs. 1979-89, pres. 1984-86), Swedish Med. Soc., Swedish Christian Med. Soc. (bd. dirs. 1972-88, pres. 1983-88), Am. Heart Assn., N.Y. Acad. Scis., Nat. Found. for Advancement of Arts, Internat. Assn. Christian Physicians (exec. com. 1975-86). Home: 1367 La Loma Ave Berkeley CA 94708 Office: SuperGen 4140 Dublin Blvd Ste 200 Dublin CA 94568

METTLER, GERALD PHILLIP, reliability engineer; b. Ft. Wayne, Ind., Oct. 24, 1936; s. Joseph Lucian and Dorothy Louise (Bixler) M.; m. Patricia Parent Mettler, May 23, 1959; children: James Anthony, Kenneth Joseph, Lisa Catherine, Charles Matthew. BS in Physics, Ill. Benedictine Coll. (now Benedictine U.), 1958; MS in Mgmt. Engring., George Washington U., 1972. Engr. Sperry Gyroscope Co., Great Neck, N.Y., 1958-66; reliability engr. ARINC Rsch. Corp. subs. Aero. Radio INC, Annapolis, Md., 1966-77; founder, pres. Reltem Rsch., Paw Paw, Mich., 1977-80; prin. reliability engr. Gould Ocean Systems, Cleve., 1980-83; staff reliability engr. Tactical Def. Sys. Lockheed Martin, Akron, Ohio, 1983—. Presenter in field. Contbr. articles to symposiums. Cath. youth orgn. advisor St. Piux X Ch., Ft. Worth, 1960-62; tchr. Sunday sch. Sacred Heart Ch., Warner Robins, Ga., 1962-65; instnl. rep. Boy Scouts Am., Bowie, Md., 1972-77. Mem. IEEE, Am. Soc. Qualtiy Control, Motivators Square Dance Club (pres. 1992—). Roman Catholic. Achievements include research in predictive technology. Office: Lockheed Martin 1210 Massillon Rd Akron OH 44315-0002

METTLER, IRVIN JACOB, science administrator, research scientist; b. Bakersfield, Calif., Sept. 11, 1950; s. Raymond Jacob and Lydia Hilda Mettler; m. Janice Marie Mettler, Aug. 19, 1972; 1 child, Michael. BS, U. Calif., Davis, 1972, MS, 1974; PhD, U. Calif., Riverside, 1977. Postdoctoral rschr. U. Calif., Santa Cruz, 1977-81; rsch. scientist Stauffer Chem. Co., Richmond, Calif., 1981-87; sr. rsch. scientist Sandoz Crop Protection, Palo Alto, 1987-92; dept. head Northrup King Co., Stanton, Minn., 1992-97; mgr. tech. Seminis Vegetable Seed, Woodland, Calif., 1998-99, dir. biotech., 2000—. Cons. Mettler Biotech., El Sobrante, Calif., 1997-98; bd. dirs. Biotech. R&D Corp., Peoria, Ill. Patentee in field; contbr. articles to sci. jours. Mem. AAAS, Am. Soc. Plant Physiologists, Phi Kappa Phi, Sigma Xi. Avocations: photography, woodworking, fishing. Office: Seminis Vegetable Seed 37437 State Hwy 16 Woodland CA 95695

METTLER, NORMA EVANGELINA, research scientist; b. Larroque, Entre Rios, Argentina, Jan. 26, 1932; d. Ernesto Rodolfo and Catalina Geronima (De Merlier) M. MD, U. Buenos Aires, 1958, PhD in Medicine, 1960; MPH, Yale U., 1968, DPH, 1970. Med. diplomate, Argentina. Med. practitioner Children's Hosp., Buenos Aires, 1953-58; asst. to chief practical work U. Buenos Aires, 1954-66; ind. rschr. Conicet, Buenos Aires, 1962-66; postdoctoral fellow Govt. Med. Sci./U.S.A./Yale, New Haven, 1966-69; mem. faculty Yale U., 1969-71; rschr. CIC Buenos Aires Province, 1978-96. Cons. virology Pan Am. Health Orgn./WHO, Chile, Brazil, Venezuela, 1971-77; prof. virology Universidad Nacional Centro Pro Vincia Buenos Aires, Tandil, Argentina, 1977-84; prof. immunology Facultad Ciencias Veterinarias-U. Buenos Aires, 1984-87; bd. dirs. dept. microbiology Facultad Medicina/U. Buenos Aires, 1989-96; cons. infectious disease dr. Florencio Escardo Pediatric Svc., Children's Hosp., Ricardo Gutierrez, 1963-66. Author: Argentine Hemorragic Fever, 1969, Los Virus en Medicine Humana y Veterinaria, 12 parts, 1978-83, Virus Trasmitidos al Hombre por Alimentos, 1990, El Universo, 1992; author over 70 publs. in profl. jours. Recipient fellowship Conicet/Argentina, Rockefeller Inst., 1960-62, grante Rockefeller Found., 1962. Fellow Royal Soc. Health; mem. AAAS, Argentine Assn. Microbiology (life), Argentine Med. Assn., Assn. Former Internat. Civil Servants (life), Am. Soc. Microbiology, N.Y. Acad. Scis. Roman Catholic. Avocations: card games, writing poetry, readings. Home: M Larumbe (Ex-San Juan) 571 1640 Buenos Aires Martinez Argentina also: Cordoba 2077 2o A 1120 Buenos Aires Argentina

METTLIN, CONNIE ANN, social worker, educator; b. LaPorte City, Iowa, Aug. 21, 1951; d. Shelby and W. Eileen (Loveless) Bellinger; m. William D. Mettlin, Sr., Apr. 21, 1993; children: Lori Ann Curran Harvey, David Randal Hess, Aerial Lynn Hess; stepchildren: William D. Jr., Brenda, Kevin, Kirk. BA, U. No. Iowa, 1984, postgrad.; MSW, U. Iowa, 1987, postgrad., Drake U., Morningside Coll.; postgrad. Upper Iowa U. Sch. social worker Area Edn. Agy. 4, Sioux Center, Iowa, 1987-92; therapist Luth. Social Svcs., Sioux City and Spencer, 1989-92, Waterloo, 1992-94; family therapist Four Oaks, 1994-95; med. social worker Va. Gay Hosp., Vinton, 1995-97; therapist Washburn, 1997-2000; adj. prof. Hawkeye Cmty. Coll., Waterloo, 1996—2000; adj. instr. Upper Iowa U., 1992—. Adj. instr. Hawkeye C.C., 1997, Kirkwood C.C., 1998. Mentor Ia. Invests Mentor Program, Waterloo; chmn. fellowship ch. Mem.: NASW, Iowa Sch. Social Work Assn. (pub. rels., co-editor newsletter 1987—92). Lutheran. Avocations: reading, camping, garage sales, biking, raising and breeding paint horses. Home: PO Box 128 Hudson IA 50643-0128 E-mail: cmettlin@aea6.k12.id.us., aerial@iawatelecom.net.

METZ, ADAM S. real estate executive; Bachelor, Cornell U.; M of Mgmt., Northwestern U. Corp. lending officer 1st Nat. Bank Chgo., 1983-87; v.p. Capital Markets Group, JMB Realty, 1987-93; treas., CFO, exec. v.p, dir. acquisitions Urban Shopping Ctrs., Inc., 1993-2000, pres., 2000—. Mem. Internat. Coun. Shopping Ctrs. Office: Urban Shopping Ctrs Inc 900 N Michigan Ave Chicago IL 60611-1542

METZ, ANTHONY J., III, federal judge; Bankruptcy judge U.S. Dist. Ct. (so. dist.) Ind., Indpls., 1997—. Office: 317 US Courthouse 46 E Ohio St Indianapolis IN 46204-1903 E-mail: anthony_metz@insb.uscourts.gov.

METZ, CHARLES EDGAR, radiology educator; b. Bayshore, N.Y., Sept. 11, 1942; s. Clinton Edgar and Grace Muriel (Schienke) M.; m. Maryanne Theresa Bahr, July, 1967 (div. 1988); children: Rebecca, Molly. BA, Bowdoin Coll., 1964; MS, U. Pa., 1966, PhD, 1969. Instr. radiology U. Chgo., 1969-71, asst. prof., 1971-75, assoc. prof., 1976-80, dir. grad. programs in med. physics, 1979-85, prof., 1980—, prof. structural biology, 1984-86. Mem. diagnostic rsch. adv. group Nat. Cancer Inst., 1980-81; mem. sci. com. Nat. Coun. on Radiation Protection and Measurements, 1982-95, Internat. Commn. on Radiation Units and Measurements, 1988-96, chmn. sci. com., 1992-99; cons. and lectr. in field. Assoc. editor: Radiology Jour., 1986—91, assoc. editor: Med. Physics Jour., 1992—95, mem. editl. bd.: Med. Decision Making, 1980—84; contbr. over 200 articles to sci. jours. and chpts. to books, software analysis used in more than 5000 labs. worldwide. Mem. Radiol. Soc. N.Am., Am. Assn. Physicists in Medicine, Soc. Med. Decision Making, Assn. Univ. Radiologists, Soc. for Health Svcs. Rsch. in Radiology, Phi Beta Kappa, Sigma Xi. Office: U Chgo Dept Radiology MC2026 5841 S Maryland Ave Chicago IL 60637-1463 E-mail: c-metz@uchicago.edu.

METZ, CRAIG HUSEMAN, business executive; b. Columbia, S.C., Aug. 26, 1955; s. Leonard Huseman and Annette (Worthington) M.; m. Karen Angela McCleary, Aug. 11, 1984; 1 child, Preston Worthington. BA, U. Tenn., 1977; JD, U. Memphis, 1986; cert., U.S. Ho. of Reps. Rep. Leadership Parliamentary Law Sch., 1987. Bar: S.C., D.C., U.S. Ct. Claims, U.S. Supreme Ct., U.S. Ct. Appeals (4th cir.). Canvass coord., liaison Campaign to Re-elect Congressman Floyd Spence, 1978; del., chmn. Shelby County Del. to 1983 Tenn. Young Rep. Fedn. Conv.; vice chmn. Shelby County Young Reps., 1983-84, chmn., 1984-85; Shelby County adminstr., asst. to Tenn. state exec. dir. Reagan-Bush Campaign, 1984; field rep. Campaign to Re-elect Congressman Floyd Spence, 1986; spl. asst. to Congressman Floyd Spence, 1986-88; counsel com. on labor and human resources U.S. Senate, 1988-90; commr.'s counsel U.S. Occupational Safety and Health Rev. Commn., Washington, 1990-91; spl. asst. to asst. sec. for legis. and congl. affairs; dep. asst. sec. for congl. liaison U.S. Dept. Edn., Washington, 1991-93; asst. dir. Divsn. Congl. Affairs AMA, 1993; chief of staff Congressman Floyd Spence, 1993—2001; adminstr. Office of the Second Congl. Dist. of S.C., U.S. Ho. of Reps., 2001; govt. rels. mgr. EMC Corp., Arlington, Va., 2001—. Judge nat. writing competition U.S. Constn. Bicentennial, S.C. 1987-88; mem. Ch. of the Ascension and Saint Agnes, Washington. Recipient award of merit Rep. Party of Shelby County, 1985, Outstanding Leadership award Shelby County Young Reps., 1985, Meritorious Svc. medal Mil. Dept. S.C., Legis. award Res. Officers Assn. U.S.; mem. Order of Palmetto. Mem. Rep. Nat. Lawyers Assn. (state chmn. S.C. chpt. 1987-90), Freedoms Found. Valley Forge, Va. Hist. Soc., Assn. for Preservation Va. Antiquities, Va. Geneal. Soc., U. South Caroliniana Soc., Palmetto Trust for Historic Preservation, Lowcountry Heritage Soc., Orangeburg County Hist. Soc., Nat. Trust for Hist. Preservation (assoc. Capital region), SAR, St. David's Soc., St. Andrew's Soc. Washington, St. George's Soc. of Balt., Mil. Soc. War of 1812, Vet. Corps Arty. State of N.Y., Gen. Soc. War of 1812, Mil. Order Loyal Legion of U.S., Order of St. John (Hospitaller), SCV, Mil. Order Stars and Bars, Sons and Daus. Colonial and Antebellum Bench and Bar 1565-1861, Sons of the Revolution, Ky. Col., Nat. Cathedral Assn., U. Tenn. Nat. Alumni Assn., Sigma Alpha Epsilon, Phi Alpha Delta (v.p. McKellar chpt., Outstanding Svc. award 1983). Republican. Episcopalian. Home: 8505 Westown Way Vienna VA 22182-2513 Office: Crystal Park III Ste 500 2231 Crystal Dr Arlington VA 22202

METZ, EMMANUEL MICHAEL, investment company executive, lawyer; b. Pitts., Sept. 19, 1928; s. Solomon and Gertrude (Krieger) M.; m. Janine Spaner, Apr. 3, 1964. BA, Dartmouth Coll., 1949; LLB, Harvard U., 1952; LLM, NYU, 1958. Bar: N.Y. 1952. Atty. ABC, N.Y.C., 1956-58; security analyst Standard & Poor's, 1958-68; mng. dir. CIBC Oppenheimer Corp., 1968—. Author: Street Fighting at Wall and Broad, 1982. Lt. USN, 1952-56. Home: 150 E 56th St New York NY 10022-3631 Office: CIBC Oppenheimer Corp 622 Third Ave New York NY 10017 E-mail: mike.metz@us.cibc.com.

METZ, HELEN CHAPIN, retired Middle East analyst; b. Beijing, China, Apr. 13, 1928; d. Selden and Mary Paul (Noyes) Chapin; m. Ronald Irwin Metz, July 14, 1951; children: Mary Selden Metz Evans, Helen Winchester Metz Ketchum, Grace Chapin Metz. AB, Vassar Coll., 1949; MA, Am. U., Beirut, 1954; postgrad., Berkeley Div. Sch. of Yale U., 1966-69. Hostess to The Honorable Selden Chapin, U.S. Amb. to the Netherlands, The Hague, 1950; instr. Beirut Coll. for Women (now Beirut Univ. Coll.), 1954-55, Madeira Sch., Greenway, Va., 1959-60; rsch. analyst Arabian Am. Oil Co., Dhahran, Saudi Arabia, 1956-58, 63-66; administrv. asst. Office Anglican Archbishop, Jerusalem, 1969-75; instr. Mercyhurst Coll., Erie, Pa., 1977-79; exec. dir. Internat. Inst., 1978-81; dep. head, devel. officer Brent Internat. Sch., Baguio, Philippines, 1981-82; analyst, sr. analyst Fed. Rsch. div. Libr. of Congress, Washington, 1983-87, supr. Middle East, North Africa, 1987-90, supr. Middle East, Africa, Latin Am., 1990-99. Editor: Libya: A Country Study, 1989, Iran: A Country Study, 1989, Iraq: A Country Study, 1990, Israel: A Country Study, 1990, Jordan: A Country Study, 1991, Egypt: A Country Study, 1992, Nigeria: A Country Study, 1992, Sudan: A Country Study, 1992, Somalia: A Country Study, 1993, Saudi Arabia: A Country Study, 1993, Persian Gulf States: Country Studies, 1994, Algeria: A Country Study, 1995, Indian Ocean: Five Island Countries, 1995, Turkey: A Country Study, 1996, Dominican Republic and Haiti: Country Studies, 2002. Mentor Edn. for Ministry St. Margaret's Ch., Washington, 1984-92, 99—; mem. mission devel. adv. com. Diocese Washington, 1987-90, mem. evangelism com., 1990-93. Vassar Coll. fellow, 1954-55. Mem. Middle East Studies Assn., Middle East Inst., Phi Beta Kappa (prize, 1949). Democrat. Episcopalian. Avocations: reading, double-crostics. Home: 3001 Veazey Ter NW Apt 334 Washington DC 20008-5455 E-mail: hchapinmetz@aol.com.

METZ, JAMES ROBERT, mathematics educator; b. Springfield, Ill., June 1, 1949; s. Leonard Thomas and Mary Agnes (Erley) M. BA, St. Louis U., 1971; MA, U. Ill., Springfield, 1977. Cert. tchr. Tchr. math. Griffin H.S., Springfield, 1971-79, Damien H.S., Honolulu, 1979-87; tchr. trainer U.S. Peace Corps, Philippines, 1987-90; tchr. math. Maryknoll H.S., Honolulu, 1990-94, Mid-Pacific Inst., Honolulu, 1994-97, Kapi'olani C.C., Honolulu, 1997—. Editorial cons. U. Hawaii, Honolulu, 1986-87, 90; editorial cons. Instrnl. Materials Corp., Philippines, 1989-90. Contbr. articles to profl. jours.; patentee puzzle.

Vol. Results, 1994—. Recipient Excellence in Math. Teaching, Soc. for Indsl. and Applied Math., 1984. Mem. Nat. Coun. Tchr. Math., Ill. Coun. Tchrs. Math., Hawaii Coun. Tchrs. Math. (v.p. 1981-82, pres. 1982-83, sec. 1998—), Phi Beta Kappa, Pi Mu Epsilon. Democrat. Roman Catholic. Avocations: hiking, writing, water sports. Home: 1630 Makiki St Apt C-105 Honolulu HI 96822-4434 Office: Kapi'olani C C 4303 Diamond Head Rd Honolulu HI 96816-4421 E-mail: metz@hawaii.edu.

METZ, LARRY EDWARD, lawyer; b. Phila., Mar. 20, 1955; s. Harry Franz and Joan (Nye) M.; m. Mariko Tomisato, Mar. 26, 1980; children: Marla Jo, Christina Jill. BA, U. Fla., 1976; JD with high honors, Fla. State U., 1983. Bar: Fla. 1983, U.S. Dist. Ct. (so., mid. and no. dists.) Fla. 1984, U.S. Ct. Appeals (11th cir.) 1984, U.S. Supreme Ct. 1987. Assoc. Fleming, O'Bryan & Fleming, Ft. Lauderdale, Fla., 1983-86; atty. Westinghouse Electric Corp., Coral Springs, 1986-88; pvt. practice Ft. Lauderdale, 1988-91, Coral Springs, 1991-93; assoc. Herzfeld & Rubin, Miami, 1993-96, ptnr. Ft. Lauderdale, 1996-99; assoc. Unger, Acree, Weinstein, Marcus, Merrill, Kast & Metz, P.L., Orlando, Fla., 1999-2000; ptnr. Unger, Acree, Weinstein, Marcus, Merrill, Kast & Metz, PL, 2000—. Area leader, sign co-chmn., spkr. George Bush for Pres. Broward County (Fla.) Victory Com., 1988; pres. Broward County Regional Rep. Club, 1991, 95; mem. exec. com. Broward County Rep. Party, 1988-91, 93-96, Lake County Rep. Party, 1999—; Rep. nominee U.S. Ho. Reps. 19th dist., Fla., 1992; mem. Fla. Guardian Ad Litem program, 1991-97; mem. Cmty. Ch. Howey-in-the-Hills, Fla., 1999—, chmn. stewardship and finance com., 2000—. Capt. USMC, 1976-82. Recipient Outstanding Mem. of Yr. award Broward Lawyers Care, 1989, 90. Mem. ABA, Lake County Bar Assn., Order of Coif, Marine Corps League (judge advocate North Lake Detachment, Fla. 2000—). Office: Unger, Acree Weinstein et al 701 Peachtree Rd Orlando FL 32804-6847 E-mail: Lmetz@ungerlawfirm.com.

METZ, MARY SEAWELL, foundation administrator, retired academic administrator; b. Rockhill, S.C., May 7, 1937; d. Columbus Jackson and Mary (Dunlap) Seawell; m. F. Eugene Metz, Dec. 21, 1957; 1 dau., Mary Eugena. BA summa cum laude in French and English, Furman U., 1958; postgrad., Institut Phonetique, Paris, 1962-63, Sorbonne, 1962-63; PhD magna cum laude in French, La. State U., 1966; HHD (hon.), Furman U., 1984; LLD (hon.), Chapman Coll., 1985; DLT (hon.), Converse Coll., 1988. Instr. French La. State U., 1965-66, asst. prof., 1966-67, 1968-72, assoc. prof., 1972-76, dir. elem. and intermediate French programs, 1966-74, spl. asst. to chancellor, 1974-75, asst. to chancellor, 1975-76; prof. French Hood Coll., Frederick, Md., 1976-81, provost, dean acad. affairs, 1976-81; pres. Mills Coll., Oakland, Calif., 1981-90; dean of extension U. Calif., Berkeley, 1991-98; pres. S.H. Cowell Found., San Fransisco, 1999—. Vis. asst. prof. U. Calif.-Berkeley, 1967-68; mem. commn. on leadership devel. Am. Coun. on Edn., 1981-90, adv. coun. Stanford Rsch. Inst., 1985-90, adv. coun. Grad. Sch. Bus., Stanford U.; bd. dirs. PG&E, SBC Comms., Inc., Union Bank, Longs Drug Stores, S.H. Cowell Found. Author: Reflets du monde francais, 1971, 78, Cahier d'exercices: Reflets du monde francais, 1972, 78, (with Helstrom) Le Francais a decouvrir, 1972, 78, Le Francais a vivre, 1972, 78, Cahier d'exercices: Le Francais a vivre, 1972, 78; standardized tests; mem. editorial bd. Liberal Edn., 1982— . Trustee Am. Conservatory Theater. NDEA fellow, 1960-62,, 1963-64; Fulbright fellow, 1962-63; Am. Council Edn. fellow, 1974-75 Mem. Western Coll. Assn. (v.p. 1982-84, pres. 1984-86), Assn. Ind. Calif. Colls. and Univs. (exec. com. 1982-90), Nat. Assn. Ind. Colls. and Univs. (govt. rels. adv. coun. 1982-85), So. Conf. Lang. Teaching (chmn. 1976-77), World Affairs Coun. No. Calif. (bd. dirs. 1984-93), Bus.-Higher Edn. Forum, Women's Forum West, Women's Coll. Coalition (exec. com. 1984-88), Phi Kappa Phi, Phi Beta Kappa. Address: PO Box 686 Stinson Beach CA 94970-0686 also: 9 Regulus Ct Alameda CA 94501-1015 Office: SH Cowell Found 120 Montgomery St San Francisco CA 94104-4303

METZ, PATRICIA ANNE, school social worker; b. Detroit, May 10, 1936; d. Hugh William and Frances (Alvord) Harris; m. Floyd A. Metz, Aug. 23, 1958 (div. Mar. 1990); children: Marcia Anne Metz Hickman, Kevin Harris Metz. BA, Albion (Mich.) Coll., 1958; MSW, Wayne State U., 1960. Cert. social worker; lic. marriage and family therapist; sch. social work specialist. Intake worker Wayne County Juvenile Ct. Clinic for Child Study, Detroit, 1960-65; intake supr. N.W. Child Guidance Ctr., Garden City, 1965-66; exec. sec. Met. Detroit chpt. NASW, Detroit, 1967-71; dir. of counseling Friends Sch., 1970-74; sch. social worker Detroit Pub. Schs., 1977-97; clin. social worker Family Svc. Detroit and Wayne County, Livonia, Mich., 1985-97; ind. practice child and family therapy, 1997-99; adj. faculty Sch. Social Work, Wayne State U., Detroit, 1996—2002; adj. faculty Sch. Social Work U. Mich., Ann Arbor, 2002—. Treas. Midwest Sch. Social Work Coun., 1987-91, mem., 1987—l mem. spl. edn. adv. com. State of Mich., 1999—. Bd. dirs. Children's Mus. Friends, Detroit, 1976-82, vol. 1976—; sr. arbitrator Better Bus. Bur., Detroit, 1986-95; mem. Lafayette Clinic Adv. Coun., Detroit, 1984-92; pres. Travelers' Aid Soc., 1983-84, life mem., 1984—; elder 1st Presbyn. Ch., 1994—. Named Spirit of Detroit, City Coun., 1990, 1997; recipient Career Achievement award, Midwest Sch. Social Work Coun., 2001. Mem.: NASW (Mich. chpt. com. in inquiry 1979—84, mem. commn. on edn. 1990—92, profl. stds. com. 1990—94, chmn. nat. sch. social work credential com. 1994—99, licensure work group 2001—), Children with Attention Deficit Disorders, Mich. Assn. Emotionally Disturbed Children, Mich. Assn. Sch. Social Workers (bd. dirs. 1982—89, state pres. 1983—84, conf. treas. 1986, 1987, 1990—91, bd. dirs. 1993—, pres. Region A 2002—, Sch. Social Worker of Yr. Region D 1989). Democrat. Avocations: bridge, golf, reading, theatre, choir. Home: 3754 Audrey Rae Ln Howell MI 48843

METZ, ROBERT ROY, publisher, editor; b. Richmond Hill, N.Y., Mar. 23, 1929; s. Robert Roy, Sr. and Mary (Kissel) M.; m. Susan Lee Blair, 1984; children: Robert Sumner, Christopher Roy. BA, Wesleyan U., Middletown Conn., 1950. Copyboy N.Y. Times, 1951, asst. fgn. news desk, 1952; rewriteman cable desk I.N.S., 1953, overnight cable editor, 1954-56, asst. feature editor, 1956-58; asst. news editor Newspaper Enterprise Assn., 1958, news editor, 1959-63, mng. editor, 1963-66, exec. editor, 1966-68, v.p., 1967-71, editorial dir., 1968-71, pres., editor, dir., 1972-94; dir. Berkeley-Small Inc., 1974-77; chmn. Berkley-Small Inc., 1976-77; v.p., dir. United Feature Syndicate, 1976-77, pres., editor, 1978; pres., editor, dir. United Media, 1978-93, chmn., 1993-94; media cons., 1994—. Pres. Peter Pan Children's Fund, 1997—. Mem.: Union League (N.Y.C.). Lutheran. Home: 170 E 77th St New York NY 10021-1912

METZ, RONALD IRWIN, retired priest, addictions counselor; b. Walthill, Nebr., Aug. 11, 1921; s. Harry Elmer and Emma Rilla (Howe) M.; m. Helen Chapin, July 14, 1951; children: Mary Selden Metz Evans, Helen Winchester Metz Ketchum, Grace Chapin Metz Hunton. BA in Chinese and Far Ea. Studies, U. Calif., Berkeley, 1945; MA in Mid. Ea. Studies, Am. U., Beirut, 1954; M Div., Yale U., 1969, STD, 1975. Ordained priest Episcopal Ch., 1969. Intelligence officer various govtl. intelligence agys., Far East and Washington, 1944-52; exec. Arabian/Am. Oil Co., Dhahran and Riyadh, Saudi Arabia, 1954-66; deacon Grace Cathedral, San Francisco; priest St. George's Cathedral, Jerusalem, 1969; exec. asst. to archbishop Jerusalem and Mid. East Archbishopric, 1969-75; rector Ch. of the Holy Spirit, Erie, Pa., 1976-81; chaplain Brent Sch., Baguio, Philippines, 1981-82; counselor of chemically dependent Washington, from 1982. Addictionologist, vol. New Beginnings Treatment Ctr., P.I.W. Hosp., Washington, 1989-90, Found. Next Step Outpatient Treatment Ctr., Washington, 1991-92; adj. clergy St. Margaret's Ch., Washington; mem. D.C. Diocesan Commn. on Alcohol and Drug Abuse, Washington, 1982-89. Bd. dirs. Mid. East Inst., Washington, 1959-60, Pub. Broadcasting System, n.w. Pa., 1976-81; mem. adv. bd. Children's Aid Internat., 1988-89. Served to col. U.S. Army, 1942-45, CBI, OSS. Decorated Bronze Star. Mem. Iran Diocesan Assn. U.S.A, Phi Beta Kappa, Sigma Chi (chaplain D.C. alumni assn. 1982-99). Democrat. Avocations: home movies, double crostics. Home: Washington, DC. Died Aug. 25, 2002.

METZ, STEVEN KENT, federal agency administrator, writer; b. Charleston, W.Va., June 30, 1956; s. David N. and Carolyn Ann (Powell) M.; m. Jayne Godwin Nelson, Aug. 14, 1977; children: Rachel Elizabeth, Stephanie Eleanor. BA, U. S.C., 1977, MA, 1981; PhD, Johns Hopkins U., 1985. Vis. prof. polit. sci. Va. Tech, Blacksburg, Va., 1984-87; prof. internat. rels. U.S. Army Command and Gen. Staff Coll., Ft. Leavenworth, Kans., 1987-91; prof. low intensity conflict and Third World studies Air War Coll., Maxwell AFB, Ala., 1991-93; rsch. prof. nat. security affairs Strategic Studies Inst. U.S. Army War Coll., Carlisle Barracks, Pa., 1993-2000, Henry L. Stimson prof. mil. studies, 1993-95, dir. rsch., chmn. regional strategy and planning dept., 2001—. Lectr., cons. in field. Contbr. articles to profl. jours., chpts. to books. Republican. Home: 5 Countryside Dr Carlisle PA 17013-9036 Office: Strategic Studies Inst US Army War Coll Carlisle Barracks PA 17013 E-mail: steven.metz@carlisle.army.mil.

METZ, STEVEN WILLIAM, small business owner; b. Inglewood, Calif., Nov. 30, 1946; s. Glenn Ludwig and Kathleen Martha (Peterson) M.; m. Michelle Marie McArthur, Aug. 11, 1989; 1 child, Glenn Christian. Student, Fullerton Coll., Calif. Supt. Oahu Interiors, Honolulu, 1969-71, Hackel Bros., Miami, Fla., 1971-73; exec. v.p. Tru-Cut Inc., Brea, Calif., 1974-82; gen. mgr. The Louvre', Grass Valley, 1983-85; mfg. engring. mgr. Rexnord Aerospace, Torrance, 1986-87; pres., founder Metz/Calcoa Inc., 1987—. Mfg. rep. consul Orange County Spring, Anaheim, 1987—, TALSCO, 1994—, Precision Resources, 1994—, GEMTECH, 1994—; mfg. rep. consul Alard Machine Products, Gardena, Calif., 1988—, v.p. spl. projects, 1997—. Charter mem. Rep. Presdl. Task Force, 1991—; mem. L.A. Coun. on World Affairs, 1991-92. With U.S. Army, 1966-68. Recipient Appreciation awards DAV, 1968, Soc. Mfg. Engrs., 1991. Fellow Soc. Carbide Engrs.; mem. Soc. Carbide and Tool Engrs. (chpt. pres. 1980-82, Appreciation award 1981), Rep. Presdl. Legion of Merit. Avocations: golf, swimming, riding, boating.

METZ, T(HEODORE) JOHN, librarian, consultant; b. Erie, Pa., Nov. 5, 1932; s. Theodore John and Dorothy Pearl (Schutte) M.; m. Dorothy Page Neff, June 11, 1955; 1 child, Margaret Elizabeth MusB, Heidelberg Coll., 1954; MA in Music, Miami U., Oxford, Ohio, 1955; MLS, U. Mich., 1959. Libr. II U. Wis., Madison, 1959-61; asst. libr. Lawrence U., Appleton, Wis., 1961-67; dir. librs. U. Wis.-Green Bay, 1967-75; exec. dir. Midwest Region Library Network, Evanston, Ill., 1975-79; coll. libr., assoc. prof. Carleton Coll., Northfield, Minn., 1979-97, coll. libr. emeritus, 1998—. Speaker, participant, coord. numerous confs. and insts., 1969—; chmn. several state libr. groups, 1971-76; mem. several nat. libr. adv. coms., 1974-80; bldg. cons. Carleton Coll., others, 1978—; mem. Citizen Amb. Rsch. Librs. del. to Ea. Europe, 1992. Author: MIDLNET Symposium Report, 1976 Chmn. Green Bay Symphony, 1971-76; mem. various bds. coms., relating to mus. activities; performer Green Bay and other orchs., 1955— Library Service scholar U. Mich., 1957; Library Service fellow U. Mich., 1958 Mem. ALA, Assn. Coll. Rsch. Librs., Internat. Fedn. Libr. Assns. Avocations: musical activities; hunting; fishing; gardening. E-mail: tmetz@carleton.edu.

METZ, WILLIAM CLINTON, program manager; b. Leominster, Mass., Oct. 13, 1944; s. William Dewitt and Clarice Styles (McKenney) M.; m. Carol Ann Giles; children: William Christopher, Jennifer Giles. B of History, Bates Coll.; M in Geography, U. R.I.; PhD in Geography, U. Pitts., 1974; MBA, Dowling Coll., 1985; M of Info. Scis., Aurora U., 1987. Sr. scientist Westinghouse, Pitts., 1974-78; prin. investigator Brookhaven Nat. Lab., Upton, N.Y., 1978-84; program mgr. Argonne (Ill.) Nat. Lab., 1984—, deputy to divsn. dir., 1990-93. Contbr. articles to profl. jours. Avocations: American history, antique cars, hiking. Office: Argonne Nat Lab 9700 Cass Ave Bldg 900 Argonne IL 60439-4803

METZENBAUM, HOWARD MORTON, former senator, consumer organization official, advocate; b. Cleve., June 4, 1917; s. Charles I. and Anna (Klafter) M.; m. Shirley Turoff, Aug. 8, 1946; children: Barbara Jo, Susan Lynn Hyatt, Shelley Hope, Amy Beth. BA, Ohio State U., 1939, LLD, 1941. Chmn. bd. Airport Parking Co. Am., 1958-66, ITT Consumer Services Corp., 1966-68, ComCorp, 1969-74; U.S. senator State of Ohio, 1974, 1977-94; chmn. Consumer Fedn. Am., Washington. Mem. War Labor Panel, 1942-45, Ohio Bur. Code Rev., 1949-50, Cleve. Met. Housing Authority, 1968-70, Lake Erie Regional Transit Authority, 1972-73, Ohio Ho. of Reps., 1943-46, Ohio Senate, 1947-50; chmn. anti-trust sub-com., labor sub-com. U.S. Senate; mem. intell com., budget com., environ. and pub. works com., judiciary com., labor and human resources, energy and natural resources, dem. policy com. Trustee Mt. Sinai Hosp., Cleve., 1961—73, treas., 1966—73; nat. co-chmn. Nat. Citizen's Com. Conquest Cancer; former vice chmn. fellows Brandeis U.; chmn. Am. Friend Rabin Ctr., Tel Aviv; past bd. dirs. Coun. Human Rels., United Cerebral Palsy Assn., Nat. Coun. Hunger and Malnutrition, Karamu House, St. Vincent Charity Hosp., Cleve., St. Jude Rsch. Hosp., Memphis. Mem. Order of Coif, Phi Eta Sigma, Tau Epsilon Rho. Home: 5610 Wisconsin Ave Bethesda MD 20815-4415

METZER, PATRICIA ANN, lawyer; b. Phila., Mar. 10, 1941; d. Freeman Weeks and Evelyn (Heap) M.; m. Karl Hormann, June 30, 1980. BA with distinction, U. Pa., 1963, LLB cum laude, 1966. Bar: Mass. 1966, D.C. 1972, U.S. Tax Ct. 1988. Assoc., then ptnr. Mintz, Levin, Cohn, Glovsky and Popeo, Boston, 1966-75; assoc. tax legis. counsel U.S. Treasury Dept., Washington, 1975-78; shareholder, dir. Goulston & Storrs, P.C., Boston, 1978-98; stockholder Hutchins, Wheeler & Dittmar, P.C., 1998—. Lectr. program continuing legal edn. Boston Coll. Law Sch., Chestnut Hill, Mass., spring, 1974; lectr. grad. tax program Boston U. Law Sch., 2001—; mem. adv. com. NYU Inst. Fed. Taxation, N.Y.C., 1981—87; mem. practitioner liaison com. Mass. Dept. Revenue, 1985—90; spkr. in field. Author: Federal Income Taxation of Individuals, 1984; mem. adv. bd. Corp. Tax and Bus. Planning Review, 1996—; mem. editl. bd. Am. Jour. Tax Policy, 1995-98; contbr. articles to profl. jours., chpts. to books. Bd. mgrs. Barrington Ct. Condominium, Cambridge, Mass., 1985-86; bd. dirs. University Road Parking Assn., Cambridge, 1988—; trustee Social Law Libr., Boston, 1989-93. Mem. ABA (tax sect., vice-chair publs. 2000-2002, mem. coun. 1996-99, chmn. subcom. allocations and distbns. partnership com. 1978-82, vice chmn. legis. 1991-93, chmn. 1993-95, com. govt. submissions, vice liaison 1993-94, liaison 1994-95, North Atlantic region, co-liaison 1995-96, N.E. region, regional liaison meetings com.), FBA (coun. on taxation, chmn. corp. taxation com. 1977-81, chmn. com. partnership taxation 1981-87), Mass. Bar Assn. (coun. tax sect. 2001-), Boston Bar Assn. (coun. 1987-89, chmn. tax sect. 1989-91), Am. Coll. Tax Counsel (bd. regents 1999—), Boston Estate Planning Coun. (exec. com. 1975, 79-82). Avocation: vocal performances (as soloist and with choral groups). Office: Hutchins Wheeler & Dittmar PC 101 Federal St Boston MA 02110-1817

METZGER, ALLAN LAWRENCE, physician, laboratory director; b. Denver, July 25, 1942; s. Jerry Mortimor and Bernice Metzger; children: Brad, Alison; m. Sondra Scerca, Oct. 18, 1987. BA, Wash. U.; MD cum laude, U. Colo. Diplomate Am. Bd. Internal Medicine, Am. Bd. Rheumatology. Intern, resident U. Chgo.-Billings Hosp., 1968-69; NIH fellow NIAMDD, Phoenix, 1970-72; fellow in rheumatology UCLA Med. Ctr., 1972-74; pvt. practice Beverly Hills, Calif., 1974—. Lab. dir. Rheumatology Diagnostics Lab, Inc., L.A., 1977—; prof. medicine UCLA. Author 4 chpts. to books; contbr. more than 50 articles to profl. jours. Col. USPHS, 1970-72. Fellow ACP, Am. Coll. Rheumatology. Fax: 310-652-2482.

METZGER, BOYD ERNEST, endocrinologist, educator; b. Hills, Minn., June 13, 1934; m. Lois N., Aug. 30, 1959; children: Beth Lynn, Gail Elaine, Gregory Boyd. MD, U. Iowa, 1959. Asst. prof. endocrinology Northwestern U., Evanston, Ill., 1968-72, assoc. prof., 1972-77, prof., 1977-2000, Tom D. Spies prof., 2000—. Contbr. articles to profl. jours. With USPHS, 1963-65. Rsch. grantee NIH, Bethesda, Md., 1990—. Fellow AAAS, Am. Diabetes Assn. (bd. dirs. 1981-84). Home: 23 The Landmark Northfield IL 60093 Office: Northwestern U Med Sch Tarry Bldg 15-735 303 E Chicago Ave Chicago IL 60611-3072 E-mail: bem@northwestern.edu.

METZGER, BRUCE MANNING, clergyman, educator; b. Middletown, Pa., Feb. 9, 1914; s. Maurice Rutt and Anna Mary (Manning) M.; m. Isobel E. Mackay, July 7, 1944; children— John Mackay, James Bruce. AB, Lebanon Valley Coll., 1935, DD, 1951; ThB, Princeton Theol. Sem., 1938, ThM, 1939; AM, Princeton U., 1940, PhD, 1942; LHD (hon.), Findlay U., 1962; DD (hon.), St. Andrews U., Scotland, 1964; DTheol (hon.), Münster U., Fed. Republic Germany, 1970; DLitt (hon.), Potchefstroom U., South Africa, 1985. Ordained to ministry Presbyn. Ch. USA, 1939. Teaching fellow N.T. Princeton Theol. Sem., 1938-40, mem. faculty, 1940—, prof. N.T. lang. and lit., 1954-64, George L. Collord prof. N.T. lang. and lit., 1964-84, emeritus, 1984—. Vis. lectr. Presbyn. Theol. Sem. South, Campinas, Brazil, 1952, Presbyn. Theol. Sem. North, Recife, Brazil, 1952; mem. Inst. Advanced Study, Princeton, 1964-65, 73-74; scholar-in-residence Tyndale House, Cambridge, 1969; vis. fellow Clare Hall, Cambridge, 1974, Wolfson Coll., Oxford U., 1979, Macquarie U., Sydney, Australia, 1982, Caribbean Grad. Sch. of Theology, Jamaica, 1990, Seminario Internacional Teológico Bautista, Buenos Aires, 1991, Griffith Thomas Lectrs., Dallas Theol. Sem., 1992; mem. mng. com. Am. Sch. Classical Studies, Athens, Greece; mem. Standard Bible com. Nat. Coun. Chs., 1952—, chmn., 1975—; mem. seminar N.T. studies Columbia U., 1959-80; mem. Kuratorium of Vetus-Latina Inst., Beuron, Germany, 1959—; adv. com. Inst. N.T. Text Rsch., U. Münster, 1961—, Thesaurus Linguae Graecae, 1972-80; Collected Works of Erasmus, 1977—; chmn. Am. com. versions Internat. Greek N.T., 1950-88; participant internat. congresses scholars, Aarhus, Aberdeen, Bangor, Basel, Bonn, Brussels, Budapest, Cairo, Cambridge, Copenhagen, Dublin, Exeter, Frankfurt, Heidelberg, London, Louvain, Manchester, Milan, Munich, Münster, Newcastle, Nottingham, Oxford, Prague, Rome, St. Andrews, Stockholm, Strasbourg, Toronto, Trondheim, Tübingen; mem. Presbytery, N.B. Author: The Saturday and Sunday Lessons from Luke in the Greek Gospel Lectionary, 1944, Lexical Aids for Students of New Testament Greek, 1946, enlarged edit., 1955, A Guide to the Preparation of a Thesis, 1950, An Introduction to the Apocrypha, 1957, Chapters in the History of New Testament Textual Criticism, 1963, The Text of the New Testament, Its Transmission, Corruption, and Restoration, 1964, 3d enlarged edit., 1992, (with H.G. May) The Oxford Annotated Bible with the Apocrypha, 1965, The New Testament, Its Background, Growth, and Content, 1965, Index to Periodical Literature on Christ and the Gospels, 1966, Historical and Literary Studies, Pagan, Jewish, and Christian, 1968, Index to Periodical Literature on the Apostle Paul, 1960, 2nd edit., 1970, A Textual Commentary on the Greek New Testament, 1971, 2d edit., 1994, The Early Versions of the New Testament, 1977, New Testament Studies, 1980, Manuscripts of the Greek Bible, 1981, The Canon of the New Testament, 1987, (with Roland Murphy) The New Oxford Annotated Bible with the Apocrypha, 1991, (with M.D. Coogan) The Oxford Companion to the Bible, 1993, Breaking the Code-Understanding the Book of Revelation, 1993, Reminiscences of an Octogenarian, 1997, (with Coogan) The Oxford Guide to People & Places of the Bible, 2001, (with Coogan) The Oxford Guide to Ideas and Issues of the Bible, 2001, The Bible in Translation, Ancient and English Versions, 2001; mem. editorial com.: Critical Greek New Testament, 1956-84; chmn. Am. com., Internat. Greek New Testament Project, 1970-88; sec. com. translators: Apocrypha (rev. standard version); editor: New Testament Tools and Studies, 30 vols, 1960-2000, Oxford Annotated Apocrypha, 1965, enlarged edit., 1977; Reader's Digest Condensed Bible, 1982; co-editor: United Bible Societies Greek New Testament, 1966, 4th edit., 1993; compiler: Index of Articles on the New Testament and the Early Church Published in Festschriften, 1951, supplement, 1955, Lists of Words Occurring Frequently in the Coptic New Testament (Sahidic Dialect), 1961, Annotated Bibliography of the Textual Criticism of the New Testament, 1955, (with Isobel M. Metzger) Oxford Concise Concordance to the Holy Bible, 1962, (with R.C. Dentan and W. Harrelson), The Making of the New Revised Standard Version of the Bible, 1991, (with Coogan) The Oxford Guide to People and Places of the Bible, 2001; contbr. articles to jours. Chmn. standard bible com. Nat. Coun. Chs., 1977-2000. Recipient cert. Disting. Svc. Nat. Coun. Chs., 1957, Disting. Alumnus award Lebanon Valley Coll. Alumni Assn., 1961, citation of appreciation Laymen's Nat. Bible Assn., 1986, Disting. Alumnus award Princeton Theol. Sem., 1989, lit. competition prize Christian Rsch. Found., 1955, 62, 63, E.T. Thompson award, 1991. Mem. Am. Philos. Soc., Soc. Bibl. Lit. (pres. 1970-71, past del. Am. Coun. Learned Socs.), Am. Bible Soc. (bd. mgrs. 1948—, chmn. com. transls. 1964-70), Am. Philol. Assn., Studiorum Novi Testamenti Societas (pres. 1971-72), Cath. Bibl. Assn., N.Am. Patristic Soc. (past pres.), Soc. Textual Scholarship (pres. 1995), Am. Soc. Papyrologists; hon. fellow, corr. mem. Higher Inst. Coptic Studies, Cairo; corr. fellow Brit. Acad. (Burkitt medal in Bibl. studies 1994). Republican. Home: 20 Cleveland Ln Princeton NJ 08540-3050 Office: Princeton Theol Sem 64 Mercer St Princeton NJ 08542-0803 E-mail: denise.schwalb@ptsem.edu.

METZGER, DELORES VIRGINIA, social services professional; b. Balt., Feb. 25, 1952; d. Arthur Willard and Delores Fredricka Maxwell; m. Albert Timothy Metzger, Apr. 15, 1972; children: Brian Timothy, Damien Phillip. AA degrees, Dundalk C.C., 1975, 89; BA, U. Balt., 1992; MSW, U. Md., 1994. Lic. social worker. Child support enforcement agt. Dept. Human Resources, Balt., 1983-85, adminstrv. reviewer Family Investment Adminstrn., 1985-87, asst. field supr., 1987-90, field supr., 1990-95, program mgr., 1995-96, mgmt. analyst, 1997-99, program analyst Social Svcs. Adminstrn., 1999—. Chair hospitality com. PTA High Point Elem. Sch., 1980-90; ch. vol. Our Daily Bread, Balt. Mem. Loyal Order of the Moose. Avocations: reading, bowling; contestant on Wheel of Fortune. Office: Dept Human Resources 311 W Saratoga St Baltimore MD 21201-3500

METZGER, ERNEST HUGH, aerospace engineer, scientist; b. Nurnberg, Germany, Oct. 22, 1923; came to U.S., 1939, naturalized, 1943; s. Paul Arthur and Charlotte Babette (Kann) M.; m. Sarah Temple Grinnell, Nov. 19, 1956; children: Lisa Metzger Dunning, Charlotte Bennett, George Grinnell. BS, CCNY, 1949; MS, Harvard U., 1950. Automatic control engr. Bell Aerospace Co. div. Textron, Buffalo, 1950-54, tech. dir. inertial nav. systems, 1954-60, chief engr., inertial instruments, 1960-70, chief engr., gravity gradiometer systems, 1970-83, dir. gravity sensor systems, 1983-86, exec. dir. engring., 1986-89, cons., 1989-95, Bell Geospace Inc., Buffalo, 1995—. Mem. panel future navigation systems Nat. Acad. Sci., com. on geodesy NRC, 1988-89, accelerator criteria com. NASA, tech. com. navigation guidance and control, AIAA, 1989—; vis. lectr. dept. aernautics and astronautics Stanford U., 1990 Contbr. articles to profl. jours.; patentee in field Served with AUS, 1943-46 Recipient Aerospace Pioneer award Niagara Frontier sect. AIAA, 1977; named to Niagara Frontier Aviation Hall of Fame, 1992. Mem. IEEE, Inst. Navigation (Thurlow award for outstanding contbn. to sci. navigation 1983), AAAS, Air Force Assn., N.Y. Acad. Scis., Explorers Club, Sigma Xi, Tau Beta Pi, Eta Kappa Nu Clubs: Harvard, Buffalo Ski. Home: 90 High Park Blvd Buffalo NY 14226-4209

METZGER, FRANK, management consultant; b. Mainz, Fed. Republic Germany, Feb. 27, 1929; came to U.S., 1938; s. Paul Alfred and Anna (Daniel) M.; m. Lore Lichter, Dec. 21, 1952; children: Peter D., Mark S. BS in Indsl. Edn., N.Y. State Tchrs.'s Coll., 1951; MS in Psychology, Carnegie Mellon U., 1953, PhD in Indsl. Psychology, 1954. Lic. psychologist, N.Y., Ill. Supr. tech. adminstrn. Gen. Electric., Lynn., Mass., 1956-58; dir. mgmt. devel. Raytheon, Newton, 1958-59; asst. dir. personnel ITT, N.Y.C., 1959-69; sr. v.p. adminstrn. Nytronics Inc., Pelham, N.Y., 1969-71; sr. v.p. corp. and orgn. devel. CNA Fin. Corp., Chgo., 1971-75; pres. Metzger and Co. Inc., 1975-76; sr. v.p. adminstrn. Bairnco Corp., N.Y.C., 1976-88; prin. Metzger & Co., Rye, N.Y., 1988—. Bd. dirs. Genlyte Group Inc., Louisville. Contbr. articles to profl. jours. Mem. Pres. Com. on Equal Employment Opportunity, Washington, 1962-65. Served with signal corps. U.S. Army, 1954-56. Office: Metzger & Co 16 Norman Dr Rye NY 10580-2250

METZGER, HENRY, federal research institution administrator; b. Mainz, Germany, Mar. 23, 1932; came to U.S., 1938; naturalized, 1945; s. Paul Alfred and Anne (Daniel) M.; m. Deborah Stashower, June 16, 1957; children: Eran D., Renée V., Carl E. MD, Columbia U., 1957. Chief chem. immunology sect. Nat. Inst. Arthritis & Musculoskeletal & Skin Disease/NIH, Bethesda, Md., 1973—; br. chief USPHS, 1983-94, sci. dir., 1987-98, med. officer grade VI, 1975-98; with Sr. Biomed. Rsch. Svc., 1999—. Carl Prausnitz Meml. lectr., 1982; Ecker Meml. lectr. Case Western Res. U., Cleve., 1984; Harvey Soc. lectr., 1984; Eli Nadel Meml. lectr. St. Louis U., 1987; Rodney Porter Meml. lectr., 1993; Burroughs-Wellcome lectr., 1994; R.E. Dyer lectr., 1995; mem. health rsch. coun. BMFT, German Govt., 1994-97. Editor: Fc Receptors & the Action of Antibodies, 1990; assoc. editor Ann. Rev. Immunology, 1982-96; contbr. numerous articles to profl. jours.; mem. editorial bd. numerous sci. jours. Recipient Meritorious Svc. award USPHS, 1978, Disting. Svc. award, 1985, 97, Joseph Mather Smith prize Columbia U., 1984. Fellow AAAS, Am. Acad. Allergy and Immunology; mem. NAS, Am. Assn. Immunologists (pres. 1991-92), Am. Soc. Biol. Chem. Molecular Biology, Am. Soc. Cell Biology, Internat. Union Immunol. Soc. (pres. 1992-95), Found. for Advanced Edn. in the Scis. (pres. 1990-92), Alpha Omega Alpha. Home: 3410 Taylor St Chevy Chase MD 20815-4024 Office: NIH 9000 Rockville Pike Rm 9n228 Bethesda MD 20892-1820 E-mail: metzgerh@exchange.nih.gov.

METZGER, H(OWELL) PETER, writer; b. N.Y.C., Feb. 22, 1931; s. Julius Radley and Gertrude (Fuller) M.; m. Frances Windham, June 30, 1956 (div. July 1987); children: John, James, Lisa, Suzanne; m. Valerie A. Farnham, Jan.

12, 1990 (div. Sept. 1995). BA, Brandeis U., 1953; PhD, Columbia U., 1965. Host radio talk show KTLN, Denver, 1966-68; mgr. advanced programs Ball Bros. Rsch. Corp., Boulder, 1968-70; rsch. assoc. dept. chemistry U. Colo., 1966-68; sr. rsch. scientist N.Y. State Psychiat. Inst., N.Y.C., 1965-66; syndicated columnist N.Y. Times Syndicate, 1972-74, Science Critic, Newspaper Enterprise Assn., 1974-76; sci. editor Rocky Mt. News, Denver, 1973-77. Mgr. public affairs planning Public Svc. Co. Colo., Denver, 1977-96; cons. Environ. Instrumentation, 1970-72; dir. Colspan Environ. Sys., Inc., Boulder, Colo., 1969-72. Author: The Atomic Establishment, 1972; contbr. articles in field to profl. jours., nat. mags. Pres. Colo. Com. for Environ. Info., Boulder, 1968-72; mem. Colo. Gov.'s State Health Planning Coun., 1969-72, Colo. Gov.'s Adv. Com. on Underground Nuc. Explosions, 1971-74; mem. spl. project on energy policy mgmt. Heritage Found., 1980; mem. 1981 U.S. Presdl. Rank Rev. Bd., U.S. Office Pers. Mgmt., 1981; bd. dirs. Wildlife-2000, 1970-72, Colo. Def. Coun., 1972-75. USPHS fellow, 1959-65; prin. investigator, 1968; archivee Hoover Instn. Stanford U., 1982 Mem. ACLU (state bd. dirs. 1968-71), Am. Alpine Club, Sigma Xi, Phi Lambda Upsilon. Address: 2595 Stanford Ave Boulder CO 80305-5332 E-mail: petemetzger@msn.com.

METZGER, JEFFREY PAUL, lawyer; b. Oct. 13, 1950; s. John E. and Ellen J. M; m. Stephanie Ann Stahr, Dec. 27, 1977. BA magna cum laude, Amherst Coll., 1973; JD, Georgetown U., 1976. Bar: D.C. 1977. Legis. asst. U.S. Senator Joseph Biden, Jr., Del., 1973; assoc. Collier, Shannon, Rill and Scott, Washington, 1976-79, Cole and Groner PC, Washington, 1979-82; trial atty. comml. litigation br. civil divsn. U.S. Dept. Justice, 1982-85; mem. prof. staff Pres.'s Blue Ribbon Commn. on Def. Mgmt., 1985-86; asst. gen. counsel Unisys Corp., McLean, Va., 1986-88, v.p., assoc. gen. counsel, 1989—. Mem. ABA. E-mail: jmetz10771@aol.com.

METZGER, JOHN MACKAY, lawyer; b. Princeton, N.J., Mar. 8, 1948; s. Bruce Manning and Isobel Elizabeth (Mackay) M.; m. Sandra Kay Wellington, May 8, 1999. BA cum laude, Harvard U., 1970; JD, NYU, 1973; postgrad., London Sch. Econs., 1973-74. Bar: Pa. 1976, N.J. 1976, U.S. Dist. Ct. N.J. 1976, U.S. Tax Ct. 1977, D.C. 1978, U.S. Ct. Appeals (fed. cir.) 1982. Tax adminstr. N.J. Div. Taxation, Trenton, 1976-86, 88—; atty. McCarthy & Schatzman PA, Princeton, 1986-88. Mem. N.J. Econ. Devel. Coun., 1987-90. Contbr. articles to profl. jours. Pres., trustee Friends of N.J. State Libr., 2000—. Mem. ABA, Am. Soc. Internat. Law, Harvard Club of N.Y.C., N.J. Hist. Soc., Supreme Ct. Historical Soc. Republican. Home: 52 Coriander Dr Princeton NJ 08540-9434 Office: 50 Barrack St Trenton NJ 08695-0269 E-mail: MetzgerEsq@aol.com.

METZGER, KATHLEEN ANN, computer systems specialist; b. Orchard Park, N.Y., Aug. 4, 1949; d. Charles Milton and Anna Irene (Matwijow) Wetherby; m. Robert George Metzger, Aug. 29, 1970 (div. June 1988). BS in Edn. cum laude, SUNY Coll., Buffalo, 1970; postgrad., SUNY, Fredonia, 1975. Cert. secondary tchr. Math. tchr. Crestwood High Sch., Mantua, Ohio, 1970-71; sec., bookkeeper Maple Bay Marina, Lakewood, N.Y., 1972; math., bus. tchr. Falconer (N.Y.) High Sch., 1972-76; bookkeeper Darling Jewelers, Lakewood, 1977-78; computer operator Ethan Allen Inc., Jamestown, N.Y., 1978-79, So. Tier Bldg. Trades, Jamestown, 1979; program analyst TRW Bearings Divsn., Inc., 1980-82; cons. Fla. Power Corp., St. Petersburg, 1982-2000; lead IT analyst Progress Energy, 2000—. Campaign advisor United Way, St. Petersburg, 1985; Beachfest vol. Suncoast Children's Dream Fund, 1988-92; vol. Christmas Toy Shop. Mem. Assn. Info. Tech. Profls. (sec.), St. Petersburg Second Time Arounders Marching Band Color Guard, Kappa Delta Pi. Republican. Roman Catholic. Avocations: travel, photography, boating, watching football and hockey, driving Corvette. Home: 8701 Blind Pass Rd Apt 110 Saint Petersburg FL 33706-1463 Office: Fla Power Corp 100 Central Ave Saint Petersburg FL 33701-3324

METZGER, LEWIS ALBERT, brokerage house executive, financial consultant; b. Mobile, Ala., Sept. 24, 1952; s. Albert A. and Carolyn (Simon) M.; m. Peggy Brooks, Aug. 24, 1985; children: Michelle, Austin. BS in Commerce and Business, U. Ala., 1974, MBA, 1976. Registered securities broker, N.Y. Stock Exch., Am. Stock Exch., N.Am. Securities Dealers; commodities and commodities options broker Chgo. Mercantile Exch., Chgo. Bd. Trade, N.Y. Futures Exch.; real estate and life ins. broker, Tex.; debt instruments options, fgn. currency options broker. Mdse. mgr. Electrotex, Houston, 1976-79; 1st v.p. Drexel Burnham Lambert, Inc., 1979-89; sr. v.p., sr. investment mgmt. cons. Salomon Smith Barney Inc., 1989—. Active Houston Big. Bros., 1979; apptd. to Ala. Citizen's Task Force on Higher Edn., 1974; bd. dirs. Gulf Coast Conservatin Assn., 1988-92, Bus. Romorrow Conf., 1973, St. Francis Episcopal Children's Ctr., 1988-92; mem. pres.'s cabinet U. Ala., 2000—; bd. dirs. Nat. Acad. Fin., Spring Br. Ind. Sch. Dist., 2000—. Mem. Assn. Profl. Investment Consultants, U. Ala. Nat. Alumni Assn. (pres. and bd. dirs. Houston chpt., dist. v.p. 1982-86), Commerce Exec. Soc. U. Ala. (bd. dirs. 1999-2000), Jaycees (mem. various coms.), Houston Options Soc., Zeta Beta Tau Fraternity (bd. trustees 1974-78), Omicron Delta Kappa, Alpha Kappa Psi. Avocations: hunting, fishing, water sports, coin collecting. Home: 11201 Claymore Rd Houston TX 77024-6704 Office: Salomon Smith Barney 5065 Westheimer Rd Ste 900 Houston TX 77056-6645 E-mail: lewis.a.metzger@rssmb.com.

METZGER, PHILIP WILLIAM, artist, author; b. Bklyn., Oct. 9, 1931; s. Jacob and Marie Barbara (Friedle) M.; m. Barbara Ann Hance, May 1, 1954; children: Jeffrey, Cindy, Lori, Scott. BS, Union Coll., 1953. Programming mgr. IBM, Gaithersburg, Md., 1955-71; ret., 1971. Art instr., Rockville, Md., 1972-81; mgmt. instr. IBM, 1968-71. Author: Managing a Programming Project, 1973, 3d edit., 1996, Managing Programming People, 1987, Perspective Without Pain, 1992, Enliven Your Paintings with Light, 1993, North Light Guide to Materials and Techniques, 1996; exhibited at numerous art shows (numerous awards). With USAF, 1953-55. Avocations: racquetball, gardening. Home: PO Box 10746 Rockville MD 20849-0746

METZGER, ROBERT STREICHER, lawyer; b. St. Louis, Sept. 27, 1950; s. Robert Stanley and Jean Harriet (Streicher) M.; m. Stephanie Joy Morgan, Nov. 16, 1980; children: Michael, Kristen, Marisa. BA, Middlebury Coll., 1974; JD, Georgetown U., 1977. Bar: Calif. 1978, D.C. 1978. Legis. aide U.S. Rep. Robert F. Drinan, Washington, 1972-73; legis. asst. U.S. Rep. Michael J. Harrington, 1973-75; rsch. fellow Ctr. for Sci. and Internat. Affairs Harvard U., Cambridge, Mass., 1977-78; assoc. Latham & Watkins, L.A., 1978-84, ptnr., 1984-90, Kirkland & Ellis, L.A., 1990-93, Troop, Meisinger, Steuber & Pasich and predecessor, L.A., 1993-97, Gibson, Dunn & Crutcher LLP, L.A., 1997—. Chmn. Aerospace and Govt. Practice Group, 1997—, Telecomms. Practice Group, 2000–; cons. Congl. Rsch. Svc., Washington, 1977-78. Contbr. articles to profl. jours. Mem. ABA (litigation pub. contracts sect.), Internat. Inst. for Strategic Studies, Jonathan Club. Office: Gibson Dunn & Crutcher LLP 333 S Grand Ave Los Angeles CA 90071-3197

METZGER, SIDNEY, retired communications engineer; b. N.Y., Feb. 1, 1917; m. Miriam Lipstein; children: David, Sally, Philip. BSEE, N.Y. Univ., 1937; MEE, Polytech. Inst. Bklyn., 1950. Engr. U.S. Signal Corps. Lab., NJ, 1939—45; head radio relay divsn. Fed. Telecommunications Labs. Internat. Tel. & Tel. Corp., 1945—54; mgr. communications engring. Astro Elect. Prod. Divsn. RCA, 1954—63; mgr. engring. divsn. Communications Satellite Corp., 1963-67, asst. v.p. and chief engr., 1968-72, asst. v.p. and chief scientist, 1972-80, v.p. and chief scientist, 1980-82; cons. engr., 1982—93; ret., 1993. Recipient Aerospace award Aerospace & Elec. Systems Soc., 1975, Internat. Communication award IEEE, 1976, Koji Kobayashi Computers & Communication award, 1985, Aerospace Communication award Am. Inst. Aeronaut. & Astronaut., 1984. Fellow IEEE, AIAA; mem. Nat. Acad. Engring, Sigma Xi. Address: Apt N-206 700 John Ringling Blvd Sarasota FL 34236-1500 Home: Apt N206 700 John Ringling Blvd Sarasota FL 34236-1500 E-mail: mimsid7@comcast.net.

METZGER, VERNON ARTHUR, management educator, consultant; b. Baldwin Park, Calif., Aug. 13, 1918; s. Vernon and Nellie C. (Ross) Metzger; m. Beth Alrene Metzger, Feb. 19, 1955; children: Susan, David1 stepchild Linda. BS, U. Calif., Berkeley, 1947, MBA, 1948. Estimating engr. C.F. Braun & Co., 1949; prof. mgmt. Calif. State U., Long Beach, 1949-89, prof. emeritus, 1989—, founder Sch. of Bus. Mgmt. cons. Mem. Fire Commn., Fountain Valley, Calif., 1959—60; mem. mgmt. task force to promote modern mgmt. in Yugoslavia, U.S. State Dept., 1977; mem. State of Calif. Fair Polit. Practices Commn., Orange County Transit Com.; pres. Orange County Dem. League, 1967—68. With USNR, 1942—45. Recipient Outstanding Citizen award, Orange County. Fellow: Soc. Advancement Mgmt. (life, dir.); mem.: Orange County Indsl. Rels. Rsch. Assn. (v.p.), Acad. Mgmt., Tau Kappa Upsilon, Alpha Kappa Psi, Beta gamma Sigma. Home: 1938 Balearic Dr Costa Mesa CA 92626-3513 Office: 1250 N Bellflower Blvd Long Beach CA 90840-0006

METZGER, W. JAMES, JR. physician, researcher, educator; b. Pitts., Oct. 30, 1945; s. Walter James Sr. and Marion Smith (Vine) M.; m. Carol Louise Hughes, Sept. 14, 1968; children: James Andrew, Joel Robert, Anne Elizabeth. BA, Stanford U., 1967; MD, Northwestern U., Chgo., 1971. Intern, resident Northwestern U. Sch. of Medicine, Chgo., 1971-74, rsch. fellow, 1974-76; asst. prof. medicine U. Iowa Coll. of Medicine, Iowa City, 1978-84; assoc. prof., sect. head East Carolina U. Sch. of Medicine, Greenville, N.C., 1984-90, prof., sect. head, 1990—, vice chmn medicine for rsch., 1993—, asst. dean clin. rsch., chmn. med. rsch., 1989-96, disting. rsch. prof. medicine, 1998—. Mem. study sect. merit rev. Nat. VA Rsch. Com., 1991-94; mem. sci. adv. bd. Epi Genesis, Inc. Co-editor: Drugs and the Lung, 1994; mem editl. Allergy Procs., 1989-93, Jour. of Allergy and Clin. Immunology, 2000; contbr. chpts. to books, papers to med. jours. Forum leader Jarvis Meml. United Meth. Ch., Greenville, 1985-98. NIH grantee, Bethesda, Md., 1988-92. Fellow ACP, Am. Coll. Chest Physicians; mem. Am. Acad. Allergy Rsch. Coun. (vice chair 1988-92, 93-95, chair 1995-97), Am. Acad. Allergy Asthma (chair bronchoalveolar lavage com. 1994-95), Rhinitis, Respiratory Diseases (chair interest sect. 1991-92), Chilean Lung Soc. (hon.). Achievements include 3 patents; research in allergic diseases; Dx and management, principles and practice in allergy, immunology and allergy clinics, immunopharmacology and investigation and classification of drugs. Office: 1400 Jackson St Denver CO 80206-2761

METZGER, YALE HYDER, lawyer, educator; b. Adrian, Mich., Oct. 20, 1959; s. John Andrew and Shirley Jane Metzger; m. Susan E. Richmond, May 19, 1995. BA in Justice, U. Alaska, 1987; JD cum laude, Gonzaga U., 1995. Bar: Alaska 1995, U.S. Dist. Ct. Alaska 1996. Law clk. to magistrate judge U.S. Dist. Ct., 1995-96; atty. in pvt. practice Anchorage, 1995—. Mem. paralegal edn. adv. com. U. Alaska, Anchorage, 1989—; adj. prof. U. Alaska, Anchorage, 1996—. With USAF, 1982-85. Mem.: ATLA, Whittier Boat Owners' Assn., S.Am. Explorers Club, Anchorage Inn of Ct. (sec. 1999—2000, treas. 2000—02). Avocations: exploration of Amazon rainforest in Ecuador, sailing in Prince William Sound, SCUBA diving, hunting big game in Alaska and Africa. Office: 425 G St Ste 510 Anchorage AK 99501-2160

METZINGER, TIMOTHY EDWARD, lawyer; b. L.A., Aug. 21, 1961; s. Robert Cole and Mary Jean (Cusick) M.; m. Cynthia Lee Stanworth, Nov. 16, 1991. BA, UCLA, 1986; JD, U. San Francisco, 1989. Bar: Calif. 1989, U.S. Dist. Ct. (ctrl., so., ea. and no. dists.) Calif. 1989, U.S. Ct. Appeals (9th cir.) 1989, U.S. Supreme Ct. 1994. Assoc. Bronson, Bronson & McKinnon, L.A., 1989-93; ptnr. Price, Postel & Parma, Santa Barbara, Calif., 1993—. Editor Santa Barbara Lawyer, 1999—. Bd. dirs. Santa Barbara County Bar Assn. Mem. Santa Barbara County Bar Assn. (bd. dirs., CFO), Santa Barbara Mus. Natural History (bd. advisors), Santa Barbara Barristers Club (pres.), Order of Barristers, Am. Inns. Ct. Avocations: diving, moutaineering, sailing. Office: Price Postel & Parma 200 E Carrillo St Ste 400 Santa Barbara CA 93101-2190

METZLER, DWIGHT FOX, civil engineer, retired state official; b. Kans., Mar. 25, 1916; s. Ross R. and Grace M. (Fox) Metzler; m. Lela Ross, June 1941 (dec. Jan. 1991); children: Linda Diane, Brenda Lee, Marilyn Anne, Martha Jean; m. Helen C. Telfel, Sept. 5, 1998. BSCE, Kans. U., 1940, CE, 1947; SM, Harvard U., 1948. Registered Kans., N.Y. Asst. engr. Kans. Bd. Health, 1940—42, san. engr., 1946—48; chief engr. Topeka, 1948—62; assoc. prof. dept. civil engring. U. Kans., 1948—59, prof., 1959—66; exec. sec. Kans. Water Resources Bd., Topeka, 1962—66; dep. commr. N.Y. State Dept. Health, Albany, 1966—70, N.Y. State Dept. Environ. Conservation, Albany, 1970—74; sec. Kans. Dept. Health and Environment, Topeka, 1974—79, dir. water supply devel., 1979—84, ret., 1984; pres. Metzler Group, from 1999. Cons. sanitary engring. Fed. Pub. Housing Authority/USPHS, 1943—46; housing cons. Chgo.-Cook County Health Survey, 1946; cons. water supply and water pollution control USPHS, 1957—66; advisor Govt. of India, 1960; ofcl. exchange to USSR on environ. health rsch. and practice, 62; advisor WHO, 1964—84; cons., expert witness Occidential Chem. Co., Love Canal, 1990—91; mem. water Pollution Bd; mem. water pollution bd. Internat. Joint Commn., 1967—74; mem. Assembly of Engring. NRC, 1977—80. Mem. editl. bd.: Internat. Jour. Water Pollution Rsch.; contbr. articles to profl. jours. Chmn. Kans. Bible Chair Bd., 1957—66; chmn. com. for new bldg. U. Kans. Sch. Religion. With USPHS, 1943—46. Recipient Disting. Svc. award, U. Kans., 1970, Disting. Engring. Svc. award, 1984, Wisdom award, Wisdom Hall of Fame, 1999. Fellow: ASCE (sec. sanitary engring. divsn. 1959—61, chmn. 1963), APHA (former mem. governing coun., exec. bd., pres., chmn. action bd., Centennial award 1972, Sedgwick medal 1981), Royal Soc. Health Gt. Britain (hon.); mem.: Kans. Rural Water Assn. (Conger award 1990, Wisdom award 1999), Nat. Acad. Engring., Kans. Engring. Soc. (Outstanding Engr. award 1978), Kans. Pub. Health Assn. (Crumbine award 1965), Am. Water Works Assn. (Fuller award 1954, Purification Divsn. award 1958), Water Pollution Control Fedn. (hon. Bedell award 1963), Tau Beta Pi, Sigma Xi. Home: Topeka, Kans. Died Oct. 30, 2001.

METZLER, ERIC HAROLD, retired state agency administrator, researcher; b. Albion, Mich., Nov. 13, 1945; s. Clarence Harold and Lois Marian (Bastian) M.; m. Patricia Ann (Trescott), Aug. 26, 1967; children: Meredith Gene, Hisa Shigematsu. BS, Mich. State U., 1968. Ops. mgr. ODNR div. Watercraft, Columbus, Ohio, 1973-80, dep. chief, 1980-96; owner Eric H. Metzler Rsch. Assocs., 1996—. Rsch. assoc. Ohio Agrl. Rsch Ctr., Wooster, 1974-78, Ohio Biol. Survey, Columbus, 1980-84, Fla. State Collection Arthropods, Gainesville, 1985—, Cleve. Mus. Natural History, 1985—, Carnegie Mus. Natural History, 1992—; assoc. mus. biol. diversity Ohio State U. Contbr. articles to profl. jours. Mem., dir. Wedge Entomol. Rsch. Found., 1994—, sec., 1998—; pres. Columbus Matural History Soc., 1981, treas. 1985-2000; trustee Midwest Biodiversity Inst., 1998-2000, treas., 1999-2000. Mem. Ohio Parks and Recreation Assn. (treas. 1978-80, 3d v.p. 1981), Ohio Lepidopterist (sec. treas. 1979, pres. 1980, newsletter editor 1980—), Lepidopterists Soc. (treas. 1985-87, pres. 1996-97). Home: 1241 Kildale Sq N Columbus OH 43229-1306

METZLER, JERRY DON, retired nursing administrator; b. Mishawaka, Ind., Mar. 6, 1935; s. Gerald Donald and Cleota Christabell (Dowell) M.; m. Dorothy J. Masters, Aug. 18, 1962. BS, Ariz. State U., 1962, MEd, 1967; BSN, San Diego State U., 1973; MS, U. Ariz., Tucson, 1980. Tchr. sci. Washington Sch., Sanger, Calif., 1963-68; tchr. biology San Jacinto (Calif.) H.S., 1968-70; staff nurse Maricopa County Hosp., Phoenix, 1973-76, St. Luke's Hosp., Phoenix, 1976-77; instr. nursing, dept. head Gila Pueblo Coll., Globe, Ariz., 1977-78; nurse educator, asst. dir. nursing USPHS Indian Hosp., Tuba City, 1980-84; asst. nursing svc. mgr. Phoenix Indian Med. Ctr., 1984-85, pub. health educator, 1985-88; dir. nursing USPHS Indian Hosp., Owyhee, Nev., 1988-90; sr. project officer USPHS, Dallas, 1990-97; ret., 1997. With USN, 1956-60, USPHS, 1990-97. Mem. ANA, Res. Officers Assn., Commd. Officers Assn. USPHS, Masons, Sigma Theta Tau. Republican. Methodist. Home: 3413 N 44th Pl Phoenix AZ 85018-6025 E-mail: jdmetzler@juno.com.

METZLER, PAUL RAYMOND, electrical engineer, consultant; b. St. Louis, Sept. 19, 1949; s. Raymond Herman and Rita Fanny (Morton) M.; m. Barbara Mary Dolan, May 18, 1974 (div. Dec. 1985); children: Tammi Marie, Julie Lynn, Brian Keith; m. Roxy Susan Clark, Dec. 20, 1987. BSEE, U. Mo., Rolla, 1973. Registered profl. engr., Tenn., Nev., Mo., Ill. Elec. engr. Titanium Pigment div. NL Industries, St. Louis, 1974-76, Reynolds Elec. & Engring. Co., Inc., Las Vegas, Nev., 1983-88; sr. elec. engr. Carborundum Environ. Systems div. Kennecott Corp., Knoxville, Tenn., 1976-81; instrument and control project engr. Chem. Separations Corp., 1981-82; cons. engr. PM Engring. Assocs., 1982-84; quality control engr. C.R. Fedrick, Inc., Kaneohe, Hawaii, 1988-89; cons. PM Engring. Assocs., Pearl City, 1989-92, Lawton, Okla., 1992-94; v.p. Pacific Rim Cons. & Inspection Corp., Aiea, Hawaii, 1991-92; elec. inspector Sverdrup-CRSS Jacob Facilities, Inc., St. Louis, 1996-2000; cons. engr. Criterium-McMahon Engrs., 2000—; office mgr., elec. engr. Selective Site Cons., Inc., Creve Coeur, 2001—. Mem. vestry Grace Episcopal Ch., Kirkwood, Mo., 1999-2001, jr. warden, 2001. Fellow: Internat. Biog. Assn. (life); mem. NSPE, Illuminating Engring. Soc. N.Am. (assoc.), Silver State Computer Users Group (v.p. 1984-86, libr. 1986-88), Instrument Soc. Am., Nat. Fire Protection Assn., Brotherhood of St. Andrew Inc. (life), Mo. Soc. Profl. Engrs., Order of Engr. (charter), Nat. Model R.R. Assn. (editor Rail Post Office 1997-2001), Big Bend R.R. Club (pres. 2001—), Kirkwood R.R. Assn. (pres. 1997—). Home: 5404 Medalton Way Saint Louis MO 63128-3531 Office: 13503 Coliseum Dr Chesterfield MO 63017 E-mail: pmetzler@swbell.net.

METZLER, ROBERT J., II, lawyer; b. Allentown, Pa., Feb. 5, 1948; s. Robert J. and Jean (Rockey) M.; m. Deborah Anne Tamoney, Aug. 21, 1976; children: Melissa, Robert III, Margot, Matthew. BA, Princeton U., 1970; JD, U. Conn., 1973. Bar: N.Y. 1974, Conn. 1976, U.S. Dist. Ct. (so. and ea. dists.) N.Y. 1974, U.S. Ct. Appeals (2d cir.) 1976. Atty. N.Y.C. Law Dept., 1973-75; law clk. to Hon. Thomas J. Meskill U.S. Ct. Appeals (2d cir.), N.Y.C. and New Britain, Conn., 1975-76; assoc. atty. Tyler, Cooper & Alcorn, LLP, New Haven, 1976-81, ptnr. New Haven and Hartford, 1982—. Dir. Common Ground Youth Leadership Forum, Hartford, 1987-98, W. Hartford Youth Hockey Assn., 1988-93, United Way Capital Region, Hartford, 1989—, United Way Conn., 1997—. Fellow Am. Coll. Investment Counsel; mem. Nat. Assn. Stock Plan Profls., Conn. Bar Assn. (chmn. pub. utility law sect. 1982-84). Office: Tyler Cooper & Alcorn City Pl Fl 35 185 Asylum St Hartford CT 06103 E-mail: metzler@tylercooper.com.

METZLER, RUTH HORTON, genealogical educator; b. Eden, N.Y., Aug. 4, 1927; d. John Morris and Bernice Louise Horton; m. Henry George Metzler, Sept. 4, 1948; children: Kathleen, Ronald, Janice, Margaret. Student, Wheaton Coll., 1945-48; AB cum laude, Wilmington Coll., 1956; MLS, SUNY, Geneseo, 1962. Cert. tchr., libr. media specialist, N.Y. Cataloging typist Peoria (Ill.) Pub. Libr., 1949-52; cataloging asst. Wilmington (Ohio) Coll. Libr., 1953-56; sch. libr. K-12 Nunda (N.Y.) Cen. Sch., 1956-65; head Libr. Media Ctr. Irondequoit H.S., Rochester, 1965-84; pres. Rochester (N.Y.) Geneal. Soc., 1989-93; instr., lectr. Rochester Mus. and Sci. Ctr., 1990—. Author several family histories. Organizing instr. Genealogy Workshops, Rochester Mus. and Sci. Ctr; contbg. lectr. Nat. Geneal. Conf. in Rochester, 1990, others. Mem. N.Y. Libr. Assn., N.Y. State Tchr.'s Retirement System, New Eng. Hist. and Geneal. Soc., Kodak Geneal. Soc., N.Y. State Coun. of Geneal., Genealogy Round Table of Monroe County (del. 1996—), Rochester Geneal. Soc., Geneal. Educators (organizing mem. 1996). Republican. Baptist. Avocations: family history photography, geneal. rsch., writing.

METZNER, BARBARA STONE, university counselor; b. St. Louis, June 9, 1940; d. Wendell Phillips and Lois Custer (Rake) Metzner. AB, Ind. U., 1962, MS, 1964, EdD, 1983; BA, Purdue U., 1979. Asst. dean students U. Ill., Urbana, 1964-68; undergrad. advisor UCLA, 1968-69; asst. dean students Ohio State U., 1969-72; student affairs officer San Diego State U., 1972-76; sr. counselor Ind. U. - Purdue U., Indpls., 1976—. Supr. Ednl. Testing Svc., Indpls., 1980-90; cons. editorial bd. Nat. Acad. Advising Assn., Manhattan, Kans., 1987-93; adj. prof. Ind. U., 1987—; mgr. Info. Svcs., Ind. U.-Purdue U., 1989-91. Contbr. articles to profl. jours., chpts. to books. Mem. Marion County Precinct Election Bd., 1980-92; mem. exec. com. Ind. Allied Health Assn., 1983-84; VIP escort Pan Am. Games, 1987. Spencer Found. grantee, 1985. Mem. AAAS, APA, Am. Edn. Rsch. Assn., Assn. Instl. Rsch., Kappa Alpha Theta (vol. charity benefits 1980-90), Phi Beta Kappa. Avocations: tennis, Chinese cooking, fine arts. Office: IUPUI 815 W Michigan St Indianapolis IN 46202-5199

METZNER, CHARLES MILLER, federal judge; b. N.Y.C., Mar. 13, 1912; s. Emanuel and Gertrude (Miller) M.; m. Jeanne Gottlieb, Oct. 6, 1966. AB, Columbia U., 1931, LL.B., 1933. Bar: N.Y. 1933. Pvt. practice, 1934; mem. Jud. Council State N.Y., 1935-41; law clk. to N.Y. supreme ct. justice, 1942-52; exec. asst. to U.S. atty. Gen. Herbert Brownell, Jr., 1953-54; mem. firm Chapman, Walsh & O'Connell, 1954-59; judge U.S. Dist Ct. (so. dist.) N.Y., 1959—. Mem. Law Revision Commn. N.Y. State, 1959; chmn. com. adminstrn. magistrates system U.S. Jud. Conf., 1970-81; chmn. Columbia Coll. Coun., 1965-66. Pres. N.Y. Young Republican Club, 1941; Trustee Columbia U., 1972-84, trustee emeritus, 1984—; bd. dirs. N.Y.C. Ctr. Music and Drama, 1969-74. Recipient Lawyer Div. of Joint Def. Appeal award, 1961, Columbia U. Alumni medal, 1966, Founders award Nat. Coun. U.S. Magistrates, 1989. Mem. ABA, Am. Law Inst., Fed. Bar Coun. (cert. Disting. Jud. Svc. 1989).

METZNER, RICHARD, advertising executive; Grad., Harvard U. Fin. analyst Am. Airlines; co-founder TMSI, 1985; sr. v.p. strategy Brierly & Ptnrs., Dallas, 1990-95, pres., 2000—; v.p., mktg Continental Airlines, 1995-2000. Named Marketer of Yr. Brandweek, Marketing 100 Advt. Age. Office: Brierley & Ptnrs 8401 N Central Expressway. Ste 1000 Dallas TX 75225*

METZNER, RICHARD JOEL, psychiatrist, psychopharmacologist, educator; b. L.A., Feb. 15, 1942; s. Robert Gerson and Esther Rebecca (Groper) M.; children: Jeffrey Anthony, David Jonathan; m. Leila Kirkley, June 26, 1993. BA, Stanford U., 1963; MD, Johns Hopkins U., 1967. Diplomate Am. Bd. Psychiatry and Neurology. Intern Roosevelt Hosp., N.Y.C., 1967-68; resident in psychiatry Stanford U. Med. Ctr., 1968-71; staff psychiatrist divsn. manpower and tng. NIMH-St. Elizabeths Hosp., Washington, 1971-73; chief audiovisual edn. sys. VA Med. Ctr. Brentwood, L.A., 1973-79; from asst. prof. psychiatry to assoc. clin. prof. UCLA Neuropsychiat. Inst., 1980-96, clin. prof., 1996—. Lectr. Sch. Social Welfare, 1975-84; pvt. practice medicine specializing in psychiatry, Bethesda, Md., 1972-73, L.A., 1973—, Sedona, Ariz., 1997—; dir. Western Inst. Psychiatry, L.A., 1977—; pres. Psychiat. Resource Network, Inc., 1984-90. Contbr. articles to profl. jours.; prodr., writer numerous films and videotapes. With USPHS, 1968-71. Recipient 6 awards for film and videotape prodns., 1976-80. Fellow: Am. Psychiat. Assn.; mem.: UCLA Psychiat. Clin. Faculty Assn. (pres. 2001—), Mental Health Careerists Assn. (chmn. 1972—73), So. Calif. Psychiat. Soc., Phi Beta Kappa (pres. 2001—02). Democrat. Jewish. Office: 916 N Foothill Rd Beverly Hills CA 90210 also: 60 Cindercone Cir Sedona AZ 86336 E-mail: rmetzner@ucla.edu., rmetzner@earthlink.net.

MEUNIER, MONIQUE, dancer; b. L.A. Studied with Irena Komoskova, studied with Yvonne Mounsey; student, Sch. Am. Ballet, 1988. Mem. corps de ballet N.Y.C. Ballet, 1990—97, soloist, 1997—98, prin., 1998—. Dancer (ballets) Agon, Apollo, Harlequinade, The Nutcracker, Swan Lake, Tschaikovsky Piano Concerto No. 2, Vienna Waltzes, The Sleeping Beauty, Ash, Delight of the Muses, A Schubert Sonata, Slavonic Dances. Office: NYC BAllet NY State Theatre 20 Lincoln Ctr Plz New York NY 10023-6913*

MEUNIER, PASCAL CHARLES, research scientist, educator; b. Quebec City, Can., Nov. 19, 1964; came to U.S., 1993; s. Maurice and Marielle (Cleroux) M.; m. Frances G. Christman, Oct. 27, 1990. BS in Physics, U. Laval, Quebec, 1986; PhD in Biophysics, U. Quebec, 1991. Postdoctoral fellow U. Cambridge, Eng., 1991-92; rsch. asst. Purdue U., West Lafayette, Ind., 1993—. Horizon Counselor, 1995-97, Quick Start Faculty mem., 1994, Purdue U., West Lafayette, Ind. Author: (freeware program) Chlorophyll, 1996, Sing-a-password, 1998; contbr. articles to profl. jours. Recipient Postdoctoral fellowship, 1991, Grad. Student fellowship, 1986-90, Natural Scis. and Engring. Rsch. Coun. Can. Mem. AAAS, MacSciTech, Am. Soc. Computing Machinery. Achievements include an improved model of the water oxidation (s-state) mechanism in photosynthesis; the interaction of respiration and photosynthesis producing oxygen signals; model of the adaptation and regulation mechanisms of photosynthesis in diazotrophic cyanobacteria; model of the regulation of photosynthesis in diazotrophic cyanobacteria. Office: Purdue U Dept Computer Scis Purdue University IN 47907

MEUNIER, ROBERT RAYMOND, research electrical engineer, optical engineer; b. Hollywood, Calif., Mar. 27, 1957; s. Raymond Robert and Anna Marie (Rapp) M; m. Janet E. Bost. ASD in Laser Electro-Optics, Pasadena (Calif.) City Coll., 1984; BS in Mgmt., Pepperdine U., 1993. Lab. asst. Jet Propulsion Lab., Pasadena, Calif., 1984-85; rsch. engr. satellite sys. Rockwell Internat., Seal Beach, 1985-89; electro-optical engr. Cymbolic Scis. Internat., Irvine, 1989-90; project engr. OCA Applied Optics, Garden Grove, 1990-92; owner, program mgr. Integrated Scientific, Mission Viejo, 1992-96; sr. sys. test engr. Rocketdyne Corp., Granada Hills, 1994-96; prog. mgr. Newport Corp.,

Irvine, 1996—. Mem. Laser Inst. Am., Soc. Photo-optical Instrumentation Engrs., L.A. Collegiate Coun. (alumnus), Inter Orgnl. Coun. (founder, chmn. 1981-82), Nat. Mgmt. Assn., Internat. Platform Assn., Lions Club, Inventors Forum, Sigma Pi. Republican. Four Square Evangelical Protestant.

MEURLIN, KEITH W. airport manager; BA, Univ. of Vermont, 1972; MS, Univ. of Southern California, 1977. Served in U.S. Air Force and Nat. Guard, 1972—; now gen. mgr. Washington Dulles Internat. Airport; mobilization asst. Langley AFB, Va. Recipient Meritorious Service Medal, Air Force Outstanding Unit Award, National Defense Srvc. Medal. Office: Washington Dulles Internat Airport PO Box 17045 Washington DC 20041-7045 also: Hdq Air Reserve Personnel Cntr Office of Public Affairs Denver CO 80280*

MEURY, VERONICA KMEC, medical foundation manager; b. Pitts., Mar. 18, 1946; d. Andrew William and Veronica Constance (Rudzik) Kmec; m. John Nicholas Meury, Jr., Oct. 29, 1966; children: John III, Matthew, Mark. BA, U. Pitts., 1963-68. Bus. office supr. Pacific Telephone, L.A., 1969-71; asst. dir. svcs. Honolulu Club, 1981-84; nat. coord. Second Chance Hot-Line, Pitts., 1985-86; project chmn. Internat. Organ Transplant Forum, 1985-87; exec. dir. Transplant Recipients Internat., 1987-93; dir. membership & devel. Helen Clay Frick Found., 1993-94; mgr. Soc. Automotive Engrs. Found., Warrendale, Pa., 1994—. Bd. dirs. AIDS Task Force, Pitts., Family Resources, Pitts., Industry, Univ. roundtable for enhancing Engring. Edn., Garrett Morgan Tech. and Transportation Futures Prog., DOT, Wash. Pres. Mt. Lebanon Dem. Women's Forum, Pitts., 1987—; campaign coord. June Delano for Commr., Pitts., 1989; bd. dirs. Jr. League Pitts., 1986—; pres. Symphony Guild of Honolulu, 1983-84; grad. Leadership Pitts., Class 6, 1989; assoc. vol. The Nat. Ctr., Washington, 1989; adv. mem. Mt. Lebanon Sch. Dist., Pitts., 1987; ordained elder Presbyn. Ch. Recipient Outstanding Svc. award Sta. KDKA-TV and Presbyn. U. Hosp., 1985, Anne D. Johnston award Jr. League Pitts., 1992. Mem. Am. Coun. Transplantation (bd. dirs.), Assn. of Jr. Leagues Internat. (area pub. rels. liaison), ACT Patient & Family Forum, Mt. Lebanon Garden Arts (program chair 1987-88). Avocations: gardening, travel, reading, gourmet cooking. Office: Soc Automotive Engrs Found 400 Commonwealth Dr Warrendale PA 15086-7511

MEUSER, FREDRICK WILLIAM, retired seminary president, church historian; b. Payne, Ohio, Sept. 14, 1923; s. Henry William and Alvina Maria (Bouyack) M.; m. Jeanne Bond Griffiths, July 29, 1951; children: Jill Martha, Douglas Griffiths. AB, Capital U., 1945, BD, 1948, DD (hon.), 1989; STM, Yale U., 1949, MA, 1953, PhD, 1956; DD (hon.), Tex. Luth. Coll., 1980, Capital U., 1989; LHD (hon.), Augustana Coll., 1985. Ordained to ministry Am. Lutheran Ch., 1948; asst. pastor 1st Luth. Ch., Galveston, Tex., 1948, Christ Luth. Ch., North Miami, Fla., 1949-51; campus minister Yale U., 1951-53; prof. ch. history Luth. Theol. Sem., Columbus, Ohio, 1953-78, dean grad. studies, 1963-69, pres., 1971-78, Trinity Luth. Sem., Columbus, 1978-88; exec. sec. div. theol. studies Luth. Council in U.S.A., 1969-71; del. World Council Chs., 1968, Luth. World Fedn., 1970; v.p. Am. Luth. Ch., 1974-80; mem. Commn. for a New Luth. Ch., 1982-86; asst. pastor St. Paul Luth. Ch., Westerville, Ohio, 1995-97. Author: The Formation of the American Lutheran Church, 1958, Luther the Preacher, 1983; author: (with others) Church in Fellowship, 1963, Lutherans in North America, 1975; translator: (with others) What Did Luther Understand by Religion, 1977, The Reconstruction of Morality, 1979; editor and author: (with others) Interpreting Luther's Legacy, 1967. Recipient Disting. Churchman's award Tex. Luth. Coll., 1972, Joseph Sittler award Trinity Luth. Sem., 1990; named Outstanding Alumnus Capital U., 1977; Am. Assn. Theol. Schs. fellow, 1961-62 Home: 6392 Claypool Ct Columbus OH 43213-3435 Office: 2199 E Main St Columbus OH 43209-3913 E-mail: fredmeuser@aol.com.

MEVEC, EDWARD ROBERT, lawyer, funeral director; b. Binghamton, N.Y., Aug. 27, 1958; s. Edward John and Margaret B. (Puskar) M.; m. Barbara Ann Vines, May 14, 1988; children: Benjamin A. Vines-Mevec, Daniel L. Vines-Mevec. BS summa cum laude, St. Thomas Aquinas Coll., Sparkill, N.Y., 1985; JD, U. Bridgeport, Conn., 1988. Bar: N.Y. 1990, U.S. Dist. Ct. (so. dist.) N.Y. 1992, U.S. Dist. Ct. (ea. dist.) N.Y. 1994, U.S. Ct. Appeals for the Armed forces 1995, U.S. Ct. Appeals (2d cir.), 1996, U.S. Supreme Ct. 1996. Atty. The Legal Aid Soc., Bronx, N.Y., 1988-89; assoc. Bruce W. Braswell, Esq., Peekskill, 1989-91, Michael T. Ridge, Esq., Bronx, 1991-92; trial atty. Gerlad G. Cowen, Esq., Elmsford, 1992. Arbitrator small claims N.Y.C. Civil Ct., Bronx, 1996—; hearing officer N.Y. State Supreme Ct., White Plains, 1996—; panel mem. Surrogate Decision Making Com., New City, N.Y., 1996—; arbitrator Lemon Law-AAA. Mem. Zoning Bd. Appeals, Peekskill, 1997; adv. legal affairs com. Youth Bd., Peekskill, 1997. Mem. Am. Judges Assn., Def. Assn. N.Y., N.Y. State Dispute Resolution Assn., N.Y. State Bar Assn., Westchester County Bar Assn. (grievance com. 1997), N.Y. State Trial Lawyers Assn., Assn. Small Claims Arbitrators, Alpha Sigma Lambda. Republican. Roman Catholic. Office: Gerald G Cowen Esq 570 Taxter Rd Elmsford NY 10523-2337

MEVERS, FRANK CLEMENT, state archivist, historian; b. New Orleans, Oct. 10, 1942; s. Lloyd F. and Mary Ashley (Collins) M.; m. Kathryn Ann Hayes, Dec. 23, 1967; children: John F., Lauren K. BA in History, La. State U., 1965; PhD in Am. History, U. N.C., 1972; MA, La. State U., 1967. Editor Papers of James Madison, Charlottesville, Va., 1972-74, Papers of Josiah Bartlett, Concord, N.H., 1974-77, Papers of William Plumer, Concord, 1977-79; state archivist State of N.H., 1979—. Editor, author: New Hampshire: State That Made US a Nation, 1989. Mem. Pub. Libr. Bd. Trustees, Concord, 1979-99. With U.S. Army, 1967-69, Korea. Episcopalian. Avocation: stamp collecting. Home: 29 Bradley St Concord NH 03301-6432 Office: NH State Archives 71 S Fruit St Concord NH 03301-2410 E-mail: fmevers@sos.state.nh.us, eatright@attbi.com.

MEW, CALVIN MARSHALL, advertising executive; b. Oakland, Calif., Oct. 27, 1947; s. Thomas Bing and May (Jan) M. BA, Yale U., 1969; MDiv, Union Theol Sem., 1973; postgrad., Columbia U., 1973-79, Harvard U., 1984. Tutor Union Theol. Sem., 1973-77; adj. lectr. Hunter Coll., 1977-79; market analyst Kenyon & Eckhart Advt., Inc., N.Y.C., 1979-82, v.p. market plans, 1982-83, rev. v.p. strategic plan, 1983-85, v.p. strategic mktg. svcs., 1985-88, sr.v.p. strategic and forward planning, 1988-90; sr. v.p., mng. dir. Bozell, Inc., 1990-93, exec. v.p., mng. dir., 1993—. Gen. mgr. Bozell Austria, 1994; exec. v.p., regional dir. L.Am. Bozell Worldwide, Inc., 1996; dir. Capritauro Investments, Ltd., 2002. Contbr. articles to profl. jours. Bd. dirs. Union Theol. Sem., 1984—, vice chmn., 1992—. Recipient Cogswell award Yale U., 1969; Columbia U. fellow, Rockefeller Bros. Fund fellow. Mem. Am. Acad. Religion, Soc. Bibl. Lit. Presbyterian. Home: 895 W End Ave New York NY 10025-3500 Office: Bozell Inc 40 W 23rd St New York NY 10010-5215

MEW, THOMAS JOSEPH, III (TOMMY MEW), artist, educator; b. Miami, Fla., Aug. 15, 1942; s. Thomas Joseph and Maude Edith (Perry) M.; m. Mary Ann Kelley, June 17, 1966; 1 son, Thomas Joseph IV. BS, Fla. State U., 1962, MA, 1964; PhD, N.Y. U., 1966. Grad. instr. Fla. State U., 1963; asst. prof. art Troy State U., 1966-68, Jacksonville U., 1968-70; prof., chmn. dept. art Berry Coll., 1970—, Dana prof. art. Juror art shows: vis. artist; lectr. in field, cons. art; dir. Fluxus West/Southeast; dir. Moon Gallery. Exhibited in one-man shows Parkway Gallery, Miami, 1962-63, 319 Gallery, N.Y.C., 1968, Meridian (Miss.) Mus., 1976, C.D.O. Gallery, Parma, Italy, 1978, Calif. State U., Sacramento, 1979, Miss. Mus. Art, Jackson, 1979, Art Inst. for Permian Basin, ITex, Arte Studio, Bergamo, Italy, Queen Street Gallery, Belfast, No. Ireland; group shows include High Mus., Atlanta, 1971, 72, 74, New Reform Gallery, Aalst, Belgium, 1975, U. Guelph, Ont., Can., 1975, Neuberger Mus., Purchase, N.Y., 1978, Arte Fiera, Bologna, Italy, 1979; represented in permanent collections Kansas City Art Inst., Mildura Art Centre, Australia, Wichita Art Mus., Jacksonville (Fla.) Art Mus., Macon Mus. Art, AT&T, Harn Mus., U. Iowa; host: Cable TV show Art: The Mew View, 1978— ; Filmmaker, 1966-69; contbr. articles to profl. jours. Bd. dirs. Rome Arts Council, 1984— ; bd. dirs. Interface. Recipient Gellhorn award N.Y. U., 1966; Cowperthwaite grantee, 1972; Lilly Found. grantee, 1975; Gulf Life grantee, 1977. Mem. Southeastern Coll. Art Conf., Coll. Art Assn. Am., Am. Fedn. Arts, Nat. Art Edn. Assn., Am. Assn. Art Dealers. Home: Rosewood Cottage PO Box 495028 Mount Berry GA 30149-5028 Office: Berry Coll Art Dept Mount Berry GA 30149 E-mail: tmew@berry.edu. *I've always moved in the direction of my dreams . . . always tried to make the great dream a reality.*

MEWANI, RAJSHREE RAMCHAND, researcher; b. Bombay, India, Apr. 3, 1969; s. Naraindas and Neena Kotwani; life ptnr. Ramchand Mewani, Dec. 13, 1999. BS, Jai Hind Coll. U. Bombay, 1989; diploma med. lab. tech., S.I.E.S. Coll. U Bombay, 1990; Master degree, Seth G.S. Med. Coll. U. Bombay, 1994, PhD, 1999. Jr. rsch. fellow Seth G.S. Med. Coll. and K.E.M. Hosp., Bombay, 1990-94, sr. rsch. fellow, 1994-99; parasitologist Inst. of Medicine, Kathmandu, Nepal, 1999-2000; rsch. fellow Georgetown U. Med. Ctr., Washington, 2000—. Contbr. articles to profl. jours.; patentee in field. Home: Apt 2 4520 MacArthur Blvd NW Washington DC 20007 Office: Georgetown U Med Ctr W201 TRB 3970 Reservoir Rd NW Washington DC 20007 Fax: 202-687-2221. E-mail: dr_rajshreek@yahoo.com., rrm6@georgetown.edu.

MEWBORN, WILLIE MAE, publisher, editor, author; b. Dover, NC, May 26, 1959; d. Joshua and Bertha Mattie Ruth M. BA in English, Atlantic Christian Coll., 1982. Author: Through the Storms & Through the Rain, 2000, Resting in God's Love, 2000; pub.: What Do You Do Once God Delivers You? Avocations: reading, writing, publishing, volunteering. Home: 1528 London Cir Durham NC 27701-2738 Office: Triumphant Through Faith Ministries PO Box 11616 Durham NC 27703

MEWHINNEY, BRUCE HARRISON NICHOLAS (MATTHEW WALKER), screenwriter, internet publisher; b. Charlottesville, Va., Apr. 15, 1949; m. Elyse Tager, June 5, 1982. BA, Antioch Coll., 1971. Assoc. editor MacUser Mag., Foster City, Calif., 1990-93; pres. Diosa Design, Alameda, 1993—; tech. mgr. AOL forum of Preview Travel, San Francisco, 1995-96. Pub. online svc. Apple Computer, Cupertino, Calif., 1993—94; web prodr. EllieMae.com, 1999—2001. Author, photographer: Down Below: Aboard the World's Classic Yachts, 1980, Welcome Aboard: Inside the World's Greatest Yachts, 1998. Avocations: sailing, screenwriting, multimedia devel. Office: Diosa Design 3028 Alta Vista Alameda CA 94502-6804 E-mail: info@diosa.com.

MEWHINNEY, LEN EVERETTE, lawyer; b. Temple, Tex., Sept. 16, 1958; s. Cindy Mayfield Mewhinney, May 28, 1983; children: Lauren Lynn, Jacob Cole. BBA in Acctg., Tex. Tech. U., 1981, JD cum laude, 1984. Bar: Tex. 1984. Assoc. Daugherty Kuperman Golden & Morehead, Austin, 1984—87, Johnson & Wortley f/k/a Johnson & Gibbs, Austin, 1987—95; shareholder Kuperman Orr Mouer & Albers, 1995—96; v.p., legal sec., gen. counsel McLane Co. Inc., Temple, Tex., 1996—. Mem. ABA, Am. Corp. Counsel Assn., State Bar Tex.

MEY, JACOB LOUIS, linguistics educator; b. Amsterdam, The Netherlands, Oct. 30, 1926; arrived in Denmark, 1952; s. Jacob Louis and Wynanda (Meyer) M.; m. Kari Lothe, July 15, 1957 (div. 1964); m. Inger Hansen, Sept. 18, 1965; children: Kari Anne, Sara Katrine, Jacob Louis IV, Inger Elise, Alexandra Rebecca, Kristianna Henrikke. Lic. in philosophy, U. Nymegen, The Netherlands, 1951; PhD, U. Copenhagen, 1960; PhD (hon.), U. Zaragoza, Spain, 1993. Lectr. linguistics Oslo U., 1960-66; assoc. prof. U. Tex., Austin, 1966-72; prof. Odense (Denmark) U., 1972-96, J.W. Goethe U., Frankfurt, Germany, 1996-97, U. Campinas, Brazil, 1997, U. Haifa and Haifa Technion, Israel, 1998, Södertörns U. Coll., Stockholm, 1999, U. de Brasilia, 2000. Vis. assoc. prof. Georgetown U., Washington, 1967; rsch. fellow Rand Corp., Santa Monica, Calif., 1963; rsch. scientist Charles U., Prague, Czechoslovakia, 1965; vis. fellow Yale U., New Haven, 1979, Northwestern U., Evanston, Ill., 1989, 94-95, Warwick (Eng.) U., 1991; vis. scientist City U., Hong Kong, 1993-94. Author: La Catégorie du Nombre en Finnois Moderne, 1961, Whose Language: A Study in Linguistic Pragmatics, 1985, Pragmatics: An Introduction, 1993, 2d edit., 2001, When Voices Clash: A Study in Literary Pragmatics, 1999, 2000, As Vozes da Sociedade, 2001; editor: Pragmalinguistics: Theory and Practice, 1979; co-editor: Encyclopedia of Language and Linguistics, 1995; editor-in-chief Jour. Pragmatics, Amsterdam, 1977—, RASK Internat. Jour. Lang. and Comm., Odense, 1996—, Internat. Jour. Cognition and Tech., 2000—; assoc. editor-in-chief: Concise Ency. of Pragmatics, 1998; mem. adv. bd. Pragmatics, 1988—, Discourse and Soc., 1990—, Psyke & Logos, 1988—, Revue de Sémantique et Pragmatique, 1997—, Text, 1998—, Miscellanea (Zaragoza), 1997—. Japan Found. scholar Tsukuba U., Ibaraki, Japan, 1983; fellow Sloane Found., 1979, Sasakawa Found., 1985, Andersen Cons., 1993. Mem. Linguistic Cir. Copenhagen, Linguistic Soc. Am., Internat. Pragmatics Assn. (mem. cons. bd. 1987—), Cognitive Technology Soc. (v.p. 2000—). Roman Catholic. Avocations: outdoor activities, water sports, bicycling, music, Japanese calligraphy. Address: 1100 W 29th St Austin TX 78703-1915 Office: U of So Denmark Inst Lang & Comm Campusvej 55 DK-5230 Odense Denmark E-mail: jam@language.sdu.dk.

MEY, RINDY, physician assistant; b. Battombong, Cambodia, Feb. 20, 1963; came to U.S., 1983; d. Dam Nong and Lach Sung; m. Chriya Phan, Feb. 12, 1994; children: Samuel Visoth, Maylia Angela. BA, Southwestern Advantist U., Keene, Tex., 1989, ASN, RN, Southwestern Advantist U., Keene, Tex., 1990. Cert. physician asst. Physician asst. West Hosp., Wes, Tex., 1996-97, Hillcrest, Waco, 1997—, Rural Family Health Clinic, Rosebud. Fellow: Tex. Acad. Physician Assts., Am. Acad. Physician Assts. Home: 475 Dal Paso Dr Waco TX 76706-5155 Office: Rural Family Health Clinic 320 E Ave F Rosebud TX 76520 E-mail: samuelnong@yahoo.com.

MEYBERG, BERNHARD ULRICH, entrepreneur; b. Norden, Germany, Aug. 29, 1917; s. Peter Bernhard and Katharine (v. Oterendorp) M.; m. Lotte Essig, Mar. 17, 1949; children: Horst Eugen, Ursula Eugenie, Gabriele Christine. Student, U. Greifswald/Pommern, 1943-45. Apprentice Savingsbank, Norden, 1935-37, employee, 1937-38; collaborator Eug Essig, Ludwigsburg, Fed. Republic Germany, 1948-70; pvt. practice Möglingen, Fed. Republic Germany, 1970—. Contbr. essays to newspapers. 1st lt. German Air Force, 1938-45, prisoner of war, 1945-47. Mem. Internat. Furniture-Carpet-Purchase Assn. (mem. exec. com.), Chamber Industry and Trade (mem. com.), Italian Chamber Trade for Germany (mem. com.). Lutheran. Avocations: sports, tennis, sailing. Home: Max-Ostheimerstrasse 6 87534 Oberstaufen Germany Office: Eugen Essig Daimlerstrasse 62 Moglingen Germany

MEYBURG, ARNIM HANS, transportation engineer, educator, consultant; b. Bremerhaven, W. Ger., Aug. 25, 1939; came to U.S., 1965; s. Friedel and Auguste (Kleeberg) M.; m. Ruth Meyburg; 1 child, Jennifer Susan. Student, U. Hamburg, 1960-62, Free U. Berlin, 1962-65; MS (Fulbright travel grantee), Northwestern U., 1968, PhD, 1971. Research assoc. Transp. Center, Northwestern U., 1968-69; asst. prof. transp. engring. Cornell U., 1969-75, assoc. prof., 1975-78, prof., 1978—, acting chmn. dept., 1977-78, chmn. dept., 1980-85, dir. Sch. Civil and Environ. Engring., 1988-98, chmn. bd. Univ. Transp. Rsch. Ctr., 1992-95; dir. Transp. Infrastructure Rsch. Consortium, 1995—. Vis. mem. faculties U. Calif., Irvine, Tech. U. Munich, Germany, (Fulbright lectr.) U. Sao Paulo, Brazil, 1984, Tech. U. Brunswick, W. Ger., 1985-86; Humboldt Found. research fellow, 1978-79; prin. investigator projects Dept. Transp., NSF, Nat. Coop. Hwy. Research Program, N.Y. State Dept. Transp., U.S. Dept. Transp. Author: (with others) Urban Transportation Modeling and Planning, 1975, Transportation Systems Evaluation, 1976, Survey Sampling and Multivariate Analysis for Social Scientists and Engineers, 1979, Survey Methods for Transport Planning, 1995; co-editor: (with others) Behavioral Travel-Demand Models, 1976, New Horizons in Travel-Behavior Research, 1981, Selected Readings in Transport Survey Methodology, 1992; contbr. articles to profl. jours., chpts. to books. NSF Research Initiation grantee, 1973; recipient Humboldt U.S. Sr. Scientist award, 1984, Fulbright sr. lectr. award, 1984. Mem. ASCE, AAUP, Transp. Rsch. Bd., Transp. Rsch. Forum, Sigma Xi, Chi Epsilon. Office: Cornell U 220 Hollister Hall Ithaca NY 14853-3501 E-mail: ahm2@cornell.edu.

MEYE, ROBERT PAUL, retired seminary educator, administrator, writer; b. Apr. 1, 1929; s. Robert and Eva (Pfau) Meye; m. Mary Cover, June 18, 1954; children: Marianne Meye Thompson, Douglas, John. BA in English Lit., Stanford U., 1951; BD, Fuller Theol. Sem., 1957; ThM in N.T., 1959; DTheol magna cum laude, U. Basel, Switzerland, 1962; DD, Eastern Bapt. Theol. Sem., 1990. Prof. No. Bapt. Theol. Sem., Lombard, Ill., 1962-77, dean, 1971-77, Sch. Theology, Fuller Theol. Sem., Pasadena, Calif., 1977-90, dean emeritus, 1992—. Assoc. provost for Ch. Rels. and Christian Community, 1990-92, prof.N.T. interpretation, 1977-92, prof. emeritus, 92—. Author: Jesus and the Twelve, 1968; co-editor: Studies in Old Testament Theology, 1992; contbr. articles to profl. jours., dictionaries, and encys. Served to lt. (j.g.) USN, 1946-47, 51-54, Korea. Mem.: Inst. Bible Rsch., Soc. Bibl. Lit., Chgo. Soc. Bibl. Rsch., Studiorum Novi Testamenti Societas, Nat. Assn. Bapt. Profs. Religion. Republican. Home: 1170 Rubio St Altadena CA 91001-2027 Office: Fuller Theol Sem 135 N Oakland Ave Pasadena CA 91182-0001 E-mail: rmeye@aol.com.

MEYENHOFER, JUDITH, public relations and marketing professional; b. Basel, Switzerland, June 3, 1967; came to U.S., 1969; d. Markus Franz and Esther Meyenhofer. BA with honors, Rutgers U., 1989. Asst. to v.p., pub. affairs dir. Internat. Flavors & Fragrances, Union Beach, N.J., 1987; intern, rsch. asst. Holt, Ross & Yulish, Inc., Edison, 1987-89; registration specialist Hoechst AG, Frankfurt am Main, Germany, 1989-90; sr. account exec. Myers CommuniCounsel, Inc., Edison, N.J., 1990-94, DHM Group, Inc., Holmdel, 1994-95; v.p. Patrice Tanaka & Co., Inc., N.Y.C., 1995—. Mem. solid waste adv. com. Monmouth County (N.J.). Recipient Steuben award Steuben Soc., 1989. Mem. Pub. Rels. Soc. Am. Avocations: travel, photography. Home: 114 Kings Hwy Middletown NJ 07748-2024 Office: Patrice Tanaka & Co Inc 320 W 13th St Fl 7 New York NY 10014-1200 E-mail: jmmusa@ptanaka.com.

MEYER, ALBERT JAMES, educational researcher; b. Cleve., Sept. 24, 1929; s. Jacob Conrad and Esther Agnes (Steiner) M.; m. Mary Ellen Yoder, Aug. 21, 1954; children: Richard, Anne, Kathryn, Barbara, Elaine. BA, Goshen Coll., 1950; MA, Princeton U., 1952, PhD, 1954. Asst. in teaching and rsch. Princeton (N.J.) U., 1950-53; fellow U. Basel, Switzerland, 1953-54, rsch. assoc. Switzerland, 1956-57; dir. for France, rep. European peace sect. Mennonite Ctrl. Com., 1954-57; asst. prof. physics Goshen (Ind.) Coll., 1958-61, prof., rsch. prof., 1967-89, adj. rsch. prof., 1989—; acad. dean, prof. Bethel Coll., North Newton, Kans., 1961-66, Menno Simons lectr., 1993; exec. sec., pres. Mennonite Bd. Edn., Elkhart, Ind., 1967-95; vis. fellow Princeton (N.J.) U., 1995-96. Exec. for secretariat Puidoux Theol. Confs., 1955-57; former mem. staff Mennonite Student Svcs. Com.; former coord. com. on liberal arts edn. North Ctrl. Assn. Colls. and Secondary Schs.; vis. rsch. scientist U. Paris, 1974-75; vis. rschr. New Coll. Berkeley, 1986-87; presenter in field; former cons. Conrad Grebel Coll., U. Waterloo, Ont., Can.; mem. peace and social concerns com. Mennonite Ch., 1959-71; former mem. Continuation Com. of Hist. Peace Chs. Contbr. articles to denominational periodicals and sci. jours. Princeton U. exch. fellow and Charles Foster Kent fellow Nat. Coun. for Religion in Higher Edn., 1953-54. Mem. Denominational Execs. for Ch.-Related Higher Edn. (chmn. 1984-86), Am. Assn. for Higher Edn., Am. Assn. Physics Tchrs. Avocations: tennis, hockey, hiking. Home: 708 Emerson St Goshen IN 46526-3904

MEYER, ALDEN MERRILL, environmental association executive; b. Buffalo, Mar. 21, 1952; s. Arthur Merrill Meyer and Susan (Rogers) Meyer Markle BA, Yale U., 1975; MS, Am. U., 1990. Energy policy analyst Conn. Citizen Action Group, Hartford, 1975-78, Environ. Action Found., Washington, 1979-82; exec. dir. Environ. Action, Inc., 1983-85, League Conservation Voters, Washington, 1985-88; dir. climate change and energy policy Union of Concerned Scientists, 1989-92, legis. dir., 1992-95, dir. govt. rels., 1995—. Bd. dirs. Ams. for Environment, Washington, 1983-87, chmn., 1985-87; bd. dirs. Urban Environment Conf., Washington, 1984-87, Zero Population Growth, 1989-98; pres. bd. dirs. Safe Energy Communication Council, Washington, 1980-85; chmn. U.S. Climate Action Network, 1990-2000; mem. state and local adv. bd. U.S. Dept. Energy, 1994-2000, mem. elec. syss. reliability task force, 1997-99; mem. Sec. Energy Adv. Bd., 1999—. Mem. Yale Whiffenpoofs, 1975. Democrat. Avocations: hiking, camping, skiing, singing. Home: 15 Montgomery Ave Takoma Park MD 20912-4614 Office: Union of Concerned Scientis 1707 H St NW # 600 Washington DC 20006-3919 E-mail: ameyer@ucsusa.org.

MEYER, ALICE VIRGINIA, state official; b. N.Y.C., Mar. 15, 1921; d. Martin G. and Marguerite Helene (Houzè) Kliemand; m. Theodore Harry Meyer, June 28, 1947; children: Robert Charles, John Edward. BA, Barnard Coll., 1941; MA, Columbia U., 1942. Tchr. pub. schs., Elmont, N.Y., 1942-43; tchr. Fairlawn (N.J.) High Sch., 1943-47; office mgr., sales rep. N.Y.C., 1948-55; substitute tchr. Pub. Schs., Easton, Conn., 1965-72; state rep., asst. minority leader Conn. State Legislature, Hartford, 1976-93. Mem. Ct. Bd. of Govs. for Higher Edn., 1993—, vice-chair, chair. bd. govs. for higher edn. Mem. Edn. Commn. of the States, 1985—87; life trustee Discovery Mus., 1980—; trustee United Way Regional Youth Substance Abuse Project, Bridgeport, 1983—93; vice chmn. Easton Rep. Town Com., 1970—78; mem. strategic planning com. Town of Easton, 1993—; vice chmn. ct. adv. coun. on intergovtl. rels., 1988—; mem. Conn. Commn. on Quality Edn., 1992—93; supporter Conn. Small Towns, 1988; mem. Conn. Humanities Coun., 1974—76, Conn. Film Commn., 1985—88; co-chair Com. on State Plan of Conservation and Devel., 1985—87; mem. Lt. Gov.'s Commn. on Mandate Reduction, 1995; sec. Easton Free Sch. Scholarship Fund, 1980—; pres. Barnard Class of 1941, 1996—; justice of the peace, 2001—; ct. adv. coun. career and vocat. edn., 1980—88; bd. dirs. 3030 Park, 1993—; Fairfield County Lit. Coalition Bridgeport, 1988—94. Named Legislator of Yr. Conn. Libr. Assn., 1985; Guardian Small Bus. grantee Nat. Fedn. Ind. Bus., 1987; honoree Fairfield YWCA Salute to Women, 1988; named grant to AAUW Fellowship Fund, Bridgeport Br., 1970, Conn. State AAUW, 1974; recipient Disting. Rep. award Easton Rep. Town Com., 2000. Mem.: LWV, AAUW (local pres. 1976, bd. dirs. 1982), Nat. Order Women Legislators (regional dir. 1987—, past pres. Conn. chpt.), Conn. Assn. Sch. Adminstrs. (hon.), Bus. and Profl. Women. Congregationalist. Avocations: swimming, sailing, bridge. Home: 18 Lantern Hill Rd Easton CT 06612-2218

MEYER, ANDREA PEROUTKA, small business owner; b. Prague, Czechoslovakia, Nov. 29, 1963; came to U.S. 1970; d. George and Alena Peroutka; m. Dana Charles Meyer, Oct. 16, 1983. BA in Liberal Arts, U. Tex., 1985, M in Libr. of Info. Sci., 1986. Libr. IBM, Austin, Tex., 1985-86; rsch. specialist Career Track Seminars, Boulder, Colo., 1986-88; founder, pres. Working Knowledge, 1988—. Project mgr. Interesting Orgns. Database for MIT, 1995—; cons. The Tom Peters Group, Palo Alto, Calif., 1989-95. Author: (workbooks) Stress Management Strategies, 1987, How to Give Presentations, 1988; co-author: (audio tape) How to Set Up a Corporate Library, 1989; co-editor Briefing Book for Inventing the Organizations of the 21st Century, 1995-96; assoc. editor Inside Decisions, 1995-96; contbr. chpts. to 3 books. Recipient Ray C. Janeway scholarship, Tex. Libr. Assn., 1985; Philip Morris scholarship, 1981-85. Mem. Planning Forum (v.p. comm., bd. dirs. Denver chpt.), Product Devel. and Mgmt. Assn. (newsletter editor), Toastmasters, Mensa (chmn. scholarship com.), Pres.'s Assn., European Consortium of Info. Cons., Phi Beta Kappa. Avocations: reading, hiking, writing, travel. Home and Office: 515 Forest Ave Boulder CO 80304-2550 E-mail: dcmeyer@knewbiquity.com.

MEYER, ANDREW HOYT, physician; b. Red Bank, N.J., June 19, 1963; s. Henry Robert and Lynn (Marks) M.; m. Kellen Leigh Meyer, Apr. 12, 1997; 1 child, Brynkly. BS, Stanford U., 1985; MD, Baylor Coll. Medicine, 1989. Diplomate in internal medicine and cardiovasc. diseases Am. Bd. Internal Medicine. Intern in internal medicine Duke U., Durham, N.C., 1989-90, resident in medicine, 1990-92; fellow in cardiology Emory U., Atlanta, 1992-95; cardiologist Yuma (Ariz.) Regional Med. Ctr., 1995—. Fellow Am. Coll. Cardiology; mem. ACP, AMA. Avocation: photography. Office: Yuma Heart Inst 2503 S Avenue A Ste 2 Yuma AZ 85364-7174

MEYER, ARMIN HENRY, retired diplomat, author, educator; b. Ft. Wayne, Ind., Jan. 19, 1914; s. Armin Paul and Leona (Buss) M.; m. Alice James, Apr. 23, 1949; 1 dau., Kathleen Alice. Student, Lincoln (Ill.) Coll., 1931-33; AB, Capital U., 1935, LL.D., 1957; MA, Ohio State U., 1941, LL.D., 1972, Wartburg Coll., S.D. Sch. Mines and Tech., 1972. Faculty Capital U., Columbus, Ohio, 1935-41; staff OWI, Egypt, Iraq, 1942-46; U.S. pub. affairs officer Baghdad, Iraq, 1946-48; pub. affairs adviser U.S. Dept. State, 1948-52; sec. Am. embassy, Beirut, Lebanon, 1952-55; dep. chief mission Kabul, Afghanistan, 1955-57; dep. dir. Office South Asian Affairs Dept. State, 1957-58, dep. dir. Office Near Eastern Affairs, 1958-59, dir. Office Nr. Ea. Affairs, 1959-61, dep. asst. sec. of state for Nr. Ea. and South Asian Affairs, 1961; US ambassador to Lebanon, 1961-65, Iran, 1965-69, Japan, 1969-72; spl. asst. to sec. state, chmn. Cabinet Com. to Combat Terrorism, 1972-73. Vis. prof. Am. U., 1974-75; dir. Ferdowsi project Georgetown U., 1975-79, adj. prof. diplomacy, 1975-86; Woodrow Wilson vis. fellow, 1974—; cons. internat. bus. and environment, 1975—. Author: Assignment Tokyo: An Ambassador's Journal, 1974; co-author: Education in Diplomacy, 1987. Hon.

mem. Lincoln Sesquicentennial Commn., 1959; bd. dirs. Washington Inst. Fgn. Affairs, 1979—, pres., 1988-98. Recipient Meritorious Svc. award Dept. State, 1958, Superior Honor award, 1973; decorated Order of Rising Sun, 1st class (Japan), 1982; inducted into Hall of Excellence Ohio Fedn. Ind. Colls., 1989. Mem. Sigma Psi. Lutheran. Home: 4610 Reno Rd NW Washington DC 20008-2941 Fax: (202) 237-7721. E-mail: 70117.2165@compuserve.com. *Faith in God; where there is a will there is a way; if a job is worth doing it is worth doing well; and the Golden Rule.*

MEYER, AUGUST CHRISTOPHER, JR. broadcasting company executive, lawyer; b. Champaign, Ill., Aug. 14, 1937; s. August C. and Clara (Rocke) M.; m. Karen Haugh Hassett, Dec. 28, 1960; children: August Christopher F., Elisabeth Hassett. BA cum laude, Harvard U., 1959, LLB, 1962. Bar: Ill. 1962. Founding ptr. Meyer-Capel, Champaign, Ill., 1962-77, of counsel, 1977—; owner, dir., officer Midwest TV, Inc., Sta. KFMB-TV-AM-FM, San Diego, Sta. WCIA-TV, Champaign, Ill. , Sta. WMBD-TV-AM, WMXP, Peoria, 1968—, pres., 1976—. Bd. dirs. BankIll., Main St. Trust Inc.; spl. asst. atty. gen. State of Ill., 1968-76. Chmn. bd. trustees Carle Found. Hosp., Urbana, Ill. Mem. Ill. Bar Assn., Champaign County Bar Assn. Clubs: Champaign Country. Home: 1408 S Prospect Ave Champaign IL 61820-6837 Office: Midwest TV Inc PO Box 197 100 W University Ave # 401 Champaign IL 61824-0197 also: Sta KFMB PO Box 85888 7677 Engineer Rd San Diego CA 92111-1515

MEYER, B. FRED, small business executive, home designer and builder, product designer; b. Long Island, N.Y., Jan. 6, 1918; s. Barthold Fred and Edna May (Clark) M.; m. Mary E. Carman, July 18, 1951; children: Patricia Meyer Sauer, Susan Meyer Sachs. Student, Pratt Inst., 1935-39, Johns Hopkins U., 1946-48, Wayne State U., 1954-55. Registered builder, Fla. Project engr. Lear, Inc., Grand Rapids, Mich., 1948-51; engring. exec. GM Corp., Warren, 1951-75; pres. BFM Assocs., Inc. (name Fred Meyer, Inc. 1990), Sarasota, Fla., 1975—. Patentee on pendulum type seat belt retractor, power window switch, power window actuator, 6-way seat switch, 6-way seat actuator, rear trunk pull-down mechanism, numerous others. Capt. USAAF, 1942-46, ETO. Mem. Oaks Country Club (Osprey, Fla.). Avocations: golf, computers, travel. Home and Office: 4753 Antler Trail Sarasota FL 34238 E-mail: bfredm@hotmail.com.

MEYER, BERNARD STERN, lawyer, former judge; b. Balt., June 7, 1916; s. Benjamin and Josephine Meyer; m. Elaine Strass, June 25, 1939 (div.); children: Patricia, Susan; m. Edythe Birnbaum, Apr. 18, 1975; m. Hortense Fox, Oct. 29, 1991. BS, Johns Hopkins U., 1936; LLB, U. Md., 1938; LLD, Hofstra U., 1980, Western State U., 1982, Union U., 1984. Bar: Md. 1938, D.C., N.Y. 1947. Assoc. Fisher & Fisher, Balt., 1938-41; with Office Gen. Counsel Treasury Dept., Washington, 1941-43; pvt. practice N.Y.C., 1948-54; ptnr. Meyer, Fink, Weinberger & Levin, 1954-58; justice N.Y. State Supreme Ct., 1959-72; of counsel Fink, Weinberger, Fredman & Charney, PC, N.Y.C., 1973-79; ptnr. Meyer, English & Cianciulli, PC, Mineola, N.Y., 1975-79; assoc. judge N.Y. Ct. Appeals, Albany, 1979-86; dep. atty. gen. in charge spl. Attica investigation State of N.Y., 1975; ptnr. Meyer, Suozzi, English & Klein PC, Mineola, 1987—. Assoc. spl. counsel Moreland Commn. To Study Workmen's Compensation Adminstrn. and Costs, 1955-57; mem. com. on govt. integrity State of N.Y., 1987-90; mem. Com. for Modern Cts., 1987—. Author: Judicial Retirement Laws of the Fifty States and the District of Columbia, 1999; contbr. articles to profl. jours. Founder United Fund L.I.; past adv. bd. Commn. Law and Social Action, Am. Jewish Congress; chmn. Task Force on Permanency Planning for Foster Children, 1986-91; past pres., bd. dirs. Health and Welfare Coun. Nassau County; past bd. dirs. Nassau-Suffolk region NCCJ, Nassau County coun. Boy Scouts Am., Nat. Ctr. for State Cts.; mem. Coalition for Effective Govt., 1991—. Lt. USNR, WWII. Recipient Disting. Svc. award L.I. Press, Presdl. medal Hofstra U., Disting. Svc. award Legal Aid Soc. Nassau County, N.Y., Johns Hopkins U. Disting. Alumnus award. Mem. ABA (adv. com. on fair trial free press, vice chmn. sr. lawyers divsn. judiciary com.), Am. Bar Found., Am. Coll. Trial Lawyers, Am. Law Inst., N.Y. Bar Assn. (chmn. jud. sect., com. on legis. policy), N.Y. Bar Found., Bar of City of N.Y. (chmn. libr., matrimonial, election law com.), Nassau County Bar Assn. (Disting. Svc. medallion 1982), Nat. Conf. State trial Judges (exec. com., past chmn.), Nat. Coll. State Jud. (bd. dirs.), Assn. Supreme Ct. Judges (past pres., chmn. pattern jury instrn. com. 1962-79), Supreme Ct. Hist. Soc., Com. Modern Cts., Nassau County Lawyers Assn. (award), Scribes, Order of Coif, Omicron Delta Kappa. Office: Meyer Suozzi English & Klein PC 1505 Kellum Pl Mineola NY 11501-4824 E-mail: bmeyer@msek.com.

MEYER, BILL, newspaper publisher, editor; b. Pratt, Kans., Aug. 6, 1925; s. Otto William and Ruth Clarinda (Jones) M.; m. Joan Aileen Wight, Sept. 11, 1949; 1 child, Eric Kent. BS in Journalism, U. Kans., 1948. News editor Marion County Record, Hoch Pub. Co., Inc., Marion, Kans., 1948-67, editor, pub., 1967—; owner Cottonwood Valley Agy., 1990-98, Hoch Pub. Co., Inc., Marion, 1998—. Editor 99th Inf. Divsn. Assn., Marion, 1971—, pres., 1998-99; lectr. media law Wichita (Kans.) State U., 1985; polit. interviewer St. KPTS-TV, Wichita, 1983-98; bd. dirs. Ctrl. Nat. Bank, Junction City, Kans.; mil. cons., travel agt. Battlefield Tours, Slidell, La., 1990—. Past pres. Marion Sch. dist. Bd. Edn., Marion County Hosp. Dist.; bd. dirs. Marion Manor Nursing Home, Kans. Hist. Soc., 1985-94; trustee, past pres. William Allen White Found., Lawrence, Kans. With U.S. Army, 1943-45, ETO. Recipient commendation Kans. Ho. of Reps., 1982, 99th Inf. Div. Assn., 1986, 89, named Kans. Master Editor, recipient Clyde Reed Kans. Master Editor award Kans. Newspaper Found., 1997, Cerus award Internat. Soc. Weekly Newspaper Editors; named Hon. Col. Kans. Calvary, 1987, Hon. Ky. Col., 1990. Mem. Nat. Newspaper Assn., Kans. Press Assn. (pres. 1982-83, Boyd Community Svc. award 1979, Outstanding Mentor award 1999), Marion C. of C. (past bd. dirs.), Marion Country Club, Masons, Shriners, Kiwanis (pres. Marion 1957), 99th Inf. Divsn. Assn. (pres. 1998), Soc. Profl. Journalists. Republican. Methodist. Avocation: military history. Home: PO Box 99 Marion KS 66861-0099 Office: Hoch Pub Co Inc 117 S 3rd St Marion KS 66861-1621 E-mail: bill@99div.com., editor@marionrecord.com.

MEYER, BILLIE JEAN, special education educator; b. Kansas City, Mo., July 27, 1943; d. Charles William and Dorothy Ellen (Alt) Emerson; m. Kenneth Lee Morris, Aug. 24, 1963 (div. Oct. 1985); 1 child, Darla Michele Morris Stewart; m. Gordon Frederick Meyer, June 1, 1986 (dec. May 1994); stepchildren: Ardith Helmer, Susan Stanford, Gary, Geneace, Patti Draughon, Shari Mohr. BS in Edn., Northeastern State U., 1965, M in Tchg., 1968. Cert. tchr., Okla.; cert. visually impaired, Braille. Substitute tchr. Muskogee (Okla.) Pub. Schs., 1965; elem. tchr. Okla. Sch. for the Blind, Muskogee, 1965-67, elem. tchr., computer tchr., 1969-98, visually impaired cons., 1998—. Adj. lectr. Northeastern State U., Tahlequah, summers 1990-92, 94-2002; on-site team mem. Nat. Accreditation Coun., 1987; mem. com. revision cert. stds., State of Okla., 1982, adj. lectr., 1998, Braille taks force mem. 1996-98; adv. com. mem. nat. evaluation systems Inc. Okla. Educators Cert. Exams Author: A Sequential Math Program for Beginning Abacus Students, 1979. Mem. Assn. of Edn. and Rehab. of the Blind and Visually Impaired, Okla. Assn. of Ednl. Rehab. of the Blind and Visually Impaired (pres.-elect 1985-86, pres. 1986-87, sec. 1993-97), Computer Using Educators, Epsilon Sigma Alpha (state pres. 1981-82, Girl of Yr. 1971, 98.). Avocations: stained glass, photo preservation, gardening, traveling, bird watching. Office: 814 N F St Muskogee OK 74403-2611 E-mail: jmijer@yahoo.com.

MEYER, BRIAN LEE, psychologist; b. Cass Lake, Minn., July 2, 1958; s. George Gotthold and Paula Sonia (Saslaw) M.; m. Sharla Janine Kerr, Sept. 12, 1987; children: David Kerr, Rachel Elise, Jessica Ann. AB magna cum laude, Harvard U., 1980; MA, Duke U., 1985, PhD, 1990. Lic. psychologist, N.Mex. Psychology intern Cambridge (Mass.) Hosp., 1988-89; postdoctoral fellow Harvard Cmty. Health Plan, Boston, 1989-90; child/family therapist Franciscan Children's Hosp., 1990-92; assoc. dir. adolescent unit U. N.Mex. Mental Health Ctr., Albuquerque, 1993-96; dep. clin. dir. protective svcs. divsn. M.Mex. Children, Youth and Families Dept., Santa Fe, 1996-99; exec. dir. Albuquerque Fam. and Child Guidance Ctr., Albuquerque, 2000—02, Va. Treatment Ctr. for Children, Richmond, Va., 2002—. Adj. asst. prof. U. N.Mex., Albuquerque, 1995—2002; asst. prof. dept. psychiatry Va. Commonwealth U., 2002—; ad hoc reviewer Jour. Clin. Child Psychology, 1995—96; reviewer NIH SBIR grants, 2000—. Contbr. chpt. to book: Advances in Behavioral Assessment of Children, Vol 5, 1991. Cons. Durham (N.C.) Mental Health Assn., 1985. Mem. APA, Nat. Assn. Counsel for Children. Office: Virginia Treatment Ctr for Children 515 North 10th St PO Box 980489 Richmond VA 23298-0489

MEYER, BRUD RICHARD, retired pharmaceutical company executive; b. Waukegan, Ill., Feb. 22, 1926; s. Charles Lewis and Mamie Olive (Broom) M.; m. Betty Louise Stine (dec. 1970); children: Linda (Mrs. Gary Stillabower), Louise (Mrs. Donald Knochel), Janet (Mrs. Gerald Cockrell), Jeff, Karen, Blake, Amy; m. Barbara Ann Hamilton, Nov. 26, 1970. BS, Purdue U., 1949. With Eli Lilly & Co., Indpls., 1949-87, indsl. engr., 1949-56, supr. indsl. engr., 1956-59, sr. personnel rep., 1960-64, personnel mgr. Lafayette, Ind., 1964-67, asst. dir., 1967-69, dir. adminstrn., 1969-79, dir. personnel and public relations, 1980-87, ret., 1987. Bd. dirs. Lafayette Home Hosp., 1977— , Hanna Community Ctr., 1983—, Tippecanoe Hist. Corp., 1985—; bd. dirs. United Way Tippecanoe County, 1970-76, pres., 1974; bd. dirs. Legal Aid Soc. Tippecanoe County, 1973—, Jr. Achievement, pres., 1979; bd. dirs. Lilly Credit Union, 1969-75, pres., 1973-74; mem. Citizen's Com. on Alcoholism, 1966-72; bd. dirs. Greater Lafayette Cmty. Ctrs., 1975-79, pres., 1977-78; bd. dirs. Tippecanoe County Child Care, 1990—, pres., 1998-99; mem., mng. dir. Battle Tippecanoe Outdoor Drama Bd. With USAAF, 1943-45. Mem. Pi Tau Sigma, Lambda Chi Alpha, C. of C. Greater Lafayette (bd. dirs., v.p. 1969-73), Battleground Hist. Soc. Methodist. Home: 4217 Trees Hill Dr Lafayette IN 47909-3451 Office: Eli Lilly & Co PO Box 7685 Lafayette IN 47903-7685

MEYER, CARL BEAT, chemical consultant, lawyer; b. Zurich, Switzerland, May 5, 1934; came to U.S., 1960; s. Karl and Alice (Wegenstein) M.; m. Elizabeth Anne Cousins, Feb. 26, 1960; 1 child, Birgit Franziska. Matura, Kantonsschule, Zuerich, Switzerland; PhD in Chemistry, U. Zurich, 1960; JD, Calif. Western Sch. Law, 1988. Bar: Nev. 1988, Calif. 1989. Postdoctoral fellow U. Calif., Berkeley, 1961-64; from asst. prof. to prof. chemistry U. Wash., Seattle, 1964-86; cons. San Diego, 1986—; pvt. practice, 1988—. Cons. Lawrence Berkeley Lab., U. Calif., Berkeley, 1964-88, U.S. Consumer Product Safety Commn., Washington, 1980-83. Author: Sulfur, Energy and Environment, 1976, Urea-Formaldehyde Resins, 1978, Indoor Air Quality, 1984; contbr. 118 articles to profl. jours. Recipient Nathan Burkan Meml. Competition award ASCAP, 1988. Fellow Am. Inst. Chemists; mem. ASTM (vice chair com. D-22.05 1986-96), ABA, Am. Chem. Soc. (chmn.-elect divsn. chemistry and law 2001, chmn., 2002), Am. Phys. Soc., Calif. Bar Assn., Nev. Bar Assn. Achievements include 2 patents in field. Office: 704 Rand Ave Oakland CA 94610-2269 E-mail: cbmeyer@msu.com.

MEYER, CARL JAMES, music educator; b. Chgo., Apr. 17, 1954; s. John William and Lorraine Emily Meyer; m. Janice Corrine Hunter, July 30, 1977; children: Katie, Jeffrey, Emily; children: , . MusB Edn., Western Ill. U., 1976; MFA, U. Iowa, 1981. Band dir. Princeville Sch. Dist. #326, Ill., 1976, Yorkwood Unit Sch. Dist. #225, Monmouth, 1976—79; orch. grad. asst. U. Iowa, Iowa City, 1979—81; orch. condr. Glenbrook H.S. Dist. #225, Glenview, Ill., 1981—. Music arranger Glenbrook North Variety Show, Northbrook, Ill., 1981—; condr. Western Springs Sch. Talent Edn., Ill., 1982—; string orch., ensemble coach Music Arts Sch., Highland Park, Ill., 1982—88; adv. bd. Chgo. Youth Symphony Orch., 1983—85; music dir. Glenview Cmty. Theatre, 1999—. Musician: Tri-City Music Festival, 1982, U. Ill. Music Consortium, 1997, Sinfonietta Accompanied All-State Chorus, 1998, Orch. Hall Anniversary Concert, 2001. Ch. organist St. Thomas Becket, Mount Prospect, Ill., 1983—2002; ch. youth choir accompanist First Congl. Ch., Des Plaines, 1986—2000; benefit performance Northbrook Rotary, Northbrook, 1988. Recipient Gold Medal, Internat. Festival of Music, 1988, Glenbrook Symphony Orch. Performance award, Midwest Internat. Band and Orch. Clinic, 2002. Mem.: Am. String Tchrs. Assn., Ill. Music Educators Assn. (band divsn. chair dist. #2 1996—98), Kappa Delta Pi, Phi Kappa Phi. Avocations: water-skiing, swimming, bicycling. Office: Glenbrook North High Sch 2300 Shermer Rd Northbrook IL 60062 E-mail: cmeyer@glenbrook.k12il.us.

MEYER, CARL SHEAFF, management consultant; b. Mineola, N.Y., Dec. 19, 1932; s. William Herman and Dorothy Gertrude (Anderson) M. BA in Arch., U. Va., 1956. Archtl. specialist govt. sales coord. metals divsn. Olin Corp., 1958-60; sales adminstr., advt. mgr. Gen. Bronze Corp., 1960-61; mng. assoc., v.p. Lester B. Knight & Assocs., N.Y.C., 1968-77; pres. William H. Meyer & Assocs., Inc., Sarasota, Fla., 1977—, Glen Rock, N.J., 1977—. Chief Plandome (N.Y.) Fire Dept., 1965-67, life mem.; mem. Knight Order St. John. With USN, 1956-58, Capt. Res., ret. 1958-80. Mem. N.Y. Yacht Club, Meadow Brook Hounds, Abington Hills Hunt Club, Reedy Creek Hunt Club, Theta Chi. Office: William H Meyer & Assocs 5110 Brywill Cir Sarasota FL 34234-2708

MEYER, CAROL FRANCES, retired pediatrician, allergist; b. Berea, Ky., June 2, 1936; d. Harvey Kessler and Jessie Irene (Hamm) Meyer; m. Daniel Baker Cox, June 5, 1955 (div. Apr. 1962). AA, U. Fla., 1955; BA, Duke U., 1957; MD, Med. Coll. Ga., 1967. Diplomate Am. Bd. Pediatrics, Am. Bd. Allergy and Immunology. Intern in pediat. Med. Coll. Ga., Augusta, 1967-68; resident in pediat. Gorgas Hosp., Canal Zone, 1968-69; fellow in pediat. respiratory disease Med. Coll. Ga., 1969-71, instr. pediat., 1971-72; med. officer pediat. Canal Zone Govt., 1972-79, Dept. of Army, Panama, 1979-82, med. officer allergy, 1982-89, physician in charge allergy clinic, 1984-89; asst. prof. pediat. and medicine Med. Coll. Ga., Augusta, 1990-2000, med. dir. Telemedicine Ctr., 2000-01; ret. Mem. Bd. of Canal Zone Merit Sys. Examiners, 1976-79. Contbr. articles to profl. jours. Mem. First Bapt. Ch. Orch., 1992-2000; founding mem., violoncello Curundu Chamber Ensemble, 1979-89. Recipient U.S. Army Exceptional Performance awards, 1985, 86, 89, Merck award Med. Coll. Ga., 1967; U. Fla. J. Hillis Miller scholar, 1954. Mem.: Am. Lung Assn. (Ga. East Ctrl. br. exec. bd. 1990—98), Ga. Ornithol. Soc., Panama Canal Soc. Fla., Am. Acad. Pediat., Am. Acad. Allergy, Asthma and Immunology, Am. Coll. Allergy, Asthma and Immunology, Ga. Pediat. Soc., Hispanic-Am. Allergy and Immunology Assn., Allergy and Immunology Soc. Ga., Am. Coll. Rheumatology, Willow Run Homeowner's Assn. (pres. 1994—99), Augusta Audubon Soc., Nat. Assn. Ret. Fed. Employees, Nature Conservancy, Am. Assn. Ret. Persons, Royal Soc. for Preservation Birds, Nat. Audubon Soc., Hawks Nest Village Assn. (1st v.p. 2000—01), Alpha Omega Alpha.

MEYER, CHARLES WILLIAM, economics educator; b. Joliet, Ill., Mar. 15, 1932; s. George Frank and Nona (Bargreen) M.; m. Donelle Sedgley, Sept. 4, 1964; 1 child, Eric. BA, U. Ill., 1954, MA, 1955; PhD, Johns Hopkins U., 1961. Asst. prof. econs. Iowa State U., Ames, 1961-64, assoc. prof., 1964-67, prof., 1967—. Rsch. coord. Gov.'s Study Iowa Tax System, Des Moines, 1965-66; vis. scholar Social Security Adminstrn., Washington, 1973-74. Author: Social Security Disability Insurance, 1979; co-author: Principles of Public Finance, 1983; editor: Social Security, 1987; contbr. articles to profl. jours. 1st lt. U.S. Army, 1955-58. Mem. Am. Econ. Assn., Phi Beta Kappa, Phi Kappa Phi. Home: 4227 Stone Brooke Rd Ames IA 50010-4113 Office: Iowa State U Dept Econs Ames IA 50011-0001

MEYER, CHARLOTTE LOIS, retired clinical social worker; b. Chelsea, Mass., June 15, 1932; d. James and Anne (Berson) Sampson; m. Irving Meyer; children: Fredric B., Marc H., James S. BS, Simmons Coll., 1952, MS in Social Work, 1954. Cert. Acad. Cert. Social Workers; bd. cert. diplomate; lic. ind. clin. social worker, Mass. Social worker Jewish Nursing Home of Western Mass., Longmeadow, Mass., 1972-73, dir. social work, 1873—2002. Avocation: art.

MEYER, CHRISTOPHER HAWKINS, lawyer; b. Springfield, Mo., Sept. 29, 1952; s. Richard DeWitt and Nancy (Hawkins) M.; m. Karen Anne Adams, Aug. 8, 1987; 1 child, C. Andrew Meyer. BA in Econs. magna cum laude, U. Mich., 1977, JD cum laude, 1981. Bar: D.C. 1981, U.S. Ct. Appeals (D.C. cir.) 1982, U.S. Ct. Appeals (9th cir.) 1983, Colo. 1985, U.S. Ct. Appeals (10th cir.) 1985, Idaho, U.S. Ct. Appeals (8th cir.). Counsel water resources program Nat. Wildlife Fedn., Washington, 1981-84, assoc. prof. adjoint, counsel Rocky Mountain Natural Resources Clinic Boulder, Colo., 1984-91; ptnr. Givens Pursley, Boise, 1991—. Contbr. articles to profl. publs. Mem. steering com. Idaho Environ. Forum; bd. dirs. Land Trust of the Treasure Valley. Recipient Lawyer of Yr. award Environ. Policy Inst., 1984, Water Conservationist of Yr. Nebr. Wildlife Fedn., 1989. Mem. Phi Beta Kappa. Democrat. Roman Catholic. Home: 3443 S Millspur Way Boise ID 83716-8648 Office: Givens Pursley LLP 277 N 6th St Ste 200 Boise ID 83702-7720

MEYER, SIR CHRISTOPHER J.R. diplomat; b. Beaconsfield, Eng., Feb. 22, 1944; m. Catherine Laylle; 2 sons, 2 stepsons. Student, Lancing Coll., Eng., Peterhouse, Cambridge, Eng., Paul Nitze Sch., Bologna, Italy. Joined Diplomatic Svc., London, 1966-68, with Moscow, 1968-70, Madrid, 1970-73; head Soviet sect. East European and Soviet dept. Fgn. and Commonwealth Office, London, 1973-76; speech-writer to fgn. sec. policy planning staff Diplomatic Svc., 1976-78; mem. UK rep. to European Comtys., Brussels, 1978-82; polit. counselor British Embassy, Moscow, 1982-84; fgn. office spokesman, press sec. to fgn. sec. Fgn. and Commonwealth Office, London, 1984-88, min. Washington, 1989-92; min., dep. head mission British Embassy, 1992—93, govt. spokesman, press sec. to prime min., 1994-97, Brit. amb. to Fed. Rep. Germany, 1997; Brit. amb. to U.S. Washington, 1997—. Vis. fellow Harvard U. Ctr. for Internat. Affairs, 1988-89. Named Knight Comdr. of the Order of St. Michael and St. George, 1998. Avocations: tennis, watching soccer, listening to jazz music. Office: Embassy of the UK of Gt Britain and No Ireland 3100 Massachusetts Ave NW Washington DC 20008-3689 Fax: 202-588-7870.

MEYER, CHRISTOPHER RICHARD, lawyer; b. Springfield, Ohio, June 18, 1952; s. Eugene Francis and Marilyn Crawford (Hopping) M.; m. Sharman Elizabeth, Sept. 8, 1973; children: Elizabeth Ann, Emily McClead, Timothy Joseph. BA summa cum laude, Ohio State U., 1974, JD, 1977. Bar: Ohio, U.S. Dist. Ct. (so. and no. dists.) Ohio, U.S. Supreme Ct. Ptnr. Reese, Pyle, Drake & Meyer, Newark, 1977—. Legal counsel Licking Meml. Hosp., Newark Ohio, 1983—, State Farm Ins. Co., Bloomington, Ill., 1977—, St. Paul Ins. Co., Columbus, Ohio, 1977—, spl. coun. Ctrl. Ohio Tech. Coll. Mem. Ohio State Bar Assn. (negligence com., litigation sect.), Ohio Assn. Civil Trial Attys., Soc. Ohio Hosp. Attys., Phi Beta Kappa. Home: 976 Briarhill Dr Newark OH 43055-2249 Office: Reese Pyle Drake & Meyer 36 N 2d St PO Box 919 Newark OH 43058-0919 E-mail: cmeyer@rpdm.com.

MEYER, DANIAL RONALD, entrepreneur, association executive; b. Cape, South Africa, May 2, 1955; s. Victor Leonard and Katerina Aletta (Steyn) M.; m. Theadora Gysberta Maria Froon, Sept. 1, 1979; children: Danial, Elizabeth, Jonathan, Malcolm, Heidi. Diploma in mktg. mgmt., Cape Tech., Cape Town, South Africa, 1977; EDP, U. Zimbabwe, Harare, 1988; diploma, Inst. Dirs., 2002. Mgmt. trainee Protea Med., Cape Town, 1974-77; sales mgr. Glaxo Surg., 1977-78; gen. mgr. Eschmann, Harare, 1978-82; mng. dir., CEO Surgimed, 1982—. Chmn. Trinidad Industries, Harare, 1996—, Meymed Holdings Ltd., Harare, 1989—; chmn. Danny Meyer Family Trust, 1994—; dir. Zimbabwe Investment Ctr., Harare, 1996—; mem. faculty of com. adv. U. Zimbabwe; bd. dirs. Suburban Med. Ctr., 1996—. Mem. Harare City Coun., 1991-2002. Recipient Industrialist of Yr. Confedn. Zimbabwe Industries, 1993, Mktg. Man. of Yr. Inst. Mktg. Mgmt., 1988. Fellow Inst. Dirs., Inst. Personal Mgmt.; mem. African, Pacific and Caribbean Assoc. C. of C. (pres.), Zimbabwe Nat. C. of C. (pres. 1995-98), Rotary Club Harare (pres. 1994-95), Royal Harare Golf Club, Harare Club. Roman Catholic. Avocations: regional politics, golf, reading, community service, outdoor activities. Home: PO Box 5908 Harare Zimbabwe E-mail: dannymeyer@mango.zw.

MEYER, DANIEL KRAMER, real estate executive; b. Denver, July 15, 1957; s. Milton Edward and Mary (Kramer) M. Student, Met. State Coll., Denver, 1977-78, U. Colo., 1978-80. Ptnr., developer RM & M II (Ltd. Partnership), Englewood, Colo., 1981-87; pres. Centennial Mortgage and Investment, Ltd., 1984-87; prin. Capriole Properties, Greenwood Village, 1983—. Alumni mem. bd. trustees Kent Denver Country Day Sch., 1981-83; sec. dist. 37 ctrl. and vacancy com. Colo. Ho. of Reps., 1991-92. Recipient Pamela Davis Beardsley devel. award Kent Denver Sch., 1995. Mem. Greenwood Athletic Club. Republican. Avocations: climbing, rollerblading, political economy, 20th century English lit., metaphysics.

MEYER, DAVID DOUGLAS, lawyer, educator; b. Grinnell, Iowa, Nov. 4, 1961; s. Richard DeWitt and Nancy Meyer; m. Amy Gajda, Aug. 29, 1986; children: Michael, Matthew. BA, U. Mich., 1984, JD, 1990. Bar: Mich. 1992, Ill. 1995, U.S. Ct. Appeals (7th cir.) 1995. Spl. asst. U.S. Senator Chas McC. Mathias, Washington, 1984-87; judicial law clk. D.C. Cir. Ct., 1990-91, U.S. Supreme Ct., Washington, 1992-93; assoc. Sidley & Austin, Chgo., Washington, 1991-92, 94-96; legal advisor Iran-U.S. Claims Tribunal, The Hague, The Netherlands, 1993-94; asst. prof. law U. Ill., Champaign, 1996-2000, assoc. prof. law, 2000—. Editor-in-chief Mich. Law Rev., Ann Arbor, 1989-90. Mem. ABA. Office: U Ill Coll Law 504 E Pennsylvania Ave Champaign IL 61820-6909 E-mail: dmeyer@law.uiuc.edu.

MEYER, DENNIS IRWIN, lawyer; b. Dayton, Ohio, Oct. 20, 1935; s. Luther Edward and Mary (McGee) M.; m. Rita Murray, June 23, 1962; children: Matthew, Michael, Rita Catherine, Peter, Denise, Abigail. BS, U. Dayton, 1957; LLB, Georgetown U., 1960, LLM, 1962. Bar: Ohio 1960, D.C. 1962. Atty.-advisor U.S. Tax Ct., Washington, 1960—62; sr. counsel Baker & McKenzie, 1965—. Bd. dirs. United Fin. Banking Cos., Vienna, Va., Oakwood Homes, Greensboro, N.C. Mem. ABA, Internat. Fiscal Assn., Met. Club, Belle Haven Country Club, Avenel Golf Club, Robert Trent Jones Golf Club. Roman Catholic. Office: Baker & McKenzie 815 Connecticut Ave NW Washington DC 20006-4004 E-mail: dennis.i.meyer@bakernet.com.

MEYER, DOROTHY, social worker; b. St. Paul, June 9, 1921; d. Morris and Ida (Torodor) Fisher; m. Elmer Marvin Meyer, Mar. 9, 1947 (dec. Dec. 1992); children: Michelle, Nancy, Laurie, Elizabeth. BA, MSW, U. Minn. Family counselor domestic rels. divsn. Dept. Ct. Svcs., Mpls.; social worker I; sr. social worker; prin. social worker; pvt. practice marriage counselor Mpls., 1986-90. Mem. AAUW. Home: 3531 Oakton Dr Apt 3008 Minnetonka MN 55305-4438

MEYER, DUANE RUSSELL, civil and cost engineer, consultant; b. Stambaugh, Mich., Mar. 31, 1948; s. Donald Gordon and Marilyn Lorraine (Zyskowski) Ml; m. Theresa Winifred Oliver, Aug. 21, 1971; children: Jennifer, Christopher, Jonathan, Melissa. BSCE, Mich. Technol. U., 1970. Registered profl. engr., Mich., Wis., Ohio. Staff design engr. McNamee, Porter and Seeley, Ann Arbor, Mich., 1970-72, asst. resident engr., 1973-75, project mgr., 1976-81; mgr. cost estimating CH2M Hill, Milw., 1981-92; project mgr. Cinergy (formerly PSI Energy), Plainfield, Ind., 1993—. Presenter papers on importance of ethics in engring. at profl. confs. Contbr. to profl. publs. Mem. Am. Assn. Cost Engrs. (pres. Wis. sect. 1985-87, Cost Engr. of Yr. 1991), Mich. Soc. Profl. Engrs. (Young Engr. of Yr. Ann Arbor chpt. 1981), Wis. Soc. Profl. Engrs. (chair ethics com. 1991—), Riverside Toastmasters (pres. 1986). Republican. Roman Catholic. Office: Cinergy 1000 E Main St Plainfield IN 46168-1765

MEYER, EDMOND GERALD, energy and natural resources educator, resources scientist, entrepreneur, former chemistry educator, university administrator; b. Albuquerque, Nov. 2, 1919; s. Leopold and Beatrice (Ilfeld) M.; m. Betty F. Knobloch, July 4, 1941; children: Lee Gordon, Terry Gene, David Gary. BS in Chemistry, Carnegie Mellon U., 1940, MS, 1942; PhD, U. N.Mex., 1950. Chemist Harbison Walker Refractories Co., 1940-41; instr. Carnegie Mellon U., 1941-42; asst. phys. chemist Bur. Mines, 1942-44; chemist research div. N.Mex. Inst. Mining and Tech., 1946-48; head dept. sci. U. Albuquerque, 1950-52; head dept. chemistry N.Mex. Highlands U., 1952-59; dir. Inst. Sci. Rsch., 1957-63; dean Grad. Sch., 1961-63, Coll. Arts and Sci., U. Wyo., 1963-75, v.p., 1974-80, prof. energy and natural resources, 1981-89, prof. and dean emeritus, 1989—. Exec. cons. Diamond Shamrock Corp., 1980; bd. dirs. Carbon Fuels Corp., First Nat. Bank, Laramie; sci. adviser Gov. of Wyo., 1964-90; pres. Coal Tech. Corp., 1981—; cons. Los Alamos Nat. Lab., NFS, HHS, GAO, TVA, Wyo. Bancorp; contractor investigator Rsch. Corp., Dept. Interior, AEC, NIH, NSF, Dept. Energy, Dept. Edn.; Fulbright exch. prof. U. Concepcion, Chile, 1959; chmn. Advanced Coal Tech., 2001. Co-author: Chemistry-Survey of Principles, 1963, Legal Rights of Chemists and Engineers, 1977, Industrial Research & Development Management, 1982; contbr. articles to profl. jours.; patentee in field. Chair, Laramie Regional Airport Bd., 1989-93, treas., 1994-97, chair; active Laramie City Coun., 1997-2001, vice mayor, 1998-2001. Lt. comdr. USNR, 1944-46, ret. Recipient Disting. Svc. award Jaycees; rsch. fellow U. N.Mex., 1948-50. Fellow AAAS, Am. Inst. Chemists (hon. fellow; pres. 1992-93, chmn. 1994-95); mem. Assoc. Western Univs. (chmn. 1972-74), Am. Chem. Soc. (councilor 1962-90, chmn. Wyo. sect. 1997, 2002), Am. Inst. Chem. Engrng., Biophys. Soc., Coun. Coll. Arts and Scis. (pres. 1971, sec.-treas. 1972-75), dir.

Washington office 1973), Laramie C. of C. (pres. 1984), Sigma Xi. Home: 1058 Colina Dr Laramie WY 82072-5015 Office: U Wyo Coll Arts Scis Laramie WY 82071-3825 E-mail: egmeyer@uwyo.edu.

MEYER, EDWARD HENRY, advertising agency executive; b. N.Y.C., Jan. 8, 1927; s. I.H. and Mildred (Driesen) M.; m. Sandra Raabin, Apr. 26, 1957; children: Margaret Ann, Anthony Edward. BA with honors in Econs, Cornell U., 1949. With Bloomingdale's div. Federated Dept Stores, 1949-51, Biow Co. (agy.), 1951-56; with Grey Advt., Inc., N.Y.C., 1956—, exec. v.p., 1963-68, pres., chief exec. officer, 1968—, chmn. bd., 1970—. Bd. dirs. Ethan Allan Interiors Inc., Harman Internat. Industries, Inc., JIm Pattison Group, Inc. Trustee Am. Mus. Natural History, Guggenheim Mus., NYU Med. Ctr., Film Soc. of Lincoln Ctr. With USCGR, 1945-47. Mem. Econ. Club (N.Y.C.), Univ. Club (N.Y.C.), Harmonie Club (N.Y.C.), Century Country Club, Atlantic Golf Club. Office: Grey Global Group Inc 777 3rd Ave New York NY 10017-1401

MEYER, ELLEN ADAMS, arts and small business development specialist; b. Sacramento, Nov. 1, 1947; d. Joseph Robert Hobson and Mary Ellen (Adams) Fort; m. Jeffrey Norman Meyer, June 18, 1966 (div. 1975); children: Zoe Ingrid, Lara Alixandra; m. Glenn Charles Madrid, June 12, 1991; 1 child, Zachary Adams Cabezuela Madrid. BFA in Studio Painting, U. Oreg., 1979; MBA in Mgmt., Sul Ross State U., 1999. Artist Studio in a Sch. Assn., N.Y.C., 1982-84; mng. dir. for artist Donald Judd, 1984-91; exec. dir. Byrd Hoffman Found., N.Y.C., 1991-92; dir. Akira Ikeda Gallery, 1992-94; arts cons. N.Y.C. and Marfa, Tex., 1994—; with Sml. Bus. Devel. Ctr. Sul Ross State U., Alpine, 2000—. Adj. prof. depts. bus. adminstrn. and art Sul Ross State U., 2000. Exhbns. include U. Oreg.-Gallery 141, 1978, Photography Gallery, N.Y.C., 1979, Pub. Image, N.Y.C., 1980, A's, N.Y.C., 1981, Interart Gallery, N.Y.C., 1982, City Gallery, N.Y.C., 1983, Artist's Space, N.Y.C., 1984, Sul Ross State U., Alpine, Tex., 1996, Nueva Vida Gallery, Alpine, 1997. Sec. City Zoning Adjustment, Marfa, 1997, alt. bd. mem., 2000; bd. dirs. Watermill Found., N.Y.C., 1991—93, Pub. Image Gallery, N.Y.C., 1981—84, Marfa Studio of Arts, 2001; sec. bd. dirs. Chinati Found., 1988—91. Democrat. Episcopalian. Office: PO Box 278 Marfa TX 79843-0278 E-mail: elenadam@yahoo.com.

MEYER, ELLEN L. academic administrator; Pres. Atlanta Coll. Art, 1992—. Office: Atlanta Coll Art Office of President 1280 Peachtree St NE Atlanta GA 30309-3502

MEYER, EUGENE CARLTON, retired editor; b. McGregor, Iowa, Dec. 10, 1923; s. Gilbert Nelson and Christine Winnifred (Henkes) M.; m. Maxine Beth Mallory, June 1, 1947; children— Bruce, Mary Lynn, John BS, Iowa State U., 1946. Farm news editor Sta. WHO, Des Moines, 1947-48; assoc. editor Hoard's Dairyman, Fort Atkinson, Wis., 1948-72, mng. editor, 1972-88. Trustee Fort Atkinson Meml. Hosp., 1966-81, pres. bd. trustees, 1976-81. Navigator, USAAF, WWII. Recipient Disting. Service award Am. Dairy Sci. Assn., 1980, Disting. Grad. award Iowa State Dairy Sci. Club, Iowa State U., 1981, Agrl. Leadership award Alpha Gamma Rho, 1982, Award of Distinction U. Wis.-Madison, 1982, Disting. Citizen of Agr. Nat. Milk Producers, 1988, Henry A. Wallace award Iowa State U., 1989, Richard E. Lyng award, 1989, Econ. Contribution award Ft. Atkinson C. of C., 1982, Nat. Assn. Animal Breeders Disting. Svc. award, 1988, Disting. Svc. award for Cmty. Svc. Ft. Atkinson Lions Club, 1995; named Industry Person of Yr. World Dairy Expo, 1988. Mem. Nat. Dairy Shrine (pres. 1980, Guest of Hon. 1986) Republican. Methodist. Home: 524 Jackson St Fort Atkinson WI 53538-1356

MEYER, F. WELLER, bank executive; b. Washington, Dec. 15, 1942; s. Martin William and Sallie Rita (Weller) M.; m. Brenda Burton, Sept. 27, 1972; children: F. Weller Jr., Brandon Michael. BS, U. Md., 1977. V.p. W.S. Steed Mortgage Co., Wheaton, Md., 1970-73; asst. dir. Mortgage Bankers Assn. Am., Washington, 1973-77; mng. dir. Mortgage Systems Corp., Bethesda, Md., 1977-83; pres., CEO Westmark Mortgage Corp., Rockville, 1983-87, Acacia Fed. Savs. Bank, Falls Church, Va., 1987—. Dir. Acacia Fed. Svcs. Bank, Acacia Svc. Corp., Falls Church, Calvert Group Ltd., Am.'s Cmty. Bankers; former pres. Thrift Instns. Adv. Coun. to the Fed. Res., Fed. Nat. Mortgage Assn. Depositors Instns. Adv. Coun. Co-author: Residential Mortgage Underwriting, 1981, Consturction Lending—Residential, 1981, Construction Lending—Residential Income Property, 1981, Income Property Underwriting, 1981. Dir. Make-A-Wish Found. of the Mid-Atlantic, 1991-97, No. Va. Cmty. Found., Fairfax, Va., 1989; mem. Citizen's Housing Adv. Com., Montgomery County, Md., 1988-90. 1st lt. U.S. Army, 1967-70, Vietnam. Mem. Optimists (pres. Washington 1978-79). Republican. Roman Catholic. Avocations: golf, hunting, jogging. E-mail: weller.meyereafsb.com. Home: 9809 Kendale Rd Rockville MD 20854-4246

MEYER, FERDINAND CHARLES, JR. lawyer; b. San Antonio, Sept. 30, 1939; Student, Tulane U.; BBA, U. Tex., 1961, LLB, 1964. Bar: Tex. 1966, U.S. Dist. Ct. (we. dist.) Tex. 1969, U.S. Ct. Appeals (5th cir.) 1971, U.S. Supreme Ct. 1975, U.S. Ct. Appeals (11th cir.) 1979, D.C. 1986. V.p., gen. counsel CSW Svcs.; ptnr. Matthews & Branscomb, San Antonio; v.p. asst. gen. counsel CSW Corp., 1986-88; v.p., gen. counsel Ctrl. & S.W. Corp., 1988-90, sr. v.p., gen. counsel, 1990-98, gen. counsel, 1990-2000, exec. v.p., gen. counsel, 1998-2000. Instr. trial advocacy St. Mary's Sch. Law, 1980-86. Capt. USAR. Fellow Am. Coll. Trial Lawyers, Tex. Bar Found.; mem. ABA, Am. Bd. Trial Advs. (adv.), State Bar Tex., Dallas Bar Assn., San Antonio Bar Assn., Internat. Assn. Def. Counsel, Phi Alpha Delta. Office: PO Box 7616 Dallas TX 75209-7616

MEYER, FRANCES CHRISTINE, freelance/self-employed editor; b. Lebanon, Ind., Mar. 6, 1949; d. Willis Edgar and Alma Pearl (Boesl) Meyer; m. John Robert Barry, Aug. 29, 1991; children: Chris Barry, Raymond Barry, Maria Barry. BA, George Washington U., 1981, MA, 1984. Editl. asst. Sen. Sam Nunn, Washington, 1981—84; staff asst. Sen. Howell Heflin, 1984—87; rschr. Rufus Lusk & Son, Silver Spring, Md., 1987—97; freelance editor Rockville, 1997—. Vol. Rockville Animal Shelter, 1997—98. Fellow Tchg., George Washington U., 1981—84. Democrat. Methodist. Avocations: animals, sketching, computer art, therapy. Home: 1617 Lewis Ave Rockville MD 20851

MEYER, FRANCES MARGARET ANTHONY, elementary and secondary school educator, health education specialist; b. Stella, Va., Nov. 15, 1947; d. Arthur Abner Jr. and Emmie Adeline (Murray) Anthony; m. Stephen Leroy Meyer, Aug. 2, 1975. BS, Longwood Coll., 1970; MS, Va. Commonwealth U., 1982, PhD, 1996. Cert. tchr., Va. Health, phys. edn., and dance tchr. Fredericksburg (Va.) City Pub. Schs., 1970-89; AIDS edn. coord. Va. Dept. Edn., Richmond, 1989-90, health edn. specialist, 1990-94, comprehensive sch. health program specialist, 1994—. Mem. rev. bd. Nat. Commn. for Health Edn. and Credentialing, Inc., conf. and profl. devel. rev., 1996-2000. Author (with others): Elementary Physical Education: Growing through Movement-A Curriculum Guide, 1982; contbr. articles to profl. jours. Mem. pub. edn. coun., comprehensive sch. health edn. team Va. affiliate Am. Cancer Soc., Richmond, 1990—; mem. pub. edn. coun., comprehensive sch. health edn. team Va. Alliance for Adolescents and Sch. Health, 1990—; dir. Va. Children's Dance Festival, 1981—96, 1997—; vol. ARC, 1976—84, 1997—2001, Va. affiliate AHA, 1982—93, 1999—2001; mem. ctrl. steering com. Health, Mental Health and Safety in Schs. Nat. Guidelines Project, Am. Acad. Pediat., 2000—; bd. dirs. ARC, Va. HIV/AIDS Network, 1997—2001. Recipient gov.'s medal for substance abuse and prevention edn. State of Va., 1997, Alumni Cmty. Svc. award Va. Commonwealth U., 1998. Mem.: AAPHERD (chmn. divsn. 1970—, past v.p., nominating com., social justice com., strategic planning com., So. Dist. honor award 1995, 1999, pres.'s recognition award 1997, svc. award 1997, nat. honor award 1999), NEA, ASCD, AAUW (com. 1989—90, 1995—), Dance Edn. Orgn. (charter mem.), Va. Assn. for Health, Phys. Edn., Recreation and Dance (various coms. 1970—, health edn. editor Va. Jour. 1994—, past pres., Tchr. of Yr. 1983, Va. Honor award 1988), Va. Alliance for Arts Edn. (adv. bd. 1980—83, 1989—90, 1995—96), Am. Coll. Health Assn. (curriculum and tng. rev. panel 1992—94), Soc. State Dirs. Health, Phys. Edn. and Recreation (legis. affairs com. 1994—98, mem. applied strategic planning com. 1994—2001, pres.-elect 1997, pres. 1998, past pres. 1999, think tank chair 2000—02, Presdl. award 1996, Presdl. Recognition award 1997, 2000, Simon A. McNeely Honor award 2000), Va. Health Promotion and Edn. Coun. (bd. dirs. 1990—96), Internat. Coun. for Health, Phys. Edn., Recreation, Sport and Dance (internat. commns. for health edn. and commn. for dance and dance edn., mem. jour. articles rev. com.), Va. Alliance for Arts Edn., Va. Mid. Sch. Assn., Va. Edn. Assn., Nat. Mid. Sch. Assn., Nat. Dance Assn. (bd. dirs. 1996—, pres. 2001—, Presdl. citation 1998, svc. award 1998, 2000, Pres.'s Merit award 2001), Nat. Network for Youth Svcs. (adv. bd. 1994—98, rev. panel), Longwood Coll. Alumni Coun. (bd. dirs. 1987—90), Delta Kappa Gamma (pres. Beta Eta chpt. 1988—90). Baptist. Avocations: travel, dancing, swimming, reading, theatrical performances.

MEYER, FRED ALBERT, JR. political science educator; b. Milw., Oct. 7, 1942; s. Fred Albert and Rose Henrietta (Hafemann) M. BA, U. Wis., 1964; MA, U. Wis., Milw., 1966; PhD, Wayne State U., 1974. Instr. Carroll Coll., Waukesha, Wis., 1970-71; prof. Polit. Sci. Ball State U., Muncie, Ind., 1971—. Editor Ind. Jour. Polit. Sci. Co-editor: Determinants of Law Enforcement Policies, 1979, Evaluating Alternative Law Enforcement Policies, 1979; co-author: The Criminal Justice Game, 1980; co-editor: State Policy Problems, 1993. Chair adv. com. on sex discrimination Ind. Civil Rights Commn., 1983-84; chair Ind. Sexual Harassment Task Force, 1989-92; chair Gender Fairness Coalition of Ind., Indpls., 1988-93, sec., 1994-97, chair 1998; chair Ind. Found. on Gender-Based Edn., Indpls., 1988-93, 1998-2001, Gender Fairness Found. Ind., 2001—; sec. Healthy Mothers Healthy Babies of Delaware County, 1995—; mem. coun. Policy Studies Orgn., 1994-2000; bd. dirs. LWV Ind., 1998-2000, Ind. Pro-Choice Action League, 1984-90. Recipient grant to produce videotape on access to prenatal care in Delaware County, Ind. Hoosier Heartland chpt. March of Dimes, Muncie, 1990; Ford Found. Legis. fellow Mich. Senate, 1965-66. Mem. Am. Polit. Sci. Assn., Policy Studies Orgn., Midwest Polit. Sci. Assn., Western Polit. Sci. Assn., So. Polit. Sci. Assn., Audubon Soc., Sierra Club. Avocations: reading, art history, listening to music, animal welfare. Office: Polit Sci Dept Ball State U Muncie IN 47306-0001 E-mail: fmeyer@gw.bus.edu.

MEYER, FRED JOSEF, financial executive; b. Zurich, Switzerland, Jan. 1, 1931; came to U.S., 1959; s. Josef and Claire (Lehmann) M.; m. Beverly Ruth Carter, Apr. 9, 1961 (div. Feb. 1975); children: Fred Jay, Marcus Clinton, Michael Josef; m. Marie-Noelle Vigneron, Oct. 30, 1975. MS, Fed. Inst. Tech., Zurich, 1956; MBA, Harvard U., 1961; LLD (hon.), Sacred Heart U., 1981. V.p. planning & adminstrn. Sandoz, Inc., Hanover, N.J., 1971-73, exec. v.p., chief fin. officer, 1973-78; pres., CEO Sandoz U.S., Inc., Greenwich, Conn., 1978-81; mng. dir., CEO Wander Ltd., Berne, Switzerland, 1981-82; sr. v.p., chief fin. officer CBS, Inc., N.Y.C., 1982-88; chief fin. officer Omnicom Group, Inc., 1988-98, vice chmn., 1998-99, spl. advisor exec. office, 2000—. Bd. dirs. Zurich Life Ins. Co. N.Y., N.Y.C., First Eagle SoGen Funds, Inc., N.Y.C., Actelion Ltd., Basle, Novartis Corp., Summit, N.J., Ptnrs. Group USA Inc., N.Y.C. Mem. Fin. Execs. Inst., Econ. Club, Harvard Club (N.Y.C.), Greenwich Country Club. Republican. Congregationalist. Office: Omnicom Group Inc 437 Madison Ave New York NY 10022-7001

MEYER, FRED WILLIAM, JR. memorial parks executive; b. Fair Haven, Mich., Jan. 7, 1924; s. Fred W. and Gladys (Marshall) M.; m. Jean Hope, Aug. 5, 1946; children— Frederick, Thomas, James, Nancy. AB, Mich. State Coll., 1946. Salesman Chapel Hill Meml. Gardens, Lansing, Mich., 1946-47; mgr. Roselawn Meml. Gardens, Saginaw, Mich., 1947-49; dist. mgr. Sunset Meml. Gardens, Evansville, Ind., 1949-53; pres., dir. Memory Gardens Mgmt. Corp., Indpls., Covington Meml. Gardens, Ft. Wayne, Ind., Chapel Hill Meml. Gardens, Grand Rapids, Mich., Forest Lawn Memory Gardens, Indpls., Lincoln Memory Gardens, Indpls., Chapel Hill Meml. Gardens, South Bend, Ind., Mercury Devel. Corp., Indpls., Quality Marble Imports, Indpls., Quality Printers, Indpls., Am. Bronze Craft, Inc., Judsonia, Ark. Mem. C. of C., A.I.M., Am. Cemetery Assn., Sigma Chi, Phi Kappa Delta. Clubs: Columbia, Meridian Hills Country, Woodland Country. Home: 110 E 111th St Indianapolis IN 46280-1051 Office: 3733 N Meridian St Indianapolis IN 46208-4305

MEYER, GAIL BARRY, retired real estate broker; b. Athens, Ga., Oct. 13, 1940; d. John Carlton and Addie Lorene (Harris) Barry; m. Leo Marcus Meyer Jr., July 2, 1960; Rand Marcus, Brian Kevin, Kelli Paige. Cert., Grad. Realtors Inst., 1979. Cert. residential specialist, cert. rape counselor. Assoc. broker, owner So. Realty, Statesboro, Ga., 1977-80; assoc. broker Zetterower-Olliff Realty, 1980-84, Century 21, Johnny Cobb Realty, Statesboro, 1984-99. Pres., v.p., treas. Citizens Against Crime, Statesboro, 1990—; pres. Victim Witness Assistance Program, Statesboro, 1990—; mem. Georgians for Victims Justice, Parents and Childrens Counsel. Recipient Deen Day Smith award C. of C. and Statesboro Herald News, 1989. Mem. NOW (pres. 1980—, v.p., treas.), MADD. Roman Catholic. Avocation: reading. Home: 274 Parkway Dr Athens GA 30606-4950 E-mail: gail586@charter.com.

MEYER, GEORGE HERBERT, lawyer; b. Detroit, Feb. 19, 1928; s. Herbert M. and Agnes F. (Eaton) M.; m. Carol Ann Jones, 1958 (div. 1981) children: Karen Ann, George Herbert Jr.; m. Katherine Palmer White, Nov. 12, 1988. AB, U. Mich., 1949; JD, Harvard U., 1952; cert., Oxford (Eng.) U., 1955; LLM in Taxation and Labor Law, Wayne State U., 1962. Bar: D.C. bar 1952, Mich. bar 1953. Assoc. firm Fischer, Franklin & Ford, Detroit, 1956-63, mem. firm, 1963-74; established firm George H. Meyer, 1974-78; sr. mem. firm Meyer and Kirk, 1978-85; sr. mem. Meyer, Kirk, Snyder & Safford PLLC, Bloomfield Hills and Detroit, Mich., 1985-99; mng. mem. Meyer, Kirk, Snyder & Lynch PLLC, Bloomfield Hills, 2000—. Curator Step Lively exhibit Mus. Am. Folk Art, N.Y.C., 1992; lectr. Am. Folk Art. Author: Equalization in Michigan and Its Effect on Local Assessments, 1963, Folk Artists Biographical Index, 1986, American Folk Art Canes: Personal Sculpture, 1992. Chmn. Birmingham (Mich.) Bd. Housing Appeals, 1964-68; vice chmn. Birmingham Bd. Zoning Appeals, 1966-69; mem. Birmingham Planning Bd., 1968-70; trustee, Bloomfield Village, Mich., 1976-80, pres., 1979-80; trustee Mus. Am. Folk Art, N.Y.C., 1987—; mem. exec. bd. Detroit Area coun. Boy Scouts Am., 1976—, counsel, 1986-95,v.p., 1996—; mem. nat. adv. bd. Folk Art Soc. Am., 1994—; trustee Detroit Sci. Ctr., 1985-99. 1st lt. JAG, USAF, 1952-55, maj. Res. ret. Recipient Silver Beaver award Detroit Area coun. Boy Scouts Am., 1989. Mem. ABA, Detroit Bar Assn., Oakland County Bar Assn., State Bar Mich., Harvard Law Sch. Assn. Mich. (dir. 1959—, pres. 1970-78), Detroit Sci. Mus. Soc. (pres. 1961-74, chmn. 1974-76), Am. Folk Art Soc. (pres. 2000—), Prismatic Club,(pres. 2002-), Scarab Club, Harvard Club (N.Y.C.), Detroit Athletic Club, Masons, Rotary, Phi Beta Kappa, Alpha Phi Omega, Pi Sigma Alpha. Republican. Unitarian Universalist. Office: Meyer Kirk Snyder & Lynch PLLC 100 W Long Lake Rd Ste 100 Bloomfield Hills MI 48304-2773 E-mail: info@meyerkirk.com.

MEYER, GEORGE WILBUR, internist, health facility administrator; b. Cleve., Apr. 30, 1941; s. George Wilbur and Emily Fuller (Campbell) M.; m. Carolyn Edwards Garrett, Apr. 8, 1967; children: Robert James, Elizabeth Jackson, Dobro Goodale. BS, MIT, 1962; MD, Tulane Med. Sch., 1966. Intern So. Pacific Hosps. Inc., San Francisco, 1966-67; resident Pacific Presbyn. Med. Ctr., 1969-72; commd. 1st lt. USAF, advanced through grades to col., 1980; fellow in gastroenterology David Grant USAF Med. Ctr., Travis AFB, Calif., 1974-76; asst. chair dept. medicine USAF Med. Ctr., Keesler AFB, Miss., 1976-78; asst. prof. dept. medicine Uniformed Svcs. Univ., Bethesda, Md., 1978-80; chair dept. medicine Wright Patterson AFB, Dayton, Ohio, 1980-82; chief of medicine Wilford Hall USAF Med. Ctr., Lackland AFB, Tex., 1982-86; chief clin. svcs. USAF Acad., Colo., 1986-88; comdr. 1st Med. Group, Langley AFB, Va., 1988-89, 86th Med. Group, Ramstein AFB, Germany, 1989-92; program dir. internal medicine Ga. Bapt. Med. Ctr., Atlanta, 1993-97; assoc. clin. prof. medicine U. Calif., Davis, 1998-2001, clin. prof. medicine, 2001—. Cons. Walter Reed Army Med. Ctr., Washington, 1978-80, Nat. Naval Med. Ctr., Bethesda, 1978-80; assoc. prof. Wright State U. Sch. Medicine, Dayton, 1980-82; cons. Dayton VA Med. Ctr., 1980-82; clin. assoc. prof. medicine U. Tex. Health Sci. Ctr., San Antonio, 1982-86, Med. Coll. Ga., Augusta, 1993-97; cons. dept. corp. med. divsn. State of Calif., 1997-98. Mem. editl. bd. Gastrointestinal Endoscopy, 1993-97, OnLine Jour. of Digestive Health, 1998-2000, Practical Gastroenterology, 1999—; book review editor Practical Gastroenterology, 1999—; contbr. articles and revs. to profl. jours. and chpts. to books. Mem. leadership com. Am. Cancer Soc., Ramstein AFB, 1989-93, bd. dirs. Atlanta City Unit, 1995-97, Ga. divsn. 1996-97, El Paso Teller Unit, Colorado Springs, 1986-88, Bexar Metro Unit, San Antonio, 1984-86; adv. com. United Health Svcs., Dayton, 1980-82. Fellow ACP (Laureate award 2001), Am. Coll. Gastroenterology; mem. Am. Soc. for Gastro Endoscopy, Am. Gastrointestinal Assn. Avocations: squash, tennis, scuba, stamps. E-mail: geowmeyer1@earthlink.net.

MEYER, GREG CHARLES, psychiatrist; b. Bismarck, N.D., Aug. 17, 1935; s. Oscar Clarence and Agnes Josephine (Pearson) M. Degree in profl. engring., Colo. Sch. Mines, 1958, Alexander Hamilton Bus. Inst., 1960; MME, U. So. Calif., 1965; MD, Marquette U., 1970. Diplomate Am. Bd. Psychiatry and Neurology, Am. Bd. Forensic Medicine, Am. Bd. Disability Analysts, Am. Bd. Forensic Examiners. Engr. Minuteman-Thiokol, Brigham City, Utah, 1958-61; sr. engr. Saturn S-II N.Am. Aviation, Downey, Calif., 1962-65; design specialist Titan-Martin, Denver, 1965-66; rotating intern Weld Country Gen. Hosp., Greenly, Colo., 1970-71; psychiatric resident Ariz. State Hosp., Phoenix, 1971-74, psychiatrist, 1974-76; pvt. practice Mesa-Tempe, Ariz., 1975-94; psychiatrist Ariz. Ctrl. Med. Ctr., 1995-99; med. dir. Ctrl. Ariz. Med. Ctr., 1997-99. Chmn. psychiatry Desert Samaritan Hosp., Mesa, 1982-86, 90-94, chmn. joint mental health, 1981-83, mem. edn. com., 1979-82, quality assurance com., 1979; exec. com. Desert Vista Hosp., Mesa, 1988-94, chief of staff, 1989; chmn. psychiatry Mesa Luth. Hosp., 1984-85, exec. com., 1984-85; mng. ptnr. Desert Samaritan Med. Bldg. II, Mesa, 1985-86; rsch., edn. com. East Valley Camel Back Hosp., 1989-90, quality assurance com., 1985; med. dir. Ctrl. Ariz. Med. Ctr., 1997-99. Co-discoverer Larson-Meyer Transform. Coach Pop Warner Football, 1974. With USMCR, 1953-59. Fellow Am. Bd. Disability Analysts; mem. AMA, Am. Psychiat. Assn., Ariz. Med. Assn., Ariz. Psychiat. Assn., Phoenix Psychiat. Coun., Maricopa County Med. Assn., Christian Med./Dental Assn., Triple Nine Soc., SCV, Wingfield Family Soc. Republican. Lutheran. Avocations: multi engine instrument pilot, sailing, computers, canoeing, photography.

MEYER, HARRY MARTIN, JR. retired health science facility administrator; b. Palestine Tex., Nov. 25, 1928. s. Harry Martin and Marjory Isabel (Griffin) M.; m. Mary Jane Martin, Aug. 19, 1949 (div. 1966); children: Harry, Mary, David; m. Barbara Story Chalfant, Nov. 21, 1966. BS Hendrix Coll., 1949, MD U. Ark., 1953; Diplomate Am. Bd. Pediatrics, 1960. instr. biology Little Rock Coll., 1949, intern. Walter Reed Army Hosp., Washington, 1953-54, med. officer dep. virus and rickettsial diseases, Walter Reed Army Inst. Rsch., 1954-57. asst. resident dep. pediatrics, N.C. Meml. Hosp., Chapel Hill, 1957-59, head virology sect. div. biologics standards, NIH, Bethesda, Md., 1959-64, chief lab. of viral immunol., div. biologics standards, NIH, 1964-72, dir. bur. biologics FDA, Bethesda, 1972-82, dir. Ctr. for Drugs & Biologics FDA, Rockville, Md., 1982-86, pres. med. research div. Am. Cyanamid Co., Pearl River, N.Y., 1986-93; retired 1993. Served to rear admiral USPHS, 1959-66, capt. U.S. Army, 1953-57. Mem. AMA, Am. Epidemiol. Soc., Am. Acad. Pediatrics, Am. Pediatric Soc. Protestant. Avocations: sailing, scuba diving, skiing, back packing. Contbr. articles to profl. jours.; patentee in field. E-mail: hanksji@interislend.net

MEYER, HELEN BERNADINE, financial services company executive; b. Ireton, Iowa, Mar. 2, 1929; d. Adolph J. and Haldora J. (Barnes) Opdahl; m. W. Thomas Logan, Nov. 19, 1955 (div. Mar. 1961); 1 stepchild Thomas C. Logan ; m. William James Meyer, Oct. 19, 1968 (dec. Aug. 1993); 1 adopted child H.B. Kris. Student, Sch. Mpls. Inst. Art, 1946-49. NASD registered rep., Iowa, Minn. Advt. artist, writer, mgr. Lawton Co., Cinn., 1949-51; illustrator, acct. exec. Simons Advt., N.Y.C., 1951—53; asst. advt. mgr. Max Wiesen & Sons, Inc., 1953-54, Mays Dept. Store, Bklyn., 1954-55; advt. and pub. rels. dir. Dayton's-Fantle's, Sioux Falls, S.D., 1955-66; comml. illustrator Meyer Advt., Worthington, Minn., 1967-69, comml. and continuity writer electronic media, 1970-76; regional promotions dir. shopping mall devel. Developers Diversified, Cleve., 1977-79; fin. svcs. exec. Meyer Ins. and Investment, Worthington, 1980—. Charter mem. Advt. Artist Guild, 1960-66, dir., 1963-64. Charter treas., pres. Zonta Internat., Sioux Falls, 1957-66; pub. rels., promotions staff Am. Cancer Soc., Worthington, 1972-77. Lutheran. Achievements include patent pending for surgical support. Avocations: photography, birding, chasing lighthouses and seashores. Home: 29744 290 St Worthington MN 56187

MEYER, HENRY LEWIS, III, banker; b. Cleve., Dec. 25, 1949; s. Henry Lewis and Anne (Taylor) M.; m. Jane Kreamer, July 15, 1978; children: Patrick Harrison, Andrew Taylor, Christopher Bicknell. BA, Colgate U., 1972; MBA, Harvard U., Boston, 1978. Asst. v.p. Soc. Nat. Bank, Cleve., 1972-76, v.p., 1978-81, sr. v.p., 1981-83; exec. v.p. Soc. Bank, Dayton, Ohio, 1983-85, pres., chief operating officer, 1985-87; sr. exec. v.p. Soc. Nat. Bank, Cleve., 1987-89, vice chmn. bd., 1989-90, pres., COO, 1990-93, pres., CEO, 1993-94, chmn. bd., CEO, 1994-95; exec. v.p. Soc. Corp., 1987-91, vice chmn. bd., 1991-94; exec. v.p. KeyCorp (formerly Soc. Corp.), 1994-95, sr. exec. v.p., COO, 1995-96, vice chmn. bd., COO, 1996-97, pres., COO, 1997—; pres., CEO KeyCorp, 2001—; exec. v.p. KeyCorp (formerly Soc. Corp.), 1994-95. Bd. dirs. Key Corp, The Lincoln Elec. Co. Trustee Am. Cancer Soc. (Cuyahoga County Unit), Cleve. Mus. Nat. History; vis. com. Case Western Res. U. Weatherhead Sch. Mgmt.; active The Holden Arboretum, Inroads, Northeast Ohio Coun. Higher Edn., Univ. Sch.; chmn. bd. trustees Sta. WVIZ-TV; mem. exec. com., bd. dirs. U. Hosps. Health Sys., Inc. Mem.: Kirtland Country (Cleve.), The Union (Cleve.), Cleve. Skating, Pepper Pike (Cleve.), Club at Key Ctr. (Cleve.). Republican. Episcopalian.*

MEYER, HORST, physics educator; b. Berlin, Germany, Mar. 1, 1926; BS, U. Geneva, 1949; PhD in physics, U. Zurich, 1953. Fellow Swiss Assn. Rsch. Physics and Math. Studies, Oxford, Eng., 1953-55; Nuffield fellow Clarendon Lab. U. Oxford, 1955-57; lectr., rsch. assoc. dept. engring. and applied physics Harvard U., Cambridge, Mass., 1957-59; from asst. prof. to prof. Duke U., Durham, N.C., 1959-84, Fritz London prof. physics, 1984—. Vis. prof. Technische Hochschule, Federal Republic of Germany, 1965, Tokyo U., 1980, 81, 83; traveling fellow Japanese Soc. for Promotion Sci., 1971, vis. scientist, 1979; guest scientist Inst. Laue-Langevin, France, 1974, 75; Yamada Found. fellow, Japan, 1986; guest scientist USSR Acad. Sci., 1988; guest prof. Toyota Inst. Tech., Nagoya, Japan, Oct. 1998; chmn. Gordon Conf. on Solid H2, 1990; western chmn. conf. quantum crystals, Almaty, Kazakhstan, 1995. Editor Jour. Low Temperature Physics, 1992—, mem. editorial bd., 1988-92; contbr. articles to profl. jours. Alfred P. Sloan fellow, 1961-65. Fellow Am. Phys. Soc. (Jesse Beams prize, 1982, Fritz London prize 1993). Achievements include exptl. rsch. on the properties of liquid and solid helium, critical phenomena in fluids, solid hydrogen and deuterium, magnetic insulators, critical phenomena. Office: Duke U Dept Physics PO Box 90305 Durham NC 27708-0305

MEYER, HOWARD ROBERT, JR. military officer, research and development; b. Bolling AFB, Md., Nov. 16, 1955; s. Howard Robert Meyer and Mamie Irene (Blackwell) Franceschini; stepfather Walter Adrian Franceschini; m. Mary Evelyn Corley, June 4, 1977; children: Rachel Eileen, Hannah Ruth, Amy Evelyn. BS, USAF Acad., 1977; MS in Chemistry, U. Wyo., 1983, PhD in Analytical Chemistry, 1990. Commd. 2d lt. USAF, 1977, advanced through grades to lt. col., 1993, retired, 1999, alt. command post missile crew comdr. Wyo., 1977-80, chief code handler tng. br. Strategic Missile Wing, 1981—82; instr. chemistry USAF Acad., Colo., 1983-86, asst. prof., 1986-87, chief environ. rsch. & develop., 1990—; dir. environ. quality info. analysis ctr. Air Force Civil Engring. Support Agy., Tyndall AFB, Fla., 1992—; dep. chief scientist AF Rsch. Lab, Kirtland AFB, N.Mex., 1993—95; dep. dir. Airborne Laser Sys. Program Office, 1996; dep. dir. spl. programs, 1997; dep. dir. Counterproliferation Support Program, Pentagon, Washington, 1998; chief program Integration Office, Counterproliferation Directorate, Def. Threat Reduction Agy., 1999; sr. analyst, scientific advisor Sci. Applications Internat. Corp., 1999—. Supporting staff to the Deputy Asst. Sec. of the Army for Rsch. & Tech. and the Chief, Future Concepts Devel., Dir. of Programs and Plans, Hdqs., USAF. Scholar U. Wyo., 1986; grad. rsch. scholar Air Force Inst. Tech., U. Wyo., 1987-90. Mem. AAAS, Am. Chem. Soc., Am. Sci. Affiliation. Republican. Southern Baptist. Avocations: science education, science and faith issues, swimming. Home: 4745 Shadow Woods Ct Dumfries VA 22026-1067 E-mail: psiigii@home.com., howard.meyer@pentagon.af.mil.

MEYER, IRWIN STEPHAN, lawyer, accountant; b. Monticello, N.Y., Nov. 14, 1941; s. Ralph and Janice (Cohen) M.; children: Kimberly B., Joshua A. BS, Rider Coll., 1963; JD, Cornell U., 1966. CPA NJ; bar: NY 1966. Tax mgr. Lybrand Ross Bros. & Montgomery, N.Y.C., 1966-71; mem. Ehrenkranz, Ehrenkranz & Schultz, 1971-74; prin. Irwin S. Meyer, 1974-77, 82-96; mem. Levine, Honig, Eisenberg & Meyer, 1977-78, Eisenberg, Honig & Meyer, 1978-81, Eisenberg, Honig, Meyer & Fogler, 1981-82, Janow & Meyer, LLC., 1997—. With U.S. Army, 1966—71. Mem. ABA, N.Y. Bar Assn., Am. Assn. Atty.-CPA, N.Y. Assn. Atty.-CPA, N.J. Soc. CPA. Office: 1 Blue Hill Plz Ste 1006 Pearl River NY 10965-3100 E-mail: irwin@janow-meyer.com.

MEYER, J. THEODORE, lawyer; b. Chgo., Apr. 13, 1936; s. Joseph Theodore and Mary Elizabeth (McHugh) M.; m. Marilu Bartholomew, Aug. 16, 1961; children: Jean, Joseph. BS, John Carroll U., 1958; postgrad., U. Chgo.; JD, DePaul U., 1962. Bar: Ill. 1962. Ptnr. Bartholomew & Meyer, Chgo., 1963-83; mem. Ill. Gen. Assembly, Ho. of Reps. 28th Legis. Dist., 1966-72, 74-82. Chmn. House environ. study com., 1968; chmn. energy environ. com. and natural resources com.; mem. appropriations and exec. com.; chmn. Joint House/Senate com. to review state air and water plans, 1968; mem. Fed. State Task Force on Energy; chmn., founder Midwest Legis. Coun. on Environ., 1971; mem. Joint Legis. Com. on Hazardous Waste in Lake Calumet Area, 1987; chmn. Gov.'s adv. com. to streamline the Ill. environ. protection act, 1999-2001, Ill. Regulatory Revision Commn., 1999-2001; mem. Ill. Pollution Control Bd., Chgo., 1983-98, Ill. EPA, 1998-99; lectr. in field. Recipient Appreciation award Ill. Wildlife Fedn., 1972, Environ. Quality award Region V, EPA, 1974, Pro Bono Publico award Self-Help Action Ctr., 1975, Merit award Dept. Ill. VFW, 1977, Environ. Legislator of Yr. award Ill. Environ. Coun., 1978-79; named Disting. Lawyer Legislator of Yr., Hon. Tex. Citizen, hon. lt. aide-de-camp Ala. State Militia. Fellow Chgo. Bar Found.; mem. ABA, Ill. Bar Assn., Chgo. Bar Assn., Nat. Rep. Legis. Assn., Nat. Trust Hist. Preservation, Nat. Wildlife Fedn., Ill. Hist. Soc. Republican. Roman Catholic.

MEYER, JACK EDWARD, radiologist, educator; b. Davenport, Iowa, Oct. 21, 1939; s. Russell and Ellen Meyer; m. Mary Jean Meyer, Jan. 9, 1966; children: Heather, Hilary. BA, Grinnell (Iowa) Coll., 1961; MD, Cornell U., 1965; MS (hon.), Harvard U., 1991. Diplomate Am. Bd. Radiology; lic. physician, Mass., Calif., Mich. Intern San Francisco Gen. Hosp., 1965-66; resident in radiology U. Mich., Ann Arbor, 1968-69, Mass. Gen. Hosp., Boston, 1969-71, asst. radiation medicine, 1971-72, head oncologic diagnostic radiology, 1979-85; chief diagnostic radiology Pondville Hosp., Walpole, 1972-78, chief radiology, chief staff, 1978-79; prof., chmn. dept. radiology U. Louisville, Ky., 1985-87; acting dir. diagnostic radiology Brigham and Women's Hosp., Boston, 1987-88, dir. diagnostic radiology, 1989-99; dir. breast imaging Dana-Farber Cancer Inst., 2001—. Asst. prof. radiology Boston U., 1972-74, assoc. clin. prof., 1974-79; asst. prof. U. Mass., Boston, 1976-77, assoc. prof. radiology, 1977-79; asst. prof. radiology Harvard Med. Sch., Boston, 1979-82, assoc. prof. radiology, 1982-85, 87-91, prof. radiology, 1991—; dir. diagnostic oncoradiology Dana-Farber Cancer Inst., Boston, 1991-99; dir. breast imaging, Brigham and Womens Hosp, Boston, 1999—. Author: (with others) Interventional Radiology, 1981, Cancer: A Manual for Practitioners, 6th edit., 1982, Lymphatic Imaging, 2d edit., 1985; cons. to editorial bd. jours.; contbr. numerous articles and abstracts to profl. jours. Examiner Am. Bd. Radiology, 1992—. Capt. USAF, 1966-68. Fellow Am. Coll. Radiology, Mass. Med. Soc., Mass. Radiol. Soc., Radiol. Soc. N.Am., Assn. Univ. Radiologists, Soc. Breast Imaging, Cancer Imaging Soc. Office: Brigham and Womens Hosp Dept Diagnostic Radiology 75 Francis St Boston MA 02115-6106 E-mail: jmeyer@partners.org.

MEYER, JAMES HENRY, university chancellor emeritus; b. Fenn, Idaho, Apr. 13, 1922; s. Carl A. and Anita (de Coursey) M.; m. Alice Bell, May 18, 1996; children by previous marriage: Stephen J., Susan T., Gary C., Joan K., Teresa A. BS in Agr, U. Idaho, 1947; MS in Nutrition (fellow Wis. Alumni Research Found.), U. Wis., 1949, PhD, 1951. Research asst. U. Wis., 1949-51; faculty U. Calif., Davis, 1951-87, prof. animal husbandry sci., 1960-87, chmn. dept., 1960-63, dean Coll. Agrl. and Environment Scis., 1963-69, univ. chancellor, 1969-87, chancellor emeritus, 1987—. Mem. Commn. Undergrad. Edn. in Biology, 1964-69 Editorial bd.: Jour. Animal Sci, 1961-65. Mem. Western Coll. Sr. Accrediting Commn., 1982-88, Western Schs. Accrediting Commn., 1987-90. With USMCR, 1942-46. Recipient Am. Feed Mfr.'s award in nutrition, 1960 Fellow AAAS; mem. Am. Soc. Animal Prodn., Nat. Assn. State Univs. and Land Grant Colls., Western Coll. Assn. (exec. com. 1971-74), Sigma Xi.

MEYER, JEFF (GEORGE JEFF MEYER), real estate executive; b. New Brunswick, N.J., Mar. 25, 1965; s. George F. and Barbara Knight (Flach) M. BS in Mech. Engring. Tech., Trenton State Coll., 1987; MBA, Rutgers U., 1992. Realtor assoc. Max E. Spann Realtors, Bedminster, N.J., 1987-88; constrn. estimator Stony Brook Constrn., Somerville, 1988-91; land acquisition analyst K. Hovnanian of Cen. N.J., North Brunswick, 1992, asst. dir. land acquisitions Branchburg, N.J., 1993, dir. land acquisitions North Brunswick, 1994—. Bd. dirs. Keep Middlesex Moving, New Brunswick, 1994. Bd. dirs. Trenton State Coll. Devel. Corp., Ewing, N.J., 1994. Home: 72 Welton St New Brunswick NJ 08901-2531 Address: PO Box Cn7825 Edison NJ 08818-7825

MEYER, JOAN MARIE, drug researcher; b. July 15, 1956; BA, St. Mary's U., Winona, Minn., 1978; MS, U. Ill., 1982, PhD, 1986. Staff scientist Procter & Gamble, Cin., 1986-90, head arthritis rschr., 1990-96, assoc. dir. arthritis new drug devel., 1996—. Bd. dirs. Ohio River Valley Arthritis Found., 1995. Office: 8700 S Mason Montgomery Rd Mason OH 45040-9760 E-mail: meyerjm@pg.com.

MEYER, JOHN ROBERT, economist, educator; b. Pasco, Wash., Dec. 6, 1927; s. Philip Conrad and Cora (Kempter) M.; m. Lee Stowell, Dec. 17, 1949; children: Leslie Karen, Ann Elizabeth, Robert Conrad. Student, Pacific U., 1945-46; BA, U. Wash., 1950; PhD (David A. Wells prize), Harvard U., 1955. Jr. fellow Harvard U., 1953-55, asst. prof., 1955-58, assoc. prof., 1958-59, prof. econs., 1959-68, prof. transportation and logistics, 1973-83; prof. Yale U., 1968-73; Harpel prof. capital formation and econ. growth Harvard U., 1983-96, prof. emeritus, 1997—. Vice chmn. Union Pacific Corp., 1982-83, dir., 1978-99; trustee Pacific U. Author: (with others) The Investment Decision—An Empirical Inquiry, 1957, Economics of Competition in the Telecommunications Industry, 1980, Autos, Transit and Cities, 1981, Deregulation and the Future of Intercity Passenger Travel, 1987, Going Private: The International Experience with Transport Privatization, 1993, Moving to Market: Restructuring Transport in the Former Soviet Union, 1996, other books; contbr. articles to profl. jours. Mem. Presdl. Task Forces on Transp., 1964, 80, Presdl. Commn. on Population Growth and Am. Future, 1970-72; pres. Nat. Bur. Econ. Research, 1967-77. Served with USNR, 1946-48. Guggenheim fellow, 1958. Fellow Am. Acad. Arts and Scis., Econometric Soc.; mem. Am. Econ. Assn. (mem. exec. com. 1971-73), Council Fgn. Relations, Econ. History Assn. Home: 572 Kinzie Island Ct Sanibel FL 33957-5021 Office: Harvard U Ctr Bus & Govt 79 Jfk St Cambridge MA 02138-5801 E-mail: jrobtmeyer@aol.com.

MEYER, JOHN ALBERT, lawyer; b. Sioux Falls, S.D., Dec. 6, 1946; s. John Richard Meyer and Beryl Geneva (Birkland) Ritz; m. Donna Rae Finch, Jan. 21, 1983; 1 child, Elizabeth Ann. BS, Iowa State U., 1969; JD, U. Iowa, 1972. Bar: Iowa 1972, Ill. 1972, U.S. Dist. Ct. (no. dist.) Ill. 1972, U.S. Supreme Ct. 1977, U.S. Tax Ct. 1981. Asst. U.S. atty. U.S. Atty's Office U.S. Dist. Ct. (no. dist.) Ill., Chgo., 1972-77; ptnr. Johnson & Colmar, 1977-83, Bortman, Meyer & Barasa, Chgo., 1983—. Recipient Disting. Svc. award FBI, 1975. Mem. Chgo. Bar Assn., Ill. State Bar Assn., ABA. Office: 20 S Clark St Ste 2210 Chicago IL 60603-1805 E-mail: chgolegal@aol.com.

MEYER, JOHN EDWARD, nuclear engineering educator; b. Pitts., Dec. 17, 1931; s. Albert Edward and Thelma Elizabeth (Brethauer) M.; m. Gracyann Lenz, June 13, 1953; children: Susan Meyer Heydon, Karl, Karen Meyer Gleasman, Thomas. BS, MS, Carnegie Inst. Tech., 1953, PhD (ASME Student award 1955), 1955. Engring. and mgmt. positions Westinghouse Bettis Atomic Power Lab., West Mifflin, Pa., 1955-75; vis. lectr. U. Calif., Berkeley, 1968-69; prof. nuclear engring. MIT, 1975-98, ret., 1998. Cons. in field. Author papers in field. Recipient Bettis Disting. Service award, 1962, Outstanding Tchr. award nuclear engring. M.I.T., 1979, Alumni Merit award Carnegie Mellon U., 1987. Fellow Am. Nuclear Soc.; mem. ASME, Sigma Xi.

MEYER, JOHN FREDERICK, engineering and computer science educator, researcher, consultant; b. Grand Rapids, Mich., July 26, 1934; s. Frederick Albert and Harriet (Stibbs) M.; m. Nancy Shaw Briggs, July 4, 1959; children: John, Patricia, James. BS, U. Mich., 1957; MS, Stanford U., 1958; PhD, U. Mich., 1967. Data systems engr. Douglas Aircraft Corp., Santa Monica, Calif., 1957; research engr. Caltech, Jet Propulsion Lab., Pasadena, 1958-67; asst. prof. U. Mich., Ann Arbor, 1968-71, assoc. prof., 1971-76, prof. elec. engring. and computer sci., 1976—, dir. Computing Research Lab., 1984-89. Cons. Calif. Inst. Tech. Jet Propulsion Lab., 1979—, Indsl. Tech. Inst., Ann Arbor, 1985—, CIMSA, Paris, 1992, Bendis Advanced Tech. Ctr., Columbia, Md., 1977-85, Thomson CSF, Paris, 1975, Italtel, Milan, 1990—, Applied Scis. Corp., Reading, Mass., 1993. Patentee Time Division Multiplexer, 1963 (NASA Inventions award 1964). Precinct chmn. 3d ward Democratic Party, Ann Arbor, 1971-74. Recipient Disting. Service Award U. Mich., 1964; IBM fellow, 1957 Fellow IEEE; mem. IEEE Computer Soc. (Cert. of Appreciation 1981, 95, Meritorious Svc. award 1985), AAAS, Assn. Computing Machinery. Home: 1946 Ridge Ave Ann Arbor MI 48104-6306 Office: U Mich 2114B EECS Bldg Ann Arbor MI 48109-2122

MEYER, JOHN MARK, political scientist, educator; b. Chgo., Aug. 29, 1962; s. Leon Jacob and Barbara Gene M.; m. Carolyn Ann Benson, Aug. 14, 1988; children: Jacob Reid, Emelia Paua. BA, Colo. Coll., 1984; MA, U. Wis., 1991, PhD, 1997. Organizer, canvass dir. Colo. Pub. Interest Rsch. Group, Denver, 1984-87; exec. dir. Ohio Pub. Interst Rsch. Group, Columbus, 1987-90; asst. prof. Humboldt State U., Arcata, Calif., 1998—, grad. coord. social scis., 2000—. Vis. lectr. Victoria U. Wellington, New Zealand, 1997; faculty advisor Campus Ctr. Appropriate Tech., Arcata, 2000—. Author: Political Nature, 2001; editor: American Indians and U.S. Politics, 2002; contbr. articles to profl. jours. Mem. Internat. Soc. Environ. Ethics, Am. Polit. Sci. Assn., Western Polit. Sci. Assn. Jewish. Office: Dept Govt Politics Humboldt State U 1 Harpst St Arcata CA 95521 E-mail: jmm7001@humboldt.edu.

MEYER, JOHN STIRLING, neurologist, educator; b. London, Feb. 24, 1924; came to U.S., 1940; s. William Charles and Alice Elizabeth (Stirling) M.; m. Wendy Haskell, July 20, 1947 (dec. 1986); children: Jane, Anne, Elizabeth, Helen, Margaret; m. Katharine Sumner, Aug. 2, 1987; m. Cora Bess Parks, Apr. 6, 1996. BSc, Trinity Coll., Hartford, Conn., 1944; MD, CM, McGill U., Montreal, Que., 1948, MSc, 1949. Diplomate Am. Bd. Neurology and Psychiatry. Intern Yale-New Haven Hosp., 1948-49, resident neurology, 1949-50, Boston City Hosp., 1950-52, resident neurophysiology, 1952-53, fellow neurophysiology, 1954-55; instr. rsch. assoc. Harvard Med. Sch., Boston, 1955-57, resident neurophysiology, 1952-53; prof., chair dept. Wayne State U., Detroit, 1957-69, Baylor Coll. Medicine, Houston, 1969-75, prof. neurology, 1976—; demonstrator neuropathology and teaching fellow neurology Harvard U. Med. Sch., 1950-52; sr. rsch. fellow USPHS, 1952-54; instr. medicine Harvard U. Med. Sch., 1954-56; assoc. vis. physician neurology Boston City Hosp., 1956-57; cons. and lectr. neurology U.S. Naval Hosp., Chelsea, Mass., 1957; prof. neurology and chmn. dept. sch. medicine Wayne State U., 1957-69, chmn. dept., 1969-76; prof. neurology, dir. stroke lab. Baylor Coll. Medicine, Houston, 1976—; with Va. Med. Ctr. Chair stroke panel Pres.' Commn. on Heart Disease Cancer & Stroke, Washington, 1964-65; mem. nat. adv. coun. Nat. Inst. Neurol. Diseases & Stroke, Bethesda, Md., 1965-69. Author 29 books; contbr. over 879 articles to profl. jours. Mem. jury Albert Lasker Med. Rsch. Awards, N.Y.C., 1965-69. Lt. (s.g.) Med. Corps USN, 1953-55, Korea. Recipient Harold G. Woff award, Am. Assn. for Study of Headache, 1977, 78, 79, Baylor Coll. Medicine award, Houston, 1980, 85, 90, 95, 2000, Mihara award Mihara Found., Tokyo, 1987, Bertha Lecture award Salzburg Conf., Washington, 1992. Mem. Am. Heart Assn. (bd. dirs. 1968-70, chair coun. on stroke 1968-70). Republican. Episcopalian. Achievements include development of xenon contrast method for measuring cerebral blood flow using computerized tomography. Office: VA Med Ctr Rm 225 2002 Holcombe Blvd Bldg 110 Houston TX 77030-4211 Fax: 713-794-7583. E-mail: jmeyer@bcm.tsu.edu.

MEYER, JOHN STRAUCH, JR. lawyer; b. St. Louis, June 12, 1958; s. John Strauch Meyer and Margaret (Bragdon) Shepley; m. Laura Lewis, May 29, 1983; children: Emily H., Julia E. AB, Yale U., 1980; JD, Washington U., St. Louis, 1984. Bar: Mo. 1984. Legis. asst., corr. to Sen. John C. Danforth Washington, 1980-81; summer assoc. Greensfelder, Hemker, St. Louis, 1982, Bryan Cave LLP, St. Louis, 1983, assoc., 1984-92, ptnr., 1993—. Mem. panel of arbitrators Am. Arbitration Assn., N.Y.C., 1994; dir. City Mus. Inc., 2001—. Co-author: (desk book) Mechanic's Liens and Construction Bonds under Missouri Law, 1991, rev. edits. Dir., past pres., past treas. Planned Parenthood of St. Louis Region, 1989-98, 99—; dir., treas., past v.p. of devel., pres. The Forsyth Sch., St. Louis, 1994-2002, pres., 1998-2001; mem. St. Louis 2004 Urban Devel. Taskforce, 1997-98. Mem. ABA, Bar Assn. of Met. St. Louis, Robert Burns Club of St. Louis (pres. 1994), Noonday Club. Unitarian Universalist. Avocations: outdoor activities, travel, exercise, fine food, single malt whiskeys. Office: Bryan Cave LLP 211 N Broadway Saint Louis MO 63102-2733 E-mail: JSMeyer@BryanCave.Com.

MEYER, JON KEITH, psychiatrist, psychoanalyst, educator; b. Springfield, Ill., May 6, 1938; s. Samuel Barclay and Finela Hermoine (Roehl) M.; m. Eleanor Fumie Yamashita, June 6, 1964; children: David Christopher, Laura Tamiko. AB summa cum laude, Dartmouth Coll., 1960; MD, Johns Hopkins U., 1964; grad., Washington Psychoanalytic Inst, 1980. Intern internal medicine Johns Hopkins Hosp., Balt., 1964-65, resident in psychiatry, 1965-67, 69, St. Elizabeth's Hosp., Washington, 1968; spl. asst. to dir. NIMH, Bethesda, Md., 1969-71; asst. prof. psychiatry Johns Hopkins Med. Sch., Balt., 1971-76, assoc. prof., 1976-83; prof. psychiatry Med. Coll. Wis., Milw., 1983—, prof. psychoanalysis, 1996—, prof. family medicine, 1990—; tng. and supervising analyst Chgo. Inst. for Psychoanalysis, 1987—2002; vice chmn. Dept. of Psychiatry, 1993—; chief psychiatry Froedtert Meml. Luth. Hosp., Milw., 1994-97; tng. and supervising analyst Wis. Psychoanaltic Inst., 2001—. Med. dir. Wis., Psychoanalytic Found., Milw., 1987-91, sec. bd. dirs., 1988-91. Author books; editl. bd. Jour. Am. Psychoanalytic Assn., 1991-94; nat. editor: The American Psychoanalyst, 1997-2001; contbr. chpts. to books, numerous articles to profl. jours. Comdr. USPHS, 1967—71. Recipient Daniel Webster Nat. scholarship, Dartmouth Coll., 1956—60, sr. fellowship, 1959—60, Dennison rsch. prize, Johns Hopkins Med. Sch., 1964; scholar Erik Erikson scholar-in-residence, Austen Riggs Ctr., Stockbridge, Mass., 1991—92, Ctr. Advanced Psychoanalytic Studies, 1998—. Fellow: Am. Coll. Psychiatrists, Am. Coll. Psychoanalysts, Am. Psychiat. Assn.; mem.: Wis. Psychoanalytic Soc. (pres. 1989—91), Assn. for Child Psychoanalysis (candidate councilor 2001—), Am. Psychoanalytic Assn. (exec. councilor 1993—97, chmn. com. on exec. coun. structure and function 1995—98, sec. 1997—2001, adminstrv. bd. Jour. Am. Psychoanalytic Assn. 1997—2001, exec. com. 1997—2001, chmn. com. on cmty. clinics 1997—2002, com. on insts. 1998—2002, com. on bylaws 2001—02, pres.-elect 2002—04, exec. com. 2002—, adminstrv. bd. Jour. Am. Psychoanalytic Assn. 2002—, Edith Sabshin Tchg. award 1999), Internat. Psychoanalytic Assn. (com. on constn. and by-laws 1997—2001, com. on procedural codes 1997—2001, mem. task force on structure and mission 1997—2001, ho. dels. 1998—2001, chair ho. of dels. 1999—2000). Avocations: photography, hiking, kayaking. Office: Med Coll Wis 4th Fl Rm 436 2025 E Newport Ave Milwaukee WI 53211-2906

MEYER, JON HOWARD, utility executive, consultant; b. Islip, N.Y., Jan. 5, 1962; s. Howard Charles and Betty Alice Meyer; m. Janet Hope Kinder, Jan. 14, 1984; children: Benjamin, Derek. Constrn. laborer Gulf Constructors, Sarasota, Fla., 1981-82; wastewater plant operator City of Ft. Meade, 1982-84; asst. chief operator Polk County Utilities, Bartow, 1984-96; mgr. wastewater Severn Trent-Avatar Utility Svcs., Fort Myers, 1996-2001; project mgr. Fla. Water Svcs., Marco Island, Fla., 2001—. Recipient Ops. of Excellence award Fla. Dept. Environ. Protection, 1996, 97, 98, Lakeside Outstanding Plant award Lakeside Equipment, 1999, Leroy Henry Scott award Fla. Water Environ. Fedn., 1999, Earle B. Phelps award 2000, William D. Hatfield award, 2001. Mem. Fla. Water & Pollution Control Operators Assn. (sec., treas. 1998-99),. Fla. Water Environment Assn. (ops. rsch. com. 1996-2001). Home: 4020 SW 6th Pl Cape Coral FL 33914 Office: Fla Water Svcs 960 Collier Blvd Marco Island FL 34145 E-mail: dodoguru@yahoo.com.

MEYER, JOSEPH B. state official, former academic administrator; b. Casper, Wyo., 1941; m. Mary Orr; children: Vincent, Warren. Student, Colo. Sch. Mines; BA, U. Wyo., 1964, JD, 1967; postgrad., Northwestern U., 1968. Dep. county atty. Fremont County, Wyo., 1967-69; assoc. Smith and Meyer, 1968-71; asst. dir. legis. svc. office State of Wyo., Cheyenne, 1971-87, atty. gen., 1987-95; spl. asst. to pres. Univ. Wyo., Laramie, 1995-98; sec. of state State of Wyoming, 1999—. Conductor numerous govt. studies on state codes including Wyo. probate, criminal, state adminstrn., banking, domestic rels., game and fish, state instn., employment security, worker's compensation, motor vehicle, others; conductor legis. rev. of adminstrv. rules; negotiator with Office of Surface Mining for Wyo. state preemption; instr. Wyo. Coll. Law, fall 1986; lectr. Rocky Mountain Mineral Law Found., 1977; chmn. Conf. Western Atty. Gen., 1992-93; mem. exec. com. Nat. Assn. Attys. Gen. Bd. dirs. Cheyenne Jr. League, 1982-85, Jessup PTO, 1980-81; instr. Boy Scouts Am. Mem. Rotary. Congregationalist. Avocations: golf, tennis, gardening, wood carving, rock hunting. Office: State Capital Bldg Cheyenne WY 82002-0001 E-mail: jmeyer3@state.wy.us.

MEYER, KARIN ZUMWALT, pharmacist, consultant; b. Buffalo, Aug. 17, 1953; d. Robert F. and Mildred (Oswald) Zumwalt; m. Jimmy E. Meyer, Aug. 12, 1994. BS in Pharmacy, Purdue U., 1976; MBA in Healthcare, Cleve. State U., 1987. Registered pharmacist, Ohio. Pharmacist Cleve. Clinic, 1982-87, Caremark, Mayfield Hts., Ohio, 1987-88; dir. pharmacy Careplus, Beachwood, 1988-89; pharmacy mgr. Kaiser Permanente, Cleve., 1989-93; dir. pharmacy Homedco Infusion, Valley View, Ohio, 1993-95; relief pharmacist, cons. RPh On the Go, Solon, 1995-96; pediat. pharmacist Cleve. Clinic Children's Hosp. for Rehab., 1996—. Adj. instr. Cuyahoga C.C., Cleve., 1990-93; clin. mgmt. team Careplus, Beachwood, 1988-89. Satellite planning com. Cleve. Clinic Found., 1982-87. Mem. Am. Pharm. Assn., Am. Soc. Health-Sys. Pharmacists (membership com. 1996-97), USTA, Cleve. Metro Ski Coun., Purdue Club Cleve., Iota Sigma Pi. Avocations: skiing, tennis, windsurfing, travel, music. Home: 8549 Settlers Passage Brecksville OH 44141-1749 E-mail: jimkarinmeyer@msn.com.

MEYER, KARL ERNEST, journalist; b. Madison, Wis., May 22, 1928; s. Ernest Louis and Dorothy (Narefsky) M.; m. Sarah Nielsen Peck, Aug. 12, 1959 (div. 1972); children— Ernest, Heather, Jonathan; m. Shareen Blair Brysac, Jan. 6, 1989. BA, U. Wis., 1951; M.P.A., Princeton U., 1953, PhD, 1956. Reporter N.Y. Times, N.Y.C., 1952, mem. editorial bd., 1979-98; editorial writer Washington Post, 1956-65, chief London Bur., 1965-70, N.Y.C. corr., 1970-71; Washington corr. New Statesman, 1961-65; sr. editor, TV critic Saturday Rev., N.Y.C., 1975-79; corr. in residence Fletcher Sch. Law and Diplomacy, Tufts U., 1979; editor World Policy Jour., N.Y.C., 2000—. Vis. journalist fellow Duke U., Durham, NC, 1988; vis. prof. Yale U., 1983, 90; McGraw prof. in writing Princeton (N.J.) U., 1993—94; vis. prof. Bard Coll., NY, 2002. Author: The New America, 1961, (with Tad Szulc) The Cuban Invasion, 1962, Fulbright of Arkansas, 1963, The Pleasures of Archaeology, 1971, The Plundered Past, 1973, Teotihuacán, 1975, The Art Museum: Power, Money, Ethics, 1979, Pundits, Poets and Wits: An Omnibus of American Newspaper Columns, 1990, (with Shareen Brysac) Tournament of Shadows: The Great Game and Race for Empire in Central Asia, 1999. Recipient citation for excellence Overseas Press Club, 1961, Bronze medal for editl. writing Sigma Delta; George Foster Peabody Broadcasting award 1983, Disting. Achievement award Sch. Journalism, U. Wis., 1985; Davenport Coll. of Yale U. fellow; Wisenschaftskolleg Inst. Adv. Studies (Berlin) fellow, 1994-95, Reuter fellow Oxford (Eng.) U., 1996-97. Mem. PEN Club Internat., Coun. on Fgn. Rels., NYU Soc. Fellows, Century Assn., Authors League Am. Home: 50 W 96th St New York NY 10025-6526 Office: World Policy Jour 66 5 Th Ave Ste 900 New York NY 10011 E-mail: kmeyer@webquill.com.

MEYER, KARL WILLIAM, retired university president; b. Ft. Wayne, Ind., May 8, 1925; s. K.W. and L. (Hofacker) M.; m. Margery R. Hamman, Apr. 15, 1950; children— Mary, William, Frederick, Ann, Jean. AB, Valparaiso U., 1948; M.F.S., U. Md., 1949; PhD, U. Wis., 1953; postgrad., U. Basel, Switzerland, 1948-49; postdoctoral fellow, U. Mich., 1958-59. Faculty Valparaiso U., 1952-53, Augustana Coll., 1953-55, Wis. State U., 1955-58; dean instrn., dir. grad. studies Wayne State Coll., 1959-63; asst. dir. bd. regents Wis. State Colls., Madison, 1963-64; pres. U. Wis.-Superior, 1964-87. Author: Karl Liebknecht: Man Without a Country, 1957; Contbr. articles to profl. jours. Served with USAAF, 1943-46, ETO. Home: W7861 Homestead Ct Holmen WI 54636-9440

MEYER, KATHLEEN MARIE, gifted education educator, writer; b. St. Louis, Oct. 29, 1944; d. Richard Henry and Leonora (Moser) Bailey; m. Thomas A. Meyer, Dec. 26, 1966; children: Richard, Amy, Mindy, Heidi. BA, Webster Coll., Webster Groves, Mo., 1966; MA, Fla. Atlantic U., 1981; postgrad., No. Ill. U., 1982—. Cert. secondary tchr., tchr. of gifted, Mo., Ill. Tchr. English Notre Dame High Sch., St. Louis, 1966-67; tchr. English, chmn. dept. Rosary High Sch., Aurora, Ill., 1981-91; instr. English DeKalb Coll. (now Ga. Perimeter Coll.), Decatur, Ga., 1992—2001, tchr. gifted program, 1999—; instr. English North Metro Tech., 2001, Kennesaw State U., 2002—. Editor, writer; mem. adv. bd. Univ. High Sch.; mem. joint enrollment coun. DeKalb Coll. Freelance editor, writer, consultant. Mem. ASCD, Nat. Coun. Tchrs. English. E-mail: kmeyer1029@yahoo.com.

MEYER, KEVIN MICHAEL, communication executive; b. Jersey City, May 28, 1962; s. Donald Steven and Joan Grace (Hurley) M.; m. Kathleen Anne Nixon, Nov. 16, 1991. BA in English, N.J. State U. (now Jersey City State Coll.), 1986. Editor-in-chief Hudson Reporter, Inc., Hoboken, N.J., 1985-89; editor, assoc. pub. Hudson County Mag., Jersey City, 1989-92; sr. comm. specialist N.J. Transit, Newark, 1992-97; dir. real estate comm. and pub. affairs Cendant Corp., Parsippany, 1997—2001, v.p. comm., real estate svcs. divsn., 2001—. Contbg. author: Musichound World, The Essential Album Guide, 1999. Mem. Pub. Rels. Soc. Am. (Pyramid award 1998), Internat. Assn. Bus. Communicators (IRIS award Excellence 1996), N.J. Press Assn. (Feature Writing 2d Pl. award 1987). Avocations: reading, writing, music, film, exercise. Office: Cendant Corp 1 Campus Dr Parsippany NJ 07054-3826 Fax: 800-322-8791. E-mail: kevin.meyer@cendant.com.

MEYER, LASKER MARCEL, retail executive; b. Houston, Jan. 8, 1926; s. Lasker M. and Lucille (Dannenbaum) M.; m. Beverly Jean Goldberg; children: Lynn Meyer Brown, Susan Meyer Sellinger. Student, Rice U., 1942-43. Pres. Foley's, Houston, 1979, chmn., chief exec. officer, 1982-87, Abraham and Straus, Bklyn., 1980-81; vice chmn. bd. Splty. Retailers, Inc., Houston, 1989-93. Past chmn. bd. United Way Tex. Gulf Coast. Mem. Bentwater Yacht and Country Club. Jewish.

MEYER, LAURENCE HARVEY, federal official; b. Bronx, N.Y., Mar. 8, 1944; BA magna cum laude, Yale U., 1965; PhD in Econs., MIT, 1970. Co-founder, pres. Laurence H. Meyer and Assocs., St. Louis, 1982-96; bd. govs. Fed. Res. Sys., Washington, 1996—. Prof. econs. Washington U., St. Louis, 1969-96, rsch. assoc. Ctr. for Study of Am. Bus., former chmn. econs. dept.; economist Fed. Res Bank, N.Y.; vis. scholar Fed. Res. Bank, St. Louis. Author textbook on macroeconomic modeling; contbr. numerous articles to profl. jours. Named Top Forecaster for Yr., Bus. Week mag., 1986; recipient Ann. Forecast award, 1993, 96. Office: Bd of Gov of Fed Res Sys 20th & C Sts NW Washington DC 20551-0001

MEYER, LAWRENCE GEORGE, lawyer; b. East Grand Rapids, Mich., Oct. 2, 1940; s. George and Evangeline (Boerma) M.; children from previous marriage: David Lawrence, Jenifer Lynne; m. Linda Elizabeth Buck, May 31, 1980; children: Elizabeth Tilden, Travis Henley. BA with honors, Mich. State U., 1961; JD with distinction, U. Mich., 1964. Bar: Wis., 1965, Ill. 1965, U.S. Supreme Ct. 1968, D.C. 1972. Assoc. Whyte, Hirschboeck, Minahan, Hardin & Harland, Milw., 1964-66; atty. antitrust div. U.S. Dept. Justice, Washington, 1966-68; legal counsel U.S. Senator Robert P. Griffin, Mich., 1968-70; dir. policy planning FTC, 1970-72; ptnr. Patton, Boggs & Blow, Washington, 1972-85, Arent, Fox, Kintner, Plotkin & Kahn, Washington, 1985-96, Gadsby & Hannah, 1996-2001; pvt. practice Washington, 2001—. Contbr. articles on antitrust and trial practice to law jours.; asst. editor. U. Mich. Law Rev., 1960-61. Bd. dirs. Hockey Hall of Fame, Toronto, 1993-99, Woodrow Wilson House, 1997—. Recipient Disting. Svc. award FTC, 1972. Mem. ABA, D.C. Bar Assn., Wis. Bar Assn., Ill. Bar Assn., U.S. Senate Ex S.O.B.s Club, City Tavern Club, Sulgrave Club, Congl. Country Club. E-mail: lawlgm.com. Home: 8777 Belmart Rd Potomac MD 20854-1610

MEYER, LEONARD B. musician, educator; b. N.Y.C., Jan. 12, 1918; s. Arthur S. and Marion (Wolff) M.; m. Janet M. Levy; children: Marion L., Carlin, Erica Cecile. Student, Bard Coll., 1936-37; BA, Columbia, 1940, MA, 1948; PhD, U. Chgo., 1954; LHD, Grinnell Coll., Loyola U., Chgo., Bard Coll., U. Chgo., Ohio State U. Faculty U. Chgo., 1946-75, head humanities sect., 1958-60, prof. music, 1961-75, chmn. music dept., 1961-70, Phyllis Fay Horton disting. svc. prof., 1972-75; Benjamin Franklin prof. music U. Pa., 1975-88, Benjamin Franklin prof. emeritus, 1988—. Fellow Ctr. for Advanced Studies, Wesleyan U., Middletown, Conn., 1960-61, Ctr. for Advanced Study in Behavioral Scis., Stanford, Calif., 1994; Ernest Bloch prof. music U. Calif., Berkeley, 1971, sr. fellow Sch. Criticism and Theory, 1975-88; resident scholar Bellagio Study and Conf. Ctr., 1982; Tanner lectr. Stanford U., 1984; Patten lectr. Ind. U., 1985; Martin Barnstein lectr. NYU, 1996. Author: Emotion and Meaning in Music, 1956, (with G.W. Cooper) The Rhythmic Structure of Music, 1960, Music, the Arts and Ideas, 1967, Explaining Music: Essays and Explorations, 1973, Style and Music: Theory, History and Ideology, 1994, The Spheres of Music: A Gathering of Essays, 2000; gen. editor: Studies in the Criticism and Theory of Music, 1980-96; mem. editl. bd. Critical Inquiry, 1974-96, Music Perception, 1983—, 96; contbr. articles to profl. jours. Guggenheim fellow, 1971-72 Fellow AAAS, Am. Acad. Arts and Scis.; mem. Am. Musicological Soc. (hon.), Soc. Music Theory, Soc. Music Perception and Cognition, Phi Beta Kappa. Home: 165 W End Ave Apt 23M New York NY 10023-5513 Office: U of Pa Music Dept Philadelphia PA 19104

MEYER, LINDA CORRINE SMITH, employment and training operations executive; b. Monroe, Mich., June 5, 1949; d. William Lambert and Marion Adelia (Hopkins) S.; m. Rodney William Meyer, Sept. 7, 1969 (div. Nov. 1979); children: Jason William, Megan Kathleen. BS in Mgmt., U. South Fla., 1992. Cert. employment and tng. adminstr. Ambulance attendant, unit mgr. emergency room Jackson Meml. Hosp., Dade City, Fla., 1967-69; unit mgr. ob-gyn. Glens Falls (N.Y.) Hosp., 1969-71; unit mgr. phys. occupational speech therapy Mass. Gen. Hosp., Boston, 1971-74; grant coord. Boston U., 1971-74; unit adminstr. ob./infirtility Mass. Gen. Hosp., 1974-77; divsn. mgr. Pasco County Bd. County Commrs., Dade City, 1977-83; divsn. mgr. greater N.Y.C. comm. consulting Henkels & McCoy, Inc., Blue Bell, Pa., 1983-87; v.p. client svcs. and tng., ops. mgr. Withlacoochee Pvt. Industry Coun., Ocala, Fla., 1992-94; mgmt. cons. Fla. Dept. Labor and Employment Security, Tallahassee, 1994—. Mem. vocat. edn. coord. com. Dist. Sch. Bd. Pasco County, Fla.; mem. edn. coord. com. Pasco-Hernando C.C., Fla. Editor Henkels & McCoy Tng. Svcs. Newsletter. Mem. legis. com. vocat. rehab. coun. and chairing coun. State of Fla.; mktg. mgr. USF Univ. Singers; vol. counselor San Antonio Boys Village; instr. LDS Ch., chorister women's orgn., ch. chorister, ch. choir dir., homemaking counselor, homemaking leader, pres. relief soc., sec. stake relief soc., sec. sunday sch.; active community dinner theatre, Broomall, Pa. Mgmt. scholar USF Coll. Bus. Adminstrn., 1992. Mem. Am. Soc. Tng. and Devel., Nat. Assn. Female Execs., Nat. Assn. Counties, Nat. Assn. County Employment and Tng. Adminstrs (legis./issues com., chmn. recipient population subcom.). Southeastern Employment & Tng. Assn. (pres. Fla. chpt., ad hoc com., keynote speaker fall conf.), Fla. Tng. Inst. (sec. exec. com., bd. dirs.), Fla. Employment and Tng. Assn., Inc. (life, pres., incorporating officer 1983), Bay Area Consortium for Women (founding mem., charter sec.), East Pasco Bus. and Profl. Women (charter, past pres.), Women in Cable, Phila. Cable Club, Gold Key Nat. Honor Soc. Independent. Avocations: swimming, reading, writing, music.

MEYER, LOIS KATHRYN, graphic artist; b. Bellingham, Wash., Mar. 19, 1926; d. William Sam and Coralie Anne (Johnson) M. BA, Western Wash. State U., 1963. Graphic artist Whatcom County Pub. Libr., Bellingham, Wash., 1963-78; studio painter, print-maker, 1963-79, San Diego, Pismo Beach, Calif., 1982—. One-woman shows include Gallery West and Gallery 217, Bellingham, Panaca Gallery, Bellevue, Wash., Choice, Inc., San Francisco, Whatcom Mus. of Art, Bellingham; group shows include Seattle Art Mus., Nat. Watercolor Exhibn., Pacific N.W. Arts and Crafts, Bellevue, N.W. Wash. Regional Artists Traveling Exhibit, Whatcom Mus. History and Art Invitational Exhibn., Anacortes (Wash.) Arts and Crafts Exhibit; works in pvt. collections Western Wash. State U., Bellingham, Skagit Valley Coll., Mt. Vernon, Wash., First Fed. Bank, Burlington, Wash. Home: 470 Solar Way Apt B Pismo Beach CA 93449-2723

MEYER, MARA ELLICE, special education consultant, principal; b. Chgo., Oct. 28, 1952; d. David and Harriett (Lazar) Einhorn; m. Leonard X. Meyer, July 20, 1986; children: Hayley Rebecca, David Joseph. BS in Speech and Hearing Sci., U. Ill., 1974, MS in Speech Pathology, 1975, postgrad., 1990—. Cert. speech and lang. pathologist, spl. edn. tchr., reading tchr. Speech and lang. pathologist Macon-Piatt Spl. Edn. Dist., Decatur, Ill., 1975-76; speech and lang. pathologist, reading specialist, learning disabilities coord. Community Consolidated Sch. Dist. # 59, Arlington Heights, 1976-87; test cons. Psychol. Corp., San Antonio, 1987-89; adj. prof. Nat.-Louis U., Evanston, Ill., 1985-87; ednl. cons. The Psychol. Corp., 1987-89, Am. Guidance Svc., Circle Pines, Minn., 1989-94; pvt. practice ednl. cons. Deerfield, Ill., 1994—. Project dir. Riverside Pub. Co., Chgo., 1993-94; mem. adv. coun. to Headstart, Dept. Human Svsc., City of Chgo., 1990-99; cons. Spl. Edn. Dist. of Lake County, 1995—. Waukegan (Ill.) Pub. Schs., 1997; cons. Lake Zurich Pub. Schs., 1996-98; asst. prin., inclusion coord. Mundelein (Ill.) Sch. Dist., 1999-2001; spl. edn. adminstr. Wilmette Schs., 2001—. Area coord. Dem. Party, Lake County, Ill., 1978—; pres. Park West Condo Assn., Lake County, 1983-88. Mem. NEA, ASCD, Nat. Assn. Elem. Prins., Nat. Family Partnership Network, Am. Speech-Lang. and Hearing Assn., Ill. Prins. Assn., Internat. Reading Assn., Coun. on Exceptional Children. Avocations: swimming official, leisure reading, technical reading. Home: 1540 Central Ave Deerfield IL 60015-3963 E-mail: mara52_1999@yahoo.com., einhornl@earthlink.net., meyerm@nttc.org.

MEYER, MARGARET ELEANOR, microbiologist, educator; b. Westwood, Calif., Feb. 8, 1923; d. Herman Henry and Eleanor (Dobson) M. BS, U. Calif., Berkeley, 1945; PhD, U. Calif., Davis, 1961. Pub. health analyst USPHS, Bethesda, Md., 1945-46; swine Brucellosis control agt. Dept. Agr., Davis, 1946-47; bacteriologist U. Calif., 1947-61; research microbiologist U. Calif. (Sch. Vet. Medicine), 1961-77, prof. vet. pub. health and microbiologist exptl. sta., 1977—; research microbiologist U. Calif. Med. Sch., Los Angeles, 1961-77; supr. Brucella identifications lab. WHO, U. Calif.-Davis, 1964—, prof. vet. pub. health, 1973—; also dir. M.A. program in preventive vet. medicine. Cons. subcom. on Brucella Internat. Com. Bacterial Taxonomy, 1962—, mem., 1966—; mem. 5th Pan Am. Congress Veterinary Medicine, Venezuela, 1966; mem. Internat. Congress Microbiology, Moscow, 1966, Mexico City, 1970, Munich, Ger., 1978, mem., officer, Eng., 1986; mem. Internat. Conf. Culture Collections, Tokyo, 1968; mem. adv. com. to Bergey's Manual Determative Bacteriology, 1967; cons. in resident Pan Am. Health Orgn., Zoonoses Lab., Buenos Aires, 1968; mem. brucellosis tech. adv. com. U.S. Animal Health Assn., 1977; FAO cons. on brucellosis control in dairy animals, Tripoli, Libya, 1981, mem. 3d internat. brucellosis symposium, Algiers, 1983; cons. Alaska Dept. Fish and Game, 1976, FAO, Libya, 1981, Bering Straits Reindeer Herders Assn., Nome, Alaska, 1981; invited speaker Internat. Symposium on Advances in Brucellosis Rsch., Tex. A&M U., 1989, Internat. Bison Conf.; resident cons. on brucellosis control in sheep and goats Am. Near East Refugee Aid, East Jerusalem, 1989; cons. on brucellosis in Yellowstone Nat. Pk., Nat. Pk. Svc., 1991—; invited mem. nat. symposium on brucellosis in the Greater Yellowstone Area, Jackson Hole, Wyo., 1994; cons. on brucellosis control in livestock for Armenia, 1994—. Contbr. articles to profl. jours. Bd. dirs. Carmichael Park and Recreation Dist., Calif., 1975; mem. Sacramento County Grand Jury, 1999-2000. Recipient Research Career Devel. award USPHS-NIH, 1963 Fellow Am. Pub. Health Assn., Am. Acad. Microbiology; mem. Soc. Am. Microbiologists, N.Am. Conf. Animal Disease Research Workers, Am. Coll. Vet. Microbiologists (hon. affiliate), U.S. Animal Health Assn. (chmn. brucellosis tech. advisory com. 1978-79), Internat. Assn. Microbiol. Socs. (mem. 1st intersect. congress 1974), AAUW, No. Calif. Women's Golf Assn., U. Calif. Alumni Assn., Sigma Xi. Clubs: U. Calif. Faculty (Davis); El Dorado Royal Country (Shingle Springs, Calif.); Reno Women's Golf. Home: 5611 Fair Oaks Blvd Carmichael CA 95608-5503 Office: U Calif Sch Vet Medicine Dept Epidemiology & Preventive Medicine Davis CA 95616

MEYER, MARGARET VAUGHAN, librarian, educator; b. Phila., Mar. 13, 1919; d. Clifford and Fannie (Lehman) Vaughan; m. Donald Robert Meyer, Sept. 3, 1949 (dec. Mar. 2002); children: Karen, Frederick E., Julie Meyer Ramos. BEd, UCLA, 1942; MLS, U. So. Calif., 1967. Elem. tchr. Indio Sch. Dist., Indio, Calif., 1942-43, Lawndale Sch. Dist., Lawndale, 1943-44, L.A. Unified Schs., 1946-53; program libr. City of Pasadena Libr., Pasadena, Calif., 1965-85. Co-author (Spanish-English): Centeno Collection-Annotated, 1977; author (biog. and notes, 2 CDs): Clifford Vaughan classical music. Organizer, chmn. libr. com. PTA, L.A., 1961—64, hon. life mem., 1964; vol. Com. Solidarity People of El Salvadore, 1985—97; mem. Citizens Com. Save Elysian Park, 1987—, L.A. County Mus. Art, 1986—, Friends of Pasadena Pub. Libr., 1986—. Mem.: ALA (del. 1967—80), L.A. Pub. Libr., Libr. Found. (charter mem.), Calif. Libr. Assn., Am. Fedn. Tchrs. (exec. bd. L.A. chpt.), Denishawn Repertory Dancers (hon. bd. dirs.), Sierra Club. Avocations: music, reading, swimming, gardening, games. Home: 1911 Cerro Gordo St Los Angeles CA 90039-3934

MEYER, MARSHALL WARNER, management and sociology educator; b. Washington, June 24, 1942; s. Richard Sol and Mildred (Warner) M.; m. Judith Pinsof, Mar. 20, 1966; children: Joshua Micah, Gabriel Sol. BA, Columbia U., 1964; MA, U. Chgo., 1965, PhD, 1967; MA, U. Pa., 1987. Instr., lectr. Harvard U., Cambridge, Mass., 1967-69; asst. prof. Cornell U., Ithaca, N.Y., 1969-73; assoc. prof. U. Calif., Riverside, 1973-75, prof. sociology, 1975-87; vis. prof. UCLA, 1985-86; vis. prof. mgmt. Yale U. Sch. Mgmt., New Haven, 1986-87; prof. mgmt. and sociology Wharton Sch., U. Pa., Phila., 1988—. Vis. scholar Russell Sage Found., N.Y.C., 1993-94; vis. prof. mgmt. Hong Kong U. Sci. and Tech., 1996. Author: Bureaucracy in Modern Society, 1972, 87, Permanently Failing Organizations, 1989, Finding Performance, 1995; assoc. editor Adminstrv. Sci. Quar., 1987—. Cons. L.A. Police Commn., 1979-80. Mem. Acad. of Mgmt., Am. Sociol. Assn. Avocations: computers, music, bicycling. Office: U Pa Wharton Sch Dept Mgmt Philadelphia PA 19104

MEYER, MARTIN JAY, lawyer; b. Wilkes-Barre, Pa., Aug. 1, 1932; s. Max and Rose (Wruble) M.; m. Joan Rosenthal, Aug. 24, 1954; children: Leah, Gary. BA, Wilkes Coll., 1954; postgrad., U. Miami, 1956-57; LLB, Temple U., 1959. Bar: Pa. 1960, U.S. Dist. Ct. (mid. dist.) Pa. 1961, U.S. Ct. Appeals (3d cir.) 1966, U.S. Supreme Ct. 1978. Assoc. Mack, Kasper & Meyer, Wilkes-Barre, 1961-66, Mack & Meyer, Wilkes-Barre, 1966-68, ptnr., 1968-80; sr. ptnr. Meyer & Swatkoski, Kingston, Pa., 1980—. Chmn. disciplinary hearing com. Pa. Supreme Ct.; apptd. spl. trial master State Ct., 1995; apptd. cert. mediator U.S. Dist. Ct. (mid. dist.) Pa., 2000; mem. Million Dollar Advocates Forum. Contbr. articles to profl. jours. Chmn. Muscular Dystrophy Assn., 1960; co-chmn. March of Dimes, 1962; trustee Temple Israel Wilkes-Barre; bd. dirs. Jewish Home Scranton, Family Svc. Assn.; arbitrator U.S. Arbitration and Mediation of N.E., Inc., Am. Arbitration Assn., Million Dollar Advocates Forum. With U.S. Army, 1955-56. Fellow Pa. Bar Found.; mem. DAV, ATLA, Am. Arbitration Assn., Pa. Soc., Pa. Bar Assn. (former co-chmn., adoption com. family law sect., alt. dispute resolution com.), Nat. Conf. Bar Pres.'s, Pa. Trial Lawyers Assn. (lectr.), Luzerne County Bar Assn. (pres. 1984-85), NE Pa. Lawyers Assn., Elks (trustee), Masons (32 degree), B'nai Brith (pres. 1967), Tau Epsilon Rho. Republican. Office: 405 3rd Ave Kingston PA 18704-5802 Fax: 570-288-1003. E-mail: mslawyers@earthlink.net.

MEYER, MAX EARL, lawyer; b. Hampton, Va., Oct. 31, 1918; s. Earl Luther and Winifred Katherine (Spacht) M.; m. Betty Maxwell Dodds, Sept. 22, 1945; children— Scott Maxwell, Ann Culliford. AB, U. Nebr., 1940, JD, 1942. Bar: Nebr. 1942, Ill. 1946. Assoc. firm Lord, Bissell & Brook, Chgo., 1945-53, ptnr., 1953-85; chmn. Chgo. Fed. Tax Forum, 1965, U. Chgo. Ann. Fed. Tax Conf., 1972; mem. Adv. Group to Commr. of IRS, 1967. Lectr. in field Bd. dirs. Music Acad. of the West, chmn. 1993-94. Mem. ABA (mem. council tax sec. 1969-72), Ill. Bar Assn. (mem. council tax sect. 1973-76), Nebr. Bar Assn., Chgo. Bar Assn. (chmn. taxation com. 1959-61), Am. Coll. Tax Counsel Clubs: Legal, Law (Chgo.); Valley Club of Montecito, Birnam Wood Golf. Lodges: Masons. Republican. Presbyterian.

MEYER, MICHAEL, automobile company executive; b. Derby, Conn., Sept. 15, 1958; s. Samuel and Margaret Lorraine (Slivinski) M. BA, U. Conn., 1980; MBA, Coll. of William and Mary, 1982. Auditor supr. Anheuser Busch Entertainment, Williamsburg, Va., 1981-82; dist. mgr. Ford Motor Co., Falls Church, 1982-85; reg. consumer svc. mgr. BMW of N.Am., Inc., Woodcliff Lake, N.J., 1985-90; regional mgr. Rolls-Royce Motor Cars, Inc., Paramus, NJ, 1991—99; v.p. Elegant USA LLC, Totown, 1999—. Office: Rolls Royce Motor Cars Inc 100 Demont Pl Totowa NJ 07512 Home: 16 Vaughn Dr Ramsey NJ 07446-1044

MEYER, MICHAEL C. diversified company executive; b. Phoenix, Apr. 4, 1956; s. John H. and Lee (Booher) M. BS in Mgmt., Ariz. State U., 1982; postgrad., U. N.Mex., 1983-84. Adminstr. bldg. and grounds Internat. Tel. & Tel., Phoenix, 1976-80; bldg. supr. Intel, Albuquerque, 1982-83, mgr. info. systems, 1983-84; ops. mgr. MCM & Assocs., Phoenix, 1984-86; pres., bd. dirs. Facility Ops. Group (FOG), Tempe, Ariz., 1986—, chief exec. officer, 1988—. Sr. ptnr. MCM & Assocs. Internat. Cons. Co.; bd. dirs. Digicom. Mem. Internat. Facility Mgmt. Assn. (bd. dirs.), Telecommunications Assn., Tempe C. of C., Phoenix C. of C., Rotary. Avocations: sailing, golf, camping. Office: Facility Ops Group 2730 S Hardy Dr Tempe AZ 85282-3354

MEYER, MICHAEL EDWIN, lawyer; b. Chgo., Oct. 23, 1942; s. Leon S. and Janet (Gorden) M.; m. Catherine Dieffenbach, Nov. 21, 1982; children: Linda, Mollie, Patrick, Kellie. BS, U. Wis., 1964; JD, U. Chgo., 1967. Bar: Calif. 1968, U.S. Supreme Ct. 1973. Assoc. Lillick & McHose, L.A., 1967-73, ptnr., 1974-90, mng. ptnr., 1986-87; ptnr. Pillsbury Madison Sutro, 1990—, mem. mgmt. com., 1990-92, chmn., 1999—. Judge pro tem Beverly Hills Mcpl. Ct., Calif., 1976-79, Los Angeles Mcpl. Ct., 1980-86; lectr. in field. Bd. dirs. Bldg. Owners and Mgrs. Assn. Greater L.A., L.A. coun. Boy Scouts Am., L.A. Sports and Entertainment Commn.; pub. counsel United Way Greater L.A., Los Angeles County Bar Found., trustee, 1997—, Reviving Baseball in Inner Cities; mem. L.A. County Sheriff Youth Found. Recipient Good Scout award L.A. coun. Boy Scouts Am., 1992, Man of Yr. award United Way, 1996. Mem. ABA, Am. Arbitration Assn. (arbitrator), Calif. Bar Assn., Los Angeles County Bar Assn. (trustee 1997—), L.A. Bar Assn., U. Chgo. Alumni Assn. So. Calif. (pres. 1980-82), Calif. Club, U. L.A. Club (dir. 1979-85, pres. 1984-85), L.A. Country Club. Jewish. Home: 759 31st St Manhattan Beach CA 90266-3456 Office: Pillsbury Winthrop 725 S Figueroa St Los Angeles CA 90017-5524 E-mail: mmeyer@pillsburywinthrop.com.

MEYER, MILTON EDWARD, JR. lawyer, artist; b. St. Louis, Nov. 26, 1922; s. Milton Edward and Jessie Marie (Hurley) M.; m. Mary C. Kramer, Nov. 5, 1949; children: Milton E. III, Melanie M. Meyer Francis, Daniel K., Gregory N. BS in Bus. Adminstrn, Washington U., 1943; LL.B., St. Louis, U., 1950; LL.M., N.Y. U., 1953. Bar: Mo. 1950, Colo. 1956. Trust adminstr. Mississippi Valley Trust Co., St. Louis, 1946-50; assoc. firm Burnett, Stern & Liberman, 1953-56; founding partner firm Hindry & Meyer, Denver, 1956-79, chmn. bd., 1970-79; spl. counsel Schmidt, Elrod & Wills, and predecessors, 1979-83, pres., 1980-82; sec. C.A. Norgren Co., Littleton, Colo., 1960-78, dir., 1971-78. Contbr. articles to profl. jours. Chmn. Denver Rotary's Artists of Am. Exhbn., 1990—92; bd. dirs. Nat. Club Assn., 1971—91, pres., 1976—78; bd. dirs. Denver Cmty. Concert Assn., 1960—64, Sewall Rehab. Ctr., Denver, 1965—68, Carl A. Norgren Found., 1960—70; Denver Leadership Found., 1983—93, Found. Colo. Women's Coll., 1982—86, chmn., bd. dirs., 1984—86; bd. dirs. Conf. Pvt. Orgns., 1982—89, chmn., bd. dirs., 1984—88. Officer, U.S. Airborne Infantry U.S. Army, 1943—46, World War II, officer, U.S. Airborne Infantry U.S. Army, 1950—52, Korean War. Recipient Wisdom Soc. award of honor. Mem. ABA, Colo. Bar Assn., Denver Bar Assn., Greater Denver Tax Counsels Assn. (founder, chmn. 1957, Denver Estate Planning Coun. (founder, pres. 1958), Am. Coll. Probate Counsel, Knickerbocker Artists, Pastel Soc. Am., Pastel Soc. West Coast (Disting. Pastellist award), Internat. Assn. Pastel Socs. (founder, dir. 1994—), Salmagundi Club, Cherry Hills Country Club, Pinehurst Country Club (pres. 1979-80), Denver Execs. Club, Hundred Club Denver, Rotary (bd. dirs. 1991-93), Phi Eta Sigma, Beta Gamma Sigma, Omicron Delta Kappa, Beta Theta Pi. Republican. Roman Catholic. Home: 5784 E Oxford Ave Cherry Hills Village CO 80111 E-mail: MiltonMeyer@att.net.

MEYER, MILTON WALTER, history educator; b. Capiz, The Philippines, Aug. 7, 1923; came to U.S., 1941; s. Frederick Willer and Ruth Violet (Schacht) M. BA, Yale U., 1947; M Internat. Affairs, Columbia U., 1949; PhD, Stanford U., 1959; DLit honoris causa, Ctrl. Philippine U., 2000. Fgn. svc. officer U.S. Dept. of State, Jakarta, Indonesia, 1951-53, Hong Kong, 1953-55; prof. history Calif. State U., L.A., 1959-94, prof. emeritus, 1994—. Author: Diplomatic History of the Philippine Republic, 1965, history books on Southeast Asia, 1965, 71, South Asia, 1968, 76, Japan, 1966, 76, 93, Asia, 1972, 97, China, 1978, 94. Mem. adv. bd. Pacific-Asia Mus., Pasadena, Calif., 1998—, mem., lectr., 1960—; founder Meyer Asian Collection, Ctrl. Philippine U., 1974. With U.S. Army, 1943-45. UN summer intern Columbia, 1948. Mem. Assn. Asian Studies, China Soc. So. Calif., OSS Soc., OSS Detachment 101 (Presdl. Unit citation), Burma Star Assn., Alumni Club Yale, Alumni Club Columbia, Alumni Club Stanford U., Phi Beta Kappa. Episcopalian. Avocations: travel, writing, playing piano, nature walks, photography. Home: 239 S Madison Ave Apt 20 Pasadena CA 91101-2841

MEYER, PAUL JAMES, communications company executive; b. San Mateo, Calif., May 21, 1928; s. August Carl and Isabel (Rutherford) M.; m. Jane Gurley, Nov. 26, 1971; children: Paul James Jr., Larry, Bill, Janna, Leslie. DAviation Edn. (hon.), Embry-Riddle Aero. U., 1956; LHD (hon.), Ft. Lauderdale U., 1957; LittD (hon.), East Tex. Bapt. U., 1989. Mgr. sales Word, Inc., Waco, Tex., 1958-60; founder, chmn. bd. dirs. SMI/USA, Inc., 1960—; also Leadership Mgmt., Inc. Bd. dirs. Waco Boys Club, 1970—; mem. Nat. Rep. Fin. Com. With airborne U.S. Army, 1946-48. Mem. Am. Mgmt. Assn., Internat. Franchise Assn., Nat. Speakers Bur. Baptist. Avocations: tennis, snow skiing, scuba diving, bicycling, mountain hiking, flying. Office: PO Box 7411 Waco TX 76714-7411

MEYER, PAUL REIMS, JR. orthopedic surgeon; b. Port Arthur, Tex. s. Paul Reims and Evelyn (Miller) M.; m. Lesa W. Meyer; children: Kristin Lynn, Holly Dee, Paul Reims III, Stewart Blair. BA, Va. Mil. Inst., 1954; MD, Tulane U., 1958; MA of Mgmt., J.L. Kellogg Grad. Sch. of Mgmt. (Northwestern U.), 1992. Dir. Spine Injury Ctr. Northwestern U., Chgo., 1972—, prof. orthopaedic surgery, 1981—. Cons. Nat. Inst. Disability and Rehab. Rsch. VA, Washington, 1978-2000; clin. prof. surgery Dept. Surgery, USUHS; mem. adv. com. World Rehab. Fund, 1990—; mem. bd. councilors Am. Acad. Orthopaedic Surgeons, 1993-96. Author: Surgery of Spine Trauma, 1988; patentee cervical orthosis. Col. M.C., USAR. Fellow ACS, Am. Acad. Orthop. Surgeons; mem. Sociéé Internationale de Chirurgie Orthopédique et de Traumatologie, Internat. Med. Soc. Paraplegia, Am. Trauma Soc. (bd. dirs. 1988—), Am. Orthop. Assn., Am. Spinal Injury Assn. (past pres.), Soc. Med. Cons. to Armed Forces, Mid-Am. Orthop. Assn. Roman Catholic. Avocations: photography, fishing, ham radio, aviation, boating. Office: Northwestern Meml Hosp 250 E Superior St Ste 619 Chicago IL 60611-2950 also: Northwestern Meml Hosp Ste 11-245 201 E Huron Chicago IL 60611 E-mail: Interspace@nwu.edu.

MEYER, PAUL RICHARD, lawyer; b. St. Louis, Apr. 12, 1925; s. Abraham Paul and Adele (Rosenfeld) M.; m. Alice Turtledove, Mar. 16, 1958; David Paul, Sarah Elizabeth, Andrea Ruth. BA, Columbia U., 1949; JD, Yale U., 1952. Bar: Oreg. 1953, Calif. 1953, N.Y. 1953, U.S. Dist.Ct. Oreg. 1953, U.S. Dist. Ct. (no. dist.) Calif. 1953, U.S. Ct. Appeals (9th cir.) 1953, U.S. Supreme Ct. 1958, U.S. Ct. Claims 1958, U.S. Tax Ct. 1958, U.S. Ct. Appeals (fed. cir.) 1958. Assoc. law sch. U. Calif., Berkeley, 1952-53; assoc. King, Miller et al, Portland, Oreg., 1953-60; ptnr. Kobin & Meyer, 1960-85; pvt. practice law, 1985—. Mem. Bd. of Mediators and Arbitrators, Am. Arbitration Assn., NASD. Mem. nat. bd., exec. com. ACLU, N.Y.C., 1971-93, ACLU nat. adv. coun., 1993—. With U.S. Army, 1943-46, ETO. Decorated Purple Heart, Bronze Star. Home and Office: 1325 SW Myrtle Dr Portland OR 97201-2274 Fax: (503) 295-2884. E-mail: paulalice@aol.com.

MEYER, PAUL WILLIAM, arboretum director, horticulturist; b. Cin., Aug. 30, 1952; s. Edward F. and Dorothy (Schroeder) M.; m. Debra L. Rodgers, May 16, 1990. BSc, Ohio State U., 1973; MSc, U. Del., 1976; diploma, U. Edinburgh, 1988. Curator Morris Arboretum U. Pa., Phila., 1976-91, dir., 1991—. Bd. dirs. The Henry Found., 1992-2000; chair Springfield Twp. planning com., Montgomery County, Pa., 1993. Mem. Am. Assn. Bot. Gardens and Arboreta (bd. dirs. Montgomery County Land Trust, Montgomery County Open Space). Avocations: bicycling, swimming, backpacking, rowing, gardening. Office: Morris Arboretum of Univ Pa 9414 Meadowbrook Ave Philadelphia PA 19118-2697

MEYER, PEARL, executive compensation consultant; b. N.Y.C. d. Allen Charles and Rose (Goldberg) Weissman; m. Ira A. Meyer. BA cum laude, postgrad., NYU. Statis. specialist, exec. comp. div. Gen. Foods Corp., White Plains, N.Y.; exec. v.p. and cons. Handy Assocs., Inc., N.Y.C.; founder, pres. Pearl Meyer & Ptnrs., 1989—. Lectr. on exec. compenstation at confs. and seminars. Contbr. numerous articles to profl. jours. Recipient Entrepreneurial Woman award Women Bus. Owners N.Y. Mem. Am. Mgmt. Assn., Worldat-Work, Soc. for Human Resources Mgmt. (cert. accredited pers. diplomate), Women's Econ. Roundtable, Pers. Accreditation Inst., Women's Forum, Sedgewood Club, Sky Club, Phi Beta Kappa, Pi Mu Epsilon, Beta Gamma Sigma. Office: Pearl Meyer & Partners Inc 445 Park Ave New York NY 10022-2606

MEYER, PETER BERT, economist, urban policy educator; b. N.Y.C., Sept. 14, 1943; s. Fred A. and Nina D. (Lewin) M.; m. Goldee E. Hecht, Jan. 22, 1967 (div. Nov. 1983); children: Lewis A., Aviva B.; m. Kristen R. Yount, Sept. 11, 1993. BA, Swarthmore Coll., 1965; PhD, U. Wis., 1970. Asst. prof. econ. planning Pa. State U., State College, 1968-75, assoc. prof., 1975-87; prof. urban policy and econs. U. Louisville, 1988—, dir. Ctr. for Environ. Policy and Mgmt., 1992—. Pres. The E.P. Systems Group, Inc., Louisville, 1980—; rsch. assoc. ABA, Washington, 1976-77; sr. rsch. assoc. CEI Cons., Ltd., London, 1985-89; cons. The Planning Exch., Glasgow, Scotland, 1985-89. Author: Drug Experiments on Prisoners, 1976; co-author: Local Jails, 1977, Contaminated Lands: Problem-Reclamation, Redevelopment and Re-Use, 1995, Reclamation and Economic Regeneration of Brownfields, 2000; contbr. articles to profl. jours. Committeeman Centre County (Pa.) Dem. Com., 1972-84, vice chmn., 1974-76; cons. community devel. orgns., Pa., N.Y., Ky., Md., W.Va., 1973—; policy strategist Bill Wachob for Congress Campaign, Centre County, 1984, 86. Grantee Nat. Endowment for Arts, 1979, Nat. Ctr. for Environ. Rsch., EPA, 2002. Mem. Am. Econs. Assn., Am. Planning Assn., Policy Studies Orgn., Urban Affairs Assn., Union for Radical Polit. Econs. (editor 1972-84, exec. com. 1975-76), Conf. Socialist Economists (U.K.) (steering com. 1985-86), Sports Car Club Am. (flagging and comm. worker). Jewish. Avocations: scuba diving, hiking, reading, traveling. Office: 426 W Bloom St Louisville KY 40208

MEYER, PHILIP GILBERT, lawyer; b. Louisville, June 26, 1945; s. Henry Gilbert and Adele (Gutermuth) M.; m. Jackie Darlene Watson, Jan. 30, 1971 (div. Apr. 1976); m. Sylvia Saunders, Oct. 9, 1976. BBA, U. Mich., 1967; JD, U. Tex., 1970. Bar: Tex. 1970, Mich. 1971, U.S. Tax Ct. 1972, U.S. Dist. Ct. (ea. dist.) Mich. 1971, U.S. Ct. Appeals (6th cir.), 1972, U.S. Dist. Ct. (no. dist.) Ohio 1976, U.S. Dist. Ct. (we. dist.) Mich. 1993, U.S. Dist. Ct. (no. dist.) Ill. 1998. Law clk. Wayne County Cir. Ct., Detroit, 1970-72; atty. Leonard C. Jaques, 1972; assoc. Christy & Robbins, Dearborn, Mich., 1972-73; ptnr. Foster, Meadows & Ballard, Detroit, 1973-79; of counsel Christy, Rogers & Gantz, Dearborn, 1979-81, Rogers & Gantz, Dearborn, 1981-86; prin. Philip G. Meyer and Assocs., Farmington Hills, 1986—. Adj. prof. U. Detroit Sch. Law, 1979. Mem. ABA (com. vice chmn. rules and procedure 1982-88), Maritime Law Assn. U.S., Mich. Bar Assn. (vice chmn. admiralty sect. 1978), Tex. Bar Assn., Detroit Bar Assn. (vice chmn. admiralty com. 1991-93, chmn. admiralty sect. 1993-95), Propeller-Port of Detroit Club (pres. 1984-85). Republican. Home: 5905 Independence Ln West Bloomfield MI 48322-1854 Office: Ste 113 30300 Northwestern Hwy Farmington Hills MI 48334-3212

MEYER, PRISCILLA ANN, Russian language and literature educator; b. Aug. 26, 1942; d. Herbert Edward and Marjorie Rose (Wolff) M.; m. William L. Trousdale, Sept. 15, 1974; 1 dau., Rachel V. BA, U. Calif., Berkeley, 1964; MA, Princeton U., 1966; PhD, 1971. Lectr. in Russian lang. and lit. Wesleyan U., Middletown, Conn., 1968-71; asst. prof., 1971-75; assoc. prof., 1975-88; prof., 1988—. Vis. asst. prof. Yale U., 1973, adv. coun. dept. Slavic lang. and lit. Princeton U., 1998-2002. Co-editor: Dostoevsky and Gogol, 1979; editor: Life in Windy Weather (by Andrei Bitov), 1986, author: Find What the Sailor Has Hidden: Vladimir Nabokov's Pale Fire, 1988; co-editor: Essays on Gogol: Logos and the Russian Word, 1992; co-editor: Nabokov's World, 2001; translator stories; mem. editl. bd. Slavic and East European Jour., 1999—; contbr. articles to profl. jours. Scholar Internat. Rsch. and Exch. Bd., 1973; grantee Ford Found., 1964-68, 70; hon. vis. fellow Sch. Slavonic and East European Studies London U., 1997, 2001. Mem. Am. Coun. Tchrs. Russian (dir. 1983-86), Am. Assn. Tchrs. Slavic and East European Studies, Vladimir Nabokov Soc. (v.p. 1983-85, 2002—), Tolstoi Soc., Dostoevsky Soc., Conn. Acad. Arts and Scis. Office: Russian Dept Wesleyan U Middletown CT 06459-0001 E-mail: pmeyer@wesleyan.edu.

MEYER, PUCCI, newspaper editor; b. N.Y.C., Sept. 1, 1944; d. Charles Albert and Lollo (Offer) M.; m. Michael V. McGill, Oct. 28, 2001. BA, U. Wis., 1966. Asst. editor Look mag., N.Y.C., 1970-71, editorial asst. Paris, 1967-69; reporter Newsday, Garden City, L.I., N.Y., 1971-73; style editor N.Y. Daily News Sunday Mag., N.Y.C., 1974-76, assoc. editor, 1977-82, editor, 1983-86; sr. editor Prodigy, White Plains, N.Y., 1987; spl. projects editor N.Y. Post, N.Y.C., 1988-89, style editor, 1990-92, food editor, 1992-93, assoc. features editor, 1993—, travel editor, 1994—. Contbr. articles to various nat. mags. Recipient Pulitzer prize as mem. Newsday investigative team that wrote articles and book The Heroin Trail, 1973. Office: NY Post 1211 6th Ave New York NY 10036-8790 E-mail: pmeyer@nypost.com.

MEYER, RACHEL ABIJAH, foundation director, artist, theorist, poet; b. Job's Corners, Pa., Aug. 18, 1963; d. Jacob Owen and Velma Ruth (Foreman) M.; children: Andrew Carson, Peter Franklin. Student, Lebanon Valley Coll. Restaurant owner Purcy's Place, Ono, Pa.; restaurant mgr. King's Table Buffet, Citrus Heights, Calif.; product finalizer TransWorld Enterprises, Blaine, Wash.; dir., support svcs. adminstr. Tacticar Found., Sacramento, 1991—; tchr. Tacticar Inst., 1995; chair Coniterms, Sacramento, 1996—. Author: Year of the Unicorn, 1994. Avocations: researching, writing, painting. Studio: 2013 Kathryn Way Sacramento CA 95821-5517

MEYER, RAYMOND JOSEPH, former college basketball coach; b. Chgo., Dec. 18, 1913; s. Joseph E. and Barbara (Hummel) M.; m. Margaret Mary Delaney, May 27, 1939 (dec. 1985); children— Barbara (Mrs. Gerald Starzyk), Raymond Thomas, Patricia (Mrs. Thomas Butterfield), Merianne (Mrs. James McGowan; dec. 1997), Joseph, Robert. AB, U. Notre Dame, 1938. Asst. coach U. Notre Dame, 1941-42; basketball coach DePaul U., Chgo., 1942—. Author: How To Play Winning Basketball, 1960, Basketball as Coached by Ray Meyer, 1967, Ray Meyer, 1 Coach, 1980, Coach, 1987. Named Coach of Yr. Chgo. Basketball Writers, 1943, 44, 48, 52, Coach of Yr. Nat. Assn. Basketball Coaches, 1978-79, Sportwriters Coach of Yr., 1978, Salvation Man of Yr., 1990; recipient Marine Corps Sportsman of Yr. award, 1979, Bunn award, 1981, Victor award, 1981, Lincoln Acad. award, 1988, Nat. Basketball Coach's Golden Jubilee award, Notre Dame Lifetime Achievement award 1998; inducted into Basketball Hall of Fame, 1979, Basketball Hall of Fame Chgo., 1981, Basketball Hall of Fame Ill., Golden Anniversay award Nat. Basketball Coaches, 1992, Naismith Found. Good Sportsman's award, 1998. Mem. Nat. Basketball Coaches Assn. Roman Catholic. Home: 2518 W Cedar Glen Dr Arlington Heights IL 60005-4336 Office: 100 Turner Ave Elk Grove Village IL 60007-3933

MEYER, RICHARD CHARLES, microbiologist, educator; b. Cleve., May 2, 1930; s. Frederick Albert and Tekla Charlotte (Schrade) M.; m. Carolyn Yvonne Patton, Apr. 6, 1963; children: Frederick Gustav, Carl Anselm. B.Sc., Baldwin-Wallace Coll., 1952; M.Sc., Ohio State U., 1957, PhD, 1961. Teaching and research asst. Ohio State U., 1956-61, research assoc., 1961-62; microbiologist Nat. Cancer Inst., NIH, Bethesda, Md., 1962-64; asst. prof. vet. pathology and hygiene and microbiology U. Ill., Urbana-Champaign, 1965-68, assoc. prof., 1968-73, prof., 1973-89, prof. emeritus, 1989—. Served with C.E. U.S. Army, 1952-54. Mem. Am. Acad. Microbiology, AAAS, Am. Inst. Biol. Sci., Am. Soc. Microbiology, Gamma Sigma Delta, Phi Zeta. Republican. Lutheran. Home: 1504 S Buckthorn Ln Mahomet IL 61853-3632 Office: Dept Vet Pathobiology U Ill at Urbana-Champaign Urbana IL 61801

MEYER, ROBERT ALAN, consultant; b. N.Y.C., Mar. 20, 1946; s. Leonard and Mildred M.; m. Gail Rein, Oct. 29, 1967; children: Jonathan, Caroline. BA in Econs., Am. Internat. Coll., 1967; MBA, NYU, 1973. 2nd v.p., mgr. mcpl. bond research Smith Barney Harris Upham and Co., Inc., N.Y.C., 1973-76; 1st v.p., dir. mcpl. bond research E.F. Hutton and Co. Inc., 1976-82; v.p., mgr. mcpl. bond research Merrill Lynch Pierce Fenner and Smith Inc., 1982-84; pres. Bond Investors Guaranty Ins. Co., 1984-90; pres., chief exec. officer Greig Fester Fin. Guaranty Brokers, Inc., 1991-94; prin. Meyer Cons. Group Inc., Holmdel, N.J., 1994-98; chmn., pres., CEO RAM Reinsurance Co. Ltd., Hamilton, Bermuda, 1998-2001; prin. Meyer Cons. Group Inc., Holmdel, N.J., 2001—. Mem. India House. Office: 20 Stoney Brook Rd Holmdel NJ 07733 E-mail: mcgramgm@msn.com.

MEYER, ROBERT ALLEN, human resource management educator; b. Wisconsin Rapids, Wis., May 31, 1943; s. Charles Harold and Viola Bertha (Stoeckmann) M.; 1 child, Timothy Charles. BA, Valparaiso (Ind.) U., 1966; MA, Mich. State U., 1967, PhD, 1972, postgrad., 1981. Asst. prof. Muskingum Area Tech. Coll., Zanesville, Ohio, 1972-74; adj. prof. U. Fla., Gainesville, 1974-80; dean acad. affairs Santa Fe Community Coll., 1974-80; asst. prof. Purdue U., W. Lafayette, Ind., 1982-84, Ga. State U., Atlanta, 1985-89; assoc. prof., program coord. U. N. Tex., Denton, 1989-91; Fulbright profl. scholar, Bangkok, 1991-92; coord. travel, tourism, hotel, restaurant mgmt. program U. Hawaii Manoa Campus, Honolulu, 1992-97; dir. distance edn., coord. travel, hotel & restaurant mgmt. SPCA, St. Petersburg, Fla., 1997—. Investor, asst. mgr. LaSiene Restaurant, Ann Arbor, Mich., 1970-72; investor, cons. Cafe Brittany St. Thomas, U.S. V.I., 1974-80, owner, operator, Houston, 1980; pres. RTM Cons., Honolulu, Hawaii, 1989—; educator World Tourism Orgn., 1993—; mem. vis. ind. coun. C. of C., 1993—; club mgr. Assn. Am., 1994—; dir. edn. Am. Assoc. Real Estate License Law Officials. Contbr. articles to profl. jours. Founding mem. Fla. Distance Learning Consortium, 1998—; bd. dirs., founder Fla. Virtual Campus, 1998—, dir. hospitality program, 1998—. Recipient White House Commendation for Partnerships with Industry and Higher Edn.,1984, George Washington Medal of Honor for innovations in higher edn., Freedoms Found., 1985, 86, Achievement award in hospitality edn. Coun. of Hotel, Restaurant & Instl. Edn., 1987. Mem. Assn. Real Estate Lic. Law Ofcls. (distance edn. coun. bd. mem. 1999—), Tarrant County Hotel and Motel Assn., Dallas Hotel Assn., Am. Soc. Tng. and Devel., Travel Ind. Assn. Tex., Hotel Sales & Mktg. Assn. (bd. dirs. 1985-89), Coun. of Hotel, Restaurant and Instl. Edn. (grad. com. 1989-90). Home: 6135 Bayou Grande Blvd NE Saint Petersburg FL 33703-1803 Office: St Petersburg Coll PO Box 13489 Saint Petersburg FL 33733-3489 E-mail: rmeyer1@tampabay.rr.com.

MEYER, ROBERT LEE, secondary education educator; b. St. Joseph, Mo., July 9, 1952; s. Robert James and Jerry Lee (Patterson) M.; m. Barbara Anita Stickles, Aug. 2, 1986. BS in Edn., Mo. Western State Coll., 1974; MA in Edn., U.S. Internat. U., 1988. Cert. tchr., Calif., Mo.; cert. specialist learning handicapped, resource specialist cert., adminstr., Calif. Spl. edn. tchr., learning handicapped Mann Jr. High Sch., San Diego, 1978-80, Serra High Sch., San Diego, 1980-84, Morse High Sch., San Diego, 1984-85; magnet seminar tchr. Bell Jr. High Sch., 1985-91; project resource tchr., dir. student activities Serra High Sch., 1991-94, resource specialist, 1994-95; magnet coord. Ctr. for Sci., Math. and Computer Tech. Samuel Gompers Secondary Sch., 1995-97; dean of students, attendance coord. Scripps Ranch H.S., non-athletic event coord., 1997-98; asst. prin. Mountain Empire Jr./Sr. H.S., 1998—2001; dean of students Gompers Secondary Sch., 2001—. Chmn. resource com. Western Assn. Schs. & Colls. accreditation Serra High Sch., San Diego, 1995, chmn. process com. Western Assn. Schs. and Colls. accreditation Gompers Secondary Sch., San Diego, 1996-97, sch. site coun., 1992-97, gov. team mem., 1992-95, chair spl. edn. dept., 1983, mem. sch. leadership team, 1992-95, sr. class advisor, 1994-95, liaison Partnerships in Edn., 1996-97; monitor City Schs. Race Human Rels. Monitoring Team, 1991-92, African Am. students pupil advocate program adv. coun., 1995-97; restructuring coord. Senate Bill 1274 Grant, 1993-95, resource specialist, 1994-95; chmn. process com. Western Assn. Schs. and Colls. accreditation Gompers Sec. Sch., adv. com. mem. African Am. students program; co-chmn. race/human rels. com. Scripps Ranch H.S., 1997-98. Contbr.: (book) History of Andrew Meyer Family, 1989. Alternate del. Dem. Party 6th Dist. and State Conventions, Holt County, Mo., 1976; mem. Nat. Conf. Minitown Race/Human Rels. Camp Coord., Scripps Ranch H.S. Recipient star adminstr. award Calif. FFA, 2000. Mem. Assn. Calif. Sch. Adminstrs., Optimist Club, Delta Chi. Democrat. Roman Catholic. Avocations: collecting political buttons, antiques, travel. E-mail: meyer@adcoe.k12.ca.us.

MEYER, ROBERTA, mediator, communication consultant; b. San Francisco, July 27, 1936; d. Theodore Robert and Virginia (Organ) Meyer; m. G. William Sheldon; children: Megan McDougall Radeski, Deborah Ann Guerra. Student, U. Utah, 1974. Cert. mediator. Founder, pres., exec. dir. Roberta Meyer Communication Cons., Inc., San Francisco, 1977—. Presenter numerous workshops in alcoholism and communication; nat. spkr. Nat. Found. Alcoholism Comm.; keynote spkr. Calif. Women's Comm. Alcoholism, 1981; mem. adv. bd. Soviet Am. Alliance Alcoholism and Other Addictions; founder Youth Dance Experience, 1999. Author: (book) Facts About Booze and Other Drugs, 1980, The Parent Connection: How to Communicate with Your Child about Alcohol and Other Drugs, 1984, Listen to the Heart, 1989, (screenplays) Understanding Addition, 1988, Better Relationships Through Effective Communication, 1991; numerous radio and TV appearances; dir.: Meyer Method Dance Program for ballroom dancers, One Meyer Method Dance Training Video, 1998. Mem. adv. bd. Marin Svcs. Women, 1980; vol. Calif. Pacific Med. Ctr., San Francisco Ballet Aux.; mem. N.Y.C. and San Francisco Ballet Cos., 1950—56, San Francisco Ballet Sch., 1956—65; founder, dir. Ballet Arts San Francisco, 1965—78, San Francisco Ballroom Dance Theatre and the accelerated dance programs, 1994—. Named 56th Point of Light, Pres. Bush, 1990; recipient award, Optimists Club. Mem.: Childrens Theatre Assn., Nat. Coun. Alcoholism and Drug Dependence Calif. (pres. 1988—91), San Francisco Womens Rehab. Assn. (pres. 1975—76, dir., founder Youth Dance Project 1999), Nat. Coun. Alcoholism (co-chmn. pub. info. com. 1985—, v.p. Bay area 1988—, bd. dirs. Teen Kick Off 1987—, Alcoholism and Drug Rsch. Comm. Ctr. 1990—, pres. 1988—, creator, cons. youth aware program 1974—), Nat. Collaborative Planning and Cmty. Svc. (cert.), San Francisco C. of C.

MEYER, ROGER ALBERT, surgeon; b. Hoquiam, Wash., June 23, 1937; m. Shelby Jean Phillips, Dec. 28, 1963 (dec.); children: Kirsten, Jennifer, Darin; m. Sheila Mary Hanley, Sept. 29, 1996. DDS, U. Wash., 1961, MS, 1967; MD, Creighton U., 1975. Diplomate Am. Bd. Oral and Maxillofacial Surgery. Dental intern USPHS Hosp., Norfolk, Va., 1961-62; dental surgeon and clin. investigaor NIDR/NIH, Bethesda, Md., 1962-63; resident oral and maxillofacial surgery U. Wash. Affiliated Hosps., Seattle, 1963-67; resident gen. surgery U. Vt. Med. Ctr., Burlington, 1975-76; clin. assoc. prof. dept. surgery Oreg. Health Scis. U., Portland, 1976-79; assoc. prof., chmn. oral and maxillofacial surgery Emory U. Sch. Dentistry, Atlanta, 1979-86; clin. asst. prof. plastic surgery Emory U. Sch. Medicine, 1981—. Cons. cleft lip, palate and craniomaxillofacial surgery State of Ga. Dept. Human Resources, Atlanta, 1981—. Author numerous chpts. in surg. textbooks and articles in profl. jours. Fellow Am. Coll. Surgeons; mem. AMA, ADA, Am. Assn. Oral and Maxillofacial Surgeons, Am. Soc. Maxillofacial Surgeons, Alpha Omega Alpha. Avocations: music (piano), tennis, skiing, running, white water kayaking. Office: East Cobb Surg Ctr Bldg H 1000 Johnson Ferry Rd Marietta GA 30068-5420

MEYER, ROGER ARNOLD, management consultant, writer; b. Jacksonville, Ill., Jan. 23, 1943; s. Arnold Henry Meyer and Hazel Elizabeth; m. Elizabeth Lynn, Mar. 22, 1969; children: Roger Matthew, Erin Elizabeth. BA, Milligan Coll., 1966; MA, La. State U., 1972, PhD, 1974. mgmt. cons. Clin. intern in psychology Southwestern Med. Sch., Dallas, 1973-74; Clay County dir. Smoky Mountain Mental Health Ctr., Marble, 1974-76, clin. dir. inpatient unit Franklin, N.C., 1976-78; clin. psychologist Valley Psychiat. Hosp., Chattanooga, 1979-80; clin. dir. Hiwassee Mental Health Ctr., Cleveland, Tenn., 1980-84; clin. psychologist Brainerd Psychol Svcs., Chattanooga, 1980-95; dir. counseling svc. Chattanooga Bible Inst., 1982-95; mgmt. cons. Brainerd Cons. Svcs., Chattanooga, 1996—. Cons. clin. hypnosis Am. Soc. Clin. Hypnosis, 1994. Contbr. articles to profl. jours. Program chmn. Brainerd Kiwanis Club, Chattanooga, 1982-95; bd. dirs. T-Cap, Nashville, 1992-94. Lt. USN, 1966-69. Mem. ASTD (program chair), Chattanooga Human Resources Assn., Chattanooga C. of C. (br. bd. dirs., v.p. 1999—), Chattanooga Assn. for Clin. Pastoral Care (pres. 1984-85, treas. 1988), Inst. for Mgmt. Cons. Democrat. Presbyterian. Avocations: woodworking, wood carving, gardening, hiking, canoeing. Office: Brainerd Cons Svcs 6074 E Brainerd Rd Chattanooga TN 37421-3908

MEYER, ROGER JESS CHRISTIAN, pediatrics educator; b. Olympia, Wash., May 14, 1928; s. Paul Eugene and Martha Bell Rogers Meyer; m. Joyce Langley, Mar. 14, 1959; children: Paul, John, William, Douglas, Nancy, Liz. BS in Chemistry, U. Wash., Seattle, 1951; MD, Washington U., St. Louis, 1955; MPH, Harvard U., 1959. Cert. pediatric bds. eligible rehab., preventive medicine, family practice. Instr. pediat. Harvard Med. Sch., Boston, 1959-62; asst. prof. U. Vt. Coll. Medicine, Burlington, 1962-65; assoc. prof. U. Va. Sch. Medicine, Charlottesville, 1965-68, Northwestern U., Chgo., 1968-76; asst. dean U. Ill. Sch. Pub. Health, 1974-76; prof. pediat. and pub. health Sch. Medicine U. Wash., Seattle, 1976—; with U.S. Army Res. Med. Corps, 1982; advanced through grades to col. U.S. Army, 1986. Chair, bd. dirs. community pediatrics sect. Am. Acad. Pediatrics, Evanston, Ill., 1973-74; pres. Child and Family Health Found., 1976—; bd. dirs. Nat. Com. Prevention Child Abuse, Chgo., 1974-76. Author 140 books and articles. Bd. dirs. N.W. orgn. ARC, Miller Bay Estates and Indianola Land Trust, Unitarian Universalist Ch.; chief pub. health Pacific Rim, U.S. Army Med. Corps 364 Civil Affairs, 1986-93; staff Madigan Army Med. Ctr.; faculty Def. Dept. JMRTC. Decorated Army Achievement medal (2) for disting. svc. 1988-89; recipient NIMH Social Sci. in Medicine award Harvard U., 1961, Children's Hosp. Ann. award, Boston, 1959; Shaller scholar U. Wash., 1950-51, NIMH Health scholar U. Rochester, 1957-58; Oxford fellow, 1992. Mem. APHA, Am. Acad. Pediat. (sect. on child devel., ethics, pediat. mil.), Marine Sci. Soc. Pacific N.W. (N.W. global epidemiology com., pres.), N.W. Pediat. Soc., Res. Officers Assn., Harvard U. Alumni Assn., Washington U. Alumni Assn. Home: 22125 Apollo Dr NE Poulsbo WA 98370-6710 E-mail: RJCMeyer@aol.com.

MEYER, ROGER PAUL, physician; b. Atlanta, Mar. 30, 1950; s. Leonard Arthur and Janet Elanor (Miller) M.; m. Marria Antonietta Skoko; children: Seth E., Hilary R. BA in Psychology with honors, U. N.C., 1972; MD, Med. Coll. Ga., 1976; postgrad., U. N.Mex., 1980. Physician in pvt. practice Carson Med. Group, Carson City, Nev., 1980—; chief of staff Carson Tahoe Hosp., 1986-87, chmn. dpt. ob-gyn., 1990-91. V.p. Nev. Physicians Rev. Orgn., 1987; dir. Physicians Managed Care IPA; sec. Nev. First Care Ins. Co. Fellow Am. Coll. Ob.-Gyn. (Nev. legislature liaison 1991); mem. Am. Acad. Reproductive Medicine, Am. Coll. Physician Execs. Jewish. Avocations: skiing, fishing, golf, motorcycle touring. Office: Carson Med Group 1200 Mountain St Carson City NV 89703-3821

MEYER, RON, agent; b. 1944; m. Kelly Chapman; children, Jennifer, Sarah, Carson, Eli. With Paul Kohner Agency, 1964-1970; agent William Morris Agency, Beverly Hills, CA, 1970-1975; co-founder, pres. Creative Artists Agency, Inc., 1975-95; pres., COO Universal Studios Inc., Universal City, 1995—; pres./COO Vivendi Universal Entertainment. Served with USMC. Office: Universal Studios Inc 100 Universal City Plz Universal City CA 91608 E-mail: susan.fleishman@unistudios.com.

MEYER, ROSALIND MAE, community volunteer; b. Fremont, Nebr., Jan. 7, 1927; d. Elwood A. P. and Emma Prince Murray; m. Richard P. Meyer, June 11, 1950; children: Susan Eldredge, Kimberly Landaal, William Meyer. BA in Psychology, U. Denver, 1949. Tchr. Denver Pub. Schs., 1949-51; journalist, columnist Trenton (Mich.) Times, 1971-79. Photographer Grosse Ile Golf and Country Club, Mich., 2000. Pres. Downriver Coun. Arts, Wayne County, Mich., 2000—; mem. steering com. Grosse Ile Libr. campaign, 1999—. Named Outstanding Woman in Arts, Hist., and Culture, Wayne County, 1999, Citizen of Yr. Grosse Ile Rotary, 1979, Woman of Yr. Grosse Ile Jaycettes, 1972, Women of Achievement Yr. Downriver Profile, 2000. Mem. Detroit Symphony Coffee Concert (founding mem.), Downriver Town Hall (founding mem.), Grosse Ile Founders Soc. (founding mem.), Grosse Ile Nature and Land Conservancy (founding mem.), Grosse Ile Questers, Book Club and Musicale. Republican. Presbyterian. Avocations: family, travel, photography, music, gardening. Home: 20769 Thorofare Rd Grosse Ile MI 48138-1248

MEYER, RUTH KRUEGER, museum administrator, educator, art historian; b. Chicago Heights, Ill., Aug. 20, 1940; d. Harold Rohe and Ruth Halbert (Bateman) Krueger; m. Kenneth R. Meyer, June 15, 1963 (div. 1978); 1 child, Karl Augustus BFA, U. Cin., 1963; MA, Brown U., 1968; PhD, U. Minn., 1980. Lectr. Walker Art Ctr., Mpls., 1970—72; instr. U. Cin., 1973—75; curator Contemporary Arts Ctr., Cin., 1976—80; dir. Ohio Found. Arts, Columbus, 1980—83, Taft Mus., Cin., 1983—93; prof. Miyazaki (Japan) Internat. Coll., 1994—2001, Art Acad. Cin., 2002—. Adj. prof. The Union Inst., Cin., 1994. Pub. Dialogue Mag., Columbus, 1980-83; author: (exhbn. catalogues) Sandy Rosen Vestal Vases, 1986, Oblique Illusion: An Installation by Rick Paul, 1986, David Black an American Sculptor, 1985, Brad Davis: The Pines, 1984, The American Weigh, 1983, New Epiphanies, 1982, (with others) The Tafts Collection: The First Ten Years of Its Development, 1988, The Tafts of Pike St., 1988, (exhbn. catalogue) The History of Travel: Paintings by William Wegman, 1985-90, 1990, The Artist Face to Face: Two Centuries of Self-Portraits from the Paris Collection of Gerald Shurr, 1989, Tributes to the Tafts, 1991, The Taft Museum: Its Collection and Its History, 1995; (with Madeleine Fidell-Beaufort) Collecting in the Gilded Age: Art Patronage in Pittsburgh, 1997, Water de Gruyter BErlin, 2000, others; contbr. articles to profl. jours. Recipient rsch. award Kress Found., 1967, 76; named Chevalier in the Order of Arts and Letters, Govt. of France, 1989. Mem. Internat. Assn. Art Critics, Coll. Art Assn. Democrat. E-mail: ruthkmeyer@yahoo.com.

MEYER, SANDRA PALMER, financial executive; b. Hobbs, N.Mex., Nov. 26, 1954; d. Aubrey King and Elizabeth (Robertson) P.; m. Gerald Edward Meyer, Dec. 16, 1978; children: Gerald P., Patrick A. B in Acctg., La. State U., 1976; AMP-ISMP Mgmt. Devel. Cert., Harvard Bus. Sch., 1995. CPA, Tex., N.C. Corp. contr. Tex. Ea. (merged with Pan Handle), Houston, 1988; dir. statements and reports Pan Handle Ea., contr. v.p. planning and controls, v.p., contr.; v.p. treas., contr. Pan Energy (merged with Duke Power); v.p. group bus. ops. Duke Energy Corp., Charlotte, N.C., v.p. planning and fin., v.p., corp. contr., 1999-2001, sr. v.p. retail svcs., 2001—. Dir. Tex. Soc. CPAs, Houston, 1995-97; pres. Fin. Execs. Inst., Houston, 1995-96. Bd. dirs. Child Care Resources, Inc., Charlotte, 1997-2000; pres. ESCAPE Family Resource Ctr., Houston, 1995-96, bd. dirs., 1993-99. Mem. AICPAs, N.C. Assn. CPAs, Fin. Execs. Internat. (pres. S.C. 2000-01). Fax: 704-373-4749. E-mail: spmeyer@duke-energy.com.

MEYER, SHELDON, publisher; b. Chgo., June 8, 1926; s. Arthur Christof and Hester Truslow (Sheldon) M.; m. Margaret Mary Kirk, July 29, 1964; children: Arabella Christina, Andrew Kirk. AB summa cum laude, Princeton U., 1949; MA (hon.), U. Oxford, 1993. With Funk & Wagnalls Co., 1951—55; assoc. editor Grosset & Dunlap, 1955-56; with Oxford Univ. Press, N.Y.C., 1956-96, editor, 1956-70; exec. editor Trade Books, 1970-82, v.p., 1974-79, sr. v.p., 1982-96, consulting editor, 1997—. Mem. Am. Assn. Univ. Presses (bd. dirs. 1969-71, 79-82, v.p. 1979-80), Am. Hist. Assn., Orgn. Am. Historians, Inst. Early Am. History and Culture (bd. dirs. 1985-87), Nat. Bd. Rev. Motion Pictures, Century Assn., Phi Beta Kappa. Home: 180 Riverside Dr New York NY 10024-1021

MEYER, STEPHAN SCHÜTZMEISTER, physics educator; b. Chgo., Mar. 29, 1953; s. Peter and Luise (Schutzmeister) M.; m. Sharon Caroline Salveter, Oct. 6, 1984; children: Samantha, Niels. BA, U. Wis., 1974; MA, Princeton U., 1976, PhD, 1979. Postdoctoral fellow MIT, Cambridge, 1979-84, asst. prof. physics, 1984-92; prof. dept. astronomy and astrophysics dept. physics U. Chgo., 1993—. Recipient Class of 1942 Career Devel. Professorship, MIT, 1988. Mem. Am. Astron. Soc. Home: 5247 S University Ave Chicago IL 60615-4405 E-mail: meyer@uchicago.edu.

MEYER, SUSAN MOON, speech language pathologist, educator; b. Hazleton, Pa., Mar. 8, 1949; d. Robert A. and Jane W. (Walters) Moon; m. John C. Meyer Jr., Feb. 16, 1989; children: Chris, Scott. BS, Pa. State U., 1971, MS, 1972; PhD, Temple U., 1983. Cert. tchr., Pa. Speech-lang. pathologist, instr. Elmira (N.Y.) Coll., 1973-74; speech-lang. pathologist Arnot-Ogden Hosp., Elmira, 1973-74; supr. Sacred Heart Hosp. Speech and Hearing Ctr., Allentown, Pa., 1974-75; speech-lang. pathology instr. Kutztown (Pa.) U., 1975-78, asst. prof., 1978-82, assoc. prof., 1982-85, prof., 1985—. Owner Speech and Lang. Svcs., Allentown, 1975-87; cons. Vis. Nurses Assn., Allentown, 1975-85, Home Care, Allentown, 1975-85. Author: Survival Guide for the Beginning Speech-Language Clinician, 1998. Mem. Am. Speech-Lang.-Hearing Assn. (cert., councilor 1986-89, Continuing Edn. award 1982, 85, 88, 91, 93-97, 99, 2001-02), Pa. Speech-Lang.-Hearing Assn. (cert., v.p. profl. preparation 1985-89, Appreciation award 1987-89, 2001), Northea. Speech and Hearing Assn. Pa. (pres. 1984-86, Outstanding Dedication award 1985, Honors of the Assn. award 1999), Coun. Suprs. Speech-Lang. Pathology and Audiology. Avocations: family activities, cross-country skiing, British sports cars, reading. Bus. Office: Kutztown U Dept Speech-Lang Kutztown PA 19530 E-mail: smeyer@kutztown.edu., sjmeyer@msn.com.

MEYER, THOMAS J. mathematics educator; b. Rochester, Minn., Aug. 14, 1949; s. Donald Joseph and Jean Ann (Gerleman) M.; m. Nancy Mae Lewis, Jan. 3, 1986. BS, Ea. Mich. U., 1971, MA, 1974, 83. Tchr. math. Van Buren Schs., North Jr. High Sch., Belleville, Mich., 1972-83, Belleville High Sch., 1983—, chmn. math. dept., 1989—. Mem. Nat. Council Tchrs. Math., Mich. Council Tchrs. Math., Math. Assn. Am., Van Buren Edn. Assn. (trustee 1974-86, crisis com. chmn. 1982-85). Avocations: gardening, miniature roses. Home: 708 Collegewood St Ypsilanti MI 48197-2133 Office: Van Buren Pub Schs 501 W Columbia Ave Belleville MI 48111-2611

MEYER, WARREN GEORGE, vocational educator; b. Plymouth, Wis., May 12, 1910; s. charles Martin and Lillie Margaret (Liese) M.; m. Marion Magdaline Lehmann, June 19, 1939; children: Karen Rhem, Stephen George. BA, U. Wis., 1932; MS, NYU, 1933. Asst. buyer Mandel bros., Chgo., 1933-34, The Davis Store, Chgo., 1934-35; divsn. head Sears Roebuck & Co., Lansing, Mich., 1935-36, Detroit, 1936-37; mktg. instr. Vocat. Adult Sch., West Allis, Wis., 1937-38; adult field instr. Wis. Vocat. Schs., 1938-41; state supr. Dept. Vocat. Edn., Topeka, 1941-46; prof. vocat. edn. U. Minn., Mpls., 1946-76, vocat. prof. emeritus, 1976—. Vocat. edn. cons. U.S. Dept. State, Frankfurt, Germany, 1951; mktg. edn. cons. Va. Poly. Inst. and State U., Blacksburg, 1960-70, U. Mass., Amherst, 1966; adv. coun. mem. Nat. Ctr. for Vocat. Edn., Columbus, Ohio, 1965-75. Lead author: Retail Marketing Principles and Practices, 1964-82 edits.; co-author: Coordination in Cooperative Vocational Education, 1975; lead author: Retail Marketing, 1988; editor: Vocational Education and Nations Economy, 1977. Lt. (s.g.) USNR, 1944-46. Recipient Tchr. Edn. Acad. award Coun. for Distributive Tchr. Edn., 1969, Horace Morse Standard Oil award U. Minn., 1972, John Robert Gregg award Nat. Bus. Edn. Assn., 1973. Mem. Am. Vocat. Assn. (hon. life), Lions (sec. 1980-98), Men of Yorke, Delta Pi Epsilon. Home: 7500 York Ave S Edina MN 55435-5633 E-mail: warmeyer@aol.com.

MEYER, WILLIAM DANIELSON, retired department store executive; b. Mpls., May 5, 1923; s. J.A. and Florence (Danielson) M.; m. Betty Ann McBride, May 28, 1950; children— Patricia Ann, Janet Elizabeth, Jean Louise. BS, UCLA, 1947. With actuarial dept. Prudential Ins. Co. Am., L.A., 1948-53; with Carter Hawley Hale Stores, Inc., 1953-93; ret., 1993; asst. sec. Carter Hawley Hale Stores, Inc., 1962-64, sec., 1964-73, dir. employee benefits, asst. sec., 1973-93. Bd. dirs. Profit Sharing Coun., chmn., 1984-86; bd. dirs. Travelers Aid Soc., L.A., pres., 1976-77; trustee Profit Sharing Rsch. Found.; v.p. U.S. Diving, 1982-84, 90-94; trustee U.S. Diving Found., 1994—. Mem. Am. Soc. Corp. Secs., Personnel and Indsl. Relations Assn., Los Angeles C. of C., Gold Key, Sigma Pi (Founder's award 1992), Alpha Kappa Psi, Phi Phi. Republican. Presbyterian. Home: 1725 Durklyn Ct San Marino CA 91108-2035

MEYER, WILLIAM MICHAEL, mortgage banking executive; b. Fort Wayne, Ind., Oct. 21, 1940; s. Henry and Lola Mae (Leedy) M.; m. Phyllis Ann Ruetschilling, Aug. 12, 1961; children: Michael Dean, Blaine Aaron, Nathan Daniel, Andrea Rene. Degree in Bus., Ind. U., 1970. V.p. Waterfield Mortgage Corp., Fort Wayne, 1963-73, First Nat. Bank, Colorado Springs, Colo., 1973-78, Underwood Mortgage Co., Lawrenceville, N.J., 1978-79, Mortgage Serv. South Bend, Ind., 1979-82; sr. v.p. Irwin Mortgage Corp., Indpls., 1982—. Bd. dirs. Ctrl. Ind. Quality Leadership Forum, Indpls. Bd. dirs. Edyvean Repertory Theatre, 1996-99. Mem. Mortgage Bankers Assn. (mem. com. 1979—), Ind. Mortgage Bankers (bd. dirs. 1992—), Rotary (Zionsville bd. dirs. 1990-93). Republican. Roman Catholic. Avocations: skiing, gardening, swimming, golf. Home: 12071 Sail Place Dr Indianapolis IN 46256-9441

MEYER-BAHLBURG, HEINO F.L. psychologist, educator; b. Hamburg, Germany, Feb. 26, 1940; came to U.S., 1969; s. Wilhelm and Marie Luise Meyer-B. Vordiplom in Psychology, U. Hamburg, 1963, Diplom Psychology, 1966; D in Natural Scis., U. Düsseldorf, 1970. Sci. asst. U. Düsseldorf, 1970; rsch. asst., then rsch. assoc. prof. psychiatry and pediatrics SUNY Med. Sch., Buffalo, 1970-77; rsch. scientist N.Y. State Psychiat. Inst., N.Y.C., 1977—; from assoc. clin. prof. med. psychology to prof. clin. psychology in psychiatry

Columbia U. Coll. Physicians and Surgeons, 1978—; pediat. behavioral endocrinologist Presbyn. Hosp., N.Y.C., 1978-90, prof. psychologist in psychiat. svc., 1990—. Contbr. numerous articles to profl. publs. Recipient Disting. Sci. Achievement award Soc. for Sci. Study of Sex, 1993; grantee NIMH, NICHD. Mem. AAAS, APA, Soc. Pediat. Psychology, Internat. Acad. Sex Rsch., German Sexual Rsch. Soc., Internat. Soc. Psychoneuroendorinology, Soc. Sci. Study Sex, Soc. Rsch. Child Devel., Soc. Sexual Therapy and Rsch., Lawson Wilkins Pediat. Endocrine Soc., Harry Benjamin Internat. Gender Dysphoria Assn., Internat. AIDS Soc. Office: Columbia U Dept Psychiatry 1051 Riverside Dr Unit 15 New York NY 10032-2695 E-mail: meyerb@childpsych.columbia.edu.

MEYERHOFF, ERICH, librarian, administrator; b. Braunschweig, Germany, Nov. 24, 1919; came to U.S., 1935; s. Karl and Irma Meyerhoff; m. Inge Zuber; children— Tina, C. Michael BS, CCNY, 1943; MS, N.Y. Sch. Social Work, 1949; MSLS, Columbia U., 1951, cert. advanced librarianship, 1974. Social worker various orgns., to 1951; reference librarian Columbia U. Med. Library, N.Y.C., 1951-57; librarian, asst. prof. Downstate Med. Ctr., SUNY, Bklyn., 1957-61; dir. Med. Library Ctr. N.Y., 1961-67; librarian Health Scis. Library, SUNY-Buffalo, 1967-70, Cornell U. Med. Coll., N.Y.C., 1970-86, asst. dean, 1977-86; chief library service VA Med. Ctr., 1986-88; archives librarian NYU Med. Ctr., 1980-91; asst. curator Ehrman Med. Libr.-Archives, NYU Sch. Medicine, 1991—. Adj. instr. biomed. comms. Columbia U., 1976-81; cons. U. Mich., Ann Arbor, 1968, N.Y. Met. Reference and Rsch. Libr. Agy., 1968-69, Coll. Physicians of Phila., 1969-70. Fellow AAAS, Med. Library Assn. (cert., bd. dirs. 1972-76, chmn. various coms. 1968-72, 78-81, Inst. for Sci. Info. award 1981-82, Janet Doe lectr. 1977, Marcia C. Noyes award 1997), N.Y. Acad. Medicine; mem. AAUP, Spl. Libraries Assn., Archons of Colophon, am. Assn. for the History of Medicine, Am. Printing History Assn., Met. New York Archivists Roundtable. Avocations: traveling, hiking. Home: 90 La Salle St New York NY 10027-4719 Office: NYU Med Ctr Archives 550 1st Ave New York NY 10016-6402 E-mail: meyere01@library.med.nyu.edu.

MEYERHOFF, JACK FULTON, financial executive; b. Joliet, Ill., May 15, 1926; s. Charles F. and Helen (Ferguson) M.; m. Mary Margaret Williams, Jan. 2, 1949; children— Keith F., Greg H., Deborah S., Todd C. BS, Miami U., Oxford, Ohio, 1947; postgrad., Ohio Wesleyan U., 1944-45; grad. Advanced Mgmt. Program, Harvard U., 1968. C.P.A., Ohio, Ill. Mgr. Arthur Andersen & Co., Chgo., Cin., Cleve., 1947-59; treas. MacGregor Sports, Cin., 1959-63; v.p., corp. controller Brunswick Corp., Chgo., 1963-77, chief fin. officer, 1972-77, v.p. corp. affairs, 1977-80, v.p. human resources, 1980-81; chmn., chief exec. officer MarJac Assocs., Nokomis, Fla., 1981—; pres., dir. Charles Oxford Corp., 1984—. Bd. dirs. Sherwood Med. Industries, Inc., Old Orchard Bank & Trust Co., Tech: Time Inc., Nokomis; organizer, vice chmn. bd. trustees Caldwell Trust Co. and Trust Cos. Am., Venice, Fla., 1993—. Treas., bd. dirs. Cove Schs.; bd. dirs., pres. Skokie Valley Cmty. Hosp., No. Ill. Indsl. Assn.; v.p., bd. dirs. Jr. Achievement; bd. dirs. Chgo. Responsibility Growth, Gulf Area Med. Properties; chmn. bd. Bon Secours-Venice Hosp., Venice Hosp. Found.; bd. dirs. J. Clifford MacDonald Handicapped Ctr. of Tampa, Sarasota Com. of 100, Triangle Econ. Devel. Coun., Manatee C.C. Found., Boys and Girls Club of Venice; mem. adv. coun. Miami U., Georgetown U., U. So. Fla. With USNR, 1944-46. Mem. Am. Inst. C.P.A.s, Ohio Soc. C.P.A.s, Ill. Soc. C.P.A.s, Fin. Execs. Inst., Nat. Assn. Accts., Harvard Bus. Sch. Alumni Assn., Miami U. Exec. Alumni Council (bd. dirs., treas.), Venice Area C. of C. (bd. dirs.), Sigma Alpha Epsilon, Delta Sigma Pi, Beta Alpha Psi, Beta Gamma Sigma Clubs: Venice Yacht, Mid America, Economic, Misty Creek Country. Lodges: Masons, Rotary. Methodist. Home: 20 Inlets Blvd Nokomis FL 34275-4108 Office: MSW Assocs PO Box 1326 Nokomis FL 34274-1326 E-mail: meyerhoffjm@comcast.net.

MEYERINK, VICTORIA PAIGE, film producer, actress; b. Santa Barbara, Calif., Dec. 27, 1960; d. William Joseph Meyerink and Jeanne Baird; m. Lawrence David Foldes, Apr. 24, 1983. Student, U. So. Calif., 1978-80. Actress, 1962—; v.p. Star Cinema Prodn. Group, Inc., 1981-85; pres. Star Entertainment Group, Inc., L.A., 1985—. Mem. faculty Internat. Film & TV Workshops, 1991—; lectr. colls. & film festivals. Prodr. (motion pictures) The Great Skycopter Rescue, 1982, Young Warriors, 1984, Night Force, 1987, Prima Donnas, 1996, Finding Home, 2002; actress (TV series) The Danny Kaye Show, Green Acres, My Three Sons, Family Affair, The FBI, Adam 12, (motion pictures) Speedway, Night of The Grizzly, Seconds, Brainstorm, The Littlest Hobo, (TV spl.) It Isn't Easy Being a Teenage Millionairess, numerous commls. Recipient Mayoral Proclamation for Outstanding Achievement, City of L.A., Cert. of Recognition for 25 Yrs. Outstanding Contbns. to the Entertainment Industry, City of L.A., Outstanding Achievement award Acad. Family Films & TV. Mem. Acad. Motion Picture Arts & Scis. (exec. com. Student Acad. Awards 1996—), L.A. Film Tchrs. Assn. Avocations: languages, travel, music, scuba diving, gourmet cooking.

MEYEROWITZ, ELLIOT MARTIN, biologist, educator; b. Washington, May 22, 1951; s. Irving and Freda (Goldberg) M.; m. Joan Agnes Kobori, June 17, 1984; 2 children. AB, Columbia U., 1973; MPhil, Yale U., 1975, PhD, 1977. Rsch. fellow Stanford U., Calif., 1977-79; asst. prof. biology Calif. Inst. Tech., Pasadena, 1980-85, assoc. prof., 1985-89, prof., 1989—, chair, 2000—. Mem. editl. bd. Trends in Genetics, Current Biology, Cell, Devel., Genome Biology; contbr. articles to profl. jours. Recipient LVMH Sci. pour l'Art Sci. prize, 1996, Internat. prize for biology, Japan, 1997, Mendel medal, U.K., 1997, Wilbur Cross medal Yale U., 2001; Jane Coffin Childs Meml. fund fellow, 1977-79, Sloan Found. fellow, 1980-82. Fellow: AAAS; mem.: NAS (Lounsbery award 1999), Academie des Scis. (fgn. mem./France), Internat. Soc. for Plant Molecular Biology (pres. 1995—97), Genetics Soc. Am. (pres. 1999, medal 1996), Bot. Soc. Am. (Pelton award 1994), Am. Soc. Plant Biologists (Gibbs medal 1995), Am. Acad. Arts and Scis., Am. Philos. Soc. Office: Calif Inst Tech Divsn Biology Pasadena CA 91125-0001 E-mail: meyerow@caltech.edu.

MEYEROWITZ, HAYA LOUISE ORLOVE, weaver, educator; b. N.Y.C., Mar. 20, 1935; arrived in Israel, 1973; d. Robert and Francis (Cohen) Orlove; m. Yosef Meyerowitz, Sept. 1, 1956; children: Aaron-David, Daniel-Shem, Avram-Raphael, Sara-Sofia. BS in Bklyn. Coll., CUNY, 1956; MS, U. Iowa, 1959. Instr. U. Iowa, Iowa City, 1956-59; tchr. biology U. Ill., Urbana, 1959-61, Cornell U., Ithaca, N.Y., 1962-64, Rice U., Houston, 1964-66; weaving tchr. Contemporary Art Mus., 1970-73; head weaving edn. Israel Mus., Jerusalem, 1973-97, Arts Ctr., Beer-Sheba, Israel, 1983-86; tchr. folk-craft and religion Project Oded, Jerusalem, 1992-96. Mem. Handweavers Guild Am. (internat. rep. 1973—), Israel Weavers Guild (chair 1983—). Home: Sulam Yaakov 1/10 Ramot Jerusalem Israel 97729 E-mail: sf_haya@bezeqint.net.

MEYERROSE, DALE WILLIAM, career officer; BS in Econs., USAF Acad., 1975; MBA, U. Utah, 1978. Commd. 2d lt. USAF, 1975, advanced through grades to brig. gen., 1998; maintenance officer 4th Combat Comms. Group, Altus AFB, Okla., 1976-77; aide-de-camp, asst. exec. officer to the comdr. European Comms. Divsn., Kapuan Air Sta., West Germany, 1977-79; aide-de-camp to the comdr. Air Force Comms. Command, Scott AFB, Ill., 1979-80; chief of maintenance 1974th Comms. Group, 1980-82; mem., air staff tng. program officer Sec. of the Air Pers. Coun., The Pentagon, Washington, 1982-83; various assignments Hdqrs. USAF, The Pentagon, 1983-85, chief future concepts, dep. chief of staff, 1990-91; comdr. 2048th Comms. Squadron, Carswell AFB, 1985-87; comms. support officer Nat. Mil. Command Ctr. the Joint Staff, the Pentagon, Washington, 1987-90; comdr. 3rd Combat Comms. Group, Tinker AFB, Okla., 1992-94; dir. comms. Operation Southern Watch, Riyadh, Saudi Arabia, 1993; dir. comms. and info. Hdqrs. USAF in Europe, Ramstein AB, Germany, 1994-96, Hdqrs. Air Combat Command, Langley AFB, Va., 1996—. Brig. gen., U.S. Base Command, Peterson AFB, Colorado Springs. Decorated Legion of Merit. Office: US Base Command J6 250 S Peterson Blvd # J6 Colorado Springs CO 80914-3285

MEYERS, ABBEY S. foundation administrator; b. Bklyn., Apr. 11, 1944; m. Jerrold B. Meyers, Oct. 23, 1966; children: David, Adam, Laura. AAS, N.Y.C. Community Coll., 1962; LHD (hon.), Alfred U., 1994. Comml. artist various advt. agys., N.Y.C., 1962-65; dir. patient svcs. Tourette Syndrome Assn., Bayside, N.Y., 1980-85; exec. dir., founder Nat. Org. for Rare Disorders, Danbury, Conn., 1985—, pres., 1995—. U.S. commr. Nat. Commn. on Orphan Diseases, Washington, 1986-89; mem. subcom. Human Gene Therapy NIH, Bethesda, Md., 1989-92; mem. recombinant DNA adv. com. NIH, 1992-96; mem. Health Care Payor Adv. Commn. on Conn. Commn. on Hosps. and Health Care, 1992-94; mem. FDA Biol. Response Modifiers Com., 1995-99; mem. DHHS Nat. Human Rsch. Protection Adv. Com., 2000—. Author: (with others) Orphan Drugs and Orphan Diseases: Clinical Reality and Public Policy, 1983, (with others) Cooperative Approaches to Research and Development of Orphan Drugs, 1985, (with others) Tourette Syndrome: Clinical Understanding and Treatment, 1988, (with others) Physicians Guide to Rare Diseases, 1992. Bd. dirs. Nat. Orphan Drug and Device Found., N.Y.C., 1982-85; leader Coalition to Pass Orphan Drug Act of 1983, 1979-82. Recipient Pub. Health Svc. award HHS, 1985, Commr.'s Spl. citation FDA, 1988. Mem. Nat. Health Coun. (bd. dirs. 1989-94), Alliance of Genetic Support Groups (bd. dirs. 1987-89), European Orgn. for Rare Disorders (hon. pres. 1997—). Avocations: reading, horseback riding. Office: Nat Org for Rare Disorders PO Box 1968 Danbury CT 06813- 196 E-mail: orphan@rarediseases.org.

MEYERS, ALBERT IRVING, chemistry educator; b. N.Y.C., Nov. 22, 1932; s. Hyman and Sylvia (Greenberg) M.; m. Joan Shepard, Aug. 10, 1957; children: Harold, Jill, Lisa BS, NYU, 1954, PhD, 1957. Rsch. chemist Cities Svc. Oil Co., Cranbury, N.J., 1957-58; asst., assoc. prof., prof. La. State U., New Orleans, 1958-70, Boyd prof., 1969; prof. Wayne State U., Detroit, 1970-72, Colo. State U., Fort Collins, 1972—, disting. prof., 1986—, John K. Stille prof. chemistry, 1993—. Spl. postdoctoral fellow Harvard U., Cambridge, 1965-66; cons. G.D. Searle Co., Skokie, Ill., 1972-84, Mid-West Rsch. Inst., Kansas City, Mo., 1974-77, NIH, Bethesda, Md., 1977-79, 85-89, Bristol-Myers Squibb Co., 1983-95, Roche Bioscience, 1989—, GlaxoSmith-Kline Beecham Co., 1994—; mem. sci. adv. bd. Trega Bioscis., La Jolla, Calif., Avanir Bioscis., La Jolla. Editor Jour. Am. Chem. Soc., 1979-85; mem. editl. adv. bd. Jour. Organic Chemistry, 1990-95, Tetrahedron, 1990—, Jour. Chem. Soc. Perkin, 1993, Jour. Chem. Soc. Chem. Commn., 1996, Heterocycles, 1974—; contbr. over 450 articles to profl. jours. Recipient Alexander von Humboldt award Fed. Republic of Germany, 1984, Disting. Alumni award NYU, 1990, award in synthetic chemistry Am. Chem. Soc., 1985, A.C. Cope Scholar award, 1987, Yamada prize, Japan, 1996, award Internat. Soc. Heterocyclic Chemistry, 1997; named Man of Yr., New Orleans Jaycees, 1968, Boyd Prof. La. State U., 1969; recipient pioneer award Am. Insts. Chemists, 1998. Fellow AAAS, Nat. Acad. Sci.; mem. Royal Soc. Chemistry (silver medalist 1982), Phila. Organic Chemistry Soc. (Allan Day award 1987). Home: 1500 Hepplewhite Ct Fort Collins CO 80526-3822 Office: Colo State Univ Dept Chemistry Fort Collins CO 80523-0001 E-mail: aimeyers@lamar.colostate.edu.

MEYERS, ALBERT THOMAS MARIE, academic counsellor; b. Luxembourg, Luxembourg, May 31, 1946; s. Hubert and Annelise (Jansen) M.; m. Angela Maria Delahaye, June 5, 1971; children: Annette, Christiane, Philippe, Catherine. Mech. Engring. Diploma, Tech. Coll. Aachen, Germany, 1970; Dr.Ing., U. Bochum, Germany, 1976. Sci. employee U. Bochum, 1970-76, acad. counsellor, 1976-77, sr. acad. counsellor, 1977—. Guest lectr. Tongji U., Shanghai, 1983; lectr. U. Bremen, Germany, 1987-89. Reviewer Applied Mechanics Revs., 1983-85; contbr. articles to profl. jours. Mem. GAMM. Avocations: classical music, church organ. Home: Maischützenstr 1 D-44805 Bochum Germany Office: Univ of Bochum Universitaetsstr 150 D-44780 Bochum Germany E-mail: meyers@web.de., meyers@tm.bi.ruhr.uni-bochum.de.

MEYERS, ALLAN D. archaeologist; b. Louisville, Aug. 18, 1971; s. Dale E. and Leona F. Meyers. BA, Centre Coll. Ky., 1993; PhD, Tex. A&M U., 1998. Registered profl. archaeologist. Adj. prof. U. Houston-Clear Lake, 1999; vis. asst. prof. Centenary Coll., Shreveport, La., 1999-2000; asst. prof. anthropology U. Wis. Colls., Janesville, 2000—02, Eckerd Coll., St. Petersburg, Fla., 2002—. Contbr. articles to profl. jours. Recipient Rsch. award So. region Inst. Internat. Edn., 1996; L.T. Jordan fellow Tex. A&M U., 1997; grad. student rsch. grantee Tex. A&M U., 1997. Mem. Soc. for Am. Archaeology, Soc. for Hist. Archaeology, Southeastern Archaeol. Conf., Sigma Xi, Phi Kappa Phi. Home: 2822 11th St N Saint Petersburg FL 33704 Office: Eckerd Coll Comparative Cultures Collegium 4200 54th Ave S Saint Petersburg FL 33711 Office Fax: 608-758-6554. E-mail: ameyers@uwc.edu.

MEYERS, AMY, museum director; m. Jack Meyers; 1 child Rachel. BA, U. Chgo.; PhD in Am. Studies, Yale U. Rschr. Dumbarton Oaks; rschr. Ctr. for Advanced Study in Visual Arts, Nat. Gallery; curator Am. Art, Henry E. Huntington Libr., Art Collections and Bot. Gardens, San Marino, Calif.; dir. Yale Ctr. for Brit. Art; prof. art Yale U. Adj. faculty Calif. Inst. Tech.; vice chair, Huntington rep. Assn. Rsch. Insts. in History of Art, 1995—2000. Co-editor (with Margaret Pritchard): Empire's Nature: Mark Catesby's New World Vision; co-editor: (with Alan Trachtenberg and Neil Gray Jr.) Classic Essays on Photography. Office: Yale Ctr for Brit Art PO Box 208280 1080 Chapel St New Haven CT 06520-8280

MEYERS, ANN ELIZABETH, sports broadcaster; b. San Diego, Mar. 26, 1955; d. Robert Eugene and Patricia Ann (Burke); m. Donald Scott Drysdale, Nov. 1, 1986; children: Donald Scott Jr., Darren John, Drew Ann. Grad., UCLA, 1978. Profl. basketball player N.J. Gems, 1979-80; profl. basketball player Ind. Pacers NBA, 1979; sports broadcaster Ind. Pacers, 1979-80; sportscaster men's basketball U. Hawaii, Honolulu, 1981-82; sportscaster men's and women's basketball UCLA, 1982-84, 89—; sportscaster volleyball, basketball, softball, tennis ESPN, 1981—; sportscaster Olympic Games ABC, L.A., 1984; sportscaster volleyball, softball, tennis, basketball, soccer Sportsvision, 1985-87; sportscaster volleyball, basketball, softball Prime Ticket, 1985-97; sportscaster CBS-TV, 1991—, ESPN Women's Basketball, Fox Women's Basketball, WNBA-NBC World Championships; sportscaster Olympic Games NBC, Sydney, Australia, 2000. Sportscaster Goodwill Games, WTBS, 1986, 90; sportscaster basketball NBC and ESPN, 1996-97, WNBA, NBA, ESPN, 1996—. Winner Silver medal Montreal Olympics, 1976, Gold medal Pan Am. Games, 1975, Silver medal, 1979, All-Am. UCLA, 1975, 76, 77, 78; 1st woman named to Hall of Fame UCLA, 1987; named to Women's Sports Hall of Fame, 1987, Orange County Sports Hall of Fame, 1985, Calif. H.S. Hall of Fame, 1990, Basketball Hall of Fame, 1993, Nat. H.S. Hall of Fame, 1995, NBC Hoop It Up, 1995, 96, 97, Cath. Youth Orgn. Hall of Fame, 1996, Women's Basketball Hall of Fame, 1999. Office: c/o Lampros and Roberts 16615 Lark Ave Ste 101 Los Gatos CA 95032-7645

MEYERS, ARTHUR SOLOMON, library director; b. N.Y.C., Dec. 14, 1937; s. Nathan and Selma (Leeser) M.; m. Marcia Indianer, June 11, 1961; children: Naomi, Ruth. AB in History, U. Miami, 1959; MS in LS, Columbia U., 1961; MA in English, U. Mo., St. Louis, 1980; MA in History, Ball State U., Muncie, Ind., 1987. Cert. libr. I, Ind. Young adult libr. N.Y. Pub. Libr., N.Y.C., 1959-61; adult and young adult libr. Detroit Pub. Libr., 1963-67; adult and young adult specialist Enoch Pratt Free Libr., Balt., 1967-73; mgr. brs. and cmty. svc. St. Louis Pub. Libr., 1973-80; dir. Muncie Pub. Libr., 1980-86, Hammond (Ind.) Pub. Libr., 1986-97, Russell Libr., Middletown, Conn., 1997—. Condr. workshops and insts. in field; presenter in field Contbr. articles to profl. jours. With U.S. Army, 1961-63. Mem. ACLU, NAACP, ALA (pres. reference and adult svcs. divsn. 1989-90), Freedom To Read Found., Soc. Historians of the Gilded Age, New Eng. Hist. Assn. Jewish. Avocations: local and family history research, ethnic heritage research, reference book reviewing. Home: 854 Long Hill Rd Middletown CT 06457-5063 Office: Russell Libr 123 Broad St Middletown CT 06457-3350 E-mail: marciarthur@msn.com., ameyers@biblio.org.

MEYERS, CAROLYN WINSTEAD, mechanical engineer, educator; b. Hampton, Va., May 11, 1946; d. John Selner and Eva Carroll (Tonsler) Winstead; divorced; children: Timothy C. III, Leslie C., Lisa A.; m. James E. Cofield, Jr. BSME, Howard U., 1968; MSME, Ga. Inst. Tech., 1979, PhD in Metallurgy, 1984. Steam generator analyst Machinery Apparatus Operation div. Machinery Apparatus Ops. div. GE, Schenectady, 1968; systems analyst Info. Svcs. div. Info. Svcs. div. GE, Bethesda, Md., 1969; instr. Atlanta U. Ctr. Corp., 1972-77; instr. mech. engring. Ga. Inst. Tech., Atlanta, 1979-84, asst. prof., 1984-90, assoc. prof., 1990-96; dir. SUCCEED Coalition Ctr. for Profl. Success, 1992-93; assoc. dean rsch. Coll. Engring. Ga. Inst. Tech., Atlanta, 1993-96; prof. mech. engring. NCAIT N.C. A&T State U., Greensboro, 1996—, dean Coll. Engring., 1996, prof. mech. engring., 1996—, v.p. acad. affairs, 2000—, provost, 2001—. Summer faculty fellow USAF Materials Lab., Wright-Patterson AFB, Ohio, 1988; program officer NSF, 1996-99. Contbr. articles to profl. jours. Chmn. waste volume reduction subcom. Atlanta Mayor's Commn. on Solid Waste Disposal, 1989-92; trustee Westminster Schs., Atlanta, 1989-93; program dir. divsn. undergrad edn. NSF, 1997-99, divsn. human resources devel., Arlington, V., 1999—. Recipient Faculty award for women NSF, 1991, Disting. Alumni award Atlanta-Howard U. Alumni Assn., 1992; named Black Engr. of Yr. in Higher Edn. U.S. Black Engr. Mag. and Coun. Engring Deans, 1990; Pres. Young Investigator grantee NSF, 1988; inducted to Acad. of Disting. Engring. Alumni Ga. Tech. U., 1996; honored alumna in edn. on Charter Day Howard U., 1997. Fellow ASME (Engr. of Yr. 1990); mem. AIME, SAE (Ralph Teetor Ednl. award 1986), Foundry Ednl. Found. (key prof. 1985-95), Soc. Women Engrs. (state pres. Atlanta sect. 1987-90), Am. Foundrymen's Soc. (sponsor student sect. 1987-95, aluminum divsn. sci. merit award 1994), Soc. Black Engrs. (Golden Torch award 2002), Links (pres. Atlanta chpt. 1987-89), Moles, Jack and Jill Am., The Girl Friends, Sigma Xi, Tau Beta Pi, Phi Kappa Phi, Alpha Kappa Alpha. Roman Catholic. Office: NC AT&T State U 1601 Market St Greensboro NC 27411 Address: 200 Lucas Park Dr Greensboro NC 27455-1459 E-mail: cmeyers@ncat.edu.

MEYERS, CHARLES JEROME, history educator; b. Chgo., Sept. 26, 1944; s. Joseph and Charlotte Pevan Meyers; m. Sylvia Drelich, Oct. 20, 1968; 1 child, Caryn. BA in History, DePaul U., 1966; MAT in Social Studies, U. Ill., 1970. Cert. tchr. 6-12, Ill. Tchr., instr. North Park Coll., Chgo., 1988-95; tchr. Grove Jr. H.S., Elk Grove Village, Ill., 1970-74, Washburne Sch., Winnetka, 1974-2000. V.p. Ave. of the Righteous, Glencoe, Ill., 1989—; cons., sr. program assoc. Facing History and Ourselves, Chgo., 1987—; tchr. exch. Fulbright/USIA, Washington, 1979-80. Bd. dirs. Raoul Wallenberg Com., Chgo., 1988-95. Named Tchr. of Yr., Winnetka C. of C., 1999; Mandel Tchr. fellow U.S. Holocaust Mus., Washington, 1997-98 E-mail: Chuck_Meyers@facing.org.

MEYERS, DAVID GEORGE, internist, cardiologist, educator; b. Muscatine, Iowa, Oct. 5, 1950; BS, Loras Coll., 1972; MD, U. Iowa, 1976; MPH, Med. Coll. Wis., 1998. Intern Creighton U., 1976-77, resident medicine, 1977-79; fellow cardiology Med. Coll. Va., 1979-81; from asst. prof. internal medicine to assoc. prof. Neb. U. Med. Ctr., Omaha, 1981-93; mem. faculty U. Kans. Med. Ctr., Kansas City, 1994, prof. internal medicine and preventive medicine, 1994—, dir. of preventive Cardiology, 1994—. Fellow ACP, Am. Coll. Cardiology, Am. Coll. Chest Physicians, Am. Heart Assn., Am. Coll. Preventive Medicine; mem. Am. Coll. Epidemiology, Am. Soc. Preventive Cardiology. Office: U Kans Med Ctr 3901 Rainbow Blvd Kansas City KS 66160-0001 E-mail: dmeyers@kumc.edu.

MEYERS, DAVID W. lawyer, writer, educator; b. Hobart, Tasmania, Australia, July 19, 1942; came to U.S., 1946; s. Philip T. and Margaret M. Meyers; m. Jane Arthur Meyers, Dec. 27, 1969; children: Duncan, Vanessa. BA magna cum laude, U. Redlands, 1964; JD, U. Calif., Berkeley, 1967; LLM, U. Edinburgh, Scotland, 1968. Bar: Calif. 1968, U.S. Dist. Ct. (no. dist.) Calif. 1971, U.S. Ct. Appeals (10th cir.) 1994, U.S. Supreme Ct. 1976. Tutor dept. comparative law U. Edinburgh, Scotland, 1967-68; assoc. Rutan & Tucker, Santa Ana, Calif., 1968-71; ptnr. Dickenson, Peatman, Fogarty, Napa, 1972—. Adj. lectr. U. Calif. Med. Sch., San Francisco, 1985-87; vis. fellow U. Edinburgh, Scotland, 1999, U. Tasmania, 2000-02. Author: Human Body and the Law, 1972, rev. edit., 1990, Medical-Legal Implications of Death & Dying, 1981; contbr. chpts. to books, articles to profl. jours. Pres. Napa Valley Coll. Found., 1997-99; trustee Queen of the Valley Hosp., 1987-93, pres., 1990-93. Mem. State Bar Calif., Napa County Bar Assn. (pres. 1986), Am. Inns of Ct. Democrat. Avocations: writing, bicycling, skiing, sailing, travel. Office: Dickenson Peatman & Fogarty 809 Coombs St Napa CA 94559-2994

MEYERS, DONALD WOOD, editor, columnist; b. New Brunswick, N.J. s. Harold Irving Meyers and Doris Eleanor Force; m. Margaret Ann Morris, Apr. 20, 1988; children: Marie, Nathaniel, Joseph, Samuel. AA, Brookdale C.C., Lincroft, N.J., 1985; student, Brigham Young U., 1987. Reporter Register, Shrewsbury, N.J., 1988-89, Suburban, East Brunswick, 1989-93, Daily Herald, Provo, Utah, 1993-98, opions page editor, 1998—. EMT East Brunswick Rescue Squad, 1983-92; v.p. Utah Found. Open Govt., 2001. Named Most Enterprising Reporter Daily Universe, 1985, Best Column Utah Press Assn., 1994, Best Editor's Column 1995; recipient Environ. Excellence award U.S. EPA Region VIII, 1996, 3d pl. Utah-Idaho-Spokane AP, 1999. Mem. Soc. Profl. Journalists (pres. Utah headliners chpt. 2002). Mem. Lds Ch. Avocations: photography, writing, desktop publishing, cycling, historical research. Office: Daily Herald 1555 N Freedom Blvd Provo UT 84604 Office Fax: 801-344-2985. E-mail: dmeyer@heraldextra.com.

MEYERS, ERIC MARK, religion educator; b. Norwich, Conn., June 5, 1940; s. Karl D. and Shirlee M. (Meyer) M.; m. Carol Lyons, June 25, 1964; children: Julie Kaete, Dina Elisa. AB, Dartmouth Coll., 1962; MA, Brandeis U., 1964; PhD, Harvard U., 1969. Lerner prof. religion, archeol., bibl. study, ancient hist. Duke U., Durham, N.C., 1969—, dir. grad. program in religion, 1979-86, 2001—; dir. Annenberg Inst., Phila., 1991-92. Pres. Am. Schs. of Oriental Rsch., Balt., 1990-96; commentator on biblical archaeology; dir. 8 digs Israel, Italy, 1970-2000. Author: 10 books; co-author: The Cambridge Companiion to the Bible, 1997; editor (in chief): The Oxford Encyclopedia of Archaeology in the Near East, 5 vols., 1997; contbr. articles more than 350 to profl. jours.; frequent guest (TV series) A&E channel, Discovery channel. Jewish. Avocations: singing (baritone), golf, the arts, travel. Home: 3202 Waterbury Dr Durham NC 27707-2416 Office: Duke U 118 Gray Bldg PO Box 90964 Bldg Durham NC 27708-0964 E-mail: emc@duke.edu.

MEYERS, GERALD CARL, educator, author, expert witness, consultant; b. Buffalo, Dec. 5, 1928; s. Meyer and Berenice (Meyers) M.; m. Barbara Jacob, Nov. 2, 1958. BS, Carnegie Inst. Tech., 1950, MS with distinction, 1954. With Ford Motor Co., Detroit, 1950-51, Chrysler Corp., Detroit and Geneva, 1954-62; with Am. Motors Corp., Detroit, 1962-84, v.p., 1967-72, group v.p. product, 1972-75, exec. v.p., 1975-77, pres., 1977-84, COO, 1977, chmn., CEO, 1977-82, ret., 1984; Ford disting. prof. Grad. Sch. Indsl. Adminstrn. Carnegie Mellon U., Pitts., 1985-96; prof. U. Mich. Bus. Sch., Ann Arbor, 1995—. Pres. Gerald C. Meyers Assocs., Inc., West Bloomfield, Mich.; adj. prof. Sch. Bus. U. Mich., Ann Arbor. Author: When It Hits the Fan, Managing the Nine Crises of Business; co-author: Dealers, Healers, Brutes and Saliors; bus. commentator Nat. Pub. Radio, Fox News Cable TV, CNBC TN Network; contbr. articles to N.Y. Times, Wall St. Jour., L.A. Times. 1st lt. USAF, 1951-53. Decorated Legion of Honor (France). Mem. Econ. Club Detroit, Tau Beta Pi, Phi Kappa Phi, Omicron Delta Kappa. Address: U Mich Bus Sch D 3246 701 Tappan Ave Ann Arbor MI 48109-1217 Office: 5600 W Maple Rd Ste B216 West Bloomfield MI 48322-3787

MEYERS, HOWARD CRAIG, lawyer; b. Chgo., Nov. 15, 1951; s. Spencer M. and Joyce L. (Dresdner) M. BA in English, Ariz. State U., 1973, JD, 1977. Bar: Ariz. 1977, N.Mex. 2000; cert. bus. bankruptcy specialist, cert. creditors rights specialist Am. Bd. Cert.; cert. bankruptcy specialist State Bar Ariz. Of counsel Burch & Cracchiolo, P.A., Phoenix. Mem. ABA, Comml. Law League of Am., Am. Bankruptcy Inst., State Bar Ariz. (debtor-creditor com.), Maricopa County Bar Assn.(profl. devel. com., alternative dispute resolution com.), Internat. Council of Shopping Ctrs. Home: 6711 E Camelback Rd Unit 65 Scottsdale AZ 85251-2067 Office: Burch & Cracchiolo PA 702 E Osborn Rd Ste 200 Phoenix AZ 85014-5234 E-mail: hmeyers@bcattorneys.com.

MEYERS, HOWARD L. lawyer; b. Dec. 22, 1948; BS, U. Del., 1970; JD, U. Va., 1973. Bar: Pa. 1973. Sr. ptnr. in bus. and fin. sect., mng. ptnr. Phila. office Morgan, Lewis & Bockius. Bd. dirs. Greater Phila. 1st Corp. Mem. ABA, Phila. Bar Assn., Greater Phila. C. of C. (mem. exec. com., bd. dirs., gen. counsel). Office: Morgan Lewis & Bockius 1701 Market St Philadelphia PA 19103-2903

MEYERS, JAMES FRANK, electronics engineer; b. Binghamton, N.Y., Sept. 9, 1946; s. Edwin Fox and Louise (Okrepkie) M. BEE, U. Louisville, 1969, ME, 1972; postgrad., George Washington U. Instr. elec. engring. lab. U. Louisville, 1968-69; engring. coop. technician Langley Research Ctr., NASA, Hampton, Va., 1966-69, aerospace technologist, 1969—. Contbr. articles to profl. jours.; patentee in field. Mem. IEEE (sect. chmn. 1975), Turnberry Two

Owners Assn. (pres., dir. 1979-82), Sports Car Club Am. (div. rallye exec. 1982-86), Eta Kappa Nu, Tau Beta Pi, Sigma Tau. Office: NASA Langley Rsch Ctr Mail Stop 493 Hampton VA 23681-0001 E-mail: James.F.Meyers@larc.nasa.gov.

MEYERS, JERRY IVAN, lawyer; b. McKeesport, Pa., Mar. 26, 1946; s. Eugene J. and Gladys Claire (Rubenstein) M.; m. Judith Drake Aughenbaugh, June, 26, 1971; 1 child, Lindsey Drake. BA in Philosophy and Rhetoric, U. Pitts., 1972; JD cum laude, U. Miami, 1975. Bar: Pa. 1975, U.S. Dist. Ct. (we. dist.) Pa. 1975. Assoc. Berger & Kapetan, Pitts., 1975-78; ptnr. Meyers, Rosen, Louik & Perry P.C., 1978—. Mem. Assn. Trial Lawyers Am., Pa. Trial Lawyers Assn. (past pres. western Pa. chpt., bd. govs. legis. policy com., med.-legis. com.), Acad. Trial Lawyers Allegheny County. Office: Meyers Rosen Louik & Perry PC The Frick Building Ste 200 Pittsburgh PA 15219-6002 E-mail: meyers@meyersmedmal.com.

MEYERS, JOHN ALLEN, magazine publisher; b. Winnetka, Ill., Feb. 21, 1929; s. Fred W. and Ruth B. (Burras) M.; m. Jane Bowers, Sept. 18, 1954; children: Jennifer, Katherine, John. BA, Mich. State U., 1951, Litt.D. (hon.), 1978; postgrad., Columbia U., 1965. Mgr. Cleve. Time mag., 1960-63, mgr. Chgo., 1963-65, mgr., 1965-68, worldwide advt. sales dir., 1968-72; v.p. Time, Inc., publisher Sports Illustrated mag., 1972-78; pub. Time mag., 1978-85; chmn. Time Inc. Mag. Co., 1985-88; chmn. emeritus Time Inc., 1988—. Appointed presdl. bd. adv. on Pvt. Sector Initiatives; chmn. J.A.M. Enterprises. Editor-in-chief Contitution mag. Bd. dirs. Sr. Mcht. Watch, U.S. Hist. Soc.; pres., Found. for the U.S. Constn. Served with USMC, 1951-53. Decorated Purple Heart. Office: Time & Life Bldg 1221 Avenue Of The Americas New York NY 10020-1001

MEYERS, KAREN DIANE, lawyer, educator, corporate officer; b. Cin., July 8, 1950; d. Willard Paul and Camille Jeannette (Schutte) M.; m. William J. Jones, Mar. 27, 1982. BA summa cum laude, Thomas More Coll., 1974; MBA, MEd, Xavier U., 1978; JD, U. Ky., Covington, 1978. Bar: Ohio 1978, Ky. 1978; CLU; CPCU. Clk. to mgr. Baldwin Co., Cin., 1970-78; adj. prof. bus. Thomas More Coll., Crestview Hill, Ky., 1978—; adj. prof. bus. CSSC U. Notre Dame, 1994; asst. sec., asst. v.p., sr. counsel The Ohio Life Ins. Co., Hamilton, 1978-91; prin. KD Meyers & Assocs., 1991; v.p. Benefit Designs, Inc., 1991-96, Little, Meyers, Garretson & Assocs., Ltd., Cin., 1996—; adj. prof. Miami U., 1998—. Bd. dirs. ARC, Hamilton, 1978-83, vol., 1978—; bd. dirs. YWCA, Hamilton, 1985-91. Gardner Found. fellow, 1968-71; recipient Ind. Progress award Bus. & Profl. Women, 1990. Fellow Life Mgmt. Inst. Atlanta; mem. ABA, Soc. Chartered Property Casualty Underwriters (instr. 1987—), Cin. Bar Assn., Butler County Bar Assn., Ohio Bar Assn., Ky. Bar Assn. Roman Catholic. Avocations: aerobics, jogging, crafts. Home: 7903 Hickory Hill Ln Cincinnati OH 45241-1363

MEYERS, KIMBERLY SUE, physical therapist; BS magna cum laude, Western Mich. U., 1978; cert. phys. therapy, Mayo Sch. Allied Health, 1981; M in Orthopedic Phys. Therapy, U. Indpls., 1996. Cert. neurodevelopmental treatment/adult hemiplegia. Staff phys. therapist Foote Hosp., Jackson, Mich., 1981-82, Borgess Hosp., 1982-89; clin. mgr. Borgess GNA, 1989-95; dept. head S.W. Mich. Rehab. GNA, 1995; clin. mgr. Borgess Woodbridge GNA, 1996-2000, Borgess Health and Fitness at Woodbridge, 2000—. Mem. Am. Phys. Therapy Assn., Orthopedic divsn.

MEYERS, LOUISA ANN, business and communications consultant; b. Omaha, July 5, 1956; d. V. William and Darinka Stephania (Shuput) M. BA in Liberal Studies magna cum laude, U. Nebr., Omaha, 1983. Wardrobe asst. Royal Shakespeare Theatre, Stratford-upon-Avon, Eng., 1977-78, asst. adminstr. Eng., 1978-79; stage/asst. co. mgr. Omaha Cmty. Playhouse, Nebr. Theatre Caravan, 1979-80; stage/prodn. mgr. Firehouse Dinner Theater, Omaha, 1980-81; pers. benefits technician Bergan Mercy Hosp., 1981-82, unit sec., 1981-83; planning mgr. Mercy Health Sys. of Midlands, 1984-85; staff asst. Omaha City Coun., 1985-86; mayoral aide City of Omaha, 1986-87, cmty. devel. mgr., 1987-89, mayor's spl. projects mgr., 1989; exec. dir. Neighborhood Housing Svcs., Omaha, 1989-90; dir. Office Comms., legis. liaison Nebr. Dept. Health, Lincoln, 1993-95; co-founder, mng. ptnr. Mercury Bus. Comms., Omaha, 1989—. Presenter on pub. policy to various comty. orgns.; flood disaster coord. Nebr. Dept. Health, 1993; state rep. Nat. Pub. Health Info. Coalition, 1993-95; film. commr. City of Omaha, 1986-89, rep. to League of Nebr. Municipalities, 1986-87; festival coord. City of Omaha, 1985-86; adminstr. City of Omaha Cable TV, 1985-86; writer various grants, reports for City of Omaha; mem. efficiency task force City of Omaha; dog obedience instr., 1998—. Contbr. articles to profl. jours.; reporter Gateway newspaper, 1982; author, co. mgr., stage mgr. dramatic touring prodn. Nebraska Heritage, 1974-75; columnist, contbr. PC Guide, Kidz!, Drug-Free Athletes, Today's Omaha Woman. Mem. chancellor's adv. com. U. Nebr., Omaha, 1974, bicentennial com., 1975; chair Joslyn Chamber Music Series, 1986-87; coord. fundraiser Queen Elizabeth Hosp., Birmingham, Eng., 1979; exec. dir. Omaha Coalition for Homeless, 1990-91; campaign mgr. Horgan for Legislature, Omaha, 1990; vol. Jesse Rasmussen for Legislature Campaign, Omaha, 1994; mem. City of Omaha Efficiency Commn., 1996-98; bd. dirs. Black Student Cath. Scholarship Fund, fin. and scholarship com., 1996-98; coord. Omaha Dog Park, 1996-98. Medill Sch. Journalism scholar, 1973, Margaret Builta scholar, 1983; recipient Admiralty award Nebr. Navy, 1993. Mem. LWV, NOW, Nebr. Nursing Assn., Nat. Mus. Women in Arts (charter mem.), Therapy Dogs Internat., Phi Kappa Phi, Alpha Psi Omega. Avocations: dog obedience training competition, property restoration and renovation, design. Home: 4927 Pinkney St Omaha NE 68104-3663 Office: Mercury Bus Comms PO Box 31397 Omaha NE 68131-0397

MEYERS, MARLENE O. retired hospital administrator; m. Eugene Meyers; children: Lori, Lisa, Dean. BSN, U. Sask., 1962; postgrad., U. Oslo, Norway, 1973; MSc, U. Calgary, Alta., Can., 1976; postgrad., Harvard U., 1980, Banff Sch. Mgmt., 1985, U. Western Ont., Can., 1993; EMT-B, Scottsdale C.C., 2000. RN, Ariz. Various nursing positions, Alta. and B.C., Can., 1962-69; instr., chair Mount Royal Coll. Allied Health, Calgary, 1969-82; asst. exec. dir. Rockyview Hosp., 1982-85; v.p. patient svcs. Calgary Gen. Hosp., 1985-91, pres., CEO, 1991-95, Meyers and Assocs. Health Care Mgmt. Cons., Calgary, 1995—; now ret. Surveyor Can. Coun. on Health Facilities Accreditation, 1986-97; mem. adv. com. for south caucasus health info. project, Can. Adv. Com. Named Calgary Woman of Yr. in field of Health, 1982; recipient Heritage of Svc. award, 1992. Mem. Alta. Assn. RNs (hon. mem., 1996), Can. Coll. Health Svcs. Orgn., Can. Exec. Svcs. Orgn., Can. Soc. for Internat. Health (bd. dirs. 1997-2001), Rotary Internat. Home and Office: 244 Osprey Cir Hope ID 83836-9664 also: 10464 E Cannon Dr Scottsdale AZ 85258-4929 E-mail: marlyo@yahoo.com.

MEYERS, MARSHA LYNN, retired social worker; b. Springfield, Ohio, Dec. 3, 1948; d. Dennis Wathan and Juanita E. (Ratliff) Easterling; m. Wade Trent Meyers, Oct. 5, 1974; children: Lindsay Dionne, Whitney Jane. BA in Sociology, Olivet Nazarene U., 1972. Lic. social worker, Ohio. Formerly social work coord. Mercy Meml. Hosp. and Home Health Care, Urbana, Ohio. Former bd. dirs. Champaign County chpt. Am. Cancer Soc.; mem. adv. bd. Mercy Meml. Hosp. Home Health Care Hospice. Named Social Worker of the Yr. for excellence in small depts. Ohio Soc. Hops. Social Workers, 1995, Social Worker of Yr., Cedarville U. chpt. Phi Alpha Theta, 2000. Mem. Nat. Assn. Social Workers, Soc. of Hosp. Social Work Dirs., Nat. Assn. Christian Social Workers (past v.p.). Home: 223 College St Urbana OH 43078-2405

MEYERS, MARY ANN, writer, consultant; b. Sodus, N.Y., Sept. 30, 1937; d. Harold Galpin and Clarice Mildred (Daniel) Dye; m. John Matthew Meyers, Aug. 22, 1959; children: Andrew Christopher, Anne Kathryn. BA magna cum laude, Syracuse U., 1959; MA, U. Pa., 1965, PhD, 1976. Editorial asst. Ladies' Home Jour., Phila., 1959-62; editor, asst. dir. news bur. U. Pa., 1962-65, asst. to pres., 1973-75, univ. sec., lectr. Am. civilization, 1980-90; contbg. writer The Pennsylvania Gazette, 1965—; dir. coll. rels., editor Haverford Horizons, lectr. in religion Haverford (Pa.) Coll., 1977-80; pres. The Annenberg Found., St. Davids, Pa., 1990-92; v.p. for external affairs Moore Coll. Art and Design, Phila., 1995-97; sr. fellow The John Templeton Found., Radnor, Pa., 1997—. Vis. com. dept. biology U. Pa., 1996—; mem. bd. advisors The Peter Gruber Found., St. Thomas, Vt., V.I. Author: A New World Jerusalem, 1983; contbg. author: Death in America, 1975, Gladly Learn, Gladly Teach, 1978, Coping with Serious Illness, 1980, Religion in American Life, 1987; contbr. articles to profl. jours. Judge recognition program Coun. for Advancement and Support Edn., Washington, 1977—78, chair creative editing and writing workshop, 1978; mem. Picker Found. Program on Human Qualities in Medicine, N.Y.C., Phila., 1980—83; del. Phila.-Leningrad Sister Cities Project, 1986; trustee U. Pa. Press., 1985—; vice chmn. U. Pa. 250th Anniversary Commn., 1990—92; mem. steering com. of bd. trustees U. Pa., Annenberg Sch. for Comm., 1990—92; mem. adv. bd. U. Pa., Annenberg Ctr. for the Performing Arts, 1990—98; mem. bd. overseers U. Pa., Sch. Arts and Scis., 1990—97; mem. steering com. of bd. trustees Annenberg Ctr. for Comm., U. So. Calif., L.A., 1990—92, The Annenberg Washington PRogram in Comm. Policy Studies of Northwestern U., Washington, 1990—92; dir., sec. Am. Acad. Polit. and Social Sci., 1992—, World Affairs Coun. Phila., 1990—95; dir. Diagnostic and Rehab. Ctr., Phila., 1993—2002; bd. advisors Peter Gruber Found., St. Thomas, 2001—. Recipient Excellence award Women in Communications, Inc., 1973-74, award for pub. affairs reporting Newsweek/Coun. for Advancement and Support Edn., 1977, Silver medal Coun. for Advancement and Support Edn., 1986. Mem. Cosmopolitan Club, Sunday Breakfast Club, Phi Beta Kappa (mem. steering com. Delaware Valley chpt. 1995-97). Roman Catholic. Avocations: reading, theater, classical music, biking. Home: 217 Gypsy Ln Wynnewood PA 19096-1112

MEYERS, MORTON ALLEN, physician, radiology educator; b. Troy, N.Y., Oct. 1, 1933; s. David and Jeanne Sarah (Dunn) M.; m. Beatrice Applebaum, June 1, 1963; children— Richard, Amy. MD, SUNY, Upstate Med. Coll., 1959. Diplomate: Am. Bd. Radiology. Intern Bellevue Hosp., N.Y.C., 1959-60; resident in radiology Columbia-Presbyn. Med. Ctr., 1960-63; fellow Am. Cancer Soc., 1961-63; prof. dept. radiology Cornell U. Med. Center, N.Y.C., 1973-78; prof., chmn. dept. radiology SUNY Sch. Medicine, Stony Brook, 1978-91, prof. dept. radiology, 1991-98, disting. prof. medicine, 1998—. Vis. investigator St. Mark's Hosp., London, 1976; spkr. Radiol. Soc. N.Am., 1986. Author: Diseases of the Adrenal Glands: Radiologic Diagnosis, 1963, Dynamic Radiology of the Abdomen: Normal and Pathologic Anatomy, 1976, 5th edit., 2000, Iatrogenic Gastrointestinal Complications, 1981; series editor: Radiology of Iatrogenic Disorders, 1981-86; editor: Computed Tomography of the Gastrointestnal Tract: Including the Peritoneal Cavity and Mesentery, 1986, Neoplasms of the Digestive Tract: Imaging, Staging, and Management, 1998; founding editor in chief Abdominal Imaging, 1976—; mem. editl. bd. Iatrogenics, Surg. and Radiol. Anatomy; contbr. chpts. to med. textbooks, articles to profl. jours.; speaker in field. Served to capt. M.C. U.S. Army, 1963-65. Fellow Am. Coll. Radiology, Am. Coll. Gastroenterology, European Soc. Gastrointestinal and Abdominal Radiology; mem. Radiol. Soc. N.Am., Am. Roentgen Ray Soc., Am. Gastroenterol. Assn., Soc. Uroradiology, Soc. Gastrointestinal Radiologists, Assn. Univ. Radiologists, N.Y. Roentgen Ray Soc., N.Y. Acad. Gastroenterology, European Assn. Radiology (hon.), Alpha Omega Alpha. Home: 14 Wainscott Ln East Setauket NY 11733-3816 Office: SUNY Health Scis Ctr Sch Medicine Dept Radiology Stony Brook NY 11794-0001

MEYERS, PAUL ANDREW, physician, educator; b. Somerville, N.J., May 3, 1949; s. Harold H. and Ina Stuart (Szabad) M.; m. Maria Luisa Padilla, Nov. 24, 1973; children: Rachel, Sarah, Carla. BA cum laude, Brown U., 1970; MD, Mt. Sinai Sch. Medicine, N.Y.C., 1973. Diplomate Am. Bd. Pediatrics; lic. physician, N.Y., N.J. Intern then resident in pediat. Mt. Sinai Hosp., N.Y.C., 1973-76; fellow pediat. hematology and oncology N.Y. Hosp., 1976-79; spl. fellow Meml. Sloan-Ketting Cancer Ctr., 1977-79, asst. attending pediatrician, 1979-92, assoc. attending pediatrician, 1992-2001, vice-chmn. dept. pediat., 1993—, attending pediatrician, 2001—. Rsch. fellow Sloan-Kettering Inst., N.Y.C., 1977-80; asst. attending pediatrican Cornell Med. Ctr., N.Y.C., 1979-85; asst. prof. pediatrics Cornell U. Med. Coll., N.YU.C., 1979-85, assoc. prof. clin. pediatrics, 19785; med. dir. Happines-Is Camping, Bronx, N.Y., 1982—. Recipient Upjohn Achievement award, 1973; fellow Smith-Harris, 1976-78, Am. Cancer Soc., 1979; Young Investigator Rsch. grantee, 1980. Fellow Am. Acad. Pediatrics; mem. Am. Soc. Clin. Oncology, Am. Soc. Pediatric Hematology/Oncology, N.Y. Soc. Study of Blood, Alpha Omega Alpha. Office: Meml Sloan-Kettering Cancer Ctr 1275 York Ave New York NY 10021-6094 E-mail: meyersp@mskcc.org.

MEYERS, RICHARD JAMES, landscape architect; b. Columbus, Ohio, Jan. 25, 1940; s. Ralph Joseph and Margaret Mary (Kruse) M.; m. Mary Igoe, Jan. 12, 1963; children: Gregory James, Helen Marie, Andrew James. B.Landscape Arch., Ohio State U., 1961. Registered landscape architect, Ohio, Mich., Fla., Ind.; cert. Council Landscape Archtl. Registration Bds. Jr. planner Columbus Planning Commn. (Ohio), 1960-62; landscape architect Behnke-Nes & Assocs., Cleve., 1962-65, Arthur Hills & Assocs., Toledo, 1965-67; ptnr. Mortensen-Meyers Assocs., 1967-69; prin. MMSS Inc., 1969-71, The Collaborative, Inc., Toledo, 1973-99; bd. dirs., past pres. Council Landscape Archtl. Registration Bd., Syracuse, N.Y., 1978-86, Ohio Bd. Landscape Architect Examiners, 1975-83. Adv. bd. Ohio State U. Land Architecture, 1999—, Toledo Mcpl. Cemetery Commn., 1999—; bd. dirs. Toledo Botanical Gardens, 2000—. Active St. Vincent Hosp. and Med. Ctr. Assocs., Toledo, 1978-83; bd. dirs. Family Svcs. Greater Toledo, 1977-82, Toledo Central City Neighborhood, 2001—; com. mem. Toledo Met. Area Coun. of Govt., 1972-79, 87-89, Toledo Bot. Gardens Design Rev. Bd., 1988-90, Downtown Toledo Vision, Inc., 1988-99; chmn. Toledo Lucas County Plan Commn., 1989-99; chmn. Toledo Adminstrv. Bd. Zoning Appeals, 1994-99, Met. Parks Com. of 25, 1991, 1997; chmn. campaign divsn. United Way, 1991; adv. bd. U. Toledo-Stranahan Arboretum, 1994—, Scenic Ohio, 1996—; trustees adv. coun. Schedel Arboretum & Gardens, 2000—. Dumbarton Oaks Jr. summer scholar, 1960; recipient First Honor Design award Am. Assn. Nurserymen, 1974; named Disting. Alumnus, Ohio State Univ. Coll. Engring., 1996. Fellow Am. Soc. Landscape Architects (merit design award Ohio chpt. 1975, 81, 83, 85, Outstanding Svc. to Profession award 1983, Ohio Chpt. medal 1984); mem. AIA, Ohio Chpt. of Am. Soc. Landscape Architects (v.p. 1974-76), Urban Land Inst., Soc. for Coll. and Univ. Planning, Am. Forestry Assn., Am. Planning Assn., Rails to Trails Conservancy, Ohio Pks. and Recreation Assn., Heatherdowns Country Club (bd. dirs. 1983). *I am fortunate to be part of a profession dedicated to improving and beautifying our physical environment through the preservation and protection of our natural resources and by the sensitive blending of economic and social needs with these natural systems. Landscape architecture provides me with a great deal of personal satisfaction.*

MEYERS, ROBERT ALLEN, chemist, publisher; b. L.A., May 15, 1936; s. Jack B. Meyers and Pearl (Cassell) Thorpe; m. Roberta Lee Hart, June 24, 1961 (div. 1976); children: Tamara, Robert Jr.; m. Ilene Braun, Feb. 27, 1977; children: Jenifer, Jacalyn. BA, San Diego State U., 1959; PhD, UCLA, 1963. Postdoctoral fellow, mem. faculty Calif. Inst. Tech., Pasadena, 1963-64; rsch. scientist Bell & Howell Rsch. Ctr., Sierra Madre, Calif., 1965; project mgr. TRW Def. & Space, Redondo Beach, 1966-81; bus. area mgr. TRW Energy Group, 1981-86; mgr. process devel. TRW Def. & Space, 1986-88, mgr. new projects devel., 1988-95; pres. Ramtech Ltd., Tarzana, Calif., 1995—. Del. U.S.-USSR Working Group, Washington and Moscow, 1973-80; chmn. adv. bd. Guide to Nuclear Power Tech., N.Y.C., 1982-84; mem. adv. coun. chemistry dept. UCLA, 1991—. Author: Coal Desulfurization, 1977; editor: Coal Handbook, 1981, Coal Structure, 1982; editor: Handbook of Petroleum Refining Processes, 1986, 2nd edit., 1996, Handbook of Synfuels Technology, 1984, Handbook of Energy Technology and Economics, 1983, Handbook of Chemicals Production Processes, 1986, others; editor-in-chief Ency. of Phys. Sci. and Tech., 1987, 92, 2001, Ency. of Modern Physics, 1990, Ency. of Lasers and Optics, 1991, Ency. of Telecom., 1989, Molecular Biology and Biotech., 1995, Ency. of Molecular Biology and Molecular Medicine, 1995, Ency. of Environ. Analysis and Remediation, 1998, Ency. of Environ. Pollution and Control, 1999, Ency. of Analytical Chemistry, 2000. Mem. Am. Chem. Soc., Am. Inst. Chem. Engrs. Avocations: swimming, bicycling, tennis, golf. Office: Ramtech Ltd 3715 Gleneagles Dr Tarzana CA 91356-5622

MEYERS, SHARON MAY, sales executive; b. Whittier, Calif., Feb. 8, 1946; d. Hubert Miller and Garnet May (Prater) Jones; m. Gary Lee Klink, June 18, 1966 (div.); children: Robert Douglas, Jeffrey Loren; m. Carl Eugene Meyers, Dec. 16, 1989. Student, Pasadena Coll. (scholar), 1963-65; AA, Rio Hondo Coll., 1978; student, Calif. State U., Fullerton, 1978; BSBA, U. Redlands, 1982. Sec. Armorlite Lens Co., Pasadena, 1963-64, James, Pond & Clark, Pasadena, 1964-65; sales sec. Fiberboard Paper, Commerce, Calif., 1965-67; instr. aide East Whittier Sch. Dist., 1974-78; sales rep. Gen. Can Co., Montebello, 1978-86, Brouse-Whited Creative Packaging, Marina del Rey, 1986; br. mgr. Gen. Can Inc., Hayward, 1986-88; bus. banking mgr. Wells Fargo Bank NA, San Jose, 1988-89; sales rep. Moore Bus. Products, Colorado Springs, Colo., 1990-93, Assoc. Bus. Products, Santa Rosa, Calif., 1993-94, Advantage Bus. Forms, Oreg., 1994-96, Tekprinting Svcs., Inc., Medford, 1996—. Sec. ch. bd. Ch. of the Nazarene, 1973-76, childrens dir., 1965-69; youth dir. Womens Christian Temperance Union, 1965-69; treas. PTA, 1977-79; bd. dirs. Bay ARea Crisis Nursery, Concord, Calif.; vol. Valley Meml. Nosp. Emergency Rm., Livermore, Calif., vol. lunch buddy program Washington Elem. Sch., 1999—. Named Sales Rep of Yr. Moore Bus. Products, 1991. Republican. Avocations: writing, cooking. Home: PO Box 1413 Shady Cove OR 97539-1413

MEYERS, STUART IRWIN, real estate developer; b. N.Y.C., Aug. 7, 1941; s. Herman and Helen Noah Meyeroff; m. Carol Ann Goldstein, Sept. 26, 1964 (div. Apr. 1970); m. Arlene Merryl Meyers, June 20, 1976 (div. Sept. 1978); children: Wendy Jill Meyers-Crabb, Jeffrey Brian Meyers. BS in Econs., Wharton Sch. U. Pa., 1963; MBA in Acctg., Columbia U., 1964. CPA, N.Y., Fla. Sr. auditor Price Waterhouse & Co., N.Y.C., 1964-68; dir. corp. devel. mergers and acquisitions ITT Corp., 1969-73; staff v.p. mergers and acquisitions RCA Corp., 1973—75; v.p. controller/CFO trucks equipment div. Hertz Corp., 1975—76; v.p. mergers and acquisitions Kraft Inc., Glenview, Ill., 1976-81; sr. v.p. mergers and acquisitions United Brands Corp., 1981-84; sr. v.p. devel. The Related Cos., Miami, Fla., 1985-93; chmn., CEO, founder, prin. The Cornerstone Group, Coral Gables, 1993—. Bd. dirs. Affordable Housing Tax Credit Coalition, Washington, 1995—, Greater Miami Svc. Corp., 1998—; bd. dirs., founder Coalition of Affordable Housing Providers, Tallahassee, 1997—; bd. dirs., trustee Nat. Assn. Home Builders Multifamily Coun., Chgo., 1997. Mem. AICPA, Fla. CPA Soc., N.Y. State CPA Soc., Wharton Sch. Club South Fla. (bd. dirs. 1983—), Dade Alumni Club U. Pa. (bd. dirs. 1983—), The Penn Club., LaGorce Country Club (founder). Jewish. Avocations: piano, golf, ranching, skiing, yachting. Office: The Cornerstone Group Penthouse 2121 Ponce De Leon Blvd Coral Gables FL 33134

MEYERS, TEDSON JAY, lawyer; b. Bayonne, N.J., May 6, 1928; s. Irving and Norma Miriam (Anson) M.; m. Patricia Elizabeth Sullivan, Apr. 10, 1965 (div. Apr. 1978); children: Mary, John, Katherine; m. Lynn Scholz, Aug. 6, 1978 (div. Oct. 1992); m. Arden Schell, Dec. 27, 2000. Student, Ohio State U., 1945-47; BA, NYU, 1949, MA, 1950; JD, Harvard U., 1953. Bar: D.C. 1953, N.Y. 1957, U.S. Supreme Ct. 1971. Asst. counsel Office Gen. Counsel, Dept. Navy, Washington, 1955-56; assoc. Liebman, Eulau & Robinson, N.Y.C., 1956-58; staff counsel for govt. regulations ABC, 1958-61; adminstrv. asst. to chmn. FCC, Washington, 1961-62; asst. to dir., dir. overseas ednl. TV projects Peace Corps, 1962-68; pvt. practice, 1968-70; ptnr. Sullivan Beauregard Meyers & Clarkson, 1970-74, Peabody Lambert & Meyers, Washington, 1974-84, Reid & Priest, Washington, 1984-96, Coudert Brothers, Washington, 1996—. Adj. prof. comm. San Diego State U., 1993—; founding pres. Harvard Legis. Rsch. Bur., 1952—53; mem. White House Task Force on Ednl. TV Overseas, 1966—68; trustee Global Legal Info. Network Found., 2001—; mem. adv. panel on internat. telecomm. law U.S. State Dept., 1987—; bd. govs. Internat. Coun. for Computer Comm., 1986—, pres., 2000—; bd. dirs. Cyber Century Forum. Contbr. conf. papers and articles to profl. publs. Mem. City Coun. Washington, 1972-75; bd. govs. Met. Washington Coun. Govts., 1973-75; chmn. Bicycle Fedn. of Am., 1977—; bd. dirs. U.S. Coun. for World Comm. Yr. 83, 1982-84; dir. The Arthur C. Clarke Found. of the U.S. Inc., 1987—. Lt. USMC, 1953-55, Korea. Rsch. fellow Carnegie Found., 1949. Fellow: Am. Bar Found.; mem.: ABA (co-founder and chmn. internat. telecomm. com., sect. sci. and tech. 1982—85, coun. mem. sect. sci. and tech. 1983—87, chmn. standing com. law libr. congress 2000), Soc. Satellite Profls., Pacific Telecomm. Coun., Royal TV Soc., Internat. Inst. Comm., Fed. Comm. Bar Assn., Potomac Boat Club, Cosmos Club Found. (trustee, chmn. 1985—88, 1990—), Cosmos Club (pres. 1988—90), Alpha Epsilon Pi. Avocations: bicycling, motorcycling, computers, sculling, military music. Office: Coudert Brothers Ste 1200 1627 I St NW Washington DC 20006-4007 E-mail: tmeyers@tedson.com.

MEYERS, THEDA MARIA, textile company executive; b. Bremen, Germany, Feb. 16; came to U.S. 1957; d. Johann-Friedrich and Christophina E.L.J. (Fentrohs) Ficke; m. Laurence Jay Meyers, Oct. 2, 1960 (div. 1970); 1 child, Jayson Bennett. Dipl., U. Bremen, 1956; student, Fashion Inst. Tech., N.Y.C., 1960. Artist-stylist Rosewood Fabrics, N.Y.C., 1960-62; textile stylist Belding Corticelli, 1962-65; chief designer Jerry Mann of Calif., L.A., 1969-74; fashion designer Sunbow Ltd., Prisma Corp., 1974-81, Frig & Frag Inc., L.A., 1981-83, Jonathan Martin, L.A., 1983-85; textile stylist, v.p. design E.M.D.A.Y., Inc., 1985-92; cons. Theda Meyers Consultancy, 1993—. Part-time tchr. Fashion Inst. of Design & Merchandising, L.A., to 1974; part-time judge Trade Tech. Coll., L.A. to 1981; textile designer extensive nat. and internat. experience in womenswear apparel design and textile design. Designer Calif. apparel. Mem. NAFE. Avocations: fine arts, theater.

MEYERS, WAYNE MARVIN, microbiologist; b. Huntingdon County, Pa., Aug. 28, 1924; s. John William and Carrie Venca (Weaver) M.; m. Esther Louise Kleinschmidt, Aug. 26, 1953; children: Amy, George, Daniel, Sara. BS in Chemistry, Juniata Coll., 1947; diploma, Moody Bible Inst., 1950; MS Med. Microbiology, U. Wis., 1953, PhD Med. Microbiology, 1955; MD, Baylor Coll. Medicine, 1959; DSc (hon.), Juniata Coll., 1986. Instr. Baylor Coll. Medicine, 1955-59; intern Conemaugh Valley Meml. Hosp., Johnstown, Pa., 1959-60; staff physician Berrien Gen. Hosp., Berrien Ctr., Mich., 1960-61; missionary physician Am. Leprosy Missions, Congo/Zaire, Burundi, 1961-73; prof. pathology Sch. Medicine U. Hawaii, Honolulu, 1973-75; chief microbiology divsn. Armed Forces Inst. Pathology, Washington, 1975-89, chief mycobacteriology, 1989—, registrar leprosy registry, 1975—; mem. leprosy panel U.S.-Japan Coop. Med. Sci. Program, 1976-83; mem. sci. adv. bd. Leonard Wood Meml., 1981-85, sci. cons. dir., 1985-87, sci. dir., 1987-90; cons., 1990—; rsch. affiliate Tulane U., 1981—. Corp. bd. dirs. Gorgas Meml. Inst. Tropical and Preventive Medicine, Inc. Bd. dirs. Internat. Jour. Leprosy, 1978-93; contbr. numerous chpts. and articles on tropical medicine to textbooks and jours. Adv. bd. Damien-Dutton Soc. for Leprosy Aid, Inc., 1983-96, corp. bd. dirs., 1996—; adv. bd. Am. Leprosy Missions, Inc., 1979-88, chmn. bd., 1985-88, program cons. to bd., mem. bd. reference, 1988—; mem. Hansen's Disease Rsch. Adv. Com., Gillis W. Long Hansen's Disease Ctr., Carville, La., 1985-92, chmn., 1985-92; mem. Buruli Ulcer Task Force WHO, 1998—. With U.S. Army, 1944-46. Allergy Found. Am. fellow, 1957, 58; WHO rsch. grantee, 1978-87. Mem. Internat. Leprosy Assn. (councillor 1978-88, pres. 1988-93), Internat. Acad. Pathology, Internat. Soc. Tropical Dermatology, Am. Soc. Tropical Medicine and Hygiene, Am. Soc. Microbiology, Binford-Dammin Soc. Infectious Disease Pathologists (sec.-treas. 1988-91, pres. 1995-96), Internat. Soc. Travel Medicine, Sigma Xi. Achievements include researching human and experimental leprosy, and other mycobacterial diseases. Office: Armed Forces Inst Pathology Washington DC 20306-6000 E-mail: wmekmeyers@erols.com.

MEYERSICK, SHARON KAY, nurse, insurance administrator; b. Waynesville, Mo., Mar. 19, 1945; d. James Monroe and Fannie Mae (Williams) Atkinson; m. Bernard William Meyersick Jr., July 27, 1974 (dec. May 1992). ADN, Mercamec C.C., St. Louis, 1970; BSN, Tarkio Coll., Mo., 1983; postgrad., Webster Coll., St. Louis, 1988. From nurse to instr. nursing edn. Normandy Osteo. Hosp., St. Louis, 1970-81; quality assurance nurse Barnes Hosp., 1981-84; review analyst Blue Cross-Blue Shield of Mo., 1985-87, supr. program review, 1987-91; appeals coord. Aetna US Healthcare, 1991—2002; pre-authorization coord. Group Health Plan, 2002—. Office: Group Health Plan 1111 Corporate Office Dr Ste 1100 Saint Louis MO 63045 E-mail: smeyerick@juno.com.

MEYERSON, CHRISTOPHER CORTLANDT, lawyer; b. Princeton, N.J., July 7, 1962; s. Dean and Beatrice Meyerson; m. Megumi Kawaguchi; 1 child, Kenneth. BA in Govt. magna cum laude, cert. in L.Am. studies, MA in History, Harvard U., 1985; MPhil in Polit. Sci., Columbia U., 1993; LLM, Kyoto (Japan) U., 1994; JD, Columbia U., 2001. Bar: D.C. 2001, D.C. 2001. Intern Bur. Inter-Am. Affairs, Office Policy Planning/Coord. U.S. State Dept., Washington, summer 1982; rsch. asst. Harvard U., 1982-83; intern, rschr. macro econ. rsch. dept. Banco Itau, São Paulo, 1983-84; human rights intern Coalition for Homeless, N.Y.C., summer 1988; legal intern gen. counsel Mus. Modern Art, summer 1989; law clk. Office of Chief Counsel for Internat. Commerce U.S. Commerce Dept., Washington, summer 1991; editl. asst. Kyoto Comparative Law Ctr., summer 1994, 95; vis. scholar Associated Kyoto

Program, 1996. Summer assoc. Venable, Baetjer, Howard & Civiletti, Washington, 1998; law clk. Office of Chief Counsel for Import Adminstrn., U.S. Commerce Dept., Washington, 1999-2000. Contbr. articles to bus. jours., Columbia Internat. Affairs Online. Scholar, Japanese Govt., 1991—97. Mem. ABA, Am. Soc. Internat. Law, Soc. Legislation Comparee, Am. Polit. Sci. Assn. (presenter papers ann. meetings), Internat. Studies Assn. (Internat. Polit. Economy Jr. Scholar award 2000, presenter papers ann. meetings). Episcopalian. Home: 7306 Summit Ave Chevy Chase MD 20815-4030

MEYERSON, LAWRENCE BERNARD, physician; b. Columbus, Ohio, Feb. 4, 1941; s. Joseph Randall and Minnie (Lemel) M.; m. Harriet Seldon, June 14, 1964; children: Michael, Jeffery, Daniel. BA, Ohio State U., 1962, MD, 1965. Diplomate Am. Bd. Dermatology. Intern Tripler Gen. Hosp., Honolulu, 1965-66; resident Brooke Gen. Hosp., San Antonio, 1966-69; chief of dermatology Walson Army Hosp., Ft. Dix, N.J., 1969-71; pres. Dermatology Ctr. PA, Irving, Tex., 1971—. Asst. clin. prof. U. Tex. S.W. Med. Sch., Dallas, 1971—. Contbr. articles to profl. jours. Maj. U.S. Army, 1965-71. Fellow Acad. Dermatology, Soc. of Laser Medicine and Surgery, Soc. Dermatol. Surgery; mem. Dallas County Med. Soc., Tex. Dermatologic Soc., Dallas Dermatologic Soc. (past pres.), Alpha Omega Alpha. Avocations: photography, skiing, boating. Office: Dermatology Ctr PA 2015 W Park Dr Irving TX 75061-2113

MEYERSON, MARGY ELLIN, urbanist, civic volunteer; b. Washington, Feb. 25, 1923; d. Arthur and Frieda (Langer) Lazarus; m. Martin Meyerson, Dec. 31, 1945; children: Adam, Laura (dec.), Matthew. BA, U. Chgo., 1943; postgrad., Harvard U., 1947-48, U. Pa., 1953-56; MA, Bryn Mawr Coll., 1953, U. Pa., 1993. Field investigator Bur. Labor Stats., 1944; asst. to gen. counsel Pa. Postwar Planning Commn., 1944-45; assoc. Phila. Housing Assn. and Citizens Council on City Planning, 1945; mgmt. staff Chgo. Housing Authority, 1946. Cons. Ill. Postwar Planning Commn., 1948; assoc. Com. on Nat. Policy, Yale U., 1948-49; lectr. social scis. Drexel U., 1956-57, city and regional planning U. Calif., Berkeley, 1965-66; bd. dirs., exec. com. Phila. Housing Assn., 1952-57; v.p., treas. Community Devel Co., Inc., 1957-63; bd. dirs., exec. com. Niagara Frontier Housing Devel., 1967-70; co-chmn. Cathedral Pk. Devel., Buffalo, 1968-70; commr. Phila. City Planning Commn., 1971-81; bd. dirs. Tensiodyne, Inc., Girard Bank Co-editor: Urban Housing, 1966, Japanese translation 1975; co-editor abstracts sect. Jour. Am. Inst. Planners, 1952-60. Trustee Oakland (Calif.) Mus., 1965-66; trustee Rosenbach Found., Rosenbach Mus. and Library, 1975—, chmn. 1979-92; trustee Presby.-U. Pa. Med. Ctr., 1983-95, exec. com. 1985-95; trustee Lewis Stevens Community Trust, 197785, v.p. 197985; mem. Pa. Humanities Council, 1981-86; adv. council Hampshire Coll., 1981—; bd. dirs. World Affairs Council, Am. Coll. in Paris Found., 1982-87; trustee Presbyn. Found. Phila., 1995-, New Courtland Elder Svcs., 1985-; overseer U. Pa. Libr., 1990-, co-chmn. Friends of the Libr., 1990-. Recipient Susan B. Anthony prize Bryn Mawr Coll., 1953, ann. award for best paper Nat. Hwy Rsch. Bd., 1953; named Disting. Dau. of Pa., 1982; Martin and Margy Meyerson Professorship named in their honor U. Pa., 1995, Martin and Margy Meyerson chair fgn. affairs named in their honor Philippine Women's U., Manila. Mem. Nat. Assn. Housing and Devel. Ofcls., Phila. Art Alliance, Prytanean Soc., Cosmopolitan Club (Phila.). Address: 2016 Spruce St Philadelphia PA 19103-6524

MEYERSON, MARTIN, university educator, urban and regional planner; b. N.Y.C., Nov. 14, 1922; s. Samuel and Etta (Berger) M.; m. Margy Ellin Lazarus, Dec. 31, 1945; children: Adam, Laura (dec.), Matthew. BA, Columbia U., 1942; MCP, Harvard U., 1949; LLD, U. Pa., 1970, Queen's U., Can., 1968, Shiraz U., Iran, 1973, U. Edinburgh, 1976; PhD honoris causa, Hebrew U., 1987; also 18 other hon. doctorates including ScD, LHD, LittD, DFA, DHum, 1967-98. Mem. staff Michael Reese Hosp., Chgo., 1945-47; asst. prof. coll. and grad. social scis. U. Chgo., 1948-52; assoc. prof., dept. chair city and regional planning U. Pa., 1952-56, prof., 1956-57, pres., 1970-81, pres. emeritus, 1981—, chmn. U. Pa. Press, chmn. adv. bd. Inst. Rsch. Higher Edn., Fels Ctr. Govt., 1981—, bd dirs. Lauder Inst. Mgmt. and Internat. Studies, co-chmn. Commn. for U. Pa. 250th Anniversary, 1987-90, Univ. prof., 1977—; exec. dir. action Am. Coun. to Improve Our Neighborhoods, 1955-56, trustee, 1956-66; Frank Backus Williams prof. city planning and urban rsch. Harvard U., 1957-63, acting dean Grad. Sch. Design, 1963; founding dir. Joint Ctr. for Urban Studies, MIT and Harvard U., 1958-63; dean, prof. urban devel. Coll. Environ. Design, U. Calif., Berkeley, 1963-66; interim chancellor U. Calif., 1965; pres., prof. public policy SUNY, Buffalo, 1966-70; prof. Inst. Urban Rsch. U. Pa.; dir. visitor Inst. for Advanced Study, Princeton, N.J., 1983-84; pres. U. Pa., 1986-99. Dir. Real Estate Rsch. Corp., 1961-67, Marine Midland Bank, 1966-70, 1st Fidelity Bancorp. (now First Union), Scott Paper Co., Penn Mut. Life, Saint Gobain Corp., Certain Teed, Norton, Avatar, Universal Health Svcs.; cons. to govts., pvt. firms U.S. and abroad, UN missions, urban/econ. devel. to, Japan, Indonesia and South Asia, Yugoslavia, 1958-65; sr. advisor urban and regional pub. and pvt. devel. Arthur D. Little, Inc., 1958-66; cons. Sears Roebuck Found., 1958-69; chmn. bd. Western N.Y. Nuclear Rsch. Ctr., 1966-70; adv. coun. NASA, 1960-65; White House presdl. task forces, urban policy, 1960-69; mem. coun. Electric Power Rsch. Inst., 1973-77; mem. U.S. del. UN Conf. on Sci. and Tech. for Less Developed Areas, 1963. Author: (with E. C. Banfield) Politics, Planning and the Public Interest, 1955, Housing, People and Cities, 1962, Face of the Metropolis, 1963, Boston, 1966, Gladly Learn and Gladly Teach, 1978; editor: Conscience of the City, 1970, McGraw-Hill Series on Cmty. Devel.; mem. editorial bd. Ency. Britannica, 1980-98, Daedalus, 1972-90. Mem. Air Conservation Commn., 1962-66; mem. Bay Area Conservation and Devel. Commn., 1965-66; chmn. Assembly Univ. Goals and Governance, 1969-74; commr. N.Y. State Commn. on Post-Secondary Sch. Edn., 1976-77; hon. prof. Nat. U. Asuncion, 1969—, Beijing U., 1996—; bd. dirs. Phila. Bicentennial Corp., 1970-76, Greater Phila. Partnership, 1973-81, Afro-Am. Film Found., 1966-70, Niagara U., 1968-70, Center for Community Change, 1968-72, Acad. Religion and Mental Health, 1970-78, Center for Ednl. Devel., 1967-70, Phila. Mus. Art, 1974—, Nat. Urban Coalition, 1969-78; trustee, Niagara U., 1968-70, Am. Coll., 1982-92, Curtis Inst. Music, 1987-94, United World Coll.N. Mex., 1984—, Am. Schs. Oriental Rsch., 1985—, Tel Aviv U., Coll. Bd., 1986-92, Hebrew U., Internat. House Ctr., Monell Chem. Senses Ctr., chmn., 1993—, Fgn. Policy Rsch. Inst., 1981—, Panasonic Found., 1982—, Ctr. for Visual History, U.S. Com. on the Constl. System; founding dir. Internat. Centre for Study East Asian Devel. Japan; Inst. for Internat. Edn., 1971—, chmn., 1981-85; bd. dirs. Internat. Council Ednl. Devel., 1971-94, Am. Council Financial Aid to Edn., 1975-81, Open Univ. Found., U.K., 1979-82; chmn. council pres. Nat. Accelerator Lab., 1972-73; co-chmn. Images (French TV), 1976-79, Salzburg Seminar Bd., 1978—, sr. fellow, 1997—; co-chmn. Marconi Internat. Fellowship Found., chair exec. com., 1978-96, chmn. bd. dirs., 1996—; Internat. gov. Center Environ. Studies, London, 1966-84; mem. sr. exec. council Conf. Bd., 1970-77; trustee Aspen. Inst., 1976-96; chair coun. UN Centre for Regional Devel., Nagoya, Japan, 1983-93; chair internat. selection commn. Phila. Liberty Medal, 1988—; bd. overseers Koc Univ., Bosphorus, Turkey, 1994—; bd. dirs. Internat. Literacy Inst., 1995—. Decorated commendatore Knight-Commdr. (Italy); chevalier de l'Ordre Nat. de Mérite (France); Order of the Rising Sun Emperor of Japan; recipient Einstein medal Am. Technion Soc., 1976, Disting. Achievement award U. Calif. Berkeley, 1984, John Jay award Columbia U., 1982, Disting. Educator award Assn. Collegiate Schs. of Planning, 1996; overseas fellow Churchill Coll. Urban Planning, Cambridge U., 1983; hon. fellow Soc. for Tech. Communication, 1988; Wheelwright fellow Harvard U.; Meyerson Hall named in his honor U. Pa. Grad. Sch. Fine Arts; Martin and Margy Meyerson Professorship named in honor U. Pa., 1995, Philippine Women's U., Manila. Fellow Am. Acad. Arts and Scis., Royal Soc. Arts (Franklin fellow), Buckminster Fuller Inst. of Design Scis. (founder), Am. Philos. Soc. (exec. com.), Nat. Acad. Edn.; mem. Am. Soc. Planning Ofcls. (past dir., aide to exec. dir.), Am. Inst. Planners (past gov., spl. award winner), Internat. Assn. Univs. Paris (Am. dir. 1975— , head 1982-85, hon. pres. 1985—), Coun. Fgn. Rels., European Acad. Arts, Scis. and Letters (academician), Phi Beta Kappa. Clubs: Philadelphia, Century (N.Y.C.), Cosmos (Washington), U. Pa. (N.Y.C.). Office: Univ Pa 225 Van Pelt Library Philadelphia PA 19104

MEYERSON, MARTIN, aerospace engineer; b. East Orange, N.J., Oct. 22, 1927; s. Max and Anna (Slobodin) M.; children: Mark Lawrence, Jann Lesley Sidorov, Jack David. BSEE, N.J. Inst. Tech., 1948, MSEE, 1951. Asst. project engr. Kay Electric Co., Pinebrook, N.J., 1949-50; program mgr. U.S. Army Signal Engring. Labs., Fort Monmouth, 1950-57; with Martin Marietta Corp., 1957-79, dir. programs, 1977-79; dep. program dir. Fairchild Rep. Co., Farmingdale, N.Y., 1979-87; dir. bus. analysis Allied Signal Aerospace Co., Arlington, Va., 1987-88; dir. bus. planning Ford Aerospace Corp., McLean, 1988-90; asst. to pres., dir. bus. devel. Elec. Systems div. Grumman Corp., Great River, N.Y., 1990-94; v.p. bus. devel. electronics and sys. integration divsn. Northrop Grumman, Bethpage, 1994-95; cons. to aerospace industry, 1995—. Mem. faculty, lectr. Dept. Def. Weapon Systems Mgmt. Ctr., Dayton, Ohio, 1967-71; mem. study panel, cons. Congl. Commn. on Govt. Procurement, Washington, 1971-72; mem. seminar team on environ. quality U.S. Dept. Commerce, Prague, Czechoslovokia, 1972; chmn. environ. quality Md. Gov.'s Science Adv. Coun., Annapolis, Md., 1957-77. Author articles, reports in field. Mem. by-laws com. Admiralty Bd. dirs., Bay Shore, N.Y., 1983-85. Fellow AIAA (assoc.), IEEE (sr.). Democrat. Jewish. Avocations: golf, walking, reading. Home: The Promenade Apt 1801S 5225 Pooks Hill Rd Bethesda MD 20814-2052 E-mail: martinmsquared@aol.com.

MEYERSON, MATTHEW, pathologist, educator, researcher; b. Boston, June 4, 1963; s. Martin and Margy Ellin Meyerson; m. Sandra Milu Hoenig, Jan. 2, 1988; children: Sophia, Olivia, Jacob, Phoebe. AB, Harvard U., Cambridge, Mass., 1985; MD, Harvard U., Boston, 1993; PhD, Harvard U., Cambridge, 1994. Diplomate Am. Bd. Pathology. Clin. and rsch. fellow Mass. Gen. Hosp., Boston, 1993-98, cons. in pathology, 2000—; Runyon-Winchell Cancer Rsch. Found. rsch. fellow Whitehead Inst. for Biomed. Rsch., Cambridge, 1995-98; asst. prof. pathology Dana-Farber Cancer Inst., Harvard U. Med. Sch., 1998—, sci. dir. Belfer Ctr. for Cancer Genomics, 1999—. Cons. Novartis AG, Switzerland, 2001—. Contbr. articles on cancer biology to med. jours., including Cell, Nature, Nature Biotech., Nature Genetics, Nature Medicine, Procs. NAS. Scholar in biomed. scis. Pew Found., 1999-2003. Mem. AAAS, Coll. Am. Pathologists, Am. Assn. for Cancer Rsch, Office: Dana-Farber Cancer Inst 44 Binney St Boston MA 02115

MEYERSON, MORTON, communications executive; b. N.Y.C., Jan. 16, 1935; s. Rachel (Lochmond) M.; m. Roberta, Jan. 3, 1959; children: James, William, Jennifer, Alexander. BA, NYU, 1956. Reporter, editor Fairchild News Svc., N.Y.C., 1956-58, AP, N.Y.C., 1958-59; assoc. editor Biddle Survey, 1961-65; editor, writer Eastman Dillon, 1965-66; dir. communications Coopers & Lybrand, 1966-83; nat. dir. comm. Arthur Young, 1983-89; bd. dirs. Ernst & Young. With USAFR, 1952-59. Mem. Overseas Press Club. Office: Ernst & Young 787 7th Ave Fl 14 New York NY 10019-6085 Address: 10240 67th Rd Apt 5F Forest Hills NY 11375-2644

MEYERSON, SEYMOUR, retired chemist; b. Chgo., Dec. 4, 1916; s. Joseph and Rena (Margulies) M.; m. Lotte Strauss, May 22, 1943; children: Sheella, Elana. SB, U. Chgo., 1938, postgrad., 1938-39, 47-48, George Williams Coll., 1939-40; DSc (hon.), Valparaiso Univ., Ind., 1995. Inspector powder & explosives Kankakee Ordnance Works, Joliet, Ill., 1942; chemist Deavitt Labs., Chgo., 1941-42; from chemist to rsch. cons. Standard Oil Co. (Ind.) Rsch. Dept. (now BP Amoco Corp.), Whiting, Ind.-Naperville, Ill., 1946-84. Mem. indsl. adv. coun. chemistry dept. U. Okla., Norman, 1967-69; Frontiers in Chemistry lectr. Wayne State U., 1965; invited spkr. James L. Waters Symposium, Pitts. Conf., Chgo., 1995. Charter mem. editl. adv. bd. Organic Mass Spectrometry, 1968-87, Mass Spectromony Revs., 1980-87; author, co-author 190 sci. publs. 2d lt. AUS, 1943-46, ETO. Mem. Am. Chem. Soc. (Frank H. Field and Joe L. Franklin award for outstanding achievement in mass spectrometry 1993), Am. Soc. for Mass Spectrometry. Achievements include many contributions to systematic chemistry of gas-phase organic ions; 2 patents in field. Home: 43 Vermont Ct Unit A1 Asheville NC 28806-3058 E-mail: meyerson43@hotmail.com.

MEYER-TISCHLER, JÖRG RUDOLF ERICH, pharmaceutical company executive; b. Pfarrkirchen, Bavaria, Germany, Aug. 1, 1944; s. William Peter Heinrich and Maria Anna Erna (Pfaller) M.-T.; m. Sybille Schmidt, July 2, 1982; children: Marian, Tobias, Gregor. Dipl.-Biochem., U. Tuebingen, Germany, 1973, Dr.rer.nat., 1977. Scientist Schering AG/Sci. Secretariate, Berlin, 1978-85; sr. auditor Schering AG/Corp. Auditing, 1986-92; R & D controller, dept. head Schering AG/Internat. Project Mgmt., 1992—2000; Corp. R&D Controlling and Reporting Schering , 2001—. Cons. in field. Capt. German Army/Signal Corps, 1964-66. Mem. Gesellschaft Deutscher Chemiker, Oesterreichischer Alpenverein, Potsdamer Golf Club, Vereinigung Angestellter Akademiker. Roman Catholic. Avocations: golf, skiing, mountain climbing, photography. Home: Heilbronner Str 12 D-10779 Berlin Germany Office: Schering AG D-13342 Berlin Germany E-mail: joerg.meyertischler@schering.de.

MEYER WEISGERBER, MARTHA LINDSEY, account executive; b. Summit, N.J., May 28, 1955; d. William Harold and Hattie Griffin (Ward) Meyer; m. James Curtis Weisgerber, June 22, 1991; 1 child, Emily Griffin. BA, Wake Forest U., 1977. Sales-mfrs. rep. Philip Morris Tobacco Co., Winston-Salem, 1977-82; pharm. sales rep. USV Pharm. Divsn.-Revlon Corp., 1982-84, Upjohn Pharms., N.J., 1984-89; hsop. sales rep., med. sys. mgr., area account mgr. Lederle Labs. divsn. Am. Cyanamid, 1989—. Deacon, elder First Presbyn. Ch., Cranford, N.J., 1995—. Mem. Jr. League Elizabeth Plainfield (bd. mem. 1991-92). Republican. Avocations: swimming, gardening. Home: 313 N Union Ave Cranford NJ 07016-2414 Office: Wyeth Ayerst Pharm PO Box 7447 Philadelphia PA 19101-7447

MEYLER, MARK ZINOVYEVICH, dentist; b. Odessa, Ukraine, June 6, 1948; came to U.S., 1989; s. Zinoviy and Liya (Keselman) M.; m. Anna Zilberman, Feb. 19, 1955; 1 child, Zinovy. D Stomatology, Odessa Med. Inst., 1971; Stomatologist, Surgeon 1st Degree, Ukraian Inst. Doctors, Kharkov, 1984; DDS, NYU, N.Y.C., 1991. Stomatologist, surgeon Stomatology Clinic #7, Odessa, 1971-88; dentist Beach Haven Dental Office, Bklyn., 1992-94, M/M Dental, Bklyn., 1994—. Inventor New Americans collected sci. reports, 1991. Mem. ADA. Office: M/M Dental 50 Shore Blvd Brooklyn NY 11235-4057

MEYLER, WILLIAM ANTHONY, financial executive; b. Newark, Oct. 29, 1944; s. Raymond Francis and Margaret (Loveless) M.; BS, St. Joseph's Coll., 1966; MBA, Fairleigh Dickinson U., 1974; m. Dana Irene Brennan, May 3, 1975; children: Daniel, Diana. CPA, N.J. Sr. acct. Ernst & Young, Trenton, N.J., 1970; dir. acctg. Baker Industries, Inc., Parsippany, N.J., 1971-72; mgr. corp. acctg. Witco Chem. Corp., N.Y.C., 1973-75, asst. to controller, 1976-79, asst. controller world-wide ops., 1977-82, asst. controller mgmt. info. systems, 1982-84; ptnr. Letters, Meyler & Co., CPAs, 1984-91; cons., exec. v.p. Investment Techs., Inc., Edison, N.J., 1985-91, also bd. dirs.; pvt. practice, Middletown, N.J., 1991—; exec. v.p., CFO Gateways to Space, Inc., 1994-96, also bd. dirs.; adj. prof. Monmouth Coll., 1983-85. Fellow N.J. Soc. CPA's; mem. AICPA, Am. Acctg. Assn., Middletown C. of C., Rotary. Home: 30 Southview Ter S Middletown NJ 07748-2415 Office: One Arin Park 1715 Highway 35 Middletown NJ 07748-1867

MEYRICH, STEVEN, arbitrator, mediator; b. Woodmere, N.Y., Oct. 31, 1951; s. Fred and Geraldine (Ehrman) M.; m. Mary Ann Shea, Dec. 24, 1984. BA, U. Rochester, 1973; JD, U. Colo., 1976. Bar: Colo. 1976, U.S. Ct. Appeals (10th cir.) 1976. Dep. dist. atty., Boulder, Colo., 1977-79; assoc. Snyder Neuman Enwall, 1979-80; pvt. practice, 1981-85; assoc. Lamm and Young, 1985-86; ptnr. Lirtzman, Nehls and Meyrich, 1986-89; sr. program mgr. CDR Assocs., 1988-90; pvt. practice, 19990—. Counsel Coloradans for David Staggs, Boulder Cunty, 1987-89. Mem. Boulder County Bar Assn. (trustee 1987-90, chmn. ethics com. 1984-87), Colo. Bar Assn. (bd. govs. 1990-94), Acad. Family Mediators, Am. Arbitration Assn., Soc. Profls. in Dispute Resolution, Nat. Assn. Securities Dealers. Jewish. Avocations: horseback riding, cross-country skiing. Office: 190 Arapahoe Ave Boulder CO 80302-4954

MEYSENBURG, MARY ANN, principal; b. L.A., Sept. 16, 1939; d. Clarence Henry and Mildred Ethel (McGee) Augustine; m. John Harold Meysenburg, June 17, 1967; children: Peter Augustine, Amy Bernadette. BA magna cum laude, U. So. Calif., 1960; MA Pvt. Sch. Adminstrn. magna cum laude, U. San Francisco, 1995. Cert. elem. tchr., Calif. Auditor, escrow officer Union Bank, L.A., 1962-64; v.p., escro mgr. Bank of Downey, Calif., 1964-66; cons., tchr. Santa Ana (Calif.) Coll. Bus., 1964-66; elem. tchr. St. Bruno's Sch., Whittier, Calif., 1966-70, Pasadena (Calif.) Unified Sch. Dist., 1971-84, Holy Angels Sch., Arcadia, Calif., 1985-89; vice prin., computer coord. Our Mother of Good Counsel, L.A., 1989-93; prin. St. Stephen Martyr, Monterey Park, Calif., 1993-2000, Holy Trinity Sch., L.A., 2000—. Eucharistic min. Holy Angels Ch., Arcadia, Calif.; mem. Writing to Read Bd.; tnr. Riordan Found., 1998—; master catechist religious edn. L.A. Archdiocese, 1988—. Author: History of the Arms Control and Disarmament Organization, 1976; organizer, editor newsletter Cath. Com. for Girl Scouts and Campfire. Eucharistic min. Our Mother of Good Counsel, 1989-95; sec. of senatus Legion of Mary, 1980-85; counselor Boy Scouts Am., 1985—; mem. Cath. com. for Girl Scouts U.S.A. and Campfire, vice chmn. acad. affairs L.A. Archdiocese, 1985-90; chair L.A. archdiocese WASC; bd. dirs. Alumni Assn., Immaculate Heart H.S., 1999—. Recipient Pius X medal L.A. Archdiocese, 1979, St. Elizabeth Ann Seton award Cath. Com. for Girl Scouts, 1988, St. Anne medal Cath. Com. for Girl Scouts, 1989, Bronze Pelican award Cath. Com. for Boy Scouts, 1989; grantee Milken Family Found., 1989, 92. Mem.: Phi Kappa Phi, Phi Delta Kappa (historian 1991—92, founds. rep. 1992—93, treas. 1993—94, 1st v.p. 1994—95, pres. 1995—96, advisor 2001—02, Svc. award 1999), Phi Beta Kappa. Avocations: tennis, walking, swimming, reading. Home: 6725 Brentmead Ave Arcadia CA 91007-7708

MEYSTEL, MICHAEL A. Internet executive; b. Moscow, Feb. 12, 1973; came to the U.S., 1978; s. Alexander M. and Marina M. (Selitsky) M.; m. Robin L. Weiss, May 25, 1997; 1 child, Jacob. Student, Drexel U., 1989-94. Sys. and network adminstr. Drexel U., Phila., 1991-94; sr. sys. analyst Bell Atlantic, Malvern, Pa., 1994-95; pres., CEO Cognisphere, Inc., West Chester, 1995—; sr. sys. analyst Decision One Corp., Malvern, 1995-96; cons., application developer Shared Med. Sys., 1996-97, Conectiv Energy, Newark, 1997-98, Anderson BDG, Inc., Allentown, Pa., 1998; cons./tech. lead The Vanguard Group, Valley Forge, 1998—. Sys. cons. ADREM, Inc., Bala, Pa., 1991-94; rsch. asst. Siemens Corp. Rsch., Princeton, N.J., 1992; pres., CEO ICSC Corp., West Chester, 1995-2000. Achievements include inventor/patentee apparatus for text structuring. Office: Cognisphere Inc PO Box 2591 West Chester PA 19380

MEZEY, ANDREW PETER, pediatrician, educator; b. Budapest, Hungary, Apr. 28, 1937; MD, NYU, 1960. Diplomate Am. Bd. Pediat. Intern then resident Bronx Mcpl. Hosp. Ctr., N.Y.C., 1960—64; mem. staff Jacobi Med. Ctr., 1966—98, Montefiore Med. Ctr., NY, 1966—, North Ctrl. Bronx Hosp., 1979—98; prof. Albert Einstein Coll. Medicine, 1994—, assoc. dean grad. medicine edn. and affilate, 1994—; chmn. dept. pediat. Beth Israel Med. Ctr., St. Luke's-Roosevelt Hosp. Ctr., 1998—2000; vice chmn. dept. pediat. Maimonides Med. Ctr., Bklyn., 2001—. Mem. Am. Acad. Pediat. Office: Maimonides Med Ctr Dept Pediatrics 1301 57th St Brooklyn NY 11219 E-mail: amezey@maimonidesmed.org.

MEZEY, JUDITH PAUL, social worker; b. N.Y.C., Nov. 14, 1946; d. Chester Eugene and Shirley (Bagley) Paul; m. Robert Joseph Mezey, Apr. 6, 1968; children: Jennifer Robin, Barry Paul. BS, Boston U., 1968; EdM, Columbia U., 1972; MSW, Barry U., 1980. Lic. social worker; RN. Pediatric staff nurse Albert Einstein Coll., N.Y.C., 1967-69; clin. instr. Morrisania-Montefiore Hosp., 1969-71; grad. student nursing Tchrs. Coll., Columbia U., 1971-72; clin. instr. Pace U., 1972-74, U. Miami, 1976-77, Fla. Internat. U., Miami, 1978-79, Barry U., Miami, 1979-86, social work grad. student, 1987-90; psychotherapist A&A Profl. Assocs., South Miami, 1991-93; pvt. practice Miami, Fla., 1993—. Facilitator support group Bapt. Hosp., Miami, 1991—. Bd. dirs. Dave and Mary Alper Jewish Cmty. Ctr., Miami, 1986—, chmn. spl. needs com., Miami, 1988—; founding chairperson Spl. Needs Program, 1988. Recipient Fed. Nurse Traineeship grant U.S. Govt., 1970. Mem. NASW. Democrat. Jewish. Avocations: tennis player, orchid grower, duplicate bridge. Home: 6740 SW 99th Ter Miami FL 33156-3240 Office: 9260 Sunset Dr Ste 203 Miami FL 33173-3255

MEZEY, ROBERT, poet, educator; b. Phila., Feb. 28, 1935; s. Ralph and Clara (Mandel) M.; m. Olivia Simpson (div.); children: Naomi, Judah, Eve. Student, Kenyon Coll., 1951-53; BA, U. Iowa, 1959; postgrad., Stanford U., 1960-61. Lectr. Western Res. U., Cleve., 1963-64, Franklin & Marshall Coll., Lancaster, Pa., 1965-66; asst. prof. Fresno (Calif.) State U., 1967-68, U. Utah, Salt Lake City, 1973-76; prof., poet-in-residence Pomona Coll., Claremont, Calif., 1976-99; ret., 1999. Author: (poems) The Lovemaker, 1960 (Lamont award), White Blossoms, 1965, The Door Standing Open, 1970, Selected Translations, 1981, Evening Wind, 1988 (Bassine citation, PEN prize 1989), Collected Poems 1952-1999, 2000 (Poets prize 2002); editor Naked Poetry, 1968, Poems from the Hebrew, 1973, Collected Poems of Henri Coulette, 1990, Selected Poems of Thomas Hardy, 1998, The Poetry of E.A. Robinson, 1999; translator: Tungsten (César Vallejo), 1987. With U.S. Army, 1953—55. Fellow Ingram Merrill, 1973, 89, Guggenheim Found., 1977, Stanford U., 1960, NEA, 1987; recipient Poetry prize Am. Acad. Arts and Letters, 1982. Avocations: tennis, chess. Home: 1663 Chattanooga Ct Claremont CA 91711-2917 Office: Pomona Coll Dept English 140 W 6th St Claremont CA 91711-6335 E-mail: rmezey@pomona.edu.

MEZGHEBE, HAILE MICHAEL, surgeon; b. Senafe, Eritrea, Feb. 12, 1948; came to U.S., 1966; MD, U. Colo., 1979. Diplomate Am. Bd. Surgery, Am. Bd. Surg. Critical Care. Intern Howard U. Hosp., Washington, 1979-80, resident in gen. surgery, 1980-84; fellow in trauma and critical care medicine Md. Inst. Emergency Med. Svcs. Sys., Balt., 1985-86; assoc. prof. surgery, assoc. dir. trauma Howard U. Coll. Medicine, Washington, 1986—, surg. dir., 1986-2000. Mem. staff Howard U. Hosp., Washington, Providence Hosp., Washington Adventist Hosp. Mem. ACS, AMA, Eritrean Med. Assn., Nat. Med. Assn., Soc. Critical Care Medicine. Address: 1305 Holly St NW Washington DC 20012-1552 Office: 2041 Georgia Ave NW Washington DC 20060-0001

MEZVINSKY, EDWARD M. lawyer; b. Ames, Iowa, Jan. 17, 1937; m. Marjorie Margolies; 11 children. BA, U. Iowa, 1960; MA in Polit. Sci., U. Calif., Berkeley, 1963, JD, 1965. State rep. Iowa State Legislature, 1969-70; U.S. congressman 1st Dist., Iowa, 1973-77; U.S. rep. UN Commn. on Human Rights, 1977-79; chmn. Pa. Dem. State Com., 1981-86. Author: A Term to Remember; contbr. articles to law jours. Mem. Pa. Bar Assn., Bar of the Supreme Ct. of U.S., Omicron Delta Kappa. Office: 535 Greystone Rd Merion Station PA 19066-1807

MIAH, ABDUL MALEK, electrical engineer, educator; b. Dhaka, Bangladesh, Feb. 14, 1948; came to U.S., 1985; s. Abdur Rahim Miah and Monjuman Begum; m. Meherunnesa Begum, Dec. 11, 1972; children: Tanveer Ahmed, Rudia Begum. BSEE, Bangladesh U. Engring. & Tech., 1969, MSEE, 1981; PhD in Elec. Engring., Wayne State U., 1992. Asst. works mgr. Bangladesh Ordnance Factories, Ghazipur, 1972-76; asst. prof. Bangladesh U. Engring. and Tech., Dhaka, 1976-82; elec. engr. SWS Engring., Inc., Birmingham, Mich., 1989; asst. prof. S.C. State U., Orangeburg, 1990-95, assoc. prof., 1995—. Mem. IEEE. Avocations: reading, watching tv, travel. E-mail: miah@sets.scsu.edu.

MIAN, AHMAD ZIA, economist; b. Panjab, Pakistan, Aug. 8, 1942; came to U.S., 1971; children: Tauneel, Michael. BA with honors, Punjab U., Lahore, Pakistan, 1960; MA, Punjab U., 1962; LLB, Karachi U., Pakistan, 1970; MS, U. W.I., Kingston, Jamaica, 1979; postgrad., U. Pa., 1988; MS in Database Design/System Devel., Oracle Edn., 1999. Cert. Microsoft sys. engr., 1999. Staff economist Pakistan Inst. Devel. Econ., Karachi, 1962-65; investment analyst Esso Ea. Inc. (Exxon), 1965-70; systems specialist Ins. Svc. Office, N.Y.C., 1971-72; sr. indsl. economist Govt. Jamaica, Kingston, 1972-74, energy planner, 1974-78; energy advisor UN, N.Y.C., 1978-80; sr. ops. officer The World Bank, Washington, 1980-99; energy advisor Govt. Jamaica, Kingston, 1990-94; pres. Ibex Bus. Sys., Inc., Mc Lean, Va., 1999-2000; project mgr. telecomm. info. sys. Inter Am. Devel. Bank and World Bank, 1999-2000; ind. cons. info. tech. systems, privatization and regulatory framework for utilities and infrastructure devel., 2000—. Author various energy, infrastructure, telecom. and tech. reports; contbr. articles to profl. jours. Mem. rev. com. task force on energy Trilateral Commn., 1978. Named Ky. col. Commonwealth of Ky., 1989. Mem. Am. Econ. Assn. Office: 9158 Richmond Hwy Fort Belvoir VA 22060 E-mail: mian_zia@hotmail.com., zmian@worldnet.att.net.

MIAN, GUO, electrical engineer; b. Shanghai, Feb. 6, 1957; came to U.S., 1987; s. Wenseng Mian and Guorong Sun; m. Ann Wang, Nov. 1, 1989. BS in Physics, Shanghai U. Sci. & Tech., 1982; MS in Physics, Western Ill. U., 1989;

DSc in Elec. Engring., Washington U., 1992. Mgr. Rec. Media Lab. Magnetic Rec. Ctr., Shanghai (China) Ctrl. Chem. Ltd., 1982-85; vis. scientist materials sci. lab. Keio U., Yokohama, Japan, 1985-87; sr. rsch. elec. engring. Quantum Corp., Milpitas, Calif., 1992-93, Conner Peripherals, San Jose, 1993-95; sr. mgr. HDD R&D Ctr. Samsung Info. Sys. Am., 1995—. Contbr. articles to Jour. Materials Sci., IEEE Trans. Magnetics, Jour. Magnetism & Magnetic Materials, Jour. Applied Physics, Japanese Jour. Applied Physics, Jour. Japanese Magnetic Soc. Recipient C & C Promotion award Found. for C & C Promotion, Tokyo, 1986. Mem. IEEE, IEEE Magnetics Soc., IEEE Computer Soc., Am. Phys. Soc. Achievements include discovery of transverse correlation length in magnetic thin film media, a linear relationship between correlation function of media noise and an off track displacement of a recording head, an algorithm to determine an autocorrelation signal to noise ratio for an arbitrary data sequence in time domain, an algorithm to determine a nonlinear bit shift in high density magnetic storage by a time domain correlation analysis which has been implemented in Lecory 7200 and 9350 digital scopes, an in-situ measurement of exchange coupling of magnetic thin film, mechanism of residual stress forming and releasing in electronic ceramics processing; inventor in field. Home: PMB 18 43494 Ellsworth St Fremont CA 94539-5819

MIAN, LAL SHAH, entomologist, educator; b. Pakistan, Mar. 4, 1945; s. Mohammad Shah M.; m. Judith Anne Conatser, Dec. 26, 1983; children: David Shah and Adam Shah. BSc in Agrl. with honors, U. Peshawar, 1967, MSc in Agrl. with honors, 1972; MS in Agrl., Am. U., Beirut, Lebanon, 1974; PhD in Entomology, U. Calif., Riverside, 1982. Registered Environ. Health Specialist. Tech. asst. forest entomology Forest Rsch. Inst., Peshawar, 1967-68; instr. entomology U. Peshawar, 1969-72, lectr. entomology, 1974-77; vector ecologist San Bernardino (Calif.) County Vector Control Program Pub. Health Dept., 1986-99; adj. lectr. dept. health sci. and human ecology Calif. State U., San Bernardino, 1993, 95, 98, asst. prof., 1999—. Mem. San Bernardino County Africanized Honey Bee Task Force, Africanized Honey Bee Steering Com. Author (with others): Distribution, Transport and Fate of the Insecticides Malathion and Parathion in the Environ. , 1981, Interagency Guidelines for the Surveillance and Control of Selected Vector-borne Pathogens in California, 1995, Inland Empire Environ. Quality Paradigm, 2000; reviewer Environ. Entomology , jour. Econ. Entomology , annals. Entomological Soc. Am., 1980—85, jour. Am. Mosquito Control Assn., 2000, assoc. edt. Bull. Soc. Vector Ecology, 1991—92, editl. bd. Wing Beats, 1992—94, jour. Bull./Soc. Vector Ecology, 1992—; contbr. articles over 70 artricles to profl. jours. Elected mem. U. Senate Lectrs. Constituency, 1976-77, U. Syndicate 23-mem Governing Body, 1976-77; mem. Curriculum Com. Faculty Agrl., 1975-76, Resident Dir. Tchr. Student Ctr., 1975-77, Chancellor's Search Com. for Dean Coll. Natural and Agrl. Scis. U. Calif., 1981, Grad. Student Coun. U. Calif., 1981, Student Mini-Grant Adv. Com. U. Calif. Coop. Ext., 1981-82. Recipient postdoctoral fellow in mosquito rsch. U. Calif., 1982-83, 84-85, 85-86; assistantship in mosquito rsch. U. Calif., 1981-82; Dawood Found. scholar U. Peshawar, 1962-63, Directorate of Edn. scholar, U. Peshawar, 1962-67, Dept. Agrl. scholar U. Peshawar, 1964-67, U.S. Aid scholar Am. U., 1972-74, Ctrl. Overseas scholarship U. Calif., 1977-82; cmty. univ. partnership fellow Calif. State U., 2000, 01, summer rsch. faculty fellow, 2000, mini-grant award fellow, 2000, 01. Mem.: AAAS, Big Bear Valley (coordinated resource mgmt. plan group 1993—94, mem. univ. diversity com. 2000—, cmty.-univ. partnershis forum 2001), Soc. Vector Ecology (local arrangements com. 1993, program com. endl. programs in vector control com. 1993, pubs. com. 1998, 2000—), Entomol. Assn. So. Calif., Nat. Environ. Health Assn., Calif. Environ. Health Assn., Mosquito and Vector Control Assn. Calif. (disease control subcom. vector control com. 1990—93, pubs. com. 1990—94, tng. and cert. 1991—, chem. control com. 1993—97, Africanized honey bee ad hoc com. 1993—99, procs. 1997, 1998—2000), N.Y. Acad. Scis., Entomol. soc. Am., Am. Mosquito Control Assn. (recertification and tng. com. 1992—94, recertification com. 1994—95, pub. rels., edn. com. 1998—), Am. Registry Profl. Entomologists, Internat. N.W. Conf. Diseases in Nature Communicable to Man, Sigma Xi. Democrat. Office: Calif State Univ Dept Health Sci/Human Ecol San Bernardino CA 92407-2397 E-mail: lmian@csusb.edu.

MIANO, LOUIS STEPHEN, arts advisor; b. N.Y.C., July 28, 1934; s. Louis Clyde and Zefira (Palombo) M. BA, Dartmouth Coll., 1955; MA, Columbia U., 1958. Writer Look Mag., N.Y.C., 1960-61; editor Show Mag., N.Y.C. and L.A., 1961-63; assoc. producer ABC-TV, 1963-66; vice-chmn., dir. creative services AC&R Advt., N.Y.C., 1966-90. Sec. EEE Theatrical Ventures, N.Y.C., 1974—; cons. in field. Co-producer plays: Design for Living, Corpse, The Seagull, Legends, Inner Voices, 1974-86 Trustee Marymount Manhattan Coll., N.Y.C., 1980—; cons. Home Box Office, 1991-92; bd. dirs. The Nat. Bd. of Rev. of Motion Pictures, 1995—; bd. dirs., sec. Circle-in-the Square; mem. gen. dirs. coun. N.Y.C. Opera, 1998, 99, 2000, 01; mem. adv. com. Henry St. Chamber Opera. Mem. Century Assn. Home and Office: 430 E 57th St New York NY 10022-3061

MIAO, JIE, mathematics educator; PhD in math., Mich. State U., 1992—98. Asst. prof. math. Ark. State U., Jonesboro, Ark., 1998—2002. Contbr. articles to profl. jour. Home: PO Box 472 State University AR 72467 Office: Ark State U PO Box 70 State University AR 72467

MIAO, RONGSHENG, mechanical and thermal engineer; b. Chengdu, China, June 16, 1952; s. Yuqin Miao and Qiaolian Zhang; m. Rong Wang, Aug. 13, 1983; 1 child, Qing Miao. M of Engring., Chengdu U. Sci. and Tech., 1985; D of Engring., Tianjin U., 1990; PhD in Mech. Engring., U. Ill., Chgo., 1997. Lectr. Chengdu U. Sci. and Tech., China, 1982-87, sr. lectr. China, 1990-92; vis. asst. prof. La. State U., Baton Rouge, 1992-93; rsch. engr. U. Ill., Chgo., 1993-97; mech. and thermal engr. IntraAction Corp., Bellwood, 1997—2001; sr. mech. engr. Agere Systems, Irwindale, Calif., 2001—. Cons. Air-Liquide Inc., Countryside, Ill., 1998, U. Ill. at Chgo., 1998—. Contbr. articles to profl. jours. Mem. ASME, AIChE, ASHRAE, N.Y. Acad. Sci. Office: Agere Sys 4920 Rivergrade Rd Irwindale CA 91706 E-mail: rmiaol@hotmail.com.

MIAO, WEIWEN, mathematician, educator; b. Changsha, Hunan, China, Feb. 6, 1967; m. Xi Qin, May 24, 1990; children: Michelle Qin. BS, Beijing Univ., Beijing, China, 1988; PhD, Tufts Univ., Medford, MA, 1995. Asst. prof. Mt. Holyoke Coll., South Hadley, Mass., Colby Coll., 1997—99; statistician Computer Task Group, 1999—2000; asst. prof. Macalester Coll., 2000—02. Contbr. scientific papers to journals. Mem.: Am. Stats. Assn. Office: Macalester College 1600 Grand Ave Saint Paul MN 55105

MIAOULIS, IOANNIS NIKOLAOS, mechanical engineer, educator; b. Athens, Greece, July 24, 1961; came to U.S., 1980; s. Nikolaos Ioannis and Titika Photini (Kokkinopoulou) M.; m. Beth Karen, Sept. 23, 1984; children: Marina, Katrina. BSME, Tufts U., 1983, MA in Econs., 1986, PhD, 1987; SMME, MIT, 1984. Asst. prof. mech. engring. Tufts U., Medford, Mass., 1987-93, assoc. prof., 1993-97, prof., 1997—, assoc. dean engring., 1993-94, dean Sch. Engring., 1994—, interim dean Sch. of Arts and Scis, 2001—. Cons. in field. Contbr. over 95 articles to sci. jours. Elected mem. Mass. Tech./Engring. Edn. Adv. Bd., 1999—, chair 2000—; elected mem. Mass. Math. & Sci. Edn. Bd., 1995-99, Tufts Alumni Coun., Medford, 1994—; elected coun. mem. Pompositticut Sch., Stow, Mass., 1993-98. Recipient Presdl. Young Investigator award NSF, 1991, Inventor's Assn. award, New. Eng., 1990, William P. Desmond award Citizen's Edn. Resource Ctr., Mass., 1996, Cmty. & Leadership award Toastmasters Internat., Mass., 1995, Jaycees Outstanding Young Leader award, 1999. Mem. ASME, AAAS, Am. Soc. Engring. Edn., Materials Rsch. Soc. Achievements include 2 U.S. patents; research in area of heat transfer in materials processing, microscale heat transfer, comparative biomechanics. Office: Tufts U Coll Engring Anderson Hall Medford MA 02155

MIARROSTAMI, RAMEEN M. internist; b. Chalus, Mazandaran, Iran, Dec. 31, 1959; came to U.S., 1978; Married July 1, 1985; children: Nicole, Nadia. BS in Biochemistry, Okla. State U., 1982; MD, Univ. Muncial Dominicana, 1985. Diplomate Am. Bd. Internal Medicine, Am. Bd. Pulmonary Diseases. Attending internist N.Y. Meth. Hosp., Bklyn., 1993—, Maimonides Med. Ctr., Bklyn., 1996—, Victory Meml. Hosp., Bklyn., 1993—. Fellow ACP, Am. Coll. Chest Physicians; mem. AMA, Am. Thoracic Soc., Soc. Critical Care Medicine. also: 263 7th Ave Ste 5H Brooklyn NY 11215-3690 Office: 7124 18th Ave Brooklyn NY 11204-5203

MICA, JOHN L. congressman; b. Binghamton, N.Y., Jan. 27, 1943; s. John and Adeline Resciniti M.; m. Patricia Szymanek, 1972; children: D'anne, Clark. AA, Miami-Dade C.C., 1965; BA, U. Fla., 1967. Chief of staff U.S. Senate, Washington; mem. Fla. Ho. of Reps., 1976-80, mem. appropriations com., mem. ethics com., mem. elections com., mem. cmty. affairs com.; mem. U.S. Ho. of Reps. from 7th Fla. Dist., Washington, 1993—. Mem. transp. and infrastructure com., govt. reform and oversight com., chmn. subcom. on aviation, 1993—. Author: Factor affecting local government reorganization efforts in Florida, Urban and Environmental Issues. Active Beth Johnson Mental Health Bd., PTA Bd., Zora Neale Hurston Meml. Com. Recipient Outstanding Svc. award Fla. Conservative Union, Outstanding Svc. award Fla. Cancer Soc., Outstanding Svc. award Sertoma, Outstanding Young Men of Am. award; named one of five outstanding Young Men in Fla. Mem. Kiwanis, Winter Park Jaycees (Good Govt. award 1972), Fla. Jaycees Statewide (Good Govt. award 1973), Tiger Bay. Republican. Episcopal. Office: PO Box 756 Winter Park FL 32790-0756 also: US House of Reps 2445 Rayburn Bldg Washington DC 20515-0005 E-mail: john.mica@mail.house.gov.

MICALE, FRANK JUDE, lawyer; b. Pitts., Jan. 10, 1949; s. Frank Jacob and Catherine Anna (Wagner) M.; m. Jane Sincler Czak. BA, Duquesne U., 1971, JD, 1977. Bar: Pa. 1977, U.S. Dist. Ct. (we. dist.) Pa. 1977, U.S. Ct. Appeals (3rd cir.) 1978. U.S. Supreme Ct. 1986; cert. Nat. Bd. Trial Advocacy. Law clk. to judge U.S. Ct. Appeals (3rd cir.), 1977-78, U.S. Dist. Ct. (we. dist.) Pa., 1978-79; assoc. Egler & Reinstadtler, Pitts., 1979-80; dep. atty. gen., sr. dep. atty. gen. in charge torts litigation sect. western region Office of Atty. Gen. Commonwealth of Pa., 1980-92; pvt. practice, 1992—. Mem. ABA, Am. Arbitration Assn., Pa. Bar Assn., Allegheny County Bar Assn., Acad. Trial Lawyers Allegheny County. Home: 5521 Claybourne St Pittsburgh PA 15232-1634 Office: 11269 Perry Hwy Ste 400 Wexford PA 15090 E-mail: frankmac@msn.com.

MICALE, JOSEPH NICHOLAS, internist; b. Atlantic City, May 23, 1936; s. Filippo and Antonina (Emanuele) M.; m. Edith W. Tortora, June 10, 1962; children: Jo Anne Micale Foody, Philip Louis. BS, Rutgers U., 1957; MD, George Washington U., 1962. Diplomate Nat. Bd. Med. Examiners, Am. Bd. Internal Medicine; cert. med., N.Y., N.J., Fla., cert. pharmacy, N.Y., N.J. Pharm. intern, 1957-58; med. intern Montefiore Hosp. and Med. Ctr., Bronx, 1962-63, resident in internal medicine, 1963-64, 66-67; resident in gastroenterology VA Hosp., 1967-68, attending in gastroenterology, 1968-73; jr. asst. attending in medicine Christ Hosp., Jersey City, 1968-72, sr. asst. attending in medicine, 1972-80, chief gastroenterology divsn., 1975-2000, assoc. attending in internal medicine, 1980-82, attending in medicine, 1982—. Treas. med. staff Christ Hosp., Jersey City, 1974-75, sec. med. staff, 1976-77, v.p. med. staff, 1978-79, pres. med. staff, 1980-81, sec. med. exec. com., 1980, chmn. med. exec. com., 1986-87, bd. govs., 1979—, dir. dept. medicine, 1982-90, asst. v.p. med. affairs, 1995-98; asst. vis. in medicine St. Mary's Hosp., Hoboken, N.J., 1968-79, cons. privileges in gastrointestinal disease, 1968-79, assoc. attending with full cons. privileges dept. medicine, 1969-79; asst., attending in medicine Palisade Gen. Hosp. (formerly North Hudson Hosp.), North Bergen, N.J., 1979, chief gastroenterology, 1979-2000; chief gastroenterology Riverside Gen. Hosp., Secaucus, N.J., 1976-83; Med. Soc. N.J. del. U.S. Pharmacopeial Conv., 1988—. Capt. U.S. Army, 1964-66. Recipient Ernest Little award, N.J. Pharm. Assn. award. Fellow Am. Coll. Gastroenterology, Acad. Medicine N.J. (bd. trustees 1988—); mem. AMA (Physicians' Recognition award), ACP (coun. N.J. chpt. 1981-85), Am. Heart Assn. (bd. dirs. Hudson County divsn., N.J. affiliate 1973-74), Am. Soc. Internal Medicine, N.J. Gastroenterology Soc., N.J. Soc. Internal Medicine (bd. trustees 1988—), Med. Soc. N.J. (treas. 1987-89, chmn. coun. pub. rels. 1988-90, 2d v.p. 1990-91, 1st v.p. 1991-92, pres.-elect 1992-93, pres. 1993-94), Hudson County Med. Soc. (treas. 1979-80, sec. 1980-81, pres.-elect 1981-82, pres. 1982-83. bd. trustees 1983—), Hudson County Stds. Rev. Orgn., Rho Chi, Alpha Omega Alpha, Smith-Reed-Russell Med. Honor Soc. Home: 7855 Boulevard E Apt 7C North Bergen NJ 07047-5928

MICARELLI, ANGEL, advertising executive; m. Joseph Micarelli; children: Ray, Noelle. BA, Regis Coll.; grad. in Spl. Studies, Harvard U. Copy dir. Acom Healthcare, Hingham, Mass., 1997—.

MICEK, ISABELLE, music educator; b. Shelby, Nebr., July 28, 1922; d. Thomas Adolph and Julia Lucy (Triba) M. MusB in Piano Performance, St. Louis Inst. Music, 1943; postgrad., Peabody Conservatory, 1971; MusM in Piano Pedagogy, St. Louis Inst. Music, 1972. Instrumental/vocal tchr. various elem. and secondary schs., Hull, Ill., 1943-45, Oakland, Iowa, 1945-46; pvt. piano/vocal/theory instr. Columbus, Nebr., 1946—. Participated internat. workshops, Honolulu, 1980, Calgary, 1990, Graz, Austria, 2000. Pres. N.E. Dist. Nebr. Music Tchrs. Assn., 1949-56, Cmty. Concert Assn., Columbus, 1965-67; advisor Birthright Columbus, 1992—. Recipient Medallion of Merit award Art Publ. Soc., St. Louis, 1957; scholar U. Mexico, Mexico City, 1950, Royal Conservatory, London, 1952, Staatlichen Hochschule, Munich, 1963, St. Cecilia Conservatory, Rome, 1966, Manuel de Falla Conservatore, Buenos Aires, 1974. Mem. Music Tchrs. Nat. Assn., Nebr. Music Tchrs. Assn., Nat. Guild (adjudicator 1993-98). Democrat. Roman Catholic. Avocations: gardening, reading, concerts, speaker for modern problems high school classes. Home: 2115 18th St Columbus NE 68601-4531

MICELI, MOTHER IGNATIUS, retired nun, missionary; b. N.Y.C., Mar. 14, 1918; d. Joseph and Cecelia (Torre) M. BS, Regis Coll.; MEd, Loyola U., New Orleans; M Religious Edn., Seattle U.; postgrad., U. Denver, 1968-69. Cert. abrini Missionary Sisters 1942. Various housemother/missionary assignments Orphanage, West Park, N.Y., 1942-44; tchr. St. Donato's Sch., Phila., 1944-48, local sch., Scranton, Pa., 1948-52, Cabrini H.S., N.Y.C., 1952-54; prin. sch./orphanage, Denver, 1954-65; coordinator religious programs All Souls Ch., Englewood, Colo., 1968-71, dir. home instr. for adults, 1971-72, dir. adult edn., 1972—. Dir. religious edn. Assumption, Welby, Colo., 1973-77, Holy Cross, Thornton, Colo., 1971-73; instr. religion various missions, 1968—. Author: (poems) Leaves Of Thought, 1978, Random Thoughts and Meditations, 1975, Colorado and St. Francis Xavier Cabrini, M.S.C., 1980, (poetry and photography book) Life's Seasons, 1989, Short History of Cabrini Shrine, 1992, Cabrini Colorado Missions, 1996, Welcome to My World, 1996, Reprieve, Poetry and Prayer; (VCRs) Welcome to Colorado, 1971, The Life of St. Frances Xavier Cabrini, 1986, The History and Meditations on the Rosary, 1990, Reprise-A Compilation of Poetry, 2002. Mem. Internat. Bibl. Assn., Religious Edn. Assn. U.S., Religious Edn. Assn. Can., Nat. League Am. Pen Women, Kappa Delta Pi. Avocations: photography, camping, hiking, fishing, jeeping. Office: All Souls Ch Religious Edn Office 435 Pennwood Cir Englewood CO 80110-6921 Home: Apt 312 2850 Columbine Rd Denver CO 80221-7600

MICHA, DAVID ALLAN, chemistry and physics educator; b. Argentina, Sept. 12, 1939; came to U.S., 1966, naturalized, 1974; s. Simon David and Catalina (Cohen) M.; m. Rebecca Stefan, 1991; children: Michael F., Anna K. MS, U. Cuyo, Bariloche, Argentina, 1962; DSc, U. Uppsala, Sweden, 1966. Rsch. assoc. Theoretical Chemistry Inst. U. Wis., Madison, 1966-67; asst. rsch. physicist Inst. Pure and Applied Sci. U. Calif., La Jolla, 1967-69; assoc. prof. chemistry and physics U. Fla., Gainesville, 1969-74, prof., 1974—, dir. Ctr. Chem. Physics, 1982-91, head phys. chem. divsn., 1999—. Vis. prof. U. Gothenburg, Sweden, 1970, Harvard U., 1972, 90, 98, 2000, 01, Max-Planck Inst., Göttingen, Germany, 1976, 96, Imperial Coll., London, 1977, U. Calif., Santa Barbara, 1982, U. Colo. and Weizmann Inst., Israel, 1983, U. Buenos Aires, 1988, 95, Supercomputer Inst., Fla. State U., 1991; mem. adv. panel div. advanced sci. computing NSF, 1990-92, Max-Planck Inst. Astrophysik, Munich, Germany, 1996, 97. Mem. editl. bd. Internat. Jour. Quantum Chemistry, 1979-88, Few-Body Systems, 1985—; editor Finite Systems and Multiparticle Dynamics, 1990—, symposium procs.; contbr. several book chpts., numerous articles to sci. jours. Recipient U.S. Sr. Scientist award A. Von Humboldt Found., 1976, Sr. Faculty Rsch. award Sigma Xi, 1985; Alfred P. Sloan Found. fellow, 1971-74; Nat. Bur. Standards JILA fellow, 1983. Fellow Am. Phys. Soc. (vice chmn. topical group on few body sys. and multi-particle dynamics 1986-88, chmn. 1988-89); mem. Am. Chem. Soc., Sigma Xi. Office: U Fla 2318 New Physics Bldg Gainesville FL 32611-8435

MICHAEL, ALFRED FREDERICK, JR. physician, medical educator; b. Phila. s. Alfred Frederick and Emma Maude (Peters) M.; m. Jeanne Jones; children: Mary, Susan, Carol. MD, Temple U., 1953. Diplomate: Am. Bd. Pediatrics (founding mem. sub-bd. pediatric nephrology, pres. 1977-80). Diagnostic lab. immunology and pediatric nephrology intern Phila. Gen. Hosp., 1953-54; resident Children's Hosp. and U. Cin. Coll. Medicine, 1957-60; postdoctoral fellow dept. pediatrics Med. Sch., U. Minn., Mpls., 1960-63, assoc. prof., 1965-68, prof. pediatrics, lab. medicine and pathology, 1968-88, dir. pediatric nephrology, 1997, Regents' Prof., 1986—, head Dept. Pediatrics, 1986-97, interim dean, 1996-97, dean, 1997—. Established investigator Am. Heart Assn., 1963-68. Past mem. editl. bd. Internat. Yr. Book of Nephrology, Am. Jour. Nephrology, Kidney Internat., Clin. Nephrology, Am. Jour. Pathology; contbr. articles to profl. jours. Served with USAF, 1955-57. Recipient Alumni Achievement award in clin. scis. Temple U. Sch. Medicine, 1988; NIH fellow, 1960-63; Guggenheim fellow, 1966-67; AAAS fellow, 1995. Mem. AAAS, AMA, Am. Soc. Clin. Investigation, Assn. Am. Physicians, Am. Pediat. Soc., Soc. for Pediat. Rsch., Am. Assn. Investigative Pathology, Am. Soc. Cell Biology, Ctrl. Soc. for Clin. Rsch., Am. Soc. Nephrology (coun., pres.-elect 1992—, pres. 1993), Internat. Soc. Nephrology, Soc. for Exptl. Biology and Medicine, Am. Fedn. Clin. Rsch., Minn. Med. Assn. Home: 1986 Lower Saint Dennis Rd Saint Paul MN 55116-2820*

MICHAEL, ANN DOZIER MARINO, real estate broker; b. Durham, N.C., Apr. 22, 1944; d. Walter Joseph and Ellen G. (Cheek) Dozier; m. John Harrison Marino, Oct. 15, 1966 (div. Jan. 1981); children: John Harrison Jr., Ann Southerlyn; m. G. Revell Michael, July 4, 1998. BA, Salem Coll., 1966. Sales assoc. Rector Assocs. Realtors, Alexandria, Va., 1984-96, Pardoe and Graham, Alexandria, 1997—2002; assoc. broker McEnearney Assocs. Realtors, 2002—. Vol. Jr. League, Chgo., 1970-74; bd. dirs. Jr. League, Washington, 1979-95, Vol. Clearing House, Washington, Project Open Rd., Chgo., Fire and Burn Inst., Washington; mem. parents coun. Burgundy Farm Sch., 1983; mem. parish coun. St. Mary's, Alexandria, 1977-80. Recipient Rookie of Yr. award No. Va. Bd. Realtors, 1985, Lifetime Top Prodr. Club, Lifetime Million Dollar Club, No. Va. Bd. Realtors, 1985-2002. Mem.: Fairfax Hunt Club, Salem Coll. Alumnae Club (pres. Chgo. chpt. 1970—73). Republican. Roman Catholic. Office: McEnearney Assocs 109 S Pitt St Alexandria VA 22314

MICHAEL, CECIL FRANCIS, JR. pediatrician; b. Albuquerque, June 3, 1950; s. Cecil F. and Gene (Clairmont) M.; m. Karen Sara Dworkin, June 28, 1975; children: Kristen, Jonathan. BA in Chemistry, U. N.M., 1972, MD, 1976. Resident in pediats. Phoenix Affiliated Pediat. Program, 1976-79; pvt. practice Cactus Children's Clinic, Glendale, Ariz., 1979—. Chmn. pediat. dept. Thunderbird Samaritan Hosp., Glendale, 1981-83; mem. grievance com. Maricopa County Med. Soc., Phoenix, 1987. Contbr. article to profl. jour. Recipient Top Doctor Nurse's List award, Phoenix Mag. Poll, 1997, Top Doctor Doctor's Poll, 1998. Fellow Am. Acad. Pediats.; mem. AMA, Ariz. Med. Assn., Maricopa County Med. Soc. Democrat. Roman Catholic. Avocations: golf, exercise, gardening, mountain biking. Office: Cactus Childrens Clinic 5310 W Thunderbird Rd Ste 300 Glendale AZ 85306-4710

MICHAEL, CHARLES JOSEPH, lawyer; b. Natchitoches, La., July 31, 1939; s. Faris Edgar and Mamie (Solomon) M.; m. Margo Farrer, Aug. 25, 1965; children: Charles J. II, Jonathan Laird. BA, Northwestern State U., 1961; JD, U. Houston, 1965. Bar: (Tex.) 1965; cert. family law Tex. Bd. Legal Specialization. Pvt. practice, Houston. Office: 16874 Royal Crest Dr Houston TX 77058-2529 E-mail: cmlaw@wt.net.

MICHAEL, CREIGHTON, artist, educator; b. Knoxville, Tenn., Jan. 12, 1949; s. James Eugene and Genetha Draughon (Duffey) M.; m. Leslie Cecil, Sept. 10, 1989; 1 child, Balin Cecil. BFA with honors, U. Tenn., Knoxville, 1971; MA in Art History, Vanderbilt U., 1976; MFA in Painting/Multi-Media, Washington U., St. Louis, 1978. Vis. prof. painting SUNY, Buffalo, 1985; vis. artist U. Alaska, Anchorage, 1986, Washington U., St. Louis, 1987, SUNY, Purchase, 1988, Muhlenberg Coll., Allentown, Pa., 1986, 91, Va. Commonwealth U., 1991, 99, Haverford (Pa.) Coll., 1993, Princeton U., 1998, 2000, 2001, Purchase Coll, SUNY, 2001, others; adj. faculty R.I. Sch. Design, Providence, 1986-98; critic Pa. Acad. Fine Arts, Phila., 1995-96. Solo exhbns. include David Beitzel Gallery, N.Y.C., 1988, Haines Gallery, San Francisco, 1990, Pence Gallery, Santa Monica, Calif., 1988, 90, Ruth Siegel Gallery, N.Y.C., 1991, San Antonio Art Inst., 1992, High Mus. Art, Atlanta, 1987, Katonah Mus. Art, N.Y., 1994, Vanderbilt U., Nashville, 1996, Kim Foster Gallery, N.Y.C., 1996, 97, 99, Robischon Gallery, Denver, 1990, 92, 94, 97, 99, Birke Art Gallery, Marshall U., Huntington, W.Va., 1998, Queens Mus. Art Bulova Corp. Ctr., 1998, Galerie Trois Points, Montreal, Que., 1999, Reynolds Gallery, Richmond, Va., 1999, Elmhurst (Ill.) Art Mus., 2000, Neuberger Mus., 2001, Freedman Gallery, Albright Coll., Reading, Pa., 2001; exhibited in group shows at Muhlenberg Coll., Allentown, Pa., Rosa Esman Gallery, N.Y.C., N.J. Ctr. for Visual Arts, Summit, L.I. U., Bklyn., Mandeville Gallery/U. Calif., San Diego, Morris Mus., Morristown, N.J., Denver Art Mus., Weatherspoon Art Gallery/U. N.C., Greensboro, Ark. Arts Ctr., Little Rock, Hopper House Art Ctr., Nyack, N.Y., Kiang Gallery, Atlanta, Albright-Knox Art Gallery, Buffalo, N.J., Neuberger Mus. Art, Purchase, N.Y., Robert Kidd Gallery, Birmingham, Mich., Islip Art Mus., West Islip, N.Y., others; represented in collections at Bklyn. Mus., Denver Art Mus., High Mus. Art, NYU, Pfizer, Inc., Progressive Corp., Vanderbilt U., R.I.S.D. Mus. Art, Am. Express Neuberger Mus. Art., Weatherspoon Art Gallery, Nat. Gallery Art, Washington, others; subject of numerous articles. Edward Albee Found. fellow, 1985; Pollock-Kranser Found. grantee, 1985; N.Y. Found. for Arts fellow, 1987; Golden Found. grantee, 2000. Home: 41 Deer Knl Mount Kisco NY 10549-4706 E-mail: lc19cm@aol.com.

MICHAEL, DIANN DEE, psychologist, educator; b. Charleston, W.Va., July 19, 1947; d. Esber John Michael and Asma Deebie Radwan; 1 child, Gianna Christiane. BA, W.Va. State Coll., 1969; PhD, U. Akron, 1978; DEA, U. Paris The Sorbonne, 1984. Lic. psychologist, Fla. Psychologist, dir. Ea. Mahoning County Mental Health Ctr., Youngstown, Ohio, 1971-77; psychologist Youngstown Psychol. Assocs., 1977-81, Fla. Mental Health Inst., Tampa, 1981-83; mem. faculty European divsn. U. Md., Heidelberg, Brussels, Turkey, 1984-91; psychologist in pvt. practice Paris, 1984-91; psychologist, clin. dir. Fla. Biodyne, Ft. Lauderdale, 1991-94; mem. faculty Nova Southeastern U., 1994—; psychologist Child and Family Psychologists, 1996—. Co-chmn. adv. bd. Tropical Elem. Sch., Plantation, 1997—98; mem. success team Seminole Mid. Sch., Plantation, 2000—01. Active St. Philip Orthodox Ch. Mem.: APA (assoc. divsn. humanistic psychology, divsn. ind. practice), Broward Psychol. Assn. (newsletter editor 2000—02, pres. 2001), Fla. Psychol. Assn. (exec. coun., child, adolescent and family divsn., Outstanding Psychologist child, adolescent and family divsn. 2002), Soc. St. Ignatius, Kfeirian Reunion Found. (newsletter editor 1995—2001, pres. bd. dirs. 1999—2001, Reunion scholar 1964—65). Avocations: painting, writing, photography, travel. Office: Child and Family Psychologists 7520 NW 5th St Plantation FL 33317

MICHAEL, DOROTHY ANN, nursing administrator, naval officer; b. Lancaster, Pa., Sept. 20, 1950; d. Richard Linus and Mary Ruth (Hahn) M.; m. Juan Roberto Morales, July 15, 1995. Diploma, RN, Montgomery Hosp. Sch. Nursing, Norristown, Pa., 1971; BSN, George Mason U., 1980; MSN, U. Tex. Health Sci. Ctr., 1985. Commd. ensign USN, 1970, advanced through grades to capt. Nurse Corps, 1994, staff nurse Nat. Naval Med. Ctr. Md., 1971-73, charge nurse Naval Hosp. Guantanamo Bay, Cuba, 1973-74, charge nurse Naval Regional Med. Ctr. Phila., 1974-76, charge nurse Naval Hosp. Keflavik, Iceland, 1977, Bethesda, Md., 1980-84; sr. nurse, asst. officer-in-charge Br. Med. Clinic Naval Weapons Ctr., China Lake, Calif., 1986-89; coord. quality assurance Naval Hosp., Oakland, 1989-92, assoc. dir. inpatient nursing, 1992-93; divsn. officer USNS Mercy, Persian Gulf, 1990-91; assoc. dir. surg. nursing Naval Hosp., Oakland, 1993-95, dir. nursing svc. Great Lakes, Ill., 1995-98; dep. comdr. Naval Ambulatory Care Ctr., Newport, R.I., 1998-2001; ret. Splty. advisor to dir. Navy Nurse Corp., Navy Med. Command, Washington, 1983-84. V.p. Deepwood Homeowners Assn., Reston, Va., 1978-82; advisor, com. mem. Reston Found., 1979. Decorated Navy Commendation medal, Meritorious Svc. medal, Legion of Merit; recipient R.W. Bjorklund Mgmt. Innovator award, Kern County, Calif., 1988, Comdr.'s award for outstanding professionalism in pub. health support, 1988. Mem. ANA (cert. nursing adminstrn.), VFW, Vietnam Vets. Am., Orgn. Nurse Execs., Am. Legion, Sigma Theta Tau. Roman Catholic. Home: 3324 Susquehanna Rd Dresher PA 19025 E-mail: dotjuan@aol.com.

MICHAEL, DOUGLAS CHARLES, law educator; b. Omaha, Dec. 8, 1957; s. B.B. and Arleen M. (Heinz) M.; m. Susan Lindsey, Jan. 11, 1986; children: Stuart Douglas, Amanda Lindsey. AB, Stanford U., 1979; MBA, U. Calif., Berkeley, 1982, JD, 1983. Bar: Calif. 1984, D.C. 1988. Staff atty. SEC, Washington, 1983-85, commr.'s counsel, 1985-87; assoc. Arnold and Porter, 1987-89; asst. prof. U. Ky. Coll. Law, Lexington, 1989-93, assoc. prof., 1993-97, prof., 1997—. Vis. prof. law U. Fla., 2000. Contbr. articles to legal jours.; author: Legal Accounting: Principles and Applications, 1997. Mem. ABA, Order of Coif. Office: U Ky Coll Law Lexington KY 40506-0048 Home: 1224 Sebring Ln Lexington KY 40513 E-mail: michaeld@uky.edu.

MICHAEL, DOUGLAS JOHN, playwright, cartoonist; b. Columbus, Ohio, Oct. 14, 1956; s. George Richard Michael; children: Billie Rae. B.Cinema, Ohio State U., 1982. Author: (play) The Original Last Wish Baby, 1995 (Best Short Am. Play of 1995/96, 1996). Home: PO Box 986 New York NY 10024 Personal E-mail: fishbein@juno.com.

MICHAEL, ERNEST ARTHUR, mathematics educator; b. Zurich, Switzerland, Aug. 26, 1925; came to U.S., 1939; s. Jakob and Erna (Sondheimer) M.; m. Colette Verger Davis, 1956 (div. 1966); children: Alan, David, Gerard; m. Erika Goodman Joseph, Dec. 4, 1966; children: Hillary, Joshua. BA, Cornell U., 1947; MA, Harvard U., 1948; PhD, U. Chgo., 1951. Mem. faculty dept. math. U. Wash., Seattle, 1953—, asst. prof., 1953-56, assoc. prof., 1956-60, prof., 1960-93, prof. emeritus, 1993—. Mem. Inst. for Advanced Study, Princeton, 1951-52, 56-57, 60-61, 68, Math. Research Inst., E.T.H., Zürich, 1973-74; vis. prof. U. Stuttgart, Ger., 1978-79, U. Munich, Fed. Republic Germany, 1987, 88, 92-93. Editor: Procs. Am. Math. Soc., 1968-71, Topology and Its Applications, 1972-94, Set-Valued Analysis, 1993—; contbr. articles to profl. jours. Served with USNR, 1944-46. Grantee AEC; Grantee Office Nav. Research; Grantee NSF; Grantee Guggenheim Found.; Grantee Humboldt Found. Mem. Am. Math. Soc., Math. Assn. Am., ACLU, Amnesty Internat. Jewish. Home: 22200 Chinook Rd Woodway WA 98020-7200 Office: U Washington Dept Math Box 354350 Seattle WA 98195-4350

MICHAEL, GARY G. retired retail supermarket and drug chain executive; b. 1940; married. BS in Bus., U. Idaho, 1962. Staff acct. Ernst & Ernst, CPA's, 1964-66; with Albertson's, Inc., Boise, Idaho, 1966—, acct., 1966-68, asst. controller, 1968-71, controller, 1971-72, v.p., controller, 1972-74, sr. v.p. fin., treas., 1974-76, exec. v.p., 1976-84, vice chmn., CFO, corp. devel. officer, 1984-91, chmn., CEO, 1991—2001. Bd. dirs. Questar Inc., Boise Cascade, Food Mktg. Inst., Clorox. Served to 1st lt. U.S. Army, 1962-64. Office: Clorox 1221 Broadway Oakland CA 94612*

MICHAEL, HENRY N. geographer, anthropologist; b. Pitts., July 14, 1913; s. Anthony M. and Albina (Dubska) M.; m. Ida Nemez, June 18, 1943; children: Susan Shelley, Richard Carleton, Andrew Paul. BA, U. Pa., 1948, MA, 1951, PhD, 1954. Instr. geography U. Pa., 1948-54; faculty Temple U., 1958-80, prof. geography, chmn. dept., 1965-73, prof., 1965-80. Research assoc. Univ. Mus., Phila., 1959-82, sr. fellow, 1982— ; mem. Bi-Nat. Commn. on Social Scis. and Humanities, Am. Council Learned Socs./Acad. Scis. USSR, 1975—. Editor: Anthropology of the North, 1959-72; editor, author: Dating Techniques for the Archaeologist, 1971, 73, 82; translator, editor various archaeol. and ethnographic works; mem. adv. publs. com. Mus. Applied Sci. Ctr. for Archaeology, U. Pa., Anthropology and Archaeology of Eurasia-A Jour. of Transls., Alaska-Siberia Rsch. Ctr.; mem. editorial bd. Expedition-The Univ. Mus. Mag. Archaeology and Anthropology, U. Pa.; contbr. articles to profl. jours. Served to 1st lt. AUS, 1942-45. Decorated Purple Heart; recipient Dir.'s award U. Pa. Mus. Archaeology and Anthropology, 2000. Fellow Am. Anthrop. Assn., Arctic Inst. N.Am.; mem. Phila. Anthrop. Soc. (coun. 1954-90), Delaware Valley Assn. Geographers, Assn. Am. Geographers, Sigma Xi. Home: 2712 Pine Valley Ln Ardmore PA 19003-1719 Office: Univ Museum U Pa Philadelphia PA 19104

MICHAEL, JAMES DANIEL, computer scientist; b. Peoria, Ill., May 27, 1957; s. Thomas Proctor and Mary Lou (Wagner) M.; m. Susan Marie Weiler, July 17, 1999. BS in Psychology, U. Calif., Davis, 1978. Teller Bank of Am., Davis, 1978-79, Fresno, Calif., 1979; computer operator Fresno County Computer Svcs., 1979-81; computer programmer Gesco Corp., Fresno, 1981-83, systems programmer, 1983-89; mgr. IBM operating systems Calif. State U., 1989-99, assoc. dir. operating sys. svcs., 2000—. Co-author: The Porter Tract - An Historical and Architectural Survey, 1990; contbr. articles to profl. publs. Mem. Fresno City and County Hist. Soc., 1989—; founding mem. Landmarks Preservation Coun., Fresno, 1991—, Tree Fresno, 1987—; mem. Fresno Zool. Soc.; commr. City of Fresno Hist. Preservation Commn., 1994-2001. Mem. Assn. for Computing Machinery, Nat. Systems Programmer Assn. Democrat. Avocations: historic home restoration, music, Irish language studies, gardening. Office: Calif State U CCMS 2225 E San Ramon Ave Fresno CA 93740-8029 E-mail: jim_michael@csufresno.edu.

MICHAEL, JERROLD MARK, public health specialist, former university dean, educator; b. Richmond, Va., Aug. 3, 1927; s. Joseph Leon and Esther Leah M.; m. Lynn Y. Simon, Mar. 17, 1951; children: Scott J., Nelson L. BCE, George Washington U., 1949; MSE, Johns Hopkins U., 1950; MPH, U. Calif., Berkeley, 1957; DrPH (hon.), Mahidol U., 1983; ScD (hon.), Tulane U., 1984. Commd. ensign USPHS, 1950, advanced through grades to rear adm., asst. surgeon gen., 1966; ret., 1970; dean Sch. Pub. Health, U. Hawaii, Honolulu, 1971-92, prof. pub. health, 1971-95; emeritus prof. pub. health U. Hawaii, 1995—; adj. prof. internat. health George Washington U., 1997—. Bd. dirs. Nat. Health Coun., 1967-78, Nat. Ctr. for Health Edn., 1977-90; mem. nat. adv. coun. on health professions edn., 1978-81; chmn. bd. dirs. Kuakini Med. Ctr., Honolulu; sec., treas. Asia-Pacific Acad. Consortium Pub. Health; vis. prof. U. Adelaide, 1993, George Washington, 1994; hon. prof. Beijing Med. U., 1994; adj. prof. internat. pub. health Goerge Washington U., 1997—. Contbr. articles to profl. jours.; assoc. editor Jour. Environ. Health, 1958-80, Asia-Pacific Jour. of Pub. Health, 1986-95. Pres. Commissioned Officers Found., 2000—. Served with USNR, 1945-47. Decorated Meritorious Svc. medal, comdr. Royal Order of Elephant (Thailand); recipient Walter Mangold award, 1961, J.S. Billings award for mil. medicine, 1964, Gold medal Hebrew U., Jerusalem, 1982, San Karcil Gold medal, Malaysia, 1989, Disting. Svc. award Pacific Island Health Officers Assn., 1992, USPHS awards, Commd. Officers Assn. Brutsche award, 1999, others. Fellow Am. Public Health Assn.; mem. Am. Acad. Health Adminstrn., Am. Soc. Cert. Sanitarians, Nat. Environ. Health Assn., Am. Acad. Environ. Engrs. Clubs: Masons. Democrat. Jewish. Home: 16736 Gooseneck Ter Olney MD 20832-2456

MICHAEL, JOHN WILLIAM, prosthetist orthotist; b. Indpls., Aug. 28, 1949; s. Floyd Donald and M. Helen (White) M.; m. Linda Louise Olson, Sept. 5, 1970; children: David William, Kathryn Louise. BS, Mich. State U., 1971; MEd, U. Ill., 1982. Cert. prosthetist orthotist. Psychiatric caseworker Wabash Valley Hosp., West Lafayette, Ind., 1971-75; prosthetist Scheck & Siress, Oak Park, Ill., 1976-78, 81-82; asst. dir. Prosthetic and Orthotic Ctr. Northwestern U., Chgo., 1978-81; dir. prostetic svcs. North Shore Orthopedics, Highland Park, Ill., 1982-85; asst. prof., dir. prosthetic and orthotic dept. Duke U., Durham, N.C., 1985-92; dir. Otto Bock USA, Mpls., 1992-99; pres. CPO Svcs., Inc., Chanhassen, Minn., 1999—. Adv. bd. mem. Amputee Coalition Am., Knoxville, Tenn., 1995—; advisor Latin Am. Prosthetist and Orthotists Assn., 1996—. Co-editor: Atlas of Limb Prosthetics, 1992; contbr. chpts. in books. Fellow Internat. Soc. Prosthetics and Orthotics (chmn. U.S. Soc. 1993-95), Am. Acad. Orthotists and Prosthetists (pres. Midwest chpt. 1983-84; pres. 1989-90, Outstanding Clinician award 1992, Disting. Practitioner award 1997), Am. Orthotic and Prosthetic Assn. (coding com. 1995—). Avocations: horticulture, disability dolls, antique automobiles. Office: 2005 Wild Rose Trl Portage IN 46368-1683

MICHAEL, JONATHAN EDWARD, insurance company executive; b. Columbus, Ohio, Mar. 19, 1954; BA, Ohio Dominican Coll., 1977. CPA, Ohio. Acct. Coopers & Lybrand, Columbus, Ohio, 1977-82; chief acct. RLI Ins. Co., Peoria, Ill., 1982-84, controller, 1984-85, v.p. fin., CFO, 1985—, exec. v.p., 1991-94, pres., COO, 1994-2000, pres., CEO, 2001—, chmn. bd., 2002—. Mem.: Mt. Hawley Country (Peoria). Roman Catholic. Avocation: golf. Office: RLI Ins Co 9025 N Lindbergh Dr Peoria IL 61615-1499

MICHAEL, M. BLANE, federal judge; b. Charleston, S.C., Feb. 17, 1943; AB, W.Va. U., 1965; JD, NYU, 1968. Bar: N.Y. 1968, U.S. Dist. Ct. (so. and ea. dists.) N.Y. 1968, W.Va. 1973, U.S. Ct. Appeals (4th cir.) 1974, U.S. Dist. Ct. (so. dist.) W.Va. 1981. Counsel to Gov. W.Va. John D. Rockefeller IV, 1977—80; atty. Jackson & Kelly, Charleston, W.Va., 1981—93; fed. judge U.S. Ct. Appeals (4th cir.), 1993—. Mem.: ABA, Kanawha County Bar Assn., W.Va. Bar Assn., Phi Beta Kappa. Office: US Circuit Judge Robert C Byrd US Courthouse 300 Virginia St E Rm 7404 Charleston WV 25301-2504*

MICHAEL, M. TODD, university educator; b. Champaign-Urbana, Ill., Oct. 3, 1967; s. Michael F. Walter, Dianne L. Walter; m. Christa Diane Salmon, Jan. 2, 1999. BS, Cornell U., 1990, Masters, 1991; PhD, Wash. State U., 1995. Cert. engr. Rsch. assoc., instr. Cornell U., Ithaca, NY, 1995—98, sr. rsch. assoc., 2001—; asst. prof. U. Alaska S.E., Juneau, Alaska, 1999—2001, affiliate asst. prof., 2001—. Adj. hydrologist Cornell U./Princeton U., 1996—. Mem.: ASAE, ASCE, Am. Geophys. Union. Achievements include research in hydrology and water resources related topics including watershed-wide hydrological processes, fluid dynamics, chemical and contaminant transport. Avocations: music, fly fishing, running, canoeing, cross country skiing. Office: Cornell Univ Biological and Environmental Engring Ithaca NY 14853-5701 Office Fax: 607-255-4080. Personal E-mail: mtw5@cornell.edu. Business E-Mail: mtw5@cornell.edu.

MICHAEL, PHYLLIS CALLENDER, composer; b. near Berwick, Pa., Dec. 24, 1908; d. Bruce Miles and Emma (Harvey) C.; m. Arthur L. Michael, Aug. 21, 1933; children: Robert Bruce, Keith Winton. Grad., Bloomsburg Coll., 1928; MusB, U. Extension Conservatory, Chgo., 1953. Tchr. Berwick (Pa.) Elem. Schs., 1928-33; substitute tchr. Shickshinny and N.W. Area, Pa., 1954-66; tchr. N.W. Area H.S., 1966-71; tchr. piano, organ, theory and voice pvt. practice, Shickshinny, Pa., 1943-89; hymn writer, poet, author, composer, 1943—. Author: Poems for Mothers, 1963, Poems from My Heart, 1964, Beside Still Waters, 1970, Fun To Do Showers, 1971, Bridal Shower Ideas, 1972, Is My Head on Straight, 1976, This is Christmas, 1985, Quotes, 1986, Hi, Lord!, 1987, Bright Tomorrows, 1989, Home Sweet Home, 1991, Reach for the Rose, 1992, God Promised, 1992, Why Me, Lord, 1993, Golden Gems, 1993, Oops, 1994, Mountains, Molehills and Mustard Seed, 1995, Surely Goodness and Mercy, 1995, Some Golden Daybreak, 1995, When Petals Fall, 1996, Peace in the Valley, 1996, Snippets from Mother's Diary, 1997, God Cares, 1998; contbr. songs, gospel songs, anthems, articles, poems to books, hymn-books, booklets, mags. and other nat. and internat. publs. Adv. mem. MBLS. Recipient first place in Nat. Favorite Hymns contest for Take Thou My Hand, 1953, cert. of merit for disting. svc. to composition of outstanding hymns, 1967. Mem. Nat. Ret. Tchrs. Assn., Internat. Platform Assn., Nat. Soc. Lit. and the Arts, Hymn Soc. Am. Address: Berwick Retirement Village 901 E 16th St Rm 725 Berwick PA 18603-2440

MICHAEL, ROBERT ROY, lawyer; b. Washington, Dec. 28, 1946; s. Colin Lamar and Mary Elva (Wilson) M.; m. Carolyn Ann Sandberg, Dec. 20, 1975; children: Shawn Robert, Erika Rae, Andrew Jon. BA, George Washington U., 1968, JD, 1971. Bar: Md. 1972, D.C. 1972, U.S. Dist. Ct. Md. 1972, U.S. Dist. Ct. D.C. 1972, U.S. Ct. Appeals (4th cir.) 1972, U.S. Supreme Ct. 1973. Assoc. A.D. Massengill, Esq., Gaithersburg, Md., 1972-73, Massengill & Jersin, Gaithersburg, 1973-74; ptnr. Massengill, Jersin & Michael, 1974-77; pres. Robert R. Michael, Chartered, Bethesda, Md., 1977-84; ptnr. Shadoan & Michael L.L.P., Rockville, 1984—. Lectr. continued profl. edn. of lawyers Md. Inst., Balt., 1984—, continuing legal edn., Rockville, 1984—, continuing legal edn. of Montgomery and Prince George's Counties; lectr. various schs. and bar assns., 1983—. Author: Videotape Depositions, 1987, Comparative Liability; co-author: Automobile Accident Deskbook; co-editor: The Annual Review of Maryland Case Law, 1983; contbr. Product Liability in Maryland, articles to profl. jours. Mem. legis. taskforce product liability, Annapolis, 1980; trustee Redland Bapt. Ch.; founder Trial Lawyers for Pub. Justice, 1982. Named Sect. Chmn. of Yr., Montgomery County, 1986-87. Mem. ABA, ATLA (gov. 1984-86, del. 1982-83), Md. Trial Lawyers Assn. (pres. 1982-83, lectr.), Montgomery County Bar Assn. (jud. selections com. chmn. 1990-91, exec. com. 1991-93, trial cts. jud. nominating commn., 1992-94, adminstrn. of Justice Comm., 1993-94, pres. 1995), Montgomery County Bar Assn. Found. (pres. bar leaders 1996-97), Am. Bar Assn. Found., Assn. Plaintiffs Trial Lawyers Met. Washington, Civil Justice Found. (trustee 1987-89), Md. State Bar (jud. selections com. 1988-94, litigation sect. coun. 1989—, chair 1997—), Am. Inns Ct. (exec. com. 1988—, chpt. LXI program chmn. 1988-89, organizer, pres. 1990, bd. govs., founder Montgomery chpt. program chair 1989-90, pres. 1990-91), Nat. Inst. Advocacy (lectr.), Am. Bd. Trial Advocates, Am. Coll. Trial Lawyers, Internat. Acad. Trial Lawyers, Inner Cir. Advs. Democrat. Baptist. Home: 8921 Brink Rd Gaithersburg MD 20882-1013 Office: Shadoan & Michael LLP 108 Park Ave Rockville MD 20850-2694

MICHAEL, SANDRA DALE, medical educator, medical researcher; b. Sacramento, Jan. 23, 1945; d. Gordon G. and Ruby F. (Johnson) M.; m. Dennis P. Murr, Aug. 12, 1967 (div. 1974). BA, Calif. State Coll., Sonoma, 1967; PhD, U. Calif., Davis, 1970. NIH predoctoral fellow U. Calif., Davis, 1967-70, NIH postdoctoral fellow, 1970-73, asst. rsch. geneticist, 1973-74; asst. prof. SUNY, Binghamton, 1974-81, assoc. prof., 1981-88, prof. reproductive endocrinology, 1988—, dept. chair, 1992-2000. Adj. prof. dept. ob-gyn. SUNY Health Scis. Ctr., Syracuse; mem. NIH Reproductive Endocrinology Study Sect., 1991-95; cons., presenter in field; grant reviewer NIH, NSF, USDA and others. Contbr. articles to profl. jours. Vice chair Tri Cities Opera Guild, Binghamton, 1987-90, chair, 1990-92; mem. Harpur Forum, Binghamton, 1987—, SUNY Found., Binghamton, 1990-96. Fulbright Sr. scholar Czech Republic, 1994; grantee NIMH, 1976-79, Nat. Cancer Inst., 1977-80, 83-87, Nat. Inst. Environ. Health Scis., 1979-80, NSF, 1981-83, NIH, 1987—. Fellow: AAAS; mem.: N.Y. Acad. Sci., Soc. for Exptl. Biology and Medicine, Women in Endocrinology, Am. Soc. for Immunology of Reprodn. (editl. bd.), Soc. for Study of Fertility, Soc. for Study of Reprodn., Endocrine Soc., Sigma Xi. Avocations: golf, skiing, bridge, opera, literature. Office: State Univ of NY Dept Biol Scis Binghamton NY 13902

MICHAEL, STEVEN CRAIG, business educator; b. Washington, May 26, 1959; m. Melanie Alper, July 25, 1993; children: Elizabeth Nancy, Claire Marie, Annemarie Bridget, Madeline Therese. BA, Rice U., 1980; M of Engring., U. Va., 1981; M of Mgmt., Northwestern U., 1987; PhD, Harvard U., 1993. Asst. prof. George Mason U., Fairfax, 1993—97; assoc. prof. bus. adminstrn. U. Ill., Champaign, 1997—. Contbr. articles to profl. jours. Trustee St. John's Chapel, Champaign, 1998—2002. Mem.: Acad. of Mgmt. Office: U Ill 1206 S 6th St Champaign IL 61820 Office Fax: 217-244-7969. Personal E-mail: smichael@uiuc.edu.

MICHAEL, TERRY P. foundation executive, educator; b. Mt. Vernon, Ill., June 9, 1947; s. Floyd Harris and Helen LaVerne Pigg. BS in Journalism, U. Ill., 1969. News reporter Mt. Vernon Register-News, 1969-70, Champaign (Ill.) News-Gazette, 1970-72; press sec. to Dem. leader and mems. Ill. Ho. of Reps., Springfield, 1973-74; press sec. to Congressman Paul Simon Ill., 1975-79; press sec. Ill. Kennedy for Pres. Com., Chgo., 1980; press sec. for Congressman Robert Matsui Calif., 1981-83; dep. dir. comms. Dem. Nat. Com., 1983, dir. conv. comms., 1984, press sec., 1985-87; dir. comms. Paul Simon for Pres. Com., Washington, 1987-88; ops. mgr. press office Dem. Nat. Conv., Atlanta, 1988; press spokesman Ohio Dukakis for Pres. Campaign, Cleve., 1988; supr. press office ops. and vols. Dem. Nat. Conv., N.Y., 1992; v.p., dir. media svcs. Ogilvy Pub. Rels. Worldwide, Washington, 1991-92; exec. dir. Washington Ctr. for Politics and Journalism, 1988—. Adj. prof. Sch. Media and Pub. Affairs, George Washington U., Washington, 1997—; guest lectr. in field. Recipient Disting. Svc. award DC chpt. Soc. Profl. Journalists, 2000; named a Rising Star in Dem. Politics, Campaigns and Elections mag., 1988. Mem. Assn. House Dem. Press Assts. (founder, 1st pres. 1977). Office: Washington Ctr Politics and Journalism PO Box 15201 Washington DC 20003-0201 E-mail: terrymichael@wcpj.org.

MICHAEL, WILLIAM BURTON, psychologist, educator; b. Pasadena, Calif., Mar. 6, 1922; s. William Whipple and Helen Augusta (Schultz) M.; m. Martha Walker Hennessey, Aug. 30, 1947 (dec. 1959); m. Joan Yvonne Johnson, Aug. 26, 1966 AB, UCLA, 1943; MS in Edn., U. So. Calif., Los Angeles, 1945, MA in Psychology, 1946, PhD, 1947. Lectr. engring. math. Calif. Inst. Tech., Pasadena, 1942-45; lectr. math., psychology and edn. U. So. Calif., L.A., 1944-47; asst. prof. psychology Princeton U., N.J., 1947-50; rsch. assoc. Rand Corp., Santa Monica, Calif., 1951-52; dir. testing bur. U. So. Calif., L.A., 1952-62, prof. edn. and psychology, 1957-62, 1967—, U. Calif., Santa Barbara, 1962-67. Cons. in field. Author: Teaching for Creative Endeavor, 1967; co-author: Psychological Foundations of Learning and Teaching, 2d edit., 1974, Handbook in Research and Evaluation, 3d edit., 1995 (standardized tests) Study Attitudes and Methods Survey, Dimensions of Self-Concept; editor Ednl. and Psychol. Measurement, 1985-95; cons. editor Jour. Pers. Evaluation in Edn., Ednl. Rsch. Quar., Spanish Jour. Psychology; contbr. chpts. to books and articles to profl. jours. Mem., bd. dirs. Neuro-Psychiat. Clinic, L.A. and Pasadena, 1958— ; mem. L.A. Philharm. Assn., 1965— ; advisor Sch. of Comm., Arcadia, Calif., 1981—. Fellow APA; mem. Am. Ednl. Rsch. Assn. (exec. com., editor Rev. Edn. Rsch. 1962-65), Western Psychol. Assn., Northeastern Ednl. Rsch. Assn., Nat. Coun. on Measurement in Edn., Calif. Ednl. Rsch. Assn. (pres. 1965), Phi Beta Kappa, Sigma Xi, Phi Kappa Phi, Psi Chi, Phi Delta Kappa. Congregationalist. Avocations: Music; travel; reading; ice cream gourmet. Home: 325 Callita Pl San Marino CA 91108-2311 Office: U So Calif Sch Edn Los Angeles CA 90089-0031

MICHAELIDES, CONSTANTINE EVANGELOS, architect, educator; b. Athens, Greece, Jan. 26, 1930; came to U.S., 1955, naturalized, 1964; s. Evangelos George and Kalliopi Constantine (Kefallonitis) M.; m. Maria S. Canellakis, Sept. 3, 1955; children: Evangelos Constantine, Dimitri Canellakis. Diploma in Architecture, Nat. Tech. U., Athens, 1952; M.Arch., Harvard U., 1957. Practice architecture, Athens, 1954-55, St. Louis, 1963—; asso. architect Carl Koch, Jose Luis Sert, Hideo Sasaki, Cambridge, Mass., 1957-59, Doxiadis Assos., Athens and Washington, 1959-60, Hellmuth, Obata & Kassabaum, St. Louis, 1962; instr. Grad. Sch. Design Harvard U., 1957-59, Athens Inst. Tech., 1959-60; asst. prof. architecture Washington U., St. Louis, 1960-64, assoc. prof., 1964-69, prof., 1969-94, assoc. dean Sch. Architecture, 1969-73; dean Washington U., Sch. Architecture, 1973-93, dean emeritus, 1993—; Ruth and Norman Moore vis. prof. Washington U., St. Louis, 1995. Vis. prof. (Sch. Architecture), Ahmedabad, India, 1970; counselor Landmarks Assn. St. Louis, 1975-79 Author: Hydra: A Greek Island Town: Its Growth and Form, 1967; contbr. articles to profl. jours. Mem. Municipal Commn. on Arts, Letters, University City, Mo., 1975-81. Served to lt. Greek Army Res., 1952-54. Fellow AIA (Rsch. award 1963-64, Presdl. Citation 1992); mem. Tech. Chamber of Greece, Soc. Archtl. Historians, Modern Greek Studies Assn., Hellenic Soc. St. Louis (pres. 1991, 95, 96). Home: 735 Radcliffe Ave Saint Louis MO 63130-3139 Office: Washington U Sch Architecture 1 Brookings Dr Saint Louis MO 63130-4899

MICHAELIDES, DOROS NIKITA, internist, medical educator; b. Nicosia, Cyprus, Jan. 7, 1936; came to U.S., 1969; s. Nikita P. and Elpinike (Taliadorou) M.; m. Eutychia J. Loizides, Feb. 27, 1965; children: Nike-Elsie, Joanna-Doris. MD magna cum laude (Royal Greek Govt., Scholar) U. Athens, 1962; DTM and H (Greek State Scholarship, Found. Scholar) U. Liverpool, Eng., 1967; MSc in Clin. Biochemistry (Greek State, Scholarship Found. Scholar), U. Newcastle-upon-Tyne (Eng.), 1969. Diplomate Am. Bd. Family Practice, Am. Bd. Allergy and Immunology; qualified Am. Bd. Internal Medicine; cert. in infectious diseases and immunochemistry, Eng. Clk., intern U. Uppsala, Sweden, 1962; resident Nicosia Gen. Hosp., 1963-66; fellow U. Liverpool Hosps., 1967; fellow internal and clin. medicine Royal Infirmary, U. Edinburgh, 1967-68; rsch. fellow Royal Victoria Infirmary, U. Newcastle-upon-Tyne, 1968-69; resident internal medicine Bapt. Meml. Hosp., Memphis, 1969-72; fellow in chest diseases Western Ola. Chest Disease Hosp., 1970-71; chief clin. immunology/respiratory care ctr. Erie, Pa.; chief respiratory care ctr. Va. Med. Ctr., 1972-84, acting chief dept. medicine, 1980-81; asst. clin. prof. medicine Hahnemann U. Sch. Medicine, Phila., 1977—, Gannon U., Erie, 1977—. Mem. staff internal medicine Hamot Med. Ctr., immunology and chest diseases Metro Health Ctr., Erie; preceptor medicine St. Vincent's Health Ctr.; affiliate staff Cleveland Clinic Found.; vol. physician Greek Nat. Guard, Cyprus, 1964. Author: The Occurrence of Proteolytic Inhibitors in Heart and Skeletal Muscle, 1969; Blood Gases, Acid-Base and Electrolytes Disturbances, 1980; Immediate Hypersensitivity: The Immunochemistry and Therapeutics of Reversible Airway Obstruction, 1980; The Equivalent Potency of Corticosteroid Preparations used in Reversible Airway Obstruction, 1981; contbr. articles to med. jours. Recipient citation for outstanding svcs. to vets. DAV, 1975, citation Adminstr. U.S. Vets. Affairs, 1978. Fellow ACP (life), Am. Assn. Cert. Allergists, Am. Coll. Allergy and Immunology (com. autoimmune diseases), Am. Assn. Clin. Immunology and Allergy (pulmonary com.), Am. Coll. Chest Physicians (life; critical care com.), Royal Soc. Medicine, Am. Coll. Angiology, N.Y. Acad. Scis., Am. Coll. Clin. Pharmacology, Am. Assn. Cert. Allergists. Greek Orthodox. Home: 4107 State St Erie PA 16508-3129 Office: Allergy Immunology & Chest Diseases 1611 Peach St Ste 220 Erie PA 16501-2121 E-mail: dnm777@pol.net.

MICHAELIDES, EFSTATHIOS EMMANUEL, mechanical engineer; b. Thessaloniki, Greece, Feb. 13, 1955; s. Emmanuel Efstathios and Eleni M.; m. Maria-Laura Garcia, July 31, 1982; children: Emmanuel Alexandros, Dimitris Nicolas, Eleni Guadalupe. BA, Oxford U., 1977, MA honoris causa, 1983; MS, Brown U., 1979, PhD, 1980. Asst. prof. U. Del., Newark, 1980-85, assoc. prof., 1985-89, acting chmn., 1985-86; head of mech. engring. Tulane U., New Orleans, 1990-92, prof., 1990—, assoc. dean, 1992—, sr. Fulbright fellow, 1997, Leo S. Weil prof. mech. engring., 1998—. Cons. DuPont, Chevron, Exxon, TASA; chair Internat. Conf. on Multiphase Flow-2001. Editor nine books, presenter more than 100 conf. papers; contbr. more than 80 articles to profl. jours.; patentee in field. Mem. ASME, ASEE, Am. Phys. Soc. Avocation: stained glass windows/master craftsman. Office: Sch Engring Tulane Univ New Orleans LA 70118 E-mail: emichael@tulane.edu.

MICHAELIS, ARTHUR FREDERICK, health care company executive; b. N.Y.C., July 24, 1941; s. Paul F. and Rose (Landsberry) M.; m. Judith Anne Gordy, June 7, 1964; children: Bradley, Jennifer. BS, Bucknell U., 1963; MS, U. Wis., 1965, PhD, 1967; MBA, Fairleigh Dickinson U., 1976. Sr. scientist Hoffmann LaRoche, Inc., Nutley, N.J., 1967-70; dir. quality control Sandoz, Inc., E. Hanover, 1970-71, dir. pharmacy and analytical rsch., 1971-77, dir. pharm. devel. N.J., 1977-79; pres., applied tech. div. KV Pharm. Corp., St. Louis, 1979-80; dir., rsch. and devel. McNeil Consumer Products, Ft. Washington, Pa., 1980-81; v.p., rsch. and devel. Menley and James Lab, Phila., 1981-85; pres. Controlled Therapeutics, Malvern, 1985-91; mng. dir. Pharm. Cons. Assocs., Devon, 1995—2001; v.p. therapeutics ActivBiotics, Inc., 2001—. Chmn., dir. Polysystems Healthcare Ltd., E. Kilbride, Scotland, 1986-91, Controlled Therapeutics-Scotland, 1985-91; pres., dir. Advanced Med., Inc., 1989-91; founder, chmn., CEO Gt. Valley Pharms., Malvern, Pa., 1991-95, Oakmont Pharms., Inc., Wayne, Pa., 1995-99. Mem. editl. bd. Analytical Profiles of Drug Substances; contbr. articles to profl. jours. Capt. U.S. Army, 1968-69. Fellow Am. Inst. Chemists; mem. AAAS, Am. Pharm. Assn., Acad. Pharm. Scis., N.J. Pharm. Quality Control Assn., N.Y. Acad. Scis., Chester Valley Golf Club (Malvern, Pa.). Avocations: golf, woodworking, photography, fishing, fine wines. E-mail: artmich@verizon.net.

MICHAELIS, KAREN LAUREE, law educator; b. Milw., Mar. 30, 1950; d. Donald Lee and Ethel Catherine (Stevens) M.; m. Larry Severtson, Aug. 2, 1980 (div. Aug. 1982); 1 child, Quinn Alexandra Michaelis. BA, U. Wis., 1972, BS, 1974; MA, Calif. State U., L.A., 1979; MS, U. Wis., 1985, PhD, 1988, JD, 1989. Bar: Wis., U.S. Dist. Ct. (we. dist.) Wis. Asst. prof. law Hofstra U., Hempstead, N.Y., 1990-93; assoc. prof. law Ill. State U., Normal, 1993-95, Wash. State U., Pullman, 1995—2002; atty. pvt. practice, Madison, Wis., 2002—. Author: Reporting Child Abuse: A Guide to Mandatory Requirements for School Personnel, 1993, Theories of Liability for Teacher Sexual Misconduct, 1996, Postmodern Perspectives and Shifting Legal Paradigms: Searching For A Critical Theory of Juvenile Justice, 1998; Student As Enemy: A Legal Construct of the Other, 1999; editor Ill. Sch. Law Quarterly, 1993-95; mem. editl. bd. Nat. Assn. Profs. of Ednl. Adminstrn., 1994-95, Planning and Changing, 1993-95, Jour. Sch. Leadership, 1991-99, People & Education: The Human Side of Edn., 1991-96. Mem. ABA, State Bar of Wis., Nat. Coun. Profs. Ednl. Adminstrn. (program com. 1994-95, morphet fund com. 1993-2000), Nat. Orgn. Legal Problems in Edn. (publs. com. 1993-2001, program com. 1995, exec. bd.), Edn. Law Assn. (bd. dirs. 1998-2000, co-chair publs. com. 1998—).

MICHAELIS, MICHAEL, management and technical consultant; b. Berlin, June 8, 1919; s. George and Martha (Bluth) M.; m. Diana Ordway Tead, Sept. 11, 1954; children: Ordway Peter, David Tead; m. Cintra McIlwain Williams, Mar. 19, 1966 (div. Nov. 1975); m. Caroline Crutcher Bishop, Mar. 17, 1984 BSc in Engring., U. London, 1941. Rsch. asst., group leader Rsch. Labs. Gen.

Electric Co., Ltd., U.K., 1935-45, staff physicist and cons., 1945-49; dir. physics divsn. Radiochem. Centre, U.K. Atomic Energy Authority, 1949-51; cons. Arthur D. Little, Inc., Cambridge, Mass., 1951-52, staff cons., 1952-61, sr. asso., 1957-61, head nuclear mgmt. cons. services, 1956-61, internat. bus. devel. services, 1959-61, policy adviser to several large corps, 1954-61, mgr. Washington ops., 1963-72, sr. cons., 1972-81; pres., CEO Partners In Enterprise, Inc., 1981—2000. Cons. to Pres.'s Spl. Asst. Sci. and Tech., The White House, 1961-63; exec. sec. The White House Panel on Civilian Tech., 1961-63; exec. dir. rsch. mgmt. adv. panel, com. on sci. and tech. U.S. Ho. of Reps., 1963-67; dep. coord. then Pres.-elect Carter's Task Force on Sci. and Tech. Policy, 1976; mem. tech. adv. bd. to U.S. Sec. Commerce, 1978-81; mem. citizens adv. coun. Congl. Caucus for Sci. and Tech., 1983-86; mem. nat. com. Am. Goals and Resources, Nat. Planning Assn., 1964-67, mem. adv. com. sci., tech. and economy, 1966-68; vice chmn. com. internat. affairs Atomic Indsl. Forum, 1958-60; assoc. with Anglo-Am. Radar Rsch. Project, World War II. Editor, project dir.: Federal Funding of Civilian Research and Development, 1976; Contbr. articles to profl. jours. Fellow AAAS (chmn. engring. sect. 1980-82, exec. dir. sr. scientists and engrs. program 1989-90); mem. IEEE (sr.), Sci. Film Assn. (founder 1943, sec. 1943-48, v.p. 1948-51), Am. Nuclear Soc., Boston Com. Fgn. Rels., Royal Inst. Physics and Phys. Soc., Soc. Internat. Devel., Royal Instn. Elec. Engrs., Assn. Hosp. Physicists, Nat. Planning Assn., World Future Soc. (dir.), U.S. C. of C. (chmn. com. on govt.-industry rels. in sci. and tech. 1963-64), Interdisciplinary Comm. Assocs. Inc. (dir. 1969-79), Am. Econ. Assn., Am. Soc. Cybernetics, Am. Soc. for Pub. Adminstrn., Atlantic Coun. U.S., Cosmos Club (Washington, sec. 1994-97, v.p. 1997-98, pres. 1998-99), Harvard Faculty Club. Home and Office: 6812 Meadow Ln Chevy Chase MD 20815-5018 E-mail: zmichael@bellatlantic.net. *The Constitution of the U.S. diffuses power so as to better secure liberty. But it also intends that practice will integrate the dispersed powers into a workable government. It confers upon its branches autonomy but also reciprocity, separateness but also interdependence. It is incumbent on each of us to help make this system work, and to make it responsive to the human needs of our country and the world.*

MICHAELIS, PAUL CHARLES, engineering physicist executive; b. Bronx, N.Y., June 18, 1935; s. Paul Fredrick and Rose (Landsbury) M.; m. Geraldine A. DeCuollo, June 29, 1958; 1 son, Paul Charles. BS in Elec. Engring, Newark Coll. Engring., 1964, MS in Physics, 1967. With AT&T Bell Labs., Murray Hill and Whippany, N.J., 1953-96; assoc. mem. tech. staff Bell Telephone Labs., 1963-67, mem. tech. staff, 1967-82, tech. mgr., 1982-96, ret., 1996; founder P.C. Michaelis Tech. Cons. Inc., Watchung, N.J., 1996—. Lectr. USSR Acad. Scis., 1972 Contbr. articles to profl. jours.; patentee in optics, magnetics, mechanics and electronics. Mem. IEEE (life; Morris N. Liebmann award 1975), AAAS, Am. Phys. Soc., U.S. Naval Inst., Am. Soc. Naval Engrs., Lions (past pres. Watchung club), Raritan Yacht Club (sec.). Home: 103 High Tor Dr Watchung NJ 07069-5424 also: 151 Amherst Dr Bayville NJ 08721 Office: P C Michaelis Tech Cons Inc 103 High Tor Dr Watchung NJ 07069-5424 E-mail: paul@michaelis.com.

MICHAELS, ALAN J. safety, occupational health and training executive, environmental services administrator, human resources specialist; b. Stowe, Pa., Nov. 29, 1946; s. Joseph and Helen (Arena) Pavelish; m. Glenda Jo Becton Lewis; children: Catherine Michaels, Victoria Anne Desiré Michaels. AA with high honors, Mesa Community Coll., 1967; BA with high honors, Ariz. State U., 1970; MS with highest honors, Colo. State U., 1979. Cert. safety profl. Tchr. Phoenix Area Pub. Schs., 1970—78; supr. safety and tng. Amax Inc., Greenwich, Conn., 1980—84; supr. employee rels. and safety Colowyo Coal Co., Meeker, Colo., 1984—86; corp. dir. safety and tng. Tenneco/Echo Bay Minerals, Reno, 1986—88; mgr. safety and human resources various locations Occidental Chem. Corp., 1979—80, 1988—94; dir. safety, fire protection, indsl. hygiene, security, pub. rels. Rayon divsn. Courtaulds/Acordis Cellulosics Fibers Inc., Axis, Ala., 1994—98; temporary assignment Dunlop Tire Corp., Huntsville, 1998—99; dir. of safety-health Lafarge Constrn. Materials, Denver, 1999—2000; mgr. safety, health, environ. and tng. Genesis Crude Oil, LLP, Houston, 2001—. Mem. exec. bd. Copper Devel. Assn., N.Y., 1980-82; mem. exec. safety com. Fla. Phosphate Coun., Orlando, 1989-90; mem. exec. com safety and health Tex. Chem. Coun., 1990-91; mem. The Pipeline Group, 2001—. Contbr. articles to profl. jours. Mem. steering com. Drug Free Mobile Coalition, 1993-94; mem. Mobile Area Tng. and Edn. Symposium, 1992-95, S.E. Consortium for Minorities in Engring., 1991-98, Edn. 2000, 1996-98; mem. adv. coun. Dist. Magnet Sch., 1994; pres. Alhambra Sch. Dist. of Classroom Tchrs., 1973-74; mem. LeMoyne Cmty. Adv. Panel, 1994-98; mem. transp. safety com. LeMoyne Indsl. Park, 1997-98. Recipient Medallion of Merit, Ariz. State U., 1967; NIOSH fellow, 1978-79. Mem. AARP, Am. Soc. Safety Engrs. (prof., Pres. Cir. 1990, Mobile chpt. sec. 1995-96, treas. 1997-98, v.p. 1998), Bus. Coun. Ala., Indsl. Pers. Assn. Mobile, Chickasaw C. of C. (pres. 1994), Ala. Textile Mfg. Assn. (health and safety sect. 1994-98), Colo. Contractors Assn., Colo. Ready Mix Concrete Assn., Colo. Rock Prodrs., Joseph Holmes Safety Assn. (founding mem. corp. chpts. 1984, 86, 99), Colo. State U. Alumni Ambassadors, Mensa. Avocations: comic classical movies, music (writing song parodies), restoring old automobiles, pet animals, sports trivia. Home: 17602 Surreywest Ln Spring TX 77379 Office: 500 Dallas St Ste 2500 Houston TX 77002 E-mail: amichaels@genesiscrudeoil.com.

MICHAELS, CINDY WHITFILL (CYNTHIA G. MICHAELS), educational consultant; b. Plainview, Tex., Aug. 31, 1951; d. Glenn Tierce and Ruby Jewell (Nichols) Whitfill; m. Terre Joe Michaels, July 16, 1977. BS, W. Tex. State U., 1972; MS, U. Tex., Dallas, 1976; postgrad. cert., E. Tex. State U., 1982; Grad., Garland Citizens Police Acad., 2000. Registered profl. ednl. diagnostician, Tex.; cert. supr. (gen. and spl. edn.), elem. edn. tchr., K-8 English tchr., spl. edn. tchr. (generic and mental retardation), Tex. Gen. and spl. edn. tchr. Plano (Tex.) Ind. Sch. Dist., 1972-76; dependents' sch. tchr. U.S. Dept. Def., Office of Overseas Edn., Schweinfurt, West Germany, 1976-77; asst. dir. edn. dept. spl. edn. Univ. Affiliated Ctr., U. Tex., Dallas, 1977-80; asst. to acting dir. edn., dept. pediatrics, Southwestern Med. Sch. Univ. Affiliated Ctr., U. Tex. Health Sci. Ctr., 1980-82; dir. Collin County Spl. Edn. Coop., Wylie, Tex., 1982-89; dir. spl. svcs. Terrell (Tex.) Ind. Sch. Dist., 1989-92; cons. for at-risk svcs. instrnl. svcs. dept. Region 10 Edn. Svc. Ctr., Richardson, Tex., 1992-93, cons. for staff devel., 1993-95; cons. Title I Svcs., 1995-96; ind. rep. Am. Communications Network, 1995—; owner Strategic Out-Source Svcs., Garland, Tex., 1996—. Self-employed ednl. cons. Strategic Outsource Svcs., 1996—; regional cons. presenter and speaker Region 10 Adminstrs. Spl. Edn., Dallas, 1982-92; state conf. presenter and speaker Tex. Assn. Bus. Sch. Bds., Houston, 1991, Tex. Edn. Agy., Austin, 1992, grant reveiwer, 1984; cons. S.W. regional tng. program educators U. So. Miss., 1992-93; regional coord. H.S. mock trial competition State Bar Tex., 1993; regional liaison Tex. Elem. Mentor Network, 1993-96; state presenter Tex. Vocat. Educators Conf., 1994. Active Dance-A-Thon for United Cerebral Palsy, Dallas, 1986; area marcher March of Dimes, 1990, Park Cities Walkathon for Multiple Sclerosis, 1994, 1995; bd. dirs. New Beginnings Ctr. Domestic Violence Agy., 2001—. Grantee Job Tng. & Partnership Act, 1991, Carl Perkins Vocat. Program, 1991, Tex. Edn. Agy., 1990, 91, 92; named Outstanding Young Woman in Am., Outstanding Young Women in Am., 1981. Mem. Tex. Coun. Adminstrs. Spl. Edn. (region 10 chairperson 1985-87, state conf. presenter 1989, 92), Garland Citizens Police Acad. Alumnae, Alpha Delta Pi (Richardson alumnae, philanthropy chair 1988, v.p. 1989, 90, 91, 94-00, v.p./sec. 1993-94). Avocations: aerobics, snow skiing, travel, dancing. Home: 2613 Oak Point Dr Garland TX 75044-7809 also: 232 Broadmoor Alto NM 88312

MICHAELS, ELISE See GILLEM, ELISE MARIE

MICHAELS, JENNIFER ALMAN, lawyer; b. N.Y.C., Mar. 1, 1948; d. David I. and Emily (Arnow) Alman; 1 child, Abigail Elizabeth. BA, Douglas Coll., 1969; JD, Cardozo Sch. of Law, 1990. Ptnr. Alman & Michaels, Highland Park, N.J., 1990—. Author, composer: (record) Music for 2's and 3's, 1981; producer, writer: (film) Critical Decisions in Medicine, 1983. Mem. ABA, Middlesex County Bar Assn., N.J. State Bar Assn., Am. Trial Lawyers Assn., Phi Kappa Phi. Avocations: aviculture, sailing. Office: 48 Timber Trce Ballston Spa NY 12020-3720

MICHAELS, JENNIFER TONKS, foreign language educator; b. Sedgley, England, May 19, 1945; d. Frank Gordon and Dorothy (Compston) Tonks; m. Eric Michaels, 1973; children: Joseph, David, Ellen. MA, U. Edinburgh, 1967, McGill U., 1971, PhD, 1974. Teaching asst. German dept. Wesleyan U., 1967-68; instr. German dept. Bucknell (Pa.) U., 1968-69; teaching asst. German dept. McGill U., Can., 1969-72; prodn. asst. Pub. TV News and Polit. program, Schenectady, N.Y., 1974-75; from asst. prof. to assoc. prof. Grinnell (Iowa) Coll., 1975-87, prof., 1987—. Vis. cons. German dept. Hamilton Coll., 1981; cons. Modern Lang. dept. Colby Coll.; panelist NEH, 1985; spkr. in field. Author: D.H. Lawrence, The Polarity of North and South, 1976, Anarchy and Eros: Otto Gross' Impact on German Expressionist Writers, 1983, Franz Jung: Expressionist, Dadaist, Revolutionary and Outsider, 1989, Franz Werfel and the Critics, 1994; contbr. numerous articles, revs. to profl. jours. Mem. MLA, Am. Assn. Tchrs. of German, Soc. Exile Studies, German Studies Assn. (sec. treas. 1991-92, v.p. 1992-94, pres. 1995-96, numerous coms.). Democrat. Avocations: music, travel, reading. Office: Grinnell Coll German Dept PO Box 805 Grinnell IA 50112-0805 E-mail: michaels@grinnell.edu.

MICHAELS, JOHN G. mathematics educator; b. Rochester, N.Y., Jan. 31, 1942; BA, Fordham U., 1963; MA, U. Rochester, 1966, PhD, 1968. Postdoctoral fellow and rsch. assoc. Carnegie-Mellon U., Pitts., 1968-70; asst. prof. of math. SUNY, Brockport, 1970-73, assoc. prof. math., 1973-80, prof. math., 1980—, chmn., dept. math., 1995-97. Co-editor: (book) Applications of Discrete Mathematics, 1991; co-author: (books) Intermediate Algebra, 1982, Linear Algebra, 1977; author: (videotape series) Calculus, 1984-85; project editor: Handbook of Discrete and Combinatorial Mathematics, 2000; co-author (website) Discrete Math. and Its Applications, 4th edit., 1999. Mem. Math. Assn. Am., Phi Beta Kappa, Sigma Xi. Office: SUNY Brockport Dept Math 350 New Campus Dr Brockport NY 14420-2914 E-mail: jmichael@brockport.edu.

MICHAELS, JOHN PATRICK, JR. investment banker, media broker; b. Orlando, Fla., May 28, 1944; s. John Patrick and Mary Elizabeth (Slemons) M.; 1 child, Kimberly Lynn. Grad., Jamaica Coll., Kingston, 1961; BA magna cum laude, Tulane U., 1966; MA in Comm. (ABC fellow), U. Pa., 1968; MA (hon.), St. Leo Coll., 1981. With Times Mirror Co., 1968-72; v.p. mktg. and devel. TM Comms. Co., 1968-72; v.p. Cable Funding, N.Y.C., 1973; founder, chmn. Comms. Equity Assocs., 1973—. Tulane scholar, 1962-66; Tulane fellow, 1963-66. Fellow Inst. Dirs. (London), Royal Overseas Club (UK), Royal Dublin Soc. (Ireland); mem. Master of Fox Hounds, Nat. Cable TV Assn., Cable TV Pioneers, Broadcast Pioneers, Knights St. Patrick, Phi Beta Kappa, Phi Eta Sigma, Sigma Chi (Significant SIG). Home: 5117 S Nichol St Tampa FL 33611-4132 Office: 101 E Kennedy Blvd Ste 3300 Tampa FL 33602-5151

MICHAELS, LORNE, television writer, producer; b. Toronto, Ont., Can. Grad., U. Toronto, 1966. Former prodr. CBC, Toronto; writer Rowan and Martin's Laugh-In, NBC, also other TV series, L.A., 1968-75; chmn. bd. Broadway Video, N.Y.C. Creator, exec. producer: Saturday Night Live, NBC, 1975-80, 85—, Late Night with Conan O'Brien, 1993—; writer, co-producer: 3 Lily Tomlin spls., Paul Simon spl.; exec. producer: (HBO spl.) Simon and Garfunkel, Concert in the Park, Paul Simon Born at the Right Time in Cen. Park, 1991, (ABC-TV spl) Rolling Stone's 30 Years of Rock 'n' Roll, 1988; exec. producer: (TV series) Night Music, NBC, Kids in the Hall, HBO, (spl.) Stones Retro., HBO; exec. producer and producer: (spl.) Saturday Night 15th Anniversary Spl., 1989; producer: I (spl.), Wayne's World; prodr. comedy and music spls. for Steve Martin, The Rutles, Flip Wilson, Rolling Stones, Beach Boys, Randy Newman, Neil Young, and Simon and Garfunkel in Central Park; producer, co-writer: Steve Martin's Best Show Ever 81; prodr. movies Wayne's World II, Tommy Boy, A Night at the Roxbury, Superstar; co-writer, prodr. movie Three Amigos, Coneheads, Black Sheep, Kids in the Hall: Brain Candy, Lassie; co-writer, prodr. movie Three Amigos; prodr., dir. Gilda Radner Live from New York, also prodr. movie Gilda Live. Recipient 4 awards Writers Guild Am., 8 Emmy awards NATAS; named Broadcaster of Yr. Internat. Radio and TV Soc., 1992; recipient George Foster Peabody award for Saturday Night Live, 1990; named to TV Acad. Hall of Fame, 1999; received star on Hollywood Walk of fame. Office: Broadway Video 1619 Broadway Fl 9 New York NY 10019-7463

MICHAELS, MARION CECELIA, writer, editor, news syndicate executive; b. Black River Falls, Wis. d. Leonard N. and Estelle O. (Payne) Doud; m. Charles Webb (div.); children: Charles, David, Robert; m. Mark J. Michaels (div.); 1 child, Merry A. Student, MIT, 1962-64, U. Wis., 1971-76, BS in Bus. Edn., 1978, MS in Spl. Edn., 1981. Mgr., instr. bus. program Blackwell Job Corps Ctr., 1987-89; mgr. Michaels Secretarial Svc., Black River Falls, Wis., 1979-83; columnist, editor Michaels News, 1983—, pres., 1989—. Hon. appt. rsch. bd. advisors Am. Biog. Inst., 1996-2001. Author: The Little Cowboy: Pursuing Dana's Dream, 1998; columnist: Single Parenting, 1983-94, Parenting Plus, 1990—; editor, contbr. (column) Surviving Single, 1990-95, To Read or Not, Report From Planet Earth, 1989—, Travel Tidbits, 1991-95, Surviving Sane, 1995-98. Chmn. Brockway Community Orgn., 1969-71; chair, counselor Brockway Youth Group, 1970-72; chmn. labor com. Dem. Platform Com., Wis., 1975-76; candidate State Assembly, 1978, 82; co-founder Franklin Delano Roosevelt Meml., 1997. Nominee Poet of the Yr., 2002; named to Internat. Poetry Hall of Fame, 1997. Mem.: AAUW, Physicians for Social Responsibility, Union Concerned Scientists, Internat. Soc. Poets (Poet of Yr. nominee 1997, 1999, 2000, 2001, 2002, Internat. Poet of Merit award 1999), Wilson Ctr., Friends of the Earth, Nat. Geog. Soc., Nat. Trust for Pub. Edn., Co-op Am., Pub. Citizen, Internat. Platform Assn., Am. United, Nat. Parks, Wis. Environ. Decade, So. Poverty Law Ctr., Natural Resources Def. Coun., Amnesty Internat., Inst. for Noetic Sci., Save the Redwoods League, League of Conservation Voters, Peale Ctr. for Positive Living, Phi Delta Kappa, Pi Omega Pi. Avocations: singing, dancing, walking, swimming, travel. Office: Michaels News RR 5 Box 367 Black River Falls WI 54615-9160

MICHAELS, RICHARD EDWARD, lawyer; b. Chgo., June 10, 1952; s. Benjamin and Lillian (Borawski) Mikolajczewski; m. Karen Lynn Belau Michaels, May 17, 1980; children: Jonathan R., Timothy R., Matthew R. BS in Commerce summa cum laude, DePaul U., 1973; JD, Northwestern U., 1977. Bar: Ill. 1977, U.S. Dist. Ct. (no. dist.) Ill. 1977, U.S. Ct. Appeals (7th cir.) 1977; CPA, Ill. Acct. Touche Ross & Co., Chgo., 1973-74; assoc. Schuyler, Roche & Zwirner and predecessor firm Hubachek & Kelly Ltd., 1977-83; ptnr. Schuyler, Roche & Zwirner, 1983—, pres., 1994—. Mem. Northwestern U. Law Rev., 1976-77. Chmn. Maine South H.S., 2001—02; mem. adv. bd. Greater Chgo. agy. Luth. Brotherhood, 1999—; vice chmn. congregation St. Andrew's Luth. Ch., Park Ridge, Ill., 1990—92, chmn. congregation, 1992—94. Mem. ABA, Internat. Bar Assn., Ill. Bar Assn., Chgo. Bar Assn., DePaul U. Alumni Assn., DePaul U. Boosters, Chgo. Athletic Assn., Northwestern Club, C.A.A. Club, Beta Gamma Sigma, Pi Gamma Mu, Beta Alpha Psi. Lutheran. Avocations: photography, golf. Home: 808 Elm St Park Ridge IL 60068-3312 Office: Schuyler Roche & Zwirner 130 E Randolph St Ste 3800 Chicago IL 60601-6342 E-mail: rmichaels@srzlaw.com.

MICHAELS, RICHARD MORTON, transportation and human factors consultant; b. Boston, Jan. 19, 1927; s. Harry Louis and Edith Sylvia (Ginsburg) M.; 1 child from previous marriage, Glenn Alan; m. Penny Sue Simon, Jan. 18, 1974. BS, Bates Coll., 1948; MA, George Washington U., 1953, PhD, 1958. Rsch. psychologist U.S. Naval Rsch. Lab., Washington, 1953-58, U.S. Bur. Pub. Rds., Washington, 1958-63, sci. advisor, 1963-68; dir. utilities tech. U.S. HUD, 1968-69; dir. rsch. transp. ctr. Northwestern U., Evanston, Ill., 1969-74; dir. urban systems lab. U. Ill., Chgo., 1974-79, assoc. dean Grad. Coll., 1979-90; v.p. PIR Michaels Assocs., 1993—. Co-author: Public Policy Development, 1974; editor: Transportation Planning and Policy Decision Making, 1980. Mem. Chgo. Civic Fedn., 1989, Met. Planning Coun., Chgo., 1990. Mem. Am. Psychol. Assn., AAAS, Inventors Coun. (v.p. 1989—, Pikarsy Meml. award 1989), Sigma Xi. Office: 6455 N Sheridan Rd # 2301 Chicago IL 60626-5345

MICHAELS, WILLARD A. (BILL MICHAELS), retired broadcasting executive; b. Omaha, May 13, 1917; s. Gus M. and Bessie (Kerstine) M.; m. Helen Louise Mintel, Nov. 20, 1938 (dec. Sept. 2000); children: Marcella, Lawrence Richard, Betty Michaels Westbrook BA, Trinity U., 1940. Asst. sports editor San Antonio Express, 1937-40; sports announcer, sales mgr., gen. mgr. KABC, San Antonio, 1940-53; gen. mgr. KGBS-TV, 1954; v.p. WJBK-TV, Detroit, 1955-61; dir. Storer Broadcasting Co., Miami Beach, Fla., 1960-85, TV v.p., 1961-66, exec. v.p., 1966-67, pres., 1967-74, chmn., 1974-82, ret., 1982. Chmn. New Boston Garden Corp. (Boston Bruins), 1972-75; dir., mem. exec. com. Northeast Airlines, 1965-72, pres., 1970-72; dir. Delta Airlines, 1972-90, adv. dir., 1990—. Trustee Storer Found. Home: 154 Manchester Way Shavano Pk San Antonio TX 78249

MICHAELSEN, HOWARD KENNETH, lawyer; b. Odessa, Wash., May 1, 1927; s. Henry Emil and Anna Marie (Ropte) M.; m. Fayetta Mable Moulton, May 27, 1929; children: Barbara Ann, Howard David, Steven Hardy, Angelia Jean. BA in Social Studies, Wash. State U., 1952; JD, Gonzaga U., 1958. Bar: Wash. 1959, U.S. Dist. Ct. (ea. dist.) Wash. 1959. Tchr. Spokane (Wash.) Sch. Dist. 81, 1954-60; pvt. practice law Spokane, 1960—. Dir. Spokane Lilac Festival Assn., 1974. With U.S. Army, 1945-47, 1950-52. Mem. Wash. Bar Assn. (arbitrator), Wash. Trial Lawyers Assn., Lions, Masons, Shriner. Democrat. United Ch. of Christ. Avocations: fishing, hiking, swimming. E_mail. Home: 8004 N Fox Point Dr Spokane WA 99208-6430 Office: 320 W Spofford Ave Spokane WA 99205-4750 E-mail: corfin@icehouse.net.

MICHAELSEN, NIELS HENRIK, painter, illustrator; b. Newark, June 23, 1924; s. James and Henrikke (Münster) M.; m. Dorothy Anne Salmons, 1954 (div. 1962); children: Hedrich Tomlin, N. Kristian. Cert. in Painting, Newark Sch. Fine & Indsl. Art, 1949. Illustrator, designer tech. publs., advt. and pub. rels. materials for govt. and industry. One-person shows include Gallery 91, Bklyn., 1976; exhibited in group shows at Newark Pub. Libr., 1946, Montclair (N.J.) Art Mus., 1947, Addison Gallery, Andover (Mass.) Acad., 1947, Rabin and Krueger Gallery, Newark, 1948, March Gallery, N.Y.C., 1960, Kornblee Gallery, N.Y.C., 1969, Atlantic Gallery, Bklyn., 1973, U.S. Courthouse at Foley Square, N.Y.C., 1980, UCCCA, Oneonta, N.Y., 1990, 94, 95, 96, 97, Bremer Farm, Otego, N.Y., 1992, 94, 97, Roberson Mus., Binghamton, 1993, Del. Hist. Assn., Delhi, N.Y., 1993, Susquehanna Art Soc., Selinsgrove, Pa., 1994, Art Assn. Harrisburg, Pa., 1994, Doshi Ctr., Harrisburg, 1995, Art Assn. Harrisburg, 1996, Lycoming Coll., Williamsport, Pa., 1997, Art Mission, Binghamton, N.Y., 1998, Chautauqua Instn., 1998, Cooperstown Art Assn., 2000, Food for Thought, 2001, The Art Mission, 2002. With U.S. Army, 1942-45. Avocations: fishing, walking, hunting. Home: 54 Cedar St Oneonta NY 13820-1645

MICHAELSON, ARTHUR M. lawyer; b. N.Y.C., May 16, 1927; s. Samuel H. and Augusta L. M.; m. Arline L. Kahn, June 30, 1957; children: Barbara L., Sarah E., David N. AB, Columbia U., 1947; LLB, Yale U., 1950. Bar: N.Y. 1950, U.S. Supreme Ct 1964. Partner Wachtel & Michaelson, N.Y.C., 1957-66; v.p. McCrory Corp., 1966-68, Glen Alden Corp., N.Y.C., 1968-73; partner Miller, Singer, Michaelson & Raives, 1973-84; counsel Hofheimer Gartlir & Gross, 1984—. Author: (with J. Blattmachr) Income Taxation of Estates and Trusts, 1980, 85, 89, 95, 96, 98. Bd. dirs., mem. exec. com. Amnesty Internat. of U.S.A., Inc., 1972-81, vice chmn., 1975-76. Served with USN, 1945-46. Mem. ABA, Assn. Bar City N.Y. Office: 530 5th Ave New York NY 10036-5101

MICHAELSON, HERBERT BERNARD, technical communications consultant; b. Washington, Dec. 29, 1916; B in Physics, N.Y. Univ., 1955. Head tech. info. Sylvania Elec., Bayside, N.Y., 1951-56; assoc. editor IBM Jour. Rsch. & Devel. IBM Corp. Headquarters, Armonk, 1956-84; cons. tech. communications Jackson Heights, 1984-92. Cons. IBM Corp., 1985-91. Author: How to Write and Publish Engineering Papers and Reports, 1992; editor: IRE Transactions on Engineering Writing and Speech, 1961; assoc. editor: IBM Journal of Research and Development, 1956-84; contbr. articles to profl. jours. With U.S. Army Signal Corps., 1943-46. Recipient IEEE Goldsmith award, 1991, IBM Corp. Div. award, 1979. Fellow Soc. Tech. Communication; mem. Soc. Tech. Communication (bd. dirs), IRE Profls. Group (treas.), IEEE Profl. Communication Soc. (adminstr. bd.), IEEE (sr. mem.). Achievements include several published papers on periodicities of the electronic work function in the table of the elements. Home: 33-50 74th St Jackson Heights NY 11372-1156

MICHAELSON, MARTIN, lawyer; b. Boston, Apr. 12, 1943; s. Eliot D. and Charlotte (Selib) M.; m. Anne Taylor, Aug. 30, 1987; children: Andrew M., Daniel M.; stepchildren: Rachel T., Hannah T. BA, U. Chgo., 1965; JD, Boston Coll., 1968. Bar: N.Y. 1968, D.C. 1973, U.S. Supreme Ct. 1973, Mass. 1983, U.S. Dist. Ct. N.Y. 1969, D.C. 1973, U.S. Ct. Appeals (1st, 2d, 3d, 4th, 6th and 9th cirs.). Atty. Cravath, Swaine & Moore, N.Y.C., 1968-71; legis. asst. Congressman Robert F. Drinan, Washington, 1971-73; atty. Hogan & Hartson, 1973-76, ptnr., 1976-83, 89—. Dep. gen. counsel Harvard U., Cambridge, Mass., 1983-88, univ. counsel, 1989, lectr. Harvard Grad. Sch. of Education, 1999. Columnist Trusteeship mag. Fellow: Nat. Assn. Coll. and Univ. Attys. Office: Hogan & Hartson Columbia Square 555 13th St NW Ste 800E Washington DC 20004-1161 E-mail: mmichaelson@hhlaw.com.

MICHAELSON, PETER LEE, lawyer; b. N.Y.C., Aug. 29, 1952; BS in Elec. Engring. and Econs., Carnegie-Mellon U., 1974, MSEE, 1975; JD, Duquesne U., 1979; LLM in Trade Regulation, NYU, 1985; postgrad., Harvard U., 1993, 96, 97, postgrad., 96, 97, 99. Bar: Pa. 1979, N.J. 1980, (U.S. Patent and Trademark Office) 1980, (U.S. Dist. Ct. N.J.) 1980, (U.S. Ct. Claims) 1980, (U.S. Ct. Mil. Appeals) 1980, (U.S. Tax Ct.) 1980, (U.S. Ct. Appeals (3d cir.)) 1981, (U.S. Ct. Appeals (fed. cir.)) 1983, N.Y. 1986, (U.S. Supreme Ct.) 1986, Alaska 2000, cert.: Ctr. Effective Dispute Resolution (mediator). Electronics project engr. Control Systems Research, Inc., Pitts., 1975-76; electronics devel. engr. Aluminum Co. Am., Alcoa Tech. Ctr., Prodn. Equip. Lab., Pitts., 1976-77, Rockwell Internat. Corp., Pitts., 1977-79; corp. patent atty., mem. patent and legal staff Bell Telephone Labs., Holmdel, N.J., 1979-82; patent atty. Pennie & Edmonds, N.Y.C., 1982-84; founding, sr. ptnr. Michaelson & Wallace, Counsellors at Law, Red Bank, N.J., Santa Clara, Calif., 1984—. Mem. disting. panel neutrals tech. ICANN domain names and Y2K panels CPR Inst. Dispute Resolution, N.Y.C.; accredited mediator Centre for Effective Dispute Resolution, London; approved mediator/arbitrator in intellectual property and ICANN domain name and keyword disputes World Intellectual Property Orgn., Geneva; arbitrator ICANN domain name and keyword disputes, arbitrator/mediator on-line disputes eResolution, Montreal, Que., Canada; arbitrator ICANN domain name disputes Nat. Arbitration Forum, Mpls.; arbitrator, mediator U.S. Dist. Ct. (ea. dist.) N.Y.; arbitrator London Ct. Internat. Arbitration, N.Am. Coun., Internat. C.of C., Paris, Internat. Ct. Arbitration, U.S. Coun. for Internat. Bus., N.Y.C.; mediator N.J. Superior Ct.; mem. CPR Inst. Dispute Resolution; master Justice Marie Garibaldi Am. Inn of Ct. for Alternative Dispute Resolution; sponsoring mem. Am. Arbitration Assn.; mem. CEDR, London. Contbr. articles to profl. jours. Mem. Sch. Budget Adv. Com., Rumson, NJ, 1981—85, Zoning Bd. Adjustment, Rumson, 1988—93. Mem.: AIPPI, Assn. Conflict Resolution, Chartered Inst. Arbitrators, N.J. Intellectual Property Law Assn., Am. Intellectual Property Law Assn., Am. Arbitration Assn. (arbitration-tech. panel, N.Y.C.). Home: 15 Holly Tree Ln Rumson NJ 07760-1950 Office: Michaelson & Wallace 328 Newman Springs Rd Parkway 109 Office Ctr PO Box 8489 Red Bank NJ 07701-8489 E-mail: pmichaelson@mandw.com.

MICHAELS-PAQUE, JOAN MARIE, artist, educator; b. Menominee, Mich., July 24, 1936; d. Frank E. and Gertrude (Pfotenhauer) Michaels; m. Henry Paul Paque, July 13, 1957; children: Juliann Marie, Elaine Marie. Student, Layton Sch. of Art, 1955-58, Marquette U., 1955-58. Art tchr. Kawashima Sch., Kyoto, 1983, Bellas Artes, San Miguel de Allende, Mex., 1985, Am. U., Washington, 1992, Peters Valley Craft Ctr., Layton, N.J., 1993-94, Cardinal Stritch U., Milw., 1990-95, Milw. Inst. Art & Design, 1993—, The Clearing Sch. of Arts, Nature and Humanities, Ellison Bay, Wis., 1995-98, 2002; art tchr., lectr. Peninsula Art Sch., Fish Creek, 1997-98; bd. dirs. Artists Working in Edn., Inc., 2000—02. Mem. adv. bd. Women's Caucus for Art, Madison, Wis. Designer Craftsmen, Milw.; mem. artists' adv. bd. Milw. Art Mus., 1993; artist advisor, co-chair Milw. AIDS Project, 1991-92; vis. artist Australia, 1989, 98, 2001, 02, Arrowmont Sch. Arts & Crafts, Gatlinburg, Tenn., 1999, 2001, Wis. Designer Crafts Coun. 75th Invitational Exhbn., Luth. Coll., Milw., 1998. One-person shows include St. Norbert Coll., De Pere, Wis., 1991; one-person shows (sculptural portraits) include Wis. Layton Gallery of Cardinal Stritch U., Milw., 1998, Wis. Luth. Coll., Milw., 2000, 01; exhibited in group shows U. Wollongong, NSW, Australia, 1989, Artworks, Milw. Art Mus., 1992, H2O Gallery, Milw., 1999, SOFA, Navy Pier, Chgo., 2000, Brisbane, Melbourne, 2001, Geelong, Australia, 2001, Cedarburg, Wis. Art Mus., 2002; author, pub.: (books) Visual Instructional Knotting, 2d edit., 1971, Design Principals/Fiber Techniques, 2d edit., 1973, A Creative/Conceptual Analysis of Textiles, 2d edit., 1979; writer, reviewer Fiberarts Mag., 1970-2002; featured in Northshore Lifestyle, 2002. Jurist Cancer Care Ctr., Milw., 1991; artist cons. African Am. Childrens Theatre, Milw., 1997-2002; artist, jurist Wis. State Fair, Milw., 1994-97, 2000; donated time and art works Women's Exptl. Theatre, Milw., 1994-2000; vis. artist, lectr. Australian Nat. U. Canberra Sch. Art, 2001. Named Most Interesting Person, Milw. Mag., 1986; grantee Internat. Forum of Arts, 1998, 2001, Eli Lilly grantee, 1993, grantee Roundy's Corp. Arts Grant, 2000. Mem. Internat. Sculpture Ctr., Australian Forum for Textile Arts (vis. artist, writer, reviewer Textile Fiber Forum 1989-2002), Arrowmont Sch. Arts and Crafts (vis. supporter, tchr. 1970-99, 2001), Shuttle Spindle and Dypot Handweavers Guild of Am., Inc. (writer, reviewer Shuttle mag. 1984-93), Milw. Art Mus. (exhibitor, bd. dirs.). Avocations: travel, learning, swimming, meeting new people, dog. Home: JMP Atelier 4455 N Frederick Ave Milwaukee WI 53211-1653 E-mail: joanmichaels@paque.com.

MICHALAK, CRAIG LANCE, real estate executive, consultant; b. Milw., Oct. 23, 1947; s. Edward J. and Gladys D. (Stevens) Michalak; m. Sarah C. Long, Aug. 21, 1971; children: Russell Steevens, William David. AB in Psychology, U. Calif., Santa Cruz, 1969; MBA with honors, UCLA, 1971. Cert. instr. real estate, brokerage mgmt., ethics and stds. of law, taxation and fin. Prin. Craig Michalak-Fine Photography, Los Gatos, Calif., 1965—71; asst. mgr. S.S. Kresge Co., L.A., 1971—72; dir. adminstrn., lectr. U. Calif., Riverside, 1972—79; chair U. Calif. Acad. Bus. Officers, 1977; v.p. Radford & Co., Bellevue, Wash., 1979—81; br. mgr., assoc. Broker Kidder Mathews & Segner, Inc., 1981—83; chmn., pres. Craig L. Michalak, Inc., comml. real estate, 1983—. Qualified expert witness State of Wash.; keynote spkr. Real Estate Investment Forum, Am. Assn. Univ. Adminstrs.; panel of experts Cain & Scott Investment Study; lectr. photography U. Calif., Santa Cruz, 1969; prin. Comml. Investment Real Estate Mktg. Network; spkr. in field. One-man shows include U. Calif., Santa Cruz, 1969, exhibited in group shows at Internat. Pedestrian Conf., 1990 (Citation award of merit); editor: Managing Tomorrow's University, 1977; mem. rev. bd. Comml. Investment Real Estate Jour., 1992—94, contbr. Crittendon Newsletter Nat. Real Estate Jour., Puget Sound Bus. Jour., Comml. Investment Real Estate Jour., Realtor News. Named Comml. Real Estate Salesman of Yr., Bellevue (Wash.) C. of C., 1981, Wash. State Comml. Real Estate Broker of Yr., 1990; named to Register of Top 4000 Americans Under Age of 40, Esquire Mag., 1985, Primary Real Estate Market Makers, Standard & Poors; recipient various awards, Boy Scouts Am. Mem.: Wash. Assn. Realtors, Nat. Assn. Realtors (disting. svc. award 1988), Comml. Real Estate Brokers Assn. (chmn. 1986—88), Comml. Investment Brokers Assn., Wash. Comml. Investment Real Estate Coun. (Disting. Svc. award 1988, Trans. of Yr. 1991, Pres.'s award 1992, Trans. of Yr. 1993, pres. 1989, exec. bd. 1985—88), Seattle King County Bd. Realtors (Pres.'s award 1986, v.p. 1986, comml. Realtor of the Month 1992, comml. investment coun., bd. dirs., lease evaluation task force), Comml. Investment Real Estate Inst. (sr. instr. Wash. 1985—, regional v.p. N.W. region 1991—93, cert. comml. investment mem. number 1920, Person of Yr. N.W. region 1992), Am. Arbitration Assn. (mem. N.W. adv. coun. 1994—, panel arbitrators), U. Calif. Santa Cruz Alumni Assn. (governing com. Rainer chpt. 1991—94). Office: Craig L Michalak Inc 1263 Chandler Dr Ste 200 Salt Lake City UT 84103-4241 Fax: 801-521-6345.

MICHALAK, EDWARD FRANCIS, lawyer; b. Evanston, Ill., Sept. 6, 1937; s. Leo Francis Michalak and Helen Sophie (Wolinski) Krakowski. BSBA, Northwestern U., 1959; LLB, Harvard U., 1962. Bar: Ill. 1962. Assoc. McDermott, Will & Emery, Chgo., 1963-69, ptnr., 1969—. Served to sgt. USAR, 1962-68. Mem. Ill. Bar Assn., Chgo. Bar Assn., Beta Gamma Sigma, Beta Alpha Psi. Roman Catholic. Avocations: golf, opera. Home: 3455 Harrison St Evanston IL 60201-4953 Office: McDermott Will & Emery 227 W Monroe St 47th Fl Chicago IL 60606-5096 E-mail: emichalak@mwe.com.

MICHALAK, JANET CAROL, reading education educator; b. Buffalo, Mar. 22, 1949; d. Theodore and Thelma Ruth (Roesch) Vukovic; m. Gerald Paul Michalak, June 19, 1971; children: Nathan, Justin. BS in Edn., SUNY Coll. at Buffalo, Buffalo, 1970; MS in Edn., SUNY, Buffalo, 1971, EdD, 1981. Cert. tchr. nursery, kindergarten, grades 1-6, reading tchr., English tchr. grades 7-12, N.Y. Reading tchr. Tonawanda (N.Y.) Sch. System, 1971-80; instr. Niagara County C.C., Sanborn, N.Y., 1980-82, asst. prof., 1982-85, assoc. prof., 1985-91, prof., 1991—; adj. lectr. SUNY, Buffalo, 1990-91. Recipient Pres.'s award for Excellence in Teaching, Niagara County C.C., 1990, Nat. Inst. for Staff & Orgnl. Devel. Excellence award, 1991, SUNY Chancellor's award for Excellence in Teaching, 1991. Mem. Coll. Reading Assn., Internat. Reading Assn., N.Y. Coll. Learning Skills Assn., Niagara Frontier Reading Coun. (bd. dirs. 1986-88, 97—). Republican. Avocation: reading. Home: 184 Montbleu Dr Getzville NY 14068-1329 Office: Niagara County CC 3111 Saunders Settlement Rd Sanborn NY 14132-9487

MICHALEK, THOMAS J, music educator; b. Denver, Oct. 10, 1968; s. Ronald D and Delores T Michalek; m. Amy L From, May 26, 1995. MusM, U. of Nebraska-Lincoln, Lincoln, Nebraska, 1992—97, Bachelors of Music Edn., 1986—91. Kodaly Concept of Music Education Orgn. of Am. Kodaly Educators, 2001. Music edn. specialist Bellevue Pub. Schools, Bellevue, Nebr., 1991—; condr. Nebr. Children's Chorus, Omaha, 1996—; music edn. instr. Peru State Coll., Peru, 1997—. Recipient Champion for Children, Bellevue, Nebr. Pub. Schools, 1997, Up and Coming Music Educator, Music Educators Nat. Conf., 2000. Mem.: Music Educators Nat. Conf., Am. Fedn. of Musicians, Am. Orff Schulwerk Assn., NEA, Orgn. of Am. Kodaly Educators (nat. bd. mem., local chpt. present 2000—02). Roman Catholic. Avocations: music, travel, gardening, woodworking.

MICHALIK, JOHN JAMES, legal educational association executive; b. Bemidji, Minn., Aug. 1, 1945; s. John and Margaret Helen (Pafko) M.; m. Diane Marie Olson, Dec. 21, 1968; children: Matthew John, Nicole, Shane. BA, U. Minn., 1967, JD, 1970. Legal editor Lawyers Coop. Pub. Co., Rochester, N.Y., 1970-75; dir. continuing legal edn. Wash. State Bar Assn., Seattle, 1975-81, exec. dir., 1981-91; asst. dean devel. and cmty. rels. Sch. of Law U. Wash., 1991-95; exec. dir., CEO Assn. Legal Adminstrs., Vernon Hills, Ill., 1995—. Fellow Coll. Law Practice Mgmt.; mem. Am. Soc. Assn. Execs., Am. Mgmt. Assn., Nat. Trust Hist. Preservation, Coll. Club Seattle. Lutheran. Office: Assn Legal Adminstrs #325 175 E Hawthorn Pkwy Ste 325 Vernon Hills IL 60061-1460 E-mail: jmichalik@alanet.org.

MICHALOWICZ, KAREN DEE, secondary education educator; b. Garrett, Ind., Nov. 7, 1942; d. Perry Linsey and Irene Veronica (Viers) Shuman; children: Joleen, Michael. AB, Cath. U., 1964; MA in Ednl. Psychology, U. Va., 1990. Tchr. St. Anthony Sch., Falls Church, Va.; math. coord., tchr. Queen of Apostles Sch., Alexandria; chair math. dept., tchr. Langley Upper Sch., McLean. Adj. prof. George Mason U.; leader, spkr. numerous workshops; VQUEST lead tchr./trainer. Contbr. articles to profl. jours. Named AAUW Tchr. of the Yr., 1994, Presdl. Award in Math., 1994; Woodrow Wilson fellow, 1991, SCIMAT/NSF, 1992; Yale U. scholar, summer 1987. Mem.: Women and Math. Edn. (pres.), Va. Assn. Ind. Schs., Va. Mid. Sch. Assn., Va. Assn. for Supervision and Curriculum Devel., Math. Assn. Am., Va. Coun. Tchrs. math. (Va. Outstanding Math. Tchr. 1992), Nat. Coun. Tchrs. Math., ASCD. Office: The Langley Sch 1411 Balls Hill Rd Mc Lean VA 22101-3415

MICHALOWSKI, RADOSLAW LUCAS, civil engineer, researcher; b. Poznan, Poland, Dec. 9, 1951; came to the U.S., 1986; s. Przemyslaw and Maria (Rutkowska) M.; m. Karella Louise Trabold, Feb. 19, 1983; children: Christopher, Laura. MS, Tech. U. Poznan, 1974, PhD, 1980. Asst. prof. Tech. U. Poznan, 1980-86; rsch. assoc. U. Minn., Mpls., 1986-90; asst. prof. Johns Hopkins U., Balt., 1990-93, assoc. prof., 1993-99; prof. U. Mich., Ann Arbor, 1999—. Contbr. articles to profl. jours. Fulbright fellow, 1981-84. Fellow ASCE (mem. editl. bd. jour. 1990-98, editor 1998-), Am. Acad. Mechanics, Internat. Soc. Soil Mechanics and Found. Engring., Internat. Geosynthetics Soc. Office: U Mich Civil & Environ Engring 2340 G G Brown Bldg Ann Arbor MI 48109-2125 E-mail: rlmich@umich.edu.

MICHALS, LEE MARIE, travel agency administrator; b. Chgo., June 6, 1939; d. Harry Joseph and Anna Marie (Monaco) Perzan; children: Debora Ann, Dana Lee, Jami. BA, Wright Coll., 1959. Cert. travel specialist and cons., destination specialist. Internat. travel sec. E.F. MacDonald Travel, Palo Alto, Calif., 1963-69; pres. Travel Experience, Santa Clara, 1973-88; ptnr. Cruise Connection, Mountain View, 1983-85; travel specialist Allways Travel, Sunnyvale, 1992-98; adminstrv. asst. Ventures Extraordinaire, Inc., San Mateo, 1998—. Former stars rep. Hertz, Ritz Carlton, Marriott Hotels, various airlines and tour cos. Mem. Am. Soc. Travel Agts., Inst. Cert. Travel Agts., Bay Area Travel Assn., Pacific Area Travel Agts., San Jose Women in Travel (organizing pres. 1971, 1st v.p. 1989, del. to internat. fedn. women's travel orgn. 1997-99). Office: Sutter Travel 693 E Remington Dr #A Sunnyvale CA 94087

MICHALSKI, GREGORY VINCENT, project manager, researcher; b. Evergreen Park, Ill., Apr. 26, 1958; , naturalized, Canada, 1997, naturalized, U.S.A. s. Frank Joseph Michalski, Lorraine Michalski; m. Betty Joyce Johnson; children: Destin. AA, Richard J. Daley Coll., Chgo., Ill., 1978; BS with hons., So.Ill. U., 1981; MS, Va.Polytechnic Inst.& State U.; MA, We. Mich.U., 1992; PhD, U.Ottawa, Ontario, Canada, 1999—99. Cert. Level 3 Hockey Coach USA Hockey, 2001, CHA Professional Trainer Canadian Hockey Assn., 1995. Instr. Ill. Technical Coll., Chgo., 1984—86; mgr. Zenith Computer Group, St. Joseph, Mich., 1986—87; sr. ednl. media designer Heathkit, Inc., Benton Harbor, 1987—90; tng. engr. Zenith Data Sys., St. Joseph, 1990—93; sr. project mgr. Nortel Networks, Ottawa, Canada, 1993—2000; program devel. associate ACT, Inc., Iowa City, 2000—. Adj. instr. Lake Mich. Coll., Benton Harbor, Mich., 1987—93, Jordan Coll., Benton Harbor, 1990—93. Co-author: Sustaining Distance Training, 2000; contbr. articles to profl. jours. Cmty. vol. Irish Youth Hockey Assn., South Bend, Mich., 1990—93; youth vol. West Carleton Minor Hockey Assn., Carp, Canada, 1993—94; cmty. vol. Arnprior Minor Hockey Assn., Arnprior, Canada, 1994—2000. Mem.: Am.Ednl. Rsch. Assn., Am.Evaluation Assn., Internat. Soc. for Performance and Instruction, Hawkeye Youth Ice Skating Assn. (assoc.; cmty. vol. 2000—, sr. webmaster). Office: ACT, Inc. 2255 N. Dubuque Rd. Iowa City IA 52243 Office Fax: 319-339-3020. Business E-Mail: michalsg@act.org.

MICHALSKI, JEANNE ANN, human resources professional; b. Tampa, Fla., Nov. 7, 1958; d. Enrique and Mary Ellen (Bandi) Escarraz; m. Michael John Michalski, Nov. 24, 1984. BA in Psychology, U. South Fla., 1979, MA in Indsl. Psychology, 1983, PhD in Indsl. Psychology, 1990. Human resource coord. GTE Data Svcs., Tampa, 1984-86, mgmt. cons., 1986-87, mgr. human resource planning, employment office, 1987-88, mgr. human resource, 1988-89; mgr. testing and performance mgmt. GTE Telephone Ops., Irving, Tex., 1989-90, mgr. continuity planning and performance mgmt., 1990-94; asst. v.p. human resources planning Burlington No., Fort Worth, 1994-95; asst. v.p. staffing and devel. Burlington No. Santa Fe, 1995—. Cons. Herb Meyer Assocs./TECO, Tampa, 1983-84, Mail Prescriptions, Tampa, 1989-90. Campaign worker Dem. state legislator election, St. Petersburg, Fla., 1980; mem. Polit. Action Com., Irving, 1989-90. Grad. fellowship scholar U. South Fla., 1979. Mem. APA, Soc. for Indsl./Orgnl. Psychologists, Dallas/Ft. Worth Indsl. Orgn. Psychologist Group, Human Resource Planning Soc. Roman Catholic. Home: 505 Woodland Trl Keller TX 76248-2634 Office: Burlington No 3000 Continental Plz Fort Worth TX 76161

MICHALSKI, MARK MARIAN MATEUSZ, consulting company executive; b. Slomniki, Poland, Apr. 5, 1955; came to U.S., 1979; s. Jozef and Helena (Jurek) M.; m. Judith Anders, July 21, 1979; children: Sarah, Emily, Anders, Peter. AB, Acad. Econ., Krakow, 1975, Stockholm U., 1979; postgrad., Cath. U. Am., 1984; MBA, Southeastern U., 1985; PhD in Telecom Policy, MPhil in Pub. Policy, GW U., 1995. Rsch. economist World Bank, Washington, 1982-87; sr. trade advisor Australian Embassy, 1987-90; project dir. Nat. Telephone Coop. Assn., 1990-91; cons. European Bank, London, 1992; asst. prof. Jagiellonian U., Krakow, Poland, 1993—; cons. World Bank, Washington, 1991—; pres. Michalski & Assocs., 1984—. V.p. Polish-Am. Congress, Washington, 1984-86, sec., 1982-84; economist Am. Enterprise Inst., Washington, 1981-82; UNDP cons. and advisor to local govt. in Poland, 1994-96. Contbr. chpts. to books; corr. Nowy Dziennik (Polish Daily News), N.Y.C., 1982-86; asst. editor Perspectives Jour., 1987-89. Sabre Found. fellow, 1991. Mem. Polish Inst. Arts & Scis., Assn. Pub. Policy Analysis & Mgmt., Phi Beta Kappa. Democrat. Roman Catholic. Avocations: swimming, poetry, philosophy. Home: 1209 Lincoln Ave Falls Church VA 22046-2532

MICHALSKI, THOMAS JOSEPH, city planner, developer; b. Waukesha, Wis., Jan. 28, 1933; s. Thomas and Anna (Benca) M. B.Arch., U. Mich., 1956, M.City Planning, 1959; postgrad., Magdalene Coll., U. Cambridge, Eng., 1988—. Urban renewal planner City of Milw., 1956-57; land planner, urban designer Baltimore County, Md., 1959-60; planning cons. City of N.Y., 1961-77; project mgr. Yanbu Indsl. Complex, Royal Comm., Saudi Arabia, 1980-83; cons. UN Ctr. for Human Settlements, Habitat Nairobi, Kenya, 1984—; bd. Community Housing Initiative Trust, 1993-98; faculty U. Mich., 1994; bd. dirs., cons. EMTEL, Inc., 2000—. Mem. faculty NYU, 1965-66, CUNY, 1970-71, Rollins Coll., 1992—; town planning cons. new town in Iran, 1977; mem. Community Bd. 8, N.Y.C., 1972-76, chmn. landmarks com.; cons. Islamic Devel. Bank, 1989—, Fla. Solar Energy Ctr. Affordable Living Conf., 1991. Author: In Search of Purpose: Essays on Planning the Human Environment, 1961, Human Values and the Emerging City, 1967 Founding mem. Friends of Cen. park; 1000 Friends of Fla., 1987—; pres. Brevard 21 Inc., 1988—; bd. govs. Coll. Architecture and Urban Planning, U. Mich., 1984-88; bd. ACLU, 1993—. Wis. Architects Found. scholar, 1953-56; Vincent Astor Found. grantee, 1971, World Wildlife Fund Successful Communities grantee, 1991. Fellow Am. Hort. Soc.; mem. Am. Planning Assn. (charter), Am. Inst. Cert. Planners, Royal Town Planning Inst., Town and Country Planning Assn., Internat. Fedn. Housing and Planning, Nat. Trust for Historic Preservation, Wis. Soc. Archtl. Historians, Mich. Urban Planning Alumni Soc. (bd. dirs. 1984-88), Audubon Soc. Fla. (chmn. conservation com. 1987-91), Assn. for Asian Studies, Worldwatch Inst., English-Speaking Union (London), Brevard County (Fla.) Democratic exec. com., So. Poverty Law Ctr., U. Mich. Club (N.Y.C.), Sierra Club, Delta Chi (Morrey Outstanding Alumnus award 1984). Roman Catholic. Home: 1925 Greenway Dr Apt I1 Melbourne FL 32901-4446 E-mail: tjmichalski1@aol.com. *The educated person prepares mightily to do something constructive about that which is displeasing, to sustain that which is good, and to discriminate the one from the other.*

MICHALSKI, WACŁAW (ŻUR-ŻUROWSKI WACŁAW MICHALSKI), adult education educator; b. Pierzchnica, Poland, Sept. 14, 1913; came to the U.S., 1951; s. Antoni and Józefa (Skrybuś) M.; m. Urszula Lewandowska, Nov. 12, 1959 (dec. 1986); 1 child, Anthony Richard. MA, Tchr.'s Coll., Poland, 1934; grad., Officer's Mil. Sch., Poland, 1934-35; postgrad., U. Wis. M.A.T.C., 1951-55. Lic. real estate broker, Wis. Tchr. jr. high sch., Poland, 1936-39; mgr. acctg. Ampco Metal Co., Milw., 1951-84; tchr., educator Marquette U., U. Wis. Ext., 1962-90, Milw. Area Tech. Coll., 1963—. Real estate agt. ShoreWest Realtors, Milw., 1955—. Contbr. articles to profl. jours. Archivist Holy Cross Brigade and Nat. Armed Forces of Poland, 1991-96. With underground resistance, Poland, 1939-45; officer Holy Cross Brigade, Poland, 1944-55, which joined U.S. 3rd Army, Czechoslovakia, 1945; Polish guard U.S. Army, Germany, 1945-47; officer Internat. Refugee Orgn., Germany, 1947-51. Recipient Polish Heritage award Pulaski Coun. Milw., 1992, Cert. of Appreciation State Hist. Soc. Wis., 1987, Vol. Svc. award Inner Agy. Coun. Volunteerism, 1986, Cert. of Commendation for Exemplary Work as an Older Worker in Our Community Milw. Com. for Nat. Older Work Week, 1995. Mem. Polish Am. Congress, N.Am. Polish Ctr. Study, Polish Western Assn. Am. (Diploma of Merit 1988), Vets. Orgns. WWI, WWII. Roman Catholic. Avocations: chess, bridge. Home: 5505 Bentwood Ln Greendale WI 53129-1314 Office: Shorewest Realtors 5300 S 108th St Hales Corners WI 53130-1368 E-mail: wmichalski@shorewest.com.

MICHAUD, CHARLES A. library director, writer; b. Salem, Mass., Jan. 6, 1950; s. Arthur and Mary Frances (Bergeron) M.; m. Rosemary M. Lynch, May 26, 1969; 1 child, Jennifer. BA, Gettysburg Coll., 1972; MLIS, Simmons Coll., 1975. Reference libr. Brockton (Mass.) Pub. Libr. System, 1976-79; libr. dir. Topsfield (Mass.) Town Libr., 1979-82, Turner Free Libr., Randolph, Mass., 1982—. Pres. adult svc. round table Mass. Libr. Assn., 1983-87. Contbr. articles to profl. jours. Mem. Arts Coun., Randolph, 1987-94. Mem. ALA, Phi Beta Kappa. Office: Turner Free Library 2 N Main St Randolph MA 02368-4604

MICHAUD, CHRISTOPHER, journalist; b. Fall River, Mass., Oct. 27, 1958; s. Albert Joseph and Claire Alice (Gauthier) M. BS, Cornell U., 1980. Editl. asst. Matthew Bender, N.Y.C., 1980—81; copy editor Playboy Enterprises, 1981; news asst. Reuters News Svc., 1982—89, journalist, 1989—96, correspondent, 1996—2001, writer, 2002—. Writer: The New York Times, 1989-93, The Advocate, 1988-94. Mem. Comms. Workers Am. Avocations: motorcycling, scuba diving, gardening, cooking, travel. Home: 784 Carroll St Apt 7 Brooklyn NY 11215-1458 Office: Reuters 19th Fl 3 Times Sq New York NY 10036

MICHAUD, GEORGES JOSEPH, astrophysics educator; b. Que., Can., Apr. 30, 1940; s. Marie-Louis and Isabelle (St. Laurent) M.; m. Denise Lemieux, June 25, 1966. BA, U. Laval, Que., 1961, BSc, 1965; PhD, Calif. Tech. Inst., Pasadena, 1970. Prof. U. Montreal, Can., 1969—; dir. Ctr. Rsch. en Calcul Appliqué, 1992-96, assoc. dean of grad. studies, 1997-2000. Recipient Steacie prize NRC, 1980, Medaille Janssen, Acad. Scis., Paris, 1982, Prix Vincent, ACFAS, 1979; Killam fellow Conseil des Arts, 1987-89. Office: Universite de Montreal Dept de Physique Montreal QC Canada H3C 3J7 E-mail: georges.michaud@umontreal.ca.

MICHAUD, J.P. entomologist, researcher; b. Chapleau, Ontario, Canada, Nov. 22, 1956; s. Barbara Allan; life ptnr. Angela Kaye Grant; children: Sophia, Rosalind. PhD, Simon Fraser U., Burnaby, Can., 1994. Rsch. assoc. U. Fla., Lake Alfred, 1995—2002; asst. prof. Kans. State U., 2002—. Contbr. articles to profl. jours. Mem.: Entomol. Soc. Am. Avocations: cycling, volleyball. Office: Univ Fla 700 Experiment Station Rd Lake Alfred FL 33850 Office Fax: 863-956-4631. E-mail: jmichaud@oznet.edu.

MICHAUD, MICHAEL HERMAN, state legislator; b. Millinocket, Maine, Jan. 18, 1955; s. James Leroy and Jean (Morrow) M. Grad., Schenck H.S., 1973; student, U. Maine, 1979. Papermaker Gt. No. Paper Co., 1973-80, mem. staff finishing dept., 1981—; mem. dist. 134 Maine Ho. of Reps., Augusta, 1991-96, mem. regional conf. task force on environment, chmn. energy and natural resources com., spkr. pro tem, chmn. appropriations and fin. affairs com., mem. legis. svc. com.; mem. Dist. 3 Maine Senate, Augusta, 1996—, pres. pro tem. Mem. com. Eastmill Fed. Credit Union, 1979—; area coord. Merril for Gov. campaign, 1978; v.p. Maine Young Dems., 1978-80, del. state conv., 1980, 82, 84, del. nat. conv., 1979. Mem. Nat. Conf. State Legislators, Katahdin Friend of Retarded Children Assn., East Br. Snow Rovers, KC. Address: 111 Main St East Millinocket ME 04430-1034 Office: Great Northern Paper Co Bowater, Main St East Millinocket ME 04430 also: State House 3 State House Station Augusta ME 04333 Home Fax: 207-746-3304.*

MICHAUD, NORMA ALICE PALMER, probation administrator, paralegal, real estate investor; b. Concord, N.H., May 6, 1946; d. Leon Charles and Goldie May (Maxfield) Palmer (both dec.); m. Bob Michaud, July 21, 1973; 1 child, Derrick Charles. AAS in Bus. Mgmt., Mississippi County C.C., 1994; student, State Tech., Memphis, 1994-99. With United Life & Accident Ins. Co., Concord, N.H., 1965-68, 71-74; data processor Blue Cross/Blue Shield, 1968-71; adminstr. U.S. Govt., 1976-92; house renovator, real estate owner Blytheville, Ark., 1986—. Dep. cir. clk., 1994; with Daniel Law Firm, 1994-95, Walter Lee Bailey & Assocs., 1996-98, Shuttleworth, Williams, Harper, Waring & Derrick, 1999, U.S. Probation Office, Western Dist., Tenn., 2000-. Mem. FPCC, Nat. Wildlife Assn., Nat. Geog. Soc., Bus. Profls. Am. (chpt. v.p. 1994), Phi Theta Kappa. Methodist. Avocations: camping, traveling, reading, painting.

MICHAUDON, ANDRÉ FRANCISQUE, physicist; b. Cavaillon, Vaucluse, France, May 14, 1929; s. Maurice Louis and Jeanne Francoise (Chatal) Michaudon; children: Claire Hello, Helene Caron. Engring. degree, Ecole Supérieure Ingenieurs Arts et Métiers, Paris, 1951, Ecole Supérieure Electricite, 1953; DSc, U. Paris, 1964. Rsch. engr. Le Materiel Teléphonique, Boulogne, France, 1954-56; group leader Commissariat à Energie Atomique, Cen Saclay, France, 1956-64, 65-72; theorist MIT, Cambridge, 1964-65; div. head Commissariat à Energie Atomique, Bruyeres le Chalel, France, 1972-79; dept. dept. head Commissariat à l'Energie Atomique, Limeil, France, 1979-83; French co-dir. Inst. Laue Langevin, Grenoble, France, 1983-89; prof. Inst. Nat. des Scis. et Techniques Nucléaires, Saclay, Orsay, France, 1969-84; physicist Los Alamos Nat. Lab., 1989—. Mem. exec. coun. European Sci. Found., Strasbourg, France, 1987—90; mem. adv. coun. Census Bur. for Nuc. Measurements, European Union, Geel, Belgium, 1990—95; cons. Orgn. for Econ. Cooperation and Devel., Paris, 1989—92. Contbr. articles to profl. jours.; author (author, editor): (book) Nuclear Fission, 1981; editor (co-gen. editor): Neutron Sources, 1983, Neutron Radiative Capture, 1984, Probability & Statistics, 1991. Lt. French Navy, 1953-54. Named knight, Order of Merit, Paris, 1984; recipient written congratulations, Minister of the Navy, France, 1954, award, Acad. des Scis., Paris, 1980. Fellow: Am. Nuclear Soc., Am. Phys. Soc.; mem.: N.Y. Acad. Scis., Francaise de Physique. Avocations: music, tennis, skiing, golf, hiking. Home: 333 Otero St Unit 6 Santa Fe NM 87501-6212 Office: Los Alamos Nat Lab Lansce Do Ms H 845 Los Alamos NM 87545-0001 E-mail: michaudon@lanl.gov.

MICHEL, ANTHONY NIKOLAUS, electrical engineering educator, researcher; b. Rekasch, Romania, Nov. 17, 1935; came to U.S., 1952; s. Anton Michel and Katharina (Metz) Malsam; m. Leone Lucille Flasch, Aug. 17, 1957; children: Mary Leone, Katherine Jean, John Peter, Anthony Joseph, Patrick Thomas. BSE.E., Marquette U., 1958, MS in Math., 1964, PhD in Elec. Engring., 1968; D.Sc. in Math., Tech. U. Graz (Austria), 1973. Registered profl. engr., Wis. Engr. in tng. U.S. Army C.E., Milw., 1958-59; project engr. AC Electronics div. Gen. Motors Corp., 1959-62, sr. research engr., 1962-65; asst. prof. elec. engring. Iowa State U., Ames, 1968-69, assoc. prof., 1969-74, prof., 1974-84; prof. elec. engring. U. Notre Dame, Ind., 1984-87, chmn. dept. elec. and computer engring., 1984-88, Frank M. Freimann prof. engring., 1987—, dean coll. engring., 1988-98. Cons. Houghton Mifflin Co., 1975, Acad. Press, 1983; cons. editor William C. Brown Co. Pubs., Dubuque, Iowa, 1982-83. Author: (with others) Qualitative Analysis of Large Scale Dynamical Systems, 1977, Mathematical Foundations in Engineering and Science, 1981, Ordinary Differential Equations, 1982, Applied Linear Algebra and Functional Analysis, 1993, (with Derong Liu) Dynamical Systems with Saturation Nonlinearities, 1993, (with Kaining Wang) Qualitative Theory of Dynamical Systems, 1994, (with Kaining Wang) Qualitative Theory of Dynamical Systems, 2d edit., revised and expanded, 2001, (with Panos J. Antsaklis) Linear Systems, 1997, (with Derong Liu) Qualitative Analysis and Synthesis of Recurrent Neural Networks, 2002; contbr. articles to profl. jours., chpts. to books. Research grantee NSF, 1972— ; research grantee Dept. Def., 1968-72; Fulbright fellow Tech. U. Vienna, Austria, 1992; recipient Alexander von Humboldt Rsch. award U.S. Sr. Scientists, 1998. Fellow IEEE (mng. editor Trans. on Cirs. and Sys. 1981-83, Best Trans. Paper award 1978, 83, 93, Centennial medal 1984, Millenium medal 2000); mem. IEEE Cirs. and Sys. Soc. (pres.s 1989, Myril B. Reed Outstanding Paper award 1993, Tech. Achievement award 1995, Golden Jubilee medal 1999), IEEE Control Sys. Soc. (Disting. Mem. award 1998), Russian Acad. Engring. (hon.), Sigma Xi, Eta Kappa Nu, Pi Mu Epsilon, Phi Kappa Phi. Home: 17001 Stonegate Ct Granger IN 46530-6948 Office: U Notre Dame Dept Elec Engring Coll Engring Notre Dame IN 46556 E-mail: anthony.n.michel.1@nd.edu.

MICHEL, BERNARD, civil engineering educator, consultant; b. Chicoutimi, Que., Canada, May 31, 1930; s. Joseph Williams and Jeanne (Tremblay) M.; m. Mariette Boivin, Sept. 7, 1954; children: Marianne, Francois, Luc, Jacques, Charles, Christine. B.Applied Sci., Laval U., 1954; Dr. Engring., Grenoble U., 1962. Registered profl. engr., Que. Research engr. Lasalle Hydraulic Lab., Quebec, 1956-60; head dept. civil engring. Laval U., 1960-63, prof., 1963—; chmn., CEO Cameco Corp., Saskatoon, Can. V.p. Arctec Can. Ltd., Ottawa, Ont., 1973-78; cons. Recherches Bermic, Inc., Quebec, 1978— Author: Ice Mechanics, 1978; patentee in field. Recipient Gzowski medal Engring. Inst. Can., 1963 Fellow Engring. Inst. Can., Can. Soc. Civil Engring. (Keefer medal 1977, 81, Prix Camille A. Dagenais 1983); mem. Royal Soc. Can., mem. Internat. Assn. Hydraulic Research (chmn. com. ice problems 1970-76) Office: Cameco Corp 2121 11th St W Saskatoon SK Canada S7M 1J3 *The biggest challenge in research is the understanding of natural processes, particularly in the field of glaciology. Nothing is so worthwhile to mankind as to follow up with engineering applications.*

MICHEL, C. RANDALL, judge, lawyer; b. Meridian, Miss., May 21, 1949; s. Arnaud Simon and Maureen Mabel (White) M.; m. Shelley Elaine Cooper, Jan. 4, 1971; children: Mark Michael, Natalie Marie. BA, Baylor U., 1971; MS, U. Okla., 1972; JD, U. Ky., 1979. Bar: Ky. 1980, U.S. Ct. Appeals (6th cir.) 1982, Tex. 1983, U.S. Dist. Ct. (we. dist.) Ky. 1988, U.S. Dist. Ct. (we., ea. and so. dists.) Tex. 1988, U.S. Ct. Appeals (5th cir.) 1993; bd. cert. Tex. Bd. Legal Specialization, Nat. Bd. Trial Advocacy. Assoc. E.R. Gregory & Assocs., Bowling Green, Ky., 1980-81; ptnr. Gregory & Michel, 1981-83; assoc. D. Brooks Cofer Jr. Inc., Bryan, Tex., 1983-84, Vance, Bruchez & Goss, Bryan, 1984-86, ptnr., 1987-90; ptnr., shareholder Bruchez, Goss, Thornton Meronoff, Michel & Hawthorne, P.C., 1990-98; judge County Ct. at Law #1, Brazos County, 1999—. Mediator Nat. Mediation Arbitration Svcs., Inc., Dallas, 1993-96; bd. dirs. Brazos County Legal Aid, Bryan, 1990-95; judge Mcpl. Ct., City of College Station, Tex., 1992-98; mediator Am. Arbitration Assn., 1990-95, mem. grievenace com. dist. 8A, 1996—. Commn. Planning and Zoning Commn., City of College Station, 1988-92; dir. Brazos Food Bank, Bryan-College Station, 1990-95, Am. Diabetes Assn., Bryan-College Station, 1984-85. Capt. USAF, 1973-77. Decorated Commendation medal, 1st oak leaf cluster; recipient Pro Bono award Brazos County Bar Assn., Bryan, 1990. Fellow Tex. Bar Found.; mem. ABA, ATLA, Def. Rsch. Inst., Am. Judicature Soc., State Bar Tex., Ky. Bar Assn., Brazos County Bar Assn. (pres.-elect 1995-96, pres. 1996-97), Omicron Delta Kappa. Avocations: computers, golf, reading, political cartooning, refinishing antiques. Office: County Ct at Law #1 300 E 26th St Ste 210 Bryan TX 77803-5360

MICHEL, CLIFFORD LLOYD, lawyer, investment executive; b. N.Y.C., Aug. 9, 1939; s. Clifford William and Barbara Lloyd (Richards) M.; m. Betsy Shirley, June 6, 1964; children: Clifford Fredrick, Jason Lloyd, Katherine Beinecke. AB cum laude, Princeton U., 1961; JD, Yale U., 1964. Bar: N.Y. 1964, U.S. Dist. Ct. (so. dist.) N.Y. 1968, U.S. Ct. Appeals (2d cir.) 1967, U.S. Supreme Ct. 1972. Assoc. Cahill Gordon & Reindel, N.Y.C., 1964-67, Paris, 1967-69, N.Y.C., 1969-71, ptnr. Paris, 1972-76, N.Y.C., 1976-2001, sr. counsel, 2001—. Bd. dirs. Alliance Capital Mgmt. Mut. Funds, Placer Dome Inc. Bd. dirs. Jockey Hollow Found., Michel Found., St. Mark's Sch., Morristown Meml. Hosp., Meml. Health Found., Atlantic Health Sys. Mem. ABA, FBA, N.Y. State Bar Assn., New York County Lawyers Assn., Am. Soc. Internat. Law, Racquet and Tennis Club, River Club, The Links, Shinnecock Hills Golf Club, Somerset Hills Country Club, Essex Hunt Club, Sankaty Head Golf Club (Mass.), Golf de Morfontaine (France), Travellers Club (Paris), Loch Lomond Club (Scotland), Nantucket Golf Club, Mayacama Golf Club. Republican.

MICHEL, DANIEL JOHN, broadcast educator, writer, photographer, artist; b. New Orleans, June 18, 1949; s. Nolan Joseph and Evelyn Marie (Breaux) M. Diploma, Sta. WKG-TV, 1986; BA in Mktg. Mgmt., Kensington U., 1989; cert. diploma photography, Media West, 1990; cert., Art Instrn. Schs. Inc., 1991, Brit.-Am. Sch. of Writing, 1991. Instr. English East Baton Rouge Sch. Bd., 1982-84; instr. broadcast prodn. Sta. WKG-TV, Baton Rouge, 1986—; freelance writer, 1987—; technician, photographer Evangeline Downs Race Track. Announcer Nat. Sports Festival, Baton Rouge, 1985. Writer song lyrics including I've Sat So Long, Now I Became Lonely, stage plays, works in Libr. of Congress, 1982—. Camera dir. La. Pub. Broadcasting Fund Raising, Baton Rouge, 1986—; instr. TV broadcasting Boy Scouts Am., Baton Rouge, 1986—. Mem. Lafayette Art Assn. (2d v.p. 1994). Roman Catholic.

MICHEL, DONALD CHARLES, editor; b. Ventura, Calif., Nov. 17, 1935; s. Charles J. and Esther Caroline (Heilert) M.; m. Loretta Perron, May 4, 1963; children: Edwin, Robert, Christopher. BA, UCLA, 1958, MS, 1959. Editor San Fernando (Calif.) Sun, 1958-60; successively reporter, weekend editor, mng. editor Valley Times Today, North Hollywood, Calif., 1960-63; feature editor Houston Chronicle, 1963-68; asst. mng. editor features Chgo. Daily News, 1968-77; exec. v.p., editor Chgo. Tribune-N.Y. News Syndicate, 1977-84; v.p. adminstrn. and editl. devel. L.A. Times Syndicate, 1984-93, dir. book devel., 1993-97; cons. L.A. Times Syndicate, 1998-99; ret. Home: 3000 Adornos Way Burbank CA 91504-1609 E-mail: donmichel@earthlink.net.

MICHEL, ELIZABETH CHENEY, educational consultant; b. Pitts., Feb. 11, 1951; d. George Philip and Charlotte Elizabeth (Cowser) Cheney; m. Raymond Joseph Michel, Oct. 21, 1973 (div. June 1997); children: Keith Raymond, Grant Petersen. BA, Rollins Coll., 1973; M in Comm., U. Ctrl. Fla., 1988, PhD, 1992. Vis. prof. Univ. Ctrl. Fla., Orlando, Fla., 1989-92; assoc. prof., chair comm. program Mars Hill (N.C.) Coll., 1993-99; comms. cons., v.p. Comms. Strategies-Healthcare.com. Corp., 1999-2000; dir. change mgmt. Ga. Tech. Authority, 2001—. Pres. Kairos Commn. Strategies, Atlanta, 1998—; bd. dirs. Biltmore Inst., 1997—, cons., 1996—; bd. dirs. Commn. on Industries of the Mind, Atlanta; vice-chair 21st Century Comm., 1996—; project coord. for joint comm. with Chinese Acad. Social Scis., China; del. to Consortium for Global Edn., China, 1998; vis. prof. comm. Kennesaw State U.; mem. internat. del. to Conf. on Environ. Sustainability, Shanghai, 2000, Implementation Strategies for SMEs, Networking 2000, Paris, 2000; v.p. Systems and Strategies; mem. bd. advisor Atlantic U. Chinese Medicine, 2000—, chair bd. dirs., 2001—. Author: 4 Simple Steps to Communications that Connect! and Kairos Community Strategies Interactive CD-ROM, 2000; chief editor: An Orchestra of Voices: Making the Argument for Press and Speech Freedom in the People's Republic of China, 2000; contbr. articles to mag. Mem. edn. com. Industries of the Mind, 1999—; bd. dirs. Atlanta Women's Network, 2000—01. Internat. Rsch. grant Appalachian Coll. Assn., 1994, 96, 97, Mellon Found., 1994, 95, 96, 97; Vis. Rsch. fellow Chinese Acad. Social Scis., 1996, 97. Mem.: Women's Network, Brit. Am. Bus. Group, Am. Educators Journalism and Mass Comm., Nat. Comm. Assn., Atlanta Coun. on Internat. Rels., Dem. Women's forum, Metro Atlanta C. of C., Women's Commerce Club, Ga. Exec. Women's Network, Atlanta Women's Network-Strategic Planning, Kappa Delta Phi, Phi Kappa Phi. Presbyterian. Avocations: acting. music, postmodernism.

MICHEL, HARTMUT, biochemist; b. Ludwigsburg, Germany, July 18, 1948; m. Ilona S. Leger, 1979; 2 children. Doctorate, U. Wurzburg, 1977. With Max Planck Inst. Biochemistry, Martinsried, ermany, 1979-87. Co-recipient Nobel prize for chemistry, 1988. Office: Max Planck Inst Biophysics Heinrich-Hoffmann Str 7 60528 Frankfurt Germany E-mail: michel@mpibp-frankfurt.mpg.de.

MICHEL, MARY ANN KEDZUF, nursing educator; b. Evergreen Park, Ill., June 1, 1939; d. John Roman and Mary Kedzuf; m. Jean Paul Michel, 1974. Diploma in nursing, Little Company of Mary Hosp., Evergreen Park, 1960; BSN, Loyola U., Chgo., 1964; MS, No. Ill. U., 1968, EdD, 1971. Staff nurse Little Co. of Mary Hosp., 1960-64; instr. Little Co. of Mary Hosp. Sch. Nursing, 1964-67, No. Ill. U., DeKalb, 1968-69, asst. prof., 1969-71; chmn. dept. nursing U. Nev., Las Vegas, 1971-73, prof. nursing, 1975—, dean Coll. Health Scis., 1973-90; pres. PERC, Inc.; mgmt. cons., 1993—95. Mgmt. cons. Nev. Donor Network, 1993; mem. So. Nev. Health Manpower Task Force, 1975; mem. manpower com. Plan Devel. Commn., Clark County Health Sys. Agy., 1977-79, mem. governing body, 1981-86; mem. Nev. Health Coordinating Coun., Western Inst. Nursing, 1971-85; mem. coordinating com. assembly instnl. adminstrs. dept. allied health edn. and accreditation AMA, 1985-88; mem. bd. advisors So. Nev. Vocat. Tech. Ctr., 1976-80; sec.-treas. Nev. Donor Network, 1988-89, chmn. bd., 1988-90. Contbr. articles to profl. jours. Trustee Desert Spring Hosp., Las Vegas, 1976-85; bd. dirs. Nathan Adelson Hospice, 1982-88, Bridge Counseling Assocs., 1982, Everywoman's Ctr., 1984-86; chair Nev. Commn. on Nursing Edn., 1972-73, Nursing Articulation Com., 1972-73, Yr. of Nurse Com., 1978; moderator Invitational Conf. Continuing Edn., Am. Soc. Allied Health Professions, 1978; mgmt. cons. Nev. Donor Network, 1994-95, Donor Organ Recovery Svc., Transplant Recipient Internat. Orgn., S.W. Eye Bank, S.W. Tissue Bank. Named Outstanding Alumnus, Loyola U., 1983; NIMH fellow, 1967-68. Fellow Am. Soc. Allied Health Professions, 1991, (chair nat. resolutions com. 1981-84, treas. 1988-90, sec's. award com. 1982-83, 92-93, nat. by-laws com. 1985, conv. chair 1987); mem. AAUP, Am. Nurses Assn., Nev. Nurses Assn. (dir. 1975-77, treas. 1977-79, conv. chair 1978), So. Nev. Area Health Edn. Coun., Western Health Deans (co-organizer 1985, chair, 1988-90), Nat. League Nursing, Nev. Heart Assn., So. Nev. Mem. Hosps. (nursing recruitment com. 1981-83, mem. nursing practice com. 1983-85), Las Vegas C. of C. (named Woman of Yr. Edn.) 1988, Slovak Catholic Sokols, Phi Kappa Phi (chpt. sec. 1981-83, pres.-elect 1983, pres. 1984, v.p. Western region 1989-95, editl. bd. jour. Nat. Forum 1989-93), Alpha Beta Gamma (hon.), Sigma Theta Tau, Zeta Kappa. Office: U Nev Las Vegas 4505 S Maryland Pky Las Vegas NV 89154-9900

MICHEL, NANCY CLAIRE, physician assistant; b. Balt., June 2, 1958; d. Louis Joseph Coleman and Ethel Eleanor (Emge) Tilden; m. Dennis James Michel, Aug. 5, 1984; children: Paul Edward, Elizabeth Claire. BA cum laude, U. Md., 1980; Physician Asst., Essex C.C., Balt., 1994. Cert. physician asst. Physician asst. in neurology Sinai Hosp. of Balt., 1994-97; physician asst. adult epilepsy program Hershey (Pa.) Med. Ctr., 1997—. Lectr. Essex Cmty. Coll., 1996—, Pa. Tech. Coll., 1999—. Fellow Am. Assn. Physician Assts. (Pa. chpt.). Avocations: bicycling, camping, gardening, skiing. Office: Hershey Med Ctr PO Box 850 Hershey PA 17033-0850

MICHEL, PAUL REDMOND, federal judge; b. Philadelphia, Pa., Feb. 3, 1941; s. Lincoln M. and Dorothy (Kelley) Michel; m. Sally Ann Clark, 1965 (div. 1987); children: Sarah Elizabeth, Margaret Kelley; m. Elizabeth Morgan, 1989. BA, Williams Coll., 1963; JD, U. Va., 1966. Bar: Pa. 1967, U.S. Supreme Ct. 1970. Asst. dist. atty. Dist. Atty.'s Office, Phila., 1967—71, dep. dist. atty. for investigations, 1972—74; asst. spl. prosecutor Watergate investigation Dept. Justice, Washington, 1974—75, dep. chief pub. integrity sect., Criminal div. and prosecutor "Koreagate" investigation, 1976—78, assoc. dep. atty. gen., 1978—81, acting dep. atty. gen., 1979—80; asst. counsel intelligence com. U.S. Senate, 1975—76, counsel and adminstrv. asst. to Sen. Arlen Specter, 1981—88; judge U.S. Ct. Appeals (Fed. cir.), Washington, 1988—. Instr. appellate practice and procedure George Washington U. Nat. Law Ctr., 1991—; instr. appellate advocacy John Marshall Law Sch., Chgo., 1991—. 2d lt. USAR, 1966—72. Office: US Ct Appeals Fed Cir 717 Madison Pl NW Washington DC 20439*

MICHEL, SANDRA SEATON, writer; b. Hancock, Mich., Jan. 30, 1935; d. Donald Wylie and Mary Lucille (Finlayson) Seaton; m. Philip Raymond Michel, July 28, 1956; children: John Donald, David Duncan, Timothy Douglas, Kristin. BA, Leland Stanford Jr. U., 1980. Adminstr. Concordia Luth. Ch., Wilmington, 1985-89; tchr., jr. high Coast Episcopal Schs., Pass Christian, Miss., 1982-84; editor Lenape Pub., Wilmington, 1972-78. Resident artist Art Edn. Program Del. Divsn. Arts & Nat. Endowment Arts, 1974-78, 85—; bd. dirs. Spinnaker Fin., Wilmington, 1985—, Highland Pub. House, 1997—. Author: (books) My Name is Jaybird, 1972, No More Someday, 1973, From the Peninsula, South, 1980, Thomas, My Brother, 1981, Visions to Keep, 1990. Bd. dirs. Concordia Pre-Sch., Wilmington, 1985-97; mem. Delaware Hist. Soc., 1985—; bd. dirs., pres. Luth. Cmty. Svcs., Wilmington, 1988-95; bd. dirs. Citizen Adv. Com., Alfred I. DuPont Dist., 1975-79, Tech. Relocation Svcs., Inc., Wilmington, 1989-94. Disting. Svc. awards Luth. Cmty. Svcs. Bd., Wilmington, 1991, 95; master poet Alfred I. DuPont Sch. Dist. Mem. Nat. Soc. Children's Book Writers and Illustrators, Diamond State Br. (br. pres. 1994-96), Nat. League Am. Pen Women (Del. state pres. 1996-98), Nat. Fedn. Press Women. Lutheran. Home: 3 Lanark Dr Wilmington DE 19803-2611 E-mail: sandramichel@att.net.

MICHEL, SHARON LEE, systems and information technology director; b. Waterloo, Wis., Dec. 23, 1946; d. Charles Raymond and Harriet Agatha (Sheridan) M. BS, U. Wis., Stevens Point, 1969. Systems analyst Employee Trust Funds State of Wis., Madison, 1976-79, dir. systems mgmt. bur., 1979-84, chief applications devel. Natural Resources, 1984-97, IT dir., 1997—. Vice chmn. orgn. Dem. Party Dane County, Madison, 1986, co-chmn., 1987-88; mem. elections com. Dem. Party Wis., 1988-2001; elected ward committeewoman Dem. Party, 1989-2000; co-chmn. Polit. Action Com., 1989, candidate recruitment, 1990; vice chair fin. devel. Nat. Women's Polit. Caucus-Wis. State Policy Coun., 1991—, co-chair, 1992-93. Mem. NAFE, NOW, Data Processing Mgmt. Assn. (v.p., sec. so. Wis. chpt. 1983, v.p0. 1984, Individual Performance award 1985, 91, 94, exec. v.p. 1989, pres. 1990). Democrat. Roman Catholic. Avocation: photography. Home: 4849 Sheboygan Ave Apt 319 Madison WI 53705-2934 Office: Dept Natural Resources State Wis PO Box 7921 Madison WI 53707-7921

MICHEL, STEPHEN LEWIS, physician; b. Chgo., Aug. 16, 1938; MD, U. Chgo.-Pritzker Sch. Med., 1962. Intern UCLA Med. Ctr., 1962-63; resident gen. surgery Cedars-Sinai Med. Ctr., L.A., 1963-67, fellow oncology, 1966-67, assoc. dir. surgery, 1976-90; assoc. clin. prof. surgery UCLA. Office: PO Box 811027 Boca Raton FL 33481-1027 E-mail: slmmd@adelphia.net.

MICHELEN, OSCAR, lawyer; b. Santo Domingo, Dominican Republic, May 1, 1960; came to U.S., 1962; s. Nasry and Marie (Armaly) M.; m. Christine Nicolaou, June 14, 1987; children: Steven, Marcus, Peter. BA, SUNY, 1982; JD, NYU, 1985. Bar: N.Y. 1986, N.J. 1986, U.S. Dist. Ct. (so. and ea. dists.) N.Y. 1986, U.S. Dist. Ct. N.J. 1986. Trial atty. Corp. Counsel of N.Y.C. Torts, 1985-86, sr. trial atty. tort divsn., 1986-87, sr. trial specialist spl. litigation unit, 1987-89; assoc. Sandback & Birnbaum, Mineola, N.Y., 1989-95; ptnr. Sandback, Birnbaum & Michelen, 1995—. Contbr. articles to profl. jours.; rsch. editor N.Y. Law Sch. Law Rev., 1984-85. Mem. parish coun. Archangel Michael Greek Orthodox Ch., Roslyn, N.Y., 1996. Office: Sandback Birnbaum & Michelen 200 Old Country Rd Mineola NY 11501-4235

MICHELI, FRANK JAMES, lawyer; b. Zanesville, Ohio, Mar. 23, 1930; s. John and Theresa (Carlini) M.; m. Doris Joan Clum, Jan. 9, 1954; children: Michael John, James Carl, Lisa Ann, Matthew Charles. Student, John Carroll U., Cleve., 1947-48, Xavier U., Cin., 1949-50; LL.D., Ohio No. U., Ada., 1953. Bar: Ohio 1953. Since practiced in, Zanesville; partner Leasure & Micheli, 1953-65, Kincaid, Micheli, Geyer & Ormond, 1965-75, Kincaid, Cultice, Micheli & Geyer (and predecessor), 1982-92; ptnr. Micheli, Baldwin, Bopeley & Northrup, 1992—. Instr. bus. law Meredith Bus. Coll., Zanesville, 1956; lectr. on med. malpractice, hosp. and nurse liability. Dir. Public Service for, City of Zanesville, 1954. Mem. Internat. Assn. Ins. Counsel, Def. Rsch. Inst., Ohio Def. Assn., Am. Ohio bar assns., Am. Judicature Soc., Am. Arbitration Assn. (mem. nat. panel), Am. Bd. Trial Advs. (bd. dirs. Ohio chpt. 1991-95, pres. 1997). Clubs: Elk. Home: 160 E Willow Dr Zanesville OH 43701-1249 Office: PO Box 788 3808 James Ct Ste 2 Zanesville OH 43702-0788 E-mail: micheli@cyberzane.net.

MICHELINI, SYLVIA HAMILTON, auditor; b. Decatur, Ala., May 16, 1946; d. George Borum and Dorothy Rose (Swatzell) Hamilton; m. H. Stewart Michelini, June 4, 1964; children: Stewart Anthony, Cynthia Leigh. BSBA summa cum laude, U. Ala., Huntsville, 1987. CPA, Ala.; cert. govt. fin. mgr., fraud examiner. Acct. Ray McCay, CPA, Huntsville, 1987-88; auditor Def. Contract Audit Agy., 1989-92; auditor-office of inspector general George C. Marshall Space Flight, Center, Ala., 1992-97; contr. Hamilton Hotels, Inc., 1997-2001. Exec. bd. Decatur City PTA, 1976-78; pres., v.p. Elem. Sch. PTA, Decatur, 1977-79; leader Girl Scouts U.S. and Cub Scouts, Decatur, 1972-77; active local ARC, 1973-77. Mem. AICPA, AAUW (chpt. treas. 1988-90), Nat. Assn. Accts. (dir. community svc. 1987-88, v.p. adminstrn. and fin. 1988-89, pres. 1989-90, nat. com. on ethics 1990-91), Nat. Notary Asns., Am. Soc. Women Accts. (chpt. treas. 1989-90, dir. chpt. devel. 1989-90), Assn. Govt. Accts. (sec. 1992-93, chmn. pub. rels. 1993-94), Ala. Soc. CPAs (profl. ethics com. 1993-94), Inst. Internal Auditors (dir. awards and recognition 1996-97, sec. 1999-2001), Inst. Mgmt. Accts. (v.p. comms., dir. program book 1991-94, Dixie coun. dir. newsletters 1992-93, dir. ednl. programs 1992-93, 93-94, nat. com. ethics, 1990-97, nat. fin. com. 1997-98), Ala. Soc. CPAs (govtl. acctg. and auditing com. 1994-95), Inst. Mgmt. Accts. (nat. bd. dirs. 1994-97, nat. fin. com. 1997-98), Phi Kappa Phi. Baptist. Avocations: reading, walking, sewing, research, music. Home and Office: 2801 Sylvia Dr SE Decatur AL 35603-5643 E-mail: michelin@hiwaay.net.

MICHELL, AURIEL BIN, lawyer, writer; b. Miami, Fla., Apr. 8, 1948; s. Sylva Rivkah Mazoulay and Arie Stepthen Michell. LLM, Clearwater Coll. of Law; DD, Hamilton State U., 1975; ThD, Slidell Bapt. Sem., 1989; JD, Kensington U., 1993. Tax lawyer City of Refuge, El Paso, Tex., 1994—; gen. counsel Intl Inst. for Health & Wellness, Orem, Utah, 1999—. Author: (book) Let's Talk Jewish, 1998 (religious best seller, 2000), Visions, 2000 (New Poet of the Yr. award, 2001), (poetry) From Deep Inside My Soul, 2001 (Internat-.Poet of Merit award, 2002). Bd. of dirs. Tampa (Fla.) Food Bank, 1982—85. Maj. U.S. Army, 1967—73. Mem.: Fed. Bar Assn. Democrat. Jewish. Avocation: travel, writing, speaking. Office: City of Refuge c/o Rio Verde University POBox 971166 Orem UT 85097 Home Fax: 915-833-4667; Office Fax: 810-274-1829. Personal E-mail: ctyrfugedu@hotmail.com. E-mail: ctyrfugedu3@hotmail.com.

MICHELS, DALE E. physician; b. Wayne, Nebr., Mar. 24, 1948; s. R.B. and Florence A. (Peterson) M.; m. Roylene C. Gustafson, Jan. 25, 1969; children: Gretchen, Sheila, Joel. BA in Medicine, U. Nebr., 1969; MD, U. Nebr., Omaha, 1973. Diplomate Am. Bd. Family Practice with added qualifications in geriatrics. Practicing family physician Lincoln (Nebr.) Family Med. Group, 1974—. Med. cons. Comm. Blood Bank of LCMS, Lincoln, 1992—; v.p. Wellmark Health Plan of Nebr., Lincoln, 1996-2000; vice-chair bd. trustees Back to the Bible, Lincoln, 1986—; sec.-treas. Family Care, P.C., Lincoln, 1986-97. Pres. Lancaster County Med. Soc., Lincoln, 1991-92, Nebr. Acad. of Family Physicians, Omaha, 1987, Nebr. Heart Assn., 1983, Lincoln Christian Sch. Bd., Lincoln, 1990-97. Recipient J.J. Hanigan award Lincoln Lancaster Comm. Health Dept., 1994, Pub. Health Leadership awrd, 2000; named Family Physician of Yr., Nebr. Acad. Family Physicians, 1999. Mem. AMA, Am. Med. Dirs. Assn., Lancaster County Med. Soc., Nebr. Acad. Family Physicians (Family Physician of Yr. 1999), Christian Med. Dental Soc., Am. Acad. Family Physicians, Nebr. Med. Assn. (pres. 1999-00). Republican. Avocations: flying, photography, gardening. Office: Lincoln Family Med Group PC 7441 O St Ste 400 Lincoln NE 68510-2466 E-mail: daromichels@cs.com.

MICHELS, DIA LOREN, publishing executive, writer; b. L.A., Oct. 22, 1958; d. Lawrence Michels and Elaine Phyllis Cooper; m. John Anthony Gualtieri, Oct. 13, 1985; children: Akaela Michels-Gualtieri, Zaydek Michels-Gualtieri, Miralah Michels-Gualtieri. BA in Econ., Brandeis U., 1980. Pres. Platypus Media, LLC, Washington, 1998—. Guest spkr. Turning the Pages, Washington, 2001—; guest expert RIFNet, Washington, 2002—; guest instr. Smithsonian Resident Associates Program, Washington, 1999—; guest commentator Pub. Radio Internat., Washington, 1997—. Author: (book) Look What I See! Where Can I Be? At Home, 2002, Look What I See! Where Can I Be? With My Animal Friends, 2002, If My Mom Were A Platypus: Animal Babies and Their Mothers, 2001, Zack in the Middle, 2001, Breastfeeding at a Glance: Facts, Figures and Trivia about Lactation, 2001, Look What I See! Where Can I Be? In the Neighborhood, 2001, Breastfeeding Annual International 2001, 2001, Milk, Money & Madness: The Culture and Politics of Breastfeeding, 1995 (Winner Book award Am. Med. Writer's Assn., 1997), A Woman's Guide to Yeast Infections, 1992. Creative dir. Watkins After-Sch. Enrichment Program, Washington, 1996—2001. Mem.: Small Press Assn. of N.Am., Publishers' Mktg. Assn., Wash. Ind. Writers, Woman's Nat. Book Assn., Am. Soc. of Journalists and Authors. Office Fax: 202-546-2356. E-mail: dia@platypusmedia.com.

MICHELS, JOSEPH B. military officer, dean; b. Spokane, Wash., Dec. 6, 1952; BS in Elec. Engring., Weber State U., Ogden, Utah, 1976; MS in Systems Mgmt., U.S.C., 1978; PhD Indsl. Engring., Tex. A&M, Coll. Sta., 1982. Registered profl. engr., Tex., 2000. Commd. 2d lt. USAF, 1976, advanced through grades to col., 1999; Chief electronics. and workload control divsns. Comm. and Installation Group USAF, Norton AFB, Calif., 1977—80; test engr. USAF, Scott AFB, Ill., 1980—81, test dir. Wright AFB, Dayton, Ohio, 1981—82; chief logistics mgmt. systems modernization USAF Pentagon, Washington, 1986—88, chief logistics spares analysis, 1988—89; maintenance supr. USAF Equipment Maintenance Squadron, Aircraft Generation Squadron, Moody AFB, Ga., 1989—90; commdr. USAF Equipment Maintenance Squadron, 1990—92; mem. chief of staff ops. group Hdqtrs. USAF Pentagon, Washington, 1992; mgr. joint program elec. commerce, elec. data interchange Hdqtrs, Defense Logistics Agy., Cameron Sta., Va., 1992—95; dir. logistics 12th Space Warning Squadron, Thule AFB, Greenland, 1995—96; chief support svcs. br. Albuquerque (N. Mex.) Field Ops. Def. Threat Reduction Agy., Kirkland (N.Mex.) AFB, 1997—99; cmmdr. logistics group USAF 11th Wing, Bolling AFB, Washington, DC, 1999—2001; dean Sch. of Systems and Lighting Air Force Inst. Tech., Wright- Patterson AFB, Dayton, Ohio, 2001—. Recipient Legion of Merit, James D. Forrestal award, U.S. Naval War Coll., 1996. Mem.: Soc. Logistics Engrs. (cert. profl. logistician 1985), Inst. Cost Analysts (cert. 1984). Office: Air Force Inst Tech Office Pub Affairs Wright Patterson AFB Dayton OH 45433-7765

MICHELS, KEVIN HOWARD, lawyer; b. Newark, Dec. 30, 1960; s. Herbert Phillip and Alice Barbara Michels; m. Kathryn Ann Hockenjos, Oct. 6, 1990. BA with honors, Rutgers U., 1983, JD, 1986. Bar: N.J. 1986, U.S. Dist. Ct. N.J. 1986, U.S. Ct. Appeals (3d cir.) 1966, U.S. Tax Ct. 1990. Law clk. N.J. Supreme Ct., Morristown, 1986-87; assoc. Pitney, Hardin, Kipp & Szuch, 1987-88, Herold and Haines, Liberty Corner, N.J., 1988-90; pvt. practice Stirling, 1990—; ptnr. Michels & Hockenjos, P.C. Mem. commn. on rules of profl. conduct N.J. Supreme Ct., 2001. Author: New Jersey Attorney Ethics, 2002; rsch. editor Rutgers Law Rev., 1985-86. Mem. ABA, N.J. Bar Assn., Phi Beta Kappa. Office: 1390 Valley Rd Stirling NJ 07980-1346

MICHELS, ROBERT, psychiatrist, educator; b. Chgo., Jan. 21, 1936; s. Samuel and Ann (Cooper) M.; m. Verena Sterba, Dec. 23, 1962; children—Katherine, James. BA, U. Chgo., 1953; MD, Northwestern U., 1958. Intern Mt. Sinai Hosp., N.Y.C., 1958-59; resident in psychiatry Columbia Presbyn.-N.Y. State Psychiat. Inst., 1959-62; mem. faculty Coll. Physicians and Surgeons, Columbia U., 1964-74, assoc. prof., 1971-74; psychiatrist student health service Columbia U., 1966-74; supervising and tng. analyst Columbia U. Center for Psychoanalytic Tng. and Research, 1972—; attending psychiatrist Vanderbilt Clinic, Presbyn. Hosp., N.Y.C., 1964-74; Barklie McKee Henry prof. psychiatry Cornell U. Med. Coll., 1974-93, chmn. dept. psychiatry, 1974-91, Stephen and Suzanne Weiss dean, 1991-96; provost for med. affairs Cornell U., 1991-96, Walsh McDermott U. prof. of medicine, 1996—, univ. prof. psychiatry, 1996—; psychiatrist-in-chief N.Y. Hosp., 1974-91, attending psychiatist, 1991—. Attending psychiatrist St. Luke's Hosp. Ctr., N.Y.C., 1966—. Co-author: The Psychiatric Interview in Clinical Practice, 1971; contbr. articles to profl. jours. Served with USPHS, 1962-64. Mem. Am. Psychiat. Assn., Am. Coll. Psychiatrists, N.Y. Psychiat. Soc., Royal Medico-Psychol. Assn., Psychiat. Rsch. Soc., Assn. Rsch. in Nervous and Mental Diseases, Assn. Acad. Psychiatry, Am. Psychoanalytic Assn., Internat. Psychoanalytic Assn., Ctr. Advanced Psychoanalytic Studies, N.Y. Acad. Scis., Alpha Omega Alpha. Office: Cornell U Med Coll 418 E 71st St New York NY 10021-4894

MICHELS, WILLIAM CHARLES, management consultant; b. White Plains, N.Y., July 10, 1948; s. Rudolf Karl and Ilse (Gruner) M. SB in Mgmt., MIT, 1970, SM in MGmt., SM in Computer Sci., 1972. Mgr. Tech. Mgmt. Inc., Cambridge, Mass., 1972-76; sr. v.p. Booz Allen & Hamilton, N.Y.C., 1976-2001, pres. Tokyo, 1995-99, chmn. Seoul, 1996-2000; dir. Integral Inc., Boston, 2001—. Editor: Computer Systems, 1971, Market Segmentation, 1992; co-author: Vision Korea, 1997. Mem. Tokyo Am. Club. Avocations: sailing, skiing, scuba diving, tennis, mountain climbing. Office: Integral Inc 111 Huntington Ave Boston MA 02199

MICHELSEN, CHRISTOPHER BRUCE HERMANN, surgeon; b. Boston, Aug. 18, 1940; s. Jost Joseph and Ingeborg Elizabeth (Dilthey) M.; children: Heidi Elizabeth, Matthew Christopher, Joshua Jost. BA, Bowdoin Coll., 1961; MD, Columbia U., 1969. Diplomate Am. Bd. Orthop. Surgery, Am. Bd. Forensic Medicine. Intern Columbia Presbyn. Med. Ctr., N.Y.C., 1969-70, resident, 1970-71; orthop. resident N.Y. Orthop. Hosp., 1971-73, jr. Anne C. Kane fellow, 1973-74, sr. Anne C. Kane fellow and hip fellow, 1974-75, traveling fellow, 1975-76; intenrat. A-O fellow, postgrad. fellow in biomechanics Case Western Res. U., instr. biomed. engring.; prof. clin. orthop. surgery, orthop. surgeon Columbia Coll. Physicians and Surgeons, 1976—; chief orthop. svc. Allen Pavillion, Columbia Presbyn. Med. Ctr., 1993—, chief orthop. spine surgery svc., 1998—. Col. USAR, ret. Fellow ACS, Am. Assn. for Surgery of Trauma, Am. Orthop. Assn., N.Am. Spine Soc., Am. Acad. Orthop. Surgeons, Internat. Coll. Surgeons, N.Y. Acad. Medicine; mem. AMA, Am. Coll. Physicians Execs., Orthop. Rsch. Soc., Am. Soc. Bone and Mineral Rsch., Royal Soc. Medicine (affiliate). Home: 102 Shearwater Ct E Jersey City NJ 07305-5483 Office: 5141 Broadway New York NY 10034-1159

MICHELSEN, DIANE, lawyer; b. Jersey City; BA in Social Sci., U. Calif., Berkeley, 1968; MSW, San Francisco State U., 1974; JD, Golden Gate U., 1979. Bar: Calif. 1980, Hawaii 2002. Therapist, adoption and surrogacy related issues Family Systems; cons. adoption and foster care State of Calif. Dept. Social Svcs.; social worker, adoption worker internat. and ind. adoptions State of Calif.; adoption worker L.A. County; lawyer, practice limited to family formation matters Lafayette, Calif., 1986—. Contbr. various mags., including Barrister Mag., Fair, Conceive Mag., ADOPT Net, Resolve, Parent's Monthly. Mem. Am. Acad. Adoption Attys. (v.p. 1995, pres. 1997, bd. dirs. 1990-95), Acad. Calif. Adoption Attys. (pres. 1987-93). Office: Law Office Diane Michelsen 3190 Old Tunnel Rd Lafayette CA 94549-4198

MICHELSEN, W(OLFGANG) JOST, neurosurgeon, educator, retired; b. Amsterdam, Holland, Aug. 20, 1935; came to U.S., 1936; s. Jost Joseph and Ingeborg Mathilde (Dilthey) M.; m. Constance Richards, Sept. 21, 1963 (div. 1987); children: Kristina, Elizabeth, Ingrid; m. Claude Claire Grenier, Mar. 30, 1988 (div. Oct. 1992); m. Martha Reed, Sept. 21, 1996. AB magna cum laude, Harvard U., 1959; MD, Columbia U., 1963. Diplomate Am. Bd. Neurol. Surgery. Intern in surgery Case Wester Res. U. Hosps., Cleve., 1963-64; asst. resident in neurology Mass. Gen. Hosp., Boston, 1964-65; asst. resident, then chief resident neurol. surgery Columbia-Presbyn. Med. Ctr., N.Y.C., 1965-69; from instr. to assoc. prof. neurosurgery Columbia U. Coll. Physicians and Surgeons, 1969-89, prof. clin. surgery, 1990—; fellow in neurosurgery Presbyn. Hosp., 1969-71, dir. neuro vascular surgery, 1989-90; dir. neurosurgery St. Luke's Roosevelt Hosp. Ctr., 1990—; prof. and chmn. dept. neurological surgery Albert Einstein Coll. Medicine, Bronx, N.Y., 1992-97; dir. neurosurgery Montefiore Med Ctr, 1992-97; ret., 1997. Asst. attending in neurosurgery, St. Luke's Hosp. Ctr., 1970—; cons. neurosurgeon Nyack (N.Y.) Hosp., 1972—, Englewood (N.J.) Hosp., 1972—; vis. prof. neurosurgery Tufts U., 1975, Emery U., 1977, Presbyn.-St. Luke's Hosp. Ctr., Chgo., 1978, Yale U., 1980; guest faculty Northwestern U., 1977, 78, U. Chgo., 1977, Colby Coll., 1980; mem. numerous panels on neurosurgery. Contbr. articles to profl. publs. 1st lt. U.S. Army, 1954-57. Grantee NIH, USPHS. Fellow ACS, Am. Heart Assn.; Mem. AMA, Am. Assn. Neurol. Surgeons (mem. sect. pediatric neurosurger), Neurosurg. Soc. Am. (v.p. 1984-85, pres. 1987-88), Congress Neurol. Surgeons, N.Y. Neurosurg. Soc., Neurosurg. Soc. State N.Y., N.Y. Acad. Scis., Assn. Rsch. in Nervous and Mental Diseases, Internat. Neurosurg. Soc., Internat. Pediatric Neurosurg. Soc., N.Y. State Med. Soc., N.Y. County Med. Soc. Office: 330 Borthwick Ave Ste 108 Portsmouth NH 03801

MICHELSOHN, MARIE-LOUISE, mathematician, educator; b. N.Y.C., Oct. 8, 1941; d. Marcel and Lucy Friedmann; children: Didi, Michelle. BS, U. Chgo., 1962, MS, 1963, PhD, 1974. Asst. prof. U. Calif. San Diego, La Jolla, 1974-75; lectr. U. Calif., Berkeley, 1975-77; mem. Inst. des Hautes Études Scientifiques, Bures sur Yvette, France, 1977-78; asst. prof. SUNY, Stony Brook, 1978-82, assoc. prof., 1982-88, prof., 1988—. Visitor Inst. Matematica Pura e Aplicada, Rio de Janeiro, 1980, Rsch. Inst. for Math. Scis., Kyoto, Japan, 1986, Tata Inst., Bombay, 1986-87; vis. mem. Inst. des Hautes Études Scientifiques, Bures-sur-Yvette, 1983-84, 93, 99-2000; dir. grad. program Dept. of Math SUNY, Stony Brook; rsch. prof. Math. Scis. Rsch. Inst., 1993-94. Author: Spin Geometry, 1989; contbr. articles to Am. Jour. Math., Acta Mathematica, Inventiones Mathematicae, Procs. London Math. Soc., Jour. Algebraic Geometry. Grantee NSF. Mem. Am. Math. Soc. Achievements include research in complex geometry, characterization of balanced spaces, Clifford and spinor cohomology, the geometry of spin manifolds and the Dirac operator, riemannian manifolds of positive curvature, the theory of algebraic cycles. Office: SUNY Dept Math Stony Brook NY 11794-0001

MICHELSON, BRUCE DAVID, information scientist; b. Indpls., May 8, 1952; s. Sidney and Evelyn Michelson; m. Victoria Louise Macy, July 30, 1950; children: Charles, Andrew. BS in Bus., Ind. U., Indpls., 1974. Staff auditor Arthur Andersen & Co., Indpls., 1974—75; dealer data processing rep. Caterpillar Tractor, Peoria, Ill., 1975—77; sales mgmt./customer svc. rep. Xerox Corp., Elmhurst, Ill. and Boston, 1978—85; various sales, mgmt. positions Digital Equip. Corp., Boston, 1985—98; svcs. mgr. Compaq Computer Corp., 1998—2000, dir. lifecycle planning N.Y.C., 2000—. Adv. bd. Xcell Image, Hartford, Conn., 2000—, Sales Mgrs. Troubleshooter by Charlie Romeo, Waltham, Mass., 1997—98. Author: Closed Loop Lifecycle Planning, 1998—99. Named TCO Cert. Expert, The Gartner Group, 1999; recipient Cert. of Achievement, TRB Cons., 1999.

MICHELSON, EDWARD HARLAN, retired medical educator; b. St. Louis, June 6, 1926; s. Leo and Bess (Levitt) M.; m. Carole Joy Fenias Benoit, Feb. 14, 1952 (div. 1967); children: Estelle, Sheryl, Robin; m. Louise Alice Desmond, Aug. 8, 1982. BS, U. Fla., 1949, MS, 1951; PhD, Harvard U., 1956. Instr. Cambridge (Mass.) Jr. Coll., 1951-53; rsch. assoc. to assoc. prof.Sch. Pub. Health Harvard U., Cambridge, 1953-83; prof. Uniformed Svcs. Sch. Health Scis., Bethesda, Md., 1983-95; prof. emeritus, 1995. Cons. in field. Editorial bd. Malacological Rev., 1984—; contbr. articles to profl. jours., chpts. to books. With USN, 1944-46; ATO. Mem. Am. Soc. parasitologists, Am. Soc. Tropical Medicine, Malacological Soc. London, Am. Inst. Biol. Scis., Am. Malacological Union, Phi Beta Kappa, Phi Kappa Phi. Avocations: chess, stamp collecting, collecting old jazz recordings. Home: 9735 SW 92nd Ct Apt D Ocala FL 34481-8635

MICHELSON, GERTRUDE GERALDINE, retired retail company executive; b. Jamestown, N.Y., June 3, 1925; d. Thomas and Celia Rosen; m. Horace Michelson, Mar. 28, 1947 (dec. Apr. 2002); children: Martha Ann (dec.), Barbara Jane. BA, Pa. State U., 1945; LL.B., Columbia U., 1947; LLD with honors, Adelphi U., 1981; DHL with honors, New Rochelle Coll., 1983; LLD with honors, Marymount Manhattan Coll., 1988; PhD in Policy Analysis, Rand Grad. Sch. With Macy's N.Y., N.Y.C., 1947—, mgmt. trainee, 1947-48, various mgmt. positions, v.p. employee personnel, 1963-70, sr. v.p. for labor and consumer relations, 1970-72, dir., mem. exec. com., 1970—; sr. v.p. pers. labor and consumer rels. Macy & Co., Inc., 1972-79, sr. v.p. external affairs, 1979-80, R.H. Macy & Co., Inc., 1980-92, sr. advisor, 1992-94; ret., 1995. Bd. dirs. GE Co. Chmn. Helena Rubenstein Found.; ret. bd. dirs. Markle Found.; chmn. emeritus bd. trustees Columbia U.; life trustee Spelman Coll.; pres. bd. overseers Tchrs. Ins. and Annuity Assn. of Am. Coll. Retirement Equities Fund, ret. Recipient Disting. Svc. medal Pa. State U., 1969. Mem. N.Y.C. Ptnrship. (vice chmn.), Women's Forum, Econ. Club N.Y. Home: 70 E 10th St New York NY 10003-5102 Office: Federated Dept Stores Inc 151 W 34th St New York NY 10001-2101

MICHELSON, LILLIAN, motion picture researcher; b. Manhattan, N.Y., June 21, 1928; d. Louis and Dora (Keller) Farber; m. Harold Michelson, Dec. 14, 1947; children: Alan Bruce, Eric Neil, Dennis Paul. Vol. Goldwyn Libr., Hollywood, Calif., 1961-69; owner Former Goldwyn Rsch. Libr., 1969—; ind. location scout, 1973—. Mem. Motion Picture Libr. Found., 2002—, Friends of L.A. Pub. Libr. Mem.: Acad. Motion Picture Arts and Scis. Office: c/o Dreamworks SKG Rsch Libr 1000 Flower St Glendale CA 91201-3007 Fax: 818-695-4326. E-mail: hmichelson@dreamworks.com.

MICHELSON, SETH GARY, biomathematician; b. Miami Beach, Fla., Aug. 29, 1950; s. Bernard and Estelle Leah (Palay) M.; m. Carole Elizabeth Coleman, Mar. 12, 1978. BS, Tulane U., 1972; MA, U. Calif., Berkeley, 1974; MS, UCLA, 1980, PhD, 1987. Asst. prof. dept. radiation biology Brown U., Providence, 1984-87; sr. biomathematician Syntex Drug Discovery, Palo Alto, Calif., 1988-90, head dept. biomath., 1990-94, dir. basic rsch. sci. support, 1994—95; dir., prin. scientist rsch. support and info. svcs. Roche Bioscis., 1995—2001; v.p. Insilico R and D Entelos, Inc., Menlo Pk., Calif., 2001—. Adj. assoc. prof. radiation medicine Brown U., 1988—, U. Calif. Extension, Berkeley, 1992—; mem. faculty PMA Edn. and Rsch. inst., Maclean, Va., 1992—; guest lectr. Soviet Acad. Scis., 1988, Beijing Med. U., 1989, Russian Acad. Scis., 1990. Contbr. over 50 articles to profl. jours. Vol. Spl. Olympics, L.a., 1983. Grantee Ocean State Gov.'s Rsch. Fund, 1987, 88, Am. Cancer Soc., 1985-87; O'Donnell rsch. scholar in oncology, 1987-88. Mem. Soc. Math. Biol. (assoc.). Democrat.

MICHELSON, SONIA, music educator, author; b. L.A., Feb. 14, 1928; d. Maurice and Elizabeth (Jacobs) Saeta; m. Irving Michelson, Apr. 4, 1954 (div. Aug. 1982); children: Ann Michelson Shoham, Louis E., Hadassah Zelman, Zahava Waldman, Elisheva Levin, Eliyahu Michaeli, Yaacov. BA, U. Calif., Berkeley, 1949. Instr. in guitar Suzuki Music Acad. of Chgo., 1980-81, Music Arts Sch., Highland Park, Ill., 1973-82; dir. in classical guitar Michelson Classic Guitar Studio, Chgo., 1973-88, dir. L.A., 1988—. Cons. Music Educators Nat. Conf., Atlantic City, N.J., 1976; columnist Guitar Found. of Am., L.A., 1984—. Author: Easy Classic Guitar Solos, 1977, Classical Guitar Study, 1982, New Dimensions in Classical Guitar for Children, 1984, Young Beginner's First Repertoire for Classical Guitar, 1996; contbr. articles to profl. jours. Mem. Am. String Tchrs. Assn. (spl. cons. 1977-85), Chgo. Classical Guitar Soc. (pres. 1978-88), Guitar Found. of Am. (mem. editorial bd. 1972—), Suzuki Assn. Am., Nat. Music Tchrs. Assn., Music Tchrs. Assn. Calif. Democrat. Jewish. Avocations: Hebrew and Israeli language studies, reading, gardening, writing. Home: 1465 Reeves St Los Angeles CA 90035-2945

MICHELSTETTER, STANLEY HUBERT, lawyer; b. Milw., July 8, 1946; s. Donald Lee and Gloria (Menke) M.; m. Joyce Bladow, Apr. 29, 1972; children: Chad S., Chris E. BA in Math., U. Wis., 1968, JD, 1972. Bar: Wis. 1972, U.S. Dist. Ct. (we. dist.) Wis. 1972. Staff atty. Wis. Employment Rels. Commn., Milw., 1972-80; pvt. practice, 1980—; adminstrv. law judge, equal rights div. adminstrat. Wis. Dept Industry, Labor & Human Rels., 1992-93. Chmn. North Shore Rep. Club, Milw., 1984-86. Served to 2d lt. Wis. N.G., 1968-74. Mem. Wis. Bar Assn. (chmn. 1993), Milw. Bar Assn., Nat. Acad. Arbitrators, Indsl. Rels. Rsch. Assn. (bd. dirs. 1987—), Rotary. Republican. Jewish. Home: 1500 W Green Brook Rd Milwaukee WI 53217-1515 Office: 1749 N Prospect Ave Milwaukee WI 53202-1966 also: PMB 37 5185 Broadway Gary IN 46409-2708 E-mail: stan@expcpc.com.

MICHENER, CHARLES DUNCAN, entomologist, researcher, entomologist, educator; b. Pasadena, Calif., Sept. 22, 1918; s. Harold and Josephine (Rigden) Michener; m. Mary Hastings, Jan. 1, 1941; children: David, Daniel, Barbara, Walter. BS, U. Calif., Berkeley, 1939, PhD, 1941. Tech. asst. U. Calif., Berkeley, 1939-42; asst. curator Am. Mus. Natural History, N.Y.C., 1942-46, assoc. curator, 1946-48, research assoc., 1949—; assoc. prof. U. Kans., 1948-49, prof., 1949-89, prof. emeritus, 1989—, chmn. dept. entomology, 1949-61, 72-75, Watkins Disting. prof. entomology, 1959-89, acting chmn. dept. systematics, ecology, 1968-69, Watkins Disting. prof. systematics and ecology, 1969-89; dir. Snow Entomol. Museum, 1974-83, state entomologist, 1949-61. Vis. rsch. prof. U. Paraná, Curitiba, Brazil, 1955—56. Author (with Mary H. Michener): (book) American Social Insects, 1951; author: (with S. F. Sakagami) Nest Architecture of the Sweat Bees, 1962, The Social Behavior of the Bees, 1974; author: (with M. D. Breed and H. E. Evans) The Biology of Social Insects, 1982; author: (with D. Fletcher) Kin Recognition in Animals, 1987; author: (with R. McGinley and B. Danforth) The Bee Genera of North and Central America, 1994, The Bees of the World, 2000; contbr. articles to profl. jours.; editor: (book) Evolution, 1962—64; Am. editor: Insectes Sociaux, 1954—55, Am. editor: , 1962—90, assoc. editor: Ann. Rev. Ecology and Systematics, 1970—90. Served to capt. San Corps AUS, 1943—46. Recipient Disting. Rsch. medal, Internat. Soc. Hymenopterists, 2002; fellow Guggenheim, U. Paraná, 1955—56, Africa, 1966—67, Fulbright, U. Queensland, 1958—59; scholar Rsch., U. Costa Rica, 1963. Fellow: AAAS, Royal Entomol. Soc. London, Am. Acad. Arts and Scis., Am. Entomol. Soc., Entomol. Soc. Am. (C. V. Riley award 1999); mem.: NAS, Kans. Entomol. Soc. (pres. 1950), Linnean Soc. London (corr.), Soc. Systematic Zoologists (hon.; pres. 1969), Russian Entomol. Soc. (hon.), Brazilian Acad. Scis. (corr.), Internat. Union Study Social Insects (pres. 1977—82,), Am. Soc. Naturalists (pres. 1978), Soc. Study Evolution (pres. 1967). Home: 1706 W 2nd St Lawrence KS 66044-1016 Office: U Kans Snow Hall 1460 Jayhawk Blvd Lawrence KS 66045-7523 E-mail: michener@ku.edu.

MICHENER, JAMES LLOYD, medical educator; b. Dec. 19, 1952; m. Gwendolyn Curtis Murphy; children: Rebecca Liane, Joshua Kieran. BA, Oberlin (Ohio) Coll., 1974; MD, Harvard Med. Sch., 1978. Diplomate Am. Bd. Family Practice. Resident in family medicine Duke U. Med. Ctr., Durham, N.C., 1978-81, Kellogg fellow, 1981-82, clin. prof. dept. cmty. and family medicine, 1994—, chmn. dept. cmty. and family medicine, 1994—. V.p. Durham Health Care, Inc., 1985-86. Co-author: Nutrition in Practice, 1990, 2d edit., 1992; contbr. numerous articles to med. pubs. including Academic Medicine, The Jour. of Family Practice, Medical Care, others; mem. editl. bd. Rx Nutrition, 1989-91; presenter in field. Bd. dirs. N.C. Med. Soc. Found., 1995—; STFM rep. resource com. on nutrition edn. Am. Acad. Family Practice Found., 1987-91. Grantee The Fullerton Found., Inc., The Josiah Macy, Jr. Found., U.S. Dept. Health and Human Svcs., Kate B. Reynolds Charitable Trust. Mem. AMA, Assn. Am. Med. Colls. (exec. coun. 2001—), Assn. Tchrs. of Preventive Medicine, Am. Acad. of Family Physicians Found., Am. Heart Assn. (del. Nat. Cholesterol Edn. Program 1987), N.C. Acad. Family Physicians (bd. dirs. 1995—), Assn. Dept. Family Medicine (bd. dirs. 1997—, sec. 1998—), Coun. Acad. Socs. (adminstrn. bd. 2000—), World Orgn. Nat. Colls., Acads. and Academic Assn. Gen. Practitioners and Family Physicians, Assn. Am. Med. Colls., Am. Austrian Founds. Internat. Health Forum (mem. steering com.). Home: 4011 Duck Pond Trail Chapel Hill NC 27514-9758 Office: Duke U Med Ctr PO Box 2914 Durham NC 27710-0001 E-mail: miche001@mc.duke.edu.

MICHENFELDER, ALBERT A. lawyer; b. St. Louis, July 21, 1926; s. Albert A. and Ruth Josephine (Donahue) M.; m. Lois Barbara Sullivan, Sept. 03, 1949 (div. May 2, 1967); children: Michael J., Ann C. Michenfelder Yancey, Elizabeth D. Michenfelder Brown; m. Ramona Jo Dysart, July 12, 1968 (dec. Jan. 2, 1998); 1 child, Julie D. Michenfelder Wolfe. B of Naval Sci., Marquette U., 1946; LLB, St. Louis U., 1950. Bar: Mo. 1950, U.S. Dist. Ct. (ea. dist.) Mo. 1950, U.S. Supreme Ct. 1975. Assoc. Flynn & Challis, St. Louis, 1950-54; pvt. practice, 1954-55; of counsel Husch & Eppenberger LLC. Mem. 21st Cir. Jud. Commn., St. Louis, 1981-87. Contbr. articles to profl. jours. City atty. City of Webster Groves, Mo., 1966-79; mem. John Marshall Club, St. Louis. Lt. (j.g.) USNR, 1944-47. Mem. Mo. Bar Assn., Bar. Assn. Met. St. Louis, St. Louis County Bar Assn. (pres. 1966), Westborough Country Club. Republican. Avocations: golf, tennis. Office: Husch & Eppenberger LLC 190 Carondelet Plz Ste 600 Saint Louis MO 63105-3441 Office Fax: 314-480-1505. E-mail: al.michenfelder@husch.com.

MICHENFELDER, JOHN DONAHUE, anesthesiology educator; b. St. Louis, Apr. 13, 1931; s. Albert A. and Ruth J. (Donahue) Michenfelder; m. Margaret Grey Nick, Oct. 22, 1955 (dec. Dec. 1971); children: Carol, David, Joseph, Paul, Matthew, Laura; m. Mary Monica Milroy, Aug. 11, 1972; 1 child Patrick. BS, St. Louis U., 1951, MD, 1955. Diplomate Am. Bd. Anesthesiology. Intern Presbyn. St. Luke's Hosp., Chgo., 1955—56, resident in internal medicine, 1956; resident in anesthesiology Mayo Clinic, Rochester, Minn., 1958—61, cons. in anesthesiology, 1961—93; prof. anesthesiology Mayo Med. Sch., 1976—93, emeritus prof., 1993—. Author: Anesthesia and the Brain, 1988, Clinical Neuroanesthesia, 1990. Fellow Faculty Anaesthetists, Royal Coll. Surgeons Ireland, 1982, Royal Coll. Surgeons Eng., 1988; grantee NIH, 1966—89, 1991—95. Mem.: Assn. Univ. Anesthetists (councilman 1975—78), Inst. Medicine, Am. Soc. Anesthesiologists (Excellence in Rsch. award 1990, Disting. Svc. award 1990). Avocations: upland game bird hunting, gardening, reading, writing. Home: 325 1st Ave NW Oronoco MN 55960-1410 Office: Mayo Clinic Emeritus Office 200 1st St SW Rochester MN 55905-0002 E-mail: am31@pitel.net.

MICHENFELDER, JOSEPH FRANCIS, public relations executive; b. Webster Groves, Mo., Mar. 30, 1929; s. Albert Aloysius and Ruth Josephine (Donahue) M.; m. Audrey Laurine Glynn, Aug. 8, 1970. BA, N.Y. State U., N.Y.C., 1951, STB, 1954, MRE, 1955; MS in Journalism, Columbia U., 1958. Projects dir. Maryknoll Headquarters, Ossining, N.Y., 1955-57, communications dir., 1958-62; dir., chief exec. officer Noticias Aliadas, S.A., Lima, Peru, 1962-69; pub. rels. dir. Pub. Affairs Analysts, Inc., N.Y.C., 1970-72, exec. v.p., 1973-89; sr. v.p. Napolitan Assocs./PAA, Inc., N.Y.C., 1989-95; pres., CEO, 1995—. Pres. IDOC/N.Am., Inc., N.Y.C., 1976—. Mng. Editor (polit. quarterly) POLITEIA, 1970-73; co-producer: TV documentary A Quiet Revolution, 1987. Trustee The Fund for Peace, 1994—, Coun. on Hemispheric Affairs, Washington, 1980—; cons. UNESCO WHO, Bogota, Lima, 1964-66; bd. dirs. Jobs for Youth, Inc., N.Y.C., 1978-84. Mem. Internat. Pub. Relations Assn., Internat. Assn. Polit. Cons., Columbia U. Journalism Alumni Fed. (pres. 1971-74), Ovrses Press Club, Columbia Club. Democrat. Avocations: theater arts, film, creative writing, ecology, Third World affairs. Office: Napolitan Assocs PAA Inc 55 5th Ave New York NY 10003-4301 E-mail: pancomm@aol.com.

MICHERO, WILLIAM HENDERSON, retired retail trade executive; b. Fort Worth, June 19, 1925; s. William Alvin and Lela Belle (Henderson) M.; m. Nan Elaine Henderson, July 9, 1948; children— Jane Elaine Michero Christie, William Sherman, Thomas Edward. BS in Commerce, Tex. Christian U., 1948. Sec. Tandy Corp., Fort Worth, 1960-75, v.p., 1970-75; with Tandycrafts, Inc., Fort Worth, 1975-90, sr. v.p., sec., dir., 1979-83, chmn. bd., 1983-90, ret., 1990. Sec. B.F. Johnston Found., Fort Worth, 1962-90. Bd. dirs. David L. Tandy Found., Fort Worth, 1968-99, Oakwood Cemetery Assn., 1979-89, Panther Boys Club, 1974-78, Fort Worth Mus. Sci. and History, 1973-75, pres. 1975, United Way; chmn. Distributive Edn. Council, 1970. Served with U.S. Navy, 1943-46. Mem.: Fort Worth, Colonial Country. Home: 4705 Shady Ridge Ct Fort Worth TX 76109-1803

MICHIE, DANIEL BOORSE, JR. lawyer; b. Phila., July 28, 1922; s. Daniel Boorse and Mae (Mueller) M.; m. Barbara F. Maddox, Aug. 29, 1970. BS, Harvard U., 1943; LLB, U. Va., 1948. Bar: Pa. 1949. Lawyer, Phila., 1949-94; assoc. Harry J. Alker (Esq.), 1949, Kephart & Kephart, 1950-51, Fell & Spalding, 1952-53, ptnr., 1954-68, Fell, Spalding, Goff & Rubin, 1969-82, Fell & Spalding, 1982-94; of counsel Richard W. Stevens, Esq., Jenkintown, Pa., 1994-2001; spl. master U.S. Ct. Appeals (3d cir.), 1970—; solicitor Twp. Abington, Pa., 1958-78. Pres. Phila. Council Internat. Visitors, 1957-60, chmn., 1979-81; pres. Phila. Crime Commn., 1960-63, Phila. Fellowship Commn., 1970-71; chmn. Pa. Adv. Com. on Probation, 1966-92, Bd. Phila. Prisons, 1968-71 Pres. Nat. Assn. Citizens Crime Commns., 1961-62, Unitarian Universalist Svc. Com., 1969-72; regional co-chmn. NCCJ, 1967-71, nat. bd. govs., 1971-80, nat. trustee, 1968-98, nat. exec. bd., 1981-88, nat. advisor, 1998—; vice chmn. Southeastern Pa. chpt. ARC, 1978-82; bd. dirs. Urban League Phila., 1981-83; bd. dirs. Valley Forge coun. Boy Scouts Am., 1955-84, adv. bd., 1984-96, adv. coun. Cradle of Liberty coun., 1996-2001; mem. St. Andrew's Soc., counselor, 1989-95; mem. Friendly Sons of St. Patrick, counselor, 1989-98. Lt. USNR, 1943-46. Mem. ABA (chmn. organized crime com. 1964-65), Phila. Bar Assn. (gov. 1970-72), Pa. Bar Assn. (ho. of dels. 1971-2000), Am. Coll. Real Estate Lawyers, Fed. Bar Assn., Am. Judicature Soc., Navy League (dir. Phila. 1967-73, v.p. 1973-76, pres. 1976-78, nat. dir. 1977-83). Republican. Unitarian Universalist (ch. pres. 1961-62, dist. pres. 1966-69). Home and Office: 104 Sunset Dr Marathon FL 33050-2940 *The most important standard of conduct I have attempted to follow is to respect the individuality and dignity of every person— including myself. Early in the practice of law I learned I could best represent my client in a business matter by gaining an understanding of the motivations and needs of the persons on the other side. Only then could I determine whether an agreement or settlement was feasible— as it almost always was. I found this same approach invariably helpful in other human endeavors.*

MICHIGAN, ALAN, lawyer; b. N.Y.C., May 26, 1945; s. Norman and Miriam (Cooper) M.; m. Teri Ruth Samach, June 29, 1980; 1 child, Edward. BA, Hobart Coll., 1966; JD, Fordham U., 1974. Bar: N.Y. 1975, U.S. Dist. Ct. (so. and ea. dists.) N.Y. 1975. Atty. Met. Life Ins. Co., N.Y.C., 1974-76; assoc. Dreyer and Traub, 1976-77, Trubin, Sillcocks, Edelman & Knapp, N.Y.C., 1977-79, Gordon, Hurwitz, Butowsky, Baker, Weitzner & Shalov, N.Y.C., 1979-81; ptnr. Brauner, Baron, Rosenzweig & Klein, LLP, 1981—. Mem. N.Y.C. Mayor's Commn. for Vietnam Vets. Meml., 1984; founder, bd. dirs. N.Y. Vietnam Vets. Leadership Program, N.Y.C., 1982-97. Lt. USN, 1968-71, USNR, 1971-79. Mem. N.Y. State Bar Assn. Democrat. Jewish. Avocations: military history, old house restoration, antique autos. Home: 626 James St Pelham Manor New York NY 10803 Office: Brauner Baron Rosenzweig & Klein LLP 61 Broadway New York NY 10006-2701 E-mail: amichigan@braunerbaron.com.

MICHLER, ROBERT E. heart surgeon; b. July 8, 1956; m. Sally Radcliffe Sandercock, May 28, 1983; children: Alexandra Keats, Sarah Radcliffe, Elizabeth Tamsin. BA magna cum laude, Harvard U., 1978; MD, Dartmouth U., 1981. Diplomate Am. Bd. Surgery, Am. Bd. Thoracic Surgery, Am. Bd. Surgery-Critical Care. Intern Columbia-Presbyn. Med. Ctr., N.Y.C., 1981-82, resident gen. surgery, 1982-86, chief resident gen. surgery, 1986-87, resident cardiothoracic surgery, 1987-88, chief resident cardiothoracic surgery, 1988-89; chief resident pediat. cardiothoracic surgery Boston Children's Hosp., Harvard Med. Sch., 1989-90, attending surgeon, 1990-97, dir. cardiac transplant svc., 1993-97; assoc. prof. surgery Columbia U., 1990-97, dir. cardiac transplantation rsch. lab., 1991-97; Karl P. Klassen prof. surgery, chief thoracic surgery Ohio State U., Columbus, 1997—; dir. cardiothoracic transplantation and rsch. Ohio State U. Med. Ctr., 1997—, co-dir. heart and lung inst., 1997—; dir. Heart Hosp., 2000—. Rsch. fellow cardiopulmonary transplantation Columbia U., Coll. Physicians and Surgeons, N.Y.C., 1984-85; presenter and lectr. in field; founder, chmn. Heart Care Internat., 1994—. Contbr. chpts. to books and articles to profl. jours. Exec. coun. mem. Second Congl. Ch., Greenwich, Conn., 1994—. Recipient Claire Lucille Pace Humanitarian award, 1996; named Person of Week, ABC World News Tonight, 1995; Leopold Schepp scholar Dartmouth Med. Sch., Hanover, N.H., 1981. Fellow ACS, Am. Coll. Cardiology, Am. Coll. Chest Physicians; mem. AMA, Am. Bd. Surgery, Am. Bd. Thoracic Surgery, Soc. Thoracic Surgeons, Internat. Soc. for Heart and Lung Transplantation, Soc. Pediat. Cardiac Surgery, Soc. Critical Care Medicine, Am. Soc. for Artificial Internal Organs, N.Y. Soc. for Thoracic Surgery, N.Y. Transplantation Soc., Riverside Yacht Club (Greenwich, Conn.). Avocations: sailing, sculling, squash, tennis. Home: 135 Preston Rd Bexley OH 43209 Office: Ohio State U Med Ctr Doan Hall N825 410 W 10th Ave Columbus OH 43210-1228

MICHNICH, MARIE E. health facility administrator, consultant, educator; M Health Svs. Adminstrn., PhD Health Svs. Rsch. , UCLA. Asst. prof. health svs. U. Washington; sr. exec. v.p. Health Policy, Am. Coll. Cardiology Clin. Practice and Sci. Svs. Divsn.; dir. Health Policy Programs and Fellowships Nat. Acad. Scis. Inst. Medicine, 2002—. Cons, spkr. in field; legis. asst. health policy Medicare, Medicaid, maternal and child health; legis. asst. Peer Rev. Orgns. U.S. Senate Majority Leader, Robert Dole (R-KS); staff liaison Exec. br., Ho. and Senate offices, health profl. and trade assns. ; mem. several nat. health policy groups. Editor 2 news pubs. Fellow Robert Wood Johnson Health Policy . Mem.: Am. Coll. Cardiology (assoc., sr. assoc. exec. v.p.), Am. Pharm. Assn. Found. (1st pub. mem. bd. dirs. 2002—), Robert Wood Johnson Health Policy Fellows Program (mem. adv. bd., dir.), Health Care Quality Alliance (former chmn.). Office: Office Health Policy Programs & Fellowsh 500 5th St NW Washington DC 20001*

MICHOD, CHARLES LOUIS, JR. lawyer; b. Champaign, Ill., July 19, 1943; s. Charles Louis Sr. and Florence Wise Michod; m. Susan Alexander, Aug. 16, 1969; children: Alexander, Richard, Michael. AB, Princeton U., 1995; JD, U. Mich., 1968. Bar: N.Y. 1968, Ill. 1969. Assoc. Shearman & Sterling, N.Y.C., 1968-69, Hopkins & Sutter, Chgo., 1969-72; ptnr. Martin, Craig, Chester & Sonnenschein, 1972-94, Kelly, Olson, Michod, De Haan & Richter, Chgo., 1995—. Ptnr. DePaul Devels., Chgo., 1986—, Carpenter Ventures, Chgo., 1989—; bd. dirs. Bouquet Assocs., Chgo. and St. Gallen, Switzerland. Bd. govs. Sch. Art Inst., Chgo., 1990—; chmn. Oxbow, Inc., Saugatuck, Mich., 1995—. Recipient Cert. of Appreciation, Law Club of the City of Chgo., 1997, Cert. of Merit, Ill. Dept. Conservation, 1980. Mem. ABA, Chgo. Bar Assn., Univ. Club Chgo., Law Club (pres. 1996-97), Lawyers Club, Coral Creek Club, Point O'Woods Country Club. Avocations: golf, squash, art, jazz. Office: Kelly Olson Michod De Haan Richter 30 S Wacker Dr Ste 2300 Chicago IL 60606 E-mail: cmichod@komdr.com.

MICHOPOULOS, ARISTOTLE V. humanities educator, researcher; b. Kotylion, Arcadia, Peloponnesos, Greece, Apr. 22, 1944; s. Vassilios A. Michopoulos and Anastasia D. Papazafeiropoulos; m. Despina Dimitropoulos (div. Jan. 30, 1996). BA, U. of Athens, Athens, Greece, 1967; MA, Grad. Ctr. of C.U.N.Y., New York, NY, 1976; PhD, Fla. State U., Tallahassee, FL, 1980. Translator Greek Orthodox Archdiocese of N. & S. Am., New York, NY, 1970—71; translator and adminstr. Hellenic indsl. Devel. Corp., 1972—74; h.s. tchr. Bd. of Edn. of NYC, 1975—76; adj. instr. Fla. State U., Tallahassee, 1977—78, asst. project dir. and curriculum writer, 1978—80; asst. prof. U. of Fla., Gainesville, 1980—87; prof. of greek studies and dir. Hellenic Coll., Brookline, Mass., 1987—. Dean Hellenic Coll., Brookline, Mass., 1995—, greek studies dept. dir., Mass., 1987—; translator, cons. Various Organizations, Many, 1980—. Rep. to u.s. dept. of edn. Greek Orthodox Archdiocese, New York, NY, 1992—98; del., com. mem. Coun. on Hellenes Abroad, Chicago, Ill., 1995—2002; nat. coord. Paideia project, Greece, 1999—2002. Recipient Fulbright Award, Fulbright Program, 1977, Socratic Award, U. of Fla., 1997; fellow Fellowship by U.S. Dept. of H.E.W., U.S. Dept. of H.E.W., 1976-1979. Mem.: Kotylion Syllogos (cons. 1980—2002, Merit Award 2000),

Am. Hellenic Edn. Assn. (AHEPA), Modern Greek Studies Assn. Avocations: tennis, swimming, backgammon, traveling. Office: Hellenic College 50 Goddard Ave Brookline MA 02445

MICHRINA, BARRY PAUL, chemist, educator; b. Spangler, Pennsylvania, May 28, 1947; s. Francis Paul and Anna Mae Michrina. BS in Chemistry, St. Francis Coll., 1969; MS in Chemistry, Colo. State U., 1971; PhD of Agronomy, Pa. State U., 1980; PhD of Anthropology, SUNY Binghamton, 1991. Rsch. chemist Eastman Kodak Co., Rochester, NY, 1971—77; rsch. assoc. Cornell U., Ithaca, 1981—83; instr. Indiana U. of Pa., 1990; prof. anthropology Mesa State Coll., Grand Junction, Colo., 1990—. Dir., chair Victor Turner Prize, 2000—01. Author: Pennsylvania Mining Families, 1993, Person to Person, 1996, Mines, Memories and More, 2000; contbr. Adv. student orgn. Native Am. Coun., Grand Junction, 1999—. Grantee Rsch. grant, Mesa State Coll. Found., 1997. Mem.: Soc. for Anthropology of Consciousness (editor 1995—97), Soc. for Humanistic Anthropology (bd. dirs.), Am. Anthrop. Assn. Office: Mesa State Coll 1100 North Ave Grand Junction CO 81501-7605

MICK, DEBORAH WEST FAIRCHILD, elementary education educator; b. Lorain, Ohio, Feb. 3, 1952; d. Harold Cole and Carolyn Elaine (Fordyce) West; m. Bruce Allen Fairchild, June 22, 1974 (div. 1986); children: Stephanie, Jared, Elizabeth; m. Alvin R. Mick, Oct. 12, 2001. BA in Music and Sociology, Houghton Coll., N.Y., 1974; student, U. N. Ala., Florence, 1984-85; BS in Elem. Edn., Ashland Coll., Ohio, 1987; MEd in Curriculum and Instrn., Ashland U., 1991. Cert. tchr., Ohio, adminstr. Music tchr. Yamaha Sch. Music, Newbury, N.Y., 1975-76; pvt. piano tchr. Petersburg, Va., 1976-79; jr. high reading tchr. Clearview Schs., Lorain, Ohio, 1987—; tchr. Durling Elem. Clearview, Vincent Elem./Kindergarten, 1989-90; kindergarten tchr. Erieview Elem. Sch., Avon Lake, Ohio, 1990-91; 3rd grade tchr. Westview Elem. Sch., 1991-92, tchr. primary, 1992—. Games club advisor Clearview Jr. High, Lorain Ohio 1987--; spelling bee advisor Clearview jr. high, Lorain Ohio 1987—; student coun. advisor Westview Elem., 1998-2001, choir pianist, 1998—. FLOWC Advt. Com. Fort Lee Officer's Wives Club, Va. 1978-79; OWC Sec. Finger Lakes Officer's Wives Club, Seneca N.Y. 1981-82; OWC V.P. Fla. Officers Wives Club, Seneca Army N.Y., 1982-83; Choir Pianist Faith Baptist Ch., Amherst Ohio 1986--. Mem. NEA, Ohio Edn. Assn., Kappa Delta Pi. Democrat. Baptist. Avocations: music, reading, water sports, swimming, boating, water skiing. Home: 2633 Vassar Ave Lorain OH 44053-2359 Office: Westview Elem Sch 155 Moore Rd Avon Lake OH 44012-1127

MICK, MARGARET ANNE, communications executive; b. Phila., Apr. 24, 1947; d. Charles Philip and Helen Margaret (Amig) Maurer; m. Donald Kenneth Mick, Sept. 8, 1979. BS with honors, Pa. State U., 1969; MA, NYU, 1972. Assoc. producer Visual Edn. Corp., Princeton, N.J., 1972-73; program devel. specialist AEtna Life & Casualty, Hartford, Conn., 1973-78, sr. program devel. specialist, 1978-81, mgr. audiovisual communications, 1981-82, dir. audiovisual and mktg. communications, 1982-84, dir. mktg. communications, 1984-86, dir. bus. devel., 1986-88, asst. v.p. customized communications, 1988-96; pres. Sachem Comm., Guilford, Conn., 1996-97; cons. Watson Wyatt Worldwide, 1997—. Juror EFLA Am. Film Festival, Hartford, 1977-79. Writer, dir., producer TV films including (ednl.) PAC-Man in the Money Works. Recipient Apex award Conn. Women's Heritage Trail, 2000. Mem. Info. Film Producers Am. (chmn. 1981, treas. 1982, Conn. Valley Chpt.), Internat. TV Assn. (chmn. 1983), Hartford Women's Network, Mature Market Inst., Bus. and Profl. Advt. Assn. Republican. Avocations: gardening, reading, dance. Home and Office: 483 Colonial Rd Guilford CT 06437-3127

MICK, THOMAS CHARLES, radiologist; b. Hamilton, Ohio, Feb. 13, 1937; BS, U. Dayton, 1959; MD, U. Cin., 1963. Diplomate Am. Bd. Radiology. Intern Miami Valley Hosp., Dayton, Ohio, 1963-64; resident radiology U. Va., Charlottesville, 1969-71, chief resident, 1970-71, fellow radiology, 1972-73; radiologist Good Samaritan Hosp., Dayton, Ohio, 1973-92, sect. chief spl. procedures, 1982-87, chmn. dept. radiol. svcs. and med. imaging, 1986-87, vice chmn., 1987-89; courtesy pvt. Wayne Hosp., Greenville, 1973-92, St. Elizabeth's Hpsp., Dayton, 1973-92; active duty USNR Newport Naval Hosp., R.I., 1964-66; resident U. Cin., 1967-69; assoc. clin. prof. radiology Wright State U.; ret., 1992. Mem. AMA, Am. Coll. Radiology, Ohio State Radiol. Soc., Radiol. Soc. N.Am., Alpha Omega Alpha. Home: 107 Forestview Dr Dayton OH 45459-2842

MICKEL, EMANUEL JOHN, foreign language educator; b. Lemont, Ill., Oct. 11, 1937; s. Emanuel John and Mildred (Newton) M.; m. Kathleen Russell, May 31, 1959; children: Jennifer, Chiara, Heather. BA, La. State U., 1959; MA, U. N.C., 1961, PhD, 1965. Asst. prof. U. Nebr., Lincoln, 1965-67, assoc. prof., 1967-68, Ind. U., Bloomington, 1968-73, prof., 1973—, dir. Medieval Studies Inst., 1976-91, chmn. French and Italian, 1984-95. Cons. NEH; French advisor Soc. Rencesvals, 1995-98; adv. bd. mem. Nineteenth Century French Studies, 1995—. Author: Marie de France, 1974, Eugene Fromentin, 1982, Ganelon Treason and the Chanson de Roland, 1989, Jules Vernes Complete Twenty Thousand Leagues Under the Sea, 1992, Enfances Godefroi and Retour de Cornumarant, 1999. Capt. U.S. Army, 1963-65. Grantee NEH, Washington, 1978-84; Lilly Open fellow Lilly Found., Indpls., 1981-82; Chevalier dans l'Ordre des Palmes Academiques, 1997. Avocations: music, theater, sports, travel, ancient literature. Office: French & Italian Dept Indiana Univ 642 Ballantine Hall Bloomington IN 47401-5020 E-mail: mickel@indiana.edu.

MICKEL, JOSEPH THOMAS, lawyer; b. Monroe, La., Nov. 12, 1951; s. Toufick and Ruth Ella (Phelps) M.; m. Carlene Elise Nickens, Dec. 10, 1981 (div.); children: Thomas, Matthew. BA, La. State U., 1975; postgrad., Tulane U., 1977-78; JD, So. U., 1979. Bar: La. 1979, U.S. Dist. Ct. (mid. dist.) La. 1981, U.S. Ct. Appeals (5th cir.) 1981, U.S. Dist. Ct. (we. dist.) La. 1983, U.S. Ct. Mil. Appeals 1985, U.S. Supreme Ct. 1985. Staff atty. Pub. Defenders Office, Baton Rouge, 1979-80; assoc. Law Offices of Michael Fugler, 1981; asst. dist. atty. La. 4th Jud. Dist. Atty.'s Office, Monroe, 1982-89; ptnr. Bruscato, Loomis & Street, 1984-85; Asst. U.S. Atty. Western Dist., U.S. Atty.'s Office, Lafayette, 1989—. Adj. prof. Northeast La. U., Monroe, 1988; mem. U.S. Dept. Justice Organized Crime Drug Task Force, 1992-93; instr. Acadiana Law Enforcement Tng. Acad., U. Lafayette La., 1995—; asst. bar examiner, com. on bar admissions Supreme Ct. State of La. Elder Presbyn. Ch., 1995—. Republican. Avocations: trapshooting, skeetshooting, bird hunting, fishing. Home: PO Box 91961 Lafayette LA 70509-1961 Office: US Atty Office 800 Lafayette St Ste 2200 Lafayette LA 70501-6865 E-mail: joseph.nickel@usdoj.gov.

MICKELSON, CLAUDIA ANN, biosafety officer, scientist; b. Detroit, Mar. 8, 1944; d. Gordon Francis and Virginia Randall Roberts; m. Michael Jay Mickelson, Sept. 1966; 1 child, David Paul. PhD, U. Rochester, 1974. Rsch. fellow U. Glasgow, Scotland, 1979-81; sr. rsch. fellow U. Melborne, Victoria, Australia, 1981-86; mem. xenotransplantation adv. bd. FDA, Washington, 1998—. Author: (book. chpt.) Principles of Biosafety, 2000. Recipient William J. O'Brian award Tufts U., 1995. Mem. AAAS (DOSER adv. bd. 1998-2001). Avocations: hiking, gardening, traveling. Office: MIT 77 Massachusetts Ave 56-255 Cambridge MA 02139-4307 Office Fax: (617) 258-5856.

MICKELSON, H(ERALD) FRED, electric utility executive; b. Pratt, Kans., Oct. 4, 1938; s. Herald E. and Arvilla (Knight) M.; m. D. Joan Mickelson, Feb. 21, 1958; children: Mikel Tod, Janet Lynn. BS in Mgmt. Sci., Pepperdine U., 1974; postgrad. Mgmt. Policy Inst., U. So. Calif., 1978. Dist. mgr. So. Calif. Edison, Santa Ana, 1982-84, mgr. corp. communications Rosemead, 1984-85, div. ops. mgr. Santa Ana, 1985-86, San Bernardino, 1986-87, mgr. mktg. Rosemead, 1987-91, regional v.p. Santa Ana, 1992—. Officer, bd. dirs. Calif. divsn. Am. Cancer Soc., chmn. bd. Calif. divsn., 1993-94, nat. bd. dirs., bd. dirs. N.W. divsn., chmn. nat. bd. dirs., 2001-2002; officer, mem. exec. com., bd. dirs. United Way of Orange County, chmn. bd., 1995, chmn. bd., 1995; bd. dirs. ARC of Orange County, St. Joseph's Hosp. of Orange; chmn. Orange County Econ. Devel. Commn., 1993-94; adv. bd. St. Jude's Hosp. of Fullerton, Sch. Bus. and Econs. Chapman U.; officer, bd. dirs. Nat. Conf. Christians and Jews, presiding co-chmn., 1994—; officer, bd. dirs. Orange County Bus. Com. for the Arts, Orgn. Unified Concerned Homeowners; bd. govs. Orange County Human Rels. Coun.; mem. Indsl. League Orange County, Orange County Transp. Coalition. Recipient Field Svcs. Builder award Am. Cancer Soc., 1992, Humanitarian award Orange County Human Rels. Commn., 1993, Comty. Leadership award Orange County Black C. of C., 1994; named one of Top 25 Bus. Leaders in Orange County, Orange County Bus. Jour., 1993-95. Mem. Edison Electric Inst. (customer svc. and mktg. bd. dirs.), Pacific Coast Electric Assn. (customer svc. and mktg. exec. com.), Orange County C. of C. (bd. dirs., exec. com., chmn. bd. 1994), Orange County Bus. Coun. Republican. Mem. First Bapt. Ch. Avocations: carpentry, vocal musician, gardening, sports car restoration, antiques.

MICKELSON, STACEY, state legislator; BA, Minot State U., 1994. Govt. rels. dir. Artspace Projects, Inc.; rep. Dist. 38 N.D. Ho. of Reps., 1994-2000, mem. fin. and taxation com., vice-chmn. transp. com. Mem. interim taxation, adminstrv. rules coms. Bowhay Inst. for Legis. Leadership and Devel. fellow. Mem. Am. Coun. Young Polit. Leaders, Darden Program Emerging Polit. Leaders, Flemming Fellows. Home: 410 Groveland Ave #702 Minneapolis MN 55403

MICKENS, RONALD ELBERT, applied mathematician, physics educator; b. Petersburg, Va., Feb. 7, 1943; s. Joseph Persival and Daisy (Brown) M.; m. Maria Kelker, Aug. 13, 1977; children James Williamson, Leah Maria. BA, Fisk U., 1964; PhD, Vanderbilt U., 1968. NSF postdoctoral fellow MIT, Cambridge, 1968-70, vis. prof., 1973-74; prof. physics Fisk U., Nashville, 1970-81, Clark Atlanta U., 1982—, Callaway prof., 1986. Vis. prof. Morehouse Coll., Atlanta, 1979-80, Joint Inst. for Lab. Astrophysics, Boulder, Colo., 1981-82; cons. adv. bd. NSF, Nat. Urban Coalition, Nat. Rsch. Coun., Am. Inst. Physics and a variety of univs. and nat. labs. Author: Nonlinear Oscillations, 1981, Difference Equations, 1987, Difference Equations: Theory and Applications, 1990, Nonstandard Finite Difference Models of Differential Equations, 1994, Oscillations in Planar Dynamical Systems, 1996; editor: Mathematics and Science, 1990, Applications of Nonstandard Finite Difference Schemes, 2000, Edward Bouchet: The First African American Doctorate, 2002; contbr. numerous rev. articles, abstracts and gen. articles to publs. Fellow Woodrow Wilson Found., Danforth Found., UNCF, Joint Inst. for Lab. Astrophysics; grantee ARO, NSF, DOE, NASA, NIH, 1968—. Fellow Am. Phys. Soc. (con., adv. bd.); mem. AAAS, European Phys. Soc., Soc. Indsl. and Applied Math., Am. Math. Soc. Achievements include construction of new finite-difference schemes for numerical solution of differential equations; new perturbation techniques for nonlinear difference and differential equations; construction of global methods for nonlinear oscillatory systems; investigation of properties of rate constants for third-order chemical react. Office: Clark Atlanta U Physics Dept Atlanta GA 30314 E-mail: rohrs@math.gatech.edu.

MICKIEWICZ, ELLEN PROPPER, political and social science educator; b. Hartford, Conn. d. George K. and Rebecca (Adler) Propper; m. Denis Mickiewicz; 1 son, Cyril. BA, Wellesley Coll.; MA, Yale U., PhD, 1965. Lectr. dept. polit. sci. Yale U., 1965-67; asst. prof. dept. polit. sci. Mich. State U., East Lansing, 1967-69, assoc. prof., 1969-73, prof., 1973-80; prof. dept. polit. sci. Emory U., Atlanta, 1980-88, dean Grad. Sch. Arts and Scis., 1980-85, Alben W. Barkley prof. polit. sci., 1988-93; James R. Shepley prof. pub. policy, prof. polit. sci. Duke U., Durham, N.C., 1994—, dir. DeWitt Wallace Ctr. for Comm. and Journalism Terry Sanford Inst. Pub. Policy, 1994—. Vis. prof. Kathryn W. Davis Chair Wellesley Coll., 1978; vis. com. dept. Slavic lang. and lit. Harvard U., 1978-85, vice chmn. vis. com. Russian Rsch. Ctr., Harvard U., 1986-92; mem. subcom. on comms. and society Am. Coun. Learned Socs./Soviet Acad. Scis., 1986-90; mem. com. on internat. security studies, Am. Acad. Arts and Scis., 1988-90; fellow The Carter Ctr., 1985—, dir. Commn. on Radio and TV Policy; mem. area adv. com. for Ea. Europe and USSR, Coun. for Internat. Exch. Of Scholars, 1987-90; mem. acad. adv. coun. The Kennan Inst. for Advanced Russian Studies, 1989-93; mem. bd. overseers Internat. Press Ctr., Moscow, 1995; dir., commr. Commn. Radio and TV Policy, 1990. Author: Soviet Political Schools, 1967, Media and the Russian Public, 1981, Split Signals: Television and Politics in the Soviet Union, 1988 (Electronic Book of Yr. award Nat. Assn. Broadcasters and Broadcast Edn. Assn. 1988); co-author: Television and Elections, 1992, Television/Radio News and Minorities, 1994, Changing Channels: Television and the Struggle for Power in Russia, 1997, revised and expanded edit., 1999; editor: Soviet Union Jour., 1980-90; co-editor: International Security and Arms Control, 1986, The Soviet Calculus of Nuclear War, 1986; editor, contbr.: Handbook of Soviet Social Science Data, 1973; mem. editl. bd. Jour. Politics, 1985-88, Harvard Internat. Jour. Press/Politics, 1995—, Polit. Comms., 1996—, Polit. Comm., 1995—. Founder, 1st chmn. bd. dirs. Opera Guild of Greater Lansing, Inc., 1972-74. Recipient Outstanding Svc. to Promote Dem. Media in Russia award Journalists Union of Russia, 1994; Ford Found. Fgn. Area Tng. fellow, 1962-65, Guggenheim fellow, 1973-74; Sigma Xi grantee, 1972-74, John and Mary R. Markle Found. grantee, 1984-88, 94-96, 95—, Ford Found. grantee, 1985, 88-91, 92—, Rockefeller Found. grantee, 1985-87, W. Alton Jones Found. grantee, 1987-88, Eurasia Found. grantee, 1993-94, Carnegie Corp. of N.Y. grantee, 1996—. Mem. Am. Assn. for Advancement Slavic Studies (bd. dirs. 1978-81, mem. awards com., mem. endowment com. 1984-86, pres. 1987-88), Am. Polit. Sci. Assn.,Internat. Studies Assn. (v.p. N.Am. 1983-84), Dante Soc. Am., So. Conf. Slavic Studies (exec. com. 1983-84), Counc. Fgn. Rels. Office: Duke U Sanford Inst Pub Policy PO Box 90241 Durham NC 27708-0241

MICKLE, MARLIN HOMER, electrical engineer, educator; b. Windber, Pa., July 5, 1936; s. Howard T. and Ruth Elma (Corle) M. BS, U. Pitts., 1961, MS, 1963, PhD, 1967. Jr. engr. IBM, 1962; engr. Westinghouse Co., 1964; mem. faculty U. Pitts., 1962—, assoc. prof. elec. engring., 1968-75, prof., 1975—, dir. computer engring. program, 1982-84, Nickolas A. DeCecco prof., 2001—. Program dir. system theory & applications NSF, 1974-75; cons. NSF, Batelle, Contraves-Goerz, TASC, Westinghouse, AMSCO, Tex. Instruments, Inc., Compunetics, others; pres. Mickle Computer Techs., Inc., Pitts., 1979-85; v.p., dir. Power Resources, Inc., Pitts., 1980-84; dir. Univ. Rsch. & Devel. Assocs., Inc. Author: (with T.W. Sze) Optimization in Systems Engineering, 1972; mem. editl. bd. Jour. Interdisciplinary Modeling and Simulation, 1978-80; editor-in-chief Internat. Jour. Paralle and Distributed Systems and Networks, 1997-2002; contbr. articles to profl. jours. Dist. lay leader Pitts. dist. United Meth. Ch., 1971-73; bd. dirs. Asbury Heights, Pitts., 1982—, Wesley Hills of Mt. Lebanon, Pitts., 1985-86; chmn. bd. dirs. Emory Sr. Housing, Pitts., 2000—. With USAF, 1954-58. Fellow IEEE. Republican. Home: 4601 5th Ave Apt 723 Pittsburgh PA 15213-3657 Office: U Pitts Dept Elec Engring Pittsburgh PA 15261-0001

MICKLISH, CLARA JO, acute care nurse practitioner; b. Ellwood City, Pa., Nov. 25, 1948; d. Joseph Micklish and Clara Oczkowski-Micklish. Diploma, St. Joseph's Hosp. Of Nurse Anesthesia, Omaha, 1977—79. Registered RN 1969. Mem.: Am. Assn. of Nurse Anesthetists, Intertel, Am. Mensa. Avocation: reading, gardening, cooking, raising dogs. Personal E-mail: cl3mc@aol.com.

MICKLITSCH, CHRISTINE NOCCHI, health care administrator; b. Hazleton, Pa., Oct. 23, 1949; d. Nicholas Edmund and Matilda Nocchi; m. Wayne D. Micklitsch, May 20, 1972; children: Sarah N., Emily M. BS, Pa. State U., State College, 1971; MBA, Boston U., 1979. Blood bank med. technologist The Deaconess Hosp., Boston, 1971-73; sr. blood bank med. technologist Tufts New Eng. Med. Ctr., 1973-76, environ. svcs. coord., 1976-78; adminstrv. resident Joslin Diabetes Found., 1978-79; sr. analyst Analysis, Mgmt. & Planning, Inc., Cambridge, Mass., 1979-80; adminstrv. dir. Hahnemann Family Health Ctr., Worcester, 1980-84; exec. dir. Swampscott (Mass.) Treatment & Trauma Ctr., 1984-85; dir. practice mgmt., instr. U. Mass. Med. Ctr., Worcester, 1985-91; dir. adminstrv. svcs. The Fallon Clinic, 1991-94; mgr. physician network devel. The Fallon healthcare Sys., 1994-97; dir. physician edn. and svcs. Fallon Cmty. Health Plan, 2000. Co-author: Physician Performance Management: Tool for Survival and Success, 1996. Incorporator, pres. Newton (Mass.) Highlands Cmty. Devel. Corp., 1981-82; treas. Patriot's Trail coun. Girl Scouts U.S., Newton, 1993-98; Christian edn. instr. Newton Highlands Congl. Ch., 1987-94. Recipient The Fred Graham award for Creativity and Innovation, Am. Coll. of Med. Practice Execs., 2000, Award of Excellence as Outstanding Physician Educator in Primary Care, 2001; fellow Kellogg, Ctr. for Rsch. an Ambulatory Health Care Adminstrn., Denver, 1979; grantee in grad. tng. in family medicine HHS, U. Mass. Med. Sch., Worcester, 1989. Fellow: Am. Coll. Med. Practice Execs. (state coll. forum rep. 1989—99, ea. sect. coll. forum rep. 1993—, named Disting. Life fellow 2001); mem.: Mass. Med. Group Mgmt. Assn. (pres. 1987—89, newsletter editor 1984—), Am. Coll. Med. Practice Execs. (mem. chair 1995—96), Boston U. Health Care Mgmt. Program Alumni Assn., Alpha Omicron Pi (parlimentarian Epsilon Alpha chpt. 1969—70). Avocations: classic cars, real estate. Home: 320 Lake Ave Newton MA 02461-1212

MICKLOS, JANET M. state agency administrator, human services director; b. Jacksonville, Fla., July 24, 1947; d. Thomas Anthony and Yolanda Mae (Murphy) Micklos; married; children: Shawn E. Satterthwaite, Ryan W. Satterthwaite; m. Terry Mercer Maisey, May 28, 1988. BA, U. No. Colo., 1969; MA disting. grad., Webster U., 1985; grad., N.H. Part-Time Police Acad., 1995. Phys. edn. tchr. Terrell Wells Mid. Sch., San Antonio, 1969-70; fitness instr./gymnastic coach Victor Valley C.C., Apple Valley, Calif., 1977-79; dir. phys. dept. Victor Valley YMCA, Victorville, 1978-79; secretarial support joint U.S. mil. mission aid to Turkey Ankara, Turkey, 1981-82; secretarial support U.S. Logistics Group, 1982-83; pub. edn. dir. Alamo Area Rape Crisis Ctr., San Antonio, 1986-88; admissions coord. Horizon Hosp., 1988; psychiat. counselor Portsmouth (N.H.) Pavilion, 1988-89; dir. human svcs. Rockingham County (N.H.) Dept. of Corrections, Brentwood, 1989—. Mem. adv. task force N.H. Coun. Chs., 1992; mem. gov.'s coun. on volunteerism, Seacoast, 1990-93; chmn. outreach commn. 1st United Meth. Ch., Portsmouth, 1990-93; mem. task force on victim restitution Rockingham County, 1992—; spl. dep. Rockingham County Sheriff's Dept., 1995-2000; police officer Newfields Police Dept., 1996-99; bd. trustees Newfields Cmty. Ch. Mem. Am. Correctional Assn., Am. Jail Assn., Rockingham County Law Enforcement Officers Assn. Methodist. Avocations: archery, gardening, reading, skiing. Office: Rockingham County Dept Corrections 99 North Rd Brentwood NH 03833-6613

MICKO, ALEXANDER S. financial executive; b. Munich, May 8, 1947; came to U.S., 1952, naturalized, 1957; s. Zygmunt and Maria (Huber) M.; m. Sharon E. Judge, June 7, 1969; 1 child, Brian A. BS, LaSalle U., 1969. CPA, N.J., Pa. Audit mgr. Price Waterhouse, Phila., 1970-77; asst. chief fin. investigations div. of Casino Gaming Enforcement, State of N.J., Trenton, 1977-79; v.p. fin. TeleScis., Inc., Mt. Laurel, N.J., 1979-87; v.p. fin., chief fin. officer, asst. sec. Dechert, Price & Rhoads, Phila., 1987-89; v.p. fin., treas., sec. NET Atlantic, Inc., Thorofare, N.J., 1989-92; v.p., contr. AAA Mid-Atlantic, Inc., Phila., 1992—. Owner AM Fin. Services, Medford, N.J., 1986—; cons. United Computer Services, Berlin. N.J., 1982—; lectr. in field. Bd. dirs. Forest Hills Civic Assn., Williamstown, N.J., 1976. With USMC, 1969-75. Recipient Michael A. DeAngelis Outstanding Profl. Achievement award, LaSalle U., Phila., 1985. Mem. AICPA, N.J. Soc. CPAs, Pa. Inst. CPAs, Fin. Execs. Inst., Nat. Assn. Accts. Roman Catholic. Avocations: skiing, golf. Home: 5 Huntington Cir Medford NJ 08055-3315 Office: AAA Mid Atlantic Inc PO Box 820884 Philadelphia PA 19182-0884

MICOZZI, MARC STEPHEN, health executive, physician, educator; b. Norfolk, Va., Oct. 27, 1953; s. Edio Dominic and Huguette (Picon) M.; m. Carole Ann O'Leary, Oct. 8, 1982; 1 child, Alicia Madeleine. Cadet, USAF Acad., 1971-72; BA, Pomona Coll., 1974; MD, U. Pa., 1979, PhD, 1986. Diplomate Am. Bd. Pathology. Rsch. fellow City of Hope Nat. Med. Ctr., Duarte, Calif., 1973; chem. engr. Gould Corp., El Monte, 1974; Luce Found. scholar Mindanao, The Philippines, 1976-77; clin. applications chemist McDonnell-Douglas Corp., Pasadena, Calif., 1978; postdoctoral fellow Allied Inst. Environ. Health, Princeton, N.J., 1979; resident in pathology Pa. Hosp., Phila., 1980-83; med. examiner Dade County Med. Examiner's Office, Miami, Fla., 1983-84; sr. investigator Nat. Cancer Inst., Bethesda, Md., 1984-86; dir. Nat. Mus. Health and Medicine, Washington, 1986-95; exec. dir. Coll. Physicians' of Phila., 1995—. Adj. prof. Uniformed Svcs. U. Health Scis., Bethesda, 1986-95, U. Pa. Sch. Medicine, 1996—; vis. lectr. Georgetown U. Sch. Medicine, Washington, 1986—, Johns Hopkins U. Sch. Medicine, Balt., 1988—; adj. prof. dept. phys. medicine U. Pa., 1996—. Editor: Nutrition and Cancer, 1989; assoc. editor Health Care, Jour. Human Orgn., 1983-89; contbr. chpts. to books and numerous articles to profl. jours. Del. White House Conf. on Youth, Estes Park, Colo., 1971, UN Conf. on Human Environ., Stockholm, 1972, NATO Advanced Study Inst., Brussels, 1982; mem. Calif. Gov.'s Adv. Com., 1972-74. Fellow Human Biology coun., Soc. for Applied Anthropology, Am. Anthrop. Assn.; Am. Acad. Forensic Scis., Am. Pub. Health Assn., N.Y. Acad. Scis. Roman Catholic. Office: Coll Physicians 19 S 22nd St Philadelphia PA 19103-3001

MICUCCI, DANA ANN, writer; b. Pitts., Feb. 26, 1961; d. Joseph E. and Mary Jo (Marcoly) M. BA in English, Northwestern U., 1983, MA in English summa cum laude, 1987; cert. French, Sorbonne, Paris, 1988; cert. creative writing, Columbia U., 1990. Sr. account exec. Golin Harris Comms., Chgo., 1985-87; sr. publicist Christie's, N.Y.C., 1988-90; journalist Paris, N.Y.C., 1987—. Author: Artists in Residence, 2001, Best Bids: The Insider's Guide to Buying at Auction, 2002, Collector's Jour., 2002; contbr. Architectural Digest, Harper's Bazaar, Internat. Herald Tribune, Chgo. Tribune, The N.Y. Times, Town and Country, others; N.Y. corr. Art & Antiques. Sr. writing fellow Columbia U., 1990. Democrat. Avocations: travel, literature, art, theatre, film.

MICZEK, KLAUS ALEXANDER, psychology educator; b. Burghausen, Bavaria, Germany, Sept. 28, 1944; came to U.S., 1967; s. Erich and Irene (Wirthl) M.; m. Christiane Baerwaldt, Aug. 8, 1970; 1 child, Nikolai A. Tchrs. cert., Paedagogische Hochschule, Berlin, 1966; PhD, U. Chgo., 1972. Asst. prof. Carnegie-Mellon U., Pitts., 1972-74, assoc. prof., 1974-79, Tufts U., Medford, Mass., 1979-83, prof., 1983-93, Moses Hunt prof. psychiatry, psychology, pharmacology and neuroscience, 1993—. Cons. Solvay-Pharma v.b., Weesp, The Netherlands, 1984-99, NIH, Rockville, Md., 1984—; Boerhaave prof. U. Leiden, The Netherlands, 1987; mem. panel on violence, NAS, 1989-92. Editor: Ethopharmacology, 1983, Ethopharmacological Aggression Research, 1984; field editor, coord. editor Behavioral Pharmacology, Jour. Psychopharmacology; contbr. articles on psychopharmacology, 1973—. Rsch. grantee Nat. Inst. Drug Abuse, 1973—, Nat. Inst. Alcoholism and Alcohol Abuse, 1981—; recipient Solvay-Duphar award APA, 1993, Bundesverdienstkreuz Cross of Merit, Fed. Republic of Germany, 1996. Fellow APA (program chmn. 1981, pres. div. psychopharmacology 1990-91, master lectr. 1999), Behavioral Pharmacol. Soc. (pres. 1992-94), Internat. Soc. for Rsch. on Aggression (councilor 1987); mem. Soc. Neurosci., N.Y. Acad. Scis., Internat. Primatol. Soc. Office: Tufts U Dept Psychology 530 Boston Ave Medford MA 02155-5532

MICZUGA, MARK NORBERT, dairy official; b. Chgo., Feb. 14, 1962; s. Norbert and Rita (Kamper) M.; m. Maria Del Carmen Caballero, Sept. 19, 1992; children: Angelica Pamela, Henry, Luis. BS, DePaul U., 1984, MBA, 1989. Mgr. steel products Mitsubishi Internat. Corp., Chgo., 1985-93; v.p. sales MC Fabrication Industries, Inc., Oak Brook Terrace, 1993-97; account mgr. Westech. Svcs., Inc., Lombard, 1997-99; branch mgr. Hygeia Dairy, 1999; customer svc. mgr. Suiza Foods/Hygeia Dairy, McAllen, Tex., 2000; customer svc. specialist B.L. Downey, Broadview, Ill., 2001—02; tech. sales rep. Pate Co., 2002—. Mem. Assn. MBA Execs. Office: Pate Co 2625 S 21st Ave Broadview IL 60155

MIDDAUGH, JACK KENDALL, II, management educator; b. Springfield, Ill., Oct. 8, 1949; s. Jack Kendall and Mildred Viola (Davis) M.; m. Maureen Ann Tewey, Aug. 7, 1976; children: Cheryl Lynn, Allison Helen. BBA in Acctg., George Washington U., 1973, MBA, 1975; PhD in Acctg., Ohio State U., 1981. Instr. Ohio State U., Columbus, 1975-80; asst. prof. U. Va., Charlottesville, 1980-87; assoc. dean, assoc. prof., dir fulltime MBA program Wake Forest U., Winston-Salem, N.C., 1987—, assoc. dean for mgmt. edn. Cons. IBM, Armonk, N.Y., 1981—, Amtrak, Washington, 1982-85, U.S. Postal Svc., Washington, 1984-85, Ernst & Whinney, Cleve., 1985-87, U.S. Civil Svc. Commn., 1973-76, Digital Equipment Corp., 1985, Armstrong World Industries, 1989—; dir. 1st Soviet-Am. Mgmt. Devel. Program, 1989; lectr. selected Soviet cities, 1989. Contbr. articles to profl. jours. Dir. Ptnrs. in Edn., 1990-91. Recipient commendation Ohio Ho. of Reps., 1978, Sara Lee award for excellence, 1990; named Outstanding Tchr. of Yr., Pacesetters of Ohio State U., 1977, 78. Mem. Am. Acctg. Assn., Decision Sci. Inst., Beta Gamma Sigma. Avocations: golf, tennis, computers. Home: 8016 Kilcash Ct Clemmons NC 27012-8666 Office: Wake Forest U Babcock Grad Sch Mgmt 7659 Reynolds Sta Winston Salem NC 27109

MIDDAUGH, RICHARD, information systems analyst, researcher; b. Tampa, Fla., Dec. 18, 1951; s. Donald Blair and Leona (Johnson) M.; m. Brenda M. Mitchell, June 10, 1990; 1 child, Richard W. Jr.; 1 stepchild, Nathan Wade Mitchell. AA with honors, Hillsborough C.C., 1973; BA in

Psychology, U. South Fla., 1975, MA in Edn., 1979. Psychometrist Divsn. Student Svcs. Hillsborough C.C., Tampa, 1975-79, rsch. analyst Office Instl. Rsch. and Computer Svcs., 1979-82, coord. Office Instl. Rsch. and Computer Svcs., 1982-84; sys. cons. Sweda Internat. div. Litton Industries, Miami, Fla., 1984-87; assoc. dir. Office Instl. Rsch. and Planning U. South Ala., Mobile, 1987-90; dir. Office Instl. Rsch. Sam Houston State U., Huntsville, Tex., 1990—, presenter workshop for dept. chairs and dirs., 1991-92. Workshop presenter City Cultural Planning Coun., 1992; cons. City of Huntsville, 1992, Huntsville-Walker County Tourism Coun., 1991, Stephen F. Austin State U., 1993, Trinity Valley C.C., 1993; panelist Tex. Assn. Instnl. Rsch., 1993, presenter, 1994; presenter Assn. for Instnl. Rsch. Ann. Forums, 1994. Editor: Resource Director for Texas Higher Education, 1994-95. Bd. dirs. Huntsville Leadership Inst., 1992-94, chmn., 1993; bd. dirs. Huntsville-Walker County United Way, v.p., 1992-93, campaign chmn. U. South Ala., 1908-89. Mem. Huntsville-Walker C. of C., Ala. Assn. Instnl. Rsch. (sec.-treas. 1990), Lions (bd. dirs. Huntsville chpt. 1991-93, v.p., pres.-elect 1991-92). Democrat. Avocations: sailing, tennis, golf. Office: Sam Houston State U Office Instnl Rsch Huntsville TX 77341

MIDDAUGH, ROBERT BURTON, artist; b. Chgo., May 12, 1935; s. John Burton and Mae Knight (Crooks) M. Student, U. Chgo., 1960-64; BFA, Art Inst. Chgo., 1964. Curator art collection 1st Nat. Bank Chgo., 1971-83. Designed, executed ednl. display, Prehistoric Project at Oriental Inst. of U. Chgo., 1968; One-man shows include, Kovler Gallery, Chgo., 1965, 67, 69, Martin Schweig Gallery, St. Louis, 1970, 72, 79, 83, U. Wis., 1976, 81, 82, Fairweather Hardin Gallery, Chgo., 1977, 80, 83, 85, Rockford Art Mus., 1987, Zaks Gallery, Chgo., 1992, 93, 97; group shows, including, Art Inst. Chgo., 1964, 66, 78, 79, Evanston (Ill.) Art Center, 1966, Joslyn Art Mus., Omaha, 1968, U. Notre Dame, 1969, Va. Mus. Fine Arts, Richmond, 1966; represented in permanent collections, Art Inst. Chgo., Boston Mus. Fine Arts, Fine Art Mus. of South, Mobile, Ala., Los Angeles County Mus., Phoenix Art Mus., Worcester (Mass.) Art Mus., Ill. State Mus., Springfield. Served with U.S. Army, 1958-60. Archivist, Chgo. Park Dist., 1998—. Mem. Arts Club Chgo.

MIDDELKAMP, JOHN NEAL, pediatrician, educator; b. Kansas City, Mo., Sept. 29, 1925; s. George H. and Clara M. (Ordelheide) M.; m. Roberta Gill, Oct. 3, 1949 (div. 1970); children— Sharon Ann, Steven Neal, Susan Jean, Scott Alan; m. Lois Harper, Mar. 1, 1974 BS, U. Mo., 1946; MD, Washington U., St. Louis, 1948. Diplomate Am. Bd. Pediatrics. Intern D.C. Gen. Hosp., Washington, 1948-49; resident St. Louis Children's Hosp., 1949-50, 52-53; instr. pediatrics Washington U., 1953-57, asst. prof. pediatrics, 1957-64, assoc. prof., 1964-70, prof., 1970-98, prof. emeritus, 1998—; dir. ambulatory pediatrics St. Louis Children's Hosp., 1974-91. Author: Camp Health Manual, 1984; contbr. articles, chpts. to profl. publs. Served to comdr. M.C., USNR, 1943-66. NIH postdoctoral fellow, 1961-62 Mem. Am. Acad. Pediatrics, Am. Soc. Microbiology, Infectious Diseases Soc. Am., Am. Pediatric Soc., Ambulatory Pediatric Assn., Sigma Xi, Alpha Omega Alpha Home: 8845 Paragon Cir Saint Louis MO 63123-1114 Office: 1 Childrens Pl Saint Louis MO 63110-1002

MIDDENDORF, ALICE CARTER, volunteer; b. Balt., Dec. 7, 1940; d. John William and Alice Temple (Carter) M. BA, Wellesley Coll., 1963, Oxford U., Eng., 1972. Libr. Boston Athenaeum Libr., 1963-66; editor Houghton Mifflin Co., Boston, 1966-69; bd. dirs. Balt. Zool. Soc., 1976; cons. Nat. Zoo, Washington, 1976-77, G. Ward & Assocs., Ridgefield, Conn., 1976-79; from bd. dirs. to bd. govs. Nat. Aquarium in Balt., 1976-88, sec. bd. govs., 1987-88, chmn. animal policy com., 1982-88; bd. dirs. Total Health Care (merger Constant Care and West Balt. Cmty. Health Ctrs.), Balt., 1981—; sec. bd. dirs. Total Health Care (merger Constant Care Med. Ctr. and West Balt. Constant Health Ctr.), 1990-93, 97-98; treas., 1998. Adv. bd. Nat. Aquarium in Balt., 1989-94, 99—, bd. govs., 1994-99, sec. bd. govs., 1995-99; bd. dirs. Constant Care Med. Ctr., Balt., Park Heights Street Acad., Balt., sec., 1988-90; pres. Fulmar Corp., Cayman Islands, Brit. West Indies, 1991-99; pres., chmn. bd. dirs. Lystra Hill Farms, Inc., Goleta, Calif., 1996-97. Bd. dirs. Scenic Md., 2002—. Recipient Pres.'s Citation, Pres. City Coun. Balt., 1974, 76, Award of Appreciation, Mayor of Balt., 1981. Avocations: scuba, underwater photography, marine biology, malacology, travel, reading. Home and Office: 1301 Hillside Rd Stevenson MD 21153-2019

MIDDENDORF, GERAD D. sociology educator; b. St. Louis, Aug. 15, 1965; s. Paul G. and Jeanette C. Middendorf; m. B. Jan Holt, Oct. 24, 1992; children: Andre Charles, Sarah Marie. BS in Econs. and Fin., So. Ill. U., 1987; MA in Internat. Affairs, Ohio U., 1992; postgrad., Mich. State U. Vol. Peace Corps, Honduras, 1988-90; pub. info. specialist U.S. Soil Conservation Svc., Athens, Ohio, 1992; project asst. Ohio Program of Intensive English, Ohio U., 1992; project supr. Visions Internat., Tortola, Brit. V.I., 1993; tchg. asst. Mich. State U., East Lansing, 1993, rsch. asst., 1993—, rsch. assoc., 1997-98. Rschr. Internat. Svc. for Nat. Agrl. Rsch., Panama and Ecuador, 1997-98. Contbr. articles to profl. jours. Active Eastminster Child Devel. Ctr., East Lansing, 1997—. Fgn. Lang. and Areas Studies fellow U.S Dept. Edn., 1999-2000, 2000—, Walker-Hill Internat. scholar, 1995. Mem. Am. Sociol. Assn., Rural Sociol. Soc., Latin Am. Studies Assn., Soc. for Internat. Devel., Soc. for Social Studies of Sci., Phi Kappa Phi. Avocations: literature, distance running, guitar. Home: 2601 Tulane Dr Lansing MI 48912-4552 Office: Mich State U Dept Sociology 316 Berkey Hall East Lansing MI 48824-1111 Fax: 517-432-2856.

MIDDENDORF, J. WILLIAM, II, investment banker; b. Balt., Sept. 22, 1924; m. Isabelle Paine, Mar. 7, 1953; children: Frances, Amy, John W. IV, Ralph Henry. B in Naval Sci., Holy Cross Coll., 1945; AB, Harvard U., 1947; MBA, NYU, 1954; LLD (hon.), Troy State U.; LittD (hon.), Sch. of Ozarks, Am. Christian Coll.; D. Social Scis. (hon.), Netherlands-Am. Inst. Commd. ensign USN, 1945, advanced through grades to lt. (j.g.), ret., 1946; with credit dept. Chase Manhattan Bank, 1947-52; ptnr. Wood Struthers and Co., 1958-61; sr. ptnr. Middendorf, Colgate and Co., 1962-69; ambassador to The Netherlands, 1969-73; sec. USN, 1974-77; pres., CEO Fin. Gen. Bankshares, Inc., 1977-81; ambassador to Orgn. Am. States, 1981-85, European Communities, 1985-87; chmn. Middendorf & Assocs., Inc., 1989—. Chmn. presdl. task force Project Econ. and Social Justice, 1986-90; mem. U.S. Del. to supervise elections in Suriname, 1988; treas. Internat. Rep. Inst. Composer 8 symphonies, 100 marches, (opera) King Richard, nat. independence march for Belize, other compositions for Latin Am. countries; guest condr. Boston Pops, St. Louis Symphony, Ind. U., others; contbr. articles to profl. jours. Mem. U.S. Olympic com., 1979-89, U.S. Olympic Selection com. for field hockey; judge field hockey Olympics, Rome, 1960; former mem. vis. com. dept. Am. paintings Met. Mus. Art, N.Y.C., vis. com. dept. Am. Art, Mus. Fine Arts, Boston; hon. v.p. Naval Hist. Found.; treas. Goldwater for Pres. com., 1962-64, Presdl. Transition com. 1968, Rep. Nat. Com., 1964-69; alt. del. for Gov. Reagan, 1980; del. State of Conn., 1964, 68, State of Va., 1996; co-chmn. Virginians for Reagan, 1980, fin. com. Va. GOP, 1980-81; coord. internat. econ. and naval adv. com. Reagan for Pres. campaign, 1980; chmn. Congl. Boosters com., 1978-81; chmn. CIA Transition Team, 1980-81; chmn. fin. com. Pres. Reagan's 1981 Inaugural com.; trustee Naval War Coll. Found., Heritage Found., Washington; past trustee Hoover Instn. for War Revolution and Peace, Corcoran Gallery, N.Y. Hist. Soc., Balt. Mus. Art, Greenwich Hist. Soc., Boston Symphony, Middlesex Sch., Concord, Mass., Nat. Symphony Orch., Mass. Gen. Hosp., Boys Club N.Y.; bd. electors Ins. Hall of Fame; bd. dirs. Georgetown U., John Philip Sousa Meml. Found., Newport Art Mus. and Mariners' Mus., Norfolk, Va.; chmn. bd. dirs. council statesmen Ludwig von Mises Inst.; chmn. Com. for Monetary Rsch. and Edn. Inc., Netherlands-Am. Amity Trust, Def. Forum Found., Navy League Awards com., 1977—; former mem. com. Dept. State Fine Arts Com.; founding chmn. U.S. Navy Meml. Found.; past chmn. Netherlands-Am. Inst., Wolf Trap Farm Park, John Carter Brown Library Assocs., Providence, Asian Composers Expo., European Council of Boy Scouts. Decorated Grand Master Order of Orange Nassau (Netherlands), Order of Arab (Republic Egypt), Grand Master of Order of Naval Merit (Republic Brazil); recipient Superior Honor award Dept. State, 1974, Disting. Pub. Svc. award Dept. Def., 1975, 76, Navy Disting. Pub. Svc. award, 1976, Naval Disting. Svc. medal Republic Brazil, 1976, Ludwig von Mises Free Market award, 1985, Inter-Am. Music Coun. award, 1985, Edwin Franko Goldman award Am. Bandmasters Assn., 1987, Assn. Harvard Clubs Am. award, Disting. Svc. medal Purdue Univ. Bands, Netherlands Soc. Phila. Gold medal, Good Citizenship medal Nat. Soc. SAR, Medal of Honor, Midwest Nat. Band Assn., Invest in Am. Am. Eagle award, 1988, Eugene J. Keogh Disting. Pub. Svc. award NYU, 1989, Nat. Commendation award Pres.' Coun. Phys. Fitness and Sports, 1989, Leadership award Am. Friends of Turkey, 1989, Adm. Arleigh Burke Leadership award, 1998, Arleigh Burke award 1998; named Alumnus of Yr. NYU, 1978; Nat. Masters Sculling champion, 1979, Gold medal The Holland Soc. Mem. Am. Antiquarian Soc., Harvard Alumni Assn. (permanent class com. 1947), Soc. Cin. (hon.), ASCAP, Walpole Soc., Co. Mil. Historians, Mil. Order Loyal Legion, SAR, Soc. of SAR, Field Hockey Assn. Am. (past pres., player/mgr. nat. team 1963), U.S. Naval Inst., Navy League. Clubs: Angler's, Downtown Assn., Union (N.Y.C.); Army-Navy, Capitol Hill, Met., Potomac Boat (Washington); Sakonnet Golf (Little Compton, R.I.); Somerset (Boston). Office: Middendorf & Assocs Inc PO Box 1040 Little Compton RI 02837

MIDDENDORF, JOHN HARLAN, English literature educator; b. N.Y.C., Mar. 31, 1922; s. George Arlington and Margaret (Hofmann) M.; m. Beverly Bruner, July 14, 1943 (dec. 1983); children: Cathie Jean Middendorf Hamilton, Peggy Ruth Middendorf Brindisi; m. Maureen L. MacGrogan, Jan. 31, 1986. AB, Dartmouth Coll., 1943; AM, Columbia U., 1947, PhD, 1953. Lectr. English CCNY, 1946, Hunter Coll., 1946-49; faculty Columbia, 1947—, prof. English, 1965-89, prof. emeritus, 1990—, dir. grad. studies, 1971-74, vice-chmn., 1976-80. Chmn. English test com. Coll. Entrance Exam. Bd., 1967-69 Contbr. articles, revs. to profl. jours.; Editor: English Writers of the Eighteenth Century, 1971; asst. editor: Johnsonian News Letter, 1950-58; co-editor, 1958-78, editor, 1978-90; assoc. editor: Yale edit. Works Samuel Johnson, 1962-66; gen. editor, 1966— . Served to lt. (j.g.) USNR, 1943-46. Faculty fellow Fund Advancement Edn., 1951-52; grantee Coun. Rsch. Humanities, 1958-59, Am. Philos. Soc., 1962, Am. Coun. Learned Socs., 1962, NEH, 1976-88. Mem. Johnsonians (sec.-treas. 1958-68, chmn. 1969, 79), Univ. Seminar on 18th Century European Culture (chmn. 1973-75, 85-87), Oxford Bibliog. Soc., Grolier Club, English Inst. (mem. supervisory com. 1963-66), Modern Lang. Assn., Soc. Sr. Scholars, Soc. Textual Scholarship (adv. bd.), Am. Soc. 18th Century Studies, Phi Beta Kappa. Home: 404 Riverside Dr New York NY 10025-1861 Office: Columbia U Dept English New York NY 10027

MIDDLEBROOK, DIANE WOOD, English language educator, writer; b. Pocatello, Idaho, Apr. 16, 1939; d. Thomas Isaac and Helen Loretta (Downey) Wood; m. Jonathan Middlebrook, June 15, 1963 (div. 1972); 1 child Leah Wood ; m. Carl Djerassi, June 21, 1985. BA, U. Wash., 1961; MA, Yale U., 1962, PhD, 1968; LittD (hon.), Kenyon Coll., 1999. Asst. prof. Stanford (Calif.) U., 1966-73, assoc. prof., 1973-83, prof., 1983-2001, D, dir. Ctr. for Rsch. on Women, 1977-79, prof. emerita, 2002—. Author: (book) Walt Whitman and Wallace Stevens, 1974, Worlds into Words: Understanding Modern Poems, 1980, Anne Sexton, A Biography, 1991, Suits Me: The Double Life of Billy Tipton, 1998, (poetry) Gin Considered as a Demon, 1983; editor: (book) Coming to Light: American Women Poets in the Twentieth Century, 1985. Founding trustee Djerassi Resident Artists Program, Woodside, Calif., 1980—83, chair, 1994; trustee San Francisco Art Inst, 1993. Finalist Nat Book Award, 1991; recipient Yale Prize for Poetry; fellow Independent Study, NEH, 1982—83, Bunting Inst, Radcliffe Col, 1982—83, Guggenheim Found, 1988—89, Rockefeller Study Ctr, 1990. Mem.: MLA, Authors Guild, Internat. Assn. U. Profs. English, Biographers Club. Avocations: collecting art, theater. Home: 1101 Green St Apt 1501 San Francisco CA 94109-2012 Office: Agent Georges Borchardt 136 E 57th St New York NY 10022 E-mail: dwm@stanford.edu.

MIDDLEBROOK, STEPHEN BEACH, lawyer; b. Hartford, Conn., 1937; BA, Yale U., 1958, LLB, 1961. Bar: Conn. 1961. Counsel Aetna Life and Casualty Co., Hartford, Conn., 1969-71, asst. gen. counsel, 1971-78, corp. sec., 1973-83, v.p., gen. counsel, 1981-88, sr. v.p., gen. counsel, 1988-90, sr. v.p., exec. counsel, 1990-94; spl. counsel Day, Berry & Howard, 1995—. Vis. fellow Rand, Santa Monica, Calif., 1994. Office: Day Berry & Howard City Place I Hartford CT 06103-3499 E-mail: sbmiddlebrook@dbh.com.

MIDDLEBROOKS, DELORIS JEANETTE, nurse, educator; b. Cedar Rapids, Iowa, Apr. 9, 1931; d. Harland R. and Rosa V. (Anderson) Hickey; m. Johnnie L. Middlebrooks, Apr. 25, 1963 (dec.); children: James, Kathleen. Diploma, Evang. Hosp. Sch. Nursing, 1956; BSN, State U. Iowa, 1958; MS in Nursing, U. Calif., San Francisco, 1960; EdD, U. Nev., Las Vegas, 1985. Instr., coord. Nev. State Hosp. Sch. Practical Nursing, Sparks, 1963-66; staff nurse St. Mary's Hosp., Reno, 1968; instr., coord. Reno VA Sch. Practical Nursing, 1968-72; instr., coord. health occupations Wooster High Sch., 1972-73; nursing faculty Truckee Meadows C.C., 1973-94, ret., 1994; intermittent staff nurse VA Hosp., 1984-86; instr., review course Stanley Kaplan Ednl. Ctr., 1987-89; clin. nursing faculty Western Nev. C.C., Carson City, 1987, Northern Nev. C.C., Elko, 1979-93; guest assoc. prof. nursing Lewis-Clark State Coll., Lewiston, Idaho, 1989. Cons. Irish Bd. Nursing, Dublin, Ireland, 1985. Nominated Nev. Voc. Tchr. of Yr., 1975, 79, 88, 89; Recipient March of Dimes Community Leadership award, 1990. Mem.: ANA, Nev. Nurses Assn., Phi Kappa Phi, Sigma Theta Tau. Home: 1385 Ebbetts Dr Reno NV 89503-1918

MIDDLEBROOKS, EDDIE JOE, environmental engineer; b. Crawford County, Ga., Oct. 16, 1932; s. Robert Harold and Jewell LaVerne (Dixon) M.; m. Charlotte Linda Hardy, Dec. 6, 1958; 1 child, Linda Tracey. BCE, U. Fla., 1956, MS, 1960; PhD, Miss. State U., 1966. Registered profl. engr., Ariz., Miss., Utah, Wash., Colo.; registered land surveyor, Fla. Asst. san. engr. USPHS, Cin., 1956-58; field engr. T.T. Jones Constrn. Co., Atlanta, 1958-59; grad. teaching asst. U. Fla., 1959-60; research asst. U. Ariz., 1960-61; asst. prof., then assoc. prof. Miss. State U., 1962-67; research engr., asst. dir. San. Engring. Research Lab., U. Calif.-Berkeley, 1968-70; prof. Utah State U., Logan, 1970-82, dean Coll. Engring., 1974-82; Newman chair natural resources engring. Clemson U., 1982-83; provost, v.p. acad. affairs Tenn. Tech. U., 1983-88, U. Tulsa, 1988-90, prof. chem. engring., 1988-92, Trustees prof. chem. engring., 1990-92, acting pres., 1990; prof. civil engring. U. Nevada, Reno, 1992-97. Mem. nat. drinking water adv. council EPA, 1981-83; cons. EPA, UN Indsl. Devel. Orgn., Calif. Water Resources Control Bd., City and County of San Francisco, State of Colo., South Fla. Water Mgmt. Dist. (Everglades), also numerous indsl. and engring. firms. Author: Modeling the Eutrophication Process, 1974, Statistical Calculations-How To Solve Statistical Problems, 1976, Biostimulation and Nutrient Assessment, 1976, Water Supply Engineering Design, 1977, Lagoon Information Source Book, 1978, Industrial Pollution Control, Vol. 1: Agro-Industries, 1979, Wastewater Collection and Treatment: Principles and Practices, 1979, Water Reuse, 1982, Wastewater Stabilization Lagoon Design, Performance and Upgrading, 1982, Reverse Osmosis Treatment of Drinking Water, 1986, Pollution Control in the Petrochemicals Industry, 1987, Natural Systems for Waste Management and Treatment, 1988, 2d edit., 1995; mem. editl. adv. bd. Lewis Pubs. Inc., Environment Internat., Environ. Abstracts; contbr. tech. articles to profl. jours. Fellow ASCE; mem. AAAS, Water Environment Fedn. (dir. 1979-81, 91-92), Eddy medal 1969), Assn. Environ. Engring. Profs. (pres. 1974), Utah Water Pollution Control Assn. (pres. 1976), Internat. Assn. on Water Quality, Am. Soc. Engring. Edn., Am. Acad. Environ. Engrs. (diplomate, trustee 1992-95, v.p. 1995, pres. 1997-98), Sigma Xi, Omicron Delta Kappa, Phi Kappa Phi (Disting. mem.), Tau Beta Pi, Sigma Tau. Home and Office: 360 Blackhawk Ln Lafayette CO 80026-9392 E-mail: Joemiddle@aol.com.

MIDDLEDITCH, LEIGH BENJAMIN, JR. lawyer, educator; b. Detroit, Sept. 30, 1929; s. Leigh Benjamin and Hope Tiffin (Noble) M.; m. Betty Lou Givens, June 27, 1953; children: Leigh III, Katherine Middleditch McDonald, Andrew B. BA, U. Va., 1951, LLB, 1957. Bar: Va. 1957. Assoc. James H. Michael, Jr., Charlottesville, Va., 1957-59; ptnr. Battle, Neal, Harris, Minor & Williams, 1959-68; legal adviser U. Va., 1968-72; ptnr. McGuire, Woods, Battle & Boothe (now McGuire Woods LLP), 1972-99, of counsel, 2000—; v.p. McGuire Woods Cons. LLC, 2001—. Lectr. Grad. Bus. Sch., U. Va., Charlottesville, 1958-94, lectr. Law Sch., 1970-90. Co-author: Virginia Civil Procedure, 1978, 2d edition, 1992; contbr. articles to profl. jours. Chmn. U. Va. Health Svcs. Found., 1988-97; bd. mgrs. U. Va. Alumni, 1994—, pres., 2000-01; bd. dirs., chmn. Va. Health Care Found., 1997-98; trustee Claude Moore Found., 1991—; mem. Va. Health Planning Bd., 1989—; bd. visitors U. Va., 1990-94; trustee Thomas Jefferson Meml. Found., Monticello, 1994—. Fellow Am. Bar Found., Va. Bar Found., Am. Coll. Tax Counsel; mem. ABA (bd. govs. 1999—), Va. State Bar (coun., chmn. bd. govs. various sects.), Charlottesville-Albemarle Bar Assn. (pres. 1979-80), U. Va. Law Sch. Alumni Assn. (pres. 1979-81), U.S. C. of C. (bd. dirs. 1998—), Va. C. of C. (pres. 1988-90), Omicron Delta Kappa. Episcopalian. Office: McGuire Woods LLP PO Box 1288 Charlottesville VA 22902-1288

MIDDLEKAUFF, ROBERT LAWRENCE, history educator, administrator; b. Yakima, Wash., July 5, 1929; s. Harold and Katherine Ruth (Horne) M.; m. Beverly Jo Martin, July 11, 1952; children: Samuel John, Holly Ruth. BA, U. Wash., 1952; PhD, Yale U., 1961. Instr. history Yale U., New Haven, 1959-62; asst. prof. history U. Calif., Berkeley, 1962-66, assoc. prof., 1966-70, prof., 1970-80, Margaret Byrne prof. history, 1980-83; dir. Huntington Library, Art Gallery and Bot. Gardens, San Marino, Calif., 1983-88; emeritus prof. U. Calif., Berkeley, 2000—, prof. history, 1988-92, Preston Hotchkiss prof., 1992—; Harmsworth prof. history Oxford (Eng.) U., 1996-97. Mem. council Inst. Early Am. History and Culture, Williamsburg, Va., 1974-76, 85-88. Author: Ancients and Axioms, 1963, The Mathers, 1971, The Glorious Cause: The American Revolution, 1763-1789, 1982, Benjamin Franklin and His Enemies, 1996. Served to 1st lt. USMC, 1952-54, Korea. Recipient Bancroft prize, 1972; recipient Commonwealth Club Gold medal, 1983; fellow Am. Council Learned Socs., 1965, NEH, 1973, Huntington Library, 1977 Fellow Am. Acad. Arts and Scis.; mem. Am. Hist. Assn., Orgn. Am. Historians, Am. Philos. Soc., Soc. Am. Historians, Am. Antiquarian Soc., Assocs. Early Am. History and Culture (mem. exec. com.), Colonial Soc. Mass. (corr.) Home: 5868 Ocean View Dr Oakland CA 94618-1535 Office: Univ Calif Dept History Berkeley CA 94720-0001 E-mail: rlmiddlek@juno.com.

MIDDLETON, ANTHONY WAYNE, JR. urologist, educator; b. May 6, 1939; s. Anthony Wayne and Dolores Caravena (Lowry) M.; m. Carol Samuelson, Oct. 23, 1970; children: Anthony Wayne, Suzanne, Kathryn, Jane, Michelle. BS, U. Utah, 1963; MD, Cornell U., 1966. Intern U. Utah Hosps., Salt Lake City, 1966-67; resident in urology Mass. Gen. Hosp., Boston, 1970-74; practice urology Middleton Urol. Assocs., Salt Lake City, 1974—. Mem. staff LDS Hosp., chmn. divsn. urology, 1995—, Salt Lake Regional Med. Ctr., 1977—79, 1984—86; assoc. clin. prof. surgery U. Utah Med. Coll., 1977—; vice-chmn. bd. govs. Utah Med. Self-Ins. Assn., 1980—81, 1996—, chmn. , 1985—87; chmn. med. adv. bd. Uroquest Co., 1996—99; med. dir. Uromed, prostate microwave co., 1999—2000, Utah divsn. Rocky Mountain Prostate, 2001—, Utah-Idaho Lithotripsy, 2001—. Editor: (monthly publ.) AACU-FAX, 1992—; assoc. editor Millenial Star Brit. LDS mag., 1960-61; contbr. articles to profl. jours. Mem. U. Utah Coll. Medicine Dean's Search Com., 1983—84; bd. dirs. Utah Symphony, 1985—2002, Primary Children's Found., 1989—96; mem. Utah Crime Reparations Bd., 2000—, chmn., 2002—; bd. dirs. U.S. Olympic Com. Doping Control M.D., 2000—02; vice chmn. Utah Med. Polit. Action Com., 1978—81; chmn. Utah Physicians for Reagan, 1983—84; del. Utah State Rep. Conv., 2000—01; chmn. Utah Med. Polit. Action Com., 1981—83; bishop, later stake presidency Ch. Jesus Christ Latter-day Saints; bd. dirs. Utah chpt. Am. Cancer Soc., 1978—86; bd. dirs. Utah Symphony and Opera, 2002—. Capt. USAF, 1968—70. Mem.: AMA (del. to Ho. of Dels. 1998—, chmn. ref. com. I 2001, mem. governing coun. SSS 2002—, alt. del. to Ho. of Dels., 1987-88, 89-92, 94, 96-98), ACS, Am. Assn. Clin. Urologists (bd. dirs. 1989—90, nat. pres.-elect 1990—91, pres. 1991—92, nat. bd. chmn. urologic polit. action com. UROPAC 1992—98, Disting. Svc. award 2000), Salt Lake Surg. Soc. (treas. 1977—78), Utah Urol. Assn. (treas. 1977—78, pres.), Salt Lake County Med. Assn. (sec. 1965—67, pres. liaison com. 1980—81, pres.-elect 1981—83, pres. 1984), Am. Urologic Assn. (socioecons. com. 1987—90, chmn. western sect. socioecons. com. 1989—90, chmn. western sect. health policy com. 1990—, pres.-elect western sect. 1999—2000, pres. 2000—01), Utah Med. Assn. (pres. 1987—88, Disting. Svc. award 1993), Beta Theta Pi (chpt. pres. Gamma Beta 1962), Alpha Omega Alpha, Phi Beta Kappa. Republican. Home: 2798 Chancellor Pl Salt Lake City UT 84108-2835 Office: 1060 East 1st South Salt Lake City UT 84102-1520 E-mail: miduro@xmission.com.

MIDDLETON, CHARLENE, retired medical and surgical nurse, educator; b. Ennis, Tex., Sept. 13, 1922; d. Charles Silvester and Harriet Eugenia (Ford) M. Diploma, Scott and White Hosp., Temple, Tex., 1945; AA, Temple Jr. Coll., 1947; BA, U. Tex., Austin, 1956. Nurse coord., ambulatory care svcs. Naval Regional Med. Ctr., Long Beach, Calif.; instr. nursing arts Scott and White Hosp., evening supr.; now ret. Lt. comdr. U.S. Navy, 1957-77. Mem. Scott and White Alumni Assn. (past pres. Dist. 7).

MIDDLETON, CHARLES JAMES, priest; b. St. Louis, Nov. 19, 1925; s. Charles John Middleton, Martha Margaretta (Rother) Middleton. Attended, Kenrick Sem., 1948—51. Ordained priest Cath. Diocese Wichita. Assoc. pastor St. Mary's Cathedral, Wichita, Kans., 1951—53; pastor St. Philip Neri, Franklin, 1954—55, St. Teresa, Madison, 1956—58, St. Louis, Waterloo, 1959—63, St. Aloysius, Greenbush, 1964—67, St. Rose, Columbus, 1967—75, St. Joseph, Arma, 1975—87, St. Patrick, Harper, 1987—93, Galena, 1993—. Home and Office: Saint Patrick Ch 207 Galena Ave Galena KS 66739-0290

MIDDLETON, CHRISTOPHER, Germanic languages and literature educator; b. Truro, Cornwall, Eng., June 10, 1926; came to U.S., 1966; s. Hubert Stanley and Dorothy May (Miller) M. BA, U. of Oxford, Eng., 1951, PhD, 1954. Lectr. King's Coll., London, 1955-65; prof. Germanic langs. and lit. U. Tex., Austin, 1966-98. Author: Selected Writings, 1989, Andalusian Poems, 1993, The Balcony Tree, 1992, Intimate Chronicles, 1996, Twenty Tropes for Doctor Dark, 2000, The Word Pavilion and Selected Poems, 2001, Jackdaw Jiving: Essays on Poetry and Translation, 1998, In the Mirror of the Eighth King, 1999, Faint Harps and Silver Voices-Selected Translations, 2000. Recipient trans. prize Schlegel-Tieck/Govt. Fed. Republic Germany, 1985, Anglo-Swiss Cultural Rels. prize Max Geilinger Stiftung, Zurich, Switzerland, 1987; Guggenheim Found. poetry fellow, 1974-75, NEA poetry fellow, 1980. Mem. Akademie der Künste Berlin. Office: U Tex Dept Of Germanic Langs Austin TX 78712

MIDDLETON, DAVID, physicist, applied mathematician, educator; b. N.Y.C., Apr. 19, 1920; s. Charles Davies Scudder and Lucile (Davidson) M.; m. Nadea Butler, May 26, 1945 (div. 1971); children: Susan Terry, Leslie Butler, David Scudder Blakeslee, George Davidson Powell; m. Joan Bartlett Reed, 1971; children: Christopher Hope, Andrew Bartlett, Henry H. Reed. Grad., Deerfield Acad., 1938; AB summa cum laude, Harvard U., 1942, AM, 1945, PhD in Physics, 1947. Tchg. fellow electronics Harvard U., Cambridge, Mass., 1942, spl. rsch. assoc. radio rsch. lab., 1942-45, NSF predoctoral fellow physics, 1945-47, rsch. fellow electronics, 1947-49, asst. prof. applied physics, 1949-54; cons. physicist, 1954—, Concord, Mass., 1957-71, N.Y.C., 1971—; adj. prof. elec. engring. Columbia U., 1960-61; adj. prof. applied physics and comm. theory Rensselaer Poly. Inst., Hartford Grad. Ctr., 1961-70; adj. prof. communication theory U. R.I., 1966—; adj. prof. math. scis. Rice U., 1979-89. U.S. del. internat. conf. Internat. Radio Union, Lima, Peru, 1975; lectr. NATO Advanced Study Inst., Grenoble, France, 1964, Copenhagen, 1980, Luneburg, Germany, 1984; mem. Naval Rsch. Adv. Com., 1970-77; mem., cons. Inst. Def. Analyses; mem. sci. adv. bd. Supercomputing Rsch. Ctr., 1987-91; cons. physicist since 1946, orgns. including Johns Hopkins U., SRI Internat., Rand Corp., USAF, Cambridge Rsch. Ctr., Comm. Satellite Corp., Lincoln Lab., NASA, Raytheon, Sylvania, Sperry-Rand, Office Naval Rsch., Applied Rsch. Labs., U. Tex., GE, Honeywell Transp. Sys. Ctr. of Dept. Transp., Dept. Commerce Office of Telecom., NOAA, Office Telecom. Policy of Exec. Office Pres., Nat. Telecom. and Info. Adminstrn., Sci. Applications Inc. (SAIC), Naval Undersea Warfare Ctr., Lawrence Livermore Nat. Labs., Planning Rsch. Corp., Applied Physics Labs. U. Wash., 1992—, Kildare Corp., 1995—, Karmanos Cancer Inst., 1997-2001, others. *During the war (1942-45) he was special research assistant to Professor J.H. Van Vleck (Nobel Laureate in Physics), with whom he took his PhD in 1947 from Harvard University, where he also did postdoctoral studies with Professor Leon Brillouin (1948). Current emphasis is on (I) random processes, signal detection, and extraction theory (1942—), (II) Statistical Physics-propagation and scattering in random media with radar and sonar applications (1960—), (III) Electromagnetic Compatibility (EMC) nongaussian noise, interference models, and processing (1968—). Other areas of current interest are optimal system design, and special applications in remote sensing and signal processing.* Author: Introduction to Statistical Communication Theory, 1960, 3d edit., 1996, Russian edit. Soviet Radio Moscow, 2 vols., 1961, 62, Topics in Communication Theory, 1965, 87, Russian edit., 1966; sci. editor English edit. Statistical Methods in Sonar (V.V. Ol'shevskii), 1978; mem. editl. bd. Info. and Control,

Advanced Serials in Electronics and Cybernetics, 1972-82; contbr. articles to tech. jours. Recipient award (with W.H. Huggins) Nat. Electronics Conf., 1956; Wisdom award of honor, 1970; First prize 3d Internat. Symposium on Electromagnetic Compatibility Rotterdam, Holland, 1979; awards U.S. Dept. Commerce, 1978 Fellow AAAS, IEEE (life, awards 1977, 79), Am. Phys. Soc., Explorers Club, Acoustical Soc. Am., N.Y. Acad. Scis., Electromagnetics Acad. MIT; mem. Am. Math. Soc., NAE, Author's Guild Am., Harvard Club (N.Y.C.), Cosmos Club (Washington), Dutch Treat (N.Y.C.), Phi Beta Kappa, Sigma Xi. Achievements include research in radar, telecommunications, underwater acoustics, oceanography, seismology, systems analysis, electromagnetic compatibility, communication theory; pioneering research in statistical communication theory. Home and Office: 127 E 91st St New York NY 10128-1601 Address: MIND 48 Garden St Cambridge MA 02138-1561

MIDDLETON, DAWN E. education educator; b. Pottstown, Pa. d. William H. and Sara G. Bowman; m. Stephen R. Mourar, June 1983; children: William Middleton, Shelly Mourar. AA in Early Childhood Edn., Montgomery Community Coll., 1972; BS in Elem. Edn., West Chester State Coll., 1974; MA in Edn. Curriculum and Instrn. Edn., Pa. State U., 1982, DEd, 1984. Instr. Continuing Edn. Pa. State U., University Park; dir. specialized early childhood programs and svcs. Wiley House, Bethlehem, Pa.; dir. Children's Sch. of Cabrini Coll., Radnor; dept. chmn., prof. edn. Cabrini Coll. Home: 208 Bethel Rd Spring City PA 19475-3200

MIDDLETON, DENISE, restaurant owner, real estate agent, educator; b. Camden, N.J., Apr. 28, 1954; d. Anthony Elton and Geraldine Lucille (Merritt) Vail; m. Robert Warner Middleton Jr., Jan. 11, 1975; children: Robert III, Ryan, Ashley. BA in Elem. Edn., Glassboro State Coll., 1976; nursery cert., Glassboro State U., 1982, reading cert., 1984. Owner Larry's Restaurant, Vineland, N.J., 1975-88, Larry's II Restaurant, Vineland, 1987—; tchr. Edgarton Meml. Sch., Newfield, N.J., 1976-77; substitute tchr. Vineland (N.J.) Pub. Schs., 1991-97; real estate agt. Coldwell Banker McClain Heller, Vineland, 1994—. Mem. Vineland (N.J.) Dist. steering com., 1991, U.N. Day Com., Vineland, 1991, Quality Edn. Act., Com., Vineland, 1991. Mem. Vineland Jaycettes, 1975-78; den leader South Jersey coun. Boy Scouts Am., Vineland; coach, pub. rels. Vineland Soccer Assn., 1984-89; referee U.S. Soccer Fedn., 1986-91; v.p. Vineland Mcpl. Alliance, 1990-91, edn. chair, 1987-92; mem. governing bd. Christian and Missionary Alliance Ch., 2001-, trustee, 2002-. Mem. Vineland (N.J.) C. of C. (edn. chairperson 1987-92, Pres.' award 1987, Outstanding Chairperson award 1991, Small Bus. of Yr. award 1992). Mem. Christian and Missionary Alliance Ch. Avocations: golf, music, theatre, reading. Office: Larrys II Restaurant 907 N Main Rd Bldg A Vineland NJ 08360-8200

MIDDLETON, GARY, county official; b. Goodland, Kans., June 15, 1953; s. Glen and Twyla Middleton; m. Sarah Metcalf, Feb. 2001. BA, Washburn U., 1976. Cert. emergency mgr., Kans. Mgr. Shawnee Couny Emergency Mgmt., Topeka, 1991—. Bd. dirs. Kans. Capital Area chpt. ARC, Topeka, 1988-2001. Recipient Vol. of Yr. award Kans. Capital Area chpt. ARC, 1988. Mem Kans. Emergency Mgmt. Assn. (bd. dirs.). Avocation: outdoor activities.

MIDDLETON, GEORGE, JR. clinical child psychologist; b. Houston, Feb. 26, 1923; s. George and Bettie (McCrary) M.; m. Margaret MacLean, Nov. 17, 1953. BA in Psychology, Birmingham-Southern Coll., 1948; MA in Psychology, U. Ala., Tuscaloosa, 1951; PhD in Clin. Psychology, Pa. State U., 1958. Lic. psychologist, La.; diplomate Am. Coll. Forensic Examiners, Am. Bd. Psychol. Specialities. Asst. clin. psychology Med. Coll. Ala., Birmingham, 1950-52; dir. dept. psychology Bryce Hosp., Tuscaloosa, 1952-54; instr. counseling Coll. Bus. Adminstrn. Pa. State U., 1956-58; asst. prof. spl. edn. McNeese State U., 1962-65, assoc. prof. spl. edn., 1962-65; dir. La. Gov.'s Program for Gifted Children, 1963—; prof. spl. edn. McNeese State U., 1965-73, prof. psychology, 1973-74; pvt. practice clin. psychology and neuropsychology, 1974—; cons. psychologist Calcasieu Parish Sch. Bd., 1975—. Vis. scholar U. Victoria, BC, Can., 1970-71. Mem. Am. Psychol. Assn., Nat. Acad. Neuropsychology, Internat. Neuropsychol. Soc., La. Psychol. Assn. (pres. 1973-74), La. Sch. Psychol. Assn., S.W. La. Psychol. Assn. (pres. 1965, 73, 84), La. State Bd. Examiners Psychologists (chmn. 1977-78), Coun. for Exceptional Children, Am. Coll. Forensic Examiners, 1996. Assn. for the Gifted. Episcopalian. Home and Office: 2001 Southwood Dr Ste A Lake Charles LA 70605-4139

MIDDLETON, HARRY JOSEPH, library administrator; b. Centerville, Iowa, Oct. 24, 1921; s. Harry J. and Florence (Beauvais) M.; m. Miriam Miller, Oct. 29, 1949; children— Susan, Deborah, James Miller, Jennifer. Student, Washburn U., 1941-43; BA, La. State U., 1947. Reporter AP, N.Y.C., 1947-49; news editor Archtl. Forum mag., 1949-52; writer March of Time, 1952-54; free lance writer, author, film dir., 1954-66; staff asst. to Pres. Lyndon B. Johnson, Washington, 1966-69, spl. asst. Austin, Tex., 1969-70; dir. Lyndon Baines Johnson Libr., U. Tex., 1970—2002; exec. dir. Lyndon Baines Johnson Found., 2002—. Author: Compact History of the Korean War, 1965, LBJ: The White House Years, 1990, Lady Bird Johnson: A Life Well-Lived, 1992. With AUS, 1943—46, With AUS, 1950—52. Mem. Sigma Delta Chi. Office: Lyndon Baines Johnson Found 2313 Red River St Austin TX 78705-5702 Home: Apt 8C 1801 Lavaca St Austin TX 78701-1306

MIDDLETON, HERMAN DAVID, SR. theater educator; b. Sanford, Fla., Mar. 24, 1925; s. Arthur Herman and Ruby Elmerry (Hart) M.; m. Amelia Mary Eggart, Dec. 1, 1945; children— Herman David, Kathleen Hart. BS, Columbia U., 1948, MA, 1949; PhD, U. Fla., 1964; postgrad., N.Y. U., 1950, Northwestern U., 1951. Instr., dir. drama and speech Maryville (Tenn.) Coll., 1949-50; instr., designer, tech. dir. theatre U. Del., 1951-55; asst. prof., head dept. drama U. N.C., Greensboro, 1956-59, assoc. prof., head dept. drama and speech, 1959-65, prof., head dept., 1965-74, prof., 1974-79, Excellence Fund prof. dept. communication and theatre, 1979-90, prof. emeritus, 1990. Designer Chucky Jack, Great Smokey Mountains Hist. Soc., Gatlinburg, Tenn., 1956, designer, dir., 1957; communications cons. N.C. Nat. Bank, 1968, Jefferson Standard Life Ins. Co., Greensboro, N.C., 1969, Gilbarco, Inc., Greensboro, 1969-70, 73 Drama critic, columnist: Sunday Star, Wilmington, Del., 1952; theatre editor: Players Mag, 1959-61; theatre columnist: Sunday editions Greensboro Daily News, 1959-62; contbr. articles to profl. jours. Mem. N.C. Arts Council Commn., 1964-66, Guilford County Bi-Centennial Celebration Commn., 1969-70; pres. Shanks Village Players, Orangeburg, N.Y.C., 1947-48, Univ. Drama Group, Newark, Del., 1954-55; bd. dirs. Broadway Theatre League Greensboro, 1958-60, Greensboro Community Arts Council, 1964-67, 69-72, Greensboro Community Theatre, 1983-86, Carolina Theatre Commn., 1990—; organizer-cons. The Market Players, West Market St. United Meth. Ch., 1979-82. Served with USN, 1943-46. Recipient O. Henry award Greensboro C. of C., 1966, Gold medallion Amoco Oil Co., 1973, Suzanne M. Davis award Southeastern Theatre Conf., 1975, Marian A. Smith Disting. Career award N.C. Theatre Conf., 1990. Mem. Am. Nat. Theatre and Acad. (organizer, exec. v.p. Piedmont chpt. 1957-60), Am. Theatre Assn. (chmn. bd. nominations 1971-72), Am. Coll. Theatre Festival (regional festival dir. 1973, 80, regional dir., mem. nat. com. 1978-80), Assn. for Theatre in Higher Edn. (founding mem. 1986-87), Speech Communication Assn. Am., Nat. Collegiate Players, Southeastern Theatre Conf. (bd. dirs. 1963-68, 87-92, pres. 1965, pres. pro-tem 1966), Carolina Dramatic Assn. (bd. dirs. 1958-59), N.C. Drama and Speech Assn. (pres. 1966-67), N.C. Theatre Conf. (co-organizer 1971, bd. dirs. 1984-92, pres. 1987-88), Assn. for Theater in Higher Edn., Phi Delta Kappa, Phi Kappa Phi, Theta Alpha Phi, Alpha Psi Omega. Democrat. Methodist. Home: 203 Village Ln Unit A Greensboro NC 27409-2517 E-mail: mid4@triad.rr.net.

MIDDLETON, IDA LAVELLE, dairy executive, comptroller; b. Hopkins County, Tex., Mar. 14, 1937; d. Wayland and Zetta Ruth (Galloway) Woodard; m. Bobby Wayne Middleton Sr., July 17, 1954; 1 child, Bobby Wayne Jr. Grad. h.s., Sulphur Springs, Tex. Clk. N.Y. Life Ins. Co., Dallas, 1954-57; sec. Republic Nat. Bank, 1958-59, N.Y. Life Ins. Co., Dallas, 1959-62, E-Systems, Inc., Greenville, 1962-72, adminstrv. asst., 1973—78; co-owner Bob Middleton Dairy, Point, 1978-99, comptroller, 1999—. Mem. employee adv. bd. E-Systems, Inc., Greenville, Tex., 1975-78. Co-author: In Their Footsteps, 1992. Bd. mem. Rains County Appraisal Tax Rev. Bd., Emory, Tex., 1982-87; mem. historian com. Clifton Cemetery Assn., Hopkins County, Tex., 1990; co-tchr. Rains County Pre-sch. Assn., Emory, 1992-93, 99-2000. Mem. Hopkins County Genealogy Soc., Tex. Farm Bur., Hopkins-Rains Counties. Avocations: genealogy, travel, gardening (flower and vegetable), antiques. Home: 650 CR 4410 Point TX 75472-5540 E-mail: midleton@koyote.com.

MIDDLETON, JAMES ALLEN, music educator; b. Woodbine, Kans., Feb. 17, 1925; s. James William and Elizabeth Barbara Middleton; m. Doris Ione Gugler, Dec. 15, 1946; children: Stephanie, Brian, Christine, Julie. BM Ed., So. Nazarene Univ., Bethany, OK, 1950; MM Ed., Univ. Okla., Norman, OK, 1954, DM Ed., 1967. Cert. Music Ed. State of Okla. Educator Deer Creek Ind. Sch. 6, Edmond, Okla., 1949—55; band instr. Norman, OK Jr. and Sr. HS, Norman, 1955—68; asst. prof. music ed. Tulsa Univ., Tulsa, 1968—73; choir dir. Asbury Meth. Ch., 1968—73; assoc. prof. music ed. Univ. Mo., Columbia, 1973—77; prof. & dir. grad. studies, music ed. UMC, 1977—87; prof. emeritus Univ. Mo., 1987—. Pres. Okla. Music Edn. Assn., Oklahoma City, 1968—70, SW Div. MENC, 1972—74; rsch. cmte. MENC, 1975—77. Co-author (book) The Complete School Band Progam, The Symphonic Band Winds, The Band Director's Companion. Mem. AF&L Musicians Union, Tulsa, Okla., 1969—73. Master sargeant U.S. Army, 1945—46, Japan. Recipient Tchr. of the Yr., Okla. Edn. Org., 1968, Bandmaster award, Okla. Bandmasters Assn., 1980. Mem.: Mo. Music Edn. Assn., Music Educators Nat. Assn. R-Liberal. Methodist. Achievements include development of co-developer, with William Robinson, of the Breath Impulse Technique of Instrumental Music instruction. Avocation: gardening. Home: 104 Dayspring Drive Columbia MO 65203 Personal E-mail: jmiddletond@cs.com.

MIDDLETON, JAMES ARTHUR, oil and gas company executive; b. Tulsa, Mar. 15, 1936; s. James Arthur and Inez (Matthews) M.; m. Victoria Middleton; children: Robert Arthur, James Daniel, Angela Lynn; stepson: Andrew Davis Fitzhugh. BA, Rice U., 1958, BS in Mech. Engring., 1959. With Atlantic Richfield Co., 1959-96; design engr. Dallas, 1962-67; tech. planner, 1967-69; mgr. shale devel. Grand Junction, Colo., 1969-72; mgr. engring. dept. Los Angeles, 1972-74; mgr. Prudhoe Bay project Pasadena, Calif., 1974-80; v.p., mgr. corp. planning Los Angeles, 1980-81; pres. ARCO Coal Co., Denver, 1981-82; sr. v.p. ARCO Oil and Gas Co., Dallas, 1982-85, pres., 1985-90, sr. v.p. parent co., 1981-87, exec. v.p. parent co., 1987-94, also bd. dirs.; chmn., CEO Crown Energy Corp., Salt Lake City, 1996-2000. Bd. dirs. Tex. Utilities Co., Dallas., ARCO Chem. Co., Berry Petroleum Co. Corp. rep. Circle Ten coun. Boy Scouts Am.; bd. dirs. L.A. coun. Boy Scouts Am., United Way Met. Dallas, Dallas Coun. on World Affairs, Jr. Achievement So. Calif. 2d lt. C.E., AUS, 1959-60 Reicpient ASME Petroleum div. Oil Drop award. Mem. Soc. Petroleum Engrs. of AIME, Tex. Mid-Continent Oil and Gas Assn., Am. Petroleum Inst., Rocky Mountain Oil and Gas Assn., We. States Petroleum Assn. (chmn. bd. dirs.), Nat. Gas Suppliers Assn. (chmn.), L.A. C. of C. (bd. dirs.), L.A. Music Ctr. Founders, Ctr. for Strategic and Internat. Studies (CSIS)-Dallas Round Table, Am. Enterprise Forum Chief Execs. Round Table, Dallas Petroleum Club, Tower, Northwood, Calif. Club, Bel-Air Country Club, L.A. Country Club. Office: 574 Chapala Dr Pacific Palisades CA 90272-4429

MIDDLETON, JAMES BOLAND, retired lawyer; b. Columbus, Ga., Aug. 19, 1934; s. Riley Kimbrough and Annie Ruth (Boland) M.; 1 child, Cynthia. BA in Psychology, Ga. State U., 1964; JD, Woodrow Wilson Coll. Law, 1972. Bar: Ga. 1972, U.S. Patent Office. Draftsman, paralegal and office mgr. to patent atty., Atlanta, 1955-68; draftsman, paralegal and office mgr. Jones & Thomas, 1968-72, assoc., 1972-76; pvt. practice intellectual property Decatur, Ga., 1976-98; ret., 1998. Mem. editl. bd. Atlanta Lawyer, 1973-82, assoc. editor, 1978-81, editor-in-chief, 1981-82. Dir. arts coun. Unitarian-Universalist Congregation Atlanta, 1989-91; bd.d irs. Unitarian-Universalist Endowment Fund, 1993-96, vice chair, 1994-95, sec., 1995-96; bd. dirs., sec. Decatur Arts Alliance, 1990-94; bd. dirs. Life Enrichment Svcs., Inc., 2002-. With U.S. Army, 1957-59. Mem. ABA, Am. Intellectual Property Law Assn., Am. Arbitration Assn. (comml. panel 1983-94), DeKalb Bar Assn., State Bar Ga. (editl. bd. jour. 1985-92, patent trademark and copyright sect. 1972-2000, chmn. 1982-83, pub. rels. com. 1982-88), Fed. Cir. Bar Assn.

MIDDLETON, JOHN ALBERT, retired communications executive; b. Bradford, Yorkshire, Eng., Mar. 20, 1915; came to U.S., 1922; s. Albert Henry and Priscilla (Lambert) Ml; m. Marjorie Frances Crossett, May 29, 1942; children: John Gary, Pamela Mary, Gregory Chester, Susan Jeanne. Grad. H.S., Manchester Ctrl. H.S., Manchester, 1934. Repair supr. New Eng. Telephone, Claremont, N.H., 1946-77; ret., 1977. City councilor, Claremont, 1986-94, asst. mayor, 1987-88, 90, 93-94, mayor, 1991; state rep., Concord, N.H., 1989-92; Justice of the Peace, N.H., 1990—; vice-chair fin. Sullivan County Delegation, N.H., 1989-92; mem. Sullivan County Econ. Devel. Coun., 1986-95; mem. Claremont Indsl. Devel. Authority, 1994, chmn. traffic com., 1987-90; chmn. health com., Claremont, 1993-94; mem. strategic planning com. Claremont Sch. Dist., 1994-95; sr. warden Union Ch., Claremont; grand marshall Independence Day Parade, July 4, 1997. With U.S. Army, 1942-46, PTO. Mem. VFW (life), Am. Legion (life), Am. Vets. (life), Shrine Legion of Honor (life), Hist. Soc. (writer historical document Civil War Tablets at City Hall 1987), Telephone Pioneers Am. (pres. 1985-86, 95), Anniversary Lodge (charter), William Pitt Tavern Lodge (charter), Sullivan Hugh-De Payens (treas. 1979-89), Hiram Lodge (Master Hiram # 9, 1963,83, 84, 85, 86, sec. 1987-89), Masons (Maj. Gen. John Sulivan medal, Disting. Svc. award 1986, Cheshire/Webb chpt. # 4 High Priest 1987-88, Columbian/St. Johns chpt. # 2 master 1983-90). Republican. Episcopalian. Avocation: woodworking. Home: 4 S Park St Claremont NH 03743-2842

MIDDLETON, JOHN EDISON, management consultant; b. Sunnyside, Wash., May 1, 1947; s. John Willbey Middleton and Marion (Brignic) Hoage; children: William Arthur, Rachel Ranee. BBA, UCLA, 1968; MBA, NYU, 1989, PhD, 1987; PhD (hon.), Oxford (Eng.) U., 1988. Dir. Ramic Prodn., N.Y.C., 1973-75; v.p. Nelson Berry, 1975-79, CEO, 1984-87; exec. v.p. Investment Internat., 1980-84, Am. Video, N.Y.C., 1987-89; pres. JBL Assocs., 1989-92; CEO LBJ Assocs. Ltd., 1992—. Exec. dir. National Coalition for Civil Rights. Col. U.S. Army, 1968-72 (Green Beret). Named Big Brother of Yr. Big Bros. N.Y., 1979. Mem. Assn. Pub. Pay Phones (pres. 1991—), Masons, Scottish Rite, Shriners, Am. Purple Heart. Republican. Jewish. Avocations: scuba diving, sky diving. Office: 50 Court St Ste 501 Brooklyn NY 11201-4859 E-mail: nccr004@aol.com.

MIDDLETON, MARC STEPHEN, corporate insurance risk manager; b. Louisville, Dec. 7, 1950; s. Joseph Scott and Virginia Marie (Schuler) M.; m. Carmen Teresa Fauscette, Feb. 22, 1969; 1 child, Marc Christopher. AA, Dalton Jr. Coll., 1970; BBA, U. Ga., 1972. Sr. risk analyst Deere and Co., Moline, Ill., 1973-78, mgr. corp. claims, 1978-79, mgr. corp. ins. dept., 1980-86; v.p. risk mgmt. svcs. John Deere Ins. Group, 1987-91; dir. risk mgmt. Deere and Co., 1992—. V.p. bd. dirs. Tahoe Ins. Co., Reno, 1981-83, Sierra Gen. Life Ins. Co., Reno, 1981-83, Continental Guaranty, Ltd., Hamilton, Bermuda, 1981-83; v.p. John Deere Ins. Co., Rock River Ins. Co., Tahoe Ins. Co., 1990-91, John Deere Life Ins. Co., Sierra Gen. Life Ins. Co., 1991; mem. M200 Risk Mgmt. Forum; mem. FM Global Risk Mgmt. Exec. Coun. Mem. Citizen's Adv. Council to East Moline (Ill.) Sch. Bd., 1978-80; coach YMCA Youth Basketball, Moline, 1978. Mem. Risk and Ins. Mgmt. Soc., Risk Mgmt. Council of Mfrs. Alliance (formerly Machinery and Allied Products Inst.), Captive Ins. Cos. Assn., ESIS (Delphi panel 1985—), Internat. Platform Assn. Roman Catholic. Avocations: tennis, hunting, fishing, woodworking. Home: PO Box 369 6 Eagle Pointe Pass Rapids City IL 61278 Office: Deere & Co 1 John Deere Pl Moline IL 61265-8098 E-mail: middletonmarcs@johndeere.com.

MIDDLETON, MICHAEL JOHN, civil engineer; b. N.Y.C., May 14, 1953; s. Vincent Aloysius and Mary Hilda (Lehane) Middleton. BS in Civil Engring., U. Calif., Davis, 1975. Registered profl. engrl., Calif., Wash., Hawaii. Project mgr. G.A. Fitch & Assoc., Concord, Calif., 1975-78, v.p., 1978-80; project mgr. Santina & Thompson, Inc., 1980-83, dir. engring., 1983-88, sr. v.p., 1988—98, sr. project mgr., 1998—. Scholar, Calif. Scholarship Fedn., 1971. Roman Catholic. Home: 1409 Bel Air Dr Apt A Concord CA 94521-5348 Office: Santina & Thompson Inc 1355 Willow Way Ste 280 Concord CA 94520-8113 Business E-Mail: mikem@santina-thompson.com.

MIDDLETON, NORMAN GRAHAM, social worker, psychotherapist; b. Jacksonville, Fla., Jan. 21, 1935; s. Norman Graham and Betty (Quina) M.; m. Judy Stephens, Aug. 1, 1968; stepchildren: Monty Stokes, Toni Stokes. BA, U. Miami (Fla.), 1960; MSW, Fla. State U., 1962. Casework counselor Family Svc., Miami, 1962-64; psychiat. social worker assoc. firm Drs. Warson, Steele, Wiener, Sarasota, Fla., 1964-66; psychotherapist, 1966—. Instr. Manatee Jr. Coll., Bradenton, Fla., 1973-76. Author: The Caverns of My Mind, 1985, Imaginative Healing, 1993, Spirited Imagination, 2002. Pres. Coun. on Epilepsy, Sarasota, 1969-70. Served with USAF, 1954-58. Fellow Fla. Soc. Clin. Social Work (pres. 1978-80); mem. Am. Group Psychotherapy Assn., Am. Assn. Sex Educators and Counselors (cert. sex educator). Democrat. Episcopalian. Home: 16626 Winburn Dr Sarasota FL 34240-9221 Office: 1257 S Tamiami Trail Sarasota FL 34239-2219 E-mail: fallenpine@aol.com.

MIDDLETON, TERESA MUIR, finance company executive, researcher; b. London, Eng. ; d. Francis Robert and Marjorie Banwell Muir; children: Christopher, Andrew, Claire. BSc, Syracuse U., 1978; MBA, Pepperdine U., 1982. Rschr. SRI Internat., Menlo Park, Calif., 1970—90; program mgr. SRI Intern., 1990—94; assoc. dir. SRI Internat., 1994—98, assoc. dir. emeritus, 1998—; pres. PatchWorx, Inc., 1998—. Founding dir. Nat. Cristina Found., Greenwich, 1989—; mem. com. Nat. Conf. Tech. and Disabilities, Northridge, 1989; chmn. Virtual Reality Conf., Menlo Park, 1991; rschr. in field. Editor: Virtual Worlds: Real Challenges, 1991. Dir. telecom. for the deaf Deafnet Dissemination Project, 1984. Recipient Mimi award, SRI Internat., 1997. Avocations: swimming, music, travel. Office: Patchworx Inc 333 Ravenswood Ave Bn318 Menlo Park CA 94025 Personal E-mail: tmiddleton@aol.com. Business E-Mail: tmiddleton@patchworx.org.*

MIDDLETON, WANDA KAREN LEE, composer, poet; b. Balt., Mar. 13, 1958; d. Willie James and Dorothy Lee Middleton; children: Ryan Kurtis, Willie Lee, Russell Lee, DaWayne Lee, Rashell Lee. Student, Bay Coll. Md., 1976—78, Balt. C.C., 1979—80; cert. in early childhood edn., Stratford Career Inst., 2001; cert. in nutrition and fitness, Profl. Career Inst., 2001. Home health aide Kelly Health Care, Towson, Md., 1976—78; recreation worker Fed. Hill Nursing Home, Balt., 1979—80; vol. St. Joseph Hosp., Towson, 1981—83; clk. Def. Investigative Svc., Washington, 1984—86; dietary asst. Amu Retirement Home, Montgomery County, Md., 1987—. Recipient Editors Choice award, Nat. Libr. Poetry, 1996, Pub. award, Cander Publs., 1996. Mem.: English Conversation Club. Avocations: writing, travel, Bible study, exercise, family games. Address: PO Box 1817 Rockville MD 20849

MIDDLETON-DOWNING, LAURA, psychiatric social worker, artist, small business owner; b. Edinburg, Ind., Apr. 20, 1935; d. John Thomas Jr. and Rowene Elizabeth (Baker) Middleton; m. George Charles Downing, 1974 (div. 1986). BA in English Lit., U. Colo., 1966, MFA, 1969, BA in Psychology, 1988; MSW, U. Denver, 1992; Doctor of Clin. Hypnotherapy, Am. Inst. Hypnotherapy, 1995. Cert. clin. hypnotherapist, Calif., Colo.; cert. past life therapist, Colo., In ternat. Bd. for Regression Therapy-Level II cert. Profl. artist, Silver Plume and Boulder, Colo., 1965—; profl. photographer Silver Plume, Boulder, 1975—; art tchr. U. Colo., Boulder and Longmont, 1971-73; mem. survey crew Bur. of Land Mgmt., Empire, Colo., 1984-85; cons. social work and psychotherapy Boulder, 1992—; psychiat. and med. social worker Good Samaritan Health Agy., 1993-97; pvt. practice clin. hypnotherapy, 1995—; pvt. practice past-life therapist, 1995—. Ind. distbr. Super Blue Green Algae, 1996—; pres. Phoenix LG, Inc., 1998—. Author, photographer Frontiers, Vol. IV, No. 1, 1979; works exhibited in 15 one-woman shows, 1969—; numerous group exhbns. including group exhbn., Colo. History Mus., Denver, 1997-98. Trustee Town of Silver Plume, Colo., 1975-84; co-founder, pres. Alma Holm Rogers Nat. Orgn. Women, Clear Creek County, 1975-82; mem. Ctrl. Mountain Coun., Clear Creek County, 1980; chairperson Mary Ellen Barnes Cmty. Ctr. Project, Silver Plume, Colo., 1983; vol. Rape Crisis Team, Boulder, 1989-90, Child & Family Advocacy Program, Boulder, 1992-97; adv. bd. mem. Good Samaritan Agy., Boulder, 1993-97; caring minister vol. First Congl. Ch., Boulder, 1995-98; founding mem. Front Range Women in the Visual Arts, Boulder, Colo., 1974. Recipient Juried Exhbn. Merit award Colo. Women in the Arts, 1979; Women's Incentive scholar U. Colo., Boulder, 1989; Grad. Sch. Social Work scholar U. Denver, 1991; Colo. Grad. grantee U. Denver, 1992. Mem. AAUW, NASW, DAR, Colo. Advs. for Responsible Mental Health Svcs., Eye Movement Desensitization Reprocessing Network, Internat. Assn. for Regression Rsch. and Therapies, Inc. (Ecocycle, Colo. block leader), Natural Resources Def. Coun., The Nature Conservancy, World Wildlife Fedn., Bus. Women's Leadership Group, Sierra Club, Defender of Wildlife, Psi Chi. Avocations: inline skating, skipping, photography, travel, volunteerism. Office: PO Box 2312 Boulder CO 80306-2312

MIDDLEWOOD, MARTIN EUGENE, technical communications specialist, writer, consultant; b. Galesburg, Ill., Mar. 21, 1947; s. Martin and Bernetta Maxine (Henderson) M.; m. Mona Marie Jarmer, Sept. 10, 1971; children: Erin, Martha, Emily, Margaret. BA, Ea. Wash. U., 1973, MA, 1980. Writer tech. manuals Tektronix, Inc., Beaverton, Oreg., 1976-77, tech. writer, 1977-79, sr. tech. writer, 1979-82, supr. pub. rels., 1982-84, mgr. pub. rels., 1984-85, mgr. mktg. communications Vancouver, Wash., 1985-86; dir. info. strategy and svcs. Waggener Edstrom, Portland, Oreg., 1986-98; pub. Cognizer Report, 1990-94. Chmn. adv. bd. sci. and tech. writing, Clark Coll., Vancouver, 1984—; owner communications cons. firm, Vancouver, 1978-98; pres., owner Frontline Strategies, Inc., 1998—. Author: (ednl. brochure series) Oscilloscope Measurements, 1979 (award of excellence Willamette Valley chpt., Network Svcing., won Awd. of Distinction, 1980, Soc. Tech. Communication, 1980); contbr. articles to profl. jours. Served with USMC, 1967-70. Recipient cert. recognition Clark Coll., Vancouver, 1984, 86, 89, 92-99, award of excellence Pacific N.W. chpt. Internat. Assn. Bus. Communicators, 1985. Mem. Soc. Tech. Communication (sr., pres. Willamette Valley chpt. 1983-85, award of recognition 1986, chpt. pub. achievement award 1985, awards of distinction, 1980, 81). Avocations: photography, martial arts. Home and Office: 1107 SE 98th Ave Vancouver WA 98664-4119 E-mail: martinm@pacific.com.

MIDELFORT, HANS CHRISTIAN ERIK, history educator; b. Eau Claire, Wis., Apr. 17, 1942; s. Peter Albert and Gerd (Gjems) M.; m. Corelyn Forsyth Senn, June 16, 1965 (div. Dec. 1981); children: Katarina, Kristian; m. Cassandra Clemons Hughes, May 25, 1985 (div. April 1996); 1 child, Lucy; m. Anne L. McKeithen, June 22, 1996. BA, Yale U., 1964, MPhil, 1967, PhD, 1970. Instr. Stanford (Calif.) U., 1968-70; asst. prof. U. Va., Charlottesville, 1970-72, assoc. prof., 1972-87, prof., 1987—, Charles Julian Bishko prof. history, 1996—. Vis. prof. Harvard U., Cambridge, Mass., 1985, Univ. Stuttgart, Germany, 1988, Univ. Bern, Switzerland, 1988; prin. Brown Coll., U. Va., 1996-2001. Author: Witch Hunting in Southwestern Germany, 1972 (Gustave Arlt prize 1972), Mad Princes of Renaissance Germany, 1994 (Roland H. Bainton prize 16th Century Studies Conf. 1995), A History of Madness in 16th Century Germany, 1999 (Ralph Waldo Emerson prize, Phi Beta Kappa, 1999, Roland H. Bainton prize 16th Century Studies Conf. 2000); editor: Johann Weyer, On Witchcraft, 1998; translator: Imperial Cities and the Reformation (Bernd Moeller), 1972, Revolution of 1525 (Peter Bickle), 1981, Shaman of Oberstdorf (Wolfgang Behringer), 1998. Mem. Soc. Reformation Rsch. (pres. 1992-93). Office: U Va Dept History Charlottesville VA 22903 E-mail: hemFe@virginia.edu.

MIDGLEY, JOHN W. civil engineer, consultant; b. Jackson, Mich., July 23, 1950; s. John R. and Beverly A. Midgley; m. Diana L. Midgley, June 20, 1970; children: Kelly L. Sheppard, John B. BS in Civil Engring., Tri-State Coll., Angola, Ind., 1972; MBA, Spring Arbor (Mich.) Coll., 1996. Registered profl. engr., Mich., Ind. Engr. Ind. State Hwy. Commn., Indpls., 1972-73, Mich. Dept. Transp., Lansing, 1973-74, asst. project engr., 1974-77, railroad crossing program engr., 1977; asst. county hwy. engr. Jackson County Rd. Commn., Jackson, 1977-79, dir. engring., 1979-2001; cons. engr. self employed, Parma, Mich., 1991—; mng. dir. Ingham County Rd. Commn., Mason, 2001—. Mem. policy com. Jackson Area Comprehensive Transp. Study, 1987-2001, chmn. tech. adv. com., 1987—; bd. advisors Nat. Work Zone Safety Info. Clearinghouse, Washington, 1998—. Recipient Merit award County Rd. Assn. Mich., 1994, Engr. of the Yr. award, 2002. Fellow ASCE; mem. NSPE, Mich. Soc. Profl. Engrs. (Engr. of the Yr. Jackson chpt. 2001), Nat. Assn. County Engrs., Inst. Transp. Engrs., Am. Road and Transp. Builders Assn. (pres. transp. ofcls. divsn. 1992-93, safety adv. coun. 1992—, bd. dirs. 1991—, chmn. 2000-2001, Ralph R. Bartelsmeyer award 1996, 2001). Avocations: golf, camping, horses. Home: 6440 Rogers Rd Parma MI 49269-9624 Office: Ingham County Rd Commn PO Box 38 Mason MI 48854-0038

MIDKIFF, KIMBERLY ANN, paralegal; b. Kingsport, Tenn., Nov. 27, 1958; d. Harold Douglas and Mary Lou (Carden) M. Student, U. Tenn., 1976-80, 94—. Cert. legal asst. Nat. Assn. Legal Assts. Legal sec. Gilreath & Rowland, Knoxville, Tenn., 1981-83, Tenn. State Atty. Gen.'s Office, Knoxville, 1983-84, Bond, Carpenter & O'Connor, Knoxville, 1984; paralegal Gilreath & Assocs., 1984-89, Lewis, King, Krieg, Waldrop & Catron, P.C., Knoxville, 1989—. Active Westminster Presbyn. Ch., Knoxville. Mem. Nat. Assn. Legal Assts., Tenn. Paralegal Assn., Knoxville Paralegal Assn., Delta Gamma Alumnae Assn., Golden Key Nat. Honor Soc., Phi Kappa Phi, Phi Alpha Theta. Democrat. Presbyterian. Avocations: vocal and piano music, horseback riding, reading, theater, hiking. Office: Lewis King Krieg Waldrop & Catron PC One Centre Square 5th Fl 620 Market St Knoxville TN 37902-2231

MIDKIFF, ROBERT RICHARDS, financial and trust company executive, consultant; b. Honolulu, Sept. 24, 1920; s. Frank Elbert and Ruth (Richards) M.; m. Evanita Sumner, July 24, 1948; children: Mary Lloyd, Robin Starr, Shelley Sumner, Robert Richards Jr., David Wilson. BA, Yale U., 1942; grad. Advanced Mgmt. Program, Harvard U., 1962; LHD, U. Hawaii, 2002. Asst. sec. Hawaiian Trust Co., 1951-56, asst. v.p., 1956-57, v.p., 1957-65; dir. Am. Factors, Ltd., 1954-65; v.p. Amfac, Inc., 1965-68; exec. v.p., dir. Am. Security Bank, Honolulu, 1968-69, pres., dir., 1969-71; pres., CEO, dir. Am. Trust Co. Hawaii, 1971-93; chmn. bd. dirs. Bishop Trust Co. Ltd., 1984-93; pres., CEO Am. Fin. Svcs. of Hawaii, 1984-93. Bd. dirs. Persis Corp., Honolulu. Co-chmn. Gov.'s Archtl. Adv. Com. on State Capitol, 1960-65; co-chmn. Gov.'s Adv. Com. on Fine Arts for State Capitol, 1965-69; past chmn., bd. dirs. Hawaii Visitors Bur.; past pres., bd. dirs. Downtown Improvement Assn., Lahaina Restoration Found., Hawaii Cmty. Found.; bd. dirs., pres. Atherton Family Found.; past chmn. Profit Sharing Rsch. Found.; past bd. dirs. Coun. on Founds.; chmn. past bd. dirs. Hawaii Theatre Ctr.; chmn. bd. dirs. Good Beginnings Alliance. Mem. Coun. on Founds., Profit Sharing Coun. Am. (past bd. dirs.), Small Bus. Coun. Am. (past bd. dirs.), ESOP Assn. Am. (past bd. dirs.), Pacific Club, Waialae Golf Club, Phi Beta Kappa. Democrat. Episcopalian. Office: 4477 Kahala Ave Honolulu HI 96816-4924 Fax: 808-737-9007. E-mail: rrmhi@aol.com.

MIDLARSKY, MANUS ISSACHAR, political scientist, educator; b. N.Y.C., Jan. 28, 1937; s. Max and Rachel (Potechin) M.; m. Elizabeth Steckel, June 25, 1961; children— Susan, Miriam, Michael. BS, CUNY, 1959; MS, Stevens Inst. Tech., 1963; PhD (Ford Found. fellow), Northwestern U., 1969. Instr. polit. sci. U. Colo., Boulder, 1967-68, asst. prof., 1968-71, assoc. prof., 1971-74, prof., 1974-89, dir. Ctr. Internat. Relations, 1983-89; Moses and Annuta Back prof. internat. peace and conflict resolution Rutgers U., New Brunswick, N.J., 1989—. Cons. USAF, 1968 Author: On War: Political Violence in the International System, 1975, The Disintegration of Political Systems: War and Revolution in Comparative Perspective, 1986, The Onset of World War, 1988, The Evolution of Inequality: War, State Survival, and Democracy in Comparative Perspective, 1999; editor: Inequality and Contemporary Revolutions, 1986, Handbook of War Studies, 1989, 93, The Internationalization of Communal Strife, 1992, (with J. Vasquez and P. Gladkov) From Rivalry to Cooperation: Russian and American Perspectives on the Post-Cold War Era, 1994, Inequality, Democracy and Economic Development, 1997, Handbook of War Studies II, 2000. Faculty fellow Richardson Inst. Conflict and Peace Research, London, 1977-78; faculty fellow Council Research and Creative Work, U. Colo., 1977-78; NSF grantee, 1973-76, 81-83, 83-85, 86-89; Nat. Endowment Humanities grantee, 1980, 83, U.S. Inst. of Peace grantee, 1997-98. Mem. Am. Polit. Sci. Assn. (pres. conflict processes sect. 1985-88) Internat. Studies Assn. (pres. West 1980-81, v.p. 1986-87), Am. Soc. Polit. and Legal Philosophy, Inter-Univ. Seminar in Armed Forces and Soc. Office: Rutgers U Dept Polit Sci Hickman Hall New Brunswick NJ 08903

MIDTHUN, DAVID ERIC, physician, consultant; b. Mpls., Apr. 10, 1958; s. Norman Edward and Jean Roslyn (Johnson) M.; m. Vivien Jane Williams, Aug. 15, 1991; children: Edward Norman, William Robert. BA, St. Olaf Coll., Northfield, Minn., 1980; MD, U. Minn., 1985. Diplomate in internal medicine and pulmonary medicine Am. Bd. Internal Medicine. Intern, resident Mayo Grad. Sch. Medicine, 1985-88, fellow, 1988-91; cons. pulmonary disease and internal medicine Mayo Clinic, Rochester, Minn., 1991—; asst. prof. Mayo Med. Sch., 1994-2000, assoc. prof., 2000—. Contbr. chpts. to books, articles to profl. jours. Active Oronoco (Minn.) Presbyn. Ch., 1994—. Fellow ACP, Am. Coll. Chest Physicians; mem. Am. Thoracic Soc., Phi Beta Kappa. Office: Mayo Clinic 200 2nd St SW Rochester MN 55905-0016

MIEL, JAN, humanities educator; b. Wayne, Pa., Oct. 10, 1930; s. Charles Jan and Mary (Long) M.; m. Elizabeth MacKiernan, Sept. 10, 1960; children: Persephone, Justin. AB, Harvard U., 1952; MA, Princeton U., 1960, PhD, 1965. Instr. Goucher Coll., Towson, Md., 1960-62; asst. prof. MIT, Cambridge, Mass., 1962-64, Wesleyan U., Middletown, Conn., 1964-70, assoc. prof., 1970-78, prof., 1978-99. Author: Pascal and Theology, 1970, Pascal and Theology (Japanese transl), 2000; contbr. Mem. exec. coun. Diocese of Conn., Hartford, 1999—. Cpl. U.S. Army, 1953-55. Fellow Johns Hopkins U., 1968, NEH, 1976, Guggenheim Found., 1977. Mem. MLA, N.Am. Soc. for 17th Century French Lit. Anglican. Home: 29 Gordon Pl Middletown CT 06457 Office: Wesleyan U Coll Letters Middletown CT 06459

MIEL, VICKY ANN, city official; b. South Bend, Ind., June 20, 1951; d. Lawrence Paul Miel and Virginia Ann (Yeagley) Hernandez. BS, Ariz. State U., 1985. Word processing coordinator City of Phoenix, 1977-78, word processing adminstr., 1978-83, chief dep. city clk., 1983-88, city clk. dir., 1988—. Assoc. prof. Phoenix Community Coll., 1982-83, Mesa (Ariz.) Community Coll., 1983; speaker in field, Boston, Santa Fe, Los Angeles, N.Y.C. and St. Paul, 1980—. Author: Phoenix Document Request Form, 1985, Developing Successful Systems Users, 1986. Judge Future Bus. Leaders Am. at Ariz. State U., Tempe, 1984; bd. dirs. Fire and Life Safety League, Phoenix, 1984. Recipient Gold Plaque, Word Processing Systems Mag., Mpls., 1980, Green Light Productivity award City of Phoenix, 1981, Honor Soc. Achievement award Internat. Word Processing Assn., 1981, 1st Ann. Grand Prize Records Mgmt. Internat. Inst. Mcpl. Clks., 1990, Olsten Award for Excellence in Records Mgmt., 1991, Tech. Award of Excellence, 1995. Mem. ASPA, Assn. Info. Systems Profls. (internat. dir. 1982-84), Internat. Inst. Mcpl. Clks. (cert., 2d v.p. 1996-97, 1st v.p. 1997-98, pres. 1998-99, tech. award of excellence 1995, immediate past pres. 1999-2000), Am. Records Mgrs. Assn., Assn. Image Mgmt., Am. Mgmt. Assn. Office: City Phoenix 200 W Washington St Ste 1500 Phoenix AZ 85003-1611

MIELE, ALFONSE RALPH, former government official; b. N.Y.C., Jan. 6, 1922; s. Angelo and Alesia (Laudadio) M.; m. Gloria I. Litrento, Nov. 22, 1942 (dec. Dec. 1977); children: Richard Lynn, Barbara Jo, Steven Arnold; m. Ann Carlino Valerio, Mar. 31, 1979 (dec. June 1988); m. Dorothy A. McGowan, July 7, 1990. AB in Litteris Gallicis with honors, Fordham U., 1942; postgrad., U. Nancy, France, 1945; MA, Columbia U., 1947, PhD, 1958. Commd. 2nd lt. U.S. Army, 1942; advanced through grades to col. USAF, 1961; served in 377th Automatic Weapons Bn., 1942-45; ret., brig. gen.; instr. French and pub. speaking Fordham Prep. Sch., N.Y.C., 1946-47; asst. prof. French and Russian U.S. Naval Acad., 1949-52; exec. officer to NATO comdrs., 1953-55; teaching asst. Columbia U., 1955-58; assoc. prof. French USAF Acad., 1958-60, prof., head dept. fgn. langs., 1960-67, assoc. dean, chmn. divsn. humanities, 1967-68; exec. v.p. Loretto Heights Coll., Denver, 1968-70; pres. Coll. St. Rose, Albany, 1970-72; prof. gen. edn. Schenectady County C.C., Schenectady, N.Y., 1972-73; dep. asst. adminstr. internat. aviation affairs FAA, Washington, 1973-75, edn. specialist, 1976—;, 1968. Asst. dir. pub. affairs U.S. Dept. Interior, Washington, 1975-76; chief negotiator civil aviation tech. agreement with USSR, 1973-75; project dir. Nat. Aviation Edn. Program for Am. Indians, 1978; asst. dir. Union County (N.J.) Coord. Agy. for Higher Edn., 1979-82; rep. Eckhart Assocs., 1983-88; relocation specialist Bradley/Wildman Co., Monument, Colo., 1989-92. Mem. Westfield (N.J.) Bd. Edn., 1985-88; bd. dirs. Pike's Peak chpt. ARC, 1990-93; pres. Colorado Springs World Affairs Coun., 1993-95; bd. dirs. and patron Tri-Lakes Ctr. for the Arts, 1998—. Decorated Bronze Star for heroism in ground combat, Legion of Merit (2) with oak leaf cluster, Belgian Fourragère; chevalier Palmes Academiques France; recipient Encaenia award Fordham Coll., 1962 Mem. Monument C. of C. (bd. dirs. 1992-94). Home: PO Box 321 Monument CO 80132-0321 *Be ever curious and willing to dare. The sweet becomes even sweeter when the bitter is overcome. Each living moment is a learning experience and adds to the anticipation of better tomorrows. The journey of life is exciting— live with that thought in mind.*

MIELE, ANGELO, engineering educator, researcher, consultant, author; b. Formia, Italy, Aug. 21, 1922; arrived in U.S., 1952, naturalized, 1985; s. Salvatore and Elena (Marino) Miele. DCivil Engring., U. Rome, Italy, 1944, DAero. Engring., 1946; DSc (hon.), Inst. Tech., Technion, Israel, 1992. Asst. prof. Poly. Inst. Bklyn., 1952- 55; prof. Purdue U., 1955-59; dir. astrodynamics Boeing Sci. Rsch. Labs., 1959-64; prof. aerospace scis., math. scis. Rice U., Houston, 1964-88, Foyt Family prof. engring., 1988-93, Foyt prof. emeritus engring., aerospace scis., math. scis., 1993—, rsch. prof., 2001—. Cons. Douglas Aircraft Co., 1956—58; cons. Allison divsn. GM Corp., 1956—58; cons. U.S. Aviation Underwriters, 1987, Boeing Comml. Airplane Co., 1989; Breakwell Meml. lectureship Internat. Astron. Fedn., 1994; Gaspare Santangelo Meml. lectureship Italian Assn. of Aeronautics and Astronautics, 2001. Author: Flight Mechanics, 1962; editor: Theory of Optimum Aerodynamic Shapes, 1965, Applied Mathematics in Aerospace Science and Engineering, 1994; contbr. Pres. Italy in Am. Assn., 1966—68. Decorated knight comdr. Order Merit Italy; recipient Levy medal, Franklin Inst. of Phila., 1974, Brouwer award, AAS, 1980, Schuck award, Am. Automatic Control Coun., 1988. Fellow: Am. Astronautical Soc., AIAA (hon.), Franklin Inst.; mem.: Nat. Acad. Engring. of Argentina (corr.), Acad. Scis. Turin (corr.), Internat. Acad. Astronautics, Russian Acad. Scis. (fgn.), NAE. Home: 3106 Kettering Dr Houston TX 77027-5504 Office: Rice Univ MS-322 Aero-Astronautics Group 6100 Main St Houston TX 77005-1827 Fax: 713 348-5407. E-mail: miele@rice.edu.

MIELE, JOEL ARTHUR, SR. civil engineer; b. Jersey City, May 28, 1934; s. Jene Gerald Sr., and Eleanor Natale (Bergida) M.; m. Faith Roseann Trombetta, July 21, 1952 (div. 1954); m. 2d Josephine Ann Cottone, Feb. 14, 1959; children: Joel Arthur, Jr., Vita Marie, Janet Ann. B.C.E., Poly. Inst. Bklyn., 1955. Registered profl. engr. N.Y., N.J., Fla.; profl. planner N.J.; chartered engr., U.K. Civil engr. Yudell & Miele, Queens, N.Y., 1955-57; chief engr. Jene G. Miele Assocs., 1960-68; prin., CEO Miele Assocs., 1968-94; commr. City Planning Commn., N.Y., 1990-94; commr. Dept. of Bldgs. City of N.Y., 1994-96; commr. Dept. Environ. Protection, N.Y., 1996—. Mem. N.Y. State Bd. for Engring. and Land Surveying, 1997—. Patentee masonry wall constrn. Mem. Cmty. Bd. 10, Queens, 1971-90, chmn., 1978-90; mem. bd. visitors Creedmoor State Hosp., 1978—, pres., 1979—; trustee Queens Borough Pub. Libr., 1979—, pres., 1995-96; bd. dirs. Peninsula Hosp. Ctr., 1984—, chair, 1990—; bd. mem. Peninsula Gen. Nursing Home, 1985—, chair, 1990—; bd. mem. Queens County Overall Econ. Devel. Corp., 1989-94, pres., 1991-94; trustee, treas. Queens Pub. Comm. Corp., 1983—; exec. v.p. Queens County and mem. Nat. Coun. Boy Scouts Am., 1991—; bd. mem. Am. Parkinson Disease Assn., 1985—, mem. exec. com., 1987—, v.p., 1996—; pres. Internat. Parkinsons Found., The Netherlands, 1997—; dir. Queens Libr. Found., 1997—; dir. Com. Assn. Met Water Agys., 1997—, Assn. Met. Sewerage Agys., 1997; mem. N.Y. State Bd. Engring. & Land Surveying, 1997—, Nat. Coun. Examiners engring. & Surveying, 1997. Lt. (j.g.) USN, 1957-60; capt. USNR, 1960-88, ret., 1988; RADM LH N.Y. Naval Militia, 1998—. Named Italian-Am. of Yr. Ferrini Welfare League, Queens, 1980, Hon. Mem. of Queens Chpt. AIA, 1994, Prof. Affiliated Mem. (Hon.), N.Y. Soc. Architects, 1994; recipient Outstanding Cmty. Leader award Boy Scouts Am., 1987, Pride of Queens award, 1990, Pub. Servant Extraordinaire award United Cerebral Palsy of Queens, 1994, Good Scout award Greater N.Y. Coun. Boy Scouts Am., 1994, Nat. Silver Beaver Court of Honor award, Boy Scouts of America, 1997, United Hosp. Funds Disting. Trustee award for Extraordinary Svc., 1997, NYSSPE Outstanding PE Mgr. of the Year, 1997, Disting. Alumni award, Polytech. U., 1998, Humanitarian of Yr. award Guide Dog Found., 2000. Fellow ASCE; mem. ASTM, NSPE (trustee polit. action com. 1990-96), N.Y. State Soc. Profl. Engrs. (v.p. 1984-86, pres. 1988-89, nat. dir. 1987-90, Engr. of Yr. 1983), Soc. Am. Mil. Engrs., N.Y. State Assn. of Professions (founding), Nat. Coun. Examiners for Engring. and Surveying, Assn. Met. Water Agys. (bd. dirs.). Democrat. Congregationalist. E-mail: jmiele2@nyc.rr.com.

MIELEC, ROGER, aerospace engineer; BS Engring. Mechanics, U. Ill., Champaign-Urbana, 1971; M Engring. in Indsl. Engring., Tex. A & M, 1973; grad., Logistics Tng. program in Maintainability Engring., Texarkana, Tex., 1973. Aerospace engr. NASA Hdqrs. Office Safety and Mission Assurance, 1990—. Gen. engr. U.S. Army, 1971—90. Office: NASA Hdqrs Mail Code Q 300 E St SW Washington DC 20546*

MIELKE, ANGELA DENISE, shop owner, emergency medical technician; b. Van Nuys, Calif., May 10, 1968; d. Joseph Kenneth Davis and Susan Marie (Derrickson) Shoemaker; m. Tyrel Marke Mielke, Jan. 20, 1996 (div. Apr. 2002); children: Samantha Jo, Summer Rose. Cert. emergency med. technician Wash. State E.M.S. Coun. Mngr. Living Well Fitness, Tacoma, 1986—90; weight loss counselor Jenny Craig, 1990—91; prin., owner Superior Cleaning Svc., Belfair, 1994—; EMT Mason County, Tahuya, 2000—, Olympic Ambulance, Bremerton, 2001—. Vol. fire fighter Mason County Fire Protection, Tahuya, 2000—. Contbr. articles to profl. jours. and mags. Avocations: writing, studying for paramedicine, outdoor activities, music, arts. Home: NE 18910 Northshore Rd Tahuya WA 98588 Office: Supeior Cleaning Svc PO Box 701 Belfair WA 98528-0701

MIELKE, DONALD EARL, lawyer, lobbyist; b. Chgo., Oct. 5, 1944; s. Martin Edward and Mildred Hedwig (Bieresdorf) M.; m. Susan Joyce Hobbs, Aug. 12, 1978. BS in Aerospace and Sci. Engring., U. Mich., 1967; JD, U. Denver, 1973; MEngring., Pa. State U., King of Prussia, 1974. Bar: Colo. 1973, U.S. Dist. Ct. Colo. 1973, U.S. Ct. Appeals (10th cir.) 1973, U.S. Supreme Ct. 1989. Sys. engr. GE Missile & Space Co., King of Prussia, 1967-69, Martin Marietta Aerospace, Denver, 1969-73; assoc. Holley, Boatright & Villano, Wheat Ridge, Colo., 1973-75; ptnr. Mielke & Mielke, Lakewood, 1975-77; pvt. practice, 1977-80, 93-98; of counsel Leabrand & Scheffel, 1981-86, Watrous & Ehlers, Lakewood, 1993-98; dist. atty. 1st Jud. Dist., Golden, Colo., 1986-93; ptnr. Watrous, Ehlers, Mielke & Goodwin, Lakewood, 1998—. Mem. Nat. Conf. Commn. on Uniform State Laws, Chgo., 1983-93, 2001—; instr. real estate law Red Rocks C.C., Golden, 1976-79, Araraphoe C.C., Littleton, Colo., 1976-79; instr. bus. law Regis Coll., Denver, 1979-82; mem. Commn. on Jud. Performance for 1st Jud. Dist., 1993—. Mem. Colo. Ho. of Reps., Denver, 1981-86, mem. judiciary com., 1995-86; mem. Nat. Environ. Enforcement Coun., Washington, 1988-92, chmn., 1992; mem. Colo. Tourism Bd., Denver, 1983-86; pres., treas., chmn. bldg. coms. Bethlehem Luth. Ch., Lakewood, 1969-95; mem. bd. Colo. Luth. H.S., Denver, 1973-80; dist. capt. Jefferson County Rep. Com., Golden, 1993—. Named Legislator of Yr., 1981-86; recipient certs. of merit, 1986-93, innovative mgmt. awards Nat. Assn. Counties, 1986-93. Mem. ABA (vice chmn. environ. crimes and nat. resoruce sect. 1988-90), Am. Acad. Forensic Sci., Nat. Dist. Attys. Assn. (bd. dirs. 1988-93). Avocations: travel, antiques, grandchildren. Home: 7037 S Miller Ct Littleton CO 80127-2950 Office: Watrous Ehlers Mielke Et Al Ste 100 7472 S Shaffer Ln Littleton CO 80127 also: 7472 S Shaffer Ln Ste 100 Littleton CO 80127

MIELKE, JAMES EDWARD, geochemist; b. Toledo, Oct. 6, 1940; s. Herbert Edward and Naomi Hilletje (Raabe) M.; m. Laurie Beth Retter, Dec. 19, 1966; children: Erin Christine, Emily Jane. BS, MIT, 1962; MS, U. Ariz., 1965; PhD, George Washington U., 1974. Mine geologist potash exploration N.S. Rsch. Found., 1962; geologist S.W. field party Smithsonian Engring. Corp., Boston, 1963-64; geochemist C-14 dating lab. Smithsonian Instn., Washington, 1964-73; specialist in marine and earth scis. Congl. Rsch. Svc./Libr. of Congress, 1973-2000, retired, 2000. Liaison to Nat. Materials Adv. Bd., Nat. Rsch. Coun., Washington, 1981-86. Author more than 170 publs. including articles in profl. jours., com. prints, Congl. Rsch. Svc. reports; co-author: Strategic and Critical Materials, 1985, Review of Research in Modern Problems in Geochemistry, 1979. Pres. Home Buyers, Inc., Washington, 1976-83. Smithsonian Instn. Rsch. grantee, 1966-69. Mem. AAAS, Am. Geophys. Union, Marine Tech. Soc., Internat. Marine Minerals Soc. Republican. Lutheran. Avocation: folk dancing. Home: 2803 Washington Ave Chevy Chase MD 20815-3009

MIELKE, PAUL WILLIAM, JR. statistician, consultant; b. St. Paul, Feb. 18, 1931; s. Paul William and Elsa (Yungbauer) M.; m. Roberta Roehl Robison, June 25, 1960; children: William, Emily Spear, Lynn. BA, U. Minn., 1953, PhD, 1963; MA, U. Ariz., 1958. Teaching asst. U. Ariz., Tucson, 1957-58, U. Minn., Mpls., 1958-60, statis. cons., 1960-62, lectr., 1962-63; from asst. to assoc. prof. dept. statistics Colo. State U., Fort Collins, 1963-72, prof. dept. statistics, 1972—. Co-author: Permutation Methods: a Distance Function Approach; contbr. articles Am. Jour. Pub. Health, Jour. of Statis. Planning and Inference, Ednl. and Psychol. Measurement, Biometrika, Earth-Sci. Revs., Weather and Forecasting, Jour. Behavioral and Ednl. Stats. Capt. USAF, 1953-57. Recipient Banner I. Miller award Am. Meteorological Assn., 1973. Fellow Am. Statis. Assn.; mem. Am. Meteorol. Soc. (Banner I. Miller award 1994), Biometric Soc. Achievements include proposal that common statistical methods (t test and analysis of variance) were based on counter intuitive geometric foundations and provided alternative statistical methods which are based on appropriate foundations. Home: 736 Cherokee Dr Fort Collins CO 80525-1517 Office: Colo State U Dept Stats Fort Collins CO 80523-1877

MIELKE, SUSAN KAY, mental health nurse; b. Saginaw, Mich., Apr. 4, 1963; d. Walter John Jr. and Sally Jane (Spiekerman) Hetzner; m. Gary Alan Mielke, Aug. 16, 1986; children: Caroline, Elizabeth, Trevor, Julia. BSN, Mich. State U., 1985. Staff nurse Weight Loss Clinic, Saginaw, 1987, St. Mary's Hosp., Saginaw, 1985-88; nurse mgr. 13 supr. psychiat. nursing Caro (Mich.) Ctr., 1987—2002; co-dir., co-owner CM Med.-Legal Cons. Inc, Saginaw, 1990—; agy. nurse Catalyst Healthcare, 2001—. Mem. Mich. State U. Nursing Alumni Assn. Lutheran. Avocations: redecoration, traveling. Office: Catalyst Healthcare Group 2052 S Dye Rd Flint MI 48532

MIELKE, WILLIAM JOHN, civil engineer; b. Waukesha, Wis., May 20, 1947; s. John Horace and Lois Margaret (Trakel) M.; m. Barbra Jean Mahnke, Dec. 28, 1968; 1 child, Anne Marie. BS in Civil Engring., U. Wis., 1971. Registered profl. engr., land surveyor Wis.; diplomate Am. Acad. Environ. Engrs., 1992. Field engr. Wis. Dept. Nat. Resources, Madison, 1968-70; civil engr. Ruekert & Mielke, Inc., Waukesha, 1971—, chief exec. officer, 1982—, pres., 1990—. Bd. dirs. Mut. Savs. Bank; pres. Wis. Underground Related Materials and Systems, 1990. Mem. Legis. Study Com. Milw. Sewerage Dist., 1985-86; mem. Southeastern Wis. Regional Planning Commn. Com., Waukesha, 1986; mem. League of Wis. Municipalities Com., Madison, 1986-90; apptd. to Govs. Clean Water Task Force, 1987-88; apptd. to legis. com. on land use policies State of Wis., 1997; vice chair Wis. Land Coun., 1998—; apptd. mem. Govs. Task Force on State and Local Govt. Fellow Am. Consulting Engrs. Coun.(chmn. profl. procurement com., 1991-93) mem. Nat. Soc. Profl. Engrs. (chmn. profl. selection com., 1986-92, del. to com. Fed.procurement archl. engring. services 1987-92) Profl. Engrs. in Private Practice Merit award, 1989, nat. award for outstanding engr.in private practice, 1993), Nat. Profl. Engrs. in Pvt. Practice, Wis. Soc. Profl. Engrs. (pres. Waukesha chpt., 1981-82, Wis. Young Engr. Yr. 1982, Wis. Engr. Yr., 1991), Wis. Profl. Engrsin Private Practice (chmn. 1986-87, Wis. Engr. of Yr. in Pvt. Practice 1988), Wis. Assn. Cons. Engrs. (pres. 1988, chmn. QBS com. 1988-91, mem. legis. com. 1992—, chmn. 1993, Pres. award 2001), Am. Pub. Works Assn., Am. Waterworks Assn., Coun. Fed. Procurement Archtl/Engring. Svcs. (chmn. elect 1994, chmn. 1995), Joint Architect/Engr. Com. Fed. Constrn. (chmn. 1994). Republican. Episcopalian. Avocations: private pilot, scuba diving, sports. Home: 640 W Glenview Ave Oconomowoc WI 53066-2710 Office: Ruekert & Mielke Inc W233 N2080 Ridgeview Pky Waukesha WI 53188-1020

MIERA, LUCILLE CATHERINE MIERA, artist, retired educator; b. Socorro, N.Mex., Nov. 25, 1931; d. Stephen Maurice and Carmen Rosela (Baca) Miera; m. Vito Modesto Miera Jr., Aug. 22, 1953; children: Stephanie Lucille Miera Mansfield, Jennifer Ann Miera Eberhart. BA, U. N.Mex., 1973, MA, 1976, Ednl. Specialist Sch. Adminstrn., 1984. Cert. tchr., adminstr., N.Mex. Apprentice land surveying and draftsmen Stephen M. Miera, Regional Land Surveyor, Albuquerque, 1946-49; typist Albuquerque Abstract & Title, 1950; typist, engring. draftsman U.S. Army Corps Engrs., Albuquerque, 1950-57; engring. draftsman U.S. Dept. Interior, 1957-59; art tchr., art dept. chair Albuquerque Pub. Sch. Sys., 1973-93, reviewer curriculum devel. plan jr. high schs.; reviewer mid. schs.; ret. Prof. asst. U. N.Mex., Albuquerque, 1974; mid. sch. articulation rep. Taylor Middle Sch., Albuquerque, 1974-83; art rep. North Ctrl. Evaluation Middle Sch., Albuquerque, 1978; pres., art tchr. N.Mex Art League, Albuquerque, 1996, 97, 99; founder art program Emeritus Acad., Tech. Vocat. Inst., 1997, art. tchr., bd. dirs. 1997—. Exhibitions include Mus. Art, Toledo, Ohio, 1964, Kirtland AFB Officers Club, Albuquerque, 1967—68, U. N.Mex., 1969—76, 1999—2000, Albuquerque Pub. Schs. Adminstrn. Bldg., 1973—93, United Bank N.Mex., 1982, Albuquerque C. of C., 1999, exhibited in group shows at N.Mex. State Fair Fine Arts Gallery, N.Mex. State Fair Hispanic Art Gallery, Scottsdale Village Cir. Art Gallery, Old Town Albuquerque De Colores Soaring Eagle and La Hacienda Galleries, Coronado Airport Gallery. Mem., flyer distbr. Rep. Party, Albuquerque, 1954; poll clk. Bernalillo County, Albuquerque, 1960; leader Campfire USA, Albuquerque, 1966, 80; treas. Manzano Band, Albuquerque, 1977; pres. Glenwood Neighborhood Assn., Albuquerque, 1984-87; pres., nat. area dir. Res. Officers Assn. Ladies, Washington, 1989-91. Mem. Nat. Mus. Women's Art (charter), Nat. Hist. Soc., N.Mex. Assn. Educators Ret., N.Mex. Watercolor Soc., N.Mex. Res. Officer Ladies (pres.), N.Mex. Archdiocesan Coun. Cath. Women (pres. 1974), Epsilon Sigma Alpha. Avocations: travel, instructing and displaying art to promote art in the community. Home: 4405 Glenwood Hills Dr NE Albuquerque NM 87111-4260 E-mail: lmierart@aol.com.

MIERNOWSKI, JAN, foreign language educator; b. Warsaw, Poland, Apr. 24, 1959; s. Stanislaw and Ewa (Fedorów) M.; m. Ewa Filipczyńska, June 16, 1979; children: Marysia, Tomek, Michal. M, U. Warsaw, 1980; Doctorat, U. Paris X-Nanterre, 1988. Lectr. U. Warsaw, 1980-83, asst. prof., 1983-89, assoc. prof., 1996—; asst. prof. U. Wis., Madison, 1989-94, assoc. prof. French and Italian, 1994-99, prof., 1999—. Author: Dialectique et Connaissance dans La Sepmaine Du Bartas, 1992, Signes Dissimilaires. La quête des noms divins dans la poésie française, 1997, Le Dieu Néant. Théologies négatives à l'aube des temps modernes, 1998, L'Ontologie de la contradiction suptique. Pour l'etude de la métaphysique des Essais, 1998, Piekne banialuki, ku najlepszej prawdzie wylozone, czyli alegoria jako prowokacja w literaturze starofrancuskiej, 2000; co-editor: Anteros, 1994. Mem. Solidarność, Poland, 1980-89. NEH fellow, 1994-95; KBN grantee, Komitet Badań Naukowych, 1997-98. Mem. Société Française des Seiziémistes, Renaissance Soc. Am. Roman Catholic. Home: Lowicka 51 M 7 02-535 Warsaw Poland Office: U Wis Madison Dept French and Italian 1220 Linden Dr Dept And Madison WI 53706-1525 E-mail: jmiernow@facstaff.wisc.edu.

MIERZEJEWSKI, ALFRED CARL, history educator, author; b. New Bedford, Mass., Aug. 26, 1953; BA, Southeastern Mass. U., North Dartmouth, 1978; MA, U. N.C., 1981, PhD, 1985. Asst. prof. Norwich U., Northfield, Vt., 1985-87; command historian U.S. Army Test and Experimentation Command, Ft. Hood, Tex., 1987-90; asst. prof. history Athens (Ala.) State U., 1990-96, assoc. prof. history, 1997—2002, U. North Tex., 2002—. Author: Collapse of the German War Economy, 1988, Most Valuable Asset of the Reich, vol. 1, 1999, vol. 2, 2000. Fulbright rsch grantee, Germany, 1992-93. Mem. Am. Hist. Assn., Hist. Soc., Bus. History Conf., German Studies Assn. Home: 569 Inca Pl Highland Village TX 75077-7206 E-mail: acmierzeje@aol.com.

MIERZWA, JOSEPH WILLIAM, lawyer, legal communications consultant; b. Chgo., Nov. 21, 1951; s. Joseph Valentine and Betty Ann (Ray) M.; m. Rolana Conley, May 18, 1974. BA, U. Kans., 1981, JD, 1985. Bar: Kans. 1985, U.S. Dist. Ct. Kans. 1985. Pvt. practice, Prairie Village, Kans., 1985-86; gen. counsel Hyatt Legal Svcs., Kansas City, Mo., 1986-87; corp. counsel NLS Corp., Inc., Lakewood, Colo., 1988; owner, mgr. Joseph W. Mierzwa Cons., 1988-92; pres. Prose Assocs., Inc., Highlands Ranch, Colo., 1991—. Cons. Nat. Legal Shield, Lakewood, 1988-92, Reader's Digest Assn., Pleasantville, N.Y., 1988—, Hyatt Legal Svcs., Cleve., 1988-94, USLaw.com, 2000—, CompPsych, 2001—, others; editor OverDrive Sys., Inc., Cleve., 1990-95. Author: The 21st Century Family Legal Guide, 1994. Mem. ABA, Kans. Bar Assn. Avocations: cooking, travel, creative writing. Office: 9889 S Spring Hill Dr Highlnds Ranch CO 80129-4349 E-mail: paibooks@aol.com.

MIES, JOHN CHARLES, internet industry executive; b. Peoria, Ill., Aug. 24, 1946; s. Ernest Gregory and Clara Emma (Reese) M. BS, Ea. Ill. U., 1968. Tchr. Centennial High Sch., Champaign, Ill., 1969-74; ptnr. The Leather Shop, 1974-78, The Waterbed Shop, Champaign, 1978-82; pres., CEO Mies Corp., 1982—. Mem. adv. bd. Bedroom mag., 1991-93; v.p./gen. mgr. AdvanceNet, 1996; pres. Online Svcs.; gen. mgr. Cambert Ltd., 1997, COO, 1999; owner Monticello Computer; ptnr. Ravecomm, LLC. Editor-in-chief The Sleep Connection newsletter; columnist Bedroom Industry Newsletter. Faculty rector Flotation Healthcare Found., chmn. bd., 1996. Mem. Nat. Waterbed Retailers Assn. (exec. com. 1987-92, sec.-treas. 1988-89, pres. 1991, chmn. long-range planning com., co-chmn. liaison com., joint pub. rels. com., named to Waterbed Hall of Fame 1992), Ctrl. State Mktg. Group (pres. 1986-89, 93, sec.-treas. 1990-92, sec. 1994-98, editor New Bedding Vision newsletter), Urbana C. of C. (chmn. leadership planning com.), Monticello C. of C. (bd. dirs. 1998, treas. 2001-02), Champaign C. of C., Waterbed Advt. Coun. (com. mem., bd. dirs. 1990-91), Waterbed Coun. (com. mem., bd. dirs. 1990-91), Waterbed Coun. (bd. dirs. 1994, sec. 1994, dir. pubs. 1995, pres. 1996). Avocations: computers, motorcycle. Office: Mies Corp 201 W Springfield Ave Champaign IL 61820-4834

MIES, RICHARD W. career officer; b. Chgo. m. Sheila McCann; children: Rachel Anne, Sara Elizabeth. BS, U.S. Naval Acad., 1967; M, Harvard U., 1982. Commd. USN, 1967, advanced through grades to adm., 1998; comdr. in chief U.S. Strategic Command. Office: 901 SAC Blvd Offutt A F B NE 68113-6000

MIESING, PAUL, university educator, consultant, researcher; b. Traunstein, Germany, Mar. 15, 1947; s. Irving and Nina Miesing; children: Debra B., Marc L. PhD, University Of Colorado, Boulder, Co, 1972—76. Assoc. prof. State University Of New York at Albany, Albany, Ny, 1979—. Mem.: Academy of Management. Office: State University Of New York At Albany 1400 Washington Ave. Albany NY 12222 Personal E-mail: paul.miesing@albany.edu.

MIFFLIN, FRED JOHN, Canadian government official; b. Bonavista, Nfld., Can., 1938; m. Gwenneth Davies; children: Cathy, Mark, Sarah. Grad., Can. Navy's Venture Tng. Program, U.S. Naval War Coll., Nat. Def. Coll., Kingston, Ont. Enlisted Can. Navy, 1954, advanced through ranks to rear admiral, 1985, head nat. def. secretariat; mem. parliament Canadian Govt., 1988-96, parliamentary sec. to min. nat. def. & vet. affairs, 1993, min. fisheries & oceans, 1996-97; min. vet. affairs and sec. of state Atlantic Can. Opportunities Agy., 1997-99. Avocations: country music, cooking. Office: Confederation Bldg, Rm 207 Ho of Commons Ottawa ON Canada K1A OA6

MIFFLIN, THEODORE EDWARD, clinical biochemistry educator; b. Zion, Ill., Aug. 4, 1946; s. Edward Kenneth and Doris (Kleeb) M.; m. Mary Louise Epperson, May 19, 1973; children: Jonathon, Jennifer, Christopher. BS in Chemistry, Weber State Coll., 1968; PhD in Biochemistry, Utah State U., 1984. Cert. clin. chemist Nat. Registry in Clin. Chemistry; diplomate Am. Bd. Clin. Chemistry. Chemist Southwest Bioclin. Lab., San Antonio, 1974-77; grad. rsch. asst. Utah State U., Logan, 1977-83; rsch. fellow med. ctr. U. Va., Charlottesville, Va., 1983-86, rsch. asst. prof. med. ctr., 1986-90; assoc. prof. U. Pitts. Med. Ctr., 1991—. Instr. Utah State U., Logan, 1980; dir. molecular probe lab., med. ctr. U. Va., Charlottesville, 1988-90; sect. chief molecular diagnostic divsn./genetics Presbyn. U. Hosp., Pitts., 1991—. Author: Use of Nucleic Acid Probes in the Clinical Laboratory, 1988; contbr. articles to profl. jours.; mem. editorial adv. bd. Clin. Chem. News, 1987-92. With U.S. Army, 1968-73, staff sgt., 1972-73. Recipient Young Invest award Acad. Clin. Lab. Physicians and Scientists, 1986. Assoc. fellow Nat. Acad. Clin. Biochemistry; mem. Am. Assn. for Clin. Chemistry (E. Cotlove award 1985), AAAS, Am. Chem. Soc. Avocation: aviation piloting. Home: 36-2 Mount Pine Ter Reading PA 19606-3908 Office: Presbyn U Hosp Rm 5845 Main Tower 200 Lothrop St Pittsburgh PA 15213-2546

MIFSUD, JOHN C. housing specialist, writer; b. Sliema, Malta, Oct. 5, 1951; s. John Felix and Stella Mary Mifsud; 1 child Zen Jefferson 1 child Sukie Jefferson 1 child Nadine Pierre-Louis Rawls. BS, Ea. Mich. U., 1973. Cert. diversity trainer. Dir. mut. housing Capitol Hill Housing Improvement Program, Seattle, 1991—94; dir. coop. housing Cmty. Devel. Svcs., Yakima, 1994—96; exec. dir. Next Step Housing, Wash., 1994—. Freelance trainer, cons. Mifsud and Assocs., Seattle, 1996—; lead trainer Affordable Housing Mgmt. Assn. Wash., Seattle, 1995—. Dir.: (documentary film) Speaking For Ourselves, 1994 (Golden Eagle Award, CINE Festival, Washington DC, 1994); contbr. anthology. Recipient 2001 award for creative nonfiction, Jack Straw Found., 2001, Silver award for excellence in ind. TV programming, Corp. for Pub. Broadcasting, 1996, N.W. Regional Emmy nomination, Regional Affiliated Broadcasters Assn., 1996, Silver Apple award, Nat. Ednl. Media Network, 1996, Silver award, Worldfest Charleston, 1996, Bronze award, Worldfest Houston, 1996, Bronze Award, Columbus Internat. Film Festival, 1996, Nat. Innovations award, Internat. Red Cross, 1990. Office: Next Step Housing PO Box 784 Yakima WA 98907

MIGALA, LUCYNA J. broadcast journalist, arts administrator, radio station executive; b. Krakow, Poland, May 22, 1944; came to U.S., 1947, naturalized, 1955; d. Joseph and Estelle (Suwala) M.; m. Frank A. Cizon, Oct. 9, 1998. Student, Loyola U., Chgo., 1962-63, Chgo. Conservatory of Music, 1963-70; BS in Journalism, Northwestern U., 1966. Radio announcer, prodr. Sta. WOPA, Oak Park, Ill., 1963-66; writer, reporter, prodr. NBC News, Chgo., 1966-69, 69-71; prodr. NBC local news, Washington, 1969; prodr., coord. NBC network news, Cleve., 1971-78, field prodr. Chgo., 1978-79; v.p. Migala Comms. Corp., 1979—. Program and news dir., on-air personality Sta. WCEV, Cicero, Ill, 1979—; lectr. City Colls., Chgo., 1981, morton Coll., 1988. Columnist Free Press, Chgo., 1984-87. Founder, artistic dir., gen. mgr. Lira Ensemble (formerly The Lira Singers), Chgo., 1965—, Artist-in-residence, Loyola U., Chgo.; mem., chmn. various cultural coms. Polish Am. Congress, 1970-80; bd. dirs. Nationalities Svcs. Ctr., Cleve., 1973-78; bd. dirs., v.p. Cicero-Berwyn Fine Arts Coun., Cicero, Ill., 1980-87; mem. City Arts I and II panels Chgo. Office of Fine Arts, 1986-89, 94; v.p. Chgo. chpt. kosciuszko Found., 1983-86; bd. dirs. Polish Women's Alliance Am., 1983-87, Ill. Humanities Coun., 1983-89, mem. exec. com., 1986-87; bd. dirs. Ill. Arts Alliance, 1989-92; founder, gen. chmn. Midwest Chopin Piano Competition (now Chgo. Chopin Competition), 1984-86; founding mem. ethnic and folk arts panel Ill. Arts Coun., 1984-87, 92-94; mem. Polonia Census 2000 Com.; bd. dirs. Am. Leadership Initiative, Chgo., 2001—. Recipient AP Broadcasters award, 1973, Emmy award NATAS, 1974, Cultural Achievement award Am. Coun. for Polish Culture, 1990, award of merit Advocates Soc. Polish Am. Attys., 1991, Human Rels. Media award City of Chgo., 1992, Outstanding Achievement in Polish Culture award Minister of Fgn. Affairs, Rep. of Poland, 1994, Civic Achievement award Polish Am. Hist. Assn., 2000; decorated Cavalier's Cross of Merit govt. of Poland, 1996; Washington Journalism Ctr. fellow, spring 1969. Mem. Soc. Profl. Journalists. Office: Sta WCEV 5356 W Belmont Ave Chicago IL 60641-4103 also: The Lira Ensemble 6525 N Sheridan Rd # Sky905 Chicago IL 60626-5344

MIGAS, ROSALIE ANN, social worker; b. Stevens Point, Wis., Apr. 18, 1951; m. Raymond Fonck, Aug. 22, 1977. BA in Social Work and Polit. Sci., U. Wis., 1973, MSSW, 1975. Cert. clin. ind. social worker. House fellow U. Wis., Madison, 1974-75; social worker Kenosha (Wis.) Sch. Dist., 1975-76, Bethesda Luth. Home, Watertown, Wis., 1976-78; supr. coding dept. Gallup Orgn., Princeton, N.J., 1979; supr. casework svcs. Big Bros./Big Sisters Mercer County, Trenton, 1985-86; social worker Bordentown (N.J.) Sch. Dist., 1979-85, 86-89; AODA/SAP coord. Wis. Heights Sch. Dist., Mazomanie, 1989-91; project dir. Wis. Assn. on Alcohol and Other Drug Abuse, Madison, 1993-96; program dir. Children's Svc. Soc. Wis., 1997—. Active Big Bros./Big Sisters Mercer County, 1986-87. NIMH fellow, 1974. Mem.: NASW (nat. leadership identification com. 1995, chair south ctrl. br. 1998—2001, pres. 2001—). Avocations: ice skating, hiking, cross country skiing. Home: 5913 S Hill Dr Madison WI 53705-4447 E-mail: romigas@mailbag.com.

MIGDOL, KENNETH M. labor relations consultant, industrial psychologist; b. Bklyn., Apr. 30, 1947; s. Lester and Sylvia (Schutzer) M.; m. Judith Strent; children: Michael, Melanie, Marissa. BA, Hofstra U., 1970; MA in Indsl. Psychology, New Sch., 1972, PhD in Indsl./Orgnl. Psychology, 1974; JD in Labor Law, Southland U., 1978. Cert. labor arbitrator. Mediator form labor rels. Electrophonics, Stamford, Conn., 1969-72; prin., pres. Ramm Assocs., 1972—; v.p. human resources IPCO Corp., Long Island, N.Y., 1975, corp. bd. dirs., educator academics and co. tng., 1978—. Mem. ASTD, Am. Arbitration Assn., Adminstrv. Mgmt. Soc., Am. Compensation ASsn. Office: Ramm Assocs PO Box 1150 Jupiter FL 33468-1150 E-mail: kenmigdol@rammassoc.com.

MIGDOL, MARVIN JACOB, public relations and marketing executive, consultant; b. Rochester, N.Y., Jan. 11, 1937; s. Frank and Dorothy (Krieger) M.; m. Frances Scheiner, June 13, 1959 (div. June 1970); children: Helene Ellen, Steven Gary, Larry Jay; m. Grace Miron, Dec. 26 1970 (div. Aug. 1986); children: Michael Alan, Susan Renee, Honi Faith; m. Roni Habel, June 30, 1991 (div. Dec. 1992). BA in Sociology, U. Buffalo, 1959; postgrad., U. Miami, 1959-60; MS in Communications, Boston U., 1961. Dir. pub. rels. United Fund, Reading, Pa., 1961-63, Rensselaer Poly. Inst., Troy, N.Y., 1963-64, Touro Infirmary, New Orleans, 1964, Hamot Hosp., Erie, Pa., 1964-65, United Jewish Fedn., Buffalo, 1965-68; pres. Marvin J. Migdol Inc., Dallas, 1968—. Instr. Boston U., 1962—, Pa. State U., 1962—, U. Tex., 1962—, Collin County Community Coll., Plano, 1990-91. Author: Public Relations Handbook, 1963, Comics as a Public Relations Tool in Communications, 1971, The Migdol Manual, 1972, Success in the 1990's, 1987, Greater Virility: Overcoming Impotence, 1993; contbr. numerous articles to profl. jours. Reporter Rep. Nat. Conv., Dallas, 1964; asst. dist. commr. Boy Scouts Am., Dallas, 1980-85; exec. bd. dirs. EPCOT Resorts, Lake Buena Vista, Fla., 1992—. Recipient Pub. Rels. award Coun. Jewish Welfare Funds & Fedn., N.Y.C., 1967, Am. Contract Bridge League, Memphis, 1983-87, Nat. Bus. League, West Palm Beach, Fla., 1968; Entrepreneur of the Year Venture mag., Dallas, 1987; Award of Merit Big Brothers & Sisters, Dallas, 1987, major league volleyball, San Jose, Calif., 1987. Mem. U.S. Profl. Mktg. Assn. (pres. 1990—), Am. Assn. Indsl. Editors (bd. dirs. 1967-70), Am. Coll. Pub. Rels. Assn. (bd. dirs. 1964-66), Inst. for Info. and Communications (bd. dirs. 1971—), Dallas Belles (dir. mktg. and pub. rels. 1987—), Jewish Nat. Fund (area dir.), Dallas Bridge Assn. (chmn. publicity), Dallas C. of C. (mem. econ. and internat. coun.), U. Buffalo Alumni Assn. We. Pa., 1964-65, Temple Shalom (vice chmn. bldg. fund 1971-72, mem. Brotherhood bd. 1985-86), Jewish Community Ctr., Alpha Epsilon Pi (gov., 1970-79), Phi Delta Phi, (v.p. 1959-60, treas. 1960—). Jewish. Avocations: writer, lecturer, baseball and softball umpire, Boy Scout leader. Home: 6816 Saddletree Trl Plano TX 75023-1348 Office: CAREington Internat Corp 7400 Gaylord Pkwy Frisco TX 75034

MIGEON, BARBARA RUBEN, pediatrician, geneticist; b. Rochester, N.Y., July 31, 1931; d. William Saul and Sara (Gitin) Ruben; m. Claude Jean Migeon, Apr. 2, 1960; children: Jacques Claude, Jean-Paul, Nicole. BA, Smith Coll., 1952; MD, SUNY, Buffalo, 1956. Diplomate Am. Bd. Pediatrics; cert. in med. genetics. Pediatric residency The Johns Hopkins U., Balt., 1956-59; fellow in endocrinology Harvard U. Med. Sch., Boston, 1959-60; fellow in genetics The Johns Hopkins Sch. Medicine, Balt., 1960-62, assoc. prof. pediatrics, 1970-79, joint appointment in biology, 1978—, prof. in pediatrics, 1979—, dir. PhD program in human genetics, 1979-89. Mem. Genetics Study Sect., NIH, Bethesda, Md., 1975-77, Mammalian Genetics Study Sect., NIH, Bethesda, 1977-79, Human Genome Study Sect., NIH, Bethesda, 1991-93. Contbr. more than 100 rsch. papers to profl. publs. Named Prin. Investigator NIH grant, 1971—; recipient Outstanding Woman Physician award Med. Coll. Pa.; Vis. investigator Carnegie Instn. of Washington, 1975, Exch. prof. Guys Hosp., 1986. Mem. Am. Pediatric Soc., Am. Soc. Human Genetics. Office: Inst Genetic Medicine CMSC 10-04 The Johns Hopkins U Baltimore MD 21287-0001

MIGEON, CLAUDE JEAN, pediatrics educator; b. Lievin, Pas-De-Calais, France, Dec. 22, 1923; came to U.S., 1950, naturalized, 1967; s. André and Pauline (Descamps) M.; m. Barbara Lou Ruben, Apr. 2, 1960; children: Jacques, Jean-Paul, Nicole. MD, Sch. Medicine, U. Paris, 1950. Fellow dept. pediatrics Sch. Medicine, Johns Hopkins U., 1950-52, asst. prof., 1954-60, asso. prof., 1960-71, prof. pediatrics, 1971—; instr. biochemistry U. Utah, 1952-54; pediatrician Johns Hopkins Hosp., 1954—. Mem. diabetes and metabolism tng. grants com. NIH, 1963-67, gen. clin. research centers com., 1968-71, mem. endocrinology study sect., 1974-78; cons. Med. Research Council Can., 1969-85, others; vis. prof. Maadi Armed Forces Hosp., Cairo, 1985, Guy's Hosp., London, 1986. Co-editor: (textbook) The Diagnosis and Treatment of Endocrine Disorders in Childhood and Adolescence, 4th edit., 1994; mem. editl. bd.: Johns Hopkins Med. Jour., 1970-72, Jour. Clin. Endocrinology and Metabolism, 1971-77, Hormone Rsch., 1979—; contbr. articles to profl. jours. Fulbright fellow, 1950; Am. Field Service fellow, 1950-51; Andre and Bella Meyer fellow, 1951-52; recipient research career award NIH, 1964-85. Fellow AAAS; mem. Endocrine Soc. (coun. 1971-74, chmn. pub. affairs com. 1974-91, Ayerst award, Williams award), Soc. Pediatric Rsch. (emeritus), Am. Pediatric Soc., Lawson Wilkins Pediatric Endocrine Soc. (founding pres. 1972), Am. Soc. Clin. Investigation (emeritus), Am. Physiol. Soc., Japanese Pediatric Endocrine Soc. (hon.), Found. for Am. Meml. Hosp. (bd. dirs. 1985—, v.p. 2001-), Soc. Francaise d'Endocrinologie (fgn. corr. mem.). Home: 502 Somerset Rd Baltimore MD 21210-2720 Office: Johns Hopkins Hosp Park 211 600 N Wolfe St Baltimore MD 21287-2520 E-mail: cmigeon@jhmi.edu.

MIGHELL, KENNETH JOHN, lawyer; b. Schenectady, N.Y., Mar. 17, 1931; s. Richard Henry and Ruth Aline (Simon) M.; m. Julia Anne Carstarphen, Aug. 24, 1961; children: Thomas Lowry, Elizabeth Anne. BBA, U. Tex., 1952, JD, 1957. Bar: Tex. 1957. Assoc. Scurry, Scurry, Pace & Wood, Dallas, 1957-61; asst. U.S. Atty. Justice Dept., 1961-77; 1st asst. No. Dist. Tex., 1974-77; U.S. Atty. No. Dist., Tex., 1977-81; ptnr. Cowles & Thompson, Dallas, 1981-96, of counsel, 1996—. Chmn. bd. mgmt. Downtown Dallas YMCA, 1974-76; pres. Dallas Area Am. Lung Assn., 1985-87; bd. dirs. YMCA Met. Dallas, 1987—; chmn. adv. bd. Southwestern Law Enforcement Inst., 1994-98; mem. SW Legal Found. (CLE adv. com. 1999—). With USN, 1952-54; capt. USNR, 1954-78. Mem.: FBA, Nat. Assn. Former U.S. Attys. (pres. 1995), State Bar Tex. (bd. dirs. 1994—95), Dallas Bar Found. (trustee 1994—, vice chmn. 1999—2000, chmn. 2001—02), Dallas Bar Assn. (bd. dirs. 1984—89, chmn. 1989, v.p. 1990—91, pres. 1993). Democrat. Methodist. Office: Cowles & Thompson 901 Main St Ste 4000 Dallas TX 75202-3793 E-mail: kmighell@cowlesthompson.com.

MIGL, DONALD RAYMOND, therapeutic optometrist, pharmacist; b. Houston, Sept. 18, 1947; s. Ervin Lawrence and Adele Marie (Boenisch) M.; m. Karen S. Coale, Mar. 23, 1974; children: Christopher Brian, Derek Drew, Monica Michelle. BS in Pharmacy, U. Houston, 1970, BS, 1978, OD, 1980, cert., 1992; postgrad., U. Ala. Med. Ctr., Birmingham, 1974-76, Stephen F. Austin State U., Nacogdoches, Tex., 1987-88. Registered pharmacist; cert. Nat. Bds. Examiners Optometry, Treatment & Mgmt. Ocular Disease; cert. therapeutic optometrist. Pharmacist Tex. Med. Ctr., Houston, 1967-69, St. Luke's and Tex. Childrens Hosp., 1967-69, Meml. Hosp., 1969-70, Ben Taub (Harris County) Hosp., 1970-71, Shades Mountain Pharmacy, Birmingham, 1974-76, Westbury Hosp., Houston, 1976-81; instr. pharmacology lab. Coll. Optometry U. Houston, 1980; pvt. practice, Nacogdoches, Tex., 1981—; pharmacist Nacogdoches Med. Ctr. Hosp., 1997-98. Mem. interdisciplinary health teams, 1977; charter advisor publ. Contact, CIBA Vision Corp., 1988-89. Judge health sci. div. Houston Area Sci. Fair, 1970. Recipient svc. award Houston Community Interdisciplinary Health Screening Programs, 1977, Spl. Academic Achievement award in pharmacy and optometry U. Houston, 1980. Mem. Am. Optometric Assn. (Optometric Recognition Award 1985-2001, Recognition Cert. for 25 yr. membership 2000), Tex. Optometric Assn. (recognition cert. 1979), Piney Woods Optometric Soc. (pres. 1984), Am. Pharm. Assn. (recognition cert. 1970), Tex. Pharm. Assn., Am. Soc. Hosp. Pharmacists, U.S. Jaycees, Gold Key, Omicron Delta Kappa. Lodges: Rotary (Paul Harris Fellow 1987, Pres. award Outstanding Svc., 1991-92). Methodist. Office: Eagle Eye 20/20 Plus Vision 4122 Ridgebrook Dr Nacogdoches TX 75965-2217

MIGLIARO, MARCO WILLIAM, electrical engineer; b. N.Y.C., Mar. 29, 1948; s. Marco Salvatore and Anna (Dalton) M.; children: Kristen Marie, Meredith Anne, Marie Angela, Marco Thomas; m. Jasoda Badlu, Nov. 19, 1988. BEE, Pratt Inst., 1969; postgrad., N.J. Inst. Tech., 1970-72. Registered profl. engr., N.Y., N.J., Pa., Mass., Fla. Engr. Am. Electric Power, N.Y.C., 1969-78; staff engr. Gibbs & Hill, Inc., 1978-81; sr. cons. engr. Ebasco Svcs., Inc., 1981-88; tech. mgr. ABB Impell Corp., Melville, N.Y., 1988-90; sr. staff specialist for nuc. engring. Fla. Power & Light, Juno Beach, 1990-96, chief elec./I&C engr., 1996—. Developer seminar on stationary batteries, 1987. Contbg. author: Handbook of Power Calculations, 1984, 99, Standard Handbook for Electrical Engineers, 1999; also articles. Recipient Meritorious Svc. award Am. Nat. Standards Inst., 1994. Fellow IEEE (pres. 2001—, stds. assn. bd. govs. 1998—, bd. dirs. 1990-92, 2001, fin. com. 1990-92, dir. stds. 1990-91, mem. exec. com. 1992, v.p. stds. activities, 1992, 2001, Stds. medal 1986, Stds. Bd. Disting. Svc. award 1993, Charles Proteus Steinmetz award 1996, Third Millennium medal 2000); mem. IEEE Power Engring. Soc. (Disting. Svc. award 1988, 92), Industry Standards and Tech. Orgn. (bd. dirs. 2000—, chmn. 2000—). Avocations: fishing, travel, music. Home: PO Box 9253 Jupiter FL 33468-9253 Office: Fla Power & Light ENG/JB PO Box 14000 Juno Beach FL 33408-0420

MIGLIORELLI, KARA MARIE, television news producer; b. Worcester, Mass., Sept. 10, 1975; d. Thomas Emil and Suzanne Marie M. Cert. in book and mag. publ., NYU, 1997; BA cum laude, Coll. of Holy Cross, 1997; M in Journalism cum laude, Columbia U., 2001. Intern Worcester Telegram and Gazette, 1997; editor Hippocrene Books Inc., N.Y.C., 1997-2000; TV news prodr. KAMR-TV (NBC), Amarillo, Tex., KCIT-TV (Fox), Amarillo. Freelance writer, poet, 1997—. Editor: (series) Illustrated Histories of Countries, 2000. Big sister mentor to inner-city kids Holy Cross Coll., Worcester, 1995—97; mem., vol. Nat. Honor Soc., Holden, 1991—93. Recipient Dominick Lepare Poetry award, Acad. of Am. Poets, 1997, Poetry prize 1st pl., The Landmark, 1997, Elmer Ream Sportmanship award, Wachusett Regional H.S., 1993, Women in Sports award, Nat. Women in Sports, 1993. Mem. Soc. of Profl. Journalists, Acad. of Am. Poets, Sigma Tau Delta (Nu Chi chpt.), Holy Cross Club of N.Y. Roman Catholic. Avocations: theatre, music, running, travel. E-mail: kara_migliorelli@hotmail.com.

MIGLIORI, JOSEPH LOUIS, physician; b. Providence, July 31, 1944; s. Joseph and Anna (Cardi) M. BA, Boston U., 1966; MD, U. Bologna, Italy, 1971. Diplomate Am. Bd. Ophthalmology. Intern St. Francis Hosp., Hartford, Conn., 1972-73; pvt. practice St. Joseph Hosp., Providence, 1973-74; basic sci. ophthalmology Harvard Med. Sch., Boston, 1974; resident in ophthalmology Sinai Hosp. of Detroit, 1974-77; pvt. practice Cranston, R.I., 1977—. Neuro ophthalmology instr. St. Joseph Hosp., Providence, 1979-83, mem. ambulatory care com., 1999; mem. utilization rev. com. Blue Cross/Blue Shield, Providence, 1980-86. Mem. Cranston C. of C., 1987—; mem. Met. Opera Assn. Fellow Am. Acad. Ophthalmology; mem. AMA (physician's recognition award 1993, 99), Providence Med. Assn., R.I. Med. Soc., New Eng. Ophthalmol. Soc., R.I. Soc. Eye Physicians & Surgeons. Roman Catholic. Avocations: piano, architecture. Office: 1150 Reservoir Ave Cranston RI 02920-6068

MIGNACCA, RITA M. American literature educator; b. Syracuse, N.Y., Nov. 2, 1955; d. Paul Joseph and Natalie (Alia) M.; m. Donald Furiuso, Sept. 6, 1971. BA, SUNY, Oswego, 1971; MA, U. Rochester, 1985; postgrad., U. Albany, 1997—. Cert. tchr., N.Y. Faculty dept. English Nazareth Coll. of Rochester, N.Y., 1985-90, SUNY, Brockport, 1990-97. Cons., workshop coord. SUNY, Brockport, 1991, 93. Active Habitat for Humanity, U. Rochester Alumni chpt., 1993—. Recipient Poet's award Dominican Coll. of Blauvelt, 1968. Mem. AAUW, MLA, Coll. English Assn. Avocation: research in immigrant literatures. Home: 86 Cottage Ave Albany NY 12203-2621 Office: U Albany SUNY Albany NY 12222-0001 E-mail: RM8900@albany.edu.

MIGNOGNA, JACALYN CORRINE, library administrator, librarian; b. Greensburg, Pa., May 7, 1957; d. Robert William and June Romayne (Gongaware) Harper; m. Michael Charles Mignogna, Nov. 14, 1981; children: Lydia Grace, Elias Charles. BFA, Edinboro U. Pa., 1979; MLS, U. Pitts., 1991, cert. advanced study preservation mgmt., 1992. Preservation intern Carnegie Natural History Mus. Libr., Pitts., 1991, preservation grant adminstr., 1994; preservation intern Pitts. Regional Libr. Ctr., 1992; cataloging intern Nat. Gallery Art Libr., Washington, 1992; Mellon intern preservation Columbia U., N.Y.C., 1992-93; children's libr. Norwin Pub. Libr., Irwin, Pa., 1995-96, libr. dir., 1996-99; preservation mgr. Carnegie Libr. of Pitts., Pitts., 1999-2000; libr. Carnegie Libr., 2000—. Preservation cons. VOLUTE Preservation Mgmt. Assn., Pitts., 1993-94. Owens fellow U. Pitts., 1990, U. Microfilms Internat. preservation fellow, 1991. Mem. ALA. Democrat. Lutheran. Home: 1193 Mica Dr North Huntingdon PA 15642-4363 Office: Carnegie Libr Pitts Pennsylvania Dept 4400 Forbes Ave Pittsburgh PA 15213-4007 E-mail: mignognaj@carnegie.library.org.

MIGNONE, MARIO B. Italian studies educator; b. Benevento, Italy, July 26, 1940; came to U.S., 1960; m. Lois Dolores Pontillo, June 29, 1968; children: Pamela Anne, Cristina Maria, Elizabeth Maria. BA, CCNY, 1967; MA, Rutgers U., 1969, PhD, 1972. Disting. prof. Italian lang. SUNY, Stony Brook, 1970—, dir. undergrad. studies, 1976-83, dir. grad. studies, 1983-87; founder, exec. dir. Ctr. for Italian Studies, chmn. French and Italian dept., 1988—98. Author: The Theater of Eduardo De Filippo, 1974, Abnormality and Anguish in the Narrative of Dino Buzzati, 1981, Eduardo De Filippo, 1984, Pirandello in America, 1988, Columbus: Meeting of Cultures, 1993, Italy Today: A Country in Transition, 1995, Italy Today: At the Crossroads of the New Millennium, 1998; assoc. mng. editor Forum Italicum, 1986-94, editor, 1994—; contbr. articles to profl. jours. Mem. Am. Assn. Tchrs. Italian (pres. 1982-84), Assn. Italian Am. Educators (pres. 1997—). Home: 17 Salt Meadow Ln Stony Brook NY 11790-1109 Office: SUNY Dept European Langs Lits Stony Brook NY 11794-3359 E-mail: mmignone@notes.cc.sunysb.edu.

MIGUE, JEAN LUC, economics educator; b. Montreal, Que., Can., Apr. 13, 1933; s. Joseph Alfred and Marie Laurence (Venne) M.; m. Renee Caron, Sept. 13, 1958; children: Paule, Pascal, Nicolas. BA in Econs, U. Montreal, 1953, MA, 1956; PhD in Econs, Am. U., 1968. Researcher Bank of Can., 1957-58; prof. Laval U., 1962-70; prof. econs. Nat. Sch. Public Adminstrn., Quebec, 1970-99. Mem. staff Econ. Coun. Can., 1973-74 Author: The Price of Health, 1974, Le Prix du Transport, 1978, Nationalistic Policies of Canada, 1979, L'Economiste et La chose Publique, 1979, The Public Monopoly of Education, 1989, Federalism and Free Trade, 1993, Etatisme et Declin du quebec, 1999, Le Monopole de La Santé, 2001. Fellow Massey Found., 1956, sr. fellow, The Fraser Inst. Fellow Royal Soc. Can.; mem, Mont Pelerin Soc. Roman Catholic. E-mail: jlmigue@sympatico.ca.

MIGUEZ-BURBANO, MARIA-JOSE, immunologist; b. Bogota, D.C., Colombia, Nov. 7, 1963; d. Jose Miguez and Gloria Burbano; m. Arturo Perez; children; Carolina. MD, J.N. Corpas Sch. Medicine, Colombia, 1988. Cert. in chiropractic acupuncture, 1989. Assoc. physician Dept. Immunology and Allergy, Bogota, 1995-97; sr. asst. rsch. prof. U. Miami Sch. Medicine, 1996-2001. Prof. Bogota Health Dept., Bogota, 1995-97; editor, rscr. in field, 2001. Recipient post-doctoral fellow rsch. award Am. Coll. Clin. Pharmacology, 1994; grantee U. Miami Comprehensive AIDS Program, 2002-2003. Office: U Miami Sch Medicine 1400 NW 10th Ave 6th Fl (D21) Miami FL 33136 Fax: 305-243-4687. E-mail: mmiguez@med.miami.edu.

MIHAILESCU, MANUELA, marketing executive; b. Bucharest, Romania, May 25, 1950; came to U.S. 1980; d. Luca and Elena Livia (Papadopol) M.; m. Jon Dogar Marinesco, June 17, 1980. Student, U. Bucharest, 1969-71; MA, Film/Theater Inst., Bucharest, 1974; MBA, CUNY, 1988. Dir. mktg./advt. Theater I. Creanga, Bucharest, 1974-79; v.p. mktg. Point Blank, Inc., N.Y.C., 1988-99, pres., 1999—. Contbr. articles to profl. jours. Recipient lst prize award 18th ann. Philip Morris Mktg./Communications Competition, 1987. Mem. Beta Gamma Sigma. Eastern Orthodox. Avocations: film, theater, travel, photography. Office: Point Blank Inc PO Box 740049 Rego Park NY 11374-0049 E-mail: manuela525@aol.com.

MIHAL, SANDRA POWELL, distance learning specialist; b. Balt., Dec. 15, 1941; d. Sanford William and Mary Louise (Barry) Powell; m. James George Anderson, June 15, 1963; children: Robin Marie, James Brian, Melissa Lee, Derek Clair; m. Charles Turner Barber, Apr. 18, 1978; stepchildren: Gretchen Jayco, Katrina Hope; m. Ladislaw Paul Mihal, May 25, 1991; stepchildren: Alexander Paul, Suzie May, Natasha Elizabeth, Rudy Darius. BA, Mt. St. Agnes Coll., 1963; MA, N.Mex. State U., 1970, Purdue U., 1975; EdD, Vanderbilt U., 1990. Cert. tchr., Md. Tchr. Ridgely-Dulaney Jr. H.S., Towson, Md., 1964; grad. asst. N.Mex. State U., Las Cruces, 1967-69; acad. advisor, instr. polit. sci. Purdue U., West Lafayette, Ind., 1974-78; prof., acad. sys. analyst U. So. Ind., Evansville, 1978-82; assoc. prof., chair dept. computer info. sys. Henderson (Ky.) C.C., 1982-88; prof. computer tech., divsn. chair Anne Arundel C.C., Arnold, Md., 1988-91; computer sys. analyst Immigration & Naturalization Svc., Dept. of Justice, Washington, 1991-92, Glynco, Ga., 1995—. Bd. dirs. Ind. Polit. Sci. Assn., Muncie, 1984-88, Internat. Studies Assn.-Midwest, Chgo., 86-88; pres. Ky. Acad. Computer Users' Group, Lexington, 1985-86; mem. telecom. adv. bd. C.C. Sys., Annapolis, Md., 1990-91; computer syst. network analyst CLARC Svcs., Pt. Charlotte, Fla., 92-95; adj. prof. history and polit. sci. Edison C.C., Punta Gorda, Fla., 1993-95. Author: Learning By Doing BASIC, 1983, Computers Learning By Doing, 1984; contbr. to several profl jours. 1980-90; author, spkr. series Faculty/Staff Edison CC 94, Ednl. Tech. Nova U., 1995. Block coord. several neighborhood assns.; mem. Henderson County Sch. Computer Adv. Bd. 1982-88; chmn. Newburgh (Ind.) Youth Orgn., 78-86; judge Sci. Fair, Annapolis, 1988-90; mem. nomination bd. Ky. Higher Edn. Assn., 1989-91; mem. Charlotte Chorale, Port Charlotte, 1992-94, Peace River Power Squadron, Port Charlotte, 1994-96. Coast Guard Aux., 1995-97. Md. State Tchr. Bd. Edn. scholar, 1960-63; fellow Sloan Found., 1973-75, U. Ky., 1984. Mem, Soc. Applied Learning Tech., Assn. Computing Machinery (v.p. 85—), Am. Legion, Pi Gamma Mu. Democrat. Mem. Ch. Of Christ. Avocations: sailing, singing, swimming, cooking, playing the dulcimer. Home: 112 Oak Ridge Rd Brunswick GA 31523-9741

MIHALAS, DIMITRI MANUEL, astrophysicist, educator; b. Los Angeles, Mar. 20, 1939; s. Emmanuel Demetrious and Jean (Christo) M.; children: Michael Demetrious, Alexaudra Genevieve. BA with highest honors, UCLA, 1959; MS, Calif. Inst. Tech., 1960, PhD, 1964. Asst. prof. astrophys. scis. Princeton U., 1964-67; asst. prof. physics U. Colo., 1967-68; asso. prof. astronomy and astrophysics U. Chgo., 1968-70, prof., 1970-71; adj. prof. astrogeophysics, also physics and astrophysics U. Colo., 1972-80; sr. scientist High Altitude Obs., Nat. Center Atmospheric Research, Boulder, Colo., 1971-79, 82-85; G.C. McVittie prof. astronomy U. Ill., 1985-98; astronomer Sacramento Peak Obs., Sunspot, N.Mex., 1979-82; staff mem. Los Alamos Nat. Lab., 1998—. Cons. Los Alamos Nat. Lab, 1981-98; vis. prof. dept. astrophysics Oxford (Eng.) U., 1977-78; sr. vis. fellow dept. physics and astronomy Univ. Coll., London, 1978; mem. astronomy adv. panel NSF, 1972-75 Author: Galactic Astronomy, 1969, 2d edit, 1981, Stellar Atmospheres, 1970, 2d edit., 1978, Theorie des Atmospheres Stellaires, 1971, Foundations of Radiation Hydrodynamics, 1984; assoc. editor Astrophys. Jour, 1970-79, Jour. Computational Physics, 1981-87, Jour. Quantitative Spectroscopy, 1984-94; mem. editorial bd. Solar Physics, 1981-89. NSF fellow, 1959-62; Van Maanen fellow, 1962-63; Eugene Higgins vis. fellow, 1963-64; Alfred P. Sloan Found. Research fellow, 1969-71; Alexander von Humboldt Stiftung sr. U.S. scientist awardee, 1984. Mem. U.S. Nat. Acad. Sci., Internat. Astron. Union (pres. commn. 36 1976-79), Am. Astron. Soc. (pub. bd. 1995-99, mem. coun. 2000—, Helen B. Warner prize 1974), Astron. Soc. Pacific (dir. 1975-77) Home: 3202 Woodland Rd Los Alamos NM 87544-0806 Office: Los Alamos Nat Lab X-3 MS-D413 Los Alamos NM 87545-0001 E-mail: dmihalas@lanl.gov.

MIHALIK, PHYLLIS ANN, consulting company executive, educator, public speaker; b. Cleve., Mar. 11, 1952; d. Henry Arvon and Dorothy (Markovich) Trepal; m. John P. Mihalik, Aug. 5, 1972. AA, Lakeland Coll., 1982; BS in Computer Sci., Lake Erie Coll., 1986; Exec. Masters in Bus. Adminstrn., Case Western Res. U., 1992. Acct. Picker Internat., Highland Heights, Ohio, 1977-80, programmer, analyst, 1980-82, fin. systems analyst, 1982-83; sr. systems analyst Harris, Solon, 1983-84, mgr. systems and programming, 1984-86, dir. internal audit, 1986-88; pres., owner Productivity & Mgmt. Cons., Chardon, 1988—2001; pres. Eden;s Keepers, Inc., 2002—. Faculty mem. Lakeland Coll., Mentor, Ohio, 1987—. Author: Introduction to PC's, 1989, Managing the PC Work Environment, 1989. Mem. Data Processing Mgmt. Assn., Assn. for Systems Mgmt., Women Bus. Owners. Avocations: horticulture, travel, stained glass, interior design. Office: Productivity and Mgmt Cons 11457 Fowlers Mill Rd Chardon OH 44024-8720

MIHALOPULOS, GUS, JR. accountant; b. Christopher, Ill., July 17, 1937; s. Gus Mihalopulos Sr. and Elizabeth Urbain; m. Jacquelyn Smith, Oct. 16, 1965; children: Michael T., Jennifer E. BS, U. Ill., 1960. Ptnr. Laventhol & Horwath, Carbondale, Ill., 1960-90, Kerber, Eck & Braeckel LLP, Carbondale, 1992—2000. Mem. coun. St. Francis Xavier, Carbondale; mem. bd. advisors Coll. Bus. Adminstrn., So. Ill. U., Carbondale. Mem. AICPA, Ill. CPA Soc. (healthcare com.), Healthcare Fin. Mgmt. Assn. (mem. com., William G. Follmer award 1980, 81, Reeves Silver merit award 1991, Muncie Gold Merit award, 1999). Avocations: bicycling, photography, golf, walking, hunting. Home: 500 S Emerald Ln Carbondale IL 62901-2143

MIHALY, EUGENE BRAMER, corporate executive, consultant, writer, educator; b. The Hague, The Netherlands, Nov. 11, 1934; s. Eddy and Cecile (Bramer) Kahn; stepson of Eugene Mihaly; m. Stacey Beth Pulner, Apr. 21, 1996; children: Lisa Klee, Jessica; stepchildren: Stephanie Pulner, Andrew Pulner. AB magna cum laude, Harvard U., 1956; PhD, London Sch. Econs. and Polit. Sci., 1964. Aviation/space editor Hartford (Conn.) Courant, 1960-61; internat. economist AID, Washington, 1964-65; dep. dir. Peace Corps, Tanzania, 1966, dir. Tanzania, 1967-68, dep. dir. East Asia/Pacific bur., 1969, dir. office program devel., evaluation and rsch., 1969-70; assoc. dir. Inst. Internat. Studies, U. Calif., Berkeley, 1970-72; pres. Mihaly Internat. Corp., 1972—; chmn. bd. Mihaly Internat. Can., Ltd., 1992—; sr. lectr. Haas Sch. Bus. U. Calif., Berkeley, 1991-95. Adj. prof. Amos Tuck Sch. Dartmouth Coll., 1997-2001. Author: Foreign Aid and Politics in Nepal: A Case Study, 1965; contbr.: Political Development in Micronesia, 1974, Management of the Multinationals, 1974; also articles to various publs. Chmn. emeritus Calif.-S.E. Asia Bus. Coun.; chmn. Global R.I.; pres. Found. for Ocean State Pub. Radio; chmn. R.I. Com. for the Humanities. Mem. Coun. on Fgn. rels., Signet Soc. Home: 4 Half Mile Rd Barrington RI 02806

MIHAN, RICHARD, retired dermatologist; b. Dec. 20, 1925; s. Arnold and Virginia Catherine (O'Reilly) M. MD, St. Louis U., 1949. Diplomate Am. Bd. Dermatology. Intern L.A. County Gen. Hosp., 1949-51, resident in dermatology, 1954-57; pvt. practice in dermatology L.A., 1957-95; prof. emeritus U. So. Calif., 1989—. Lt. Comdr. USNR, 1951-53. Fellow ACP; mem. AMA, Pacific Dermatol. Assn. (exec. bd. 1971-74), Am. Acad. Dermatol., Calif. Med. Assn. (chmn. dermatol. sect. 1973-74), L.A. Met. Dermatology Soc. (pres. 1975-76), L.A. Acad. Medicine (pres. 1988-89), Order of St. John of Jerusalem, of Rhodes, and of Malta, Order of St. Lazarus (comdr.), Calif. Club. Roman Cath. Home: 3278 Wilshire Blvd Apt 503 Los Angeles CA 90010-1431

MIHELICH, EDWARD DAVID, chemist; b. Coeur D'Alene, Idaho, June 24, 1950; s. Joseph Anthony and Alma Josephine (Folden) M.; m. Loren Marie O'Connor, May 20, 1972; children: Christopher Colin, Patrick Joseph. BS, Ill. Inst. Tech., Chgo., 1972; PhD, Colo. State U., 1975. Postdoctoral rsch. assoc. Harvard U., Cambridge, Mass., 1975-77; chemist Procter & Gamble Co., Cin., 1977-83; rsch. scientist Eli Lilly and Co., Indpls., 1983-90, sr. rsch. scientist, 1991—. Contbr. articles to profl. jours. Bd. dirs. Sycamore Sch., 1993-96. Mem. Am. Chem. Soc. Office: Lilly Rsch Labs DC 4816 Lilly Corp Ctr Indianapolis IN 46285-0001

MIHM, JOHN CLIFFORD, chemical engineer; b. Austin, Tex., July 28, 1942; s. Clifford Henry and Adeline (Cleary) M.; m. Janet Eleanor Skales, May 29, 1964; 1 child, Mary Lynn, 1 granddaughter, Cassandra. AA, Frank Phillips Coll., 1962; BSChemE, Tex. Tech. U., 1964. Registered profl. engr., Tex. With Phillips Petroleum Co., 1964—, v.p. corp. engring. Okla., 1987-92, v.p. R & D, 1992-93, sr. v.p. corp. tech., 1993-99, sr. v.p. tech. and project devel., 1999—; engr. mgr. E & P Phillips Petroleum Co., Stavanger, Norway, 1977-82. Adv. bd. Tex. Tech. U., Lubbock, Tex., 1985—, pres. deans coun., 1996-98. Bd. dirs. Boy Scouts Am., Bartlesville, 1986—, area III pres., 1998-2002. Mem. ASME (ind. adv. bd. 1989—), NSPE (mem. adv. bd. 1994—), AIChE (ECC divsn., bd. dirs. 1989-93, chmn. 1992-93), Okla. Soc. Profl. Engrs. (Outstanding Engr. in Mgmt. award 1991), Soc. Profl. Engrs., Okla. Engring. Found. (bd. dirs., pres. 1993-97). Republican. Roman Catholic. Office: 411 S Keeler Ave Phillips Petroleum Co 260 Rf Bartlesville OK 74004-0001

MIHM, MARTIN CHARLES, JR. pathologist, educator; b. Pitts. s. Martin Charles and Cecilia Matilda (Hepp) M. AB, Duquesne U., 1955; MD, U. Pitts., 1961; MA (with honors), Harvard U., 1989. Diplomate Am. Bd. Dermatology, Am. Bd. Pathology. Intern Mt. Sinai Hosp., N.Y.C., 1961-62, resident in medicine, 1963-64; resident in dermatology Mass. Gen. Hosp., Boston, 1964-67, resident in Pathology, 1968-72, chief dermatopathology, 1973-94; asst. prof. pathology Harvard U. Med. Sch., 1972-75, assoc. prof., 1975-79, chief dermatopathology, 1982-93; prof. pathology Mass. Gen. Hosp.-Harvard U., 1980-93; prof., chief dermatopathology, dermatology Albany (N.Y.) Med. Coll., 1993—. Adj. prof. pathology Vanderbilt U., 1989—; chmn. pathology com. Intergroup Melanoma Study, 1983—; pathologist Malignant Melanoma Coop. Group, 1972-77; chief sr. adminstr. Wellman Labs., Mass. Gen. Hosp., 1985-93; cons. WHO, 1985—, chmn. pathology standing com., 1991—; vis. prof. pathology Harvard Med. Sch., 1993-96; clin. prof. pathology Harvard Med. Sch., 1996; sr. dermatopathologist and pathologist, Mass. Gen. Hosp., 1996—. Author: Primer of Dermatopathology, 1984, 2d edit., 1992, Problematic Pigmented Lesions, 1990; co-author: Melanoma and Nevi, 1997; editor: Lymphoproliferative Disorders of the Skin, 1986, Pathbiology and Recognition Malignant Melanoma, 1988; contbr. articles to med. jours. Served to comdr. USPHS, 1967-69. Fellow ACP, Am. Acad. Dermatology, Am. Soc. Dermatopathology; mem. AMA (Harvard Med. Sch. rep. to med. sch. sect. 1991), Harvard Dermatology House Officer's Assn. (pres. 1982), Harvard Club (Boston, N.Y.C.), Fat Orange Club, Alpha Omega Alpha, Pi Gamma Mu. Democrat. Roman Catholic. Home: 8 Whittier Pl Apt 16C Boston MA 02114-1410 Office: Albany Med Coll 47 New Scotland Ave Albany NY 12208-3412 also: Mass Gen Hosp 275 Charles St Boston MA 02114-3002

MIHM, MICHAEL MARTIN, federal judge; b. Amboy, Ill., May 18, 1943; s. Martin Clarence and Frances Johannah (Morrissey) M.; m. Judith Ann Zosky, May 6, 1967; children— Molly Elizabeth, Sarah Ann, Jacob Michael, Jennifer Leah BA, Loras Coll., 1964; JD, St. Louis U., 1967. Asst. prosecuting atty. St. Louis County, Clayton, Mo., 1967-68; asst. state's atty. Peoria County, Peoria, Ill., 1968-69; asst. city atty. City of Peoria, 1969-72; state's atty. Peoria County, Peoria, 1972-80; sole practice, 1980-82; U.S. dist. judge U.S. Govt., 1982—; chief U.S. dist. judge U.S. Dist. Ct. (ctrl. dist.) Ill., 1991-98. Chmn. com. internat. jud. rels. U.S. Jud. Conf., 1994—96, mem. exec. com., 1995—97, mem. com. jud. br., 1987—93, mem. com. internat. jud. rels., 1998—; mem. Supreme Ct. Fellows Commn., 2000—; adj. prof. law John Marshall Law Sch., 1990—. Past mem. adv. bd. Big Brothers-Big Sisters, Crisis Nursery, Peoria; past bd. dirs. Salvation Army, Peoria, W.D. Boyce council Boy Scouts Am., State of Ill. Treatment Alternatives to Street Crime, Gov.'s Criminal Justice Info. Council; past vice-chmn. Ill. Dangerous Drugs Adv. Council; trustee Proctor Health Care Found., 1991-2002. Recipient Good Govt. award Peoria Jaycees, 1978 Mem. Peoria County Bar Assn. Roman Catholic. Office e-mail: michael. Office: US Dist Ct 204 Federal Bldg 100 NE Monroe St Peoria IL 61602-1003

MIHRAM, GEORGE ARTHUR, mathematician; b. Norman, Okla., Sept. 21, 1939; s. Russell George and Ella Lee (Stanaland) M.; m. Danielle Redibaum, Dec. 22, 1965. BS summa cum laude, U. Okla., 1960; postgrad., Wash. State U., Pullman, 1960-61; MS, Okla. State U., 1962, PhD, 1965. Operational rschr. Ops. Rsch., Inc., Silver Spring, Md., 1965-66; systems analyst Joint Chiefs Staff, Washington, 1966-68; asst. prof. U. Pa., Phila., 1968-74; mem. faculty U. So. Calif., University Park, 1978-79. Cons. IBM Corp., East Fishkill, N.Y., 1973, Acad. Ntural Scis., Phila., 1970-71, Office Asst. Sec. Def., 1969, Hdqrs. USAF, 1968-69. Author: Simulation: Statistical Foundations and Methodology, 1972, An Epistle to Dr. Benjamin Franklin, 1975, A Critique of World Models, 1975; co-author: Human Knowledge: Role of Models, Metaphors, and Analogy, 1974, Religion: Man's Earliest Science, 1978, Credibility: Every Computer Programme is a Simulation Model, 1985, Tele-cybernetics: Implications for the International Marketplace, 1988, Telecybernetics: Inferences from Living Systems to Both Science and Political Science, 1994, The Enhanced Electronic Postmark, 1997, Resolving Two Congressional Duties, 2000; assoc. editor: Simulation, 1973-75, Internat. Jour. Gen. Systems, 1973—, Modeling and Simulation, 1974-92. Mem. peer rev. panels NSF, Washington, 1974, 82. Capt. U.S. Army, 1966-68. Decorated Joint Svcs. Commendation medal; recipient award Conf. Simulation of Large Systems, Bielefeld, Fed. Republic Germany, 1980; Fulbright scholar U. Sydney, Australia, 1964-65; NSF rsch. initiation grantee, 1970-72, internat. travel grantee, 1975, NATO grantee, 1977. Mem. AAAS (fellow nominee 1974, profl. socs. ethics group 1987-95, program liaison com. 1992-94), Am. Philos. Assn., Soc. Study Social Problems, Internat. Soc. Sys. Sci., Soc. Computer Simulation (chmn. tech. com. on verification and validation 1974-75), Soc. Lit. and Sci., Internat. Assc. Statis. Computing, Internat. Assn. Cybernetics, Am. Math. Soc., Am. Statis. Assn., Biometric Soc., Can. Math. Soc., Assn. Computing Machinery, Interface (of Computer Sci. and Stats.) Found., Ops. Rsch. Soc. Am. (ethics and profl. practice com. 1983-95), Math. Assn. Am., Sigma Xi, Phi Beta Kappa, Pi Mu Epsilon, Phi Eta Sigma. Avocation: mankind's search for truth mimes nature's biochemical process ensuring survival. Home and Office: PO Box 1188 Princeton NJ 08542-1188

MIILLER, SUSAN DIANE, artist; b. N.Y.C. d. Charles and Alyce Mary (Gebhardt) Knapp; m. Craig Smith, Jan. 13, 2002. BFA, SUNY, 1988; MFA, U. North Tex., 1992. Scenic designer Forestburgh (N.Y.) Playhouse, 1989; adj. prof. Tex. Christian U., Ft. Worth, 1992-94; lectr. U. Tex., Dallas, 1995-99, SUNY, New Paltz, 1999—. Treas. mem. 500X Gallery, Dallas, 1991-92. One-woman shows include Western Tex. Coll., 1993, Brazos Gallery, Richland Coll., 1993, Women & Their Work Gallery, 1995 (Gallery Artists Series award, 1995), A.I.R. Gallery, 1996, Milagros Contemporary Art, 1996, Pentimenti Gallery, Pa., 1997, Plano Art Ctr., 1999, Orange County C.C., 2000, Continental Gallery, 2001, Marie Park Studios, 2001; resident artist Weir Farm Nat. Hist. Trust. Recipient 4th Nat. Biennial Exhbns. Grand Purchase award, 1991, Mus. Abilene award, 1992, Lubbock Art Festival Merit award, 1992, 2d pl. award, Matrix Gallery, 1995, Hon. Mention award 3d Biennial Gulf of Mex. Exhbn., 1995, 1st place award, Soho Gallery, 1996, Juror's Choice award, Bucking the Texan Myth Exhbn., 1998, hon. mention, Susquehanna Art Mus., 1998, 1999, Faculty Devel. award, 2001. Mem. Coll. Art Assn. Office: PO Box 775 Sparrow Bush NY 12780-0775

MIJOVIC, JOVAN, chemical engineering educator; b. Belgrade, Sept. 4, 1948; s. Slobodan and Gordana Mijovic; m. Cecilia Ochoa, Sept. 27, 1979; 1 child, Lisa Aleksandra. BS in Chem. Engring., Faculty of Tech., Belgrade, 1972; MS in Chem. Engring., U. Wis., 1974, PhD in Chem. Engring., 1978. Asst. prof. chem. engring. Polytech. U., Bklyn., 1978-83, assoc. prof., 1983-93, prof., 1993—, head dept. chem. engring., 1995-96. Adj. prof. materials and prodn. engring., U. Naples, Italy, 1996—, vis. prof. chem. engring., 1991, 92, 93, 94, 95; vis. prof. chem. engring. U. San Sebastian, Spain, 1997, 2000, Inst. Chem. Tech., U. Perugia, Italy, 1994, 96, 2000 Contbr. articles to sci. and profl. jours. Avocations: music, tennis, languages. Office: Polytech U 6 Metrotech Ctr Brooklyn NY 11201 E-mail: jmijovic@poly.edu.

MIKA, JOSEPH JOHN, library school director, educator, consultant; b. McKees Rocks, Pa., Mar. 1, 1948; s. George Joseph and Sophie Ann (Stec) M.; m. Marianne Hartzell; children: Jason-Paul Joseph, Matthew Douglas, Meghan Leigh. BA in English, U. Pitts., 1969, MLS, 1971, PhD in Libr. Sci., 1980. Asst. libr., instr. Ohio State U., Mansfield, 1971-73; asst. libr., asst. prof. Johnson State Coll., Vt., 1973-75; grad. asst., tchg. fellow Sch. Libr. and Info. Sci., U. Pitts., 1975-77; asst. dean, assoc. prof. libr. svc. U. So. Miss., Hattiesburg, 1977-86; dir. libr. and info. sci. program Wayne State U., 1986—95, 2002—, prof., 1994—2001. Cons. to libraries; co-owner Libr. Jobs Network, Libr. Tng. Network. Editor Jour. of Edn. for Libr. and Info. Sci., 1995—. Col. USAR. Decorated DSM. Mem. ALA (councilor 1983-86, 98-2001, chmn. constrn. and bylaws com. 1985-86), Assn. Libr. and Info. Sci. Edn. (chmn. membership com. 1982-83, chmn. nominating com. 1982, exec. bd. 1986), Miss. Libr. Assn. (pres.-elect 1985), Mich. Libr. Assn. (chair libr. edn. com. 1989), Leadership Acad. (oversight com. 1989-95), Assn. Coll. and Rsch. Librs. (chmn. 1982-83, chmn. budget com. 1982-83), Soc. Miss. Archivists (treas., exec. bd. 1981-83), Mich. Ctr. for the Book (chair 1994-2001), Kiwanis (Hattiesburg), Beta Phi Mu (pres.-elect 1987-89, pres. 1989-91), Phi Delta Kappa. E-mal. Home: 222 Abbott Woods Dr East Lansing MI 48823-1995 Office: Wayne State U Libr and Info Sci Program 106 Kresge Library Detroit MI 48202 E-mail: aa2500@wayne.edu.

MIKALOW, ALFRED ALEXANDER, II, deep sea diver, marine surveyor, marine diving consultant; b. N.Y.C., Jan. 19, 1921; m. Janice Brenner, Aug. 1, 1960; children: Alfred Alexander, Jon Alfred. Student, Rutgers U., 1940; MS, U. Calif., Berkeley, 1948; MA, Rochdale U. (Can.), 1950. Owner Coastal Diving Co., Oakland, Calif., 1950—, Divers Supply, Oakland, 1952—; dir. Coastal Sch. Deep Sea Diving, 1950—. Capt. and master rsch. vessel Coastal Researcher I; mem. Marine Inspection Bur., Oakland. marine diving contractor, cons. Mem. adv. bd. Medic Alert Found., Turlock, Calif., 1960—. Author: Fell's Guide to Sunken Treasure Ships of the World, 1972; (with H. Rieseberg) The Knight from Maine, 1974. Lt. comdr. USN, 1941-47, PTO, 1949-50, Korea. Decorated Purple Heart, Silver Star. Mem. Divers Assn. Am. (pres. 1970-74), Treasury Recovery, Inc. (pres. 1972-75), Internat. Assn. Profl. Divers, Assn. Diving Contractors, Calif. Assn. Pvt. Edn. (no. v.p. 1971-72), Authors Guild, Internat. Game Fish Assn., U.S. Navy League, U.S. Res. Officers Assn., Tailhook Assn., U.S. Submarine Vets. WWII, Explorer Club (San Francisco), Calif. Assn. Marine Surveyors (pres. 1988—), Soc. Naval Archs. and Marine Engrs. (assoc.), Masons, Leions, Am. Legion, VFW. Office: 52 Mira Loma Rd Orinda CA 94563-2332

MIKALSON, JON DENNIS, classics educator; b. Milw., Aug. 1, 1943; s. John Martin and Evelyn Kathryn (Heuser) M.; m. Mary Helen Villemonte, Aug. 28, 1966; children: Melissa, Jacquelyn. BA, U. Wis., 1965; postgrad., Am. Sch. Classical Studies, Athens, Greece, 1968-69; PhD, Harvard U., 1970. Asst. prof. classics U. Va., Charlottesville, 1970-75, assoc. prof., 1975-84, prof., 1984—, William R. Kenan Jr. prof. classics, 1999—, chmn. dept. classics, 1978-90. Dir. Echols Scholar Program, 1997-2000; vis. scholar Corpus Christi Coll., Cambridge, Eng., 1977-78; mem. Inst. for Advanced Study, Princeton, N.J., 1984-85; Whitehead prof. Am. Sch. Classical Studies, 1995-96. Author: The Sacred and Civil Calendar of the Athenian Year, 1975, Athenian Popular Religion, 1983, Honor Thy Gods: Popular Religion in Greek Tragedy, 1991, Religion in Hellenistic Athens, 1998; contbr. articles to profl. and scholarly jours. James Rignall Wheeler fellow Am. Sch. Classical Studies, 1968-69, NEH fellow, 1977-78, Herodotus fellow Inst. for Advanced Study, 1984-85. Mem. Am. Philol. Assn., Am. Sch. Classical Studies, Archeol. Inst. of Am., Classical Assn. of Middle West and South (pres. so. sect. 1988-90), Classical Assn. of Va., Phi Beta Kappa, Phi Eta Sigma, Phi Kappa Phi, Omicron Delta Kappa. Clubs: Lions. Home: PO Box 664 Crozet VA 22932-0664 Office: University of Virginia Dept of Classics 453 Cabell Hall Charlottesville VA 22903-3196 E-mail: jdm9x@virginia.edu.

MIKATA, YOZO, mechanical engineer, software engineer; b. Nichinan, Miyazaki, Japan, Jan. 29, 1956; came to U.S., 1981; s. Chotaro and Fumiko (Kato) M. BS in Civil Engring., U. Tokyo, 1979, MS in Civil Engring., 1981; PhD in Mech. Engring., U. Del., Newark, 1984. Postdoctoral fellow Northwestern U., Evanston, Ill., 1984-87; postgrad. rsch. engr. U. Calif. San Diego, LaJolla, Calif., 1987-89; rsch. assoc. U. Ill., Urbana-Champaign, 1989-90; asst. prof. Old Dominion U., Norfolk, Va., 1990-96; sr. rsch. scientist ICAM, NASA Langley Rsch. Ctr., Hampton, 1996-99; software engr. Bell Atlantic Network Svcs., Silver Spring, Md., 1999-2000; structural mechanics engr. Lockheed Martin Co., Schenectady, N.Y., 2000—. Contbr. articles to profl. jours. Rsch. grantee Engring. Found., Washington, 1992, NASA Langley Rsch. Ctr., Hampton, 1993, 94. Mem. ASME, Soc. Indsl. and Applied Math., Am. Acad. Mechanics. Achievements include research on micromechanics of coated fiber composite materials providing analytical solutions, and thereby contributed to the understanding of local mechanical behavior of coatings; research on wave propagation, fracture mechanics, dynamic phase transformation; avocations: tennis, swimming, jazz, astronomy, number theory. Office: Lockheed Martin Co PO Box 1072 Schenectady NY 12301

MIKAWA, TAKASHI, biomedical science educator; b. Kobe, Japan, Apr. 7, 1951; came to U.S., 1988; s. Yoshihiko and Kazuko M.; m. Yukie Mori, Apr. 7, 1977; children: Yuki, Tomoko, Jun. BS, Kobe (Japan) U., 1975; MS, Kyoto (Japan) U., 1977, PhD, 1980. Postdoct. dept. pharmacology Coll. Medicine U. Tokyo, 1980-81, asst. prof. dept. pharmacology Coll. Medicine, 1981-83; asst. prof. dept. neurochemistry Nat. Inst. Physiol. Scis., Okazaki, Japan, 1983-86, acting assoc. prof. dept. neurochemistry, 1986-90; asst. prof. dept. cell biology and anatomy Med. Coll. Cornell U., 1990-97, assoc. prof. dept. cell biology and anatomy Med. Coll., 1997—. Vis. asst. prof. dept. cell biology and anatomy Med. Coll., Cornell U., 1988-90, asst. prof. cell biology and genetics program Grad Sch. Med. Scis., 1991-97; mem. tri-institutional MD/PhD program Med. Coll. Cornell U./Rockefeller U./Sloan-Kettering Inst. Cancer Rsch., 1992; mem. rev. panel com. musculoskeletal cell culture biol. flight experiments NASA, 1993, human embriology and devel. 2 study sect. NIH, 1996—; external rev. cardiology merit rev. VA Affairs Merit Rev. Bds. Med. RSch. Svc. VA, 1993, 95; lectr., spkr. in field Peer reviewer: The Proceedings of the Nat. Acad. Scis. USA, Devel. Dynamics, Am. Jour. Physiology, Devel. Biology; contbr. numerous articles to profl. jours. Pre-doct. fellow Japan Soc. Promotion Sci., 1979-80, postdoct. fellow, 1980-81; Irma T. Hirschl scholar, 1996—. Mem. AHA (investigator N.Y.C. affiliate 1991-93, mem. review panel cardiovascular devel. study sect. 1997—). Achievements include discovery of origin of the cardiac conduction system, identification of a mitogen for cardiac muscle cells, origin of coronary vascular system. Home: 329 Weaver St Larchmont NY 10538-1719 Office: Cornell U Med Coll Dept Cell Biology & Anatomy 1300 York Ave New York NY 10021-4805

MIKEL, THOMAS KELLY, JR. laboratory administrator; b. Aug. 27, 1946; s. Thomas Kelly and Vrazo Anne (Katherine) M.. BA, San Jose State U., 1973; MA, U. Calif., Santa Barbara, 1975. Asst. dir. Santa Barbara Underseas Found., 1975—76; marine biologist PJB Labs., Ventura, Calif., 1981—88; lab. dir. ABC Labs., 1988—. Instr. oceanography Ventura Coll., 1980—81; chair joint task group, sect. author 20th edit. Stds. Methods Exam. Water & Wastewater APHA, 1996; biol. coord. Anacapa Underwater Natural trail U.S. Nat. Park Svc., 1976; designer ecol. restoration program of upper Newport Bay, Orange County, Calif., 78; rsch. contbr. 3d Internat. Artificial Reef Conf., Newport Beach, Calif., 1983, Ann. Conf. Am. Petroleum Inst., Houston. With U.S. Army, 1968—70. Mem.: ASTME (rsch. contbr. 10th ann. symposium 1986), Soc. Environ. Toxicology and Chemistry (bd. dirs. 2000—), Soc. Population Ecologists, Assn. Environ. Profls. Democrat.

MIKELL, FRANK LEONARD, cardiologist; b. Augusta, Ga., Apr. 26, 1947; s. Frank Leonard and Mary (Herndon) M.; three children. BA, Emory U., 1969; B in Med. Scis., Dartmouth Med. Sch., 1972; MD, Emory U. Med. Sch., 1974. Asst. prof. medicine U. Minn., Mpls., 1979-82; interventional cardiologist Prairie Cardiovasc. Cons., Springfield, Ill., 1982—. Clin. assoc. prof. medicine So. Ill. U. Med. Sch., Springfield, 1987—. Fellow Am. Coll. Cardiology, Am. Coll. Chest Physicians, Am. Coll. Physicians, Soc. Cardiac Angiography & Intervention, Coun. Clin. Cardiology Am. Heart Assn. Avocations: golf, hunting. Office: Prairie Cardiovasc Cons PO Box 19420 Springfield IL 62794-9420

MIKELS, RICHARD ELIOT, lawyer; b. Cambridge, Mass., July 14, 1947; s. Albert Louis and Charlotte Betty (Shapiro) M.; m. Deborah Gwen Katz, Aug. 29, 1970; children: Allison Brooke, Robert Jarrett. BS in Bus. Adminstrn., Boston U., 1969, JD cum laude, 1972. Bar: Mass. 1972, U.S. Dist. Ct. Mass. 1974, U.S. Ct. Appeals (1st cir.) 1978. Legal examiner ICC, Washington, 1972-74; ptnr. Riemer & Braunstein, Boston, 1974-80; ptnr., chmn. comml. law sect. Peabody & Brown, 1980-88; mem., chmn. comml. law sect. Mintz, Levin, Cohn, Ferris, Glovsky and Popeo, P.C., 1988—. Contbr. articles to profl. jours. Tng. adv. com. Jewish Vocat. Svc., Boston, 1991, 95, 96, bd. dirs., 1995-99, vice chair microenterprise adv. com. 1997; vice-chair lawyers com. Combined Jewish Philanthropies, 1994, 95. Fellow Am. Coll. Bankruptcy; mem. ABA, Am. Bankruptcy Inst. (bd. dirs. 2000—), Assn. Comml. Ins. Attys., Comml. Law League Am., Mass. Bar Assn., Boston Bar Assn., Boston U. Law Alumni Assn. (mem. exec. com., v.p. exec. com. 1999-2002, pres. exec. com. 2000-01). Office: Mintz Levin Cohn Ferris Glovsky & Popeo PC 1 Financial Ctr Fl 39 Boston MA 02111-2657

MIKE-NARD, BEVERLY JEAN, nurse; b. Youngstown, Ohio, Nov. 3, 1957; d. Michael Ablen and Marion Charlotte (Saba) Mike; children: Stacy Nicole, Kenneth Robert Jr. Nursing diploma, St. Elizabeth Hosp. Med. Ctr., 1978; student, Youngstown State U., 1988-89; BSN, Pa. State U., 1991; MSN, Case Western Res. U., 1993. RN, Ohio; cert. hosp. based neonatal resuscitation program instr., cert. CPR instr., cert. neonatal nurse practitioner; cert. PALS instr.; cert. Nat. Certification Corp. Nurse asst. St. Elizabeth Hosp. Med. Ctr., Youngstown, 1977-78, nurse orthopaedic dept., 1978-81, nurse neonatal ICU, 1982-93, asst. coord. apnea home monitor program, CPR instr., 1993-96, neonatal nurse practitioner, 1994-96, coord. RespiGam program, 1996. Sec. Color My World Day Care Ctr., 1986-92; first Neonatal Nurse Practitioner in

Mahoning, Trumbull, Columbiana, Mercer and Lawrence County; RespiGam coord., neonatal nurse practitioner Forum Health Tod Children's Hosp., Poland, Ohio, 1989—; RSV prophylaxis clinic/synagis RespiGam coord., 1997—; pediatric clin. instr. Case Western Res. U.-Frances Payne Bolton Sch. nursing, 1999—; pediatric clin. instr. Kent State U., 1999—; mentor for grad. nursing students Youngstown State U., 1998-2000. Active PTA, Austintown, Ohio, 1985-89, Poland, Ohio, 1989—; mem. parish coun. St. Maron Ch., 1994-96, CCD tchr., 1994-95. Mem. ANA, NAACOG (cert.), Ohio Nurses Assn., Nat. Assn. Neonatal Nurses, Nat. Apstolate Maronites (bd. dirs. 1999—). Democrat. Maronite Catholic. Avocations: golf, biking, swimming. Home: 3330 Partridge Park Dr Poland OH 44514-2807 Fax: 330-757-8851. E-mail: bjmikenard@aol.com.

MIKESELL, JANICE HARLAN, writer, poet; b. St. Louis, Feb. 23, 1935; d. John Lawrence Harlan and Ruth Esther Bedwell; m. James Roderick Weber, July 30, 1955 (div. June 1974); m. Ritchie Patterson Mikesell, Sept. 9, 1978; children: James, Stephen, David, Mary. Student, S.D. State U., 1981-85. RN, Colo. Author: A Survivor's Manual, 1989, Fate Worse than Dealth, 1995, Some People Don't Know that Barns Have Faces, 1998, No Redeeming Social Merit, 2000; contbg. editor Johnny Harlan, the Irish Boy, 1993; contbg. co-editor Women, Houses and Homes, 1988. Mem. S.D. Humanities Counil Spkrs. Bur., 2002—. Recipient PEN Syndicated Fiction award Nat. Endowment for the Arts, 1984, Schultz Werth award S.D. State U., 1985; S.D. Arts Coun. fellowship, 1985. Mem. Poets and Writers, Siouxland Creative Writers (past v.p., co-pres.), Phi Kappa Phi. Roman Catholic. Avocations: photography, swimming, art films, antiques, fine dining. Office: PO Box 87945 Sioux Falls SD 57109-7945

MIKESELL, JOHN L. economics educator; b. Bloomington, Ind., Oct. 23, 1942; s. R.M. and Minnie (Shigley) M.; m. Karen Roberts, June 13, 1964; children: Elizabeth, Tom, Dan. BA in Econs., Wabash Coll., 1964; MA in Econs., U. Ill., 1965, PhD in econ., 1969. Asst. prof. econs. W.Va. U., Morgantown, W.Va., 1968-72; assoc. prof. sch. pub. and environ. affairs Ind. U., Bloomington, 1973-78, prof., 1978—, assoc. dean acad. affairs, 1986—. Author: Fiscal Administration, 1990; co-author: (with J. Due) Sales Taxation (outstanding acad. book 1984); contbr. articles to profl. jours. Mem. Phi Beta Kappa, Omicron Delta Epsilon. Home: 5930 E Lampkins Ridge Rd Bloomington IN 47401-9726 Office: Ind U 300 Sch of Pub Environ Affairs Bloomington IN 47405

MIKESELL, MARVIN WRAY, geography educator; b. Kansas City, Mo., June 16, 1929; s. Loy George and Clara (Wade) M.; m. Reine-Marie de France, Apr. 1, 1957. BA, UCLA, 1952, MA, 1953; PhD, U. Calif.-Berkeley, 1959. Instr. to prof. geography U. Chgo., 1958—, chmn. dept. geography, 1969-74, 83-86. Del. U.S. Nat. Commn. for UNESCO Author: Northern Morocco, 1961; editor: Readings in Cultural Geography, 1962, Geographers Abroad, 1973, Perspectives on Environment, 1974. Fellow Am. Geog. Soc. (hon.); mem. Assn. Am. Geographers (pres. 1975-76, Disting. Career award 1995). Clubs: Quadrangle. Home: 1155 E 56th St Chicago IL 60637-1530 Office: Com Geog Studies 5828 S University Ave Chicago IL 60637-1583 E-mail: mmikesel@uchicago.edu.

MIKESELL, PAMELA PRESTWOOD, guidance counselor; b. Waukegan, Ill., May 16, 1945; d. Robert Milton and Ann Sandra (Subotka) Prestwood; m. Jan Erwin Mikesell, Dec. 25, 1965; children: Danielle Marie, Lisa Michelle. Grad., Western Ill. U., 1967, Western Md. Coll., 1975. Dir. Fairfield (Pa.) Sch. Bd., 1988-92; councilwoman Carroll Valley (Pa.) Boro, 1996—. Mem. NEA, Pa. Edn. Assn., Littlestown Edn. Assn. (pres. 1985-87, 91-93, 2002-), Pa. Sch. Counselors Assn., Delta Kappa Gamma (pres. 1996-98). Democrat. Episcopalian. Home: 6 Meadow Trl Fairfield PA 17320-8220

MIKESELL, RAYMOND FRECH, economics educator; b. Eaton, Ohio, Feb. 13, 1913; s. Otho Francis and Josephine (Frech) M.; m. Desyl DeLauder, 1937 (div.); children: George DeLauder and Norman DeLauder (twins); m. Irene Langdoc, 1957 (dec.); m. Grace Schneiders, 1997. Student, Carnegie Inst. Tech., 1931-33; BA cum laude, MA, Ohio U., 1935, PhD, 1939. Asst. prof. econ. U. Wash., 1937-41; economist OPA, Washington, 1941-42, U.S. Treasury Dept., 1942-46, rep. Egypt, 1943-44, cons., 1946-47; on Middle East affairs FOA, 1953; chief fgn. minerals div. Pres.'s Materials Policy Commn., 1951-52; mem. staff Fgn. Econ. Policy Com. (Randall Com.), 1953-54; mem. U.S. Currency Mission to Saudi Arabia, 1948; spl. U.S. rep. to Israel, summer 1952; mem. U.S. mission to Israel, Ethiopia, summer 1953; prof. econs. U. Va., 1946-57; W.E. Miner prof. econs. U. Oreg., 1957-87, prof. econs., 1987—; dir. Inst. Internat. Studies and Overseas Adminstrn., 1958-60; assoc. dir. Inst. Internat. Studies and Overseas Adminstrn. U. Oreg., 1960-68; vis. prof. Grad. Inst. Internat. Studies, Geneva, 1964. Sr. staff mem. Council Econ. Advisers, Exec. Office of Pres., 1955-56, cons. to Council Econ. Advisers, 1956-57; cons. Pan Am. Union, 1954-63, Dept. State, 1947-53, 63-67, 71-83, Ford Found., 1962, Dept. Commerce, 1962-64, ICA, 1952-53, 61-62, OAS, 1963-73, AID, 1964-71; mem. UN Econ. Commn. for Latin Am. working group on regional market, 1958; cons. Senate Fgn. Relations Com., 1962, 67, World Bank, 1968, Inter-Am. Devel. Bank, 1968-75; mem. panel advisers Sec. Treasury, 1965-69; sr. fellow Nat. Bur. Econ. Research, 1972-73 Author: U.S. Economic Policy and International Relations, 1952, Foreign Exchange in the Postwar World, 1954, The Emerging Pattern of International Payments, 1954, Foreign Investments in Latin America, 1955, Promoting United States Private Investments Abroad, 1957, Agricultural Surpluses and Export Policy, 1958, U.S. Private and Government Investment Abroad, 1962, (with M. Trued) Arabian Oil, 1949, (with H. Chenery) Postwar Bilateral Payments Agreements, 1955, (with J. Behrman) Financing Free World Trade with the Sino-Soviet Bloc, 1958, Public International Lending for Development, 1966, (with R.W. Adler) Public External Financing of Developing Banks, 1966, Public Foreign Capital for Private Enterprises in Developing Countries, 1966, The Economics of Foreign Aid, 1968, Financing World Trade, 1969, (with others) Foreign Investment in the Petroleum and Mineral Industries, 1971, (with H. Furth) Foreign Dollar Balances and the International Role of the Dollar, 1974, Foreign Investment in the Copper Industry, 1975, The World Copper Industry, 1979, New Patterns of World Mineral Development, 1979, The Economics of Foreign Aid and Self-Sustaining Development, 1983, Foreign Investment in Mining Projects, 1983, Petroleum Company Operations and Agreements in the Developing Countries, 1984, Stockpiling Strategic Materials, 1986, Nonfuel Minerals: Foreign Dependence and National Security, 1987, (with John W. Whitney) The World Mining Industry: Investment Strategy and Public Policy, 1987, The Global Copper Industry: Problems and Prospects, 1988, (with Lawrence F. Williams) International Banks and the Environment, 1992, Economic Development and the Environment, 1992, The Bretton Woods Debates, 1994, (with Richard Auty) Sustainable Development in Mineral Economies, 1998, Foreign Adventures of an Economist, 2000; mem. editl. adv. bd. Middle East Jour., 1947-58; mem. bd. editors: Am. Econ. Rev., 1953-55. Home: 2290 Spring Blvd Eugene OR 97403-1860

MIKESELL, RICHARD HUGH, writer; b. South Bend, Ind., Sept. 20, 1938; s. Kenneth Leroy and Marion Helena (Pittenger) M. BA, U. Calif., Berkeley, 1964; JD, U. Calif., San Francisco, 1967; MA, Calif. State U., 1969. Teaching asst. U. Calif., Berkeley, 1960-64; purchase officer Faber Enterprises, Santa Monica, Calif., 1967-69; freelance writer, 1969—; shipping officer EMME Clothing, Culver City, Calif., 1971-74; buyer Santos Imports, Rome, 1975-79; pub. rels. officer Cri-Help, Inc., North Hollywood, Calif., 1983-93; exec. v.p. The Loan Network, Venice, 1993—. Cons. in field. Author: The Flame in the Flesh, 1971, (ghost writer) One Flew Over the Cuckoos Nest, 1974; author of poems, 1960—. With U.S. Army, 1958-60. Independent. Avocation: skiing, pocket billiards, chess. Home: 707 Marr St Apt 205 Venice CA 90291-4790

MIKESELL, RICHARD LYON, lawyer, financial counselor; b. Corning, N.Y., Jan. 29, 1941; s. Walter Ray and Clara Ellen (Lyon) M.; m. Anna May Creese, Mar. 16, 1973; 1 child, Joel. BSChemE, U. Calif., Berkeley, 1962; LLB, Duke U., 1965; BA in Liberal Studies, UCLA, 1977. Bar: U.S. Supreme Ct. 1971, Ohio 1965, Calif. 1967, U.S. Ct. Appeals (9th cir.) 1982, U.S. Ct. Appeals (2d cir.) 1993, U.S. Patent Office 1967. Patent atty. Procter & Gamble, Cin., 1965-66, Rocketdyne divsn. N.Am. Aviation, L.A., 1966-69; pvt. practice law, 1969-81; prin. Law Offices of R.L. Mikesell, 1981—. Fin. counselor L.A. Police Dept., 1986—; arbitrator Am. Arbitration Assn., L.A., 1980—. Pres. San Fernando Valley Fair Housing Coun., L.A., 1969-72, Valley Women's Ctr., L.A., 1990; line res. officer L.A. Police Dept., 1969-72. Named Res. Officer of Yr. L.A. Police Dept., 1990, 98; recipient 1st Place award Nat. SPAM Recipe Contest, 1998. Avocation: high power rifle shooting. Office: 14540 Hamlin St Ste B Van Nuys CA 91411-4147 E-mail: richlyon@worldnet.att.com.

MIKIEWICZ, ANNA DANIELLA, marketing and international business exporter; b. Chgo., Dec. 22, 1960; d. Zdislaw and Lucy (Magnusweska) M. BS in Mktg., Elmhurst Coll., 1982; postgrad., Triton Coll. Asst. to midwestern regional mgr. Melster Pub. Co., Chgo., 1983; sales rep. First Impressions, Elk Grive, Ill., 1984; asst. to Midwestern dist. mgr. Airco Ind. Gases, Broadview, Carol Stream, 1985; customer svc. & ops. mgr. Yamazen USA, Inc., Schaumburg, 1985-88; nat. sales & mktg. coord. Kitamura Machinery U.S.A. Inc., 1988-95; mktg. mgr. Beth Lee Boutique, 1995-97; internat. bus. export control sales coord. MHI Machine Tool USA, Inc. subs. Mistubishi Heavy Industries, 1997-99; internat. bus. asst. to exec. v.p. sales America Excel, Inc., Palatine, Ill., 1999—; internat. bus. Brazil Market JST Sales Am., Inc., 2000—. Named Chgo. Polish Queen Polish Am. Culture Club, 1983-84. Mem. NAFE. Republican. Roman Catholic.

MIKITA, JOSEPH KARL, broadcasting executive; b. nr. Richmond, Va., Oct. 3, 1918; s. John and Catherine (Wargofcak) M.; m. Mary Therese Benya, Nov. 26, 1942; children: Patty-Jane Mikita McGlynn, Michael, M. Noel Mikita Garagiola. BS, Fordham U., 1939; MS, Columbia U., 1940. Treas., controller Capital Cities Broadcasting Co., Albany, N.Y., 1955-58; controller Westinghouse Broadcasting Co., Inc., N.Y.C., 1958-60, v.p. fin., 1960-64, v.p. fin. and adminstrn., 1964-65, sr. v.p., 1965-69, 1975—; also dir., exec. v.p. Westinghouse Electric Corp. for Broadcasting, Learning and Leisure Activities, 1969-75. Dir. Sutro Tower, Inc. Author: (with others) The Business of Broadcasting, 1964. Bd. dirs. Fordham U. Council, Albany County Workshop, Albany County Heart Assn., Citizens For Reasonable Growth, Boca Raton; chmn. bd. Instructional TV. Served to maj. AUS, 1940-45, ETO. Recipient Order of Merit (Silver), Westinghouse Electric Corp., Disting. Service Alumni award Fordham U., 1969. Mem. AICPA, Internat. Radio and TV Soc., N.Y. Soc. CPAs, Fin. Execs. Inst. (dir., past pres. Manhattan chpt.), Inst. Broadcasting Fin. Mgmt. (past dir.), Town Club, Westchester Country Club, Boca Raton Club, M.G.A., JDM Country Club, Royal Palm Yacht and Country Club, Palm Beach Country Club, Golden Harbour Yacht Club (commodore), Rotary (1st v.p. N.Y.). Home: 3125 NE 7th Dr Boca Raton FL 33431-6906 Office: 90 Park Ave New York NY 10016-1301 E-mail: 8jmikita@bellsouth.net.

MIKITKA, GERALD PETER, investment banker, financial consultant; b. Chgo., July 7, 1943; s. Michael and Helen (Cuprisin) M.; m. Nancy Lee Parker, Mar. 6, 1977; children: Richard, Jeffrey, Jennifer. BSBA in Fin., Roosevelt U., 1966, postgrad., 1967. Diplomate: registered investment advisor. Sr. investment exec. Shearson Hammill & Co., Chgo., 1967-73; chmn., pres. Capital Directions, Inc., 1973—. Pres. CDI Fin. Advisors, Chgo., 1974—, CDI Properties, Chgo., 1974— , CDI Communications, Inc., Chgo., 1978—, A.B. Properties Inc., Chgo., 1986—. Am. Eagle Realty Inc., Chgo., 1988—, Grand Caribbean Properties Inc., Chgo., 1988, Cain Estates Inc., Chgo., 1988—, Caribbean Sea Properties Inc., Chgo., 1989—. Served with U.S. Army, 1967-69. Mem. Nat. Assn. Securities Dealers, Securities Investment Protection Assn., Broadcast Fin. Mgmt. Assn., Nat. Radio Broadcast Assn., Internat. Assn. Fin. Planning. Lodges: Rotary.

MIKKELSON, DEAN HAROLD, geological engineer, writer; b. Devils Lake, N.D., July 25, 1922; s. John Harold and Theodora (Eklund) M.; m. Delphene Doss, May 30, 1946; 1 child, Lynn Dee Hoffman. Student, N.D. State Coll., 1940-41; midshipman, U.S. Naval Acad., 1942-45; BS in Geological Engring., U. N.D., 1956. Registered profl. engr., Okla. 2d officer U.S. Lines, Quaker Lines-States Lines, Portland, Oreg., 1945-48; ptnr. J.I. Case Farm Machinery & Packard Automobile Franchises, Devils Lake, N.D., 1948-52; oil and gas lease broker, 1952-54; geologist Sohio Petroleum Co., Oklahoma City, 1956-58; geol. engr. Petrobras, Belem do Para, Brazil, 1958-60; pvt. practice Oklahoma City, 1961-78; pres., owner Dogwatch Petroleum, Inc., 1978-98; owner Spindrift Press, 1998—. Agrl. pilot, N.D., Mont., Tex., N.Mex., summers, 1952-56. Author: (as Dee Geo) Danny; contbr. articles to profl. jours. Candidate Okla. Rep. State Legislature, Oklahoma City, 1958; del. various county and state conv., N.D. and Okla., 1948-68. With N.D. N.G., 1938-40, U.S. Army Air Corps., 1942. Mem. Oklahoma City Geol. Soc., Masons, Shriners, Jesters, Am. Legion, Sportsmans Country Club. Republican. Avocations: hunting, fishing, golf, oil painting, singing. Office: Spindrift Press 4430 NW 50th St Ste C2 Oklahoma City OK 73112-2295

MIKKELSON, ERIC T. lawyer; b. Madison, Wis., July 27, 1967; s. Gerald E. Mikkelson and Ruth Elaine Lee. AB, Stanford U., 1990; JD, U. Kans., 1994. Bar: Kans. 1994, Mo. 1995. Pvt. practice, 1994-97; judge, 1996-97; assoc. Shook, Hardy & Bacon LLP, Kansas City, 1997—. Mem. ABA (tax sect.), Mo. Bar, Kans. Bar Assn. Avocations: sports, travel, arts. Office: Shook Hardy & Bacon PO Box 15607 Kansas City MO 64106-0607

MIKLES, DEVIN ALARIC, physician; b. Ft. Belvoir, Va., Dec. 19, 1949; s. Truman Fredrick and Dorothy Jean (Reed) M.; m. Lisa Wecker Sparks, 1970 (div. 1974); 1 child, Ian Alaric; m. Beverly Maguire Will, 1975 (div. 1979); 1 child, Christiane Alexandra; m. Patricia Lee McMullen, Mar. 16, 1986; 1 child, Lee Schuyler. BA magna cum laude, U. Colo., Colorado Springs, 1979; MD with honors in Neuroanatomy, U. Colo. Health Scis. Ctr., 1984. Diplomate Am. Bd. Internal Medicine. Intern Presbyn./St. Lukes Med. Ctr., Denver, 1984-85, resident in internal medicine, 1985-87, attending physician internal medicine Denver and Aurora, Colo., 1987-91, Presbyn./St. Lukes Healthcare Ctr., Aurora, 1988-91; pvt. practice internal medicine Centennial Healthcare Ctr., Englewood, 1989-91, Verde Valley Med. Ctr., Cottonwood, Ariz., 1991-99; lectr. internal medicine Marcus J. Lawrence Med. Ctr., 1991-99, mem., advisor cmty. edn. com., 1995—; med. dir. Centerpath: Inst. Integrative Health and Healing Sedona (Ariz.) Med. Ctr., 1997-98; pres., founder Interdisciplinary Cmty. Healing Systems Cons., 1997—. Founder, chmn. David G. Wells MD Meml. Libr.; med. dir. No. Ariz. Healthcare Home Health/Hospice, Cottonwood, 1996—, mem. profl. adv. com., 1995—; founding mem. Bd. Massage Examiners, Colorado Springs, 1977-79. Recipient Excellence in Broadcasting award KKFM Radio Sta., Colorado Springs, 1974. Mem. AMA, ACP, Verde Valley Ind. Practice Assn. (pres., founder, 1994-97), Verde Healthcare Alliance (pres., co-founder 1996-99), Phi Beta Kappa. Avocations: perma culture, organic gardening, mountain running and climbing, travel, weight lifting. Office: Choices Integrative Healthcare Sedona 2935 Southwest Dr Sedona AZ 86336-3725

MIKLOS, TOMÁS, management consultant, future studies and education consultant; b. Mexico City, May 29, 1938; s. Tiburcio and Edith Miklos; m. Monique Landesmann, Feb. 4, 1965; children: David, Vanessa. Chem. engr., Facultad de Química, Mexico City, 1959; PhD, MSc, Sorbonne, Paris, 1963; Clin. Degree, Instituto Mexicano de Psicología, Mexico City, 1980; M in Psychoanalysis, Centro de Investigaciones y Estudios Psicoanalíticos, Mexico City, 1985. Cert. engr. Budget mgr. Syntex Corp., 1970-75; sr. cons. Cresap, McCormick & Paget, 1975-80; gen. dir. T.M. Consultores, 1980-82; dir. literacy program Instituto Nacional para la Educación de los Adultos, Mexico City, 1982-85; gen. dir. Fund. Javier Barros Sierra Inst. on Prospective, 1985-89, Latin Am. Regional Edn. Ctr., Patzcuaro, Mexico, 1989-92, Inst. Nac. Asesoria Especializada, Mexico City, 1992-93; gen. coord. evaluation, internal advisor planning, adult edn. network Ministry of Edn., 1993—; ednl. cons. Coun. for Human and Social Devel. and Latin Am. Edn. Comm. Inst., 2001—. Tchr. U.N.A.M.-U. Mexico, Mexico City, 1958—93, U.I.A.-U. Iberoamericana, Mexico City, 1985—93, Lassalle U., U. Tlaxcala, U. Morchs; advisor, cons., 1980—93; psychoanalyst, 1987—93. Author: Ten Encounters With..., 1975, Planning for Change, 1980, Prospective Planning, 1989, Interactive Planning, 1993, The Political Decisions, 2000. Fellow Nat. History and Geography Soc., Mexican Acad. Engring. (sec. 1985-93), Sociedad Mexicana de Geografía y Estadística; mem. AAAS, Mexican Acad. History, World Future Soc., N.Y. Acad. Scis. Home: Cda del Rayo 20 53920 La Herradura Mexico City Mexico Office: Inst Nac de Asesoria Schiller 148 11560 Mexico City Mexico

MIKLOVIC, DANIEL THOMAS, research executive; b. St. Louis, Oct. 1, 1950; s. John Joseph and Ruby Irene (Cloyd) M.; m. Linda Lois Pinkley, July 12, 1975; 1 child, Aimee Linette. AS in Nuclear Tech., Air Force Community Coll., Randolph AFB, Tex., 1977; BSEE, U. Mo., 1979; MS in Systems Mgmt., U. So. Calif., 1986. Engr. Weyerhaeuser, Raymond, Wash., 1979-82, Scott Paper, Skowhegan, Maine, 1982-83; from rschr. to mgr. corp. planning Weyerhaeuser, Tacoma, 1983-92; marketing dir. Indsl. Sys., Inc., Bothell, Wash., 1992-95; v.p. Gartner Group, Stamford, Conn., 1995—. Owner Mfg. Integration Planning Svcs., Issaquah, Wash., 1992—. Author: Real-Time Control Networks, 1993; contbr. monthly columnn Mfg. Comms., Automation and Control, Jour. Inst. of Measurement and Control publs.; co-host (with Alexander Haig) World Bus. Rev., 1997—, CNBC. Chmn. Pierce Coll. Vocat. Adv. Com., Puyallup, Wash., 1985-91. Staff sgt. USAF, 1973-77. Mem. Indsl. Computing Soc. (fellow chpt. bd. dirs., pres.), Tau Beta Pi, Eta Kappa Nu, Delta Tau Delta. Office: Gartner Group 56 Top Gallant Rd Stamford CT 06902-7700

MIKLUSAK, THOMAS ALAN, psychiatrist, psychoanalyst; b. Cherry Point, N.C., Mar. 25, 1946; s. Alex Frank and Betty Ann (Baker) M.; m. Chris G. Wolski, June 21, 1969; children: Courtney, Ryan. BA, U. Notre Dame, 1968; MD, Ind. U., Indpls., 1972; PhD in Adult Psychoanalysis, So. Calif. Psychoanalytic Inst, Beverly Hills, 1990. Intern Santa Barbara (Calif.) Cottage and Gen. Hosps., 1972-73; resident adult psychiatry UCLA/Brentwood VA, Westwood, Calif., 1973-76; fellow child psychiatry UCLA, 1975-77; adult psychoanalysis clin. assoc. So. Calif. Psychoanalytic Inst., Beverly Hills, 1982-90, child psychoanalysis clin. assoc., 1985-91; pvt. practice child and adult psychiatry and psychoanalysis Pasadena, Calif., 1977—. Asst. prof. child psychiatry U. So. Calif. Med. Sch., 1984-97. Mem. Am. Psychoanalytic Assn., Am. Psychiat. Assn., So. Calif. Psychoanalytic Soc., Soc. Calif. Psychiat. Soc. Office: 180 S Lake Ave Ste 255 Pasadena CA 91101-4737

MIKO, MARY V. personnel director; b. Detroit, June 2, 1949; d. George and Mary C. (Karpach). BA, Oglethorpe U., 1989; MBA, Mich. State U., 1992. Clerical GM, Mich., 1968-75, quality control/insp., 1975-84, support mfg.. Ga., 1984-88, support engring. Mich., Ga., 1989-96, staff planner Mich., 1997—. Rsch. Fed. Credit Union, Warren, Mich, 1994-98, Dir. Mich. State Alumni, Troy, 1995-98. Avocations: boating, golf, travel, reading. Home: 39785 Mount Elliott Dr Clinton Township MI 48038-4041 Office: GM 30001 Van Dyke Ave Warren MI 48093-2350

MIKOLAJCZAK, BOLESLAW, computer science educator, researcher, consultant; b. Poznan, Poland, June 30, 1946; came to U.S., 1986; s. Walenty and Maria (Piechocka) M; m. Urszula Hajdrowska, Aug. 14, 1971; children: Maciej, Wojciech Rafal. MS in Control Engring. summa cum lauda, Tech. U., Poznan, 1970, PhD, 1974, Dr.Habilitis in Computer Sci., 1979; MS in Math., Adam Mickiewicz U., Poznan, 1972. Lectr. Inst. Control Engring., Poznan, 1970-74, asst. prof., 1974-79, assoc. prof., 1980-85, Computer Sci. Ctr., Poznan, 1985-86; vis. lectr. dept. computer sci. Southea. Mass. U. (now U. Mass.), Dartmouth, 1986-87, assoc. prof., 1987-91; assoc. prof. dept. computer and info. sci. U. Mass. (formerly Southeastern Mass. U.), 1991—; prof. computer sci. U. Mass., 1993—, chmn. computer and info. sci. dept., 1995—. Sci. cons. Elana, Torun, Poland, 1980-85, Tekoma, Warsaw, Poland, 1982-84, Lenin's Steelwork, Cracow, Poland, 1984-85, Mercomp, Warsaw, 1985-86; vis. scholar Cornell U., Ithaca, N.Y., 1976-77. Author: Transformations of Automata and Computational Complexity of Some Problems in Automata Theory, 1988, Algebraic and Structural Automata Theory, 1989, Algebraic and Structural Automata Theory Eng. edit., 1991; others; contbr. articles to profl. jours.; patentee in field. Active Polish Tchrs. Assn., 1964-80, Trade Union Solidarnosc, 1980—. Recipient award Ministry of Sci. and Tech., 1980, Gen. Tech. Orgn., 1980, Polish Acad. Scis., 1981, 84, Ministry of Higher Edn., 1982. Mem. Am. Math. Soc., Computer Soc. of IEEE, Polish Math. Soc., Assn. for Computing Machinery, Polish Computer Soc., Mass. Tchrs. Assn., Math. Revs. (reviewer 1976—). Roman Catholic. Achievements include patents for digital systems; research in algebraic and structural automata theory, in computational complexity of some problems in automata theory, in analysis and design of parallel algorithms, analysis and design of distributed software systems using Patri nets. Office: U Mass Old Wesport Rd Dartmouth MA 02747

MIKOLYZK, THOMAS ANDREW, librarian; b. Kenosha, Wis., Sept. 9, 1953; s. Andrew John and Charlotte Elaine (McIver) M.; m. Ann J. Moyer, May 26, 1973 (div. June 1981); children: Kari, Emily; m. Amy L. Kessel, Sept. 4, 1982; 1 child, Alice; 1 stepchild, David. BA in English and Elem. Edn., Beloit (Wis.) Coll., 1982; MA in Libr. Sci., U. Chgo., 1986; cert. in advanced study, Concordia U., 1995. Libr. asst. Beloit Coll., 1980-82; sports writer Beloit Daily News, 1981-83; tchr. Turner Mid. Sch., Beloit, 1983; tchr., libr. Horizon's Edge Sch., Canterbury, N.H., 1983-85; libr. U. Ill., Chgo., 1985-86, Lake Forest (Ill.) Coll., 1986-89, Dist 62, Des Plaines, Ill., 1989-93; libr., dir. summer program Avery Coonley Sch., Downers Grove, 1993-97; libr. Prevention First, Inc., Chgo., 1999—. Dir. ednl. cons., 1993—. Author: Langston Hughes-A Bio-Bibliography, 1990, Oscar Wilde: An Annotated Bibliography, 1993. Campaign mgr. United Way, Delavan, Wis., 1978-79; deacon 1st Congregation Ch., Des Plaines, 1990. Mem. Ill. Sch. Libr. Assn., Ind. Sch. Assn. Ctrl. States, U.S. Chess Fedn. Avocations: chess, bibliography, book collecting, sailing. Home: 7361 Prescott Ln La Grange IL 60525-5037 Office: 720 N Franklin St Chicago IL 60610-7214

MIKULSKI, BARBARA ANN, senator; b. Balt., July 20, 1936; d. William and Christine (Kutz) M. BA, Mt. St. Agnes Coll., 1958; MSW, U. Md., 1965; LLD (hon.), Goucher Coll., 1973, Hood Coll., 1978, Bowie State U., 1989, Morgan State U., 1990, U. Mass., 1991; DHL (hon.), Pratt Inst., 1974. Tchr. Vista Tng. Ctr. Mount St. Mary's Sem., Balt.; social worker Balt. Dept. Social Services, 1961-63, 66-70; mem. Balt. City Council, 1971-76, 95th-99th Congresses from 3d Md. Dist., 1977-87; U.S. senator from Md., 1987—; sec. Dem. Conf. 104th-106th Congress. Adj. prof. Loyola Coll., 1972-76; mem. U.S. Senate labor and human resources com., 1987—, ranking mem. subcom. on aging, 1993—; mem. appropriations com., 1987, ranking mem. subcom. on vets., housing, and ind. agys., 1987—. Bd. visitors U.S. Naval Acad. Recipient Nat. Citizen of Yr. award Buffalo Am.-Polit. Eagle, 1973, Woman of Yr. Bus. & Profl. Women's Club Assn., 1973, Outstanding Alumnus U. Md. Sch. Social Work, 1973, Govt. Social Responsibility award, 1991. Mem. LWV.*

MIKULSKI, JOHN MICHAEL, music educator; b. Buffalo, May 9, 1957; s. John Michael and Lena Mikulski; m. Marguerite Mary Denton, May 3, 1980; children: John F., Richard M., Andrew R. MusB in Edn., Shenandoah Conservatory Music, WInchester, Va., 1979; MusM in Edn., SUNY, Buffalo, 1985. Cert. tchr. N.Y. Music tchr. St. Gregory the Gt. Sch., Amherst, NY, 1979—80; tchr. Oakfield (N.Y.)-Alabama Ctrl. Sch., 1981—. Solo adjudicator N.Y. State Sch. Music Assn., 1985—; music parade judge Genesee Vally Judging Assn., Batavia, NY, 1983—; guest condr. Perry (N.Y.) Ctrl. Sch. Named Tchr. of the Yr., Wal-Mart Corp., 2002. Mem.: Internat. Clarinet Assn., Internat. Assn. Jazz Educators, Music Educators Nat. Conf. Home: 1129 Boncliff Dr Alden NY 14004 Office: Oakfield Alabama Ctrl Sch 7001 Lewiston Rd Oakfield NY 14125 Personal E-mail: olddays57@aol.com.

MIKUS, ELEANORE ANN, artist; b. Detroit, July 25, 1927; d. Joseph and Bertha (Englot) M.; m. Richard Burns, July 6, 1949 (div. 1963); children: Richard, Hillary, Gabrielle. Student, Mich. State U., 1946-49, U. Mex., summer 1948; B.F.A., U. Denver, 1957, MA, 1967; postgrad., Art Students League, 1958, NYU, 1959-60. Asst. prof. Cornell U., Ithaca, N.Y., 1979-80, assoc. prof., 1980-92, prof. art, 1992-94, prof. emerita, 1994—. Asst. prof. art Monmouth Coll., West Long Branch, N.J., 1966-70, prof. Cornell, Rome, 1989; vis. lectr. painting Cooper Union, N.Y.C., 1970-72, Central Sch. Art and Design, London, 1973-77, Kensington Inst., London, 1974-77, Harrow (Eng.) Coll. Tech. and Art, 1975-76. Exhibited in 22 one-person shows at Pace Gallery, N.Y.C. and O.K. Harris Gallery, N.Y.C., Baskett Gallery, Cin., 1982, 84, 85, Claudia Carr Gallery, 1998, 99—, Mitchell Algus Gallery, N.Y.C., 1998; represented in permanent collections including Mus. Modern Art, N.Y.C., Whitney Mus., N.Y.C., Los Angeles County Mus., Cin. Mus., Birmingham (Ala.) Mus. Art, Norton Simon Mus., Pasadena, Bklyn. Mus., Honolulu Acad. Arts, Indpls. Mus. Art, Nat. Gallery Art, Washington, Victoria and Albert Mus., London, Libr. of Congress, Washington; subject of book Eleanore Mikus, Shadows of the Real (by Robert Hobbs and Judith Bernstock), 1991. Guggenheim fellow, 1966-67; Tamarind fellow, summer 1968; MacDowell fellow, summer 1969. Mem. AAUP. Home: PO Box 4775 Ithaca NY 14852-4775 Office: Cornell U Dept Art Tjaden Hall Ithaca NY 14853 also: 270 Luce Rd Groton NY 13073-9747

MIKVA, ABNER JOSEPH, lawyer, retired federal judge; b. Milw., Jan. 21, 1926; s. Henry Abraham and Ida (Fishman) M.; m. Zoe Wise, Sept. 19, 1948; children: Mary, Laurie, Rachel. JD cum laude, U. Chgo., 1951; DL (hon.) , U. Ill., 1980, Am. U., 1991, Northwestern U., 1991, Tulane U., 1993, Ill. Inst. Tech., 1997, Santa Clara U., 2000, Wm. Mitchell Coll. Law, 2001; DHL (hon.) , Hebrew U., 1989, U. Wis., 1995. Bar: Ill. 1951, D.C. 1978. Law clk. to Hon. Sherman Minton U.S. Supreme Ct., 1951; ptnr. Devoe, Shadur, Mikva & Plotkin, Chgo., 1952-68, D'Ancona, Pflaum, Wyatt & Riskind, 1973-74; lectr. Northwestern U. Law Sch., Chgo., 1973-75, U. Pa. Law Sch., 1983-85, Georgetown Law Sch., 1986-88, Duke U. Law Sch., Durham, N.C., 1990-91, U. Chgo. Law Sch., 1992-93; mem. Ill. Gen. Assembly from 23d Dist., 1956-66, 91st-92d Congresses from 2d Dist. Ill., 94th-96th Congresses from 10th Dist. Ill.; mem. ways and means com., judiciatry com. ways and means com., judiciary com.; chmn. Dem. Study Group; resigned, 1979; from judge to chief judge U.S. Circuit Ct. Appeals D.C., 1979-94, chief judge, 1991-94; counsel to the President The White House, Washington, 1994-96; arbitrator JAMS, Inc., 1997—. Vis. prof., Walter Schaefer chair in pub. policy U. Chgo., 1996-98; vis. prof. U. Ill. Coll. Law, 1998-2000, U. Chgo., 2000—. Author: The American Congress: The First Branch, 1983, The Legislative Process, 1995, An Introduction to Statutory Interpretation, 1997. With USAAF, WWII. Sr. fellow Inst. Govt. & Pub. Affairs U. Ill., 1998-2000; recipient Page One award Chgo. Newspaper Guild, 1964, Best Legislator award Ind. Voters Ill., 1956-66, Alumni medal U. Chgo., 1996, Paul Douglas Ethics in Govt. award, 1998; named one of ten Outstanding Young Men in Chgo., Jr. Assn. Commerce and Industry, 1961. Fellow AAAS; mem. ABA, Chgo. Bar Assn. (bd. mgrs. 1962-64), D.C. Bar Assn., Am. Law Inst., U.S. Assn. Former Mems. Congress, Order of Coif, Phi Beta Kappa. Home: Ph 6 5020 S Lake Shore Dr Chicago IL 60615-3253 E-mail: amikva@law.uchicago.edu.

MILAM, JOHN DANIEL, pathologist, educator; b. Kilgore, Tex., May 22, 1933; s. Ott G. and Effie (White) M.; m. Carol Jones Milam, Aug. 1, 1959; children: Kay, Beth, John Jr., Julie. BS, La. State U., 1955, MS, 1957, MD, 1960. 189attending pathologist St. Luke's Episcopal Hosp., Houston, 1967—89; cons. in pathology Tex. Children's Hosp., 1979—99, emeritus, 2000—; prof. lab. medicine M.D. Anderson Cancer Ctr., U. Tex., 1990—; prof. pathology and lab. medicine U. Tex. Med. Sch., 1989—; chief pathology Lyndon B. Johnson Gen. Hosp., 1995—2001. Trustee Am. Bd. Pathology, 1985—96, pres., 1995. Contbr. numerous articles to profl. jours., chpts., abstracts to books. Bd. dirs. Harris County chpt. ARC, 1978—, bd. dir., 1978—. Mem.: Am. Soc. Clin. Pathologists (Israel Davidsohn award for disting. svc. 2001), Tex. Soc. Pathologists (George T. Caldwell award 1981, 1981), Am. Assn. Blood Banks (pres. 1984, 1984, Disting. Svc. award 1988). Republican. Baptist. Home: 11927 Arbordale Ln Houston TX 77024-5001 Office: U Tex Houston Med Sch Dept Pathology 6431 Fannin St Rm 2.022 Houston TX 77030-1501 E-mail: john.d.milam@uth.tmc.edu.

MILAM, JUNE MATTHEWS, life insurance agent; b. Preston, Ga., Mar. 27, 1931; d. Curtis J. and Mary (Doster) Matthews; m. James Cage Lowry, Dec. 20, 1952 (dec.); m. Walker Hinton Milam, Jr., June 15, 1957; children: James L., Melinda K., Lisa W. Ary, Matthew W. BA, La. State U., 1952. Agt. N.Y. Life Ins. Co., Metairie, La., 1966—; alderman City of Harahan, 1980-86, mayor pro-tem, 1982-84. Guest spkr. to industry in 26 states, 1968—; charter leader N.Y. Life Ins. Women's Network, N.Y.C., 1981-83. Contbr. articles to profl. and trade jours. Mem. adv. bd. Battered Women's Program, New Orleans, 1978-84, Jefferson Parish Econ. Devel. Coun., 1988-92, sec., 1990; co-founder Met. Battered Women's program, 1984; bd. dirs. Abused Children's Advocacy Ctr., 1990—, pres. 1997-2001; bd. dirs. Extra Mile, Inc., 1995-98, sec., 1995-96, pres., 1996-97; co-founder, charter pres. Jefferson 25 Women's Polit. Orgn., 1991-95; chairperson JEDCO Citizen's Adv. Group, 1993; mem. East Jefferson Gen. Hosp. Found. Planned Giving Com., 1994—. Named Boss of Yr. Am. Bus. Women's Assn., Metairie, 1976, Man of Yr. New Orleans Assn. Life Underwriters, La. State Assn. Life Underwriters, 1976; recipient Nat. Quality award 25 yrs.; Quality of Life grantee MDRT Found., 1990, 99; recipient N.Y. Life Ins. Co. New Orleans First Life Time Achievement award, 1999. Mem. Nat. Assn. Fin. and Ins. Advisors, La. Assn. Fin. and Ins. Advisors, New Orleans Assn. Fin. and Ins. Advisors, Womens Bus. Owners Assn. (adv. bd. 1984-88), Million Dollar Round Table, New Orleans Top Twenty Study Group, Jefferson C. of C. (charter mem.). Republican. Presbyterian. Avocation: gourmet cooking. Office: NY Life Ins Co 3333 W Napoleon Ave Ste 200 Metairie LA 70001-2897 E-mail: jmilam@ft.newyorklife.com.

MILAM, WILLIAM BRYANT, ambassador, economist; b. Bisbee, Ariz., July 24, 1936; s. Burl Vivian and Alice Vera (Pierce) M.; step-children: Erika, Fred. AB, Stanford U., 1959; MA, U. Mich., 1970; postgrad., Am. U., 1973. Polit. officer Dept. State, Washington, 1967-69; fin. economist Dept. State and Am. Embassy, Washington and London, 1970-75; energy economist Dept. State, Washington, 1975-77, dep. office dir., 1977-80, office dir., 1980-83; dep. chief of mission Am. Embassy, Yaounde, Cameroon, 1983-85; dep. asst. sec. Dept. State, Washington, 1985-90; U.S. amb. to Bangladesh, 1990-93; spl. negotiator oceans environ. sci. Dept. State, Washington, 1993-95; chief of mission Am. Embassy, Monrovia, Liberia, 1995-98, U.S. amb. to Pakistan, Islamabad, 1998-2001. Calif. State scholar, 1956-59; recipient James Clement Dunn award Dept. of State, 1981, Superior Honor award, 1983, Pres.'s Meritorious Svc. award U.S. Govt., 1990, Pres. Outstanding Svc. award, 1991. Avocations: reading, golf.

MILAN, MARJORIE LUCILLE, early childhood education educator; b. Ludlow, Colo., June 24, 1926; d. John B. and Barbara (Zenonian) Pinamont; m. John Francis Milan, June 18, 1949; children: Barbara, J. Mark, Kevin. BA, U. Colo., 1947, MA, 1978; PhD, U. Denver, 1983. Cert. tchr., adminstr., supt., Colo. Tchr. Boulder (Colo.) Pub. Schs., 1947-49, Denver Pub. Schs., 1949-51, 67—; adminstr. T. Tot Kindergarten, Denver, 1951-55; tchr. Colo. Women's Coll., 1956-57; adminstr. Associated Schs., 1956-67. Adv. bd. George Washington Carver Nursery, Denver, 1960-85. Mem. Assn. Childhood Edn. (state bd. 1960—, Hall of Excellence 1991), Rotary (pres. chpt. 1994-95), Philanthropic Ednl. Orgn., Phi Delta Kappa, Delta Kappa Gamma. Avocations: swimming, music. Home: 1775 Lee St Lakewood CO 80215-2855

MILANDER, HENRY MARTIN, educational consultant; b. Northampton, Pa., Apr. 17, 1939; s. Martin Edward and Margaret Catherine (Makovetz) M.; children: Martin Henry, Beth Ann. BS summa cum laude, Lock Haven U., Pa., 1961; MA, Bowling Green (Ohio) State U., 1962; EdS (Future Faculty fellow 1964), U. No. Iowa, 1965; EdD, Ill. State U., Normal, 1967. Instr. Wartburg Coll., Waverly, Iowa, 1962-64; asst. prof. Ill. State U., 1966-67; dean instrn. Belleville (Ill.) Area Coll., 1967-69; v.p. acad. affairs Lorain County Community Coll., Elyria, Ohio, 1969-72; pres. Olympic Coll., Bremerton, Wash., 1972-87, Northeastern Jr. Coll., Sterling, Colo., 1988-95; edn1. cons., 1995—. Pres. Bremers, Inc., 1986-87. Contbr. articles to profl. jours. Pres. Kitsap County Comprehensive Health Planning Council, 1975-76; pres. Logan County Colo. United Way, 1992-93. Recipient Faculty Growth award Wartburg Coll., 1963, Community Service award, 1975, Chief Thunderbird award, 1985. Mem. Am. Assn. C.C., Am. Assn. Sch. Adminstrs., N.W. Assn. Cmty. and Jr. Colls., Wash. Assn. C.C. (pres. 1984-85), Wash. C.C. Computing Consortium (chmn. bd. dirs. 1985-87), Puget Sound Naval Bases Assn. (pres. 1982-86), Wash. Assn. C.C. Pres. (pres. 1984-85), Bremerton Area C. of C. (pres. 1977-78), Colo. Assn. C.C. Pres. (pres. 1993-94), Rotary (pres. Sterling Club 1992-93), Kappa Delta Pi, Phi Delta Kappa. Lutheran. Home: 1290 Raven Creek Dr NW Bremerton WA 98311-9042

MILANICH, JERALD THOMAS, archaeologist, museum curator; b. Painesville, Ohio, Oct. 13, 1945; s. John Joseph and Jean Marie (Bales) M.; m. Maxine L. Margolis, Dec. 20, 1970; 1 child, Nara Bales. BA, U. Fla., 1967, MA, 1968, PhD, 1971. Fellow Smithsonian Inst., Washington, 1971-72; asst. prof. anthropology U. Fla., Gainesville, 1972-75; asst. curator Fla. Mus. Natural History, 1975-77, assoc. curator, 1977-81, chmn. dept. anthropology, 1981-83, 91-94, curator, 1981—. Editl. bd. Archaeology Mag., 1992-2002, contbg. editor, 2002--. Author: (with Samuel Proctor) Tacachale -- Essays on the Indians of Florida and Southeastern Georgia During the Historic Period, 1978; (with Charles Fairbanks) Florida Archaeology, 1980; McKeithen Weeden Island, 1984; Early Prehistoric Southeast, 1985; (with Susan Milbrath) First Encounters, Spanish Explorations in the Caribbean and the United States, 1492-1570, 1989; The Hernando de Soto Expedition, 1990; Earliest Hispanic-Native America Interactions in the Greater American Southwest, 1991; (with Charles Hudson) Hernando de Soto and the Indians of Florida, 1993, Archaeology of Precolumbian Florida, 1994, Florida Indians and the Invasion of Europe, 1995, The Timucua, 1996, Archaeology of Northern Florida, 1997, Florida Indians From Ancient Times to the Present, 1998, Laboring in the Fields of the Lord: Spanish Missions and Southeastern Indians, 1999, Famous Florida Sites: Mount Royal and Crystal River, 1999. Recipient Ripley P. Bullen award, 1980, Rembert Patrick Book award, 1994-95; grantee NSF, 1970-71, 73-75, 77-82, Wentworth Found., 1976-77, 81-84, 91, NEH, 1985, 87-89, Fla. Divsn. Hist. Resources, 1981, 83-89, 91, 96-97, 2000-02. Mem. Soc. Am. Archaeology (exec. bd. 1990-93), Soc. Profl. Archeologists (cert., pres. 1981-82), So. Anthrop. Soc., S.E. Archeol. Conf. (pres. 1986-88). Office: Fla Mus Natural History Gainesville FL 32611-7800

MILANO, BERNARD JOSEPH, professional services company executive; b. Pennsauken, N.J., May 20, 1940; s. Joseph and Mildred Lucy (Casey) M.; m. Mary Nicolina Fitzgerald, Sept. 29, 1962 (div. 1985); children: Diane, Lisa, Karen, Michael; m. Sharon Gay Pierson, Aug. 2, 1985; children: Matthew, Adam. BS in Acctg., Temple U., 1961; D (hon.), N.C. A&T State U., 1998. Auditor Peat Marwick, Phila., 1961-75, with N.J., 1975; ptnr. univ. rels., diversity and alumni programs KPMG Peat Marwick, Montvale. Exec. dir., bd. trustee KPMG Found.; mem. Human Resources Leadership Team, KPMG Peat Marwick; bd. dirs. Students Free Enterprise, Episcopal Ch. Found., Leadership Edn. and Devel. Program in Bus., Inc., Adminstrs. Acctg. Programs Group, Project Equality, 1995, Nat. Consortium Ednl. Access, Inc., 1993-96, Fedn. Schs. Acctg., 1988-90; bd. govs. Sigma Phi Epsilon Nat. Found.; dean's adv. bd. U. Ariz., James Madison U., Temple U. (Outstanding Alumnus Bus. Sch. award 1992); acctg. adv. bd. Brigham Young U., Fla. State U., Fordham U., U. N.C.; pres.'s bd. govs. Ramapo Coll.; mem. corp. adv. bd. Golden Key Nat. Honor Soc. (Pres.' award 1993), Consortium Grad. Study Mgmt; bd. dirs. Am. Assembly Collegiate Schs. Bus., 1992-95, nominating com., 1992, 93, 95, exec. com., 1973-75, acctg. visitation com., 1989-90, acctg. accreditation com., 199-91, strategic issues com., 1991-92. Founding mem., trustee, v.p. Allendale (N.J.) Found. Ednl. Excellence, Inc.; mem. audit com. Episcopal Diocese Newark, past mem. commn. ministry; bd. dirs. N.J. chpt. ARC, 1995; past mem. bd. edn. City of Darien, Conn.; treas. Ch. Epiphany, Allendale, 1988-92, jr. warden, 1993, sr. warden, 1994, chair rector search com., 1989, mem. search com., 1995. Mem. Assn. Corp. Recruiting Execs., Am. Acctg. Assn. (v.p. 1992-95, exec. com. 1992-95, fin. com. 1992-95, chmn. 1993-94, edn. adv. com. 1987-92), Beta Alpha Psi (pres.-elect). Office: KPMG Peat Marwick LLP 3 Chestnut Ridge Rd Montvale NJ 07645-1842

MILANOVICH, NORMA JOANNE, training and development company executive; b. Littlefork, Minn., June 4, 1945; d. Lyle Albert and Loretta (Leona) Drake; m. Rudolph William Milanovich, Mar. 18, 1943 (dec.); 1 child, Rudolph William Jr. BS in Home Econs., U. Wis., Stout, 1968; MA in Curriculum and Instrn., U. Houston, 1973, EdD in Curriculum and Program Devel., 1982. Instr. human svcs. dept. U. Houston, 1971-75; dir. videos project U. N.Mex., Albuquerque, 1976-78, dir. vocat. edn. equity ctr., 1978-88, asst. prof. occupational edn., 1982-88, coord. occupational vocat. edn. programs, 1983-88, dir. consortium rsch. and devel. in occupational edn., 1984-88; pres. Alpha Connection Tng. Corp., 1988—; exec. dir. Trinity Found., 1991—; pres. Athena Leadership Ctr., 1999—. Adj. instr. Cen. Tng. Acad., Dept. Energy, Wackenhut; mem. faculty U. Phoenix; adj. faculty So. Ill. U., Lesley Coll., Boston. Author: Model Equitable Behavior in the Classroom, 1983, Handbook for Vocational-Technical Certification in New Mexico, 1985, A Vision for Kansas: Systems of Measures and Standards of Performance, 1992, Workplace Skills: The Employability Factor, 1993; editor: Choosing What's Best for You, 1982, A Handbook for Handling Conflict in the Classroom, 1983, Starting Out...A Job Finding Handbook for Teen Parents, Going to Work...Job Rights for Teens; author: JTPA Strategic Marketing Plan, 1990, We, The Arcturians, 1990, Sacred Journey to Atlantis, 1991, The Light Shall Set You Free, 1996; editor: Majestic Raise newsletter, 1996—, Celestial Voices newsletter, 1991—. Del. Youth for Understanding Internat. Program, 1985—90; mem. adv. bd. Southwestern Indian Poly. Inst., 1984—88; com. mem. Region VI Consumer Exch. Com., 1982—84; ednl. lectures, tng., tour dir. internat. study tours to Japan, Austria, Korea, India, Nepal, Mex., Eng., Greece, Egypt, Australia, New Zealand, Fed. Republic Germany, Israel, Guatemala, Peru, Bolivia, Chile, Easter Island, Tibet, China, Hong Kong, Turkey, Italy, Russia, Ukraine, Sweden, Norway, France, Kenya, Tanzania, Zimbabwe, North Pole Arctic Region, Antarctica, Argentina, Ireland, Scotland, New Zealand, Fiji, Australia, Bali, Palau, The Amazon, Galapagos Islands, Ethiopia, Mongolia, Gobi Desert, Portugal, Spain, Poland, Austria, Sicily, U.S.; facilitator, dir. Ann. Worldwide Confs., 1999, 2000; keynote spkr., workshop tng. presenter worldwide; coord. Worldwide Conf. for Peace on Earth in Portugal, India, 1999, India, 2000, Rome, 2001, Jordan, 2002, Washington, 2002, Bahamas, 2002; Bd. dirs. Albuquerque Single Parent Occupational Scholarship Program, 1984—86. Grantee N.Mex. Dept. Edn., 1976-78, 78-86, 83-86, HEW, 1979, 80, 81, 83, 84, 85, 86, 87. Mem. ASTD, Am. Vocat. Assn., Vocat. Edn. Equity Coun., Nat. Coalition for Sex Equity Edn., Am. Home Econs. Assn., Inst. Noetic Scis., N.Mex. Home Econs. Assn., N.Mex. Vocat. Edn. Assn., N.Mex. Adv. Coun. on Vocat. Edn., Greater Albuquerque C. of C., NAFE, Phi Delta Kappa, Phi Upsilon Omicron, Phi Theta Kappa. Democrat. Roman Catholic. Office: Athena Leadership Ctr Scottsdale AZ 85259 E-mail: info@athenalctr.com.

MILASKI, JOHN JOSEPH, business transformation industry consultant; b. Johnson City, N.Y., Sept. 16, 1959; s. John Walter and Nellie Joan (Panaro) Milaski; m. Ann Mildred Caldwell, Jan. 22, 1994; children: Ian Alexander, Isaac Nicholas. AAS, Broome C.C., 1979; BSEE, Rochester Inst. Tech., 1984; MBA, Syracuse U., 1991. Registered engr., N.Y.; cert. bus. transformation cons. Design engr. IBM, Endicott, N.Y., 1979-84, systems engr., 1984-85, mktg. cons., 1985-91, cons. Cons. & Sys. Integration Svcs. upstate N.Y., 1992-94, cons. Worldwide Document Mgmt. Solutions Group, 1995-96, con. Worldwide Cons. Svcs., 1996-99; prin. IBM WW BT Cons. Svcs., 2000—. Ga. state advisor to Nat. Rep. Senatorial Com., 1997. Inventor. Vol. IBM Olympic Force Team 1996 Summer Olympics; trust mgr. Nat. Trust for Hist. Preservation; charter mem. Statue of Liberty-Ellis Island Found., Inc.; founding mem. Nat. Wall of Tolerance. Recipient Utilities Industry Mktg. Excellence award IBM Systems Engring. Symposium, 1989, 91. Mem. IEEE (sr.), ASME (sr.), Am. Mgmt. Assn., Am. Prodn. and Inventory Control Soc. (sr.), Internat. Platform Assn., Computer and Automated Sys. Assn., N.Y. State Sheriff's Assn., Ga. State Sheriff's Assn., Ga. State Troopers Assn., U.S. Holocaust Meml. Mus. (charter mem.), IBM 100 Percent Club, U.S. C. of C., Internat. Directory of Disting. Leadership, Nat. Mus. of the Am. Indian (charter), Nat. WWII Meml. Soc. (charter), Am. Battle Monuments Commn. (charter), Libr. of Congress (charter), Nat. Trust for Historic Preservation, Centennial Olympic Pk. in Atlanta (constructing donor). Republican. Roman Catholic. Avocations: skiing, travelling, boating. Home: 2315 Sagamore Pl Cape Coral FL 33914-2571

MILAVSKY, HAROLD PHILLIP, real estate executive; b. Limerick, Sask., Can., Jan. 25, 1931; s. Jack and Clara M. B in Commerce, U. Sask., Saskatoon, Can., 1953; LLD (hon.), U. Sask., 1995, U. Calgary, 1995. Chief acct., treas., controller Loram Internat. Ltd. div. Mannix Co. Ltd., Calgary, Alta., Can., 1956-65; v.p., chief fin. officer Power Corp. Devels. Ltd., Can., 1965-69; exec. v.p., bd. dirs. Great West Internat. Equities Ltd. (name now Trizec Corp. Ltd.), Can., 1976-94; pres. Trizec Corp. Ltd., Can., 1976-86, bd. dirs. Can., 1976-94, chmn. Can., 1986-93, Quantico Capital Corp., Calgary, 1994—. Bd. dirs. Consol. Properties Ltd., Citadel Diversified Mgmt., Ltd., Calgary, ENMAX Corp., Prime West Energy Inc., Calgary, Aspen Properties, Ltd., Calgary, Torode Realty, Ltd., Calgary. Past dir. Conf. Bd. Can., Terry Fox Humanitarian Award Program; past gov. Acctg. Edn. Found. Alta.; hon. col. 14th Svc. Battalion, Calgary; bd. dirs. Tennis Can., chmn., 2001—. Recipeint B'nai Brith award of merit, 1952, Commemorative medal 125th Birthday of Can., 1992. Fellow Inst. Chartered Accts. Alta.; mem. Inst. Chartered Accts. Sask., Can. Inst. Pub. Real Estate Cos. (past pres., bd. dirs.), Can. C. of C. (past chmn.), Internat. Profl. Hockey Alumni (founding dir.), Petroleum Club, Ranchmen's Club. Avocations: skiing, tennis, horseback riding. Office: Quantico Capital Corp 1920-855 Second St SW Calgary AB Canada T2P 4J7

MILBANK, JEREMIAH, foundation executive; b. N.Y.C., Mar. 24, 1920; s. Jeremiah and Katharine (Schulze) M.; m. Andrea Hunter, July 19, 1947 (dec. Oct. 1982); children: Jeremiah III, Victoria Milbank Whitney, Elizabeth Milbank Archer, Joseph H.; m. Rose Jackson Sheppard, May 4, 1991 (dec. Feb. 1998); m. Mary G. Rockefeller, Jan. 25, 1999. BA, Yale U., 1942; MBA, Harvard U., 1948; L.H.D. (hon.), Ithaca (N.Y.) Coll., 1976, Sacred Heart U., Conn.; LL.D., Manhattan Coll. With J.M. Found., N.Y.C., pres., 1971—. Pres. Turkey Hill Corp., 1972—. Author: First Century of Flight in America, 1942. Chmn. emeritus Boys and Girls Clubs Am.; hon. pres. Internat. Ctr. for the Disabled, 1991—; fin. chmn. Rep. Nat. Com., 1969-72, 75-77. Lt. USNR, 1943-46. Mem. River Club (N.Y.C.), Round Hill Club (Greenwich), Yale Club. Republican. Home: 84 Grandview Ave Rye NY 10580-2007 Office: 60 E 42nd St New York NY 10165-0006

MILBOURNE, WALTER ROBERTSON, lawyer; b. Phila., Aug. 27, 1933; s. Charles Gordon and Florie Henderson (Robertson) M.; m. Georgena Sue Dyer, June 19, 1965; children: Gregory Broughton, Karen Elizabeth, Walter Robertson, Margaret Henderson. AB, Princeton U., 1955; LL.B., Harvard U., 1958. Bar: Pa. 1959. Assoc. firm Pepper, Hamilton & Sheetz, Phila., 1959-65, Obermayer, Rebmann, Maxwell & Hippel, Phila., 1965-67, ptnr., 1968-84, Saul, Ewing, Remick & Saul, 1984-2000, of counsel, 2001—. Bd. dirs. Pa. Lumbermen's Mut. Ins. Co., Phila. Reins. Corp.; co-chmn. Nat. Conf. Lawyers and Collection Agys., 1979-90; chmn. bus. litigation com. Def. Rsch. Inst., 1986-89, mem. law instsn. com., 1989-95. Chmn. mental health budget sect. Phila. United Fund, 1967—70; pres. Found. Internat. Assn. Def. Counsel, 1997—2001. Fellow: Am. Coll. Trial Lawyers (mem. internat. com. 1992—96); mem.: ABA, Internat. Assn. Def. Counsel (exec. com. 1985—88), Phila. Bar Assn., Pa. Bar Assn., Phila. Lawn Tennis Assn. (pres. 1969—70), Merion Cricket Club. Republican. Home: 689 Fernfield Cir Wayne PA 19087-2002 Office: Saul Ewing Remick & Saul 3800 Centre Sq W Philadelphia PA 19102 E-mail: Waltermilb@aol.com.

MILBRATH, MARY MERRILL LEMKE, quality assurance professional; b. Evanston, Ill., Aug. 13, 1940; d. William Frederick and Martha Merrill (Slagel) Lemke; m. Gene McCoy Milbrath, Aug. 22, 1964; children: Elizabeth Ann, Sarah Toril Jeanne. BA in Biology, Albion Coll., 1962; MS in Plant Pathology, U. Ariz., 1966. Microbiologist Abbott Labs., North Chicago, Ill., 1962; toxicologist U. Ariz., Tucson, 1965-67, U. Ill., Urbana, 1976-77, entomologist, 1978; plant pathologist State of Oreg., Salem, 1979, chemist, 1980-82; quality auditor Siltec Corp., 1983-84, quality control supr., 1985-91, quality auditing mgr., 1992-97, implementor ISO 9002, 1995, implementor ISO 9001 Quality Std., 1996, quality assurance dir., 1997—; implementor ISO 14001 Siltec Corp., 1998. Active Ill. Emergency Svcs.toxic sub task force U. Ill., Urbana, 1978; mem. Responsible Corp. Citizens Com., Salem, 1989-96. Mem. citizens adv. com. Sch. Bd., Urbana, 1976-78; campaigner Oreg. 5th Dist. Race, Salem, 1984, Oreg. Nat. Abortion Rights Assn. League, Salem, 1986; bd. dirs. Tribute to Outstanding Women, YWCA, 1992, 93, 94, 95; vol. Tree Giving, 1991, 92. NDEA fellow U.S. Dept. Def., 1962; elected Woman of Achievement, YWCA, 1997. Mem. AAUW (chmn. interest group), Am. Soc. for Quality (cert. quality auditor exam writing com. 1993, 95, exam rev. 1996, 98, 2002, spkr. nat. conf. 1999), Willamette U. House Corp. (treas. 1982-85, v.p. 1991-96, mem.-at-large 2000—, treas. 2001--), Delta Gamma (treas. Salem Alumnae chpt. 1981-85, pres. Salem Alumnae chpt. 1987-89, scholarship advisor Willamette U. chpt. 1986-90). Avocations: family activities, travel, painting. Office: Mitsubishi Silicon Am 1351 Tandem Ave NE Salem OR 97303-4105

MILBRATH, ROBERT HENRY, retired petroleum executive; b. Apr. 17, 1912; s. Paul and Mabel (Volkman) M.; m. Margaret Ripperger, Jan. 19, 1940; children: Robert S., Constance, Susan. BS, U.S. Naval Acad., 1934. With Standard Oil Co. N.J., 1934-74; v.p., gen. mgr. Esso Sociedad Anonima Petrolera Argentina, 1938-42, 45-50; area contact East Coast South Am., mktg. coordination, 1950-52; dir. Internat. Petroleum Co., 1954—, v.p., 1956; v.p., dir. Esso Export Corp. N.Y., 1957-59, exec. v.p., dir., 1959-61; pres., dir. chmn. exec. com. Esso Internat., Inc. (formerly Esso Export Corp.), 1961-66; exec. v.p. Esso Europe, 1966-68; logistics coordinator Standard Oil Co. (N.J.) (now Exxon Corp.), 1968-69, dir., v.p., 1969-70, dir., sr. v.p., 1970-73, ret., 1974. Cons. Boys Clubs Am., 1978-84. Served to lt. comdr. USNR; asst. naval attache 1942, Buenos Aires; chief Latin Am. sect. Army-Navy Petroleum Bd. 1943-45, Washington. Mem. U.S. Naval Acad. Alumni Assn. Clubs: University (N.Y.C.), Ponte Vedra Club. Republican. Home: 13847 Silkvine Ln Jacksonville FL 32224-9621

MILBURN, RICHARD HENRY, physics educator; b. Newark, June 3, 1928; s. Richard Percy and Lucy Elizabeth (Karr) M.; m. Nancy Jeannette Stafford, Aug. 25, 1951; children— Sarah Stafford, Anne Douglas. AB, Harvard U., 1948, A.M., 1951, PhD, 1954. Instr. Harvard U., Cambridge, Mass., 1954, 56-57, asst. prof., 1957-61; assoc. prof. physics Tufts U., Medford, 1961-65, prof., 1965-98, John Wade prof., 1990-98, rsch. prof., 1998—. Fulbright lectr., India, 1984 Trustee Cambridge Friends Sch., 1989-95. With U.S. Army, 1954-56. Sheldon travelling fellow, 1948-49; NSF fellow, 1952-53; Guggenheim fellow, 1960 Fellow Am. Phys. Soc. (past chmn. New Eng. sect.); mem. Am. Assn. Physics Tchrs., AAAS, AAUP. Achievements include research on high energy and elementary particles physics. Home: 1 Plymouth Rd Winchester MA 01890-3620 Office: Tufts Univ Medford MA 02155

MILBURY-STEEN, SALLY LOUISE (SARAH MILBURY-STEEN), not-for-profit association administrator, advocate; b. Wilmington, Del., Jan. 25, 1943; d. Frank Douglas and Lillian Alice Jasa Milbury; m. John Norvel Steen, May 3, 1974; 1 child, Blythe Rebecca. BA in Comparative Lit., U. Wis., 1965; MA in Comparative Lit., Ind. U., 1970, PhD in Comparative Lit., 1975. Tchr. English as Fgn. Lang. U.S. Peace Corps, Sangmélima, Cameroun, 1965-67; tchr. English Western H.S., Washington, 1970-72; asst. instr. Comparative Lit. Dept. Ind. U., Bloomington, 1968-70, 72-74; Fulbright Hayes sr. lectr. Nat. U. of Gabon, Libreville, Gabon, 1975-77; coord. Freeze Voter, Wilmington, Del., 1984; adminstrv. asst. Physicians for Social Responsibility, 1985; exec. dir. De Pacem in Terris, Inc., 1985—. Author: (book) European and African Sterotypes in Twentieth Century Fiction, 1980; editor (newsletter) Delmarva Peacework, 1990—. Peace cons. New Castle Presbytery, Newark, Del., 1985—, Bd. Ch. and Society Peninsula-Del. Conf. United. Meth. Ch., Dover, Del, 1985-2000; co-clk. Friends Peace Com., Phila., 1991-98; founder, officer Del. Citizens Opposed to Death Penalty, Wilmington, 1992—; co-facilitator Healing Our Nation, Wilmington, 1997—; mem. Civil Rights Commn., Wilmington, 1993-95, 96-97; v.p. bd. Newark Ctr. for Creative Learning. Recipient Spirit of the Am. Woman, J.C. Penney Co., Pa., Del., N.J. Region, 1990, Cmty. Builder award Nat. Conf. for Cmty. and Justice, Wilmington, 1996; named Paul Harris fellow Rotary Club Caesar Rodney chpt., Wilmington, 1997. Mem. Soc. Friends. Avocations: hanging clothes on the line, reading and travel. Office: De Pacem in Terris 1304 N Rodney St Wilmington DE 19806-4227 E-mail: pinterris@aol.com.

MILDER, DAVID GEOFFREY, oral and maxillofacial surgeon; b. Shaw AFB, S.C., Mar. 24, 1960; s. Jay Joel Milder and Laurel Lynn Tamkin; m. Theresa Tsai, Dec. 22, 1985; children: Melissa, Megan. BS, U. Calif., Irvine, 1981; DDS, UCLA, 1986; MD, U. Mo., Kansas City, 1991. Surg. intern Truman Med. Ctr., 1992, resident in oral and maxillofacial surgery, 1987-92; med. technologist UCLA Hosp., 1982-87; pvt. practice as dentist Hawthorne, Calif., 1986-87; pvt. practice as oral and maxillofacial surgeon San Diego, 1993—. Bd. trustees Mission Bay Hosp., San Diego, 1998-2000. Mem. ADA, San Diego County Dental Soc. (bd. dirs. 1996—, chair dental care coun. 1997-2000), Am. Assn. of Oral and Maxillofacial Surgeons, Calif. Dental Assn., Acad. of Osseointegration, Calif. Med. Assn., Phi Beta Kappa, Alpha Omega Alpha, Omicron Delta Upsilon. Avocations: running, biking, rollerblading. Office: 3737 Moraga Ave Ste B216 San Diego CA 92117-5495 E-mail: dmilder@pol.net.

MILDVAN, DONNA, infectious diseases physician; b. Phila., June 20, 1942; d. Carl David and Gertrude M.; m. Rolf Dirk Hamann; 1 child, Gabriella Kay. AB magna cum laude, Bryn Mawr Coll., 1963; MD, Johns Hopkins U., 1967. Diplomate Am. Bd. Internal Medicine and Infectious Diseases. Intern, resident Mt. Sinai Hosp., N.Y.C., 1967-70, fellow, infectious diseases, 1970-72; asst., assoc. prof. clin. medicine Mt. Sinai Sch. Medicine, 1972-87; prof. clinical medicine Dept. Medicine, Mt. Sinai Sch. Medicine, 1987-88, prof. medicine, 1988-94; physician-in-charge infectious diseases Beth Israel Med. Ctr., 1972-79, chief, div. infectious diseases, 1980—; prof. medicine Albert Einstein Coll. of Medicine, 1994—. Mem. AIDS charter rev. com., NIH/Nat.

Inst. Allergy and Infectious Diseases, Bethesda, 1987—; cons. FDA, Rockville, 1987—, Ctrs. for Disease Control, Atlanta, 1985-86; among first to describe AIDS, "Pre-AIDS", AIDS Dementia, 1982, among first to study AZT, 1986; Keynote speaker, II Internat. Conf. on AIDS, Paris, 1986 and other achievements in field; Sophie Jones Meml. lectr. in infectious diseases U. Mich. Hosps., 1984. Contbr. numerous articles to profl. jours; co-editor two books, several book chpts. and abstracts on infectious diseases and AIDS. Grantee N.Y. State AIDS Inst., 1986-87; Henry Strong Denison scholar Johns Hopkins U. Sch. Medicine, 1967; recipient Woman of Achievement award AAUW, 1987; contract for antiviral therapy in AIDS, Nat. Cancer Inst./Nat. Inst. Allergy and Infectious Diseases, 1985-86, subcontract Nat. Inst. Allergy and Infectious Diseases, ACTU, 1987-99, prin. investigator, 2000—. Fellow Infectious Diseases Soc. Am.; mem. Am. Soc. Microbiology, AAAS, Harvey Soc., Internat. AIDS Soc. Democrat. Jewish. Avocation: old movies. Office: Beth Israel Med Ctr 1st Ave New York NY 10003-7903

MILEDI, RICARDO, neurobiologist; b. Mexico City, Sept. 15, 1927; m. Ana Mela Garces, Dec. 17, 1955; 1 child, Rico. BSc, Instituto Cientifico y Literario, Chihuahua, Mex., 1945; MD, U. Nacional Autonoma de Mex., 1955; Doctor Honoris Causa, Universidad del Pais Vasco, 1992, U. Trieste, Italy, 2000, U. Chihuahua, Mex., 2000. Researcher Instituto Nacional de Cardiologia, Mex., 1954-56; fellow John Curtin Sch. Med. Res., Canberra, Australia, 1956-58; mem. faculty U. Coll., London, 1959-85, Foulerton research prof. of Royal Soc., 1975-85, head dept. biophysics, 1978-85; Disting. prof. dept. neurobiology and behavior U. Calif., Irvine, 1984—. Editor Archives of Med. Rsch. Trustee PEW L.Am. Fellows Program. Recipient Principe de Asturias prize, Spain, 1999. Fellow Royal Soc. London (Royal medal 1999), Am. Acad. Arts and Scis.; mem. AAAS, NAS, 3d World Acad. Scis., (titular) European Acad. Arts, Scis., Humanities, N.Y. Acad. Scis., Hungarian Acad. Scis. (hon.), Mex. Acad. Scis., Mex. Acad. Medicine. Home: 9 Gibbs Ct Irvine CA 92612-4032 Office: U Calif Dept Neurobiology Behavior 2205 Bio Sci Ii Irvine CA 92697-4550 E-mail: rmiledi@uci.edu.

MILES, ARTHUR J. financial planner, consultant; b. N.Y.C., Sept. 2, 1920; s. Levi and Rachel Goldsworthy (Hiscock) M.; m. Pearl Cooper, Nov. 27, 1947; children: Beverly Miles Kerns, Douglas Robert. BBA, Pace U., 1958; MBA, NYU, 1963; postgrad., Dartmouth Coll., 1966, Brown U., 1970-71. Instr. Brown U., Providence, 1970-71; with Dime Savs. Bank, N.Y.C., 1938-81, exec. v.p., treas., 1975-78, sr. exec. v.p., treas., 1978-81; pres. AJM Assocs., Floral Park, N.Y., then Sarasota, Fla., 1981—. Newscaster Sta. WUSF-FM, Tampa, Fla.; bd. dirs. Cultural Instns. Retirement System, N.Y.C., 1968—; fin. cons. Bklyn. Inst. Arts and Scis., 1972—. Trustee, nat. treas. Alcoholics Anonymous, N.Y.C., 1970-79; tech. adviser N.Y.C. Fin. Liason Com., 1975-76. Served to sgt., inf. U.S. Army, 1942-45, Philippines. Fellow Fedn. Fin. Analysts; mem. Nat. Assn. Bus. Economists, Internat. Assn. Fin. Planners, Broadcast Pioneers, NYU Club, Marco Polo Club (N.Y.C.), Tournament Players Club. Republican. Office: AJM Assocs 8325 Shadow Pine Way Sarasota FL 34238-5624

MILES, BRIAN JOHN, urologist; b. Belfast, Ireland, Nov. 8, 1946; s. William Livingston and Kathleen (Jamison) M.; m. Renee' Gig DeBlaise, Sept. 15, 1990. BS, Mich. State U., 1967; MS in Engring., U. Mich., 1968, MD, 1974. Diplomate Am. Bd. Urology. Intern surgery Georgetown U., Washington, 1974-75; resident urology Walter Reed Army Med. Ctr., 1978-82; instr. Dept. of Urology Mich. Army Med. Ctr., Tacoma, 1982-84; instr. Dept. of Surgery U. Washington, Seattle, 1982-84; staff physician Dept. of Surgery Henry Ford Hosp., Detroit, 1984-91; assoc. prof. U. Mich., Ann Arbor, 1984-93; dir. resident edn. Henry Ford Hosp., Detroit, 1987-93, dir. urologic oncology, 1988-93; assoc. prof. Scott Dept. of Urology, Houston, 1993-2000; prof. Scott Dept. Urology, 2000—; chief of urology VA Med. Ctr., 1993-98, St. Luke's Episcopal Hosp., Houston, 1993—. Assoc. editor: (book) Comprehensive Textbook of Genitourinary Oncology, 1995. Ltc. Army Med. Corp, 1975-84. Mem. ACS, Am. Urologic Assn. (Prostate Cancer Outcomes Analysis Grant 1995, 96), Soc. Urologic Oncology, Soc. of Univ. of Urologist, Societe' Internat. d'Urologie. Avocations: history, sports, reading. Home: 3781 Farbar St Houston TX 77005-3713 Office: Scott Dept of Urology 6560 Fannin St Ste 2100 Houston TX 77030-2769

MILES, CHRISTINE MARIE, museum director; b. Madison, Ind., Mar. 2, 1951; d. Leland Weber and Mary Virginia (Geyer) M. BA, Boston U., 1973; MA, George Washington U., 1982; postgrad., Mus. Mgmt. Inst., 1985. Curatorial asst. Mus. City of N.Y., 1973-75; art gallery dir. South Street Seaport Mus., N.Y.C., 1975-77; rschr. The Octagon, AIA Found., Washington, 1978-80; dir. Fraunces Tavern Mus., 1980-86, Albany (N.Y.) Inst. History and Art, 1986—. Bd. dirs. SUNY-Albany Found. Author, writer/coordinator, compiler of catalogs in field. Mem. Arts Commn. City of Albany; pres. Gallery Assn. N.Y. State, 1991-93, Mus. Assn. N.Y. State. Mem. Am. Assn. Mus. Office: Albany Inst History and Art 125 Washington Ave Albany NY 12210-2296

MILES, DAVID MICHAEL, lawyer; b. Jackson, Mich., Aug. 5, 1954; s. Richard George and Joann Marie (Stefanoff) M.; m. Noelle Suzanne McHugh, Sept. 6, 1986; children: Amy Elizabeth, Margaret Noelle, Lane McHugh. Student, U. Mich., 1972-74; BA cum laude, Clark U., 1976; JD magna cum laude, George Washington U., 1979. Bar: D.C. 1979, U.S. Ct. Appeals (4th cir.) 1980, U.S. Dist. Ct. Md. 1980, U.S. Dist. Ct. D.C. 1983, U.S. Supreme Ct. 1983, U.S. Ct. Appeals (D.C. cir.) 1981, U.S Ct. Appeals (9th cir.) 1984, U.S. Ct. Appeals (2d cir.) 1986. Law clk. to Chief Judge Edward Northrop, U.S Dist. Ct. Md., 1979-80; law clk. to Cir. Judge George MacKinnon U.S. Ct. Appeals, Washington, 1980-81; assoc. Fried, Frank, Harris, Shriver & Jacobson, 1981-86, ptnr., 1986-92, Sidley & Austin, Washington, 1992—. Co-author: The Law of Financial Services, 1988; contbr. articles to profl. jours. Democrat. Roman Catholic. Home: 5229 Westpath Way Bethesda MD 20816 Office: Sidley, Austin, Brown & Wood 1501 K St NW Washington DC 20005 E-mail: DavidM9876@aol.com., dmiles@sidley.com.

MILES, DAVID R. lawyer; b. Richmond, Ind., Apr. 13, 1955; s. John R. and Joyce L. M.; m. Mary E. McMorrow, Apr. 17, 1982; children: Julie, Kathleen. BA in Polit. Sci., Wittenberg U., 1977; JD, U. Toledo, 1980. Bar: Ohio 1981, U.S. Dist. Ct. (so. dist.) Ohio 1981. Pvt. practice, Fairborn, Ohio, 1981—. Editor Dayton Bar Assn. Mem. S.W. Ohio Assn. Businessmen, Phi Gamma Delta. Avocation: sports. Office: 125 W Main St Ste 201 Fairborn OH 45324-4749

MILES, DONALD ORVAL, clinical microbiologist; b. Callaway, Nebr., May 29, 1939; s. Kermit Lester and Pearl Merna (Johnson) M.; m. Paula Dee Ragsdale, June 12, 1960 (div. Nov. 1982); 1 child, Jennifer Lynne; m. Vicki Dee Dillow, Nov. 23, 1988; stepchildren: Denise Rene Chamness Steck Vargas, Ricky Lee Chamness (dec.), Rhonda Len Chamness. BA, Hastings (Nebr.) Coll., 1964; student, U. Nebr., 1957-60, MS, 1967, PhD, 1972. Cert. specialist in pub. health and med. microbiology; cert. massage therapist; cert. in med. herbalism. Instr. dept. microbiology U. Nebr., Lincoln, 1972; postdoctoral fellow dept. oral biology Coll. Dentistry, U. Nebr., 1973; asst. prof. Sch. Health Scis. Grand Valley Colls., Allendale, Mich., 1973-76; chief sect. microbiology and immunology, dept. pathology St. Mary's Hosp., Grand Rapids, 1976-81; clin. microbiologist, sect. supr. lab. dept. St. Francis Med. Ctr., Cape Girardeau, Mo., 1981—; established Caring Touch Massage Therapy Ctr., 1992. Adj. faculty dept. biology S.E. Mo. U., Cape Girardeau, 1983—; researcher S.E. Mo. Coop. Lyme Disease Rsch. Group, 1989-95. Editorial cons. Biol. Abstracts, RRM Med. and Clin. Microbiology, Phila., 1984—; contbr. articles to profl. jours. Bd. dirs. West YMCA, Grand Rapids, 1981; bd. dirs., vol. ARC, Cape Girardeau, 1982-89; mem. choir St. Mary's Ch., Anna, Ill., 1988-94. Comdr. USNR, 1956-92, ret. Nat. Inst. Dental Rsch. fellow, 1973. Mem. Am. Soc. for Microbiology, Nebr. Acad. Sci. (emeritus), Am. Soc. Clin. Pathologists, South Ctrl. Assn. Clin. Microbiology, Soc. Healthcare Epidemiologists Am., Am. Herbalist Guild, Am. Body Workers and Massage Profls., Sigma Xi. Avocations: walking/jogging, singing, home wine, bread making and medical herbalism, growing herbs. Home: 350 State Highway Y Jackson MO 63755-7744 Office: Lab Dept St Francis Med Ctr 211 Saint Francis Dr Cape Girardeau MO 63703-5049

MILES, DONNA REGINA, educator, researcher; b. Albuquerque, Dec. 17, 1969; d. John Herman Gieske, Helen Edith Gieske; m. Thomas Raymond Miles; children: Ashleigh, Brittany, Madeline. BS, U. N.Mex., 1991; PhD, U. Colo., 1997. Postdoctoral fellow Nat. Inst. on Drug Abuse, Balt., 1997—98, Inst. for Drug and Alcohol Studies, Va. Commonwealth U., Richmond, 1998—2001; asst. prof. dept. human genetics Va. Commonwealth U., 2001—. Fellow, U. Colo., Boulder, 1992—93; scholar Bldg. Interdisciplinary Rsch. Careers in Women's Health award scholar, 2001. Mem.: Behavioral Genetics Assn., Phi Beta Kappa. Office: Va Commonwealth Univ PO Box 980003 Richmond VA 23298 Business E-Mail: dmiles@hsc.vcu.edu.

MILES, DORIS COOPER, bank executive; b. Camp Le June, N.C., Jan. 16, 1963; d. Thomas Wayne and Linda Gene (DuVall) Cooper; 1 child J. Brian. Sales and mktg. sec. Hawthorne at Leesburg, Fla., 1989—91; contr. to Delta Techop and Credit Union Norrell Svcs., Atlanta, 1991—93; workers compensation adminstr. Riscorp, Maitland, Fla., 1995—96; sales and leasing adminstr. Jaymark Bldrs., Clermont, 1996—98; EAS contr. to IBM Norrell Spherion, Atlanta, 1998—2000, Orlando, Fla., 2000—01; dealer fin. sec. Independent Bank, Cleveland, Tenn., 2001—. Author: (booklet) To the Policy Holder, 1994, (book) Mommy and the Masher, 1996, The Storm's Heart, 1998, Between Love and Duty, 2001. Avocations: motivational speaking, travel, photography. Home: 2941 Eastview Ter SE Cleveland TN 37323

MILES, FRANK CHARLES, retired newspaper executive; b. Detroit, Jan. 1, 1926; s. Nelson and Ethel Jane (Mennill) M.; m. Catharine Estelle Coleman, Sept. 4, 1948; children: Barbara Ann, Diana Estelle. Student, Westervelt Bus. Coll., 1947-48. With Thomson Newspapers Ltd., Cambridge, Ont., Can., 1950-52, 54-55; bus. mgr. Sarnia (Ont.) Obs., 1952-54; gen. mgr. Pembroke (Ont.) Obs., 1956-58, Moose Jaw (Sask.) Times-Herald, Can., 1958-62; pub. Austin (Minn.) Daily Herald, 1962-66; sr. v.p., gen. mgr. Thomson Newspapers Inc., Des Plaines, Ill., 1966-89, exec. v.p. acquisitions, 1990-91, ret., 1991, also bd. dirs. Vol. assignments Internat. Media Fund, Baltics, Albania, 1992-93; Knight fellowship Moscow, 1994, Ctrl. for Ind. Journalism, Bucharest, Romania, 1995, Kocise Slovakia, 1996, Internat. Rsch. & Exch. Corp., Zagreb, Croatia, Belarus, 1997, Brest, Minsk, Belarus, 1997-98. Mem. Sigma Delta Chi. Republican. Mem. United Ch. of Christ. Home: 3892 Bordeaux Dr Punta Gorda FL 33950

MILES, GAVIN WENTWORTH, lawyer; b. Cambridge, Mass., Sept. 10, 1960; s. Perry Ambrose and Kathleen (McCartney) B.; m. Sarah Jane Berger, Jan. 16, 1995; 1 child: Benjamin. BA in Pol. Sci., Columbia Coll., 1982; JD, Emory U., 1989. Bar: N.Y. 1990. Asst. dist. atty. King's County (N.Y.) Dist. Atty's. Office, Bklyn., 1989-94, sr. asst. dist. atty., 1994-96, spl. counsel, rackets, 1996-2000, dep. bur. chief, rackets, 2000-01, 1st dep. bur. chief, rackets, 2001—. Mem. N.Y.C. Bar Assn. (criminal cts. com. 1996-98). Avocation: history. Office: Kings County DA'S Office 350 Jay St Brooklyn NY 11201-2900

MILES, HARRY LEHMAN, lawyer, educator; b. May 4, 1944; s. Sidney and Beatrice (Lehman) M. AB, Dartmouth Coll., 1965; JD, Bklyn. Law Sch., 1969; MA in Comms., U. Mass., Amherst, 1972. Tchr. James Madison H.S., Bklyn., 1966-70; instr. U. Mass., Amherst, 1970-72; practice law, 1971-75; asst. dist. atty. Northwestern Dist., Mass., 1975-79, 1st asst. dist. atty., 1979-80; ptnr. Growhoski, Callahan & Miles, Northampton, 1980-94, Green, Miles, Lipton, White & Fitz-Gibbon, Northampton, 1994—. Past adj. prof. law Western New Eng. Coll. Sch. Law; v.p., dir. Western Mass. Legal Services Corp. Mem. Shutesbury (Mass.) Bd. Health, 1972-74, Shutesbury Fin. Com., 1973-74. Fellow Am. Acad. Forensic Scis. (jurisprudence sect.), Am. Coll. Trial Lawyers, Mass. Bar Found.; mem. ABA, Mass. Bar Assn., Hampshire County Bar Assn., Franklin County Bar Assn., Mass. Assn. Criminal Defense Lawyers, Dartmouth Lawyers Assn. Democrat. Office: Green Miles Lipton White Fitz-Gibbon 77 Pleasant St PO Box 210 Northampton MA 01060-0210 E-mail: harrymiles@aol.com.

MILES, JACK (JOHN RUSSIANO), journalist, educator; b. Chgo., July 30, 1942; s. John Alvin and Mary Jean (Murphy) M.; m. Jacqueline Russiano, Aug. 23, 1980; 1 child, Kathleen. LittB, Xavier U., Cin., 1964; PhB, Pontifical Gregorian U., Rome, 1966; student, Hebrew U., Jerusalem, 1966-67; PhD, Harvard U., 1971. Asst. prof. Loyola U., Chgo., 1970-74; asst. dir. Scholars Press, Missoula, Mont., 1974-75; postdoctoral fellow U. Chgo., 1975-76; editor Doubleday & Co., N.Y.C., 1976-78; exec. editor U. Calif. Press, Berkeley, 1978-85; book editor L.A. Times, 1985-91, mem. editl. bd., 1991-95; dir. Humanities Ctr. Claremont (Calif.) Grad. U., 1995-97; Mellon vis. prof. Calif. Inst. Tech., 1997-98; sr. advisor to pres. J. Paul Getty Trust, L.A., 1999—. Contb. editor Atlantic Monthly, 1995—. Author: Retroversion and Text Criticism, 1984, God: A Biography, 1995, Christ: A Crisis in the Life of God, 2001; contbr. learned and popular articles to various periodicals; book reviewer. Recipient Pulitzer prize for biography, 1996; Guggenheim fellow, 1990-91. Mem. PEN, Nat. Book Critics Circle (pres. 1990-92), Am. Acad. Religion, Amnesty Internat. Episcopalian. Office: J Paul Getty Trust 1200 Getty Center Dr Ste 1100 Los Angeles CA 90049-1688

MILES, JESSE MC LANE, retired accounting company executive; b. De Funiak Springs, Fla., June 17, 1932; s. Percy Webb and Dora (Pippin) M.; m. Catherine Rita Eugenio, July 18, 1959; children: Jesse Jr., Catherine, Teresa, John, Thomas, Robert BSBA, U. Fla., 1954. C.P.A., N.Y. Mem. staff, mgr., prin. Arthur Young & Co., N.Y.C., 1954-63, ptnr., 1963-89, dep. chmn.-internat., 1985-89; chmn. Arthur Young Internat., 1985-89; ptnr. Ernst & Young, 1989-92; co-chmn. Ernst & Young Internat., 1989-92; ret., 1992. Mem. AICPA, N.Y. Inst. CPAs, Burning Tree Country Club (Greenwich, Conn.), Blind Brook Club (Rye Brook, N.Y.), Boca Pointe Country Club (Boca Raton, Fla.). Home: 7077 Via Mediterrania Boca Raton FL 33433

MILES, JIM, state official; Prof. of law Greenville Tech. Coll.; Sec. of State State of S.C., 1991—. Mem. Soc. Internat. Bus. Office: Sec of State PO Box 11350 Columbia SC 29211-1350*

MILES, JOHN BILL, accountant, tax advisor; b. Knox County, Ky., Sept. 18, 1931; s. John Ishmael and Allie Arizona (Engle) M.; m. Mary Patricia Wilson, May 25, 1963; children: Melanie, Jennifer, Dennis. BSC, Salmon P. Chase Coll., Highland Heights, 1962; BS in Acctg., U. Cin., 1972; MBA, Lincoln Grad. Sch. Mgmt., Des Moines, 2001. CPA; accredited tax advisor; enrolled agt. Cost acct. Avco Corp., Cin., 1956-58; chief auditor Pepsi-Cola Bottling Co., 1958-64; property acct. Monsanto Co., Addyston, Ohio, 1964-66; sec.-treas. Shur-Good Biscuit Co., Inc., Cin., 1966-79; acct. Fabritec Internat. Corp., Cold Spring, Ky., 1980-98; ind. practice acctg. Cheviot, Ohio, 1999—. Lt. Col. Ohio Mil. Res. Mem.: NRA, AICPA, Ohio Assn. Ind. Accts., Nat. Soc. Accts., Ohio Soc. CPAs, Honorable Order Ky. Cols., Am. Legion, Assn. U.S. Army, Fur Takers of Am., Accts. for Pub. Interest, Ohio Mil. Res. Assn., Cheviot Rep. Club. Home: 3816 Roswell Ave Cincinnati OH 45211-3329

MILES, JOHN CARLEN, II, dental company executive; b. Portland, Maine, Feb. 22, 1942; s. John Carlen and Dorothy Clare (Hanson) M.; m. Anna Maria Chico, Sept. 10, 1977; children— Karen, Shirley, Lawrence, Suzanne BSI.E., Lehigh U., 1964; MBA, NYU, 1971. Mfg. mgr. Permacel div. Johnson & Johnson, New Brunswick, N.J., 1964-71; prodn. planning mgr. Coty div. Pfizer, Inc., Sanford, N.C., 1971-73; v.p.-gen. mgr. FDI Inc., Edison, N.J., 1973-78; sr. v.p., gen. mgr. Rhone-Poulenc, Inc., Monmouth Junction, 1978-85; chmn., CEO Dentsply Internat. Inc., York, Pa., 1986—96, chmn., CEO, 1996—. Bd. dirs. Respironics Inc. Bd. dirs. Nat. Found. Dentistry for the Handicapped. Recipient Clause V. Swank award Johnson & Johnson, 1967 Mem.: Am. Dental Trade Assn. (bd. dirs.), Bonita Bay Country Club (Fla.), Country Club of York. Republican. Presbyterian. Avocations: golf, boating, reading. Home: 3700 Springetts Dr York PA 17402-9027 Office: Dentsply Internat Inc 570 W College Ave York PA 17404-3880

MILES, JOHN FREDERICK, retired manufacturing company executive; b. Fredericton, N.B., Can., Aug. 13, 1926; s . Ralph Edward and Hazel Jean (Young) M.; m. Frances Power, Oct. 2, 1950; children: John F., Robert D., Dalyce J., Leytha J. Sr. Matric, U. N.B., 1944; B.Sc. in Chem. Engring., Queen's U., Kingston, Ont., Can., 1948. Prodn. mgr. Dominion Steel & Coal Corp. Ltd., 1948-65, jr. engr., 1948-49, battery foreman coke ovens, 1949-51, gen. foreman coke ovens, 1951-56, rsch. engr. coke ovens and blast furnaces, 1956-57, asst. supt. blast furnace dept., 1957-58, asst. to gen. supt., 1958-60, asst. works mgr. Sidney Works, 1960-62, gen. mgr. Etobicoke Works, 1962-65; works mgr. Slater Steels—Hamilton Splty. Bar Div. (div. Slater Industries), Hamilton, Ont., Can., 1965-66, Can., 1966-71, v.p. mfg. Can., 1971-86, div. pres. Can., 1986-91, pres., CEO Can., 1991-93, bd. dirs. Can., 1991-99. Mem. Assn. Profl. Engrs. Ont., Assn. Iron and Steel Engrs. E-mail: johnmiles73@hotmail.com.

MILES, KENNETH ONTARIO, academic program director; b. Washington; s. Lessie Olivia Walker. BA, U. Va., 1992, MEd, 1998. Tchr., coach Gonzaga Coll. High Sch., Washington, 1993-95; acad. lifeskills coord. U. Va., Charlottesville, 1995-97; coord. acad. support football Syracuse (N.Y.) U. Athletic Dept., 1997—2002; dir. student svcs. Sch. Info. Studies Syracuse (N.Y.) U., 2002—. Mem. Black Coaches Assn., Nat. Assn. Advisors Athletics (chmn. ethnic concerns com. 1999-2000). Democrat. Baptist. Avocation: weight training. Office: Syracuse U Sch Info Studies 4-206 Ctr for Sci and Tech Syracuse NY 13244-4100 Fax: 315-443-5673. E-mail: komiles@syr.edu.

MILES, LELAND WEBER, university president; b. Balt., Jan. 18, 1924; s. Leland Weber and Marie (Fitzpatrick) M.; m. Mary Virginia Geyer, July 9, 1947; children: Christine Marie, Gregory Lynn. AB cum laude, Juniata Coll., 1946; MA, U. N.C., 1947, PhD, 1949; postgrad., Duke U., 1949; DLitt (hon.), Juniata Coll., 1969; LHD (hon.), Rosary Hill Coll., 1970; LLD (hon.), Far East U., 1979; DHC (hon.), U. Guadalajara, Mex., 1984; Order of Merit, Alfred U., 1986. Assoc. prof. English Hanover Coll., 1949-50, prof., chmn. English dept., 1950-60; assoc. prof., asst. to head English dept. U. Cin., 1960-63, prof., 1963-64, founder humanities reading program for engrs., 1961; dean Coll. Arts and Scis., U. Bridgeport, Conn., 1964-67; pres. U. Bridgeport, 1974-87; founder U. Bridgeport Sch. Law, 1977; pres. emeritus U. Bridgeport, 1987—; pres. Alfred U., 1967-74. Bd. dirs. United Illuminating, 1978-94, chmn. audit com., 1992-94, Grolier, 1984-88, Wright Managed Investment Funds, 1988—, Internat. Peace Acad., 1982-90, mem. adv. coun., 1990—; Danforth scholar Union Theol. Sem., 1956; Lilly fellow Sch. Letters Ind. U., 1959; Am. Council Learned Socs. fellow Harvard, 1963-64; Sr. Fulbright Research scholar Kings Coll. U. London, 1964, vis. scholar, 1972; seminar leader, deans and presidents insts. Am. Council on Edn., 1973-79; chmn. bd. Acad. Collective Bargaining Info. Service, Washington, 1977-79; producer, moderator Casing the Classics CBS Sta. WHAS-TV, Louisville, 1958-61; moderator Aspen (Colo.) Inst. for Humanistic Studies, 1969-70; lectr. Keedick Lecture Bur., N.Y.C., 1956-83. Author: John Colet and the Platonic Tradition, 1961; editor: St. Thomas More's Dialogue of Comfort Against Tribulation, 1965, Where Do You Stand On Linquistics?, 1964, revised, 1968; sr. editor: (with Stephen Graubard and later Stephen B. Baxter) Studies in British History and Culture, 1965-79, Provoking Thought: What Colleges Should Do For Students, 2001; contbg. editor Nat. Forum, 1983-91, editl. advisor, 1991-94; contbr. articles to learned jours., chpts. in books. Trustee Western N.Y. Nuclear Rsch. Ctr., 1967-73; chmn. bd. Coll. Ctr. Finger Lakes, 1968-71; vice-chmn. bd. Empire State Found., 1969-71, chmn., 1971-73; mem. New Eng. Bd. Higher Edn., 1985-87, Ambs. Roundtable, 1986-92, Fuld Found./Nat. League Nursing Adv. Coun. on Accreditation, 1986-88; chmn. Ettinger scholarship com. Ednl. Found. Am., 1987-93; bd. dirs. Conn. Grand Opera, 1978-89, Bridgeport Bus. Coun., 1982-88; bd. dirs. Save the Children, 1988-95, chmn. adv. coun., 1990-95. 1st lt. USAAF, 1944-45; capt. USAFR. Decorated DFC with oak leaf cluster, Crown Decoration of Honor 3rd Order Iran, 1978; chevalier l'Ordre des Palmes Académique (France), 1984; recipient Rosa and Samuel Sachs prize Cin. Inst. Fine Arts, 1961, Cultural medal Republic of China, 1983, Disting. Svc. award Greater Bridgeport Bar Assn., 1986, Outstanding Civilian Svc. medal Dept. Army, 1988; Miles scholars Alfred U., 1995—. Fellow Royal Soc. Arts, Manufactures and Commerce (life); mem. Renaissance Soc. Am., English Speaking Union (bd. dirs. Greenwich, Conn. chpt. 1998—), Internat. Assn. Univ. Pres. (pres. 1981-84, pres. emeritus 1984—, chief UN mission 1988-97, World Peace award 1987, chmn. UN commn. on arms control edn. 1991-96, mem. coun. sr. advisers 1992—), Knights of Malta (order of the Orthodox Knights Hospitaller of St. John of Jerusalem, Russian orthodox br.), Phi Kappa Phi. Clubs: Univ. (N.Y.C.); Country of Fairfield (Conn.). Episcopalian. Home: 87 Field Point Dr Fairfield CT 06430-6329

MILES, RAY, technology executive; b. Sarajevo, Bosnia-Herzegovina, Mar. 24, 1952; arrived in U.S., 1996; BSc in elec. engring. and computer sci., U. Sarajevo, 1974; MSc in elec. engring. and computer sci., U. Zagreb, Croatia, 1981; PhD in elec. engring. and computer sci., U. Sarajevo, 1987; MBA, So. Meth. U., 1999. Prof. computer sci. U. Sarajevo, Bosnia-Herzegovina, 1987—92; divsn. dir. mktg. and engring. Energoinvest, Bosnia-Herzegovina, 1977-92; sr. rsch. fellow, mgr. tech. alliances, mgr. internat. bus. devel. British Telecom, London, 1992—96; branch mgr., COO Deutsche Telekom/Sun Consortium, 1996—2001; bus. mgr. Tex. Instruments, Dallas, 1996—2001; pres. comm. svcs. Electronic Data Sys., Plano, 2001—. Mem. bd. dirs. U. Sarajevo, 1989-91, CERD, Sarajevo, 1989-92, World Affairs Coun. of Greater Dallas, 1998-, MCC, Austin, Tex., 1998-2000; prin. info. tech. adv. Dept. Defense, Belgrade, former Yugoslavia, 1987-92; mentor, StarTech, Richardson, Tex.; mem. Dallas Com. on Fgn. Affairs. Author: Programming in Pascal, 1986, Programming in Macro-II, 1987, Global Currency, 1995; editor: Experience with Management of Software Projects, 1990; adv. editor Engring. Applications of Artificial Intelligence-Elsevier, 1988-95. Lt. Navy, 1979-80. Mem. IEEE (sr.), Am. Coun. on Germany. Avocations: classical music, art, skiing, photography, hiking.

MILES, RAYMOND EDWARD, former university dean, organizational behavior and industrial relations educator; b. Cleburne, Tex., Nov. 2, 1932; s. Willard Francis and Wilma Nell (Owen) M.; m. Lucile Dustin, Dec. 27, 1952; children: Laura, Grant, Kenneth. BA with highest honors, U. North Tex., 1954, MBA, 1958; PhD, Stanford U., 1963. Clk. Santa Fe R.R., Gainesville, Tex., 1950-55; instr. mgmt. Sch. Bus. U. North Tex., Denton, 1958-60; asst. prof. organizational behavior and indsl. relations Sch. Bus. Adminstrn. U. Calif.-Berkeley, 1963-68, assoc. prof., 1968-71, prof., 1971—, assoc. dean Haas Sch. of Bus., 1978-81, dean, 1983-90; dir. Inst. Indsl. Relations, 1982-83; cons. various pvt., pub. orgns. Author: Theories of Management, 1975, (with Charles C. Snow) Organization Strategy, Structure and Process, 1978, (with Charles C. Snow) Fit, Failure, and the Hall of Fame, 1994; co-author: Organizational Behavior: Research and Issues, 1976; co-editor, contbg. author: Organization by Design: Theory and Practice, 1981. Served to 1st. lt. USAF, 1955-58. Mem. Indsl. Relations Research Assn., Acad. Mgmt. Democrat. Unitarian Universalist. Home: 8640 Don Carol Dr El Cerrito CA 94530-2733 Office: U Calif Walter A Haas Sch Bus Berkeley CA 94720-0001 E-mail: miles@haas.berkeley.edu.

MILES, RICHARD BRYANT, mechanical and aerospace engineering educator; b. Washington, July 10, 1943; s. Thomas Kirk and Elizabeth (Bryant) M.; m. Susan McCoy, May 14, 1983; children: Thomas, Julia. BSEE, Stanford U., 1966, MSEE, 1967, PhD in Elec. Engring., 1972. Rsch. assoc. elec. engring. dept. Stanford (Calif.) U., summer 1972; asst. prof. mech. and aerospace engring. dept. Princeton (N.J.) U., 1972-78, assoc. prof., 1978-82, prof., 1982—, chmn. engring. physics program, 1980-96. Lectr. Northwestern Poly. U., Xian, China, 1987; rsch. scientist CNRS; vis. prof. U. Marseilles, France, 1995; acting dept. chmn. Princeton U., 2002.. Contbr. articles to profl. publs., chpt. to book Advances in Fluid Mechanics Measurements, 1989; patentee in field. Bd. dirs. Fannie and John Hertz Found., Livermore, Calif., 1989—. Fannie and John Hertz Found. fellow, 1969-72. Fellow AIAA (Aerodynamic Measurement Tech. TC award 2000) Optical Soc. Am.; mem. IEEE (sr.), Am. Phys. Soc. Office: Princeton U Mech & Aerospace Engring D-414 Eng Quad Olden St Princeton NJ 08544-0001

MILES, RICHARD R. writer, curator; b. Tokyo, Apr. 1, 1938; s. Robert Henri and Eleanor Alfrida Perreau-Saussine; m. Xuong-Hong Quach, Feb. 1, 1994. BA, Georgetown U., 1958, UCLA, 1960, MFA, 1980. Cert. tchr., Calif.; cert. adminstrv., Calif. Actor, L.A., 1945-60; novelist, 1965-72; pres. Burbank (Calif.) Tchrs. Assn., 1977-79; dir. Meilinki Enterprises Ltd., L.A., 1982—. Author: (novels) That Cold Day In The Park, 1965, Angel Loves Nobody, 1969, The Moon Bathers, 1972, (non-fiction) Prints of Paul Jacoulet, 1980, Watercolors of Paul Jacoulet, 1988, Elizabeth Keith-The Printed Works, 1992, Printmaker in Paradise: Charles W. Bartlett, 2001. Recipient Samuel Goldwyn award, UCLA, 1979, 80. Mem. Writers Guild Am., New England Appraisers Assn. Avocations: reading.

MILES, RICHARD ROBERT, art historian, writer; b. Tokyo, Apr. 1, 1939; s. Robert Henri and Eleanor Alfrida (Child) Perreau-Saussine. BA, UCLA, 1972. Novelist, screenwriter various, 1965-72; dir. Meilinki Enterprises Ltd.,

1980—. Bd. dirs. Balcom Trading Co., Tokyo, 1979-82. Author: That Cold Day in the Park, 1965 (Dell Book award 1965), Angel Loves Nobody, 1967 (Samuel Goldwyn award UCLA, 1969); (art history) Prints of Paul Jacoulet, 1982, Elizabeth Keith-The Prints, 1989, The Watercolors of Paul Jacoulet, 1992, Printmaker in Paradise: Charles W. Bartlett, 2001, others. Mem. Internat. Soc. of Fine Art Appraisers, New Eng. Appraisers Assn., Writers Guild of Am. West, Acad. of Am. Poets. Office: Meilinki Enterprises Ltd 214 N Bowling Green Way Los Angeles CA 90049-2816

MILES, ROBERT HENRY, management consultant, educator; b. Norfolk, Va., Mar. 10, 1944; s. Henry Bateman and Mildred Verda (Cuthrell) M.; m. Jane Irving Calfee, Aug. 27, 1966; children: Alexander Bateman, Holen Irving. BS, U. Va., 1967; PhD, U. N.C., 1974. Ops. analyst Ford Motor Co., Norfolk, 1968; project mgr. Advanced Rsch. Projects Agy. Office Sec. Def., Washington, 1970-71; asst. prof., co-founder Mgmt. Inst., U. Ala. Grad. Sch. Bus., Tuscaloosa, 1974-75; asst. prof. Sch. Orgn. and Mgmt. Yale U., New Haven, 1975-78; assoc. prof. Harvard Bus. Sch., Boston, 1978-85; vis. prof. Stanford Exec. Inst., Palo Alto, Calif., 1987-95; Isaac Stiles Hopkins prof. orgn. & mgmt. Goizueta Bus. Sch. Emory U., Atlanta, 1987-89; dept. dean Emory U. Bus. Sch., 1989-90, dean of faculty, 1990-93, Hopkins fellow, 1995—; mem. sec.'s adv. bd. U.S. Dept. Energy, Washington, 1993-96; prin. Corp. Transformation Resources, Atlanta and Boston, 1996—. Adv. bd. orgn. effectiveness programs The Conf. Bd., N.Y.C., 1994—; mem. adv. bd. McIntire Sch. Commerce, U. Va., Charlottesville, 1987-95; mem. exec. adv. bd. Ivan Allen Coll., Ga. Inst. Technology, 1997—. Author: Macro Organizational Behavior, 1980; (with J.R. Kimberly) The Organizational Life Cycle: Issues in the Creation, Transformation, and Decline of Organizations, 1980, Managing the Corporate Social Environment: A Grounded Theory, 1987; (with K.S. Cameron) Coffin Nails and Corporate Strategies, 1982, (with A. Bhambri) The Regulatory Executives, 1983; (with W.A. Randolph) The Organization Game: A Simulation, 1979, 83, 93, Corporate Comeback: The Renewal and Transformation of National Semiconductor, 1996, Leading Corporate Transformation: A Blueprint for Business Renewal, 1997; mem. edit. bd. Adminstrv. Sci. Quar., 1978-86, Mgmt. Sci., 1979-82. 1st lt. U.S. Army, 1969-71. Recipient Disting. Svc. award Emory U., 1993. Mem. Acad. Mgmt. (chmn. orgn. and mgmt. theory divsn. 1984-85), Strategic Mgmt. Soc., Harvard Club (Boston), Commerce Club (Atlanta), Cherokee Town Club (Atlanta), Beta Gamma Sigma. Unitarian Universalist. Avocations: boating, tennis. Home: # 4 177 Fox Hill Rd # 4 Chatham MA 02633-1413 also: 177 Fox Hill Rd Chatham MA 02633-1413

MILES, RUBY ALICE BRANCH, librarian, consultant; b. Houston, Sept. 6, 1941; d. Richard A. and Ernestine (Phelps) Branch; m. Emerson Edward Miles, Apr. 18, 1970 (dec. Mar. 1971). BS in Edn., Prairie View U., 1963; MSLS, Atlanta U., 1969. Cert. librarian, Tex. Sch. librarian Aldine Ind. Sch. Dist., Houston, 1963-65, Houston Ind. Sch. Dist., 1965-68, 77—; children/young adult librarian Atlanta Pub. Libr. Sys., 1969-71, br. librarian III, 1971-77; campus librarian Houston C.C. Sys., 1985-998; reference med. libr. Houston Acad. of Medicine - Tex. Med. Ctr. Libr., 1998—; libr. Houston C.C. Sys., 1985—. Libr. cons. Internat. Christian Inst., Houston, 1991-95. Vol. storyteller Tex. Children's Hosp., Houston, 1991-97. Mem. ALA (mem. com. 1990-96), Tex. Libr. Assn. Democrat. Methodist. Avocations: reading, travel. Office: Michael E DeBakey HS for Health Professions 3100 Shenandoah St Houston TX 77021-1042 Fax: 713-746-5211. E-mail: rmiles@houstonisd.org.

MILES, RUBY WILLIAMS, secondary education educator; b. Petersburg, Va., Jan. 19, 1929; d. Richard Allen and Elizabeth (Penny) Williams; m. John Oscar Miles, Jan. 7, 1950 (div. 1966); children: Karen Jonnia Miles George, Steven Ricardo. BA, Va. State Coll., Petersburg, 1971, MA, 1977. Cert. high sch. tchr., Va. Tchr. English Dinwiddie (Va.) Sch., 1971-78, Clarksville (Tenn.) Sch., 1978-80, Petersburg Pub. Schs., 1982—, head English dept., 1991-96, ret., 1996; instr. St. Paul's Coll., Lawrenceville, Va., 1981-82; asst. prof. St. Leo Coll., Ft. Lee, 1988; instr. english/speech Bethany Baptist Church, Petersburg, VA, 1998—. Tchr., counselor Upward Bound project Va. State U., summer, 1974; tchr. Hopewell Pub. Schs., Va. summer 1983—; instr. John Tyler C.C., Fort Lee Va., 1992—; adj. prof. Richard Bland Coll., Coll. William and Mary, Va., 2001—. Songwriter: A Day in September. Bd. dirs. Playmaker Fellows Ltd., Petersburg, 1983; co-dir. Exclusively Youth Models, 1984-85. Recipient Leadership award Va. Edn. Assn., 1985. Mem. Petersburg Edn. Assn. (past pres.), Am. Bus. Women's Assn., Nat. Orgn. for Women, Nat. Assn. Female Execs., NEA, Nat. Coun. Tchrs. English, Jr. Civic League, Delta Sigma Theta. Avocations. writing, traveling. Home: 2733 Rollingwood Rd Petersburg VA 23805-2317

MILES, SAMUEL I(SRAEL), psychiatrist, educator; b. Munich, Mar. 4, 1949; came to U.S., 1949; s. Henry and Renee (Ringel) M.; m. Denise Marie Robey, June 26, 1977; children: Jonathan David, Justin Alexander. BS, CCNY, 1970; MD, N.Y. Med. Coll., 1974; PhD, So. Calif. Psychoanalytic Inst., 1986. Diplomate Am. Bd. Psychiatry and Neurology with added qualifications in forensic psychiatry and addiction psychiatry. Intern D.C. Gen. Hosp., Washington, 1974-75; resident in psychiatry Cedars-Sinai Med. Ctr., Los Angeles, 1975-78; practice medicine specializing in psychiatry, 1978—; ind. med. examiner Calif. Dept. Indsl. Relations, 1984-91, qualified med. examiner, 1991—. Asst. clin. prof. psychiatry UCLA Sch. Medicine, 1978-97, assoc. clin. prof., 1998—; assoc. clin. chief dept. psychiatry Cedars-Sinai Med. Ctr., 1998-99; mem. faculty So. Calif. Psychoanalytic Inst., 1986—; mem. psychiat. panel Superior Ct. Los Angeles County, 1990—, Fed. Ct., 1990—. Fellow Am. Psychiat. Assn., Am. Acad. Psychoanalysis, Am. Orthopsychiat. Assn.; mem. Acad. Psychiatry and the Law, Am. Coll. Legal Medicine, Am. Coll. Addiction Psychiatry, Calif. Psychiat. Assn. (mem. managed care com. 1991-96), So. Calif. Psychiat. Soc. (coun. rep. 1985-88, 92-95, chairperson pvt. practice com. 1988-92, sec. 1991-92, 2002—, mem. worker's compensation com. 1992—, treas. 1997-98), So. Calif. Psychoanalytic Inst. (pres. clin. assocs. orgn. 1981-82, mem. admissions com. 1988—, mem. ethics stds. com. 1991-92, chair ethics stds. com. 1993-98, mem. exec. com. 1993-98). Jewish. Avocations: aviation, swimming. Office: 8631 W 3rd St Ste 425E Los Angeles CA 90048-5908

MILES, THOMAS CASWELL, aerospace engineer; b. Atlanta, Mar. 21, 1952; s. Franklin Caswell and Eugenia Frances (Newsom) M.; m. Linda Susan Duggleby, Aug. 10, 1980. BMET, So. Poly. State U., 1977; postgrad., Troy State U., 1978-80. Assoc. engr. aircraft design Lockheed Martin Aero. Co., Marietta, Ga., 1980-82, engr., aircraft design, 1982-85, sr. engr., aircraft design, 1985-89, group engr., 1989-90, specialist engr., 1990-98, sr. specialist engr., 1998-2001, staff engr., 2001—. Mem. SAE-A-6 Mil. Aircraft & Helicopter Panel, 1987-91, SAE-A-10 Aircraft Oxygen Equipment Com., 1996—. Mem. AIAA, (assoc. fellow), ASME, ASTM, Nat. Mgmt. Assn. (bd. dirs. 1996-2000), Soc. Automotive Engrs. (SAE co. rep., SAE Atlanta sect. vice chmn. aircraft), Oxygen Standardization Coord. Group, Assn. Fraternity Advisors (affiliate), Wick's Lake Homeowners Assn. (pres. 1995, v.p. 1996, 97), Tau Kappa Epsilon (Providence advisor 1999—, dist. pres. 1987-88, dist. v.p. 1984-99, chpt. advisor 1980-87, key leader 1985, 90, So. Order of Honor 1989). Avocations: sailing, screen printing. Home: 1926 Wicks Ridge Ln Marietta GA 30062-6777 E-mail: tekezeke@aol.com.

MILES, TRAVIS ANTHONY, state senator; b. Dec. 6, 1937; s. Paul McDill and Stella (McCrary) M.; 1 dau., Laura Lynne Maxwell. Student, Phillips U., 1954-59. Mem. Ark. Senate, 1981—94; pres. Miles, Beals & Assocs. Advt. Agy., Inc., Ft. Smith, 1961—2001; ret., 2001. Served with U.S. Army, 1953-64. Pres. Coun. Boy Scouts Am., 1977-78; pres. Ft. Smith Girl's Club, 1979-81, hon. girl, 1979. Named Outstanding Young Man, Jaycees, 1967; recipient Silver Beaver award Boy Scouts, 1968, disting. svc. award, 1979, outstanding svc. award St. Edward Med. Ctr., 1979, Svc. to Mankind award Sertoma Club, 1982. Rep. Pioneer award Ark. Rep. Party, 1996, numerous civic profl. and govtl. awards. Mem. Fort Smith/Van Buren Advt. Fedn. (pres. 1972-73), Old Ft. Christian Bus. Men (chmn. com. 1976-78), Kiwanis (past pres.). Mem. Christian Ch. (Disciples Of Christ). Home: 5426 Highland Dr Fort Smith AR 72903-1414

MILES, WENDELL A. federal judge; b. Holland, Mich., Apr. 17, 1916; s. Fred T. and Dena Del (Alverson) M.; m. Mariette Bruckert, June 8, 1946; children: Lorraine Miles, Michelle Miles Kopinski, Thomas Paul. AB, Hope Coll., 1938, LLD (hon.), 1980; MA, U. Wyo., 1939; JD, U. Mich., 1942; LLD (hon.), Detroit Coll. Law, 1979. Bar: Mich. Ptnr. Miles & Miles, Holland, 1948-53, Miles, Mika, Meyers, Beckett & Jones, Grand Rapids, Mich., 1961-70; pros. atty. County of Ottawa, 1949-53; U.S. dist. atty. Western Dist. Mich., Grand Rapids, 1953-60, U.S. dist. judge, 1974—, chief judge, 1979-86, sr. judge, 1986—. Cir. judge 20th Jud. Cir. Ct. Mich., 1970-74; instr. Hope Coll., 1948-53, Am. Inst. Banking, 1953-60; adj. prof. Am. constl. history Hope Coll., Holland, Mich., 1979— ; mem. Mich. Higher Edn. Commn.; apptd. Fgn. Intelligence Surveillance Count, Washington, 1989—. Pres. Holland Bd. Edn., 1952-63. Served to capt. U.S. Army, 1942-47. Recipient Liberty Bell award, 1986. Fellow Am. Bar Found.; mem. ABA, Mich. Bar Assn., Fed. Bar Assn., Ottawa County Bar Assn., Grand Rapids Bar (Inns of Ct. 1995—), Am. Judicature Soc., Torch Club, Rotary Club, Masons. Office: US Dist Ct 236 Fed Bldg 110 Michigan St NW Ste 452 Grand Rapids MI 49503-2363 E-mail: miles@miwd.uscourts.gov.

MILES, WILLIAM TRICE, state legislator; b. Fulton, Miss., Jan. 6, 1938; s. Ira Matison and Ellen Ozema (Webb) M.; m. Patricia Ann Reed, May 16, 1957; William T. Jr., Pattie Miles Cox. BA, U. Miss., 1959. Journalist Itawamba Times, Fulton, Miss., 1954-56; pub. rels. exec. Miss. State U., Starkville, 1958-59; journalist Tupelo (Miss.) Jour., 1959-63; journalism instr. Itawamba C.C., Fulton, 1959-69; CEO Bill Miles Assocs., Inc., Tupelo, 1963-95; editor, publisher, owner The Amory (Miss.) Advertiser, 1972-80, The Nettleton (Miss.) News, 1975-80; rep. 21st dist. Miss Ho. of Reps., Jackson, Miss., 1996—. Author: (manual) How to Gain and Maintain Public Confidence for Police Organizations, 1968 Mem. Itawamba County Devel. Coun., Fulton, Miss., 1985—. Mem. Sigma Delta Chi. Democrat. Mem. Ch. of Christ. Avocation: golf. Home: PO Box 246 Fulton MS 38843-0246

MILES-LA GRANGE, VICKI, judge; b. Oklahoma City, Sept. 30, 1953; d. Charles and Mary (Greenard) Miles. BA, Vassar Coll., 1974; LLB, Howard U., 1977; cert., U. Ghana, West Africa; DHL (hon.), Oklahoma City U., 1995. Legis. aide Spkr. House Rep. Carl Albert, 1974-76; law clerk Judge Woodrow Seals U.S. Dist. Ct. (so. dist.), Tex., 1977-79; fellow, atty. criminal divsn. U.S. Dept. Justice, Washington, 1979-83; asst. dist. atty. Dist. Atty.'s Office, Oklahoma County, 1983-86; pvt. practice Oklahoma City, 1986-93; mem. Okla. Senate (Dist. 48), 1987-93; U.S. atty. U.S. Dept. Justice, Oklahoma City, 1993-94; judge U.S. Dist. Ct. (we. dist.), 1994—. Bd. trustees Vassar Coll. Mem. ABA, Nat. Bar Assn., Okla. Bar Assn., Am. Inns Ct. Democrat. Baptist. Office: US Dist Judge US Courthouse 200 NW 4th St Ste 5011 Oklahoma City OK 73102-3031

MILETICH, IVO, library and information scientist, bibliographer, educator, linguist, literature research specialist; b. Pucisca, Yugoslavia, Apr. 18, 1936; came to U.S., 1966, naturalized, 1972; s. Josip and Mandina (Bagich) M.; m. Mira Pilja, Mar. 11, 1967; children: George Edward, Marina Julie. AB, Acad. Edn., Split, Yugoslavia, 1960; AM in History, U. Skopje, Macedonia, Yugoslavia, 1966; cert. advanced study, English Inst., Chgo., 1969; MA in Libr. Sci., Rosary Coll., River Forest, Ill., 1971. Cert. libr., Va. Tchr. various schs., Yugoslavia, 1959-65; asst. bibliographer Slavic langs. and lit. Joseph Regenstein and Sam Harper Librs., U. Chgo., 1967-71; tchr. Croatian lang. co-edn. YMCA Community Coll., Chgo., 1969-71, 74—; bibliographer Old Dominion U., Norfolk, Va., 1971-74; assoc. prof. libr. sci., bibliographer Chgo. State U., 1974—. Translator, interpreter English, Latin, Croatian, Serbian, Macedonian, Bulgarian, Old Ch. Slavic, Slovene, 1969—; interpreter Berlitz Trans. Ctr. Sch. Langs.; lectr. South Slavonic langs., lit., history and culture, Balkan states culture, heritage and folk lit., transl. techniques; lectr. in field. Contbr. various confs., seminars, workshops, jours., transl. of articles, studies, work on dictionary, Berlitz Transl. Svc. transl. and interpretion. Recipient cert. of appreciation YMCA C.C., Chgo., 1976, cert. Beta Phi Mu, U. Pitts., 1972, Am. Translators Assn., 1980, Assn. Coll. and Rsch. Librs., 1986. Mem. ALA, Am. Fedn. Tchrs., Assn. Coll. and Rsch. Librs., Chgo. Acad. Libr. Coun. Libr. of Congress (assoc.), Soc. Scholarly Publishing, Beta Phi Mu. Home: 618 Exchange Ave Calumet City IL 60409-3903 Office: Chgo State U Rm Lib 203 95th St at King Dr Chicago IL 60628

MILETTO, DAVID GREGORY, artist; b. Elmhurst, Ill., July 28, 1949; s. Angelo and Evelyn (Cingolane) M. BFA, Sch. Art Inst. Chgo., 1972. Author: The White Rose, 1994; exhibited at Nina Owen Ltd., Chgo., 1986, Sioux City (Iowa) Art Ctr. Biennial, 1987, N.Am. Sculpture Exhbn., Golden, Colo., 1988, 39th Ilmoiain Midwest Art Show, Quincy, Ill., 1989, Gallery La Movida, Chgo., 1989, Chgo. Internat. Sch. Art Auction, 1988, Midwestern Sculpture Exhbn., South Bend, Ind., 1990, Gallerie Stephanie, Chgo., 1993, others. Mem. Internat. Sculptures of Washington, Chgo. Artists' Coalition. Home: 167 Briarwood Ln Palatine IL 60067-7501

MILEWSKI, BARBARA ANNE, pediatrics nurse, neonatal intensive care nurse; b. Chgo., Sept. 11, 1934; d. Anthony and LaVerne (Sepp) Witt; m. Leonard A. Milewski, Feb. 23, 1952; children: Pamela, Robert, Diane, Timothy. ADN, Harper Coll., Palatine, Ill, 1982; BS, Northern Ill. U., 1992; postgrad., North Park Coll. RN, Ill.; cert. CPR instr. Staff nurse Northwest Community Hosp., Arlington Heights, Ill., Resurrection Hosp., Chgo.; nurse neonatal ICU Children's Meml. Hosp.; day care cons. Cook County Dept. Pub. Health. CPR instr. Stewart Oxygen Svcs., Chgo.; instr., organizer parenting and well baby classes and clinics; vol. Children's Meml. Hosp.; health coord. CEDA Head Start; cons. day care Cook County Dept. Pub. Health; mem. adv. bd. Cook County Child Care Resource and Referral. Vol. first aid instr. Boy Scouts Am.; CPR instr. Harper Coll., Children's Meml. Hosp.; dir. Albany Park Cmty. Ctr. Head Start, Chgo.; day care cons. Cook County Dept. Pub. Health. Mem. Am. Mortar Bd., Sigma Theta Tau.

MILEY, GEORGE HUNTER, nuclear and electrical engineering educator; b. Shreveport, La., Aug. 6, 1933; s. George Hunter and Norma Angeline (Dowling) M.; m. Elizabeth Burroughs, Nov. 22, 1958; children: Susan Miley Hibbs, Hunter Robert. BS in Chem. Engring., Carnegie-Mellon U., 1955; MS, U. Mich., 1956, PhD in Chem.-Nuclear Engring., 1959. Nuclear engr. Knolls Atomic Power Lab., Gen. Electric Co., Schenectady, 1959-61; mem. faculty U. Ill., Urbana, 1961—, prof., 1967—, chmn. nuclear engring. program, 1975-86, dir. Fusion Studies Lab., 1976—, fellow Ctr. for Advanced Study, 1985-86; dir. rsch. Rockford Tech. Assocs. Inc., 1990-94; pres., dir. rsch. NPL Assocs., 1994—. Vis. prof. U. Colo., 1967, Cornell U., 1969-70, U. New South Wales, 1986, Imperial Coll. of London, 1987; mem. Ill. Radiation Protection Bd., 1988—; mem. Air Force Studies Bd., 1990-94; chmn. tech. adv. com. Ill. Low Level Radioactive Waste Site, 1990-96; chmn. com. on indsl. uses of radiation Ill. Dept. Nuclear Safety, 1989—. Author: Direct Conversion of Nuclear Radiation Energy, 1971, Fusion Energy Conversion, 1976; editor Jour. Fusion Tech., 1980-2001; U.S. assoc. editor Laser and Particle Beams, 1982-86, mng. editor, 1987-91, editor-in-chief, 1991-2002; U.S. editor Jour. Plasma Physics, 1995—. Served with C.E. AUS, 1960. Recipient Western Electric Tchg.-Rsch. award, 1977, Halliburton Engring. Edn. Leadership award, 1990, Edward Teller medal, 1995, Scientist of Yr. award Jour. New Energy, 1996; Inst. for New Energy 1996 Scientist of the Yr.; NATO sr. sci. fellow, 1975-76, Guggenheim fellow, 1985-86, Japanese Soc. Promotion of Sci. fellow, 1994. Fellow IEEE, Am. Nuclear Soc. (dir. 1980-83, Disting. Svc. award 1980, Outstanding Achievement award Fusion Energy divsn. 1992), Am. Phys. Soc.; mem. Am. Soc. Engring. Edn. (chmn. energy conversion com. 1967-70, pres. U. Ill. chpt. 1973-74, chmn. nuclear divsn. 1975-76, Outstanding Tchr. award 1973), Sigma Xi, Tau Beta Pi. Presbyterian. Achievements include research on fusion, energy conversion, reactor kinetics. Office: U Ill 214 Nuclear Engring Lab 103 S Goodwin Ave Urbana IL 61801-2901 E-mail: georgehm@aol.com. *My professional goal has been to insure that future generations have a plentiful supply of economical, readily available energy such as offered by fusion. Not only should this insure a continued improvement in the standard of living for persons in all nations, but it should help maintain peace which is threatened by the struggle to obtain and control limited natural sources of energy.*

MILFORD, FREDERICK JOHN, retired research company executive; b. Cleve., July 1, 1926; s. Frederick Charles and Florence M.; m. Jean Irene Olson, Sept. 8, 1951; 1 child, Cheryl Lynn. BS in Physics, Case Inst. Tech., 1949; PhD in Physics, M.I.T., 1952. Instr. Case Inst. Tech., Cleve., 1952-56, asst. prof., 1956-59; div. cons. Battelle Columbus Labs., 1959-62, div. chief, 1962-64, sr. fellow, 1964-66, dir. research in phys. scis., 1966-73, scientist, 1973, dept. mgr., 1973-76, assoc. dir., 1976-85, chief scientist, 1985-87, v.p. spl. programs, 1987-89, ret., 1989. Vis. prof. physics U. Wash., 1969 Author: (with J.R. Reitz) Foundations of Electromagnetic Theory, 1960, 4th edit., 1993. Emeritus mem. adv. bd. Central Ohio Salvation Army. Served with USNR, 1945-46. George Eastman fellow, 1951-52; Focke scholar, 1948-49 Fellow Am. Phys. Soc.; mem. Masons, Army and Navy Club, Kit Kat Club. Home: 1411 London Dr Columbus OH 43221-1543

MILFORD, MURRAY HUDSON, retired soil science educator; b. Honey Grove, Tex., Sept. 29, 1934; s. Murray Lane and Vivian Ione (Hudson) M.; m. Marsha Ann Rasmussen, July 21, 1961; children: Rebecca Ione, Murray Daniel. BS in Agronomy, Tex. A&M, 1955, MS in Agronomy, 1959; PhD in Soil Science, U. Wis., 1962. Cert. profl. soil scientist. Rsch. assoc. Cornell U., Ithaca, N.Y., 1962-63, asst. prof., 1963-68, assoc. prof., 1968, Tex. A&M U., College Station, 1968-74, prof., 1974-2001; ret., 2001. Author: (lab. manual) Soils and Soil Science-Lab. Exercises, 1970. 1st lt. USAR, 1955-57. Recipient so. region award for excellence in coll. and univ. tchg. in food and agrl. scis. Nat. Assn. State Univs. and Land Grant Colls., Higher Edn. Program, USDA, 1995. Fellow AAAS, Am. Soc. Agronomy (pres. Tex. chpt. 1982-83, Resident Edn. award 1978), Soil Sci. Soc. Am. (Edn. award 1988); mem. Soil and Water Conservation Soc. (pres. Tex. coun. of chpts. 1987). Democrat. Presbyterian. Home: 3606 Tanglewood Dr Bryan TX 77802-3320 E-mail: mmilford@tca.net.

MILFORD, STEPHEN ALAN, management consultant; b. New Haven, Nov. 16, 1955; BA, Hamilton Coll., 1977; MBA, U. Va., 1981. Acct. Price Waterhouse, Stamford, Conn., 1977-79; inventory analyst Nat. Supply, Houston, 1981-82; CFO Enterprise Techs., 1982-84; merger and acquisition cons. Arthur Young, Washington, 1984-87; treas. Cosma/Magna Internat., Brampton, Ont., Can., 1987-89; v.p. corp. devel. Laidlaw Waste Systems, Burlington, Can., 1989-91; CEO Milford Consulting Assocs., Vt., 1991—. V.p. fin. Sovcan Star Satellite, Montreal, Que., Can., 1992-93; CFO, v.p. fin. Vt. Teddy Bear Co., Shelburne, 1995; bd. dirs. Chgo. Bicycle Co., Burlington, Vt., 1996-98; chmn., CEO, City Web, Inc., 1998-2000; gen. mgr. Elysium Power Solutions, Pensacola, Fla., 2000--. Office: Elysium Power Solutions 5603 N W St Pensacola FL 32505

MILGRAM, JEROME H. marine and ocean engineer, educator; b. Phila., Sept. 23, 1938; s. Samuel J. and Fannie M. BSEE, BS in Naval Architecture and Marine Engring., MIT, 1961, MS, 1962, PhD in Hydrodynamics, 1965. Registered profl. engr., Mass. With Scripps Inst. Oceanography, San Diego, summer 1961; project engr. Block Assocs., Cambridge, Mass., 1961-67; asst. prof. MIT, 1967-70, assoc. prof., 1970-77, prof. ocean engring., 1977-89, William I. Koch prof. marine tech., 1989—. Rsch. assoc. in biophysics Harvard U. Med. Sch., 1974-76; vis. prof. in naval architecture and marine engrng. U. Mich., 1988-89; design dir. Am. 3 Found., 1991-95; guest investigator Woods Hole Oceanog. Instn., 1996—; vis. prof. Johns Hopkins U., 1996-97. Contbr. articles to profl. jours.; patentee in field. Recipient Am. Bur. Shipping award, 1961, Alan Berman Outstanding Rsch. Publ. award U.S. Naval Rsch. Lab., 1990, AT&T Design Innovation award, 1992. Fellow Soc. Naval Archs. and Marine Engrs. (life); mem. NAE (life), Nat. Rsch. Coun. (marine bd. 1998-2001). Home: 20 Blossom Hill Rd Winchester MA 01890-3455 Office: MIT 77 Massachusetts Ave Rm 5-318 Cambridge MA 02139-4307 E-mail: jmilgram@mit.edu.

MILGRAM, JUDITH LEE, art educator, administrator, artist; b. Holyoke, Mass. d. Robert Henry Kirley and Beatrice Bertha Hebert; m. Richard Myron Milgram; children: Rhonda Beth Longo, Gary David. Diploma, Art Inst. Boston. Cert. art instr., Conn. Illustrator Erving (Mass.) Paper Co.; advt. artist Kennedy's of New England, Boston, 1965; illustrator McLaughlin & Reilly Pub. Co.; art instr. Art Inst. Boston; designer Compugraphic Corp., Wilmington, Mass.; dir. art Shoreline Sch. Art, Music, Inc., Branford, Conn., 1978—. Cons. for tech. sch. evaluation, Conn. Dept. Edn., Hartford, 1985-88; art judge Jr. C. of C., Madison, Conn., 1982-87; presenter TV, art leagues, pub. and pvt. schs., Conn. Numerous exhbns. librs., schs., galleries, including Berkshire Mus., Pittsfield, Mass. Art lectr. pub. access TV, Branford; vol. lectr. cmty. art shows and fairs, Guilford, Conn. Mem. Conn. Art Tchrs. Assn., Arts Coun. Greater New Haven. Avocation: equestrianism. Office: Shoreline Sch Art & Music 482 E Main St Branford CT 06405-2919 E-mail: shoreline.school@snet.net.

MILGRAM, RICHARD MYRON, music school administrator; b. Moultrie, Ga. s. Bernard Byron and Libbie Elaine M.; m. Judith Lee Milgram; children: Rhonda Beth, Gary David. MusB, Berklee Coll. Music, Boston; MusM, Boston U. Cert. tchr. Mass., Conn. Tchr. Norwood (Mass.) Pub. Schs., 1969-72; asst. prof. Merrimack Coll., North Andover, Mass., 1972-75; tchr. Guilford (Conn.) Pub. Schs., 1975-77; pres., co-founder Shoreline Sch. Art and Music, Branford, Conn., 1978—. Mem. music edn. coun./student tchr. practicum com. Westfield (Mass.) State Coll., 1978-81, New Haven Arts Coun.; judge various music competitions; performance Carnegie Hall, 1997, Quick Ctr. for the Arts/Fairfield U., 1998; guest condr. Conn. Symphonic Band, 1997. Contbr. revs. to music jours. Mem. Phi Mu Alpha Sinfonia. Office: Shoreline Sch Art and Music Inc 482 E Main St Branford CT 06405-2919

MILGRIM, DARROW A. insurance broker, recreation consultant; b. Chgo., Apr. 30, 1945; s. David and Miriam (Glickman) M.; m. Laurie Stevens, Apr. 15, 1984; children: Derick, Jared, Kayla. BA, Calif. State U., San Bernardino, 1968; postgrad., U. So. Calif., 1972. Accredited ins. adv.; cert. ins. counselor; cert. sch. adminstr. Tchr. Rialto (Calif.) Unified Sch. Dist., 1969-70, Las Virgenes Unified Sch. Dist., Westlake Village, Calif., 1970-78; instr. Calif. State U., Northridge, 1980-84; pres. Darrow Milgrim Ins. Svcs., Inc.; ins. broker, dir. Speare Ins. Brokers, Blade Ins. Svcs., Sherman Oaks, Calif., 1984—. Dir. Calamigos Star C Ranch Summer Camp, Malibu, Calif., Calamigos Environ. Edn. Ctr., Malibu. Editor: Legislation and Regulations for Organized Camps, 1987. Pres. Calif. Camping Adv. Coun., Long Beach, 1985-87, 99-2000; bd. dirs. Calif. Collaboration for Youth, Sacramento, 1985—, Camp Ronald McDonald for Good Times, 1989-95; commr. dept. parks and recreation City of Agoura Hills, Calif., 1987-93; cons. Ronald McDonald House Charities, S.C., L.A., 1986-95, ACA Legis Task Force and Nat. Pub. Policy Com. Mem. Am. Camping Assn. (bd. dirs. So. Calif. sect., mem. nat. pub. policy com. Martinsville, Ind., 1980-98, nat. bd. dirs. 1990-95, legis. liaison, regional honor 1986), Ins. Brokers and Agts. of L.A. Coun., Agts. and Brokers State Legis. Coun. Office: Speare and Co Ins Brokers 15303 Ventura Blvd Ste 600 Sherman Oaks CA 91403 E-mail: dmilgrim@speare.com.

MILGRIM, FRANKLIN MARSHALL, merchant; b. N.Y.C., Aug. 24, 1925; s. Charles and Sally (Knobel) M.; m. Carol E. Kleinman, Sept. 2, 1945; children: Nancy Ellen, Catherine. Grad. with honors, Woodmere (N.Y.) Acad., 1943; BS in Econs. with honors, Wharton Sch. U. Pa., 1949. Asst. mgr. Milgrim, Cleve., 1949-50; merchandiser, buyer H. Milgrim Bros., Inc., N.Y.C., 1950-52, v.p., dir., gen. merchandiser, 1952-57; pres., dir. Milgrim, Inc., Cleve. and Columbus, Ohio, 1957—. V.p., dir. Milgrim, Inc. (Mich.), Detroit, 1962-66, The 9-18 Corp., Cleve., 1969— ; pres., treas., dir. Milgrim Suburban, Inc., 1963— , Milo, Inc., Columbus, 1966— , The Milgrim Co., Cleve., 1966— ; pres., dir. Frankly Paul Bailey Inc., Cleve., 1965— ; Dir., v.p. M and M Receivers Assn., Cleve., 1959-68 Pres. Severance Center Mchts. Assn., Cleveland Heights, 1963-66; Pres., bd. dirs. Greater Cleve. Area chpt. Nat. Council on Alcoholism, 1973— ; chmn. bd. Alcoholism Services of Cleve., 1977— ; fin. chmn. adv. council Salvation Army Harbor Light Complex, 1976— , chmn. bd. adv. council, 1981— ; mem. Greater Cleve. adv. bd. Salvation Army, 1981— ; founding bd. dirs. Sister Mary Ignatia Gavin Found.; foreman Cuyahoga County Grand Jury, 1986. Served with USNR, 1943-46. Mem. Oakwood Country Club (Cleve.), Cleve. Mid-Day Club, City Club (Cleve.), Cleve. Playhouse, Turnberry club (North Miami Beach, Fla.). Home: 4000 Towerside Ter Apt 1908 Miami FL 33138-2240 Address: Apt 1908 4000 Towerside Ter Miami Shores FL 33138-2240

MILGRIM, ROGER MICHAEL, lawyer; b. N.Y.C., Mar. 22, 1937; s. Isreal and Iola (Lash) M.; m. Patricia Conway, July 10, 1971; children: Justin. BA, U. Pa., 1958; LLB, NYU, 1961, LLM, 1962. Bar: N.Y., U.S. Supreme Ct. Assoc. Baker & McKenzie, Paris, 1963-65, Nixon Mudge et al, N.Y.C., 1965-68; mem. Milgrim Thomajan & Lee P.C., 1968-92; ptnr., chmn. intellectual property group Paul, Hastings, Janofsky & Walker LLP, 1992—, chmn. litigation dept., 1999-2000. Adj. prof. sch. law NYU, N.Y.C., 1974—; bd. dirs. Colfexip Stone Offshore S.A., 1999—2001; bd. suprs. Technip Coflexip S.A., 2001—. Author: Milgrim on Trade Secrets, 1968, supplement,

2002, Milgrim on Licensing, 1990, supplement, 2002. Trustee Coll. Wooster, 1994-97, Bklyn. Hosp., 1982-91; bd. dirs. Fulbright Assn., 1998—, chmn. Fulbright Prize com., 1999-01; bd. advs. UniStates LLC. Mem. Knickerbocker Club, Phila. Cricket Club. Republican. Home: 301 E 52nd St New York NY 10022-6319 Office: Paul Hastings Janofsky & Walker LLP 75 E 55th New York NY 10022-3205 E-mail: rogermilgrim@paulhastings.com.

MILGRIM, SAMUEL G. television producer; b. Phila., Apr. 4, 1953; s. I. Jerome and Shirley Jane (Gorson) M.; m. Maggie Ellen Melia, Oct. 19, 1997. BS magna cum laude, Ithaca Coll., 1976. Prodr. Exec. Pictures, Universal City, Calif., 1976-78; exec. prodr. Mort Kasman Prodns., N.Y.C., 1978-80, Marstellar Advt., N.Y.C., 1980-84; v.p. exec. prodr. Temerlin McClain, Irving, Tex., 1984—. Office: Temerlin McClain 6555 Sierra Dr Irving TX 75039-2479

MILGROM, FELIX, immunologist, educator; b. Rohatyn, Poland, Oct. 12, 1919; came to U.S., 1958; naturalized, 1963; s. Henryk and Ernestina (Cyryl) M.; m. Halina Miszel, Oct. 15, 1941; children: Henry, Martin Louis. Student, U. Lwow, Poland, 1937-41, U. Lublin, 1945; MD, U. Wroclaw, Poland, 1947; MD (hon.), U. Vienna, Austria, 1976, U. Lund, Sweden, 1979, U. Heidelberg, Fed. Republic Germany, 1979, U. Bergen, Norway, 1980; DSc (hon.), U. Med. Dent., N.J., 1991. Rsch. assoc., prof. dept. microbiology Sch. Medicine U. Wroclaw, 1946-54, chmn. dept., 1954; prof., head dept. microbiology Sch. Medicine, Silesian U., Zabrze, Poland, 1954-57; rsch. assoc. Svc. de Chime Microbienne, Pasteur Inst., Paris, 1957; rsch. assoc. prof. dept. bacteriology and immunology U. Buffalo Sch. Medicine, 1958-62; assoc. prof., then prof. and disting. prof. microbiology Sch. Medicine, SUNY, Buffalo, 1962—, chmn. dept., 1967-85. Author: Studies on the Structure of Antibodies, 1950; co-editor: International Convocations on Immunology, 1969, 75, 79, 85, Principles of Immunology, 1973, 2d edit., 1979, Principles of Immunological Diagnosis in Medicine, 1981, Medical Microbiology, 1982; editor in chief Internat. Archives of Allergy and Applied Immunology, 1965-91; contbg. editor Vox Sanguinis, 1965-76, Transfusion, 1966-73, Cellular Immunology, 1970-83, Transplantation, 1975-78; contbr. numerous articles to profl. jours. Recipient Alfred Jurzykowski Found. prize, 1986, Paul Ehrlich and Ludwig Darmstaedter prize, 1987. Mem. Am. Assn. Immunologists, Transplantation Soc. (v.p. 1976-78), Am. Acad. Microbiology, Coll. Internat. Allergologicum (v.p. 1970-78, pres. 1978-82, hon. mem. 1990—), Polish Acad. Arts and Scis., Sigma Xi. Achievements include research on the serology of syphillis, Tb, rheumatoid arthritis, organ and tissue specificity including blood groups, transplantation and autoimmunity. Home: 474 Getzville Rd Buffalo NY 14226-2555

MILHORAT, THOMAS HERRICK, neurosurgeon; b. N.Y.C., Apr. 5, 1936; s. Ade Thomas and Edith Caulkins (Herrick) M.; m. Edith Mostile, 1961; children: John Thomas, Robert Herrick. BA, Cornell U., 1957, MD, 1961. Intern, asst. resident in gen. surgery N.Y. Hosp.-Cornell Med. Ctr., 1961—63, asst. resident, chief resident in neurosurgery, 1965—68, asst. neurosurgeon NIH, 1968—71; clin. assoc., dept. surg. neurology Nat. Inst. Neurol. Diseases and Blindness, Bethesda, 1963—65; assoc. prof. neurol. surgery, assoc. prof. child health and devel. George Washington U. Sch. Medicine, Washington, 1971—74; prof. child health and devel. George Washington U., 1974—81, prof. neurol. surgery, 1974—81; chmn. dept. neurosurgery Children's Hosp. Nat. Med. Ctr., 1971—81; prof. neurol. surgery, dept. chmn. SUNY Health Sci. Ctr., Bklyn., 1982—2001; chmn. dept. neurosurgery North Shore/L.I. Jewish Health System, 2002—; dir. Chiari Ctr. North Shore Univ. Hosp., 2002—; prof. neurol. surgery N.Y.U. Sch. Medicine, 2002—. Neurosurgeon-in-chief Kings County Hosp. Ctr., 1982—2001; regional chmn. neurol. surgery L.I. Coll. Hosp., 1986—2001, Coney Island Hosp., 1986—2001; program dir. Neurosurgery Rsch. Tng. Program, 1982—2001; mem. Nat. Coun. Scientists NIH, 1969—82. Author: Hydrocephalus and Cerebrospinal Fluid, 1972, Pediatric Neurosurgery, 1978, Cerebrospinal Fluid and the Brain Edemas, 1987; (with M.K. Hammock) Cranial Computed Tomography in Infancy and Childhood, 1981; mem. editl. bd. Neurosurgery, 1997—, Neurosurg Focus: Syringomyelia, 2000—; contbr. more than 325 articles to profl. jours. Lt. USNR, 1942—45. Recipient 1st prize in pathology, Cornell U. Med. Sch. Dept. Ob-Gyn., 1960, Charles L. Horn prize Cornell Med. Sch., 1961, Best Paper award ann. combined meeting N.Y. Acad. Medicine/N.Y. Neurosurg. Soc., 1965, Pudenz award for Excellence in CSF Physiology, 1994, E. Jefferson Browder award for excellence in Neurosurgery, 1986, Arthur A. Kaplan award for excellence in neurosurgery, 1999; named one of N.Y.'s Best Doctors, N.Y. Mag., 1992-2001. Mem. AAAS, Internat. Soc. Pediat. Neurosurgery, Am. Assn. Neurol. Surgery (pediat. sect.), Am. Syringomyelia Alliance Project (chmn. med. adv. bd. 1996—), Am. Acad. Pediat. (surg. sect.), Soc. Pediat. Rsch., N.Y. Acad. Medicine, N.Y. Soc. Neurosurgery (pres. 1988-90), Bklyn. Neurologic Soc. (pres. 1988-95), Soc. Neurosci., Internat. Soc. Neurosci., Soc. Neurol. Surgeons, Med. Club Bklyn., Sigma Xi. Avocations: golf, billiards, gardening. E-mail: bkneurosx.aol.com. Office: Chiari Ctr 300 Community Dr Manhasset NY 11030 Fax: 516-562-3030. E-mail: tmilhora@nshs.edu.

MILHOUS, DAVID MATTHEW, film and television editor; b. Pomona, Calif., July 9, 1967; s. Paul Ballard and Mary Ann (Bollinger) M.; m. Karyn Lynn Cook, May 29, 1993; children: James Paul, Collin Bernard. Student, U. So. Calif., 1987-88; BFA in Film Prodn., NYU, 1991; MFA, Am. Film Inst. Exec. prodr. Bond Films, Ft. Lauderdale, Fla., 1992-94; network editor CNN, Atlanta, 1995-99; film editor, 1999—. Recipient Founders Day award NYU, 1992. Fellow Am. Film Inst. Republican. Avocations: screenwriting, musical composition, sailing. Office: Paramount Pictures 5555 Melrose Ave Hollywood CA 90038

MILHOUSE, PAUL WILLIAM, bishop; b. St. Francisville, Ill., Aug. 31, 1910; s. Willis Cleveland and Carrie (Pence) M.; m. Mary Frances Noblitt, June 29, 1932; children: Mary Catherine Milhouse Hauswald, Pauline Joyce Milhouse Vermillion, Paul David. AB, U. Indpls. (formerly Ind. Cen. U.), 1932; D.D., U. Ind. (formerly Ind. Cen. U.), 1950; B.D., Am. Theol. Sem., 1937, Th.D., 1946; L.H.D., Westmar Coll., 1965; S.T.D., Oklahoma City U., 1969; D.D., So. Meth. U., 1969. Ordained to ministry United Brethren Ch., 1931; pastor Birds, Ill., 1928-29, Elliott, 1932-37, Olney, 1937-41, 1st Ch., Decatur, 1941-51; asso. editor Telescope-Messenger, 1951-58; exec. sec. gen. council Evang. United Brethren Ch., 1959-60, bishop, 1960-68, United Meth. Ch., 1968—. Presiding bishop Southwestern Area, Evang. United Brethren Ch., 1960-68; presiding bishop United Meth. Ch., Okla., 1968-80; pres. Coun. United Meth. Bishops, 1977-78; bishop-in-residence Oklahoma City U., 1980-91, U. Indpls., 1992-97; mem. commn. to unite Evang. United Brethren Ch. and Meth. Ch., 1960-68. Author: Enlisting and Developing Church Leaders, 1946, Come Unto Me, 1946, Lift Up Your Eyes, 1955, Doorways to Spritual Living, 1950, Except the Lord Build the House, 1949, Christian Worship in Symbol and Ritual, 1953, Laymen in the Church, 1957, At Life's Crossroads, 1959, Phillip William Otterbein, 1968, Nineteen Bishops of the Evangelical United Brethren Church, 1974, Organizing for Effective Ministry, 1980, Theological and Historical Roots of United Methodists, 1980, Detour Into Yesterday, 1984, Okla. City U., Miracle at 23d and Blackwelder, 1984, Transforming Dollars into Service, A History of Methodist Manor, 1987, St. Lukes of Oklahoma City, 1988, Franklin United Methodist Community, (a brief history), 1999; also articles; editor: Facing Frontiers, 1960. Trustee United Theol. Sem., 1959-68, hon. life trustee, 1980—, hon. chmn. capital fund campaign, 2001; trustee Westmar Coll., 1960-68, Western Home, 1960-68, So. Meth. U., 1968-80, Oklahoma City U., 1968-80, hon. life trustee, 1980-99, emeritus trustee, 1999—, Francis E. Willard Home, 1968-80, Meth. Manor, 1968-80, Boys Ranch, 1968-80, Last Frontier coun. Boy Scouts Am., 1968-80. Recipient Disting. Alumnus award Ind. Ctrl. U. (now U. Indpls.), 1978, Gene and Joanne Sease award, 2000, Disting. Friend award Oklahoma City U., 1979, Disting. Svc. award, 1980, Top Hand award Oklahoma City C. of C., 1980, Bishop Paul W. Milhouse award Oklahoma City U., 1990, Disting. Svc. award for contbns. to United Meth. history Gen. Commn. on Archives and History, 1996, Johson County Health Found. Pres. Circle award, 2001. Mem. Mark Twain Writers Guild, Epsilon Sigma Alpha, now Alpha Chi. *Life is a gift to be lived in harmony with the purpose of God, who holds us accountable for the way we live.*

MILI, ALI, information technology educator, scientist; b. Jemmal, Monastir, Tunisia, Jan. 31, 1953; came to U.S., 1995; s. Taieb Mil and Aisha Ben Bnina; 1 child, Noor. Grad., U. Joseph Fourier, Grenoble, France, 1978, Doctorat D'etat, 1985; PhD, U. Ill., 1981. Prin. scientist Honeywell Inc., Mpls., 1980-81; asst. prof. Tex. A&M U., College Station, 1981-82, Laval U., Que., Can., 1982-84; prof. U. Tunis, Tunisia, 1984-91, U. Ottawa, 1991-97; sr. scientist Inst. for Software Rsch., Fairmont, W.Va., 1997—; prof. W.Va. U., Morgantown, 1997—. Vis. scientist U. Queensland, Brisbane, Australia, 1989; vis. prof. Fudan U., Shanghai, China, 1985; guest prof. U. Klagenfurt, Austria, 1987-99; vis. lectr. U. Oran, Algeria, 1986-89. Author: Program Verification, 1985, Fault Tolerance, 1990, Program Construction, 1994; co-author: Program Specification, 1989.

MILIAN, SHARON M. journalist, nurse; b. Louisville, Jan. 9, 1955; d. Norman Lawrence and Dolores Juanita (Hayes) Brotzge; m. Carl A. LaFave, Oct. 5, 1974 (div. 1982); m. William Henry Milian, Nov. 4, 1983; children: Lisa Marie, Steven Hayes. A in Nursing, Jefferson C.C., 1979; AA, St. Petersburg Jr. Coll., 1997; BA, U. So. Fla., 1999. RN, Fla.; cert. gerontol. nurse, med. coder. Nurse St. Anthony Hosp., Louisville, 1979-82, Mease Hosp., Dunedin, Fla., 1982-83, Nursefinders and other agys., PalmHarbor, 1983-94, Morton Plant Hosp., Clearwater, 1994-98; journalist Palm Harbor, 1997—. Contbr. articles to nursing jours. Vol., newsletter editor Friends of Brooker Creek Preserve, Tarpon Springs, Fla., 1997-2001; vol. Pinellas County Schs., 1989—, Oldsmar (Fla.) Little League, 1993—. Coll. scholar St. Petersburg campus U. South Fla., 1999, Tampa campus, 1999. Mem. Am. Med. Writers Assn. (sec., co-editor), Assn. Late-Deafened Adults (newsletter contbr.), Soc. Prof. Journalists (treas. U. South Fla. chpt. 1998-2000, newsletter editor), Friends Deaf Svc. Ctr. (bd. dirs.), U. South Fla. Alumni Assn. Democrat. Roman Catholic. Avocations: scuba diving, crafting, bicycling. Office: 1880 Eagle Trace Blvd Palm Harbor FL 34685 E-mail: smilian@tampabay.rr.com.

MILIC-EMILI, JOSEPH, physician, educator; b. Sezana, Slovenia, May 27, 1931; arrived in Can., 1963; s. Joseph Milic-Emili and Giovanna Milic-Emili Perhavec; m. Ann Harding, Nov. 2, 1957; children: Claire, Anne-Marie, Alice, Andrew. MD, U. Milan, 1955; Dr. honoris causa, U. Louvain, Belgium, 1987, Kunming Med. Coll., China, 1987, U. Montpellier, France, 1994, U. Ferrara, Italy, 1996, U. Athens, Greece, 1998, U. Ljubljana, Slovenia. Asst. prof. physiology and exptl. medicine McGill U., Montreal, Que., Can., 1963-65, assoc. prof. Can., 1965-69, prof. Can., 1970-97, prof. emeritus Can., 1998—, dir. Meakins-Christie Labs. Can., 1979-94. Vis. prof. Lab. de Physiologie Faculte de Medecine Saint-Antoine, Paris, Svc. de Pneumologie Hosp. Beaujon, Paris, 1978-79, 94-95, chmn. dept. physiology, 1973-78; vis. cons. medicine Royal Postgrad. Med. Sch., London, 1969-70; vis. cons. Aeronautics Imperial Coll. Tech., London, 1969-70; asst. prof. physiology U. Liege, Belgium, 1958-60; asst. prof. U. Milan, 1956-58. Mem. editl. bd. Jour. Applied Physiology, 1970-76, Rev. Française des Maladies Respiratories, 1979-96, Rivista de Biologia, 1979-86, Am. Rev. Respiratory Disease, 1982-89, Reanimation, Soins Intensifs, Medicine d'Urgence, 1984-95. Mem. applied physiology and bioengrig. study sect. NIH, 1975-78. Decorated Order of Can.; recipient Gold medal C. Forlanini U. Pavia, Italy, 1982, Am. Coll. Chest Physicians medal, 1984, 98, Harry Wunderly medal Thoracic Soc. Australia, 1988, medal Italian Sch. Mil. Medicine, 1990, medal Med. Sch. Brest, 1997, medal Med. Sch. Ferrara, 1997, medal Med. Sch. Bologna; author of one of 100-most cited articles in clin. rsch. of 1960s; named one of 1,000 most-cited contemporary scientists, 1965-78, 1998 Presdl. award European Respiratory Soc., 1998 Dist. Lectr. in Physiology Am. Col. Chest Physicians Soc. Med. Clin. Bononiensis Sci., 2001. Fellow Royal Soc. Can., Slovenian Acad. Sci. (fgn. corr.); mem. Am. Physiol. Soc., Can. Physiol. Soc., Can. Thoracic Soc., Med. Rsch. Coun. (mem. grants com. 1980), Soc. Pneumologie Belge (hon.), Brazilian Physiol. Soc. (hon.), Hellenic Thoracic Soc. (hon.), Polish Pneumological Soc. (hon.), Chilean Resp. Soc. (hon.). Home: 4394 Circle Rd Montreal QC Canada H4W 1Y5 Office: McGill U Meakins-Christie Labs 3626 St Urbain St Montreal QC Canada H2X 2P2 E-mail: milic@meakins.lan.mcgill.ca.

MILIO, LOUIS ROMOLO, retired law educator, social worker; b. Balt. s. Placido and Rose (Pirrotti) M.; m. Ellenor K. Stafford, July 8, 1978 (dec. Sept. 1990). LLB, U. Balt., 1948, LLM, 1950, JD, 1972; LLD (hon.), We. U., 1951. Cert. social worker asst., Md. Copy boy Balt. Sun, 1943; cost acct. Continental Can Co., Balt., 1945; tax bailiff City Bur. Collections, 1946-49; atty. City Bur. Recreation, 1948—, social worker/drug counselor, 1970—; staff dept. welfare City of Balt., 1964-65; case worker Hdqrs. Office, Balt., 1965-66. Instr. Italian and pub. speaking YWCA, Balt., 1944; prof. law Ea. Coll. of Commerce, Balt., 1950-51; prof. philosophy Johns Hopkins Univ., Balt.; pres. Milio Cometics Co., Internat., Lady Eleanor Beauty Soap. Author: Faith, Hope & Charity, 1949; patent pending Milio Aviation Safety Sys. Co-founder, sec. Good Neighbor League, Balt., 1948; candidate U.S. Congress, 1946, 50; candidate Mayor Balt. City, 1952, 56, 59; candidate gov. Md., 1966-74. Pvt. 1st Class Md. State Guard, 1943-94. Mem. Star Spangled Banner Flag House Assn (last living resident). Dem. Roman Cath. Avocations: swimming, walking, bowling, cooking, gardening. Home and Office: Village of Cross Keys 2 Cross Keys Rd Apt C Baltimore MD 21210-1719

MILIORA, MARIA TERESA, chemist, psychotherapist, psychoanalyst, educator; b. Somerville, Mass., June 29, 1938; d. Andrew and Maria Civita (Gallinaro) Migliorini. BA cum laude, Regis Coll., 1960; PhD, Tufts U., 1965; MSW, Boston U., 1985. Rsch. asst. Tufts U., Medford, Mass., 1960-64, rsch. assoc., 1965-66; assoc. prof. Suffolk U., Boston, 1965-68, 1968-71, prof., 1971—, chmn. dept. chemistry, 1972-84, presdl. search com., 1980, faculty rep. strategic planning com., 1992—; faculty Boston Inst. for Psychotherapy, 1992-96, Tng. and Rsch. Inst. for Self Psychology, N.Y.C., 1994—. Rsch. assoc. Bio-Research Inst., Cambridge, Mass., 1968. Author: Narcissism, the Family, and Madness, 2000; contbr. articles to profl. jours. Faculty rep. to trustees Joint Coun. on Univ. Affairs, Suffolk U., 1973-77, 79-81; convenor Pres.'s Commn. on Status of Women, 1974-78, speaker ednl. policy com., 1972-73; chair cultural diversity CLAS Curriculum, 1991—. Mem. AAUP (chpt. pres. 1970), NASW, Am. Chem. Soc. (alt. councillor 1976-82, councillor 1979-82, bd. dirs. Northeastern sect. 1976-80, chmn. pub. rels. sect. 1977-79), Mass. Acad. Clin. Social Work, Nat. Assn. for Advancement Psychoanalysis, Nat. Membership Com. on Psychoanalysis, Sigma Xi (chpt. pres. 1972-73), Sigma Zeta (chpt. sect. 1970-80), Alpha Lambda Delta, Delta Epsilon Sigma. Home: 41 Irving St Newton MA 02459-1611 Office: Suffolk University Beacon Hill Boston MA 02114

MILIOZZI, PAOLO, electrical engineer; b. Macerata, Italy, Nov. 22, 1967; s. Antonio and Teresa Miliozzi; m. Ana Maria Isabel Hernandez, July 19, 1997. Laurea summa cum laude, U. Bologna, Italy, 1992; PhD, U. Padova, Italy, 1996. Grad. student rschr. U. Padova, 1992-94, U. Calif., Berkeley, 1994-95, rsch. engrng. fellow, 1995-96; design automation engr. Rockwell Internat., Newport Beach, Calif., 1996-98; sr. staff design automation engr. Conexant Systems, 1999—. Contbr. articles to profl. jours. Lt. Italian Air Force, 1993-94. Recipient scholarship Edn. Abroad Program, U. Calif., 1994. Mem. IEEE. Roman Catholic. Avocations: photography, volleyball, scuba diving, swimming. Office: Conexant Systems Inc 4311 Jamboree Rd #MC E03301 Newport Beach CA 92660-3007 E-mail: paolo.miliozzi@conexant.com.

MILITELLO, SAMUEL PHILIP, lawyer; b. Buffalo, Dec. 16, 1947; s. Samuel Anthony and Katherine (Pesono) M.; m. Anne Little, May 27, 1972; children: Matthew Samuel, Rebecca Anne, Caitlin Frances. BA, Canisius Coll., 1969; JD, SUNY, Buffalo, 1972. Bar: N.Y. 1972, U.S. Ct. Mil. Appeals 1973, U.S. Army Ct. of Mil. Rev. 1976, U.S. Ct. Claims 1977, U.S. Supreme Ct. 1977, U.S. Dist. Ct. (we. dist.) N.Y. 1986, U.S. Dist. Ct. (no. dist.) N.Y. 1987, U.S. Dist. Ct. (ea. dist.) N.Y. 1994, U.S. Ct. Appeals (2d cir.), 1990. Assoc. Williams & Katzman, Watertown, N.Y., 1978-79; legal counsel, mgr. of litigation Parsons Corp., Pasadena, Calif., 1979-84; gen. counsel, sec. Envirogas, Inc., Hamburg, N.Y., 1984-86; assoc. Bond, Schoeneck & King, Watertown, 1987-88; mng. ptnr. The Militello Law Office, P.C., Watertown, 1989—; counsel Parsons Gilbane, New Orleans, 1979-81; gen. counsel The Stebbins Engrng. and Mfg. Co. and subs., 1986—. Capt. JAGC, U.S. Army, 1973-78. Decorated Army Commendation medal with one oak leaf cluster, Meritorious Service medal. Mem. ABA (pub. contracts sect.), N.Y. State Bar Assn., N.Y. Criminal and Civil Cts. Bar Assn., Bar Assn. of Erie County (N.Y.), Bar Assn. of Jefferson County (N.Y.), No. N.Y. Builders Exchange, Assoc. Gen. Contractors Am., Am. Legion, K.C. (adv. 1978-79). Roman Catholic. Office: PO Box 6800 1619 Ohio St Watertown NY 13601-3032

MILK, JARED MARC, real estate company executive, writer; b. Gt. Neck, N.Y., Dec. 24, 1969; s. Richard H. Milk and Hattie (Fuld) Milk Solymosy. AA in Bus., SUNY, 1990; BA in Theater & Comms., SUNY, Old Westbury, 1992; AA in Bus., Nassau C.C. Real estate sales N.Y., real estate broker N.Y. Broker Surf Realty, 1995-96; owner Milk and Assocs., 1996—, Hamajama Wood Boxes and Bags, 1996—, Castlecove Vending Machines, 1988—, ATM Credit Card Machines, 1999—, Ads-in-Motion, 2000—, Jared's Nuts , Cedarhurst, NY, 2001—, Driving Sch., Cedarhurst, 2001—; broker Candie's, 2002. Author: Flying Feathers, 1993; co-author: (book-on-cassette) Cinderella Cockroach, 1990, A Christmas Tale, 1994, A Chanukah Tale, 1995, The Mystery of the Old Fishing Shack, 1999, Legally Raped, 1999, Confessions on the Psycho Lane, 1999. Mem. N.Y. State Real Estate Assn., Nassau Rep. Club. Democrat. Jewish. Avocations: tennis, collecting, ice-skating, golf, travel, antiques. Office: PO Box 24 Cedarhurst NY 11516

MILKEY, JAMES R. environmental lawyer; b. Hartford, Conn., Dec. 17, 1956; s. Robert K. and Ruth M. Milkey; m. Cathie Jo Martin, July 7, 1990; children: Julian M., Jonathan R. AB magna cum laude, Harvard U., 1978; M City Planning, MIT, 1983; JD magna cum laude, Harvard U., 1983. Bar: Mass. 1983, U.S. Ct. Appeals (1st cir.) 1984, U.S. Dist. Ct. Mass. 1984, U.S. Supreme Ct. 1990. Law clk. Mass. Appeals Ct., Boston, 1983-84; asst. atty. gen. Office of the Atty. Gen., 1984-94, 95—, dep. chief environ. protection divsn., 1990-94, dir. land use and environ. protection, 1995-96, chief environ. protection divsn., 1996—. Vis. assoc. prof. Pace Law Sch., White Plains, N.Y., 1994-95; seminar instr. Harvard U., Cambridge, 1990, 92; mem. Bronnfields Adv. Group, Boston, 1999—. Author: (book chpt.) Massachusetts Environmental Law, 1991, 93, 96, 99. Mem. Mass. Bar Assn., Boston Bar Assn. (mem. environ. steering com. 1996—), Environ. League of Mass. (Unsung Hero award 1998), Mass. Audubon Soc., Mass Pub. Interest Rsch. Group, Environ. League of Mass. Home: 34 Woodcliff Rd Newton MA 02461-1825 Office: Office of Atty Gen 200 Portland St Boston MA 02114-1722 E-mail: jim.milkey@ago.state.ma.us.

MILKEY, VIRGINIA A. state legislator; b. Brattleboro, Vt., Jan. 27, 1950; BA, Middlebury Coll., 1972. Mem. Vt. Ho. of Reps., Montpelier, 1991—. Dir. Ret. and Sr. Vol. Program of Windham County.; co-founder, bd. dirs. Bonnyvale Environ. Edn. Ctr.; bd. dirs. Alliance for Bldg. Cmty.; mem. Brattleboro Agrl. Adv. Com.; mem., exec., health, property and casualty and lifen and state/fed. rels. coms. of Nat. Conf. Ins. Legislators. Rep. Brattleboro Town Meeting; corporator Brattleboro Meml. Hosp. Mem. Nat. Assn. Ret. and Sr. Vol. Program Dirs., New Eng. Assn. Ret. and Sr. Vol. Program Dirs., Vt. Nat. Sr. Svc. Corps. Dirs. Assn. Home: 266 Meadowbrook Rd Brattleboro VT 05301-2581

MILKMAN, MARIANNE FRIEDENTHAL, retired city planner; b. Berlin, May 13, 1931; arrived in US, 1957; d. Ernst Leopold and Margarethe (Goldschmidt) Friedenthal; m. Roger Dawson Milkman, Oct. 18, 1958; children: Ruth, Louise, Janet, Paul. BA, Cambridge (Eng.) U., 1952, MA, 1956; teaching diploma, London U., 1953. Tchr. biology Milham Ford High Sch., Oxford, Eng., 1953-57; teaching fellow, rsch. asst. U. Mich., Ann Arbor, 1957-59; sci. dir. Children's Sch. Sci., Woods Hole, Mass., 1971-72; planning technician dept. planning and program devel. City of Iowa City, 1975-76, planner I, 1976-79, assoc. planner, 1979-85, coord. comty. devel., 1986-96; ret., 1996. Bikeways chmn Project Green, Iowa City, 1968—75. Fellow, English Speaking Union, 1957—58; scholar State, Cambridge Univ and London Univ, 1949—53, Fulbright Traveling, Univ Mich, 1957. Mem.: Nat Community Develop Asn, Nat Asn Housing and Redevelopment Offs, Am Planning Asn (secy-treas Iowa chpt 1982—84, vpres 1984—86, pres 1986—88, chmn univ relations comt 1987—91, Pres's Award 1988). Jewish. Avocations: mountain hiking, wild flowers, music. Home: 12 Fells Rd Falmouth MA 02540-1626

MILKMAN, MARTIN IRVING, economics educator; b. Annapolis, Md., Sept. 8, 1960; s. Joseph and Beatrice Milkman. BA cum laude, Brandeis U., 1982; MS, U. Oreg., 1985, PhD, 1989. Asst. prof. econs. Gonzaga U., Spokane, Wash., 1987-88; assoc. prof. econs. Murray (Ky.) State U., 1988—98, prof., 1998—, dir. Buf. Bus. and Econ. Rsch.; economist U.S. Dept. Energy, Washington, 1990-91. Cons. Southwestern Pub. Co., Cin., 1989, U.S. AID, Belize, 1990, Pub. Citizen, 1993, Ky. Ctr. for Workforce Devel., 1993-99, West Ky. Ednl. Coop., 1999-, Ky. Cmty. and Tech. Coll. Sys., 1998-, Ky. Dept. Edn., 1999-. Contbr. articles to profl. jours. Mem. Am. Econ. Assn., Ky. Econ. Assn. Democrat. Avocations: tennis, hiking, golfing. Office: Murray State U Dept Econs and Fin Murray KY 42071

MILKMAN, ROGER DAWSON, genetics educator, molecular evolution researcher; b. N.Y.C., Oct. 15, 1930; s. Louis Arthur and Margaret (Weinstein) M.; m. Marianne Friedenthal, Oct. 18, 1958; children: Ruth Margaret, Louise Friedenthal, Janet Dawson Milkman Lussenhop, Paul David. AB, Harvard U., 1951, A.M., 1954, PhD, 1956. Student, asst., instr., investigator Marine Biol. Lab., Woods Hole, Mass., 1952-72, 88-96; instr., asst. prof. U. Mich., Ann Arbor, 1957-60; assoc. prof., prof. Syracuse U., N.Y., 1960-68; prof. biol. scis. U. Iowa, Iowa City, 1968-2001, prof. emeritus, 2001—, chmn. univ. genetics PhD program, 1992-93. Vis. prof. biology Grinnell (Iowa) Coll., 1990; mem. genetics study sect. NIH, 1986-87; NSF panelist, 1996-99. Translator: Developmental Physiology, 1970; editor: Perspectives on Evolution, 1982, Experimental Population Genetics, 1983, Evolution jour., 1984-86; mem. editl. bd. Jour. Bacteriology, 1998-2000; contbr. articles to profl. jours. Sec. Soc. Gen. Physiologists, 1963-65, Am. Soc. Naturalists, 1980-82; alumni rep. Phillips Acad., Andover, Mass., 1980-94. NSF grantee, 1959— ; USPHS grantee, 1984-87. Fellow AAAS; mem. Am. Soc. for Microbiology, Genetics Soc. Am., Corp. Marine Biol. Lab., Soc. for Gen. Microbiology (U.K.), Soc. Study Evolution, Soc. Molecular Biology and Evolution, Internat. Soc. for Molecular Evolution. Jewish. Avocation: mountain hiking. Home: 12 Fells Rd Falmouth MA 02540-1626 Office: Marine Biol Lab Lillie 503 Woods Hole MA 02543-1015

MILL, JETH, performing company executive; Exe. dir. Des Moines Symphony. Office: Des Moines Symph 221 Walnut St Des Moines IA 50309*

MILLAN, ALVIN, speech pathology/audiology services professional, educator; b. San Juan, P.R., May 28, 1968; s. William Millan and Aura Fuentes; m. Norma Rodriguez, Dec. 19, 1992; children: Liz C., Kenneth X. B in Speech Therapy, U. P.R., 1990, M in Speech Lang. Pathology, 1992, cert. in early intervention devel. deficiencies, 1996. Cert. speech lang. pathologist P.R., assistive tech. cert. prof. speech lang. and comm. disorders U. P.R. Med. Scis. Campus, San Juan, 1991—. Contbr. articles to profl. jours. Fellow: Assn. Reading Devel., Assn. Curriculum Devel.; mem.: Am. Speech and Lang. Assn. (advocacy spkrs. bur. 1999—2001), P.R. Orgn. Speech-Lang. Pathology and Audiology (pres. adv. bd. 1996—99, v.p. 1999—2000, sec. 2000—). Avocations: reading, writing, meditation, spirituality, travel. Home: Calle San Patricio aa-15 Alturas de San Pedro Fajardo PR 00738 Office: Ctr Rehab del Habla Lenguaje Ave Gen Valero 313-B Fajardo PR 00738

MILLAR, GORDON HALSTEAD, mechanical engineer, agricultural machinery manufacturing executive; b. Newark, Nov. 28, 1923; s. George Halstead and Dill E. (McMullen) M.; m. Virginia M. Jedryczka, Aug. 24, 1957; children: George B., Kathryn M., Juliet S., John G., James H. B.M.E., U. Detroit, 1949, D.Sc. (hon.), 1977; PhD, U. Wis., 1952; L.H.D., West Coast U., 1984; D.Sc. (hon.), Western Mich. U., 1986. Registered profl. engr., Fla., Ill., Iowa, Mich., Minn., Ohio. Supr. new powerplants Ford Motor Co., 1952-57; engring. mgr. Meriam Instrument Co., Cleve., 1957-59; dir. new products McCulloch Corp., Los Angeles, 1959-63; with Deere & Co., 1963-84, v.p. engring. Ill., 1972-84; exec. assoc. Southwest Research Inst., 1987. Mem. Fed. Adv. Com. Indsl. Innovation, 1979; chmn. West Ctrl. Ill. Ednl. Telecom. Corp.; pres. Accreditation Bd. for Engring. and Tech., 1983-85; pres., fellow Accreditation Bd. for Engring. and Tech. Contbr. articles to profl. jours.; patentee in field. Chmn. Quad Cities chpt. United Way, 1976-77; bd. dirs.; adv. council Bradley U. Coll. Engring. and Tech.; mem. exec. com. Illowa council Boy Scouts Am., 1977-79. Served with U.S. Army, World War II. Decorated Purple Heart; recipient Alumnus of Year award U. Detroit, 1976, Comdrs. medal for pub. svc. Dept. Army, 1989 Fellow ASME (hon. life mem.), Soc. Automotive Engrs. (pres. 1984, bd. dirs. 1984-86, mem. nat. nominating com.); mem. NAE, NSPE, Engrs. Joint Coun., Indsl. Rsch.

Inst., Engring. Soc. Detroit, Am. Soc. Agrl. Engrs., Ill. Soc. Profl. Engrs., Moline C. of C., Aviation Coun. E-mail: N5644&@aol.com. Home: 1840 Wiley Post Trl Daytona Beach FL 32128

MILLAR, JAMES F. pharmaceutical executive; Exec. v.p. No. Group Cardinal Health Inc., Dublin, with distbn., pres. drug wholesaling opers., exec. v.p., Pharm. Distbn. and Med. Products. Office: Cardinal Health Inc 7000 Cardinal Pl Dublin OH 43017-1092*

MILLAR, JAMES ROBERT, economist, educator, university official; b. San Antonio, July 7, 1936; s. James G. and Virginia M. (Harrison) M.; m. Gera Ascher, July 4, 1965; children: Leo Schaeg (dec.), Mira Gail. BA, U. Tex., 1958; PhD in Econs., Cornell U., 1965. Asst. prof. dept. econs. U. Ill., Urbana, 1965-70, assoc. prof., 1970-72, prof., 1973-89, assoc. vice chancellor for acad. affairs, 1984-89, dir. internat. programs and studies, 1984-89; prof. econs. and internat. affairs George Washington U., Washington, 1989—, dir. Inst. for European, Russian and Eurasian Studies, 1989-01, assoc. dean Elliott Sch. Internat. Affairs, 1989-95, acting dean, 1994. Mem. acad. coun. Kennan Inst. Advanced Russian Studies, 1975-84; young faculty exchangee Moscow State U., 1966; cons. to congressmen and various U.S. govt. depts., 1972—; dir. Soviet Interview Project, 1981-88; sec., bd. dirs. Midwest Univs. Consortium for Internat. Activities, 1984-88, chmn. bd., 1988-89; bd. dirs. IREX. Author: The ABCs of Soviet Socialism, 1981 (non-fiction award Soc. Midland Authors, 1981), The Soviet Economic Experiment, 1990; editor, contbr. The Soviet Rural Community, 1971; editor: Slavic Rev., Am. Quar. Soviet and East European Studies, 1975-80, Problems of Post-Communism, 1996—; editor, contbr. Politics, Work and Daily Life, A Survey of Former Soviet Citizens, 1987; editor, contbr. Cracks in the Monolith: Party Power in the Brezhnev Era, 1992, The Social Legacy of Communism, 1994; contbr. articles on studies on Soviet/Russian economy and econ. history to scholarly jours. Served with Q.M.C. U.S. Army, 1960. Ford Found. fgn. area fellow, 1961-64; sr. scholar rsch. travel grantee to USSR, 1972; Am. Coun. Learned Socs./USSR Acad. Scis. travel exchangee, 1979; fellow Woodrow Wilson Internat. Ctr. for Scholars, 1988-89, Guggenheim fellow, 1995-96; IREX advanced rsch. grantee, 1996. Mem. AAAS, Internat. Coun. Ctrl. and East European Studies, Econ. History Assn., Assn. Evolutionary Econs., Am. Assn. Advancement Slavic Studies (del. Am. Coun. Learned Soc. 1992-98, bd. dirs. 1995-2001, v.p. 1998-99, pres. 1999-2000, chair coun. of member insts. 1995-99), Am. Coun. Learned Soc. (treas., bd. dirs. 1996-2002, sec. 1994-96, mem. exec. com. del., chair 1992-95, mem. joint com. with Social Sci. Rsch. Coun. 1990-95), N.Y. Acad. Sci., Phi Beta Kappa (pres. Alpha chpt. 1998-01). Home: 2801 New Mexico Ave NW Apt 1215 Washington DC 20007-3942 Office: George Washington U Inst Eur Russ Eurasian Studies 2013 G St NW Ste 402 D Washington DC 20052-0001 E-mail: millar@gwu.edu.

MILLAR, JEFFERY LYNN, writer; b. Houston, July 10, 1942; s. Daniel Lynn Millar and Betty Ruth (Shove) Coons; m. Lynne McDonald, Dec. 21, 1964 (div. Aug. 1983); m. Peggy V. Watson, Apr. 1, 1994. BA, U. Tex., 1964. Reporter Houston Chronicle, 1964-65, film critic, 1965-2000, columnist, 1972-2000. Writer, co-creator: (comic strip) Tank McNamara, Universal Press Syndicate, Kansas City, 1974—.

MILLAR, JOHN DONALD, occupational and environmental health consultant, speaker; b. Newport News, Va., Feb. 27, 1934; s. John and Dorothea Virginia (Smith) M.; m. Joan M. Phillips, Aug. 17, 1957; children: John Stuart, Alison Gordon, Virginia Taylor. BS, U. Richmond, 1956; MD, Med. Coll. Va., 1959; D.T.P.H., London Sch. Hygiene and Tropical Medicine, 1966; D of Pub. Svc. (hon.), Greenville (Ill.) Coll., 1994. Cert. specialist in Gen. Preventive Medicine, 1969. Intern U. Utah Affiliated Hosps., Salt Lake City, 1959-60, asst. resident in medicine, 1960-61; chief Epidemic Intelligence Svc., Ctr. for Disease Control, USPHS, HEW, Atlanta, 1961-63, dep. chief surveillance sect. epidemiology br., 1962-63, chief smallpox unit, 1963-65, dir. smallpox eradication program, 1966-70, dir. Bur. State Svcs., 1970-78, asst. dir. Ctr. for Disease Control for Pub. Health Practice, 1979-80; dir. Nat. Ctr. Environ. Health, 1980-81, Nat. Inst. for Occupation Safety and Health, Atlanta, 1981-93, chmn. exec. com. Nat. Toxicology Program, 1989-93; pres. Don Millar & Assocs., Inc., 1993—. Adj. prof. occupational and environ. health Sch. Pub. Health Emory U., Atlanta, 1988-98; cons. on smallpox, smallpox eradication, immunization programs and occupational and environ. health WHO; mem. WHO expert adv. panel on occupational health; bd. dirs. Farm Safety 4 Just Kids, 1993-98; tech. adv. bd. Ctr. Protect Workers' Rights, 1993; disting. fellow, vice chmn. Pub. Health Policy Adv. Bd., Inc., Washington, 1998—. Mem. editl. bd. Am. Jour. Indsl. Medicine, 1985—, Am. Jour. Occupl. Psychology, 1993—, Am. Jour. Preventive Medicine, 1993—; contbr. articles to profl. jours. Recipient Surgeon Gen's. Commendation medal, 1965, Okeke prize London Sch. Hygiene and Tropical Medicine, 1966, Presdl. award for mgmt. improvement, 1972, W.C. Gorgas medal Assn. Mil. Surgeons U.S., 1987, Lucas lectr. Faculty Occupational Medicine Royal Coll. Physicians, London, 1987, Outstanding Med. Alumnus award Med. Coll. Va., 1988; also recipient Equal Employment Opportunity award, 1975, Medal of Excellence, 1977, Joseph W. Mountin lectr. award, 1986, Alexander D. Langmuir MD Meml. lectr. award, 2001, all from Ctrs. for Disease Control, Disting. Svc. medal USPHS, 1983, 88, Exemplary Svc. medal Surgeon Gen. U.S., 1988, Giants in Occupational Medicine lectr. U. Utah, 1989, William S. Knudsen award Am. Coll. Occupational Medicine, 1991, presdl. citation APA, 1991, William Steiger Meml. award Am. Conf. Govtl. Indsl. Hygienists, 1993, Health Watch award for outstanding contbns. toward improving health of minority popyulations, 1992, Award of Merit Minerva Edn. Inst., 1993, Alumni Disting. Svc. award U. Richmond, 1993; named to Order Bifurcated Needle, World Health Orgn., 1978, Faculty Occupational Medicine, Royal Coll. Physicians, London, 1990; elected Safety and Health Hall of Fame Internat., Nat. Safety Coun., 1997. Mem. Am. Indsl. Hygiene Assn. (hon.), Am. Coll. Occupl. and Environ. Medicine, Am. Epidemiol. Soc., Collegium Ramazzini, Am. Assn. Pub. Health Physicians., Assn. Mil. Surgeons U.S., Pub. Health Svc. Commissioned Officers Assn., Alpha Omega Alpha.

MILLAR, RICHARD WILLIAM, JR. lawyer; b. L.A., May 11, 1938; LLB, U. San Francisco, 1966. Bar: Calif. 1967, U.S. Dist. Ct. (cen. dist.) Calif. 1967, U.S. Dist. Ct. (no. dist.) Calif. 1969, U.S. Dist. Ct. (so. dist.) Calif. 1973, U.S. Supreme Ct. Assoc. Iverson & Hogoboom, Los Angeles, 1967-72; ptnr. Eilers, Stewart, Pangman & Millar, Newport Beach, Calif., 1973-75, Millar & Heckman, Newport Beach, 1975-77, Millar, Hodges & Bemis, Newport Beach, 1979—. Fellow: Am. Bar Found.; mem.: Orange County Bar Assn. (sec. 1999, treas. 2000, pres. 2002, chmn. bus. litig. sect. 1981, chmn. judiciary com. 1988—90, dir. charitable fund 2000), Calif. Bar Assn. (lectr. CLE), ABA (litigation sect. trial practice com., ho. of dels. 1990—), Palm Valley Country Club (Palm Desert, Calif.), Pacific Club, Bohemian Club (San Francisco), Balboa Bay Club. Home: 71 Hillsdale Newport Beach CA 92660 Office: Millar Hodges & Bemis One Newport Pl Ste # 900 Newport Beach CA 92660 E-mail: millar@mhblaw.net.

MILLAR, ROBERT JAMES, social science educator; b. Abington, Pa., Feb. 15, 1951; s. Robert Eugene and Louise Ruth (Mitsch) M.; m. Lynn C. Harding, May 18, 1974; children: Nancy, Reed, Scotty. BS in Social Studies, Kutztown U., 1973, MEd in Social Sci., 1978. Tchr. social studies Hatboro (Pa.)-Horsham Sch. Dist., 1973-75, Fleetwood (Pa.) Area Sch. Dist., 1975-77; assoc. prof. social sci. Reading (Pa.) Area Community Coll., 1977—. Instr. archeaology Kutztown (Pa.) U., 1985-92; instr. social sci. Alvernia Coll., Reading, 1986-88; resource person in anthropology and archaeology Berks County Intermediate Unit, Reading, 1984—; cons. archaeologist Borough of Shillington, Pa., 1985-92. Producer, host local TV program, ACLU Presents, 1981-88, Alternative News Show, 1991—; editor: Prehistoric Artifacts of the Schuylkill Valley, 1983. Bd. dirs. Health Systems Coun. S.E. Pa., Allentown, 1982-86; chmn. pub. affairs com. Planned Parenthood Ea. Pa., Reading, 1987-90; vice chmn. Sierra Club Berks County, Kutztown, 1988-96; chmn. Dem. Socialists Club; v.p. Dem. Coun. Berks County, 1987-89; pres. Berks County sect. ACLU, 1981-84, 86-92, bd. dirs. Pa. chpt., 1980-84; mem. Berks County Planning Commn., 1991-95. Mem. Soc. Pa. Archaeology, Schuylkill Valley Archaeology Soc. (pres. 1976-77, 81-87), Eastern States Archaeol. Fedn., Archaeol. Soc. N.J., N.Y. Archaeol. Soc. Avocations: political Americana, gardening, collecting rare books. Home: 19 Spring Ln Fleetwood PA 19522-9027 Office: Reading Area CC PO Box 1706 Reading PA 19603-1706 E-mail: lbrsmillar@earthlink.net.

MILLAR, ROGER MARTIN, JR. civil engineer, planner, consultant; b. Ft. Belvoir, Va., Apr. 21, 1959; s. Roger Martin Millar and Sara Elizabeth Boulden; m. Stephanie Jean Lawson, Apr. 17, 1998; children: Madeleine, Roger III. BSCE, U. Va., 1982. Registered profl. engr., Oreg., Wash., Idaho, Wyo., Colo., Pa. Rsch. asst. Va. Hwy. and Transp. Rsch. Coun., Charlottesville, 1978-81; constrn. engr. Haley, Chisholm, and Morris, 1982; project mgr. Office of Transp., City of Portland, Oreg., 1983-86, prin. engr., divsn. mgr., 1986-90; dir. transp. and environ. svcs. Otak, Lake Oswego, 1990-95, prin., 1995-98, prin., regional dir. Carbondale, Colo., 1998—. Project mgr. urban design River Dist. Devel. Plan, Portland, 1994; project mgr. engring. Portland Central City Streetcar; vice chair Tualatin Valley Econ. Devel. Corp., Tigard, Oreg., 1996-98. Sec. Columbia Corridor Assn., Portland, 1994-97; bd. dirs. Oreg. Trout, Portland, 1997-2001. Recipient Dave Fredrikson Meml. award Columbia Corridor Assn., 1993. Fellow ASCE (chair Pacific N.W. Coun. 1997-98, named Outstanding Young mem. Oreg. sect. 1990); mem. Am. Consulting Engrs. Coun., Am. Inst. Cert. Planners, Am. Planning Assn. Presbyterian. Avocations: fly fishing, skiing. Office: Otak 36 N 4th St Carbondale CO 81623

MILLAR, SALLY GRAY, nurse; b. Madison, Wis., Dec. 8, 1946; d. William Llewellyn and Janet Josephine (Dean) M. Student, U. Iowa, 1964-65; R.N., St. Joseph Hosp. Sch. Nursing, 1968; MBA, Simmons Coll. Grad. Sch. Mgmt., 1985. Staff nurse Bryn Mawr (Pa.) Hosp., 1968-69; team leader, cardiac surg. intensive care unit Mass. Gen. Hosp., Boston, 1969-78, head nurse, respiratory/surg. intensive care unit, 1978-81, clin. nurse leader, intensive care nursing service, 1981-85, project dir. patient classification system, 1985-86, dir. nursing info. systems, 1986-97, dir. integrated clin. support svcs., 1997—. Editor: Focus on Critical Care, 1978-80; editor-in-chief: Methods in Critical Care, 1980, Procedure Manual for Critical Care, 1985. Mem. Am. Assn. Critical Care Nurses (pres. 1980-81, dir. 1976-82), Soc. Critical Care Medicine. Republican. Roman Catholic. Home: 849 Boston Post Rd E Apt 3E Marlborough MA 01752-3700 Office: Mass Gen Hosp 32 Fruit St Boston MA 02114-2620

MILLARD, CHARLES PHILLIP, manufacturing company executive; b. Janesville, Wis., Apr. 21, 1948; s. Duane Francis and Mary Lou (Ganley) M.; m. Mary Franzen, Oct. 7, 1967 (div. June 13, 1990); children: Katherine, Laura. Student, U. Wis., Janesville, 1966-67. Spot welder Gen. Motors Corp., Janesville, 1966-67; plant mgr. Insta-Foam Products, Addison, Ill., 1967-72; warehouse mgr. Ram Golf Corp., Elk Grove, 1972-77; master scheduler Gandalf Data Inc., Wheeling, 1977-84, corp. mfg. coord., 1984-85; corp. mktg. coord. Gandalf Technologies Inc., 1985-87, corp. strategist, 1988-89; internat. rsch. analyst Gandalf Data Inc., 1989-90; asst. mgr. safety/security Fellowes Mfg. Co., Itasca, Ill., 1990-93; process specialist, cons. Janesville, Wis., 1993-94; asst. mgr. Janesville Travel Ctr., 1994-95; prodn. material coord. Alliant TechSystems, 1995-96; prodn. inventory control mgr. fabrication divsn. Freedom Plastics, 1997-99; armed security staff U.S. Attys. Office, Fed. Cthse. & FEMA Facilities, Madison, 2000. Patrol Officer Des Plaines (Ill.) Police Res., 1987-89; vol. with Alzheimer patients, 1999-2000. Mem. Am. Mgmt. Assn., Am. Mktg. Assn., Furniture Workers Union, Am. Fedn. Police, Nat. Rifle Assn. Avocations: physical fitness, motorcycling, home improvements, auto mechanics.

MILLARD, CHARLES WARREN, III, museum director, writer; b. Elizabeth, N.J., Dec. 20, 1932; s. Charles Warren and Constance Emily (Keppler) M. AB magna cum laude, Princeton U., 1954; MA, Harvard U., 1963, PhD, 1971. Asst. to dir. Fogg Art Mus. Harvard U., Cambridge, Mass., 1963-64; asst. to dir. Dumbarton Oaks, Washington, 1965-66; dir. Washington Gallery Modern Art, 1966-67; teaching fellow Harvard U., 1968-69; curator 19th Century European art L.A. County Mus. Art, 1971-74; chief curator Hirshhorn Mus. and Sculpture Garden Smithsonian Instn., Washington, 1974-86; adj. prof. Johns Hopkins U., Balt., 1983-86; dir. Ackland Art Mus. U. N.C., Chapel Hill, 1986-93, adj. prof., 1986-93; chmn. vis. com. to fine arts dept. Boston U., 1977-80. Chmn. nat. adv. bd. Ackland Art Mus., 2000—. Author: The Sculpture of Edgar Degas, 1977, La Vie d'Auguste Preault, Auguste Preault Sculpteur Romantique, 1809-1879, 1997; art editor Hudson Rev., 1972-87; contbr. articles to profl. jours. With USN, 1956-59.

MILLARD, ESTHER LOUND, foundation administrator, educator; b. Metaline, Wash., June 10, 1909; d. Peter S. and Emily Christine (Dahlgren) Lound; m. Homer Behne Millard, Apr. 25, 1951 (dec. May 1962). BA, U. Wis., 1933, MA, 1935. Cert. tchr., Oreg., Wis. Instr. U. Hawaii, Honolulu, 1938-43; joined USN, 1943, advanced through ranks to lt. commdr., resigned, 1952; dir. Millard Sch., Bandon, Oreg., 1954-81; pres. Millard Found., 1984—. Trustee Falcon Found., Colorado Springs, Colo., 1986—; established scholarship fund for med. sch. students, U. Wis, Millard honors program benefitting cadets at USAF Acad. Mem. Bascom Hill Soc. (U. Wis.), Women's Meml. Found. (charter), Phi Beta Kappa. Republican. Avocations: reading, music, gardening. Home: 56557 Tom Smith Rd Bandon OR 97411-6309

MILLARD, HERBERT DEAN, dentist; b. Grayling, Mich., May 22, 1924; s. Harold Herbert and Hulda Helen (Phoebe) Millard; m. Dolores Helen Pyers, June 19, 1948; children: Mary Helen Mayo, Thomas Alan, Alice Lynn McCormick;1 child Anna Elizabeth. DDS, U. Mich., 1952, MS, 1956; FDS (hon.) , Royal Coll. Physicians & Surgeons, Glasgow, Scotland, 2000. Emeritus prof. of dentistry U. Mich., Ann Arbor, 1989—; editor Am. Acad. Oral Medicine, N.Y.C., 1989—94, Mich. Dental Assoc., Lansing, Mich., 1967—72; prof. of dentistry U. Mich., 1956—89. Mem. council Dental Therapeutic Am. Dental Assoc., Chgo., 1968—74. Co-author: (textbook) Oral Diagnosis 6 edition , 1959—83. Cpl. Army Air Corp, 1943—45, Italy. Mem.: Ann Arbor Rotary Club (pres. 1986—87, Paul Harris fellow 1995). Avocations: singing, golf, bowling. Home: 1205 Glen Leven Rd Ann Arbor MI 48103 Office: U Mich 1011 N U Ave Rm 303 Ann Arbor MI 48109-1078 E-mail: hdean@umich.edu.

MILLARD, JAMES KEMPER, marketing executive; b. Lexington, Ky., Oct. 28, 1948; s. Lyman Clifford and Cora (Carrick) M.; m. Madelyn Hooper, Nov. 26, 1983; children: Lyman Clifford III, Sean Duffy, James Kemper Jr., Caroline Carrick. BA, Transylvania U., Lexington, Ky., 1971. Writer AP, Lexington, 1970—71; asst. news. dir. Sta. WLEX-TV, FM, 1971—76; producer Ky. Dept. Pub. Info., Frankfort, 1973; dir. univ. rels. Transylvania U., Lexington, 1973—79; acct. supr. Abbott Advt., Inc., 1979—85; mktg. dir. Steak N' Shake, Inc., Indpls., 1985; field mktg. mgr. Blue Bell, Pa., 1985—86; field mktg. dir. Nutri/System Inc., 1986—88, v.p. communications, 1988—90, sr. v.p. mktg., 1990—91; pres. Mktg. Comm. Overview, Inc., Exton, 1991—93, Waterwild Mktg., Lexington, Ky., 1993—94; dir. promotion and devel. Sta. WKYT-TV, 1994—99; exec. cons. eCorporation, 1999—2000; pres. ConnectedCampus.com., 1999—2000; sr. v.p. devel./strategy Equity Technologies and Resources, Inc., Lexington, 2000—02, pres., CEO, 2002—; pres. ETCR Mergers and Acquisitions, Inc., 2001—; COO, Verified Prescription Safeguards, Inc., 2002—. Mem. acad. adv. com. Ea. Ky. U., Richmond, 1983-87; treas. Bluegrass Integrated Pest Mgmt., Lexington, 1983-85; case study spkr. Radio Advertisers Bur., 1989, 90. Author: C&O Streamliners, 1994. Mem. Comdr.-in-Chief Leadership Circle, 1990—; pres. Swan Kitchen Car Co., 1990—; mem. Am. Assn. Pvt. R.R. Car Owners, 1990—, R.R. Passenger Car Alliance, 1990—, Hon. Order Ky. Cols., 1976—; cons. Jr. Achievement; mem. campaign cabinet United Way of Bluegrass, 1995, mem. dream team, 1998—99; mem. devel. coun. Midway Coll., 1995—; deacon Ctrl. Christian Ch., Lexington, 1984—86, 1994—2001; bd. dirs. Chesapeake and Ohio Ry. Hist. Soc., Clifton Forge, Va., 1983—98, v.p., 1994—97; bd. dirs. Found. for Affordable Housing, 1995—, Friends of McConnell Springs, 1998—, chmn., 2002—; bd. dirs. Bluegrass Trust for Hist. Preservation, 1998—, v.p., 1999, pres., 2000—02; trustee Lexington (Ky.) History Mus., 2000—; chmn. Friends of McConnell Springs. Recipient Great Menu award Nat. Restaurant Assn., 1982, Key Man award Jerrico Inc., 1981, Silver and Bronze ADDY Awards Lexington Advt. Club, 1982, Gold Award Fla. Restaurant Assn., 1984, Innovative Idea award Ky. Broadcasters Assn., 1995. Mem. Rotary Internat., Delta Sigma Phi (pres. U. Ky. corp. bd. 1994-97). Democrat. Mem. Christian Ch. (Disciples Of Christ). Address: Waterwild Farm PO Box 12012 Lexington KY 40579-2012 E-mail: jmillard@mis.net.

MILLARD, MAX, pathologist; b. London, Apr. 8, 1921; came to U.S., 1952; s. Morris and Annie (Zlotover) M.; m. Heather Millard, Apr. 4, 1951; children— Lesley Ann, Gillian Linda. M.D., U. Dublin, 1944, M.A. (hon.), 1952. Diplomate Am. Bds. Clin. Anat. Pathology. Resident, Jackson Meml. Hosp., Miami, Fla., 1952-55; assoc. prof. U. Miami Sch. Medicine, 1960-72; asst. pathologist Jackson Meml. Hosp., 1955-64, dir. surg. pathology, 1964-72; cons. pathologist Bromley & Farnborough Hosps., London, 1972-76; dir. dept. pathology South Miami Hosp., 1976— . Served to capt. M.C., Royal Army, 1948-49. Fellow Royal Soc. Medicine, Royal Coll. Pathologists, Royal Coll. Physicians Ireland; mem. Internat. Acad. Pathology. Author: Autopsy Pathology, 1953; contbr. chpts. to books. Office: South Miami Hosp 6200 SW 73rd St Miami FL 33143-4679

MILLARD, NEAL STEVEN, lawyer; b. Dallas, June 6, 1947; s. Bernard and Adele (Marks) M.; m. Janet Keast, Mar. 12, 1994; 1 child, Kendall Layne. BA cum laude, UCLA, 1969; JD, U. Chgo., 1972. Bar: Calif. 1972, U.S. Dist. Ct. (cen. dist.) Calif. 1973, U.S. Tax Ct. 1973, U.S. Ct. Appeals (9th cir.) 1987, N.Y. 1990. Assoc. Willis, Butler & Schiefly, Los Angeles, 1972-75; ptnr. Morrison & Foerster, 1975-84, Jones, Day, Reavis & Pogue, Los Angeles, 1984-93, White & Case, L.A., 1993—. Instr. Calif. State Coll., San Bernardino, 1975-76; lectr. Practising Law Inst., N.Y.C., 1983-90, Calif. Edn. of Bar, 1987-90; adj. prof. USC Law Ctr., 1994—. Citizens adv. com. L.A. Olympics, 1982-84; trustee Altadena (Calif.) Libr. Dist., 1985-86; bd. dirs. Woodcraft Rangers, L.A., 1982-90, pres., 1986-88; bd. dirs. L.A. County Bar Found., 1990-2000, pres., 1997-98; mem. Energy Commn. of County and Cities of L.A., 1995-99; bd. dirs. Inner City Law Ctr., 1996-99; mem. jud. procedures commn. L.A. County, 1999—, chair, 2000—. Mem. ABA, Calif. Bar Assn., N.Y. State Bar Assn., L.A. County Bar Assn. (trustee 1985-87), Pub. Counsel (bd. dirs. 1984-87, 90-93), U. Chgo. Law Alumni Assn. (pres. 1998-2001), USC Inst. for Corporate Counsel (advisory bd. 1998—), Calif. Club, Phi Beta Kappa, Pi Gamma Mu, Phi Delta Phi. Office: White & Case 633 W 5th St Ste 1900 Los Angeles CA 90071-2087 E-mail: nmillard@whitecase.com.

MILLARD, RICHARD STEVEN, lawyer; b. Pasadena, Calif., Feb. 6, 1952; s. Kenneth A. and Kathryn Mary (Paden) M.; m. Jessica Ann Edwards, May 15, 1977; children: Victoria, Elizabeth, Andrew. AB, Stanford U., 1974; JD magna cum laude, U. Mich., 1977. Bar: Calif. 1977, Ill. 1985. Assoc. Heller, Ehrman, White & McAuliff, San Francisco, 1977-81, Mayer, Brown & Platt, Chgo., 1982-83, ptnr., 1984-99, Weil, Gotshal & Manges, Redwood Shores, Calif., 1999—. Mem. ABA, Order of Coif. Office: Weil Gotshal & Manges 201 Redwood Shores Pkwy Redwood City CA 94065 E-mail: richard.millard@weil.com.

MILLAY, KATHLEEN KRINER, communication disorders educator; b. Chambersburg, Pa., May 12, 1946; d. Ray R. and Janet (Groft) Kriner; m. Robert H. Millay, Sept. 2, 1967; children: Timothy, Meredith, Tyler. BA, Wittenberg U., 1968; MA, Mich. State U., 1969; PhD, U. Tex.-Dallas, Richardson, 1984. Assoc. prof. comm. disorders Tex. Woman's U., Denton, 1989—; co-dir. Ft. Worth Cleft Palate Program, 1995—. Cons. Ft. Worth Lost Chord Club, 1994—; co-dir. distance learning grad. program Tex. Edn. Assn., Mt. Pleasant, 1994-97. Mem.: Tex. Speech, Lang. and Hearing Assn., Am. Speech, Lang. and Hearing Assn. (cert. clin. competence in audiology and speech-lang. pathology). Avocations: cycling, horseback riding. Home: 318 N Rosemont Ave Dallas TX 75208-5415 Office: Tex Woman's U Dept Comm Scis-Disorders PO Box 425737 Denton TX 76204-5737 E-mail: F_Millagy@twu.edu.

MILLENDER-MCDONALD, JUANITA, congresswoman, school system administration; b. Birmingham, Ala., Sept. 7, 1938; d. Shelly and Everlina (Dortch) M.; m. James McDonald III, July 26, 1955; children: Valeria, Angela, Sherryll, Michael, Roderick. BS, U. Redlands, Calif., 1980; MS in Edn., Calif. State U., L.A., 1986; postgrad., U. So. Calif. Manuscript editor Calif. State Dept. Edn., Sacramento; dir. gender equity programs L.A. Unified Sch. Dist.; mem. U.S. Congress from 37th Calif dist., Washington, 1996—; mem. small bus. com., transp. and infrastructure com. City councilwoman, Carson; bd. dirs. S.C.L.C. Pvt. Industry Coun. Policy Bd., West Basin Mcpl. Water Dist., Cities Legis. League (vice chmn.; mem. Nat. Women's Polit. Caucus; mem. adv. bd. Comparative Ethnic Tng. U. So. Calif.; founder, exec. dir. Young Advocates So. Calif. Mem. NEA, Nat. Assn. Minority Polit. Women, NAFE, Nat. Fedn. Bus. and Profl. Women, Assn. Calif. Sch. Adminstrs., Am. Mgmt. Assn., Nat. Coun. Jewish Women, Carson C. of C., Phi Delta Kappa. Democrat. Office: US House Reps 125 Cannon Bldg Washington DC 20515-0537*

MILLEPIED, BENJAMIN, ballet dancer; b. Bordeaux, France; Studied with Michel Rahn, Conservatoire Nat., Lyon, France; studied, Sch. Am. Ballet, 1992—93. Mem. corps de ballet N.Y.C. Ballet, 1995—98, soloist, 1998—. Dancer (ballets) 2 & 3 Part Inventions, prin. roles Agon, Ballo Della Regina, Chaconne, Coppelia, Divertimento from "Le Baiser de la Fee", Jewels, A Midsummer Night's Dream, The Nutcracker, La Sonnambula, La Source, Stars and Stripes, Symphony in C., Bournonville Divertissements, Brandenburg, Les Noces, numerous others. Recipient Prix de Lausanne award, 1994, Mae L. Wien award, 1995; scholar, French Ministry, 1993. Office: NYC Ballet NY State Theatre 20 Lincoln Ctr Plz New York NY 10023-6913*

MILLER, AARON E. neurologist; b. Balt., June 19, 1943; s. Isadore H. Miller and Florence Kovitz; m. Ellen Sue Goldstein, Sept. 10, 1978; children: Alexandra Michelle, Caroline Julie. BA, Brandeis U., 1964; MD, NYU, 1968. Asst. prof. neurology Albert Einstein Coll. Medicine, Bronx, N.Y., 1978-81; dir. divsn. neurology Maimonides Med. Ctr., Bklyn., 1981—. Prof. clin. neurology SUNY-Health Sci. Ctr., Bklyn., 1992-2001; clin. prof. neurology Mt. Sinai Sch. Medicine, 2001—. Author: (with others) Handbook of Neurology, 2001; contbr. articles to profl. jours. Lt. comdr. USN, 1971-73. Fellow Am. Acad. Neurology (chmn. multiple sclerosis sect. Mpls. chpt. 1996-97, co-chmn. edn. com. Mpls. chpt. 1997—); mem. Nat. Multiple Sclerosis Soc. (chmn. profl. edn. com. 1993-2001, chief med. officer and chmn. med. adv. bd. 2002—), Alpha Omega Alpha, Phi Beta Kappa. Bus. Office: Maimonides Med Ctr 4802 10th Ave Brooklyn NY 11219-2844 E-mail: amiller@maimonidesmed.org.

MILLER, ADAM DAVID, poet, publishing executive; b. St. George, Calif., Oct. 8, 1922; s. Adam and Margaret Ann (Butler) M.; m. Betty Jean Brown (div.); children: Robin Kate, Pemba Sadas; m. Sharon Elise Peeples. BA, U. Calif., Berkeley, 1948, MA, 1952. Cert. cert. tchr. Calif. Tchr. Vallejo (Calif.) High Sch., 1955, Oakland (Calif.) Tech. High Sch., 1957—59, San Francisco State Coll., 1962—67, Tuskegee (Ala.) Inst., 1965, Laney C.C., Oakland, 1967—68, U. Calif., Berkeley, 1987—91. Author: poems (Naomi Long Madgett poetry award). Commr. Pub. Arts Commn., Berkeley, 1997—. OM class 3 USN, 1942—46. Recipient Naomi Long Madgett poetry award; fellow fellowship, NEA, 1973—74, Bay Area Writing Project, 1978, 1994. Mem.: Nat. Writers Union, PEN USA. Office: Eshu House Publishing PO Box 162 Berkeley CA 94701-0162 E-mail: eshuhouse@yahoo.com.

MILLER, ADELE ENGELBRECHT, educational administrator; b. Jersey City, July 31, 1946; d. John Fred and Dorathea Kathryn (Kamm) Engelbrecht; m. William A. Miller, Jr., Dec. 21, 1981. BS in Bus. Edn., Fairleigh Dickinson U., 1968, MBA magna cum laude, 1974; cert. in pub. sch. adminstrn. and supervision, Jersey City State Coll., 1976. Bus. tchr. Jersey City Bd. Edn., 1967-99, coord. coop. bus. edn. programs, 1973-99, acting v.p., 1985-86, prin. of summer sch., 1986, chmn. dept., 1996-99. Adj. instr. St. Peter's Coll., 1974-75; curriculum cons. Cittone Bus. Sch., 1981-82; mem. adv. coun. Dickinson H.S., 1973-99, chmn., 1978-80; organizer, bd. dirs. Frances Nadel and Cooke-Connolly-Coffey-Witt Faculty Meml. Scholarships, 1978-99; trustee Dickinson H.S. Parents Coun., 1985-88. Co-author: New Jersey Cooperative Business Education Coordinators Resource Manual, 1984; author coop. bus. edn. study course Jersey City Pub. Schs., 1980, 84. Mem. Citizens Adv. Coun. to Mayor of Jersey City, 1968—71; organizer, dir. Jersey City Youth Week, 1970—72; chmn. juv. conf. com. Hudson County Juv. Ct., 1978—; v.p., sec., trustee, chmn. dinner-musicale Jersey City Coll.-Comty. Orch., 1979—88; explorer scouting adv. bd. Hudson-Hamilton coun. bd. Scouts Am., 1985—88; trustee YWCA of Hudson County, 1988—99; dir. CREATE Charter High Sch., 2001—. Recipient Dickinson H.S. Key Club Tchr. of Yr. award 1971, Merrill-Lynch Outstanding Performance in Edn. award, 1995; named Educator of Yr. Dickinson H.S. Parents Coun., 1987-88. Mem.: AAUW (edn. chmn., sec. N.J. divsn., del. to White House briefing on edn., women's issues, arms control, dist. coord., chmn. nominations, historian), NEA, Jersey City Woman's Club (scholarship chmn., adviser Jr. Woman's Club), N.J. Fedn. Women's Clubs, Vocat. Edn. Assn. N.J., N.J. Bus.

Edn. Assn., N.J. Coop. Bus. Edn. Coords. Assn. (pres., v.p., sec., treas. 1991—92, Coop. Edn. Coord. of Yr.), Jersey City Edn. Assn. (bldg. dir.), N.J. Edn. Assn., Jersey City Rotary Club (dir., Interact Club advisor, program chmn., sec., v.p., pres., gov.'s rep., Vocational Svc. award 2001, Paul Harris Fellow, Walter Head Fellow), Coll. Club Jersey City (pres., v.p., sec.), Lake Hopatcong Yacht Club, Rotary (internat. dist. 7490), Phi Delta Kappa. Home: 91 Sherman Pl Jersey City NJ 07307-3729 E-mail: millerassoc@nac.net.

MILLER, AILEEN ETTA MARTHA, medical association administrator, nutritionist; b. Sullivan, Ind., Oct. 4, 1924; d. Arthur Henry and Alice Maria (Michael) Dettmer; m. Robert Charles Miller, Sept. 1, 1945; children: Robert Conrad, Debra Carol, Theresa Marie. D of Chiropractic, Palmer Coll. Chiropractic, 1945. Sec. Soroptomist Internat., East Detroit, Mich., 1951-52, Mich. State Chiropractic Assn. Dist. 1, East Detroit, 1957-58, Macomb County Chiropractic Assn., East Detroit, 1982-86, pres. Warren, 1986-87. Cons. Chiropractic Physicians, Roseville, 1986—. Min. United Metaphysical Ch., Shelby Township, Mich. Mem.: Atlas Orthogonal Chiropractic Assn., Macomb County Chiropractic Assn., Mich. State chiropractic Assn., Ind. Assn. Spiritualists, Found. Chiropractic Edn. and Rsch., Roy Sweat Rsch. and Edn. Found., Palmer Coll. Alumni Assn. (Humanitarian and Svc. award 1995), Divine Dimensions Inst. (minister), Assn. Rsch. and Enlightenment, Order Ea. Star. Avocations: travel, bible study. Office: 13831 Treeland Dr Shelby Township MI 48315-6058

MILLER, ALAN, software executive, management specialist; b. Bklyn., Apr. 20, 1954; s. Michael and Lillian Charlotte (Garment) M.; m. Zelda Sara Bochlin, Nov. 16, 1974; children: Michael Glenn, Dara Jennifer. BS in Computer Sci. magna cum laude, SUNY, 1975; MBA in Mgmt. with honors, Adelphi U., 1982. Tech. svcs. mgr. Guardian Life Ins. Co., N.Y.C., 1977-81; project mgr. Mfrs. Hanover Trust Co., 1981-83; asst. v.p. Bankers Trust Co., 1983-86; v.p., MIS dir. Bank Am. Trust Co. of N.Y., 1986-87; assoc. John Diebold and Assocs., 1987-89; mgr. banking practice AGS Info. Svcs., 1989-90; v.p. mktg. and bus. devel., product mgr. global trade fin. BIS Banking Systems, 1990-93; sr. cons. Computer Scis. Corp., 1994-95; solution exec. global fin. industries IBM Software Solutions, Somers, NY, 1995—98; client exec. Goldman Sachs Group IBM Corp., N.Y.C., 1998—. Chmn. Sch. Dist. Adv. Com., Plainview, N.Y., 1981-83; exec. producer Oklahoma prodn. Patio Players, Plainview, 1990-91; bd. dirs. men's club Plainview Jewish Ctr., 1986-95. Mem. Delta Mu Delta. Jewish. Avocations: softball, theater, games shows, volleyball. Home: 21 Beaumont Dr Plainview NY 11803-2507 Office: IBM 33 Maiden Ln New York NY 10038-4598 E-mail: Alan.Miller@us.ibm.com.

MILLER, ALAN B. hospital management executive; b. N.Y.C., Aug. 17, 1937; s. Daniel and Mary (Blumenthal) M.; m. Jill K. Stein, Oct. 5, 1968; children: Marc Daniel, Marni Elizabeth, Abby Danielle. BA, Coll. William and Mary, 1958; MBA, U. Pa., 1960. V.p. Young & Rubicam, Inc., N.Y.C., 1964-69; sr. v.p. Am. Medicorp., Inc., L.A., 1970, pres., chief exec. officer Phila., 1973-77, chmn. bd., 1977, Hosp. Underwriting Group, 1977-78; founder, pres., chmn. bd. Universal Health Svcs., King of Prussia, Pa., 1978—; chmn., founder UHT-Real Estate Trust, 1986—. Formerly health care adviser Fed. Mediation and Conciliation Svc.; chmn., pres. Universal Health Svcs. Real Estate Investment Trust, N.Y. Stock Exch., 1986—; bd. dirs. CDI Corp., Broadlane, Penn Mut. Life Ins.; mem. exec. bd. Wharton Sch., U. Pa. Chmn. Opera Co. of Phila. Capt. USAR. Mem. Phila. C. of C. (bd. dir.). Home: 57 Crosby Brown Rd Gladwyne PA 19035-1512 Office: Universal Health Svcs Inc 367 S Gulph Rd King Of Prussia PA 19406

MILLER, ALAN GILMORE, psychiatrist; b. Port Townsend, Wa., Apr. 3, 1931; s. Horace G. and Anastasia B. (Skeith) M.; m. Marilyn Waters, Aug. 11, 1954 (div. June 1962); children: Kenneth A., Richard R.; m. Brenda Sullivan, Mar. 26, 1966 (div. Feb. 1983); children: Kathleen A., Kerry H.; m. Marilyn Wilkerson, May 26, 1989; children: Teresa Wilkerson, John Wilkerson. BA, Willamette U., 1952; MD, U. Oreg., 1955. Diplomate Am. Bd. Psychiatry and Neurology in psychiatry. Commd. lt. (j.g.) USN, 1956, advanced through grades to capt., 1970, ret., 1977; intern Sacramento County Hosp., 1955-56; resident psychiatry Naval Hosp., Oakland, Calif., 1957-60; psychiatrist 3rd Mar Divsn. FMF, Okinawa, 1960-62; chief psychiatry svc. Naval Hosp., St. Albans, N.Y., 1962-71; asst. chief psychiatry svc. Nat. Naval Med. Ctr., Bethesda, Md., 1971-73; psychiatrist Naval Acad., Annapolis, 1973-76; pvt. practice, 1977-82; staff psychiatrist VA Med. Ctr., Reno, 1982-86, dir. outpatient mental health svcs. Perry Point, Md., 1986—. Fellow Am. Acad. Psychoanalysis; mem. Am. Group Psychotherapy Assn., Am. Psychiat. Assn. (life). Avocation: golf. Office: VA Med Ctr PO Box 26 Perry Point MD 21902-0026

MILLER, ALAN JAY, rare book dealer, author; b. Bklyn., July 11, 1936; s. Louis and Claire (Maltz) M.; m. Susan Ruth Morris, Oct. 29, 1961; children—Laurie Ann, Adam Louis. BA, Cornell U., 1957. Chartered fin. analyst. Pres. Analysis-in-Depth Inc., N.Y.C., 1965-67; mng. editor Value Line Investment Survey, 1967-68; rsch. dir. Emanuel Deetjen & Co., 1968-69; exec. v.p., dir. Intersci. Capital Mgmt. Corp., 1969-71; pres., dir. ICM Equity Fund Inc., 1970-71, ICM Fin. Fund Inc., N.Y.C., 1970-71; v.p., assoc. rsch. dir. Bache & Co., Inc., 1972, G.H. Walker & Co., Inc., N.Y.C., 1972-73; 1st v.p., assoc. rsch. dir. Blyth Eastman Dillon & Co. Inc., 1974-76; dir. rsch. E.F. Hutton & Co., Inc., 1976-81, sr. v.p., 1976-80, exec. v.p., 1981-88; dir. Hutton Investment Mgmt., 1976-88; mng. dir. SLH Asset Mgmt. Shearson Lehman Hutton, Inc, N.Y.C., 1988-90; sr. v.p. Martin E. Segal Co., 1990-92. Adj. assoc. prof. Columbia U. Grad. Sch. Bus., 1978-79; mem. faculty N.Y. Inst. Fin., 1977-98; adj. prof. Adelphi U. Coll., 1993-98; rare book dealer, 1998—. Author: Socially Responsible Investing: How to Invest with Your Conscience, 1991, Standard and Poor's 401(k) Planning Guide, 1995. Mem. N.Y. Soc. Security Analysts, Fin. Analysts Fedn. E-mail: alan@alansbooks.com.

MILLER, ALAN M. editor, educator, writer; b. N.Y.C., July 24, 1934; s. Philip and Sylvia (Lubash) M.; children: Neil, Peter, Stephanie, Douglas; m. Sharon A. Tanenbaum, Aug. 29, 1996; step-children: Holly Harouche, Becky Theodoratos. AB, Syracuse U., 1955, LLB, 1958, JD, 1968. Asst. counsel 3 joint legis. coms. N.Y. State Legislature, 1968-70; counsel to minority Nassau County Bd. Suprs., 1974-75; prin. atty. editor West Group, Westbury, N.Y., Eagan, Minn., 1985—. Adj. faculty screenwriting Mpls. Coll., 1999—, Hofstra U., 1990-97, Discovery Ctr., 1990-94, N.Y. Inst. Tech., Old Westbury, 1987-89; presenter 2nd ann. Internat. Conf. on Law and Psychiatry, Jerusalem, 1986; judge Screenwriting competition, 2000—. Columnist South Shore Record, Woodmere, N.Y., Another Viewpoint, 1985-99 (awards N.Y. Press Assn. 1988, 89, 94, Best column award 1992), Single-Minded, 1991-92, N.Y. Bowler, 1991-93 (Bowling Mag. awards 1990-93, Best column award 1992), Nostalgia Mag., 1990-91; writer-editor USCAdvantage, 1995-99 (Immy awards 1996, 97); editor: Beyond the Bar, West Group, 2000-02; contbr. numerous articles to publs., including N.Y. Times, Newsday, Newsday Mag., Mpls. Star-Tribune, Nat. Press Assn. Assembly dist. leader N.Y. State Dem. Com., 1965-76; commn. chair Village of Woodsburgh, N.Y., 1980, chair telecommn. com. City of Eagan, Minn., 2000—; mem. citizens adv. com. for Minn. Twins, 2000—; elected to bd. of dirs. Minn. Assn. Cable TV Adminstrs.; host Access to Democracy cable TV show, 2001—. Recipient awards for coverage of Persian Gulf War from Israel, 1991, nat. coun. Jewish Women, 1991, Five Towns Sr. Couns. Mem. Am. Film Inst., Screenwriters Workshop. Jewish. Home: 4316 Aries Ct Eagan MN 55123-1825 Office: 610 Opperman Dr Eagan MN 55123-1340 Fax: 651-905-1980. E-mail: alan.miller@earthlink.net.

MILLER, ALBERT J. cardiologist, internist; b. Chgo., 1922; MD, Northwestern U., 1946. Diplomate Am. Bd. Internal Medicine, Am. Bd. Cardiovascular Diseases. Intern Michael Reese Hosp., Chgo., 1945-46, resident in medicine, 1950, fellow in cardiology rsch. Cardiovascular Inst., 1948-50; resident in medicine VA Hosp., Hines, Ill., 1950-51; attending physician Northwestern Meml. Hosp., Chgo.; prof. clin. medicine, cardiology Northwestern U. Med. Sch. Author: The Lymphatics of the Heart, 1982, Diagnosis of Chest Pain, 1988; has done basic rsch. on lymphatics of the heart. Fellow ACP, Am. Coll. Cardiology, Am. Fedn. for Clin. Rsch., Ctrl. Soc. for Clin. Rsch. Office: Clin Cardiol Group Ltd 676 N Saint Clair St Ste 1930 Chicago IL 60611-2956 E-mail: ajm057@northwestern.edu.

MILLER, ALBERT JAY, retired library and information sciences director; b. Beaver Falls, Pa., Dec. 7, 1927; s. Joseph Jefferson and Alberta Fae (Shaffer) M. BS, Geneva Coll., 1952; MLS, Rutgers U., 1958; postgrad., U. Chgo., 1960-61, U. Pitts., 1963-68, U. Mich., 1969. Libr. West Allegheny Jr. H.S., Imperial, Pa., 1959-60, Butler (Pa.) Area Sr. H.S., 1962-67, Pa. State U., New Kensington, 1969-89, tchr.-libr. continuing edn. dept., 1970-89, ret. libr. and info. svcs. dir. emeritus, 1989, prof. emeritus. Author: A Selective Bibliography of Existentialism in Education and Related Topics, 1969, Confrontation, Conflict and Dissent, 1972, Death: A Bibliographical Guide, 1977; book and media rev. editor: Learning Today, 1978— , mem. editorial bd., 1979— . Instr. water safety ARC, New Kensington, 1969—, Citizens Gen. Hosp., 1971-72; active Boy Scouts Am., 1970—; bd. dirs. Westmoreland County, Butler County mental health assns.; mem. Allegheny-Kiski Human Rels. Coun., 1976-77; bd. dirs. Allegheny-Kiski Sr. Citizens Center, 1976-77, fund raising chmn., 1989-90; 2nd v.p., 1997-98, pres., 1998—; bd. corporators Geneva Coll., Beaver Falls, Pa., 1987—; Sunday Sch. tchr. Manchester Ref. Presbyn. Ch., 1970—, elder, 1984—, clk. of session, 1984—, Sabbath Sch. supt., 1990, elder emeritus; mem., pub. rels. dir. Twirling Unltd., Akron, Ohio; baton twirler Kensington Firemens Band; entrepreneur Al's Terrific Twirling Tricks-Catch It; tchr., judge Nat. Baton Twirling Assn., 1998; book reader People's Libr. New Kensington, Pa. N.Y. State Hall of fame Twirling Champion, 1999. Mem. NEA (life), Pa. Edn. Assn. (life), ALA, Pa. Lib. Assn., U.S. Twirling Assn. (profl. mem.). Democratic. Home: 160 Crosswynds Dr Beaver Falls PA 15010-1182

MILLER, ALLAN JOHN, lawyer; b. Beachwood, Ohio, Oct. 17, 1921; s. Carl Frederick and Rhoda (Warren) M.; m. Marjorie Hewitt Pirtle, Aug. 10, 1946; children: James W., Patricia Anne. BBA, Fenn Coll., 1946; LL.B., Western Res. U., 1948; D. (hon.), Dyke Coll., Cleve., 1986. Bar: Ohio 1948. With Standard Oil Co., Ohio, 1948-77, treas., 1967-77; mem. firm Kiefer, Knecht, Rees, Meyer & Miller, Cleve., 1977-81. Dir. United Screw & Bolt Corp., 1977-97. Chmn. bd. dirs. Luth. Med. Ctr., Cleve., 1967-82; pres. Luth. Med. Ctr. Med. Staff Found., 1979-85; bd. dirs. Christian Residencies Found., 1972-77, St. Luke's Hosp. Assn., 1973-84; chmn. bd. trustees Dyke Coll., Cleve., 1971-86. With AUS, 1943-46, PTO. Mem. Cleve. Treas.'s Club. Clubs: Capri Isles Golf Club (Venice, Fla.). Presbyterian. Home: Apt 531 900 Tamiami Trl S Venice FL 34285-3627 E-mail: ajmvenice@cs.com.

MILLER, ALLEN RICHARD, retired mathematician; b. Bklyn., 1942; BS, Bklyn. Coll., 1965; MA, U. Md., 1971. Mathematician U.S. Naval Rsch. Lab., Washington, 1968-93; prof. George Washington U., 1992-95; ret. Contbr. articles to profl. jours. With U.S. Army, 1965-67. Achievements include research in special functions and applied mathematics.

MILLER, ALLEN TERRY, JR. lawyer; b. Alexandria, Va., Sept. 19, 1954; s. Allen Terry and Eleanor Jane (Thompson) M.; m. Maureen Ann Callaghan, June 22, 1985; children: Brendan Allen, Patrick Joseph, Brigit Eleanor. BA, U. Va., 1977; JD, Seattle U., 1982. Bar: Wash. 1982, U.S. Dist. Ct. (we. dist.) Wash. 1982, U.S. Ct. Appeals (9th cir.) 1985, U.S. Dist. Ct. (ea. dist.) Wash. 1986, U.S. Dist. Ct. (no. dist.) N.Y. 1990, U.S. Dist. Ct. (we. dist.) Mich. 1990, U.S. Supreme Ct. 1990, U.S. Ct. Appeals (2d and 6th cirs.) 1991. Legis. asst. Congressman Paul N. McCloskey Jr., Washington, 1978-79; asst. atty. gen. State of Washington, Olympia, 1982-92; prin. Connolly, Tacon & Meserve, 1992—. Adj. prof. environ. law Seattle U., 1991—2001. Commr. Olympia Planning Commn., 1987-92, vice-chair, 1991, chair, 1992; mem. North Capitol Campus Heritage Pk. Devel. Assn., 1989—, sec., 1989-90, pres., 1991—; pres. Olympia Chorale and Light Opera Co., 1984-85; mem. St. Michael's Sch. Bd., 1993-96, chair, 1994-96; bd. dirs. South Sound YMCA, 1996—, Olympia Symphony, 1999-2001, Olympia Sch. Dist. Found., 1998—; pres. bd. dirs. United Way Thurston County, 1998—, pres. 2000-02; pres. Olympia Yashiro Sister City Assn., 2001-02. Recipient Merit award Am. Planning Assn., 1989, 92, Citizen of Yr. award Thurston County, 1998. Mem. ABA, Wash. Bar Assn. (mem. environ. law sect. 1984—, ct. rules com. 1985-89, jud. recommendation com. 1991-94, legis. com. 1994-97, ct. improvement com. 1997-2000), Thurston County Bar Assn., Leadership Thurston County, Olympic-Thurston C. of C. (trustee 1996-00, pres.-elect 1997, pres. 1998), Rotary (Olympia, bd. dirs. 2002—). Democrat. Roman Catholic. Avocations: mountaineering, kayaking, tennis, piano. Home: 1617 Sylvester St SW Olympia WA 98501-2228 Office: Heritage Bldg 5th and Columbia Olympia WA 98501-1114

MILLER, ALWIN VERMAR, educational advisor, consultant; b. Dardanelle, Ark., Oct. 12, 1922; s. William Marshall and Ollie Vernice (Green) M.; m. Patricia Jane Knox, Dec. 31, 1945; children: Carol, Alwin, William, Nitiya, Thomas. AA, Ark. Poly. Inst., 1939; BS, BA with honors, UCLA, 1947, MEd, 1948, EdD, 1956; cert., Internat. Inst. Ednl. Planning, (UNESCO), 1967-68. Instr. Chico (Calif.) State Coll., 1948-49; assoc. prof. So. Oreg. Coll., Ashland, 1949-57; edn. advisor AID, Washington, 1957-75; cons. on internat. devel. Upper Marlboro, Md., 1975—. Lt. col. USAF, 1942-46. Mem. ASTD, Soc. Internat. Devel., Internat. Soc. Ednl. Planning, Res. Officers Assn. (v.p. D.C. dept. 1986-87, treas. 1991-97, pres.-elect 1997-98, pres. 1998-99, Reilly Meml. Scholarship com. 1999-2002, retirement com. 2002-), Am. Legion (post comdr. 1995-96, 99-2000, dept. vice comdr. 1996-97, dept. comdr. 1997-98, vice chmn. nat. security 1999--), Mil. Order World Wars (chpt. pres. 1999-2002, nat. security com. 2002-, nat. legis. com. 2002-), Nat. Sojourners, Mil. Order of Temple of Jerusalem, Forty and Eight (grand conducteur 2000-2001), Lions, Masons, Shriners, K.T., Phi Delta Kappa. Democrat. Office: 8107 Bird Ln Greenbelt MD 20770-2104 E-mail: avmiller46@cs.com.

MILLER, ANDREA LYNN, library science educator; b. Warren, Pa., Sept. 25, 1957; d. Harlan Kermit and Hazel Adeline Samuelson; m. Michael Edward Miller, oct. 16, 1953; 1 child, Lena. BS in Edn., Clarion U., 1978, MA in English, 1982, MSLS, 1991; PhD in Info. Scis., U. Pitts., 1997. English tchr. Redbank Valley Sch. Dist., New Bethlehem, Pa., 1979-86, sch. libr. media specialist, 1986-92; assoc. prof. libr. sci. Clarion (Pa.) U., 1992—, dir. Inst. for Study and Devel. of Sci. Libr. Info. Ctrs., 2000—, dept. chair and program dir. dept. libr. sci., 2002—. Distance edn. trainer Cmty. Agile Ptnrs. in Edn., Bethlehem, 1999—, Ctr. for Distance Edn., Pa. State Sys. Higher Edn., Harrisburg, 1999—. Contbg. author: Powerful Public Relations with Full-time Results, 2d edit., 2001; author profl. devel. workshop in field. Trustee Clarion Free Pub. Libr., 1993-99. Recipient Laura Braun scholarship, 1993; grantee Pa. State Sys. Higher Edn., 1999. Mem. ALA, ASCD, Assn. Libr. and Info. Sci. Edn., Pa. Assn. Ednl. Comms. and Tech., Assn. Pa. State Coll. and Univ. Facilities (chmn. nominating com. 1995-97), Assn. Libr. Svc. to Childen, Young Sch. Librarians (chmn. Highsmith rsch. grant award 1999-2001), Pa. Sch. Librarians Assn. (co-chmn. state curriculum com. 1998-2002), Internat. Assn. Sch. Librarians, Assn. Ednl. Comms. and Tech., Delta Kappa Gamma. Democrat. Baptist. Avocations: travel, golf, biking. Home: 35 Ross St Clarion PA 16214 Office: Clarion U Pa 840 Wood St Clarion PA 16214 Fax: (814) 393-2150. E-mail: amiller@clarion-net.com., amiller@clarion.edu.

MILLER, ANDREW DAVID, physician; b. Allentown, Pa., Oct. 2, 1953; s. Morton and Judith (Farmer) M.; m. Lynne H. Ruff, 1981; children: Rebecca, Lisa. AB, Princeton U., 1975; MD, Columbia U., 1979; MPH, Harvard U., 1982. Bd. cert. Am. Bd. Preventive Medicine. Dir. chronic disease svcs. N.J. Dept. Health, Trenton, 1982-84, dir. local health devel. svcs., 1984-92, dir. pub. health residency program, 1990-95, med. dir., family health svcs., 1992-95; project dir. Medicaid managed care Peer Rev. Orgn. N.J., East Brunswick, 1995—. Contbr. articles to profl. jours. Fellow Am. Coll. Preventive Medicine; mem. APHA, N.J. Pub. Health Assn. Jewish. Avocation: running. Office: Peer Rev Orgn NJ 557 Cranbury Rd Ste 21 East Brunswick NJ 08816-5419 E-mail: central.amiller@pronj.org.

MILLER, ANDREW KENNETH, management consultant; b. Washington, Oct. 3, 1960; s. Martin Kenneth and Rosemary Miller; m. Theresa Luk, Feb. 18, 1989; children: Elizabeth, Olivia. BA in Econs., U. Chgo., 1983; MBA, Duke U., 1985. Assoc. McLean (Va.) Group, 1985-86; project leader E.F. Hutton, N.Y.C., 1986-88; project mgr. Chem. Bank, 1988-92; lead cons. Booz Allen & Hamilton, Singapore, 1992-94; mng. assoc. Coopers & Lybrand, N.Y.C., 1994-97; sr. mgr. Ernst & Young, 1997-99; pres., CEO Milluk, Inc., 1999—; sr. v.p. Pacific Delight Tours, 2002—. Fellow Duke U. Sch. Bus., 1984-85. Mem. Nat. Eagle Scout Assn., N.Y. Rep. Club. Republican. E-mail: andrew k. Home: 201 E 87th St Apt 16d& New York NY 10128-3203 Office: Milluk Inc 201 E 87th St Apt 69 D and E New York NY 10128 E-mail: andrew_k_miller@yahoo.com.

MILLER, ANDREW PICKENS, lawyer; b. Fairfax, Va., Dec. 21, 1932; s. Francis Pickens and Helen (Hill) M.; m. Penelope Farthing, Nov. 18, 1990; children: Julia Lane, Andrew Pickens, Elise Givhan, Winfield Scott, Lucia Holcombe. AB magna cum laude, Princeton U., 1954; postgrad., New Coll., Oxford (Eng.) U., 1954-55; LLB, U. Va., 1960. Bar: Va. 1960, U.S. Supreme Ct. 1967, D.C. 1979. Asso. Penn, Stuart & Stuart, 1960-62; partner Penn, Stuart & Miller, Abingdon, Va., 1963-69; atty. gen. State of Va., 1970-77; partner Mays, Valentine, Davenport & Moore, Richmond, Va., 1977-78, Dickstein, Shapiro, Morin & Oshinsky, LLP, Washington, 1979—. Pres., Young Democratic Clubs Va., 1966-67; chmn. Washington County Dem. Com., 1967-69; Dem. nominee for U.S. Senate from Va., 1978; bd. dirs. Barter Found., 1962-69; trustee King Coll., 1966-74; mem. adv. bd. Ams. for Effective Law Enforcement, 1973-77, Center for Oceans Law and Policy, 1975-79; vice-chmn. Va. Bd. Corrections, 1983-86. Served to 1st lt. AUS, 1955-57. Fellow Am. Bar Found.; mem. ABA (ho. dels. 1971-76, action commn. to reduce ct. costs and delay 1979-84, commn. on pub. understanding about the law 1992-95), So. Conf. Attys. Gen. (vice chmn. 1972-73, chmn. 1973-74), Nat. Assn. Attys. Gen. (exec. com. 1973-74, chmn. antitrust com. 1971-76, Wyman Meml. award 1976), Va. Bar Assn. (chmn. young lawyers sect. 1967-68, exec. com. 1985-88), Am. Judicature Soc. (bd. dirs. 1973-76, exec. com. 1974-76), Soc. of Cin. (Va. standing com. 1986-89, 93-96, asst. sec., 1992-95, sec. gen. 1995-98), The John Marshall Found. (pres. 1987-89), Phi Beta Kappa, Omicron Delta Kappa. Presbyterian. Home: 1503 35th St NW Washington DC 20007-2729 Office: Dickstein Shapiro Morin & Oshinsky LLP 2101 L St NW Washington DC 20037-1526

MILLER, ANNE KATHLEEN, training company executive, technical marketing consultant; b. Denver, Sept. 15, 1942; d. John Henry and Kathryn Elizabeth (Doherty) Meyer; m. Edgar Earle Miller, Aug. 20, 1966 (div. Aug. 1976); children: Sheila Anne, Rebecca Elizabeth; m. Warren Ross Landry, Dec. 11, 1982 (dec. Oct. 1990) BS in Chemistry, St. Mary Coll., Leavenworth, Kans., 1964. Cert. jr. coll., secondary tchr., Calif. Lectr. San Jose (Calif.) State U., 1978-82; product mgr. Jasco Chem., Mountain View, Calif., 1979-82; v.p., gen. mgr. Micropel, Hayward, 1982-84; product mktg. mgr. Cambridge Instruments, Santa Clara, 1984-86, KLA Instruments, Santa Clara, 1986-87; pres., owner Meyland Enterprises, Redwood City, Calif., 1987—, Semiconductor Svc. Tng. Orgn., Redwood City, 1988—. Inventor formation of optical film. Mem. Soc. Photo Optical Instrumentation Engrs., Am. Chem. Soc., Semiconductor Industry Equipment Materials Internat., Am. Electronics Assn. Office: Semiconductor Svcs 735 Hillcrest Way Redwood City CA 94062-3453 E-mail: millerak@aol.com.

MILLER, ANNETTE K. See MATEMA, ZSUN-NEE KIMBALL

MILLER, ANNIE MOSELEY, real estate broker; b. Conyers, Ga., June 24, 1921; d. Felix Jefferson and Essie Mae (Brewer) Moseley; m. James C. Miller, Jr., July 23, 1939; children: James C. III, John K., Jerry A., Jack T., Jennifer A., Julie A. Student, U. Ga., 1969, Atlanta (Ga.) Tech. Sch., 1970, Johnson Real Estate Inst., 1974, DeKalb Coll., Decatur, Ga., 1979. Pvt. practice interior decorating, Conyers, 1970-74; sales agt. C-21 Dickson Realty, 1974-79; broker, prin. Annie Miller Realty, Inc., 1979—. Landscape appraisor Rockdale County Schs., Conyers, 1940-74, Rockdale County Chs., Conyers 1970-74; pres. bldg. com. Conyers Ch., 1969; lectr. real estate seminars Rockdale County schs. Conyers, 1979. Recipient Tri-Color Ribbons Conyers Garden Club, 1968-70. Mem. Rockdale Bd. Realtors (profl. standards com. 1985—, million dollar award 1967, 69, 70), Nat. Bd. Realtors, Ga. Bd. Realtors, Conyers-Rockdale C. of C. (Mrs. Rockdale County 1968). Republican. Presbyterian. Avocations: gardening, sewing, needlework, teaching seminars, ecology. Home: 1671 Canterbury Pointe SE Conyers GA 30013-6412 Office: 1453 Klondike Rd SW # B Conyers GA 30094-5103

MILLER, ANTHONY BERNARD, physician, medical researcher; b. Woodford, Eng., Apr. 17, 1931; married, 1952; 5 children. BA, U. Cambridge, 1952, MB, BChir, 1955. House officer Oldchurch Hosp., Romford, Eng., 1955-57; med. registrar Luton and Dunstable Hosp., Eng., 1959-62; mem. sci. staff Med. Research Council Tb and Chest Disease Unit, London, 1962-71; assoc. prof. preventive medicine and biostats. U. Toronto, 1972-76, prof., 1976-96, chmn. dept., 1992-96, dir. grad. program in epidemiology, 1986-91; dir. epidemiology unit Nat. Cancer Inst. Can., Toronto, 1971-86; dir. Nat. Breast Screening Study, 1980—, WHO Collaborating Ctr. on Evaluation of Screening for Cancer, 1991-2000; prof. emeritus, 1997—. Nat. Health scientist, 1988-93; mem. working cadre Bladder Cancer Project, U.S., 1973-75; mem. epidemology com. Breast Cancer Task Force, U.S., 1973-77, chmn., 1975-77; mem. Fed. Task Force Cervical Cytol. Screening, Can., 1974-76, 80-81, Union Internat. Contre le Cancer com., controlled therapeutic trials, 1978-82, Multidisciplinary project breast cancer, 1978-82, chmn. project on screening, 1982-93; mem. sci. council Internat. Agy. Research Cancer, Lyon, 1981-85, chmn., 1985; mem. com. on diet, nutrition and cancer NRC of U.S., 1980-83, mem. oversight com. radioepidemiologic tables, 1983-84, com. on diet and health, 1986-89, com. on dietary guidelines implementation, 1988-91, chmn. com. on environmental epidemiology, 1990-94; chmn. Ont. Task Force on Primary Prevention of Cancer, 1994-95. Served with RAF, 1957-59. Mem. Can. Oncology Soc. (sec.-treas. 1975-79, pres. 1980-81), Soc. Epidemiology Research, Internat. Epidemiology Assn., Am. Soc. Preventive Oncology (pres. 1983-85), Am. Coll. Epidemiology (bd. dirs. 1987-89). Office: DKFZ Divsn Clin Epidemiology Im Neuenheimer Feld 280 D-69120 Heidelberg Germany E-mail: a.miller@dkfz-heidelberg.de.

MILLER, ARJAY, retired university dean; b. Shelby, Nebr., Mar. 4, 1916; s. Rawley John and Mary Gertrude (Schade) M.; m. Frances Marion Fearing, Aug. 18, 1940; children: Kenneth Fearing, Ann Elizabeth (Mrs. James Olstad). BS with highest honors, UCLA, 1937; LL.D. (hon.), 1964; postgrad., U. Calif.-Berkeley, 1938-40; LL.D. (hon.), Washington U., St. Louis; LL.D., Whitman Coll., 1965, U. Nebr., 1965, Ripon Coll., 1980. Teaching asst. U. Calif. at Berkeley, 1938-40; research technician Calif. State Planning Bd., 1941; economist Fed. Res. Bank San Francisco, 1941-43; asst. treas. Ford Motor Co., 1946-53, controller, 1953-57, v.p., controller, 1957-61, v.p. finance, 1961-62, v.p. of staff group, 1962-63, pres., 1963-68, vice chmn., 1968-69; dean Grad. Sch. Bus., Stanford U., 1969-79, emeritus, 1979—. Former chmn. Automobile Mfrs. Assn., Econ. Devel. Corp. Greater Detroit; councillor The Conf. Bd.; past chmn., life trustee Urban Inst.; mem. Public Adv. Commn. on U.S. Trade Policy, 1968-69, Pres.'s Nat. Commn. on Productivity, 1970-74. Trustee Internat. Exec. Svc. Coirps.; hon. trustee The Brookings Instn.; dir. emeritus S.R.I. Internat.; dir. Pub. Policy Inst. Calif.; former pres. Detroit Press Club Found.; former chmn. Boy Area Coun. Capt. USAAF, 1943-46. Recipient Alumnus of Year Achievement award UCLA, 1964; Distinguished Nebraskan award, 1968; Nat. Industry Leader award B'nai B'rith, 1968 Fellow Am. Acad. Arts and Scis. Clubs: Pacific Union, Bohemian. Presbyterian.

MILLER, ARNOLD, electronics executive; b. N.Y.C., May 8, 1928; s. Sam and Mina (Krutalow) M.; m. Beverly Shayne, Feb. 5, 1950; children: Debra Lynn, Marla Jo, Linda Sue BS in Chemistry, UCLA, 1948, PhD in Phys. Chemistry, 1951. Registered profl. engr., Calif. Rsch. phys. chemist Wrigley Rsch. Co., Chgo., 1951; supr. phys. chemistry Armour Rsch. Found., 1951-54, mgr. chemistry and metals, 1954-56; chief materials sci. dept. Borg-Warner Rsch. Ctr., Des Plaines, Ill., 1956-59; dir. rsch. Rockwell Corp., Anaheim, Calif., 1959-66, dir. microelec. ops., 1967-68; group exec. materials ops. Whittaker Corp., L.A., 1968-70; pres. Theta Sensors, Orange, Calif., 1970-72; mgr. xeroradiography Xerox Corp., Pasadena, 1972-75, corp. dir. rsch. and adv. devel. Stamford, Conn., 1975-78, El Segundo, Calif., 1978-81, v.p. electronics div., 1981-84, pres. electronics div., 1984-87, corp. officer Stamford, 1984-87; pres. Tech. Strategy Group, Fullerton, Calif., 1987—. Bd. dirs. Spectro Diode Labs, San Jose, Calif., Semicondr. Rsch. Corp., Colorep Inc., Carlsbad, Calif.; bd. dirs., chair audit com. Merisel Computer Products, El Segundo, Calif., lead dir., 1989—; mem. vis. com. on materials sci. U. So. Calif., L.A., 1966-68; mem. State of Calif. Micro Bd., 1984-2000. Editorial adv. bd. Advances in Solid State Chemistry; co-editor Electronics Industry Development; contbr. numerous articles to profl. jours. and monographs; patentee in field. Mem. civilian adv. group Dept. Commerce, 1959-60; mem. 5th decade com., also adv. com. on engrng. and mgmt. program UCLA, 1984—; mem. com. on scholarly commn. with People's Republic of China, Tech. Transfer Task Force, Nat. Acad. Sci., Washington, 1985; bd. dirs. Orange County Pacific Symphony, Fullerton, Calif., 1982—; mem. univ.'s adv. bd.

Calif. State U.-Fullerton, 1986—, chair, 1991—; v.p., bd. dirs. Heritage Pointe Home for the Aging, 1987-97; chmn. Indsl. Assocs. sch. engring. and computer sci. Calif. State U., 1987-97, trustee continuing learning ctr., 1993—; mem. Overseas Devel. Coun., 1988—; mem. Nat. Com. U.S.-China Rels., 1990—; trustee So. Calif. Coll. of Optometry, 1996—, sec.-treas. 1997—; bd. mem. Cmty. Found., 1995—, v.p., 1997—. Recipient Sci. Merit award Navy Bur. Ordnance/Armour Rsch. Found., 1952, IR-100 award, 1964, 69; named hon. alumnus Calif. State U., Fullerton, 1996, Univ. medal. Inst. Gerontology Calif. State U., Fullerton, 2002. Fellow AAAS; mem. IEEE, AIME, Am. Chem. Soc., So. Calif. Coalition Edn. Mfg. Engring. (bd. dirs. 1994-98), Elec. Industry Assn. (past chmn. microelectronics), Phi Beta Kappa, Sigma Xi, Phi Lamda Upsilon Home: 505 Westchester Pl Fullerton CA 92835-2706 Office: Tech Strategy Group PO Box 5769 Fullerton CA 92838-0769 E-mail: amiller@fullerton.edu.

MILLER, ARNOLD, retired newspaper editor; b. Cleve., May 24, 1931; s. Ben and Fanny (Keller) M.; m. Loretta Cooney, June 29, 1957 (div. 1977); children: Adrienne, Evan, Bryn, Alyssa. BS in Journalism, Kent State U., 1956. Copy editor News-Sentinel, Fort Wayne, Ind., 1956; asst. city editor Beacon Jour., Akron, Ohio, 1957-65; mng. editor Morning Herald, Hagerstown, Md., 1965-69; reporter, columnist, asst. news editor Cleve. Press, 1969-72; mng. editor Chronicle-Telegram, Elyria, Ohio, 1972-97, ret., 1997. With U.S. Army, 1953-54. Mem. Assoc. Press Mng. Editors Assn., Md.-Del. Press Assn., Ohio UPI Editors Assn. (pres. 1978), Assoc. Press Soc. Ohio (adv. bd. 1992-93). Jewish. Home: 1550 Cedarwood Dr Apt D Cleveland OH 44145-1811

MILLER, ARTHUR, playwright, author; b. N.Y.C., Oct. 17, 1915; s. Isadore and Augusta (Barnett) M.; m. Mary Grace Slattery, Aug. 5, 1940 (div. 1956); children: Jane Ellen, Robert; m. Marilyn Monroe, June 1956 (div. 1961); m. Ingeborg Morath, Feb. 1962; children: Rebecca Augusta, Daniel. AB, U. Mich., 1938, LHD, 1956; LittD (hon.), Oxford U., 1995, Harvard U., 1997, Brandeis U., 1998. Assoc. prof. drama U. Mich., 1973-74. Author: (plays) Honors at Dawn, 1936 (Avery Hopwood award for playwriting U. Mich.), No Villain: They Too Arise, 1937 (Avery Hopwood award for playwriting U. Mich.), Man Who Had All the Luck, 1944 (Nat. prize Theatre Guild), That They May Win, 1944, All My Sons, 1947 (N.Y. Drama Critics Circle award, Tony award best play, Donaldson award), Death of a Salesman, 1949 (N.Y. Drama Critics Circle award, Tony award, Donaldson award, Pulitzer prize in drama), The Crucible, 1953 (Tony award, Donaldson award, Obie award 1958), A View from the Bridge, 1955 (Antoinette Perry award Best Revival), A Memory of Two Mondays, 1955, After the Fall, 1964, Incident at Vichy, 1964, The Price, 1968, Fame, 1970, The Reason Why, 1970, The Creation of the World and Other Business, 1972, Up From Paradise, 1974, The Archbishop's Ceiling, 1976, The American Clock, 1980, Some Kind of Love Story, 1983, Elegy for a Lady, 1983, Playing for Time, 1986, Danger: Memory!, 1986, The Last Yankee, 1990 (BBC Best Play award 1992), The Ride Down Mt. Morgan, 1991, Broken Glass, 1994 (Olivier award London 1995), Mr. Peter's Connections, 1998, Resurrection Blues; (play adaptation) Enemy of the People (Ibsen), 1950; (screenplays) The Story of G.I. Joe, 1945, The Misfits, 1961, The Hook, 1975, Everybody Wins, 1990, The Crucible, 1995; (teleplays) Death of a Salesman, 1966, The Price, 1971, Fame, 1978, Playing for Time, 1980 (George Foster Peabody award 1981, Outstanding Writing Emmy award 1981), All My Sons, 1987, An Enemy of the People, 1990, The American Clock, 1994; author: Situation Normal, 1944, Focus, 1945, Jane's Blanket, 1963, I Don't Need You Anymore, 1967, In Russia, 1969, In the Country, 1977, The Theatre Essays of Arthur Miller, 1978, Chinese Encounters, 1979, Salesman in Beijing, 1987, Timebends: A Life, 1987, The Misfits and Other Stories, 1987, (novella) Homely Girl, 1994; exec. prodr. Death of a Salesman, 1985 (Outstanding Drama/Comedy Spl. Emmy award 1985). Recipient Bur. New Plays prize Theatre Guild, 1938, Nat. Assn. Ind. Schs. award, 1954, Gold Medal for drama Nat. Inst. Arts and Letters, 1959, Anglo-Am. award, 1966, Creative Arts award Brandeis U., 1970, Lit. Lion award N.Y. Pub. Libr., 1983, John F. Kennedy Lifetime Achievement award, 1984, Algur Meadows award So. Meth. U., 1991, Antoinette Perry Lifetime Achievement award, 1999, Prix Molière, 1999, Dorothy and Lillian Gish award, 1999, Praemium Imperiale award, Japan.

MILLER, ARTHUR HAROLD, lawyer; b. Plainfield, N.J., Sept. 21, 1935; s. Leon Daniel and Bertha Zelda (Madoff) M.; m. Lynn Fieldman, Aug. 24, 1958; children: Jennifer, Jonathan. BA, Princeton U., 1957; JD, Columbia U., 1960. Bar: N.Y. 1961, U.S. Supreme Ct. 1965, N.J. 1969. Assoc. Wachtel & Michaelson, N.Y.C., 1961-65, Netter, Lewy, Dowd, N.Y.C., 1965-67, Dannenberg Hazen & Lake, N.Y.C., 1967-69; ptnr. Clarick, Clarick & Miller, New Brunswick, N.J., 1971-78, Miller, Miller & Tucker PA, New Brunswick, 1979—. Chmn. Middlesex County Legal Svcs. Corp., New Brunswick, 1975-83. Active Sch. Bd. Highland Park, N.J., 1981-84. Mem. N.J. Bar Assn. (chmn. availibility legal svcs. com. 1983-85, lawyer referral com. 1986-88), MIddlesex County Bar Assn. (pres. 1993-94, lawyer achievement award 1996), Middlesex County Bar Found. (pres. 1997-98), Middlesex County C. of C. (trustee and legal counsel 1990-93). Democrat. Jewish. Home: 145 N 9th Ave Highland Park NJ 08904-3627 Office: Miller Miller & Tucker 96 Paterson St New Brunswick NJ 08901-2109 E-mail: amiller@millerandmiller.com.

MILLER, ARTHUR MADDEN, lawyer, investment banker; b. Greenville, S.C., Apr. 10, 1953; s. Charles Frederick and Kathryn Irene (Madden) M.; m. Roberta Beck Connolly, Apr. 17, 1993; children: Isabella McIntyre Madden, Roberta Beck Connolly. AB in History, Princeton U., 1973; MA in History, U. N.C., 1976; JD with distinction, Duke U., 1978; LLM in Taxation, NYU, 1982. Bar: N.Y. 1979, U.S. Dist. Ct. (so. dist.) N.Y. 1979. Assoc. Mudge Rose Guthrie Alexander & Ferdon, N.Y.C., 1978-85; v.p. pub. fin. Goldman, Sachs & Co., 1985—. Mem. adv. bd. Mary Baldwin Coll., Staunton, Va., 1982-86; trustee Princeton U. Rowing Assn., N.J., 1980—, pres., 1986-95; trustee Rebecca Kelly Dance Co., N.Y.C., 1984-86; mem. Power Ten, N.Y., steward, 1992-95. Mem. ABA (tax sect. com. on tax exempt financing 1985—), Nat. Assn. Bond Lawyers (lectr. 1985—), Pub. Securities Assn. (cons. 1985—), Practising Law Inst. (lectr. 1980, editor/author course materials 1980—), Bond Attys. Workshop (editor/author course material 1983—, lectr. 1983—), Princeton Club. Office: Goldman Sachs & Co 85 Broad St New York NY 10004-2456 E-mail: arthur.miller@gs.com.

MILLER, ARTHUR P., JR. journalist, writer; b. Washington, Apr. 6, 1924; s. Arthur Patterson and Bertha Cecilia (Redifer) Miller; m. Marjorie Lyman Miller, Apr. 16, 1955; children: Susan Smith, Kathryn Thomas, Janet Martin, Nancy Brown. BA, Pa. State U., 1947; MA, Columbia U., 1948. News editor All Hands Mag., Navy Dept., Washington, 1948—50; writer Internat. Press Svc. U.S. Info. Agy., 1950—55; writer, editor for Geographic Sch. Bulletin Nat. Geographic Soc., 1955—74; pub. affairs officer Mid Atlantic Region Nat. Park Svc., Phila., 1974—88. Lectr. in field. Author: (novels) Weekend Journeys, 1995, Pennsylvania Battlefields and Military Landmarks, 2000; contbr. articles to profl. jours., chapters to books. Singer Bryn Mawr Mainliners. With USN, 1943—45, PTO. Mem.: Outdoor Writers Assn., Soc. Profl. Journalists, Soc. Preservation and Encouragement of Barbershop Quartet Singing in Am., Delaware County Press Club (bd. dirs.), Nat. Press Club (bd. dirs., fin. sec. 1963—65). Republican. Methodist. Home: 12 Grant Ln Wayne PA 19087-2505 Personal E-mail: ammiller12@aol.com.

MILLER, ARTHUR RAPHAEL, law educator; b. N.Y.C., June 22, 1934; s. Murray and Mary (Schapin) Miller; m. Ellen Monica Joachim, June 8, 1958 (div. 1978); 1 child Matthew Richard ; m. Marilyn Tarmy, 1982 (div. 1988); m. Sandra L. Young, 1992 (div. 2001). AB, U. Rochester, 1955; LLB, Harvard U., 1958; student, Bklyn. Coll., 1952, 55, CCNY, 1955. Bar: N.Y. 1959, U.S. Supreme Ct. 1959, Mass. 1983. With Cleary, Gottlieb, Steen & Hamilton, N.Y.C., 1958-61; assoc. dir. Columbia Law Sch. Project Internat. Procedure, 1961-62; instr. Columbia U. Law Sch., 1961-62; asso. prof. U. Minn. Law Sch., 1962-65; prof. law U. Mich. Law Sch., 1965-72; vis. prof. Harvard U. Law Sch., 1971-72, prof., 1972-86, Bruce Bromley prof., 1986—. Rsch. assoc. Mental Health Research Inst., 1966-68; dir. project computer assisted instn. Am. Assn. Law Schs., 1968-75; spl. rapporteur State Dept. concerning chpt. II of Hague Conv., 1967; del. U.S.-Italian Conf. Internat. Jud. Assistance, 1961, 62; chmn. task force external affairs Interuniv. Communications Council, 1966-70; mem. law panel, com. sci. and tech. info. Fed. Council Sci. and Tech., Pres.'s Office Sci. and Tech., 1969-72; mem. adv. group Nat. Acad. Sci. Project on Computer Data Banks, 1970-78; mem. spl. adv. group to chief justice Supreme Ct. on Fed. Civil Litigation; mem. com. on automated personal data systems HEW, 1972-73; chmn. Mass. Security and Privacy Council, Mass. Commn. on Privacy; mem. U.S. Commn. New Technol. Uses Copyrighted Works, 1975-79; reporter U.S. Supreme Ct.'s Adv. Com. on Civil Rules, 1978-86, mem. 1986-91; faculty Fed. Jud. Ctr.; reporter study on complex litigation Am. Law Inst.; bd. dirs. Research Found. on Complex Litigations, 1975-80; bd. overseers Rand Inst. on Civil Justice, 1998—. Author: The Assault on Privacy: Computers, Data Banks, and Dossiers, 1971, Miller's Court, 1982; (with others) New York Civil Practice, 8 vols., Civil Procedure Cases and Materials, 7th edit., 1997, Federal Practice and Procedure: Civil, 34 vols., 1969—, CPLR Manual, 1967; host syndicated TV shows in Context, Miller's Law, Miller's Court, Headlines on Trial; legal expert Good Morning America. Served with AUS, 1958-59. Recipient Nat. Emmy award for The Constitution, That Delicate Balance. Mem. Am. Law Inst. Office: Harvard U Harvard Law Sch Cambridge MA 02138

MILLER, AUDREY THORNTON, retired educational administrator; b. Glassboro, N.J., June 22, 1937; d. Aubrey and Rebecca Thornton; m. Kenneth C. Miller, Sr., Nov. 20, 1967; children: Yvette A. Rudd, Kenneth C. Jr. BS, Cheyney U., 1963; MEd, Rutgers U., 1974; EdD, Nova Southeastern U., 1998. Cert. prin., supr. N.J. Tchr. Camden (N.J.) Bd. Edn., 1963-74, asst. to prin., 1974-97, vice prin. H.C. Sharp Sch., 1997-2000; ret., 2000. Advisor Theta Chi City Wide chpt. Rowan U., 1980-85, Sharp Sch. Safety Patrol, Camden, 1991-95, Network III Drug Program, Camden, 1993-96; adv. bd. Carter's Psychol. Svc., Camden County, 1995—; SJ area rep. Cheyney U. Alumni, 2000-02. Author: Using the Writing Process to Enchance Elementary Students Writing Proficiency and Teachers' Instructional Strategies, 1998. V.p. Garden City Alumnae of Delta Sigma Theta Sorority, Inc., Sicklerville, N.J., 1989-91; chairperson Career Women's Ministry, St. Matthews Bapt. Ch. Williamstown, N.J., 1993-96. Recipient Set a Good Example award Gov. Christie Whitman, Trenton, 1994, Disting. Achievement award, Camden Bd. Edn., 1994, 96, Proclamation, Bd. Chosen Freeholders, Camden County, 2000. Mem. NAACP, AFL-CIO, Black Women's Edn. Alliance (Educator's award 1992), Camden City Fedn. Sch. Adminstrs., N.J. Fedn. Colored Women's Club (Outstanding Svc. in Edn. award 2000), Cheyney U. Alumni Assn. (life), Nova Southeastern U. Alumni Assn., Rutgers U. Alumni, Delta Sigma Theta Sorority (life), Kappa Delta Pi. Democrat. Avocations: interior decorating, travel, tennis. Home: 4 Pierson Pl Sicklerville NJ 08081-2006 E-mail: milerau@.aol.com.

MILLER, B. JACK, investment company executive; b. N.Y.C., Mar. 1, 1945; s. Bertram Jackson and Charlotte (Kea) M.; m. Lynsie Schaberg; children: Molly, Andrew. AB, Princeton U., 1966; MBA, U. Mich., 1968. Various positions Eli Lilly and Co., Indpls., 1968-80, dir. benefit plan investments, 1980-88; v.p. benefit investments Philip Morris Cos. Inc., N.Y.C., 1988-89, v.p., corp. contr., 1989-92; v.p. J.P. Morgan Investment Mgmt., 1992-98; v.p. bus. devel. GM Investment Mgmt. Corp., 1998—. Served with M.I., USAR, 1968-74. Mem. Fin. Execs. Internat. Avocations: golf, bridge. Office: GM Asset Mgmt Corp 767 5th Ave New York NY 10153-0023 E-mail: jack.miller@gm.com.

MILLER, BARBARA KENTON, retired librarian; b. N.Y.C., Sept. 21, 1934; d. Robert Alfred and Kathleen Hope (Levy) Kenton; m. John Arnold Miller, June 15, 1955; children: Valerie Ann Galef, Jennifer Karen Kraft. BA with distinction, Finch Coll., 1960; MLS, C.W. Post, 1976. Cert. libr., N.Y. Libr., cons. archivist Coun. Fgn. Rels., N.Y.C., 1977-2000; ret., 2000. Cons. archivist Coun. on Fgn. Rels. Mem. Spl. Librs. Assn., Beta Phi Mu. Avocations: dogs, golf, tennis. Office: Coun Fgn Rels 58 E 68th St New York NY 10021-5953 E-mail: bkmiller55@aol.com.

MILLER, BARBARA STALLCUP, development consultant; b. Montague, Calif., Sept. 4, 1919; d. Joseph Nathaniel and Maybelle (Needham) Stallcup; m. Leland F. Miller, May 16, 1946; children: Paula Kay, Susan Lee, Daniel Joseph, Alison Jean. BA, U. Oreg., 1942. Women's editor Eugene (Oreg.) Daily News, 1941-43; law clk. to J. Everett Barr, Yreka, Calif., 1943-45; mgr. Yreka C. of C., 1945-46; Northwest supr. Louis Harris and Assocs., Portland, Oreg., 1959-62; dir. pub. rels. and fund raising Columbia River coun. Girl Scouts U.S.A., 1962-67; pvt. practice pub. rels. cons. Portland, 1967-72; adviser of student publs., asst. prof. comms. U. Portland, 1967-72, dir. pub. rels. and info., asst. prof. comms., 1972-78, dir. devel., 1978-79; exec. dir. devel., 1979-83; assoc. dir. St. Vincent Med. Found., 1983-88; dir. planned giving Good Samaritan Found., 1988-95; planned giving cons., 1995—. Contbr. articles to profl. jours. Pres. bd. dirs. Vols. of Am. of Oreg., Inc., 1980-84, pres. regional adv. bd., 1982-84; chmn. bd. dirs. S.E. mental Health Network, 1984-88; nat. bd. dirs. Vols. of Am., Inc., 1984-96; pres., bd. dirs. Vol. Bur. Greater Portland, 1991-93; mem. U. Oreg. Journalism Advancement Coun., 1991—. Named Oasis Sr. Role Model, 1992, pres. Oasis adv. coun., 2000—, pres. Ont. Presdl. Citation, Oreg. Communicators Assn., 1973, Matrix award, 1976, 80, Miltner award U. Portland, 1977, Communicator of Achievement award Oreg. Press Women, 1992, Willamette Valley Devel. Officers award, 1992 (Barbara Stallcup Miller Profl. Achievement award 1992). Mem. Nat. Coast Trail Assn. (pres. bd. dirs. 1997—), Nat. Soc. Fundraising Execs., Nat. Planned Giving Coun., Women in Comm. (NW regional v.p. 1973-75, Offbeat award 1988), Nat. Fedn. Press Women, Oreg. Press Women (dist. dir.), PRSA (dir. local chpt., Marsh award 1989), Oreg. Fedn. Womens Clubs (comms. chmn. 1978-80), Alpha Xi Delta (found. trustee, editor 1988-95), Portland Zenith (pres. 1975-76, 81-82, 2002—). Unitarian Universalist. Home and Office: 1706 Boca Ratan Dr Lake Oswego OR 97034-1624 E-mail: bmiller@teleport.com.

MILLER, BARRY, research administrator, psychologist; b. N.Y.C., Dec. 25, 1942; s. Jack and Ida (Kaplan) M.; m. Susan Hallermeier; children: Eric, Arianne, Kristina, Barrie. BS in Psychology, Bklyn. Coll., 1965; MS in Psychology, Villanova U., 1967; PhD in Psychiatry, Med. Coll. Pa., 1971. Instr. psychology Villanova (Pa.) U., 1971-73; asst. dir. dept. behavioral sci., med. rsch. scientist Ea. Pa. Psychiatric Inst., Phila., 1971-73, sr. med. rsch. scientist, 1973-80; dir. Pa. Bur. Rsch. and Tng., Harrisburg, 1973-81; asst. prof. psychology U. Pa. Med. Sch., Phila., 1975-78, asst. clin. prof. psychology, 1978—; assoc. prof. psychiatry Med. Coll. Pa., 1981-90, rsch. assoc. prof. medicine, 1983-90, assoc. dean for rsch., 1981-90; dir. for rsch. devel. Albert Einstein Healthcare Network, 1990-95; dir. The Permanente Med. Group Rsch. Inst., Oakland, Calif., 1995-99; adj. assoc. prof. psychiatry Med. Coll. Pa., Phila., 1990—; rsch. assoc. prof. psychiatry Temple U. Sch. Med., 1990—; asst. dir. rsch. planning and devel. Divsn. Rsch., Oakland, Calif., 1999—. Mem. sci. and tech. task force Pa. Econ. Devel. Partnership, Harrisburg, 1987-88, adv. com. Clin. Rsch. Ctr. Psychopathology of Elderly, Phila., 1985-88; mem. cancer control prgram Pa. Dept. Health, 1994; vis. rsch. assoc. prof. Med. Coll. Pa., Phila., 1991—. Contbr. articles to profl. jours.; mem. editorial bd. Jour. Mental Health Adminstrn., 1988—, assoc. editor, 1989—. Bd. dirs. Community Mental Health Ctr. 6A, Phila., 1969-73, Northwest Jewish Youth Ctrs., Phila., 1974-75; mem. Lafayette Hill Civic Assn., 1973-86, Citizens Coun. Whitemarsh (Pa.) Twp., 1975-86; pres., bd. dirs. Golden Eagle Luxury Homeowners Assn., Pleasanton, Calif., 1995-97. Grantee HHS, NIH. Mem. AAAS, Am. Psychol. Assn., Assn. Mental Health Adminstrs., Assn. Univ. Tech. Mgrs., Soc. Rsch. Adminstrs., Calif. Psychol. Assn. Avocation: tennis. Office: Divsn Rsch 2000 Broadway Oakland CA 94612-3429

MILLER, BARRY M. child care administrator; b. Balt., Sept. 14, 1952; s. Charles M. and Sonia F. (Weiner) M. BA in Sociology, U. Md., 1975; MS in Child Devel., W.Va. U., 1978. With Am. Rsch. Bur., Beltsville, Md., 1973-77; dir. child devel. Scotts Run Settlement House, Osage, W.Va., 1978-84; v.p. provider svcs. Family Cen. Inc., Ft. Lauderdale, Fla., 1985—. Cons. in field. Mem. Nat. Assn. Edn. of Young Children, Nat. Assn. Family Child Care Credential (validator), Child and Adult Care Sponsors Assn. (former state rep.), So. Assn. Children Under Six, Broward Assn. for Edn. Young Children, Broward County Family Day Care Assn. (founder), Phi Upsilon Omicron. Democrat. Jewish. Home: 9640 NW 7th Cir 2013 Plantation FL 33324 Office: Family Central 840 SW 81st Ave N Fort Lauderdale FL 33068-2001 E-mail: bmiller@familycentral.org.

MILLER, BEATRICE ELLEN, communications executive; b. Washington, Oct. 19, 1946; d. I. Roy and Marie (Pratt) M. Assoc. BS, Point Park Coll., 1966. Asst. prodr. Fuller/Smith Ross Advt., Pitts., 1966-69; project assoc. Time-Life, Inc., N.Y.C., 1970; exec. v.p. Communicators/Pitts. Inc., 1971-82; dir. comms. Pet Inc., St. Louis, 1983-95; dir. comm. Mallinckrodt Med. Inc., 1995-97; prin. Miller Comm., 1997—. Mem. Pub. Rels. Soc. Am., Bus. Mktg. Assn. (bd. dirs. 1988—, chmn. profl. assistance network com. 1988, v.p. profl. devel. 1989—, pres. 1990—, cert.), Food Mktg. Communicators, Ad Club St. Louis, Press Club St. Louis. Home: 16054 S 14th Dr Phoenix AZ 85045-0613 E-mail: beamilcom@cs.com.

MILLER, BEBE, choreographer; b. N.Y.C., Sept. 20, 1950; BA in Fine Arts, Earlham Coll., 1971; MA in Dance, Ohio State U., 1975. Owner Bebe Miller Co., N.Y.C., 1985—; prof. dance Ohio State U., 2002—. Bd. dirs. Dance USA, Dance Theater Workshop, Danspace Project; tchr. U. Ill., Champaign/Urbana, UCLA, NYU, Mt. Holyoke Coll., Movement Rsch., N.Y.C., Sarah Lawrence Coll., U. Minn., Mills Coll., Middlebury Coll., Va. Commonwealth U., Tex. Women's U., Cal Arts and Stanford U. Choreographer (theatre) Tiny Sisters in the Enormous Land, 1995, Going to the Wall, 1998, (original works) Oreg. Ballet Theatre, Boston Ballet, Dayton Contemporary Dance Co. and others. Recipient 2 Bessie awards, award, Am. Choreographer, 1988, Young Artists Recognition award, Dewars, 1990; fellow, Creative Artists Pub. Svc., 1984, Nat. Found. for Arts, 1984, Nat. Endowment for Arts, 1985—88, John Simon Guggenheim Found., 1988. Office: Bebe Miller Co 54 W 21st St Ste 502 New York NY 10010*

MILLER, BENJAMIN HENRY, priest, human rights advocate; b. New Orleans, Aug. 11, 1925; arrived in Sri Lanka, 1948; s. Charles Tessier M. and Margaret Effie Smith. BS in Physics, Spring Hill Coll., 1947, PhL, 1948; S.T.L., De Nobili Coll., Pune, India, 1955. Joined S.J., 1941. Rector St. Michael's Coll., Batticaloa, Sri Lanka, 1959-70; pastor Diocese Trinco, Sri Lanka, 1972-76; supt. Kalkudah (Sri Lanka) Estate, 1977—2002; dir., founder, pres. Ea. Tech. Inst., Batticaloa, Sri Lanka, 1990-95. Treas. Jesuit Fathers, Batticaloa, Sri Lanka, 1960-96; founder, v.p. Ea. Fisherises Enterprise, Batticaloa; spkr. environ. sem. Ea. U. Sri Lanka, 1992; founder, mem. Coun. Religions, Batticaloa, 1960-2002; founder, mem. Peace Com., Batticaloa, compiler record missing persons, victims ethnic civil war; mem. adv. bd. Human Rights Task Force, Batticaloa, 1996; govt. monitor Sri Lanka Monitoring Mission of Norwegian Ceasefire Agreement, 2002. Founder, vice chmn. Red Cross Branch, Batticaloa, Sri Lanka, 1990; v.p., life mem. Batticaloa branch Cancer Soc., 1988. Mem. Batticaloa Rotary Club (pres. 1979-80, charter mem. Nat. Coun. Peace and Harmony 1980-83, chmn. nat. com. overseas vols. 1987). Avocations: environmental activity, afternoons at the beach, motorcycling. Home: 1 Jesuit St Batticaloa Sri Lanka Office: Jesuit Residency 1 Jesuit St Battilacoa Sri Lanka

MILLER, BENJAMIN K. retired state supreme court justice; b. Springfield, Ill., Nov. 5, 1936; s. Clifford and Mary (Luthyens) M. BA, So. Ill. U., 1958; JD, Vanderbilt U., 1961. Bar: Ill. 1961. Ptnr. Olsen, Cantrill & Miller, Springfield, 1964-70; prin. Ben Miller-Law Office, 1970-76; judge 7th jud. cir. Ill. Cir. Ct., 1976-82, presiding judge Criminal div., 1977-81, chief judge, 1981-82; justice Ill. Appellate Ct., 4th Jud. Dist., 1982-84, Ill. Supreme Ct., Springfield, 1984-2001, chief justice, 1991-93, ret., 2001. Adj. prof. So. Ill. U., Springfield, 1974—; chmn. Ill. Cts. Commn., 1988-90; mem. Ill. Gov.'s Adv. Coun. on Criminal Justice Legis., 1977-84, Ad Hoc Com. on Tech. in Cts., 1985—. Mem. editorial rev. bd. Illinois Civil Practice Before Trial, Illinois Civil Trial Practice Pres. Cen. Ill. Mental Health Assn., 1969-71; bd. govs. Aid to Retarded Citizens, 1977-80; mem. Lincoln Legals Adv. Bd., 1988—. Lt. USNR, 1964-67. Mem. ABA (bar admissions com. sect. of legal edn. and admissions to bar 1992—), Ill. State Bar Assn. (bd. govs. 1970-76, treas. 1975-76), Sangamon County Bar Assn., Ctrl. Ill. Women's Bar Assn., Am. Judicature Soc. (bd. dirs. 1990-95), Abraham Lincoln Assn. (bd. dirs. 1988-98). Address: 1918 Jeanette Ln Springfield IL 62702

MILLER, BERTIN, priest, social administrator; b. Joliet, Ill., May 15, 1936; s. William Sumner Ellsworth and Mary Marguerite (Hanrahan) M. BA, Quincy Coll., 1960; STB, Antonianum, Rome, 1964. Ordained priest Roman Cath. Ch., 1964. Chaplain Mo. State Correction Farmington/Pacific, Hillsboro, Mo., 1988-92; exec. dir. Evergreen Hills Homes, Dittmer, 1973—; dir. Il Ritiro, 1977—; spiritual dir. St. Michael's Inst., Sunset Hills, Mo., 1986-88. Lectr. Marsh, Curtis, McCall, St. Louis, 1986—. Chaplain Cedar Hill (Mo.) Fire Dept., 1989-92; assoc. mem. Nat. Coun. on Sexual Addiction, Inc.; founder, exec. dir. RECON, Inc., 1992—; Cath. chaplain Jefferson County Sheriff's Dept., 1995—. Mem. Lions, Elks, KC (4th deg.). Home: PO Box 400 Dittmer MO 63023-0400 Office: PO Box 220 Dittmer MO 63023-0220 E-mail: bwem@nightowl.net.

MILLER, BETTY BROWN, freelance writer; b. Altus, Ark., Dec. 21, 1926; d. Carlos William and Arlie Gertrude (Sublett) Brown; m. Robert Wiley Miller, Nov. 15, 1953; children: Janet Ruth, Stephen Wiley. BS, Okla. State U., 1949; MS, U. Tulsa, 1953; postgrad., Am. U., 1966-68. Tchr. LeFlore (Okla.) H.S., 1947-48, Osage Indian Reservation H.S., Hominy, Okla., 1948-50, Jenks (Okla.) H.S., 1950-51; instr. Sch. Bus. U. Tulsa, 1950-51; tchr. Tulsa pub. schs., 1951-54; instr. Burdette Coll., Boston, 1954-55; reporter Bethesda-Chevy Chase Tribune, Montgomery County, Md., 1970-73; freelance writer, contbr. newspapers and mags., 1973—. V.p. Kenwood Park (Md.) Citizens Assn., 1960; mem. Ft. Sumner Citizens Assn., editor newsletter, 1969; mem. Md. State PTA, editl. coord. leadership conf., 1973-74; founder, chair Montgomery County Forum Edn., 1970-75; trustee Friends Valley Forge Nat. Hist. Park; bd. dirs. Friends Curtis Inst. Music; mem. Nat. Mus. Women in the Arts, Musical Fund Soc. Phila.; trustee adv. Help the Aged. Mem.: DAR, PEO, Union League Phila. (past mem. ladies com., mem. ladies adv. com.), The Nat. Gravel Soc., Internat. Platform Assn., Montgomery County Press Assn., Nat. Soc. Arts & Letters (past editor mag., bd. dirs. pub rels., past nat. corr. sec.), Huguenot Soc. Pa. (v.p. 1989—92, pres. 1993—95, past bd. dirs., hon. v.p. 1997—), Nat. League Am. Pen Women (former budget chmn., past nat. treas.), Soc. Descendants of Washington's Army at Valley Forge (past. nat. comdr. in chief, past inspector gen. Nat. Huguenot Soc., past. mem. gen. coun.), Acorn Club Phila., Sedgeley Club (pres. Phila. 1985—88), Washington Club, U.D.C., Adventures Unltd. (chmn. Washington chpt.), Capital Spkrs. Club Washington (past pres.), Melba T. Croft Music Club, Order Ea. Star (life). Republican. Address: PO Box 573 Valley Forge PA 19481-0573

MILLER, BETTY SUE, counselor; b. Hopkinsville, Ky., June 11, 1960; d. Gerald and Mable (Lee) M. AA, Hopkinsville C.C., 1980; BS, Murray (Ky.) State U., 1982; MEd, U. North Tex., 1987; M of Ednl. Counseling, U. Phoenix, 1995. Cert. tchr., Colo.; cert. spl. svcs., Colo.; cert. K-12 counselor. Tchr. Dallas Ind. Sch. System, 1982-89, Jefferson County Sch. Dist., Wheat Ridge, Colo., 1989-96, sch. counselor Littleton, 1996—; counselor Karlis Family Ctr., Lakewood, 1995—. Instr. Colo. State U., Denver, 1992; lic. profl. counselor. Editor The Round Table Literary mag., 1980. Mem. ACA, Am. Assn. of Christian Counselors, Jefferson County Edn. Assn., Jefferson County Internat. Reading Assn. (bldg. rep. 1991-96), Am. Sch. Counselor Assn. Avocations: drama, reading, arts and crafts, decorating. Office: Summit Ridge Middle Sch 11809 W Coal Mine Ave Littleton CO 80127-4849

MILLER, BEVERLY, marketing consultant; b. Osaka, Japan, Sept. 22, 1952; d. Aldee and Helen Miller. BA magna cum laude, U. Md., 1976; JD, Georgetown U., 1982. Corp. devel. officer Folger Shakespeare Libr., Washington, 1982-83; nat. mktg. cons. Blue Cross Blue Sheild Assns., 1983-86; change mgmt. cons. Sewell Mktg. and Promotions, Göteborg, Sweden, 1986-87; CEO Tng. Connexion/Market Mgmt. Spectrum, 1987—; chmn., CEO Absormatic, The Connexion Internat., Stockholm, 1997—. Adj. prof. Internat. Bus. Coll., Göteborg campus Johnson & Wales U., 1994—; fundraising cons. Swedish Jr. C. of C., Göteborg, 1987-90; orgnl. cons. Götaverken Energy/Kvaerner Pulping Techs., Karlstad, Sweden, 1991-93; internal mktg. cons. Neste/Borealis, Copenhagen, 1993-97. Host, scriptwriter corp. promotional film: SKF: The Constant Quest, 1997 (2d pl. Silver Screen award Internat. Film and Video Festival 1998); author: (manuals) A Guide to Strategic Interpersonal Communications, 1987, Coaching, Communicating and Marketing for Excellence, 1997. Fundraiser Washington City Coun. campaign, 1982, campaign mgr., 1990; vol. Big Sisters Nat. Capitol Area, Washington, 1985-86. Recipient Cert. of Achievement and Appreciation, FINA/Swedish Swimming Fedn., 1996, Cert. of Achievement and Outstanding Contbn., Corp. Pub. Affairs-SKF, 1997. Mem. Swedish-Am. C. of C., Am. Mktg. Assn., Am. Mgmt. Assn., European Assn. Internat. Edn.

MILLER, BEVERLY WHITE, past college president, education consultation; b. Willoughby, Ohio; d. Joseph Martin and Marguerite Sarah (Storer) White; m. Lynn Martin Miller, Oct. 11, 1945 (dec. 1986); children: Michaela Ann, Craig Martin, Todd Daniel, Cass Timothy, Simone Agnes. AB, Western Res. U., 1945; MA, Mich. State U., 1957; PhD, U. Toledo, 1967; LHD (hon.), Coll. St. Benedict, St. Joseph, Minn., 1979; LLD (hon.), U. Toledo, 1988. Chem. and biol. researcher, 1945-57; tchr. schs. in Mich., also Mercy Sch. Nursing, St. Lawrence Hosp., Lansing, Mich., 1957-58; mem. chemistry and biology faculty Mary Manse Coll., Toledo, 1958-71, dean grad. div., 1968-71, exec. v.p., 1968-71; acad. dean Salve Regina Coll., Newport, R.I., 1971-74; pres. Coll. St. Benedict, St. Joseph, Minn., 1974-79, Western New Eng. Coll., Springfield, Mass., 1980-96, pres. emerita, 1996—. Higher edn. cons., 1996—; cons. U.S. Office Edn., 1980; mem. Springfield Pvt. Industry Coun./Regional Employment Bd., exec. com., 1982-94; mem. Minn. Pvt. Coll. Coun., 1974-79, sec., 1974-75, vice chmn., 1975-76, chmn., 1976-77; cons. in field. Author papers and books in field. Corporator Mercy Hosp., Springfield, Mass. Recipient President's citation St. John's U., Minn., 1979; also various service awards; named disting. alumna of yr. U. Toledo, 1998. Mem. AAAS, Am. Assn. Higher Edn., Assn. Cath. Colls. and Univs. (exec. bd.), Internat. Assn. Sci. Edn., Nat. Assn. Ind. Colls. and Univs. (govt. rels. adv. com., bd. dirs. 1990-93, exec. com. 1991-93, treas. 1992-93), Nat. Assn. Biology Tchrs., Assn. Ind. Colls. and Univs. of Mass. (exec. com. 1981-96, vice chmn. 1985-86, chmn. 1986-87), Nat. Assn. Rsch. Sci. Tchg., Springfield C. of C. (bd. dirs.), Am. Assn. Univ. Adminstrs. (bd. dirs. 1989-92), Delta Kappa Gamma, Sigma Delta Epsilon. Office: 6713 County Road M Delta OH 43515-9778

MILLER, BILL See PISTORIUS, ALVIN WILLIAM JR.

MILLER, BONNIE SEWELL, marketing professional, writer; b. Junction City, Ky., July 24, 1932; d. William Andrew and Lillian Irene (McCowan) Sewell; m. William Gustave Tournade Jr., Nov. 5, 1950 (div. 1974); children: Bonnie Sue Tournade Zaner, William Gustave III, Sharon Irene Tournade Leach; m. Bruce George Miller, Nov. 15, 1981. BA, U. South Fla., 1968, MA, 1973. Cert. tchr., Fla. Chair dept. English Tampa (Fla.) Cath. H.S., 1972-78; tchr. Clearwater (Fla.) H.S., 1978-80; mgr. prodn. svcs. Paradyne Corp., Largo, Fla., 1980-83; freelance writer, cons. Tampa, 1983-84; mgr. product documentation PPS, Inc., Largo, 1984-86, mgr. mktg. comm., 1986-87; writer Nixdorf Computer Corp., Tampa, 1988-89; mktg. dir. Suncoast Schs. Fed. Credit Union, 1989-98; co-owner, v.p., writer, cons. Need-A-Writer, Inc., 1998—. Instr. English, Hillsborough C.C., Tampa, 1975—87; cons. bus. writing Coronet Instrnl. Media Writing Project, Tampa, 1976, Nat. Mgmt. Assn., Tampa, 1981—87; adj. instr. profl. writing U. South Fla., 1993; adj. instr. tech. writing U. Tampa, 2002, English instr., 2002—. Author: Youth Financial Literacy, 1999, Effective Business Writing for Credit Unions, 2000; contbr. articles to profl. jours. Bd. dirs. SERVE, Tampa, Credit Union Mktg. Assn. Coun., Sing Parent Displaced Homemakers Group; legis. chair Tampa PTA, 1965; judge speech contest Am. Legion, Tampa, 1976; vol. North Tampa Vol. Libr., 1988. NEH fellow, 1975. Mem. NAFE, Soc. Tech. Communicators, Am. Assn. Bus. Women, Kappa Delta Pi. Democrat. Baptist. Avocations: writing, sewing, gardening, exotic birds, travel, decorating. Home and Office: 516 2d Ave SE Lutz FL 33549 Office Fax: 813-948-8251.

MILLER, BRADLEY ADAM, economist; b. Plainfield, N.J., Sept. 14, 1959; s. H. Glen and Betty (Woodruff) M.; m. Lynne Patricia Sutton, 1994. BS Physics, Computer Sci., Purdue U., 1981; MS Pub. Policy Analysis, U. Rochester, 1983; PhD in Econs., U. Calif., Berkeley, 1988. Teaching asst. dept. physics Purdue U., West Lafayette, Ind., 1980-81; vis. rsch. fellow Lunar & Planetary Inst, NASA, Houston, 1980, 81; dept. instr. dept. polit. sci. U. Rochester, Rochester, N.Y., 1982; grad. rsch. resident Argonne Nat. Lab., Washington, 1982, 83; regulatory impact analyst U.S. Dept. Energy, 1983-84; grad. rsch. asst. dept. econs. law sch. U. Calif., Berkeley, 1985-88, grad. student instr. dept. econs., 1986; ind. cons., 1984-88; sr. assoc. Charles River Assocs., Boston, 1988-94, prin., 1994-99, v.p., 2000—. Co-author: Oil Import Quotas in the Context of the International Energy Agency Sharing Agreement, 1988; author several conf. papers. Flood fellow U. Calif., Berkeley, 1984-85, grad. student fellow U. Rochester, 1982-83, pub. svc. fellow U.S. Dept. Edn., 1981-82. Mem. Internat. Assn. Energy Econs., Am. Econ. Assn., Ops. Rsch. Soc. Am., Sigma Pi Sigma. Avocations: running, softball, tennis, coin collecting., racquetball. Office: Charles River Assocs 200 Clarendon St Fl 33 Boston MA 02116-5092

MILLER, BRENDA SUZANNE, editor; d. Jimmy H. and Sylvia A. Miller. BA, Coe Coll., 1998; M in Profl. Writing, U. of So. Calif., 2002. Asst. to the editor Jour. of Mktg., L.A., 1999—. Copyeditor U. of So. Calif., L.A., 1999—. Mem.: Phi Kappa Phi. Personal E-mail: bmiller_54@hotmail.com.

MILLER, BRUCE NORMAN, lawyer, retired podiatrist; b. N.Y.C., Dec. 18, 1944; s. Michael and Florence M.; m. Ann Pauline Hills, Aug. 1982 (div. 1989); 1 child, Michael Frank; m. Nancy Denise Davis, Oct. 15, 1994; 1 child, Laura MacKenzie. AS, L.I. U., 1966; D in Podiatric Medicine, Ohio U., Cleve., 1970; JD, BS in Law, U. W. L.A., 1986. Bar: Calif. 1987, U.S. Dist. Ct. (cen. dist.) Calif. 1987. Podiatric physician, surgeon, L.A. and Marina Del Ray, Calif., 1972-83; assoc. Law Offices Bruce Fagel, Beverly Hills, 1987, Law Offices Ralph S. Hemer, Glendale, 1987-94; sr. assoc. Gittler & Bradford, L.A., 1994—. Editor-in-chief U. W. L.A. Law Jour., 1985-86. Mem.: ABA. Avocations: hockey, working out, reading, camping. Office: Gittler & Bradford 11620 Wilshire Blvd Ste 800 Los Angeles CA 90025-1793 E-mail: BMiller@gblaw.net.

MILLER, BRUCE RICHARD, employee benefits executive; b. Hazleton, Pa., Mar. 16, 1944; s. Robert Joseph and Marguerite Marie (Fritz) M.; BA in Polit. Sci., Pa. State U., 1971. Supr. salary adminstrn. Govt. Employees Ins. Co., Chevy Chase, Md., 1971-73; asst. to personnel dir. MCI Telecommunications, Inc., Washington, 1973-74; wage and salary adminstr. Kay Jewelers, Inc., Alexandria, Va., 1974, dir. personnel, 1974-84, div. v.p. personnel, 1981-85; founder, pres., chief exec. officer Employee Benefits Corp. Am., Fairfax, 1984-89, McLean, Va., 1989—. Pa. State U. Presdl. assoc.; contbr. articles to profl. jours. Mem. Alexandria Human Rights Commn., 1982-85; Active Back the Lions Club; mem. cmty. adv. coun. Ctr. for Performing Arts, Coll. of the Liberal Arts Devel. Coun. Served with U.S. Army, 1966-70. Mem. Soc. Human Resource Mgmt., Pa. State U. Alumni Assn., Pa. State U. Nittany Lion Club (bd. dirs., mem. adv. council), Pa. State U. Club of Greater Washington, Nat. Capital Area Nittany Lion (pres.), Nat. Assn. Life Underwriters, Nat. Assn. Health Underwriters, No. Va. Assn. Life Underwriters, Assn. Health Ins. Agts. Home: 12312 Blair Ridge Rd Fairfax VA 22033-1800 Office: 1420 Spring Hill Rd Ste 620 Mc Lean VA 22102-3030

MILLER, BRYANE KATHERINE, artist, writer; b. Front Royal, Va., Dec. 26, 1949; d. Carl Bryan and Gertrude (Erbe) M. AA, Marymount U., 1970; BA, Lynchburg Coll., 1972. Dir. arts City of Lynchburg (Va.), 1972-73; adminstrv. asst. to dir. Va. State Water Control Bd., Richmond, 1973-76; tchr. art St. Mary's Sch., 1974-76; mgr., buyers asst. Hecht's (formerly Miller and Rhoad's Corp.), 1976-77, divsn. store mgr., 1976-79; mgr. Dunhill Temps., Inc., Richmond, 1979-84; freelance artist, 1984—. Publicity cons. Trinity Hist. House Tour, Little Washington, Va., 1992%; mem. Christmas Decorating com. Belle Grove Plantation, Middletowqn, Va., 1992; lectr. in field, pub. speaker. Author: Dignified Departure, 1993; exhibited in group show Shenandoah Valley Va., Richmond. Bd. dirs. Richmond Urban League, 1980-84, Lynchburg Pub. Works, 1973; bd. dirs. Am. Heart Assn., Gochland County, Va., 1990-91, cmty. chmn. Manakin Sabot, Va., 1987-90; vol. radio broadcaster weekly program for blind The Va. Voice, 1980-87; history chmn. Rep. Women's Club, Gochland County, 1989-90, 3d v.p., 1987-89; arts coun. del. Cath. Parochial Schs., Richmond, 1974-77; v.p. Blue Ridge Arts Coun., 1994—, bd. dirs., 1993—. Mem. Shenandoah Valley Artists Assn., Shenandoah Valley Writer's Guild, Front Royal C. of C., Bus. and Profl. Women, Women of Washington (charter), Older Women's League (del. to White House), Garden Club Warren County (corr. sec., flower chmn. Hist. Garden Week in Va.), Thomas Jefferson Garden Club (bd. dirs. 1989-91), Ibebana (1st v.p. 1990-91, 2d v.p. 1989-90, bd. dirs. 1989-91, planning bd. 1987-90). Home and Office: PO Box 1171 Front Royal VA 22630-1171

MILLER, BRYANT DAVIS, healthcare administrator; b. Oct. 15, 1951; BS, U. So. Miss., 1973; MRE, New Orleans Bapt. Theol. Sem., 1988. Cert. master addition counselor, clin. supr. Pastor Milford Bapt. Ch., Leary, Ga., 1990-94; substance abuse outpatient dir. Middle Flint Behavioral Health Care, Americus, 1993-95; program dir. Penfield Christian Home Ga. Bapt. Conv., Union Point, 1995—. Author/editor: Christian Recover (6 wk. rehab. curriculum), 1995, Family Addiction and recovery (4 hr. seminar), 1995. Counselor ch. ministry with addicted families, 2000—. Mem. Ga. Addiction Counselors Assn. (mem. cert. bd. 1998—), Ga. Assn. of Recovery Residences (edn. com. 1997-98. Home: 1050 Cemetary Rd Union Point GA 30669-2201 Office: 1061 Mercer Cir Union Point GA 30669-2205

MILLER, BUFFY, dancer; b. Atlanta; Studies with, Patricia Bromley; student, New Ballet Sch. Mem. Feld Ballet Tech. Soc., 1986—97; with Ballet Tech., 1997—. Office: c/o Ballet Tech 890 Broadway 8th Fl New York NY 11222*

MILLER, C. ARDEN, physician, educator; b. Shelby, Ohio, Sept. 19, 1924; s. Harley H. and Mary (Thuma) Miller; m. Helen Meihack, June 26, 1948; children: John Lewis, Thomas Meihack, Helen Lewis, Benjamin Lewis. Student, Oberlin Coll., 1942—44; MD cum laude, Yale, 1948. Intern, then asst. resident pediatrics Grace-New Haven Community Hosp., 1948—51; faculty U. Kans. Med. Center, 1951—66, dir. childrens rehab. unit, 1957—60, dean Med. Sch., dir., 1960—66; prof. pediatrics and maternal and child health U. N.C., Chapel Hill, 1966—98, emeritus, 1998—, vice chancellor health scis., 1966—71, chmn. dept. maternal and child health, 1977—87. Chmn. exec. com. Citizens Bd. Inquiry into Health Svcs. for Am., 1968—71. Mem. editl. bd.: Jour. Med. Edn., 1960—66; contbr. articles to profl. jours. Trustee Appalachian Regional Hosps., 1974—84, Planned Parenthood Fedn.; chmn. Alan Guttmacher Inst., 1978—84, 1986—. Recipient Robert H. Felix Disting. Svc. award, St. Louis U., 1977, Martha Mae Eliot award in pub. health, 1984, O. Max Gardner award, U. N.C., 1987; scholar Am. Markle scholar in med. scis., 1955—60. Fellow: Royal Soc. Health (hon.), Clare Hall Cambridge (Eng.) U. (life); mem.: APHA (chmn. action bd. 1972—75, pres. 1974—75, Sedgewick Meml. medal 1986), Inst. of Medicine NAS, Assn. Am. Med. Colls. (v.p. 1965—66), Soc. Pediat. Rsch., Delta Omega, Alpha Omega Alpha, Sigma Xi. Home: 908 Greenwood Rd Chapel Hill NC 27514-3910 E-mail: Arden_Miller@unc.edu.

MILLER, CALLIX EDWIN, manufacturing executive, consultant; b. South Bend, Ind., Mar. 27, 1924; s. Callix Edwin and Marguerite Cash (Sweeney) M.; m. Theresa Ann Pirchio, June 25, 1949; children: Madeline, Callix, John, David, Thomas. BS in Archtl. Engring., U. Notre Dame, 1949. Mgr. engring. Internat. Mining and Chem. Corp., Chgo., 1951-61; exec. dir. Sperry Rand Corp., N.Y.C., 1961-64; v.p. Internat. Minerals & Chem. Corp., Chgo., 1964-72, Assocs. Corp. N.Am., Dallas, 1972-78; corp. v.p. tech. resources Clark Equipment Co., Buchanan, Mich., 1978-85. Consulting services covering design, planning, feasibility studies, econ. devel.; adj. prof. arch U. Notre Dame, 2000-01. Bd. dirs. Chgo. Area coun. Boy Scouts Am., 1967-70, Alexian Bros. Hosp., Chgo., 1966-68. Served with USNR, 1943-45. Mem. AIA, ASCE, Soc. Am. Mil. Engrs., Am. Concrete Inst., Knollwood Country Club (Northbrook, Ill.), Sport Club, Faculty Club (U. Notre Dame), Elks, K.C. Republican. Roman Catholic. Home: 16174 Baywood Ln Granger IN 46530-9716 E-mail: calyxeia@prodigy.net.

MILLER, CANDICE S. state official; b. May 7, 1954; m. Donald G. Miller; 1 child, Wendy Nicole. Student, Macomb County C.C., Northwood U. Sec., treas. D.B. Snider, Inc., 1972-79; trustee Harrison Twp., 1979-80, supr., 1980-92; treas. Macomb County, 1992-95; sec. of state State of Mich., Lansing, 1995—. Mem. Lake St. Clair Blue Ribbon Commn. Chair John Engler for Gov. campaign, Macomb County; del. Rep. Nat. Conv., 1996; co-chair Rep. Platform Com., 1996, Dole/Kemp Presdl. Campaign, Mich., 1996, Bush/Cheney Presdl. Campaign, Mich., 2000; mem. Carehouse-Macomb County Child Adv. Ctr., Selfridge Air Nat. Guard Base Cmty. Coun., Detroit Econ. Club; mem. adminstrv. bd. Mich. State, mem. safety commn. Avocations: boating, yacht racing. Office: Treasury Building 430 W Allegan Fl 1 Lansing MI 48918-0001 E-mail: candicem@sosmail.state.mi.us.

MILLER, CARL F. secondary school educator; b. Pitts., Mar. 25, 1967; s. Robert A. and Joanne N. Miller; m. Molly C. Moyer, June 16, 1990 (div. Jan. 2001); children: Caroline, Emily. BS in Music Edn., Indiana U. Pa., 1989. Dir. of bands Crawford Ctrl. Sch. Dist.-Cochranton (Pa.) H.S., 1990—. Music/visual adjudicator Pa. Fedn. Contest Judges, Pitts., 1993—, Allegheny Judges Assn., Erie, Pa., 1994—. Deacon First Presbyn. Ch., Meadville, Pa., 2000—01. Mem.: NEA, Lakeshore Marching Band Assn. (v.p.), Crawford Ctrl. Edn. Assn., Pa. State Edn. Assn., Pa. Music Educators Assn., Music Educators Nat. Conf. Republican. Avocations: golf, computers. Office: Cochranton HS 127 Second St Cochranton PA 16314

MILLER, CAROL LYNN, librarian; b. Kingsville, Tex., Mar. 31, 1961; d. Walter Edward Jr. and Emma Lee (Nelson) M. BS in Early Childhood Edn., So. Nazerene U., 1985; M in Early Childhood Edn., Ala. A & M U., 1987; MLS, U. Ala., 1993. Office worker Salvation Army, Huntsville, 1979-83; libr. Madison (Ala.) Branch Library, 1985; sub. tchr. Huntsville (Ala) City and Madison County Sch. System, 1986-87; br. head Madison Br. Libr., 1987-92, Madison Square Mall Br. Libr., Huntsville, 1992-2000; head adult svcs./reference, asst. br. mgr. Madison Pub. Libr., 2000—02; librn. supr. Bold and Cool Satellite Librs. Ft. Worth Pub. Libr., 2002—. Mem. Upbeat Vol. Program. Mem. ALA. Office: Ft Worth Pub Libr 1801 North/South Fwy Fort Worth TX 76102

MILLER, CAROLE ANN LYONS, editor, publisher, video and marketing specialist; b. Newton, Mass. d. Markham Harold and Ursula Patricia (Foley) Lyons; m. David Thomas Miller, July 4, 1978. BA, Boston U., 1964; bus. cert., Hickox Sch., Boston, 1964; cert. advt. and mktg. profl., UCLA, 1973; cert. retail mgmt. profl., Ind. U., 1976. Editor Triangle Topics, Pacific Telephone, L.A.; programmer L.A. Ctrl. Area Spkrs. Bur., 1964-66; mng. editor, mktg. dir. Teen mag., L.A. and N.Y.C., 1966-76; advt. dir. L.S. Ayres & Co., Indpls., 1976-78; v.p. mktg. The Denver, 1978-79; founder, editor, pub. Clockwise mag., Ventura, Calif., 1979-85; mktg. mgr., mgr. pub. rels. and spl. events Robinson's Dept. Store, L.A., 1985-87; exec. v.p., dir. mktg. Harrison Svcs., L.A., San Francisco, 1987-93; pres. divsn. Miller & Miller MillerMania, Video Image and Mktg., Camino, Calif., 1993—. Instr. retail advt. Ind. U., 1977-78. Recipient Pres.'s award Advt. Women of N.Y., 1974; Seklemian award, 1977; Pub. Svc. Addy award, 1978. Mem. Advt. Women N.Y., Retail Advt. and Mktg. Assn., Fashion Group Internat., Bay Area Integrated Mktg., San Francisco Fashion Group, UCLA Alumni Assn. (life, Sacramento chpt.), Media Coms. (Sacramento chpt.), Assn. Image Cons. Internat. E-mail: 2m@compuserve.com.

MILLER, CAROLINE, editor-in-chief; Exec. editor Variety mag., N.Y.C., 1989-92; editor-in-chief Lear's mag., 1992-94, Seventeen mag., N.Y.C., 1994-96, New York mag., N.Y.C., 1996—. Office: New York Mag 444 Madison Ave Fl 14 New York NY 10022-6999

MILLER, CARROLL GERARD, JR. (GERRY MILLER), lawyer; b. San Antonio, Dec. 12, 1944; s. Carroll Gerard Sr. and Glyn (Roddy) M.; m. Sylvia Louise Mertins, Mar. 7 1971 (dec. 1982); children: Glyn Marie Bennett, Roddy Gerard, Gina Louise. AS, Del Mar Coll., 1965; BS, U. Houston, 1967; JD, Tex. Tech. U., 1970. Bar: Tex. 1970, Colo. 1987, D.C. 1989, U.S. Dist. Ct. (so. dist.) Tex. 1971, U.S. Ct. Appeals (5th cir.) Tex. 1973, U.S. Supreme Ct. 1974, U.S. Ct. Appeals (D.C. 1986); bd. cert. in criminal law. Assoc. Allison, Madden, White & Brin, Corpus Christi, Tex., 1970-71; asst. city atty. City of Corpus Christi, 1971; asst. dist. atty. Nueces County Dist. Attys. Office, Corpus Christi, 1971-73; asst. city atty. civil div. City of Corpus Christi, 1973-74; atty. Corpus Christi Police Dept.-City of Corpus Christi, 1974-77; pvt. practice Corpus Christi, 1973—. Adj. prof. Bee County Coll., Beeville, Tex., 1973-74, Tex. A & I U., Corpus Christi, 1975-76. Past treas. and diaconate First Presbyn. Ch., Corpus Christi; bd. dirs., incorporator Iron Curtain Outreach; 20/20 coun. Open Doors. Mem. SAR, SCV, Assn. Trial Lawyers Am., Tex. Criminal Def. Lawyers Assn., Nat. Criminal Def. Lawyers Assn., Coll. State Bar Tex., Sons of Republic Tex., Crime Stoppers, Inc. (past dir.), Bay Yacht Club (dir.). Republican. Avocations: sailing, scuba diving, photography, astronomy. Home: 1209 Sandpiper Dr Corpus Christi TX 78412-3821 Office: 1007 Kinney St Corpus Christi TX 78401-3009 E-mail: lawgmiller@aol.com.

MILLER, CATHERINE ANN, nursing administrator; b. Cin., Mar. 27, 1954; BS in Biology and Chemistry, Mary Washington Coll., 1976; AD in Nursing cum laude, Raymond Walters Gen. Tech. Coll., 1981; BS in Mgmt., Coll. Mt. St. Joseph, Cin., 1987; MBA, Century U., 1993. Cert. nephrology nurse. Hemodialysis staff St. Barnabas Dialysis, Pinebrook, 1975-77, Ltd. Care Dialysis, Cin., 1977-81; hemodialysis nurse ICU Bethesda Hosp., Inc., 1981-89, continuing edn. instr., 1984-87, basic life support instr., 1985-86; adminstr. Dialysis Ctrs. Dayton, 1989-93; ctr. mgr. REN Ctr.-Crestview Hills, Ky., 1993-97; clin. mgr. Gambro Healthcare South Hill, Southgate, 1997—2001; ctr. dir. Gambro Health Care, Silverton, Ohio, 2001—. Mem.: Am. Nephrology Nurses Assn., Nat. Renal Adminstrs. Assn. Avocation: swimming and soccer officiating. Home: 828 Dorgene Ln Cincinnati OH 45244 Office: Gambro Healthcare Silverton 6929 Silverton Ave Cincinnati OH 45236 E-mail: miller_cathy@hotmail.com.

MILLER, CHARLES, business management market research consultant; b. Crowley, La., Nov. 1, 1959; s. Rufus Paul and Rose (Lacombe) M.; m. Monica Lynn Habetz, Aug. 10, 1985; children: Monique L., Paul T. BS, La. State U., 1981, MS, 1985; PhD, Ohio State U., 1989. Rsch. asst. horticulture dept. La. State U., Baton Rouge, 1977-78, La. State Soil Testing Lab., Baton Rouge, 1978-81; rsch. assoc. La. Rice Rsch. Sta., Crowley, 1982; agriculture tchr. Acadia Parish Sch. Bd., Crowley and Iota, 1982-87; rsch. assoc. Ohio State U., Columbus, 1987-89, asst. prof., 1989-92; prin., dir. relationship assessment practice S4 Cons. Inc., Powell, Ohio, 1992-98; co-founder, sr. v.p. Insight MAS, Dublin, 1998—; co-founder, pres. Iota (La.) Trucking, 2000—. Co-author: (with D.C. Swaddling) Customer Power: How to Grow Sales and Profits in a Customer-Driven Marketplace, 2001. Minister, lector St. John Neumann Ch., Sunbury, Ohio, 1992—. Recipient project grant for tchr. prep. program U.S. Dept. Edn., 1990, Am. Farmer award Nat. Future Farmers Am., 1979. Mem. Am. Mktg. Assn., Am. Soc. for Quality, Omicron Tau Theta (editor 1991-92, Outstanding Svc. award 1992), Phi Delta Kappa, Gamma Sigma Delta, Alpha Zeta. Democrat. Roman Catholic. Avocation: woodworking. Office: Insight MAS 4230 Tuller Rd Dublin OH 43017-5065 E-mail: Cmiller@insightmas.com.

MILLER, CHARLES WALLACE, historian, environmental geologist, educator; b. Phoenix, July 7, 1946; s. Charles W. and Emabel O. Miller; m. Connie Raschke, June 3, 1972; 1 child, Geoffrey Wallace. BA, U. Md., 1969; MA, U. Tex., 1970; BS, SUNY, Albany, 1978; PhD, Union Inst., 1990. Tchr. pub. schs., San Antonio, 1971-76; instr. San Antonio Coll., 1972-78, St. Mary's Univ., San Antonio, 1976-78, Cochise Coll., Sierra Vista, Az., 1989-90; environ. geologist U.S. Geol. Survey, Metairie, La., 1978-80; field geologist U.S. Bur. Land Mgmt., Moab, Utah, 1980-84; historian U.S. Bur. Reclamation, Salt Lake City, 1990-94; environ. scientist USAF, Tucson, 1994—. Mineral cons., Tucson, 1984-89; instr. Pima C.C., 1998—. Author: Stake Your Claim! The Tale of America's Enduring Mining Law, 1991, The Spirit of the Pioneers Still Rules, 1997, The Automobile Gold Rushes, 1998. Vol. Christ Cmty. Ch., Tucson, also various youth orgns. including Boy Scouts and one-on-one mentoring program for troubled youth; group coord. Combined Fed. Campaign. Mem. Nat. Eagle Scout Assn., Mining History Assn., James Madison Brigade for Preservation of the U.S. Constn., Mensa, Hist. Soc., Golden Key, Phi Alpha Theta, Pi Sigma Alpha. Avocations: backpacking, scuba diving, photography. Home: 136 S Shadow Creek Pl Tucson AZ 85748-3278 Office: USAF 355 CES CEVA Davis Monthan A F B AZ 85707

MILLER, CHARLES A. lawyer; b. Oakland, Calif., Feb. 7, 1935; s. Frank and Janice (Greene) M.; m. Jeanette Segal, Sept. 27, 1964; children: Jennifer Fay Haight, Charlotte Irene Marvin, Ira David. AB, U. Calif., Berkeley, 1955, LLB, 1958. Law clk. to assoc. justice U.S. Supreme Ct., Washington, 1958-59; assoc. Covington & Burling, 1959-67, ptnr., 1967—, chmn. mgmt. com., 1991-95. Mem. criminal justice coordinating bd., Washington, 1977-78; chmn. hearing com. Bd. on Profl. Responsibility, Washington, 1980-86. Pres. U. Calif. Alumni Club, Washington, 1962-70; mem. various coms. and adv. bds. Washington Pub. Sch. System, 1972-79; chmn. lawyers com. Washington Performing Arts Soc., 1984-86; bd. dirs. Dumbarton Concert Series, Washington, 1986—, chmn., 1990—; trustee Fed. City Coun.; chair D.C. Citizens Welfare Transformation Com., 1996-97; co-chair Task Force on D.C. Governance, 1996—; mem. Mayor's Commn. on Juvenile Justice, Washington, 2001-2002. Fellow Am. Coll. Trial Lawyers; mem. ABA, D.C. Bar Assn., U. Calif. Alumni Assn. (trustee 1989-92). Clubs: Burning Tree (Bethesda, Md.). Democrat. Jewish. Office: Covington & Burling 1201 Pennsylvania Ave NW PO Box 7566 Washington DC 20044-7566 E-mail: cmiller@cov.com.

MILLER, CHARLES E. (CHUCK MILLER), judge; b. Washington, Sept. 26, 1944; s. Charles Edward Miller and Mary (Cox) M.; divorced; 1 child, Samantha Mcgill Cox. BA, So. Meth. U., 1971, JD, 1972. Bar: Tex. 1972. Assoc. Roseborough & Curlee, Dallas, 1972-77; judge County Criminal Ct. #7, 1977-82, Ct. Criminal Appeals, Austin, Tex., 1983-94; state judge at large State of Tex., 1995—. Arbitrator comml., employment and labor panels Am. Arbitration Assn., 1995—; adj. prof. criminal law So. Meth. U. Law Sch., Dallas, 1980—82. Author and lectr. in field. Mem. nat. adv. coun. Nat. victim Ctr., N.Y.C. and Washington; mem. nat. steeringcom. Victims Constitutional Amendment Network; mem. adv. bd. victims Organized to Ensure Rights and Safety; mem. victim assistancecom. Tex. Young Lawyers Assn.; parliamentarian state exec. bd. People Against Violent Crime. With U.S. Army, 1966-70. Named Disting. Mil. Grad., Officer Candidate Sch., Ft. Sill, Okla., 1968, Best Dallas Misdemeanor Ct. Judge, Dallas Bar Assn., 1982, Best Dallas Criminal Ct. Judge, Dallas County Criminal Bar Assn., 1982; decorated Army Commendational medal, 1970; recipient Sunny von Bulow Nat. Victim Advocacy Ctr. Appreciation cert., 1987, U.S. Dept. Justice Victims of Crime Appreciation cert., 1992, Victims Organized to Ensure Rights and Safety Advocate for Justice award, 1993, People Against Violent Crime Appreciation cert., 1993. Mem. SAR, State Bar Tex. (chmn. criminal law sect. 1981-82, course dir. advanced criminal law course 1990, chmn. crime victim com. 1992-94, crime victim & witness, 1994, cert. specialist in criminal law), Coll. State Bar Tex., Tex. Bar Found. Republican. Home and Office: 1701 Foggy Glen Cv Austin TX 78733-1541 E-mail: judgechuckmiller@att.net.

MILLER, CHARLES EDMOND, retired library administrator; b. Bridgeport, Conn., Aug. 3, 1938; s. Edmond and Irene Ovelia (Boudreaux) M.; m. Alice Ann Phillips, June 2, 1962; children— Alison, Charles Edmond, Catherine, Susan. Student, U. Hawaii, 1957-58; BA, McNeese State U., 1964; MS in L.S., La. State U., 1966. Tchr. Lake Charles (La.) High Sch., 1964-65; mem. staff La. State U. Library, Baton Rouge, 1966-69; asso. dir. Tulane U. Library New Orleans, 1969-73; dir. Fla. State U. Library, Tallahassee, 1973-2000; ret., 2000. Vis. coms. So. Assn. Colls. and Schs.; bd. dirs. SOLINET, 1979-81, 85-86, corp. v.p., vice chmn., 1980-81; cons. in field; adv. com. state Libr. Fla.; bd. dirs. Ctr. for Rsch. Librs., 1976-77, 91-97, sec., 1993-96; mem. policy bd. Fla. Libr. Network; pres. Assn. Southeastern Rsch. Librs., 1982-84; mem. rsch. libr. adv. com. Online Computer Libr. Ctr., Inc., Dublin, Ohio, 1993-98. Asst. editor: La. Library Assn. Bull, 1967; contbr. articles to library sci. jours.; book revs. to Southeastern Librarian. Served with USMCR, 1956-59. Mem. ALA, Fla. Libr. Assn. (dir. 1979-81), Southeastern Libr. Assn., Assn. Coll. and Rsch. Librs., Assn. Rsch. Librs. (bd. dirs. 1985-90, v.p., pres.-elect 1987-88, pres. 1988-89), Fla. Ctr. Libr. Automation (chmn. bd. dirs. 1985-96), Rsch. Librs. Group (exec. com. 1988-90, bd. dirs. 1991-94), Phi Kappa Phi, Beta Phi Mu, Sigma Tau Delta.

MILLER, CHARLES HAMPTON, lawyer; b. Southampton, N.Y., Jan. 25, 1928; s. Abraham E. and Ethel (Simon) M.; m. Mary Fried, Aug. 26, 1956; children: Cathy Lynn, Steven Scott, Jennifer Lee. BA, Syracuse U., 1949; LLB, Columbia U., 1952. Bar: N.Y. 1952, Republic of Korea 1954, U.S. Ct. Appeals (2d cir.) 1958, U.S. Supreme Ct. 1969, U.S. Ct. Appeals (3d cir.) 1972, U.S. Ct. Appeals (7th cir.) 1973, U.S. Ct. Appeals (9th cir.) 1995; cert. mediator and early neutral evaluator (so. and ea. dists.) N.Y., 1994, mediator Supreme Ct. N.Y. County, 1996; arbitrator Ea. dist. N.Y., 1993. Asst. counsel Waterfront Commn., N.Y. Harbor, 1954-56; asst. atty. U.S. Atty. for So. Dist. N.Y., 1956-58; assoc. Cole & Deitz, N.Y.C., 1958-61, Marshall Bratter Greene Allison & Tucker, N.Y.C., 1961-64, ptnr., 1964-82, Hess Segall Guterman Pelz Steiner & Barovick, N.Y.C., 1982-86, Loeb & Loeb LLP, N.Y.C., 1986-2000, counsel, 2000—. Mem. faculty Continuing Legal Edn., Columbia U. Law

Sch., 1976-82. With U.S. Army, 1952-54. Fellow Am. Bar Found.; mem. Assn. Bar City of N.Y. Home: 171 Ralph Ave White Plains NY 10606-3813 Office: Loeb & Loeb LLP 345 Park Ave Fl 18 New York NY 10154-1895 E-mail: cmiller@loeb.com.

MILLER, CHARLES JAY, dentist; b. Pitts., Nov. 10, 1924; s. I. Franklin and Ella (Abrams) M.; m. Barbara Thorpe, May 30, 1975; children: Sandi, Wayne, Wendy, John Thorpe. BS, U. Pitts., 1948, DDS, 1950. Diplomate Am. Acad. Osseointegration. Dentist Miller, Werrin, Gruendel, P.A., Pitts., 1950—. Chmn. Council Dental Health, Odontological Soc. Wester Pa., Pitts., 1974; clin. prof. fixed partial prosthodontics Grad. Sch. Dental Medicine, U. Pitts., 1981—. Author: Inlays, Crowns and Bridges, 1962 (translated into German, Portuguese and Spanish, 1965-67); editor: Restorative Dentistry, 1972, (with others) Electrosurgery, 1989, Cosmetic Dentistry, 1987. Bd. dirs. United Jewish Fedn., Pitts., 1981-83; chmn. alumni giving fund U. Pitts., 1990—. 1st lt. USAAF, 1944-45, ETO. Decorated Air medal with 5 silver oak leaf clusters, Presdl. Citation, European campaign ribbon, Victory ribbon; recipient Disting. Alumnus award U. Pitts., 1988; plaque commemorating funding and bldg. Edward J. Forrest Ctr. for Continuing Edn., U. Pitts., 1996. Fellow Am. Coll. Dentists, Internat. Coll. Dentists; mem. Am. Acad. Dentistry (bd. dirs. Pitts. chpt., v.p. 1996-97), Greater N.Y. Acad. Prosthodontics, Internat. Congress Oral Implantologists, Am. Acad. Esthetic Dentistry (charter, mem. 1998-99), U. Pitts. Sch. Dental Medicine Alumni Assn. (pres. 1998-99), Concordia Club (pres. 1984-86), Kiwanis (pres. Pitts. 1965), Omicron Kappa Upsilon. Democrat. Office: 3506 5th Ave Pittsburgh PA 15213-3310 E-mail: miller@usaor.net.

MILLER, CHARLES LOUIS, II, consultant; b. Bethesda , Md., Mar. 1, 1952; s. Charles Louis and Patricia Ann (Fox) Miller; m. Lucia Leondina Balos (div. May 25, 1995); 1 child Catherine Theresa. BA, SUNY, Buffalo, 1975, MA, 1977; PhD, 1994; JD, U. Buffalo Law Sch., 2002. Contract archaeologist Allegheny Nat. Forest, Warren, Pa., 1983—84; ptnr. Wood & Miller, Buffalo, 1989—90; v.p. Butterbaugh & Miller, 1990—91; sole propietor Miller & Assocs., 1991—. Grad. asst. SUNY , Bufffalo, 1979—83; exec. prodn. editor Buffalo Intellectual Property Law Jour., 1999—2002; grad. rsch. asst. U. Buffalo Law Sch., 2001—02. Mem.: Phi Alpha Delta. Avocation: martial arts. Home and Office: Buffalo Intell Law Jour 103 Heath St Buffalo NY 14214 E-mail: clmiller14214@yahoo.com.

MILLER, CHARLES MAURICE, lawyer; b. L.A., Sept. 7, 1948; BA cum laude, UCLA, 1970; postgrad., U. So. Calif., L.A., 1970-71; JD, U. Akron, 1975. Bar: Ohio 1975, Calif. 1978, U.S. Dist. Ct. (cen. dist.) Calif. 1978, U.S. Ct. Appeals (9th cir.) 1978, U.S. Supreme Ct. 1981. Gen. atty. U.S. Immigration & Naturalization Svc., U.S. Dept. Justice, L.A., 1976-79; ptnr. Miller Law Offices, 1979—. Adj. prof. law U. West L.A., 1989-90. Co-editor: The Visa Processing Guide: Process and Procedures at U.S. Consulates and Embassies, 8th edit., 2000; articles editor U. Akron Law Rev., 1974-75. Mem. Calif. Bd. Legal Specialization, San Francisco, 1988-89. Mem. Bar of Calif. (chmn. immigration splty. 1988-89, commr. immigration splty. 1987-90), Am. Immigration Law Found. (bd. trustees 1995-98), Am. Immigration Lawyers Assn. (bd. dirs. 1998-2001, mem. bd. govs., chair So. Calif. chpt. 1993-94, INS headquarters liaison com. 1997-98, co-chair mentor program 1990-91, co-chair visa office liaison 1991-92, vice chair 1994-95, co-chair consular rev. task force 1993-95, Jack Wasserman Meml. award for excellence in immigration litigation 1995). Office: Miller Law Offices 12441 Ventura Blvd Studio City CA 91604-2407

MILLER, CHARLES RICKIE, thermal and fluid systems analyst, engineering manager; b. New Albany, Ind., Oct. 4, 1946; s. Marshall Christian and Thelma Virginia (Martin) M.; m. Janel Howell, Nov. 24, 1968; children: Kimberly, Brian, Audrey, Rachel. BA in Physics, DePauw U., 1969; postgrad., Rice U., 1969-70, U. Houston, 1972-76. Tech. editor ITT/Fed. Electric Corp., Houston, 1970-71, LTV/Svc. Tech. Corp., Houston, 1971; sys. safety engr. Boeing Aerospace Corp., 1971-76; thermal analyst space sys. divsn. Rockwell Internat. Corp., 1976-89; mgr. thermal and fluid sys. for space shuttle payloads Space Shuttle Program, Office NASA/L.B. Johnson Space Ctr., 1989—. Mem. edtl. team Apollo 14, 15 preliminary sci. reports, 1971-72; mem. sys. integration negotiating team for Space Shuttle to Mir Space Sta. rendezvous and docking missions, 1993-98, chmn. negotiating team for Space Shuttle to Mir Space Sta. water preparation and transfer, 1994-98, space shuttle program co-chmn. for shuttle/internat. space sta. program joint tech. working groups for thermal control, environ. control and life support sys., 1996—. Bd. dirs. Space City Aquatic Team, Houston, 1990-91. Rector scholar DePauw U., 1964-68; Rice fellow Rice U., 1969-70. Mem. AIAA, ASME, Nat. Space Soc., Air Force Assn., Am. Inst. Physics, Planetary Soc., Sigma Pi Sigma. Avocations: children's sports, jogging, science fiction, military history. Home: 806 Walbrook Dr Houston TX 77062-4030 Office: NASA Mail Code MS2 LB Johnson Space Ctr Houston TX 77058 E-mail: cmiller@ems.jsc.nasa.gov.

MILLER, CHERYL DEANN, former professional basketball coach, broadcaster; b. Riverside, Calif., Jan. 3, 1964; BA in Broadcast Journalism, U. So. Calif., 1985. Basketball player Jr. Nat. Team, 1981, U.S. Nat. Team, 1982, U.S. Olympics, 1984; commentator ABC Sports; head coach women's basketball U. So. Calif., 1993-94; commentator TNT Sports, Atlanta, 1996; gen. mgr., head coach Phoenix Mercury, 1997—2000. Player JC Penney All-Am. Team Five, U. So. Calif. Women's Basketball Team, World Championship Team, 1983. Recipient Sports Illustrated Player of Yr., 1986, Naismith Player of Yr. award, Kodak All-Am. award, more than 1,140 trophies and 125 plaques including Nat. Sports Festival, 1981, Pan Am. Games, 1983, FIBA World Championship, Goodwill Games, gold medal 1984 Olympic Games; elected to Naismith Basketball Hall of Fame, 1995.*

MILLER, CHERYL MARIE, special education educator, business owner; b. Syracuse, N.Y., Sept. 3, 1969; d. Lawrence J. and Georgia Ann (Smith) Gola; m. Wendell L. Miller, June 8, 1991; 1 child, Ian William. BS in Edn., SUNY, Geneseo, 1991; MS in Edn., SUNY, Oswego, 1995. Cert. spl. edn. tchr., reading tchr., N.Y. Spl. edn. tchr. South Jefferson Ctrl. Sch., Adams Center, N.Y., 1991-93; mental health case mgr. Oswego County Health Dept., Oswego, 1994-98; spl. edn. aide Sandy Creek (N.Y.) Ctrl. Sch., 1998-99; spl. edn. tchr. Rehab Resources, Oswego, 1999—. Mem. Coun. for Exceptional Children, Internat. Reading Assn. Avocations: reading, archery. Home: 391 Kehoe Rd Sandy Creek NY 13145-2172

MILLER, CHRISTINE MARIE, marketing executive, public relations executive; b. Williamsport, Pa., Dec. 7, 1950; d. Frederick James and Mary (Wurster) M.; m. Robert M. Ancell, Mar. 30, 1985. BA, U. Kans., 1972; MA, Northwewstern U., 1978, PhD, 1982. Pub. rels. asst. Bedford County Commr., Bedford, Pa., 1972-73; teaching asst. Northwestern U., Evanston, Ill., 1977-80; asst. prof. U. Ala., Tuscaloosa, 1980-82, Loyola U., New Orleans, 1982-85; vis. prof. Ind. U. Sch. Journalism, Bloomington, 1985-86; mktg. dir. Nat. Inst. Fitness & Sport, Indpls., 1986-88; program dir. Nat. Entrepreneurship Acad., Bloomington, 1986-88; mgmt. assoc. community and media rels. Subaru-Isuzu Automotive, Inc., Lafayette, Ind., 1988-91; dir. pub. rels. Giddings & Lewis, Fond Du Lac, Wis., 1991-93; v.p. comm. and enrollment mgmt. Milton Hershey (Pa.) Sch., 1993-94, dir. adminstrn., 1994-95; mktg. comms. mgr. WorldCom Govt. Markets, McLean, Va., 1995—. Co-author: The Biographical Dictionary of World War II General and Flag Officers, 1996; contbr. articles to profl. jours. Bd. dirs. Indpls. Entrepreneurship Acad., 1988-91, Area IV Agy., Greater Lafayette Mus. Art, 1989-91. With USN, 1973-77, capt. USNR, 1977—. Mem. Armed Forces Comm. Electronics Assn., Pub. Rels. Soc. Am., Naval Order of the U.S. (nat. pub. affairs com.), U.S. Naval Pub. Affairs Alumnae Assn. (bd. dirs.), Naval Res. Assn., Res. Officers Assn. Presbyterian. Avocations: cooking, swimming, reading, travel, cycling. Home: 7406 Salford Ct Alexandria VA 22315-4728 Office: WorldCom Def Markets Ste 7055 1945 Old Gallows Rd Vienna VA 22182-3931 E-mail: christine.m.miller@wcom.com.

MILLER, CHRISTINE ODELL COOK, judge; b. Oakland, Calif., Aug. 26, 1944; m. Dennis F. Miller; 2 children. BA in Polit. Sci., Stanford U., 1966; JD, U. Utah, 1969. Bar: D.C., Calif. Law clk. to Hon. David T. Lewis U.S. Ct. Appeals (10th cir.), Salt Lake City; trial atty. Dept. Justice, U.S. Ct. Claims; team leader atty. FTC; atty. Hogan & Hartson, Washington; spl. counsel Pension Benefit Guaranty Corp.; dep. gen. counsel U.S. Ry. Assn.; ptnr. Shack & Kimball, Washington; judge U.S. Ct. Fed. Claims, 1982—. Comment editor Utah law Rev. Scholar U. Utah Coll. Law. Mem. D.C. Bar Assn., Calif. State Bar, Order of Coif, Univ. Club (bd. govs.), Cosmos Club. Avocation: geneology. Office: US Ct Fed Claims 717 Madison Pl NW Ste 617 Washington DC 20439-0002

MILLER, CHRISTINE TALLEY, physical education educator; b. Wilmington, Del., Sept. 11, 1959; d. Willard Radley and Anna Rose (Oddo) Talley; m. Jeffrey Lynch Miller, Nov. 14, 1987; children: Radley Edward, Rebecca Anna. BS in Phys. Edn., U. Del., 1981, MS in Phys. Edn., 1984. Cert. phys. edn. tchr., Del. Phys. edn. tchr. Pilot Sch. Inc., Wilmington, 1981-85; EKG technician Christiana Care Health Sys., Newark, 1978—; phys. edn. tchr. Red Clay Consol. Sch. Dist., Wilmington, 1985—. Mem. stds. revision com. Del. Dept. Pub. Instrn., 1991; mem. stds. rev. com. Red Clay Consol. Sch. Dist., 1993-94, curriculum revision com., 1988-92; coach spl. olympics, 1985-88. Contbg. author: A Legacy of Delaware Women, 1987. Jump Rope for Heart coord. Am. Heart Assn., Newark, 1994—; mem. Gov.'s Coun. for Lifestyles and Fitness, State of Del., 1991-93. Recipient Gov.'s Cup award for outstanding phys. edn. program Gov. Mike Castle, Del., 1991, Gov.'s award for health and fitness, 1999. Mem. AAHPERD, Del. Assn. for Health, Phys. Edn., Recreation and Dance (sec. 1981-86, v.p. health, treas. 1999-2001, Outstanding Phys. Edn. Tchr. of Yr. 1986, 99). Home: 1206 Arundel Dr Wilmington DE 19808-2137

MILLER, CHRISTOPHER EDWARD, investment advisor; b. July 20, 1958; m. Joan Martin; children: Daniel, Benjamin, Samuel. BA in Math., Econs. with hons., Hobart Coll., Geneva, N.Y., 1980. V.p. Citibank, NA, N.Y.C., 1980-89, Bankers Trust Co., N.Y.C., 1989-96; ptnr. Roanoke Asset Mgmt., 1996-99; pres. Apple Securities, LLC, 1998-99; sr. v.p. Fleming Asset Mgmt., N.Y.C., 1999-2000; dir. Credit Suisse First Boston, 2000—01; exec. dir. Morgan Stanley Capital Internat., 2001—. Home: 38 Old Mill Rd Weston CT 06883-1542

MILLER, CLAIRE CODY, lawyer, mediator; b. Staten Island, N.Y., Feb. 17, 1961; d. William Michael Jr. and Elvira (Cavallaro) C.; m. Bradley Noah Miller, Sept. 25, 1988; children: Rachael F., Brian W. BA, SUNY, Albany, 1983; JD, N.Y. Law Sch., 1986. Assoc. Bruce G. Behrins & Assoc., Staten Island, 1987-90; pvt. practice Claire Cody Miller, Esq., 1990—. Mediator Edgewater Mediation, Staten Island, 1995; com. mem. character and fitness com. appellate divsn. 2nd dept. Supreme Ct. N.Y., 1997. Del. to jud. nominations Richmond County Dem., Bklyn., 1992, 94, 95, 96, 97, 98. Mem. Staten Island Women's Bar (pres. 1991-93), Women's Bar Assn. N.Y. (del. 1992, 94, co-chair working mother's com. 1995—), Richmond County Bar Assn. (mem. grievance com. 1993—), Assn. Bar City of N.Y. (mem. matrimonial com.). Office: Claire Cody Miller Esq 1 Edgewater Plz Ste 201 Staten Island NY 10305-4900

MILLER, CLAIRE ELLEN, writer, editor, educator; b. Milw., July 17, 1936; d. Emil George Benjamin and Phyllis Dorothy (Rahn) Holtzen; m. Gerald Ray Miller, June 21, 1958; children: Karin Miller O'Callaghan, Russell Bruce Miller. BS in Edn., Concordia U., 1961. Catalog clk. U. Ill. Libr., Urbana, 1960-61; tchr. Grace Episcopal Day Sch., Silver Spring, Md., 1971-77, The Norwood Sch., Bethesda, 1977-79; writer Media Materials, Balt., 1980; project editor Ednl. Challenges, Alexandria, Va., 1981; asst. mng. editor Ranger Rick Mag., Nat. Wildlife Fedn., Vienna, 1981-87, mng. editor, 1988-2001, contbg. editor, 2002—; propr. Claire Ellen Miller, Writer and Editor, Rockville, Md., 2001—. Author numerous activity books for presch. thru jr. high, 1979-80; project editor 6 vocabulary books, 1981; author numerous children's stories to mag. Mem. Assn. Ednl. Pubs., Md. Ornithol. Soc. Democrat. Lutheran. Avocation: birding. Home and Office: 17501 Kirk Ln Rockville MD 20853-1033 E-mail: clairemiller@erols.com.

MILLER, CLIFF, engineer; b. Griffin, Ga., Aug. 8, 1958; s. Isaiah and Marline Miller; m. Charlotte Lenoir Free, Aug. 9, 1986. BS in Gen. Engring., U.S. Mil. Acad., 1982. Commd. 2d lt. U.S. Army, 1982, advanced through grades to capt., 1985; resigned, 1987; mgr. level 1, Procter & Gamble, Mehoopany, Pa., 1987-91, mgr. level 2, 1991-94; market mgr. Pepsico/Tricon, Overland Park, Kans., 1994-99; with Citigroup/Saloman Smith Barney, Kansas City, Mo., 1999—. Diversity trainer By Visions, Boston; leader Black Mgrs. Work Team, Mehoopany, 1988-89. Mem. Northeastern Networking, Tunkhannock Jaycees. Avocations: reading, writing, jogging. Office: Citigroup Salomon Smith Barney 4520 Main St Fl 8 Kansas City MO 64111-1816 Home: 4100 Highway 45 N Meridian MS 39301-1203

MILLER, CLIFFORD ALBERT, merchant banker, business consultant; b. Salt Lake City, Aug. 6, 1928; s. Clifford Elmer and LaVeryl (Jensen) M.; m. Judith Auten, Sept. 20, 1976; 1 child, Courtney; children by previous marriage, Clifford, Christin, Stephanie. Student, U. Utah, 1945-50, UCLA, 1956. Pres. Braun & Co., L.A., 1955-82, chmn., 1982-87; exec. v.p. Gt. Western Fin. Corp., Beverly Hills, Calif., 1987-91; chmn. Clifford Group, Inc., bus. cons., 1992—; mng. dir. Shamrock Holdings, Inc., 1992—, Shamrock Capital Advisors, L.P., 1992—. Bd. dirs. Frontier Bank, Park City, Utah, Triad Broadcasting Co., Inc. Monterey, Calif.; cons to White House, 1969-74. Trustee Harvey Mudd Coll., Claremont, Calif., 1974—, chmn. bd. trustees, 1991-98; chmn. bd. dirs. L.A. Master Chorale, 1989-93, chmn. emeritus, 1993; mem. chmn.'s coun. Music Ctr. Unified Fund Campaign; bd. trustees Keck Grad. Inst. Applied Life Scis., Claremont, 1997—. Mem. Calif. Club, Wilshire Country Club, Park Meadows Country Club, Pi Kappa Alpha. Office: Shamrock Holdings Inc 4444 W Lakeside Dr PO Box 7774 Burbank CA 91510-7774

MILLER, CLIFFORD JOEL, lawyer; b. L.A., Oct. 31, 1947; s. Eugene and Marian (Millman) M. BA, U. Calif., Irvine, 1969; JD, Pepperdine U., 1973. Bar: Calif. 1974, Hawaii 1974, U.S. Dist. Ct. Hawaii 1974. Ptnr. Rice, Lee & Wong, Honolulu, 1974-80, Goodsill Anderson Quinn & Stifel, Honolulu, 1980-89, McCorriston Miller Mukai MacKinnon, Honolulu, 1989—. Mem. ABA, Calif. Bar Assn., Hawaii Bar Assn., Am. Coll. Real Estate Lawyers. Avocations: sailing, volleyball, swimming, history. Office: McCorriston Miller Mukai MacKinnon 5 Waterfront Plz 500 Ala Moana Blvd Ste 400 Honolulu HI 96813-4920 E-mail: cmiller@m4law.com.

MILLER, CONNIE JOY, real estate analyst, broker; b. Martinez, Calif., May 7, 1949; d. Lee Issac James and Lela Martha (Carter) James Poe; m. Avery Jared Miller Oct. 22, 1967 (div. Mar. 1988); children: Elaine Paula Miller Bond, Alfred Saul Jacob Miller. AA, Contra Costa Coll., San Pablo; BA, St. Mary's Coll. Lic. real estate broker. Acct. AT&T, San Francisco, 1967; real estate broker, mgr. Berkeley and El Cerrito, 1979-93; CFO A.J. Miller & Assocs., Berkeley, 1978-87; auditor UCOP, Oakland, 1987-88, benefits acct., 1988, exec. asst. to assoc. v.p., 1988—94, sr. real estate analyst, 1994—2001, asst. real estate officer, 2001—. Chair Cmty. Resources for Children; past pres. El Cerrito Soccer, Tilden chpt. ORT; past v.p. Berkeley Hadassah. Mem. NAR, Calif. Assn. Realtors, Berkeley Assn. Realtors, Am. Real Estate Assn. Jewish. Avocations: gardening, golf, travel, art. Home: 7300 Pomona Ct El Cerrito CA 94530 Office: UC Office of Pres 1111 Franklin St 6th Fl Oakland CA 94607-5200

MILLER, CORBIN RUSSELL, investment company executive; b. Huntington, W.Va., Apr. 6, 1948; s. Corbin Russell and Ernestine (Thorne) M.; m. Kathryn Ann Anderson, Sept. 16, 1978. AB cum laude, Princeton (N.J.) U., 1971. Trainee Morgan Guaranty Trust Co., N.Y.C., 1972-74, asst. treas., 1974-77; assoc. Wm. Sword & Co. Inc., Princeton, 1977-79; v.p. J. Henry Schroder Corp., N.Y.C., 1979-83, J. Henry Schroder Bank & Trust, N.Y.C., 1983-87; sr. v.p. IBJ Schroder Bank & Trust Co., 1987-90; chmn. Koala Techs. Corp., Pleasanton, Calif., 1990-91; mng. dir. Regent Ptnrs. Inc., N.Y.C. and Denver, 1991-92; exec. v.p. S.N. Phelps & Co., Greenwich, Conn., 1992-95; exec. v.p., CFO, dir. Carey Internat., Inc., Washington, 1995-96; pres. Lombard North Am. Inc., San Francisco, 1997-99; sr. ptnr. Continuum Ventures LLC, N.Y.C., Calif., 2000—. Bd. dirs. Lombard Investments, Inc., San Francisco. Bd. dirs. Met. Opera Guild, N.Y.C., 1994—. Mem. Am. Soc. Order St. John of Jerusalem (chancellor 1999—), Met. Opera Club (pres. 1992-94), Knickerbocker Club, Rockaway Hunting Club, Racquet and Tennis Club, The Brook. Republican. Episcopalian. Avocation: golf. Home: 1165 5th Ave New York NY 10029-6931 Office: Continuum Ventures LLC 300 Park Ave Fl 17 New York NY 10022-7402

MILLER, CREIGHTON HERBERT, music educator; b. Philadelphia, Tenn., 1950; s. Herbert Clarence and Carolyn Anna Miller. BMAS, U. of Del., Newark,DE, 1968—88. Band dir. Beech H.S., Hendersonville, Tenn., 1990—2002, T.W. Hunter Mid. Sch., Hendersonville, 1990—2002; band director ST. Marks H.S., Wilmington, Del., 1988—90; band dir. Gold Coast Christian Sch., FT. Lauderdale, Fla., 1981—85, Sunrise Mid. Sch., FT. Lauderdale, GM, 1981—85; brass dir. Lauderdale Lake Mid. Sch., Fla., 1982—84. Trombonist Gen. Jackson Showboat, Nashville, 1992—2002, Opryland Theme Pk., Nashville, 1991—99, Free Lance& Rec., Nashville, 1990—2002. Trombonist (film) The Road - Shelby Lynne. Mem. Nat. Rifle Assiciation, Washington, 1976—2002; charter founder Second Amendment Task Force, Fairfax, Va., 1976; mem. NRA Inst. For Legislative Action, 2000—02. Recipient Renaissance Tchr. Award, Summer County Sch. , Fairfax,VA, 1992. Mem.: NRA Inst. for Legislative Action (assoc.), Music Educator Nat. Confrence (assoc.), Am. Fedn. of Mucician (assoc.; 1970 2002). Freedom. Episcopalian. Avocations: shooting, hunting, horseback riding. Home: 3126 Long Hollow Pike Hendersonville TN 37075 Personal E-mail: creightonmiller@hotmail.com.

MILLER, CYNTHIA ELLEN, visual artist; b. Fond du lac, Wis., Mar. 18, 1953; d. Sherman Rowe and Sheila Ann Finn Miller; m. Charles Haskell Alexander, Nov. 8, 1986; children: Katherine Clare, Nora Julia. BFA, San Francisco Art Inst., 1977; MFA, U. Ariz., 1981. Art instr. Tucson Mus. of Art Sch., 1981—, U. Ariz., Tucson, 1998—. Co-founder Dinnerware Artists Coop., Tucson, 1979—85; bd. dirs. Chax Press, Tucson, visual artist book cover illustrations, 1986—2002. Exhibited in group shows at Tucson Mus. Art, U. Ariz. Gallery and Art Mus., Etherton Gallery, Scottsdale Ctr. for the Arts, Mesa S.W. Mus., Yuma Art Ctr., Pima C.C. Art Gallery, Eleanor Jeck Gallery, Tucson. Bd. dirs. Tucson/Pima Arts Coun., 1988-92. Painting fellowship Ariz. Commn. on the Arts, 1989; recipient Diamond Addy award Nashville Advt. Fedn., 1989; named Disting. Ariz. Artist Tucson Cmty. Found., 1991. Studio: 101 W 6th St Ste 6 Tucson AZ 85701-1000

MILLER, D. DOUGLAS, retired music educator, conductor; b. Algona, Iowa, July 2, 1941; s. Donald Bruce and Dorothy A. (Orms) M.; m. Grace Ann Fogle, June 6, 1964; children: David, Kristin Michele. BMusEd, Drake U., 1963, MMus, 1965; DMus, Ind. U., 1973. Music libr. Des Moines Pub. Libr., 1963-65; instr., grad. asst. Ind. U., Bloomington, 1965-68; instr. music U. Maine, Gorham, 1968-69; from assoc. prof. to prof. music Pa. State U., University Park, 1969-2001; ret., 2001. Music dir. various choirs, 1960-68, State Coll. Choral Soc., 1971-99, Pa. Chorale, State College, 1984-2000, Pa. Chamber Chorale, 1993-2001. Co-author: Heinrich Schutz, A Bibliography, 1986 (Choice Outstanding Acad. book award 1986). Mem. Am. Choral Dirs Assn. (Pa. pres. 1993-95, 96-97, pres. ea. divsn. 2000-2002), Am. Musicological Soc., Soc. 17th Century Music, Internat. Heinrich Schütz Soc. (nat. sec., treas. 1988-90), Coll. Music Soc., Music Educators Nat. Conf., Chorus Am. Mem. Soc. Of Friends. Avocations: gardening, construction. Home: 330 Henderson Rd Julian PA 16844-8102 E-mail: ddm8@psu.edu.

MILLER, DALE THOMAS, investment executive; b. Murray, Utah, Nov. 8, 1968; s. Thomas Hudelson and Arlene Jones M.; m. Kari Edgren, May 25, 1991; children: Grace, Ethan, Connor, Elsa, Caelen. BA, Willamette U., 1991. Assoc. JW Gant, Washington, 1991; sr. claims rep. State Farm Ins., Milwaukee, Oreg., 1992-93; assoc. investment banker Cort Mackenzie, Portland, 1993-94; v.p. Smith Barney, Seattle, 1994-96; v.p.. Merrill Lynch, 1996—2001; founder, dir. eBallot.net Inc., 1997—2000; sr. v.p. UBS, 2001—. Author: (pseudonym John C. Hudelson) Sleeping Like A Baby, 1998. Mem. Emerald City Philharm. Symphony, prin., 1997-98; precinct officer Rep. Party, Bellevue, Wash., 1996; scoutmaster Boy Scouts Am., 1991-94; mem. alumni bd. Willamette U., Salem, Oreg., 1997-98; bd. dirs. YMCA, Seattle, 1998; chair Willamette Forum, 1999; bd. dirs. MIT Enterprise Forum, 1999. Named Program Vol. of Yr., YMCA, 1998. Mem. Lds Ch. Avocations: trap, angling, Colonial furniture construction, French horn. Home: 10235 NE 58th St Kirkland WA 98033-7440 Office: 500 108th Ave NE Ste 2000 Bellevue WA 98004-5552

MILLER, DAN, congressman; b. Mich., May 30, 1942; m. Glenda Darsey; children: Daniel, Kathryn. Grad., U. Fla., 1964; MBA, Emory U., 1965; PhD, La. State U., 1970. Ptnr. Miller Enterprises, Bradenton, Fla.; restaurant owner Twin Dolphin Marina Grille, 1977—; instr. Ga. State U., U. South Fla., Sarasota; mem. 103rd-106th Congresses from 13th Fla. Dist., 1993—; mem. appropriations com. Mem. govt. reform com.; chmn. subcom. on the Census. Mem. Manatee C. of C. Episcopalian. Office: US Ho of Reps 127 Cannon Hob Washington DC 20515-0001*

MILLER, DANIEL LEE, surgeon; b. Ashland, Ky., Jan. 31, 1959; s. Rexal J. and Ruth K. Miller; m. Pamela Farrell, July 26, 1986; children: Meagan Meredith, Jordan Nicholas, Jackson Daniel, Madelyn Grace. BS in Chemistry, Biology cum laude, Georgetown Coll., 1981; MD, U. Ky., 1985. Diplomate Am. Bd. Surgery, Am. Bd. Thoracic Surgery. Jr. asst. resident Georgetown U. Hosp., Washington, 1985-86, resident, 1986-87, clin. ECMO fellow, 1987-88, sr. asst. resident, 1988-89, asst. chief resident, 1989-90, chief resident, 1990-91; cardiothoracic surgery fellow Mayo Med. Ctr., Rochester, Minn., 1991-94, sr. asst. cons., assoc. prof. surgery, edn. coord. divsn. thoracic surgery, 1997—2002; chief thoracic surgery, asst. prof. U. Louisville, Ky., 1994-97; surg. dir. thoracic oncology program Emory U. Clinic, 2002—; assoc. prof. surgery Emory U. Sch. Medicine, 2002—. Robert W. Philip Meml. lectr. Royal Coll. Physicians Edinburgh, Scotland, 1996. Guest reviewer Chest, So. Med. Jour., Annals Thoracic Surgery, European Respiratory Jour., Am. Jour. Surgery, Asian Cardiovasc. and Thoracic Annals, Jour. Thoracic and Cardiovasc. Surgery, Annals of Surgery; contbr. articles to profl. jours. Recipient 1st pl. Washington Acad. Surgeons, 1990, Alumni Achievement award Georgetown Coll., 2001; Presdl. scholar Georgetown Coll.; Summer Rsch. fellow NIH, 1982, 83; Biomed. Rsch. Support grantee Georgetown U. Sch. Medicine, 1988-89, 89-90. Fellow ACS (2d pl. Resident Trauma Competition Va. chpt. 1989), Am. Coll. Chest Physicians (1st pl. Case Presentations 1993); mem. AMA, Am. Thoracic Soc., Assn. Acad. Surgeons, Soc. Thoracic Surgeons, Am. Fedn. Clinic Rsch., Mayo Clinic Thoracic Soc., Mayo Clinic Priestley Soc., Robert B. Wallace Soc. (charter), N. Ctrl. Cancer Treatment Group, So. Thoracic Surg. Assn., Gen. Thoracic Surg. Club, Am. Assn. Thoracic Surgery, Beta Beta Beta. Avocations: cycling, football, squash. Office: Emory Univ Clinic 1365 Clifton Rd Atlanta GA 30322 Office Fax: 404-778-4346. E-mail: daniel_miller@emoryhealthcare.org.

MILLER, DANIEL RAYMOND, prosecutor; b. Evansville, Ind., Sept. 20, 1963; s. Daniel Edgar and Virginia Sue (Baumgart) M. BA magna cum laude, DePauw U., 1985; JD cum laude, Ind. U., 1989. Bar: Ind. 1989. Clk. to Hon. William I. Garrard, Ind. Ct. of Appeals, Indpls., 1989-90; dep. pros. atty. Vanderburgh County Pros.'s Office, Evansville, 1990—. Pres. Substance Abuse Coun. Vanderburgh County, 1997-98; chmn. pastoral coun. St. John Cath. Ch., Evansville, 1995-98; mem. Diocese of Evansville Pastoral Coun., 1997-2000; pres. 4-H Coun., 1999. Meml. Ind. Bar Assn., Ind. Drug Enforcement Assn., Nat. Dist. Attys. Assn., 4-H Club Assn. (bd. dirs. 1995-2001, leader Energetics club 1991—, treas. 2000-2001, pres. Vanderburgh County 4-H Leaders 2001-02), St. Vincent DePaul Soc. (pres. 1994, sec. conf. 1995—) Vanderburgh County Coop. Ext. Svc. (bd. dirs. 2000—). Republican. Roman Catholic. Avocations: gardening, church choir. Home: 13521 N Green River Rd Evansville IN 47725-9769 Office: Vanderburgh Co Pros Office Rm 108 City County Adm Bldg Evansville IN 47708 E-mail: drmprosec@aol.com.

MILLER, DARCY M. publishing executive; b. Glen Ridge, N.J., June 17, 1953; d. Paul Richardson and Susan (Alling) Miller; m. James R. Donaldson III, Feb. 6, 1988 (div.); 1 child Zoe Alling Donaldson. Co-founder, assoc. pub. Mus. Mag., N.Y.C., 1979-83; pub. Crop Protection Chemicals Reference, 1983-85; assoc. pub. Chief Exec. Mag., 1986-87, pub., 1987-89, exec. v.p., 1989-96; pub. Stagebill, 1996-97; group pub. Am. Baby Group, 1997-2000, pres., 2000—01; pres. corp. sales Primedia Inc., N.Y.C., 2001—. Mem. ASCAP, Advt. Women of N.Y. Democrat. Episcopalian. Office: Primedia Inc 261 Madison Ave New York NY 10016

MILLER, DAVID WILLIAM, historian, educator; b. Coudersport, Pa., July 9, 1940; s. Arthur Charles and Kathryn Marie (Long) M.; m. Margaret Vick Richardson, Aug. 22, 1964; 1 child, Roberta Neal. BA, Rice U., 1962; MA, U. Wis., 1963; PhD, U. Chgo., 1968. Instr. history Carnegie Mellon U., Pitts.,

1967-68, asst. prof., 1968-73, assoc. prof., 1973-80, prof., 1980—. Author: Church, State and Nation in Ireland, 1898-1921, 1973, Queen's Rebels: Ulster Loyalism in Historical Perspective, 1978; editor: Peep o'Day Boys and Defenders: Selected Documents on the Disturbances in County Armagh, 1784-1796, 1990; co-editor: Piety and Power in Ireland, 1760-1960, 2000; assoc. editor: New Dictionary of National Biography, 1994—, Encyclopedia of Ireland, 2001—; prin. developer: (interactive atlas) Great American History Machine, 1994. Sr. research fellow Inst. Irish Studies Queen's U., Belfast, Northern Ireland, 1975-76. Mem. Am. Hist. Assn., Am. Conf. for Irish Studies. Democrat. Presbyterian. Avocations: walking, singing. Office: Carnegie Mellon Univ Dept of History Schenley Park Pittsburgh PA 15213 E-mail: dwmiller@cmu.edu.

MILLER, DAVID A. lawyer; b. Charleroi, Pa., Dec. 7, 1952; s. Francis E. and Betty L. Miller. A. in Specialized Tech., Pa. Tech. Inst., Pitts., 1975; BA, George Mason U., 1982; JD, U. Va., 1985. Bar: Va. 1985, Pa. 1987. Svc. engr. Compugraphic Corp., 1975-80; assoc. Roeder, Durrette & Davenport, Fairfax, Va., 1985-86; law clk. Hon. David L. Gilmore, Washington, 1986-87; assoc. Karlowitz, Hoffman, McCall & Kane, Pitts., 1987-89, Amatangelo, Baisley & Rega, Donora, 1989—. Mem. Pa. Bar Assn., Va. State Bar (assoc.), Washington County Bar Assn., Westmoreland County Bar Assn., Allegheny County Bar Assn. Avocations: golf, skiing, computers. Office: 100 4th St Donora PA 15033-1541

MILLER, DAVID ALLEN, air force officer; b. Galion, Ohio, Sept. 3, 1963; s. Richard Allen and Dorothy S. (Stoyanovich) M.; m. Regina Denise Fulkerson, Mar. 16, 1987; 1 child, Christopher David. BS, Bowling Green (Ohio) U., 1985, Tex. A&M U., 1987; MS, U. Md., 1994. Commd. 2d lt. USAF, 1986, advanced through grades to maj., 1998, ret., 1996; comdr., dir., chief fin. officer Palehua Solar Obs., Honolulu, 1996-99; observatory dir. Palehua Solar Observatory, 1996-99. Team chief Air Force Space Forecast Ctr., Falcon, Colo., 1994-96, v.p. booster club, 1995. Contbg. author, editor: Maryland Pilot Earth Science and Technology Education Network, 1994. Vol. St. Andrew's Epis. Cathedral, Honolulu, 1996-99, Camp Timberline, Hawaii, 1999; earth sci. instr. Md. High Sch. Tchrs., 1993-94; clean air forecaster U. Md., College Park, 1993-94, trooper, stable mgr. cavalry, 1993; sailor Pacific Yacht Club, Hickam AFB, 1997. Decorated Commendation medal, first oak leaf, Meritorious Svc. medal. Mem. AAAS, Air Force Space Command Officers Club, Am. Phys. Soc. Achievements include development of technique to forecast spacecraft internal charging conditions. Office: Palehua Solar Obs 14 AF/A33W 747 Nebraska Ave Ste 302 Vandenberg AFB CA 93437-6249 Home: 7462 Gadsby Sq Alexandria VA 22315-5288

MILLER, DAVID ANTHONY, lawyer; b. Linton, Ind., Oct. 6, 1946; s. Edward I. and Jane M. (O'Hern) M.; m. Carol E. Martin, Aug. 9, 1970; 1 child, Jennifer Rose. Student, Murray State U., 1965; BS, Ind. State U., 1969; JD, Ind. U., Indpls., 1973. Bar: Ind. 1973, U.S. Dist. Ct. (so. dist.) Ind. 1973, U.S. Supreme Ct. 1981, U.S. Ct. Appeals (7th cir.) 1982. Dep. atty. gen. State of Ind., Indpls., 1973-76, dir. consumer protection divsn. office atty. gen., 1976-93, asst. atty. gen., 1977-80, chief counsel office atty. gen., 1981-93; prin. Hollingsworth, Meek, Miller and Minglin, 1993—. Youth dir. Emmanuel Luth. Ch., Indpls., 1981-85, exec. dir., 1988-90; chmn. bd. Chambers Found., 1994—; pres. bd. Lutheran H.S., 1996-2002; bd. dirs., vice chmn. Greater Indpls. Rep. Fin. Com.; pres. Perry Twp. Firefighter Found., Inc. Mem. ABA, Ind. State Bar. Assn., Indpls. Bar Assn., Ind. State U. Alumni Assn., Columbia Club, Lambda Chi Alpha. Republican. Avocations: numismatics, golfing. Home: 6454 Forrest Commons Blvd Indianapolis IN 46227-7105 Office: 7550 S Meridian St Ste A Indianapolis IN 46217

MILLER, DAVID CHRISTOPHER, psychologist, researcher; b. Warwick, R.I., Dec. 7, 1968; s. Edmund Wilbur and Joyce Delores Miller; m. Jacquelyn Marie Grady, June 24, 1995; children: Alexander Thomas, Dominic Christopher. BA, Assumption Coll., 1990; MA, U. Md., 1995, PhD, 2000. Program mgr. S. Worcester County Rehab. Ctr., Webster, Mass., 1990—93; rsch. analyst Am. Inst. Rsch., Washington, 1999—. Contbr. articles to profl. jours. Recipient Crown & Shield award, Assumption Coll., 1990; fellow Tchg. fellow, U. Md., 1993—95. Mem.: APA, Am. Edn. Rsch. Assn., Kappa Delta Pi (life). Avocations: gardening, cooking, college sports, home projects. Office: American Inst Rsch Education Stats Svcs Inst 1990 K St NW Ste 500 Washington DC 20006 Home: 4901 Iroquois St College Park MD 20740 Fax: 202-737-4918. E-mail: dmiller@air.org.

MILLER, DAVID EDMOND, physician; b. Biscoe, N.C., June 6, 1930; s. James Herbert and Elsie Dale (McGlaughon) M.; m. Marjorie Willard Penton, June 4, 1960; children: Marjorie Dale, David Edmond. AB, Duke U., 1952, MD, 1956. Diplomate Am. Bd. Internal Medicine (subspecialty bd. cardiovascular disease). Internmed. ctr. Duke U., Durham, N.C., 1956-57, resident in internal medicine, 1957-58, 59, 60, research fellow cardiovascular disesase, 1958-59, 61, assoc. internal medicine and cardiology, 1963-79, clin. asst., prof. medicine cardiology, 1979-91; practice medicine specialising in internal medicine and cardiology, 1964-2000; attending physician internal medicine div. cardiology Watts Hosp., 1964-76, chief medicine, 1975-76; attending physician cardiology divsn. internal medicine Durham Regional Hosp. (formerly Durham County Gen. Hosp.), 1976-2000, chmn. dept. internal medicine, 1976-82, pres. med. staff, 1980-81, ret., 2000. Adv. com. Duke Med. Ctr. Contbr. articles to profl. jours. Council clin. cardiology N.C. chpt. Am. Heart Assn., 1963—. Served to lt. comdr. USNR, 1961-63. Fellow ACP, Am. Coll. Cardiology, Royal Soc. Medicine, Royal Soc. Health; mem. AMA, So. Med. Assn., N.C. Med. Soc. (del. ho. of dels. 1981, 82, 83), N.C. Durham-Orange County Med. Soc., Am. Soc. Internal Medicine, N.C. Soc. Internal Medicine (exec. coun. 1984-92), Am. Fedn. Clin. Rsch. Clubs: Capitol, Hope Valley Country, Univ., Duke Faculty, Carolina Yacht. Methodist. Home: 1544 Hermitage Ct Durham NC 27707-1680

MILLER, DAVID EMANUEL, physics educator, researcher; b. Bethel, Vt., Aug. 30, 1943; s. Manuel Southworth and Lucille (Shurtleff) M. BA, U. Vt., 1965; MA, SUNY, Stony Brook, 1967, PhD, 1971; Habilitation in Theoretical Physics, U. Bielefeld, Germany, 1978. Instr. physics SUNY, Stony Brook, 1970-71; Wissenschaftlicher asst. Freie U., Berlin, 1972-75; scientist U. Bielefeld, 1975-78, Heinrich-Hertz Stipendium, 1977-78; privat dozent U. Bielefeld, 1978-83, univ. prof., 1987—; asst. prof. of physics Pa. State U., Hazleton, 1983-86, assoc. prof., 1986-92, prof., 1992—. Recipient Heinrich-Hertz stipendium, 1977-78, Fulbright award U. Wroclaw, Poland, 1997. Mem. Am. Phys. Soc., Am. Assn. Physics Tchrs., Fulbright Assn., Deutsche Physikalische Gesellschaft, Deutscher Hochschulverband, N.Y. Acad. Sci., Am. Math. Soc., Phi Beta Kappa, Sigma Xi. Home: PO Box 611 Conyngham PA 18219-0611 Office: Pa State U High Acres Hazleton PA 18201 E-mail: om0@psu.edu., dmiller@physik.uni-bielefeld.de.

MILLER, DAVID GROFF, insurance agent; b. Kansas City, Kans., Aug. 17, 1949; s. Vincent G. and Ruth (Whitton) M.; m. Marjorie Zwiers, 1979. BA, U. Kans., 1972. CLU. Press aide to U.S. Senator James B. Pearson, 1974-75; fed. grant adminstr. Kans. Gov. Robert Bennett, 1975-78; brokerage rep. Paul Revere Co., Overland Park, Kans., 1979-85; prin. Miller Agy., Inc., Eudora, 1985—. Rep. dist. 43 Kans. State Reps., 1981-91; chmn. Kans. State Rep. Party, 1995-98. Mem.: Ind. Ins. Agts., Omicron Delta Kappa. Methodist. Office: Miller Agy Inc PO Box 460 Eudora KS 66025-0460

MILLER, DAVID W. lawyer; b. Indpls., July 1, 1950; s. Charles Warren Miller and Katherine Louise (Beckner) Dearing; m. Mindy Miller, May 20, 1972; children: Adam David, Ashley Kay, Amanda Katherine Kupfer. BA, Ind. U., Bloomington, 1971; JD summa cum laude, Ind. U., Indpls., 1976. Bar: Ind. 1977. Investigator NLRB, Indpls., 1971-76; assoc. Roberts & Ryder, 1977-80, ptnr., 1981-86, Baker & Daniels, Indpls., 1986—. Bd. dirs. Everybody's Oil Corp., Anderson, Ind. Bd. dirs. S. Madison Cmty. Found., Pendleton, Wis. Mem. Ind. Bar Assn. (chmn. labor law sect. 1981-82). Republican. Office: 300 N Meridian St Ste 2700 Indianapolis IN 46204-1750

MILLER, DAWN MARIE, meteorologist; b. Hartford, Conn., Sept. 17, 1963; d. Eugene E. Miller and Audrey E. (Flagg) Laurel; m. Dennis James Miller, Sept. 9, 1989; children: Zackarey, Amanda. BS in Meteorology, SUNY, Oneonta, 1985. Customer support specialist WSI Corp., Bedford, Mass., 1985-87, from media TV mktg. to product mktg. specialist-data svcs. Billerica, 1987-97, sr. meteorologist, product mktg. specialist, 1997-99, sr. meteorologist, assoc. product mgr., 1999—2001, sr. meteorologist, media mktg. and promotion, 2001—. Mem. Oneonta Alumni Assn., Nat. Arbor Day Found., Nat. Audubon Soc., The Am. Horticultural Soc., The Nature Conservancy, Am. Meteorol. Soc., Nat. Weather Assn. Republican. Episcopalian. Avocations: meteorology, astronomy, photography, gardening, bird watching, NASCAR (Joe Gibbs Racing # 18 and # 20). Home: 37 Wren Dr Litchfield NH 03052-2540 Office: WSI Corp 4 Federal St Billerica MA 01821-3569 E-mail: dmmiller17@hotmail.com.

MILLER, DEANE GUYNES, salon and cosmetic studio owner; b. El Paso, Tex., Jan. 12, 1927; d. James Tillman and Margaret (Brady) Guynes; m. Richard George Miller, Apr. 12, 1947; children: J. Michael, Marcia Deane. Degree in bus. adminstrn., U. Tex., El Paso, 1949. Owner four Merle Norman Cosmetic Studios, El Paso, 1967-96; pres. The Velvet Door, Inc., 1967-96. Salon and cosmetic studio owner; b. El Paso, Tex., Jan. 12, 1927; d. James Tillman and Margaret (Brady) Guynes; degree in bus. adminstrn. U. Tex., El Paso, 1949; m. Richard George Miller, Apr. 12, 1947; children: J. Michael, Marcia Deane. Owner four Merle Norman Cosmetic Studios, El Paso, 1967-96; pres. The Velvet Door, Inc., El Paso, 1967-96; dir. Mountain Bell Telephone Co. Pres. bd. dirs. YWCA, 1967; v.p. Sun Bowl Assn., 1970; bd. dirs. El Paso Symphony Assn.; bd. dirs., treas. El Paso Mus. Art, pres., trustee, 1990, pres., 1991-93; chmn. bd. El Paso Internat. Airport; bd. dirs., sec. Armed Services YMCA, 1987, 1st v.p., 1990. Named Outstanding Woman field of civic endeavor, El Paso Herald Post. Mem. Women's C. of C. (pres. 1969), Pan Am. Round Table (dir., pres. 1987), Internat. Assn. for Visual Arts (v.p. 2000). Pres., bd. dirs. YWCA, 1967; v.p. sun Bowl Assn., 1970; bd. dirs. El Paso Symphony Assn.; bd. dirs., treas. El Paso Mus. Art, trustee, 1990, pres., 1990-93; chmn. bd. El Paso Internat. Airport; bd. dirs., sec. Armed Svcs. YMCA, 1987, 1st v.p., 1990. Named Outstanding Woman field of civic endeavor El Paso Herald Post. Mem. Women's C. of C. (pres. 1969), Pan Am. Round Table (dir., pres. 1987), Internat. Assn. for Visual Arts (v.p. 1998, 2000). Home: 1 Silent Crest Dr El Paso TX 79902-2160 Office: 1211 Montana Ave El Paso TX 79902

MILLER, DEBORAH JEAN, computer training and document consultant; b. Elmhurst, Ill., Oct. 2, 1951; d. Thomas Francis and Ruthe Conn (Johnston) M. BFA, Ill. Wesleyan U., 1973; MA, Northwestern U., 1974. Pres. Miller & Assocs., Evanston, Ill., 1980—. Mem. AAUW, NOW, Internat. Interactive Comm. Soc., Soc. Tech. Comm., Ind. Writers Chgo. (bd. dirs. 1985-86), Chgo. Coun. Fgn. Rels., Internat. Soc. Performance and Instrn. (Chgo. chpt.), Northwestern U. Alumni Assn. Office: 814 Mulford St Evanston IL 60202-3355 E-mail: doc1train@aol.com.

MILLER, DECATUR HOWARD, lawyer; b. Balt., June 29, 1932; s. Lawrence Vernon and Katherine Louise (Baum) M.; m. Sally Burnam Smith, Nov. 23, 1963; 1 dau., Clemence Mary Katherine. BA, Yale U., 1954; LL.B., Harvard U., 1959. Bar: Md. 1959. Assoc. Piper & Marbury, Balt., 1959-62, 1963-66, ptnr., 1967-94, ptnr. emeritus, 1995—, mng. ptnr., 1974-87, chmn., 1987-94; Md. Securities commr., 1962-63. Bd. dirs. MSD&T Funds. Trustee Enoch Pratt Free Libr., 1975—, v.p., 1977—85, pres., 1985—89; trustee Calvert Sch., Balt., 1976—89, pres., 1982—87; trustee Walters Art Gallery, 1987—91; mem. bd. sponsors Sellinger Sch. Bus. and Mgmt. Loyola Coll., 1990—98; mem. Mayor's Bus. Adv. Coun., 1993—99; mem. bd. visitors U. Md. Balt. County, 1994—2000; mem. bus. sch. adv. coun. Morgan State U., 1994—96; chmn. Equal Justice Coun., 1999—; bd. dirs. Balt. Symphony Orch., 1970—; v.p., 1978—86, Balt. Symphony Orch., 1988—90, pres., 1990—92; bd. dirs. United Way Ctrl. Md., 1988—91, The Leadership, 1990—93, Empower Balt. Mgmt. Corp., 1995—, Coll. Bound Found., 1990—2001, chmn., 1994—96; bd.dirs. Greater Balt. Com., 1988—96, chmn., 1992—94; bd. dirs. U. Md. Found., 2000—. With U.S. Army, 1954—56. Mem. ABA, Md. Bar Assn., Balt.Bar Assn., Am. Law Inst., Am. Bar Found., Md. Bar Found., Elkridge Club, 14 W. Hamilton St. Club, Ctr. Club, Elizabethan Club, Lawyers Round Table. Home: 3704 N Charles St Apt 1305 Baltimore MD 21218 Office: Piper Rudnick LLP 6225 Smith Ave Baltimore MD 21209-3600

MILLER, DENNIS DIXON, economics educator; b. Chillicothe, Ohio, May 1, 1950; s. Kermit Baker and Martha (Ralston) M. BA, Heidelberg Coll., 1972; MA, U. Colo., 1979, PhD, 1985; D (hon.), Ternopil Acad. Nat. Economy, Ukraine, 2000. Instr. in econs. Am. U., Cairo, Egypt, 1982-84; internat. economist USDA, Washington, 1985-86; prof. Baldwin-Wallace Coll., Berea, Ohio, 1987—. Rsch. assoc. Internat. Ctr. Energy and Econ. Devel., Boulder, Colo., 1979-82, Inst. Behavioral Sci., Boulder, 1979-82, 84-85; vis. scholar Hoover Instn., Stanford U., Palo Alto, fall 1986; acad. advisor Heartland Inst., Chgo., 1988—, Buckeye Ctr.; book reviewer Choice mag., 1984—; manuscript reviewer Dryden Press, 1994-96; pub. policy advisor Heritage Found.'s Listing, Washington, 1991—, econ. cons. gen., 1991—; vis. prof. Mithibai Coll., U. Bombay, India, summer and fall 1991; coord. agy. Air Quality Pub. Adv. Task Force, 1993; v.p. Adam Ferguson Inst., 1996—; vis. prof. The U. of the Autonomous Regions of the Caribbean Coast of Nicaragua, Bluefields, fall 1996; vis. prof. The Ternopil Acad. of Nat. Economy Ukraine, 1997; Fulbright sr. specialist Discipline Peer Rev. Com., 2001. Earhart Found. fellow, 1977-78; Fulbright scholar, 1999-2000. Mem. AAAS, Am. Econs. Assn., Cleve. Coun. on World Afairs, Assn. Pvt. Enterprise Edn., Ohio Assn. Economists and Polit. Scientists (v.p. 2000-01, pres. 2001-02), Intertel, Middle East Inst., Sierra Club, Nature Conservancy, Mensa, Eagle Scout. Avocations: running, tennis, reading, travel. Home: 12 Adelbert St Apt 2 Berea OH 44017-1753 Office: Baldwin Wallace Coll Dept Of Econs Berea OH 44017 E-mail: dmiller@bw.edu.

MILLER, DENNIS EDWARD, health medical executive; b. Detroit, Dec. 21, 1951; m. Deborah Ann Keith, Feb. 12, 1977. BS, Austin Peay State U., 1973; MBA, U. South Fla., 1981. CPA. Chief exec. officer Hosp. Corp. of Am., Bennettsville, S.C., 1976-84; div. v.p. Westworld Community Healthcare, Waco, Tex., 1984-86; group v.p. Nat. Healthcare, Inc., Dothan, Ala., 1986-87; COO Healthcare Connections, Brentwood, Tenn., 1988; cons. VHA Physician Svcs., Inc., Dallas, 1988-90; asst. adminstr., CFO Clarksville (Tenn.) Meml. Hosp., 1990; Franklin, Tenn., 1990; sr. v.p., COO Eastside Ventures, Inc., Birmingham, Ala., 1990-93; sr. v.p. Ea. Health System, Inc., 1993—2003; CEO Williamson Med. Ctr., Franklin, 2002—. Chmn. Minority Leadership Task Force, Ea. Health System, Inc., 1994-95. Sec. Ala. Health Svcs. Bd.; mem. Literacy Coun. Ala., Ala. Hosp. Assn. State Legis. Com., future directions com.; chmn. Birmingham Regional Healthcare Exec. Forum; chmn. friends of scouting campaign Boy Scouts Am., 1996. Fellow Am. Coll. Healthcare Execs. (chmn diplomate credentials com., Ala. Regent's award for exec. excellence 1995), Hosp. Fin. Mgmt. Assn. (Follmer Bronze Merit award for outstanding svc.); mem. AICPA, Tenn. Soc. CPAs, Ala. Soc. CPAs (chmn. state legis. com.), Ala. Hosp. Assn. (future directions com.), Birmingham C. of C. (chmn. memberhsip com.), Birmingham East Rotary Club (pres., chmn. membership com.), Mensa, Shriners, Masons, Birmingham Touchdown Club, Sigma Chi. Avocations: hunting, fishing, gardening, antique collecting. Office: Williamson Med Ctr 2021 Carothers Rd Franklin TN 37067 E-mail: dmiller@wmed.org.

MILLER, DENYCE KARLINA, tax specialist; b. Chicago, Ill., July 2, 1963; d. Sidney Miller, Vera Miller. BS in Commerce, DePaul U., 2001; M in Acctg., Kellstadt Grad. Sch. Bus. DePaul U., 2002. Tax cons. Denyce Miller Tax Svc., Bellwood, Ill., 2001—; postal employee devel. tng. technician USPS, Chgo., 1985—2002. Fin. com. mem. Am. Postal Workers Union, Chgo., 2001—. Author: Blind Love, 1996. Coord. hearing impaired Am. Postal Workers Union, Chgo., 1992—94; combined fed. campaign key worker USPS, 1989; dir. clk. craft Am. Postal Workers Union, Chgo ., 2001—02. Recipient Taekwondo First Dan award, Kukkiwon World Taekwondo Hdqs., 1996. Mem.: AICPA (assoc.; Associate Member 2001—02, Scholarship award 2001), Inst. Mgmt. Accts. (Member 2001—02, Scholarship award 2001), Ill. Cert. Pub. Accts. Soc. (assoc.; Associate Member 2001—02). Democrat. Apostolic. Avocation: Tae Kwon Do. Home: 1012 Marshall Bellwood IL 60104-2322 Home Fax: (708) 544-8419. Personal E-mail: denyce@wans.net.

MILLER, DIANE DORIS, executive search consultant; b. Sacramento, Jan. 18, 1954; d. George Campbell and Doris Lucille (Benninger) M. BA, U. Pacific, 1976, Golden Gate U., 1985, MBA, 1987. Mgr. A.G. Spanos, Sacramento, 1977-81, Lee Sammis, Sacramento, 1981-83; v.p. Consol. Capital, San Francisco, 1983-86; pres. Wilcox Miller & Nelson, Sacramento, 1986—. Bd. dirs. Sacramento Symphony En Corps, 1982-84, Sacramento Ballet, 1983-84, 86-92, Sacramento Symphony Assn., 1988-92, Oakland Ballet, Calif., 1984-85, Sacramento Symphony Found., 1994-98, Sacramento Reg. Found., 1996-99; chmn. bd. Sacramento Met. C. of C., 1998-2002; mem. Golden Gate U., 1995-97. Named Vol. of Yr., Jr. League, 1983; recipient award, Bus. Jour., 2002. Mem. U. Pacific Alumni Assn. (bd. dirs. 1978-85), Sacramento Metro. C. of C. (bd. dirs., Bus. Vol. in the Arts 1989). Republican. Avocations: ballet, water sports. E-mail: dmiller@wilcoxcareer.com.

MILLER, DIANE WILMARTH, human resources director; b. Clarinda, Iowa, Mar. 12, 1940; d. Donald and Floy Pauline (Madden) W.; m. Robert Nolen Miller, Aug. 21, 1965; children: Robert Wilmarth, Anne Elizabeth. *Husband Robert N. Miller, BA 1962 Cornell College, JD 1965 University of Colorado Law School, Boulder, is currently a partner in the law firm LeBoeuf, Lamb, Green & MacRae, He is a past U.S. Attorney for the District of Colorado. Son Robert Wilmarth Miller, BA 1996 Hasting College, JD 1999 University of Wyoming College of Law, Laramie, is currently employed as a deputy district attorney in the DA's office in Greeley, Colorado. Daughter, Anne Elizabeth Miller, BA 1999 University of Denver, was awarded Denver University's prestigious Pioneer Award and is currently manager of inflight services for Frontier Airlines in Denver.* AA, Colo. Women's Coll., 1960; BBA, U. Iowa, 1962; MA, U. No. Colo., 1994. Cert. tchr., Colo.; vocat. credential, Colo.; cert. sr. profl. in human resources. Sec.-counselor U. S.C. Rep., Myrtle Beach AFB, 1968-69; instr. Coastal Carolina Campus U. S.C., Conway, 1967-69; tchr. bus. Poudre Sch. Dist. R-1, Ft. Collins, Colo., 1970-71; travel cons. United Bank Travel Svc., Greeley, 1972-74; dir. human resources Aims Community Coll., 1984—2001. Instr. part-time Aims Cmty. Coll., 1972—89. Active 1st Congl. Ch., Greeley. Mem.: Philanthropic Ednl. Orgn. (pres. 1988—89), Women's Panhellenic Assn. (pres. 1983—84), Questers (pres. 2002—), WTK Club, Scroll and Fan Club (pres. 1985—86). Home: 3530 Wagon Trail Pl Greeley CO 80634-3405

MILLER, DON ROBERT, surgeon, educator; b. Highland, Kans., July 6, 1925; s. Pleasant V. and Lucy Anna (Hammond) M.; m. Geraldine Ellen Nelson, Sept. 6, 1947; children: Don R., Laurie, Todd, Marcia, Kristen, Felicia. AB, Westminster Coll., 1944; MD, U. Kans., 1948. Mem. faculty U. Kans., Kansas City, 1957-73, prof. surgery, 1970-73, U. Calif. Irvine, 1973-92, prof. emeritus, 1992—, vice chmn., chief dept. surgery, pres. med. staff, 1989-91. Dir. surgery Orange County (Calif.) Med. Center, 1973-77. Contbr. articles to profl. jours. Gov. 1988-92. Served with USNR, 1943-45, 50-52. Spl. research fellow Zurich, Switzerland, 1965-66 Fellow A.C.S., Am. Coll. Cardiology; mem. Am. Soc. Univ. Surgeons, Am. Surg. Assn., Soc. Vascular Surgery, Am. Assn. Thoracic Surgery, Am., Central, Western surg. assns., Internat. Cardiovascular Soc., Sigma Xi, Alpha Omega Alpha. Achievements include research on extracorporeal circulation, myocardial function. Home: 743 Louisiana St Lawrence KS 66044-2339

MILLER, DON WILSON, nuclear engineering educator; b. Westerville, Ohio, Mar. 16, 1942; s. Don Paul and Rachel (Jones) M.; m. Mary Catherine Thompson, June 25, 1966; children: Amy Beth, Stacy Catherine, Paul Wilson Thompson. BS in Physics, Miami U., Oxford, Ohio, 1964, MS in Physics, 1966; MS in Nuclear Engring., Ohio State U., 1970, PhD in Nuclear Engring., 1971. Rsch. assoc. Ohio State U., Columbus, 1966-68, univ. fellow, 1968-69, tchg. assoc., 1969-71, asst. prof. nuclear engring., 1971-74, assoc. prof., 1974-80, chmn. nuclear engring. program, 1977-97, prof., 1980—, dir. nuclear reactor lab., 1977—. Sec., treas. Cellar Lumber Co., Westerville, Ohio, 1972-84, 85—; cons. Monsanto Rsch. Corp., Miamisburg, Ohio, 1979, NRC, Washington, 1982-84, 99—, Scantech. Corp., Santa Fe, 1984-95, Neoprobe Corp., Columbus, 1990, Electric Power Rsch. Inst., Palo Alto, Calif., 1992-94; mem. adv. com. on reactor safeguards Nuclear Regulator Commn., 1995-99. Patentee in field; contbr. articles to profl. jours. Mem. Westerville Bd. Edn., 1976-91, pres., 1977-78, 86-88; mem. Ohio Sch. Bd.'s Assn., Columbus, 1976-91; mem. fed. rels. com. Nat. Sch. Bd.'s Assn., Washington, 1984-86. With USAR, 1960-68. Named Tech. Person of Yr. Columbus Tech. Coun., 1979; named to All Region Bd. Ohio Sch. Bd's. Assn., 1981, 86, Westerville South H.S. Hall of Fame, 1996; recipient Coll. of Engring Rsch. award Ohio State U., 1984, Disting. Alumnus award, 1999; Achievement award Mid Ohio Chpt Multiple Sclerosis Soc., 1988. Fellow Am. Nuclear Soc. (chmn. edn. divsn. 1986-87, bd. dirs. 1989-91, chair human factors divsn. 1993-94, v.p./pres. elect 1995-96, pres. 1996-97, Cert. Appreciation 1991); mem. IEEE (sr. mem.), Am. Soc. Engring. Edn. (chmn. nuclear engring. divsn. 1978-79, Glenn Murphy award 1989), Instrument Soc. Am. (sr. mem.), Nuclear Dept. Heads Orgn. (chmn. 1985-86), Westerville Edn. Assn. (Friend of Edn. award 1992), Rotary (Courtright Cmty. Svc. award 1989), Kiwanis, Hoover Yacht Club, Alpha Nu Sigma (chmn. 1991-93). Avocations: sailing, Am. history, traveling, amateur radio (extra class license). Home: 172 Walnut Ridge Ln Westerville OH 43081-2464 Office: Ohio State U Dept Mech Engring Nuclear Engring Program 206 W 18th Ave Columbus OH 43210-1189 E-mail: miller.68@osu.edu.

MILLER, DONALD EDWIN, physician; b. Phila., Mar. 25, 1933; s. Percy Edwin and Mary Isabel (Baumgartner) M.; m. Jeanne Lynn Plequette; children: Natalie Ann, Jeffrey Edwin, Jennifer Mary. AB, Princeton (N.J.) U., 1955; MD, Hahnemann Med. Coll., 1959. Intern in ob.-gyn. Abington (Pa.) Meml. Hosp., 1959-60, Albany (N.Y.) Med. Coll., 1962-64; pres. Middlesex Ob-Gyn. Assocs., Middletown, Conn., 1964-2000; chmn. dept. ob-gyn. Middlesex Meml. Hosp., 1980-88. Cons. Conn. Valley Hosp., Middletown, 1966-2000, Elmcrest Psychiat. Inst., Portland, Conn., 1970-95. Capt. M.C., USAF, 1960-62. Capt. USAF, 1959-61. Mem. Conn. State Med. Soc., Middlesex County Med. Soc. Republican. Presbyterian. Avocations: antiques, fluorescent minerals, gardening. Home: PO Box 120 Haddam CT 06438-0120 Office: Middlesex Ob-Gyn Assocs 540 Saybrook Rd Ste 360 Middletown CT 06457-4723 E-mail: djmillerhaddam@aol.com.

MILLER, DONALD EUGENE, aerospace executive; b. Providence, Mar. 20, 1947; s. Meyer Samuel and Beatrice (Wattman) M.; m. Deborah Neary Miller, Mar. 14, 1987. BA, Boston U., 1968; JD, U. Pa., 1972. Law clk. Assoc. Justice Alfred H. Joslin Supreme Ct., Providence, 1972-73; prin., lawyer Temkin, Merolla & Zurier, 1973-81, Temkin & Miller, Ltd., Providence, 1981-91; exec. v.p., gen. counsel, corp. sec. The Fairchild Corp., Dulles, Va., 1991—. Author: (treatise) Buying and Selling a Small Business, 1987. Mem. R.I. Bar Assn., Mass. Bar Assn. Avocation: dog breeding and exhibition. Home: 10704 Riverwood Dr Potomac MD 20854-1332 Office: Fairchild Corp 45025 Aviation Dr Ste 400 Dulles VA 20166-7516

MILLER, DONALD KEITH, venture capitalist, asset management executive; b. Akron, Ohio, Feb. 2, 1932; s. Clinton Raymond and Hazel Elizabeth (Curl) M.; m. Barbara Dewees Duff, Sept. 25, 1971 (div. 1983); children: Prescott Clinton, Barclay St. John; m. Priscilla Corwith Barker, Sept. 17, 1988. BS, Cornell U., 1954; MBA, Harvard U., 1959. Asst. treas. Chase Manhattan Bank, N.Y.C., 1959-62; asst. to v.p. Electric Bond & Share, 1962-66; gen. ptnr. G.H. Walker & Co. Inc., 1966-74; sr. v.p. White Weld & Co., 1974-77; mng. dir. Blyth Eastman Paine Webber Inc., 1978-86; chmn. Greylock Fin., 1987-98, Christensen Boyles Corp., Salt Lake City, 1987-95; chmn., CEO, Thomson Adv. Group L.P., Stamford, Conn., 1990-93, vice chmn., 1993-94; pres., CEO, TAG Inc., 1994-97; pres. Presbar Corp., Greenwich, Conn., 1998—; chmn. Axiom Internat. Investors, LLC, N.Y.C., 1999—. Bd. dirs. RPM, Inc., Medina, Ohio, chmn. audit com.; bd. dirs. Huffy Corp., Dayton, Ohio, Dallas, Layne Christensen, Mission Woods, Kans. 1st lt. U.S. Army, 1954-57. Avocation: tennis, squash. Home: 588 Round Hill Rd Greenwich CT 06831-2724

MILLER, DONALD KENNETH, engineering consultant; b. St. Louis, Oct. 18, 1925; s. Henry Edward and Ernestine Elizabeth (Schmeer) M.; m. Arline Louise Heckman, Feb. 27, 1953; children: Garry Edwin, Kristine Louise Miller Morris. BSChemE, Mo. U., 1950. Registered profl. engr., Pa. Application engr. York (Pa.) Corp., St. Louis, Houston, York, 1951-62; mgr. quality control York divsn. Borg Warner Corp., 1962-65, chief engr., 1965-85; refrigeration specialist York Internat. Corp., 1985-88; pres. MDK Engring. Corp., York, 1988—. Author: (with others) Plant Engineering Handbook, 1959, ASHRAE Handbook, 1981-94, Applied Thermal Design, 1989; contbr. articles to ASHRAE Jour. and IIR/IIF Internat. Congress Procs.; inventor desuperheater control in a refrigeration apparatus. With USNR, 1944—46. Mem. AIChE, ACS, NSPE, ASHRAE (life mem., cen. Pa. chpt., sec. 1972-73, treas. 1973-74, v.p. 1974-75, pres. 1975-76, Disting. Svc. award 1992), U.S.

Nat. Com. Internat. Inst. Refrigeration, RSvc. Corps of Ret. Execs., otary. Avocations: sketching, computers. Office: MDK Engring Corp 391 Greendale Rd York PA 17403 E-mail: mdkche50@aol.com.

MILLER, DONALD LANE, publishing executive; b. Pitts., May 14, 1918; s. Donald Edwin and Arvilla (Lane) M.; A.B., Kenyon Coll., 1940; Russian interpreter cert. U. Colo., 1946; postgrad. U. Pitts., 1947-48; m. Norma Reno, Feb. 2, 1951. Reporter, Pitts. Sun-Telegraph, 1940-42, Washington Post, 1946; with pub. rels. dept. Westinghouse Electric Corp., Pitts., 1947-51; reporter Billboard and Tide, 1953; pub. rels. dir. Nat. Agrl. Chem. Assn., Washington, 1954-58; sec. Donald Lerch & Co., Washington, 1958-61; pres. Asso. Pub. Rels. Counselors, Washington, 1961-77; chmn. Braddock Comm., Inc.; chmn. emeritus Children's Aid Internat.; exec. dir. All Am. Conf., Washington, 1962-75. Editor GOP Nationalities News, Rep. Nat. Com., 1960; pub. rels. nationalities div. Rep. Nat. Com., 1964; coord. life underwriters sect. Citizens for Nixon-Agnew, 1968; co-pub. Cmty. Forum, 1996—. Served from ensign to lt., USNR, 1942-46; from lt. to lt. comdr., 1951-53. Decorated Knight of Europe. Mem. English Speaking Union, SAR, Phi Beta Kappa, Delta Tau Delta. Clubs: Nat. Press. Author: Strategy for Conquest, 1966, George to George: 200 Years of Presidential Quotations, 1989, Call of the Northern Neck, 1992. Home: 428 Fleets Bay Rd PO Box 1978 Kilmarnock VA 22482-1978 Office: PO Box 710720 Herndon VA 20171-0720

MILLER, DONALD LESESSNE, publishing executive; b. N.Y.C., Jan. 10, 1932; s. John H. and Mamie (Johnson) M.; m. Ann Davie, Aug. 12, 1951 (div. 1981); children: Lynn, Mark; m. Gail Aileen Wallace, June 27, 1981. BA, U. Md., 1967; cert., Harvard Grad. Sch. Bus. Adminstrn., 1969. Enlisted U.S. Army, 1948, advanced through grades to maj., 1966, ret., 1968; spl. asst. to pres., mgr. corp. recruitment Inmont Corp., N.Y.C., 1968-70; v.p. indsl. relations Seatrain Shipbldg. Corp., 1970-71; dep. asst. sec. def. U.S. Dept. Def., Washington, 1971-73; v.p. personnel mgmt. Columbia U., N.Y.C., 1973-78; dir. personnel devel. and adminstrn. Internat. Paper, 1978-79; v.p. employee relations Consol. Edison N.Y., 1979-86, Dow Jones & Co., Inc., N.Y.C., 1986-95; CEO, pub. Our World News. Bd. dirs. Bank of N.Y., Bank of N.Y. Co. and Schering-Plough Corp. Author: An Album of Black Americans in the Armed Forces, 1969. Chmn. bd. emeritus Associated Black Charities, N.Y.C., 1982-94. Decorated Legion of Merit; decorated Commendation Medal; recipient Disting. Civilian Service medal Dept. Def., 1973, Disting. Alumnus award U. Md., 1977 Mem. Alpha Sigma Lambda, Pi Sigma Alpha, Phi Kappa Phi, Alpha Phi Alpha, Sigma Pi Phi.

MILLER, DONALD MUXLOW, accountant; b. Luverne, Minn., Feb. 21, 1924; s. Henry Clay and Mildred Eva (Muxlow) M.; m. Eunice Jean Gibson, Feb. 19, 1944; children: SueRilla M., Donna Jean Eichten, Patsy Ann Pushee. Student, Metro State, St. Paul, 1973-84. Lic. pub. acct. Mgr. Hines & Paulus, CPA, Worthington, Minn., 1952-65; commandant Minn. Vets. Home, Mpls., 1965-68; prin. D.M. Miller, Acct., 1968-70, 76-78; asst. sec. Minn. State Senate, St. Paul, 1970-72; comptr. Western Oil Co., Mpls., 1972-76; commr. Dept. VA, State of Minn., St. Paul, 1978-81; pres. D.M. Miller & Assoc., Ltd., Mpls., 1981-97; chief exec. officer MARD, Inc., 1985-95; v.p. Miller, Micketts & Assocs. Ltd., 1993-96; pres. D.M. Miller Ltd., Worthington, 1997—. Trustee Heart Professorship Found., 1987-91; pres. Legionville Sch. Patrol Camp, Brainerd, Minn., 1963-64; pres. bd. govs. Big Island Vets. Camp, Mpls., 1986-88. 2nd lt. USAAC, 1942-46; 1st lt. USAF, 1951-52. 2d lt. USAAC, 1942—46, 1st lt. USAF, 1951—52. Recipient Volunteer of the Year award Kidney Found., 1975. Mem. VFW, Nat. Soc. Pub. Accts., Minn. Assn. Pub. Accts. (dist. dir.), Nat. Assn. State Vets. Homes (hon. life mem., reg. v.p. 1967-68), Nat. Assn. State Dirs. Vets Affairs (reg. v.p. 1978-79), Minn. Gaming Assn. (exec. sec. 1987-92), Am. Legion (hon life mem., comdr. Minn. 1962-63, nat. com. chmn. 1980-84, pres. Minn. Found. Bd. 1990-91). Presbyterian. Avocation: golf.

MILLER, DONALD R. pharmacist, educator; b. Nov. 15, 1954; BSc in Pharmacy, U. Man., 1976; Cert. of Residency in Hosp. Pharmacy, U. Hosp. Sask., Saskatchewan, 1978; PharmD, U. Mich., 1978. Lic. pharmacist N.D., Man. Summer rsch. fellow U. Man., 1975; pharmacy resident Univ. Hosp., Saskatoon, Sask., 1977-78; asst. prof. pharmacy practice and dir. Drug Info. Ctr. N.D. State U., Fargo, 1978-85, assoc. prof. pharmacy practice, 1985-99, chmn. dept. pharmacy practice, 1997—, prof. pharmacy practice, 1999—; clin. pharmacist Dakota Med. Ctr., 1983-90, VA Med. Ctr., Fargo, 1990—2001. Mem. expert adv. panel on rheumatology/clin. immunology USP Com. on Revision, 1995—. Contbr. articles to profl. jours.; referee for manuscripts Am. Jour. Health Sys. Pharmacy, 1995—, Clin. Pharmacy, 1982—94, Annals of Pharmacotherapy, 1987—, Annals Internal Medicine, 1999—; : mem. editl. adv. bd. Arthritis Today, 1995—. Nat. chmn. pharmacy program task force Arthritis Found., 1986-87, bd. dirs. Dakota chpt., 1981-88, 90-95, v.p., 1982-83, pres. 1984-85, chmn. rsch. subcom. 1986-88, bd. dirs. north ctrl. chpt., 2001—. Recipient Upjohn Pharmacy Rsch. award N.D. Soc. Hosp. Pharmacists, 1990, Vol. Svc. citation Arthritis Found., 1987, Achievement award, 1982, Roche award Can. Soc. Hosp. Pharmacists, 1979, Dr. D. McDougall Meml. award U. Man., 1976; grantee N.D. State U., 1980, 82, VA Western Regional Office, 1980, , 82, Riker Pharms., 1980, Arthritis Found., 1982, Smith Kline & French, 1983, 84-85, 86, 87, Sterling-Winthrop Rsch. Inst., 1984, Merck, Sharpe & Dohme Co., 1984, Ayerst Labs., 1985-89, SKF Co., 1986, Emmes Corp., 1988-91, Winthrop Pharms., 1988, 88-92, Rhone-Poulenc Pharms., 1989, McNeil Pharms., 1989-90, N.D. State U. Devel. found., 1998, Dakota Med. Found., 1999, 2002. Fellow: Am. Soc. Health-System Pharmacists; mem.: Am. Coll. Clin. Pharmacy, Am. Pharm. Assn., Arthritis Health Profl. Assn., Am. Assn. Colls. Pharmacy (chair task force on curricular outcomes 1997—98, chair task force on classroom assessment 1998—99), N.D. Pharm. Assn., N.D. Soc. Health System Pharmacists (sec.-treas. 1981—83, profls. affairs com. 1994—96). Home: 1101 42d Ave N Fargo ND 58102 Office: Pharmacy Practice Dept PO Box 5055 Fargo ND 58105-5055 Fax: 701-231-7606. E-mail: donald.miller@ndsu.nodak.edu.

MILLER, DONALD ROSS, management consultant; b. Huntington, N.Y., Aug. 5, 1927; s. George Everett and Ethel May (Ross) M.; m. Constance Higgins, 1948 (div. 1955); children: Donald Ross Jr., Cynthia Lynn, Candace Lee; m. Janet Heyman Behr, Apr. 15, 1965; children: Jeffrey Lawrence, Wendy Lorraine. BS/BEA, MIT, 1950. Cert. mgmt. cons. Inst. of Mgmt. Cons. Staff engr. Stop & Shop, Inc., Boston, 1950-56; v.p., dir. Cresap, McCormick and Paget, Inc., N.Y.C., 1956-76; mng. dir. Donald R. Miller Mgmt. Cons., Palm Desert, Calif., 1977—. Pres., CEO Carl Fischer Inc., N.Y.C., 1996; bd. dirs. Nash Finch Co., Mpls., chmn. bd. dirs., 1995-2000; bd. dirs. Michael Anthony Jewelers, Inc., Mt. Vernon, N.Y., Western Horizon Resorts, Inc., Gunnison, Colo. Author: Management Practices Manual, 3 vols., 1963, (booklet) Management of Managerial Resources, 1969. Bd. dirs. Queens Mus. Art, Flushing, N.Y., 1982-93, pres., 1988-92; pres. Lexington House, Forest Hills, 1984-2001; mem. MIT Alumni Adv. Coun., Cambridge, Mass., 1955-75; bd. govs. Alumni Ctr. N.Y.C., 1965-75, chmn., 1968-72; bd. dirs. Vol. Cons. Group, N.Y., 1969-79; trustee Queens Theatre in the Park, Flushing Meadow, N.Y., 1976-82. With U.S. Maritime Svc., 1945-46, ETO, U.S. Army, 1946-48. Mem. Nat. Assn. Corp. Dirs., Inst. Mgmt. Cons., Sky Club. Episcopal. Avocations: tennis, reading. Home: Shadow Mountain #171 73850 Fairway Dr Box 10 Palm Desert CA 92260 Office: PO Box 649 Forest Hills NY 11375-0649

MILLER, DORIS MAYHILL, accountant; b. Arkansas City, Kans., Apr. 30, 1947; d. Samuel Walter and Ferne Etta (Nellis) M.; m. James M. Dent, Aug. 3, 1971 (div. Dec. 31, 1982); m. Albert Raymond Miller, July 1, 1984; stepchildren: Michelle, Debra, Lynda. BS in Elem. Edn., Kans. State U., 1969; M in Sec. Edn., Emporia State U., 1980; math. student, Johnson County C.C., Lenexa, Kans., 1975-83; bus. and acctg. student, Cowley County C.C., Arkansas City, Kans., 1984-91. Cert. tchr., Kans. Tchr. 5th grade Olath (Kans.) Unified Sch. Dist., 1969-70; tchr. Shawnee Mission (Kans.) Unified Sch. Dist., 1970-84; field trip coord., counselor Live and Learn Group Home Boys, Olathe, summer 1983; tchr. jr. h.s. Arkansas City Unified Sch. Dist., Arkansas City, 1984-86; instr., bookkeeper, office mgr. H&R Block Profl. Bus. Svc., 1986-88; acct. Winfield (Kans.) Correctional Facility, 1988—. Mem. tng. adv. bd. Winfield Correctional Facility, Winfield, 1990—. Singer ch. and cmty. choirs, Lenexa, Olathe, Arkansas City, 1973—; vol. youth diversion Cmty. Accountability Bd., Olathe, 1982-84; 4-H judge Coop. Ext. Coun., Sedgwick County, 1991—; bd. dirs., trustee, treas. Meth. Ch., 1993-94, acct., treas., 1994—. Avocations: singing, crafts, healthy exercise, grandchildren, roller skating.

MILLER, DOROTHEA HELEN, retired educator and librarian; b. Macedonia, Iowa, Mar. 10, 1925; d. Carl Hamilton and Dorothy Marie (Wilson) Stempel; m. Ruben Roy Miller, Sept. 30, 1945 (dec. May 1987); children: Cecilia Rogge, Catherine Miller-King, Constance Miller. Student, U. Denver, 1942-45, State U. Iowa, 1960; BA with honors, Kearney (Nebr.) State Coll., 1966; ME, U. Nebr., 1970. Cert. media specialist Nebr. Libr. Oakland (Iowa) Pub. Libr., 1956-61; elem. libr. Grand Island (Nebr.) Pub. Schs., 1962-65, elem. libr. supr., 1965-78, media specialist, 1978-86; ret., 1986. Cons. N.D.E.A. Inst. for Advanced Study in Ednl. Media Concordia Coll., 1967. Vol. Denver Mus. of Natural History, 1994-96, Nat. Def. Edn. Act Inst. Libr. Materials for Minority Students, Queens Coll., N.Y. Named Outstanding Educator in Am. Acad. of Am. Educators, 1973-74. Mem. AAUW, Nat. Cherry Creek Woman's Club (treas. 2002—), Nebr. Congress Parents and Tchrs. (hon. life), Nat. Mus. Women in Arts, Order Ea. Star (assoc. matron). Democrat. Methodist. Avocations: genealogy, watercolors, calligraphy, poetry. Home: 13991 E Marina Dr Apt 303 Aurora CO 80014-3788 E-mail: TheaMil03@aol.com.

MILLER, DOROTHY ELOISE, education educator; b. Ft. Pierce, Fla., Apr. 13, 1944; d. Robert Foy and Aline (Mahon) Wilkes. BS in Edn., Bloomsburg U., 1966, MEd, 1969; MLA, Johns Hopkins U., 1978; EdD, Columbia U., 1991. Tchr. Cen. Dauphin East H.S., Harrisburg, Pa., 1966-68, Aberdeen (Md.) H.S., 1968-69; asst. dean of coll., prof. Harford C.C., Bel Air, Md., 1969—. Owner Ideas by Design, 1995—; mem. accreditation team Mid. States Commn., 1995— ; statewide writing skills assessment com., statewide English stds. com. Md. Higher Edn. Commn. 1997-2001, English composition com., 1997—; adj. prof. U. Balt., 2001. Editor: Renewing the American Community Colleges, 1984; contbr. articles to profl. jours. Pres. Harlan Sq. Condominium Assn., Bel Air, 1982, 90-96, Md. internat. divsn. St. Petersburg Sister State Com., 1993-2001; edn. liaison AAUW, Harford County, Md., 1982-92; cen. com. mem. Rep. Party, Harford County, 1974-78; crusade co-chair Am. Cancer Soc., Harford County, 1976-78; mem. faculty adv. com. Md. Higher Edn. Commn., 1993-96; people's adv. coun. Harford County Coun., 1994—. Recipient Nat. Tchg. Excellence award Nat. Inst. for Staff and Orgn. Devel., U. Tex.-Austin, 1992. Mem. Nat. Mus. Women in the Arts (charter). Republican. Methodist. Avocations: skiing, swimming, golf, reading, image consulting. Office: Harford Community Coll 401 Thomas Run Rd Bel Air MD 21015-1627 E-mail: demiller@harford.cc.md.us.

MILLER, DREW, financial management company executive; b. West Chester, Pa., Aug. 1, 1958; s. Raymond and Carol (Canfield) M.; m. Annabeth D.; 1 child, Anna Clarice. BS, USAF Acad., Colo., 1980; M in Pub. Policy, Harvard U., 1982, PhD, 1985. Cert. mgmt. acct., cert. fin. planner. Intelligence officer USAF, 1980-87; mgr. Con Agra, Inc., 1987-94; pres. Heartland Mgmt. Cons. Group, Papillion, Nebr., 1994—. Fin. Continuum, LLC, 1998-2000; mergers and acquisitions advisor, 2001—. V.p. Fin. Dynamics, Inc., Papillion, 1997-98. County commr. Sarpy County, Nebr., 1990-94; mem. Bd. Regents U. Nebr., 1994—. Republican. Home: 1904 Barrington Pkwy Papillion NE 68046-4152 E-mail: drmiller@drewmiller.com.

MILLER, DUANE KING, health and beauty care company executive; b. N.Y.C., Mar. 1, 1931; s. Henry Charles and Helen Marion (King) M.; m. Nancy L. Longley, June 6, 1954; children: Cheryl L., Duane L. AB in Econs. and Fin., NYU, 1951. V.p. mktg. Warner-Chilcott divsn. Warner Lambert Co., Morris Plains, N.J., 1970-72, pres. divsn., 1973-77; exec. v.p. Am. Optical div., pres. Am. Optical Internat div. Warner Lambert Co., Southbridge, Mass., 1978; pres. biol. and proprietary products divsn., v.p. Revlon Health Care Group, Revlon Corp., Tuckahoe, N.Y., 1978-80, pres. ethical, proprietary and vision care divsns., 1981-82, corp. v.p. parent co., 1982, pres. Revlon Health Care Group, 1983-92, corp. exec. v.p. parent co., 1984-92, pres. Revlon Health Beauty Care and Internat. Group, 1988-92, ret., 1992; pres. DKL Properties, health care cons., Promedex Techs., 1992—. Author: (with otners) Marketing Planning for Chief Executives and Planners, 1966. Mem. Rep. Nat. Com. Mem. Princeton Club N.Y., Cripple Creek (Del.) Golf Club, Masons, Shriners. Home: 8 Western Dr Colts Neck NJ 07722-1271 Office: 483 Rte 520 Marlboro NJ 07746

MILLER, DWIGHT RICHARD, professional hair care industry executive, cosmetologist, consultant; b. Johnstown, Pa., Jan. 24, 1943; Grad., Comer & Doran Sch., San Diego; DSci. (hon.), London Inst. for Applied Rsch., 1973. Cert. aromatherapist; lic. cosmetologist., instr.; Brit. Mastercraftsman. Styles dir. Marinello-Comer, Hollywood, Calif., 1965-67; expert Pivot Point Internat., Chgo., 1967-68; styles dir. Lapins, L.A., 1969; dir. Redken, 1970, Vidal Sassoon, London, 1971-74; world amb. Pivot Point, New Zealand and Australia, 1974-75, internat. artistic dir., 1975-78; internat. dir., co-founder Hair Artists Inst. & Registry, 1978-81; internat. artistic dir. Zotos Internat., Darien, Conn., 1981-87, Matrix Essentials, Inc., Solon, Ohio, 1987-92; bd. dirs., founder, v.p. creative Anasazi Exclusive Salon Products, Inc., Dubuque, Iowa, 1992-96; pres. Anasazi Salon Sys., Santa Fe, 1996-98; cons., 1998—. Judge hairdressing competitions including Norwegian Masters, Australian Nat. Championships; pres. Intercrimpers, London, 1974-75; cons. Amos, Clairol, John Frieda, John Sahag, J.C. Penney, NCA, Matrix, Zotos/ISO, 1998—, Hairworld; celebrity stylist Doris Day, 1960's, Monica Seles, 1990's. Author: (book) Sculptic Cutting Pivot Point 75, Prismatics, 1983, Milady's Standard System of Salon Skills, 1998, Amos Master Cutting System, 2000; prodr.(and dir.): (documentaries, 15), (numerous tech. and industry videos); contbr. articles and photographs to popular mags.; mem. editl. bd.: Shades mag., mem. editl. bd.: Launchpad mag. Cons. American Crew; with USMC, 1960-64. Named Artistic Dir. Yr. Am. Salon mag., Intercoiffure Educator of the Century; presented with Order of White Elephant, 1976; recipient London Gold Cup for Best Presentation London Beauty Festival, 1982, Dr. Everett G. McDonough award for Excellence in Permanent Waving, World Master award Art and Fashion Group, 1992, N.Am. Hairstylist of the Yr. award, 2000. Mem. Cercle des Arts et Techniques de la Coiffure, Intercoiffure, Haute Coiffure Franchaise, Soc. Cosmetic Chemists, Hair Artists Great Britain, Internat. Assn. Trichogists, Nat. Cosmetologists Assn. (HairAmerica, cert. instr.), Am. Soc. Phytotherapy and Aromatherapy, HairChicago (hon.), Art and Fashion Group (pres. 1993), 'Dressers MC (pres. 1990—), London's Alternative Hair Club (patron), The Salon Assn., Am. Beauty Assn., Beauty and Barber Suppy Inst. Achievements include development of several profl. product lines including Vidal Sassoon-London, Design Freedom, Bain de Terre, Ultra Bond, Vavoom!, Systeme Biolage. Home and Office: 707 Don Gaspar Ave Santa Fe NM 87505-2629 E-mail: dwight@DwightMiller.com.

MILLER, DWIGHT MERRICK, archivist, historian; b. Keosauqua, Iowa, July 25, 1932; s. Leo Albert and Beryl Irene (Merrick) M.; m. Frances Florine Olney, Nov. 19, 1961 (dec. Sept. 1977); 1 child, Dianne; m. Judith Spencer, 1979 (div. 1988); m. Pauline K. Leaverton, 1999. BA, U. Iowa, Iowa City, 1959; MA, Truman State U., Kirksville, 1961; attended, The American U., Washington, 1963-64. Asst. archivist Manuscript Divsn., Library of Congress, Washington, 1961-64; sr. archivist Herbert Hoover Presdl. Libr., West Branch, 1964-99. Compiler, asst. editor: The Public Papers of the Presidents: Herbert Hoover; 1929-1933 (6 vols.), 1974-77; co-editor: Herbert Hoover and Harry S. Truman: A Documentary History, 1992, Historical Materials in the Herbert Hoover Presidential Library, 1996, Herbert Hoover and Franklin D. Roosevelt: A Documentary History, 1998; editor: Laura Ingalls Wilder and the American Frontier: Five Perspectives, 2002. Co-chmn. Iowa Sesquicentennial Commn. Cedar Cty., Tipton, 1995-97. Mem. Herbert Hoover Presdl. Libr. Assn., Univ. Athletic Club, Friends of the Univ. of Iowa Libraries (adv. bd. 1976-81), Manuscript Soc., Ft. Ticonderoga Assn. (adv. bd. 1991—). Presbyterian. Avocations: book collecting, historical Iowa pottery. Home: 10 Rita Lyn Ct Iowa City IA 52245-3504

MILLER, EDMOND TROWBRIDGE, civil engineer, educator, consultant; b. Pitts., Dec. 9, 1933; s. George Ellsworth and Billie Sue (Watson) M.; m. Nancy Lee Cooper, July 21, 1956; children: Carol Anne, Nancy Ruth, Laura Elizabeth. B.C.E., Ga. Inst. Tech., 1955, MSC.E., 1957; C.E., MIT, 1963; PhD, Tex. A&M U., 1967. Registered profl. engr., Ala., Fla. Asst. prof. civil engring. U. Ala., Tuscaloosa, 1963-64, assoc. prof., 1967-71, prof., 1971-75; v.p. William S. Pollard Cons., Memphis, 1976-77; chmn. dept. civil engring. U. Louisville, 1977-81; prof. U. Ala., Birmingham, 1981-96, chmn. dept. civil engring., 1981-90, interim dean Sch. Engring., 1984; ret., 1996. Instr. civil engring. Tex. A&M U., 1964-67. Served to capt. C.E. AUS, 1956-57. Automotive Safety Found. fellow, 1964-65; recipient Outstanding Achievement in Edn. award Ky. Soc. Profl. Engrs., 1980 Fellow ASCE (dist. 9 council 1978-80), Inst. Transp. Engrs.; mem. Am. Soc. Engring. Edn., Transp. Research Bd., Sigma Xi, Phi Kappa Phi, Tau Beta Pi, Chi Epsilon Christian Scientist. Home: 2566 Dalton Dr Pelham AL 35124-1448 Mailing: PO Box 158 Pelham AL 35124-0158

MILLER, EDMUND KENNETH, retired electrical engineer, educator; b. Dec. 24, 1935; s. Edmund William and Viola Louise (Ludwig) M. ; Patricia Ann Denn, Aug. 23, 1958; children: Kerry Ann, Mark Christopher. BSEE, Mich. Tech. U., 1957; MS in Nuclear Engring., U. Mich., 1958; MSEE, 1961, PhD in Elec. Engring., 1965. Rsch. assoc. U. Mich., Ann Arbor, 1965-68; sr. scientist MD Assocs., San Ramon, Calif., 1968-71; group leader engring. rsch. div. Lawrence Livermore Lab., Livermore, 1971-78; leader engring. rsch. div., 1978-83; leader nuclear energy sys. div., 1983-85; regents prof. elect. and computer engring. U. Kans., 1985-87; mgr. electromagnetics Rockwell Sci. Ctr., Thousand Oaks, Calif., 1987-88; dir. electromagnetics rsch. op. Gen. Rsch. Corp., Santa Barbara, 1988-89; group leader MEE div. Los Alamos (N.Mex.) Nat. Lab., 1989-93; ret., 1993. Editor: Time Domain Measurements in Electromagnets, 1986; past assoc. editor Radio Sci.; assoc. editor IEEE Potentials, 1985-91, 94—, editor, 1992-94; assoc. editor IEEE AP-S mag.l co-editor (with L. Medgyesi-Mitschang and E.H. Newman) Computational Electromagnetics, 1991; edtl. bd. Internat. Jour. Numerical Modeling, 1990—, Computer Applications in Engring. Edn., 1992—; editorL Jour. Electromagietic Waves and Applications, 1991—, Jour. of Applied Computational Electromagnetics Soc., IEEE Computer Soc. Mag. Computational Scu. and Engring., 1994—; contbr. 140 articles to profl. jours. Stocker vis. prof. of elec. and computer engring., Ohio U., Athens, 1994-95. Fellow IEEE (mem. pres. bd. 1991-93); mem. Optical Soc. Am., Acoustical Soc. Am., Am. Soc. Engring. Edn., Electromagnetics Soc. (pas bd. dirs.) Internat. Sci. Radio Union (past chmn. U.S. Commn. A), Applied Computational Electromagnetics Soc. (past pres.)(IEEE Third Millennium medal 2000). Home: 3225 Calle Celestial Santa Fe NM 87506-1213

MILLER, EDWARD BOONE, lawyer; b. Milw., Mar. 26, 1922; s. Edward A. and Myra (Munsert) M.; m. Anne Harmon Chase Phillips, Feb. 14, 1969 (dec. Dec. 2001); children by previous marriage: Barbara Miller Anderson, Ellen Miller Gerkens, Elizabeth Miller Lawhun, Thomas; stepchildren: T. Christopher Phillips, Sarah Phillips Parkhill. BA, U. Wis., 1942, LL.B., 1947; student, Harvard Bus. Sch., 1942-43. Bar: Wis. 1947, Ill. 1948. With firm Pope, Ballard, Shepard & Fowle, Chgo., 1947-51, 52-70, ptnr., 1953-70, 75-93, mng. partner, 1979-82, chmn. labor and employment law dept., 1975-76, 87-88, 90-91; of counsel Seyfarth Shaw, 1994—. Mem. adv. com. Ctr. for Labor Mgmt. Dispute Resolution, Stetson U., 1984—, Inst. Indsl. Rels., Loyola U., 1987-91, Kent Pub. Employee Labor Rels. Conf., 1988—, Ill. Ednl. Labor Rels. Bd., 1988—; exec. asst. to industry mems. Regional Wage Stblzn. Bd., Chgo., 1951-52, industry mem., 1952; chmn. NLRB, Washington, 1970-74; mem. panel of labor law experts Commerce Clearing House, 1987—; dir. Chgo. Wheel & Mfg. Co., 1965-70, 75-88, Andes Candies, Inc., 1965-68, 75-80 Mem. Gov. Ill. Commn. Labor-Mgmt. Policies for Pub. Employees, 1966-67; chmn. Midwest Pension Conf., 1960-61; mem. labor relations com. Ill. C. of C., 1953-70; bd. dirs. Am. Found. Continuing Edn., 1960-69. Served to lt. USNR, 1943-46. Mem. ABA (NLRB practice and procedures com., internat. labor law com.), Ill. Bar Assn., Wis. Bar Assn., Chgo. Assn. Commerce and Industry (chmn. labor relations com. 1980-86, bd. dirs. 1987-97), Am. Employment Law Coun. (mem. adv. bd. 1995—), Coll. Labor and Employment Lawyers (emeritus mem.), Order of Coif. Clubs: Legal (Chgo.), Law (Chgo.), Cliff Dwellers (Chgo.). Republican. Congregationalist. Home: 632 Chatham Rd Glenview IL 60025-4402 Office: 55 E Monroe St Chicago IL 60603-5713 E-mail: milleed@seyfarth.com.

MILLER, EDWARD CARL WILLIAM, physician; b. Norfolk, Va., Mar. 4, 1952; s. Yale M. and Virginia (Getz) M.; m. Jayne R. Sternal, Dec. 28, 1974; children: Jamie, Sara, Joni. BA, Northwestern U., 1973; MD, U. Ill.-Chgo., 1977. Physician U. Ill. Health Svcs., Urbana, 1980-81; emergency physician Mercy Hosp., 1981-85, St. Michael Hosp., Milw., 1985—, St. Francis Hosp., Milw., 1998—. Fellow Am. Coll. Emergency Physicians, Am. Acad. Family Physicians. Republican. Lutheran. Avocations: sailing, woodworking, computers. Home: 3926 W Le Mont Blvd Mequon WI 53092-5226 Office: St Michael Hosp 2400 W Villard Ave Milwaukee WI 53209-4999 E-mail: edm3565592@yahoo.com.

MILLER, EDWARD DANIEL, financial services executive; b. 1940; married. Grad., Pace U. With Mfrs. Hanover Trust Co., N.Y.C., 1961-91, pres., vice chmn. Chemical, 1991-95; sr. vice chmn., bd. dir. Chase Manhattan Corp., 1995-97; dir., chmn, CEO Equitable Life Assurance Soc., 1997—; sr. exec. v.p., mem. exec. com. AXA, 1997—2001; pres., CEO AXA Financial, 1997—2001, supervisory bd., 2001—. Office: AXA Financial Inc Rm 3403 1290 Avenue Of The Americas Fl 16 New York NY 10104-0101*

MILLER, EDWARD DORING, anesthesiologist; b. Rochester, N.Y., Feb. 1, 1943; s. Edward D. and Natalie (Sidam) Miller; m. Leslie Coombs, June 15, 1968 (dec. Apr. 1987); children: Sara Davenport, Katherine Coombs; m. Lynne Root, Apr. 30, 1988; children: Lawrence Root, Elizabeth Root Fusco. AB, Ohio Wesleyan U., 1964; MD, U. Rochester, 1968. Diplomate Am. Bd. Anesthesiology, Am. Coll. Anesthesiology; cert. critical care medicine. Surg. intern Univ. Hosp., Boston, 1968-69; anesthesia resident Peter Bent Brigham Hosp., 1969-71; fellow in physiology Harvard Med. Sch., 1971-73; dir. anesthesia research Brooke Army Med. Ctr., Ft. Sam Houston, Tex., 1973-75; asst. prof. anesthesiology U. Va. Med. Ctr., Charlottesville, 1975-79, assoc. prof. anesthesiology, 1979-82, prof. anesthesiology, 1982-83, prof. anesthesiology, surgery, 1983-86; E.M. Papper prof. anesthesiology, chmn. dept. Columbia U. Coll. Physicians and Surgeons, N.Y.C., 1986-94; Mark C. Rogers prof., chmn. dept. anesthesiology Johns Hopkins U., Balt., 1994—, interim dean med. faculty, v.p. medicine Sch. Medicine, 1996-97, dean Sch. of Medicine, 1997—, CEO, 1997—. Sr. scientist physiology, pharmacology Hosp. Necker, Paris, 1981-82; examiner Am. Bd. Anesthesiology; v.p. clin. faculty U. Va., 1983-85, pres. 1985-86. Editor Anesthesia and Analgesia, 1982-92; contbr. numerous articles to profl. jours. Pres. Barracks-Rugby-Preston Neighborhoods, Va., 1977-79; vestry Christ Episc. Ch., Va., 1985-86. Served to maj. M.C., U.S. Army, 1973-75. Recipient Research Career Devel. award Nat. Inst. Gen. Med. Scis., 1978-83; NIH grantee, 1977-87, Inst. Nat. de la Sante et de la Recherche Medicale grantee, 1981-82. Mem. Assn. U. Anesthetists (sec. 1984-87), Am. Soc. Anesthesiologists, Am. Physiol. Soc., Internat. Anesthesia Research Soc. (trustee 1988—), Soc. Critical Care Medicine, Soc. Cardiovascular Anesthesiologists, Assn. Univ. Anesthesiologists (pres. 1990-92), Found. for Anesthesia Edn. and Rsch. (bd. dirs. 1986—), Up Med. Bd. Presbyn. Hosp. Home: 15 Meadow Rd Baltimore MD 21212-1022 Office: Johns Hopkins U Sch Med SOM 100 720 Rutland Ave Baltimore MD 21205-2196

MILLER, ELDON EARL, corporate business publications consultant, retired manufacturing company executive; b. Hutchinson, Kans., Jan. 1, 1919; s. Robert Dewalt and Martha Velva (Stauffer) M.; m. Margaret Borgsdorf, Mar. 26, 1950. BA, UCLA, 1941. Formerly newspaper editor, mag. editor, pub. relations cons., polit. writer; with Purex Industries, Inc., Lakewood, Calif., 1950-85, asst. sec., 1971-72, v.p. corp. relations, 1972-85, cons. bus. publs., corp. relations, 1985—. Republican. Presbyterian. Home and Office: 26685 Westhaven Dr Laguna Hills CA 92653-5767

MILLER, ELEANOR, English language and literature educator; b. Mill Valley, Calif. BA with honors, U. Nev., 1966, PhD in English with honors, 1970. Instr. English Valley Coll., San Bernardino, Calif., 1983-84, Crafton Hills Coll., Redlands, 1984-86, Coll. of the Desert, Palm Springs, 1986-90; prof. English Composition & Literature So. Nev. C.C., Las Vegas, 1990—. Chair teaching-learning excellence com. So. Nev. C.C., Las Vegas, 1991-94, new faculty mentor, 1995—. Author: English Placement Grading, 1991, CCSN Writing Across the Curriculum, 1994, New Faculty Mentoring, 1997, Teaching Excellence, 1998. Advisor/participant Women's Re-entry Ctr., Palm Springs/Las Vegas, 1989-94; vol. Womyn's Festival Com., U. Nev., Las Vegas, 1994—; mem. adv. bd. Collegiate Press, 1998—. Mem. AAUW, Nat. Coun. Tchrs. English, Nev. State Tchrs. English, Nev. Adult Edn. Assn., Nev. Humanities Com., Mountain Plains Adult Edn. Assn., U. Nev. Alumni Assn., Women in Comm., Phi Kappa Phi. Avocations: reading, travel. Office: So Nev CC 3200 E Cheyenne Ave North Las Vegas NV 89030-4228

MILLER, ELIZABETH HEIDBREDER, academic administrator; b. Kansas City, Mo., Dec. 17, 1948; d. Walter Morris and Gunborg Elizabeth (Janson) Heidbreder; m. Thomas Edmund Poley, Jan. 30, 1971 (div. Oct. 1984); children: Brent Matthew Poley, Andrew Morris Poley; m. James Robin Miller, Nov. 24, 1989. BS, Kans. State U., 1970; MS, Emporia State U., 1973; EdD, U. N.Mex., 1996. Tchr. Concordia (Kans.) H.S., 1973-74; coord., tchr. Kilian C.C., Sioux Falls, S.D., 1980-81; office mgr. Dr. Jess Koons, Liberal, Kans., 1984-86; instr. bus. tech. U. N.Mex., Gallup, 1986-96, dean instrn., 1996—2002, interim exec. dir., 2002—. Tchr. Jefferson County Adult Edn., Wheatridge, Colo., 1982-83, Seward County C.C., Liberal, 1984-86; adv. bd. Sch.-to-Work, Gallup, 1996-98, Ft. Wingate H.S. Acads., 2000—. Bd. dirs. Gallup McKinley County C. of C., 1993-96, 2001--; mem. Leadership McKinley, 1996-97, steering com., 1992-2000; mem. Gallup Pub. Libr. Bd., 1997-2001, U. N.Mex.-G Ambs., 1995—; alt. rep. N.Mex. Coun. of Tech. in Edn., N.Mex. Senate Joint Meml. 40 Study Com., Regional Econ. and Edn. Partnership Bd., 1996-97, McKinley Devel. Found. Bd., 1999—; trustee Rehoboth McKinley Christian Health Care Svcs., 1998—, Leadership N.Mex., 2001-02, Harvard Inst. for Mgmt. and Leadership in Edn., 2000; mem. exec. com. Navajo Nat. Rural Systemic Initiative, 2000—. Mem. Assn. for Career and Tech. Edn., Nat. Bus. Edn. Assn., N.Mex. Coun. Chief Instrnl. Officers, Delta Pi Epsilon (bus. hon.). Avocations: walking, reading, gardening, piano. Office: U N Mex 200 College Rd Gallup NM 87301-5603 E-mail: schlbeth@gallup.unm.edu.

MILLER, ELIZABETH JANE, secondary education educator; b. Kline, S.C., Aug. 24, 1936; d. William Donleigh and Pearl (Ayer) Barker; m. Ronald Earl Miller, June 4, 1960 (div. Aug. 1978); 1 child, Burton Ronald. BS in Secondary Edn., Newberry (S.C.) Coll., 1959. Qualified nat. tchr. exam. Classroom tchr. Lexington (S.C.) Elem. Sch., 1959-60, Springfield (Ga.) Elem. Sch., 1960-61, Winter Pk. (Fla.) Elem. Sch., 1961-63, Allendale-Fairfax (S.C.) H.S., 1963-67; classroom tchr., dept. head Bamberg (S.C.)-Ehrhardt H.S., 1969-71, Andrew Jackson Acad., Ehrhardt, S.C., 1971-81; classroom tchr. Smoaks (S.C.) Mid. Sch., 1981-83, Wade Hampton H.S., Hampton, S.C., 1983-98; ret., 1998. Editor: History of Bamberg County, 1997; contbr. articles to profl. jours. Bd. dirs. Barnwell County Mus., 1996—; mem. Bamberg County Hist. Soc., 1970—. Mem. DAR (state historian 1979-82, state chmn. pub. rels. 1982-85), NEA, Nat. Coun. Tchrs. of English, Nat. Soc. U.S. Daus. 1812 (corr. nat. sec. 1976-79, state pres. 1970-73, nat. historian 1973-76), UDC (chpt. pres. 1997—). Avocation: researching state historic markers and National Register nominations. Home: 3022 Big Fork Rd Barnwell SC 29812-7016

MILLER, ELLEN S. marketing communications executive; b. Indpls., June 28, 1954; d. Harold Edward and Lilian (Gantner) M. BA, DePauw U., 1976; postgrad., Sch. Visual Arts, N.Y.C., 1981-82. Editorial asst. Daisy mag., N.Y.C., 1976-77; asst. dept. mgr., Christmas hiring mgr. Bloomingdale's, 1978; sales rep. Rosenthal USA Ltd., 1979, mktg. asst., 1980-81, dir. mktg. comms., 1982-90; mgr. consumer mktg. Creamer Dickson Basford, Providence, 1990, v.p., 1991-94; prin. E.S. Miller Comm., 1994—. Instr. Learning Connection. Editor Community Prep. Sch. newsletter, 1993. Trustee Cmty. Prep Sch., Providence, 1993—, mem. exec. com., 1997—. Recipient Bell Ringer award New Eng. Pub. Club, 1992, 93, Iris award N.J. chpt. Internat. Assn. Bus. Communicators, 1993, Silver Quill award Dist. I, 1993, Holland award Ctrl. Mass. Advt. Club, 1997. Mem. Pub. Rels. Soc. Am., Nat. Tabletop Assn. (com. chair 1989), Internat. Tabletop Awards (bd. dirs. 1989), Rotary Club. Republican. Presbyterian. E-mail: ellensmiller@att.net.

MILLER, ELLIOTT CAIRNS, retired bank executive, lawyer; b. Cambridge, Mass., May 4, 1934; s. James Wilkinson and Mary Elliott (Cairns) M.; m. Mary Killion, July 2, 1960; children: Jonathan Vaill, Stephen Killion. AB, Harvard Coll., 1956; JD, U. Mich., 1961; LLM, Boston U., 1970. Bar: Conn. 1962. Assoc. Robinson & Cole, Hartford, Conn., 1961-66, ptnr., 1967-72; v.p., counsel Soc. for Savs., 1972-73, sr. v.p., 1973-78, exec. v.p., 1978, pres., CEO, dir., 1979-90; pres., CEO Soc. for Savs. Bancorp Inc., 1987-90. Bd. dirs. nat. council Savs. Inst., Washington, 1984-88. Trustee, chmn. Kingswood-Oxford Sch., West Hartford, 1977-87; trustee Coordinating Coun. on Founds., 1987-90; bd. dirs. Downtown Coun., Hartford, 1975-90; trustee Greater Hartford Arts Coun., 1980-88; trustee Wadsworth Atheneum, 1990-99; trustee Hartford Stage Co., 1973-85, hon. trustee, 1985—; corporator Hartford Hosp., Inst. of Living; mem. transition com. Conn. State Treas. Denise Nappier, 1998-99. With U.S. Army, 1956-58. Mem. Conn. Bar Assn., The 1892 Club (Hartford), Monday Evening Club (Hartford), Dauntless Club (Essex, Conn.), Ferrari Club Am., Bernese Mountain Dog Club. Methodist. Home: 9 Champlin Sq Essex CT 06426-1101

MILLER, EMILIE F. former state senator, consultant; b. Chgo., Aug. 11, 1936; d. Bruno C. and Etta M. (Senese) Feiza; m. Dean E. Miller; children: Desireé M., Edward C. BSBA, Drake U., 1958. Asst. buyer Jordan Marsh Co., Boston, 1958-60, Carson, Pirie, Scott & Co., Chgo., 1960-62; dept. mgr., asst. buyer Woodward & Lothrop, Washington, 1962-64; state labor coord. Robb Davis Daliles Joint Campaign; legis. aide Senator Adelard Brandt, Va., 1980-83; fin. dir. Saslaw for Congress, 1984; legis. cons. Va. Fedn. Bus. Profl. Women, 1986-87, 98-00; senator Va. Gen. Assembly, Richmond, 1988-92; cons. apptd. by Gov. Wilder to bd. dirs. Innovative Tech. Authority, 1992-94, Ctr. for Innovative Tech., 1992-94; cons., 1992—; sr. mgr. Thompson, Cobb, Brazilio & Assocs., 1998—. Bus. tng. seminars Moscow, Nizhny Novgorod, Russia, 1993, Novgorod, St. Petersburg, 1995; cons. in field. Guest editl. writer No. Va. Sun, 1981; host, prodr. weekly TV program, Channel 61. Mem. State Ctrl. Com. Dem. Party Va., Richmond, 1974—, steering com., 2000—, chair 11th congrl. dist., 2001—; mem. Fairfax County Dem. Com., 1968—, chair, 1976-80, 98-2000, Presdl. Inaugural Com., 1977, 1992 Dem. Nat. Platform Com., Va. mem. on temp. coms., Dem. Adv. Com. Robb-Spong Commn., 1978-79; chair 11th Congrl. Dist. Dem. Com., 2001; founder, chair Va. Assoc. Dem. County and City Chmn., 1976-80, Fairfax County Dem. Com., 1976-80; chair 11th Congl. Dist. Dem. Com., 2001; security supr. 1980 Dem. Nat. Conv.; v.p. Va. Fedn. Dem. Women, 1992-94; bd. dirs. Stop Child Abuse Now, 1988, Ctr. Innovative Tech., 1992-94, Ct. Apptd. Spl. Advs., 1993-96; nat. alumni bd. J.A. Achievement, BRAVO adv. com. for the first Gov.'s Awards for Arts in Va., 1979-80; lay tchr. St. Ambrose Cath. Ch., 1963-80; del. to White House Conf. on Children, 1970; chair Va. Coalition for Mentally Disturbed, 1992-94; mem. com. of 100, Va. Opera Bd., 1994-99; bd. dirs. Social Action Linking Together. Recipient Disting. Grad. award Jr. Achievement, 1973, Woman of Achievement award Fairfax (Va.) Bd. Suprs. and Fairfax County Commn. for Women, 1982, Cmty. Svc. award Friends of Victims Assistance Network, 1988, Founders award Fairfax County Coun. of Arts, 1989, Mental Health Assn. of Northern Va. Warren Stambaugh award, 1991, Ann. Svc. award Va. Assn. for Marriage and Family Therapy, 1991, Psychology Soc. of Washington Cmty. Svc. award, 1993, pacesetter award So. Women in Pub. Leadership Conf., 1996. Mem. NOW, Nat. Mus. Women in the Arts, Va. Assn. Female Execs. (mem. adv. bd., bd. dirs., v.p. 1992—), Va. Assn. Cmty. Svc. Bds. (chmn. 1980-82), North Va. Assn. Cmty. Bds. (chmn. 1978-79, 95-98), Fairfax County Coun. Arts (v.p. 1980—, mem. exec. com. internat. children's festival, Founders award 1989), Fairfax County C. of C. (mem. legis. com.), Greater Merrifield Bus. and Profl. Assn., Mental Health Assn. No.Va. (bd. dirs.), Ctrl. Fairfax C. of C., Falls Church C. of C., Bus. and Profl. Women's Fedn. Va., Mantua Citizens Assn. (exec. bd.), Bus. and Profl. Women's Club (pres. Falls Church chpt. 1994-96, Woman of Yr. award 1990), Women's Nat. Dem. Club (past v.p., mem. bd. govs.), Downtown Club (Richmond), Va. Assn. Female Execs. (bd. dirs. 1992—), Phi Gamma Nu. Roman Catholic. Avocations: Cubs fan, tennis, art. Home: 8701 Duvall St Fairfax VA 22031-2711 Office: PO Box 249 Merrifield VA 22116-0249 E-mail: EmilieMiller@cs.com.

MILLER, ERIC NATHAN, neuropsychologist; b. Oceanside, Calif., Nov. 21, 1955; s. David and Nancy Miller; 1 child, Bryan Scott. BA in Psychology, U. Va., 1977; MS in Psychology, U. Wis., 1981, PhD in Clin. Psychology, 1986. Lic. clin. psychologist, Calif. Fellow neuropsychology UCLA, 1986-88, asst. rsch. neuropsychologist, 1988-94, assoc. rsch. neuropsychologist, 1994—, assoc. clin. prof., 1996-2000, clin. prof., 2000—. Owner, propr. Norland Software, L.A., 1983—; project dir. divsn. epidemiology UCLA, 1987—; reviewer jours. in field. Contbr. articles to profl. jours. Fellow Wis. Alumni Rsch. Fund. Mem. APA, Internat. Neuropsychol. Soc., Phi Beta Kappa. Office: UCLA Neuropsychiat Inst 760 Westwood Plz Rm C8747 Los Angeles CA 90095-8353

MILLER, ERNEST CHARLES, management consultant; b. Bronx, N.Y., July 14, 1925; s. Ernest Philip and Elizabeth (Hellwig) M.; m. Edith Grosvenor Porterfield, Nov. 11, 1947 (div. Oct. 3, 1963); children: Laura Lee, Marcy Rogers, Ernest Charles; m. Tung-fen Lin, Jan. 8, 1985. AB, Yale U., 1945; MA, U. Pa., 1949. Lic. psychologist, N.Y. Instr. U. Pa., 1947-51, cons., 1950-53; br. mgr., bd. dirs. Richardson, Bellows, Henry & Co., Inc., 1953-55; mgr. personnel tech. Am. Standard, Inc., 1955-59; mng. prin. Hellwig, Miller & Assos., Westport, Conn., 1959-61; sr. assoc. Cresap, McCormick & Paget, Inc., N.Y.C., 1961-63; with Am. Mgmt. Assns., 1964-83, pres. AMACOM div., 1978-81, group v.p. AMA Publs. Group, 1981-83; pres. Miller, Hellwig Assocs., 1984—. Author works in strategic planning, orgn. devel., human resources, exec. compensation and mgmt. Bd. dirs. La Jolla Inst. for Allergy and Immunology; mem. Columbia U. All-Univ. Seminar, China Internat. Bus. Orgn. and Mgmt. NEH fellow, 1980 Mem. APA, Soc. Indsl. and Orgnl. Psychology. Episcopalian. Office: Miller Hellwig Assocs 150 W End Ave New York NY 10023-5713 E-mail: millerhelwig@earthlink.net.

MILLER, ESTHER SCOBIE POWERS, appraiser, water colorist, gallery owner; b. Peninsula, Ohio, Apr. 16, 1929; d. John Henry and Hazel Blanche (Appleton) Scobie; m. Elmer Duane Powers, June 13, 1948 (div. 1965); m. Kenneth Ward Miller, Aug. 26, 1980; children: Terrance, Michael, Susan, Jennifer. Student, Kansas City (Mo.) Art Inst., 1948-50, Bethel Coll., 1965-67, Ind. U., South Bend, 1965-67. Designated SRA-real estate appraiser. Owner brokerage Powers Realty, Culver, Ind., 1967-76; pvt. practice fee appraising South Bend, 1978-84, Culver, 1984-88, Plymouth, Ind., 1988-90; profl. watercolorist, owner Painter & Poet Gallery, Culver. Mem. St. Joe Valley Water Color Soc. Methodist. Avocations: piano and organ playing, reading. E-mail: info@painterandpoet.com.

MILLER, ETHAN, computer science educator; b. Mass., 1966; s. Ralph and Avis M. Miller; m. Lisa Miller, 1996; children: Sabrina, Zachary. BS, Brown U., 1987; MS, PhD, U. Calif., Berkeley, 1994. Software engr. BBN Labs., Cambridge, Mass., 1987-88; asst. prof. U. Md., Balt., 1994-2000, U. Calif., Santa Cruz, 2000—. NSF fellow, 1988-92. Mem. IEEE, Assn. Computing Machines, Sigma Xi. Office: U Calif 1156 High St Santa Cruz CA 95064 E-mail: elm@cs.ucsc.edu.

MILLER, EUGENE, university official, business executive; b. Chgo., Oct. 6, 1925; s. Harry and Fannie (Prosterman) M.; m. Edith Sutker, Sept. 23, 1951 (div. Sept. 1965); children: Ross, Scott, June; m. Thelma Gottlieb, Dec. 22, 1965; stepchildren: Paul Gottlieb, Alan Gottlieb. BS, Ga. Inst. Tech., 1945; AB magna cum laude, Bethany Coll., 1947, LLD, 1969; diploma, Oxford (Eng.) U., 1947; MS in Journalism, Columbia U., 1948; MBA, NYU, 1959; postgrad., Pace U., 1973—. Reporter, then city editor Greensboro (N.C.) Daily News, 1948-52; S.W. bur. chief Bus. Week mag., Houston, 1952-54, assoc. mng. editor N.Y.C., 1954-60; dir. pub. affairs and communications McGraw-Hill, Inc., 1960-63, v.p., 1963-68; sr. v.p. pub. rels. and investor rels., exec. com. N.Y. Stock Exch., N.Y.C., 1968-73; sr. v.p. CNA Fin. Corp., Chgo., 1973-75; chmn. Eugene Miller & Assos., Glencoe, Ill., 1975-77; v.p. USG Corp., Chgo., 1977-82, sr. v.p., 1982-85, mem. mgmt. com., 1982-91, exec. v.p., CFO, 1985-87, elected vice chmn., CFO, 1987-91, mem. exec. com., also bd. dirs.; prof., exec.-in-residence Coll. Bus. Fla. Atlantic U., 1991—; chmn., CEO Ideon Group, Inc., Jacksonville, Fla., 1996. Adj. prof. mgmt. NYU, 1963-65; prof. bus. adminstrn. Fordham U., 1969-75; prof. fin., chmn. dept. Northeastern Ill. U., 1975-78; lectr. to bus. and ednl. groups; bd. dirs. MRFI, Inc., Chgo., bd. dirs., mem. adv. bd. dirs. Nationwide Acceptance Corp., Chgo.; cons. to sec. Dept. Commerce, 1961-66; editor-in-residence U. Oreg., 1992; exec.-in-residence U. Ill., 1991, U. Wis., 1991, U. Toronto, 1992; exec.-in-residence, POHL fellow U. Wyo., 1992; mem. adv. bd. CFO mag., 1991-99; bd. dirs. RJD Holdings, Inc., Chgo.; bd. dirs. Tutor Time Learning Systems, Inc., Boca Raton, 1997—; cons. Arthur Andersen & Co., Chgo., 1992-97; mem. adv. bd. GotTrouble.com, Inc., Sherman Oaks, Calif.; bd. dirs. Niche Directories, Inc., Boca Raton, Fla.; mng. dir. ICA Advisors LLC, Boca Raton. Author: Your Future in Securities, 1974, Barron's Guide to Graduate Business Schools, 1977, 12th edit., 2001; contbg. editor: Public Relations Handbook, 1988, Boardroom Reports, 1986—; writer syndicated bus. column., 1964-86; mem. editl. bd. IRQ mag., 1997—. Trustee Bethany Coll., 1970—; mem. alumni bd. Columbia U. Sch. Journalism. Comdr. USNR, World War II, ret. Recipient outstanding achievement award Bethany Coll., 1963, 50th anniversary award Sch. Journalism Columbia U., also honors award, 1963, Sch. Journalism Ohio U., 1964, disting. svc. award in investment edn. Nat. Assn. Investment Clubs, 1980, Roalman award Nat. Investor Rels. Inst., 1987. Fellow Pub. Rels. Soc. Am.; mem. Nat. Assn. Bus. Economists, Soc. Am. Bus. Editors and Writers (founder), Fin. Execs. Inst., Arthur Page Soc., St. Andrew's Country Club, Sigma Delta Chi, Alpha Sigma Phi. Home: 7351 Ballantrae Ct Boca Raton FL 33496-1423 Office: Fla Atlantic U 777 Glades Rd Boca Raton FL 33431-6424 Fax: 561-852-1814. E-mail: Gene160@aol.com.

MILLER, FRANK LEWIS, lawyer, writer; b. Denver, Feb. 1, 1951; s. Frank Lewis III and Lucille Alice (McBride) M.; m. Janice Brenner, Nov. 26, 1987 (div. July 1996); children: Jessica Jean, Alexander Palani; m. Etsuko Tatsuta, June 21, 1997; 1 child, Kai Lewis Tatsuta. BA, U. Hawaii, Manoa, 1973; JD, U. Santa Clara, 1978. Bar: Hawaii, 1978, U.S. Dist. Ct. Hawaii, 1978. Vista atty. Life of Land, Honolulu, 1978-79; dep. pub. defender Hawaii Office Pub. Defender, Kealakekua, 1979-80, Honolulu, Capt. Cook, Hawaii, 1984-95; staff writer West Hawaii Today, Kailua-Kona, 1980-83, 84; pvt. practice, 1995—. Contbr. poems, short stories to profl. mags. Avocations: running, surfing, photography. Office: PO Box 415 Kealakekua HI 96750 E-mail: frankiv@kona.net.

MILLER, FRANKLIN G. bioethicist; b. Washington, July 15, 1948; BA, Columbia Coll., 1971; PhD, Columbia U., 1977. From asst. prof. to assoc. prof. med. edn. U. Va., Charlottesville, 1990-99; spl. expert NIMH, Bethesda, Md., 1999—. Mem. instnl. rev. bd. NIMH, Bethesda, 1991—; mem. ethics com. NIH Clin. Ctr., Bethesda, 1990—. Contbr. articles to profl. jours. Home: 3910 Underwood St Chevy Chase MD 20815-5030 E-mail: fgm3910@aol.com.

MILLER, FREDERICK, pathologist; b. N.Y.C., Apr. 5, 1937; s. Alex and Sarah Miller; m. Emilie J Kronish, June 2, 1962; children: David, Allison. BS, U. Wis., 1956; MD, N.Y. U., 1961. Diplomate Am Bd Pathology. Intern Bellevue Hosp., N.Y.C., 1961-62, resident, 1962-63; practice medicine specializing in pathology, 1965—; clin. assoc., attending physician Nat. Inst. Arthritis and Metabolic Diseases, 1963-65; resident chief pathology dept. NYU Med. Ctr., 1965-67; attending pathologist Bellevue and Univ. Hosps., N.Y.C., 1967; asst. prof. pathology NYU, 1967-70, assoc. prof., 1970, SUNY, Stony Brook, 1970-75, prof., 1975—, chmn. dept. pathology, 1973-2000, Marvin Kuschner prof. pathology, 1991—, dir. lab. for arthritis and related diseases, 1976—; dir. labs. Univ. Hosp., 1978—, pathologist-in-chief, 1979—. Mem Nat Bd Med Examiners Pathology, 1996—98. Contbr. articles to profl jours. With USPHS, 1963—65. Recipient Bausch and Lomb Medal for Research, 1961, Pres's Award, SUNY, Stony Brook, 1990, Chancellor's Award, 1990, Aesculapius Award, 1993, Golden Apple Award, ASMA, 1995; grantee NIH, 1963—87. Mem.: AAAS, Suffolk Orchid Soc, Asn Pathology Chairmen, Am Asn Immunologists, NY Acad Sci, Int Acad Pathology, Am Soc Clin Pathologists (award 1961), Soc Clin Immunology, Harvey Soc, Alpha Omega Alpha (counselor 2000—), Sigma Xi. Home: 46 Manchester Ln Stony Brook NY 11790-2826 Office: Univ Hosp USB L2-743B Stony Brook NY 11794-7025 E-mail: fmiller@notes.cc.sunysb.edu.

MILLER, FREDERICK ROBESON, banker; b. Oakland, Calif., Oct. 11, 1927; s. Charles Lennon and Juliet Robeson (Chamberlain) M.; m. Nancy McDaniel, July 19, 1952; children: Susan Chase Miller Clark, Stephen Robeson, Elizabeth Rockwell BA, Yale U., 1952. With J.P. Morgan & Co., Inc., 1952-54; v.p. Phila. Nat. Bank, 1954-69; pres. Waterbury Nat. Bank, Conn., 1969-71, City Nat. Bank, Bridgeport, 1971-72, Conn. Nat. Bank, Bridgeport, 1973-83, also chief exec. officer, vice chmn.; vice chmn. Hartford Nat. Corp., until 1984. Served with U.S. Army, 1946-47. Mem. Sons of the Revolution, Tubac Golf Resort, Yale Club N.Y.C. Republican. Episcopalian. Home: PO Box 1503 Tubac AZ 85646-1503 E-mail: milltubac@worldnet.att.com.

MILLER, FREDERICK STATEN, retired music educator, academic administrator; b. Lima, Ohio, Dec. 12, 1930; s. Donald Frederick and Esther Lillian (Moore) Miller; m. Florence Dorothy Mistak, June 20, 1959; children: Jennifer Leigh Greene, John Staten. B of Music Edn., Northwestern U., 1957, M in Music, 1958; D of Music Performance, U. Iowa, 1974. Mem. music faculty U. Ark., Fayetteville, 1958-64; asst. dir. bands Northwestern U., Evanston, Ill., 1964-70, assoc. dean, sch. music, 1970-76; dean, sch. music DePaul U., Chgo., 1976-95, ret., 1995. Bd. dirs., Concertante de Chgo.; accreditation evaluator North Ctrl. Assn., Boulder, Colo., 1982—91, Nat. Assn. Schs. Music, Washington, 1981—91; mem. bd. edn. New Trier H.S., 1997—2001. Composer/arranger numerous pub. works for band; editor music publs. Served with USN, 1948-52. Mem. ASCAP, Nat. Assn. Schs. Music (hon. life, regional chmn. 1982-84, instl. rep., treas. 1984-88, v.p. 1988-91, pres. 1991-94), John P. Paynter Found., Pi Kappa Lambda (bd. regents 1970-74), Phi Kappa Phi. Clubs: University (Chgo.); Sheridan Shore Yacht (Wilmette, Ill.). Roman Catholic. Avocations: sailing, cooking, jazz performance. Home: 1322 Greenwood Ave Wilmette IL 60091-1624

MILLER, G. WAYNE, writer; b. Melrose, Mass., June 12, 1954; s. Roger Linwood and Mary Maraghey Miller; m. Alexis Magner Miller, 1980; children: Rachel Magner, Katherine Linwood, G. Calvin. BA, Harvard U., ., 1976. Staff writer Providence Jour., 1981—. Author: (book) Thunder Rise, 1989, The Work of Human Hands, 1993, Coming of Age, 1995, Toy Wars, 1998, King of Hearts, 2000, Men and Speed, 2002. Pres. bd. trustees Jesse Smith Meml. Libr., Burrillville, RI, 1997; sec. facilities com. Burrillville Libr., 2000; mem. schs. com. Harvard-Radcliffe Club of RI, Providence, 1992; sec. Burrillville Jr. Hockey League, 2002. Recipient Disting. Writing award, Am. Soc. of Newspaper Editors, 1992, Sword of Hope Judges award, Am. Cancer Soc., 1999, Excellence in Journalism award, Nat. Marrow Donor Program, 2000. Mem.: Am. Med. Writers Assn., Providence Newspaper Guild, Authors Guild, Mystery Writers of Am., Harvard Club of Boston. Home: 350 Eagle Peak Road Pascoag RI 02859 Office: Providence Journal 75 Fountain St Providence RI 02902 Home Fax: 401-679-0030; Office Fax: 401-277-7346. Personal E-mail: gwmiller@ids.net. E-mail: gwmiller@projo.com.

MILLER, GALE TIMOTHY, lawyer; b. Kalamazoo, Sept. 15, 1946; s. Arthur H. and Eleanor (Johnson) M.; m. Janice Lindvall, June 1, 1968; children: Jeremy L., Amanda E., Timothy W. AB, Augustana Coll., 1968; JD, U. Mich., 1971. Bar: Mich. 1971, Colo. 1973, U.S. Dist. Ct. Colo. 1973, U.S. Ct. Appeals (10th cir.) 1979, U.S. Supreme Ct. 1997. Trial atty. FTC, Washington, 1971-73; assoc. Davis Graham & Stubbs LLP, Denver, 1973-77, ptnr., 1978—, chmn. exec. com., 1998—2001. Bd. dirs. Sr. Housing Options, Inc., 1980-93, Colo. Jud. Inst., 1999—; chair Colo. Lawyers Com., 1989-91, bd. dirs., 1987—, Individual Lawyer of Yr., 1994. Recipient Cmty. Svc. award Colo. Hispanic Bar Assn., 1996. Mem. ABA (antitrust sect. task force on model civil antitrust jury instrns.), Colo. Bar Assn. (chair antitrust sect. 1996-98), Denver Bar Assn. Democrat. Lutheran. Office: Davis Graham & Stubbs LLP 1550 17th St Ste 500 Denver CO 80202

MILLER, GARFIELD LANKARD, III, investment banker; b. Buffalo, Apr. 8, 1950; s. Garfield Lankard and Johanne (Cunningham) M.; m. Martha Ellen McGarry, Aug. 24, 1974; 1 child, Cornelia Lawton. BBA, Middlebury (Vt.) Coll., 1972; MBA, U. Pa., 1975. Account mgr. Citibank, N.A., N.Y.C., 1975-79; ltd. ptnr. Bear, Stearns & Co., 1979-85; mng. dir. CS First Boston, Inc., 1985-91, Salomon Bros. Inc., N.Y.C., 1991-94; pres. Aegis Energy Advisors Corp., 1994—. Office: Aegis Energy Advisors Corp 152 W 57th St 29th Fl New York NY 10019-3310 E-mail: glmiller@aegisenergy.com.

MILLER, GARY DOUGLAS, urban planning consultant, former aerospace company executive; b. Cleve., Dec. 14, 1942; s. Wells Winton and Ruth Alyce (Noreen) M.; m. Julia Ann Walraven, Aug. 7, 1988; children: Eric, Brooke. AA, Moorpark (Calif.) Coll., 1975; BA in Math. summa cum laude, Calif. State U., Northridge, 1977, MBA in Ops. Rsch. summa cum laude, 1979. Tech. maintenance staff Hughes Aircraft Co., El Segundo, Calif., 1965-72, project dir. tech. pubs., 1972-75, mgr. logistics support, 1975-88, mgr. non-def. initiatives, 1988-94, mgr. internat. studies, 1994-99; urban demographics rschr. City of L.A., 1999—. Tech. dir. Sys. Engring. Network, El Segundo, 1993-95; dir. Inst. for Nat. Drug Abuse Rsch., Austin, Tex., 1989-92, Sys. Engring. Adv. Coun., U. So. Calif., L.A., 1993—. Contbr. numerous articles to profl. jours. Sgt. USAF, 1960-64. Mem. AAAS, Am. Def. Preparedness Assn., Nat. Security Indsl. Assn., Internat. Coun. on Sys. Engring., Inst. for Ops. Rsch./Mgmt. Sci., Intertel, Internat. Soc. for Philos. Inquiry, Archaeol. Inst. Am., Mensa, Phi Kappa Phi. Avocations: archaeology, golf. Home: 1857 Love Cir Simi Valley CA 93063-4322 Office: City of LA 205 S Broadway Ste 508 Los Angeles CA 90012

MILLER, GARY EVAN, psychiatrist, mental health services administrator; b. Cleve., Aug. 19, 1935; s. Henry M. and Mollie (Price) M.; m. Karen Ann Marie Barrett, Sept. 16, 1972; children: Anna Charis, Rebecca Elizabeth. MD, U. Tex., Galveston, 1960. Diplomate in psychiatry, addiction psychiatry, and geriatric psychiatry Am. Bd. Psychiatry and Neurology. Intern Montefiore Hosp., N.Y.C., 1960-61; resident in psychiatry U. Hosps. Cleve., 1961-62, Austin State Hosp., Tex., 1963-65; dep. commr. mental health services Dept. Mental Health and Mental Retardation, 1967-70; dir. Rio Grande State Center for Mental Health and Mental Retardation, Dept. Mental Health, Harlingen, 1966-67; asst. commr., dir. Rochester regional office State Dept. Mental Hygiene, N.Y., 1970-72; clin. asst. prof. psychiatry U. Rochester Sch. Medicine and Dentistry, 1970-72; asst. clin. prof. psychiatry SUNY, Buffalo, 1970-72; cons. mental health Ga. Dept. Human Resources, Atlanta, 1972, dir. div. mental health, 1972-74; clin. prof. psychiatry Emory U. Sch. Medicine, Atlanta, 1972-74; vice chmn. Ga. State Planning and Adv. Council for Devel. Disabilities Services and Constrn., 1972-73; cons. mental health services orgn. and adminstrn., 1974-76; dir. mental health and devel. services State of N.H. Concord, 1976-82; commr. Tex. Dept. Mental Health and Mental Retardation Austin, 1982-88; clin. prof. psychiatry U. Tex. Health Sci. Ctr., Houston, adj. assoc. prof. psychiatry San Antonio, 1984-95; dir. profl. svcs. HCA Gulf Pines Hosp., Houston, 1988-94, chief of staff, 1993; clin. dir. adult psychiatry Cypress Creek Hosp., 1994-2000, med. dir., 2000—, pres. med. staff, 1996; assoc. clin. psychiatry Post Oak Psychiatric Assocs., 1988-90; pres. Alternative Svcs. Network, 1990—. Dir. state alcoholism program in Ga., 1972—74; dir. state alcoholism program in South Tex. region, 1966—67; mem. faculty U. S.C. Sch. Alcohol and Drug Studies, 1975; mem. quality assurance com. Aetna U.S. Healthcare Pharmacy, 1999—2001. Contbr. articles to profl. jours. Served as capt. M.C., U.S. Army, 1962-63. Recipient Cert. of Recognition, Ga. Psychol. Assn., 1973. Fellow Am. Psychiat. Assn. (life, cert. in adminstrv. psychiatry, com. on psychiat. adminstrn. and mgmt. 1999—); mem. AMA, Am. Soc. Clin. Psychopharmacology (cert. in clin. psychopharmacology), Am. Soc. Addiction Medicine (cert. alcoholism and other drug dependencies), Am. Acad. Addiction Psychiatry, N.H. Psychiat. Soc. (pres. 1981-82), Nat. Assn. State Mental Health Program Dirs. (bd. dirs. 1984-88, sec. 1986-88), N.H. Med. Soc., Am. Acad. Psychiatry and the Law, Am. Assn. Psychiat. Adminstrs. (pres. Tex. chpt. 1986), Tex. Med. Assn., Tex. Soc. Psychiat. Physicians, Mental Health Assn. Houston and Harris County (bd. dirs. 1989-95, v.p. advocacy 1990-95), Alpha Omega Alpha. Home: 5314 Westminster Ct Houston TX 77069-3338 Office: 530 Wells Fargo Dr Ste 110 Houston TX 77090-4026

MILLER, GARY G. congressman; b. Huntsville, Ark., 1948; m. Cathy, 1972; 4 children. Student, Mt. San Antonio C.C. Founder G. Miller Devel. Co.; mem. U.S. Congress from 4th Calif. dist., Washington, 1999—; mem. budget com., fin. svcs. com., sci. com. Bd. dirs. Sonrise Christian Sch., 1982; appointed to Diamond Bar (Calif.) Mcpl. Adv. Coun., 1988; elected to 1st Diamond Bar City Coun., 1989; mayor, 1992; elected to Calif. State Assembly, 1995 (chmn. budget com. and banking and fin. com., vice chmn. transp. com.). With U.S. Army. Republican. Achievements include proposing 24 bills signed into law, successfully negotiated funding of 1st class size reduction program, and produced balanced budget that reduced the bus. tax. to 1973 levels while maintaing a $310 million reserve. Office: US Ho Reps 1037 Longworth Ho Office Bldg Washington DC 20515-0001*

MILLER, GARY H. lawyer; b. New Orleans, Mar. 11, 1957; s. Leo Jr. and Suzanne Robinowitz (Meltzer) M.; m. Ellen Baldwin Hoffman, Oct. 18, 1986; children: Matthew Hilliard, Katherine Elise. BA magna cum laude, New Eng. Coll., 1979; JD cum laude, Tulane U., 1982. Assoc. Jones Walker, New

Orleans, 1982-89, ptnr., 1990—. Mem. moot ct. bd. Tulane U. Sch. Law, 1980-82; lectr in field. Bd. dirs. Golden Retriever Club Greater New Orleans, Inc., 1980, Burtheville Cmty. Assn., Inc., 1997—; class agt. New England Coll. Mem. La. Bar Assn. (treas. consumer protection, lender liability and bankruptcy sect. 1990-91, chmn. consumer protection, lender liability and bank sect. 1991-92), Phi Tau Beta. Democrat. Jewish. Avocations: Retriever and obedience training, fishing, hunting, guitar. Office: Jones Walker 201 Saint Charles Ave Ste 5200 New Orleans LA 70170-5100 E-mail: fisher31157@msn.com., gmiller@joneswalker.com.

MILLER, GARY J. political economist; b. Urbana, Ill., Jan. 2, 1949; s. Gerald J. and Doris Elaine (Miner) M.; m. Anne Colberg, Jan. 29, 1971; children: Neil, Ethan. BA, U. Ill., 1971; PhD, U. Tex., 1976. Asst. prof. Calif. Inst. Tech., Pasadena, 1976-79; assoc. prof. Mich. State U., East Lansing, 1979-86; Taylor prof. polit. economy Washington U., St. Louis, 1986-97; assoc. dean for acad. affairs Olin Sch. Bus., 1995-96, prof. polit. sci. Author: Cities by Contract, 1981, Reforming Bureaucracy, 1987, Managerial Dilemmas, 1992. NSF grantee, 1981, 83, 92. Mem. Phi Beta Kappa, Phi Kappa Phi (Disting. Faculty award 1994). Democrat. Office: Washington U Dept Polit Sci 1 Brookings Dr Dept Polit Saint Louis MO 63130-4899 E-mail: gjmiller@artsci.wustl.edu.

MILLER, GAY DAVIS, lawyer; b. Florence, Ariz., Dec. 20, 1947; d. Franklin Theodore and Mary (Belshaw) Davis; m. John Donald Miller, May 15, 1971; 1 child, Katherine Alexandra. BA, U. Colo., 1969; JD, Am. U., 1975. Bar: D.C. 1975. Atty., spl. asst. to gen. counsel, sr. counsel corp. affairs Inter Am. Devel. Bank, Washington, 1975-78, 83—; atty. Intelsat, 1978-80. Articles editor: Am. U. Law Rev., 1974—75, contbg. author: The Inspection Panel of the World Bank: A Different Complaints Procedure, 2001. Bd. dirs. Hist. Mt. Pleasant, Inc., Washington, 1985-86, Washington Bridle Trails Assn., 1992—. Mem.: ABA, Am. Soc. Internat. Law, Inter Am. Bar Assn. Office: Inter Am Devel Bank 1300 New York Ave NW Washington DC 20577-0001 E-mail: gaym@iadb.org.

MILLER, GENE EDWARD, newspaper reporter and editor; b. Evansville, Ind., Sept. 16, 1928; m. Electra Sonia Yphantis, Apr. 13, 1952 (dec. May 1993); children: Janet Irene, Theresa Jean, Thomas Raphael, Roberta Lynn; m. Caroline Heck, Mar. 1, 1998. AB in Journalism, Ind. U., 1950, LL.D. (hon.), 1977; Nieman fellow, Harvard U., 1967-68. Reporter Jour.-Gazette, Ft. Wayne, Ind., 1950-51, Washington Bur. Wall St. Jour., 1953-54, Richmond (Va.) News Leader, 1954-57, Miami (Fla.) Herald, 1957—. Author: Invitation To A Lynching, 83 Hours Till Dawn. Served with AUS, 1951-53. Recipient Pulitzer prize for local reporting, 1967, 76 Office: 1 Herald Plz Miami FL 33132-1609

MILLER, GENEVIEVE, retired medical historian; b. Butler, Pa., Oct. 15, 1914; d. Charles Russell and Genevieve (Wolford) M. AB, Goucher Coll., 1935; MA, Johns Hopkins U., 1939; PhD, Cornell U., 1955. Asst. in history medicine Johns Hopkins Inst. History of Medicine, Balt., 1943-44, instr., 1945-48, rsch. assoc., 1979-94; asst. prof. history of sci. Case Western Res. U. Sch. Medicine, Cleve., 1953-67, assoc. prof., 1967-79, assoc. prof. emeritus, 1979—; rsch. assoc. med. history Clevel. Med. Libr. Assn., 1953-62; curator Howard Dittrick Mus. Hist. Medicine, 1962-67, dir., 1967-79. Corr. mem. fgn. socs. history of medicine. *The desire to see as much of the world as possible and to retrace its past adds enormously to the richness and pleasure of life. Her MA degree from Johns Hopkins in 1939 was the first degree to be awarded in the United States for graduate studies in the history of medicine.* Author: William Beaumont's Formative Years: Two Early Notebooks 1811-1821, 1946; The Adoption of Inoculation for Smallpox in England and France, 1957 (William H. Welch medal Am. Assn. History Medicine 1962), Bibliography of the History of Medicine of the U.S. and Canada, 1939-1960, 1964, Bibliography of the Writings of Henry E. Sigerist, 1966, Letters of Edward Jenner and Other Documents Concerning the Early History of Vaccination, 1983; assoc. editor Bull. of History of Medicine, 1944-48, acting. editor, 1948, mem. adv. editl. bd., 1960-92; mem. bd. editors Jour. History of Medicine & Allied Scis., 1948-65; editor Newsletter Am. Assn. History of Medicine, 1986-96; contbr. articles to profl. jours. Alumna trustee Goucher Coll., Balt., 1966-69; trustee Judson Retirement Cmty., Clevel., 1993-99, Am. Coun. Learned Socs. fellow, 1948-50, Dean Van Meter fellow, Goucher Coll., 1953-54. Fellow Cleve. Med. Libr. Assn. (hon.); mem. Am. Assn. History Medicine (pres. 1978-80, mem. coun. 1960-63, Lifetime Achievement award 1999), Am. Hist. Assn., Internat. Soc. History of Medicine, Soc. Archtl. Historians, Phi Beta Kappa. Democrat. Home and Office: Judson Manor Apt 616 1890 E 107th St Cleveland OH 44106-2251

MILLER, GEOFFREY, child neurologist; b. Manchester, Eng., Feb. 1, 1947; came to U.S., 1988; s. Erwin and Cynthia Sarah Miller; m. Patricia Sarah Craigie, June 21, 1985; children: Joanne, Sally, Alethea. BA, MB, ChB, BAO, Trinity Coll., Dublin, Ireland, 1972, MA, 1982; MD, U. Western Australia, 1985, PharmM, 2002. Diplomate Am. Bd. Psychiatry and Neurology, Am. Bd. Child Neurology, Am. Bd. Neurodevelopmental Disabilities. Fellow Royal Postgrad. Med. Sch., London, 1982-83; devel. pediatrician Princess Margaret Hosp. for Children, Perth, Australia, 1983-85; med. dir. Sir David Brand Ctr. for Cerebral Palsy, Australia, 1983-84; assoc. prof. pediat. Pa. State U., Hershey, 1988-92; co-dir. Muscular Dystrophy Assn. Clinic, 1988-92, clinic physician Houston, 1998—; prof. pediat. and neurology Baylor Coll. Medicine, 1992—, chief devel. pediat. sect., 2000—; dir. Meyer Ctr. Devel. Pediat., Tex. Childrens Hosp., 2000—. Vis. specialist West Australian Soc. for Crippled Children, Perth, 1983; investigator Neuromuscular Rsch. Inst., Perth, 1984-87. Editor: Static Encephalopathies, 1992, Cerebral Palsies, 1998; contbr. articles to jours. in field. Capt. Royal Army Med. Corps, 1970-78. Elected and inducted into Am. Neurol. Assn., 1996. Fellow Royal Coll. Physicians, Royal Coll. Australasian Physicians; mem. Royal Coll. Physicians (London), Child Neurology Soc. (membership com. 1996-97, internat. affairs com. 1997—), Internat. Child Neurology Soc., Soc. for Devel. Pediat., Am. Acad. Cerebral Palsy and Devel. Medicine (outcomes com. 2001—). Avocations: playing rugby and soccer for university, Irish Med. Sch. and Royal Army Med. Corps. Office: Tex Childrens Hosp 6621 Fannin St Houston TX 77030-2303 E-mail: gmiller@bcm.tmc.edu.

MILLER, GEORGE, congressman; b. Richmond, Calif., May 17, 1945; s. George and Dorothy (Rumsey) M.; m. Cynthia Caccavo, 1964; children: George, Stephen. BA, San Francisco State Coll., 1968; JD, U. Calif., Davis, 1972. Legis. counsel Calif. senate majority leader, 1969-73; mem. U.S. Congress from 7th Calif. dist., 1975—; mem. edn. and workforce resources com. Chmn. subcom. on oversight and investigations, 1985—, chmn. subcom. on labor stds., 1981-84, chmn. select com. on children, youth and families, 1983-91, chmn. com. on natural resources, 1991-94; mem. com. on edn. and lab., dep. majority whip, 1989-94; vice chair Dem. Policy Com., 1995—. Mem. Calif. Bar Assn. Office: House of Reps 2205 Rayburn Ho Office Bldg Washington DC 20515-0001*

MILLER, GEORGE ARMITAGE, psychologist, educator; b. Charleston, W.Va., Feb. 3, 1920; s. George E. and Florence (Armitage) M.; m. Katherine James, Nov. 29, 1939 (dec. Jan. 1996); children: Nancy, Donnally James. BA, U. Ala., 1940, MA, 1941; AM, Harvard U., 1944, PhD, 1946; PhD (hon.), U. Louvain, 1976; D Social Sci. (hon.), Yale U., 1979; DSc (hon.), Columbia U., 1980, U. Sussex, 1984, New Sch. Social Rsch., 1993; LittD (hon.), Charleston U., 1992; DSc (hon.), DSc (hon.), New Sch. Social Rsch., 1993, Princeton U., 1996, Williams Coll., 2000. Instr. psychology U. Ala., 1941-43; rsch. fellow Harvard Psycho-Acoustic Lab., 1944-48; asst. prof. psychology Harvard U., 1948-51, assoc. prof., 1955-58, prof., 1958-68, chmn. dept psychology, 1964-67, co-dir. Ctr. for Cognitive Studies, 1960-67; prof. Rockefeller U., N.Y.C., 1968-79, adj. prof., 1979-82; prof. psychology Princeton U., 1979-90, James S. McDonnell Disting. prof. psychology, 1982-90, James S. McDonnell Disting. prof. psychology emeritus, 1990—, program dir. McDonnell-Pew Program in Cognitive Neurosci., 1989-94; assoc. prof. MIT, 1951-55. Vis. Inst. for Advanced Study, Princeton, 1972-76, 82-83, mem., 1950, 70-72; vis. prof. Rockefeller U., 1967-68, MIT, 1976-79, group leader Lincoln Lab., 1953-55; fellow Ctr. Advanced Study in Behavioral Scis., Stanford U., 1958-59; Fulbright research prof. Oxford (Eng.) U., 1963-64; Sesquicentennial prof. U. Ala., 1981. Author: Language and Communication, 1951, (with Galanter and Pribram) Plans and the Structure of Behavior, 1960, Psychology, 1962, (with Johnson-Laird) Language and Perception, 1976, Spontaneous Apprentices, 1977, Language and Speech, 1981, The Science of Words, 1991; editor Psychol. Bulletin, 1981-82. Recipient Disting. Service award Am. Speech and Hearing Assn., 1976, award in behavioral scis. N.Y. Acad. Scis., 1982, Hermann von Helmholtz award Cognitive Neurosci. Inst., 1989, Nat. Medal Sci. NSF, 1991, Gold Medal Am. Psychological Found. 1990, Nat. Medal of Sci. 1991, Louis E. Levy medal Franklin Inst., 1991, John P. Govern award, Am. Assn. for Advancement of Sci., 2000; Guggenheim fellow, 1986, William James fellow Am. Psychological Soc., 1989; Fondation Fyssen Priz Internat. for cognitive sci., 1992. Fellow Brit. Psychol. Assn. (hon.); mem. NAS, AAAS (chmn. sect. J 1981, John P. McGovern award 2000), Am. Psychol. Assn. (pres. 1968-69, Disting. Scientific Contbn. award 1963, William James Book award divsn. gen. psychology 1993), Eastern Psychol. Assn. (pres. 1961-62), Acoustical Soc. Am., Linguistic Soc. Am., Am. Statis. Assn., Am. Philos. Soc., Am. Physiol. Soc., Psychometric Soc., Soc. Exptl. Psychologists (Warren medal 1972), Am. Acad. Arts and Scis., Psychonomic Soc., Royal Netherlands Acad. Arts and Scis. (fgn.), Sigma Xi. Home: 16 Willow St Princeton NJ 08542-6923 Office: Princeton Univ Dept Psychology Green Hall Princeton NJ 08544

MILLER, GEORGE DAVID, retired military officer, retired not-for-profit developer; b. McKeesport, Pa., Apr. 5, 1930; s. George G. and Nellie G. (Cullen) M.; m. Barbara Aex; 1 child from previous marriage: George David Jr.; stepchildren: Jason Dunn, Elizabeth Dunn. BS, U.S. Naval Acad., 1953; MS in Aerospace Engring, Air Force Inst. Tech., 1966; postgrad., Nat. War Coll., 1970-71. Commd. 2d lt. U.S. Air Force, 1953, advanced through grades to lt. gen., 1981; ops. officer, comdr. 22d Spl. Ops. Squadron, Nakhon Phanom Royal Thai AFB, Thailand, 1970-71; dep. comdr. for ops., vice comdr., comdr. 55th Strategic Reconnaissance Wing, Offutt AFB, Nebr., 1971-74; comdr. 17th Air div., 307th Strategic wing, U-Tapao Airfield, Thailand, 1974-75; comdr. 57th Air Div. Minot AFB, N.D., 1975-76; asst. dep. chief staff ops. hdqrs. SAC, Offutt AFB, Nebr., 1976-77; dep. dir. single integrated operational plan Joint Strategic Target Planning Staff, Joint Chiefs of Staff, 1977-79; dir. plans, dep. chief of staff ops., plans and readiness Hdqrs. USAF, Washington, 1979-80, asst. dep. chief staff ops., plans and readiness, 1980-81; vice comdr.-in-chief SAC, Offutt AFB, Nebr., 1981-84; exec. dir., sec.-gen. U.S. Olympic Com., 1984-87. Pres., exec. dir. Morris Animal Found., 1989-92; pres., CEO Nat. Fire Protection Assn., 1992-2002, chmn. bd. NFPA Rsch. Found., 1992-2002; chmn. Internat. Confederaton of Fire Protection Assns. (CFPA_I), 1992-2002; vice chair, The Retired Officers Assn.; trustee U.S. Naval Acad. Found. Decorated Def. D.S.M., Air Force DSM, Legion of Merit, D.F.C. with 3 oak leaf clusters Air medal with 18 oak leaf clusters, others. Mem. VFW, Air Force Assn., Am. Legion, Masons, Scottish Rite, Shriners, Daedalians, Retired Officers Assn. (bd. dirs.), NFPA, Metro Fire Chiefs Assn. Lutheran. Home: 20 Phillips Pond Natick MA 01760-5643

MILLER, GEORGE DEWITT, JR. lawyer; b. Detroit, Aug. 20, 1928; s. George DeWitt and Eleanor Mary Miller; m. Prudence Brewster Saunders, Dec. 28, 1951; children: Margaret DeWitt, Joy Saunders. BA magna cum laude, Amherst Coll., 1950; JD with distinction, U. Mich., 1953. Bar: Mich. 1953, U.S. Dist. Ct. (so. dist.) Mich. 1953, U.S. Ct. Appeals (6th cir.) 1960, U.S. Tax Ct. 1960. Assoc. Bodman, Longley & Dahling, Detroit, 1957-61, ptnr., 1962—. Trustee, mem. Matilda R. Wilson Fund, 1993—, pres., 1998—; trustee Maplegrove Ctr./Kingswood Hosp., Henry Ford Health Sys., 1995—. Capt. USAF, 1953-56. Recipient Commendation medal. Fellow Mich. State Bar Found.; mem. ABA, State Bar Mich., Detroit Bar Assn., Detroit Athletic Club, Orchard Lake Country Club, Order of Coif, Phi Beta Kappa. Episcopalian. Avocations: yacht racing, shooting, gardening. Home: 320 Dunston Rd Bloomfield Hills MI 48304-3415 Office: Bodman Longley & Dahling 100 Renaissance Ctr Ste 34 Detroit MI 48243-1001

MILLER, G(EORGE) WILLIAM, merchant banker, business executive; b. Sapulpa, Okla., Mar. 9, 1925; s. James Dick and Hazle Deane (Orrick) M.; m. Ariadna Rogojarsky, Dec. 22, 1946. BS in Marine Engring., U.S. Coast Guard Acad., 1945; JD, U. Calif., Berkeley, 1952; hon. degree, Babson Coll, Boston U., Brown U., Bryant Coll., Fairfield U., Fla. State U., R.I. U. Bar: Calif. 1952, N.Y. 1953. Asst. sec. Textron Inc., 1956-57, v.p., 1957-60, pres., 1960-74, COO, 1960-67, CEO, 1967-78; chmn. Fed. Res. Bd., Washington, 1978-79; sec. of Treasury, 1979-81; chmn. G. William Miller & Co. Inc., 1981—; chmn., CEO Federated Dept. Stores, Inc., 1990-92; chmn. bd. HomePlace of Am., Inc., 1995-2001, The H. John Heinz III Ctr. Sci., Econ., Environ., 2000—. Bd. dirs. Repligen Corp., GS Industries, Inc., Simon Property Group, Inc.; past chmn. adv. coun. Pres.'s Com. EEO, 1963-65; mem. coun. Nat. Found. Humanities, 1966-67; bd. dirs. USCG Acad. Found., 1969-78, pres., 1973-77, chmn., 1977-78; chmn. U.S. Indsl. Payroll Savs. Bond Com., 1977, Pres.'s Com. HIRE, 1977; co-chmn. Polish-U.S. Econ. Coun., 1977-78, U.S.-USSR Trade and Econ. Coun., 1977-78, Pres.'s Cir. NAS, 1989-92. Bd. dirs. Washington Opera; bd. trustees Marine Biological Laboratory, Woods Hole, Mass. U. Calif. fellow, Berkeley. Mem. State Bar Calif., Nat. Alliance Businessmen (bd. dirs. 1968-78, chmn. 1977-78), Conf. Bd. (trustee 1972-78, chmn. 1977-78), Bus. Coun., Lyford Cay Club (Nassau), Acoaxet Club (Westport, Mass.), Brook Club (N.Y.C.), Burning Tree Club, Chevy Chase Club, Order of Coif, Phi Delta Phi. Office: 1215 19th St NW Washington DC 20036-2401 E-mail: miller@gwmco.com.

MILLER, GERALD CECIL, immunologist, laboratory administrator, educator; b. Wichita, Kans., Dec. 20, 1944; s. Cecil William and Mildred Ester (Carlisle) M.; m. Josephine Buller, June 1, 1968; children: Nathan Gerald, Natalie Buller. BA, Emporia (Kans.) State U., 1967, MS, 1969; PhD, Kans. State U., 1972. Diplomate Am. Bd. Med. Lab. Immunology. Rsch. fellow Mayo Med. Sch. and Mayo Found., Rochester, Minn., 1972-75; sr. scientist Health Cen. Rsch. Found., Mpls., 1975-77; grad. tchg. and rsch. asst. Emporia State U., 1967-69, Kans. State U., Manhattan, 1969-70, NIH predoctoral fellow, 1970-72; asst. prof. microbiology and immunology Oral Roberts U. Sch. Medicine, Tulsa, 1977-82; owner, dir. Immuno-Diagnostics Lab. Inc., 1982-94; adj. assoc. prof. Oral Roberts U. Sch. Medicine, 1986-90; mem. ancillary med. staff Children's Med. Ctr., 1979—2000; chief immunology, microbiology and flow cytometry Regional Med. Lab., 1994—; clin. lab. immunologist Pathology Lab. Assocs., 1994—. Adj. asst. prof. U. Okla. Med. Coll., Tulsa, 1986—; adj. assoc. prof. Okla. State U. Osteo. Med. Sch., 1999—, lectr. Nat. Med. Rev./Kaplain Med., 1991—. Mem. editl. bd. Jour. Clin. Lab. Analysis, Clin. and Diagnostic Lab. Immunology; contbr. articles and abstracts to sci. jours. Trustee 1st United Meth. Ch., 1994-97, 99-2001, mem. adminstrv. bd., 1978—; bd. dirs. Brush Creek Boys Ranch, 1996-98; cert. ofcl. USA Track and Field, 1986-2000. Mem. AAAS, Am. Soc. Microbiology, Assn. Med. Lab. Immunologists (treas. 1997-2001), Clin. Immunology Soc., N.Y. Acad. Scis., Sigma Xi. Avocations: hunting, hiking, canoeing, backpacking, fly fishing. Office: Regional Med Lab 1923 S Utica Ave Tulsa OK 74104-6520

MILLER, GERALD MILTON, II, management consultant; b. Reading, Pa., July 12, 1962; s. Gerald Milton and Diane Mae M.; m. Laurie Ann Rozzi, Nov. 24, 1984 (div. Nov. 1988); m. Gretchen Elise Bendorf, May 19, 1992; children: Calvin Thomas, Drew Alan. BA in Econs., Pa. State U., 1984; MA in Econs., George Washington U., 1987; PhD in Econs., George Mason U., 1989. Cert. integrated resource mgmt., mgmt. acct. Asst. mgr. Heister Corp., State Coll., Pa., 1981-84; mathemat. economist U.S. Dept. Commerce, Washington, 1984-86; sr. analyst Synergy, Inc., 1986-89; ptnr. Deloitte Cons., Parsippany, N.J., 1989-98, mng. dir. Munich, Germany, 1999—. Author: Antitrust and Industrial Performance, 1993. Nat. grad. fellow NSF, 1986. Mem. Am. Prodn. and Inventory Control Soc., Inst. Mgmt. Accts. (cert. mgmt. acct.), Inst. Mgmt. Accts. Republican. Avocations: canoeing, weight training, golf, hiking. Home: PO Box 820 Ten Westport Rd Wilton CT 06897-0820 Office: Deloitte Cons Isartorplatz 8 Munich 80331 Germany

MILLER, GERALDINE B. music educator; b. Johnstown, Pa., Sept. 30, 1917; d. Samuel George Felton and Jennie Aurora Ling; m. Walter Randolph Miller, Mar. 19, 1916; children: W. Bruce, Diane Miller Jackson. BA, Ursinus Coll., 1939; MusB, Phila. Conservatory of Music, 1964. Piano tchr. Lancaster County Conservatory of Music, Lancaster, pa., 1959-62; pvt. piano tchr. Bala Cynwyd, Pa., 1959—. Recipient 1st prize winner Tri-Concerts Assn., 1968, 2d prize Pa. Music Tchrs. Assn., 1977. Mem. Phila. Music Tchrs. Assn. (v.p. 1986-90, pres. 1990-92, publicity chmn.), Musical Coterie of Wayne (jr. coterie chmn. 1969-87), Music Study Club. Avocations: sewing, needlework, gardening. Home: 3300 Darby Rd #2210 Haverford PA 19041-1068

MILLER, G(ERSON) H(ARRY), research institute director, mathematician, computer scientist, chemist; b. Phila., Mar. 2, 1924; m. Mary Alexa Heath, Jan. 28, 1961; children: Byron, Alexandra. BA, Pomona Coll., 1949; MEd in Counseling and Pers., Temple U., 1951; PhD. in Ednl. Psychology, U. So. Calif., 1957; MS in Math., U. Ill., 1982, postgrad., 1963-65. Jr. high sch. and jr. coll. instr. math. L.A. Sch. Dist., 1953-57; assoc. prof. Western Ill. U., Macomb, 1957-60; prof. Towson State U., Balt., 1960-61; prof. math. and edn. Parsons Coll., Fairfield, Iowa, 1961-65; prof. Tenn. Technol. U., Cookeville, 1966-89; prof. math. and computer sci. Edinboro (Pa.) U., 1968-71, 81-89, asst. dir. Institutional Rsch., 1972-80, emeritus prof., 1999—; dir. Studies On Smoking, Inc. and SOS Stop Smoking Clinic, Edinboro, 1972—. Spkr. state, nat. and internat. profl. meetings; condr. seminars on smoking and health London, Fed. Republic Germany, Alaska, New Brunswick, N.J., Chgo., Costa Rica, Nice, Washington, Alexandria, Va., Boston; dir. Nat. Study Math. Requirements for Scientists and Engrs., 1966-73; condr. Nat. Symposium for Am. Inst. Biol. Scis., Am. Chem. Soc. and Am. Soc. Engring. Educators, 1970-75; dir. Math. for Industry Confs. Contbr. numerous articles to profl. jours. Pres. Edinboro YMCA, 1972-83; bd. dirs. Common Cause, Harrisburg, Pa., 1975-80; Sgt. USAAF, 1943-46, PTO. Grantee U.S. Office Edn., 1968, 70, No Other World, 1973, NAS, 1980, ITT Life Ins. Corp., 1983, Erie Comty. Found., 1987. Fellow Am. Inst. Chemists (cert. profl. chemist), AAAS; mem. APHA, Am. Assn. World Health, Am. Chem. Soc., Am. Soc. Engring. Edn., Internat. Assn. Pure and Applied Chemists, Internat. Soc. for Preventive Oncology, Math. Assn. Am., Am. Diabetes Assn., Nat. Coun. Tchrs. Math., Sch. Sci. and Math. Assn., N.Y. Acad. Scis. (hon.), Acad. Sr. Profls. (hon.). Home and Office: Studies on Smoking Inc 125 High St Edinboro PA 16412-2552 also: 25 Crescent Pl S Saint Petersburg FL 33711-5118 E-mail: drghmiller@aol.com.

MILLER, GORDON DAVID, lawyer; b. Huntington, N.Y., May 6, 1940; s. Gordon Stanley and Marie Christine (Smith) Miller; m. Leueen Mary O'Connor, Aug. 6, 1966; children: Christine Victoria, Heather Leueen, Winston Gordon Malachie. AB cum laude, Colgate U., 1962; LLB, Harvard U., 1965; LLM, NYU, 1974. Bar: N.Y. 1966, U.S. Dist. Ct. (so. and ea. dists.) N.Y. 1968. Sr. atty. N.Y. Life Ins. Co., N.Y.C., 1966—69; assoc. Winthrop Stimson Putnam & Roberts, 1969—70; atty. Pfizer Inc., 1970—73; legal officer, asst. sec. Internat. Nickel Co. Inc., 1973—85; assoc. Bruce Clark & Assocs., 1985—88; asst. corp. counsel City of New York, 1988—. Mem. exec. com. Colgate U. Ann. Fund, 1970—84; bd. dirs. Colgate U. Alumni Corp., 1976—80, chmn. nom. com., 1978—80. Recipient Maroon citation, Colgate U. Alumni Corp., 1977. Mem.: N.Y. County Lawyers Assn., Harvard Club. Home: 360 1st Ave New York NY 10010-4912 Office: Office of Corp Counsel 100 Church St New York NY 10007

MILLER, GREEN RUSSELL, economist, educator; b. Kenvir, Ky., Mar. 10, 1939; s. Clifford Wesley and Lorene (Farmer) M.; m. Carolyn Sue Blackburn, Oct. 7, 1966; children: Laura Marie, Russell Wesley. BA, U. Tex., El Paso, 1969; MA, U. Oreg., 1971; PhD, U. Ky., 1985. Asst. prof. Sch. Pub. Affairs, Ky. State U., Frankfort, 1977; instr. Transylvania U., Lexington, 1973-79; 1999prof. econs., dir. Ctr. for Econ. Edn. Morehead (Ky.) State U., 1979. Bd. dirs. Ky. Council Econ. Edn., Louisville, 1979-96; cons. to various law firms, Ky., 1973—. Contbr. numerous articles to profl. jours. Coach Little League Baseball, Morehead, 1982-85, Youth Soccer League, 1985-86; bd. dirs. St. Albans Ch., Morehead, 1979-82, Gethsemane Luth. Ch., 1989-97; vol. One-on-One program Dept. of Corrections, Lexington, 1973-82. Mem. Midwest Econ. Assn., Ky. Econs. Assn., Mo. Valley Econ. Assn. (Jerome F. Schwier merotorious svc. award 1997), So. Econ. Assn., Ky. Assn. Ednl. Opportunity Program Pers., Joint Coun. on Econ. Edn., Nat. Assn. Econ. Educators, Ky. Coun. on Econ. Edn. (bd. dirs. 1979-96, Outstanding Ctr. Dir. 1981-82), Assn. Ky. Econ. Educators (charter, mem. original bylaws com., nominating com. 1985-93), Nat. Assn. Forensic Econs. (charter, bd. dirs. 1986-87, bus. editor Jour. of Econs. 1990-97, chair acctg.-econs.-fin. 1988-2002). Democrat. Lutheran. Avocations: hiking, reading. Home: 1240 Rodburn Hollow Rd Morehead KY 40351-9092 Office: Morehead State U UPO 1280 222 Combs Morehead KY 40351

MILLER, GREG M. secondary school educator; b. Tiffin, Ohio, June 8, 1975; s. Charles A. and Carol A. Miller; m. Christina K. Hammon, June 27, 1998. MusB Edn., Ohio State U., 1998. Cert. tchr. music K-12 Ohio, 1998. Instrumental music tchr. Liberty Union-Thurston Schs., Balt., 1998—2000, Gahanna-Jefferson Pub. Schs., Gahanna, 2000—. Bass sect. leader, adult choir North Broadway United Meth. Ch., Columbus, Ohio, 1998—; percussionist, sect. leader Heisey Wind Ensemble (cmty. band), Granville, Ohio, 2000—02. Named Most Inspirational Bandsman, Ohio State U. Marching Band, 1997. Mem.: Music Educators' Conf. Ohio, Music Educators' Nat. Conf. United Methodist. Avocations: reading, golf, fantasy baseball. Home: 950 Timothy Dr Gahanna OH 43230 Office: Gahanna Middle Sch South 349 Shady Spring Dr Gahanna OH 43230 Office Fax: 614-337-3734. Personal E-mail: millergregm@yahoo.com.

MILLER, GREGORY ALLEN, psychology educator; b. St. Louis, Dec. 28, 1952; s. H. Glen and Betty A. (Woodruff) M.; m. Margarita Ham, Aug. 22, 1981. AB magna cum laude, Harvard U., 1975; MS, U. Wis., 1978, PhD, 1982. Lic. clin. psychologist, Ill. Intern in clin. psychology Rush-Presby. St. Luke Med. Ctr., Chgo., 1981-82; asst. prof. psychology U. Ill., Champaign, 1982-87, assoc. prof., 1987-93, prof., 1993—. Editor Psychophysiology; contbr. articles to profl. jours. Mem. Soc. for Psychophysiol. Rsch. (past pres.), Soc. for Rsch. Psychopathology, Am. Psychol. Soc. Office: U Ill Dept Psychology 603 E Daniel St Champaign IL 61820-6232

MILLER, GREGORY KENT, structural engineer; b. Anaconda, Mont., July 6, 1951; s. Robert Bruce and Lois Patricia (Arvish) Miller. BS in Civil Engring./Engring. Mechanics, Mont. State U., 1973, MS in Engring. Mechanics, 1974. Project engr. U.S. Energy R&D Adminstrn., Idaho Falls, Idaho, 1974-77; structural engr. EG&G Idaho, Inc., 1977-93, supr., 1993-94, Lockheed Martin Idaho Technologies Co., Idaho Falls, 1994-99, BBWI, Idaho Falls, 1999—. Contbr. articles to profl jours. Mem.: ASME (comd mem boiler and pressure vessel code sect III 1995—), Phi Kappa Phi (Sr of Yr 1973), Tau Beta Pi. Achievements include research in advanced modeling and analysis methods for evaluating failure of fuel particles in high-temperature gas-cooled reactors; contributed to technology for evaluating complex material behavior in pressure vessels; advanced methods for evaluating containers bearing nuclear materials for impact loads associated with accidental drop events. Office: BBWI Technologies Co PO Box 1625 Idaho Falls ID 83415-3765 E-mail: gkm@inel.gov.

MILLER, GREGORY R. lawyer; Chief asst. U.S. atty. Dept. Justice, Tallahassee, U.S. atty., 1993-98; asst. U.S. atty. Dept Justice, 2000—02, U.S. atty, 2002—; assoc. Fowler, White, Gillen, Boggs, Villareal and Banker, PA, 1998-2000. Office: US Atty's Office 111 N Adams St Tallahassee FL 32301

MILLER, GUY M. critical care physician and anesthesiologist; b. Phila., July 21, 1958; s. Harold and Sylvia (Levin) M. BS, George Washington U., 1980; PhD in Chemistry, U. Va., 1986; MD, Med. Coll. Pa., 1988. Intern in surgery U. Chgo., 1989-91; resident Johns Hopkins U., Balt., 1991-92, fellow, 1993; chmn., CEO Galileo Labs., Inc., Santa Clara, Calif., 1994—; clin. instr. Stanford (Calif.) U. Sch. Medicine, 1996—. Asst. prof. Johns Hopkins U., Balt., 1994-95, adj. asst. prof., 1995-96; bd. dirs. Bonny Doon Vineyard; adj. prof., mem. dean's adv. bd. U. NC Sch. Pub. Health, Chapel Hill, 2001-; mem. sci. adv. bd. EAS Inc., 2001-. Office: Galileo Labs Inc 5301 Patrick Henry Dr Santa Clara CA 95054-1114 E-mail: gmiller@GalileoLabs.com.

MILLER, H. TODD, lawyer; b. Buffalo, Sept. 19, 1947; s. Henry Opel and Irene Teresa (Hauck) M.; m. June Diehl Lancaster, Aug. 1, 1970; children: Catharine Maclay, Todd Lancaster, Peter Hanes. BA, SUNY, Buffalo, 1969; JD, Duke U., 1971. Bar: N.C. 1971, D.C. 1973. Jud. clerk to Hon. Charles R. Simpson U.S. Tax Ct., Washington, 1971-73; assoc. atty. Hogan & Hartson LLP, 1973-78; ptnr. Hogan & Hartson, 1979—. Mem. Phi Beta Kappa, Order of the Coif. Episcopalian. Office: Hogan & Hartson Columbia Sq 555 13th St NW Ste 800E Washington DC 20004-1161

MILLER, HAROLD ARTHUR, lawyer; b. St. Marie, Ill., Aug. 18, 1922; s. Arthur E. and Luletta (Noé) M.; m. Michele H. Rogivue, Nov. 21, 1947; children: Maurice H., Jan Leland, Marc Richard. BS in Acctg., U. Ill., 1942, JD, 1950. Bar: Ill. 1950, U.S. Dist. Ct. Ill. 1950, U.S. Tax Ct. 1950. Fgn. svc.

officer U.S. State Dept., Paris, France, 1945-48; ptnr. Filson, Williamson & Miller, Champaign, Ill., 1950-60, Williamson & Miller, Champaign, 1960-72, Miller & Hendren, Champaign, 1972—. Atty. Christie Clinic Found., Champaign, 1960—; atty. pub. schs. dists., Champaign & Vermilion Counties, Ill., 1960—; atty. for municipalities in Champaign County, Ill., 1970—. Author: Estate Planning for Doctors, 1961, Intervivos Trusts Alternative to Probate, 1996. Bd. dirs., officer Urbana Ill. Sch. Dist., 1957-69; chmn., trustee Parkland Coll., Champaign, 1971-91; founding bd. mem. CCDC Found., Champaign-Urbana Ednl. Found., Moore Heart Found., Christie Found.; life mem. PTA. With inf. U.S. Army, 1942-45, ETO. Mem. ABA, Am. Judicature Soc., Ill. and Local Bar Assns., Ill. Trial Lawyers Assn., Alpha Kappa Psi. Presbyterian. Office: Miller & Hendren Attys 30 E Main St #200 Champaign IL 61820-3629 E-mail: ham@mhlawoffice.com.

MILLER, HAROLD EDWARD, retired manufacturing conglomerate executive, consultant; b. St. Louis, Nov. 23, 1926; s. George Edward and Georgenia Elizabeth (Franklin) M.; m. Lilian Ruth Gantner, Dec. 23, 1949; children—Ellen Susan, Jeffrey Arthur. BSBA, Washington U., St. Louis, 1949. Vice pres. Fulton Iron Works Co., St. Louis, 1968-71, pres., 1971-79, chmn. bd., 1979-90; v.p. Katy Industries Inc., Elgin, Ill., 1976-77, exec. v.p., 1978-90, also dir., to 1990; pres. HM Consulting, Palatine, Ill., 1990—. Internat. cons. Vigel Spa, Italy; v.p. Vigel U.S.A. Inc., 1996—. Served with U.S. Army, 1945-46. Mem. Barrington Tennis Club, Inverness Golf Club. Presbyterian. E-mail: hmillercons84@cs.com.

MILLER, HAROLD WILLIAM, nuclear geochemist; b. Walton, N.Y., Apr. 21, 1920; s. Harold Frank and Vera Leona (Simons) M. BS in Chemistry, U. Mich., 1943; MS in Chemistry, U. Colo., 1948, postgrad. Control chemist Linde Air Products Co., Buffalo, 1943-46; analytical research chemist Gen. Electric Co., Richland, Wash., 1948-51; research chemist Phillips Petroleum Co., Idaho Falls, Idaho, 1953-56; with Anaconda (Mont.) Copper Co., 1956; tech. dir., v.p. U.S. Yttrium Co., Laramie, Wyo., 1956-57; tech. dir. Colo. div. The Wah Chang Co., Boulder, Colo., 1957-58; analytical chemist The Climax (Colo.) Molybdenum Co., 1959; with research and devel. The Colo. Sch. of Mines Research Found., Golden, 1960-62; cons. Boulder, 1960—; sr. research physicist Dow Chem. Co., Golden, 1963-73. Bd. dirs. Sweeney Mining and Milling Corp., Boulder; cons. Hendricks Mining and Milling Co., Boulder; instr. nuclear physics and nuclear chemistry Rocky Flats Plant, U. Colo. Contbr. numerous articles to profl. jours. Recipient Lifetime Achievement award Boulder County Metal Mining Assn., 1990. Mem. Sigma Xi. Avocations: mineralogy, western U.S. mining history. Home and Office: PO Box 1092 Boulder CO 80306-1092

MILLER, HARRY, mechanical engineer; b. Detroit, July 11, 1915; s. Isaac William Miller and Rose Pineles; m. Thelma Osinoff, July 15, 1944; children: Jeffrey, Arlene. BSME, CCNY, 1937. Registered profl. engr., N.Y., Ariz. Engr. Master Wire Die Corp., N.Y.C., 1937-39; marine engr. Bklyn. Navy Yard, 1939-45; cons. Machinpak Co., 1945-48; dept. head Sperry Corp., Lake Success, N.Y., 1948-59; tech. dir. Sperry Flight Sys., Phoenix, 1959-85; freelance cons., 1985-89; ptnr. Space Saver Parking Sys., 1992-99. Cons. Honeywell Inc., Delta Airlines, Spensley, Horn, Jubas and Lubitz, Neuman, Williams, Anderson and Olsen, Donovan and Olsen Contbr. articles to profl. publs. Recipient Airlines Pioneer award Airlines Avionics Inst., Paris, 1985. Democrat. Jewish. Achievements include 47 patents in field. Home: 5136 N 68th Pl Scottsdale AZ 85253-7007

MILLER, HARRY B(ENJAMIN), lawyer; b. Lexington, Ky., Jan. 4, 1924; s. Harry Benjamin Miller and Ann (Walcutt) Winn; m. Patricia Griffin, Mar. 22, 1946 (dec.); children: Thomas, Robin, John, Harry Benjamin III. LLM, U. Ky., 1948. Bar: Ky. 1948, U.S. Dist. Ct. (ea. dist.) Ky. 1948, U.S. Ct. Appeals (6th cir.) 1952, U.S. Supreme Ct. 1962. Pres. Miller, Griffin & Marks, P.S.C., Lexington, 1962—. Mng. editor U. Ky. Law Rev., 1948. Treas. Ky. Dem. State Party, Frankfort, 1960-68. Mem. Order of Coif. Presbyterian. Avocation: golf. Home: 111 Woodland Ave Lexington KY 40502-6415 Office: Miller Griffin & Marks PSC Security Trust Bldg Ste 600 Lexington KY 40507-1232

MILLER, HARRY BRILL, scenic designer, actor, director, acting instructor, lyricist, interior designer; b. Jersey City, Jan. 26, 1924; s. Max Joseph Miller and Lillian (Hirsch) Grodjesk. BA, U. Mich., 1946; MA, Smith Coll., 1948. Set designer, asst. scenic designer various Broadway, Off Broadway and summer shows, N.Y.C., 1948-72; scenic designer NBC-TV, 1950-63; art dir. MPO-Video Prodns., 1962; scenic designer CBS-TV, 1963-91. Indsl. show designer Norelco, Thompson CSF, Engelhard, N.Y.C., 1958-75; interior designer Interior Comml. Constrn. Assocs., Hialeah, Fla., 1969-70; dir., writer Miramar Minstrels, N.Y.C., 1979—; dir. PACT Theatres, N.Y.C., 1995-98; acting tchr. Emmanuel Midtown Young Men and Young Women's Hebrew Assn., N.Y.C., 1989-90. Set designer (TV shows) Princeton '54, '55, '56 (Peabody 1954, 55), The Price is Right, 1962-63, Jackie Gleason Show, 1969-70, CBS News and Special Events, 1986-91, (mus. show) Nashville at the Garden, 1972; art dir. (TV show) Guiding Light, 1978-86 (2 Emmys 1984, 85), The Edge of Night, 1964-69; prodn. designer TV show Captain Kangaroo, 1970-78 (various Peabody awards); set design asst. (Broadway mus.) Funny Girl, 1964, (Broadway play) Sign in Sidney Brustein's Window; actor Kaye Playhouse, N.Y.C., 1998. Sgt. U.S. Army, 1943-46. Recipient Teaching Assistanship French Govt., Paris, 1948. Mem. United Scenic Artists, Miramar Ski Club (trip chair 1991-93, v.p. 1997-98, pres. 1999-2000). Avocations: skiing, dancing, swimming, painting, acting. Address: 333 W 56th St Apt 7B New York NY 10019-3770

MILLER, HARRY FREEMAN, university administrator; b. Vallejo, Calif., Aug. 27, 1946; s. Theodore Harry and Grace (Eubank) M.; 1 child, Charissa Rainie. BA, Howard U., 1969; JD, U. Calif., Davis, 1972; cert., Harvard U., 1989, U. Chgo., 1998. Assoc. gen. sec. Stanford U., Palo Alto, Calif., 1973-79; asst. dean, lectr. law Syracuse (N.Y.) U., 1979-81; dir. devel. Georgetown U. Law Ctr., Washington, 1981-83; v.p. instnl. advt. Morgan State U., Balt., 1983-91; assoc. v.p., dir. planned giving U. South Fla., Tampa, 1991-95; assoc. v.p. devel. Tex. So. U., Houston, 1996—. Host Lou Rauls Telethon for United Negro Coll. Fund, Syracuse, 1981, mem. adv. com., Tampa, 1993-95; mem. Nat. Sports Festival Com., Syracuse, 1981. Mem. Nat. Soc. Fund Raising Execs., Assn. Fund Raising Officers (bd. dirs. 1984-90), Am. Inst. Parliamentarians, Tampa Urban League (bd. dirs. 1993-95), Phi Alpha Delta. Office: Tex So U Office of Devel 3100 Cleburne St Houston TX 77004-4501

MILLER, HARRY GEORGE, education educator; b. Waukesha, Wis., Feb. 15, 1941; s. Harry Fricke and Ethel Ruth (D'Amato) M.; m. Mary Frances Shugrue, June 20, 1964; children: Alicia, Michael, Anne, Dierdre, Courtney. BA, Carroll Coll., 1963; M.Ed., U. Nebr., 1967, Ed.D., 1970. Tchr. Westside Community Schs., Omaha, 1964-67; demonstration tchr. East Edn. Complex, Lincoln (Nebr.) Pub. Schs., 1967-68; instr. curriculum research Tchrs. Coll., U. Nebr., Lincoln, 1968-70; faculty So. Ill. U., Carbondale, 1970—, asso. prof. edn., dept. secondary edn., 1972—, chmn. dept. secondary edn., 1973-75, prof., chmn. dept. ednl. leadership, 1975—; dean, prof. Coll. Tech. Careers, 1980-89; assoc. v.p. acad. affairs So. Ill. U., 1989-92; dean, prof. Ctr. Adult and Continuing Edn. The Am. U., Cairo, 1992—. Rsch. prof. Min. Edn., Thailand, 1978, vis. prof., Malaysia, 80, Republic of Korea, 85, PRC, 1991; cons. to various orgsn. and instns., 1969—74. Author: Beyond Facts: Objective Ways to Measure Thinking, 1976, Adults Teaching Adults, 1977, Responsibility Education, 1977, The Adult Educator: A Handbook for Staff Development, 1978, An Introduction to Adult and Continuing Education, 1979, The Education of Adults, 1981, The Life-long Learning Experience, 1986, Grassroots, 1992, Veiled Voices, 1993, Come, Sit Awhile, 1995, Assalaamu Aleikum, 1997, Mazmaza, 2000; also monographs; mem. editorial bd. Traning, 1976. Exec. dir. Mid. East Assn. of Nat. Schs., 1999—; mem. Ill. Migrant Coun., 1974; mem. adv. bd. Evaluation and Devel. Ctr., Rehab. inst., Carbondale, 1974—80; bd. dirs. St. Joseph's Hosp., Overseas Ednl. Svcs., 1997—, Am. Ednl. Network, 1998—, Cairo Am. Coll., 1996—. Fulbright grantee Republic of Togo, 1982 Mem. Pub. Adult and Continuing Edn. Assn., Rural Edn. Assn., Ill. Coun. for Social Studies (hon.), Community Svcs. Assn. Cairo (bd. dirs. 1994-96), Greater Cleve. Coun. for Social Studies (hon.), Ednl. Coun. fo 100 Inc., Coll. of Cons. Clubs: K.C. Democrat. Roman Catholic. Office: Am U Ctr Adult and Cont Educ PO Box 2511 113 Sharia Kass Aini Cairo Egypt E-mail: harrymlr@aucegypt.edu.

MILLER, HARVEY R. lawyer, bankruptcy reorganization specialist; b. Bklyn., Mar. 1, 1933; married Grad., Columbia U. Law Sch., 1959. Sr. ptnr. Weil Gotshal and Manges LLP, N.Y.C. Adj. prof. law NYU Law Sch.; lectr. law Columbia U. Law Sch. Office: Weil Gotshal & Manges LLP 767 5th Ave Fl 29 New York NY 10153-0023 E-mail: harvey.miller@weil.com.

MILLER, HARVEY S. SHIPLEY, foundation trustee, private investor; b. Phila., Sept. 28, 1948; s. Frank Leroy and Betty Charlotte (Elfont) M. BA, Swarthmore Coll., 1970; JD, Harvard U., 1973. Bar: N.Y. 1973. Assoc. Debevoise & Plimpton, N.Y.C., 1973-75; curator and dir. dept. collections and spl. exhbns. Franklin Inst., Phila., 1975-81; v.p. Energy Solutions, Inc., N.Y.C., 1982-84; pres., chief exec. officer, dir. Daltex Med. Scis., Inc., 1983-86, dir. exec. com., 1983-94, chief operating officer, vice chmn., 1986-91, pres., chief operating officer, 1991-93; trustee The Judith Rothschild Found., 1993—. Author: Milton Avery: Drawings and Paintings, 1976, It's About Time, 1979; author, editor: New Spaces: Exploring the Aesthetic Dimensions of Holography, 1979; co-author: Rapid Inactivation of Infectious Pathogens by Chlorhexidine-coated Gloves, 1992; contbr. articles to profl. jours. Mem. vis. com. on photography George Eastman House, Rochester, N.Y., 1976-78; trustee Milton and Sally Avery Arts Found., N.Y.C., 1983—, sec., 1996—; trustee The Franklin Inst., Phila., 1993-95, Phila. Mus. Art, 1985—, exec. com., 1993-96; assoc. trustee U. Pa., 1981-95; trustee Arcadia U., 2002-; bd. govs. Print Club, Phila., 1976-87; bd. overseers U. Pa. Sch. Nursing, 1981—, Edith C. Blum Art Inst. Bard Coll., 1984-87; bd. dirs., mem. corp. MacDowell Colony, N.Y.C., 1982-85; exec. bd. dirs. Fabric Workshop, Phila., 1976-86; mem. prints and drawings and photographs trustees adv. com. Phila. Mus. Art, 1974—, trustee, 1985—, investment com., 1989-95, exec., devel. and exhbn. coms., 1993-96; mem. vis. com. modern Art Met. Mus. Art, 1998—; bd. assocs. Swarthmore Coll. Librs., Phila., 1978-86; treas., dir. Arcadia Found., Norristown, Pa., 1981—; chmn. adv. bd. Inst. Contemporary Art U. Pa., 1982-84; trustee, vice chmn. coms. on instrn. Pa. Acad. Fine Arts, 1982-91, trustee emeritus, 1991—, chmn. collections and exhbns. com., 1985-87; trustee N.Y. Studio Sch., 1974-80, U. of the Arts, 1979-86; mem. exec. bd. Citizens for Arts in Pa., 1980; adv. bd. The Highlands Hist. Soc., 1999—; bd. dirs. Once Gallery, Inc., 1974-75, Wildlife Preservation Trust Internat., Inc., 1990-95; mem. Mayor's Cultural Adv. Coun., Phila., 1987-91; chair Mayor's Art-in-City Hall Program, Phila., 1992-94; trustees coun. Nat. Gallery Art, Washington, 1995-2000, 2001—; mem. collections com. Hist. Soc. Pa., 1991-93, councilor trustee, 1992-93; mem. vis. com. photographs Met. Mus. Art, 1996—, vis. com. modern art, 1998—; mem. trustees' com. on drawings Mus. Modern Art, 1996—, Prints and Illustrated Books, Museum of Modern Art, 2001—; mem. photography accessions com. San Francisco Mus. of Modern Art, 1997—; arts adv. com. Fund for the Waterworks, 1999—. Fellow The Pierpont Morgan Libr.; mem. ABA, Assn. of Bar of City of N.Y., Athenaeum, Libr. Co. Phila., Am. Philos. Soc., Hist. Soc. Pa., Phila. Art Alliance, Union League of Phila., Harvard Club of N.Y.C., Swarthmore Club Phila., Phi Sigma Kappa. Republican. Home: Plumlyn 7036 Sheaff Ln Fort Washington PA 19034-2017 Office: 1110 Park Ave New York NY 10128-1201

MILLER, HENRY FRANKLIN, lawyer; b. Phila., May 19, 1938; s. Lester and Bessie (Posner) M.; m. Barbara Ann Gendel, June 20, 1964; children: Andrew, Alexa. AB, Lafayette Coll., 1959; LLB, U. Pa., 1964. Bar: Pa. 1965. Law clk. U.S. Dist. Ct. Del., Wilmington, 1964-65; assoc. Wolf, Block, Schorr & Solis-Cohen, Phila., 1965-71, ptnr., 1971—. Pres. Soc. Hill Synagogue, Phila., 1978-79, Big Brothers/Big Sisters Assn. of Phila., 1980-81, Jewish Family & Children's Agy., Phila., 1986-88. 1st lt. U.S. Army, 1959-60. Mem. Am. Coll. Real Estate Lawyers. Avocations: swimming, hiking, cycling, reading. Office: Wolf Block Schorr & Solis-Cohen 1650 Arch St Fl 21 Philadelphia PA 19103-2029 E-mail: hmiller@wolfblock.com.

MILLER, HERBERT DELL, petroleum engineer; b. Oklahoma City, Sept. 29, 1919; s. Merrill Dell and Susan (Green) M.; m. Rosalind Rebecca Moore, Nov. 23, 1947; children: Rebecca Miller Wheeler, Robert Rexford. Registered profl. engr., Okla., Tex. Field engr. Amerada Petroleum Corp., Houston, 1948-49, Hobbs, N.Mex., 1947-48, dist. engr. Longview, Tex., 1949-57, sr. engr. Tulsa, 1957-62; petroleum engr. Moore & Miller Oil Co., Oklahoma City, 1962-78; owner Herbert D. Miller Co., 1978—. Maj., F.A., AUS, 1941-47; ETO. Decorated Bronze Star with oak leaf cluster, Purple Heart (U.S.); Croix de Guerre (France). Mem. AIME, Oklahoma City Golf. Republican. Episcopalian (pres. Men's Club 1973). Home and Office: 1819 W Wilshire Blvd Oklahoma City OK 73116-4115

MILLER, HERBERT ELMER, accountant; b. DeWitt, Iowa, Aug. 11, 1914; s. Elmer Joseph and Marian (Briggs) M.; m. Lenore Snitkey, July 1, 1938; 1 dau., Barbara Ruth. AB, State U. Iowa, 1936, MA, 1937; PhD, U. Minn., 1944; Dr. h.c., Free U. Brussels, 1982; D.H.L. (h.c.), De Paul U., 1983. C.P.A., Iowa. Acctg. prof. U. Minn., U. Mich., Mich. State U., 1938-70; ptnr. Arthur Andersen & Co., Chgo., 1970-78; dir. Sch. Acctg., U. Ga., Athens, 1978-83. Co-author: Finney-Miller accounting series, 1950-70; editor, contbr.: C.P.A. Rev. Manual, 1951-79. Mem. AICPA (bd. dirs. 1968-70), Am. Acctg. Assn. (pres. 1965-66), Federated Schs. Acctg. (pres. 1982), Beta Gamma Sigma, Beta Alpha Psi (nat. pres. 1961-62) Home: 145 S Stratford Dr Athens GA 30605-3025

MILLER, HERBERT H. lawyer; b. Balt., May 24, 1921; s. Louis Miller and Rebecca Platt; m. Irene R. Rosen, Aug. 27, 1944; children: Rose, Marjorie, Fran. JD cum laude, U. Balt., 1942; ABA in Acctg., Balt. Coll. of Commerce, 1947. Bar: Md. 1943, U.S. Dist. Ct. Md. 1944, U.S. Supreme Ct. 1986; notary pub., Md. Law clk. Rubenstein and Rubenstein, Balt., 1938-39, Joel J. Hochman, Balt., 1939-40, Feikin & Talkin, Balt., 1940-42; atty. Sherbow, Harris & Medwedeff, 1942-43, Harris & Medwedeff, Balt., 1943-45; pvt. practice Balt. and Towson, Md., 1946—. Mem. inquiry panel Atty. Grievance Com. Md., Balt. County, 1985—; panel chmn. Health Claims Arbitration, Balt., 1994—. Bd. trustees Balt. Coll. Commerce, 1948-52, Beth El Congregation, Balt. County, 1990-94; youth advisor B'nai B'rith, Balt., 1943-88, mem. B'nai B'rith Youth Orgn., pres., 1940-42. Mem. Md. State Bar Assn., Balt. City Bar Assn., Balt. County Bar Assn., Mensa Internat. (arbitrator Md.). Avocations: reading, handyman work, walking. Office: 200 E Joppa Rd Ste 205 Towson MD 21286-3107

MILLER, HERMAN LUNDEN, retired physicist; b. Detroit, Apr. 23, 1924; s. Josiah Leonidas and Sadie Irene (Lunden) M.; m. Dorothy Grace Sack, Sept. 15, 1951. BS in Engring. Physics, U. Mich., 1948, MS in Physics, 1951. Registered profl. engr., Mich. Physicist Ethyl Corp., Ferndale, Mich., 1948-49, Dow Chem. Co., Denver, 1950-55; mem. project rsch. staff Princeton (N.J.) U., 1955-65; physicist Bendix Aerospace, Ann Arbor, Mich., 1965-72; nuclear engr. Commonwealth Assocs., Jackson, 1973-80. Author: Lewiston in the Lumbering Era, 1992, Lumbering in Early Twentieth Century Michigan, The Kneeland-Bigelow Company Experience, 1995.; contbr. articles to profl. jours. With USAF, 1943-46, PTO, lt. col. Res. Mem. IEEE, Am. Phys. Soc., Am. Nuclear Soc.

MILLER, HOPE RIDINGS, author; b. Bonham, Tex. d. Alfred Lafayette and Grace (Dupree) Ridings; m. Clarence Lee Miller, Sept. 26, 1932 (dec. Jan. 1965). BA, U. Tex.; MA, Columbia; D.Litt., Austin Coll. Society editor Washington Post, 1938-45; Washington corr. Town and Country mag., 1944-46, The Argonaut mag., 1945-49; Washington columnist Promenade mag., 1945-51; syndicated column McNaught, 1945-50; asso. editor Diplomat mag., 1952-55, editor in chief, 1956-66; television prodn. staff Metromedia, Inc., 1966-70; Washington editor Antique Monthly, 1976-89. Mem. editorial adv. bd. Horizon mag., 1978-89. Author: Embassy Row: The Life and Times of Diplomatic Washington, 1969, Great Houses of Washington, 1969, Scandals In The Highest Office: Facts and Fictions in the Private Lives of Our Presidents, 1973; script for cassette tape Circling Lafayette Square, 1976. Mem. women's bd. Columbia Hosp., Friends of the Folger Library, Washington Heart Assn. Mem. Nat. Press Club, Hist. Soc. Washington, Friends of LBJ Libr., Am. News women's Club, The Circle of the Nat. Gallery of Art, Stephen F. Austin Soc., Am. Archives of Art, Smithsonian Assocs., Nat. Mus. Women in the Arts, Sulgrave Club. Home: 1868 Columbia Rd NW Washington DC 20009-5183

MILLER, IRIS ANN, landscape architect, urban designer, educator; b. Pitts., Jan. 6, 1938; d. Bernard and Sadye (Topel) Ress; m. Lawrence Alan Miller, Jan. 24, 1959; children: Bradley Stuart, Richard Lyle, Stefan Ress. BS cum laude, U. Pitts., 1959, MEd in Secondary Edn., 1961; postgrad. in psychology and counseling, U. Md., 1962-68; MArch, Cath. U. Am., 1979. Tchr. various pub. and pvt. schs., Pitts., Monroeville, Pa., Montgomery County, Md., 1959-61, 63-64; free lance landscape design Washington, 1965-81; architecture design and research O'Neil and Manion Architects, Bethesda, Md., 1979, 81; architecture design and drawing Frank Schlesinger Architects/Planners, Washington, 1979-80; prin. Iris Miller Urbanism and Landscape Design, 1982—; cons. architecture design Washington, 1982—. Vis. lectr. Cath. U. Am., Washington, 1983-86, vis. asst. prof., 1987-93, adj. asst. prof., 1993-96, adj. assoc. prof., 1997—, dir. landscape, arch. studies, 1986-89, dir. landscape studies, 1990—; urban design cons. Techworld, Washington, 1984-86; devel. dir. Tech. 2000 Mus., 1985-86; dir., presenter lectr. series resident assoc. program Smithsonian Instn., Washington, 1982, 83, 85, 87, 89, 98; dir., founder 7th, 8th and 9th Sts. Group Streetscape project, Washington, 1986-89, others; founder Charrette urban design seminar, Washington, Dallas, Alexandria, Va., St. Louis and Cleve., 1982-89; initiator, participant Sarasota (Fla.) Regional Urban Design Assistance R/UDAT Team, 1983, seminar Nat. Gallery Art, Washington, 1984, Nat. Arboretum, 1988, symposia Cath. U. Am., 1987—; invited jury panel, Fulbright Travel Awards, 1997-99; Lambda Alpha Internat. Hon. Soc., 1998—;facilitator/panel North Capital St./Fruxton Circle Charette, 2001; invited panel Japan Triennial Echigo-Tsumari, 1999, 2000; spkr., team leader McMillan Reservoir Charrette, Washington, 1999; apptd. mem. D.C. Downtown Partnership Streetscape subcom., 1989-91, D.C. Interactive Downtown Task Force Streetscape and Traffic subcom., 1996; D.C. Stakeholder Signage Subcommittee, 1997—, D.C. Stakeholder Traffic Subcommittee, 1998, D.C. Stakeholder Streetscape Subcom., 1999; co-founder, co-chmn. Brookland/CUA Neighborhood Improvement Partnership, 1999—; founder, co-dir. symposium. Libr. of Congress, 1995; dir. symposium D.C. Interagy. Task Force Seminar on Streetscape and Signage, 1995; dir., mem. steering com. numerous confs. in field; invited participant Congress for New Urbanism, 1994—; program spkr. U.S. Embassy Amman, Jordan, 1992, ICOMOS, 1992, 93, U. Va., 1993, Ecole Nationale Superieure du Paysage/Versailles, France, 1993, U. Osaka, Japan, 1993, 95, 96, 97 Tokyo Inst. Tech. U., 1993, Chiba Inst. Tech., Japan, 1998, SUNY, Buffalo, 1994, U. Colo., Denver, 1994, Mayors Inst. on City Design, St. Louis, 1994, Tongji U., Shanghai, China, 1995, 97, Tsinghua U., China, 1995, 98; jury critic Cath. U. Am., 1980-99, U. Puerto Rico, U. Va., 1993, Tsinghua U., China, 1998; instr. ceramics, Bethesda, Md., 1975-76. Author, co-editor: (book) Urban Design: Visions and Reflections, 1991, Capital Visions: Reflections on a Decade of Urban Design Charrettes and a Look Ahead, 1995, (map and text) Visions of Washington: Composite Plan of Urban Interventions, 1991; author: D.C. Streetscape & Signage Resource Manual, 1996; co-author: Retrospective Catalogue: Collegiate Exhibition for Excellence in Urban Design, 1997, Washington In Maps, 2002; contbr. articles to profl. jours.; landscape design featured in major landscape archtl. jours. in US and Japan, 1998, 2000; featured nationally in Assoc. Press articles on fragrant landscapes, 1999; curator, author exhbn. and catalogue on Washington Maps Sumner Sch. Mus., 1987, 92, U. Md., 1993, Embassy of France, 1993, SUNY Buffalo, 1994, U. Calif., Berkeley, 1994, U. Toronto, Can., 1995; curator, author exhbn. ACSA Ann. Meeting, Montreal, 1994; co-curator, author exhbn. and catalogue Octagon Mus., 1987; project dir., curator Paris-Washington Exhbn., 1987—; exhibitor, installation, Tokyo, Japan, 1997; recent residential and other landscape projects include Univ. Club. Wash., 1997-98, Salle de Fete Site Plan, Francheville, France, 1993, Kahn Residence, Arlington, Va., 1993-94, Marks Residence, Silver Spring, Md., 1993, Nesse, Lewis Residence, Silver Spring, 1992, Friedman Residence, Washington, 1992, Drysdale Hershon Residence, Washington, 1991, Miller Residence, Washington, 1990—, Sexton Residence, Kenwood, Chevy Chase, Md., 1990, 95, Romano Residence, Fairfax Station, Va., 1989, Mushinski Residence, Bethesda, Md., 1989, 8th St. Mall Washington, 1987-88, Mishkin, Jennis Residence, Bethesda, 1988, Cramer Residence, Bethesda, 1988; recent home design and renovations include Sexton Residence, Chevy Chase, 1994, Miller Jayapal Residence, San Francisco, 1993, Marks Residence, Silver Spring, 1993, Miller Residence, 1991, Washington, Mishkin Jennis Residence, Bethesda, 1988. Co-chmn. stamp com. Bicentennial Washington, 1987-90; founding mem. Washington Network, 1986-89; mem. adv. panel L'Enfant Forum, Washington, 1987-90, Hist. Georgetown Found., 1989-90; trustee John J. Sexton Fund for Local Govt. Studies, Sch. Pub. Affairs, U. Md., College Park, 1983-93; dir., founder Pub.-Pvt. Partnership and Univ. Scholarship Outreach Inner-City H.S. Program, Cath. U. Am., Washington Pub. Schs., 1985—; dir., founder Intern Exch. Program Landscape Architecture France-U.S.A., Cath. U. Am., U. Va., Friends of Vieilles Maisons Francaises, 1991-98, study-travel Asia Arch./Landscape Scholarship Fund, 1998—; dir., co-founder Intern Exch. Program Landscape Architecture China-U.S.A., Cath. U. Am., Tongji U., Shanghai, 1995—, Osaka U., Japan, 1996—, Chiba Inst. Tech., Japan, 1998-99; historic landscape com. U.S./Internat. Coun. on Monuments and Sites, 1990—; active Cultural Alliance Greater Washington, Nat. Trust Historic Preservation, Ikebana Internat., His. Soc. Washington, Nat. Mus. for Bldg. Arts; alumni coun. Sch. Architecture and Planning, Cath. U. Am., 1986—; mem. com. on environment Congress for New Urbanism, 1994—. Travel rsch. grantee Cath. U. Am., 1978, 79; grantee Govt. France, 1985, NEA (2), 1982, 92; recipient Program Devel. award Cath. U. Am., 1978. Mem. AIA (assoc., nat., regional and urban design exhbn. and panel, chmn. edn. subcom. 1987-96, sec. edn. subcom. 1997—, chmn., founder data base on design edn. and urban design, chmn. edn. conf. 1983, chmn. newsletter 1993, edn. com. D.C. chpt. 1981-83, Charrette co-chmn., program devel. award 1982), Assn. Collegiate Schs. Architecture (spkr. N.E. region conf. 1989, spkr. ann. meeting 1991-92, chmn. panel 1989—, chair Collegiate Exhbn. for Excellence in Urban Design 1990—, author conf. procs. 1991-93, Citation for Urban Design 1993, 95), Am. Soc. Landscape Architects (Potomac chpt. strategic planning com. 1994-95), Am. Planning Assn., U.S.-Internat. Coun. on Monuments and Sites (program spkr. 1987, 92, 93, hist. landscapes com.), Friends Vieilles Maisons Francaises (program spkr. 1987, 92), Friends of Vieilles Maisons Francaises, Congress for New Urbanism (com. on environment 1994—), Alpha Epsilon Phi (pres. D.C. alumni 1965-67). Avocations: photography, Japanese flower arranging, tennis, jogging. Home: 3820 52nd St NW Washington DC 20016-1924

MILLER, IRVING FRANKLIN, chemical engineering educator, biomedical engineering educator, academic administrator; b. N.Y.C., Sept. 27, 1934; s. Sol and Gertrude (Rochkind) M.; m. Baila Hannah Milner, Jan. 28, 1962; children: Eugenia Lynne, Jonathan Mark. BS in Chem. Engring., NYU, 1955; MS, Purdue U., 1956; PhD, U. Mich., 1960. Rsch. scientist United Aircraft Corp., Hartford, 1959-61; from asst. prof. to prof., head chem. engring. Poly. Inst. Bklyn., 1961-72; prof. bioengring., head bioengring. program U. Ill., Chgo., 1973-79, acting head sys. engring. dept., 1978-79, assoc. vice chancellor rsch., dean Grad. Coll., 1979-85, prof. chem. engring., head chem. engring., 1986-95, dir. Ctr. for Advanced Edn. and Rsch., 1989-90, dir. Office of Spl. Projects, 1990-92, dir. bioengring. program, 1992-95; dean Coll. Engring. U. Akron, Ohio, 1995-98, prof. biomed. engring., 1998-2000; dir. tech. con. svc. BioTechPlex Corp., 2002—. Cons. to industry; cons. NAS, NIH; dir. distance learning programs Ohio Aerospace Inst., 1998—2000. Editor: Electrochemical Bioscience and Bioengineering, 1973; contbr. articles profl. jours. Mem. AIChE, AAAS, Am. Chem. Soc., Biomed. Engring. Soc., N.Y. Acad Scis. Home: 1746 N Larrabee St Chicago IL 60614-5634 E-mail: ifmiller@uic.edu.

MILLER, ISADORE, television executive, consultant; b. Montreal, Quebec, Can. s. Michael S. and Mollie M.; m. Lilly, Nov. 10, 1952; children: Laura Lee, Elise Wendy Debra. BBA, CCNY, 1952, MBA, 1957; LLB, LaSalle Extension U., 1970. Various positions CBS, N.Y.C., 1954-70; mgr. spl. projects Entertainment div. CBS, 1970-72, assoc. dir. bus. affairs, 1972-77, dir. children's programming, 1977-80; mgr. prodn. ctr. Operations div. CBS, 1980-81; v.p. bus. adminstrn. D'Arcy Masius Benton & Bowles, 1981-88; sr. v.p. Riverview Prodns. Inc. subs. D'Arcy Masius Benton & Bowles, 1983-88. Bd. dirs. Riverview Prodns., Inc., 1985-88; cons. various orgns. N.Y.C and L.A., 1980-88; pres. Izzy Miller Enterprises, Inc., 1988-95, Millennium III, Inc., 1991-93; pres., bd. dirs. Prime Life Network, 1995. Vol. Jewish Family Service of No. Middlesex County, Edison, N.J., 1983— (cert. of Appreciation for Outstanding and Dedicated Service 1986). Served with U.S. Army, 1952-54, Korea. Mem. NATAS (gov. N.Y. chpt. 1984, 91—, trustee 1985-90, nat. treas. 1986-90, 94-96, 1st v.p. 1987-88, head nat. fin. com., nat. award com.), Internat. Radio and TV Soc., B'nai B'rith, Am. Jewish Congress, Mus. Broadcasting, Zimerlu Mus. Democrat. Jewish. Home: 411 Genista Plz # A Jamesburg NJ 08831-3910

MILLER, JACK (JACK MILLER), publishing company executive; b. Middletown, Ohio, Sept. 11, 1931; s. John William and Helena Bernice (Pendleton) M.; m. Barbara Elaine Stutsman, Jan. 19, 1952; children: Stacy Lynn, John Dewey, Tamara Leigh, Mark Douglas, Matthew Scott, Delano Mitchell. BS in Civil Engring., Wash. State U., Pullman, 1958. Sales engr. Armco Steel Corp., Middletown, Ohio, 1958-64; v.p., dir. mktg. Mes-Tex, Houston, 1964-67, Kirby Bldg. Sys., Houston, 1967-69; pres. Group Comm., Inc., 1969-81, chmn. bd. dirs., 1981—. Lectr. in field; condr. seminars in field. Author: Selling Building Systems, 1970, Profitable Management Techniques for Contractors, 1973, A Professional Approach to Marketing for the Construction Industry, 1977, Design/Build, Build/Lease, and Financing Building Projects, 1977, Human Stress ... How to Turn It Into Success, 1978, Advanced Negotiating Skills and Strategies, 1979, The Jack Miller Reports, 1985, Rules You Should Know About Investing, 1988, 16 Opportunities in Build/Lease, 1988, Rules You Should Know About Motivation, 1988, Rules You Should Know to be a Better Manager, 1988, Rules You Should Know About Investing in Real Estate, 1988, Rules You Should Know About Time Management and Speed Reading/Speed Learning, 1988, The Important Steps that Take You to Health, Wealth and Happiness, 1992, Rules You Should Know Before You Build Your Important Project, 1993, Total Quality Management for the Construction Industry, 1993, Guide Manual for a Win/Win Negotiator, 1999. Elder Pines Presbyn. Ch., Houston, 1996—. With USAF, 1950-54. Mem. ASCE, Associated Builders and Contractors, Associated Gen. Contractors, Am. Soc. for Quality, The Jack Miller Network, Tau Beta Pi, Phi Kappa Phi. Republican. Presbyterian. Office: Group Comm 10417 Rockley Rd Houston TX 77099-3565

MILLER, JACK DAVID R. radiologist, physician, educator; b. Johannesburg, South Africa, Apr. 15, 1930; s. Harold Lewis and Inez (Behrman) M.; m. Miriam Sheckter, Dec., 1988. B.Sc., M.B., Ch.B., U. Witwatersrand, Johannesburg, 1956. Diplomate: Am. Bd. Radiology. Intern Coronation Hosp., Johannesburg, 1957-58; resident in radiology Passavant Meml. Hosp., Chgo., 1959-62, Wesley Meml. Hosp., Chgo., 1959-62; fellow in radiology Northwestern U. Med. Sch., 1962-63; chmn. dept. radiology U. Hosp., Edmonton, Alta., Can., 1971-83; prof. emeritus radiology U. Alta., 1997—. Clin. prof. radiology U. Alta., 1971— Fellow Royal Coll. Physicians Can., Am. Coll. Radiology. Office: U Alberta Dept Radiology Edmonton AB Canada

MILLER, JACQUELINE ELAINE, accountant; b. Rochester, N.Y., Sept. 9, 1963; d. Lawrence Michael and Evelyn Ann Wager; m. Daniel James Miller, June 25, 1986; children: Daniel Joseph, Mark Gregory. BS, Rochester Inst. of Tech., 1985. CPA, N.Y. Supr. Pinto, Mucenski and Watson, Potsdam, N.Y., 1986—. Mem. N.Y. Soc CPAs. Avocations: playing accordion, skiing. Office: 42 Market St Potsdam NY 13676-1747

MILLER, JACQUELINE WINSLOW, library director; b. N.Y.C., Apr. 15, 1935; d. Lynward Roosevelt and Sarah Ellen (Grevious) W.; 1 child, Percy Scott. BA, Morgan State Coll., 1957; MLS, Pratt Inst., 1960; grad. profl. seminar, U. Md., 1973. Cert. profl. librarian. With Bklyn. Pub. Libr., 1957-68; head extension svcs. New Rochelle (N.Y.) Pub. Libr., 1969-70; br. adminstr. Grinton Will Yonkers (N.Y.) Pub. Libr., 1970-75; dir. Yonkers Pub. Libr., 1975-96. Mem. adj. faculty grad. libr. studies Queens Coll., CUNY, 1989, 90. Mem. commr.'s com. Statewide Libr. Devel., Albany, N.Y., 1980; mem. N.Y. Gov.'s Comm. on Librs., 190, 91; bd. dirs. Community Planning Coun., Yonkers, N.Y., 1987; mem. Yonkers Black Women's Polit. Caucus, 1987; pres. bd. Literacy Vols. of Westchester County, 1991-92; mem. fair campaign practices com. LWV, 1996—. Recipient Yonkers Citizen award Ch. of Our Saviour, 1980, 2d Ann. Mae Morgan Robinson award Yonkers chpt. Westchester Black Women's Polit. Caucus, 1992, 3d Ann. Equality Day award City of Yonkers, 1992, African-Am. Heritage 1st award YWCA, 1994; named Outstanding Profl. Woman Nat. Assn. Negro Bus. and Profl. Women's Clubs Inc., 1981. Mem. ALA (councilor 1987-91), N.Y. State Libr. Assn., Pub. Libr. Dirs. Assn. (exec. bd.), N.Y. State Pub. Libr. Dirs. Assn., Westchester Libr. Assn., Yonkers C. of C. (bd. dirs. 1992-95), Rotary (Yonkers chpt.).

MILLER, JAMES ALFRED LOCKE, JR. (JIM MILLER), aircraft maintenance technician; b. Freeport, N.Y., June 6, 1943; s. James Alfred Locke and Leila James (Wootten) M. AA in Paralegal Tech., Ctrl. Carolina Tech. Inst., 1976; AA in Aviation Maintenance, Wayne C.C., 1981; BS in Aviation Mgmt., So. Ill. U., Carbondale, 1989. Lic. aircraft mech. FAA. Ramp serviceman Eastern Air Lines, Raleigh-Durham, N.C., 1965-71; U.S. Customs warehouse officer R.J. Reynolds Tobacco Co., Winston-Salem; seaman/helmsman USNS Mizar T-AGOR 11, 1972; mech. Naval Air Depot, Cherry Point, N.C., 1981-87, Piedmont Airlines, Winston-Salem, 1987; FAA/FCC tech. US Air, N.C., 1987-98; mechanic US Airways/Charlotte Airport, 1998—. Mem. SAR, Assn. Former Intelligence Officers, Profl. Aviation Maintenance Assn., Internat. Assn. Machinist and Aerospace Workers, N.C. A. Philip Randolph Inst., Soc. Indsl. Archaeology, U.S. Horse Cavalry Assn. Republican. Episcopalian. Avocations: genealogy, history. Home: 11427 Fox Hill Dr Charlotte NC 28269-3166 Office: US Airways 5535 Wilkinson Blvd Charlotte NC 28208-5451 E-mail: jalmillerjr@worldnet.att.net.

MILLER, JAMES CLIFFORD, III, economist; b. Atlanta, June 25, 1942; s. James Clifford and Annie (Moseley) M.; m. Demaris Humphries, Dec. 22, 1961; children: Katrina Demaris, John Felix, Sabrina Louise. BBA, U. Ga., 1964; PhD in Econs., U. Va., 1969; LLD (hon.), U. of Pacific, 1987; PhD (hon.), Kennesaw Coll., 1988. Asst. prof. Ga. State U., Atlanta, 1968-69; economist U.S. Dept. Transp., Washington, 1969-72; assoc. prof. econs. Tex. A&M U., College Station, 1972-74; economist U.S. Coun. Econ. Advs., Washington, 1974-75; asst. dir. U.S. Council Wage and Price Stability, 1975-77; resident scholar Am. Enterprise Inst., 1977-81; adminstr. Office Info. and Regulatory Affairs, Office Mgmt. and Budget and exec. dir. Presdl. Task Force on Regulatory Relief, Washington, 1981; chmn. FTC, 1981-85; dir. Office Mgmt. and Budget, 1985-88; disting. fellow, chmn., counsellor Citizens for a Sound Economy, 1988—2002; disting. fellow Ctr. for Study of Pub. Choice George Mason U., 1988—2002. Pres., chmn. bd. Econ. Impact Analysts, Inc., 1978-2002; chmn. Cap Analysis Group, 2002-; chmn. The Capital Group of Howrey Simon Arnold & White, 2002-. Author: Why the Draft?: The Case for a Volunteer Army, 1968, Economic Regulation of Domestic Air Transport: Theory and Policy, 1974, Perspectives on Federal Transportation Policy, 1975, Benefit-Cost Analyses of Social Regulation: Case Studies from the Council on Wage and Price Stability, 1979, Reforming Regulation, 1980, The Economist as Reformer, 1989, Fix the U.S. Budget: Urgings of an "Abominable No-Man," 1994, Monopoly Politics, 1999. Candidate for Rep. nomination for U.S. Senate for Va., 1994, 96. Thomas Jefferson fellow, 1965-66, DuPont fellow, 1966-67, Ford Found. fellow, 1967-68. Mem. Am. Econ. Assn., Pub. Choice Soc., So. Econ. Assn. (exec. com. 1980-81, v.p. 1990-91), Adminstrv. Conf. U.S. (vice chmn. 1987-88). Republican. Presbyterian. Office: The Cap Grp 1299 Pennsylvania NW Ste 300 Washington DC 20004 E-mail: millerj@howrey.com.

MILLER, JAMES EDWARD, computer scientist, educator; b. Lafayette, La., Mar. 21, 1940; s. Edward Gustave and Orpha Marie (DeVilbis) M.; m. Diane Moon, June 6, 1964; children: Deborah Elaine, Michael Edward. BS, U. La., Lafayette, 1961, PhD, 1972; MS, Auburn U., 1964. Systems engr. IBM, Birmingham, Ala., 1965-68; asst. prof. U. West Fla., Pensacola, 1968-70, chmn. systems sci., 1972-86; grad. rschr. U. La., Lafayette, 1970-72; computer systems analyst EPA, Washington, 1979; prof., chmn. computer sci. and stats. U. So. Miss., Hattiesburg, 1986-92, prof., 1992—; program evaluator Computer Sci. Accreditation Commn., 1986-92. Cons., lectr. in field; co-dir. NASA/Am. Soc. Engring. Edn. Faculty Fellowship Program-Stennis Space Flight Ctr., 1990—. Author numerous articles for tech. publs. Mem. Computer Soc. of IEEE, Assn. Computing Machinery (editor Computer Sci. Edn. spl. interest group bull. 1982-97), Data Processing Mgmt. Assn. (dir. edn. spl. interest group 1985-86), Internat. Assn. Math. and Computer Modeling. Democrat. Methodist. Office: U So Miss Computer Sci & Stat PO Box 5106 Hattiesburg MS 39406-1000 E-mail: jim.miller@usm.edu.

MILLER, JAMES GEGAN, research scientist, physics educator; b. St. Louis, Nov. 11, 1942; s. Francis John and Elizabeth Ann (Caul) M.; m. Judith Anne Kelvin, Apr. 23, 1966; 1 child, Douglas Ryan. AB, St. Louis U., 1964; MA, Washington U., 1966, PhD, 1969. Asst. prof. physics Washington U., St. Louis, 1970-72, assoc. prof., 1972-77, prof. physics, 1977—, dir. lab. for ultrasonics, 1987—, rsch. asst. prof. medicine, 1976-81, rsch. assoc. prof. medicine, 1981-88, rsch. prof. medicine, 1988-2000, prof. biomed. engring., 1998—, Albert Gordon Hill prof. physics, 1999—, prof. medicine, 2000—. Contbr. articles to profl. jours.; patentee in field. Recipient I-R 100 award Indsl. Research Devel. Mag., 1974, 78; NIH, NASA grantee, NIH Merit Award, 1998. Fellow IEEE (sr., gov. com. Ultrasonics, Ferroelectrics and Frequency Control Soc. 1978-80,86-88, 92-94), Am. Inst. Ultrasound in Medicine, Acoustical Soc. Am., Am. Inst. Med. and Biol. Engring.; mem. Am. Phys. Soc., Sigma Xi (nat. lectr. 1981-82). Home: 444 Edgewood Dr Saint Louis MO 63105-2016 Office: PO Box 1105 Saint Louis MO 63188-1105

MILLER, JAMES MCCALMONT, pediatrician; b. Springfield, Mass., Sept. 25, 1938; s. John Haynes and Josephine (Darrah) M.; m. Jane Rose, July 7, 1975; children: John, Charlotte, Willard. AB, Hamilton Coll., 1960; MD, Cornell U., 1964. Resident U. Colo. Med. Ctr., Denver, 1964-67; staff pediatrician Kaiser Permanente Med. Ctr., Walnut Creek, Calif., 1969-87, chief pediatrician, 1971-82, Pleasanton, 1982-87; staff pediatrician Appalachian Regional Health, Hazard, Ky., 1987-92, N.W. Pediat. Ctr., Centralia, Wash., 1992—. Clin. assoc. U. N.Mex., Albuquerque, 1967-69; instr. U. Calif., San Francisco, 1969-87, U. Ky., Lexington, 1988-92. With U.S. Army, 1967-69. Fellow Am. Acad. Pediat.; mem. Wash. State Med. Assn. Office: Northwest Pediatric Ctr 908 S Scheuber Rd Centralia WA 98531-9027 E-mail: jmiller@localaccess.com.

MILLER, JAMES MONROE, lawyer; b. Owensboro, Ky., Apr. 20, 1948; s. James Rufus and Tommie (Melton) M.; m. Patricia Kirkpatrick, Nov. 28, 1975; children: Marian Elizabeth, James Graham. Student, George Washington U., 1966-67; BE, U. Ky., 1970, JD, 1973. Bar: Ky. 1973, U.S. Dist. Ct. Ky. 1973, U.S. Ct. Appeals (6th cir.) 1976, U.S. Supreme Ct. 1976. Law clk. to chief judge U.S. Dist. Ct. (we. dist.) Ky., Louisville and Owensboro, 1973-74; mng. ptnr. Sullivan, Mountjoy, Stainback & Miller, P.S.C., Owensboro, 1974—. Mem. Leadership Ky., 1988, Leadership Owensboro, 1986; bd. dirs. Leadership Ky. Found., 2002--; sec., bd. dirs. Wendell Foster Ctr. Endowment Found., Inc., Owensboro; sec. Owensboro-Daviess County Indsl. Found., Inc. Mem. ABA, Ky. Bar Assn. (chmn. Law Day/Spkrs. Bur. com. 1989-91), Daviess County Bar Assn., Ky. Coun. on Higher Edn. (chmn. programs com. 1991-93, chmn. 1993-96), Coun. Postsecondary Edn., Gov.'s Higher Edn. Rev. Commn. (chmn. 1993), Gov.'s Task Force on Tchr. Edn. Democrat. Methodist. Avocations: fishing, hunting, hiking, golf, skiing. Home: 1920 Sheridan Pl Owensboro KY 42301-4525 Office: Sullivan Mountjoy Stainback & Miller PSC PO Box 727 100 Saint Ann St Owensboro KY 42303-4144

MILLER, JAMES RICHARD, public health physician; b. North Adams, Mass., Oct. 11, 1949; s. Joseph Michael and Vera Joan Miller; m. Shelagh Marie Clancy, 1984 (div. 1998); children: Emily, Alexander. AB, Colgate U., 1974; MPH, Tulane U., 1975; MD, SUNY, Buffalo, 1979. Diplomate Am. Bd. Preventive Medicine. Physician, dir. Mid-Ohio Valley Health Dept., Parkersburg, W.Va., 1983-85; commr. of health Onondaga County Health Dept., Syracuse, N.Y., 1985-95; dir. parasitic disease surveillance N.Y.C. Depts. Health and Environ. Protection, 1995-2000; coord. vector borne disease surveillance and control N.Y.C. Dept. Health, 2000—; mem. indoor air quality task force U.S. EPA Region 2, NY, 2002; mem. Lower Manhattan Air Quality Task Force, N.Y.C., 2002—. Mem. working group on health care provider outreach and edn. Nat. Drinking Water Adv. Coun., Washington, 1998-99; chair residency adv. com., gen. preventive medicine N.Y.C. Dept. Health, 1996-99; clin. asst. prof. dept. preventive medicine SUNY Health Sci. Ctr., Syracise, 1986-95. Contbr. articles to profl. jours. Vol., Peace Corps, Lomé, Togo, 1971-72. Mem. APHA, Am. Water Works Assn., Am. Mosquito Control Assn., Phi Beta Kappa. Avocations: family history, map collecting. Office: NYC Dept Health and Mental Hygiene 125 Worth St Rm 326 New York NY 10013-4006 E-mail: jmiller@health.nyc.gov.

MILLER, J(AMES) ROBERT, chemistry educator; b. Milford, Nebr., July 2, 1922; s. Chris J. and Ruth M. (McClure) M.; m. Jean T. MacArthur; children: Robert, James, Susan, David, Stephen, Sarah. BS, Iowa State U., 1943; PhD, Syracuse U., 1950; DSc (hon.), Hartwick Coll., 1998. Jr. rsch. chemist Parke, Davis & Co., Detroit, 1943-47; asst. prof., then assoc. prof. chemistry Hartwick Coll., Oneonta, N.Y., 1950-53, prof. chemistry, 1954-84, chmn. dept. chemistry, 1952-66, prof. emeritus, 1985—. Lab. cons. Fox Hosp., Oneonta, 1958-59. Contbr. rsch. articles to profl. jours. Mem. Am. Chem. Soc., Am. Ornithol. Union, Cooper Ornithol. Soc., Wilson Ornithol. Soc., Caribbean Ornithol. Soc., Assn. Field Ornithologists. Home: 636 County Highway 35 Maryland NY 12116-1915

MILLER, JAMES RUMRILL, III, finance educator; b. Phila., Dec. 21, 1937; s. James Rumrill and Elizabeth Pleasants (King) M.; m. Bettie M. Studer, May 1, 1989; children from previous marriage: Elizabeth, Katharine, Kerry. AB, Princeton U., 1959; MBA (Woodrow Wilson fellow), Harvard U., 1962; PhD, M.I.T., 1966. Sys. analyst MITRE Corp., Bedford, Mass., 1962-67; asst. prof. bus. adminstrn. Stanford (Calif.) U., 1967-69, assoc. prof., 1970-73, prof., from 1973; Walter and Elise Haas prof. bus. adminstrn. Stanford U., 1977-97, assoc. dean Bus. Sch., 1974-76, Walter and Elise Haas prof. bus. adminstrn. emeritus, 1997—. Cons. in field. Author: Professional Decision Making, 1970; contbr. numerous articles to profl. jours. Mem. Phi Beta Kappa. Republican. Episcopalian. Office: PO Box 169 Chapman AL 36015-0169 E-mail: mdmsinc@aol.com.

MILLER, JAMES VINCE, university president; b. Waynetown, Ind., July 16, 1920; s. J. Vince and Hazel B. (Spore) M.; m. Mildred Mae Hockersmith, June 13, 1943; children: Maryllyn Jean, Rachel Katherine. BA in Philosophy and English, U. Indpls., 1942; M.Div. in History and Lit., United Sem., Dayton, Ohio, 1945; postgrad., Earlham Coll., 1945-46; PhD in Philosophy, Boston U., 1955; LL.D. (hon.), Otterbein Coll., 1971, U. Indpls., 1979. Ordained to ministry Evang. United Brethren Ch., 1945; pastor Greensfork, Ind., 1944-46, Stow, Mass., 1946-48; faculty dept. philosophy and religion Bates Coll., Lewiston, Maine, 1950-64, prof., 1960-64, chmn. dept., 1958-64; acad. dean Otterbein Coll., Westerville, Ohio, 1964-68, v.p. for acad. affairs, acad. dean, 1968-71; pres. Pacific U., Forest Grove, Oreg., 1971-83, pres. emeritus, 1983—; pres. Nat. Coll. of Naturopathic Medicine, Portland, 1989-93, pres. emeritus, 1993—. Adj. prof. Union Grad. Sch., 1970-78, San Francisco Theol. Sem., 1979-86; chmn. N.W. Assn. Pvt. Colls. and Univs., 1974-76; treas. Oreg. Ind. Coll. Assn., 1974-75, 76-78, chmn., 1978-79; adv. com. Oreg. Ednl. Coordinating Commn., 1976-79; chmn. council for higher edn. United Ch. Bd. Homeland Missions, 1975-76; former mem. adv. com. Gov.'s Listening Post; former mem. spl. com. on future of edn. in Oreg., Oreg. Ednl. Coordinating Commn.; mem. Oreg. Bd. Optometry, 1988-92. Mem.: Rotary. Methodist. Address: 1633 Mowry Sq Richland WA 99352-2612

MILLER, JANE ANDREWS, accountant; b. Nashville, Aug. 14, 1952; d. Joseph Raymond Andrews and Allison (Bartlett) Fang; m. Thomas C. Heselton, June 22, 1970 (div. 1978); 1 child, Elizabeth Lyn; m. Keith Evan Miller, Apr. 14, 1984. Degree in Bus. Typing and Computers, Fairfax (Va.) Bus. Sch., 1974. Cert. notary public. Adminstrv. asst. T.J. Fannon & Sons, Alexandria, Va., 1973-79; distbn. clk., adminstrv. asst. U.S. Post Office, Merrifield, 1980-83; acct., sec., treas. Aux. Electric Power Co., Fairfax, 1983—. Pvt. practice, investment counselor, Fairfax; sec., treas. AEPCO, Inc., K & J, Inc., 1990—. Mem. Friends of Calypso; assoc. mem. Smithsonian Instn.; v.p. Grand Masters Bowling League, 1994-95; founder Millers Doubles League, 1995, sec., 1995-96; founder Ebonite Open; founder Scotch Doubles Tournament, 1999; sec. Mels Diner League, 1999—, pres. Mels Diner Summer League, 1999—. Mem. Millers Doubles (sec. 1996-97), Fla. State 600 Club, Mels Diner League (sec. 1999—, pres. summer league 1999-2000, tournament dir.), Monday Doubles (sec. 2001—). Republican. Avocations: gardening, music, interior design, drama, bowling.

MILLER, JANEL HOWELL, psychologist; b. Boone, N.C., May 18, 1947; d. John Estle and Grace Louise (Hemberger) Howell; m. C. Rick Miller, Nov. 24, 1968; children: Kimberly, Brian, Audrey, Rachel. BA, DePauw U., 1969; postgrad., Rice U., 1969; MA, U. Houston, 1972; PhD, Tex. A&M U., 1979. Lic. clin. psychologist, sch. psychologist, Tex. Assoc. sch. psychologist Houston Ind. Sch. Dist., 1971-74; rsch. psychologist VA Hosp., Houston, 1972; assoc. sch. psychologist Clear Creek (Tex.) Ind. Sch. Dist., 1974-76; instr. psychology, counseling psychology intern Tex. A&M U., 1976-77; clin. psychology intern VA Hosp., Houston, 1977-78; coord. psychol. svcs. Clear Creek Ind. Sch. Dist., 1978-81, assoc. dir. psychol. svcs., 1981-82; pvt. practice Houston, 1982—. Faculty U. Houston-Clear Lake, 1984—; adolescent suicide cons., 1984—. DePauw U. Alumni scholar, 1965-69; NIMH fellow U. Houston, 1970-71. Mem. APA, Am. Assn. Marriage and Family Therapists, Soc. for Personality Assessment, Am. Coll. Forensic Examiners, Internat. Rorschach Soc., Tex. Psychol. Assn., Tex. Assn. Marriage and Family Therapists, Houston Psychol. Assn. (media rep. 1984-85), Houston Assn. Marriage and Family Therapists. Home: 806 Walbrook Dr Houston TX 77062-4030 Office: 16854 Royal Crest Dr Houston TX 77058-2529 E-mail: shrinkskate@sbcglobal.net.

MILLER, JANISE LUEVENIA MONICA, lawyer; b. Atlanta, Dec. 25, 1956; d. James Thomas and Vera Luevenia (Brown) M.; 1 child, Brandyn Matthew Cooper. BA, Spalding U., 1976; JD, John Marshall Law Sch., 1979. Bar: Ga. 1982, U.S. Ct. Appeals (11th cir.) 1989. Mental health law specialist Ga. Legal Svcs., Atlanta, 1987-88; atty., paralegal Rogers & Sparks, 1980-82; staff counsel Ga. Dept. Med. Assistance, 1982-83; assoc. atty. Cuffie, Mitchell & Assocs., 1983-84, Cuffie & Assocs., Atlanta, 1984-85; pvt. practice, 1985-86; of counsel Albert A. Mitchell & Assocs., 1987-92, A.A. Mitchell & Assocs., Atlanta, 1987-92; pvt. practice, 1993—. Judge pro hac vice Atlanta Mcpl. Ct. 1989-91. Assoc. editor Nexus, 1980. Chairperson, pres. United Schleroderma Found., Atlanta, 1991-92. Fellow Ga. Bar Found.; mem. State Bar of Ga., Ga. Assn. of Black Women Attys. (Svc. award 1986), Atlanta Bar Assn. (chairperson, seminar com. 1987-88, sec./treas. criminal law sect. 1988-89), Nat. Bar Assn. (chairperson Gertrude Rush Dinner 1992), Gate City Bar Assn. (pres. 1987, editor newsletter 1992). Democrat. Roman Catholic. Avocations: reading, writing, swimming, cooking. Office: PO Box 11229 Atlanta GA 30310-0229 E-mail: JLMMIL@aol.com.

MILLER, JAY ALAN, retired civil rights association executive; b. Cleve., Feb. 8, 1928; s. Herbert Phillip Miller and Ruth Weisbach; m. Joyce Dannen, Feb. 1, 1952 (div. Oct. 1964); children: Joshua, Adam, Rebecca; m. Mary Lou Edelstein Kaplan, Dec. 2, 2000. BSc, U. Ill., 1950. Organizer Amalgamated Clothing Workers, Chgo., 1950-52, bus. agt., edn. dir. Wilkes-Barre, Pa., 1956-61; organizer United Packing House Workers, Chgo., 1952-53; reporter Cleve. Press, 1954-56; peace edn. dir. Am. Friends Svc. Com., Chgo., 1961-65; exec. dir. ACLU of Ill., 1965-71,78-2001, ACLU of No. Calif., San Francisco, 1971-74; assoc. dir. legis. office ACLU, Washington, 1975-78. Pres. AFL-CIO Labor Coun., Hazelton, Pa., 1959-61, mem. trade union delegation to USSR, 1960; chmn. Turn Toward Peace, Chgo., 1962-64; coord. Com. for a Test Ban Treaty, Ill. and Wis., 1962-63; dep. dir. Ill. Rally for Civil Rights, Chgo., 1964. With U.S. Army, 1946-48, PTO.

MILLER, JEAN PATRICIA SALMON, art educator; b. Little Falls, Minn., Sept. 28, 1920; d. Albert Michael and Wilma (Kaestner) Salmon; m. George Fricke Miller, Sept. 8, 1951 (dec. Apr. 1991); children: Victoria Jean, George Laurids. BS, St. Cloud State Tchrs. Coll., 1942; MS, U. Wis., Whitewater, 1976. Lic. cert. secondary English, art, Wis. Tchr. elem. and secondary art Pub. Schs. Sauk Center, Minn., 1943; tchr. secondary art Bd. Edn., Idaho, 1945; tchr. elem. and secondary art Elkhorn (Wis.) Area Schs., 1950-78; tchr. art adult edn. Kenosha Tech. Coll., Elkhorn, Wis., 1969; cooperating tchr., supr. art majors in edn. U. Wis., Whitewater, 1970-77. Coord. Art Train Project, Walworth County. Represented in permanent collections Irwin L. Young Auditorium, U. Wis., Whitewater. Sec. Walworth County Needs of Children and Youth, Williams Bay, Wis., 1956-57; co-chair, sponsor Senate Bill 161-art requirement for h.s. grad., 1988-89. Recipient Grand award painting Walworth County Fair, 1970, 3rd award painting Geneva Lake Art Assn., Lake Geneva, Wis., Acrylic Painting First award Badlants Art Assn., 1994. Mem. Nat. Art Edn. Assn., Wis. Women in Arts, Wis. Art Edn. Assn., Wis. Regional Artists Assn. (co-chmn. Wis. regional art program 1992, 93, corr. sec. 1992—), Walworth County Art Assn. (bd. dirs. 1979-94, pres. 1986-87), Badlands Art Assn., Kiwanis, Elks, Alpha Delta Kappa (pres. Theta chpt. Wis. 1968-70), Delta Kappa Gamma (Iota chpt.). Home and Office: 215 5th St N Richardton ND 58652-7107

MILLER, JEANNE-MARIE ANDERSON (MRS. NATHAN J. MILLER), English language educator, academic administrator; b. Washington, Feb. 18, 1937; d. William and Agnes Catherine (Johns) Anderson m. Nathan John Miller, Oct. 2, 1960. BA, Howard U., 1959, MA, 1963, PhD, 1976. Instr. dept. English Howard U., Washington, 1963-76, asst. prof., 1976-79, assoc. prof., 1979-92, prof., 1992-97, prof. emeritus, 1997—, asst. dir. Inst. Arts and Humanities, 1973-75, asst. acad. planning, office v.p. for acad. affairs, 1976-90. Cons. Am. Studies Assn., 1972-75, Silver Burdett Pub. Co., Nat. Endowment for Humanities, 1978—; adv. bd. D.C. Libr. for Arts, 1973—, John Oliver Killens Writers Guild, 1975—, Afro-Am. Theatre, Balt., 1975—. Editor, Black Theatre Bull., 1977-86; Realism to Ritual: Form and Style in Black Theatre, 1983; assoc. editor Theatre Jour., 1980-81; contbr. articles to profl. jours. Mem. Washington Performing Arts Soc., 1971—, Friends of Sta. WETA-TV, 1971—, Mus. African Art, 1971—, Arena Stage Assocs., 1972—, Washington Opera Guild, 1982—, Wolf Trap Assocs., 1982—, Drama League N.Y., 1995, Shakespeare Theatre, 2001—, Met. Opera Guild, 2002—. Ford Found. fellow, 1970-72, So. Fellowships Fund fellow, 1973-74; Howard U. rsch. grant, 1975-76, 94-97, ACLS grant, 1978-79, NEH grant, 1981-84. Mem.: LWV (D.C. chpt.), MLA, ACLU, AAUP, Folger Shakespeare Libr., Acad. Am. Poets, Am. Theatre and Drama Soc., Studio Mus. Harlem, Nat. Mus. Women in Arts, Nat. Bldg. Mus., Winterthur Guild, Hist. Soc. Washington, D.C. Preservation League, Nat. Trust Historic Preservation, Zora Neale Hurston Soc., Langston Hughes Soc., Ibsen Soc., Friends of Kennedy Ctr. for Performing Arts, Am. Assn. Higher Edn., Coll. Lang. Assn., Common Cause, Am. Assn. Higher Edn., Am. Studies Assn., Coll. English Assn., Nat. Coun. Tchrs. English, Sierra Club, Pi Lambda Theta. Democrat. Episcopalian. Home: 504 24th St NE Washington DC 20002-4818

MILLER, JEFF, congressman; b. Fla., 1959; m. Griswold Vicki Miller; 2 children. BA, U. Fla., 1984. State rep. Dist. I, 1998, 2000; Congressman Fla. Dist. 1, 2002—. Past chmn. Escambia County Legislative Del., 1999—2000. Mem. Fla. Hist. Soc., various areas of C. of C., Elizabeth Chapel United Meth. Ch., Chumuckla; mem. bd. dirs. Santa Rose County United Way; Pregnancy Resource Ctr. Milton Milton; Gulf Coast Coun. Boy Scouts Am.; Fla. FFA Found. Mem.: Coun. Ready Infrastructure, Com. on Rules, Ethics and Elections, Com. on Gen. Govt. Appropriations, Congl. Redistricting Com., Utilities and Telecommunications Com. (chmn.), Com. on Vet. Affairs, Ho. Armed Svcs. Com. Office: Congress 127 Cannon HOB Washington DC 20515-0901*

MILLER, JEFFREY CLARK, lawyer; b. Boston, Aug. 17, 1943; s. Andrew Otterson and Jeanne (White) M.; m. Susanne Jackson, Oct. 23, 1970; children: Gordon, Andrew, Katharine, Eric. BA, Yale U., 1965; JD, Cornell U., 1968. Bar: N.Y. 1970. Assoc. Miller, Montgomery, Spalding & Sogi, N.Y.C., 1968-69; sec. Jamaica Water & Utilities Inc., Greenwich, Conn., 1969-72; assoc. Reid & Priest, N.Y.C., 1972-86, ptnr., 1986-93; asst. gen. coun. Northeast Utilities Svc. Co., Berlin, 1993—. Bd. dirs. Wilson Point Property Owners Assn., Norwalk, Conn., 1972-74, pres., 1988-92; trustee St. Luke's Sch., New Canaan, Conn., 1992—, chmn., 1995-97; sec. Yale U. Class 1965, 1990-2000. Mem. ABA, N.Y. State Bar Assn. (sec. pub. utility com. 1983-87). Home: 1 Valley Rd Norwalk CT 06854-5010 Office: Northeast Utilities Svc Co PO Box 270 Hartford CT 06141-0270 E-mail: millejc@nu.com.

MILLER, JEFFREY DAVID, allergist; b. N.Y.C., Oct. 19, 1947; s. Leonard and Ruth Miller; children: Andrew, Amy. AB cum laude, CUNY, 1967; MD, NYU, 1971. Diplomate Am. Bd. Pediat., Am. Bd. Allergy and Immunology, Nat. Bd. Med. Examiners. Intern in pediat. Bronx (Mcpl.) Hosp. and Albert Einstein Hosp., 1971-72, jr. resident in pediat., 1972-73, jr. resident, 1973-74; fellow in allergy and clin. immunology Roosevelt Hosp., N.Y.C., 1974-76; pvt. practice, Danbury, Conn., 1976—; CEO, Mission: Allergy, Inc. Attending physician Danbury Hosp. Contbr. articles to med. jours.; patentee in field. Fellow Am. Acad. Allergy Immunology, Am. Acad. Pediat; mem. New Eng. Soc. Allergy, Conn. Allergy Soc. (pres. 1995-96), N.Y. Allergy Soc. (sec. 1991-94), Fairfield County Med. Assn., Phi Beta Kappa, Alpha Omega Alpha. Office: Allergy and Asthma Assocs 107 Newtown Rd Danbury CT 06810-4146

MILLER, JEFFREY MICHAEL, architect; b. Washington, Sept. 24, 1943; s. Henry J. and Margaret M. (Paxton) M.; children: Christine, Ellen. BArch, Cath. U., 1969. Registered architect, Md. Architect Richard P. Browne Assoc., Columbia, Md., 1970-74; pres. Jeffrey M. Miller Arch., 1974-75; project mgr. TCSB, Silver Spring, Md., 1975-79, Lockman Assocs., Washington, 1979-83, Mark Beck Assocs., Columbia, 1983-84, CHK Architects, Silver Spring, Md., 1984-87; sr. assoc. Design Collective, Balt., 1987—. With USN, 1963-65. Mem. AIA. Office: Design Collective 100 E Pratt St Fl 14 Baltimore MD 21202-1013 E-mail: jeffmiller@designcollective.com.

MILLER, JENNIFER RENEE, music educator, composer, writer; b. North Little Rock, Ark., June 19, 1960; d. Victor F. Moore Sr. and Clara June Magness-Moore; m. Dale G. Miller, June 21, 1989. Student, Ind. Bapt. Coll. Owner, piano instr. Jennifer Miller Piano Studio, 1987—; owner, composer, arranger, lyricist Signature Songs, Washington, 1992—. Freelance writer Guideposts' Angels on Earth Mag., Family Connection Mag., Pekin, Ill., 1997, Maple Lawn Homes, Eureka, Ill., 1998-99, Meadows Mennonite Retirement Cmty., Chenoa, Ill., 1999—; pianist, organist, dir. children's choir, dir. worship team, songwriter, arranger various chs., Ark., Tenn., Tex., so. and no. Calif., Ill., 1987—; advisor, cons. to new piano tchrs. and songwriters, Washington. Author, composer, arranger, lyricist contemporary Christian songs; contbr. articles to mags. Group piano for pre-kindergarten. Mem. Am. Coll. Musicians-Nat. Guild Piano Tchrs., Ill. State Music Tchrs. Assn., Music Tchrs. Nat., Christian Copyright Licensing Agy., Peoria Area Music Tchrs. Assn. (editor, art dir. 1996—). Avocations: graphic arts, books, cinema. Home: 702 Eldridge St Washington IL 61571-2818 Office: Signature Songs Jennifer Miller Piano Studio 702 Eldridge St Washington IL 61571-2818 E-mail: jenmusic2@insightbb.com.

MILLER, JERRY BRIAN, radio broadcaster; b. Gallipolis, Ohio, Apr. 19, 1961; s. Robert Edward and Joan Avonne (Null) M.; 1 child, Kaitlin Jean. Grad. high sch., Ironton, Ohio. Weekend on-air personality Sta. WGNT, Huntington, W.Va., 1976-79, afternoon on-air personality, 1979-80, morning on-air personality, 1980-86; staff booth announcer Sta. WOWK-TV, 1977-88; morning on-air personality Sta. WKEE, 1986-87, Sta. WAMX-FM, Huntington, 1987-88, host Miller at Midday, 1988; host evening talk show Sta WKRC, Cin., 1988-90; host morning talk show WODJ-FM, Grand Rapids, Mich., 1990-93; promotion dir., afternoon air personality WTCR, Huntington, W.Va., 1993-96; morning air personality WKEE-FM, 1996—. Designer Huntington post card Skyline, 1985. Chmn. Walk-Am. March of Dimes, Huntington, 1982; organizer food collection Clarksburg (W.Va.) flood victims, 1985, local bus. rallies, 1984; active unemployed workers projects, Huntington, 1983; fund raiser Huntington Child Devel. Shelter, 1986—; advisor Huntington area United Way, 1986—. Recipient Key to City of Huntington, 1984, Outstanding Achievement in Media award Tri-State Achievers Club, 1986, Presdl. Thanks from George Bush for Help in Dessert Storm, 1991; named Outstanding West Virginian Gov. Jay Rockefeller, 1984, Best Disc Jockey in Huntington, Huntington Herald Dispatch Readers Poll, 1988; J.B. Miller St. named in his honor, Huntington, 1985; radio show featured in USA Today, People mag., Life, New Woman, Donohue, 1989; named to Huntington Wall Fame, 1991. Republican. Methodist. Avocations: video movie collecting, photography, restoring old radios, swimming, weight lifting. Home: 2731 S 10th St Ironton OH 45638-2758 Office: WKEE-FM 134 4th Ave Huntington WV 25701-1253 E-mail: jbmiller@zoomnet.net.

MILLER, JERRY HUBER, retired university chancellor; b. Salem, Ohio, June 15, 1931; s. Duber Daniel and Ida Claire (Holdereith) M.; m. Margaret A. Setter, 1958; children: Gregory, Joy, Carol, Beth, David. BA, Harvard U., 1953; MDiv., Hamma Sch. Theology, 1957; DD (hon.), Trinity Luth. Sem., 1981. Ordained to ministry Luth. Ch., 1957. Research assoc., intern Cornell U., Ithaca, N.Y., 1955-56; instr. Wittenberg U., Springfield, Ohio, 1956-57; parish pastor Ch. of Good Shepherd, Cin., 1957-62; asst. to pres. Ohio Synod Luth. Ch. Am., 1962-66; sr. campus pastor, dir. campus ministry U. Wis., Madison, 1966-69; regional dir. Nat. Luth. Campus Ministry, 1969-76, exec. dir. Chgo., 1977-81; pres. Calif. Luth. U., Thousand Oaks, 1981-92, chancellor, 1992-94, pres. emeritus, 1994—; ret. Ventura County Maritime Mus., Channel Islands Harbor, Calif., 1993-95. Chmn. Los Robles Bank, Thousand Oaks, 1987-2000; mem. exec. com. Coun. Ind. Colls., Washington, Assn. Ind. Calif. Colls. and Univs., 1981-92, Coun. Luth. Colls., Luth. Ednl. Conf. N.Am., 1977-94; vice chair bd. behavioral sci. State Calif.; bd. dirs. Santa Barbara Bank and Trust. Editor: The Higher Disciplines, 1956; contbr. articles to profl. jours. Bd. dirs. Wittenberg U., Augustana Coll., Rock Island, Ill., United Way, Thousand oaks, Ventura County chpt. ARC, Thousand Oaks, YMCA; chmn. bd. dirs. Los Robles Hosp.; vice chair Stagecoach Inn Mus. Found., 1998—; bd. trustees Ventura County Maritime Mus., 1993—. Named Man of Yr., Salem, 1975, Man of Yr. Conejo Valley, 1999; Siebert Found. fellow, 1975. Mem. Am. Assn. Higher Edn., Council Advancement and Support Edn., Harvard Alumni Assn., Western Coll. Assn. (bd. dirs.), Conejo Valley C. of C. (bd. dirs.), Conejo Symphony Orch. (bd. dirs.), Conejo Valley Hist. Soc. (bd. dirs. 1995—). Clubs: Harvard (Ill., Ohio, Wis., Calif.), YMCA (regional bd. dirs., vice chair 1996-99), Rotary. Avocations: skiing, golfing, hiking, travelling. E-mail: msmjhm@aol.com.

MILLER, JILL LEE, lawyer; b. Framingham, Mass., Aug. 22, 1966; d. Robert F. and Harriet (Leventhal) M. BS, Cornell U., 1988, JD cum laude, 1991; LLM in Taxation, NYU, 1996. Bar: N.Y. 1992, Mass. 1992. Assoc. Stroock & Stroock & Lavan, N.Y.C., 1991-93; ct. intern Surrogates Ct., 1993-94; assoc. Rosenman & Colin, 1994-95, Riker, Danzig, Morristown, NJ, 1995-96; mgr. trusts/estates dept. Morea & Schwartz, N.Y.C., 1996—2002; ptnr. and dept. head of trusts and estate Kostelanetz & Fink, LLP, 2002—. Chair, founder Trusts and Estates Discussion Group, N.Y.C., 1997—. Mem. N.Y. State Bar Assn. (chair subcom. women in the profession 1994-97), Cornell Club, Cornell Law Assn. Avocations: foreign travel, painting, photography, horticulture. Home: 23 Halfmoon Isle Jersey City NJ 07305 Office: Kostelanetz & Fink LLP 530 Fifth Ave New York NY 10036 E-mail: jmiller@KFLaw.com.

MILLER, JILL MARIE, psychoanalyst; b. Denver, Mar. 1, 1953; d. Wilbur C. and Viretta Ann (Shaw) M. BA, U. Denver, 1974, MSW, 1979; grad. child and adolescent psychoanalyst, Anna Freud Ctr., London, 1989; PhD, U. London, 1993; grad. adult psychoanalyst, Denver Psychoanalytic Inst., 1996. Cert. child, adolescent, adult psychoayst Am. Psychoanalytic Assn.; tng. and supervising analyst, Denver Psychoanalytic Inst., 2002—. Clin. social worker Cath. Cmty. Svcs., Denver, 1979-83, Mt. Airy Psychiat. Hosp., Denver, 1983-85; pvt. practice clin. social worker, 1982-85; pvt. practice psychoanalyst, 1991—. Faculty mem. Denver Psychoanalytic Inst., Colo. Ctr. for Psychoanalytic Studies, 1991—; clin. instr. dept. psychiatry U. Colo. Med. Sch., Denver, 1994-98, asst. clin. prof. 1998—. Contbr. to books. Recipient prize for outstanding clin. paper The Anna Freud Ctr., London, 1987, Brandt Steele award The Denver Inst. for Psychoanalysis, 1998; Dorothy Burlingham scholar The Anna Freud Ctr., London, 1989, 90. Mem. Assn. Child Psychoanalysis (bd. mem., councillor 1996-99), Denver Inst. for Psychoanalysis (assoc. dir. child and adolescent tng. 1995-98, dir. 1998—). Avocation: outdoor activities. Office: 240 Saint Paul St Denver CO 80206-5126

MILLER, JILL THOMPSON, sales support; b. Murray, Ky., June 16, 1964; d. Rex Allen and Ann Thompson; m. Kenneth R. Miller Jr., Aug. 8, 1987. BA, William Woods Coll., 1986; MBA, Washington U., St. Louis, 1988. Property mgr. Pantheon Corp., St. Louis, 1987-89; account exec. Lane/Mazzone & Assocs., Paducah, Ky., 1989-91; mem. IS dept. Airgas, Lexington, 1993—. Mng. editor Western Ky. Sr. Sourcebook, 1989; asst. editor Paducah Life, 1989. Area rep. Am.-Scandinavian Internat. Student Exch. program, Lexington, 1990-97. Avocations: reading, movies, crafts, pets, gardening. Office: Airgas 500 Codell Dr Lexington KY 40509-1016 E-mail: jill.miller@airgas.com.

MILLER, JO CAROLYN DENDY, family and marriage counselor, educator; b. Gorman, Tex., Sept. 16, 1942; d. Leonard Lee and Vera Vertie (Robison) Dendy; m. Douglas Terry Barnes, June 1, 1963 (div. June 1975); children: Douglas Alan, Bradley Jason; m. Walton Sansom Miller, Sept. 19, 1982. BA, Tarleton State U., 1964; MEd, U. North State, 1977; PhD, Tex. Woman's U., 1993. Tchr. Mineral Wells (Tex.) High Sch., 1964-65, Weatherford (Tex.) Middle Sch., 1969-74; counselor, instr. psychology Tarrant County Jr. Coll., Hurst, Tex., 1977-82; pvt. practice family and marriage counseling Dallas, 1982—. Author: (with Velma Baker, Jeannene Ward) Becoming: A Human Relations Workbook, 1981. Mem. ACA, Tex. State Bd. Examiners Profl. Counselors, Tex. State Bd. Marriage and Family Therapists, Tex. Counseling Assn., North Ctrl. Tex. Counseling Assn., Dallas Symphony Orch. League, Nat. Coun. Family Rels., Tex. Mental Health Counselors Assn., Internat. Assn. for Marriage and Family Counselors. Methodist. Office: 8222 Douglas Ave Ste 777 Dallas TX 75225-5938

MILLER, JOAN LEFF, artist; b. N.Y.C., Nov. 9, 1930; d. Sydney and Rita (Zion) Leff; m. Alfred Miller; children: Wendy, Paul. BFA, Temple U., 1952. Mem. Graphic Eye Gallery, Port Washington, N.Y., 1975-81, Phoenix Gallery, N.Y.C., 1981-88. Painter: Las Rojas Mexicanas, 1993 (cash award Nat. Assn. Women Artists 1994); Corcoran Gallery, Washington, Palazzo Vecchio, Florence, Italy, Parrish Mus., Southampton, N.Y., others. Tutor N.Y. City Learning Leaders, 1994— Avocations: swimming, kayaking. Home: 1192 Park Ave New York NY 10128-1314 E-mail: joanmillerart@aol.com.

MILLER, JOHN, mechanical engineer; BS in Aerospace Engring., MS in Mech. Engring., U. Md. Project engr. Pratt & Whitney Aircraft Co., West Palm Beach, Fla., 1969—71; from mem. staff to assoc. dir. U.S. Army Rsch. Lab., Adelphi, Minn., 1971—98, assoc. dir. plans, programs & budget, 1998—. Office: US Army Research Laboratory Attn: AMSRL CS EA PA 2800 Powder Mill Rd Adelphi MD 20783-1197*

MILLER, JOHN NELSON, banker; b. Youngstown, Ohio, Sept. 15, 1948; s. W. Frederic and Julia Elizabeth (Lohman) M. MusB in Cello, Westminster Coll., 1970; MBA in Fin., U. Pa., 1974. Asst. br. mgr. Mahoning Nat. Bank, Youngstown, 1970-72; asst. dir. fin. svcs. dept. Mellon Bank N.Am., Pitts., 1974-76; v.p., head cash mgmt. divsn. Md. Nat. Bank, Balt., 1976-78; v.p., mgr. corp. cash mgmt. divsn. N.Y. Bank of Am., N.Y.C., 1978-80; dir. cash mgmt., strategic planning, product mgmt. and tng. Bank of Am. S.F., 1980-81; v.p., global account officer for utilities/telecomm. Bank of Am., N.Y.C., 1981-84, team leader, CFO, corp. payment divsn. large corp. sales, 1984-87, mgr. credit preparation and analysis unit N.Am. divsn., 1987-88; v.p.,eastern region mgr. cash mgmt. divsn. Wells Fargo Bank of N.Y., 1988-90, v.p., mgr. Eastern, Midwestern, Rocky Mt., Pacific & nat., 1990-93; v.p. and group sales mgr. Bank of Am., NT and SA Fgn. Currency Svcs., San Francisco, 1993-94; v.p., regional sales mgr. Bank of Am. Global Payment Svcs., Bank of Am., 1994-99, sr. v.p., 1999—. Lectr. Wharton Grad. Sch., U. Pa., Am. Mgmt. Assn. cash mgmt. seminars, Bank Adminstrn. Inst.; speaker Payment Sys. Inc., Corp. EFT Seminar, Atlanta, Nat. Conf. Treasury Mgmt. Assn.; mem. Corp. Payment Task Force, N.Y.C., Corp. EFT Cost-Benefit Task Force. Chmn. ann. giving program Wharton Grad. Sch., 1977-79; trustee San Francisco Performances, 1993-99. Mem. Wharton Grad. Sch. Alumni Assn., (pres. local club, rep., nat. dir., mem. exec. com.), Bank Adminstrn. Inst. (mem. subcom. interindustry commn.), Am. Nat. Standards Inst. (subcom. interindustry optical scan standards) Cash Mgmt. Inst. (dir.), Omicron Delta Kappa, Mchts. Club Balt., Univ. Club Pitts., Rotary. Office: CA4-706-06-01 1850 Gateway Blvd Concord CA 94520-3282

MILLER, J(OHN) WESLEY, III, lawyer, writer; b. Springfield, Mass., Oct. 3, 1941; s. John Wesley Jr. and Blanche Ethel Miller. AB, Colby Coll., 1963; AM, Harvard U., 1964, JD, 1981. Bar: Mass. 1984, U.S. Dist. Ct. Mass. 1984, U.S. Supreme Ct. 1993. Instr. English Heidelberg Coll., Tiffin, Ohio, 1964-69, U. Wis., 1969-77; real estate broker, 1977-84. Founder Miller-Wilson Family Papers, U. Vt., Madison (Wis.) People's Poster and Propaganda Collection, St. Hist. Soc. Wis. Author: History of Buckingham Junior High School, 1956, The Millers of Roxham, 1958, Symphonic Heritage, 1959, Community Guide to Madison Murals, 1977, Aunt Jennie's Poems, 1986, Blanche and John's Fernbank: A Wilbraham Camping Experience, 2001; founding editor: Hein's Poetry and the Law Series, 1985—; editor: Curiosities and Law of Wills, 1989, Lawyers Alcove, 1990, Famous Divorces, 1991, Legal Laughs, 1993, Coke in Verse, 1999, Law and Lawyers Laid Open, 2002; founding editor: Law Libr. Microform Consortium Arts Law Letters Collection, 1991—; exhibitor A Salue to Street Art, State Hist. Soc. wis., 1974; contbr. Poems of Ambrose Philips, 1969, Oxford English Dictionary, 1995—. Recipient Cmty. Activism award Bay State Objectivist, 1993, 94, 95; fellow Wisdom Hall of Fame, 2000, Samuel Victor Constant fellow, 2001. Mem. MLA, Am. Philol. Assn., Milton Soc., New Eng. Historic Geneal. Soc., Vt. Hist. Soc., Wis. Acad. Scis., Arts and Letters, Pilgrim Soc., Ancient and Hon. Arty. Co., Mayflower Soc., Soc. Colonial Wars, Sons and Daus. of the Victims of Colonial Witch Trials, Mensa, Springfield Renaissance Group. Office: 5 Birchland Ave Springfield MA 01119-2708 *The advancement of learning is my goal. Professionalism is the standard, and nothing else will do.*

MILLER, JOHN ALBERT, university educator, consultant; b. St. Louis County, Mo., Mar. 22, 1939; s. John Adam and Emma D. (Doering) M.; m. Eunice Ann Timm, Aug. 25, 1968; children: Michael, Kristin. AA, St. Paul's Coll., 1958; BA with high honors, Concordia Sr. Coll., 1960; postgrad., Wash. U., St. Louis, 1960-64; MBA, Ind. U., 1971, DBA in Mktg., 1972. Proofreader, editor Concordia Pub. House, St. Louis, 1960-62, periodical sales mgr., 1964-68; asst. prof. Drake U., Des Moines, 1971-74; cons. FTC, Washington, 1974-75; vis. assoc. prof. Ind. U., Bloomington, 1975-77; assoc. prof. U. Colo., Colorado Springs, 1977-79, prof., 1977-86, prof. mktg., resident dean, 1980-84; v.p. market devel. Peak Health Care Inc., 1984-85; dean Valparaiso (Ind.) U., 1986-96, prof. mktg., 1986—. Cons. and rschr. govt. and industry; dir. health maintenance orgn.; bd. dirs. Ind. Acad. Social Scis., 1988-90; adv. bd. N.W. Ind. Small Bus. Devel. Ctr., 1989-91; consulting dean USIA project to form Polish Assn. of Bus. Schs., 1995. Author: Labeling Research The State of the Art, 1978; contbr. articles to profl. jours. Mem. Colorado Springs Symphony Orch. Coun., 1980-86; cons. Citizens Goals of Colorado Springs, 1985-86, Jr. League Colorado Springs, 1981-82; bd. dirs. Christmas in April-Valparaiso, 1991-96, Assn. Luth. Older Adults, 1998—. With U.S. Army, 1962-64. U.S. Steel fellow, 1970-71. Mem. Assn. Consumer Rsch. (chmn. membership 1978-79), Am. Mktg. Assn. (fed. govt. liaison com. 1975-76), Am. Acad. Advt., Ind. Acad. Social Scis. (bd. dirs. 1988-90), Greater Valparaiso C. of C. (accreditation com. 1991, planning com. 1989-92, chair 1992), Am. Assembly Collegiate Schs. Bus. (internat. affairs com. 1991-93, mem. peer rev. team 1994, 96, com. mem., seminar leader, faculty mem., program chair for New Deans seminar and other workshops 1992—), Beta Gamma Sigma, Alpha Iota Delta. Lutheran. Avocations: racquetball, jogging, walking. Home: 1504 Del Vista Dr Valparaiso IN 46385-3322 Office: Valparaiso U Dept Mktg Valparaiso IN 46383

MILLER, JOHN D, literature educator; b. Porthsmouth, Va., 1974; s. William Harvey Miller and Marilyn Ann Carlson. BA English Lit., Va. Commonwealth U., Richmond, VA, 1997; m.a. english lit., Auburn U., Auburn, AL, 2002. Tchg. asst. Auburn U., Auburn, Ala., 2000—02; account exec. Dave I wans & Associates, Norfolk, Va., 1997—2000. Mem.: Nat. Coun. Of Tchr. Of English (assoc.), Am. Assoc.of U. Profess (assoc.). Home: 362 West Magnolia Avenue Apt2 Auburn, AL AL 36832 Personal E-mail: go28go@yahoo.com.

MILLER, JOHN DAVID, manufacturing company executive; b. Utica, N.Y., Mar. 24, 1945; s. David Gordon and Eleanor Katherine (Brant) M., m. Ann Geraldine Johnston, Feb. 25, 1968; children: Shannon, Adra. BSME, Rochester Inst. Tech., 1968. Jr. engr. Pall Corp., Cortland, N.Y., 1968-70; staff engr., 1970-71; group leader Pall Corp., Cortland, N.Y., 1971-76, mgr. filter design, 1976-78, v.p., tech. dir., 1978-86, sr. v.p., dir. R&D, 1986-2000, chief tech. officer, 2000—. Patentee filter equipment. Mem. ASME. Unitarian Universalist. Avocations: song writing, sculpture, rowing, squash. Home: 3945 48th St Long Island City NY 11104-1021 Office: Pall Corp 25 Harbor Park Dr Port Washington NY 11050-4664

MILLER, JOHN E. cardiovascular surgeon; b. Cochranville, Pa., Apr. 25, 1918; s. John Wilbur and Esther Elizabeth (Cunningham) M.; m. Nov. 25, 1945; children:Bradford, Toy, Kim, Garth. BA, Pa. State, 1938; MD, Jefferson Med. Coll., 1942. Diplomate Am. Bd. General Surgery, Am. Bd. Thoracic Surgery. Fellow thoracic surgery U. Mich., Ann Arbor, 1948-50; chief thoracic and vascular surgery Md. Gen. Hosp., Balt., 1950-86, St. Joseph's Hosp., Towson, Md., 1974-86; ret., 1986. Trustee Bon Secours Hosp., Balt., 1988-96. Capt. USAR, 1943-46. Fellow Am. Coll. Surgeons (Md. chpt. pres. 1966-67), Am. Coll. Chest Physicians; mem. AMA, Am. Thoracic Soc., Am. Heart Assn., Am. Lung Assn. (pres.), So. Assn. Thoracic Surgery, Md. Thoracic Soc. (pres. 1965-67), Md. Lung Assn. (pres. 1977-78), Balt. City Med. Soc., Soc. Thoracic Surgeons, Am. Trauma Soc. (founding mem.). Home: 723 Chapel Ridge Rd Lutherville Timonium MD 21093-1807 E-mail: jmi2767980@aol.com.

MILLER, JOHN EDDIE, lawyer; b. Wayne, Mich., Nov. 14, 1945; s. George Hayden and Georgia Irene (Stevenson) M.; m. Nancy Carol Sanders, Jan. 7, 1968; children: Andrea Christine, Matthew Kit. BA, Baylor U., 1967; JD, U. Memphis, 1973; LLM, U. Mo., 1980. Bar: Mo. 1974, U.S. Dist. Ct. (we. dist.) Mo. 1974, Tex. 1982. Asst. prof. Central Mo. State U., Warrensburg, 1973-74; sole practice Sedalia, Mo., 1974-79; sr. contract adminstr. Midwest Research Inst., Kansas City, 1979-81, Tracor Inc., Austin, Tex., 1981-84; contract negotiator Tex. Instruments, 1984-86; sr. contract adminstr. Tracor Aerospace Inc., 1986-87, Radian Corp., Austin, 1987-96; counsel., asst. co. sec. Radian Internat. LLC, 1996—. Corp. sec. Radian Southeast Asia (SEA) Ltd., Bangkok, 1995—, dir. Radian Southeast Asia (SEA) Ltd., Bangkok, 1996—; corp. sec. Radian Internat. Overseas Mgmt. Co., 1996—; instr. bus. law State Fair Community Coll., Sedalia, 1974-79, Austin Community Coll., 1983-84. Bd. dirs. Legal Aid Western Mo., 1977—79, Boy's Club, Sedalia, 1974—79. Served with U.S. Army, 1968—71. Mem.: U.S. Tennis Assn., Tex. Bar Assn. (intellectual property law sect., internat. law sect., computer law sect.), Mo. Bar Assn. (internat. law com., patent, trademark and copyright law com., tech. law com.), Phi Alpha Delta. E-mail: johnemiller@excite.com.

MILLER, JOHN EDWARD, army officer, technology executive, educational administrator; b. Paragould, Ark., May 8, 1941; s. Wardlow Knox and Anna Mae (Danford) M.; m. Joan Carolyn Capano, Oct. 5, 1968; children: C. Claire, J. Andrew, JoAnna M., Mary Ellen. BS in Math., S.W. Mo. State U., 1963; MS in Ops. Rsch., Ga. Inst. Tech., 1971; postgrad., Yale U., 1991. Commd. 2d lt. U.S. Army, 1963, advanced through grades to lt. gen., 1993; student, then author, instr., grad. studies faculty mem. U.S. Army Command and Gen. Staff Coll., Ft. Leavenworth, Kans., 1974-77; bn. comdr. 4th Brigade, 4th Inf. Divsn., Wiesbaden, Fed. Republic Germany, 1977-79; ops. and tng. officer 8th Inf. Div., Badkreuznach, Fed. Republic Germany, 1979-81; student U.S. Army War Coll., Carlisle, Pa., 1982; divsn. chief Office Dep. Chief of Staff for Rsch. Devel. and Acquisition, Dept. Army, Washington, 1982-84; brigade comdr., chief of staff 9th Inf. Divsn., Ft. Lewis, Wash., 1984-87; asst. for combat devels. U.S. Army Tng. and Doctrine Command, Ft. Monroe, Va., 1987-88; asst. div. comdr. for ops. and tng. 8th Inf. Divsn., Baumholder, Fed. Republic Germany, 1988-89; dep. comdt. U.S. Army Command and Gen. Staff Coll., Ft. Leavenworth, 1989-91; comdr. 101st Airborne Divsn., Ft. Campbell, Ky., 1991-93; U.S. army command, gen. staff coll. U.S. Army, Ft. Leavenworth, 1993-95; dep. comdg. gen. U.S. Army Tng. and Doctrine Command, Ft. Monroe, Va., 1995-97; exec. dir. learning solutions Oracle Corp., Reston, 1997—2000, exec. dir. defense bus. operations, v.p. bus. develop, 2000—02. Apptd. mem. Am. U. MBA adv. bd., 1999; apptd. chair exec. bd. Nat. Academies, Army Sci. and Tech., 2001, Army Sci. Bd., 1999; selected guest lectr. Def. Experts Exch., JFK Sch. Govt., Harvard U. and Peoples Liberation Army, China. Decorated Disting. Svc. medal U.S. Army; recipient Outstanding Alumni award, S.W. Mo. State U., 1993. Mem. Assn. U.S. Army, Disabled Am. Vets Assn., 101st Airborne Divsn.Assn. Republican. Avocations: tennis, skiing, sailing. Office: 1910 Oracle Way Reston VA 20190-4733

MILLER, JOHN GRIDER, writer; b. Annapolis, Md., Aug. 23, 1935; s. John Stanley and Ruby Corinne (Young) M.; m. Susan Bradner Bailey, Oct. 26, 1974; children: Kerry, John, Alison. BA, Yale U., 1957. Commd. 2d lt. USMC, 1957, advanced through grades to col., inf./ops. advisor Vietnamese Marine Corps., 1970-71, prin. speechwriter for Commandant, 1971-76, commd. officer Battalion Landing Team, 1977-78, asst. chief of staff ops. and plans III Amphibious Force, 1982-83, dep. dir. Marine Corps History Washington, 1983-85, ret., 1985; mng. editor Procs. and Naval History U.S. Naval Inst., Annapolis, Md., 1985-2000. Author: The Battle to Save the Houston, 1985, (Pocket Books edit., 1992, Bluejacket edit., 2000), The Bridge at Dong Ha, 1989, (Dell edit. 1990, Bluejacket edit., 1996, Audiobook edit., 1997), Punching Out: A Guide to Post-Military Transition, 1994, The Co-Vans: U.S. Marine Advisors in Vietnam, 2000. Decorated Legion of Merit with gold star, Bronze Star with combat V, Cross of Gallantry, Vietnamese Marine Corps.; recipient Author of Yr. award Naval Inst., 1990, Alfred Thayer Mahan award Navy League of U.S., 2002. Mem. Marine Corps. Hist. Found. (bd. dirs., Gen. Wallace M. Greene Jr. Book award 1989, Disting. Svc. award 1998), Mil. Order of World Wars (past chpt. comdr., chmn. nat. mag. com.), Civitan Internat. (past chpt. pres.), Washington Naval and Maritime Corrs.' Cir., New Providence Club, Annapolis Chorale. Avocations: music, piano, choral singing, boating. Home: 21 Sands Ave Annapolis MD 21403-4426 E-mail: millerjgsands@cs.com.

MILLER, J(OHN) KENT, lawyer, educator; b. Chanute, Kans., Mar. 9, 1944; s. Ernest William and Margery (Olson) M.; m. Toni R. Taff, June 5, 1965 (div. Apr. 1975); children: Gentry, Callan; m. Leslie J. Jaffe, Sept. 14, 1979; children: Todd, Morgan. BS, U. Kans., 1966; JD, U. Denver, 1970. Bar: Colo. 1970, U.S. Dist. Ct. Colo. 1970, U.S. Supreme Ct. 1975. Mng. ptnr. Anderson, Campbell & Langesen, Denver, 1970-83; v.p. Gerash, Robinson, Miller & Miranda, 1984-87; pres. Miller & McCarren, PC, 1988-94, of counsel, 1994—. Adj. prof. U. Denver Sch. Law, 1990—. Author: (with others) Annual Survey Colorado Law, 1982-2000; author (2 vols.) Colorado Personal Injury Practice, 1989, 2d edit. (4 vols.), 2000. Mem. ABA, ATLA, Am. Bd. Trial Advs. (adv.), Colo. Trial Lawyers Assn. (bd. dirs. 1984-87), Denver Bar Assn., Colo. Bar Assn., Def. Rsch. Inst., Colo. Def. Lawyers Assn. Avocations: skiing, squash, performance driving instructor. Office: Miller & McCarren PC 2150 W 29th Ave Ste 500 Denver CO 80211-3844

MILLER, JOHN LEED, lawyer; b. Geneva, May 7, 1949; s. John Axel and Martha Mary (Masilunis) M.; m. Roosy Yanti, Jan. 2, 2001. BA, Northwestern U., 1971; JD, U. Chgo., 1975. Bar: Ill. 1975, U.S. Dist. Ct. (no. dist.) Ill., U.S. Ct. Appeals (7th and 8th cirs.). Assoc. counsel Profl. Ind. Mass-Mktg. Adminstrs., Chgo., 1975-76; legis. counsel to minority leader Ill. Ho. of Reps., Chgo. and Springfield, Ill., 1977-80, chief legal counsel, 1980, chief counsel to spkr., 1981-83; ptnr. Shaw and Miller, Chgo., 1981-84, Theodore A. Woerthwein, Chgo., 1984-85, Woerthwein & Miller, Chgo., 1985—. Statewide chmn. Ill. Young Voters for the Pres., 1972; dir. Ill. Ho. Rep. campaign com., 1976, 78, cons., 1982; pres. Newberry Pla. Condominium Assn., 1989-94. With ISNG, 1969-75. James scholar, 1970. Mem. Lawyers for the Creative Arts, Primitive Art Soc. Chgo. (treas. 1984-86, v.p. 1987, pres. 1988-89), Indonesia-Am. Assn. Ill. (bd. dirs.), Adventurers Club (participant first descent of Boh River, Borneo), Phi Eta Sigma, Phi Beta Kappa. Lutheran. Home: 1030 N State St Apt 9D Chicago IL 60610-5484 Office: Woerthwein & Miller PO Box A 3612 Chicago IL 60690-3612

MILLER, JOHN PETER (JACK MILLER), journalist; b. Peterborough, Ont., Can., Aug. 3, 1928; s. Wesley and Margaret (Baker) M.; ed. Welland and Toronto; m. Helen DeMars, July 30, 1949; children: Candice (dec.), Gregory (dec.). Sports editor to front page editor Welland Evening Tribune, 1949-53; with Hamilton (Ont.) Spectator, 1953-71, radio and TV columnist, 1955-71; radio and TV columnist Toronto Daily Star, 1971-78, comm. editor, 1979-85, sci. columnist, 1982-85, sci. writer, 1985-89, sci. editor, 1989-91, sci. corr., 1991-95; prof. journalism Niagara Coll., 1996—; frequent TV and radio appearances. Recipient writing awards CSWA 1985 (2), 87, 88 (2), 89. Mem. Can. Sci. Writers Assn., Nat. Sci. Writers Assn. Contbr. stories to mags. Office: 162 Martindale Rd Apt 103 Saint Catharines ON Canada L2S 3S4

MILLER, JOHN R. accountant; b. Wilkes-Barre, Pa., Nov. 28, 1946; s. John Turner and Elsie May (Johns) M.; children: Stephen, Jo-El. BS in Commerce and Fin., Wilkes U., 1968. CPA, Pa., N.Y.; cert. govt. fin. mgr. Audit exec. Com. of Pa., Harrisburg, 1971-73; sr. acct. KPMG LLP, Phila., 1968-71, mgr. Harrisburg, 1973-76, sr. mgr. N.Y.C., 1976-79, ptnr., 1979—, ptnr.-in-charge Metro N.Y. govt. practices, 1993-95, also bd. dirs., ptnr.-in-charge of nat. assurance and resource mgmt. practices, 1995-97; northeast regional ptnr.-in-charge KPMG Cons., 1997—; nat. mng. ptnr. pub. svcs. mgmt. com. KPMG LLP, 1997-98, vice chmn. health care and public sector, 1998—; vice-chmn. KPMG N.Y. Found., 1997—. Mem. U.S. Auditing Standards Adv. Coun., Washington, 1990-93, 97-98, chair, 2001—; chair Govtl. Auditing Standards Adv. Coun., Norwalk, Conn., 2001, mem., 1987-91. Bd. dirs. Rye (N.Y.) YMCA, 1988-97, Osborn Retirement Community, 1991—, Wilkes U., 1999—; mem. Nat. Civic League, Denver, 1985—; trustee Citizens Budget

Commn., N.Y.C., 1985—; Prin. Coun. for Excellence in Govt., Washington, 1987—; bd. advisors Chariot Capital; vestry mem. Trinity Ch.; trustee Cath. of St. John, The Durne. Recipient Ellis Island medal of honor, 2002. Mem. AICPA (chmn. govt. acctg. and auditing com. 1987-90, chmn. audit quality 1991-95, chmn. govt. and nonprofit expert panel 2000—), Pa. Inst. CPAs (Leadership award 1968), N.Y. State Soc. CPAs, Masons, Coveleigh Club, Sky Club, Assn. of Govt. Accts. (Einhorn-Gary Outstanding Contbn. award 2000, Andy Barr award for leadership excellence 2001), Soc. of Magi. Episcopalian. Avocations: travel, reading, sports. Office: KPMG LLP 345 Park Ave New York NY 10154-0004

MILLER, JOHN RICHARD, interior designer; b. Washington, Feb. 11, 1927; s. John Henry and Helen (Vermillion) M.; m. Audrey Gene Owens, Nov. 6, 1946; children: Pamela Dawn, Felicity Amanda, Timothy John. Diploma in interior design, Colbert Inst., Washington, 1950. Designer Hollidge Interiors, Washington, 1950-51; pres. Miller's Interiors Inc., Temple Hills, Md., 1951—. Bd. dirs. St. Barnabas Venture, Temple Hills. Author: Training for Design Related Trades, 1976; columnist Washington Star, 1971-79. Mem. Pres.'s Com. on Employment of Handicapped, 1978-82, White House Design Com., 1969-74, Presdl. Barrier Free Design Com., 1972-80. With USN, 1944-46, PTO. Fellow Am. Soc. Interior Designers (pres. Potomac chpt. 1973-80, nat. dir. 1960-74, chmn. opportunity guidance coun. 1972-74); mem. Nat. Soc. Interior Designers (pres. Potomac chpt. 1974-76), Tantallon Country Club (Oxon Hill, Md.). Democrat. Episcopalian. Avocations: tennis, reading. Home: 13710 Piscataway Dr Fort Washington MD 20744-6634 Office: Millers Interiors Inc PO Box 441711 Fort Washington MD 20749-1711

MILLER, JOHN ROBERT, oil industry executive; b. Lima, Ohio, Dec. 28, 1937; s. John O. and Mary L. (Zickafoose) M.; m. Karen A. Eier, Dec. 30, 1961; children: Robert A., Lisa A., James E. BSChE with honors, U. Cin., 1960, D.Comml. Sc. hon., 1983. With Standard Oil Co., Cleve., 1960-86, dir. fin., 1974-75, v.p. fin., 1975-78, v.p. transp., 1978-79, sr. v.p. tech. and chems., 1979-80, pres., COO, 1980-86; bd. dirs.; pres., CEO TBN Holdings, 1986-2000; chmn., CEO Petroleum Ptnrs., 2000—. Bd. dirs. Cambrex Corp., Eaton Corp., Riverwood Holding, Inc.; former chmn. Fed. Res. Bank, Cleve.; mem. adv. bd. 5iTech. Mem. Pepper Pike Club, The Country Club, Chagrin Valley Hunt Club, Tau Beta Pi. Office: Petroleum Ptnrs Inc 29325 Chagrin Blvd Ste 301 Cleveland OH 44122 E-mail: office@johnrmiller.com.

MILLER, JOHN RONALD, minister; b. L.A., Jan. 4, 1938; s. Clarence Raymond and Yolanda Sarah (Capenaro) M.; m. Madelon Louise Tetaz, Mar. 26, 1966; children: Sarah Louise, John Ronald. BA, Southwestern Coll., 1960; MDiv, Drew U., 1963; MA, Rutgers U., 1966. Ordained to ministry United Meth. Ch., 1965, United Ch. Christ, 1966. Pastor Burden (Kans.) Meth. Ch., 1958-60; min. Wilson Meml. Union Ch., Watchung, N.J., 1961—. Mem. Consultation on Ch. Union, Princeton, N.J., 1982—, com. on disabled United Ch. of Christ, Montclair, N.J., 1982—. Chmn. Dorthea Dix Chapel Bldg. Program; pres. Trenton Psychiat. Hosp.-State of N.J., 1985; mem. N.J. State Bd. Human Svcs., 1996—. Southwestern Coll. scholar, 1960, Tipple scholar, 1960. Mem. Nat. Coun. Chs. of Jesus Christ (governing bd. 1985—), Internat. Coun. Community Chs. (moderator ecumenical commn. 1984—, regional trustee, exec. bd. 1987, v.p. exec. bd. 1991, pres. communion 1995-97), Optimists. Office: Mary E Wilson Meml Union Ch 7 Valley Rd Watchung NJ 07069-6034

MILLER, JOHN T. , JR. lawyer, educator; b. Waterbury, Conn., Aug. 10, 1922; s. John T. and Anna (Purdy) M.; children: Kent, Lauren, Clare, Miriam, Michael, Sheila, Lisa, Colin, Margaret. AB with high honors, Clark U., 1944; JD, Georgetown U., 1948; Docteur en Droit, U. Geneva, 1951; postgrad., U. Paris, 1951. Bar: Conn. 1949 (inactive), D.C. 1950, U.S. Ct. Appeals (2d, 3d, 5th, 10th, 11th and D.C. cirs.), U.S. Supreme Ct. 1952. With Econ. Cooperation Adminstn. Am. Embassy, London, 1950-51; assoc. Covington & Burling, 1952-53, Gallagher, Connor & Boland, 1953-62; pvt. practice Washington, 1962—. Adj. prof. law Georgetown U. Law Ctr., Washington, 1959—; mem. Panel on Future of Internat. Ct. Justice. Co-author: Regulation of Trade, 1953, Modern American Antitrust Law, 1958, Major American Antitrust Laws, 1965; author: Foreign Trade in Gas and Electricity in North America: A Legal and Historical Study, 1970, Energy Problems and the Federal Government: Cases and Material, 8th edit., 1996, Deregulating the Interstate Natural Gas and Electric Power Industries, 3d edit., 2002; contbr. articles, book revs. to legal publs. Trustee Clark U., 1970-76; bd. trustees De Sales Sch. of Theology, 1993-97; bd. advisors Georgetown Visitation Prep. Sch., 1978-94, bd. trustees, 1994-96, emeritus trustee, 1996—; former fin. chmn. troop 46 Nat. Capital Area coun. Boy Scouts Am.; pres. Thomas More Soc. Am., 1996-97. 1st lt. U.S. Army, 1943-46, 48-49. Decorated Bronze Star; recipient 10 yr. teaching award Nat. Jud. Coll., 1983. Mem. ABA (coun., chmn. adminstrv. law sect. 1972-73, ho. dels. 1991-93), AAUP, D.C. Bar Assn., Fed. Energy Bar Assn. (pres. 1990-91), Congl. Country Club, Army and Navy Club (bd. govs. 2000—), DACOR, Prettyman-Leventhal Am. Inn of Ct. (master 1988-99, pres. 1995-96), Sovereign Mil. Order of Malta (knight). Republican. Roman Catholic. Home: 4721 Rodman St NW Washington DC 20016-3234 Office: 1001 Connecticut Ave NW Washington DC 20036-5504 E-mail: jtmillerjr@erols.com.

MILLER, JOLENE K. healthcare educator; b. Evansville, Ind., Apr. 5, 1955; d. Joe B. and Geraldine (Phillips) Daniel; m. Larry J. Miller, May 17, 1974; children: Benjamin D., Joshua J. AS, U. So. Ind., Evansville, 1974; BS, U. St. Francis, Joliet, Ill., 1986; MS in Edn., Purdue U., 1992. Registered respiratory therapist. Respiratory therapist Meml. Hosp., Jasper, Ind., 1975-76; respiratory therapist, asst. dept. chair King's Daus. Hosp., Ashland, Ky., 1977-81; mem. faculty Ivy Tech. State Coll., Lafayette, Ind., 1982-90, chair health divsn., 1990—. Mem. adv. bd. respiratory care Shawnee State Coll., Portsmouth, Ohio, 1978-81. Commr. Commn. Accreditations Allied Health Edn. Programs, 1995—. Mem.: Nat. Network for Allied Health Programs in Two-Yr. Coll. (treas. 2001—), Lafayette C. of C. (com. chmn. 1995—99). Christian. Office: Ivy Tech State Coll PO Box 6299 Lafayette IN 47903-6299 E-mail: jomiller@ivy.tech.edu.

MILLER, JON PHILIP, marketing and business development professional, pharmaceutical executive; b. Moline, Ill., Mar. 30, 1944; s. Clyde Sheldon and Alice Lenora (Taes) M.; m. Shirley Ann Hymes, Aug. 21, 1965; children: Melissa, Elizabeth. AB, Augustana Coll., 1966; PhD, St. Louis U., 1970; MBA, Pepperdine U., 1983. Rsch. assoc. to sr. biochemist ICN Pharm., Inc., Irvine, Calif., 1970-72, leader molecular pharmacology group, 1972-73, head molecular pharmacology/drug metabolism dept., 1973-76, dir. biology div., 1975-76; dir. SRI-NCI liaison group SRI Internat. (formally Stanford Rsch. Inst.), Menlo Park, 1976-78, sr. bioorganic chemist, 1978-80, head medicinal biochemistry program, 1980-84, dir. biotech. rsch. dept., 1982-85, dir. biotech. and biomed. rsch. lab., 1985-92, assoc. dir. life scis. div., 1989-92; dir. bus. devel., strategic mktg. MDS Panlabs, Inc., Bothell, Wash., 1992-98; dir. pharm. mktg. Applied Biosystems, Foster City, Calif., 1998—2001; dir. corp. devel. ACLARA Bioscis., Mountain View, 2001—. Office: ACLARA Bioscis 1288 Pear Ave Mountain View CA 94043

MILLER, JONATHAN LEWIS, lawyer, computer consultant; b. Boston, Dec. 9, 1947; s. Harold Irving and Maida (Rosenberg) M.; m. Arleen Garfinkle, Nov. 2, 1985; 1 child, Jonah Maxwell. BA in Sociology, Colby Coll., 1973; BS in Physics, U. Washington, 1980; JD, U. Denver, 1994. Bar: Colo. 1994. Proprietor, cons. J. Miller & Assoc., Colo., 1982-85; pres., atty. J. Miller & Assoc., Inc., Boulder, 1985-95; assoc. Martin & Mehaffy LLC, 1995—. Mng. editor: Transp. Law Jour., 1992-94; author: Legal Software Reviews, Orange County Lawyer, 1998. Avocations: skiing, biking, flying, reading, horseback riding. Home: 173 Wild Tiger Rd Boulder CO 80302-9263 Office: 1113 Spruce St Boulder CO 80302-4011 E-mail: jonmesq@aol.com.

MILLER, JONATHAN WOLFE, theater and film director, physician; b. London, July 21, 1934; s. Emanuel Miller; m. Helen Rachel Collet, 1956; 3 children. Ed., St. John's Coll., Cambridge U.; MB Ch, Univ. Coll. Hosp. Med. Sch., London, 1959; DLitt (hon.), U. Leicester, 1981, Cambridge U., 1996; Dr. (hon.), Open U., 1983. Dir. Nottingham Playhouse, 1963-69; assoc. dir. nat. Theatre, 1973-75; mem. Arts Coun., 1975-76; artistic dir. Old Vic, 1988-90; lectr. Nat. Gallery, 1995, Met. Mus., N.Y.C., 1995; curator major exhbn. Nat. Gallery, London, 1998. Vis. prof. drama Westfield Coll., U. London, 1977-78; lectr. wide variety of subjects. Co-author, actor in Beyond the Fringe, 1961-64; dir. Under Plain Cover Royal Ct. Theatre, 1962, The Old Glory, N.Y.C., 1964, Prometheus Bound, Yale Drama Sch., 1967, Oxford and Cambridge Shakespeare Co. prod. of Twelfth Night, on tour in U.s., 1969; dir. for Nat. Theatre, London: The Merchant of Venice, 1970, Danton's Death, 1971, The School for Scandal, 1972, The Marriage of Figaro, 1974; other prodns. include: The Tempest, London, 1970, Prometheus Bound, London, 1971, The Taming of the Shrew, Chichester, Eng., 1972, The Seagull, Chichester, 1973, The Malcontent, Nottingham, Eng., 1973, The Family in Love, 1974, The Importance of Being Earnest, 1975, All's Well That Ends Well, Measure For Measure, Greenwich Season, 1975, Three Sisters, 1977; dir. operas Arden Must Die, 1973, Sadler's Well Theatre, 1974, The Cunning Little Vixen, Glyndebourne, 1975, 77, Marriage of Figaro, Vienna State Opera, 1991, Robert Devereux, Monte Carlo, 1992, Die Gezeichnete, Zurich, 1992, Maria Stuarda, Monte Carlo, 1993, the Secret Marriage, Opera North, 1993; dir. for English Nat. Opera: The Marriage of Figaro, 1978, The Turn of the Screw, 1979, 91, Arabella, 1980, Othello, 1981, Rigoletto, 1982, 85 (alwo at Met. Opera, N.Y.C.), Fidelio, 1982, 83, Don Giovanni, 1985, The Magic Flute, 1986, Tosca, 1986, The Mikado, 1986, 88, The Barber of Seville, 1987, Cosi fan Tutte, 1995, Carmen, 1995; dir. for Kent Opera: Cosi Fan Tutte, 1975, Rigoletto, 1975, Orfeo, 1976, Eugene Onegin, 1977, La Traviata, 1979, 96, Falstaff, 1980, 81, Fiedlio, 1982, 83, 88; dir. for La Scala Milan: La Fanciulla del West, 1991, Manon Lescaut, 1992; dir. for Maggio Musicale, Florence: Don Giovanni, 1990, Cosísi fan Tutte, 1991, 94, Marriage of Figaro, 1992, La Bohéme, 1994, La Bohéme, which transfered to La Bastille, 1995, dir., Strass Ariadne auf Naxos, 1997; dir. Met. Opera, N.Y.: Katya Kabanova, 1991, Pelléas et Mélisande, 1995; dir in co-prodn. with L.A. Music Ctr. and Houston Grand Opera House Der Rosenkavalier, 1994; dir. Broadway play Long Day's Journey Into Night, 1986, The Taming of the Shrew at Royal Shakespeare Co., Stratford, 1987, Andromache, One Way Pendulum, Bussy D'Ambois, all at Vic, 1988, The Tempest, 1988, Turn of the Screw, 1989, Kimg Lear, 1989, The Liar, 1989; films include: Take a Girl Like You, 1969; TV films include: Whistle and I'll Come to You, 1967, Alice in Wonderland, 1967, The Body in Question Series, 1978, Henry the Sixth, part I, 1983, States of Mind Series, 1983; exec. prodr. Shakespeare TV series, 1979-81; author (TV) McLuhan, 1971, The Body in Question, 1978, States of Mind, The Facts of Life, Subsequent Performances, 1986, Who Cares, Born Talking, Museums of Madness, Anthropology, Opera Works; editor: Freud: The Man, His World, His Influence, 1972, The Don Giovanni Book, 1990; actor (TV) Jonathan Miller on Reflection, 1998, (TV mini-series) The Talk Show Story, 2000. Decorated Order of Brit. Empire; named Dir. of Yr., Soc. West End Theatre Awards, 1976; recipient Silver medal Royal TV Soc., 1981; fellow Univ. Coll. London; hon. fellow St. John's Coll., Cambridge U.; rsch. fellow in history of medicine Univ. Coll., London U., 1970-73. Fellow Royal Coll. Physicians (London and Edinburgh); mem. AAAS (fgn. mem.). Office: care IMG Artists 616 Chiswick High St London W45RX England

MILLER, JOSEPH AARON, lawyer, musician; b. Bklyn., Oct. 24, 1961; s. Bernard and Caroline (Ashe) M. BA, Emory U., Atlanta, 1984; JD, Coll. William and Mary, Williamsburg, Va., 1987. Atty. Miller & Bondurant, Portsmouth, Va., 1988-99; with Accidental Injury Advocates, Norfolk, 1999—. Mem. ABA, ATLA, Va. Trial Lawyers Assn., N.C. Bar Assn., N.C. Acad. Trial Attys. Office: Accidental Injury Advocates Ltd 4101 Granby St Ste 206 Norfolk VA 23504 E-mail: joe@accidentalinjurylaw.com.

MILLER, JOSEPH ANTHONY, healthcare executive, psychotherapist; b. Patterson, N.J., June 4, 1959; s. George Jr. and Margaret Marie Miller; m. Susan H. Miller, May 25, 1985; children: Brian, Lauren. BA, William Paterson U., Wayne, N.J., 1982; MSW, NYU, 1984, PhD, 1999. Cert. social worker. Psychotherapist in pvt. practice, Wayne, 1982—; dir. child psychiatry Bergen Regional Med. Ctr., Paramus, N.J., 1986-93; regional clin. dir. Merit Behavioral Care Corp., N.Y.C., 1993-96; asst. v.p. F.E.G.S., 1996—. Clin. adv. MCC Behavioral Care, Parsippany, N.J., 1998—; mem. clin. faculty Fordham U., N.Y.C., 1999—, UMDNJ-Tech. Assistance Ctr., New Brunswick, 1988—. Trustee Wayne P.A.L., 1998—, asst. commr. football, 1997—. Recipient Cert. of Commendation, County of Bergen, N.J., 1992, Bergen County Exec., 1992. Roman Catholic. Avocations: golf, sailing, reading, arts, coaching. Home: 75 Harrison Rd Wayne NJ 07470-4514 Office: FEGS 315 Hudson St Fl 9 New York NY 10013-1009 E-mail: JMiller@FEGS.org.

MILLER, JOSEPH ARTHUR, retired manufacturing engineer, educator, consultant; b. Brattleboro, Vt., Aug. 28, 1933; s. Joseph Maynard and Marjorie Antoinette (Hammerberg) M.; m. Ardene Hedwig Barker, Aug. 19, 1956; children: Stephanie L., Jocelyn A., Shana L., Gregory J. BS in Agrl., Andrews U., Berrien Springs, Mich., 1955; MS in Agrl. Mechs., Mich. State U., 1959; EdD in Vocat. Edn., UCLA, 1973. Constrn. engr. Thornton Bldg. & Supply, Inc., Williamston, Mich., 1959-63, C & B Silo Co., Charlotte, 1963-64; instr. and dir. retraining Lansing (Mich.) C.C., 1964-68; asst. prof./prog. coord./coop coord. San Jose State U., 1968-79; mfg. specialist Lockheed Martin Missiles and Space (and predecessor cos.), Sunnyvale, Calif., 1979-81, rsch. specialist, 1981-88, NASA project mgr., 1982-83, staff engr., 1988-96, rsch. staff engr., 1996-98, coord. flexible mfg. system simulation project, 1994-96, team mem. federally funded AIMS Agile Mfg. project, 1995-97, team mem. corp funded machining outsource initative project, 1995-97, coord. productivity improvement program, 1996-98; engring. and constrn. cons., Berry Creek, 1998—. Agrl. engring. cons. USDA Poultry Expt. Sta., 1960-62; computer numerical control cons. Dynamechtronics, Inc., Sunnyvale, 1987-90; machining cons. Lockheed, Space Sys. Div., 1986-96; instr. computer numerical control DeAnza Coll., Cupertino, Calif., 1985-88, Labor Employment Tng. Corp., San Jose, Calif., 1988-93; instr. computer-aided mfg. and non traditional machining San Jose (Calif.) State U., 1994-97; team leader Pursuit of Excellence machine tool project Lockheed Martin Missiles and Space, Sunnyvale, Calif., 1990-95, coord. safety award program, 1997-98, mem. quality awareness program screening com., 1998. Author: Student Manual for CNC Lathe, 1990; contbr. articles to profl. jours. Career counselor Pacific Union Coll., Angwin, Calif., 1985-92. UCLA fellow, 1969-73. Mem. Soc. Mfg. Engrs. (sr. mem. 1980-92, chmn. edn. com. local chpt. 1984-85, career guidance counselor 1986-88), Nat. Assn. Indsl. Tech. (pres. industry divsn. 1987-88, bd. cert. 1991-92, mem., chmn. accreditation visitation teams 1984—), Calif. Assn. Indsl. Tech. (pres. 1974-75, 84-85), Am. Soc. Indsl. Tech. (pres. 1980-81). Seventh-day Adventist. Avocations: violin, camping, designing and building homes, traveling. Home: PO Box 190 Berry Creek CA 95916-0190

MILLER, JOSEPH IRWIN, automotive manufacturing company executive; b. Columbus, Ind., May 26, 1909; s. Hugh Thomas and Nettie Irwin (Sweeney) M.; m. Xenia Ruth Simons, Feb. 5, 1943; children: Margaret Irwin, Catherine Gibbs, Elizabeth Ann Garr, Hugh Thomas, II, William Irwin. Grad., Taft Sch., 1927; AB, Yale U., 1931, MA (hon.), 1959, LHD (hon.), 1979; MA, Oxford (Eng.) U., 1933; LLD, Bethany Coll., 1956, Tex. Christian U., Ind. U., 1958, Oberlin Coll., Princeton, 1962; LL.D., Hamilton Coll., 1964, Columbia, 1968, Mich. State U., 1968, Dartmouth, 1971, U. Notre Dame, 1972, Ball State U., 1972, Lynchburg Coll., 1985; L.H.D. (hon.), Case Inst. Tech., 1966, U. Dubuque, 1977; Hum.D., Manchester U., 1973, Moravian Coll., 1976. Assoc. Cummins Engine Co., Inc., Columbus, Ind., 1934—, v.p., gen. mgr., 1934-42, exec. v.p., 1944-47, pres., 1947-51, chmn. bd., 1951-77, chmn. exec. com., 1977-95; dir., 1995-97; hon. chmn. Cummins Engine, 1997—. Pres. Irwin-Union Bank & Trust Co., 1947-54, bd. dir., 1937—, chmn., 1954-75; chmn. exec. com. Irwin Union Corp., 1976-90, hon. chmn., 1997—; bd. dirs. Irwin Fin. Corp., 1990—; mem. Commn. Money and Credit, 1958-61, Pres.'s Com. Postal Reorgn., 1968, Pres.'s Com. Urban Housing, 1968; chmn. Pres.'s Com. on Trade Rels. with Soviet Union and Eastern European Nations, 1965, Nat. Adv. Commn. on Health Manpower, 1966; vice chmn. UN Commn. on Multinat. Corps., 1974; adv. council U.S. Dept. Commerce, 1976; mem. Study Commn. on U.S. Policy Toward So. Africa, 1979-81. Pres. nat. Coun. Chs. of Christ U.S.A., 1960-63; trustee Nat. Humanities Ctr., 1978-90, Carnegie Instn., Washington, 1988-91; mem. cen. and exec. coms. World Coun. Chs., 1961-68; trustee Ford Found., 1961-79, Yale Corp., 1959-77, Urban Inst., 1966-76, Mayo Found., 1977-82; fellow Branford Coll. Recipient Rosenberger award U. Chgo., 1977, 1st MacDowell Colony award, 1981; hon. fellow Balliol Coll., Oxford (Eng.) U.; Benjamin Franklin fellow Royal Soc. Arts. Fellow Am. Acad. Arts and Scis., Royal Inst. Brit. Architects (hon.); mem. AIA (hon.), Am. Philos. Soc., Ind. Acad., Bus. Coun., Conf. Bd. (sr.), Phi Beta Kappa, Beta Gamma Sigma. Mem. Christian Ch. Office: 301 Washington St Columbus IN 47201-6743

MILLER, JOSEPH J. research scientist; b. Schenectady, N.Y., Dec. 14, 1958; s. James J. and Venera R. Miller; m. Christen A. Bonacci, Aug. 30, 1986; 1 child, Luke Joseph. BSc, McGill U., Montreal, Can., 1981; MS, U. R.I., 1983; PhD, SUNY, Brooklyn, 1989. Postdoctoral assoc. MIT, Cambridge, 1989-91; rsch. scientist Organon Teknika, Rockville, Md., 1991-94; sr. scientist Instrumentation Lab., Inc., Lexington, Mass., 1994-98; asst. prof. chemistry Ithaca (NY) U., 1998—. Home: 413 N Geneva St Ithaca NY 14850-4111 E-mail: jmiller@ithaca.edu.

MILLER, JOSEPH MATTHEW, retired surgeon; b. Yonkers, N.Y., 1911; s. Adolph and Katherine (Becker) M.; m. Mary Alice Case, Dec. 18, 1940; children: Joseph M. Jr., Dorcas S., Karl S., John M. AB, Columbia U., 1931; MD, Columbia Coll. P&S, 1935; MS in Surgery, U. Minn., 1939. Diplomate Am. Bd. Surgery. Intern St. John's Riverside Hosp., Yonkers, 1935-36; resident Mayo Found. for Med. Edn. Rsch., Rochester, Minn., 1936-40; fellow in surgery Mayo Found., 1936-40; chief surg. svcs. VA Hosp., Ft. Howard, Md., 1946-70; ret., 1988. Asst. prof. surgery emeritus Johns Hopkins Sch. Medicine; clin. prof. surgery Meharry Med. Coll. Contbr. articles to profl. jours. Fellow ACS; mem. Md. chpt. ACS, Balt. Acad. Surgery (founding mem.), Priestly Soc., Johns Hopkins Med. and Surg. Soc., Alumni Assn. Mayo Found. for Med. Edn. and Rsch.

MILLER, JOSEPH MORTON, internist; b. Boston, Nov. 9, 1921; s. Benjamin and Esther (Sugar) M.; m. Betty Jean Harris, Sept. 17, 1976; children: Beth, Keith, Eric, Gregory, Coralia. AB, Harvard Coll., 1942; MD, Harvard Med. Sch., 1945; MPH, Harvard Sch. Pub. Health, 1960. Diplomate Am. Bd. Internal Medicine, Preventive Medicine. Intern Mt. Sinai Hosp., N.Y.C., 1945-46; resident Cushing VA Hosp., Framingham, Mass., 1949-50; cons. occupl. health Durham, N.H., 1980—. Cons. environ. and toxicology. Capt. U.S. Army, 1946-48. Mem. APHA, Am. Coll. Environ. and Occupl. Medicine. Home and Office: 13 Burnham Ave Durham NH 03824-3010

MILLER, JP (JAMES PINCKNEY MILLER), screenwriter, novelist, playwright; b. San Antonio, Dec. 18, 1919; s. Rolland James and Rose Jetta (Smith) M.; m. Ayers Elizabeth Fite, May 16, 1942 (div. 1947); 1 child, James Jr.; m. Juanita Marie Currie, Nov. 20, 1948 (div. 1962); children: John, Montgomery; m. Julianne Renee Nicolaus, Nov. 24, 1965; children: Lia, Anthony, Sophie. BA, Rice U., 1941; postgrad., Yale U., 1946-47, Am. Theater Wing, N.Y.C., 1951-53. Pres. Kingwood Enterprises, Inc., N.Y. and N.J., 1965—. Chmn. N.J. Motion Picture Commn., 1980-81; adj. prof. playwriting Drew U., 1993. Screenwriter: (TV) Days of Wine and Roses, The People Next Door (Emmy award 1969), The Rabbit Trap, Hide and Seek, Yellow Jack, Old Tasslefoot, The Pardon-Me Boy, Flight Report, The Catamaran, Your Money or Your Wife, The Lindbergh Kidnapping Case, Helter Skelter (Edgar Allan Poe award 1977), I Know My First Name is Steven (Emmy nomination 1989); (feature film) Days of Wine and Roses, The Rabbit Trap, The Young Savages, Behold a Pale Horse, The People Next Door, Helter Skelter; novelist: The Race for Home, 1968, Liv, 1972, The Skook, 1984, Surviving Joy, 1995; (play) Days of Wine and Roses, Privacy, Is There Anybody There?. Mem. Bd. Adjustments Kingwood Twp., N.J., 1972-75. Served to Lt. USNR, 1942-46, PTO. Decorated Purple Heart, Presdl. Unit citation. Mem. Acad. Motion Picture Arts and Scis., PEN Am. Ctr., Dramatists Guild, Authors Guild, Writers Guild Am., West. Democrat. Avocations: sports, traveling, poetry.

MILLER, JUDITH ROSALIND, mathematician, educator; b. Northampton, Mass., Nov. 15, 1967; AB in Math., Havard U., Cambridge, Mass., 1989; PhD, U. Mich., 1994. Vis. mem. Courant Inst. NYU, N.Y.C., 1994—95; vis. asst. prof. Simon Fraser U., Burnaby, Canada, 1995—97; asst. prof. Georgetown U., Washington, 1997—. Contbr. articles to profl. jours. Office: Georgetown Univ Math Dept Washington DC 20057 E-mail: miller@math.georgetown.edu.

MILLER, JUDITH WOLFE COHEN, consultant; b. Boston, Aug. 19, 1928; d. Benjamin and Charlotte Frances (Wolfe) Cohen; m. Sanford Arthur Miller, Aug. 17, 1958; children: Wallis Jo, Debra Lauren. BS, Northeastern U., 1949. Research technician Mass. Gen. Hosp., Boston, 1949-51, NE Med. Ctr., Boston, 1951-52; spl. asst. MIT, Cambridge, 1952-61; v.p., treas. S.A. Miller and Assoc., Inc., San Antonio, Washington, 1987—. Cons. 9th internat. symposium on the U.S. Constitution Smithsonian Inst., Washington, 1987. Chmn. MIT Matrons, 1972, New Eng. Consevatory Prep. Sch. Parents' Assn., Boston, 1976, First Bicentennial '87 Symposium "The Constitution", Washington, 1985; Montgomery County chmn. Nat. Symphony Orch. Womens' Com., Washington, 1979-81; boutique chmn. Decorators' Showhouse Nat. Symphony Orch., Washington, 1981, 86; docent Nat. Archives Vols., Washington, 1979—; co-chmn. Am. Newspaper Pub. Assn. Found. Colloquium, Washington, 1985; pres. Nat. Archives Vols., Washington, 1983-84; vice-chmn. Constitution Study Group at Nat. Archives, Washington, 1982-87; docent Inst. Texan Culture, San Antonio, 1988-91; program chmn. U. Tex. Health Sci. Ctr. Club, San Antonio, 1988-89; White House vol. Presdl. Student Correspondence, 1996-2001. Mem.: Welcome to Washington. Home and Office: SA Miller & Assocs Inc 5450 Whitley Park Ter Apt 704 Bethesda MD 20814-2066 Fax: 301-897-0888.

MILLER, JUDSON FREDERICK, lawyer, former military officer; b. Tulsa, Dec. 5, 1924; s. Herbert Frederick and Martha (Davidson) M.; m. June Hirakis, Aug. 4, 1967; children by previous marriage: Kathleen, Shelley, Douglas, Judson Frederick. BS, U. Md., 1961; postgrad., Army War Coll., 1961-62; MA, George Washington U., 1962; JD, U. Puget Sound, 1980. Bar: Wash. 1981. Commd. 2d lt. U.S. Army, 1943, advanced through grades to maj. gen., 1975; platoon leader, co. comdr. 4th Cav. Group, Europe, 1944-46, 82d Airborne Div., 1947-50; with 187th Airborne RCT and Hdqrs. 8th Army, 1950-52; instr. Armored Sch., 1953-56; bn. comdr. 14th Armored Cav., 1958-60; with Hdqrs. U.S. Strike Command, 1963-65; brigade comdr., chief of staff 4th Inf. Div., Vietnam, 1966-67; mem. gen. staff Dept. Army, 1967-68; dep. comdg. gen. Ft. Ord, Cal., 1968-69; asst. chief of staff Hdqrs. Allied Forces Central Europe, 1969-71; asst. comdr. 3d Inf. Div., Germany, 1971-73; chief of staff I Corps Group, Korea, 1973-75; dep. comdg. gen. VII Corps, Germany, 1975-77; ret., 1977; assoc. F.G. Enslow and Assocs., Tacoma, 1981—. Decorated Silver Star, Legion of Merit, Bronze Star with V device and oak leaf cluster, Joint Service Commendation medal, Air medal with 8 oak leaf clusters, Purple Heart, Vietnamese Gallantry Cross with palm; named to Okla. Mil. Acad. Hall of Fame, 1988. Mem. ABA, Assn. U.S. Army. Clubs: Tacoma Country, Lakewood Racquet. Home: 8009 75th St SW Tacoma WA 98498-4817 Office: Tacoma Mall Office Bldg 4301 S Pine St Ste 205 Tacoma WA 98409-7205

MILLER, JUDY E. social worker, researcher; b. Denver, July 20, 1950; d. Benjamin K. Miller and Marianne (Winter) Cohn. BA, Loretto Heights Coll., U. Without Walls, Denver, 1974; MA, U. Denver, 1977; MSW., La. State U., 1985. Case mgr. New Orleans Adolescent Hosp., 1987—. Writing, research on various subjects; author: Dove Over the Edge, 1972. Bd. dirs. Found. for Health Edn., New Orleans, 1984; rsch. writer Sun King catalog La. State Mus., New Orleans, 1984; librarian, vol. New Orleans Mus. Art, 1981-83. Mem. Nat. Assn. for Social Workers (community svc. 1987).

MILLER, KAREN K. social worker; BA, Kent State U., 1974; MS in Social Work, U. Tex., Austin, 1983. Lic. clin. social worker. Caseworker Children Svcs. Bd. Summit County, Akron, Ohio, 1975-76; transitional svcs. coord. Massillon (Ohio) State Hosp., 1976-78, social program coord., 1976-82; grad. intern U. Tex., Austin, 1980-83; asst. dir. outpatient svcs. Cen. Mental Health, Canton, Ohio, 1983—; pvt. practice, 1990—. Mem. Nat. Assn. Social Workers, Psi Chi.

MILLER, KARL A. management counselor; b. Reading, Pa., Feb. 27, 1931; s. Harvey and Kathleen Schwartz (Bechtel) M.; m. Carol Joann Mickle, July 28, 1956; children: Dawn Alison, Kevin Bryan. BS in Indsl. Engring., Pa. State U., 1953; MS in Indsl. Mgmt., MIT, 1963. Bus. mgr. GE, Evendale, Ohio, 1953-55, Lynn, Mass., 1956-63; asst. to pres. Burns & Roe, N.Y.C., 1964-65; cons. George Armstrong Co., 1966-68; sr. cons. H.B. Maynard Co., 1968-70; mng. ptnr. Kamid Assocs. Mgmt. cons. to newspapers, electronic media, agribus., govt., architects, engrs., constrn., mfg. and health care delivery firms, Yonkers, N.Y., 1971—; owner David Goliath Ltd.; developer, owner joint tech. projects serving Pacific Rim Aircraft Maintenance Sta., 1990—; ptnr. Power Jets Unltd., 1992—, Pegasus Power Prodrs. Ltd., 1994—;

arbitrator Better Bus. Bur. of N.Y.C., 1982-84; lectr. fin. profitability and mktg. Bucknell U., Pa., Mercy Coll., N.Y., Dominican Coll., Blauvelt, N.Y., 1981-82; speaker in field. Author: Estimating: A Management Process for SEMS at Surrey University, England, 1998, Networking in Jet Engine Retrofitting, 1963, The Farm Machinery Market, 1973; editor Jet Engine Newsletter, 1955-56; contbr. articles to profl. jours. Pres. men's brotherhood Collegiate Ch. N.Y.C., 1970-72; pres. Westchestertowne Houses Condominium, Yonkers, 1971-76, Coun. Condominiums N.Y. State, 1972-76; commr. of deeds City of Yonkers, 1976, chmn. citizens budget adv. com., 1975-76. Recipient Speak Up award Peabody (Mass.) Jr. C. of C., 1960, Minuteman citation, 1960, Henry B. Kane award MIT, 1990. Mem.: Triangle Frat., Internat. Platform Assn., Westchester Personal Computer Users Group, Chinese-Am. MIT, Nat. Mus. Naval Aviation Found. (Pensacola), Air Force Assn. (Gen. Carl A. Tooey Spaatz chpt. 251 pres. 1995—2001, N.E. region pres. 2001—, pres. N.E. region 2001—), Yonkers C. of C. (pres.'s club 1975—78), U.S. Naval Inst. (life), MIT Alumni Ctr. N.Y.C. (gov. 1970—81), U.S. Naval Meml. Found. (nat. adv. coun. 1993—), Army/Navy Club Washington, Am. Legion (life; vice-comdr. 1995, post comdr. 1996—99), Sigma Tau. Republican. Mem. Protestant Dutch Reformed Ch. Home: Unit 21 412 N Broadway Yonkers NY 10701-1938 Office: PO Box 63 Yonkers NY 10703-0063 E-mail: vze2t5zq@verizon.net.

MILLER, KARL FREDERICK, insurance professional; b. White Plains, N.Y., Oct. 30, 1963; s. Robert Bernard Miller and Elizabeth Hendricks Miller; m. Corinne Simpson Miller, Oct. 20, 1990; children: Kevin, Bridget, Kerry. BA in History, U. Fla., 1985. Chartered property casualty underwriter; assoc. risk mgmt. Adjuster Prudential, Fort Lauderdale, Fla., 1987-94; supr. Transp. Fin. Group, 1994-97; supr., program mgr. CCC Consumer Svcs., 1997-2000; ins. mgr. Sunbeam Corp., 2000—. Author: A Warning, 1990; contbr. fiction and poetry to numerous periodicals; inventor. Committeeman Broward Dem. Exec. Com., Ft. Lauderdale, 1992-95; v.p. Coral Springs Improvement Dist., 1995—. Mem. CPCU Soc., Nat. Cath. Edn. Assn., Fla. Rosary (pres. 1991—), Fla. Youth Soccer Assn., Dems. for Life of Am. Roman Catholic. Avocations: guitar, running, coaching soccer. Home: 1999 NW 83rd Dr Coral Springs FL 33071-6271

MILLER, KEITH ALLAN, judge, lawyer; b. Jacksonville, N.C., Aug. 21, 1953; s. Paul V. Miller and Ruth E. Vanderpool; m. Ivanna D. Long, Dec. 24, 1981; children: Esther, Gail, Joel, Jared, Isaac. BS in Phys. Scis., Pacific Union Coll., Angwin, Calif., 1978; JD, Syracuse U., 1990; postgrad., Willamette U., 1991-94. Bar: Oreg. 1992, U.S. Ct. Vet. Appeals 1992, U.S. Supreme Ct. 1999. Orchadist Miller Farms, Umqua, Oreg., 1981-85; pvt. practice atty. Sublimity, 1992-95, Sweet Home, 1996—; peer ct. judge Linn County Cts., 1998—. Dir. guardian ad-litem program ABA, Chgo., 1983. Columnist Horse Cents, 1993. Dir. John Anderson for Pres., Douglas County, Oreg., 1980, Multiple Sclerosis Soc. Douglas County, Roseburg, Oreg., 1980; organizer, pres. Dallas Mobile Home Pk. Renters Assn., 1992-94; Dem. candidate Oreg. State Rep. Dist. 34, 1992, 94. Petty officer USN, 1979-80. Scholar Am. United Separation Ch. and State, 1985. Mem. Oreg. Criminal Def. Lawyers Assn. Democrat. Avocations: auto restoration, stamp collecting, boat building. Office: 1262 Main St Sweet Home OR 97386-1608 Fax: 541-367-4209.

MILLER, KEITH LLOYD, lawyer; b. Harvey, N.D., July 27, 1951; s. Lloyd Vernie and Marian A. (Leintz) M.; m. Linda Suzanne Nelson, Aug. 7, 1971; children: Christopher Nelson, ann Elizabeth. BA, Concordia Coll., Moorhead, Minn., 1972; JD, U. N.D., 1975. Bar: Minn. 1976, U.S. Dist. Ct. Minn. 1976, U.S. Ct. Appeals (8th cir.) 1976, N.D. 1982, U.S. Dist. Ct. N.d. 1982. Assoc. Stefanson, Landberg & Alm, Moorhead, 1976-78; ptnr. Miller, Norman & Assocs., Ltd., 1978—. Cons. Nat. Legal Svcs. Corp., Washington, 1984-86; dir. Northwestern Minn. Legal Svcs. Corp., Moorhead, 1981-87, chmn. bd., 1983-86. Contbr. articles to profl. jours. Bd. dirs. Clay County Dem. Farm Labor Party, Moorhead, 1984-86; advisor Nat. Moot Trial Competition Team, Concordia Coll., 1986-96; mem. organizing com., 1st pres. Judge Ronald N. Davies Inn of Ct., 1996-97. Mem.: ATLA, Acad. Cert. Trial Lawyers Minn., Am. Arbitration Assn. (arbitrator 1980—), State Bar Assn. N.D., N.D. Trial Lawyers Assn., Minn. State Bar Assn. (mem. civil litigation sect. governing coun. 2002—), Minn. Trial Lawyers Assn. (bd. govs. 1987—, treas. 1995—96, sec. 1996—97, v.p. 1997—98, pres.-elect 1998, pres. 1999—2000, contbr. to jour.). Lutheran. Office: Miller Norman & Assocs 403 Center Ave Ste 201 Moorhead MN 56560-1900 E-mail: klmiller@mnalaw.com.

MILLER, KEITH WILLIAM, computer science educator; b. New York, Ill., Feb. 12, 1952; s. Herman Frank Miller, Dorothy Helen Miller; m. Bethany June Spielman; children: Eric Miller-Spielman, Noah Miller-Spielman. BSEd, Concordia Tchrs. Coll., 1973; MS in Math., Coll. William & Mary, 1976; PhD in Computer Sci., U. Iowa, 1983. Prof. computer sci. U. Ill., Springfield, 1993—. Contbr. articles. Mem.: ACM SIGCAS (vice chair 2001—02), IEEE Computer Soc., ACM. Office: Univ IL Springfield Comp Sci 4900 Shepherd Rd Springfield IN 62703 Uzbekistan

MILLER, KEN, state legislator; b. Fort Collins, Colo., Feb. 1, 1957; m. Peggy Miller. Student, Ft. Collins VoTech. Farmer; roofing and wood mfg. contractor; mem. Mont. Senate, Dist. 11, Helena, 1994—; chair bills and jour. com., vice chair local govt. com. Mont. Senate; mem. joint appropriations subcom. on edn./cultural resources Mont. State Senate, mem. natural resources com., mem. fin. and claims com.; adminstr. polit. orgn., state chmn. Ma. Republican Party, 2001—. Republican. Home: PO Box 186 Laurel MT 59044-0186 Office: 1419-B Helena Ave Helena MT 59601 E-mail: Ken@cw2.com.*

MILLER, KEN LEROY, religious studies educator, consultant, writer; b. San Antonio, July 29, 1933; s. Eldridge and Paskel Dovie (Vick) M.; m. Eddie Juanell Crawford, June 14, 1953 (dec. Apr. 1981); children: Kimberly Miller Stern, Kerry, Karen Miller Davis; m. Carolyn Gayle Conatser, May 4, 1982; children: Sheila Stanley, Keith Conatser. BA, Abilene Christian U., 1958; MEd, Trinity U., 1965; EdD, Ariz. State U., 1975. Cert. tchr., Tex. Tchr. SAn Antonio Ind. Sch. Dist., 1957-58; tchr., adminstr. N.E. Ind. Sch. Dist., San Antonio, 1958-69; min. edn. MacArthur Park Ch. of Christ, 1960-69; prin. Ralls (Tex.) Ind. Sch. Dist., 1969-70; minister of edn. S.W. Ch. of Christ, Phoenix, 1970-74; adminstr., tchr. Lubbock (Tex.) Christian Sch./U., 1974-77; minister of edn. Sunset Ch. of Christ, Lubbock, 1977-87; prof. religious edn. Harding U., Searcy, Ark., 1987-98, ret., 1998. Curriculum cons. Sweet Pub. Co., Ft. Worth, 1988-98; leader internat. and nat. religious edn. workshops and seminars. Author: Moral and Religious Stages of Development, 1975, (curriculum) Old Testament Personalities, 1980, Organization, Administration, Supervision of the Bible School, 1993, Recruiting, Training, Retaining Teachers in the Bible School, 1993, Curriculum for the Bible School, 1993; editor: Recipes for Living and Teaching, 1982, (curriculum) Growing in Knowledge, 1977-90, The MINNITH series, 1991-2001; guest editor, contbr. Christian Family 1984. With U.S. Army, 1954-56. Mem. Christian Educators, Christian Edn. Assn., Religious Edn. Assn., Assn. Secondary Schs. and Colls., Alpha Psi Omega, Sigma Tau Delta. Republican. Mem. Ch. of Christ. Avocations: fishing, hunting, reading, travel, writing, poetry readings. Home: 1417 Thames Dr Plano TX 75075-2734 E-mail: klmillerplano@hotmail.com.

MILLER, KENNETH EDWARD, mechanical engineer, consultant; b. Weymouth, Mass., Dec. 24, 1951; s. Edward Francis and Lena Joan (Trotta) M.; m. Eunice Gayle Gooch, Dec. 21, 1996; children: Nicole Elizabeth, Brent Edward. BSME, Northeastern U., 1974; MS in Systems Mgmt., U. So. Calif., 1982. Registered profl. engr., Fla., N.Y., N.H., Ariz., Nev.; registered land surveyor, Ariz. Test engr. Stone & Webster Engring., Boston, 1974-76; plant engr. N.Y. State Power Authority, Buchanan, 1976-80; maintenance engr. Pub. Service Co. of N.H., Seabrook, 1980-82; cons. engr. Helios Engring. Inc., Litchfield Park, Ariz., 1982-87; sr. supervisory service engr. Quadrex Corp., Coraopolis, Penn., 1987-89; cons. engr. Helios Engring., Inc., Litchfield Park, Ariz., 1989-95, Sun Tech. Svcs., Inc., Mission Viejo, Calif., 1995-96, Cataract, Inc., Pennsauken, N.J., 1996-97, Chapdelaine & Assocs., Inc., Hurst, Tex., 1998, Fla. Power Corp., Crystal River, 1998—. Republican. Roman Catholic. Avocations: piloting, scuba diving. Address: PO Box 10187 Brooksville FL 34603-0187

MILLER, KENNETH EDWARD, sociologist, educator; b. N.Y.C., June 17, 1929; s. Joseph F. and Irene (Edersheim) M.; m. Andrée Nora Barthelemy, Feb. 14, 1959 (div. Nov. 1984); children: Jennifer Andrée, Christopher Kenneth; m. Janet Sue Daniels, May 21, 1990. BA, U. Ala., 1953, MA, 1956; PhD, Duke, 1965; MS, Drake U., 1986. Asst. to pres., dir. devel. Jacksonville (Fla.) U., 1957-60; dir. Health Council, asso. dir. Community Planning Council, Birmingham, Ala., 1960-62; asst. prof. sociology Emory U., Atlanta, 1966-70, acting chmn. dept., 1969-70; prof. sociology Drake U., Des Moines, 1970-96, chmn. dept., 1970-79, 82-88, asst. to dean for grad. studies, 1991-92, prof. emeritus, 1996—. Research sociologist U. Ala., 1956-57; research asso. U.S. Civil Service Commn., summer 1968. Served with USN, 1946-48. Postdoctoral research fellow Duke, 1965-66. Mem. Midwest Sociol. Soc. Home: 2129 NW 140th St Clive IA 50325-8730

MILLER, KENNETH GREGORY, retired air force officer; b. Bryan, Tex., July 28, 1944; s. Max Richard and Catherine Mae (Sultzman) M.; m. Ann Marguerite Perpich, Nov. 25, 1966; children: Keith G., Deborah J., Craig S. BS in Aero. Engring., Purdue U., 1966; MS in Systems Mgmt., U. So. Calif., 1970; grad., Nat. War Coll., Washington, 1986; postgrad., U. Va., 1988. Commd. 2d lt. USAF, 1966, advanced through grades to brig. gen., 1995; with Office Sec. Def., Washington, 1980-81; various positions to dir. field ops. F-16 System Program Office, Wright-Patterson AFB, Ohio, 1981-86; chief engring. div. Sacramento Air Logistics Ctr., McClellan AFB, Calif., 1986-87; dir. materiel mgmt. Ogden Air Logistics Ctr., Hill AFB, Utah, 1987-89; vice comdr. Acquisition Logistics Div., Wright-Patterson AFB, 1989-90; comdr. Air Force Contract Mgmt. Divsn., Kirtland AFB, N.Mex., 1990; comdr. western dist. Def. Contract Mgmt. Command, L.A., 1990-91; dir. C-17 Program Office, Wright-Patterson AFB, 1991-93; dep. asst. sec. for acquistion USAF, Washington, 1993-94, dir. supply hdqrs., 1994-95; v.p. for gulf ops. BDM Fed., 1995-96; group v.p. for advanced tech. svcs. group RJO Enterprises, Inc., 1997; sr. v.p. Dayton ops. CACI, Inc., 1997-99; group v.p. Air Force programs Anteon Corp., 1999—. Mem. engring. bd. visitors Purdue U. Decorated Disting. Svc. medal, Legion of Merit (2), Def. Superior Svc. medal; recipient award of merit Freedom Found; named Outstanding Aerospace Engr., Purdue U., Disting. Engring. Alumnus, Purdue U., 2001; named to ROTC Hall of Fame, 2001. Mem. Nat. Contract Mgmt. Assn. (bd. advisors 1990-92), Soc. Logistics Engrs., Nat. Def. Indsl. Assn. Office: 1560 Wilson Blvd Ste 800 Arlington VA 22209 E-mail: kmiller@anteon.com.

MILLER, KENNETH MICHAEL, electronics executive, director; b. Chgo., Nov. 20, 1921; s. Matthew and Tillie (Otto) M.; m. Dolores June Miller, Jan. 16, 1943 (dec. Dec. 1968); children: Barbara Anne Reed, Nancy Jeanne Hathaway, Kenneth Michael, Roger Allan; m. Sally J. Ballingham, June 20, 1970. Student, Ill. Inst. Tech., 1940-41, UCLA, 1961. Electronics engr. Rauland Corp., Chgo., 1941-48; gen. mgr. Lear, Inc., Santa Monica, Calif., 1948-59; v.p., gen. mgr. Motorola Aviation Electronics, Inc., Culver City, 1959-60; v.p., gen. mgr. instrument divsn. Daystrom, Inc., L.A., 1961; gen. mgr. metrics divsn. Singer Co., L.A. and Bridgeport, Conn., 1962-65; v.p., gen. mgr. Lear Jet Corp., 1965-66; pres., dir. Infonics, Inc., 1967-68; v.p., gen. mgr. Computer Industries, Inc., 1968-69; dir. ops., tech. products group Am. Std. Corp., McLean, Va., also v.p., gen. mgr. Wilcox Elec. divsn. Kansas City, Mo., 1969-71; pres. Wilcox Elec., Inc. subs. Northrop Corp., 1971-72; v.p., dir. World Wide Wilcox, Inc. subs., McLean, 1971-72; pres., CEO, dir. Penril Corp., Rockville, Md., 1973-86; pres. K-M Miller and Assocs., 1986—. Dir. George Mason Bank, NA, Washington, Palmer Nat. Bank, Washington. Mem. adv. bd. Washington Bus. Jour.; contbr. articles to profl. jours. Mem. regional planning coun. Cmty. Mental Health Svcs., Bridgeport, 1964; mem. Bridgeport Capital Fund Com.; trustee Park City Hosp.; vice dir. Montgomery County Arts Coun.; bd. dirs. U. Bridgeport; mem. Md. State Com. High Tech. Recipient Job Makers award Mfrs. Assn. Bridgeport, 1963. Fellow Radio Club Am. (dir., chmn grants-in-aid com.); mem. AIAA, IEEE, Aircraft Owners and Pilots Assn., Am. Mgmt. Assn., Armed Forces Comm. and Electronics Assn. (life), Electronic Industries Assn., Instrument Soc. Am. (life), Nat. Aero. Assn., Soc. Non-Destructive Testing, Soc. Automotive Engrs., Air Force Assn., Am. Radio Relay League (life), Amateur Satellite Corp. (life), Am. Def. Preparedness Assn. (life), Aero. Elec. Soc. (life), Nat. Capital DX Assn. (pres. 1987-88), Assn. Old Crows (life), Mfrs. Assn. Bridgeport (dir.), Bridgeport Engring. Inst., Bridgeport C. of C. (pres. 1964), Quarter Century Wireless Assn. (life, Disting. Svc. award 1994), Soc. Wireless Pioneers, Rolling Hills Country Club (Wichita), Algonquin Club (Bridgeport). Home and Office: 16904 George Washington Dr Rockville MD 20853-1128 E-mail: kmm@prodigy.net.

MILLER, KENNETH ROYE, JR. financial planner, educator; b. Charleston, S.C., Aug. 19, 1965; s. Kenneth Roy and Cheryl (Allred) M.; m. Jill Thompson, Aug. 8, 1987. BA in Polit. Sci., Westminster Coll., Fulton, Mo., 1987; MPA, U. Ky., 1993, PhD in Pub. Adminstrn., 1995. Fin. planner Waddell and Reed, St. Louis, 1987-88; stockbroker Paine Webber, Paducah, Ky., 1988-90; rschr. U. Ky., Lexington, 1990-95; chief policy analyst State Auditors Office, Frankfort, Ky, 1995-99; ptnr. Kissling Orgn., 1999-2000; ChFC Jefferson Pilot Fin., 2000—. Prof. Ea. Ky. U., 1999-2000, U. Ky., 2000—. Capt. U.S. Army, 1998—. Mem. ASPA (treas. 1994-99). Avocations: reading, weight-lifting, biking, movies.

MILLER, KENNETH WILLIAM, II, research and development engineering executive; b. Cleve., May 11, 1951; s. Kenneth William and Margaret Mary Miller; m. Joan Ellen Pattillo, Aug. 12, 1972 (div. Oct. 1992); children: Kenneth William III, Victoria Joan, Christopher John. BSEE, MIT, 1974, MS in Mgmt. of Tech., 1983; postgrad., Am. U. Paris, 1994-95, Harvard U., 1997. From process engr. to sr. equipment engr. Corning (N.Y.) Glass Works, 1974-78, supr. process engring., 1978-80, sr. mkt. devel. analyst, 1980, sr. project engr., 1980-81; product engring. mgr. Duracell Divsn. Gillette, Lexington, N.C., 1983-85; mgr. advanced tech. Gen. Dynamics Advanced Tech., Greensboro, 1985; v.p., bd. dirs. Frey Holdings, Inc., Mansfield, 1985-89; v.p. Intellogistics, Inc., Columbus, Ohio, 1989, Zack's Investment Rsch., Chgo., 1991; pres., treas. New Video Holdings, Malden, Mass., 1995—. Computer programmer Fed Res Bank Boston, 1972—74; lectr mgt sci Ohio State Univ, 1988. Author: International Technology Strategy, 1983, GATT, 1994 (Cetus Paribus), Our Future Welfare, 1995, Godspace 2084, 2002; contbr. articles to profl. jours. Rep cand state rep, Richard County, Ohio, 1988; Rep cand Richland City Coun, 1989; mem exec comt Ohio Reps; head usher Harvard-Epworth United Meth Ch, 1999—. Mem.: SAR (Mass. bd. mgrs. 2001—, v.p. Boston chpt.), IEEE (sr.), MIT Alumni Assn., Ohio Acad. Sci. (life; judge), Eagle Scout Assn. (life). Avocations: camping, personal computing, international travel. Home and Office: 115 Washington St Apt 5 Malden MA 02148-3718 Personal E-mail: kwmillerII@aol.com.

MILLER, KERRY LEE, city manager; b. Nov. 30, 1950; m. Pamela Miller. BA, Brigham Young U., 1974, MPA, 1976. Asst. to city mgr. City of Las Vegas, 1978-80; ct. adminstr. Mcpl. Ct., Las Vegas, 1980-82; city mgr. City of Sanger (Calif.), 1982-87, City of South Lake Tahoe (Calif.), 1987-99, City of Encinitas (Calif.), 1999—. Home and Office: 505 S. Vulcan Ave Encinitas CA 92024-3633 E-mail: kmiller@ci.encinitas.ca.us.

MILLER, KERRY LEE, lawyer; b. West Palm Beach, Sept. 11, 1955; s. Clyde Howard and Alice (Hummel) M.; m. Myrna Patricia Garza, June 9, 1979; children: Alexander James, Eric Anthony. BA, George Mason U., 1977; JD, Cath. U., 1981. Bar: D.C. 1981, Va. 1982, U.S. Dist. Ct. (D.C. dist.) 1982, U.S. Ct. Appeals (D.C. and 4th cirs.) 1982, U.S. Ct. Appeals (fed. cir.) 1989, U.S. Ct. Claims 1989, U.S. Supreme Ct. 1989, U.S. Dist. Ct. (ea. and we. dists.) Va. 1993. Asst. gen. counsel Office Gen. Counsel U.S. Govt. Printing Office, Washington, 1981-87, assoc. gen. counsel contracts and procurement, 1987-99; adminstrv. law judge Bd. Contract Appeals U.S. Govt. Printing Office, 1999—. Mem. Fed. Bar Assn. (mem. chpt. coun. Capitol Hill chpt.), Bd. Contract Appeals Judges Assn., Computer Law Assn., Contract Appeals Bar Assn. Office: US Govt Printing Office Office Bd Contract Appeals 732 N Capitol St NW Washington DC 20401-0001 E-mail: kmiller@gpo.gov.

MILLER, KEVIN CLARK, heavy equipment operator, writer; b. Spokane, Wash., Dec. 26, 1961; s. Clark Allen and Myrtle Alena Miller; m. Maria Elaina Celli; children: Brandon. Heavy equipment operator, mechanic Faulkner Walsh Constructors, Bethel, Alaska, 1996—98; supt., heavy equipment operator Alaska Complete Tank, Anchorage, 2000—02. Author: Visions: Book One, 2001, The Lone Birch, 2002, (eBook) Interior Survival, 2000. Home: PO Box 243446 Anchorage AK 99524 Personal E-mail: mkbmiller@aol.com.

MILLER, KEVIN ROBERT, employee benefit consultant; b. Miller, S.D., Sept. 7, 1961; s. Robert Leo and Norma Cecelia (Pottebaum) M.; m. Ellen Susan Arends, Sept. 21, 1985; children: Collin John, Tyler Jordan, Jacob Robert. BS in Bus. Mgmt. and Mktg., No. State Coll., 1983. CLU The Am. Coll.; cert. fund specialist Inst. Cert. Fund Specialists, chartered fin. cons. The Am. Coll., chartered mutual fund counselor Coll. for Fin. Planning. Credit rep. Citibank S.D., NA, Sioux Falls, 1983-84; terr. mgr. Cosmair Inc., Mankato, Minn., 1984-86; employee benefit cons., retirement planner Arends Assocs., Inc., Albert Lea, 1986-90; employee benefits cons. Fringe Benefits Design, Eden Prairie, 1990-94, pres., CEO Bloomington, 1995—. Mem. Kiwanis. Republican. Roman Catholic. Office: Fringe Benefits Design 7900 Xerxes Ave S Ste 700 Bloomington MN 55431-1127

MILLER, L. MARTIN, accountant, financial planning specialist; b. N.Y.C., Sept. 17, 1939; s. Harvey and Julia (Lewis) M.; m. Judith Sklar, Jan. 21, 1962; children: Philip, Marjorie. BS, Wharton Sch., U. Pa., 1960; M Taxation, Villanova U., 2001. CPA; CFP; accredited fin. planning specialist. Jr. acct. Deloitte, Haskins & Sells, N.Y.C., 1960-62, sr. acct. Phila., 1962-64; mng. ptnr. Cogen, Sklar LLP, 1964—. Treas. Coronet Container Co., Inc., Phila., Val Mar Realty Corp., N.Y.C.; dir. Penn Internat. Trading Co., Phila.; mng. dir. CPA Tax Forum, 1966-69; underwriting mem. Lloyds of London, 1978-95, chmn. Mid-Atlantic region, 1991-92; mem. faculty Wharton Sch. U. Pa., 1992-99; lectr., discussion leader on fin. and taxation; columnist Montgomery and Bucks County Dental News. Author: Accountants Guide to S.E.C. Filings, 1968, Salaries, Penn. Non-Profit Report, 1997, Worker Compensation, Practical Tax Strategies, 2000; contbr. articles to profl. jours. Mem. Phila. Rep. Com., 1963-67, treas. Daerr-Bannon for state rep. com., 1997; chmn. Lower Merion Twp. scholarship fund, 1975-78; bd. dirs. Main Line Br. ARC, 1997-2000; bd. dirs. Penn Valley Civic Assn., 1973-79, Gladwyne Civic Assn., 1992-95; mem. Lower Merion Planning Commn., 1978-82, Gov.'s Tax Study Commn.; pres. Mensa Edn. and Rsch. Found., 1984-86; mem. SEC Forum on Small Bus. Capital Formation, 1983, Pa. Impact, 1995; apptd. to Pa. State Bd. Accountancy, 1985-94, chmn., 1990-91; elected sch. bd. dir. Lower Merion Twp., 1993-97, also chmn. fin. com. Served with U.S. Army, 1961-62. Recipient Outstanding Achievement award Germantown Civic Assn., 1965. Mem. Pa. Inst. CPAs (edn. com. 1975-78, bd. dirs. 1979-81, by-laws chmn. 1980-83, mem. non-profit orgns. com. 1995-99), Nat. Assn. State Bds. Accountancy (edn. com. 1987, nominating com. 1989, experience com. 1990, continuing edn. com. 1995—), Cert. Fin. Planner (bd. ethics 1995-97), AICPAs (nat. tax commn. 1979-82, exec. com. self regulation divsn. for CPA firms 1984-87, acctg. and rev. svcs. com. 1985-88, long range planning com., ethics divsn. 1985-88, specialization bd. 1989-90, ethics exec. com. 1990-93, mem. curriculum and acctg. edn. 1993-96, chmn. fin. assistance task force 1995, bd. dirs. Estate Planning Coun. 1998—, nomination com. 1999), Little 10 Acctg. Assn. (edn. chmn. 1980-84), Main Line C. of C. (govt. affairs com. 1991-99), Mensa (internat. fin. officer 1970-74), Masons (past master), Plays and Players Club (treas. 1978-79), Beta Alpha Psi. Home: 204 Dove Ln Haverford PA 19041-1902 Office: Cogen Sklar LLP 150 Monument Rd Bala Cynwyd PA 19004-1702

MILLER, LARRY JOE, evangelist; b. Huntingburg, Ind., Mar. 17, 1954; s. Gordon Russel and Nona Maxine (Wininger) M.; m. Jolene Kay Daniel, May 17, 1974; children: Benjamin Daniel, Joshua Joe. BS, Ky. Christian Coll., 1981. Ordained to ministry Christian Ch., 1981. Chaplain asst. Ky. Christian Coll., Grayson, 1977-78; youth min. Beech Street Christian Ch., Ashland, Ky., 1979-80; facilities mgr., dir. sch. shop Ind. Children's Christian Home, Ladoga, 1981-86; elder, evangelist New Market (Ind.) Christian Ch., 1982; min. Waveland (Ind.) Christian Ch., 1987-89; elder, evangelist Brady Lane Christian Ch., Lafayette, Ind., 1990—. Owner, operator Miller Constrn., Grayson, 1979-81; human resources rep. Subaru-Isuzu Automotive, Lafayette, 1989-96; corp. trainer N.Am. Lighting, Flora, Ill., 1996-97; owner Larry's Home Improvement, 1997-98; adj. faculty, bus. and industry tng., Ivy Tech State Coll., Lafayette, Ind., 1997-2000; owner Property Plus, 2000-. Democrat. Home: 3419 Coventry Ln Lafayette IN 47909-2960 *Life is short, and must be used to its fullest potential for His glory.*

MILLER, LARRY THOMAS, accountant; b. Omaha, Oct. 24, 1940; s. Elmer Thomas and Lucile Valentine (Hammon) M. Student, U. Omaha, 1958-63. With acctg. dept. Union Pacific R.R. Co., Omaha, 1959-92, tax acct., 1969—; prin. Doyle Distbg., 1996—. Author: (song lyrics) for country albums America, Bad Girl Problem, Fire Fool, 1997, HillTop Country, Love is Sweet, Holman Hollow, 1998; co-author: (how-to book) Bowling Our way, 1996. Served with U.S. Army, M.P., 1965-67. Mem. Am. Acctg. Assn. Republican. Home: 2353 N 92nd Ave Omaha NE 68134-5930 Office: Doyle Distributing 2353 N 92nd Ave Apt 14 Omaha NE 68134-5930 E-mail: dyldstrb@mitec.net.

MILLER, LAURA, mayor, journalist; b. Balt., Nov. 18, 1958; m. Steven Wolens; children: Alex, Lily, Maxwell. Grad., U. Wis., Madison. Mem. Dallas City Coun.; mayor City of Dallas, 2002—. Columnist, investigative reporter Dallas Observer, metro columnist Dallas Times Herald, New York Daily News, The Dallas Morning News, The Miami Herald. Recipient H.L. Mencken Writing award, Balt. Sun, 1995, 6 Katie awards, Dallas Press Club, 2 Tex. Headliner awards, 2 Philbin awards, Dallas Bar Assn., cert. of merit, ABA. Office: Dallas City Hall 1500 Marilla St Rm 5EN Dallas TX 75201-6390*

MILLER, LENORE WOLF DANIELS, speech-language pathologist; b. N.Y.C., Mar. 9, 1937; d. Samuel D. and Sarah (Reisman) Wolf; m. Marshall Nelson Daniels, Mar. 30, 1958 (div. Jan. 1965); m. Macey I. Miller, Dec. 11, 1977; 1 child, Suzanne Hayley. BA, CUNY, 1958, MA, 1961; ScD, Boston U., 1983. Sr. speech pathologist L.I. Coll. Hosp., N.Y.C., 1959-68; supr. speech-lang. pathology Tufts-New England Med. Ctr., Boston, 1968-87, dir. speech-lang. pathology, 1987-95, co-dir dept. speech-lang. pathology, 1987-95; pvt. and cons. practice speech-lang. pathology, Newton, Mass., 1995—. Asst. prof. depts. otolaryngology and rehab. medicine Tufts U. Sch. Medicine, 1992—96, asst. prof. dept. child psychiatry, 1995—96; adj. faculty Emerson Coll., 1993, Northeastern U., 1994, Boston U., 1993—, Mass. Gen. Hosp. Inst. Health Professions, 1998, 2002; specialist in areas of cranio-facial anomalies, voice disorders, dysfluency, lang. and motor-speech disorders, pediat. , adult and geriatric; presenter in field. Contbr. articles to profl. jours. Mem. Am. Fedn. Musicians, 1965—80; del. Mass. Health Coun., Boston, 1974, 1975; mem. Tanglewood Festival Chorus, 1971—75, Newton Singers, 2001—; former actor Ivy Tower Playhouse, Spring Lake, NJ, Bklyn. Heights Repertory Co. Theatre, Bklyn. Nat. Office Edn. grantee, 1980. Mem.: Boston Area Voice Interest Group, Mass. Speech-Lang.-Hearing Assn. (pres. elect 1976—77, pres. 1977—78, sr. chair govtl. affairs 1988—91, honors 1979), Am. Cleft Palate-Craniofacial Assn. (pub. rels. com. 1973—74, by-laws com. 1977—78), Am. Assn. Pvt. Practice Speech Pathology and Audiology, Am. Speech-Lang.-Hearing Assn. (legis. coun. 1973—75, chair com. spl. rules 1974—75). Avocations: singing, drama, gourmet cooking, biking, tennis.

MILLER, LEO PERCY, investor, writer; b. Murray, Iowa, Mar. 16, 1926; s. Percy Henry Miller and Edna Marie Luce-Miller; m. Lucille Patterson; 1 child Cheryl Miller-Larson 1 child Monty 1 child Terry. M in Bible Theology(hon.) , Internat. Bible Inst. & Sem., 1985. Lic. real estate realtor Calif., 1986. Freelance writer, Sanger, Calif., 1975—. Author: No Dirt In My Face, 2000. Pvt. first class U.S. Army, 1944—48, Europe. Mem.: Christian Writers Guild (mem. 1999—2002, None N/A). Southern Baptist. Avocation: volunteer religious ministries.

MILLER, LEROY PAUL, JR. secondary English educator; b. Holyoke, Mass., Feb. 21, 1949; s. Leroy Paul Sr. and Rose Marie (Danehey) M. AA, Northampton (Mass.) Jr. Coll., 1972; BA, U. New. Eng., Biddeford, Maine, 1974; MEd, Springfield (Mass.) Coll., 1977; postgrad., Am. Internat. Coll., Springfield. Cert. elem. tchr., English tchr., guidance counselor, Mass. Sch. adjustment counselor Holyoke Pub. Schs., 1978-79, ednl. programmer, 1979-80, tutor Chpt. I, 1980-81; tutor Amherst (Mass.) Pub. Schs., 1982-84; tchr. West Springfield (Mass.) Pub. Schs., 1985-86; tchr. English Springfield Pub. Schs., 1986—. Fundraiser M. Marcus Kiley Mid. Sch.; alumni counselor U. New Eng., 1977—. Mem. NEA, ASCD, Nat. Coun. Tchrs. English, Mass. Tchrs. Assn., Springfield Edn. Assn. (faculty rep. 1986—), U. New Eng. Alumni Assn. (v.p. 1990—), Elks, Psi Chi. Democrat. Roman Catholic. Avocations: reading, bowling. Home: 2 Gerard Way Holyoke MA 01040-1204 Office: M Marcus Kiley Mid Sch 180 Cooley St Springfield MA 01128-1108 E-mail: lmill55169@aol.com.

MILLER, LESLIE ANNE, lawyer; b. Franlin, Ind., Nov. 4, 1951; d. G. Thomas and Anne (Gaines) Miller; m. Richard B. Worley, Feb. 14, 1987. AB cum laude, Mt. Holyoke Coll., South Hadley, Pa., 1973; MA in Polit. Sci., Eagle Inst. Politics Rutgers U., New Brunswick, N.J., 1974; JD, Dickinson Sch. of Law, Carlisle, Pa., 1977; LLM with honors, Temple U., 1994. Bar: Pa. 1977, U.S. Dist. Ct. (ea. dist.) Pa. 1977, U.S. Ct. Appeals (3d cir.) 1980, U.S. Dist. Ct. (ea. dist.) Pa. 1987. Assoc. LaBrum & Doak, Phila., 1977-81, ptnr., 1982-86, Goldfein & Joseph, Phila., 1986-95, McKissock & Hoffman, P.C., Phila., 1995—. Bd. dirs. WHYY-TV, 1996—; del. Third Circuit Jud. Conf., 1981, 82, 85; mem. Jud. Inquiry and Rev. Bd., 1990-94, chair, 1993-94; mem. faculty trial advocacy program Dickinson Sch. Law, 1992, 94; mem. hearing com., disciplinary bd. Supreme Ct. Pa., 1996—; mem. faculty Acad. Advocacy Temple U., 1994—; judge pro tem Ct. of Common Pleas. Mem. acad. ball com. Phila. Orch., 1986-87, 89-91, 95-96, mem. acad. music com. 1998—; mem. Open Space Task Force Com., Lower Merion Twp., Pa., 1990, bd. dirs., 1990-94, mem. counsel, 1990, Lower Merion Conservancy, 1995-97, 2000—, others; bd. dirs. Med. Coll. Pa., 1985-96, sec., 1987-92, chair presdl. search com., 1993, chair presdl. inauguration, 1987, chair com. on acad. affairs, 1989-95, chair dean's search com., 1994-95, chair nomenclature com., 1996; bd. dirs. Med. Coll. Hosps., 1991-96, Allegheny Health Edn. and Rsch. Found., 1993-96, Hahnemann U. Med. Sch., 1994-96, Pa. Ballet, 1994—, St. Christopher's Hosp. for Children, 1991-94, vice chair, 1990-94; bd. dirs. Phila. Free Libr., 1997—; trustee Mt. Holyoke Coll., 2000—; bd. govs. Dickinson Sch. Law, Pa. State U., 2001—. Recipient Mary Lyon award, Mt. Holyoke Alumni Assn., 1985, Alumnae Medal of Honor, 1988, Hon. Alumnae award, 1989, Pres.'s award Med. Coll. Pa., 1993, Sylvia Rambo award Dickinson Sch. of Law, 1997, Star award Forum of Exec. Women, 1998, Ann Alpern award PBA Women in the Profession, 1999, Sandra Day O'Connor award Phila. Bar Assn., 1999, Outstanding Leadership in Support of Legal Svcs. award Pa. Legal Svcs., 1999; named to Pa. Honor Roll of Women, 1996, Disting. Dau. of Pa., Gov. Tom Ridge, 1999. Fellow Am. Bar Found., Pa. Bar Found.; mem. ABA, Phila. Bar Assn. (mem. exec. com. divsn. young lawyers 1982-85, mem. bicentennial com 1986-87, bd. govs. 1990-93, mem. gender bias task force 1993-97, chair com. on jud. selection and retention 1987-89, vice chair 1985-87, investigative divsn. 1982-85, chair Andrew Hamilton Ball 1989, trustee Phila. Bar Found. 1990-97, co-chair century three commn. 1995-97, others), Pa. Bar Assn. (found. ho. dels. life fellow, bd. govs. 1980-83, 84-87, 91-93, chair young lawyers divsn. 1982-83, mem. long range planning com. 1985-87, mem. com. on professionalism, 1987-91, vice chmn. jud. inquiry and rev. bd. study com. 1989-91, sec. 1984-87, chair ho. dels. 1991-93, chair commn. on women in the profession 1993-95, v.p. 1996-97, pres. 1998-99, immediate past pres. 1999—, apptd. mem. ct. jud. discipline 1999), Pa. Bar Inst. (mem. faculty, course planner), Phila. Assn. Def. Counsel (mem. exec. coun. 1987-90, 94, mem. joint trial demonstration with Phila. Trial Lawyers Assn. 1993), Def. Rsch. Inst. (spkr. toxic torts seminar 1983), Phila. Bar Edn. Advocacy Women Litigators (course planner, mem. faculty 1995), Women's Assn. Women's Alternatives (bd. dirs. 1983-94, vice chair 1985-94), Phila. Forum Exec. Women, Pa. Women's Forum, Com. of Seventy, Mt. Holyoke Alumnae Assn. (bd. dirs. 1986-89). Democrat. Lutheran. Avocations: collecting Am. antiques, gardening, running. Office: McKissock & Hoffman PC 1700 Market St Ste 3000 Philadelphia PA 19103-3933 E-mail: millesq@aol.com.

MILLER, LIA VERENA REYES, management services executive; b. Pasay City, Manila, Philippines, Sept. 1, 1966; d. Rudy San Pedro and Cecilia San Pedro (Suarez) Reyes; m. Thomas Michael Miller, Oct. 3, 1998; stepchildren: Michael Bradley, Brenton Joseph. BS, Marymount Coll., 1988. Creative dir. Pacific Design, Indpls., 1989-91; v.p. ops. Park Kwik Corp. of Am., 1988-92; self-employed parking cons. N.Y.C., 1992-95; dir. Internat. Parking Profls., Singapore, 1997—; pres. ParkAsia, Inc., Philippines, 1995—. Parking Co. Asia, Philippines, 1999—. Cons. Fort Bonifacio Devel. Corp., Manila, Philippines, 1995-99, Kerry Properties, Hong Kong, 1997-98, Metro Pacific Land Corp., Manila, Philippines, 1997, Totsuka Station, Japan, 1997. Chmn. Bus. Encouraging Students for Tomorrow, Ind., 1989-90 (recipient Leadership award 1990); vol. Kiwanis Club Indpls., 1986; counselor, leader Eli Lilly Project Leadership, Ind., 1984; mem. Women's Round Table, Ind., 1989-92, Commn. for Downtown Indpls., 1989-91. Mem. Nat. Parking Assn., Internat. Parking Inst. Avocations: scuba diving, drawing and painting, tennis, traveling.

MILLER, LILLIE M. nursing educator; b. Atlanta, Nov. 16, 1937; d. George W. and Lillie M. (Reese) McDaniel; m. Harold G. Miller, June 30, 1962; children: Daren K., Lisa K. Diploma in nursing, Jewish Hosp. of Cin., 1959; BSN, U. Cin., 1961; MEd, Temple U., 1970; MSN, Villanova U., 1987. RN, Pa.; cert. sch. nurse, cert. clin. specialist in med.-surg. nursing ANCC. Instr. sch. nursing Jewish Hosp. Cin., 1959-62; instr. Phila. Gen. Hosp. Sch. Nursing, 1962-67; sch. nurse Norristown (Pa.) Area Sch. Dist., 1967-70; nursing instr. Villanova U., Villanova, Pa., 1988; asst. prof. Montgomery County C.C., Blue Bell, 1983-93, assoc. prof, 1993-98, prof., 1998—. Advisor Student Nurses Assn. Pa. Recipient Pi Tau Delta scholarship, Chapel of Four Chaplains. Mem.: ANA, Pa. Med. Soc. (patient adv. bd. 2001—), Villanova U. Alumni Assn., Temple U. Alumni Assn., Jewish Hosp. Alumni Assn., Pa. League for Nursing, Nat. League for Nursing, Sigma Theta Tau. E-mail: lmiller@mc3.edu.

MILLER, LINDA B. political scientist; b. Manchester, N.H., Aug. 7, 1937; d. Louis and Helene (Chase) M. AB cum laude, Radcliffe Coll., 1959; MA, Columbia U., 1961, PhD, 1965. Asst. prof. Barnard Coll., 1964-67; rsch. assoc. Princeton U., 1966-67, Harvard U., 1967-71, 76-81, lectr. polit. sci., 1968-69; assoc. prof. Wellesley (Mass.) Coll., 1969-75, prof. polit. sci., 1975—, chmn. dept., 1985-89. Vis. prof. rsch. Watson Inst., Brown U., 1997, vis. prof. political sci., Brown Univ., 1997; adj. prof. internat. rels. Watson Inst., Brown U., 1998-2000, sr. fellow, 2000—. Author: World Order and Local Disorder: The United Nations and Internal Conflicts, 1967, Dynamics of World Politics: Studies in the Resolution of Conflicts, 1968, Cyprus: The Law and Politics of Civil Strife, 1968; co-author, co-editor: Ideas and Ideals: Essays on Politics in Honor of Stanley Hoffmann, 1993; editor Internat. Studies Rev., 1999-2002; contbr. articles to profl. jours. Internat. Affairs fellow Coun. Fng. Rels., 1973-74, Rockefeller Found. fellow, 1976-77, Oceanographic Instn. sr. fellow, 1979-80, 82-83, NATO social sci. rsch. fellow, 1982-83. Mem. Inst. Strategic Studies, Internat. Studies Assn., Coun. Fgn. Rels., Phi Beta Kappa. Home: PO Box 415 South Wellfleet MA 02663-0415 Office: Wellesley Coll Dept Polit Sci Wellesley MA 02482 also: Watson Inst Brown U PO Box 1970 Providence RI 02912-1970 E-mail: Linda_Miller@brown.edu.

MILLER, LINDA KAREN, educator; b. Kansas City, Jan. 22, 1948; d. Bennie Chris and Thelma Jane (Richey) M. B of Secondary Edn., U. Kans., 1970; M of Secondary Edn., U. Va., 1978, EdD, 1991. Tchr. social studies Pierson Jr. High Sch., Kansas City, 1970-72; substitute tchr. Fairfax (Va.) Pub. Schs., 1972-73; reading aide Lake Braddock Secondary Sch., Burke, Va., 1973-74; tchr. social studies Mark Twain Intermediate Sch., Alexandria, 1974-75, Herndon (Va.) Intermediate Sch., 1975-78, Fairfax High Sch., 1978-86, 87—. Cons. in field. Named Pre-Collegiate Tchr. of Yr., Orgn. Am. Historians, 1996, Secondary Tchr. of Yr., Nat. Coun. for Social Studies, 1996, U. Va., 1997, Outstanding Secondary Tchr., Va. Hist. Soc., 1998, Va. Geography Tchr. of Yr., 1999, Global Technet Tchr. of Yr., Nat. Peace Corps Assn., 1999, Nat. Peace Educator, 2002; recipient George Washington medal, Valley Forge Freedom Found., 1988, Excellence in Tchg. award, U. Kans. Sch. Edn., 1999, Celebrating Tchg. Excellence award, Am. Coun. Tchrs. Russian, 1998; fellow, Korean Soc., 2000, Am. Revolution fellow, N.Y. Hist. Soc., 2001. Mem. Nat. Coun. Social Studies (curriculum com. 1991-94), Am. Legal History Soc., Orgn. Am. Historians, Va. Coun. Social Studies, Washington Area Women Historians, U. Va. Alumni Assn. Republican. Episcopalian. Avocation: doll collecting. Office: Fairfax High Sch 3500 Old Lee Hwy Fairfax VA 22030-1888

MILLER, LINDA LOU, education administrator, communications specialist; b. Pottsville, Pa., Feb. 5, 1955; d. Cletus Isaac and Erma Ruth (Brown) M.; m. William Joseph Murray Jr., July 23, 1989; 1 stepchild, Nathan Andrew. BA, Shippensburg (Pa.) U., 1977; MEd, Pa. State U., 1998. Copywriter, media buyer Williams & Assocs., Harrisburg, Pa., 1977-78; dir. communications Pa. Newspaper Pub.'s Assn., 1978-82; dir. alumni affairs Shippensburg U. Pa., 1982-85; exec. v.p. Pa. Soc. Assn. Execs., Harrisburg, 1985-90; dir. communications The Milton Hershey (Pa.) Sch., 1990—2001; adj. instr. Shippensburg (Pa.) U., Lebanon Valley Coll.; sales coord. Messiah Villaga/Grantham Heights, 2001—; dir. major gifts Shippensburg U. Found., 2002—. Sec. Kimberley Meadows Civic Assn., Mechanicsburg, Pa., 1990; adv. coun. Shippensburg U., 1990; pers. chair Chapel Hill United Ch. of Christ, 1992-94, ops. commn., 1992-94; mem. Milton Hershey Postage Stamp Celebration Com., 1995; editor 100th Ann. Memories Book, St. Peter's UCC, Pine Grove, Pa., 2000-01. Recipient Disting. Alumnus award, Pien Grove Area Alumni Assn., 2002, Outstanding Achievement award, U. Pa. Shippensburg, 1998. Mem. PRSA, NAFE, Pa. Soc. Assn. Execs., Ctrl. Pa. Assn. Profl. Women, Coun. for Advancement and Support of Edn., Am. Soc. Assn. Execs. (bd. dirs. 1989, cert.), Conf. Assn. Soc. Execs. (pres. 1988-89), Allied Socs. Coun. (chmn. 1988-89), Exec. Club of Ctrl. Pa. (bd. dirs. 1988-90), Rotary Club. Avocations: reading, walking, travel, recreational sports, desktop publishing. Home: 27 Conway Dr Mechanicsburg PA 17055-6136 Office: Shippensburg Univ Found 1871 Old Main Dr Shippensburg PA 17257

MILLER, LISA FRIEDMAN, psychology educator; b. Iowa City, July 25, 1966; m. Philip Roger Miller. BA, Yale U., 1988; PhD, U. Pa., 1994. Asst. prof. Tchrs. Coll. Columbia U., N.Y.C., NY, 1998—, asst. prof. Coll. Physicians and Surgeons, 1998—. Contbr. articles to profl. jours., chapters to books. Grantee, William T. Grant Found., N.Y.C., 1999—, NIMH, N.Y.C., 1999—. Mem.: APA (exec. com. divsn. 36 2001—02, WT Grant Faculty Scholars Award 1999-2003). Avocations: running, theater , museums. Office: Tchrs Coll Columbia U 525 W 120th St New York NY 10027 Business E-Mail: drlfm@yahoo.com.

MILLER, LLOYD DANIEL, real estate agent; b. Savannah, Mo., May 25, 1916; s. Daniel Edward and Minnie (Wiedmer) M.; m. Mabel Gertrude Kurz, June 9, 1939; children: Sharon Miller Schumacher, Donna Miller Bodinson, Rosemary Rae Miller, Jeffrey Lloyd. BS in Agrl. Journalism, U. Mo., 1941. Reporter, feature writer, photographer, market editor Corn Belt Farm Dailies, Chgo., Kansas City, Mo., 1941-43; asst. agrl. editor U. Mo., 1946; dir. pub. relations Am. Angus Assn., Chgo., 1946-67, St. Joseph, Mo., 1967, asst. sec., dir. pub. relations, 1968, exec. sec., 1968-78, sr. cons., 1978-81; realtor The Prudential Summers Realtors, 1978—. Mem. U.S. Agrl. Tech. Adv. Com. on Livestock and Livestock Products for Trade Negotiations, 1975-79. Bd. dirs. Mo. Western State Coll. Found., 1976-82, pres., 1978-79; deacon Wyatt Park Bapt. Ch.; chmn. Heartland Ctr., Heartland Hosp. West, 1987-89, bd. dirs. 1987-95. With AUS, 1943-45. Recipient Silver Anvil award Pub. Relations Soc. Am., 1962, Faculty-Alumni award U. Mo.-Columbia, 1975 Mem. Nat. Assn. Realtors, St. Joseph Area C. of C. (pres. 1969, dir., chmn. agri-bus. coun. 1971), St. Joseph Regional Bd. Realtors (pres. 1986), Realtors Land Inst. (v.p. Mo. chpt. 1987-90), Am. Angus Heritage Found., Masons (32 deg.), Shriners, Kiwanis, Sigma Delta Chi. Home: 3302 N Woodbine Rd Apt 10 Saint Joseph MO 64505-9323 Office: 1007 E Saint Maartens Dr Saint Joseph MO 64506-2993

MILLER, LORETTA MARIE, protective services official, writer; b. Seattle, Jan. 15, 1957; d. Louis Joseph and Doreen Marie M.. Diploma, E. Detroit High Sch., Eastpointe, Mich., 1975. Sec. Grace Hosp., Detroit, 1975—77; 9-1-1 dispatcher City of Warren (Mich.) Police, 1977—. Chairperson adv. bd. Clemis, Pontiac, Mich., 1999—; intern Comcast Cable, Detroit; camera and editing maching operator; EMD, CTO instr. Warren Police. Author: Whispers of the Wind, 1999, poems; performer (voice over): CD Demo, 2001. EMT vol. Richmond-Lenox (MIch.) EMS, 1977—81; vol. Royal Oak (Mich.) React, 1977. Recipient Civilian Citation, City of Warren. Avocations: short story and script writing, cross country skiing, music, tv, theater .

MILLER, LORING ERIK, insurance agent, broker; b. N.Y.C., Apr. 6, 1951; s. Martin and Frances (Kaufman) M.; m. Ilene Jane Cook, Dec. 18, 1983; children: Justin, Jennifer, Mallory. Student, L.I. U., 1968-72; diploma, GM Sch. Dealership Mdse./Mgmt., 1977. Treas. Dial Chevrolet Inc., Westbury, N.Y., 1970-77, v.p., owner, 1977-88; pres. Middle Country Brokerage Inc., 1984-87, Loring E. Miller Agy. Inc., Mineola, N.Y., 1978—. Bd. dirs., pres. Nassau County Police Res. Assn., 1985—; chmn. bd. dirs., founder Suffolk County Police Res., 1997—; assoc. dir. N.Y.C. Police Res. Assn., 1986—, N.Y. Finest Found.; state trustee, lodge pres. N.Y. State Fraternal Order of Police.; bd. dirs., Suffolk County Crime Stoppers; scoutmaster Boy Scouts Am., 1994-97; hon. mem. Nassau County Police Dept.; dir. N.Y. Law Enforcement Found. Mem.: Profl. Ins. Agts. N.Y., Nassau County Soc. Prevention Cruelty to Animals (detective and peace officer divsn. law enforcement). Office: 398 Willis Ave Mineola NY 11501-1819

MILLER, LOUIS HOWARD, biologist, researcher; b. Balt., Feb. 4, 1935; s. David and Daisy (Arenson) Miller; m. Nancy Jo Harned, Sept. 26, 1959; 1 child Jennifer. BS, Haverford Coll., 1956; MD, Washington U., St. Louis, 1960; MS in Parasitology, Columbia U., 1964. Asst. prof. then assoc. prof. Coll. of P & S, Columbia U., N.Y.C., 1967—71; head malaria sect. NIAID, NIH, Bethesda, Md., 1971—92, chief lab. parasitic diseases, 1992—. Contbr. articles. Capt. U.S. Army, 1965—67. Recipient Paul Ehrlich/Ludwig Darmstaedter prize, 1989, Award for Disting. Achievement in Infectious Disease Rsch., Bristol-Myers Squibb, 1996, Commonwealth award in sci. and invention, 1999. Fellow: ACP, Queensland Inst. Med. Rsch., Royal Soc. Tropical Medicine and Hygiene; mem.: Assn. Am. Physicians, Inst. of Medicine, NAS, Am. Soc. Tropical Medicine and Hygiene (pres. 1988). Office: NIH Rm 126 Bldg 4 Bethesda MD 20892-0001

MILLER, LOUIS E. airport terminal executive, accountant; b. Salt Lake City, Apr. 24, 1948; Student , U. Utah; grad., Stevens Henager Bus. Coll. CPA. Responsible fin. and adminstrn. Airport Authority; dep. dir. airports Salt Lake City; ptnr. pub. acctg. firm; internal auditor Salt Lake City Corp.; promoted to exec. dir., CEO Salt Lake City Airport Authority; CPA; exec. dir., CEO Tampa Internat. Airport , 1996—. Pres. Westshore alliance; mem. bd. Tampa Bay Conv. & Visitors Bur. (TBCVB); mem. bd. dirs. Tampa Bay Partnership, Met. Planning Orgn., Greater Tampa C.of C.; mem. bd. dirs. Policy Com. Com. of One Hundred. Served U.S. Army. Named to Utah Travel Coun.'s Tourism Hall of Fame ; recipient Freedom of Enterprise award, Utah Assn. Cert. Pub. Accts., Svc. to Industry award, Associated Gen. Contractors of Am. Utah chpt. . Mem.: Airports Coun. Internat. (chmn. N.Am. region 1994). Office: PO Box 22287 Tampa FL 33622*

MILLER, LOUIS H. lawyer; b. Lampeter, U.K., Apr. 22, 1945; m. Diane Matuszewski, Dec. 31, 1973; children: Margaret, Anthony. BA in History, Rutgers Coll., 1967; JD, Temple U., 1970. Bar: N.J. 1970, U.S. Dist. Ct. N.J. 1970, U.S. Supreme Ct. 1996. Law clk. to Judge Thomas Beetel Hunterdon County Ct., Flemington, N.J., 1970-71; law clk. to Judge Baruch Seidman Superior Ct. N.J. Chancery, Trenton, 1971-72; assoc. Jefferson, Jefferson & Vaida, Flemington, 1972-75; ptnr. Vaida & Miller, 1975-78; pvt. practice, 1978-81, 88—; judge Superior Ct. N.J., 1981-88; of counsel Levinson Axelrod Wheaton & Grayzel, 1990-97. Spl. dep. atty. gen. N.J. Hunterdon County Prosecutor Office, Flemington, 1972-73; condemnation commr. Appt. Superior Ct. N.J., Flemington, 1988—, N.J. Assembly spkrs. commr.; commr. N.J. State Commn. Investigation, Trenton, 1993-97; arbitrator U.S. Fed. Dist. Ct. N.J., 1989—. Twp. committeeman Alexandria Twp. Com., R.D. Milford, N.J., 1978-81. Mem. Am. Judges Assn., Am. Judicature Soc., N.J. State Bar Assn. (mem. dist. ethics com. 1980-81, mem. mcpl. ct. practice com. 1996—), Hunterdon County Bar Assn., Consular Law Soc., Welsh Am. Geneal. Soc., Welsh North Am. C. of C. (bd. dirs.), USF Constellation Mus. Republican. Avocations: paleontology, traveling, hiking. Office: PO Box 850 40 Main St Flemington NJ 08822-1411 E-mail: millerlh@earthlink.net.

MILLER, LOUISE DEAN, writer, retired journalist; b. Lubbock, Tex., Dec. 10, 1921; d. Arlie David and Ludie Lee (Hart) Dean; m. Mickey Lester Miller, Aug. 30, 1946; children: Linda Miller Kelly, Lee Miller Parks, Lynne Miller Carson. BA in Journalism, BS in Journalism, Tex. Woman's U., 1943. Gen. reporter Vernon (Tex.) Daily Record, 1943-4; feature gen. reporter Tinker AFB Paper, Oklahoma City, 1944-46; women's editor Albuquerque Tribune, 1946-48; writer Albuquerque Pub. Schs., 1967-68; program dir. Young Women's Christian Assn., Albuquerque, 1970-72; newspaper columnist Albuquerque Jour., 1972-87. Author, editor: The Book of Windows, 1990; co-author, editor: Administration of Secondary Athletics, 1991. Sec.-treas. El Vado (N.Mex.) Cabin Owners Assn., 1977-95. Mem. AAUW (pres. 1964-66, sec. N.Mex. div. 1989-93), Soc. Profl. Journalists, Assn. Women in Comms. (Albuquerque chpt. pres. 1968-70). Democrat. Methodist. Avocations: painting, genealogy, sewing, music. Home: 1201 Richmond Dr NE Albuquerque NM 87106-2023

MILLER, LYNN BRECKENFELDER, health and physical education educator; b. Milw., Dec. 2, 1964; d. Roy Arthur and Nancy Lee (Sobocinski) B.; m. Brian L. Miller. BS, Winona State U., 1987; MPH, Ill. Benedictine Coll., Lisle, 1992; postgrad., No. Ill. U. Tchr. health and phys. edn. Newark (N.Y.) Cen. Sch. Dist., 1987-88, Wheaton (Ill.) Warrenville Dist. 200, 1988—; coach track and volleyball Wheaton Warrenville South High Sch., 1989-94. Coach track West Chicago H.S., 1997-2000, Hubble Mid. Sch., 1999—; coach volleyball, Hubble Mid. Sch., 1995—. Vol. Wheaton Recycling Ctr., 1990-94. Named Acad. All Am. U.S. Achievement Acad., 1987, outstanding student major, Nat. Assn. Sport and Phys. Edn., 1987; recipient traineeship USPHS, 1989. Mem. NEA, AAHPERD, Ill. Edn. Assn., Ill. Assn. Health, Phys. Edn., Recreation and Dance, Kappa Delta Pi. Democrat. Avocations: softball, volleyball, crafts, floral arranging, golf. E-mails. Home: 2 S 573 Continental Dr Warrenville IL 60555 Office: Hubble Mid Sch 603 S Main St Wheaton IL 60187-5240 E-mail: coachbreck@aol.com., blmiller@aol.com.

MILLER, LYNNE MARIE, environmental company executive; b. N.Y.C., Aug. 4, 1951; d. David Jr. and Evelyn (Gulbransen) M. AB, Wellesley Coll., 1973; MS, Rutgers U., 1976. Analyst Franklin Inst., Phila., 1976-78; dir. hazardous waste div. Clement Assocs., Washington, 1978-81; pres. Risk Sci. Internat., 1981-86; CEO, Environ. Strategies Corp., Reston, Va., 1986—. Bd. dirs. Scana Corp., Adams Nat. Bank. Editor: Insurance Claims for Environmental Damages, 1989, editor-in-chief Environ. Claims Jour.; contbr. chpts. to books. Named Ins. Woman of Yr. Assn. Profl. Ins. Women, 1983. Mem. Am. Cons. Engrs. Coun., Wellesley Bus. Leadership Coun. Office: Environ Strategies Corp 11911 Freedom Dr Ste 900 Reston VA 20190-5631 E-mail: lmiller@escva.com.

MILLER, LYNNE MARIE, critical care nurse, administrator; b. Chgo., Apr. 7, 1947; d. Michael John and Helen (Eckardt) Patzek; m. Harry James Miller, Aug. 10, 1968; children: Gretchen Hope, Gary Rutherford. Diploma, Abington (Pa.) Meml. Hosp., 1968; BS, Phila. Coll. Textile and Sci., 1993; MSN, Gwynedd Mercy Coll., 1997. RN, Pa.; cert. nurse adminstr.; cert. managed care adminstr.; cert. case mgmt. Pediatric staff nurse Fitzgerald Mercy Hosp., Darby, Pa., 1968-69; vis. nurse Community Nursing Svc., Lansdowne, 1969-72; staff critical care nurse ICU Doylestown (Pa.) Hosp., 1972-80, night supr., 1980-86, nurse mgr. med./surg., telemetry, ventilator care and cardiac rehab., 1986-90, clin. system mgr., 1990-93, dir. oper. rm. and surg. svcs., 1993-98; dir. care mgmt. Bucks County Physician Hosp. Alliance, Doylestown, Pa., 1998-2000; dir. wound care ctr. Doylestown (Pa.) Hosp., 1998-2000, chief adminstr. officer Health and Wellness Ctr., 2000—. Coll. educator, orgnl. spkr. Contbg. editor Springhouse Corp, FA Davis. Mem. AACN, AORN, Am. Orgn. Nurse Execs. Pa. Orgn. Nurse Leaders, Southeastern Pa. Orgn. Nurse Leaders, Sigma Theta Tau-Iota Kappa (cert.). Office: Doylestown Hosp 595 W State St Doylestown PA 18901-2597 also: 847 Easton Rd Warrington PA 18976

MILLER, M. SAMMYE, history educator; b. Phila., Feb. 23, 1947; s. Herman S. and Sammye Elizabeth (Adams) M.; m. Gloria J. Sellman, Aug. 9, 1991; children: Tashia, Tanisha. BA, Del. State U., 1968; MA, Trinity Coll., 1970; PhD, Cath. U. Am., 1977. Tchr. D.C. Pub. Schs., 1969-70; historian svc. program NEH, Washington, 1978-81; exec. dir. Assn. for the Study Afro-Am. Life and History, 1983-84; editor Negro History Bull., 1983-84; chair dept. history and govt. Bowie (Md.) State U., 1971—, dean Sch. Arts and Scis., asst. to provost, 2001—. Contbr. articles to profl. jours. Recipient Rsch. Achievement award Nat. Assn. for Equal Opportunity in Higher Edn., 1984. Mem. K.C., Kappa Alpha Psi, Kappa Delta Pi, Phi Alpha Theta. Democrat. Roman Catholic. Home: 7709 Wingate Dr Glenn Dale MD 20769-2010 Office: Bowie State U Office of the Dean 14000 Jericho Park Rd Dept And Bowie MD 20715-3319 E-mail: Smiller@bowiestate.edu.

MILLER, MALCOLM HENRY, manufacturing sales executive, real estate developer; b. Elgin, Ill., Feb. 6, 1934; s. Carl Theodore and Alice Lucy (Garbisch) M. BA, U. Wis., 1957; postgrad., Am. Inst. Fgn. Trade, 1961, U. N.Mex., 1963. Sales engr. Fairbanks Morse Corp., Beloit, Wis., 1962; pvt. practice real estate Albuquerque, 1964-75; supt., v.p. Walworth Foundries, Inc., Darien, Wis., 1959-61, exec. v.p. sales, co-owner, 1975—; v.p. sales, co-owner Waukesha Specialty Co., Inc., 1975—. Treas. Fastcast, Inc., Albuquerque, 1993—. Loan advisor, developer Community Assn. for Sr. Housing, Albuquerque, 1967-70; Rep. candidate for state senator N.Mex., 1970; active fin. com. Bernalillo County Reps., N.Mex., 1970-80, Walworth County Reps., Wis., 1976-77. Served to 1st lt. U.S. Army, 1957-59. Mem. Am. Foundrymen's Assn., Dairy Food Industries Supply Assn., Dairy Food Industries Supply Assn. (bd. dirs. 1992-95), Santa Fe Opera Guild, Big Foot Country Club, Nat. "W" Club, Masons, The Madison Club, Sigma Alpha Epsilon. Republican. Episcopalian. Avocations: health activities, cinema, opera. Home: 223 Fremont St PO Box 37 Walworth WI 53184-0037 Office: Walworth Foundries Inc PO Box 160 Hwy 14 and Hwy 15 Interchange Darien WI 53114

MILLER, MARGARET ALISON, education educator; b. L.A., Dec. 17, 1944; d. Richard Crump and Virginia Margaret (Dudley) M.; m. Spencer Hall, Aug. 21, 1967 (div. 1977); 1 child, Justin Robinson; m. Alan Blair Howard, Oct. 7, 1990. BA in English summa cum laude, UCLA, 1966; postgrad., Stanford U., 1966-67; PhD in English, U. Va., 1971. Instr. English U. Va., Charlottesville, 1971-72; from asst. prof. to assoc. prof. U. Mass., Dartmouth, 1972-83, prof. English, 1983-86, co-dir. women's studies program North Dartmouth, 1981-83, asst. to dean arts and scis., 1983-85, asst. to pres., 1985-86; acad. affairs coord. State Coun. Higher Edn. for Va., Richmond, 1986-87, assoc. dir. for acad. affairs, 1987-97; pres. Am. Assn. for Higher Edn., Washington, 1997-2000; pres. emerita Am. Assn. Higher Edn., 2000—; prof. higher edn. policy U. Va., Charlottesville, 2001—. Head English sect. transitional summer program Brown U., 1976; instr. honors program Va. Commonwealth U., 1991-93; cons. Coun. Rectors, Budapest, 1993, Minn. State U. System, Mpls., 1992, U.S. Dept. Edn., Washington, 1990—, S.C. Higher Edn. Commn., 1989-90, Edn. Commn. States, Denver, 1994-2000; presenter in field; participant UNESCO World Conf. on Higher Edn., 1998; adv. commr. Edn. Commn. of the States, 1998-2000; chair steering com. Washington Higher Edn. Secretariat, 1997-2000; mem. Nat. Postsecondary Edn. Cooperative, 1997-2000; cons. Nat. Ctr. for Pub. Policy and Higher Edn., 1998—; bd. dirs. Nat. Ctr. for Edn. Mgmt. Sys., 2001—, Edn. Direct; participant Aspen Inst., 1998; exec. editor Change mag., 2000—; judge Tchrs. Ins. Annuity Assn./Coll. Retirement Equity Fund Hesburgh awards, 1999—. Contbr. articles to profl. jours. Mem. Am. Assn. Higher Edn. (leadership coun.), Am. Coun. on Edn. (exec. com. identification program in Va. 1988-97, participant nat. identification program's 41st nat. forum for women leaders in higher edn. 1989, adv. bd. Inst.), Phi Beta Kappa. Avocations: reading, gardening, travel. Home: 2176 Lindsay Rd Gordonsville VA 22942-1620 Office: Curry Sch Edn U Va 405 Emmett St S Charlottesville VA 22903 E-mail: pmiller@virginia.edu.

MILLER, MARGERY SILBERMAN, psychologist, speech pathologist, medical educator; b. May 7, 1951; d. Bernard and Charlotte Silberman; m. Donald F. Moores; children: Kip Lee, Tige Justice. BA, Elmira Coll., 1971; MA, NYU, 1972; EdS, MS, SUNY-Albany, 1975; MA, Towson State U., 1987; PhD, Georgetown U., 1991. Lic. speech pathologist, N.Y., Md.; lic. psychologist, Md.; cert. tchr. nursery-6th grades, spl. edn., N.Y.; nationally cert. sch. psychologist. Speech and lang. pathologist Mental Retardation Inst. Flower and Fifth Ave. Hosp., N.Y.C., 1971—72; cmty. speech/lang. pathologist, dir. speech and hearing svc. N.Y. State Dept. Mental Hygiene, Troy, 1972—74; instr. comm. disorders dept. Coll. St. Rose, Albany, NY, 1975—77; clin. supr. U. Md., College Park, 1978; speech/lang. pathologist Md. Sch. for Deaf, Frederick, 1978—84; auditory devel. specialist Montgomery County Pub. Schs., Rockville, Md., 1984—87; coord. Family Life program Nat. Acad. Gallaudet U., Washington, 1987—88, interim dir., 1988—89; dir. Counseling & Devel. Ctr. N.W. Campus, 1989—93; prof. psychology, coord. psychology internship program Gallaudet U., 1993—; lic. practicing psychologist Bethesda, Md., 1998—. Instr. sign lang. program Frederick C.C.; dance instr. for deaf adolescents; diagnostic cons. on speech pathology. Author: It's O.K. To Be Angry, 1976; contbr. chpt. to Cognition, Education, and Deafness:

Directions for Research and Instruction, 1985; mem. editl. rev. com. Gov.'s Devel. Disabilities Coun. Md., 1984; presenter at confs.; contbr. articles to profl. jours. Vol., choreographer Miss Deaf Am. Pageant, 1984. Office of Edn. Children's Bur. fellow, 1971. Mem. Am. Speech, Lang. and Hearing Assn. (cert. clin. competence in speech/lang. apthology), Nat. Assn. of Deaf, Nat. Assn. Sch. Psychologists, Am. Psychol. Assn. Jewish. Office: Gallaudet U 800 Florida Ave NE Washington DC 20002-3660 Home: 12311 Stoney Creek Rd Potomac MD 20854 E-mail: margery.miller@gallaudet.edu.

MILLER, MARILYN JOANE, retired social worker; b. Beaverton, Mich., Oct. 22, 1939; d. Ellis Justin and Alma (Witkoske) LeVee; m. Richard Bruce Miller, 1998. BA, Olivet Nazarene U., Kankakee, Ill., 1961; MSW, U. Mich., 1967. Diplomat Am. Bd. Clin. Social Work. Rsdl. area supr./counselor Adrian (Mich.) Tng. Sch., 1961-73; clin. supr. Sunny Ridge Home for Children, Wheaton, Ill., 1973-76; prevention specialist Focus Prog., CEI CMHB, 1976-81; sr. mental health therapist Southland Counseling Ctr., 1981-88, supr., 1988-89; dir. Comprehensive Substance Abuse Treatment Prog., Lansing, 1989-91; program supr. Southland Counseling Ctr., 1991-2000; ret., 2000. Cert. case presentation method evaluator CRC/AODA, 1988—2000. Sec. bd. Lansing First Ch. of Nazarene, 1984-89; bd. dirs. Parkwood YMCA, 1984-87. Mem. NASW, Nat. Assn. Christians in Social Work, Acad. Cert. Social Workers. Lutheran.

MILLER, MARILYN LEA, library science educator; AA, Graceland Coll., 1950; BS in English, U. Kans., 1952; AMLS, U. Mich., 1959, PhD of Librarianship and Higher Edn., 1976. Bldg.-level sch. libr. Wellsville (Kans.) H.S., 1952-54; tchr.-libr. Arthur Capper Jr. H.S., Topeka, 1954-56; head libr. Topeka H.S., 1956-62; sch. libr. cons. State of Kans. Dept. of Pub. Instrn., 1962-67; from asst. to assoc. prof. Sch. Librarianship Western Mich. U., Kalamazoo, 1967-77; assoc. prof. libr. sci. U. N.C., Chapel Hill, 1977-87, prof., chair dept. libr. and info. studies Greensboro, 1987-95, prof. emeritus, 1996—. Vis. faculty Kans. State Tchrs., Emporia, 1960, 63, 64, 66, U. Minn., Mpls., 1971, U. Manitoba, Winnipeg, Can., 1971; vis. prof. Appalachian State U., Boone, N.C., 1987; adv. bd. sch. libr. media program Nat. Ctr. for Edn. Stats., 1989, user rev. panel, 1990; chair assoc. dean search com. Sch. Edn., 1988, coord. Piedmont young writers conf., 1989-94, 97-99, chair race and gender com., 1990-93, SACS planning and evaluation com., 1990-91, learning resources ctr. adv. com., 1991-93; hearing panel for honor code U. N.C. Greensboro, 1988-91, assn. women faculty and administrv. staff, 1987-95, faculty coun., 1987-95, chair, 1994-95, univ. libr. com., 1987-88, com. faculty devel. in race and gender scholarship, 1990-92; lectr. and cons. in field. Mem. editl. bd. The Emergency Librarian, 1981-97, Collection Building: Studies in the Development and Effective Use of Library Resources, 1978-96; contbr. chpts. to books, articles to profl. jours. Selected as one of four children's libr. specialists to visit Russian sch. and pub. librs., book pubs., Moscow, Leningrad, Tashkent, 1979; hon. del. White House Conf. on Libr. and Info. Svcs., Washington, 1991; head del. Romanian Summer Inst. on Librarianship in U.S., 1991; citizen amb. People to People Internat. Program, People's Republic of China, 1992, Russian and Poland, 1992, Russia, 1994, Barcelona, 1995; exec. bd. dirs. Friends of Greensboro Pub. Libr., 1996-99, chair gift shop and coffee shop adv. com., 1996—; chmn. Citizens Materials Adv. com., 1999, Citizens Strategic Long Range Planning com., 2001-02, Sch. Pub. Libr. com., 2002. Recipient Freedom Found. medal, 1962, Disting. Svc. to Sch. Librs. award Kans. Assn. Sch. Librs., 1982, Disting. Svc. award Graceland Coll., 1992, Disting. Alumnus award Sch. Libr. and Info. Studies, U. Mich., 1988, Contribution to Libr. Info. Sci. award Assn. Libr. Info. Sci., 1999; Delta Kappa Gamma scholar, 1972. Mem.: ALA (awards com. 1971—72, chair Chgo. conf. resolutions 1972, chair 1973—75, resolutions com. 1976—78, adv. com. Nat. Ctr. Ednl. Stats. 1984, standing com. libr. edn. 1987—91, yearbook adv. com. 1988—90, chair 1989—90, pres. 1992—93, exec. dir. 1994, chair rsch. com., Disting. Svc. award Am. Assn. Sch. Librs. 1993), Friends of N.C. Pub. Librs. (bd. dirs. 2000—), So. Assn. Colls. and Schs. (accreditation team 1988), Southeastern Libr. Assn. (chair libr. educators sect. 1990—92), N.C. Assn. Sch. Librs., Assn. Libr Svc. to Children (bd. dirs. 1976—81, pres. 1979—80, rsch. com. 1982—85, chair nominating com. 1984, chair 1984—85), Assn. Ednl. Comms. and Tech., Am. Assn. Sch. Librs. (nominating com. 1980, pub. com. 1981—82, chair search com. exec. dir. 1985, v.p., pres.-elect 1985—86, pres. 1986—87, coord. coms. nat. stds. vision and implementation 1995—98), N.C. Libr. Assn. (life; edn. libr. com. 1978—80, 1982—86, bd. dirs. 1987—99, exec. bd. status women roundtable 1989—, chmn.-elect 1995—97, chmn. 1997—99, commn. on status of sch. librs. 1999—2000).

MILLER, MARK KARL, journalist; b. Meadville, Pa., Aug. 5, 1953; s. Richard Karl and Ellener Louise (Zimber) M. BA in Comms. and Journalism, Shippensburg U. of Pa., 1975. Editl. asst. Broadcasting mag., Washington, 1975, staff writer, 1976—77, asst. editor, 1977—80, sr. news editor, 1980—87, asst. mng. editor, 1987—91; mng. editor Broadcasting & Cable mag., 1991—98, Digital TV mag., Washington, 1999; freelance editor, writer, photographer, rschr., 2000—. Mem. editl. adv. bd. Shippensburg U. of Pa., 1989-94, mem. profl. adv. bd. comm./journalism dept., 1994-96. Recipient Outstanding Alumnus award Shippensburg U., 1992. Mem. Soc. Profl. Journalists, Art Deco Soc. of Washington (bd. dirs., publs. chair 1986-97), Nat. Press Club. Home and Office: 2425 Valley Way Cheverly MD 20785-2956 E-mail: mkmiller@comcast.net.

MILLER, MARK WILLIAM, investment advisor, writer; b. Kansas City, Mo., Mar. 23, 1964; s. William Joseph and Arden (Roberts) M.; m. Kelly Lyn Macklin, Sept. 18, 1998. BS in Polit. Sci. and Econs., Kans. U., 1987. Registered investment advisor, Kans.; registered in. cons. Fin. planner IDS/Am. Express, Overland Park, Kans., 1987-89; registered rep. Stern Bros. and Co., Kansas City, 1989-91; mut. fund mgr. DST Systems, Inc., 1993; pres. Sensible Saver Publs., Inc., 1993—; CEO, cons. Miller Capital Mgmt., Inc., Overland Park, 2000—. Author: The Sensible Saver, 1996, The Complete Idiot's Guide to Being a Cheapskate, 1999. Vol. Birchwood Ch., Independence, Mo., 2000. Avocations: golf, flying. Office: Miller Capital Mgmt Inc 4650 College Blvd Ste 210 Overland Park KS 66211 Fax: (913) 327-7374. E-mail: millercapital@cs.com.

MILLER, MARSHALL LEE, lawyer; b. Chattanooga, Oct. 18, 1942; BA, Harvard U., 1964; student, Oxford U., Eng., Heidelberg U., Germany; JD, Yale U., 1970. Bar: D.C. 1971, U.S. Supreme Ct. 1979. Spl. asst. to adminstr. U.S. EPA, 1971-73; assoc. dep. atty. gen. U.S. Dept. Justice, 1973-74; asst. sec. labor (acctg.), dep. adminstr. OSHA, 1975-76; ptnr. Baise & Miller, Washington. Bd. editors: Yale Law Jour.; Soviet Mil. editor: Armed Forces Jour., 1983-87; author books internat. and environ. topics. Bd. dirs. Bulgarian-Am. Enterprise Fund, Electronic Warfare Assocs., Am. Coun. of Internat. Living, Am. Assn. Advancement Sci. Office: Baise & Miller 1020 19th St NW Ste 400 Washington DC 20036-6101 Home: PO Box 1311 Bethany Beach DE 19930-1311

MILLER, MARTIN EUGENE, school system consultant, negotiator, lobbyist; b. Decatur, Ill., May 14, 1945; s. Floyd Homer and Vivian LaVerne (Gould) M.; m. Sherry Kay Bandy, May 25, 1968; children: Liane, Laura. BS, U. Ill., 1968; MEd, U. North Fla., 1974. Cert. math. tchr.; cert. ednl. adminstrn. and supervision. Tchr. Decatur (Ill.) Pub. Schs., 1968, Clay County Sch. Bd., Orange Park, Fla., 1970-74, coordinator cert. personnel Green Cove Springs, 1974-77, dir. instructional personnel, 1977-78, dir. personnel services, 1978-81, asst. supt. for human resources and labor rels., 1981-93, dir. cmty. and govtl. rels., 1993-97. Past mem. Edn. Stds. Commn., Tallahassee, 1985-93, vice chmn., 1988-92; past mem. Blue Cross-Blue Shield Adv. Coun., Jacksonville, Fla.; past mem. Fla. Ednl. Leaders Forum. Served as staff sgt. USAF, 1968-70. Mem. Am. Assn. Sch. Adminstrs., Fla. Assn. Sch. Adminstrs., Fla. Pub. Employer Labor Rels. Assn., Fla. Edn. Negotiators (past pres.), Fla. Ednl. Legis. Liaisons (pres.), Phi Delta Kappa. Democrat. Presbyterian. Avocations: home computers, music, swimming. Home: 1612 Bay Cir W Orange Park FL 32073-4746 E-mail: martinmiller@MillerConsultingGroup.com.

MILLER, MARY HOTCHKISS, lay worker; b. Washington, Dec. 4, 1936; d. Neil and Esther LeMoyne (Helfer) H.; m. Ronald Homer Miller, May 20, 1961; 1 child, Timothy Ronald. BA, Western Md. Coll., 1958; MRE, Union Theol. Sem, 1960; Cert., Windham House, N.Y.C., 1960. Dir. Christian Edn. Bruton Parish ch., Williamsburg, Va., 1960-61; dir. Christian Edn. (part-time) All Saints Episcopal Ch., Bklyn., 1961-62; adminstrv. and program asst., Christian Social Rels. Dept., Exec. Coun. Episcopal Ch. U.S.A. Episcopal Ch. Ctr., N.Y.C., 1967-72; nat. treas., mem. bd., chmn. Episcopal Peace Fellowship, Washington, N.Y.C. and Chgo., 1972-88, exec. sec. Washington, 1989-2001; mem. Standing Commn. on Anglican and Internat. Peace with Justice, Epis. Ch., 2001—; ret., 2001. Bd. dirs., exec. com. Nat. Campaign for Peace Tax Fund, Washington, 1989—91; bd. dirs. Ctr. on Conscience and War/Nat. Interreligious Svc. Bd. for Conscientious Objectors, Washington, 1989—96, Washington, 2001—; coord. The Consultation. Contbr. articles to Witness mag. and jours., newsletters in field; editl. bd. ISSUES of Gen. Convs. of Episcopal Ch., 1973-91; designer ch. vestments and banners. Democrat. E-mail: mary.miller@ecunet.org.

MILLER, MARY JEANNETTE, office management specialist; b. Washington, Sept. 24, 1912; d. John William and David Evengeline (Hill) Sims; m. Cecil Miller, June 17, 1934 (dec.); children: Sylvenia Delores Doby, Ferdi A., Cecil Jr. (dec.). Student, Howard U., 1929-30, U. Ill., 1940-42, Dept. Agr. Grad. Sch., 1957-59, U. Md., 1975; cert. in Vocat. Photography, Prince George's C.C., 1986. Chief mail processing unit Bur. Reclamation, Washington, 1940-57; records supr. AID, Manila, Korea, Mali, Guyana, Dominican Republic, Indonesia, Laos, 1957-71; office engr. Bechtel Assocs., Washington, 1976-79; real estate assoc; tchr. English as 2d lang. Ministry of Edn., Seoul, Korea, 1960-61, Ministry of Fin., Laos, 1968-70; cons. to Ministry of Fin. Royal Lao Govt., 1971-74; cons. AID missions to Yemen, Sudan, Somalia, 1982; records mgmt. cons. AID, Monrovia, Liberia, 1980-81, Sri Lanka, 1984; docent Mus. African Art Smithsonian Inst., Washington, 1986-89; circulation asst. Prince George County Meml. Libr. System, Hyattsville, Md., 1987-91, ret.; mem. Friends of Internat. Edn. Com., 1985-92; sec./treas., bd. dirs. Miller Transitional, Inc. Author handbooks on office mgmt.; publs. to travel book. Mem. NAFE, Am. Assn. Ret. Persons (bd. mem. Fla. chpt. 1357), Mayor's Internat. Adv. Coun. Mem. AARP (bd. dirs.), Soc. Am. Archivists, Am. Mgmt. Assn., Montgomery County Bd. Realtors, Am. Fgn. Svc. Assn., Nat. Trust Hist. Preservation, Assn. Am. Fgn. Svc. Women's Writer Group, Consumer Mail Panel, Zeta Phi Beta. Roman Catholic. Home: 5597 Seminary Rd Apt 510S Falls Church VA 22041-3520

MILLER, MARY KATHERINE, management consultant; b. Dunmore, Pa., Sept. 19, 1959; d. Philip Joseph and Madeline (Calomino) Miller; 1 child, Nathan Michael Garbrandt. BA, Case Western Res. U., 1982; MBA, Ashland U., 1996. Lic. social worker, Ohio. Workshop dir. Stark County Bd. Mental Retardation/Devel. Disabilities, Canton, Ohio, 1988-90; residential dir. Apple Creek (Ohio) Devel. Ctr., 1990-91; program dir. Stark County Out of Poverty Partnership, Inc., Canton, 1991-96; pres. MKM & Assocs., Dover, Ohio, 1995—. Charter mem. bd. trustees Harbor House, Inc., New Philadelphia, Ohio, 1986-91. Mem. NASW, Inst. Mgmt. Cons., Acad. Family Mediators, Ohio Provider Resources Assn. Avocations: parenting, motorcycling, gardening, research and writing on religions, spiritual and social issues. Home: 505 S Tuscarawas Ave Dover OH 44622-2343 Office: MKM & Assocs 505 S Tuscarawas Ave Dover OH 44622-2343

MILLER, MARY LOIS, retired nurse midwife; b. Altoona, Pa., Feb. 21, 1933; d. Isaac Emory and Lucinda Jane (Brumbaugh) Miller. Diploma, West Suburban Hosp. Sch., 1953; BSN, Wheaton (Ill.) Coll., 1955; MRE, Grace Theol. Sem., 1957; nurse midwife, Frontier Nursing Svc., 1959. Cert. nurse midwife. Nurse obstetrics Delnor Hosp., St. Charles, Ill., 1953-55; head nurse McDonald Hosp., Warsaw, 1955-57; med. missionary Fgn. Missionary Soc. Grace Brethren Ch., Winona Lake, 1959-79; cert. nurse midwife Lewistown (Pa.) Hosp., 1979-97; ret., 1997. Organist, pianist Kish Valley Grace Brethren Ch., 1986-98; pianist, digital pianist Altoona Grace Brethren Ch., 1998—. Recipient Ordre du Merit du Chevalier, Ctrl. African Rep., 1972. Mem. Am. Coll. Nurse Midwives (sec.). Home: 1007 N 2nd St Juniata Altoona PA 16601-5613

MILLER, MAURICE DEAN, design engineer; b. Iowa, June 1, 1936; s. Orville K. and Sarah M. (Bachman) M.; m. Deanna M. Hummon, Mar. 13, 1960; children: Gerald M., Rhonda Miller Masiliones. BS, Iowa State U., 1958; MS, Kans. U., 1968. Bridge engr. Howard, Needles, Tammen & Bergendoff, Kansas City, Mo., 1958-68, chief bridge designer Chgo., 1968-72, structional engr. Rio de Janerio, Brazil, 1972-75, project mgr. Chgo., 1975-76, chief bridge designer Kansas City, Mo., 1976-90, assoc., 1990—. Contbr. articles to profl. jours. Fellow ASCE; mem. NSPE, Am. Inst. Steel Constrn., Internat. Assn. Bridge & Structual Engrs. Achievements include design of 6 Mississippi River and 3 Missouri River bridges. Home: 12906 W 77th Ter Shawnee Mission KS 66216-3212 Office: Howard Needles Tammen & Bergendoff 9200 Ward Pky Kansas City MO 64114-3308

MILLER, MAX DUNHAM, JR. lawyer; b. Des Moines, Oct. 17, 1946; s. Max Dunham and Beulah (Head) M.; m. Melissa Ann Dart, Jan. 10, 1969 (div. July 1975); 1 child, Ann Marie Victoria; m. Caroline Jean Armendt, Sept. 19, 1981 (div. Dec. 2001); children: Alexander Bradshaw, Benjamin Everrett. BS with high honors, Mich. State U., 1968; postgrad., George Washington U., 1970-71; JD, U. Md., 1975. Bar: Md. 1976, U.S. Dist. Ct. Md. 1976, U.S. Ct. Appeals (4th cir.) 1981, U.S. Supreme Ct. 1982. Engr. U.S. Dept. of Def., Aberdeen Proving Ground, Md., 1968-72; law clk. to presiding judge Md. Cir. Ct., Higinbothom in Bel Air, 1975-76; asst. county atty. Harford County, Bel Air, 1976-79; assoc. Lentz & Hooper P.A., Balt., 1979-81; ptnr. Miller, Olszewski & Moore, P.A., Bel Air, 1981-94; prin. Law Offices of Max D. Miller, P.A., 1994—. County atty. Harford County, Md., 1983-88. Mem. Md. Bar Assn., Assn. Trial Lawyers Am., Md. Trial Lawyers Assn., Harford County Bar Assn., Phi Kappa Phi, Phi Eta Sigma. Avocations: golf, sailing, canoeing, bicycling, ice and roller hockey. Home: 308 Whetstone Rd Forest Hill MD 21050-1332 Office: 5 S Hickory Ave Bel Air MD 21014-3732

MILLER, MAX WILLIAM, emergency physician; b. Walnut Creek, Calif., Nov. 27, 1955; m. Ramona Lynn Miller; 1 child, Aaron. BA in Biology cum laude, Lewis and Clark Coll., 1978; MD, Med. Coll. Wis., 1984. Diplomate Am. Bd. Internal Medicine, Am. Bd. Emergency Medicine. From intern to chief resident San Joaquin Gen. Hosp., Stockton, Calif., 1984-88, attending physician emergency medicine, 1987-91; pvt. practice internal medicine, 1988-90; attending physician emergency medicine Stanislaus Med. Ctr., Modesto, Calif., 1989-97, St. Joseph's Hosp., 1993-94, Barton Meml. Hosp., South Lake Tahoe, Calif., 1994-95; emergency medicine physician Dameron Hosp., Stockton, 1996-2000; attending physician emergency medicine Health Care Svcs. Stanislaus County, Urgent Care, 1997-98; emergency medicine physician St. Dominic's Hosp., Manteca, Calif., 2000—. Dir. home health svcs. Sutter Tracy Cmty. Hosp., Tracy, Calif., 1989—, co-dir. intensive care unit, 1989, internal medicine com., 1989; emergency dept. com. Stanislaus Med. Ctr., Modesto, 1989-97, emergency dept. liaison to surgery com., 1990-97. Mem. Am. Coll. Internal Medicine (diplomate), Am. Assn. Physician Specialists-Emergency Medicine (diplomate). Home: 1852 W 11th St # 600 Tracy CA 95376-3736 Office: St Dominics Hosp Emergency Dept 1777 W Tosemite Ave Manteca CA 95337-5130

MILLER, MAYNARD MALCOLM, geologist, educator, research institute director, explorer, legislator; b. Seattle, Jan. 23, 1921; s. Joseph Anthony and Juanita Queena (Davison) M.; m. Joan Walsh, Sept. 15, 1951; children: Ross McCord, Lance Davison. BS magna cum laude, Harvard U., 1943; MA, Columbia U., 1948; PhD (Fulbright scholar), St. John's Coll., Cambridge U., Eng., 1957; student, Naval War Coll., Air War Coll., Oak Ridge Inst. Nuclear Sci.; D of Sci. (hon.), U. Alaska, 1990. Registered profl. geologist, Idaho. Asst. prof. naval sci. Princeton (N.J.) U., 1946; geologist Gulf Oil Co., Cuba, 1947; rsch. assoc., coord., dir. Office Naval Rsch. Juneau Icefield Rsch. Project, Am Geog. Soc., N.Y.C., 1948-53; staff scientist Swiss Fed. Inst. for Snow and Avalanche Rsch., Davos, 1952-53; instr. dept. geography Cambridge U., 1953-54, 56; assoc. producer, field unit dir. film Seven Wonders of the World Cinerama Corp., Europe, Asia, Africa, Middle East, 1954-55; rsch. assoc. Lamont Geol. Obs., N.Y.C., 1955-59; sr. scientist dept. geology Columbia U., 1957-59; asst. prof. geology Mich. State U., East Lansing, 1959-61, assoc. prof., 1961-63, prof., 1963-75; dean Coll. Mines and Earth Resources U. Idaho, Moscow, 1975-88, prof. geology, dir. Glaciological and Arctic Scis. Inst., 1975—; dir., state geologist Idaho Geol. Survey, 1975-88; rep. Legislature of State of Idaho, Boise, 1992-2000. Prin. investigator, geol. cons. sci. contracts and projects for govt. agys., univs., pvt. corps., geographic socs., 1946—; geophys. cons. Nat. Park Svc., NASA, USAF, Nat. Acad. Sci.; organizer leader USAF-Harvard Mt. St. Elias Expdn., 1946; chief geologist Am. Mt. Everest Expdn., Nepal, 1963; dir. Nat. Geographic Soc. Alaskan Glacier Commemorative Project, 1964—; organizer field leader Nat. Geographic Soc. Joint U.S.-Can. Mt. Kennedy Yukon Meml. Mapping Expdn., 1965, Muséo Argentino de Ciencias Naturales, Patagonian expdn. and glacier study for Inst.. Geologico del Peru & Am. Geog. Soc., 1949-50, participant adv. missions People's Republic of China, 1981, 86, 88, 98, geol. expdns. Himalaya, Nepal, 1963, 84, 87, USAF mission to Ellesmere Land, North Pole and Polar Sea, 1951; organizer, ops. officer USN-LTA blimp geophysics flight to Ice Island T-3 and North Pole area for Office Naval Rsch., 58; prin. investigator U.S. Naval Oceanographic Office sea and pack ice Rsch. Ice Island T-3 Polar Sea, 1967-68, 70-73; dir. lunar field sta. simulation program USAF-Boeing Co., 1959-60; co-prin., prin. investigator Nat. Geographic Soc. 30 Yr. Remap of Lemon, Taku and Cathedral Massif Glaciers, Juneau Icefield, 1989-2000; exec. dir. Found. for Glacier and Environ. Rsch., Pacific Sci. Ctr., Seattle, 1955-95, 1997—, chmn., 1992—, pres., 1955-85, trustee, 1960—, organizer, dir. Juneau (Alaska) Icefield Rsch. Program (JIRP), 1946—; cons. Dept. Hwys. State of Alaska, 1965; chmn., exec. dir. World Ctr. for Exploration Found., N.Y.C., 1968-71; dir., mem. adv. bd. Idaho Geol. Survey, 1975-88; chmn. nat. coun. JSHS program U.S. Army Rsch. Office and Acad. Applied Sci., 1982-90; sci. dir. U.S. Army Rsch. Office and DOD Nat. Sci. and Humanities Symposia program, 1991—; disting. guest prof. China U. Geoscis., Wuhan, 1981—, Changchun U. Earth Scis., People's Republic of China, 1988—; adj. prof. U. Alaska, 1986—. Author: Field Manual of Glaciological and Arctic Sciences; co-author books on Alaskan glaciers and Nepal geology; contbr. over 200 reports, sci. papers to profl. jours., ency. articles, chpts. to books, monographs; prodr., nat. lectr. films and videos. Past mem. nat. exploring com., nat. sea exploring com. Boy Scouts Am.; past mem. nat. adv. bd. Embry Riddle Aero. U.; bd. dirs. Idaho Rsch. Found.; pres. state divsn. Mich. UN Assn., 1970-73; mem. Centennial and Health Environ. Commns., Moscow, Idaho, 1987—. With USN, 1943-46, PTO. Decorated 11 campaign and battle stars; named Leader of Tomorrow Seattle C. of C. and Time mag., 1953, one of Ten Outstanding Young Men U.S. Jaycees, 1954; recipient commendation for lunar environ. study USAF, 1960, Hubbard medal (co-recipient with Mt. Everest expdn. team) Nat. Geog. Soc., 1963, Elisha Kent Kane Gold medal Geog. Soc. Phila., 1964, Karo award Soc. Mil. Engrs., 1966, Franklin L. Burr award Nat. Geog. Soc., 1967, Commendation Boy Scouts Am., 1970, Disting. Svc. commendation plaque UN Assn. U.S., Disting. Svc. commendation State of Mich. Legis., 1975, Outstanding Civilian Svc. medal U.S. Army Rsch. Office, 1977, Outstanding Leadership in Minerals Edn. commendations Idaho Mining Assn., 1985, 87, Nat. Disting. Tchg. award Assn. Am. Geographers, 1996; recipient numerous grants NSF, Nat. Geog. Soc., NASA, ARO, M.J. Murdock Trust, others, 1948—. Fellow Geol. Soc. Am., Arctic Inst. N.Am., Explorers Club; mem. councilor AAAS (Pacific divsn. 1978-88), AIME, Am. Geophys. Union, Internat. Glaciological Soc. (past councilor), ASME (hon. nat. lectr.), Assn. of Am. State Geologists (hon.), Am. Legis. Exchange Coun., Am. Assn. Amateur Oarsmen (life), Am. Alpine Club (past councilor, life mem.), Fulbright Assn., Alpine Club (London), Appalachian Club (hon. corr.), Brit. Mountaineering Assn. (hon., past v.p.), The Mountaineers (hon.), Cambridge U. Mountaineering Club (hon.), Himalyan Club (Calcutta), English Speaking Union (nat. lectr.), Naval Res. Assn. (life), Dutch Treat Club, Circumnavigators Club (life), Adventurers Club N.Y. (medalist), Am. Legion, VFW, Harvard Club (N.Y.C. and Seattle), Sigma Xi, Phi Beta Kappa (pres. Epsilon chpt. Mich. State U. 1969-70), Phi Kappa Phi. Republican. Methodist. Avocations: skiing, mountaineering, photography. Home: 514 E 1st St Moscow ID 83843-2814 Office: U Idaho Coll Sci Moscow ID 83844-3022 also: Found Glacier & Environ Rsch 4470 N Douglas Hwy Juneau AK 99801-9403 E-mail: jirp@uidaho.edu.

MILLER, MELVIA FLORENCE, writer, consultant; b. Muncie, Ind., Dec. 27, 1948; d. Melvin John and Elizabeth Ann Miller; children: Malik Price, Mikal Price. BA, Ball State U.; MA, U. Mich.; PhD (hon.) , Columbia U.; DD (hon.) , Holistic U. Instr. Ball State U., Muncie, Ind., 1970—71, U. Mich., Ann Arbor, Mich., 1971—80; tng. mgr. AT&T, Southfield, 1981—83. Tng. mgr. Chrysler Corp., Detroit, 1979—81; cons. E.T.D. Cons., Ann Arbor, 1976—85; writer Mothership Publ., San Diego, 1997—99; staff writer, cons. AHREA, Las Vegas, 1999—; spkr. in field. Author: Mail Order Marketing 101, 1999, Ebony & Ivory, 2002, (game) New & Different Friends, 2002; contbr. columns in newspapers. Office: Write On Consulting Firm PO Box 31043 Las Vegas NV 89103 E-mail: getpaid77@hotmail.com.

MILLER, MERRILY DALE, special education educator; b. Yonkers, N.Y., Mar. 3, 1943; d. Stanley and Pearl Sylvia (Colin) Dulman; m. Edward Miller, Dec. 24, 1964 (div. July 23, 1990); children: Logan, Sloan, Dane. AB cum laude, Vassar Coll., 1965; MA, Memphis State U., 1968; MEd, Columbia U., 1972, EdD, 1974. Tchr., Yonkers, 1968-72; dir. edn. Massive Econ. Neighborhood Devel. Corp., N.Y.C., 1973-74; dir. rsch. The Door, 1974-75; asst. prof. Fordham U., 1976-84, assoc. prof., 1984-88, Mount St. Mary Coll., Newburgh, N.Y., 1990-94, prof., 1994—, chairperson divsn. of edn., 1995-97. Cons. schs. and families, Westchester, N.Y., 1980—, Conn. State Dept. Edn., Bridgeport, 1987-89, N.Y. State Dept. Edn., Albany, 1989-91, N.Y. Sch. Deaf, White Plains, 1987—. Advisor Coalition for Family Justice, Irvington, N.Y., 1990—; mem. alumni coun. Vassar Coll. Office: 330 Powell Ave Newburgh NY 12550-3412

MILLER, MICHAEL, physician, educator; b. Queens, N.Y., June 19, 1957; s. Irving Maltz and Lenore (Goldstein) Miller; m. Lisa L. Miller; children: Avery Lauren, Ilana Frieda. BA, Rutgers U., 1979; MD, Robert Wood Johnson Med. Sch., 1983. Diplomate Am. Bd. Internal Medicine, Am. Bd. Cardiovascular Disease, Nat. Bd. Med. Examiners. Intern dept. medicine Med. Ctr. U. Cin., 1983-84, resident internal medicine, 1984-86; lipoprotein metabolism fellow Sch. Medicine Johns Hopkins U., Balt., 1986-89, cardiovascular disease fellow, 1988-91; dir. ctr. preventive cardiology U. Md. Med. Sys., 1991—; assoc. prof. medicine divsn. cardiology Sch. Medicine U. Md., 1991—; asst. prof. medicine divsn. cardiology Sch. Medicine Johns Hopkins U., 1991—; adj. asst. prof. dept. medicine Baylor Coll. Medicine, Houston, 1992—. Tchr. Sch. Medicine U. Md., 1994—, Johns Hopkins U., 1993—, Balt. Pub. Sch. Sys., 1991—; lectr. in field. Author: The Practice of Coronary Disease Prevention, 1996; contbr. numerous chpts. to books and articles to profl. jours.; reviewer numerous jours.; featured in ednl. recordings, 1990—; columnist drkoop.com. Mem. Gov.'s Task Force Cardiovasc. Disease Prevention. Grantee Parke-Davis, 1989—, NIH/Am. Heart Assn., 1989—, Bristol-Myers Squibb, 1991-93, Sandoz, 1992-93, Pfizer, 1992—, Merck, 1997—; recipient Robert Galbraith award, 1979, William F. Grupe award, 1983, Samuel Kaslev award, 1994. Fellow Am. Coll. Cardiology (co-author Preventive Cardiology, 1998—), Am. Heart Assn. Coun. Arteriosclerosis; mem. AAAS, Am. Soc. Preventive Cardiology, Am. Heart Assn. Coun. Epidemiology, Phi Beta Kappa. Jewish. Avocations: skiing, tennis, hiking. Home: 4301 Norwood Rd Baltimore MD 21218-1119 Office: U Md Divsn Cardiology 22 S Greene St Baltimore MD 21201-1544 E-mail: llmmmiller@aol.com., mmiller@heart.umaryland.edu.

MILLER, MICHAEL, literary arts researcher, writer; b. Colo., May 19, 1949; s. Bryan and Lorraine (Cull) M.; m. Marie Antoinette Montez; 1 child, Estrella Claudine. Student, Inst. Allende, San Miguel, Mex., 1968; BA in History, N.Mex. Highlands U., 1972; MA in Info. Sci., U. Denver, 1974. Mem. faculty N.Mex. Highlands U., Las Vegas, 1974-76; dir. LRC U. N.Mex. No. br., Santa Cruz, 1976-80; archivist N.Mex. State Archives, Santa Fe, 1980-86, dir., 1986-90; dir., asst. prof. Ctr. S.W. Rsch. U. N.Mex., Albuquerque, 1990-95; dir. rsch. and lit. arts N.Mex. Hispanic Cultural Ctr., 1995—. Mem. editl. adv. bd. S.W. Heritage, Hobbs, 1980-86, N.Mex. Almanac, Santa Fe, 1990-93; mem. hist. adv. bd. State of N.Mex., 1994—; part-time faculty No. N.Mex. C.C., 1998; mem. adv. bd. N.Mex. Hist. Records, 1998. Author: Monuments of Adobe, 1992 (award of merit), New Mexico Scrapbook, 1991; editor: Hispanic Heroes, 1993, New Mexico: Celebrating 400 Years of History, 1998, (with others) Enduring Cowboys, 1999, Flow of the River, 2000, Barelas: A Traves de los Años, 2001; editor: A Hispanic Timeline of New Mexico History, 2002. Mem. N.Mex. Cuarto Centennial Com.; commr. La Puebla Cmty. Ditch, 1995—; mem. La Communidad de la Puebla, 1994—; bd. dirs. Santa Fe-Pojoaque Soil and Water Conservation Dist., 1998; chair edn. and pub. rels. N.Mex. Assn. Conservation Dists. Grantee Nat. Endowment for Arts, 1990, N.Mex. Arts Coun., 1994; recipient award of excellence Tex. Graphics, 1992, Offcl. Quincentennial Publ. award Archdiocese of Santa Fe,

1992. Mem. N.Mex. Hist. Soc., N.Mex. Libr. Assn., Soc. S.W. Archivists, Chimayó Cultural Preservation Assn., N.Mex. Preservation Alliance (founder). Democrat. Roman Catholic. Avocations: fly fishing, archery hunting. Home: PO Box 22 Santa Cruz NM 87567-0022 Office: NMex Hispanic Cultural Ctr PO Box 12317 Albuquerque NM 87195-0317

MILLER, MICHAEL D. psychologist; b. Mar. 5, 1957; BA, Marquette U., Milwaukee, 1979; PhD/MS, Purdue U., W. Lafayette, Ind., 1984. Clin. psychologist Marshfield Clin., Wisc., 1989—, Arnett Clin., Lafayette, Ind., 1984-89; clin. intern U. Okla. Children's Hosp., Oklahoma City, 83-84. Contbr. articles to profl. jours. Mem. OLP sch. bd., Marshfield, Wisc., 1997—; speaker Marshfield Clin. Speakers Bureau, 1989—. Office: Marshfield Clin Dept Psyc 1000 N Oak Ave Marshfield WI 54449-5703

MILLER, MICHAEL DAVID, gynecologist, obstetrician; b. Nyack, N.Y., Feb. 12, 1935; s. Joseph Samuel Arluck and Sarah Elizabeth (Carpin) M.; m. Merle Judith Jablin, Aug. 16, 1959; children: Nicole Gabrielle, Steven Paul. BSc, Union Coll., Schenectady, N.Y., 1957; MD, Albert Einstein U., 1962. Diplomate Am. Bd. Ob-Gyn, Am. Bd. Med. Examiners. Intern, then resident in ob-gyn Downstate Med. Ctr., N.Y.C., 1962-1967; obstetrician, gynecologist Permanente Med. Group, San Francisco, 1969-96, perinatologist, 1979-96; assoc. clin. prof. U. Calif., 1994—. Mem. former chmn. Kaiser Found. Hosp. perinatal rev. com. (former chmn.), San Francisco, 1969-96; lectr. in field. Former chair med. adv. com. City and County of San Francisco Perinatal Forum. Served to maj. U.S. Army, 1967-69. Fellow: Am. Coll. Obs.-Gyn.; mem.: San Francisco Med. Soc., Hellman Obs.-Gyn. Soc., Soc. Maternal-Fetal Medicine. Avocations: harpsichord, photography, tennis, skiing, hiking. Home: 26 Mount Wittenburg Ct San Rafael CA 94903-1058 E-mail: mdmillermd@aol.com.

MILLER, MICHAEL JEFFREY, editor, columnist; b. Chgo., Dec. 10, 1958; s. Kenneth Maynard and Joan (Callner) M.; m. Joan A Slobin, Oct. 18, 1987. BS in Computer Sci., Rensselaer Poly., Troy, N.Y., 1979; MS in Journalism, Northwestern U., Evanston, Ill., 1980. Sr. editor Bldg. Design and Constrn., Chgo., 1980-83; west coast bur. chief Popular Computing, San Francisco, 1983-85; exec. editor InfoWorld, Menlo Park, Calif., 1985-89, editor, 1989-90, editor-in-chief, 1991, PC Mag., N.Y.C., 1991—; exec. v.p., editl. dir. Ziff-Davis Pub., 1997—. Mem. Am. Soc. Technion, Soc. Profl. Journalists. Office: PC Mag 28 E 28th St New York NY 10016-7930

MILLER, MICHAEL JON, survey engineer, local government manager; b. Parkers Prairie, Minn., Mar. 17, 1950; s. Buford Kenneth and Gretchen Cena (Sharp) M.; m. Terry Lynn Peck, May 20, 1972; children: Livia Mica, David Peter. BS, U. Wis., Platteville, 1972; M of Pub. Adminstrn., Ariz. State U., 1988. Cert. profl. land surveyor, Wis., Ariz., soil tester, Wis. Chief of surveys Hovelsrud Cons. Assn., Richland Ctr., Wis., 1972-78; ops. mgr. Tech. Advisors, Inc., Phoenix, 1978-82; profl. surveyor Coe and Van Loo, Inc., 1982-83; survey engr. City of Phoenix, 1983—. Land surveyor mem. Ariz. Bd. Tech. Registration, 1989-97, emeritus mem., 1997—, sec., 1990-91, vice chmn., 1991, chmn., 1991-92, vice chmn. 1993-94, chmn. 1994-95; mem. Enforcement Adv. Com., 1997—. Content editor The Ariz. Surveyor; contbr. articles to profl. jours. Dep. registrar Dem. Party of Ariz., Phoenix, 1983-94; clk. Phoenix Friends Meeting, 1985-86; recording clk. Intermountain Yearly Meeting of Religious Soc. of Friends, 1984-85. Fellow Am. Congress on Surveying and Mapping (membership chmn. 1987-88); mem. Nat. Soc. Profl. Surveyors (gov. for Ariz. 1985-89), Western Fedn. Land Surveyors (state del. 1988-89), Ariz. Profl. Land Surveyors (sec. 1983-84, pres. 1985-86, Outstanding award 1981, life mem. award 1996), Nat. Coun. Examiners for Engrs. and Surveyors (chmn. western zone nominating com. 1998), Am. Pub. Works Assn., Am. Soc. for Pub. Adminstrn. (bd. dirs. Ariz. chpt. 2000—, pres.-elect 2002--, comm. dir. sect. for historic, artistic and reflective expression), World Clown Assn., Internat. Jugglers Assn., Greater Ariz. Bicycle Assn. Democrat. Avocations: hist. research, writing, juggling, bicycling. Home: 4026 E Campbell Ave Phoenix AZ 85018-3709 E-mail: mjm4449@excite.com., michael.miller@phoenix.gov.

MILLER, MICHAEL PATIKY, lawyer; b. Huntington, N.Y., Apr. 16, 1944; s. George J. and Alida (Patiky) Miller; m. Dorothy Denn, Dec. 25, 1966; children: Lauren M. Golubtchik, Jonathan M., Rachel Miller Lazarus. AB, Rutgers U., 1965; JD, NYU, 1968. Bar: N.J. 1968, U.S. Dist. Ct. N.J. 1968, Calif. 1975, U.S. Dist. Ct. (no. dist.) Calif. 1975, U.S. Tax Ct. 1977, U.S. Ct. Appeals (9th cir.) 1977, U.S. Ct. Appeals (fed. cir.) 1984, U.S. Dist. Ct. (cen. dist.) Calif. 1982, U.S. Supreme Ct. 1983, U.S. Claims Ct. 1986. Atty. Electric Power Research Inst., Palo Alto, Calif., 1974-77; assoc. Weinberg, Ziff & Kaye, 1977-78; ptnr. Weinberg, Ziff & Miller, 1978—, mng. ptnr., 1990-98; lectr. on tax and estate planning U. Calif. Extension, 1980—. Author: Creditor Rights in Proceedings Outside Estate Adminstrn., 1995, rev., 1999, revised edit., 2002, Estate Planning for Foreign Nationals in Silicon Valley, 2000; co-author: Decedents Estate Practice, 2001, Trust Administration, 2d edit., 2001; contbg. author: California Wills and Trusts, 1991, Estate Planning for Unmarried Couples, 1998, California Trust Administration, 1999; contbr. chpts. in books and articles to profl. jours. Treas. No. Calif. region United Synagogue Am., 1985-89, pres., 1992-95. Capt. U.S. Army, 1969-74, Vietnam, Ethiopia. Recipient Lion of Judah award, 1984, Cert. Merit U. Judaism, 1992. Mem. ABA (chmn. region VI pub. contract law sect. 1975-78, commn. tax practice in small law firms, com. on taxation of trusts, estates, taxation sect. 1986—), N.J. State Bar, State Bar of Calif. (commr. tax law adv. commn. 1989-92, 93-95, chair 1994-95, mem. bd. legal specialization 1994-95), Santa Clara County Bar Assn. (chmn. estate planning, probate and trust sect. 1982, trustee 1983-84), Silicon Valley Bar Assn. (pres. 2000—). Office: Weinberg Ziff & Miller 400 Cambridge Ave Palo Alto CA 94306-1507 Fax: 650-324-2822.

MILLER, MICHAEL STRATTON, lawyer; b. Cin., May 12, 1958; s. Karl Stratton and Sari Elizabeth (Derby) M.; m. Susan Beth Spector; children: Stefannie A., Jamie E., Jessica L., Christopher D. BA, U. Cin., 1981; JD, Ohio State U., 1984. Bar: Ohio. Atty. Wolske & Blue, Columbus, Ohio, 1984-94, Palmer Volkema Thomas, Columbus, 1995—. Contbr. articles to profl. publs. Mem. ATLA, Ohio Acad. of Trial Lawyers (trustee 1996—, chair constitutional challenge com. 1997-99, editor Trial mag. 1997—, editor Adv. 1998—), Franklin County Trial Lawyers (trustee 1998—, chair negligence law com. 1995-97, 99-00), Ohio State Bar Assn., Columbus Bar Assn. Office: Palmer Volkema Thomas 140 E Town St Ste 1100 Columbus OH 43215-5183 E-mail: mmiller@pvtlaw.com.

MILLER, MICHAEL THOMAS, lawyer; b. Mpls., Jan. 22, 1959; BA, U. Minn., 1981, JD, 1985. Bar: Minn. 1985, U.S. Dist. Ct. Minn. 1985, U.S. Ct. Appeals (8th cir.) 1987, U.S. Ct. Appeals (10th cir.) 1996, U.S. Supreme Ct. 1989. Law clk. Hon. Peter S. Popovich Minn. Ct. Appeals, St. Paul, 1985-87; assoc. Briggs & Morgan, P.A., Mpls., 1987-92, shareholder, 1992—. Contbr. articles to profl. jours. Office: Briggs & Morgan 2400 IDS Ctr Minneapolis MN 55402

MILLER, MICKEY LESTER, retired school administrator; b. Albuquerque, July 26, 1920; s. Chester Lester and Myra Easter (Cassidy) M.; m. Louise Dean Miller, Aug. 30, 1946; children: Linda Miller Kelly, Lee Miller Parks, Lynne Miller Carson. BS, U. N.Mex., 1944; MS, Columbia U., 1949. Coach, tchr. math. Jefferson Jr. H.S., Albuquerque, 1946-49; coach, dept. chair, athletic dir. Highland H.S., 1949-64, asst. prin., 1964-70; dist. program coord. Albuquerque Pub. Schs., 1970-90; ret., 1990. Author: Guide to Administration of Secondary Athletics, 1990; author brochures, handbooks, articles. Pub. mem. N.Mex. Bd. Dentistry, 1992—. With USN, 1942-46. Recipient Honor award S.W. Dist. Am. Alliance Health, Phys. Edn., Recreation and Dance, 1971, N.Mex. Coaches Assn., 1981, Hall of Fame award N.Mex. Activities Assn., 1985; named Retiree of Yr., S.W. Dist. Am. Alliance Health, Phys. Edn., Recreation and Dance, 1994; named to U. N.Mex. Alumni Lettermen Hall of Honor, 1994; named to Albuquerque Sports Hall of Fame, 1995. Mem. AAHPERD (life, budget/nominating rep. 1985, honor award 1999), U. N.Mex. Alumni Assn., U. N.Mex. LOBO Lettermen Club (pres., treas. 1972). Democrat. Methodist. Avocations: golf, travel, baseball scouting. Home: 1201 Richmond Dr NE Albuquerque NM 87106-2023

MILLER, MILTON ALLEN, lawyer; b. L.A., Jan. 15, 1954; s. Samuel C. and Sylvia Mary Jane (Silver) Miller; m. Mary Ann Toman, Sept. 10, 1988; 1 child Mary Ann. AB With distinction and honors in Econs., Stanford U., 1976; JD with honors, Harvard U., 1979. Bar: Calif. 1979, U.S. Ct. Appeals 9th cir.) 1979, U.S. Supreme Ct. 1989, Calif. (U.S. Dist. Ct. (cen., no. and so. dists.)) 1981. Law clk. U.S. Ct. Appeals (9th cir.), Sacramento, 1979—80; assoc. Latham & Watkins, L.A., 1979—87, ptnr., 1987—. Chmn. ethics com. Latham & Watkins, L.A., 1986—. Author: (non fiction) Attorney Ethics, 1993; editor: Harvard Law Rev., 1978—79; contbr. articles to profl. jours. Mem.: ATLA, ABA, L.A. County Bar Assn. (chmn. profl. responsibility and ethics com.), Calif. State Bar Assn. (mem. com. on profl. responsibility), Am. Cancer Soc. (L.A. chpt.), Phi Beta Kappa. Office: Latham & Watkins 633 W 5th St Ste 4000 Los Angeles CA 90071-2005 E-mail: milt.miller@lw.com. *Notable cases include Raquel Welch vs. MGM Corp.; served as trial and insurance counsel in San Juan Dupont Plaza Hotel Fire litigation.*

MILLER, MORGAN LINCOLN, textile manufacturing company executive; b. New Rochelle, N.Y., Feb. 11, 1924; s. Harry H. and Belle M.; m. Marjorie Leff, June 8, 1952; children— Betsy, Harry Robert, Amy, Cindy. BA, Lehigh U., Bethlehem, Pa., 1947. With Nat. Spinning Co., Inc., 1959—, exec. v.p., 1964—, vice chmn., 1990—; pres. Jr. Accent Dress Mfg. Co., 1956—, Coquet Bathing Suit Mfg. Co., 1954—. Bd. dirs. BHC Comm., Inc. V.p. Westchester (N.Y.) Reform Temple, 1971, Westchester Jewish Cmty. Svcs., White Plains, 1970; trustee Beth Israel Med. Ctr. With USNR, 1942—45. Named Industry Man of Year United Jewish Appeal, 1980. Mem.: Quaker Ridge Golf Club. Republican. Office: 111 W 40th St New York NY 10018-2506

MILLER, NANCY A. nursing administrator; b. Lehighton, Pa., Apr. 6, 1942; d. Calvin Erck and Mabel Rosetta (Burkett) Geiger; children: Michael Todd Miller, Nicole Ann Miller. Diploma, St. Luke's Sch. Nursing, Bethlehem, Pa., 1962. RN, Pa. Staff nurse Vis. Nurse Assn., Stroudsburg, 1981-89; dir. community health svcs. Home Health Schs., Pa.; adminstr. Home Care Affiliates; DON Stroud Manor, East Stroudsburg, Pa., 1989-91, Brookmont Health Care Ctr. Inc., Effort, 1991-97; case mgr. Riverside Rehab., Mt. Pocono, 1997-98; DON Pocono Med. Ctr., East Stroudsburg, 1998-99; RN supr. Stroud Manor, 1999-2001; RN assessment coord. Pleasant Valley Manor, 2001—. Office: Pocono Med Ctr Stroudsburg PA 18360 E-mail: rowdy@ptj.net.

MILLER, NANCY ELLEN, computer consultant; b. Detroit, Aug. 30, 1956; d. George Jacob and Charlotte M. Miller. BS in Computer and Comm. Scis. (hons.), U. Mich., 1978; MS in Computer Scis., U. Wis., 1981. Product engr. Ford Motor Co., Dearborn, Mich., 1977; computer programmer Unique Bus. Sys., Inc., Southfield, 1978; tchg. asst. computer scis. dept. U. Wis., Madison, 1978-82; computer scientist Lister Hill Nat. Ctr. Biomed. Commns., Nat. Libr. Medicine NIH, Bethesda, Md., 1984-88; pvt. practice West Bloomfield, Mich., 1993—. *Nancy E. Miller's professional interests in the field of artificial intelligence include: expert systems, default logic, planning, knowledge-based systems, case-based reasoning, logic programming, agents, fuzzy logic, neural networks, and genetic programming. She is also interested in object-oriented programming and design. Ms. Miller is highly skilled in the following computer languages, systems, and tools: Lisp, Prolog, C++, C, Pascal, UNIX, Windows, Framekit, etc. She has used rapid prototyping and structured programming methodologies. Ms. Miller has worked in many facets of computer science, from research and development to end-user applications, in academia, government and industry, and on all sizes of computers.* Active Nat. Abortion and Reproductive Rights Action League, Washington, 1984—, Nat. Women's Polit. Caucus, Washington, 1984—, Planned Parenthood Fedn. Am., NY, 1986--, Jewish Fedn. Met. Detroit, Bloomfield Hills, 1991--, Dem. Nat. Com., Washington, 1984—, Hadassah: The Women's Zionist Org. of Am., Inc., N.Y., 1992—. Recipient Jour. of Am. Soc. for Info. Sci. Best Paper award, 1988. Mem. Assn. for Computing Machinery (sec. S.E. Mich. spl. interest group on artificial intelligence 1993-94), Am. Assn. for Artificial Intelligence and Spl. Interest Groups in Mfg. and Bus., Assn. for Logic Programming, U. Wis. Alumni Assn. (life), U. Mich. Alumni Assn. (life). Home and Office: 6220 Village Park Dr Apt 104 West Bloomfield MI 48322-2146 E-mail: NancyMiller588@msn.com.

MILLER, NANCY K. literature educator; PhD, Columbia U. Prof. City U. N.Y., N.Y.C. Contbr. articles. Office: CUNY Grad Ctr PhD Program in Eng 365 5th Ave New York NY 10016-4309 Office Fax: 212-817-8336. E-mail: nmiller@gc.cuny.edu.*

MILLER, NEIL SCOTT, lawyer; b. N.Y.C., Jan. 2, 1969; BA in Polit. Sci., U. Vt., 1991; JD, Bklyn. Law Sch., 1994. Assoc. Agins, Siegel & Reiner, N.Y.C., 1995-97, Graham & James, N.Y.C., 1997-99, Greenberg Traurig, N.Y.C., 1999—. Office: Greenberg Traurig 200 Park Ave New York NY 10166 E-mail: millern@gtlaw.com.

MILLER, NEIL STUART, advertising executive; b. N.Y.C., July 30, 1958; s. Irving Israel Maltz and Lenore (Goldstein) M.; m. Karen Joyce Salomon, Nov. 22, 1987; children: Lindsay Alexandra, Jacqueline Olivia, Sara Allison. BS, SUNY, Buffalo, 1980; MBA, SUNY, Binghamton, 1982. CPA, N.Y. Staff auditor Peat Marwick Mitchell & Co., N.Y.C., 1982-83; ops. auditor Gulf & Western Industries, 1983-84; spl. projects acct. Mickelberry Comms., 1984-86; v.p. fin. Ptnrs. & Shevack Inc. (subs. Mickelberry Comms. Inc.), 1986-87, sr. v.p. fin., 1987-89, exec. v.p., CFO, 1989-96, exec. v.p., COO, 1996-98; sr. v.p., fin. dir. McCann Erickson New York (subs. Interpublic Group of Cos.), 1998-2000; CFO N.Am. MindShare (subs. WPP Group PLC), 2000; COO TN Media (subs. True North Comm./Interpublic Group of Cos.), NYC, 2000—01; CFO N.Am. Foote, Cone & Belding, N.Y.C., 2001—. Mem. AICPA, Am. Mgmt. Assn., N.Y. State Soc. CPA's (past mem. com. CFOs and advt.), Advt. Agy. Fin. Mgmt. Group, Fin. Execs. Inst. Avocations: skiing, motorcycling, golf. Home: 594 W Saddle River Rd Upper Saddle River NJ 07458-1115 Office: Foote Cone & Belding 150 E 42nd St New York NY 10017-5612

MILLER, NEWTON EDD, JR. communications educator; b. Houston, Mar. 13, 1920; s. Newton Edd and Anastasia (Johnston) M.; m. Edwina Whitaker, Aug. 30, 1942; children: Cathy Edwina, Kenneth Edd. BS, U. Tex., 1939, MA, 1940; PhD, U. Mich., 1952; LL.D., U. Nev., Reno., 1974. Tutor U. Tex., Austin, 1940-41, instr., 1941-45, asst. prof. speech, 1945-47; research asst. Navy Conf. Research, 1947-52; mem. faculty U. Mich., Ann Arbor, 1947-65, successively lectr., instr., asst. prof. speech, 1947-55, assoc. prof., 1955-59, prof., 1959-65, asst. dir. summer session, 1953-57, assoc. dir., 1957-63, asst. to v.p. acad. affairs, 1963-65; chancellor U. Nev., Reno, 1965-68, pres., 1968-73, U. Maine, Portland-Gorham, 1973-78; chmn. communications dept. No. Ky. U., 1978-87, emeritus, 1987—, interim gen. mgr. Sta. WNKU, 1985-86. Mem. adv. com. to commr. of edn. U.S. Office of Edn., Accreditation and Instl. Eligibility, 1976-79, acting chmn., 1977-78; mem. Judicial Edn. Study Group Am. Univ. Law Inst., 1977-78; mem. Nat. Accreditation Commn. for Agys. Serving Blind and Physically Handicapped, 1988-97, pres., 1991-92, bd. dirs., 1999—. Author: Post War World Organization, Background Studies, 1942, (with J.J. Villareal) First Course in Speech, 1945, (with W.M. Sattler) Discussion and Debate, 1951, Discussion and Conference, 2d edit., 1968, (with Stephen D. Boyd) Public Speaking: A Practical Handbook, 1985, 2d edit., 1989; co-editor: Required Arbitration of Labor Disputes, 1947. Pres. bd. dirs. Perry Nursery Sch., 1956-57, Sierra Cmty. Orch., 1989-94; mem. Ann Arbor Bd. Edn., 1959-65, Washtenaw County Bd. Edn.; sec. bd. dirs. Behringer Crawford Mus.; bd. dirs. Siera Arts Found., 1992—; pres. Reno/Sparks Theater Cmty. Coalition, 1994-96; mem. Nev. Humanities Com., 1994-2001. Mem. Mich. Assn. Sch. Bds. (dir.), N.W. Assn. Colls. and Secondary Schs. (chmn. higher commn. 1971-73), Am. Forensic Assn. (pres. Midwest sect. 1950-53), Central States Speech Assn. (pres. 1958-59), Mich. Speech Assn. (exec. sec. 1950-55), Speech Communication Assn. (chmn. fin. bd.), Assn. Western Us. (chmn. 1971-72), Coun. on Naturopathic Med. Edn., Delta Sigma Rho (nat. v.p. 1948-52), Phi Kappa Phi. Address: 1480 Ayershire Ct Reno NV 89509-5248

MILLER, NORMAN CHARLES, JR. retired journalism educator; b. Pitts., Oct. 2, 1934; s. Norman Charles and Elizabeth (Burns) M.; m. Mollie Rudy, June 15, 1957; children— Norman III, Mary Ellen, Teri, Scott BA, Pa. State U., 1956. Reporter Wall Street Jour., San Francisco, 1960-63, reporter N.Y.C., 1963-64, bur. chief Detroit, 1964-66, Washington corr., 1966-72, Washington Bur. chief, 1973-83; nat. editor Los Angeles Times, 1983-97; lectr. journalism U. So. Calif., 1997—2001; ret., 2001. Author: The Great Salad Oil Swindle, 1965 Served to lt. (j.g.) USN, 1956-60. Recipient Disting. Alumnus award Pa. State U., 1978; George Polk Meml. award L.I. U., 1963; Pulitzer Prize, 1964 Mem.: Gridiron (Washington). Roman Catholic. Avocation: tennis.

MILLER, ORLANDO JACK, physician, educator; b. Oklahoma City, May 11, 1927; s. Arthur Leroy and Iduma Dorris (Berry) M.; m. Dorothy Anne Smith, July 10, 1954; children: Richard Lawrence, Cynthia Kathleen, Karen Ann. BS, Yale U., 1946, MD, 1950. Intern St. Anthony Hosp., Oklahoma City, 1950-51; asst. resident in obstetrics and gynecology Yale-New Haven Med. Center, 1954-57, resident, instr., 1957-58; vis. fellow dept. obstetrics and gynecology Tulane U. Service, Charity Hosp., New Orleans, 1958; hon. research asst. Galton Lab., Univ. Coll., London, 1958-60; instr. Coll. Physicians and Surgeons Columbia U., N.Y.C., 1960, asso. dept. obstetrics and gynecology, 1960-61, asst. prof., 1961-65, asso. prof., 1965-69, prof. dept. human genetics and devel., dept. obstetrics and gynecology, 1969-85; asst. attending obstetrician, gynecologist Presbyn. Hosp., 1964-65, assoc., 1965-70, attending obstetrician and gynecologist, 1970-85; prof. molecular biology, genetics and ob-gyn. Wayne State U. Sch. Medicine, Detroit, 1985-94, prof. Ctr. for Molecular Medicine and Genetics, 1994-96, prof. emeritus, 1996—, chmn. dept. molecular biology and genetics, 1985-93, dir. Ctr. for Molecular Biology, 1987-90. Bd. dirs.Am. Bd. Med. Genetics, 1983-85, v.p., 1983, pres., 1984, 85. Author: (with E. Therman) Human Chromosomes, 2000; editor Cytogenetics, 1970-72; assoc. editor: Birth Defects Compendium, 1971-74, Cytogenetics and Cell Genetics, 1972-97; mem. editl. bd. Cytogenetics, 1961-69, Am. Jour. Human Genetics, 1969-74, 79-83, Gynecologic Investigation, 1970-77, Teratology, 1972-74, Cancer Genetics and Cytogenetics, 1979-84, Jour. Exptl. Zoology, 1989-92, Chromosome Rsch., 1994-99; mem. editl. bd. com. Genomics, 1987-93, assoc. editor, 1993-96; mem. adv. bd. Human Genetics, 1978-98; cons. Jour. Med. Primatology, 1977-94; consulting editor McGraw-Hill Yearbook of Sci. and Tech., 1995—, Encyclopedia of Science and Technology, 1997—; contbr. chpts. to textbooks and articles to med. and sci. jours. Mem. sci. adv. com. on rsch. Nat. Found. March of Dimes, 1967-96, mem. sci. com., 1996—; mem. sci. rec. com. Basil O'Connor starter grants, 1973-77, 86-94; mem. human embryology and devel. study sect. NIH, 1970-74, chmn., 1972-74; mem. com. for study of inborn errors of metabolism NRC, 1972-74; mem. sci. adv. com. virology and cell biology Am. Cancer Soc., 1974-78, mem. sci. adv. com. cell and devel. biology, 1986-90; mem. human genome study sect. NIH, 1991-94; U.S. rep. permanent com. Internat. Congress of Human Genetics, 1986-91. With AUS, 1951-53. James Hudson Brown Jr. fellow Yale U., 1947-48; NRC fellow, 1953-54; Population Council fellow, 1958-59; Josiah Macy Jr. fellow, 1960-61; NSF sr. postdoctoral fellow U. Oxford, 1968-69; vis. scientist U. Edinburgh, 1983-84; Disting. vis. fellow, Fogarty Internat. fellow LaTrobe U., Melbourne, Australia, 1992; recipient Pres. Disting. Scientist award Soc. for Gynecol. Investigation, 1999. Fellow AAAS; mem. AAAS, Am. Genetic Assn., Am. Soc. Cell Biology, Am. Soc. Human Genetics (bd. dirs. 1970-73, 86-90), Genetics Soc. Am., Genetics Soc. Australia, Human Genome Orgn., Acad. Scholars, Wayne State U. (life, pres. 1996-97), Sigma Xi. Presbyterian. Home: 1915 Stonycroft Ln Bloomfield Hills MI 48304-2339 Office: 540 E Canfield St Detroit MI 48201-1928 E-mail: ojmiller@cmb.biosci.wayne.edu.

MILLER, OSCAR, economics educator; b. Chgo., Oct. 1, 1920; s. Meyer and Dina (Shenfeld) M.; m. Esther Bromberg, June 10, 1945; children: Lauren, Sharon, Ira. MA, U. Chgo., 1948. Instr. econs. U Ill., Chgo., 1948—, prof. econs., 1972—, dean students, assoc. vice chancellor, 1979-83. Lectr. on politics and econs. in free mkt. Mem. econ. adv. bd. U.S. Israel C. of C., Chgo., 1990—. Lt. USN, 1942-45. Recipient Pepper award Claude Pepper, 1993, Alumni award of Disting. Tchg. Coll. Bus. Adminstrn., U. Ill., Chgo., 1993. Jewish. Avocation: U.S.-Israel relations. Home: 7201 N Lincoln Ave Apt 201 Lincolnwood IL 60712-1822 Office: U Ill at Chicago 601 S Morgan St # Mc144 Chicago IL 60607-7100 E-mail: oemiller@attglobal.net.

MILLER, PAMELA GUNDERSEN, mayor; b. Cambridge, Mass., Sept. 7, 1938; d. Sven M. and Harriet Adams Gundersen; m. Ralph E. Miller, July 7, 1962; children: Alexander, Erik, Karen. AB magna cum laude, Smith Coll., 1960. Feature writer Congl. Quar., Washington, 1962-65; dir. cable TV franchising Storer Broadcasting Co., Louisville, Lexington, Ky., 1978-80, 81-82; mem. 4th dist. Lexington Fayette county Urban Coun., 1973-77; councilwoman-at-large, 1982-93; vice mayor, 1984-86, 89-93; mayor, 1993—. Dep. commr. Ky. Dept. Local Govt., Frankfort, 1980-81; pres. Pam Miller, Inc., 1984-94, Community Ventures Corp., 1985—. Mem. Fayette County Bd. Health, 1975-77, Downtown Devel. Commn., 1975-77; alt. del. Dem. Nat. Conv., 1976; bd. dirs. YMCA, Lexington, 1975-77, 85-90, Fund for the Arts, 1984-93, Council of Arts, 1978-80, Sister Cities, 1978-80; treas. Prichard Com. for Acad. Excellence, 1983—. Named woman of achievement YWCA, 1984, outstanding Woman of Blue Grass, AAUW, 1984. Mem. LWV (dir. 1970-73), Profl. Women's Forum, NOW, Land and Nature Trust of the Bluegrass. Home: 140 Cherokee Park Lexington KY 40503-1304 Office: 200 E Main St Lexington KY 40507-1310

MILLER, PATRICK DWIGHT, JR. religion educator, minister; b. Atlanta, Oct. 24, 1935; s. Patrick Dwight and Lila Morse (Bonner) M.; m. Mary Ann Sudduth, Dec. 27, 1958; children: Jonathan Sudduth, Patrick James. AB, Davidson Coll., 1956; BD, Union Theol. Sem., Va., 1959; PhD, Harvard U., 1964. Ordained to ministry Presbyn. Ch., 1963. Pastor, minister Trinity Presbyn. Ch., Traveler's Rest, S.C., 1963-65; asst. prof. Bibl. studies Union Theol. Sem., Richmond, Va., 1966-68, assoc. prof., 1968-73, prof., 1973-84, dean of faculty, 1979-83; Charles T. Haley prof. of Old Testament Theology Princeton (N.J.) Theol. Sem., 1984—. Author: The Divine Warrior in Early Israel, 1973, The Hand of the Lord, 1977, Sin and Judgment in the Prophets, 1982, Interpreting the Psalms, 1986, Deuteronomy, 1990, They Cried to the Lord, 1994, The Religion of Ancient Israel, 2000, Israelite Religion and Biblical Theology, 2000; editor: Theology Today, 1990—. Mem. Soc. of Bibl. Lit. (sec.-treas. 1987-88, pres. 1998), Rev. Std. Version Translation Com. Democrat. Presbyterian. Office: Princeton Theol Sem PO Box 821 Princeton NJ 08542-0803

MILLER, PATRICK WILLIAM, research administrator, educator; b. Toledo, Sept. 1, 1947; s. Richard William and Mary Olivia (Rinna) M.; m. Jean Ellen Thomas, Apr. 5, 1974; children: Joy, Tatum, Alex. BS in Indstrl. Edn., Bowling Green State U., 1971, MEd in Career Edn. and Tech., 1973; PhD in Indstrl. Tech. Edn., Ohio State U., 1977; Master's cert. Govt. Contract Adminstrn., George Washington U., 1995. Tchr. Montgomery Hills Jr. High Sch., Silver Spring, Md., 1971-72, Rockville (Md.) High Sch., 1973-74; asst. prof. Wayne State U., Detroit, 1977-79; assoc. prof., grad. coord. indstrl. edn. and tech. Western Carolina U., Cullowhee, N.C., 1979-81; assoc prof. U. No. Iowa, Cedar Falls, 1981-86; dir. grad. studies practical arts and vocat.-tech. edn. U. Mo., Columbia, 1986-89; devel. editor Am. Tech. Pubs., Homewood, Ill., 1989-90; proposal mgr. Nat. Opinion Rsch. Ctr. U. Chgo., 1990-96; dir. grants & contracts City Colls. Chgo., 1996-99; assoc. v.p. acad. affairs Prairie State Coll., 1999—2001, also dean workforce devel. and career edn., 1999—2001; ret., 2001. Pres. Patrick W. Miller and Assocs., Munster, Ind., 1981—; presenter, advisor and cons. in field. Author: Nonverbal Communication: Its Impact on Teaching and Learning, 1983, Teacher Written Tests: A Guide for Planning, Creating, Administering and Assessing, 1985, Nonverbal Communication: What Research Says to the Teacher, 1988, How To Write Tests for Students, 1990, Nonverbal Communication in the Classroom, 2000, Nonverbal Communication in the Workplace, 2000, Grant Writing: Strategies for Developing Winning Proposals, 2d edit., 2002, Test Development: Guidelines, Practical Suggestions and Examples, 2001; mem. editl. bd. Jour. Indsl. Tchr. Edn., 1981-88, Am. Vocat. Edn. Rsch. Jour., 1981-85, 94—, Tech. Tchr., 1982-84, Jour. Indsl. Tech., 1984—, Jour. Vocat. and Tech. Edn., 1987-90, Human Resource Devel. Quar., 1989—; also articles. Sec. U. No. Iowa United Faculty, Cedar Falls, 1983-84, pres., 1984-86. Lance cpl. USMC, 1966-68, Vietnam. Recipient editl. recognition award Jour. Indsl. Tchr. Edn., 1984, 86, 88; named One of Accomplished Grads. of Coll. Tech., Bowling Green State U., 1995. Mem. ASTD, Am. Ednl. Rsch. Assn., Assn. for Career and Tech. Edn., Am. Vocat. Edn. Rsch. Assn., Nat. Assn. Indsl. Tech. (chmn. rsch. grants 1982-87, pres. industry divsn. 1991-92, chmn. exec. bd. 1992-93, past pres. 1993-94, Leadership award 1992, 93), Nat. Assn. Indsl. and Tech. Tchr. Educators (pres. 1988-89, past pres. 1989-90, trustee 1990-93, Outstanding Svc. award 1988, 90), Internat. Tech. Edn. Assn., Coun. Tech. Tchr. Edn., Epsilon Pi Tau, Phi Delta Kappa. E-mail: miller9147@aol.com., pwmiller@online.com.

MILLER, PAUL AUSBORN, adult education educator; b. East Liverpool, Ohio, Mar. 22, 1917; s. Harry A. and Elizabeth (Stewart) M.; m. Catherine Spiker, Dec. 9, 1939 (dec. Dec. 1964); children— Paula Kay, Thomas

Ausborn; m. Francena Lounsbery Nolan, Jan. 15, 1966. BS, U. W.Va., 1939; MA, Mich. State U., 1947, PhD, 1953. County agrl. agt. in, W.Va., 1939-42; extension specialist sociology and anthropology Mich. State U., East Lansing, 1947-55, asst. prof., 1947-52, assoc. prof., 1953, prof., 1953-61, dir. coop. ext. svc., 1954-58, provost, 1959-61; pres. W.Va. U., 1962-66; asst. sec. for edn. HEW, Charlotte, 1966-68; disting. prof. edn., dir. univ. planning studies U. N.C., 1966-68; prof. adult edn. N.C. Sate U. at Raleigh, 1668-69; pres. Rochester (N.Y.) Inst. of Tech., 1969-79, pres. emeritus, 1979—, prof., 1979-83. Sr. program cons. W.K. Kellogg Found., 1979-83; adj. prof. rural sociology U. Mo.-Columbia, 1994—. Author: Community Health Action, 1953; co-author: Patterns for Lifelong Learning, 1973; contbr. to publs. in field. Mem. Colombian Commn. Higher Edn., 1960-61. Served as 1st lt. USAAF, 1942-46. Named to the Internat. Adult and Continuing Edn. Hall of Fame. Fellow Am. Sociol. Assn.; mem. Rural Sociol. Soc., Phi Kappa Phi, Epsilon Sigma Phi. Home: 1909 Walden Ct Columbia MO 65203-5407 E-mail: rursocpm@showme.missouri.edu.

MILLER, PAUL GEORGE, computer company executive; b. Louisville, Dec. 13, 1922; s. George Moore and Pauline Louise (Koob) M.; m. Doris Kahl Ingram, Feb. 17, 1979; children: George, James, Randolph. B.M.E., Purdue U., 1948; BS, U.S. Naval Acad., 1946; BS in Electronics Engring., postgrad. in Nuclear Sci., Mass. Inst. Tech., 1949. Gen. mgr. control systems div. Daystrom (later acquired by Control Data Corp.), La Jolla, Calif., 1957-65; v.p., gen. mgr. communications and spl. systems group Control Data Corp., Mpls., 1965-67, v.p., group gen. mgr. computer systems and devel., 1967-69, sr. v.p., mktg. group exec., 1970-72, sr. v.p., 1973—; pres. Control Data Mktg. Co.; chmn., chief exec. officer Comml. Credit Co., 1977-83. Bd. dirs. LSC, Inc. Served to lt. USN, 1946-57. Recipient Distinguished Alumnus award Purdue U., 1968 Mem. IEEE (sr.), Sigma Xi, Tau Beta Pi, Eta Kappa Nu, Delta Tau Delta. Home: ll203 Falls Rd Lutherville MD 21093 Office: PO Box 725 Brooklandville MD 21022-0725

MILLER, PAUL J. lawyer; b. Boston, Mar. 27, 1929; s. Edward and Esther (Kalis) M.; children— Robin, Jonathan; m. Michal Davis, Sept. 1, 1965; children— Anthony, Douglas BA, Yale U., 1950; LL.B., Harvard U., 1953. Bar: Mass. 1953, Ill. 1957. Assoc. Miller & Miller, Boston, 1953-54; assoc. Sonnenschein Nath & Rosenthal, Chgo., 1957-63, ptnr., 1963—. Bd. dirs. Oil-Dri Corp. Am., Chgo. Trustee Latin Sch. of Chgo., 1985-91. 1st lt. JAGC, U.S. Army, 1954-57. Fellow Am. Bar Found.; mem. Tavern Club, Saddle and Cycle Club, Law Club, Phi Beta Kappa. Avocation: sailing. Office: Sonnenschein Nath & Rosenthal 233 S Wacker Dr Ste 8000 Chicago IL 60606-6491 E-mail: pjm@sonnenschein.com.

MILLER, PAUL MCGRATH, JR. executive search consulting company executive; b. Oct. 31, 1935; s. Paul McGrath and Lena D. (Carr) M.; m. Charlene F. Russnak, Sept. 12, 1970 (div.); children: Andrew McGrath, Christopher Paul; m. C. Sue Whitehouse, Aug. 12, 1989 (div.). BMechE, Cornell U., 1958; MBA, Harvard U., 1966. Foreman Procter & Gamble, Cin., 1958-60; market analyst United Aircraft Co., Sunnyvale, Calif., 1963-64; asst. to chmn. bd. Boise Cascade Corp. (Idaho), 1966, gen. mktg. mgr. Insulite divsn., 1966-67, nat. sales mgr. Lumber and Plywood, 1967-68, asst. to exec. v.p. Paper Group, 1968-69; group dir. mktg. Am. Std., Inc., N.Y.C., 1969-71; dir. corp. comms. Indian Head, Inc., 1971-74; v.p. mktg. Ball & Socket Mfg. Co., Cheshire, Conn., 1975, Cory Coffee Svc., Chgo., 1976, v.p., gen. mgr., 1977-80; v.p., ptnr. Korn/Ferry Internat., 1980-87; ptnr. LAI, Inc. (formerly Lamalie Assocs. Inc.), 1987-99, TMP Exec. Search, Lexington, Va., 1999-2001, Stratford Group, Lexington, 2001—. Mem. Winnetka (Ill.) Caucus, 1980. Capt. USAF, 1960-63. Mem. Racquet Club (Chgo.), Harvard Club (N.Y.C.), Harvard Bus. Sch. Club (Chgo., dir.), Harvard U. Club (Chgo., dir.). Presbyterian.

MILLER, PAUL S(AMUEL), lawyer; b. Paterson, N.J., Apr. 8, 1939; s. Louis and Etta (Wolff) M.; m. Carol Plesser, Mar. 26, 1961; children: Nicole F., Margo H., Jason E. BA, Rutgers U., 1960, JD magna cum laude, 1962. Bar: N.Y. 1963. Assoc. Kaye, Scholer, Fierman, Hayes & Handler, N.Y.C., 1962-63, Rubin, Baum & Levin, N.Y.C., 1964; ptnr. Fishman, Miller & Zimet, 1964-70; counsel Leasing Cons., Inc., Rosyln, N.Y., 1970-71; with Pfizer Inc., N.Y.C., 1971—2002, assoc. gen. counsel, v.p., gen. counsel, 1986-92, sr. v.p., gen. counsel, 1992-99, exec. v.p., gen. counsel, 1999—2002; spl. counsel Kaye Scholer LLP, 2002—. Ofcl. corr. Pharm. Mfrs. Assn., mem., chmn. exec. com. law sect., 1989-90. Mem. United Jewish Appeal Com., Essex County, 1981-83, co-chmn. Livingston sect., 1982; chmn. bd. dirs. Citizens Crime Commn. of N.Y.C., Inc.; bd. dirs. Am. Israel Pub. Affairs Com., Am. Jewish Congress, Jewish Theol. Sem., U.S. C. of C., chmn. Nat. Chamber Litigation Coun.; mem. bus. adv. coun. Touro Law Sch.; mem. bd. overseers Inst. Civil Justice, RAND. Albert Einstein Coll. Medicine, Jaffee Inst. Strategic Studies at Tel Aviv U. Mem. ABA (antitrust law sect., corp. banking and bus. law sect., natural resources law sect., sci. and tech. sect., mem. health law forum com.), N.Y. State Bar Assn. (antitrust law sect., food and drug law sect.). Office: Kaye Scholer OOP 425 Park Ave New York NY 10022

MILLER, PEGGY GORDON ELLIOTT, university president; b. Matewan, W.Va., May 27, 1937; d. Herbert Hunt and Mary Ann (Renfro) Gordon; m. Robert Lawrence Miller, Nov. 23, 2001; children from previous marriage: Scott Vandling Elliott III, Anne Gordon Elliott. BA, Transylvania Coll., 1959; MA, Northwestern U., 1964; EdD, Ind. U., 1975. Tchr. Horace Mann H.S., Gary, Ind., 1959-64; instr. English Am. Inst. Banking, 1969-70, Ind. U. N.W., Gary, 1965-69, lectr. Edn., 1973-74, asst. prof. edn., 1975-78, assoc. prof., 1978-80, supr. secondary student tchg., 1973-74, dir. student tchg., 1975-77, dir. Office Field Experiences, 1977-78, dir. profl. devel., 1978-80, spl. asst. to chancellor, 1981-83, asst. to chancellor, 1983-84, acting chancellor, 1983-84, chancellor, 1984-92; pres. U. Akron, Ohio, 1992-96, S.D. State U., 1998—. Sr. fellow Nat. Ctr. for Higher Edn., 1996-97; vis. prof. U. Ark., 1979-80, U. Alaska, 1982; bd. dirs. Lubrizol Corp., A. Schulman Corp., First Nat. Bank Brookings, Commn. on Women in Higher Edn., Akron Tomorrow, Ohio Aerospace Consortium, Ohio Super Computer Com.; holder VA Harrington disting. chair in edn., 1994-96, Charles G. Herbrich chair in leadership mgmt., 1996— Author: (with C. Smith) Reading Activities for Middle and Secondary Schools: A Handbook for Teachers, 1979, Reading Instruction for Secondary Schools, 1986, How to Improve Your Scores on Reading Competency Tests, 1981, (with C. Smith and G. Ingersoll) Trends in Educational Materials: Traditionals and the New Technologies, 1983, The Urban Campus: Educating a New Majority for a New Century, 1994, also numerous articles. Bd. dirs. Meth. Hosp., N.W. Ind. Forum, N.W. Ind. Symphony, S.D. Art Mus., Boys Club N.W. Ind., Akron Symphony, NBD Bank, John S. Knight Conv. Ctr., Inventure Pl., Akron Roundtable, Cleve. Com. Higher Edn. Recipient Disting. Alumni award Northwestern U., UA Disting. Alumni award, 1994, numerous grants; Am. Council on Edn. fellow in acad. adminstrn. Ind. U., Bloomington, 1980-81. Mem. Assn. Tchr. Educators (nat. pres. 1984-85, Disting. Mem. 1990), Nat. Acad. Tchrs. Edn. (bd. dirs. 1983—), Ind. Assn. Tchr. Educators (past pres.), North Ctrl. Assn. (mem. commn. at large), Am. Assn. State Colls. and Univs. (sr. fellow 1996-98, acting v.p. divsn. acad. and internat. programs 1997, bd. dirs.), Am. Coun. Edn. (bd. dirs.), Leadership Devel. Coun. ACE, Ohio Inter Univ. Coun. (chairperson), Internat. Reading Assn., Akron Urban League (bd. dirs.), P.E.O., Cosmos Club, Phi Delta Kappa (Outstanding Young Educator award), Delta Kappa Gamma (Leadership/Mgmt. fellow 1980), Pi Lambda Theta, Pi Kappa Phi, Chi Omega. Episcopalian. Avocation: music. Home: 929 Harvey Dunn St Brookings SD 57006-1347 Office: South Dakota State Univ Office of the Pres Adminstrn Bldg 201 Brookings SD 57007-0001 E-mail: Peggy_Miller@sdstate.edu.

MILLER, PEGGY A(NN), lawyer; b. Bklyn., July 22, 1952; d. Milton and Edythe (Koffler) M. BS summa cum laude, Union Coll., 1974; JD, Harvard U., 1977. Bar: N.Y. 1978, D.C. 1980. Assoc. Martin, Obermaier & Morvillo, N.Y.C., 1977-80, Kaye, Scholer, Fierman, Hays & Handler, Washington, 1980-84; assoc. gen. counsel, exec. dir. Prodigy Svcs. Co., White Plains, N.Y., 1985-95; of counsel LeBoeuf, Lamb, Greene & MacRae LLP, N.Y.C., 1995—. Bd. dirs. Internet Alliance, Washington, Info. Industry Assn., Washington, asst. treas., 1992-93, exec. com. 1992-94, Leadership award, 1995; bd. advisors Internet Alliance/DMA. Author: Information Executive's Guide to Intellectual Property Rights, 1985, Guide to Database Distribution, 1987. Classroom vol. Jr. Achievement, Elmsford, N.Y., 1995—. Mem. Harvard Multimedia Club, Phi Beta Kappa. Avocations: horseback riding, tennis, travel, music, photography. Office: LeBoeuf Lamb Greene & MacRae LLP 125 W 55th St New York NY 10019-5369 E-mail: pamiller@llgm.com.

MILLER, PEGGY MCLAREN, retired management educator; b. Tomahawk, Wis., Jan. 12, 1931; d. Cecil Glenn and Gladys Lucille (Bame) McLaren; m. Richard Irwin Miller, June 25, 1955; children: Joan Marie, Diane Lee, Janine Louise. BS, Iowa State U., 1953; MA, Am. U., 1959; MBA, Rochester Inst. Tech., 1979; PhD, Ohio U., 1987. Instr. Beirut Coll. for Women, 1953-55, U. Ky., Lexington, 1964-66, S.W. Tex. State U., San Marcos, 1981-84; home economist Borden Co., N.Y.C., 1955-58; cons. Consumer Cons., Chgo., Springfield, Ill., 1972-77; sr. mktg. rep. N.Y. State Dept. Agr., Rochester, 1978-79; asst. prof., coord. bus. and mgmt. Keuka Coll., Keuka Park, N.Y., 1979-81; lectr. mgmt. Ohio U., Athens, 1984-2000; ret., 2000. Home: 17 Briarwood Dr Athens OH 45701-1302 E-mail: pmmiller@aol.com.

MILLER, PHILIP EFREM, librarian; b. Providence, Feb. 18, 1945; s. Jacob and Natalie (Rouslin) M.; m. Zenia Weiner, Dec. 20, 1969; 1 son, Paul Jeremy. BSL., Georgetown U., 1967; MS, U. Mich., 1968, A.M.L.S., 1973; PhD, NYU, 1984. Asst. libr. Hebrew Union Coll., N.Y.C., 1973-76, acting libr., 1976-78, librarian, 1978—. Author: Karaite Separatism in 19th Century Russia, 1993. Mem. Assn. Jewish Libraries (pres. 1982-84), Jewish Book Coun. (exec. bd. 1977-2000), Am. Soc. for Jewish Music (exec. bd. 1990-98). Home: 56 Truman Dr Marlboro NJ 07746-1122 Office: Hebrew Union Coll-Jewish Inst of Religion Klau Libr 1 W 4th St New York NY 10012-1105

MILLER, PHILIP GRAY, artist; b. Seattle, Aug. 18, 1947; s. Robert Chester and Angnes Minto (Weston) M. Student, Whitman Coll., Walla Walla, Wash., 1965-69. Artist, musician Gallery Functional Art, Santa Monica, L.A., 1970—. Furniture maker Sonrisa Bernice Steinbaum Gallery, N.Y.C.; cons. Inner Cities Murals Project, L.A., 1992—, Met. Transp. Agy., L.A., 1993-94. Author (novella) Death Valley Girls, 1989, (screenplay) Hurt By Love, 1993, (book) Cynic's Guide to Spiritual Awakening, 1993; curator Punch Gallery, L.A., 1993; permanent exhibhibn., a Colony for AVT Nespelem, Washington, 1997—, writer, actor, film maker; works represented in permanent collections Conrado Terasas City Coun., L.A., Laguna Beach (Calif.) Mus., Venice (Calif.) Family Clinic, AIDS Project L.A.; represented in group shows Punch Gallery, 1996, Gallery Function al Art, 1997; Plates of the Vain pictorial book, 1999. Min. Universal Life Ch., Seattle, L.A., 1969—. Recipient Design 100 award Met. Home, 1989. Avocations: yoga, cats, gardening, basketball. Office: Philip Miller Design 11100 Cumpston St Ste 11 North Hollywood CA 91601-2713

MILLER, PHILIP WILLIAM, sales executive; b. Elkhart, Ind., Feb. 5, 1948; s. William Philip and Ruth (Putman) M. BS, USAF Acad., 1971; MBA, U. No. Colo., 1977. Commd. 2d lt. USAF, 1971, advanced through grades to capt., 1975; instr. pilot 49th Tactical Fighter Wing, Alamogordo, N.Mex., 1976-79, King Abdulaziz Air Base, Dhahran, Saudi Arabia, 1979-81; ret., 1981; br. mgr. flight ops. support McDonnell Douglas, Dhahran, 1981-83; owner Miller Enterprises, Denver and Hickory, N.C., 1984-87; pres. Cannon Aviation Inc., Hickory, 1985, Miller Theatres, Inc., Elkhart, 1987-90; owner Main St. Prodn., Inc., 1991-92; mgr. Elkhart Mcpl. Airport, 1992-94; pres. SkyQuest Flight Ctr., Inc., Elkhart, Ind., 1995-96; v.p., towmaster Wiers Mfg., Plymouth, 1996-2000; nat. sales mgr. Newmar Corp., Nappanee, 2000—. Bd. dirs. Elkhart Ctr., Inc. Author ednl. materials. Bd. dirs. Downtown Merchant's Assn., Elkhart, 1987-88; chmn. Elkhart Jazz Festival, 1987-90. Mem. Am. Assn. Airport Execs., Nat. Bus. Aircraft Assn., Exptl. Aircraft Assn., Aircraft Owners and Pilots Assn., Internat. Aerobatic Club, Elks. Republican. Methodist. Office: Newmar Corp PO Box 30 Nappanee IN 46550-0030 E-mail: philmiller@hotmail.com.

MILLER, PHILLIP EDWARD, environmental scientist; b. Waterloo, Iowa, May 29, 1935; s. Joe Monroe and Katherine Elva (Groom) M.; m. Cathy Ann Love, Sept. 15, 1962; children: Eric Anthony, Bryan Edward, Stefan Patrick, Gregory Joseph. BA in Sci. Edn., U. No. Iowa, 1961; MA in Sci. Edn., U. Iowa, 1964; postgrad., U. Wis., 1966-68. Physics and chemistry tchr. Millersburg (Iowa) Community High Sch., 1961-62; supervising tchr. NSF Insvc. Inst. U. Iowa, Iowa City, 1962-64; instr. biology, area coord. Office Equal Opportunity Western Ky. U., Bowling Green, 1964-66; sci. editor, journalism instr.-sci. and tech. Mich. State U., East Lansing, 1968-74; asst. prof. agr., forestry and home econs. U. Minn., St. Paul, 1974-77; sr. editor atomic energy div. E.I. du Pont de Nemours and Co., Aiken, S.C., 1977-89; sr. scientist environ. protection dept. Westinghouse Savannah River Co., 1989-99; pres. Agy. for Book Authors, Collectors and Understanding of Sci., 1994—. Radiol. air and drinking water program owner environ./govt. group Morrison Knudsen Corp., Aiken, 1999-2000; prin. scientist Washington Group Internat., Inc., Aiken, 2000-01; environ. engr. Resource Conservation and Recovery Act, 2001—; panelist 26th Internat. Tech. Comm. Conf., L.A., 1979; participant Dept. Energy/Westinghouse Sch. for Environ. Excellence, Cin., 1991; invited contbr. to proceedings of the 1st Tatarstan Symposium on Energy, Environment and Econs., Kazan, Tatarstan, Russia, 1992. Mem. publs. com. Cen. Assn. Sci. and Math. Tchrs., Iowa City, 1969-72; editor Nat. Task Force on Agrl. Energy R&D, Washington, 1976; editor, contbr. Minn. Sci. Mag., 1974-77; contbr. several hundred med., sci. and engring. articles including to Procs. of Iowa Acad. Scis., Sch. Sci. and Math., Am. Biology Tchrs., Procs. of Internat. Communication Conf., and Procs. of Westinghouse Computer Symposium. Pres. Savannah River Rifle & Pistol Club, Aiken, 1981-82, Aiken Toastmasters, 1984; judge speech contests Optimist and 4-H Club Contests, Aiken, 1985-86. Sgt. U.S. Army, 1955-58. Decorated Disting. Marksman Badge gold medal; recipient 1st place sci. writing Argonne Labs. Assn., 1973, Profl. Achievement Permanent Profl. cert. Iowa State Bd. of Pub. Instrn., 1974, Blue Ribbon, Am. Assn. Agrl. Coll. Editors, Tex. A&M, 1976. Achievements include research in the causes and timing of pre-adolescent initial interest in science; discovery that low-zinc root environment causes delay of development and acceleration of senescence in tobacco plants; creation of publicity for the MSU discovery of platinum drugs-among the most widely used cancer drugs. E-mail: phillip.miller@srs.gov.

MILLER, PHYLLIS KADEN, communications administrator; b. Bklyn., July 12, 1938; d. Kelman M. Hoffman and Mary Sillman; m. Charles Kaden, Sept. 16, 1956 (dec. Mar. 1966); 1 child, Inger Kaden; m. Kalman I. Miller, Aug. 18, 1968; 1 child, Justin Brett. BA in Polit. Sci. with honors, Rutgers U., 1971, MA in Polit. Sci., 1972. Media coord., pub. info. officer Protective Svcs. Resource Inst. U. Medicine and Dentistry N.J., Piscataway, 1975-76; writer/editor Office of Publs. Rutgers U., New Brunswick, 1979-80; assoc. dir. pub. affairs N.J. Inst. Tech., Newark, 1980-83, dir. pub. rels., 1983-90; dir. comm. Montclair State U., Upper Montclair, N.J., 1990—. Editor Rutgers Newsletter, Tech. & Soc., 1987 (Silver medal for periodicals), Mensa Rsch. Jour.; co-prodr. (radio series) Child Abuse and Neglect, 1976; writer, co-prodr. (video) Reaching Out, 1988 (Am. Cancer Soc. Nat. award for comm. 1988), (TV) New Jersey, the Garbage State, 1989 (Cable award for programming excellence 1989); exec. editor Insight newsletter, 1991-96 (Silver medal CASE 1996), (student recruitment viewbook) Choices and Challenges, 1991, (student recruitment viewbook) Montclair State, 1993-94 (Silver award 1993 Admissions Mktg. Competition 1993, award for comm. excellence Internat. Assn. Bus. Communicators 1994), (student recruitment video) As We See It, 1996 (Gold award Admissions Mktg. competition 1996); reporter, copy editor, entertainment editor Daily Home News, New Brunswick, N.J. Bd. trustees Am. Cancer Soc. (N.J. divsn.), Am. Mensa Edn. and Rsch. Found., editor Mensa Rsch. Jour. Recipient award Coll. Sports Info. Dirs. Assn., 1997, award of distinction Communicators Awards, 1997, Iris Award IABC, 1999, Best in Nation award Coll. Sports Info. Dirs. Assn., 1997, numerous Communicators Awards, 1997-2002, Iris award IABC, 1999, Bronze medal CASE, 1998, Disting. Svc. award Mensa Edn. and Rsch. Found., 2001, award of excellence IABC, 2002, award of merit IABC, 2002, awards NJ Advt. Club, 2001-02. Mem. Internat. Assn. Bus. Communicators, Coun. for Advancement and Support of Edn., Pub. Rels. Soc. Am. (Cert. of Commendation 1997), N.J. Press Assn., Edn. Writers Assn. Home: 23 Lexington Rd Somerset NJ 08873-1725 E-mail: millerp@mail.montclair.edu.

MILLER, R. WARBURTON, psychologist, citrus farmer; b. Bellefonte, Pa., Nov. 23, 1921; s. Joseph Frederick and Mary Warburton Miller; m. Joyce Larayne Miller; children: Pamela Joyce, Page Layne. AB, Pa. State U., 1942; MA, U. of the Redlands, 1951; PhD, U. So. Calif., 1957; postgrad., San Bernardino Valley Coll., Columbia U., U. Mich., U. Minn., L.A. State Coll., U. Internat., Saltillo, Coah, Mex., Inst. Mex. Cultura Internat., Guadalajara; JD, Loma Linda Coll. Law, 1985. Lic. clin. psychologist, marriage, family and child counselor, clin. speech pathologist. Capt. USN, 1942-44, 51-53; officer USNR, 1942-74; staff psychologist San Bernardino County Med. Ctr., 1968-74; forensic psychologist/clin. psychologist; pvt. practice with Dr. Joyce Miller. Mem. psychology examining com. State Bd. Med. Examiners, 1970-74; dir. Mojave Valley Coordinating Coun. Family Mental Health, 1971-72; lectr. U. So. Calif., U. Redlands, Loma Linda U.; chmn. bd. dirs. AVORA Corp., 1981—; bd. dirs., v.p. East Pioneer Mut. Water Co.; cons. hosps.; expert witness in forensic psychology. Author (with wife Joyce): Dealing with the Behavioral Problems in the Elementary School, 1968, A Layman's Handbook for Aphasic Rehabilitation, 1973; contbr. articles to profl. jours. Bd. dirs. State of Calif. Psychologists Polit. Action Com.; past pres. Carriage Club, Civic Light Opera Assn., San Bernardino chpt. City of Hope Hosp. # 434, San Bernardino County Navy League; bd. dirs., past pres. Goodwill Industries of the Inland Counties; pres. San Bernardino Libr. Found., 1995—. Recipient George Washington medal Freedoms Found. at Valley Forge, 1970, 72, 73, honor cert., 1974, Disting. Citizens Lifetime Achievement award Calif. Inland Empire Coun., Boy Scouts Am., 2000. Fellow Am. Assn. Marriage Counselors; mem. SAR (past pres. So. Calif. chpt. at Riverside, past pres. State of Calif., nat. trustee 1970-74, v.p. gen. nat. soc. western dist. 1972-74, chmn. nat. soc. Ind. Day com. 1971-73, nat. exec. com. 1973-74, sec. gen. nat. soc. 1974-76), Calif. State Psychol. Assn., Inland So. Calif. Soc. Clin. Psychologists, Naval Res. Assn., San Bernardino Area C. of C. (bd. dirs. 1990—, pres. 1999), Masons, Hon. Order Ky. Cols., Rotary (Paul Harris award), Tau Kappa Alpha, Pi Delta Sigma, Kappa Sigma. Avocation: travel. Home and Office: 6836 Palm Ave Highland CA 92346-2513 E-mail: drbob@omnivision.com.

MILLER, RANDAL HOWARD, health science association administrator; b. Fostoria, Ohio, Apr. 11, 1947; s. Richard Paul and Michaline (Tinkovicz) M.; m. Patricia June Smith, May 29, 1970 (div. Apr. 1978); 1 child, Rhett Howard; m. Angel Jo Belfiore, May 27, 1978; 1 child, Shea Michal. BS, Bowling Green (Ohio) U., 1970. Chief labs. dept. health City of Cleve., 1975-78; coordinator lab. projects St. Vincent Charity Hosp., Cleve., 1980-83; pres. Trace Elements Analysis, Inc., Richfield, Ohio, 1979-88; asst. dir. clin. pathology Univ. Hosps., Cleve., 1988-92; adminstr. and mktg. dir. Univ. Med. Labs., 1992-96; pres. Howard Miller Assocs., 1995—. Corp. sec. Midwest LabLink, Ltd., Ohio, 1995—. Served to sgt. U.S. Army, 1970-76. Mem. Clin. Lab. Mgmt. Assn., Am. Soc. Clin. Pathologists, Med. Group Mgmt. Assn., Ohio Pub. Lab. Dirs., Greater Cleve. Hosp. Assn. (vice-chmn. lab. com. 1986-89, chmn. lab. com. 1989-90), Alpha Sigma Phi. Roman Catholic. Avocation: music. Office: Howard Miller Assocs 4011 Timber Trail Medina OH 44256

MILLER, RAYMOND EDWARD, computer science educator; b. Bay City, Mich., Oct. 9, 1928; s. Martin Theophil and Elizabeth Charlotte (Zierath) M.; m. Marilyn Lueck, June 18, 1955; children: Patricia Ann, Laura Jean, Donna Lyn, Martha Eileen. BS in Mech. Engring., U. Wis., 1950; BEE, U. Ill., 1954, MS in Math., 1955, PhD in Elect. Engring., 1957. Design engr. IBM, Endicott, Poughkeepsie, N.Y., 1950-51, mem. rsch. staff Yorktown Heights, 1957-81; dir., prof. Ga. Inst. Tech., Atlanta, 1980-89, prof. emeritus, 1989—; dir. Ctr. Excellence in Space Data and Info. Scis. NASA, Greenbelt, Md., 1988-93; prof. U. Md., College Park, 1989—. Pres. Computing Scis. Accreditation Bd., N.Y.C., 1985-87. Author: Switching Theory, Vols. I and II, 1965; editor: (with J.W. Thatcher) Complexity of Computer Computation, 1972; patentee in field. Lt. USAF, 1951-53. Fellow AAAS, IEEE; Assn. for Computing Machinery, IEEE Computer Soc. (v.p. edn. acts 1991-92). Lutheran. Avocations: tennis, fishing. Office: U Md Dept of Computer Sci A V Williams Bldg College Park MD 20742-0001 E-mail: miller@cs.umd.edu.

MILLER, RAYMOND JARVIS, agronomy educator; b. Claresholm, Alta., Can., Mar. 19, 1934; came to U.S., 1957, naturalized, 1975; s. Charles Jarvis and Wilma Macy (Anderson) M.; m. Frances Anne Davidson, Apr. 28, 1956; children: Cheryl Rae, Jeffrey John, Jay Robert. BS (Fed. Provincial grantee 1954-56, Dan Baker scholar 1954-56), U. Alta., Edmonton, 1957; MS, Wash. State U., 1960; PhD, Purdue U., 1962; Doctorate (hon.), Moscow State Agro Engring. U., 2000. Mem. faculty N.C. State U., 1962-65, U. Ill., 1965-69; asst. dir., then asso. dir. Ill. Agrl. Expt. Sta., 1969-73; dir. Idaho Agrl. Expt. Sta., 1973-79; dean U. Idaho Coll. Agr., 1979-85, v.p. for agr.; dean Coll. Agr. and Coll. Life Sci. U. Md., College Park, 1986-89, vice chancellor agr. and natural resources, 1989-91; pres. Md. Inst. for Agrl. and Natural Resources, 1991-93, prof. agronomy, 1986—, dir. internat. program agrl. natural resources, 1998—. Internat. expert in areas of agrl. sci. and edn. with spl. emphasis on Russia, former Soviet Union, East Europe, China, Latin Am. and the Pacific Rim. Author numerous papers in field. Pres. Idaho Rsch. Found., 1980-85; bd. govs. Agrl. Rsch. Inst., 1979-80; chmn. legis. subcom. Expt. Sta. Com. on Policy, 1981-82; chmn. bd. div. agr. Land Grant Assn., 1985-86; co-chmn. Nat. Com. Internat. Sci. Edn. Joint Coun., USDA, 1991-94; bd. dirs. C.V. Riley Found., 1985-93; chmn. budget com. Bd. Agr., Nat. Assn. State Univs. and Land Grant Colls., 1993; mem. U.S./Russian Subcom. on Agrl. Rsch., Edn. and Ext., 1996—. Grantee Internat. Congress Soil Sci., 1960, Purdue U. Research Found., summers 1960, 61 Fellow AAAS, Am. Soc. Agronomy, Soil Sci. Soc. Am.; mem. Internat. Soc. Soil Sci., Clay and Clay Minerals Soc., Am. Chem. Soc., Am. Soc. Plant Physiolotists, Elks, Lions, Sigma Xi, Phi Kappa Phi, Gamma Sigma Delta, Alpha Zeta. Home: Apt 716 9348 Cherry Hill Rd College Park MD 20740 Office: Symons Hall Univ Md College Park College Park MD 20742 E-mail: rm33@umail.umd.edu.

MILLER, RAYMOND VINCENT, JR. lawyer; b. Providence, July 1, 1954; s. Raymond Vincent and Mary Eunice (Mullen) M.; m. Elizabeth Ann White, May 31, 1980; children: Travis, Charles. BA, U. R.I., 1976; JD cum laude, U. Miami, 1981. Bar: Fla. 1981, U.S. Dist. Ct. (so. dist.) Fla. 1981, U.S. Ct. Appeals (11th cir.) 1986, U.S. Dist. Ct. (mid. dist.) Fla. 1987. Area supr. job devel. and tng. div. R.I. Dept. Econ. Devel., Providence, 1977-78; assoc. Thornton & Herndon, Miami, Fla., 1981-83, Britton, Cohen et al, Miami, 1983-85, Edward A. Kaufman, P.A., Miami, 1985-88; ptnr. Kaufman, Miller, Dickstein & Grunspan, 1988-2000; shareholder Gunster, Yoakley & Stewart, P.A., 2000—. Mem. ABA, Fla. Bar Assn., Nat Order Barristers, Soc. Bar and Gavel, Acad. Fla. Trial Lawyers (chair comml. law sect. 1993-95). Office: Gunster Yoakley & Stewart PA 2 S Biscayne Blvd Ste 3400 Miami FL 33131 E-mail: RMiller@gunster.com.

MILLER, REGINALD WAYNE, professional basketball player; b. Riverside, Calif., Aug. 24, 1965; Student, UCLA. Profl. basketball player Indiana Pacers, 1987—. Named to NBA All-Star Team, 1990, 94, Dream Team I, 1994, Dream Team II, 1996. Achievements include being a holder of NBA Playoff record most three-point field goals in one quarter (5), 1994, co-holder NBA Playoff record most three-point field goals in one half (6), 1994, 95; first Pacers player to surpass 15,000 career points/5 time all star. Office: c/o Indiana Pacers Market St Arena 300 E Market St Fl 1 Indianapolis IN 46204-2603*

MILLER, RENE HARCOURT, aerospace engineer, educator; b. Tenafly, N.J., May 19, 1916; s. Arthur C. and Elizabeth M. (Tobin) M.; m. Marcelle Hansotte, July 16, 1948 (div. 1968); children: Christal L., John M.; m. Maureen Michael, Nov. 20, 1973. BA, Cambridge U., 1937, MA, 1954. Registered profl. engr., Mass. Aero. engr. G.L. Martin Co., Balt., 1937-39; chief aero. and devel. McDonnell Aircraft Corp., St. Louis, 1939-44; mem. faculty aero. engring. MIT, Cambridge, 1944—, prof., 1957-86, Slater prof. flight transp., 1962-86, head dept. aeros. and astronautics, 1968-78, prof. emeritus, 1986—; v.p. engring. Kaman Aircraft Corp., Bloomfield, Conn., 1952-54. Mem. tech. adv. bd. FAA, 1964-66; mem. Aircraft panel Pres.'s Sci. Adv. Com., 1960-72, Army Sci. Adv. Panel, 1966-73; chmn. Army Aviation Sci. Adv. Group, 1963-73; mem. Air Force Sci. Adv. Bd., 1959-70; com. on aircraft aerodynamics NASA, 1960-70 Contbr. articles to profl. jours. Recipient U.S. Army Decoration for Meritorious Civilian Service, 1967, 70; recipient L.B. Laskowitz award N.Y. Acad. Scis., 1976 Fellow Am. Helicopter Soc. (hon. tech. dir. 1957-59, editor jour. 1957-59, Klemin award, Hon. Nikolski lectr. 1983), AIAA (hon., pres. 1977-78, Sylvanus Albert Reed award), Royal Aero. Soc. (Great Britain); mem. Nat. Acad. Engring., Internat. Acad. Astronautics, Academie National de L'Air et de L'Espace France. Home: San Jose New Rd Penzance Cornwall TR18 4PN England Office: MIT Dept Aeros & Astronautics 33-320 Cambridge MA 02139 E-mail: renmiller@compuserve.com.

MILLER, REUBEN GEORGE, economics educator; b. Phila., Mar. 28, 1930; s. George and Edna (Fuchs) M.; m. Sylvia Raigla, June 9, 1955. BA, LaSalle Coll., 1952; diploma, U. Stockholm, 1954; MA, U. Mont., 1956; PhD, Ohio State U., 1966. Asst. instr. Ohio State U., 1954-57; acting asst. prof. Oberlin (Ohio) Coll., 1957-58; asst. prof. U. Mass., Amherst, 1959-67; assoc. prof. econs. Smith Coll., Northampton, Mass., 1967-70; Charles A. Dana prof. econs., chmn. dept. Sweet Briar Coll., 1970—, chmn. div. social scis. Mem. adv. staff Computer Sci. Corp., Washington; cons. Dept. Def.; Fulbright-Hayes lectr. econs. Coll. Law, Nat. Taiwan U., Republic China, 1965-66 Contbr. articles to profl. jours. Am.-Scandinavian Found. fellow, 1952-53; Research Tng. fellow Social Sci. Research Council, 1958-59 Mem. Am. Econ. Assn., Am. Fin. Assn., Royal Econ. Soc. Office: Sweet Briar Coll Dept Econs Sweet Briar VA 24595

MILLER, RICHARD ALAN, economist, educator; b. Springfield, Ohio, Feb. 25, 1931; s. Ross and Beatrice Miller; m. Joan Taylor Walton, July 7, 1956; children: Carol Elizabeth, Jean Anne, Eric Ross. BA, Oberlin Coll., 1952; MA, Yale U., 1957; MA (hon.), Wesleyan U., 1972; PhD, Yale U., 1962. Mem. faculty Wesleyan U., Middletown, Conn., 1960—, chmn. dept. econs., 1968-69, 71-73, 75-76, 92-94, Andrews prof., 1995-98. Vis. lectr. Yale U., New Haven, 1961-62, vis. assoc. prof., 1967-68, vis. prof., 1973, 83, 85, 95; vis. assoc. prof. U. Calif., Berkeley, 1969-70; vis. prof. U. Adelaide, Australia, 1981; vis. lectr econs. U. Conn., Storrs, 1983; economist Econ. Policy Office, Antitrust Div., U.S. Dept. Justice, Washington, 1973-74, cons., 1974-75; cons. antitrust sect. State Conn., 1980, 82; dir. Kawanhee, Inc., Maine, 1975-81, 82-86 Contbr. articles on indsl. orgn. and antitrust econs. to profl. jours. Mem. cert. adv. coun. Dept. Edn., State Conn., 1982-86; mem. coms. Bd. for State Acad. Awards. State Conn., 1978-97; dean faculty of Cons. Examiners., 1985-87; trustee Conn. Joint Coun. Econ. Edn., 1982-85. Served to lt. (j.g.) USNR, 1952-55. Ford Found. fellow Yale U., 1958-59; NSF fellow MIT, 1964-65, Wesleyan U., 1965-69; Shelby Cullom Davis Found. grantee Wesleyan U., 1979-82; Fulbright fellow N.Z. Inst. Econ. Research, 1986, 88. Mem. Am. Econs. Assn., Indsl. Orgn. Soc. Congregationalist. Home: 83 Paterson Dr Middletown CT 06457-5138 Office: Wesleyan U Dept Econs Middletown CT 06459-0001 E-mail: ramiller@wesleyan.edu.

MILLER, RICHARD ALLAN, lawyer; b. N.Y.C., Oct. 28, 1947; s. Harold B. and Helen (Schwartz) M.; m. Karen R. Mangold, July, 5, 1970; children: David, Matthew. BA, SUNY, Buffalo, 1969; MA, Ohio State U., 1970; JD, NYU, 1973. Bar: N.Y. 1974, U.S. Dist. Ct. (so. and ea. dists.) N.Y. 1974, U.S. Ct. Appeals (2d cir.) 1977, U.S. Supreme Ct. 1980. Assoc. Paul Weiss et al, N.Y.C., 1973-75; asst. dist. atty. N.Y. County, 1975-77; ptnr. Newman, Tannenbaum et al, 1980-91, Katten Muchin & Zavis, N.Y.C., 1992-96, White & Case, 1996—2002; v.p., corp. counsel Prudential Fin., 2002—. Staff counsel Presdl. Task Force on Market Mechanisms, 1987-88; speaker Internat. Conf. Futures Money Mgmt., 1990-92. Editor, pub. Futures & Derivatives L. Rpt., 1981—, Securities Arbitration Commentator, 1988—. Mem. Assn. of the Bar of the City of N.Y. (chair futures regulations com.). Jewish. Avocation: golf. Home: 22 Roosevelt Rd Maplewood NJ 07040-2116 Office: White & Case 1155 Ave Americas New York NY 10036 E-mail: rmiller@whitecase.com.

MILLER, RICHARD BRUCE, electronics company executive; b. Bryn Mawr, Pa., Jan. 2, 1947; s. Robert and Kathryn (Marks) M; m. Nedra Lynn Herbert, Aug. 28, 1971; children: Sean Patrick and Ryan Cameron. BA in Polit. Sci., Shippensburg State U., 1969, MA in Polit. Sci., 1975. Asst. city mgr. City of Chambersburg, Pa., 1970-72; city mgr. City of New Cumberland, 1972-76, Montgomery Twp., N.J., 1976-78; from internal control mgr. to contr. Xerox Corp., Harrisburg, Pa., 1978-83, field adminstrn. ops. mgr. Stamford, Conn., 1983-85; ctr. mgr. City of N.Y.C., N.Y.C., 1985-88; transition mgr. bus. ops. Stamford, Conn., 1988-89; mgr., ops. support Ea. region, 1989-90; mgr. quality/customer satisfaction Xerox Corp., Stamford, 1990-91, mgr. customer svc. ops. Conn., 1991-92, mgr. sys. products adminstrn. Rochester, N.Y., 1992-93, mgr. customized solutions adminstrn., 1993-94, market to collection, 1994-95; from infrastructure delivery mgr. to applications mgr. Office Document Products, 1995-97, applications mgr., 1997; applications framework mgr. Year 2000 Program Office Xerox Corp. Info. Mgmt., Rochester, 1997-2000; mgr. productivity office Xerox Corp., 2000-01, mgr. fin. outsourcing N.Am. info. mgmt., 2001—. Mem. All Star Club Xerox Corp., 1982-83, 85-86, 87-88, 89-90, grad. Astronaut VII, 1987, chief info. officer Leadership award, 1995. Bd. dirs. So. Conn. Child Guidance Ctr., 1988-90, Child Care Ctrs., Stamford, 1990-92; cubmaster Boy Scouts Am., Fairport, N.Y., 1994-95; youth sports coach Southeast YMCA, Pittsford, N.Y., 1993-96, Fairport Youth Lacrosse, 1994-2000; registrar Perinton Youth Hockey, 1998-2000. Republican. Roman Catholic. Avocations: tennis, boating, amateur radio, reading. Home: 800 Phillips Rd Webster NY 14580-9720 Office: 800 Phillips Rd Webster NY 14580-9720 E-mail: bmiller5@rochester.rr.com., bruce.miller@usa.xerox.com.

MILLER, RICHARD JOSEPH, lawyer; b. San Diego, Jan. 20, 1941; s. Daniel Preston and June (Beissel) M.; divorced, 1972; 1 child, Shelli Renee; m. Paula Anne English, May 29, 1982. BA, U. Tex., Arlington, 1970; M of Pub. Adminstrn., So. Meth. U., Dallas, 1974; JD, Baylor U., 1983. Bar: U.S. Dist. Ct. (we. dist.) Tex. 1988. Officer, supr. Dallas Police Dept., 1963-75; program coord. Tex. Organized Crime Prevention Council, Austin, 1975-76; chief of police Killeen (Tex.) Police Dept., 1976-79; tng. cons. Tex. Commn. on Law Enforcement Officer Standards and Edn., Austin, 1979-80; chief of police Denton (Tex.) Police Dept., 1980; sole practice Killeen, 1983-88; ptnr. Kleff, Lewis, Miller & Assocs., 1989; pvt. practice Tex., 1989-92; elected county atty. Bell County (Tex.), Bell County, 1993—. Author: The Train Robbing Bunch, 1981, Texas Firemen's and Policemen's Civil Service Law, 1987, Bounty Hunter, 1988, Bloody Bill Longley, 1996, Sam Bass & Gang, 1999. Vice chmn. Leon Valley dist. Boy Scouts Am., 1987-88; bd. dirs. Killeen Crimestoppers, Inc., 1986-91, Killeen Literacy Coun., 1987-90; mem. Bell County Hist. Commn., 1988-91. With U.S. Army, 1958-61. Fellow Tex. Bar Found.; mem. Bell-Lampasas-Mills Counties Bar Assn., Tex. Dist. and County Attys. Assn., Nat. Assn. Outlaw and Lawman History (bd. dirs. 1986—), Western Writers of Am., Rotary. Avocations: Old West research, jogging, cartooning. Office: PO Box 1127 Belton TX 76513-5127 Home: 1917 Sutton Pl Trl Harker Heights TX 76548-6043

MILLER, RICHARD KIDWELL, artist, actor, educator; b. Fairmont, W.Va., Mar. 15, 1930; s. Maurice Entler and Lillian (Reed) M.; m. Teresa Marie Robinson, Apr. 27, 1957. Student, Pa. Acad. Fine Arts, 1948-49; BA, Am. U., 1953; MFA, Columbia U., 1956. Instr. painting Scarsdale (N.Y.) Community Sch., 1970-75; asst. prof. Kansas City Art Inst., 1968-69. Participated extensively in profl. theater as actor and singer including roles in Broadway Prodn. Baker Street, Oliver, Funny Girl, Wonderful Town, Illya, Darling, Indians, Rise and Fall of the City of Mahogonny; actor stock cos. including Fiddler on the Roof; one-man art shows include Trans-Lux Gallery, Washington, 1951, Bader Gallery, Washington, 1954, Balt. Mus. Art, 1955, Graham Gallery Ltd., N.Y.C., 1960, 62, 65, Argas Gallery, Madison, N.J., 1966, Jefferson Place Gallery, Washington, 1966, Albrecht Kemper Mus. Art, St. Joseph, Mo., 1969, L.I. U., 1973, Aaron Berman Gallery N.Y.C., 1983, Westbeth Gallery, N.Y.C., 1982, John Jay Gallery, N.Y.C., 1998, 2000, JCC of Mid-Westchester, 2001; group shows include Corcoran Gallery Art., 1950-51, 53, Pa. Acad. Fine Arts, 1951, 64, Carnegie Internat., 1961, Salon de National, Paris, 1954, Whitney Mus., 1958, U. Nebr., 1963, Martha Jackson Gallery, N.Y.C., 1973, Nat. Acad. Design, N.Y.C., 1996, Art of the Northeast, New Caanan, Conn., 1996, others; represented in permanent collections Albrecht Kemper Mus. of Art, St. Joseph, Mo., Hirshorn Mus. and Sculpture Garden, Washington, Phillips Collection, Washington, Rochester Mus. Art, U. Ariz. Mus. of Art, Tucson, Watkins Gallery Collection, Wshington, also numerous private collections; featured in Jan. edit. Am. Artist Mag., 1988, Christian Sci. Monitor, 1990,, World Artists (Claude Marks), 1991. Washington Times Herald scholar, 1944, 45, 46; Gertrude Whitney scholar, 1948-53, 55-56; Fulbright fellow, 1953-54 Address: 222 W 83d St Apt 8C New York NY 10024-4913 *I have an insatiable need to express myself— I suppose I was born with it. I was given more than one talent to satisfy this need, and for that I thank God. I have endeavored to use these talents to the absolute best of my ability. I can do no more than that. Some times I have succeeded, and many times I have failed, but the real joy and meaning is in the doing. All the pain has been worth it.*

MILLER, RICHARD LAWRENCE, dermatologist; b. Toledo, Jan. 6, 1944; s. William and Ernestine (Neulicht) M.; m. Joyce Margaret Karsh, Dec. 17, 1967; children: Jennafer Lynn, Aaron Mark, Stephanie Michelle. AB, Franklin and Marshall U., 1965; MD, Duke U., 1968. Intern Maimonides Med. Ctr., Bklyn., 1968-69; pvt. practice Setauket, N.Y., 1975—; chief dermatology J.T. Mather Meml. Hosp., Port Jefferson; asst. prof. dermatology SUNY Hosp., Stony Brook. Lt. comdr. USNR, 1969-75. Fellow L.I. Dermatology Soc., N.Y. State Dermatology Soc., Am. Acad. Dermatology, AMA, Suffolk Dermatology Soc. (pres. 1981-82). Office: 200 Main St Ste 5 Setauket NY 11733-2918

MILLER, RICHARD LYNN, pharmaceutical scientist; b. Stevens Point, Wis., Sept. 27, 1945; s. Gordon L. and Jean Ellen (Leary) M.; divorced; children: Analiese, Colin, Autumn. BS in Biology, U. Wis., Stevens Point, 1967; PhD in Microbiology, U. Minn., 1974. Rsch. asst. microbiology U. Minn., Mpls., 1970-74; postdoctoral fellow Pa. State U., Hershey, 1975-77; sr. microbiologist 3M Riker, St. Paul, 1977-79, rsch. specialist, 1979-86, sr. rsch. specialist, 1986-87; mgr. pharmacology 3M Pharms., 1987-97, divsn. scientist, 1998-2000, corp. scientist, 2000—. Contbr. articles and abstracts to profl. jours. With U.S. Army, 1968-70. NIH postdoctoral fellow. Mem. AAAS, N.Y. Acad. Sci., Internat. Soc. Antiviral Rsch., Inflammation Rsch. Assn. Avocations: gardening, hiking, fishing. Office: 3M Pharmaceuticals 270 2S 06 3M Ctr Saint Paul MN 55144-0001 E-mail: rlmiller1@mmm.com.

MILLER, RICHARD MCDERMOTT, sculptor; b. New Philadelphia, Ohio, Apr. 30, 1922; s. J. Harry and Clela Belle (McDermott) M.; m. Audrey F. Miller, 1942; 1 dau., Sue Ann (Mrs. Kenneth Hartz); m. Gloria B. Bley, Mar. 18, 1961. Student, Cleve. Inst. Art, 1940-42, 49-51. Prof. emeritus Queens Coll., CUNY. One man shows include Peridot Gallery, N.Y.C., 1964, 66, 67, 69, Washburn Gallery, N.Y.C., 1971, 74, 75, 77, Canton (Ohio) Art Inst., 1980, 20-yr. retrospective Artists Choice Mus., N.Y.C., 1984, Springfield (Mo.) Mus. Art, 1985, Friends of Figurative Sculpture Gallery, N.Y.C., 1987-99, 2002, Philharm. Ctr., Naples, Fla., 1991, J.J. Brookings Gallery, San Francisco, 1997, Barnet Park, Spartanburg, S.C., 1999, Brookgreen Gardens, S.C., 2001; represented in numerous pub. and pvt. collections; author: Figure Sculpture in Wax and Plaster, 1971. Served with AUS, 1942-46. Mem. NAD (pres. 1989-92), Sculptors Guild, Nat. Sculpture Soc. (pres. 1997-2000), Century Assn. Address: 53 Mercer St New York NY 10013-2617 E-mail: sohosculpt@aol.com.

MILLER, RICHARD N. medical association administrator; b. Jan. 27, 1938; m. Janet Olin, 1966; children: Margaret, Julia. Grad., Loras Coll.; MD, U. Iowa, 1963; MPH, Harvard U., 1967. Diplomate Am. Bd. Preventive Medicine. Intern Washington Hosp. Ctr., 1963-64; resident Walter Reed Army Inst. Rsch., Washington, 1967-69; pub. health officer Third Civil Affairs Detachment U.S. Army, Canal Zone, Republic of Panama, 1964-66, chief preventive medicine activity USARSUPTHAL Bangkok, Thailand, 1970-72, chief preventive medicine activity USAMEDDAC Frankfurt, Germany, 1972-75, regional preventive medicine cons. Ft. McPherson, Ga., 1975-79; dir. divsn. preventive medicine Walter Reed Inst. Rsch., Washington, 1979-93, dir. residency program in gen. preventive medicine, 1979-88, 91-93, dir. WRAIR ann. tropical medicine course, 1979-93; asst. prof. preventive medicine and biometrics USUHS, 1981-93; dir. Med. Follow-up Agy. Inst. of Medicine, 1993—. Contbr. articles to profl. jours. Mem. Am. Coll. Epidemiology, Am. Soc. for Tropical Medicine and Hygiene, Soc. for Epidemiology Rsch., Infectious Disease Soc. Am. Office: Inst of Med Med Follow-up Agy 2101 Constitution Ave NW Washington DC 20418-0007*

MILLER, RICHARD SHERWIN, law educator; b. Boston, Dec. 11, 1930; s. Max and Mollie Miller; m. Doris Sheila Lunchick, May 24, 1956; children: Andrea Jayne Armitage, Matthew Harlan. BSBA, Boston U., 1951, JD magna cum laude, 1956; LLM, Yale U., 1959. Bar: Mass. 1956, Mich. 1961, Hawaii 1977. Pvt. practice law, Boston, 1956-58; assoc. prof. law Wayne State U., Detroit, 1959-62, prof., 1962-65, Ohio State U., Columbus, 1965-73, dir. clin. and interdisciplinary program, 1971-73; prof. U. Hawaii, Honolulu, 1973-95, prof. emeritus, 1995—, dean, 1981-84. Vis. prof. law USIA/U. Hawaii, Hiroshima U. Affiliation Program, Japan, fall 1986, Victoria U., Wellington, N.Z., Spring 1987; del. Hawaii State Jud. Conf., 1989-92; cons. Hawaii Coalition for Health, 1997—. Author: Courts and the Law: An Introduction to our Legal System, 1980; editor: (with Roland Stanger) Essays on Expropriations, 1967; editor-in-chief: Boston U. Law Rev., 1955-56; contbr. articles to profl. jours. Mem. Hawaii Substance Abuse Task Force, 1994-95; arbitrator Hawaii Ct. Annexed Arbitration Program, 1995-99; bd. dirs. Drug Policy Forum Hawaii, 1996—; mem. Save our Star-Bulletin Com., 1999-2001; mem. Citizens for Competitive Air Travel, 2002-. 1st lt. USAF, 1951-53. Sterling-Ford fellow Yale U., 1958-59; named Lawyer of Yr. Japan-Hawaii Lawyers Assn., 1990; recipient Cmty. Svc. award Hawaii Med. Assn. Alliance, 1999. Mem. ABA, Hawaii State Bar Assn., Hawaii ACLU, Am. Inn of Ct. IV (emeritus founding mem., master of the bench), Am. Law Inst., Honolulu Cmty-Media Coun. (pres. 1994-98, v.p. 1998-2000, treas. 2000—). Office: U Hawaii Richardson Sch Law 2515 Dole St Honolulu HI 96822-2328

MILLER, RICHARD STEVEN, lawyer; b. Mt. Vernon, N.Y., Dec. 5, 1951; s. Norman and Mildred (Curtis) M. BA, U. Pa., 1974; JD, NYU, 1977. Bar: N.Y. 1978, U.S. Dist. Ct. (so. and ea. dists.) N.Y. 1978, U.S. Ct. Appeals (2d cir.) 1978. Asst. dist. atty. Kings County, N.Y., 1977-79; with Hahn & Hessen, N.Y.C., 1979-82, Levin & Weintraub & Crames, N.Y.C., 1982-87; counsel, then ptnr. Rogers & Wells, 1987-91; ptnr. Dewey Ballantine LLP, 1991-2001; prin. shareholder Greenburg Traurig LLP, 2001—, co-chmn. nat. reorgn., bankruptcy and restructuring practice, 2001—. Mem. ABA, Internat. Bar Assn., Am. Bankruptcy Inst. Office: Greenberg Traurig 200 Park Avenue 15th Fl New York NY 10166 Office Fax: 212-801-6400. E-mail: millerrs@gtlaw.com.

MILLER, RICHARD WALTER, consulting engineer; b. Greenfield, Mass., Feb. 16, 1935; s. Wilfred E. and Ruth B. (Booker) M.; m. Barbara J. Mushovic, May 2, 1960; children: Pamela J., Brenda M., Jennifer E. BS, Northeastern U., 1958, MS, 1960. Registered profl. engr., Mass. Design engr. Walworth Co., Braintree, Mass., 1960-62; sr. flow cons. The Foxboro Co., Foxboro, 1962—; cons., pres. R.W. Miller & Assocs., 1988-98, R.W. Miller & Assocs., Inc., Venice, Fla., 1998—. Author: Flow Measurement Engineer Handbook, 1983, 87, 96; contbr. tech. papers to profl. jours. Recipient Outstanding Alumni award Northeastern U., 1983; Bristol fellow The Foxboro Co., 1987. Fellow ASME (chmn. 1980—, Dedicated Svc. award 1985, v.p. 1986-89). Achievements include patents in field on an inline powered viscometer, a vortex flowmeter, an annular target flowmeter, and a mass flowmeter apparatus. Avocations: sailing, golf, oil painting. Home and Office: 512 Pennyroyal Pl Venice FL 34293-7233

MILLER, RICHARDS THORN, naval architect, engineer; b. Jan. 31, 1918; s. Herman Geistweit and Helen Buckman (Thorn) M.; m. Jean Corbat Spear, Sept. 13, 1941 (dec.); children: Patricia (Mrs. Charles G. Fishburn), Linda (Mrs. John X. Carrier); m. Alice Johnson Houghton, May 19, 1984. BS in Naval Arch. and Marine Engring., Webb Inst. Naval Arch., 1940; Naval Engr., MIT, 1951. Registered profl. engr. Commd. ensign USN, 1940, advanced through grades to capt., 1960; head preliminary design br. Bur. Ships, 1960-63; dir. Mine Def. Lab., Panama City, Fla., 1963-66; dir. ship design Naval Ship Engring. Ctr., 1966-68; specialized work design oceanographic rsch. ships, mine sweepers, torpedo boats, destroyers; ret., 1968. Mgr. ocean engring. Oceanic divsn. Westinghouse Electric Corp., 1969-75, adv. engr., 1975-79; cons. naval arch. and engr., 1968—; arbitrator admiralty and ship bldg. contract cases, 1978—; mem. com. naval arch. Am. Bur. Shipping, 1960-63, mem. tech. com., 1978-92; mem. ship structure com., 1966-68. Author: (with R.G. Henry) Sailing Yacht Design, 1963, (with K.L. Kirkman) Sailing Yacht Design—A New Appreciation, 1990; also sects. in books, articles. Decorated Navy Legion of Merit; recipient William Selkirk Owen award Webb Alumni Assn., 1983. Fellow Soc. Naval Archs. and Marine Engrs. (chmn. S.E. sect. 1965-66, chmn. marine sys. com. 1970-77, chmn. tech. and rsch. steering com. 1977-78, chmn. small craft com. 1983-87, v.p. tech. and rsch. 1979-81, hon. life v.p. 1981—, mem. coun. 1976—, mem. exec. com. 1977-81, Capt. Joseph H. Linnard prize 1964, Disting. Svc. award 1988); mem. Am. Soc. Naval Engrs. (mem. coun. 1976-78), U.S. Naval Inst., Christie Soc., Md. Bd. for Profl. Engrs., N.Y. Yacht Club, Annapolis Yacht Club, Sailing Club of the Chesapeake, Sigma Xi. Home and Office: 957 Melvin Rd Annapolis MD 21403-1315

MILLER, RITA, personnel consultant, diecasting company executive; b. Bklyn., Jan. 15, 1925; d. Joseph and Etta M.; BA, Bklyn. Coll., 1947; MA, Boston U., 1949; children: Erika Greenwald, Roy Barnet Glickman. Personnel officer, sec. to pres. Marine Elec. Corp., Bklyn., 1943-47; script writer Song Debut, Boston, 1949-50; dir. Writers' Workshops, interviewer pub. opinion surveys, New Rochelle, N.Y., 1962-64; mgr. employee relations Dynacast div. Coats & Clark, Inc., Yorktown Heights, 1966-89. Mem. Am. Soc. Personnel Adminstrn., Westchester Personnel Mgmt. Assn. (dir.), Personnel Council New Rochelle, Bus. and Profl. Women U.S.A., Nat. Sociology Hon. Soc. Editor: The Management Consultant (George Kenning), 1965; contbr. articles to profl. jours. Home: 16 Congress St New Rochelle NY 10801-1902

MILLER, ROBERT, advertising executive; b. N.Y.C., June 2, 1923; s. Samuel and Adele (Elswit) M.; m. Frances Fitzgerald, June 10, 1944 (dec. 1978); children: Marc Robert, William Fitzgerald, Daniel Bates, Ellen Minette (Mrs. John Meyer); m. Sandra Gold, 1980; 1 child, Richard Scott. Student, NYU, 1940-42, Syracuse U., 1943. Newsroom employee N.Y. Daily Mirror, 1942; with Miller Advt. Agy., Inc., N.Y.C., 1946—, v.p., 1948-54, chmn. bd., 1954-57, pres., 1958—, Miller Advt. Service Corp., 1956-62, Miller Advt. Agy. Ill., Inc., 1965-73, also bd. dirs. Bd. dirs. Hereford Ins. Co., Inc., 1988-94. Contbg. editor Madison Avenue mag., 1975-78. Bd. govs. Roslyn Democratic Club, 1957-61, 68-73; mem. Nassau County Dem. Com., 1958-61, 68-73; Bd. dirs. Shalom Peace Found., 1970-89. Served to 1st lt. USAAF, 1942-46. Mem. Am. Legion, Jewish War Vets. Home: 301 E 52nd St New York NY 10022-6319 also: 17 Shelly Dr Ellenville NY 12428-1809 Office: Miller Advt Agy Inc 71 Fifth Ave New York NY 10003-3004 E-mail: bobmiller@miller.aa.com.

MILLER, ROBERT ALLEN, hotel executive; b. Chgo., Nov. 26, 1945; m. Diana Marie Hall, Dec. 29, 1967; children: David, Allison, Brian. BSBA, U. Fla., 1967. CPA, Fla. Auditor, acct. Arthur Young & Co., Tampa, Fla., 1967-72; chief fin. officer Fleetwing Corp., Lakeland, 1972-78; pres. Am. Resorts Corp., 1978-84; v.p. Marriott Internat., Bethesda, Md., 1984—. Office: Marriott Internat 1 Marriott Dr Washington DC 20058-0001

MILLER, ROBERT ALLEN, software engineer, consultant; b. Batavia, N.Y., Aug. 18, 1946; s. Wilford Earl and Mildred A. (Faith) M. BA, DePauw U., 1968. Cert. data processor, cert. systems profl. Software engr. AT&T, Alpharetta, Ga., 1972-95, instr. Bell Labs. Tech. Edn. Ctr., 1988-94. Vol. ARC, Atlanta, 1992. Sgt. USAF, 1968-72. Mem. Assn. for Computing Machinery. Office: AT&T 300 N Point Pkwy Alpharetta GA 30005-4116

MILLER, ROBERT ARTHUR, former state supreme court chief justice; b. Aberdeen, S.D., Aug. 28, 1939; s. Edward Louis and Bertha Leone (Hitchcox) Miller; m. Shirlee Ann Schlim, Sept. 5, 1964; children: Catherine Sue, Scott Edward, David Alan, Gerri Elizabeth, Robert Charles. BSBA, U. S.D., 1961, JD, 1963. Asst. atty. gen. State of S.D., Pierre, 1963—65; pvt. practice law Philip, 1965—71; state atty. Haakon County, 1965—71; city atty. City of Philip, 1965—71; judge State of S.D. (6th cir.), Pierre, 1971—86, presiding judge, 1975—86; justice S.D. Supreme Ct., 1986—2001, chief justice, 1990—2001, ret., 2001—. Bd. dirs. Nat. Conf. of Chief Justices, 1996—97, State Justice Inst., 1998—, chair, 1998—; trustee S.D. Retirement Sys., Pierre, 1974—85, chmn., 1982—85; mem. faculty S.D. Law Enforcement Tng. Acad., 1975—85; bd. dirs. U. S.D. Law Sch. Found., 1990—. Mem. S.D. State Crime Commn., 1979—86; mem. adv. commn. S.D. Sch. for the Deaf, 1983—85, Comm. Svcs. to Deaf, 1990—92; cts. counselor S.D. Boy's State, 1986—, Nat. Awards Jury Freedoms Found., 1991. Mem.: S.D. Judge's Assn. (pres. 1974—75), State Bar of S.D., Elks. Roman Catholic. Avocations: golf, hunting. Office: SD Supreme Ct State Capitol Bldg 500 E Capitol Ave Pierre SD 57501-5070*

MILLER, ROBERT CARL, real estate developer; b. Schenectady, N.Y., June 14, 1943; s. Carl B. and Mary Grace (Messitt) M.; m. Marcia Reilly, Aug. 3, 1968; children: Alison, Robert, Jonathan, Timothy, Geoffrey, Emily. BBA, Siena Coll., 1965; JD, Albany Law Sch., 1968; LLM, NYU, 1974. Bar: N.Y. 1969, U.S. Tax Ct. 1971; CPA, N.Y. Ptnr. Tate, Tate. Miller & Ruthman, Albany, N.Y., 1970-80; pres. Miller, Seeley & Segel, P.C., 1980-85, Windsor Devel. Group, Inc., Albany, 1985—. Bd. dirs. Lake George Opera Co., Glen Falls, N.Y., 1986—, Schenectady Mus. Art Com., 1984-93, Cerebral Palsy Ctr. for Disabled, 1988—, Albany Symphony Orch., 1989—; trustee Albany Law Sch., 2002--. Roman Catholic. Home: 8 Cardinal Ct Clifton Park NY 12065-2731 Office: Windsor Devel Group Inc 15 Park Ave Clifton Park NY 12065-2924 E-mail: rmiller@windsorrealtygroup.com.

MILLER, ROBERT CARL, retired library director; b. May 9, 1936; m. Jeanne M. Larson. BS in History and Philosophy, Marquette U., 1958; MS in Am. History, U. Wis., 1962; MA in Libr. Sci., U. Chgo., 1966. Head telephone reference Library of Congress, Wash., 1959-60; reference librarian Marquette U., Milw., 1960-62, acquisition librarian, 1962-66; head tech. services/librarian Parsons Coll., Fairfield, Iowa, 1966-68; head acquisitions dept. U. of Chgo. Library, Ill., 1968-71, assoc. dir (reader services), 1971-73; assoc dir (gen. service) U. of Chgo., 1973-75; dir. of libraries U. Mo., St. Louis, 1975-78; dir of libraries U. of Notre Dame, Ind., 1978-97, ret., 1997. Vis. prof. IBIN-U. Warsaw, Poland, 1992, 93, 97, 2000, 02. Contbr. to prof. jour. Fellow Woodrow Wilson Found. (sr.), Coun. on Libr. Resources; mem. ALA, Polish Inst. of Arts and Letters of Am. Roman Catholic. Home: 27752 Woodland Dr Chicago City MN 55103 E-mail: miller.1@nd.edu.

MILLER, ROBERT CHARLES, retired physicist; b. State College, Pa., Feb. 2, 1925; s. Lawrence P. Miller and Eva Mae (Gross) Wiedemann; m. Virginia Callaghan, Aug. 30, 1952; children: Robin Kingon Storey, Jeffrey Lawrence Miller, Lauren Wray Lynch. AB, Columbia U., 1948, MA, 1952, PhD, 1956. Staff mem. Johns-Manville Research Ctr., Finderne, N.J., 1948-49; teaching asst. in physics Columbia U., N.Y.C., 1949-51, lectr. in physics, 1951-53; mem. tech. staff Bell Telephone Labs., Murray Hill, N.J., 1954-63, head solid state spectroscopy research dept., 1963-67; staff mem. Inst. Defense Analyses, Arlington, Va., 1967-68; head optical elec. research dept. Bell Telephone Labs., Murray Hill, 1968-77; mem. tech. staff AT&T Bell Labs., 1977-84, disting. mem. tech. staff, 1984-88, ret., 1988. Cons. Office of Sec. Def., Arlington, Va., 1968-75. Inventor (with Dr. J.A. Giordmaine) Optical Parametric Oscillator, 1965 (co-recipient R.W. Wood prize, 1986); contbr. articles to profl. jours. Served with U.S. Army, 1943-46, ETO. RCA predoctoral fellow Columbia U., 1953-54. Fellow Am. Phys. Soc.; mem. AAAS, N.Y. Acad. Scis., Sigma Xi. Avocations: sailing, sports cars, tennis. Home: 65 Eaton Ct Cotuit MA 02635-2908 E-mail: rvcmiller@prodigy.net.

MILLER, ROBERT EARL, engineer, educator; b. Rockford, Ill., Oct. 4, 1932; s. Leslie D. and Marcia V. (Jones) M. BS, U. Ill., 1954, MS, 1955, PhD, 1959. Asst. prof. theoretical and applied mechanics U. Ill., Urbana, 1959-61, assoc. prof., 1961-68, prof., 1968-94, prof. emeritus, 1994—. Cons. in field to industry U.S. Army; in various positions in industry, summers, 1963-68 Contbr. articles to profl. jours. Mem. AIAA, Am. Soc. Engring. Edn. (Disting. Engring. award 1991), ASCE. Office: U Ill 216 Talbot Lab 104 S Wright St Urbana IL 61801-2935 E-mail: rem@uiuc.edu.

MILLER, ROBERT EDVIN, environmental education specialist, researcher, industrial hygienist; b. Lancaster, Pa., May 8, 1935; s. Grant Edvin and Regina (Keller) M.; m. Nancy Jean Gustafson, May 29, 1982; children: Lenore Ruth, David Robert, Robert E. Jr., Stacy JoAnn, Regina Louise. BA, U. Millersville, 1966; MS, U. Md., 1976. Tchr. pub. schs., Lancaster, Pa., 1966-68, Pottstown, 1968-70; faculty rsch. asst. U. Md., Solomons, 1970-76, environ. specialist III Cambridge, 1971-81, environ. specialist IV, 1982-90; fisheries biologist Horn Point Environ. Labs., 1981-83. Prof. Wor-Wic Tech. Nursing Sch., Cambridge, 1981-83; referee Fishery Bull., Cmbridge, 1982-83, Bull. of Marine Sci., Cambridge, 1983—. Narrator and cons. ednl. film Chesapeake Blues, 1974 (Golden Eagle award 1975); contbr. articles to profl. jours. Mem. ways and means com. United Fund of Dorchester County, Cambridge, 1982-85; tchr. Dorchester County Adult Edn. and Queen Anne County Adult Edn., Kent Island, Md., 1983. Grantee Power Plant Siting Program, 1979-81, Univ. Md., 1983-84, Waddell Found., 1983. Mem. Roddy Sci. Soc. (pres. 1965), Atlantic Estuarine Rsch. Soc. (membership com. 1973), Estuarine Rsch. Soc., Nat. Marine Edn. Assn., Nat. Sci. Tchrs. Assn. (comm. com., evaluation com., safety officer U. Md., 1996—, ind. hyg. IV, gov. advisery coun. for controlled hazardous substances, 1999—). Republican. Home: 5531 Whitehall Rd Cambridge MD 21613-3443 Office: Horn Point Environ Labs PO Box 775 Cambridge MD 21613-0775

MILLER, ROBERT ELMER, management consultant; b. Kansas City, Mo., Sept. 4, 1920; s. Harold Elmer and Henrietta Mary (Mersch) Miller; m. Louise Isabelle Hartman, Nov. 3, 1940; children: Sharron Louise Miller Hughes, Antoinette Lynn Miller, Theresa Beth Miller Maun. Student, Am. U., 1949-50, Kans. U., 1951-52, U. N.Mex., 1953-54; grad., U.S. Army Command/Gen. Staff. Enlisted as pvt. U.S. Army, 1940; commd. Corps. Engrs., 1942; advanced through grades to col., 1964; ret., 1968; with Atomic Energy Commn., Las Vegas, Nev., 1952-57, nuclear test planner ops., dep. mgr., 1957-59, mgr. nuclear tests ops., 1969-72; mem. AEC On-Off Continent Test Planning Bd., 1962-69; v.p. plans Resource Scis. Corp., Tulsa, 1972-73, exec. v.p., 1974-79; gov.'s enveron. advisor State of Nev., 1970-72. Former mem. various bd. dirs.; exec. v.p. William Bros. Engring. Co., 1979; v.p. U.S. Filter Corp., 1980-81, ret. 1982. Decorated Bronze Star, Purple Heart. Mem. Am. Nuclear Soc., Assn. Ret. Officers Assn., Indian Springs Country Club. Republican. Home: 841 Millwood Rd Broken Arrow OK 74011-8619

MILLER, ROBERT FRANK, retired electronics engineer, educator; b. Milw., Mar. 30, 1925; s. Frank Joseph and Evangeline Elizabeth (Hamann) M.; m. La Verne Boyle, Jan. 10, 1948 (dec. 1978); children: Patricia Ann, Susan Barbara, Nancy Lynn; m. Ruth Winifred Drobnic, July 26, 1980. BSEE, U. Wis., 1947, MSEE, 1954, PhD in Elec. Engring., 1957. Profl. engr., Wis. Instr. physics Milw. Sch. Engring., 1949-53; sr. engr. semicondr. Delco Electronics/GMC, Kokomo, Ind., 1957-67, asst. chief engr., 1967-70, mgr. product assurance, 1970-73, dir. quality control, 1973-85; asst. prof. elec. engring. tech. Purdue U., 1986-90; ret., 1990. Ind. cons., Kokomo, 1990—; mem. Ind. Microelectronics Commn., Indpls., 1987—. Author tech. papers; co-author lab. manuals. Bd. dirs. Howard Community Hosp. Found., Kokomo, 1974—; trustee YMCA, Kokomo, 1990—, bd. dirs., 1967-90. Named Disting. Alumnus U. Wis., Madison, 1980, 90. Mem. IEEE (life), Am. Soc. Quality Control (bd. dirs. sect. 0918, advisor Cen. Ind. sect. bd. 1988—), Sigma Xi, Tau Beta Pi, Phi Kappa Phi, Eta Kappa Nu. Presbyterian. Home: 3201 Susan Dr Kokomo IN 46902-7506

MILLER, ROBERT G. drug store chain company executive; b. 1944; With Albertson's Inc., 1961-89, exec. v.p. retail ops., 1989-91; chmn. bd., pres., CEO Fred Meyer Inc., Portland, Oreg., 1991-99; COO Kroger Co., Cin., 1999; chmn. and CEO Rite Aid Corp., Camp Hill, Pa., 1999—. Office: Rite Aid Corp 30 Hunter Ln Camp Hill PA 17011-2410*

MILLER, ROBERT HAROLD, otolaryngologist, educator; b. Columbia, Mo., July 2, 1947; s. Harold Oswald and Ruth Nadine (Ballew) M.; m. Martha Guillory, Apr. 18, 1981; children: Morgan Guillory, Reed Thurston. BS in Biology, Tulane U., 1969, MD, 1973; cert. in otolaryngology-head/neck surg., UCLA Med. Ctr., 1978; MBA, Tulane U., 1996. Diplomate Am. Bd. Otolaryngology. From asst. prof. to assoc. prof. otolaryngology-HNS Baylor Coll. Medicine, Houston, 1978-87; prof., chmn. otolaryngology-HNS Tulane Sch. Medicine, New Orleans, 1987-98, vice-chancellor for clin. affairs, 1997-99; dean U. Nev. Sch. Medicine, 1999—2001, prof., 1999—. Bd. dirs. Am. Bd. Otolaryngology; chief of staff Tulane Hosp., 1995-96. Mem. editl. bd. Archives of Otolaryngology, 1986—, Head & Neck Surgery, 1987—, Laryngoscope '96. Named Outstanding Young Man, Houston C. of C., 1980; Robert Wood Johnson Health Policy fellow, 1996-97. Fellow ACS, Am. Soc. Head & Neck Surgery, Am. Acad. Oto-Head & Neck Surgery (Disting. Svc. award 1994, Honor award 1991), Triological Soc. (exec. sec. 1992-97). Avocations: tennis, computers. Office: Univ Nevada Sch Medicine 2040 W Charleston Blvd Ste 400 Las Vegas NV 89102-2249

MILLER, ROBERT JAMES, educational association administrator; b. Mansfield, Ohio, Jan. 27, 1926; s. Dennis Cornelius and Mabel (Snyder) M.; m. Jerri Ann Burran, June 5, 1952; children: Robert James Jr., Dennis Burran. Student, Heidelberg Coll., 1946-47; BS, U. N.Mex., 1950, MA, 1952; postgrad., Miami U., Oxford, Ohio, 1951-55; MBA, Fla. Atlantic U., 1978. Asst. exec. sec. Phi Delta Theta Hdqrs., Oxford, 1951-54, adminstrv. sec., 1954-55, exec. v.p., 1955-91; pres. Phi Delta Theta Found., 1984-96; bus. mgr. The Scroll, 1955-91; cons., 1997—. Dir. Interfrat. Found., 1995—. Editor: Phikeia—The Manual of Phi Delta Theta, 1951, 19 edits., 1989, Phis Sing, 1958, Constitution and General Statutes of Phi Delta Theta, Fraternity Education Foundations, 1962, Directory of Phi Delta Theta, 1973. Chmn. United Appeal, Oxford, 1960; bd. dirs. U. N.Mex. Alumni Assn., 1961-68, Work Devel. Assn., 1999—; pres. Fedn. of Clubs, Oxford, 1964, McGuffey PTA, 1971, Miami U. Art Mus., 1993-94, McCullough-Hyde Hosp., Oxford, 1966, chmn. endowment adv. com., 1988-89; vol. leader Boy Scouts Am., Oxford, 1966-79. Recipient citizen of yr. award City of Oxford, 1968, citation Theta Chi, 1967, Order of Interfrat. Svc. Lambda Chi Alpha, 1994, interfrat. leadership award Sigma Nu, 1994, accolate for intrafraternity svc. Kappa Alpha, meritorious svc. award Boy. Scouts Am., 1977, others; Interfrat. Inst. fellow Ind. U., 1988. Mem. Nat. Intrafraternity Conf. (various coms. 1954-96, gold medal 1992), Am. Soc. Assn. Execs. (cert.), Cin. Soc. Assn. Execs., Fraternity Execs. Assn. (pres. 1962-63, disting. svc. award 1991), Edgewater Conf. (pres. 1978-79), Summit Soc., Country Club Oxford (bd. dirs.), Order of Symposiarchs, Order of Omega, Rotary (founder Oxford club 1965, pres. 1966, merit award 1974, dist. gov. S.W. Ohio 1978-79, study group exch. leader South Africa 1992), Blue Key, Phi Delta Kappa, Omicron Delta Kappa. Home: 170 Hilltop Rd Oxford OH 45056-1572 Office: Phi Delta Theta Ednl Found 2 S Campus Ave Oxford OH 45056-1801

MILLER, ROBERT JAMES, fundraising company executive; b. Rochester, Minn., Nov. 8, 1944; s. Robert Harrison and Beverly Anne (Vaughn) M.; m. Donna M. Hofner, June 17, 1967 (div. 1987); children: Laura Anne, Stephen James; m. Josephine M. Rose, Oct. 8, 1988; 1 child, Erica Rose Miller. BA, Alfred U., 1967; MBA, CUNY, 1970. Grants specialsit U.S. Dept. Health & Human Svcs., Washington, 1972-76; pres. Robert J. Miller & Assocs. Inc., Buffalo, 1976—; commd. 2d lt. U.S. Army, 1967, advanced through grades to Maj., 1976, resigned, 1977. Lectr. on grant devel., 1977—. Author (text) Personnel Administration, 1973, Program Evaluation, 1974; contbg. author Newsletter for Nat. Soc. of Fundraising Execs. Bd. Trustees Clarence (N.Y.) Ctrl. Schs., 1976-80. Recipient Bronze Star U.S. Army, Vietnam, 1970. Mem. Nat. Soc. of Fund Raising Execs. (bd. dirs. 1993—), Jr. Achievement Western N.Y. (bd. dirs. 1992—). Republican. Avocations: private pilot, skiing. Home: 41 Summershade Ct East Amherst NY 14051-1677 Office: Robert J Miller & Assocs 124 Delaware St Tonawanda NY 14150-3421

MILLER, ROBERT LOUIS, university dean, chemistry educator; b. Chgo., Jan. 26, 1926; s. Sam P. and Ida (Reich) M.; m. Virginia Southard, Oct. 26, 1947 (dec. Sept. 1973); children: Ruth, Stephen, Martin, Andrew; m. Bonnie Seay Berard, Nov. 28, 1975; children: Edouard, Derek. PhB, U. Chgo., 1947, BS, 1949, MS, 1951; PhD, Ill. Inst. Tech.; PhD (NSF Sci. faculty fellow), 1963. Mem. faculty U. Ill. Chgo. Circle Campus, 1953-67, asst. dean Coll. Liberal Arts and Scis., 1963-65, assoc. dean Coll. Liberal Arts and Scis., 1965-67; prof. chemistry U. N.C.-Greensboro, 1968-98, dean arts and scis., 1968-85, acting dean Grad. Sch., 1989-91, spl. asst. to the provost, 1993-94, acting assoc. provost, 1994-96, spl. asst. to provost, 1996-97, interim head dept. math. scis., 2001—. Am. Council Edn. adminstrv. intern SUNY-Binghamton, 1967-68 Mem. exec. com. of com. environ. affairs Piedmont Council Govts., 1971-76; mem. Greensboro Task Force on Energy; chmn. residential and transp. subcom Greensboro Energy Commn.; mem. Bd. Edn., Oak Park, Ill., 1965-66; bd. dirs. Hospice at Greensboro, 1981-87, pres., 1982-84, vol. 1988-89; vol., mem. bd. dirs. Cities in Schs., 1988-92; bd. dirs. Gilbert Pearson Audubon Soc., Greensboro Civil Liberties Union, Weatherspoon Gallery, 1981-85. Served with AUS, 1944-46, ETO. Mem. AAAS, Sigma Xi (treas. chpt.). Home: 4020 Watauga Dr Greensboro NC 27410-4502

MILLER, ROBERT NOLEN, lawyer; b. Monmouth, Ill., May 30, 1940; s. Robert Clinton and Doris Margaret (Nolen) M.; m. Diane Wilmarth, Aug. 21, 1965; children: Robert Wilmarth, Anne Elizabeth. BA, Cornell Coll., Mt. Vernon, Iowa, 1962; JD, U. Colo., 1965. Bar: Colo. 1965. Assoc. firm M. Quiat, Denver, 1965-66, Fischer & Beaty, Ft. Collins, Colo., 1969-70; dist. atty. Weld County Dist. Atty's. Office, Greeley, 1971-81; U.S. atty. U.S. Dept. Justice, Denver, 1981-88; chief counsel litigation and security US West Inc., Englewood, Colo., 1988-93; of counsel Patton, Boggs & Blow, Denver, 1993-94; ptnr., head litigation LeBoeuf, Lamb, Greene & Mac Crae, 1994—. Instr. bus. law Am. U., U. S.C., Myrtle Beach, 1966-69; mem. Gov.'s Commn. for Columbine and Civil Justice Reform, 1999—; mem. Supreme Ct. Nominating Commn., 1999—. Co-author: Deathroads, 1978 Bd. dirs. Boys Club, Greeley, 1974-78, 1st Congl. Ch., Greeley, 1975-78; Rep. candidate for atty. gen. Colo., 1977-78. Capt. USAF, 1966-69. Recipient Citizen of Yr. award Elks Club, Greeley. Mem. Fed. Bar Assn. (pres. Colo. chpt. 1983-84), Colo. Dist. Atty's Coun. (pres. 1976-77), Colo. Bar Assn., Weld County Bar Assn., Rotary (pres. local chpt. 1980-81). Republican. Avocations: fishing, hunting, golf, tennis, reading. Office: LeBoeuf Lamb Greene MacRae 633 17th St Ste 2000 Denver CO 80202-3620

MILLER, ROBERT REESE, trade association executive; b. Cin., Nov. 14, 1934; s. Louis and Lucille D. (Cantwell) M.; m. Jimmie Lorraine Mote, Aug. 15, 1965; children: Tracy Lou, Kimberly Kristin. BS, U. Okla., 1959. Ter. mgr. Walker div. Tenneco, Shreveport, La., 1961-64; dist. mgr. Garlock, Inc., Chgo., 1964-68; regional mgr. Ideal Corp., Bklyn., 1968-69, nat. sales mgr., 1970-73, v.p., 1973-74; group v.p. Parker Hannifin Automotive, 1975-86; pres. Gen. Automotive Splty., North Brunswick, N.J., 1986-89; v.p. Wagner div. Cooper Industries, Parsippany, 1989-91; chmn. Motor and Equipment Mfrs. Assn., Englewood Cliffs, 1985-87, pres., CEO, Research Triangle Park, N.C., 1991—. Chmn. Automotive Anti-Counterfeiting Task Force, 1983-87; mem. auto parts adv. com. U.S. Dept. Commerce, Washington, 1993-95; responsible for achieving passage of trade mark counterfeit bill making product counterfeiting a criminal offense. Contbr. articles to profl. publ. Bd. dirs. Automotive Hall of Fame, 1998—; mem. adv. bd. Northwood U.; chm. bd. Am. Hwy. Users Alliance; trustee Automotive Warehouse Distbrs. Found. Recipient Pursuit of Excellence award Automotive Warehouse Distbrs. Assn., 1991. Mem. Automotive Sales Coun. (pres. 1985-87), Fedn. N.Am. Automotive Parts Mfrs. (sec.-gen. 1993-95, 99—), Durham C. of C. (bd. dirs. 1995—), Treyburn Country Club (bd. dirs., treas.), Univ. Club, Detroit Soc. Clubs. Avocations: reading, golf, deep sea fishing, tennis. Office: Motor-Equipment Mfrs Assn PO Box 13966 Research Triangle Park NC 27709

MILLER, ROBERT SCOTT, mental health administrator, social worker; b. Seattle, Dec. 12, 1947; s. Bert Lester and Carol Theresa (Gustafson) M.; m. Karen Ann Staake, Nov. 12, 1977; children: Sarah, Megan, Emily. BA in Sociology cum laude, Seattle Pacific U., 1970; AM in Social Work, U. Chgo., 1972; MA in Human Resources Mgmt., Pepperdine U., 1977. LCSW Washington. Br. supr. Wash. State Dept. Social and Health Svcs., Oak Harbor and Anacortes, 1975-78, supr. casework Everett, 1973-75; lectr., coord. rural community mental health project U. Wash., Seattle, 1978-83; exec. dir. Armed Svcs. YMCA, Oak Harbor, 1984-86; area dir. United Way of Island County, 1986-88, exec. dir., 1988-92, Saratoga Community Mental Health, Coupeville, Wash., 1992-93; outpatient therapist, attention-deficit/hyperactivity disorder mental health specialist Cath. Cmty. Svcs. Northwest, Oak Harbor, 1993-96, dir., 1996—2001, Mount Vernon, 1996-99, clin. dir. Everett, 1998—; practicum instr. sch. social work Ea. Wash. U., 2001; pvt. practice counseling, 2001—. Internship supr., counseling program, Seattle U., 1998-99, Bastyr U., 2000-01; part-time instr. sociology Chapman U. Naval Air Sta. Whidbey Island, Orange, Calif., 1988-95. *Robert Miller researched with J. Ray: Rural Community Mental Health: The Scope of Practice, Worker Satisfaction, and Implications for Training, University of Washington (1982). He presented paper The Role Transition of Professionals Moving to Rural Locales, NATO Symposium on Role Transitions, University Wisconsin, 1982. He designed first crisis nursery in Washington (1983). One of first two male presidents of a Business & Professional Women's club (1986). He received McDonald's Program Achievment Awards for YMCA latchkey program, and community indoctrination tour for Whidbey Island Naval Air Station personnel (1986).* Contbr. articles to profl. jours. Bd. dirs. Puget Sound chpt. Huntington's Disease Soc. Am., 1989-93, pres., 1991, fundraising chmn., 1989-91, v.p., 1990; mem. adv. bd. United Ways Wash., 1991-92; chmn. Island County bd. emergency food and shelter program Fed. Emergency Mgmt. Agy.; vice chmn. Cmty. Resource Network, Oak Harbor, 1991; mem. steering com. Greater Oak Harbor Econ. Summit, 1991; mem. strategic planning com. Whidbey Gen. Hosp., Coupeville, 1992-93; mem. exec. com. Mt. Baker coun. Boy Scouts Am., 1993; bd. dirs. Opportunity Coun., Bellingham, 1993-94; bd. dirs. Concerts on the Cove, Coupeville, 1993-96, v.p., 1994-95; mem. Oak Harbor Citizen's Comprehensive Plan Task Force, 1994; mem. Readiness to Learn Coupeville Cmty. Team, 1996; risk mgmt. subcom. chair Assoc. Provider Network, 1997-98; mem. child study team Island County, 1996-99, child protective team, 1997-99; mem. health adv. bd. Head Start, Mt. Vernon, Wash., 1999—. Recipient outstanding svc. award Armed Svcs. YMCA of U.S., Dallas, 1985, two program merit awards McDonald's Corp., Oak Harbor, 1986; named Alumni of a Growing Vision, Seattle Pacific U., 1991, Diplomat of Yr. Greater Oak Harbor C. of C., 1991. Mem. NASW (bd. dirs. Wash. chpt. 1982-85), Wash. Assn. Social Welfare (pres. 1975-76), Acad. Cert. Social Workers, Sunrise Rotary Club (sec. Oak Harbor chpt. 1998-99). Roman Catholic. Avocations: reading, genealogy, fishing, computers. Home: 2450 S Rocky Way Coupeville WA 98239-9610 Office: Ste B206 275 SE Cabot Dr Oak Harbor WA 98277 E-mail: robertmiller@counsellor.com.

MILLER, ROBERT STEVEN, secondary school educator; b. Van Nuys, Calif., Aug. 9, 1963; s. Frederick Earl and Mary (Brash) M. AA, L.A. Valley Coll., 1984; BSBA, Calif. State U., 1987, MA in History, 1990. Cert. substitute tchr., 1993-96. Study group leader, study skills researcher Ednl. Opportunity Program Calif. State U., L.A., 1989-93, faculty mem. History Dept., lectr., 1990-92; sec., treas. Agate/Amethyst World, Inc., Van Nuys, Calif., 1986-91, v.p., 1992-96; with Summer Bridge Program Calif. State U., L.A., 1994-96; tchr. history Chatsworth (Calif.) H.S., 1996—. Mng. editor jour. Perspectives, 1990, editor-in-chief, 1991. Jake Gimbel scholar, 1989. Mem. Am. Historians Assn., The Soc. for Historians of Am. Fgn. Rels., Phi Alpha Theta (v.p. 1990, pres. 1991, Eta Xi chpt., Ledeboer Family scholar 1989), Pi Sigma Epsilon (v.p. 1986-87, pres. 1988 Phi chpt.), Mu Kappa Tau (pres. and founder 1989, Calif State U. LA chpt.). Democrat. Roman Catholic. Home: 13750 Runnymede St Van Nuys CA 91405-1515 Office: Chatsworth HS 10027 Lurline Ave Chatsworth CA 91311-3153

MILLER, ROBERT W. music educator, musician; b. Iron Mountain, Mich., Dec. 25, 1950; s. Walter Harry and Caroline Louise Miller. BMus, U. Mich., 1973; MMus, Peabody Conservatory of Music, Balt., 1974; Dr.Musical Arts, Peabody Inst. of Johns Hopkins U., Balt., 1979. Full prof. of music, artist-in-residence East Stroudsburg U. of Pa., 1977—. Adj. prof. music Essex C.C., Balt., 1975—77; piano faculty Interlochen Ctr. of Arts, Mich., 1978—80; summer faculty Mansfield Coll./Oxford U., England, 1986—89, IFK U. of Salzburg and Cultural Studies Acad., Austria, 1991—; guest artist N.Y. Philharm. Ensembles, N.Y.C., 1998, N.Y.C., 2002; solo and chamber music recitals Weill Recital Hall at Carnegie Hall, N.Y.C., 1998—2002; rehearsal pianist Van Cliburn at Interlochen Ctr. for the Arts, 1975—80. Musician: (solo piano recital) Salle Cortot, 1992, 2000, Weill Recital Hall at Carnegie Hall, 2000, (piano concerto soloist) World Youth Symphony, (piano concert soloist) Peabody Symphony, Montclair Chamber Ensemble, Pine Mountain Music Festival; recording artist Media Rite Prodns., Educo Records. Founder, artistic dir. Carter Chamber Music Series, East Stroudsburg, 1993—; competition judge Pa. Gov.'s Sch. of Arts, Tatamy, 1978—. Named to Outstanding Young Men of Am., 1980; recipient Disting. Prof. award, East Stroudsburg U., 2002; scholar F. Lammot Belin Arts scholar, Waverly, Pa., 1991. Mem.: Assn. of Pa. State Coll. and Univ. Faculty, Music Tchrs. Nat. Assn., Am. Liszt Soc. Avocations: swimming, scuba diving, water skiing, hiking. Mailing: East Stroudsburg Univ Dept Music Fine Arts Bldg East Stroudsburg PA 18301

MILLER, ROBERTA ANN, gastroenterology nurse; b. Saginaw, Mich., Mar. 5, 1955; d. Frank William and Elizabeth Martha (Zimmerman) Carelli; m. Mark Clifford Miller, July, 1977; children: Matthew Gerald, Sarah Rose. BSN, No. Mich. U., 1977. RN, Mich.; cert. gastroenterology clinician. Staff nurse med./surg. unit St. Anthony Med. Ctr., Columbus, Ohio, 1977-78, staff nurse surg. ICU, 1978-85, staff nurse vascular lab., 1985-86, gastroenterology clinician, 1986-92; supr. digestive disease ctr. Grant Med. Ctr., 1994—. Contbr. articles to profl. jours. Mem. Hosp. Mgmt. Assn., Soc. Gastroenterology Nurses ans Assocs. (mem. rsch. com., dir. edn. 1998—), Ohio Soc. Gastrointestinal Nurses and Assocs. (pres. 1993-98). E-mail: b.miller@ohiohealth.com.

MILLER, ROBERTA BALSTAD, science administrator; b. Mpls., June 25, 1940; d. Gerhard Oliver and Laverne K. (Anderson) Balstad; m. Gary David Lange, Nov. 26, 1959 (div. 1968); m. Floyd John Miller, June 15, 1969; 1 child, Aaron Gerhard. BA, U. Minn., 1964, MA, 1970, PhD, 1973. Rsch. assoc. AIA, Washington, 1974; staff assoc. Social Sci. Rsch. Coun., 1975-81; exec. dir. Consortium Social Sci. Assns., 1981-84; divsn. dir. NSF, 1984-93; pres., CEO Consortium for Internat. Earth Sci. Info. Network (CIESIN), University Center, Mich., 1993-98; adj. prof. natural resources policy and behavior U. Mich., 1993-97; sr. rsch. scientist, dir. CIESIN Columbia U., N.Y.C., 1998—. Guest scholar Woodrow Wilson Internat. Ctr. Scholars, 1994; sr. assoc. mem. St. Anthony's Coll., U. Oxford, Eng., 1991-92; mem. chmn. NATO adv. panel on Advanced Sci. Insts./Advanced Rsch. Workshops, Brussels, 1988-91, chmn. steering com. space applications & commercialization Nat. Rsch. Coun., 1999—; mem. exec. com. Space Studies Bd. Nat. Rsch. Coun., 1995-2000; mem. U.S. Nat. Com. IIASA, 1995—; chmn. adv. bd. Luxembourg Income Survey, 1987-91; mem. climate rsch. com. Nat. Rsch. Coun., 1997-99; mem. com. on global change rsch. Nat. Rsch. Coun., 1999-2002. Author: City and Hinterland, 1979; editor (with Harriet Zuckerman) Science Indicators: Implications for Research and Policy, 1979; contbr. articles to profl. jours.; translator poetry of Jorge Luis Borges, 1989, 90, 91, N.P. von Wyk Louw, 1998. Bd. trustees Newport Schs., Kensington, Md., 1986-91, St. Anthony's Coll. Trust, 1994—, sec., 1997-2000, chair, 2000—; adv. trustee Environ. Rsch. Inst. Mich., 1995-98. Recipient NSF Meritorious Svc. award, 1993. Fellow AAAS (com. mem., chmn. 1987-93); mem. U.S. Man in the Bioshphere Program (com., chmn. 1989-91), Internat. Social Sci. Coun. (com. 1991-95, v.p. 1992-94), Am. Lit. Translators Assn., Coun. on Fgn. Rels., Cosmos Club. Lutheran. Home: 3909 Jocelyn St NW Washington DC 20015-1905 Office: CIESIN Columbia U PO Box 1000 Palisades NY 10964-8000

MILLER, ROBERTA SELWYN, communications director; b. Bklyn., Aug. 15; d. Phillip Gordon and Lillian (Blumin) Selwyn; m. Stuart Miller, Sept. 3, 1956 (div. May 1977); children: Eric, Nancy Miller Cook, Leslie. Student, Bennington (Vt.) Coll., 1953-56; BS, Barry U., 1981. Lic. real estate broker, Fla. Owner Fabulous Finds, Miami, Fla., 1975-85; real estate brokerage Deco Dr. Realty, Miami Beach, 1985-90; dir. corp. comms. Interaxx Network, Inc., Miami, 1990—. Owner Image Inc., Miami, 1975-85. Pres. Chopin Found., Miami, 1988. Avocations: traveling, music.

MILLER, ROCHMANNA, secondary school educator; b. Bklyn., July 18, 1953; d. Nathaniel and Betty (Thayler) M. BA in English and Lit., U. Calif., Irvine, 1976; postgrad., UCLA; MA in English, Calif. State U., L.A., 1992. Cert. secondary tchr., Calif. With Navigator Press, L.A.; tchr. English, Roosevelt High Sch. Coord. curriculum and advanced placement Humanitas Tng. Ctr. Fellow Coun. for Basic Edn., 1989; various grants. Mem. Nat. Coun. Tchrs. English. Mem. Calif. Coun. Humanities. Home: 7660 Beverly Blvd Apt 325 Los Angeles CA 90036-2743

MILLER, ROGER ALLEN, physicist; b. Chillicothe, Ohio, June 27, 1934; s. Joseph Perrin and Mary Josephine (Sowers) M.; m. Barbara Pauline Rice, Aug. 31, 1957; children: Erich Rice, Gretchen Rice, Carl Rice. BS, Ohio U., 1956; PhD, Case Inst., 1963. Rsch. assoc. Case Inst., Cleve., 1963-64; rsch. physicist Corning (N.Y.) Inc., 1964-71, sr. rsch. physicist, 1971-79, devel. assoc., 1979-87, sr. rsch. assoc., 1987—. Spl. lectr. physics Elmira Coll., N.Y., 1966-69; mem. edit. bd. Fiber and Integrated Optics, Pasadena, Calif., 1976-86, mem. adv. bd. 1986-88. Contbr. articles to profl. jours. AART award Assn. for the Advancement Radiation Tech., 1990. Mem. Am. Phys. Soc., Optical Soc. Am., Am. Assn. Physics Tchrs., Sigma Xi, Phi Beta Kappa, Phi Kappa Phi. Achievements include contributions to the development of lead free Steuben crystal; development of optical waveguide coatings and coating applicators; design and development of the first, all dielectric, low-loss optical waveguide cable; patentee in field. Office: Corning Inc Sullivan Pk Sp Fr 03 # 1 Corning NY 14831-0001

MILLER, RONALD BAXTER, English language educator, author; b. Rocky Mount, N.C., Oct. 11, 1948; s. Marcellus Cornelius and Elsie (Bryant) M.; m. Jessica Garris, June 5, 1971 (div. 1998); 1 child, Akin Dasan; m. Diana L. Ranson, Sept. 3, 2000. BA magna cum laude, N.C. Ctrl. U., 1970; AM, Brown U., 1972, PhD, 1974. Asst. prof. English Haverford Coll., Haverford, Pa., 1974-76; assoc. prof. English, dir. Black lit. program U. Tenn., Knoxville, 1977-81, prof. English, dir. Black lit. program, 1982-92, Lindsay Young prof. liberal arts and English, 1986-87; prof. English, dir. Inst. for African Am. Studies U. Ga., Athens, 1992—. Instr. summer sch. Roger Williams Coll., Bristol, R.I., 1973; lectr. SUNY, 1974; Mellon prof. Xavier Univ., New Orleans, 1988; Irvine Found. visiting scholar Univ. San Francisco, 1991. Author: (reference guide) Langston Hughes and Gwendolyn Brooks, 1978, The Art and Imagination of Langston Hughes, 1989 (Am. Book award, 1991), (monograph) Southern Trace in Black Critical Theory: Redemption of Time, 1991; editor, contbr.: Black American Literature and Humanism, 1981, Black American Poets Between Worlds, 1940-60, 1986; co-editor: Call and Response The Riverside Anthology of African American Literary Tradition, 1998, Collected Works of Langston Hughes, 2001; mem. editl. bd. Tenn. Studies in Lit., 1991-93, Black Fiction Project (Yale-Cornell-Duke-Harvard), 1985—, U. Ga. Press, 1994-97; contbr. numerous articles and revs. to profl. jours. Recipient award Am. Coun. of Learned Socs., 1978, Golden Key Faculty award Nat. Golden Key, 1990, 95, Alpha award for disting. svc. U. Ga. Athens, 1993, Am. Book award, 1991, Langston Hughes prize, 2001; Lilly Sr. Tchg. fellow U. Ga. Athens, 1994, Nat. Rsch. Coun. sr. fellow, 1986-87, NDEA fellow, 1970-72, Ford Found. fellow, 1972-73, NEH fellow, 1975; Nat. Fellowships Fund dissertation grantee, 1973-74, others. Mem. MLA (exec. com. Afro-Am. Lit. Discussion Group 1980-83, chair 1982-83, mem. del. assembly 1984-86, 97-99, com. on langs. and lits. of Am. 1993-97, chair 1996), Langston Hughes Soc. (pres. 1984-90, exec. editor Langston Hughes Review 1993—). Office: U Ga Inst African Am Studies Athens GA 30602 E-mail: rbmiller@arches.uga.edu., rbmiller6@home.com.

MILLER, RONALD EUGENE, regional science educator; b. Seattle, Sept. 1, 1933; s. Eugene H. and Nellie A. (Myers) M. BA, Harvard U., 1955; MA, U. Wash., 1957; PhD, Princeton U., 1961. Asst. prof. regional sci. U. Pa., Phila., 1962-65, assoc. prof., 1965-71, prof., 1971-95, chmn. dept., 1981-84, prof. emeritus, 1995—. Author: Input-Output Analysis, 1985, Optimization, 2000; Dynamic Optimization and Economic Applications, 1979; also articles; editor Jour. Regional Sci., 1965— . Mem. Regional Sci. Assn. Home: 137 Elfreths Aly Philadelphia PA 19106-2005 Office: U Pa Regional Sci Program 3718 Locust Walk Philadelphia PA 19104-6209 E-mail: remiller@ssc.upenn.edu.

MILLER, RONALD GRANT, writer, critic; b. Santa Cruz, Calif., Feb. 28, 1939; s. Fred Robert and Evelyn Lenora Miller; m. Darla-Jean Irene Rode, Nov. 2, 1963. AA, Monterey Peninsula Coll., 1958; BA, San Jose State U., 1961. Reporter Santa Cruz (Calif.) Sentinel, 1959-62; reporter, chief news bur. San Jose (Calif.) Mercury News, 1962-77, editor T.V., 1977-99; syndicated TV columnist Knight Ridder Syndicate, 1978-99; journalist, author, 1998—. Commentator, critic Sta. KLOK, San Jose, 1981-83; nat. judge Cableace awards, 1987; adj. instr. Whatcom C.C., Bellingham, Wash., 2001--, We. Wash. U., 2002—; instr. Whatcom C.C., 2001—, West Washington U., 2003—. Author: (foreword) Les Brown's Encyclopedia of Television, 1992; co-author: Masterpiece Theatre, 1995, Author: Mystery! A Celebration, 1996 (Agatha, Anthony, and Macavity award nominee 1996-97); contbr. articles and short fiction to various mags.; columnist, mng. editor TheColumnists.com website, 1999—; mystery columnist Alibris.com. website, 2000, PBS mystery.com website, 2001-2002; writer, co-exec. prodr. Dark Corridors: The Curious History of Mystery. Recipient Nat. Spot News Photo award Sigma Delta Chi, 1961, Outstanding Alumnus award San Jose State U. Dept. Journalism and Mass Comm., 1985, Nat. Headline award Press Club Atlantic City, 1994. Mem. TV Critics Assn. (nat. pres. 1981). Democrat. Home and Office: 5437 Canvasback Rd Blaine WA 98230

MILLER, RONALD K. real estate broker, educator; b. Penn Yan, Ny, Apr. 8, 1948; s. Harold and Helen Miller; m. Marguerite Miller, July 16, 2001; children: Jennifer McKay, Kristoffer; m. Jane Miller, Jan. 2, 1970 (div. May 1, 2001). BA, MacMurray Coll., Jacksonville, Illinois, 1970; MA, Elmira Coll., Elmira, NY, 1975. Educator Canandaigua Schools, Canandaigua, NY, 1970—71, Dundee Schools, Dundee, 1972—. Assoc. broker Keuka Shoreline

Properties, Penn Yan, NY, 1992—. Choir dir. First Presbyn. Ch., Penn Yann, NY, 1970—2002. Avocations: gardening, woodworking. Office: Dundee Central School 55 Water Street Dundee NY 14837

MILLER, RONALD WRIGHT, pharmaceutical scientist; b. Pottstown, Pa., Dec. 8, 1947; s. Wright Reninger and Marcelle (Scholler) M.; m. Carol Catherine Grove, Mar. 27, 1971. BS in Chemistry, Lebanon Valley Coll., 1970; MBA, Temple U., 1977, PhD in Pharmaceutics, 1988. Asst. to prodn. mgr. Glenbrook Labs. Divsn., Sterling Drug, Trenton, 1971-74; asst. prodn. mgr. Elkins-Sinn Co., Cherry Hill, N.J., 1974-75; sr. compounding supr. Richardson-Merrell Co., Hatboro, Pa., 1975-80; sr. rsch. scientist Whitehall Labs. Divsn., Am. Home Products, Hammonton, N.J., 1980-88; assoc. dir. Worldwide Pharm. Tech. Bristol-Myers Squibb Co., New Brunswick, 1988—. Lt. col. USAR, 1970-95, ret. Mem. Am. Chem. Soc. (cert.), Am. Assn. Pharm. Scientists. Achievements include patents for coated aspirin tablets decomposition inhibited by incorporation of citric, alginic and glutamic acid mixtures thereof, for enteric coated aspirin tablets rendered shock-insensitive by providing a protective coat of hydroxypropyl methylcellulose of at least 1.5% by weight of the tablet core; pharmaceutical research on compaction with vacuum deparation system and its technological advantages and NIR spectroscopy in-process mapping of roller compaction. Home: 126 Fox Hollow Dr Langhorne PA 19053-2492 Office: Bristol-Myers Squibb PO Box 191 New Brunswick NJ 08903-0191

MILLER, ROSEMARY MARGARET, accountant; b. Jersey City, Jan. 3, 1935; d. Joseph John and Marguerite (Delatush) Corbin; m. James Noyes Orton, 1956 (div. 1977); m. Julian Allen Miller, Oct. 14, 1978 (dec. 1993); children: Alexandria Lynn Hayes, Jennifer Ann Orton Cole. Student Barnard Coll., 1953-54, Rutgers U., Newark, 1954-56, Howard U., 1962-63, No. Va. Community Coll., 1976-83; AA, Thomas A. Edison State Coll., 1981; BS in Acctg., U. Md., 1987; cert. H & R Block, 1981; cert. tax profl. Am. Inst. Tax Studies. Bookkeeper Gen. Electronics, Inc., Washington, 1970-73; cost acct. Radiation Systems, Inc., Sterling, Va., 1973-80; acct. Bilsom Internat., Inc., Reston, Va., 1980-83; sales mgr. Bay Country Homes, Inc., Fruitland, Md., 1984; sr. staff acct. Snow, Powell & Meade, Salisbury, Md., 1985-86; acct. Meadows Hydraulics, Inc., Fruitland, Md., 1987-88; acct. Porter & Powell CPAs, Salisbury, 1988-93; owner, prin. RCOM Cons., acctg., bookeeping, taxes, Princess Anne, Md. Mem. Accreditation Council for Accountancy (accredited 1981), Nat. Soc. Public Accts., Inst. Mgmt. Accts., Nat. Soc. Tax Profls. (cert. tax profl. 1994). Democrat. Lutheran. Address: 9057 N 47th Dr Glendale AZ 85302-3651

MILLER, ROSS HAYS, retired neurosurgeon; b. Ada, Okla., Jan. 30, 1923; s. Harry and Helen (Rice) M.; m. Catherine Railey, May 2, 1943; children—Terry Hays, Helen Stacy. BS, East Central State Coll., Ada, 1943; MD, U. Okla., 1946; MS in Neurosurgery, U. Minn., 1952. Diplomate: Am. Bd. Neurol. Surgery (chmn. exam. com. 1978-84). Intern St. Luke's Hosp., Cleve., 1946-47; fellow in neurosurgery Mayo Clinic, Rochester, Minn., 1950-54; instr. in neurosurgery Mayo Med. Sch., 1954-63, asst. prof. neurosurgery, 1963-73, asso. prof., 1973-75, prof., chmn. dept. neurosurgery, from 1975, now ret. Vis. prof. neurol. surgery Med. Coll. Ga., Augusta Contbr. numerous articles to med. publs. Trustee East Central State U. Found. Served as capt., M.C. U.S. Army, 1947-49, Korea. Named to Okla. Hall of Fame, 1977, Athletic Hall of Fame, East Central U. Okla., 1977; recipient Disting. Alumnus award East Central U. Okla., 1974, Mayo Found. Disting. Alumnus award, 1992. Mem. AMA, ACS, Am. Assn. Neurol. Surgeons (chmn. com. profl. practice 1976-79, dir. 1976-79, v.p. 1979, rep. to Council Med. Splty. Socs. 1980-84), Congress Neurol. Surgeons (exec. com. 1963-65), Minn. Soc. Neurol. Scis., Neurosurg. Soc. Am. (v.p. 1975), Soc. Neurol. Surgeons (v.p. 1983), Sigma Xi.

MILLER, ROSS M. financial services company executive; b. Greenville, S.C., Jan. 6, 1954; s. Milton Gerald Miller and Sara Stein; m. Mary M. O'Keeffe, July 20, 1979; children: Alison, Catherine. BS, Calif. Inst. Tech., 1975; AM, Harvard U., 1977, PhD, 1979. Asst. prof. U. Houston, 1979-82, Calif. Inst. Tech., Pasadena, 1981, Boston U., 1981-89; sr. staff scientist GE Corp. R&D, Schnectady, N.Y., 1989-95; sr. v.p. Natwest Markets and dir. rsch. NatWest Investment Mgmt., Boston, 1995-96; pres. Miller Risk Advisors, Niskayuna, N.Y., 1996—. Mem. program com. Internat. Conf. on Artificial Intelligence Applications on Wall St. and Internat. Workshop on Artificial Intelligence in Econs. and Mgmt.; cons. MAC Group, Cambridge, Mass., 1983-85, FTC, Washington, 1982-85, Millipore, Inc., Bedford, Mass., 1983-84, U.S. Dept. State, Washington, 1987. Author: Computer-Aided Financial Analysis, 1990; contbr. articles to profl. jours. Achievement Rewards for Coll. Scientist fellow, 1973, Grad. fellow Harvard U., 1975, Lock Soc. Hon. fellow Boston U., 1984. Mem. Am. Econs. Assn., Am. Fin. Assn., Econometric Soc., Boston Security Analysts Soc., Boston Econ. Club.

MILLER, ROSS MICHAEL, medical association administrator, pediatrician; b. L.A., Feb. 21, 1954; s. Alvin Abraham and Sylvia (Steinholtz) M.; m. Eva Paul, June 27, 1987; children: Sofie, Eliot. BSc, Stanford U., 1975; MD, U. So. Calif., 1980; MPH, UCLA, 1998. Diplomate Am. Bd. Pediats. Sys. analyst Kaiser Permanente, L.A., 1975-76, pediatrician, 1982-88; intern, resident Children's Hosp., 1980-83, pediatrician, 1980-88, physician advisor, 1988-95; emergency physician Intercare, 1983-88; med. dir. Cigna Healthcare, Glendale, Calif., 1995—. Asst. prof. U. So. Calif., L.A., 1988-95; adv. bd. UCLA Health Scis., 1996—, Nat. Managed Health Care Congress, Boston, 1996—, Modern Beverly Homecare, Monrovia, Calif., 1996—; cons. Olsten Health Svcs., Melville, N.Y., 1996—. Nation chief YMCA Indian Guides, L.A., 1997—. Mem. Nat. IPA Coalition, Am. Coll. Physician Execs., Am. Coll. Healthcare Execs., L.A. Pediat. Soc., Pacific Bus. Group on Health, Phi Delta Epsilon (western regional coord. 1976-80). Avocations: baseball, music. Office: Cigna Healthcare 400 N Brand Blvd Glendale CA 91203-2311 E-mail: ross.miller@cigna.com.

MILLER, ROY RAYMOND, optician, oculist; b. Delta, Ohio, Sept. 20, 1929; s. Roy Draton and Ethel Bernice (Shaffer) M.; m. Evelyn Frances Birsen, Jan. 16, 1954; children: Stephanie, Christopher, Neil Benjamin. Student, Burnham High Sch., Sylvania, Ohio. Lic. Optician. Optician Miller Opticians Inc., Lima, Ohio, 1961—; pres. Miller Opticians and Miller, 1961—, Artificial Eye Lab., Toledo, 1961-88; lic. ocularist Miller Artificial Eye Lab. Appointed to Ohio Optician and Oculorist Bd., Gov. Vonivoich, 1995. Lectr. Nat. Convention, 1978, 1987. Candidate U.S. Congress, Lima 1984, zoning appeals bd. Shawnee Twp., 1980-88, lic. bd. Ohio Optical Dispensing Bd., 1979-85, reapptd., 2000. Cpl. US Army, 1951-52. Recipient award Nat. Acad. Achievements, 1995; inducted into The Internat. Poetry Hall of Fame, 1998. Fellow Nat. Acad. Opticianry (Contbn. to Edn. of Opticianry award 1995), Internat. Acad. Opticians; mem. Am. Soc. Ocularists, Opticians Assn. Am. (diplomate, past bd. dirs., Optician of Yr. 1995, finalist Entrepreneur of Yr. nomination 1995), Guild Prescription Opticians of Am. (bd. dirs.), Optician Assn. Ohio (past pres.), Sertoma (pres. 1983-84), Kiwanis (pres. 1973-74). Republican. Roman Catholic. Avocations: marathon runner, snow skiing, bicycling. Office: Miller Opticians Inc 825 W Market St Ste 202 Lima OH 45805-2794

MILLER, RUTH LOYD, lawyer, author; b. Ida, La., May 29, 1922; d. Cecil A. and Gladys (Means) Loyd; m. Minos D. Miller, Jr., Dec. 22, 1942; children: Bonner M. Cutting, Minos D. III, James Valcour. BA in Speech, La. State U., 1942; MA in English, U. La., 1987. Bar: La. 1957. Sole practice, Jennings, La., 1957—; sec. Jennings Gas Co., 1959—. Author, editor: Shakespeare Identified, 3rd edit., 1975, Hidden Allusions in Shakespeare's Plays, 3rd edit., 1975, A Hundreth Sundrie Flowers, 2d edit., 1975. First v.p. La. Constnl. Conv., 1973; mem. La. Mineral Bd., 1972-73; mem. bd. suprs. La. State Univ. Sys., 1974-88, chmn., 1983-84; active polit. campaigns, La. Named Nat. Woman of Yr., Delta Zeta, 1983. Mem. ABA, La. State Bar Assn. Republican. Methodist. Home: PO Box 1309 Jennings LA 70546-1309

MILLER, SAM SCOTT, lawyer; b. Ft. Worth, July 26, 1938; s. Percy Vernon and Mildred Lois (MacDowell) M.; m. Mary Harrison FitzHugh, May 10, 1969. BA, Mich. State U., 1960; JD, Tulane U., 1964; LLM, Yale U., 1965. Bar: La. 1965, N.Y. 1966, Minn. 1969. Assoc. Simpson Thacher & Bartlett, N.Y.C., 1965-68; sr. counsel Investors Diversified Services, Mpls., 1968-73; ptnr. Ireland Gibson Reams & Miller, Memphis, 1973-74; gen. counsel Paine Webber Group, Inc., N.Y.C., 1974-87, sr. v.p., 1976-87; ptnr. Orrick, Herrington & Sutcliffe, 1987—. Adj. prof. NYU Law Sch., 1986-90; vis. lectr. Yale Law Sch., 1980-85, Inst. for Internat. Econs. and Trade, Wuhan, China, 1983, U. Calif., 1986; trustee Omni Mut., Inc., 1988-; ombudsman Kidder Peabody Group, 1988-, Charles Schwab & Co., 1991-, Gruntal & Co., 1995-. Contbr. articles to profl. jours.; editor-in-chief: Tulane Law Rev, 1964-65; bd. editors Securities Regulation Law Jour., 1982—. Bd. dirs. Guthrie Theatre Found., Mpls., 1971-74; bd. dirs. Minn. Opera Co., 1971-74, Yale U. Law Sch. Fund., 1981—; bd. govs. Investment Co. Inst., 1980-87. Fellow Fgn. Policy Assn.; mem. ABA (chmn. subcom. market regulation 1985-93, vice chmn. com. fed. regulation of securities 1995-98, chmn. subcom. electronic comm. 1999—), Assn. Bar City N.Y. (treas. and mem. exec. com. 1994-96, chmn. broker-dealer investment co. and regulations subcom. 1982-83), Internat. Bar Assn., Securities Industry Assn. (chmn. fed. regulation com. 1976-78), Down Town Assn., Knickerbocker Club, Order of Coif, Omicron Delta Kappa. Democrat. Baptist. Office: Orrick Herrington & Sutcliffe 666 5th Ave Rm 203 New York NY 10103-1798

MILLER, SANDRA ANN, communications consultant; b. Bklyn., Sept. 15, 1948; d. Milton Arthur and Etta (Heit) Katz; m. Julian Jay Miller, Jan. 26, 1992. BA, Queens Coll., 1970; MBA, Baruch Coll., 1986. Asst. divsn. mgr. Hukapoo, N.Y.C., 1975-84; sales mgr. Petticord Enterprises, 1984-86; dir. exec. edn. Baruch Coll., 1986-88; cons. McAlinden Assocs., 1988-92; owner, founder ICT Impact Comms. Techniques, 1992—. Adj. lectr. NYU, N.Y.C., 1994—. Contbr. articles to profl. publs. Mem. Am. Mktg. Assn. (co-chair 1994-95), Profl. Svcs. Mktg. Leadership Coun., Nat. Law Firm Mktg. Assn. (chair spkrs. bur. Met. N.Y. chpt. 1994-95), Beta Gamma Sigma. Office: ICT Impact Comms Technique 301 E 22nd St Apt 5R New York NY 10010-4824

MILLER, SANFORD ARTHUR, academic administrator, biochemistry educator; b. Bklyn., May 12, 1931; s. Howard and Lillian (Kenter) Epstein; m. Judith W. Cohen, Aug. 17, 1958; children: Wallis Jo, Debra Lauren. BS in Chemistry and Biology, CCNY, 1952; MS in Psychology and Biochemistry, Rutgers U., 1956, PhD, 1957. Jr. chemist electronics br. Army Chem. Ctr., Edgewood, Md., summer 1951, chemist applied rsch. br., 1952; asst. to chief toxicology Army Med. Ctr., Washington, 1953-54; tchg. asst. in physiology and biochemistry Rutgers U., 1955-57; rsch. assoc. dept. food tech. MIT, 1957-59, asst. prof. nutritional biochemistry, 1959-65, assoc. prof., 1965-70, prof., dir. tng. program in oral sci., 1970-83; dir. Ctr. Food Safety and Applied Nutrition FDA, Washington, 1978-87; prof. biochem. and medicine, dean grad. sch. biomed. scis. U. Tex. Health Sci. Ctr., San Antonio, 1987-2000, prof., dean emeritus, 2000—. Sr. fellow, prof. Ctr. for Food and Nutrition Policy, Georgetown Univ., Wash., 1999—; vis. lectr. in nutrition Tufts U. Sch. Dental Medicine, 1963-85, Boston U. Sch. Medicine, 1963-87, Harvard U. Sch. Medicine, 1963-87; sr. lectr. MIT, 1983-84; cons. to food and drug cos., U.S. and abroad; chmn. ad hoc com. Nat. Inst. Neurol. Disease and Stroke, 1972-77; mem. meetings com. Fedn. Am. Socs. Exptl. Biology, 1972, chmn. conf., 1973, expert com. on generally recognized as safe substances, 1972-78; mem. com. on maternal and child health Nat. Inst. Child Health and Human Devel., 1973-77, com. on contraceptive steroids, 1973-81, com. on growth and devel., 1972-76; mem. adv. com. on nutrition Nat. Inst. Dental Rsch., 1973-78; bd. sci. advs. FDA, 1972-78; mem. Food Update Bd. Govs. Food and Drug Law Inst., 1978-82; trustee toxicology forum; mem. Nat. Adv. Environ. Health Scis. Coun., 1988-92, U.S. Nestle Adv. Bd., 1990, Food Forum, Inst. Med., Nat. Acad. of Scis., 1993—; co-chmn. USDA-FDA working group on food safety legis., 1980-87; coord. nutrition initiatives for Pub. Health Svc., 1982-87; co-chmn. Cancer Risk Assessment Task Force, 1984-87; U.S. co-coord. Codex Alimentarius, 1984-87; chair dietary ref. intakes on macronutrients Nat. Acad. Sci., 2000, com. on agrl. biotech., health and the environment, 2000, roundtable on environ. health scis., rsch. and medicine, 2000. Contbr. numerous articles , revs., chpts. to profl. publs.; mem. editl. bd. Drug-Nutrient Interactions, 1981— Cpl. U.S. Army, 1953-54. Recipient Outstanding Tchr. of Yr. award MIT, 1975, Pub. Health Svc. Superior Svc. award, 1982, Award of Merit, FDA, 1987, Esther Peters Conumer Svc. award Food Mktg. Inst., 1988, Disting. Svc. award FDA, 2000; recipient numerous grants and fellowships including Nat. Acad. Scis., 1959, NIH, 1960-78, AEC, 1965, Disting. Svc. award HHS, 1983. Fellow Mark L. Morris Animal Care Panel (hon.); mem. Am. Chem. Soc. (Sterling B. Hendricks award 1989), W.O. Atwater Meml. Lectureship, Agrl. Rsch. Svc., Glenn W. Kilpatrick Meml. Address, Assn. of Food and Drug Offcls. (nat. councilor 1966-69, nat. chmn. com. on nutrition edn. 1969-72, Babcock-Hart award 1991), Animal Care Panel, Am. Inst. Nutrition (chmn. fellows com. 1977-78, chmn. biochem. nutrition com. 1967-69, nat. program com. 1967-72, chair pub. affairs com. 1989-91, Conrad Elvehjem award 1981), Soc. Teratology, Perinatal Rsch. Soc., Am. Inst. Dental Rsch., Soc. Pediatric Rsch., Gordon Rsch. Confs. (chmn. 1973, vice chmn. 1972), Western Hemisphere Nutrition Congress (program com. 1977, chair WHO-FAO joint food safety com. 1990, world food conf. planning commn. 1990-92), Commn. on Health and Environ. (panel on food and agriculture 1990 Jewish. Office: Georgetown Univ Ctr for Food/Nutrition Pol 3240 Prospect St Washington DC 20057

MILLER, SANFORD MARVIN, anesthesiology educator; b. Phila., Dec. 28, 1932; AB, U. Chgo.; MD, Jefferson Med. Coll., 1957. Diplomate Am. Bd. Anesthesiology. Intern Jefferson Hosp., Phila., 1957-58, resident in anesthesiology, 1958-60; fellow Westminster Hosp., London, 1960-61; attending anesthesiologist, asst. prof. NYU Med. Ctr., N.Y.C., 1975-2000, assoc. prof., 2000—; attending anesthesiologist Bellevue Hosp., 1975—. Mem. AMA, Am. Soc. Anesthesiologists, Am. Coll. Anesthesiologists. Office: NYU Med Ctr 560 1st Ave New York NY 10016-6402 E-mail: sanford.miller@med.nyu.edu.

MILLER, SARABETH, secondary education educator; b. Kouts, Ind., Apr. 6, 1927; d. Clayton Everett and Eva Margaret (Noland) Reif; m. Lloyd Melvin Miller, Dec. 2, 1944; children: Virginia, Shirley, Judith, John, Nola, Steven. BA, Valparaiso U., 1972, MA in L.S., 1977, postgrad., Purdue U., 1983, Ind. U., 1986, 91, Art Inst. Ft. Lauderdale, Fla., 1992, Ind. State U., 1996, 97, St. Joseph U., 1998. Lic. tchr., Ind.; cert. in data processing. Office employee Porter County Herald, Hebron, Ind., 1954-55, Little Co. of Mary Hosp. and Home, San Pierre, Ind., 1960-65, Jasper County Co-op, Tefft, Ind., 1965-69, Hannon's, Valparaiso, 1969-72; tchr. art DeMotte (Ind.) elem. sch., 1972-76, Kankakee Valley High Sch., Wheatfield, Ind., 1976—; participant Lilly Creative Tchr.'s Workshop. Past sponsor (art and lit. mag.) Mirage; leader 4-H Club, Kouts, participant North Cen. Regional Forum, 1991, 92, 93; mem., elder Kouts Presbyn. Ch.; mem. adv. com. for secondary sch. showcase Valparaiso U. Recipient various prizes Lake Central Fair (Ind.), 1975, 80, photography award Ind. Dept. Tourism, 1976, Porter County Fair, 1989, 96, 98, 2000, 01, Gainer Bank Calendar award; Lilly Endowment fellow Lilly Extending Tchr. Creativity Inst., 1987, 94, 95, 96, 2002, 4-H 45 yr. leader tenure award, 1994; grantee Nat. Gallery of Art, 1993. Mem. NEA, Nat. Art Edn. Assn., Ind. Tchrs. Assn., Ind. Art Edn. Assn., Kankakee Valley Tchrs. Assn., North Ctrl. Assn. Secondary Schs. (mem. evaluation team). Presbyterian. Contbr. articles and photographs to various local publs. Home: 1056 S Baums Bridge Rd Kouts IN 46347-9712

MILLER, SHEILA, state legislator; d. Vernon and Mildred M.; m. Michael Miller; 1 child, Emilie C. BS cum laude, Pa. State U., 1974. Rep. dist. 129 State of Pa., 1993—. Bd. dirs. Berks County Farmland Preservation. Mem. Nat. Cattlemens Assn., Berks Farm Bur., Berks Cattlemens Assn., Pa. Cattlemens Assn., Heidelberg Heritage Soc., Berks County Rep. Women, Phi Kappa Phi, Gamma Sigma Delta Agrl. Alumni Soc. Office: Pa Ho of Reps B13 Main Capitol Bldg PO Box 202020 Harrisburg PA 17120-2020

MILLER, SHELBY ALEXANDER, chemical engineer, educator; b. Louisville, July 9, 1914; s. George Walter and Stella Katherine (Cralle) M.; m. Jean Adele Danielson, Dec. 26, 1939 (div. May 1948); 1 son, Shelby Carlton; m. Helen Adare Kennedy, May 29, 1952 (dec. Feb. 1971). BS, U. Louisville, 1935; PhD, U. Minn., 1943. Registered profl. engr., Del., Kans., N.Y. Asst. chemist Corhart Refractories Co., Louisville, 1935-36; teaching, rsch. asst. chem. engring. U. Minn., Mpls., 1935-39; devel. engr., rsch. chem. engr. E.I. duPont de Nemours & Co., Inc., Wilmington, Del., 1940-46; assoc. prof. chem. engring. U. Kan., Lawrence, 1946-50, prof., 1950-55; Fulbright prof. chem. engring. King's Coll. Durham U., Newcastle-upon-Tyne, Eng., 1952-53; prof., chem. engring. U. Rochester, 1955-69, chmn., 1955-68; assoc. lab. dir. Argonne (Ill.) Nat. Lab., 1969-74; dir. Ctr. Ednl. Affairs, 1969-79, sr. chem. engr., 1969-84, ret., cons., 1984—. Vis. prof. chem. engring. U. Calif., Berkeley, 1967-68; vis. prof. U. of Philippines, Quezon City, 1986; cons. in field. Editor: Chem. Engring. Edn. Quar, 1965-67; sect. editor: Perry's Chem. Engrs.' Handbook, 5th edit., 1973, 6th edit., 1984, 7th edit. 1997; contbr. to McGraw-Hill Ency. Sci. and Tech., 5th edit., 1982, 6th edit., 1987, 7th edit., 1992; contbr. articles to profl. jours. Sec. Kans. Bd. Engring. Examiners, 1954-55; mem. adv. com. on tng. Internat. Atomic Energy Agy., 1975-79; treas. Lawrence (Kans.) League for Practice Democracy, 1950-52; sec. Argonne Credit Union, 1994-97. Fellow AAAS, Am. Inst. Chemists, Am. Inst. Chem. Engrs. (past chmn. Kansas City sect.); mem. Am. Chem. Soc. (past chmn. Rochester sect.), Soc. Chem. Industry, Am. Soc. Engring. Edn. (past chmn. grad. studies div.), Am. Nuclear Soc., Filtration Soc., Triangle, Sigma Xi, Sigma Tau, Phi Lambda Upsilon, Tau Beta Pi, Alpha Chi Sigma. Presbyterian. Home: 825 63rd St Downers Grove IL 60516-1962 Office: Argonne Nat Lab Chem Tech Divsn Argonne IL 60439-4837 E-mail: millers@cmt.anl.gov.

MILLER, STANFORD, retired reinsurance executive, lawyer; b. Kansas City, Mo., Nov. 15, 1913; s. Hugh and Gertrude Anna (Kraft) M.; m. Gloria Goble, July 11, 1942 (div. 1958); 1 child, Hans Hugh; m. Beverly Breuer, Apr. 19, 1962; 1 son, Bradford Channing. BA, U. Kans., 1934; JD, U. Chgo., 1938. Bar: Mo. 1938. Former chmn., CEO, Employers Reins. Corp. Lectr. in field. Author: (with Robert D. Brown) Health Insurance Underwriting, 1962; also articles. Trustee emeritus U. Mo. Kansas City; trustee Kans. chpt. Nature Conservancy. Mem. Mo. Bar Assn., Reins. Assn. Am. (past chmn.), Health Ins. Assn. Am. (former sec., dir.), Phi Alpha Delta, Alpha Tau Omega. Clubs: Rotary, Profl. Men's, Mission Hills Country. Home: 2709 Tomahawk Rd Shawnee Mission KS 66208-1827 E-mail: smiller@blitz-it.net.

MILLER, STEPHEN RALPH, lawyer; b. Chgo., Nov. 28, 1950; s. Ralph and Karin Ann (Olson) M.; children: David Williams, Lindsay Christine. m. Sheila L. Krysiak, Feb. 2, 1998. BA cum laude, Yale U., 1972; JD, Cornell U., 1975. Bar: Ill. Assoc. McDermott, Will & Emery, Chgo., 1975-80, income ptnr., 1981-85, equity ptnr., 1986—, mgmt. com. mem., 1992-95. Mem. spl. task force on post-employment benefits Fin. Acctg. Standards Bd., Norwalk, Conn., 1987—91. Contbr. articles to profl. jours. Mem. Chgo. Coun. on Fgn. Rels., 1978—, devel. com., 1997-2002, chair devel. subcom., 1999-2002, external rels. com.; trustee police pension bd., Wilmette, Ill., 1992-98; trustee Seabury We. Theol. Sem., Evanston, Ill., 1994-2002, chancellor, 1996-97, chair trusteeship com., 2000-02. Mem.: ABA, Lawyers' Club of Chgo., Yale Club Chgo. Avocations: sailing, water-skiing, cross country skiing. Office: McDermott Will & Emery 227 W Monroe St Ste 4700 Chicago IL 60606-5096 E-mail: smiller@mwe.com.

MILLER, STEPHEN WARREN, dean; b. Rockville Centre, N.Y., July 23, 1954; s. Warren Harding Miller and Carol Simon; m. Laurie Robin Hogan (div. July 1988); 1 child, James Warren. AA, Indian River C.C., 1974; BS, Fla. State U., 1977, MS, 1982. Cert. career devel. facilitator master instr. Nat. Occupl. Info. Coord. Com.; cert. instr. Zenger/Miller Tng. Corp. Sports reporter WECA/ABC, Tallahassee, 1976-77, WXLT/ABC, Sarasota, 1980-82; 7th and 8th grade sci. tchr. St. Anastasia Sch., Ft. Pierce, 1978-80; dir. student life Macon (Ga.) C.C., 1981-86; assoc. dean continuing edn. Fla. Atlantic U., Ft. Lauderdale, 1986—. Bd. dirs. Am. Coll. Testing, Iowa City, Iowa, 1995—; bd. advisors PACE Ctr. for Girls, Ft. Lauderdale, 1996—. Contbr. to book: High Technology and the 3 Rs, 1985; contbr. articles to profl. jours. Mem. Broward Rep. Leadership, Ft. Lauderdale, 1997—; bd. dirs. SAILS Found., Macon and Ft. Lauderdale, 1995—; chpt. advisor Phi Delta Kappa, Boca Raton, 1988-89; mem. career adv. bd. Broward County Sch. Bd., Ft. Lauderdale, 1991—; chmn. Broward County Americorp., 1995-96; mem. bus. devel. com. Broward Econ. Devel. Bd., 1988—, pres. A Child is Missing. Named Disting. Pres., Kiwanis Internat., 1985, Kiwanian of Yr., 1984, Outstanding Young Man of Am. U.S. Jaycees, 1983. Mem. Ft. Lauderdale C. of C. (bd. govs. 1995-97, Proclamation award). Republican. Episcopalian. Avocations: jet skiing, golf, guitar, reading. Office: Fla Atlantic U 1515 W Commercial Blvd Fort Lauderdale FL 33309-3095 Fax: (954) 351-4176.

MILLER, STEVEN, medical administrator; Grad., U. Mo., Kansas City. Hosp. staff, faculty Wash. U., 1990—, nephrology fellow, 1988, assoc. prof., 1997—, dir. hypertension clinic divsn. nephrology; med. dir. systemwide renal network Barnes-Jewish Hosp.; chief med. officer Wash. U. Sch. Medicine-Barnes Jewish Hosp., 1999—. Mem.: Internat. Soc. Nephrology, ACP.*

MILLER, STEVEN H. museum director; b. Phila., 1947; m. Jane McClure Pelson; children: Andrew Steven, Katherine Ann. BA, Bard Coll., 1970; cert. in conservation sci., Internat. Ctr. for Study of Preservation and Restoration of Cultural Property, Rome, 1978. Asst. to sr. curator Mus. of City of N.Y., N.Y.C., 1971-72, asst. curator paintings, prints and photographs, 1973-77, curator prints and photographs, 1977-79, curator, dept. head fine art collections, history and spl. collections, 1979-85, sr. curator, 1985-87; asst. dir. Maine State Mus., 1987-91; dir. of mus. Western Res. Hist. Soc., Cleve., 1991-95; exec. dir. The Bennington (Vt.) Mus., 1995—2001, Morris Mus., Morristown, NJ, 2001—. Adj. prof. mus. studies Case Western Res. U., 1991-94; lectr. NYU, 1978-87, Columbia U., N.Y.C., 1981, 82, New Sch. for Social Rsch., N.Y.C., 1978, 83, Maine State Mus., 1987-91. Author catalogs; contbr. articles to profl. jours. Charter and former mem. hist. preservation com. City of Gardiner, Maine; mem. Williamstown Art Conservation Ctr.; bd. govs. Bard-St. Stephen's Alumni Assn.; bd. trustees Hist. Deerfield, Mass.; past bd. dirs. Vt. Mus. and Gallery Alliance; former mem. landmarks preservation com. Shaker Heights, Ohio; former mem. adv. com. Blaine House Restoration, Maine; former mem., art adv. com. Gracie Mansion Conservancy, N.Y.C.; former mem. adv. coun. Mus. Moving Image, Astoria, NY. Mem.: NARAS (assoc.), Maine Assn. Mus. (co-founder, charter coun. mem.), Am. Assn. Mus. (mem. mus. advocacy team, mem. mus. accreditation vis. com.), Park Ave. Club (Morristown), Nat. Arts Club. Home: 45 Washington Ave Morristown NJ 07960-5622

MILLER, STEVEN MAX, humanities educator; b. Portland, Ind., Feb. 9, 1950; s. J. Max and Belva Kathryn (Kitty Booher) M.; m. Fran Felice Koski, May 30, 1985 (div. 1992). BA in English with high honors, Coll. of William and Mary, 1972; MA in English Lang. and Lit., Ind. U., 1975, PhD in English Lang. and Lit., 1985. Sr. libr. asst. cataloger rare books and spl. collections Lilly Libr., Bloomington, Ind., 1972-76; prof. English Millersville (Pa.) U., 1985—; dir. univ. honors program Millersville (Pa.) U., 1999-2001, dir. Honors Coll., 2001—. Cons. women writers project Brown U., Providence, 1990-95. Contbr. articles to profl. jours. Grantee NEH, 1991, 92. Mem. MLA, John Donne Soc. Am., Spenser Soc. Episcopalian. Avocation: gardening. Office: Millersville U Dept English PO Box 1002 Millersville PA 17551-0302

MILLER, STEVEN SCOTT, lawyer; b. N.Y.C., May 28, 1947; s. Stanley Irwin and Corinne (Mass) M.; m. Nina Catherine Augello, Apr. 24, 1983. BA cum laude, U. Pa., 1967; JD cum laude, NYU, 1970. Bar: N.Y. 1971, U.S. Dist. Ct. (so. and ea. dists.) N.Y. 1972, U.S. Ct. Appeals (2d cir.) 1974. Law clk. to judge U.S. Dist. Ct. (so. dist.) N.Y., N.Y.C., 1970-71; assoc. Proskauer Rose Goetz & Mendelsohn, 1971-78, Rosenman & Colin, N.Y.C., 1978-81, ptnr., 1981-92; v.p., asst. gen. counsel J.P. Morgan Chase & Co. (formerly Chase Manhattan Bank), 1992—. Editor NYU Law Rev., 1968-70. Mem.: NY State Bar Assn., NYU Law Sch. Alumni Assn. (pres. 2000—02). Home: 135 E 83rd St New York NY 10028-2408 Office: JP Morgan Chase & Co 1 Chase Manhattan Plz Fl 26 New York NY 10081-0001

MILLER, STUART A. real estate executive, lawyer; Grad., Harvard U.; JD, U. Miami, 1982. Various positions homebuilding divsn. Lennar Corp., Miami, Fla., pres. homebuilding divsn. and former investment divsn., 1991—97, pres., CEO, 1997—, also bd. dirs. Bd. dirs. Union Bank Fla. Office: Lennar Corp 700 NW 107th Ave Ste 400 Miami FL 33172-3154*

MILLER, SUSAN ANN, school system administrator; b. Cleve., Nov. 24, 1947; d. Earl Wilbur and Marie Coletta (Hendershot) M. BS in Edn., Kent State U., 1969; MEd, Cleve. State U., 1975; PhD, Kent State U., 1993. Cert. supt.; cert. elem. prin., cert. elem. supervisor; cert. Learning Disabled/Behavior Disabled tchr.; cert. tchr. grades 1-8; cert. sch. counselor; lic. counselor. Tchr., guidance counselor, interim prin. North Royalton City Schs., Ohio, 1969-84; dir. elem. and spl. edn., acting supt., asst. supt. Ednl. Svc. Ctr. of Cuyahoga County , Valley View, 1984—. Contbr. articles to profl. jours. Grantee Latchkey Program, State Dept. Edn., North Coast Leadership Forum, Peer Assistance and Rev., Entry Yr. Program, Alt. H.S. Mem. ASCD,

Coun. Exceptional Children, Phi Delta Kappa. Office: ESC Cuyahoga County 5700 W Canal Rd Valley View OH 44125-3326 Home: 7236 Morning Star Trail Sagamore Hills OH 44067 E-mail: susan.a.miller@lnoca.org.

MILLER, SUSAN JANET, business educator, researcher; b. Hillingdon, Middlesex, Eng., 1955; d. Ronald Frank and Joyce Pamela (West) M. BA with honors, Bradford & Ilkley Coll., 1985; MBA, Bradford U., 1986, PhD, 1990. Various positions in adminstrn. in pub. and pvt. orgns. BBC and Taylor Woodrow, 1974-85; rschr. Bradford (Eng.) U., 1990-91; sr. lectr. Durham (Eng.) U., 1991—. Co-author, contbr.: Handbook of Organization Studies, 1996, Encyclopedic Dictionary of Organization Behavior, 1995; contbr. articles to profl. jours. including Am. Behavioral Scientist and Exec. Devel. Jour. (MCB Press Lit. award 1993). Grantee U.S. Army, Rsch. Isnt., 1995. Avocations: walking, badminton. Office: Durham U Bus Sch Mill Hall Ln Durham DH1 3LB England E-mail: susan.miller@durham.ac.uk.

MILLER, SUSAN PETERSON, special education educator; b. Cheyenne, Wyo., Jan. 12, 1956; d. Robert Ernest and Geraldine Lanore Peterson; m. Steven Michael Miller, May 24, 1991. BS, Fla. So. Coll., 1978; MEd, U. Fla., 1981, PhD, 1987. Tchr. Alachua County Schs., Gainesville, Fla., 1978-85; cons. tchr., program mgr. Multidisciplinary Diagnostic and Tng. Program, 1985-87; vis. asst. prof. U. Fla., 1987-91; asst. prof. spl. edn. U. Nev., Las Vegas, 1991-94, assoc. prof., 1994-00, prof., 2000—. Learning strategy trainer Ctr. for Rsch. on Learning, Lawrence, Kans., 1990—; cons. editor Action in Tchr. Edn. Jour., 1992—, Intervention in Sch. and Clinic Jour., 1994—; mem. adv. bd. New Horizons Acad., Las Vegas, 1998—; participant, presenter numerous spl. edn. confs., 1982—. Author: Validated Practices for Teaching Students with Diverse Needs and Abilities, 2002; co-author: Strategic Math Series, 7 curricular books, 1991-94; contbr. over 40 articles to profl. jours., chpts. to books. Named Nev. Prof. of Yr., Nat. Carnegie Found., 1999. Mem. Divsn. for Learning Disabilities (exec. bd., treas. 1997-99, v.p. 2001-02), Coun. for Exceptional Children. Democrat. Avocation: bowling. Office: U Nev PO Box 453014 Las Vegas NV 89154-3014

MILLER, SUSAN SMITH, state official; b. York, Pa., Aug. 25, 1941; d. Howard LaRue and Ruth Marietta (Kisiner) S.; m. David Roswell Miller, Aug. 13, 1961 (div. June 1974); children: Justine Elisabeth, Matthew David. BA in Psychology, Sociology, Lebanon Valley Coll., 1963. Tchr. fourth and fifth grade Morongo Unified Sch. Dist., Twenty-nine Palms, Calif., 1963-64; caseworker Children's Svcs. of York County, Pa., 1965-67; personnel mgr. Max Eckardt Shiny-Brite, Inc., York, 1974-75; health svcs. coord., social svcs. worker Crispus Attucks Early Learning Ctr., 1975-76; mgr. Bookland, Inc., 1976-77; from licensing rep. to chief licensing Pa. Dept. Pub. Welfare, Daycare, Harrisburg, Pa., 1977—2002; chief licensing & program activities & subsidized child day care program ops. Pa. Dept. Pub. Welfare, 2002—. Group leader Base Nursery, Twenty-nine Palms, 1964-65, social svcs. vol. ARC, Twenty-nine Palms, 1964-65; mem. testing/group counseling divsn. Mental Health Clinic, Hanover, Pa., 1968-69; citizens adv. bd. York County Assistance Office, 1968-89; bd. dirs. Red Lion (Pa.) VNA, 1969-70; organizer Red Lion Area Women's Club, 1968-71; mem. Red Lion Mobil Foods Bd., 1995—; county chair, sec., bd. dirs. Lebanon Valley Coll. Alumni Assn., 1969-75, others. Mem. Nat. Assn. Regulatory Adminstrn., Pa. Govt. Assn. for the Regulation of Lic. Facilities. Avocations: reading, sewing, making Ukranian eggs, gardening.

MILLER, SUZANNE MARIE, state librarian; b. Feb. 25, 1954; d. John Gordon and Dorothy Margaret (Sabatka) M.; 1 child, Altinay Marie. BA in English, U. S.D., 1975; MA in Library Sci., U. Denver, 1976, postgrad. in law, 1984. Librarian II U. S.D. Sch. of Law, Vermillion, 1977-78; law libr. U. LaVerne, Calif., 1978-85, instr. in law, 1980-85; asst. libr. tech. svcs. McGeorge Sch. Law, 1985-99, prof. advanced legal rsch., 1994-99; state librarian S.D. State Library, Pierre, S.D., 1999—. Co-author (with Elizabeth J. Pokorny) U.S. Government Documents: A Practical Guide for Library Assistants in Academic and Public Libraries, 1988; contbr. chpt. to book, articles to profl. jours. Pres. Short Grass Arts Coun., 2001—03; bd. dirs. Black Hills Playhouse Bd., 1999—, S.D. Ctr. for the Book Bd., 2002—. Recipient A. Jurisprudence award Bancroft Whitney Pub. Co., 1983. Mem.: Western Pacific Assn. Law Librs. (sec. 1990—94, pres. elect 1994—95, pres. 1995—96, local arrangements chair 1997), No. Calif. Assn. Law Librs. (mem. program com., inst. 1988), Mt. Plains Libr. Assn. (S.D. rep. to exec. bd. 2001—), So. Calif. Assn. Law Librs. (arrangements com. 1981—82), Am. Assn. Law Librs., S.D. Libr. Assn., ALA. Roman Catholic. Home: 505 N Grand Ave Pierre SD 57501-2014 Office: SD State Library 800 Governors Dr Pierre SD 57501-2235 E-mail: suzanne.miller@state.sd.us.

MILLER, TAMARA DEDRA, psychologist; b. Cleve., Jan. 13, 1961; d. Taswill Taylor and Ethel (Midgett) M.; stepd. Gwendolyn (Hicks) M. BA in Psychology, Wittenberg U., 1982; D in Psychology, Wright State U., 1987. Lic. clin. psychologist, Ohio. Chief psychol. svc. USAF, Altus, Okla., 1987-89, chief psychol. testing Dayton, Ohio, 1989-92; dir. PTSD program Dept. VA, 1992—; clin. prof. Wright State U., 1992—. Cons. Jackson County Youth, Altus, 1987-89, Ctr. for Retardation, Altus, 1987-89; adj. prof. Ctrl. State U., Wilberforce, 1991—; mem. panel Women's Fed. Program, Dayton, 1991; clin. advisor Les Femmes Concerned Citizens for Cancer, Dayton, 1992—. Consulting editor: Professional Psychology: Research and Practice, 1994. Capt. USAF, 1986-89. Mem. Nat. Coun. Negro Women Inc., VA Psychologists, Delta Sigma Theta. Avocations: reading, theatre, dance, aerobics, modeling. Home: 5670 Olive Tree Dr Dayton OH 45426-1313 Office: Dept VA Affairs Med Ctr 4100 E 3rd St Dayton OH 45403-2244

MILLER, TED ROBERT, policy analyst; b. Sept. 17, 1947; s. Marvin Lester and Carolyn Ruth Miller; m. Valerie Sue Nelkin. BS in Engring., Case Western Res. U., 1968; MS in Ops. Rsch., U. Pa., 1971, M in City Planning, 1970, PhD in Regional Sci., 1975. Ops. rsch. analyst U.S. Dept. Commerce, Nat. Bur. Stds. and HEW, Washington, 1971-75; staff dir. task force on Nat. Blood Data Ctr. Am. Blood Commn., Rosslyn, Va., 1975-77; asst. dir. urban and econ. devel. Nat. Inst. Advanced Studies, Washington, 1977-78; v.p. Granville Corp., 1978-84; sr. rsch. assoc. Urban Inst., 1984-93; dir. Children's Safety Network Econ. and Ins. Rsch. Ctr., 1992—. V.p. Nat. Pub. Svcs. Rsch. Inst., Calverton, Md., 1993-96, pres., 1997—; prin. rsch. scientist Pacific Inst. Rsch. and Evaluation, Calverton, 1997—. Mem. bd. editors Jour. Safety Rsch., 1991—, Jour. Forensic Econs., 1991—, Acc. Analysis and Prevention, 1993—, Inf. Prev., 2002-; contbr. articles to profl. jours. Mem. Bd. Proprs. Ea. N.J., 1974-98; pres. Adelphi Ter. Condo. Assn., 1979-81. Recipient Nationwide on Your Side Hwy. Safety award, 1996. Fellow Assn. Advt. Automotive Medicine, Am. Inst. Cert. Planners; mem. AAAS, APHA (Excellence in Sci. award injury control sect. 1999), So. Regional Sci. Assn. (exec. coun. 1990-92), Am. Econ. Assn., Pi Delta Epsilon. Democrat. Office: 11701 Beltsville Dr Ste 300 Beltsville MD 20705

MILLER, TERRY ALAN, chemistry educator; b. Girard, Kans., Dec. 18, 1943; s. Dwight D. Miller and Rachel E. (Detjen) Beltram; m. Barbara Hoffmann, July 16, 1966; children: Brian, Stuart. BA, U. Kans., 1965; PhD, Cambridge (Eng.) U., 1968. Disting. tech. staff Bell Telephone Labs, 1968-84; vis. asst. prof. Princeton U., 1968-71; vis. lectr. Stanford U., 1972; vis. fgn. scholar Inst. Molecular Sci., Okazaki, Japan, summer 1983; Ohio eminent scholar, prof. chemistry Ohio State U., Columbus, 1984—. Chair Molecular Spectroscopy Symposium, Columbus, 1992—. Mem. editl. bd. Jour. Chem. Physics, 1978-81, Jour. Molecular Spectroscopy, 1982-87, Laser Chemistry, 1986—, Rev. of Sci. Instruments, 1986-89, Jour. Phys. Chemistry, 1989-95, Jour. Optical Soc. Am., 1989-95, Chemtracts, 1989-90, Ann. Revs. Phys. Chemistry, 1989-94, Jour. Molecular Structure, 1996—; contbr. more than 250 articles to profl. jours. Recipient Bourke medal Royal Soc. Chemistry, 1998; Marshall fellow Brit. Govt., 1965-67, NSF fellow, 1967-68. Fellow Optical Soc. Am. (Meggars award 1993), Am. Phys. Soc. (H.P. Broida award 1999); mem. Am. Chem. Soc. (councilor), Coblentz Soc. (Bomen-Michaelson award 1995). Office: Ohio State U 120 W 18th Ave Columbus OH 43210-1106

MILLER, TERRY MORROW, lawyer; b. Columbus, Ohio, Mar. 11, 1947; s. Robert E. and Elizabeth Jane (Morrow) M.; m. Martha Estella Johnson, Mar. 20, 1976; 1 child, Timothy. BS, Ohio State U., 1969, JD, 1975. Bar: Ohio 1975, U.S. Ct. Appeals (6th cir.) 1979, U.S. Supreme Ct. 1980. Asst. atty. gen. State of Ohio, Columbus, 1975-77; ptnr. Miller & Noga, 1977-81; assoc. Vorys, Sater, Seymour and Pease, 1981-85, ptnr., 1986—. Trustee Columbus Literacy Coun., 1997—. Sgt. U.S. Army, 1969-71, Okinawa. Mem. Ohio State Bar Assn., Columbus Bar Assn., Little Turtle Country Club (mems. coun. 1997-2000, pres. 1998-2000). Avocations: golf, Ohio history. Home: 288 E North Broadway Columbus OH 43214-4114 Office: Vorys Sater Seymour et al PO Box 1008 52 E Gay St Columbus OH 43215-3108 E-mail: tmmiller@vssp.com.

MILLER, THERESA L. library director; b. Port Huron, Mich., Apr. 2, 1959; d. David R. Miller and Mary Louise Preininger. AA, AS, St. Clair County C.C., Port Huron, Mich., 1990; BS, Wayne State U., 1992, MLIS, 1994. Support tutor St. Clair County C.C., 1988-89, master tutor, 1989-91; circulation supr. Baker Coll. of Port Huron, 1992-95, faculty math., 1998; pub. spkr. Mich., 1988—; investigative asst. Huffmaster Cos., Port Huron, 1998-2000; libr. dir. Baker Coll. of Pt. Huron, 1995—. Baker coll. rep. County Tech. Adv. Com., St. Clair County, 1997—; adv. bd. mem. Baker Coll. of PH Career Svcs., 1998—2001; judge Bus. Profs. of Am., St. Clair County, 1994—2000, Port Huron H.S. Writing Competition, 1997—. Editor: (newsletter) Baker Beacon, 1997; author: (newsletter) LUC News, 1993-96; author: (book) A Reference Librarians User Guide to the Internet, 1993. Recorder for the blind, Libr. of Mich., Lansing, 1996—; mem. gov. bd. Seaway Cmty. Freenet, St. Clair County, 1995-96; pres., founding bd. First Night of Port Huron, 2001—. Mem.: Internat. Libr. Support Group (founder 1999—, chmn.), Librs. Using Computers/Mich. (chair 1994—96), Mich. Libr. Assn., Optimists (Port Huron bd. dirs. 1997—99, pres. Pt. Huron chpt. 2000—01, lt. gov. Mich. 2001—03), Phi Theta Kappa (treas. 1989—90, founding alumni pres. St. Clair C.C. chpt. 1991). Avocations: profl. singing, jewelry collecting, auctions, theater, investing. Office: Baker Coll Port Huron Libr 3403 Lapeer Rd Port Huron MI 48060 E-mail: theresa.miller@baker.edu.

MILLER, THERESA VALENTINI, social worker, psychotherapist; b. N.Y.C., Nov. 23, 1951; d. Fermin George and Dorothy (Lindeborg) Valentini; m. Matthew Neil Miller, Oct. 25, 1981; children: Marisa, Elisabeth. BS, SUNY, Stony Brook, 1973; MSW, SUNY, Albany, 1975. Bd. cert. diplomate clin. social work Am. Bd. Examiners in Clin. Social Work. Med. social worker Nursing Sisters Home Vis. Svc., Bklyn., 1975-78, Meth. Hosp., Bklyn., 1978-82; psychotherapist 5th Ave. Ctr. for Counselling and Psychotherapy, N.Y.C., 1978-80; social work supr. Meth. Hosp., 1982-88; dir. social work Coney Island Hosp., Bklyn., 1988-92; pvt. practice psychotherapy, 1980—. Sch. social worker N.Y.C. Bd. Edn., 1999—. Bd. dirs. Park Slope Geriatric Day Ctr., Bklyn., 1988-97. Mem. NASW, Acad. Cert. Social Workers (cert. diplomate in clin. social work). Avocations: ice skating, gardening, art. Home: 10002 160th Ave Howard Beach NY 11414-3833

MILLER, THOMAS J. state attorney general; b. Dubuque, Iowa, Aug. 11, 1944; s. Elmer John and Betty Maude (Kross) Miller; m. Linda Cottington, Jan. 10, 1981; 1 child Matthew. BA, Loras Coll., Dubuque, 1966; JD, Harvard U., 1969. Bar: Iowa 1969. With VISTA, Balt., 1969—70; legis. asst. to U.S. rep. John C. Culver, 1970—71; legal edn. dir. Balt. Legal Aid Bur., part-time faculty U. Md. Sch. Law, 1971—73; pvt. practice McGregor, Iowa, 1973—78; city atty., 1973—79, Marquette; atty. gen. of Iowa, 1978—90, 1994—; ptnr. Faegre & Benson, Des Moines, 1991—95. Chmn. Microsoft case exec. com.; co-chmn. Airline Competition Working Group; pres. 2d Dist. New Dem. Club , Balt., 1972. Mem.: NAAG (pres. 1989—90, chmn. consumer protection, ins., budget, and antitrust coms., Wyman award 1990), ABA, Iowa Bar Assn., Common Cause. Roman Catholic. Office: Office of the Atty Gen Hoover State Office Bldg 1305 E Walnut St Des Moines IA 50319-0112*

MILLER, THOMAS EUGENE, lawyer, writer; b. Bryan, Tex., Jan. 4, 1929; s. Eugene Adam and Ella Lucille (Schroeder) M. BA, BS, Tex. A&M U., 1950; MA, U. Tex., 1956, JD, 1966; postgrad., U. Houston, 1956-58, U. Calif., 1983. Bar: Tex. 1966. Rsch. technician M.D. Anderson Hosp., Houston, 1956-58; claims examiner trainee Social Security Adminstrn., New Orleans, 1964; trademark examiner U.S. Patent and Trademark Office, Washington, 1966; editor Bancroft-Whitney Co., San Francisco, 1966-92. Author: (under pseudonym Millard Thomas) Home From 7-North, 1984; contbr. to numerous legal publs. Contbg. mem. Dem. Nat. Com., 1981—; mem. Celebrate Bryan Com. Mem. ABA, World Lit. Assn., World Inst. Achievement, United Writers Assn. India, Nat. Trust for Hist. Preservation, Tex. Bar Assn., African Wildlife Found., World Wildlife Fund, Internat. Platform Assn., Nat. Writers Assn., Scribes, Acad. Polit. Sci., Press Club, Commonwealth Club, Rotary Club (Paul Harris fellow, Found. fellow), Menninger Soc., Tex. A&M U. Faculty Club, Phi Kappa Phi, Psi Chi, Phi Eta Sigma. Methodist. Home: 101 N Haswell Dr Bryan TX 77803-4848 *Personal philosophy: Use your experience and abilities not only to understand life and to succeed, but also to help others' journeys through life.*

MILLER, THOMAS ROBBINS, lawyer, publisher; b. Chgo., Mar. 8, 1938; s. William Whipple and Helen (Robbins) M.; m. Tran Tuong Nhu, July 3, 1974; children: Toby, Teddy, Nathalie, Gabriella. BA, Yale U., 1960; LLB, Stanford U., 1965; cert., Parker Sch. Fgn. and Comparative Law, Columbia U., 1966. Bar: N.Y. 1966, Calif. 1974. Assoc. Webster & Sheffield, N.Y.C., 1965-68; sole practice, 1968-74, Berkeley, 1974-89; pub. Lancaster Miller Pubs., 1974-89; sr. ptnr. Miller & Ngo, PLC, Oakland, Calif., 1989—. Founder, pres. Internat. Children's Fund, Berkeley, 1974—; cons. Peace Corps, Washington, 1961, Ctr. for Constl. Rights, UNICEF, N.Y.C., 1973-76; dep. dir. Calif. Rural Legal Assistance, San Francisco, 1977-79. Named 1 of 10 Outstanding Young Men in U.S., U.S. Jaycees, 1974 Democrat. Office: 725 Washington St Oakland CA 94607-3924 E-mail: viasco@aol.com.

MILLER, THOMAS V. MIKE, JR. state legislator; b. Clinton, Md., Dec. 3, 1942; married; 5 children. BS, U. Md., 1964, JD, 1967. Mem. Ho. of Dels., 1971-75; atty.; mem. Dist. 27 Md. Senate, 1975—, pres., 1987—, co-chmn. legis. policy com., mem. rules and spending affordability com., mem. joint com. on legis. ethics, mem. adv. coun. lead poisoning, mem. Md. housing policy commn., mem. State House Trust, 1987—, mem. vet. home commn., 1987, mem. state commn. on capital city, 1987—. Mem. Md. 1992 Commn., 1989, Gov.'s Task Force on Trees and Forests, 1990—; pres. So. State Senate Leaders Conf., 1988; mem. Surratts, Brandywine, Nottingham, Ft. Washington and Upper Marlboro Dem. Clubs; pres. Senate Pres. Forum. Named Disting. Alumnus of Yr., U. Md., 1988, Outstanding Citizen, Prince George's County Bd. Trade, Outstanding Legislator, Md. Mcpl. League, Legislator of Yr. Md. Retailers Assn., 1998; recipient William P. Coliton Cmty. Svc. award Johns Hopkins U., Pub. Svc. award Local 400 AFL-CIO, Outstanding K.C. award, Bulger award for legis. excellence. Mem. ABA, Md. Bar Assn., Prince George's County Bar Assn. Office: State House, H-107 Annapolis MD 21401-1991*

MILLER, THOMAS WILLIAM, psychologist; b. Rochester, N.Y., Feb. 7, 1943; s. William J. Miller and Evelyn A. Weber; m. Jean Alderson, June 17, 1967; children: David T., Jeanine M. BS, St. John Fisher, Rochester, 1965; MS, U. Scranton, 1967; PhD, SUNY, Buffalo, 1971. Lic. clin. psychologist Ky., Mich., Pa., Conn. Psychologist Buffalo Psychiat. Ctr., 1965-70; asst. prof. Rosary Hill Coll., Williamsville, N.Y., 1970-74; v.p. student affairs Daemen Coll., Amherst, 1974-75; psychologist VA Med. Ctr., Buffalo, 1975-80, chief psychology svc. Lexington, Ky., 1980-96; prof. dept. psychiatry U. Ky., 1980—; prof. Murray (Ky.) State U., 1996—, U. Conn. Sch. Allied Health, 2000—. Vice-chmn. State Psychology Bd., Frankfort, Ky., 1983-86. Author: Stressful Life Events, 1989, Chronic Pain, 1990, Manual of Sexual Abuse, 1991, Clinical Handbook of Child Abuse, 1995, Theory and Assessment of Stressful Life Events, 1996, Clinical Disorders and Stressful Life Events, 1997, Children of Trauma, 1998, Clinical Handbook of Adult Exploitation and Abuse, 1998. Bd. dirs. Nat. Kidney Found., Lexington, 1982—, Big Bros. Big Sisters Calloway County; mem. exec. bd. Bluegrass coun. Boy Scouts Am., Lexington, 1983. Named Outstanding Alumnus, SUNY, Buffalo, 1988; recipient recognition award Ky. Dept. Human Resources, 1993, RHR Internat. award, 1996, Outstanding Psychologist award, 1997, Disting. VA Rsch. award, 1997, Rsch. Excellence award, 2000. Fellow Am. Psychol. Assn. (pres. dvsn. psychology in pub. svc.), Am. Psychol. Soc.; mem. Ky. Psychol. Assn. (pres. 1986), Assoc. VA Chief Psychologists (pres. 1985-89). Office: U of Conn School of Allied Hlth 358 Mansfield Rd U-101 Storrs Mansfield CT 06269-2101

MILLER, THORMUND AUBREY, lawyer; b. Pocatello, Idaho, July 14, 1919; s. Roy Edmund and Lillian (Thordarson) M.; m. Hannah A. Flansburgh, Feb. 10, 1946; children: Karen Lynette Van Gerpen, Christine Alison Westall. BA, Reed Coll., 1941; LLB, Columbia U., 1948; grad., Advanced Mgmt. Program, Harvard Bus. Sch., 1961. Bar: Calif. 1949, D.C. 1951, U.S. Supreme Ct. 1960. Assoc. McCutchen, Thomas, Matthews, Griffiths & Greene, San Francisco, 1948-50; atty. So. Pacific Transp. Co., Washington, 1950-56, asst. gen. atty., 1956-59, gen. atty., 1959-66, sr. gen. atty., 1966-75, gen. solicitor, 1975-79, gen. commerce counsel, 1979-83, dir., mem. exec. com., 1983-87, v.p., gen. counsel, 1983-89; gen. counsel So. Pacific Communications Co., 1970-79, dir., 1970-81; pvt. practice law Atherton, Calif., 1989-96. Pres. Wood Acres Citizens Assn., Bethesda, Md., 1955-56; mem. exec. com. Holbrook Palmer Recreation Park Found., 1979—, pres., 1982-84; bd. dirs. Atherton Civic Interest League, 1981—, pres., 1992-94; mem. Atherton Park and Recreation Commn., 1991-95; mem. alumni bd. Reed Coll., 1971-72, trustee, 1987-2002, campaign com., 1995-2000; bd. dirs. Assocs. of U. Calif. Press, 1994—; mem. San Mateo Civil Grand Jury, 1997. Lt. USNR, 1942-46. Mem. ABA, Calif. Bar Assn., World Trade Club. Presbyterian.

MILLER, TIMOTHY EARL, planning company executive; b. Johnstown, Pa., Dec. 21, 1952; s. Gene E. and Ives (Stibich) M.; m. Donna Marie Tiffany, Sept. 22, 1985. BS in Environ. Resource Mgmt., Pa. State U., 1974. Project mgr. Earth Metrics, Inc., Palo Alto, Calif., 1975-77; asst. dir. mktg. Environ. Sci. Assn., San Francisco, 1977-81; sr. planner Wagstaff-Brady, Berkeley, Calif., 1981-82; regional dir. ESA-Urbitran, N.Y.C., 1982-84; pres. Hudson Ptnrship., Inc., N.Y.C. and New Brunswick, N.J., 1984-86; prin., pres. Tim Miller Assocs., Inc., Cold Spring, N.Y., 1986—. Contbr. articles to profl. jours. Active Big Bros./ Big Sisters, San Francisco, 1980-82, Bklyn. Heights Assn., 1985-87. Mem. Am. Inst. Cert. Planners (cert.), Am. Planning Assn., N.Y. State planning Fedn., Regional Plan Assn., Urban Land Inst., Hudson Valley Builder's Assn. Democrat. Avocations: fishing, skiing, golf, basketball. Office: 10 North St Cold Spring NY 10516-3023

MILLER, TOMMY EUGENE, federal judge; b. 1948; BA, U. Va., 1970; JD, Coll. of William and Mary, 1973. Bar: Va. 1973, U.S. Dist. Ct. (ea. dist.) Va. 1973, U.S. Ct. Appeals (4th cir.), U.S. Supreme Ct. Asst. commonwealth's atty. Commonwealth of Va., Norfolk, 1974-80; asst. U.S. Atty. U.S. Dist. Ct. (ea. dist.) Va., 1980-87, magistrate judge, 1987—. Adj. prof. Coll. of William and Mary Law Sch., 1999—; mem. Jud. Conf. Adv. Com. on Criminal Rules. Office: US Courthouse 600 Granby St Ste 173 Norfolk VA 23510-1915 Fax: 757-222-7027.

MILLER, TONI M. ANDREWS, critical care nurse, educator; b. Webb City, Mo., July 20, 1949; d. John F. and Gettius M. (Short) Henry; div.; children: Bradley Ardrey, Mischa Andrews, Paul Andrews. ADN, Mo. So. Coll., Joplin, 1973, BSN, 1995. Cert. ACLS, TNCC. Asst. insvc. dir. Kirksville (Mo.) Osteo. Hosp., 1975-76; charge nurse, unit program supr. St. Louis Devel. Disabilities Treatment Ctr., 1983-85; clin. supr. ICU Oak Hill Osteo. Hosp., Joplin, 1986-95; emergency room/ICU nurse Fitzgibbon Hosp., Marshall, Mo., 1997, house supr., 1998, 2000—, primary nurse utilization rev. and patient edn., 1998-2000. Recipient Joseph P. Kennedy award, 1966. Mem. AACN. Home: 865 S Salt Pond Ave Apt 3C Marshall MO 65340-2566

MILLER, VALERIE CAROL, journalist; b. Chgo. d. V. Heinz and Arlene Elizabeth Miller. A in Gen. Studies, C.C. So. Nev.; BA Comms., U. Nev., 1998. Travel coord. Great Escape Travel, Las Vegas, 1996—97; staff writer, reporter U. Nev. Las Vegas Rebel Yell Students Newspaper, 1997—98; travel coord. World Travel and Accessories, Las Vegas, 1998—2000; reporter, freelance writer, intern Las Vegas Sun Newspaper, 1998—2000; broadcaster, disk jockey Sta. KLAV AM 1230, Las Vegas, 1997—; reporter, staff writer Las Vegas Bus. Press Newspaper, 2000—. Vol. Shade Tree Shelter, Las Vegas, 2002; vol. writer Nev. Times Newspaper, 1995, 1997. Recipient 2002 Small Bus. Journalist of Yr. award for Nev., U.S. Small Bus. Adminstrn., 2001, Best Feature Story 3rd place award, Nev. Press Assn., 2001. Fellow: Soc. for the Advanced Placement of Materials, Working in Comms., Soc. Profl. Journalists, 3rd Wave Nev., Tortois Group; mem.: Phi Lambda Eta. Avocations: traveling, writing poems and song lyrics, learning guitar, watching movies. Home: 613 Mosswood Dr Henderson NV 89015-8329 Office: Las Vegas Bus Press 1385 Pama Ln Ste 111 Las Vegas NV 89119

MILLER, VEL, artist; b. Nekoosa, Wis., Jan. 22, 1936; d. Clarence Alvin Krause and Celia Mae (Houston) Clark; m. Warren Eugene Miller, Apr. 30, 1955; children: Jennifer, Andrea, Matthew, Stuart. Student, Valley Coll., Art League L.A. Exhbns. include Stamford (Tex.) Art Found., Haley Libr., Midland, Tex., Peppertree Ranch, Santa Ynez, Calif., Mountain Oyster Club, Tucson, Cowboy Gathering, Paso Robles, Cattlemans Show, San Luis Obispo, Calif., West Lives On Gallery, Jackson, Wyo., Shared Visions Gallery, Boca Raton, Fla., Judith Hale Gallery, Los Olivos, Calif., Western Interpretations Gallery, Atascadero, Calif.; represented in permanent collections at Home Savings and Loan L.A., Glendale (Ariz.) Coll., Cavalry Mus., Samore, France; also pvt. collections. Recipient Best of Show award San Fernando Valley Art Club, San Gabriel Art Assn., Death Valley Invitational Show, numerous others. Mem. Am. Woman Artist (founder), Oil Painters Am. E-mail: velmiller@tcsn.net.

MILLER, VELVET G. healthcare administrator; b. Reading, Pa., Aug. 16, 1945; d. Louis L. and Pattee J. Miller; m. Calvin E. Davis, Sept. 14, 1991; 1 child Toby L. C. Davis. BSN, Wagner Coll., 1967; MEd, Temple U., 1976; MPA, Harvard U., 1984; PhD, Boston U., 1997. RN. Assoc. commr. Mass. Dept. Pub. Welfare, Boston, 1988-89, Mass. Dept. Health, Boston, 1989-91; v.p. Wagner Coll., S.I., 1991-92; Medicaid dir. N.J. Dept. Human Svcs., Trenton, 1994-96, dep. commr., 1996-98; exec. dir. Children's Futures N.J., Princeton, 1998-99; ptnr. Davis Miller Group, Trenton, 1991—; pres., CEO Horizon/Mercy, 2001—. Mem. adv. bd. Urban Inst., Washington, 1996—, Finding Common Ground, Columbia U., N.Y.C., 1997—. Co-author: (book) Renegotiating Healthcare, 1995 (ANA CPR inst. award, 1995, ANA CPR inst. award, 1996); contbr. articles and reports to profl. jours. Bd. dirs. FAmilies USA, Washington, 1993—99. Recipient Pub. Svc. award, N.J. Pub. Policy Rsch. Inst., 1998, Caballo award for excellence in pub. svc., Commonwealth of Mass., 1988. Fellow: Am. Acad. Nursing; mem.: ANA, APHA. Democrat. Presbyterian. Home: 219 Cornwall Ave Trenton NJ 08618-3321 Office: Horizon Mercy 275 Phillips Blvd Trenton NJ 08618 E-mail: dmg219@msn.com.

MILLER, VERNON DALLACE, minister; b. McClure, Ill., Sept. 27, 1932; s. Homer Lee and Marie Kathleen (White) M.; m. Alice Elizabeth Wright, July 25, 1954; children: Ronald, Philip, Elizabeth, Annette, Douglas. Student, Moody Bible Inst., 1950-53, S.E. Mo. State, 1954, So. Ill. U., 1956-57; BA, Cedarville Coll., 1963, LittD, 1988. Ordained to min. Bapt. Ch., McClure, 1953. Pastor Camp Creek Bapt. Ch., Murphysboro, Ill., 1953-54, Bible Fellowship Bapt. Ch., Carterville, 1954-57, Faith Bapt. Ch., Mattoon, 1957-60, Immanuel Bapt. Ch., Arcanum, Ohio, 1961-63; editor, bus. mgr. Regular Bapt. Press, Chgo., 1963-70; pres. Ch. Bldg. Cons., 1971-87; exec. editor, treas. Gen. Assn. of Regular Bapt. Chs., Schaumburg, 1987-97; min. christian edn. Berean Bapt. Ch., Portage, Mich., 2002—. Exec. bd. Awana Youth Assn., Streamwood, Ill., 1965-83, Grand Rapids (Mich.) Bapt. Coll. and Sem., 1981-91, Shepherds Bapt. Ministries, Union Grove, Wis., 1965-96. Editor: (mag.) The Baptist Bulletin, 1987-97. Del. Ill. Small Bus. Com., Springfield, Ill., 1984. Mem. Christian Ministries Mgmt. Assn. Republican.

MILLER, VICKIE GAIL, writer; b. Waco, Tex., Aug. 14, 1955; d. Selvia Miller and Irene Washington; children: Leroy Ellis III, Shamon Deondre, Shanna Shaneke, Taya Shante, Malcolm Jamal. Student, Midland (Tex.) Coll., 1973-77. Nurses aide, Odessa, Tex. Author: Doris Miller, 1997, A Long Road to Survive, 1997; creator WWI Doris Miller Action Figure doll, 2000.

MILLER, VINCENT PAUL, JR. geography and regional planning educator; b. Swissvale, Pa., May 11, 1932; s. Vincent Paul and May Eleanor Miller; m. Alida Field Ward, July 23, 1960; 1 child, Bradley Cleland. BS, Muskingum Coll., 1954; MS, Pa. State U., 1957; PhD, Mich. State U., 1970. Social sci. asst. Quartermaster R&D Comdt., Natick, Mass., 1957-59; instr. Coll. of Wooster, Ohio, 1959-60; asst. instr. Mich. State U., East Lansing, 1961; assoc. prof. Indiana (Pa.) U., 1962-70, prof., 1970-98, prof. emeritus, 1999—. Author: Project Ebenezer: Modeling Holistic Missions, 1981, Central Place Hierarchy & Access to Services, 1985; editor/author: The Future at the Bicentennial, 1977, Planning Issues in Marginal Areas, 1991, Technology, Landscape, and Arrested Development: Essays on the Geography of Marginality, 1997; editor: The Pa. Jr. Geographer, 1965-66, The Pa. Geographer, 1966-75. Dir. rsch. Ministries in Action, Miami, Fla., 1980—, dir. holistic curriculum devel., 1999—; bd. mem. Birthright, Indiana, United Ministry Indiana U. of Pa., pres. bd. 1997; mem. com. Diaconal Ministries Com., Kiskiminitas Presbytery, chair self-devel. of people com., 2002—; cons. Iona Study Ctr., Ministries in Action; co-founder PIMA (Planning Marginal Areas), 1989. Ctrl. Pl. Rsch. grantee, 1985, Travel grantee U. Presbyn. Ch., 1995. Mem. AAAS, Assn. Am. Geographers (bd. rural devel. splty. group 1984-88, sec. treas. 1984-86, pres. 1986-88), Assn. Pub. Justice, Pa. Geog. Soc. (pres. 1979-80), Soc. for Advancement of Scandinavian Studies, Sigma Xi (pres. Ind. chpt. 1977-78). Avocations: music, writing, photography, yard work. Home: 111 View St Indiana PA 15701-1547 Office: Indiana U of Pa Dept Geography & Regional Pl Indiana PA 15705-0001

MILLER, W. DENISE SAUNDERS, community health nurse; b. Camden, N.J., Feb. 28, 1954; d. John Francis and Mary Lou (Decker) Saunders; m. Irvin Miller, Aug. 29, 1987. Diploma, Del. Valley Acad., 1973; AAS, Mercer County C.C., 1978; BSN, SUNY, Albany, 1984. RN, N.J. Nurse clinician III, Deborah Heart & Lung Ctr., Browns Mills, N.J., 1978-81; charge nurse CCU, Zurbrugg Meml. Hosp., Riverside, 1981-82, clin. coord. ICU/CCU Willingboro, 1982-84; asst. head nurse MICU, Fawcett Meml. Hosp., Port Charlotte, Fla., 1984-86; part-time staff nurse ICU, Venice (Fla.) Hosp., 1986-89; paramed. ins. nurse examiner Port Charlotte, 1987-92; clin. dir. Nursefinders, 1992-94; dir. staff edn. Housecall Home Health, Sarasota, Fla., 1994-95, dir. staff devel. and tng. Port Charlotte, Ft. Myers, 1995-96, clin. care mgr., 1996-97; staff devel. coord. DeSoto Mem. Home Health, Arcadia, 1998; care mgr. Shore Care Home Health, Somers Point, N.J., 1999—. Instr. intravenous therapy Deborah Heart & Lung Ctr., 1980; instr. BCLS Zurbrugg Meml. Hosp., 1981-84; ACLS provider Am. Heart Assn., Burlington County, N.J., 1979-84, BCLS instr., 1980-84; citizen advisor Sta. WBBH-TV, Ft. Myers, 1987-89; pres. Charlotte County Home Health Network, 1993-94. Pres. S.W. Lupus Found. of Fla., Port Charlotte, 1992; active Arthritis Found., Juvenile Diabetes Found.; edn. chairperson Charlotte County Home Health Network, 1995-96; membership chairperson Charlotte Elder Affairs Network, 1993. Mem. VFW Aux., 42d Rainbow Divsn. Aux. Republican. Methodist. Avocations: fishing, ballroom dancing, theater, reading, antiquing. Home: 4719 Boxwood Pl Mays Landing NJ 08330-2820 Office: Shore Care Home Health 1 New York Ave Somers Point NJ 08244 E-mail: dsmrn@yahoo.com.

MILLER, W. MARSHALL, II, insurance broker; b. Roanoke, Va., Feb. 3, 1953; s. Warren M. and Anne (Cooper) M; m. Paige Timberlake. BA, Coll. William and Mary, 1975. CLU, ChFC. Spl. agt. Prudential Ins. Co., Newport News, Va., 1976—; owner and pres. Ins. Consultants of Va., Inc., 1979—. Mem. Soc. Fin. Svc. Profls., Advanced Assn. Life Underwriters, Internat. Assn. Fin. Planners, Peninsula Estate Planning Coun., Peninsula Chartered Life Underwriters (v.p. 1982-83), PRUSER Group, Million Dollar Round Table. Lutheran. Avocations: golf, photography, travel, gardening, bridge. Office: Ins Consultants of Va Inc 825 Diligence Dr Ste 201 Newport News VA 23606-4272 E-mail: marshall@insurance-icv.com.

MILLER, WALKER DAVID, judge; m. Susanne Hauk; 3 children. LLB, U. Colo., 1963; M in Comparative Law, U. Chgo., 1965. Bar: Colo., 1963. Asst. prof. Sch. Law, U. Kans., Lawrence, 1966-69; ptnr. Miller & Ruyle, Greeley, Colo., 1969, Miller, Ruyle, Steinmark & Shade, Greeley, 1970-74; solo practice, Colo., 1974-92; ptnr. Karowsky, Witwer, Miller and Oldenburg, 1992-96; judge U.S. Dist. Ct. Colo., Denver, 1996—. Office: US Dist Ct Colo 1929 Stout St Rm C-530 Denver CO 80294-1929

MILLER, WALTER EDWARD, physical scientist, researcher; b. St. Johns, Ariz., Oct. 15, 1936; s. Walter Edward and Geraldine Marie (Sides) M.; m. Emma Lee Nelson, June 10, 1960; children: Carol Lynn, Brenda Kay Miller Flowers, Melissa Joy Johnson Williams. BS in Natural Sci. magna cum laude, Bethany Nazarene Coll., 1958; postgrad., Vanderbilt U., 1958-59, U. Ala., 1964-69. Cert. math. tchr., Tenn. Aviator, flight leader USMC, 1959-64; math. tchr. Trevecca High Sch., Nashville, 1958-59; physicist Electromagnetics Lab U.S. Army Missile Command, Redstone Arsenal, Ala., 1964-68; rsch. physicist RD & E Ctr. Army Missile Command, 1968-90, supr., phys. scientist, 1991-99; sr. electro-optics cons. Dynetics, Inc., Huntsville, 1999—. Quality control chemist S.W. Fertilizer Mfg., Bethany, Okla., 1957-58; tech. cons. D-7 panel NATO, Brussels, 1972, 4 power working group, Paris, 1983; test dir. Joint U.S.-German Laser Expt., Graffenwoehr, 1979; prin. investigator Hypervelocity Missile/LOSAT, Advanced Sensors, U.S. Army Missile Command, Redstone Arsenal, 1984-94; mem. Tri-Svc. Working Group U.S. Experts on optical guidance, 1986-96; mem. long term sci. study on combat ID, panel 1 NATO Def. Rsch. Group, 1994-95. Contbr. numerous articles to scholarly and profl. jours.; patentee 33 U.S. and 3 fgn. patents, 3 patents pending. Speaker, mem. Gideons Internat., 1980—; mem. governing bd. Mastin Lake Nazarene Ch., 1975-99. Capt. USMC, 1960-64, Cuba. Recipient Svc. award Mastin Lake Nazarene Ch., 1985, Army-wide R & D award, 1968, 74, 83. Mem. Phi Delta Lambda. Achievements include research in U.S. laser beam rider missile guidance (principal investigator), 1970-85; development of TOW2 missile IR guidance, 1976-79, TOW2B remote target sensor, 1985-90, laser guidance for hypervelocity missile, 1989-94, very low cost SCATTER-RIDER guidance technique, 1993-98, and miniature 3-D LADAR Seeker, 1997-99, Micro-Missile Tech., 1998-99. Office: Dynetics Inc PO Box 5500 Huntsville AL 35814-5500 E-mail: ednemma@hotmail.com.

MILLER, WALTER JAMES, English and humanities educator, writer; b. McKee City, N.J., Jan. 16, 1918; s. Walter Theodore and Celestia Anna (Simmons) Miller; children: Naomi, Jason, Robin, Jared, Elizabeth. BA, CUNY, 1941; MA, Columbia U., 1952. Instr. English Poly. Inst. Brooklyn, N.Y., 1946-53, asst. prof., 1953-55; asst. prof. English and modern langs. Colo. State U., Ft. Collins, 1955-56; assoc. prof. English NYU, N.Y.C., 1958-66, prof. English, 1966-84, prof. emeritus, 1984—. Dir. Summer Writers Conf. Hofstra U., Hempstead, N.Y., 1972-79, NYU, N.Y.C., 1983-85. Author: Engineers as Writers, 1953, Making an Angel: Poems, 1977, 1001 Ideas for English Papers, 1994, Love's Mainland: New and Selected Poems, 2001, Joseph in the Pit: A Verse Drama, 2002; author, translator: Annotated Jules Verne, 1995; editor, translator: Verne's 20,000 Leagues Under the Sea, 1993; contbg. editor Simon and Schuster, 1969-97. Recipient Spl. award, Engrs. Coun. Profl. Devel., 1966, Charles Angoff award, The Lit. Rev., 1983, Gt. Tchr. award, NYU Alumni Assn., 1980, Fisher Second Harvest award, CUNY Alumni Assn., 1997; fellow, Ruttenberg Found., 1999—2002. Democrat. Office: NYU 50 W 4th St Rm 330 New York NY 10012-1165 E-mail: wjm2@nyu.edu.

MILLER, WALTER LUTHER, pediatrician, educator; b. Alexandria, Va., Feb. 21, 1944; s. Luther Samuel and Beryl (Rinderle) M. SB, MIT, 1965; MD, Duke U., 1970. Diplomate Am. Bd. Pediatrics. Intern, then resident Mass. Gen. Hosp., Boston, 1970-72; staff assoc. NIH, Bethesda, Md., 1972-74; sr. resident U. Calif., San Francisco, 1974-75, rsch. fellow, 1975-78, asst. prof. pediatrics, 1978-83, assoc. prof., 1983-87, prof., 1987—, dir. Child Health Rsch. Ctr., 1992—, faculty biomed. scis. grad. program, 1982—, faculty genetics grad. program, 1998—, assoc. prof. metabolic rsch. unit, 1983-87, prof., 1987—, chief divsn. endocrinology, 2000—. Editor DNA and Cell Biology Jour., 1983—; mem. editl. bds. numerous sci. jours.; contbr. articles to profl. jours. Del. Dem. Nat. Conv., N.Y.C., 1976. Served with USPHS, 1972-74. Recipient Nat. Rsch. Svc. award NIH, 1975, Clin. Investigator award, 1978, Albion O Bernstein award N.Y. Med. Soc., 1993, Clin. Endocrinology Trust medal Brit. Endocrine Soc., 1993, Henning Andersen prize European Soc. Pediatric Endocrinology, 1993, Samuel Rosenthal Found. prize for excellence in acad. pediatrics, 1999. Fellow: AAAS, Molecular Medicine Soc.; mem.: Lawson Wilkins Pediat. Endocrine Soc. (edn. com. 1992—96, coun. 1995—96, corp. adv. bd. 1998—2002), Am. Soc. Clin. Investigation, Am. Soc. Human Genetics, Endocrine Soc. (fin. com. 1999—2002, Edwin B. Astwood lecture award 1988), We. Soc. Pediat. Rsch. (Ross Rsch. award 1982), European Soc. for Paediatric Endocrinology (hon.), Japanese Soc. for Pediat. Endocrinology (hon.), Soc. Pediat. Rsch., Am. Pediat. Soc., Am. Acad. Pediats., Assn. Am. Physicians, Am. Soc. for Microbiology, Theta Delta Chi. Office: U Calif Med Ctr Dept Pediat 1466 4th Ave San Francisco CA 94122-2656

MILLER, WALTER NEAL, insurance company consultant; b. N.Y.C., Nov. 26, 1929; s. Morton and Kathryn (Gersten) M.; m. Nancy Louise Clapp, Sept. 11, 1954; children— Scott, Timothy, David, Kathryn Wallace, Amy Tully. BA, Swarthmore Coll., 1951. With N.Y. Life Ins. Co., N.Y.C., 1951-86; v.p., actuary Prudential Ins. Co., Newark, 1986-93; sr. v.p., chief actuary Prudential Preferred Fin. Svcs., Liberty Corner, N.J., 1993-94; pvt. practice cons., 1994—. Author: (with others) Analysis of Actuarial Theory for Variable Life Insurance, 1969; contbr. (with others) articles to profl. jours. Mem. Soc. Actuaries (bd. dirs.), Am. Acad. Actuaries (bd. dirs., v.p.), Actuarial Stds. Bd. (chmn.). Home: 48 Eagle Ridge Dr Essex CT 06426-1370 E-mail: walterm746@aol.com.

MILLER, WALTER RICHARD , JR. banker; b. N.Y.C., Nov. 20, 1934; s. Walter Richard and Ann M. (Phelan) M.; m. Joan M. Groark; children: Kathryn A., Margaret E., Jennifer M., Walter Richard III. AB, Dartmouth Coll., 1955; MBA, Columbia U., 1957; PhD, NYU, 1965. Dir. mktg., v.p. Mellon Nat. Corp., Pitts., 1965-78; sr. v.p. First Atlanta Corp., 1979-81; exec. v.p. Norwest Corp., Mpls., 1981-86; pres., chief exec. officer First Constn. Fin. Corp., New Haven, 1987-91, also bd. dirs.; pres., CEO First Constn. Bank, 1987-90; pres. Fin. Mktg. and Planning Co., Whitneyville, Conn., 1990—. Exec.-in-residence Quinnipiac Coll., 1990-91, prof. fin. and mktg., 1991-95; pres. CIRRUS Sys., Inc.; exec. dir. Wright Investors' Svc., Milford, Conn., 1995—. Contbr. articles, chpts. to profl. pubs. Bd. dirs. St. Paul Chamber Orch., Minn. Pub. Radio, Sci. Mus. Minn., Quinnipiac Coll., Hamden, Conn., Quinnipiac Coun. Boy Scouts Am., The Mus. of AM. Theatre; chmn. bd. Orchestra New England. With USAF, 1958. Teaching fellow NYU, N.Y.C., 1960; Ford Found. fellow NYU, 1962 Mem. Interbank Card Assn. (internat. chmn., bd. dirs.), Am. Mktg. Assn. (contbg. editor), Bank Mktg. Assn. (bd. dirs., chmn. mktg. planning council, chmn. mktg. mgmt. council), Somerset Club, New Haven County Club, Quinnipiack Club, Lawn Club. Home and Office: 470 Whitney Ave Apt B1 New Haven CT 06511

MILLER, WARREN LLOYD, lawyer; b. Bklyn., July 18, 1944; s. Allan and Ella Miller; m. Jana Lee Morris, May 13, 1978; children: Lindsey Beth, Alan Gregory, William Brett. BA with high honor, Am. U., 1966; JD with honors, George Washington U., 1969. Bar: Va., 1969, D.C., 1969, U.S. Supreme Ct., 1981. Law clk. to Hon. Edward A. Beard Superior Ct. D.C., 1968-69; asst. U.S. atty. for D.C., 1969-74; ptnr. Stein, Miller & Brodsky, 1974-85; pres. Warren L. Miller, P.C., 1986—; of counsel Reed, Smith, Shaw & McClay, 1986-93. Lectr. Georgetown U. Law Sch., 1970-71, Am. U., 1971-72; guest spkr. various radio & TV programs and legal forums; mem. Jud. Conf. D.C. Cir., 1984—; pres. Asst. U.S. Attys. Assn. of D.C., 1983-84. Contbr. articles to profl. jours. Parliamentarian credentials and rules coms. Rep. Nat. Conv., 1984; mem. D.C. Law Revision Commn., 1987-91 (apptd. by Pres. Reagan), mem. U.S. Commn. for Preservation of Am.'s Heritage Abroad, 1992— (apptd. by Pres. Bush, reapptd. by Pres. Clinton 1996, 99), now chmn. (apptd. by Pres. Bush) 2001—; bd. dirs. Found. for Buchenwald and Mittelbau-Dora Memls., 1994—; spkr. ceremonies commemorating 50th anniversary of liberation of Buchenwald Concentration Camp, Buchenwald, Germany, 1995, Ceremony Dedicating Little Camp Meml., Buchenwald, Germany, 2002; spkr. U.S. Holocaust Meml. Mus., 1995, 2002; fundraiser for Rep. Nat. Com. and Pres. Bush, 1988-92; co-chmn. dinner for V.P. Bush, 1988; vice-chmn. Pres.'s Dinner, 1989; co-chmn. Pres.'s Club, Washington, 1990-92; chmn. fundraiser for U.S. Senator Christopher Bond, 1992, 97; chmn., fundraiser U.S. Senator John Warner, 1996; vice-chmn., fundraiser Senator Bob Dole, 1996; co-chmn., fundraiser Gov. George W. Bush Presdl. Exploratory Com., 1999, mem. host com., fundraiser for Gov. George W. Bush, 2000, U.S. Sen. John Warner, 2001, Gov. Jeb Bush, 2002. Mem. Congl. Country Club (Bethesda, Md.), Phi Delta Phi, Omicron Delta Kappa, Pi Gamma Mu. Office: 2300 N St NW Washington DC 20037-1122

MILLER, WAYNE, actor, designer, producer, impresario; b. N.Y.C., Apr. 5, 1951; s. Charles E. and Agnes (Dunigan) M.; m. Donna D'Ermilio, Dec. 30, 1979. Pres. Carriage Trade, Inc., Howell, N.J., 1984-95; prin. Stage Door Theatrical, S.I., N.Y., 1991—. Scenic and lighting designer, N.Y.C., 1976—; dir. Snug Harbor Cultural Ctr., 1998—; pres. lighting designer Staten Island Shakespearean Theatre, 1996—. Acting roles include (cable TV show) Walking the Dog, 1990, Cranial Crunch, 1998-01, (TV show) Guiding Light, 1984, (classical play) Richard III, 1984, Macbeth, 1984, (mus. play) Anything Goes, 1985, Annie, 1986, La Cage Aux Folles, 1988, Showboat, 1988, Mame, 1989, Chicago, 1990, 42d St., 1990, Love Letters, 1993, Mr. Roberts, 1994, Mack and Mabel, 1994, All My Sons, 1995, Laughter on the 23d Floor, 1996; scenic and lighting designer Oklahoma, 1984, On Borrowed Time, 1985, Carousel, 1986, Is There Life After High Sch., 1988, Chicago, 1995, The Miser, 1995, The Crucible, 1996, The Blue Angel, 1998, also concerts and revs.; prodr. The Blue Angel, N.Y. premier, 1998. V.p. S.I. Civic Theatre, 1984-89; bd. dirs. S.I. Coun. on Arts, 1988. Mem. Snug Harbor Cultural Ctr., N.Y.C. Opera Guild. Home: 208 Kissel Ave Staten Island NY 10310-1669

MILLER, WAYNE CLAYTON, student services administrator, notary public; b. Columbus, Ohio, Feb. 23, 1949; s. Eugene H. and Beulah M. (Stoll) M. BA, Owosso Coll., 1971; MA, Mich. State U., 1979. Mgr. adminstrv. svcs. John Wesley Coll., Owosso, Mich., 1972-75, instr., social sci., 1975-78, dir., career planning, 1978-79; acad. advisor Spring Arbor (Mich.) Coll., 1979-81, instr., history, 1979-81; acad. counselor Franklin U., Columbus, 1981-83, asst. dir. acad. advising, 1983-85, dir., acad. advising, 1985-92, instr. Film Appreciation, 1985—, asst. dir., student svcs., 1992-97, dir., student svcs., 1997-2000, asst. v.p. student svcs., 2000—. Advisor Franklin U. Student Senate, Columbus, 1982-84; inst. creative activities program Ohio State U., Columbus, 1990-98; discussion panelist Educable TV-25 Worl d Film Classics series, 1990—; juror social issues category The Columbus Internat. Film and Video Festival, 1994, chair edn. category, 1995—; mem. spkrs. bur. Franklin U. Editor: (newsletter) New Directions, 1985-91; assoc. editor: Movies on Media Handbook. Bd. trustees Film Coun. of Greater Columbus; co-host: Columbus Museum of Art Film series, 1996; scholar, researcher Westerville Civic Symphony, 1997, competition judge Future Bus. Leaders of Am. State Conf. 1997—; judge Miss East-Ctrl. Ohio Scholarship program, 2000, Bus. and Profl. Women of Ohio State Speakoff Competition, 2001, Miss Mansfield Ohio Scholarship Program, 2001. Named one of Outstanding Young Men in Am., 1982, 85. Mem. Nat. Acad. Advising Assn. (cert. of merit award 1986, Outstanding Instnl. Advising award 1994), Nat. Film Soc. (life), Nat. Nominating com. 1997 Outstanding Young Women Am. and Young Men Am., Am. Film Inst., Ohio Coll. Pers. Assn., Ohio Notary Assn., Nat. Euchre Players Assn. (dir. adminstrn.), Columbus Kiwanis (chair career guidance com.), Future Bus. Leaders Am., Phi Beta Lambda. Avocations: film studies, history, Sherlock Holmes memorabilia, charitable activites, playing cards. Home: 2729 Brittany Oaks Blvd Hilliard OH 43026-8575 Office: Franklin U 201 S Grant Ave Columbus OH 43215-5399

MILLER, WILBUR HOBART, business diversification consultant; b. Boston, Feb. 15, 1915; s. Silas Reuben and Muriel Mae (Greene) M.; m. Harriett I. Harmon, June 20, 1941; children: Nancy Iber Miller Harray, Warren Harmon, Donna Sewall Miller Davidge. BS, U. N.H., 1936, MS, 1938; PhD, Columbia U., 1941. Rsch. chemist Am. Cyanamid Co., Stamford, Conn., 1941-49, Washington tech. rep., 1949-53, dir. food industry devel., 1953-57, tech. dir. products for agr. Cyanamid Internat. N.Y.C., 1957-60; sr. scientist Dunlap & Assos., Darien, Conn., 1960-63, sr. assoc., 1963-66; coord. new product devel. Celanese Corp., N.Y.C., 1966-67, mgr. comml. rsch., 1967-68, dir. corp. devel., 1969-84; bus. diversification cons., 1984—. Lectr. on bus. and soc. Western Conn. State Coll., 1977-79. Contbr. sci. papers to profl. jours.; patentee in field. Chmn. Stamford Forum for World Affairs, 1954-87, hon. chmn., 1987—; mem. adv. bd. Ctr. for Study of Presidency, 1980-99; bd. dirs. Stamford Symphony, 1974-80, v.p., 1978-80; bd. dirs. Stamford Hist. Soc., 1988, v.p., 1991-92, pres., 1993-95; pres. Coun. for Continuing Edn. Stamford, 1963, bd. dirs., 1960-70; elder United Presbyn. Ch., nominating com., 1960-63; pres. Interfaith Coun. of Stamford, 1973; internat. fellow U. Bridgeport, 1985-88; mem. pres.'s coun. U. N.H., 1982—; bd. dirs. Stamford Sr. Ctr., 1997—, vice chmn., 2002—. Recipient outstanding achievement award Coll. Tech., U. N.H., 1971, Am. Design award, 1948, Golden Rule Award J.C. Penney & Co., 1986; Univ. fellow Columbia U., 1940-41. Fellow AAAS, Am. Inst. Chemists (councillor N.Y. chpt. 1984-85); mem. Am. Chem. Soc. (news svc. adv. bd., 1948-53), N.Y. Acad. Scis., Société de Chimie Industrielle (v.p. fin. Am. sect. 1980-84, dir. 1984—), Inst. Food Tech., Soc. for Internat. Devel., Am. Acad. Polit. and Social Scis., Stamford Hist. Soc., Chemists Club (N.Y.C., treas. 1982-84), Sigma Xi, Alpha Chi Sigma, Phi Kappa Phi. Home: 122 Palmers Hill Rd #1111 Stamford CT 06902-2134

MILLER, WILBUR RANDOLPH, university educator and administrator; b. Elsberry, Mo., Nov. 12, 1932; s. Charles Clifton and Pauline Jean (Dryden) M. Student, SE Mo. U., 1951-53; BEd, U. Mo., 1954, MEd, 1955, EdD, 1960. Cert. secondary tchr., Mo. Tchr. indsl. arts Hazelwood Sch. Dist., St. Louis, 1955-56, U. Lab. Sch., Columbia, Mo., 1956-60; indsl. tchr. educator Purdue U., West Lafayette, Ind., 1960-63; asst. prof. U. Mo., Columbia, 1963-67, assoc. prof. and chmn. dept. coll. edn., 1967-76, prof. and assoc. dean coll. edn., 1976-86, dean coll. edn., 1986-91, prof., dean emeritus, 1992; cons. Rep. of Turkey, 1993, 94; v.p. for devel. Auburn U., 1996—. Chmn. adv. coun. Fed. Rsch. Ctr. in Vocat. Edn., Ohio State U., Columbus, 1981-84; internat. edn. cons. 1992—; edn. adv. bd. DeVry Inc., Oakwood Terrace, Ill., 1986—; mem. pvt. post-sec. tech. sch. accreditation commn. Accrediting Commn. Career Schs. and Colls. Tech., 1994-98. Author: Teaching Children Through Construction Activities, 1985, Instructors and Their Jobs, 1998, The Golf Primer, 1991, Handbook for College Teaching, 1997; editor: (series) Basic Industrial Arts, 1978; contbr. more than 40 articles to profl. jours. Pres., bd. dirs. Lenoir Inc., Columbia, 1977-84; mem. Woodhaven Sch. Bd., Columbia, 1982-83. With USNR, 1955-63. Recipient U. Mo. Faculty/Alumni award, 1985. Mem. Nat. Assn. Indsl. Tchr. Educators (pres., officer 1965-74), Am. Indsl. Arts Assn. (v.p. 1980), Mo. Vocat. Assn. (pres. 1974-75), Mo. Assn. Colls. for Tchr. Edn. (pres. 1987-90), Am. Vocat. Assn. (Outstanding Svc. award 1979), U. Mo. Faculty Club (officer 1977-82), Kiwanis. Mem. Christian Ch. (Disciples Of Christ). Avocations: golf, travel, home maintenance. Office: PO Box 2683 Auburn AL 36831-2683

MILLER, WILLARD, JR. mathematician, educator; b. Ft. Wayne, Ind., Sept. 17, 1937; s. Willard and Ruth (Kemerly) Miller; m. Jane Campbell Scott, June 5, 1965; children: Stephen, Andrea. S.B. in Math., U. Chgo., 1958; PhD in Applied Math. U. Calif.-Berkeley, 1963. Vis. mem. Courant Inst. Math. Scis., NYU, 1963-65; mem. faculty U. Minn., 1965—, prof. math., 1972—, head Sch. Math., 1978-86; co-prin. investigator Inst. Math. and its Applications, 1980-94, assoc. dir., 1987-94, dir., 1997—2001; assoc. dean Inst. of Tech., 1994-97; acting dean Inst. of Tech., 1995. Author: Lie Theory and Special Functions, 1968, Symmetry Groups and Their Applications, 1972, Symmetry and Separation of Variables, 1977; assoc. editor Jour. Math. Physics, 1973-75, Applicable Analysis, 1978-90. Mem. AAAS, Soc. Indsl. and Applied Math. (mng. editor Jour. Math. Analysis 1975-81), Am. Math. Soc., Sigma Xi. Home: 4508 Edmund Blvd Minneapolis MN 55406-3629 Office: Univ Minn Sch Math Minneapolis MN 55455

MILLER, WILLIAM, library administrator; b. Phila., Jan. 9, 1947; s. Julius and Norma (Frank) M.; m. Anne Hendry Hickok, July 20, 1983; children: Jessica, Miriam. BA, Temple U., 1968; PhD, U. Rochester, 1974; MLS, U. Toronto, Ontario, Canada, 1976. Reference libr. Albion (Mich.) Coll., 1976-80; head reference and govt. documents Mich. State U. Libr., East Lansing, Mich., 1980-84; assoc. dean of librs. Bowling Green (Ohio) State U., 1984-87; dir. librs. Fla. Atlantic U., Boca Raton, 1987—. Editor: College Librarianship, 1981, Academic Research on the Internet: Options for Scholars and Libraries, 2001; contbr. articles to profl. jours. Recipient Ontario Libr. Assn. Prize, Toronto, 1976, Libr. Instrn. Grant, Earlham Coll., Nat. Sci Found., 1978. Mem. ALA (chair editorial bd. Choice mag. 1980-82, other offices), Assn. Coll. and Rsch. Librs. (pres. 1996-97). Home: 8595 Brody Way Boca Raton FL 33433-7647 Office: Fla Atlantic U Libr PO Box 3092 Boca Raton FL 33431-0992 E-mail: miller@fau.edu.

MILLER, WILLIAM RICHEY, JR. lawyer; b. Oklahoma City, Apr. 4, 1947; s. William Richey and Edna Rosalind (Nielsen) M.; m. Susan Hammond, Aug. 2, 1970; children: Brooke, Karen. BA, Pomona Coll., Claremont, Calif., 1969; MA, Claremont Grad. Sch., 1972; JD, Lewis and Clark Coll., 1975. Bar: Oreg. 1975, U.S. Dist. Ct. Oreg. 1976, U.S. Ct. Appeals (9th cir.) 1976. Staff atty. Oreg. Ct. Appeals, Salem, 1975-76; with firm Griffith, Bittner, Abbott & Roberts, Portland, Oreg., 1976-83; ptnr. Davis Wright Tremaine, 1983—. Adj. prof. Lewis and Clark Law Sch., 1975-78. Bd. dirs. Portland Civic Theatre, 1988-91, Am. Lung Assn. Oreg., Portland, 1985-88, Oreg. Bus. Com. for the Arts, Portland, 1991-93. Mem. Oreg. State Bar (sect. chair 1990-91), Comml. Fin. Assn., Oreg. Bankers Assn., Lewis and Clark Alumni Assn. (bd. dirs. 1989-92). Presbyterian. Home: 843 Lakeshore Rd Lake Oswego OR 97034-3704 Office: Davis Wright Tremaine 1300 SW 5th Ave Ste 2300 Portland OR 97201-5682

MILLER, WILLIAM ALVIN, clergyman, author, lecturer; b. Pitts., Jan. 1, 1931; s. Christ William and Anna Ernestine (Wilhelm) M.; m. Marilyn Mae Miller, Aug. 8, 1953; children: Mark William, Eric Michael. BA, Capital U., 1953; MDiv, Luth. Theol. Sem., Columbus, Ohio, 1957; MST, Andover Newton Theol. Sch., Newton Centre, Mass., 1958, D of Ministry, 1974. Ordained to ministry Luth. Ch.; lic. marriage & family therapist, Minn.; cert. chaplain Assn. of Profl. Chaplains. Pastor St. James Luth. Ch., Balt., 1958—66; chaplain Fairview Hosp., Mpls., 1966—73, dir. dept. religion & health, 1973—87; instr. Fairview Sch. Nursing, 1967—75, Luther Northwestern Theol. Sem., St. Paul, 1973—85; pres. Woodland Pub. Co., Wayzata, 1979—2000; dir. Woodland Pastoral Assocs., Mpls., 1987—96; assoc. pastor Cen. Luth. Ch., 1989—94. Chair bd. dirs. Luth. Social Svcs. Md., Balt., 1963-65; adminstr. Dialogue 88, Mpls., 1987-88; marriaage & family therapist emeritus, Minn. Author: Why Do Christians Break Down?, 1973, Big Kids' Mother Goose, 1976, When Going to Pieces Holds You Together, 1976, You Count, You Really Do!, 1976, Mid Life, New Life, 1978, Conversations, 1980, Make Friends With Your Shadow, 1981, Prayers at Mid Point, 1983, The Joy of Feeling Good, 1986, Your Golden Shadow, 1989, 91, Meeting the Shadow, 1991; assoc. editor Jour. Pastoral Care, Decatur, Ga., 1984-88, editl. cons., 1988—; contbr. articles to profl. jours. Chaplain, Jr. C. of C., Randallstown, Md., 1962-64; bd. dirs. Am. Protestant Health Assn., Schaumburg, Ill., 1983-89; clin. mem. Am. Assn. Marriage & Family Therapy, 1989-96, Minn. Assn. Marriage & Family Therapy, 1989-96. Fellow Coll. Chaplains (pres. 1985-87), Assn. Mental Health Clergy (Anton T. Boisen award 1989); mem. Assn. Clin. Pastoral Edn. (supr. emeritus 2000—), Am. Assn. Marriage and Family Therapy, Minn. Assn. Marriage and Family Therapy. Avocations: cabinetmaking, publishing, construction. Home and Office: 2005 Xanthus Ln N Minneapolis MN 55447-2053

MILLER, WILLIAM CHARLES, theological librarian, educator; b. Mpls., Oct. 26, 1947; s. Robert Charles and Cleithra Mae (Johnson) M.; m. Brenda Kathleen Barnes, July 24, 1969; children: Amy Renee, Jared Charles. BA, Ind. Wesleyan U., 1968; MLS, Kent State U., 1974, PhD, 1983; postgrad., U. Kans., 1984; MA in Religious Studies, Ctrl. Bapt. Theol. Sem., 1988; MBA, MidAm. Nazarene U., Olathe, KS, 1997; STM, Nashotah House, 2001. Ordained to ministry Ch. of Nazarene, 1986. Libr. technician Kent State U., 1972-74; catalog libr. Mt. Vernon Nazarene Coll., Ohio, 1974-76, catalog and acquisitions libr., 1976-78; dir. libr. svcs., prof. theol. bibliography Nazarene Theol. Sem., Kansas City, Mo., 1978—, dean for adminstrn., 1996-98, 99—. Adj. rsch. assoc. U. Kans., 1984-85; adj. prof. MidAm. Nazarene U., Olathe, Kans., 1994-2000; bd. dirs. Small Libr. Computing Inc.; pres. Mo. Libr. Network Corp., St. Louis, Mo., 1998-2001. Author: Holiness Works: A Bibliography, 1986; editor TUG Newsletter, 1984-87, bd. dirs., 1985-88; editor Jour. Religious and Theol. Info., 1990-98. With U.S. Army, 1968-72. Mem. ALA, Am. Assn. Higher Edn., Assn. Study Higher Edn., Bibliog. Soc. Am., Bibliog. Soc. London, Kansas City Met. Libr. Network (coun. mem. 1987-89), Am. Theol. Libr. Assn. (bd. dirs. 1985-88), Kansas City Theol. Libr. Assn. (pres. 1985-89), Wesleyan Theol. Soc., Ch. Eng. Record Soc., Beta Phi Mu. Home: 18290 W 155th Ter Olathe KS 66062-6718 Office: Nazarene Theol Sem 1700 E Meyer Blvd Kansas City MO 64131-1246 E-mail: wcmiller@nts.edu.

MILLER, WILLIAM CHARLES, lawyer; b. Jacksonville, Fla., Aug. 6, 1937; s. Charles and Mary Elizabeth (Kiger) M.; m. Hadmut Gisela Larsen, June 10, 1961; children: Monica Lee, Charles Andreas. BA, Washington and Lee U., 1958, LLB, 1961; LLM, NYU, 1963; postgrad., Harvard U., 1978. Bar: Fla. 1961, Calif. 1984, Ind. 1987, U.S. Supreme Ct. 1968. Counsel to electrochem., elastomers and internat. depts. E.I. duPont de Nemours & Co., Wilmington, Del., 1963-66; counsel S. Am. ops. Bristol-Myers Co., N.Y.C., 1967-69; internat. counsel Xerox Corp., Stamford, Conn., 1969-79, assoc. gen. counsel, 1979-80; v.p., gen. counsel, sec. Max Factor & Co., Hollywood, Calif., 1981-85, Boehringer Mannheim Corp., Indpls., 1985-92; v.p., gen. counsel Collagen Corp., Palo Alto, Calif., 1992-95, Gen. Probe Inc., San Diego, 1995-96, Safeskin Corp., San Diego, 1996-98; exec. v.p. Lipomatrix

Inc., Neuchatel, Switzerland, 1998-99; gen. counsel Turbostar Comm. Corp., 2000—02. Bd. dirs. Aesthetic and Reconstructive Techs., Inc., 2002—. Bd. dirs. Southwestern Legal Found., 1975-85. Fulbright scholar, 1959-60; Ford Found. fellow, 1961-62; Hague Acad. fellow, 1963; German Govt. grantee, 1962-63; Kappa Sigma scholar, 1959. Mem. Internat. Bar Assn., ABA, Calif. Bar Assn., Fla. Bar Assn., Ind. Bar Assn., Masons, Elks, Phi Beta Kappa, Phi Eta Sigma, Delta Theta Phi. Republican. Mem. Christian Ch. Home: 3516 Villanova Ave San Diego CA 92122-2313

MILLER, WILLIAM CHARLES, college dean, architect; b. San Francisco, May 11, 1945; s. Francis Leland and Ethel Lorene (Britt) M.; m. Beverly Jean McConnell, Dec. 22, 1968; children: Britt A., David A. BArch, U. Oreg., 1968; MArch, U. Ill., 1970. Registered architect, Ariz., Kans., Utah. Architect various firms, San Francisco, Sacramento, Calif., Tucson and Oak Harbor, Wash.; asst. prof. Coll. Architecture U. Ariz., Tucson, 1970-73, 74-77; assoc. prof. dept. architecture Kans. State U., Manhattan, 1977-86, prof., 1986-92, head dept., 1990-92; prof. Grad. Sch. Architecture U. Utah, Salt Lake City, 1992—, dean, 1992—2002. Guest lectr. over 40 schs. architecture; presenter numerous profl. socs. and orgns.; dir. west ctrl. region Assn. Collegiate Schs. Architecture, 1988-91, chair theme paper sessions ann. meeting, San Francisco, 1990, chair regional paper sessions ann. meeting, Washington, 1991, co-chair adminstrv. conf., Milw., 1995; bd. dirs. Nat. Archtl. Accrediting Bd., 1996-99; mem. Utah Architects Lic. Bd., 2000—. Author: Alvar Aalto: An Annotated Bibliography, 1984; co-editor: The Architecture of the In-Between, 1990, Architecture: Back to Life, 1991; contbr. articles to profl. jours., chpts. to books. Bd. dirs. Assist, Inc., Artspace, Inc., Contemporary Arts Group. Recipient Svc. awards Assn. Collegiate Schs. Architecture, Nat. Coun. Archtl. Registration Bds., Nat. Archtl. Accrediting Bd. Fellow AIA (pres-elect Flint Hills, treas. Utah, exec. com., treas., exec. com. Western Mountain region, elected coll. of fellows 1997); mem. Am.-Scandinavian Found., Soc. for Advancement Scandinavian Studies, Tau Sigma Delta. Office: U Utah Grad Sch Architecture Salt Lake City UT 84112 E-mail: miller@arch.utah.edu.

MILLER, WILLIAM FREDERICK, research company executive, educator, business consultant; b. Vincennes, Ind., Nov. 19, 1925; s. William and Elsie M. (Everts) M.; m. Patty J. Smith, June 19, 1949; 1 son, Rodney Wayne. Student, Vincennes U., 1946-47; BS, Purdue U., 1949, MS, 1951, PhD, 1956; DSc (hon.), 1972. Mem. staff Argonne Nat. Lab., 1955-64, assoc. physicist, 1956-59, dir. applied math. div., 1959-64; prof. computer sci. Stanford U., Palo Alto, Calif., 1965-97, Herbert Hoover prof. pub. and pvt. mgmt. emeritus, 1997—, assoc. provost for computing, 1968-70, v.p. for rsch., 1970-71, v.p., provost, 1971-78; mem. Stanford Assocs., 1972—; pres., CEO SRI Internat., Menlo Park, Calif., 1979-90; chmn. bd., CEO SRI Devel. Co., David Sarnoff Rsch. Ctr., Inc., Princeton, N.J. Chmn. bd. dirs. Borland Software; bd. dirs. XPEED, Inc., Data Digest; chmn. bd. dirs. Sentris Corp.; professorial lectr. applied math. U. Chgo., 1962-64; vis. prof. math. Purdue U., 1962-63; vis. scholar Ctr. for Advanced Study in Behavioral Scis., 1976; fellow McKenna Group; mem. adv. coun. BHP Internat., 1990-97; computer sci. and engring bd. NAS, 1968-71; mem. Nat. Sci. Bd., 1982-88; corp. com. computers in edn. Brown UU., 1971-79; mem. policy bd. EDUCOM Planning Coun. on Computing in Edn., 1974-79, chmn., 1974-76; mem. ednl. adv. bd. Guggenheim Meml. Found., 1976-80; com. postdoctoral and doctoral rsch. staff NRC, 1977-80, computer sci. and telecom.; dir. Fund Am., 1977-91, Fireman's Fund Ins., 1977-91, Wells Fargo Bank and Co., 1996-97, Varian Assocs. Inc., 1973-96, Veo Systems Inc., 1996-99. Mem. editl. bd. Pattern Recognition Jour, 1968-72, Jour. Computational Physics, 1970-74. Served to 2d lt. F.A. AUS, 1943-46. Recipient Frederic B. Whitman award United Way Bay Area, 1982, Sarnoff Founders medal, 1997, David Packard Civic Entrepreneurship Team award, 1998, Robert K. Jaedicke Silver Apple award Stanford U. Bus. Sch. Alumni, 1998, The Dongbaeg medal Order of Civil Merit, The Rep. of Korea, 2000, The Okawa prize, The Okawa Found. for Info. and Telecoms., 2000; named to Silicon Valley Engring. Hall of Fame, 2001. Fellow IEEE, Am. Acad. Arts and Scis., AAAS; mem. Am. Math. Soc., Am. Phys. Soc., Soc. Indsl. and Applied Math., Assn. Computing Machinery, Nat. Acad. Engring., Sigma Xi, Tau Beta Pi (Eminent Engr. 1989). Office: Stanford U Grad Sch Bus Stanford CA 94305

MILLER, WILLIAM GREEN, ambassador; b. N.Y.C., Aug. 15, 1931; m. Suzanne Lisle; 2 children. BA, MA, Oxford U., U.K.; postgrad., Harvard U. Tutor Winthrop House Harvard U., 1956-59; with Fgn. Svc., 1959; vice consul, polit. officer Isfahan, Iran, 1959-62; polit. officer Tehran, Iran, 1962-64; line officer, exec. secretariat Dept. of State, 1965-66; mem. Sr. Interdepartmental Group, 1966-67; spl. asst. fgn. affairs and def. Senator John Sherman Cooper, 1967-73; staff dir. Senate Select Com. Emergency Powers, 1973-75, Senate Select Com. to Study Govtl. Ops. with Respect to Intelligence Communities, 1975-76, Senate Select Com. Intelligence, 1976-81; assoc. dean, adj. prof. internat. politics Fletcher Sch. Law and Diplomacy, 1981-83, rsch. assoc., 1983-85; faculty assoc. Harvard Ctr. Middle Eastern Studies, 1983-86; pres. Am. Com. U.S.- Soviet Rels., 1986-92; U.S. amb. to Ukraine, 1993-98. Cons. D.H. Sawyer and Assocs., Ltd., N.Y.C., 1985; bd. dirs. Internat. Found., pres. 1986-92; pres. Com. Am.- Russian Rels., cons. Catherine T. MacArthur Found., 1992-93. Contbr. articles to profl. jours. Bd. dirs. The Andrei Sakharov Found., 1998—, Inst. Social Action and Renewal in Eurasia, 1998—. Rsch. fellow Harvard Ctr. Sci. and Internat. Affairs, 1984-86, John F. Kennedy Sch. of Govt. fellow Harvard U., 1986. Fellow Rsch. Inst. of Politics; mem. Nat. Acad. Pub. Diplomacy, Nat. Acad. Pub. Adminstrn., Internat. Inst. Strategic Studies, Coun. Fgn. Rels., Children of the 21st Century, Middle East Inst., Soc. Iranian Studies, Search For Common Ground. Office: Woodrow Wilson Internat Ctr Scholars 1 Woodrow Wilson Plaza 1300 Pennsylvania Ave NW Washington DC 20004-3002 E-mail: wmiller@igc.org.

MILLER, WILLIAM HUGHES, theoretical chemist, educator; b. Kosciusko, Miss., Mar. 16, 1941; s. Weldon Howard and Jewel Irene (Hughes) M.; m. Margaret Ann Westbrook, June 4, 1966; children: Alison Leslie, Emily Sinclaire. BS, Ga. Inst. Tech., 1963; AM, Harvard U., 1964, PhD, 1967. Jr. fellow Harvard U., 1967-69; NATO postdoctoral fellow Freiburg (Germany) U., 1967-68; asst. prof. chemistry U. Calif., Berkeley, 1969-72, assoc. prof., 1972-74, prof., 1974—, dept. chmn., 1989-93, chancellor's prof., 1998—, Kenneth S. Pitzer disting. prof., 1999—. Fellow Churchill Coll., Cambridge (Eng.) U., 1975-76; hon. prof. Shandong U., People's Republic of China, 1994. Alfred P. Sloan fellow, 1970-72; Camille and Henry Dreyfus fellow, 1973-78; Guggenheim fellow, 1975-76, Christensen fellow St. Catherine's Coll., Oxford, 1993; recipient Alexander von Humboldt-Stiftung U.S. Sr. Scientist award, 1981-82, Ernest Orlando Lawrence Meml. award, 1985, Hirschfelder prize in theoretical chemistry, U. Wis., 1996, Alumni Achievement award Ga. Inst. Tech., 1997, Spiers medal Faraday divsn. Royal Soc. Chemistry, London, 1998. Fellow AAAS, Am. Acad. Arts and Scis., Am. Phys. Soc. (Irving Langmuir award 1990); mem. NAS, Am. Chem. Soc. (Theoretical Chemistry award 1994, Ira Remsen award 1997, Peter Debye awrd in phys. chemistry 2003), Internat. Acad. Quantum Molecular Sci. (Ann. prize 1974). Office: U Calif Dept Chemistry Berkeley CA 94720-0001

MILLER, WILLIAM IRWIN, finance company executive; b. Columbus, Ind., Apr. 30, 1956; s. Joseph Irwin and Xenia Ruth (Simons) M.; m. Lynne Marie Maguire, Oct. 29, 1983; children: Katherine Maguire, Laura Marie, Emily Elizabeth. BA, Yale U., 1978; MBA, Stanford U., 1981. Sect. mgr. Cummins Engine Co., Inc., Charleston, S.C., 1978-79; assoc. Warburg Pincus Capital Corp., N.Y.C., 1981-83; pres. Irwin Mgmt. Co., Inc., Columbus, 1984-90, also bd. dirs.; chmn. Irwin Fin. Corp., 1990—. Chmn. Irwin Mgmt. Co. and Tipton Lakes Co., Columbus, 1984—; bd. dirs. Cummins Inc., Irwin-Sweeney-Miller Found., Columbus, Tennant Co., Mpls., New Perspective Fund, L.A., New World Fund, L.A. Trustee The Taft Sch., Watertown, Conn., 1979—, Christian Theol. Sem., Indpls., 1988-94, Europacific Growth Fund, L.A., 1992—; bd. dirs. Cummins Found., Columbus, Ind., 1989—, Irwin Fin. Found., Columbus, 1991—, The Heritage Fund of Bartholomew County, Columbus, 1998—; mem. investment com. Yale U., New Haven, 1995-99, 2000—; mem. Ctrl. Ind. Corp. Partnership, Indpls., 1999—, Nat. Bldg. Mus., 2001—. Office: Irwin Fin Corp 500 Washington St PO Box 929 Columbus IN 47202-0929

MILLER, WILLIAM JACOB, public relations executive; b. Providence, Apr. 28, 1952; s. Gerald Howard and Eunice Ruth (Gomberg) M. BS, Emerson Coll., 1974. Theatrical publicist Cameron Mackintosh, Inc., N.Y.C., to date. Mgr. Theatre of Performing Arts, Miami Beach, Fla., 1986-87; adv. dir. Same Time, Next Year touring prodn. 1978, 79; press rep. numerous theatrical prodns. including Miss Saigon, 1993-2000, The Phantom of the Opera, 1991—, Les Miserables, 1988—, Cats, 1987-88, Sugar Babies, 1979, 82-85, Colette, 1982, Fiddler on the Roof, 1981-82, Lolita, 1980-81, Deathtrap, 1980, others. Mem. Assn. Theatrical Press Agts. and Mgrs., League Am. Theatres and Prodrs. Home: 50 Park Ave Apt 16C New York NY 10016-3081

MILLER, WILLIAM LEE, JR. minister; b. Mammoth Spring, Ark., Dec. 27, 1926; s. William L. and Janie Katherine (Murrell) M.; m. Marion Evelyn O'Neal, Mar. 23, 1947 (div. 1976); children: Georgia Katherine Miller Beach, William Lee III; m. Judith Ann Bell, Nov. 28, 1977 (dec. July 1997); m. Delores Bryan, Dec. 27, 1998. AB, Phillips U., 1950, LittD, 1968; postgrad., U. Ark., 1951-52, Tex. Christian U., 1958, U. Ky., 1961; BD, Lexington Theol. Sem., 1961, MDiv, 1997. Ordained to ministry Christian Ch. (Disciples of Christ), 1950. Pastor 1st Christian Ch., Rogers, Ark., 1952-59, Rogers Heights Christian Ch., Tulsa, 1961-62; v.p. Bd. Higher Edn., Indpls., 1962-68; pres. Bd. Higher Edn. Christian Ch. (Disciples of Christ), 1968-77; v.p. devel. Nat. City Christian Ch. Corp., Washington, 1977-82; upper Midwest regional min., pres. Christian Ch. (Disciples of Christ), Des Moines, 1982-93; pres. Miller Devel. Assocs. Dir. Christian Ch. Found., Indpls., 1968-77, 84-93; trustee Bethany Coll., W.Va., 1972-85, Culver Stockton Coll., 1970-77, 82-94, Tougaloo Coll., Jackson, Miss., 1970-76, Christian Theol. Sem., Indpls., 1987-94. Precinct committeeman Dem. Party, Indpls., 1968-72; mem. Reagan First Inaugural Religious Com.; bd. dris. St. Louis Christian Home, 1956-59; chmn. Coop. Coll. Registry, Washington, 1963-70; mem. Disciples of Christ Ch., Disciples Soc. for Faith & Reason; bd. dirs., exec. com. Christian Ch. D.C., N.C., 1995-98; pres. Friends of Dare County (N.C.) Librs., 1997-99; v.p. North Dare County Ministerial Assn., 1998-99. Mem. Disciples of Christ Hist. Soc., Coun. Christian Unity (exec. com. 1968-77), Nat. Evangelistic Assn. (bd. dirs. 1983-86), Am. Assn. Higher Edn., Masons, KT, NAACP, Sigma Chi, Am. Legion, Interfaith Alliance, Amnesty Internat., Sierra Club. Mem. Christian Ch. (Disciples Of Christ). Home and Office: Miller Devel Assocs 1710 W Long Blvd Raymore MO 64083-9116

MILLER, WILLIAM NAPIER CRIPPS, lawyer; b. Long Branch, N.J., June 7, 1930; adopted s. Julia (Erwin) M.; m. Carolyn Anderson, Jan. 19, 1951 (div. 1963); children: Bruce Douglass, Jennifer Erwin; m. Hannelore Steinbeck, Dec. 4, 1970 AA, Coll. Marin, 1949; student, U. Calif.-Berkeley, 1949-51, JD, 1955. Bar: N.Y., Calif. 1956, U.S. Supreme Ct. 1983. Assoc. Mudge, Stern, Baldwin & Todd, N.Y.C., 1955-58, Pillsbury, Madison & Sutro, San Francisco, 1959-65, ptnr., 1966—; staff NYU Law Sch., 1957-58; ct. adv. com. Calif. State Assembly Judiciary Com., 1979-80. Author: Long Pig, 2002. Bd. dirs. Laguna Honda Hosp., San Francisco, 1966— ; bd. visitors U. Calif.-Hastings Law Sch. Served with USAF, 1951-52. Recipient Bur. Nat. Affairs award U. Calif.-Hastings, 1955; recipient Thurston Soc. award, 1953. Fellow Am. Coll. Trial Lawyers; mem. ABA, San Francisco Bar Assn., Order of Coif, St. Francis Yacht Club, Silverado Country Club. Home: 16 George Ln Sausalito CA 94965-1890 Office: Pillsbury Winthrop LLP PO Box 7880 San Francisco CA 94120-7880

MILLER, WILLIAM RAY, retired aircraft manufacturing executive; b. Seattle, Nov. 2, 1935; s. Jack William and Mary Leona (Johnson) M.; m. Maralyn Rae Edwards, Oct. 12, 1957; children: Brian Thomas, Kathleen Louise Miller Ancel. BS, Iowa State U., 1962. Facilities resource mgr. Boeing Comml. Airplane Co., Renton, Wash., 1957-94. Mem. Masons (grand master Wash., 1989-90, supreme coun. Scottish Rite, sovereign grand inspector gen. Orient of Wash., 1993—), DeMolay Internat. (supreme coun. 1989—). Presbyterian. Avocations: photography, reading, travel. Home: 30725 21st Ave SW Federal Way WA 98023-7801

MILLER, WILMA HILDRUTH, education educator; b. Dixon, Ill., Mar. 8, 1936; d. William Alexander and Ruth Karin (Hanson) M. BS in Edn., No. Ill. U., DeKalb, 1958, MS in Edn., 1961; DEd, U. Ariz., 1967. Cert. reading specialist. Elem. tchr. Dist. 170, Dixon, Ill., 1958-63, Dist. 1, Tucson, 1963-64; asst. prof. edn. Wis. State U., Whitewater, 1965-68; assoc. prof. edn. Ill. State U., Normal, 1968-72, prof., 1972-98, prof. emeritus, 1998—. Author: Diagnosing and Correcting Reading Difficulties in Children, 1988, Reading Comprehension, 1990, Complete Reading Disabilities Handbook, 1993, Alternative Assessment Techniques in Reading and Writing, 1995, Reading and Writing Remediation Kit, 1997, The Reading Teacher's Survival Kit, 2001, Reading SKills Problem Solver, 2002, others; contbr. over 225 articles to profl. jours. Altar Guild, usher, greeter, communion asst. Our Saviour Luth. Ch., Normal, 1990—. Recipient Outstanding Contbn. to Edn. award No. Ill. U., 1998. Mem. Internat. Reading Assn. (parent and reading com. 1972-74, editl. adv. bd. 1995-98, Outstanding Dissertation award 1968), Mid-State Reading Coun. (editl. adv. bd. 1991-98), Alpha Upsilon Alpha (advisor Reading chpt. 1993-98), Pi Lambda Theta, Kappa Delta Pi, Phi Delta Kappa. Avocations: travel, Wisconsin Northwoods, writing, animals. Home: 302 N Coolidge St Normal IL 61761-2435 E-mail: whmille@ilstu.edu., whmille@centurytel.net.

MILLER, YVONNE BOND, state legislator, educator; b. Edenton, N.C. d. John and Pency Bond. BS, Va. State Coll., Petersburg, 1956; postgrad., Va. State Coll., Norfolk, 1966; MA, Columbia U., 1962; PhD, U. Pitts., 1973; postgrad., CCNY, 1976. Tchr. Norfolk Pub. Schs., 1956-68; asst. prof. Norfolk State U., 1968-71, assoc. prof., 1971-74, prof., 1974-88, head dept. early childhood/elem. edn., 1984-87; mem. Va. Ho. Dels., Richmond, 1984-87, mem. edn. com., health, welfare and instns. com., militia and police com., 1983-87; mem. Va. Senate, 1987—. Commerce and labor com., gen. laws com., transp. com., rehab. and social svcs. com. Va. Senate, HIV subcom., remediation subcom., unemployment compensation act subcom., infants and toddlers with disabilities subcom.; mem. intergovtl. coop. commn., youth commn., disability commn., Va. Coun. Coord. Prevention commn.; cons. in field. Commr. Ea. Va. Med. Authority; adv. bd. Va. Div. Children; active C.H. Mason Meml. Ch. of God in Christ. 1st black woman to be elected to Va. Legislature, 1983, 1st black woman to be elected to Va. Senate, 1987. Mem. Nat. Alliance Black Sch. Educators (bd. dirs.), Va. Assn. for Early Childhood Edn., Nat. Assn. Dem. Chairs, Zeta Phi Beta (past officer). Office: 2539 Corprew Ave Norfolk VA 23504-3909 also: Va Senate Gen Assembly Bldg Rm 318 Richmond VA 23219 Fax: 757-627-7203., 757-640-0577. E-mail: senmiller@acninc.net., ybmiller1@aol.com.

MILLER, ZELL BRYAN, senator, former governor; b. Young Harris, Ga., Feb. 24, 1932; s. Stephen Grady and Birdie (Bryan) M.; m. Shirley Carver, Jan. 14, 1954; children: Murphy Carver, Matthew Stephen. Student, Young Harris Coll.; AB, MA, U. Ga. Dir. Ga. Bd. Probation, 1965-66; dep. dir. Ga. Dept. Corrections, 1967-68; exec. sec. to gov. Ga., 1968-71; mem. State Bd. Pardons and Paroles, Atlanta, 1973-75; lt. gov. State of Ga., 1975-90, gov., 1990-98; prof. polit. sci. and history U. Ga., 1999—; U.S. senator from Ga., 2000—. Prof. Young Harris Coll., 1959-64, Emory U., Young Harris Coll., U. Ga.; bd. dirs. various corps., including Overseas Pvt. Investment Corp. (OPIC), Ga. Power, Gray Comms., Ezgov.com, Post Properties, Kollmann USA. Author: The Mountains Within Me, 1985, Great Georgians, 1983, They Heard Georgia Singing, Corps Values, 1996, 2d edit., 1997. Mem. Ga. Senate, 1960-64; mayor Young Harris, 1959; exec. dir. Democratic Com. Ga., 1971-72; pres. Coun. State Govts., 1991—; vice chmn. So. Gov.'s Assn., 1991—; bd. dirs. Towns County Hosp. Authority. Served with USMC, 1953-56. Mem. Ga. Sch. Food Services Assn. (life), Ga. Peace Officers Assn. (life), Gridiron Soc. U. Ga., Blue Key, Lions Club. Methodist. Address: US Senate 257 Dirksen Senate Office Bldg Washington DC 20510*

MILLER, ZOYA DICKINS (MRS. HILLIARD EVE MILLER JR.), civic worker; b. Washington, July 15, 1923; d. Randolph and Zoya Pavlovna (Klementinovska) Dickins; m. Hilliard Eve Miller, Jr., Dec. 6, 1943; children: Jeffrey Arnot, Hilliard Eve III. Grad., Stuart Sch. Costume Design, Washington, 1942; student, Cochran Galleries of Fine Arts, 1942, Sophie Newcomb Coll., 1944, New Eng. Conservatory Music, 1946, Colo. Coll., 1965; grad., Internat. Sch. Reading, 1969; student, Cochran Galleries of Fine Arts, 1942. Lic. pvt. pilot. Instr. Stuart Summer Sch. Costume Design, Washington, 1942; fashion coord. Julius Garfinckel, 1942-43; fashion coord., cons. Mademoiselle mag., 1942-44; star TV show Cowbelle Kitchen, 1957-58, Flair for Living, 1958-59; model mags. and comml. films, also nat. comml. recs., 1956-80; dir. rsch. devel. Webb-Waring Inst. for Cancer, Aging and Antioxidant Rsch., Denver, 1973—. Contbr. articles, lectr. on health care sys. and fund raising. Mem. exec. com., bd. dirs. El Paso County chpt. Am. Lung Assn. Colo., 1965-84, bd. dirs., 1965-87, chmn. radio and TV coun., 1963-70, mem. med. affairs com., 1965-70, pres., 1965-66, procurer found. funds, 1965-70; developer nat. radio ednl. prodns. for internat. use Am. Lung Assn., 1963-70, coord. statewide pulmonary screening programs Colo., other states, 1965-72; chmn. benefit fund raising El Paso County Cancer Soc., 1963; co-founder, coord. Colorado Springs Debutante Ball, 1967—; coord. Nat. Gov.'s Comprehensive Health Planning Coun., 1967-74, chmn., 1971-72; chmn. Colo. Chronic Care Com., 1969-73, chmn. fund raising, 1970-72, chmn. spl. com. conl. studies on nat. health bills, 1971-73; mem. Colo.-Wyo. Regional Med. Program Adv. Coun., 1969-73; mem. Colo. Med. Found. Consumers Adv. Coun., 1972-78; mem. decorative arts com. Colorado Springs Fine Arts Ctr., 1972-75; founder, state coord. Nov. Noel Pediat. Benefit Am. Lung Assn., 1973-87; founder, chmn. bd. dirs. Newborn Hope, Inc., 1987—; mem. adv. bd. Wagon Wheel Girl Scouts, 1991-94, Cmty. in Schs., 1995—; mem. cmty. adv. coun. Beth-El Nursing Sch., 1998—; bd. dirs. Episcopal Columbarium Assn., 2001, The Family Attachment Ctr., Inc. Zoya Dickins Miller Vol. of Yr. award established Am. Lung Assn. of Colo., 1979; recipient James J. Waring award Colo. Conf. on Respiratory Disease Workers, 1963, Nat. Pub. Rels. award Am. Lung Assn., 1979, Gold Double Bar Cross award, 1980, 83, Jefferson award Am. Inst. Pub. Svc., 1991, Thousand Points of Light award The White House, 1992, Recognition award So. Colo. Women's C. of C., 1994, Silver Spur Cmty. award Pikes Peak Range Riders, 1994, Silver Bell award Assistance League Colorado Springs, 1996, Svc. to Mankind award Centennial Sertoma Club, 1997, Help Can't Wait award Pikes Peak chpt. ARC, 1997, Cmty. Weaver award The Independent News, 1997, Apgar award Colo. March of Dimes, 1998; named Humanitarian of Yr., Am. Lung Assn. of Colo., 1987, One of 50 Most Influential Women in Colorado Springs by Gazette Telegraph Newspaper, 1990, One of 5 Leading Ladies Colo. Homes & Lifestyles Mag., 1991. Mem.: Nat. Soc. Fund Raising Execs., Denver Round Table for Planned Giving, Colo. Assn. Fund Raisers, The Family Attachment Ctr., Nat. Cowbell Assn. (El Paso county pres. 1954, TV chmn., chmn. nat. Father of Yr. contest Colo. 1956—57), Garden of the Gods Club, Cheyenne Mountain Country Club. Home: 74 W Cheyenne Mountain Blvd Colorado Springs CO 80906-4336

MILLER CALANDRA, LINDA MARGUERITA, pediatric nurse practitioner; b. Lansdale, Pa., June 7, 1957; d. Clarence P. and Ruth E. (Priester) Miller; m. Robert T. Calandra Jr.; 1 child, Lindsey. BSN, U. Del., 1979; MSN, U. Pa., 1986. Lic. nurse, Pa.; PNP, ANA; cert. otorhinolaryngology nurse Nat. Certifying Bd. Otorhinolaryngology and Head-Neck Nurses. Assoc. nurse Children's Hosp. Phila., 1979-80, primary surg. nurse, 1980-82, clin. nurse specialist in pediat. otorhinolaryngology, 1983-86, PNP in otorhinolaryngology, 1986—. Mem. Nat. Cert. Bd. of Otorhinolaryngology, Head and Neck Nurses, 1991-97; clin. preceptor Sch. Nursing, U. Pa., 1992-2000; presenter Neonatal Nursing Conf., Boston, 1988, Nat. Nurse Practitioner Debate, Balt., 1992, U. Pa., 1993, various profl. assn. confs. Mem. editl. adv. bd. ADVANCE for Nurse Practitioners, 1993—; contbr. articles to profl. jours. Mem. Nat. Assn. Pediat. Nurse Assocs. and Practitioners, Soc. Ear, Nose and Throat Advances in Children (mem. com. on coms. 1993-95, mem. liaison com. 1993-95, sec. 1999-2002), Soc. Otorhinolaryngology and Head and Neck Nurses (co-chairperson edn. com. 1993-95, v.p. 1999—, pres.-elect 2001-02, pres. 2002—), Pa. Acad. Otorhinolaryngology, Sigma Theta Tau. Home: 2120 Jenkintown Rd Glenside PA 19038-5314 Office: Childrens Hosp PA 34th Civic Center Blvd Philadelphia PA 19104 E-mail: calandra@email.chop.edu.

MILLER DAVIS, MARY-AGNES, social worker; b. Montgomery, Ala., Jan. 21; d. George Joseph and Mollie (Ingersoll) M.; m. Edward Davis, Sept. 20, 1941. BA, Wayne State U., 1944; MSW, U. Mich., 1970. Lic. social worker, Mich. Social caseworker Cath. Family Ctr., Detroit, 1946-48; foster homes worker Juvenile Ct., 1953-57; youth svc. bur. League of Cath. Women, 1957-59; mayor's cmty. action for youth com. worker City of Detroit, 1963; instr. urban sociology Madonna Coll., Livonia, Mich., 1968; pers. cons. Edward Davis Motor Sales, Detroit, 1963-70; exec. cons. Edward Davis Assocs., Inc., from 1975. Founder Co-Ette Club, Inc., Detroit, 1941—, Met. Detroit Teen Conf. Coalition, Detroit, 1983—; program chair Wayne State U.-Merrill Palmer Inst., Detroit, 1976—, founder Met. Detroit Teen Conf. Editor Girl Friends, Inc. Mag., 1960-62; contbr. articles to profl. jours. Life mem. NAACP, League of Cath. Women, ARC; charter mem. Meadowbrook Summer Music Festival, com. of Oakland (Mich.) U.; adv. bd. Women for the Detroit Symphony Orch.; mem./patron Founder's Soc. the Detroit Inst. of Arts; bd. dirs., other offices ARC, Detroit, 1974—; active The Detroit Hist. Soc., Heart of Gold Coun., Women for United Found. (named to Heart of Gold coun. 1968), Friends of the Detroit Libr., Mich. Opera Theatre; mem. nat. hon. com./nat. vol. week United Cmty. Svc. and Nat. Vol. Ctr., Washington, 1990—; former bd. dirs. United Community Svcs. Women's Com., Campfire Girls, LWV, Neighborhood Svcs. Orgn., Cath. Interracial Coun. and others; founder Met. Detroit Teen Conf. Coalitions Merrill Palmer Inst. Wayne State U. Recipient Nat. Cmty. Leadership award Nat. Coun. Women of U.S., Inc., 1984, Am. Human Resources award Am. Bicentennial Rsch. Inst., 1976, Heart of Gold award United Way, 1968, Nat. Leadership award United Negro Coll. Fund, 1963, Recognition award Westin Hotel, 1991, Top Ladies of Distinction award, 1994, Civic award Am. Assn. Bus. Women, 1998, Youth Leadership award Merrill Palmer Inst. of Wayne State U., 1999, Cmty. Leadership award, 1999, Civic/Social Vol. Leadership award Automobile Industry and Edward Davis Found./Edn. and Scholarships for Youth, 2001; named one of Mich. Outstanding Women City of Detroit, 1976, Michiganer of the Yr., Detroit News Newspaper, 2001; Heart of Gold 25th Anniversary honoree United Way Southeastern Mich., 1992; Vassar Summer Seminar scholar NCCJ, 1953, Notre Dame Summer Seminar scholar, 1960; named one of Most Outstanding Women of Decade, Nordstrom's Dept. Store, 1996. Mem. NASW, ARC (bd. dirs. 1973—, life), Nat. Conf. of Social Work, The Cons. Club of Detroit (adv. bd. edn. com.), Detroit Econ. Club (adv. com.). Home: Detroit, Mich. Died Apr. 18, 2001.

MILLER-HANCE, WANDA C. anesthesiologist; b. N.Y.C., July 11, 1956; d. Juan R. Miller and Julia Hance. Student, U. P.R., 1974-77; MD, U. Wis., 1981. Diplomate in pediatrics and pediatric cardiology Am. Bd. Pediatrics; diplomate Am. Bd. Anesthesiology. Intern, resident in pediats. U. Tex. SW Med. Ctr., Dallas, 1981-84, rsch. fellow, 1985-87; fellow in pediat. cardiology Baylor Coll. Medicine, Houston, 1987-90; asst. prof. U. Calif., San Diego, 1991-93; resident in anesthesia Mass. Gen. Hosp., Boston, 1993-96; asst. prof. U. Calif., San Francisco, 1996-99; assoc. prof. Baylen Coll., 2002—. Author: Critical Care Secrets, 1998, Cardiology Clinics, 2000; contbr. articles to profl. jours. Bugher Found. fellow Am. Heart Assn., 1991, grantee, 1992; recipient investigator award NIH, San Diego, 1991, Found. for Anesthesia Edn. and Rsch., San Francisco, 1999. Fellow Am. Coll. Cardiology; mem. Am. Coll. Cardiology, Am. Soc. Anesthesiologists, Am. Soc. Echocardiography, Internat. Anesthesia Rsch. Soc., Soc. Cardiovasc. Anesthesiologists, Soc. for Pediatric Anesthesia. Office: Tex Children's Hosp Div Pediat Cardiovasc Anes 6621 Fannin St 19345H Houston TX 77030

MILLER-LANE, BARBARA See LANE, BARBARA MILLER

MILLER-PIERCE, DIANA LYNN, artist, psychotherapist; b. Kokomo, Ind., May 11, 1954; d. John Allen and Velma Marie Miller; m. Donald Ray Pierce, July 21, 1979. MSW, Ind. U., 1978. Cert. ACSW. Pvt. practice Choice Makers Counseling, Ft. Wayne, Ind., 1987—. Exhibited in group shows Am. Watercolor Soc. Show, 1989. Recipient 3d Pl. award Windsor Newton Internat. Art Goes on Holiday, 1998, Ind. Artist Club Merit award, 1998, Watercolor Soc. Ind. Merit award, 1992, Hoosier Salon Merit awards. Mem. Watercolor Soc. Ind. (signature mem.), Hoosier Salon (exhibiting mem., Merit award 1994), Ind. Artist Club. Office: Trillium Studio 8231 Sakaden Pkwy Fort Wayne IN 46825 E-mail: dianapierce@msn.com.

MILLER-ROSEMAN, LINDA SARAH, critical care, emergency room nurse; b. Flushing, N.Y., Jan. 27, 1952; d. Raymond P. and Mary Rosaleen (Heaney) M. Diploma, Lenox Hill Hosp. Sch. Nursing, N.Y.C., 1973; BA, Marymount Manhattan Coll., 1991. Staff nurse, ICU Lenox Hill Hosp., 1973-76, sr. staff nurse, open heart unit, 1976-79, staff nurse, emergency rm., 1979-84, staff nurse, invasive cardiology lab., 1984-87, sr. staff nurse emergency rm., 1987-90, staff nurse ambulatory surgery, 1990-91, clin. instr. med./surg., 1991-92, staff nurse interventional cardiology/progressive coronary care unit, 1992—. Home: 310 E 65th St Apt 4F New York NY 10021-6741

MILLER-SANBORN, NANCY JANET, insurance agent; b. Champaign, Ill., Sept. 14, 1954; d. Allan Stephen and Janet Margaret (Worth) Miller; m. David W. Sanborn, Nov. 24, 1990; 1 child Katherine Janet Sanborn. BA cum laude, U. Mass., 1976. CLU, ChFC. Spl. agt. Prudential Ins. Co. Am., East Longmeadow, Mass., 1976—98, fin. planner, 1998—. Broker various ins. cos., East Longmeadow, 1980-2001, Longmeadow, 2001-. Bd. dirs. Hampden County Estate Planning Coun., 2001—. Recipient Nat. Sales Achievement award for 10 yrs. Nat. Assn. Life Underwriters, 1989; selected one of 125 Univ. of Mass. grads. to watch. Mem. Am. Soc. CLUs, Am. Soc. Chartered Fin. Cons., Western Mass. CLU and ChFC Soc. (v.p. 1994-95, pres.- elect 1995-96, pres. 1996-97), Springfield Assn. Life Underwriters (v.p. 1985-86, pres. 1987-88), Springfield C. of C. (Breakfast Club com. 1986-89), East Longmeadow C. of C. (clk. 1989-90, pres. 1991-92). Avocations: swimming, Stairmaster, Cybex. Office: 666 Bliss Rd #5 Longmeadow MA 01106

MILLER-YOUNG, CORRIENE CALHOUN, nursing educator; b. N.Y.C., Oct. 22, 1959; d. Timothy E. Calhoun and Suzetta Franklin; children: Christopher, Jeremy, James, Aja. BSN, Rutgers U., Newark, 1982; postgrad., Memphis State U., 1992—. RN, N.J., Tenn.; cert. wound ostomy nurse; cert. wound and ostomy specialist. Staff nurse Muhlenberg Hosp., Plainfield, N.J., 1981-86, Kimberly Nurses, Union, 1986-89; health coord. Neighborhood House, Plainfield, 1989-91; staff nurse/nurse clinician Bapt. Meml. Hosp., Memphis, 1991-2000; LPN instr. Tenn. Tech. Ctr., 1994—. Named Nurse of Month, Kimberly Nurses, 1987. Mem. ANA, Kappa Delta Pi.

MILLET, CRAIG STEVEN, music educator; b. Alexandria, La., Nov. 8, 1966; s. Sherwood and Ramona Millet; m. Julie Elizabeth Fore, Mar. 31, 1990; children: Lindsey, Matthew. BA, La. Tech U, Ruston, LA, 1984—89. Asst band dir. St Amant H.S., Ruston, La., 1990—99, band dir. St Amant, 1999—. Pres. Dist. IV Band Directors, St Amant, La., 1995—97. Recipient La. Tech U Bandmaster of the Yr., La. Tech U music faculty, 2001. Avocations: music, fishing. Home: 18496 Oakwood Dr Prairieville LA 70769 Office: St Amant High School 12035 Hwy 431 Saint Amant LA 70774 Personal E-mail: craigmillet@hotmail.com.

MILLET, JOHN BRADFORD, retired surgeon; b. Buffalo, Aug. 8, 1916; s. John Alfred Parsons and Alice Jeannette (Murrell) M.; m. Constance Hopkins Dallas, Nov. 1974; children: John Bradford Jr., David Francis, Polly Watson. BS, Harvard U., 1938, MD, 1942. Diplomate Am. Bd. Surgery. Surg. intern Mass. Gen. Hosp., Boston, 1942-43, surg. resident, 1946-49; chief thoracic surgery, partner Slocum Dickson Clinic, Utica, N.Y., 1949-55; pvt. practice medicine specializing in surgery, 1955—; sr. attending surgeon St. Luke's Meml. Hosp. Ctr., 1955-81, chief dept. surgery, 1969-70; sr. attending surgeon St. Elizabeth's Hosp., 1955—, Faxton Hosp., 1979-86; ret., 1985; asst. to pres. Mohawk Metal Products Inc., 1989-91; pres. Miltel divsn. Millwheel, Inc., 1992-94. Former cons. surgeon Herkimer Meml. Hosp., Rose Hosp., Rome, N.Y., Marcy (N.Y.) State Hosp.; former med. adv. to Vis. Nurse Assn.; former dir. Health Systems Agy. Cen. N.Y., Med. Securities Fund, 1964-65, Med. Funds Mgmt. Corp., 1964-65, Digimetrics Inc., M.V. Hockey Inc., Millwheel Inc., IEX Inc., JDC Resources, Inc., B.F.I. Telecommunications Co. Inc., Utica Disposables Inc., Input Specialists Inc., LJB Ventures Inc.; pres. White Birch Home of Utica, Inc.; adminstrv. asst. U.S. Bur. Census, 2000, H&R Block, 2001. Former med. adv. com. Planned Parenthood of Mohawk Valley; pres. Midstate Com. on Area Wide Health Planning, 1966-72; co-chmn. citizens com. on devel. of med. sch. in Utica area; co-developer Brookside Racquet Club, Wedgewood Apartments, Treadway Resort, Meadows. Maj. M.C. AUS, 1943-46. Fellow ACS, Am. Coll. Chest Physicians; mem. AMA, Am. Thoracic Soc., Coll. Angiology, Central N.Y. Surg. Soc., Mohawk Valley Surg. Soc. (pres., 1968-69), Central N.Y. Acad. Medicine, Oneida County (chmn. edn. com., 1968-69), N.Y. State Soc. Surgeons (bd. dirs. 1970-85), N.Y. State Med. Soc. (com. for homeless), Pan-Am. Med. Assn., Pan Pacific Surg. Assn., Utica Med. Club (pres. 1960-61), Med. Soc. N.Y. State (com. on homeless), Night Stick Club (chief 1965-66), Harvard Club of Mohawk Valley (pres. 1951-66), Harvard Coll. Alumni Club (Fund area chmn.), Ft. Schuyler Club, Sadaquada Golf Club, Adirondack League Club, Ideal Flying Club, Rotary, Masons, Shriners (potentate 1981-82). Republican. Episcopalian. Home: 1642 York St Utica NY 13502-4959 E-mail: bmillet111@aol.com.

MILLETT, KATE (KATHERINE MURRAY MILLETT), political activist, sculptor, artist, writer; b. St. Paul, Sept. 14, 1934; m. Fumio Yoshimura, 1965. BA magna cum laude, U. Minn., 1956; postgrad. with 1st class honors, St. Hilda's Coll. Oxford, Eng., 1956-58; PhD with distinction, Columbia U., 1970. Instr. English U. N.C. at Greensboro, 1958; file clk. N.Y.C.; kindergarten tchr., 1960-61; sculptor, Tokyo, 1961-63; tchr. Barnard Coll., 1964-70; tchr. English Bryn Mawr (Pa.) Coll., 1970. Disting. vis. prof. Sacramento State Coll., 1972—73; adj. prof. NYU, N.Y.C.; founder Women's Art Colony Farm, Poughkeepsie, NY; rep. as non-govtl. orgn. on behalf of human rights UN. Author: Sexual Politics, 1970, The Prostitution Papers, 1973, Flying, 1974, Sita, 1977, The Basement, 1979, Going to Iran, 1982, The Loony Bin Trip, 1990, The Politics of Cruelty, 1994, A.D., 1995, Mother Millett, 2001; co-prodr., co-dir. film Three Lives, 1970; one-woman shows Minami Gallery, Tokyo, Judson Gallery, N.Y.C., 1967, Noho Gallery, N.Y.C., 1976, 79, 80, 82, 84, 86, 93, 99, Women's Bldg., L.A., 1977; drawings Andre Wanters Gallery, Berlin, 1980, Courtland Jessup Gallery, Provincetown, Mass., 1991, 92, 93, 94, 95, 98, 99, Retrospective Exhbn., U. Md., 1997, Hunter Coll., 1998, Northampton Ctr. for the Arts, 1998, John Jay Coll., N.Y.C., 1998. Mem. Congress of Racial Equality; chmn. edn. com. NOW, 1966; active supporter gay and women's liberation groups, also mental patients liberation and political prisoners; UN rep. for polit. prisoners. Mem. Phi Beta Kappa. Office: 295 Bowery New York NY 10003-7104

MILLETT, STEPHEN MALCOLM, futurist, consultant, historian; b. N.Y.C., Feb. 22, 1947; s. John David and Catherine (Letsinger) M.; m. Sherry Richards, Sept. 2, 1989; children: Jennifer Jane, Ann E. AB, Miami U., Oxford, Ohio, 1969; MA, Ohio State U., 1970, PhD, 1972. Rschr. Battelle, Columbus, Ohio, 1979—. Mgr. tech. forecasts incl. Strategic Technologies 2005 and 2020 and Energy Innovations 2010. Author: Manager's Guide to Technology Forecasting, 1991, Scottish Settlers of America, 1996; pub. and editor U.S. Scots, 1992-97. Capt. USAF, 1973-79. Mem. Phi Delta Theta. Avocations: Scottish history and culture, antiques. Home: 3673 Tillbury Ave Columbus OH 43220-5068 Office: Battelle 505 King Ave Columbus OH 43201-2693 E-mail: milletts@battelle.org.

MILLEV, YONKO TIMCHEV, physicist, researcher, educator; b. Balchik, Bulgaria, Oct. 14, 1956; came to U.S., 2000; s. Timcho Alexandrov and Veska Dimitrova (Vitanova) M.; m. Nadya Eugenieva Leyarovska, Sept. 8, 1982 (div. 1984); 1 child, Lambrina; m. Izolda Ivanova Pashmakova, Oct. 10, 1986; 1 child, Vihren. Diploma higher edn., Sofia (Bulgaria) U., 1982; PhD in Physics, Bulgarian Acad. Scis., Sofia, 1988. Physicist Bulgarian Acad. Scis., 1982-84; lectr. Tech. U., Sofia, 1984-88, sr. lectr., 1988-92; rsch. assoc. Max Planck Inst., Stuttgart, Germany, 1992—, fellow Germany, 1995—, Alexander von Humboldt fellow Germany, 1992-94. Hon. rsch. fellow Queen's U. Belfast, No. Ireland, 1994. Contbr. articles to sci. jours. With Bulgarian Army, 1975-77. Rsch. grantee Germ. Acad. Exch. Svc., 1991, E Cmty. Commn., 1994. Mem. Am. Phys. Soc. Orthodox. Avocations: soccer, badminton, books. Office: Calif State U 1250 Bellflower Long Beach CA 90840 E-mail: imilev@csulb.edu.

MILLGATE, JANE, language professional; b. Leeds, Eng., June 8, 1937; d. Maurice and Marie (Schofield) Barr; m. Michael Millgate, Feb. 27, 1960. BA with honors, Leeds U., Eng., 1959, MA, 1963; PhD, U. Kent, Eng., 1970. Instr. U. Toronto, Ont., Can., 1964-65, lectr. Can., 1965-70, asst. prof. Can., 1970-72, assoc. prof. Can., 1972-77, prof. English Can., 1977-97, prof. emeritus Can., 1997—, vice-dean arts and scis. Can., 1983-87. Mem. bd. regents Victoria U., Toronto, 1981-86. Author: Macaulay, 1973, Walter Scott, 1984, 2d edit., 1987, Scott's Last Edition: A Study in Publishing History, 1987; editor: Editing 19th Century Fiction, 1978; contbr. articles to profl. jours. Doctoral fellow Can. Coun., 1968-70; rsch. fellow Can. Coun., 1972, 74-75, Social Scis. and Humanities Rsch. Coun. Can., 1980-81, 85-87, 88-90, 91-94, 95-98, 98—, Connaught Rsch. fellow, 1995-96; recipient Rose Mary Crawshay prize Brit. Acad., 1988. Fellow Royal Soc. Can., Royal Soc. Edinburgh; mem. Victorian Studies Assn. (pres. 1978-80), Assn. Can. Univ. Tchrs. English (pres. 1980-82), Can. Fedn. for Humanities (exec. 1981-83, 95-96), Assn. Scottish Lit. Studies, Soc. for History of Authorship, Reading, and Pub., Bibliog. Soc. Home: 1 Balmoral Ave Apt 809 Toronto ON Canada M4V 3B9 Office: Victoria Coll U Toronto Toronto ON Canada M5S 1K7

MILLGATE, MICHAEL (MICHAEL HENRY MILLGATE), retired English educator; b. Southampton, Eng., July 19, 1929; arrived in Can., 1964; s. Stanley and Marjorie Louisa (Norris) M.; m. Jane Barr, Feb. 27, 1960. BA, Cambridge U., 1952, MA, 1956; postgrad., U. Mich., Ann Arbor, 1956-57; PhD, U. Leeds, 1960. Tutor Workers' Ednl. Assn., Eng., 1953-56; lectr. English lit. U. Leeds, 1958-64; prof., chmn. dept. English York U., Ont., Can., 1964-67; prof. English U. Toronto, 67-94, univ. prof., 87-94, univ. prof. emeritus, 1994—. Carpenter lectr. Ohio Wesleyan U., 1978; vis. scholar Meiji U., 1985. Author: William Faulkner, 1961, American Social Fiction, 1964, The Achievement of William Faulkner, 1966, Thomas Hardy: His Career as a Novelist, 1971, Thomas Hardy: A Biography, 1982, Testamentary Acts: Browning, Tennyson, James, Hardy, 1992, Faulkner's Place, 1997; editor: Tennyson: Selected Poems, 1963, Thomas Hardy: The Life and Work of Thomas Hardy, 1985, William Faulkner Manuscripts, 20 (4 vols.), 21 (2 vols.), 22 (4 vols.), 23 (2 vols.), 1986, New Essays on Light in August, 1987, Thomas Hardy: Selected Letters, 1990, Letters of Emma and Florence Hardy, 1996, Thomas Hardy's Public Voice, 2001; co-editor: Transatlantic Dialogue, 1966, Lion in the Garden, 1968, The Collected Letters of Thomas Hardy, Vol. I, 1978, Vol. II, 1980, Vol. III, 1982, Vol. IV, 1984, Vol. V, 1985, Vol. VI, 1987, Vol. VII, 1988, Thomas Hardy's Studies, Specimens, Etc. Notebook, 1994. Mem. ednl. adv. bd. JOhn Guggenhiem Meml. Found., 1994—2002. Can. Coun. leave fellow, 1968-69, S.W. Brooks fellow U. Queensland, 1971; Killam sr. rsch. scholar, 1974-75; John Simon Guggenheim Meml. fellow, 1977-78, Connaught sr. fellow, 1979-80; Social Sci. and Humanities Rsch. Coun. Can. leave fellow, 1981-82, grantee, 1977—; Can. Coun. grantee, 1973-77; Killam rsch. fellow, 1986-88. Fellow Royal Soc. Lit., Royal Soc. Can. (Pierre Chauveau medal 1999); mem. MLA (adv. com. Ctr. for Edit. Am. Authors 1971-74, com. on scholarly edits. 1985-89), Victorian Studies Assn. Ont. (pres. 1970-72), Thomas Hardy Soc. (v.p. 1973—), Bibliog. Soc. Am., Soc. for Study So. Lit. (exec. coun. 1972-76, 81-83), Soc. Textual Scholarship, Tennyson Soc. Home: 1 Balmoral Ave Apt 809 Toronto ON Canada M4V 3B9 E-mail: michael.millgate@utoronto.ca.

MILLIAN, KENNETH YOUNG, public policy consultant; b. Washington, Sept. 29, 1927; s. John Curry and Myrtle (Young) M.; m. Alva Randolph Clarke, Sept. 10, 1949; children: J. Randolph, Kenneth Y. Jr., Kathleen M. Gilbert, Elizabeth M. Allen. BA, U. Md., 1951; MA in Internat. Rels., George Washington U., 1969; Diploma, Nat. War Coll., Washington, 1969; MS in Bus., Columbia U., 1980. Officer U.S. Fgn. Svc., 1951-76; corp. exec. W.R. Grace & Co., N.Y.C, 1976-93, corp. v.p., dir. govt. rels. Washington, 1982-88, corp. v.p., dir. environ. policy N.Y.C., Fla., 1988-93; ret., 1993; pres. Millian Assocs. LLC, Washington, 1993-2000; chmn. Millian Byers Assocs. LLC, 2000—. Pres. Found. for Pres. Pvt. Sector Survey on Cost Control (Grace Commn.), 1986-92. Bd. govs. Wesley Theol. Sem., Washington, 1988—, Nat. Dem. Club, Washington, 1998-02. Democrat. Methodist. Avocations: sailing, golf. Office: Millian Byers Assocs LLC 1090 Vermont Ave NW Ste 300 Washington DC 20005-4966 E-mail: kym@milbya.com.

MILLIARD, ALINE, social worker; b. Portage, Maine, Nov. 18, 1937; d. Alderic and Ida (Dionne) M. MSW, Adelphi U., 1976; diploma social work supervision, Hunter Coll., 1986. Bd. cert. diplomate, clin. cert. social worker. Nurses' aide Good Samaritan Hosp., West Islip, N.Y., 1964-65, admitting office clk., 1965-70, social svc. asst.; intake worker Maryhaven Diagnostic & Guidance Ctr., Port Jefferson, 1972-74; coord. marriage counseling program Diocesan Human Rels. Svcs., Portland, Maine, 1975-77, family svc. worker, 1977-79; sch. social worker Sanford (Maine) Pub. Sch. Dept., 1979-81; campus social worker Green Chimneys Childrne Svcs., Brewster, N.Y., 1982-85, dir. group homes, 1985-88; social worker Fletcher Allen Health Care, Burlington, 1989—. Mem. Acad. Cert. Social Workers, NASW. Home: 64 1/2 Howard St Burlington VT 05401-4814 Office: FAHC Colchester Ave Burlington VT 05401 E-mail: Aline.Milliard@vtmednet.org.

MILLICAN, KIRK, architect; b. Ft. Worth, Oct. 4, 1951; s. Harold F. and Georgia N. (Williams) M.; m. Marian McKeever, Oct. 25, 1986; 1 child, Carter McKeever. BA, Washington U., 1973, MArch, 1976. Designer Growald Architects, Ft. Worth, 1977-78; architect S.I. Morris Assocs., Houston, 1978-79; sr. v.p., prin. project designer, mgr., dir. transp. Hellmuth, Obata & Kassabaum, Dallas, 1979—. Bd. dirs. HOK Planning Group, 2000. Archtl. designs include Cedars Sta., 1996 (Honor award Tex. Soc. Architects 1996), Tarrant County Jail, Dallas Area Rapid Transit (Dallas Planning award 1996, Nat. Honor award for design 2000); exhbns. include Mus. Fine Arts Houston, 2001; pub. art commns. include City of Ft. Worth, 2002—. Founder, treas. Urban Strategies, Ft. Worth, 1991—; bd. dirs. Arts Coun. Ft. Worth, 1994—2001, James L. West Spl. Care Ctr., 1999—2002; founder, bd. dirs. Contemporary Art Ctr., Ft. Worth, 1995—99, pres., 1999; mem. urban design com. Downtown Ft. Worth, 1992—99, City of Ft. Worth Pub. Art Commn., 2002—. Recipient Streams and Valleys, Inc. award, 1993, Leadership Arts award Dallas Bus. Com. for the Arts, 1993. Mem.: AIA (exec. com. 1991—94, nat. chmn. interiors com. 1994, spkr. 1995—2002), Tex. Soc. Architects (state chmn. interiors com. 1986—91, spkr. 2000, spkr. 2001, Honor award 1997, Dallas Planning award 1998), Ft. Worth Club. Methodist. Avocations: running, skiing.

MILLICHAP, JOSEPH GORDON, neurologist, educator; b. Wellington, Eng., Dec. 18, 1918; came to U.S., 1956, naturalized, 1965; s. Joseph P. and Alice (Fiello) M.; m. Mary Irene Fortey, Feb. 25, 1946 (dec. Oct. 1969); children: Martin Gordon, Paul Anthony; m. Nancy Melanie Kluczynski, Nov. 7, 1970 (dec. Apr. 1995); children: Gordon Thomas, John Joseph. M.B. with honors in Surgery, St. Bartholomew's Med. Coll., U. London, Eng., 1946, MD in Internal Medicine, 1951, diploma child health, 1948. Diplomate: Am. Bd. Pediatrics, Am. Bd. Neurology and Child Neurology, Am. Bd. Electroencephalography. Intern, resident St. Bartholomew's Hosp., 1946-49, Hosp. Sick Children, London, 1951-53, Mass. Gen. Hosp., Boston, 1958-60; pediatric neurologist NIH, 1955-56; USPHS fellow neurology Mass. Gen. Hosp., Boston, 1958-60; cons. pediatric neurology Mayo Clinic, 1960-63; pediatric neurologist Children's Meml. Hosp., Northwestern Med. Center, Chgo., 1963—; prof. neurology and pediatrics Northwestern U. Med. Sch., 1963—. Cons. surgeon gen. USPHS; mem. med. adv. bds. Ill. Epilepsy League, Muscular Dystrophy Found., Cerebral Palsy Found., 1963—; vis. prof. Gt. Ormond St. Hosp., U. London, 1986-87. Author: Febrile Convulsions, 1967, Pediatric Neurology, 1967, Learning Disabilities, 1974, The Hyperactive Child with MBD, 1975, Nutrition, Diet and Behavior, 1985, Dyslexia, 1986, Progress in Pediatric Neurology, 1991, Vol. II, 1994, Vol. III, 1997, Environmental Poisons in Our Food, 1993, A Guide to Drinking Water, Hazards and Health Risks, 1995, Attention Deficit Hyperactivity and Learning Disorders, 1998, (with G.T. Millichap) The School in a Garden, 2000; editor Jour. Pediatric Neurology Briefs; contbr. articles to profl. jours., chpts. to books. Chmn. research com. med. adv. bd. Epilepsy Found., 1965— . Served with RAF, 1949-51. Named New Citizen of Year in Met. Chgo., 1965; recipient Americanism Medal D.A.R., 1972, Brennemann award Chgo. Pediat. Soc., 1998; USPHS research grantee, 1957 Fellow Royal Coll. Physicians; mem. Am. Neurol. Assn., Am. Pediatric Soc., Am. Soc. Pediatric Research, Am. Acad. Neurology, Am. Soc. Pharmacology and Exptl. Therapeautics, Soc. Exptl. Biology and Medicine, Am. Bd. Psychiatry and Neurology (asst. examiner 1961—), A.M.A. Episcopalian. Home: PO Box 11391 Chicago IL 60611-0391 Office: Children's Meml Hosp Box 51 2300 N Childrens Plz Chicago IL 60614-3394

MILLIGAN, ARTHUR ACHILLE, retired banker; b. Oxnard, Calif., Oct. 29, 1917; s. John Leslie and Julia (Levy) M.; m. Jeanne Welch, Dec. 12, 1942; children: Michael S., Marshall C. BA, Stanford U., 1938. Pres., CEO Bank of A. Levy, Oxnard, Calif., 1955-82, chmn. bd. dirs., 1982-87, chmn. exec. com., 1988-95; dir. Oxnard Frozen Foods Corps., 1958-90; chmn. Real Estate Investment Trust of Calif., Santa Monica, 1968-87, ret. Lt. USN, 1942-45. Mem. Ind. Bankers So. Calif. (pres. 1958), Western Ind. Bankers (pres. 1961), Calif. Bankers Assn. (pres. 1964), Am. Bankers Assn. (pres. 1978), Valley Club (Montecito, bd. dirs. 1969-72, 85-87, 88—, pres. 1990-92), Elks, Rotary (pres. 1949—). Republican.

MILLIGAN, CYNTHIA HARDIN, university dean, lawyer; BA, U. Kans., 1967; JD, George Washington U., 1970. Bar: D.C. 1970, Nebr. 1977. Assoc. Arent, Fox, Kintnor, Plotkin & Kahn, Washington, 1970-77; ptnr. Rembolt, Ludtke, Milligan & Berger, Lincoln, Nebr., 1977-87; dir. Nebr. Dept. Banking and Fin., 1987-91; pres. CMA, 1991-98; dean U. Nebr. Coll. Bus. Adminstrn., 1998—. Bd. dirs. Wells Fargo & Co., San Francisco, Gallup Orgn., Princeton, N.J., Calvert Funds, Bethesda, Md. Trustee W.K. Kellogg Found., Battle Creek, Mich. Fellow Nebr. Bar Found.; mem. Nebr. Bar Assn. Office: U Nebr Coll Bus Adminstrn PO Box 880405 Lincoln NE 68588-0405

MILLIGAN, DONALD BRUCE, physician, educator; b. Belleville, Kans., Sept. 25, 1948; s. Samuel Wayne and Fern (Cunningham) M.; m. Katherine Phyllis Lee, Aug. 21, 1971 (div. Nov. 1992); children: Heather Lee, Patrick Sean; m. Linda Louise (Ralston) Milligan, June 10, 1995. BA cum laude, Sterling Coll., 1970; MD, Johns Hopkins U., 1974. Diplomate Am. Bd. Family Practice. Resident in family practice Kans. U. Med. Ctr., Kansas City, 1974-77, instr., 1982-93, 98—; pvt. practice Olathe, Kans., 1977-82, 97-98; urgent care physician Oak Pk. Health Svcs., Overland Pk., 1993-97; asst. prof. Kans. U. Med. Ctr., 1998—. Legal cons., Kansas City, 1982—. Recipient Alumni award Sterling Coll., 1993. Presbyterian. Avocations: Kansas City Symphony Chorus, travel, reading. Office: Kans U Med Ctr 3901 Rainbow Blvd Kansas City KS 66160-0001 E-mail: dmilligan@kumc.edu.

MILLIGAN, GLENN EDWARD, poet; b. Detroit, Aug. 21, 1949; s. George Edwin and Doris Ann M. BBA in Econ., Western Mich. U., Kalamazoo, 1984. Disabled american vet., 1974—. Author: Lust, Love, Life, 1986, Nocturnes, 1988, Beyond Bamboo, 1998, Passage, 1999, Lament, 2000. Mem. Disabled Am. Vets., Battle Creek, Mich., 1979—. Home: 1430 W Territorial Rd Battle Creek MI 49015

MILLIGAN, GLENN WESLEY, business educator; b. Enid, Okla., June 11, 1949; s. Donald Lee and Wanda Lee Milligan. BA, U. So. Calif., 1971; MA, Calif. State U., 1974; PhD, Ohio State U., 1978. Cert. quality engr. Prof., chair Fisher Coll. of Bus., Ohio State U., Columbus, 1978—. Dept. chair Fisher Coll. of Bus., Columbus, 1996—, undergrad. programs chair, 1994-96. Contbr. articles to profl. jours. With U.S. Army, 1971-78. Mem. Classification of N.Am. (bus. mgr. 1987-90), Am. Soc. for Quality, Am. Psychol. Assn. Democrat. Avocations: music, travel. Office: Fisher Coll of Bus Ohio State U Columbus OH 43210

MILLIGAN, JOHN DRANE, historian, educator; b. N.Y.C., Oct. 11, 1924; s. Carl Glover and Hazel Gray (Drane) M.; m. Joyce Mary Jervis, Nov. 16, 1946; children: Jacqueline M., Paula J., Mary M., Elizabeth Y. BA, U. Mich., 1952, MA, 1953, PhD, 1961. Tchg. asst. U. Mich., 1951-52, tchg. fellow, 1954-56; from asst. prof. to prof. history SUNY, Buffalo, 1962-2000, dir. grad. programs in history, 1963-68, 94-95, dir. undergrad. programs in history, 1979-86, acting dept. chmn., summers, 1977, 78-80, 88, prof. emeritus, 2000. Vis. prof. McMaster U., Hamilton, Ont., Can., summer 1964, 69-70 Author: Gunboats Down the Mississippi, 1965, From the Fresh-Water Navy, 1861-1864, 1970; also chpts. in books, articles in jours., encys. Mem. Ann Arbor chpt. NAACP, exec. bd., 1956-61; mem. ACLU, exec. bd., 1959-61; mem. campaign coms. for various candidates for local and nat. office, 1960-76; mem. Buffalo NAACP, Buffalo Housing Opportunities Made Equal, Citizens Council on Human Relations, Physicians for Social Responsibility, Common Cause, Amnesty Internat.; faculty chmn. United Fund dr., 1977; active Foster Parents Plan, 1955-70; adoptive parent Internat. Social Services; founder charitable trust for minority coll. scholarships. Served with USAAF, 1943-46, USAFR, 1946-56. James B. Angell scholar U. Mich.; grantee Research Found. SUNY; grantee U.S. Naval Inst.; Citation of Civil War Round Table; Moncado Award of Am. Mil. Inst. Mem. Am. Hist. Assn., Assn. Am. Historians, So. Hist. Assn., Buffalo and Erie County Hist. Soc., Afro-Am. Hist. Soc., Soc. Civil War Historians, Buffalo Coun. for Responsibility in Fgn. Policy (founding), Soaring Soc. Am., Aircraft Owners and Pilots Assn., Niagara Soaring Club, Cambria Flying Soc., Silver Wings Assn., Civil War Round Table, SUNY Buffalo Pres.'s Assocs., SUNY Buffalo Founders' Soc., Tau Sigma Delta, Phi Kappa Phi, Phi Alpha Theta. Home: 21 Allenhurst Rd Buffalo NY 14214-1201 *If an individual cannot influence for the better the course of humankind, one can sometimes influence for the better the life of another individual.*

MILLIGAN, KAREN LITTLE, education educator; b. Maryville, Tenn., Mar. 20, 1957; d. Joe Neil and Gladys Louise (Cole) Little; m. Thomas Braden Milligan, Jr., July 10, 1982; children: David Lloyd, Meredith Claire. BA, Carson-Newman Coll., 1978; MS, U. Tenn., 1981, PhD, 1998. Coord. of program for gifted students Jefferson County Schs., Jefferson City, Tenn., 1980-83, tchr. 6th grade, 1984-94; grad. tchg. asst. COE U. Tenn., Knoxville, 1994-96; asst. prof. tchr. edn. Carson-Newman Coll., Jefferson City, 1996—. Tchr. cons. Nat. Geographic Soc., Washington, 1987. Troop leader Girl Scouts of Am., Jefferson City, 1994. Named to Outstanding Young Women of Am., 1985; grantee Tenn. State Dept. Edn., 1991. Mem. ASCD, Assn. for Advancement of Computing in Edn., Internat. Soc. for Tech. in Edn. Baptist. Avocations: camping, bicycling, organist, handbell choir mem. Office: Carson-Newman Coll Box 71874 Jefferson City TN 37760

MILLIGAN, SISTER MARY, theology educator, religious consultant; b. Los Angeles, Jan. 23, 1935; d. Bernard Joseph and Carolyn (Krebs) M. BA, Marymount Coll., 1956; Dr. de l'Univ., U. Paris, 1959; MA in Theology, St. Mary's Coll., Notre Dame, Ind., 1966; STD, Gregorian U., 1975; D. honoris causa, Marymount U., 1988. Tchr. Cours Marymount, Neuilly, France, 1956-59; asst. prof. Marymount Coll., Los Angeles, 1959-67; gen. councillor Religious of Sacred Heart of Mary, Rome, 1969-75, gen. superior, 1980-85; asst. prof. Loyola Marymount U., Los Angeles, 1977-78, provost, 1986-90, prof., 1990—, dean liberal arts, 1992-97, provincial superior, 1997—. Pres. bd. dirs. St. John's Sem., Camarillo, Calif., 1986-89; mem. exec. com. Internat. Union Superiors Gen., Rome, 1983-85; mem. planning bd. spiritual renewal program Loyola Marymount U., Los Angeles, 1976-78. Author: That They May Have Life, 1975; compiler analytical index Ways of Peace, 1986; contbr. articles to profl. jours. Vis. scholar Grad. Theol. Union, Berkeley, 1986. Mem. Calif. Women in Higher Edn., Coll. Theology Soc., Cath. Biblical Assn. Democrat. Roman Catholic. Home: 3216 Eagle St Los Angeles CA 90063-3121 E-mail: marymilligan@earthlink.net.

MILLIGAN, MICHAEL EDWARD, insurance services company executive; b. Fullerton, Calif., Aug. 28, 1952; s. Edward Scott Milligan and Patricia Ann (Shirk) Madson; m. Diane Marie Mascaro, June 21, 1974; children: Robert Michael, Lauren Alicia, Stefanie Diane. BS, U.S. Mil. Acad., 1974; MS, U. So. Calif., 1979. Commd. 2d lt. U.S. Army, 1974, advanced through grades to capt., 1979, comdr. Europe, 1974-79; resigned, 1979; various positions to group leader product devel. Procter & Gamble, Cin., 1979-85; mgr. product devel. and tech. svcs., then div. mgr. engring. Pepsi Cola USA, Purchase, N.Y., 1985-87; div. mgr. stratetic planning ops. Pepsi Cola Co., Somers, 1987-88; dir. mktg., sales and devel. Gen. Analysis Corp., Norwalk, Conn., 1988-89; dir. market planning and devel. Ins. Svcs. Office subs. ISOTEL, N.Y.C., 1989-91; asst. v.p. mktg. and product devel. Ins. Svcs. Office, Inc., 1991-98; v.p. mktg., bus. devel. and strategic planning Chirapoint, Alpharetta, Ga., 1998—. Republican. Roman Catholic. Avocation: golf.

MILLIGAN, MICHAEL LEE, dentist; b. Kenton, Ohio, Sept. 5, 1952; s. Robert L. and Lena R. (Chiesa) M.; m. Karen S. Nice, Sept. 20, 1975; children: Kristen, Patrick, Lyndsey, Marisa. BS, U. Houston, 1975; DMD, So. Ill. U., 1978. Gen. practice dentistry, Bloomington, Ill., 1978—. Co-developer Eastland Profl. Bldg., Bloomington, 1987-88. Co-founder World Golf Tour, 1997; founder Nat. Competitive Golf Tour, 2001. Ill. Men's Golf Champion, 1974, Ill. Men's Match Play Golf Champion, 1977, Chgo. Dist. Golf. Champion, 1973, 74, 77, Butler Nat. Amateur Golf Champion, 1994. Mem. ADA, Ill. Dental Soc., McLean County Dental Soc. (pres. 1987-88). Lodges: KC. Home: 208 Grandview Dr Normal IL 61761-3135 Office: 1404 Eastland Dr Ste 101 Bloomington IL 61701-7904

MILLIGAN, RENEÉ ANN, nursing educator, researcher; b. Ft. Wayne, Ind., Sept. 17, 1952; d. Richard Kenneth and Ramona Ann (Eme) Smith; m. David Lee Milligan, Aug. 28, 1972; children: Rachel, Sarah. BS, Ball State U., 1974, MA, 1977; PhD, U. Md., Balt., 1989. Asst. prof. Ind.-Purdue U.; dir. nursing activities Northwestern State U.; staff RN Holy Cross Hosp., Silver Spring, Md.; lectr. U. Md., Balt.; Robert Wood Johnson clin. nurse scholar U.

Rochester (N.Y.); assoc. prof., acting dir. rsch. Georgetown U., Washington, 1998-99, assoc. prof., 1996—. Adj. prof. Johns Hopkins U., 2000—. Dir. rsch. and evaluation Pregnancy Aid Ctr., College Park, Md., 2000—. Mem. ANA, Assn. Women's Health Obstetric and Neonatal Nurses, Ea. Nursing Rsch. Soc., Sigma Theta Tau. E-mail: milligar@gunet.georgetown.edu.

MILLIGAN, TERRY WILSON, business and product development consultant; b. Hackensack, N.J., Aug. 29, 1935; s. Wilson McLeish and Mildred B. (Dabinett) M.; m. Doris Carol Jachtman, Aug. 31, 1957; children: Scott, Peter, Susan. BS, Marietta (Ohio) Coll., 1956; PhD in Chemistry, U. Ill., 1959. From scientist to mktg. mgr. sci. markets Polaroid Corp., Cambridge, Mass., 1959-88, tech. dir. conventional film, 1989-98, bus. devel. mgr. Wayland, 1999—2001. Contbr. articles to sci. mags.; patentee in field. Chmn. Town Warrant Com., Belmont, Mass., 1987—. Grantee NSF, 1958; recipient fellowship U. Ill., Champaign, 1956-59. Mem. AAAS, Am. Chem. Soc., Phi Beta Kappa. Unitarian Universalist. Avocations: fishing, gardening, travel. E-mail: terrywmilligan@aol.com.

MILLIKAN, CLARK HAROLD, physician; b. Freeport, Ill., Mar. 2, 1915; s. William Clarance and Louise (Chamberlain) M.; m. Gayle Margaret Gross, May 2, 1942 (div. Apr. 1966); children: Terri, Clark William, Jeffry Brent; m. Janet T. Holmes, July 21, 1966 (div. Dec. 1987); m. Nancy Futrell, Dec. 28, 1987. Student, Parsons (Kans.) Jr. Coll., 1935; MD, U. Kans., 1939. Diplomate Am. Bd. Psychiatry and Neurology. Intern St. Luke's Hosp., Clev., 1939-40, asst. resident medicine, 1940-41; from resident neurology to asst. prof. neurology State U. Iowa, Iowa City, 1941-49; staff Mayo Clinic, Rochester, Minn., 1949—, cons. neurology, 1958—; dir. Mayo Center for Clin. Rsch. in Cerebrovascular Disease; prof. neurology Mayo Sch. Medicine; physician-in-chief pro tem Cleve. Clinic, 1970; prof. neurology U. Utah Sch. Medicine, Salt Lake City, 1976-87, U. Miami (Fla.) Sch. Medicine, 1987-88; scholar in residence, dept. neurology Henry Ford Hosp., Detroit, 1988-92; prof. neurology Sch. of Medicine Creighton U., Omaha, 1992-94; clin. prof. neurology Med. Coll. Ohio, Toledo, 1994-97; dir. acad. affairs Intermountain Stroke Rsch. Found., Salt Lake City, 1997—. Asst. chmn., editor trans. 2d Princeton Conf. Cerebrovascular Disease, 1957, chmn. confs., 1961, 64; chmn. com. classification and nomenclature cerebrovascular disease USPHS, 1955-69; mem. council Nat. Inst. Neurologic Diseases and Blindness, NIH, USPHS, 1961-65, div. regional med. program, 1965-68; A.O.A. lectr. Baylor U., Waco, Tex., 1952; James Mawer Pearson Meml. lectr., Vancouver, B.C., Can., 1958; Conner Meml. lectr. Am. Heart Assn., 1961; Peter T. Bohan lectr. U. Kans., 1965, 73 Editor: Jour. Stroke, 1970-76, assoc. editor, 1976—. Recipient Outstanding Alumnus award U. Kans., 1973 Fellow ACP, Am. Acad. Neurology (founding chmn. sect. on stroke and vascular neurology 1994), Royal Soc. Medicine; mem. AMA, AAUP, AAAS, Assn. Rsch. Nervous and Mental Disease (pres. 1961), Am. Neurol. Assn. (1st v.p. 1969-70, pres. 1973-74), Minn. Med. Assn., Four County Med. Soc. South Minn., Cen. Neuropsychiat. Assn., N.Y. Acad. Sci., Am. Heart Assn. (chmn. coun. cerebrovascular disease 1967-68, Gold Heart award 1976, Spl. Merit award 1981), Nat. Stroke Assn. (pres. 1986, editor Jour. Stroke and Cerebrovascular Disease 1990—), Sigma Xi. E-mail: clarkmillikan@yahoo.com.

MILLIKAN, JAMES ROLENS, cleaning service executive, musician, composer, fitness consultant; b. Beaumont, Tex., Jan. 15, 1950; s. George Lee and Gertrude Louise (Mann) M.; m. Dorothy Jane Albright, Apr. 22, 1989. BFA, U. Houston, 1968; MFA, Juilliard Sch., 1971. Mgr., ptnr. Edward, Bankers & Co., Houston, 1971-73; prop. gen. Max M. Kaplan Properties, San Antonio, 1973-75; gen. bldg. mgr. Property Mgmt. Systems, Atlanta, 1975-79; dir. real estate Sun Life Group Am., 1979-81; prin. The Millikan Cos., 1981-85, J.R. & Co., Atlanta, 1985-87; sr. v.p., gen. mgr. east coast Nat. Cleaning Contractors, Inc., 1987-93; prin., pres. Master Bldg. Cleaners Inc., 1993—; owner Atlanta Kicksport. Owner ATlanta Kicksport; cons., Sun Life Group Am., 1982-84, McFaddin Ventures, Houston, 1983-84. Composer: Crystal Blue Persuasion (gold record 1969), Crimson & Clover (gold record 1969), Mony Mony (gold record 1969), I Love You More Today than Yesterday (gold record 1970), 1900 Yesterday (gold record 1971), others; instrumentalist for orchs. of Duke Ellington, Count Basie, Buddy Rich, Woody Herman and Glenn Miller, 1965-68; drummer, arranger, conductor for recording artist Petula Clark, 1968-71, leader J.R. and Co., Jazz Ensemble. Founder, pres., St. Luke's Econ. Devel. Corp., Atlanta, 1979, bd. dirs.; bd. dirs. St. Jude's House, Atlanta, 1984, Am. Suicide Found., chmn. Southeastern Divsn. Nat. Bd. Am. Found. for Suicide Prevention; mem. Home Bldg. with Habitat for Humanity. With U.S. Army, 1970-76. Mem. Bldg. Owners and Mgrs. Atlanta, Am. Mktg. Assn., Am. Suicide Found. (bd. dirs.), Bldg. Svc. Contractors Assn. Internat. Democrat. Episcopalian. Avocations: music, golfing, skiing, white water rafting, running, kick boxing. Home and Office: Master Bldg Cleaners Inc 2722 Vinings Oak Dr SE Atlanta GA 30080

MILLIKAN, LARRY EDWARD, dermatologist; b. Sterling, Ill., May 12, 1936; s. Daniel Franklin and Harriet Adeline (Parmenter) M.; m. Jeanine Dorothy Johnson, Aug. 27, 1960; children: Marshall, Rebecca. BA, Monmouth Coll., 1958; MD, U. Mo., 1962, postgrad. in Medicine, 1985—2001. Intern Great Lakes Naval Hosp., Ill., 1962-63; housestaff in tng. U. Mich., Ann Arbor, 1967-69, chief resident, 1969-70; asst. prof. dermatology U. Mo., Columbia, 1970-74, assoc. prof., 1974-81; chmn. dept. dermatology Tulane U., New Orleans, 1981—. Cons. physician Charity Hosp., New Orleans, Tulane U. Hosp., New Orleans, Riley Hosp., Anderson Hosp., Rush Hosp., all Meridia, Miss.; mem. bd. trustees Sulzberger Inst. for Dermatological Edn., 1995-99; chmn. cont. med. edn. com. La. State Med. Soc., 1994-97. Assoc. editor Internat. Jour. Dermatology, 1980-99; mem. editl. bd. Current Concepts in Skin Disorders, Am. Jour. Med. Scis.; contbr. articles to med. jours. Bd. dirs. Women's Dermatol. Assn., 1994-99. With USN, 1960-67. Recipient Andres Bello awrd Govt. of Venezuela, 1989, citation of merit Sch. Medicine, U. Mo., 1993, Faculty Alumnus award U. Mo., 1997; named Disting. Alumnus, Monmouth Coll., 1990; Nat. Cancer Inst. grantee, 1976-84. Fellow ACP; mem. AAAS, AMA, Am. Acad. Dermatology (bd. dirs. 1986-90), Am. Dermatol. Assn., Am. Dermatol. Soc. for Allergy and Immunology (pres., bd. dirs.), Soc. for Investigative Dermatology (past pres. South sect.), So. Med. Assn. (vice chmn. dermatology sect. 1984, chmn. 1994), Coll. Physicians Phila., Assn. Profs. Dermatology (bd. dirs. 1984-86), Orleans Parish Med. Soc., La. Med. Soc., Pan Am. Med. Assn., Internat. Soc. Dermatology (dep. sec. gen. 1989—), Mo. Allergy Assn. (past pres.), Am. Coll. Cryosurgery, Assn. Acad. Dermatol. Surgeons, Internat. Soc. Dermatol. Surgery, Internat. Acad. Cosmetic Dermatology (sec. gen. 1996—), Dermatol. Found. Leaders Soc. (state chmn. 1993-97). Office: Tulane Univ Sch Medicine Dept of Dermatology 1430 Tulane Ave TB36 New Orleans LA 70112-2699

MILLIKAN, RUTH GARRETT, philosophy educator; b. Phila., Dec. 19, 1933; d. Milan Wayne and Eunice (Peterson) Garrett; m. James D. Millikan, Dec. 28, 1961 (div. July 1969); children: Aino, Natasha; m. Donald P. Shankweiler, June 27, 1972. BA, Oberlin Coll., 1955; PhD, Yale U., 1969. Instr. U. Conn., Storrs, 1962-64, assoc. prof. philosophy, 1983-89, prof. philosophy, 1989-2001, Bd. Trustees Disting. prof., 2001—; asst. prof. Berea (Ky.) Coll., 1969-71, U. We. Mich., Kalamazoo, 1971-72; prof. philosophy U. Mich., Ann Arbor, 1994-96. Lectr. in numerous countries. Author: Language, Thought and Other Biological Categories, 1984, White Queen Psychology, 1993, On Clear and Confused Ideas, 2000; contbr. articles to jours. Recipient Jean Nicod prize, Republic of France, 2002. Home: 406 Wormwood Hill Rd Mansfield Center CT 06250 Office: U Conn Philosophy Dept Storrs CT 06269

MILLIKEN, CHARLES BUCKLAND, lawyer; b. New Haven, June 2, 1931; s. Arthur and Susan Lord (Buckland) M.; m. Sandra Stewart, July 6, 1957; children: Susan S., Andrew S. BA, Yale U., 1952; JD, Harvard U., 1957. Bar: Conn. 1957. Assoc. Shipman & Goodwin, Hartford, Conn., 1957-60, ptnr., 1961-92, counsel, 1993—. Lectr. law corp. taxation U. Conn. Contbr. articles to profl. jours. Trustee Westminster Sch., Simsbury, Conn., 1969—, sec., 1970-74, chmn., 1974-80; bd. dirs. Hartford Symphony, 1959-74, 1980—, sec., 1960-62, pres., 1962-64; bd. dirs. Greater Hartford Arts Council, 1971-90; trustee Hartt Sch. Music, 1980-94, 95—, chmn., 1980-99; regent U. Hartford, 1988-94. With U.S. Army, 1952-54. Fellow Am. Coll. Trust and Estate Counsel, Am. Coll. Tax Counsel; mem. ABA, Conn. Bar Assn. (chmn. tax sect. 1979-82), Hartford County Bar Assn. Home: 56 Ely Rd Farmington CT 06032-1707 Office: 1 American Row Hartford CT 06103-2819

MILLIKEN, DOUGLAS GORDON, financial consultant, municipal official; b. Denver, June 13, 1957; s. J. Gordon and Marie (Machell) M. M in Acctg. and Fin. Mgmt., U. Denver, 1980. CPA, 1980. Ind. fin. cons., Centennial, Colo., 1990—. Elected treas., City of Centennial, 2001. Bd. mem., Colo. Legal Initiatives Project, Denver, 1993-96. Mem. Colo. Soc. CPAs, Rocky Mountain Wrestling Club (founding mem. 1994). Avocation: amateur wrestling. Home: 5315 S Nepal Way Centennial CO 80015-2143 Office: City of Centennial Ste 200 12503 E Euclid Dr Centennial CO 80111-6400 Office Fax: 720-408-0933. E-mail: doug@dougmilliken.com.

MILLIKEN, JEFFREY, cardiothoracic surgeon; b. Wyandotte, MI, Mar. 15, 1956; s. Francis and Nancy Milliken; m. Julie Mills, Oct. 24, 1998; children: Sarah, Amanda. Biomedical sci., U. Mich., 1974—77; med. degree, Univ. Mich. Med. Sch., 1976—80. Cert. Nat. Bd. Med. Examiners 1981, Am. Bd. Thoracic Surgery 1989, Am. Bd. Thoracic Surgery, Recertification 1998, Am. Bd. Surgery 1987. Surgery internship UCLA, L.A., Calif., 1980—81, resident in surgery, 1981—82, rsch. fellow cardiothoracic surgery, 1982—84, sr. residency surgery, 1984—85, chief resident gen. surgery, 1985—86, chief resident cardiothoracic surgery, 1986—88; sr. registrat cardiac surgery Victorian Pediat. Cardiac Surgical Unit Royal Children's Hosp., Victoria, Australia, 1988—89; asst. prof. surgery UCLA Coll. Medicine, Harbor-UCLA Med. Ctr., Torrance, Calif., 1989—95, chief div. cardiothoracic surgery, 1989—95; clin. assoc. prof. surgery UCI Coll. Medicine, UCI Med. Ctr., Orange, 1995—99, chief div. cardiothoracic surgery, 1995—, clinical prof. surgery, 1999—. Office: UCI Med Ctr Hosp 101 The City Dr Bldg 53 Rm 117 Orange CA 92868 Office Fax: 714-456-8870. Business E-Mail: jcmillik@uci.edu.

MILLIKEN, JOHN GORDON, research economist; b. Denver, May 12, 1927; s. William Boyd and Margaret Irene (Marsh) M.; m. Marie Violet Machell, June 13, 1953; children: Karen Marie, Douglas Gordon, David Tait, Anne Alain. BS, Yale U., 1949, BEng, 1950; MS, U. Colo., 1966, PhD, 1969. Registered profl. engr., Colo. Engr. U.S. Bur. Reclamation, Denver, 1950-55; asst. to plant mgr. Stanley Aviation Corp., 1955-56; prin. mgmt. engr., dept. mgr. Martin-Marietta Aerospace Divsn., 1956-64; mgmt. engr. Safeway Stores, Inc., 1964-66; sr. rsch. economist, prof., assoc. div. head U. Denver Rsch. Inst., 1966-86; pres. Univ. Senate, 1980-81; prin. Milliken Chapman Rsch. Group, Inc., Littleton, Colo., 1986-88, Milliken Rsch. Group, Inc., Littleton, 1988—. Vis. fellow sci. policy rsch. unit U. Sussex, Eng., 1975-76; cons. mgmt. engr. Author: Aerospace Management Techniques, 1971, Federal Incentives for Innovation, 1974, Recycling Municipal Wastewater, 1977, Water and Energy in Colorado's Future, 1981, Metropolitan Water Management, 1981, Technological Innovation and Economic Vitality, 1983, Water Management in the Denver, Colorado Urban Area, 1988, Benefits and Costs of Oxygenated Fuels in Colorado, 1990, Water Transfer Alternatives Study, 1994, Colorado Springs Water Resources Plan Alternative Assessment Study, 1995, Colorado Springs Utilities Wastewater Infrastructure Alternatives Study, 1998; contbr. articles to profl. jours. Bd. dirs. S.E. Englewood Water Dist., 1963—, South Englewood San. Dist., 1965—; bd. dirs. South Suburban Pk. and Recreation Dist., 1971-96, chmn., 1990-92; v.p. South Suburban Land and Facilities Corp., 2001—; chmn. Dem. Com. of Arapahoe County, 1969-71, 5th Congl. Dist. Colo., 1972-73, 74-75; mem. exec. com. Colo. Faculty Adv. Coun., 1981-85; mem. Garrison Diversion Unit Commn., 1984; trustee Colo. Local Govt. Liquid Asset Trust, 1986—, chmn., 1991-93; bd. dirs. Colo. Spl. Dist. Assn. Property and Liability Pool, 1989—, pres. 1997-98. With M.C., U.S. Army, 1945-46. Recipient Adlai E. Stevenson Meml. award, 1981, cert. of Appreciation for svc. to Nation, U.S. Sec. Interior, 1984, hon. title "Amicus Universitatis," U. Denver, 1994, Disting. Svc. award Spl. Dist. Assn. Colo., 1995; Milliken Park named in his honor for svcs. to Littleton cmty., 1996. Mem. Acad. Mgmt., Nat. Assn. Bus. Economists, Yale Sci. and Engring. Assn., Am. Water Works Assn., Sigma Xi, Tau Beta Pi, Beta Gamma Sigma, Sigma Iota Epsilon. Congregationalist. Home and Office: 6502 S Ogden St Centennial CO 80121-2561 E-mail: jgordonmil@aol.com.

MILLIKEN, PETER ANDREW STEWART, legislator; b. Nov. 11, 1946; BA in Polit. Studies & Econs. with honor, Queen's U. Kingston, 1968; BA, U. Oxford, 1970, MA, 1978; LLB, Dalhousie U., 1971. Bar: Ont., 1973; solicitor Supreme Ct. Ont. Asst. Hon. George J. McIlraith, 1967-68; solicitor Cunningham, Little, Bonham, Milliken, Kingston, Ont., 1973-78; ptnr. Swan, Carty, Little & Bonham, 1978-89; elected mem. Parliament Kingston and Islands, 1988—, apptd. dep. chmn. Coms. Whole Ho., 1996-97, apptd. dep. spkr., chmn. coms., 1997—. Chair standing com. procedure and house affairs, 1994-96, co-chair spl. joint com. code conduct, 1995-97, Bd. Internal Economy, 1997—; part-time lectr. Bus. Law, Sch. Bus. Queen's U., Kingston, 1973-81. Contbr. articles to profl. jours. Office: 558D Center Block Ottawa ON K1A OA6 Canada E-mail: milliken@peter.milliken.org.

MILLIKEN, ROGER, textile company executive; b. N.Y.C., Oct. 24, 1915; s. Gerrish and Agnes (Gayley) M.; m. Justine V. R. Hooper, June 5, 1948; children: Justine, Nancy, Roger, David, Weston. Student, Groton Sch., 1929-33; AB, Yale U., 1937; LLD (hon.) , Wofford Coll., Rose-Hulman Inst. Tech., Phila. Coll. Textiles and Sci., Brenau Coll., The Citadel; D. Textile Industry (hon.) , Clemson U.; DHL (hon.) , Converse Coll.; D. Bus. admin. (hon.) , U. S.C., Spartanburg; LLD (hon.) , LaGrange Coll., Furman U.; HHD (hon.) , Presbyterian Coll. CEO Milliken & Co., N.Y.C., 1947-83, chmn., chief exec. officer, 1983—. Chmn. bd. Inst. Textile Tech., 1948-97; bd. dirs. S.C. Textile Mfrs. Assn. Chmn. Greenville-Spartanburg Airport Commn.; trustee Wofford Coll., S.C. Found. Ind. Coll. Named to, Nat. Bus. Hall of Fame, 2000. Mem. AIA (hon.), Bus. Council, Textile Inst. (Eng.) (companion mem.) Clubs: Union League, Links, Augusta Nat. Golf, Yeamans Hall. Office: Milliken & Co PO Box 1926 Spartanburg SC 29304-1926

MILLIMET, ERWIN, lawyer; b. N.Y.C., Oct. 7, 1925; s. Maurice and Henrietta (Cohen) Millimet; children: Robert, James, Rachel, Sarah. BA magna cum laude, Amherst Coll., 1948; LLB cum laude, Harvard U., 1951. Bar: N.Y. 1952. Formerly sr. ptnr., chmn. exec. com. Stroock & Stroock & Lavan, N.Y.C.; ret., 1991. Mem. faculty Grad. Sch. Mgmt., U. Mass. Mem. bd. visitors U. San Diego Law Sch.; mem. Five Coll. Libr., Northhampton, LI; active Nat. Support Group for Africa; founder Citizens for Am., Washington, 1984; mem. Rep. Presdl. Task Force. Mem. N.Y. State Bar Assn., Assn. of Bar of City of N.Y., Fed. Bar Assn., Rep. Club (N.Y.C. and Washington), Phi Beta Kappa. E-mail: emill@gis.net.

MILLIMET, JOSEPH ALLEN, retired lawyer; b. West Orange, N.J., July 23, 1914; s. Morris and Dorothy (McBlain) M.; m. Elizabeth Gray Gingras, Jan. 10, 1942 (dec. 1995); children: Madlyn Ann (Mrs. Angus Deming), Lisa Gray, Rebecca Allen, Peter Joseph (dec.). AB, Dartmouth Coll., 1936; LLB, Yale U., 1939; LLD (hon.), U. N.H., 1992. Bar: N.H. 1939. Pvt. practice, Concord and Manchester, N.H.; sr. ptnr. Devine, Millimet, Stahl & Branch, and predecessors (now Devine Millimet & Branch), Manchester, 1947-93, ret., 1993; with FCC, 1941-42. Mem. N.H. Bd. Bar Examiners, 1953-61, legislative counsel to, gov. N.H., 1963-66; chmn. Commn. to Revise N.H. Constn., 1964, 74, 84; mem. Commn. Uniform State Laws, 1965-73. With USCG, 1942-45. Fellow Am. Coll. Trial Lawyers; mem. N.H. Bar Assn. (pres. 1962-63), ABA. Democrat. Home: 100 Alliance Way Apt 281 Manchester NH 03102-8402 Office: Devine Millimet & Branch 111 Amherst St Manchester NH 03101-1809 E-mail: jmillimet@mediat.net.

MILLING, BERT WILLIAM, JR. magistrate judge; b. Mobile, Ala., Mar. 5, 1946; s. Bert William and Marjorie Ann (Smith) M.; m. Priscilla Pitman, Apr. 15, 1966; children: Brooks Pitman, Jeremy Bacon, Maran Celeste. AB in Philosophy, The Coll. of William and Mary, 1968; JD, U. Ala., 1971. Bar: Ala. 1971. Legal officer 212th Arty. Group, Fort Lewis, Wash., 1971-72; legal asst. officer Judge Advocate Gen.'s Office, Ft. Sill, Okla., 1972-74; spl. asst. atty. gen. Dist. Atty.'s Office, Mobile, 1974-75, asst. dist. atty., 1977-78; assoc. Sintz, Pike, Campbell & Duke, 1975-77; ct. referee Juvenile Div. of Cir. Ct., 1978-81; counsel U.S. Senate Com. on Jud., Subcom. on Security & Terrorism, Washington, 1981-83; asst. U.S. atty. Justice Dept., Mobile, 1983-86; U.S. magistrate judge U. S. Dist. Ct. So. Dist. Ala., 1986—. Capt. U.S. Army, 1971-74; maj. N.G., USAR, 1975-87. Mem. Ala. Bar Assn., Mobile Bar Assn., Fed. Magistrate Judges Assn., Christian Legal Soc. Anglican. Avocations: photography, music, reading, exercising, family activities. Office: US Courthouse 113 Saint Joseph St Mobile AL 36602-3606

MILLING, MARCUS EUGENE, SR. geologist; b. Galveston, Tex., Oct. 8, 1938; s. Robert Richardson and Leonora Mildred (Currey) M.; m. Sandra Ann Dunlay, Sept. 11, 1959; 1 child, Marcus Eugene Jr. BS in Geology, Lamar U., 1961; MS in Geology, U. Iowa, 1964, PhD in Geology, 1968. Cert. petroleum geologist. Rsch. geologist Exxon Prodn. Rsch. Co., Houston, 1968-76; prodn. geologist Exxon Co. U.S.A., Kingsville, Tex., 1976-78, dist. exptl. geologist New Orleans, 1978-80; mgr. geol. rsch. Arco Oil and Gas Co., Plano, Tex., 1980-86, chief geologist Dallas, 1986-87; assoc. dir. Bur. Econ. Geology U. Tex., Austin, 1987-92; exec. dir. Am. Geol. Inst., Alexandria, Va., 1992—. Vice-chmn. Offshore Tech. Conf., Dallas, 1984-87; dir. Geosci. Inst. for Oil and Gas Recovery Rsch., Austin, 1988-91. NSF fellow, 1966. Fellow Geol. Soc. Am. (councilor 1986-89); mem. Am. Assn. Petroleum Geologists, Soc. Petroleum Engrs., Am. Inst. Profl. Geologists (Ben H. Parker Meml. medal 1997), Blue Key, Sigma Xi. Home: 11457 Hollow Timber Ct Reston VA 20194-1980 Office: Am Geol Inst 4220 King St Alexandria VA 22302-1507 E-mail: mmilling@dgiweb.org.

MILLINGTON, MICHELE, musician, business owner; b. Wilkes-Barre, Pa., Dec. 6, 1958; d. Milton Rowe and Ann (Williams) M.; m. Martin L. Wentz, Dec. 31, 1994. BA in Music, Wilkes U., 1980; MA in Musicology, Marywood U., Scranton, Pa., 1986; postgrad., Cath. U. Am., 1990. Cert. music tchr. Music tchr. St. Ignatius Sch., Kingston, Pa., 1991, St. Anthony's Sch., Washington, 1991-93; choral dir. Kings Coll., Wilkes-Barre, 1994-98; pvt. tchr. piano, Mountaintop, Pa., 1980—; music faculty Wilkes U., Wilkes-Barre, 1998—, Pa. State U., 2000—. Music dir. Bloomsburg (Pa.) Theatre Ensemble, 1998, Little Theatre, Wilkes-Barre, 1998, 2000, Music Box Theatre, Swazersville, Pa., 1990. Mem. Pa. Music Tchrs. Assn. (bd. dirs., certification chair 1997-99), Am. Coll. Musicians (faculty). Avocations: cello, roller skating. Home: 101 Pine View Est Mountain Top PA 18707-9029 Office: Bassler Equipment Co 1300 Wyoming Ave Forty Fort PA 18704-4155

MILLLER, SARI ELIZABETH (SALLY DERBY), writer; b. Dayton, Ohio, July 1, 1934; d. Wallene Russell Derby and Hildred (Chester) Derby; m. Karl Stratton Miller, Dec. 10, 1955; children: David, Michael, Steven, Philip, Matthew, Sarah. BA, Western Coll., Oxford, Ohio, 1956. Author: (Juvenile fiction) My Steps, 1996, Taiko on a Windy Night, 2001, Hannah's Bookmobile Christmas, 2001. Home: 770 Southmeadow Cir Cincinnati OH 45231 E-mail: smiller50@earthlink.net.

MILLMAN, ARTHUR EDWARD, internist, cardiologist, educator; b. N.Y.C., Oct. 12, 1943; MD, Albert Einstein Coll. Medicine, 1969. Diplomate Am. Bd. Internal Medicine, Am. Bd. Cardiology. From intern to resident in medicine Mt. Sinai Hosp., N.Y.C., 1969-72, resident in cardiology, 1974-76; chief of cardiology St. Elizabeth Hosp., N.J.; med. staff St. Michael's Med. Ctr., Newark, Beth Israel Med. Ctr., Newark; assoc. prof. medicine Seton Hall Sch. Grad. Med. Edn.; asst. clin. prof. medicine U. Medicine and Dentistry, Newark; pvt. practice Elizabeth. Fellow Am. Coll. Cardiology, Soc. Cardiac Angiography and Intervention, Am. Heart Assn.; mem. Am. Soc. Echocardiology, N.Y. Heart Assn., Am. Soc. Cardiology, Union County N.J. Med. Soc. (Union county divsn.). Office: 240 Williamson St Ste 502 Elizabeth NJ 07202-3673

MILLMAN, ARTHUR LANCE, oculoplastic surgeon; b. N.Y.C., Feb. 8, 1958; BSN, MD, Northwestern U., Evanston, Ill. Diplomate Am. Bd. Ophthalmology and Eye Plastic Surgery. Dir. Manhattan Ctr. Facial Plastic Surgery; asst. prof. N.Y. Eye and Ear Infirmary; fellow Heed & Knapp Found.; chief plastic surgery Lenox Hill Hosp. Author: (textbook) Facial Plastic Surgery; contbr. articles to profl. jours. Mem. N.Y. Acad. Medicine (William Warner Happin award), N.Y. Facial Plastic Soc. (founding). Avocations: golf, hist. scale modelling, music.

MILLMAN, BRUCE RUSSELL, lawyer; b. Bronx, N.Y., June 4, 1948; s. Meyer and Garie (Solomon) M.; m. Lorrie Jan Liss, Aug. 12, 1973; children: Noemi, Avi. AB, Princeton U., 1970; JD, Columbia U., 1973. Bar: N.Y. 1974, U.S. Dist. Ct. (ea. and so. dists.) N.Y. 1975, U.S. Ct. Appeals (2d dir.) 1978, U.S. Supreme Ct. 1978. Assoc. Rains & Pogrebin and predecessors Rains, Pogrebin & Scher, Mineola, N.Y., 1973-79, ptnr., 1980—. Arbitrator Nassau County Dist. Ct., Mineola, 1981-83. Contbr. New York Employment Law, 1995, Labor and Employment Law for the Corporate Counselor and General Practitioner, 1994, Updating Issues in Employment Law, 1986, Public Sector Labor and Employment Law, 1988. Bd. dirs. West Side Montessori Sch., N.Y.C., 1984-90, sec., 1985-87, pres., 1987-90. Harlan Fiske Stone scholar Columbia U. Law Sch., N.Y.C., 1971, 73. Mem. ABA, N.Y. State Bar Assn. (chair labor and employment law sect. 1997-98), Nassau County Bar Assn., Indsl. Rels. Rsch. Assn. (bd. dirs. L.I. chpt. 1984—, pres. 1995-96). Home: 60 Riverside Dr New York NY 10024-6108 Office: Rains & Pogrebin PC 210 Old Country Rd Ste 12 Mineola NY 11501-4288 also: 375 Park Ave New York NY 10152-0002 E-mail: bmillman@rainslaw.com.

MILLMAN, IRVING, microbiologist, educator, retired inventor; b. N.Y.C., May 23, 1923; BS, City Coll. N.Y., 1948; MS, U. Ky., 1951; PhD, Northwestern U., 1954. Asst. prof. Northwestern U., 1954; formerly with Armour & Co., Pub. Health RSch. Inst. of N.Y.C., Merck Inst. Therapeutic Rsch.; adj. prof. Hahnemann U., Phila. Inducted Nat. Inventors Hall of Fame, 1993. Fellow Am. Acad. Microbiology; mem. N.Y. Acad. Scis., AAAS, Am. Soc. Microbiology. Achievements include development of test to identify Hepatitis B in blood samples. Office: Nat Inventors Hall Fame 221 S Broadway St Akron OH 44308-1505 also: Sch of Med MCP Hahnemann U 2900 W Queen Ln Philadelphia PA 19129-1033*

MILLMAN, JODE SUSAN, lawyer; b. Poughkeepsie, N.Y., Dec. 28, 1954; d. Samuel Keith and Ellin Sadenberg (Bainder) M.; m. Michael James Harris, June 20, 1982; children: Maxwell, Benjamin. BA, Syracuse U., 1976, JD, 1979. Bar: N.Y. 1980, Mich. 2001, U.S. Dist. Ct. (so. and ea. dists.) N.Y. 1982, U.S. Supreme Ct. 1983. Asst. corp. counsel City of Poughkeepsie, 1979-81; assoc. Law Office of Lou Lewis, Poughkeepsie, 1981-85; pvt. practice, 1985—; pres. Seats Pub. Co., 2001—. Staff counsel City of Poughkeepsie Office of Property Devel., 1990—; gen. mgr. WCZX-Comms. Corp. Author: (novels) (children's books) Birthday Wishes and Rock'n Roll Dreams, The Firebird Ballet, Goldie Lox and the Three Behrs, (non-fiction) SEATS: Your Guide to the Best Seats in the House; author: (contbg. author) Kaminstein Legislative History of the Copyright Law, 1979. Pres. Dutchess County (N.Y.) Vis. Bur., 1980—82; mem. assigned counsel program Dutchess County Family Ct.1985, 1985—; trustee Greater Poughkeepsie Libr. Dist., 1991—94, Poughkeepsie Day Sch., 1995—2002; bd. dirs. Poughkeepsie Ballet Theater1982, 1982, Jewish Cmty. Ctr., 1988. Mem.: Washtenaw County Bar Assn., Mich. Bar Assn., Dutchess County Bar Assn. (grievance com. 1994—2001), N.Y. State Bar Assn. Democrat. Jewish. Office: 3997 Preserve Dr Dexter MI 48130 E-mail: jodem54@aol.com.

MILLMAN, RICHARD GEORGE, architect, educator; b. St. Johns, Mich., Feb. 12, 1925; s. Harold Fildew and Elizabeth Hill (Van Deusen) M.; m. Mary Louise Manley, June 17, 1950; children: John Richard, Ruth Barbara. BArch, U. Mich., 1951, MArch, 1962. Registered architect, Mich., Ohio, Ala. Job capt. Smith Hinchman & Grylls, Detroit, 1951-52; designer assoc. Eliot Robinson, AIA, Birmingham, Mich., 1952-55; designer Eero Saarinen Assocs., Bloomfield Hills, 1955-56; assoc. Chas. W. Lane Assocs. Inc., Ann Arbor, 1956-59; prin. Kainlauri, MacMullan, Millman, 1959-62; assoc. prof. Ohio U., Athens, 1962-68; prof. Auburn (Ala.) U., 1968—, head architecture dept., 1968-73, 84-85, head indsl. design dept., 1988-89. Prof. Mid. East Tech. U., Ankara, Turkey, 1966-67,King Faisal U., Dammam, Saudi Arabia, 1979-81. One man shows include Dhahran Art Group, Saudi Arabia, 1981, Peet Gallery, Auburn U., 1983, 91, Heritage Hall Mus., Talladega, Ala., 1998; author: Washtenaw Community Coll., 1962, Auburn U. Tour Guide, 1990. With U.S. Army, 1943-46, ETO, PTO. Decorated Bronze Star; recipient Cert. of Honor Ala. Hist. Commn., 1977; Alumni scholar U. Mich., 1961; Fulbright lectr. Exch. Com., Mid. East Tech. U., 1966. Mem. AIA (treas. Ala. coun. 1969, v.p. 1970, pres. 1972, emeritus 1990, Auburn chpt. pres. 1970, emeritus), Nat. Coun. Archtl. Registration Bd. (cert.), Auburn Arts Assn., Ga. Watercolor Soc. (signature mem.), Watercolor Soc. of Ala. (signature mem.), So. Watercolor Soc. (signature mem.). Avocations: painting, photography. Home: 736 Brenda Ave Auburn AL 36830-6038 E-mail: millmmm@charter.net.

MILLNER, ROBERT B. lawyer; b. N.Y.C., Apr. 20, 1950; s. Nathan and Babette E. (Leventhal) M.; m. Susan Brent, June 5, 1983; children: Jacob, Daniel, Rebecca. BA, Wesleyan U., 1971; JD, U. Chgo., 1975. Bar: Ill. 1975. Law clk. to Hon. George C. Edwards U.S. Ct. Appeals for 6th Cir., Cin., 1975-76; with Sonnenschein Nath & Rosenthal, Chgo., 1976—, ptnr., 1982—. Mem. Panel of Bankruptcy Trustees, Chgo., 1992-97. Editorial bd. Jour. Corp. Disclosure and Confidentiality, 1989-92; contbr. articles to profl. jours. Trustee Anshe Emet Synagogue, Chgo., 1990-93; v.p. Am. Jewish Cong. midwest region, 1995—. Fellow: Am. Bar Found.; mem.: Comml. Bar Assn. (hon. overseas mem.), Chgo. Bar Assn., Am. Bankruptcy Inst., ABA (co-chair bankruptcy and insolvency com. litigation sect. 1992—95, 2001—), Wesleyan Alumni Club Chgo. (pres. 1988—90), Std. Club, Legal Club, Phi Beta Kappa. Office: Sonnenschein Nath & Rosenthal 8000 Sears Tower Chicago IL 60606

MILLON, HENRY ARMAND, fine arts educator, architectural historian; b. Altoona, Pa., Feb. 22, 1927; s. Henri Francois and Louise (de Serent) M.; m. Emily Dees, June, 1953; m. Judith Rice, Dec. 27, 1966; children: Henri, Hadrian, Phoebe, Aaron. BA, Tulane U., 1947, BS, 1949, BArch, 1953; AM, Harvard U., 1954, MArch, 1955, PhD, 1964; LHD (hon.), Tulane U., 1995. Asst. prof. MIT, Cambridge, 1960-69, prof., 1969-80, vis. prof., 1981—, pres. univ. Film Study Ctr., 1972-73, trustee Film Study Ctr., 1967-73; dean Ctr. for Advanced Study in Visual Arts, Nat. Gallery Art, Washington, 1979-2000, dean emeritus, 2000—. Mem. bd. visitors Fine Arts Sch. Boston Mus., 1972-78; mem. rsch. grants panel NEH, 1972-73, rsch. tools panel, 1983; dir. Am. Acad. in Rome, 1974-77, trustee, 1977-96, vice chmn., 1982-96; mem. adv. coun. Sch. Architecture, Princeton U., 1970-73, 97—, adv. coun. dept. art and archeology, 1972-73, 80-84; mem. cons. com. Nat. Survey Historic Sites and Bldgs., Nat. Pk. Svc. div. U.S. Dept. Interior, 1969-80; vice chmn. Boston Landmarks Commn., 1970-73; panelist Gladys Kriebel Delmas Found., 1979—; chmn. adv. bd. architecture and design TV series Guggenheim Prodns., 1980-88; vis. com. Dept. Fine Arts Harvard U., 1982-84, Sch. Hist. Studies Inst. Advanced Study, 1978, Arthur M. Sackler Gallery Smithsonian Instn., 1986-92; mem. U.S. Nat. Com. History of Art, 1980-2000; alt. del. Internat. Com. Hist ory of Art, 1981-85, del., 1985-96, sci. sec. working group Thesaurus Artis Universalis, 1983-89; hon. mem. Boston Archtl. Ctr., 1982—; chmn. sr. fellows com. history of landscape architecture program Dumbarton Oaks, 1983-89, convenor archtl. drawing adv. group, 1983-87; mem. adv. com. Getty Art Hist. Info. Program, 1983-91, mem. internat. repertory of lit. of art history, 1985-90, adv. com. Bibliography of the History of Art, 1986—; vice chmn. Coun. Am. Overseas Rsch. Ctrs., 1984-90; pres. Found. for Documents of Architecture, 1987-93; trustee Nat. Bldg. Mus., 1988-94. Author: Baroque and Rococo Architecture, 1962, Key Monuments in the History of Architecture, 1964; author: (with Andreina Griseri, Sarah McPhee and Mercedes Viale Ferre) Filippo Juvarra: Drawings from the Roman Period, 1704-1714, Part I, 1984, Part II, 1999; author: (with Craigh Hugh Smyth) Michelangelo Architect, 1988; author: (with Linda Nochlin) Art and Architecture in the Service of Politics, 1978; author: Studies in Italian Art and Architecture 15th through 18th Centuries, 1980; co-editor: The Renaissance from Brunelleschi to Michelangelo, 1994; editor: Triumph of the Baroque-Architecture in Europe, 1999. Trustee Clark Art Inst., 1996—, Phillips Collection, 2001—, St. Paul's Ch., Rome, 2000—. With USNR, 1944—46. Recipient citation for excellence Internat. Archtl. Book Publ., AIA, 1994, Prix Hercule Catenacci, Inst. de France, 1995, A.H. Barr award Coll. Art Assn., 1996, Centennial medal Am. Acad. in Rome, Sesquicentennial medal Tulane U., 1997, others; Hon. Mem. Accademia di San Luca, 1995; Fulbright fellow, Italy, 1957, Am. Acad. Rome fellow, 1957-60. Mem. Soc. Archtl. Historians (pres. 1968-70), Coll. Art Assn. (bd. dirs. 1982-85), AIA Found. (mem. octagon com. 1986-88), Renaissance Soc., Am. Acad. Arts and Scis., Am. Philos. Soc. (curator 1998—), Deputazione Subalpina di Storia Patria, Soc. Preservation New Eng. Antiquities, Am. Inst. Archeology, Am. Soc. 18th Century Studies, Academia delle Scienze di Torino, Am. Co. Learned Soc. (fellows' adv. coun. 1998-2000). Home: 8051 Parkside Ln NW Washington DC 20012-2252 E-mail: judithmil@aol.com.

MILLOY, FRANK JOSEPH, JR. surgeon; b. Phoenix, June 26, 1924; s. Frank Joseph and Ola (McCabe) M. BS, Notre Dame U., 1946; MS, Northwestern U., 1949, MD, 1947. Diplomate Am. Bd. Surgery and Thoracic Surgery. Intern Cook County Hosp., Chgo., 1947-49, resident, 1953-57; practice medicine, specializing in surgery Lake Forest, Ill., 1958—. Hon. attending staff Presbyn.-St. Lukes Hosp.; former mem. attending staff Cook County Hosp.; mem. staff U. Ill. Rsch. Hosp.; clin. assoc. prof. surgery, U. Ill. Med. Sch.; assoc. prof. surgery Rush Med. Sch. Contbr. more than 35 articles to profl. jours., chpts. to books. Cons. West Side Vet. Hosp. Served as apprentice seaman USNR, 1943-45; lt. M.C., USNR, 1950-52; PTO. Mem.: ACS, Soc. Med. History Chgo. (pres.), Cook County Hosp. Surg. Alumni Assn., Karl Meyer Surg. Soc. (sec.), Warren Cole Surg. Soc. (past sec.), Ill. Thoracic Surg. Soc. (past pres.), Soc. Thoracic Surgeons, Am. Coll. Chest Physicians, Internat. Soc. Surgery, Chgo. Surg. Soc., Univ. Club (Chgo.), Met. Club, Phi Beta Po. Home: 574 Jackson Ave Glencoe IL 60022-2036

MILLS, AGNES EUNICE KARLIN, artist, printmaker, sculptor; b. N.Y.C., Apr. 2, 1915; d. Herman Karlin and Celia (Ducoffe) Karlin; m. Saul Mills, May 10, 1938 (dec. Nov. 1993); children: Karen, Marghe. Grad., Cooper Union Art Sch., N.Y.C., 1938; BFA, Pratt Inst., 1975; student, NYU. One-woman shows include Carus Gallery, N.Y.C., Unitarian Soc., Manhasset, N.Y., Harbor Gallery, Cold Spring Harbor, N.Y., North Truro Art Gallery, Cape Cod, Mass., Alfredo Valente Gallery, N.Y.C., Robbins Gallery, East Orange, N.J., Nuance Galleries, Tampa, Friends of Tampa Ballet, Graphic Eye Coop Gallery, Pt. Washington, N.Y., City Ctr. Gallery, N.Y.C., Lincoln Ctr. Art Gallery, N.Y.C., North Shore Cmty. Arts Ctr., Great Neck, N.Y., Delray Beach Works in Progress Gallery, Boca Raton Cmty. Ctr., Palm Beach Pub. Libr., Gramercy Park Armory, N.Y.C.; exhibited in group shows at Alfredo Valente Gallery, N.Y.C., Audubon Soc., N.Y.C., Bowdoin Coll. Mus. Art, Brunswick, Maine, Brandeis U., Waltham, Mass., Bklyn. Mus. Art, Brown U., Providence, Butler Inst. Am. Art, Youngstown, Ohio, Colgate U. Libr., Hamilton, N.Y., Cornell U., Ithaca, N.Y., East Hampton (N.Y.) Guild Artists, Gallery K, Woodstock, N.Y., Graphic Eye Coop Gallery, Port Washington, N.Y., Heckscher Mus., Huntington, N.Y., Hunterdon County Mus., Clinton, N.J., Joan Avnet Gallery, Great Neck, N.Y., Lincoln Ctr. Libr. Performing Arts, N.Y.C., Madison Gallery, N.Y.C., Boca Raton City Hall, Boca Raton Cmty. Ctr., Boca Raton Libr.; represented in permanent collections at Boca Raton Mus. Art, Nat. Women in the Arts Mus. Home: 1070 SW 22nd Ave Villa 13#3 Delray Beach FL 33445-6030

MILLS, BELEN COLLANTES, early childhood education educator; b. Philippines; s. Ricardo and Epifania (Tomines) C.; children: Belinda Mills Keiser, Roger A. BSE, Leyte Normal Coll., Tacloban, Leyte, Philippines, 1954; MS in Edn., Ind. U., 1955, EdD, 1967. Prof. early childhood edn. Fla. State U., Tallahassee. Early childhood cons. to ednl. agys. and orgns. Author books on early childhood edn., phonics-based children's books and acad. readiness computer programs; contbr. articles to profl.jours. Smith-Mundt Fulbright scholar. Mem. Nat. Assn. for the Edn. of Young Children, Nat. Assn. of Early Childhood Tchr. Edn., World Coun. for Curriculum and Instruction, Assn. of Childhood Edn. Internat. Home: PO Box 20023 Tallahassee FL 32316-0023 E-mail: raintown@polaris.net.

MILLS, BOB, member of parliament; b. Young, Sask., Can. m. Nicole Mills; children: Ken, Kari Anne, Melinda, Rosanno, Ric, Amanda. BA in Sci. and Edn., U. Saskatchewan. Tchr. biology Lindsay Thurber Comprehensive H.S., 1965-79; founder Mills Travel, Ltd., 1979—; elected to House of Commons, Red Deer, Alberta, Can., 1993—, reelected to Can., 1997, 2000—. Parliamentary activities include mem. steering com. on fgn. affairs and internat. trade, Ofcl. Opposition Fgn. Affairs Critic, Opposition Health Critic, 2000—, mem. standing com. on health, chief environ. critic. gen., 2001—. Mem. Am. Express Network (recipient Travel Hall of Fame award 1992). Avocations: farming, gardening, photography, travel. Office: Rm 920 Confed Ottawa ON Canada K1A 0A6 E-mail: millsb@parl.gc.ca.

MILLS, BRADFORD, merchant banker; b. N.Y.C., Dec. 16, 1926; s. Dudley Holbrook and Louise (Morris) M.; m. Cheryl Ann Di Paolo; children: Elizabeth Lee, Bradford Alan, Barbara Louise, Ross Dudley. BA cum laude in Econs, Princeton U., 1948; postgrad., Oxford (Eng.) U., 1950-51. Asst. to dir. overseas ters. div. ECA, Paris, 1948-50; assoc. corp. fin. dept. F. Eberstadt & Co., N.Y.C., 1954-62, ptnr., 1960-62; mng. ptnr. N.Y. Securities Co., 1962-70; chmn., dir. Specialized Svcs., Inc., Atlanta, 1968-85; pres., CEO Overseas Pvt. Investment Corp., Washington, 1971-73, dir., 1971-75; chmn. bd., dir. F. Eberstadt & Co. Internat., 1973-74; mng. ptnr. Bradford Assocs., 1974-92; ltd. ptnr. Bradford Investment Ptnrs. Ltd., 1992-96. Past chmn. Diamond Glass, MMX Corp., HWC Corp., Chgo., Stock Tab Corp., O.S. Kelly Co., Filtration Scis., Overseas Pvt. Investors Ltd., Overseas Pvt. Equities, Overseas Equity Investors, Inc., Specialized Svcs., Inc., U.S. Precision Glass, Inc.; chmn. Princeton Investment Group, HDMR Discovery Inc.; bd. dirs. The Princeton Packet, Stonecare Internat. Pres. Mills Found.; trustee, vice chmn. Millbrook (N.Y.) Sch., 1978—; trustee, mem. fin., investment and strategic planning coms. Med. Ctr. Princeton, chmn. nominating com., 1995—. Mem. Coun. Fgn. Rels., Blooming Grove Club (Pa.), Links Club, Leash Club, Anglers Club N.Y., Nassau Club (trustee 1998—), Bedens Brook Club, Amwell Valley Conservancy, Inc., TPC at Jasna Polona. Home: 15 Van Kirk Rd Princeton NJ 08540-4207 Office: Bradford Investment Group Inc 44 Nassau St Ste 365 Princeton NJ 08542-4511 E-mail: patchesteddy@msn.com.

MILLS, CAROL ANDREWS, mental health administrator; b. North Dighton, Mass., Feb. 12, 1943; d. Francis Freeman Grant and Julia Catherine (Trond) Andrews; divorced; 1 child, Judith Caroline. Cert. in AMA mgmt., Bristol C.C., 1991. From jr. clk. to program coord. Commonwealth of Mass. Dept. of Mental Health, 1961—2002; ret., 2002. Selectman Town of Berkley, Mass., 1996—, chmn. Bd. of Selectmen, 1997-99; mem. exec. bd. Bristol County Adv. Bd.; mem. Mass. Dem. State Com., 1987—; mem. Dem. Town Com., Berkley, 1968—; del. Dem. Nat. Convention from Mass., 1996; mem. Berkley Scholarship Com., 1989—; pres., bd. trustees Bristol County Agrl. H.S., 1987-93; justice of the peace, notary public. Mem. DAR, Berkley Hist. Soc. (pres. 1991-95), Mass. Orgn. Genealogists, Bristol County Selectman's Assn. (v.p. 1998-2000, pres. 2000-2002), Daus. Am. Colonists, Mayflower Soc. Roman Catholic. Avocations: politics, genealogy. Home: 540 Berkley St Berkley MA 02779-1002

MILLS, CAROL MARGARET, business consultant, public relations consultant; b. Salt Lake City, Aug. 31, 1943; d. Samuel Lawrence and Beth (Neilson) M. BS magna cum laude, U. Utah, 1965. With W.S. Hatch Co., Woods Cross, Utah, 1965-87, corp. sec., 1970-87, traffic mgr., 1969-87, dir. publicity, 1974-87, cons. various orgns., 1988—. Dir. Hatch vc. Corp., 1972-87, Nat. Tank Truck Carriers, Inc., Washington, 1977-88; bd. dirs. Intermountain Tariff Bur. Inc., 1978-88, chmn., 1981-82, 1986-87; bd. dirs. Mountainwest Venture Group. Fund raiser March of Dimes, Am. Cancer Soc., Am. Heart Assn.; active senatorial campaign, 1976, gubernatorial campaign, 1984, 88, congl. campaign, 1990, 92, 94, vice chair voting dist., 1988-90, congl. campaign, 1994, chmn. 1990-92, chmn. party caucus legis. dist.; witness transp. com. Utah State Legislature, 1984, 85; apptd. by gov. to bd. trustees Utah Tech. Fin. Corp., 1986—, corp. sec., mem. exec. com., 1988—; mem. expdn. to Antarctica, 1996, Titanic '96 expdn.; mem. Iceland and Greenland expdn., 2001; mem. Pioneer Theatre Guld, 1985--. Recipient Svc. awards W.S. Hatch Co., 1971, 80; VIP chpt. Easter Seal Telethon, 1989, 90, Outstanding Vol. Svc. award Easter Seal Soc. Utah, 1989, 90. Mem. Nat. Tank Truck Carriers, Transp. Club Salt Lake City, Am. Trucking Assn. (mem. pub. rels. coun.), Utah Motor Transport Assn. (bd. dirs. 1982-88), Internat. Platform Assn., Traveler's Century Club, Titanic Internat., Beta Gamma Sigma, Phi Kappa Phi, Phi Chi Theta. Home: HC 11 Box 329 Kamiah ID 83536-9410 Office: PO Box 1495 Kamiah ID 83536-1495

MILLS, CELESTE LOUISE, credit manager, hypnotherapist, professional magician; b. L.A., May 16, 1952; d. Emery John and Helen Louise (Bradbury) W.; m. Robert Richardson Feigel, Apr. 11, 1971 (div. 1973); m. Peter Alexander Mills, June 12, 1991. (div. 1992). BBA, Western State U., Doniphan, Mo., 1987; PhD in Religion, Universal Life Ch. Univ., 1987; grad., Hypnotism Tng. Inst., Glendale, Calif., 1990. Cert. hypnotherapist. Credit mgr. accounts receivable Gensler-Lee Diamonds, Santa Barbara, Calif., 1973-74, Terry Hinge and Hardware, Van Nuys, 1975-78; credit mgr., fin. analyst Peanut Butter Fashions, Chatsworth, 1978-82; personal mgr. Charter Mgmt. Co., Beverly Hills, 1982-83; co-owner, v.p. Noreen Jenney Communicates, 1983-85; corp. credit mgr., fin. analyst Ctrl. Diagnostic Lab., Tarzana, Calif., 1985-89; credit mgr., fin. analyst Metwest Clin. Lab., Inc., 1989-90; pvt. practice, clin. hypnotherapist Sherman Oaks, 1990—. Cons. Results Now, Inc., Tarzana, 1986-87; profl. magician Magic Castle, Hollywood, 1989—, Prodr., host (TV) Brainstorm, 1993—. Media spokesperson Am. Cancer Soc., 1990—. Mem. NAFE, NOW, Nat. Humane Ednl. Found., Credit Mgrs. Assn. Trade Groups (bd. govs. 1988-89), Nat. Clin. Lab. Trade Group (chmn. 1988-89), Med. and Surg. Suppliers Trade Group (vice chmn. 1988-89, chmn. 1989-90), Soc. Am. Magicians, Acad. Magical Arts, Internat. Brotherhood of Magicians, Assn. Advanced Ethical Hypnosis, Am. Coun. Hypnotist Examiners. Avocations: scuba diving, sailing.

MILLS, CHARLES ANTHONY, structural engineer, consultant; b. Martinsville, Va., Jan. 13, 1965; s. William Albert and Edith Ruth (Adams) M. BS in Mech. Engring., N.C. State U., 1988, MS, 1991. Registered profl. engr., Mich. Mech. engr. Carolina Power & Light Co., New Hill, N.C., 1985; project engr. Burroughs Wellcome Co., Greenville, 1987-88; teaching asst. N.C. State U., Raleigh, 1989-91; product design engr. Ford Motor Co., Dearborn, Mich., 1991-94; youth counselor Cameron (N.C.) Boys Camp/Bapt. Children's Home, 1994-95; pres. Tech. Imperatives, Inc., Cary, N.C., 1996-98; sr. project engr. Johnson Controls, Inc., Holland, Mich., 1998—. Author: Collaborative Engineering and the Internet: Linking Product Development Partners Via the Web, 1998. Active Rutherford Inst., Charlottesville, Va., 1993—; Citizens for Family Values, Ann Arbor, Mich., 1993-94. GTE Gold Leadership scholar, 1990, scholar N.C. Acoustical Soc., 1989, Turrentine Meml. scholar N.C. State U., 1986. Mem. ASME (assoc.), Soc. Mfg. Engrs., Computer and Automated Sys. Assn., Rapid Prototyping Assn., Soc. Concurrent Engring., CAD Soc., Pi Tau Sigma. Avocations: bicycling, hiking, canoeing, rock-climbing, audio. Office: Johnson Controls Inc One Prince Ctr Holland MI 49423

MILLS, CHARLES GARDNER, lawyer; b. Griffin, Ga., Feb. 29, 1940; s. Charles G. and Marguerite (Powell) M. AB, Yale U., 1962; JD, Boston Coll., 1967; LLM, Touro Coll., 2002. Bar: N.Y. 67, U.S. Dist. Ct. (so. and ea. dists.) 72, U.S. Ct. Appeals (2d cir.) 75, U.S. Supreme Ct. 77, U.S. Ct. Fed. Claims 91, U.S. Ct. Appeals for Vets. Claims 96, U.S. Dist. Ct. (no. dist.) N.Y. 99. Assoc. Smart & McKay, N.Y.C., 1967-68, Smart & Mills, N.Y.C., 1969-71, Eaton & VanWinkle, N.Y.C., 1971-82, Payne, Wood & Littlejohn, Glen Cove and Melville, N.Y., 1982-91; pvt. practice, Glen Cove, 1991—. With U.S. Army, 1962-64, ETO. Mem. Assn. Bar City N.Y., Nassau County Bar Assn., Rotary (pres. Glen Cove Club 1989-90), Am. Legion (comdr. Locust Valley, N.Y. post 1988-90, comdr. Nassau County com. 1995-96, N.Y. Judge Advocate, 1998—), Soc. Colonial Wars, SCV, Order of the Arrow. Republican. Roman Catholic. Office: 56 School St Glen Cove NY 11542-2512

MILLS, DALE DOUGLAS, journalist; b. Seattle, Oct. 4, 1930; d. Donald Emery and Antoinette (Kinleyside) Douglas; m. William Russell Mills, Aug. 13, 1955; children: Lida Susan, William Tad Jr., Peter Donald, Jane Douglas. BA, U. Wash., 1952. Reporter Seattle Times, 1954-55, 74-83; asst. libr. Harvard U., 1955-56; editor Puget Soundings mag., 1968-71. Author: (satire) Deliver Us From Squid Roe, 1995. Mem. com. sign control Seattle City Coun., 1970-72; rsch. dir. City Coun. campaign, 1971; bd. mgrs. King County Juvenile Ct.; trustee Allied Arts Seattle; bd. dirs. King County Coun. for Prevention of Child Abuse and Neglect. Recipient awards for excellence in reporting Wash. Press Assn., Nat. Fedn. Press Women, Allied Daily Newspapers, C.B. Blethen Meml. award for disting. investigative reporting, Excellence award Soc. Profl. Journalists/Sigma Delta Chi. Mem.: Jr. League Seattle, Seattle Times Stars, Helen T. Bush Children's Hosp Guild., Sunset Club, Seattle Yacht Club, Kappa Kappa Gamma.

MILLS, DANIEL QUINN, business educator, consultant, author; b. Houston, Nov. 24, 1941; s. Daniel Monroe and Louise (Quinn) M.; divorced; children: Lisa Ann, Shirley Elizabeth. BA, Ohio Wesleyan U., 1963; MA, Harvard U., 1965, PhD, 1968. Prof. MIT, Cambridge, 1968-75, Harvard Bus. Sch., Boston, 1976—. Impartial umpire Plan to Settle Disputes in Constrn., 1973-79, Trans-Alaska Pipeline, 1975-78, AFL-CIO Internal Disputes Plan, 1975-82; commr. Nat. Commn. on Employment Policy, Washington, 1982-86. Author: Industrial Relations in Construction, 1971, Labor, Government and Inflation, 1975, Labor-Management Relations, 1978, 5th edit., 1993, The New Competitors, 1985, Not Like Our Parents: The Baby-Boom Generation, 1987, The IBM Lesson, 1988, The Rebirth of the Corporation, 1990, The GEM Principle, 1994, Broken Promises: What Went Wrong at IBM, 1996, e-Leadership, 2000, Buy, Lie and Sell High: How Investors Lost Out on Enron and The Internet Bubble, 2002. Mem. Am. Econ. Assn., Indsl. Relations Research Assn., Phi Beta Kappa Mem. United Ch. of Christ. Office: Harvard U Harvard Bus Sch Soldiers Field Rd Allston MA 02163

MILLS, DAVID HARLOW, psychologist, association executive; b. Marshalltown, Iowa, Dec. 26, 1932; s. Harlow Burgess and Esther Winifred (Brewer) M.; m. Janet Louise Anderson, June 15, 1957 (div. 1984); children: Ross Harlow, Anne Louise; m. Susan S. Greene, Aug. 3, 1984. BS, Iowa State U., 1955, MS, 1957; PhD, Mich. State U., 1964. Postdoctoral fellow USPHS U. Ill., Champaign, 1964-65; from asst. prof. psychology to assoc. prof. Iowa State U., Ames, 1965-69, asst. dir. counseling ctr., 1967-69; faculty U. Md., College Park, 1969-81, prof. psychology, 1972-81, asst. dir. counseling center, 1969-81; adminstrv. officer Am. Psychol. Assn., Washington, 1981-86; pvt. practice Bangor, Maine, 1989—, Blue Hill, 1990—. Cons. Iowa Women's Reformatory, 1966-69, VA, Rockwell City, Iowa, 1966-69; rsch. assoc. Nat. Register Health Svcs. Providers in Psychology; mgmt. cons. Ctr. Creative Leadership U. Md., 1980—; mem. Maine Bd. Psychologists; mem. exam com. Assn. State and Provincial State Psychology Bds., 1995-98; mem. Maine State Bd. Examiners Psychologists, 1994—, chair, 1996-99. Contbr. articles to profl. jours. Pres. Woodmoor-Pinecrest Citizens Assn., Silver Spring, Md., 1973-74; mem. com. higher edn. Allied Civic Group Montgomery County, 1974, sr. fellow Consortium of Univs. of the Washington D.C. Met. Area., 1987—. Served with U.S. Army, 1957-61. Fellow APA (bd. dirs. 1986-90, dir. ethics 1986—, ethics cons. 1990—); mem. Internat. Assn. Counseling Svcs. (accrediting bd. 1972-74, v.p. 1975-77, pres. 1977-79). Democrat. Unitarian Universalist. Home: RR 1 Box 323A Little Deer Isle ME 04650-9714 Office: PO Box 108 Little Deer Isle ME 04650-0108 E-mail: bigskye@acadia.net.

MILLS, DENNIS JOSEPH, member of parliament; b. ; m. Victoria Upper; children: Stephanie, Jennifer, Craig, Andrea. Student, St. Thomas's U., York U. Owner Chmn. Mills, 1968-80; past corp. v.p., officer Magna Internat., 1984-86; chmn. Bus. Opportunities of Can., 1986-87; former sr. advisor to Hon. James Fleming Min. of Multiculturalism, 1980; former advisor to Hon. Marc Lalonde Min. of Energy, 1980-81; former sr. policy advisor Cabinet Com. on Comms. Prime Min. of Can., 1982-84; former parliamentary sec. Min. of Industry, Hon. Jon Manley, 1994-96; M.P. for Toronto-Danforth House of Commons, 1988—. Keynote spkr. USA-USSR Citizens Summit on the Environment, Moscow, 1990; chmn. Campaign for Can.; co-chmn. Our World, The Summit on the Environment, Toronto, 1989. Author: A Life Less Taxing, 1989, The Single Tax, 1990; co-author: Taking Care of Small Business, Sport in Canada: Everybody's Business, 1989. Chmn. United Way, York region, 1985, Youth Network, 1986; co-chmn. Magna for Can. Scholarship Fund, 1995-96; govs. Ont. Hockey League. Inducted into The Order of St. Michael's. Office: House of Commons Rm 264 West Block Ottawa ON Canada K1A 0A6 E-mail: dennismills@parl.gc.ca.

MILLS, DON HARPER, pathology and psychiatry educator, lawyer; b. Peking, China, July 29, 1927; came to U.S., 1928; s. Clarence Alonzo and Edith Clarissa (Parrett) M.; m. Lillian Frances Snyder, June 11, 1949; children: Frances Jo, Jon Snyder. BS, U. Cin., 1950, MD, 1953; JD, U. So. Calif., 1958. Diplomate Am. Bd. Law in Medicine. Intern L.A. County Gen. Hosp., 1953-54, admitting physician, 1954-57, attending staff pathologist, 1959—; pathology fellow U. So. Calif., L.A., 1954-55, instr. pathology, 1958-62, asst. clin. prof., 1962-65, assoc. clin. prof., 1965-69, clin. prof., 1969—, clin. prof. psychiatry and behavioral sci., 1986—. Asst. in pathology Hosp. Good Samaritan, L.A., 1956-65, cons. staff, 1962-72, affiliating staff, 1972-91; dep. med. examiner Office of L.A. County Med. Examiner, 1957-61; instr. legal medicine Loma Linda (Calif.) U. Sch. Medicine, 1960-66, assoc. clin. prof. humanities, 1966-95; cons. HEW, 1972-73, 75-76, Dept. of Def., 1975-80; bd. dirs. Am. Bd. Law in Medicine, Inc., Chgo., 1980-86; med. dir. Profl. Risk Mgmt. Group, 1989-2001; med. dir., Octagon Risk Svcs., Inc., 2001—. Column editor Newsletter of the Long Beach Med. Assn., 1960-75, Jour. Am. Osteopathic Assn., 1965-77, Ortho Panel, 1970-78; exec. editor Trauma, 1964-88, mem. editl. bd., 1988—; mem. editl. bd. Legal Aspects of Med. Practice, 1972-90, Med. Alert Comms., 1973-75, Am. Jour. Forensic Medicine and Pathology, 1979-87, Hosp. Risk Control, 1981-96; contbr. numerous articles to profl. jours. Bd. dirs. Inst. for Med. Risk Studies, 1988—; mem. adv. bd. Pacific Ctr. for Health Policy and Ethics, 1997—, chmn., 1999—. Recipient Ritz Heerman award Calif. Hosp. Assn., 1986, Disting. fellow Am. Acad. Forensic Scis., 1993, Genesis award Pacific Ctr. for Health Policy and Ethics, 1993, Founder's award Am. Coll. Med. Quality, 1994. Fellow Am. Coll. Legal Medicine (pres. 1974-76, bd. govs. 1970-78, v.p. 1972-74, chmn. malpractice com. 1973-74, jour. editl. bd. 1984—, gold medal 1999), Am. Acad. Forensic Sci. (gen. program chmn. 1966-67, chmn. jurisprudence sect. 1966-67, 73-74, exec. com. 1971-74, 84-88, v.p. 1984-85, pres. 1986-87, ethics com. 1976-86, 91-2001, chmn. ethics com. 1994-2001, long-term planning com. 1990—, jour. editl. bd. 1965-79); mem. AMA (jour. editl. bd. 1973-77), AAAS, ABA, Am. Coll. Med. Quality (hon. life), Calif. Med. Assn., L.A. County Med. Assn., L.A. County Bar Assn., Am. Soc. Hosp. Attys., Calif. Soc. Hosp. Attys. Home: 700 E Ocean Blvd Unit 2606 Long Beach CA 90802-5039 Office: 911 N Studebaker Rd Ste 250 Long Beach CA 90815-4959 E-mail: Don.Mills@octagonrs.com.

MILLS, DOROTHY ALLEN, investor; b. New Brunswick, N.J., Dec. 14, 1920; d. James R. and Bertha Lovilla (Porter) Allen; m. George M. Mills, Apr. 21, 1945; children: Dianne Adele McKay, Dorothy Louise Sphatt. BA, Douglass Coll., New Brunswick, N.J., 1943. Investment reviewer Cen. Hanover Bank, N.Y.C., 1943-44; asst. to dir. of admissions and sec. undergrad. yrs. Douglass Coll., New Brunswick, 1944-45; sec., regional dir. O.P.A., Ventura, Calif., 1945-46; corp. sec. George M. Mills Inc., Highland Park, N.J., 1946-75; pvt. investor N. Brunswick, 1975—. Sr. v.p. Children Am. Revolution, N.J., 1965; active alumni com. Douglass Coll., 1990—. Recipient Douglass Alumni award, 1992. Mem. AAUW, New Brunswick Hist. Soc., DAR, English Speaking Union, Rutgers Alumni Faculty Club, Woman's League of Rutgers U., Princeton-Douglass Alumni Club, N. Brunswick Women's Club, Auxiliary Robert Wood Johnson Hosp. and Med. Sch. Republican. Mem. Dutch Reformed Ch. Avocations: travel, gardening, bridge. Home: 1054 Hoover Dr New Brunswick NJ 08902-3244

MILLS, DOROTHY JANE (DOROTHY Z. SEYMOUR), writer; b. Cleve., July 5, 1928; d. Henry Zander and Katherine Helen Reinert; m. Harold Seymour, May 21, 1949 (dec. Sept. 25, 1992); m. Roy Elburt Mills, Feb. 15, 1995. Student, Cleve. State U., 1946—49; BS, Case-Western Res. U., 1950, MA, 1952. Cert. elem. and H.S. tchr. Ohio, N.Y. Tchr. Cleve. Pub. Schs., 1950—66, Parma Heights (Ohio) Pub. Schs., 1950—66, Pelham (N.Y.) Pub. Schs., 1950—66, Warwick (N.Y.) Pub. Schs., 1950—66; sr. editor Ginn & Co., Pubs., Boston, Lexington, Mass., 1967—73, Lexington, 1979—81; freelance writer, editor, cons., 1981—; owner Patricia Publs., Naples, Fla., 1998—. EAH cons. Stillpoint Pub., Walpole, NY, 1987—; freelance editor, 1987—95; lectr. in field. Author: (children's textbooks) Bill and the Fish, 1965, Brad and Nell, 1965, Stop Pretending, 1965, Ballerina Bess, 1965, Ann Likes Red, 1965, The Rabbit, 1965, The Tent, 1965, The Sandwich, 1965, Big Beds and Little Beds, 1965, (edn. text) Toad Charts, 1987, (novels) The Sceptre, 1998, 1999, Meatless Meat: A Book of Recipes for Meat Substitutes, 2001; co-author, editor: Fear Not to Sow Because of the Birds, 1988; ; co-author (with Harold Seymour): Baseball: The Early Years, 1960, Baseball: The Golden Age, 1971, Baseball: The People's Game, 1990; co-author: (edn. text) Word Recognition, 1987, author short stories; contbr. articles to publs. Mem.: NASSH, SABR, AAUW. Avocations: piano playing, singing, traveling. Home and Office: Patrician Publs 300 Pier A Naples FL 34112

MILLS, EDWIN SMITH S. economics educator; b. Collingswood, N.J., June 25, 1928; s. Edwin Smith and Roberta (Haywood) M.; m. Barbara Jean Dressner, Sept. 2, 1950; children: Alan Stuart, Susan Dorinda; m. Margaret M. Hutchinson, Jan. 22, 1977. BA, Brown U., 1951; PhD, U. Birmingham, Eng., 1956. Asst. lectr. Univ. Coll. North Staffordshire, Eng., 1953-55; instr. Mass. Inst. Tech., 1955-57; mem. faculty Johns Hopkins, Balt., 1957-70, prof. econs., 1963-70, chmn. dept. econs., 1966-69; prof. econs. and pub. affairs, Gerald L. Phillippe prof. urban studies Princeton U., 1970-75, prof. econs., 1975-87, chmn. dept., 1975-77; Gary Rosenberg prof. real estate and fin. Kellog Sch. Mgmt. Northwestern U., Evanston, Ill., 1987—. Vis. research fellow Cowles Found., Yale, 1961; sr. profl. staff Council Econ. Advisers, 1964-65 Author: The Burden of Government, 1986. Served to 2d lt. AUS, 1946-48. 2d lt. U.S. Army, 1946—48. Grantee Many rsch. grants and contracts, 1960—95. Mem. Am. Econ. Assn., Phi Beta Kappa. Home: 1 Calvin Cir Apt B105 Evanston IL 60201-1953 Office: Northwestern U Ctr Real Estate Rsch Kellogg Graduate School 2001 Sheridan Rd Evanston IL 60208-0814

MILLS, ELIZABETH ANN, retired librarian; b. Cambridge, Mass., Apr. 1, 1934; d. Ralph Edwin and Sylvia Elizabeth (Meehan) McCurdy; m. Albert Ernest Mills, July 6, 1957; 1 child, Karen Elizabeth. BA, Duke U., 1956; MS, Simmons Coll., 1973; postgrad., Boston Coll., Framingham State U., Bridgewater State U. Sec. Lowell House, Harvard U., Cambridge, Mass., 1956-57; substitute libr., tchr. Wellesley (Mass.) H.S., 1972-73, Needham (Mass.) H.S., 1972-73; libr. Tucker Sch. Media Ctr., Milton (Mass.) Pub. Schs., 1973-94, chmn. computer curriculum com., 1982, mem. computer study com., 1988-91, bldg. coord. gifted program, 1981-94; libr. Milton (Mass.) H.S., 1994-98; ret., 1998. Contbr. articles to profl. jours. Active Girl Scouts U.S.A., U.S. Power Squadron, Gt. Blue Hill, Mass., 1974-94. Mem. ALA, Am. Assn. Sch. Librs., Assn. Libr. Svc. Children, Mas. Assn. Ednl. Media, Mass. Sch. Libr. Assn., Beta Phi Mu, Kappa Delta, Delta Kappa Gamma. Republican. Episcopalian. Home: 177 Jarvis Cir Needham MA 02492-2034

MILLS, ELIZABETH SHOWN, genealogist, editor, writer; b. Cleve., Dec. 29, 1944; d. Floyd Finley Shown and Elizabeth Thulmar (Jeffcoat) Carver; m. Gary B. Mills, 1963; children: Clayton Bernard, Donna Rachal, Daniel Garland. BA, U. Ala., 1980. Cert. genealogist, geneal. lectr. Profl. geneal. writer, educator, 1972—; editor Nat. Geneal. Soc. Quar., Arlington, Va., 1987—. Faculty Samford U. Inst. of Genealogy and Hist. Rsch., Birmingham, Ala., 1980—; trustee Assn. for Promotion of Scholarship in Genealogy, N.Y., 1984-90; contract dir., cons. U. Ala., 1985-92; faculty Nat. Inst. of Geneal. Rsch., 1985-97. Author, editor, translator Cane River Creole Series, 6 vols.; author: Evidence: Citation and Analysis for the Family Historian, 1997, Professional Genealogy: A Manual for Researchers, Writers, Editors, Lecturers, and Librarians, 2001; contbr. articles to profl. jours. Trustee Nat. Bd. Certification Genealogists, 1984—, v.p., 1989-94, pres., 1994-96; trustee Assn. Profl. Genealogists, 1984-90, 92-94, regional v.p., 1988-89. Named Outstanding Young Women of Am. Jaycees, Gadsden, 1976, Outstanding Alumna award U. Ala. New Coll., Tuscaloosa, 1990. Fellow Am. Soc. Geneal.ogy(sec. 1992-95, v.p. 1995-98, pres. 1998-2001), Nat. Geneal. Soc. (councilor 1987-92), Utah Geneal. Assn., Grady McWhiney Rsch. Found. (sr.); mem. Assn. Profl. Genealogists (Smallwood Svc. award, 1989). Republican. Roman Catholic. Office: Nat Geneal Soc Quarterly 1732 Ridgedale Dr Tuscaloosa AL 35406-1942

MILLS, EUGENE SUMNER, college president; b. West Newton, Ind., Sept. 13, 1924; s. Sumner Amos and Lela (Weatherly) M.; m. Dorothy Frances Wildman, Oct. 22, 1945; children: David Walden, Sara Anne. AB, Earlham Coll., 1948; MA, Claremont Grad. U., 1949, PhD, 1952; Spl. Postdoctoral Auditor, Harvard, 1958-59; LLD (hon.), N.H. Coll., 1979, U. N.H., 1988; LHD (hon.), Earlham Coll., 1987. Instr. psychology Whittier (Calif.) Coll., 1950, asst. prof., chmn. dept., 1952-55, assoc. prof., chmn. dept., 1955-60, prof. psychology, chmn. dept., 1960-62; faculty U. N.H., Durham, 1962-79, prof. psychology, 1962-79, chmn. dept., 1962-65, dean Grad. Sch., coordinator research, 1963-67; dean U. N.H. (Coll. Liberal Arts), 1967-70, acad. v.p., 1970-71, provost, 1971-74, provost, acting pres., 1974, pres., 1974-79, Whittier (Calif.) Coll. and Whittier Coll. Sch. of Law, 1979-89; prof. psychology Whittier (Calif.) Coll., 1979-89, emeritus prof. psychology, pres. emeritus, 1989—. Vis. prof. U. Victoria, B.C., summers 1958, 60; bd. dirs. Elderhostel, Inc., 1977-97, chmn., 1984-90, vice chmn., 1996-97; bd. dirs. Fedco Inc., vice-chmn., 1996-98; interim pres. Earlham Coll., 1996-97; bd. dirs. Fedco Charitable Found., 2001—, New Eng. Bd. Higher Edn., 1974-79; mem. N.H. Psychol. Assn., 1962-79, pres., 1969-70, bd. dirs., 1967-70; trustee Earlham Coll., 1966-69, hon. lifetime trustee, 1997—. Author: George Trumbull Ladd: Pioneer American Psychologist, 1969, The Story of Elderhostel, 1993; contbr. articles to profl. jours. Danforth Found. grantee; NSF grantee. Fellow Am. Psychol. Assn.; mem. Western Psychol. Assn., Sigma Xi, Phi Kappa Phi., Omicron Delta Kappa Mem. Soc. Of Friends.

MILLS, FREDERICK VANFLEET, art educator, educator, watercolorist; b. Bremen, Ohio, June 5, 1925; s. Frederick William and Juanita Ellen (VanFleet) M.; m. Lois Jean Rademacher; children: Mark Steven (dec.), Michael Sherwood, Mollie Sue, Merre Shannon, Randal Dean, Susan Lynn, Todd Patrick, Shondra Marie. BS, Ohio State U., 1949; MS, Ind. U., 1951, EdD, 1956; postgrad., U.S. Army Staff and Command Coll., 1973-76. Tchr. art, supr. Celina (Ohio) Pub. Schs., 1949-51; instr. univ. h.s. Ind. U., 1951-55, prof. art, art edn., chmn. dept. art edn., 1959-65; vis. prof. U. Tex.-Austin, 1965; chmn. dept. related arts, crafts and interior design U. Tenn., Konxville, 1966-68; prof. art, chmn. dept. art Ill. State U., 1968-85, prof. emeritus, 1985—; dist. prof. art Lincoln Coll., Normal, 1986—. Rsch. reader humanities HEW, 1968-69; resource person arts, edn. and Ams. panel Rockefeller Report Am Coun. Arts in Edn., 1977-78; cons. Latin Am. Fulbright Scholarship Program Harvard U., 1981-82; mem. com. Ill. Fine Arts Rev. for Capital Devel. Bd., 1987—, planning com. Nat. Inst. Advanced Studies in Art and Design and Archives of Am. Art Sch., 1988—, rsch. com. Nat. Sch. Art and Design. One-man shows include McLean County Arts Ctr., Bloomington, Ill., Lincoln (Ill.) Coll., Ill. Agriculture Assn. Credit Union Art Exhbn. Series, Bloomington, Suzette Schochet Gallery, Newport, R.I.; represented in permanent collections Ill. State U. Credit Union, Normal, Ill. State U. Computer Lab., Normal, Mid-Ill. Credit Union, Bloomington, I Wonderlin Gallery, Normal, Ill., State Farm Ins. Co., Kemper Fin. Securities/Kemper Fin. Fund, First of Am. Bank, Ill., Diamond Star Motors Corp., Easter Seal Assn., City of Vladimir, Russia, City of Asahikawa, Hokkaido, Japan, County of McLean, City of Bloomington, Town of Normal; author, editor: The Status of the Visual Arts in Higher Education, 1976, New Perspectives in Visual Arts Administration, 1977, Issues in the Administration of Visual Arts, 1978, Politics and the Visual Arts, 1979, The Visual Arts in the Ninth Decade, 1980; editor Western Arts Bull., 1958-62; featured in 12 part ser. As An Artist Sees local pub. access; contbr. to profl. jours. Pres. Ill. Alliance Art Edn., 1975-77, Ill. Task Force for Arts Edn. in Gen. Edn., 1976-77; mem. Tenn. Arts Commn., 1967-68, Nat. Alliance Arts Edn./Kennedy Ctr., 1975-77; charter trustee Ill. Summer Sch. for Arts, v.p., v.p. Found. Bd., 1988-94; bd. dirs., co-founder Sugar Creek Arts Festival, Normal, 1985—; chair major gifts com. Normal Theater Restoration Project, 1992—; bd. dirs., v.p. McLean County Arts Ctr., Bloomington, 1980-90, sponsor Skilled Crafts award, 1968—. Served to maj. USAR; Col. Ill. Militia. Recipient Recognition award Alliance for Arts Edn., 1984, Outstanding Svc. award Ill. Alliance Arts Edn., 1984, 1994 Ornament of Yr./Artist of Yr. award, Ill. State U. Alumni Assn. Svc. Awd.; subject articles, TV interviews Mem. Nat. Council Art Adminstrs. (charter, sr. rsch. editor bd. dirs. 1973-81), Nat. Assn. Schs. Art (instnl. del. 1974-84, nominating com. 1977-78, rsch. com. 1976-77), Western Arts Assn. (pres. 1962-64), Coll. Art Assn., Nat. Art Edn. Assn. (dir. 1964-66), Scabbard and Blade, Phi Delta Kappa, Delta Tau Delta, Delta Phi Delta. Clubs: Rotary Internat. Home: 25306 Arrowhead Lne Hudson IL 61748-9414 *As I reflect on my life and career up to this point, I feel that consistency and humaneness are two words that come to mind. It seems extremely important to be consistent when a person relates to others, and if that is coupled with humaneness and consideration of the value of others, being aware of their strengths and weaknesses, their likes and dislikes, it becomes easier to relate to them in this most complex world of ours.*

MILLS, GARY BERNARD, history educator; b. Marshall, Tex., Sept. 10, 1944; s. Harold Garland and Hazel Cecilia (Rachal) M.; m. Elizabeth Shown; children: Clayton Bernard, Donna Rachal, Daniel Garland. BA in History and Bus. Adminstrn., Delta State U., 1967; MA in History, Miss. State U., 1969, PhD in History, 1974. Instr. history McNeese State U., Lake Charles, La., 1969-72, U. Ctr., Jackson, Miss., 1972-75; asst. prof. U. Ala., Gadsden, 1976-79, assoc. prof., 1979-82, Tuscaloosa, 1982-83, prof. history, 1984[0089]. Cons. in field. Author numerous books; co-editor Nat. Geneal. Soc. Quar., 1987+; contbr. numerous articles to profl. jours. Del. Am.-Russian Archival Adv., Washington, Moscow, Minsk, 1989-91; mem. adv. bd. Archive Am. Minority Cultures, U. Ala., 1983-90. Fellow Huntington Libr., San Marino, Calif., 1988. Fellow Grady McWhiney Hist. Rsch. Found. (sr.); mem. Nat. Geneal. Soc., Am. Hist. Assn., Ala. Hist. Assn., La. Hist. Assn. (bd. dirs. 1972-94), Orgn. Ala. Historians, So. Hist. Assn. (various coms. 1981-86), St. George Tucker Soc. (fellow 1992+). Independent. Roman Catholic. Avocations: music, genealogy. Home: Tuscaloosa, Ala. Died Jan. 26, 2002.

MILLS, GEORGE ALEXANDER, retired science administrator; b. Saskatoon, Sask., Can., Mar. 20, 1914; s. George Robison and Leafa (Johnson) M.; m. Roberta Walker Mills, June 15, 1940; children: Richard, Sandra, Marilyn, Janice. B.Sc., U. Sask., 1934, M.Sc., 1936; PhD, Columbia U. Instr., Dartmouth Coll., 1939-40; with Houdry Process Co., 1940-68, U.S. Bur. Mines, 1968-75, chief coal div., 1968-75; dir. fossil energy research ERDA, 1975-77; dir. internat. programs fossil energy Dept. Energy, Washington, 1977-81; exec. dir. Ctr. Catalytic Sci. and Tech., U. Del., Newark, 1981-84, sr. scientist Ctr. Catalytic Sci and Tech., 1984-95. Contbr. numerous articles to profl. jours.; patentee in field. Mem. NAE, AIChE, AAAS, Am. Inst. Chemists (Pioneer award), Am. Chem. Soc. (Storch award, Murphree award), Catalysis Soc. Presbyterian. Home: Cokesbury Village 726 Loveville Rd Apt 406 Hockessin DE 19707-1508 E-mail: galexmills@compuserve.com.

MILLS, GEORGE MARSHALL, insurance consultant; b. Newton, N.J., May 20, 1923; s. J. Marshall and Emma (Scott) M.; m. Dorothy Lovilla Allen, Apr. 21, 1945; children: Dianne (Mrs. Thomas McKay III), Dorothy L.A. (Mrs. Edward Sphatt). BA, Rutgers U., 1943; MA, Columbia U., 1951. CLU, CPCU; chartered fin. cons.; cert. govt. fund mgr. Pres. George M. Mills Inc., North Brunswick, N.J., 1946-75; pres. CORECO, Inc., Newark, 1960-78; risk mgr. N.J. Hwy. Authority, Woodbridge, 1976-95; pres. Assoc. Risk Mgmt., North Brunswick, N.J., 1995—. Cons. Govs.'s Com. on Bus. Efficiency in Pub. Schs., 1979-80; cons. Risk Mgmt. Ins., Real Estate. Bd. dirs. Alpha Chi Rho Ednl. Found., vice-chmn. 1991-95; workshop Easter Seal Soc.; mem. Gov.'s Task Force on Sound Mcpl. Govt., 1981-82; pres. Nat. Interfrat. Conf., 1979-80. With USNR, 1943-46. Mem. Am. Coll. Life Underwriters, Am. Coll. Property Liability Underwriters, Internat. Bridge Tunnel and Turnpike Assn. (chmn. risk mgmt. com. 1980-95, mem. bus. ins. risk mgmt. bd. 1988-95, Matthew J. Lenz Jr. medal 1989, Paul K. Addams award 1992), New Brunswick Hist. Soc., English Speaking Union, Rutgers Club, Alpha Chi Rho (nat. councillor 1964-70, nat. pres. 1970-73, nat. treas. 1975-78), Kappa Kappa Psi, Tau Kappa Alpha, Phi Delta Phi. Mem. Reformed Ch. Am. Home: 1054 Hoover Dr New Brunswick NJ 08902-3244

MILLS, GLORIA ADAMS, energy service consultant; b. Chgo., Mar. 1, 1940; d. Edward Charles and Olive Margaret (McCarty) Adams; m. Peter Mills, Dec. 29, 1962 (div. July 1986). BA, Rosary Coll., River Forest, Ill., 1962, MALS, 1970; MBA, U. Chgo., 1976. Lit. chemist UOP, Inc., Des Plaines, Ill., 1962-70, supr. patent libr., 1970-77, mktg. engr., 1977-81, mgr. project devel., 1981-83; v.p. mktg. Covanta Waste to Energy, Inc., Fairfield, N.J., 1983-87, sr. v.p. mktg., 1987-89, exec. v.p. mktg. NJ, 1989-94; exec. v.p. bus. devel. Ogden Waste to Energy, Inc., N.J., 1994-01, ret., 2001. Chmn. of bd. Ambiente 2000 S.r.l., 1998-01, mem. indsl. adv. bd. So. Ill. U. Coll. Engring. and Tech., Carbondale, 1985-90, 2000—. Contbr. articles to profl. jours. Mem. ASME (solid waste processing div., medal of achievement 2001), Am. Chem. Soc. Avocations: travel, reading.

MILLS, HELENE AUDREY, education educator; b. Oct. 6, 1933; d. Paul Albert and Mabel Meister; m. Ray Mills, Apr. 17, 1954; children: Keith, Katherine (dec.), Kevin. BS in Family Life Edn., Wayne State U., 1954, MEd in Human Resources, 1965, EdD in Gen. Adminstrn., 1980. Supr., instr. Wayne State Coll. Edn., 1958-67; tchr. life studies, health edn. Seaholm H.S., Birmingham, Mich., 1967-72, 74-77, asst. to prin., 1974-77, asst. prin., 1978-79, prin., 1990-97, Derby Mid. Sch., Birmingham, 1980-90; asst. prof. Oakland U., Rochester Hills, Mich., 1997—. Adj. prof. Wayne State U., Detroit, 1989-91, Oakland U., Rochester, 1985-89, asst. prof., 1997—. Consulting editor Clearing Ho., 1985-97; contbr. articles to profl. jours. Mem. steering com. Meadowbrook Leadership Acad., 1984-87; mem. Detroit Strategic Planning Task Force, 1986-88; mem. exec. bd. Oakland County Youth Assistance, 1987-90; program chairperson women's group Northbrooke Ch., 1997-99, mem. adult minstries purpose com., 1998-99. Recipient PTSA Coun. Pres. award, 1982, Celebration of Women award Greater Detroit Coun. NA'AMAT USA, 1986, Exemplary Secondary Sch. award State Mich., 1991. Mem. NASCD, Nat. Staff Devel. Assn., Nat. Secondary Prins. Assn., Mich. Assn. Supervision and Curriculum Devel., Mich. Coun. Family Rels., Mich. Secondary Prins. Assn., Oakland County Secondary Prins. Assn. (pres. 1983-85, Prin. of the Yr. 1991), Phi Delta Kappa (chmn. mem. Oakland br. 1998—). Office: Oakland U 311 Odowd Hall Rochester Hills MI 48309-4423 E-mail: mills@oakland.edu.

MILLS, HUGH MILTON, JR. retired college president; b. Albany, Ga., Oct. 24, 1922; s. Hugh Milton Mills Sr. and Johnie Lamar West; m. Evelyn Heath, Oct. 6, 1944 (dec. Aug. 1994); children: Hugh Milton III, Ralph West, Rebecca Ann. AA, N. Ga. Coll., 1943; BS in Edn., U. Ga., 1945, MEd, 1947, EdD, 1956; LLD (hon.), Brenau Coll., 1983. Cert. prof. tchr., Ga. Tchr., coach Rockmart (Ga.) H.S., 1945-47, Albany (Ga.) H.S., 1947-48; from instr. to asst. prof. U. Ga., Athens, 1948-51, from asst. prof. to assoc. prof., 1953-65; supervising prin. Rockmart Pub. Schs., 1951-53; pres. Gainesville (Ga.) Jr. Coll., 1965-84; interim pres. Brenau Coll., Gainesville, 1985; pres. emeritus Gainesville Coll., 1985—. Cons. Ga. Dept. Vocat. Rehab., Atlanta, 1955-65. With U.S. Army Air Corp, 1942-43. Named Ga. Man of the Yr. Conservation Dist. Ga., 1986. Mem. Phi Beta Kappa, Phi Kappa Phi, Kappa Delta Pi, Phi Delta Kappa. Baptist. Avocation: woodworking. Office: Gainesville Coll PO Box 1358 Gainesville GA 30503

MILLS, INGA-BRITTA, artist; b. Eskilstuna, Sweden, Sept. 14, 1925; came to U.S., 1954; d. Gerhard Valdemar and Märta Kristina (Söderberg) Stenhäll; m. Mogens Schiött, June, 1950 (div. 1952); m. Victor Moore Mills, June 6, 1956; children: Karl-Olof, Victoria Inga Kristina. Attended, U. Gothenburg, Sweden, 1946-48; BA, MA, Montclair State Coll., 1979; postgrad., Temple U., 1980-82. Sec. to port dir. Port Authority, Gothenburg, Sweden, 1952-54; adminstrv. asst. UN, N.Y.C., 1954-55. One-person shows include Montclair (N.J.) Pub. Libr., 1977, UN Food and Agr. Orgn., Rome, 1979, Libr. Arts Ctr., Newport, N.H., 1984, Ariel Gallery, Soho, N.Y.C., 1986, Stamford Mus. and Nature Ctr., 1989, Burnham Libr., Bridgewater, Conn., 1991, Westover Sch., Middlebury, Conn., 1993, Roxbury Libr., 1995, Gallery AE, Gothenburg, Sweden, 1995, Conn. Housing Fin. Authority, Rockyhill; exhibited in group shows including Am. Women's Assn. of Rome, 1982, Marian Graves Mugar Gallery, Colby-Sawyer Coll., New London, N.H., 1984, Artworks Gallery, Hartford, Conn., 1986, Greene Gallery, Guilford, Conn., 1989, The Discovery Mus., Bridgeport, Conn., 1990, Silvermine Galleries, New Canaan, Conn., 1990, Ward-Nasse Gallery, Soho, 1991, 92, Internat. Juried Print Exhibit, Somers, N.Y., 1992, Grand Prix Fine Art de Paris, 1993, Stamford Hist. Soc., 1993, Montserrat Gallery, Soho, 1994, Internat. Print Biennial, Cracow, Poland, 1994, Trenton (N.J.) State Coll., 1995, New Haven Paint and Clay Club, 1995, Conn. Women Artists, New Britain Mus. Am. Art, 1995, Internat Print Triennial, Cracow, Polant, 1997, 4th Ann. Internat. Graphics Addiction, Stockholm, 1997; represented in collections Conning & Co., N.Y.C., New Haven Paint and Clay Club, Somerstown Gallery, Somers; represented in pvt. collections, U.S., Europe, Japan, and Australia. Recipient Marjorie Frances Meml. award Stamford (Conn.) Mus. and Nature Ctr., 1990, Faber-Birren Color award Stamford Art Assn., 1990. Mem. Wash. Art Assn. Democrat. Avocations: gardening, reading, music, theatre.

MILLS, JAMES LOUIS, medical researcher, pediatric epidemiologist; b. N.Y.C., Nov. 7, 1947; s. James and Edith Alice Mills; m. Gayle Linda Countryman, Oct. 2, 1974; children: Andrew Ross, Ian Philip. BA, U. Pa., 1969, MS in Epidemiology, 1979; MD, N.Y. Med. Coll., 1973. Diplomate Am. Bd. Pediatrics, Am. Bd. Pediatric Endocrinology. Resident Cornell U., N.Y.C., 1973-75; fellow in pediat. endocrinology Children's Hosp., Phila., 1975-79; fellow Nat. Insts. Health, Bethesda, Md., 1979-82, rsch. med. officer, 1982-90, chief pediat. epidemiology sect., 1990—, with sr. biomed. rsch. svc., 2000—. Assoc. epidemiology Johns Hopkins U., Balt., 1985—; invited spkr. Biomed Rsch. Caucus, U.S. Congress, 1995; med. rschr. in birth defects and pregnancy. Contbr. articles to profl. jours. Mem. med. ethics commn. Episcopal Diocese Wash., 1994-99. Recipient Dir.'s award NIH, 1989, 2000, Leader award Parenting Mag., 1997. Fellow Am. Coll. Epidemiology; mem. Am. Epidemiol. Soc., Am. Pediat. Soc., Soc. Pediat. Rsch. Episcopalian. Avocations: hiking, art, music, oriental rugs. Home: 11906 Oden Ct Rockville MD 20852-4341 Office: Nat Insts Health 6100 Building Rm 7bo3 Bethesda MD 20892-0001 E-mail: jamesmills@nih.gov.

MILLS, JERI, gynecologist; b. Cleve., Nov. 25, 1954; d. Jake and Ida (Langeman) M. DVM, Ohio State U., 1980; MD, Am. U. of Caribbean, Montserrat, 1987. Diplomate Am. Bd. Ob-gyn. Intern, resident SUNY, Buffalo, 1987-91; physician Appalachian Ob-gyn. Assocs., Kingsport, Tenn., 1991-93; staff physician CIGNA Health Plan, Tucson, 1993-96; owner, pvt. practice Green Valley Women's Health Care Integrative Medicine, Ariz., 1997—. Reiki master tchr. Author: Tapestry of Healing, 2001; contbr. articles to The Health Times, The Desert Voice. Avocations: training dogs and horses, ballroom dancing, sculpting, making jewelry. Office: Green Valley Womens Health Care Ste 40 170 N La Cañada Dr Green Valley AZ 85614 E-mail: jeri@tapestryofhealing.com.

MILLS, JERRY WOODROW, lawyer; b. Springfield, Mo., July 17, 1940; s. Woodrow Wilson and Billie Louise M.; m. Marion Cargile, Mar. 27, 1964; children: Eric E., Brendon W. BSEE, Tex. A&M U., 1963; JD, Georgetown U., 1967. Bar: Tex. 1967, U.S. Patent Office 1967. Ptnr. Richards, Harris & Hubbard, Dallas, 1970-82, Baker, Mills & Glast, Dallas, 1982-90; sr. ptnr. Baker & Botts, 1990—. Adj. prof. So. Meth. U. Law Sch., 1994-97. Bd. dirs. Dallas Legal Svcs. Project, 1972-75. Fellow Tex. Bar, Dallas Bar; mem. ABA, Tex. State Jr. Bar Assn. (treas. 1975, dir.), Dallas Jr. Bar Assn. (pres. 1971, Outstanding Young Lawyer award 1975), Dallas Bar Assn. (bd. dirs. 1983-85). Methodist. Office: Baker & Botts 800 Trammell Crow Ctr 2001 Ross Ave Ste 900 Dallas TX 75201-2917 E-mail: jmills@bakerbotts.com.

MILLS, JON K. psychologist, educator, philosopher; AS in Criminal Justice, Parkland Coll., 1985; BS in Psychology with honors, So. Ill. U., 1987, MA in Rehab. Counseling with honors, 1988; PsyD in Clin. Psychology, Ill. Sch. Profl. Psychology, 1992; MA in Philosophy, Vanderbilt U., 1998, PhD in Philosophy, 1999. Cert. rehab. counselor; cert. psychologist, Ont. Crisis intervention trainer, hotline supr. Synergy Crisis Intervention Agy., Carbondale, Ill., 1986-87, individual and family counselor, 1987; individual and group therapist Evaluation and Devel. Ctr., 1987-88, Youth Options: Substance Abuse Svcs., Marion, 1988; intern Jackson County Community Mental Health Ctr., Carbondale, 1988; diagnostic extern Elgin (Ill.) State Mental Health Ctr., 1989-90; staff therapist Davis Ctr. for Emotional Devel., Glen Ellyn, Ill., 1989-90; therapy extern Roosevelt U., Chgo., 1990—; counselor coord. Copley Weight Mgmt. Copley Meml. Hosp., Aurora, Ill., 1989—; predoctoral intern Michael Reese Hosp. and Med. Ctr., Chgo., 1991; asst. prof. dept. psychology Lewis U., Romeoville, Ill., 1992—; staff psychologist Inst. for Behavioral Svcs., Oak Brook, 1993—. Adj. faculty dept. psychology Waubonsee C.C., Sugar Grove, Ill., 1990—, Coll. of Dupage, Naperville, 1989—; faculty mem. social sci. dept. Joliet (Ill.) Jr. Coll. , 1990—; asst. prof. psychology Tenn. State U., 1994—96; faculty Capella U., 1998—2000, Adler Sch. of Profl. Psychology, Toronto, 1999—, U. Toronto, 2000; staff psychologist, internship coord., clin. supr. Mental Health Program Lakeridge Health Corp., Oshawa; bd. dirs. Ethics Rsch. Rev. Bd., 1999—; assoc. Rsch. Inst. at Lakeridge Health. Editor: Philosophy and Psychology; assoc. editor: Value Inquiry Book Series; reviewer Psychoanalytic Psychology; contbr. numerous articles to profl. jours. Tchg. fellow Vanderbilt U. Dept. Philosophy, Nashville, 1994—; Fulbright scholar U. Toronto, York U., 1996-97, others. Mem. APA, Can. Philos. Assn., Can. Soc. for Philos. Practice (bd. dirs. 1999—), Ill. Group Psychotherapy Soc., Chgo. Assn. for Psychoanalytic Psychology, Phi Kappa Phi, Gamma Beta Phi. Avocations: vocal, guitar, harmonica. Home: 600 E Monroe St Ste 319 Springfield IL 62701-1674 E-mail: jmills@processpsychology.com.

MILLS, JOSHUA REDMOND, financial executive; b. Lynn, Mass., Aug. 30, 1936; s. Joshua and Adelaide (Redmond) M.; m. Annette Aliferis Perillo, May 29, 1965; children: Carlotta, Anastasia AB, Harvard U., 1957; postgrad., NYU, 1960-65. Cert. employee benefits specialist. With Chase Manhattan Bank, N.Y.C., 1960-63; With Continental Bank Internat., 1963-66; v.p. Amerconsult Corp., N.Y.C. and Peru, 1966-74; pres. Joshua Mills & Co., North Stonington, Conn., 1974—, Fin. Counsel Corp., Westerly, R.I., 1984—. Chmn. strategy com., mem. gen. council Presbytery of N.Y.C., 1976-81; rep. to Town Meeting, Greenwich, Conn., 1981-83; mem. steering com. Tri-State Urban Conf., Fairfield County 2000 Task Force (conf.) Mem. Harvard Club (N.Y.C.), Mason's Is. Yacht Club. Republican. Office: 183 Providence New London Tpke North Stonington CT 06359-1721

MILLS, KEVIN LEE, information technology researcher; b. Frederick, Md., Oct. 21, 1951; s. John Lee and Doris Jean (Comer) M.; m. Karen June Davis, Dec. 30, 1972; children: Colin Walter, Elizabeth Anne. BS in Polit. Sci. and Econs., Frostburg (Md.) State U., 1973; MS in Tech. Mgmt., Am. U., 1979; PhD in Info. Tech., George Mason U., 1996. Sr. computer analyst System Devel. Corp., McLean, Va., 1976-81; project mgr. Tesdata Systems Corp., 1981-82; computer scientist Nat. Bur. of Stds., Gaithersburg, Md., 1982-84, group leader, 1984-87; divsn. chief Nat. Inst. Stds. and Tech., 1987-95; program mgr. Def. Advanced Rsch. Projects Agy., Arlington, Va., 1996-98; adj. prof. George Mason U., 1996—; divsn. chief Nat. Inst. Standards & Technology, Gaithersburg, Md., 1999-2001, sr. rsch. scientist, 2001—. Cons. in field, 1980-82. Contbr. articles to jours. Capt. USMC, 1972-78. Mem. IEEE (sr.), Assn. for Computing Machinery. Avocations: hiking, writing, reading, photography. E-mail: kmills@nist.gov.

MILLS, KEVIN PAUL, lawyer; b. Detroit, Oct. 1, 1961; s. Raymond Eugene and Helene Audrey M.; m. Holly Beth Fechner, June 15, 1986. BA, Oberlin Coll., 1983; JD, U. Mich., 1987. Bar: Mich. 1988. High sch. tchr., asst. dir. summer environ. inst. The Storm King Sch., Cornwall-on-Hudson, N.Y., 1983-84; staff atty. E. Mich. Environ. Action Coun., Birmingham, Mich., 1987-90; assoc. Tucker & Rolf, Southfield, 1988-89; sr. atty., pollution prevention program dir. Environ. Def., Washington, 1990—. Low-level radioactive waste cons. State Mich., Lansing, 1988; founder Pollution Prevention Alliance, 1991, co-founder Great Printer's Project, 1992, co-founder Clean Car Campaign, 1999, staff to co-chair eco-efficiency Pres. Coun. Sustainable Devel., 1993-95, Auto Pollution Prevention adv. group, 1994-98, EPA Auto Mfr. CSI, 1994-97; mem. adv. bd. Nat. Pollution Prevention Roundtable, 1996—; mem. adv. com. Working Group on Cmty. Right-to-Know, 1997—; mem. Nat. Adv. Coun. on Environ. Policy and Tech., 1997-2002. Bd. dirs., v.p. Ea. Mich. Environ. Action Coun., Birmingham, 1985-87; pres. Environ. Law Soc., Ann Arbor, Mich., 1986-87. Recipient Outstanding Achievement award Environ. Def., 2000. Mem. State Bar Mich. Office: Environ Def 1875 Connecticut Ave NW Washington DC 20009-5728

MILLS, LAUREL, writer; b. Farmington, Maine, Jan. 19, 1946; d. Lewis Bradley and Doris Elizabeth (Brown) Lothrop; m. Thomas Waman Mills, Sept. 3, 1965 (div. Mar. 1982); children: Beth Mills, Marissa Mills. AA in English, U. Wis., Fox Valley, 1982; BS in English, U. Wis., Oshkosh, 1984, MA in Humanities, 1989. Outreach libr. Eliza D. Smith Pub. Libr., Menasha, Wis., 1984-87; lectr. in English U. Wis. - Fox Valley, 1988—. Tchr. of writing poetry, The Clearing, Ellison Bay, Wis., 1994-2000; instr. of creative writing, U. Wis., Oshkosh, 1988—, Fox Valley, 1986-97. Editor: Fox Cry Rev., 1997—; author: (novel) Undercurrents, 2001, (poetry books) Canada Geese Coming Home, 1986 (Writers award Coun. for Wis.), The Gull Is My Divining Rod, 1985 (Outstanding Achievement Honors Wis. Libr. Assn. 1985), Troika IV: Hidden Seed, 1992 (Posner Poetry award), I Sing Back, 1997 (Pippistrelle Best of Small Press award); contbr. to literary mags., anthologies and songs. Named Outstanding Young Alumni U. Wis., Oshkosh, 1990; recipient Writers Residency, Ragdale Found., Lake Forest, Ill., 1997, 2000, 2001. Mem. Wis. Fellowship of Poets (sec. 1986-87). Democrat. Avocations: swimming, reading, bicycling. Home: 1437 Deerwood Dr Neenah WI 54956-1801 Office: U Wis-Fox Valley 1478 Midway Rd Menasha WI 54952-1297 E-mail: lmills@uwc.edu., writemills@prodigy.net.

MILLS, LAWRENCE, lawyer, business and transportation consultant; b. Salt Lake City, Aug. 15, 1932; s. Samuel L. and Beth (Neilson) M. BS, U. Utah, 1955, JD, 1956. Bar: Utah 1956, ICC 1961, U.S. Supreme Ct. 1963. With W.S. Hatch Co. Inc., Woods Cross, Utah, 1947-89, gen. mgr., 1963-89, v.p., 1970-89, also dir. Bd. dirs. Nat. Tank Truck Carriers, Inc., Washington, 1963—, pres., 1974-75, chmn. bd., 1975-76; mem. motor carrier adv. com. Utah State Dept. Transp., 1979—; keynote speaker Rocky Mountain Safety Suprs. Conf., 1976; mem. expedition to Antartica, 1996, Titanic Expedition,

1996. Contbr. articles to legal and profl. jours. and transp. publs. Del. to County and State Convs., Utah, 1970-72; v.p. Utah Safety Coun., 1979-82, bd. dirs., 1979—, pres., 1983-84; mem. Utah Gov's Adv. Com. on Small Bus.; capt. Easter Seal Telethon, 1989, 90; state vice chmn. High Frontier, 1987—; mem. adv. com. Utah State Indsl. Commn., 1988—, chmn. com. studying health care cost containment and reporting requirements 1990—; mem. expdn. to Antarctica, 1996, Titanic '96 expedition, Iceland expedition, 2001, Greenland expedition, 2001. Recipient Safety Dir. award Nat. Tank Carriers Co., 1967, Outstanding Svc. and Contbn. award, 1995, Trophy award W.S. Hatch Co., 1975, Disting. Svc. award Utah State Indsl. Commn., 1992, Outstanding Svc. award Utah Safety Coun., 1994. Mem. Salt Lake County Bar Assn., Utah Motor Transport Assn. (dir. 1967—, pres. 1974-76, Outstanding Achievement Award 1989), Utah Hwy. Users Assn. (dir. 1981—), Indsl. Rels. Coun. (dir. 1974—), Salt Lake City C. of C., U.S. Jaycees (life Senator 1969—, ambassador 1977—, pres. Utah Senate 1979-80, Henry Giessenbier fellow 1989), Nat. Petroleum Coun., Utah Associated Gen. Contractors (assoc. 1975-77, 88—), Silver Tank Club, Hillsdale Coll. President's Club, Traveler's Century Club. Home: HC 11 Box 329 Kamiah ID 83536-9410 Office: PO Box 1495 Kamiah ID 83536-1495 *Personal philosophy: Excessive government regulation stifles individual initiative. We should learn from the downfall of communism.*

MILLS, LINDA GAYLE, social work and law educator; b. L.A., Oct. 21, 1957; d. Harold and Anne Mills; m. Peter Goodrich, Dec. 25, 1996; 1 child, Ronnie Mills Goodrich. JD, U. Calif., San Francisco, 1983; MSW, San Francisco State U., 1986; PhD, Brandeis U., 1994. Bar: Calif.; lic. clin. social worker, Calif. Exec. dir., founder The Hawkins Ctr. Law and Svcs. for People with Disabilities, Richmond, Calif., 1986-91; sr. program officer Echoing Green Found., N.Y.C., 1993-94; asst. prof. UCLA, 1994-98, assoc. prof., 1998-99, NYU, N.Y.C., 1999-2001, prof., 2001—. Rsch. assoc. Brandeis Health Policy Inst., Waltham, Mass., 1993; cons. U.S. Gen. Acctg. Office, Washington, 1992. Author: The Heart of Intimate Abuse: New Interventions in Child Welfare Criminal Justice and Health Settings, 1998, A Penchant for Prejudice: Unraveling Bias in Judicial Decisionmaking, 1999; contbr. articles to profl. jours. and editls. to newspapers. PEW Charitable Trust fellow, 1991-94; NSF grantee, 1993; prin. investigator U.S. HHS, 1995-2000, Calif. Social Wk. Edn. Ctr., 1996-97, 98-2000. Jewish. Office: New York Univ Sch Social Wk One Washington Sq N #201A New York NY 10003 E-mail: linda.mills@nyu.edu.

MILLS, LOIS JEAN, company executive, former legislative aide, former education educator; b. Chgo., Oct. 20, 1939; d. Martin J. and Annabelle M. (Hrabik) Rademacher; m. Frederick V. Mills, Dec. 1, 1974; children: Todd, Susan, Randal, Merre, Mollie, Michael, Mark (dec.). BS in Edn., Ill. State U., Normal, 1962, MS in Edn., 1969. Lectr. elem. curriculum Ill. State U., 1973-90; in-svc. advisor for elem., gifted, critical thinking and study skills, coop. learning Title I State Bd. Edn., Springfield, Ill., 1969-90; elem. tchr., supr. Metcalf Lab. Sch. Ill. State U., 1962-72; legis. aide to Asst. Majority Leader Senator John Maitland, Jr., Ill. Gen. Assembly, 1990-95; pres., ptnr. Mills Design Assocs., 1996—. Mem. state rep. Dan Rutherford's house task force for statute repeal, 1995—, adv. roundtable, 1995—, legis. task force for cmty. residential svcs. deaf adults, 1995—; campaign coord. Asst. Majority Leader Senator John Maitland, Jr., 1995—; county campaign ccord. for Ill. Comptroller Loleta Didrickson, 1994-98. Contbr. articles to profl. jours. Pres. Leadership Ill., 1994—, pres.-elect, 1993-94; past pres. governing bd. Lake Bloomington Assn., v.p., 1993-94, pres., 1994-95; mem. mgmt. com. McLean County 21st Century commn., 1991-92, vice chair cmty. rels., 1991-92; commr. McLean County Regional Planning commn., vice chair 1994-95; charter bd. govs. Ill. Lincoln Excellence in Pub. Svc. Series, 1994—, charter bd. dirs., Save the Patient health edn. and resources orgn., other civic activities; mem. Ill. steering com. Beijing-UN Women's Conf. One Yr. Later, 1996; mem. gov.'s commn. on status of women, Econ. Opportunities Working Group, 1998-, State U. Annuitants Assn. and Found. Social Security Equity/Offset. Recipient Exemplary Tchr. awards Ill. State U. Student Elem. Edn. Bd., Women of Distinction award YWCA of McLean County, Ill. State Univ. Alumni Assn. Svc. Awd. Mem. NAFE, Ill. State U. Alumni Assn. (bd. dirs. 1982—, internat. pres. 1992-94, 1994—), McLean County Rep. Women's Club (v.p. 1986, pres. 1987, past pres. 1988), Ill. Rep. Committeewoman's Roundtable, Ill. Fedn. Rep. Women, Nat. Fedn. Rep. Women, Internat. Platform Assn. Home: K-162 Lake Bloomington 25306 Arrowhead Ln Hudson IL 61748-9414

MILLS, LORI LYNNE, psychologist, educator; b. Mattoon, Ill., Nov. 11, 1966; d. Roy Edward and Lorna Sue Gibson; m. Cort Alfred Mills, Dec. 16, 1995; children: Gibson Thomas, Cooper Joseph. BA, Milligan Coll., 1988; MA, U. Louisville, 1991, PhD, 1995. Lic. clin. psychologist, health svc. provider, Tenn. Assoc. prof. Milligan Coll., Tenn., 1993—; therapist Frontier Health, Johnson City, 1996-2000. Mem. APA. Office: Milligan Coll PO Box 500 Milligan College TN 37682 E-mail: lmills@milligan.edu.

MILLS, NANCY ELLYN, hematologist, oncologist; b. N.Y.C., May 17, 1962; BA magna cum laude, Harvard U., 1983; MD, Mt. Sinai Sch. Medicine, 1987. Diplomate Am. Bd. Internal Medicine, Am. Bd. Hematology, Am. Bd. Oncology, Nat. Bd. Med. Examiners. Intern, resident in internal medicine Mt. Sinai Med. Ctr., N.Y.C., 1987-90; fellow hematology/oncology NYU Med. Ctr., 1990-93; instr. medicine NYU Sch. Medicine, 1993-96, clin. asst. prof., 1996—2001; asst. attending physician Meml. Sloan Kettering Cancer Ctr., N.Y.C., 1996—2001; attending physician Phelps Meml. Hosp. Ctr., 1996—; asst. attending Meml. Sloan-Kettering Cancer Ctr., 1996—2001, assoc. clin. attending, 2001—, clin. assoc. attending physician, 2001—. Fellow ACP; mem. Am. Assn. Cancer Rsch., Am. Fedn. Clin. Rsch., Am. Soc. Clin. Oncology, Am. Soc. Hematology, Internat. Assn. Study Lung Cancer, N.Y. Soc. Study Blood. Office: Meml Sloan Kettering Cancer Ctr 777 N Broadway Ste 102 Sleepy Hollow NY 10591-1019

MILLS, NICOLAUS, American studies educator, writer; b. Cleve., Dec. 2, 1938; s. Nicolaus and Muriel Mills. AB, Harvard U., 1960; PhD, Brown U., 1966. Asst. prof. English. U. Mich., Ann Arbor, 1965-70; rschr. Ctr. for Urban and Minority Studies Columbia U. Tchrs. Coll., N.Y.C., 1970-72; prof. Am. studies Sarah Lawrence Coll., Bronxville, N.Y., 1972—. Author: American and English Fiction in the Nineteenth Century, 1973, The Crowd in American Literature, 1986, Like a Holy Crusade: Mississippi 1964, 1992, The Triump of Meanness: America's War Against Its Better Self, 1997; Editor: Comparisons: A Short Story Anthology, 1972, The Great School Bus Controversy, 1973, The New Journalism, 1974, Busing USA, 1979, Culture in the Age of Money, 1990, Forty Years of Dissent, 1994, Agruing Immigraton, 1994, Debating Affirmative Action, 1994; co-editor: The New Killing fields: Massacre and the Politics of Intervention, 2002; mem. editl. bd. Dissent, 1980-; Sunday mag. columnist Cleve. Plain Dealer, 1998-99; contbr. articles to mags. and newspapers, including N.Y. Times, L.A. Times, Newsday, Chgo. Tribune, San Francisco Chronicle, Nation, New Republic, Yale Rev., Dissent. Woodrow Wilson fellow, 1960, Rockefeller Found., 1980; grantee Am. Coun. Learned Socs., 1971, Hewlett-Mellon grantee Sarah Lawrence Coll., 1996; sr. scholar Woodwor Wilson Internat. Ctr., Washington, 2001-2002. Mem. PEN. Democrat. Office: Sarah Lawrence Coll One Mead Way Bronxville NY 10708 E-mail: nmills@slc.edu.

MILLS, OLAN, II, photography company executive; b. 1930; married. Grad., Princeton U., 1952. With Olan Mills, Inc., Chattanooga, 1955—, now chmn., sec., also bd. dirs. Office: Olan Mills Inc Gen Offices 4325 Amnicola Hwy Chattanooga TN 37406-1014

MILLS, PATRICIA JAGENTOWICZ, political philosophy educator, writer; b. Newark, Mar. 18, 1944; d. Alexander A. and Louise A. (Breunig) Jagentowicz; 1 child, Holland Mills. BA, Rutgers U., 1973; MA, SUNY, Stony Brook, 1975; PhD, York U., Toronto, Ont., Can., 1984. Lectr. U. Toronto, 1984-85, vis. scholar, 1985-86, asst. prof. philosophy, 1986-88; asst. prof. polit. theory U. Mass., Amherst, 1988-91, assoc. prof. polit. theory, 1991—. Vis. scholar Pembroke Ctr. for Tchg. and Rsch. on Women, Brown U., 1999-2000; lectr. philosophy dept. Smith Coll., spring 1992; manuscript referee Social Scis. and Humanities Rsch. Coun. Can., 1985-86, 87-88, 91-92, Polity: Jour. of Northeastern Polit. Sci. Assn., 1990, 91; invited spkr. New Sch. for Social Rsch., 1990, Coll. Holy Cross, 1991, NEH seminar, Mt. Holyoke Coll., 1992, U. Pitts., 1993, Antigone Conf., SUNY Buffalo, 1997; presenter paper 20th World Congress Philosophy, 1998. Author: Woman, Nature, and Psyche, 1987; editor: Feminist Interpretations of G.W.F. Hegel, 1996; author, contbr.: (book chpts.) The Sexism of Social and Political Theory: Women and Reproduction from Plato to Nietzsche, 1979, Ethnicity in a Technological Age, 1988, Taking Our Time: Feminist Perspectives on Temporality, 1989, Renewing the Earth: The Promise of Social Ecology, 1990, The Future of Continental Philosophy and the Politics of Difference, 1991, Ecological Feminist Philosophies, 1996, The Phenomenology of Spirit Reader, 1998; contbr. articles to profl. jours. Dir. Drop-In Ctr., Newark, 1972-73; mem. N.J. Abortion Project, 1971-73; mem. Fortune Soc., N.J., 1972; grassroots organizer against the war in Vietnam, N.J., 1970-71; grassroots organizer women's movement, N.J. and N.Y., 1971-73. Recipient Disting. Tchg. award Delta Lambda chpt. Pi Sigma Alpha Honor Soc., U. Mass., 1997; postdoctoral fellow Social Scis. and Humanities Rsch. Coun. Can., 1983-85; scholar York U., 1975; faculty grantee for tchg. U. Mass., 1991-92. Mem. Am. Philos. Assn. (conf. presenter 1995 meeting), Soc. for Phenomenology and Existential Philosophy (presenter conf. papers 1988, 91, 92), Hegel Soc., Ancient Philosophy Soc., Soc. for the Study of Women Philosophers. Office: U Mass Thompson Hall Dept Polit Sci Amherst MA 01003 E-mail: pjmills@polsci.umass.edu.

MILLS, PAUL J. psychiatry educator; b. Phila., Apr. 11, 1955; s. William L. and Bernice C. Mills; m. Kim B. Mills, May 26, 1983; 1 child, Marian K. PhD, Maharishi Internat. U., Fairfield, Iowa, 1987. Asst. prof. U. Calif., San Diego, 1990—96, assoc. prof., 1996—2002, prof., 2002—. Dir. clin. rsch. labs. U. San Diego, 1996—. Contbr. over 180 articles to profl. jours., chpts. to books. Patient care vol. San Diego Hosp., 1995—; pres. bd. dirs. Waldorf Sch. of San Diego, 1993-94. Mem. Am. Psychosomatic Soc. (co-chair membership com. 1998—, chair awards com. 2000—), Soc. Behavioral Medicine (program com. 1999-2000). Avocation: surfing. Office: U Calif San Diego Med Ctr 200 W Arbor Dr San Diego CA 92103-0804 E-mail: pmills@ucsd.edu

MILLS, RICHARD HENRY, federal judge; b. Beardstown, Ill., July 19, 1929; s. Myron Epler and Helen Christine (Greve) M.; m. Rachel Ann Keagle, June 16, 1962; children: Jonathan K., Daniel Cass. BA, Ill. Coll., 1951; JD, Mercer U., 1957; LLM, U. Va., 1982. Bar: Ill. 1957, U.S. Dist. Ct. Ill. 1958, U.S. Ct. Appeals 1959, U.S. Ct. Mil. Appeals 1963, U.S. Supreme Ct. 1963. Legal advisor Ill. Youth Commn., 1958-60; state's atty. Cass County, Virginia, Ill., 1960-64; judge Ill. 8th Jud. Cir., 1966-76, Ill. 4th Dist. Appellate Ct., Springfield, Ill., 1976-85, U.S. Dist. Ct. (cen. dist.) Ill., Springfield, 1985—. Adj. prof. So. Ill. U. Sch. Medicine, 1985—; mem. adv. bd. Nat. Inst. Corrections, Washington, 1984-88, Ill. Supreme Ct. Rules Com., Chgo., 1963-85. Contbr. articles to profl. jours. Pres. Abraham Lincoln coun. Boy Scouts Am., 1978-80. With U.S. Army, 1952-54, Korea, col. res.; maj. gen. Ill. Militia. Recipient George Washington Honor medal Freedoms Found., 1969, 73, 75, 82, Disting. Eagle Scout Boy Scouts Am., 1985. Fellow Am. Bar Found.; mem. ABA, Nat. Conf. Fed. Trial Judges (chmn. 1999-00), Ill. Bar Assn., Chgo. Bar Assn., Cass County Bar Assn. (pres. 1962-64, 75-76), Sangamon County Bar Assn., 7th Cir. Bar Assn., Am. Law Inst., Fed. Judges Assn., Army and Navy Club (Washington), Sangamo Club, Masons (33 degree), Lincoln-Douglas Am. Inn of Ct. 150 (founding, pres. 1991-93). Republican. Office: US Dist Ct 600 E Monroe St Ste 117 Sprngfield IL 62701-1659

MILLS, ROBERT LEE, president emeritus; b. Erlanger, Ky., Nov. 13, 1916; s. John Clifford and Dixie Lee (Morris) M.; m. Mildred Sizer, June 24, 1942; children: Robert Lee, Dixie Louise, Barbara Jean. AB in Math. and Physics, U. Ky., 1938, MA in Ednl. Adminstrn, 1941, Ed.D., 1951; LLD, William Jewell Coll., 1971. Tchr. Covington (Ky.) pub. schs., 1938-41; head hydraulics br. Air Force Tech. Sch., Lincoln, Nebr., 1942-44; mem. supervisory staff electromagnetic plant Oak Ridge, 1944-48; research asst. U. Ky., Lexington, 1948-51, dean admissions, registrar, 1954-57; dir. research, head bur. adminstrn. and finance Ky. Dept. Edn., 1951-54; chmn. dept. ednl. adminstrn. U. Tex., Austin, 1957-59; pres. Georgetown (Ky.) Coll., 1959-78, chancellor, 1978-86, pres. emeritus, 1987—. Exec. sec. Ky. Adv. Commn. Ednl. Policy, 1952-54; v.p. Ky. Assn. Colls. and Secondary Schs., 1962-63, exec. com., 1959-64, pres., 1963-64; chmn. exec. com. Ky. Ind. Coll. Found.; mem. Ky. Commn. on Higher Edn., 1967-70, Ky. Govt. Council, 1968-72; adviser Texas Assn. Sch. Bds., 1957-59 Contbr. articles to profl. jours. Cons. Pres.' Com., White House Conf. Edn., 1955; mem. Ky. Devel. Council, 1961-65, Ky. Constn. Revision Assembly, 1964-66. Recipient Distinguished Alumni award U. Ky., 1963, Centennial award, 1964 Mem. Nat., Ky. edn. assns., Newcomen Soc., So. Assn. Bapt. Colls. (pres. 1965-66), Bapt. World Alliance (mem. exec. com. 1965-70, chmn. men's dept. 1965-67), So. Assn. Colls. and Schs. (commn. on colls. 1971-77), Kappa Delta Pi, Phi Delta Kappa, Phi Kappa Tau. Lodges: Kiwanis. Democrat. Baptist.

MILLS, RUSSELL ANDREW, newspaper publisher; b. St. Thomas, Ont., Can., July 14, 1944; s. Gerald Armond and Phyllis Marie (Hulse) M.; m. Judith Elizabeth Zimmerman, Mar. 25, 1967; children: Lara, Colin, Patrick. BA, U. Western Ont., London, 1967, MA, 1968. Reporter London (Ont.) Free Press, 1964-67; city editor The Oshawa (Ont.) Times, 1970; asst. city editor, night editor, asst. mng. editor The Ottawa (Ont.) Citizen, 1971-85, exec. editor, 1975-76, editor, 1977-84, gen.mgr., 1984-86, pub., 1986-89, pres., publ., 1992—; pres. Southam Newspaper Group, Toronto, Ont., 1989-92. Office: Ottawa Citizen 1101 Baxter Rd Ottawa ON Canada K2C 3M4

MILLS, S. LOREN, product safety manager, engineer; b. Manassas, Va., Oct. 31, 1946; s. James Bryan and Charlatta Ruth (Holland) M.; m. Nancy Jane Mathews, Apr. 7, 1979; children: Tyler, Mitchell, Molly. BS, Western Mich. U., Kalamazoo, 1975. Cert. product safety mgr. Internat. Product Safety Mgmt. Cert. Bd.; cert. safety specialist in product safety World Safety Orgn. Cert./Accreditation Bd. Sr. staff engr. Clark Equipment Co., Battle Creek, Mich., 1966-86; engrng. mgr. Hayes Machine Co., Marshall, 1986-88; product safety cons. Mills Cons., 1988-89; product safety mgr. Van Dorn Demag Corp., Strongsville, Ohio, 1989—. V.p., bd. dirs. Insulation Wholesale Supply Co., Battle Creek, 1981-2000. Co-author: Product Safety Management Handbook, 1994. Mem. Nat. Safety Coun., 1995—. With U.S. Army, 1968-74. Mem. ASME (Am. Nat. Stds. Inst. B56.1 stds. devel. com. 1981—), Soc. Plastics Industry (chmn. risk mgmt. com. 1992-98), Assn. Mfg. Tech. (mem. capital goods stds. coalition U.S. Tag ISO/TC199 com. 1992—), Am. Soc. Plastics Industry (mem. Am. Nat. Stds. Inst. B151.1 stds. devel. com. 1989—, Am. Nat. Stds. Inst. B151.27 stds. devel. com. 1991—, Am. Nat. Stds. Inst. B151.29 stds. devel. com. 2000—), Nat. Elec. Mfrs. Assn. (Am. Nat. Stds. Inst. Z535 stds. devel. com. 1991—, Am. Nat. Stds. Inst./Nat. Fire Protection Assn. 79 std. devel. com. 1997—), Soc. Automotive Engrs., Am. Soc. Safety Engrs., Nat. Safety Coun. (Am. Nat. Stds. Inst. Z244 lockout/tagout of energy sources, stds. devel. com. 1998—), Nat. Safety Coun. (mem. rubber and plastics sect. 1998—). Avocations: tennis, boating, fishing. Home: 19813 Winding Trl Strongsville OH 44149-8741 Office: Van Dorn Demag Corp 11792 Alameda Dr Strongsville OH 44149-3000

MILLS, SANFORD LEWIS, writer; b. Toccoa, Ga. s. Arthur Pardee and Dora Evelyn Mills; m. Janet Elaine Mills, June 23, 1956; children: Linda Ann, Russell Paris. BBA, U. Ga., Atlanta, GA, 1953—56; UGStudies, Fla. State U., Eglin Field, Fl, 1950—51; Grad. Work, U. Cin., Cincinnati, OH, 1959—59, Clemson U., Clemson, SC, 1974—74, Prinston Ext., Prenston, NJ, 1975—75. Tel. comm. craft. At & T, Atlanta, 1952—58, engr. Cincinnati, Ohio, 1958—62, Atlanta, 1962—65, engr. staff supr. New York, NY, 1965—68; tech. writing supr. Western Electric Co., Winston-Salem, NC, 1968—80; adult edn. instr. Forsyth Tecnincal Collete, 1970—79; contract writer Belcore, 1986—87, At &T, Winston-Salem, 1988—93; pres. Sanford Mills Associates, Inc., 1991—; pub. Salem Star News Paper, 1991—. Author: Techniques of Guidance & Counseling for Supervisors, Papa's Poems. Staff sargent USAF, 1949—52. Mem.: Scottish Rite FreeMasons, Masonic Lodge # 289. Avocations: painter, poet, writer, counselor. Home: 2911 Hope Valley Rd Winston Salem NC 27106 Office: 2911 Hope Valley Rd Winston Salem NC 27106 Office Fax: 336-768-5851. E-mail: sanfordmills@aol.com.

MILLS, STEPHEN, artistic director; Prin. dancer Ballet Austin, 1987, choreographer, 1988, resident choreographer, 1992, assoc. artistic dir., 1999—, artistic dir. Instr. Internat. Theatrical Inst., Cyprus; master tchr. Booker T. Washington H.S. for the Performing Arts, Dallas, Va. Sch. of the Arts, New Orleans Ctr. for Creative Arts, Stephens Coll., Mo., Point Park Coll., Pitts., Ballet Austin. Choreographed works have been shown at Ballet Builders at Lincoln Ctr., 1998, Rencontres Chorégraphiques Internat. des Seine-Saint-Denis, Paris, Cuballet, Havana, The Dayton Ballet, The Sarasota (Fla.) Ballet, Ballet Pacifica, Dallas Black Dance Theatre, Dance Kaleidoscope, Ontario Ballet Theatre, Toronto, Icelandic Ballet Co., Reykjavik0; performing mem. Harkness Ballet, Am. Dance Machine, Cin. Ballet, Indpls. Ballet Theatre, Balanchine Repertoire. Office: Ballet Austin 3002 Guadalupe St Austin TX 78705-2818*

MILLS, STEVEN A. information technology executive; Sales trainee, mktg. rep. IBM, N.Y.C., 1974—80, mem. bus. planning staff divsn. data processing, 1981—82, mgr. bus. planning staff, 1982—84, adminstrv. asst. to v.p. and asst. group exec. plans and controls, 1984—85, dir. planning info. sys. and comm. group, 1985—88, dir. fin. planning, 1988—89, dir. ops. programming sys., 1989—90, asst. gen. mgr. fin. and planning, 1990—92, gen. mgr. Santa Teresa lab., 1992—95, gen. mgr. software group strategy and solutions, 1995—2000, sr. v.p., group exec. software, 1974—. Mem. ops. com. IBM, mem. worldwide mgmt. coun., mem. corp. tech. com. Office: IBM 1133 Westchester Ave White Plains NY 10604*

MILLS, TEHERAN L. (TERRY MILLS), sociology educator; b. N.Y.C., Feb. 5, 1949; s. Lehman R. and Shirley Marie MIlls; m. Antonia Allen, Feb. 10, 1968; children: Brion K., Dion L. BA in Polit. Sci., L.I. U., 1974; MA in Sociology, U. So. Calif., 1995, PhD in Sociology and Gerontology, 1996. Asst. prof. U. Fla., Gainesville, 1996—. Editl. bd. Jour. Family Issues, Gainesville. Faculty advisor Alpha Kappa Delta Sociology Honor Soc., Gainesville. Avocations: hiking, golf, travel. Office: U Fla PO Box 117330 Gainesville FL 32611-7330 Fax: (352) 392-6568. E-mail: tlmills@soc.ufl.edu.

MILLS, WILLIAM HAROLD, JR. construction company executive; b. St. Petersburg, Fla., July 24, 1939; s. William Harold and Caroline (Bonfoey) M.; m. Sylvia Ludwig, Jan. 4, 1962 (div. 1975); children— William Harold III, Robert Michael, Leslie Anne; m. Kimberly Keyes, May 4, 1985 (div. 1988); m. Gigi Alice Schmidt, Aug. 1, 1990. Grad., Woodberry Forest Sch., 1954-57; BS in Civil Engring., U. Fla., 1961. Cert. Class A gen. contractor, Fla. V.P. bus. devel. Mills & Jones Constrn., St. Petersburg, Fla., 1964-68; v.p. Wellington Corp., Atlanta, 1968-71; exec. v.p. Mills & Jones Constrn., St. Petersburg, Fla., 1971-79; pres., chmn. Federal Constrn. Co., 1979-88, vice chmn., 1988—; pres., chair Univ. Housing Svcs., Inc. Mem. adv. com. St Petersburg Port, 1993—. Pres. St. Petersburg Progress, Inc., 1986-87; active mem. Suncoasters, St. Petersburg, 1974—, St. Anthony's Devel. Found., St. Petersburg, 1983-86; past chmn. Pinellas Marine Inst., St. Petersburg, Blue Ribbon Zoning Com., City of St. Petersburg; former mem. Pinellas County Constrn. Licensing Bd., Tampa Bay Aviation Adv. Com., United Fund Pinellas County; former mem. U. South Fla. Campus Adv. Bd. Named Hon. Royal Navy Liaison Officer Her Majesty's Royal Navy, 1984— Mem. ASCE, NSPE, Am. Mgmt. Assn., Mensa, St. Petersburg Area C. of C. (bd. govs. 1983-85), Fla. Sports Adv. Coun., Order of Salvador/Salvador Dali Mus., St. Petersburg Yacht Club, Dragon Club, Les Ambassadeurs Club (London), Annabel's Club (London), Useppa Island Club (past bd. govs.), Sigma Alpha Epsilon, U.S. Croquet Assn., Univ. Fla. Pres.'s Coun. (life). Republican. Episcopalian. Home: 1260 Brightwaters Blvd NE Saint Petersburg FL 33704-3728 Office: 25 2d St N Ste 400 Saint Petersburg FL 33701 E-mail: wmillsjr@uhsi.com.

MILLS, WILLIAM HAYES, lawyer; b. Gordo, Ala., Mar. 30, 1931; s. Early S. and Bama (Cameron) M. LL.B., U. Ala., 1956. Bar: Ala. 1956. Since practiced in Birmingham; partner Rogers, Howard, Redden & Mills, 1961-79, Redden, Mills & Clark, 1979—. Arbitrator Fed. Mediation and Conciliation Service, Am. Arbitration Assn. Served with AUS, 1948-50, 50-51. Mem. ABA, Ala., Birmingham bar assns., Am., ATLA. Baptist. Home: 2105 Williamsburg Way Birmingham AL 35223-1740 Office: Redden Mills & Clark 940 Regions Bank Bldg Birmingham AL 35203-3209 E-mail: whm@rmclaw.com.

MILLSAPS, FRED RAY, investor; b. Blue Ridge, Ga., Apr. 30, 1929; s. Samuel Hunter and Ora Lee (Bradshaw) M.; m. Audrey Margaret Hopkins, June 22, 1957; children: Judith Gail, Stephen Hunter, Walter Scott. AB, Emory U., 1951; postgrad., U. Wis. Sch. Banking, 1955-57, Harvard Bus. Sch., 1962; LLD, Fla. So. Coll., 1991. V.p. Fed. Res. Bank, Atlanta, 1958-64; fin. v.p. Fla. Power & Light Co., 1965-69; chmn., pres. Landmark Banking Corp. of Fla., Ft. Lauderdale, 1969-78. Bd. dirs. Franklin Templeton Mut. Funds, Mut. Shares Funds. Chmn. South Fla. Coordinating Coun., 1976-78, WPBT Cmty. TV Found. of South Fla., 1973-75, Fla. So. Coll., Lakeland, 1976-95, Broward Performing Arts Authority, Honda Classic, Broward Workshop, Holy Cross Health Corp.; mem. Fla. Coun. of 100. Mem. Coral Ridge Country Club. Methodist.

MILLSPAUGH, MARTIN LAURENCE, real estate developer, urban development consultant; b. Columbus, Ohio, Dec. 16, 1925; s. Martin Laurence and Elisabeth (Park) M.; m. Meredith Plant, May 10, 1952; children: Elisabeth, M. Laurence, Meredith, Thomas. AB summa cum laude, Princeton U., 1949. Reporter, columnist Richmond News Leader, Va., 1949-53; urban affairs writer Balt. Evening Sun, 1953-57; asst. commr. Urban Renewal Adminstrn., Washington, 1957-60; dep. gen. mgr. Charles Ctr., Balt., 1960-65; pres., chmn., CEO Charles Ctr.-Inner Harbor Mgmt., Inc., 1965-85; exec. v.p., pres., vice chmn. Enterprise Devel. Co., Columbia, Md., 1985—, also bd. dirs.; pres. Enterprise Internat. Devel. Co., 1988-91, vice chmn., 1991—, Enterprise Real Estate Svcs., Inc., 1996—. Adv. bd. Ctr. for Balt. Studies/U. Balt.; cons. to pvt. developers and local pub. agys., Mass., Va., S.C., Fla., Calif., Sydney, 1981—; conducted seminars in Nagasaki and Kagoshima, Japan, 1991-92; lectr. Columbia U., Princeton U., Johns Hopkins U., U. Md., U. New Orleans, NYU, Acad. Polit. Sci., AAAS, Lambda Alpha Internat., 1991, 95, U.K. Inst. Travel and Tourism, 1993, Can. Water Resources Assn., 1991, Nat. Bldg. Mus., 1995, Internat. Property Market, Cannes, 1996, others; appeared on USIA Worldnet TV Dialogue, Montevideo, Uruguay, 1990, Recife and Rio de Janeiro, 1995. Author: (with others) The Human Side of Urban Renewal, 1958; author, editor (monograph) Baltimore's Charles Center, 1964; author (newspaper series) Design for Living (hon. mention Heywood Broun award 1957); profl. appearances include VOA, 1994, CBS Sunday News, 1994; contbr. articles to profl. jours. Trustee Enoch Pratt Free Libr., Balt., 1965-85, Gilman Sch., 1975-80, Bryn Mawr Sch. for Girls, 1978-81; bd. dirs. Planned Parenthood Assn. Md., 1962-65, Roland Park Civic League, 1962-64, sec., 1963-64, Blue Cross of Md., Inc., 1970-80, Balt. Symphony Orch. Assn., 1974-78, YMCA of Greater Balt. area, 1977-81; Md. Internat. Coun., Balt., 1992-96, mem. long range planning com., 1994-96, sec., 1995-96; mem. chair nominating com. World Trade Ctr. Inst., 1996—; mem. task force Twentieth Century Fund, N.Y.C., 1984-85; mem. adv. coun. real estate devel. program Columbia U. Grad. Sch. Architecture and Planning, 1985-94; bd. advisors Fight-Blight Fund, Balt., 1961-62, Waterfront Ctr., Washington, 1987-90; adv. bd. Nat. Aquarium, Balt., 1988-2001, Sch. Bus. Mgmt. Morgan State U., 1993-94, Real Estate Inst., Sch. Continuing Studies Johns Hopkins U., 1994—, chair, 2000—; pres.'s adv. bd. U. Md. Balt. County, 1989-94; mem. adv. panel Ctr. Strategic and Internat. Studies, Washington, 1993-94; mem. Md. Transp. Real Estate Adv. Group, 1996; mem. U.S. Senate Productivity Award Selection Com. for Md., 1987. Served to sgt. USAF, 1944-46, PTO. Recipient Disting. Svc. award U.S. Housing and Home Fin. Agy., Washington, 1960, Urban Planning award The Waterfront Ctr., 1995, Awd. for Civic Accomplishment Greater Baltimore Comm., 1981, Prix of Excellence Awd. Internat. Real Estate Fedn., 1997, Awd. of Excellence and Honorary Life Counc. Awd., Urban Land Inst., 1980, 95. Mem. Urban Land Inst. (exec. group internat. coun., 1989—, vice chmn. internat. coun. 1995-96, chair adv. panel for city of Harrisburg, Pa., 1984, internat. com. 1987-88, 96-97, Balt. dist. coord. 1987-91, vice-chmn. dist. coun. 1991-94; mem. adv. panel for Oklahoma City, 1995, awards com. 1995-97), Internat. Real Estate Fedn., Greater Balt. Com. (urban affairs coun. 1982-84, Coun. on Urban Econ. Devel., Internat. Downtown Assn., Internat. New Town Assn. (mem. adv. panel for waterfront devel. for City of Malmo, Sweden 1987), Phi Beta Kappa, Lambda Alpha. Clubs: Center, Balt., 14 W Hamilton St (Balt.); Ivy (Princeton, N.J.). Democrat. Episcopalian. Home and Office: 203 Ridgewood Rd Baltimore MD 21210-2538 Office: Enterprise Devel Co 600 American City Bldg Columbia MD 21044 E-mail: martinmillspaugh@ereserve.com.

MILLSTEIN, DAVID J. lawyer; b. N.Y.C., Apr. 15, 1953; s. Stanley and Irma (Klein) M. AB, U. Calif., Berkeley, 1975, JD, 1979. Bar: Calif. 1979, U.S. Dist. Ct. (no. dist.) Calif. 1979, U.S. Dist. Ct. (ea. dist.) Calif. 1984. Assoc. Bostwick & Tehin, San Francisco, 1991-93; asst. dist. atty. San

Francisco Dist. Atty.'s Office, 1993—; pvt. practice San Francisco, 1982-95, 97—; ptnr. Millstein & Doolittle, 1996-97; chief asst. dist. Atty. City and County of San Francisco, 1996; ptnr. Millstein & Assocs., San Francisco, 1997—. Judge pro tem San Francisco Mcpl. Ct., 1983—; probation monitor Calif. State Bar, 1995—; panelist Calif. Psychol. Assn.; lectr. San Francisco Gen. Hosp., Stanford U., 1994, Boalt Hall Sch. of Law, U. Calif., Berkeley, 1995-96; adj. prof. Hastings Coll. Law, San Francisco, 1993-96, co-chair advocacy sect., 1994-95; legal analyst KBO-ABC News, San Francisco, 1995—, KTVV-Fox News, Oakland, Calif., 1994—; chief asst. dist. atty. City and County of San Francisco, 1996. Author supplement to How to Prepare For, Take and Use a Deposition, 1995; contbr. articles to law jours. Office: 580 California St Ste 500 San Francisco CA 94104-1000

MILLSTEIN, HERBERT SYDNEY, management consultant; b. Chgo., May 17, 1920; s. John and Bessie (Friedman) M.; m. Karen Annette Edwards, Aug. 21, 1971; children: Merle, Randy, Howard; stepchildren: David, Daniel, Dale, Douglas, Daren. BS, U. Ill., 1942; MBA, UCLA, 1960. Tng. officer, contbg. negotiator VA, East St. Louis, Ill., 1947-48; indsl. engr. Arthur K. Meyer Co., L.A., 1948-52; radar test engr. Hughes Aircraft, 1952; chief prodn. divsn., spl. asst. ballistic missiles and space, chief ballistic missle logistics mgmt. div. USAF L.A. Air Procurement Dist., 1952-59; mem. tech. staff Intellectronics Lab., TRW, Canoga Park, Calif., 1959-60; v.p. Ops. Rsch., Inc., Santa Monica, 1960-62; v.p., co-founder Mgmt. Tech., Inc., L.A., 1962-68; pres., dir. Mktg. Scis. Corp., Washington, 1968-74; dir. nat. productivity group, acctg. and fin. mgmt. divsn. GAO, 1974-86; pres. TRM, 1986-90, Millins Corp., Oviedo, Fla., 1990—. Adj. prof. Am. U. Contbr. articles to profl. jours. Vice pres. Chancellor Farms Civic Assn., Springfield, Va., 1979-80. With USAAF, 1944-46. Mem. AAAS, AIAA, Ops. Rsch. Soc. Am., Inst. Mgmt. Scis., Assn. Govt. Accts (cert. govt. fin. mgr.), Ind. Acad. Sci., Inst. Applied Pub. Fin. Mgmr. (co-founder). Home and Office: 3449 Sterling Lake Cir Oviedo FL 32765-5168 Fax: 407-977-6414. E-mail: HandKMillins@prodigy.net.

MILLSTEIN, IRA M. lawyer, lecturer; b. N.Y.C., Nov. 8, 1926; s. Harry M. and Birdie E. (Rosenbaum) M.; m. Diane G. Greenberg, July 3, 1949; children: James Eliot, Elizabeth Jane. BS, Columbia U., 1947, LL.B., 1949. Bar: N.Y. 1949, U.S. Supreme Ct. 1973. Atty. antitrust div. Dept. Justice, Washington, 1949-51; assoc. firm Weil Gotshal & Manges, N.Y.C., 1951-57, ptnr., 1957—. Fellow faculty govt. John F. Kennedy Sch. Govt., Harvard U., 1983-87; Eugene F. Williams Jr. vis. prof. in competetive enterprise and strategy, mem. adv. bd. Yale Sch. Mgmt., 1996—; chmn. pvt. sector adv. group on corp. governance World Bank/OECD-Paris, Washington, 1999—; counsel, bd. dirs. Lower Manhattan Devel. Corp., 2002--; sponsor Global Corp. Governance Forum. Author: (with Katsh) The Limits of Corporate Power, 1981; contbr. articles to profl. jours. Mem. Nat. Commn. on Consumer Fin., 1969-72, chmn., 1971-72; chmn. exec. com. bd. overseers Albert Einstein Coll. Medicine, Yeshiva U., Bronx, N.Y., 1981—; former chmn. bd. trustees Cen. Pk. Conservancy, 1990-99; co-chair NYSE, NASD Blue Ribbon com. on improving audit coms., 1999. Decorated chevalier Nat. Order of Merit, France. Mem. Am. Acad. Arts and Scis. (elected), ABA (chmn. antitrust law sect. 1977-78), N.Y. State Bar Assn. (chmn. antitrust law sect. 1967-68), Nat. Assn. Corp. Dirs. (bd. dirs. 1994—), Met. Club, Quaker Ridge Golf Club. Home: 1240 Flagler Dr Mamaroneck NY 10543-4601 Office: Weil Gotshal & Manges 767 5th Ave Ste 3201 New York NY 10153-0023 E-mail: ira.millstein@weil.com.

MILLSTONE, DAVID JEFFREY, lawyer; b. Morgantown, W.Va., 1946; AB, Johns Hopkins U., 1968; JD, U. W.Va., 1971. Bar: Ohio 1971. Ptnr. Squire, Sanders & Dempsey LLP, Cleve., intrnat. coord. labor and employment practice. Co-author: (book) Wage Hour Law--How to Comply, 2001; editor: (manual) Ohio and Fed. Employment Law Manual, 2001. Mem.: ABA. Office: Squire Sanders & Dempsey 4900 Key Tower 127 Public Sq Ste 4900 Cleveland OH 44114-1304 E-mail: dmillstone@ssd.com.

MILMAN, ALYSSA WHITE, lawyer, educator; b. Bklyn., Jan. 16, 1969; d. Leon Arthur and Barbara Lee (Hoops) M. Grad., U. Mass., 1989; JD, Calif. Western U., San Diego, 1992. Bar: Calif. 1992, U.S. Ct. Appeals (9th cir.) 1992. Asoc. Angelo & Assocs., Newport Beach, Calif., 1992-97; ptnr. Angelo & Milman, Irvine, 1999—. Adj. prof. Whittier Law Sch., Costa Mesa, Calif., 1998. Editor Calif. Western Law Rev./Internat. Law Jour., 1991-92. Vol., Shortshop, Orange County, 1995—, VIP, Orange County, 1995—. Mem. ABA, Orange County Bar Assn. Avocations: running, tennis, skiing. Office: Angelo and Milman 18111 Von Karman Ave Irvine CA 92612 Fax: (949) 660-0018. E-mail: alyssa@milmanlaw.com.

MILMAN, PERRY JAY, physician, gastroenterologist; b. Bklyn., Dec. 26, 1948; s. Joseph and Shirley (Edelstein) M.; m. Sheryl Marsha Solomon, Sept. 22, 1974; children: Jara Kendall, Darin Brent. BS in Biology cum laude, Bklyn. Coll., CUNY, 1969; MD magna cum laude, SUNY, Bklyn., 1973. Intern, resident in internal medicine L.I. Jewish Med. Ctr., New Hyde Park, N.Y., 1973-76, chief resident in internal medicine, 1976; fellow in gastroenterology N.Y. VA Hosp./NYU, N.Y.C., 1976-78; acting chief gastroenterology SUNY/Northport VA Hosp., Stony Brook, 1978-79; chief gastroenterology divsn. Flushing (N.Y.) Hosp. Med. Ctr., 1985-97. Contbr. articles to profl. jours. Fellow ACP, AGA, ASGE, NYSGE, LI Gastro, Am. Coll. Gastroenterology, Sigma Xi, Alpha Omega Alpha. Jewish. Avocations: piano, biking, skiing. Office: 2001 Marcus Ave Lake Success NY 11042-1011 E-mail: pmilman@msn.com.

MILMED, PAUL KUSSY, lawyer; b. Newark, Oct. 15, 1944; s. Leon Sidney and Bella (Kussy) M.; m. Debra R. Anisman, Oct. 23, 1988; children: Laura, Julia. AB, Amherst Coll., 1966; MSc, U. London, 1968; EdM, Harvard U., 1969; JD, NYU, 1975. Bar: N.J. 1975, N.Y. 1976, U.S. Ct. Appeals (2d cir.) 1975, U.S. Dist. Ct. N.J. 1975, U.S. Dist. Ct. (so. dist.) N.Y. 1976, U.S. Dist. Ct. (ea. dist.) N.Y. 1994. Law clk. Hon. Alan B. Handler N.J. Superior Ct. Appellate Divsn., Newark, 1975-76; assoc. Weil, Gotshal & Manges, N.Y.C., 1976-83; asst. U.S. atty. U.S. Atty.'s Office, So. Dist. N.Y., 1983-93, chief environ. protection unit, 1990-93; of counsel White & Case, 1993—. Ct.-apptd. mediator U.S. Dist. Ct., So. Dist. N.Y., 1996—. Rsch. editor NYU Rev. of Law and Social Change, 1974-75; editl. adv. bd. Fordham Environ. Law Jour., 1993—; contbr. articles to profl. jours. Mem. bd. trustees The Town Sch., N.Y.C. Mem. ABA, Assn. Bar City of N.Y. Avocation: photography. Home: One Gracie Terr New York NY 10028 Office: White & Case 1155 Avenue Of The Americas New York NY 10036-2787 E-mail: pkm@post.harvard.edu.

MILMOE, PATRICK JOSEPH, retired lawyer; b. Oct. 2, 1939; s. Hugh A. Milmoe and Mary Francis (O'Connell) Steenken; m. Carolyn Mann, Nov. 30, 1963; children: Mary Kaye Chrysicas, Caroline Pugh, Hugh. BA, Coll. William and Mary, 1959; JD, U. Va., 1962. Bar: N.Y. 1962, Va. 1962, Fla. 1989. With Davis & Polk, N.Y.C., 1965-72; ptnr. Hunton & Williams, Richmond, Va., 1972-2001, ret., 2001—. Chmn. DARE Marina, Inc., Grafton, Va., 1992—, States Roofing Corp., Norfolk, Va., 1994—, Virginia Beach Marlin Club, Inc., 1980—. Trustee Village of Atlantic Beach, N.Y., 1965-72; bd. dirs. St. Joseph's Villa, Richmond, Va., 1985-91, Hanover Tavern Found., 1998-2001. Capt. U.S. Army, 1963-65. Mem. Am. Coll. Real Estate Lawyers. Avocations: boating, fishing. Office: Hunton & Williams Riverfront Plz East Tower 951 E Byrd St Ste 200 Richmond VA 23219-4074 E-mail: pmilmoe@hunton.com.

MILNE, CHRISTOPHER MCQUISTON WILMOTH, photographer, journalist; b. N.Y.C., June 6, 1934; s. C. Lee Wilmoth and Helen Milne; m. Vesta Seymour, Jan. 6, 1999; children: Bruce, Milne, Geoffrey, David, James, Kevin. BA, Geneva Coll., 1956; studied color photography, Roman Vishniak, Montreal, 1973; MA, U. Fla., 1985. Writer U.S. Steel, Pitts., 1957-61; writer, owner Interpel Corp., 1961—; founder Fisherman's Life Mus., HFX, Canada, 1978; writer, corr. U.P.I., Washington, 1969-87; pub., editor Ea. Shore Echo, Halifax, N.S., Can., 1976-77; instr. various colls., 1988—; publ. Safe Harbour Press, Crescent, Pa., 1989—; owner, pres. Milne Inst., 1999—. Spl. investigator Scranton commn. investigating killings Kent State U., 1971. Editor: RR Stations of Pennsylvania, 1967; author: Ethics for Journalists, 2000; contbr. articles & photographs to Official Railway Guide, 1978-79; photographer traveling exhibit A Brutal Season—Northern Ireland, 1988-, When Trains Were King, 1992—; asst. editor Can. Nat. Rlwys., 1978; official photographer CPR, 1974. Active Christ Ch. at Grove Farm; counselor House Trailer Com. on Aging, 1970; spl. investigator Agy. for Social Concerns of United Meth. Ch., 1972; founder Fishermen's Life Mus., Halifax, Can. Mem. SAR, VFW, Soc. Profl. Journalists, Train Collectors Assn., Profl. Photographers Am., Elks, Nat. Multiple Sclerosis Soc. Mem. Soc. Of Friends. Office: Milne Inst PO Box 331 Crescent PA 15046

MILNE, CLARK ROGER, civil engineer; b. Harvey, Ill., Apr. 17, 1951; s. Donald Yule and Martha Mary (Clarke) M.; m. Ruiz Ann Sample Garrett, May 6, 1978 (div. July 1982); 1 child, Tana Raimi; m. Karen Ann Moutrey, Aug. 28, 1983; children: Abraham, Sarah. BS in Indsl. Engring., Cornell U., 1973; MS in Engring. Mgmt., M in Civil Engring., U. Alaska, 1977. Registered profl. engr., Alaska. Indsl. engr. Eaton Corp., Inc., Cleve., 1973-75; project engr. Interstate Constrn., Anchorage, 1977; heavy constrn. supt. Peter Kiewit Sons, Co., 1977-80; bldg. supt. Kiewit Constrn., Co., Fairbanks, Alaska, 1981-83; constrn. mgr. Jordan Constrn., 1984; chief civil engr. Fairbanks North Star Borough, 1985-88; regional mgr. Arctic Slope Cons. Group, Fairbanks, 1988-91; maintenance dir. Alaska Dept. Transp. & Pub. Facilities, 1991-95; ops. mgr., sr. engr. Dames & Moore-FAI, 1995-98; sr. engr. Nortech Engring., 1998—. Mem. Alaska Soc. Profl. Engrs. (state math. counts coord. 1998, Engr. of Yr. award 1993, state pres. 1999), Greater Fairbanks C. of C. (chmn. transp. commn. 1996-98). Avocations: math counts, family, beekeeping. Home: 1119 Coppet St Fairbanks AK 99709-4722 E-mail: milne@mosquitonet.com., cmilne@nortechengr.com.

MILNE, EDWARD LAWRENCE, biomedical engineer; b. Ottawa, Ont., Can., June 20, 1948; came to U.S., 1985; s. Roderick Francis and Mary Angela (Massiah) M.; m. Pamela Mary Sklenka, Aug. 23, 1975; children: Marc Aaron, Adam Daniel. BSc, Dalhousie U., 1971. Rsrch. asst. Tech. U. N.S., Halifax, Can., 1973-76; technologist Dalhousie U., 1976-85; tech. dir. orthopedic rsch. Mt. Sinai Med. Ctr., Miami Beach, Fla., 1986—. Contbr. articles to profl. jours. Avocations: computers, reading, fresh water fishing, gardening. Office: Mt Sinai Med Ctr 4300 Alton Rd Miami Beach FL 33140-2800 E-mail: tmilne@msmc.com., tmilne@bellsouth.net.

MILNE-KUHN, MICHELLE DAWN, artist; b. Bloomington, Minn., June 23, 1967; d. William and Karen Jean Milne; m. Daniel James Kuhn, June 29, 1995. Grad., U. Wis., 1991; postgrad., Art Inst. of Chgo. Artist, Ariz., 1994-99. Vol. U.S. Peace Corps, Zambia, Africa, 1995-96; artistic dir. The Many Faces of HIV/AIDS, Phoenix. Creator: The Many Faces of HIV/AIDS presentation, 1998 (Vibrant Arts grantee). Mem. Internat. Sculpture Ctr.

MILNER, BRENDA ATKINSON LANGFORD, neuropsychologist; b. July 15, 1918; arrived in Can., 1944; d. Samuel and Leslie (Doig) Langford. BA, Cambridge (Eng.) U., 1939, MA, 1949, ScD, 1972; PhD, McGill U., 1952, DSc (hon.), 1991; LLD (hon.), Queen's U., 1980, U. Man., 1982, U. Lethbridge, 1986, Mt. Holyoke Coll., 1986, U. Laval, 1987, U. Toronto, 1987; LHD (hon.), Mt. St. Vincent U., 1988; Hon. D., U. de Montréal, 1988; Dsc (hon.), Wesleyan U., 1991, Acadia U., 1991, U. St. Andrews, 1992, U. Hartford, 1997, McMaster U., 1999; LLD (hon.), Cambridge U., 2000. Exptl. officer U.K. Ministry of Supply, 1941-44; prof. agrégé Inst. Psychology U. Montreal, 1944-52; rsch. assoc. psychology dept. McGill U., Montreal, 1952-3, lectr. dept. neurology and neurosurgery, 1953-60, from asst. prof. to assoc. prof. to prof. psychology, 1960-93; Dorothy J. Killam prof. Montreal Neurol. Inst., 1993—. Head neuropsychology rsch. unit Montreal Neurol. Inst., 1953-90; Clothworkers fellow Girton Coll., Cambridge, 1972-73; hon. fellow Newnham Coll., Cambridge, 1989—. Mem. editl. bd. Neurpsychologia, 1973-93, Behavioral Brain Rsch., 1980-88, Hippocampus, 1990-96. Decorated officer Order of Can., officer Nat. Order of Que., 1985; Career investigator Med. Rsch. Coun. Can., 1964-99; recipient Kathleen Stott prize Newnham Coll., 1971, Karl Spencer Lashley award Am. Philos. Soc., 1979, Izaak Walton Killam Meml. prize Can. Coun., 1983, Hermann Von Helmholtz prize Cognitive Neurosci. Inst., 1984, Penfield award Can. League Against Epilepsy, 1984, Wilder Penfield prize Province of Que., 1993, Neural Plasticity prize Found. IPSEN, Paris, Met. Life Found. award, 1996; named Gt. Montrealer, 1987; named to Can. Med. Hall of Fame, 1997; William James fellow Am. Psychol. Soc., 1989 Fellow APA (Disting. Contbn. award 1973), AAAS, Royal Soc. London, Royal Soc. Can. (McLaughlin medal 1995), Can. Psychol. Assn.; mem. NAS (fgn. assoc.), Am. Epilepsy Soc. (William G. Lennox award 1974, 95), Am. Neurol. Assn., Association de Psychologie Scientifique de Langue Française, Brit. Soc. Exptl. Psychology, Exptl. Psychol. Soc., Psychonomic Soc., Ea. Psychol. Assn., Internat. Neuropsychology Symposium, Internat. Brain Rsch. Orgn. (exec. sec. 1993-97), Soc. Neurosci. (Ralph W. Gerard prize 1987), Am. Acad. Neurology (assoc.), Assn. Rsch. in Nervous and Mental Diseases (assoc.), Royal Soc. Medicine (affiliate), European Brain and Behavior Soc. (hon.), Sigma Xi. Office: Montreal Neurol Inst 3801 University St Montreal QC Canada H3A 2B4 E-mail: bmilner@bic.mni.mcgill.ca.

MILNER, CHARLES FREMONT, JR. manufacturing company executive; b. Durham, N.C., July 21, 1942; s. Charles Fremont and Eloyse (Sargent) M.; m. Molly Franc Wakefield, Aug. 28, 1965; children: Bernadette Ann Milner Gardner, Eloyse Lee. BA, Guilford Coll., 1963; MBA, Harvard U., 1965. Asst. to comptroller Harvard U., 1965-66; instr. Northeastern U., Boston, 1965-66; with Burlington Hosiery Co. divsn. Burlington (N.C.) Industries, 1966-71, asst. v.p., 1970-71; exec. v.p. Parklane Hosiery Co., Inc., New Hyde Park, N.Y., 1971-74; pres. Rudin & Roth, Inc. divsn. NCC Industries, N.Y.C., 1974-75; v.p. apparel group M. Lowenstein and Sons, 1975-76; pres., CEO BBC, Inc. and Camp Industry divsns. Genesco, Inc., 1976-80; gen. mgr. Johnston and Murphy Shoe Co. divsn., 1979—; gen. mgr. footwear mktg. and mfg. Genesco, Inc., 1980-81, v.p., 1981-82; pres., CEO Hope Hosiery Mills and C.M. Industries, Inc., Adamstown, Pa., 1983—. Trustee Friends Acad., Locust Valley, N.Y., 1974-79, Guilford Coll., 1982-97, vice chmn., 1989, chmn., 1990-97; mem. class chief fund agt. Harvard Bus. Sch., 1986-91, alumni bd., 1992-2001, v.p., 1995-97, pres., 1997-99, past pres., 1999-2001. Mem. Nat. Assn. hosiery Mfrs. (dir. 1978-82, 87—, exec. com. 1989-93, 99—, 2d vice chmn. 1991-92, vice chmn. 1992, chmn. 1993), Lancaster Country Club, Hamilton Club, Moselem Springs Golf Club. Home: 158 Hamilton Rd Lancaster PA 17603-4734 Office: 205 Washington St Denver PA 17517 E-mail: mmilner@socksmyway.com.

MILNER, CLYDE A., II, historian; b. Durham, N.C., Oct. 19, 1948; s. Charles Fremont and Eloyse (Sargent) M.; m. Carol Ann O'Connor, Aug. 14, 1977; children: Catherine Carol, Charles Clyde. AB, U. N.C., 1971; MA, Yale U., 1973, MPhil, 1974, PhD, 1979. Admissions counselor Guilford Coll., Greensboro, N.C., 1968-70; acting instr. Yale U., New Haven, 1974-75; research fellow McNickle Ctr., Chgo., 1975-76; instr. Utah State U., Logan, 1976-79, asst. prof., 1979-82, assoc. prof., 1982-88, prof., 1988—2002; dir. Mountain West Ctr. for Regional Studies, 1997-2000; dir. PhD program in heritage studies Ark. State U., 2002—, prof., 2002—. Reader of manuscripts History Book Club, Inc., 1986—; exec. dir. Am. Studies program, Utah State U., 1997-2000. Author: With Good Intentions, 1982; editor: Major Problems in the History of the American West, 1989, co-editor 2d edit., 1997; editor: A New Significance: Re-envisioning the History of the American West, 1996; assoc. editor The Western Hist. Quar., 1984-87, co-editor, 1987-89, editor, 1990-97, exec. editor, 1998-2002; co-editor: Churchmen and the Western Indians, 1985, Trails: Toward a New Western History, 1991, Oxford History of the American West, 1994 (Western Heritage award for non-fiction Nat. Cowboy Hall of Fame 1994, Caughey Western History Assn. award for best book on history of Am. West 1995). Recipient Paladen Writing award The Montana Mag. Western History, 1987, Faculty Svc. award Associated Students Utah State U., 1987, Outstanding Social Science Researcher award Utah State U., 1983, (with Carol A. O'Connor) Charles Redd prize Utah Acad. Scis., Arts and Letters, 1996. Mem. Western History Assn., Orgn. Am. Historians, Phi Alpha Theta, Phi Beta Kappa. Mem. Soc. Of Friends. Home: 1306 E Country Club Terr Jonesboro AR 72401-4325 Office: Ark State U Heritage Studies PhD Program PO Box 69 State University AR 72467 E-mail: cmilner@hass.usu.edu.

MILNER, HAROLD WILLIAM, hotel executive; b. Salt Lake City, Nov. 11, 1934; s. Kenneth W. and Olive (Schoettlin) M.; m. Susan Emmett, June 19, 1959 (div. 1976); children— John Kenneth, Mary Sue; m. Lois Friemuth, Aug. 14, 1977; 1 dau., Jennifer Rebecca. BS, U. Utah, 1960; MBA, Harvard, 1962. Instr. Brigham Young U., Provo, Utah, 1962-64; v.p. Gen. Paper Corp., Mpls., 1964-65; dir. finance Amalgamated Sugar Co., Ogden, Utah, 1965-67; corp. treas. Marriott Corp., Washington, 1967-70; pres., chief exec. officer, trustee Hotel Investors, Kensington, Md., 1970-75; pres., chief exec. officer Americana Hotels Corp., Chgo., 1975-85, Kahler Corp., Rochester, Minn., 1985-97; pres., CEO The Kensington Co., Salt Lake City, 1997—. Trustee Baron Asset Funds, 1987—. Author: A Special Report on Contract Maintenance, 1963. Served as lt. AUS, 1960. Mem. Minn. Bus. Partnership (dir. 1991—). Mem. Lds Ch. Office: The Kensington Co 2293 Morning Star Dr Park City UT 84060-6725 E-mail: hmilner@aol.com.

MILNER, IRVIN MYRON, lawyer; b. Cleve., Feb. 5, 1916; s. Nathan and Rose (Spector) M.; m. Zelda Winograd., Aug. 15, 1943 AB cum laude, Western Res. U. (now Case Western Res. U.), 1937, JD, 1940, LL.M., 1970. Bar: Ohio 1940, U.S. Dist. Ct. (no. dist.) Ohio 1946. Pvt. practice, Cleve., 1946—. Exec. sec., counsel Men's Apparel Club Ohio, Cleve., 1947-48; adj. instr. Sch. Law, Case Western Res. U., 1965-66; spl. counsel Ohio Office Atty. Gen., 1960-70; legal counsel Korean Am. Assn. Greater Cleve., 1973-95. Mem. Cleve. Fgn. Consular Corps., 1970-96, hon. consul Rep. of Korea for Cleve., 1970-96; bd. dirs. Internat. Human Assistance Programs, Inc., 1973-79, voting corp. mem., 1980-88; mem. Republican Nat. Com. Served with U.S. Army, 1941-45, ETO. Decorated Order Diplomatic Svc. Merit-Heung-in medal (Republic of Korea), 1975; named to Disting. Alumni Hall of Fame, Cleveland Heights (Ohio) High Sch., 1983. Fellow Internat. Consular Coll., Ohio Bar Found.; mem. ABA (small bus. com., corp. bus. law sect. 1971-74), Greater Cleve. Bar Assn., Cuyahoga County Bar Assn. (pres. 1975-76, co-chmn. jud. standards com. 1987-88, life trustee, award of Special Merit 1976, Pres.' award 1988), Ohio State Bar Assn. (coun. dels., 1976-86, com. on legal ethics and profl. conduct 1984-97), Cuyahoga County Bar Found. (sec.-treas. 1980-84, bd. dirs. 1984—), Cuyahoga County Coun. Ohio VFW (comdr. 1958, Merit award 1958), Am. Security Coun. (nat. adv. bd.), Cleve. Coun. on World Affairs, Western Res. Coll. Alumni Assn. (bd. dirs. 1982-88), Cleve. City Club, Masons (32 deg.), Tau Epsilon Rho (chancellor Cleve. Grad. chpt. 1987-88), Delta Phi Alpha. Jewish.

MILNER, KENNETH PAUL, lawyer; b. Phila., June 2, 1951; s. Stanley O. and Marcia Elva Milner; m. Ruth Marie Kosonovich, June 16, 1973; children: Zachary Stanton, Adrienne Nicole. BA, U. Pa., 1973; JD, Boston U., 1976. Bar: Pa. 1976, U.S. Dist. Ct. (ea. dist.) Pa. 1976, U.S. Supreme Ct., 2000. Assoc. Law Office of Donald Joel, Phila., 1976-77; assoc. counsel, gen. counsel Cottman Transmission System, Inc., Ft. Washington, Pa., 1977-82; owner Law Office of Kenneth P. Milner, Phila., 1982-88; ptnr. Gold & Bowman, 1988-90, Starfield & Payne, P.C., Ft. Washington, 1990-94; dir., shareholder McTighe, Weiss, O'Rourke & Milner, P.C., Norristown, Pa., 1994-00; ptnr. Masterson, Braunfeld & Milner LLP, 2000—. Sec., vice chair, chair Montgomery County Realtor/Atty. Joint Liaison Com., 1996—. Contbr. articles to profl. jours. Counsel, mem. exec. bd. Montgomery County Literacy Network, 1996—; co-chair diversity Upper Dublin (Pa.) Strategic Planning Com., 1993-96. Recipient Chmn.'s award Am. Heart Assn., Eastern Montgomery, Pa., 1996. Mem. ABA, Pa. Bar Assn., Montgomery Bar Assn. (chair franchise law com. 1994-98, mem. long range planning com. 1998-00, bd. dirs. 1999—, mem. exec. com. 1999), Upper Dublin Soccer club (bd. dirs., sec. 1990-96). Office: Masterson Braunfeld & Milner LLP 702 One Montgomery Plz Norristown PA 19401 E-mail: kmilner@masterbraun.com.

MILNER, MATTHEW A. supervisor; s. Joel Thomas and Frances Mildred Milner; m. Anne Marie Babovec, June 8, 1991; children: Taylor Hardy, Madisson. D in Musical Arts, U. Houston, 2000. Cert. instrumental tchr., adminstrn. mid - mgmt. Elem. music tchr. Ft. Bend Ind. Sch. Dist., Sugar Land, Tex., 1989—94, orch. dir., 1994—2000, coord. performing arts, 2000—. Cons. Ctr. Educator Devel. Fine Arts, San Antonio, 2001—. Coach Upward Basketball First United Meth. Ch., Sugar Land, 1999—2002. Mem.: Coll. Music Soc., Tex. Assn. Sch. Adminstrs., Music Educators Nat. Conf., Tex. Orch. Dirs. Assn., Tex. Music Educators Assn. Avocations: reading, exercise. Office: Fort Bend Ind Sch Dist 16431 Lexington Blvd Sugar Land TX 77479 Office Fax: 281-634-1716. Personal E-mail: m.milner@att.net. E-mail: matthew.milner@fortbend.k12.tx.us.

MILNER, MAX, food and nutrition consultant; b. Edmonton, Alta., Can., Jan. 24, 1914; came to U.S., 1939, naturalized, 1944; s. Morris Abram and Rose (Lertzman) M.; m. Elizabeth Banen, Aug. 9, 1942; children— Ruth Sharon, Marcia Ann. B.Sc., U. Sask., 1938; LL.D. (hon.), 1979; MS, U. Minn., 1941, PhD, 1945. Research chemist Pillsbury Mills Inc., Mpls., 1939-40; prof. grain sci. and industry Kans. State U., Manhattan, 1947-59; sr. food technologist UNICEF, N.Y.C., 1959-71; chief nutrition br. AID, 1966-67; dir. secretariat protein calorie adv. group UN, 1971-75; assoc. dir. internat. nutrition program M.I.T., 1975-78; exec. officer Am. Inst. Nutrition, Bethesda, Md., 1978-84; mem. U.S. Wheat Industry Council, 1980-83; mem. expert evaluation panel Bd. Internat. Food and Agrl. Devel., 1983—. Chmn. Gordon Research Conf. Food and Nutrition, 1968; Gen. Food Co. (Can.) disting. internat. lectr., 1975 Co-author: Protein Resources and Technology, 1978, Postharvest Biology and Biotechnology, 1978; Editor: Protein-enriched Cereal Foods for World Needs, 1969, Nutrition Improvement of Food Legumes by Breeding, 1975; Contbr. articles to profl. jours., chpts. to monographs. Bd. dirs., exec. com. Meals for Million/Freedom From Hunger Found., 1975-83, cons. in field. Fellow AAAS, Inst. Food Technologists (Internat. award 1968, lectr. sci. series 1971-72, Disting. Food Service award N.Y. sect. 1975), Am. Soc. Nutritional Scis.; mem. Am. Chem. Soc., Am. Assn. Cereal Chemists Home: Apt 212 8100 Connecticut Ave Chevy Chase MD 20815 E-mail: bbmilner@aol.com. *As a child of immigrant parents with minimal formal education, my career, like that of many Americans with this kind of background, is a testimonial to the unique role of the Canadian and American system of open higher education, available to all able to qualify for admission. It is to such institutions that I owe a profound debt.*

MILNER, PETER MARSHALL, psychology educator; b. Silkstone Common, Eng., June 13, 1919; s. David William and Edith Anne (Marshall) M.; m. Susan Walker, Oct. 13, 1970; 1 son, David Elliot. BS, Leeds U., 1941; MS, McGill U., PhD, 1954. Sr. sci. officer U.K. Ministry Supply, 1941-48; research asso. physics McGill U., 1948-50, research asst., prof. dept. psychology, 1950-92, prof. emeritus, 1992—, chmn. dept., 1980-83. Author: Physiological Psychology, 1970, The Autonomous Brain, 1999. Fellow APA., Can. Psychol. Assn.; mem. Sigma Xi. Home: 2255 Chomedey St # 15 Montreal QC Canada H3H 2B1 Office: McGill U Dept Psychology 1205 Dr Penfield Ave Montreal QC Canada H3A 1B1 E-mail: peter.milner@mcgill.ca.

MILNER, RICHARD GERARD, physicist; b. Cork, Ireland, Dec. 2, 1956; s. William and Maura (McGrath) M.; m. Eileen Troy, June 21, 1980; children: William, Samuel, David. BS with honors, Univ. Coll. Cork, 1978, MS, 1979; PhD, Calif. Inst. Tech., 1985. Rsch. assoc. Calif. Inst. Tech., 1985-88, rsch. scientist, 1988; asst. prof. MIT, Cambridge, 1988-93, assoc. prof., 1993-98, prof., 1998—, dir. of Bates Linear Accelerator Ctr., 1998—. Recipient Presdl. Young Investigator award NSF, 1989. Office: Bates Linear Accelerator MIT 77 Massachusetts Ave Cambridge MA 02139-4301 E-mail: milner@mitlns.mit.edu.

MILNER, WESLEY TYRE, political science educator; b. Ft. Worth; s. E.R. and Sue Milner; married. BA in Econs. and German, U. Tex., 1986; MA in Internat. Affairs, George Washington U., 1993; PhD in Polit. Sci., U. North Tex., 1999. Govtl. liaison Advanced Power Techs., Inc., Washington, 1987-93; instr. U. North Tex., Denton, 1994-98; asst. prof. polit. sci., dir. internat. studies U. Evansville, Ind., 1999—. Contbr. articles to profl. jours. Mem. Am. Polit. Sci. Assn., Midwest Polit. Sci. Assn., So. Polit. Sci. Assn., Internat. Studies Assn. Methodist. Office: U Evansville 1800 Lincoln Ave Evansville IN 47722 Fax: (812) 479-2282. E-mail: wm23@evansville.edu.

MILNES, ARTHUR GEORGE, electrical engineer, educator; b. Heswall, Eng., July 30, 1922; came to U.S., 1957, naturalized, 1964; s. George and Marion (Teasdale) M.; m. Mary Laverne Wertz, Dec. 4, 1955; children: Sheila Rae, Brian George, John Teasdale. BSc, U. Bristol, Eng., 1943, MSc, 1947, DSc, 1956. With Royal Aircraft Establishment, 1943-57, prin. sci. officer, 1952-57; mem. faculty Carnegie-Mellon U., Pitts., 1957-87, prof. elec. engring., 1960-87, assoc. head dept., 1966-69, Buhl prof., 1973-87, prof. emeritus, 1987—. Cons. to industry on semiconductor devices, 1957 Author: Transductors and Magnetic Amplifiers, 1957, (with D.L. Feucht) Heterojunctions and Metal-Semiconductor Junctions, 1972, Deep Impurities in Semiconductors, 1973, Semiconductor Devices and Integrated Electronics, 1979;

contbr. articles to profl. jours. FOA rsch. fellow NAS-Royal Soc. London, 1954. Fellow IEEE (J.J. Ebers award 1982, van der Ziel award 1993), Am. Phys. Soc., Instn. Elec. Engrs. (London). Home: 1417 Inverness St Pittsburgh PA 15217-1157

MILNIKEL, ROBERT SAXON, lawyer; b. Chgo., Aug. 17, 1926; s. Gustav and Emma Hazel (Saxon) M.; m. Virginia Lee Wylie, July 26, 1969; children: Robert Saxon Jr., Elizabeth Wylie. AB, U. Chgo., 1950, JD, 1953. Bar: Ill. 1953, U.S. Dist. Ct. 1954. Assoc. Traeger, Bolger & Traeger, Chgo., 1953-57, Heineke, Conklin & Schrader, Chgo., 1958-66; ptnr. Peterson & Ross, 1966—. With USN, 1944-46, PTO. Mem. Beta Theta Pi (pres. chpt. and alumni assn.), Cliffdwellers Club (bd. dirs. Arts Found.) Republican. Lutheran. Home: 601 Ridge Rd Kenilworth IL 60043-1042 Office: Peterson & Ross 200 E Randolph St Ste 7300 Chicago IL 60601-7012 E-mail: milnikel@enteract.com.

MILNOR, HAZEL, nurse; b. Marble, Ark., Apr. 2, 1921; d. Andrew Jackson and Laura Jane (Davis) Spencer; m. John Champion Milnor, June 21, 1951 (dec. Aug. 1989); children: Mary Christine, Jean Ann Laura. RN, Calif., Hawaii. Nurse pvt. duty, Calif., 1942—; surg. nurse Queen's Hosp., Hawaii, 1944-46; flight attendant United Airlines, San Francisco, 1946-51. Author: poems. Founding pres. Sgt. Angels Ministry, Hawaii. Inducted Internat. Poetry Hall of Fame. Mem. Assn. Retarded Citizens (bd. dirs., mem. com.), Angel Collector's Club Am., Clipped Wings (mem.-at-large, mem. coms.), Internat. Soc. Poets (disting.), Oahu Country Club. Republican. Episcopalian. Avocations: collecting angels, travel.

MILNOR, WILLIAM ROBERT, physician; b. Wilmington, Del., May 4, 1920; s. William Robert and Virginia (Sterling) M.; m. Gabriella Mahaffy, Aug. 19, 1944; children— Katherine Alexander, William Henry. AB, Princeton U., 1941; MD, Johns Hopkins U., 1944. Diplomate: Am. Bd. Internal Medicine. Intern, resident Johns Hopkins Hosp., 1944-46; research fellow Nat. Heart Inst., 1949-51; physician-in-charge heart sta. Johns Hopkins Hosp., 1951-60, physician, 1952—; mem. faculty Johns Hopkins Med. Sch., 1951—, prof. physiology, 1969—. Vis. fellow St. Catherine's Coll., Oxford (Eng.) U., 1968; mem. med. adv. panel Am. Inst. Biol. Scis., 1971— ; assessor Nat. Med. Research Council of Australia, 1976— Author: Hemodynamics, 2d edit., 1989, Cardio-vascular Physiology, 1990; contbr. articles to med. textbooks, med. jours. Served to capt. M.C. USAAF, 1946-48. Fellow A.C.P.; mem. Am. Physiol. Soc., Am. Fedn. Clin. Research, Biomed. Engring. Soc., Am. Heart Assn. (chmn. research com. 1966), Heart Assn. Md. (past pres.) Clubs: L'Hirondelle, Princeton, 14 W Hamilton St.

MILONAS, MINOS, artist, designer, poet; b. Heraklion, Crete, Greece, Apr. 28, 1936; came to U.S., 1964, naturalized, 1968; s. Stavros and Maria (Kaplantzis) M.; m. Arlene Watson, Dec. 23, 1963 (div. 1970); m. Sarah Brown, Dec. 1973 (div. 1974); m. Elaine Mauceli, May 26, 1988. BA, Calif. State U., Northridge, 1970; MFA with hons., U. Wash., Seattle, 1972. Freelance writer and poet, Athens, 1960-64; freelance artist L.A., 1964-66; instr. U. Wash., 1971-72, Studio Milonas, Seattle, 1972-76, artist N.Y.C., 1977—, textile designer, 1984-94. One man shows include Second Story Gallery, Seattle, 1971, Henry Art Gallery, Seattle, 1972, Polly Friedlander Gallery, Seattle, 1973, Stavrakakis Gallery, Crete, Greece, 1977, West Broadway Gallery, N.Y.C., 1979, 81, 82, Heraklion Art Gallery, Crete, 1983, Kreonides Gallery, Athens, 1983, 84, Doma Gallery, N.Y.C., 1988, Hellenic Cultural Ctr., N.Y., 1990, 93, Cypriot Consulate, N.Y.C., 1990; exhibitions in group shows at Calif. State U., Northridge, 1968-69, Mcpl. Art Gallery, L.A., 1969, U. Wash. Libr., Seattle, 1971, 72, Panaca Gallery, Bellevue, Wash., 1973, Mercer Island Art Gallery, Seattle, 1973, Henry Art Gallery, Seattle, 1973, Tacoma Art Mus., 1973, 75, N.W. Watercolor Soc., 1974, Gordon Woodside Gallery, Seattle, 1974, Coll. of the Cisciyous, Calif., 1975, Laguna Gloria Art Mus., Austin, Tex., 1975, Redmonds (Wash.) Arts Festival, 1975, Univ. Dist. Arts Festival, Seattle, 1976, Bellevue Art Mus., 1976, Sunne Savage Gallery, Boston, 1976, Cretan Artists, Stavrakakis Gallery, Heraklion, Crete, 1978, Internat. Drawing Biennale, Cleveland, Eng., 1981-82, Bowes Mus., Barnard Castle, Eng., 1982, Shipley Art Gallery, Gateshed, Eng., 1982, House of Commons, London, 1982, Haggin Mus., Stockton, Calif., 1985-86, U. N.D., Grand Forks, 1987, Greek Cultural Ctr., Springfield, Mass., 1987, 89, Del Bello Gallery, Toronto, Ont., Can., 1987, Ball State U., Muncie, Ind., 1989, Morin-Miller Galleries, N.Y.C., 1989-90, Columbia (Md.) Coll., 1989, Grand Prospect Hall, Bklyn., 1990, Kenneth Raymond Gallery, Boca Raton, Fla., 1993-96; author: The Small Caravan, 1962; author of short stories; author of numerous poems; videos include Multimedia Artist, 1988, 500 Definitions--Art Is, 1991. Recipient 4 Sculpture awards Summer Art Festivals, 1970-76, 2 Merit awards Greek Cultural Ctr., 1987; U. Wash. grantee, 1970; U. Wash. scholar, 1971. Mem. Nat. Artists Equity Assn., Inc., N.Y. Artists Equity Assn., Inc., Poetry Soc. Am., Greek-Am. Writers Assn. Democrat. Home and Office: 790 11th Ave Apt 39A New York NY 10019-3521

MILONE, FRANCIS MICHAEL, lawyer; b. Phila., June 18, 1947; s. Michael Nicholas and Frances Theresa (Fair) Milone; m. Maida R. Crane, Nov. 25, 1991; children: Michael, Matthew. BA, LaSalle Coll., 1969; MS, Pa. State U., 1971; JD, U. Pa., 1974. Bar: Pa. 1974, U.S. Dist. Ct. (ea. dist.) Pa. 1974, U.S. Dist. Ct. (mid. dist.) Pa. 1979, U.S. Dist. Ct. (ea. dist.) Mich. 1983, U.S. Ct. Appeals (3d cir.) 1978, U.S. Ct. Appeals (4th and 5th cirs.) 1979, U.S. Supreme Ct. 1979. Assoc. Montgomery, McCracken, Walker & Rhoads, Phila., 1974—77; ptnr. Morgan, Lewis & Bockius, 1981—. Mem.: ABA (labor and litig. sects.), Phila. Bar Assn., Pa. Bar Assn. Home: 912 Field Ln Villanova PA 19085-2003 Office: Morgan Lewis & Bockius 1701 Market St Philadelphia PA 19103-2903 E-mail: fmilone@morganlewis.com.

MILORO, PROTOPRESBTER FRANK, church official, religious studies educator; b. Wilmington, Del., Jan. 26, 1947; m. Constance Ann Evanisko, Apr. 20, 1969; children: Alexandra, Stephanie, Christopher. Grad. summa cum laude, Saviour Sem., 1969; grad. with high honors, St. Vincent Coll., 1972; attended, U. Pitts. Ordained to Diaconate and Priesthood, 1969. Assigned St. John's Ch., Ligonier, Pa., 1969-72, St. Stephen's Ch., Latrobe, 1969-72, St. John's Ch., Rahway, N.J., 1972-76; dir. Camp Nazareth, diocesan dir. youth, 1976-86; dean Christ the Saviour Sem.; elevated to dignity of Very Rev., 1985; sec. to bishop; instr. homiletics and parish administn.; diocesan chancellor Am. Carpatho-Russian Orthodox Diocese, 1990—; dean Christ the Savior Cathedral, 1997—. Chaplain Ea. Orthodox residents Polk Ctr., Commonwealth Pa., established chapel. Assoc. editor The Ch. Messenger. Office: 312 Garfield St Johnstown PA 15906-2122

MILOY, LEATHA FAYE, university program director; b. Marlin, Tex., Mar. 12, 1936; d. J. D. and Leola Hazel (Rhudy) Hill; m. John Miloy, June 20, 1960; children: Tyler Hill, David Reed, Nancy Lee. BA, Sam Houston State U., 1957; MS, Tex. A&M U., 1967, PhD, 1978. Dir. pub. affairs Gulf Univs. Rsch. Corp., College Station, Tex., 1966-69; asst. dir. Ctr. for Marine Resources Tex. A&M U., 1974-76, dir. edn. svcs., 1974-78; dir. info. and spl. svcs. Tex. Woman's U., Denton, 1978-79; asst. v.p. univ. advancement S.W. Tex. State U., San Marcos, 1979-83, asst. to pres., 1983-84, v.p. student and instl. rels., 1984-90, v.p. univ. advancement, 1990-93, dir. capital campaign, 1993-98. Vis. lectr. humanities and sea U. Va., 1972-73; cons. Office Tech. Assessment, Washington, 1976-86, Tex. A&M U., Galveston, 1979-82, Bemidji State U., Glassboro State Coll., 1984; mem. Task Force on Edn. and Pub. Interest, 1987-88. Editor: The Ocean From Space, 1969; author, editor Sea Grant 70's, 1970-79 (Sea Grant award 1973-74); contbr. articles to profl. jours. Ad hoc mem. Marine Resources Coun. Tex., Austin, 1971-72, Tex. Energy Adv. Coun., 1974-75; chmn. United Way, Bryan, Tex., 1976; com. mem. various local elections, 1974-78. NSF grantee, 1970-78; recipient Marine Resources Info. award NSF, 1969-71, Tex. Energy Info. award Gov.'s Office, 1974-75, Tex. Water Info. award Dept. Interior, 1977-79. Mem. Nat. Soc. Fundraising Execs., Coun. for the Advancement and Support Edn. (bd. dirs. 1979-81, Disting. Achievement award 1998), Coun. Student Svcs. (v.p. Tex. 1988-90). Avocations: reading, painting, fishing. Home: PO Box 752 Buchanan Dam TX 78609-0752 E-mail: lmiloy@tstar.net.

MIL'SHTEIN, SAMSON, semiconductor physicist; b. Vinitza, USSR, Aug. 6, 1940; came to U.S., 1982; s. Khaim and Golda (Tzukerman) M.; married; children: Mark, Valery. MS, State U., Odessa, USSR, 1963; PhD, U. Jerusalem, 1976. Lectr. Jr. Coll., Kherson, USSR, 1963-65; staff Inst. Marine Engrs., Odessa, 1965-67, Inst. Solid State Physics, Moscow, 1967-72; lectr. U. Jerusalem, 1974-76; sr. lectr. Ben-Gurion U., Beer-Shera, Israel, 1976-82; vis. scientist Bell Labs., Murray Hills, N.J., 1982-83; sr. scientist Semiconductors Group, Cabot Corp., Billeria, Mass., 1984-86; prof. elec. and computer engring. U. Mass., Lowell, 1987—, dir. Advanced Electronic Tech. Ctr., 1990—. Asst. dean for rsch., 1998-99; presenter in field. Contbr. more than 190 articles to profl. jours., patentee in field. Recipient 1st prize for sci. achievements Inst. Solid State Physics of Acad. Scis. USSR, 1971. Mem. IEEE, Materials Rsch. Soc., Elec. Micros. Soc. Jewish. Avocations: classical music, jazz, art, table tennis.

MILSOM, ROBERT CORTLANDT, banker; b. Butler, Pa., Dec. 15, 1924; s. Robert C. and M. Ethel (Leyland) M. BS, John Carroll U., 1948. With PNC Bank (formerly Pitts. Nat. Bank), 1948-90; asst. sec., asst. cashier customer relations div. PNC Bank, 1953-56, asst. v.p. loan div., 1956-60, v.p. charge comml. loan group, 1960-65, sr. v.p. charge comml. banking div., 1965-68, exec. v.p., 1968-72, pres., 1972-85, chmn., CEO, 1985-90, also bd. dirs., 1972—; vice chmn., dir. PNC Bank Corp, 1972-90. Bd. dirs. PNC Bank N.A., PNC Equity Mgmt. Corp., Exec. Svc. Corps., Foxwall Med. Svc.; chmn. bd. trustees Mercy Hosp. Pitts., 1994—. Bd. dirs. Pitts. Mercy Health System, Inc., Pitts. Ballet Theatre, Regional Indsl. Devel. Corp.; hon. trustee John Carroll U., Cleve.; mem. adv. bd. Mon Valley Renaissance program California U. Pa. Mem. Duquesne Club of Pitts., Fox Chapel Golf Club of Pitts., Laurel Valley Golf Club, Rolling Rock Club. Office: PNC Bank 5th Ave & Wood St Pittsburgh PA 15222 also: PNC Bank NA P1-POPP-23-3 1 Pnc Plz Pittsburgh PA 15222-2709

MILSTEAD, JOHN DAVID, reporter; b. Rock Hill, S.C., Feb. 28, 1972; s. John William and Marlene S. Milstead. BA, Oberlin Coll., 1994. Reporter Cin. Bus. Courier, 1994-96; editor Small Bus. News, Dayton, Ohio, 1996-97; bus. editor The Herald, Rock Hill, 1997-2000, city editor, 1999; staff reporter Wall Street Jour., Charlotte, N.C., Southeast Jour., 2000; reporter Denver Rocky Mountain News, 2001—. Bd. dirs. York County Teen Pregnancy Prevention Coun., 1997-2001, Cmtys. in Schs., 1999-2001. Recipient 1st place award for beat reporting S.C. Press Assn., 1998. Mem. Soc. Am. Bus. Editors and Writers. Office: Rocky Mountain News 400 W Colfax Ave Denver CO 80204-0004 E-mail: jdmilstead@world.oberlin.edu.

MILSTED, AMY, biomedical educator; BSEd, Ohio State U., 1967; PhD, CUNY, 1977. Lectr. Hunter Coll./CUNY, 1970-76; instr. Carnegie-Mellon U., Pitts., 1976-77; postdoctoral fellow Muscular Dystrophy Assn./Carnegie-Mellon U., 1978-79; rsch. assoc. Case Western Res. U., Cleve., 1979-82; rsch. chemist VA Med. Ctr., 1982-87; project staff The Cleve. Clin. Found., 1987-89; asst. staff dept. brain and vascular rsch. Cleve. Clinic Found., 1989-93; grad. faculty Sch. Biomed. Scis. Kent (Ohio) State U., 1995—; assoc. prof. dept. biology U. Akron, Ohio, 1993-2000, prof. biology, 2000—. Adj. faculty biology dept. Cleve. State U., 1991-97. Contbr. articles to profl. jours. Mem. Am. Heart Assn., Inter-Am. Soc. Hypertension, Am. Chem. Soc., Endocrine Soc., AAAS, Assn. Women in Sci. Office: University of Akron Dept of Biology Asec 279 Akron OH 44325-3908 E-mail: milsted@uakron.edu.

MILSTEIN, ELLIOTT STEVEN, law educator, academic administrator; b. Oct. 19, 1944; s. Samuel M. and Mildred K. Milstein; m. Bonnie Myrun, Oct. 1, 1967 (div. Oct. 1992); 1 child, Jacob. BA, U. Hartford, 1966, LLD (hon.) , 1997; JD, U. Conn., 1969; LLM, Yale U., 1971; LLD (hon.) , Nova Southeastern U., 2001. Bar: conn. 1969, D.C. 1972, U.S. Dist. Ct. Conn. 1969, U.S. Ct. Appeals (D.C.) 1972. Lectr. law U. Conn. Clin. Program, 1969-70; staff counsel New Haven Legal Assistance Assn., 1971-72; asst. prof. law, dir. clin. programs Washington Coll. Law Am. U., 1972-74, assoc. prof., dir. clin. programs, 1974-77, prof., dir. clin. programs, 1977-88, interim dean, 1988-90, dean, 1990—. Prof. law, Washington Coll. Law Am. U., 1995—; co-dir. Nat. Vets. law Ctr., 1978-84; cons. Calif. Bar Bd. of Bar Admissions, Nat. Conf. Bar Examiners, law tng. Practising Law Inst., N.Y.C.; chmn. D.C. Law Students in Ct. Program, 1982-83; mem. Law Tchrs. for Legal Svcs. Bd. dirs. Alliance for Justice, 1996-97. Ford Urban Law fellow, 1971-72. Mem. ABA (skills tng. com. 1983-85, govt. rels. com. 1992—), ACLU, Soc. Am. Law Tchrs., Assn. Am. Law Schs. (chmn. sect clin. edn. 1982, accreditation com. 1984-86, chmn. standing com. clin. edn. 1993—, exec. com. 1996-2001, pres.-elect 1999, pres. 2000). Democrat. Home: 3216 Brooklawn Ct Bethesda MD 20815-3941 Office: Am U Washington Coll Law 4801 Massachusetts Ave NW Washington DC 20016-8196

MILSTEIN, LAURENCE BENNETT, electrical engineering educator, researcher; b. Bklyn., Oct. 28, 1942; s. Harry and Sadie (Kaplan) M.; m. Suzanne Barbara Hirschman, Oct. 3, 1969; children— Coreen Roxanne, Renair Marissa B.E.E., CUNY, 1964; MSE.E., Poly. Inst. Bklyn., 1966, PhD in Elec. Engring., 1968. Mem. tech. staff Hughes Aircraft Co., El Segundo, Calif., 1968-69, staff engr., 1969-72, sr. staff engr., 1972-74; asst. prof. Rensselaer Poly. Inst., Troy, N.Y., 1974-76, U. Calif.-San Diego, La Jolla, 1976-79, assoc. prof., 1979-82, prof. elec. engring., 1982—, chmn. dept., 1984-88. Cons. Hughes Aircraft Co., Culver City, Calif., 1976—78, Lockheed Missiles and Space Co., Sunnyvale, Calif., 1978—93, Motorola Satellite Comm., 1992—96, InterDigital Comm. Corp., 1992—96, Golden Bridge Tech., 1995—99; cons. various govt. agys., pvt. cos., 1975—. Co-editor: Tutorials in Modern Communications, 1983; Spread Spectrum Communications, 1983; contbr. articles to profl. jours. Recipient Outstanding Tchr. award Warren Coll., U. Calif.-San Diego, La Jolla, 1982, Disting. Tchg. award, 1999; grantee Army Rsch. Office, 1977-80, 81-84, 86-89, 91-94, 95—, Office of Naval Rsch., Arlington, Va., 1982—, TRW, San Diego, 1983-89, 92-97, NSF, 1993-96, 97—. Fellow IEEE (Millennium medal 2000, Edwin Armstrong Achievement award 2000, MILCOM long term tech. achievement award 1998), IEEE Coms. Soc. (bd. govs. 1983, 85-87, 93-95, v.p. for tech. activities 1990-91), IEEE Info. Theory Soc. (bd. govs. 1989-94). Jewish. Office: U Calif San Diego Dept Elec Computer Engring La Jolla CA 92093 E-mail: milstein@ece.ucsd.edu.

MILSTEIN, RICHARD SHERMAN, lawyer; b. Westfield, Mass., May 9, 1926; s. Abraham and Sarah (Yudman) M. BA, Harvard U., 1948; JD, Boston U., 1952. Bar: Mass. 1952, U.S. Supreme Ct. 1959. Ptnr. Ely & King, Springfield, Mass., 1954-95, Chaplin & Milstein, Boston, 1984-91; sr. counsel Robinson, Donovan, Madden & Barry P.C., Springfield, 1995-98. Dir. Mass. Continuing Legal Edn., 1969-80; cons. dir., 1980—. Commr. Springfield Parking Authority, 1984-90; trustee Comty. Music Sch., Springfield, 1994-96, Springfield Symphony Orch., 1995-99, Springfield Libr. Mus. Assn., Baystate Hosp. Found., 2001-; overseer Mass. Supreme Jud. Ct. Hist. Soc., 1995—, Boston Lyric Opera, 2002-; trustee, life mem. Sta. WGBY-TV, pub. TV, Springfield; mem. adv. com. Springfield Fine Art Mus., 1988-90, 95-2000, chmn., 1988-90, mem. collections com., 2000—; trustee Baystate Hosp., v.p., 1995-97; vice chmn. Westfield Acad., 1980-99; chmn. Horace Smith Fund, 1977-93; bd. dirs., v.p. Boston Ctr. for Adult Edn., 1998—; bd. overseers Huntington Theater, Boston, 1999—; overseer Boston Lyric Opera; mem. vis. com. Mus. Fine Arts, Boston; trustee Baystate Health Found., Inc., 2001—. Lt. comdr. USCGR, 1952-64. Recipient Am. Law Inst.-ABA Harrison Tweed Spl. Merit award for contbn. to CLE, 1997, Mass. Bar Cmty. Svc. award, 1998, William Pynchon award for Cmty. Svc. City of Springfield, 1999. Fellow Am. Coll. Trust and Estate Counsel, Mass. Bar Found. (life); mem. Am. Law Inst. (life), Am. Bar Found. (life). Home: 300 Boylston St Boston MA 02116-3923 also: Mass Continuing Legal Edn 10 Winter Pl Boston MA 02108-4733 Home (Winter): 330 S Ocean Blvd Apt 2E Palm Beach FL 33480 E-mail: rsmilstein@aol.com.

MILSTEN, ROBERT B. lawyer; b. Tulsa, Nov. 6, 1932; s. Travis I. and Regina (Jankowsky) M.; m. Jane Herskowitz, June 24, 1956; children: Stuart Paul, Leslie Jane. BS, Ind. U., 1954; LL.B., U. Okla., 1956; postgrad., So. Meth. U., 1959. Bar: Okla. 1956, U.S. Ct. of Appeals 1956, U.S. Tax Ct 1956. Practiced in, Oklahoma City, 1962—; govt. atty. Office Chief Counsel, IRS, 1958-62; atty. Fuller, Smith, Mosburg & Davis, 1962-63; sr. counsel Andrews, Davis, Legg, Bixler, Milsten & Price, Inc., 1964—, mem. firm, 1966—, dir., 1977-82, 96-98. Mem. S.W. region IRS/Bar Liaison Com., 1994-97. Past pres., trustee Temple B'nai Israel. Served as lt., JAGC USAF, 1956-58. Mem. ABA (com. civil and criminal tax penalties sect. taxation 1962—98), Okla. Bar Assn., Fed. Bar Assn. (2d v.p. local chpt. 1976), Econ. Club Okla., Quail Creek Golf and Country Club, Men's Dinner Club , Phi Delta Phi (treas. 1955-56)

MILSTONE, LEONARD MATTHEW, physician, educator, researcher; b. Newark, Oct. 19, 1944; s. Jacob Haskell and Vivian Kaufman M.; m. Ellen Block, Aug. 21, 1967; children: Jenya, Aaron Michael. BS in Chemistry, Yale Coll., 1966; MD, Yale U., 1970. Diplomate Am. Bd. Dermatology. Resident U. Oreg. Med. Sch., Portland, Oreg., 1970-71, 71-72; rsch. assoc. NIH, Bethesda, Md., 1972-75; resident Yale-New Haven Hosp., New Haven, 1975-77, attending physician, 1978—; faculty, prof. Yale U. Sch. of Medicine, New Haven, 1977-93, 93—; staff physician VAMC, West Haven, Conn., 1981—, chief, dermatology svc., 1988—. Cons. Alcide Corp., Farmingdale, N.Y., 1982-86, Novartis Pharm., East Hanover, N.J., 1997—; vis. prof. Ben Gurion U., Beersheva, Israel, 1990. Editor: Endocrine, Metabolic and Immunologic Functions of Keratinocytes, 1988; assoc. editor Jour. Investigative Dermatology, 1992—; contbr. over 75 articles to profl. jours. Bd. dirs. Congregation Mishken Israel, Hamden, Conn., 1980-83; chmn. med. adv. bd. Found. for Ichthyosis and Related Skin Types, Ardmore, Pa., 1989—, bd. dirs. Lt. comdr. USPHS, 1972-75. Recipient Anna Fuller Faculty award Yale U. Sch. Medicine, 1977-80; rsch. grantee NIH, Bethesda, 1986—, Vet.'s Adminstrn., Washington, 1980-90. Fellow Am. Acad. Dermatology; mem. AAAS, Soc. Investigative Dermatology, Soc. for Molecular Medicine, Am. Soc. Gene Therapy, Am. Dermatol. Assn. Jewish. Avocations: sports, gardening, music, breadmaking.

MILTON, CAROL LYNNE, artist; b. N.Y.C., June 23, 1947; d. August William Thiel and Ruth Elizabeth Gilbert; m. Thomas Macon Milton, Mar. 31, 1973; 1 child, Nicholas John. Sec. Herndon (Va.) Oldtown Gallery, 1989-90, treas., 1990-91; pres. Reston (Va.) Arts Gallery, 1991-92, treas., 1992-93; v.p. Vienna (Va.) Arts Soc. Inc., 1994-95, pres., 1995-98, bd. dirs., 1998-2001. Art program provider Gt. Falls. (Va.) Womens Club, Mobil Wife's Club; chair VAS Gallery, 2000-01, dir., 2001—. Watercolor painter, 1993—; exhbns. include Herndon (Va.) Old Town Gallery, 1988, Reston (Va.) Art Gallery, 1991, 92, Reston Health Club, 1992, Patrick Henry Libr., Vienna, Va., 1991, 97, 99, Reston Cmty. Art Ctr., 1992, Cameron Glenn Ctr., Reston, 1992, Vienna Town Hall, 1995, Hannabils Coffee House, Vienna, 1996, Thomas Jefferson Libr., Falls Church, Va., 1996. Art show provider Arts in Pub. Places, metro D.C. area, 1989—; mural painter Our Lady of Good Coun., Vienna, 1996; calendar artist Town of Vienna, 1998, mem. mural project com. Town of Vienna, 1999. Avocations: gardening, gourmet cooking, antiquing, traveling. Studio: 10311 Yellow Pine Dr Vienna VA 22182-1344 E-mail: miltons@newstreet.com.

MILTON, CATHERINE HIGGS, social service entrepreneur; b. N.Y.C., Jan. 6, 1943; d. Edgar Homer and Josephine (Doughty) Higgs; m. A. Fenner Milton (div.); m. Thomas F. McBride, Aug. 25, 1974; children: Raphael McBride, Luke McBride. BA, Mt. Holyoke Coll., 1964, PhD (hon.), 1992. Reporter, travel writer Boston Globe, 1964-68; with Internat. Assn. Chiefs Police, Washington, 1968-70; asst. dir. Police Found., 1970-75; spl. asst. U.S. Treasury Dept., 1977-80; project staff Spl. Com. Aging/Senate, 1980-81; spl. asst. to pres., founder/exec. dir. Stanford (Calif.) U. Haas Ctr. for Public, 1981-91; exec. dir. Commn. for Nat. and Cmty. Svc., Washington, 1991-93; v.p. Corp. for Nat. Svc., 1993-95; exec. dir. Presidio Leadership Ctr., 1995-96; exec. dir. U.S. Programs Save the Children, Westport, Conn., 1996—. Mem. U.S. Atty. General's Task Force on Family Violence, 1981-82; chair nat. forum Kellogg Found., 1990. Author: Women in Policing, 1972, Police Use of Deadly Force, 1976; co-author: History of Black Americans, 1965, Team Policing, Little Sisters and the Law, 1970. Bd. mem. Youth Svc. Calif., L.A., 1986-91, Trauma Found., San Francisco, 1982-90; spl. advisor Campus Compact, 1986-91 Nat. Kellogg Found. fellow, Battle Creek, Mich., 1985-88; recipient Dedication and Outstanding Efforts award Bd. Suprs., Santa Clara, Calif., 1989, Outstanding Vol. Contbn. award Strive for Five, San Francisco, 1991, Dinkelspiel award Stanford U., 1991; named Outstanding Campus Adminstr. COOL, 1987. Avocations: backpacking, skiing, hiking, travel. Home: 4 Anchor Ln Westport CT 06880-3602 Office: Save the Children PO Box 950 Westport CT 06881-0950

MILTON, CHAD EARL, lawyer; b. Brevard County, Fla., Jan. 29, 1947; s. Rex Dale and Mary Margaret (Peacock) M.; m. Ann Mitchell Bunting, Mar. 30, 1972; children: Samuel, Kathleen, Kelsey. BA, Colo. Coll., 1969; JD, U. Colo., 1974; postgrad., U. Mo., 1976-77. Bar: Colo. 1974, Mo. 1977, U.S. Dist. Ct. Colo. 1974, U.S. Dist. Ct. (we. dist.) Mo. 1977. Counsel Office of Colo. State Pub. Defender, Colo. Springs, 1974-76; pub. info. officer, counsel Mid-Am. Arts Alliance, Kansas City, Mo., 1977-78; claims counsel Employers Reinsurance Corp., 1978-80; sr. v.p. Media/Profl. Ins., 1981-2000; sr. v.p. nat. practice leader, intellectual property & media Marsh, 2000—. Reporter, photographer, editor Golden (Colo.) Daily Transcript, 1970; investigator, law clk. Office of Colo. State Pub. Defender, Denver, Golden, 1970-74; participant Annenberg Project on the Reform of Libel Laws, Washington, 1987-88; adj. prof., comm. and advt. law Webster U., 1989-93; lectr. in field. Pres. bd. dirs. Folly Theater, 1992-94. Mem. ABA (chair intellectual property law com. of the torts and ins. practice sect., forum com. on comm. law, ctrl. and Ea. European law initiative), Mo. Bar Assn., Kansas City Met. Bar Assn., Libel Def. Resource Ctr. (editorial bd., exec. com.). Avocations: tennis, golf, skiing, sailing, antique maps. Home: 8821 Alhambra St Shawnee Mission KS 66207-2357 Office: Marsh 2405 Grand Blvd Kansas City MO 64108-2510 E-mail: chad.e.milton@marsh.com.

MILTON, DONALD KIRBY, occupational and environmental health researcher; b. Mineola, N.Y., Mar. 27, 1951; s. Clare Leon and Chloe Milton; m. Diane Dolle Teichert, Aug. 1979; children: Alexa, Ross. BA in Chemistry cum laude, U. Md., 1976; MD, Johns Hopkins U., 1980; M Occupl. Health, Harvard U., 1985, DPH, 1989. Resident in internal medicine Grady Meml. Hosp., Atlanta, 1980-82, Univ. Hosp., Boston, 1983-84; clin. rsch. fellow Emory U. Sch. Medicine, Atlanta, 1982-83; resident in occupl. medicine Sch. Pub. Health Harvard U., Boston, 1984-86, fellow occupl. health Sch. Pub. Health, 1986-88; rsch. assoc. Sch. Pub. Health, Harvard U., 1988-90, asst. prof., 1990-97, assoc. prof., 1997—. Bioaerosols com. Am. Conf. Govt. Ind. Hygienists, Cin., 1988, vice-chair, 1995-97, chair, 1998-2001; occupl. health cons. Fallon Clinic, Worcester, Mas., 1986—. Contbr. articles to profl. jours. Recipient Lloyd Hyde Rsch. award, Emory U. Sch. Medicine, 1983, Best Paper award, Indoor Air Jour., 2002. Mem. Am. Thoracic Soc., Am. Coll. Occupational and Environ. Medicine. Achievements include rsch. in measure occupational asthma incidence in U.S., correlation of outdoor air supply and absence rate among office workers; first to show that endotoxin, instilled in animal lungs causes emphysema; description of acute exposure-response relation for endotoxin and pulmonary function among non-agricultural workers. Office: Harvard Sch Pub Health 665 Huntington Ave Boston MA 02115-6021 E-mail: dmilton@hsph.harvard.edu.

MILTON, JOHN CHARLES DOUGLAS, nuclear physicist, researcher; b. Regina, Sask., Can., June 1, 1924; s. William and Frances Craigie (McDowall) M.; m. Gwendolyn Margaret Shaw, Oct. 10, 1953; children: Bruce F., Leslie J.F., Neil W.D., Theresa M. A.M. in Music, U. Man., 1943, B.Sc. with honors, 1947; MA, Princeton U., 1949, PhD in Physics, 1951. Asst. rsch. officer Atomic Energy Can., Ltd., Chalk River, Ont., 1951-57, assoc. rsch. officer, 1957-62, sr. rsch. officer, 1962-70, prin. rsch. officer, 1970-91, head nuclear physics br., 1967-83, dir. physics div., 1983-85, v.p. physics and health scis., 1986-90, researcher emeritus, 1990-97. Vis. scientist Lawrence Berkeley Lab., 1960-62, Centre de Recherches, Strasbourg & Bruyeres-le-Chatel, 1975-76; chmn. nuclear physics grants Natural Sci. and Engring. Research Council, 1977-82; adv. bd. TRIUMF 1984-92; bd. dirs. Can. Fusion Fuels Tech., 1986-90, Tokamak de Varennes, 1986-90. Pres. Deep River Hort. Assn., 1997-98. Fellow Royal Soc. Can., Am. Phys. Soc.; mem. Can. Assn. Physicists (pres. 1992). Home: 3 Alexander Pl Deep River ON Canada K0J 1P0

MILTON, JOHN P. ecologist, educator, author, photographer; b. Jersey City, Nov. 30, 1938; s. John Jr. and Barbara (Potter) M. BS, U. Mich., 1962, MS, 1963. Dir. internat. programs divsn. Conservation Found., Washington, 1963-72; pres., chmn. Threshold Found., 1973—. Vis. scholar Woodrow Wilson Internat. Sch. for Scholars, Washington, 1972-73; vis. prof. U. Ill., Springfield, 1978-80; pres. Sacred Passage and the Way of Nature, Bisbee, Ariz., 1985—. Author: Future Environments of North America, 1966, Nameless Valleys, Shining Mountains, 1970, The Careless Technology: Ecology and International Development, 1972, Ecological Principles for Economic Development, 1973, Alaska, The Last Great Wilderness, 1973, The Future of America, 1977, The Galapagos, 1980, Ecological Planning in the Nepalese Terai, 1981, Sky Above, Earth Below, 1999. Mem. NAS (com. mem.), Am.

Assn. Scis. (com. mem.), Ecol. Soc. Am. Avocations: camping, hiking, canoeing, meditation, vision quest. Office: Sacred Passage & The Way of Nature PO Box CZ Main St Bisbee AZ 85603

MILTON, JOSEPH PAYNE, lawyer; b. Richmond, Va., Oct. 24, 1943; s. Hubert E. and Grace C. Milton; children: Michael Payne, Amy Barrett, David King; m. Cela Cabler Milton, Apr. 8, 1989. BS in Bus. Adminstrn., U. Fla., 1967, JD, 1969. Bar: Fla. 1969, U.S. Ct. Appeals (5th cir.) 1971, U.S. Supreme Ct. 1972, U.S. Ct. Appeals (11th cir.) 1981. Assoc. Toole, Taylor, Moseley & Gabel, Jacksonville, 1969-70; ptnr. Toole, Taylor, Moseley, Gabel & Milton, 1971-78, Howell, Liles, Braddock & Milton, Jacksonville, 1978-89, Milton & Leach, Jacksonville, 1990-95, Milton, Leach & D'Andrea, Jacksonville, 1996—. Mem. Mayor's Blue Ribbon Task Force; mem. Law Ctr. Coun., U. Fla. Coll. Law, 1972-78, mem. alumni coun., 1995—; campaign chmn. N.E. Fla. chpt. March of Dimes, 1973-74, v.p., 1974-75; pres. Willing Hands, 1974-75; chmn. attys.' divsn. United Way, 1977; pres. Civic Round Table of Jacksonville, 1980-81; mem. exec. com. Jacksonville Area Legal Aid, Inc., 1982-83; chmn. pvt. bar involvement com. Legal Aid Bd. Dirs., 1982-83. Recipient Outstanding Svc. award for individual contbns. in support of legal svcs. for the poor, 1981. Fellow: Soc. Lawyers for Pub. Svc., Southeastern Admiralty Law (com., dir. Port, Jacksonville 1996—99), Am. Bar Found., Internat. Soc. Barristers; mem.: ATLA, Am. Judicature Soc., Acad. Fla. Trial Lawyers, Maritime Law Assn. U.S. (mem. com. professionalism 1996—), Nat. Assn. R.R. Trial Counsel (exec. com. 1979—, v.p. southeastern region 1984—86, pres.-elect 1989—90, pres. 1990—91), Jacksonville Assn. Def. Counsel (pres. 1981—82, lectr. CLE programs, guest lectr. U. Fla. Nat. Assn. R.R. Trial Counsel), Fla. Coun. Bar Assn. Pres. (exec. com. 1982—88, v.p. 1984, pres. 1985—86), Fla. Bar (bd. cert civil trial lawyer, bd. cert. admiralty and maritime law , grievance com. 1975—77, chmn. grievance com. 1976, 4th jud. cir. nominating commn. 1980—82, mem. exec. coun. for trial sect. 1982—89, voluntary bar liaison com. 1982—83, chmn.-elect 1986—87, chmn. 1987, 1988, bd. govs. 1988, charter mem. admiralty and maritime law bd. cert. 1996—2000, chmn. 1998, chmn. 4th jud. cir. professionalism com. 1998—, recipient Outstanding Professionalism Program 1999, 2001), Jacksonville Bar Assn. (pres. 1980—81, young lawyers sect. 1974—75, Lawyer of Yr. award 1999), Am. Bd. Trial Advs. (charter, pres. Jacksonville chpt. 1997, FLABOTA bd. mem. 1997—, treas. 1999, pres.-elect 2000, nat. bd. mem. 1999—, chpt. selected as Best in Nation 1997, Jacksonville chpt. Trial Lawyer of Yr. 2000, selected as Fla. Trial Lawyer of Yr. 2000), Fla. Chpt. Am. Bd. Trial Advs. (treas. 1999, mem. exec. com. 1997—), Country Club Sapphire Valley (N.C.), Gulf Life Tower Club, Univ. Club, San Jose Country Club. Republican. Home: 4655 Corrientes Cir N Jacksonville FL 32217-4329 Office: Milton Leach D'Andrea & Ritter 815 S Main St Ste 200 Jacksonville FL 32207-8181 E-mail: jmilton@mld-law.com.

MILTON, RICHARD HENRY, retired diplomat, children's advocate; b. Bowling Green, Ky., Sept. 30, 1938; s. Lester Thomas and Rose Ann (Jesse) M.; m. Evy M. Miller, Aug. 28, 1964; children: Christopher, Ann. Student, W.Va. U., 1956-57; BA, Marshall U., 1960, MA, 1964. Tchr., Columbus, Ohio, 1960-61; tchr. Sidney, 1964-65; fgn. svc. officer U.S. Dept. State, Washington, 1965-94; dep. asst. dir. ACDA, 1982-83; consul gen. U.S. consulate gen., Guayaquil, Ecuador, 1984-87; polit. advisor U.S. Space Command, Peterson AFB, Colo., 1987-90, 92-94; v.p. Am. Fgn. Svc. Assn., U.S. Dept. State, Washington, 1990-91. Vis. prof. USCG Acad., New London, Conn., 1977-79. Ct. apptd. spl advocate Colo. 4th Jud. Dist., 1993—, Cmty. Partnership for Child Devel., 1995—, Protect our Children Coalition, 1996; bd. dirs. Colo. State Office of the Child's Rep., 2000—. Served to 1st lt. U.S. Army, 1961-63 Congl. fellow Am. Polit. Sci. Assn., 1974-75; recipient Dist. Vol. of Yr. award Ct. Apptd. Spl. Advocate, 1998, State Vol. of Yr. award, 1999, Nat. C.A.S.A. Vol. of Yr. award, 2000. Mem. Am. Fgn. Svc. Assn., Consular Officers Assn. (pres. 1983-84). Avocation: antique automobiles. Home: 2022 Devon St Colorado Springs CO 80909-1618

MILTON, ROBERT A. air transportation executive; BS in Indsl. Mgmt., Ga. Inst. Tech., 1983. Founder, pres., CEO air carrier svc., 1983—88; founding ptnr. Air Eagle Holdings, Inc., Atlanta, 1991—92; from cons. to sr. v.p. mktg. and in-flight svc. Air Canada, Inc., Saint-Laurent, Canada, 1992—95, exec. v.p., COO Canada, 1996—99, pres., CEO Canada, 1999—. Cons. in field. Named Can. Top 40 Under 40 award, Maclean's Mag., 1999. Office: Air Canada Inc Air Canada Ctr 773 Cote Verta W Saint-Laurent H4Y 1H4 Canada*

MILUNAS, J. ROBERT, health care organization executive; b. Aug. 7, 1947; s. Joseph John M.; m. Glenetta Graham; children: Amy, Joseph, Anna Kate. BS, Tulane U., 1969; postgrad., Samford U., 1973; MBA, Ga. State U., 1977. Mgr. internal and govt. reporting, corp. contr.'s staff Arvin Industries Inc., Columbus, Ind., 1977-80; mgr. consol. acctg., corp. contr.'s staff Mattel Inc., Hawthorne, Calif., 1980-82; asst. contr. Times Mirror Cable TV Inc., Irvine, 1982-83; Western Div. contr. SCA, Santa Ana, 1983-84; v.p., corp. contr. Tchrs. Mgmt. Investment Corp., Newport Beach, 1984-86; v.p., chief fin. officer Beech St. Inc., Irvine, 1987-89; v.p. fin. and adminstrn. Consumer-Health Inc., Newport Beach, Calif., 1989-93; pres. Aegis Consulting Svcs., Dana Point, 1993—. 1st lt. U.S. Army Transp. Corps., 1969-71. Decorated Bronze Star. Home: 33461 Galleon Way Dana Point CA 92629-1610 *Life is a precious gift to be nurtured daily through interaction with friends and family and helping others achieve their potential.*

MILUNSKY, AUBREY, geneticist, pediatrician, medical educator; b. Johannesburg, South Africa, Nov. 3, 1936; came to U.S., 1969; 1 child, Jeffrey M. MB, BCh, U. Witwatersrand, Johannesburg, 1960, DSc, 1982; postgrad., Gt. Ormond St. Hosp., London, 1965. Diplomate Am. Bd. Pediatrics, Am. Bd. Med. Genetics. Intern Johannesburg Gen. Hosp./Baragwanath Hosp., Johannesburg, 1961; resident in internal medicine and pediat. Baragwanath Hosp., 1961-64; pediat. registrar Queen Mary's Hosp. for Children, Surrey, Eng., 1965-66; asst. pediatrician New England Med. Ctr. Tufts U., Boston, 1966-70, from instr. to asst. prof. pediat. Sch. Medicine, 1966-70; rsch. fellow and assoc. in neurology Mass. Gen. Hosp./Harvard Med. Sch., 1969-70; dir. Birth Defects and Genetics Clinic Mass. Gen. Hosp., 1971-73, asst. pediatrician, 1971-82, assoc. dir. Cystic Fibrosis Clinic, 1975-79; asst. prof. pediatrics Harvard Med. Sch., 1971-81; prof. pediatrics and ob-gyn. Sch. Medicine, dir. Ctr. for Human Genetics, assoc. physician Univ. Hosp. Boston U., 1981—, prof. pathology, 1985—, Endowed chair human genetics, 1991—; pediatrician Boston City Hosp., 1981—. Mem. Mass. State Genetics Adv. Bd., 1983-84; profl. adv. bd. Nat. Tuberous Sclerosis Assn., 1990-93; quality assurance com. New England Regional Genetics Group, 1990-96. Author: The Prenatal Diagnosis of Hereditary Disorders, 1973, Know Your Genes, 1977, How to Have the Healthiest Baby You Can., 1987, Choices, Not Chances: An Essential Guide to your Heredity and Health, 1989, Heredity and Your Family's Health, 1992, Your Genetic Destiny: Know Your Genes, Secure Your Health, Save Your Life, 2001; editor: Clinics in Perinatology, Vol. II, 1974, The Prevention of Genetic Disease and Mental Retardation, 1975, Genetic Disorders and the Fetus: Diagnosis, Prevention and Treatment, 1979, 4th edit., 1998, Coping with Crisis and Handicap, 1981, (with G.J. Annas) Genetics and the Law I, 1976, Genetics and the Law II, 1980, Genetics and the Law III, 1986, (with E.A. Friedman and L. Gluck) Advances in Perinatal Medicine, 1981, Vol. II, 1982, Vol. III, 1983, Vol. IV, 1985, Vol. V, 1986; mem. editl. bd. Am. Jour. Law and Medicine, 1974-93, Am. Jour. Med. Genetics, 1977-94, Bioethics Digest, 1977-78, Prenatal Diagnosis, 1980-90, 92—, Intelligence Reports in Ob-Gyn., 1982-88, Fetal Therapy, 1986—; peer reviewer New England Jour. Medicine, Pediatrics, Am. Jour. Med. Genetics, Am. Jour. Ob-Gyn., Am. Jour. Law and Medicine, Am. Jour. Pub. Health, Prenatal Diagnosis, Fetal Therapy, Ob-Gyn., Epidemiology, Jour. Pediatrics; contbr. over 300 articles to profl. jours. Recipient First Place Film award Nat. Coun. Family Rels. Media Awards Co., 1990, Tinsley Harrison award So. Soc. for Clin. Investigation, 1991; Aubrey Milunsky Endowed Chair in Human Genetics named in his honor Boston U., 1991. Fellow Am. Coll. Med. Genetics (founding), Royal Coll. Physicians (diploma in child health 1965); mem. Am. Pediat. Soc., Am. Soc. Human Genetics (social issues com. 1983-87), Am. Soc. Law and Medicine (v.p. 1982-83, pres.-elect 1983-85, pres. 1985-86, bd. dirs. 1986-88, 90-93), Soc. for Pediat. Rsch., Mass. Med. Soc. Office: Boston U Sch Medicine Ctr for Human Genetics 715 Albany St Boston MA 02118-2307

MIMMS, THOMAS BOWMAN, JR. lawyer; b. Atlanta, Oct. 11, 1944; s. Thomas Bowman and Alice Buehl Mimms; m. Alison Hayward, July 22, 1967; children: Karen Mimms Swift, Christina Mimms Couret. BA, U. N.C., 1965; JD, Columbia U., 1969. Bar: Fla. 1969, Ga., 1999, U.S. Dist. Ct. (mid. dist.) Fla. 1972, U.S. Supreme Ct. 1973, U.S. Ct. Appeals (11th cir.) 1981 Ga. Supreme Ct., 2000. Assoc. atty. Fleming O'Bryan, Fort Lauderdale, Fla., 1969-72; shareholder Macfarlane Ferguson & McMullen, Tampa, 1972-99. Fellow Am. Bar Found.; mem. Fla. Bar Assn. (exec. coun. bus. law sect. 1987-99, chair bus. law legislation com. 1995-99, chair bus. law bankrupty/UCC com. 1988-89, chair fin. instns. com. 1993-94), Tampa Bay Bankruptcy Bar Assn. (pres. 1992-93), Columbia U. Alumni Club (dir. 1991-99). Democrat. Episcopalian. Office: Mimms Enterprises 85A Mill St Ste 100 Roswell GA 30075-4952 E-mail: legal@mimms.org.

MIMS, WILLIAM CLEVELAND, state legislator, lawyer; b. Harrisonburg, Va., June 20, 1957; s. David Lathan and Lurleen Shirley (Stovall) M.; m. Jane Ellen Rehme, Dec. 20, 1980; children: Katherine Grace, Emily Anne, Sarah Joy. AB, Coll. of William & Mary, 1979; JD, George Washington U., 1984; LLM, Georgetown U., 1986. Bar: Va. Legis. asst. Congressman Paul Trible, Washington, 1981-82; dep. legis. dir. Senator Paul Trible, 1983-85; chief of staff Congressman Frank Wolf, 1986-87; atty. Hazel & Thomas, P.C., Leesburg, Va., 1987-91, Worcester, Mims & Atwill, P.C., 1993—2002, Mims, Atwill & Leigh, P.C., Leesburg, 2002—; mem. Va. Gen. Assembly, Richmond, 1991—, del., 1992-98, senator, 1998—. Adj. prof. law George Mason U., 2002--; mem. Va. Housing Study Commn., 1994—, chmn. 2000—; mem. Va. Code Commn., 2000, No. Va. Transp. Commn., 2000—. Bd. dirs. Dulles Area Transp. Assn., Herndon, Va., 1994—, Marshall Home Preservation Fund, Leesburg, 1992—, Youth for Tomorrow, 1995-97; treas., bd. dirs. Loudoun Bar Assn., Leesburg, 1988-89; active Nat. Eagle Scout Assn., 1992--. Flemming fellow, 1995-96. Mem. Va. Bar Assn. (Boyd-Graves Conf. 1996—, bd. govs. 2002--), Va. Trial Lawyers Assn., Christian Legal Soc. Republican. Episcopalian. Office: Mims Atwill & Leigh PC PO Box 741 Leesburg VA 20178-0741

MIN, BALSHIK, pathologist; b. Seoul, Jan. 15, 1942; s. Young-Ock and Yang-Hee (Kim) M.; m. Jungsoon Ahn, Apr. 25, 1970; children: James, Susan. MD, Seoul Nat. U., 1966. Pathologist Faxton-St. Luke's Healthcare, Utica, N.Y., 1978—, dir. of labs., 1984—; pathologist Centrex Clin. Labs., New Hartford, N.Y., 1978—. Dir. of labs. Centrex Clin. Labs., New Hartford, 1990-96, bd. dirs. Capt. Korean Army, 1966-70. Fellow Coll. of Am. Pathologists; mem. AMA, Am. Soc. Clin. Pathology, Nat. Soc. Histotechnology, Cen. N.Y. Acad. Medicine. Avocations: reading, classical music, gardening, golf. Office: Faxton-St Lukes Healthcare 1676 Sunset Ave Utica NY 13502-5416

MIN, HOKEY, business educator; b. Seoul, South Korea, June 28, 1954; s. Byungjoo and Hangwon (Seo) M. BA, Hankuk U. of Fgn. Studies, Seoul, South Korea, 1978; MBA, Yonsei U., Seoul, South Korea, 1980, U. S.C., 1982; PhD, Ohio State U., 1987. Freelance writer Chas. E. Merrill Pub. Co., Columbus, Ohio, 1983; teaching assoc. Ohio State U., 1983-87; asst. prof. U. New Orleans, 1987-89, Northeastern U., Boston, 1989-92, Auburn U., 1992-98; exec. dir. Logistics and Distbn. Inst./U. Louisville, 1998—; prof. mgmt. and mktg. U. Louisville. Cons. Shoe Corp. Am., Columbus, 1983-84, Nationwide Ins. Co., 1984, Russell Athletic Wear, Master Lock, Westpoint Stevens, 1997, Briggs and Stratten, 1998. Contbr. articles to profl. jours. Recipient Most Outstanding Rsch. award Coll. Bus. at Auburn U., 1993, 98, Citation of Excellence award, 1997. Mem. Decision Scis. Inst., Inst. Mgmt. Scis., Ops. Rsch. Soc. Am., Am. Prodn. and Inventory Soc., Coun. of Logistics Mgmt., Southeastern Decision Scis. Inst. (Hon. Mention 1986), Southeastern TIMS (Best Student Paper 1986). Republican. Avocations: portrait painting, ice skating, golf, science fiction. Office: Univ Louisville Louisville KY 40292-0001

MIN, PYONG GAP, sociologist, researcher; b. Choongnam, Korea, Feb. 18, 1942; s. Hong Sik Min and Nam Hee Song; divorced; children: Jay, Michael, Tony; m. Young Oak Kim. BA, Seoul Nat. U., Korea, 1970; MA, Ga. State U., 1975, PhD, 1979, PhD, 1983. Gen. reporter Korea Herald, Seoul, 1970-71; instr., rsch. assoc. Ga. State U., Atlanta, 1983-86; from asst. to assoc. prof. Queens Coll., N.Y.C., 1987-96, prof., 1996—. Prof. grad. ctr. CUNY, 1993—. Author: Korean Small Business in Atlanta, 1988, Caught in the Middle, 1996 (Nat. Book award 1997, 98), Korean Immigrant Families in New York, 1998; editor: Asian Americans, 1995, The Second Generation, 2002, Mass Migration in the United States, 2002; co-editor: Struggle for Ethnic Identity, 1999, Religions in Asian America, 2002; mem. editl. bd. Jour. Am. Ethnic History, 1997—, Devel. and Soc., 1997—, Amerasia Jour., 1998—, Internat. Migration Rev., 2001-. Exec. bd. dirs. Korea Global Found., 2001—. Fellow, Social Sci. Rsch. Coun., 2000—01; grantee, NSF, 1986—87. Mem. Am. Sociol. Assn. (coun. mem. internat. migration sect. 1996-99). Democrat. Home: 205-14 50 Ave Oakland Gardens NY 11364 Office: Dept Sociology Queens Coll Flushing NY 11367 E-mail: min@troll.soc.ac.edu.

MIN, SUNG SIK, accountant; b. Seoul, Republic of Korea, June 30, 1942; came to U.S., 1972. s. Young Zai and Kyung Hun M.; m. Jane Eunice Yoo; children: Daniel, David, Douglas, John. BA, Korea U., Seoul, 1965, MBA, 1969, NYU, 1978. CPA, N.Y. Sec., contr. Edward A. Viner & Co., Inc., N.Y.C., 1985-88; dir. fin. Royal Alliance Assocs., Inc./Broad, Inc., 1988-90; CFO, sec. Reich & Co., Inc., Iselin, N.J., 1990—; pres. Classic Georgian Furnishings, Inc., 1989—. Mem. Nat. Assn. Securities Dealers (chief fin. officer 1985—). Home: 17 Everett Ave Staten Island NY 10309-3538 Office: 1008 Baker Rd High Point NC 27263-2130

MINA, JOHN LOUIS (IVAN MINEA), religious studies educator, archivist; b. Nancy, France, Jan. 31, 1950; came to U.S. 1951; s. Albert and Mila (Koenig) M. BA with highest honors, U. Calif., Santa Barbara, 1972; MA, U. Calif., Berkeley, 1974, PhD, 1979. Lectr. Centre D'Etudes Russes, Meudon, France, 1984-85; vis. asst. prof. U. Ky., Lexington, 1987-88; prof. Sts. Cyril and Methodius Sem., Pitts., 1990-95; archivist Met. Archdiocese of Pitts., Byzantine Rite, 1997—. Contbr. articles to profl. jours. Mem. Cath. Hist. Soc. West Pa., Pitts. Recipient Dobro Slovo, U. Calif., Berkeley, 1980; U. Calif. Regents scholar, 1968; Fulbright fellow, 1972. Mem. Assn. Cath. Diocesan Archivists, KC (4th degree), Phi Beta Kappa. Byzantine Catholic. Avocations: travel, foreign affairs. Home: 318 Park Ave Clairton PA 15025-1758 Office: 66 Riverview Ave Pittsburgh PA 15214-2253 E-mail: ivanmin@attglobal.net.

MINAHAN, DANIEL FRANCIS, lawyer, retired manufacturing executive; b. Orange, N.J., Dec. 3, 1929; s. Alfred A. and Katherine (Kelly) M.; m. Mary Jean Gaffney, May 2, 1953; children: Daniel F. Jr., John A. AB magna cum laude, U. Notre Dame, 1951; JD magna cum laude, U. Conn., 1964; grad., Advanced Mgmt. Program, Harvard, 1975. Bar: Conn. 1964, U.S. Supreme Ct 1969, U.S. Ct. of Appeals (2d cir.), U.S. Dist. Ct. Conn. 1971. Mgr. indsl. engring. Uniroyal, Inc., Naugatuck, Conn., 1952-59, mgr. indsl. relations, 1959-64, dir. labor relations N.Y.C., 1964-66; v.p. indsl. relations and labor counsel Phillips Van Heusen Corp., 1966-69; v.p. personnel-adminstrn. Broadway-Hale Stores, Inc., L.A., 1969-70; v.p. employee relations, sec. Magnavox-N.Am., Philips Corp., 1970-73, v.p. ops., group exec., 1973-83, sr. v.p. adminstrn., 1984-89, exec. v.p., 1989-93, vice-chmn., 1991-93; vice-chmn. nat. found. bd. Robert Anderson Sch. Mgmt., U. N.Mex., 1993-98; pvt. practice, 1998—. Trustees adv. coun., Fairfield U., mem. dean's coun. Grad. Sch. Bus. Co-author: The Developing Labor Law, 1971. Chmn. bd. Internat. Fedn. Keystone Youth Orgns., London and Chgo., 1984-88; vice-chmn. nat. found. bd. Anderson Sch. Mgmt., U. N.Mex., 1993-98. With USMC. Mem. The Forum for World Affairs, Conn. Bar Assn., Harvard Club, Club Internat. (Chgo.).

MINAI, OMAR AHMAD, physician; b. Lahore, Pakistan; s. Idris Ahmad and Riaz Fatima Minai; m. Beena Ahmad, Dec. 7, 1998. MB BS, Aga Khan U., Karachi, Pakistan, 1990. Diplomate Am. Bd. Internal Medicine, Am. Bd. Pulmonary Medicine, Am. Bd. Critical Care Medicine, Am. Bd. Sleep Medicine. Intern in internal medicine U. Conn., Farmington, 1992-93, resident in internal medicine, 1992-96; fellow in pulmonary and critical care medicine Cleve. Clin. Found., 1996-99, staff physician in pulmonary and critical care medicine, 1999—. Contbr. Mem.: ACP, Am. Thoracic Soc., Am. Coll. Chest Physicians. Office: Cleve Clinic Found 9500 Euclid Ave Ste A-90 Cleveland OH 44195-0001

MINAMI, ROBERT YOSHIO, artist, graphic designer; b. Seattle, May 1, 1919; s. Kichitaro and Suma (Fujita) M.; m. Shizu Tashiro, May 30, 1953; 1 child, Ken. Artist; student, Art Inst., Chgo., 1957, Am. Acad. Art, 1980-81. Graphic artist Filmack Studios, Chgo., 1945-48, S. Taylor & Leavitt Assocs., Chgo., 1949-50; head graphic designer NBC-TV, 1950-82; fine artist Robert Minami's Studio, Oceanside, Calif., 1983—. Artist Goodman Theatre Design, Chgo., 1955-56; mem. Oceanside Mus. Art Exhbn. Com.; art instr. Mus. Sch. Art, Oceanside, 1997-98, 99. Exhibits include Oceanside Mus. Art, 1996. Active Supporters for City Couns., Oceanside, 1984—. Recipient Merit award Artist Guild Chgo., 1956, People's Choice award Carlsbad Oceanside Art League, 1986, Dick Blick award, 1992, 1st place award Mixed Media Collage, 1993, Nat. Watercolor award Watercolor West, 1994, Best of Watercolor Painting, Texture award, 1997. Mem. San Diego Watercolor Soc., United Scenic Artists (life), Am. Fine Art Connection, San Diego Art Inst., Nat. Watercolor Soc. (assoc.), Watercolor West Juried Assn., Internat. Soc. Exptl. Art, San Diego Artists Guild, San Diego Mus. Fine Arts. Avocations: painting, travel, movies, concerts, opera.

MINAR, PAUL G. design consultant; b. Phoenix, July 12, 1932; s. Aaron Crowther and Ione Anna (Schmid) Mortensen. Student, Ariz. State U., 1950-54, John F. Kennedy U., 1978-80, Antioch West U., 1980. Sound effects technician, TV stage mgr. Sta. KHJ-AM-TV, L.A., 1955-63; displayer W.&J. Sloane Furniture Co., Beverly Hills, Calif., 1963-66, Bullock's Dept. Store, L.A., 1966-68, Macy's Dept. Store, San Francisco, 1968-70; interior designer Lloyd's Furniture Co., San Diego, 1970-71, Bonynge's Furniture Co., Oakland, Calif., 1971-72, Breuner's Furniture Co., Oakland, 1972-74; design cons. The Other Artist, San Francisco, 1974—. Archival rschr. and conservation Petaluma Hist. Mus., 1994—; profl. numerologist; lectr. in onomatology. Author: At One with the Numbers, 1997; writer, producer (documentary) The Modern Nursing Home, 1959. Vol. talent agt. San Francisco Symphony Black and White Ball, 1983; bd. dirs. Akasha Personal Projects; mem. Fine Arts Mus. of San Francisco. Mem. Inst. Noetic Scis., Petaluma Mus. Assn., Interant. Assn. Numerologists. Democrat. Roman Catholic. Avocations: wilderness exploration, tennis, classical music, parapsychology, world history. Office: The Other Artist 3200 Buchanan St San Francisco CA 94123-3517

MINARCZIK, JENNIFER ANN, communications company executive; b. Parma, Ohio, Oct. 23, 1973; d. Dennis Alan and Martha Lee (Mason) M. BS in Latin Am. and Leadership Studies, U. Richmond, Va., 1995. Coord. Joint Rep. Campaign, Richmond, 1995; legis. aide Senator Emmett Hanger, 1996; dep. campaign mgr. Friends of Richard Cullen, 1996; comm. coord. Dole/Kemp '96, 1996; polit. affairs coord. GTE Corp., Washington, 1996-98, staff mgr. govt. advocacy planning, 1998—. Mem. Henrico County Rep. Com., Richmond, 1995-97, Arlington County (Va.) Rep. Com., 1997. Gov.'s fellow, Richmond, 1995. Mem. Women in Govt. Rels. Avocations: golf, running, swimming. Office: GTE 1850 M St NW Ste 1200 Washington DC 20036-5893

MINARDI, RICHARD A., JR. lawyer; b. Mobile, Ala., Aug. 15, 1943; s. Richard A. and Martha F. (Beck) M.; m. Frances Archer Guy, Oct. 21, 1989. BA, Yale U., 1965, LLB, 1968. Bar: Va. 1969. Assoc. McGuire Woods & Battle, Richmond, Va., 1968-71; ptnr. Staples, Greenberg Minardi & Kessler, 1971-86, Mays & Valentine, Richmond, 1986-2000, Troutman Sanders LLP, Richmond, 2001—. Mem. ABA, Va. Bar Assn., Richmond Bar Assn. Home: 211 Santa Clara Dr Richmond VA 23229-7152 Office: Mays & Valentine PO Box 1122 Richmond VA 23218-1122 E-mail: rick.minardi@troutmansanders.com.

MINARIK, ELSE HOLMELUND (BIGART MINARIK), author; b. Aarhus, Denmark, Sept. 13, 1920; d. Kaj Marius and Helga Holmelund; m. Walter Minarik, July 14, 1940 (dec.); 1 child, Brooke Ellen; m. Homer Bigart, Oct. 3, 1970 (dec.). BA, Queens Coll., 1942. Tchr. 1st grade, art Commack (N.Y.) Pub. Schs., 1950-54. Author children's books: Little Bear, 1957, Father Bear Comes Home, 1959, Little Bear's Friend, 1960, Little Bear's Visit, 1961, No Fighting, No Biting, 1958, Cat and Dog, 1960, The Winds That Come From Far Away, 1960, The Little Giant Girl and the Elf Boy, 1963, A Kiss for Little Bear, 1968, What If, 1987, Percy and the Five Houses, 1988, It's Spring, 1989, The Little Girl and the Dragon, 1991, Am I Beautiful, 1992. Mem. PEN Club. Home: 30 Gebig Rd Nottingham NH 03290 Office: care Greenwillow Books 1350 Ave Americas New York NY 10019

MINASIAN, LORI, internist, oncologist, educator; b. Anchorage, Apr. 17, 1960; MD, George Washington U., 1987. Diplomate Am. Bd. Internal Medicine, Am. Bd. Oncology. Intern Case Western Res. U., 1987-88, resident in internal medicine, 1988-90; fellow in med. oncology Meml. Sloan-Kettering Cancer Ctr., N.Y., 1990-93, appointed staff, 1993, Nat. Cancer Inst. divsn. Cancer Prevention and Control, Potomac, Md.; staff Med. Coll. Ga., Augusta, 1994-96, chief cmty. oncology and rehab. br., 1997, Nat. Cancer Inst. divsn. Cancer Prevention, Bethesda, Md., 1999—. Mem. ACP, Am. Soc. Clin. Oncology. Office: 6130 Executive Blvd Rm 2017 Bethesda MD 20892-0001

MINASYAN, GEORGIY R. acoustical engineer, computer programmer; b. Tbilisi, Ga., USSR, Oct. 31, 1962; arrived in U.S., 1997; s. Robert G. Minasyan and Valentina D. Podlesnova; 1 child. MsD, Moscow Inst. Radio Engring. Electronics and Automation, 1986; PhD Acoustics Inst., Russian Acad. Scis., Moscow, 1994. Engr., rschr. Acoustics Inst., 1986-91, scientist, 1991-94, sr. scientist, 1994-97, Telefactor Corp., West Conshokochen, Pa., 1997—. Contbr. chpt. to book: Full Field Inversion Methods, 1995; contbr. articles to profl. jours. Small Bus. Rsch. grant NIH, 1998. Mem. IEEE, Computer Soc. of IEEE, Engring. in Medicine and Biology Soc., Acoustical Soc. Am., Signal Processing Soc., Internat. Neural Network Soc. Avocations: chess, automobiles, music. E-amil. Home: 2042 Spring Mill Rd Lafayette Hill PA 19444-2110 Office: Telefactor Corp 1094 New Dehaven St West Conshohocken PA 19428-2713 E-mail: gminasyan@yahoo.com.

MINC, HENRYK, mathematics educator; b. Lodz, Poland, Nov. 12, 1919; s. Izrael and Haja (Zyngler) M.; m. Catherine Taylor Duncan, Apr. 16, 1943; children: Robert Henry, Ralph Edward, Raymond. MA with honors, Edinburgh (Scotland) U., 1955; PhD, 1959. Tchr. Morgan Acad., Dundee, Scotland, 1956-58; lectr. Dundee Tech. Coll., 1957-58, U. B.C., Vancouver, Can., 1958-59, asst. prof. Can., 1959-60; assoc. prof. U. Fla., Gainesville, 1960-63; prof. U. Calif., Santa Barbara, 1963-90; emeritus, 1990—. Vis. prof. Technion Isreael Inst. Tech., Haifa, 1969-80. Author: A Survey of Matrix Theory and Matrix Inequalities, 1964, Russian translation, 1972, Chinese translation, 1990, Introduction to Linear Algebra, 1968, Spanish translation, 1968, Modern University Algebra, 1966, Elementary Linear Algebra, Spanish translation, 1971, New College Algebra, 1968, Elementary Functions and Coordinate Geometry, 1969, Algebra and Trigonometry, 1970, College Algebra, 1970, College Trigonometry, 1971, Integrated Analytic Geometry and Algebra with Circular Functions, 1973, Permanents, 1978, Russian translation, 1980, Chinese translation, 1991, Nonnegative Matrices, 1988, Chinese translation, 1991; contbr. over 80 rsch. articles to math. jours., 9 rsch. papers to archaeol. and ancient numismatic jours., articles to Burns Chronicle; referee and reviewer math. jours. 2nd lt. Polish Army, 1940-48, France, U.K. Recipient Lester Ford award Math. Assn. Am., 1966, rsch. contract Office Naval Rsch., 1985-88, Air Force Office Sci. Rsch. grantee, 1960-83, Lady Davis fellow, 1975-78. Fellow: Soc. Antiquaries of Scotland; mem.: Saltire Soc., Scots. Lang. Soc., Scottish Soc. Santa Barbara (past chieftain), Robert Burns World Fedn. (hon. pres.), Am. Math. Soc., James Hogg Soc., L.A. Burns Club. Democrat. Home: 4076 Naranjo Dr Santa Barbara CA 93110-1213 Office: U Calif Dept Math Santa Barbara CA 93106 E-mail: hmincburns@cox.net.

MINCER, JACOB, economics educator; b. Tomaszow, Poland, July 15, 1922; came to U.S., 1948; s. Isaac and Dora (Eisen) M.; m. Flora Kaplan, 1951; children: Deborah, Carolyn. BA, Emory U., 1950; PhD, Columbia U., 1957; LLD honoris causa, U. Chgo., 1991. Asst. prof. CUNY, 1954-59; assoc. prof. Columbia U., N.Y.C., 1960-62, prof. econs., 1962—. Mem. research staff Nat. Bur. Econ. Research, N.Y.C., 1960—. Author: Schooling, Experience and Earnings, 1974, Studies in Human Capital, 1993, Studies in Labor Supply, 1993; author, editor: Economic Forecasts and Expectations, 1969. Contbr. numerous articles to profl. publs. Postdoctoral fellow U. Chgo., 1957-58; Guggenheim fellow, N.Y.C., 1971. Fellow Am. Statis. Assn., Econometric Soc., Am. Econ. Assn. (Disting.); mem. NAS, Am. Acad. Arts and Scis., Nat. Acad. Edn. Home: 448 Riverside Dr New York NY 10027-6801 Office: Columbia U Dept Econs 118th St at Amsterdam Ave New York NY 10027

MINCH, JEFFREY LEONARD STEPHEN, real estate developer; b. Somerville, N.J., Feb. 7, 1951; s. Leonard Clarence and Rita Marie (Brennan) M.; m. Tempe Elizabeth Yarborough Carlton, Dec. 1, 1979; children: Leonard Jeffrey, Elizabeth Yarborough. BS in Civil Engring., VMI, Lexington, Va., 1973; MBA in Fin., Monmouth Coll., Fair Lawn, N.J., 1977. Registered profl. engr., Tex. Project mgr. Mobil Corp., Chgo. and Rochester, N.Y., 1977-81; ptnr. Rust Properties, Austin, Tex., 1981-84; mng. ptnr. Norwood Properties, 1984—. Bd. mem. Capital Met. Transp. Authority, Austin, 1988-90. Capt. U.S. Army, 1973-77. Mem. Va. Mil. Inst. Alumni Assn. (pres. Centex chpt. 1987—, bd. mem. Lexington 1987—), Barton Creek Country Club, Univ. Club, Met. Club. Republican. Roman Catholic. Avocations: sailing, fishing, skiing, golfing.

MINCHEW, JOHN RANDALL, lawyer; b. Washington, July 31, 1957; s. John Richard and Lucile Elizabeth (Shaw) M. AB, Duke U., 1980; JD, Washington & Lee U., 1984; Cert. in Jurisprudence, Oxford U., 1982. Bar: Va. 1984, U.S. Dist. Ct. (ea. dist.) Va. 1985, U.S. Ct. Appeals (4th cir.) 1985, U.S. Supreme Ct. 1997. Jud. clk. Supreme Ct. Va., 1984-85; mng. ptnr. Loudoun County Office, Walsh, Colucci, Stackhouse, Emrich & Lubeley, P.C., Leesburg, Va., 1998—. V.p., dir. devel. The Minchew Corp., Fairfax, Va., 1985—; chmn. Loudoun County Econ. Devel. Commn., 1996-98; pres. Va. Shelter Corp. Adminstrv. editor: Washington & Lee Law Rev., 1984. Pro bono caseworker Legal Aid Soc. Roanoke Valley, Lexington, Va., 1982-84. Mem. ABA, Va. State Bar (mem. Commn. on Unauthorized Practice of Law 1994-98), Fairfax Bar Assn., Loudoun Bar Assn. (pres. 1995-96), Phi Delta Phi. Avocations: scuba diving, aviation, rugby. Home: 330 W Market St Leesburg VA 20176-2601 Office: Walsh Colucci Stackhouse Emrich & Lubeley PC 1 E Market St Ste 3 Leesburg VA 20176-3014 Fax: 703-737-3633.

MINCKLEY, CARLA BETH, lawyer; b. N.Y.C., Mar. 3, 1957; d. Jerome J. and Estelle (Franklin) Landsman; m. Steven D. Minckley, May 10, 1985; children: Taylor F., Amanda K. BA magna cum laude, U. Albany, N.Y., 1979; JD, U. Denver, 1987. Bar: Colo. 1988, U.S. Dist. Ct. Colo. 1988, U.S. Ct. Appeals (10th cir.) 1992. Asst. compliance officer Integrated Resources Equity Corp., Englewood, Colo., 1981-85; law clk. Tallmadge, Tallmadge, Wallace & Hahn, P.C., Denver, 1985-88; assoc. Law Office of Fay Matsugage, 1988-90, Brega & Winters, P.C., Denver, 1990-95; pvt. practice Englewood, 1995—97; ptnr. Birge & Minckley P.C., Denver, 1998—. Mem. ABA, Colo. Bar Assn., Denver Bar Assn. Democrat. Avocations: aerobics, boating, skiing. Office: 1700 Broadway #1501 Denver CO 80290

MINDE, EDITH GABRIELE, music educator, conductor; b. Brno, Czechia, May 30, 1936; came to U.S., 1968; d. Ottokar and Hildegard (Petzny) Halla; m. Stefan Minde; children: Matthias, Bernd. M in Performing Arts, State Conservatory, Nurnberg, Germany, 1958. Choir conductor Children's Choir, Nurnberg, Germany, 1956-59, Portland, Oreg., 1977-81; choir dir., music instr. Cath. Sch. Dist., 1981—. Choir conductor Liedertafel Harmonie Choir, Portland, 1994-96, Liederkreis, Portland, 1996—; founder German Children's Choir, Portland. Avocations: watercolor, painting, hiking, reading.

MINDELL, EARL LAWRENCE, nutritionist, writer; b. St. Boniface, Man., Can., Jan. 20, 1940; came to U.S., 1965, naturalized, 1972. s. William and Minerva Sybil (Galsky) M.; m. Gail Andrea Jaffe, May 16, 1971; children: Evan Louis-Ashley, Alanna Dayan. BS in Pharmacy, N.D. State U., 1963; PhD in Nutrition, Pacific We. U., 1985; master herbalist, Dominion Herbal Coll., 1995. Pres. Adanac Mgmt. Inc., 1979—; instr. Dale Carnegie course; lectr. on nutrition, radio and TV. Author: Earl Mindell's Vitamin Bible, Parents Nutrition Bible, Earl Mindell's Quick and Easy Guide to Better Health, Earl Mindell's Pill Bible, Earl Mindell's Shaping Up With Vitamins, Earl Mindell's Safe Eating, Earl Mindell's Herb Bible, Mindell's Food as Medicine, Earl Mindell's Soy Miracle, 1995, Anti-Aging Bible, 1996, Secret Remedies, 1997, Supplement Bible, 1998, Nutrition and Health for Your Dog, 1998, Prescription Alternatives, 1998, 2d edit., 1999, Vitamin Bible for the 21st Century, 1999, Dr. Earl Mindell's Secrets of Natural Health, 2000, Arthritis Miracle, 2000, Peak Performance Bible, 2000, Diet Bible, 2002; columnist: Let's Live mag., columnist: The Vitamin Supplement, columnist: The Vitamin Connection, columnist: Health 'N Fit, columnist: Unsafe at Any Meal, 2002; contbr. articles on nutrition to profl. jours. Fellow Brit. Homeopathic Inst., Scottish Inst. Homeopathy; mem. Beverly Hills, Rancho Park, Western Los Angeles (dir.) regional chambers commerce, Calif., Am. Med. Assn., Am. pharm. assns., Am. Acad. Gen. Pharm. Practice, Am. Inst. for History of Pharmacy, Am. Nutrition Soc., Internat. Coll. Applied Nutrition, Nutrition Found., Nat. Health Fedn., Orthomolecular Med. Assn., Internat. Acad. Preventive Medicine. Clubs: City of Hope, Beverly Hills Rotary, Masons, Shriners. E-mail: drearlmindell.com. Home and Office: 621 N Palm Dr Beverly Hills CA 90210-3414

MINDELL, EUGENE ROBERT, surgeon, educator; b. Chgo., Feb. 24, 1922; s. Leon and Tillie (Rosenthal) M.; m. June A. Abrams, Sept. 19, 1945; children: Barbara, Ruth, David, Douglas. BS, U. Chgo., 1943, MD, 1945. Diplomate Am. Bd. Orthopaedic Surgery (bd. dirs. 1977-84, pres. 1983-84). Resident in orthopaedic surgery U. Chgo. Clinics, 1948-52; instr. U. Chgo., 1952; mem. faculty dept. orthopaedic surgery Sch. Medicine SUNY, Buffalo, 1953—, prof. Sch. Medicine, 1964—; chmn. dept. SUNY Sch. Medicine, 1964-88, dir. orthopaedic oncology Sch. Medicine, 1988—. Mem. bd. mgrs. Erie County Med. Ctr., 1990-96. Assoc. editor Jour. Bone and Joint Surgery, 1984-88, trustee, 1991—; dep. editor Clin. Orthopaedics and Related Rsch. representing Musculoskeletal Tumor Soc., 1997—; contbr. articles to profl. jours. Lt. (j.g.) M.C. USNR, 1946-48. Eugene R. Mindell Endowed Chair of Orthopaedic Surgery established in his honor SUNY, Buffalo, 1996; recipient Disting. Svc. award Alumni U. Chgo. Sch. Medicine, 1990, award for achievement in health care D'Youville Coll., 2002; NRC fellow, 1949-50. Fellow ACS; mem. Am. Acad. Orthopaedic Surgeons (bd. dirs. 1991-92), Am. Orthopaedic Assn. (v.p. 1990-91), Assn. Orthopaedic Chmn., Am. Assn. Surgery of Trauma, Am. Orthopaedic Rsch. Soc. (pres. 1972-73, residency rev. com. 1985-91), Musculoskeletal Tumor Soc. (pres. 1989-90), Coun. Musculoskeletal Specialty Socs. (chmn. elect 1991, chmn. 1992). Jewish. Home: 85 Depew Ave Buffalo NY 14214-1509 Office: 100 High St Buffalo NY 14203-1126

MINDES, GAYLE DEAN, education educator; b. Kansas City, Mo., Feb. 11, 1942; d. Elton Burnett and Juanita Maxine (Mangold) Taylor; m. Marvin William Mindes, June 20, 1969 (dec.); 1 child, Jonathan Seth. BS, U. Kans., 1964; MS, U. Wis., 1965; EdD, Loyola U., Chgo., 1979. Tchr. pub. schs., Newburgh, N.Y., 1965-67; spl. educator Ill. Dept. Mental Health, Chgo., 1967-69; spl. edn. supr. Evanston (Ill.) Dist. 65 Schs., 1969-74; lectr. Loyola U., Chgo., 1974-76, Coll. St. Francis, Joliet, 1976-79; asst. prof. edn. Oklahoma City U., 1979-80; prof. sch. edn. DePaul U., 1993-99, acting dean, 1998-99, prof. edn., dir. edn. program, 1999—, dir. EdD program, 2000—02. Lectr. Northeastern Ill., U. Chgo. 1974, North Park Coll., Chgo., 1978; vis. asst. prof., rsch. assoc. Roosevelt U. Coll. Edn., Chgo, 1983-87, Albert A. Robin campus prof., dir. R&D dir. tchr. edn., dir. early childhood, dir. grad. edn. ctr., 1993; search com. multicultural student affairs, v.p. advancement, DePaul U.; chair Roosevelt U. Senate, 1986-89; trustee Roosevelt U., 1987-93; co-chair ILAEYC Bldg. Bridges; alt. rep. faculty coun. DePaul U. Sch. Edn., faculty adv. com. to univ. plan. and info. tech., panel on grievances, 1995-99, comprehensive pers. devel. com., 1995-99; tng. sub-com. adv. Ill. Dept. Children & Family Svcs., 1993-95; panel of advisers comprehensive pers. devel. sys. Ill. State Bd. Edn., 1995-99; mentor, cons. to partnerships project tng. early intervention svcs. U. Ill., Champaign; panelist Ill. Initiative for Articulation between Ill. Bd. Higher Edn. and Ill. Cmty. Coll. Bd., Early Childhood Assessment Sys.; co-chair, panelist Bansenville Pub. Schs.; cons. in field; project evaluator Chgo. Tchr. Collaborative, Dept. Edn., 1999—; chair U. Tchg. Learning Tech. com., 2001—. Author: (with Marie Donovan) Building Character: Five Enduring Themes for a Stronger Early Childhood Curriculum PK-3, 2000; editor: DePaul U. Sch. Edn. Newsletter; co-author: Planning a Theme Based Curriculum for 4's or 5's, 1993, Assessing Young Children: 1996, Encyclopedia of Children's Play, 1997; mem. editl. bd. Ill. Sch. R&D, Ill. Divsn. Early Childhood Edn. Adv. Com. to Ill. Bd. Edn.; contbr. articles to profl. jours. Bd. dirs. North Side Family Day Care, 1981; northside affiliate Mus. Contemporary Art, 1991-96; active Gov's Task Force on Alternative Rts. to Cert., 1999—; edn. adv. com. Okla. Dept. Edn., 1979-80; adv. bd. bilingual early childhood program Oakton C.C.; adv. bd. early childood tech. assistance project Chgo. Pub. Schs., Lake View Mental Health, 1986-90; planning com. Lake View Citizens Coun. Day Care Ctr., 1978-79; local planning coun. Ill. Dept. Child and Family Svcs.; childcare block grant tng. sub. com.; chair teen com. Florence G. Heller JCC, membership com.; adv. bd. Harold Washington Coll. Child Devel., regional tech. assistance grant LICA; mem. parents. com. Francis W. Parker Sch.; mem. assessment task force Dept. Human Svcs., City of Chgo., 2001—; trustee Congregation Kol Ani. U. Kans. scholar, 1960, Cerebral Palsy Assn. scholar, 1965; U. Wis. fellow in mental retardation, 1964-65. Fellow: Am. Orthopsychiat. Assn.; mem.: ASCD, APA, AAUP, Found. for Excellence in Tchg. (selection com. Golden Apple 1989—94), Soc. for Rsch. in Child Devel., Coun. on Children with Behavioral Disorders, Ill. Assn. for Edn. Young Children (co-chair bldg. bridges project), Ill. Coun. for Exceptional Children, Coun. for Exceptional Children, Am. Ednl. Rsch. Assn., Nat. Assn. for Edn. Young Children (tchr. edn. bd. 1990—94), Pi Lambda Theta, Phi Delta Kappa, Alpha Sigma Nu. Office: DePaul Univ Sch Of Edn Chicago IL 60614 E-mail: gmindes@codor.depauledu.

MINDIN, VLADIMIR YUDOVICH, information systems specialist, chemist, educator; b. Tbilisi, Georgia, USSR, June 6, 1939; came to U.S., 1992; naturalized U.S. citizen, 1997; s. Yuda Isaakovich and Sofia Markovna (Ioffe) M.; m. Irina Alexandrovna Pleshivaia, July 1, 1964; children: Liya, Yakov. MS, Georgian Tech. U., Tbilisi, 1961, PhD, 1969. Sr. rsch. scientist Georgian Tech. U., 1970-80, assoc. prof. phys. chemistry, 1980-92; founder, head computational chemistry lab. Georgian Acad. Sci., Tbilisi, 1980-92; investigator Beltran Inc., Bklyn., 1993-94, prin. investigator, 1994-95; statistician AFP, Inc., Manhasset, N.Y., 1995-98, info. systems dir., 1998-2001; prof. dept. computer sys. and math. Globe Inst. Tech., N.Y.C., 2001—. Cons. DNS Sci., Inc., Bklyn., 1992-97; chief scientific officer, BioNova, Inc., Forest Hills, N.Y., 1997-2001, v.p. info. sys., 2001—. Author: (with A.G. Morachevskii and A.S. Avaliany) Liquid Cathodes, 1978, (with A.V. Sarukhanishvily and J.S. Galuashvily) Inorganic Substances Thermodynamic Parameters Calculation on Computers by Landia Method, 1987; (with S.M. Mazmishvily and D.V. Eristavy) Album of Compositions of Condensed and Gaseous Phase of Silica-Carbon System, 1988 (Georgian Chem. soc. award 1989), (with A.V. Sarukhanishvily) Chemical Thermodynamics, 1990; (with D.V. Eristavy) Investigation on Thermodynamics of Interaction in Boron and Silicon Containing Systems By Means of Digital Chemistry Methods, 1994; contbr. articles to profl. jours. Grantee Dept. Def., 1994-95. Mem. Am. Statis. Assn., Minerals, Metals, Materials Soc., Assn. Engrs. and Scientists for New Ams. (assoc. exec. dir. 1993-94). Achievements include co-development of the first complete phase diagram of the silica-carbon system; patents (with others): method of manganese salt solutions obtaining, method of manufacturing of porous electrodes, method of manganese obtaining, device for electrochemical measurement during electrolysis of melted media, working of sulphur ores, nonferrous metals aulphate ores roasting process, unhydrous manganese chloride producing process, a way of working sulphide ores containing nonferrous metals, furnace charge for silicomanganese obtaining, the batch for the medium carbonic ferromanganese smelting. Home: 70 Dahill Rd Apt 5A Brooklyn NY 11218-2232 Office: BioNova Inc 102-05 63 Rd Ste #1 Forest Hills NY 11375 also: Globe Inst Tech 291 Broadway 2d Fl New York NY 10007 E-mail: vmindin@Ibionova.com., vmindin@aol.com.

MINDLIN, PAULA ROSALIE, retired reading educator; b. N.Y.C., Nov. 27, 1944; d. Simon S. and Sylvia (Naroff) Bernstein; m. Alfred Carl Mindlin, Aug. 14, 1965; 1 child Spencer Douglas. BA in Edn., Bklyn. Coll., 1965; MS in Edn., Queens Coll., 1970, Specialist Sch. Adminstrn, 1973. Tchr. Dist. 16 Pub. Sch., Bklyn., 1965-68; reading tchr. Dist. 29 Pub. Sch. and Dist. 16, 1968-85; instr. insvc. courses Comty. Sch. Dist. 29, Queens Village, N.Y., 1984-93, reading coord. Reading/Comms. Arts Program Queens, 1985-90; dir. reading Cmty. Sch. Dist. 29, Queens Village, 1990-94. Adj. lectr. York Coll., 1989; dir. Chpt. 1 Program (Nat. Recognition 1994, U.S. Sec. of Edn.); curriculum cons., 1997—98. Recipient svc. award N.Y. State Reading Assn. Coun., 1996. Mem. Internat. Reading Assn., Queensboro Reading Coun. (pres. 1994-96, Educator of Yr. award 1994). Avocations: reading, gardening.

MINDT LONG, W. KAYE, clinical social worker; b. St. Paul, Feb. 22, 1953; d. Erwin Etmor and Wanda (Goodwin) Mindt; 1 child, Jennifer Nicole. BS, BSW, Nebr. Wesleyan U., 1980; MSW, U. Nebr., Omaha, 1988. LCSW, lic. mental health practitioner. Protective svcs. worker Nebr. Dept. Social Svcs., Grand Island, 1980-85, permanency reviewer, 1985-88; pvt. clin. social worker, 1988—. Tng. cons. Dept. Social Svcs., Lincoln, 1981-88; cons. Hall County Children's Village, Grand Island, 1986—. Mem. Com. Against Sexual Child assault, Grand Island, 1984-87; mem. Nat. Coalition Against Sexual Assault, 1990-93; AIDS educator Train the Trainer Prog., 1990—; critical incident stress debriefer team Region 3, State Nebr., 1989-91. Scholar P.E.O., 1989. Mem. Nat. Assn. Social Workers. Democrat. Methodist. Avocations: walking, bicycle riding, photography. Office: 1811 W 2nd St Ste 330 Grand Island NE 68803-5464

MINEA, IVAN See **MINA, JOHN LOUIS**

MINEHART, JEAN BESSE, tax accountant; b. Cleve., Nov. 8, 1937; d. Ralph and Augusta Besse; m. Ralph Conrad Minehart, Aug. 28, 1959; children: Patricia Minehart Miron, Deborah Minehart Rust, Elizabeth, Stephen. BA, Mass. Wellesley Coll., 1959; MEd, U. Va., 1971. Rsch. assoc. Age Ctr. of New Eng., Boston, 1959-61; substitute tchr. Charlottesville (Va.) Sch. System, 1976-81; tax acct. H&R Block, Charlottesville, 1982-94, Huey & Bjorn, Charlottesville, 1994—. Past pres. Ephphatha Village Housing for the Deaf, Charlottesville, 1984-87; bd. dirs. Tues. Evening Concert Series, Charlottesville, 1990-94; sec., bd. dirs. Family Svc., Inc., Charlottesville, 1987-91; bd. dirs. Westminster Organ Concert Series; elder Westminster Presbyn. Ch., 1979-81, 94-96. Mem. LWV (v.p., treas. 1991-95) Blue Ridge Wellesley Club (pres. Charlottesvillechpt. 1989-91, dorm rep. 1996—). Avocations: reading, music. Home: 1714 Yorktown Dr Charlottesville VA 22901-3034 Office: Huey & Bjorn 408 E Market St Ste 207 Charlottesville VA 22902-5261

MINER, EARL ROY, literature educator, educator; b. Marshfield, Wis., Feb. 21, 1927; s. Roy Jacob and Marjory M.; m. Virginia Lane, July 15, 1950; children: Erik Earl, Lisa Lane. BA summa cum laude, U. Minn., 1949, MA, 1951, PhD, 1955. Instr. English Williams Coll., 1953-55; mem. faculty dept. English UCLA, 1955-72, prof., 1964-72; prof. English Princeton U., 1972-74, Townsend Martin prof. English and comparative lit., 1974-2000, Townsend Martin prof. emeritus, 2000—. Vis. fellow U. Canterbury, 1985; mem. joint com. for Japanese Studies Social Sci. Rsch. Coun., 1979-83; disting. vis. prof. Emory U., 1989; vis. prof. UCLA, 1990, Stanford U., 1994; mem. Com. on Scholarly Comm. with Peoples Republic China, 1983-87. Author numerous books including The Japanese Tradition in British and American Literature, 1958, The Metaphysical Mode from Donne to Cowley, 1969, The Restoration Mode from Milton to Dryden, 1974, The Princeton Companion to Classical Japanese Literature, 1985, Comparative Poetics, 1991, Naming Properties, 1996; co-author: Literary Transmission and Authority, 1993; assoc. editor The New Princeton Ency. of Poetry and Poetics, 1993; assoc. gen. editor Calif. edit. Works of John Dryden, 1964-72, editor 3 vols.; author articles. Decorated Order of the Rising Sun with Gold Rays and Neck Ribbon Japanese Govt.; named a Fulbright Scholar, Kyoto and Osaka U., 1960—61, Oxford U., 1966—67, Chinese U. of Hong Kong, 1985—86, John Garrett vis. fellow, U. Canterbury, New Zealand, 1985; named disting. lectr., Taiwan, 1985, vis. prof., Internat. Rsch. Ctr. for Japanese Studies, 1993—94; recipient Yamagata Banto prize, Osaka Prefectural Govt., 1987, Koizumi Yakumo prize, 1991; fellow, Am. Coun. Learned Socs., 1962—63, Guggenheim Found., 1977—78, Woodrow Wilson Internat. Ctr. for Scholars, 1982—83, U. Calif. Humanities Rsch. Inst., 1990. Mem. Am. Soc. for 18th Century Studies (pres. 1981-82, Clifford lectr. 1997), Milton Soc. Am. (pres. 1982-83), Am. Comparative Lit. Assn. (mem. adv. bd. 1977-80, 86-89), Internat. Comparative Lit. Assn. (mem. exec. coun. 1986-88, pres. 1988-91). Office: Princeton U 22 McCosh Hall Princeton NJ 08540-5627 E-mail: eminer@princeton.edu.

MINER, JACQUELINE, political consultant; b. Mt. Vernon, N.Y., Dec. 10, 1936; d. Ralph E. and Agnes (McGee) Mariani; B.A., Coll. St. Rose, 1971, M.A., 1974; m. Roger J. Miner, Aug. 11, 1975; children: Laurence, Ronald Carmichael, Ralph Carmichael, Mark. Ind. polit. cons., Hudson, N.Y.; instr. history and polit. sci. SUNY, Hudson, 1974-79. Rep. county committeewoman, 1958-76; vice chmn. N.Y. State Ronald Reagan campaign, 1980; candidate for Rep. nomination for U.S. Senate, 1982; co-chair N.Y. state steering com. George Bush for Pres. campaign, 1986-88; vice chmn. N.Y. State Rep. Com., 1991-93; del. Rep. Convention, 1992; chmn. Coll. Consortium for Internat. Studies; mem. White House Outreach Working Group on Central Am.; co-chmn. N.Y. State Reagan Roundup Campaign, 1984-86; mem. nat. steering com. Fund for Am.'s Future, 2d cir. Hist. Com. Mem. U.S. Supreme Ct. Hist. Soc., P.E.O. Address: 1 Merlins Way Hudson NY 12534-4157

MINER, JOHN BURNHAM, industrial relations educator, writer; b. N.Y.C., July 20, 1926; s. John Lynn and Bess (Burnham) M.; children by previous marriage: Barbara, John, Cynthia, Frances; m. Barbara Allen Williams, June 1, 1979; children: Jennifer, Heather. AB, Princeton U., 1950, PhD, 1955; MA, Clark U., 1952. Lic. psychologist, N.Y. Rsch. assoc. Columbia U., 1956-57; mgr. psychol. svcs. Atlantic Refining Co., Phila., 1957-60; mem. faculty U. Oreg., Eugene, 1960-68; prof., chmn. dept. orgnl. sci. U. Md., College Park, 1968-73; rsch. prof. Ga. State U., Atlanta, 1973-87, Disting. prof., 1974; pres. Orgnl. Measurement Systems Press, Eugene, Oreg., 1976—; prof. human resources SUNY, Buffalo, 1987-94, chmn. dept. orgn. and human resources, 1989-92; profl. practice Eugene, Oreg., 1995—. Cons. McKinsey & Co., N.Y.C., 1966-69; vis. lectr. U. Pa., Phila., 1959-60; vis. prof. U. Calif., Berkeley, 1966-67, U. South Fla., Tampa, 1972; researcher on orgnl. motivation, theories of orgn., human resource utilization, bus. policy and strategy, entrepreneurship. Author many books and monographs including Personnel Psychology, 1969, Personnel and Industrial Relations, 1969, 73, 77, 85, The Challenge of Managing, 1975, (with Mary Green Miner) Policy Issues Personnel and Industrial Relations, 1977, (with George A. Steiner) Management Policy and Strategy, 1977, James A. Hamilton-Hosp. Adminstrs. Book award 1982, 86), (with M.G. Miner) Employee Selection Within the Law, 1978, Theories of Organizational Behavior, 1980, Theories of Organizational Structure and Process, 1982, People Problems: The Executive Answer Book, 1985, The Practice of Management, 1985, Organizational Behavior: Performance and Productivity, 1988, Industrial-Organizational Psychology, 1992, Role Motivation Theories, 1993, (with Donald P. Crane) Human Resource Management: The Strategic Perspective, 1995, The 4 Routes to Entrepreneurial Success, 1996, (with Michael H. Capps) How Honesty Testing Works, 1997, A Psychological Typology of Successful Entrepreneurs, 1997, Organizational Behavior: Foundations, Theories and Analyses, 2002; contbr. numerous articles, papers to profl. jours. Served with AUS, 1944-46, ETO. Decorated Bronze Star, Combat Infantryman's badge. Fellow APA, Acad. of Mgmt. (editor Jour. 1973-75, pres. 1977-78), Soc. for Personality Assessment, Am. Psychol. Soc.; mem. Soc. for Human Resource Mgmt., Indsl. Rels. Rsch. Assn., Internat. Coun. for Small Bus., Strategic Mgmt. Soc., Internat. Pers. Mgmt. Assn., Human Resource Planning Soc. Republican. Home and Office: 34199 Country View Dr Eugene OR 97408-9440

MINER, JOHN RONALD, bioengineer; b. Scottsburg, Ind., July 4, 1938; s. Gerald Lamont and Alice Mae (Murphy) M.; m. Betty Katheron Emery, Aug. 4, 1963; children: Saralena Marie, Katherine Alice, Frederick Gerald. BS in Chem. Engring, U. Kans., 1959; MSE. in San. Engring, U. Mich., 1960; PhD in Chem. Engring. and Microbiology, Kans. State U., 1967. Lic. profl. engr., Kans., Oreg. San. engr. Kans. Dept. Health, Topeka, 1959-64; grad. research asst. Kans. State U., Manhattan, 1964-67; asst. prof. agrl. engring. Iowa State U., 1967-71, assoc. prof., 1971-72; assoc. prof. agrl. engring. Oreg. State U., 1972-76, prof., 1976—. head dept., 1976-86, acting assoc. dean Coll. Agrl. Sci., 1983-84, assoc. dir. Office Internat. Research and Devel., 1986-90, extension water quality specialist, 1991—; environ. engr. FAO of UN, Singapore, 1980-81. Fulbright scholar U. Malawi, 1997-98; internat. cons.; cons. to livestock feeding ops., agrl. devel. firms. Co-author 2 books on livestock waste mgmt.; author 3 books of children's sermons; contbr. numerous articles on livestock prodn., pollution control, control of odors associated with livestock prodn. to profl. publs. Fellow Am. Soc. Agrl. Engrs. (bd. dirs. 1985-87); mem. Water Pollution Control Fedn., Sigma Xi, Gamma Sigma Delta, Alpha Epsilon, Tau Beta Pi. Presbyterian. Office: Oreg State U Dept Bioengring Corvallis OR 97331 E-mail: minerj@engr.orst.edu.

MINER, LYNNE SHIRLEY, nurse midwife, educator; b. Portland, Maine, July 31, 1950; d. Raymond H. Sweetsir and Agnes Marion (Stevens) Racine; m. Dwight F. Hasler, Aug. 14, 1999; children: Alexander Sean Perry, Lindsey Scarlett. BSN, U. Maine, 1979; MSN, U. Fla., 1986; cert. nurse midwife, Am. Coll. Nurse Midwives. Nurse midwife Turner & Muir MD PA, Cocoa Beach, Fla., 1987-94; clin. dir., nurse midwife Renaissance Birth and Women's Ctr., Palm Bay, 1994-97, Health First, Melbourne, 1997-2000, Hibiscus Nurse-Midwifery Svcs, Melbourne, 2000—. Adj. faculty U. Fla., Jacksonville, 1994—. Chairperson healthy start pub. rels. Prenatal and Infant Health Care Coalition, Cocoa, Fla., 1993—99. Named Healthy Start Person of Yr., Prenatal and Infant Health Care Coalition, 1996. Mem.: Fla. Perinatal Assn., Am. Coll. Nurse Midwives (v.p. chpt. 1997—2001, pres. 2001—), Sigma Theta Tau. Office: Hibiscus Nurse-Midwifery Svcs 1326 S Pine St Melbourne FL 32901-3231

MINER, ROGER JEFFREY, judge; b. Apr. 14, 1934; s. Abram and Anne M. Miner; m. Jacqueline Mariani; 4 children. BS, SUNY; LLB cum laude, N.Y. Law Sch., 1956; postgrad., Bklyn. Law Sch., Judge Advocate Gen.'s Sch., U. Va.; LLD (hon.), N.Y. Law Sch., 1989, Syracuse U., 1990, Albany Law Sch./Union U., 1996; attended, Emory U. Bar: N.Y. 1956, U.S. Ct. Mil. Appeals 1956, Republic of Korea 1958, U.S. Dist. Ct. (so. and ea. dists.) N.Y. 1959. Ptnr. Miner & Miner, Hudson, NY, 1959—75; corp. counsel City of Hudson, 1961—64; asst. dist. atty. Columbia County, 1964, dist. atty., 1968—75; justice N.Y. State Supreme Ct., 1976—81; judge U.S. Dist. Ct. (no. dist.) N.Y., 1981—85, U.S. Ct. Appeals (2d cir.), Albany, NY, 1985—, now sr. judge. Adj. assoc. prof. criminal law State U. Sys., NY, 1974—79; adj. prof. law N.Y. Law Sch., 1986—96, Albany Law Sch. Union U., 1997—; lectr. state and local bar assns.; lectr. SUNY, Albany, 1985; with N.Y. Law Sch. Bd. Trustees, 1991—96; mem. jud. coun. 2d Cir., 1992—96; chmn. 2d Cir. Com. on Hist. and Commemorative Events, 1989—94; with Cameras in the Courtoom Com., 1993—96, No. Dist. Hist. Com., 1981—85, State, Fed. Jud. Coun. of N.Y., 1986—91, chmn., 1990—91, Jud. Conf. on U.S. com. on fed.-state jurisdiction, 1987—92; trustee Practicing Law Inst., 1995—2002. Mng. editor: N.Y. Law Sch. Law Rev.; contbr. articles to law jours. 1st lt. JAGC U.S. Army, 1956—59, capt. USAR, ret. Named Columbia County Man of Yr., 1984; recipient Dean's medal for disting. profl. svc., N.Y. Law Sch., Disting. Alumnus award, Charles W. Froessel award for Valuable Contbn. to Law, Albany Jewish Fedn. award, Abraham Lincoln award, Cmty. Svc. award, Kiwanis, others, Ellis Island medal of honor. Mem.: ATLA, ABA, Columbia County Magistrates Assn., Am. Soc. Writers on Legal Subjects, Fed. Bar Coun., Fed. Judges Assn., Am. Judicature Soc., Am. Law Inst., Columbia County Bar Assn., Assn. of Bar of City of N.Y., N.Y. State Bar Assn., B'nai Brith, N.Y. Law Sch. Alumni Assn. (hon.; bd. dirs.), Supreme Ct. Hist. Soc., Columbia County Hist. Soc., Elks (past exalted ruler). Jewish. Office: US Ct Appeals 445 Broadway Ste 414 Albany NY 12207-2926

MINER, THELMA SMITH, retired American literature educator; b. Ocean City, N.J., Jan. 15, 1915; d. Benjamin Franklin Smith and Myrtle Estelle Simkins; m. Ward Lester Miner, Oct. 27, 1950. BA, Dickinson Coll., 1935; MA, U. Pa., 1942, PhD, 1945. Tchr. 5th grade, Ocean City, 1935-42; instr. Temple U., Phila., 1945-48; asst. prof. Dickinson Coll., Carlisle, Pa., 1948-51; from asst. prof. to prof. Youngstown (Ohio) State U., 1953-76. Co-author: Transatlantic Migration, 1955; editor: Uncollected Poems of J.R. Lovell, 1950; contbr. articles to profl. jours. Mem. Ams. for Dem. Action, Youngstown, 1957-76. Scholar Fulbright Found., 1960-61. Mem. MLA, AARP, NOW, ACLU, Nat. Abortion and Reproductive Rights Orgn., Sanibel-Captiva Conservation Found., "Ding" Darling Wildlife Soc., Audubon Soc. Democrat. Avocations: reading, travel. Home: Shell Point Village 1631 King's Crown Fort Myers FL 33908-1625

MINER, THOMAS HAWLEY, international entrepreneur; b. Shelbyville, Ill., June 19, 1927; s. Lester Ward and Thirza (Hawley) M.; m. Lucyna T. Minciel, July 22, 1983; children: Robert Thomas, William John. Student, U.S. Mil. Acad., 1946-47; BA, Knox Coll., 1950; JD, U. Ill., 1953. Bar: Ill. 1954. Atty. Continental Ill. Nat. Bank & Trust Co., Chgo., 1953-55; pres. Harper-Wyman Internat. (S.A.), Venezuela and Mex., 1955-58, Hudson Internat. (S.A.), Can. and Switzerland, 1958-60, Thomas H. Miner & Assoc., Inc., Chgo., 1960—; chmn. Miner, Fraser & Gabriel Pub. Affairs, Inc., Washington,

1982-88, Miner Systems, Inc., 1981—. Bd. dirs. Lakeside Bank, Worldschool, Bright Oceans Internat. Corp.; chmn. Ill. dist. export coun. U.S. Dept. Commerce, 1971—; sec. Consular Corps. Chgo., 1986—88; chmn. Mid-Am. China Mgmt. Tng. Ctr., Global Software Source. Chmn. bd. dirs. Sch. Art Inst. Chgo., 1977-81; bd. govs., life mem., sustaining fellow Art Inst. Chgo.; former chmn. UN Assn., Chgo.; founder, chmn. Mid-Am. Com., 1968—; former mem. bd. dirs. UNICEF, NAM, Internat. Trade Policy Com. and Working Group on Commonwealth of Ind. States and Ea. Europe; trustee 4th Presbyn. Ch., Chgo., Roosevelt U., Chgo., 1996; bd. advisors Mercy Hosp.; vice chmn. Chgo. Sister Cities; mem. adv. bd. Internat. Inst. Edn.; bd. dirs. Internat. Sister Cities. With USNR, 1945-46; mem. Pres. Coun. U. Ill. Found. Capt. U.S. Army, 1946-47. Decorated commendatore Ordine al Merito della Repubblica Italiana; recipient Alumni Achievement award Knox Coll., 1974, Gold Medallion award Internat. Visitors Ctr. Chgo., 1989; named One of Chgo.'s 10 Outstanding Young Men, 1962, Chicagoan of Year Chgo. Assn. Commerce and Industry, 1968, Alumni of Month Coll. Law U. Ill., Nov. 1970, Aug. 1984; hon. consul Republic of Senegal, 1970-88. Mem. Am. Mgmt. Assn., Chgoland C. of C., Mid-Am. Arab C. of C. (founder, former pres.), Chgo. Bar Assn., Chgo. Com., Chgo. Coun. Fgn. Rels. (past dir.), Coun. of the Ams., Internat. Trade Club (past dir., pres.), Japan-Am. Soc., Nat. Coun. U.S.-China Trade, Nat. Acad. Scis. (pres. coun.), English Speaking Union (dir., past chmn.) Trade and Econs. Coun. USA-CIS (dir.), U.S.-Russia Bus. Coun., Mus. Contemporary Art, Newcomen Soc. N.Am., U.S.-China Bus. Coun., U.S.-Arab C. of C. (bd. dirs.), U.S.-Mex. C. of C. (bd. dirs.), Thomas Minor Soc., Chgo. Club, Econ. Club, Grant Park Concerts Soc., Chgo. Farmers Club, Mid-Am. Club, Univ. Club (Washington), Univ. Club (Milw.), Hillsboro Club (Fla.), Tryall Golf and Beach Club (Jamaica), Rotary, Phi Delta Phi, Phi Gamma Delta. Office: 150 N Michigan Ave Chicago IL 60601-7553 also: 2400 Virginia Ave NW Washington DC 20037-2612 also: Miner Farms Shelbyville IL 62565 E-mail: ltminer@aol.com.

MINER, VALERIE J. literature educator, writer; b. N.Y.C., Aug. 28, 1947; life ptnr. Helen E. Longino, Mar. 18, 1981. BA, U. Calif., Berkeley, 1969, M of Journalism, 1970. Tchg. asst., tchr., counselor Upward Bound program U. Calif., Berkeley, 1967—69; tchg. asst. speech dept. Laney Coll., Oakland, Calif., 1969—70; instr. English and journalism depts. Centennial Coll., Toronto, Canada, 1972—74; instr. York U., Canada, 1973; instr. English and creative writing depts. U. Toronto, 1972—74; lectr. dept. mass comm. Calif. State U., Hayward, 1977; lectr. dept. journalism San Francisco State U., 1977—78; lectr. dept. English Mills Coll., Oakland, Calif., 1980—81; lectr. English, mass comm., humanities and field studies depts. U. Calif., Berkeley, 1977—89; asst. prof. dept. English Ariz. State U., Tempe, 1990—92; assoc. prof. dept. English U. Minn., Mpls., 1992—95, prof. dept. English, 1995—. Writer-in-residence Colls. of Advanced Edn., South Australia and Western Australia, 1988. Author: Blood Sisters, 1982, Movement, A Novel in Stories, 1985, Murder in the English Department, 1982, Winter's Edge, 1985, All Good Women, 1987, Trespassing and Other Stories, 1989, Rumors from the Cauldron: Selected Essays, Reviews, and Reportage, 1992, A Walking Fire, 1994, Range of Light, 1998, The Low Road, 2001; co-author: numerous books; contbr. chpts. to books, articles to profl. jours. Mem.: MLA. Avocations: hiking, attending dance and theatre performances. Office: Univ Minn Dept English 207 Church St SE Minneapolis MN 55455

MINES, DENISE CAROL, law librarian; b. Phila., June 20, 1956; d. Alexander Abraham and Shirley (Gelman) M.; m. Ivan Bell, Nov. 18, 1990. BA, George Washington U., 1978; M of Librarianship, Emory U., 1979. Asst. libr. Alston Miller & Gaines, Atlanta, 1979-81; libr. Smith Cohen Ringel Kohler & Martin, 1981-84; asst. libr. Schnader Harrison Segal & Lewis, Phila., 1984-87; libr. Reed Smith Shaw & McClay, 1987-90, Mesirov Gelman Jaffe Cramer & Jamieson, Phila., 1990—. Mem. Am. Assn. Law Librs., Greater Phila. Law Librs. Assn. (sec. 1986-87, v.p. 1993-94, pres. 1994-95). Office: Mesirov Gelman Jaffe Cramer & Jamieson 1735 Market St Ste 3901 Philadelphia PA 19103-7503

MINES, MICHAEL, lawyer; b. Seattle, May 4, 1929; s. Henry Walker and Dorothy Elizabeth (Bressler) M.; m. Phyllis Eastham, Aug. 24, 1957; children: Linda Mines Elliott, Sandra, Diane Paull, Michael Lister. BA, U. Wash., 1951, JD, 1954. Bar: Wash. 1954, U.S. Dist. Ct. (we. dist.) Wash. 1957, U.S. Dist. Ct. Mont. 1970, U.S. Ct. Appeals (9th cir.) 1961, U.S. Supreme Ct. Assoc. Skeel, McKelvy, Henke, Evenson & Uhlman, Seattle, 1956-66, ptnr., 1966-68, Hullin, Roberts, Mines, Fite & Riveland, Seattle, 1968-75, Skeel, McKelvy, Henke, Evenson & Betts, Seattle, 1975-79, Betts, Patterson & Mines, 1978—. Moderator Wash.-No. Idaho conf. United Ch. of Christ, 1975-76; trustee Plymouth Housing Group, 1991-97; chair adult edn. bd. Plymouth Congl. Ch., Seattle, 1998-2001. With U.S. Army, 1954-56. Mem. ABA, Wash. State Bar Assn., Seattle-King Bar Assn., Am. Coll. Trial Lawyers (state chair 1984-85), Internat. Acad. Trial Lawyers (bd. dirs. 1991-96), U. Wash. Law Sch. Alumni Assn. (trustee, pres. bd. dirs. 1995-97). Home: 2474 Crestmont Pl W Seattle WA 98199-3714 Office: Betts Patterson Mines PS One Convention Ctr Ste 1400 700 Pike St Seattle WA 98101-3927 E-mail: mpmines@aol.com., mmines@bpmlaw.com.

MINES, RICHARD OLIVER, JR. civil and environmental engineer; b. Hot Springs, Va., July 23, 1953; s. Richard Oliver and Dreama Irene (Blankenship) M. BSCE, Va. Mil. Inst., 1975; ME in Civil Engring., U. Va., 1977; PhD, Va. Poly. Inst., 1983. Instr. Va. Mil. Inst., Lexington, 1977-79; project engr. William Matotan & Assocs., Albuquerque, 1979; grad. asst. Va. Poly. U., Blacksburg, 1980-83; asst. prof. U. South Fla., Tampa, 1983-85, Va. Mil. Inst., 1985-86; project engr. CH2M Hill, Gainesville, Fla., 1986-90; sr. process engr. Black & Veatch, Tampa, 1990-92; asst. prof. U. South Fla., 1992-98; assoc. prof., program dir. environ. engring. Mercer U., Macon, Ga., 1998—. Adj. prof. Santa Fe Community Coll., Gainesville, 1989, U. South Fla., 1990—. Contbr. chpt. to book, articles to profl. jours. Capt. USAF, 1977. Engring. Found. grantee, 1985. Mem. ASCE (Student chpt. prof. of the yr. award 1995, 87), Water Environ. Fedn., Am. Water Works Assn., Chi Epsilon, Kappa Alpha. Baptist. Achievements include research on oxygen transfer studies in the completely mixed activated sludge process and biological nutrient removal studies. Office: 1400 Coleman Ave Macon GA 31207-0001 E-mail: mines_ro@mercer.edu.

MINETA, NORMAN YOSHIO, federal agency administrator; b. San Jose, Calif., Nov. 12, 1931; s. Kay Kunisaku and Kane (Watanabe) M.; m. Danealia; children: David, K., Stuart S.; stepchildren: Robert M. Brantner, Mark Brantner. BS, U. Calif.-Berkeley, 1953; D of Pub. Svc., Santa Clara U., 1989; HHD (hon.), Rust Coll., 1993. Agt./broker Mineta Ins. Agy., San Jose, 1956-89; mem. adv. bd. Bank of Tokyo in Calif., 1961-75; mem. San Jose City Council, 1967-71; vice mayor City of San Jose, 1969-71, mayor, 1971-75; mem. 94th-104th Congresses from 13th (now 15th) Calif. dist., 1975-95; subcom. surface transp., 1989-92; former dep. Dem. whip; ranking minority mem. transp. and infrastructure com.; sr. v.p., mng. dir. transp. sys. & srvs. Lockheed Martin, Washington, 1995-2000; sec. U.S. Dept. Commerce, 2000-2001; secy. transp. U.S. Dept. Transp., Washington, 2001—. Chmn. fin. com. Santa Clara County (Calif.) Council Chs., 1960-62; commr. San Jose Human Relations Commn., 1962-64, San Jose Housing Authority, 1966— Precinct chmn. Community Theater Bond Issue, 1964; mem. spl. gifts com. Santa Clara County council Boy Scouts Am., 1967; sec. Santa Clara County Grand Jury, 1964; bd. dirs. Wesley Found., San Jose State Coll., 1956-58, Pacific Neighbors, Community Council Cen. Santa Clara County, Japan Soc., San Francisco, Santa Clara County chpt. NCCJ, Mexican-Am. Community Services Agy.; mem. exec. bd. No. Calif.-Western Nev. dist. council Japanese Am. Citizens League, 1960-62, pres. San Jose chpt., 1957-59; bd. regents Smithsonian Instn., 1979-95 ; chmn. Smithsonian vis. com. for Freer Gallery, 1981-95; mem. bd. regents Santa Clara U.; chmn. Nat. Civil Aviation Rev. Commn., 1997; mem. Smithsonian Nat. Bd., 1996—. Served to lt. AUS, 1954-56. Mem. Greater San Jose C. of C., Nat. Assn. Indsl. Ins. Agts., Calif. Assn. Indsl. Ins. Agts., San Jose Assn. Ind. Ins. Agts. (dir. 1960-62), North San Jose Optimists Club (pres. 1956-58), Jackson-Taylor Bus. and Profl. Assn. (dir. 1963). Methodist. Office: US Dept Transp 400 Seventh St SW Washington DC 20590 Office Fax: 202-366-7202. *Personal philosophy: My two greatest responsibilities are accountability and accessibility to everyone I represent, and to anyone who comes to me for help.**

MINETREE, JAMES LAWRENCE, III, retired military officer, educator; b. Balt., Feb. 21, 1937; s. James Lawrence and Rhoda (Blossom) M.; m. Martha Milling, Apr. 9, 1983; children: James Lawrence IV, Peter Milling, Jennifer Grace, Margaret Warner; stepchildren: Rachael, Aubrilyn. B, U. Nebr., Omaha, 1971; MA, U. So. Calif., L.A., 1973. Commd. 2d lt. U.S. Army, 1964, advanced through grades to lt. col., 1979; mem. Nat. Intelligence Coun. CIA, Langley, Va., 1979-82; ret. U.S. Army, 1982; with GE Aerospace Sys., Reston, Va., 1982-85; dir. Crisis Mgmt. Info. Sys. BDM, Tysons Corner, 1985-86; pres. Analytical Scis. Inc., Vienna, 1986-90; founder Nat. Inst. for Urban Search and Rescue, Santa Barbara, Calif., 1982—; prof. U. Md. U. Coll., College Park, 1992—; founder, pres. Wilson Inst. for Humanitarian Assistance, Springfield, Va., 1998—. Trustee Nat. Assn. for Search and Rescue, Fairfax, Va., 1984-88; mem. nat. adv. bd. Congl. Fire Svcs. Inst., Washington, 1990-96. Author. Disaster mgmt. officer Fed. Emergency Mgmt. Agy., Washington, 1993-2000; U.S. Govt. rep. European Coun., Athens, Greece, 1990; conceived U.S. Nat. and Internat. Urban Search and Rescue Teams, 1987; bd. dirs. Downtown Benefits Dist., Balt., 1993; tchr. disadvantaged inner-city youth. Decorated Legion of Merit (2), Bronze Star (2), Air medal, Meritorious Svc. medal, Army Commendation medal (3), Vietnam Cross of Gallantry, Civic Action medal, others, Dominican Republic and Republic of Vietnam; recipient Presdl. citation Pub. Svc. The White House, Washington, 1995. Mem. VFW, Nat. Def. Exec. Res., Assn. U.S. Army, Am. Legion. Republican. Episcopalian. Avocations: humanitarian assistance, education, sailing, skiing, pastoral ministry. Home: 7513 Candytuft Ct Springfield VA 22153-1803 E-mail: peteminetree@cox.rr.com.

MINEY, MAUREEN ELIZABETH, middle school educator; b. Bklyn., Nov. 12, 1946; d. Patrick F. and Grace A. (Dillon) M. BS, St. Thomas Aquinas Coll., 1968; MA, Manhattan Coll., 1973; postgrad., N.Y.U., Montclair State Coll. Tchr. Nanuet (N.Y.) Pub. Schs., 1968—, acad. team leader, 1985—. Supt. tchr. coun. Nanuet Pub. Schs., 1973-75, camp instr. 6th grade, 1975—; mem. middle sch. curriculum com., 1987—, computer adv. com., 1987—, middle sch. improvement com., 1988—, dist. writing com., 1989—, middle sch. adv. com.; dist. lang. arts com., 1994—, dist. math. task force, dist. leadership team, 2001—; dist. mentor, 2001-; presenter NCTE nat. conv. N.J. Sci. Tchrs. Assn., N.Y. State Mid. Sch. Assn. Active Nanuet PTA. Mem. ASCD, Nat. Mid. Sch. Assn., N.J. Assn. for Middle Level Edn., N.Y. State Middle Sch. Assn., Nat. Coun. Tchrs. Math., Am. Fedn. Tchrs., Nat. Coun. Tchrs. English, Am. Mus. Natural History, Met. Mus. Art, N.Y. State United Tchrs., N.Y. Zool. Soc., N.Y. Bot. Garden, N.J. Coun. Tchrs. English, N.J. Sci. Tchrs. Assn., N.Y. Outdoor Edn. Assn., Hudson Valley Orienteering, U.S. Orienteering Fedn., Liberty Sci. Ctr., Nanuet Tchrs. Assn., Internat. Reading Assn. (presenter), Delta Kappa Gamma. Avocations: walking, reading, bicycling, arts and crafts. Office: A MacArthur Barr Mid Sch 143 Church St Nanuet NY 10954-3030

MING, SI-CHUN, pathologist, educator; b. Shanghai, China, Nov. 10, 1922; came to U.S., 1949, naturalized, 1964; s. Sian-Fan and Jan-Teh (Kuo) M.; m. Pen-Ming Lee, Aug. 17, 1957; children: Carol, Ruby, Stephanie, Michael, Jeffrey, Eileen. MD, Nat. Central U. Coll. Medicine, China, 1947. Resident in pathology Mass. Gen. Hosp., Boston, 1952-56; assoc. pathologist Beth Israel Hosp., 1956-67; asst. prof. pathology Harvard U. Med. Sch., 1965-67; assoc. prof. U. Md., 1967-71; prof. Temple U., Phila., 1971-93, prof. emeritus, 1993—, acting chmn. dept. pathology, 1978-80, dep. chmn. dept. path., 1980-86. Mem. Internat. Study Group on Gastric Cancer; mem. coun. Internat. Gastric Cancer Assn.; U.S. rep. WHO Collaborating Ctr. for Primary Prevention, Diagnosis and Treatment of Gastric Cancer, 1984-98; hon. prof. Tianjin Med. Coll., Shanghai Second Med. U., Fourth Mil. Med. U., China, 1988—. Author: Tumors of the Esophagus and Stomach, 1973, supplement, 1985, Precursors of Gastric Cancer, 1984, Pathology of the Gastrointestinal Tract, 1992, 2d edit., 1998; mem. editl. bd. World Jour. Gastroenterology, 1998—, Gastric Cancer, 1998—. Nat. Cancer Inst. sr. fellow Karolinska Inst. Stockholm, 1964-65; named hon. prof. Tianjin Med. U., Shanghai Second Med. U. and Fourth Mil. Med. U., China, 1988—. Mem. AAAS, U.S. Canadian Acad. Pathology, Am. Soc. Investigative Pathology, Am. Gastroenterol. Assn., N.Y. Acad. Scis. Achievements include development of classification method for stomach carcinoma based on the growth pattern of the cancer. Office: 3400 N Broad St Philadelphia PA 19140-5104 E-mail: ming@astro.ocis.temple.edu.

MINGE, DAVID, former congressman, lawyer, law educator; b. Clarkfield, Minn., 1942; m. Karen Aaker; children: Erik, Olaf. BA in History, St. Olaf Coll., 1964; JD, U. Chgo., 1967. Atty. Faegre & Benson, Mpls., 1967-70; prof. law U. Wyo., 1970-77; atty. Nelson, Oyen, Torvik, Minge & Gilbertson, 1977-93; mem. 103d-106th Congresses from 2nd Minn. Dist., 1993-2001; judge Minn. Ct. Appeals, Minn., 2002—. Cons. Ho. Jud. Com., Subcom. Adminstrv. Law U.S. Congress, 1975; chair Agrl. Law Sect., Minn. State Bar Assn. 1990-92, adv. bd. Western Minn. Legal Svcs., 1978-84; bd. dirs. Legal Advice Clinics, Ltd., Hennepin County, Western Minn. Vol. Atty. Program; lectr. U. Minn., Morris, 2001-02 Clk. Montevideo Sch. Bd., 1989-92; dir. Montevideo Community Devel. Corp.; steering com. Clean Up the River Environ., 1992 ; co-coord. Montevideo area CROP Walk for the Hungry, Multi-church Vietnamese Refugee Resettlement Com., Montevideo, 1978-90; bd. dirs. Montevideo United Way, Model Cities Program, Kinder Kare; chair AFS Montevideo chpt. Fellow Kellogg Found. Food and Soc. fellow, 2002; scholar, Woodrow Wilson Ctr. for Internat. Studies, 2002. Mem. Minn. Bar Assn., Chippewa County Bar Assn. (chair), Montevideo C. of C., Kiwanis (pres.) Address: 25 Constitution Ave Saint Paul MN 55155

MINGER, TERRELL JOHN, public administration and natural resource institute executive; b. Canton, Ohio, Oct. 7, 1942; s. John Wilson and Margaret Rose M.; m. Judith R. Arnold, Aug. 7, 1965; 1 child, Gabriella Sophia. BA, Baker U., 1966; MPA, Kans. U., 1969; postgrad., MIT, 1975; Loeb fellow, Harvard U., 1976-77; postgrad, Stanford U., 1979; MBA, U. Colo., 1983. Asst. dir. admissions Baker U., 1966-67; asst. city mgr. City of Boulder, Colo., 1968-69; city mgr. City of Vail, 1969-79; pres., CEO Whistler Village Land Co., Vancouver, B.C., Can., 1979-81; v.p., gen. mgr. Cumberland S.W. Inc., Denver, 1981-83; exec. asst. dep. chief of staff to Gov. Colo., 1983-87; pres., CEO Sundance (Utah) Inst. for Resource Mgmt., 1986—, Sundance Enterprises Ltd., 1988-91. Adj. prof. grad. sch. pub. affairs U. Colo., 1983—, Sch. Bus. U. Denver, 1992—; bd. dirs. Colo. Open Lands, Inc.; participant UN Conf. on Environment and Devel., Rio de Janeiro, 1992; chmn. environ. adv. bd. Wal-Mart, Inc., 1990—; co-chmn. task force sustainable consumption World Bus. Coun. Sustainable Devel.; co-chmn. N.Am. Telecom./Environ. Taskforce; chmn. Environ. Excellence Task Force Telecomm. Industry; environ. advisor Salt Lake City Olympic Com. Editor: Greenhouse/Glasnost-The Global Warming Crisis, 1990, Val Symposium Papers, 1970-79; author, editor: Growth Alternatives for Rocky Mountain West, 1976, Future of Human Settlements in the West, 1977. Spl. del. UN Habitat Conf. Human Settlements, spl. rep. to UN Environ. Program, 1992, coord. UN Global Youth Forum, 1993-94, co-chmn. conf. on environ. and mktg., N.Y.C., 1993; founder Vail Symposium, advisor UN Environ. Program Telecom. Charter, Nairobi, Kenya, 1999; co-founder, bd. dirs. Colo. Park Found., 1985—; chair World Alpine Championship Conf., Vail, Colo., 1999; founding mem. Greenhouse/Glasnost U.S./USSR Teleconf. with Soviet Acad. Scis., 1989—; mem. pres. task force Commn. on Sustainable Devel., 1994—; co-chmn. Golf and Environ. Conf., Pebble Beach, Calif., 1995; founder, pres. Western Rendezvous, 1995—; bd. dirs. Piton Found., 1996. Nat. finalist White House Fellowship, 1978; recipient Colo. Soc. Landscape Arch. award, 1999; named one of B.C.'s Top Bus. Leaders for the '80s, 1980. Mem. Urban Land Inst., Colo. Acad. Pub. Adminstrn. (charter, founding mem. 1988), Colo. City Mgmt. Innovation award 1974-76), Western Gov.'s Assn. (staff coun., chmn. adv. com. 1985-86), Flatirons Athletic Club. Home: 785 6th St Boulder CO 80302-7416 Office: Ctr for Resource Mgmt 1410 Grant St Ste 307C Denver CO 80203-1846

MINGES, JOHN FRANKLIN, III, non-profit management consultant; b. Greenville, N.C., Mar. 27, 1963; s. John Franklin II and Thorburn (Whitehurst) M.; m. Sarah Jo Poindexter, Aug. 2, 1986. BSW, East Carolina U., 1986. Adminstr. pers. and pub. rels. Pepsi-Cola Bottling co., Greenville, 1986-89, v.p., 1990-98; non-profit mgmt. cons. Minges & Assocs., 1998—. Exec. dir. The Greater Greenville Found., 1999—2001. Mem. Gov.'s Crime Commn., Raleigh, 1995—2001; bd. dirs. Pitt-Greenville Crime Stoppers, Greenville Industries Bd., Greenville Cmty. Shelter, 1996—2000. Recipient Outstanding Cmty. Svc. award Greenville City Coun., 1988, Outstanding Svc. to N.C. award Gov. N.C., 1995, Medallion for Unusually Devoted Svc. to Youth Boys and Girls Clubs Am., 1993; named Civitan Citizen of Yr. Greenville Civitan, 1990, Greenville C. of C., 1996. Mem. Greenville-Pitt County C. of C. (bd. dirs.), Rotary Internat. (Paul Harris fellow 1991). Avocations: metal detecting, coin collecting. E-mail: john@minges.com.

MINGLE, JAMES JOHN, lawyer; AB in English, St. Joseph's Coll., Phila., 1968; JD, U. Va., 1973. Bar: Md. 1974, Va. 1990, N.Y. 1996. Asst. to pres. Frostburg State Coll., 1973-77, adj. prof. bus. law, 1975-77; asst. atty. gen. State of Md., 1977-89; chief counsel state univ. and coll. sys. U. Md., Md. Pub. TV, 1981-89; gen. counsel U. Va., Charlottesville, 1989-95, lectr. law, 1994-95; gen. counsel, sec. corp., adj. prof. law Cornell U., Ithaca, N.J., 1995—. Adj. prof. law U. Md., 1984-88; asst. to bus. mgr. Phila. 76ers NBA Club, 1968-69; city atty. City of Frostburg, Md., 1974-76. Mem. Nat. Assn. Coll. and Univ. Attys.

MINGO, JAMES WILLIAM EDGAR, lawyer; b. Halifax, N.S., Can., Nov. 25, 1926; s. Edgar Willard and Lila Theresa (McManus) M.; m. Edith Peppard Hawkins, July 6, 1953; children: Sarah M. (Mrs. J.P. Camus), James A., Johanna E., Nancy S. (Mrs. S.J. Overgaard-Thomsen), Charles H. BA, Dalhousie U., Halifax, 1947, LL.B., 1949; LL.D. (hon), Dalhousie U., 1998; LL.M., Columbia U., 1950; LL.D. (hon.), St. Mary's U., 1981. Bar: N.S. 1950, Queen's counsel 1966. Ptnr. Stewart, McKelvey, Stirling & Scales (and predecessors), Halifax, 1958—, assoc., 1950-57, chmn. exec. com., 1979-92. Pres., dir. Canning Investment Corp. Ltd., Halifax; Minas Basin Pulp & Power Co. Ltd., Hantsport, N.S., Minas Basin Holdings Ltd., Hantsport, The Great Eastern Corp. Ltd., Charlottetown, P.E.I. and Halifax, Onex Corp., Toronto, Oxford Frozen Foods Ltd., Oxford, N.S.; trustee Forum for Young Canadians. Mem. Halifax-Dartmouth Port Commn., 1955-83, chmn., 1960-83; chmn. Halifax Grammar Sch., 1971-73; mem. Halifax Port Authority, 1972-84; chmn. nat. treasury com. Liberal Party Can., 1976-85; dir. N.S. Legal Aid, 1977-80; mem. Med. Research Council Working Group on Human Experimentation, 1977-78. Mem. Can. Bar Assn. (exec. com. 1973-76, spl. com. on legal ethics 1969-75, 84-87), N.S. Barristers Soc. (pres. 1975-76). Clubs: Halifax, Saraguay, Royal N.S. Yacht Squadron, Ashburn. Office: Box 997 Tower I Purdy's Wharf Halifax NS Canada B3J 2X2

MINGUS, MATTHEW SCOTT, public administration educator; b. Presque Isle, Maine, May 12, 1966; s. Monte Ceary Mingus and Gail Marie Beck; m. Tabitha Terese Young, Aug. 10, 1991; 1 child, Rene Elizabeth. BA, U. Denver, 1988; MPA, U. Victoria, B.C., Can., 1991; PhD, U. Colo., Denver, 1999. Asst. prof. pub. adminstrn. Western Mich. U., Kalamazoo, 1998—. Editor: Part of the Solution, 1994; contbr. articles to profl. jours. Speech critic, judge H.S. speech and debate tournaments, Colo. and Mich., 1988—. Grad. fellow U. Victoria, 1988-91; Harry S. Truman scholar, 1986-91; U. Denver honors program scholar, 1984-88. Mem. ASPA, Inst. Noetic Scis., Am. Pub. Policy and Mgmt. Assn., Pub. Adminstrn. Theory Network, Phi Beta Kappa. Avocations: photography, running, showshoeing. Home: PO Box 19845 Kalamazoo MI 49019-0845 E-mail: Matthew.Mingus@wmich.edu.

MINI, ANNE ALEXANDRA APOSTOLIDES, writer, educator; b. Oakland, Calif., Sept. 30, 1966; d. Norman and Kleo Varvara (Apostolides) M. AB, Harvard U., 1988; MA, U. Chgo., 1991; PhD, U. Wash., 1995. Founding ptnr. Decidedly You Counseling Svc., Seattle, 1995-99; freelance-writer, 1995—; pres. Thesisadvisor.com, 2000—. Lectr., tchg. asst. U. Wash., Seattle, 1991-95, Nancy Hartsock Rotating Chair, 1995. Author: The General Strike of 1934, 1988, Alexis de Tocqueville in Historical Context, 1991, An Expressive Revolution, 1995, Security Issues, 1996, Favorite Son, 1999, Background Noise, 2001. Precinct com. officer Seattle Dem. Com., 1996—; del. King County Dem. Ctrl. Com., Seattle, 1996—, mem. bylaws com., 1999; polit. campaign cons., 1998—; mem. Wash. State Dem. Platform Com., 1998, 2000; Wash. state del. Dem. Nat. Conv., 2000. Radcliffe scholar, 1984-88; grantee U. Wash., 1995, 90, U. Chgo., 1989-91, Norcroft Writing Fellowship, 2002. Avocations: 18th and 19th century French liberalism, gourmandry, viticulture. E-mail: authoress1@foxinternet.com.

MINICHELLO, DENNIS, lawyer; b. Cleve., June 9, 1952; s. Ernest Anthony and Mary Theresa (Rocci) M.; m. Janine Stevens, Feb. 14, 1987. BA in Econs., MA in Econs., Ohio U., 1974; JD, Northwestern U., 1978. Bar: U.S. Dist. Ct. (no. dist.) Ill., U.S. Ct. Appeals (7th cir.), Supreme Ct. Ill., U.S. Supreme Ct. Assoc. Haskell & Perrin, Chgo., 1978-84; ptnr. Tribler & Marwedel, 1984-89, Keck, Mahin & Cate, Chgo., 1989—. Contbr. articles to profl. jours. Bd. dirs. Great Lakes Naval and Maritime Mus. Fulbright scholar, 1974-75. Mem. ABA, Ill. State Bar Assn., Chgo. Bar Assn. (mem. transp. com.), Maritime Law Assn. (proctor), Casualty Adjusters Assn. Chgo., The Propeller Club U.S. (pres. 1983-84), Port Chgo., Met. Club. Roman Catholic. Avocations: sailing, reading, running. Office: Marwedel Minichello & Reeb PC 10 S Riverside Plz Ste 660 Chicago IL 60606-3709

MINICK, MICHAEL, publishing executive; b. Albany, N.Y., Mar. 26, 1945; s. Jason and Ruth Isabelle (Solomon) M. Student, U. Va., 1963-66; BA in History, L.I. U., 1968. Editorial dir. Mag. Mgmt., N.Y.C., 1969-73; mng. editor Gentlemen's Quarterly, 1975-76; pub., ptnr. Beauty Digest, 1978-90; pub. Pa. Ofcl. Wine and Liquor Quar., 1985—, Ohio Liquor Quar., 1990—. Author: The Kung Fu Exercise Book-Health Secrets of Ancient China, 1974, The Wisdom of Kung Fu, 1974; contbr. numerous articles to popular mags. Mem. 25 Yr. Club of Ind. Distbrs., Pa. Wine and Spirit Assn. Democrat. Home: 440 W 22nd St New York NY 10011-2526

MINICUCCI, RICHARD FRANCIS, lawyer, former hospital administrator; b. N.Y.C., Jan. 16, 1947; s. Daniel Michael and Marie Felice (Trotta) M.; m. Nancy Jean Moran, Aug. 16, 1969; children: Jonathan, Elizabeth, Richard. BA, Rutgers Coll., 1969; MHA, Duke U., 1971; JD, Memphis State U., 1976. Bar: Tenn. 1977, N.Y. 1978. Adminstrv. asst. Duke Hosp., Durham, N.C., 1971; health planner Mid-South Med. Ctr. Coun., Memphis, 1971-73; dir. adminstrn. Memphis & Shelby County Hosp. Authority, 1973-77; assoc. Hayt Hayt & Landau, Great Neck, N.Y., 1977-81, ptnr., 1981-89, Nixon Peabody LLP (Nixon Hargrave Devans & Doyle, LLP), Garden City, 1989—. Lectr. various health law assns. Editor: New York Environmental Law Handbook, 2d edit.; author: Residency Training Program Accreditation, 1st-5th edits.; editor-in-chief Accreditation Alert. Co-chmn. fund raising Luth. High Sch., Brookville, N.Y., 1991. Capt. U.S. Army, 1971-79. Mem. Am. Acad. Hosp. Attys., N.Y. State Bar Assn., Nassau Bar Assn., Am. Health Lawyers Assn. Republican. Roman Catholic. Avocations: tennis, skiing, hockey, travel. Office: Nixon Peabody LLP 990 Stewart Ave Ste 350 Garden City NY 11530-4838

MINICUCCI, ROBERT A. business executive; b. Waterbury, Conn., May 7, 1952; s. Arnold A. and Mary (Garafola) M.; m. Jill Hanau, June 18, 1988; children: Robert A. Jr., Alexandra H. BA, Amherst (Mass.) Coll., 1975; MBA, Harvard U., 1979. CPA. Staff acct. Price Waterhouse, Boston, 1975-77; assoc. Lehman Bros., N.Y.C., 1979-82, v.p., 1982-85, sr. v.p., 1985-88, mng. dir., 1988-91; sr. v.p., treas. Am. Express Co., 1991-92; CFO First Data Corp., N.Y.C., 1992-93; gen. ptnr. Welsh, Carson, Anderson & Stowe, 1993—. Bd. dirs. Amdocs Ltd. Inc., Attachmate Corp., Global Knowledge Network Inc., BancTec, Inc., Alliance Data Systems, Inc. Home: 7 Hilltop Rd S Norwalk CT 06854-5001 Office: Welsh Carson Anderson Stowe 320 Park Ave Ste 2500 New York NY 10022-6815

MINIEAR, J. DEDERICK, software company executive, consultant; b. Columbia City, Ind., Oct. 10, 1959; s. Gary Allen and Mallory Virgean (Dederick) M.; m. Lisa Anne Lattimer, July 30, 1983 (div. May 1991); 1 child, Andrew Ross. BA in Econs. and Computer Studies, Northwestern U., 1982. Head data processing Holcomb & Hoke, Mfg., Indpls., 1982-85; systems engr. Elec. Data Systems, Kokomo, Ind., 1985-87; cons. Healthcare Adminstrv. Systems, Indpls., 1987-89, Software Synergy Inc., Indpls., 1989-90, Indecon, Inc., Indpls., 1990-94, Source Cons., Indpls., 1994-97; founder, owner, CEO Aerosoft, Inc., 1989—. Computer cons. Ind. Basketball Hall of Fame, New Castle, 1989-90. Author, found. mem.: Northwestern Rev., 1982; author PC graphics, advt. diskettes, fitness log, screen saver software and video. Pvt. promoter Pres.'s Coun. on Phys. Fitness and Sport, Indpls., 1991—, Nat. Assn. Gov.'s Couns. on Phys. Fitness and Sports. Mem. Christian Coalition (press liaison 1995-96), Full Gospel Businessmen Fellowship Internat. (local sec. 1991—), Gideons Intenat. (local v.p. 2000—). Methodist. Avocations: jogging, weightlifting, basketball. Office: Aerosoft 6827 Kentland Dr Indianapolis IN 46237-9410

MINIGH, HOWARD L. pharmaceutical executive; b. W.Va. m. Carole Minigh; 2 children. BS in Chemistry and Math., Glenville State Coll.; PhD in Organic Chemistry, W.Va. U. Process chemist Am. Cyanamid Co., 1974—78, various sales, mktg. and ops. mgmt. positions, 1978—91, v.p. agrl. div., 1991—92, pres. agrl. div., 1992—94; pres. Am. Cyanamid Global Agrl. Products, 1994—2000; group v.p. DuPont Agriculture & Nutrition, 2000—. Mem. pres.'s adv. group CropLife Internat.; past bd. mem. Am. Crop Protection Assn., FFA Sponsors Bd. Office: DuPont Corp Info Ctr Barley Mill Plz PIO Wilmington DE 19880-0010*

MININBERG, DAVID T. pediatric urology surgeon, educator; b. N.Y.C., May 28, 1936; s. Benjamin and Mildred (Zellermayer) M.; m. Anne Wikler, June 16, 1957; children: Gustav, Julien. BA, Yale U., 1957; MD, N.Y. Med. Coll., 1961. Intern Beth Israel Hosp., N.Y.C., 1961-62; resident in surgery East Orange (N.J.) Vets. Hosp., 1962-63; resident in urology N.Y. Med. Coll., N.Y.C., 1963-66; Ferdinand Valentine fellow N.Y. Acad. Medicine, 1966-67; instr. urology, pediatrics N.Y. Med. Coll., N.Y.C., 1967-69, asst. prof. urology, pediatrics, 1969-74, assoc. prof. urology, pediatrics, 1974-77; assoc. prof. surgery/urology Cornell U. Med. Coll., 1977—, dir. pediatric urology, 1977—. Trustee Nat. Kidney Found., chmn.-elect sect. pediatric urology nephrology, 1994-96, chmn. 1996-98; bd. chmn. Nat. Enuresis Soc., 1992-93; mem. exec. com. Am. Acad. Pediatrics/Urology, 1985-91. Recipient Sprague Carleton award N.Y. Med. Coll., 1961, Ferdinand Valentine fellow N.Y. Adac. Medicine, 1966-67. Mem. Urology Am. Acad. Pediatrics (pres. sect. 1990). Home: 860 5th Ave New York NY 10021-5856

MINISH, ROBERT ARTHUR, lawyer; b. Mpls., Dec. 25, 1938; s. William Arthur and Agnes Emilia (Olson) M.; m. Marveen Eleanor Allen, Sept. 16, 1961; 1 child, Roberta Ruth. BA, U. Minn., 1960, JD, 1963. Bar: Minn. 1963. Assoc. Popham, Haik, Schnobrich & Kaufman, Ltd., Mpls., 1963-67, 1967-97; ptnr. Hinshaw & Culbertson, 1997—. Bd. dirs. Braas Co., Mpls. Mem. ABA, Minn. Bar Assn. Avocations: fishing, traveling. Home: 331 Pearson Way NE Minneapolis MN 55432-2418 Office: Hinshaw & Culbertson 3100 Piper Jaffray Tower 222 S 9th St Minneapolis MN 55402-3389

MINISI, ANTHONY S. lawyer; b. Sept. 18, 1926; s. Anthony F. and Leonora (Petoia) M.; m. Rita Marie Hentz, Jan. 8, 1949; children: Claire, Anthony J., Joseph J., Brian A. BS, U. Pa., 1948, JD, 1952. Player N.Y. Giants NFL, 1948; law clk. to presiding judge Ct. of Common Pleas #6, Phila., 1952-54; counsel Wolf, Block, Schorr and Solis-Cohen, 1954—. Past pres., vice chmn. Robert E. Maxwell Meml. Football Club, Eastern Assn. Intercoll. Football Ofcls. Past chmn. Com. of Seventy, Phila.; former mem., past pres. Bd. of Edn., Tredyffrin/Easttown Joint Sch. Dist.; mem., chmn. bd. supr. Easttown Twp.; past v.p. Cmty. Svcs. Planning Coun., Phila.; trustee U. Pa.; trustee, mem. exec. com. U. Pa. Health Sys.; chmn. Clin. Care Assocs. U. Pa. Health Sys.; former mem., vice-chmn. Pa. State Bd. Law Examiners. Served to maj. USAR. Mem. ABA (ho. of dels.), Pa. Bar Assn., Phila. Jr. Bar Assn. (past pres.), Def. Lawyers Am., Assn. Trial Attys. Am., Phila. Bar Assn. (bd. of govs., past chmn.), Phila. Trial Lawyers Assn., Fed. Bar Assn., Lawyers Club (past pres.), Justinian soc., Union League (Phila.). Republican. Roman Catholic. Office: Wolf Block Schorr & Solis-Cohen SE Corner 15th & Chestnut Sts Philadelphia PA 19102

MINK, MAXINE MOCK, real estate company executive; b. Lakeland, Fla., Jan. 17, 1938; d. Idus Frank and Elizabeth (Warren) Mock; student Fla. So. Coll.; children: Lance Granger, Justin Chandler. With Union Fin. Co., Lakeland, Fla., 1956-62; ptnr./owner S & S Ent. & Arrow Lake Mobile Home Pk., Lakeland, 1957-66; head bookkeeper Seaboard Fin., Lakeland, 1964-68; ptnr. Custom Chem., Inc., Lakeland, 1968-75, Don Emilio Perfumers, Newport Beach, Calif., 1978-79; owner Maxine Mink Public Relations, Newport Beach, 1978-83; fine homes and relocation specialist Merrill Lynch Realty, Newport Beach, 1985-90, Tarbell Realtors, Newport Beach, 1990-93, Prudential Calif. Realty, Newport Beach, 1993-95, Grubb & Ellis Real Estate, 1996-97, Prudential Calif. Realty, Newport Beach, 1997-2001, Mink Realty, Newport Beach, 2002—. Bd. dirs. Guild of Lakeland Symphony Orch., 1972-75; mem. Lakeland Gen. Hosp. Aux., 1974-76, Mus. Modern Art. Mem. NAFE, Newport Beach C. of C., Hoag Hosp. Aux., Orange County Music Center Guild. Republican. Clubs: Balboa Bay, Sherman Library and Gardens, The 552. Office: PO Box 1262 Newport Beach CA 92659-0262

MINK, MICHAEL DUANE, community education consultant; b. Radford, Va., Nov. 10, 1966; s. Duane and Phyllis Mink. BA, Coll. William and Mary, 1989; MPA, U. N.C., 1994. Dir. quality assurance Pvt. Industry Coun., Phila., 1994—99; assoc. dir. Ga. Inst. Tech., Atlanta, 1999—2000; project coord. Atlanta Cmty. Food Bank, 2001—. Co-founder Midtown Writers Cir., Atlanta, 2000—01. Sec., founding mem. Friends Classical Music, Phila., 1997—99. Scholar Merit scholar, U. NC, Chapel Hill, 1993—94. Democrat. Avocations: classical music performance, organic cooking, reading, historic renovation. Personal E-mail: mink_m@bellsouth.net.

MINK, RONALD DEAN, music educator; b. Springfield, Mo., Apr. 19, 1950; s. Ronald Victor and Doris Ellen Mink; m. Bonnie Marie Miller, Dec. 27, 1972; children: Jessica, Grant. BS, SW Mo. State U., Springfield, MO, 1972; MM, Pitts. State U., Pittsburgh, 1979. Band dir. Braymer C-4 Pub. Sch., Braymer, Mo., 1972—75; dir. music Ft. Scott USD 245 Pub. Sch., Fort Scott, Kans., 1975—84; music coord. Gt. Bend USD 428 Pub. Sch., Great Bend, 1984—. Choir and music dir. First Christian Ch., Great Bend, Kans., 1990—2002. Mem.: Phi Beta Mu Internat. Band Frat. (exec. seer 1988—2002), Kappa Kappa Psi (charter pres. 1970), Phi Mu Alpha. D-Liberal. Christian. Avocation: arranging. Home: 3012 16th Street Great Bend KS 67530

MINKEL, HERBERT PHILIP, JR. lawyer; b. Boston, Feb. 11, 1947; s. Herbert Philip and Helen (Sullivan) M. BA, Holy Cross Coll., 1969; JD, NYU, 1972. Bar: Mass. 1973, N.Y. 1976, U.S. Dist. Ct. Mass. 1973, U.S. Dist. Ct. (so. dist.) N.Y. 1976. Law clk. U.S. Dist. Ct. Mass., Boston, 1972-73; assoc. Milbank, Tweed, Hadley & McCloy, N.Y.C., 1973-79; ptnr. Fried, Frank, Harris, Shriver & Jacobson, 1979-94; mem. adv. com. on bankruptcy rules Jud. Conf. U.S., 1987-93; sr. ptnr. Minkel and Assocs., N.Y.C., 1994—. Adj. assoc. prof. NYU Law Sch., 1987-94. Contbg. author: American Bankers Assn. Bankruptcy Manual, 1979; contbg. editor: 5 Collier on Bankruptcy, 15th edit., 1979-96; contbr. articles to profl. jours. Bd. advisors Internat. Yacht Restoration Sch., Newport, R.I., Spl. Olympics, Spl. Smiles. Root-Tilden scholar NYU, 1969-72. Mem. ABA, Nat. Bankruptcy Conf., Assn. Bar City of N.Y. Home: 68 Bumps River Rd Osterville MA 02655-1525 Office: Minkel and Assocs Ste 2217 1270 Avenue Of The Americas New York NY 10020-1801 also: 112 Revere St Boston MA 02114

MINKER, JACK, computer scientist, educator; b. Bklyn., July 4, 1927; s. Harry and Rose (Lapuck) M.; m. Rita Goldberg, June 24, 1951 (dec. Oct. 11, 1988); children: Michael Saul, Sally Anne; m. Johanna Cartee Weinstein, Jan. 19, 1997. BA cum laude with honors in Math., Bklyn. Coll., 1949; MS in Math., U. Wis., 1950; PhD in Math., U. Pa., 1959. Grad. teaching asst. U. Wis., 1949-50; tchr. math. Erasmus Hall High Sch., Bklyn., 1950-51; engr. Bell Aircraft Corp., Buffalo, 1951-52; mgr. info. tech. sect. RCA, Bethesda, Md., 1952-63; dir. tech. staff Auerbach Corp., Washington, 1963-67, tech. cons., 1967-72; mem. Faculty NIH Grad. Sch., 1965-66; vis. mem. faculty U. Md., 1967-68, assoc. prof. computer sci., 1968-71, prof., 1971-98, prof. emeritus, 1998—, 1st chmn. dept. computer sci., 1974-79; cons., speaker, lectr. in field; cons. NSF, 1979-82, chmn. adv. bd. on computer sci., 1980-82. Prof. Inst. Advanced Computer Studies, 1986—; vice-chmn. Com. Concerned Scientists, 1973—; past mem. U.S. Nat. Com. for Fedn. Info. Documentalists. Author: (with H. Gallaire and J.M. Nicolas) Logic and Data Bases a Deductive Approach, 1984; editor: (with H. Gallaire and J.M. Nicholas) Advances in Data Base Theory, vol. 1, 1980, vol. 2, 1984, (with H. Gallaire) Logic and Data Bases, 1978, Foundations of Deductive Databases and Logic Programming, 1988, (with J. Lobo and A. Rajasekar) Foundations of Disjunctive Logic Programming, 1992, Logic-Based Artificial Intelligence, 2000; founding editor-in-chief Theory and Practice of Logic Programming, 2000-2001; contbr. numerous articles to profl. publs.; publs. reviewer; mem. editl. bd. numerous jours. Vice chmn. Com. Concerned Scientists, 1972—. With U.S. Army, 1945-46. Recipient U. Md. Presdl. medal, 1996; named Disting. Scholar-Tchr. U. Md., 1997-98. Fellow AAAS, ACM, IEEE (editl. bd. Expert Info. Sys. jour.), Am. Assn. Artificial Intelligence (founding); mem. Assn. Computing Machinery (chmn. nat. program com. 1968-69, vice chmn. com. on sci. freedom and human rights 1979-89, Outstanding Contbn. award 1985). Jewish. Office: U Md Dept Computer Sci Inst Advanced Computer College Park MD 20742-0001 E-mail: minker@cs.umd.edu.

MINKOFF, ALICE SYDNEY, interior designer, showroom owner; b. Washington, Jan. 29, 1948; d. Lawrence and Ellen (Altman) Glassman; children: Adam Pollin, Shane Pollin, Jacob, Sam. Student, U. Md. Owner Fredrick, Miley & Assocs., Inc., 1983—, Showroom at Washington Design Ctr. Interior designer for homebuilders, 1975-82; interior designer high end residential homes and hotel interiors, 1980—. Vol. Food and Friends, Washington, 1991—; chair Heartstrings, 1990; active AIDS Awareness. Mem. NOW, ACLU, Nat. Trust Hist. Preservation, Nature Conservancy, Amagansett Village Improvement Soc., Human Rights Campaign. Avocations: gourmet cooking, travel, collecting antique dolls and quilts. Home: PO Box 7064 Amagansett NY 11930-7064 also: 3018 New Mexico Ave NW Washington DC 20016 Office: Matches at Miley 300 D St SW Ste 401 Washington DC 20024-4705

MINKOFF, EVELYN WEINSTEIN, volunteer; b. Madison, Wis., Nov. 23, 1925; d. Max and Freida (Blachman) Weinstein; m. Ben Minkoff, Oct. 20, 1946 (dec. Oct. 1984); children: David Ira, Joel Stewart, Fredlyn Sue, Marc J. Student, U. Wis., 1943-46. Bd. dirs. Coun. Jewish Fedns., exec. com., 1995—; pres. Madison Jewish Cmty. Coun., 1992-94, Disting. Svc. award, 1995; profl. vol. Op. Headstart, Nat. Kidney Found. Recipient Golda Meir award State of Israel Bonds, 1990. Mem. Hadassah (life, past pres. local, past pres. Great Lakes region). Democrat. Avocation: travel.

MINKOFF, JACK, economics educator; b. N.Y.C., Jan. 29, 1925; s. Isidore and Yetta (Fine) M.; m. Anne B. Johnson, June 19, 1948; children— Ellen, Paul. AB, Cornell U., 1948; A.M., Columbia U., 1950, PhD (Ford Found. fellow), 1960. Instr. econs. Western Res. U., 1952-53; instr. econs. Sarah Lawrence Coll., 1959-60; prof. econs., chmn. dept. social sci. Pratt Inst., Bklyn., 1960—, acting dean Sch. Liberal Arts and Scis., 1985-86, dean, 1986-93, acting provost, 1993-95; prof. econs., 1996—. Served with USAAF, 1943-45. Fellow Social Sci. Research Council, 1950-51 Mem. Phi Beta Kappa. Home: 57 Ruxton Rd Great Neck NY 11023-1528 Office: Pratt Inst Economics Dept Brooklyn NY 11205

MINKOFF, JOHN, applied mathematics, signal processing and engineering educator; b. Bklyn. s. Alvin Minkoff and Mollie Schwartz; m. Susan Alder, Nov. 19, 1966; 1 child, John. BSEE, Columbia U., 1962, MSEE, 1963, PhD, 1967. Rsch. engr. Columbia U., N.Y.C., 1964-67, rsch. assoc., 1967-73; mgr. analysis activities Riverside Rsch. Inst., 1973-77; mem. tech. staff Bell Telephone Labs., Whippany, N.J., 1977-86; disting mem. tech. staff ATT/Lucent Techs. Bell Labs., 1986—2001; staff scientist ITT Aerospace Comm. Divsn., 2001—. Adj. prof. elec. enging. Polytech. U. N.Y., 1989-90; adj. prof. applied math. NYU, N.Y.C., 1990-95. Author: Signals Noise and Active Sensors, 1992, Signal Processing Fundamentals and Applications for Communications and Sensing Systems, 2002; contbr. articles to profl. jours. Music dir. Hawthorne (N.J.) Symphony Orch. NSF grantee, 1975. Mem. Am. Phys. Soc. Jewish. Avocation: music. Home: 578 Jones Rd Englewood NJ 07631 Office: ITT Aerospace Comm Divsn 100 Kingsland Rd Clifton NJ 07014 Fax: 973-284-4778. E-mail: john.minkoff@itt.com.

MINKOFF, KENNETH MARK, psychiatrist; b. Bklyn., Dec. 26, 1948; s. Arnold and Phyllis Betty (Filzer) M.; m. Maxine Linda Roth, Dec. 12, 1971 (div. Jan. 1988); children: Alison, Rebecca, Michael; m. Linda Mary Swain, July 24, 1988; children: Alexander, Sarah. BA, Harvard U., 1968; MD, U. Pa., 1973. Diplomate Am. Bd. Psychiatry and Neurology, with additional qualifications in Addiction Psychiatry. Intern Grad. Hosp., Phila., 1973; resident in psychiatry U. Calif., San Diego, 1973-76; faculty dept. psychiatry Cambridge Hosp., Harvard Med. Sch., 1976—, asst. clin. prof., 1994—; med. dir. day treatment Somerville (Mass.) Mental Health Clinic, 1976-78, clinic dir., 1978-84; pvt. practice Woburn, Mass., 1984—; chief psychiatry Choate-Symmes Health Svcs., 1984-90, Choate Health Systems, Woburn, 1990-97; med. dir. Arbour-Choate Health Mgmt., 1997—. Cons., tchr., 1987—; med. dir. Arbour Fuller Hosp., 1998-99; chair CMHS panel on co-occurring psychiat. and substance disorders, 1996—; nat., state and county cons. on integrated systems of care for individuals with co-occurring disorders, 1998—. Co-editor: Dual Diagnosis of Serious Mental Illness and Substance Disorder, 1991, Public Sector Managed Health Care: A Survival Manual, 1997; contbr. articles to med. jours., chpts. to books. Recipient clin. excellence award Mass. Alliance for Mentally Ill, 1988. Mem. Am. Psychiat. Assn., Group for Advancement Psychiatry (chmn. Com. on Psychiatry and Cmty. 1986-93), Am. Assn. Addiction Psychiatrists, Am. Hosp. Assn. (gov. coun. sect. on psychiatry and substance abuse 1993-94), Am. Assn. Cmty. Psychiatrists (bd. dirs. 1990—, chair healthcare sys. com. 1993—). Jewish. Avocations: bird-watching, biking, fishing, gardening. Home: 12 Jefferson Dr Acton MA 01720-3104 Office: Arbour-Choate 500 W Cummings Park Ste 3900 Woburn MA 01801-6500 E-mail: kminkov@aol.com.

MINKOFF, MICHAEL, computational and computer scientist, educator; b. Chgo., Oct. 20, 1944; s. Sol M. and Ann Minkoff; m. Ruth N. (Rosner) M., Dec. 5, 1982; 1 child, Michelle E. BS, U. Wis., 1966, MS, 1970, PhD, 1973; MS in Engring., Princeton U., 1968. Prin. applications scientist Argonne (Ill.) Nat. Lab., 1973—. Asst. prof. No. Ill. U., DeKalb, 1973-75, adj. prof., 1989-92; mem. adj. faculty Harper Coll., Palatine, Ill., 1989—; mem. exec. com. Nat. Energy Rsch. Sci. Computing Users Group, Berkeley, Calif., 1997—. Contbr. over 70 articles to sci. jours. Mem. Soc. for Indsl. and Applied Math. (vis. lectr. to U.S. colls. 1996—). Office: Argonne Nat Lab 9700 S Cass Ave Argonne IL 60439 E-mail: minkoff@anl.gov.

MINKOWITZ, DONNA, writer, journalist; b. Bklyn., May 8, 1964; BA, Yale U., 1985; grad. in comparative lit., Cornell U., 1987. Columnist, feature writer Village Voice, N.Y.C., 1987-95; columnist The Advocate, L.A., 1991—93, 1994—96. Cons. episodes and script PBS documentar, PBS/ITVS Series, N.Y., 1993; lectr. Yale U., Cornell U., Pace U., ALA, others, 1987—; performer, reader Iowa Pub. Radio, PEN, L.A., KGB Bar, others, 1995—; tchr. writing workshops N.Y.C. Lesbian and Gay Cmty. Ctr.'s In Our Own Write Program: The Kitchen performance space; tchr. pvt. workshops, 1998—. Author: (memoir) Ferocious Romance: What My Encounters with the Right Taught Me About Sex, God and Fury, 1998 (Lambda Lit. award, Best Book on Religion and Spirituality 1998); prodr.: (performances) Violent/Christ, 2000, Holy! Holy! Holy! Holy and Cruel, 2000; freelance writer Salon mag., The Nation, N.Y. Mag., N.Y. Newsday; contbr. articles and essays to books and textbooks including The Elements of Argument, America Now, To Be Real: Telling the Truth and Changing the Face of Feminism; guest: (TV and radio shows) The Charlie Rose Show, Nat. Pub. Radio's Talk of the Nation, NBC Nightly News, Nightline, The Bob Grant Show, CNN Morning News, 1990—. Recipient Exceptional Merit Media award Radcliffe Coll., 1996, Award for Outstanding Journalism, Nat. Lesbian and Gay Journalists Assn., 1992, Award for Outstanding Local News Corr., GLAAD Media Awards, 1991, Bklyn. award Lambda Ind. Dems. of Bklyn., 1994, Award for Best Gay Coverage in Non-Gay Publ., Gay and Lesbian Press Assn., 1991; finalist Quality Paperback Book Club's New Visions award Quality Paperback Book Club, 1998, Pulitzer prize nominee, 1991; Andrew D. White fellow in comparative lit. Cornell U., 1986-87. Mem. Nat. Lesbian and Gay Journalists Assn.

MINKOWITZ, MARTIN, lawyer, former state government official; b. Bklyn., 1939; s. Jacob and Marion (Kornblau) M.; m. Carol L. Ziegler; 1 son from previous marriage, Stuart Allan. AA, Bklyn. Coll., 1959, BA, 1961; JD, Bklyn. Law Sch., 1963, LLM, 1965. Bar: N.Y. 1963, U.S. Supreme Ct. 1967, U.S. Tax Ct. 1974, all four U.S. Dist. Cts. N.Y. Ptnr. Minkowitz, Hagen & Rosenbluth, N.Y.C., 1964-76; gen. counsel State of N.Y. Workers' Compensation Bd., 1976-81; dep. supt. and gen. counsel State of N.Y. Ins. Dept., 1981-88; instr. CUNY, 1975; ptnr. Stroock & Stroock & Lavan, N.Y.C., 1988—. Adv. bd. Coll. Ins., 1987-90; adj. prof. law N.Y. Law Sch., N.Y.C., 1982—; lectr. ABA, N.Y. C. of C., Practicing Law Inst., N.Y. State Bar Assn., Nat. Assn. Ins. Commrs., Nat. Conf. Ins. Legis.; hearing officer N.Y.C. Transp. Dept., 1970-75; cons. City Coun. N.Y.C. 1969. Author: (with others) Rent Stabilization and Control, 1973; (with others) Handling the Basic Workers' Compensation Law Case, 1996; co-author: Workers Compensation, Insurance and Law Practice-The Next Generation, 1989; commentaries to McKinney's Consol. Laws, 1982—; mem. editl. bd. Jour. Occupl. Rehab. U. Rochester, 1991—; contbr. articles to profl. jours. Bd. dirs., sec. Kingsbay YM-YWHA, Bklyn., 1978-99, elected dir. emeritus, 1999—; pres. bd. dirs. Shore Terrace Co-op., Bklyn., 1982-83; co-chmn. exec. bd., met. coun., nat. v.p. Am. Jewish Congress, N.Y.C., 1983-91; bd. dirs. Met. Coord. Coun. on Jewish poverty, 1993—, Nat. Conf. for Cmty. and Justice (bd. dir. N.Y. divsn. 1994-2001, nat. bd. trustees 1995-2001, chair N.Y. divsn. 1998-2001). Recipient cert. meritorious svc. Bklyn. Law Sch., Outstanding Pub. Svc. award Ind. Ins. Agt. Assn., citation outstanding performance State of N.Y. Workers' Compensation Bd., Disting. Leadership award N.Y. Claims Assn., City of Peace award State of Israel Bonds, Brotherhood award NCCJ. Fellow N.Y. State Bar Found.; mem. N.Y. County Lawyers Assn. (chmn. unlawful practice of law com. 1982-86, mem. profl. ethics com. 1985-91, chair worker's compensation com. 1988-91, bd. dirs. 1997-2001, chair profl. ethics com. 2001—), N.Y. State Bar Assn. (mem. ho. of dels., chmn. unlawful practice of law com. 1981-83, mem. com. on profl. ethics 1981-84, chmn. com. profl. discipline 1988-92, Sustaining Mem. of Yr. award 1995), Soc. Ins. Receivers, Bklyn. Law Sch. Alumni Assn. (v.p. bd. dirs. 1984-92, pres. elect 1993-94, pres. 1995-96). Office: Stroock Stroock & Lavan 180 Maiden Ln Fl 17 New York NY 10038-4937 E-mail: mminkowitz@stroock.com.

MINKOWYCZ, W. J. mechanical engineering educator; b. Libokhora, Ukraine, Oct. 21, 1937; came to U.S., 1949; s. Alexander and Anna (Tokan) M.; m. Diana Eva Szandra, May 12, 1973; 1 child, Liliana Christine Anne BS in Mech. Engring., U. Minn., 1958, MS in Mech. Engring., 1961, PhD in Mech. Engring, 1965. Asst. prof. U. Ill., Chgo., 1966-68, assoc. prof., 1968-78, prof., 1978—. Cons. Argonne Nat. Lab, Ill., 1970-82, U. Hawaii, Honolulu, 1974-94. Founding editor-in-chief (jour.) Jour. Numerical Heat Transfer, 1978—; editor: Internat. Jour. Heat and Mass Transfer, 1968-, Rheologically Complex Fluids, 1972, Internat. Comms. in Heat and Mass Transfer Jour., 1974-, Handbook of Numerical Heat Transfer, 1988—, Advances in Numerical Heat Transfer, Vol 1, 1997, Vol. 2, 1999, (book series) Computational and Physical Processes in Mechanics and Thermal Sciences, 1979-, Advances in Numerical Heat Transfer, 1996-, Vol. 1, 1997, Vol. 2, 1999—; contbr. articles to profl. jours. Recipient Silver Circle for Excellence in Teaching, U. Ill.-Chgo., 1975, 76, 81, 86, 90, 94, Harold A. Simon award Excellence in Teaching, 1986, Ralph Coats Roe Outstanding Tchr. award Am. Soc. Engring. Edn., 1988, U. Ill. Disting. Tchr. award, 1989. Fellow ASME (Heat Transfer Meml. award 1993); mem. Sigma Xi, Pi Tau Sigma. Republican. Ukrainian Catholic. Office: U Ill Dept Mech Engring Mail Code 251 842 W Taylor St Chicago IL 60607-7021 E-mail: wjm@uic.edu.

MINKUS, RAYMOND DAVID, communications and public relations executive; b. Chgo., Aug. 8, 1953; s. Fred and Roslyn Minkus; BS in Journalism, U. Mo., Columbia, 1975; m. Sara Anthony, June 26, 1977; children: Stephanie Raye, Evan Andrew. Reporter, asst. sect. editor Fairchild Publs., N.Y.C., 1975, Chgo.-Midwest editor, 1976; fin. news columnist Milw. Sentinel, 1976-78; sr. communications specialist, mgr. media rels. Miller Brewing Co. Milw., 1978-81; pres. Weiser Minkus Walek Communications, 1981-91; pres. Minkus & Dunne Communications, Inc., 1992—; chmn. ArakNet Comm., 1995—. Bd. dirs. Future Milw., 1980-81; mem. mktg. com. Milw. United Performing Arts Fund, 1980-81; communication task force Chgo. Area Cen. Com., 1984—; legis. asst. Mo. Ho. of Reps., 1974-75; bd dirs. Mental Health Assn. Ill., 1993—, Cystic Fibrosis Found., 1986-92. Recipient Outstanding Corp. Publ. award Bus. and Profl. Adv. Assn. Milw. Mem. Chgoland C. of C. (bd. dirs.), Pub. Rels. Soc. Internat. Assn. Bus. Communicators. Am., Chgo. Assn. Commerce and Industry (communications com., bd. dirs., exec. coms., div. v.p., Vol. of Yr. 1988). Contbr. articles to Common Stock Reporter, Women's Wear Daily, Chgo. Tribune, Commerce Mag., Prentice-Hall Exec. Action Report, others. Home: 2292 Sheridan Rd Highland Park IL 60035-2015 Office: Minkus & Dunne Comm Inc 150 S Wacker Dr Chicago IL 60606-4103

MINNA, MARIA, member of parliament; b. Pofi, Frosinone, Italy, Mar. 14, 1948; arrived in Can., 1957. Grad. in Sociology with honors, U. Toronto. Policy advisor to former Ont. Premier David Peterson; pres. COSTI-IIAS Immigrant Svcs.; v.p. pub. affairs cons. co., Toronto; M.P. from Beaches-Woodbine dist. Ho. of Commons, 1993-97, MP from Beaches-East York dist. Ottawa, Ont., Can., 1997—; apptd. parliamentary sec. Min. Citizenship and Immigration, 1996; re-apptd., 1997; chmn. to social policy com. Nat. Libertarian Caucus, 1998-99, min. for internat. cooperation, 1999—2002. Life-long liberal, mem. Nat. Platform Com., 1988; apptd. vice chair standing com. Human Resources Devel., 1994. Contbr. reports on cmty. devel. and provision of svcs. to immigrants and minority groups. Former mem. campaign cabinet United Way Gtr. Toronto; former dir. Nat. Coun. Welfare Mem. Nat. Congress Italian-Canadians (former exec. dir. Toronto dist., former pres.). Office: House of Commons 406 West Block Ottawa ON Canada K1A 0A6 Fax: 613-996-7942.

MINNEMAN, KENNETH PAUL, pharmacology educatir; b. Sacramento, Sept. 1, 1952; s. John Jesse and Esther Annette Minneman; children: Jennifer, Rebecca, Jeffrey. BS, MIT, 1974; PhD, U. Cambridge, England, 1977. Asst. prof. pharm. Emory U., Atlanta, 1980-85, assoc. prof. pharm., 1985-90, prof. pharm, 1990-2000, Charles Howard Candler prof. pharm., 2000—. Author: Human Pharmacology: Molecular to Clinical, 1998 (Excellence award PhRMA Found. 2000). Biomed. rsch. grantee NIH, 1981—; postdoctoral fellow U. Colo. Med. Ctr., Denver, 1977-80. Mem. AAAS, Am. Soc. Pharm. & Exptl. Therapeutics (exec. coun. 1999-2002), Soc. Neurosci., Internat. Soc. Neurochem. Home: 206 Eleventh St Atlanta GA 30309 Office: Emory U 1510 Clifton Rd Atlanta GA 30322 Fax: 404-727-0365. E-mail: kminneman@pharm.emory.edu.

MINNER, RUTH ANN, governor; b. Milford, Del., Jan. 17, 1935; m. Roger Minner (dec.). Student Del. Tech. and Community Coll. Office receptionist Gov. of Del., 1972-74; mem. Del. Ho. of Reps., 1974-82; mem. Del. Senate, 1982-92; lt. gov. State of Del., Dover, 1993-2001, gov., 2001—. Mem. Dem. Nat. Com., 1988. Office: Office Gov William Penn St Tatnall Bldg 3d Fl Dover DE 19901

MINNER, THOMAS O. marketing executive; b. Chgo., Jan. 3, 1956; s. Robert Schermerhorn and Arleen Minner; m. Mary Anderson; children: Allison, Brent, Courtney, Drew, Summer, Annie. BS in Bus. Adminstrn., U. Ill., 1978; MBA, Northwestern U., 1980. Mktg. mgmt. trainee PPG Industries, Inc., Pitts., 1978-79; market devel. mgr. Gould Inc., Mpls., 1980-89; v.p., gen. mgr. Automotive Battery Div. GNB, Inc., Atlanta, 1990-96; pres., CEO GNB Technologies, Inc., 1997-2000; pres. Transp. Bus. Group, Exide Tech., 2000—02, Champion Performance Products, LLC, 2002—. Bd. dirs. Students in Free Enterprise. Mem. Battery Coun. Internat. (bd. dirs.). Home: 3485 Newport Bay Dr Alpharetta GA 30005-7820 Office: Champion Performance Products LLC 13000 Deerfield Pkwy Alpharetta GA 30004

MINNERLY, ROBERT WARD, retired headmaster; b. Yonkers, N.Y., Mar. 21, 1935; s. Richard Warren and Margaret Marion (DeBrocky) M.; m. Sandra Overmire, June 12, 1957; children: Scott Ward, John Robert, Sydney Sue. AB, Brown U., 1957; MAT, U. Tex., Arlington, 1980. Tchr., coach Rumsey Hall Sch., Washington, 1962-64, Berkshire Sch., Sheffield, Mass., 1964-70, asst. head, 1969-70, headmaster, 1970-76; dir. Salisbury (Conn.) Summer Sch. Reading and English, 1970; prin. upper sch. Ft. Worth Country Day Sch., 1976-86; headmaster Charles Wright Acad., Tacoma, 1986-96; edn. cons. The Edn. Group, 1996-2000; interim dir. Harold E. LeMay Mus., 2001—02. Cons. Tarrant County Coalition on Substance Abuse, 1982-84; mem. mayor's task force Tacoma Edn. Summit, 1991-92. Contbr. articles to profl. jours. Bd. dirs. Tacoma/Pierce County Good Will Games Art Coun., 1989, Multicare Found., Tacoma, 2002; mem. exec. com. Am. Leadership Forum, 1991-95; bd. dirs. Broadway Ctr. for Performing Arts, Tacoma, 1988-94, 96-98, mem. exec. com., 1990-93; elected Wash. State Bd. Edn., 1996-2001; bd. dirs. Tacoma Youth Choir, 2000—. Named Adminstr. of Yr. Wash. Journalism Edn. Assn., 1991; recipient Columbia award, Wash. Fedn. Ind. Schs., 2000. Mem. Pacific N.W. Assn. Ind. Schs. (chmn. long-range planning com. 1989-92, exec. com. 1990-92, 91, v.p. 1994). Republican. Presbyterian. Home and Office: 4214 39th Avenue Ct NW Gig Harbor WA 98335-8029

MINNERS, HOWARD ALYN, physician, research administrator; b. Rockville Center, N.Y., Sept. 1, 1931; s. Howard A. and Marie Henriette (Soberski) M.; m. Gretchen Paffenbarger, Oct. 25, 1958; children: Todd, Bradford. AB, Princeton U., 1953; MD, Yale U., 1957; MPH, Harvard U., 1960. Diplomate Am. Bd. of Preventive Medicine; cert. Nat. Bd. of Med. Examiners. 2d. lt. USAF, 1956; intern Wilford Hall USAF Hosp., San Antonio, 1957-58; resident

Sch. of Aerospace Medicine, USAF, Brooks AFB, Tex., 1960-62; advanced through grades to maj. USAF, 1966; advanced through grades to rear adm. USPHS, ret., 1987; dir. office rsch. promotion and devel. WHO, Geneva, Switzerland, 1977-80; dir. Office of Sci. Advisor Agy. Internat. Devel., Washington, 1981-91; dep. dir. Office Internat. Health USPHS and Asst. Surgeon Gen., 1980-81. Assoc. dir. NIH Nat. Inst. of Allergy and Infectious Diseases, 1966-77; astronaut flight surgeon NASA, Houston, 1962-66. Pres. Model A Ford Found., 1994-2000. Fellow World Acad. Art and Sci., Am. Coll. Preventive Medicine; mem. AAAS, Internat. Found. Sci. Stockholm (pres., chmn. bd. trustees 1991-97). Avocations: antique automobile restoration, advertising history. E-mail: Minndax@aol.com.

MINNESTE, VIKTOR, JR. retired electrical company executive; b. Haapsalu, Estonia, Jan. 15, 1932; s. Viktor and Alice (Lembra) M. BSEE, U. Ill., 1960. Elec. engr. Bell & Howell Co., 1960-69; microstatics divsn. A-M Co., 1969-71, multigraphics divsn., 1972-73; elec. engr. bus. products group Victor Comptometer Co. (merged with Walter Kidde Corp.), Chgo., 1973-74, svc. mgr. internat. group, 1974-75, supr. elecs. desing group, 1975-82; project engr. Warner Electric, 1982-84; systems engr. Barrett Elecs., 1984-85; phone engr. Williams Elecs., 1986-88; cons. engr., 1988-92; ind. contractor, 1993-95; ret., 1995. Pub. Motteid/Thoughts, 1962-68. Chmn. Estonian-Ams. Polit Action Com., 1968-72. With AUS, 1952-54. Home and Office: 3134 N Kimball Ave Chicago IL 60618-6856

MINNICH, DIANE KAY, legal association administrator; b. Iowa City, Feb. 17, 1956; d. Ralph Maynard Minnich and Kathryn Jane (Obye) Tompkins. BA in Behavioral Sci., San Jose State U., 1978. Tutorial program coord./instr. Operation SHARE/La Valley Coll., Van Nuys, Calif., 1979-81; field exec. Silver Sage Girl Scout Coun., Boise, Idaho, 1981-85; continuing legal edn. dir. Idaho State Bar/Idaho Law Found. Inc., 1985-88, dep. dir., 1988-90, exec. dir., 1990—. Mem. adv. bd. legal asst. program Boise State U. Mem. Assn. CLE Adminstrs., Chgo., 1985-90; bd. dirs. Silver Sage coun. Girl Scouts, Boise, 1990-93, 99-2001, mem. nominating com., 1990-94, 97-2001, chair nominating com., 1991-92; mem. legal asst. program adv. bd. Boise State U. Named one of Outstanding Young Women in Am., 1991. Mem. Nat. Orgn. Bar Execs. (membership com. 1992-97, chair 1996-97), Zonta Club Boise (pres. 1991-92, bd. dirs. 1989-93), Rotary Club Boise (chair mem. com. 1994-97, bd. dirs. 1996-97, 99—). Avocations: softball, jogging, golf. Office: Idaho State Bar Idaho Law Found PO Box 895 525 W Jefferson St Boise ID 83702-5931

MINNICH, NELSON HUBERT JOSEPH, historian, educator; b. Cin., Jan. 15, 1942; s. Hubert Jakob Matthäus and Alberta Mary Rosella (Pfadt) M. AB in Philosophy, Boston Coll., 1965, MA in History, 1969; STB in Theology, Gregorian U., 1970; PhD in History, Harvard U., 1977. Instr. Loyola Acad., Wilmette, Ill., 1966-68; teaching fellow, asst. Harvard U., Cambridge, Mass., 1972-76; instr. Cath. U. of Am., Washington, 1977, asst. prof., 1977-83, assoc. prof., 1983-93, prof., 1993—. Chmn. Dept. Ch. History, 1978-79, 87-89, 98—. Co-editor: Studies in Catholic History in Honor of John Tracy Ellis, 1985; author: The Fifth Lateran Council (1512-17): Studies on Its Membership, Diplomacy, and Proposals for Reform, 1993, The Catholic Reformation: Council, Churchmen, and Controversies, 1993; assoc. editor The Cath. Hist. Rev., 1977-90; editor Melville Studies in Church History, 1988—; assoc. editor: (for ch. history materials) The Encyclopedia of the Renaissance, 6 vols., 1999; contbr. chpts to books, articles to profl. jours. Grantee, Soc. Internat. Historiae Conciliorum Investigandae, 1982, 84, 86, 87, 90, 97, Am. Philos. Soc., 1984, NEH, 1978, Am. Coun. Learned Socs., 1986, Cath. Univ. Am. faculty rsch., 1981, 90, 93-97, 01; sr. scholar, Renaissance Soc. Am., 2001; travelling fellow Harvard U., 1973-74, Villa I Tatti: The Harvard U. Ctr. for Italian Renaissance, 1979, Am. Acad. in Rome, 1979-80, Am. Coun. Learned Socs., 1979-80, 1990, NEH, 1986; tchg. scholar Harvard U., 1971-76, Richard Krautheimer, 1980, Carl Meyer prize, 1977. Mem. Am. Cath. Hist. Assn., Gesellschaft zur Herausgabe des Corpus Catholicorum, Erasmus of Rotterdam Soc., Sixteenth Century Studies Conf., Renaissance Soc. Am. Avocations: dancing, local politics, gardening, travel, genealogy. Home: 5713 37th Ave Hyattsville MD 20782-3821 Office: Cath U of Am 417 Caldwell Hl Washington DC 20064-0001 E-mail: minnich@cua.edu.

MINNICK, BRUCE ALEXANDER, lawyer; b. New London, Conn., Apr. 16, 1943; s. Robert Wood Minnick and Nedra Louise (Alexander) Wiesman; m. Judith Anita Saxon, Sept. 23, 1967 (div. 1981); children: Audra Anne, Lisa Michelle; m. Charlotte Ann Springfield, Apr. 10, 1983 (div. 1991); 1 child, Matthew Alexander; m. Debra C. Williams, July 3, 1997; 1 stepchild, Brandy Michelle Williams. AA, Broward Community Coll., 1970; BS with honors, Fla. State U., 1971, JD, 1977. BarL Fla. 1978, U.S. Dist. Ct. (no. dist.) Fla. 1979, U.S. Dist. Ct. (mid. and so. dists.) Fla. 1982, U.S. Supreme Ct. 1981, U.S. Ct. Appeals (11th cir.) 1982, U.S. Tax Ct. 1983, U.S. Ct. Claims 1983, U.S. Dist. Ct. (ea. dist.) Mich. 1990. Staff dir., counsel rules com. Fla. Ho. Reps., Tallahassee, 1976-78; v.p., gen. counsel Fla. Credit Union League, 1978-80; asst. atty. gen. dep. legal affairs State of Fla., 1981-86; ptnr. Mang, Rett & Collette, P.A., 1986-93, Mang, Rett & Minnick PA, Tallahassee, 1994-95; pvt. practice Bruce A. Minnick PA, 1996—. Chief adv. Fla. Commn. on Ethics, 1995-96; lectr. state agys., 1982—, Fla. Bar, 1986—; v.p. for fin., gen. counsel UCompass.com, Inc.. Mem. Leon County Dist. Adv. Com., 1980-82, 92-94; mem. exec. com. Leon County Dems., 1984-2000.—. Mem. ABA (labor sect., local govt. and law sect.), Fla. Bar Assn. (chmn. com. labor sect. 1987-91, mem. exec. coun. labor sect. 1989-93, founding chmn. Fed. Ct. practice com. 1990-92, del. to 11th Cir. Jud. Conf. 1990-92, com. chmn. govt. lawyer sect. 1991-2000—, rep. mem. pub. rels. com. 1991-93), Tallahassee Bar Assn., Fa. Govt. Bar Assn., Fla. Women Lawyers Assn., Fed. Bar Assn. (pres.-elect Tallahassee chpt. 1995, pres. 1996), Govs. Club, Univ. Ctr. Club, Golden Eagle Country Club, Phi Alpha Delta. Christian Scientist. Avocations: golf, astronomy, writing. Home: 9017 Eagles Ridge Dr Tallahassee FL 32312-4046 Office: 3116 Capital Cir NE Ste 10 PO Box 15588 Tallahassee FL 32317-5588 Fax: 850-385-8414. E-mail: minnicklaw@prodigy.net.

MINNICK, DAVID MICHAEL, lawyer; b. Las vegas, Nev., Apr. 24, 1956; s. Carl Wallace and Myrtle Ada (Perry) M.; m. Nancy Sue Grosse. BS in Agrl. Journalism, U. Mo., 1978, JD, 1981. Agt. real estate and ins. Phillips Petroleum Co., Odessa, Tex., 1981; asst. cir. atty. Cirt. Atty.'s Office, St. Louis, 1982-85; pvt. practice Troy, Mo., 1985-86; asst. pros. atty., 1985-86; litigation counsel, assoc. v.p. A.G. Edwards & Sons, St. Louis, 1986-90; mng. dir., gen. counsel Morgan Keegan & Co., Memphis, 1990-98; pvt. practice Kansas City, Mo., 1998-2000; sr. regional atty. NASD Regulation, Inc., 2000—. Arbitrator NASDR, N.Y. Stock Exch., Am. Stock Exch., 1995—; litigation adv. com. The Bond Mkt. Assn., 1997—. Contbr. articles to profl. jours. Bd. dirs. YMCA, Memphis, 1993-96; vol. Teach for a Day Programs, Memphis Ptnrs., 1994-96. Mem. Securities Industry assn. (legal and compliance div.), Econ. Club of Memphis, Masons, Shriner. Avocations: ranching, farming, running, hunting, college football. Office: NASD Regulation Inc 120 W 12th St Ste 900 Kansas City MO 64105

MINNICK, GEORGE RICHARD, retired dentist; b. Akron, Ohio, Nov. 13, 1928; s. George Harold and Mildred (May) Minnick; m. Norma Lee Hicks, Feb. 20, 1931; 1 stepchild Thomas Hicks Downs. DDS, U. Md., 1954. Lic. dentist Colo., Md. Pvt. practice, Denver, 1954—56, Williamsport, Md., 1958—94; ret., 1994. Author: The Wald, 1998, Poor Pockets, 1998, Tyler, 1998, The Bugle Calls, 1999, Shandrydan, 2000. Capt. U.S. Army, 1956—58. Mem.: Antique Automobile Club Am. (life; sec.-treas. 1972—74). Republican. Methodist. Avocations: antique cars, writing. Home: 124 Village Oak Dr Salisbury MD 21804

MINNICK, MALCOLM DAVID, lawyer; b. Indpls., July 5, 1946; s. Malcolm Dick and Frances Louise (Porter) M.; m. Heidi Rosemarie Klein, May 24, 1972. BA, U. Mich., 1968, JD, 1972. Bar: Calif. 1972, U.S. Dist. Ct. (cen. dist.) Calif. 1972, U.S. Ct. Appeals (9th cir.) 1984, U.S. Dist. Ct. (no. dist.) Calif. 1986, U.S. Supreme Ct. 1986. Assoc. Lillick McHose & Charles, Los Angeles, 1972-78; ptnr. Lillick & McHose, 1978-91, Pillsbury Winthrop LLC, San Francisco, 1991—. Group mgr. Creditors Rights and Bankruptcy Group, 1993-98; panelist Calif. Continuing Edn. of Bar, L.A., 1982-86, 88, Practicing Law Inst., 1992, 93, 94, Banking Law Inst., 1999, 2000; bd. govs. Fin. Lawyers Conf., L.A., 1981-84; mem. exec. com. Lillick & McHose, 1982-85. Co-author: Checklist for Secured Commercial Loans, 1983. Pres. Ross Sch. Found., 1997-98. Mem. ABA (corp., banking and bus. law sect.), Calif. Bar Assn. (Uniform Comml. Code com. 1983-86), L.A. County Bar Assn. (exec. com. comml. law and bankruptcy sect. 1987-90), Bar Assn. San Francisco (comml. law and bankruptcy sect.), L.A. Country Club, Univ. Club (bd. dirs. 1983-86, pres. 1985-86). Avocation: golf. Office: Pillsbury Winthrop LLC 50 Fremont St San Francisco CA 94105-2230 E-mail: dminnick@pillsburywinthrop.com.

MINNIGH, JOEL DOUGLAS, library director; b. Greenville, Pa., Apr. 9, 1949; s. Wendell Ellsworth and Frances Alene (Hyde) M.; m. Margaret Beth Crowther, Dec. 26, 1972; children: Bradley Dean, Douglas Knox. BA, Allegheny Coll., 1971; MLS, U. Pitts., 1975. Cert. libr., Pa. Asst. libr. Wilkinsburg (Pa.) Pub. Libr., 1976-77, head libr., 1977—. Bd. dirs. Goodwill Industries Pitts., 1980-90, Mulberry Sr. Citizens Ctr., Wilkinsburg, Pa., 2001--; vice chmn. bd. dirs. Bach Choir Pitts., 1984-87; sec., bd. dirs. United Meth. Ch. Union, Pitts., 1987-88; elder, deacon Fox Chapel Presbyn. Ch., 1987—, soloist, 1998—. Recipient honor Goodwill Industries Pitts., 1990, citation Pa. Senate, 1991. Mem. Pa. Libr. Assn. (treas. S.W. chpt. 1988-89), Allegheny County Libr. Assn. (pres. librs. adv. coun. 2001-02, bd. dirs. 2002--), Wilkinsburg C. of C. (dir. 1998—, sec. 1999—). Republican. Avocations: travel, cooking, gardening, music, reading. Home: 1009 Blackridge Rd Pittsburgh PA 15235-2719 Office: Wilkinsburg Pub Libr 605 Ross Ave Pittsburgh PA 15221-2145

MINNIX, BRUCE MILTON, television and theatre director; b. Hendersonville, N.C., Apr. 26, 1923; s. Bruce Milton and Jane Irene (Leverett) M.; m. Corinne McClure, Aug. 5, 1950; 1 child, Tracy Logue. BA, U. N.C., 1948. Mem. faculty New Sch., N.Y.C., 1977-80; adj. prof., Bklyn., 1985; AT&T sales tng. program, 1987. Dir. numerous TV shows including: U.S. Steel Hour, 1961-62, Merchant of Venice, 1962, Essay on Doors, 1963, Never Too Young, 1965-66, On Being Black, 1969, The Haggadah Oratorio, 1981, Search for Tomorrow, 1968-74, All My Children, 1978-79, Another World, 1981, Texas, 1981-82, Body Talk, 1983, As the World Turns, 1985-86; The Cradle Will Rock, 1986 (Emmy nomination), Minolta Tng. series Minolta Info. Network, 1980-81; dir. Citibank, 1984, N.J. Bell (AT&T), 1985; dir. Victorian Cape May A Video Visit to a Town out of Time, 1988 (medal Houston Film Festival), dir. Pitney Bowes Copier Intro 1992, Time Warner Cable 1991; producer, writer: Mt. Washington Valley, A Video Visit in Four Seasons, 1990; Actor: Music Video by Little Texas What Might Have Been, 1993. Mayor, City of Cape May, N.J., 1972-76; founding mem., 3-term pres. Mid-Atlantic Center for Arts. Served with USN, 1943-45. Mem. Dirs. Guild Am.

MINO, MICHAEL GEORGE, engineering executive; b. Buffalo, Oct. 9, 1954; s. George Michael and Rita Cecilia (DiGennaro) M.; m. Lynn Ann Barone, Apr. 12, 1986. BSEE, Rensselaer Polytechnic Inst., 1975, MSEE, 1976; MBA in Fin., Rochester Inst. Tech., 1978. Registered profl. engr., N.Y. Engr., supr. Eastman Kodak Co., Rochester, N.Y., 1974-82; exec. v.p., founder Ormec Systems Corp., 1982-90, also bd. dirs., chmn.; exec. v.p., gen. mgr. Vinton Inc., Henrietta, N.Y., 1990-92; v.p. engring. and quality Hansford Mfg. Corp., Rochester, 1992-99; CEO Object Factory, Greenville, S.C., 1999—. Chmn. investment rev. com. Tech Ventures; entrepreneur in residence Clemson Spiro Ctr., 2000—. Vice-chmn. Rensselaer Exec. Bd., Troy, N.Y., 1976; coord. Kodak Jr. Achievement, Rochester, 1980-82. Mem. IEEE, Rensselaer Alumni Assn. (pres. 1980-83), Jaycees (vice chmn. Rochester br., Key Leader award), Phalanx, Tau Beta Pi, Eta Kappa Nu. Avocations: alpine skiing, sailing, amateur radio (1st class radiotelephone lic.). Home: 110 Merrifield Ct Greenville SC 29615-3434 Office: Clemson U Box 341345 165 Sirrine Hall Clemson SC 29634-1345 E-mail: minom@attglobal.net.

MINOCHA, ANIL, physician, educator, researcher; b. India, Feb. 4, 1957; Came to U.S., 1982; s. Ram Saroop and Kamla Devi M. Pre-med. diploma, Punjab U., India, 1974; MD, Med. Coll., Rohtak, India, 1980; postgrad. studies in pharmacology, Baylor Coll. Medicine, 1982-84. Diplomate Am. Bd. Internal Medicine, Am. Bd. Gastroenterology, Am. Bd. Forensic Medicine, Am. Bd. Geriatric Medicine. House officer depts. ophthalmology and dermatology Med. Coll. Hosp., Rohtak, India, 1980-81; med. officer State Health Svcs. Govts. of Punjab and Haryana, India, 1981-82; rsch. asst. Baylor Coll. Med., Houston, 1982-84; fellow clin. pharmacology U. Va., Charlottesville, 1984-86; resident physician Franklin Square Hosp., Balt., 1986-89; fellow gastroenterology Mich. State U., East Lansing, 1989-91; asst. prof. U. Louisville, 1991-95; assoc. prof. medicine U. Okla., Oklahoma City, 1995-99, mem. faculty ctr. of toxicology, 1997-99, assoc. prof. geriatric medicine, 1998-99; chief gastroenterology So. Ill. U. Sch. Medicine, Springfield, 1999—2002; dir. divsn. digestive diseases U. Miss. Med. Ctr., Jackson, 2002—. Instr. dept. medicine Mich. State U., 1989-91; staff physician dept. medicine VAA Med. Ctr., Louisville, 1991-95; mem. credentials com. Humana Hosp., U. Louisville, 1992, other coms., 1992-94; mem. R&D com. VA Hosp., 1992-95; presenter in field; mem. pharmacy and therapeutics com. Heartland Health Plan, Oklahoma City, 1996—; mem. R&D com. VA Med. Ctr., Oklahoma City, 1996—, chmn. med. record com., 1996—; mem. world lit. rev. panel Am. Jour. Gastroenterology, 1996; mem. Formulary Adv. Coun. of the Okla. State Bd. of Nursing, 1997—. Author: The Gastroenterology Resident Pocket Survival Guide, 1999, Minocha's Guide to Digestive Diseases, 2000, How to Stop Heartburn, 2001; contbr. numerous articles to profl. jours. Prin. investigator Gulf Biosystems, Charlottesville, 1985; biomed. rsch. grantee Mich. State U., 1990; sch. medicine rsch. grantee U. Louisville, 1993. Fellow ACP, Am. Coll. Gastroenterology, Am. Coll. Forensic Examiners; mem. Am. Gastroenterol. Assn., Am. Assn. for Study of Liver Disease. Office: U Miss Med Ctr Divsn Digestive Diseases 2500 N State St Jackson MS 39216 Office Fax: 601-984-4548. E-mail: docwrite@aol.com.

MINOGUE, ROBERT BROPHY, retired nuclear engineer; b. Covington, Ky., Jan. 31, 1928; s. Joseph and Catherine Ann (Brophy) M.; m. Marie Joan Clarke, June 12, 1954; children: Patrick, Margaret, Marie, Francis. BS, Thomas More Coll., 1949; MS, U. Cin., 1951; grad., Oak Ridge Sch. Reactor Tech., 1952. Nuclear engr., then head nuclear tech. sect. naval reactors br. AEC, Washington, 1952-56; head research reactor design and engring., then head nuclear power plant engring. sect. Gen. Atomic div. Gen. Dynamics Corp., 1957-67; chief spl. projects br. div. reactor standards AEC, Washington, 1967-72, asst. dir., then dep. dir. regulatory standards, 1972-74; dir. office standards devel. Nuclear Regulatory Commn., 1975-80, dir. office research, 1980-86; pvt. practice Temecula, Calif., 1986—. U.S. mem. sr. adv. group Safety Standards IAEA, 1974-86; mem. Com. on Interagy. Radiation Research and Policy Coordination, 1982-86. Author: Reactor Shielding Design Manual, 1956; patentee: Triga Research Reactor. Served with AUS, 1946-48. Recipient Bernard F. Langer award, ASME, 1982. Roman Catholic. Home and Office: 29743 Marhill Cir Temecula CA 92591-1809

MINOR, CLARA MAE, election judge; b. Altapass, N.C., Dec. 3, 1931; d. David Wilkerson Sullins, and Carrie Mae Schism; m. Lawrence Alfred Minor, Oct. 27, 1950; children: Lawrence, Charles, Beverly, John. Grad. h.s., Canton, Ohio, 1949. Sales clk. JC Penney Co., Canton, 1973-80; presiding judge Stark County Election Bd., 1983—. Pres., mem. PTA, Hubbard, Ohio, 197-72. Mem. DAR, Daus. Am. Colonists, Daus. War of 1812. Republican. Methodist. Avocations: reading, collector ladies antique watches and compacts.

MINOR, EDWARD COLQUITT, paper company executive, lawyer; b. Balt., Dec. 1, 1942; s. Edward Essau and Mary Newell (Schultz) Minor; m. Joan Slade, Aug. 29, 1964; 1 child Elizabeth Colquitt. AB in Econ., Western Md. Coll., 1964; LLB cum laude, Boston U., 1967. Bar: Md. 1967, Ga. 1972, Va. 1974, U.S. Supreme Ct. Assoc. Semmes Bowen & Semmes, Balt., 1967-68; judge adv. U.S. Army, Savannah and Vietnam, 1968-72; assoc. Connerat Dunn & Hunter, Savannah, 1972-73; gsr. atty. Kraft Paper Union Camp Corp., 1973, asst. gen. counsel, asst. sec Fine Paper Franklin, Va., 1974-85, assoc. gen. counsel, asst. sec. Fine Paper, 1985-99, mgr. Fine Paper, 1988-95, divsn. procurement mgr. purchasing Fine Paper, 1995-99. Mem. citizens adv. bd. Va. Dept. Environ. Qualtiy. Mem. Gov.'s Commn. Efficiency, 1988; chmn. Franklin Constl. Bicentennial Commn.; chmn. bd. dirs. Southampton Acad., Courtland, Va., 1985—88; dep. mem. Va. Bus. Coun., 1985—88; chmn. citizens adv. bd. Va. Dept. Air Pollution Control, 1992, mem., 1993—99, Roundtable Environ. Standing, 1991; mem. exec. bd. Diocese S.E. Va., Episcopal Ch., 1985—89; vestryman Emmanual Episcopal Ch., Franklin, 1985, 1987, 1991; bd. dirs. Tidewater Heart Assn., Norfolk, Va., 1980—86, Future of Hampton Rds., Inc., Rawles Mus. Arts, 1992—93. Decorated Bronze Star. Fellow: Royal Soc. Encouragement Arts Am.; mem.: Va. Mfrs. Assn. (chmn. environ. affairs com. 1985—99, bd. dirs. 1994—95), Ga. BAr Assn., Md. Bar Assn., Va. Bar Assn. (co-chmn. corp. counsel sect. 1990—92, bd. govs. adminstrv. law sect., jud. com. 1997, bd. govs. copr. counsel sect. 1998—), Va. State BAr (chmn. environ. sect. 1990—91), Town Point Club, Norfolk Yacht Club, Rotary (pres.Franklin 1992—93). Home: 23456 Thomas Cir Courtland VA 23837-1336 E-mail: jminor@beldar.com.

MINOR, GEORGE GILMER, III, drug and hospital supply company executive; b. 1940; married. BA, Va. Mil. Inst., 1963; MBA, U. Va., 1966. With Owens & Minor, Inc., Richmond, Va., 1963—, mgr. sales Acme Candy Co. div., 1966-68, mgr. retail mktg., 1968-73, div. mgr. wholesale drug br., 1973-77, v.p., 1977-80, exec. v.p., 1980-81, pres. 1981-1999, chmn. 1994-, CEO, 1981—, also bd. dirs. Office: Owens & Minor Inc 4800 Cox Rd Glen Allen VA 23060-6292*

MINOR, JOSEPH EDWARD, civil engineer, educator; b. Corpus Christi, Tex., June 2, 1938; s. William Smoot Jr. and Irene (Schiller) M.; m. Treva Ann Edmiston, Sept. 3, 1960; children: Joseph Edward Jr., Sharon Diane. BSCE, Tex. A&M U., 1959, M of Engring., 1960; PhD, Tex. Tech U., 1974. Registered profl. engr., Tex., Mo., Fla. Sr. rsch. engr. Southwest Research Inst., San Antonio, 1962-69; P. Whitfield Horn prof. Tex. Tech U., Lubbock, 1969-88; Thomas Reese prof., chmn. dept. civil engring. U. Mo., Rolla, 1988-93, rsch. prof., 1993—. Pres. Insulating Glass Cert. Council, N.Y., 1986-89. Contbr. articles to profl. jours. Served with USAR. Recipient Disting. Engr. award Tex. Tech U., 1989, Disting. Svc. award Nat. Hurricane Conf., 1999; Nat. Def. fellow, 1959-60; Fulbright scholar, 1978. Fellow ASCE (pres. Tex. sect. 1984-85); mem. Nat. Soc. Profl. Engrs., Am. Meteorol. Soc. Presbyterian. Avocation: fishing. Office: Joseph E Minor PE Consulting Engineer PO Box 603 Rockport TX 78381-0603 E-mail: joeminor@dbstech.com.

MINOR, JOYCE DONALDSON, marketing professional; b. Traverse City, Mich., Aug. 5, 1949; BA in English, Cen. Mo. State U., 1991. Various journalism positions to mktg. coord. Kimley-Horn Engrs., Dallas, 1993—97; mag. editor U. Ala. Law Sch., Tuscaloosa, 1998—2000; mktg. comms. profl. AFFLINK, 2000—. Editor: (books) Glossaries of Video Terms, 1995; contbr. articles. Baptist. Avocation: praise team singer, internet entrepreneur, freelance writer.

MINOR, LISA, research scientist; b. New London, Conn., May 25, 1956; d. Alfred and Doris Webb; m. Keith Demarest. PhD, Penn. State U., Hershey, 1979—85. Postdoctoral fellow Med. Coll. of Penn., Philadelphia, 1986—89; sr. scientist RWJohnson PRI, Raritan, NJ, 1989—94; prin. scientist Johnson & Johnson Pharm. R & D, 1994—. Sci. advisor IBC, Boston, 2001. Mem.: Soc. Biomolecular Screening (coun. mem. 2000), Endocrine Soc., Am. Soc. Diabetes. Office: Johnson and Johnson Pharm R & D Welsh and McKean Rds Spring House PA 19477-0776

MINOR, MARIAN THOMAS, elementary and secondary school educational consultant; b. Richmond, Va., Apr. 16, 1933; d. James Madison and Florence Elwood (Edwards) M. BS, U. Va., 1955; MEd, William and Mary Coll., 1968; postgrad., Va. Commonwealth U., 1987-88. Cert. guidance, health and phys. edn. Educator Richmond (Va.) Pub. Schs., 1955-90, ednl. cons., 1990—. Educator Sch. Nursing Med. Coll. Va., Richmond, 1958-68; camp dir. Manakin, Va., 1956-68; nat. basketball ofcl. Richmond (Va.) Bd. Ofcls., 1952-77; mem. faculty adv. com. Albert Hill Middle Sch., Richmond, 1965-90, dept. chmn., 1960-90, Tchr. of Yr., 1980; textbook adoption Richmond (Va.) Pub. Sch., 1975, 85, curriculum planner, 1978-79, 82-83, 84-85; PTA coord. Albert Hill Middle Sch., Richmond, 1985-89, chmn. self-study and accreditation team, 1987-88. Mem. Sherwood Park Civic Assn., Richmond, 1960-98; v.p. alumni weekend Mary Washington Alumni Assn., Fredericksburg, Va., 1965, 66, v.p. annual giving, 1967; chmn. basketball ofcl. examiners Richmond Bd. Women Ofcls., 1966-76; bd. dirs., homeowner adv., constrn. crewman, family svcs. com. Habitat for Humanity, 1994-2002, Blitz Build 2000 adv. chmn.; mem. exec. com. Northminster Bapt. Ch., 1991-94, 99-2002, deacon, clk., 97-99, worship team, 1999—, promises chair, 1991-94, mem. by-laws revision com., 1986, 98, 99, srs. task force chmn., v.p., sr. fellowship, regional Befriender Ministry adv. coun. Recipient J.C. Penney Golden Rule award, 1996, Outstanding Vol. award Habitat for Humanity, 1998, Outstanding Svc. award Albert Hill PTA, 1988. Mem. AAUW, AAHPERD, Va. Health Phys. Edn. Assn., Va. Ret. Tchrs. Assn., Train Collectors Assn., King and Queen Hist. Soc., Mortar Bd., Alpha Phi Sigma, Kappa Delta Pi. Republican. Avocations: gardening, genealogy, local history, historical preservation, antiques. Home and Office: 1507 Brookland Pky Richmond VA 23227-4707

MINOR, ROBERT ALLEN, lawyer; b. Washington, Oct. 20, 1948; s. Robert Walter and Joan (Allen) M.; m. Sue Ellyn Blose, June 13, 1981; children: Robert Barratt, Sarah Allen. AB in English, Duke U., 1970; JD, Ohio State U., 1975. Bar: Ohio 1975, U.S. Dist. Ct. (so. dist.) Ohio 1976, D.C. 1979. Assoc. Vorys, Sater, Seymour & Pease, LLP, Columbus, Ohio, 1975-82, ptnr., 1982—. Author seminar articles. With U.S. Army, 1970-72. Mem. Ohio Bar Assn., Columbus Bar Assn., Athletic Club Columbus, Scioto Country Club. Republican. Presbyterian. Office: Vorys Sater Seymour & Pease LLP PO Box 1008 52 E Gay St Columbus OH 43215-3161

MINOR, RONALD RAY, minister; b. Aliceville, Ala., Nov. 3, 1944; s. Hershel Ray and Minnie Ozell (Goodson) M.; m. Gwendolyn Otella Newsome, July 25, 1970; 1 child, Rhonda Rene. BA in Ministerial, Southeastern Bible Coll., 1971, BA in Secondary Edn., 1973; DDiv, Southern Bible Coll., 1984. Ordained to ministry Pentecostal Ch. of God, 1968. Gen. sec. Pentecostal Ch. of God, Joplin, Mo., 1979—, dist. supt. Philadelphia, Miss., 1975-79, pastor Bartow, LaBelle, Fla., Orient Park Tabernacle, Tampa. Pres. Pentecostal Young People's Assn., Fla. and Miss.; sec. Gen. Bd. Pentecostal Ch. of God, Joplin, 1979; bd. dirs. Nat. Assn. Evangs., Wheaton, Ill., 1981-96; adv. coun. Am. Bible Soc., N.Y.C., 1979—; sec. Commn. Chaplains, Washington, 1991-95. Home: 2625 Markwardt Joplin MO 64801-5353 Office: Pentecostal Ch of God 4901 Pennsylvania Ave Joplin MO 64804-4947

MINOR, WILLIAM HENNING, lawyer; b. Washington, May 23, 1967; s. Robert Center and Carole Jean (Swanson) M.; m. Christine E. Enemark, Oct. 10, 1998. BA magna cum laude, Tufts U., 1989; JD, Columbia U., 1995. Bar: Md. 1995, D.C. 1996. Legis. asst. to Rep. Edward J. Markey, Washington, 1989-92; assoc. Verner, Liipfert, Bernhard, McPherson & Hand, 1995—. Editor-in-chief Columbia Jour. Law & Social Problems, 1994-95. Mem. ABA, Md. Bar Assn., Bar Assn. D.C. Democrat. Presbyterian. Office: Verner Liipfert Bernhard McPherson & Hand 901 15th St NW Ste 600 Washington DC 20005-2306

MINOR, WILLIE, college department chair; b. Navasota, Tex., Jan. 31, 1951; s. Carl Jr. and Marjorie (Williams) M. BS, Prairie View A&M U., 1973, MS, 1974; MA, U. Phoenix, 1980; EdD, Ariz. State U., 1976. Assoc. prof. bus. Prairie View (Tex.) A&M U., 1976-77; coord., prof. bus. Phoenix Coll., Phoenix, 1977-87, prof. bus., dept. chair, 1987-89, assoc. dean of instrn., 1989-96. Pres. Maricopa C.C. Faculty Exec. Coun., 1999-2000. Bd. dirs. Jr. Achievement, Phoenix, 1995-96, Future Devel. Edn. & Performing Arts Acad., Phoenix, 1995-96. Mem. Ariz. Occupational Adminstrn. Coun. (pres. 1989—), Maricopa Coun. on Black Am. Affairs, Phi Delta Kappa, Delta Mu Delta, Pi Omega Pi, Phi Beta Lambda. Democrat. Avocations: reading, hunting, fishing. Home: 6442 W Fremont Rd Laveen AZ 85339-9772 Office: Phoenix Coll 1202 W Thomas Rd Phoenix AZ 85013-4208 E-mail: willie.minor@riomail.maricopa.edu.

MINOSHIMA, SATOSHI, radiologist, researcher; b. Tokyo, Japan, Nov. 23, 1962; s. Ichiro and Shizuko Minoshima; m. Yoshimi Anzai, July 11, 1991; 1 child Erika. MD, Chiba U. Sch. of Medicine, Japan, 1987; PhD, Chiba U. Sch. of Medicine, 1994. Diplomate Japanese Bd. of Medicine 1987, cert. ECFMG 1993, diplomate Japanese Bd. of Radiology 1993, Am. Bd. of Nuc. Medicine 1998. Asst. prof. internal medicine U. of Mich., Ann Arbor, 1994—98, assoc. prof. of internal medicine, 1998—2000; prof. of radiology U. of Wash., Seattle, 2000—02; adj. prof. of radiology U. of Mich., Ann Arbor, 2000—. Cons. Nuclearmed. Cliniic and Polytech Clinic, U. Munich, Germany, 1993—2000, Hamamatsu Med. Ctr. / Advanced Med. Imaging Ctr., Hamamatsu, Shizuoka, Japan, 1997—2002. Recipient Young Scientist Travel Award, Organizing Com. of Internat. Symposium on Quantification of Brain Function, 1993, Best 10 Abstract Award, Dept. Internal Medicine, U. of Mich.,

1993, Disting. Achievement Award, Divsn. Nuc. Medicine, U. of Mich., 1994, Henry Wagner, Jr. Award, Inst. Advanced Med. Tech., 1999. Mem.: AMA, Japanese Radiol. Soc., Japanese Soc. Nuc. Medicine (33d Nuc.Medicine award 1995), Soc. of Nuc. Medicine (Tetelman award 1996). Office: Univ Wash 1959 N.E. Pacific Street, Box 356004 Seattle WA 98195-6004 Office Fax: 206-598-4192. Business E-Mail: minoshim@u.washington.edu.

MINOT, STEPHEN, writer; b. Boston, May 27, 1927; s. William and Elizabeth Howard Chapman M.; m. Mollie Minot, 1949 (div. 1952); 1 child, Reid; m. Virginia S. Minot, Feb. 18, 1955; children: Nicholas William, Chrystos Bailey. AB, Harvard Coll., 1951; MA, Johns Hopkins U., 1955. Instr. Bowdoin Coll., Brunswick, Maine, 1955-57, asst. prof., 1957-58; vis. asst. prof. U. Conn., Hartford, 1958-59, Trinity Coll., Hartford, 1959-61, lectr., 1961-65, asst. prof., 1965-69, adj. assoc prof., 1969-72, assoc. prof. part-time, 1972-77, prof. part-time, 1977-89; prof., chair U. Calif., Riverside, 1990-95, prof. emeritus, 1995—. Author: Chill of Dusk, 1964, Three Genres, 1965, Ghost Images, 1979, Surviving the Flood, 1981, Reading Fiction, 1984; co-editor: Three Stances of Modern Fiction, 1965; author many short stories; contbr. articles to profl. jours. With Army Air Corps, 1945-46. Recipient Atlantic First The Atlantic Monthly, 1962; Saxton Meml. fellowship Eugene F. Saxton Meml. Found., 1963, fellowship for writing Nat. Endowment for the Arts, 1976-77, 81-82. Mem. Authors Guild. Democrat. Avocations: forest management, boating. Home: 2225 Mt Vernon Ave Riverside CA 92507 Office: Dept Creative Writing U Calif Riverside CA 92521 E-mail: s.minot@juno.com.

MINOTTI, DIANA LYNN, art appraiser, consultant; b. Bronx, Aug. 30, 1964; d. Joseph John and Carol Diana (Kavanaugh) M. BFA, Coll. New Rochelle, 1986; MA, Fashion Inst. Tech., 1989. Salesperson Art & Blueprint, New Rochelle, N.Y., 1982; adminstrv. asst. Gracie Mansion Gallery, N.Y.C., 1984-86; exec. asst. A.R.E. Fine Art, Scarsdale, N.Y., 1985-87; v.p. mktg., cons. appraiser Fine Art Resources, Inc., N.Y.C., 1987-94; pres., cons., appraiser DMG Fine Art, Inc., 1993—; asst. dir. New World Art Ctr., 1997—; adj. prof. Coll. of New Rochelle. Instr. Pelham (N.Y.) Art Ctr., 1994—, Westchester Conservatory Music, White Plains, N.Y., 1996—; bd.dirs. Castle Gallery, Coll. New Rochelle; lectr. in field; licensed by city of N.Y. Dept. of Consumer Affairs, Sightseeing Tour Guide. Presenter of Art Appreciation Slide Lecture Series Art Theory at area nursing homes. Mem. NAFE, Profl. Picture Framers Assn., Guides Assn. N.Y. Avocations: dancing, food, history, fashion of cultures. Home: Beauchamp Gardens 151 Centre Ave New Rochelle NY 10805-3040 Office: Diana Minotti Fine Art Inc 111 E 14th St # 183 New York NY 10003-4103 E-mail: dmfa183@aol.com.

MINOTTI, MARK ANTHONY, chemistry educator; b. S.I., N.Y., July 23, 1974; s. Frank Thomas and Christine Marie (Palma) M. BS in Chemistry, Wagner Coll., 1996, MS in Edn., 1998; diploma in ednl. adminstrn./supervision, St. John's U., 1999, EdD in Instructional Leadership, 2001. Assoc. dir. music St. Charles Ch., S.I., 1992—; tchg. asst. Wagner Coll., 1993-96; instr. chemistry St. Joseph-by-the-Sea H.S., 1996-99; asst. prin. St. Francis de Sales and St. Lucy Acad., N.Y.C., 1999—. Author website Chemtacular.com, 1997. Asst. coord. St. Charles Sports Program, S.I., 1992—; mem. young people's forum Archdiocese N.Y., 1994. Megerle Sci. scholar Wagner Coll., 1993-96, Alumni scholar, 1996-98. Fellow Internat. Union Pure and Applied Chemistry; mem. ACS, ASCD, Nat. Sci. Tchrs. Assn., Nat. Assn. Secondary Sch. Prins. Republican. Roman Catholic. Avocation: music, piano, travel, reading, education. Office: St Francis de Sales and St Lucy Acad 116 E 97th St New York NY 10029-7201

MINOW, JOSEPHINE BASKIN, civic volunteer; b. Chgo., Nov. 3, 1926; d. Salem N. and Bessie (Sampson) Baskin; m. Newton N. Minow, May 29, 1949; children: Nell, Martha, Mary. BS, Northwestern U., 1948. Asst. to advt. dir. Mandel Brothers Dept. Store, Chgo., 1948-49; tchr. Francis W. Parker Sch., 1949-50; vol. in civil and charitable activities, 1950—; bd. dirs. Juvenile Protective Assn., Chgo., 1958—, pres., 1973-75. Bd. dirs. Parnham Trust, Beaminster, Dorset, Eng. Author: Marty the Broken Hearted Artichoke, 1997. Founder, coord. Children's div. Hospitality and Info. Svc., Washington, 1961-63; mem. Caucus Com., Glencoe, Ill., 1965-69; co-chmn. spl. study on juvenile justice Chgo. Community Trust, 1978-80; chmn. Know Your Chgo., 1980-83; bd. dirs. Chgo. Coun. Fgn. Rels.; trustee Chgo. Hist. Soc., Ravinia Festival Assn.; mem. women's bd. Field Mus., U. Chgo.; founding mem., v.p. women's bd. Northwestern U., 1978; bd. govs. Chgo. Symphony, 1966-73, 76— ; mem. Citizens Com. Juvenile Ct. of Cook County, 1985-96; exec. com. Northwestern U. Libr. Coun., 1974-96; co-chair grandparents' adv. com. Chgo. Children's Mus., 1999; bd. dirs. Jane Addams Juvenile Ct. Found. Recipient spl. award Chgo. Sch. and Workshop for Retarded, 1975, Children's Guardian award Juvenile Protective Assn., 1993. Mem. Hebrew Immigrant Aid Soc. (bd. dirs. 1977-98, award 1988), Friday Club, Northmoor Country Club, The Arts Club. Democrat. Jewish. Office: Chgo Hist Soc Clark St at North Ave Chicago IL 60614

MINOW, NEWTON NORMAN, lawyer, educator; b. Milw., Jan. 17, 1926; s. Jay A. and Doris (Stein) M.; m. Josephine Baskin, May 29, 1949; children: Nell, Martha, Mary. BS, Northwestern U., 1949, JD, 1950, LLD (hon.), 1965, U. Wis., Brandeis U., 1963, Columbia Coll., 1972, Govs. State U., 1984, De Paul U., 1989, RAND Grad. Sch., 1993, U. Notre Dame, 1994, Roosevelt U., 1996, Barat Coll., 1996, Santa Clara U. Sch. Law, 1998. Bar: Wis. 1950, Ill. 1950. With firm Mayer, Brown & Platt, Chgo., 1950-51, 53-55; law clk. to chief justice Fred. M. Vinson, 1951-52; adminstrv. asst. to Ill. Gov. Stevenson, 1952-53; spl. asst. to Adlai E. Stevenson in presdl. campaign, 1952, 56; ptnr. firm Stevenson, Rifkind & Wirtz, Chgo., N.Y.C. and Washington, 1955-61; chmn. FCC, Wash., 1961-63; exec. v.p., gen. counsel, dir. Ency. Brit., Chgo., 1963-65; ptnr. Sidley Austin Brown & Wood, 1965-91, counsel, 1991—. Former trustee, past chmn. bd., adv. trustee Rand Corp.; past chmn. Chgo. Ednl. TV; chmn. pub. rev. bd. Arthur Andersen & Co., 1974-83; chmn. bd. trustees Carnegie Corp. of N.Y., 1993-97, trustee, 1987-97; Annenberg U. prof. com. policy and law Northwestern U., 1987—; dir. Annenberg Washington Program, 1987-96. Author: Equal Time: The Private Broadcasters and the Public Interest, 1964; co-author: Presidential Television, 1973, Electronics and the Future, 1977, For Great Debates, 1987, Abandoned in the Wasteland: Children, Television, and the First Amendment, 1995; contbr.: Aw We Knew Adlai. Trustee Notre Dame U., 1964-77, 83-96, life trustee, 1996, Mayo Found., 1973-81; trustee Northwestern U., 1975-87, life trustee, 1987—; co-chmn. presdl. debates LWV, 1976, 80, presdl. debate commn., 1993—; bd. govs. Pub. Broadcasting Svc., 1973-80, chmn. bd., 1978-80; chmn. bd. overseers Jewish Theol. Sem., 1974-77; trustee Chgo. Orchestral Assn., 1975-87, life trustee, 1987—. With AUS, 1944-46. Named 1 of Am.'s 10 Outstanding Young Men 1961; recipient George Foster Peabody Broadcasting award, 1961; Ralph Lowell award, 1982 Fellow Am. Bar Found., Am. Acad. Arts and Scis.; mem. Northwestern U. Alumni Assn. (medal 1978), Comml. Club (pres. 1987-88), Chgo. Club, Century Club (N.Y.C.). Democrat. Office: Sidley Austin Brown & Wood Ste 4800 10 S Dearborn St Chicago IL 60603 E-mail: nminow@sidley.com.

MINSHALL, GREG, computer programmer; b. Carmel, Calif., Apr. 21, 1952; s. Glenn Almon and Martha Jane (Hardesty) M.; m. Maria Concepción Gonzalez, Dec. 30, 1976 (div. Jan. 1984); children: Matthew, Cecilia; m. Carol Ann Mendel, Oct. 4, 1987 (div. Feb. 1992); children: Oriana, Jacob. BA in Math., U. Calif., Berkeley, 1985. Computer programmer Stanford Linear Accelerator Ctr., Menlo Park, Calif., 1969-70, 72-73; computer programmer/engr. Inst. for Advanced Computation, Sunnyvale, 1978-80; computer programmer U. Calif., Berkeley, 1980-88; cons., 1984-88; computer programmer Novell, Inc., Walnut Creek, Calif., 1988-95, Ipsilon Networks, Inc., Mountain View, 1995—97; founder Siara Sys., 1998—2002. Mem. IEEE, Internet Engring. Task Force, Assn. for Computing Machinery, Usenix.

MINSKY, AARON GARR (AARON VON CELLO), musician, composer; b. Bklyn., Jan. 28, 1958; s. Harold Bernard and Pearl Gilda (Tisman) M.; m. Karen Susan Oberman, June, 27, 1998. MusB, Manhattan Sch. Music, N.Y.C., 1980, MusM, 1981. Performing guitarist. 1968—; performed as cellist with orchestras including Nat. Orchestral Assn., 1985, Va. Opera, 1983-84, Va. Philharmonic, 1983-84, Am. Philharmonic, 1982, Filarmonica de Caracas, Venezuela, 1981, (Broadway) Cats, Woman of the Year; performed as classical chamber cellist in venues including Carnegie Hall, N.Y.C., 1981, and WNCN N.Y. radio station, 1984; performing pop cellist with performers such as Tony Bennet, Roberta Peters and Mel Torme, and has performed for leaders of govt., industry, and the arts; performing rock cellist in venues such as SUNY, Potsdam, 2000, World Cello Congress III, Towson U., 2000, New Dirs. Cello Fest., U. Conn., 1998, 2000, 1982—; composing cellist, 1988—; conductor: Dirs. Orchestra N.Y. State Sch. Music Assn., Albany, 2001; author: A Rational Basis for the Traditional Jewish Faith; composer (music books): Ten American Cello Etudes, 1988, Three American Cello Duets, 1989, Three Concert Etudes for unaccompanied cello, 1990, Three American Pieces for unaccompanied viola, 1991, Young American Ensembles for violins and guitars, violas, and cellos and basses, 1995, Pacific Northwest Suite for guitars, violins, violas, cellos, basses, 1998, (video) So, You're Having a Baby (two-time Nova award), (documentary film) Dream City (Silver award for exptl. film in Houston Film Festival, 1989, Jury award in N.Y. Expn. short film and video, 1989) ; composer, singer, musician, prodr.(CDs): Breaking the Sound Barriers, 2000, Von Cello Rules, 2002; music included in curriculum of Associated Bd. Royal Schs. Mus, U.K., 1999, N.Y. State Sch. Music Assn., 1997, A Guide to the Standard Cello Repertoire, 2000. Mem. Com. for Accuracy in Reporting on the Middle East in Am., 2001; composer theme song Mothers March Against AIDS, Washington, 1994, S.I. Pageant, 1999, ten shows for Theatre Rehab. for Youth Theatre Co., 1983—99. Recipient two certs. merit song contest Billboard Mag., 1989, ASCAPLUS award ASCAP, 2000, 01. Mem.: NARAS (voting mem.), New Directions Cello Assn. (steering com.), Violoncello Soc., Am. Soc. Composers and Pubs., Am. Fedn. Musicians, Nat. Acad. Popular Music/Songwriters Hall of Fame, Friends of the Earth, Physicians for Social Responsibility. Avocations: hiking, reading, traveling. E-mail: voncello@voncello.com.

MINSKY, BRUCE WILLIAM, lawyer; b. Queens, N.Y., Sept. 28, 1963; m. Jill R. Heinter, May 1992; children: Aryeh Hanan, Elisheva Yael, Calev Betzalel, Refael Akiva. BA in Polit. Sci., Boston U., 1985; JD, Southwestern U., 1988; LLM in Am. Banking, Boston U., 1989. Bar: Calif. 1988, Conn. 1989, N.Y. 1990, U.S. Dist. Ct. (ea. and so. dist.), U.S. Ct. Appeals. Assoc. Quirk & Bakalor, N.Y.C., 1989-91; house counsel, v.p. Banco Popular N.Am., 1991—, Banco Poplur N. Am., 1999. Atty. Monday Night Law Pro Bono Svcs., N.Y.C. Mem. Assn. of Bar of City of N.Y. (mem. young lawyers com. 1993-95). Avocations: music, sports, literature. Office: 7 W 51st St New York NY 10019-6910

MINTCHELL, GARY ALAN, editor; b. Sidney, Ohio, Nov. 19, 1947; s. Jacque Eugene and Sandra Irene (Zwiebel) M.; m. Beverly Kay Moseley, June 12, 1970; children: Heather Lorelle, Derek Travis. BA, Ohio Northern U., 1969; postgrad., La. State U., 1970-71. Tchr. Delphos (Ohio) St. John Schs., 1969-70; product mgmt. Airstream div. Beatrice, Jackson Ctr., Ohio, 1971-80; quality assurance mgr. Questor Corp., Piqua, 1980-81; mgr. product devel. GLO Internat., Dayton, 1981-84; v.p. mktg. Cardinal Tool Corp., Engelwood, 1984-88; mgr. Eograph div. Eotron Corp., Dayton, 1988-89; pres. Success Solutions, Sidney, 1989-98; sr. editor Control Engring. mag., Oak Brook, Ill., 1998—. Mem. Sidney Sch. Bd., 1982-90. Mem. The Planning Forum, Sidney Jaycees (Outstanding Cmty. Svc. Award 1981), Soc. Mfg. Engrs. (sr.), Indsl. Computing Soc., Machine Vision Assn. Democrat. Methodist. Avocations: computers, golf, running, soccer official. Home: 1227 Colonial Dr Sidney OH 45365-3457 Office: Control Engring CPE Sidney OH 45365

MINTER, ALAN HUNTRESS, lawyer; b. San Antonio, Feb. 21, 1939; s. Merton Melrose Minter and Katherine Logan Huntress; m. Patricia West, May 31, 1964; children: Katherine Ruth, Patricia West. Student, Brown U., 1957-59; BA, U. Tex., 1962, JD, 1965. Bar: Tex., U.S. Supreme Ct., U.S. Tax Ct., U.S. Ct. Claims, U.S. Ct. Mil. Appeals, U.S. Ct. Customs and Patent Appeals, U.S. Ct. Appeals (5th cir.), U.S. Dist. Ct. (no., we., ea., so. dists.) Tex. Asst. atty. Atty. Gen.'s Office, State of Tex., Austin, 1965-71; pvt. practice, 1971—. Mem. nat. adv. com. Deganawidah Quetzalcoatl U., Davis, Calif., History Aviation Collection U. Tex., Austin; bd. dirs. Young Man's Bus. League, Austing, 1972, St. Andrew's Episcopal Sch. Austin, 1973-76, Tex. Hist. Found., 1983-85, Les Patrons Paramount Theatre Performing Arts, 1978-82; mem. ad hoc hist. zoning com. City of Austin, 1973; mem. citizen adv. com. Tex. Constl. Revision Com., 1973; bd. dirs. Austin Heritage Soc., 1974-81, chmn. properties com., 1975-76, co-chmn. properties com., 1976-77, 2d v.p., 1978-79; mem. steering com. Tex. Heritage Coun. Tex. Hist. Found., 1977-80, 81-83, v.p. edn., 1978-80; mem. adv. coun. Winedale Hist. Ctr. U. Tex., 1978-87, treas., 1984-85; vice-chmn. City Austin Tex. Libr. Commn., 1980-81, chmn., 1981-84; trustee Elisabet Ney Mus. Assn., 1980-81. Fellow Tex. Bar Found.; mem. ABA (vice chmn. 1981-85, hist. preservation and easement com. real property, probate and trust law sect.), ATLA, SCV, Comml. Law League Am., State Bar Tex., Sheriff's Assn. Tex. (assoc.), Tex. Old Fts. and Missions Restoration Assn., Old Trail Drivers Assn. Tex., State Assn. Tex. Pioneers, Sons Republic Tex., Travis County Bar Assn. (bd. dirs. chmn. estate planning and probate law sect. 1994-2001, bd. dirs. estate planning and probate law sect. 1995-96, bd. dirs. bankruptcy law sect. 2001—), Order Alamo, Order Sons Hermann State Tex., German Club, Phi Alpha Delta. Avocations: hunting, fishing, travel, reading, writing. Home: 1602 W Lynn St Austin TX 78703-3446

MINTER, DAVID LEE, English literature educator; b. Midland, Tex., Mar. 20, 1935; s. Kenneth Cruse and Frances (Hennessy) M.; m. Cynthia Caroline Sewell, Dec. 22, 1957; children: Christopher Sewell, Frances Elizabeth. BA, N. Tex. State U., 1957, MA, 1959; BD, Yale U., 1961, PhD, 1965. Univ. lectr. Hamburg (W. Ger.) U., 1965-66; lectr. Yale U., 1966-67; asst. prof. Rice U., Houston, 1967-69, assoc. prof., 1969-74, prof., 1974-80; prof. English Emory U., Atlanta, 1981-89, Asa G. Candler prof. Am. lit., 1989-90, dean Coll. Arts and Scis., 1981-90, v.p. arts and scis., 1984-90; Libbie Shearn Moody prof. English Rice U., Houston, 1990-99, interim vice provost, univ. libr., 1995-96, interim provost, 1999-2000, Bruce and Elizabeth Dunlevie prof. English, 1999—. Author: The Interpreted Design as a Structural Principle in American Prose, 1969, William Faulkner: His Life and Work, 1980, 82, 91, 97, French edit., 1984, Korean editn., 1999, A Cultural History of the American Novel: Henry James to William Faulkner, 1994, 96, Faulkner's Questioning Narratives: Fiction of the Major Phase, 2001; editor: Twentieth-Century Interpretations of Light in August, 1969, The Norton Critical Edit. of The Sound and the Fury, 1987, 93; co-editor: The Harper American Literature, 1986, 93, 96, 97, The Columbia Literary History of the United States, 1987 (Italian edit. 1990, Chinese edit. 1994, Japanese edit. 1997); also articles and revs. Fulbright Travel fellow, 1966; Nat. Endowment for Humanities fellow, 1969-70; Am. Council Learned Socs. grantee, 1975; Fred Harris Daniels fellow, 1980 Mem. MLA, Am. Lit. Group, Am. Studies Assn., Phi Beta Kappa. Methodist. Home: 2145 Swift Houston TX 77030-1215 Office: Rice U Dept English PO Box 1892 Houston TX 77251-1892

MINTER, GREGORY BYRON, lawyer, educator; b. Omaha, Dec. 6, 1940; s. Byron H. and Martha E. (Nelson) M.; m. Jane A. Baumhover, June 15, 1999; children: Deborah Anne, Brian Thomas, David Barton, Timothy J., Rhea A., Jordanna F. BSBA, Mcpl. U. Omaha, 1964; JD, Creighton U., 1965. Bar: Nebr. 1965, U.S. Supreme Ct. 1972. Assoc. Fitzgerald, Schorr, Barmettler & Brennan, P.C., Omaha, 1965-71, ptnr., 1971—. Adj. prof. Creighton U. Sch. Law, 1969—, U. Nebr. Sch. Law, 1981-86; dir., 1980-2000, v.p.-pres. elect, 1984-86, pres., 1986-88, chmn. curriculum com., publs. com., 1988-2000. Nebr. Continuing Legal Edn., Inc., 1980-86; dir. Nebr. Jud. Coll., chmn. seminars com., 1985-88; cons. U.S. Dept. Justice, 1981; mem. faculty SEC, 1969-98. Author legal publs. Pres. Omaha Ballet Soc., 1982-83, bd. dirs., 1980-84; v.p., sec. Omaha Symphony Coun., 1980-83, pres. 1983-84; bd. dirs. Omaha Symphony Assn., 1984-93, v.p. 1985-88, sec. 1988-90, pres. 1990-92; chairperson cmty. adv. bd. Sta. KVNO Pub. Radio, 1983-84; mem. Nebr. House of Dels., 1990—. Served to capt. JAGC, U.S. Army, 1967-78. Fellow Nebr. State Bar Found. (Outstanding Legal Educator award 1997); mem. Nebr. Bar Assn., Omaha Bar Assn., Nat. Assn. Bond Lawyers, Am. Immigration Lawyers Assn., Alpha Sigma Nu. Republican. Presbyterian. Home: 2331 N 53rd St Omaha NE 68104-4231 Office: Ste 400 13220 California St Omaha NE 68154-5228 E-mail: gminter@fitzlaw.com.

MINTER, JERRY BURNETT, electronic component company executive, engineer; b. Ft. Worth, Oct. 31, 1913; s. Claude Joe and Roxie (Ayers) M.; m. Monica Rose Hanlon, Mar. 2, 1940; children: Claude, Mark (dec.), Byron, Claire, Maureen. BSEE, MIT, 1934. Engr. Boonton (N.J.) Radio Corp., 1935-36, Ferris Instruments Co., Boonton, 1936-39; v.p., chief engr. Measurements Corp., 1939-53; pres. Components Corp., Denville, N.J., 1946—. Contbr. numerous articles to tech. jours; 23 patents in field. Pilot CAP, Morristown, N.J., 1947-50. Fellow IEEE (life, past chmn. No. N.J. sect.), Audio Engring. Soc. (past pres.), Radio Club Am. (life, pres. emeritus, past pres., Armstrong medal 1968); mem. AIAA, Am. Soc. for Metals (life), N.Y. Acad. Scis., Soc. Motion Picture and TV Engrs. (life), Internat. Soc. Photo-Optical Instrumentation Engrs., Quiet Birdmen. Home: 48 Normandy Heights Rd Morristown NJ 07960-4613 Office: Components Corp 6 Kinsley Pl Denville NJ 07834 E-mail: compcorp@garden.net.

MINTER, JIMMIE RUTH, accountant; b. Greenville, S.C., Sept. 28, 1941; d. James C. and Lois (Williams) Jannino; m. Charles H. Minter, Nov. 3, 1972; 1 child, Regina M.; stepchildren: Rhonda, Julie, Gregg; adopted child, Michael Minter. BS in Acctg., U. S.C., 1962. Asst. controller Package Supply & Equipment Co., Greenville, 1964-70, Olympia Knitting Mills, Spartanburg, S.C., 1970-72; controller Diacou Knitting Mills, 1972-74; adminstr. Atlanta Med. Specialists, P.C., Riverdale, Ga., 1974-79; adminstr., corp. sec. David L. Cooper, M.D., P.C., 1979-89; acct. Ted L. Griffin Enterprises, Jonesboro, Ga., 1988—; chief tax acct. Clayton County Tax Commn., 1993—. Program chmn. 4th of July Celebration and Beauty Pageant, City of Riverdale; mem. exec. com. Clayton County Dem. Party, 1987—; Ga. State Dem. treas.; active Clinton Campaign Com.; active local and state election campaign fund raising; bd. dirs. Clayton County Human Rels. Coun., Clayton County Alzheimer's Support Svcs.; chairperson Gold Sword Annual Ball Am. Cancer Soc. Home: 1244 Branchfield Ct Riverdale GA 30296-2148

MINTER, KENDALL ARTHUR, lawyer; b. N.Y.C., May 24, 1952; s. William Arthur and Jerolyn (Johnson) M.; m. Revola Fontaine, Sept. 29, 1954; children: Kamali, Namik, Amani. BA, Cornell U., 1974; JD, 1976; postgrad., U. Pa.Wharton Sch. Fin., 1977. Bar: N.Y. 1977, D.C. 1978, U.S. Dist. Ct. (ea. and so. dists.) N.Y. 1978. Disk jockey, newscaster, salesman, dir. black affairs dept. WKTO and WVBR-FM, 1970-76; founder, chmn. bd. Full Circle Enterprises, Inc., 1972-76; corp. counsel, dir. broadcasting Fairchild Industries, Inc., Germantown, Md., 1976-78, Burns, Jackson, Miller, Summit and Jacoby, N.Y.C., 1978-80; sole practice, 1980-88; ptnr. Minter and Gay, P.C., 1988-92; of counsel Phillips, Nizer, Benjamin Kirm and Ballon (N.Y.C.), Lewin & Rosenthal (Boston), 1992-95, Golden Goodloe & Assocs., Atlanta, 1995—, Rudolph & Beer, Atlanta, 1997—. Chmn. bd. trustees Rhythym and Blues Found.; bd. dirs. Living Legends Found. Mem.: ABA (forum com on entertainment and sports industry), N.Y. State Bar Assn., Black Entertainment and Sports Lawyers Assn. (founding mem. past exec. dir., gen. counsel), Internat. Bar Assn., Nat. Bar Assn., Order of St. John, Knights of Malta. Avocations: SCUBA diving, boating, golf, skiin. Office: Golden and Assocs PC 5398 E Mountain St Stone Mountain GA 30083-3079

MINTER, PHILIP CLAYTON, retired communications company executive; b. Sydney, Australia, Aug. 9, 1928; came to U.S., 1957; s. Roy Dixon and Adeline Claire (Bradly) M.; m. Mary Bashford Schettler, Jan. 24., 1959 (dec. July 1999); children: Elizabeth C., Margaret S. BSc with honours, U. Sydney, 1951; MS, U. Wyo., 1958; PhD, U. Wis., 1960. Tchr. King's Sch., Parramatta, Australia, 1951-57; mng. dir. Motivational Rsch. Assocs., Sydney, 1960-62; dir. rsch. Nat. Fund Raising Coun., 1962-65; project dir. USDA, Ft. Collins, Colo., 1965-67; chief info. pesticides program USPHS, Atlanta, 1967-68; mgr. data bases div. Pa. Rsch. Assocs., Phila., 1968-70; pres. EDL Communications Inc., King of Prussia, Pa., 1970-94. Pres. Svc. Tng. Ltd., Kenilworth, Eng., 1976-88; cons. Westinghouse Learning Corp., 1972. Author: Handbook for Pesticide-Chemicals Program Coordinators, 1967. Recipient Terry Magill award Australia Soc., N.Y., 1994. Mem. Soc. Automotive Engrs., Sci. Rsch. Soc. Am., Royal Heritage Soc. (bd. dirs.), U. Wis. Alumni Assn. (bd. dirs. Delaware Valley br.), Australian/Am. C. of C. Phila. (exec. dir.), Union League, Brit. Officers Club Phila. (pres. 1992-93), Sloane Club (London), Sigma Xi. Republican. Episcopalian. Home: 1576 Stapler Dr Yardley PA 19067-4214

MINTON, DWIGHT CHURCH, manufacturing company executive; b. North Hills, N.Y., Dec. 17, 1934; s. Henry Miller and Helen Dwight (Church) M.; m. Marian Haven Haines, Aug. 4, 1956; children: Valerie Haven, Daphne Forsyth, Henry Brewster. BA, Yale U., 1959; MBA, Stanford U., 1961. With Church & Dwight Co., Inc., Princeton, N.J., 1961—, asst. v.p., 1964-66, v.p., 1966-67, pres., 1967-81, chief exec. officer, 1969-95, chmn., 1981—, chmn. bd., 1966—2001, chmn. emeritus NJ, 2001—. Bd. dirs. Crane Corp. Trustee Atlanta U., 1971-88, Morehouse Coll., 1971—, Spelman Coll., 1971-80; v.p., bd. dirs. Greater Yellowstone Coalition, 1991-99. With U.S. Army, 1956-57. Mem. Chem. Mfrs. Assn. (bd. dirs. 1980-83), Grocery Mfrs. Am. (dir. 1983-87). Clubs: Racquet and Tennis, Yale, Lotos. Office: Church & Dwight Co Inc 469 N Harrison St Princeton NJ 08540-3510

MINTON, HENRY LEE, psychology educator; b. N.Y.C., Nov. 20, 1934; s. Irving and Sophie (Shapiro) M.; m. Sheila Gay Cohen, Jan. 27, 1963 (div. Dec. 1983); 1 child, Gregory. BA, NYU, 1956; MA, So. Ill. U., 1958; PhD, Pa. State U., 1962. Asst. prof. Calif. State U., L.A., 1963-65, SUNY, Albany, 1965-67; assoc. prof. Miami U., Oxford, Ohio, 1967-70; prof. psychology U. Windsor, Ont., Can., 1970-2000, prof. emeritus Can., 2000—. Author: Differential Psychology, 1980, Lewis M. Terman, 1988, Currents of Thought in American Social Psychology, 1991, Departing from Deviance, 2002. Grantee Social Sci. and Humanities Rsch. Coun., Ottawa, Ont., 1995-98. Fellow APA; mem. Cheiron Soc. Avocations: painting, travel. Home: 670 Camden Ct Rochester Hills MI 48307-4590 E-mail: hlminton@aol.com.

MINTON, JENNIFER, information technology executive; Various positions audit divsn. Arthur Andersen LLP, 1983; various fin. positions including asst. corp. controller Oracle Corp., Redwood City, Calif., 1989—98, corp. controller, 1998—, v.p., 1995, sr. v.p., 2000—. Office: acle Corp 500 Oracle Pkwy Redwood City CA 94085*

MINTON, JERRY DAVIS, lawyer, consultant, former banker; b. Ft. Worth, Aug. 13, 1928; s. Robert Bruch and Anna Elizabeth (Davis) M.; m. Martha Drew Fields, Nov. 28, 1975; children: Marianne, Martha, John Morgan. BBA, U. Tex., Austin, 1949, JD, 1960; grad. cert., Nat. Trust Sch., Northwestern U., 1960. Of counsel Michener, Larimore, Swindle, Whitaker, Flowers et al., 1991-98; adv. dir. Kanaly Trust Co., Houston, 1992-2000. Vice chmn. 1st Nat. Bank Ft. Worth, 1982-84; chmn., CEO 1st City Bank Ft. Worth, 1986-91. Pilot USAF, 1951-55, pilot Tex. Air N.G., 1955-57; capt. USAFR Ret.). Decorated D.F.C., Air medal with 3 oak leaf clusters. Mem. State Bar Tex., Tarrant County Bar Assn., Mil. Order World Wars, Soc. Descs. of Washington's Army at Valley Forge, Mil. Order Stars and Bars, SAR, SCV, River Crest Country Club, Breakfast Club, Sigma Iota Epsilon, Phi Delta Phi. Episcopalian. Home: 5404 El Dorado Dr Fort Worth TX 76107-3236

MINTON, JOHN DEAN, historian, educator; b. Cadiz, Ky., July 29, 1921; s. John Ernest and Daisy Dean (Wilson) M.; m. Betty Jo Redick, June 8, 1947; children— John Dean, James Ernest. AB in Edn, U. Ky., 1943, MA in History, 1947; PhD, Vanderbilt U., 1959. Instr. history U. Miami, Fla., 1951; tchr. Broward County Pub. Sch. Sys., U. Miami evening divsn., 1951-53; prin. Trigg County (Ky.) H.S., 1953-58; prof. history We. Ky. U., Bowling Green, 1958-86, ret., dean Grad. Coll., 1964-71, v.p. for adminstrv. affairs, 1970-79, interim pres., 1979, v.p. for student affairs, 1981-86, part-time prof., 1986-96. Author: The New Deal in Tennessee, 1932-1938, 1979; contbr. articles to profl. jours. Mem. Gen. Bd. Discipleship, United Meth. Ch.; mem. Louisville Bd. Discipleship; lay spkr. Louisville Conf. Meth. Ch.; bd. dirs. Higher Edn. Found., Meth. Ch., Jesse Stuart Found. Served with USNR, 1943-46. Mem. NEA, Ky. Edn. Assn., So. Hist. Assn., Ky. Hist. Soc., Bowling Green C. of C. (bd. dirs.), Civitan Club (pres. Cadiz 1956), Phi Alpha Theta, Phi Eta Sigma, Kappa Delta Pi Home: 645 Ridgecrest Way Bowling Green KY 42104-3818

MINTON, JOSEPH PAUL, retired safety organization executive; b. Houston, Oct. 20, 1924; s. Joseph Marion and Stella (Fite) M.; m. Nancy Fettig, June 19, 1948; children: Joan M., Michael J., Jean A., Mary B., John E., Diane C. BS in Air Transp., Purdue U., 1949; Grad., U.S. Air Force Air Command and Staff Coll., 1958. Commd. 2d lt. USAF, 1944, advanced through grades to col., 1966, combat Burma, World War II, assigments in crew, staff and command, ret., 1967; v.p. Purdue Airlines Inc., Lafayette, Ind., 1967-68, pres., CEO, 1969-71; mng. dir., chief exec. officer Saber Air Ltd., Singapore, 1971-73; sr. v.p. Brit. Caledonian Airways, N.Y.C., 1974-76; mng. dir. Nat. Transp. Safety Bd., Washington, 1977-78; exec. dir. Nat. Safety Coun.,

1978-88. Decorated D.F.C. with oak leaf cluster, Air medal with 3 oak leaf clusters, 3 battle stars, Air Force Commendation medal with oak leaf cluster. Republican. Roman Catholic. Address: 1720 Lake Shore Crest Dr Apt 15 Reston VA 20190-3243

MINTON, MELANIE SUE, neuroscience nurse; b. Cin., Apr. 3, 1950; d. Lester L. and Wanda (Harman) M. Diploma, The Christ Hosp. Sch. Nursing, 1971; BS in Nursing, Prairie View U. A&M, 1982; MBA in Health Care Mgmt., Our Lady of Lake U., Houston, 1995. RN, Tex.; CNRN, ACLS instr., BCLS instr., bd. cert. neurosci. Staff, charge nurse The Christ Hosp., Cin., 1971—72, Barnes Hosp, St. Louis, 1972; asst. head nurse The Christ Hosp., Cin., 1972—74; relief nurse supr. The Meth. Hosp., Houston, 1975—87, clin. educator, 1989—2000; trauma rehab. nurse Inst. for Rehab. & Rsch., 1987—89; nurse specialist neurosurg., neurol. and otolaryn. ICUs Meth. Hosp., 1989—2000; coord. continuing edn. U. Tex. Sch. Nursing, 2000—; lead bus. faculty LeTourneau U., 1997—; dir. neurosci. nursing Meml. City Hosp., 2002—. Presenter, speaker in field. Co-editor, contbg. author: Neuroscience Nursing for the New Millennium—Nursing Clinics of North America, 1999. Mem. Am. Assn. Neurosci. Nurses, S.E. Tex. Chpt. Am. Assn. Neurosci. Nurses, World Fedn. Neurosci. Nurses. Home: 2021 Spenwick Dr Apt 210 Houston TX 77055-1546

MINTON, MICHAEL HARRY, lawyer, business exec.; b. Indpls., May 14, 1946; s. Bernard Jerome and Dorothy Louise (Groene) M.; children— Melanie, Michael, Morgan, Annie. B.A., U. Notre Dame, 1968; intermediate degree London Sch. Econs., 1970; J.D., Northwestern U., 1971. Bar: Ill. 1971, U.S. Dist. Ct. (no. dist.) Ill. 1971, U.S. Supreme Ct. 1980; cert. civil trial advocacy specialist Nat. Bd. Trial Advocacy. Assoc. Biestek & Facchini, Arlington Heights, Ill., 1971-74; ptnr. Facchini & Minton, Schaumburg, Ill., 1974-85; sole practice, Chgo., 1985—. Trustee Village of Mt. Prospect (Ill.), 1974-78, chmn. fire and police com. 1977-78, bldg. com. 1978. Mem. ABA, Ill. Bar Assn., Chgo. Bar Assn. (matrimonial law com. 1972—), DuPage County Bar Assn., N.W. Suburban Bar Assn. (chmn. family law sect. 1979—), Assn. Trial Lawyers Am., Ill. Trial Lawyers Assn. Roman Catholic. Clubs: Meadow (Rolling Meadows, Ill.); Union League (Chgo.). Mem. bd. editors Fair Share, Newsletter of Divorce, 1981; author: What Is a Wife Worth?, 1983; contbr. numerous articles to legal jours. Home: 1020 Blackburn Dr Palatine IL 60067-4218 Office: 222 N La Salle St Ste 1950 Chicago IL 60601-1102 E-mail: minton@mintonoffices.com.

MINTON, YVONNE FAY, mezzo-soprano; b. Sydney, Australia; d. Robert Thomas and Alice Violet M.; m. William Barclay, Aug. 24, 1965; children— Malcolm Alexander, Alison Elizabeth. Ed., Sydney Conservatorium of Music, 1960-61. Mezzo-soprano with all maj. orchs. in, Australia, 1958-61; moved to, London, 1961, joined, Royal Opera House, Covent Garden, 1965-70, guest artist, Cologne (Germany) Opera, 1969— , U.S. debut as Octavian in Der Rosenkavalier, 1970; appeared, with Lyric Opera, Chgo., 1970, Met. Opera, N.Y.C., 1973, San Francisco Opera, 1974, Paris Opera, 1974, Bayreuth, 1974, Salzburg, 1978; sings regularly with maj. symphony orchs. throughout world, 1968— ; recs. include The Knot Garden, 1970, Cosi Fan Tutte, 1971, Lulu, 1979; maj. vocal works include Mahler songs with, Chgo. Symphony. Comdr. Order Brit. Empire, 1980 Hon. mem. Royal Acad. Music. Office: care Ingpen & Williams 26 Wadham Rd London SW15 2LR England

MINTS, GRIGORI EFROIM, mathematics specialist; b. Leningrad, USSR, June 7, 1939; s. Efroim B. and Lea M. (Novick) M.; m. Marianna Rozenfeld, July 21, 1987; 1 child, Anna. Diploma, Leningrad U., 1961, PhD, 1965, ScD, 1989. Rsch. assoc. Steklov Inst. Math., Leningrad, 1961-79; with Nauka Pubs., 1979-85; sr. rsch. assoc. Inst. Cybernetics, Tallinn, Estonia, 1985-91; prof. dept. philosophy Stanford (Calif.) U., 1991—. Mem. ed. bd. Jour. Symbolic Logic, 1987-90; program orgn. com. Logic in Computer Sci., 1991-94, ASL mtg., CSLI Workshop on Logic, Language and Computation. Author: (book) A Short Introduction to Modal Logic, 1992, Selected Papers in Proof Theory, 1992, A Short Introduction to Intuitionistic Logic, 2000; editor: Mathematical Investigation of Logical Deduction, 1967, COLOG-88, 1989, Logic Colloquium, 1996; mem. editl. bd.: jour. Jour. Philos. Logic, mem. editl. bd.: jour. Jour. of Logic and Computation, mem. editl. bd.: jour. IGPL; contbr. articles to profl. jours. Mem. Assn. Symbolic Logic (mem. coun. 1990-93), Internat. Union History and Philosophy and Sci. (assessor 1991-95).

MINTZ, ALBERT, lawyer; b. New Orleans, Oct. 19, 1929; s. Morris and Goldie (Goldblum) M.; m. Linda Barnett, Dec. 19, 1954; children— John Morris, Margaret Anne. BBA, Tulane U., 1948, JD, 1951. Bar: La. 1951; cert. tax specialist, estate and adminstrn. specialist. Since practiced in, New Orleans; ptnr. Montgomery, Barnett, Brown, Read, Hammond & Mintz, Hurwitz-Mintz Realty Cos., New Orleans. Bd. dirs. Strauss Distbrs., Avrico, Inc. Mem. bd. editors Tulane Law Rev. Adv. bd. Law Sch. Tulane U.; chmn., dir. adv. bd. Tulane Summer Lyric Theater; bd. dirs. Tulane Ctr. Stage Talent and Shakespearean Theatre; bd. dirs. Jewish Cmty. Ctr., New Orleans, 1965-72, Jewish Fedn., 1968—, Home for Jewish Aged, 1968-71, Jewish Family Svc., New Orleans, 1968-72; trustee, bd. mgrs. Touro Infirmary Hosp. and Found. chosen as the 1999 recipient of the Judah Touro Society Awd. for his outstanding contribution to the hosp. and its foundation; trustee Jewish Endowment Found.; charter mem. La. Hist. Assn. Recipient Tulane Outstanding Alumnus award, Class of 1951, 2001. Mem. ABA, La. Bar Assn. (lectr., publ. on corp., tax, real estate law), New Orleans Bar Assn. (exec. com. 1971-74), Am. Law Inst., U.S. Hist. Assn., New Orleans C. of C. (chmn. com. civic affairs and state legis. 1968-69), City Energy Club, Tulane Bus. Sch. Emeritus Club, Exec. comm. of the Tulane Emeritus Club; Phi Delta Phi, Omicron Delta Kappa, Zeta Beta Tau. Jewish. Home: 1915 State St New Orleans LA 70118-6251 Office: 3200 Energy Ctr 1100 Poydras St New Orleans LA 70163-1101 E-mail: amintz@monbar.com.

MINTZ, DALE LEIBSON, health education executive; b. Bronx, July 28, 1944; d. Jack and Martha (Tobin) Leibson; m. Stephen Allan Mintz, June 19, 1966; children: Eric Michael, Jaclyn Leibson. BA, SUNY, Purchase, 1982; MPA, Bernard M. Baruch Coll., 1991. Cert. health edn. specialist. Corp. art cons. Merryl Wilson Assoc., N.Y.C., 1982-85; asst. to CEO New Am. Libr., 1985-86; estates coord. Sotheby's, 1986-87; program dir. Am. Heart Assn., Purchase, 1987-94; field svcs. exec. Nat. Hemophilia Found., N.Y.C., 1994-95; nat. health edn. dir. Hadassah, Women's Zionist Orgn. of Am., 1995—. Chair task force COMMIT, Yonkers, N.Y., 1988-93. Trustee Comty. Synagogue, Rye, N.Y., 1975-78, Rye Arts Ctr., 1980-89, Rye Hist. Soc., 1994-97. Mem. Nat. Assn. Exec. Women, Assn. Women's Health Profls., N.Y. State Profl. Health Educators. Avocations: reading, volunteering. Office: Hadassah 50 W 58th St New York NY 10019-2590

MINTZ, DANIEL HARVEY, endocrinologist, educator, academic administrator; b. N.Y.C., Sept. 16, 1930; s. Jacob A. and Fannie Mintz; m. Dawn E. Hynes, Jan. 15, 1961 (dec.); children: David, Denise, Debra; m. Marge Kleinman, Nov. 30, 1996. BS cum laude, St. Bonaventure Coll., 1951; MD, N.Y. Med. Coll., 1956. Diplomate Am. Bd. Internal Medicine. Intern Henry Ford Hosp., Detroit, 1956-57; resident Georgetown med. div. D.C. Gen. Hosp., Washington, 1957-59, Georgetown U. Hosp., Washington, 1958-59; fellow medicine Nat. Inst. Arthritis and Metabolic Diseases, 1959-60, Am. Diabetes Assn., 1960-61; practice medicine, specializing in diabetes and endocrinology U. Miami. (Fla.) Sch. Medicine, prof. medicine, 1969—, Mary Lou Held prof. medicine, 1981-96, chief div. endocrinology and metabolism, dept. medicine, 1969-80, Sci. dir. Diabetes Research Inst., 1980-96, sci. dir. emeritus, 1996—; asst. prof. medicine Georgetown U. Sch. Medicine, 1963-64; assoc. prof. medicine U. Pitts. Sch. Medicine, 1964-69; chief svc. Georgetown U. Med. div. D.C. Gen. Hosp., Washington, 1963-64; chief medicine Magee-Women's Hosp., Pitts., 1964-69. Guest prof. U. Geneva, 1976—77. Contbr. articles to profl. jours. Fellow: ACP; mem.: Am. Assn. Physicians, So. Soc. Clin. Investigation, Ctrl. Soc. Clin. Investigation, Am. Soc. Clin. Investigation, Am. Fedn. Clin. Rsch., Am. Diabetes Assn., Endocrine Soc. Office: U Miami Diabetes Rsch Inst PO Box 016960 R-77 Miami FL 33101-6960

MINTZ, HERMAN, adult education educator; b. Trenton, Sept. 19, 1931; s. Solomon and Rose (Shulman) M.; children: Victor, Elisheva. BS, Trenton State Coll., 1953, MA, 1962. Cert. tchr. K-12; cert. bus. edn. Tchr. Ewing Twp. Pub. Schs., Trenton, 1953-93, Princeton (N.J.) Twp. Schs., 1957-58, Ewing Adult Sch., Trenton, 1990—. Author: Discovering Business 1000 Plus, 1985, Career Skit Kit, 1992, Telephone Use Activity Pack, 1992, Fit to Teach, 1993. Bd. dirs. Jewish Cmty. Ctr. of Delaware Valley, N.J., 2000—. Served U.S. Army, 1953-55. Honorable Mention N.J. Coun. Econ. Edn., 1991. Mem. Knights of Pythias (chancellor commdr. Fortitude Lodge 1993—), Jewish War Veterans (quartermaster post 156 1955—). Jewish. Avocations: dancing, public speaking, nutrition. Home: 41 Laurel Ave Trenton NJ 08618-4015 E-mail: mintz45@msn.com.

MINTZ, JEFFRY ALAN, lawyer, consultant; b. N.Y.C., Sept. 15, 1943; s. Aaron Herbert and Lillian Betty (Greenspan) M.; m. Susan Politzer, Aug. 22, 1979; children: Jennifer, Melanie, Jonathan. AB, Tufts U., 1964; LLB, Rutgers U., 1967; postgrad., U. Pa. Law Sch., 1968-70. Bar: D.C. 1968, N.Y. 1970, U.S. Supreme Ct. 1972, N.J. 1973, Pa. 1983; registered mediator, N.J. Law clk. to judge U.S. Ct. Appeals, New Orleans, 1967-68; asst. defender Defender Assn. Phila., 1968-70; asst. counsel NAACP Legal Def. and Ednl. Fund, N.Y.C., 1970-74; dir. Office Inmate Advocacy, N.J. Dept. Pub. Adv., Trenton, 1974-81; pvt. practice Haddonfield and Medford, N.J., 1982; ptnr. Stein & Shapiro, Medford, 1982-83, Cherry Hill, N.J., 1983-84, Mesirov, Gelman, Jaffe, Cramer & Jamieson, Cherry Hill, Phila., 1984-90, Schlesinger, Mintz & Pilles, Mt. Holly, N.J., 1990-92; pvt. practice, 1992—. Trustee Congregation M'hor Shalom, Cherry Hill, 1990-97; mem. Burlington County and Mt. Laurel Dem. Coun. Com., 1993-95, 2002--; chair Moorestown Dem. Com., 1995-2001. Mem. ATLA, N.J. Bar Assn. (del., gen. coun. 1986-88, 89-91), D.C. Bar Assn., Camden County Bar Assn., Burlington County Bar Assn. (trustee 1989-92), Assn. Trial Lawyers N.J. (bd. govs. 1990-95), Barrister, Burlington Am. Inn of Ct. (founding mem. dist. fee arbitration com., vice chmn., 1999-2000, chmn. 2000-01). Jewish. Home: 22 Lexington Ct Mount Laurel NJ 08054-3701 Office: 129 High St Mount Holly NJ 08060-1401 E-mail: mhlaw@eticomm.net.

MINTZ, JOEL ALAN, law educator; b. N.Y.C., July 24, 1949; s. Samuel Isaiah and Eleanor (Streichler) M.; m. Meri-Jane Rochelson, Aug. 25, 1975; children: Daniel Rochelson, Robert Eli. BA, Columbia U., 1970, LLM, 1982, JSD, 1989; JD, NYU, 1974. Bar: N.Y. 1975, U.S. Dist. Ct. (so. and ea. dists.) N.Y. 1982, U.S. Ct. Appeals (2d cir.) 1982. Atty. enforcement div. EPA, Chgo., 1975-76, chief atty. case devel. unit, 1977-78, policy advisor to regional adminstr., 1979; sr. litigation atty. Office Enforcement, EPA, Washington, 1980-81; asst. prof. environ. law Nova U. Law Ctr., Ft. Lauderdale, Fla., 1982-85, assoc. prof., 1985-87, prof., 1987—. Author: State and Local Government Environmental Liability, 1994, Enforcement At the EPA: High Stakes, 1995; author: (with others) Environmental Law, 4th edit., 2000, State and Local Taxation and Finance In A Nutshell, 2nd edit., 2000; contbr. articles to legal jours. and treatises. Mem. ABA, Environ. Law Inst. Assocs., Fla. Bar (assoc.), Internat. Coun. Environ. Law, Internat. Union for Conservation of Nature (commn. on environ. law), Assn. Am. Law Schs. (exec. com., state and local govt. law sect.), Phi Alpha Delta. Avocations: reading, fitness walking, canoeing. Home: 2060 NE 209th St Miami FL 33179-1628 Office: Nova Southeastern U Law Ctr 3305 College Ave Fort Lauderdale FL 33314-7721 E-mail: mintzj@nsu.law.nova.edu.

MINTZ, KENNETH ANDREW, librarian; b. Plattsburgh, N.Y., Mar. 15, 1951; s. Max Manuel and Mildred Patricia (O'Rourke) M.; m. Melinda Lou Harris, Jan. 12, 1974 (div. Oct. 31, 1975). BA, U. Redlands, 1973; MLS, So. Conn. State U., 1978. Cert. profl. libr., N.J. Temporary cataloger Medford (Mass.) Pub. Libr., 1980; libr. Bayonne (N.J.) Pub. Libr., 1980-88; cataloger Hoboken (N.J.) Pub. Libr., 1991-99, head tech. svcs. dept., 1999—, newsletter editor, 1999—2000. Book reviewer Libr. Jour., N.Y.C., 1988-93; head drama group Community Ch. of N.Y., N.Y.C., 1993—2002. *Kenneth Mintz published book reviews in the Riverside, California Times-Picayune in 1974. In 1979, he published a booklet entitled How the Library Can Help You, bought by the British Library, Columbia University Libraries and libraries in Connecticut, Massachusetts and New Jersey. He has had short stories published in Nightly Sounds, Entertain, New Voices, and Cochran's Corner; poems in the Connecticut River Review, American Libraries, and Quill Books. His 1991 $1,000 Quill Poetry award was for "Decscending Jacob's Ladder". His plays have been produced by the Greenhouse Theater and the Community Church in Manhattan, the Attic Ensemble in Jersey City, and the Bayonne Playhouse.* Author: The Holy Ghost, 1980; (plays) O'Reilly and the Banshee, 1981, Coffee, 1983, The Trial Balloon, 1983, 84, Politics in New Jersey, 1984, Das Khristmas Karol, 1986, The Lagoon, 1989, Black Fire in the Chalice, 2000; newsletter editor Unitarian Soc. Rutherford, N.J., 1984-85; asst. newsletter editor First Unitarian Soc. New Haven, 1979-80; contbr. book revs. to Am. Book Rev., Wilson Libr. Bulletin, Libr. and Culture. Mem. ch. coun. Cmty. Ch. of N.Y., 1988—90. Recipient Quill Poetry award Quill Books, 1991, Essay prize Hudson County Writing Festival, Bayonne, 1994, Bayonne Writers Legion of Honor award, 1989, 98, Editor's Choice award Nat. Libr. Poetry, 1989, 96, Garden state writing Challenge Poetry award, 1998, awards N.J. Superbowl of Writing, Halloween Story, 1995, Playwriting, 1995, Essay, 1996, 97, Short Story, 1997, Bayonne Writers Spl. Legion award, 1996, Christmas Story prize Hudson County Writing Festival, Bayonne, 1997, Bayonne Writers Group Founder's Comp. award, 1997, Garden State Writing Challenge Essay award, 1997, N.J. Olympics of Writing essay award, 1998; N.J. Olympics of Writing playwriting award, 1998, Legion of Honor award Bayonne Poetry Writers', 1997, Legion of Honor award Bayonne Essay Writers, 1998, award Bayonne Writers Group Short Story Reading Competition, 1998, award Bayonne Writers Group Short Story Reading competition, 1999, Essay Writer of Yr. award Bayonne Writers' Group, 1999, 2000, others; named Poet of Yr., 1994, Writer of Yr., 1995, N.J. Essay Writer of Yr., 1997; named to Bayonne Writers' Wall of Fame, 1996, Honor Soc. Bayonne Writer's Group, 1997. Mem.: ALA, The Woodrow Wilson Internat. Ctr. for Scholars, Am. friends of Shakespeare's Globe, Peabody Essex Mus., Nation Assocs., House Seven Gables Settlement Assn., Poets Guild, Poets House, N.Y. Acad. Scis., Modern Poetry Assn., Acad. of Am. Poets, Bayonne Writers Group (v.p. 1986), Poetry Soc. of Am., N.J. Libr. Assn., Friends of Dickens NY, Mark Twain House, Friends of the N.Y. Pub. Libr., Irish Am. Partnership, Irish Am. Cultural Inst. Democrat. Unitarian Universalist. Avocations: history, piano, chess, bowling, fishing. Office: Hoboken Pub Libr 500 Park Ave Hoboken NJ 07030-3906 E-mail: kmintz351@aol.com.

MINTZ, LENORE CHAICE (LEA MINTZ), human resources consultant; b. N.Y.C., Aug. 6, 1925; d. Abraham and Eva (Kornblith) Chaice; m. Lewis R. Mintz, July 4, 1944 (dec. Aug. 1996); children: Richard Lewis, Alan Lee, Douglas Chaice. Student, U. Mich., 1942-44; BA magna cum laude, U. Bridgeport, 1976. Cert. personnel cons. Office mgr., personnel cons. Golden Door, Inc., Norwalk, Conn., 1970-78; v.p. permanent div. Aubrey Thomas, Inc., Stamford and Norwalk, 1978-84; sr. v.p. Aubrey Thomas Temps., N.Y., N.J., Conn., Pa., 1984-88; area v.p. Mid-Atlantic div. Talent Tree Personnel Svcs., 1988-89; v.p. bus. devel. Human Resources, Inc., Norwalk, Stamford, Statford and North Haven, 1989-90; prin. Lea Mintz & Assocs., Norwalk, 1990—. Spkr., panel mem., condr. workshop and seminars in field; justice of peace , Fairfield County, Conn., 1954—94; mem. adv. bd. Norwalk Savs. Soc., 1987—98, U.S. Surg. Corp. (now Tyco Corp.), 1991—; mem. adv. bd. Instl. Animal Care and Use Com. Bayer Corp., 2002; mem. Instl. Animal Care and Use Com. Loaned exec. United Way of Norwalk & Wilton, Conn., 1991-92; mem., chmn. Norwalk Bd. Edn., 1966-72; mem. Norwalk Planning and Zoning Commn., 1971-73, Conn. Edn. Coun., 1979-83, Conn. Small Bus. Adv. Coun., 1984-86; mem. regional adv. coun. Norwalk Cmty. Tech. Coll., 1988-90; past pres. Norwalk Cmty. Tech. Coll. Found., 1988-90, bd. dirs. 1964-94, life hon. bd. dirs., 1995—; del. numerous Dem. state and county convs.; Clinton del. Dem. Nat. Conv., 1992; mem. adv. coun. displaced homemakers Bridgeport YWCA, 1988-90; v.p. Greater Norwalk Cmty. Coun., 1973-75; life mem. Women's Aux. Jewish Home for Aged in Conn.; cmty. rels. cons. Family & Children's Aid Mid-Fairfield County, Conn., 1992—; active numerous other orgns. Recipient numerous awards including Woman of Yr. award Norwalk Bus. and Profl. Womens Club, 1984, Outstanding Woman of Decade award UN Assn. Conn., 1987, Outstanding Svc. award Conn. Cmty. and Tech. Coll. Bd. Trustees, 1991 (1st honoree), Successful Aging award Conn. Cmty. Care Inc., 1999, Woman of Substance award Conn. Post Newspaper, 2000. Mem. Women in Mgmt. (pres. 1990, Ann. Recognition award Conn. and Met. N.Y. area 1988), Internat. Assn. Personnel Women, Greater Norwalk C. of C. (bd. dirs. 1980-84, 1st Athena award 1986), Nat. Coun. Jewish Women (life), LWV, Midday Club Stamford, B'nai B'rith (life), Alpha Sigma Lambda. Avocations: reading, knitting, travel, golf. Home and Office: Silvermine 4 May Dr Norwalk CT 06850-1033 E-mail: leamintz@aol.com.

MINTZ, M. J. lawyer; b. Phila., Oct. 29, 1940; s. Arthur and Lillian (Altenberg) Mintz; m. Judith E. Held; children: Robert A., Christine L. BS, Temple U., 1961, JD, 1968. CPA Pa., D.C.; bar: D.C. Atty. adv. to judge U.S. Tax Ct., Washington, 1968-70; asst. gen. counsel Cost of Living Coun. Exec. Office of Pres., 1971-73; ptnr. Dickstein, Shapiro & Morin, 1973—. Adj. prof. George Mason U. Law Sch., Va., 1974—78; advisor U.S. Sec. Labor, Employee Ret. Income Security Act, 1974, Adv. Coun., Washington, 1982—85. Contbr. articles to profl. jours. Apptd. by Pres. Ronald Reagan to adv. com. Pension Benefit Guaranty Corp., 1987, reapptd. and designated chmn. by Pres. George Bush; apptd. by Gov. George Allen of Va. Bd. Va. Pub. Bldg. Authority, 1996—2001, reapptd. by Gov. James Gilmore, 2001—; Rep. candidate Fairfax County Bd. Suprs., 1971. Fellow: Nat. Assn. Watch & Cook Collectors, Freeman of the Worshipful Co. of Clockmakers (London); mem.: AICPA, ABA, Antiquarian Horological Soc. (London), Naval Club (London), Chappaquiddick Beach Club, Met. Club (Washington), Belle Haven Country Club, Cosmos Club. Avocation: antiquarian horologist.

MINTZ, MARSHALL GARY, lawyer; b. Detroit, May 28, 1947; BA, UCLA, 1968, JD, 1971. Bar: Calif. 1972. Law clk. appellate dept L.A. County Superior Ct., 1971-72; ptnr. Kelly Lytton Mintz & Vann, LLP, L.A., Calif., 1995-2001; of counsel Sidley & Bell LLP, 2001—. Moderator, panelist Calif. Continuing Edn. of Bar, 1980—; mem. arbitration adminstrv. com. L.A. County Superior Ct., 1979, mem. 1984 Olympics spl. settlement panel; mem. arbitration panel L.A. Superior Ct., 1999—. Mem. ABA, State Bar Calif., L.A. County Bar Assn. (arbitrator arbitration and client rels. com. 1978-99), Assn. Bus. Trial Lawyers (bd. govs. 1976-77, program chmn. 1976). Office: Sidley & Bell LLP 2940 Westwood Blvd 2d Fl Los Angeles CA 90064 E-mail: mgmintz@earthlink.net.

MINTZ, MAX M. historian; b. London, Aug. 21, 1919; came to U.S., 1920; s. Samuel and Janie (Stein) M.; widowed; 1 child, Kenneth Andrew. BSS, CCNY, N.Y.C., 1941; MA, NYU, N.Y.C., 1947, PhD, 1957. Tchg. asst. NYU, N.Y.C., 1946-48; prof. history State U. N.Y., Plattsburgh, 1948-51; tool engr. Internat. Bus. Machines, Poughkeepsie, N.Y., 1951-63; from asst. prof. to prof. history So. Conn. State U., New Haven, 1963-85, prof. emeritus history, 1985—. Author: Gouverneur Morris, 1970, Generals of Saratoga, 1990, Seeds of Empire, 1999. With U.S. Army, 1944—46, ETO. Grantee NEH, 1983, Am. Philosophical Soc., 1983; John Adams fellow U. London, 1996; Eccles Ctr. fellow Brit. Libr., 1996. Mem. Orgn. Am. Historians. Democrat. Unitarian Universalist. Avocations: woodworking, walking. Home: 104 Norman Rd Hamden CT 06514 Office: So Conn State U 501 Crescent St Hamden CT 06515

MINTZ, MORTON ABNER, author, former newspaper reporter; b. Ann Arbor, Mich., Jan. 26, 1922; s. William and Sarah (Solomon) M.; m. Anita Inez Franz, Aug. 30, 1946; children— Margaret Ruth, Elizabeth Diane (dec.), Roberta Joan, Daniel Robert. AB in Econs, U. Mich., 1943. Reporter St. Louis Star-Times, 1946-50; reporter, asst. city editor St. Louis Globe-Democrat, 1951-58; reporter Washington Post, 1958-88. Author: The Therapeutic Nightmare, 1965, By Prescription Only, 1967, The Pill: An Alarming Report, 1969, At Any Cost: Corporate Greed, Women, and the Dalkon Shield, 1985, (with Jerry S. Cohen) America, Inc.: Who Owns and Operates the United States, 1971, Power, Inc.: Public and Private Rulers and How to Make Them Accountable, 1976, (with others) In the Name of Profit: Profiles in Corporate Irresponsiblity, 1972, More Bucks, Less Bang: How the Pentagon Buys Ineffective Weapons, 1983. Recipient Heywood Broun, Raymond Clapper, George Polk awards for journalism, 1962, A.J. Liebling award, 1974, Worth Bingham Meml. award, 1976, Columbia Journalism award, 1983, Hugh M. Hefner First Amendment award for lifetime achievement, 1996. E-mail: mintzm@earthlink.net.

MINTZ, NORMAN NELSON, investment banker, educator; b. N.Y.C., Sept. 18, 1934; s. Alexander and Rebecca (Nelson) M.; m. Marcia Lynn Belford, Aug. 27, 1960; children: Geoffrey Belford, Douglas Nelson. AB, Bucknell U., 1955; PhD, NYU, 1966. Asst. gen. mgr. Ross Products Inc., N.Y.C., 1957-59; media analyst Benton & Bowles Inc., 1960; asst. prof. fin. Syracuse U., 1965-69; asst. prof. econs. Columbia U., N.Y.C., 1968-72, assoc. dean Grad. Sch. Arts and Scis., 1972-77, dep. provost, 1977-80, acting provost, 1978-79, sr. v.p., 1980-82, exec. v.p. for acad. affairs, 1982-89, exec. v.p., ret., 1990—; mng. dir. Loeb Ptnrs. Corp., 1990—. Economist U.S.-P.R. Commn. on Status of P.R., 1965-66; bd. dirs. Loeb Holding Corp., Loeb Ptnrs. Corp., Sr. Network, Inc., Comm. Mgmt. Sys., Inc., Exxel/Atmos, Inc., Evare, L.L.C., Intersections, Inc., Loeb Arbitrage Fund. Author: Monetary Union and Economic Integration, 1970; contbr. articles to profl. jours. Dir. Citizens Budget Commn., Conf. on Jewish Social Studies, 1975—94, N.Y.C. Coun. on Econ. Edn., 1993—. 1st lt. Signal Corps. U.S. Army, 1955—57. Earhart Found. fellow, 1963-65 Mem. Am. Econ. Assn., Am. Fin. Assn., Royal Econ. Soc., India House Club, Phi Beta Kappa, Omicron Delta Epsilon. Office: care Loeb Ptnrs 61 Broadway New York NY 10006-2701 E-mail: nmintz@loebpartners.com.

MINTZ, RONALD STEVEN, lawyer, photojournalist; b. Bklyn., Aug. 16, 1947; s. Herbert and Phoebe (Gilman) M.; children: Raymond, Gloria. JD, Western State U., Fullerton, Calif., 1978. Bar: Calif. 1978, U.S. Dist. Ct. (no., so., ea. and cen. dists.) Calif. 1978, U.S. Ct. Appeals (9th cir.) 1979, U.S. Supreme Ct. 1982. Pvt. practice law, Berkeley, Calif., 1978-80, Canyon Country, 1980-83, Chino, 1983-84, Ontario, 1984-88, Pomona, 1988-91, San Fernando, 1991-92; pvt. practice Joshua Tree, 1993-94, Hollywood, 1994-2001, L.A., 2001—. Founder legal aid orgn. to protect civil rights Tactical Law Command. Producer film on air pollution: State of Emergency, 1971, videotape documentary: America-A True Glimpse, 1987; publisher opposition newspaper: Ten Penny Press. Recipient Am. Jurisprudence awards Bancroft Whitney Law Book Pub. Co., 1977, 78. Mem. Lawyers in Mensa (charter), State Bar Calif. (criminal law sect. 1983-84, police misconduct lawyer referral service), Mensa. Avocations: photography, film, video, guns, cars. Office: 2007 Wilshire Blvd #602 Los Angeles CA 90057 Fax: 323-733-3768. E-mail: taclawcom@netzero.net.

MINTZ, SAMUEL ISAIAH, English language educator, writer; b. N.Y.C., Nov. 20, 1923; Nathan and Anna (Sheinkman) M.; m. Eleanor Streichler, Mar. 2, 1947; children: Joel Alan, Jonathan. BA, Bklyn. Coll., 1948; MA, Columbia U., 1949, PhD, 1958. Prof. City Coll. N.Y., N.Y.C., 1948-86, prof. doctoral faculty, 1965-86, prof. emeritus, 1986—, CUNY Grad. Ctr., N.Y.C., 1986—. English faculty Cambridge U., Eng., 1964-65; vis. prof. Columbia U., N.Y.C., 1969-70, Barnard Coll., N.Y.C., 1987-89; vis. fellow Wolfson Coll. Oxford U., 1973. Author: The Hunting of Leviathan, 1962, 2d edit., 1996; editor: From Smollett to Henry James, 1980; founder, editor History Ideas Newsletter, N.Y.C., 1954-60; contbr. articles to profl. jours. With Army Air Force, 1943-46. Fulbright fellow Cambridge U., 1956-57, rsch. scholar, 1964-65, Guggenheim fellow, 1964. Office: City U NY Grad Sch 365 5th Ave New York NY 10016-4309

MINTZ, SEYMOUR STANLEY, lawyer; b. Newark, Mar. 7, 1912; AB, George Washington U., 1933, JD, 1936. Bar: D.C. 1936. Atty. Office of Undersec. of Treasury, 1937-38, Office of Chief Counsel, IRS, 1938-42; assoc. Hogan & Hartson, Washington, 1946-49, ptnr., 1949-84, counsel, 1985—. Contbr. articles to profl. jours. Fellow Am. Coll. Tax Counsel; mem. ABA, D.C. Bar Assn., Am. Law Inst., Order of Coif. Office: Hogan & Hartson 555 13th St NW Ste 800E Washington DC 20004-1161

MINTZ, SHLOMO, conductor, violist, violinist; b. Moscow, Oct. 30, 1957; came to U.S., 1974; s. Abraham and Eve (Labko) M.; m. Corina Ciacci; children: Elav David, Alexander. Studied with Ilona Feher; Diploma, Juilliard Sch. Music, 1979. Judge internat. Tchaikovsky Competition, Moscow, 1990; juror queen Elisabeth Internat. Music Competition, Brussels, 1993. Concerto debut with Israel Philharm.; violin solo recordings include Violin Concertos by Mendelssohn and Bruch (Grand prix du Disque Diapason d'or), 1981, Complete Sonatas and Partitas for Solo Violin by J.S. Bach, The Miraculous Mandarin-Two Portraits (with Abbado/Chicago Symphony Orchestra) by Bartok, Compositions and Arrangements (with Clifford Benson, piano) by

Kreisler, Violin Concerto; also Bruch: Violin Concerto Number 1 (with Abbado/Chgo. Symphony Orchestra) by Mendelssohn, Twenty-Four Caprices by Paganini, Two Violin Concertos (with Abbado/London Symphony Orchestra) by Prokofiev, The Four Seasons (with Stern, Perlman, Mehta) by Vivaldi, Vivaldi violin concertos, Vols. I & II (with Israel Chamber Orch.), 1992, Collection String Symphonies, Vol. III to X, (with Israel Chamber Orch., 1992, Violin and Viola Sonatas by Chostakovich (with V. Postnikova); apptd. music advisor, chief condr., soloist Israel Chamber Orch., 1989-93; artistic advisor, prin. guest condr. Limburg Symphony Orch., Maastricht, The Netherlands, 1994; condr. London Symphony Orch., Berlin Radio Symphony, Balt. Symphony, Detroit Symphony, Rotterdam Philharm.; soloist with Montreal Symphony, Nat. Symphony, Washington, Carnegie Hall, Tonhalle Orch. of Zurich, Spanish Nat. Orch., Israel Philharm., others. Recipient Premio Accademia Musicale, Chigiana Siena, Italy, 1984. Uses Zahn violin made by Stradivarius, and a Carlo-Guiseppe Testrove viola. Office: ICM Artists Inc 40 W 57th St Fl 16 New York NY 10019-4098

MINTZ, SIDNEY WILFRED, anthropologist; b. Dover, N.J., Nov. 16, 1922; s. Solomon and Fromme Leah (Tulchin) M.; m. June Mirken, May 1952 (div. Dec. 1962); children: Eric Daniel, Elizabeth Rachel; m. Jacqueline Wei, June 6, 1964. BA, Bklyn. Coll., 1943; PhD, Columbia U., 1951; MA, Yale U., 1963. Mem. faculty dept. anthropology Yale U., New Haven, 1951-74, prof., 1963-74; prof. anthropology Johns Hopkins U., Balt., 1974-97, prof. emeritus, 1997—. Vis. prof. anthropology MIT, 1964-65, Princeton U., 1975-76; directeur d'études associé E.P.H.E., Paris, 1970-71; professeur associé. Coll. de France, Paris, 1988; editor Yale U. Press Caribbean Series, 1957-74; Lewis Henry Morgan lectr. U. Rochester, 1972; Christian Gauss lectr. Princeton U., 1979; Harry Hoijer lectr. UCLA, 1981; Duijker Found. lectr., Amsterdam, 1988; Rodney lectr. U. Warwick, 1993. Author: (with others) People of Puerto Rico, 1956, Worker in the Cane, The Life History of a Puerto Rican Sugar Cane Worker, 1960, Caribbean Transformations, 1974, Sweetness and Power, 1985, (with Richard Price) The Birth of African-American Culture, 1992, Tasting Food, Tasting Freedom, 1996. Served with USAAF, 1943-46. Recipient William Clyde DeVane medal Yale U., 1972, Huxley medalist Royal Anthrop. Inst., 1994, disting. lectr. award Am. Anthrop. Assn., 1996; named Social Sci. Rsch. Coun. Faculty Rsch. fellow, 1958-59, Guggenheim fellow, 1957, Fulbright fellow, 1966-67, 70-71, NEH fellow, 1978-79, Smithsonian Inst. Regents' fellow, 1986-87. Fellow Am. Anthrop. Assn.; mem. Am. Ethnol. Soc. (v.p., pres.-elect 1967-68), Royal Anthrop. Soc. Gt. Britain and Ireland, Am. Acad. Arts and Scis., Sigma Xi. Office: Johns Hopkins U Dept Anthropology Baltimore MD 21218 E-mail: swmintz@aol.com.

MINTZ, SUSAN ASHINOFF, apparel manufacturing company executive; b. N.Y.C., Dec. 7, 1949; d. Lawrence Lloyd and Thelma B. (Rubens) Ashinoff; m. Robert Mintz, June 18, 1983; children: Geoffrey Mintz , Tyler Mintz. BA, Finch Coll., 1971; MPA, NYU, 1977. Menswear advt. asst. New Yorker Mag., N.Y.C., 1971-72; assoc. Staub Warmbold & Assocs., Inc., exec. search co., 1972-80; exec. v.p. Muhammad Ali Sportswear, Ltd., 1980-81; pres. Forum Sportswear, Ltd., N.Y.C. and Portsmouth, Va., 1981—; group v.p., bd. dirs. Coronet Group, Portsmouth, 1985—. Trustee Dean Jr. Coll. Named to Outstanding Young Women in Am., U.S. Jaycees, 1980. Mem.: Beacon Hill Club. Office: 2615 Elmhurst Ln Portsmouth VA 23701-2736

MINTZ, WALTER, investment company executive; b. Vienna, Austria, Feb. 23, 1929; came to U.S., 1938, naturalized, 1945; s. Maximilian and Ilse (Schueller) M.; m. Sandra Jane Earl, Aug. 27, 1971. BA, Reed Coll., 1950; postgrad. in econs, Columbia, 1950—51, postgrad. in econs, 1953—54. Asso. editor Barrons mag., 1951-53, 54-56; with Shearson Hammill Co., 1956-70, dir. research, 1962-69, exec. v.p. charge investment div., 1965-70; partner Cumberland Assocs., investment mgmt., 1970-85; spl. ltd. ptnr. Cumberland Ptnrs., investment ptnrship., 1982—. Bd. dirs. Merrill Lynch Phoenix Fund, Merrill Lynch Fed. Securities Trust. Trustee Reed Coll., 1971—, vice chmn. bd. trustees, 1991-98, chmn. bd. trustees, 1998-2002; trustee Manhattan Inst., 1990-2002, vice chmn., 1994—; bd. dirs. Citizens Union Found. of N.Y.C., 1985—. Mem. N.Y. Soc. Security Analysts (bd. dirs. 1969-75) Home: 2 E 88th St New York NY 10128-0555 Office: Cumberland Assocs Rm 3803 1114 Avenue Of The Americas New York NY 10036-7775

MINTZER, DAVID, physics educator; b. N.Y.C., May 4, 1926; s. Herman and Anna (Katz) M.; m. Justine Nancy Klein, June 26, 1949; children: Elizabeth Amy, Robert Andrew. BS in Physics, Mass. Inst. Tech., 1945, PhD, 1949. Asst. prof. physics Brown U., 1949-55; research asso. Yale U., 1955-56, assoc. prof., dir. lab. marine physics, 1956-62; prof. mech. engring. Northwestern U., Evanston, 1962-91, prof. physics and astronomy, 1968-91, prof. emeritus mech. engring., prof emeritus physics and astronomy, 1991—; assoc. dean McCormick Sch. Engring. and Applied Sci., 1970-73, acting dean, 1971-72, v.p. for rsch., dean sci., 1973-86, spl. asst. to pres., 1986-87, prof. emeritus mech. engring., physics and astronomy, 1991—. Mem. mine adv. com. Nat. Acad. Sci.-NRC, 1963-73; mem. Ill. Gov.'s Commn. on Sci. and Tech., 1987-88; mem. adv. bd. Applied Rsch. Lab. Pa. State U., 1976-82, chmn., 1980-81. Contbr. numerous chpts. to books, papers to profl. publs. Trustee EDUCOM interuniv. communications coun., 1975-83, vice chmn., 1977-78, chmn., 1978-81; trustee Adler Planetarium, 1976-92, life trustee, 1992—; bd. dirs. Rsch. Park, Inc., Evanston, 1986-92, treas., 1986-91; trustee Ill. Math. and Sci. Acad., 1986-97, mem. exec. com., 1989-95, chmn. alliance coun., 1991-93; chmn. bd. dirs. Heartland Venture Capital Network, Inc., 1987-90; bd. dirs. Tech. Innovation Ctr., Inc., 1990-92, treas., 1990-92. Fellow Am. Phys. Soc., Acoustical Soc. Am.; mem. ASME, Am. Astron. Soc., Sigma Xi, Tau Beta Pi, Pi Tau Sigma. Achievements include research on underwater acoustics and rarefied gas dynamics. Office: 332 Villena Way Palm Desert CA 92260-2172 E-mail: dmin@northwestern.edu.

MINTZER, JACOBO E. physician, researcher; b. Argentina; m. Olga Brawman; children: Jonathan, Adam. BA, Latin Am. Rabbinical Sem., Buenos Aires, 1978; MD, Buenos Aires U., 1978. Diplomate Am. Bd. Psychiatry & Neurology, Am. Bd. Gen. Psychiatry, Israel Bd. Psychiatry & Neurology. Intern, resident Hadassah-Hebrew U., Jerusalem, 1979-85; fellow in geriatric psychiatry UCLA, 1985-87; asst. prof. U. Miami (Fla.) Sch. Medicine, 1987-91; assoc. prof. Med. U. S.C., Charleston, 1991-98, prof., 1998—. Dir. gero-psychiatry fellowship program, dir. geriatric psychiatry program Med. U. S.C., Charleston, 1991—; co-dir. Alzheimer's Rsch. & Clin. Program, 1997—; mem. clin. ctrs. and spl. projects rev. com. NIMH, 1997-99. Contbr. articles to profl. jours. Scholar geriatric psychiatry edn. scholar, Med. U. S.C. Found. Mem.: Am. Assn. Geriatric Psychiatrists, Am. Assn. Geriatric Psychiatry, Am. Psychiatric Assn. (chairperson com. ethnic minority elderly 1996—99, coun. on aging 2001). Jewish. Office: Med U SC Alzheimer's Rsch and Clin Programs 5900 Core Rd Ste 203 North Charleston SC 29406-6076 E-mail: mintzerj@musc.edu.

MINUDRI, REGINA URSULA, librarian, consultant; b. San Francisco, May 9, 1937; d. John C. and Molly (Halter) M. BA, San Francisco Coll. for Women, 1958; MLS, U. Calif., Berkeley, 1959. Reference libr. Menlo Park (Calif.) Pub. Libr., 1959-62; regional libr. Santa Clara County (Calif.) Libr., 1962-68; project coord. Fed. Young Adult Libr. Svcs. Project, Mountain View, Calif., 1968-71; dir. profl. svcs. Alameda County (Calif.) Libr., 1971, asst. county libr., 1972-77; libr. dir. Berkeley Pub. Libr., 1977-94; city libr. San Francisco Pub. Libr., 1997-2000. Lectr. U. San Francisco, 1970-72, U. Calif., Berkeley, 1977-81, 91-93, San Jose State U., 1994-97; cons., 1975-90; mem. adv. bd. Miles Cutter Ednl., 1992-98. Author: Getting It Together, A Young Adult Bibliography, 1970; contbr. articles to publs. including Sch. Libr. Jour., Wilson Libr. Bull. Bd. dirs. No. Calif. ACLU, 1994-96, Cmty. Memory, 1989-91, Berkeley Pub. Libr. Found., 1996-99; bd. dirs. Berkeley Cmty. Fund, 1995-99, chair youth com., 1994-96; mem. bd. mgrs. ctrl. br. Berkeley YMCA, 1988-93. Recipient proclamation Mayor of Berkeley, 1985, 86, 94, Citation of Merit, Calif. State Assembly, 1994; named Woman of Yr., Alameda County North chpt. Nat. Women's Polit. Caucus, 1985, Outstanding Alumna, U. Calif. Sch. Libr. and Info. Scis., Berkeley, 1987, Lifetime Achievement award Berkeley Cmty. Fund, 2001. Mem. ALA (pres. 1986-87, exec. bd. 1980-89, coun. 1979-88, 90-94, Grolier award 1974), Calif. Libr. Assn. (pres. 1981, coun. 1965-69, 79-82), LWV (dir. Berkeley chpt. 1980-81, v.p. comm. svcs. 1995-97). Office: Reality Mgmt 836 The Alameda Berkeley CA 94707-1916

MINUS, EDWARD RICHELIEU, English language educator, writer; b. Greenville, S.C., Aug. 15, 1938; s. Edward Richelieu and Miriam (Marchant) M. BA, Presbyn. Coll., 1960; MA, Boston U., 1969. Tchr. English, Clover (S.C.) H.S., 1962-64, Roanoke Rapids (N.C.) H.S., 1964-65; instr. English, Spartanburg (S.C.) Jr. Coll., 1965-71, Wofford Coll., Spartanburg, 1972-81, Raritan Valley C.C., Somerville, N.J., 1982—. Author: (novel) Kite, 1986; contbr. numerous stories to Atlantic Monthly, Yale Rev., Tri Quar., Gettysburg Rev., also others; contbr. poetry to New Republic, Boston Phoenix, New Eng. Rev., Ga. Rev., also others. Grantee NEH, 1971-72, S.C. Arts Commn., 1980-81, N.J. Council Arts, 1988-89. Democrat. Avocations: reading, chess, theatre, movies, walking. Home: PO Box 135 Somerville NJ 08876

MINZNER, DEAN FREDERICK, aviation company executive; b. July 20, 1945; s. Frederick Louis and Winifred (Hughes) M. BA, Franklin and Marshall Coll., 1967; MBA, Columbia U., 1972. Dist. exec. Greater N.Y. couns. Boy Scouts Am., N.Y.C., 1972-76; sales exec. Coast Avia, Long Beach, Calif., 1976-78, Performance Aircraft, Inc., Hayward, 1978; owner, pres. Western Aviation Consultants, Inc., 1978-82, Cal-Pacific Assocs., Inc., Hayward, 1979—, Cal-Pacific Enterprises, Hayward, 1982—. Mem. Assn. MBA Execs., Columbia U. Grad. Sch. Bus. Alumni Assn., Aircraft Owners and Pilots Assn. Office: PO Box 6206 Hayward CA 94540-6206 E-mail: dminz@hotmail.com.

MINZNER, PAMELA BURGY, state supreme court justice; b. Meridian, Miss., Nov. 19, 1943; BA cum laude, Miami U., 1965; LLB, Harvard U., 1968. Bar: Mass. 1968, N.Mex. 1972. Pvt. practice, Mass., 1968—71, Albuquerque, 1971—73; adj. prof. law U. N.Mex., 1972—73, asst. prof., 1973—77, assoc. prof., 1977—80, prof. law, 1980—84; judge N.Mex. Ct. Appeals, 1984—94, chief judge, 1993—94; justice N.Mex. Supreme Ct., Santa Fe, 1994—, chief justice, 1999—2001. Mem. faculty Inst. Preparativo Legal U., N.Mex. Sch. Law, 1975, 79; participant NEH Summer Seminars for Law Tchrs. Stanford Law Sch., 1982, U. Chgo. Law Sch., 1978. Author (with Robert T. Laurence): A Student's Guide to Estates in Land and Future Interests: Text, Examples, Problems & Answers, 1981, 2d edit., 1993. Mem.: ABA, State Bar N.Mex. (co-editor newsletter 1979—83, bd. dirs. 1978—79, 1983—84, sect. on women's legal rights and obligations), Gamma Phi Beta. Democrat. Avocations: reading, bridge, movies. Office: Supreme Ct Bldg 237 Don Gaspar Ave Santa Fe NM 87501-2178

MIOTKE, DAVID ROY, music educator; b. Appleton, WI, Nov. 30, 1956; s. George Charles and Mary Mae Miotke; m. Sherril Grace Miotke, Oct. 23, 1982. BS, Carroll Coll., 1979. Band dir., music tchr. Reedsburg (Wis.) Sch. Dist., 1979—. Instrumental dir. Choraliers Show Choir, Reedsburg, 1981—; tech. coord. Cal Ctr., Reedsburg, 1999—. Composer: (full band commn.) Shiva Dance, 1989, March for Bosiphus, 1989. Hand bell choir dir. St. John Luth. Ch., Reedsburg, 1992—. Mem.: Wis. Youth Band Dirs. Assn. (pres.), Music Educators Nat. Conf. Avocation: working puzzles, writing music, painting. Office: Webb Mid Sch 707 N Webb Ave Reedsburg WI 53959

MIOTKOWSKI, IRENEUSZ, physicist; b. Magdeburg, Germany, Dec. 5, 1945; s. Wladyslaw and Melania Miotla; m. Stanislawa Jadwiga Bylok; children: Malgorzata Malinowska, Agata Miotkowska. PhD, Inst. Physics Polish Acad. Scis., Warsaw. Sr. rsch. scientist Purdue U., West Lafayette, Ind., 1991—. Contbr. articles. Mem.: Am. Phys. Soc. Home: 2421 N Armstrong Dr #1D West Lafayette IN 47906 Office: Purdue Univ 1396 Physics Bldg West Lafayette IN 47907 Fax: (765)-494-0706. Business E-Mail: irek@physics.purdue.edu.

MIPRO, TERRY JAMES, accountant, financial professional; b. New Orleans, Dec. 12, 1961; s. John Alfred and Linda Lorriane (Arceneaux) M. BS, U. New Orleans, 1983. CPA, La. Bookkeeper, inside salesman Sherwin-Williams Co., New Orleans, 1978-84; asst. market analyst Delta Beverage Group, Harahan, La., 1984-86, fin. control mgr., 1986-89; asst. payroll supr. Oak Tree Fed. Savs. Bank, New Orleans, 1989-90, club acct., 1990-91, fin. reporting acct., 1991-94; fin. reporting coord., banking officer Whitney Nat. Bank, 1995—. Mem. event staff Cystic Fibrosis Found., Metairie, La., 1994. Mem. AICPA, Soc. La. CPAs (new CPA com.). Avocations: volleyball, jogging, bowling. Home: 1329 Sigur Ave Metairie LA 70005-1219 Office: Whitney Nat Bank 228 Saint Charles Ave Ste 228 New Orleans LA 70130-2628

MIR, MARILYN, retired educator; b. Upland, Ind., Dec. 9, 1927; d. Robert Heavin Thompson and Lenora Hults; m. Hashem Robert Mir-Afzali, May 12, 1957 (div. 1976); children: Michael Robert Mir-Afzali, Susan Marie Farrell. BS, Ball State U., 1947; postgrad., U. Colo., 1948; MS, Ind. U., 1950; postgrad., U. Wash., 1951, U. Calif., 1952-53, San Francisco State U., 1984-85. Tchr. bus., Ind., 1947-50, Wenatchee (Wash.) High Sch., 1950-52; exec. sec. Fritzi of Calif., San Francisco, 1958-63; engring. sec. Div. of Westinghouse, 1963-68; tchr. bus. and English San Francisco Unified Schs., 1968-85, attendance coord., 1985-87, cons., 1987-90. Vol. libr. Grossmont High Sch. Dist., El Cajon, Calif., 1990—, San Carlos Pub. Libr., San Diego, 1985; ednl. missionary Utah Presbyn. Schs., 1985, N.Mex. Presbyn. Schs., 1987, N.C. Presbyn. Schs., 1989; vol. Hospice, 1997—, ARC, 1998—, Christian Cmty. Theatre, 1998—, Am. Cancer Soc., 2000—. 27342260Mem. AAUW, Alzheimer's Assn., San Carlos Women's Club (edn. com.). Democrat. Presbyterian. Home: 7912 June Lake Dr San Diego CA 92119-3120

MIRABELLA, STEPHEN GUY, artist, educator, writer; b. N.Y.C., 1955; s. Guy and Grace M.; m. Sigrid C. Mirabella; 1 child, Tamera Reisiger. Student, N.Y. Acad. of Art, 1983—84; BS in English, SUNY, 1996; MEd, U. Va., 2001. English tchr. Lynchburg (Va.) Sch. Dist., 1997—. One man shows include Manhasset, N.Y. Pub. Art Gallery, 1992, Bayville Mus., N.Y., 1993-94; exhibited in group shows at Nat. Sculpture Soc. (bronze plaque 1992), Smith Mountain Lake Art Show (3rd prize) 1998, Dialog with Death, 1997 (Spl. Arts 1st prize 1996), Staunton Va./Augusta County Regional Art Show (Best in Show, 1st Pl.), Smith Mountain Lake Art Show, Nat. Sculpture Soc., Nat. Arts Club, Lynchburg Fine Arts Ctr., Hudson Valley Art Assn., Bayville Mus., N.Y., Manhasset N.Y. Pub. Art Gallery, Sculpture Ctr., N.Y.C.; permanent collections include Sylvester Stallone Collection; sculptures include John Milton Meml., SUNY, Oneonta, 2000, Nat. Mus. Am. History, 1996, Am. Numismatic Assn. Mus. Colo. Springs, Colo., 1995, Am., Numismatic Soc. collection, NYC, 2000. Bd. dirs., publs. com. chair Friends of Sweet Briar (Va.) Coll. Libr. Grantee N.Y. State Coun. for the Arts, 1994, 95. Mem. Nat. Sculpture Soc., Allied Artists of Am. (assoc.). Avocations: electric and acoustic guitar, poetry, fiction, songwriting. Home: 1416 Indian Creek Rd Amherst VA 24521

MIRABELLI, ANTHONY JAMES, management consultant; b. Port Jefferson, N.Y., June 13, 1948; s. Anthony J. Sr. M. and Marguerite Marie Lighthall; m. Susan Marie; children: Christina M., Michael J. BS, Clemson U., 1970; MS, L.I. U; postgrad., SUNY. Dir. rsch. & devel. Harrison & Crosfield, Bronxville, N.Y., 1977-83; v.p. mktg. Indsl. Genetics, Inc., Columbia, Md., 1983-85; exec. dir. Soumen Sokerie Oy, Schaumburg, Ill., 1985-87; pres., CEO AEC Corp., Woodridge, 1987-91; dir. Indsl. Fermentation Genetics, Bencia, Calif.; v.p. Old Inlet Ptnrs., Inc., N.Y.C., 1991-2000; v.p. mergers and acquisitions Icon Capital Mgmt., Inc., Chgo., 1997—; COO mergers and acquisitions merchant banking divsn. Trident Investment Group LLC, Naperville, Ill. Bd. dirs., sec. Walnut Ridge Home Owners Corp., Naperville, Ill., 1986-88; chmn., CEO Bellport (N.Y.) Ambulance Corp., 1970-76. Anglican. Office: Trident Investment Group LLC PO Box 16 Naperville IL 60566-0016 E-mail: aj.m@usa.net.

MIRABELLI, EUGENE, English educator; b. Arlington, Mass. s. Eugene and Josephine Amarù M.; m. Margaret Anne Black; children: Francesca, Gabriella, Eugene. BA, Harvard U., 1952, PhD, 1960; MA, Johns Hopkins, 1955. Instr. Williams Coll., Williamstown, Mass., 1960-64; from asst. to assoc. prof. SUNY, Albany, 1965-94, prof., 1994-95, prof. emeritus, 1995—. Founding dir., treas. Alternative Lit. Programs, Albany, 1979—. Author: The Burning Air, 1959, The Way In, 1968, No Resting Place, 1972, The World at Noon, 1994, The Language Nobody Speaks, 1999.

MIRABELLO, FRANCIS JOSEPH, lawyer; b. Ft. Lauderdale, Fla., Mar. 2, 1954; s. Frank Guy and Mary (Sorce) M.; m. Marianna Hay O'Neal, Aug. 5, 1978; childen: Diana H., A. Paul. BS in Civil Engring., Princeton U., 1975; JD, Harvard U., 1978. Bar: Calif. 1978, Pa. 1981, Fla. 1983. Assoc. Irell & Manella, Los Angeles, 1978-81; ptnr. Morgan, Lewis & Bockius, Phila., 1981—. Lectr. law Villanova (Pa.) U. Law Sch., adj. prof. law U. Pa., Phila. Mem. ABA, ACTEC. Clubs: Merion Cricket, Phila. Skating, Commonwealth Nat. Golf. Avocations: tennis, golf. Office: Morgan Lewis & Bockius 1701 Market St Philadelphia PA 19103-2903

MIRABELLO, MARK LINDEN, history educator; b. Toledo, May 6, 1955; s. Paul Joseph and Regina Joan (Baranski) M. BA, U. Toledo, 1977; MA, U. Va., 1979; PhD, U. Glasgow (Scotland), 1988. Instr. honors program U. Toledo, 1984-87; sr. instr. European history Shawnee State U., Portsmouth, Ohio, 1987-88, asst. prof. European history, 1988-93, chair honors program, 1990—, assoc. prof. European History, 1993—; vis. assoc. prof. European history Nizhni Novgorod State U., Russia, 1994. Dir. Ian B. Cowan Award for Outstanding Work in Hist. Studies, Shawnee State U., Portsmouth, 1990—; cons. The Open Air, Shawnee State U. newspaper, Portsmouth, 1992—, The Univ. Chronicle Shawnee State Univ. Newspaper, Portsmouth, 1992—; co-founder, advisor Ar Tyr Ar Fraternity Shawnee State U., Portsmouth, 1992—. Author: The Odin Brotherhood: A True Narrative of a Dialogue with a Mysterious Secret Society, 1992, The Crimes of Jehovah: A Brief Selection from the Bible, 1996, The Cannibal Within, 2002. Co-founder, adviser Delta Tau Omega fraternity, Shawnee State U., Portsmouth, 1992—. Honored by Asatru Sogulega Bokasafn, 1996; named Hon. Ky. Col. by Gov's. Office, 1998. Mem. Am. Hist. Assn., Ohio Acad. History, Fortean Soc. (London), Internat. Fortean Orgn., Planetary Soc.. Avocation: Fortean research. Home: 940 2nd St Portsmouth OH 45662-4303 Office: Dept History Shawnee State U Portsmouth OH 45662

MIRABILE, CAROLYN ROSE, lawyer; b. Norristown, Pa., June 12, 1966; d. Paul Joseph and Norma Jean (DiFerdinando) M.; m. Richard Lawrence Giles, Sept. 26, 1992; 1 child, Gabriella Savannah. BA in Polit. Sci., Villanova U., 1988, JD, 1991. Bar: Pa. 1991, N.J. 1991. Assoc. Gultanoff & Lynch, Norristown, 1992-93, Gultanoff Lynch & Tornetta, Norristown, 1993-94; ptnr. Lynch Tornetta & Mirabile, 1994-96, Lynch & Mirabile, Norristown, 1996—. Assoc. Montgomery County Family Law Com., 1991—, Doris Jonas Freed Am. Inn of Ct., 1994—; co-chair Montgomery County Law Day, Norristown, 1993—95, Family Law Practicum, 1996. Mem.: Montgomery Bar Assn. (treas.). Avocation: golf, volleyball. Office: Lynch & Mirabile 617 Swede St Norristown PA 19401-3901 Fax: 610-277-2043.

MIRABITO, MICHAEL MARK, communications educator; b. N.Y.C., Apr. 15, 1956; s. Anthony J. and Jean (Cutrone) M. BFA in Film/TV, NYU, 1977; MS in Comm., N.Y. Inst. Tech., 1979; PhD, Bowling Green State U., 1982. Asst. prof. comm. U. Tulsa, 1982-85, Ithaca (N.Y.) Coll., 1985-93; assoc. prof., then prof. and chairperson dept. comm. Marywood Coll. Comm. Arts, Scranton, Pa., 1993—. Cons. VITA, 1983, Trigger Inc., 1993—. Author: Exploration of Space with Cameras, 1982, New Communications Technology, 1990, New Communications Technology II, III and IV, 2000; contbr. articles to profl. jours., chpt. to book. Rsch. grantee Nat. Assn. Broadcasters, 1987, Digital Equipment Corp., 1988, L2I tech. grant, 2001. Mem. Soc. Motion Picture and TV Engrs. (award com.), Nat. Space Soc., Nat. Space Club. Achievements include co-design of computer-TV facilities; development of graduate program. E-mail: mirabito@ac.marywood.edu.

MIRACLE, DORIS JEAN, retired medical/surgical nurse; b. Louisville, July 23, 1931; d. Bernard Louis and Catherine Federle; m. Earl Miracle, Aug. 31, 1951; 1 child David. Surg. nurse Norton Hosp., Louisville, Norton-Children's Hosp., Louisville. Contbr. poetry anthologies. Mem.: Ky. Writer's Coalition, Internat. Soc. of Poets, Soc. Children's Book Writers and Illustrators. Avocation: reading, writing poetry, astronomy, art, music.

MIRACLE, GORDON ELDON, advertising educator; b. Olympia, Wash., May 28, 1930; s. Gordon Tipler and Corine Adriana (Orlebeke) M.; m. Christa Stoeter, June 29, 1957; children: Gary, Gregory, Glenn. BBA, U. Wis., 1952, MBA, 1958, PhD, 1962. Case officer, civilian intelligence analyst U.S. Army, Fed. Republic Germany, 1955-57; instr. commerce U. Wis. Grad. Sch. Bus., Madison, 1958-60; instr., then asst. prof. mktg. U. Mich., Ann Arbor, 1960-66; assoc. prof. advt. Mich. State U., East Lansing, 1966-70, chmn. PhD program in mass media, 1973-74, chmn. dept., 1974-80, prof. advt., 1970-99, prof. emeritus, 1999—. Vis. prof. mktg. mgmt. N. European Mgmt. Inst., Oslo, 1972-73; cons., lectr. in field. Author: Management of International Advertising, 1966; co-author: International Marketing Management, 1970, Advertising and Government Regulation, 1979, Instructor's Manual for International Marketing Management, 1971, European Regulation of Advertising: Supranational Regulation of Advertising in the European Economic Community, 1986, Voluntary Regulation of Advertising: A Comparative Analysis of the United Kingdom and the United States, 1987, (in Korean) Cultures in Advertising: Advertising in Cultures, 1990; contbr. articles to scholarly and profl. jours.; editor: Marketing Decision Making: Strategy and Payoff, 1965, Sharing for Understanding, Proc. Ann. Conf. Am. Acad. Advt., 1977. Served with AUS, 1952-55. Recipient first Biennial Excellence in Advt. award, U. Ill., 1995; Ford Found. fellow, 1961-62, 64, Am. Assn. Advt. Agys. fellow Marsteller, Inc., 1967, Advt. Ednl. Found. fellow McCann-Erickson Hakuhodo, 1985, Fulbright rsch. fellow Waseda U., Tokyo, 1985; recipient numerous grants; recipient Viktor-Mataja medal Austrian Advt. Rsch. Assn., Vienna, 1999. Fellow: Am. Acad. Advt. (treas., exec. com. 1978—79); mem.: Internat. Advt. Assn., Internat. Advt. Assn. ((ednl. accreditation com. 1993—95, internat. advt. edn. group 1996—2001), Am. Mktg. Assn., Acad. Internat. Bus. (sec., exec. com. 1973—75), Adcraft Club Detroit. Home: 10025 Oak Island Dr Laingsburg MI 48848-8718 Office: Mich State U Dept Advt East Lansing MI 48824 E-mail: miracle@msu.edu.

MIRACLE, NANCY, foundation administrator; b. N.Y.C., Sept. 14, 1946; d. Joseph (Stepfather) and Jennie (Cusumano) Maniscalco(Stepmother), Vincent Bruno and Nancy Cusumano; Acting student with Lee Strasberg, Carnegie Hall Studios, N.Y.C., 1955—62; tutored in classical lit. and writing, N.Y.C., 1957—66; student, Manhattan C.C., N.Y.C., 1966—69; student, creative writing, New Sch. for Social Rsch., N.Y.C., 1970—74; MFA in Creative Writing, Goddard Coll., 1979; tutored, Ibiza, Spain, 1979—80. Lectr. Marymount Coll., N.Y.C., 1979; tutor CUNY, 1983; condr. workshops Women's Internat. Writing Group, 1976—82; tchr. YMCA Writing Workshops, Honolulu, 1988—89, St. Louis Sch. , Honolulu, 1993—94; tutor U. Hawaii, 2000—; pres. Marilyn Monroe Found., 1985—. Actor(lead): 2 plays, 1955—58; author: Lesser Sins, 1979, Venus Oh So Bright, 1994, Here I Am Mother, 1992; contbr. chapters to books. Republican. Avocations: dancing, theater , gym, swimming, yoga. Home: PO Box 118 New York NY 10116 Office: Marilyn Monroe Found PO Box 89676 Honolulu HI 96830

MIRACLE, PAMELA DADANT, public relations and communications consultant; b. Santa Monica, Calif., July 11, 1950; d. Philip Maurice and Helen Irene Dadant. BA in French cum laude, Santa Clara U., 1972; MA in Internat. Studies and French, postgrad., Monterey Inst. Internat. Study, 1975. Asst. mgr. Lingua Lang. Svcs., N.Y.C., 1976-78; internat. mktg. asst. Bausch & Lomb, Sunland, Calif., 1978-82; internat. advt. coord. Hydril Co., L.A., 1982-83; internat. localization mgr. Apple Computer Inc., Cupertino, Calif., 1983-85, internat. pub. rels. mgr., 1985-87; pub. rels. mgr. Apple Europe, Apple Computer Inc., Paris, 1987-88; corp. rels. mgr. Apple Pacific, Apple Computer Inc., Cupertino, 1988-92; pub. rels. and communications cons., 1992—. Mem. Pub. Rels. Soc., Internat. Assn. Bus. Communicators. Office: Miomi Valley Hospital 1 Wyoming St Dayton OH 45409

MIRACLE, ROBERT WARREN, retired banker; b. Casper, Wyo. m. Maggie Zanoni; children: Mark, John BS in Law, U. Wyo., 1951; grad. with honors, Pacific Coast Banking Sch., 1960. With Wyo. Nat. Bank (now Norwest Bank Casper N.A.), 1954-91; exec. v.p. Wyo. Nat. Bank of Casper, 1967; pres., chief exec. officer Wyo. Nat. Bank of Casper (now Norwest Bank Casper N.A.)_, 1968-87; chmn. Wyo. Nat. Bank of Casper (formerly Norwest Bank Casper N.A.), 1983-91, also bd. dirs.; pres., chief exec. officer, dir. Wyo. Nat. Bancorp. (formerly Affiliated Bank Corp Wyo.), Casper, 1970-91; mgr. Kemmerer LaBarge Royalties LLC, 1999—. Instr. bank mgmt. U. Colo., 1971-75. Bd. dirs. United Fund of Natrona County, Wyo., 1963-85, campaign co-chmn., 1973-78; trustee The Myra Fox Skelton Found., 1963—, Goodstein Found., 1992—; bd. dirs., pres. Investment in Casper, 1967-70; Wyo. treas. Radio Free Europe, 1967-72; trustee Casper Coll. Foun., 1967-91, pres., 1973-75, 85-91; trustee U. Wyo. Found., 1972-87; chmn. Casper Downtown Improvement Assn., 1974-75; bd. dirs. Cen. Wyo. Fair Bd., 1974-79, pres., 1977-78; dir. Mountain States Employers Coun., 1979-91; bd. dirs. Wyo.

Natural Gas Pipeline Authority, 1991-97; trustee Meml. Hosp. Natrona County, 1993-96, pres. 1995-96; bd. dirs. Wyo. Med. Ctr., 1996-99. Capt. USMC, 1951-53. Recipient James C. Scarboro Meml. award Colo. Sch. Banking., 1977; Disting. Service in Bus. award U. Wyo. Coll. Commerce and Industry, 1980 Mem. Wyo. Bankers Assn. (chmn. legis. com. 1969-80, pres. 1974-75), Am. Bankers Assn. (mem. governing coun. 1974-75, 81-83), Am. Mgmt. Assn., Rocky Mountain Oil and Gas Assn., Newcomer Soc. in N.Am., Casper C. of C. (pres. 1965-66, Disting. Svc. award 1981), VFW, Casper Petroleum Club, Casper Country Club (pres. 1993-94), Casper Rotary Club (hon. Rotarian award 1996-97), Masons, Lions.

MIRAGLIO, ANGELA MARIA, dietitian; b. Chgo., Sept. 12, 1944; d. Charles A. and Rose C. (Moles) M.; m. Robert S. Schwartz, Oct. 22, 1983. BS, Mundelein Coll., 1966; MS, U. Chgo., 1975. Registered dietitian. Clin. nutrition dir. West Suburban Kidney Ctr., Oak Park, Ill., 1974-78; clin. nutritionist Pediatric Outpatient Clinics U. Chgo., 1978-83; owner AMM Nutrition Services, Chgo., 1984—2001; mgr. Mktg. Comm. Monsanto Co., 1998—99; owner AMM Food and Nutrition Cons., Des Plaines, Ill., 2001—. Instr. Chgo. City-Wide Coll., 1979-81; lectr. De Paul U. Sch. Nursing, Chgo., 1978-80. Author: Food Composition Tables for Renal Diets, 1978; contbr. articles to profl. jours. Bd. dirs. Dorridge Condominium Assn., Chgo.; treas. Cons. Nutritionist Dietetic Practice Group, 1989-91. Mem. Am. Dietetic Assn., Soc. for Nutrition Edn., Ill. Dietetic Assn. (chair coun. profl. issues 1997-99, pres.-elect 1999-2000, pres. 2000-2001), Chgo. Dietetic Assn. (sec. 1969-71), Chgo. Nutrition Assn. Roman Catholic. Home and Office: 290 King Ln Des Plaines IL 60016-5976 E-mail: ammiraglio@aol.com.

MIRAMS, WILLIAM C. construction executive; b. Alhambra, Calif., Apr. 24, 1934; s. William Roy Mirams and Mary Louise Clarke; m. Judith Ann Hamilton, Feb. 20, 1956 (div. 1961); children: Deborah, Sheryl, Bruce, Lisa; m. Lisa Ann Richmond, Dec. 5, 1979. BS in Engring., Stanford U., 1956. Pres., owner various cos., Calif. & Idaho, 1961—; with Capri Builders, Inc., 1961-85, Mirams & Smith, Inc., 1961-75, Marinata Devel. Co. Inc., 1974—. Capt., USMC, 1956-60. Avocations: skiing, sailing. Office: 3835 Birch St Newport Beach CA 92660 Address: 17022 Starfish Ln Sugarloaf Key FL 33042 E-mail: mirams@sunvalley.net.

MIRAND, EDWIN ALBERT, medical scientist; b. Buffalo, July 18, 1926; s. Thomas and Lucy (Papier) M. BA, U. Buffalo, 1947, MA, 1949; PhD, Syracuse (N.Y.) U., 1951; DSc (hon.), Niagara (N.Y.) U., 1970, D'Youville Coll., Buffalo, 1974. Successively undergrad. asst., grad. asst., instr. U. Buffalo, 1946-48; teaching fellow Syracuse U., 1948-51; instr. Utica (N.Y.) Coll., 1950; mem. staff Roswell Park Meml. Inst., Buffalo, 1951—; head W. Seneca labs., 1961—, assoc. inst. dir., head dept. edn., 1967—, dir. cancer rsch., 1968-73, head dept. viral oncology, 1970-73, head dept. biol. recources, 1973—. Rsch. prof. biology Grad. Sch., prof. biochem. pharmacology Sch. Pharmacy, SUNY, Buffalo, 1955-97, dean emeritus, 1997—, dean Roswell Park grad. div. SUNY, 1967—; rsch. prof. biology Grad. Sch.; mem. human cancer virus task force, clin. cancer edn. com. NIH; sr. advisor to pres. and CEO, Roswell Park Cancer Inst., 1997—, dir. alumni, 1997—. Mem. editl. bd. Jour. Surg. Oncology, Cancer Rsch., Jour. Cancer Edn., Cancer jour.; contbr. articles to profl. jours. Mem. U.S. nat. com. Union Internat. Contra Cancer; profl. edn. com. cancer control Nat. Cancer inst.; liaison mem. Pres.'s Nat. Cancer Adv. Bd.; sec. N.Y. State Cancer Programs, Inc., 1984—; bd. dirs. Network in Aging of We. N.Y., Inc., 1986—; mem. N.Y. State Health Rsch. Coun., Gov.'s AIDS adv. coun., 1982—; trustee D'Youville Coll., 1998—. Recipient Billings Silver medal AMA, 1963, Margaret Hays Edwards award in edn., SUNY, Buffalo, 1993, Citation award in sci. coll. arts and scis., 1964, award sci. rsch. mammalian tumor viruses Med. Soc. State N.Y., 1963. Fellow: AAAS, N.Y. Acad. Sci. (life); mem.: Buffalo Fine Arts Acad., Buffalo Hist. Soc., Am. Soc. Preventive Oncology, Hematology Soc., Internat. Union Against Cancer (chmn. U.S. nat. com. 1979-2001, sec.-gen. 13th Internat. Cancer Congress), Pub. Health Cancer Assn. Am., Internat. Soc. Hematology, Am. Soc. Hematology, Buffalo Acad. Medicine, Am. Assn. for Cancer Edn., Soc. Exptl. Biology and medicine, Am. Soc. Zoologists, Radiation Rsch. Soc., Am. Assn. Cancer Rsch., Assn. Am. Cancer Insts. (sec.-treas. 1968-99), Internat. Assn. for Gnotobiology (pres. 1981-84), Assn. Gnotobiotics (pres. 1968-69, dir. 1975-78), Am. Cancer Soc. (state pub. edn. com. 1982-, naf. adv. com. on rsch. personnel 1985-), Sigma Xi. Home: 925 Delaware Ave Buffalo NY 14209 Office: Roswell Park Meml Inst Elm and Carlton Streets Buffalo NY 14263-0002

MIRANDA, CARLOS SA, food products company executive; b. Fall River, Mass., Nov. 16, 1929; s. Carlos Sa and Annette (Pratt) M.; m. Natalie Cardoso, Jan. 5, 1949; children: Carla, Lucy, John. BS in Mech. Engring., Marquette U., 1956. With internat. div. Kellogg Co., Battle Creek, Mich., 1964-65, gen. mgr. Brazil, 1965-80, Kellogg's Spain, 1983-84; v.p. Kellogg Internat., Battle Creek, 1980-89; country dir. internat. exec. svc. corps. Costa Rica, 1990-91; mediator Fla. County Cts., 1994—. Recipient Pero Vaz Caminha award, Brazil, 1976; conferred title Comdr. of Legion of Honor of Marshal Rondon, Brazil, 1971. Mem. ASME. Republican. Roman Catholic. Home: 988 Blvd of the Arts Apt 1016 Sarasota FL 34236-4840

MIRANDA, CONSTANCIO FERNANDES, civil engineering educator; b. Raia-Goa, India, Dec. 4, 1926; came to U.S., 1960, naturalized, 1966; s. Alex Fernandes and Maria Marcelina (Viegas) M.; m. Joan Mary Menezes, Mar. 3, 1957; children: Steven Alex, Christopher Gerard, Kenneth Michael, Marie Lynn. Student, Karnatak Coll., Dharwar, 1944-46; B Engring. (civil), U. Bombay, 1949; MS in Civil Engring, U. Notre Dame, 1962; PhD in Structural Engring, Ohio State U., 1964; MA in Math, U. Detroit, 1974. Registered profl. engr., Mich. With civil engring. projects Govt. Bombay, 1950-60; teaching asst., then instr. U. Notre Dame, 1960-62; instr., rsch. assoc. Ohio State U., 1962-64; mem. rsch. staff U. N.Mex., 1964-65; mem. faculty U. Detroit, 1965-88, prof. civil engring., 1966-88, chmn. dept., 1965-72, prof. structural and systems engring., 1973-88, assoc. dean Coll. Engring., acting dean, 1972-73, ret., 1989; cons. civil, structural, systems engring., applied maths. and computer applications, 1989—. Bd. dir. Profl. Adv. Svc. Ctr., 1973-75; staff engr. EPA, N.C., 1976-77. Contbr. profl. jours. Named Engring. Tchr. of Yr. Engring. Joint Coun., U. Detroit, 1967, 76; Distinguished Alumnus Ohio State U., 1973. Mem. ASCE, Am. Soc. Engring. Edn., Sigma Xi, Chi Epsilon, Tau Beta Pi, Pi Mu Epsilon. Home: 100 Silvercliff Trl Cary NC 27513-2803 E-mail: contoot@mindspring.com.

MIRANDA, MICHELE RENEE, optometrist; b. Springfield, Mass., Jan. 6, 1960; BS, Springfield Coll., 1982; OD, New Eng. Coll. Optometry, 1986; postgrad., Johns Hopkins U. Diplomate Internat. Assn. Bd. Examiners in Optometry. Resident VA Med. Ctr., Roxbury/Brockton, Mass., 1988; optometrist Med. Eye Care Assoc., Norwood, 1987-95, Bassett Healthcare, Cooperston, N.Y., 1995-96, Baystate Eye Care, PC, Springfield, Mass., 1996-99, John J. Papale, MD PC, Springfield, 1999—2000; mgr. laser vision svc. Fichman Eye Ctr., P.C., 2000—. Liaison New Eng. Coun. Optometrists, Boston, 1989-91, bd. corporators, 1991-93; spkr. in field. Recipient Alumni Assn. award New Eng. Coll. Optometry, 1986, Barnes Hind Student Recognition award New Eng. Coll. Optometry, 1986. Mem. Am. Optometric Assn., N.Y. State Optometric Assn., Mass. Soc. Optometrists (pres. 1990-91), Beta Sigma Kappa.

MIRANDA, ROBERT NICHOLAS, publishing company executive; b. Bklyn., July 9, 1934; m. Marilyn H. Pils, May 25, 1958; children: Marilyn, Robert, Susan, Lori, Jennifer AA in Acctg. and Bus. Adminstrn., SUNY-Farmingdale. Pres. Pergamon Press, Inc., Elmsford, N.Y., 1965-92; chmn., chief exec. officer Cognizant Communication Corp., 1992—; owner Miranda Press, 2002. Bd. dirs., exec. v.p., vice chmn. Soc. and Assoc. Svc. Corp., McLean, Va., 1979-82; bd. dirs., chmn. electronics com. Copyright Clearance Ctr., 1984-93. Pub. Acupuncture and Electro Therapeutics Rsch., Analgesia, Bird Behavior, Cancer Prevention Internat., Cell Transplantation, Festival Mgmt. and Event Tourism, Gene Expression, Info. Tech. and Tourism, Life Support and Biosphere Sci., Oncology Rsch., Tourism Analysis, Technology: Jour. of Regulatory Sci., Failure and Lessons Learned in Info. Tech., Pacific Tourism Rev., SSA Jour.-Jour. of Semi-Condr. Safety Assn., Tourism, Culture and Comm., Tourism Dynamic Book Series. Served with USNR, 1954-59 Mem. Council Sci. Editors, Internat. Soc. Intelligent Systems (founder, bd. dirs., fin. dir. 1992—). Avocations: hunting, fishing, horseback riding. Office: Cognizant Comm Corp 3 Hartsdale Rd Elmsford NY 10523-3701

MIRELS, HAROLD, aerospace engineer; b. N.Y.C., July 29, 1924; s. Hyman and Lily (Efron) M.; m. Nell Segal, Oct. 4, 1953; children: Lily, Laurence Franklin, Jeremy Mark. BSME, Cooper U., 1944; MSME, Case Inst. Tech., 1949; PhD in Aero. Engring., Cornell U., 1953. Sect. head NACA, Cleve., 1944-57; br. chief NASA, 1957-61; dept. head Aerospace Corp., El Segundo, Calif., 1961-78, assoc. dir., 1978-84, prin. scientist, 1984-93; cons., 1993—. Co-inventor continuous wave chem. laser. Recipient Tech. Achievement award Cleve. Tech. Socs., 1960. Fellow AIAA (Fluid and Plasmadynamics award 1988), Am. Phys. Soc.; mem. Nat. Acad. Engring. Home: 3 Seahurst Rd Palos Verdes Peninsula CA 90274-3700

MIRENBURG, BARRY LEONARD, publisher, company executive, educator; b. N.Y.C., Feb. 16, 1952; s. Fred and Mildred (Solomon) M. BS, Mercy Coll., 1979; BFA, Cooper Union, 1980; MBA, N.Y. Inst. of Tech., 1983; MA, Columbia U., 1983, postgrad., 1983—; MFA, Syracuse U., 1990; postgrad., Columbia U. Tchrs. Coll., 1997. Pres., pub. Barlenmir House, N.Y.C., 1972—; pres., owner Barlenmir House Theatres, Inc., 1978—; head Design Graphics N.Y. Inst. of Tech., 1979—; pres., creative dir. The Corp. Communications Group, 1985—, Mirenburg & Co., N.Y.C., 1985—. Instr. unranked Parsons Sch. of Design, N.Y.C., 1979—, coord. computer graphics, 1990-91; asst. prof. Fashion Inst. of Tech., N.Y.C., 1979-81; corp. art dir. Music Sales/Quick Fox, N.Y.C., 1982-85; adj. assoc. prof. Grad.. Sch. Coll. of New Rochelle, N.Y., 1985—; chmn. Restaurants Internat. Inc., 1993—. Founder, dir. Am. Health and Fitness Alliance, 1997—. Recipient more than 125 awards and honors for art and design; Fulbright scholar, 1991. Mem. AAUP, Nat. Coun. Art Adminstrs., Am. Inst. Graphic Arts, Soc. Publ. Designers, Am. Ctr. for Design, Art Dirs. Club, Soc. Indsl. Designers, Coll. Art Assn., Mensa. Home and Office: 301 E 38th St New York NY 10016-2750

MIRICK, ROBERT ALLEN, military officer; b. Kingston, N.Y., June 26, 1957; s. Harry Lawrence and Jean Alice (Erickson) Mirick; m. Pamela Ann Warburton, July 24, 1982; children: Kristen E., Kathryn A., Meredith W., Abigail S. BS in Oceanography, U.S. Naval Acad., 1979; MS in Engring. Acoustics, Naval Postgrad. Sch., 1989; MS in Nat. Security Strategy, Nat. War Coll., 2001. Commd. ensign USN, 1979, advanced through grades to capt., 2000; navigator, propulsion asst. USS McCandless, 1979-82; diving and deck officer USS Pigeon, 1983-85; exec. officer, navigator USS Bolster, 1985-87; commdg. officer USS Hoist, 1990-92; cmty. mgr., assignment and placement officer USN Spl. Ops., 1993-95; exec. officer U.S. Naval Activities, Guam, 1995-97; base ops. support officer US Naval Forces, Marianas, Guam, 1997-98; commdg. officer Mobile Diving and Salvage Unit 1, Pearl Harbor, Hawaii, 1998-99; chief staff officer, comdr. Explosive Ordnance Disposal Group One, San Diego, 1999-2000; comdg. officer Seal Beach Naval Weapons Sta., 2001—. Vol. staff diver Monterey Bay Aquarium, Calif., 1987—89, Aquarium of the Pacific, Long Beach, Calif., 2001—; field asst. Scripps Inst., San Diego, 1984—2000. Contbr. articles to profl. jours. Pres. Parents Assn. L.A., San Pedro, Calif., 1986. Decorated Meritorious Svc. medal USN; recipient Nat. Partnership for Reinventing Govt. Silver Hammer award for diving and salvage work, U.S. V.P., 1999. Mem.: U.S. Naval Order, U.S. Naval Inst., Am. Soc. Naval Engrs., Acoustical Soc. Am., Soc. Colonial Wars. Republican. Achievements include research in sediment acoustics; development of an apparatus to determine the complex mass of a viscous fluid contained in a rigid porous solid from acoustic pressure measurements; contributor to certification of USN MK2 Mod1 Deep Diving System to 850 feet; senior salvage officer and command center watch commander for survivor rescue, and search and recovery phase of KAL flight 801 disaster, Guam, 1997; senior fleet salvage officer for recovery of Alaska Air Flight 261 disaster offshore, Los Angeles area, 2000. Office: Naval Weapons Sta Seal Beach 800 Seal Beach Blvd Seal Beach CA 90740-5000 Home: 103 Hussey Rd Seal Beach CA 90740 E-mail: themiricks@earthlink.net.

MIRISOLA, LISA HEINEMANN, air quality engineer; b. Glendale, Calif., Mar. 25, 1963; d. J. Herbert and Betty Jane (Howson) Heinemann; m. Daniel Carl Mirisola, June 27, 1987; 1 child, Ian Cataldo. BSME, UCLA, 1986. Cert. engr.-in-tng., Calif. Air quality engr. South Coast Air Quality Mgmt. Dist., Diamond Bar, Calif., 1988—. Chancellor's scholar UCLA, 1981. Mem. ASME, NSPE, Soc. Women Engrs. Office: South Coast Air Quality Mgmt Dist 21865 Copley Dr Diamond Bar CA 91765-4178 E-mail: lmirisola@aqmd.gov.

MIRK, JUDY ANN, retired elementary educator; b. Victorville, Calif., June 10, 1944; d. Richard Nesbit and Corrine (Berghoefer). BA in Social Sci., San Jose (Calif.) State U., 1966, cert. in teaching, 1967; MA in Edn., Calif. State U., Chico, 1980. Cert. elem. edn. tchr., Calif. Profl. psychology trainee John F. Kennedy U., Orinda, Calif., 1997—99; tchr. Cupertino (Calif.) Union Sch. Dist., 1967-95; lead tchr. lang. arts Dilworth Sch., San Jose, 1988-90, mem. supt.'s adv. team, 1986-90, mem. student study team, 1987-95; ret. Mem. student study team, 1987-95; mem. Dilworth Sch. Site Coun., 1981-95. Mem. The Commonwealth Club of Calif, Phi Mu. Green Party. Avocations: photography, natural history, watercolors. Home: 2075 Redwood Dr Santa Cruz CA 95060-1238

MIRKIN, BERNARD LEO, clinical pharmacologist, pediatrician; b. Bronx, N.Y., Mar. 31, 1928; s. Max and Esther M.; m. Phyllis Korduner, Aug. 1954 (dec. 1982); children: Lisa Mia, Mara Rebecca; m. Sarah Solotaroff, 1986; stepchildren: Jennifer, Rachel, Jacob. AB, NYU, 1949; PhD, Yale U., 1953; MD, U. Minn., 1964. Asst. prof. pharmacology SUNY, Downstate Med. Center, 1954-60; Ford Found. postdoctoral fellow Karolinska Inst., Stockholm, 1960-61; USPHS post-doctoral fellow Yale U., 1961-62; resident in pediatrics U. Minn. Hosp., Mpls., 1964-66; asst. prof. U. Minn. Med. Sch., 1966-67, asso. prof., 1967-72; prof. pediatrics, pharmacology and biol. chemistry, dir. div. clin. pharmacology U. Minn. Health Sci. Ctr., 1972-89; prof. pediatrics and molecular pharmacology Northwestern U. Med. Sch., Chgo., 1989—; head, dir. rsch. Inst. for Edn. and Rsch. Children's Meml. Hosp., 1989—99; assoc. dean rsch. Northwestern U. Med. Sch., 1994—96; dir. rsch. emeritus Inst. for Edn. and Rsch. Children's Meml. Hosp., Chgo., 2000—. Cons. Office of Technology Assessment, U.S. Congress, WHO, U.S. Pharmacopeia, PhARMA Found., Nat. Inst. Health; fellow Jesus Coll., Oxford U., 1974. Author: Perinatal Pharmacology and Therapeutics, 1976, Clinical Pharmacology: A Pediatric Perspective, 1978. postdoctoral fellow Karolinska Inst. Stockholm 1960-61 Served with M.C. U.S. Army, 1954-56. Mem. AAAS, Soc. Pediat. Rsch., Am. Assn. Cancer Rsch., Am. Pediat. Soc., Am. Soc. Pharm. Exptl. Therapeutics, Am. Soc. Clin. Pharm. and Therapeutics. Home: 427 Greenleaf St Evanston IL 60202-1328 Office: Childrens Meml Inst Edn and Rsch Mailcode # 117 2300 N Childrens Plz Chicago IL 60614-3363 E-mail: b-mirkin@northwestern.edu.

MIRKIN, GABE BARON, allergist, pediatrician, medical writer, educator, radio personality, talk show host; b. Brookline, Mass., June 18, 1935; s. Mitchell and Vera (Baron) M.; children: Gene, Jan, Jill, Geoffrey, Kenny; m. Diana Purdie Rich, 1998. BA, Harvard U., 1957; MD, Baylor U., 1961. Diplomate Am. Bd. Pediatrics, Sub Bd. Allergy, Am. Bd. Allergy and Immunology, Am. Bd. Sports Medicine. Resident in pediatrics Mass. Gen. Hosp., Boston, 1961-63; fellow allergy, immunology, dermatology Johns Hopkins Hosp., Balt., 1963-65; allergy, immunology, dermatology, sports medicine pvt. practice, Silver Spring, Md., 1966—. Tchg. fellow in pediat., Harvard Med. Sch., 1962-63, in allergy and immunology, Johns Hopkins Med. Sch., 1963-65; asst. prof. dept. phys. edn., U. Md., College Park, 1976-83; assoc. clin. prof. dept. pediat. Georgetown U. Sch. of Medicine, 1984—; syndicated nat. talk show host on health, fitness and nutrition. Author: (books) The Sportsmedicine Book, 1978, Getting Thin, 1983, Dr. Gabe Mirkin's Fitness Clinic, 1986, The Complete Sportsmedicine Book for Women, 1985, 2d rev. edit. 1991, (with Shangold) Women and Exercise, 1988, Dr. Gabe Mirkin's Fatfree, Flavorfull Book, 1995, (with Diana Mirkin) The 20 Gram Diet, 1995, The 20/30 Fat and Fiber Diet Plan, Dr. Gabe Mirkins Rocket Guide to Fitness & Sports, (with Rich) The Whole Grains Cookbook, 1997, The Good Food Book, 2001; contbr. chpts. to 1 encyclopedia and 14 other books on Sports, Exercise or Nutrition; author (newsletter) The Mirkin Report, 1990—; columnist: syndicated weekly in N.Y. Times, 1978-89, in United Features, 1989-94; weekly column in Washington Post, 1976, weekly syndicated column on sports medicine, Singer Media Corp., 1994-99; weekly TV appearances on P.M. Mag. WDVM-TV, Washington, 1979 weekly appearance on House Party, NBC TV, 1990, monthly appearance on The Learning Channel, Cable TV; host internationally syndicated radio talk show, 1996—; daily 90 second radio spots on fitness and nutrition, CBS Radio Stations News Svc., 1979—; sporadic host talk show on health fitness and nutrition, KMOX Radio, St. Louis, 1982—; nightly talk show host NBC Washington, WRC, 1982-84, 87—, WNTR, 1984-86; Weekly 3 minute spots on fitness and nutrition for Physicians Radio Network, 1984-85; daily 3-hour talk show on health, fitness and nutrition syndicated nationally by Sun Radio Network, 1992; weekly 2-hour talk show on fitness and nutrition WEEI, Boston, 1993-94 and others; columnist and contbg. editor to numerous health and fitness mags.; contbr. to profl. jours. also. Major USAF, 1968-70. Fellow Am. Coll. Allergists, Am. Assn. Cert. Allergists, Am. Assn. for Clin. Immunology and Allergy, Am. Acad. Pediatrics, Am. Acad. Allergy and Immunology; mem. AMA, Am. Coll. Sports Medicine, Am. Med. Writers Assn., Med Chirurgical Soc. Md., Montgomery County Med. Soc. Avocation: bicycle tandem riding. Office: 10901 Connecticut Ave Kensington MD 20895-1645 E-mail: gabe@drmirkin.com.

MIRMAN, JOEL HARVEY, lawyer; b. Toledo, Dec. 3, 1941; s. Benjamin and Minnie (Krapifko) M.; children: Lisa, Julie, Benjamin. BBA, Ohio U., 1963; JD, Ohio State U., 1966. Bar: Ohio 1966, U.S. Dist. Ct. (so. dist.) Ohio 1966, U.S. Supreme Ct. 1972. Ptnr. Topper, Alloway, Goodman, DeLeone & Duffey, Columbus, Ohio, 1966-85, Benesch, Friedlander, Coplan & Aronoff, 1986-93; shareholder Buckingham, Doolittle & Burroughs, Columbus, Ohio, 1994—. Lectr. Ohio CLE Inst., Columbus, 1972—. Author direct examination CLE materials; contbr. articles to profl. jours. Mem. Ohio Elections Commn., 1976-80, vice-chmn. 1980. Mem. Capital Club, Worthington Hills Country Club, Worthington Hills Civic Assn. (pres. 1992-93), Assn. Trial Lawyers Am. (chmn. family law sects. 1993-94). E-mail: jmirman@bdblaw.com.

MIRONOVICH, ALEX, publisher; b. Brooklyn, N.Y., Nov. 30, 1952; s. Peter Mironovich and Olga Sachrina; m. Cynthia Ann Wuss, July 23, 1983; children: Britany, Nicholas. BA in psychology, City U., N.Y.C., 1970-74. Sales rep. House Beautiful mag., N.Y.C., 1976-79, Sawyer Ferguson Walker, N.Y.C., 1979-82, Creative Ideas for Living, N.Y.C., 1982-83, Parents mag. G and J, N.Y.C.; assoc. pub. Y.M. Gruner and Jahr, N.Y., 1986-88, pub., 1988; former pub. Better Homes and Gardens, N.Y.C.; pres. pub. group, exec. v.p. Playboy Enterprises Inc., Chgo., 1999—. Office: Playboy Enterprises Inc 680 N Lake Shore Dr Chicago IL 60611-4402*

MIROWITZ, SCOTT ALAN, radiologist; b. St. Louis, May 17, 1959; s. Carl L. and Helene S. (Steinman) M.; m. Jacqueline Finger, June 2, 1985; children: Jessica L., Melanie B., Adam M. BA summa cum laude, Tulane U., 1981; MD, Washington U., St. Louis, 1985; MS in Med. Mgmt., Tulane U., 1997. Certificate in med. mgmt. Am. Coll. Physician Execs., Tulane U., 1996. Radiology resident Washington U., 1989, MRI fellowship, 1990; dir. magnetic resonance imaging Jewish Hosp. at Washington U. Med. Ctr., St. Louis, 1990-93; radiologist-in-chief Mallinckrodt Inst. of Radiology, Barnes-Jewish Hosp. North, 1994-2001; assoc. prof. radiology Washington U. Sch. of Medicine, 1994-99, prof. radiology, 2000-01, U. Pitts. Sch. Medicine, 2001—, chmn. dept. radiology, 2001—. Co-dir. Body MRI, 1995—. Author: Pitfalls, Variants, Artifacts in Body MR Imaging, 1995; co-editor: Cardiovascular Magnetic Resonance Imaging, 1991; contbr. numerous articles to profl. jours; cons. editor MRI Clinics of North America, 1996—; assoc. editor MRI, Radiology, 1996—. Recipient Editor's Recognition award with Spl. Distinction Radiology, 1991, 92, 93, Joseph Whitley radiology edn. award Assn. U. Radiology, 2000. Fellow Am. Coll. Physician Execs.; mem. Radiologic Soc. of N.Am. (Roengten centellial fellowship award 1998), Am. Roentgen Ray Soc., Soc. of Magnetic Resonance (Magna Cum Laude Poster award 1991), Soc. for Computed Body Tomography and Magnetic Resonance (Winthrop award for Outstanding Paper, 1990). Office: Dept Radiology U Pitts Med Ctr 200 Lothrop St Pittsburgh PA 15213-2582

MIROWSKI, PHILIP EDWARD, economics educator; b. Jackson, Mich., Aug. 21, 1951; s. Edward and Elizabeth Mirowski; m. Pamela Margaret Cook, June 14, 1986. BA, Mich. State U., 1973; MA in Econs., U. Mich., 1976, PhD in Econs., 1979. Asst. prof. U. Santa Clara, Calif., 1978-81, Tufts U., Medford, Mass., 1981-84, assoc. prof. econs., 1984-90; Carl Koch prof. econs. and history and philosophy of sci. U. Notre Dame, Ind., 1990—. Vis. assoc. prof. Yale U., New Haven, 1987-88; vis. prof. Tinbergen Inst., Erasmus U., Rotterdam, Holland, 1991, U. Paris, 1997, U. Modena, Italy, 1998. Author: Reconstruction of Economic Theory, 1986, Against Mechanism, 1988, More Heat Than Light, 1989; Rowman & Littlefield series editor Studies in Worldly Philosophy; editor: Natural Images in Economics, 1994, Edgeworth on Chance, 1994; mem. editorial bd. History Polit. Econ., Duke U., 1986—, Social Concept, 1988-94; contbr. articles to profl. jours. Mem. Am. Econs. Assn., History Sci. Soc., History Econs. Soc., Soc. for Social Studies of Sci., Philosophy of Sci. Assn. Office: U Notre Dame Dept Econs Notre Dame IN 46556

MIRRA, CATHERINE M. social worker; b. N.Y.C., Jan. 30, 1952; AA, Rockland Community Coll., 1975; BS, Dominican Coll., 1981; MS, Columbia U., 1982. Lic. social worker, N.J. Sr. program devel. specialist State of N.J.-Judiciary, Bergen County; adminstr. County of Bergen-Youth Svcs. Commn., Hackensack. Mem. Nat. Assn. Social Workers, Acad. Cert. Social Workers.

MIRRA, SUZANNE SAMUELS, neuropathologist, researcher; BA, Hunter Coll., 1962; MD, SUNY, Bklyn., 1967. Instr. pathology Yale U. Sch. Medicine, New Haven, 1971-73; staff pathologist Atlanta VA Med. Ctr., Decatur, Ga., 1973-97; asst. prof. pathology Emory U. Sch. Medicine, Atlanta, 1973-80, assoc. prof. pathology, 1981-93, prof. pathology, 1993-97; prof., chair dept. pathology SUNY Health Sci. Ctr., Bklyn., 1997—. Dir., prin. investor Emory Alzheimer's Disease Ctr., Atlanta, 1991—97. Mem. editl. bd. Arch Pathol. Lab. Med., 1988-2000, Jour. Neuropathology Exptl. Neurology, 1991-95, Brain Pathology, 1995-99, Alzheimer's Disease Reviews, 1995-2000. Recipient Albert E. Levy Sci. Faculty Rsch. award Emory U., 1987, Disting. Alumnus Achievement award SUNY, 1992; named to Hunter Coll. Hall of Fame, 1996. Fellow Coll. Am. Pathologists (Presdl. award 1987,89, Herbert Lansky award 1990, chair neuropathology commn. 1992-95); mem. Am. Assn. Neuropathologists (v.p. profl. affairs 1992-97, pres. 1999-2000), Alzheimer's Assn. (bd. dirs. Atlanta chpt. 1987-97, nat. bd. dirs. 1997—). Office: SUNY Health Sci Ctr 450 Clarkson Ave Brooklyn NY 11203-2056 E-mail: smirra@downstate.edu.

MIRRIELEES, JAMES FAY, III, publishing executive; b. Cin., Nov. 2, 1939; s. James Fay and Alicia Lucille (Beatty) M.; m. Gillian C. Hanlon, July, 1986; 1 child, Hillary Evan, from previous marriage. BA, U. Cin. Editorial dir. McGraw-Hill Coll. Pub. Co., N.Y.C., 1975-77; v.p. Holt-Rinehart & Winston, 1977-79; pres. CBS Coll. Pub., 1979-81, 83-85, CBS Internat. Pub., 1981-83; mng. dir. European ops. Ashton-Tate, London, 1985-86; pres. Somerset House Edn. and Profl. Pubs., 1986-87; chief exec. officer Raintree Pub. Inc., 1987-88; chmn., pres. Raintree I Ltd. Partnership, 1988-91; pres. Coronet/MTI Film & Video, Deerfield, Ill., 1991-93; v.p. mktg. Edunetics Corp., Arlington, Va., 1993-95; v.p. bus. devel. Jennings & Keefe Media, 1995; pres. Blue Aegean Media, Arlington, Va., 1996—; mng. ptnr. Waterside E-Ventures, 2000—01; exec. v.p. Digital Learning Interactive, 2001—. Democrat. Home and Office: 2175 N Pierce St Arlington VA 22209-1110 E-mail: blueaegmedia@cs.com.

MIRRO, JOHN, engineering company executive; Student, MIT, Cambridge, Mass. Pres. Conmec, Inc, Bethlehem, Pa. Office: Conmec Inc 1480 Valley Center Pky Bethlehem PA 18017-2264

MIRSKY, ALLAN FRANKLIN, psychologist, researcher; b. N.Y.C., Feb. 2, 1929; s. Harry Leroy and Charlotte (Copans) M.; m. Carol Patricia Vogel, June 24, 1951 (dec. 1983); children: Laura Ann, Richard Daniel; m. Constance Catharine Duncan, July 4, 1986. BS, City Coll. N.Y., 1950; MS, Yale U., 1952, PhD, 1954. Diplomate Am. Bd. Profl. Psychology; cert. clin. Neuropsychology. Rsch. psychologist Nat. Inst. Health, Bethesda, Md., 1954-61; asst. prof. to prof. Boston U., Mass., 1961-80; chief lab. of psychology and psychopathology NIH, Bethesda, Md., 1980-95, chief sect. on clin. and exptl. neuropsychology, 1995—. Cons. NIH, NSF, NRC, Washington, 1965-93, WHO, 1992—; adj. prof. Johns Hopkins U., Balt., 1987—. Editor, author: Education and The Brain, 1978, Elements of Petit Mal Epilepsy, 1988. Comdr. USPHS, 1954-61. Rsch. grant NSF, NIH, 1961-80; recipient Career award NIMH, 1961-80, Outstanding Achievement in Psychology City Coll. N.Y., 1989. Fellow AAAS, APA (pres. divsn. comp. and physiol. psychology 1982-83, pres. divsn. clin. neuropsychology 2001—), Am. EEG Soc., Am.

Coll. Neuropsychopharmacology; mem. Internat. Neuropsychological Soc. (pres. 1972), Cosmos Club. Achievements include contributiions to the neuropsychology of attention, schizophrenia and petit mal epilepsy. Home: 5502 Spruce Tree Ave Bethesda MD 20814 Office: NIMH 5415 W Cedar Ln Ste 203B MSC 2615 Bethesda MD 20892-2615

MIRSKY, ARTHUR, geologist, educator; b. Phila., Feb. 8, 1927; s. Victor and Dorothy M.; m. Patricia Shorey, Dec. 22, 1961; 1 dau., Alexis Catherine. Student, Bklyn. Coll., 1944-45, 46-48; BA, U. Calif., 1950; MS, U. Ariz., 1955; PhD, Ohio State U., 1960. Cert. geologist, Ind. Field uranium geologist AEC, S.W. U.S., 1951-53; cons. uranium geologist Albuquerque, 1955-56; asst. dir. Inst. Polar Studies, Ohio State U., 1960-67; adj. asst. prof. geology Ohio State U., 1964-67; from asst. prof. geology to prof. Ind. U.-Purdue U., Indpls., 1967-94, prof. emeritus, 1994—, coord. geology, 1967-69, chmn. dept. geology, 1969-93. Contbr. articles to profl. jours. Served with USN, 1944-46. Mem. AAAS, AAUP, Am. Inst. Profl. Geologists, Geol. Soc. Am., Nat. Assn. Geosci. Tchrs., Am. Geol. Inst., Soc. Sedimentary Geology, Ind. Acad. Sci., Sigma Xi. Office: Indiana U-Purdue U Dept Geology 723 W Michigan St Indianapolis IN 46202-5132 E-mail: amirsky@iupui.edu.

MIRSKY, HOWARD, social services administrator, pharmacologist, pharmacist; b. Chgo., Nov. 10, 1933; s. Reuben R. and Jeanette Mirsky. BS in Pharmacy, U. Ill., 1955. Pharmacist Walgreen Co., Chgo., 1955-56, 58-59, Sol's Drugs Inc., Chgo., 1959-71; asst. exec. dir. Ill. Pharmacists Assn.; exec. dir. Citizens Alliance for Venereal Disease Awareness, Mt. Prospect, Ill., 1974—. Editor (newsletter) STD Spotlight, 1974—. With U.S. Army, 1956-58. Recipient Advtg. award U.S. TV Commls. Festival, 1975, CLIO award CLIO Found., 1978. Avocations: photography, music, hiking, communications study. Office: CAVDA Ste 128 800 WCentral Rd Mount Prospect IL 60056 E-mail: cavdarx@earthlink.net.

MIRSKY, PHYLLIS SIMON, librarian; b. Petach Tikva, Israel, Dec. 18, 1940; d. Allan and Lea (Prizant) Simon; m. Edward Mirsky, Oct. 21, 1967; 1 child, Seth (dec.). BS in Social Welfare, Ohio State U., 1962; postgrad., Columbia U., 1962-63; AMLS, U. Mich., 1965. Caseworker field placement Children's Aid Soc., N.Y.C., 1962-63; hosp. libr. hosp. and instns. divsn. Cleve. Pub. Libr., 1963-64; reference libr. UCLA Biomed. Libr., 1965-68, reference/acquisitions libr., 1968-69, head cons./continuing edn. Pacific S.W. Regl. Med. Libr. Sv., 1969-71, asst. dir. Pacific S.W. Regl. Med. Libr. Sv., 1971-73, faculty coord. Biomed. Libr. program Cen. San Joaquin Valley Area Health Edn. Ctr., 1973-77, assoc. dir. Pacific S.W. Regl. Med. Libr. Sv., 1973-79; head reference sect., coord. libr. assoc. program Nat. Libr. of Medicine, Bethesda, Md., 1979-81; asst. univ. libr., scis. U. Calif.-San Diego, La Jolla, 1981-86, acting univ. libr., 1985, 92-93, 98-99, asst. univ. libr. adminstrv. and pub. svcs., 1986-87, assoc. univ. libr. adminstrv. and pub. svcs., 1987-92, assoc. univ. libr., 1993-95; dep. univ. libr., 1995—. Guest lectr. Libr. Schs. UCLA and U. So. Calif., 1967-78, Grad. Sch. Libr. Sci. Cath. U., Washington, 1980, Grad. Sch. Libr. and Info. Sci. UCLA, 1984; mem. task force on role of spl. libr. nationwide network and coop. programs Nat. Commn. on Libr. and Info. Svcs./Spl. Libr. Assn., 1981-83; facilitator AASLD/MLA Guidelines Scenario Writing Session, L.A., 1984; mem. users coun. OCLC Online Computer Libr. Ctr., Inc., 1991-94; U. Calif.-San Diego rep. Coalition for Networked Info., 1992—; instr. Assn. Rsch. Librs., Office Mgmt. Studies, Mgmt. Inst., 1987; peer reviewer Coll. Libr. Tech. and Cooperation Grant Program U.S. Dept. Edn., 1988-94; cons. Nat. Libr. Medicine, Bethesda, Md., 1988, San Diego Mus. Contemporary Art Libr., La Jolla, Calif., 1993, Salk Inst., 1995; mem. Libr. of Congress Network Adv. Com., 1994-96, chair steering com., 1995-96. Contbr. articles to profl. jours. and bulls. Mem. fin. com. City of Del Mar, 1995-98, chair, 1997-98. NIH fellow Columbia U., 1962-63; sr. fellow UCLA/Coun. on Libr. Resources, 1987. Fellow Med. Libr. Assn. (bd. dirs. 1977-80); mem. ALA (site visitors panel com. on accreditation 1990-92, libr. adminstrn. and mgmt. assn. 1990-92), Med. Libr. Group Soc. Calif. and Ariz. (sec. 1970-71, v.p. 1971-72, pres. 1972-73), Documentation Abstracts, Inc. (bd. dirs. 1985-90, vice chair bd. dirs. 1988-90), Med. Libr. Assn. (pres. 1984-85), U. Mich. Sch. Libr. Sci. Alumni Assn. Office: U Calif San Diego U Libr 0175G 9500 Gilman Dr La Jolla CA 92093-5003

MIRTO, GREGORIO L. priest; b. Kilbo, Philippines, Dec. 20, 1941; arrived in U.S., 82; s. Gregorio Mirto and Isidra Laserna. Licentiate in Sacred Theology, U. Santo Tomas, Manila, Philippines, 1965; D Canon Law, U. St. Thomas Aquinas, Rome, 1987. Advocate Roman Rota, Vatican City, 1984—87; parochial vicar St. Joseph Parish, El Paso, Tex., 1988—90, Cathedral Parish, Denver, 1991—94, Light of the World Ch., Littleton, 1994—97; judge marriage tribunal Archdiocese of Denver, 1990—91; pastor St. William Cath. Ch., Ft. Lupton, 1997—. Mem.: KC (chaplain). Roman Catholic. Avocations: opera, musical shows, movies, classical music. Home and Office: 1025 Fulton Ave Fort Lupton CO 80621 Fax: 303-857-6643.

MIRZA, LEONA LOUSIN, educator; b. Chgo., July 1, 1944; d. Max B. and Opal Lousin; m. David B. Mirza; children: Sara Anush, Elizabeth Ann. BA in Math., North Park Coll., Chgo., 1965; MA in Edn., Western Mich. U., Kalamazoo, 1967, EdD in Edn., 1972; cert. in computer studies, North Park Coll., 1983. Specialist in elem. curriculum and adminstrn. Tchr. Kalamazoo Pub. Schs., 1965-69; prof. math. edn. North Park U., Chgo., 1969-2001, asst. acad. dean, 1999—2001; dir. Inst. for Internat. and Cultural Studies, 2001—. Editor The Ill. Math. Tchr., 1992-95; contbr. articles to profl. jours. Chmn. adv. com. on edn. in Ill., 1975-77. Mem. Nat. Coun. Tchrs. Math., Ill. Coun. Tchrs. Math., Ill. Assn. Colls. of Tchr. Edn., Ill. Assn. Tchrs. Edn. in Pvt. Colls. (officer 1974-86). Home: 5241 N Sawyer Ave Chicago IL 60625-4715 Office: 3225 W Foster Ave Chicago IL 60625-4823

MIRZA, MUHAMMAD ZUBAIR, product development company executive, researcher, engineering consultant, inventor; b. Jhelum, Punjab, Pakistan, Nov. 13, 1949; came to U.S., 1971; s. Muhammad Siddique and Shehr (Bano) M.; m. Tahira Beena, Aug. 12, 1977; children: Sarah, Nadia, Sana. Grad., Cadet Coll., Hasan Abdal, Pakistan, 1967; AS in Respiratory Therapy, St. Joseph/VA Hines Hosps., Chgo., 1974; BS in Biology, U. Ill., Springfield, 1976; MS in Product Design for Health Care, U. Ill., Chgo., 1978. Respiratory therapist St. Joseph Hosp., Chgo., 1974-79; assoc. engr. J.G.G. & Assocs., Woodbridge, N.J., 1979; product devel. engr. Becton-Dickinson Respiratory Sys., Lincoln Park, 1979-82; biomed. product devel. cons. M. Zubair Mirza Cons., Saddle Brook, 1982-86; co-founder, v.p. R & D, bd. dirs. Critichem, Inc. (acquired by Becton-Dickinson Corp. 1986), Little Falls, 1982-86; mgr. advanced devel. engring. Becton-Dickinson, Critichem Group, Fairlawn, 1986-88; dir. biomed. engring./tech. and equipment planning Shifa Internat. Hosp., Islamabad, Pakistan, 1989-90; pres. M. Zubair Mirza Cons., Wyckoff, Elmwood Park, N.J., 1988—, Natural Solutions, Inc., Wyckoff, Elmwood Park, 1991—. Rsch. asst. Sch. Medicine, So. Ill. U., Springfield, 1976; rsch. assoc. Office of Spl. Edn., Springfield, 1975-76, designer spl. edn. facility; rsch. assoc. to sr. cons. WHO, Geneva, 1977-78, designer self-health care kit. Author: Islamization of Business, 1994; patentee on respiratory monitor, 1992, respiratory monitoring device, 1993, trocar system, 1994, mechanical trocar insertion aparatus, 1995, pocket electronic spirometer, 1998, others. Trustee, v.p. Islamic Edn. Found. N.J., 1995-99, active Muslim, Jewish & Christian Dialogues, 1994—; Ameer The Spirit Medina (a comprehensive Islamic soc./inst.), 1997—; mem. Am. Islamic Arbitration Assn., 1998—, mem. various cmty. project coms. Moslem. Avocations: inventing, writing, reading, camping. Office: 22A Garden Dr Elmwood Park NJ 07407-1027 E-mail: nsi@juno.com.

MIRZA, SHAUKAT, engineering educator, researcher, consultant; b. Bhopal, India, Aug. 1, 1936; s. Mirza Afaq Beg and Birjees Jahan; m. Ferzana Beg, June 25, 1967; children: Sabah Jahan, Mazin. BSc in Engring., Aligarh U., 1956; MSCE, U. Wis., 1960, PhD in Engring. Mechanics, 1962. Sr. lectr. Delhi (India) Coll. Engring., 1962-64; prof. Indian Inst. Tech., New Delhi, 1964-69; prof. mech. engring. U. Ottawa, Ont., Can., 1969-96, vice dean R & D faculty engring. Can., 1991-94, prof. emeritus Can., 1996—; vis. engr. Westinghouse Nuclear Europe, Brussels, 1976-77, Def. Rsch. Establishment, Ottawa, 1987-88; cons. Govt. of India, New Delhi, 1967-68, Atomic Energy Can., 1974-80, Bell No. Rsch., Ottawa, 1981-82; vis. prof. Worcester (Mass.) Poly. Inst., 1994-95, prof. mech. engring., interim dir. mfg. engring., 1998-2001; prof. mech. and aerospace engring., dir. indsl. ptnrs. program N.C. State U., Raleigh, 2001—. Vis. prof. Ecole Nat. Superieur d'Ingeneur de Const. Aero., Toulouse, France, 1994; invited keynote speaker various internat. profl. confs. Contbr. rsch. articles, tech. reports to publs. Recipient President's gold medal Roorkee U., India, 1958. Fellow ASME. Office: NC State U Dept Mech and Aero Engring Broughton Hall 2601 Stinson Dr Raleigh NC 27695

MIRZA, ZAKIR HUSSAIN, aerospace company consultant; b. Jullundar, India, Dec. 15, 1947; arrived in Can., 1971, came to U.S., 1977; s. Mohammad Hussain and Kaniz Fatima Mirza; m. Naveeda J. Mirza, Aug. 26, 1977; children: Noreen, Hassan, Nadeem. BSc in Physics/Maths., U. Panjab, Lahore, Pakistan, 1968, MSc in Physics, 1970. Test engr. Bendix Corp., Windsor, Ont., Can., 1971-79; mgr. instrumentation engring. Nat. Tech. Sys., Saugus, Calif., 1979-82; sr. instrumentation engr. Wyle Labs., Norco, 1982-84; sr. test engr. Rohr Corp., Chula Vista, 1984-87; cons. various clients including Boeing Satellite Sys., El Segundo, Ledtronics, Torrance, Teledyne Continental Motors, Muskegon, Mich., FMC Corp., San Jose, Calif., Stewart and Stevenson, Houston, Thiokol Corp., Brigham City, Utah, 1987—. Fellow Inst. Advancement Engring., AIAA (past chmn. L.A. chpt.). Republican. Moslem. Avocations: flying fixed wing aircraft, swimming. Home: 4952 Blackhorse Rd Rancho Palos Verdes CA 90275 Office: Boeing Satellite Sys W/S02/D320 PO Box 92919 Los Angeles CA 90009

MISA, KENNETH FRANKLIN, management consultant; b. Jamaica, N.Y., Sept. 24, 1939; s. Frank J. and Mary M. (Soszka) M. BS in Psychology cum laude, Purdue U., 1963; PhD in Psychology, St. John's U., 1966. Cert. mgmt. cons.; lic. psychologist, Calif. Staff psychologist Rohrer, Hibler & Replogle, L.A., 1966-67; assoc. A.T. Kearney, Inc., 1968-71, sr. assoc., 1972-74, prin., 1975-78, v.p., ptnr., 1979-86; pres. HR Cons. Group, 1987—. Mem. APA, Am. Psychol. Soc., Calif. State Psychol. Assn., Soc. for Human Resources Mgmt., Human Resources Planning Soc., Indsl. Rels. Rsch. Assn., Soc. for Indsl. and Orgnl. Psychology, World Affairs Coun. L.A., Town Hall So. Calif., Glendale C. of C., Jonathan Club. Republican. Roman Catholic. Home: 804 S Orange Grove Blvd Pasadena CA 91105-1715 Office: HR Cons Group 100 N Brand Blvd Ste 200 Glendale CA 91203-2642 Fax: 626-441-9584. E-mail: kfmhrcg@aol.com.

MISCELLA, MARIA DIANA, humanities educator; b. N.Y.C., July 11, 1929; d. Nicola and Giovanna (Tangorra) Torelli; m. Emilio Miscella, Feb. 27, 1954 (dec. Sept. 30, 1996); children: Delia, Marisa, Giuliana. Tchr. Degree, Istituto Magistrale, Lecce, Italy, 1946; postgrad., U. Naples, 1946-48; BA, Hunter Coll., 1954, MA, 1972. Cert. secondary educator, N.Y. state, N.Y.C. English corr. GE Co., Rome, 1950-51; corr. Spanish & French Pettinos Import & Export Co., N.Y.C., 1952-53; tchr. Italian Harrison (N.Y.) H.S., 1967-87, St. John's U., Queens, N.Y., 1987-89; lectr. Italian various orgsn., N.Y. State, 1987—; lectr. Italian lit. and history various colls. and univs., N.Y., 1987—. Moderator of club Harrison (N.Y.) H.S., 1967-87. Mem. Little Neck (N.Y.) Civic Assn., 1970-95, Am. Assn. Ret. People, Douglaston, N.Y., 1994—; founder, treas. Italian Am. Women's Ctr., 1997—. Recipient scholarship Columbia U., 1954, Letter of Commendation, Bd. Regents, Albany, N.Y., 1980; named Woman of Yr., Consortium of L.I. Italian Am. Orgns., 1992. Mem. AAUW (hostess, v.p. 1990-93, cert. of commendation 1996), Am. Assn. Tchrs. of Italian (sec. Societa Onoraria Italica 1979-91), Ams. of Italian Heritage (bd. mem. 1982—), Sons of Italy (John Marino Lodge cultural com. mem 1994—, Merit award 1995), Assn. Italian Am. Educators (dir./historian by-laws com. 2000), N.Y. State United Tchrs., Am. Fedn. Tchrs., Nat. Italian Am. Found., Douglaston Women Club, Retirees Club. Roman Catholic. Avocations: reading, writing, travel, going to theatre, playing bridge.

MISCEO, GIOVANNI FRANCESCO, psychology educator; b. Bari, Italy, July 20, 1953; came to U.S., 1963; s. Vito and Domenica Misceo; m. Gretchen Wilbur, Mar. 22, 1984; 1 child, Domenico C. BA, BS, No. Ill. U., 1977; MS, Kans. State U., 1980, PhD, 1987. Asst. prof. Mo. Valley Coll., Marshall, Mo., 1988-90; asst. prof. psychology Benedictine Coll., Atchison, Kans., 1990-92, chair psychology dept., 1992-2000, assoc. prof. psychology, 1993—. Dir. Discovery Program, Atchison, 1995-99; mng. editor Benedictine Discovery Jour., Atchison, 1998-99; councilor Undergrad. Rsch. Coun., 1997-99. Author (chpt. in book) Advances in Psychology, 1998; contbr. articles to profl. jours. Mem. APA, Am. Psychol. Sci., Midwestern Psychol. Assn., Psychonomic Soc., Cheiron Soc., Gt. Plains Behavioral Rsch. Assn. Office: Benedictine Coll 1020 N 2d St Atchison KS 66002 E-mail: gmisco@benedictine.edu.

MISCHKE, CARL HERBERT, religious association executive, retired; b. Hazel, S.D., Oct. 27, 1922; s. Emil Gustav and Pauline Alvina (Polzin) M.; m. Gladys Lindloff, July 6, 1947; children: Joel, Susan Mischke Blahnik, Philip, Steven. BA, Northwestern Coll., Watertown, Wis., 1944; M.Div., Wis. Luth. Sem., Mequon, 1947. Ordained to ministry Evang. Lutheran Ch. Parish pastor Wis. Synod, 1947-79; pres. Western Wis. Dist. Evang. Luth. Ch., Juneau, 1964-79; v.p. Wis. Luth. Synod, Milw., 1966-79, pres., 1979-93; retired, 1993.

MISCHKE, CHARLES RUSSELL, mechanical engineering educator; b. Glendale, N.Y., Mar. 2, 1927; s. Reinhart Charles and Dena Amelia (Scholl) M.; m. Margaret R. Bubeck, Aug. 4, 1951; children: Thomas, James. BSME, Cornell U., 1947, MME, 1950; PhD, U. Wis., 1953. Lic. mechanical engr. Iowa, Kans. Asst. prof. mech. engring. U. Kans., Lawrence, 1953-56, assoc. prof. mech. engring., 1956-57; prof., chmn. mech. engring. Pratt Inst., N.Y.C., 1957-64; prof. mech. engring. Iowa State U., Ames, 1964—, Alcoa Found. prof., 1974. Author: Elements of Mechanical Analysis, 1963, Introduction to Computer-Aided Design, 1968, Mathematical Model Building, 1972; editor: Standard Handbook of Machine Design, 1996, Mechanical Engineering Design, 6th edit., 2001, 8 Mechancal Designers Workbooks, 1990, Fundamentos de Diseno Mechanico, 4 vols., 1994. Scoutmaster Boy Scouts Am., Ames. With USNR, 1944-75, mem. Res. ret. Recipient Ralph Teetor award Soc. Automotive Engrs., 1977, best book award Am. Assn. Pubs., 1986, Legis. Teaching Excellence award Iowa Assembly, 1990, Ralph Coates Roe award Am. Soc. for Engring. Edn., 1991. Fellow ASME (life, Machine Design award 1990); mem. Am. Soc. Engring. Edn. (Centennial cert. 1993), Am. Gear Mfrs. Assn., Scabbard and Blade, Cardinal Key, Sigma Xi, Phi Kappa Phi, Pi Tau Sigma. Avocations: model building, railway history, diesel locomotive engineer, B&SV railroad. Office: Iowa State U Dept Mech Engring Ames IA 50011-0001

MISCHKE, FREDERICK CHARLES, manufacturing company executive; b. Benton Harbor, Mich., Sept. 21, 1930; s. Fred William and Clara Adeline (Ruhno) M.; m. Kathleen Ann Schultz, Nov. 19, 1955 (dec. Aug. 1980); children: Stephanie Ann, Michael Frederick (dec. Oct. 12, 1996), Eric William; m. Lori Ann Leonard, Dec. 23, 1983. AA, Lake Mich. Coll., 1956; BBA, Western Mich. U., 1958. CPA, Ind., Mich. Staff acct. Lybrand, Ross Bros. & Montgomery, Chgo., 1958-63, supr. acctg. Niles, Mich., 1963-65; v.p., treas. Skyline Corp., Elkhart, Ind., 1965-91, ret., 1991. Vol. Svc. Corps. Ret. Execs., 1992—, local v.p., 1993-99, treas. 2000—; chmn. Meml. Endowment Fund Luth. Ch., 1995—. Mem. AICPA, Ind. Assn. CPAs (Civic Achievement award, 1976), Mich. Assn. CPAs, Fin. Execs. Inst. (Michiana chpt. pres. 1974-75), Nat. Assn. Accts., U.S. Power Squadron. Clubs: Elcona Country (pres. 1975). Lodges: Rotary (local pres. 1976-77). Republican. Lutheran. Avocations: photography, boating, golf. Home: 23322 Greenleaf Blvd Elkhart IN 46514-4508

MISE, JESSE SHERDEN, structural engineer, consultant; b. Jonesville, Va., July 13, 1933; s. Clabe Moss and Gladys Elizabeth (Orr) M.; m. Betty Joy Curtiss, July 8, 1984; children: Nancy Miller, Linda Andrews, Doug Hinshaw. BS in Math., Tenn. Tech, 1957. Registered profl. engr., Tenn., Mo. Road designer Va. Dept. Hwys., Petersburg, Va., 1958-64; structural designer various archtl., engring. firms, 1964-67; structural engr. Combustion Engring., Windsor, Conn., 1967-72, Tenn. Eastman, Kingsport, 1973-76, Tenn. Valley Authority, Knoxville, 1976-87, ABB Environ., Knoxville, 1988-91; cons. Jesse S. Mise, P.E., 1992—; chief engr. James Thomas Engring., 1992—. Author: Engineers Guide to Unusual Opportunities, 1972. Mem. Patriots of East Tenn., Knoxville, 1996—. Mem. ASCE, Nat. Coun. of Examiners for Engring. and Surveying, 1993—. Home and Office: 5704 Melstone Dr Knoxville TN 37912-4629

MISELSON, ALEX J. (JACOB MISELSON), portfolio manager, securities analyst, investment theorist; b. N.Y.C., Feb. 23, 1926; s. Aaron and Bertha (Guskin) M. BS in Social Sci. with honors in History, CCNY, 1947; MA in History, Columbia U., 1950; MA in Econs., Queens Coll., 1975. Instr. dept. history CCNY, 1949-55; tchr. Kearny (N.J.) High Sch., 1955-57, Uniondale High Sch., L.I., N.Y., 1957-76; reg. rep. Herzfeld and Stern, N.Y.C., 1977-81, Haas Securities Corp., N.Y.C., 1981-83, Fahnestock and Co., N.Y.C., 1983-85, Dominick and Dominick, N.Y.C., 1985; dir. rsch. A.T. Brod and Co., Inc., 1986-94, Investors Assocs., N.Y.C., 1994-96, Paragon Capital Markets, N.Y.C., 1996—2001; dir. investment strategy, 2000—. Instr. econs. Nassau Community Coll., 1969-75; head coach basketball Kearny High Sch., 1955-57; asst. coach basketball C.W. Post Coll., Greenvale, L.I., 1958-59; spl. guest TV talk shows; commentator in fin. field, 1988—. Contbr. articles to profl. publs., regularly interviewed by talk shows on special occasions, regularly interviewed by The Wall Street Transcript as part of its series on successful money managers, recognized as leading proponent of sophisticated long-term quality investing, with a unique highly unconventional selection technique and strategy. Active L.I. Coun. for Econ. Edn., Hofstra U., Hempstead, N.Y., 1968-75. With U.S. Army, 1944-45. Mem. Phi Delta Kappa, Phi Alpha Theta, Phi Beta Kappa. Avocations: reading, writing, theatre.

MISETICH, IONE HOZENDORF, business services company executive, enrolled agent, financial planner, accountant; b. Jackson, Miss., Sept. 19, 1937; d. Glenn Frederick and Ione Belle (Lowry) Hozendorf; m. Francis John Reget, Jan. 17, 1967 (div. 1986); m. Charles Drago Misetich, May 28, 1993; children: Diane Michele, Philip Francis, Michael Trahern. BA cum laude, U. Minn., 1959. CFP; CPA, Calif. Pres., Ea. Sierra Bus. Svcs., Inc., Bishop, Calif., 1980—; sec.-treas. Meyer Cookie Co., Inc. Soprano, Bishop Cmty. Chorus, 1974-78; treas. Calvary Bapt. Ch., Bishop, 1975—, choir dir., 1980—; chmn. Civic Arts Commn., City of Bishop, 1984-87; bd. dirs. Inyo Council for the Arts, 1987-90; pres. Bishop Com. Concert Assn., 1989—. Mem. Nat. Assn. Enrolled Agts., Calif. Soc. Enrolled Agts., Calif. Assn. Ind. Accts., Internat. Assn. Fin. Planners, Inst. CFP, Aircraft Owners and Pilots Assn., DAR, Mensa, Playhouse 395, Bishop Toastmasters Club, Bishop Rotary Club. Republican. Home: 325 Kempton St # 610 Spring Valley CA 91977-5810 Office: 130 Short St Bishop CA 93514-3538 Address: PO Box 728 Bishop CA 93515-0728

MISH, FREDERICK CRITTENDEN, editor; b. Hagerstown, Md., Feb. 11, 1938; s. Joseph Dubbs and Edith Louise (Crittenden) M.; m. Judith Elizabeth Solberg, Mar. 15, 1969; children— Stephen Crittenden, Andrew Dubbs, David Rogneby BA, Yale U., 1959; MA, U. Minn., 1967, PhD, 1973; LHD (hon.), York Coll., 1995. Instr. English, Severn Sch., Severna Park, Md., 1959-61, chmn. dept. English, 1963-65; teaching assoc. U. Minn., Mpls., 1965-71; asst. editor G & C Merriam Co., Springfield, Mass., 1973-74, assoc. editor, 1974, sr. editor, 1974-75, joint editorial dir, 1975-78; editorial dir. Merriam-Webster Inc., 1978-93, v.p., editor-in-chief, 1993—. Editor-in-chief: The Merriam-Webster Book of Word Histories, 1976, 6,000 Words: A Supplement to Webster's Third, 1976, Webster's School Dictionary, 1980, Webster's Beginning Dictionary, 1980, Webster's Vest Pocket Dictionary, 1981, Webster's Ninth New Collegiate Dictionary, 1983, Merriam Webster's Collegiate Dictionary, 10th Edit., 1993, 9,000 Words: A Supplement to Webster's Third, 1983, 12,000 Words: A Supplement to Webster's Third, 1986, Webster's Intermediate Dictionary, 1986, Webster's Word Histories, 1989, The New Merriam Webster Dictionary, 1989, Addenda Section 1993: A Supplement to Webster's Third, The Merriam-Webster Dictionary, 1994. Advisor Noah Webster Found., 1979—; trustee Davis and Elkins Coll., 1986-95, 96-99. With U.S. Army, 1961-63. S. H. Monk teaching fellow, 1971-72 Mem. MLA, Nat. Coun. Tchrs. English (commn. on English lang. 1981-83), Linguistic Soc. Am., Am. Dialect Soc., Am. Name Soc., Dictionary Soc. N.Am. Home: 45 Harwich Rd Longmeadow MA 01106-1207 Office: Merriam Webster Inc 47 Federal St PO Box 281 Springfield MA 01102-0281

MISHAL, DEVADATT M. obstetrician/gynecologist; b. Ratnagiri, India, Mar. 15, 1948; came to U.S., 1973; MD, Bombay U., 1973. Diplomate Am. Bd. Obstetrics and Gynecology. Intern Lower Bucks Hosp., Bristol, Calif., 1973-74; resident in obstetrics, gynecology Cooper Hosp. U. Med. Ctr., Camden, 1977-80; chmn. obstetrics, gynecology Downey (Calif.) Regional Med. Ctr., 1992-96, pres. of staff Calif.; staff Presby Inter Cmty. Hosp., Whittier, St. Francis Med. Ctr., Lynwood; mem. staff L.A. County Med. Assn.; pvt. practice, group partnership Downey, Calif., 1982—; pres. med. staff Downey Regional Med. Ctr., 1999—2001. Mem. ACOG, Am. Assn. of Gynecological Laparoscopists, Calif. Med. Assn. (L.A. chpt.), L.A. County Med. Assn. Office: 8500 Florence Ave Downey CA 90240-4015 also: 12446 Washington Blvd Whittier CA 90602-1005

MISHELEVICH, DAVID JACOB, medical company executive, consultant; b. Pitts., Jan. 26, 1942; s. Benjamin and Sarah (Bachrach) M.; m. Bonnie Gray McKim, Dec. 6, 1981; 1 child, Cory Jane. BS in Physics, U. Pitts., 1962; MD, Johns Hopkins U., 1966, PhD in Biomed. Engring., 1970. Lic., Md., Tex. Intern in medicine Balt. City Hosps., 1966-67; staff assoc. Nat. Inst. Neurol. Diseases and Stroke, NIH, Bethesda, Md., 1967-69; exec. v.p. Nat. Ednl. Consultants, Balt., 1971-72; prof., dept. chairperson, dir. med. computing resources ctr. U. Tex. Health Sci. Ctr., Dallas, 1972-82; attending physician/sr. attending physician internal med. Dallas County Hosp., Dist. Parkland Meml. Hosp., 1973-82; v.p. computer and software tech. EAN-TECH, Mountain View, Calif., 1983-84; CEO Garden Gate Software, Cupertino, 1984-86; dir., then v.p. and gen. mgr. applications and rsch. divsn. IntelliCorp, Inc., Mountain View, 1986-89; v.p. mktg. and sales Viewpoint Engring., 1989-90; v.p. engring. AirWays Med. Techs., Inc., Palo Alto, Calif., 1991-93; dir., then v.p. R&D, chief tech. officer Circadian, Inc., San Jose, 1993-95, v.p., gen. mgr. AirWays Asthma Ctrs. divsn., 1995-96; CEO Sterling Healthcare Outcomes, Inc., Cupertino, 1996—; founder, exec. v.p., chief tech. officer QENM.com, 1999-2001; chief tech. officer HealthShore, Inc., 2001—. Pres. Mishelevich Assocs., Dallas, 1982-83, Cupertino, 1990-91; mem. biomed. libr. rev. com. NIH-Nat. Libr. Medicine, 1978-82; cons. in field. Former tech. reviewer IBM Sys. Jour., Jour. of AMA; contbr. numerous articles to profl. jours.; patentee in field. V.p. Dallas chpt. Am. Jewish Congress, 1980-84, Am. Jewish Fund, 1980-81. Fellow Am. Coll. Med. Informatics; mem. AAAS, IEEE and IEEE Computer Soc. (exec. bd. tech. com. on computational medicine 1981-83), Am. Assn. for Artificial Intelligence, Assn. for Computing Machinery (chair Dallas chpt. 1974-75), Am. Med. Informatics Assn., Internat. Med. Outcomes Trust, Internat. Tandem Users Group (past pres.), Phi Beta Kappa, Omicron Kappa. Democrat. Jewish. Home and Office: 7301 Vista del Mar #B111 Playa Del Rey CA 90293 *Working with computers for some forty years has made me particularly sensitive to human needs and productivity. Two principles in which I believe are the human resources principle (maximize people's strengths and minimize or neutralize their weaknesses so they perform personally and professionally better than they would otherwise expect of themselves), and the optimality principle (I would rather do a 92% job in two weeks than a 97% job in 2 years).*

MISHELL, DANIEL R., JR. obstetrician, gynecologist, educator; b. Newark, May 7, 1931; s. Daniel R. and Helen Mishell; m. Carol Goodrich; children: Sandra, Daniel III, Tanya. BA, Stanford U., 1952, MD, 1955. Diplomate Am. Bd. Ob-Gyn. (examiner 1975-95, bd. dirs., dir. subspecialty divsn. reproductive endocrinology 1985-89, pres. 1986-90, chmn. 1990-94). Intern L.A. County Harbor Gen. Hosp., Torrance, 1955-56; resident in internal medicine Bellevue Hosp., N.Y.C., 1956-57; resident in ob-gyn. UCLA-Harbor Gen. Hosp., Torrance, 1959-63; rsch. fellow Univ. Hosp., Uppsala, Sweden, 1961-62; from asst. prof. to assoc. prof. dept. ob-gyn. UCLA Sch. Medicine, 1963-69; prof. U. So. Calif., L.A., 1969—, assoc. chmn. dept., 1972-78, chmn. dept. ob/gyn., 1978—. Editor-in-chief Contraception, 1969—; editor Jour. Reproductive Medicine, 1982—, Year Book of Obstetrics and Gynecology, 1987—, Year Book of Infertility, 1989-96; adv. com. Core Jours. in Ob-gyn., 1982—; mem. editl. bd. New Trends in Gynecology and Obstetrics, 1998—. Capt. USAF, 1957-59. Recipient Lester T. Hibbard award U. So. Calif., L.A., 1983, Joseph Bolivar DeLee Humanitarian award Chgo. Lying-In Hosp., 1985, Arthur and Edith Wippman Sci. Rsch. award Planned Parenthood Fedn. Am., 1992, Disting. Scientist award Soc. Gynecologic Investigation, 1994. Mem. Am. Gyn-Ob Soc., Am. Soc. Reproductive Medicine, Am. Coll. Obstetricians and Gynecologists, Am. Fedn. Clin. Rsch., Endocrine Soc., Soc. for Gynecologic Investigation (pres. 1985-86), L.A. Ob-Gyn. Soc. (v.p. 1984-85, pres. 1985-86), Assn. Profs. Gynecology and Obstetrics (exec. coun. 1982-85), Pacific Coast Fertility Soc. (pres. 1973-74), Salerni Collegium, L.A. Athletic Club, Phi Beta Kappa, Alpha Omega Alpha. Avocations: tennis, fishing. Office: U So Calif 1240 N Mission Rd Los Angeles CA 90033-1019 E-mail: mishell@hsc.usc.edu.

MISHIK, ANTHONY NEAL, pediatrician; b. Bklyn., May 11, 1957; s. Cornelius Paul and Marianna Francine (Gallo) M.; m. Deborah Jean De Loiselle; 3 children. BA in Biology, U. Pa., 1979; MS in Physiology, Georgetown U., 1980, MD, 1984. Diplomate Am. Bd. Pediatrics. Intern, resident Naval Hosp., Oakland, Calif., 1984-87, pediatrician Cherry Point, N.C., 1987-91, pediatrics dept. head, 1988-91; pediatrician Woodbury Pediatrics, Woodbury Heights, N.J., 1991-95; pediatrician, owner West Deptford Pediatrics, Wenonah, 1995—. Bd dirs. Children's Healthcare, P.A., Cherry Hill, N.J., sec. 1993-99; bd. dirs. Children's Health Assocs., LLC, v.p. 1998—; mem. task force on children and adolescents N.J. Dept. Health, Trenton, 1995-2000; mem. planning com. So. N.J. Perinatal Coop., Pennsauken, 1993—; clin. preceptor U. Pa. Sch. Nursing, Phila., 1992—; clin. faculty dirs. Gloucester County C. C., 1993-97; bd. dirs. So. N.J. Perinatal Coop. Contbr. article to profl. jour. Bd. dirs. So. N.J. Perinatal Coop, 1997—. Lt. comdr. USN, 1984-91. Fellow Am. Acad. Pediatrics (mem. N.J. chpt., alternate counselor 1992-96, counselor 1996-2000, fed. access legis. coord. 1994-97). Roman Catholic. Avocations: computers, reading science fiction. Office: West Deptford Pediatrics 601 Office Plz Wenonah NJ 08090 E-mail: tonymishik@cs.com.

MISHINA, MIZUHO, artist; b. Osaka, Japan, Nov. 21, 1942; came to U.S., 1979; d. Kakusen Mah and Fumiko Hayashi; m. Masanori Mishina, Mar. 14, 1968; children: Yuri, Mayu. Degree in home econs., Kawamura Women's Coll., Tokyo, 1963; BA in art, No. Ill. U., 1986. Sec. Inst. for Nuclear Study, U. Tokyo, 1965-69; gallery asst. Charles Bennett Gallery, Geneva, 1984-85; artist, 1986—. Exhbn. com. mem. Fermi Nat. Lab., Batavia, Ill., 1981-94, landscape com. mem., 1984-88, Nalwo bd. mem., 1981, 89, auditorium com. mem., 1982-84. One-person shows include Chgo. Atty. Gen. Office, 1991, Beverly Art Ctr., Chgo., 1991, Geneva (Ill.) Pub. Libr., 1991, 94, Independence Arts Coun. Gallery, Kans., 1991, Rolling Meadows (Ill.) Pub. Libr., 1992, Batavia (Ill.) Pub. Libr., 1992, Borders Books, Naperville, Ill., 1995, Glen Ellyn, 97, Geneva, 99; exhibited in group shows Fermi Nat. Lab., Batavia, Ill., 1987, Galeria Mesa, Ariz., 1988, Miami EXPO 89, Fla., 1989, Kiwshwaukee (Ill.) Coll. Art Gallery, 1993, Roberta Campbell Cultural Arts Ctr., Geneva, 1993, Art in Embossier, Majuro, Marshal Island, 1996, Borders Books, Wheaton, Ill., 1997, Coll. DuPage, Glen Ellyn, 1998, Norris Gallery, St. Charles, Ill., 1999, Internat. Libr. of Photography, Owings, Md., 1999, Geneva C. of C., 2000. Recipient jewelry award Coll. of DuPage, 1996, 97, 98. Mem. Soc. N.Am. Goldsmiths, Golden Key. Avocations: travel, snorkeling. Home: 322 Grant Ave Geneva IL 60134-1115

MISHKIN, BARBARA FRIEDMAN, lawyer; b. Phila., Feb. 19, 1936; d. Maurice Harold and Gertrude (Sanders) F.; m. Martin S. Thaler, Mar. 22, 1958 (div. 1970); children: Diane Sanders, Paul Sanders, David Emile, Amy Suzanne; m. Mortimer Mishkin, May 27, 1971. AB, Mount Holyoke Coll., 1957; MA, Yale U., 1958; JD, Am. U., 1981. Bar: D.C. 1982, U.S. Supreme Ct. 1989, U.S. Ct. Appeals (4th cir.) 1995. Research psychologist NIMH, Bethesda, Md., 1968-69; spl. asst. to chief judge U.S. Ct. Appeals (D.C. cir.), Washington, 1970-71; spl. asst. to scientific dir. Nat. Inst. Child Health, Bethesda, 1971-74; asst. staff dir. Nat. Commn. for the Protection of Human Subjects, Washington, 1974-78; staff dir. Ethics Adv. Bd. HEW, 1978-80; dep. dir. Pres.' Commn. on Ethics in Medicine and Research, 1980-83; assoc. Hogan and Hartson, 1983-89, counsel, 1990-93; ptnr. Hogan & Hartson, 1994—. Cons. Ctr. for Law and Health Scis., Boston, 1970-73; cons., lectr. Johns Hopkins U. Sch. of Medicine, Balt., 1971-73; bd. dirs. Bon Secours Health Systems, Inc., Columbia, Md., 1984-90. Contbr. numerous articles on health law, med. ethics and biomed. research to jours. in field. Mem. policy bd. Legal Counsel for the Elderly, Washington, 1984-88, vice chair, 1988-90; trustee Mt. Holyoke Coll., 1985-90; mem. Mayor's Adv. Task Force on Hospice Licensure, Washington, 1985-87; bd. dirs. Hebrew Home Greater Washington, 1987-91. Mem. ABA (chair sect. on health and environment 1988-92, chair com. on regulating rsch. 1996-98), D.C. Bar Assn. (subcom. rights of the elderly and the handicapped 1985-92, Pro Bono Atty. Yr. 1988), AAAS (com. on sci. freedom and responsibility 1986-92, AAAS/ABA Nat. Conf. Lawyers and Scientists 1992, ABA co-chair 1993-97), Am. Soc. Law, Medicine and Ethics (bd. dirs. 1995-98). Home: 5610 Wisconsin Ave Apt 402 Chevy Chase MD 20815-4429 Office: Hogan & Hartson Columbia Sq 555 13th St Washington DC 20004 E-mail: bfmishkin@hhlaw.com.

MISHKIN, PAUL J. lawyer, educator; b. Trenton, N.J., Jan. 1, 1927; s. Mark Mordecai and Bella (Dworetsky) M.; m. Mildred Brofman Westover; 1 child, Jonathan Mills Westover. AB, Columbia U., 1947, JD, 1950; MA (hon.), U. Pa., 1971. Bar: N.Y. State bar 1950, U.S. Supreme Ct. bar 1958. Mem. faculty Law Sch. U. Pa., Phila., 1950-72; prof. law U. Calif., Berkeley, 1972-75, Emanuel S. Heller prof., 1975—. Cons. City of Phila., 1953; reporter study div. jurisdiction between state and fed. cts. Am. Law Inst., 1960-65; mem. faculty Salzburg Seminar in Am. Studies, 1974; Charles Inglis Thompson guest prof. U. Colo., 1975; John Randolph Tucker lectr., 1978, Owen J. Roberts Meml. lectr., 1982; vis. fellow Wolfson Coll., Cambridge U., 1984; vis. prof. Duke U. Law Sch., 1989. Author: (with Morris) On Law in Courts, 1965, (with others) Federal Courts and the Federal System, 2d edit, 1973, 3d edit, 1988; contbr. articles to profl. jours. Trustee Jewish Publ. Soc. Am., 1966-75; mem. permanent com. Oliver Wendell Holmes Devise, 1979-87. With USNR 1945-46. Rockefeller Found. rsch. grantee, 1956; Center for Advanced Study in Behavioral Scis. fellow, 1964-65; recipient Russell Prize for Excellence in Teaching, 1996. Fellow Am. Acad. Arts Scis., Am. Bar Found.; mem. Am. Law Inst., Order of Coif, Phi Beta Kappa. Home: 91 Stonewall Rd Berkeley CA 94705-1414 Office: U Calif Sch Law Boalt Hall Berkeley CA 94720

MISHLER, CLIFFORD LESLIE, publisher; b. Vandalia, Mich., Aug. 11, 1939; s. Nelson Howard and Lily Mae (Young) M.; m. Sandra Rae Knutson, Dec. 21, 1963 (dec. July 8, 1972); m. Sylvia M. Leer, Feb. 27, 1976; children: Sheila, Sharon, Susan. Student, Northwestern U., 1957-58. Author, pub. ann. edits. Ann. Studies U.S. and Can. Commemorative Medals and Tokens, 1958-63; assoc. editor Numismatic News, Krause Publs., Iola, Wis., 1963-64, editor, 1964-66, numismatic editor all publs., 1966-75, exec. v.p., pub. all numismatic publs., 1975-78, exec. v.p., pub. all products, 1978-88, sr. v.p., pub. all Numismatic products, 1988-89, sr. v.p. ops., 1989-90; pres. Krause Publs., Iola, Wis., 1991-99. Chmn. bd. dirs. Krause Publs., 2000—; bd. dirs. First State Bank Iola, 1972-83, Scandinavia Telephone Co., 1987-91, TDS Telecom cmty. bd., 1997-2000; ex-officio dir. Iola Old Car Show, Inc., 1985—; mem. coins and medals adv. panel Am. Revolution Bicentennial Commn., 1970-75; mem. ann. assay commn. U.S. Mint, 1973. Co-author: Standard Catalog of World Coins, ann. 1972—; contbr. articles New Book Knowledge, ann. 1969-81. Bd. dirs. William R. Higgins, Jr. Found., 1991—. Recipient The Internat. Vreneli Preistrager: The "Friendly Prize" for lifetime numismatic achievements, Munzen-Revue, Basel, Switzerland, 2001. Fellow Am. Numismatic Soc. (life mem., coun. mem. 1997—); mem. Am. Numismatic Assn. (life mem., medal of merit 1983, Farran Zerbe meml. disting svc. award 1984, Glen Smedley meml. dedicated svcs. award 1991, Lifetime Achievement award 1997), Token and Medal Soc. (life mem., pres. 1976-78, editor jour. 1964-68, disting. svc. award 1966, 80), Numismatists Wis. (life mem., pres. 1974-76, meritorious svc. award 1972), Soc. Internat. Numismatics (award of excellence 1981), Blue Ridge Numismatic Assn. (life mem., hall of fame 1994), Tex. Numismatic Assn. (life mem., hall of fame 1993), Ind. State Numismatic Assn. (life mem., founders award 1993), Ctrl. States Numismatic Soc. (life mem., medal of merit 1984), Wis. Commemorative Quarter Coun., Iola Lions (Melvin Jones fellow 1996). Home: 100 Island Dr Iola WI 54945-9485 Office: 700 E State St Iola WI 54990-0001

MISHLER, JOHN MILTON (YOCHANAN MENASHSHEH BEN SHAUL), natural sciences educator, administrator, artist; b. Cairo, Sept. 25, 1946; s. John Milton and Mary Jane (Woodbury) M.; m. Mary Therese Stember, Apr. 15, 1972 (div. Nov. 1981); m. Sigrid Ruth Elizabeth Fischer, Dec. 15, 1981; 1 child, Joshua Evan. AA with honors, Orange Coast Coll., Costa Mesa, Calif., 1966; AB in Molecular Biology, U. Calif., San Diego, 1969, ScM in Engring. Scis., 1971; DPhil in Immunohematology, St. John's Coll., Oxford U., 1978. Cert. community coll. instr., Calif. Clin. coord. McGaw Labs., Costa Mesa, 1972-78; rsch. fellow Royal Postgrad. Med. Sch., Eng., 1977-78, Med. U., Cologne, Fed. Republic Germany, 1978-80; br. chief Nat. Heart, Lung and Blood Inst. NIH, Bethesda, Md., 1980-82; prof. med., basic life scis. and pharmacol. U. Mo., Kansas City, 1983-89, asst. vice chancellor, 1983-85, dir. div. basic med. scis., 1985-86, assoc. vice chancellor, 1985-89; prof. nat. scis. U. Md. Ea. Shore, Princess Anne, 1989-94, dean grad. studies and rsch., 1989-91; prof. biology Delaware Valley Coll. Sci. and Agrl., Doylestown, Pa., 1994—, dean of Coll., 1994-95. Frequent nat. and internat. lectr.; chmn. 13 nat. and internat. meeting sects. Author: Pharmacology of Hydroxyethyl Starch. Use in Therapy and Blood Banking, 1982; editor or co-editor 6 sci. monographs; mem. editorial rev. bd. Jour. Soc. Rsch. Adminstrs., 1987-91; book rev. editor Grants Mag., 1987-89; contbr. more than 100 articles to profl. jours. Bd. dirs. Ctr. for Bus. Innovation, Inc., 1987, Bucks Assn. for Retarded Citizens, 1995-96; v.p. Artsbridge, 1999-2000. Sr. rsch. fellow Alexander von Humboldt Foun. (Germany), 1978-80; recipient Outstanding Adminstrn. Svc. award U. Mo., Kansas City, 1987, Excellence award Soc. Rsch. Adminstrn., 1989, Cert. Appreciation, 1991, Silver and Bronze awards Artist Guild of Delaware Valley, 1998, Second prize Chester County Art Assn., 1998, Bd. Dirs. award Gtr. Norristown Art League, 1998, Award of Merit Westmoreland Art Nats., 1998, Perkins Ctr. for Arts, 2000, hon. mention Tyme Gallery, 1998, Sacred Mountain Ann. Art Show, 1998, Robert Ransley Outstanding Talent award, 1999, 2nd prize drawing Ctr. for the Creative Arts, 1999, 1st prize graphics Perkiomen Valley Art Ctr., 1999, Wayne Art Supply awrd Wayne Art Ctr., 2002, Pres.'s award Salmagundi Club, 2002. Fellow Internat. Soc. Haematology, Royal Coll. Pathologists; mem. Am. Soc. Hematology, German Soc. Hematology, Nat. Coun. Univ. Rsch. Adminstrn., Nat. Assn. State Univs. and Land-Grant Colls. (mem. exec. com. coun. on rsch. policy and grad. edn. 1990-91), Coun. Grad. Schs., N.Y. Acad. Scis., Sigma Xi. Jewish. Avocations: reading, abstract art painting, writing, music. Home: 475 North St Apt 6F Doylestown PA 18901-3863 Office: Delaware Valley Coll 700 E Butler Ave Doylestown PA 18901-2607 E-mail: mishlerj@devalcol.edu.

MISHLER, MARK SEAN, lawyer; b. Princeton, N.J., Oct. 18, 1956; BA, Brandeis U., 1978; JD, Boston Coll., 1981. Bar: Mass. 1981, N.Y. 1982, U.S. Dist. Ct. (no. dist.) N.Y. 1982, U.S. Ct. Appeals (2nd cir.) 1997. Dir. Student Legal Svcs., Albany, N.Y., 1981-87; assoc. Walter, Thayer & Long, 1987-88; ptnr. Walter, Thayer & Mishler, 1988—. Adj. instr. Cornell U. Sch. Indsl. and Labor Rels., 1997. Mem. exec. bd. Albany br. NAACP, 1985—; mem. Albany Cmty./Police Rels. Bd., 1986-88; candidate for Dist. Atty. of Albany County, 2000. Recipient award for disting. svc. in legal redress Albany Br. NAACP, 1986, Frederick Douglas Struggle for Justice award Ctr. for Law & Justice, Albany, 1992, Progressive Leadership award Capital Dist. Citizen Action, 1998. Mem. Nat. Lawyers Guild, N.Y. State Assn. Criminal Def. Lawyers. Office: Walter Thayer & Mishler PC 756 Madison Ave Albany NY 12208-3832

MISHLER, WILLIAM, II, political science educator; b. Miami, Fla., Oct. 14, 1947; s. William Thomas Earle and Marie Katheryn (Schmitz) M. BA, Stetson U., 1969; MA, Duke U., 1972, PhD, 1973. Asst. prof. Duke U., Durham, N.C., 1972-78; assoc. prof. SUNY, Buffalo, 1978-82, prof., chmn., 1984-86; dir. polit. sci. program NSF, Washington, 1982-84; prof., chmn. U. S.C., Columbia, 1986-89, prof., 1989-97, James F. and Maude B. Byrnes prof. govt., 1995-97; prof., head dept. polit. sci. U. Ariz., Tucson, 1997—. Vis. prof. U. Strathelyde, Glasgow, Scotland, 1976-77; vis. scientist, dir. polit. sci. program NSF, Washington, 1990-91. Author: Influence in Parliament, Political Participation in Canada, Representative Democracy in the Canadian Provinces, Resurgence of Conservatism, Controversies in Political Economy, Democracy and its Alternatives; mem. editl. bds. Jour. Politics, 1982-88, 2000—, Legis. Studies Quar., 1988-91, 99—, Electoral Studies, 1998—. Capt. U.S. Army, 1972. Mem. Am. Polit. Sci. Assn., So. Polit. Sci. Assn., Midwest Polit. Sci. Assn., Can. Polit. Sci. Assn., Internat. Studies Assn., Assn. Can. Studies (U.S. chpt.). Office: U Ariz Dept Polit Sci Tucson AZ 85721-0001 E-mail: mishler@u.arizona.edu.

MISHNE, JUDITH MARKS, social work educator, psychotherapist; b. Cleve., Feb. 21, 1932; d. Moses Isaac and Lillian (Kemelman) Marks; (div.); 1 child, Jonathan. BS, U. Wis., 1953; MSW, Case Western Res. U., 1955; cert., Inst. of Psychoanalysis, Chgo., 1974; DSW, CUNY, 1981. Caseworker Akron (Ohio) Child Guidance Ctr., 1955-56, Cleve. Child Guidance Ctr., 1956-58, Jewish Family Svc., Cleveland Heights, 1959-62; sch. social worker Orange Bd. Edn., Pepper Pike, Ohio, 1962-66; unit supr. Bellefaire of Jewish Children's Bur., Cleve., 1964-66; assoc. prof. sch. of social svcs. adminstrn. U. Chgo., 1966-76; assoc. prof. sch. social work Columbia U., N.Y.C., 1977-79; from assoc. prof. to prof. sch. social work NYU, 1979—. Summer faculty mem. sch. social work Smith Coll., Northampton, Mass., 1975-82; cons. Pritzker Children's Hosp., Chgo., 1968-74, Madden Hosp., Chgo., 1973-75, Queens Child Guidance Clinic, Jamaica, N.Y., 1979-80, Roosevelt Hosp., N.Y.C., 1983, Jewish Family Svc., Hackensack, N.Y., 1986-87; vis. lectr. U. Haifa (Israel) Sch. Social Work, 1994. Author: Clinical Work With Children, 1983, Clinical Work With Adolescents, 1986, Evolution and Application of Clinical Theory: Perspectives From Four Psychologies, 1993, The Learning Curve: Elevating Children's Academic and Social Competence, 1996; editor: Psychotherapy and Training in Clinical Social Work, 1980; co-editor: (with others) Ego and Self Psychology: Group Intervention With Children and Adolescents, 1983. Named Disting. Practitioner in Social Work Nat. Academics of Practice, 1983; recipient Spencer Found. award NYU, 1987, Spl. Achievement award PhD Alumni Assn. CUNY, 1996; Vis. scholar Bar Ilan U. Sch. of Social Work, Israel, 1993, 94. Mem. Assn. of Child and Adolescent Therapists, Nat. Fedn. Socs. for Social Work, Coun. on Social Work Edn., Nat. Acad. of Practice in Social Work, Assn. for Psychoanalytic Self Psychology. Democrat. Home: 225 W 88th St # 4E New York NY 10024-2303 Office: NYU Sch of Social Work 2 Washington Sq N New York NY 10003-6669

MISHOE, RAINELLE DIXON, educator; b. Burlington, N.C., Feb. 18, 1950; d. James Milo and Nellie (Rainey) Dixon; m. Harmon W. Mishoe Jr., Apr. 23, 1988; 1 child from previous marriage, Jessica Rainelle Tinsley. BA in English, N.C. State U., 1972. Cert. tchr., real estate broker. Tchr. Richard B. Harrison Jr. High Sch., Selma, N.C., 1972-73, Flat Rock (N.C.) Jr. High Sch., 1973-79; owner, designer The Finishing Touch, Carolina Beach, N.C., 1981-87; tchr. lang. arts Lake Forest Jr. High Sch., 1987-88; tchr. English Hoggard High Sch., Wilmington, 1988—. Chmn. curriculum com. Henderson County Bd. Edn., Hendersonville, N.C., 1978-79; mem. archtl. rev. bd. Old Chimney Homeowners Assn., 1985-86. Feature writer Hendersonville Times News, 1976-77. Pres. Hendersonville Jaycettes, 1975, treas., 1976, chmn. bd. dirs., 1977; mem. family life com. First United Meth. Ch., Hendersonville, N.C.; good neighbor com. Old Chimney Homeowners' Assn.; advisor Miss John T. Hoggard Pageant, Optimist Speech Contest, Sr. Class; membership com. mem. Country Club of Landfall. Recipient Dist. Spoke award Hendersonville Jaycettes, 1977; named Outstanding Jaycette, Hendersonville Jaycettes, 1976. Mem. Nat. Home Furnishings Assn., So. Home Furnishings Assn., Cape Fear Sales and Mktg. Assn. (social chmn. 1986), Kappa Kappa Iota (historian 1977, v.p. 1978, pres. 1979, chmn. bd. dirs. 1980-81). Clubs: Jr. Woman's (Hendersonville). Democrat. Methodist. Avocations: skiing, knitting, reading. Home: 1219 Pembroke Jones Rd Wilmington NC 28405-5203

MISHRA, ANIL KUMAR, research scientist, consultant; b. Ayer, Bihar, India, Jan. 1, 1961; s. Vishwa Nath and Prabha Mishra; m. Pranati Mishra, June 12, 1985; 1 child, Harsha. BTech in Petroleum, Indian Sch. Mines, Dhanbad, Bihar, India, 1982; MS in Petroleum, U. Tex., 1993; PhD in Hydrology, N.Mex. Inst. Mining & Tech., 1997. Asst. exec. engr. Oil and Natural Gas Commn., Bombay, 1982-85, exec. engr., 1985-88; sr. rsch. officer Planning Commn., New Delhi, 1988-90; rsch. asst. U. Tex., Austin, 1990-93, N.Mex. Tech., Socorro, 1993-97; rsch. scientist Lawrence Berkeley (Calif.) Nat. Lab., 1997—. Contbr. articles to profl. jours. including Advances in Water Resources, Jour. Math. and Geology. Recipient Student Paper awrd Internat. Assn. Hydrology, 1997. Mem. Am. Geophys. Union, Soc. Petroleum Engrs. Avocations: travel, languages, music, reading. Office: Lawrence Berkeley Nat Lab 1 Cyclotron Rd M S 90 1116 Berkeley CA 94720-0001 Home: Apt 202 1414 S Dairy Ashford St Houston TX 77077-2352

MISHRA, CHANDRA S. finance educator, consultant; b. India, Jan. 5, 1962; came to U.S., 1986; s. K.C. and S. Mishra; m. Karabi Mishra, June 23, 1985; children: Mitushi, Sachit. BS, Saurastra U., India, 1982; MS, Nat. Inst. Tng. Indsl. Engr., India, 1984; PhD, U. Tex., Dallas, 1991. Asst. prof. fin. Loyola U., Chgo., 1990-96; assoc. prof. fin. Oreg. State U., Corvallis, 1996—. Cons., Corvallis, 1996—. Home: 2415 Chinwood Trail Maitland FL 32751 Office: Crummer School of Business Rollins College Winter Park FL 32789

MISHRA, DIGAMBAR, political scientist; b. Kamalpur Village, Orissa State, India, May 8, 1938; s. Jagannath and Maguni Mishra; m. Josna Mishra; children: Anoop, Likun. MA, Utkal U., Vani Vihar, Orissa, 1967; MPA, U. Ala., 1975, PhD, 1980. Professor of Political Science Miles College, Birmingham, Ala., 1981—. Bicentennial fellow Stanford U., Palo Alto, 1983; cons. ethnographer Decision Info. Resources, Houston. Active Leadership Birmingham, 1999—2000. Master: Ala. Polit. Sci. (pres. 1995—96). Home: 1603 Shades Glen Cir Birmingham AL 35226 Office: Divsn Social and Behavioral Sci 5500 Myron Massey Blvd Birmingham AL Home Fax: 205-929-1512. Personal E-mail: mishra@mail.miles.edu.

MISHRA, MUNMAYA K. polymer scientist; b. Cuttack, India, Sept. 27, 1955; came to U.S., 1982; m. Bidulata Sar, 1983; children: Swati, Suraj. MS, Berhampur U., India, 1978; PhD, Utkal U., India, 1981. Rsch. assoc. Gaylord Rsch. Inst., Whippany, N.J., 1982, U. Akron (Ohio), 1983-86; assoc. scientist Polysar, Inc., Stow, Ohio, 1987-89; sr. scientist Texaco/Ethyl, Beacon, N.Y., 1990-96; advisor Ethyl Corp., Richmond, Va., 1996—. Author: Handbook of Radical Vinyl Polymerization, 1998; editor: Macromolecular Design Concept and Practice, 1994, Macromolecular Engineering Recent Advances, 1995, Star and Hyperbranched Polymers, 1999, Tailored Polymers and Applications, 2000; editor Jour. Macromolecular Reports, 1990-97, Jour. Designed Monomers and Polymers, 1997—, Polymer-Plastics Tech. and Engring., 1997—; contbr. articles to profl. jours.; patentee in field. Mem. Am. Chem. Soc. (Rsch. award 1995). Avocations: camping, coin collecting, travel. Office: Ethyl Corp PO Box 2158 Richmond VA 23218-2158

MISHRA, RAJIV SHARAN, metallurgical engineer, educator; b. Chapra, Bihar, India, July 15, 1961; s. Shambhu Sharan and Indu Mishra; m. Sarita Trivedi; children: Mayank, Rajit. B. Engring., U. of Rajasthan, Jaipur, India, 1982; M.Tech., Indian Inst. of tech., Kanpur, India, 1985; PhD, U. Seffield, Eng., 1988. Scientist, group leader Def. Metall. Rsch. Lab., Hyderabad, India, 1988—94; postgrad. rsch. engr. U. Calif., Davis, 1994—97, adj. asst. prof., 1997—99; asst. prof. U. Mo., Rolla, 1999—. Mem. mfg. edn. exec. com. U. Mo., Rolla, 1999—; vice-chmn. Joint ASM/TMS Com. on Mech. Behavior of Materials, Warrendale. Editor: (proceedings) Creep Behavior of Advanced Materials for the 21st Century, 1999, Ultrafine Grained Materials, 2000, Friction Stir Welding and Processing, 2001; contbr. Recipient Faculty Excellence award, U. Mo.i-Rolla, 2001, Young Metallurgist award, Indian Inst. of Metals, India, 1993, Brunton Medal, University of Sheffield, UK, 1988, ORS award, Com. of Vice-Chancellors and Prins. of UK, 1985—88; fellow Firth Pre-doctoral fellowship, U. of Sheffield, UK, 1985—88. Mem.: Am. Welding Soc., Soc. Mfg. Engrs., The Minerals, Metals and Materials Soc., Am. Soc. Metals, Indian Inst. of Metals (life). Achievements include patents for include nanocrystalline alumina-diamond composites. Office: Univ of Missouri Dept Metall Engring 1870 Miner Cir Rolla MO 65409 Office Fax: 573-341-6934. Business E-Mail: rsmishra@umr.edu.

MISHRIKI, YEHIA YOUSRI, physician; b. Cairo, Egypt, Sept. 25, 1954; s. Yousri Youssef and Galila (Boutros) M.; widowed; children: Kate Ashley, Hannah Elizabeth. BA in Chemistry, Franklin and Marshall Coll., 1976; MD, Loyola U., 1979. Diplomate in internal medicine Am. Bd. Internal Medicine. Intern in medicine to chief med. resident Winthrop Univ. Hosp., 1980-84; asst. chmn. dept. medicine Winthrop-Univ. Hosp., Mineola, N.Y., 1984-86; vice chmn. dept. medicine Lehigh Valley Hosp., Allentown, Pa., 1986-90, dir. residency program and transitional programs, 1986-90, chief divsn. ambulatory care, 1990-99; assoc. prof. clin. medicine Pa. State U. Coll. Medicine, Hershey, 1995-99, prof. clin. medicine, 1999—. Mem. arts adv. com. Lehigh Valley Chamber Orch., Allentown, 1996—. Named Tchr. of Yr., Lehigh Valley Hosp., 1989, 92, 99. Fellow ACP; mem. Soc. Gen. Internal Medicine. Libertarian. Christian. Avocations: book collecting, reading. Home: 4752 Belmont Dr Emmaus PA 18049-1227 Office: Lehigh Valley Hosp 1210 S Cedar Crest Blvd Allentown PA 18103-6255 E-mail: Yehia.Mishriki@lvh.com.

MISIEK, DALE JOSEPH, oral and maxillofacial surgeon; b. Hartford, Conn., Dec. 10, 1952; s. Joseph John and Jadwiga Magdelena (Wojtowicz) M.; m. Patricia Ann Munson, June 28, 1975; children: Matthew Bryan, Stacey Lynne, Michael Stephen. BA magna cum laude, U. Conn., Storrs, 1974; DMD, U. Conn., Farmington, 1978; cert. advanced tng. oral and maxillofacial surgery, La. State U., 1982. Diplomate Am. Bd. Oral and Maxillofacial Surgery. Resident oral surgery Charity Hosp. of La., New Orleans, 1978-82; asst. prof. dept. oral and maxillofacial surgery Sch. Dentistry, La. State U., 1984-87, assoc. prof., 1987-94; prof. dept. oral and maxillofacial surgery Sch. Dentistry La. State U., 1994-98; also mem. various coms. Sch. Dentistry, La. State U.; practice dentistry specializing in oral surgery, 1982-84; pvt. practice Charlotte, 1998—. Mem. staff Univ. Hosp., New Orleans, 1982-; courtesy staff Children's Hosp., New Orleans, 1982—; cons. VA Med. Ctr., New Orleans, 1984—, Presbyn. Med. Ctr., Charlotte, 1998—, U. Hosp., Charlotte, 1998—, Northeast Med. Ctr., Concord, 1999—; lectr. in field. Contbr. articles and abstracts to profl. jours. Recipient C.V. Mosby Book award. Fellow Am. Assn. Oral and Maxillofacial Surgeons (mem. spl. com. for devel. stds. and criteria for care 1986, spl. com. on oral and maxillofacial surgery self-assessment program 1990), Am. Coll. Oral and Maxillofacial Surgeons; mem. ADA (cons. commn. on dental accreditation 1986-2000), Am. Bd. Oral and Maxillofacial Surgery (adv. com. 1990-95, regional advisor Dist. III 1996-99), Am. Acad. Cosmetic Surgery, La. Soc. Oral and Maxillofacial Surgeons (anesthesia com. 1983-85, advanced cardiac life support com. 1986-88, sec./treas. 1991-95, v.p. 1996—), Internat. Assn. Oral and Maxillofacial Surgery, Acad. Osseointegration, Charlotte Dental Soc., 2d Dist. Dental Soc., N.C. Dental Soc., N.C. Soc. Oral and Mexillofacial Surgeons, Phi Beta Kappa, Phi Kappa Phi, Omicron Kappa Upsilon. Republican. Roman Catholic. Avocations: baseball, weightlifting, fishing. Office: 8738 University City Blvd Charlotte NC 28213-3558 E-mail: drdjm1@aol.com.

MISKA, ERIC ALEXANDER, molecular biologist, researcher; b. Bitburg, Germany, June 29, 1971; came to U.S., 2000; s. Siegfried and Gafron Erica M.; m. Ines Alvarez Garcia, Jun. 24, 2000. BA, Univ. Dublin, 1996; PhD, U. Cambridge, Eng., 2000. Rsch. assoc. Wellcome/CRC Inst. Univ. Cambridge, 1999-2000; rsch. fellow MIT, Cambridge, 2000—. Contbr. articles to profl. jours. Fellow Cambridge European Trust. Office: MIT 77 Massachusetts Ave Cambridge MA 02139 E-mail: miska@mit.edu.

MISKIEWICZ, SUSANNE PIATEK, educational administrator; b. Elizabeth, N.J., Nov. 19, 1947; d. Edward Walter and Charlotte Teresa (Kardel) Piatek; m. Randall Lee Grover; 1 child, Michelle Lee Grover Domenico; m. Raymond Richard Miskiewicz; children: Lisa Marie, Raymond Edward. BA, Newark State Coll., 1972; MA, Kean Coll., 1976. Cert. prin./supr., supr., reading specialist, elem. edn., nursery sch., N.J. Tchr. Linden (N.J.) Bd. Edn., 1973-79, 87-90, Linden Adult Sch., 1981-88, dir., 1988-90; tchr. Roselle (N.J.) Bd. Edn., 1991, New Providence (N.J.) Bd. Edn., 1991—2001, dept. head lang. arts K-12, coord. mid. coll., 1996-99, asst. adminstr., 1999—2001; edn. program devel. specialist N.J. Dept. Edn., 2002—. Cons., trainer N.J. Dept. Edn., Trenton, 1987-90; cons. Am. Guidance Svc., Minn., 1979—; mem. bd. edn. Linden, 1991-94, v.p., 1993-94; presenter NJEA Conv., 1976, Edn. Fair, Washington, 1973. Reviewer: Prep, Keymath, You and Your Small Wonder, Books 1 and 2, 1979-88. Sec., treas., v.p. PTA, Linden, 1984—92; treas. Kean U. Diversity Coun., Union , NJ, 2000—; mem., v.p. Gen. Pulaski Com., Linden, 1985—; mem., sec., v.p., treas. Linden Summer Theatre, 1978—85; leader Girl Scouts Am., Linden, 1987—91; trustee Linden Free Pub. Libr., 1999—, St. Teresa' Ch., Linden, 1970—73; advisor St. Elizabeth's Ch. Altar Server Soc., 1994—98, lector, 1998—, eucharistic min., 2000—. Scholar Holocaust Ctr. Kean U.; Jewish Labor Com. fellow. Mem. NEA, ASCD, Nat. Coun. Tchrs. English (state leader 1999—), Lang. and Literacy Assn., N.J. ASCD, Internat. Reading Assn., N.J. Reading Assn., N.J. Edn. Assn., N.J. Coun. Tchrs. English (bd. dirs. 1998—, treas. 2000), New Providence Edn. Assn. (pres. 1995-2001), diversity 2000 (treas. 1998—), Phi Delta Kappa. Roman Catholic. Avocations: reading, crafts, golf. Home: 43 Palisade Rd Linden NJ 07036-3828 Office: NJ Dept Edn 1501 Livingston Ave N New Brunswick NJ 08902 E-mail: suem908@aol.com.

MISKOWSKI, LEE R. retired automobile executive; b. Stevens Point, Wis., Mar. 27, 1932; s. Paul P. and Marie Grace (Glazer) M.; m. Billie Poulson, 1963; children: Christine, Katherine. BBA, U. Wis., 1954, MBA, 1957. V.p. Ford of Europe Ford Motor Co., Cologne, Germany, 1977-80, gen. mktg. mgr.

Ford div. Dearborn, Mich., 1980-83, v.p., gen. mgr. parts and svc. div., 1989-91, v.p., gen. mgr. Lincoln-Mercury div., 1991-94, ret., 1994. Bd. dirs. Wolverine Brass, Inc., U. Wis. MC Found., Bradford Equities. Chmn. Hospice of Mich., 1996-98; vice chmn. Hospice of Mich. Found.; chmn. bd. dirs. Mich. Parkinson Found., Detroit, 1992-94, bd. dirs. Bradford Equities, Wolverine Bradd, Autocraft, 1994-2000. With U.S. Army, 1954-56. Mem. Oakland Hills Country Club. Roman Catholic. Avocations: tennis, golf, reading, travel.

MISLOVE, MICHAEL WILLIAM, mathematics educator, theoretical computer scientist; b. Washington, Feb. 8, 1944; s. Rhoda Frank and Ellsworth Herman Grell(Stepfather); m. Marilyn Burrus, Apr. 12, 1975; children: Alan, Caroline. BA in Math., U. of the South, 1965; PhD in Math., U. Tenn., 1969. Vis. asst. prof. U. Fla., Gainesville, 1970; asst. prof. Tulane U., New Orleans, 1970—75, assoc. prof. math., 1975—79, prof. math., 1979—. Vis. prof. (one month) U. of Paris 7, Paris, 6/01—7/01, Paris, 6/99—7/99; vis. prof. Programming Rsch. Group, University of Oxford, Great Britain and Northern Ireland, 1/91—7/91; summer faculty Thomas Watson Rsch. Ctr., IBM, Yorktown Heights, NY, 6/90—7/90; vis. faculty Math. Inst., University of Oxford, Great Britain and Northern Ireland, 7/84—1/85; alexander von humboldt rsch. fellow Technische Hochschule Darmstadt, Darmstadt, Germany, 6/82—8/82, Darmstadt, 6/78—8/78, Mathematisches Institut, Universitaet Tuebingen, Germany, 1975—75. Co-author: A Compendium of Continuous Lattices, 1980; editor, founder: jour. Electronic Notes in Theoretical Computer Sci., 1975—; editor: Theoretical Computer Sci., 1985—. Named Astor Vis. Lectr., Programming Rsch. Group, U. of Oxford, 1998; recipient Scholar Travel award, Fulbright Commn., 1975; grantee (with K. H. Hofmann), NSF, 1971—81, 1998—2000, 2001—02, Office of Naval Rsch., 1988—. Avocation: sailing. Office: Tulane U Math Dept 6823 St Charles Ave New Orleans LA 70118 Office Fax: 504-865-5063 (504) 865-5063. Personal E-mail: mislove@tulane.edu.

MISLOW, KURT MARTIN, chemist, educator; b. Berlin, Germany, June 5, 1923; came to U.S., 1940, naturalized, 1946; s. Max and Ida (Bingen) M.; m. Jacqueline Ford, 1966; children: Christopher, John. BS, Tulane U., 1944, DSc (hon.), 1975; PhD, Calif. Inst. Tech., 1947; D honoris causa, Free U., Brussels, 1974, Uppsala U., 1977, Düsseldorf U., 1994. Instr. NYU, 1947-51, asst. prof., 1951-56, asso. prof., 1956-60, prof., 1960-64; Hugh Stott Taylor prof. chemistry Princeton, 1964-88, chmn. dept. chemistry, 1968-74, prof. emeritus, 1988—. Vis. prof. Stanford U., 1960, Calif. Inst. Tech., 1994; M.S. Kharasch vis. prof. U. Chgo., 1989; Univ. lectr. U. London, 1965; J.A. McRae Meml. lectr. Queen's U., 1967; H.A. Iddles lectr. U. N.H., 1972; Solvay lectr. and medalist Free U. Brussels, 1972; E.C. Lee lectr. U. Chgo.; A.A. Vernon lectr. Northeastern U., 1976; PPG lectr. Ohio U., 1977; J. Musher Meml. lectr. Hebrew U. Jerusalem, 1978; North Country lectr., 1978; Honor lectr. Ariz. State U., 1981; E. Ritchie meml. lectr. Sydney U., 1983; Fuson lectr. U. Nev., 1983; Research Scholar lectr. Drew U., 1983; McGregory lectr. Colgate U., 1984; Sandia lectr. U. Alta., 1984; Purves lectr. McGill U., 1985; Arnold lectr. So. Ill. U., 1985; Bergmann lectr. Yale U., 1986; H.C. Brown lectr. Purdue U., 1988; Irvine lectr. U. St. Andrews, 1988; Eyring lectr. Ariz. State U., 1989; Disting. Scientist lectr. Bard Coll., 1991; Syntex Disting. lectr. Colo. State U., 1991; Disting. scientist lectr. Bard Coll., 1991; J.W.T. Spinks lectr. U. Saskatchewan, 1992; Bristol-Myers-Squibb disting. lectr. Syracuse U., 1992; Churchill fellow Cambridge U., 1974-75; mem. adv. panel chemistry NSF, 1963-66; mem. panel medical and organic chemistry NIH, 1963-66. Author: Introduction to Stereochemistry, 1965; also numerous articles; bd. editors: Jour. Organic Chemistry, 1965-70; mem. editl. adv. bd. Monatshefte für Chemie, Topics in Stereochemistry, Accounts of Chem. Rsch., Chem. and Engring. News, Bull des Sociétés Chimiques Belges, Symmetry, Jour. Math. Chemistry. Recipient Prelog medal, ETH Zurich, 1986, W.H. Nichols medal, 1987, Sci. Achievement award medal CCNY, 1988, Disting. Alumni award Calif. Inst. Tech., 1990, Chirality medal, 1993, Sesquicentennial medal Tulane U., 1997, Arthur C. Cope Scholar award Am. Chem. Soc. 1995; Guggenheim fellow, 1957-58, 74-75, Alfred P. Sloan fellow, 1959-63, Sherman Fairchild disting. scholar Calif. Inst. Tech., 1990, 91, 94. Fellow AAAS, Am. Acad. Arts and Scis.; mem. NAS, AAUP, Am. Chem. Soc. (James Flack Norris award 1975), Academia Nazionale dei Lincei (fgn. mem.), Phi Beta Kappa, Sigma Xi. E-mail: kmislow@princeton.edu.

MISNER, CHARLES WILLIAM, physics educator; b. Jackson, Mich., June 13, 1932; s. Francis deSales and Madge B. (Mee) M.; m. Susanne Elisabeth Kemp, June 13, 1959; children: Benedicte Elisabeth, Francis Frithjof, Timothy Charles, Christopher Kemp. BS, U. Notre Dame, 1952; MA, Princeton U., 1954, PhD, 1957. Instr. Princeton U., (N.J.), 1956-59, asst. prof., 1959-63; assoc. prof. physics U. Md., College Park, 1963-66, prof., 1966-2000, assoc. chair physics dept., 1995-99, prof. emeritus, sr. rsch. scientist, 2000—. Vis. fellow Inst. for Theoretical Physics, U. Calif., Santa Barbara, 1980-81, All Souls Coll., Oxford, Eng., 1973, Max Planck-Albert Einstein Inst., Potsdam, Germany, 2000, 2002; vis. faculty Calif. Inst. Tech., 1972, Princeton U., 1969 Author: (with Wheeler and Thorne) Gravitation, 1973, (with Patrick J.Cooney) Spreadsheet Physics, 1991; contbr. articles to profl. jours. Recipient Sci. Centennial award U. Notre Dame, 1965, Dannie Heineman prize (with R. Arnowitt and S. Deser) for math. physics Am. Phys. Soc., 1994; NSF sr. postdoctoral fellow, 1966-67; Guggenheim fellow, 1972-73; Einstein Centennial lectr., 1979. Fellow Am. Phys. Soc., Royal Astron. Soc., Am. Acad. Arts and Scis.; mem. Philosophy of Sci. Assn., Am. Math. Soc. Fedn. Am. Scientists Democrat. Roman Catholic. Office: U Md Dept Physics College Park MD 20742-4111

MISNER, CHARLOTTE BLANCHE RUCKMAN, retired community organization administrator; b. Gifford, Idaho, Aug. 30, 1937; d. Richard Steele and Arizona (Hill) Ruckman; m. G. Arthur Misner, Jr., Aug. 29, 1959; children: Michelle, Mary, Jennifer. BS in Psychology, U. Idaho, 1959. Vol. numerous orgns., India, Mexico, The Philippines, 1962-70; sec., v.p., pres., trustee St. Luke's Hosp., Manila, 1970-84; founding mem., 3d v.p., pres. Am. Women's Club of Philippines, 1980-84; exec. dir. Friends of Oakland (Calif.) Parks and Recreation, 1986-2000, ret., 2000. Active Lincoln Child Ctr., Oakland, 1984—. Recipient Vol. Svc. award Women's Bd. St. Luke's Hosp., 1977, Mid. Sch. Vol. award Internat. Sch.-Manila, 1980. Me. Alpha Gamma Delta (alumnae treas., pres. East Bay 1985-89, province dir. alumnae 1989-98, bd. dirs. alumni devel. 1998—, mem. steering com. centennial capital campaign 1999—), Cum Laude Soc. (hon.). Home: 5304 Woodgrove Ct Concord CA 94521-5422

MISNER, LORRAINE, laboratory technologist; b. Fitchburg, Mass., June 24, 1948; d. Cedric Winfield and Pearl Erma (Hallisey) M. BA in Biology, Fitchburg State Coll., 1971; MS in Med. Tech., Anna Maria Coll., 1983. Cert. Novell engr. Lab. technologist Leominster (Mass.) Hosp., 1971-87; rsch. asst. U. Lowell Rsch. Found. (now U. Mass. Lowell Rsch. Found.), 1987-99; sys. engr. TeleSpectrum Worldwide Inc., 1999—. Piccolo Townsend (Mass.) Mil. Band, 1964-93; mem. choir United Ch. of Christ, 1961—. Mem. Am. Soc. Clin. Pathologists (assoc., registrant). Avocations: bowling, music, travel, dancing. E-mail: lorraine.misner@hp.com.

MISNER, ROBERT DAVID, electronic warfare and magnetic recording consultant, electro-mechanical company executive; b. Waynesville, Ill., May 1, 1920; s. Oscar and Elizabeth (Nyren) M.; student Ill. Wesleyan U., 1939-42; B.S. in Physics, George Washington U., 1946; postgr. U. Md., 1948; m. Virginia Fuehrer, June 4, 1949; children: Robin Beth, Christie Marie. Mem. staff U.S. Naval Rsch. Lab., Washington, 1942-44, 46—, br. head signal exploitation br., 1965-87; pres. MEMRE Co., 1987—; cons. Served in USNR, 1944-46. Recipient Disting. Civilian Service award USN, 1970; others. Mem. IEEE (sr.), Assn. Old Crows, Sigma Xi. Contbr. articles to profl. jours. Home: 7107 Sussex Pl Alexandria VA 22307-2006 Office: 4555 Overlook Ave SW Washington DC 20375-0001

MISRA, DEVESH K. engineering educator; b. Lucknow, India, Dec. 25, 1957; s. Ram Pratap and Kamla Devi Misra; m. Mamta Misra, June 19, 1987; 1 child Tanmay. PhD, U. Cambridge, Eng., 1983. Chartered engr., Eng. Scientist Metall. Rsch. Lab., Hyderabad, India, 1984—97; staff metallurgist,/engr. LTV Steel-Tech. Ctr., Independence, Ohio, 1997—2000; prof. U. La., Lafayette, 2001—. Mem.: Inst. Materials. Home: 115 Westfield Dr Lafayette LA 70503 Office: U La at Lafayette Dept Chem Engring Lafayette LA 70504-4130 Home Fax: 337-482-1220 /6688. Personal E-mail: DMISRA@LOUISIANA.EDU.

MISRA, DWIJEN CRISTOBAL, surgeon; b. Boston, Sept. 4, 1958; s. Dwijendra Kumar and Candida Rosario (Cristobal) M.; m. Nancy Ann Snider, Nov. 26, 1988; children: Benjamin, Mary Allison, Nathanial. BS, U. Mich., 1981; MD, Wayne State U., 1986. Diplomate Am. Bd. Surgery. Intern William Beaumont Hosp., Royal Oak, Mich., 1986-87, resident in gen. surgery, 1987-91; pvt. practice Troy. Mem. staff William Beaumont Hosp., Troy. Fellow ACS; mem. AMA, Am. Soc. Gen. Surgeons, Detroit Surgery Soc., Am. Hernia Soc. Office: 44199 Dequindre Rd Ste 412 Troy MI 48085-1128

MISRA, JOYA, communications educator; b. Louisville, May 16, 1967; d. Raghunath Prasad and Therese (Rettenmund) M.; m. David Mednicoff; 1 child: Amina. BA, Centenary Coll. La., 1988; MA, Emory U., 1991, PhD, 1994. Mgr. Sta. KSCL, Shreveport, 1986-88; statistical cons., 1989-92; instr. Emory U., 1992-94; asst. prof. U. Ga., Athens, 1994—99, U. Mass., Amherst, 1999—2000, assoc. prof., 2001—. Contbr. to profl. jours. Mem. ASA, SWS, GSA, CSSP, Southern Sociological Soc., Am. Sociological Assn, Sociologists for Women in Soc., Soc. for the Study of Social Problems, Ea. Sociological Soc. Office: U Mass Dept Sociology Thomson Hall Amherst MA 01003

MISRA, RAGHUNATH PRASAD, physician, educator; b. Calcutta, W. Bengal, India, Feb. 1, 1928; came to U.S., 1964; s. Guru Prasad and Anandi M.; m. Therese Rettenmund, Sept. 13, 1963; children: Sima, Joya, Maya, Tara. BSc with honors, Calcutta U., 1948; MBBS, Med. Coll., Calcutta, 1953; PhD, McGill U., Montreal, Que., 1965. Diplomate Am. Bd. Anatomical and Clin. Pathology. Asst. prof., dir. kidney lab. U. Louisville Sch. Medicine, 1964-68; asso. investigator and dir. kidney lab Mt. Sinai Hosp., Cleve., 1968-73; asst. prof. Case Western Reserve Med. Sch., 1973-76; asst. prof., dir. kidney lab. La. State U., Sch. Medicine, Shreveport, 1976-80, assoc. prof., 1980-86; prof. La. State U., Sch. of Medicine, 1986—98, emeritus prof., 1998—, dir. Ocular Pathology Lab., 1988—. Cons. VA Med. Ctr., Shreveport, 1977-98, EA Conway Meml. Hosp., Monroe, La., 1980-98. Author: Atlas of Skin Biopsy, 1983. Pres. India Assn. of Shreveport, 1979, 81. Recipient Tallisman Fellowship, Mt. Sinai Hosp., 1970-73. Fellow Am. Coll. Pathologists, Am. Soc. Clin. Pathologists, Am. Coll. of Internat. Physicians, U. Calcutta Med. Alumni Assn. Am. (pres. 1992-93), Sigma Xi (pres. 1987-89). Democrat. Hindu. Avocations: photography, travel. Office: La State U Sch Medicine 1501 Kings Hwy Shreveport LA 71103-4228 E-mail: rmisra@lsuhsc.edu.

MISRACH, RICHARD LAURENCE, photographer; b. L.A., July 11, 1949; s. Robert Laskin and Lucille (Gardner) M.; m. Debra Bloomfield, Jan. 18, 1981 (div. 1987); 1 son, Jacob Luke; m. Myriam Weisang, Apr. 17, 1989. AB in Psychology, U. Calif., Berkeley, 1971. Instr. Assoc. Students Studio, U. Calif., Berkeley, 1971-77; vis. lectr. U. Calif.-Berkeley, 1982; lectr. U. Calif.-Santa Barbara, 1984. Juror Nat. Endowment Arts, 1986; lectr. Calif. Inst. for Arts, 1990. Exhbns. include Whitney Biennial, 1981, 91, Musèe d'Art Moderne, Paris, 1979, Mus. Modern Art, N.Y.C., 1978, Grapestake Gallery, San Francisco, 1979, 81, Young-Hoffman Gallery, Chgo., 1980, Oakland Mus., 1982, 87, San Franciso Mus. Modern Art, 1983, Centre Georges Pompidou, Paris, 1983, L.A. County Mus. Art, 1984, Fraenkel Gallery, San Francsico, 1985, 89, 91, 95, 97, 99, Min Gallery, Tokyo, 1975-87, Univ. Art Mus., Berkeley, Curt Marcus Gallery, 1995, 96, 97, 2000, James Danziger Gallery, 1995, Robert Mann Gallery, N.Y., 1999, Melbourne Internat. Festival, Australia, 1995, G. Gibson Gallery, 2000, High Mus. Art, Atlanta, 2000, others; one person exhbns. at Art Inst. Chgo., 1988, Milw. Art Mus., 1988, Carpenter Ctr., Harvard U., 1988, Fotomann, Inc., N.Y., 1989, 91, Photographers Gallery, 1990, Parco Gallery, Tokyo, 1990, Arles Festival, France, 1990, Jan Kesner Gallery, 1990, 91, 94, 2000, Houston Mus. Fine Arts, 1996, Ctr. Creative Photography, Tucson, 1996, Mus. Contemporary Art, Chgo., 1997, Contemporary Mus. of Art Art, Hawaii, 1997, San Jose Mus. of Art, 1998, Diputacion de Granada, Spain, 1999; art commn. cover Time mag., July 4, 1998; books include Telegraph 3 A.M., 1974, Grapestake Gallery, 1979, (A Photographic Book), 1979, Hawaii portfolio, 1980, Graecism dye-transfer portfolio, 1982, Desert Cantos, 1987, (Internat. Ctr. of Photography award 1988), Bravo 20: The Bombing of the American West, 1990 (Pen Ctr. U.S. A. West award for nonfiction 1991), Richard Misrach, Minn. Gallery, 1988, Violent Legacies, Aperture, 1992, Crimes and Splendors, 1996, Cantos del Desierto, Di putacion de Granada, 1999, The Sky Book, 2000, Richard Misrach: Golden Gate, 2001, Pictures of Paintings, 2002. Guggenheim fellow, 1978; Ferguson grantee, 1976; NEA grantee, 1973, 77, 84, 92; AT&T commn., 1979; Eureka fellow, 1991; recipient Koret Israel prize, 1992. *Photographs are the shadows of reality much like dreams. On the one hand, they appear to literally transcribe the real world, while on the other, they defy our linear concept of time and meaning. Because the primary illusion of photography is fact, it is the most powerful art medium of our time.*

MISRACK, TANA MARIE, counselor, minister, writer; b. Toledo, July 25, 1954; d. Anthony James and Isabelle (Drinkhouse) Richards; m. Robert Aaron Misrack, June 30, 1996. AS in Interior Design, West Valley Coll., 1979. Ordained to ministry Universal Ch. of Master, 1986. Owner, designer Interiors by Tana Marie, Saratoga, Calif., 1979-88; min., profl. intuitive counselor Monterey, 1988—; CEO, cons. Strategies for Success, 1994—. Lectr., seminar leader, Monterey, 1988—; radio personality Sta. KNRY-1240 Cannery Row, Monterey, 2000—, Sta. KFNX, Phoenix, 2001—; profl. intuitive counselor. Author: Isle of Fantasies, 1995, Mating Games:Stop Playing and Start Loving, 1999, Guy Code: Understand Your Man, 2000; contbr. articles to profl. jours. Amb. San Jose (Calif.) C. of C., 1993—; mem. Mt. View (Calif.) Chamber, 1994—. Mem. Women's Fund (1st v.p. 1994-98, pres. 1998—), Monterey C. of C. Avocations: cycling, photography, writing.

MISS, ROBERT EDWARD, fundraiser; b. Frederick, Md., Oct. 14, 1937; s. Robert Edward Sr. and Anna Theresa (Pazdersky) M.; m. Lee Ann Menendez Devine, Nov. 23, 1964 (div. Feb. 1985); children; Stephen Patrick, David Edward, Sarah Ann; m. Judith F. Schwartz Millman, May 22, 1993. AB, Fordham U., 1963; MA, U. N.C., 1973. Asst. dir. pub. affairs Fordham U., Bronx, N.Y., 1963-65; editor Coun. for Advancement and Support of Edn., Washington, 1965-69; network dir. U. N.C.-TV, Chapel Hill, 1969-79; v.p. City Suburban Workshop, N.Y.C., 1979-81; dir. mktg. comm. Lighthouse, Inc., 1981-86; ptnr. Mktg. Comm. Policy Group, N.Y.C.-various, 1986-89; v.p. Heartshare Human Svcs., Bklyn., 1989-95; sr. acct. exec. Semple & Bixel, Inc., Nutley, N.J., 1996-97; ptnr. Resource Devel. Coun., Dobbs Ferry, N.Y., 1998—. Author, editor: Teacher's Resources for ETV, 1973, Corp. Strategy for Issues of Aging, 1988; author of poems. Mentor team in tng. Leukemia Soc. of Am. Recipient Gilbert Poetry prize Women in the Moon Pubs., 1995. Mem. Nat. Soc. Fundraising Execs., Acad. Am. Poets, Westchester Assn. Devel. Officers. Democrat. Roman Catholic. Avocations: poetry writing, film/video producing, road racing. Home and Office: 37 Round Hill Rd Dobbs Ferry NY 10522-3310

MISSAN, RICHARD SHERMAN, lawyer; b. New Haven, Oct. 5, 1933; s. Albert and Hannah (Hochberg) M.; m. Aileen Louise Missan; children: Hilary, Andrew, Wendy. B.A., Yale U., 1955, J.D., 1958. Bar: N.Y. 1959, U.S. Dist. Ct. (so. and ea. dists.) N.Y. 1979, U.S. Ct. Appeals (2d cir.) N.Y. 1993. Assoc. Kaye, Scholer, Fierman, Hays & Handler, N.Y.C., 1962-67; ptnr. Schoenfeld & Jacobs, N.Y.C., 1968-78, Walsh & Frisch, N.Y.C., 1979-80, Gersten, Savage & Kaplowitz, N.Y.C., 1980-87, v.p., gen. counsel, Avis, Inc., 1987-88; pvt. practice, N.Y.C., 1988—; spl. prof. law Hofstra U., 1988—; mem. panel of mediators U.S. Dist. Ct. (ea. dist.) N.Y. Revision author: Corporations, New York Practice Guide (Business and Commercial). Mem. ABA, N.Y. State Bar Assn., Fed. Bar Council, Assn. of Bar of City of N.Y. (com. on corrections, chmn. subcom. on legis., com. on juvenile justice, chmn. subcom. on juvenile facilities, com. on atomic energy, mem. com. on mcpl. affairs, com. on housing and urban devel.), Yale Club.

MISSAR, CHARLES DONALD, librarian; b. Cleve., July 16, 1925; s. Charles Frank and Genevieve Catherine (Buechele) M.; m. Margaret Mary du Fief, Feb. 17, 1962; children: Charles David, Stephen du Fief. Student, Sacred Heart Sem., Detroit, 1943-45, St. Mary's Sem., Cleve., 1945-49; BA, John Carroll U., 1951; MLS, Cath. U. Am., 1960. Referral specialist Libr. of Congress, Washington, 1963-66; ERIC info. specialist U.S. Office Edn., 1966-72; head Ednl. Reference Ctr. Nat. Inst. Edn., 1973-78, supervisory libr., 1978-85; sr. libr. U.S. Dept. Edn., 1985-86; sr. editor Computer Scis. Corp. Profl. Svcs. Group, 1986-94, Missar Assocs., Washington, 1994—. Agy. rep. Fed. Libr. Com., Washington, 1978-86; ann. lectr. Fed. Libr. Resources Workshop, Catholic U. Am., Washington, 1981-96. Editor: Management of Federally Sponsored Libraries: Case Studies and Analysis, 1995; compiler, author: A Checklist of Ohio Imprints From 1821 to 1825, 1960; editor monthly jour. Tech. Abstract Bull., 1958-60; mem. editl. bd. Online Mag., 1977-80 Bd. dirs. Shrine of the Most Blessed Sacrament St. Pius X Libr. Recipient Superior Svc. Group award U.S. Office Edn., 1968, Superior Performance award Nat. Inst. Edn., 1974, 84; inductee Spl. Libraries Assn. Hall of Fame, 1991. Mem. ALA, D.C. Libr. Assn. (treas. 1972-74), Spl. Librs. Assn. (chmn. edn. divsn. 1980-81, chmn. 1989-90), Am. Soc. Info. Sci. (chmn. info. svcs. for edn. group 1984-86), John Carroll Soc., Cleve. Club, Serra Club (pres. 1992-93, 94-96), Arimathean Club, Ohio Soc., Cosmos Club. Roman Catholic. Home: 5617 32nd St NW Washington DC 20015-1622 Fax: 202-362-5709. E-mail: cdmissar@starpower.net.

MISSIMER, DENISE LOUISE, mental health nurse; b. Glendale, Calif., June 20, 1952; d. Charles and Mary Evelyn (Morris) Hutchison; m. James Thomas Missimer, Oct. 25, 1980; children: Crystal Leigh, Heather Nicole. ADN, El Paso Community Coll., 1973; BS in Health Arts, Coll. of St. Francis, Phoenix, 1989. Psychiat. nurse Ariz. State Hosp., Phoenix, 1976-78, psychiat. nurse adminstr., 1978-82; asst. nursing mgr. St. Luke's Behavioral Health Ctr., 1982-87, nurse mgr., 1987-91; pvt. practice, 1991—. Speaker in field; legal cons. eating disorders. Mem. ARC (Ariz. state disaster chmn. 1978). Home and Office: 1397 W Courtney Ln Tempe AZ 85284-5117 E-mail: jmissime@ix.netcom.com.

MISSIMER, THOMAS MICHAEL, geologist; b. Lancaster, Pa., Mar. 10, 1950; s. Jacob M. and Lorraine L. (Bilodeau) M. AB in Geology, Franklin and Marshall Coll., 1972; MS in Geology, Fla. State U., 1973; PhD in Marine Geology and Geophysics, U. Miami, Fla., 1995. Registered profl. geologist, Fla., Ga., Ind., Va. Hydrologist U.S. Geol. Survey, Ft. Myers, Fla., 1973-75; rsch. assoc. sedimentology U. Miami, Coral Gables, 1975-76; pres. Missimer & Assocs., Inc., Cape Coral, Fla., 1976-92; vice chmn. ViroGroup, Inc., 1991-93; pres. CDM Missimer, Ft. Myers, 1993-99; v.p. Camp, Dresser & McKee, Inc., 1994—, CDM Missimer, Ft. Myers, 1999—. Mem. Bd. Fla. Profl. Geologists, 1991-97, avice chmn., 1993, chmn., 1994; apptd. by Gov. J. Bush to the Fla. Forever Adv. Coun., 1999—, vice chmn. 1993, chmn. 1994; chmn. tech. adv. com. Govt. Com. for a Substantial South Fla., 1995-98, chmn., 1996-98. Author Water supply development for membrane water treatment facilities, 1994, Lender's Guide to environmental liability management, 1996; contbr. hydrogeol. and geol. studies of Southeastern U.S. to sci. jours.; contbr. more than 180 articles to profl. jours. Mem. citizens planning adv. com. Bd. Lee County (Fla.), 1981-82, chmn., 1982-83. Recipient Best Paper award, Internat. Desalination Assn., D.C. World Conf. on Desalination, 1991, Acad. Merit award U. Miami, 1997. Mem. Geol. Soc. Am., Am. Inst. Profl. Geologists (cert. profl. geol. scienitst), Am. Water Resources Assn., Am. Water Works Assn., AAAS, Am. Inst. Hydrology (cert. profl. hydrogeologist), Am. Groundwater Assn. (cert. Hydrogeologist), Fla. Acad. Scis. (chmn. earth and planetary sci. sect. 1973-74, 95), Internat. Desalination Assn., Southeastern Geol. Soc., S.E. Desalting Assn. (bd. dirs. 1996-98). Republican. Home: 3214 Mcgregor Blvd Fort Myers FL 33901-6723 Office: CDM Missimer College Pkwy Ste 202 Fort Myers FL 33919 E-mail: Missimertom@cdm.com.

MISSIRIOTIS, IRENE, geriatric services professional, artist; b. North Charleroi, Pa., Nov. 12, 1938; d. Alexander and Athena (Stirou) M. Diploma in fashion illustration, Art Inst. Pitts., 1960; BS in Psychology-English, writing cert., U. Pitts., 1976. Artist Livingston's, Youngstown, Ohio, 1961-63; layout artist O'Neils, Akron, 1963-67; tchr. art Art Inst. Pitts., 1967-73; reporter, typographer, layout artist, illustrator Night Times, Pitts., 1973-76; art coord. Cmty. Human Svcs. Corp., 1977-78; recreation leader Pitts. Parks and Recreation Dept., summers 1979-80; program mgr. United Cerebral Palsy Assn., Pitts., 1981; adult day care attendant Hill House Assn., 1985-87; therapeutic recreation asst. Angelus Convalescent Ctr., 1987-89; activities coord. Canterbury Place, 1989-90; activities dir. The Woodwell, 1991-97, Thorpe's Personal Care Home, Charleroi, 2000—02, Cullins Health Ctr., Pitts. Freelance artist watercolors, greeting cards, brochures, booklets, flyers, 1956—. Art exhibit Pitts. by the Sea Ctr. Art Gallery, 1997. Vol. Mondale-Ferraro Presdl. Campaign, Pitts., 1984; activist mem. NOW, 1974—; Christmas bell ringer, singer Salvation Army, Pitts., 1998. Mem. Pitts. Assn. for the Arts in Edn. and Therapy, Assn. for Women in Psychology, Nat. Mus. Women in the Arts (charter), Nat. Mus. Am. Indian (charter, cert. of appreciation), Waterford Soc. (charter), World Wildlife Fund, Alpha Sigma Lambda (charter). Democrat. Greek Orthodox. Avocations: singing, cooking, collecting pandas and shells, walking. Home: 367 S Negley Ave Apt 5 Pittsburgh PA 15232

MISTHAL, HOWARD JOSEPH, retired accountant, lawyer; b. Bklyn., Feb. 16, 1940; s. Max and Evelyn (Glass) M.; m. Angela Marie Giorgio, May 7, 1975; children: Barry Jay, Robin Lyn, Sara Ann. BBA cum laude, CCNY, 1961; LLB cum laude, NYU, 1967, LLM, 1972. CPA, N.Y.; bar: N.Y. 1968. From staff mem. to sr. tax ptnr. David Berdon & Co., LLP, CPAs, N.Y.C., 1961-99; ret., 1999. Dir., chmn. audit and loan com. The Apple Bank for Savs., to 1999; lectr. Sch. of Law Summer Continuing Ednl. Program, NYU, 1990-95. Mem. AICPA, N.Y. State Soc. CPAs. Avocations: bicycling, hiking, swimming, travel.

MISULIS, KARL EDWARD, physician; b. Saranac Lake, N.Y., Aug. 6, 1953; s. Edward Victor and Ruth Aileen (Miller) M.; m. Christa Margaret Stoscheck, June 14, 1980; children: Edward Nicholas, Karl Christian. BS with honors, Queens U., 1975; PhD, SUNY, Syracuse, 1980; MD, Vanderbilt U., 1982. Diplomate Am. Bd. Psychiatry and Neurology. Chief resident, neurology Vanderbilt U., Nashville, 1984-85, resident, neurology, 1982-86, asst. prof. neurology, 1986-90, assoc. prof. neurology, 1990-98, prof. neurology, 1998—; neurologist Semmes-Murphey Clinic, Jackson, 1991—. Author: (books) Essentials of Clinical Neurophysiology, 1993, Spehlmann's Evoked Potential Primer, 1994, Neurologic Localization and Diagnosis, 1996; editor: Scientific Foundations of Neurology, 1996, Disorders of Mental Status, 1998, Confusion, 1999, Review Manual for Neurology in Clinical Practice, 2000; contbr. articles to profl. publs. Recipient CIDA award NIH. Fellow Am. Acad. Neurology (Saul Korey award); mem. So. Clin. Neurol. Soc. (v.p. 1994—), AAN (mem. com. on crit. care), Am. Acad. Clin. Neurophysiology, Alpha Omega Alpha. Office: Semmes-Murphey Clin 614 Skyline Dr Jackson TN 38301-3923 E-mail: kemisulis@hotmail.com.

MITAL, ANIL, engineering educator; b. Barabanki, India, Nov. 13, 1951; came to U.S., 1975; s. Virendra Nath and Malti (Gupta) M.; m. Chetna Gupta, June 12, 1981; children: Anubhav, Aashi. B.E., Allahabad U., 1974; MS, Kans. State U., 1976; PhD, Tex. Tech. U., 1980. Asst. prof. indsl. engring. U. Wis., Platteville, 1979-80; assoc. prof., 1984-92; prof. indsl. engring. and phys. med. and rehab., 1993—; human factors engring. grad. coord. U. Cin., 1981—. Dir. Ergonomics Rsch. Lab., 1981—. Editor-in-chief Internat. Jour. Indsl. Ergonomics, 1986—, Internat. Jour. Indls. Engring.-Theory Applications and Practice, 1994—, Elsevier Book Series in Ergonomics; exec. editor: Internat. Jour. Human Resource Devel. and Mgmt., 1999—; gen. editor: Trends in Ergonomics/Human Factors I, 1984, Applications of Fuzzy Set Theory in Human Factors, 1986, Manual Materials Handling, 1989, A Guide to Manual Materials Handling, 1993, 2nd edit., 1997, Handbook of Expert Systems in Manufacturing and Production Engring., 1994, numerous other ergonomics jours.; contbr. numerous articles to profl. jours. Mem. Big Bros.-Big Sisters, Lubbock, Tex., 1977—. Grantee Nat. Inst. Occupl. Safety and Health, 1982-85, NSF, 1993-96; rsch. grantee Nat. Inst. Disability and Rehab., 1993-97; recipient Gold Medal for performacnce Allahabad U., 1974; named Young Engr. Yr. Engrs. and Scientists Cin., 1984; Jr. Morrow Rsch. Chair, 1982-83. Fellow Human Factors and Ergonomics Soc. (Paul M. Fitts award 1996), Inst. Indsl. Egnrs.; mem. Am. Indsl. Hygiene Assn. (chmn. nat. ergonomics com. 1984-85), Human Factors Soc. Am. (editl. bd., chmn. indsl. ergonomics tech. group 1985-86, Outstanding Contbns. award Tri-State chpt. 1984), Human Factors Soc. Greater Cin. (pres. 1983-84), Inst. Indsl. Engrs. (treas. Cin. chpt. 1983-84, ergonomics divsn. 1987-88, ergonomics divsn. award 1989, Eugene L. Grante award 1988), Soc. Automotive Engrs. (faculty advisor 1987-88, Ralph R. Teetor award 1985), Internat. Soc. Occupl. Ergonomics and Safety (Disting. Accomplishment award 1993), Pi Tau Sigma, Alpha Pi Mu, Tau Beta Pi (faculty advisor 1981-85), Phi Kappa Phi, Omicron Delta Kappa, delta Phi Epsilon, Sigma Xi (Disting. Rsch. award 1984), 100 Mile Joggers. Home: 7242 Cascade Dr West Chester OH 45069-2291

MITCH, WILLIAM EVANS, nephrologist; b. Birmingham, Ala., July 22, 1941; s. William Evans and Mary Elizabeth (Ackerman) M.; m. Frances Alexandra Fisher, Aug. 21, 1965; children: Eleanor Baylor, William Armistead. BA, Harvard Coll., 1963; MD, Harvard Med. Sch., 1967. Intern Brigham & Women's Hosp., Boston, 1967-68, resident, 1968-69; clin. assoc. Nat. Inst. Health, Bethesda, Md., 1969-72; resident Johns Hopkins Hosp., Balt., 1972-73, Brigham & Women's Hosp., 1973-74; asst. prof., assoc. prof. Johns Hopkins U. Dept. Pharm., Balt., 1974-78; assoc. prof. medicine Harvard Med. Sch., Boston, 1978-87; prof. medicine Emory U. Sch. Medicine, Atlanta, 1987—2002; chmn. dept. medicine U. Tex., Galveston, 2002—. Mem. study sect. NIH, 1988-92. Editor: The Progressive Nature of Renal Disease, 1986, 2d edit., 1992, Nutrition and the Kidney, 1988, 4th edit., 2002. Pres. region II Nat. Kidney Found., 1990-92, chmn. sci. adv. bd., 1996-98; chmn. exec. coun. on kidney Am. Heart Assn. Grantee NIH, 1979—. Mem. Am. Soc. Clin. Investigation, Assn. Am. Physicians, Am. Clin. and Climatol. Assn., Am. Soc. Nephrology (exec. coun. 1998—), Internat. Soc. Nephrology (treas. 1997—). Office: U Tex Galveston 4124 John Sealy Annex 301 University Blvd Galveston TX 77555-

MITCHAM, CARL, humanities educator; b. Dallas, Sept. 20, 1941; s. J.T. and Betty (Clapp) M.; m. Marylee Daniel, Mar. 26, 1965; children: Mark, Jessica, Emilie, Anna. BA in Philosophy magna cum laude, U. Colo., 1967, MA in Philosophy, 1969; PhD, Fordham U., 1988. Instr. philosophy Berea (Ky.) Coll., 1970-72; lectr. philosophy and social sci. St. Catharine Coll., Ky., 1972-82; assoc. prof. humanities Poly. U., Bklyn., 1982-89; prof. philosophy and sci. tech. soc. Pa. State U., 1989—. Author: Philosophy and Technology: Readings in the Philosophical Problems of Technology, 1972, reprinted edit., 1983, Theology and Technology: Essays in Christian Analysis and Exegesis, 1984, Philosophy and Technology II: INformation Technology and Computers in Theory and Practice, 1986, Philosophy of Technology in Spanish Speaking Countries, 1992, Thinking Through Technology, 1994; contbr. articles to profl. jours. Grantee NSF, 1975-78, 88, 93, NEH, 1978-80, 93, Am. Coun. Learned Socs., 1981, Ky. Humanities Coun., 1981-82, Franklin J. Matchette Found. and Goethe House N.Y., 1983, Exxon Edn. Found., 1984-88, JM Found., 1986, NSF, 1988, MacArthur Found., 1988. Mem. AAAS (com. on sci. freedom and responsibility), Am. Cath. Philos. Assn., Inst. for Theol. Encounter with Sci. and Tech., Soc. for Philosophy and Tech. (bd. dirs. 1980-85, co-editor Newsletter 1982-84), Soc. for History of Tech. (Abbot Payson Usher prize 1974). Office: Pa State U STS Program 240 Sparks Bldg University Park PA 16802-5201

MITCHAM, JULIUS JEROME, accountant; b. Pine Bluff, Ark., Jan. 2, 1941; s. James Vernon and Bertha Lee (Robertson) M.; m. Janet Claire Berry, Mar. 31, 1970 (div. Sept. 1981); m. Marsha Lee Henderson, Oct. 22, 1983; 1 child, Timothy John. BBA, U. Cen. Ark., 1971. CPA, Ark.; cert. healthcare fin. mgr. Br. mgr. Comml. Nat. Bank, Little Rock, 1961-66; auditor, acctg. supr. Ark. Blue Cross and Blue Shield, 1971-77; contr. Riverview Hosp., 1977-81; pvt. practice acctg., 1981-82; contr. Henryetta (Okla.) Med. Ctr., 1982-83; fin. report supr. Am. Med. Internat., Inc., Houston, 1983; dir. corp. acctg. Ft. Myers (Fla.) Cmty. Hosp., 1984-86; contr. Med. Ctr. of Southeast Okla., Durant, 1986-87; CFO Gulf Coast Cmty. Hosp./Qualicare of Miss., Inc., 1987-88; asst. adminstr. fin. S.W. Gen. Hosp., San Antonio, 1988-89; pvt. practice, 1989-90; CFO Bapt. Meml. Hosps. of Mississippi County, Blytheville, Ark., 1991-94, Med. Arts Hosp., Texarkana, Tex., 1994-96, Healthsouth Rehab. Hosp., Texarkana, 1997-98; pres. Mitcham & Assocs., 1998—2001; CFO Muscogee (Creek) Nation Divsn. Health Adminstrn., Okmulgee, Okla., 2002—. Served with USN, 1959-61. Mem. AICPA, Ark. Soc. CPAs, Healthcare Fin. Mgmt. Assn. (cert. fellow), Lions (sec. 1985-86, 2d v.p. 1995-96), Masons. Republican. Baptist. Home: PO Box 277 Okmulgee OK 74447 Office: PO Box 400 Okmulgee OK 74447 E-mail: jerrymitcham@mail.ihs.gov.

MITCHELHILL, JAMES MOFFAT, retired civil engineer; b. St. Joseph, Mo., Aug. 11, 1912; s. William and Jeannette (Ambrose) M.; m. Maurine Hutchason, Jan. 9, 1937 (div. 1962); children: Janis Maurine Mitchelhill Leas, Jeri Ann Mitchelhill Riney; m. Alicia Beuchat, 1982. BS, Northwestern U., 1934, MSCE, 1935. Registered profl. engr., Mont., P.R., Tex. Engring. dept. C., M., St. P. & P.R.R. Co., Chgo. and Miles City, Mont., 1935-45; asst. mgr. Ponce & Guayama R.R. Co., Aguirre, P.R., 1945-51, v.p., gen. mgr., 1969-70; mgr. Ctr. Cortada, Santa Isabel, 1951-54; r.r. supt. Braden Copper Co., Rancagua, Chile, 1954-63; staff engr. Coverdale — Colpitts, N.Y.C., 1963-64; asst. to exec. v.p. Ctrl. Aguirre Sugar Co., 1964-67; v.p., gen. mgr. Coddea, Inc., Dominican Republic, 1967-68; asst. to gen. mgr. Land Adminstrn. of P.R., La Nueva Central Aguirre, 1970-71; with Centrals Aguirre Lafayette and Mercedita, 1971-72; asst. to gen. mgr. Corporacion Azucarera de P.R., 1973-76, asst. to exec. dir., 1977-79, asst. exec. dir. for environ., 1979-82, engring. cons., 1982-92; Kendall County engr., 1985-97; ret. Fellow ASCE; mem. Am. Ry. Engring. Assn., colegio de Ingenieros y Agrimensores de P.R., Explorers Club, Circumnavigators Club, Travellers Century Club, Sigma Xi, Tau Beta Pi. Home: PO Box 506 Boerne TX 78006-0506

MITCHELL, ADA MAE BOYD, legal assistant; b. Nov. 23, 1927; d. Allen T. Boyd and Marjorie (Bigger) Mills Boyd; 1 child, Joseph W. Student, NYU, 1972-73. Supr. Faberge, Inc., Mahwah, N.J.; mgr. Demostration Svcs. and Promotional Monies; mgr. accts. receivables, credit mgr. Faberge, Inc., Mahwah, N.J., 1946-89; legal asst. Wright Patterson Med. Ctr., Dayton, Ohio, 1990—. Pres. Urban League Guild, Bergen County, NJ, 1982—83, bd. dirs., 1982—83; founder N.J. Coalition of 100 Black Women, 1982; dtr. Isis Akbar Ct. # 33, 1995—; vol. WPAFB, Ohio-Legal Office/Med. Group, 1990—, Nat. Notary Assn., 1990—, Heroines of Jericho P.H.A. Burning Bush Ct., 1997, Truth Guild #2 Heroines of Temple Crusades, 1997; active Dayton Urban League Guild, 1991; treas. Bethany Presbyn. Ch., Englewood, NJ, 1975, fin. sect., 1966—67, chair bldg. and renovation com., 1978—81, choir mem., elder, 1979—. clk. of session, 1980—85; 1st Black woman moderator Presbytery of Palisades-Presbyn. Ch., 1986; mem. self devel. of people com. Presbyn. Ch. Miami Presbytery, Dayton; active Jarvis Soc. Nat. Presbyn. Ch. Mem. NAFE, NAACP, Order Eastern Star (Queen of Sheba chpt. 4, Worthy Matron 1972-73).

MITCHELL, ADELE DICKINSON, health facility administrator; b. Va., Sept. 29, 1952; d. William A. Dickinson and Nancy (McGowen) Ring; m. William L. Mitchell, May 23, 1977. BSN cum laude, U. Va., 1977. RN, Va.; cert. CPR and spl. care cons. Staff nurse emergency rm. Trauma I Ctr. Care U. Va., Charlottesville, 1976-78; coronary intensive care specialist Cmty. Hosp. Roanoke (Va.) Valley, 1978-85; adminstr. nursing/clin. nursing, clin. dir. protocol, dir. rsch. Clinician Svcs., Roanoke, 1984-92. Vol. free clinics for the working poor, 1978-85; vol. tchr. adult edn. classes, 1978-85; vol. tchr. natural childbirth, 1978-85; bd. dirs. rsch. muscle tissue regeneration in field. Named Profl. Woman of Yr., Internat. Pilot Orgn., 1991, Nat. Competition Pilot Clubs Internat., 1991. Achievements include design of templates got patent in field. E-mail: spirit623@prodigy.net.

MITCHELL, ALLAN EDWIN, lawyer; b. Okemah, Okla., May 13, 1944; m. Neva G. Ream; children: Brian E., Amy E. BA in Mass. Comm., Northwestern Okla. State U., Alva, 1991; JD, U. Okla., 1994. Bar: Okla. 1994, U.S. dist. ct. (we. and no. dists.) 1994. Asst. state mgr. Oklahomans for Right to Work, Oklahoma City, 1967-68; exec. dir. London Sq. Village, 1968-73; dist. mgr. Farmland Ins. Svc., 1974-80, Nat. Farmers Union, Oklahoma City, 1980-85; dist. agt. Prudential Ins., Cherokee, Okla., 1985-89; atty. Hughes & Grant, Oklahoma City, 1994-96, Collins & Mitchell, Cherokee, Okla., 1996—; asst. dist. atty Alfalfa County, 1996—. Mem. Cherokee Bd. Edn., 1985-90; mem. fin. com. Rep. Party of Okla., 1995, state com., 1997X; scoutmaster, 1981-86, bd. mem. Great Salt Plains Coun. Boy Scouts Am.; adult advisor Girl Scouts Am.; pres. United Way Cherokee, 1984; mem. Okla. Sch. Bd. Mems. Legis. Network, 1985-90, state com. Okla. Rep. Party, 1997; vol. Okla. Spl. Olympics, 1996, 97. Mem. Ch. of the Nazarene. Avocations: public speaking, politics, civic activities. Office: Collins & Mitchell 214 S Grand Ave Cherokee OK 73728-2030

MITCHELL, ANDREA, journalist; b. N.Y.C., Oct. 30, 1946; d. Sydney and Cecile Mitchell; m. Alan Greenspan, Apr. 6, 1997. BA, U. Pa., 1967. Polit. reporter KYW Newsradio, Phila., 1967-76; polit. corr. Sta. KYW-TV, 1972-76; corr. Sta. WTOP-TV, Washington, 1977-78; gen. assignment and energy corr. NBC News, 1978-81, White House corr., 1981-88, chief congl. corr., 1989-92, chief White House corr., 1993-94, chief fgn. affairs corr., 1995—. Co-anchor Summer Sunday, USA, NBC-TV News, 1984, substitute anchor Meet the Press, 1988–; host MSNBC The Mitchell Report, Decision 2000. Trustee U. Pa., 1995—. Recipient award for pub. affairs reporting Am. Polit. Sci. Assn., 1969, Pub. Affairs Reporting award AP, 1976, AP Broadcast award, 1977; named Communicator of the Yr., Phila. chpt. Women in Comms., 1976, Woman of the Yr., Phila. chpt. Am. Women in Radio and TV, 1989, Lucretia Mott award Woman's Way, 1991. Office: NBC News 4001 Nebraska Ave NW Washington DC 20016-2733

MITCHELL, ANDY, Canadian federal official; b. Montreal; married; 3 children. Grad., Carleton U. Mem. House of Commons, Ottawa, Ont., Can., 1993—, sec. of state (parks) Can., 1997—. Chair standing com. on natural resources, House of Commons, vice chair ind. com., chair of fed. Ont. govt. caucus task force on Access to Capital by Small Bus., ministerial task force on disability and Canadians, chair No. Ont. Liberal caucus. Active vol., foster parent Children's Aid Soc.; vol. summer theater Muskoka, Elliott Lake Arts Task Force; mem. Elliott Lake and Gravenhurst Econ. Devel. Com. Mem. Ont. C. of C. (dir.), Northeastern Ont. C. of C. (past pres.), Elliott Lake C. of C. (past pres.), Gravenhurst C. of C. (past pres.). Office: House of Commons Ottawa ON Canada K1A 0A6

MITCHELL, ANN MARGARET, mental health nurse, educator; b. Pitts. d. John G. and Joan M. RN diploma, Pa. State U., 1974, BS, 1976, MS, 1979; PhD, U. Pitts., 1987. Clin. nurse specialist Western Psychiat. Inst. and Clinic, Pitts., 1985-89; pvt. practice, traveling nurse, cons. Pa., Calif, 1989-91; rsch. asst. prof. U. Pitts. Sch. Nursing, Pitts., 1991-95, asst. prof. nursing & psychiatry, 1995—. Bd. trustees MSH, 2001. Collaborator: Interpersonal Relationship Skills Tng. Program, 1978, Rels. Tng., 1984. Mem. Exec. Women's Coun., Greater Pitts., Inc., 1992. Recipient traineeship Pa. State U., University Park, 1976-78, scholarship U. Pit ts., Pa., 1980-82; grantee faculty scholar Uppsala (Sweden) U., 1996, Keio (Japan) U., Tokyo, 1998. Mem. ANA, Am. Assn. Suicidology, Am. Found. Suicide Prevention (bd. dirs. Pa. chpt.), Psychiat. Nurse Mgrs. Pa., Inc. (hon.), Assn. Clin. Nurse Specialists, Sigma Theta Tau, Kappa Delta Pi. Home: 5826 Nicholson St Pittsburgh PA 15217-2341 Office: Univ Pitts Sch Nursing # 415 Victoria Bldg 3500 Victoria St Pittsburgh PA 15213-2543

MITCHELL, ANNIE-MARTIN, volunteer civic worker; b. Rockwood, Tenn., Apr. 8, 1921; d. Robert Amis and Ruth (Cashion) Lauderdale; m. Charles Austin Mitchell, Aug. 7, 1942; children: Virginia M. Zarka, Charles Mitchell, Jr., Robert Almont. Student, Milligan Coll., 1938-40; BS magna cum laude, U. Tenn., 1942. Active numerous civic orgns., including: trustee White County Hosp., 1992—, chair of ann. giving, U. Tenn. Alumni Assn., 1992-93; pres. U. Tenn. Alumni Assn., 1991-92, pres.-elect 1990-91; mem. Tenn. Conf. fin. and adminstrv. com., United Meth. Ch., 1988-96, adminstrv. bd. 1980—, numerous others; dist. rep. White County Dem. Com., Sparta, 1988—, ballot clk. White County Election Commn., Sparta, 1990-2000; pres. Tenn PTA, 1969-72; v.p. Nat. PTA, 1972-74; v.p. Cumberland Valley Girl Scouts USA, 1975-81. Recipient Merrill Palmer scholarship, 1941, Lewisohn fellowship, 1941-42, Chancellor's award U. Tenn., 1994, Centennial Leader award, 1997. Mem. Sparta Woman's Club (pres. 1990-92, Outstanding Club Woman 1992), Phi Kappa Phi, Omicron Nu, Delta Kappa Gamma (hon.), Omicron Delta Kappa (hon.), others. Avocations: bridge, travel, boating, reading. Home: 108 S Highland Dr Sparta TN 38583-2234

MITCHELL, BERT BREON, literary translator; b. Salina, Kans., Aug. 9, 1942; s. John Charles and Bernita Maxine (Breon) M.; m. Lynda Diane Fink, July 21, 1965; children: Kieron Breon, Kerry Archer. BA, U. Kans., 1964; PhD, Oxford U., 1968. Asst. prof. German and comparative lit. Ind. U., Bloomington, 1968-71, assoc. prof., 1971-78, prof., 1978—, assoc. dean Coll. Arts and Scis., 1975-77, chmn. comparative lit., 1977-85, dir. Wells Scholars program, 1988-98. Dir. The Lilly Libr., 2001—. Author: James Joyce and the German Novel, 1922-1933, 1976, Beyond Illustration; The Livre d'Artiste in the Twentieth Century, 1976, The Complete Lithographs of Delacroix's Faust and Manet's The Raven, 1981; editor: Literature and the Other Arts, 1978, Metamorphosis and the Arts, 1979, Paul Morand, Fancy Goods/Open All Night, 1984; translator: Heartstop (Martin Grzimek), 1984, Selected Stories (Siegfried Lenz), 1989, The Musk Deer and Other Stories (Vilas Sarang), 1990, Looking Back (Lou Andreas-Salomé), 1991, Shadowlife (Martin Grzimek), 1991, Laura's Skin (J.F. Federspiel), 1991, The Color of the Snow (Rüdiger Kremer), 1992, Knife Edge (Ralf Rothmann) 1992, In the Kingdom of Enki (Vilas Sarang), 1993, The Silent Angel (Heinrich Böll), 1994, On the Glacier (Jürgen Kross), 1996, The God of Impertinence (Sten Nadolny), 1997, The Mad Dog (Heinrich Böll), 1997, The Trial (Franz Kafka), 1998. Rhodes scholar, 1964-68; Danforth fellow, 1964-68, Woodrow Wilson fellow, 1964, Alexander-von-Humboldt fellow, 1971, Translation fellow Nat. Endowment for Arts, 1989, Mellon fellow U. Tex., 1999; recipient Frederic Bachman Lieber Meml. award for disting. teaching, 1974, hon. citation Columbia Translation Ctr., 1990, Theodore Christian Hoepfner award So. Humanities Rev., 1995, Katharine and Daniel Leab award, 2001. Mem. MLA (chair William Riley Parker prize selection com. 1994), P.E.N., Am. Comparative Lit. Assn., Am. Lit. Translators Assn. (pres. 1985-87, Alta prize for disting. translation 1992), Am. Translators Assn. (com. lit. transl. 1983-84, German Lit. prize for disting. translation 1987, chmn. honors and awards com. 1995. hon. citation for disting. transl. 1999), Nat. Coun. Tchrs. of English (chair com. on comparative and world lit. 1995-98), James Joyce Found., Franz Kafka Soc., Samuel Beckett Soc., So. Comparative Lit. Assn., Brit. Comparative Lit. Assn., Internat. Comparative Lit. Assn., Am. Antiquarian Soc. Office: BH657 Indiana U Bloomington IN 47405 E-mail: mitchell@indiana.edu.

MITCHELL, BETTIE PHAENON, religious organization administrator; b. Colorado Springs, Colo., June 6, 1934; d. Roy William and Laura Lee (Costin) Roberts; m. Gerald Mitchell, May 3, 1952; children: Michelle Smith, Laura Sweitz, Jennie Grenzer, Mohammad Bader. BS in Edn., Lewis & Clark Coll., 1954; postgrad., Portland State U., 1962-72; MA in Religion summa cum laude, Warner Pacific Coll., 1979. Cert. counselor, Oreg. Elem. tchr. Quincy Sch. Dist., Clatskanie, Oreg., 1955-56; substitute tchr. Beaverton (Oreg.) and Washington County Schs., 1956-77; tchr. of the Bible Portland (Oreg.) C.C., 1974-92; counseling and healing ministry, 1977-79; founder, exec. dir. Good Samaritan Ministries, Beaverton, 1979—2002, founder, internat. exec. dir., 1988—2002. Tchr. Christian Renewal Ctr. Workshops, 1977-2002; spkr., presenter in field; leader tours in the Mid. East; developing counselor edn. programs Spain, Ghana, Pakistan, Ukraine, Jordan, Egypt, Kenya, Uganda, Tanzania, Zambia, Malawi, South Africa, Nigeria, Burundi, Sierra Leone, India, Bangladesh, Rwanda, Singapore, Canada, Congo, Liberia, Thailand, Ghana, Palestine, Can. Author: Who Is My Neighbor? A Parable, 1988, The Power of Conflict and Sacrifice, A Therapy Manual for Christian Marriage, 1988, Good Samaritan Training Handbook, 1989, Be Still and Listen to His Voice, The Story of Prayer and Faith, 1990, A Need for Understanding - International Counselor Training Manual, 1993, The Heros of Vietnam, The Children They Touched. Mem. Israel Task Force, Portland, 1974-80; Leader Camp Fire Internat., 1962-73, elem. sch. coord., 1962-68; asst. dir. Washington County Civil Def., 1961-63; precinct committeewoman Rep. Party, 1960; bd. dirs. Beaverton Fish, 1966-74; v.p. NCCJ, Portland, 1983-85; chmn., speaker's bur. Near East Task Force for Israel; chmn. fire bond issue campaign City of Beaverton, mgr. mayoral campaign, 1960; sunday sch. tchr., speaker, organizer Sharing and Caring program Bethel Ch., 1974-79. Mem. Am. Christian Counseling Assn., Christian Assn. for Psychol. Studies, Oreg. Counseling Assn. Republican. Avocations: historical research, writing, photography. Home: 6550 SW Imperial Dr Beaverton OR 97008-5311 Office: Good Samaritan Ministries 7929 SW Cirrus Dr Ste 23 Beaverton OR 97008-5973 Fax: 503-646-8898.

MITCHELL, BETTY JO, writer, publisher; b. May 2, 1931; d. Edith Darrah McWilliams. BA, S.W. Mo. State U.; MSLS, U. So. Calif. Asst. acquisitions librarian Calif. State U., Northridge, 1967-69, librarian for pers. and fin., 1969-71, acting assoc. libr. dir., 1971-72, assoc. dir. univ. librs., 1972-81; mgr. info. sys. City Santa Monica Rent Control, 1984-93; owner Viewpoint Press, Tehachapi, Calif. Cons. We. Interstate Commn. for Higher Edn. USOE Inst. for Tng. in Staff Devel. Problem Solving; participant workshops in field; spkr. at profl. confs. in field; bd. dirs. Tehachapi Cmty. Orch. Author: ALMS: A Budget Based Library Management System, 1982, The Secret of Hilhouse: An Adult Book for Teens, 1993, The Huckenpuck Papers: The Tale of a Family's Secret and a Young Girl's Search for Self-Esteem, 2001; co-author: Cost Analysis of Library Functions: A Total System Approach, 1978, How to See the U.S. on $12 a Day; contbr. writings to profl. publs.; editor Staff Development column in Spl. Librs., 1975-76. Bd. dirs. San Fernando Valley coun. Girl Scouts U.S., 1974-77, employed pers. com., 1979-81; bd. dirs. Bear Valley Springs Condo. Owners Assn., 1978, Empyrean Found., 1978-81, Tehachapi Cmty. Orch. Found., 1998—. Mem. AAUP, AAUW, ALA (chmn. various coms.), Assn. Women in Computing (bd. dirs. 1987-89), Nat. Libr. Assn., Author's Guild, Calif. Libr. Assn., Assn. Calif. State U. profs. (sec., exec. com. 1971-72), Phi Beta Chi, Alpha Mu Gamma. Office: PMB 400 785 Tucker Rd Ste G Tehachapi CA 93561-2523 Fax: 661-821-7515. E-mail: joie99@aol.com.

MITCHELL, BEVERLY SHRIVER, hematologist, oncologist, educator; b. Balt., May 14, 1944; m. John Robert Pringle; children: Robert Mitchell, Elizabeth Greene. AB summa cum laude in Biochemistry, Smith Coll., 1965; MD, Harvard U., 1969. Hematology fellow U. Mich., Ann Arbor, 1975-77, from instr. to asst. prof. internal medicine, 1977-81, assoc. prof., 1981-87, prof. internal medicine and pharmacology, 1987-91, U. N.C., Chapel Hill, 1991—, divsn. chief hematology/oncology, 1994—; assoc. dir. Lineberger Cancer Ctr., 1994—. Vis. scientist Fred Hutchinson Cancer Ctr., Seattle, 1984; mem. bd. sci. counselors Cancer Treatment divsn. Nat. Cancer Inst., 1993-95; mem. ad hoc adv. com. NIDDK, 1993. Author: Recent Developments in Transplantation Medicine, 1994; (with others) Cecil's Textbook of Internal Medicine, 1999. Recipient Stohlman award Leukemia Soc. Am., 1988. Mem. Am. Soc. Hematology (treas. 1991-96, v.p. 1998), Phi Beta, Inst. Medicine. Achievements include the cloning of DNA for Deocycytidine Kinase. Office: U NC at Chapel Hill CB # 7305 3009 Old Clinic Bldg # 7305 Chapel Hill NC 27599-0001*

MITCHELL, BONNIE S. interior designer; b. Balt., Apr. 23, 1951; d. Bill Endicter and Ramona M. Gettings; m. Morris Edgar Nicholson, Jr. Feb. 14, 1981 (div. Sept. 1992); 1 child, Bryan Russell Sweetser; m. Michael E. Mitchell, Nov. 11, 2000. Grad., Howard H.S., Ellicott City, Md., 1969. Sales mgr. Seitz Furniture, Supplies & More, Prescott, Ariz.; owner R&B Design Interiors; retail furniture salesperson, interior designer Barrows Furniture; retail furniture salesperson R&B Furniture, Phoenix, Chesapeake Furniture, Dundalk and Towson, Md. E-mail: mbmichael@qwest.net.

MITCHELL, BRIANE NELSON, lawyer; b. Seattle, July 4, 1953; s. Robert Max and Frances Marie (Nelson) M.; m. Suzanne Harmatz; children: Brianne Nelson, Brittany Suzanne. AB, Columbia U., 1975; JD, U. Idaho, 1978. Law clk. U.S. Ct. Appeals (9th cir.), 1978-80; assoc. Debevoise & Plimpton, N.Y.C., 1980-84, Paul, Hastings, Janofsky & Walker, L.A., 1984-86, ptnr., 1986-93; with McCambridge, Deixler & Marmaro, 1994-95; ptnr. Shapiro, Mitchell & Dupont LLP, Santa Monica, 1996-2000, Manatt, Phelps & Phillips LLP, L.A., 2000—. Mem. ABA, Idaho Bar Assn., N.Y. State Bar Assn., Calif. Bar Assn. Office: Manatt Phelps & Phillips LLP 11355 W Olympic Blvd Los Angeles CA 90064-1614 E-mail: bnmitchell@manatt.com.

MITCHELL, BRUCE TYSON, lawyer; b. San Francisco, Nov. 6, 1928; s. John Robert and Lorraine C. (Tyson) M.; m. Adrienne Means Hiscox, Oct. 14, 1951; 1 son, Mark Means. AB with great distinction, Stanford U., 1949, JD, 1951. Bar: Calif. 1952, U.S. Dist. Ct. (no. dist.) Calif 1952, U.S. Ct. Appeals (9th cir.) 1952, U.S. Supreme Ct. 1971. Estate adminstr. Crocker Nat. Bank, San Francisco, 1955-57; atty. Utah Internat. Inc., 1957-87, sec., 1974-87, sr. counsel, 1961-87. Mem. non-securities panel arbitrators N.Y. Stock Exch., Pacific Stock Exchange, NASD Bd. Arbitrators. Chmn. San Mateo County Rep. Cen. Com., 1964-70; mem. Calif. Rep. Central Com., 1964-74, 77-83; alt. del. Rep. Nat. Conv., 1968; co-chmn. San Mateo (Calif.) County Pres. Ford Com., 1976; mem. bd. visitors sch. law Stanford U., 1980-83; exec. v.p., bd. dirs. San Francisco Jr. C. of C., 1961; bd. dirs. No. Calif. chpt. Arthritis Found., 1972-85, 1987-92, St. Francis Hosp. Found., San Francisco, 1992-98, 99—, hon. dir., 1998-99—. Lt. (j.g.) USNR, 1952-55, Japan. Mem. ABA, Calif. Bar Assn., San Francisco Bar Assn., Am. Judicature Soc., Am. Soc. Corp. Secs. (v.p. 1976-77, dir. 1976-79), Assn. Former Intelligence Officers, Commonwealth Club of Calif. (pres. San Francisco 1973), Stanford Assocs., Pacific Union Club, Olympic Club, Capitol Hill Club, Travelers Century Club, Masons. Congregationalist. Home: 165 Redwood Dr Hillsborough CA 94010-6971 Office: 225 Bush St Fl 16 San Francisco CA 94104-4213

MITCHELL, BURLEY BAYARD, JR. lawyer; b. Oxford, N.C., Dec. 15, 1940; s. Burley Bayard and Dorothy Ford (Champion) M.; m. Mary Lou Willett, Aug. 3, 1962; children: David Bayard, Catherine Morris. BA with honors, N.C. State U., 1966, DHL (hon.), 1995; JD, U. N.C., 1969; LLD (hon.), Campbell U., 1998. Bar: N.C. 1969, U.S. Ct. Appeals (4th cir.) 1970, U.S. Ct. Appeals (3d cir.) 2002, U.S. Supreme Ct. 1972. Asst. atty. gen. State of N.C., Raleigh, 1969-72, dist. atty., 1973-77, judge Ct. Appeals, 1977-79, sec. crime control, 1979-82; justice Supreme Ct. of N.C., Raleigh, 1982-94; chief justice Supreme Ct. of N.C., Raleigh, 1995-99; ptnr. Womble Carlyle Sandridge and Rice, 1999—; atty. Womble Carlyle Sandridge and Rice, PLLC, 2002—. Served with USN, 1958-62, Asia. Recipient N.C. Nat. Guard Citizen Commendation award, 1982 Mem. ABA, VFW, N.C. Bar Assn., Mensa, Am. Legion, Phi Beta Kappa. Democrat. Methodist. Home: 4301 City of Oaks Wynd Raleigh NC 27612-5316 Office: First Union Cptl Ctr Ste 2100 PO Box 831 Raleigh NC 27602-0831

MITCHELL, CAROL ANN, lawyer; b. New Bedford, Mass., Sept. 2, 1957; d. John E. and Edith A. (Mogensen) M. AB, Vassar Coll., 1979; JD, William and Mary Coll., 1982. Bar: D.C. 1983, U.S. Ct. Appeals (Fed. cir.) 1988, U.S. Ct. Internat. Trade 1986. Atty.-advisor Benefits Rev. Bd., Washington, 1982-83; import compliance specialist Internat. Trade Adminstrn. U.S. Dept. Commerce, 1983-85; assoc. Collier, Shannon & Scott, 1985-90, Akin, Gump, Strauss, Hauer & Feld, Washington, 1990-91, Dewey, Ballantine, Washington, 1991-94; of counsel Steptoe & Johnson, 1994—. Mem. Vassar Club. Office: 1330 Connecticut Ave NW Washington DC 20036-1704 E-mail: cmitchel@steptoe.com.

MITCHELL, CAROLYN COCHRAN, foundation administrator's executive assistant; b. Atlanta, Dec. 27, 1943; d. Clemern Covell and Agnes Emily (Veal) Cochran; m. W. Alan Mitchell, Aug. 30, 1964; 1 child, Teri Marie. AB magna cum laude, Mercer U., 1965, M in Svc. Mgmt., 1989. Caseworker Ga. Dept. Family & Children Svcs., Macon, 1965-67, Covington, 1967-69; presch. dir. Southwestern Theol. Sem., Ft. Worth, 1969-70; presch. tchr., dir. Noah's Ark Day Care, Bowden, Ga., 1970-72, First Bapt. Ch., Bremen, 1972-75, Roebuck Park Bapt. Ch., Birmingham, Ala., 1975-79; freelance office mgr. and bookkeeper Macon, 1979-84; asst. to pres. Ga. Wesleyan Coll., 1984-98; asst. to pres., CEO Medcen Cmty. Health Found., 1998—. Exec. dir. Ga. Women of Achievement, 1991-95; dir. Macon Arts Alliance, 1987-91; mem. Cultural Plan Oversight Com., 1989-90. Mem. Get Out the Vote Task Force, Macon, 1981—, Macon Symphony Guild, 1986-91; dep. registrar Bibb County Bd. Elections, Macon, 1981-95; asst. sec. Ronald McDonald House Ctrl. Ga., 1999-2000. Mem. AAUW (bd. dirs. Ga. chpt., v.p. 1991-93, chair coll.-univ. rels. com. 1993-94, bylaws com. 1991-92, v.p., sec., treas., historian, newsletter editor, Macon chpt., Named Gift Honoree 1988, 2000), NAFE, NOW, Women's Network for Change, Am. Mgmt. Assn., Presdl. Assts. in Higher Edn., Religious Coalition for Reproductive Choice, The Interfaith Alliance, Women's Polit. Orgn. Macon, Sigma Mu. Democrat. Unitarian Universalist. E-mail: mitchell.carolyn@mccg.org.

MITCHELL, CHARLES EDWARD, lawyer, arbitrator; b. Seymour, Ind., July 7, 1925; s. Edward Charles Mitchell and Lula Belle (Thompson) Browning; m. Julia Viola Sarjeant, Sept. 15, 1951; children: Charles Leonard, Albert Bascom. Student, Morehouse Coll., Atlanta, 1943-44, 46-47, NYU, 1949; JD, Temple U., Phila., 1954. Bar: D.C. 1970, U.S. Ct. Appeals (3d cir.) 1971, Pa. 1972, U.S. Supreme Ct. 1973, U.S. Ct. Appeals (6th cir.) 1984; cert. labor arbitrator, Am. Arbitration Assn., Fed. Mediation and Conciliation Svc. Tchr. City of Phila., 1954-55; mgmt. trainee Office of Dir. of Fin., Budget Bur., Phila., 1955-56; legal asst. Office of Phila. Dist. Atty., 1956-60; claims rep., claims authorizer U.S. HEW, Social Security Adminstrn., Phila., 1960-64; atty., examiner NLRB, 1964-72; mgmt. labor counsel E.I. duPont de Nemours & Co., 1972-92; pvt. practice, 1993-99. Mem. labor panel Am. Arbitration Assn.; mem. roster of arbitrators Fed. Mediation and Conciliation Svc. 1st class seaman USN, 1944-46. Mem. ABA (mgmt. mem. sect. labor and employment law, practice and procs. com. 1973-92), Fed. Bar Assn. (pres. Del.

chpt. 1974-76, nat. chpt. del. 1973-78), Indsl. Rels. Rsch. Assn. (v.p. 1970-72), Phila. Bar Assn. Democrat. Episcopalian. Avocations: golf, tennis, chess, bridge, travel. E-mail: cemitchell5500ap@aol.com.

MITCHELL, CHARLES F. lawyer; b. Washington, Oct. 18, 1963; s. John Joseph and Duane (Schwertner) M.; m. Sherrie Ilyse Braude, June 7, 1986; children: Matthew Ryan, Sydni Paige, Jake Bradley. BA, U. Md., 1985; JD, Georgetown U., 1989. Bar: Md. 1989, D.C. 1991, U.S. Ct. Md. 1990, U.S. Ct. Appeals (4th and fed. cirs.) 1991, U.S. Ct. Fed. Claims 1991. Assoc. Holland & Knight (formerly Dunnells & Duvall), Washington, 1989-93; gen. counsel John J. Kirlin, Inc., Rockville, Md., 1993—. Contbr. articles to profl. jours. Mem. Am. Inns of Ct., ABA (vice-chmn. subcontracts com. for constrn. industry 1995, mem. public contract law/litigation sects.). Avocations: golf, tennis. Home: 9814 Bald Cypress Dr Rockville MD 20850-3494 Office: John J Kirlin Inc 515 Dover Rd # 2100 Rockville MD 20850-1388

MITCHELL, CHARLES PETER, library director; b. Bklyn., May 3, 1949; s. Charles S. and Anna B. Mitchell; m. Roberta Downing, Dec. 10, 1977. BA summa cum laude, Pace U., 1971; MLS, Pratt Inst., 1972. Jr./sr./prin. libr. Paterson (N.J.) Pub. Libr., 1972-80; libr. dir. Falmouth (Maine) Meml. Libr., 1980-93, Blue Hill (Maine) Pub. Libr., 1993-95, Millinocket (Maine) Meml. Libr., 1995—. Tchr. adult edn. program Falmouth, Maine, 1992; lectr. Woman's Lit. Union, Westbrook Coll., 1986. Columnist book reviews: Katahdin Times, 1995—, Forecaster, Falmouth, Maine, 1984-92; contbr. articles to profl. jours. Chmn. So. Maine Libr. Dist., Portland, 1983-85, Libr. Prime, 1988-91, treas., 1986-88, 92-93. Recipient Nat. Libr. award, 1989. Mem. Maine Libr. Assn., Richard III Soc. Avocations: classical music, film history. Home: 25 Garden St Millinocket ME 04462-1812 Office: Millinocket Meml Library 5 Maine Ave Millinocket ME 04462-1416

MITCHELL, CHARLIE HENRY, music educator; b. Orrville, Ala., Feb. 13, 1951; s. Willie and Earlene Mitchell. BA, Stilman Coll., 1972; MME, U. Louisville, 1981; DMA, U. Ky., 1998. Music tchr. Jefferson County Bd. Edn., Louisville, 1972—99; dir. music Springdale Presbyn. Ch., 1999—. Pvt. piano tchr. Bd. dirs. Louisville Bach Soc. Mem.: Hymn Soc., Am. Guild English Handbell Ringers, Am. Guild Organists. Avocation: tennis. Home: 4310 S Church Way Louisville KY 40207

MITCHELL, CLIFTON WILKES, psychologist, educator; b. Martinsville, Va., Feb. 4, 1952; s. Talmadge and Josephine Mitchell; m. Linda L. Mitchell, July 25, 1992; children: Steve Scariot, Craig Scariot, Susan Scariot BA in Psychology, Va. Polytech. Inst., Blacksburg, 1974; MA in Clin. Psychology, We. Ky. U., Bowling Green, 1976; PhD in Counseling Psychology, Ind. State U., Terre Haute, 1992. Lic. psychologist, Ohio. Asst. prof. counseling E. Tenn. U., Johnson City, 1992—; instr. techniques lab. Ind. State U., Terre Haute, 1990, 91, instr. stats, 1990, counselor, 1991, St. Mary of The Woods Coll., Terre Haute, 1990; intern Luton Mental Health Consortium, Nashville; asst. prof. counseling East Tennessee U., Johnson City, 1992—. Presenter in field. Contbr. articles to profl. jours. Presenter to numerous civic orgns. Grantee Pres. Grant-in-Aid program, 1994, 95, Rsch. Devel. Com., 1995, Tenn. Dept. Human Svcs., 1997. Mem. APA, ACA, Tenn. Counseling Assn., Tenn. Psychol. Assn., Intermountain Psychol. Assn., So. Assn. Counselor Edn. and Supervision, Watauga Counseling Assn., Phi Kappa Phi. Office: East Tenn State U Box 70548 Johnson City TN 37614-0548

MITCHELL, DANIEL J.B. economics educator; b. Bklyn., Sept. 7, 1942; s. Alter Brady and Celia (Rosenbloom) M.; m. Alice Tolk, Aug. 28, 1966; children: Nina A., Joshua W. AB, Columbia Coll., 1964; PhD, MIT, 1968. Sr. fellow Brookings Instn., Washington, 1978-79; chief economist U.S. Pay Bd., 1972-73; prof. econs. Sch. Mgmt., UCLA, 1968—. Dir. Inst. Indsl. Rels., UCLA, 1979-90. Author: Unions, Wages and Inflation, 1980, Human Resource Management, 1990; co-author: The Pay Board's Progress, 1978; co-editor: Can California Be Competitive and Caring, 1989. Mem. Am. Econ. Assn. (program com. 1988-89, nominating com. 1981-83), Indsl. Rels. Rsch. Assn. (exec. bd. 1981-89), Human Resource Outlook Panel.

MITCHELL, DAVID SPEAR, writer, editor, publisher, science educator; b. Salem, Mass., Dec. 6, 1945; s. Neal Burgess and Jean (Doig) M.; m. Anniken Brødersen, June 30, 1971; children: Katarina, Susanne, Andréa, Nathaniel. BA in English cum laude, U. Mass., 1970; MEd, Emerson Coll., 1970; postgrad., U. Oslo, 1971, U. Heidelburg, Germany. Tchr. Steiner Skole pa Grav, Baerum, Norway, 1970-71; founder, tchr. Pine Hill Waldorf Sch., Wilton, N.H., 1972-92; faculty chmn., tchr. life sci. Shining Mountain Waldorf Sch., Boulder, Colo., 1992—. Writer, editor, pub. Assn. of Waldorf Schs. N.Am., Fair Oaks, Calif., 1996—; adj. prof. Antioch Grad. Sch. Edn., Keene, N.H., 1982-92; mem. pvt. sch. leadership com. U.S. Dept. Edn., Washington, 1990—. Author: Will-Developed Intelligence, 1999, The Riddle of America, 2001, The Wonder of Waldorf Chemistry, 2001; editor numerous books, 1988—; editor author Waldorf Sci. Newsletter, 1995—. With U.S. Army, 1965-68. Mem. Assn. Waldorf Schs. N.Am. (Ea. regional chmn. 1982-90, chmn. publs. 1990—), Nat. Assn. Sci. Tchrs., Colo. Assn. for Sci. Tchrs. Home and Office: 1158 Quince Ave Boulder CO 80304-6700 E-mail: davidm@awsna.org.

MITCHELL, DAVID WALKER, lawyer; b. Oakland, Calif., Nov. 11, 1935; s. Theodore Boyd and Helen Louise (Walker) M.; m. Carolyn Hilliard Graves, July 29, 1961; children: Sarah, Betsy. AB in History, Stanford U., 1957; JD, Harvard U., 1960. Bar: Calif. 1961. Assoc. Kindel & Anderson, L.A., 1961-65, Weir, Hopkins, Donovan, San Jose, Calif., 1965-68; ptnr. Hopkins, Mitchell & Carley, 1968-87, McCutchen, Doyle, Brown & Enersen, San Jose, 1987-93, Hoge, Fenton, Jones & Appel, San Jose, 1993-2000, of counsel, 2001—. Bd. dirs. Peninsula Open Space Trust, Menlo Park, Calif., 1982—, pres., 1984-92; bd. dirs. Cmty. Found. Silicon Valley., San Jose, 1977-94, 99—; chair bd. trustees United Way Santa Clara County, 1983-85. Fellow Am. Bar Found., Am. Leadership Forum (sr.); mem. Santa Clara County Bar Assn. (trustee 1972-75), San Jose C. of C. (bd. dirs. 1975-80). Mem. United Ch. of Christ. Avocations: music, hiking. Office: Hoge Fenton Jones Appel 60 S Market St Ste 1400 San Jose CA 95113-2396 E-mail: dwm@hogefenton.com.

MITCHELL, DONALD WAYNE, management consultant, investment manager, lawyer, writer; b. San Bernardino, Calif., Nov. 1, 1946; s. Donald Wardell and Edith Felice (Wood) M.; m. Carol Bruckner, Nov. 11, 1984; children: Donald Weyland, Mark De Saussure, Mandy Sara, Janis Felicia. AB magna cum laude, Harvard U., 1968, JD, 1971. Bar: Mass. 1971. Project mgr. Boston Cons. Group, 1971-74; dir. strategic planning Heublein, Inc., Farmington, Conn., 1974-77; chmn. Mitchell and Co., Wellesley, Mass., 1977—; pres. Mitchell Investment Mgmt. Co., Inc., 1981—. Chmn. Share Price Growth 100, 1989—, Leading CFOs, 1993—, Outstanding CEOs, 1994—; pres. Leading Exec. Orgns. 100, Inc., 1991—. Co-author: The 2,000 Percent Solution, 1999, The Irresistible Growth Enterprise, 2000, The Ultimate Competitive Advantage, 2003. Chmn. Twenty Times Progress Project, 1995—, vice chmn. law sch. class of 1971 Harvard U., Cambridge, 1981-82, chmn. law sch fund 10th ann. gift campaign, 1980-81, chmn. law sch. class of 1971 15th reunion, 1985-86, co-chmn. class of 1968 20th reunion Harvard U., 1986-88; bd. dirs. Literacy Vols. Mass., 1993-2001, v.p. strategic planning, 1999-2001. Mem. Harvard Alumni Assn. (bd. dirs. 1986-88), Harvard Law Sch. Assn. (mem. centennial com. 1984-86, treas. 1987-90, mem. bus. com. 1999—). Office: Mitchell and Co 888 Worcester St Wellesley MA 02482 E-mail: donmitch@fastforward400.com.

MITCHELL, DOROTHY HARVEY, healthcare administrator; b. Brunswick, Ga., Oct. 2, 1958; d. Hallie Tyson and Dorothy (Thornton) Harvey; m. Carroll David Mitchell, Dec. 12, 1981; children: Christin Marie, Matthew Kevin. ADN, Brunswick Coll., 1978; BS in Health Adminstrn., Columbia So. U., 1998, MS in Health Adminstrn., 1999. RN, Ga.; Cert. intensive care nurse, BCLS instr., case mgr. Nurse med. ICU, S.E. Ga. Regional Med. Ctr., Brunswick, 1978-85; nurse adminstr. Home Care Svcs., Inc., 1985-87; nurse adminstr. Brunswick div. Healthmaster Home Health Care of Ga., Inc., 1987-95; RN adminstr. Care South St. Joseph's Hosp., 1995-97; client care coord. S.E. Ga. First Choice Med., 1997-99, asst. dir profl. svcs., 1997-99; dir. quality mgmt. S.E. Ga. Regional Med. Ctr., Brunswick, 1999-2001; sys. dir. quality mgmr. S.E. Ga. Health Sys., 2001—. Mem. quality assurance bd. Hosp. of Golden Isles, Brunswick, 1989-93; mem. adv. mktg. com. Golden Isles Children Ctr., 2001—; mem. adv. bd. Glynn Brunswick Meml. Hosp. Credit Union, 2001—. Mem. NAFE, Am. Coll. Healthcare Execs., Ga. Pub. Health Assn. (chmn. home health sect. 1991-92, vice chmn. home health sect. 1990-91), Oak Grove Island Property Owners Assn. (bd. dirs. 1996-98), Nat. Assn. Health Care Quality, Ga. Hosp. Assn., Ga. Assn. Health Care Quality. Methodist. Avocations: sewing, crafts, fishing, gardening. Office: SE Ga Regional Med Ctr PO Box 1518 Brunswick GA 31521-1518 E-mail: dmitche@sghs.org.

MITCHELL, EARL NELSON, physicist, educator; b. Centerville, Iowa, Aug. 30, 1926; s. Earl Nelson and Nina (Swank) M.; m. Marlys Marie Panning, July 23, 1955. AB magna cum laude, U. Iowa, 1949, MS, 1951; PhD, U. Minn., 1955. Research scientist Sperry Rand Corp., St. Paul, 1955-58; asst. prof., then assoc. prof. physics U. N.D., Grand Forks, 1958-62; vis. assoc. prof., then assoc. prof. and prof. physics U. N.C., Chapel Hill, 1962-91, prof. emeritus, 1991—, asst. chmn. dept., 1968-76. Lectr. Hamline U., 1956, 57; cons. Sperry Rand Corp., 1958-62 Contbr. articles to profl. jours.; author textbooks. Mem. Chapel Hill Planning Bd., 1970-71; pres. Chapel Hill Concert Series, 1967-70; mem. bd. for missions to deaf Luth. Ch. Mo. Synod, 1958-64. Served in USNR, 1945-46. Mem. Am. Phys. Soc., Am. Soc. Enologists (bd. dirs. ea. sect. 1984-91, pres. elect 1988, pres. 1989, past pres. 1990), N.C. Grape Coun., N.C. Wine Growers Assn. (pres. 1994-98, past pres. 1998—), Phi Beta Kappa, Sigma Xi, Phi Eta Sigma. Democrat. Office: U NC Dept Physics Chapel Hill NC 27599-0001 E-mail: mitchell.earl.marlys@worldnet.att.net.

MITCHELL, EARL WESLEY, clergyman; b. Excelsior Springs, Mo., Mar. 16, 1931; s. Earl Van and Ora Leah (Butterfield) M.; m. Mary Lou Bell, June 8, 1956; children: Susan Yvonne, Randall Bruce. Ordained to ministry Christian Union Ch., 1971. Min. Vibbard (Mo.) Christian Union Ch., 1962-69, Liberty (Mo.) Christian Ch., 1969-77, Barwick Christian Union Ch., Cameron, Mo., 1977-80, Independence (Mo.) Christian Union Ch., 1980-95; assoc. pastor Flack Meml. Christian Union Ch., Excelsior Springs, Mo., 1995—. Former mem. state exec. bd. Christian Union Mo., 1995-98; area rep. Mo. Christian Union USA; former mem. gen. exec. bd., former editor C.U. Witness. Sgt. USAF, 1951-55. Avocations: music, woodworking, painting, photography. Home and Office: 618 Henrie St Excelsior Springs MO 64024-2022

MITCHELL, EDWARD JOHN, economist, retired educator; b. Newark, Aug. 15, 1937; s. Edward Charles and Gladys (Werner) M.; m. Mary Josephine Osborne, June 14, 1958; children: Susan, Edward. BA summa cum laude, Bowling Green State U., 1960; postgrad. (Social Sci. Research Council fellow), Nuffield Coll., Oxford U., Eng., 1963-64, PhD in Econs. (NDEA fellow 1960-63, NSF fellow 1964-65), 1966. Lectr. in econs. Wharton Sch., U. Pa., 1964-65; economist Rand Corp., 1965-68; mem. Inst. Advanced Study, Princeton, N.J., 1968-69; sr. economist Pres.'s Council Econ. Advs., Washington, 1969-72; vis. assoc. prof. econs. Cornell U., 1972-73; assoc. prof. bus. econs. U. Mich., 1973-75, prof., 1975-88, prof. emeritus bus. econs. and pub. policy, 1988—; pres. Edward J. Mitchell Inc., Ann Arbor, 1977—. Dir. nat. energy project Am. Enterprise Inst., 1974-76; pres. Fountainhead Investment Co., 1984— Author: U.S. Energy Policy: A Primer, 1974, Dialogue on World Oil, 1974, Financing the Energy Industry, 1975, Vertical Integration of the Oil Industry, 1976, The Deregulation of Natural Gas, 1983; contbr. articles to profl. jours. Home: 310 Penny Ln Santa Barbara CA 93108-2601 Office: Grad Sch Bus U Mich Ann Arbor MI 48109 E-mail: mitchell296@home.com.

MITCHELL, EHRMAN BURKMAN, JR. architect; b. Harrisburg, Pa., Jan. 25, 1924; s. Ehrman Burkman and Alice (DeCevee) M.; m. Hermine Strickler, Sept. 25, 1948; children: Eric Ehrman, Marianne. AB, U. Pa., 1947, BArch, 1948; LHD (hon.), Spring Garden Coll., 1989. Asso. architect Bellante & Clauss, 1951-58; partner Mitchell/Giurgola, Assocs., Phila., 1958-85. Dir. Wyck Assn.; lectr. Ohio State U., U. Ariz., U. Utah, Cath. U. Am., Washington U., St. Louis, U. Notre Dame, Dartmouth Coll., U. Ky., U. Md., Temple U.; Phila. lectr. U. Nebr.; lectr. Calif. Poly. State U., U. Brasilia, Boston Archtl. Ctr., Pa. State U., Clemson U., Cornell U.; bd. overseers Temple U. Arch. Sch., U. Pa. Grad. Sch. Fine Arts; arch. design rev. panels U. Pa. Prin. works Nat. hdqrs. Am. Coll. Life Underwriters, Bryn Mawr, Pa. also, Adult Learning Research Center; office bldg. Penn Mut. Life Ins. Co., Phila., Ins. Co. N.Am., Phila.; U. Wash. Law Sch. and Library, Seattle, USIS Cultural Center, Brasilia, Brazil, A.B. Volvo Co. mfg. plant, Chesapeake, Va., New Parliament House, Canberra, Australia. Pres. Citizens Coun. Whitemarch Twp., Montgomery County, Pa., 1963-65, dir., 1963-67; mem. Del. Valley Citizens Transp. Com., 1964—, Citizens Coun. Montgomery County, 1964—; mem. archtl. rev. panel U.S. Fed. Res. System; bd. regents Am. Archtl. Found. With USNR, 1943-46. Recipient Gold medal Artists Guild Phila., Hazlett award Pa. Coun. Arts, 1985, plaque honor Mexican Fedn. Architects; fellow U. Pa. Mus. Fellow Royal Archtl. Inst. Can. (hon.), Royal Australian Inst. Architects; mem. AIA (chpt. dir. Phila. 1965-68, coll. fellows 1969—, nat. dir. 1973-75, v.p. 1977, 1st v.p. 1978, pres. 1979, gold medal Phila. chpt. 1964, 72, 74, silver medal 1973, Nat. Honor award 1974, 75, archtl. firm award 1976), Pa. Soc. Architects (dir. 1966—, sec. 1966, v.p. 1967, pres. 1968, silver medal 1974, 75, 77), Am. Inst. Mgmt. (pres.'s coun. 1967), Pa. Acad. Fine Arts, Pan Am. Fedn. Architects, Nat. Acad. Designs, Societe Arquitecto Mexicanos, Beta Theta Pi. Clubs: Philadelphia, Carpenter's Co., St. Andrew's Soc. (Phila.). Home: 600 E Cathedral Rd Apt E101 Philadelphia PA 19128-1929

MITCHELL, ELIZABETH MARELLE, family nurse practitioner, nursing educator, medical, surgical nurse; b. Bemis, Tenn., Dec. 2, 1937; d. William Columbus and Ruth Marelle (Wadley) Latham, William Columbus and Ruth Marelle (Wadley) Latham; m. Thomas Alton McNatt, June 20, 1953 (dec. Mar. 1984); children: Glenn McNatt, Craig McNatt, Chris McNatt; m. Charles Leon Mitchell, Sept. 7, 1985; stepchildren: Melanie Campbell, Mike, Allyson Webb. AA in Nursing, Union U., 1965; BSN, U. Tenn., Martin, 1994; MSN, FNP, U. Tenn., Memphis, 1996. RN Tenn., cert. CNOR, BCLS, BCLS instr., BCLS instr. trainer, ACLS, ACLS instr., family nurse practitioner, ANCC. Staff nurse med.-surg. units Jackson (Tenn.)-Madison County Gen. Hosp., 1965-66; physician 1st asst. Jackson Clinic Surgeons, 1966-74; nursing instr. Jackson Area Vo-Tech Sch., 1974-78, nursing instr. supr., 1978-81; supr. oper. rm. Jackson Splty. Hosp. (acquired by Jackson-Madison County Gen. Hosp. 1983), 1981-85; instr. nurse edn. Jackson-Madison County Gen. Hosp., 1985-96; family nurse practitioner Perry County Med. Ctr., 1996—. Nursing adv. bd. mem. Jackson Area Vo-Tech Sch., 1987—96; task force nursing asst. curriculum devel. mem. State of Tenn., Nashville, 1992; clin. skills judge Health Occupations Student Assn. Tenn. State Competition, Nashville, 1992. Tchr. Sun. sch. Malesus Bapt. Ch., Malesus, Tenn., 1975—86. Mem.: ANA, West Tenn. Healthcare Edn. and Tng. Conf. Group (pres. 1987, regional rep. 1988, sec. 1994), Tenn. Nursing Assn., Am. Soc. Healthcare Edn. and Tng. (svc. rep. West Tenn. 1988, Outstanding Regional Rep. Tenn. chpt. 1988), Assn. Oper. Rm. Nurses (program com. 1993, 1994), Am. Acad. Nurse Practitioners, U. Tenn. Martin Nursing Honor Soc., Sigma Theta Tau, Phi Theta Kappa. Avocations: reading, swimming, crafts. Home: RR 3 Box 378 Linden TN 37096-9544 Office: Perry County Med Ctr 115 E Brooklyn St Linden TN 37096

MITCHELL, ELLEN CLABAUGH, investment executive; b. Omaha, Mar. 2, 1942; d. Joseph Franklin and Dorothy (Newton) Carpenter; m. Dixon L. Mitchell, Aug. 25, 1962; l child, Lara Ellen. BS in Fin. & Econs., U. Nebr., Omaha, 1965; MBA, Va. Poly. Inst., 1983. Chartered Fin. Analyst. Asst. v.p. Firstier Fin., Omaha, 1965-69, 1971-75, Bridges Investments, Omaha, 1970-71; analyst U.S. Securities and Exchange Commn., Washington, 1983-85; v.p. Nat. Bank of Washington, 1985-87, Foxhall Investment Mgmt., Washington, 1987-93; pres. Mitchell Advisors Inc., Reston, Va., 1993—. Mem. Washington Soc. Investment Analysts, Inst. Chartered Fin. Analysts, Garden Club (v.p., treas. 1980). Episcopalian. Home: 2017 Turtle Pond Dr Reston VA 20191-4045 Office: Mitchell Advisors Inc 2017 Turtle Pond Dr Reston VA 20191-4045

MITCHELL, ERIC EHRMAN, photographer, stock broker; b. Phila., Nov. 24, 1954; s. Ehrman Burkman and Hermine (Strickler) M.; m. Leslie Ann March, Aug. 18, 1984; children: Meredith Hermine, Lauren Calder. BS in Photography and Bus., Skidmore Coll., 1977. Accredited asset mgmt. specialist. Head photographer Phila. (Pa.) Mus. Art, 1978-86; freelance photographer St. Peters, Pa., 1986-94; stockbroker Montanto Securities, Bluebell, 1994-95, Boenning & Scattergood, Inc., 1996—. Photographs have appeared in various books, catalogues and mags. worldwide. Planning commr. South Coventry Twp., Chester County, Pa., 1990-96, 2001-, supr., 1992-98; mem. Fedn. No. Chester County Communities, Pa., 1992—. Mem. Am. Soc. Media Photographers, Rotary. Avocations: skiing, hiking, woodland management, technical analysis of the stock market. Office: Boenning & Scattergood 601 High St Pottstown PA 19464

MITCHELL, GARRY, management consultant, writer; b. Medicine Hat, Alberta, Can., Mar. 22, 1938; s. Archibald Hugh Mitchell and Isobel Lucielle Barber; m. Valerie Nield, Dec. 16, 1968; 1 child, Heather McCall. B in Edn., U. Alta., Edmonton, 1961; MA, CUNY, N.Y.C., 1976; PhD, NYU, 1989. Broadcaster, Medicine Hat, Edmonton, N.Y.C., 1956-80; chmn. theater dept. Victoria Composite H.S., Edmonton, 1961-64; actor in broadway, TV, movies and regional N.Y.C., 1964-72; sales rep., mgr. Eplo Chems., Holiday Magic, AB Dick, 1972-76; assoc. prof. Nassau C.C., N.Y., 1976-81; cons., spkr. GM Tng. Specialists, N.Y.C., Yarmouth Port, Mass., 1979—. Author: Total Time Management, 1985, How to Motivate Successfully, 1986, The Trainer's Handbook 1st edition, 1987, 98, The Heart of the Sale, 1996. Mem. Internat. Soc. Gen. Semantics, N.Y. Acad. Scis. Avocations: theater, reading. Home and Office: GM Tng Specialists 95 Pine Ln Barnstable MA 02630

MITCHELL, GARY EARL, physicist, educator; b. Louisville, July 5, 1935; s. Earl Raymond and Delma Kathlene (Lockard) M.; m. Carolyn Fey Stutz, Aug. 4, 1957; children: Scott Frederick, Karen Lee (dec.). BS, U. Louisville, 1956; MA, Duke U., 1958; PhD, Fla. State U., 1962. Research assoc. Columbia U., N.Y.C., 1962-64, asst. prof., 1964-68; assoc. prof. N.C. State U., Raleigh, 1968-74, prof. physics, 1974— , assoc. head physics dept., 1982-97; assoc. dir. Triangle Univs. Nuclear Lab., 1992--. Contbr. numerous articles to sci. publs. Sr. scientist Alexander Von Humboldt Found., Bonn, Fed. Republic Germany, 1975, 97. Recipient Alumni Disting. Prof. award N.C. State U. Fellow Am. Phys. Soc. (Jesse Beams award 1997); mem. numerous sci. assns. Avocation: history. Home: 2913 Harriman Dr Durham NC 27705-5423 Office: NC State U Dept Physics PO Box 8202 Raleigh NC 27695-0001

MITCHELL, GENEVA BROOKE, hypnotherapist; b. Ringgold, Tex., Feb. 15, 1929; d. Roy Banks and Willie Jewel (Lemons) Shaw; m. Roy David Mitchell, Nov. 30, 1947; children: Ronald, Donald, Joel, Pamela, Annette. D of Clin. Hypnosis, Am. Inst. Hypnotherapy, Calif., 1989. Cert. master hypnotist Hypnosis Tng. Inst., hypnotherapist, advanced investigative and forensic hypnosis. Chiropractic asst., Alamogordo, N.Mex., 1962-79; hypnotherapist Alamogordo Hypnosis and Counseling Ctr., 1980-92, M&M Horses Corp., Tularosa, N.Mex., 1985-92; mgr. Shaw Mobile Home Park, 1986-99; mng. ptnr. Shaw, Mitchell & Mallory, Albuquerque, 1986, mgr., 1987-88; owner A New Image Hyupnosis Ctr., 1992; ret., 1992. Pres. N.Mex. Chiropractic Aux., 1984-85; mem. Am. Coun. Hypnotist Examiners, 1980-85; hypnotist for tape series; instr. New Forever Trim Life Loss Program; spkr. Am. Bd. Hypnotherapy Conv., 1991. Author: Take the Power, 1991. Charter pres. La Sertoma, Alamogordo, 1957; pres. Oreg. Sch. PTA, Alamogordo, 1958, La Luz Sch. Parents Club, N.Mex., 1962; sec. N.Mex. Jr. Rodeo Assn., 1964; co-founder Pre-Sch. La Luz, 1969; active N.Mex. Govs. Coun. on Youth, 1969; bd. dirs. Otero county Jr. Rodeo Assn., N.Mex., 1968; dir. self-hypnosis sch. Recipient Spkrs. award Life Found., 1984. Mem. Am. Assn. Profl. Hypnotherapists, Ladies for Life (Appreciation award 1984, 90), N.Mex. Ladies Life Fellowship (pres. 1983, bd. dirs. 1985), S.W. Hypnotherapy Examining Bd., Internat. Chiropractic Assn. Aux. (pres. 1994—, conv. chmn. 1993), Ladies for Life Chiropractic Orgn. (pres. elect 1993). Avocations: golf, painting, swimming, martial arts, writing. E-mail: gbmitchell@aol.com.

MITCHELL, GEOFFREY BENTLEY, accountant; b. Adelaide, Australia, June 20, 1944; arrived in Eng., 1981; s. Arthur Hale and Eunice Bentley (Wood) M.; m. Diedre Maria McKenna, Jan. 26, 1967; children: Mark James, Matthew Paul, Melissa Kate. B Econs., U. Adelaide, 1965. Chartered acct. From lectr. to sr. lectr. U. Adelaide, 1966-77; reader Flinders U., Adelaide, Australia, 1977-81; sec.-gen. Internat. Acctg. Stds. Com., London, 1981-85; tech. dir. Inst. Chartered Accts. in Eng. and Wales, 1985-90; head group acctg. policies, then dir. group fin. svcs., then chief accountant Barclays PLC, 1990—. Author: Principles of Accounting, 1981. Decorated officer Order of the Brit. Empire. Fellow Inst. Chartered Accts. in Australia, Inst. Chartered Accts. in Eng. and Wales (chmn. bus. law commn., mem. coun.); mem. Garrick Club. Avocation: tennis. Home: Scriventon Oast Stockland Green Speldhurst Tunbridge Wells TN3 0TU England Office: Barclays PLC 54 Lombard St London EC3P 3AH England

MITCHELL, GEORGE CHARLES, diplomat, international consultant, mediator, educator, writer; b. Aug. 6, 1920; s. Charles Peter and Athena N. (Kapotas) Mitchell; m. Nina Catherine Chaconas, Oct. 22, 1955; children: Martina, Melinda, Marlena. BS, U. Nebr., Kearney, 1941; postgrad., U. Nebr., Lincoln, 1941-42; cert., Oxford U., 1947; MA, Georgetown U., 1947; cert., Acad. Internat. Law, The Hague, The Netherlands, 1948; PhD summa cum laude, Sorbonne U., Paris, 1949; postgrad., Inst. d'Etudes Politiques, Paris, 1947-49, George Washington U. Law Sch., 1959-61, Fgn. Svc. Inst., 1962, 69, U. Pitts., 1974, U.S. Army War Coll., 1980, U.S. Naval War Coll., 1981. News corr., Washington and Western Europe, 1946-49; polit. analyst U.S. Dept. State, Washington, 1951-54, specialist, 1954-55; dep. prin. officer, econ. com. officer, consul Am. Consulate Gen., Belfast, No. Ireland, 1955-58; fgn. rels. officer U.S. Dept. State, Washington, 1958-62; prin. officer, polit. officer, consul Am. Consulate, Arequipa, Peru, 1962-67; dean Consular Corps, 1965-66; polit.-mil. officer, lst sec. Am. Embassy, Santo Domingo, Dominican Republic, 1967-68; prin. officer, polit.-econ. officer, consul Am. Consulate, San Luis Potosi, Mex., 1968-71; chief Speakers Bur. U.S. Dept. State, Washington, 1971-72, plans officer Bur. Pub. Affairs, 1971-72; exec. dir. World Affairs Coun. Pitts., 1973-91; internat. con., mediator Pitts., 1989—; exec. dir. internat. mgmt. tng. Lang. Ctr., 1990-91. Adj. prof. grad. internat. bus. mgmt. Point Pk. Coll., 1991—; internat. mgr. U.S. Arbitration and Mediation, Pa., 1992—93; bd. dirs. Stas. KGFW and KQKY, Kearney, Stas. KKAR and KQKQ, Omaha, Stas. KXNP-KODY, North Platte, 1954—96; leader del. to China World Affairs Coun., 1978; leader del. to Taiwan and Philippines Nat. Coun. World Affairs, 1988. Author: (book) Matthew B. Ridgway: Soldier, Statesman, Scholar, Citizen, 1999; editor: World Affairs Coun. newsletter, Nat. Coun. World Affairs Orgns. newsletter; co-editor: Asian/Pacific Dynamics-Economic, Political, Security, 1984; radio interviewer on internat. affairs, judge (TV series) Battle of Wits; contbr. articles to U.S. govt. publs., profl. jours., newspapers. Founder Prescott Sch., Arequipa; mem. Western Pa. Dist. Export Coun., Pitts., 1979—92; founder, pres. Atheneum Soc., Washington, 1952; founder Am. Soc. Arequipa, 1963. Lt. (j.g.) USNR, 1942—45, ETO. Recipient Meritorious Honor award, U.S. Dept. State, 1966; scholar AHEPA, 1939, U. Nebr., 1941. Mem.: Am. Arbitration Assn., Midwest Conf. World Affairs (adv. coun. 1988—90, Disting. Svc. award 1972, 1988), Assn. Conflict Resolution, Internat. Exec. Svc. Corps, Fgn. Affairs Rels. Corps, Nat. Coun. World Affairs Orgns. (v.p. 1985—87, pres. 1987—89, bd. dirs., exec. com. 1974—91), Com. Present Danger (founding, bd. dirs.), Am. Fgn. Svc. Assn., Rotary, Mortar Bd. Avocations: reading, writing, public speaking, antiques, travel. Home and Office: 3416 Brookdale Dr Upper Saint Clair Pittsburgh PA 15241-1558

MITCHELL, GEORGE ERNEST, JR. animal scientist, educator; b. Duoro, N.Mex., June 7, 1930; s. George Ernest and Alma Thyrza (Hatley) M.; m. Billie Carolyn McMahan, Mar. 14, 1952; children: Leslie Dianne, Karen Leigh, Cynthia Faye. BS, U. Mo., 1951, MS, 1954; PhD, U. Ill., 1956. Asst. prof. animal sci. U. Ill., 1956-60; assoc. prof. U. Ky., Lexington, 1960-67, prof., 1967-98, prof. emeritus, 1998—, dir. grad. studies in animal scis., 1964-96, coord. beef cattle and sheep, 1974-90. Contbr. articles to profl. jours. Served with USAF, 1951-53. Fulbright research scholar New Zealand, 1973-74; Rsch. scholar Japan Soc. for Promotion of Sci., Japan, 1989 Mem. Am. Soc. Animal Sci. (sec. 1969-70, v.p. 1970-71, pres. So. sect. 1971-72, rsch. fellow 1989, Disting. Svc. award 1994), Am. Dairy Sci. Assn., Am. Inst. Nutrition, AAAS, Council for Agrl. Sci. and Tech., Sigma Xi, Alpha Zeta, Gamma Sigma Delta, Omicron Delta Kappa. Democrat. Methodist. Home: 690 Hill N Dale Rd Lexington KY 40503-2164 Office: U Ky 809 W P Garrigus Bldg Lexington KY 40546-0001 E-mail: gmitchel@earthlink.net.

MITCHELL, GEORGE JOHN, former senator, lawyer; b. Waterville, Maine, Aug. 20, 1933; s. George J. and Mary (Saad) M.; m. Heather MacLachlan; children: Andrea, Andrew, Claire. BA, Bowdoin Coll., 1954;

LL.B., Georgetown U., 1960. Bar: Maine 1960, D.C. 1960. Trial atty. anti-trust div. U.S. Dept. Justice, Washington, 1960-62; exec. asst. Senator Edmund Muskie, 1962-65; ptnr. Jensen, Baird, Gardner & Henry, Portland, Maine, 1965-77; U.S. atty., 1977-79; U.S. dist. judge, 1979-80; U.S. senator from Maine, 1980-95; mem. environ. and pub. works com., 1980-95; mem. vet. affairs com., fin. com., 1981-95; mem. nat. ocean policy study group, arms control observer group; ex officio mem. intelligence com.; elected majority leader U.S. Senate, Washington, 1988-95; chmn. Dem. Senatorial Campaign Com., 1984-86; special counsel Verner, Liipfert, Bernhard, McPherson and Hand, Washington, 1996—, Prati, Flaherty, Beliveau, Pachios & Haley, Portland, Maine, 1997—. Chmn. Maine Democratic Com., 1966-68; nat. committeeman, Maine, 1968-77; asst. county atty. Cumberland County, 1971; chair Internat. Com. on violence in the Middle East, 2001. Served with U.S. Army, 1954-56. Chaired Northern Ireland peace talks which led to the Good Friday Agreement, 1998. Office: Verner, Liipfert, Bernhard, McPherson and Hand 901 15th St NW Ste 600 Washington DC 20005-2306

MITCHELL, GEORGE TRICE, physician; b. Marshall, Ill., Jan. 20, 1914; s. Roscoe Addison and Alma (Trice) M.; m. Mildred Aletha Miller, June 21, 1941; children: Linda Sue, Mary Kathryn. BS, Purdue U., 1935; MD, George Washington U., 1940. Intern Meth. Hosp., Indpls., 1940-41; gen. practice medicine, Marshall, 1946—. Mem. courtesy staff Union and Regional Hosps., Terre Haute, Ind.; clin. assoc. Sch. Basic Medicine, U. Ill.; mem. recruitment and retention com. U. Ill. Coll. Medicine, Rockford; chmn. bd. dirs. 1st Nat. Bank, Marshall. Author: Dr. George-An Account of the Life of a Country Doctor, 1993. Mem. adv. coun. premedicine Eastern Ill. U., 1965-69; alt. del. Rep. Conv., 1968, del., 1972; trustee Lakeland Jr. Coll., 1978-92. Lt. col. USAAF, 1941-45. Named Health Practitioner of Yr. Ill. Rural Health Assn., 1993; recipient Disting. Svc. award, Lake Land Coll., 1992, Purdue Alumni Assn. Citizenship award, 1996. Fellow Am. Acad. Family Physicians (Family Physician of Yr. 1993); mem. AMA, Ill. Med. Soc. (2d v.p. 1980-81), Clark County Med. Soc. (pres.), Aesculapian Soc. of Wabash Valley (pres. 1965), Nat. Rural Health Assn. (Practitioner of Yr. 19951999 Disting. Svc. award), Ill. Rural Health Assn. (bd. dirs.), Clark County Hist. Soc. (pres. 1968-70), Masons (32 degree), Shriners. Methodist. Home: 15923 N Oak Crest Rd Marshall IL 62441-4332 Office: 410 N 2d St Marshall IL 62441-1010

MITCHELL, GEORGE WASHINGTON, JR. physician, educator; b. Balt., Apr. 30, 1917; s. George Washington and Katharyne Eugenia (Diggs) M.; m. Anne Jenkins Shriver, Dec. 19, 1942 (div. 1954); children: Beverly Shriver, George Washington III, Anne Jenkins, Edward Diggs; m. Mary Elizabeth McKay, Sept. 14, 1957; children— Bruce McKay, Katharyne Wilcox. AB, Johns Hopkins, 1938, MD, 1942. Diplomate: Am. Bd. Ob-Gyn (dir.). Intern Johns Hopkins Hosp., 1942, resident, 1946-49; gynecologist in chief New Eng. Med. Center Hosp., Boston, 1950-81; prof. ob-gyn Tufts U. Sch. Med., 1954-81, prof. emeritus, 1981—, chmn. dept., 1956-81; prof. ob-gyn U. Tex., San Antonio, 1981—; chief of gynecology U. Tex. Health Scis. Center, 1981-92. Cons. Surgeon Gen. Navy. Served with USNR, 1943-46. Recipient Pub. Svc. award USN, 1977; named to Soc. Scholars Johns Hopkins U., 1991. Fellow ACS, ACOG, Am. Gynecol. and Obstet. Soc.; mem. AMA, Am. Fertility Soc., Soc. Pelvic Surgeons, Mass. Med. Soc., Obstet. Soc. Boston, New Eng. Ob-Gyn. Soc., Soc. Gynecol. Oncologists, So. Atlantic, Tex. Ob-Gyn. Soc., N.Am. Ob-Gyn. Soc., S.W. Ob-Gyn. soc., Johns Hopkins Med. and Surg. Assn., Soc. of Scholars Johns Hopkins U. Office: Dept Obstetrics and Gynecology U Texas Health Sci Center San Antonio TX 78284

MITCHELL, HUGH ALLEN, JR. lawyer; b. Olney, Md., May 9, 1956; s. Ruth Anne (Waple) M.; m. Denise A. Eldridge, Aug. 19, 1979; children: Jason, Samuel, Timothy, Hugh, Kayla, Josiah, Eben, Evangeline. BA in Econs., U. Md., 1977; JD, U. Va., 1980. Bar: Md. 1980, D.C. 1982. Law clk. to Hon. Ridgely P. Melvin, Jr., Md. Ct. Spl. Appeals, Annapolis, 1980-81; assoc. Glassie, Pewett, Dudley, Beebe & Shanks, Washington, 1981-83, Law Office Ronald R. Holden, Annapolis, Md., 1983-87; dir. devel. Annapolis Area Christian Sch., 1987-91; assoc. Barr & Testa, P.A., Balt., 1991-93; ptnr. Barr & Mitchell, P.A., 1993-96, Stewart, Plant & Blumenthal, LLC, Balt., 1996—. Spkr., instr. Md. Inst. for Continuing Edn. Lawyers, Balt. and Annapolis, 1992—, Md. Assn. CPAs, Balt. and Gambrills, Md., 1995—. Contbr. articles to law publs. Elder Evang. Presbyn. Ch., Annapolis, 1985-89; founder, pres. Recreational Youth Athletic League, Annapolis, 1993-99; mem. Anne Arundel County Human Rights Adv. Com., Annapolis, 1994-97. Fellow Am. Coll. Trust and Estate Counsel; mem. Md. Bar Assn. (augmented estate com. 1994-2000, coun. elder law sect. 1994-96, coun. estates and trusts sect. 1996-98). Avocations: reading, teaching. Office: 7 Saint Paul St Ste 910 Baltimore MD 21202-1672

MITCHELL, JACK H., III, lawyer; b. Birmingham, Ala., Sept. 9, 1947; BSChE, Clemson U., 1969; JD, Vanderbilt U., 1972. Bar: S.C. Assoc. Horton Law Firm, Greenville, SC, 1973—74, John M. Dillard PA, Greenville, 1974—75; ptnr. Dillard & Mitchell, 1975—77, Dillard Mitchell & Ariail, Greenville, 1977—79, Mitchell & Ariail, Greenville, 1979—97; pvt. practice Jack H. Mitchell III, Atty., 1997—. Lt. USAF, 1972—73. Mem.: S.C. State Bar Assn., Poinsett Club, Cotillion Club. Episcopalian. Home: 128 Bridgeton Dr Greenville SC 29615-2653 Office: 119 Williams St Greenville SC 29601-3144

MITCHELL, JAMES ANDREW, education educator; b. Fort Campbell, Ky., Feb. 16, 1953; s. James Andrew and Joyce Anne (Smith) M.; m. Oana Geodoiu, Aug. 13, 1999; 1 child, Magdalena Amelie. AB, Vassar Coll., 1975; MA, Princeton U., 1979, PhD, 1985. Instr. Princeton (N.J.) U., 1981-82; asst. prof. Haverford (Pa.) Coll., 1981-82, U. Redlands, Calif., 1982-85; escort/interpreter U.S. Dept. State, Washington, 1983-86; project mgr. Delphi Internat. Group, 1986-89; asst. prof. Mt. Vernon Coll., 1989-90; assoc. prof. Calif. State U., Northridge, 1990—. Vis. faculty fellow Am. U. in Kyrgyzstan, 2001, U. Bucharest, 2001. Contbr. articles to profl. jours. Mem. African policy issues group George Bush for Pres. Campaign, Washington, 1988. Recipient J. William Fulbright fellowship CIES and USIA, U. Bucharest, 1977, fellowship NEH, Washington, 1989, John Parker Compton pre-doctoral fellow Ctr. for Internat. Studies, Princeton U., 1981, rsch. program for devel. studies grantee Woodrow Wilson Sch., Princeton U., 1989. Avocations: fitness profl., aerobic exercise. Office: Dept Polit Sci/Calif State 18111 Nordhoff St Northridge CA 91330-0001

MITCHELL, JAMES EDWIN, architect, educator; b. N.Y.C., July 27, 1942; s. Edward Elbert Mitchell and Marian Tompkins (Cowles) Botsford; m. Catherine Fairbank, Aug. 28, 1963; 1 child, Natasha. BA cum laude, Harvard U., 1965, MS, 1967; MArch, U. Pa., 1973. Registered architect, Pa., N.J., N.Y. Staff architect Robert Gorman, Architect, Phila., 1974-75; assoc. dir. Ednl. Futures, Inc., 1975-76; assoc. Robert D. Lynn Assoc. Architects, 1976-79; prin. James E. Mitchell, AIA, 1979-81; founding ptnr. Jordan, Mitchell, Inc., 1981-88; assoc. prof. Drexel U., 1988—, interim dept. head civil and archtl. engring., 1991-92, assoc. dean for undergrad. affairs Coll. of Engring., 1992-95, dir. faculty devel. ctr., 1999—. Prin. works include Ctr. for Study of Adult Devel., 1979, Columbia Med. Ctr., 1983, Spring Garden Health Ctr., 1984, TJo Sports Medicine Ctr., 1988. Bd. dirs. Better Bus. Bur. Phila., 1987-88, The Phila. Sch., 1985-97. With USPHS, 1987-89. Mem. AIA (treas. Phila. chpt. 1982-84), ASCE, Nat. Soc. Archtl. Engrs. (charter), Am. Soc. Engring. Edn. Office: 4-280H St Philadelphia PA 19124 E-mail: james.mitchell@coe.drexel.edu.

MITCHELL, JAMES KENNETH, civil engineer, educator; b. Manchester, N.H., Apr. 19, 1930; s. Richard N. and Henrietta (Moench) M.; m. Virginia D. Williams, Nov. 24, 1951; children: Richard A., Laura K., James W., Donald M., David L. BBCE, Rensselaer Poly. Inst., 1951; MS, MIT, 1953, DSc, 1956. Mem. faculty U. Calif., Berkeley, 1958-93, prof. civil engring., 1968-89, chmn. dept., 1979-84, Edward G. and John R. Cahill prof. civil engring., 1989-92, Edward G. and John R. Cahill prof. civil engring. emeritus, 1993—; Via prof. civil engring. Va. Poly. Inst. and State U., Blacksburg, 1994-99, Univ. Disting. prof., 1996-99, Univ. Disting. prof. emeritus, 1999—. Geotech. cons., 1960—. Author: Fundamentals of Soil Behavior, 1976, 2d edit., 1993; contbr. articles to profl. jours. Asst. scoutmaster Boy Scouts Am., 1975-82; mem. Moraga (Calif.) Environ. Rev. Com., 1978-80. Served to 1st lt. AUS, 1956-58. Recipient Exceptional Sci. Achievement medal NASA, 1973, Berkeley citation, 1993, Chief of Engrs. Outstanding Svc. award U.S. Army Corps Engrs., 1999. Fellow ASCE (hon., Huber prize 1965, Middlebrooks award 1962, 70, 73, 2001, Norman medal 1972, 95, Terzaghi lectr. 1984, Terzaghi award 1985, pres. San Francisco sect. 1986-87); mem. Nat. Acad. Engring., Nat. Acad. Sci., Am. Soc. Engring. Edn. (We. Electric Fund award 1979), NRC (geotech. bd. chmn. 1990-94, bd. on infrastructure and constrn. environ. 1994-96, transp. rsch. bd. exec. com. 1983-87), Internat. Soc. Soil Mechanics and Geotech. Engring. (v.p. N.Am. 1989-94, Kevin Nash Gold medal 2001), Earthquake Engring. Rsch. Inst., Japanese Geotech. Soc. (internat. hon. mem.), Brit. Geotech. Soc. (Rankine lectr. 1991), Sigma Xi, Tau Beta Pi. Office: Va Tech Dept Civil Engring Blacksburg VA 24061-0105 E-mail: jkm@vt.edu.

MITCHELL, JAMES KENNETH, geography educator; b. Londonderry, No. Ireland, Apr. 5, 1943; came to U.S., 1965; s. James and Sarah Ethel (Orr) M.; m. Elizabeth Jean McConaghy, Aug. 12, 1966; children: James Alexander, Patrick Alan. BSc with honors, Queens U. Belfast, No. Ireland, 1965; MA, U. Cin., 1965-67, M of Cmty. Planning, 1967; PhD in Geography, U. Chgo., 1973. Lectr. environ. resources Cook Coll., Rutgers U., New Brunswick, N.J., 1970-73, asst. prof., 1973-75, assoc. prof., 1975-80; prof. geography Rutgers U., 1980—, chair dept. geography, 1988-91, 94-96, dir. grad. program in geography, 1977-85, 88-91, 99-01. Chair U.S. Sci. Com. on the Outer Continental Shelf, Washington, 1979-82; mem. com. on natural disasters NRC, Washington, 1982-86; expert witness. Author: Community Response to Coastal Erosion, 1974; author, editor: The Long Road to Recovery, 1996, Crucibles of Hazard: Megacities and Disasters in Transition, 1999; founding editor Global Environ. Change, 1990-93, Environ. Hazards, 1999—. Mem. curriculum adv. com. South Brunswick (N.J.) H.S., 1986-89. Recipient Presdl. award for disting. pub. svc. Rutgers U., 1984; East-West Ctr. fellow Environment and Policy Inst., 1987; Ctr. for Critical Analysis of Contemporary Culture fellow, 1991-92. Mem.: AAAS, Internat. Geog. Union (chair study group on the disaster vulnerability of megacities 1993—97), Internat. Rsch. Com. on Disasters, Inst. Brit. Geographers, Royal Geog. Soc., Assn. Am. Geographers, Am. Geog. Soc. (coun. 1984—93), Am. Conf. for Irish Studies. Presbyterian. Office: Rutgers U Dept Geography 54 Joyce Kilmer Ave Dept Piscataway NJ 08854-8045 E-mail: jmitchell@rci.rutgers.edu.

MITCHELL, JANET ALDRICH, fund raising executive, reference materials publisher; b. Providence, Jan. 12, 1928; d. Norman Ackley and Janet Aldrich; m. Raymond Warren Mitchell, Jan. 9, 1954 (div. 1967); children: Lydia Aldrich, Polly Mitchell Ranson. AB, Smith Coll., 1949; MEd, Rutgers U., 1975. Engaged in devel. various non-profit orgns., 1954-72; dir. devel. Wilson Fellowship Found., Princeton, N.J., 1972-74; dir. spl. projects N.J. Dept. Higher Edn., Trenton, 1974-76; prin., owner Mitchell Guide, 1976—. Cons. numerous non-profit orgns., 1976-86; lectr. Adult Sch., Princeton, 1983-84. Editor: Directory of Woodrow Wilson Fellows, 1968, A Community of Scholars, 1980. Exec. officer Princeton Cmty. Dem. Orgn., 1984—86; elected Princeton Twp. Com., 1987—89; mem. NAACP Legal Def. Fund, 1980—86; trustee N.J. Hist. Soc., 1984—86, Smith Coll. Class of 1949, 1999—. Mem. Princeton Smith Coll. Club (fund agent 1964-69, pres. 1968-70), Princeton Dog Club (bd. dirs. 1962-68). Episcopalian. Avocation: breeding and showing standard poodles. Home: 810 Sturwood Way Lawrenceville NJ 08648 Office: PO Box 626 Pennington NJ 08534 E-mail: grantsnj@aol.com.

MITCHELL, JEFFREY THOMAS, health science facility administrator; b. Columbus, Ohio, Aug. 9, 1946; s. Roger Lyman and Virginia Claire (Sands); children: Lauren Claire, Spencer Thomas. BS, Wright State U., 1976; Masters in Hosp. Adminstr, Xavier U., 1978. Asst. v.p. Grandview Hosp., Dayton, Ohio, 1977-81; v.p. Wyandotte (Mich.) Gen. Hosp., 1981-85; assoc. prof. Mercy Coll. Detroit, 1981-85; v.p. Aultman Hosp., Canton, Ohio, 1985-91; adminstr., chief exec. officer The Shriner's Children's Hosp., Lexington, Ky., 1992-93; v.p. Innovative Med. Svcs., Inc., Bradenton, Fla., 1994—98; ind. cons. Mitchell & Assocs., 1998—2001; dir. continuous improvement Bon Secours St. Joseph Hosp., Port Charlotte, Fla., 2001—. Bd. dirs. Erie Shores Health Services Inc., Monroe, mem. ambulatory surgery S. Mich. Program Afford. Health, 1980-85, adminstrv. mem. S. Detroit Ongoing Med. System Council, 1981-85, ambulatory task force mem. Miami Valley Health Systems Agy., Dayton 1977-81; instr. grad. program health adminstrn. Cen. Mich. U., Mt. Clemens. Mem. United Arts Found. Stark County, Stark County Cancer Com. Mem. Am. Coll. Health Care Execs. Republican. Episcopalian. Home: 7309 13th Ave W Bradenton FL 34209-5407 Office: Innovative Med Svcs Inc 1235 Tallevast Rd Sarasota FL 34243-3271

MITCHELL, JOAN LAVERNE, research scientist; b. Palo Alto, Calif., May 24, 1947; d. William Richardson and Doris LaVerne (Roddan) M. BS in Physics, Stanford U., 1969; MS in Physics, U. Ill., 1971, PhD in Physics, 1974. Rsch. staff mem. T.J. Watson Rsch. Ctr. IBM, Yorktown Heights, N.Y., 1974-88, 96-98, mgr. T.J. Watson Rsch. Ctr., 1979-88, image tech. cons. mktg. White Plains, 1989-91, rsch. staff mem. T.J. Watson Rsch. Ctr. Hawthorne, 1991-94, mgr. T.J. Watson Rsch. Ctr., 1992-94, supplemental employee Burlington, 1994-96; vis. prof. U. Ill., Urbana, 1996; with IBM Printing Systems Divsn., Boulder, Colo., 1999—; fellow IBM, 2001—. Del. CCITT Study Group XIV, 1978-79, ISO JPEG Com., 1987-94. Co-author: JPEG Still Image Data Compression Standard, 1993, MPEG Video Compression Standard, 1997; contbr. articles to profl. jours. Xerox Indsl. fellow, 1970-71. Fellow IEEE; mem. Am. Phys. Soc., Sigma Xi (chpt. sec. 1976, v.p. 1977, pres. 1978). Democrat. Achievements include co-inventor on numerous patents. Home: 2400 17th Ave Unit 103D Longmont CO 80503-1781 Office: IBM Printing Systems Divsn 6300 Diagonal Hwy MS004N Boulder CO 80301-9270

MITCHELL, JOHN CHARLES, business executive; b. Bedford, Ind., May 25, 1947; s. John Lewis and Mary Ellen (Rowe) M.; m. Marie Elizabeth Bruland, Aug. 21, 1971; 1 child, Allison Anne. BA in Econs., Va. Mil. Inst., 1969; MBA, JD, Ind. U., 1975. Bar: Ind., 1975, Fed. Cts., 1975. Brand mgr. Procter and Gamble Co., Cin., 1975-82; group product mgr. RJR/Del Monte, San Francisco, 1982-84; dir. mktg. RJR/Nabisco, Parsippany, N.J., 1984-87, v.p. mktg., 1987-88, v.p., gen. mgr., 1988-90, pres. sales and logistics co., 1991-94, pres. Planters, Lifesavers co. Winston-Salem, N.C., 1994-96; pres. bus. printer divsn. Lexmark Internat., Inc., Lexington, Ky., 1997-99; founder The Collaborative Inst., Chapel Hill, N.C., 2001—. 1st lt. US Army, 1969-71. Inductee Va. Mil. Inst. Sports Hall of Fame, 1981. Mem. ABA. Republican. Methodist. Avocations: golf, skiing. E-mail: jandmmitchell@worldnet.att.net.

MITCHELL, JOHN DAVID, journalism educator, retired; b. Chgo., Jan. 22, 1924; m. Mila Agnes Johnston, Sept. 12, 1947 (div. 1981); children: Justin, Alexandra. AB, Oberlin Coll., 1950; MS in Journalism, Kans. State U., 1959. Sports editor Elgin (Ill.) Courier-News, 1946-47; reporter/desk man Rockford Morning Star, Ill., 1950-52, Lima News, Ohio, 1952-56; temp. instr. Kans. State U., 1956-58; asst. prof., assoc. prof. Univ. Colo., 1958-73; mag. dept. acting chair Newhouse Sch., Syracuse (N.Y.) Univ., 1973-79, newspaper dept. chair, 1973-83, journalism divsn. acting asst. dean, 1980-81, journalism prof., 1973-94, prof. emeritus, 1994—. Fulbright lectr. Thammasat Univ., Bangkok, 1962-63; exec. sec. N.Y. State Soc. of Newspaper Editors, Syracuse, 1973-80. Co-author: Mass Communication Resources in Thailand, 1965; contbr. chpt. to The Asian Newspapers Reluctant Revolution, 1971; contbr. articles to profl. jours. Mem. Assn. for Edn. in Journalism and Mass Communication (charter mem. newspaper div., head 1976-79, minorities and communications div. charter mem., sec. 1977-79), Soc. Profl. Journalists, Syracuse Press Club (Svc. award 1984). Democrat. Avocations: sports, collecting jazz, country and western music, travel. Home: 101 Sun Harbor Dr Liverpool NY 13088-4323

MITCHELL, JOHN DIETRICH, theatre arts institute executive; b. Rockford, Ill., Nov. 3, 1917; s. John Dennis Royce and Dora Marie (Schroeder) M.; m. Miriam Pitcairn, Aug. 25, 1956; children: John Daniel, Lorenzo Theodore, Barbarina Mitchell Heyerdahl. BSS, Northwestern U., 1939, MA, 1941; EdD, Columbia U., 1956; HHD (hon.), Northwood U., 1986. Dir., producer Am. Broadcasting Co., N.Y.C., 1942-46; assoc. editor Samuel French, Publ., 1946-48; assoc. prof. Manhattan Coll., 1948-58; pres. Inst. for Advanced Studies in the Theatre Arts, 1958-97. Founder, pres. Eaton St. Press, Key West, Fla., 1994, Mitchell Performing Arts Ctr., Campus Acad., Pa., 2001; bd. dirs. Beneficia Found., Jenkintown, Pa. Author: Staging Chekhov, 1990, Actors Talk, 1991, Gift of Apollo, 1992, Staging Japanese Theatre: Noh and Kabuki, 1995, Men Stand on Shoulders, 1996; author: (aka Jack Royce) The Train Stopped at Domodossola, 1993, Murder at the Kabuki, 1994, Dressed to Murder, 1997, Way to the Towers of Silence, 1997, Bewitched by the Stage, 1997, Troubled Paradise, 1998, The Wallpaper Murder, 1998, Death in the Suit of Lights, 1999, Too Beautiful to Live, 2002. Trustee emeritus Northwood U., Midland, Mich., 1972-91; patron Met. Opera, N.Y.C.; golden donor Am. Ballet Theatre. Named hon. conch Key West (Fla.) Commrs., 1994; dedication of Mitchell Performing Arts Ctr., Bryn Athyn, Pa., 2001. Mem. Met. Mus., Key West Arts and Hist. Soc., Spencer Family Assn. Mayflower Soc., Key West Literary Seminar (emeritus), Nippon Club N.Y.C. Mem. Community Ch. Avocations: Tai Chi Chuan, swimming, collecting musical recordings, books. Home and Office: Apts 105-106 W La Brisa 1901 Roosevelt Blvd Key West FL 33040 Fax: 305-296-5827. E-mail: jdm@keysdigital.com.

MITCHELL, JOHN LAURIN AMOS, biological science educator; b. Lincoln, Nebr., July 18, 1944; s. William A. and Ruth Chilla (Cobbey) M.; m. Gail Ann Kurtz, July 13, 1968; children: Jill, Todd. BA, Oberlin Coll., 1966; PhD, Princeton U., 1970. Postdoctoral fellow McArdle Inst. Cancer Rsch., Madison, Wis., 1970-73; asst. prof. No. Ill. U., DeKalb, 1973-78, assoc. prof., prof., 1983—; dir. Ctr. Biochem. Biophys. Rsch., 1997—. Inventor in field; contbr. articles to profl. jours.

MITCHELL, JOHN NOYES, JR. retired electrical engineer; b. Pownal, Maine, Dec. 16, 1930; s. John Noyes and Frances (Small) M.; m. Marilyn Jean Michaelis, Sept. 1, 1956 (dec.); children: Brian John, Cynthia Lynn Mitchell Tumbleson, Stephanie Lee Mitchell Judson; m. Jacqueline A. Starr, Sept. 10, 1999. BSEE, Milw. Sch. Engring., 1957. Registered profl. engr., Ohio. Elec. rsch. engr. Nat. Cash Register Co., Dayton, Ohio, 1957-65; sr. engr. Xerox Corp., Rochester, N.Y., 1965-70, area mgr., 1970-73, Dallas, 1973-76, El Segundo, Calif., 1976-79, tech. program mgr., 1979-85, competitive benchmarking mgr., 1985-92, quality mgr., 1992-97. With USN, 1949—53. Mem. IEEE, Mason. Republican. Episcopalian. Home: 5545 Downham Meadow Sarasota FL 34235-0971 E-mail: jnmitch3@comcast.net.

MITCHELL, JON CEANDER, music educator, conductor; b. Chgo., June 18, 1949; s. James William and Violet Linnea Mitchell; m. Ester Morales, Dec. 22, 1973; children: Monica Mitchell Finn, Lydia, David. MusB, Millikin U., 1971; MS in Music Edn., U. Ill., Champaign-Urbana, 1972, EdD in Music Edn., 1980. Asst. prof. music Hanover Coll., Ind., 1982—87; condr. wind ensemble Carnegie Mellon U., Pitts., 1987—91; asst. prof. music U. Ga., Athens, 1991—92; chair dept. music U. Mass. , Boston, 1992—. Music dir. North Pitts. Civic Symphony, Pitts., 1988—92; guest conducting various bands and orchs. Author: (book) From Kneller Hall to Hammersmith, 1990, A Comprehensive Biography of Gustav Holst, 2001; contbr. articles to profl. jours. Mem.: Coll. Band Dirs. Nat. Assn., Music Educators Nat. Conf., World Assn. Symphonic Bands and Ensembles (asst. editor newsletter 2000, editor WASBE jour. 1994), Condrs. Guild, Phi Kappa Phi. Avocations: travel, model railroading, coaster collecting. Office: Dept Music U Mass 100 Morrissey Blvd Boston MA 02125-3393

MITCHELL, JOSEPH PATRICK, architect; b. Bellingham, Wash., Sept. 29, 1939; s. Joseph Henry and Jessie Delila (Smith) M.; m. Marilyn Ruth Jorgenson, June 23, 1962; children: Amy Evangeline, Kirk Patrick, Scott Henry. Student, Western Wash. State Coll., 1957-59; BA, U. Wash., 1963, BArch, 1965. Cert. Nat. Coun. of Architectural Registration Bd. Assoc. designer, draftsman, project architect Beckwith Spangler Davis, Bellevue, Wash., 1965-70; prin. J. Patrick Mitchell, AIA & Assocs./Architects/Planners/Cons., Kirkland, 1970—. Chmn. long range planning com. Lake Retreat Camp, 1965-93; charter mem. Northshore Bapt. Ch., 1969, bldg. chmn., 1980-96, elder, 1984-90; mem. bd extension and ctrl. com. Columbia Bapt. Conf., 1977-83; del. to Bapt. World Alliance 16th Congress, Seoul, Korea, 1990, 17th Congress, Buenos Aires, 1995, 18th Congress, Melbourne, Australia, 2000; trustee Bakke Libr./Cultural Ctr., 1994-96; vice-moderator Columbia Bapt. Conf., 1995-96, moderator, 1996-97, overseer ch. ministries bd., pres., 1997-99; charter mem. Cascade Cmty. Ch., 1997—, mem. bldg. com., 1999—; mem. Deming Hist. Cemetery Assn., 1997—; tour leader numerous internat. cities, 1998-2002. Recipient Internat. Archtl. Design award St. John Vianney Parish, 1989. Mem. AIA, Constrn. Specification Inst., Interfaith Forum Religion, Art, and Architecture, Nat. Fedn. Bus., Nat. Coun. Archtl. Bds., Internat. Conference of Building Ofcls., Christian Mgmt. Assn., Christian Camping Internat., Wash. Farm Forestry Assn., Woodinville C. of C. Office: 12620 120th Ave NE Ste 208 Kirkland WA 98034-7511

MITCHELL, KAREN FRANCES, artist, jewelry designer; b. Denver, Aug. 24, 1953; d. Harry Francis and Mary Jane Margrete (Jensen-Borg) M. BFA, U. Colo., 1975; postgrad., Gemological Inst. Am., 1986, Kulicke Jewelry Arts Inst., 1988, Cecilia Bauer Studio, 1992, Fashion Inst. of Tech., 1993, Nat. Acad. Design, 1994. Tchg. cert., art specialist. Jewelry designer, pres. Karen Mitchell Design, Aspen, Colo., 1978—; cultural rschr., cons. various Italian newspapers and mags. , N.Y. and Colo., 1992-94, Italian Consulate Cultural Inst., N.Y., 1992—94. Instr. workshops in design and goldsmithing technique; apprentice Van der Schoot Disegno e Fabricazione, Milan, 1989—91. (co-designer, contbr.) 1991-1995 World Gold Coun. Jewelry Trend Book, (jewelry featured in video and exhbn.) World Gold Coun. , Aaron Faber Gallery , N.Y.C. , 2002, Yaw Gallery , Mich., SOFA, Chgo., J. Cotter Gallery , 2002. Vol. chmn. benefit com. Aspen Art Mus.; co-chmn. Benefit Com., Aspen Music Festival; mem. Les Dames d'Aspen; vol. Profl. Women's Orgn. , Italy, Am. Craft Mus., NY, 1993, Coun. Fashion Designers Am.; bd. trustees Aspen Snowmass Coun. for Arts; vol. Internat. Design Conf. of Aspen, Screening Com. Aspen Film Fest, Soprano, Aspen Choral Soc., Aspen Ski Club/U.S. Olympic Equestrian Team, 1995. Named Vol. of Yr., Aspen Art Mus., 2001. Mem. Soc. N.Am. Goldsmiths, Am. Craft Coun., Jewelry Design Profl.'s Network. Address: PO Box 4885 Aspen CO 81612-4885

MITCHELL, KATHLEEN ANN, illustrator, graphic designer; b. Cin., July 27, 1948; d. Gerald Paige and Velma Alice (Bleier) Clary; m. Terence Nigel Mitchell, Feb. 2, 1977; children: Jessica Rose, Alexander Christien. BSc in Design, U. Cin., 1971. Graphic designer Lippincott & Margulies, N.Y.C., 1971, Allied Internat., London, 1972, Moura-George Briggs, London, 1973-75; art dir., photographer Phonograph Record Mag., L.A., 1976-77; ptnr. Walter Morgan Assocs., Santa Monica, Calif., 1977-80; illustrator Artists Internat., L.A. and N.Y.C., 1983—. Illustrator: (books) Once Upon a Cat, 1983, Jane Eyre, 1983, Alice in Wonderland, 1986, The Wizard of Oz, 1987, The Secret Garden, 1987, Kittens, Kittens, Kittens, 1987, My Bible Alphabet, 1987, The Christmas Story, 1989, Silent Night, 1989, The First Christmas, 1992, Aladdin and the Magic Lamp, 1993, Cinderella, 1993, Cats, 1994, Friendships, 1994, Thoughts, 1994, Beauty and the Beast, 1995, Joseph and the Dream Coat, 1995, Dogs, 1995, My Little Flower, 1995, The Joy of Christmas, 1995, There's a Ghost in the House, 1996, Puss in Boots, 1997, My Secret Valentine, 1997, Valentine Thoughts, 1997, Sleeping Beauty, 1997, The Wild Swans, 1998, The Story of Moses, 1999, Honesty, 1999, The Secret Garden, 2000, Bible Stories from the Old Testament, 2000, Parables from the New Testament, 2000, Prince Carrots, 2001, The Magic Set, 2001, Anne of Green Gables, 2002. Democrat. Avocations: art, antiques. Home: 1040 22nd St Santa Monica CA 90403-4518 E-mail: tkmitchell@earthlink.net.

MITCHELL, KEITH CHRISTOPHER, software engineer, consultant; b. Balt., May 18, 1960; s. Jack Lawrence and Phyllis Ann (DaShiell) M.; m. Angela Meade, Mar. 22, 1994; children: Thomas, William. BS in Info. Sys., U. Md., 1982; MS in Info. Sys., U. Md., Balt., 1992, PhD in Info. Sys., 1997. Project mgr. La Jolla Mgmt., Columbia, Md., 1982-87; v.p. ops. SOLON Consulting Group, Ltd., Silver Spring, 1987-96; project mgr. specialty products group 3M Health Info. Systems (acquired SOLON Mar. 1, 1996), 1996-97, software dev. mgr., decision support products, 1997-99, tech. adv. com. mem., 1996—2001, industry stds. team lead, 1997—2001, project mgr. internat. software devel. group, 1998—2001, fin. and ops. lead internet devel. team, 1999-2001, knowledge architect, 2001—, mgr. knowledge architecture and implementation, 2002—. Corp. sec. Applied Med. Software, Inc., N.J., 1995-96. Mem. IEEE. Avocations: basketball, reading, sailboat racing, golf. Home: 8410 Sand Cherry Ln Laurel MD 20723-1090 Office: 3M Health Info Systems 12501 Prosperity Dr Silver Spring MD 20904-1689 E-mail: kcmitchell@mmm.com.

MITCHELL, KENNETH D. physiologist, medical educator; b. Musselburgh, Scotland, Mar. 5, 1959; m. Maria Heavens, Sept. 30, 1995. BSc with upper 2d class honors, U. Edinburgh, Scotland, 1981, PhD in Physiology, 1986. Physiology tutor Univ. Med. Sch., Edinburgh, 1981-84; rsch. assoc.

Dept. Physiology and Biophysics Nephrology Rsch. and Tng. Ctr. U. Ala., Birmingham, 1984-86, postdoctoral rsch. fellow, 1986-87, rsch. instr., 1987-88, scientist I, 1987-88; asst. prof. Dept. Physiology Tulane U. Sch. Medicine, New Orleans, 1988-95, assoc. prof., 1995—. Contbr. articles to profl. jours. Mem. Am. Physiological Soc., Am. Soc. Nephrology, Am. Heart Assn. (fellow Coun. High Blood Pressure Rsch. 1993—, Established Investigator award 1995-2000), Internat. Soc. Nephrology. Office: Tulane U Sch Medicine Dept Physiology SL39 1430 Tulane Ave New Orleans LA 70112-2699 E-mail: kmitche1@tulane.edu.

MITCHELL, LAURA ANNE GILBERT, family nurse practitioner; b. Anniston, Ala., Oct. 13, 1957; d. Leonard A. and Betty Joyce (Wilkinson) Gilbert; m. Lee H. Mitchell, June 20, 1981; 1 child, Joseph L. ADN, DeKalb Coll., 1987; BSN magna cum laude, Med. Coll. Ga., 1993; MSN, Ga. State U., 1997. Cert. family nurse practitioner, critical care nurse. Staff nurse, preceptor ICU and CCU Gwinnett Med. Ctr., Lawrenceville, Ga., 1987-89, charge nurse cardiac catheterization lab., 1989-97, staff nurse cardiac catheterization lab., 1997—; family nurse practitioner Promina Gwinnett Health Sys., 1997—. Mem. AACN, AANP, ANA, Phi Theta Kappa (internat.), Sigma Theta Tau. Home: 435 Clark Lake Estates Dr Grayson GA 30017-1234 E-mail: LMITCH5085@aol.com.

MITCHELL, LEE MARK, communications executive, investment fund manager, lawyer; b. Albany , N.Y., Apr. 16, 1943; s. Maurice B. and Mildred (Roth) M.; m. Barbara Lee Anderson, Aug. 27, 1966; children: Mark, Matthew. AB, Wesleyan U., 1965; JD, U. Chgo., 1968. Bar: Ill. 1968, D.C. 1969, U.S. Supreme Ct. 1972. Assoc. Leibman, Williams, Bennett, Baird & Minow, Chgo. and Washington, 1968-72, Sidley & Austin, Washington, 1972-74, ptnr., 1974-84, 92-94; exec. v.p. and gen. counsel Field Enterprises, Inc., Chgo., 1981-83, pres., CEO, 1983-84, Field Corp., 1984-92; prin. Golder, Thoma, Cressey, Rauner, Inc., Chgo., 1994-98; ptnr. Thoma Cressey Equity Ptnrs., Inc., 1998—. Chmn. Chgo. Stock Exch., Inc. Author: Openly Arrived At, 1974, With the Nation Watching, 1979; co-author: Presidential Television, 1973. Bd. visitors U. Chgo. Law Sch., 1984—86, Medill Sch. Journalism, Northwestern U., 1984—91; pres. bd. govs. Chgo. Met. Planning Coun., 1988—91; mem. midwest regional adv. bd. Inst. Internat. Edn., 1987—99; trustee Ravinia Festival Assn., 1989—97, Northwestern U., Northwestern Meml. Hosp.; U.S. del. Brit. Legis. Conf. on Govt. and Media, Ditchley Park, England, 1974; adv. com. LWV Presdl. Debates, Washington, 1979—80, 1982. Mem.: Econ. Mid-Am. Club, ABA, Comml. Club Chgo. Home: 135 Maple Hill Rd Glencoe IL 60022-1252 Office: Thoma Cressey Equity Ptnrs Sears Tower Ste 9200 233 S Wacker Dr Chicago IL 60606-6306 E-mail: LMitchell@thomacressey.com.

MITCHELL, LILLIAN ADASSA, educator; b. Oct. 20, 1951; BS in Elem. Edn., W.I. Coll., 1982; MA, Andrew's U., 1987. Asst. prin. Bklyn. Sch., 1991-97; prin. Whispering Pines Sch., Old Westbury, N.Y., 1997—. Recipient Zappara Excellence in Tchg. award, 1992. Home: 3206 Bayswater Ct Far Rockaway NY 11691-1606

MITCHELL, LINDA MARLENE, education educator; b. Atchison, Kans., June 18, 1952; d. Frank Fayne and Marlene Marie Riley; m. John Lee Mitchell Jr., Oct. 16, 1971; children: John Michael, Joseph Lee, Jessica Nicole. BA, Wichita State U., 1986, MA, 1990; PhD, U. Kans., 1997. Lic. speech lang. pathologist; cert. neonatal assessment scale; cert. legal asst. Legal asst. Woodard, Baylock & HErnandez, Wichita, 1979-87; legal asst. to corp. counsel Pizza Hut, Inc., 1987-89; infant-toddler svcs. coord., speech/lang. pathologist Rainbows United, Inc., 1990-93; rsch. asst. U. Kans., Lawrence, 1993-96; v.p. Futures Unltd., Inc., Wellington, Kans., 1996-97; asst. prof. dept. curriculum & instrn. Wichita State U., 1997—. Presenter in field. Assoc. editor: Jour. Critical Inquiry Into Curriculum and Instrn., 1998—; contbr. articles. Kans. Health Found. grantee, 1996, Wichita State U. Rsch./Creative Project grantee, 1997. Mem. ASCD, Am. Speech-Lang.-Hearing Assn., Nat. Assn. Edn. Young Children, Am. Asn. People with Disabilities, Coun. Exceptional Children, Assn. Persons With Severe Handicaps. Democrat. Avocations: walking, weight lifting, flower gardening, bird watching, hiking, crochet. Office: Wichita State U 1845 Fairmount St Wichita KS 67260-0001

MITCHELL, LUCILLE ANNE, retired elementary school educator; b. Dayton Corners, Ill., Oct. 19, 1928; d. Roy Rollin and Edna May (Whitehouse) Sheppard; m. Donald L. Mitchell; children: David, Diane, Barbara Rock, Patricia Reaves. BS in Edn., Augustana Coll., 1966; MS in Edn., Western Ill. U., 1972, Edn. Specialist, 1974. Tchr. Carbon Cliff (Ill.) Elem. Sch., 1962-65, Moline (Ill.) Bd. Edn., 1967-92. Mem. textbook selection com. Moline Bd. Edn., 1967-84; tchr. of gifted Moline Bd. Edn., 1985-87. Contbr. (poetry) Footprints Through the Forest, 2000, Best Poems and Poets of 2001, 2001. Counselor to pastor Cmty. of Christ , 2001—02, elder in priesthood. Named Ill. Master Tchr., State of Ill., 1984. Mem. Ill. Edn. Assn. (various coms.), Moline Edn. Assn. (various coms.), Delta Kappa Gamma (program chmn. 1978-79, recording sec. 1980-81). Avocations: organ, piano, oil and water color painting, writing poetry. Home: 3214 55th Street Ct Moline IL 61265-5740 E-mail: donnlucy@aol.com.

MITCHELL, MALCOLM STUART, physician, researcher; b. N.Y.C., May 6, 1937; s. Max E. and Sylvia Mitchell; m. June Kan, Aug. 14, 1976; 1 child, Ian Douglas; children by previous marriage— Jeffrey Scott, Roderick Keith, Derek James. AB magna cum laude, Harvard Coll., 1957; MD, Yale U., 1962. Diplomate Am. Bd. Internal Medicine. Instr. to assoc. prof. of medicine and pharmacology Yale U. Sch. Medicine, New Haven, 1968-78; chief of med. oncology, dir. clin. investigations U. So. Calif. Sch. Medicine and Cancer Ctr., Los Angeles, 1978-84, prof. medicine and microbiology, 1978-94; prof. medicine, dir. Ctr. for Biol. Therapy-Melanoma Rsch., U. Calif. at San Diego Sch. Medicine and Cancer Ctr., La Jolla, 1994-98; prog. leader biol. therapy, Herrick Chair cancer immunology Karmanos Cancer Inst., Detroit, 1998—, interim dir. clin. rsch., 1998—2000. Cons various panels Nat. Cancer Inst., Bethesda, Md., 1975— ; mem. adv. com. Am. Cancer Soc., N.Y.C., 1975-79, U.S. Pharmacopeia, Washington DC, 1975-80; chmn. sci. adv. com. Nat. Cancer Cytology Ctr., N.Y.C., 1981-86; mem. Expert Panel on Unprofl. Med. Conduct, Calif., 1981—, prof. med., immunology and microbiol. Author: Hybridomas in Cancer Diagnosis and Treatment, 1982, The Modulation of Immunity, 1985, Immunity to Cancer, 1985, Human Tumor Antigens and Specific Tumor Therapy, 1989, Immunity to Cancer II, 1989, Biological Approaches to Cancer Treatment: Biomodulation, 1992; editor-in-chief Yale Jour. Biology and Medicine, 1976-78; contbr. articles to profl. jours. Pres., founder Philanthropic: Am. Melanoma Found. Recipient Research Career Devel. award Nat. Cancer Inst., 1974-79; Leukemia Soc. Am. scholar, 1968-73; Fulbright scholar, Oxford, 1959-60 Mem. Am. Assn. Immunologists, Am. Soc. Clin. Investigation, Am. Soc. Clin. Oncology, Soc. Biol. Therapy (bd. dirs. 1986-89), Am. Radium Soc. (2d v.p. 1979-80), Am. Assn. Cancer Rsch., Phi Beta Kappa, Sigma Xi. Democrat. Avocations: classical and jazz piano, tennis, skiing. Office: Karmanos Cancer Inst 110 E Warren Ave Detroit MI 48201-1312 E-mail: mitchell@karmanos.org.

MITCHELL, MARCIA JEANNE, freelance/self-employed writer, events producer; b. San Jose, Calif., Feb. 20, 1932; d. Eugene Lewis Wilcox and Gladys Delphine Shoemaker; m. John Alexander Donnan (div. June 1, 1975); children: Alan James Donnan, Kristen Elizabeth Donnan; m. Thomas Francis Mitchell, June 29, 1983. Student, Colo. State U., 1965—67; BA, Norwich U., Vt. Coll., 1989. Writer, editor Rapid City (S.D.) Jour., 1968—73; cabinet officer, sec. labor S.D. State Govt., Pierre, 1973—75; sr. exec. Corp. for Pub. Broadcasting, Washington, 1975—80; assoc. dir. Am. Film Inst., Washington & L.A., 1980—87; freelance writer, prodr., 1988—. Lectr., seminar leader mgmt. strategies for women, 1980—82; lectr. Crystal Cruise Lines, 1999; motivational sem. spkr., SD, 2000; mgmt. cons. Jon Crane Watercolors, Inc., 2001. Prodr.: world premieres of maj. motion pictures, 1980—86, A Daughter's Tribute to Fred Astair, 2001; author: Cosmetics from the Kitchen, 1972, Raindance to Research, 1977, Management Strategies for Women, 1980, 1981, The Spy Who Seduced America: Lies and Betrayal in the Heat of the Cold War, 2002. Past sec. Nat. Assns. Commns. on Women; vice chair Montserrat Found. for Charitable Giving, West Indies, 1995—2001; chair spl. events Hill City (S.D.) Arts Coun., 2001; mem. Montserrat Nat. Trust, Montserrat, 2001; past chair grants com. State Fine Arts Coun., SD; past mem. State Commn. on Status of Women; mem., organizer S.D. Dem. Women, 2001—02; past bd. dirs. Women's Equity Action League, N.Y.C., NY; past chair TV broadcasting com. PBS Sta. WETA-TV, Washington. Recipient 1st pl. feature writing, S.D. Press Women, 1995. Mem.: Nat. Fedn. Press Women (Top Press Woman of Yr. 1972—73). Roman Catholic.

MITCHELL, MARY ANN CARRICO, poet; b. Louisville, Aug. 1, 1937; d. Bernard and Catherine (Steinlocker) Carrico; m. William Ray Mitchell, Aug. 25, 1962; children: Michael, Anne Marie, Katherine. RN, St. Joseph Sch. Nursing, Louisville, 1958; BSN, U. Colo., 1962. Head nurse Our Lady of Peace Hosp., Louisville, 1960; mgr. collections Point Loma Credit Union, San Diego, 1974-77; charge nurse Mercy Hosp., 1977-78; managerial sec. Gulf Oil, Denver, 1977-81; exec. sec. Phillips Petrol, 1981-82; adminstrv. asst. Reliance Petroleum, 1982-84. Mem. Nat. League Am. Pen Women (founder, pres. Bluegrass of KY branch), 2000. Author: (poems) Meeshak, 1997, My First Vertical, 1997, White Tail-a-Flyin', 1997, Friends, 1997. Mem. DAR, AAUW, Nat. League Am. Penwomen (founder, pres. Bluegrass of Ky. br.). Roman Catholic. Avocations: painting, sewing, quilting, gardening, poetry. Home: 494 Lea View Ave Campbellsburg KY 40011-7545 E-mail: macmky@aol.com.

MITCHELL, MATTHEW KYLE, lawyer; b. Phila., Mar. 12, 1968; s. Bertram Harold and Joanne (Oritsky) M. AB in Govt. and Law, Lafayette Coll., Easton, Pa., 1990; JD cum laude, U. Miami, 1993. Bar: Fla. 1993, N.J. 1993, U.S. Dist. Ct. N.J. 1994, U.S. Dist. Ct. (so. dist.) Fla. 1994, U.S. Ct. Appeals (11th and 3d cirs.) 1994, U.S. Supreme Ct. 1998. Assoc. Angones, Hunter, McClure, Lynch & Williams, Miami, Fla., 1993-95, Green, Lundgren & Ryan, Haddonfield, N.J., 1995—. Mem. ATLA, Fla. Bar Assn., N.J. Bar Assn., Camden County Bar Assn. Office: Green Lundgren and Ryan PC PO Box 70 Haddonfield NJ 08033-0085

MITCHELL, MICHAEL KIEHL, elementary and secondary education educator, minister; b. Phila., Oct. 27, 1932; s. Robert Bartow and Louise Room (Keyser) M.; m. Gloria (Nell) Wilburn, Nov. 12, 1960; children: Donald Kiehl, Robert Alan. B in Edn., U. Miami, 1955; MEd, Tex. A&M U., 1975, PhD, 1978; grad., Internat. Sch. Christian Comm., Front Sight Handgun Tng. Acad., 2000. Cert. elem. and secondary edn., Fla., Tex., Alaska; lic. comml. pilot; ordained priest Contemporary Cath. Ch., 2002. Tchr. math. Dade County Pub. Schs., Miami Springs, Fla., 1955-60; tchr. elem. Greenwood Sch. Dist., Midland, Tex., 1961-63; from tchr. social studies, English to tng. coord. Midland (Tex.) Sch. Dist., 1963-75; prin. rsch. investigator Tex. A&M U., College Station, 1977-78; project dir. Edn. Profl. Devel. Consortium, Richardson, Tex., 1978-79; sr. rsch. scientist Am. Airlines, Dallas, 1979-83; pres. North Rsch. Inc., Anchorage, 1983-84; vocat. edn. curriculum specialist Anchorage Sch. Dist., 1984-87; sci. tchr., dept. head McLaughlin Youth Ctr. Anchorage (Alaska) Sch. Dist., 1987-2001; ret., 2001. Adj. prof. U. Alaska, Anchorage, 1987-89; evaluation team N.W. Accreditation Assn., Anchorage, 1985; asst. min. United Meth. ch., 1990-94; min. Christian Cmty. Fellowship, 1994—; deacon 1st Congl. Ch., Anchorage; instr. Flight and Ground Sch.; online counselor New Hope Online Svcs. of Crystal Cathedral Ch. of Rev. Robert H. Schuller; minister Sunday ch. svcs. McLaughlin Youth Ctr., AK State Reform Sch., 1999-2001. Dir., v.p. Anchorage Cmty. Theater, 1984-89; marriage commr. 3d Jud. Dist. Alaska, Anchorage, 1989-93; vol. United Way, Anchorage, 1984-90, Tony Knowles for Gov. Campaign, Anchorage, 1990, 94, Mark Begich for Mcpl. Assembly Campaign, 1991, Cheryl Clementson for Mcpl. Assembly Campaign, 1993. With U.S. Army, 1946-47. Tex. Edn. Agy. fellow, Austin, 1975, Ednl. Profl. Devel. fellow, 1975-78. Mem. NEA, NSTA, SAG, NRA (life), Alliance for Separation of School and State, Anchorage Edn. Assn., Am. Correctional Edn. Assn., Alaska Airmans Assn. (life, bd. dirs. 1983-89), Mensa (life), Am. Legion (life), Clowns of Am., Alaska Sci. Tchrs. Assn. (life), Alaskan Aviation Safety Found., Tex. Assn. Aerospace Tchrs. (life), Former Students Assn. Tex. A&M U., Vets. Underaged Mil. Svc. (life), Am. Legion (life), Guns Am. (life), Phi Delta Kappa, Phi Kappa Phi. Libertarian. Avocations: commercial pilot, professional acting, FAA accident prevention counselor. Home: 6626 Foothill Dr Anchorage AK 99504-2620 Office: Christian Cmty Fellowship 6626 Foothill Dr Anchorage AK 99504 E-mail: michaelmitchell@gci.net. *Life has taught me: 1) Regret not the past. 2) Fear not the future. 3) Enjoy the moment.*

MITCHELL, MICHAEL SHERMAN, lawyer; b. Walla Walla, Wash., Oct. 28, 1953; s. Sherman Raley and Mary Ella (Hirsch) M.; children: Kelsey, Kyle, Ryan. AA, Walla Walla Community Coll., 1972; BA, Wash. State U., 1975; JD, Willamette U., 1978. Bar: Wash. 1978, U.S. Dist. Ct. (ea. dist.) Wash. 1981, U.S. Dist. Ct. (western dist.) Wash. 1986. Dep. pros. atty. Walla Walla County, 1978-81; assoc., ptnr. Roach, Votendahl, Monahan & Mitchell, Walla Walla, 1981-89; sole practitioner Michael S. Mitchell, Atty., 1989—. Instr. Walla Walla Community Coll., 1981. Bd. dirs. Planned Parenthood Bd., Walla Walla, 1981-82, Blue Mountain Cougar Club, Walla Walla, 1988-97, United Way Walla Walla, 1991-94, Blue Mountain Sr. Housing Group, 1993—. Mem. Wash. State Bar Assn. (corrections com. 1981-82, fee arbitration bd. 1989-91, exec. com. gen. practice sect. 1994-99, chair 1997-98), Walla Walla County Bar Assn. (sec.-treas. 1992, v.p. 1993, pres. 1994), Walla Walla Country Club. Avocation: athletics. Office: 129 W Main St Walla Walla WA 99362-2817 E-mail: msmlaw@hscis.net.

MITCHELL, MOZELLA GORDON, English language educator, minister; b. Starkville, Miss., Aug. 14, 1936; d. John Thomas and Odena Mae (Graham) Gordon; m. Edrick R. Woodson, Mar. 20, 1951 (div. 1974); children: Cynthia LaVern, Marcia Delores Woodson Miller. AB, LeMoyne Coll., 1959; MA in English, U. Mich., 1963; MA in Religious Studies, Colgate-Rochester Divinity Sch., 1973; PhD, Emory U., 1980. Instr. in English and Speech Alcorn A&M Coll., Lorman, Miss., 1960-61; instr. English, chmn. dept. Owen Jr. Coll., Memphis, 1961-65; asst. prof. English and religion Norfolk State Coll., U. Norfolk, Va., 1965-81; assoc. prof. U. South Fla., Tampa, 1981-93, prof., 1993—; pastor Mount Sinai AME Zion Ch., 1982-89; presiding elder Tampa dist. AME Zion Ch., 1988—; pastor, founder Love of Christ AME Zion Tabernacle, Branden, Fla., 1993—. Vis. assoc. prof. Hood Theol. Sem., Salisbury, N.C., 1979-80, St. Louis U., 1992-93; vis. asst. lectr. U. Rochester, N.Y., 1972-73; co-dir. Ghent VISTA Project, Norfolk, 1969-71; cons. Black Women and Ministry Interdenominational Theol. Ctr; lectr. Fla. Humanities Coun., 1994-95; Meml. lectr. Mordecai Johnson Inst., Colgate Rochester Div. Sch., 1997. Author: Spiritual Dynamics of Howard Thurman's Theology, 1985, Howard Thurman and the Quest for Freedom, Proc. 2d Ann. Howard Thurman Convocation (Peter Lang), 1992, African American Religious History in Tampa Bay, 1992;, New Africa in America: The Blending of African and American Religious and Social Traditions Among Black People in Meridian, Mississippi and Surrounding Counties (Peter Lang), 1994, also articles, essays in field; editor: Martin Luther King Meml. Series in Religion, Culture and Social Devel.; editorial bd. Cornucipia Reprint Series. Mem. Tampa-Hillsborough County Human Rels. Coun., 1987—; founder Women at the Well, Inc.; del. 7th assembly World Coun. Chs., Canberra, Australia, 1991, 17th World Meth. Coun., Rio de Janiero, 1996; del. 18th World Meth. Coun., Brighton, England, 2001; mem. connectional coun. A.M.E. Zion Ch., Charlotte, 1984—, staff writer Sunday sch. lit., 1981—, mem. jud. coun.; pres. Fla. Coun. Chs., Orlando, Fla., 1988—90, pres.-elect, 1998—, pres. exec. bd., 2000. Recipient ecumenical leadership citation Fla. Coun. Chs., 1990, Inaugural lectr. award Geddes Hanson Black Cultural Ctr. Princeton Theol. Sem., 1993; fellow Nat. Doctoral Fund, 1978-80; grantee NEH, 1981, Fla. Endowment for Humanities, 1990—, U. South Fla. Rsch. Coun., 1990—. Mem. Coll. Theology Soc., Am. Acad. Religion, Soc. for the Study of Black Religion (pres. 1992-96), Joint Ctr. for Polit. Studies, Black Women in Ch. and Soc., Alpha Kappa Alpha. Phi Kappa Phi. Democrat. Methodist. Avocations: piano, poetry, tennis, bicycling, Scrabble. Office: U South Fla 301 CPR Religious Studies Dept Tampa FL 33620 E-mail: mozellam@aol.com. *In my estimation, people are people, whatever the race, class or status. Between the front yard and the back porch of each individual dwells the real person, to whom I like to direct my approach.*

MITCHELL, NORMA TAYLOR, history educator; b. Norfolk, Va., Nov. 14, 1936; d. Orville Carson Sr. and Emma (Heal) Taylor; m. Frank Joseph Mitchell, Sept. 5, 1959; 1 child, Anne Mitchell Whisnant. BA in History, Coll. William and Mary, 1958; MA, Duke U., 1962, PhD, 1967. Instr. history and polit. sci. Union Coll., Barbourville, Ky., 1962-64; dean of women Ctrl. Meth. Coll., Fayette, Mo., 1968-70; assoc. prof. history Troy (Ala.) State U., 1970-84, prof. history, 1984-99, prof. emerita, 1999—. Mem. gen. commn. on archives and history United Meth. Ch., 1972-80, chair women's history project, 1977-80; vice chair nat. planning com. Bicentennial of Methodism in Am., 1979-80; hist. lectr. groups within United Meth. Ch., 1972—; lectr., presenter in field. Contbr. chpts. to books; author articles and revs. Lay leader United Meth. Ch., local, state and nat. levels, 1960—, including bd. dirs. United Meth. Bd. Pastoral Care and Counseling, 1984-92, bd. dirs. United Meth. Children's Homes, Ala.-West Fla., 1989-99; del. Southeastern Jurisdictional Confs., 1980; United Meth. Women conf. officer, 1976-80; conf. chair Commn. on Status and Role of Women, 1976-80. Recipient awards and honors; So. Fellowships Fund grantee, 1958-61; Cokesbury Tchg. fellow, 1964-65. Mem. AAUP, NEA, NOW, AAUW (v.p. for membership Troy br. 1995-99, honoree Ednl. Found. 1998-99), Ala. Edn. Assn., Am. Hist. Assn., So. Hist. Assn. (membership com. 1992), So. Assn. for Women Historians, Ala. Assn. Historians, Ala. Hist. Assn., North Ala. United Meth. Hist. Soc., Bread for the World, Amnesty Internat., Mothers Against Drunk Driving, Humane Soc. U.S., Phi Beta Kappa, Phi Kappa Phi, Phi Alpha Theta, Omicron Delta Kappa. Democrat. Avocation: children's and animal rights advocacy. Home: 7 Vandora Pl Durham NC 27705 Office: Troy State U Dept History Bibb Graves Hall 305 Troy AL 36082-0001 E-mail: ntmitchel@earthlink.net.

MITCHELL, ORLAN E. clergyman, former college president; b. Eldora, Iowa, Mar. 13, 1933; s. Frank E. and Alice G. (Brown) M.; m. Verlene J. Huehn, June 10, 1952; children: Jolene R., Stephen M., Nadene A., Timothy M., Mark E. BA, Grinnell Coll., 1955; B.D., Yale U., 1959, M.Div., 1965; D.Min., San Francisco Theol. Sem., 1976. Ordained to ministry United Ch. of Christ, 1959; pastor chs. Sheridan Twp., Iowa, 1954-55, New Preston, Conn., 1956-59, Clarion, Iowa, 1959-69, Yankton, S.D., 1969-77; pres. Yankton (S.D.) Coll., 1977-96; conf. minister Iowa Conf. United Ch. Christ; ret., 1996. Cons. in field. Mem. Sch. Bd., Clarion, Iowa, 1965-69, mem., Yankton, S.D., 1973-77, pres., 1976; bd. dirs. Lewis and Clark Mental Health Center. Mem. S.D. Found. Pvt. Colls., S.D. Assn. Pvt. Colls., Colls. of Mid-Am. Lodges: Kiwanis; Masons. Democrat. Office: 725 Park St Grinnell IA 50112-2235 E-mail: orlanm@pcpartner.net.

MITCHELL, PATRICK JOHN, financial executive; b. Honolulu, May 24, 1958; s. Bradford William and Frances (Cantwell) Mitchell; m. Catherine Elliott, June 15, 1985; children: Bradford Elliott, Margaret Whiting. BS in Acctg., Pa. State U., 1980. CPA, Pa. Mgr. Arthur Young & Co., Phila., 1980-89; dir. investor rels. Delphi Fin. Group, Inc., 1989—; asst. v.p. Reliance Standard Life, 1989-95; v.p., CFO & treas. Westbridge Captial Corp., Fort Worth, 1995—, pres & COO; CEO & chmn. Ascent Assurance Inc. (formerly Westbridge Captial Corp.), 1998—. Pres. Upper Merion chpt. Am. Cancer Soc., Phila., 1992; chmn. fundraising Utility Emergency Svcs. Fund, Phila., 1992. Mem. AICPA, Pa. Inst. CPAs. Republican. Roman Catholic. Home: 2713 Heritage Hills Dr Fort Worth TX 76109-5516 Office: Ascent Assurance Inc 110 W. Seventh St. Ste 300 Fort Worth TX 76102

MITCHELL, PATSY MALIER, religious school founder and administrator; b. Greenwood, Miss., Aug. 28, 1948; d. William Lonal and Lillian (Walker) Malier; m. Charles E. Mitchell, Apr. 20, 1970; children: Christopher, Kara, Angela. BS in Edn., Delta State U., 1970, MEd, 1974, Edn. Specialist, 1979; MA in Ch. Ministries, Ch. of God Sch. Theology, 1990; PhD in Psychology and Counseling, La. Bapt. U., 1994; D in Edn. Christian Sch. Adminstrn., Baptist Christian U., 1992. Cert. sch. adminstr. Youth, Christian edn. dir. Ch. of God, Minter City, Miss., 1975—, teen talent dir., 1983—, missions rep., 1975—, dist. Christian edn. dir. Cleveland, Miss., 1983-85, sch. adminstr., 1985—. Del. Ch. of God Edn. Leadership, Cleveland, Tenn., 1990; del., spkr. Christian Sch. Internat., Chattanooga, 1991. Contbr. Dir. St. Jude Children's Hosp., Memphis, 1991; vol. 4-H Club, Greenwood, Miss., 1985—91. Named Outstanding Young Women of Am., 1983, 50 Leading Bus. Women in Miss., 2001; recipient Cmty. Pride award, Chevron, 1988, Internat. Woman of Yr. award, 1993. Mem.: NAFE, Ch. of God Edn. Assn., Christian Schs. Internat., Christian Sch. Adminstrs., Gospel Music Assn., Ch. of God Sch. of Theology Alumni assn., Delta State Alumni Assn. Republican. Home: RR 1 Box 72A Minter City MS 38944-9714 *The greatest gift that God has given mankind is the capacity to love and encourage others. It is God's gift to us and our gift to others.*

MITCHELL, PAULA RAE, nursing educator, college dean; b. Independence , Mo., Jan. 10, 1951; d. Millard Henry and E. Lorene (Denton) Gates; m. Ralph William Mitchell, May 24, 1975. BS in Nursing, Graceland Coll., 1973; MS in Nursing, U. Tex., 1976; EdD in ednl. Adminstrn., N.Mex. State U., 1996. RN, Tex., Mo.; cert. childbirth educator. Instr. nursing El Paso (Tex.) C.C., 1979-85, dir. nursing, 1985—, acting divsn. chmn. health occupations, 1985-86, divsn. dean, 1998-99, dean health occupations, 1999-2000, curriculum facilitator, 1984-86, dean health occupations, math and sci., campus dean, 2000—. Ob-gyn. nurse practitioner Planned Parenthood, El Paso, 1981-86, mem. med. com., 1986-98; cons. in field. Author: (with Grippando) Nursing Perspectives and Issues, 1989, 93; contbr. articles to profl. jours. Founder, bd. dirs. Health-CREST, El Paso, 1981—85; mem. pub. edn. com. Am. Cancer Soc., 1983—84, mem. profl. activities com., 1992—93; mem. El-Paso City-County Bd. Health, 1989—91; mem. Govt. Applications Rev. Com. Rio Grande Coun. Govts., 1989—91; mem. collaborative coun. El Paso Magnet H.S. for Health Care Professions, 1992—94; co-chair health and human svcs. task force Unite El Paso Health, 1996—98, mem. steering com., 1999—2000; co-chair health taskforce El Paso Cmty. Legis. Agenda, 1997—99; mem. adv. com. Ctr. for Border Health Rsch., Paso del Norte Health Found., 1998—; mem. Leadership El Paso, 1999; bd. dirs. Border Health Inst., El Paso, 2001—. Capt. U.S. Army, 1972—78. Decorated Army Commendation medal, Meritorious Svc. medal. Named to Women's Hall of Fame, El Paso Commn., 1999. Mem. Nat. League Nursing (resolutions com. Assocs. Degree coun. 1987-89, accreditation site visitor, AD coun. 1990—, mem. Tex. edn. com. 1991-92, Tex. 3d v.p. 1992-93, Tex. 1st v.p. 1997-99, nominating com. 1999—), Am. Soc. Psychoprophylaxis Obstetrics, Nurses Assn. Am. Coll. Ob-Gyn. (cert. in ambulatory women's healthcare, chpt. coord. 1979-83, nat. program rev. com. 1984-86, corr. 1987-89), Advanced Nurse Practitioner Group El Paso (coord. 1980-83, legis. com. 1984), Am. Phys. Therapist Assn. (commn. on accreditation, site visitor for phys. therapist asst. programs 1991—), Orgn. Assoc. Degree Nursing (Tex. membership chmn. 1985-89, chmn. goals com. 1989—, mem. nat. bylaws com. 1990-95), Am. Vocat. Assn., Am. Assn. Women Cmty. and Jr. Colls., Tex. Orgn. Nurse Execs., Nat. Coun. Workforce Edn. (articulation task force 1986-89, program standards task force 1991-93), Nat. Coun. Instrnl. Adminstrs., Tex. Soc. Allied Health Profls., Tex. Nurses Assn. (pres.-elect dist. one 2002), Nat. Soc. Allied Health Profls. (edn. com. 1993-96), El Paso C. of C., Sigma Theta Tau, Phi Kappa Phi. Mem. Christian Ch. (Disciples Of Christ). Home: 4616 Cupid Dr El Paso TX 79924-1726 Office: El Paso C C PO Box 20500 El Paso TX 79998-0500 E-mail: paulam@epcc.edu.

MITCHELL, PETER KENNETH, JR. educational consultant, association administrator; b. Bklyn., June 12, 1949; s. Peter Kenneth and Joan Marie (Hayes) Mitchell; 1 child Elyse Alexandra. BA, SUNY, Geneseo, 1970; MS in French, L.I. U., 1975; cert. of French lang. proficiency, U. de Neuchatel, Switzerland, 1969. Tchr. French and Spanish Middle Country Sch. Dist., Selden, N.Y., 1972-81; tech. asst. to dir. internat. affairs dept. Am. Fedn. Tchrs., Washington, 1981-82; asst. to gen. sec. Internat. Fedn. of Free Tchrs. Unions, Amsterdam, 1982-90; exec. dir. Internat. Reading Assn., Newark, 1990-91; owner Insights Out Assocs., 1992—. Dir. mktg. Jr. Achievement Del., 1994-99. Author numerous ednl. publs. Recipient Father of Yr. award Nat. Multiple Sclerosis Soc., 1998. Mem. Blue and Gold Club, Washington U. Club, Amnesty Internat. Avocations: reading, music. Office: Insights Out Assocs PO Box 9652 Newark DE 19714-9652

MITCHELL, PETER T. family nurse practitioner; b. Phila. AS, Mpls. Community Coll., 1987; BS, U. Minn., 1994, MS, 1999. RN. Staff nurse Abbott Northwestern Hosp., Mpls.; nurse practitioner N. Suburban Family Physicians, Shoreview, Minn., Veterans Affairs Med. Ctr., Mpls. Mem. Minn. Nurses Assn. (commr. econ. and gen. welfare).

MITCHELL, PETER WILLIAM, addictions counselor; b. Queens, N.Y., Sept. 2, 1950; s. James Francis and Margaret (Tiernan) M.; m. Mary Elizabeth Brett, May 15, 1976; children: Bryan Scott, Shannon Marie, Kevin James, Michael Ryan. BS in Mktg., Fordham U., 1972; MBA, Calif. Coast U., 1984; PhD in Chem. Dependency magna cum laude, La Salle U., 1997. Cert.

criminal justice specialist, master addictions counselor. Spl. agt. FBI, Washington, 1972-77; store co-mgr. First Nat. Stores, Inc., Somerville, Mass., 1977-78; area sales mgr. H.J. Heinz Co., Indpls., 1978-83; exec. sales rep. Sandoz Nutrition Corp., Mpls., 1983-91; regional sales mgr. Fresenius Pharma USA, Inc., New Brunswick, N.J., 1991-92; sales cons. Cardinal Health/Marmac Div., East Windsor, Conn., 1992-93; primary counselor, case mgr. Sunrise House Found., Lafayette, NJ, 1993-98; clin. dir. Turning Point, Inc., Secaucus, 1998-00; sr. clinician St. Clare's Hosp., Boonton Twp., 2000—01; pres. Mitchell Addiction Cons. Svcs., Hamburg, 1992—; clinician Overlook Hosp., Summit, 2001—. Bd. mem. Vernon (N.J.) Twp. Little League, 1985-89, Vernon (N.J.) Bd. Ethics, 1991—. Recipient Capitol award Nat. Leadership Coun., Washington, 1991. Mem. Nat. Assn. Alcoholism and Drug Abuse Counselors, Am. Assn. Compulsive Gambling Counselors, Nat. Assn. Forensic Counselors. Republican. Roman Catholic. Avocations: softball, basketball, volleyball, golf. Home: 101 Greenhill Rd Hamburg NJ 07419-2100 Office: Overlook Hosp 99 Beauvoir Ave Summit NJ 07902 E-mail: drpwm@warwick.net.

MITCHELL, PHILLIP SCOTT, copy editor; b. Stuttgart, Ark., Dec. 27, 1975; s. John Millard and Gail Fleming M. BA in English, BS in Journalism summa cum laude, Ark. State U., 1998. Copy editor Ark. Dem.-Gazette, Little Rock, 1998-2000, Fort Worth Star-Telegram, 2000—. Pres. scholar Ark. State U., 1998, Spl. Merit Cert. William Randolph Hearst Found., 1998. Mem. Soc. of Profl. Journalists, Am. Copy Editors Soc. Baptist. Avocations: writing, reading, basketball. Home: Apt 109 2809 Trinity Oaks Ct Arlington TX 76006 Office: Fort Worth Star-Telegram 400 W 7th St Fort Worth TX 76102 E-mail: psmitchell198@hotmail.com.

MITCHELL, RICHARD BOYLE, security consultant; b. St. Louis, June 20, 1947; s. Samuel West and Blair (Boyle) M.; m. Sallie Jean Gear, Dec. 4, 1999; children: Rebecca, Jessica. BS in Mktg., NYU, 1969. Account exec. D.L. Blair Corp., N.Y.C., 1967-70, NW Ayer Advt. Agy., N.Y.C., 1970-74; sr. account exec. Ted Bates Agy., 1974-75; sr. v.p. DKG Advt., 1975-81, McCaffrey/McCall, N.Y.C., 1981-86; pres., CEO Marshall Jaccoma Mitchell Advt., 1986-96; sr. ptnr. Modem Media, 1996-97; mng. dir., mgmt. cons. MJM Cons., 1997—2001; pres. 911 Cons., 2001—. Commr. Wilton (Conn.) Police Dept., 1984-01. Served with USAR, 1969-74. Mem.: Wilton Riding. Democrat. Roman Catholic. Avocations: mil. history, running, weight lifting. Home: 20 Indian Hill Rd Wilton CT 06897-1319 Office: 911 Cons 521 5th Ave Fl 17 New York NY 10175-1799 Fax: 212-292-4441. E-mail: bomitchell@911consulting.net.

MITCHELL, RICHARD CHARLES, human resources executive; b. Chgo., Aug. 11, 1953; s. Joseph and Alice Mitchell; m. Anne Marie Mitchell, Oct. 3, 1981; children: Nicole Marie, Brittany Marie. Diploma in Spanish, U. Salamanca, Spain, 1977; BS in Indsl. Psychology, St. Joseph's Coll., Collegeville, Ind., 1975; MS in Indsl. Rels., Iowa State U., 1977. Compensation analyst U.S. Gypsum Co., Chgo., 1978, sr. benefits analyst, 1978-79, employee rels. supr. Balt., 1979-80, employee rels. supt. Camden, N.Y., 1980-81; area employee rels. mgr. Pepsi-Cola Bottling Group, Dallas, 1981; mgr. human resource planning Tenneco Oil, Houston, 1981-84; area mgr. labor rels. Packaging Corp. Am. subs. Tenneco, Evanston, Ill., 1984-86; mgr. human resources Tenneco Packaging subs. Tenneco, 1987-89, dir. human resources, 1989-91, dir. human resources planning, quality and mgmt. sys., 1991-93, dir. human resources planning and compensation, 1993-94, dir. human resources planning, compensation and benefits, 1994-95, dir. internat. human resources, 1995-97, v.p. internat. human resources, 1997—; v.p. compensation, benefits and orgn. effectiveness Pactiv Corp. (formerly Tenneco Packaging), Lake Forest, Ill., 1997—2000; dir. corp. compensation Compaq Computer Corp., Houston, 2001; dir. global compensation, benefits, HRIS, and corp. human resource Sauer-Danfoss, Inc., Lake Forest, Ill., 2002—. Cons. in field, Deerfield, Ill., 1984—, Lake Forest, 1990—. Co-author: Personnel & The Law, 1977. Social worker Logansport (Ind.) State Mental Hosp., 1974; probation officer County of Jaspar, Rensselaer, Ind., 1975. Mem. Human Resources Mgmt. Assn. Chgo., Soc. Human Resources Mgmt., Wellness Couns. Am. (bd. dirs., officer, treas., founder), Assn. for Fitness in Bus., Coll. Placement Coun., World at Work (mem. faculty, benefits adv. bd.), Human Resources Planning Soc. Roman Catholic. Avocations: competitive running, fishing, reading, physical fitness. Office: Sauer-Danfoss Inc 1190 Harlan Ct Lake Forest IL 60045 E-mail: dmitchell@sauer-dnfoss.com.

MITCHELL, RIE ROGERS, psychologist, counselor, educator; b. Tucson, Feb. 1, 1940; d. Martin Smith and Lavaun (Peterson) Rogers; m. Rex C. Mitchell, Mar. 16, 1961; 1 child, Scott Rogers. Student, Mills Coll., 1958-59; BS, U. Utah, 1962, MS, 1963; postgrad., San Diego State U., 1965-66; MA, PhD, UCLA, 1969. Diplomate Am. Bd. Psychology; registered play therapist, supr.; cert. sandplay therapist. Tchr. Coronado (Calif.) Unified Sch. Dist., 1964-65; sch. psychologist Glendale (Calif.) Unified Sch. Dist., 1968-70; psychologist Glendale Guidance Clinic, 1970-77; asst. prof. ednl. psychology Calif. State U., Northridge, 1970-74, assoc. prof., 1974-78, prof., 1978—. Chmn. dept. ednl. psychology, 1976-80, 2000—, acting exec. asst. to pres. Calif. State U., Dominguez Hills, 1978-79; cons. to various Calif. sch. dists.; pvt. practice psychology, Calabasas, Calif. Author: Sandplay: Past Present & Future, 1994; contbr. numerous articles to profl. jours. Recipient Outstanding Educator award Maharishi Soc., 1978, Woman of Yr. award U. Utah, 1962, Profl. Leadership award Western Assn. Counselor Edn., 1990, Disting. Tchg. award Calif. U. Northridge, 1994. Mem. APA, Calif. Assn. Counselor Edn., Supervision and Adminstrn. (dir. 1976-77), Western Assn. Counselor Edn. and Supervision (officer 1978-82, pres. 1980-81), Assn. Counselor Edn. and Supervision (dir. 1980-81, program chmn. 1981-82, treas. 1983-86, Presdl. award 1986, Leadership award 1987), UCLA Doctoral Alumni Assn. (pres. 1974-76), Am. Ednl. Rsch. Assn., Calif. Women in Higher Edn. (pres. chpt. 1977-78), Calif. Concerns (treas. 1984-86), Sandplay Therpists of Am. (fin. officer 1996-2000, bd. mem. 1993—, media chair, 1995, bylaws chair, 1994-96, exceptions com. chair, 1995-96), Pi Lambda Theta (pres. chpt. 1970-71, chairwoman nat. resolutions 1971-73). Home: 4503 Alta Tupelo Dr Calabasas CA 91302-2516 Office: Calif State U Counselor Edn Dept Northridge CA 91330-0001

MITCHELL, ROBERT CARL, physicist, educator; b. North Hero, Vt., Nov. 28, 1970; s. Richard Carl Mitchell and Eileen May Curtis. BS, St. Michael's Coll., Colchester, Vt., 1992; MS, Rensselaer Poly. Inst., 1994; PhD, U. Okla., 2001. Tchg. asst. dept. physics St. Michael's Coll., 1989—92; tchg./rsch. asst. dept. physics Rensselaer Poly. Inst., Troy, NY, 1993—94, U. Okla., Norman, 1996—2001; asst. prof. dept. physics St. Ambrose U., Davenport, Iowa, 2001—. Dir. S.G. Menke Obs. St. Ambrose U., 2001—. Mem.: Am. Astron. Soc., Quad Cities Astron. Soc., Delta Epsilon Sigma. Office: St Ambrose U Physics Dept 518 W Locust St Davenport IA 52803 Office Fax: 563-333-6243. Business E-Mail: MitchellRobertC@ambrose.sau.edu.

MITCHELL, ROBERT DALE, consulting engineer; b. Worthington, Minn., Aug. 2, 1910; s. Karl V. and Margaret Dumont (Steigleder) M.; m. Carol Sherman Northrop, June 17, 1939; children— Constance Remington, Robert Brown. BS, S.D. State U., 1932; S.M. (grad. fellow), Harvard U., 1939. Engr. J. Emberg, Madison, S.D., 1932-35; instr. S.D. State U., 1935-37; engr. Malcolm Pirnie Engrs., N.Y.C., 1939-42, project engr., ptnr., 1945-70; sr. v.p., sec., chief engr. Malcolm Pirnie, Inc., 1970-75; cons. Malcolm Pirnie Engrs., 1975—. Served to maj. San. Corps AUS, 1942-45. Recipient Distinguished Engr. award S.D. State U., 1977 Mem. ASCE, Am. Water Works Assn., Am. Cons. Engrs. Council, New Eng. Water Works Assn. (Commemorative award 1963) Home: 487 Brackett Rd Rye NH 03870-2204 Office: 104 Corporate Park Dr White Plains NY 10604-3804

MITCHELL, ROBERT JAMES, petroleum company executive; b. Montour Falls, N.Y., Mar. 16, 1925; s. Robert Bowlby and Helen (Bates) M.; m. Pearl Kohnken, Aug. 30, 1947; children: Susan E., LuAnne, Robert James II. Student, Ga. Inst. Tech., 1944, U. Richmond, 1945, Sampson Coll., 1947-48; JD, Valparaiso U., 1953. Adjuster State Farm Mut. Auto Ins., Valparaiso, 1953-54; dist. rep. life ins. Aid Assn. for Luths., Hoffman, Ill., 1954-57; with dept. devel. Valparaiso (Ind.) U., 1957-58; oil prodr. Hoffman, 1958-64; founder, pres., dir. Ego Oil Co., Inc., 1964—; founder, pres., CEO Altec Energy, Inc., 1988—. Author: Spencarian Sonnet, Of Sunshine and Dreams, 1996; The Aleutians, 1998. With USNR, 1941-46, 50-52. Mem. Ind. Petroleum Assn. Am. (dir. 1976—), Delta Theta Phi. Home: Apt 101 2201 Montgomery Park Blvd Conroe TX 77304-3549

MITCHELL, ROBERT JOSEPH, insurance executive; b. Chgo., Mar. 2, 1947; s. Charles Robert and Rita (Cagney) M.; m. Nancy Telfer, Dec. 24, 1970; children: Laura Magee, Claire Clagett. BS, Loyola U., Chgo., 1970. CLU, ChFC. Asst. cashier Mich. Ave. Nat. Bank, Chgo., 1970-74; asst. v.p. First Nat. Bank of Lake Forest, Ill., 1974-78, United Bank of Skyline, Denver, 1978-79, v.p. comml. loan adminstr., 1979-82; pres., chief exec. officer United Bank of Cherry Creek, Denver, 1982-83; exec. v.p. Capital Nat. Bank, Ft. Worth, 1983-87; ins. agt./broker, pres. Mitchell & Moroneso Ins. Svcs. & Investment Inc., 1987—; pres. The More Fin. Group. Agts. adv. coun. rep. Conn. Mut., Hartford. Bd. dirs., pres. Easter Seals, Ft. Worth, 1988-95; chmn. bd. dirs. Big Bros./Big Sisters of Tarrant County, 1987; bd. dirs., pres. Internat. Sister Cities of Ft. Worth, 1989—; mem. priorities com. United Way, 1985—; exec. com. bd. mem. Mus. Sci. and History, Ft. Worth, 1990, Boys and Girls Club Ft. Worth, exec. com., 1997, 98, 99, 2000. Recipient Nat. Quality award Nat. Assn. Life Underwriters, 1990, 91, 92, 93, Pres. Hon. award Conn. Mut. Life Ins. Co., 1990, 91. Mem. Nat. Assn. Life Underwriters, Am. Soc. CLUs, Ft. Worth Bus. and Estate Coun., Ft. Worth Million Dollar Roundtable (life, Ct. of Table 1999, 2000), Ft. Worth Rotary (sec. bd., Paul Harris fellow). Roman Catholic. Avocations: racquetball, squash. Office: Mitchell & Moroneso Ins & Investments 306 W 7th St Ste 888 Fort Worth TX 76102-4912

MITCHELL, ROGER LOWRY, retired agronomy educator; b. Grinnell, Iowa, Sept. 13, 1932; s. Robert T. and Cecile (Lowry) M.; m. Joyce Elaine Lindgren, June 26, 1955; children: Laura, Susan, Sarah, Martha. BS in Agronomy, Iowa State Coll., 1954; MS, Cornell U., 1958; PhD in Crop Physiology, Iowa State U., 1961. Mem. faculty Iowa State U., 1959-69, prof. agronomy, 1966-69, prof. charge farm operation curriculum, 1962-66; prof. agronomy, chmn. dept. U. Mo., Columbia, 1969-72, 81-83, emeritus prof., 1998—, dean agr., dir. expt. sta., 1983-98, dean extension, 1972-75, emeritus dean, 1998—; v.p. agr. Kans. State U., Manhattan, 1975-80; exec. dir. Mid-Am. Internat. Agrl. Consortium, 1981; ret., 1998. Exec. bd. divsn. agr. Nat. Assn. State Univs. and Land Grant Colls., 1978-80, 85-90, chmn., 1988-89; mem. bd. agr. NRC/NAS, 1983-86. Author: Crop Growth and Culture, 1970; co-author: Physiology of Crop Plants, 1985 Served to 2d lt. USAAF, 1954-56. Danforth fellow, 1956-61; Acad. Adminstrn. fellow Am. Council Edn., 1966-67; recipient Henry A. Wallace award Iowa State U., 1993, Sec.'s Honor award USDA, 1998. Fellow AAAS (chmn. sect. O 1980-81), Am. Soc. Agronomy (pres. 1979-80), Crop Sci. Soc. (pres. 1975-76); mem. Soil Sci. Soc. Am., Coun. Agrl. Sci. and Tech., Sigma Xi, Gamma Sigma Delta, Alpha Zeta, Phi Kappa Phi. Home: 502 W Lathrop Rd Columbia MO 65203-2804 E-mail: mitchellrj@missouri.edu.

MITCHELL, RONNIE MONROE, lawyer, educator; b. Clinton, N.C., Nov. 10, 1952; s. Ondus Corneilius and Margaret Ronie (Johnson) M.; m. Martha Cheryl Coble, May 25, 1975; children: Grant Stephen, Mitchell, Meredith Elizabeth Mitchell. BA, Wake Forest U., 1975, JD, 1978. Bar: N.C. 1978, U.S. Dist. Ct. (ea. dist.) N.C. 1978, U.S. Ct. Appeals (4th cir.) 1983, U.S. Supreme Ct. 1984. Assoc. atty. Brown, Fox & Deaver, Fayetteville, N.C., 1978-81; ptnr. Harris, Sweeny & Mitchell, 1981-91, Harris, Mitchell & Hancox, 1991-96, Harris & Mitchell, 1997-98, Harris, Mitchell, Burns & Brewer, 1998-2000, Mithchell, Brewer, Richardson, Adams, Burns and Boughman, 2000—. Adj. prof. law Norman Adrian Wiggins Sch. of Law, Campbell U; bd. dirs. Mace, Inc. Contbr. chpts. to books. Chmn. Cumberland County Bd. Adjustment, 1985-92, Cumberland County Rescue Squad, 1986-93; bd. dirs. Cumberland County Rescue Squad, Fayetteville, 1983-91. Recipient U.S. Law Week award Bur. Nat. Affairs, 1978. Mem. ABA, ATLA, Twelfth Judicial Dist. Bar Assn. (pres. 1988-89), N.C. Bar Assn. (councillor Young Lawyers divsn. 1982-85), N.C. Legis. Rsch. Commn. (family law com. 1994), Cumberland County Bar Assn. (mem. family law com., N.C. State Bar Bd. legal specialization), N.C. Acad. Trial Lawyers, Fayetteville Ind. Light Infantry Club, Dem. Men's Club (pres. 1993-94), Moose, Masons. Home: RR 1901 Water Oaks Dr Fayetteville NC 28301-9125 Office: Mitchell Brewer Richardson Adams Burns and Boughman 308 Person St Fayetteville NC 28301-5736

MITCHELL, ROY SHAW, lawyer; b. Sherwood, N.Y., Jan. 16, 1934; s. Malcolm Douglas and Ruth Landon (Holland) M.; m. Nancy Elizabeth Bishop, Aug. 27, 1955; children: Mark E., Jeffrey B., Jennifer R. BS, Cornell U., 1957; JD with honors, George Washington U., Washington, D.C., 1959. Bar: D.C. 1959, Ohio 1960, Va. 1967, U.S. Ct. Fed. Claims 1963, U.S. Supreme Ct. 1965. Atty. Squire, Sanders & Dempsey, Cleve., 1960-61, Hudson & Creyke, Washington, 1961-67, Lewis, Mitchell & Moore, Vienna, 1967-87, Morgan, Lewis & Bockius LLP, Washington, 1987-99; pres., CEO constrn. claims group Hill Internat., Inc., 1999—. Vice-chmn. Ameribanc Savs. Bank, Annandale, Va., 1980-95; trustee Ameribanc Investors Group, Annandale, 1980-95. Co-author: (with others) Handbook of Construction Law and Claims, 1982, 89; contbr. numerous articles to profl. jours. Fellow ABA (pub. contract law sect.), Am. Coll. Construction Lawyers, Va. Bar Assn., D.C. Bar Assn. Presbyterian. Avocation: boating. Home: 5 Jefferson Run Rd Great Falls VA 22066-3200 Office: Constrn Claims Group Hill Internat Inc 1225 Eye St NW Ste 601 Washington DC 20005-5961 E-mail: roymitchell@hillinti.com.

MITCHELL, RUSSELL HARRY, dermatologist; b. Erie, N.D., Oct. 19, 1925; s. William John and Anna Lillian (Sögge) M.; m. Judith Lawes Douvarjo, May 24, 1968 (dec. Mar. 2000); children: Kathy Ellen, Gregory Alan, Jill Elaine, Crystal Anne. BS, BA, U. Minn., Mpls., 1947, BM, MD, 1951; postgrad., U. Pa., 1968-69. Diplomate Am. Bd. Dermatology. Intern Gorgas Hosp., C.Z., 1951-52; commd. lt. (j.g.) M.C. USN, 1953, advanced through grades to capt., 1968, svc. in Vietnam, ret., 1981; resident in dermatology U.S. Naval Hosp., Phila., 1967-70; asst. chief out-patient dept. Gorgas Hosp., 1955-64; chief med. and surg. wards Ariz. State Hosp., Phoenix, 1965; pvt. practice Leesburg, Va., 1978—. Staff Loudoun Health Ctr., 1975—; dermatologist Nat. Naval Med. Ctr., Bethesda, Md., 1973-81; asst. prof. Georgetown U. Med. Sch., 1975-85. Contbr. articles to profl. jours. Pres. Archaeol. Soc. Panama, 1962-64. Decorated bronze star with combat V; Vietnam Gallantry Cross with Palm and clasp; Condecoration Vasco Nuñez de Balboa in orden de Caballero (Panamá). Fellow Am. Acad. Dermatology, Am. Acad. Physicians, Explorers Club; mem. AMA, Assn. Mil. Surgeons, Assn. Mil. Dermatologists (life), Am. Soc. Contemporary Medicine and Surgery, Soc. Am. Archaeology, Loudoun County Med. Soc., Dermatology Found., Marine's Meml. Club (assoc.), Phi Chi. Home: 18685 Woodburn Rd Leesburg VA 20175-9029 Office: 823 S King St Ste J Leesburg VA 20175-3916

MITCHELL, SHAWNE MAUREEN, author; b. Tacoma, Jan. 09; d. F. King and Nona Margaret Burnside (Hayes) M.; m. J.D. Cook, Spt. 4, 1982; children: Travis, Austin. BA, U. Wash., 1972; postgrad., U. Santa Monica, 1997—. CEO Adventures of the Spirit, Santa Barbara, Calif., 1994—; author, spkr. Soul Style, 1995—; columnist Feng Shui-Soul Style, Calif., 1996—. Cons. real estate, Wash., Calif., 1980—; dir. Small Luxury Hotels, L.A., 1986-87; internat. spkr., author on subject of higher consciousness; internat. spkr. on Feng Shui. Author: Soul Style, 1997, Exploring Feng Shui, Ancient Secrets and Modern Insights, 2001, Creating Home Sanctuaries with Feng Shui, 2002; editor: Home Sanctuaries mag.; contbr. articles to profl. jours. Bd. dirs. Montecito (Calif.) Ednl. Found., 1997-99, Los Positas Park Found., Santa Barbara, 1995, Nuclear Age Peace Found. Fellow Master Minds of Montecito (vice-chair); mem. DAR, Montecito Instn. Group (sec.), Womens Exec. Network, Seattle Tennis Club. Avocations: boating, hiking, sailing, traveling, music. Office: Adventures of the Spirit Inc PO Box 5765 Santa Barbara CA 93150-5765 E-mail: shawne@soulstyle.com.

MITCHELL, SHERYL LYNN, analyst, educator; b. Detroit, June 8, 1958; d. Clarence and Gladys Elizabeth Warren. BA, U. Mich., Dearborn, 1991; M in Pub. Adminstrn., Ctrl. Mich. U., 1996. Mgr. ops. control Sunflight Holidays, Dearborn, 1977-80; adminstrv. asst. Wayne County Econ. Devel. Corp., 1980-82; closing asst. Merrill Lynch Relocation Mgmt., Southfield, Mich., 1983-85; spl. projects Coun. Mem. Mel Ravitz, Detroit, 1985-97; adminstrv. analyst Oakland County Bd. Commrs., Pontiac, Mich., 1999; facilitator U. Phoenix Mich., Southfield, 1999—. Facilitator, adj. faculty St. Mary's Coll., Orchard Lake, Mich., 1999—; cons. Warren and Assocs., W. Bloomfield, Mich. Author: (booklet) Oakland County Senior Assitance Directory, 1999—. Vol. Vol. Income Tax Asst. Program, 1989—; mem. W. Bloomfield Cable Adv. Bd., 1999—; bd. dirs. Mich. Women's Campaign Fund, 1999—. Recepient Spirit Detroit award, 1997; named Outstanding Vol. Acctg. Aid Soc., 1998. Mem. Women's Action New Directions, U. Mich. Coll. Arts, Sci. and Letters Alumni (mem. bd. govs. 1996-99), U. Mich. Dearborn Alumni Soc. (mem. bd. govs. 1998—), U. Mich. Dearborn African Am. Alumni Affiliate (chairperson 1998—). Democrat. Home: 5735 Warrenshire Dr West Bloomfield MI 48322-1538 Office: Oakland County Bd Commrs 1200 N Telegraph Rd Pontiac MI 48341-1032 Fax: 248-858-1572.

MITCHELL, STEPHEN MILTON, manufacturing executive; b. Atlanta, Oct. 23, 1943; s. Judge Stephenson and Elizabeth Ruth (Morgan) M.; m. Carolyn Docia Goss, June 29, 1968; children: William Stephenson, Scott Milton, Gregory Stephen. B of Indsl. Engring. with honors, Ga. Inst. Tech., 1965, MS in Indsl. Engring., 1966. Registered profl. engr., Ga. Sr. engr. Lochkeed-Ga. Corp., Marietta, 1966-70; mgr. material control Snapper Power Equipment, McDonough, Ga., 1970-73; pres. Atlanta Processing Co., Conley, 1973-86; sr. v.p., gen. mgr. Norcom, Inc., Norcross, 1986-93; chmn., CEO Atlanta Processing B, Inc., Tucker, 1993-94; CEO Internat. Processing Corp., Atlanta, 1994, Sertec Corp., Atlanta, 1995—, also bd. dirs. Bd. dirs. Atlanta Processing Co., Conley, Ga., Norcom, Inc., Norcross, APB Inc., Tucker, Ga., IPC, Atlanta; mem. exec. com., chmn., bd. dirs. Clairmont Oaks, Inc., 1988—. Bd. dirs., treas. Common Cause, Ga., 1989—; active First Bapt. Ch. of Decatur, Ga., 1968—, chmn. bd. deacons, 1993, 95. Mem. Young Presidents Orgn., World Presidents Orgn., Ga. Tech. Alumni Assn. (trustee 1981-87). Republican. Home: 5268 Browning Way SW Lilburn GA 30047-7029 Office: Sertec Corp 2100 Powers Ferry Rd NW Ste 200 Atlanta GA 30339-5014

MITCHELL, TEDDY LEE, physician; b. Columbia, La., Feb. 24, 1962; s. Oliver Clayton nad Mary Elizabeth (Johnston) M.; m. Janet Luisa Tornelli, Apr. 9, 1988; children: Mary Katherine, Oliver Charles, Christopher Tornelli. BS in Biology, Stephen F. Austin State U., 1983; MD, U. Tex. Med. Br., 1987. Diplomate Am. Bd. Internal Medicine, Cert. of Added Qualification-Sports Medicine. Intern U. Tex. Med. Br., Galveston, 1987-88, resident, 1988-90, 90-91; staff physician Cooper Aerobics Ctr., Dallas, 1991—, med. dir. wellness program, 1991—. Mem. Rep. Sen. Inner Cir., Washington, 1993, Heritage Found., Washington, 1993. Capt. U.S. Army Res. Med. Corps, 1988-96. Fellow Am. Coll. Sports Medicine; mem. AMA, Am. Coll. Physicians (cert Merit 1990), Tex. Med. Assn., Dallas County Med. Soc. Methodist. Avocations: exercise, travel, music. Home: 3224 Lovers Ln Dallas TX 75225-7626

MITCHELL, TERENCE EDWARD, materials scientist; b. Haywards Heath, Sussex, Eng., May 18, 1937; came to U.S., 1963, naturalized, 1978; s. Thomas Frank and Dorothy Elizabeth (Perrin) M.; m. Marion Wyatt, Dec. 5, 1959; children: Robin Norman, Jeremy Neil. BA, St. Catharine's Coll., Cambridge (Eng.) U., 1958, MA, PhD in Physics, St. Catharine's Coll., Cambridge (Eng.) U., 1962; ScD, U. Cambridge, 1994. Research fellow Cavendish Lab., Cambridge, 1962-63; asst. prof. metallurgy Case Inst. Tech., 1963-66; assoc. prof. Case Western Res. U., 1966-75, prof., 1975-87, adj. prof., 1987—, chmn. dept., 1983-86, dir. high voltage electron microscopy facility, 1970-82, co-dir. materials research lab., 1982-83; vis. scientist NASA at Ames Lab., Stanford U. and Electric Power Research Inst., Palo Alto, Calif., 1975-76; scientist Ctr. Materials Sci. Los Alamos (N.Mex.) Nat. Lab., 1987—, lab fellow, 1991—; lab fellows chair Los Alamos (N.Mex.) Nat. Lab., 1993-95. Chmn. steering com. Electron Microscopy Ctr. Argonne (Ill.) Nat. Lab., 1979-83; cons. in field; mem. vis. com. metals and ceramics div. Oak Ridge Lab., 1987-91; vis. com. solid state scis. div. Ames Lab., 1987-89; sci. adv. com. Sci. and Tech. Ctr. for Superconductivity, 1989-93. Materials sci. editor Microscopy Rsch. and Technique, 1986—; sr. editor North Am., 1994—; contbr. 400 articles to profl. jours. Pres. Cleve. Ethical Soc., 1970-72; bd. dirs Am. Ethical Union, 1972-74; steward Los Alamos Unitarian Ch., 1992-94; mem. policy com. Univ. Materials Coun., 1986-89; mem. policy com. Argonne Electron Microscopy Steering Com., chmn. 1978-82. Electric Power Research Inst. fellow, 1975-76; NSF grantee, 1966-88; Dept. Energy grantee, 1970-86, 87—; NIH grantee, 1969-72; NASA grantee, 1974-77, 81-87; USAF Office Sci. Research grantee, 1974-85; U.S. Army Research Office grantee, 1970-75, 79-83, EPRI grantee, 1986-89; spl. issue in his honor Philos. Mag. A, Sept. 1998. Fellow Am. Soc. Metals, Am. Phys. Soc., Am. Ceramics Soc. (assoc. editor jour. 1989—, v.p. 1999-2000), Minerals, Metals & Materials Soc., Los Alamos Nat. Lab.; mem. Japan Soc. Promotion of Sci., Electron Microscopy Soc. Am. (program chmn. 1981-82, dir. 1984-86, pres.-elect 1994, pres. 1995, past pres. 1996), Materials Rsch. Soc., Soc. Francaise de Microscopie Electronique (sci. com. 1982-90). Office: Los Alamos Nat Lab Ctr Materials Sci Ms # G755 Los Alamos NM 87545-0001 E-mail: temitchell@lanl.gov.

MITCHELL, THOMAS, editor; m. Jo Mitchell; children: Jeffery, Jay. Grad., Colo. State U. City editor Mid-Cities Daily News, Hurst, Tex.; editor Lewisville (Tex.) Daily Leader; city editor Shreveport (La.) Jour.; asst. city editor The Miami News; mng. editor Las Vegas Rev. Jour., 1989-92, editor, 1992—. Recipient First place prize for editl. writing Best of the West journalism competition, 1990, First place prize Nev. Press Assn., 1995. Mem. Am. Soc. Newspaper Editors, Investigative Reporters and Editors. Office: Las Vegas Rev. Jour. PO Box 70 1111 W Bonanza Rd Las Vegas NV 89125*

MITCHELL, THOMAS EDWARD, JR. communications cabling executive; b. Sacramento, Apr. 12, 1946; s. Thomas Edward and Violet Mae (Southall) M.; m. Terri Kathleen Vance, Apr. 20, 1969; children: Anthony E., Brian C. BA, Nat. U., 1987, MBA, 1988. Enlisted USMC, 1966, advanced through grades to maj., 1980, retired, 1989; sr. exec. Nat. Decision Sys., Encinitas, Calif., 1989-90, Equifax Mktg. Decision Sys., San Diego, 1990-93; exec. v.p., bd. dirs. Holocomm Sys. Inc., 1993—. Bd. dirs. Cal-Pacific Steel Structure Inc., Hawaii, Calif. Contbr. articles to profl. jours.; patentee in field. Dir. Toys for Tots, L.A./ORange Counties, Calif., 1974-77. Recipient Silver Star medal U.S. Pres., 1968, Meritorious Svc. medal, Joint Chiefs of Staff Commendation medal, others. Mem. World Trade Assn. (assoc. 1989—), Am. Legion, Internat. Platform Assn. Avocations: restoring old cars, racquetball, golf, history. Home: 3264 Chase Ct Oceanside CA 92056-3809 Office: Holcomm Sys Inc 2131 Palomar Airport Rd Ste 150 Carlsbad CA 92009-1452

MITCHELL, THOMAS SOREN, urologist; b. Santa Monica, Calif., Feb. 15, 1941; s. Cyril Louis and Florence Jeanette (Mortensen) M.; m. Michal Jane Lawrence, June 19, 1963; children: Thomas Soren Jr., Lee Delphine. BA, Loma Linda U., 1962, MD, 1966. Diplomate Am. Bd. Urology. Resident U. Wash. Hosp., Seattle, 1966-67, Loma Linda (Calif.) Univ. Hosp., 1967-68; resident in urology U. Calif. Hosp., San Diego, 1970-74; pvt. practice urology Santa Monica, Calif., 1974-96; chief urology St. John's Hosp., 1990-94. Asst. clin. prof. urology UCLA Med. Sch., 1976—. Capt. USAF, 1968-70, Vietnam. Mem. Pacific Oncology Soc. (exec. bd. dirs., sec. 1994—), Am. Urol. Assn., Bay Surg. Soc. Avocations: wine making, fly fishing, tennis, hiking. Office: 2021 Santa Monica Blvd Ste 510E Santa Monica CA 90404-2218

MITCHELL, WAYNE LEE, health care administrator; b. Mar. 25, 1937; s. Albert C. and Elizabeth Isabelle (Nagel) M.; m. Marie Galletti. BA, U. Redlands, Calif., 1959; MSW, Ariz. State U., 1970, EdD, 1979. Social worker various county, state, and fed. agys., 1962-70; social worker Bur. Indian Affairs, Phoenix, 1970-77, USPHS, 1977-79; asst. prof. Ariz. State U., 1979-84; with USPHS, Phoenix, 1984—. Lectr. in field. Contbr. articles to publs. Bd. dirs. Phoenix Indian Comty. Sch., 1973-75, ATLATL, 1994-98, Partnership for Comty. Devel. Ariz. State U.-West, 1996-99, Cen. Ariz. Health Sys. Agy., 1982-85; mem. Phoenix Area Health Adv. Bd., 1975, Comty. Behavioral Mental Health Bd., 1976-80, Fgn. Rels. Com., Phoenix; trustee Heard Mus. Anthropology, Phoenix, 1996; apptd. Ariz. State Bd. Behavioral Health Examiners, 2000-2002. With USCG, 1960-62. Recipient Comty. Svc. award Ariz. Temple of Islam, 1980, Ariz. State U., 1996, Dir. Excellence award Phoenix Area IHS Dir., 1992, 93, Nat. IHS Dir.'s award for outstanding svc., 2000. Mem. NASW, Fgn. Rels. Coun., Am. Hosp. Assn., U.S.-China Assn., Kappa Delta Pi, Phi Delta Kappa, Chi Sigma Chi, Nucleus Club. Democrat. Congregationalist. Home: PO Box 9592 Phoenix AZ 85068-9592 Office: DHHS IHS Two Renaissance Sq 40 N Central Ave Phoenix AZ 85004-4424 E-mail: drwlmitch@msn.com.

MITCHELL, WILFRID BEDE, librarian; b. Bloomington, Ind., Nov. 5, 1953; s. W. Bede and Barbara Plumb Mitchell; m. Carrie N. Cornejo, May 30, 1992. BA in Philosophy, U. Mich., 1975, MLS, 1977; EdD, Mont. State U., 1989. Circulation and res. libr. Mont. State U., Bozeman, 1978-85; head circulation libr. U. N.C., Greensboro, 1985-90; assoc. univ. libr. Appalachian State U., Boone, N.C., 1990-99; dean libr. Ga. So. U., Statesboro, 1999—. Contbr. articles to profl. jours. Mem. Assn. Coll. and Rsch. Librs. (chair acad. status com. 1995-96, chair instnl. priorities and faculty rewards task force, 1996-98, bd. dirs. 2002—), Libr. Adminstrn. and Mgmt. Assn. (chair publs. and bibliography com. sys. and svcs. sect. 1997-98, mem. strategic planning implementation com. 2001-02), Phi Delta Kappa. Office: Ga So U Henderson Libr PO Box 8074 Statesboro GA 30460-1000 Fax: 912-681-0093.

MITCHELL, WILLIAM CLARK, printmaker, graphic artist; b. Holyoke, Mass., Dec. 15, 1958; s. Ronald Herbert and Ann Theresa (Clark) M.; m. Mary Margaret Malone, Jan. 7, 1984; children: Matthew and Michael (twins). BA in Studio Art, State U. Coll. at Oneonta, N.Y., 1980; student, Boston Mus. Sch., 1980-81. Graphic artist/designer SUNY Coll. at Oneonta, 1978-79; graphic artist Boston Blueprint Co., 1981-83; graphic artist/designer Right on Target, Somersworth, N.H., 1983-84; graphic artist, pre-press specialist U. N.H., Durham, 1984—; educator League of N.H. Craftsmen, Exeter, 1993—. Tchr. screenprinting and children's printmaking League of N.H. Craftsmen. Executed various commns. Mem. N.H. Art Assn., League N.H. Craftsmen, Rochester Print Club. Avocations: hiking, skiing, travel. Home: 102 Watson Rd Dover NH 03820-5801 E-mail: wcmprints@attbi.net.

MITCHELL, WILLIAM D. lawyer; b. Great Falls, Mont., June 15, 1947; s. William Howard and Dorothy Elizabeth (Lane) M.; m. Mary Claire McDonough, Aug. 15, 1973; children: James Edward, Andrew Elliott, Thomas Michael. BA cum laude, U. Wash., Seattle, 1969; MA in Econs., JD, U. Calif., Berkeley, 1976; MLT, Georgetown U., 1982. Bar: Calif. 1977, DC 1978, Del. 1982, Mont. 1981, Fla. 1983, U.S. Ct. Appeals (11th cir.) 1994, U.S. Dist. Ct. (no. dist.) Fla. 1992, U.S. Dist. Ct. (so. dist.) Fla. 1986, U.S. Dist. Ct. (mid. dist.) Fla. 1984, U.S. Dist. Ct. Mont. 1981, U.S. Tax Ct. 1992. Atty. Fed. Trade Commn., Washington, 1976-79; assoc. Koteen & Burt, 1979-80, Tipp, Hoven & Skjelset, Missoula, Mont., 1980-81, Murdoch & Walsh, Wilmington, Del., 1982-83, Carlton, Fields, Ward, Smith & Cutler, Tampa, 1983-88; of counsel Foley & Lardner, 1988-90; ptnr. Langford, Hill, Mitchell, Trybus & Whalen, Fla., 1991-92; pres. Mitchell Law Group, 1992—. Devel. bd. Sun Coast Gerentology Ctr. Co-author: (book) Employee Fringe and Welfare Benefit Plans, 1988; author: Estate and Retirement Answer Book, 1994; contbr. articles to numerous jours. Lt. U.S. Navy, 1969-72. Mem. ABA (sect. taxation, com. on employee benefits, labor and employment law sect., com. on employee benefits, MEWA subcom., mgmt. co-chair), Greater Tampa Sertoma Club (dir. 1993-96, pres. 1996-97), Tampa Bay Writers Alliance, Mensa. Lutheran. Avocations: creative writing, acting, golf, weight lifting, auto sports.

MITCHELL, WILLIAM GRAHAM CHAMPION, lawyer, business executive; b. Raleigh, Dec. 24, 1946; s. Burley Bayard and Dorothy Ford (Champion) M.; children: William Graham, Margaret Scripture. AB, U. N.C., 1969, JD with highest hons., 1975. Bar: N.C. 1975, U.S. Dist. Ct. (ea., mid. and we. dists.) N.C. 1976, U.S. Ct. Appeals (4th cir.) 1978. Ptnr. Womble, Carlyle, Sandridge & Rice, Winston-Salem, 1975-87; sr. v.p. for external affairs RJR Nabisco, Atlanta, 1987-89; exec. v.p. R.J. Reynolds Tobacco Co., Winston-Salem, 1988-89; ptnr. Howrey & Simon, Washington, 1990-94; spl. counselor to chmn. bd. True North Comm., Inc., Chgo., 1996; chmn. bd., CEO Global Exch. Carrier Co., Leesburg, Va., 1997-00; pres., CEO Global Comms. Techs. Inc., Reston, 1999-2000; chmn. bd., CEO Convergence Equipment Co., Manassas, 1999-2000; chmn. bd. Qfactor Inc., Bethesda, Md., 2000-01; exec. v.p., gen. mgr. Verisign Inc., Mountainview, Calif., 2001—. Bd. dirs. Fed. Agrl. Mortgage Corp., Washington. Mem. Pres.'s Adv. Com. on Trade Policy and Negotiations, Indsl. Policy Adv. Com., Washington, 1991—; exec. com. Nat. Assn. Mfrs., Washington, 1988-89, Nat. Fgn. Trade Coun., 1988-89; chmn. Tobacco Inst., Washington, 1988-89; bd. dirs. Washington Performing Arts Soc., 1988-92; bd. advisors Dem. Leadership Coun., 1988—; founding trustee Progressive Policy Inst., 1988—; vice chmn. fin. Bush Campaign. Mem.: ABA (vice chmn. antitrust sect., pvt. litigation com. 1987—89, chmn. FTC com. 1986), Forsyth Country Club, City Club of Washington, Georgetown Club, Order of the Coif. E-mail: cmitchell@verisign.com., Wgchamp@aol.com.

MITCHELL, WILLIAM MARVIN, pathology educator; b. Atlanta, Mar. 3, 1935; s. William Joseph and Marvin Eugenia (Peavy) M.; m. Shirley Ann Crowell, Dec. 22, 1959; children: Alexander James, Keith Townsend, Derek Loren. AS, Vanderbilt U., 1957, MD, 1960; PhD, Johns Hopkins U., 1966. Diplomate Am. Bd. Pathology. Asst. prof. microbiology and medicine Vanderbilt U., Nashville, 1966-70, assoc. prof. pathology, 1970-78, prof., 1978—. Med. dir. Specialized Assays, Nashville, 1981-91; med. dir. Vanderbilt Pathology Lab. Svcs., 1994—; med. dir. Home Health Care Am., 1998—; cons. NIH, DuPont Co., Smith Kline, others. Patentee in field; contbr. articles to profl. jours. Bd. dirs. St. Augustine's Chapel, Nashville, 1981-86, Hemispherix Biopharma, Inc., Phila., 1998—; judge Regional Sci. and Engring. Fair, Nashville, 1985, 88; judge Internat. Sci. Engring. Fair, Nashville, 1992, Birmingham, 1994. Eleanor Roosevelt Internat. Cancer fellow Internat. Union Against Cancer, 1976-77; grantee NIH. Mem. AAAS, Am. Assn. Pathology, Am. Chem. Soc., Am. Soc. Biol. Chemists, Am. Soc. Microbiology, Internat. Acad. Pathology, Am. Soc. Interferon Rsch., Am. AIDS Soc., Sigma Xi. Episcopalian. Avocations: skiing, crafts, music.

MITCHELTREE, THOMAS JAMES, secondary education educator; b. Portland, Oreg., Oct. 17, 1946; s. James Walter and Audrey Lee Mitcheltree; m. Sally Jean Eichsteadt, Nov. 21, 1975 (div. July 1988); children: Tobin, Patrick, Jennifer, Kathryn; m. Laura Struble, Aug. 15, 1993 (div. Jan. 1999). BA in English, U. Oreg., 1971, MEd, 1972. Russian interpreter, translator voice intercept U.S. Army Security Agy., 1964-68; part-time worker Register Guard, Eugene, Oreg., 1968-71; tchr. Aloha (Oreg.) H.S., 1971-72; tchr. drama, publs. and writing Woodburn (Oreg.) H.S., 1972—, chair dept. English, 1980-95; tchr. composition and creative writing Ohemeketa C.C., Salem, Oreg., 1975—. Author: Terror in Room 201, 1981, Katy's Will, 1996, Dataman, 1997, Merry Little Christmas, 2002. Bd. dirs. World Berry Players Cmty. Theater Group, Woodburn, 1990—, Woodburn Cable Access Bd., 1996-98. Democrat. Roman Catholic. Avocations: community theater productions, furniture building, model building, car restoration.

MITCHEM, CHERYL E. accounting educator; b. South Bend, Ind., June 24, 1947; d. Roy Francis and Marcella Evelyn (Chryst) Drake; m. Allen Pershing Mitchem, Jr., Nov. 28, 1969; children: Michael, Marlo, Megan, Melissa. BA, Tex. Christian U., 1969; MBA, San Diego State U., 1980; PhD, Va. Commonwealth U., 1990. CPA, Va.; cert. mgmt. acct. Vis. prof. acctg. Coll. William and Mary, Williamsburg, Va., 1986-88; adj. prof. acctg. Va. Commonwealth U., Richmond, 1988-89; asst. prof. acctg. Christopher Newport U., Newport News, Va., 1989-91, Va. State U., Petersburg, 1991-93, chair acctg., 1993—. Contbr. articles to profl. jours. Treas., Greenfield Dragons Athletic Assn., Richmond, 1988-95. Mem. AICPA, Am. Acctg. Assn., Inst. Mgmt. Accts. Mem. Christian Ch. (Disciples Of Christ). Avocations: travel, reading, family activities.

MITCHEM, MARY TERESA, publishing executive; b. Atlanta, Aug. 31, 1944; d. John Reese and Sara Letitia (Marable) Mitchem. BA in History, David Lipscomb Coll., 1966. Sch. and library sales mgr. Chilton Book Co., Phila., 1972-79; dir. market devel. Baker & Taylor Co. div. W.R. Grace, N.Y.C., 1979-81; dir. mktg. R.R. Bowker Co. div. Xerox Corp., N.Y.C, 1981-83, dir. mktg. research, 1983-85; mktg. mgr. W.B. Saunders Co. div. CBS, Inc., Phila., 1985-87; mktg. dir. Congl. Quarterly Inc., Washington, 1987-89; dir. mktg. rsch. and devel. Bur. Nat. Affairs, Inc., 1990-96; account exec. Hughes Rsch. Corp., Rockville, Md., 1996; vice pres., ptnr. The Psychological Advantage, Inc., Atlanta, 1997-2000; mktg. cons. Project Mgmt. Inst., Pub. Divsn., Newtown Square, Pa., 2000—. Mem. Book Industry Study Group, Inc. (chairperson stats. com. 1984-86), Mktg. Research Assn., Soc. Competitive Intelligence Profls. Fax: 828-648-0413. E-mail: TMitchem4mktg@aol.com.

MITCHENER, JOHN EDWARD, music educator, musician; b. Laurinburg, N.C., June 30, 1964; s. James Samuel and Sara (Carton) M.. BM, N.C. Sch. Arts, Winston-Salem, 1986; MM organ, Eastman Sch. Music, Rochester, N.Y., 1989, MM harpsichord, 1994, D.Mus. Arts, 1995. Organist The Am. Cathedral in Paris, Paris, 1989; dir. music, organist Zion Episcopal Ch., Palmyra, NY, 1991—95; grad. asst. harpsichord Eastman Sch. Music, 1991—92, assoc. instr. organ cmty. edn. divsn., 1992—95, grad. tchg. asst. in organ, 1992—95, grad. tchg. asst. in baroque ensembles, 1994—95; assoc. prof. organ and coll. organist Salem College, Winston-Salem, NC, 1995—; Kenan prof. organ N.C. Sch. of the Arts, 1995—. Organist St. Paul's Episc. Ch., Winston-Salem, NC, 2001—. Musician: (classical organ recitals and concerts) Complete organ works of Johann Sebastian Bach, 2000— (Faculty Development Grant from North Carolina School of the Arts, 2001), concerts of Am. music performed througout Europe (Austria, France, Germany, Poland, and Switzerland), 2001, (organ concerts) organ music of Bach performed throughout Europe, 2000, concerts and master classes in USA and Europe, performances heard on Nat. Pub. Radio and Austrian Nat. Radio, —, collaborative artist for 5 CD recordings, —. Mem. exec. com. bd. trustees and chmn. music com. Moravian Music Found., Winston-Salem. Recipient organ competition winner, Music Tchrs. Assn., 1986, Nat. Winner nat. organ competition, Music Tchrs. Nat. Assn., 1986, Winner music competition, N.C. Music Tchrs. Assn. (so. divsn.), 1986, Winner 3rd prize, Dublin Internat. Organ Competition, 1990, Winner Gold Medal in harpsichord, Nat. Conservatory Rueil-Malmaison, France, 1990, Winner Prix d'Excellence in Organ, 1990, Winner Prix de Virtuosité, 1991. Mem.: Am. Guild of Organists (dean Winston-Salem chpt. 1997—99, Winner AGO competition, Phila. 1987, Winner organ competition Winston-Salem chpt. 1983). Avocations: golf, reading, running, walking, hiking. Office: NC Sch Arts 1533 S Main St Winston Salem NC 27117-2189 Business E-Mail: mitchenerj@ncarts.edu.

MITCHUM, CASSANDRA, poet, writer; b. Greensboro, N.C., June 11, 1950; m. Preston Mitchum Sr., Dec. 17, 1973; children: Preston Jr., Cynthia, Vanessa. Bus. cert., Monroe Bus. Inst., 1970. Receptionist, typist Royal Nat. Bank, N.Y.C., 1970-72, Metcalf & Eddie Engrs., N.Y.C., 1972-74; sec. Bendix Internat., 1975-80; receptionist Chrysler Corp., 1980-81; sec. Nat. Assn. Securities, Washington, 1981-83; word processor, sec. Lewis, Kominers & James, Counselors-at-Law, 1983-84, 86. Author numerous poems. Recipient Merit certificate World of Poetry, Sacramento, 1990, Editor's Choice award Nat. Libr. Poetry, 1996-97; named Golden Poet, World of Poetry, Sacramento, 1991; named to Internat. Poetry Hall of Fame, 1997; named one of Best Poets of 1997, 98, Outstanding Poet of 1998. Mem. Internat. Soc. Poets. Democrat. Penecostal. Home: Apt 25 11936 Beltsville Dr Beltsville MD 20705-3151

MITELMAN, BONNIE COSSMAN, editor, writer, lecturer; b. Flint, Mich., Feb. 15, 1941; d. Maurice B. and Frieda H. (Ragir) Cossman; student U. Mich., 1958-61; BA, Northwestern U., 1969; MA, Manhattanville Coll., 1977; m. Stanley D. Lelewer, Mar. 12, 1961 (div. 1969); children: Joanne, Stephen (dec.); m. Alan N. Mitelman, July 23, 1972; 1 son, Geoffrey. Copywriter trainee Dancer-Fitzgerald-Sample, Inc., Chgo., 1956-60; advt. copywriter Spiegel, Inc., Chgo., 1961-63; freelance advt. and public relations writer, Chgo., N.Y., 1963-72; co-founder Mitelman & Assocs., Briarcliff Manor, N.Y., 1972-92, pub. rels. assoc., 1992-94, asst. dir. pub. rels., 1994-97; dir. internal comms. Anti-Defamation League, N.Y.C., 1997—; adj. lectr. dept. history Mercy Coll., Dobbs Ferry, N.Y., 1979-85; contbr. articles to N.Y. Times, Am. Experiences, Vol. II, Am. History Illustrated, Working Mother, Reform Judaism, 1977—. Mem. Am. Hist. Assn., Women in Comm., Authors Guild. Author: Mothers Who Work: Strategies for Coping; mem. editl. bd. Reform Judaism, 1977— .

MITGANG, IRIS FELDMAN, retired lawyer; b. Chgo., Sept. 2, 1937; d. Harry and Leanore (Nelson) Feldman; m. Robert Newton Mitgang, Sept. 9, 1956 (div. Dec. 1974); children: Alix Susan, Steven Ross, Jennifer Lynn. AB, U. Chgo., 1958; MA, U. Rochester, 1967; JD, U. Calif., Davis, 1976. Bar: Calif. 1976, U.S. Dist. Ct. (no. and ea. dists.) Calif.; cert. specialist family law. Ptnr. Dodge, Reyes, Brorby, Randall, Mitgang & Titmus, Walnut Creek, Calif., 1978-90; prin. Law Office Iris F. Mitgang, 1990—98, ret., 1998. Instr. legal writing Sch. Law U. Calif., Davis, 1975-76; adj. prof. family law Sch. Law John F. Kennedy U., Walnut Creek, 1977-87, Sch. Law Golden Gate U., San Francisco, 1987; mem. pro tempore judges panel Contra Costa Superior Ct.; spkr. in field. Mem. editorial bd. Law Rev. U. Calif., Davis Sch. Law, 1976; contbr. various articles to profl. jours. Bd. dirs. Leadership Conf. Civil Rights, Washington, 1979-81, ACLU, Northern Calif.; founding mem. Rape Crisis Ctr. Contra Costa County. Recipient Woman of Yr. award Bus. and Profl. Women, 1979, Women's Leadership award State of Calif., 1980. Mem. State Bar Assn. Calif., Nat. Women's Polit. Caucus (nat. chair 1979-81, nat. adv. bd. chair 1981-85, vice chair 1977-79, politic. action chair 1977-79), Am. Acad. Family Mediators, Contra Costa Bar Assn. (co-chair fam. law mediation sect. 1992—), Calif. Women Lawyers, Alameda Contra Costa Trial Lawyers (bd. dirs. 1992-95, chair mentors program), Assn. Family and Conciliation Cts., Assn. Cert. Family Law Specialists, Calif. Dispute Resolution Coun., Soc. Profls. in Dispute Resolution. Democrat. Jewish. E-mail: irismitgang@hotmail.com.

MITGANG, LEE DAVID, journalist, author, lecturer, foundation manager; b. N.Y.C., Nov. 12, 1949; s. Herbert and Shirley (Kravchick) M.; m. Gina Saporito, June 17, 1979; 1 child, Caroline. BA in Polit. Sci., U. Mich., Ann Arbor, 1971; MS in History of Polit. Thought, London Sch. Econ., 1972. Corr. bus. and Wall Street, UPI, N.Y.C., 1972-74; bus. writer AP, 1974-76, urban affairs writer, 1976-80, nat. edn. writer, 1980-91; sr. fellow Carnegie Found. for Advancement of Tchg., Princeton, N.J., 1992-97; pvt. practice cons., journalist Ridgewood, NJ, 1997-2000; dir. ednl. svcs. Wallace-Reader's Digest Funds, 2002—. Dir. comms. Wallace-Reader's Digest Funds, N.Y.C., 2000—; asst. dir. Hechinger Inst. on Edn. and Media, Tchrs. Coll., Columbia U., 1999-2000. Co-author: Building Community: A New Future for Architecture Education and Practice, 1996; prin. author: School Choice, 1992; author: Big Bird and Beyond: The New Media and The Markle Foundation, 2000; contbg. editor Archtl. Record Mag., 1997-2001; mem. editl. bd. Reaching Today's Youth Jour., 1996—. Recipient Disting. Achievement award Ednl. Press Assn., 1991, Sci.-in-Soc. award Nat. Assn. Sci. Writers, 1989, Gerald Loeb award for Disting. Bus. and Fin. Journalism, 1977, John Hancock award for Excellence in Bus. Journalism, 1976. Mem. Edn. Writer Assn. Home and Office: 216 Doremus Ave Ridgewood NJ 07450-4240 E-mail: LMitgang@wallacefunds.org.

MITIO, JOHN, III, elementary school educator; b. Michigan City, Ind., Jan. 15, 1950; s. John Mitio Jr. and Bonnie Gloria (Pearce) Morse; stepson of Eugene A. Morse; m. Judy Sena, Nov. 25, 1971 (div. 1985); m. Gail Stefl, Sept. 5, 1987 (div. 1995); 1 child, Kevin Michael. AA in Liberal Arts, N.Mex. State U., Alamogordo, 1976; BA in Anthropology, N.Mex. State U., Las Cruces, 1979. Engr. aide U.S. Civil Service, Alamogordo, 1974-75, Dynalectron Corp., Alamogordo, 1976; law enforcement campus police N.Mex. State U., Las Cruces, 1977-79; eligibility worker human svcs. dept. State of N. Mex., Albuquerque, 1984-86, medicaid planner human svcs. dept. Santa Fe, 1986-99; mgr. pub. rels. Cove Mil. Surplus, North Las Vegas, Nev., 1997-2000; rsch. cons. MRC Group Rsch. Inst., Las Vegas, 2000—01; elem. tchr. Clark County Sch. Dist., 2002—. Sgt. USAF, 1969-73, 1st lt., 79-83. Decorated Nat. Def. Svc. medal, Armed Forces Expeditionary medal, Air Force Overseas Svc. medal, Air Force Good Conduct medal. Mem. Planetary Soc., World Future Soc., Nat. Space Soc. Republican. Roman Catholic. Avocations: opera, skiing, winemaking. Home and Office: 4608 Valley Dr North Las Vegas NV 89031

MITLAK, STEFANY (STEFANY LYNN MITLAK), lawyer; b. N.Y.C., Oct. 1, 1958; d. Irwin and Karel Sondra (Sperling) Cooperman; m. Bruce H. Mitlak, Sept. 20, 1987. BS, U. Mich., 1980; JD, Western New Eng. Coll., 1983; LLM, Boston U., 1989. Bar: R.I. 1984, Mass. 1985, Md. 1986, Ind. 1996. Spl. asst. atty. gen. Atty. Gen.'s Office State of R.I., Providence, 1984-85; assoc. McCormack & Putziger, Boston, 1985-90, Fitch, Wiley, Richlin & Tourse, Boston, 1990-92; spl. asst. corp. counsel pub. facilities dept. City of Boston, 1992-95; assoc. Johnson, Smith, Densborn, Wright & Heath, Indpls., 1995-96; devel. atty. Simon Group, 1996—. Fundraiser Women's Polit. Caucus, Providence, 1984-85; chairwoman bldg. and licensing com. Neighborhood Assn. of the Back Bay, Boston, 1992. Avocations: swimming, skiing.

MITNICK, HAL, rheumatologist; BA, Lafayette Univ., 1968; MD, N.Y. Univ. Sch. Medicine, 1972. Diplomate Am. Bd. Internal Medicine, Am. Bd. Rheumatology. Mem. staff dept. rheumatology N.Y. Univ., 1978, mem. staff dept. internal medicine, 1976, clinical prof. medicine, 1995—. Fellow Am. Coll. Rheumatology. Office: 333 E 34th St New York NY 10016-4977

MITRA, AMITABHA, plastic surgeon; b. Calcutta, India, Dec. 11, 1945; came to U.S., 1978; m. Jesmin; 1 child, Avir. MBBS, U. Calcutta, 1968; MS, U. Delhi, 1976; MD, Temple U., 1984. Diplomate Am. Bd. Plastic Surgery, Am. Bd. Surgery. From instr. to prof. surgery Temple U., Phila., 1984-90, prof., dir. plastic surgery residents, 1990—, chief sect., 1999—. Dir. Temple Hand Ctr., Phila., 1990—, S.J. Hulnick Burn Ctr. and Congenital Hand Ctr., St. Christopher's Hosp., Phila., 1990-97, co-dir. cleft lip and palate, 1990-97; med. edn. com. Episcopal Hosp., 1990—. Recipient Cum Laude award Radiology Soc. N.Am., 1989, Best Paper award Am. Assn. Hand Surgery, 1996; named Best Plastic Surgeon, Phila. Mag., 1995—. Fellow Royal Coll. Surgeons; mem. Fedn. Cleft Lip/Palate Soc. (membership com. 1990—), Nat. Burn Found. (bd. dirs. 1990—), Robert H. Ivy Soc. (treas. 1997—, Best Paper award 1996, 97), Sushruta Soc. (pres. 1995—). Office: Temple Plastic Surgery Assocs 3322 N Broad St Fl 3D Philadelphia PA 19140-5185

MITRA, SANJIT KUMAR, electrical and computer engineering educator; b. Calcutta, West Bengal, India, Nov. 26, 1935; came to U.S., 1958; MS in Tech., U. Calcutta, 1956; MS, U. Calif., Berkeley, 1960, PhD, 1962; D of Tech. (hon.), Tampere (Finland) U., 1987; Academician, Acad. Finland, 2000. Asst. engr. Indian Statis. Inst., Calcutta, 1956-58; from teaching asst. to assoc. Univ. Calif., Berkeley, 1958-62; asst. prof. Cornell U., Ithaca, N.Y., 1962-65; mem. tech. staff Bell Telephone Labs., Holmdel, N.J., 1965-67; prof. U. Calif., Davis, 1967-77, prof. elec. and computer engring. Santa Barbara, 1977—, chmn. dept. elec. and computer engring., 1979-82; dir. Ctr. for Info. Processing Rsch., 1993-96. Cons. Lawrence Livermore (Calif.) Nat. Lab., 1974-95; cons. editor Van Nostrand Reinhold Co., N.Y.C., 1977-88; mem. adv. bd. Coll. Engring. Rice U., Houston, 1986-89; mem. adv. coun. Rsch. Inst. for Math. and Computing Sci., U. Groningen, The Netherlands, 1995—; mem. adv. bd. Internat. Signal Processing Ctr., Tampere U. of Tech., Finland, 1997—; external assessor Faculty of Engring., U. Putra Malaysia, Serdang, 1997—. Author: Analysis and Synthesis of Linear Active Networks, 1969, Digital and Analog Integrated Circuits, 1980; co-editor: Modern Filter Theory and Design, 1973, Two-Dimensional Digital Signal Processing, 1978, Miniaturized and Integrated Filters, 1989, Multidimensional Processing of Video Signals, 1992, Handbook for Digital Signal Processing, 1993, Digital Signal Processing: A Computer-Based Approach, 1997, 2d edit., 2000, Nonuniform Discrete Fourier Transform and Its Signal Processing Applications, 1998, Digital Signal Processing Laboratory Using MATLAB, 1999, Nonlinear Image Processing, 2000. Named Disting. Fulbright Prof., Coun. for Internat. Exch. of Scholars, 1984, 1986, 1988, Disting. Sr. Scientist, Humboldt Found., 1989; recipient Edn. award, IEEE Circuits and Sys. Soc., 1988, Mac Van Valkenburg award, 1999, Golden Jubilee medal, 1999, Blemlein-Browne-Willans premium, IEE, 2000, McGraw-Hill/Jacob Millman award, Edn. Soc., 2001, Tech. Achievement award, IEEE Signal Processing Soc., 2001, European Assn. Signal Processing, 2002, Best Paper award, IEEE Transactions on Circuits and Sys. for Video Tech., 2002. Fellow: IEEE (Golden Jubilee medal 1999, Millennium medal 2000), AAAS, Internat. Soc. Optical Engring.; mem.: Acad. of Finland, European Assn. for Signal Processing, Am. Soc. for Engring. Edn. (F.E. Terman award 1973, AT&T Found. award 1985). Achievements include patents for two-port newtorks for realizing transfer functions; non-reciprocal wave translating device; discrete cosine transform-based image coding and decoding method; method and apparatus for multipath channel shaping; method for embedding and extracting digital data in images and videos. Office: Univ Calif Dept Elec Computer Eng Santa Barbara CA 93106

MITRA, SOMENATH, environmental scientist, educator; b. Calcutta, West Bengal, India, Sept. 20, 1959; s. Arun Kumar and Bani Mitra; m. Naznin A. Rahim; children: Anjali, Kabir. MS, So. Ill. U., 1981, PhD, 1987. Nat. rsch. coun. fellow U.S. EPA, Rsch. Triangle Pk., NC, 1988—90, rsch. chemist, 1990—91; prof. N.J. Inst. of Technology, Newark, 1991—. Cons. U.S. EPA, Rsch. Triangle Pk., NC. Author: Environmental Chemical Analysis, 1998. Achievements include patents for in field. Home: 54 Huntley Way Bridgewater NJ 08807 Office: New Jersey Institute of Technology Chemistry and Environmental Science Newark NJ 07102 Fax: 973-642-7170. Business E-Mail: mitranj@yahoo.com.

MITRA, SUDEB, mathematician, educator; b. Calcutta, West Bengal, India, Aug. 3, 1960; s. Biswanath and Anjali Mitra. PhD in Math., Cornell U., Ithaca, N.Y., 1999. Grad. tchg. asst. Cornell U., Ithaca, NY, 1993—99; postdoctoral fellow U. of Conn., Storrs, 1999—2002; asst. prof. Queens Coll. CUNY, Flushing, NY, 2002—. Reviewer Math. Revs., 2000—. Contbr. articles to profl. jours. Charter mem. Amnesty Internat., Ithaca, NY, 1997—99. Grantee Hutchinson Fellowship, Dept. of Math., Cornell U., 1997, Several Grad. Fellowships, Cornell U., 1996, 1997, 1998, 1999. Mem.: Zentralblatt Math. (reviewer 2001—02), Am. Math. Soc. Avocation: reading. Office: Univ Conn Dept Math (U-9) Storrs Mansfield CT 06269-3009 Business E-Mail: mitra@math.uconn.edu.

MITRANO, JOHN R. sociology educator; b. Rochester, N.Y., Dec. 15, 1965; s. John R. and Thomasine A. Mitrano; m. Robbin E. Smith, May 26, 1990; children: Marisa, Alessandra, Matthew. BA, Northwestern U., 1988; MA, Boston Coll., 1990, PhD, 1995. Asst. prof. sociology Ctrl. Conn. State U., New Britain, 1994-99, assoc. prof. sociology, 1999—, dir. urban studies, 1997—, chmn. sociology dept., 2000—. Cons. Diversity Initiatives, West Hartford, Conn., 1995—. Contbr. articles to profl. jours. Rsch. grantee Nat. Italian-Am. Found., 1997, 98. Mem. Am. Sociol. Assn., Am. Italian Hist. Assn., Acad. Mgmt., N.Am. Soc. Study of Sport. Socialist. Roman Catholic. Office: Ctrl Conn State U Dept Sociology 1615 Stanley St New Britain CT 06053-2439

MITRANO, PETER PAUL, lawyer, engineer; b. Newton, Mass., Sept. 27, 1951; s. Peter Paul and Mary Ann (Hirrel) M.; m. Virginia Lee Kelly, Oct. 6, 1984 (div.); children: Christina Lee, Peter Paul, Christopher Louis. BS in Civil Engring., Northeastern U., 1973; JD, George Mason U., 1977. Bar: Va. 1977, D.C. 1987, N.H. 1993, Mass. 1998, U.S. Dist. Ct. (ea. dist.) Va., U.S. Dist. Ct. D.C., U.S. Dist. Ct. Mass., U.S. Dist. Ct. N.H., U.S. Ct. Fed. Claims, U.S. Patent Office, U.S. Ct. Appeals (4th cir.), U.S. Ct. Appeals (fed. cir.), U.S. Ct. Appeals (11th cir.), U.S. Ct. Appeals (D.C. cir.), U.S. Supreme Ct., U.S. Ct. Appeals 91st cir.) ; registered profl. engr., Va. Sole practice, Fairfax, Va., 1979-93, Etna, N.H., 1993—. Mem. D.C. Bar Assn., N.H. Bar Assn., Va. Bar Assn. Avocations: skiing, baby sitting.

MITRANY, DEVORA, medical writer, editor; b. Oak Park, Ill., Mar. 20, 1947; d. John Joseph and Frances Elizabeth (Kirke) Lang. BA cum laude, Beloit Coll., 1969; postgrad., Boston U., 1971-72. Elem. and presch. tchr., Boston, Oak Park, Ill., 1969-72; regional adminstr. TRW Fin. Sys., Wellesley, Mass., 1972-76; mgr. mktg. comms. Computer Sharing Svcs., Denver, 1976-82; dir. corp. comms. Corp. Mgmt. Sys., 1982-85; sr. copywriter On-Line Software Internat., Ft. Lee, N.J., 1985-86; mgr. corp. comms. Health Mgmt. Sys., N.Y.C., 1986-89; dir. pub. rels. Am. Sephardi Fedn., 1989-92; pres. The Mitrell Group, 1992-94; U.S. mktg. dir. The Best of Israel, 1994-95; publs. specialist PCS Health Sys., Inc., 1995—98; sci. publs. mgr. AdvancePCs, 1998—. Press release chmn. Nassau Region Hadassah, 1992-94; bd. dirs. Chabad Women, 1995-98, Companion Animal Assn. Ariz., 1999-2000. Bd. dirs. Talia Hadassah, 1986-94, co-pres., 1990-92; v.p. edn. Long Beach Hadassah, 1992-94; dir. pub. rels. Bus. Roundtable on Nat. Security, Colo., 1983-84. Recipient Nat. Leadership award Long Beach Hadassah, 1991-92, Nat. Leadership award Talia Hadassah, 1993-94; named Woman of Yr., Talia Hadassah, 1993. Mem.: Am. Sephardi Fedn. (edn. com. 1987—89), Colo. Conf. Communicators (Denver Advt. Fedn. liaison 1981—84), Denver Advt. Fedn. (bd. dirs. 1981—83, Alfie award 1984), Coun. Sci. Editors (program com. 2001—, sponsorship com. 2000—, chair 2002—), Am. Med. Writers Assn. (mem. ghostwriting task force 2001—). Jewish.

MITRASINOVIC, PETAR M. chemist, researcher; b. Valjevo, Yugoslavia, Nov. 15, 1968; s. Milorad P. and Milena M. Mitrasinovic; life ptnr.. BSc, Fla. State U.; MSc, PhD, U. Belgrade. Process control engr. Sumrbank Holding, Izmir, Turkey, 1991—93; rsch. asst. U. Belgrade, Ctr. Molecular Machines, Yugoslavia, 1993—95, rsch. assoc. Yugoslavia, 1995—97; rsch. asst. Fla.

State U., Tallahassee, 1997—2001; Killam postdoctoral fellow Dalhousie U., Halifax, Canada, 2001—02; rsch. fellow U. Mons, Mons, Belgium, 2002—. Rsch. asst. Fla. State U., Tallahassee, 1997—2001; rsch. associate Ctr. for Molecular Machines, U. of Belgrade, Belgrade, Serbia-Monteneg (Yugoslavia), 1995—97; rsch. asst. Ctr. for Molecular Machines, U. of Belgarde, Belgarde, Serbia-Monteneg (Yugoslavia), 1993—95; process control engr. Sumrbank Holding, Izmir, Turkey, 1991—93. Contbr. chapters to books, articles. Mem. Greek Orthodox Ch., Tallahasse, 1994—; sci. fair judge Tallahassee Region, 1997—. Fellow, Yugoslavian Found. for Young Scientists, 1988—93, Internat. Assn. for Exch. of Students, 1991, Yugoslavian Nat. Sci. Found., 1993—97, Fla. State U., 1997—2001, Killam fellow, Killam Trust, Dalhousie U., 2002. Mem.: Am. Chem. Soc., Can. Chemistry Coun. (assoc.), Can. Soc. Chemistry (assoc.), Saum (assoc.). Avocations: foreign languages, cooking, travel, history, literature. Personal E-mail: pmitrasi68@yahoo.com.

MITRE, BLIMA KIRMAYER, pathologist, educator; b. Romania, Aug. 15, 1942; came to U.S., 1968, naturalized, 1978; d. Moses and Regina Kirmayer; m. Ricardo J. Mitre, Oct. 7, 1967; children: Edward, Sandra, Marcie, Richard James. Grad., U. Mayor de San Simon, 1967. Intern Viedma Hosp., Cochabamba, Bolivia, 1967-68; resident in pathology Bapt. Meml. Hosp., Jacksonville, Fla., 1968-70; with Presbyn. Hosp., Pitts., 1970-72, Children's Hosp., Pitts., 1972-73; staff pathologist Passavant Hosp., 1990—; clin. asst. prof. pathology U. Pitts. Med. Sch., 1970—. Mem. ACMS, PMS, Internat. Acad. Pathology, Am. Soc. Clin. Pathologists, Coll. Am. Pathologists, Pa. Assn. Clin. Pathologists. Office: Passavant Hosp 9100 Babcock Blvd Pittsburgh PA 15237-5815

MITROVGENIS, JAMES WILLIAM, JR. journalist; b. McAlester, Okla., Feb. 15, 1950; s. James William Sr. and Kula Mitrovgenis; m. Brigitte Dunnebier. Student, U. Okla., 1968-72. Reporter McAlester Daily Dem., 1973-76; news editor Muskogee (Okla.) Phoenix, 1976-81; night copy editor Daily Okla., Oklahoma City, 1981-86, night news editor, 1986-91, copy editor, 1991—. Mem. NRA, AP Okla. News Execs. (bd. dirs. 1987-89, 1st pl. page one layout award 1987, 2d pl. gen. excellence award 1987, 3d pl. page one layout award 1987, 2d pl. gen. excellence award 1986). Greek Orthodox. Avocations: traveling, photography. Office: Daily Okla 9000 Broadway Ext Oklahoma City OK 73114-3799 E-mail: jmitrovgenis@oklahoman.com.

MITRY, DARRYL JOSEPH, educator, writer, strategic advisor, corporate chief executive officer; b. Pitts., Feb. 25, 1943; s. Joseph David and Lorraine Marion (Viale) de Mitry; 1 child, Eden Michelle de Mitry. BA, Calif. State U., L.A., 1967; MA, U. So. Calif., 1968, DPhil, 1971. Pres. S.M.I. Corp., L.A., 1968-70; prof. Calif. State U., San Francisco, 1970-71, U. Redlands, 1971-73, West Coast U., San Diego, 1996-97; rsch. dir. U. Ky. Med. Ctr., Lexington, 1973-76; lectr. med. econs., dir. bur. bus., econs. San Diego State U., 1976-78, 88-90; pres. Crossover Corp., L.A., 1979-85; cons. dir. Mirchandani Assocs., Beverly Hills, Calif., 1986-94; pres. Writers Web Global Internet, 1997-99; prof. Nat. U., LaJolla, Calif., 1997—, chmn. dept. bus. Sch. Bus. and Tech., 1999-00; pres., CEO Space Market Devel., 1999—. Exec. cons. StereoMedia Inc., Burbank, Calif., 1992-94; advisor Internat. Distance Edn., teleconf.-computer Internet, Extended Studies Inst. and Coop. Global Alliance, Europe, Asia, Mid.-East, N.Am., Cen. Am., S.Am., 1997-2002; univ. lead MBA program, 1998-2001, lead internat. bus.-econs. studies, 1997-2002; coun. mem., rsch. cons., fellow Reforming Economies Rsch. Inst., St. Petersburg, Russia, 1998—; internat. advisor NEXUS, Paris, 1998-99. Author: Profiles in Price Theory, 1972, Synoptic Guide in Political Economics, 1985, Strategic Initiatives, 1996; editor Bus. Inquiry jour., 1976-78; editor, co-author: Global Leadership in the 21st Century, 1998. Exec. dir. Nat. Living History Inst., San Diego, 1996; co-chair soc. club Am. Cancer Soc., San Diego, 1996; bd. dirs. Animal Rights Legal Fund, Mission Viejo, Calif., 1996. Recipient Golden Baton award San Diego Orch. Assn., 1985, Gallery Honor award Art Assn., San Diego, 1984. Mem. Omicron Delta Epsilon (Disting. Merit award 1971), Sigma Beta Delta (pres. 2000). Avocations: art exhibiting, sculpting, narrating TV and films. Home: 10840 Queen Ave La Mesa CA 91941-7124 Office: Nat U 11255 North Torrey Pines Rd La Jolla CA 92037-1011 E-mail: dmitry_usa@lycos.com.

MITSAKOS, CHARLES LEONIDAS, education educator, consultant; b. Lowell, Mass., Oct. 17, 1939; s. Leonidas A. and Vasiliki (Sampatakakis) M.; m. Stella Martakos, June 23, 1963; children: Charles L. Jr., Andria Estelle. BS in Edn., Lowell State Coll., 1961; EdM, Boston U., 1963, EdD, 1977. Tchr., team leader, social studies curriculum specialist Lexington (Mass.) Pub. Schs., 1961-67; social studies coord., cons. Chelmsford (Mass.) Pub. Schs., 1967-78; asst. supt. of schs. Andover (Mass.) Pub. Schs., 1978-83; supt. of schs. Winchester (Mass.) Pub. Schs., 1984-92; clin. faculty supr. Sch. Edn., Boston Coll., Chestnut Hill, Mass., 1992-93; prof. edn., chair dept. edn. Rivier Coll., Nashua, N.H., 1993—. Ednl. cons. to schs. and sch. dists. in 15 states, U.S. V.I., U.S. Dept. Def. Dep. Schs. and Ministries of Edn., 1970—; dir. Mid. Sch. Staff Devel. Inst. for Social Desegregation Program, Fairfield County, S.C., 1972; mem. staff, lectr. in team tchg. and social studies edn. NSF Insts., Stanford U., Ind. U., SUNY, Geneseo, Xavier U., U. N.C., Boston U., 1968-75; sr. lectr. sch. administrn. and curriculum devel. Sch. Grad. Studies, Rivier Coll., 1977-93, numerous others. Author, gen. editor: (multimedia program for elem. sch.) The Family of Man Social Studies Program, 1971-77; co-author: (textbooks) America! America!, 1977, revised 2d edit., 1987, Ginn Social Studies, 1987; author: (workbook) America! America! Workbook, 1982, (textbook) Earth's Geography and Environment, 1991; others. Mem. Coun. Tchr. Edn. N.H. Dept. Edn., Fin. Com. and Steering Com. So. N.H. Sch. to Careers Partnership; mem., bd. dirs., past pres. Social Sci. Edn. Consortium; past chmn. task force on teenagers and religious edn. Greek Orthodox Archdiocese of North and South Am.; former trustee U. Lowell; chairperson affirmative action com., chairperson com. to oversee U. Lowell Rsch. Found.; former mem. ad hoc budget com. Town of Winchester; former mem. bd. dirs., chairperson nominating com. and search com. for resident dirs. Andover Com. for A Better Chance; fund-raising chairperson, mem. edn. com., former trustee, newsletter editor local ch. Recipient Disting. Alumni award U. Lowell, Coll. of Edn., 1987. Democrat. Greek Orthodox. Avocations: writing travel articles, mosaic iconography, travel, reading. Office: Rivier Coll 420 Main St Nashua NH 03060-5043 E-mail: cmitsakos@rivier.edu.

MITSCHELE, MICHAEL DOUGLAS, concrete and aggregate company executive; b. Orange, N.J., May 15, 1956; s. Herbert James Jr. and Joyce Francis (Weber) M.; m. Elaine June Sperun, Dec. 13, 1975 (div. Dec. 1992); children: Melissa, Dawn, Daniel. Student, Seton Hall U., South Orange, N.J., 1974-75. With UPS, Parsippany, NJ, 1975-76; owner North Jersey Auto Ent., 1976-78; ops. mgr. Robert J. Baer, Inc., Roseland, N.J., 1975-82, COO, 1982-87, pres., 1987—, Baer Aggregates, Inc., Phillipsburg, N.J., 1986-93; owner Baer Concrete, Inc., 1993-99, Medada, LLC, 1995—, Stoneface, LLC, 1998—; pres. Baer Concrete Inc. (wholly owned subsidiary U.S. Concrete Inc.), 1999-2001, USC Atlantic Inc., Elmwood Park, NJ, 2001—. Chmn. N.J. Concrete Awards, 1985, 86; mem. adv. coun. The Summit Trust Co., Roseland, N.J., 1987-92; pres. Odd-A-See Enterprise, 1991—. Vice-chmn. Roseland Recreation Com., 1981-86, soccer coach, 1990-91; chmn. bd. Roseland First Aid Squad, 1987-88, 91-2000; bd. dirs. United Way North Essex, 1995-99; bd. trustees Caldwell Coll., 1998—. Mem. N.J. Concrete and Aggregate Assn. (v.p., charter bd. dirs. 1989), Am. Concrete Inst., Nat. Ready Mix Concrete Assn. (fin. mgmt. bd. 1992-95, bd. dirs. 1995-2000, chmn. membership com.), Morris County C. of C. (Man of Yr. award 1997), Rotary (pres. 1986-87, 94-95, gov.'s rep. 1988-89, Paul Harris fellow 1987, 89, chmn. 747 conf. 1991, dist. affairs com. 1995-99, chmn. 1998-99). Republican. Roman Catholic. Avocations: skiing, sailing, golf, biking, fly fishing. Office: USC Atlantic Inc Ste 300 475 Market St Elmwood Park NJ 07407

MITSCHER, LESTER ALLEN, chemist, educator; b. Detroit, Aug. 20, 1931; s. Lester and Mary Athelda (Pounder) M.; m. Betty Jane McRoberts, May 29, 1953; children: Katrina, Kurt, Mark. BS, Wayne U., 1953, PhD, 1958. Research scientist, group leader Lederle Labs., Pearl River, N.Y., 1958-67; prof. Ohio State U., Columbus, 1967-75, U. Kans., Lawrence, 1975—, chmn. dept. medicinal chemistry, 1975-92; intersearch prof. Victorian Coll. of Pharmacy, Monash U., Melbourne, Australia, 1975—. Cons. NIH, Am. Cancer Soc., Abbott Labs., Pharmacia Labs. Author: (with D. Lednicer) The Organic Chemistry of Drug Synthesis, Vol. 1, 1976, Vol. 2, 1980, Vol. 3, 1984, Vol. 4, 1990, The Chemistry of the Tetracycline Antibiotics, 1978; co-author: The Green Tea Book, 1997; editor-in-chief Medicinal Research Reviews, 1995-99; contbr. over 250 articles to profl. jours. Recipient Disting. Alumnus award Sch. Pharmacy, Wayne State U., 1980, 97, Research Achievement award Acad. Pharm. Scis., 1980, 97, Volweiler research award Am. Assn. Colls. Pharmacy, 1985, Higuchi-Simmons award U. Kans., 1986. Fellow AAAS; mem. Am. Soc. Pharmacognosy (pres. 1992-93), Am. Chem. Soc. (former chmn. councilor medicinal chemistry divsn., Bristol-Myers Smissman rsch. award 1989, Med. Chemistry award 2000), Chem. Soc. London, Japanese Antibiotics Assn., Soc. Heterocyclic Chemistry, Internat. Union of Pure and Applied Chemistry (commr. medicinal chemistry divsn.), Internat. Orgn. for Chemistry in Developing Countries (steering com.). Presbyterian. Office: Dept Medicinal Chemistry U Kans Lawrence KS 66045 E-mail: lmitscher@ku.edu.

MITSEFF, CARL, lawyer; b. Detroit, Nov. 16, 1928; s. Frank H. and Katherine (Schaffer) M.; m. Phyllis Schlitters, June 28, 1952; children: C. Randall, Bradley Scott, Julie, Emily, Faye. BS, Wayne State U., 1952, LL.B., 1955. Bar: Mich. 1956. Practiced in Detroit, 1956—; staff atty. Burroughs Corp., 1955-60; mem. firm LeVasseur, Mitseff, Egan & Capp, 1960-80, Mitseff & Baril, 1980-85, Fitzgerald, Hodgman, Cox, Cawthoren & McMahon, 1986-90, Cox & Hodgman, 1990—. Spl. asst. atty. gen. State of Mich.; lectr. in field. Named to Mich. Workers Compensation Hall of Fame, 2000. Mem. ABA, State Bar Mich., Internat. Assn. Ins. Counsel, Internat. Assn. Indsl. Accident Bds. and Commns., Detroit Athletic Club (bd. dirs.), Beavers (pres.), Lochmoor Club, Grosse Pointe Yacht Club, Pi Kappa Alpha, Delta Theta Phi. Home: 612 N Brys Dr Grosse Pointe Woods MI 48236-1247 Office: 1001 Woodward Ave Ste 1000 Detroit MI 48226-1904

MITSELMAKHER, GUENAKH, physics educator, researcher; b. Vilnius, Lithuania, Dec. 5, 1945; came to U.S., 1991; s. Viktoras and Anna (Bannikova) M.; m. Antonina Lavrova, Aug. 22, 1970; children: Irina, Victor. M Physics, Moscow State U., 1968; PhD in Physics, Joint Inst. Nuclear Rsch., Dubna, Russia, 1974; DS, USSR State Com. Higher Edn., Moscow, 1987. Staff scientist Joint Inst. for Nuclear Rsch., Dubna, Russia, 1968-91, dept. head, 1983-91, dep. dir. lab., 1987-89; staff scientist Superconducting Supercollider Lab., Dallas, 1991-94, Fermi Nat. Accelerator Lab., Batavia, Ill., 1994-98; prof. physics U. Fla., Gainesville, 1995—, dir. Inst. for High Energy Physics and Astrophysics, 2000—. Mem. adv. com. Program Fundamental Nuclear Physics, Ministry of Sci. of Russian Fedn., Moscow, 1993-2000; mem. steering com. compact muon solenoid CMS, experiement European Ctr. for Nuclear Rsch., CERN, Geneva, 1997—; cons. to dir. Joint Inst. Nuclear Rsch., Dubna, Russia, 2000—. Contbr. over 150 articles to profl. publs. Fellow: Am. Phys. Soc.; mem.: AAAS. Achievements include contributions to physics of pions and muons, study of electroweak interactions, particle detectors development. Home: 4929 SW 95th Ter Gainesville FL 32608-4189 Office: U Fla Dept Physics Gainesville FL 32611 E-mail: mitselmakher@phys.ufl.edu.

MITSUI, JAMES MASAO, retired language educator, poet, consultant; b. Skyokomish, Wash., Feb. 4, 1940; d. Minoru and Shime M.; m. Lilly Kramer, Aug. 7, 1986; children: Britt, Karen, Candy, Becky, Jacqui, Tad. BA in Edn., Ea. Wash. U., Cheney, 1963; BA in English, U. Wash., Seattle, 1973, MA in English, 1975. Cert. tchr. Wash. Tchr. English Hazen High Sch. Renton (Wash.) Sch. Dist., 1966—99, ret., 1999. Poetry cons. Scott-Foresman Publs., Glenview, Ill., 1994—. Author: (poetry books) Journal of the Sun, 1974, Crossing the Phantom River, 1978, After the Long Train, 1986, From A Three Cornered World, 1997. 1st lt. U.S. Army, 1964—65. Recipient Tchg. award, King 5 TV, 1998; grantee NEA, 1976. Mem.: NEA, Friends of the Shelter. Avocations: painting, fishing, snow-shoeing, cross country skiing. Home: 229 Sandy Dr Cocolalla ID 83813 E-mail: jim3wells@aol.com.

MITTAL, ARUN K. physician; b. Indore, M.P., India, Dec. 5, 1938; s. Govind Lal and Puran Devi M.; children: Raj, Vijay, Jyoti. Student, Holkar Coll., India, 1954-56; grad., M.G.M. Med. Coll., India, 1956-61. Cert. Am. Bd. of Surgery, Am. Bd. Thoracic Cardiovasc. Surgery, Indian Bd. of Surgery. Cardiovasc. surgeon Torrance (Calif.) Meml. Hosp., 1973—, Little Co. of Mary Hosp., Torrance, 1975—, Bay Harbor Hosp., Lomita, Calif., 1978—, UCLA, Carson, 1980—. Mem. European Assn. for Cardiothoracic Surgeons, Am. Coll. Surgeons, Am. Coll. Cardiology, Am. Soc. Artificial Internal Organs, L.A. Surg. Soc., Soc. for Thoracic Surgeons. Office: 21350 Hawthorne Blvd # 270 Torrance CA 90503

MITTAL, MANMOHAN, design and technology engineer; b. Muzaffarnagar, India, Sept. 5, 1950; came to U.S., 1981; s. Keder Nath and Prakash (Wati) M.; m. Shashi Rani, Jan. 28, 1976; children: Vivek, Vibhav. BSEE, Inst. Tech. Banaras Hindu U., Varanasi, India, 1971; MASEE, U. Ottawa, Ont., Can., 1981; PhD in Elec. and Computer Engring., Wash. State U., 1984. Electronics engr. IIMS Banaras Hindu U., 1971-73; design engr. Bharat Heavy Elecs. Ltd., Haridwar, India, 1973-79; grad. rsch./tchg. asst. Wash. State U., Pullman and U. Ottawa, 1979-84; DA mgr. CAE design automation Silicon Systems, Inc., Tustin, Calif., 1984-88; mgr. std. cell design automation Vitesse Semicondr. Corp., Camarillo, 1988-94; sole propr., cons. 2M Soft Tech. Group, Thousand Oaks, 1994-96; sr. dir. VLSI core design group C-Cube Micro Systems, Milpitas, 1996-99; sr. dir. VLSI, Excess Bandwidth Corp., Santa Clara, 1999-2000; v.p. IC design Virata Corp., 2000—01; v.p. U.S. Digital LSI Engring., Globespan Virata, Red Bone, NJ, 2001—. Contbr. tech. papers to profl. jours. U. medal Inst. Tech., Banaras Hindu U., 1972; fellow U. Ottawa, 1979-81; grantee Wash. State U., 1981-84. Mem. IEEE (sr., sec. exec. com. Orange County chpt. 1985-88, mem. tech. program. com., custom integrated cirs. conf. 1988-94, bipolar circuits and tech. conf. 1985-90), N.Y. Acad. Scis., Assn. Computing Machines, Sigma Xi, Tau Beta Pi. Hindu. Achievements include patent for Incremental Hierarchical Netlist Extraction Tool. Avocations: traveling, badminton, tennis. Office: Globespan Virata Inc 2700 San Tomas Santa Clara CA 95051 E-mail: mmittal@virata.com.

MITTEL, JOHN J. economist, corporate executive; b. L.I., N.Y. s. John and Mary (Leidolf) M.; 1 child, James C. BBA, CUNY. Rschr. econs. dept. McGraw Hill & Co., N.Y.C.; mgr., asst. to pres., Indsl. Commodity Corp., J. Carvel Lange Inc., and J. Carvel Lange Internat., Inc., 1956-64, corp. sec., 1958-86, v.p., 1964-80, exec. v.p., 1980-86; pres. I.C. Investors Corp., 1972—, I.C. Pension Adv., Inc., N.Y.C., 1977—. Bd. dir. several corps.; plan adminstr., trustee Combined Indsl. Commodity Corp. and J. Carvel Lange Inc. Pension Plan, 1962-86, J. Carvel Lange Internat. Inc. Profit Sharing Trust, 1969-86, Combined Indsl. Commodity Corp. and J. Carvel Lange Inc. Employees Profit Sharing Plan, 1977-86. Co-author: How Good a Sales Profit Are You, 1961, The Role of the Economic Consulting Firm. Mem. grad. adv. bd. Bernard M. Baruch Coll., CUNY, 1971-72. Mem. Conf. Bd., Am. Statis. Assn., Newcomen Soc. N.Am., Union League (N.Y.C.). Office: 10633 Saint Andrews Rd Boynton Beach FL 33436-4714

MITTELBACH, GARY GEORGE, research scientist, educator; b. Cedar Rapids, Iowa, Sept. 13, 1952; s. George and Dorothy Mittelbach; m. Katherine Gross, Dec. 27, 1975; children: John, Mark. PhD, Mich. State U., 1980. Rsch. scientist Ohio State U., Columbus, 1980-87; prof. Mich. State U., East Lansing, 1987—. Contbr. articles to profl. jours. Mem. Ecol. Soc. Am. (assoc. editor 1994-97). Avocations: travel, hunting, fishing, running. Office: WK Kellogg Biol Sta 3700 E Gull Lake Dr Hickory Corners MI 49060 Fax: 616-671-2104. E-mail: mittelbach@kbs.msu.edu.

MITTELSTADT, CHARLES ANTHONY, advertising executive; b. Eau Claire, Wis., Mar. 19, 1918; s. Frederick William and Pearl (White) M.; m. Angelica Farber, Feb. 20, 1957; children— Nancy Lee, Charles Anthony II, Monica, Simone. BS, U. Wis., 1942, postgrad., 1945-47; grad., Advanced Mgmt. Program, Harvard, 1960. Radio announcer sta. WIBA, Madison, Wis., 1945-47; account exec. Foote, Cone & Belding, Chgo., 1948-52, Campbell-Mithun, Chgo., 1953-54; mktg. dir. Tatham-Laird, 1955-56; exec. v.p. The Marschalk Co., N.Y.C., 1957-64, also bd. dirs.; chmn. plans bd., mgr. Interpub. Group Cos., Inc., Frankfurt, Germany, 1964-66; pres., CEO Erwin Wasey, Inc., Los Angeles, 1967-69; sr. v.p., mgr. Ctr. for Advt. Services Interpub. Group of Cos., Inc., 1969-92, cons., 1991—. Trustee, v.p. N.Y. Foundling Hosp., 1979-2001. Mem. Wis. Alumni Club, Harvard Alumni Club, N.Y. Athletic Club (N.Y.C.), Westchester Country Club, Am. Yacht Club. Home: 12 Griswold Rd Rye NY 10580-1802 *Be your own person, do your own thinking. Always give something back to those less fortunate.*

MITTELSTAEDT, ARTHUR HOWARD, JR. educational educator; b. N.Y.C., Sept. 25, 1936; m. Sue Carol Olsen, 1962; children: Kurt Arthur, Karen Maria. BS, Syracuse U., 1958; MPA, NYU, 1963, EdD, 1977. Self-employed landscape designer N.Y. State, 1954-58; asst. landscape architect N.Y.C. Housing Authority, 1959; landscape architect Nassau County Dept. Public Works, 1959-62, Office Joseph Gangemi, N.Y.C., 1959; landscape architect, planning cons. Urban Planning Assocs., Port Washington, N.Y., 1960—, Planning Assocs., Mineola, 1961—. Chmn. bd. P.A. Edn. and Recreations Cons., Inc., leisure systems planner, Hempstead, Bohemia and Ronkonkoma, N.Y., 1966—; adj. asst. prof. NYU, 1965-70, Hunter Coll., 1971, So. Conn. State Coll., 1975-77; prof. Merrimack Valley C.C., 1973; assoc. prof. C.W. Post Ctr., L.I. U., 1978-85; participant confs. in field. Contbr. numerous articles, reports to profl. publs. Exec. bd. Nassau County coun. Boy Scouts Am., 1978-84; usher, vestryman St. Stephen's Epis. Ch., Port Washington, 1975-80; corp. bd. dirs. Nassau-Suffolk YMCA, 1975-78; trustee Dikaia Found., 1977-80; trustee Sci. Mus. of L.I. Health and Safety Comm. Nat. Boy Scouts of Am.; mem. Cmty. Safety Divsn., vice-chmn. Nat. Safety Coun. Capt. USAR, 1958-65. Disting. fellow N.Y. State Recreation and Park Soc. (chmn. various coms. 1973—, pres. 1983-84); mem. Am. Soc. Landscape Architects, Am. Inst. Cert. Planners, Coun. Park and Recreation Cons. (pres.), Nat. Park and Recreation Assn., Comml. Recreation and Tourism Soc. (pres. 1992-98), AAHPER (trustee nat. found. 1974-76), Nassau Recreation, Park and Conservation Soc. (chmn. civic affairs com. 1970-84; profl., presdl. and hon. mention awards 1963-83), recipient numerous nat. awards. Office: Planning Assocs 39 Shadyside Ave Port Washington NY 11050-2416

MITTELSTAEDT, JANET RUGEN, music educator, composer; b. Port Washington, N.Y., Mar. 30, 1941; d. Chester Davis and Harriet Helen (Goodman) Rugen; m. Ronald Edward Mittelstaedt, Aug. 24, 1963; children: Edward D., Amy C. Leimbach, Thomas A. BS in Edn., Bucknell U., 1963; BA in Music, Marylhurst U., 1984; MM in Composition, U. Portland, 1993. Nat. cert. in piano and composition Music Tchrs. Nat. Assn. Tchr. 6th grade Spring Branch Sch. Dist., Houston, 1964-66; piano tchr., 1964-66, Pitts., 1967-74, Portland, Oreg., 1978—; composition tchr., 1988—; pianist, music coord. Evergreen Presbyn. Ch., 1994-2000. Dir. children's mus. Evergreen Ch., 1996, 97; participant Ernest Bloch Composers Symposium, 1993. Composer: (piano solos) Solo Snips, 1991, Splashes of Color, 1992, Sonatina for Youth, 1993, Fabric and Frills, 1994. Recipient award, Ernest Bloch Composers Symposium, 1993, spl. awards, ASCAP, 1994, 1995, 1997, 1998, 1999, 2000, 2001. Mem.: Oreg. Music Tchrs. Assn. (chair Portland program 1999—2001, Portland composition 1998—99, state composition 1992—95, chair Portland ensemble 1992—94, chair Pt. syllabus 1980s, music theory clinician 1980s, music composition clinician 1990—, composition adjudicator 1990—, syllabus adjudicator 2002—, Composer of Yr. 1994), Oreg. Fedn. of Music Clubs (chair composition 1980s). Republican. Presbyterian. Avocations: reading, travel, writing poetry. Home: 4485 NW 187th Ave Portland OR 97229-2911 E-mail: jan@sintsink.com.

MITTEMEYER, BERNHARD THEODORE, urology and surgery educator; arrived in U.S., 1944, naturalized; BS in Biology, Moravian Coll., 1952, LLD (hon.) , 1982; MD, Temple U., 1956; DSc , William Jewell Coll., 1985. Diplomate Am. Bd. Urology, Am. Bd. Quality Assurance and Utilization Rev. Physicians. Rotation intern Santa Barbara (Calif.) Cottage and County Hosps., 1956—57; advanced through grades from capt. to lt. gen. U.S. Army, 1957—81; resident in gen. surgery Fitzsimons Army Med. Ctr., Denver, 1959—61; resident in urol. surgery Tripler Army Med. Ctr., Honolulu, 1962—65; asst. chief urol. surgery svc. urol. residency tng. program Walter Reed Army Med. Ctr., Washington, 1965—68, 1971—74, chief urol. surgery svc. and urol. residency tng. program, 1974—77, chief dept. surgery, 1976—77, comdg. gen., 1980—81; surgeon gen. Dept Army, 1981—85; ret., 1985—86; sr. v.p., corp. med. dir. Whittaker Health Svcs., L.A., 1985—2002; prof. urology and surgery Tex. Tech U., Lubbock, 1986—, exec. v.p. Health Scis. Ctr., 1986—96; interim dean Tex. Tech U. Sch. Medicine, 1988—90, interim dean, 1995—96; provost Tex. Tech U., 1988—96. Clin. assoc. prof. urology George Washington U. Sch. Medicine, Washington, 1974—85; clin. prof. surgery Uniformed Svcs. U. Health Scis., Bethesda, Md., 1976—; vis. prof., guest lectr. urology U. Mo., U. Pitts., Korea U., Pa. State U., U. Mass., U. Va., Wake Forest U., Armed Forces Inst. Pathology, Walter Reed Army Inst. Rsch., 1975—; ctrl. com. of pub.-acad. liaison Tex. Dept. Mental Health and Mental Retardation, 1990—; managed health care adv. com. ex. Dept. Criminal Justice, 1993—96; presenter in field. Contbr. articles to profl. jours. Trustee Moravian Coll., 1982—86; bd. dirs. Sci. Spectrum, Lubbock, 1988—, Lubbock Symphony Orch., 1989—92, Lubbock Conv. and Visitors Bur., 1991—93. Decorated D.S.M., Legion of Merit with oak leaf cluster, DFC, Bronze Star with V device, Air medal with oak leaf cluster; recipient Comenius award, Moravian Coll., 1978, Founders medal, Assn. Mil. Surgeons, 1978, Alumni Achievement award in health policy, Temple U. Sch. Medicine, 1988. Fellow: ACS, Am. Coll. Quality Assurance and Utilization Rev. Physicians, Am. Coll. Physician Execs.; mem.: AMA (ho. of dels. 1981—85), South Ctrl. Sect. Am. Urol. Assn., Lubbock-Crosby-Garza County Med. Soc. (armed svcs. com. 1988—96), Tex. Med. Assn. (cons. coun. on med. edn. 1987—96), Assn. U.S. Army, Soc. Med. Cons. to Armed Forces, Am. Acad. Med. Dirs., Uniformed Svcs. U. Surg. Assocs., Soc. U. Urologists, Soc. Govt. Svc. Urologists, Am. Urol. Assn., Lubbock C. of C. Home: PO Box 65285 Lubbock TX 79464-5285 Office: Tex Tech U Health Sci Ctr Med Office Plz 3502 9th St Ste 260 Lubbock TX 79415-5305 E-mail: bmittemeyer@cox.net.

MITTENDORF, ROBERT, physician, epidemiologist; b. Ironton, Ohio, Aug. 6, 1943; s. Robert William and Martha Jane (Whitley) M.; m. Marguerite Jean Herschel, Nov. 10, 1979; children: Jeffrey David, Robert William II, Inga. BS, Ohio State U., 1966; MD, U. Ky., 1974; MPH, Harvard U., 1987, D Pub. Health, 1991. Diplomate Am. Bd. Ob-Gyn. Attending physician St. Margaret's Hosp., Boston, 1977-87; chief of surgery Winthrop (Mass.) Hosp., 1986-88; project dir., collaborative breast cancer study Harvard U., Boston, 1989-91; dir. Office Clin. Rsch. Tufts Sch. Medicine, 1991-92; dir. health studies, dept. ob-gyn. U. Chgo., 1992-99; assoc. prof. Loyola U. Med. Ctr., Maywood, Ill., dir. divsn. gen. ob-gyn, 2000—. Mem. sci. adv. com. anti-epileptic drugs in pregnancy registry Mass. Gen. Hosp., Boston, 1997—; cons. Nat. Ctrs. for Disease Control and Prevention, Atlanta, 1994; bd. dirs. U. Chgo. Health Plan, Chgo., Quadrangle Faculty Club, U. Chgo.; manuscript reviewer The Lancet, 1998. Author: Control of Transmissible Diseases in Health Care, 1995; contbr. articles to profl. jours. Med. dir. Cambridge Econ. Opportunity Com., 1977-78. Capt. USAF, 1966-70. Mem. AMA, Soc. Maternal Fetal Medicine, Soc. Epidemiol. Rsch. Democrat. Achievements include devel. of a linear regression model that permits the more precise determination of the estimated date of confinement in pregnant women (Mittendorf-Williams Rule); discovery that strenuous phys. activity is associated with a reduced risk of breast cancer, using a multivariable logistic regression model. Prin. investigator of the MAGnet Trial (magnesium and neurologic endpoints randomized control trial) to determine if using antenatal magnesium sulfate is associated with the prevention of severe cerebral palsy. Through statis. meta-analysis, discovered that certain prophylactic antibiotics are highly efficacious in preventing the serious infections associated with total abdominal hysterectomy. Home: 5634 S Woodlawn Ave Chicago IL 60637-1623 Office: Loyola U Med Ctr 2160 S 1st Ave Maywood IL 60153-3304 E-mail: rmitten@lumc.edu.

MITTENTHAL, PETER A. lawyer; b. White Plains, N.Y., June 16, 1953; BA, U. Fla., Gainesville, 1975; JD, U. LaVerne, 1978. Bar: Calif. 1979, U.S. Dist. Ct. (ctrl. dist.) Calif. 1980, U.S. Ct. Appeals (9th cir.) Calif. 1982, U.S. Dist. Ct. (no. dist.) Calif. 1998, U.S. Dist. Ct. (so. dist.) Calif. 1999; lic. radio broadcaster, FAA. Assoc. Snyder, Dorenfeld, Calabasas, Calif., 1996—. Prosecutor discipinary procs. (pro bono) State Bar Calif., L.A., 1988; former disc jockey and comml. voiceover announcer, Fla.; arbitrator L.A. Superior Ct. Former judge Pro Tem. L.A. Mcpl. Ct., 1985-90. Mem. ABA, So. Calif. Fraud Investigator's Assn., Am. Horse Shows Assn. Avocation: equestrian show-jumping. Office: Snyder Dorenfeld 24025 Park Sorrento Ste 150 Calabasas CA 91302-4004

MITTERAND, HENRI C. education educator, writer; b. Vault-De-Lugny, Yonne, France, Aug. 7, 1928; s. Joseph and Helene (Dangauthier) M.; m. Helene T. D'Afflitto, Dec. 24, 1955; children: Marie-Helene, Jacques-Olivier. Lic., U. Paris, 1969, Maitrise, 1950, Agregation, 1951, PhD, 1969; Hon. Degree, U. Athens, 1997. Asst. to assoc. prof. U. Besancon, France, 1957-65;

assoc. prof. U. Reims, France, 1965-68; prof. U. Paris 8, 1968-78, U. Paris 3, 1978-90, Columbia U., N.Y.C., 1990—. Vis. prof. U. Toronto, Can., 1970-93, U. Pa., 1999; editl. cons., Paris, 1971—; mem. numerous advisory bds. in field. Editor: (books) Zola, 5 Vols., 1959-67 (award 1968), Zola, 15 Vols., 1970; author: (books) Le Discours du roman, 1980, L'Illusion réaliste, 1994, Zola et le Naturalisme, 1986, Le Regard et le Signe, 1987, Le Roman à l'oeuvre, 1998, (biography) Zola I, 1999, II, 2001, III, 2002. Officier des Palmes Acads., France, 1987, Chevalier de la Legion d'Honneur, France, 1989, Grand Prix de la Ville de Paris, 2000. Mem. Royal Soc. Can., Soc. des Amis de Zola (pres. 1990—), Inst. Pierre Larousse (pres. 1990), Acad. du Morvan, Soc. of Fellows/Columbia U. Avocations: sailing, music, films, books. Office: Columbia U Broadway/116th St W New York NY 10027 E-mail: hm12@columbia.edu.

MITTERMILLER, JAMES JOSEPH, lawyer; b. Washington, Apr. 13, 1953; s. Jack and Alice Marie (Froeba) M.; m. Elizabeth Gaillard Simons, June 23, 1979; children: Samuel Stoney, Paul Andrew, Laurie Alice, Claire Mary. Student, U. Heidelberg, 1973-74; BA, Claremont McKenna Coll., 1975; JD, U. Calif. Berkeley, 1978. Bar: Calif., U.S. Dist. Ct. (so., ctrl. and ea. dists.) Calif., U.S. Ct. Appeals (9th cir.), U.S. Supreme Ct. Assoc. Sheppard, Mullin, Richter & Hampton, L.A., 1978-86, ptnr., 1986—. Panelist Calif. Continuing Edn. of Bar, L.A. and San Diego, 1984—. Dir. Legal Aid Soc. of San Diego, 1990—, pres., 1998-2000. Recipient Wiley Manuel Pro Bono award Calif. State Bar, 1992, 2001. Mem. Assn. Bus. Trial Lawyers (bd. dirs. 1998-2001), Am. Inns of Ct., Claremont McKenna Coll. Alumni Assn. San Diego (bd. dirs.). Avocations: swimming, surfing. Office: Sheppard Mullin Richter & Hampton 501 W Broadway Fl 19 San Diego CA 92101-3536

MITTL, RAINER N. ophthalmologist; b. Munich, West Germany, Mar. 19, 1939; came to U.S., 1965; s. Joseph and Maria (Schwickert) M.; m. Janice J. Janoski, June 28, 1970. MD, U. Munich, 1964. Resident in ophthalmology N.Y. Med. Coll., 1967-70; fellow Johns Hopkins Hosp., 1972-73; practice medicine, specializing in ophthalmology N.Y.C., 1973—. Mem. staff Columbia-Presbyn. Med. Ctr. Mem. AMA, ACS, Am. Acad. Ophthalmology, Internat. Coll. Surgeons, Vitreous Soc., N.Y. Athletic club, Univ. Club. Office: Suite 314 Edward S Harkness Eye Inst Columbia-Presbyn Med Center 635 W 165th St New York NY 10032 E-mail: Mittl0phNY@aol.com.

MITTLEBERG, ERIC MICHAEL, pharmaceutical executive; b. N.Y.C., Nov. 7, 1951; s. Irving Ralph and Rose (Schnieder) M.; m. Jane Susan Baumoehl, Dec. 25, 1977; children: Scott, Alyson, Lauren. BS in Pharmacy, St. Johns U., Jamaica, N.Y., 1974, MS in Ind. Pharmaceutics, 1978, PhD in Pharmaceutics, 1982. Registered pharmacist, N.Y. Assoc. scientist Hoffmann-LaRoche Inc., Nutley, N.J., 1974-78; dept. head process improvement Lederle Labs, Pearl River, N.Y., 1978-83; mgr. mfg. devel. Key Pharm., Miami, Fla., 1983-86; dir. prodn. and tech. svcs. Schering Labs, 1986-89; sr. dir. pharm. devel./tech. svcs. worldwide R.W. Johnson Pharm. Rsch. Inst., Raritan, N.J., 1989-97; v.p. sci./med. affairs Ivax Corp., 1997—. Mem. Internat. Soc. Pharm. Engrs., Acad. Pharm. Sci., Am. Pharm. Assn. Office: IVAX Pharm Inc 140 Legrand Ave Northvale NJ 07647-2403

MITTMAN, NEAL, nephrologist, medical educator; b. N.Y.C., Jan. 24, 1953; s. Arnold Mittman and Tess Blumenthal; m. Candace Clark Martin, Sept. 21, 1980; children: Alexander Clark, Zachary Wade. BA, CUNY-Queen's Coll., 1973; MD, N.Y. Med. Coll., 1977. Diplomate Am. Bd. Internal Medicine, Am. Bd. Nephrology. Intern N.Y. Med. Coll./Met. Hosp. Ctr., N.Y.C., 1977-78, resident, 1978-80; resident in nephrology Albert Einstein Coll. Medicine, Bronx, N.Y., 1980-82; asst. prof. medicine Mt. Sinai Sch. Medicine, 1982-86; assoc. chief divsn. nephrology Beth Israel Med. Ctr., N.Y.C., 1982-86, L.I. Coll. Hosp., Bklyn., 1986—; asoc. prof. clin. medicine SUNY Health Sci. Ctr., 1993—. Mem. med. adv. bd. Nat. Kidney Found. N.Y./N.J., N.Y.C., 1994—, mem. grants and fellowship rev. com., 1995—. Co-editor: Ambulatory Peritoneal Dialysis, 1990; contbr. articles to med. jours. Recipient Clin. Rsch. award NIH, 1980-82; named one of N.Y. Met. Best Drs., Castle, Connolly Med., Ltd., 1997, 98, 99, 2000. Fellow ACP; mem. Am. Soc. Nephrology, Am. Soc. Artificial Internal Organs, Am. Soc. Hypertension, Internat. Soc. Nephrology, N.Y. Soc. Nephrology (sec.-treas. 1996-97, v.p. 1997-98, pres. 1998-99), Met. Renal Care Network (bd. dirs., sec.). Avocations: country living, opera, gourmet cooking. Office: L I Coll Hosp 339 Hicks St Brooklyn NY 11201-5509

MITTON, MICHAEL ANTHONY, environmental technology company executive; b. Bremen, Germany, Mar. 13, 1947; came to U.S., 1948 (parents Am. citizens); s. Ralph Walter and Aniela (Pilarz) M.; m. Lisa Van der Veer, Mar. 7, 1986 (div. 1991); m. Marilyn Kay Bowen, Sept. 18, 1993. BS, U. Wyo., 1970. Asst. mgr. ops. Moller Steamship Co., N.Y.C., 1970-72; investment analyst Moller Industries, 1972-73; internal auditor Corning (N.Y.) Glass Works, 1973-75, supr. acctg., 1975-76; dir. acctg. Autotrain Corp., Washington, 1977-78; pres. RMA Ltd., Ft. Collins, Colo., 1978-81; contr. Purecycle Corp., Boulder, 1981-83; pres., chief exec. officer, treas. Synthetech Inc., Albany, Oreg., 1983-90, bd. dirs., chmn., 1990-95; ret., 1995; pres., CEO Chemical Biosensors, Inc., Beaverton, Oreg., 1992-95; technology entrepreneur, founder environ. tech. co., 1995—. Co-chmn. Oreg. Biotech. Industry Coun., 1989-90. Mem. Gov.'s Task Force Tech. Transfer, 1992-94. Fellow Am. Leadership Forum; mem. Soaring Soc. Am., Oreg. Biotech. Assn. (bd. dirs., chmn. 1990-91, pres. 1991-92), Multnomah Athletic Club. Avocations: flying, squash, skiing, sailing. Home: PO Box 4275 Incline Village NV 89450-4275

MITTS, MARYBETH FRAZIER, real estate company executive, consultant; b. Hartford, Conn., Sept. 4, 1963; d. Robert Lee and Patricia Ann (Casey) Frazier. m. Kevin Garry Mitts, July 14, 1990; children: Margaret, Elizabeth, Katherine. BA, Mount Holyoke Coll., Mass., 1985; M in Pub. Mgmt., U. Md., 1987. Notary Pub., Calif., 1995-97. Rehab. mgmt. specialist U.S. Dept. Housing and Urban Devel., Washington, 1987-90; budget analyst Office of the Comptr., U.S. Dept. Navy, Crystal City, Va., 1990-91; fiscal officer MCAS, U.S. Dept. Navy, Camp Pendleton, Calif., 1991, dep. comptr. Tustin, 1991-92; sr. cons. Comprehensive Housing Svcs., Fountain Valley, 1992-95; prin. Affordable Housing Profls., San Diego, 1995-97. Treas. Naval Officers Spouses Club, Okinawa, 1999—2000; mem. Lenox Elem. Sch. Coun., 2001—. Mem. Mount Holyoke Club San Diego (chmn. pres. 1995-97). Republican. Roman Catholic. E-mail: kmbmitts@hotmail.com.

MITZNER, KENNETH MARTIN, electrical engineering consultant; b. Bklyn., May 7, 1938; s. Louis Bernard and Dora (Sandler) M.; m. Ruth Maria Osorio, Dec. 26, 1968; children: Camille Lorena Mitzner Zeiter, Esther Jeannette Mitzner Lin, Sharon Michelle Mitzner Mentkowski. BS, MIT, 1958; MS, Calif. Inst. Tech., 1959, PhD, 1964. Mem. tech. staff Hughes Aircraft, Malibu, Calif., 1959-64; prin. engr. B-2 divsn. Northrop Corp., Pico Rivera, 1964-94; owner Mitzner Sci. and Tech., Oceanside, 1995—. Instr. U. Calif., Santa Barbara, 1964-65; lectr. in field. Author: (handbook) Demonstrations Against Abortion & Death Selection, 1970; contbr. articles to profl. jours. Pres. Mobilization for the Unnamed, Oceanside, Calif., 1970—; bd. dirs. Ams. United for Life, 1971-94, Nat. Right to Life Com., 1980-81, Jewish Life Issues Com., Solana Beach, 1983—; sec. Calif. Pro Life Coun., Sacramento, 1972; mem. L.A. County Select Citizens Com. on Life Support Policies, L.A., 1983-85 Named Patron of Life Calif. Pro Life Coun., 1976, Pres's award, 1979; Howard Hughes fellow, 1959-64; grantee Fullbright Found., Govt. Italy, 1961-62. Fellow IEEE; mem. U.S. Nat. Commn. Internat. Union Radio Sci. (del. to 20th gen. assembly), Electromagnetics Acad. Avocations: historic research, stamp collecting.

MIURA, AKIO, quality assurance management professional; b. Tokyo, Oct. 7, 1936; s. Takeshi and Sakiko (Andoh) M.; m. Takako Nakatani, Apr. 14, 1968; 1 child, Masahiro. BS, Waseda U., Tokyo, 1959. Cert. quality auditor; reliability engr., quality engr.; quality mgr., six sigma black belt, registered sr. auditor RAB IATCA, cert. Six Sigma Black Belt RAB IATCA. Staff mem. Mitsubishi Corp., Tokyo, 1959-75, mgr. indsl. machinery, 1975-78, asst. gen. mgr. indsl. machinery, 1984-90; exec. dir. Kinka Kikai Co., Gifu, Japan, 1978-84; sr. cons. N.C. Kist & Assocs., Inc., Naperville, Ill., 1990—; pres. Internat. Quality Sys., Inc., Tokyo, 1990—. Chair Internat. QA Inst., 1991—. Author: Guide for Preparation of Quality Manual, 1992, Practice of ISO 9000, 1994.; contbr. articles to profl. jours. Fellow Am. Soc. Quality (cert. quality mgr., internat. councilor quality audit divsn.); mem. Internat. Quality Inst. (chmn.). Avocations: baseball, chinese boxing, karate, fencing, classical music. Home and Office: 3-24-14-703 Shimo-meguro Meguroku Tokyo 153-0064 Japan Fax: 81-3-3712-3399. E-mail: a-miura-qad-iqai@mwa.biglobe.ne.jp.

MIURA, ROBERT MITSURU, mathematician, researcher, educator; b. Selma, Calif., Sept. 12, 1938; s. Richard Katsuki and Frances Yoneko Miura; m. Kathryn Bannai; children: Derek Katsuki, Brian Robert, Jared Bannai Nagae, Sean Takeo. BS, U. Calif.-Berkeley, 1960, MS, 1962; MA, Princeton U., 1964, PhD, 1966. Rsch. assoc. Princeton U. Plasma Physics Lab., 1965-67; assoc. rsch. scientist Courant Inst. Math. Sci., N.Y.C., 1967-68; asst. prof. math. NYU, 1968-71; assoc. prof. math. Vanderbilt U., 1971-75, U. B.C., Vancouver, B.C., Can., 1975-78, prof. Canada, 1978—2001; prof. math., sci., biomed. engring. N.J. Inst. Tech., 2001—. Chmn. joint com. on math. in life scis. Am. Math. Soc.-Soc. Indsl. and Applied Math., 1981-84; bd. dirs. Soc. for Math. Biology, 1995-98. Editor: Backlund Transformations, 1976, Nonlinear Phenomena in Physics and Biology, 1981, Some Mathematical Questions in Biology-Neurobiology, 1982, Muscle Physiology, 1986, DNA Sequence Analysis, 1986, Plant Biology, 1986; assoc. editor Can. Applied Math. Quar.; co-editor-in-chief: Jour. Math. Biology, 1982—99, co-editor-in-chief: Analysis and Applications, 2000—, mem. editl. bd.: Integrative Neurosci., 2001—; contbr. articles to profl. jours. Mem. steering com. Ctr. Math. Rsch., U. Montreal, 1990-94; mem. sci. adv. panel Fields Inst., Toronto. John Simon Guggenheim fellow, 1980-81; U. B.C. hon. Killam fellow, 1980-81 Fellow Royal Soc. Can.; mem. AAAS (nominating com., math. sect.), Am. Math. Soc., Soc. Indsl. and Applied Math., Can. Applied Indsl. Math. Soc., Can. Math. Soc. (internat. affairs com.), Soc. Math. Biology, Pacific Inst. Math. Sci. (interim exec. bd. 1996), Sigma Xi. Office: NJ Inst Tech Dept Math Sci University Hgts Newark NJ 07102

MIXER, RONALD WAYNE, minister; b. Mpls., Jan. 22, 1954; s. Joseph William and Faith Amour (Minor) M.; m. Glenda Renae Fjordbak, June 22, 1974; children: Rachelle Renae, Danielle Kaye. BA, North Cen. Bible Coll., 1977; M in Ministry, Internat. Bible Sem., 1983. Ordained to ministry. Dir. ch. ministry Rock River Christian Ctr., Rock Falls, Ill., 1977-79; dir. christian edn. Cen. Assembly of God, Tulsa, 1979-80; sr. pastor Manchester (Iowa) Assembly of God, 1980-83, Richmond (Mo.) Assembly of God, 1983-84, Odessa (Mo.) First Assembly of God, 1984-87; field rep. Am. Bible Soc., N.Y.C., 1988-97, program mgr. 1999 Yr. of the Bible, 1997-99, asst. dir. vol. ministries Olathe, Kans., 1999—, assoc. dir. Bible reading programs, 1999-2000; dir. church relations Cross Pointe Net., 2000; acct. dir. Grizzard, Atlanta, 2001—02; CEO Logos Media Network, Overland Park, Kans., 2002. Mem. Olathe (Kans.) Human Rels. Commn., 1990-98, chair, 1996-97. Named one of Outstanding Young Men in Am., U.S. Jaycees, 1986. Mem. Internat. Platform Assn., Assemblies of God Ministers, Toastmasters Internat. Republican. Avocation: racquetball. Office: 229 Peachtree St NE Atlanta GA 30303 E-mail: rmixer@lycos.com. *If, at the end of my life, those who have known me can say, "we could see the Fruit of the Spirit in his living", then I shall have lived well.*

MIXON, DEBORAH LYNN BURTON, elementary school educator; b. Charleston, S.C., Mar. 26, 1956; d. Harold Boyd and Peggy Wynell (Seagraves) Burton; m. Steven Douglas Schmidt (div. Mar. 1982); 1 child, Julie Ann Schmidt; m. Timothy Lamar Mixon, Oct. 11, 1982; children: Phillip Lamar, Catherine Elizabeth. BS in Edn., U. Ga., 1994. Cert. early childhood and gifted in-field educator, Ga. Office coord. Morrison's Cafeteria, Athens, Ga., 1974-76; cashier Winn-Dixie, 1976-78; data entry clk. Athens Tech. Data Ctr., 1978-79; adminstrv. sec. U. Ga., Athens, 1980-86; sec. to plant mgr. Certain Teed Corp., 1986-87; s. adminstrv. sec. U. Ga., 1987-93; tchr. 4th grade Hall County Sch. Sys., Gainesville, Ga., 1994-2000, tchr. kindergarten, 2000—. Leader Cub Scouts den Boy Scouts Am., 1993-94; troop vol. Girl Scouts U.S., 1992—; vol. leader 4-H Clarke County, Athens, 1992-94. Presdl. scholar U. Ga., 1993-94. Mem.: Ga. Assn. for Gifted Children, Ga. Assn. Educators, Kappa Delta Epsilon (perfect scholar 1994), Golden Key, Delta Kappa Gamma. Avocations: hiking, camping, swimming, canoeing, reading. Home: 171 Scottwood Dr Athens GA 30607-1338 E-mail: debbie.mixon@hallco.org., dmixon@hotmail.com.

MIXON, DONNA JO, financial analyst; b. Waco, Tex., Jan. 2, 1966; d. Weldon Clay and Joann (Richards) W.; married; three children. AAS, McLennan Community Coll., Waco, 1989; BBA, Baylor U., 1992, MBA, 1993; postgrad., U. Tex., Arlington, 1994-95, Tex. State Tech. Coll., 1997-98. Instr. acctg. Ctrl. Tex. Coll., 1994-98; sr. fin. analyst Continental Express Airlines, Houston, 1999—2000; acct. City of Austin, 1998-1999; staff acct., fin. analyst BP Amoco, Texas City, Tex., 2000—02; sr. procedures analyst Harris County Auditor's Office, Houston, 2002—. Bus. and acctg. sys. cons., 1990-98; GED instr., McLennan County, 1995-98; instr. mgmt. Tarleton State U., 1996-98; instr. acctg. Ctrl. Tex. Coll., 1994-98. Exec. bd. Woodway PTA, 1994-96; mem. exec. com. Cub Scouts Am., 1993-94; exec. bd. mem. Midway Coun. of PTAs, 1994-95; dep. treas. The Soc. for Creative Anachronism-The Shire of Emerald Keep, 1995-96, treas., 1996-97. Recipient Student Scholar award Am. Assn. Cmty. and Jr. Colls. Mem. Phi Theta Kappa (reporter 1988-89, Student Scholar award, Outstanding Acctg. Student award 1988, Outstanding Svc. award 1989). Avocations: piano playing, writing. E-mail: djmixon@houston.rr.com.

MIXON, KEVIN ANTHONY, music educator, composer; b. Huntsville, Ala., Nov. 18, 1964; s. Harold Dean Mixon and Barbara Anne McCoy; children: Chelsea, Kevin, Jr. BS, Syracuse U., 1996; MS, U. Ill., 2000; Assoc. in Applied Sci., Onondaga C.C., Syracuse, NY, 1994. Cert. tchr. NY, Ill. Instrumental music tchr. South Ctrl. Sch. Dist., Kinmundy, Ill., 1996—97, Palos Mid. Sch., Palos Park, 1997—98, Newark (NY) Mid. Sch., 1998—99, Franklin Magnet Sch. of the Arts, Syracuse, 1999—. Freelance composer/arranger ednl. and comml. works. Contbr. articles to profl. jours. Mem.: Onondaga County Music Educators Assn., NY State Band Directors Assn., Nat. Band Assn., NY State Sch. Music Assn. (cert. percussion adjudicator 1999—), Music Educators Nat. Conf., Golden Key, Phi Theta Kappa, Phi Kappa Phi, Phi Kappa Lambda. Home: 483 Cable Rd Williamstown NY 13493

MIXON, VALORIE JOHNSON, physician assistant; b. Orlando, Fla., Mar. 27, 1965; m. Myron R.D. Mixon, Mar. 13, 1988; children: Joseph S., Benjamin K. BA in Sci., Emory U., 1989. Physician asst. Planned Parenthood, Asheville, N.C., 1989-90, Paul Chang, MD, Asheville, 1990-91, Blue Ridge Bone Joint, Asheville, 1991-93, Asheville Family Health, 1993-95, Mills River Family Health Ctr., Horse Shoe, N.C., 1995-98, Dr. Paul G. Smith, D.O., 1998—. Author: Cortlandt Letter, 1997. Vol. Children's Advocacy Ctr., 2001. Mem. Am. Acad. Physician Assts. (cert.), Tenn. Acad. Physician Assts. Avocations: sewing, crafts, gardening, water sports. Home: 7123 Flagstone Dr Ooltewah TN 37363-8780 Office: Erlanger Work Force 9309 Jason Pike Ooltewah TN 37363

MIXTER, CHRISTIAN JOHN, lawyer; b. Basel, Switzerland, Mar. 13, 1953; s. Keith Eugene and Beatrice Maria (Ruf) M.; m. Linna M. Barnes, Dec. 17, 1977; children: Sara Elizabeth Barnes Mixter, Laura Ellen Barnes Mixter. BA, Ohio State U., 1974; JD, Duke U., 1977. Bar: N.Y. 1978, D.C. 1981. Assoc. Davis Polk & Wardwell, N.Y.C. and Washington, 1977-87; assoc. counsel Office Ind. Counsel (Iran/Contra), Washington, 1987-91; asst. chief litigation counsel Enforcement divsn. SEC, 1991-97, chief litigation counsel, 1997-2000; ptnr. Morgan, Lewis & Bockius LLP, 2000—. Mem. ABA (bus. law and litig. sects.), Assn. Bar City N.Y., Phi Beta Kappa, Order of the Coif. Office: Morgan Lewis & Bockius LLP 1111 Pennsylvania Ave NW Washington DC 20004 E-mail: cmixter@morganlewis.com.

MIYAGAWA, ICHIRO, physicist; b. Hiratsuka, Kanagawa, Japan, Mar. 5, 1922; s. Shigejiro and Tsuma (Itoh) M.; m. Mitsuko Yamada, Feb. 10, 1950; children: Shigeru, Haruyo, Mari. BS, Nagoya (Japan) U., 1945; DSc, U. Tokyo, 1954. Asst. prof. U. Tokyo, 1959-62; vis. asst. prof. Duke U., Durham, N.C., 1963-65; asst. prof. physics U. Ala., Tuscaloosa, 1965-66, assoc. prof., 1966-70, prof., 1970-80, Univ. Research prof. physics, 1980-92, prof. emeritus, 1992—. Contbr. articles to profl. jours. Recipient Samuel Ullman award, 1998; USPHS grantee; EPA grantee; NIH grantee. Fellow Am. Phys. Soc.; mem., AAAS, Sigma Xi. Home: 6434 Misty Ridge Dr Birmingham AL 35235-*Finding truth in any work or in any matter, however simple, is rewarding, although painful in many cases. Successful people in every spectrum of society are master discoverers of truth.*

MIYAHIRA, SARAH DIANE, research and education director, psychologist, educator; b. Wailuku, Maui, Hawaii, May 13, 1948; d. Ronald Takayoshi and Bertha Asae (Nagagaki) M.; m. Justin Masakatsu Koizumi, Sept. 7, 1974; 1 child, Jason Miyahira Koizumi. BA, U. Hawaii, 1970; MA, Ohio State U., 1973, PhD, 1976. Lic. psychologist, marriage, family and child counselor, Calif. Staff psychologist counseling svcs. U. So. Calif., L.A., 1978-81; lectr., 1978-80; assoc. dir. counseling svcs. U. So. Calif., 1981-83, dir., 1983-85; dean student svcs. Honolulu Community Coll., 1985-88; dean student affairs and open grants East-West Ctr., Honolulu, 1988-94; assoc. dir. of edn. Pacific Ctr. for PTSD, 1994-97; acting dir. Pacific Islands divsn. Nat. Ctr. for PTSD, 1997-2000; acting coord. R&D VA, Honolulu, 2000-01; dep. dir. VA Telemedicine, Hawaii, 2000—. Psychotherapist, orgnl. behavior cons., L.A., 1979-85; mem. bd. behavioral sci. examiners State of Calif., 1981-84, mem. accreditation team postsecondary edn. com., 1981; mem. commn. on status of women U. Hawaii, Honolulu, 1987, mem. com. human studies, 1994-2000, mem. clin. studies program adv. bd. dept. psychology, 1994-98. Mem. steering com. Asian Pacific Women's Network, L.A., 1980; bd. dirs. Asian Pacific Am. support group U. So. Calif., 1983-85; mem. nominating com. YWCA, Honolulu, 1986-88; mem. com. human use Tripler Army Med. Ctr., 2000—; mem. sub-com. VA. Human Subjects, Honolulu, 2000; mem. VA R&D Com., 2000—. Mem. APA (bd. ethnic minority affairs 1986-88, chmn. 1988, mem. ethics com. 1989-90, com. on women in psychology 1992-95, chmn., 1994, chair divsn. 35 continuing edn. com. 1993-96, mem. women's work group, rural health svcs. delivery task force 1995-97, com. internat. rels. in psychology 1996-98, chmn. 1998, pres. sect. 6, divsn. 12, 2001), Soc. for Study Ethnics and Minority Issues, Asian Am. Psychol. Assn., Women in Higher Edn. Adminstrn., Hawaii Network, Pacific and Asian Affairs Coun., Honolulu Com. on Fgn. Rels. Avocations: reading, travel, hiking.

MIYAMOTO, CRAIG TOYOKI, public relations executive; b. Joliet, Ill., Oct. 14, 1944; s. Robert Mitsuo Miyamoto, Dorothy Toyoko (Okumura) Miyamoto; m. Diana Chie Ueda, Mar. 24, 1966; children: James Anthony Kazuyuki, Carleton Alan Yasuo. Reporter Alhambra Post-Advocate, Alhambra, Calif., 1968—70; editor Monterey Park Californian, 1970—71; mng. editor So. Calif. Pub. Co., 1971—72; dep. pub. rels. dir. Honolulu Bd. Water Supply, 1972—76, dir. pub. rels., 1976—77; pres. Miyamoto Advt./Pub. Rels., Honolulu, 1977—87; v.p. Profl. Comm., Inc., 1987—92, exec, v,o, 1995—97; prin. Miyamoto Strategic Counsel, 1997—. Asst. prof. U. Hawaii, 1992—95, instr. pub. rels., 1978—80, 1995—, adj. prof., 1995—98, 2002; reporter Pineapple Post, Honolulu, 1977—88, Aura Publs., Honolulu, 1980—83. Author: How to Earn $2,000 or More Without Hardly Working at All, 1979, Pineapple Post Catalogue, 1984, Environmental Public Relations: A Primer on the Hottest Growth Area of the 90's, 1991, U.S. Corporate Environmental Policy: Philosophy vs Practice at the Dawn of a New Millenium, 1995, Environmental Public Relations and the PRSA Code of Ethics, 1995, Public Relations Ethics 201: Challenges We Just Can't Ignore, 1996. Pres. Honolulu Jaycees, 1975—76; mem. exec. com. 50th State Fair, 1974—76; dir. pub. rels. Hawaii Jaycees, 1974—75, Monterey Park C. of C., 1970—71; bd. dirs. San Gabriel Valley YMCA, 1971—72, Garfield Cmty. Sch. Bd., 1971—72, Am. Heart Assn. Hawaii affiliate; treas. Alzheimer's Assn. of Hawaii, 1991—92; mem. senate Jaycees Internat., 1976—. Named Man of Yr., Honolulu, 1974, Profl. of Yr., Gregg Perry Pub. Rels., 1992; recipient John Armbruster award, 1974, State Svc. award, Hawaii Jaycees, 1974. Fellow: Pub. Rels. Soc. Am. (accredited, bd. dirs. Hawaii chpt., pres., v.p., sec. Hawaii chpt., chmn. South Pacific dist., sec. environ. sect., nat. bd. dirs. 1997—98); mem.: Hawaii Advt. Fedn. (bd. dirs.), Internat. Acad. Bus. Disciplines, Am. Mktg. Assn. (v.p. comm. group Honolulu chpt. 1996—97), Am. Advt. Fedn., Hawaii Stamp and Coin Dealers Assn (pres., v.p.), Am. Philatelic Soc., Am. Topical Assn., Hawaiian Philatelic Soc., Bur. Issues Assn., Internat. Soc. Japanese Philately, Mensa. Democrat. Office: PO Box 61414 Honolulu HI 96839-1414

MIYAMOTO, CURTIS TRENT, medical educator; b. Bristol, Pa., Nov. 26, 1957; s. Sadao and Amy E. Miyamoto; m. Maria Amparo Gomez, Sept. 24, 1983; children: Maria Victoria, David James, Robert Paul. BS, Muhlenberg Coll., 1979; MD, U. Navarra, Pamplona, Spain, 1986. Lic. physician, Pa.; cert. radiation oncologist; bd. cert. radiation oncology Am. Bd. Radiology. Co-founder Brain Tumor Ctr. Med. Coll. Pa. Hahnemann U., Phila., 1994-99; assoc. med. dir. Gynecologic Oncology Ctr., 1996-99; assoc. prof., chief clin. svc. Med. Coll. Pa. Hahnemann U., 1999-2001, vice chmn., 2001—; med. educator West Mich. Cancer Ctr., Kalamazoo, 1999; prof., chmn. dept. radiation oncology Temple U. Hosp., Phila., 2001—. Bd. dir. Richard Zaloga Found., Old Forge, Pa.; former mem. risk mgmt., quality improvement com., former instnl. rev. bd. Med. Coll. Pa. Hahnemann U.; former mem. faculty Radiatin Oncology Self Assessment Program. Author: (with others) Management of Salivary Gland Lesions, 1992, Radioimmunoglobulins in Cancer Therapy, Principles and Practice of Radiation Oncology, 1996, (book chpt.) Combined Modality Therapy of Central Nervous System Tumors, 2001, radiation Therapy Principles for High Grade Gliomas, Quarterly Update: Principles and Practice of Radiation Oncology, 2001; co-author: (with others) Radiobiology in Radiotherapy, 1988, Recent Results in Cancer Research-Systemic Radiotherapy with Monoclonal Antibodies, 1996, Radioimmunoglobulins in Cancer Therapy, Principles and Practice of Radiation Oncology, 1996; contbr. articles to profl. jours. including Am. Jour. Clin. Oncology, Internat. Jour. Radiation Oncology; mem. editl. bd. Radiation Oncology Investigations; article reviewer Am. Jour. Clin. Oncology. Mem. worship com. First Presbyn. Ch., Morristown, N.J., 1996; v.p. PTA, Glenolden, Pa., 1993. Outstanding scholar Hahnemann U., 1991. Fellow AMA (Physician's Recognition award 1994), Am. Cancer Soc.; mem. Interat. Coll. Physicians & Surgeons, Coll. Physicians Phila., Am. Soc. for Therapeutic Radiology and Oncology, Alpha Phi Omega (life), Sigma Xi. Republican. Presbyterian. Achievements include extensive work with biologic response modifiers. Home: 32 Parkdale Pl Marlton NJ 08053-3852 Office: Temple Univ Hosp Dept Radiation Oncology 3401 North Broad St Philadelphia PA 19140 E-mail: miyamoc@tuhs.temple.edu.

MIYAMOTO, JUN, nuclear engineer; b. Tokushima, Japan, Feb. 15, 1968; arrived in U.S., 1985; BS, Tohoku U., Sendai, Japan, 1991; MS, U. Calif., Berkeley, 1993; PhD, U. Mich., 1997. Rsch. asst. U. Mich., Ann Arbor, 1993-97; rsch. assoc. Purdue U., West Lafayette, Ind., 1997-98, rsch. scientist, 1999—, cons., 1997. Physicist INFN, Pisa, Italy, 1999. Mem. IEEE Nuclear Sci. Office: Dept Physics Purdue U West Lafayette IN 47906

MIYAMOTO, RICHARD TAKASHI, otolaryngologist; b. Zeeland, Mich., Feb. 2, 1944; s. Dave Norio and Haruko (Okano) M.; m. Cynthia Vander-Burgh, June 17, 1967; children: Richard Christopher, Geoffrey Takashi. BS cum laude, Wheaton Coll., 1966; MD, U. Mich., 1970; MS in Otology, U.So. Calif., 1978; D in Engring. (hon.) Rose Hulman Inst. of Tech., 2001. Diplomate Am. Bd. Otolaryngology. Intern Butterworth Hosp., Grand Rapids, Mich., 1970-71, resident in surgery, 1971-72; resident in otolaryngology Ind. U. Sch. Medicine, 1972-75; fellow in otology and neurotology St. Vincent Hosp. and Otologic Med. Group, L.A., 1977-78; asst. prof. Ind. U. Sch. Medicine, Indpls., 1978-83, assoc. prof., 1983-88; prof. 1988—; chmn. 1987—, chief Otology and Neurotology dept. Otolaryngology, Head and Neck Surgery, Ind. U., 1982—, chmn. dept. Otolaryngology, 1987—, Arilla DeVault prof., 1991; chief Otolaryngology, Head and Neck Surgery Wishard Meml. Hosp., 1979—. Mem. editorial bd. Laryngoscope, Am. Jour. of Otology, Otolaryngology-Head and Neck Surgery, European archives of Oto-Rhino-Laryngology, Anales de Otorrinolaringologia Mexicana; contbr. articles to profl. jours. Mem. adv. coun. Nat. Inst. Deafness and other communication disorders, 1989-94; mem. med. adv. bd. Alexander Graham Bell Assn. for the Deaf, The Ear Found. Served to maj. USAF, 1975-77. Named Arilla DeVault Disting. investigator Ind. U., 1983. Fellow Am. Acad. Otolaryngology (gov. 1982—), ACS, Am. Otological, Rhinological, and Laryngological Soc. (Thesis Disting. for Excellence award), Am. Neurotology Soc. (pres. elect 1999-2000, pres. 2000-01), Am. Auditory Soc. (mem. exec. com. 1985—); mem. Am. Acad. Pediats., N.Y. Acad. Scis., Otosclerosis Study Group (coun. 1993—), Am. Otol. Soc. (coun. 1992—), Marines Meml. Assn., Assn. Rsch. Otol. (pres. elect 2000-2001, pres. 2001-), Wheaton Coll. Scholastic Honor Soc., Cosmos Club of Washington, Columbia Club of Ind., Royal Soc. Medicine London, Collegium Oto-Laryngologicum Amecitiae Sacrum; Alpha Omega Alpha, Psi Iote X. Office: Ind U Sch Med 702 Barnhill Dr Indianapolis IN 46202-5128

MIYASAKI, GEORGE JOJI, artist; b. Kalopa, Hawaii, Mar. 24, 1935; BFA, Calif. Coll. Arts and Crafts, 1957, MFA, 1958. Asst. prof. art Calif. Coll. Arts and Crafts, Oakland, 1958-64; mem. faculty dept. art U. Calif., Berkeley, 1964-94, prof. emeritus. John Hay Whitney fellow, 1957-58; Tamarind printing fellow, 1961; Guggenheim fellow, 1963-64; Nat. Endowment for Arts fellow, 1980-81, 85-86. Mem. NAD. Home: 2844 Forest Ave Berkeley CA 94705-1309

MIYASAKI, SHUICHI, lawyer; b. Paauilo, Hawaii, Aug. 6, 1928; s. Torakichi and Teyo (Kimura) M.; m. Pearl Takeko Saiki, Sept. 11, 1954; children: Joy Michiko, Miles Tadashi, Jan Keiko, Ann Yoshie. BSCE, U. Hawaii-Honolulu, 1951; JD, U. Minn., 1957; grad., Army War Coll., 1973. Bar: Minn. 1957, Hawaii 1959, U.S. Supreme Ct. 1980. Examiner U.S. Patent Office, 1957-59; dep. atty. gen. State of Hawaii, 1960-61; mem., dir., sec./treas. Okumura Takushi Funaki & Wee, Honolulu, 1961-90; pvt. practice, 1991—; atty. Hawaii Senate, 1961, chief counsel ways and means com., 1962, chief counsel judiciary com., 1967-70; civil engr. Japan Constrn. Agy., Tokyo, 1953-54; staff judge adv., col. USAR, Ft. DeRussy, Hawaii, 1968-79. Local legal counsel Jaycees, 1962; lectr. Nat. Assn. Pub. Accts. Hawaii Chpt. Ann. Conf., 1990, 94, Mid Pacific Inst. Found., Honolulu, 1990, Econ. Study Club of Hawaii, 1990, Meiji Life Ins. Co. Japan, 1992, Cent. YMCA, 1992, City Bank Honolulu, 1997. Legis. chmn. armed services com. C. of C. of Hawaii, 1973; instnl. rep. Aloha council Boy Scouts Am., 1963-78; exec. com., sec., dir. Legal Aid Soc. Hawaii, 1970-72; state v.p. Hawaii Jaycees, 1964-65; dir., legal counsel St. Louis Heights Community Assn., 1963, 65, 73, 91—; dir., legal counsel Citizens Study Club for Naturalization of Citizens, 1963-68; advisory bd. Project Dana Honolulu, 1991—, vice chair, 1991, 92; bd. dirs. Omote Senke Found., 1999—; life mem. Res. Officers Assn. U.S. Served to 1st lt. AUS, 1951-54. Decorated Meritorious Service medal with oak leaf cluster. Mem. ABA, Hawaii Bar Assn., U.S. Patent Office Soc., Hawaii Estate Planning Council, Rotary, Central YMCA Club, Waikiki Athletic Club, Army Golf Assn., Elks, Phi Delta Phi. Office: 1001 Bishop St Ste 1030 Honolulu HI 96813-3408 *Personal philosophy: Study hard, work hard, play hard, love hard, have time for nonsense, help others and be fair to all concerned.*

MIYATA, GEN, history of religion educator; b. Kyoto, Japan, Feb. 11, 1933; s. Zenichiro and Ine (Yoshida) M.; m. Hiroko Fujiwara, Feb. 3, 1968; children: Kenichi, Mamoru, Teizo. BA, Tokyo U., 1956, MA, 1958. Lectr. Tenri (Japan) U., 1964-70, assoc. prof., 1970-79, prof., 1979-2001, chairperson dept. religious studies, 1981-87, 89-91, 92-93, 96-98, dean faculty letters, 1987-89, 91-92, dean faculty human studies, 1993-96. Vis. prof. Ind. U., Bloomington, 1980-81. Mem. Japanese Assn. for Am. Studies (councilor 1972-2000), Japanese Assn. for Religious Studies (dir. 1989—). Tenrikyo. Office: Tenri U Somanouchi cho Tenri Nara 632-8510 Japan E-mail: g-miyata@sta.tenri-u.ac.jp.

MIYATA, KEIJIRO, culinary arts educator; b. Tokyo, Mar. 8, 1951; came to U.S., 1967; s. Yataro Miyata and Hekkiken (Liu) Choy; m. Connie Joyce Nelson, Mar. 8, 1976; children: Michelle, Kelly, Adam. Assoc. in Occupational Study, Culinary Inst. Am., Hyde Park, N.Y., 1972, cert. of nutrition, 1991; cert., Seattle Wine Sch., 1991. Cert. exec. chef; cert. culinary educator. Garde mgr. Mid-Pacific Country Club, Kailua, Hawaii, 1972; working chef Waikiki Yacht Club, Honolulu, 1972-74, Sagano Japanese Restaurant, New Rochelle, N.Y., 1974-76; asst. pastry chef Rye Town (N.Y.) Hilton Hotel, 1976-77; working chef The Explorer, Everett, Wash., 1977-79; exec. chef Holiday Inn, 1979-81, Mill Creek (Wash.) Country Club, 1981; culinary art instr. Everett Community Coll., 1981-85, North Seattle (Wash.) Community Coll., 1985-90, Seattle Cen. Community Coll., 1990—. Cons. Chalon Corp., Redmond, Wash., Chiang-Mai Restaurant, Mukilteo, Wash., 1988, Holiday Inn Crown Plaza, Seattle, Satsuma Japanese Restaurant, 1996. Participant Nagano Winter Olympic Ice Sculpture Festival, Karuizawa, Japan, 1998. Recipient Gold awards Am. Culinary Fedn., Oreg. State Chef's Assn., Portland, 1983, Gold and Bronze medals World Culinary Olympic, Frankfurt, Germany, 1984, 1988, Grand Champion award U.S. Nat. Ice Carving Contest, N.Y.C., 1986, 2d place award, All Japan Ice Carving Assn., Asahikawa, 1988, Ednl. Excellence award Oreg. and Wash. Community coll. Couns. Wash. Fedn. of Tchrs./Am. Fedn. of Tchrs./AFL-CIO, 1988, 1989, ACF Seafood Challenge State finalist, Charlotte, N.C., 1989, New Orleans, 1990, 1st place, Pacific Rim Invitational World Ice Sculpting Classic, 1989, Seymour Ice Sculpting Competition, 1991, 3d Ann. Internat. Ice Sculpting Competition, Lake Louise, Alta., Can., 1993, award of Excellence, Wash. Fedn. Tchrs./Am. Fedn. Tchrs./AFL-CIO, 1993, 1st place, Wash. State Seafood Festival Recipe Contest, Shelton, Wash., 1993, Grand Champion, 1994, 1st place, ICE ART'94 Ice Sculpting Competition, Fairbanks, Alaska, 1994, Most Artistic award Asahikawa Internat. Ice Sculpting Competition, 1996, 1st place Ice Carver's Choice, People's Choice Awards--8th Internat. Ice Carving Championship, Anchorage, Alaska, 1997, selected as Snow Sculpting Team Mem. of Sister City of Portland, Internat. Snow Sculpting Competition, Sapporo, Japan, 1997, participant, Nagano Winter Olympic Ice Sculpture Festival, Karuizawa, Japan, 1998, NICA, Gold Medal Ice Carver's Choice Awd., People's awd., Crystal Gall. of Ice, Internatl. Carving Comp., Alaska, 1999, 1st place, People's Choice Awards--7th Annual Internat. Sculpting Competition, Lake Louise, Alberta, Canada, 2000, 2d Place Hokkaido Newspaper award, Asahikawa Internat. Ice Sculpting competition, 2000, 3rd place team, Ice Alaska, Ice Art, Fairbank, Alaska, 2001, 1st place, People's Choice Award, 9th Ann. Internat. Ice Sculpting Competition, Lake Louise, Alberta. Mem. Wash. State Chefs Assn. (bd. dirs. 1982, 83, 86, 87, 88, cert. chmn. 1986-92, Chef of Yr. 1986), Am. Acad. Chefs, Nat. Ice Carving Assn. Office: Seattle Ctr Cmty Coll 1701 Broadway Seattle WA 98122-2413 E-mail: kmiyat@sccd.ctc.edu.

MIYAZAKI, KOICHI, economics educator; b. Yokohama, Japan, Dec. 7, 1949; s. Yoshikazu and Teruko (Inukai) M.; m. Mizuyo Muto, Jan. 16, 1993. BA, Yokohama Nat. U., 1972; MA, U. Tokyo, 1974. Prof. dept. econs. Hosei U., Tokyo, 1986—. Contbr. articles to profl. jours. Mem. Am. Econ. Assn., Tokyo Ctr. for Econ. Rsch., Japanese Econ. Assn. Avocation: tennis. Home: 565-10-202 Kitano-Machi Hachioji-Shi Tokyo 192-0906 Japan Office: Hosei U Dept Econs 4342 Aihara-Machi Machida-Shi Tokyo 194-0298 Japan E-mail: koichi@m.email.ne.jp.

MIYOSHI, DAVID MASAO, lawyer, international investment consultant; b. Overton, Nev., Jan. 2, 1944; s. Joseph Masaru and Jean Michiye (Horikiri) M.; m. Teruko Ochiai, July 16, 1977; children: Mark Masahiro, Brandon Kohei. BS, U. So. Calif., 1966; JD, U. Calif., San Francisco, 1973; cert. completion, Waseda U., Tokyo, 1976; MBA, Harvard U., 1978. Bar: Calif. 1973, U.S. Dist. Ct. (cen. dist.) Calif. 1973. Fgr. assoc. atty. Matsuo and Kosugi Law Offices, Tokyo, 1974-76; assoc. atty. Matsuo Law Office, 1976-78; assoc. Mori & Ota, L.A., 1978-80, Morgan, Lewis & Bockius, L.A., 1980-82; pres., chief exec. officer Trans-Continental Investment, 1982-84; sr. atty. Miyoshi Law Office, 1983—; pres. Dai-Ichi Mortgage Co., 1984-86; sr. atty. Law Offices of David Miyoshi, 1986-93; pres. Global Fin. Corp., 1988-93, Wallstreet Masters, 2000—; legal counsel Japanese Am. Med. Assn., 2000—. Bd. dirs. Global Masters, Inc., L.A.; gen. counsel Japanese Am. Med. Assn., 1999—. Author: U.S. Condominium Regulations, 1976, U.S. Real Property Investment, 1986, Gingrich, America's De Gaulle; editor: U.S. trade Laws newsletter, 1978, U.S. Real Estate Report, 1987-93; contbr. articles to profl. jours. Bd. dirs. Am. Bapt. Soc., Los Angeles, 1986, Palos Verdes (Calif.) Bapt. Ch., 1986. Served to capt. USMC, 1966-69, Vietnam. Mem. ABA, Calif. Bar Assn., L.A. County Bar Assn. Republican. Avocations: tennis, golf, flying, skiing. Office: 707 Wilshire Blvd Ste 3260 Los Angeles CA 90017-3514

MIYOSHI, KAZUHISA, senior research scientist; b. Kobe, Japan, Feb. 15, 1946; came to the U.S., 1976; s. Kintaro and Emiko (Ogawa) M.; m. Sumiko Hasegawa, July 23, 1973; children: Hiroshi, Amy D., Bradley D., Jennifer K. B in Engring., Osaka Inst. Tech., 1968; MS, Osaka U., 1970, PhD, 1975. Asst. prof. Kanazawa (Japan) U., 1970-78; rsch. assoc. Nat. Rsch. Coun./NASA, Cleve., 1976-78; rsch. scientist, sr. rsch. scientist NASA, 1979—. Cons. Hashiba Am., Inc., Akron, Ohio, 1986-94, space flight awareness, 1998; priority area rschr. Japan Soc. Promotion Sci. Invitation Fellowship program, 1995. Author (, editor): (Book) Surface Diagnostics in Tribology , 1993; author: Solid Lubrication Fundamentals and Applications, 2001, Research and Development Management Manual; editor (Assoc. editor): (Book) Advances into Storage Systems; editor: (assoc. editor) (Jour.) Diamond Films and Tech, 1995—; editor: (regional) (jour.) Tribology Internat., 1999—; contbr. articles to profl. jours., chpts. to books; mem. editl. bds., 1992—; , editor (guest) ; editl.advisor Japanese Soc. Tribologists, 1995—. Vol. tchr. Japanese Lang. Sch. Cleve., 1990—. Grantee Japanese Rsch. Coun., 1974, 75. Mem. Am. Vacuum Soc., Soc. Tribologists and Lubrication Engrs., Japanese Soc. Tribologists, Japanese Assn. N.E. Ohio (sec. 1994—). Achievements include research in advanced materials, including diamond and diamondlike carbon coatings, ceramic coatings, and composites. Home: 5541 Quail Run North Olmsted OH 44070-3979 Office: NASA Lewis Rsch Ctr 21000 Brookpark Rd Cleveland OH 44135-3191

MIYOSHI, MASAO, literature educator, writer; b. Tokyo, May 14, 1928; came to U.S., 1952; s. Katsunai Miyoshi and Hisae Takahama; m. Elizabeth Ann Lester, July 27, 1953 (div. 1977); m. Martha L. Archibald, Apr. 8, 1977; children: Kathy Michele, Owen Malcolm, Melina Cybele. BA, U. Tokyo, 1951; MA, NYU, 1955, PhD, 1963. Instr., lectr. Gakushin U., Tokyo, 1951-52, 54-55; from asst. prof. to assoc. prof. to prof. English U. Calif., Berkeley, 1963-87; Edwin O. Reischauer prof. Japanese studies Harvard U., Cambridge, Mass., 1984-85; Hajime Mori prof. lit. U. Calif., San Diego, 1986—. Vis. prof. U. Chgo., 1978-81; dir. regional seminar and Japanese studies U. Calif., Berkeley, 1980-86; dir. program for Japanese studies U. Calif., San Diego, 1989-95; dir. council on East Asian Studies U. Calif at San Diego, 1997-2000. Author: The Divided Self, 1969, Accomplices of Silence, 1975, As We Saw Them, 1979, Off Center, 1991; editor: Postmodernism and Japan, 1989, Japan in the World, 1993, The Cultures of Globalization, 1998, Learning Places, 2002, (book series) Asia-Pacific: Culture, Politics, and Society. Guggenheim fellow, 1971-72, 75-76. Mem. MLA, Assn. for Asian Studies, Internat. Comparative Lit. Assn. Office: U Calif 9500 Gilman Dr La Jolla CA 92093-5004

MIZE, JOE HENRY, industrial engineer, educator; b. Colorado City, Tex., June 14, 1934; s. Kelly Marcus and Birtie (Adams) M.; m. Betty Bentley, Mar. 16, 1966; 1 dau., Kelly Jean. BS in Indsl. Engring, Tex. Tech. Coll., 1958; MS (Research Found. grantee) in Indsl. Engring, Purdue U., 1963, PhD, 1964. Registered profl. engr., Ala., Okla. Indsl. engr. White Sands Missile Range, N.Mex., 1958-61; grad. research asst. Purdue U., Lafayette, Ind., 1961-64; asso. prof. engring. Auburn (Ala.) U., 1964-69; dir. Auburn (Ala.) U. (Computer Center), 1965-66; prof. engring. Ariz. State U., Tempe, 1969-72; prof., head Sch. Indsl. Engring. and Mgmt. Okla. State U., Stillwater, 1972-80, dir. Univ. Ctr. for Energy Research, 1980-83, Regents prof., 1982-94; v.p. Hong Kong U. of Sci. and Tech., 1994-98; prof., v.p. Hong Kong U. Sci. & Tech., 1994-98; rsch. affiliate engring. sys. divsn. MIT, 1998—. Cons. to Air War Coll., 1968-69, U.S. Army, Ops. Analysis Standby Unit, U. N.C., 1965-69, various mfg. firms, 1964—; program adv. Office of Mgmt. and Budget, Exec. Office of the President, Washington, 1974-79; adv. to NSF, 1974-94, Nat. Center for Productivity and Quality of Work Life, 1973-78; chmn. tech. adv. council So. Growth Policies Bd., 1975-77; accrediting visitor Engrs. Council for Profl. Devel., 1973-80 Author: (with J.G. Cox) Essentials of Simulation (translated into Japanese 1970), 1968, Prosim V.: Instructor's Manual, 1971, Student's Manual, 1971, (with C.R. White and George H. Brooks) Operations Planning and Control, 1971, (with J.L. Kuester) Optimization Techniques with Fortran, 1973, (with W.C. Turner and K.E. Case) Introduction to Industrial and Systems Engineering, 3d edit., 1993 (named Book of Yr., Am. Inst. Indsl. Engrs. 1979), Guide to Systems Integration, 1991; contrbr. articles to profl. jours., more. Recipient Disting. Engring. Alumnus award Purdue U., 1978 Mem. Am. Inst. Indsl. Engrs. (exec. v.p. 1978-80, pres. 1981-82, H.G. Maynard Innovative Achievement award 1977, Gilbreth Indsl. Engring. award 1990), Am. Soc. for Engring. Edn. (sec. govt. rels. com. 1975-76), Nat. Soc. Profl. Engrs., Okla. Soc. Profl. Engrs. (Outstanding Engring. Achievement award 1977, Outstanding Engr. in Okla. 1981), Inst. Mgmt. Scis., Coun. Indsl. Engring. Acad. Dept. Heads (chmn. 1975-76), NAE, Nat. Rsch. Coun., Sigma Xi, Tau Beta Pi, Alpha Pi Mu. Office: Oklahoma State U Dept Indsl Engring Stillwater OK 74078-0001

MIZEJEWSKI, GERALD JUDE, research scientist; b. Pitts., Aug. 1, 1939; s. Edward Lenard and Ann Veronica (Barnosky) M.; m. Darlene Diana Dietrich, June12, 1965; children: Steven Michael, James Gerald, William Matthew, Susan Marie, Gerald Jude Jr., Michael Christopher. BS in Biology, Duquesne U., 1961; MS in Zoology, U. Md., 1965, PhD in Zoology, 1968; post doctoral, U. Mich., 1970. Rsch. asst. veterinary science dept. U. Md., College Park, 1967-68; rsch. assoc. internal medicine dept. U. Mich., Ann Arbor, 1968-70, instr. sch. pub. health, 1970-71, rsch. physiologist VA hosp., 1970-71; asst. prof. biology dept. U. S.C., Columbia, 1971-74; rsch. scientist N.Y. State Health Dept., Albany, 1974-79; sr. rsch. scientist Wadsworth Ctr. Labs., 1979—; dir. oncofetal antigen lab. N.Y. State Dept. Health, 1984—, asst. dir. hypothyroid newborn screening lab., 1990—. Assoc. prof. SUNY, Albany, 1988—, Albany Med. Coll., 1980—, Rensselaer Poly. Inst., Troy, N.Y., 1986—, Union Coll., 1990—. Author numerous books; contbr. articles to profl. jours. Youth leader YMCA Indian Guides, Clifton Park, N.Y., 1978-84; pack leader Boy Scouts Am., Clifton Park, 1976-86. With USMC, 1961-66. Named Rsch. fellow Nat. Science Found., 1963; grantee Nat. Cancer Inst., Bethesda, Md., 1990. Mem. N.Y. Acad. Sci., Am. Fedn. Clin. Rsch. Office: Wadsworth Ctr NYS Health Dept Empire State Plz Albany NY 12223

MIZEL, MARK STUART, orthopedic surgeon; b. N.Y.C., May 23, 1945; s. Harold Henry and Irene (Adelman) M. BSME, Columbia U., 1966, MSME, 1968; MD, Tufts U., 1977. Diplomate Am. Bd. Orthopedic Surgery. Intern George Washington U. Hosp., 1977-78, resident in surgery, 1978-79; resident Mass. Gen. Hosp., Boston, 1979-82; fellow in foot and ankle surgery Dr. Roger Mann, San Francisco, 1983; practice medicine specializing in orthopedic surgery Orthopedic Ctr. of Lake Worth, Fla., 1983-91; clin. assoc. prof. orthopedics and rehab. U. Miami, 1989-91; clin. asst. prof. orthopedic surgery Tufts U., Boston, 1991-95; dir. Boston Foot and Ankle Ctr., 1991-95; asst. prof. orthopedic surgery Johns Hopkins U., Balt., 1995-97; assoc. prof. Boston U., 1997-99; assoc. prof. orthop. surgery U. Miami, 2000—02, prof. orthop. surgery, 2002—. Assoc. editor Foot & Ankle; reviewer Jour. Bone and Joint Surgery, Jour. Am. Acad. Orthop. Surgeons. Served as aviator USN, 1969-72; Vietnam. Fellow ACS, Am. Acad. Orthopedic Surgeons, Am. Orthopedic Foot and Ankle Soc. (membership com. 1988-90, orthotics and prosthetics com. 1990-91, chmn. regional rev. subcom., 1993-96). Office: 900 NW 17th St Miami FL 33136-1119 E-mail: msmmdltjg@aol.com.

MIZER, RICHARD ANTHONY, technology company executive; b. San Francisco, Jan. 7, 1952; s. Conrad Xavier and Sally Jo (Hagan) M. BA in Bioengring. and Econs., U. Calif., San Diego, 1977. Founding ptnr. Microdoctors, Palo Alto, Calif., 1974-94; mgr., ptnr. K-Family Corp. dba Harlow's Night Club, Fremont, 1977-79, Restaurants Unique Inc. dba Bourbon St., Mountain View, 1980-83; engring. mgr. Pacific Bell, San Ramon, 1983-89, tech. staff advanced tech., 1989-92, developer advanced video svcs., 1992-96; asst. v.p. Nuko Info. Sys., Inc., San Jose, Calif., 1996-98; pres., CEO Digital Ventures Diversified Inc., 1998—. Exec. prodr.: Cinema of the Future sm, 1992; assoc. prodr. Soccer Fest: World Cup Soccer Final in HDTV to Europe and U.S. theaters from Pasadena Rose Bowl, 1994; exec. in chg. prodn. 50th Anniversary of Signing of UN Charter, 1995. Mem. security staff Republican Task Force, San Francisco, 1984, tech. staff U.S. Olympic Com., Los Angeles, 1984. Mem. IEEE, Nat. Assn. Broadcasters, Soc. Motion Picture and TV Engrs. (western region gov. 1999-2000). Roman Catholic. Avocations: martial arts, auto racing, skiing, triathlon. Office: Digital Ventures Diversified Inc 990 Richard Ave Ste 112 Santa Clara CA 95050-2828 E-mail: ramizer@wmr.com.

MIZGALA, HENRY F. physician, consultant, retired medical educator; b. Montreal, Nov. 28, 1932; s. Louis and Mary (Ropeleski) M.; m. Pauline Barbara Delaney, Oct. 26, 1957; children: Paul Stephen, Cynthia Louise, Liane Mary Mizgala Sizemore, Melanie Frances Mizgala Dressler, Nancy Elizabeth Mizgala Lewis. BA magna cum laude, Loyola Coll., Montreal, 1953; MD, C.M., McGill U., 1957. Rotating intern, then resident in medicine St. Mary's Hosp., Montreal, 1957-59, asst. physician, 1963-66; resident in medicine Royal Victoria Hosp., Montreal, 1959-60; Dazian fellow cardiology Mt. Sinai Hosp., N.Y.C., 1960-61, USPHS fellow cardiology, 1961-62; resident in cardiology Montreal Gen. Hosp., 1962-63, assoc. physician, 1966-74; asst. physician, cons. cardiology Lachine (Que.) Gen. Hosp., 1964-80; cardiologist Montreal Heart Inst., also dir. CCU, 1974-80; cons. Centre Hosp. Baie des Chaleurs, Gaspe, Que., 1975-80; hon. cons. Montreal Heart Inst., 1980—; prof. medicine U. B.C., 1980-97; hon. attending med. staff, cardiologist The Vancouver (B.C.) Hosp. and Health Scis. Ctr.; cons. B.C. Cancer Agy., Vancouver, 1981—; cons. staff Univ. Hosp., U. B.C. site, 1981-94; mem. faculty McGill U. Med. Sch., Montreal, 1968-74, asso. prof. medicine, 1973-74; assoc. prof., then prof. Montreal U. Med. Sch., 1974-81; prof. medicine, head div. cardiology U. B.C., 1980-87, prof. medicine emeritus, 1998—. Mem. editl. bd. Can. Jour. Cardiol. 1988-99, Jour. Am. Coll. Cardiology, 1992-95; contbr. numerous articles to med. jours. Fellow Royal Coll. Phys. and Surg. Can., Am. Coll. Cardiology, Am. Heart Assn. (council clin. cardiology); mem. Can. Med. Assn., Can. Cardiovascular Soc. (treas. 1974-90), Que. Med. Assn., B.C. Med. Assn., B.C. and Yukon Heart and Stroke Found. (bd. dirs., sr. bd. dirs.), Alpha Omega Alpha. Office: U BC Div Cardiology Dept Med 865 W 10th Ave Vancouver BC Canada V5Z IL7 E-mail: mhenry@interchange.ubc.ca.

MIZIOLEK, ANDRZEJ WLADYSLAW, research physicist; b. Hannover, Fed. Republic Germany, Feb. 17, 1950; s. Ryszard Roman and Irena (Stasinowska) M.; m. Karen Louise Beemon, Nov. 30, 1974 (div. K.L. Beemon); children: Nicole Alicia Beemon Miziolek, Claire Elizabeth Beemon Miziolek; m. Lucy B. Biggs, Oct. 10, 1998. BS in Chemistry magna cum laude, Wayne State U., 1971; PhD in Phys. Chemistry, U. Calif., Berkeley, 1976. Postgrad. rsch. chemist U. Calif., Irvine, 1976-77, asst. rsch. chemist San Diego, 1977-81; rsch. physicist U.S. Army Ballistic Rsch. Lab., Aberdeen Proving Ground, Md., 1981—; sci. advisor Office Naval Rsch., Arlington, Va., 1989; leader applied photochemistry and laser spectroscopy team U.S. Army Ballistic Rsch. Lab., Aberdeen Proving Ground, Md., 1985-95. Chmn. Jannaf Panel on Propellant Combustion, Laurel, Md., 1988; founder/co-chmn. Topical Mtg. in Laser Applications to Chem. Analysis, 1987, 90; chmn. mtg. Internat. Conf. Laser Induced Breakdown Spectroscopy (LIBS 2002). Contbr. 50 articles to profl. jours.; patentee resonance elemental detector; author 100 govt. reports; author: (book) Halon Replacements: Technology and Science, 1995; topical editor: Jour. Applied optics, 1996—. Recipient 3 outstanding achievement awards and 1st prize Army Sci. Conf., 1986, 88, 92. Fellow Optical Soc. Am. (chair tech. group fundamental and applied spectroscopy 1991-93, U.S. Army rep. on DOD Halon Replacement Program NGP 1996—, 10 outstanding army material pers. award 1999); mem. Am. Chem. Soc., Phi Beta Kappa, Sigma Xi. Avocations: piano, tennis, skiing, photography, video. Home: 117 Margate Rd Lutherville MD 21093-5838 Office: Army Rsch Lab AMSRL-WM-BD Aberdeen Proving Ground MD 21005 E-mail: miziolek@arl.army.mil.

MIZRAHI, ABRAHAM MORDECHAY, retired cosmetics and health care company executive, physician; b. Jerusalem, Apr. 16, 1929; came to U.S., 1952, naturalized, 1960; s. Solomon R. and Rachel (Haliwa) M.; m. Suzanne Eve Glasser, Mar. 15, 1956; children: Debra, Judith, Karen. BS, Manchester Coll., 1955; MD, Albert Einstein Coll. Medicine, 1960. Diplomate: Am. Bd. Pediatrics, Nat. Bd. Med. Examiners. Intern U. N.C., 1960-61; pediatric resident Columbia-Presbyn. Med. Center, N.Y.C., 1961-63, NIH fellow in neonatology, 1963-65; assoc. dir. Newborn Service Mt. Sinai Hosp., N.Y.C.; also dir. Newborn Service Elmhurst Med. Center, 1965-67; staff physician Geigy Pharm. Corp., N.Y.C., 1967-69, head cardio-pulmonary sect., 1969-71; sr. v.p. corp. med. affairs USV Pharm. Corp., Tuckahoe, N.Y., 1971-76; v.p. health and safety Revlon, Inc., N.Y.C., 1976-89, sr. v.p. human resources, 1989-94; ret., 1994. Assoc. in pediatrics Columbia U., 1963-67; cons. in neonatology Misericordia-Fordham Med. Ctr., 1967-89; clin. affiliate N.Y. Hosp.; clin. asst. prof. Cornell U. Med. Coll., 1982—. Contbr. articles to profl. jours. Trustee Westchester (N.Y.) Jewish Center. Mem. AMA, N.Y. State and County Med. Soc., Am., N.Y. acads. medicine, Am. Soc. Clin. Pharmacology and Therapeutics, Am. Pub. Health Assn., Am. Occupational Med. Assn. Home: 7 Jason Ln Mamaroneck NY 10543-2108 *The principles that have guided my life are old Biblical concepts. Firstly, that God had created Adam and Eve and all Men are, therefore, brothers and sisters. Secondly, God created Man and, therefore every human being has a spark of God in him. It, therefore, follows that killing diminshes God's presence on earth and saving of a human being increases His presence.*

MIZRAHI, EDWARD ALAN, allergist; b. Tyler, Tex., Aug. 24, 1945; BS in Econs., U. Pa., 1967; MD, U. Fla., 1972. Diplomate Am. Bd. Internal Medicine, Am. Bd. Allergy and Immunology. Intern Med. Coll. Ga., Augusta, 1972-73, resident, 1973-75; fellow Nat. Jewish Hosp., U. Colo., Denver, 1975-77; pvt. practice Jacksonville, Fla., 1977—. Physician Bapt. Med. Ctr., Jacksonville, Meml. Med. Ctr., Jacksonville, St. Luke's Med. Ctr., Jacksonville, St. Vincent's Med. Ctr., Jacksonville, Meth. Hosp., Jacksonville, Orange Park (Fla.) Med. Ctr. Mem. Am. Coll. Allergy, Asthma and Immunology, Am. Acad. Allergy, Asthma and Immunology, Fla. Med. Assn., Fla. Allergy, Asthma and Immunology Soc., Duval County Med. Soc., Southeastern Allergy Assn. Office: 3636 University Blvd S Ste B2 Jacksonville FL 32216-4223

MIZRAHI, LILLIAN, television producer; b. N.Y.C., Feb. 10, 1942; d. Herman and Deborah (Lewis) Tobinson; m. Silvano Mizrahi (div. June 1993); children: Monique, Alexander. Grad. h.s., Bronx, N.Y., 1958. Talent exec. Hour Mag., Hollywood, Calif., 1980-85, Lifestyles of the Rich and Famous, Hollywood, 1991, 94, 95, SAG Awards TV Spls., Hollywood, 1995-96, 98—, Global Olympic Village, U.S. Olympics, Atlanta, 1996, Nickelodean Big Help-a-Thon, Santa Monica, Calif., 1996; fund raiser various TV shows and spl. events. Pres. Parents Assn., Buckley Sch., Sherman Oaks, Calif., 1989-90; vol. J. Paul Getty Mus., L.A., 1997; vol. docent Assistance League, L.A., 1992. Mem. NATAS (activities com. 1982-86, mem. Blue Ribbon Panels of Emmy voters), WIF. Democrat. Jewish.

MIZRUCHI, MARK SHELDON, sociology and business administration educator; b. New Haven, Dec. 10, 1953; s. Ephraim Harold and Ruth (Trachtenberg) M.; m. Katherine Teves, June 17, 1981 (div. June 1995); 1 child, Joshua. BA, Washington U., 1975; MA, SUNY, Stony Brook, 1977, PhD, 1980. Statis. analyst Albert Einstein Coll. of Medicine, Bronx, N.Y., 1980-83, asst. prof. psychiatry, 1981-87, supr. statis. svcs., 1983-87; asst. prof. sociology Columbia U., N.Y.C., 1987-89, assoc. prof. sociology, 1989-91; prof. sociology and bus. adminstrn. U. Mich., Ann Arbor, 1991—. Author: The American Corporate Network, 1904-1974, 1982, The Structure of Corporate Political Action, 1992; editor (with M. Schwartz) Intercorporate Relations, 1987. Recipient Presdl. Young Investigator award NSF, 1988-93; grantee NSf, 1987-88, 93-95, 94-95; invited fellow Ctr. for Advanced Study in the Behavioral Scis., 1989. Mem. Am. Sociol. Assn., Acad. Mgmt., Internat. Network for Social Network Analysis, Sociol. Rsch. Assn. Office: Dept Sociology Univ Mich Ann Arbor MI 48109-1382

MIZUGUCHI, NORMAN, state senator; b. Hilo, Hawaii, May 26, 1939; m. Harriet Mizuguchi; 1 child, Reid. BS, Springfield Coll.; MS, Mich. State U.; PhD, U. Utah. Mem. state house State of Hawaii, 1974-78, state senator, 1978—2000, pres. state senate, 1994—2000; pres. Hawaiian Emporium Inc., Sundance Circle Inc.; tchr., edn. officer Dept. of Edn. Sec. Pearl city Makule Softball League; mem. Barbers Point coun., Navy League, Hawaiian Edn. Coun., Hui Kokua Kinipopo Booster Club, Japanese Am. Citizens League Honolulu, Aiea Hongwanji. Democrat.*

MJOLSNESS, RAYMOND CHARLES, retired physicist, researcher; b. Chgo., Apr. 22, 1933; s. Raymond and Emma Pearl (McCormick) Veseth; m. Patricia M. McGeary, Oct. 6, 1957; children: Eric, Ingrid, Kirsten. BA, Reed Coll., 1953, Oxford (Eng.) U., 1955; PhD, Princeton U., 1963. Rsch. assoc. Los Alamos (N.Mex.) Nat. Lab., 1958-61; asst. prof. math. Reed Coll., Portland, Oreg., 1961-62; staff scientist GE Space Sci. Ctr., King of Prussia, Pa., 1962-63; staff mem. Los Alamos Nat. Lab., 1963-67; assoc. prof. astronomy Pa. State U., State College, 1967-69; staff mem. Los Alamos Nat. Lab., 1969-92. Adj. prof. physics Los Alamos Nat. Lab., 1983-84. Contbr. articles to profl. jours. including Phys. Rev., Physics of Fluids, Turbulent Shear Flow II. Mem. Am. Phys. Soc. Achievements include research in plasma stability theory and collision theory, electron-atom and electron-molecule collisions, cosmology, hydrodynamics (turbulence, stability theory, code development, low gravity flows), and foundations of quantum mechanics. Avocations: jogging, weightlifting, music, chess, investing. Home: 207 Dos Brazos St Los Alamos NM 87544-2426

MKHITARIAN, MARINE, chemical engineer; b. Moscow, Russia, Apr. 14, 1956; d. Artavazd and Elena Mkhitarian; m. Aleksan Martirosian, Sept. 25, 1981 (dec. Mar. 1994); 1 child, Hrachia. BS in Chem. Tech., Polytech. U., Yerevan, Armenia, 1979; MS, Mendeleev Inst. Chem. Tech., Moscow, 1991. Sr. R&D chemist Plastpolymer, Yerevan, Armenia, 1979-92; technologist

Docdata Calif., Canoga Park, 1995-99; mastering and quality control supr. Crest Nat., L.A., 1999—. Contbr. articles to profl. jours. Fellow Am. Inst. Chemists; mem. AIChE, Am. Chem. Soc., Soc. Plastics Engrs. Avocations: reading, travel, music. Home: Apt A 1528 N Harvard Blvd Los Angeles CA 90027 Office: Crest Nat 6721 Romaine St Hollywood CA 90038 E-mail: marinem@msn.com.

MKPARU, FIDELIS OKECHUKWU, cardiologist, educator, consultant; b. Onitsha, Nigeria, Mar. 18, 1959; s. Dennis and Virginia (Ezeoke) Mkparu. BS, SUNY, Albany, 1982; MD, Meharry Med. Sch., 1987. Diplomate Am. Bd. Internal Medicine, Am. Bd. Cardiovasc. Disease. Intern Ind. U., Indpls., 1987-88, resident in internal medicine, 1988-90; fellow in cardiology U. Conn., Farmington, 1990-93, NIH rsch. fellow, 1990-92; fellow in cardiology Harvard U. Med. Sch., Boston, 1993-94; assoc. dir. cardiovasc. dept., cardiovasc. cons. Procter & Gamble, Cin., 1994-95; dir. heart failure Ohio Heart Care, Inc., Canton, 1996—; asst. prof. cardiology, cardiology cons. N.E. Ohio U. Coll. Medicine, Rootstown, 1996—. Contbr. articles to med. jours. Vol. Mended Hearts, Alliance, Ohio, 1996—, Am. Heart Assn., Canton, 1996—. Recipient Merck award Merck Pharm., 1993. Fellow Am. Coll. Angiology, Am. Coll. Cardiology (travel award 1993), Am. Coll. Chest Physicians; mem. AMA, Am. Assn. Nuclear Cardiology. Roman Catholic. Avocations: soccer, photography, hiking, poetry. Home: 5821 Loma Linda Ln NE Canton OH 44721-3929 Office: 5821 Loma Linda Ln NE Canton OH 44721-3929 E-mail: fom@neoucom.edu.

MKRYAN, SONYA, geophysicist, researcher, educator; b. Beyrouth, Lebanon, Mar. 1, 1935; arrived in U.S., 1979; m. Vahram and Marie (Topalian) Faradjian; m. Karapet Mkryan, Apr. 11, 1970; children: Marine, Anahit, Lusine. MS in Physics, Pedagogical Inst., 1956; PhD in Tech. Scis., Tbilicy State U., 1970. Physics, math. tchr. H.S., Ghaltakchi, 1956-57; librarian Ores Dept., Leninakan, Armenia, 1957-60; geophycist, rschr. Inst. of Geophysics Engrng. Seismology, 1960-70; assoc. prof. of physics Polytech. Inst., Kirovakan, Armenia, 1970-79; mech. inspector Robertshaw Co., Anaheim, Calif., 1980-82; tchr. Pasadena (Calif.) Sch. Dist., 1983-86; eligibility worker, acting supr. Dept. of Pub. Svcs., Glendale, Calif., 1986-97; social worker in home supportive svcs., 1997-2001. Author: (poetry) Ups and Downs of Life, 1987, Incessant Melodies, 1992, Light and Darkness, 1997, (novels) Eternities Travelers, 1998;one-woman shows include Tekeyan Gallere, Pasadena, Calif., 1989, Pasadena Union of Marash Armenians Hall, 1982—95, exhibited in group shows at Altadena, Pasadena, Downey, Glendale, Ambassador Hotel, L.A. (2d prize, 1987), Wilshir Ebel, 1988. Bd. dirs. Sahag-Mesrob Armenian Christian Sch. Mem. Armenian Writers Union in Calif., Internat. Soc. of Poets, Nat. Libr. of Poets, Armenian Allied Arts Assn. (First prize 1982, 84, 85, 87, 91), Armenian Radio and TV Com. Avocations: writing, walking, reading, cooking, dancing. Home: 2723 N Lake Ave Altadena CA 91001-1903

MLAY, MARIAN, retired government official; b. Pitts., Sept. 11, 1935; AB, U. Pitts., 1957; postgrad., Princeton U., 1969-70; JD, Am. U., 1977. Mgmt. intern HEW, Washington, 1961-70, dep. dir. Chgo. region, 1971-72, dir. divsn. consol. funding, 1972-73; dep. dir. office policy devel. and planning USPHS, 1973-77; dir. program evaluation EPA, 1978-9, dep. dir. office of drinking water, 1979-84, dir. office of ground water protection, 1984-91, dir. oceans and coastal protection, 1991-95; sr. rsch. assoc. Nat. Acad. Pub. Adminstrn., 1995-97; ret., 1997. Contbr. articles to profl. jours., chpts. to books. Bd. dirs. D.C. United Fund, 1979-80, New Dominion Chorale, 2001--, Davis Meml. Goodwill Book Com., 1999-2002. Princeton U. fellow, 1969-70; recipient Career Edn. award Nat. Inst. Public Affairs, 1960. Mem. ABA, D.C. Bar Assn. (co-chair steering com. energy, environ. and natural resources sect.). Home: 3747 1/2 Kanawha St NW Washington DC 20015-1838 E-mail: mmlay@erols.com.

MLOCK, MARY, employee benefits professional; b. Troy, N.Y., Jan. 18, 1957; AS, Hudson Valley C.C., 1977; BBA, Siena Coll., 1979. CPA, N.Y. Tax mgr. Bollam Sheedy Torani, Albany, N.Y., 1987-94, mgr. employee benefits, 1994-96; ptnr. Oxford Assocs. LLP, 1997—. Office: Oxford Assocs LLP 26 Computer Dr W Ste 5 Albany NY 12205-1694

MLOTEK, HERMAN VICTOR, former religious education educator; b. Poland, Apr. 8, 1922; arrived in Can., 1932; came to U.S., 1939, naturalized, 1949; s. Shlomo Zalmen and Rose (Goldkind) M.; m. Estelle Weiss, Nov. 23, 1947; children: David Benjamin, Alan Steven. BS, De Paul U., 1946; postgrad., Hebrew Theol. Coll., Skokie, Ill., 1939-47, Roosevelt U., 1956-57, Nat. Coll. Edn., 1978. Ordained rabbi, 1952; cert. elem., secondary, jr. coll. tchr. and supr., Ill. Prin. Beth Itzchok Sch., Chgo., 1947-62, Albany Park Day Sch., Chgo., 1949-51, Albany Park-Beth Itzchok Sch., Chgo., 1962-64, Lincolnwood (Ill.). Jewish Congregation, 1964-73; tchr. Chgo. Pub. Schs., 1973-92, ret., 1992. Mem. Am. Fedn. Tchrs., Ill. Fedn. Tchrs., Chgo. Tchrs. Union, Religious Zionists Chgo., Agudath Isreal Ill., Associated Talmud Torah Chgo., World Jewish Congress. Avocations: chess, reading, walking. Home: 6234 N Lawndale Ave Chicago IL 60659-1104

MLSNA, KATHRYN KIMURA, lawyer; b. Yonkers, N.Y., Apr. 23, 1952; d. Eugene T. and Grace Kimura; m. Timothy Martin Misna; children: Lauren Marie, Matthew Christopher, Michael Timothy. BA, Northwestern U., 1974, JD, 1977. Bar: Ill. 1977, U.S. Dist. Ct. (no. dist.) Ill. 1977. Mng. counsel McDonald's Corp., Oak Brook, Ill., 1977—. Speaker in field. Contbr. chpt. to book. Bd. dirs. Japanese Am. Svc. Com.; mem. adv. bd. intellectual property DePaul U. Sch. Law, 1999—. Mem. ABA, Ill. Bar Assn., Chgo. Bar Assn., Asian Am. Bar Assn. (bd. dirs. 1996-98), Promotion Mktg. Assn. (v.p. 1988-92, chmn., pres. 1992-93, chmn. integrated mktg. com. 1993-94, chmn. assn. alliance com., co-chair legal and govtl. affairs com.), Northwestern U. Alumni Assn. (officer, bd. dirs. 1994-98). Office: McDonald's Corp 1 Mcdonalds Plz Oak Brook IL 60523-1911

MNYUKH, YURI, physicist; b. Moscow, Oct. 13, 1926; came to U.S., 1977; s. Vladimir K. and Ester K. (Shneidman) M.; m. Ninel Panfilova, 1960 (separated); 1 child, Anna. M. in Physics and Engrng., Physic and Engrng. Coll., Moscow, 1950; PhD in Physic and Math., Acad. of Sci., Moscow, 1959. Sr. engr. Rsch. Inst. Plastics, Moscow, 1950-54; rsch. scientist USSR Acad. of Sci. Inst. Elementoorganic Compounds, 1954-64; head of lab. USSR Acad. of Sci. Inst. Biophysics, Puschino, 1964-73; rsch. scientist NYU, N.Y.C., 1978—. Mem. sci. bd. USSR Acad. of Sci. Inst. Biophysics, Puschino, 1964-73. Contbr. articles to Jour. Physics and Chemistry of Solids, Jour. of Crystal Growth, Molecular Crystals and Liquid Crystals, Doklady of the USSR Acad. of Scis. Mem. Moscow Watch Helsinki Group, 1976-77. Mem. Am. Phys. Soc. Achievements include discovery of some basic phenomena of crystal-crystal phase transitions including growth of well-shaped single crystals in crystals, layer-by-layer mode of the rearrangements, non-anomalous nature of "lambda-anomalies"; development of general concept of solid-solid phase transitions as a variation of usual crystal growth, involving nucleation, interface, mode of molecular rearrangement, kinetics, and the relation to ferromagnetism and ferroelectricity. Office: NYU 29 Washington Pl New York NY 10003-6630

MO, LUKE WEI, physicist, educator; b. Shangtung, China, June 3, 1934; s. Si-leng and Shu-feng (Lo) M.; m. Doris Chang, Dec. 31, 1960; children: Curtis L., Alice. BS in Elec. Engrng. Nat. Taiwan U., 1955; MS in Physics, Nat. Tsinghua U., Taiwan, 1959; PhD, Columbia U., 1963. Research asso. Columbia U., N.Y.C., 1963-64; research physicist Stanford (Calif.) Linear Accelerator, 1965-69; asst. prof. physics U. Chgo., 1969-76; prof. physics Va. Poly. Inst. and State U., Blacksburg, 1976—. Contbr. articles to profl. jours. Served with Taiwan Air Force, 1955-56. Recipient Alumni Research Excellence award Va. Poly. Inst. and State U., 1980, Guggenheim fellow, 1981, NSF grantee, 1969— Fellow Am. Phys. Soc. Office: Va Poly Inst Dept Physics 315 Robeson Hall Blacksburg VA 24061-0435

MO, ROGER SHIH-YAH, electronics engineering manager; b. Shanghai, Rep. of China, Mar. 10, 1939; s. Maurice Chun-Dat and Mary (Shen) M.; m. Amy Chun-Muh Chang, June 21, 1964; 1 child, Karen Voong-Tsun. BSEE, MIT, 1962; MSEE, Northeastern U., Boston, 1964, PhD, 1967; MBA, Pepperdine U., 1980. Engr. Raytheon Corp., Sudbury, Mass., 1967-69; on tech. staff Xerox, El Segundo, Calif., 1969-74, mgr. memory, 1974-77, mgr. cirs. and subsystems, 1977-81, area mgr., 1981-87, program mgr., 1987-89, imaging systems mgr., 1989-92, systems design mgr., 1992—. Sr. lectr. West Coast U., L.A., 1978-87, chmn. acad. standards com., 1981-82. Contbr. articles to profl. jours. Bd. dirs. The Wellness Community So. Bay Cities, 1989-96, The Pacific Views Homeowners Assn., 1996—. Mem. IEEE, Chinese Am. Assn. of So. Calif. (bd. dirs. 1983-87). Lodges: Flip Flap (local chmn. 1974, nat. chmn. 1976). Democrat. Roman Catholic. Avocations: golf, table tennis, photography. Home: 6852 Verde Ridge Rd Palos Verdes Peninsula CA 90275-4638 Office: Xerox Corp 701 S Aviation Blvd El Segundo CA 90245-4898

MO, SUCHOON, psychology educator; b. Nagoya, Japan, Apr. 19, 1932; came to U.S., 1955; s. Chihyun and Oksil (Kim) M.; m. Mary Madeleine Lang; children: Blaise, Bernard; m. Judith Carol Oslick, Dec. 26, 1969; childrn: Sage, Daisy, Clifton. BS, Idaho State Coll., 1959; PhD, U. Pa., 1968. Asst. prof. U. Detroit, 1967-73; prof. U. So. Colo., Pueblo, 1973—. Avocation: Taekwondo (martial art). Home: 1158 S Yerba Santa Dr Pueblo West CO 81007-1947 Office: Psychology Dept U So Colo Pueblo CO 81001

MO, YI-LUNG, structural engineering educator; b. Taichung, Taiwan, Aug. 28, 1955; s. Tzai-Nan and In-Fang (Teng) M.; m. Grace H.C. Wu, Sept. 26, 1985; children: Steven, Sophia. BS, Nat. Cheng Kung U., 1977; MS, Nat. Taiwan U., 1979; PhD, U. Hannover, Germany, 1982; MS, DePaul U., 1989. Assoc. prof. Nat. Cheng Kung U., Tainan, 1991-94, prof., 1994-2000; rsch. asst. Nat. Taiwan U., Taipei, 1977-79, U. Hannover, 1979-82; postdoctoral rsch. assoc. U. Houston, 1982-84; structural engrng. designer Sargent & Lundy Engrs., Chgo., 1984-89, engrng. analyst, 1989-91; rsch. prof. U. Houston, 1999-2000, prof. dept. civil and environ. engrng., 2000—. Alexander von Humboldt vis. prof. U. Hannover, 1995; vis. engr. Korean Power Engrng. Co., Seoul, 1990; vis. scholar Stanford U., 1998. Author: Dynamic Behavior of Concrete Structures, 1994. Recipient Disting. Rsch. award Nat. Sci. Coun., Taiwan, 1999, Rsch. Creativity award, 2000; scholar Friedrich Ebert Stiftung, 1982, Prestressed System Inc., 1982-84; Alexander von Humboldt Rsch. fellow, Germany, 1995. Fellow Alexander von Humboldt Stiftung, Germany; mem. ASCE, Am. Concrete Inst., Am. Biog. Inst. Rsch. Assn., Internat. Assn. for Bridge and Structural Engrng., Internat. Biog. Assn. England, N.Y. Acad. Sci. Office: Dept Civil Environ Engrng U Houston Houston TX 77204-4003 E-mail: yilungmo@egr.uh.edu.

MOAG, RODNEY FRANK, language educator, country music singer; b. Warsaw, Oct. 15, 1936; s. Hugh Alexander and Imogene (Hodges) M.; m. Rachel Ann Foley, Feb. 9, 1964 (div. Aug. 1974); children: Robin Gray, Hugh Daniel, Jeffry Lee. BS, Syracuse U., 1961; MA, U. Wis., 1966, PhD, 1973. Dir. college preparatory program for visually impaired U. Mo., Columbia, 1974; vis. Fulbright prof. U. South Pacific, Suva, Fiji Islands, 1975-78; vis. assoc. prof. U. Mich., Ann Arbor, 1978-80, adj. prof., 1981, vis. assoc. prof., 1982; sr. lectr. U. Tex., Austin, 1981, 83-90, assoc. prof., 1990—. Author: (texts) Fiji Hindi, 1977, Malayalam, 1986; country music artist: several records, 3 CDs, 1995, 2000, 2002. Mng. dir. Amateur Radio Repeaters of Washtenaw, 1984-86; pres. Mich. Repeater Coun., 1985-88; v.p. Austin Amateur Radio Club, 1993-94; vol. programmer, KO-OP. Mem. Ctrl. Tex. Bluegrass Assn., Austin Amateur Radio Club, Austin Repeater Orgn., Tex. VHF FM Soc. Avocations: amateur radio, country and bluegrass music. Home: 6909 Miranda Dr Austin TX 78752-3119 Office: Univ Tex Dept Asian Studies WCH 4.134 Austin TX 78712 E-mail: rodmoag@texas.net., rmoag@mail.utexas.edu.

MOAK, ELIZABETH, performing pianist; b. Oxford, Miss. d. Franklin E. and Helen H. Moak; m. Jean-Claude Coquempot. MusB in Piano Performance, Peabody Conservatory, 1983, MusM in Piano Performance, 1985; Diplôme de Virtuosité, Neuchâtel Conservatory, Switzerland, 1989. Prof. music/piano Millsaps Coll., Jackson, Miss., 1996—. Performing classical pianist in concert series with orch., on radio, other masterclasses. Theodore Presser Found. fellow, 1993. Mem. Music Tchrs. Nat. Assn., Mu Phi Epsilon Found. (bd. dirs.), Mu Phi Epsilon (winner Internat. Competition 1995). Office: Millsaps Coll PO Box 150693 1701 N State St Jackson MS 39210-0002

MOATES, G. PAUL, lawyer; b. May 26, 1947; s. Guy Hart and Virginia Rose (Mayolett) Moates; m. Constance A. Sadler. BA, Amherst Coll., 1969; JD, U. Chgo., 1975. Bar: Ill. 1975, D.C. 1976, U.S. Ct. Appeals (D.C. cir.) 1976, U.S. Supreme Ct. 1980, U.S. Ct. Appeals (6th cir.) 1984, U.S. Ct. Appeals (3d cir.) 1991, U.S. Ct. Appeals (7th cir.) 1993. Assoc. Sidley & Austin, Washington, 1975—82, ptnr., 1982—. Contbr. articles to profl. jours. Mem.: ABA, D.C. Bar Assn., Ill. Bar Assn. Office: Sidley Austin Brown & Wood 1501 K Street NW Washington DC 20005

MOATS, PATRICK ANDREW, poet; b. Norfolk, Nebr., Jan. 5, 1958; s. Myron L. and Nylotis (Overhue) M.; children: Jessica Lynn Kugler. Student, Northeast Cmty. Coll., Norfolk, 1975, Cen. Cmty. Coll., Nebr., 1984-85, student, 1999, So. Idaho U., 2001. Foreman The Svc. Co., Lexington, Nebr., 1987-88; driver Omaha World Herald, 1988-90, Nebraskaland Express, Norfolk, 1990-91; foreman, driver Pole Maintenance Co., Columbus, 1992-98; truck driver Werner Enterprises, Omaha, 1999-2000; driver liberty Ctr., Norfolk, 2000—; cmty. support specialist S.L. Start and Assocs., Inc., Twin Falls, Idaho, 2001—. Contbr. poetry to anthologies including Am. Poetry Ann., Inspirations, Seasons of Change, Journeys, The Times News, Twin Falls, 2001—. Vol., supporter Faith for Today, Nat. ARbor Day Found., Nat. Camps for Blind Children, Native Evangelism Initiative, Family First, The Norfolk Rescue Mission, ARC, Twin Falls, 2001. Mem. Internat. Soc. Poets. Avocations: mission ministry work, reading, writing, gardening, stamp and coin collecting.

MOBASHER, MAHER ATTIA, academic administrator; b. Elsharkia, Egypt, Dec. 10, 1940; came to U.S., 1970; m. Salwa Fekry Elnakib, June 19, 1983; children: Ahmed, Samer. B in Commerce, Ain Shams U., Egypt, 1963; D in Econs. & Social Devel., Inst. Nat. Devel., Egypt, 1966; MS in acctg., L.I. U., 1975; D in Bus. Adminstrn., Nova Southeastern U., 1995. Acctg. supr. Gen. Orgn. Commerce, Cairo, 1963-70; internal auditor Emigrant Savings Bank, N.Y.C., 1970-73; bank examiner European Am. Bank, 1973-77; comptroller Cmty. Action. Com. Danbury, Conn., 1977-79; budget ops. mgr. CUNY, Bklyn., 1979-89, bus. mgr., asst. adminstr. Bronx C.C. Bronx, 1989—. Scholar Inst. Nat. Planning, 1964-66; Rsch. grantee Bronx C.C. Found., 1994. Mem. Am. Mgmt. Assn., Am. Assn. Univ. Adminstrs., Nat. Coun. C.C. Bus. Officials, C.C. Bus. Officers Assn., Assn. Coll. Adminstrn. Profls. Office: Bronx CC 181 and University Bronx NY 10453

MOBASHERY, SHAHRIAR, chemist; b. May 17, 1958; BS in Biol. Scis., U. So. Calif., L.A., 1980, BS in Chemistry, 1981; PhD, U. Chgo., 1985. Rschr. Rockefeller U., 1986-88; asst. prof. Wayne State U., Detroit, 1989-94, assoc. prof., 1994-97, chair divsn. biochemistry, dept. chemistry, 1996—, prof. chemistry, 1997—, prof. dept. pharmacology, biochemistry and molecular biology, 2000—, dir. Inst. Drug Design, 2000—. Cons. Salk Inst., 1989-92, Affymax Corp., 1996-98, Procter & Gamble Pharm., 1997-98, Aurora Bioscis., 1998-2000, Guilford Pharm., 2000—; mem. sci. adv. bd. New Biotics, Inc., 2001--; mem. adv. com. biochemistry and endocrinology Am. Cancer Soc., 1994-96, 99-2000; mem. bioorganics and natural products study sect. NIH, 2001--; chmn. numerous symposia; speaker in field. Co-author: Resolving the Antibiotic Paradox: Progress in Understanding Drug Resistance and Development of New Antibiotics, 1998; mem. editl. bd. Pharmaceutical and Medicinal Chemistry, 1995—, Jour. Antibiotics, 1998—, Antimicrobial Agents Chemotherapy, 1999—, Bioorganic Chemistry, 2000—, Organic Synthesis, 2002--, Letters Organic Chemistry, 2002--, Letters Drug Design and Discovery, 2002--, Mini Revs. in Organic Chemistry, 2002--; ad hoc reviewer numerous jours. and orgns.; contbr. articles to profl. jours.; patentee in field. Mem. AAAS, Am. Chem. Soc., Am. Soc. Microbiology, Sigma Xi. Office: Wayne State U Dept Chemistry Detroit MI 48202 E-mail: som@chem.wayne.edu.

MOBBS, SIR GERALD NIGEL, property investment executive; b. Birmingham, Eng., Sept. 22, 1937; s. Gerald Aubrey and Elizabeth (Lanchester) M.; m. Pamela Jame Marguerite Berry, Sept. 14, 1961; children: Christopher William, (twins) Virginia Elizabeth and Penelope Helen. Student, Oxford (Eng.) U., 1956-59; DSc (hon.), City Univ., London, 1988; D Univ (hon.), U. Buckingham, Eng., 1993; LLD (hon.), Reading U., 2000. Exec. Slough (Eng.) Estates plc, 1960-63, dir., 1963-71, mng. dir., 1971-76, chmn., CEO, 1976-99; chmn. Bovis Homes, 1999—. Chmn. Charterhouse Group, London, 1977-83; bd. dirs. Howard of Walden Estates, London, Barclays Bank, London, Kingfisher plc, London, chmn., 1995-96. Pres. Brit. Property Fedn., London, 1979-81; chmn. Property Services Agy., Adv. Bd., London, 1980-86, U. Buckingham, 1987-98; mem. Commonwealth War Graves Commn., London, 1988-97; mem. constrn. task force DETR, 1997-98; Lord Lt. of Buckinghamshire, 1997—; chmn. Wembley Task Force, 1999—; commnr. Royal Hosp. Chelsea, 2000—. Mem. RICS (hon.), Comm. on Corporate Governance. Office: Slough Estates plc 234 Bath Rd Slough SL1 4EE England

MOBERG, DAVID OSCAR, sociology educator; b. Montevideo, Minn., Feb. 13, 1922; s. Fred Ludwig and Anna E. (Sundberg) M.; m. Helen H. Heitzman, Mar. 16, 1946 (dec. Oct. 16, 1992); children: David Paul, Lynette, Jonathan, Philip; m. Marlys Taege, July 23, 1994. AA, Bethel Jr. Coll., 1942; AB, Seattle Pacific Coll., 1947; MA, U. Wash., 1949; PhD, U. Minn., 1952. Assoc. instr. U. Wash., Seattle, 1948-49; faculty Bethel Coll., St. Paul, 1949-68, prof. sociology, 1959-68, chmn. dept. social scis., 1952-68; prof. sociology Marquette U., Milw., 1968-91, prof. emeritus, 1991—, chmn. dept. sociology and anthropology, 1968-77. Cons. Nat. Liberty Found., 1970-71, Fetzer Inst., 1995-96; rsch. cons. Internat. Luth. Women's Missionary League, 1997-99, Bonnie Walker & Assocs., 1997-99; cons. Nat. Interfaith Coalition on Aging, 1973-75, mem. nat. adv. bd., 1980-89; guest rschr. Sociology of Religion Inst., Stockholm, summer 1978; adj. prof. San Francisco Theol. Sem., 1964-73, McCormick Theol. Sem., 1975-78, 81-82; vis. prof. U. So. Calif., 1979, Princeton Theol. Sem., 1979, So. Bapt. Theol. Sem., 1982, Soc. for Care of the Handicapped in the Gaza Strip of Palestine, 1995; mem. adv. bd. Ecumenical Ministry with Mature Adults, 1983-92; resource scholar Christianity Today Inst., 1985—; mem. bd. adv. editors Haworth Pastoral Press, 1998—. Author: The Church as A Social Institution, 1962, 2d edit. 1984, (with Robert M. Gray) The Church and the Older Person, 1962, 2d edit., 1977, Inasmuch: Christian Social Responsibility in the 20th Century, 1965, White House Conference on Aging: Spiritual Well-Being Background and Issues, 1971, The Great Reversal: Evangelism and Social Concern, 1972, 2d edit, 1977, Wholistic Christianity, 1985, Woman of God: An Assessment of the Spirituality of Women in the LCMS, 1999; also articles, chpts. in symposia.; editor: International Directory of Religious Information Systems, 1971, Spiritual Well-Being: Sociological Perspectives, 1979, Rev. Religious Research, 1968-72, Jour. Am. Sci. Affiliation, 1962-64, Adris Newsletter, 1971-76, Aging and Spirituality: Spiritual Dimensions of Aging Theory, Research, Practice, and Policy, 2001; co-editor Research in the Social Scientific Study of Religion, 1986—; assoc. editor: Social Compass, 1968—; mem. editl. bd. Christian Univ. Press, 1979-84, Perspectives on Sci. and Christian Faith, 1988—; consulting editor Calif. Sociologist, 1982-96. Fulbright lectr. U. Groningen, Netherlands, 1957-58, Fulbright lectr. Muenster U., West Germany, 1964-65. Fellow Am. Sci. Affiliation (editor jour. 1962-64, publs. com. 1984-91, social ethics com. 1985-88, program chair 1995-96), Gerontol. Soc. Am.; mem. Am. Sociol. Assn., Internat. Sociol. Assn. (sociology of religion rsch. com. 1972—), Wis. Sociol. Assn. (pres. 1969-71), Midwest Sociol. Assn. (Wis. bd. dirs. 1971-73), Assn. Devel. Religious Info. Sys. (coord. ADRIS 1971—, editor ADRIS newsletter 1971-76), Religious Rsch. Assn. (editor Rev. Religious Rsch. 1968-72, contbg. editor 1973-77, assoc. editor 1983—, bd. dirs. 1959-61, 68-72, pres. 1981-82, H. Paul Douglass lectr. 1986), Assn. for Sociology of Religion (exec. coun. 1971-73, pres. 1976-77), Soc. for Sci. Study Religion (exec. coun. 1971-74, sr. editl. cons. SSSR-RRA History Project 1995-99), Evangelicals for Social Action (planning com. 1973-75), Christian Sociol. Soc. (steering com. 1973-81, newsletter lit. reviewer 1981-93), Family Rsch. Coun. (assoc. 1985-88, rsch. network 1989-98), Psychologists Interested in Religious Issues (profl. affiliate 1984-99), Univ. Faculty for Life, Midwest Coun. for Social Rsch. on Aging (fellow 1961-64, 87—), Am. Soc. on Aging, Forum on Religion and Aging, Fairview Elder Enterprises (bd. dirs. 1989—). Home and Office: 7120 W Dove Ct Milwaukee WI 53223-2766 E-mail: david.moberg@marquette.edu. *As I try to live with eternity's values in view, my entire lifetime seems to grow ever briefer, not longer.*

MOBERLY, ELIZABETH ROSAMUND, archaeologist, educator; b. Caterham, England, Sept. 18, 1949; came to U.S., 1987; d. Robert Basil and Eliza Maria (Gitmans) M. BA with honors, Oxford U., England, 1972, MA, 1975, DPhil, 1977. Dir. psychosexual edn. & therapy BCM Internat., Upper Darby, Pa., 1989-95, dir. cancer & immune deficiency crisis project, 1995-99; archaeologist/dir. freelance, 1999—. Author: Suffering, Innocent and Guilty, 1978, Psychogenesis, 1983, Homosexuality: A New Christian Ethic, 1983, The Psychology of Self and Other, 1985; co-author: A New Dictionary of Christian Ethics, 1986, Breaking Out, 1986, Lent for Busy People, 1987, New Dictionary of Christian Ethics and Pastoral Theology, 1995; author of poems; contbr. articles to profl. jours. Mem. Am. Assn. Christian Counselors, Internat. Soc. Cryptozoology, Christian Legal Soc., Assn. Christian Therapists, Soc. Study of Indigenous Langs. of the Ams. Avocations: international and historical cuisine, poetry, languages, holistic healthcare. Home: PO Box 348 Upper Darby PA 19082-0348

MOBERLY, LINDEN EMERY, educational administrator; b. Laramie, Wyo., Jan. 4, 1923; s. Linden E. and Ruth (Gathercole) M. BS, Coll. Emporia, 1952; MS, Kans. State Tchrs. Coll., 1954; m. Viola F. Mosher, Apr. 29, 1949. Tchr. sci., Florence, Kans., 1952-54, Concordia, Kans., 1954-56, Grand Junction, Colo., 1957-60; asst. prin. Orchard Mesa Jr. High Sch., Grand Junction, 1960-66, prin., 1967-84; field cons. Nat. Assn. Secondary Sch. Prins., 1985—. Sgt. USMC, 1941-46. Recipient Outstanding Secondary Prin. award Colo. Assn. Sch. Execs., 1978. Mem. NEA, VFW, Nat. Assn. Secondary Prins. (bd. dir. 1979-83), Colo. Edn. Assn. (bd.dir. 1968-71), Colo. North Central Assn. Colls. and Secondary Schs., Colo. Assn. Secondary Sch. Prins. (bd. dir. 1974-77), Lions, Sons of the Revolution, Marine Corps League (life), VFW (life), Masons (award of Excellence 1990). Home: 2256 Kingston Rd Grand Junction CO 81503-1221

MOBLEY, CLARENCE FOWLER, retired civil engineer; b. Johnston, S.C., Apr. 24, 1921; s. Clarence Fowler Mobley and Anna Juanita (Williams) Mobley McCreight; m. Hazel Cleo Shankel, May 28, 1948 (dec. Feb. 1976); children: Richard Alan, Robert Steven; m. Annie Long Smith, Dec. 19, 1986 (dec. Apr. 1990). BSCE, U. S.C., Columbia, 1942; cert. in mgmt., USN, Monterey, Calif., 1958; MBA, U. San Francisco, 1978. Registered profl. engr., Calif. Jr. civil engr. U.S. Tenn. Authority Valley, Knoxville, Tenn., 1942; commd. ensign USN, 1943, advanced through grades to comdr., 1968; pub. works officer Civil Engr. Corps, USN, Hawthorne, Nev., 1955-58; exec. officer USN Housing Activity, Yokohama, Japan, 1960-63; asst. pub. works officer San Francisco Bay Naval Shipyard, 1965-68; asst. engr. City of Daly City, Calif., 1968-69, engr., supr. water divsn., 1969-70, city engr., 1977-78, city engr., pub. works dir., 1979-82, ret., 1982. Contbr. articles to We. Cosntrn., USN Civil Engr. Corps Bull., Engrng. News Record, The Rocket. Mem. ASCE, Soc. Am. Mil. Engrs. (treas. Seattle chpt. 1959-60), Calif. Soc. Profl. Engrs. (sec. 1970-72), Masons, Toastmasters Internat. Republican. Home: 91 Fairmont Dr Daly City CA 94015-3072

MOBLEY, CLEON MARION, JR. (CHIP MOBLEY), physics educator, real estate executive; b. Reidsville, Ga., July 14, 1940; s. Cleon M. and Lucile (Anderson) M.; m. Martha Hewlett, 1962 (div. 1970); children: Lisa Anne, Arthur Marion; m. Delia Braswell, 1997. AS, So. Poly. U., 1961; BS, Oglethorpe U., 1963; MS, U. Mo., 1966; PhD, The Union Inst. Ohio, 1987. Lic. airplane pilot. Faculty rsch. assoc. Ga. Inst. Tech., Atlanta, 1963-65; faculty fellow NASA, 1967-68; from asst. to assoc. prof. physics Ga. So. U., Statesboro, 1968-95, dir. planetarium, assoc. prof. emeritus, 1995—; pres. Mobley Sci. Co., 1993—. Pres. Assoc. Income Properties, Inc., Statesboro, 1982—, Savannah Properties Mgmt., Inc., 1983-87; sci. cons. AEC fellow, 1965; sec. Ga. Acad. Sci., 1990-94. Contbr. articles to profl. jours. NASA-ASEE fellow, 1970. Mem. Statesboro Home Builders Assn., Am. Inst. Physics, Ga. Acad. Sci., Sigma Phi Epsilon. Methodist. Office: PO Box 2053 Statesboro GA 30459-2053 E-mail: dell@frontiernet.net.

MOBLEY, EMILY RUTH, library dean, educator; b. Valdosta, Ga., Oct. 1, 1942; d. Emmett and Ruth (Johnson) M. AB in Edn., U. Mich., 1964, AM in Libr. Sci., 1967, postgrad., 1973-76. Tchr. Ecorse (Mich.) Pub. Schs., 1964-65; adminstrv. trainee Chrysler Corp., Highland Park, Mich., 1965-66, engrng. libr., 1966-69; libr. II Wayne State U., Detroit, 1969-72, libr. III, 1972-75; staff asst. GM Rsch. Labs. Libr., Warren, Mich., 1976-78, supr. reader svcs., 1978-81; libr. dir. GMI Engrng. & Mgmt. Inst., Flint, 1982-86; assoc. dir. for pub. svcs. & collection devel., assoc. prof. libr. sci. Purdue U. Librs., West Lafayette, Ind., 1986-89, acting dir. librs., assoc. prof. libr. sci., 1989, dean librs., prof. libr. sci., 1989—; Esther Ellis Norton Disting. Prof. Libr. Sci. Purdue U., 1997—. Adj. lectr. U. Mich. Sch. Libr. Sci., Ann Arbor, 1974-75, 83-86; grants reader Libr. of Mich., 1980-81; project dir. Mideastern Mich. Region Libr. Cooperation, 1984-86; cons. Libr. Coop. of Macomb, 1985-86, Clark-Atlanta U., 1990-91; search com. for new dir. of libr. Smithsonian Instn., 1988; mem. GM Pub. Affairs Subcom. on Introducing Minorities to Engring.; presenter in field. Author: Special Libraries at Work, 1984, numerous other publs.; mem. editl. bd. Reference Svcs. Rev., 1989—, Infomanage, 1993-97. Mem. corp. vis. com. for librs. MIT, 1990—, Carnegie-Mellon U., 1998—; mem. Ind. Statewide Libr. Automation Task Force, 1989-90; mem. state tech. strategy subcom. on info. tech. and telecomms. Ind. Corp. for Sci. & Tech., 1989; mem. nat. adv. com. Libr. of Congress, 1988; trustee Libr. of Mich., 1983-86, v.p., 1986, long range plan com., 1979-82, task force on document access and delivery, 1977-79; info. project mem. Rep. Nat. Conv., 1980; bd. dirs. Small Farms Assn., Southfield, Mich., Lafayette Symphony Orch., YWCA. Recipient Bausch & Lomb award for sci. achievement, 1960, Cert. for Outstanding Performance in Acad. Achievement State of Mich. Ho. of Reps., 1976, Spl. Tribute for Outstanding Contbns. Libr. of Mich. Bd. Trustees, 1986, Disting. Alumnus award U. Mich. Sch. Info. & Libr. Studies, 1989; U. Mich. Regents Alumni scholar, 1960-64; CIC doctoral fellow in libr. sci., 1973-76. Mem. ALA (com. on accreditation, subcom. to rev. 1972, standards for accreditation 1988-89, OLOS minority internship com. 1988-89, nominating com. 1992-93, mem. com. resolutions com. 1993-97), Assn. Coll. & Rsch. Librs. (task force on libr. sch. curriculum 1988-89, com. on profl. edn. 1990-92), Libr. Adminstrn. & Mgmt. Assn., Assn. Rsch. Librs. (bd. dirs. 1990-93), Spl. Librs. Assn. (pres. 1987-88, fellow 1991, com. mem.), Alpha Kappa Alpha, Phi Kappa Phi, Sigma Xi, Iron Key. Office: Purdue U Librs Stewart Ctr Lafayette IN 47907

MOBLEY, JOHN HOMER, II, lawyer; b. Shreveport, La., Apr. 21, 1930; s. John Hinson and Beulah (Wilson) M.; m. Sue Lawton, Aug. 9, 1958; children: John Lawton, Anne Davant. AB, U. Ga., 1951, JD, 1953. Bar: Ga. 1952, U.S. Dist. Ct. D.C. Ptnr. Kelley & Mobley, Atlanta, 1956-63, Gambrell & Mobley, Atlanta, 1963-83; sr. ptnr. Sutherland, Asbill & Brennan, 1983—. Chmn., Cities in Schs. of Ga.; bd. dirs. Cities in Schs.; mem. bd. visitors Emory U.; trustee Canterbury Ct. Episcopal Retirement Home of Atlanta. Capt. JAGC, USAF, 1953-55. Mem. ABA, D.C. Bar, State Bar Ga., Atlanta Bar Assn., Am. Judicature Soc., Atlanta Lawyers Club, Atlanta Athletic Club, Atlanta Country Club, Commerce Club, Piedmont Driving Club, Georgian Club, N.Y. Athletic Club, Met. Club of Washignton, Phi Delta Phi. Home: 4348 Sentinel Post Rd NW Atlanta GA 30327-3910 Office: Sutherland Asbill & Brennan 999 Peachtree St NE Ste 2300 Atlanta GA 30309-3996 Office Fax: 404-853-8806. E-mail: jhmobley@sablaw.com.

MOBLEY, NANCY ELIZABETH, artist, art educator; b. San Angelo, Tex., July 29, 1940; d. William Carl and Mary Elizabeth Fox; m. Billy Jack Wimberley, Aug. 2, 1958 (div. 1972); children: Billy Carl, John Wayne, James Bryan; m. Thomas Howard Mobley, Sept. 28, 1974. BA, Angelo State U., San Angelo, 1990. Draftsman Gen. Telephone Co., San Angelo, 1965-68, William E. Fox & Assocs., San Angelo, 1970-74; draftsman, archtl. estimator Burk Constrn. Co., 1974-76; illustrator Helenikon Air Base, Athens, Greece, 1977-80, Bitburg (Germany) Air Base, 1980-82, publicity writer, editor, 1982-83; jewelry designer Jeweler's Workshop, San Angelo, 1985-87; part-time artist, art tchr., 1976—. Vol. art tchr. Children's Art Mus., San Angelo, 1995-98. Exhibited in solo shows at Athens Art Gallery, 1979, Bitburg (Germany) Am. Express Bank, 1980, Houston Harte Univ. Ctr. Gallery, San Angelo, Tex., 1984, 85, 88, 96, Tom Green County Libr., San Angelo, 2000; group shows include Tom Green County Libr., San Angelo, 1984, Breckenridge (Tex.) Fine Arts Ctr., 1996, 97, 98, 99, Soc. Watercolor Artists, Ft. Worth, 1997, Watercolor Art Soc. Houston, 1998, Shannon Hosp., San Angelo, 1999; represented in pub. and pvt. collections. Docent San Angelo Mus. Fine Art, San Angelo, 1995-99. Recipient Bertha B. Becton scholarship Angelo State U., San Angelo, 1988, Charles Wendell art scholarship Angelo State U., San Angelo, 1990, Carr acad. scholarship Angelo State U., San Angelo, 1988-90, 1st pl. watercolors Breckenridge (Tex.) Arts Nat. Competition, 1996, 1st pl. alumni art competition Angelo State U. Alumni Assn., San Angelo, 1998, Best of Show Zeta Phi's 2nd Internat. Art Competition, San Angelo, Tex.; numerous others. Mem. San Angelo Art Club (3rd v.p. 1997-98, 1st v.p. 1998-99, 2nd v.p. 1999-02, Artist of Yr. 1998). Baptist. Avocations: reading, writing, exercising, collecting antiques. Home: 106 Churchill Blvd San Angelo TX 76903-8613 E-mail: tmobley@cox-internet.com.

MOBLEY, TONY ALLEN, foundation executive, former university dean, recreation educator; b. Harrodsburg, Ky., May 19, 1938; s. Cecil and Beatrice (Bailey) M.; m. Betty Weaver, June 10, 1961; 1 child, Derek Lloyd. BS, Georgetown Coll., 1960; MS, Ind. U., 1962, D Recreation, 1965; MRE, So. Sem., Louisville, 1963. Chmn. dept. recreation and pks. Western Ill. U., Macomb, 1965-72, Pa. State U., University Park, 1972-76; prof., chmn. recreation and pks., dean Sch. Health, Phys. Edn. and Recreation Ind. U., Bloomington, 1976—; exec. dir. Ind. U. Found., 2002—. Chair health adv. coun. White River Park Commn., State of Ind., 1979—; v.p Ind. Sports Corp., Indpls., 1983-89; bd. dirs. Nat. Inst. for Fitness and Sport, Indpls., 1984-93; J.B. Nash scholar, lectr. Am. Assn. Leisure and Recreation, Reston, Va., 1985. Contbr. over 50 articles to profl. jours. Bd. dirs. Monroe County YMCA, Bloomington, 1984-88, United Way, Bloomington, 1994—; mem. Gov.'s Coun. for Phys. Fitness and Sport, 1991—. Am. Coun. Edn. adminstrv. internship fellow, N.C. State U., 1970-71. Fellow Am. Acad. Pk. and Recreation Adminstrn. (pres. 1985-86); mem. Nat. Recreation and Pk. Assn. (pres. 1978-79, Nat. Disting. Profl. award 1981), Assn. Rsch., Adminstrn., Profl. Couns. and Socs. (pres. 1986-87, award 1987), Am. Alliance Health, Phys. Edn., Recreation and Dance (Coll. and Univ. Adminstrs. Coun. Honor award 1986, R. Tait McKenzie award 1996), Soc. Pk. and Recreation Edn. (pres. 1974-75, award 1978), Ind. Pk. and Recreation Assn. (Outstanding Profl. award 1985). Avocations: golf, travel. Office: Ind U Found PO Box 500 Bloomington IN 47402

MOBLEY, WILLIAM HODGES, management educator, researcher, author, executive; b. Akron, Ohio, Nov. 15, 1941; BA, Denison U., 1963; PhD, U. Md., 1971. Registered psychologist, Hong Kong. Mgr. employee rels. rsch. PPG Industries, Pitts., 1971-73; prof. U. S.C., Columbia, 1973-80; head dept. of mgmt. Tex. A&M U., College Station, 1980-83, dean. Coll. of Bus. Adminstrn., 1983-86, exec. dep. chancellor, 1986-88, pres., 1988-93; chancellor Tex. A&M U. Sys., 1993-94; prof. mgmt. Tex. A&M U., 1980-96; pres. PDI Global Rsch. Consortium, Ltd., Hong Kong, Dallas, London, 1996—. Vis. fellow Cornell U., 1994, vis. prof. Hong Kong U. Sci. and Tech., 1995-97, U. Hong Kong, 1998. Author: Employee Turnover, 1982, Advances in Global Leadership, vol. I, 1999, vol. II, 2001. Bd. dirs. Internat. Food and Agrl. Devel. and Econ. Coop., U.S. AID, 1992-94; mem. tri-lateral task force on N.Am. Higher Edn. Coop., USIA, 1993-95; trustee SIOP Found., 1998-2001, AMMA Found., Denison U.; mem. Pres. Bush's Commn. on Minority Bus. Devel., 1990-92, U.S. Com. of the Pacific Econ. Coop. Coun., 1995—; bd. dirs. Medici Med. Corp., 1992—, Concept Tech. Ltd., 1999—. Sr. Fulbright scholar Found. for Scholarly Exchange, Republic China, 1978-79; recipient DAAD, Rep. Germany, 1984; Fellow NDEA U.S. Dept. of Edn., 1968-71. Fellow APA, Am. Psychol. Soc.

MOCEANU, DOMINIQUE, retired gymnast, Olympic athlete; b. Hollywood, Calif., Sept. 30, 1981; Mem. Nat. Team, 1992-93, 93-94, 1994-95, 95-96, 1999; coach Gymnastics World, Ohio, 2002—. Competitions include U.S. Classic, 1991, 92, 93, U.S. Gymnastics Championships, 1992, Am. Classic, 1993, U.S. Olympic Festival, 1993, Coca-Cola Nat. Championships, 1993, 94, 95, 96, Am. Classic/World Championships, 1994, Am. Classic/Pan Am. Games, 1995, World Team Trials, 1995, U.S. Olympic Trials, 1996, John Hancock U.S. Gymnastics Championships, 1997, 98; mem. Olympic team, Sydney, Australia, 2000. Recipient Silver and Bronze medals World Championships, 1995, Gold medal team competition Olympic Games, Atlanta, 1996; placed 1st in balance beam U.S. Classic, Salt Lake City, 1991, 2d in balance beam jr. divsn. U.S. Gymnastics Championships, Columbus, 1992, 2d in all around, 1st team, vault, uneven bars and floor exercise Jr. Pan Am. Games, 1992, 1st in team and balance beam, 3rd in uneven bars Internat. Tournament of Jr. Women's Gymnastics, Charleroi, Belgium, 1993, 1st in all around, vault and team floor exercise, 3rd in uneven bars and balance beam jr. divsn. Coca-Cola Nat. Championships, Nashville, 1994, 1st in team all around, 1st in vault, 3rd in balance beam and floor exercise Am. Classic-Pan Am. Games Trials, Oakland, Calif., 1995, 1st in all around, 2d in floor exercise, 3rd in vault Coca-Cola Nat. Championships, New Orleans, 1995, 1st in all around World Team Trials, Austin, 1995, 1st in uneven bars, 3rd in balance beam Reese's Internat. Gymnastics Cup, Portland, 1995, 1st in all around, team and floor exercise, 3rd in vault and balance beam, 2nd in uneven bars Visa Challenge, Fairfax, Va., 1995, 3rd all around for team, 2d for team balance beam World Championships, Sabae, Japan, 1995; named USOC SportsWoman of Month, Apr. and Sept. 1995; named individual all-around finalist World Championships Team, 1997, gold medalist Goodwill Games, 1998. Avocations: swimming, reading, listening to music. Office: Gymnastics World 6630 Harris Rd Cleveland OH 44147*

MOCH, ROBERT GASTON, lawyer; b. Montesano, Wash., June 20, 1914; s. Gaston and Fleeta Belle (Metcalf) M.; m. Barbara M. Kent, Sept. 2, 1940 (dec.); children: Marilynn A., Michael K., Robert M.; m. LaVerne I. Miller, May 29, 1968. BA magna cum laude, U. Wash., 1936; JD, Harvard Coll., 1941. Bar: Mass. 1941, Wash. 1945. Asst. crew coach U. Wash., 1936-39; head crew coach Mass. Inst. Tech., 1939-44; practiced in Boston, 1941-44, Seattle, 1945-2000; asso. Herrick, Smith, Donald, Farley & Ketchum, 1941-44, Eggerman, Rosling & Williams, 1945-50, Weter, Roberts & Shefelman, 1950-53; ptnr. Roberts & Shefelman, 1953-87; of counsel Foster, Pepper & Shefelman, 1988-99; retired. Del. Nat. Conf. on Law and Poverty, 1965, Nat. Defender Conf., 1969; chmn. King County Pub. Defender Adv. Com., 1970 Mem. U. Wash. Crew, 1933-36. Recipient Olympic Gold medal, 1936; named to Nat. Rowing Found. Hall of Fame, U. Wash. Hall of Fame. Mem. ABA, Wash. Bar Assn., Seattle-King County Bar Assn. (past trustee, com. chmn.), U. Wash. Alumni Assn. (pres. 1978-79, Disting. Svc. award 1986), Wash. Alumni Advs. (pres. 1985-87), Rainier Club, Rotary, Phi Beta Kappa, Beta Gamma Sigma, Alpha Kappa Psi, Phi Delta Phi, Phi Gamma Delta. Mem. Christian Ch. Home: 17143 133rd Ave NE Apt 368 Woodinville WA 98072-4314

MOCHEL, MYRON GEORGE, mechanical engineer, educator; b. Fremont, Ohio, Oct. 9, 1905; s. Gustave A. and Rose M. (Minich) M.; m. Eunice Katherine Steinicke, Aug. 30, 1930 (dec. Dec. 1982); children: Kenneth R., David G., Virginia June. BSME, Case Western Res. U., 1929; MSME, Yale U., 1930. Registered profl. engr. N.Y., Mass., Pa. Devel. engr. nitrogen div. Allied Chem. Corp., Hopewell, Va., 1930-31; devel. engr. R&D dept. Mobil Corp., Paulsboro, N.J., 1931-37; design and devel. engr. gearing div. Westinghouse Electric Corp., Pitts., 1937-43; rsch. assoc. underwater sound lab. Harvard U., Cambridge, Mass., 1943-45; supr. of tng. steam turbine div. Worthington Corp., Wellsville, N.Y., 1945-49; prof. mech. engr. Clarkson U., Potsdam, 1949-71, prof. emeritus, 1971—. Lect. U. Pitts., 1938-43, N.Y. State U. Adult Edn., Wellsville, 1946-49, Oswego, 1965, N.Y. State High Sch. Enrichment Program, Potsdam, 1962-71; cons. Designers for Industry, Cleve., 1953, rsch. engr. Morris Machine Works, Baldwinsville, N.Y., 1954, design engr. Racquette River Paper Co., Potsdam, 1955. Author: Fundamentals of Engineering Graphics, 1960, Pre-Engineering and Applied Science Fundamentals, 1962, Fortran Programming, Programs and Schematic Storage Maps, 1971; co-author: (with Eunice S. Mochel) Funds For Fun, 1983, (with Donald H. Purcell) Beyond Expectations, 1985; contbr. articles to profl. jours. and on internet. Officer, vol. St. Lawrence Valley Hospice, 1983; pres. Mayfield Tenants Assn., 1989-91. Mem. ASME, Am. Soc. Engring. Edn. (advt. mgr. Jour. Engring. Graphics 1963-66, sec. 1966-67, high schs. laision on engring. graphics 1962-65, awards com. chmn. 1965-66), Am. Assn. Ret. Persons (founder St. Lawrence County chpt., income tax counselor 1988-89, medicare/medicaid assistance program counselor 1988—, pres. 1989-90). Republican. Mem. Unitarian Universalist Ch. Home and Office: 931 Mayfield Dr Potsdam NY 13676-4222

MOCK, DAVID CLINTON, JR. internist; b. Redlands, Calif., 1922; s. David Clinton and Eithel (Benson) M.; m. Marcella Enriqueta Fellin, 1952. AB, U. So. Calif., 1944; MD, M.H.D., Hahnemann Med. Coll., 1948. Intern Hahnemann Hosp., Phila., 1948-49; resident San Mateo (Calif.) County Hosp., 1949-51, 54, VA Hosp., Oklahoma City, 1954-55; research fellow in exptl. therapeutics U. Okla., 1956-57, L.N. Upjohn fellow, 1958, dir. exptl. therapeutics unit, 1959-62; dir., preceptorship program, 1968-76; assoc. prof. medicine U. Okla., Oklahoma City, 1963-72, prof., 1972-84, prof. emeritus medicine, 1984—, assoc. dean med. student affairs, 1970-76, assoc. dean postdoctoral edn., 1976-82, dir. continuing med. edn., 1980-83, dir. Transitional Yr. program, 1980-84, dir. History of Medicine program, 1982-84. Chief med. svc., Navajo Base Hosp., Ft. Defiance, Ariz., 1951-53; assoc. faculty homeopathy Royal London Homeopathic Hosp. Capt. USPHS, 1951-53, res.; now ret. Fellow ACP; mem. Am. Fedn. Medical Rsch., N.Y. Acad. Scis. Unitarian Universalist. Home: 570 Alameda Blvd Coronado CA 92118-1617

MOCK, ERIC V. lawyer; b. N.Y.C., Apr. 24, 1942; s. Vern F. and Esther G. Mock; children: Sarah, Stephen. AB, Duke U., 1963; LLB, Harvard U., 1966. Bar: N.Y. 1967. Assoc. Dewey Ballantine, N.Y.C., 1966-76; atty. Revlon, Inc., 1977-78; asst. v.p., counsel Capital Holding Corp., Louisville, 1979-87; assoc. Dornbush, Mensch, Mandelstam & Schaeffer, N.Y.C., 1987—. Avocation: bridge. Office: Dornbush Mensch Mandelstam & Schaeffer 747 3d Ave New York NY 10017 E-mail: mock@dmmslaw.com.

MOCK, FRANK MACKENZIE, lawyer; b. South Bend, Ind., May 17, 1944; s. Frank Carlton and Julia (Baughmann) M.; m. Virginia Johns, Dec. 31, 1974 (div. Feb. 1991); children: Shannon, John, Bridget; m. Christine Mall, June 1995; 1 child, Mackenzie Ann. BA, Duke U., 1966, JD, 1969. Bar: Fla. 1969. Assoc. Mahoney, Adams, Criser, Jacksonville, Fla., 1969-74, ptnr., 1977-92; gen. counsel Builders Investment Group, Valley Forge, Pa., 1974-77; ptnr. Baker & Hostetler, Orlando, Fla., 1992—. Mem. ABA, Am. Coll. Mortgage Lawyers, Duval County Bar Assn., Orange County Bar Assn., Dade County Bar Assn., Palm Beach County Bar Assn., Turnaround Mgmt. Assn. Republican. Episcopalian. Avocations: hiking, fishing, reading. Home: 2147 Santa Antilles Rd Orlando FL 32806-1533 Office: Baker & Hostetler 200 S Orange Ave Ste 2300 Orlando FL 32801-3432

MOCK, MELINDA SMITH, orthopedic nurse specialist, consultant; b. Austell, Ga., Nov. 15, 1947; d. Robert Jehu and Emily Dorris (Smith) Smith; m. David Thomas Mock, Oct. 20, 1969. ASN, DeKalb Coll., 1972. RN, Ga.; cert. orthopedic nurse specialist, orthopedic nurse. Nursing technician Ga. Bapt. Hosp., Atlanta, 1967, staff nurse, 1979; asst. corr. Harcourt, Brace & World Pub. Co., 1968-69; receptionist, sec. Goodbody & Co., 1969-70; nursing asst. DeKalb Gen. Hosp., Decatur, Ga., 1970-71; staff nurse Doctors' Meml. Hosp., Atlanta, 1972-73; staff nurse, relief charge nurse Shallowford Cmty. Hosp., 1973, charge nurse, 1973-76, head nurse, 1976-79, orthopedic nurse specialist emergency room, 1979; rehab. specialist, sr. rehab. specialist Internat. Rehab. Assocs., Inc., Norcross, Ga., 1981, rehab. supr., 1981-82; cons., founder, propr. Healthcare Cost Cons., Alpharetta, Ga., 1982-83; cons., founder, pres. Healthcare Cost Cons., Inc., 1983—. Mem. legis. com. of adv. coun. Ga. Bd. Nursing, Atlanta, 1984-85; mem. adv. coun. Milton H.S. Coop. Bus. Edn., 1986-89; mem. Nat. Fedn. Specialty Nursing Orgns. Task Force on Profl. Liability Ins., 1987-89, Congressman Patrick Swindall Sr. Citizen Adv. Coun., 1988, Congressman Ben Jones Vets. Affairs Adv. Com., 1989-92, White House Conf. on Small Bus., 1995, Congressman Newt Gingrich Small Bus. Adv. Com., 1997-99; apptd. spkr. Congl. Small Bus. Summit by Congressman Gingrich, 1998. Dep. voter registrar Fulton County, Ga., 1983-87; Rep. treas. 23d house dist., mem. Fulton County Rep. Com., 1989-2001, nominating com., 1991, 92, 93, 95, 97, chmn. polit. action com., 1993-95, asst. treas., 1994-95, sec., 1995-97; treas. 41st House Dist. Rep. Party, 1993-97; mem. state exec. com. Ga. Rep. Party, 1997-99; 1st vice chairwoman 6th Congl. Dist. Rep. Party, 1993-97, chmn., 1997-99; mem. State Com. Ga. Rep. Party, 1993-2002; del. Fulton County Rep. Conv., 1991, 92, 94, 95, 96, 97, 99, 2000; del. Ga. 4th Congl. Dist., 1991, 92, parliamentarian, 1992, credentials com., 1992; del. Ga. Rep. Conv., 1991, 92, 93, 95, 96, 97, 99, Ga. 6th Congl. Dist. Rep. Party Conv., 1993, 95, 96, 97, 99, 2000, Ga. 9th Congl. Dist. Conv., 2001, 7th Congl. Dist. Conv., 2002; alt. del.-at-large Nat. Rep. Conv., 1996; mem. Chattahoochee Rep. Women, 1989-2001, chmn. campaign com., 1992-94, rec. sec., 1995-2001; chmn. nominating com. House Dist. 23, 1990; mem. steering com. to re-elect state rep. Tom Campbell, 1990; mem. campaign staff to re-elect state senator Sallie Newbill, 1990, 92, 94; health advisor campaign to elect Matt Towery for lt. gov., 1990, health adv. campaign to elect Bob Barr U.S. Senate, 1991-92; mem. election com. Mark Burkhalter for State Rep.; vol. campaign staff to re-elect Congressman Newt Gingrich, 1992, 94, 96, 98; mem. campaign staff to elect Jim Hunt as state rep., 1996; vol. campaign to elect Tom Price to state senate, 1996, Cherokee Co. Republican Party, 2001—. Recipient Nat. Disting. Svc. Registry award, 1987; named Outstanding Young Women Am., 1984. Mem. Nat. Assn. Orthopedic Nurses (nat. policies com. 1981-82, chmn. govt. rels. com. 1987-90, nat. treas. 1991-95, nat. pres. elect 1998-99, pres. 1999-2000, nurse Washington intern 1987, 99, legis. contbr. editor news 1989, chmn. legis workshop 1989, co-chmn. legis. workshop 1990, guest editl. Orthopaedic Nursing Jour. 1988, spkr. 1990, 92, 93, 94, 98, Ann. Congress del. 1982, 91, 92, 93, 94, 96, 98, 99, 2000, 2001, Pres.'s award 1992, Outstanding Contbn. to NAON award 1996, chmn. budget and fin. com. 1991-95, nat. bylaws and policies com. 1995-98, bylaws and policies com. Atlanta chpt. 1994-96, pres-elect Atlanta chpt. 1996-97, pres. 1997-98, program dir. 2002-), Orthopedic Nurses Assn. (nat. bd. dirs. 1977-79, nat. treas. 1979-80), Coun. Splty. Nursing Orgns. Ga. (nominating com. 1976-77), Assn. Rehab. Nurses (bd. dirs. Ga. chpt. 1980-81, del. people-to-people program to China 1981), Nat. Fedn. Ind. Bus. (guardian 1988—, adv. coun. 1990—, healthcare task force chmn. 1992—, vice-chmn./fed. liaison Ga. adv. coun. 1995—), Am. Bd. Nursing Specialities (chmn. nominating com. 1993-94, 94-95, chmn. com. on specialty bd. rev. 1993-95), Ga. Jaycees (dist. 4C rep. Ga. Jaycee Legis. 1984, 85), Ga. Seatbelt Coalition, Orthopaedic Nurses Cert. Bd. (bd. dirs. 1991-96, pres. 1992-93, task force on advanced practice certification 1991-92), North Fulton C. of C. (vice chmn. health svc. effectiveness alliance 1984-85, chmn. 1985-86, co-chmn./editor periodical 1985, 3rd Quarter Workhorse award 1985), Alpharetta Jaycees (adminstrv. v.p. 1984-85, internal v.p. 1985-86), Alpharetta Jaycee Women (bd. dirs. 1983); Ga. Perimeter Coll. Nursing Alumni Assn. (bd. dirs. 2000—). Baptist. Avocations: reading, boating, community service activities. Home: 1280 Trinity Church Rd Canton GA 30115 Office: Healthcare Cost Cons Inc PO Box 466 Alpharetta GA 30009-0466

MOCK, ROBERT ALLEN, professional figure skating coach, editor; b. Pitts., Aug. 11, 1950; s. Fred Allen and Helene Marie (Sedore) M. BA in Sociology, Duquesne U., Pitts., 1971, MS in Sociology, 1978. Cert. Arena programmer, judge (gold) Ice Skating Inst. Profl. coach USFSA, 1975—; editor Am. Skating World GRP Publs., 1980—; skating dir. Ice Garden Arena, Pitts., 1987-95, Nevin Ice Arena, Greensburgh, Pa., 1989-96, Neville Ice Arena, Pitts., 1991-95, Airport Ice Arena, Pitts., 1994-95, Ctr. Ice Arena, Delmont, Pa., 1997; dir. Nat. Figure Skating Sch., 1997—. Chair coaches com. U.S. Figure Skating, 1991-95, mem. internat. com., ice dancing com., competition com. Mem. bd. regents Inst. Ice Arena Mgmt., 2000—. Recipient Top 26 Coaches award Ice Skating Inst., 1991, 92, 93, Dist. # 2 Merit award, 1994, Ritter Shumway award Figure Skating Cmty. Mem.: U.S. Figure Skating Assn. (bd. dirs. 1992—, Gold medal), Profl. Skaters Assn. Internat. (pres. 1995—98, Master rated), Mid-Atlantic Mgrs. Assn. (bd. dirs. 1981—96), Profl. Nat. Skaters Assn. (hon.). Avocation, running. Home: 505 Larimer Ave Turtle Creek PA 15145-1924 Office: Ctr Ice Arena 100 Center Ice Dr Delmont PA 15626 E-mail: mbobmock@aol.com.

MOCK, ROBERT CLAUDE, architect; b. Baden, Germany, May 3, 1928; came to U.S., 1938, naturalized, 1943; s. Ernest and Charlotte (Geismar) M.; m. Belle Carol Bach, Dec. 23, 1952 (div.); children: John Bach, Nicole Louise; m. Marjorie Reubenfeld, Dec. 20, 1964. BArch, Pratt Inst., 1950; MArch, Harvard U., 1953. Registered arch., N.Y., Conn., N.J., Nat. Coun. Archtl. Registration Bds. Arch. George C. Marshall Space Ctr., Huntsville, Ala., 1950-51; archtl. critic Columbia Sch. Architecture, N.Y.C., 1953-54; dir. facility design Am. Airlines, 1955-60; founder Robert C. Mock & Assocs., 1960—. Mem. Mayor's Panel of Archs., N.Y.C. Prin. works include: Shine Motor Inn, Queens, N.Y., 1961 (recipient 1st prize motel category Queens C. of C. 1961), temporary terminal bldg. Eastern Air Lines , La Guardia Airport, N.Y.C., 1961, cargo bldgs United Airlines and Trans World Airlines, Kennedy Airport, N.Y.C., Bridgeport (Conn.) Airport, 1961, Eastern Air Lines Med. Ctr., Kennedy Airport, 1962, ticket office Trans World Airlines Fifth Ave., N.Y.C., 1962, terminal bldgs. Eastern Air Lines and Trans World Airlines , La Guardia Airport, N.Y.C., 1963, 7 bldgs. Mfrs. Hanover Trust Co. , 1964-66, kitchen and commissary bldg. Lufthansa German Airlines, 1964, Ambassador Club, La Guardia Airport, 1964, Happyland Sch., N.Y.C., 1965, cargo bldgs. Alitalia and Lufthansa German Airlines, Kennedy Airport, 1965, FAA-Nat. Prototype Air Traffic Control Tower, 1966; Lufthansa German Airlines; Irish Internat. Airlines, El Al Israel Airlines, Varig Brazilian Airlines; passenger terminals Kennedy Airport, 1970; Swiss Air Cargo Terminal, Lufthansa German Airlines, cargo terminals El Al Israel airline cargo terminal, Kennedy Airport, 1972, passenger terminal Aerolineas Argentina, 1974, N.Am. hdqrs. Aerolineas Argentinas, N.Y.C., 1974, corp. hdqrs. Am. Airlines, 1977, N.Am. hdqrs. Varig Brazilian Airlines, N.Y.C., 1977, Norel-Ronel Indsl. Pk., Hollywood, Fla., 1979, N.Am. hdqrs. Irish Internat. Airlines , N.Y.C., 1979, corp. hdqrs. Bankers Trust Co., N.Y.C., 1980, cargo terminal Air India, cargo terminal Flying Tiger, Kennedy Airport, 1982, 2 flight kitchen bldgs. Ogden Food Corp., Kennedy Airport, 1984, 88 and LaGuardia Airport, 1987, Greenwich Assn. Retarded Citizens Sch., 1983, passenger terminal extension Varig Brazilian Airlines , 1985, 3 restaurants La Guardia Airport, 1987, residences Palm Beach, Fla., 1989-92, Bethesda, Md., 1993, 97, 98, 99, (named best custom residence in U.S., Profl. Builder Mag. 2000), Fenwick Island, Del., 1994, Potomac Falls, Md., 1995. Recipient Vol. of Yr. award United Way, 1984. Mem. Am. Arbitration Assn., Harvard Club, Admirals Cove Club. Office: 185 Byram Shore Rd Greenwich CT 06830-6909

MOCK, STANLEY CLYDE, certified financial planner, investment advisor; b. Seattle, Nov. 7, 1946; s. Darrell O. and Elsie (Broeckel) M.; m. Deloris J. Weis, June 4, 1967; children: Shannon Mock Frohardt, Kristin Ann Hagen. Student, Columbia Basin U., 1965-67; CFP, Coll. Fin. Planning, 1987. CFP, registered investment advisor, prin. Agt. Met. Life Ins. Co., Eugene, Oreg., 1969-73, sales mgr. Spokane, 1973-76, advanced underwriting advisor Bellevue, Wash., 1976, dist. sales mgr. Boise, Idaho, 1976-78; gen. agt. Ohio Nat. Fin. Svcs., 1978—; fin. planner Fin. Planning Svcs. LLC, 1978—. Author: Life Insurance Selling, 1992; contbr. articles to mags. With USNR, 1967-69. Named One of Best Fin. Planners in Am., Money Mag., 1987. Mem.: Soc. Fin. Svcs. Profls. (bd. dirs.), Fin. Planning Assn. (bd. dirs. Idaho chpt.), Soc. Fin. Planning Profls. (pres. 1988—89), Rotary, Distributive Edn. Club Am. (pres. 1965). Republican. Avocations: Harley-Davidson motorcycles, snowmobiles, shooting. Office: Fin Planning Svcs LLC 3601 N Lakeharbor Ln Boise ID 83703-6969 E-mail: stan@fps4u.com.

MOCKER, HANS WALTER, physicist; b. Teplice, Czech Republic, Feb. 22, 1929; came to U.S., 1960; s. Emil and Marie (Schubert) M.; m. Carol Virginia Vines, Feb. 13, 1981; children: Peter, Nancy. MS in Physics, Inst. Tech., Darmstadt, Germany, 1954; PhD in Physics, U. Innsbruck, Austria, 1959. Sr. rsch. scientist rsch. dept. Honeywell, Mpls., 1960-65, prin. rsch. scientist sys. and rsch., 1965-69, sect. chief sys. and rsch., 1969-78, prin. rsch. fellow sys. and rsch., 1978-93; Ctr. fellow Tech. Ctr.-Alliant Tech. Sys., 1991-93; cons. Electro-Optics Laser Sys., Dothan, Ala., 1994—. Physicist Farbenfabriken Bayer, Krefeld, Germany, 1959-60; mem. advanced group on electronic devices Undersec. of Def., Washington, 1977-78; presenter in field. Co-author: Design of Infrared and Laser Systems, 1981; contbr. articles to profl. jours. including Laser Focus, Applied Optics, Applied Physics Letters, IEEE Jour. Quant. Electr. Coach Minn. Soccer Assn., Mpls., 1981-83. Recipient H.W. Sweatt award, 1968, ir-100 award Indsl. Rsch. Mag., 1969, 77, Excellence in Oral Presentation, Soc. Automotive Engrs., 1993; named one of 7 Wonders of Engring., Minn. Soc. Profl. Engrs., 1970. Achievements include patents for apparatus for supervising proportion of magnetically active component in a fluid, for ring laser biased to permit two equal intensity transition frequencies to be generated in opposite directions, for optical system for laser doppler homodyne detection, for relaxation laser synchronizer for pulsed laser operation, for rapidly tunable laser, for method and means for removing claddings from optical fibers, for rapid wavelength switching of IR lasers with Bragg Cells, for laser doppler velocimeter using stable semiconductor or solid-state lasers, for scanning laser helmet mounted sight, for laser cavity helmet mounted sight, for solid-block homodyne interferometer, for look-ahead windshear detector by filtered Raleigh-scattered light. Avocations: skiing, travel, woodworking. Home: 204 Westbrook Rd Dothan AL 36303-2952

MOCKLER, ROBERT JOSEPH, management educator; b. St. Louis, May 23, 1932; s. Colman Michael and Veronica (McKenna) M. BA, Harvard U., 1954, MBA, 1959; PhD, Columbia U., 1961. Instr. Rutgers U., N.J., 1959-61; Joseph F. Adams prof. mgmt. St. John's U., Jamaica, N.Y., 1962—. Lectr. in field; owner Real Estate Bus., N.Y.C., 1973-84. Co-author: Strategic Management: A Methodological Approach, 4th edit., 1994, An Information Systems Plan for the Malaysian Agricultural Research and Development Inst., 1993, Expert Systems: An Introduction to Knowledge-Based Systems, 1992; author: Strategic Management: A Research Guide With Comprehensive Bibliographies, 1993, Strategic Management: An Integrative Context-Specific Process, 1993, Strategic Management Cases, 1999, Rethinking Strategic Mgmt., 1995, Multinational Cross-Cultural Management, 1997, Multcultural Strategic Alliances, 2000, Expert Knowledge Based Systems, 2002; contbr. articles to profl. jours. and books to chpts. 1st lt. Artillery, 1955-57. Recipient Fulbright award, 1993, Innovative Teaching award Decision Sci. Inst., 1990. Avocations: skiing, theater, golf, opera. Office: 114 E 90th St Ste 1B New York NY 10128-1551

MOCKLIN, KEVIN ETIENNE, physician, medical educator; b. New Orleans, May 14, 1951; s. Stephen Gilbert and Shirley Ann (Bartchy) M.; m. Cynthia Jean Scott, May 19, 1978; children: Christine, Kathleen. BS in Pharmacy, U. Miss., 1974; MD, La. State U., 1978. Diplomate Am. Coll. Physicians. Intern dept. medicine U. Miss., Jackson, 1978-79; resident dept. medicine La. State U., New Orleans, 1979-81, chief resident dept. medicine, 1981-82, clin. instr. medicine, 1982-84, clin. asst. prof. medicine, 1984—; ptnr. Internal Medicine Clinic of Lake Charles, La., 1982—. Home and Office: 2770 3rd Ave Ste 350 Lake Charles LA 70601-0404

MOCKO, GEORGE PAUL, minister; b. Little Falls, N.Y., Feb. 15, 1934; s. George and Anna (Swancara) M.; m. Elizabeth Carol Davidson, Sept. 2, 1956; children: David, Paul, Kristopher, Elissa BA, Hartwick Coll., 1956; BD, Phila. Sem., 1959, STM, 1972; DD (hon.), Gettysburg Coll., 1978. Ordained to ministry Evang. Luth. Ch. in Am., 1959. Pastor Jacob's and Outwood Chs., Pine Grove, Pa., 1959-62; assoc. pastor St Mark's Ch., Wilmington, Del., 1962-65, sr. pastor, 1965-78, Ascension Evang. Luth. Ch., Towson, Md., 1978-91; bishop Del.-Md. Synod Evang. Luth Ch. in Am., 1991-2000, ret., 2000. Author books; contbr. articles to profl. jours. Home: 501 Sussex Rd Baltimore MD 21286-7609 E-mail: GPmocko@aol.com. *Colossians speaks of Christ as the one in whom "all things hold together". I know that Christ is the one who holds me together. Proclaiming and living his life, the church holds our society together.*

MOCKUS, JOSEPH FRANK, electrical engineer; b. Chgo., Nov. 17, 1965; s. Joseph John and Jean Frances (Widmar) M. BS Gen. Engring., Washington Nat. U., 1995. Cert. engr.-in-tng. Mich., cert. quality sys. auditor. Asst. engr. C. Cretors and Co., Chgo., 1987; dir. automotive programs Andrew Corp. Wireless Products Group, Itasca, 1989—98; mgr. OEM sales Kenwood USA Corp., North Riverside, 1998; dir. bus. area Andrew Corp., Addison, 1999—. Patentee in field. Mem. ASTM, IEEE, Am. Soc. Quality Control (sr., cert. quality technician), Antennas and Propagation Soc., Vehicular Tech. Soc., Mensa. Achievements include U.S. patents on low cost, slot fed ultra high frequency glass mount antenna, 1995, 96, RF Coupler for Concealed Mobile Telecommunications Systems, 1999, Multi-band Antenna for Cellular and GPS, 2000, Transmission line terminations and junctions, 2000. Avocations: tennis, literature, music. Office: 1200 A Greenbriar Addison IL 60101

MODABBER, FARROKH ZIAOLLAH, immunologist; b. Rasht, Guilan, Iran, Feb. 27, 1940; came to U.S., 1958; s. Ziaollah and Maryam Modabber; children: Zia F., M. Ramin, Yalda Modabber. BA, UCLA, 1964, PhD, 1968. Fellow Harvard Med. Sch., Boston, 1969-72; asst. prof. Harvard U., 1974-77; assoc. prof. Pahlavi U., Shiraz, Iran, 1971-73; head dept. pathobiology Sch. Pub. Health, Teheran, 1975-77; dir. Pasteur Inst., 1978; head dept. immunology Syntex Rsch., Palo Alto, Calif., 1982-84; sci., coord. leishmaniasis rsch. and coord. strategic rsch. divns. tropical diseases WHO, Geneva, Switzerland, 1984-2000; dir. Infectious Disease Rsch. Inst., Seattle, 2000—. Expert adv. bd. on immunology WHO, 1977-83; vis. sci. Pasteur Inst., Paris, 1979-82; vis. lectr. Harvard, 1977-82; hon. prof. Karolinska, Sweden & Khartoum, Sudan. Editor: Research on Control Strategies for Leishmaniases; patentee in immunodiagnostics; contbr. articles to profl. jours. Mem. Am. Assn. of Immunologists, British Soc. for Immunology, N.Y. Acad. Sci., Am. Soc. of Microbiology, Iranian Soc. for Immunology (pres., founder). Avocation: classical Persian music. Home: 6510 108th Ave NE Kirkland WA 98033 Office: Infectious Disease Rsch Inst 1124 Columbia St Ste 600 Seattle WA 98104 Fax: (206) 381-3678. E-mail: fmodabber@IDRI.org.

MODANO, MICHAEL, professional hockey player; b. Livonia, Mich., June 7, 1970; Right wing/ctr. Minn. North Stars, 1988-93, Dallas Stars, 1993—. Player World Hockey League East All-Star Game, 1988-89, NHL All-Rookie Game, 1989-90, NHL All-Star Game, 1993; mem. Stanley Cup Championship Team, 1999. Office: Amer Airlines Ctr 2500 Victory Ave Dallas TX 75219*

MODARRES, MOHAMMAD, education educator; b. Esfahan, Iran, Aug. 11, 1952; s. Mohsen and Zahra M.; m. Susan Partovi, Jan. 25, 1984; 1 child, Ceena. BS, Tehran Polytecnic, Iran, 1974; MS, MIT, 1977, PhD, 1980. Reliability analyst Sci. Application, McLean, Va., 1980-82; prof. U. Md., College Park, 1982—; dir. Ctr. for Technology Risk Studies/U. Md., 1997—. Cons. Scientech, Corp., Rockville, Md., 1987—; expert panel mem. Nuclear Regulatory Commn., Rockville, 1991-99; cons. Energy Rsch., Inc., Rockville, 1995—; adv. bd. PLG, Inc., Irvine, Calif., 1983-84. Author: (book) What Every Engineer Should Know About Reliability and Risk Analysis, 1993; co-author: (books) Reliability Engineers and Risk Analysis: A Practical Guide, 1999, Communications Nuclear Power: Assurance Safety for the Future, 1998; contbg. author: Wiley's Ency. of Elec. and Electronics Engring., 1998. Recipient Disting. Scholar-Tchr. award U. Md., 1994-95, Inventor of Yr. award 1996. Fellow Am. Nuclear Soc. (chair human factors divsn. 1996-97, nuclear installations com. safety divsn. program 1997-98); mem. IEEE, Soc. for Risk Analysis. Office: Univ Md 2100 Marie Mount Hall College Park MD 20742-7531

MODE, CHARLES J. mathematician, educator; b. Bismarck, N.D., Dec. 29, 1927; s. Charles and Fannie E. (Hansen) M.; m. Eleanore L. Perdelwitz; 1 dau., Martha Lisa. BS in Genetics, N.D. State U., 1952; MS in Genetics, Kans. State U., 1953; PhD in Genetics, U. Calif., Davis and Berkeley, 1956; postgrad. in stats. (Univ. fellow), N.C. State U., 1956-57. Asst. prof. math. Mont. State U., 1957-59, asso. prof., 1960-62, prof., 1963-66, mem. genetics group, 1957-66; asso. prof. math. stats. SUNY, Buffalo, 1966-70; prof. math. Drexel U., 1970—. Cons. to industry. Author: (books) Multitype Branching Processes - Theory and Applications, 1971, Stochastic Processes in Demography and Their Computer Implementation, 1985, Stochatic Processes in Epidemiology, HIV/AIDS, Other Infectious Diseases and Computers, 2000; contbr. articles; editor (assoc.): (jour.) Math. Bioscis., 1975—. Mem. Inst. Math. Stats., Biometric Soc., Am. Math. Soc., AAAS, Population Assn. Am., Sigma Xi, Phi Kappa Phi, Pi Mu Epsilon. Lutheran. Home: 502 Balsam Rd Cherry Hill NJ 08003-3202 Office: Drexel Univ Dept Math Philadelphia PA 19104

MODE, DONALD G. urologist, medical director; b. Jeffersonville, Ind., Aug. 11, 1934; s. George E. and Ellen B. Mode; m. Julia A. Pfaffinger, June 25, 1955 (div. May 1981); children: Stephen C., Kevin P., Donna A., Michael A., Kathleen M.; m. Tia Teresa Trent, June 19, 1982; children: Richard Freier, Matthew Freier, Ian C., Bonnie E. AB, Ind. U., 1960; MD, Ind. U., Indpls., 1964. Intern Kern County Gen. Hosp., Bakersfield, Calif., 1964-65, resident in gen. surgery, 1966-67; resident in urology Vanderbilt U. Hosp., Nashville, 1967-70; pvt. practice urology Fullerton and Bishop, Calif., 1970-90; med. adminstr. Osbon Med. Sys., Augusta, Ga., 1993-95; med. dir. Imagyn Med. Tech., 1995-98, Timm Med. Tech., Mpls., 1998-2000; assoc. prof. urology Med. Coll. Ga., 2000. Urology cons. Spinal Cord Injury Svc., VA Med. Ctr., Augusta. Sgt. USMC, 1953-57, Korea. Fellow ACS; mem. AMA, Am. Urol. Assn., Med. Assn. Ga., Found. for Med. Care (pres. 1975-77), Inyo-Muno County Med. Soc. (pres. 1987). Republican. Baptist. Avocations: hunting, fishing, boating, travel, reading. Home: 3508 Lost Tree Ln Martinez GA 30907-8212 Office: VAMC Rm 1E-128 SCI Unit 1 Freedom Way Augusta GA 30904 E-mail: dmode9@comcast.net.

MODELL, ARTHUR B. professional football team executive; b. Bklyn., June 23, 1925; m. Patricia Breslin, July 25, 1969; stepchildren: John, David. Owner, pres. Cleve. Browns football team (now Baltimore Ravens), 1961—, owner, CEO. Pres. Nat. Football League, 1967-70 Office: Baltimore Ravens 200 Saint Paul Pl Ste 2400 Baltimore MD 21202-2003 also: Baltimore Ravens Ravens Stadium 1101 Russell Street Baltimore MD 21230*

MODELL, JEROME HERBERT, anesthesiologist, educator; b. St. Paul, Sept. 9, 1932; s. William and Frieda (Singer) M.; m. Shirley Graves, Nov. 25, 1977; children— Charles, Jack, Julie. BA, U. Minn., 1954, BS, MD, U. Minn., 1957. Intern U.S. Naval Hosp., St. Albans, N.Y., 1957-58, resident, 1958-60; practice medicine specializing in anesthesiology Gainesville, Fla., 1969—; attending staff U.S. Naval Hosp., St. Albans, 1960-61, chief anesthesiology Pensacola, Fla., 1961-63; asso. prof. dept. anesthesiology U. Miami (Fla.) Sch. Medicine, 1963-69; prof., chmn. dept. anesthesiology U. Fla. Coll. Medicine, Gainesville, 1969-92, sr. assoc. dean clin. affairs, 1990-95, exec. assoc. dean, 1996-97, interim dean, 1997; assoc. v.p. U. Fla. Health Sci. Ctr. Affiliations, 1992-96. Assoc. v.p. U. Fla. Health Sci., 1998-2000, emeritus prof. 2000—, courtesy prof. large animal scis., 1999—. Author: The Pathophysiology and Treatment of Drowning and Near-Drowning, 1971, (with others) Introduction to Life Support, 1973; also numerous scientific articles. Served to lt. comdr. USN, 1957-63. Recipient NIH Research Career Devel. award. Mem. AMA, AAAS, Assn. U. Anesthetists, Am. Soc. Anesthesiologists, N.Y. Acad. Scis., Am. Coll. Chest Physicians. Home: PO Box 14347 Gainesville FL 32604-2347 Office: U Fla Coll Medicine PO Box 100254 Gainesville FL 32610-0254

MODELL, JOHN, social sciences educator; b. N.Y.C., June 3, 1941; s. Walter and Merriam (Levant) Modell; m. Judith Schachter, June 2, 1963 (div.); children: Jennifer, Matthew Thelonious; m. Cynthia Garcia Coll, June 25, 2000. AB, Columbia U., 1962, MA, 1963, PhD, 1969; postgrad. (Social Sci. Research Council research tng. fellow), U. Pa., 1969-70. Research asst. Bur. Applied Social Research, Columbia U., 1962-65; lectr. Kingsborough Community Coll., 1965-66; dir. research Japanese Am. Research Project, UCLA, 1966-69; asst. prof. history U. Minn., 1969-72, assoc. prof., 1972-77, prof., 1977-83, Carnegie Mellon U., 1983-99, acting dean Coll. Humanities and Social Scis., 1985-87; prof. edn. and human devel., prof. sociology Brown U., Providence, 1999—. Rsch. assoc. Phila. Social History Project U. Pa., 1974—85; Cardozo vis. prof. history Yale U., 1991; mem. adv. planning com. Ctr. for Coordination of Study of Social Indicators Social Sci. Rsch. Coun., 1980—85; mem. com. child devel. rsch. and pub. policy NRC, 1981—86; mem. coun. Inter-Univ. Consortium for Polit. and Social Rsch., 1982—86; adv. com. Henry Murray Ctr. for Rsch. in Human Lives Radcliffe Coll.; mem. MacArthur Found. Rsch. Network on Successful Pathways Through Middle Childhood; mem. Network Program on Aging and Social Change Nat. Inst. Aging. Author: The Economics and Politics of Racial Accommodation: The Japanese of Los Angeles 1900-1942, 1977, Into One's Own: From Youth to Adulthood in the United States, 1920-1975, 1989; author: (with others) The Economic Basis of Ethnic Solidarity, 1981, Recent Social Trends in the United States, 1960-90, 1991; editor (, author (with others): The Kikuchi Diary: Chronicle of an American Concentration Camp, 1973; editor: (with others) Theory, Method, and Practice in Social and Cultural History, 1992, Children in Time and Place: Developmental and Historical Insights, 1993. Fellow John Guggenheim Meml., 1978—79. Home: 125 Morris Ave Providence RI 02906-2426 Office: Brown U Dept Edn Providence RI 02912-0001

MODELL, STEPHEN MARK, medical researcher, educator; b. Detroit, June 22, 1958; s. Richard Martin and Sola Jane (Hamburger) M.; m. Wanpen Prasoptham, Jan. 14, 1988; 1 child, Marrisa Lynne. AB in Philosophy, Stanford U., 1980; MD, Med. Coll. Ohio, 1984; MS in Clin. Rsch. Design/Statis.Analysis, U. Mich., 1991. Asst. coord. The Resource for Pub. Health Policy U. Mich. Sch. Pub. Health, Ann Arbor, 1987-89; rsch. asst., dept. psychiatry U. Mich., 1989-90, rsch. assoc. Genome Ethics Com., 1992-94; rsch. assoc. Coun. Genetics and Soc. U. Mich. Dept. Health Mgmt. and Policy, 1995-98, rsch. dir. genetics policy, 1999—; dissemination activities dir. Mich. Ctr. for Genomics and Pub. Health, 2000—. Mem. Pres.'s Coun., Med. Coll. Ohio, 1992—. Genome studies sect. editor Ultimate Reality and Meaning, 1995—; editor Studies in Biophilosophy, 1997. Recipient honorable mention Nellie Westerman prize competition in clin. rsch. ethics, Am. Fedn. Clin. Rsch., 1995. Mem. AMA, Am. Fedn. Med. Rsch., N.Y. Acad. Scis., Maimonides Soc., Internat. Soc. Study of Human Ideas on Ultimate Reality and Meaning (bd. dirs. 1994—, treas. 1999-2000, v.p. 2001—). Avocations: book discussion groups, water sports, jogging, hiking, travel. Home: 3086 Deer Creek Ct Ann Arbor MI 48105-9664 Office: U Mich Sch Pub Health SPH-II OCBPH M4157 109 S Observatory St Ann Arbor MI 48109-2029 E-mail: mod@umich.edu.

MODER, JOHN JOSEPH, non-profit administrator; b. St. Louis, Apr. 9, 1948; s. Helen (Freihaut) M. BA in English and Philosophy, St. Mary's U., San Antonio, 1970; MA in Philosophy, Fordham U., 1972, PhD in Philosophy, 1977; M Div, U. St. Michael's, 1979. Joined Soc. of Mary, ordained priest Roman Cath. Ch., 1979. Mem. faculty Assumption High Sch., East St. Louis, Ill., 1973—74, Vianney High Sch., St. Louis, 1975—76; faculty mem. Irish Christian Bros. Sch., Mono Mills, Canada, 1977—79; asst. prof. philosophy St. Mary's U., San Antonio, 1979—86, assoc. prof. philosophy, trustee, co-chmn. peace commn., 1986—88, pres., 1988—2000, Jr. Achievement South Tex., 2000—01; tchr. Alamo Heights H.S., 2001—02; v.p., COO Hispanic Assn. Colls and Univs., 2002—. Bd. advisors Communities-in-Schs., San Antonio, 1988-2000. Mem. Am. Cath. Philos. Assn. Avocations: hiking, reading, travel, running.

MODER, KEVIN G. rheumatologist, consultant; b. St. Louis, Jan. 30, 1961; Student, St. Louis U., 1979-83; MD, U. Mo., 1983. Cons. in rheumatology and internal medicine Mayo Clinic, Rochester, 1993—. Contbr. chpts. to books, articles to profl. publs. Mem. ACP, AMA, Am. Coll. Rheumatology, Mayo Alumni Assn. (sec.). Office: Mayo Clinic 200 1st St SW Rochester MN 55905-0002

MODERACKI, EDMUND ANTHONY, music educator, conductor; b. Hackensack, N.J., July 18, 1946; s. Edmund Joseph and Helen Theresa (Fisher) Moderacki; m. Brenda Wing Moderacki. BA, Montclair State Coll., 1968, postgrad., 1970-71; MA, Hunter Coll., 1970, postgrad., 1970-72, Newark State Coll., 1969-70, Seton Hall U., 1970, Rutgers U., 1976-78, Ctr. for Understanding Media, 1973. Tchr. music pub. schs., River Vale, N.J., 1968—; asst. condr. Ridgewood (N.J.) Symphony Orch., 1969—, trustee, pres., 1986-87, 94-95; artistic dir. Ridgewood (N.J.) Symphony, 2001—; asst. condr. Adelphi Chamber Orch., 1994-95. Tuba soloist Rutherford Cmty. Band, Ridgewood Village Band, Waldwick Band, Ridgewood Concert Band, 1978—, trustee, 1985—, guest condr., 1985, 86, 88, 93; mgr. All Bergen High Sch. Band, 1994; condr. All Bergen County High Sch. Band, 2001. Author: Images of America: River Vale. Town historian River Vale; mem. steering com. Bergen County Teen Arts, 1991—. Recipient County Exec. Vol. award, 1991, Tchr. Recognition award Gov. of State of N.J., 1990; Bergen County PTA fellow, 1976. Mem. NEA, Music Educators Nat. Conf., N.J. Orch. Assn. (trustee 1981-85), N.J. Edn. Assn. (alt. del. assembly 1983-93, mem. state membership com. 1986-2001), Music Educators Bergen County (bd. mem. at-large 1995-97, treas. 1997-2000, pres.-elect 2000-2002, pres. 2002—), River Vale Edn. Assn. (pres. 1981-83, 88-91, 2000—), Brigade Am. Revolution (bd. dirs. at large 1991-95, info. officer 1989-95, adj. 1996-2000, editor Brigade Press 2002-), Phi Mu Alpha Sinfonia, Kappa Delta Pi. Home: 740 White Birch Rd Washington Township NJ 07676 Office: Woodside Sch Rivervale NJ 07675

MODERY, RICHARD GILLMAN, marketing and sales executive; b. Chgo., Sept. 20, 1941; s. Richard Gustave Modery and Betty Jane (Gillman) Perok; m. Kay Francis Whitby, July 31, 1966 (div. July 1977); children: Stacey Lynn, Marci Kay; m. Anne-Marie Lucette Arsenault, Feb. 27, 1979. Student, Joliet (Ill.) Jr. Coll., 1959-61, Aurora (Ill.) Coll., 1963-65, Davenport Bus. Coll., Grand Rapids, Mich., 1969-71, Northwestern U., Evanston, Ill., 1987. Mktg. products mgr. Rapistan, Inc., Grand Rapids, 1964-75; mgr. estimating, project mgmt., customer svc. E.W. Buschman Co., Cin., 1975-78; exec. v.p. Metzgar Conveyor Co., Grand Rapids, 1979-84; mng. dir. Metzco Internat (cen. and S.Am.), Mich., 1981-84, Transfer Technologies, Inc., Grand Rapids, 1984-87; gen. ptnr., pres., chief exec. officer Nat. Monument Co., 1986—99; v.p. Translogic Corp., Denver, 1987-88; corp. officer, v.p. mktg., field ops. and sales S.I. Handling Systems, Inc., Easton, Pa., 1988-91; pres. Handling Concepts, Inc., Chgo., 1993—, Modery Sys., Inc., Chgo., 1997—. Agt.Muratec-Murata Automated Systems, Inc., Agent, 1997—2000. Patentee in field. Commr. City of East Grand Rapids, Mich. Traffic Commn., 1983—86; bd. dirs. Naperville (Ill.) Humane Soc., 2001—. Mem. Internat. Material Mgmt. Soc., Am. Mgmt. Assn., Material Handling Inst. Am., Material Handling Inst. (speaker nat. confs.), Am. Mktg. Assn., Conveyor Equipment Mfrs. Assn., Material Handling Equipment Distbrs. Assn., Masons (32 degree). Avocations: golf, photography, power walking, computers. Home: 2255 Palmer Cir Naperville IL 60564-5672 Office: Handling Concepts Inc 2255 Palmer Cir Naperville IL 60564-5672 also: Modery Sys Inc 2255 Palmer Cir Naperville IL 60564-5672

MODESITT, JOHN EDWARD, artist; b. Los Alamos, N.Mex., Nov. 6, 1955; s. George Edward and Lorraine Hellen Modesitt; m. Toshiko Sakamoto; children: Emily. BA, Santa Barbara City Coll., 1977. Oil painting (Christies Auction, LA). Mem.: Santa Barbara Art Assn., Calif. Art Club. Home: 707 Fresca Ct Solana Beach CA 92075 Personal E-mail: j.modesitt@worldnet.att.net.

MODIANO, ALBERT LOUIS, gas, oil industry executive; b. N.Y.C., Sept. 10, 1953; s. Sam A. and Eve Modiano; m. Carolyn Elizabeth Barker, Sept. 29, 1979; children: Aaron, Sarah Anne. BA cum laude, Hobart Coll., 1975; MA, U. Chgo., 1977; postgrad., Harvard U., 1992. Mem. U.S. Senate, 1980-81; assoc. Am. Petroleum Inst., Washington, 1981-87; dep. dir. Office of Oil Policy U.S. Dept. Energy, 1987-89; dep. dir. U.S. Minerals Mgmt. Svc., 1989-93; v.p. U.S. Oil & Gas Assn., 1993—. Mem. Phi Beta Kappa. Office: Ste 601 901 F St NW Washington DC 20004-1400

MODIC, STANLEY JOHN, business editor, publisher; b. Fairport Harbor, Ohio, Dec. 29, 1936; s. Frank and Mary (Zakrajsek) M.; m. Albina DiMichele, May 27, 1961; children— Mark Francis, Laurel Marie. BS in Commerce, Ohio U., 1958. Musician, band leader, 1953-58; Reporter The Telegraph, Painesville, Ohio, 1960-63, city editor, 1964-65; asst. editor Steel Mag., Cleve., 1965-67, news editor, 1968-70; mng. editor Industry Week (formerly Steel Mag.), Cleve., 1970-72, exec. editor, 1972; editor Industry Week, 1972-86; sr. editor Industry Week (formerly Steel Mag.), 1986-89; editor-in-chief Purchasing World Mag., 1989-90, Tooling and Prodn. Mag., 1990—. Mcpl. clk. Fairport Harbor, 1960-61; mem. Fairport Harbor Village Council, 1962-63, pres., 1962-63. Recipient G.D. Crane award Am. Bus. Press, 1991; named Slovenian Man of Yr., Fedn. Slovenian Homes, Cleve., 1998. Mem.: Press Club (pres. Cleve. chpt. 1978—79), Hungarian Culture Club, Am. Slovenian Club (Fairport Harbor) (pres. 2002—), KC, Elks, Sigma Delta Chi (pres. Cleve. chpt. 1975—76). Home: 5842 Woodhill St Painesville OH 44077-5167 Office: 6001 Cochran Rd 1st Fl Cleveland OH 44139-3310 E-mail: smodic@nelsonpub.com.

MODIGLIANI, FRANCO, economist, educator, finance educator; b. Rome, June 18, 1918; arrived in U.S., 1939, naturalized, 1946; s. Enrico and Olga (Flaschel) Modigliani; m. Serena Calabi, May 22, 1939; children: Andre, Sergio. D. Jurisprudence, U. Rome, 1939; D. Social Sci., New Sch. Social Rsch., 1944; LLD (hon.) , U. Chgo., 1967; D. honoris causa (hon.) , U. Louvain, Belgium, 1974, Istituto Universitario di Bergamo, 1979, Hartford U.; LHD (hon.) , Bard Coll., 1985, Brandeis U., 1986, New Sch. Social Research, 1989; LLD, Mich. State U., 1989; D (hon.) , U. Ill., 1990, U. Valencia, Spain, 1992; D in Managerial Engring. (hon.) , U. Naples, 1998. Instr. econs. and statistics N.J. Coll. Women, New Brunswick, 1942; instr., then asso. econs. and statistics Bard Coll., Columbia, 1942—44; lectr., asst. prof. math. econs. and econometrics New Sch. Social Rsch., 1943—44, 1946—48; rsch. asso., chief statistician Inst. World Affairs, N.Y.C., 1945—48; rsch. cons. Cowles Commn. Rsch. in Econs. U. Chgo., 1949—54; asso. prof., then prof. econs. U. Ill., 1949—52; prof. econs. and indsl. adminstrn. Carnegie Inst. Tech., 1952—60; vis. prof. econs. Harvard U., 1957—58; prof. econs. Northwestern U., 1960—62; vis. prof. econs. MIT, 1960—61, prof. econs. and finance, 1962—, Inst. prof., 1970—88, Inst. prof. emeritus, 1988—. Fellow polit. economy U. Chgo., 1948; Fulbright lectr. U. Rome, also, Palermo, Italy, 1955. Author: The Debate Over Stabilization Policy, 1986, Il Caso Italia, 1986, The Collected Papers of Franco Modigliani, 3 vols., 1980, The Collected Papers of Franco Modigliani, 4th and 5th vols., 1989; co-author: National Incomes and International Trade, 1953, Planning Production Inventories and Work Forces, 1960, The Role of Anticipations and Plans in Economic Behavior and Their Use in Economic Analysis and Forecasting, 1961, New Mortgage Designs for Stable Housing in an Inflationary Environment, 1975; co-author: (with Frank J. Fabozzi) Capital Markets: Institutions and Instruments, 1991, Mortgage and Mortgage-Backed Security Markets, 1992; co-author: (with Frank J. Fabozzi, Michael G. Ferri) Foundations of Financial Markets and Institutions, 1994; co-author: Le Avventure di un Economista: Mia Vita, Le Mie Idee, La Nostra Epoca, 1999, (English edit.) Adventures of an Economist, 2001. Named hon. citizen, Town of Modigliana, Italy, 1993, Town of Chiavari, Italy, 1996, Jan Timbergen Meml. lectr., Rotterdam, 1994; recipient Nobel prize in econ. sci., 1985, Cavaliere Di Gran Croce Repubblica Italiana, 1985, Premio Coltura for Econs., Repubblica Italiana, 1988, Premio APE award, 1988, Graham and Dodd award, 1975, 1980, James R. Killian Jr. Faculty Achievement award, 1985, Lord Found. prize, 1989, Italy Premio Columbus, 1989, Italy Premio Guido Dorso, 1989, Italy Premio Stivale D'oro, 1991, Italy Premio Campione D'Italia, 1992, Premio Scanno, 1997. Fellow: NAS, Internat. Econ. Assn. (v.p. 1977—83, hon. pres. 1983—), Am. Acad. Arts and Scis., Am. Econ. Assn. (v.p. 1971, pres. 1976), Econometric Soc. (coun. 1960, v.p. 1961, pres. 1962); mem.: Shadow Fin. Regulatory Com., Accademia Nazionale dei Lincei (Rome), Boston Security Analysts Soc. (hon.), Am. Fin. Assn. (pres. 1981). E-mail: francom@mit.edu.

MODIGLIANI, LEAH, financial analyst; b. Ann Arbor, Mich., Nov. 20, 1964; d. Andrea and Katherine M.; m. Nicky McGrane June 19, 1999. AB, Oberlin Coll., OH, 1986; MBA, Havard U., 1995. Analyst ABT Assocs., Cambridge, Mass., 1987-88; dir. operations Marsoft Inc., Boston, 1988-95; stock market analyst Morgan Stanley, N.Y.C., 1996—. Contbr. to profl. jours. Vol. Student Sponsor Partnership, 1995—; advisor, vol. Girls Inc., 1998—.

MODIN, FREDRIK, professional hockey player; b. Sundsvall, Sweden, Oct. 8, 1974; Hockey player Brynas IF, Maple Leafs, 1996-99; left wing Tampa Bay (Fla.) Lightning, 1999—. Office: Tampa Bay Lightning Ice Palace 401 Channelside Dr Tampa FL 33602*

MODISETT, JEFFREY A. lawyer, state attorney general, business executive; b. Windfall, Ind., Aug. 10, 1954; s. James Richard and Diana T. Modisett; m. Jennifer Ashworth, June 9, 1990; children: Matthew Hunter Ashworth, Haden Nicholas. BA, UCLA, 1976; MA, Oxford (Eng.) U., 1978; JD, Yale U., 1981. Bar: Ind., Calif., D.C. Clk. to Hon. R. Peckham U.S. Dist. Ct. (no. dist.) Calif., San Francisco, 1981—82; asst. U.S. atty. Office U.S. Atty. (ctrl. dist.) Calif., L.A., 1982—88; issues dir. Evan Bayh for Gov., Indpls., 1988; exec. asst. to gov. State of Ind., 1988—90; prosecutor Marion County, 1991—94; sr. counsel Ice Miller Donadio & Ryan, 1995—96; atty. gen. State of Ind., 1997—2000; dep. CEO, gen. counsel Dem. Nat. Conv., 2000; co-CEO TechNet, Palo Alto, Calif., 2000—01; ptnr. Manatt Phelps & Phillips LLP, 2001—02, Bryan Cave LLP, 2002—. Chmn. Gov. Commn. for Drug Free Ind., Indpls., 1989—, Gov. Coun. on Impaired and Dangerous Driving, Indpls., 1989—; pres. Family Advocacy Ctr., Indpls., 1991—94, Hoosier Alliance Against Drugs, Indpls., 1993—96; dir. Cmty. Couns. of Indpls., 1991—93; chmn. Ind. Criminal Justice Inst., Indpls., 1989—90, dir., 1989—; vice chmn. Juvenile Justice and Youth Gang Study Com., Indpls., 1992—94; legal analyst Sta. WTHR-TV, Indpls., 1995—96. Author: Prosecutor's Perspective, 1991—94; editor-in-chief: Yale Jour. Internat. Law, 1980—81. Co-chair Ind. State Dem. Coordinated Campaign, Indpls., 1996. Named Top Lawyer, Indpls. Monthly mag., 1993; named to Sagamore of Wabash, State of Ind., 1995; recipient Spl. Enforcement award, U.S. Customs, 1988, Child Safety Adv. award, Automotive Safety for Children, 1997, STAR Alliance Impact award, 1998, Spirit of Ind. award, Am. Lung Assn., 1999. Mem.: Indpls. Bar Assn., Ind. Bar Assn. Avocation: bicycling.

MODISETTE, LAURA JESSEN, information designer; b. Toledo, Apr. 5, 1951; d. Otto Carl Jessen and Violet Delores Stohl; s. Jean Pierre Modisette, Sept. 3, 1977. BA in Polit. Sci., Miami U., Oxford, Ohio, 1973; MA in Polit. Sci., U. Milw., 1974; MS in Future Studies, U. Houston, 1978. Asst. to dept. chair future studies U. of Houston, Clear Lake City, Tex., 1976-77; staff assoc. Rice Ctr., Houston, 1977-79; program asst. Ohio State U., Columbus, 1979-80; rsch. scientist Battelle Meml. Inst., 1980-83, prin. rsch. scientist, 1983-2001, project mgr., 2001—. Contbr. articles to profl. publs. Program specialist First Link United Way Agy., Columbus, 1982-90, site coord. Yes! program, 1992-93; grant reviewer Ohio Cmty. Svc. Coun., Columbus, 1998—; mem. single year allocation com. United Way of Franklin County, 1985-90; racewalking judge U.S.A Track and Field, 1999-2000. Univ. fellow U. Wis.,

1973-74. Mem. Project Mgmt. Inst., Internat. Soc. for Performance Improvements (membership chair 1987-88), Internat. Inst. for Info. Design, Soc. for Tech. Comm. (sr. mem., pres. Ctrl. Ohio chpt. 2000-01, chpt. of excellence award 2001, region 4 pacesetter award 2001, Mem. of Yr. 1998-99, Disting. Tech. Comm. Award of Merit 1999), Buckeye Striders (v.p. 1999-2001), BuckCHI. Avocations: racewalking, volksmarching, gardening, reading. Home: 216 Wilber Ave Columbus OH 43215-1395 Office: Battelle Meml Inst 505 King Ave Columbus OH 43201-2681

MODISHER, MELVIN WAYNE, obstetrician/gynecologist, educator; b. Sharpsville, Pa., May 9, 1916; MD, Temple U., 1943. Diplomate Am. Bd. Ob-Gyn. Intern Abington Meml. Hosp., 1944; resident in ob-gyn. Bethesda Hosp., Cin., 1946-49; mem. staff U. Hosp., San Diego. Assoc. clin. prof. reproductive medicine Med. Sch. U. Calif. San Diego. Fellow ACS. E-mail: melcor@cts.com.

MODLIN, HOWARD S. lawyer; b. N.Y.C., Apr. 10, 1931; s. Martin and Rose Modlin; m. Margot S. Modlin, Oct. 18, 1956; children: James, Laura, Peter. AB, Union Coll., Schenectady, 1952; JD, Columbia U., 1955. Bar: N.Y. 1956, D.C. 1973. Assoc. Weisman, Celler, Spett & Modlin, P.C., N.Y.C., 1956-61, ptnr., 1961-76, mng. ptnr., 1976-95, pres., 1996—. Chmn. bd. dirs., sec. Gen. DataComm Industries, Inc., Naugatuck, Conn.; bd. dirs. Am.-Book-Stratford Press, Inc., N.Y.C., Fedders Corp., Liberty Corner, NJ, Trans-Lux Corp., Norwalk, Conn. Chmn. bd. dirs. Daus. of Jacob Geriat. Ctr., Bronx, N.Y. Mem. ABA, Assn. of Bar of City of N.Y., D.C. Bar Assn. Office: Weisman Celler Spett & Modlin PC 445 Park Ave New York NY 10022-2606

MOE, ANDREW IRVING, veterinarian; b. Tacoma, Jan. 2, 1927; s. Ole Andrew and Ingeborg (Gordham) M.; m. Dorothy Clara Becker, June 25, 1950 (dec. Nov. 30, 2001); children: Sylvia Moe McGowan, Palema Moe Barker, Joyce. BS in Biology, U. Puget Sound, 1949; BA, Wash. State U., 1953, DVM, 1954. Meat cutter Art Hansem, Tacoma, 1943-48; gen. practice as vet. Baronti Vet. Hosp., Eugene, Oreg., 1956-57; vet. regulatory Calif. Animal Health br., resident vet. II Calif. Dept. Food & Agr., Modesto, 1957-64, acting vet.-in-charge Modesto Dist. office, vet. III, 1976-77, ret., 1990—. Watersafety instr. ARC, 1958-61. Capt. Vet. Corps., 1954-56, 62, Post 4144 Quartermaster, 2001—; All State Team Post quartermaster, 2001-02; comdr. 417th Med. Svc. Flight Res. (AFRES), 1965-66, 71-73; lt. col. Biomed Scis. Corps. USAF, ret., 1982. Recipient Chief Vet. badge, 1975. Mem. VFW (life, comdr. post 4144 1998-2001, quartermaster 2000—), No. San Joaquin Vet. Med. Assn. (pres. 1979), Calif. Acad. Vet. Medicine (charter), Res. Officers Assn. (life), Ret. Officers Assn. (life), Assn. Mil. Surgeons U.S. (life), Sons of Norway, Shriners (bd. dirs. Modesto Shrine 1995), Masons (Illustrious Master Modesto chpt. 1983, Allied Masonic degree, pres. Modesto Masonic Luncheon Club 1991, 98, Meritorious Svc. medal 1992, Man of Yr. award 1999), Scottish Rite (pres. Ctrl. Valley 1997, bd. dirs. 1998-2001), Presido Yacht Club Sausalito (Calif.), Theta Chi, Alpha Psi. Lutheran. Home: 161 Norwegian Ave Modesto CA 95350-3542

MOE, JAMES BURTON, pharmaceutical company executive; b. Hayfield, Minn., Oct. 4, 1940; s. James Herald and Clara Clema (DeVriendt) M.; m. Janice Naomi Nackerud, Nov. 27, 1959; children: Carolyn, Alyson, Jennifer, Bryce. BS, U. Minn., 1962, DVM, 1964; PhD, U. Calif., Davis, 1978. Pvt. vet. practice Dodge Vet. Clinic, Dodge Center, Minn., 1964-66; commd. 1st lt. U.S. Army, 1966, advanced through grades to lt. col., 1979, retired, 1986; dir. divsn. pathology Walter Reed Army Inst. Rsch., Washington, 1980-86; sr. scientist The Upjohn Co., Kalamazoo, 1986-88, dir. drug devel. toxicology, 1988-89, exec. dir. drug safety rsch., 1989-94, v.p. world wide drug safety rsch. Japan and Asia, 1994-95; v.p. world wide toxicology Pharmacia & Upjohn, Inc., Kalamzoo, Mich., 1995-2000; v.p. global toxicology Pharmacia Corp., 2000—. Contbr. articles to profl. jours., chpts. to books. Decorated Bronze Star, Legion of Merit; Calif. Lung Assn. Pulmonary Rsch. grantee, 1976. Mem. Am. Coll. Vet. Pathologists (pres. 1992-93), Soc. Toxicol. Pathologists, U.S. Can. Assn. of Pathology. Lutheran. Avocations: golf, jogging, woodworking. Home: 4450 Foxfire Trl Portage MI 49024-9540 Office: Global Toxicology Pharmacia Corp 301 Henrietta St Kalamazoo MI 49007-4940

MOE, ORVILLE LEROY, racetrack executive; b. Spokane, Wash., Nov. 26, 1936; s. Clarence Orville and Georgia Maria (Lombard) M.; m. Deonne Wesley Schultz, Jan. 11, 1953; children: Kathleen June, Susan Marie, Terry Ann. Co-owner Moe's Sudden Svc. Fuel Co., Spokane, Wash., 1956-74; sec. Gold Res. Mining Corp., 1973-89, Bonanza Gold Corp., Spokane, 1973-85; pres., founder Spokane Raceway Park, Inc., 1971—. Regional v.p. Am. Hot Rod Assn., Kansas, Mo., 1968-84, mktg. dir., 1978-84; co-producer Internat. Car Show Assn., Spokane, 1969-90. Co-producer Spokane Auto Boat Speed Show, 1964—. Mem. Nat. Rep. Senatorial Com., 1984—; mem., trustee Rep. Presdl. Task Force, mem. 1992 Presdl. Trust Rep. Nat. Com. Mem. ISCA, Eagles, Am. Hot Rod Assn. (exec. v.p. Spokane, Wash. 1986—), Internat. Footprint Assn., Am. Auto Racing Assn. (regional v.p.). Republican. Avocations: auto racing, mining, collecting and rebuilding autos, fishing, ice hockey. Office: Spokane Raceway Park Inc 101 N Hayford Rd Spokane WA 99224-9510

MOE, RICHARD PALMER, lawyer; b. Duluth, Minn., Nov. 27, 1936; s. Russell James and Virginia Mary (Palmer) M.; m. Julia Neimeyer, Dec. 26, 1964; children— Eric Palmer, Andrew Neimeyer, Alexandra Julia. BA, Williams Coll., 1959; LL.B., U. Minn., 1966. Bar: Minn. 1967, D.C. 1979, N.Y. 1991. Adminstrv. asst. to mayor, City of Mpls., 1961-62; to lt. gov. State of Minn., 1963-66; fin. dir. Minn. Democratic Farmer-Labor Party, 1967-69, chmn., 1969-72; adminstrv. asst. to Sen. Walter F. Mondale of Minn., Washington, 1972-76; chief of staff Vice Pres. Walter F. Mondale, 1977-81; counsel Davis Polk & Wardwell, Washington, 1981-85, ptnr., 1985-92; pres. Nat. Trust for Hist. Preservation, 1992—. Trustee Ford Found., 1998—. Office: Nat Trust for Hist Preservation 1785 Massachusetts Ave NW Washington DC 20036-2117

MOE, ROGER DEANE, state legislator, secondary education educator; b. Crookston, Minn., June 2, 1944; s. Melvin Truman and Matheldia (Njus) M.; m. Paulette Moe; four children. BS, Mayville State Coll., 1966; student, Moorhead State Coll., 1969, N.D. State U., 1970. Tchr. Ada (Minn.) H.S., 1966—; v.p. Coleman, Christian Advt. Agy.; mem. Minn. Senate from 2nd dist., St. Paul, 1970—; majority leader Minn. State Senate, 1981—. Chmn. rules and adminstrn. com., mem. ethics and campaign reform, edn., and higher edn. coms., Minn. State Senate. Ward del. Ada, Minn., 1970; state del. Minn. Dem.-Farmer-Labor Conv., 1970. Mem. NEA, Ada Edn. Assn., Jaycees. Office: Rt 3 Box 86A Erskine MN 56535-9532 also: State Senate 208 Capitol 75 Constitution Ave Saint Paul MN 55155-1601*

MOE, RONALD CHESNEY, public administration researcher; b. San Diego, May 28, 1937; s. Chesney R. and L. Bernice (Weston) M.; m. Carolyn Carr, May 18, 1962 (div. Feb. 1974); children: Steven, Cynthia; m. Grace Tyler, Apr. 30, 1976. BA, Claremont Coll., 1959; MA, Columbia U., 1962, PhD in Pub. Law and Govt., 1968. Asst. prof. San Diego State U., 1967-70; sr. policy advisor Office of Econ. Opportunity, Exec. Office of the Pres., Washington, 1970-71, Cost of Living Coun., Exec. Office of the Pres., Washington, 1971-73; specialist govt. orgns. and mgmt. Congl. Rsch. Svc. Libr. of Congress, 1973—. Cons. OECD, Paris, 1996—. Contbr. chpts. in books, articles to profl. jours. Mem. exec. bd. Congregational Chs. of Am., Milw., 1985-89. Capt. U.S. Army Res., 1961-63. Ctr. Study of Am. Govt. fellow Johns Hopkins U., Washington, 1993—; recipient ASPA Louis Brownlow award, 1988, 91, 95-96. Fellow Nat. Acad. Pub. Adminstrn.; mem. Acad. Polit. Sci., Cosmos Club (Washington), Phi Beta Kappa. Republican. Home: 4700 Connecticut Ave NW Apt 407 Washington DC 20008-5609 Office: Congl Rsch Svc Libr Of Congress Washington DC 20540-0001 E-mail: rmoe@crs.loc.gov.

MOE, STANLEY ALLEN, architect, consultant; b. Fargo, N.D., May 28, 1914; s. Arnold Ole and Freda Emily (Pape) Moe; m. Doris Lucille Anderson, July 25, 1937 (dec. 2000); children: Willa Moe Crouse, Myra Moe Galther; m. Reiko Izuno, Nov. 11, 2001. BArch, U. Minn., 1936; D of Engring. (hon.), U. N.D., 1993. lic. architect several states; cert. Nat. Coun. Archtl. Registration Bds. Project architect several firms in Midwest, 1936-42; project architect U.S. Army Corps Engrs.., Africa, 1942-43; ptnr. H.S. Starin, Architects & Engrs., Duluth, Minn., 1943-47; sr. ptnr. Moe & Larsen, Architects & Engrs., L.A., 1947-54; ptnr., gen. mgr., exec. v.p. Daniel, Mann, Johnson & Mendenall, 1954-71, corp. v.p., 1972-79; prin. Stanley A. Moe, AIA, 1979—. Dir. design of major mil. projects in Eritrea, Sudan, Egypt, Yemen for Allied Forces, 1942-43; chmn. control com. DMJM & Assocs., dir. design prototype, tng. & operational facilities Titan I Intercontinental Ballistic Missiles Program USAF, 1958-63; project dir. Space Shuttle facilities Kennedy Space Ctr., 1973; project dir. for design of aircraft maintenance complex Iranian Aircraft Industries, 1978; project mgr. for design of major med. facility program Min. of Def. and Aviation, Saudi Arabia, 1975-76; project mgr. design of Boufarik Internat. Airport, Algeria, 1983. Pres. San. Fernando Valley Young Reps., 1952, Van Nuys (Calif.) Jaycees, 1950. Recipient Disting. Svc. award for cmty. svc. Van Nuys Jaycees, 1949, Sioux award U. N.D. Alumni Assn., 1985, Trustees Soc. award U. Minn., 1992; inducted into N.D. Entrepreneur Hall of Fame, 2000. Mem. AIA (Calif. coun.), Rotary, Delta Tau Delta. Republican. Presbyterian. Avocations: world travel, hunting, fishing, historic restoration, woodworking. Home and Office: 447 S Plymouth Blvd Los Angeles CA 90020-4706

MOECKEL, BILL REID, retired university dean; b. Pekin, Ill., Sept. 2, 1925; s. Willis E. and Daisy M. M.; m. Pauline C. Fox, Sept. 1, 1946; children— Steven, Cindy, Nancy. BS, U. Ill., 1948, MS, 1949, PhD, 1953. Instr. mktg. U. Mo., 1949-51; asst. prof. Ga. State U., 1953-54; asso. dean Sch. Bus., Ohio State U., 1954-67; dir. USAF Sch. Logistics, 1958-65; dean Sch. Bus., Miami U., Oxford, Ohio, 1967-87. Served with AUS, 1943-46. Mem. Am. Assembly Collegiate Schs. Bus. (nat. pres. 1981-82), Air Force Inst. Tech. Assn. Grads, Beta Gamma Sigma (nat. pres. 1976-78), Alpha Delta Sigma, Omicron Delta Kappa, Alpha Kappa Psi, Pi Sigma Epsilon, Mu Kappa Tau, Beta Alpha Psi.

MOECKEL, HENRY THEODORE, architect; b. Waterbury, Conn., May 13, 1918; s. Henry Theodore and Anna Gertrude (Vest) M.; m. Beryl Bronson (div. 1949); children: Holly, Steven, Cathy, Jeffery, Henry T. III.; m. Marjorie Hollis, Nov. 2, 1963. BArch, Rensselaer Poly. Inst., 1940. Registered architect, Conn. With Henry T. Moeckel & Son, Architects, Naugatuck, Conn., 1945-60, Henry T. Moeckel & Assocs., Architects, Naugatuck, 1960-70; pres. Moeckel & Oris, Architects, 1970-94, ret., 1994. Prin. works include sch. bldgs., libraries, firehouses, town halls, housing projects for elderly, chs. Mem. AIA. Lodges: Rotary (pres. 1950, dist. gov. 1955). Republican. Congregationalist. Avocations: fishing, golf. Home: 994 Main St S Woodbury CT 06798-3801

MOEDERSHEIM, SABINE, foreign language educator; b. Freiburg, Germany, Aug. 4, 1959; came to U.S. 1998; d. Karl-Heinz and Margrit F.L. Moedersheim. DPhil, Albert-Ludwigs U., Freiburg, 1992. Asst. prof. Albert Ludwigs U., Freiburg, 1992-95; vis. asst. prof. McGill U., Montreal, Can., 1996-98; asst. prof. U. Wis., Madison, 1998—. Author: Domini Doctrina Coronat, 1994; editor: Cramer: Emblemata Sacra, 1994, Ammon: Imitatio Crameriana, 1999. Lynen fellow Alexander-von-Humboldt Found., Bonn, Germany, 1996-98. Office: U Wis Dept German 818 Van Hise Hall Madison WI 53706 E-mail: smoedersheim@facstaff.wisc.edu.

MOE-FISHBACK, BARBARA ANN, counseling administrator; b. Grand Forks, N.D., June 24, 1955; d. Robert Alan and Ruth Ann (Wang) Moe; m. William Martin Fishback; children: Kristen Ann, William Robert. BS in Psychology, U. N.D., 1977, MA in Counseling and Guidance, 1979, BS in Elem. Edn., 1984. Cert. elem. counselor, Ill. Tchr. United Day Nursery, Grand Forks, 1977-78; social worker Cavalier County Social Svcs., Langdon, N.D., 1979-83; elem. sch. counselor Douglas Sch. Sys., Ellsworth AFB, S.D., 1984-87, Jacksonville (Ill.) Sch. Sys., 1987—. Vol. Big Sister Program, Grand Forks, 1978-84; leader Pine to Prairie coun. Girl Scouts U.S., 1980-82; tchrs. asst. Head Start Program, Grand Forks, 1979. Mem. AACD, NEA, AAUW (local br. newsletter editor 1980-81, br. sec. 1981-83), Ill. Assn. Counseling and Devel., Ill. Sch. Counselor Assn., Ill. Edn. Assn., Am. Sch. Counselor Assn., Kappa Alpha Theta (newsletter, mag. article editor 1976-77), Jaycettes (dir. 1982-83). Avocations: cooking, camping, curling, ceramics, creative writing. Home: 291 Sandusky St Jacksonville IL 62650-1844 Office: Lafayette Center Dist 117 747 W Lafayette Ave Jacksonville IL 62650-1832

MOEHLE, CARM ROBERT, lawyer; b. Indio, Calif., June 10, 1948; s. Robert Rudolph Moehle and Catherine Marie Whitcraft. BSCE, U. Mo., Rolla, 1970; JD, U. Mo., 1974. Bar: Mo. 1974, Ariz. 1978, Colo. 1986, U.S. Dist. Ct. Ariz. 1978, U.S. Dist. Ct. (we. dist.) Mo. 1974, U.S. Supreme Ct. 1980. Law clk. Mo. Ct. Appeals (we. dist.), Kansas City, 1974-75; prosecuting atty. Greene County, Springfield, Mo., 1975-77; law clk. Ariz. Supreme Ct., Phoenix, 1977-78; staff atty. Ariz. Ct. Appeals, 1978-82; atty. Bosco & DiMatteo, P.C., 1983-91, Scult, Lazarus, French, Zwillinger and Smock, P.A., Phoenix, 1992-93; pvt. practice, 1994—. Chmn. bd. dirs. Ariz. Coun. Trout Unlimited, Phoenix, 1989—; trustee Maricopa County Bar Found., Phoenix, 1992-95. Mem. Ariz. Trial Lawyers Assn., Maricopa County Bar Assn. (vol. lawyers program). Avocations: backpacking, hiking, flyfishing, golf, skiing. E-mail: carm.moehle@azbar.org.

MOEHLMAN, MICHAEL SCOTT, lawyer; b. Columbus, Ohio, Apr. 11, 1938; s. Arthur Henry and Marguerite Caroline M.; m. Carol Jean Shafer, Sept. 28, 1963; 1 son, Matthew. BA, Harvard U., 1960; LLB, U. Tex., 1963. Bar: Tex. 1963. Sr. ptnr. Baker & Botts, Houston, 1963—. Bd. dirs. St. Martin's Episcopal Children's Ctr. Mem. ABA (com. bank securities), Internat. Bar Assn., Tex. Bar Assn. (com. revision corp. law), Houston Bar Assn. (judicature com.), Tex.-Mex. Bar Assn., Am. Judicature Soc., Houston Bar Found. (chmn. bd. dirs.), Phi Delta Phi. Clubs: Houston (chmn. fin. com., bd. dirs., pres.), Houston Racquet, Houston Yacht, Harvard (Boston), St. Charles Bay Hunting. Episcopalian. Office: Baker & Botts 1 Shell Plz 30th Fl Houston TX 77002 E-mail: michael.moehlman@bakerbotts.com.

MOEHLMAN, RUTH, historian, writer; b. Detroit, June 29, 1933; d. Theodore and Freda Alice (Levin) Roth; m. Albert E. Moehlman, June 5, 1956; children: Elizabeth Moehlman Guss, Laura Moehlman Golden, Denise, Theresa. BA, Wayne State U., 1955, MA, 1956. Curator Detroit Hist. Mus., 1957; writer Farmington Forum, Farmington Hills, Mich., 1965-83; writer pamphlets and articles Farmington Observer, spl. writer, 1998—. Author: If the Walls Could Talk: Heritage Homes of Farmington, 1980, 2d edit., 1993. Pres. Farmington (Mich.) Hist. Soc., 1991; sec., chmn. Farmington Hills Hist. Dist. Commn.; docent Farmington Hist. Mus.; chmn. Farmington Heritate Home Tour. Avocations: tennis, gardening. Home: 32659 Olde Franklin Dr Farmington MI 48334-1745

MOEHRING, FRED ADOLF, fastener distribution company executive; b. Bklyn., Nov. 4, 1935; s. Fred Henry Christian and Elsa Marta (Klein) M.; m. Marilyn Agnes Rieber, June 7, 1958; 1 child, Donna. Grad. high sch., Jamaica, N.Y. Salesman Miller-Charles and Co., Mineola, N.Y., 1956-63, Century Fasteners Corp., Elmhurst, 1963-65; gen. mgr. Stewart Air Industries, Syosset, 1965-70; salesman Supreme Lake Mfg. Co., Plantsville, Conn., 1971, Allmetal Screw Products Inc., Garden City, N.Y., 1971-72; cab driver Scull's Angels, Flushing, 1972-74; gen. mgr. Empire Fasteners, L.I.C., 1974-83, Mar-Lin Sales, Bklyn., 1983-97, Fred A. Moehring, Inc., Bklyn., 1998—. Mem. ASME, ASTM, NRA, ASM Internat., Soc. Automotive Engrs., Met. Fastener Distbrs. Assn. (pres. 1991-92), Steuben Soc. Am., United German-Am. Com. of U.S.A., Inc., German-Am. Steuben Parade Com. Republican. Lutheran. Avocation: golf. Office: Fred A Moehring Inc 208 N 8th St Brooklyn NY 11211-2008 E-mail: fred35@iwon.com.

MOELHMAN, AMY JO, social worker; b. Lafayette, Ind., Mar. 18, 1954; d. Charles and Marian (Young) Moelhman. BS, Ball State U., 1976; MSW, U. Denver, 1979. Lic. clin. social worker, Ind. Social worker Adolescent Crisis Team, Adams County Social Svc., Denver; counselor adolescent boys prog. Pleasant Run Children's Home, Indpls.; group therapist Mothers of Victims of Sexual Abuse, Mid-Town Mental Health; supr. foster care and counseling prog. Children's Bur.; mgr. Family Connection Ctr., 1989-90; dir. family programs Vis. Nurse Svc., Indpls., 1990-96; dir. Holy Family Svcs., Cath. Social Svcs., 1996—2001; cons. Brown County Family Access Ctr., 1999—; supr. cmty. programs Indpls. Transition Ctr. Casey Family Programs, 2001—. Chair Ind. Coalition of Family-based Svcs., 1992-94; co-chair family preservation com. Marion County Stepahead; part-time faculty masters in social work program Ind. U.-Purdue U., Indpls. Contbr. articles to profl. jours. Mem. NASW, Acad. Cert. Social Workers. Home: 818 E 53rd St Indianapolis IN 46220-3104 E-mail: amoelhman@casey.org.

MOELING, WALTER GOOS, IV, lawyer; b. Quantico, Va., Feb. 16, 1943; s. Walter Goos III and Dorothy M.; m. Nell Frances Askew, Aug. 27, 1965; children: Charles H., Christine E. BA, Duke U., 1965, JD, 1968. Bar: Ga. 1968. Assoc. Powell, Goldstein, Frazer & Murphy, Atlanta, 1968-75, ptnr., 1975—. Bd. dirs. So. Banking Law and Policy Conf., 1989-96, Southeastern Conf. for Bank Dirs., 1996—, Children's Rehab. Ctr., Atlanta, 1982—, Gatchell Home, Atlanta, 1983—; bd. dirs. Frazer Ctr., 1989—, chmn. bd. dirs., 1993. Mem. ABA (mem. banking com. 1986—), Ga. C. of C. (bd. dirs. 1998-2000), Ga. Bar Assn., Ga. Bankers Assn. (assoc., chairperson bank counsel sect. 1992-95, bd. dirs. 1998-2000), Cmty. Bankers Assn. (assoc.), Capital City Club, Willow Point Country Club. Democrat. Unitarian Universalist. Avocations: golf, fly-fishing. Office: Powell Goldstein Frazer & Murphy 191 Peachtree St NE Ste 16 Atlanta GA 30303-1740 E-mail: wmoeling@pgfm.com.

MOELLER, AUDREY CAROLYN, retired energy company executive, corporate secretary; b. Pitts., May 10, 1935; d. Nicholas William and Edith Tecla (Russman) M. Grad. high sch., Pitts. Legal sec. Equitable Resources Inc., Pitts., 1955-72, asst. corp. sec., 1972-80, corp. sec., 1980-86, v.p., corp. sec., 1986-99; also corp. sec. Equitable Resources Inc. subs.; ret., 1999. Com. mem. United Way Allegheny County, Pa., 1978, United Way Southwestern Pa., 1984. Mem.: Pa. Assn. Notaries, Am. Soc. Corp. Secs. (chmn. membership Pitts. chpt. 1995, treas. 1996, v.p and program chmn. 1997, pres. 1998, asst. sec.), Loyal Christian Benefit Assn. (nat. coun. 1993, pres. br. 331 2000, nat. auditor 2001). Democrat. Roman Catholic. Avocations: choral singing, golf, travel. Home: 1003 Cherry Hill Dr Presto PA 15142

MOELLER, DADE WILLIAM, environmental engineer, educator; b. Grant, Fla., Feb. 27, 1927; s. Robert A. and Victoria (Bolton) M.; m. Betty Jean Radford, Oct. 7, 1949 (dec. Oct. 1998); children: Garland Radford, Mark Bolton, William Kehne, Matthew Palmer, Elisabeth Anne. BSCE, Ga. Inst. Tech., 1947, MS in Environ. Engring., 1948; PhD in Nuclear Engring., N.C. State U., 1957. Commd. jr. asst. san. engr. USPHS, 1948, advanced through grades to san. engr. dir., 1961; rsch. engr. Los Alamos Sci. Lab., 1949-52; staff asst. Radiol. Health Program, Washington, 1952-54; rsch. assoc. Oak Ridge Nat. Lab., 1956-57; chief radiol. health tng. Taft San. Engring. Ctr., Cin., 1957-61; officer charge Northeastern Radiol. Health Lab., Winchester, Mass., 1961-66; assoc. dir. Kresge Center Environ. Health, Harvard Sch. Pub. Health, 1966-83, prof. engring. in environmental health, head dept. environmental health scis., 1968-83, dir. Office of Continuing Edn., 1982-84, assoc. dean continuing edn., 1985-93; environ. cons., 1993—; pres. Dade Moeller & Assocs., Inc., 1993—. Cons. radiol. health. Author: (textbook) Environmental Health, 2d edit., 1997; contbr. articles to profl. jours. Chmn. Am. Bd. Health Physics, 1967-70; mem. com. 4 Internat. Commn. on Radiol. Protection, 1978-85; chmn. nat. air pollution manpower devel. adv. com. U.S. EPA, 1972-75; mem. adv. com. reactor safeguards U.S. NRC, 1973-88, chmn., 1976, chmn. adv. com. nuclear waste, 1988-93. Named to Ga. Inst. Tech. Engring. Hall of Fame, 1999; recipient Disting. Engring. Alumnus award, N.C. State U., 2001. Fellow Am. Pub. Health Assn., Am. Nuclear Soc.; mem. AAAS, Am. Acad. Environ. Engrs., Nat. Coun. Radiation Protection and Measurements (hon.), NAE, Health Physics Soc. (pres. 1971-72). Home and Office: 257 River Island Rd New Bern NC 28562-3669 E-mail: dademoeller@cconnect.net.

MOELLER, FLOYD DOUGLAS, lawyer; b. Safford, Ariz., Aug. 16, 1949; s. Floyd Albert and Helen Lou (Posey) M.; m. Tyra Brown, Dec. 18, 1970; children: Kristin, Sam, John, Susan. BS in Police Sci., Brigham Young U., 1972, JD, 1977; MS in Mgmt., Lesley Coll., 1985, MA in Counseling Psychology, 1987; LLM in Tax, Washington Sch. Law, 1987, D of Juridicial Sci., 2001. Bar: N.Mex. 1978, U.S. Dist. Ct. N.Mex. 1978, U.S. Dist. Ct. Ariz. 1978, U.S. Ct. Appeals (10th cir.) 1979 , U.S. Tax Ct. 1981, U.S. Supreme Ct. 1981, Navajo Nation, Hopi Tribe, Jicarilla Apache Tribe, White Mountain Apache Tribe, So. Ute Tribe, Ute Mountain Tribe, So. Paiute Coun., Ft. Belknap Indian Ct., Gila River Indian Ct., Mescalaro Apache Ct., S.W. Inter Tribal Ct. Appeals, Zuni Tribal Ct. Assoc. Wade Beavers & Assocs., Farmington, N.Mex., 1978-79; ptnr. Nunn & Moeller, 1979; sole practice, 1979-80, 87—; ptnr. Moeller & Burnham, 1980-87. Mem. exec. com. Better Bus. Bur. of 4 Corners, 1978, bd. dirs., 1978—; bd. dirs. Farmington Pub. Library Bd., 1979-86, San Juan Med. Found., San Juan Pub. Library Found., Halvorson House; chmn. local troop coms. Boy Scouts Am., Farmington, 1985—. Capt. USMC, 1972-75. Named diplomat Nat. Bd. Trial Advocacy, 1986. Mem. ABA, J. Reuben Clark Law Soc., Nat. Panel Consumer Arbitrators, Am. Arbitration Assn., N.Mex. Trial Lawyers Assn., N.Mex. State Bar Assn. (CLE, fee arbitration coms. 1985, pres. trial practice sect. 1988), Navajo Nat. Bar Assn., San Juan County Bar Assn., 4 Corners Inn of Ct. Republican. Mem. Lds Ch. Avocations: reading, poetry, gardening, knot tying. Office: PO Box 15249 Farmington NM 87401-5249 Fax: (505) 362-0818. E-mail: dmoeller@acrnet.com.

MOELLER, HENRY WILLIAM, retired marine biology educator; b. Woodbury, N.J., Aug. 4, 1937; s. Henry William Moeller Sr. and Florence Thelma (Johnson) McCarthy; m. Barbara Marie Wunder, Nov. 12, 1961; children: Thomas, Russell, Charles. AB, Drew U., 1959; MS, Rutgers U., 1965, PhD, 1969. From instr. to asst. prof. marine sci. Southampton (N.Y.) Coll., L.I. U., 1965-68; from asst prof. to prof. marine sci. Dowling Coll., Oakdale, N.Y., 1969-2000, prof. emeritus, 2001—. Sci. advisor N.Y. State Assembly and U.S. Ho. of Reps., 1980's; bd. dirs. Landmarks and Historic Trusts, Southampton. Author: Unfurling the History of the Stars and Stripes, 1992, 2d edit., 1995; patentee in field. Bd. trustees Nature Conservancy, Shelter Island, N.Y., 1985-86; mem. com. apptd. by Gov. Cuomo, Aquaculture 2000, Albany, N.Y., 1987-89. With USAR, 1960-66. Recipient Suffolk County Heritage award Suffolk County Legislature, 1982, Suffolk County Vol. Recognition award 2d Legis. Dist. Suffolk County Legislature, 2001. Mem. Suffolk County Archaeol. Assn. (past pres.). Home: PO Box 995 Hampton Bays NY 11946-0905 E-mail: henrymoeller@worldnet.att.net.

MOELLER, JAMES, retired state supreme court justice; b. Valley, Nebr., Nov. 14, 1933; s. Hans and Marie Grace (Shumaker) M.; m. Nancy Lee Kiely, Dec. 16, 1961; children: Amy Jo, Linda Anne. BA, Nebr. Wesleyan U., 1954; JD with high distinction, George Washington U., 1959. Bar: Ariz. 1959, U.S. Dist. Ct. Ariz. 1959, U.S. Ct. Appeals (9th cir.) 1961. Assoc. Lewis and Roca, Phoenix, 1959-64, ptnr., 1964-70, Moeller Hover Jensen & Henry, Phoenix, 1970-77; judge Maricopa County Superior Ct., 1977-87; assoc. justice Ariz. Supreme Ct., 1987-92, vice chief justice, 1992-96, assoc. justice, 1996-98; ret., 1998—. Editor-in-chief George Washington U. Law Rev., 1958-59. Bd. dirs. Found. for Blind Children, Scottsdale, Ariz., 1964-70, Ariz. Found. Prevention of Blindness, Phoenix, 1966-70; Rep. committeeman, Phoenix and Scottsdale, 1965-69. Served with U.S. Army, 1954-56. Fellow Am. Bar Found., Ariz. Bar Found.; mem. Ariz. Bar Assn., Maricopa County Bar Assn. Presbyterian. Avocations: travel, puzzles, history.

MOELLER, JOSEPH JOHN, JR. university official; b. Jersey City, Feb. 1, 1946; s. Joseph John and Paula (Huneke) M.; m. Linda Lee Recksiek, Aug. 8, 1971. BEng, Stevens Inst. Tech., 1967, MEng, 1969, PhD, 1975. Instr. Stevens Inst. Tech., Hoboken, N.J., 1970-75, asst. prof., 1975-77, dean ednl. devel., 1977-85, mgr. personal computer program, 1983-85, assoc. provost for computing and info. systems, 1985-88, v.p. for info. systems, 1988-92, v.p. for adminstrv. and info. sys., 1992-94, v.p. grad. sch. and rsch., 1994—. Adminstr. N.J. Bus.-Industry-Sci. Edn. Consortium, Hoboken, 1985-92; adminstr. N.J. Intercampus Network, Inc., Steering Com. Adminstr., Hoboken, 1990-93, pres. 1993-97, bd. trustees, 1990—; chmn. Newark Remote Access Ctr., Hoboken, 1988-93. Contbr. articles to profl. jours., chpt. to book. Dir. Hudson County chpt. United Way, 1992-94. Named Outstanding Tchr. of Yr., Stevens Inst. Tech., 1973; honored by N.J. Gen. Assembly for meritorious svc. to edn., 1997. Mem. Assn. Ind. Colls. and Univs. (dir. 1993—), Am. Soc. for Engring. Edn., N.J. Soc. for Info. Mgmt., Sigma Xi, Tau Beta Pi (mem. adv. bd.). Avocations: travel, music. Office: Castle Point On The Hudson Hoboken NJ 07030-5906

MOELLER, MARY ELLA, retired home economist, educator, radio commentator; b. Southampton, N.Y., Mar. 11, 1938; d. Harry Eugene and Edith Leone (Reester) Parsons; m. James Myron Moeller, Aug. 5, 1961; 1 child, Mary Beth. BS in Home Econs., U. Nebr., 1960; MLS, SUNY, Stony Brook, 1977. Tchr. home econs. Port Jefferson Schs., N.Y., 1960-70; home econs.

program asst. Suffolk County Coop. Extension of Cornell U., Riverhead, 1972-82; tchr. home econs. Eastport (N.Y.) H.S., 1982-85, South County Schs., Bellport Middle Sch., N.Y., 1985-93; sch. coord. N.Y. state mentoring program Bellport Middle Sch., 1992-95. Host Ask Your Neighbor, Sta. WRIV, Riverhead, 1982-87; trainer Home Econs. Entrepreneurship N.Y. State Edn. Dept., 1986-95; mem. home and career skills regional team N.Y. State Edn. Dept., 1984-86; mem. consumer homemaking adv. bd. Bd. Coop. Edn.; friendly svc. chmn. N.Y. State Ret. Tchrs. L.I. Zone, 1995—. Contbr. monthly articles to consumer publs. Chairperson policy bd. South Country Tchrs. Ctr.; mem. East Hampton Town Citizens Adv. com. Mem.: N.Y. State Ret. Tchrs. Assn. (v.p. Friendly Svc. 2000—), Suffolk County Home Econs. Assn., Am. Home Econs. Assn. (cert. home economist), N.Y. State Home Econs. Assn., East Hampton Ladies Village Improvement Soc. (bd. dirs.), DAR (historian 1985, parliamentarian East Hampton chpt.), Daus. of the Founders and Patriots of Am. (N.Y.chpt.), Eastern Gate Garden Club, Eastern Star (matron 1970). Home: 161 Newtown Ln East Hampton NY 11937-2429 Office: Bellport Mid Sch Kreamer St Bellport NY 11713 E-mail: jasmoel@aol.com.

MOELLER, RICHARD ROBERT, political science educator; b. Euclid, Ohio, Nov. 8, 1966; m. Loralie Davis, April 9, 1994. BA, Baldwin-Wallace Coll., 1989; MA, George Washington U., 1991; PhD, U. Edinburgh, Scotland, 1995. Political analyst Schoman and Spates Internat., Silver Spring, Md., 1995—; lectr. U. Nev., Las Vegas, 1996-98; asst. prof. The Metropolitan State Coll. Denver, Colo., 1998—. Author: (with others) Political Parties and the European Union, 1996, The Internet Guide for Students of World Politics, 2000; contbr. articles to profl. jours.; creator web site U. Nev., Las Vegas, 1996-98; creator website for polit. sci. dept. Metro State Coll., Denver, 1999-2000; creator website for Golda Meir Ctr., Denver, 2000. Mem. selection team Military Acad. State of Nev., Las Vegas, 1998, State of Colo., Denver, 1999; lectr. Social Studies Council Nev., Las Vegas, 1997. Mem. Am. Political Sci. Assn., German Studies Assn., Ohio Assn. Economists Political Scientists, Lambda Chi Alpha. Office: The Metropolitan Coll Denver Political Sci PO Box 173362 Denver CO 80217-3362 Fax: 303-556-2716. E-mail: rmoeller@yahoo.com.

MOELLER, ROBERT CHARLES (BUD MOELLER), management consultant; b. Washington, Sept. 5, 1954; s. Charles Edward and Ann Joan (Federico) M.; m. Carol Elizabeth Buchanan, June 19, 1976; children: Melaine Elizabeth, Robert Kehne. BChemE, Ga. Inst. Tech., 1976; MBA, Harvard U., 1978. Cons. ERT, Concord, Mass., 1977-78; assoc. Booz, Allen & Hamilton, Bethesda, Md., 1978-81, sr. assoc., 1981-83, prin. San Francisco, 1983-88, v.p., 1988-92; mng. officer Asia/Pacfic Energy Practice, Singapore, 1992-97; ptnr. Accenture, San Francisco, 1998—. Chmn. bd. dirs. Nat. Capital YFC, Olney, Md., 1981-83. Contbr. articles to energy and bus. pubs. Chmn. bd. dirs. East Bay Youth for Christ, Concord, Calif., 1983-91; mem. Rep. Presdl. Task Force, Washington, 1984-91; advisor Montgomery County (Md.) Health Dept., 1981; mem. World Affairs Coun., San Francisco Mayor's Fiscal Adv. Com.; adv. YFC Internat., 1992-97; bd. dirs. Emerging Young Leaders, 1998-2001. Mem. Am. Inst. Chem. Engrs., Mensa, Ferrari Owners Club, Sports Car Club of Am., Harvard Bus. Sch. Club (Singapore and San Francisco). Republican. Avocation: profl. auto racing. Address: 1030 Gelston Cir Mc Lean VA 22102 Office: Accenture Spear St Tower 1 Market Plz Fl 37 San Francisco CA 94105-1196 *Personal philosophy: Nothing is ever given; it must be earned.*

MOELLER, ROBERT JOHN, management consultant, consultant; b. Mpls., July 20, 1938; s. Ben G. and Catheryn D. M.; m. Sharon Lee Holmberg, Sept. 1, 1962; children: Mark Thomas (dec.), Maria Therese. BBA, U. Minn., 1962, MBA, 1965; grad. exec. mgmt. program, Columbia U., 1972; grad. exec. internat. mgmt., Mankato U., 1990. Asst. brand mgr. toiletries Procter & Gamble, Cin., 1965-68; group product mgr. No. div. Am. Can Co., Greenwich, Conn., 1968-71, dir. mktg. Dixie div., 1971-73; v.p. mktg. and sales Tonka Toy Co., Mpls., 1973-77, Toro Co., Mpls., 1977-79, v.p. gen. mgr. outdoor appliance div., 1979-80, v.p. gen. mgr. irrigation div., 1980-84, exec. v.p. internat. and irrigation div., 1984-88; pres., COO Mackay Envelope Corp., 1988-90; sr. v.p. mktg. meat sector Cargill, Inc., 1991-94; pres. Moeller Mgmt. Cons., 1992-98. Bd. dirs. Vista Info. Solutions. Chmn. 2002, Voyageur Outward Bound Sch., 1993-99; bd. dirs. State of Minn. Prison Industries, St. Paul, 1984—; commr. Chaska (Minn.) Planning Commn., 1988-98; pres. Dist. 112 Ednl. Found., Chaska, 1987-92; pres. Chaska Civic Theatre, 1978-80; chmn. S.W. Metro Transit Commn., 1998—, Jonathan Archtl. Rev. Commn., 1976-78, Mpls. United Way, 1997-98, bd. dirs., 1999-2002. With USN, 1955-61. Recipient Crystal Achievement award for human svcs. First Nat. Bank of Chaska, 1996. Avocations: skiing, sailing, tennis, music, golf.

MOELLER, SUSAN ELAINE, artist; b. Akron, Ohio, Jan. 27, 1949; d. Guy Raymond and June Elaine (Inherst) Walker; m. Robert Allen Moeller, Aug. 13, 1988. BFA, BA in Edn., Akron U., 1972. Art tchr., dept. head Manchester Sch. Sys., Akron, 1972-79; ad exec. The Repository, Canton, Ohio, 1979-81; art dir. Vic & Walt's, Akron, 1981-85; illustrator Collector's Marketplace Mag., Atwater, Ohio, 1983-85; freelance artist, graphic designer Akron, 1985-94; fine artist, co-owner Creative Images Studio, Cuyahoga Falls, Ohio, 1994-98, Nogal, N.Mex., 1998—; owner Paz de Nogal Gallery and Studio, 1998—. Co-owner Creative Images Assocs., Cuyahoga Falls, 1986-98; Nogal, N. Mex., 1998—; graphic cons. Advanced Analytical and Computational Solutions, Inc., Cleve., 1996-97. Akron Chess Club, 1989-97; art juror Cuyahoga Falls H.S., 1997; owner, organizer Paz de Nogal Fine Art Shows, 1998—. Artist, designer: (bd. game) Barnes Publishing, 1984; contbr. poetry and drawing to Cat Fancy Mag., 1994; illustrator: (mag.) Collector's Marketplace, 1983-85, (newspaper) Canton Repository, 1979-81; exhibited N.E. Ohio Fine Art Guild shows, 1996-97. Donor of fine art to various charities, Akron, 1996-98. Recipient Hon. Mention award Kent (Ohio) Art-in-the-Park Com., 1996. Mem. ASPCA, Humane Soc. U.S., Humane Soc. Summit County, Pet Ptnrs. Rescue City (Pet Angel 1997), Lincoln County Humane Soc., Creative Connection, Ohio Arts and Crafts Guild, Cuyahoga Valley Soc. Fine Arts, Lincoln County Soc. Artists. Avocations: antiques, lapidary arts, gardening, writing. Studio: Paz de Nogal PO Box 190 Nogal NM 88341-0190

MOELLERING, HELEN S. retired social worker; b. St. Elizabeth, Mo., Dec. 6, 1939; d. James Patrick and Mildred Irene (Crane) Howard; m. Robert Kenneth Moellering, Sept. 17, 1960 (dec. Jan. 1995); children: Michael, Carla. BS in Psychology with honors, Lindenwood Coll., 1976; MSW, St. Louis U., 1978; cert., Family Therapy Inst., St. Louis, 1992. Lic. clin. social worker, Mo. Social worker Divsn. Family Svcs., St. Charles and St. Louis, 1978-89; family preservation therapist Children's Svcs., St. Charles, 1990-97; primary mental health project worker Rochester (N.Y.) Sch. 7, 1998—2002. Field instr. Washington U., St. Louis, 1989-97. Contbr. articles to profl. jours. Past leader Girl Scouts Am., Bowling Green, Ky., St. Charles Mo.; leader 4-H; vol. Sch. # 22, Rochester. Mem. Am. Assn. Marriage and Family Therapists. Presbyterian. Avocations: studying classical piano, studying writing. Home: 33 Menlo Pl Rochester NY 14620-2717

MOELLERING, JOHN HENRY, aviation maintenance company executive; b. Ft. Wayne, Ind., Feb. 4, 1938; s. Robert Charles and Irene Pauline (Nolde) M.; m. Karla Louise Fritzsche, Dec. 21, 1963; children: John Henry, Matthew C., Ann Elizabeth. BS, U.S. Mil. Acad., 1959; MS, U. Calif., Berkeley, 1962; postgrad., Army Command and Gen. Staff Coll., 1971-72, Army War Coll., 1976-77. Registered profl. engr., La. Commd. 2d lt. U.S. Army, 1959, advanced through grades to lt. gen., 1985; aide de camp Combat Devel. Command, 1961-63; command and staff 24th Inf. Div., Fed. Republic Germany, 1964-67; ops. officer Engr. Group, Vietnam, 1967-68; instr. civil engring., asst. prof. history U.S. Mil. Acad., 1968-71; with Office Army Chief of Staff, Pentagon, 1972-73; White House staff, 1973-74; bn. comdr. 101st Airborne Div., 1974-76; dist. engr. Vicksburg, Miss., 1977-79; exec. to Army Chief of Staff, Pentagon, 1979-81; asst. div. comdr. 9th Inf. Div., Ft. Lewis, Wash., 1981-82; commandant West Point, N.Y., 1982-84; comdg. gen. Ft. Leonard Wood, Mo., 1984-85; asst. to chmn. Joint Chiefs of Staff, Pentagon, Washington, 1985-87; corp. v.p. Automatic Data Processing, Inc., San Ramon, Calif., 1987-90; pres., chief exec. officer Lear Siegler Mgmt. Svcs. Corp., Oklahoma City, 1990-93; pres. UNC Aviation Svcs., Annapolis, Md., 1993-97; pres., CEO Lear Siegler Svcs., Inc., 1997—. Bd. dirs. USAA Ins. Co., Lear Sigeler Svcs., Inc., Indsl. Coll. of the Armed Forces; mem. Industry Conf. Bd. ; frequent lectr. Nat. Def. U. Editor, contbr.: Evolution of Modern Warfare, 1969, Battalion Commanders Speak Out, 1977. Mem. Sci. Def. Bd., The Pentagon; chmn. Class of '59 fund com. U.S. Mil. Acad., 1984—89. Decorated Def. DSM, Army DSM, Legion of Merit, Bronze Star; White House fellow, 1973-74. Mem.: Nat. Def. Indsl. Assn. (bd. dirs.), Phi Kappa Phi. Home: 1526 Shipsview Rd Annapolis MD 21401-5740 Office: 175 Admiral Cochrane Dr Annapolis MD 21401-7316 E-mail: johnmoellering@hotlink.com.

MOELLERING, ROBERT CHARLES, JR. internist, educator; b. Lafayette, Ind., June 9, 1936; s. Robert Charles and Irene Pauline (Nolde) M.; children: Anne Elizabeth, Robert Charles, Catherine Irene; m. Mary Jane Ferraro, July 11, 1987. BA, Valparaiso U., 1958, DSc, 1980; MD cum laude, Harvard U., 1962. Diplomate: Am. Bd. Internal Medicine. Intern Mass. Gen. Hosp., Boston, 1962-63, resident, 1963-64, postdoctoral fellow in infectious diseases, 1967-70, resident, 1966-67, mem. infectious disease unit and asst. physician, 1970-76, assoc. physician, 1976-83, hon. physician, 1983—, cons. bacteriology, 1972-87; instr. medicine Harvard U. Med. Sch., 1970-72, asst. prof., 1972-76, assoc. prof., 1976-80, prof., 1980—; chmn. dept. medicine, physician-in-chief New Eng. Deaconess Hosp., 1981-96; pres., CEO Deaconess Profl. Practice Group, 1995-98; Shields Warren-Mallinckrodt prof. rsch. Harvard U. Med. Sch., Boston, 1981-89, Shields Warren-Mallinckrodt prof. med. rsch., 1989-99, Herrman Blumgart prof. medicine, 1999—; assoc. physician-in-chief Beth Israel Deconess Med. Ctr., 1996—98, physician-in-chief, 1998—; pres. CEO Harvard Medical Fac. Phys. BIDMC, 1998—. Mem. subcom. on susceptibility testing Nat. Com. for CLin. Lab. Standards, 1976-88; mem. subcom. on antimicrobial agts. and chemotherapy, 1978-80; subcom. on antimicrobiol disc. diffusion suceptibility testing, 1980-88; chmn. data safety monitoring bd. Nat. Inst. Allergy and Infections Disease, NIH, 1997—. Mem. editl. bd. Antimicrobial Agts. and Chemotherapy, 1977-81, editor, 1981-85, editor-in-chief, 1985-95; editor European Jour. Clin. Microbial Infectious Diseases, 1990—; consulting. editor Infectious Disease Clinics N.Am., 1986—; editor Les Infections, 1983; editl. bd. New Eng. Jour. Medicine, 1977-81, European Jour.Clin. Microbiology, 1981—, Jour. Infectious Diseases, 1981-85, 89-93, Infectious Disease Alert, 1981-92, Pharmacotherapy, 1982—, Antimicrobial Agts. Ann., 1984-87, Zentralblatt Fur Bacteriologie, Microbiologie and Hygience, 1984—, Jour. of Infection, 1986—, Innovations, 1986-90, Residents Forum in Internal Medicine, 1988-90, Diagnostic Microbiology and Infectious Disease, 1989-90, Internat. Jour. Antimicrobial Agts., 1990—, Infectious Diseases in Clin. Practice, 1991-92, Jour. Infection and Chemotherapy, 1995—. Served with USPHS, 1964-66. Grantee USPHS, NIH. Fellow ACP, Am. Acad. Microbiology, Infectious Diseases Soc. Am. (v.p. 1988-89, pres. elect 1989-90, pres. 1990-91, past pres. 1991-92), Royal Coll. Physicians (hon.); mem. Am. Soc. Microbiology, Am. Clin. and Climatol. Assn., Internat. Soc. Chemotherapy, Am. Soc. Clin. Investigation, Assn. Am. Physicians, European Soc. Clin. Microbiology, Am. Fedn. Clin. Rsch., Assn. Profs. Medicine, Roxbury Clin. Records Club, Mass. Med. Soc. (councilor), Brit. Soc. Antimicrobial Chemotherapy, Coun. Biology Editors, Alpha Omega Alpha, Phi Kappa Psi. Home: 49 Longfellow Rd Wellesley MA 02481-5220 Office: Beth Israel Deaconess Med Ctr Dept Medicine 110 Francis St Boston MA 02215-5501 E-mail: rmoeller@caregroup.harvard.edu.

MOELY, BARBARA E. psychology researcher, educator; b. Prairie du Sac, Wis., July 17, 1940; d. John Arthur and Loretta Ruth (Giese) M.; children: John Jacob Moely Wiener, David Andrew Moely Wiener. Student, Carroll Coll., 1958-60; BA, U. Wis., 1962, MA, 1964; PhD, U. Minn., 1968. Asst. prof. U. Hawaii, Honolulu, 1967-71; rsch. psychologist UCLA, 1971-72; asst. prof. Tulane U., New Orleans, 1972-75, assoc. prof. psychology, 1975-85, prof., 1985—, dept. chmn., 1992-96, dir. Office of Svc. Learning, 1999—. Contbr. articles to profl. jours. Grantee U.S. Office Edn., Handicapped Pers. Preparation, 1977-80, Tulane U., 1973, 75, 77, 78, 83-84, Inst. for Mental Hygiene, City of New Orleans, 1983-84, 2000, Nat. Inst. Edn., 1983-84, La. Edn. Quality Support Fund, 1988, 89, 91, 92, 96, HUD, 1997—, Annenberg, 1997, HHS, 1997—2002, U.S. Dept. Edn., 1999—, Fund for Improvement Post-Secondary Edn., 2000—. Mem. AAUP (v.p. La. conf. 1992-93, sec. 1993-97, v.p. 1998-2000, pres. Tulane 1992-94), APA, Soc. Rsch. in Child Devel., Am. Ednl. Rsch. Assn., Southwestern Soc. for Rsch. in Human Devel. (pres. 1986-88), Phi Beta Kappa (pres. Alpha chpt. La. 1981-82, sec. 1995-99) Office: Tulane Univ Dept Psychology New Orleans LA 70118 E-mail: moely@tulane.edu.

MOEN, MARGARET, print company editor; b. Tokyo, Japan, Apr. 2, 1951; came to U.S. in 1951; d. Raymond Otis and Evelyn (Carr) M. BA in history, summa cum laude, Seattle U., 1972; MA in english, U. Minn., 1980. Assoc. editor Wanderer Printing Co., St. Paul, 1973—. Contbr. articles to profl. jours. Precinct sec. Republican party, St. Paul, Minn., 1996. Mem. U. Minn. Alumni Assn., Minn. Hist. Soc., Rebels Swing Dance Club, Smithsonian Institution. Republican. Roman Catholic. Avocations: swing and ballroom dancing, photography, italian language, genealogy. E-mail. E-mail: moeneditor@cox.net.

MOEN, RODNEY CHARLES, state legislator, retired naval officer; b. Whitehall, Wis., July 26, 1937; s. Edwin O. and Tena A. (Gunderson) M.; m. Catherine Jean Wolfe, 1959; children: Scott A., Jon C. (dec.), Rodd M., Catherine J., Daniel M. Student, Syracuse U., 1964-65; BA, U. So. Calif., 1972; postgrad., Ball State U., 1975-76. Gen. mgr. We. Wis. Comm. Coop., Independence, 1976-83; mem. Wis. Senate from 31st dist., Madison, 1983—; chair health, utilities, vets. and mil. affairs com. Wis. Senate, 1983—, asst. majority leader. Contbg. editor Govt. Photography, 1970-74. Lt. USN, 1955-76, Vietnam. Home: 18775 Dewey St Whitehall WI 54773-0215 Office: State Capitol PO Box 7882 Madison WI 53707-7882

MOENS, DAVID BRIAN, manufacturing company executive; b. Burlington, Vt., Jan. 23, 1958; s. Albert John Moens and Helen Lillian (Parsons) Wildman; m. Rebecca Marie Reilly, Oct. 1, 1983 (div. Jan. 1996); children: Kaitlyn Elizabeth, Colleen Patricia; m. Dorinda Sue Kroymann, Aug. 4, 2001. Student, U. Pa., 1975-76. Programmer Germantown Savs. Bank, Bala Cynwyd, Pa., 1977-79; sr. programmer Minicom Corp., Cherry Hill, N.J., 1979-80; ptnr. Bus. Sys. Software, Haddonfield, 1980-86; software engr. Commodore Semiconductor Sys., Norristown, Pa., 1986-87; sr. programmer, analyst Franklin Mint, Franklin Center, 1988-89; cons. Integral Systems, Inc., Albuquerque, 1989-91; sr. cons. Computer Methods Corp., Marlton, N.J., 1991-95; decision support mgr. Intel Corp., Chandler, Ariz., 1995—. E-mail: dbmoens@cox.net.

MOENS, PETER B. biology researcher and educator; b. Sukabumi, Indonesia, May 15, 1931; s. Hendrick P. and Anneke D. (Ritsema van Eck) M.; m. Marja Schröder, May 8, 1953; children: Richard, Theodore, Vivian, Cecilia, Francis. PhD, U. Toronto, 1963. Lectr. biology York U., Toronto, Ont., Can., 1963-64, asst. prof., 1964-67, asso. prof., 1967-71, prof., 1971—, chmn. dept. biology, 1981-84. Editor: Genome, 1983—, Chromosoma, 1988—2001. Fellow Royal Soc. Can.; mem. Genetics Soc. Am., Can. Soc. Cell Biology, Genetics Soc. Can. (pres. 1979), Am. Soc. Cell Biology Office: York U Dept Biology 4700 Keele St Toronto ON Canada M3J 1P3

MOENY, WILLIAM MICHAEL, research and development executive, scientist; b. Alamosa, Colo., Jan. 6, 1945; s. William Cowin and Christine Elizabeth (Wilson) M.; m. Mary Lee Hampton, Oct. 22, 1966; children: Michael James, Stephen Wallis, Susanna Marie. BS in Aerospace Engring., Northrop U., 1967; MS in Aerospace Engring., U. Wash., 1970. Aerospace engr. Boeing Co., Seattle, 1967-71, Naval Missile Ctr., Point Mugu, Calif., 1971-73; physicist Air Force Weapons Lab., Albuquerque, 1973-77; founder, pres., v.p. R&D Tetra Corp., 1977—. Bd. elders Grace Ch., Albuquerque, 1988—. Mem. AIAA, IEEE (program com. 1995), Am. Phys. Soc., N.Mex. Entrepreneurs Assn. (exec. positions 1983—). Achievements include patents in field. Avocations: surfing, traveling, hunting, exploring. Home: 12213 Vienna Dr NE Albuquerque NM 87111-2827 Office: Tetra Corp 3701 Hawkins St NE Albuquerque NM 87109-4512

MOERBEEK, STANLEY LEONARD, lawyer; b. Toronto, Ont., Can., Nov. 12, 1951; came to U.S., 1953; s. John Jacob and Mary Emily Moerbeek; m. Carol Annette Mordaunt, Apr. 17, 1982; children: Sarah, Noah. BA magna cum laude, Calif. State U., Fullerton, 1974; student, U. San Diego-Sorbonne, Paris, 1977; JD, Loyola U., 1979. Bar: Calif. 1980; cert. in internat. bus. transactions, bankruptcy and bus. rehab., and civil trial practice. From law clk. to assoc. McAlpin Doonan & Seese, Covina, Calif., 1977-81; assoc. Robert L. Baker, Pasadena, 1981-82, Miller Bush & Minnott, Fullerton, 1982-83; prin. Law Office of Stanley L. Moerbeek, 1984—. Judge pro tem Orange County Superior Ct., Calif., 1984—; notary pub., lt. gov. 9th cir. law student divsn. ABA, 1979. Mem. Heritage Found., Washington, 1989—. Calif. Gov.'s Office scholar, 1970; recipient Plaque of Appreciation, Fullerton Kiwanis, 1983. Mem. Calif. Assn. Realtors (referral panel atty. 1985—), Orange County Bar Assn. (Coll. of Trial Advocacy 1985), Calif. C. of C., Phi Kappa Phi. Roman Catholic. Avocations: history, politics, sports. Office: 1370 N Brea Blvd Ste 210 Fullerton CA 92835-4128 E-mail: slmlaw@netzero.net.

MOERDLER, CHARLES GERARD, lawyer; b. Paris, Nov. 15, 1934; came to the U.S., 1946, naturalized, 1952; s. Herman and Erna Anna (Brandwein) M.; m. Pearl G. Hecht, Dec. 26, 1955; children: Jeffrey Alan, Mark Laurence, Sharon Michele. BA, L.I.U., 1953; JD, Fordham U., 1956. Bar: NY 1956, U.S. Supreme Ct. 1962. Assoc. Cravath, Swaine & Moore, N.Y.C., 1956-65; spl. counsel coms. City of N.Y. and judiciary N.Y. State Assembly, 1960-61; commr. bldgs. City of N.Y., 1966-67; sr. ptnr., chmn. litigation dept. Stroock & Stroock & Lavan, N.Y.C., 1967—. Bd. dirs., gen. counsel, dir. N.Y. Post Co., Inc., 1987-92; cons. housing, urban devel. and real estate to Mayor of N.Y.C., 1967-73; mem. com. on character and fitness of applicants for admission to Bar, Appellate divsn. 1st Dept., N.Y., 1977—, vice chmn. 1998—; mem. disciplinary com. appellate divsn. 1st Dept., N.Y., 1998—, commr. N.Y. State Ins. Fund, 1978-97, vice chmn., 1986-94, chmn., 1995-97; mem. Mayor's Com. on Judiciary, 1994-2001; mem. N.Y.C. Housing Devel. Corp., 1997—; bd. dirs. N.Y.C. Residential Mortgage Ins. Corp., 1997—; chmn. bd. dirs. Bank Austria Creditanstalt LLC, 1999-2001; mem. N.Y.C. Bd. Collective Bargaining, 2000—. Mem. editorial bd. N.Y. Law Jour., 1985—; assoc. editor Fordham Law Rev., 1956. Asst. dir. Rockefeller nat. presdl. campaign com., 1964; adv. bd. Sch. Internat. Affairs Columbia U., 1977-80; bd. govs. L.I.U., 1966, trustee, 1985-91; chmn. Cmty. Planning Bds. 8 and 14, Bronx County, 1977-78; nat. bd. govs. Am. Jewish Congress, 1966; bd. overseers Jewish Theol. Sem. Am., 1993-95; trustee St. Barnabas Hosp., Bronx, N.Y., 1985—. Recipient Walker Metcalf award L.I. U., 1966. Mem. Am. Bar Assn., N.Y. State Bar Assn., N.Y. County Lawyers Assn., Internat. Bar Assn., Assn. of Bar of City of N.Y., Free Sons of Israel, Metro. Club. Home: 7 Rivercrest Rd Bronx NY 10471-1236 Office: Stroock Stroock & Lavan 180 Maiden Ln New York NY 10038 E-mail: cmoerdler@stroock.com.

MOERK, ALICE ANNE, music educator, composer; b. Phila., Mar. 1, 1936; d. John Carroll and Ann Marie (CArolan) M. MusB, Carthage Coll., Kenosha, Wis., 1957; MFA, Ohio U., 1959; PhD, W.Va. U., 1969. Chair music dept. Marion (Va.) Coll., 1959-63; prof. music Vardell Hall, Red Springs, N.C., 1964-65; chair music dept. Lees Coll., Jackson, Ky., 1965-67; prof. music Fairmont (W.Va.) State Coll., 1967-2000, now prof. emeritus. Tchr. W.Va. Elderhostel, Fairmont, 1981-83, W.Va. Gov.'s Honors Acad., Fairmont, 1989-90; dir. music St. Mark's Luth. Ch., Clarksburg, 1983-94; tchr. W.Va. Lifetime Learning, Fairmont, 1997-2000. Author: Perception and Music, 1989, Sonic Insights, 1991; composer: Alianor, opera in monologue, 1997, The Unicorn Weeps, opera, 1996, Harbour Symphony for Concert Band, 1997, Andy, a musical, 1995, Dialogue Between Ancients and Moderns, a cantata, 1998, Peculiarities, Byrdwatch, 1999, Ciurlionis for piano and orch, The Wise Woman, opera, 2000, The Flatwoods Monster, opera, 2001, also song cycles and chamber works. Recipient Music award, Nat. League Am. Pen Women, 2000; grantee, Fairmont State Coll., 1971, 1973, 1983, 1989, 1990, 1992, 1996, Humanities Found. of W.Va. Humanities Coun., 1990, 1992. Mem.: Nat. League Am. Pen Women, Tampa Bay Composers Forum, Popular Culture Soc., Internat. Assn. Women in Music, Sigma Alpha Iota. Lutheran. Home: PO Box 1257 Anna Maria FL 34216-1257 E-mail: amoerk@juno.com.

MOERS, JOYCE ANN, bookkeeper, day camp administrator; b. Evansville, Ind., Sept. 4, 1956; d. Lawrence Burns and Virginia Frances London; m. John Michael Moers, June 7, 1980; children: Michael J., Rachel N. Legal sec. and bus. degree, Lockyear Bus. Coll., 1976. Bookkeeper Reitz Drug Store, Evansville, Ind., 1970-75; plant mgr. sec. Carhartt Mfg., 1975-76; bookkeeper, day camp adminstr. Burdette Park, 1976—, day camp adminstr., 1989—. Recipient County Achievement award Ind. Assn. Counties, Vanderburgh County, 1992; grantee Mead Johnson, Evansville, 1992—. Mem. Nat. Assn. Concessionaires, Ind. Assn. Sch. Age Child Care (bd. mem. 1996-98), Evansville 4-C, Go-Fishin. Roman Catholic. Avocations: camping, family activities, walking. Office: Burdette Park 5301 Nurrenbern Rd Evansville IN 47712-8534 E-mail: indebt4alittle@aol.com.

MOERSCHEL, DAVID JONATHAN, biologist; b. Dover, Del., Oct. 13, 1977; s. Richard Eugene and Cynthia Ann M. BS magna cum laude, U. Ga., 1999; MS in Biology, Ga. State U., 2002. Project mgr. ACR Constrn., Kennesaw, Ga., 1995-2000; lab. mgr. dept. biology Ga. State U., Atlanta, 2000—. Webmaster Biology Grad, Student Assn., Ga. State U., 2000—, coord. Neurosci. Jour. Club, 2001—. Vol. emer. rm. Grady Health Systems, Atlanta, 2000—, physicians office Woodpark (Ga.) Med. Ctr., 2000. Mem. AAAS, Sigma Xi, Phi Beta Kappa, Phi Kappa Phi (life). Republican. Avocations: martial arts, flute, reading.

MOERY, PHILLIP WEISS, economist, educator; b. Little Rock, May 25, 1948; s. Clarence Bryan and Beatrice Frances (Weiss) M.; m. Lisa Wray Shockley, July 29, 1978; 2 children. BSA, U. Ark., 1970; PhD, George Washington U., 1980. Asst. prof. econs. Shepherd Coll., Shepherdstown, W.Va., 1981-88; exec. dir. Greater Hagerstown (Md.) Com., 1988-89; pres., Callaway prof. Brenan Coll., Gainesville, Ga., 1989—. Mem. Eastern Econ. Assn., Atlanta Econs. Club, Nat. Assn. Bus. Economists, Eastern Fin. Assn., Nat. Assn. Accts. Clubs: Army and Navy (Washington). Episcopalian. Avocation: tennis. Office: Brenan Coll Butler Hall Gainesville GA 30506

MOESCHL, STANLEY FRANCIS, electrical engineer, management consultant; b. Cin., Mar. 14, 1931; s. Stanley F. and Matilda F. (Trenkamp) M.; m. Kathleen K. Koebel, Aug. 21, 1954; children: Stanley, Melissa, Deborah, Karen. *Stanley Moeschl's son, Stanley, attended U.S. Coast Guard Academy and Duke University, BS 1977 (Computer Science). His daughter, Melissa, attended Berry College and University of South Florida, BA 1978. His daughter, Deborah, graduated from Georgetown University, BA 1980 and University of Florida Doctor Jurisprudence, 1983. Stanley's daughter, Karen, graduated from the University of Florida, BS 1982 and Doctor of Veterinary Medicine, 1986.* BSEE, Purdue U., 1957. Engr. Honeywell Space Div., St. Petersberg, Fla., 1957-60, engring. mgr., 1960-69, program mgr., 1969-77; dir. engring. Honeywell Avionics Div., Mpls., 1977-80; v.p. gen. mgr. Honeywell Space Div., St. Petersberg, 1980-82, Honeywell Avionics Div., Mpls., 1982-88; pres. Sundstrand Data Control, Redmond, Wash., 1988-92. Bd. mem. Com. of 100, St. Petersberg, 1980-82, Wash. Round Table, Seattle, 1989-92. *While at Honeywell, Mr. Moeschel was involved in designing and producing Avionics for all U.S. Manned Flight Systems, including Mercury, Gemini, Apollo, and Space Shuttle. He was also involved in providing equipment for all the A11, YF12, SR71, B52, F14, C5A, F111, B2, C17, and the Viking Lander 1976. He worked on the following Missile Programs: Bomarc, Agena, Atlas Centaur, Minuteman, and Air Launcg Cruise Missile.* Bd. dirs. Jr. Achievement, Mpls., 1983-86, Seattle, 1989-92. With USCG, 1951-54, Korea. Mem. IEEE, AIEE, Eta Kappa Nu, Tau Beta Pi. Home: 12826 Yacht Club Cir Fort Myers FL 33919-4635 E-mail: sfmoeschl@aol.com.

MOESE, MARK DOUGLAS, environmental consultant; b. Jersey City, Aug. 3, 1954; s. Harold Francis and Mary Frances (Wilk) M.; m. Elizabeth Renker Cozine, Apr. 20, 1991; children: Elizabeth Renker, Kevin Harold. BS, Fairleigh Dickinson U., 1976, MS, 1979; PhD, NYU, 1988. Rsch. asst. West Indies Lab., St. Croix, V.I., 1978-79, NYU Med. Ctr., Tuxedo, N.Y., 1980-86; staff scientist Hazen and Sawyer, PC, N.Y.C., 1982-85; supr. risk assessment EBASCO Environ., Lyndhurst, N.J., 1986-94, Foster Wheeler Environ., Lyndhurst, 1994-96, Betterchem Corp., Campbell Hall, N.Y., 1996; environ. cons. Louis Berger & Assocs., Inc., East Orange, N.J., 1996-98, Tams Cons., Inc., Bloomfield, 1998—. Cons. Taiwan Power Co., Taipei, 1987, 89, Hub River Power Co., Fauji Corp., Karachi, Pakistan, 1991-92, Chinese Rsch. Acad. Environ. Scis., 1993, Drainage Water Rsch. Inst., Cairo, 1997; human and environ. risk assessments profl. Ebasco Environ., 1986-94, Foster Wheeler Environ., Lydnhurst, N.J., 1994-96, Betterchem Corp., 1996; cons. Louis Berger & Assocs., 1996-98; TAMS Cons., Inc., 1998—. Contbr. articles to profl. jours. Sigma Xi grantee-in-aid, 1978; Grad. fellow NYU Med. Ctr.,

1980-86. Mem. Western Dredging Assn., Soc. for Risk Analysis, Soc. Environ. Toxicology and Chemistry. Office: Tams Cons Inc 300 Broadacres Dr Ste 5 Bloomfield NJ 07003-3187 E-mail: mmoese@tamsconsultants.com.

MOESER, JAMES CHARLES, university chancellor, musician; b. Colorado City, Tex., Apr. 3, 1939; s. Charles Victor and Virginia (James) M.; m. Jesse Kaye Edwards, Jan. 26, 1963 (div. July 1984); children: James Christopher, Kathryn Carter; m. Susan Kay Smith Dickerson, June 21, 1987. B.Mus., U. Tex., 1961, M.M., 1964; postgrad. (Fulbright grantee), Hochschule fur Musik, Berlin, 1961-62; D.MA (Univ. fellow), U. Mich., 1966. Chmn. dept. organ, asst. prof. organ U. Kans., 1966-69, assoc. prof., 1969-74, prof., 1974-86, dean Sch. Fine Arts, 1975-86, Carl and Ruth Althaus disting. prof. organ, 1985-86; organist, choirmaster Plymouth Congl. Ch., Lawrence, Kans., 1967-86; organist nat. conf. Music Tchrs. Nat. Assn., Portland, Oreg., 1972, L.A., 1974; dean Coll. Arts and Architecture, Pa. State U., State College, 1986-96; chancellor U. Nebr., Lincoln, Nebr., 1996—2000, U.N.C. - Chapel Hill, Chapel Hill, NC, 2000—. Concert organist, on tour, W. Ger., 1977, Lisbon (Portugal) Festival, 1978, 81, recitals for, Musica Festiva da Costa Verde, Portugal, 1981; organist concerts, W. Ger., 1982, 86, 87; world premier Paul Creston's 3d Symphony for Organ and Orchestra, Kennedy Ctr., Washington, 1982. Bd. govs. Josephson Inst. Ethics; bd. trustees N.C. Symphony Soc., Inc., 2001—; mem. vis. com. Meml. Ch., Harvard U. Recipient Palmer Christian award U. Mich., 1981, Disting. Alumnus awrd Grad. Sch. U. Tex., 2001; Kent fellow Danforth Found.; Danforth Assoc. Mem. Am. Guild Organists (past dean chpt., nat. dir. student groups 1973-75, nat. chmn. com. on profl. edn. 1983— , chmn. 2d nat. conf. on organ pedagogy 1984, 3d nat. conf. 1986, v.p. 1986—). Episcopalian. Home: 1000 Raleigh Rd Chapel Hill NC 27517-4415 Office: UNC Office of the Chancellor PO Box 9100 Chapel Hill NC 27599-0001 E-mail: james_moeser@unc.edu.

MOESSNER, HAROLD FREDERIC, allergist; b. Lincoln, Nebr., Mar. 29, 1945; s. Samuel Frederick and Helen Lucy (Larson) M.; m. Linda McLeod, Apr. 30, 1972; children: Annie Larson, John Christopher, Sarah Elizabeth. BS with distinction, U. Nebr., 1967; MD, U. Minn., 1971. Diplomate Am. Bd. Pediatrics, Am. Bd. Allergy and Immunology. Intern VA Hosp., Dallas, 1971-72; resident in pediatrics Children's Med. Ctr., 1972-74; commd. 2d lt. U.S. Army, 1974-78, advanced through the grades to col., 1980-87; pediatrician Fort Ritchie, Md., 1974-75, U.S. Army Hosp, Augsburg, Germany, 1975-78; fellow in adolescent medicine U. Tex. Health and Sci. Ctr., Dallas, 1978-79; asst. prof. pediatrics Uniformed Svcs., U. Health Scis., Bethesda, Md., 1980-83; fellow allergy and immunology Walter Reed Army Med. Ctr., Washington, 1983-85; chief allergy immunology svc., chief dept. medicine Blanchfield Army Hosp., Fort Campbell, Ky., 1985-87; pvt. practice Nashville, 1987—. Assoc. staff Williamson Med. Ctr., Franklin, Tenn. Contbr. to profl. jours. Fellow Am. Bd. Pediats., Am. Bd. Allergy and Immunology; mem. Am. Acad. Allergy and Immunology, Williamson County Med. Soc., Tenn. Soc. Allergy, Tenn. State Med. Assn., Phi Beta Kappa. Home: 5304 Otter Creek Ct Brentwood TN 37027-4126 Office: 1909 Mallory Ln Ste 308 Franklin TN 37067-8230 also: 251 Hillcrest Dr Ste 101 Clarksville TN 37043-

MOEVS, CHRISTIAN ROBERT, literature educator; b. Boston, Sept. 21, 1958; s. Robert Walter and Maria Teresa (Marabini) M. AB, Harvard Coll., 1980; MA, Columbia U., 1989, PhD with distinction, 1994. Asst. to v.p. ICM Artists, N.Y.C., 1983-85; preceptor Columbia U., 1991-92; assoc. prof. U. Notre Dame, Ind., 1994—. Co-editor: Devers Series in Dante Studies, 1995—; translator: A Catholic Priest Meets Sai Baba, 1994; contbr. articles to profl. jours. Pres. Sathya Sai Baba Ctr. South Bend, Ind., 1996—. Recipient 6 Interim awards Inst. for Scholarship in the Liberal Arts, 1995-99, Ann. award, 1997, Detur prize, Edwards-Whitaker prize Harvard Coll., 1977; NEH fellow, 1997-98; Medieval Inst. U. Notre Dame fellow, 1994—; Villa I Tatti fellow, 2001-02. Mem. MLA, Dante Soc. Am., Am. Assn. Tchrs. Italian, Am. Assn. Italian Studies, Medieval Acad. Am., Soc. Dantesca Italiana, Fox Club. Democrat. Roman Catholic. Avocations: music, philosophy, woodworking. Home: 125 W Marion St South Bend IN 46601-1030 Office: U Notre Dame 343 OShaughnessy Hall Notre Dame IN 46556 E-mail: moevs.1@nd.edu.

MOFFAT, AMY A, anthropologist, applied cultural ethnographer; b. Upland, CA, Aug. 6, 1971; d. R. Haines Moffat, S. Lynn Moffat; m. Paul Chambers. Bachelors of Art, Beloit College, Beloit, Wisconsin, 1989—93; Masters of Applied Anthropology, University of Maryland, College Park, MD, 1997—99. Instructor University of South Florida, Tampa, FL, 2000—01, Western Michigan University, Kalamazoo, 2002—02. Project Coordinator Cultural Systems Analysis Group, UMD, College Park, MD, 1998—99; Intern - Applied Anthropologist LTG Associates, Takoma Park, MD, 1998—98. Treasurer Graduate Assistants United, Tampa, FL, 1999—2001. Mem.: National Association of the Practice of Anthropology, American Anthropological Association, Society for Applied Anthropology. Personal E-mail: amymoffat@hotmail.com.

MOFFAT, MARIAN MACINTYRE, lawyer; b. Coral Gables, Fla., Apr. 15, 1947; d. James and Elinore (Tomlinson) M.; m. Thomas E. Jepson, May 26, 1972. BA, U. Mo., 1970, MPA, 1975, JD, 1977. Bar: Calif. 1979, Mo. 1978, U.S. Dist. Ct. (we. dist.) Mo. 1978, U.S. Dist. Ct. (no. dist.) Calif. 1979, U.S. Ct. Appeals (8th cir.) 1985. Staff atty. Legal Aid of Western Mo., Kansas City, 1979-81; dep. dir. Office of Human Rels. and Citizen Complaints, 1981-82; pvt. practice, 1982—. Pres. Coleman Highlands Neighborhood Assn., Kansas City, 1992-94; bd. dirs. Citizens Assn. Kansas City, 1995-97, 98, treas., PAC treas. 1999-2001, sec., 1996-97; sec. Westpoint Citizens Action Coalition, 1994-97, v.p. issues, 1997-99; alt. mem. Kansas City (Mo.) Bd. Zoning Adjustment, 1999-2001; v.p., pres. Greater Kansas City Women's Polit. Caucus, 2000. Recipient Robert C. Welch Vol. Atty. Project award Kansas City Met. Bar Assn., 1984, Bob Regan Westport Good Neighbor award, 1998, Valentine Neighborhood Assn. Love award, 2000, KC150 Neighborhood Hero award, 2000, Avocations: crossword puzzles, gardening. Home: 3333 Karnes Blvd Kansas City MO 64111-3648 E-mail: mimimoffat@lawyer.com.

MOFFAT, MARYBETH, consulting company executive; b. Pitts., July 25, 1951; d. Herbert Franklin and Florence Grafe (Knerem) M.; m. Brian Francis Soulier, Nov. 30, 1974 (div.). BA, Carroll Coll., 1973. Indsl. engring. technician Wis. Centrifugal Co., Waukesha, Wisc., 1976-77; indsl. engr. Utility Products, Inc., Milw., 1977-79; mgr. indsl. engring. Bear Automotive (divsn. SPX Corp.), Bangor, Pa., 1980-90; program mgr. Toyota Johnson Controls, Inc. Automotive Systems Group, 1990-2001; pres., CEO Moffat Enterprises, Inc., 2001—. Group home house parent Headwaters Regional Achievement Ctr., Lake Tomahawk, Wis., 1974. Mem. Am. Inst. Indsl. Engrs., MTM Assn. for Standards Rsch., Indsl. Mgmt. Soc., Alpha Gamma Delta (standards chmn. 1971-72). Republican. Methodist. Avocations: skiing, horseback riding, swimming, reading. Office: 3660 Walden Dr Ste E Lexington KY 40517 E-mail: mbmoffat123@cs.com.

MOFFAT, ROBERT JOHN, mechanical engineering educator, researcher; b. Grosse Point, Mich., Nov. 29, 1927; s. John Wesley Alexander and Annie Elizabeth (Harries) M.; m. Sylvia Jo Gladden, July, 1952 (div. 1972); 1 child, John Gladden; m. Jan K. Elliott, June 1973 (div. Dec. 1981); m. Ruth M. Taka, June 1991. BS in Mech. Engring., U. Mich., 1952; MS in Mech. Engring., Wayne State U., 1961; MS in Mechanics, Stanford U., 1966, PhD, 1967. Sr. rsch. engr. GM Rsch. Labs., Warren, Mich., 1952-62; assoc. prof. mech. engring. Stanford (Calif.) U., 1967-72, prof., 1972—, chmn. thermoscis. div., 1972-86. Pres. Moffat Thermoscis., Inc., 1984—. Contbr. over 195 articles to profl. jours.; patentee in field. Scoutmaster Boy Scouts Am., Royal Oak, Mich., 1953-55. Pvt. U.S. Army, 1946-47. Fellow ASME (Holly medal 1987, Melville medal 1987, Heat Transfer Meml. award 1989); mem. Instrument Soc. Am. (sr.). Republican. Avocations: trout fishing, bike riding/touring, scuba. Home: Apt 1 2333 Eastridge Ave Menlo Park CA 94025-6741 Office: Stanford Univ Dept Mech Engring Stanford CA 94305

MOFFAT, ROBERT W., JR. information technology executive; BS in Econs., Union Coll.; MBA in Mgmt. Info. Sys., Iona Coll. Various mgmt. positions IBM, 1978, gen. mgr. personal sys. group, sr. v.p., group exec. personal sys. and integrated supply chain, 2002—. IBM ptnr. exec. Bell South. Office: IBM 1133 Westchester Ave White Plains NY 10604*

MOFFATT, HUGH MCCULLOCH, JR. hospital administrator, physical therapist; b. Steubenville, Ohio, Oct. 11, 1933; s. Hugh McCulloch and Agnes Elizabeth (Bickerstaff) M.; m. Ruth Anne Colvin, Aug. 16, 1958; children: David, Susan. AB, Asbury Coll., 1958; cert. in phys. therapy, Duke U., 1963. Lic. in phys. therapy and health care adminstrn. Commd. officer USPHS, 1964, advanced through grades to capt., therapist, 1964-66, Sitka, Alaska, 1970-72, therapist cons. Atlanta, 1968-70, clinic adminstr. Kayenta, Ariz., 1972-73, hosp. dir. Sitka, 1973-78; therapist cons. Idaho Dept. Health, Boise, 1966-68; contract health officer USPHS, Anchorage, 1978-89, ret., 1989; phys. therapy cons. Ocean Beach Hosp., Ilwaco, Wash., 1989—, Harbors Home Health Svcs., Aberdeen, 1990—. Therapist cons. Our Lady of Compassion Care Ctr., Anchorage, 1979—, Alaska Native Med. Ctr., Anchorage, 1988—. With U.S. Army, 1955-57. Mem. Am. Phys. Therapy Assn., Commd. Officers Assn. USPHS, Res. Officers Assn., Ret. Officers Assn., Am. Assn. Individual Investors, Am. Assn. Ret. Persons, Eagles. Avocations: automobile repairs, woodworking, camping, fishing, church choir.

MOFFATT, JOYCE ANNE, performing arts executive; b. Grand Rapids, Mich., Jan. 3, 1936; d. John Barnard and Ruth Lillian (Pellow) M. BA in Lit., U. Mich., 1957, MA in Theatre, 1960; HHD (hon.), Profl. Sch. Psychology, San Francisco, 1991. Stage mgr., lighting designer Off-Broadway plays; costume, lighting and set designer, stage mgr. stock cos., 1954-62; nat. subscription mgr. Theatre Guild/Am. Theatre Soc., N.Y.C., 1965-67; subscription mgr. Theatre, Inc.-Phoenix Theatre, 1963-67; cons. N.Y.C. Ballet and N.Y.C. Opera, 1967-70; asst. house mgr. N.Y. State Theater, 1970-72; dir. ticket sales City Ctr. of Music and Drama, Inc., N.Y.C., 1970-72; prodn. mgr. San Antonio's Symphony/Opera, 1973-75; gen. mgr. San Antonio Symphony/Opera, 1975-76, 55th St. Dance Theater Found., Inc., N.Y.C., 1976-77, Ballet Theatre Found., Inc./Am. Ballet Theatre, N.Y.C., 1977-81; v.p. prodn. Radio City Music Hall Prodns., Inc., 1981-83; artist-in-residence CCNY, 1981—; propr. mgmt. cons. firm for performing arts N.Y.C., 1983—; exec. dir. San Francisco Ballet Assn., 1987-93; mng. dir. Houston Ballet Assoc., 1993-95; gen. mgr. Chgo. Music and Dance Theater, Inc., 1995—. Cons. Ford Found., N.Y. State Coun. on Arts, Kennedy Ctr. for Performing Arts.; mem. dance panels N.Y. State Coun. on Arts, 1979-81; mem. panels for Support to Prominent Orgns. and Dance, Calif. Arts Coun., 1988-92. Appointee San Francisco Cultural Affairs Task Force, 1991; chmn. bd. dirs. Tex. Inst. for Arts in Edn., 1994—; trustee Internat. Alliance of Theatrical Stage Employees Local 16 Pension and Welfare Fund, 1991-94; bd. dirs. Rudolf Nureyev Dance Found., Chgo., 1998—. Mem. Assn. Theatrical Press Agts. and Mgrs., Actors Equity Assn., United Scenic Artists Local 829, San Francisco Visitors and Conv. Bur. (bd. dirs.), Argyle Club (San Antonio). Office: Chicago Music & Dance Theater Mezz Level 203 N La Salle St Chicago IL 60601-1210

MOFFATT, KATY (KATHERINE LOUELLA MOFFATT), musician, vocalist, songwriter; b. Ft. Worth, Nov. 19, 1950; d. Lester Huger and Sue-Jo (Jarrott) M. Student, Sophie Newcomb Coll., 1968, St. John's Coll., 1969-70. Rec. artist Columbia Records, 1975-79, Permian/MCA Records, 1982-84, Enigma Records, L.A., 1985, Wrestler Records, L.A., 1987-88, Red Moon Records, Switzerland, 1988-93, Philo/Rounder Records, 1989-96, Round Tower Music, U.K., Ireland, Europe, 1993-96, Watermelon Records, U.S., 1994-96, Panther City Records, New Zealand, 1998, Hightone/HMG Records, 1998-2001, Western Jubilee/Shanachie Records, 2001—. Folksinger, Ft. Worth, 1967-68; musician, vocalist, songwriter, rec. artist: (films) Billy Jack, 1970, Hard Country, 1981, The Thing Called Love, 1993; prodn. asst. film, Sta. KIII-TV, Corpus Christi, 1970, audio engr., Sta. KRIS-TV, Corpus Christi, 1970; musician, vocalist in blues band, Corpus Christi, 1970; receptionist, bookkeeping asst., copywriter, announcer, Sta. KFWT, Ft. Worth, 1971, musician, vocalist, songwriter, Denver, 1971-72, on tour, 1973, 75—, Denver, 1974, on tour, 1976-79, European tour, 1977, Can. tour, 1984-85, on tour in Europe, U.S., Can., Asia and Australia, 1985—; albums include Katy, 1976, Kissin' In The California Sun, Am. release, 1977, internat. release, 1978, A Town South of Bakersfield, 1985, Walkin' on the Moon, European release, 1988, U.S. release, 1989, Child Bride, 1990, (duet album with brother Hugh) Dance Me Outside, 1992, (Switzerland only) Indoor Fireworks, 1992, The Greatest Show On Earth A.K.A. The Evangeline Hotel, 1994, Hearts Gone Wild, 1994, Tulare Dust, 1995, (duet album with Kate Brislin) Sleepless Nights, 1996, Midnight Radio, 1996, Angel Town, 1998, Loose Diamond, 1999, Cowboy Girl, 2001; songs include The Magic Ring, 1971; Gerry's Song, 1973, Kansas City Morning, 1974, Take Me Back To Texas, 1975, (Waitin' For) The Real Thing, 1975, Didn't We Have Love, 1976, Kissin' in the California Sun, 1977, Walkin' on the Moon, 1989. Recipient Record World Album award, 1976; named one of 4 Top New Female Vocalists, Cashbox Singles Awards, 1976; nominee for Top New Female Vocalist, Acad. Country Music, 1985; winner best singer-songwriter category Ft. Worth Weekly Mag. Music awards, 1997. Mem. AFTRA, SAG, NARAS, Am. Fedn. Musicians.

MOFFATT, MICHAEL ALAN, lawyer; b. Indpls., Feb. 22, 1964; s. James L. Kelso and Peggy A. Tackett; m. Nancy Norman, Sept. 23, 1989; children: Patricia Margaret, Michael Alan, Nicole Elizabeth, Michelle Ann. BA in Polit. Sci., Depauw U., 1986; JD, Ind. U., 1989. Bar: Ind. 1989, U.S. Dist. Ct. (so. and no. dists.) Ind. 1989, U.S. Ct. Appeals (7th cir.) 1991, U.S. Supreme Ct., 1999. Law clk., assoc. White & Raub, Indpls., 1987-94; assoc. Wooden McLaughlin & Sterner, 1994-95, Barnes & Thornburg, Indpls., 1995-2000, ptnr., 2001; shareholder Ogletree Deakins, Nash, Smoak and Stewart, P.C., 2001—. Lectr. litigation, paralegal program, Ind. U./Purdue U., Ind. CLE Forum & labor/employmemt seminars. Contbr. articles to legal jours. Co-chmn. Keep Am. Beautiful, Greencastle, Ind., 1986, bd. dirs., sec., 1990—94; v.o. Fall Creek Little League, 2002—; mem. devel. control com. Geist Harbors Property Owner's Assn., Indpls., 1993—94, cons., 1994, pres., 1997—99; bd. dirs., tournament chair Fall Creek Little League, 2001—; cons. pediatric ethics com. Meth. Hosp., Indpls., 1990—92; winners cir. mentor U.S. Auto Club. Mem.: ABA (labor and employment sect.), Indpls. Bar Assn. (exec. coun. labor law sect. 1999, vice chmn. 2000, chmn. 2001), Ind. Bar Assn. (mem. exec. coun. labor law sect. 2002—), Fed. Bar Assn., Exch. Club (pres.-elect 1997—98, pres. 1998—99, past pres. 1999—2000). Avocations: golf, basketball, softball. Office: Ogletree Deakins Nash Smoak & Stewart PC One Indiana Sq Ste 2300 Indianapolis IN 46204 Business E-Mail: mike.moffatt@odnss.com.

MOFFATT, MINDY ANN, educator, educational training specialist; b. Mpls., Aug. 3, 1951; d. Ralph Theron and La Vone Muriel (Bergstrom) M. Student, UCLA, 1972-73; BA, Calif. State U., Fullerton, 1975, MS in Edn., 1991. Cert. elem. tchr., Calif. Tchr. early childhood edn. program Meadows Elem. Sch., Valencia, Calif., 1977-78; tchr. United Parents Against Forced Busing, Chatsworth, 1978-80; founding tchr. Gazebo Two Sch. for Young Gifted and Creative Children, Summerville, S.C., 1980-81; tchr. Anaheim (Calif.) Union H.S. Dist., Anaheim, Calif., 1981-89, mentor, tchr., 1985-88; tchr. Greentree Elem. Sch., Irvine, 1989-90; with Thurston Mid. Sch., Laguna Beach, 1990-92; tng. specialist Scripps Clinics and Rsch. Found., LaJolla, 1993-94; tchr. White Hill Mid. Sch., Ross Valley Sch. Dist., San Anselmo, 1994-95, J.B. Davidson Mid. Sch., San Rafael, 1996-2000; asst. prin. Ventura (Calif.) H.S., 2000—01; lang. arts specialist in writing Ventura Unified Sch. Dist., 2001—. Cons. writing project U. Calif., Irvine, 1982—; textbook cons. McDougal, Littell & Co., Evanston, Ill., 1984-86; facilitator Summer Tech. Tng. Inst., Irvine, 1987. Co-author: Practical Ideas for Teaching Writing as a Process, 1986, 87, Thinking/Writing: Fostering Critical Thinking Through Writing, 1991, Reading, Thinking, and Writing About Culturally Diverse Literature, 1995. Mem. Our Ultimate Recreation (Orange County, Calif., chairperson social com. 1983, chairperson backpacking 1983, v.p. 1993-94). Avocations: whitewater rafting, canoeing, bicycling, skiing, backpacking. Office: Ventura Unified Sch Dist 120 E Santa Clara Ventura CA 93001 E-mail: mmoffatt@vtusd.k12.ca.us.edu.

MOFFATT, ROBERT HENRY, accountant, publisher, writer, consultant; b. June 30, 1930; s. James Bigelow and Edwige Edith Moffatt; m. Hannelore Mann, Jan. 7, 1989. Student, Loyola Coll., Montreal, 1948-52, Arcadia U., 1962, UCLA, 1970, 72. Lic. in air navigation, Can.; enrolled agt. Dept. Treasury. Mng. editor, pub. Kings-Annapolis Wings, 1961-66; pres. Valley Pubs. Ltd., Kingston, N.S., Can., 1961-67; exec. dir. Maritime Motor Transport Assn., Moncton, N.B., Can., 1967-68; editor Maritime Truck Transport Rev., Can., 1967-68; dir. custom products divsn. Wolf-Brown Inc., L.A., 1968-77; newsletter pub., writer, 1980—; pvt. practice tax acctg. L.A., 1970—. Columnist, author editls. in mags. Clk., author constn. Village of Greenwood, N.S., 1961-63; chmn. bd. commrs., 1963-66; publicity chmn. Voluntary Econ. Planning Program, province N.S., 1965-66. Lt. Can. Air Force, 1954-60. Mem. Nat. Assn. Enrolled Agts. (newsletter editor, bd. dirs.), Nat. Soc. Pub. Accts. (accredited in taxation, corp. dir.), Calif. Soc. Enrolled Agts. Home and Office: 7509 W 88th St Los Angeles CA 90045-3408

MOFFET, JANE HUMES, retired school principal; b. Phila., July 2, 1930; d. Samuel and Dorothy (Humes) M. BS, East Stroudsburg U., 1952; ME, Rutgers U., 1960. Cert. tchr., counselor, prin., N.J. Tchr. South Plainfield (N.J.) Bd. Edn., 1952-62; guidance dir. Saddle Brook (N.J.) Bd. Edn., 1962-67, sch. vice-prin., 1967-70, high sch. prin., 1971-91, acting supt., 1991-94; ret., 1994. Bd. dirs. All-Am. Girls Profl. Baseball League. Named Cooperstown Baseball Hall of Fame, 1988, East Stroudsburg Hall of Fame Field Hockey and Basketball, 1990, Pa. Sports Hall of Fame, 1998, Gloucester County Sports Hall of Fame, 1999, Pitnam H.S. Sports Hall of Fame, 1999. Mem. NEA, N.J. Edn. Assn., Nat. Assn. Secondary Prins., N.J. Prins. and Suprs. Assn. Avocations: golf, boating. Home: 1811 Monitor Dr Toms River NJ 08753-3113

MOFFET, KENNETH WILLIAM, lawyer; b. Mpls., Mar. 29, 1959; s. Donald Pratt and Sally (Hullsiek) M. BA, Denison U., 1981; JD, Am. U., 1984. Bar: Fla. 1984, U.S. Dist. Ct. (so. dist.) Fla. 1985, U.S. Ct. Appeals (11th cir.) 1987. Assoc. Fleming, O'Bryan & Fleming, Ft. Lauderdale, Fla., 1984-86, Roberts & Reynolds, P.A., West Palm Beach, 1986-89, ptnr., 1989-96; pres. Moffet & Alexander, P.A., 1997, sr. ptnr., 1997—. Bd. dirs. adv. Am. Lung Assn. S.E. Fla., 1996—. Mem. Palm Beach County Bar Assn., Fla. Def. Lawyers Assn., Phi Beta Kappa. Republican. Presbyterian. Avocations: skiing, tennis. Office: Moffet & Alexander PA 1601 Forum Pl West Palm Beach FL 33401-8101

MOFFETT, CHARLES SIMONTON, museum director, curator, writer; b. Washington, Sept. 19, 1945; s. Charles Simonton M. and Faith Atherton Locke Phelps; m. Jane Pettigrew Daniels, July 28, 1979; children: Kate Serena, Charles Locke. BA, Middlebury Coll., 1967; MA, NYU, 1970. Ford Found. fellow Nelson Gallery Art, Kansas City, Mo., 1969-70; expert Sotheby Parke Bernet, N.Y.C., 1970-71; guest asst. curator Met. Mus., 1974-75, assoc. curator, 1976-81, curator European paintings, 1981-83; curator-in-charge Fine Arts Mus. San Francisco, 1983-87, chief curator, summer 1987; sr. curator paintings Nat. Gallery Art, Washington, 1987-92; dir. The Phillips Collection, 1992-98; exec. v.p., co-chmn. impressionist, modern, contemporary art world wide Sotheby's, 1998—. Organizer mus. exhbns., author catalogues; mem. spl. exhbns. panel Nat. Endowment for Arts, 1987; project dir. publs. grant from J. Paul Getty Trust to Fine Arts Mus. San Francisco, 1987; fellow conf. on econs. of arts, presenter Salzburg (Austria) Conf., 1993; grad. Mus. Mgmt. Inst., 1990, sr. mus. assoc., 1994—. Trustee San Francisco Day Sch., 1987, Middlebury Coll., 1987-90, Sterling and Francine Clark Art Inst., 1996-98, Terra Found. for the Arts, 1997-98. Andrew Mellon fellow Met. Mus. Art, 1975; travel grantee Met. Mus. Art, 1980; recipient award for best exhbn. Soho News Arts Awards, 1978; co-recipient Prix Bernier for Manet 1832-1883, 1983, recipient Alumni Achievement award Middlebury Coll., 1985, Kaufman award Nat. Gallery Art, 1989. Episcopalian. Office: Sotheby's 1334 York Ave New York NY 10021-4806

MOFFETT, DAWN SCHULTEN, elementary education educator; b. Phila., Nov. 22, 1946; d. Emil Ferdinand and Helen Marie (McPhee) Schulten; m. Thomas Lee Moffett, July 25, 1970; children: Carolyn Dawn, Deborah Leanne, William Lee. BS, Bloomsburg U., 1968; postgrad., Temple U., 1969-71. Cert. tchr., Pa. Tchr. 4th grade Hatboro-Horsham Sch. Dist., Horsham, Pa., 1968-69, tchr. 1st grade, 1969-72; kindergarten tchr.'s aide Quantico (Va.) Sch. Dist., 1972-73; kindergarten tchr. U-Gro Learning Centres, Palmyra, Pa., 1986-87; subs. tchr. Cen. Dauphin Sch. Dist., Harrisburg, 1989-90, Lower Dauphin Sch. Dist., Hummelstown, 1989-90, Milton Hershey Sch., Hershey, 1987-90; tchr., grade 2 S.E. Elem. Sch., Lebanon, 1990-91, tchr. continuous progress program, grades 1-3, 1991—, tchr. 1st grade, 1999—. Sch. dir. Derry Twp. Sch. Dist., Hershey, 1983-87, 96-97, Dauphin County Vo-Tech Sch., Harrisburg, 1984-87; trustee First United Meth. Ch., 1988-90, mem. coun. of ministries, 1988-90, 95—, dir. higher edn., 1995—; sec. Derry Twp. Libr. Bd., 1987-93; mem. Hershey Libr. Endowment Bd., 1986—, chmn., 2000—; pres. Friends of Hershey Pub. Libr., 1986-88; active PTO. Recipient Svc. award Pa. Sch. Bds. Assn., 1987, Dauphin County Tech. Sch., 1987, Derry Twp. Sch. Dist., 1987, Award of Excellence in Edn., Lebanon Valley C. of C., 2000; inductee Lebanon County Ednl. Honor Soc., 2002. Mem. AAUW (pres. Hershey 1978-80, Outstanding Woman of Yr. 1982), NEA, Pa. State Edn. Assn., Pa. Libr. Assn., Internat. Reading Assn., Nat. Tchrs. English. Republican. Avocations: snow skiing, swimming, crocheting, counted cross-stitch, quilting. Home: 357 Laurie Ave Hummelstown PA 17036-9720 E-mail: dsmoff@aol.com.

MOFFETT, FRANK CARDWELL, architect, civil engineer, real estate developer; b. Houston, Dec. 9, 1931; s. Ferrell Orlando and Jewell Bernice (Williams) M.; m. Annie Doris Thorn, Aug. 1, 1952 (div.); children: David Cardwell (dec.), Douglas Howard; m. Darlene Adele Alm Sayan, June 7, 1985 (div.); m. Vicki Lynn Schultz Harris, May 1, 1999. BArch, U. Tex., 1958. Registered arch.; profl. engr.; cert. Nat. Council Archtl. Registration Bds., U.S. Dept. Def., Fallout Shelter Analysis, environ. engring. Arch. Seattle, Harmon, Pray & Detrich, Arnold G. Gangnes, Ralf E. Decker, Roland Terry & Assocs., 1958-64; ptnr. Heideman & Moffett, AIA, Seattle, 1964-71; chief arch. Wash. State Dept. Hwys., Olympia, 1971-77, Wash. State Dept. Transp., Olympia, 1977-87; owner The Moffett Co., WA, 1987—. Adv. Wash. State Bldg. Code Counc., 1975-95, instr. civil engrng. tech., Olympia Tech. Commty. Coll., 1975-77; adv. mem. archtl. barriers subcom. Internat. Conf. Building Ofcls.; founder, treas. T.A.A., Inc., P.S., 1988, pres., 1991—; presenter in field. Archtl. works include hdqrs. Gen. Telephone Directory Co., Everett, Wash., 1964; Edmonds Unitarian Ch., 1966; tenant devel. Seattle Hdqrs. Office, Seattle First Nat. Bank, 1968-70; Wash. State Dept. Transp. Area Hdqrs. Offices, Mt. Vernon, Selah, Raymond, Colfax and Port Orchard 1973-87; Materials Lab., Spokane, Wash., 1974; Olympic Meml. Gardens, Tumwater, Wash., 1988, City Anacortes emergency power stas., 1989, L. Albert Residence, 1990, F. Gasperetti Residence, 1991, G. Holbrook Residence, 2000; archtl. barriers cons. State of Alaska, 1978, State of Wash., 1972-94. Co-author: An Illustrated Handbook for Barrier-Free Design, 2nd edit., 1985, 3rd edit., 1987, 4th Edit., 1989, Accessibility Design for All, 1992, 2nd edit., 1995, 3d edit., 1998; Housing and Building Accessibility: The Law in Washington, 1992. Chmn. Planning Commn. of Mountlake Terr., Wash., 1963, 64, mem., 1961-67; mem. State of Wash. Govs. Task Force on Wilderness, 1972-75, Heritage Park Task Force, Olympia, Wash., 1986—; trustee Cascade Symphony Orch., 1971; incorporating pres. United Singles, Olympia, 1978-79; capt. CAP, fin. ofcr. Olympia Squadron; mem. nat. panel profl. advisors to Nat. Multiple Sclerosis Soc., 1993—; bd. dirs. Wash. Coalition Citizens with Disabilities; expert witness Ams. with Disabilities Act of 1990. With USN, 1951-54. Fellow ASCE; mem. AIA (dir. S.W. Wash. chpt. 1980-82, pres.-elect 1985, pres. 1986, dir. Wash. council 1986, archs. in govt. nat. com. 1978-87, chmn. N.W. and Pacific region conf. 1991), Am. Public Works Assn., Inst. Bldgs. and Grounds , Constrn. Specifications Inst., Am. Arbitration Assn. (invited panelist), Washington Soc./Nat. Huguenot Soc. (pres. 1978-80, 85-87, 95-99), Gen. Soc. Mayflower Descs. (gov. Wash. Soc. 1982-83, dep. gov. gen. Gen. Soc., 1998—), SAR (state treas. 1984-85), SCV Sons and Daus. of Pilgrims (gov. Wash. Soc. 1984), Baronial Order of Magna Charta, Aircraft Owners' and Pilots' Assn., Rotary (pres. Edmonds, 1969-70), Olympia, Coll. Club of Seattle. Republican. Baptist. Home and Office: PO Box 7 Hanford CA 93232-0007 E-mail: fmoffett@aol.com., taaae@aol.com.

MOFFETT, HOWARD MACKENZIE, lawyer; b. New Orleans, Dec. 26, 1943; s. Howard F. and Margaret Delphia (Mackenzie) M.; m. Karin Ingrid Henrikson, July 26, 1986 (div. Dec. 1993); a child, Anna Kristin. BA in History, Yale Coll., 1966; MA in Econ., Cambridge (Eng.) U., 1969; JD, U. Calif., Berkeley, 1975. Bar: N.H. 1975, U.S. Dist. Ct. N.H. 1975, U.S. Ct. Appeals (1st cir.) 1994. Reporter Viet Nam Guardian, Saigon, 1966-67, Newsweek, Saigon, 1966-67; legis. & adminstrv. asst. U.S. Rep. John B. Anderson, Washington, 1969-72; assoc. Orr and Reno PA, Concord, N.H., 1975-82, ptnr., 1982—, also bd. dirs. Trustee Canterbury (N.H.) Shaker Village, 1985—. Mem. N.H. Hist. Soc. (trustee 2000—). Democrat. Presbyterian. Office: Orr and Reno PA One Eagle Square Concord NH 03301

MOFFETT, J. DENNY, lawyer; b. Atlanta, Sept. 20, 1947; s. James Denny Moffett Jr. and Dorothy (Mckenzie) McCall; m. Mary F. Ray, June 6, 1987; children: David, Jenny. BA, U. Okla., 1969; JD with honors, George Washington U., 1972, LLM in Taxation, 1974. Bar: Okla. 1972, U.S. Tax Ct. 1973, Wyo. 2001. Legis. asst. U.S. Senate, Washington, 1973-74; ptnr. Conner & Winters, Tulsa, 1974-90, McKenzie, Moffett, Elias & Books, Tulsa, Oklahoma City, 1990-97, Moffett & Assocs., P.C., Tulsa, 1997—. Adj. faculty U. Tulsa Law Sch., 1978; arbitrator Nat. Assn. Securities Dealers. Commr. Ark.-Okla. River Compact Commn., 1990-94; pres. Nicholas Club Tulsa, 1984; endowment com. Trinity Episcopal Ch., 1990—. 2d lt. U.S. Army, 1972-74; bd. dirs. Am. Cancer Soc., Tulsa, 1991-94. Mem. Am. Arbitration Assn., Tulsa Tax Club (pres. 1981, 94). Republican. Home: 2132 E 32nd Pl Tulsa OK 74105-2222 Office: Moffett & Assocs PC 1722 S Carson Ave Ste 3203 Tulsa OK 74119

MOFFETT, JUDITH, writer, translator; b. Louisville, Aug. 30, 1942; d. James Selby Moffett and Margaret Lee Cowherd; m. Edward B. Irving Jr., Mar. 17, 1983 (dec. Mar. 1998). MA in English, Colo. State U., 1966; MA in Am. Civilization, U. Pa., 1970, PhD, 1971. Asst. prof. English Pa. State U., Erie, 1971-75; vis. instr. poetry U. Iowa, Iowa City, 1977-78; prof. English U. Pa., Phila., 1978-93; instr. U. Ky., Lexington, 2000—. Author: (poems) Keeping Time, 1976, Whinny Moor Crossing, 1984; (criticism) James Merrill: An Introduction to the Poetry, 1984; (novel) Pennterra, 1987, The Ragged World, 1991, Two That Came True, 1991, Time, Like an Ever-Rolling Stream, 1992, (nonfiction) Homestead Year: Back to the Land in Surburbia, 1995; translator: Gentleman, Single, Refined and Selected Poems 1937-1959 (Hjalmar Gullberg), 1979, The North! To the North! Five Swedish Poets of the Nineteenth Century, 2001. Recipient Transl. prize Swedish Acad., 1982, Theodore Sturgeon award, 1987, John W. Campbell award, 1988; Fulbright Tchg. fellow, 1967; Fulbright Travel grantee, 1973; Creative Writing grantee Ingram Merrill Found., 1976, 80, 91; Transl. grantee NEH, 1983, NEA Creative Writing fellow, 1984; grantee Swedish Acad., 1994. Avocations: mountain hiking, I Ching. Home: 2336 Glensboro Rd Lawrenceburg KY 40342 E-mail: hefngafr@aol.com.

MOFFETT, SAMUEL HUGH, retired educator, minister; b. Pyongyang, Korea, Apr. 7, 1916; (parents Am. citizens); s. Samuel Austin and Lucia Hester (Fish) M.; m. Elizabeth Barnwell Tarrant, June 30, 1942 (dec. Jan. 1955); m. Eileen Flower, Sept. 15, 1956. AB in Classics summa cum laude, Wheaton (Ill.) Coll., 1938; ThB, Princeton Theol. Sem., 1942; PhD in Religion, Ch. History, Yale U., 1945; postgrad., Coll. Chinese Studies, Peking, 1947-48; LittD (hon.), Yonsei U., Seoul, Republic of Korea, 1981; DD (hon.), King Coll., Bristol, Tenn., 1985, Gordon-Conwell Theol. Sem., 1995, Presbyn. Coll. and Sem., 1996; PhD (hon.), Soongsil U., Seoul, 1997. Ordained to ministry Presbyn. Ch. (USA), 1943. Asst. pastor 1st Presbyn. Ch., Bridgeport, Conn., 1943-44, interim pastor New Haven, 1944-45; dir. youth work Presbyn. Bd. Fgn. Missions, 1945-46; mem. faculty Yenching U., Peking, 1948-49, Nanking (China) Theol. Sem., 1949-50; vis. lectr. Princeton (N.J.) Theol. Sem., 1953-55, Henry W. Luce prof. ecumenics and mission, 1981-86, chmn. ch. history dept., 1983-86, guest prof., 1986-87, prof. emeritus, 1986—; assoc. pres. Presbyn. Theol. Sem. Korea, Seoul, 1970-81, prof. ch. history, 1960-81, dean grad. sch., 1966-70, hon. pres., 1981—. Dir. Asian Ctr. for Theol. Studies and Missions, Seoul, 1974-81, hon. pres., 1981—; bd. dirs. Yonsei U., 1957-81, Soongsil U., 1969-81, Whitworth Coll., Spokane, Wash., 1973-79; commn. rep. in Korea Presbyn. Ch. (USA), 1960-64; mem. U.S. Edn. Commn. in Korea, 1966-67; chmn. theol. consultation World Alliance Reformed Chs., Nairobi, 1971; trustee Princeton-in-Asia, 1984—. Author: Wher'er The Sun, 1953, The Christians of Korea, 1962, (with others) Joy for an Anxious Age, 1968, First Encounters: Korea 1880-1910, 1982, A History of Christianity in Asia, vol. 1, 1992; contbr. articles, book revs. to various publs. Pres. Royal Asiatic Soc., Korea, 1968, councillor, 1963-81. Decorated Order of Civil Merit Peony medal Republic of Korea, Medal of Aaron and Hur U.S. Army Chaplains. Vis. scholar Cambridge U., 1970-71, 76-77; fellow Ctr. for Theol. Inquiry, Princeton, 1986-90. Mem. Am. Soc. Ch. History, Am. Soc. Missiology (pres. 1986-87), Am. Assn. Profs. of Missions (pres. 1985-86), Nassau Club. Republican.

MOFFETT, T(ERRILL) K(AY), lawyer; b. Becker, Miss., July 11, 1949; s. Elmer C. and Mary Ethel (Meek) M.; m. Rita C. Millsaps, Mar. 11, 1972; 1 child, Tara Leigh. BS, U.S. Mil. Acad., 1971; MA in Polit. Sci., U. Hawaii, 1974; JD, U. Miss., 1979. Bar: Miss. 1979, Ala. 1998. Grad. tchr. Am. govt. U. Miss., Oxford, 1977-80; ptnr. Moffett and Thorne, Tupelo, Miss., 1980-88; owner Moffett Law Firm, 1988—; pros. atty. City of Tupelo, 1989-99. Rep. candidate for U.S. Congress 1st Miss. Dist., 1978, 80; 1st dist. coord. Reagan for Pres., 1980; co-chmn. Lee County George Bush for Pres. Com., 1988, 92; mem. Lee County Rep. Exec. Com., 1980—; chmn. Tupelo Rep. Exec. Com., 1988—; active 1st Bapt. Ch., Tupelo; bd. dirs. Sav-A-Life Tupelo, Inc. Capt. U.S. Army, 1971-76; brig. gen. USAR, 2000—, Miss. Army NG, 1999—. Harvard fellow, 1995-96. Mem. ABA, Miss. State Bar Assn., Lee County Bar Assn., Ala. State Bar Assn., Civitan, Masons, Habitat for Humanity, Phi Sigma Alpha. Avocations: music, hunting, tennis, travel. Home: 1761 N Parc Cir Tupelo MS 38804-9753 Office: Moffett Law Firm PO Drawer 1707 330 N Broadway St Tupelo MS 38802-3926

MOFFETT, THOMAS DELANO, music educator; b. Smiths, Ala., Sept. 19, 1942; s. Early Moffett and Estella Sparks; m. Gloria Jean Marshall, Dec. 22, 1968; children: Stephanie Viloria, Marlon Delano. BS, Fla. A&M U., 1963; MEd, Auburn U., 1972, EdD, 1981. Cert. tchr., Ga. Band dir. Drake High Sch., Auburn, Ala., 1963-66, Talbotton Rd. Jr. High Sch., Columbus, Ga., 1966-78; asst. prin. Waddell Elem. Sch., 1978-81; prin. St. Mary's Elem. Sch., 1981-90, Dimon Elem. Sch., Columbus, 1990; music supr. Muscogee County Sch. Dist., 1990-93; assoc. prof. music Troy (Ala.) State U., 1993—. Freelance musician. Active membership drive YMCA, Columbus, 1991; mem. adv. bd. Boy Scouts Am. Pack 120, Columbus, 1981-89; mem. bd. dirs. Southeastern U.S. Band Clinic, Youth Orch. Greater Columbus. Recipient citation Achievement in Edn., Omega Psi Phi, 1981, Past President's award Muscogee Elem. Prins. Assn., 1989, Outstanding Alumni award Fla. A&M, 1987; named Boss of Yr., Muscogee Assn. Edn. Office Personnel, 1989. Mem. NEA, Music Educators Nat. Conf., Ala. Music Educators Assn., Troy State Educators Assn., Phi Delta Kappa, Phi Mu Alpha. Democrat. Methodist. Avocations: golf, bowling, singing, saxophone. Home: PO Box 5501 Columbus GA 31906-0501 Office: Troy State U Smith Hall Troy AL 36082 E-mail: tmoffett@troyst.edu.

MOFFIE, H. STEVEN, psychiatrist; b. Chgo., May 5, 1946; s. Samuel Edward and Miriam (Misha) M.; m. Lynn Hansher, June 30, 1968; children: Stacia, Evan. MD, Yale U., 1971. Diplomate Am. Bd. Psychiatry and Neurology. Intern L.A. County-U. So. Calif. Med. Ctr., L.A., 1971-72; resident U. Chgo. Hosps. and Clins., 1972-75; clin. dir. Calhoun-Cleburne Mental Health Ctr., Anniston, Ala., 1975-77, N.W. Med. Health Ctr., Houston, 1978-89; dir. Med. and Psychol. Svcs., 1983-85; assoc. prof. Baylor Coll. Medicine, 1985-89; prof. Med. Coll. Wis., Milw., 1989—; supr. Sports Psychiat. Inst., 1990-94; chief of staff St. Mary's Hill Hosp., 1990-92. Mem. grant rev. com. NIMH, Washington, 1986; cons. Acad. Managed Care, Milw., 1990—; editor Social Psychiatry Spotlight, Milw., 1998—; chair Socio-Cultural Cmty. Coalition, 1998—. Editor: A Clinician's Manual, 1982, Psychiatry: A Problem-Oriented Approach, 1986, The Ethical Way, 1997, I Have A Vision, 1999. Bd. dirs. Tex. Com. for Humanities, 1988-89, Milw. Ethnic Coun., 1991-94, Alliance for Mentally Ill, Milw., 1993-99. Maj. U.S. Army, 1975-77. Named Exemplary Psychiatrist, Nat. Alliance for Mentally Ill, 1993. Fellow Am. Psychiat. Assn., Am. Orthopsychiat. Assn.; mem. Am. Assn. for Social Psychiatry (pres. 1998—), Am. Assn. Cmty. Psychiatrists (emeritus bd. 1997—, sponsor award for ethical practice 1998—), Wis. Psychiat. Adminstrs. (chair ethics com. 1999—), Grand Ave. Club (bd. dirs. 1999). Jewish. Avocations: family, music, art, travel, sports. Home: 1200 E Bywater Ln Milwaukee WI 53217-2840 E-mail: rustevie@earthlink.net.

MOFFITT, AUGUSTINE EDWARD, steel company executive; b. Oct. 2, 1945; s. Augustine E and Margaret (Dolores) Moffitt; m. Joanne Alexandra Klatko, Sept. 16, 1967; children: Christopher, Amy. AB cum laude, La Salle Coll., 1967; MS, Harvard U., 1969, ScD, 1973, Advanced Mgmt. Program, 1996. Sr. asst. health svcs. officer Nat. Inst. Occupational Safety & Health, Cin., 1969-71, toxicologist, 1971-72, chief biochem. pharmacology, 1972-73; sr. environ. chemist and toxicologist Bethlehem (Pa.) Steel Corp., 1973-76, dir. environ. chemistry and toxicology, 1976-80, mgr. environ. health, 1980-83, mgr. occupl. health and safety, 1983-84, mgr. human resources, 1984-94, v.p. safety, health and environment, 1994-98, sr. v.p. adminstr., 1998-200, exec. v.p., CAO, 2000—. Bd dirs Nat Safety Coun, Chicago, 1983—85, Chicago, 1998—; trustee Lehigh Valley Health Network, 1997—; bd dirs Lehigh Valley Bus-Educ Partnership, 1998—; bd gov Inst Career Develop, 1998—; chmn comt environ affairs Int Iron and Steel Inst, 1998—2000. Trustee Muhlenberg Med Ctr, 1988—. Mem.: Am Indust Hygiene Asn, Soc Toxicology, Am Iron and Steel Inst, Bethlehem Area CofC, Sigma Xi. Office: Bethlehem Steel Corp 1170 8th Ave Rm 2123 Bethlehem PA 18016-7600 E-mail: amoffitt@bethsteel.com.

MOFFITT, CAROLYN MULLINS, university official; b. Victoria, Ark. d. Jefferson Forrest and Mabel Mullins: children: James S. Crone, Jr., Jefferson Edward Crone, Laurie Kittrell. BBA, U. Memphis, 1994. Supr. Medicare billing City of Memphis Hosp., 1968-71; dir. budget and reimbursement Regional Med. Ctr., Memphis, 1971-90, bus. mgr. ambulatory svcs., 1990-91; patient accounts mgr. radiology dept. U. Tenn. Med. Group, 1992-99; mgmt. analyst, compliance officer U. Tenn. Health Sci. Ctr., 1999—. Cons. Meth. Healthcare, Memphis, 1982-84, Brannon McCullough, Primary Health Care Ctr., Memphis, 1990-92; mem. adv. bd. Porter Leath Children's Home, Memphis, 1989-92. Mem. Healthcare Fin. Mgmt. Assn. (cert., fellow, bd. dirs. 1995-96, v.p. 1996-98, pres. 1999-2000, bd. chmn. 2000-2001, compliance officers forum adv. coun. 2001—). Avocations: stained glass creations, collectibles, reading, family. Office: U Tenn Bowld Hosp Ste 706B 951 Court Ave Memphis TN 38103-2813 E-mail: cmoffitt@utmem.edu.

MOFFITT, CHARLES WILLIAM, art gallery director; b. Altoona, Pa., Mar. 24, 1932; s. Charles William and Beatrice Jeanette (Shellenberger) M.; m. Marianne Foley Potter, May 23, 1980 (dec.); children: Michelle Ann Hunt, Charles William III, Deborah K. Moffitt Russell; stepchildren: Christopher Potter, Kimberly Bryan. BA, Pa. State U., 1957. Examiner Pa. R.R., Buffalo, 1957-62; asst. to pres. White Cross Stores, Inc., Monroeville, Pa., 1962-65, sec., 1965-70, v.p. adminstrn., sec., 1970-72; dir. labor relations and legal affairs Revco D.S., Inc., Cleve., 1972-75, asst. v.p. personnel, 1974-75; pres. Fashion Wearhouse, Inc., Altoona, Pa., 1975-87; dir. Servello Gallery Art, 2002—. Owner Omega Advt. Co.; pres. Olympus I, Inc., 1980-87; agt. Prin. Fin. Group, 1988-90, Variable Annuity Life Ins. Co., 1990-2001. Co-author: Mincemeat Cartoons, Altoona Mirror Newspaper. Bd. dirs. Bedford Springs Music Festival, 1984-87, Blair County Arts Found., 1987-91. Republican. Roman Catholic. Home: RR 5 Box 2324 Altoona PA 16601

MOFFITT, CHRISTINE M. biologist, educator; PhD, U. Mass., 1978. Instr. Smith Coll., Northampton, Mass., 1978—80; postdoctoral assoc. U. Mass., Amherst, 1980—81; asst. prof. U. Idaho, Moscow, 1982—88, assoc. prof., 1989—98, prof., 1999—. Contbr. articles to profl. jours. Named Outstanding Alumna, U. Mass. Natural Resources Coll., 1999. Mem.: Am. Fisheries Soc. (pres, pres. elect, 1st vp and 2 vp 1996—2000, Meritorious Svc. award 1994). Office: Dept Fish and Wildlife Resource Univ Idaho Moscow ID 83844-1136 E-mail: cmoffitt@uidaho.edu.

MOFFITT, DAVID LOUIS, lawyer, county official, state official; b. Alexandria, Va., June 8, 1953; s. Otis Breheon and Lillian Vlasta (Svatik) M.; m. Kathleen Ann Brata, Aug. 20, 1988 (div. Nov. 1999); children: David Lachlan, Drake Lorne. BA in Philosophy, U. Mich., 1976; JD, U. Detroit, 1979. Assoc. Plunkett, Cooney, Rutt, Watters, Stanczyk and Pedersen, PC, Detroit, 1979-80, Kitch, Suhreheinrich, Smith, Saurbier and Drutchas, PC, Detroit, 1980-81, Alan R. Miller, PC, Birmingham, 1981-83; pvt. practice Bingham Farms, 1983—. Lectr. real estate law U. Mich. Grad. Sch. Bus. Adminstrn./Mich. Assn. Realtors. Contbr. articles to profl. jours. Active Oakland County Bd. Commrs., 1985—, pers. com., 1985-94, 99—, vice-chmn., 1988-89, chmn. pub. svcs. com., 1998-99, 2001—, vice-chmn., 1999-2000, chmn., 2001—, vice-chmn. majority party caucus, 1987-89, 99, vice-chmn. planning and bldg. com., 1989-91, pers. appeals bd., 1992-93; chmn. Oakland County Zoning Coordinating Bd., 1991, 93, vice-chmn., 1992, chmn. ct. reform study com., 1996-98, chmn. rules revision study com., 1998, energy evaluation task force, 1999—; exec. coun. Southeast Mich. Coun. Govts., 1993—; justice and law enforcement com. Mich. Assn. Counties, 1999-2000; pub. lands nat. policy steering com. Nat. Assn. Counties, 1996-99, vice-chmn. Payment In Lieu of Taxation subcom., 1997; mem. Environ., Energy & Land Use Nat. Policy Steering Com., 1992-96, 99—; Justice and Pub. Safety Nat. Policy Steering Com., 2001—; pub. hearing officer Oakland County Road Commn., 1983-85; adminstr. emeritus David L. Moffit Scholarships for Outstanding Legal Editl. Achievement and Outstanding Achievement in Legal Journalism, U. Detroit Mercy Sch. Law; apptd. to Mich. State Hazardous Waste Site Rev. Bd., 1995—. Named Clarence M. Burton/ Dean's scholar U. Detroit, 1979; recipient Most Disting. Brief to Mich. Supreme Ct. award Thomas M. Cooley Law Sch., 1988. Office: 30600 Telegraph Rd Ste 3250 Bingham Farms MI 48025-5701 E-mail: dlmoffittassoc@ameritech.net.

MOFFITT, RAY, social worker, consultant; b. Moline, Ill., Sept. 1, 1937; s. Ernest R. and Ida L. (Wiggins) M. BS, U. Ill., 1959, MSW, 1966; postgrad. child welfare tng. program, 1995. Cert. social worker, Ill. Social work trainee, grad. sch. field worker various Ill. agencies, 1963-66; social worker, program adminstr. Ill. Soldiers' and Sailors' Children's Sch., Normal, Ill., 1966-73; co-founder, dir. Kaleidoscope, Inc., Bloomington, 1973-74; pres., dir. Browndale/Kaleidoscope, Inc., various, 1974; field instr. Jane Addams Coll. Social Work U. Ill. at Chgo., 1975-77; social worker Village of Maywood (Ill.), 1977-82, cmty. rep., dir. cmty. rels., 1982-87; founder, dir. Explosonic Rockers Street Jazz Theatrical Troupe, 1987-92; founder, exec. prodr. MWAH! Performing Arts Troupe, 1993—; social worker DuPage County Sheriff's Dept., Wheaton, Ill., 1995—. Collaborator Chgo. Area Project and DuPage County Area Project. Mem. NASW, Acad. Cert. Social Workers, U. Ill. Alumni Assn., Child Care Assn. of Ill., Ill. Alcoholism and Drug Dependence Assn., Boy Scouts Am. (former Explorer advisor), Mental Health Assn. in Ill., Ill. Drug Edn. Alliance, Ill. Assn. Student Assistance Profls., Du Page Intergenerational Village, Alpha Zeta Alumni Assn. Home: 159 Cottage Hill Ave Apt 215 Elmhurst IL 60126-3347

MOFFITT, SUSAN RAYE, family care nurse practitioner; b. Mt. Carmel, Ill., July 22, 1964; d. Merle E. and Donna R. (Moore) Holsen; m. Tony Lee Moffitt, June 4, 1991; children: Sarah Ann, Alexander Lee. AASN, Kankakee (Ill.) Community Coll, 1984; BSN, SUNY, 1997; MSN, U. Tampa, 2000. Cert. provider, instr. ACLS, BLS; critical care RN, AACN, family nurse practitioner. Staff nurse med./surg. emergency rm. Lawrence County Meml. Hosp., Lawrenceville, Ill., 1984-87; staff nurse CCU, charge nurse Welborn Bapt. Hosp., Evansville, Ind., 1987-89; charge nurse CCU, Lakeland (Fla.) Regional Med. Ctr., 1989-96, edn. coord. med. cardiology unit, 1997-2000; staff nurse Cardiac Interventional Unit Lakeland Regional Med. Ctr., 1996-97; nurse practitioner Clark and Daughtrey Med. Group, Lakeland, 2000—02, LifePath Hospice and Palliative Care, Lakeland, Fla., 2002—. Preceptor Lakeland Regional Med. Ctr., Welborn Bapt. Hosp. Mem.: ANA, Fla. Nurses Assn., Sigma Theta Tau. E-mail: tmoffitt@tampabay.rr.com.

MOFFITT, TONY LEE, cardiology nurse practitioner; b. Vincennes, Ind., Nov. 7, 1961; s. Larry Richard Moffitt and Bonita Jean (Burrell) Shidler; m. Susan Raye Holsen, June 4, 1991; children: Sarah Ann, Alexander Lee. ADN, Olney Coll., 1987; BSN magna cum laude, U. of State of N.Y., 1997; MSN, U. Tampa, 2000. Cert. Bd. certified Family Practice ARNP, RN Fla., ACLS provider, emergency nurse, critical care nurse. Staff nurse Lawrence County Meml., Lawrenceville, Ill., 1987, Lakeland (Fla.) Regional Med. Ctr., 1987-2000, mem. recruitment and retention, 1988-90, asst. charge nurse, 1990-93; team leader Cardiac Interventional Unit, 1994-95, Cardiac Intensive Care, 1997-2000; emergency nurse South Fla. Bapt., Plant City, 1991-98, charge nurse, 1993-94; team leader Cardiac Interventional Unit, 1994-95, Cardiac Intensive Care, 1997—; advanced RN practitioner Clark & Daughtrey Cardiology, Lakeland, Fla., 2000—. Emergency med. tech. and paramedic clin. instr. Polk C.C., Lakeland, 1990—92. Named Outstanding Student award, Air Force; recipient Nursing Faculty award, U. Tampa, 2000, Achievement award, 2000. Mem.: Fla. Nurses Assn., ANA, Sigma Theta Tau. Republican. Avocation: Avocations: finance, cooking, dining, water sports, SCUBA. Home: 7843 Nature Trail Lakeland FL 33809-5079 Office: Clark & Daughtrey Cardiology 130 Pablo St Lakeland FL 33803

MOFFLIN, LIONEL HUGH (HARRY MOFFLIN), biomedical engineer, physician; b. Fremantle, Australia, Dec. 20, 1923; arrived in US, 1974; s. Horace Elgar and Ida Beatrice (Moseley) Mofflin. MB, BS, U. Adelaide, Australia, 1948; MSc in Biomed. Engrng., Case Western Res. U., 1980; cardiac tech. cert. of proficiency, Cuyahoga C.C. Engr. Cleve. Hearing & Speech Ctr., 1981-83; engr. Electronics Design Ctr. Case Western Res. U., Cleve., 1983-86; circuit designer, 1986-92; project engr. Mofflin Enterprises, Cleve., 1992—. Electronic circuit designer, 1986—98. Fellow: Royal Col Physicians (Edinburgh); mem.: ACP-ASIM. Avocations: preventive medicine, art, music. Office: Mofflin Enterprises 2727 Lancashire Rd Ste B410 Cleveland Heights OH 44106-5518

MOFFLY, JOHN WESLEY, IV, magazine publishing executive; b. Phila., Aug. 5, 1926; s. John W. III Moffly and Audrey (Kane) Chancellor; m. Donna Jeanette Clegg, July 11, 1959; children: Jonathan Wesley, Audrey Kane Lkotz. BA, Princeton U., 1949; student, Woodrow Wilson Sch. N.Y. advt. mgr. House & Home Mag. Time Inc., N.Y.C., 1962-66, N.Y. advt. exec. LIFE Mag., 1967-73, v.p. selling areas mktg. divsn., 1973-87; pres., owner Moffly Pubs., Inc., 1987—; pub. Greenwich and Westport mags. Bd. dirs. Boys and Girls Club Greenwich, United Way, Greenwich Emergency Med. Svc., Greenwich Adult Day Care; mem. Amb.'s Round Table-Forum, World Affairs. With USAAF, 1944-45. Mem. Greenwich C. of C. (chmn. bd. dirs. 1999-2000, Small Businessman of Yr. 1991), Riverside Yacht Club, Cruising Club Am., Indian Harbor Yacht Club. Republican. Episcopalian. Avocations: sailing, tennis, clay bird shooting, skiing, international studies. Home: 100 Meadow Rd Riverside CT 06878-2520 Office: Greenwich Mag 39 Lewis St Greenwich CT 06830-5558

MOGCK, DEREK LEONARD, lawyer; b. June 29, 1971; BA in Polit. Studies, Gordon Coll., 1993; MS in Pub. Affairs, U. Mass., Boston, 1998; JD, U. Conn., 2001. Bar: Conn. 2001, Fed. Dist. Conn. 2002. Asst. to pres. Ethics & Pub. Policy Ctr., Washington, 1993-95; legis. liaison Mass. Hwy. Dept., Boston, 1995-98; assoc. Shipman & Goodwin LLP, Hartford, Conn., 2001—. Home: 92 Hilltop Dr Weatogue CT 06089-9671 Office: Shipman & Goodwin LLP One American Row Hartford CT 06103-2819

MOGEL, LEONARD HENRY, writer; b. Bklyn., Oct. 23, 1922; s. Isaac and Shirley (Goldman) M.; m. Ann Vera Levy, Oct. 23, 1949; children: Wendy Lynn, Jane Ellen. BBA, Coll. City N.Y., 1947. Salesman N.Y. Printing Co., N.Y.C., 1946-48; sales mgr. Pollak Printing Co., 1948-52; advt. dir. Diners Club, Inc., 1952-56; pub. Diners Club for Signature and Bravo mags., 1956-67; pres. Leonard Mogel Assos., Inc. (nat. advt. reps.), N.Y.C., 1952-67; prin. owner San Francisco Warriors Profl. Basketball Team, 1963-64; pres. Twenty First Century Communications Inc., N.Y.C., 1967-72; pub. Cheetah and Weight Watchers mags., 1967-75; dir. Regents Pub. Co. div. Simon & Schuster, 1960-67; advt. cons. Harvard Lampoon, 1968; pub. Nat. Lampoon, 1970-86, Liberty mag., 1971-73, Ingenue mag., 1973-75, Heavy Metal mag., 1977-86. Adj. prof. NYU Sch. Continuing Edn., 1973—78; panelist Folio Mag. Pub. Conf., 1975—76. Exec. prodr.: (feature films) Heavy Metal, 1981; author: Everything You Need to Know to Make It in the Magazine Business, 1979, Making It in the Media Professions, 1988, Making It in Advertising, 1993, Making It in Public Relations, 1993, Making It in Broadcasting, 1994, Making It in Book Publishing, 1996, Creating Your Career in Communications, the Media and Entertainment, 1998, The Newspaper: Everything You Need to Know to Make It in the Newspaper Business, 2000. Sponsor Albert Einstein Med. Coll., Birch Wathen Sch., N.Y.C. Served with AUS, 1942-46, CBI.

MOGENSEN, CHARLES RAY, JR. food service administrator; b. Elizabeth, N.J., May 7, 1946; s. Charles Ray Sr. and Hellen Oakley (Holland) M.; m. Linda Diane Friezer, Apr. 25, 1970; children: Charles Ray III, Jason C., Eric S., Lindsey H. Student, Middlesex County Vocat. Coll., 1972. Cert. food executive, 1979, 1987; lic. real estate agt. NJ. Chef St. Elizabeth Hosp., Elizabeth, N.J., 1969-70; dir. food svcs. Cornell Hall Conv. Ctr., Union, 1970-96; dir. food svc. Corrections Corp. Am., Elizabeth (N.J.) Detention Ctr., 1996—; owner Charles Mogensen Antique Galleries, Ltd., Red Bank, NJ. Pres. C.R.M. Food Enterprises, Ltd., Kenilworth, N.J., 1971-89. Author: (recipes) Escargots Without Shells, 1979 (citation merit 1979). Mem. Rep. Nat. Com., Washington, 1988; mem. adv. bd. Episcopalian Program for Homeless, Elizabeth, 1990, Union County (N.J.) Coalition for Homeless, 1991. Cpl. USMC, 1964-68, Vietnam. Named N.Y. Dist. winner Gen. Foods Corp., 1981; recipient Cert. of Appreciation Roselle Park (N.J.) First Aid Squad, 1986, award of merit USNR, 1990. Mem. VFW, Vets. of Vietnam War, Am. Legion (cert. of appreciation 1999), Royal Arch Masons, Internat. Food Svc. Exec. Assn. (pres. 1977, 79, 85, 86, bd. dirs., treas. 1989-91, Royal Order of Skillet 1987, Humanitarianism award 1987), Am. Correctional Food Svc. Assn., Asia Soc. Avocations: antiques, coins, Oriental art. Home: The Harbour Club 708 Sunshine Ct Parlin NJ 08859 Office: Corrections Corp Am Elizabeth Detention Ctr 625 Evans St Elizabeth NJ 07201-2008

MOGERMAN, SUSAN, state agency administrator; Dir. State of Ill. Historic Preservation Agy., Springfield. Office: State Ill Hist Preservation Agy 500 E Madison Springfield IL 62701-1028

MOGGRIDGE, DONALD EDWARD, economics educator, author; b. Windsor, Ont., Can., May 25, 1943; s. William Robert and Doris Margaret (Livingston) M.; m. Janet Ruth Skelton, July 29, 1967 (div. 1977). B.A. with honors, U. Toronto, Ont., 1965; M.A., Cambridge U., 1968, Ph.D., 1970. Fellow Clare Coll., Cambridge, 1967-75, 79-81; asst. lectr., U. Cambridge, 1971-72, lectr., 1973-75; prof. econs. U. Toronto, 1974— , assoc. dean social scis. Sch. Grad. Studies, 1985-87, 95, 96-97, vice-dean, 1997-2000; assoc. dean social scis. faculty Arts and Scis., 1977—. Author: The Return to Gold, 1925, 1969; British Monetary Policy 1924-31, 1972; Keynes, 1975. Editor The Collected Writings of John Maynard Keynes, 24 vols., 1971-92, joint mng. editor, 1977—. Mem. Royal Econ. Soc., Am. Econ. Assn., Can. Econ. Assn., Econ. History Soc., History of Econs. Soc. (pres. 1988-89). Club: United Oxford and Cambridge (London). Home: 11 Woodstock Pl Toronto ON Canada M4X 1T7 Office: Univ Toronto Dept of Economics 150 St George St Toronto ON Canada M5S 1A1

MOGHISSI, KAMRAN S. obstetrician, gynecologist, educator; b. Tehran, Sept. 11, 1925; came to US, 1959, naturalized, 1965; s. Ahmad and Monireh (Rohani) M; m. Ida Laura Tedeschi, Jan. 2, 1952; children: Diana J., Soraya R. ChB, MB, U. Geneva, 1951; MD, 1952. Diplomate Am. Bd. Ob-Gyn., Am. Bd. Reproductive Endocrinology. Intern U. Hosp., Geneva, 1951-52, Horton Gen. Hosp., United Oxford Hosps., Banbury, Eng., 1952-53; resident in ob-gyn. Gloucestershire Royal Hosp., Eng., 1953-54, St. Helier Hosp., London, 1954-55, Leeds Regional Hosp. Bd., Yorkshire, Eng., 1955-56, Detroit Receiving Hosp., 1961, attending gynecologist, 1962; assoc. prof. ob-gyn. U. Shiraz Med. Sch., Iran, 1957-59; rsch. assoc. ob-gyn. and physiol. chemistry Wayne State U., Detroit, 1959-61, from asst. prof. to prof., 1962-2000, prof. emeritus, 2001—, dir. divsn. reproductive endocrinology and infertility, 1970-94, vice chmn., 1983-88, chmn. dept. ob-gyn., 1988-91; sr. attending physician ob-gyn. Hutzel Hosp., 1963, vice chief, 1978-82, 83-89, chief, 1982-83, 88-91, chief of staff, 1991-93; attending surgeon, chief ob-gyn. Harper-Grace Hosp., 1983-84; obstetrician, gynecologist, chief Detroit Med. Ctr., 1988-91. Developer exhibits in medicine, movies and tchg. prodns.; cons., lectr. in field. Mem. numerous editl. bds.; contbr. chpts. to books, articles to profl. jours. Fellow ACS, Am. Coll. Ob-Gyn., Am. Gynecol. and Obstetric Soc.; mem. AMA (ho. of dels. 1992—), Am. Soc. Reprodn. Medicine (formerly Am. Fertility Soc., pres. 1990-91), Soc. Study of Reprodn., Am. Soc. Andrology, Wayne County Med. Soc., Mich. Soc. Ob-Gyn., Ctrl. Assn. Ob-Gyn., Soc. Reproductive Endocrinology and Infertility (charter mem., pres. 1990), Soc. Reproductive Surgeons (charter mem.), Soc. for Assisted Reproductive Tech. (charter mem.), Soc. Gynecologic Investigation, European Soc. Human Reprodn. and Embryology, Renaissance Club. Home: 12733 Sycamore Pte Plainwell MI 49080 Office: Hutzel Hosp 4707 Saint Antoine St Detroit MI 48201-1498 E-mail: kmoghiss@med.wayne.edu.

MOGILNER, ALIJANDRA, federal official, researcher; b. Calif., Mar. 31, 1944; d. Clinton Card and Bertha Margaret Bryant; m. Geoffrey Mogilner, Aug. 15, 1972; children: Ingred Chamberlin, Tayopa, David. PhD, U. Nat. Autónoma de México, Mexico City. Inst. U. Calif., La Jolla; editor European Union news and info. svc. U. Ga., Peachtree Gopher; sr. analyst ORION Sci. Sys., McLean, Va.; pres. spl. task force on terrorism U.S. Govt., Washington,

2001—; analyst joint task force on money laundering U.S. Dept. of the Treasury: Customs, 2001—. Grad. student mentor U. Calif., La Jolla; founding mem., analyst G2i and G2-Forward OSINT projects. Contbr. articles to profl. jours.

MOGILNY, ALEXANDER, professional hockey player; b. Khabarovsk, Russia, Feb. 18, 1969; With Buffalo Sabres, 1988-95, capt., 1993-95; with Vancouver Canucks, 1995-99; right wing N.J. Devils, 1999—2001; player Toronto Maple Leafs, 2001—. Mem. gold-medal winning USSR Olympic Team, 1988. Played in NHL All-Star Game, 1992-94; named to Sporting News All-Star Second Team, 1992-93, NHL All-Star Second Team, 1992-93. Office: Toronto Maple Leafs Air Canada Ctr 40 Bay St Ste 300 Toronto ON M5J 2X2 Canada*

MOGK, JOHN EDWARD, law educator, association executive, consultant; b. Detroit, Feb. 10, 1939; s. Clifford Anthony and Evelyn Lenore (Paselk) M.; m. Lylas Heidi Good, Aug. 23, 1964; children: Marja, Tenley, Matthew. BBA, U. Mich., 1961, JD with distinction, 1964; diploma in comparative law, U. Stockholm, 1965. Bar: N.Y. 1966, Mich. 1970. Assoc. atty. Shearman & Sterling, N.Y.C., 1964-68; mem. faculty Wayne State U. Sch. Law, 1968—, dir. grad. studies, 1990-95. Pres. MERRA Rsch. Corp., 1974-94; cons. econ. and urban devel., arbitrator; vis. prof. U. Utrecht, The Netherlands, 2000. Editor Michigan International Lawyer and Utilities Law Rev.; contbr. articles to profl. jours. Chmn. Mich. TOP Task Force, 1972; vice chmn. Mich. Constrn. Code Commn., 1973; mem. exec. com. Southeastern Mich. Coun. Govts., 1970; chmn. Detroit Sch. Boundary Commn., 1970, Downtown Detroit Vacant Bldg. Com., 1991-93; mem. Detroit Bd. Edn., 1970; mgr. Detroit Empowerment Zone Proposal, 1994; project exec. New Detroit Stadium, 1995; pres. Habitat for Humanity Detroit, 1999. Named Outstanding Contbr. Internat. Law Sect., State Bar of Mich., 2001, Outstanding Wayne State U. Assoc. Prof., 1971, Outstanding Wayne Law Sch. Prof., 1977, 83, 93, 97, Outstanding Young Man in Detroit, 1972, One of Ten Outstanding Young Men in U.S., 1973, One of Four Outstanding Vols. in U.S., 1974; recipient Presdl. citation Wayne State U., 1977, State of Mich., 1988, 94; Am.-Scandinavian fellow, 1965; vis. fellow U. Warwick, Eng., 1985-86. Mem. ABA, Mich. Bar Assn. (Outstanding Achievement award Internat. Law Sect. 2001), Assn. of Bar of City of N.Y. Home: 1000 Yorkshire Rd Grosse Pointe Park MI 48230-1432

MOGOL, ALAN JAY, lawyer; b. Balt., July 29, 1946; s. Jesse and Kitty (Stutman) m.; m. Ellen Epstein, June 19, 1969; children: Andrew Stephen, Jonathan David. BA with distinction, U. Va., 1968, JD, 1971. Bar: Md. 1972, U.S. Dist. Ct. Md. 1972, U.S. Ct. Appeals (4th cir.) 1972, U.S. Supreme Ct. 1978. Assoc. Ober, Kaler, Grimes & Shriver, Balt., 1971-77, ptnr., 1978—. Chmn. comml. finance Ober, Kaler, Grimes & Shriver, Balt., 1980-81, 84-85, 91-97, 2002—, chmn. equipment leasing practice group, 1998—; lectr. on continuing edn. Md. Inst. Continuing Profl. Edn. for Lawyers, 1988-92, trustee, 1990-93; spkr. seminars Nat. Health Lawyers Assn., Washington, 1986-87, Rocky Mountain Mgmt., Denver, 1987, Med. Imaging Expo., 1995, Washington, 1995. Co-author: In Structuring the Secured Loan Agreement, 1991, Commercial Finance Guide, 1997, Equipment Leasing, 1999; contbr. articles to profl. jours. and local newspapers. Bd. dirs. Transitional Living Coun., Balt., 1972-92; bd. trustees Md. Inst. of Continuing Profl. Edn. for Lawyers, 1990-93. Fellow Md. Bar Found., Inc.; mem. ABA, Equipment Leasing Assn. Am. (lawyers com. 1986-89, program com. 1986-91, speaker seminars), Md. Bar Assn. (uniform comml. code com. 1988—, chmn. 1991-93, vice chmn. bus. sect. 1995-96, chmn. bus. sect. 1996-97). Avocation: tennis. Office: Ober Kaler Grimes & Shriver 120 E Baltimore St Ste 800 Baltimore MD 21202-1643 E-mail: ajmogol@ober.com.

MOGREN, PAUL ANDREW, librarian; b. Fort Collins, Colo., Aug. 31, 1950; s. Edwin W. and Arle Mae (Arnason) M.; m. Ann Marie Breznay, Aug. 16, 1980; 1 child, Christian Andrew. BA, Colo. State U., 1972; MA, U. Denver, 1973; PhD, U. Utah, 1980. Reference libr. Marriott Libr., U. Utah, Salt Lake City, 1973-82, head of reference, 1982-96, collection specialist, 1996—. Cons. Gov.'s Mansion Libr., Salt Lake City, 1995—, Dixie Coll. Libr., St. George, Utah, 1990; adj. prof. Emporia (Kans.) State U., 1996—; mem. Ogden Union Sta. Libr., 1997—. Mem. AAUP (pres. U. Utah chpt. 1986-89), ALA (coun. 1992-96, RUSA History Libr. of Yr. award 2000), Utah Libr. Assn. (pres. 1988-89). Avocations: gardening, travel. Office: U Utah Marriott Libr 295 S 15th East Salt Lake City UT 84112-0860

MOGULL, ROBERT G. education educator, researcher; b. N.Y.C., Aug. 16, 1939; s. Alexander A. and Shirley Mogull; m. Susan Mogull; children: Robin, Scott, Michael. PhD, W.Va. U., Morgantown, 1969. Cert. tchr., counselor N.Y. Prof. bus. stats. Calif. State U., Sacramento, 1970—. Cons. in field. Contbr. articles to profl. jours. Recipient numerous rsch. grants. Avocation: gardening. Office: Calif State U 6000 J St Sacramento CA 95819-6088 Office Fax: 916-278-6757. Business E-Mail: mogullr@csus.edu.

MOHAIDEEN, A. HASSAN, surgeon, healthcare executive; b. Ramanathapuram, India, Aug. 14, 1940; s. Abdul and Mariam (Pitchai) Kader; m. Zarina M. Meera, May 30, 1965 (dec. July 1986); children: Ahamed, Mariam, Najeeba, Azeema; m. Laurie J. Kucich, June 23, 1989; children: Yasmin Sara, Leila Jahan. MD, U. Madras, India, 1965; MBA, Wagner Coll., 1996. Diplomate Am. Bd. Surgery, Am. Bd. Quality Assurance and Utilization; cert. physician exec. Am. Coll. Physician Execs. Intern Govt. Stanley Hosp., Madras, 1965-66, Good Samaritan Hosp., West Islip, N.Y., 1967-68; resident in gen. and vascular surgery L.I. Coll. Hosp., Bklyn., 1968-73, asst. attending surgeon, 1973-76, assoc. attending surgeon, 1976-78, attending surgeon, 1978—, chief divsn. vascular surgery, 1980-93, dir. vascular lab., 1981-93; v.p. Bklyn.-Caledonian Hosp. Ctr. (affiliate of NYU), 1994-95; sr. v.p., managed care and exec. vice-chmn. dept. surgery The Bklyn.-Caledonian Hosp. Ctr. (affiliate of NYU), 1995-96; pres., CEO, Health Plan Systems, Inc., Rochelle Park, NJ, 2001—. Asst. surgeon G.H.Q. Hosp., Ramnad, India, 1966-67; assoc. attending surgeon Meth. Hosp., Bklyn., 1982-90, attending surgeon, 1991-97; asst. attending surgeon Bklyn. Caledonian Med. Ctr., 1973-85, mem. courtesy staff, 1985-94, 97—, attending surgeon, 1994-96; attending surgeon Victory Meml. Hosp., Bklyn., 1982—; vis. physician Kings County Hosp. Ctr., Bklyn., 1973-94; clin. instr. in surgery Downstate Med. Ctr., SUNY, Bklyn., 1973-78, clin. asst. prof. surgery, 1978—; mem. exec. com. of med. staff L.I. Coll. Hosp., Bklyn., 1979-93, treas. med. staff, 1982-85, pres., 1985-87, med. chmn. Guild Ball com., 1981, mem. quality assurance com. dept. surgery, 1988-94, chmn. credentials com., 1990-93, quality assurance and risk mgmt. com., 1990-93; bd. dirs. Aetna Health Plans of N.Y., AIDS adv. com., 1987-93, stds. com., 1986-94, quality assurance com.; bd. dirs. Aetna-U.S. Healthcare, 1997; mem. credentials com. Prucare, 1988-92; sr. v.p. managed care Bklyn. Hosp., 1995-96; mem. quality mgmt. com. Oxford Health Plans, 1995—; mem. quality improvement com. Chubb Health, N.Y., 1994-96, Cigna (HealthSource), 1997; ; mem. credentials com. United Healthcare, 1997—; exec. dir. Mayan Health, PPO, Atlantic Med. Assocs. IPA; pres. Health Plan Sys., Inc. Contbr. articles to med. jours. Fellow ACS (com. on Long Island dist. applicants, 1988-99, bd. dirs. Bklyn.-L.I. chpt.), Royal Coll. Physicians and Surgeons Can. (cert.), Internat. Coll. Surgeons; mem. AMA (Physician's Recognition award), AAAS, Am. Coll. Physician Execs., Med. Soc. of State of N.Y., N.Y. State Soc. of Surgeons, N.Y. Acad. of Scis., Med. Soc. of County of Kings (mediation com., 1979-85), Bklyn. Surg. Soc., Soc. for Non-Invasive Vascular Technicians, Kings Physicians I.P.A. (pres./med. dir., 1985-95), Bklyn. Physicians I.P.A. (v.p., 1985-96, pres.). Avocations: photography, computers, walking. E-mail: hassan@mohaideen.com.

MOHALLEY, PATRICIA JOANN, library media specialist; b. Lafayette, Ind., Aug. 24, 1951; d. Robert Dean and Alta Mae (Hancock) Clerget; m. Jeremiah J. Mohalley, Mar. 17, 1979; Sarah Frances and Jeremiah J. Jr. BA in Edn., Purdue U., 1973, MS in Edn., 1978. Cert. edn.-libr. media specialist, Ind., Tex. Tchr. grade 5 Crown Point (Ind.) Sch. Corp., 1973-74; tchr. grades 5 and 6 South Newton Sch. Corp., Kentland, Ind., 1974-77; dir. elem. librs. Community Sch. Corp. of Ea. Hancock County, Wilkinson, 1977-80; libr. media specialist Met. Sch. Dist. of Lawrence Twp., Indpls., 1980-81, Spring Br. Ind. Sch. Dist., Houston, 1981-89, Klein (Tex.) Ind. Sch. Dist., 1989—. Active Cypress Creek Friends Libr., Spring, Tex., 1988—; life mem. Tex. PTA, 1989—. Mem. ALA, Tex. Libr. Assn. Avocations: reading, traveling, baking. Home: 7814 Springberry Ct Spring TX 77379-4084

MOHAMADI, MASOUD, retired surgeon; b. Tehran, Iran, June 8, 1937; children: Hooman, Michele, Robert; m. Soheila Emami, 1990. MD, U. Tehran, 1961. Diplomate Am. Bd. Surgery. Intern Coney Island Hosp., N.Y.C., 1962-63; resident in gen. surgery Maimonides Med. Ctr., Bklyn., 1963-67; fellow in vasc. surgery Kings County Hosp., 1967-68. Mem. AMA, Am. Soc. Bariatric Surgery. Republican. E-mail: MMO2@msn.com.

MOHAMED, JOSEPH, SR. real estate broker, farmer; b. Omar, W.Va., Mar. 19, 1928; s. Mose and Minnie Elizabeth (Martin) M.; m. Shirley Ida Medeiros; children: Joseph Jr., John W., James R., Leslie Louise. AA in Bus. Adminstrn., Sacramento City Coll., 1950; BBA Personnel, Sacramento State U., 1952; postgrad., U. Pacific, U. Calif., Davis, Am. River Coll. Farmer, 1949—; founder comml. trucking operation Calif., 1949-52, Baja, Mex., 1953; founder Mexican Co. of Agr. and Livestock Ltd., Ensenada, Baja, Mex., 1953-57; owner Quintair, Inc., 1954—; contractor, real estate developer, 1949—; owner Joseph's Landscape Svc., Sacramento, 1952-72, Joseph Mohamed Enterprises, 1982—. Pest control adviser, Calif., 1970—. Mem. Rep. Nat. Com., Rep. Presdl. Task Force, Sacramento Regional Arts Coun., 1965—, Govs.' Emergency Drought Task Force, 1977, Civil Affairs Assn., Calif. Rental Assn., 1975—, Sacramento Apartment Assn., Calif. Apartment Assn., Nat. Apartment Assn.; dir. McClellan Aviation Museum Found., Sacramento County Sheriff's Mounted Posse, 1961—. Served with U.S. Army, 1946-48, USAR, 1949-78. Decorated Legion of Merit; recipient Master Aviator Badge. Mem. Sacramento U. Alumni Assn., Sacramento State Horseman's Assn., Calif. State Horseman's Assn., Sacramento Metro. C. of C., Navy League of U.S., Reserve Officer's Assn., Assn. of U.S. Army, Elk Grove C. of C., Sacramento Bd. of Realtors, Calif. Assn. Realtors, Nat. Assn. Realtors. Clubs: Comstock (Sacramento), Commonwealth (San Francisco). Lodges: Masons, Shriners.

MOHAMED, MUKHTAR HASSAN, public health service officer, consultant; b. Hargeisa, Waqoyi Galbeed, Somalia, Apr. 8, 1973; s. Hassan Mohamed Nur and Amina Mohamed Diriye. MA , Yale U., 2000, postgrad. Cert. World Wide Water Condition 2001. Nutrition assessor Save the Children, Kebribeyah, Ethiopia, 1991—93; vol. health and aux. assistant Internat. Com. of the Red Cross, Berbera, Somalia, 1990; registrar UN Higher Commr. for Refugees, Borama, Somalia, 1990. Advocated refugee children and child soldiers Save the Children, Kebribeyah and Hartsheik Somali Refugee Camps, Hararghe, Ethiopia, 1991—93. Fellow fellowship, Yale U., 2000-2002; grantee Ford Found. Summer Rsch. grant, 2001. Home: 68 Mansfield # 2L New Haven CT 06511 Personal E-mail: mukhamoh@yahoo.com.

MOHAMMADI, MINA, physician, researcher; b. Tehran, Iran, Nov. 5, 1965; came to the U.S., 1994; d. Jafar and Pouran Mohammadi; m. Bijan Poursharaiati, Mar. 31, 1986; children: Pegah, Meelad. BS, Mahmoodzadeh Sch., Tehran, 1982; MBBS, Ambedkar Med. Sch., Bangalore, India, 1989. Diplomate Am. Bd. Internal Medicine, Am. Bd. Pulmonary Diseases. Resident in internal medicine N.Y. Meth. Hosp., Bklyn., 1994-97; fellow in pulmonary medicine Coney Island Hosp., 1997-99; pulmonologist, med. staff mem. N. Ctrl. Bronx Hosp., Bronx, N.Y., 1999—. Faculty apptd. asst. prof. Albert Einstein Coll. Medicine. Fellow Coll. Chest Physician; mem. AMA, Am. Coll. Chest Physicians, Am. Thoracic Soc. Avocations: aerobics, horseback riding, dancing, playing chess. Home: 1040 Regency Park Dr Martin TN 38237 E-mail: mamohammadi@yahoo.com.

MOHAMMED, ABDUL-AZEEZ F. mechanical engineer; b. Madras, India, May 17, 1971; s. Fakir-Mohideen Mohammed and Farid Rahima Abulhasan; m. Sharmila I. Jamaldeen, Jan. 1, 1996. PhD, U. Ill., 1998. Mech. engr. GE Corp. R&D Ctr., Niskayuna, N.Y., 1998-99, project leader, 2000—. Contbr. articles to profl. jours. Mem. Sigma Xi. Office: GE Corp R&D Ctr 1 Research Cir Niskayuna NY 12309 Office Fax: 518-387-7292. E-mail: mohammed@crd.ge.com.

MOHAN, ANNETTE IMELDA, producer, educator; b. Bombay, India, Sept. 17, 1950; arrived in U.S., 1983; d. Joseph Alexander and Amy (Vaz) Gonsalves. BA, U. Bombay, 1971; MA, Andrews U., 1980, Norfolk State U., 1990. Prodr. Bombay TV, 1972-83; v.p. L.I.F.E., Inc., Virginia Beach, Va., 1983-98, Lathika Internat., Huntsville, Ala., 1998—. Asst. prof. Oakwood Coll., Huntsville, 1998—. Prodr.(shows): Young World, 1975—79, Magic Lamp, 1979—82; exec. prodr.(documentary): Hanged on a Twisted Cross, 1996 (Chris award Columbus (Ohio) Film Festival, 1996), (film): Nazaraana-The Gift, 1997 (Bronze award Columbus Film Festival, 1997), Father of Preachers, 2001, Here I Stand, 2001, 2001, Revolution of Conscience, 2002. Avocation: Avocations: travel, stamps, coins, cooking. Office: PO Box 5072 Huntsville AL 35814-5072 E-mail: LIFEINCVA@aol.com.

MOHAN, CHANDRA, research biochemistry educator; b. Lucknow, India, Aug. 3, 1950; came to U.S., 1977; s. Prithivi Nath and Tara Rani (Sharma) Shastri; m. Nirmala Devi Sharma, July 23, 1978; children: Deepak, Naveen. BS, Bangalore (India) U., 1970, MS, 1972, PhD, 1976. Research assoc. U. So. Calif. Med. Sch., Los Angeles, 1977-83, asst. prof., 1983-93; dir. tech. svc., sr. tech. writer CalBioChem Corp., San Diego, 1993—. Assoc. editor Biochem. Medicine, Los Angeles, 1986-93; contbr. articles to profl. jours. Recipient BRSG award U. So. Calif., 1983. Mem. AAAS, Am. Diabetes Assn., Am. Soc. for Biochemistry and Molecular Biology, N.Y. Acad. Scis., Soc. Exptl. Biology and Medicine, Am. Inst. Nutrition. Hindu. Avocations: photography, coin collecting. Home: 13638 Dicky St Whittier CA 90605-2949 Office: CalBioChem Corp 10394 Pacific Center Ct San Diego CA 92121-4340

MOHAN, JOHN J. lawyer; b. St. Louis, May 22, 1945; s. John Joseph and Virginia Loretta (Durkin) M.; m. Elaine Bronwyn Lipe, May 29, 1982; children: Bryn Elizabeth, John Burke. BS Indsl. Engring., St. Louis U., Sch. Engring. and Earth Scis., 1967; JD, St. Louis U., 1971. Bar: Mo. 1971, Ill. 1971, U.S. Dist. Ct. (we. dist.) Mo. 1971, U.S. Dist. Ct. (ea. dist.) Mo. 1980, U.S. Dist. Ct. (so. dist.) Ill. 1981, U.S. Ct. Appeals (8th cir.) 1987. Asst. prosecuting atty. St. Louis County, 1971-72; asst. cir. atty. St. Louis Cir. Atty's. Office, 1972-74; spl. asst. state's atty. St. Clair County Atty's. Office, Belleville, Ill., 1974—; assoc. Lashley, Caruthers, Theis, Rava & Hamel, St. Louis, 1979-80; ptnr. Schreiber, Tueth & Mohan, Clayton, Mo., 1981-83, Danis, Reid, Murphy, Tobben, Schreiber & Mohan, Ladue, 1983-87, Hinshaw & Culbertson, St. Louis, 1987-97, Blackwell, Sanders, Peper, Martin, St. Louis, 1998-2000, Mickes, Tueth, Keeney, Cooper, Mohan & Jackstadt, P.C., 2000—. Mem. U. Mo. Law Sch. Found. Scholarship. Mem. ABA, Am. Arbitration Assn. (cert. mediator, arbitrator 1988—), Ill. State Bar Assn., Mo. Bar, Bar Assn. Met. St. Louis, St. Clair County Bar, St. Louis County Bar, Def. Rsch. Inst., Mo. Orgn. Def. Lawyers, Pinnacle Arbitration and Mediation Svcs. (cert. mediator, arbitrator 1997—), Phi Delta Phi. Home: 529 Big Horn Basin Ct Wildwood MO 63011-4818 Office: Mickes Tueth Keeney Cooper Mohan Jackstadt PC 425 S Woods Mill Rd Ste 300 Saint Louis MO 63017

MOHAN, RAM K. engineer; b. N. Parur, Kerala, India, Mar. 16, 1966; s. C.G.R. Nair and Bharathi Devi; m. Aparna K. Mohan, Aug. 14, 1991. BS, Cochin U. Sci. and Tech., India, 1988; MS, U. R.I., 1990; PhD, Tex. A&M U., 1993. Registered profl. engr., S.c. Rsch. asst. U. R.I. Marine Geomechs. Lab., Kingston, 1988-90; rsch. asst. Hydromechanics Lab. Tex. A&M U., College Station, 1990-93; sr. cons. Coastal Sci. and Engring., Inc., Columbia, S.C., 1993-94; sr. project engr. Blasland, Bouck & Lee, Inc., Syracuse, N.Y., 1994-96; sr. engr., project mgr. Gahagan & Bryant Assocs., Inc., Balt., 1996—. Presenter in field. Editor Shipstechnic Jour., 1987-88; mem. rev. bd. Jour. Marine Environ. Engring., 1997—, Jour. Hydraulic Rsch., 1997—, Can. Geotech. Jour., 1997—, Fluid Dynamics Rsch., 1997—, Marine Geotechnique, 1997—, Marine Georesources and Geotech., 1998—, Water Environ. Rsch., 1997—, Ocean Engring., 1997—; contbr. articles to profl. jours. Mem. ASCE (com. on stds. for shore protection 1997—, ocean engring. and wave mechs. com. 1998—, com. on spill prevention 1997—, reviewer Jour. Water, Port, Coastal and Ocean Engring. 1997—, Jour. Hydraulic Engring. 1997—, Jour. Environ. Engring. 1997—), World Dredging Assn., Permanent Internat. Assn. Navigation Congresses, Coastal Edn. and Rsch. Found., Am. Shore and Beach Preservation Assn., Marine Tech. Soc., Internat. Assn. Hydraulic Rsch., Sigma Xi. Office: Gahagan & Bryant Inc 9008 Yellow Brick Rd # 0 Baltimore MD 21237-5606

MOHAN, TUNGESH NATH, television and film producer, film educator; b. Lucknow, India, Oct. 30, 1949; arrived in U.S., 1979; s. Bhola Shambu and Saraswati P. (Devi) Nath; m. Annette Gonsalves Mohan; 1 child Lathika. BS, Kampur (India) U., 1969; diploma in Cinema, Film and TV Inst. India, Poona, 1972; MA, Andrews U., 1980. Producer Bombay TV, 1972-75, 77-79; asst. prof. Film and TV Inst. India, Poona, 1975-77; TV producer 700 Club, Virginia Beach, Va., 1980-82; producer spl. projects Christian Broadcasting Network, 1982-86, Christian Broadcasting Network Cable Prodns., Inc., Virginia Beach, 1986-87; dir. Internat. CBN Producers Group, 1987-89, Internat. NorthStar Entertainment Group, L.A., 1989-92; mgr. Adventist Comm. Network, Silver Springs, Md., 1992-93; pres. TriAngel Media Corp., Thousand Oaks, Calif., 1992-94. Adj. prof. Film and TV Inst. India, Poona, 1975—79, Spicer Coll., Poona, 1975—79, Hampton (Va.) U., 1980—92; pres. Producers Unit One, Virginia Beach, 1982—, L.I.F.E. Inc., 1993—; cons. Global Comm. Assocs., Virginia Beach, 1987—88, Global TV Syndication, 1998—; dir. Telecomm. Ctr., Huntsville, 1998—. Exec. prodr.: Stand at Ease, 1989—90, A Father of Preachers, 2001; prodr.: Touching the Supernatural, 1992, Midnight Cry, 1994, Master Control, 1994, The Way We Were, 1995, Bought at a Price, 1996, Hanged on a Twisted Cross, 1996 (Chris award for best film, Bronze medal for screenplay Columbus Film Festival, 1996), Inn Keeper, 1996, The Invitation, 1997, The Gift, 1997 (Bronze Plaque for 2d pl. Columbus Internat. Film Fest, 1997), (dir.): Reaalizing the Vision, 2001; exec. prodr.: Father of Preachers, 2001; prodr.(dir.): Here I Stand, 2002, Revolution of Conscience, 2002, The Hymnmaker, 2002, In the First Steps of Martin Luther, 2002, For One English Officer, 2002, The Dawning, 2002. Mem.: NATAS, Dirs. Guild Am., Writers Guild Am., Lions. Mem. Seventh-Day Adventist. Avocation: Avocations: collecting stamps, music, camping, travel, tennis. Home: 118 Hunters Hill Trl Toney AL 35773-6947 Office: PO Box 5072 Huntsville AL 35814-5072 E-mail: lifeincva@aol.com.

MOHAN-IYENGAR, RAJ, automotive executive, researcher; b. Tiruchirapalli, India; s. Krishnaswamy and Rajalakshmi Rengarajan; married. BE, Madras U., India, 1980; ME, Indian Inst. Sci., Bangalorre, 1982; MS, Rutgers U., New Brunswick, N.J., 1985; ScM, Brown U., Providence, 1986; PhD, Brown U., 1990. Rsch. assoc. Brown U., Providence, 1990, U. Pa., Phila., 1990—91; rsch. scientist Battelle Meml. Inst., Columbus, 1991—99; sr. engr. Rouge Steel Co., Dearborn, Mich., 1999—2001, mgr. auto. platforms, 2001—. Editor: (ASME Jour.of EMT - Special Issue) Integration of Scientific and Engineering Aspects of Structural Materials in High Temperature Applications, 2000, (ASME Journal of PVP - Special Issue) Challenges and Resolution in Structural Life Prediction, 2001, (Fatigue and Fracture of EM&S -Jour.) Materials and Mechanics Issues in Structural Life Prediction, 1998, (ASME - Bound Volume PVP 413) Understanding and Predicting Material Degradation, 2000, (ASME Bound Volume - PVP 391) Advances in Life Prediction Methodology, 1999; assoc. editor Jour. of Pressure Vessel Tech., 2001—; contbr. Mem.: ASME, SAE (com. mem. ferrous 2001—), Am. Soc. Metals (Com. mem.- Materials Divsn. nd PVP Divsn. 1997—, Achievement Certificates 1998, 1999, 2000, 2001). Office: Rouge Steel Company PO Box 1631 3001 Miller Rd Dearborn MI 48121 Business E-Mail: rmohan@rougesteel.com.

MOHANROY, PRADEEP, physician; b. Madras, Tamilnadu, India, Apr. 30, 1964; came to U.S., 1994; s. Devasahayam Mohanroy and Sheila Samuel; m. Sangeetha Daniel, Apr. 4, 1994. MB, BS, Stanley Med. Coll., Madras, 1988; diploma tuber. and respir. dis. (hon.), Madras Med. Coll., 1990. Diplomate Am. Bd. Internal Medicine. Resident in pulmonary medicine Madras Med. Coll. and Hosps., 1988-90; resident in intensive care medicine Stanley Hosp., Madras, 1990; resident in internal medicine Nat. Health Svc. Hosps., U.K., 1990-93; resident in internal and pulmonary medicine U. Newcastle Upon Tyne (Eng.)/Darlington Hosp., 1993-94; resident in internal medicine Tex. Tech. U. Health Scis. Ctr., Amarillo, 1994-96; staff physician VA Med. Ctr., 1996-99, chief med. svc., 1999—. Mem. Royal Coll. Physicians (U.K.), ACP (assoc.). Avocations: music, physical fitness. Office: VA Med Ctr 6801 Amarillo Blvd W Amarillo TX 79109

MOHANTY, AMAR K. polymer scientist, educator, researcher; b. Cuttack, Orissa, India, Mar. 19, 1958; came to U.S., 1999; s. Bishnu Charan and Basania Manjari Mohanty; m. Manjusri Misra, Feb. 8, 1988. Grad., Ravenshaw Coll., Cuttack, 1976, BSc, 1978, MSc in Chemistry, 1980, PhD in Chemistry, 1987. Lectr. in chemistry Ravenshaw Coll., Cuttack, 1993-97; Alexander Von Humboldt fellow Tech. U. Berlin, 1997-99; post doctoral rsch. assoc. Iowa State U., Ames, 1999—; rsch. assoc. Mich. State U., East Lansing, 2000—, vis. assoc. prof. Contbr. articles to profl. jours. Mem.: AIChE, Am. Chem. Soc. Avocations: writing, gardening, cooking. Office: Mich State U Composite Materials and Structures Ctr 2100EB East Lansing MI 48824 Home: Apt 6 2322 Knob Hill Dr Okemos MI 48864-4569 E-mail: mohantya@egr.msu.edu.

MOHANTY, CHRISTINE ANN, retired language educator, actress; b. Coaldale, Pa., Jan. 4, 1945; d. Warren Russell and Helen Hargraves; m. Leonard Yehudi Seltzer; children: Kasmira. BA, Queens Coll., Flushing, N.Y., MS Edn., 1972; PhD, SUNY, Stony Brook, 1986. Tchr. fgn. langs. Three Village Ctrl. Sch. Dist., Setauket, NY, 1969—2000; asst. prof. Suffolk County C.C., Selden, 1994—. Dir.: (films) Deathtrap, 1992; contbr. articles to profl. jours.; actor: (films) Wuthering Heights, 2001, Arsenic and Old Lace, 2000, Phantom of the Opera, 2000, Three Blind Mice, 1999, Social Security, 1999; dir.: Snow Queen, 1995; actor: Prelude to a Kiss, 1998, Stepping Out, 1992. Recipient Educator of the Week award, NY55 WLNY-TV, 2000; scholar U. Salamanca scholarship, N.Y. State Edn. Dept., 1990. Mem.: AAUW, Am. Assn. Tchrs. of French (pres. Suffolk county 1990—93, scholarship to France 1982), Long Island Lang. Tchrs., Phi Beta Kappa. Democrat. Avocations: travel, tennis, creative writing, painting. Home: 109 Edgewater Ave Bayport NY 11705 Personal E-mail: christinemohanty@excite.com.

MOHANTY, MADHU SUDAN, economist, educator, economist; b. Chhatria, Orissa, India, Nov. 25, 1957; s. Basanti Mohanty, Nagendra Nath Mohanty; m. Gita Rani Das; children: Bibhu, Sudipta, Aditya. PhD, U. Wis., Milw., 1990. Lectr. econs. Utkal U., Bhubaneswar, 1981—86; tchg. asst., instr. U. Wis., Milw., 1986—90; prof. econs. Calif. State U., L.A., 1990—. Seminar coord. dept. econs. Calif. State U., L.A., 1992—2000, dir. Bur. Bus. and Econ. Orgn., 2000—01; vis. prof. econs. U. Calif., Riverside, 2000. Contbr. articles to profl. jours. Recipient Disting. Scholar award, Phi Kappa Phi Honors Soc., 1997. Mem.: Soc. Labor Econs., Western Econ. Assn., Am. Econ. Assn. Office: Calif State U Los Angeles 5151 State University Dr Los Angeles CA 90032 Business E-Mail: mmohant@calstatela.edu.

MOHANTY, MANOJ K. mineral engineer, mineral engineer, mineral engineer; b. Bhubaneswar, Orissa, India, Mar. 9, 1965; arrived in U.S., 1991; s. Surendra Nath Mohanty, Pramila Mohanty, Kiranbala Mohanty; m. Pragyan "Sheela" P. Mohanty; children: Anjalika. BS in Mining Engring., REC, Roankela, India, 1985; PhD, So. Ill. U., 1997. Under mgr. Coal India Ltd., Brajraj Nagar, India, 1985—91; asst. Scientist So. Ill. U., Carbondale, 1994—97, asst. prof., 2000—; sr. process engr. Richwood Industries, Huntington, W.Va., 1998—99. Contbr. articles to profl. jours. Grantee Coal Cleaning Tech. Rsch. grants, Ill. Dept. Commerce and Cmty. Affairs; Clean Coal Rev. Bd., 2000, 2001. Mem.: Soc. Mining, Metallurgy and Petroleum Engrs. (chair-elect coal preparation com 2002—, editl. bd. Coal Preparation jour.). Office: So Ill Univ Mining and Mineral Resources Engring Carbondale IL Office Fax: 618-453-7455. Business E-Mail: mohanty@engr.siu.edu.

MOHAPATRA, MANINDRA KUMAR, public affairs educator; b. Bhadrak, Orissa, India, Aug. 1, 1935; came to U.S., 1966, naturalized, 1977; s. Baishnab and Indumati Mohapatra; m. Urmila Mohanty; children— Simani, Sangram. M.P.A., U. Mich., 1967; Ph.D., U. Ky., 1971. From instr. to assoc. prof. Old Dominion U., 1969-80; prof. pub. affairs Ky. State U., Frankfort, 1980— . Author: A Study of Affluent Asian Indians in the United States, 1984. Contbr. articles to profl. jours. Mem. Am. Soc. Pub. Adminstrn., Am. Polit. Sci. Assn., Indian Inst. Pub. Adminstrn., Ky. Polit. Sci. Assn. (v.p. 1982-83, exec. sec. 1983-86). Democrat. Hindu. Home: 200 Jackboot Ct # D Terre Haute IN 47803

MOHD ZAIN, A(HMAD) ZAIDY, counselor; b. Kelantan, Malaysia, Jan. 24, 1956; came to U.S., 1979; s. Mohd Zain Abd Rahman and Siti Katijah Kechik; m. Tracey A. West; children: Andrew, Jasmine. BBA, Western Mich. U., 1980; MPA, Sangamon State U., 1983, MA in Counseling, 1989; PhD in Counseling Edn. and Supervision, Kent State U., 1995. Bank exec. Bank of Commerce BHD, Kuala Lumpur, Malaysia, 1983—85; dir. Sasquatch Group Cos., 1985—86; therapist Kemmerer Village Children's Home, Assumption, Ill., 1988—89; mental health counselor Cmty. Resource Ctr., Centralia,

1989—90; assoc. prof. behavioral scis. Delta State U., Cleveland, Miss., 1993—97; assoc. prof. counselor edn. S.E. Mo. State U., Cape Girardeau, 1997—. Part time lectr. Mara Inst. Tech., Kuala Lumpur, 1984-85. Mem. editl. bd.: Family Jour.: Counseling and Therapy for Couples and Families. Mem. ACA, Internat. Assn for Marriage and Family Counselors, Assn. for Counselor Edn. and Supervision, Chi Sigma Iota. Avocations: camping, travelling, hiking, boating, canoeing. Home: 2019 Brink Ave Cape Girardeau MO 63703-6401 Office: S E Mo State U Dept Ednl Adminstrn Coun One University Plz Cape Girardeau MO 63701-4799 E-mail: zmohdzain@semo.edu., zaidymohdzain@yahoo.com.

MOHIUDDIN, SYED MAQDOOM, cardiologist, educator; b. Hyderabad, India, Nov. 14, 1934; came to U.S., 1961, naturalized, 1976; s. Syed Nizamuddin and Amat-Ul-Butool Mahmoodi; m. Ayesha Sultana Mahmoodi, July 16, 1961; children: Sameena J., Syed R., Kulsoom S. MB, BS, Osmania U., 1960; MS, Creighton U., Omaha, 1967; DSc, Laval U., Que., Can., 1970. Diplomate Am. Bd. Internal Medcine (cardiovascular disease). Intern Altoona (Pa.) Gen. Hosp., 1961-62; resident in cardiology Creighton Meml. Hosp., also St. Joseph Hosp., Omaha, 1963-65, mem. staff, 1965—; prof. adjoint Laval U. Med. Sch., 1970; practice medicine specializing in cardiology Omaha, 1970—; prof. Creighton U. Med. Sch., 1977—, assoc. dir. div. cardiology, 1983-96; prof. pharmacy practice Creighton U. Sch. Pharmacy, 1986—; dir divsn. cardiology, 1996—; assoc. chair for acad. affairs dept. medicine, 1998—. Cons. Omaha VA Hosp. Rsch. fellow Med. Rsch. Coun. Can., 1968; grantee Med. Rsch. Coun. Can., 1970; grantee NIH, 1973. Fellow ACP, Am. Coll. Cardiology (gov. for Nebr. 1987-90), Am. Coll. Clin. Pharmacology, Am. Coll. Chest Physicians; mem. AAAS, Am. Heart Assn. (fellow coun. clin. cardiology, bd. dirs. 1973-75), Am. Fedn. Clin. Rsch., Nebr. Heart Assn. (chmn. rsch. com. 1974-76, dir. 1973—), Gt. Plains Heart Com. (Nebr. rep. 1976-84, pres. 1977-78), N.Y. Acad. Scis., Nebr. Cardiovascular Soc. (pres. 1980-81). Democrat. Moslem. Home: 12531 Shamrock Rd Omaha NE 68154-3529 Office: Cardiac Ctr Creighton U 3006 Webster St Omaha NE 68131-2027

MOHIUDDIN, YASMEEN NIAZ, economics educator; b. Aligarh, India, Feb. 25, 1948; came to U.S., 1974, naturalized, 1994. d. Niaz Ahmed Siddiqui and Bismillah Niaz Ahmed; m. Muhammad Mohiuddin Siddiqi, July 29, 1972; children: Umar Mohiuddin Siddiqi, Nazia Mohiuddin Siddiqi. BA, U. Karachi, Pakistan, 1965, MA, 1967, Vanderbilt U., Nashville, 1978, PhD, 1983. Staff economist Inst. Devel. Econs., Karachi, Pakistan, 1967-69; from asst. prof. to assoc. prof. U. Karachi, Pakistan, 1969-74, 78-81, 83-85, prof. Pakistan, 1991; tchr. asst. Vanderbilt U., Nashville, 1977-78; instr., asst. prof. U. of the South, Sewanee, 1981-83, 85-90, assoc. prof., 1990-96, prof., 1996—; chair dept. econs., 1997—; cons. World Bank, Washington, 1988—, World Food Program, Rome, Italy, 1989—, chair dept. econs., 1997—. Vis. prof. Vanderbilt Univ., summer, 1988, 97, 99; cons. Internat. Fund for Agrl. Devel., Rome, Italy, 1991—, Food and Agrl. Orgn., 1996—, UN Development Program, 1996—, U.S. Agy. Internat. Devel., 1999—; assoc. exec. editor Jour. Asian Econs., N.J., 1989—; keynote speaker Soc. for Internat. Devel., Bangladesh, 1990; apptd. by gov. to Tenn. Econ. Coun. on Women; lecturer in the field. Contbr. articles to profl. jours. Adv. bd. mem. Tenn. Network for Cmty. Econ. Devel.; bd. dirs. Appalachian Women's Guild, 1994-96, Cumberland Ctr. for Justice and Peace, 1994—; panelist AAUW. Internat. Labor Orgn. travel grantee, 1985, Soc. Internat. Devel. travel grantee, 1985, 91, Can. Internat. Devel. Agy. travel grantee, 1985, U. of South Rsch. grantee, 1986-89, 90—, U. Ky. travel grantee, 1987, 90, 95, Ford Found. fellow, 1974-78, 81, Ford Found. travel grantee, 1992, U Wis. Women's Studies fellow, 1983, fellow Transfer of Knowledge Through Expatriate Nat. UNDP programme. Mem. LWV, NOW (co-pres. Sewanee chpt. 1988-89), Nat. Social Sci. Assn., Ea. Econ. Assn., Soc. for Internat. Devel., Pakistan Fedn. of U. Women, Am. Com. on Asian Econ. Studies, Toastmasters Internat. Club, Bread for the World, Pakistan Women's Assns. Moslem. Avocations: community development work, clogging, travel, chess, reading. Home: 114 Maxon Ln Sewanee TN 37375 Office: U of the South Dept Econs Sewanee TN 37383-0001

MOHL, ALLAN S. social worker; b. Passaic, N.J., Feb. 10, 1933; s. Milton and Ruth (Meisler) M.; m. Judith Klein, Dec. 21, 1958; children: Barbara, Eric, Adam. BA, NYU, 1954, MA, 1956, MSS, 1960; PhD, Columbia Pacific U., 1991. Diplomate Clin. Social Work. Dir. residential social svcs., adminstr. Queens (N.Y.) Soc. for Prevention of Cruelty of Children, N.Y., 1977-80; psychotherapist in pvt. practice Ardsley, 1966—; cons., dir. family svcs. Tip Neighborhood House, Bronx, 1980-84; sch. social worker Com. on Spl. Edn., Dist. 28, N.Y.C., 1984—2002. Condr. workshop on incestuous families and child sexual abuse; unit dir. Children's Village, Dobbs Ferry, N.Y., 1971-77; cons. Parents Anonymous, South Bronx, N.Y., 1983-84; com. mem. Crisis Intervention Dist. 28, 1995-2002; mem. Queens regional staff devel. com., 1995-98; mem. Queens regional social work awards com., 1996-98. Contbr. articles to profl. jours. Former chmn. Gen. Social Svcs. Adv. Coun. # 6, 1982-83; active participant Bronx Task Force on Child Abuse and Neglect; group leader Project Enable, South Bronx, N.Y., 1965-67; sponsor Parents' Anonymous group, Bronx, 1982-84. With U.S. Army, 1956-58. NIMH grantee; recipient Editor's Choice award Internat. Libr. Poetry, 1999, 2000, 2002. Mem. NASW (awards com. Queens, N.Y. chpt.), Am. Assn. Marriage and Family Therapy, Am. Orthopsychiat. Assn., N.Y. State Soc. Clin. Social Wk. Psychotherapists, Internat. Assn. Counselors and Therapists, Am. Group Psychotherapy Assn. (assoc. clin. mem.), Internat. Soc. Poets (disting. mem.), N.Y. Acad. Scis. Home: 8 Shorthill Rd Ardsley NY 10502-2020

MOHLE-BOETANI, JANET CAROL, epidemiologist; b. Oakland, Calif., Dec. 23, 1958; d. Robert Henry and Denise Mohle; m. Mark S. Manasse, May 23, 1992; children, Julian and Declan. AB in Molecular Biology with honors, U. Calif., Berkeley, 1981; MD with rsch. honors, Stanford (Calif.) U., 1987; MPH, U. Calif., Berkley, 2001. Diplomate Am. Bd. Internal Medicine. Intern in internal medicine Stanford U. Hosp., 1987-88, resident in internal medicine, 1988-90; resident in preventive medicine Ctr. Disease Control and Prevention, Atlanta, 1991-92; resident preventive medicine, med. epidemiologist Santa Clara County, Calif., 1992-96; med. epidemiologist Calif. Dept. Health Svcs., Berkeley, 1996—. Instr. Field Epidemiology Tng. Program, Riyadh, Saudi Arabia, 1991, Ctr. Disease Control and Prevention, Atlanta, 1992, U. Calif. Coop. Ext., 1993, U. Calif. Berkeley, 1993-96. Contbr. articles and chpts. to profl. jours. and books. Presdl. Rsch. fellow U. Calif., Berkeley, 1980-81. Mem. Am. Coll. of Epidemiology, Soc. Epidemiologic Rsch. Office: 2151 Berkeley Way Rm 708 Berkeley CA 94704-1011

MOHLEJI, SATISH CHANDRA, electrical engineer; b. New Delhi, India, Aug. 16, 1940; came to U.S. 1970; s. Raghbir Singh and Kashmiro Devi (Sharma) M.; m. Manjula Sharma, Apr. 5, 1972; children: Anjali, Shalini, Nandita. BE with hons., U. Bombay, India, 1962; M.Engring., Tech. U. N.S., Can., 1967; PhD, U. Windsor, Can., 1970; MS in Mgmt. Sci., Am. U., Washington, 1988. Registered profl. engr., Ont., 1967-79. Asst. engr. World Wide Engrs. pvt. Ltd., New Delhi, 1962-63, Dodsal Pvt. Ltd., New Delhi, 1963-64; engr. trainee Richard Zimmerman, K.G., Stuttgart, Germany, 1964; engr. Std. Elec. Lorenz, 1964-65, Lear Siegler, Inc., Grand Rapids, Mich., 1970-71; sr. prin. engr. MITRE Corp., McLean, Va., 1971—. Contbr. articles to profl. jours. Mem. rsch. adv. panel Aviation Wk. and Space Tech. Pub., 1986-87. Fellow AIAA (assoc., chmn. aircraft ops. tech. com. 1995-97); mem. IEEE (sr.) Internat. Fedn. Automatic Control (chmn. air traffic control automation tech. com. 1993-99) RTCA (spl. com. SC-166 tech. working group, chmn. 1989-92). Avocations: photography, gardening. Home: 12324 Ox Hill Rd Fairfax VA 22033-2407 Office: The MITRE Corp 7515 Colshire Dr Mc Lean VA 22102-3480 E-mail: smohleji@mitre.org.

MOHLER, BRIAN JEFFERY, diplomat; b. Niskayuna, N.Y., May 28, 1948; s. Donald and Rosemary (Brown) M. BA, Johns Hopkins U., 1970, MA, 1972. Economist Congl. Rsch. Svc. Libr. of Congress, Washington, 1973-74; staff asst. Bur. Econ. Affairs, Dept. State, 1974-76, economist, 1979-82; consul Am. Consulate Gen., Strasbourg, France, 1976-78; desk officer European cmty. affairs Bur. European Affairs, Dept. State, Washington, 1982-84; petroleum attache Am. Embassy, Riyadh, Saudi Arabia, 1986-88, counselor for econ. affairs Saudi Arabia, 1988-90, dep. chief of mission Abu Dhabi, United Arab Emirates, 1990-93; desk officer Japanese affairs Bur. East Asian and Pacific Affairs, Washington, 1984-86; dep. dir. of econs. for Japanese affairs Bur. East Asian and Pacific Affairs, Dept. State, 1993-95; counselor for econ. affairs Am. Embassy, Tokyo, 1995-99; dir. econ. sanctions policy Bur. Econ. Affairs Dept. State, Washington, 1999-2001, dir. Japanese affairs Bur. East Asian and Pacific Affairs, 2001—. 2d lt. U.S. Army, 1972, capt. USAR, 1972-85. Recipient Superior Honor award Dept. of State, 1993, 98, Meritorious Honor award, 1987, Award Sec. of Transp., 1998. Mem.: Japan-Am. Soc. of Washington DC, Am. Fgn. Svc. Assn., Sigma Nu. Roman Catholic. E-mails. E-mail: mohlerbj@state.gov., bjmohler@hotmail.com.

MOHLER, EDWIN EUGENE, orthopedic surgeon; b. Lancaster, Pa., Apr. 8, 1943; s. Raymond Harold and Louraine Mohler; m. Maureen Costello, July 1968 (div. 1976); m. Linda Anita Reynolds, Feb. 9, 1989; children: Seth, Jared, Eamonn. BS, Mt. St. Mary's Coll., Emmitsburg, Md., 1965; MD, U. Md., Balt., 1969. Diplomate Nat. Bd. Med. Examiners, Am. Bd. Orthopedic Surgery. Intern Maimonides Med. Ctr., Bklyn., 1969-70, resident in surgery, 1970-71; resident in orthopedic surgery Kings County-Downstate Med Ctr., 1971-73, chief resident in orthopedics, 1973-74; fellow in pediatric orthopedics Newington (Conn.) Children's Hosp., 1974-75; asst. prof. orthopedics Downstate Med. Ctr., Bklyn., 1975-82; med. cons. United Cerebral Palsy, N.Y.C. and N.Y. State, 1979-82; orthopedic cons. Wassaic (N.Y.) Devel. Ctr., 1982-93; orthopedic surg. cons. in pvt. practice, Albany, N.Y., 1989—. Orthopedic surg. cons. St. Joseph's Abbey, Spencer, Mass., 1976—. Collaborative author: Low Back Pain in Monastic Community. Co-founder Christian Help in Park Slope, Bklyn., 1973—, dir. free med. clinic, 1976—; bd. dirs. County Family Svcs., Hudson, N.Y., 1984-93, Chatham (N.Y.) Ctrl. Sch. Dist., 1988-93. Lt. USN, 1967-75. Dr. Scholl's Found. grantee. Mem. Am. Acad. Orthopedic Surgery, Am. Acad. Cerebral Palsy and Devel. Medicine, Lancaster Cath. H.S. Alumni, Mt. St. Mary's Coll. Alumni, U. Md. Alumni. Christian. Avocations: golf, skiing, hiking, biking, photography. Office: 4 Airline Dr Albany NY 12205-1023 E-mail: emoler@hotmail.com.

MOHLER, GEORGIA ANN, geriatrics nurse practitioner; b. Iowa Falls, Iowa, Mar. 11, 1941; d. George Edward and Norma Dorothy (Wolf) M. Diploma, Meth.-Kahler, Rochester, Minn., 1962; BSN, U. Wash., 1971. RN, Wash.; cert. geriatric nurse practitioner. Relief charge nurse, team leader Swedish Hosp., Seattle, 1963-72; pub. health nurse Vis. Nurse Svc., 1971-72; relief charge nurse and medicare coord. Restorative Care Ctr., 1972-81; unit coord. Tacoma Luth. Home and Retirement Ctr., Tacoma, 1981-82; nurse practitioner Tacoma Luth. Home, 1983-99, dir. home health agy. and nurse practitioner, 1993-2000; nurse practitioner Caroline Kline Galland Home, Seattle, 2000—. Developer assisted living program, Tacoma. Contbr. to profl. jours. Mem. Pierce County Nurse Practitioner Group, Nat. Conf. Gerontol. Nurse Practitioners. Home: 909 N I St Apt 401 Tacoma WA 98403-2136

MOHLER, RICHARD ALBERT, JR. academic administrator, theologian; b. Lakeland, Fla., Oct. 9, 1959; s. Richard Albert Sr. and Janet Rae (Johnson) M.; m. Mary Ann Kahler, July 16, 1983; children: Mary Katherine, Christopher Albert. BA magna cum laude, Samford U., 1980; MDiv, So. Bapt. Theol. Sem., Louisville, 1983, PhD, 1989; postgrad., St. Meinrad Sch. Theology, 1985, Oxford (Eng.) U., 1986. Ordained min. So. Bapt. Ch. Pastor Union Grove Bapt. Ch., Bedford, Ky., 1982-87; asst. to pres., coord. found. support, dir. capital funding So. Bapt. Theol. Sem., Louisville, 1983-89, pres., 1993—; editor The Christian Index, Atlanta, 1989-93, prof. christian theology, 1996—. Assoc. dir. The So. Sem. Found., 1983-89; rsch. fellow Ethics and Religious Liberty Commn., 1998—; lectr. in field. Assoc. editor Preaching, 1985-93, contbg. editor, 1993—; gen. editor: The Gods of the Age of the God of the Ages?, 1993; editor-in-chief The So. Bapt. Jour. Theology, 1997—; columnist Religion News Svc., 1998—; sr. corr. World Mag., 1997—; mem. editl. bd. Salem Broadcasting, 1999—; host (radio program) Truth On the Line, 2001—; contbr. articles to profl. jours. Pres., chmn. Coun. of Sem. Pres. of So. Bapt. Conv., 1996—, chmn., Greater Louisville Billy Graham Crusade, 2001. Named one of 40 Rising Evang. Leaders, Christianity Today, 1996, one of 96 Southerners to Watch, Atlanta Jour. and Constitution, 1996, one of 50 Young Leaders Under 40 years of age TIME Mag., one of Emerging Leaders in Edn. CHANGE Mag., 1998. Mem. Am. Acad. Religion, Soc. Biblical Lit., Evang. Theol. Soc., Evang. Philos. Soc., So. Bapt. Hist. Soc., Bapt. Pub. Rels. Assn., So. Bapt. Press Assn., Evang. Press Assn., Nat. Assn. Evangs., Ga. Bapt. Hist. Soc., Rotary Internat., Phi Kappa Phi, Omicron Delta Kappa. Achievements include being named one of 50 young leaders under 40 years of age TIME Mag. Office: So Bapt Theol Sem 2825 Lexington Rd Louisville KY 40280-0001 E-mail: presoffic@sbts.edu.

MOHLER, ROBERT E. lawyer; b. Akron, Ohio, Aug. 14, 1912; s. Rueben Albert and Pearl (Carter) M.; married; children: Roger A., Jocelyn Lance, Janice Grove. AB with distinction, U. Akron, 1936, LLB, 1947; MA, Ohio State U., 1939. Bar: Ohio 1947, U.S. Dist. Ct. (no. dist.) Ohio 1958, U.S. Supreme Ct. 1971. Pvt. practice, 1946—49, 1972—2001; asst. prosecutor, then prosecutor Summit County, Ohio, 1949—52; past mem. Akron Child Guidance Ctr.; mem., past pres. Summit County Juvenile Ct. Adv. Com., 1952. Asst. counsel Firestone Tire & Rubber, 1952-70. Author publs. on history of Summit County. Active numerous civic orgns.; mem., past pres. Akron Bd. Edn., Summit County Hist. Soc.; candidate for mayor City of Akron, 1947, candidate for mcpl. judge, 1973. Democrat. Avocation: reading. Home and Office: 321 Mull Ave Akron OH 44313-7654

MOHLER, RONALD RUTT, electrical engineering educator; b. Ephrata, Pa., Apr. 11, 1931; s. David Wealand and Elizabeth (Rutt) M.; m. Nancy Alice Strickler, May 6, 1950; children: Curtis Gene, Pamela Louise, Susan Lynn, Anita Marie, John Scott, Andrew Thomas, Jennifer Lee, Lisa Nancy. BS (scholarship), Pa. State U., 1956; MS, U. So. Calif., 1958; PhD, U. Mich., 1965. Designer, trainee Textile Machine Works, Rockwell Internat. Corp., Reading, Pa., 1949-56; staff mem. Hughes Aircraft Co., Culver City, Calif., 1956-58, Los Alamos Sci. Lab., 1958-65; asso. prof. elec. engring. U. N.Mex., Albuquerque, 1965-69; prof. elec. engring./aerospace, mech. and nuclear engring. U. Okla., 1969-72, prof., chmn. info. and computing scis., 1970-72; dir. Systems Research Center, 1969-72; adj. prof. elec. engring. and nuclear engring. U. N.Mex., Los Alamos Grad. Center, 1959-65; cons. Sandia Corp., Albuquerque, 1966-69, Aerojet-Gen. Corp., Sacramento, 1966; vis. assoc. prof. system sci. UCLA, 1968-69; cons. community health project OEO, Oklahoma City, 1970-71; prof. elec. and computer engring. Oreg. State U., Corvallis, 1972-98, prof. emeritus, 1998—, head dept., 1972-79, 90; pres. Pace Tech., Inc., 1982-97. Vis. prof. U. Rome, 1973, 75, Imperial Coll., London, 1978-79, U.S. Naval Postgrad. Sch., 1983-85, Australian Nat. U., 1988, Sydney U., 1995, 98; cons. Optimization Software, L.A., 1973—, Bonneville Power Adminstrn., 1975—, Internat. Inst. Applied Systems Analysis, 1988—. Author: Optimal Control of Nuclear Reactors, 1970, Bilinear Control Processes, 1973, Nonlinear Systems: Dynamics and Control, vol. 1, 1991, Applications to Bilinear Control, vol. II, 1991, Disease Dynamics, 1993; editor: Theory and Application of Variable Structure Systems, 1972, Variable Structure Systems with Application to Biology and Economics, 1975, Recent Developments in Variable Structure Systems, Economics and Biology, 1979, Nonlinear Time Series and Signal Processing, 1988, assoc. editor Annals of Nuclear Energy, 1973-97; contbr. jours. Chmn. St. Stephens Sch. Bd., Norman, 1970-72. Recipient NATO award, 1979; rsch. grantee NSF, 1966-99, Sandia Labs., 1966-68, 96-97, ONR, 1981-92, NASA, EPRI, BPA, 1990-97; AEC fellow, 1961-65, Hughes fellow, 1956-58; Acad. Sci. exch. scientist to USSR and China, 1980, US-CIS (USSR) Commn. on Engring. Edn., 1991—. Fellow IEEE (life, local chmn. 1975); mem. Control System Soc., Sigma Xi, Tau Beta Pi, Pi Tau Sigma. Democrat. Home: 16111 Old Juniper Rd Sisters OR 97759-9654 E-mail: ronamoh@aol.com.

MOHLER, STANLEY ROSS, physician, educator; b. Amarillo, Tex., Sept. 30, 1927; s. Norton Harrison and Minnie Alice (Ross) M.; m. Ursula Luise Burkhardt, Jan. 24, 1953; children: Susan Luise, Stanley Ross, Mark Hallock. BA, MA, U. Tex., 1953, MD, 1956. Diplomate Am. Bd. Preventive Medicine. Intern USPHS Hosp., San Francisco, 1956-57; med. officer Center Aging Research, NIH, Bethesda, Md., 1957-61; dir. Civil Aeromed. Rsch. Inst., FAA, Oklahoma City, 1961-66, chief aeromed. applications divsn. Washington, 1966-78; prof.; vice chmn. dept. community medicine, dir. aerospace medicine Wright State U. Sch. Medicine, Dayton, Ohio, 1978—. Rsch. assoc. prof. preventive medicine and pub. health U. Okla. Med. Sch., 1961—; vice-chmn. Am. Bd. Preventive Medicine, 1978—, sec.-treas., 1980—. Co-editor: Space Biology and Medicine (5 vols.), 1995 (Life Scis. Book award Internat. Acad. Astronautics); contbr. articles to profl. jours. Bd. dirs. Sr. Citizens Assn. Oklahoma City, 1962— , Flying Physicians Assn., 1961—. Served with AUS, 1946-48. Recipient Gail Borden Rsch. award, Boothby award Aerospace Med. Assn., 1966, FAA Meritorious Svc. award, 1974, Cecil A. Brownlow Publ. award Flight Safety Found., 1998; co-recipient Life Scis. Book award in space, biology and medicine Internat. Acad. Astronautics, 1995. Fellow Geriatrics Soc., Aerospace Med. Assn. (pres. 1983, Harry G. Moseley award 1974, Lyster award 1984, Louis H. Bauer Founders award 1998), Am. Coll. Preventive Medicine, Gerontol. Soc.; mem. AMA, Aircraft Owners and Pilots Assn. (Sharples award 1984, Hubertus Strughold award 1991), Alpha Omega Alpha. Home: 6539 Reigate Rd Dayton OH 45459-3214 Office: Wright State U Sch Medicine PO Box 927 Dayton OH 45401-0927

MOHLER, TERENCE JOHN, psychologist; s. Edward F. and Gertrude A. (Aylward) M.; m. Carol B. Kulczak; children: Renee, John, Timothy. BE, ME, EdS, Toledo U.; PhD, Union Inst., 1979, Walden U. Lic. psychologist, Ohio. Psychologist, sr. ptnr. Psychol. Assocs., Maumee, Ohio, 1970—. Assoc. fellow Inst. for Advanced Study in Rational Psychotherapy, N.Y.C. Served in U.S. Army, 1951-53, Korea. Mem. APA, Ohio Psychol. Assn., Northwestern Ohio Psychol. Assn., Maumee Vly. Psychol. Assn., Soc. Behaviorists, Toledo Acad. Profl. Psychology, Nat. Registry Mental Health Providers, Am. Personnel and Guidance Assn., Ohio Personnel and Guidance Assn., Coun. Exceptional Children, Rotary (Paul Harris fellow), Kappa Delta Phi. Home: 1904 Glen Ellyn Dr Toledo OH 43614-3256

MOHN, MELVIN PAUL, anatomist, educator; b. Cleve., June 19, 1926; s. Paul Melvin and Julia (Jacobik) M.; m. Audrey Faye Lonergan, June 28, 1952; children— Shorey Faye, Andrew Paul AB, Marietta Coll., 1950; Sc.M., Brown U., 1952, PhD in Biology, 1955. Instr. SUNY Downstate Med. Ctr., Bklyn., 1955-59, asst. prof., 1959-63; asst. prof. anatomy U. Kans. Sch. Medicine, Kansas City, 1963-65, assoc. prof., 1965-72, prof., 1972-89, prof. emeritus, 1989—. Cons. Nat. Med. Audiovisual Ctr., Atlanta, 1972; vis. lectr. U. Miami Sch. Medicine, Fla., 1966. Bd. dirs. U. Kans. Med. Ctr. Credit Union, 1968-77, Kansas City Youth Symphony, 1972-77; mem. U.S. Pony Club, 1964-71, Med. Arts Symphony, 1965-71, 90—, Spring Hill Chorale, 1990—. Served with USN, 1944-46, PTO. McCoy fellow, 1950, Arnold biology fellow, 1954 Fellow AAAS; mem. Am. Soc. Zoologists, Am. Assn. Anatomists, Am. Inst. Biol. Sci., Phi Beta Kappa, Sigma Xi, Beta Beta Beta. Clubs: Lions, Rotary,. Lodges: Masons. Republican. Methodist. Home: Yankee Bit Farm 23595 W 223rd St Spring Hill KS 66083-4029 Office: U Kans Med Ctr Dept Anatomy 39th and Rainbow St Kansas City KS 66103

MOHN, STEPHEN MICHAEL, commodity manager; b. Plattsburg, N.Y., June 23, 1968; s. Kermit Stephen and Barbara Ann (Jacocks) M.; m. Jacqueline Lee Schuler, Jan. 18, 1992; children: Stephen Joseph, Jacob Eric. BS, Miami U., Oxford, Ohio, 1990. Cert. purchasing mgr. Buyer Dayton (Ohio) Power and Light, 1991-96; commodity mgr. Copeland Corp., Sidney, Ohio, 1996-99; sr. commodity mgr. McQuay Internat., Staunton, Va., 1999—. Vol. firefighter Washington Twp. Fire Dept., Centerville, Ohio, 1992-99. Mem.: Nat. Assn. Purchasing Mgmt. (pres. Blue Ridge chap. 2002, acad. scholarship Dayton chpt. 1995). Avocations: cycling, camping. Office: McQuay Internat PO Box 2510 Staunton VA 24402-2510 E-mail: steve.mohn@mcquay.com.

MOHNEY, NELL WEBB, religion educator, speaker, author; b. Shelby, N.C., Oct. 31, 1921; d. John Wonnie and Maude (Ferree) Webb; m. Ralph Wilson Mohney, Dec. 31, 1948; children: Richard Bentley, Ralph Wilson Jr. BA, Greensboro Coll., 1943; LHD (hon.), Tenn. Wesleyan Coll., 1982. Dir. youth work Western N.C. Conf., Salisbury, 1945-48; dir. Christian edn. 1st United Meth. Ch., Lenoir, N.C., 1943-45, Washington Pike United Meth. Ch., Knoxville, Tenn., 1952-56; dir. adult ministries 1st Centenary United Meth. Ch., Chattanooga, 1967-73, dir. membership devel., 1973-81, 1st Broad St. United Meth. Ch., Kingsport, Tenn., 1981-87; speaker, seminar leader for bus., profl., religious orgns. S.E. U.S., 1960—. Spkr. Internat. Women's Conf., Crystal Cathedral, 1991, 2001; adj. staff Bd. Discipleship Sect. on Evangelism, Nashville, 1987-96. Author: Inside Story, 1979, Single Out Singles for Ministry, 1989, Don't Put a Period Where God Put a Comma, 1993, How to be Up on Down Days, 1995, Keep on Kicking as Long as You Are Ticking, 1999, Get A Faith Lift, 2000, Develop Your Bounce Back Ability, 2000, From Eve to Esther: What Old Testament Women Say to Women Today, 2001, From Mary to Lydia, 2002; co-author: Parable Churches, 1989, Churches of Vision, 1990, 365 Meditations for Grandmothers, 1996, 365 Meditations for Women, 1997; contbr. weekly article Chattanooga Free Press, 1977—, Kingsport Times, 1981—. Recipient Freedom Founds. award for writing, Valley Forge, Pa., 1973, for speaking, 1974, Key to City of Chattanooga, 1979; named Disting. Alumnae Greensboro Coll., 1988, Woman of Distinction in Chattanooga, 1992, Woman of Distinction Hall of Fame, 1993, Tenn. Woman of Yr., 1999. Republican. Home: 1004 Northbridge Ln Chattanooga TN 37405-4214

MOHOLY-NAGY, HATTULA, archaeologist; b. Berlin, Oct. 11, 1933; arrived in U.S., 1937; d. László and Sibyl Pietzsch Moholy-Nagy; m. Roger G. Schneggenburger, June 21, 1987; m. Hans-Rudolf Hug, June 1965 (div. Mar. 1979); children: Andreas Laszlo Hug, Daniel Claude Hug. AB in History, U. Mich., 1955, PhD in Anthropology, 1994; AM in Anthropology, U. Chgo., 1958. Field lab. head Joint Casas Grandes Project of Amerind Found., Dragoon, Ariz., 1958—59; Tikal project rschr. U. Pa. Mus., Phila., 1960—, Tikal project field lab., 1960, field lab. dir., 1961—64; lectr. U. Zurich, 1971—78; rsch. assoc. U. Pa. Mus., 1994—. Reviewer anthropol. books and jours., 1960—; participant profl. meetings, 1974—; lectr. and cons. in field, 1995—. Contbr. Mem.: Catalogue Raisonné Scholars Assn., Archaeol. Inst. Am., Soc. for Am. Archaeology, Am. Anthropol. Assn. Home: 1204 Gardner Ann Arbor MI 48104-4321 E-mail: hattula@sprynet.com.

MOHR, ANTHONY JAMES, judge; b. L.A., May 11, 1947; s. Gerald Leonard and Rita Lenore (Goldstein) M. BA in Govt. cum laude with honors, Wesleyan U., 1969; JD, Columbia U., 1972; diploma with honors, Internat. Faculty for Comparative Law, 1975. Bar: Calif. 1972, U.S. Dist. Ct. (cen. dist.) Calif. 1973, U.S. Ct. Appeals (9th cir.) 1974, D.C. 1976, U.S. Supreme Ct. 1981. Law clk. to judge U.S. Dist. Ct. (cen. dist.) Calif., 1972-73; assoc. Alschuler Grossman, Stein & Kahan, 1973-75; pvt. practice L.A., 1976-94; judge L.A. Mcpl. Ct., 1994-97, L.A. Superior Ct., 1997—. Faculty atty. asst. tng. program UCLA, 1982-97, bd. dirs. internat. student ctr., 1986—, Performing Tree, 1997-2002. Mem. editl. bd. Calif. Bar Jour., 1979-80, L.A. Lawyer Mag., 1989-94; contbr. articles to profl. jours. Del. White House Conf. on Youth, 1971; faculty Ctr. Jud. Edn. and Rsch, 1997—; nat. adv. coun. Ctr. for Study of Presidency, 1974-99; mem. L.A. Dist. Atty.'s Adv. Coun., 1976-82; hearing officer L.A. County Employees Ret. Assn., 1986-94. Mem. ABA, Calif. Judges Assn., Beverly Hills Bar Assn. (bd. govs. 1975-80, chmn. litig. sect. 1983-85, chair resolutions com. 1991-92, ex. officio bd. dirs. 1998-99, 2002—, Dist. Svc. award 1992), Assn. of Bus. Trial lawyers (bd. govs. 2001—), Barristers of Beverly Hills Bar Assn. (pres. 1979-80), Am. Judicature Soc. (dir. 1982-83), L.A. County Bar Assn., Phi Beta Kappa, Phi Delta Phi. Office: LA Superior Ct 600 S Commonwealth Ave Los Angeles CA 90005 E-mail: amohr@lasuperiorcourt.org.

MOHR, BARBARA JEANNE, educator; b. Santa Monica, Calif., Jan. 26, 1953; d. Edgar Kirchner and Beatrice Jeanne (Anderson) M. BA, Calif. State U., Fullerton, 1976; MS, Calif. State U., 1982. Multiple Subject Teaching Credential, 1977, Single Subject Tchr. Credential, 1977. Substitute tchr. Fullerton (Calif.) Sch. Dist., 1977-78, tchr., 1978—, mentor, 1984-96. Tchr. calligraphy Laguna Rd. Sch., 1985-92, student coun. advisor, 1988-92, advisor Just Say No Club, 1986-94. Named Tchr. of Yr. Fullerton Sch. Dist., 1989; recipient Hon. Svc. award Laguna Rd. Sch. PTA, 1989; Weingart fellow Nat. Gallery of Art Tchr. Inst., 1996. Mem. NEA, Calif. Tchrs. Assn., Fullerton Elem. Tchrs. Assn., Calif. State U. Alumni Assn., Phi Kappa Phi. Avocations: calligraphy, gardening, travel.

MOHR, DAVID CURTIS, psychologist, educator; b. San Francisco, Nov. 10, 1957; s. Gerhard Ernst and Carolyn (Curtis) M. BA, U. Calif., Berkeley, 1980; MA, U. Ariz., 1989, PhD, 1991. Lic. psychologist, Calif. Postdoctoral fellow Calif. Pacific Med. Ctr., 1991-94; asst. prof. dept. neurology U. Calif., San Francisco, 1994—2001, asst. prof. dept. psychiatry, 2001—; dir. psychology rsch. VA Med. Ctr., 2000—. Contbr. articles to profl. jours., chpts. to books. Fulbright scholar, 1989-90. Office: VA Med Ctr 4150 Clement St (116-A) San Francisco CA 94121 E-mail: dmohr@itsa.ucsf.edu.

MOHR, DIANE LOUISE, library administrator; b. Fairbanks, Alaska, Nov. 24, 1951; d. Dean Burgette and Mary Louise (Leonard) M. BA in Black Studies, Calif. State U., 1977; MSLS, U. So. Calif., 1978; cert. pub. mgr., George Washington U., 1999. With Getty Oil Co., L.A., 1978-80; libr. L.A. County Pub. Libr. Woodcrest br., 1980-82, View Park Pub. Libr., L.A., 1982-84, Compton (Calif.) Pub. Libr., 1984-87; sociology libr. Martin Luther King Pub. Libr., Washington, 1987-89; br. libr. West End Pub. Libr., 1990; asst. coord. of adult svcs. D.C. Pub. Libr., 1991—, adult collection coord., 2001—. Mem. ALA, D.C. Libr. Assn., Black Caucus of the Am. Libr. Assn., Alpha Kappa Alpha, Phi Kappa Phi. Episcopalian. Office: DC Public Libr 901 G St NW # 417 Washington DC 20001-4531

MOHR, GARY ALAN, physician; b. Erie, Pa., Aug. 17, 1952; s. Arthur John and Sue (Richardson) M.; children: Benjamin, Nathan, Elizabeth, Katelyn, Eric. BS, Pa. State U., 1975; MD, Jefferson Med. Coll., 1979. Cert. Am. Bd. Family Practice. Intern, resident in family medicine St. Vincent Health Ctr., Erie, Pa., 1979-82; pvt. practice Canon City, Colo., 1982—. Asst. clin. prof. family medicine U. Colo. Health Scis. Ctr. Founder, treas. Jefferson Soc., Fremont County, Colo., 1991. Fellow Am. Acad. Family Physicians; mem. Fremont County Med. Soc. (past pres.), Mensa. Lutheran. Achievements include climbing Mt. Kilimajaro, Oct. 2000. Avocations: hiking, scuba, philately, numismatics, computing. Office: 730 Macon Ave Canon City CO 81212-3314

MOHR, JAY PRESTON, neurologist, educator; b. Mar. 5, 1937; s. John G. and Marguerite F. Mohr; m. Joan L. Seal, Mar. 10, 1962; children: Thea, Gregory. AB, Haverford Coll., 1958; MS, MD, U. Va., 1963. Diplomate Am. Bd. Neurology and Psychiatry. Intern then asst. resident Mary Imogene Bassett Hosp., Cooperstown, N.Y., 1963-65; asst. resident N.Y. Neurol. Inst., Columbia-Presbyn. Med. Ctr., N.Y.C., 1965-66; instr. neurology Johns Hopkins U. Med. Sch., U. Md. Med. Sch., 1969-71; assoc. neurologist Mass. Gen. Hosp., Boston, 1972-78; asst. prof. Harvard U. Med. Sch., 1972-78; prof. neurologi, chmn. dept. U. South Ala. Med. Sch., Mobile, 1978-83; Sciarra prof. clin. neurology Co,umbia U. Coll. Physicians & Surgeons, N.Y.C., 1983—. Dir. cerebrovascular research N.Y. Neurol. Inst., N.Y.C., 1983—. Contbr. articles to med. jours. Mag. M.C., U.S. Army, 1969-72. Neurology fellow Mass. Gen. Hosp., 1966-69. Fellow Am. Acad. Neurology; mem. Am. Neurol. Assn., Am. Heart Assn. (Stroke coun.), Sigma Xi. Democrat. Mem. Soc. Of Friends. Home: PO Box 1014 Shelter Island Heights NY 11965-1014 Office: NY Neurol Inst 710 W 168th St New York NY 10032-2603 also: Presbyn Hosp Columbia-Presbyn Med Ctr New York NY 10032-3784 E-mail: jpm10@columbia.edu.

MOHR, JEFFREY MICHAEL, real estate and insurance executive; b. Baton Rouge, Sept. 20, 1960; s. Lewis Thompson Sr. and Josephine (Agosta) M.; m. Lisa Juneau, Mar. 9, 1961; children: Jeffrey Michael Jr., Brittany Danielle. BS in Mgmt. Adminstrn., La. State U., 1982. CPCU; cert. assoc. in risk mgmt. Ins. agt., producer Lewis Mohr Real Estate and Ins. Agy., Inc., Baton Rouge, 1983-84, pres., 1984—. Bd. dirs. Ind. Agts. Svc. Corp. Mem. La. Edn. Adv. Coun., 1994—; bd. dirs. Baton Rouge Soccer Assn. Mem. Ind. Ins. Agts. Am. (edn. com.), Ind. Ins. Agts. La. (chmn. editorial adv. bd. 1994-96, chmn. personal lines tech. com., chmn. communications com., bd. dirs., 1998—, fin. com. 1998—), Ind. Ins. Agts. Baton Rouge (pres. 1994), Baton Rouge C. of C., Exch. Club (bd. dirs. 1985-88), Capitol Area Tigers Club (sec. 1986-90, v.p. 1990-92, bd. dirs. 1992-96), Soc. CPCU (Bayou chpt. bd. dirs. 1995), Delta Tau Delta (v.p. house corp. 1988-91, pres. 1992-2000, pres. so. divsn. house corp. 1994-2000). Republican. Roman Catholic. Avocations: football, basketball. Office: Lewis Mohr Real Estate & Ins 11051 Coursey Blvd Baton Rouge LA 70816 E-mail: jmohr@mohragency.com.

MOHR, JOHN LUTHER, biologist, environmental consultant; b. Reading, Pa., Dec. 1, 1911; s. Luther Seth and Anna Elizabeth (Davis) M.; m. Frances Edith Christensen, Nov. 23, 1939; children: Jeremy John, Christopher Charles. AB in Biology, Bucknell U., 1933; student, Oberlin Coll., 1933-34; PhD in Zoology, U. Calif., Berkeley, 1939; student, Marine Biol. Lab., Woods Hole, Mass., 1934. Research asso. Pacific Islands Research, Stanford, 1942-44; rsch. assoc. Allan Hancock Found., U. So. Calif., 1944-46, asst. prof., 1946-47, asst. prof. dept. biology, 1947-54, asso. prof., 1954-57, prof., 1957-77; chmn. dept., 1960-62; prof. emeritus, 1977—; vis. prof. summers U. Wash. Friday Harbor Labs., 1956, '57. Rsch. assoc. vertebrate zoology Natural History Mus., Los Angeles County, 1996—; marine borer and pollution surveys harbors So. Calif., 1948-51, arctic marine biol. research, 1952-71; chief marine zool. group U.S. Antarctic research ship Eltanin in Drake Passage, 1962, in South Pacific sector, 1965; research deontology in sci. and academia; researcher on parasitic protozoans of anurans, crustaceans, elephants; analysis of agy. and industry documents, ethics and derelictions of steward agy., sci. and tech. orgns. as they relate to offshore and coastal onshore oil activities, environ. effects of oil spill dispersants and offshore oil industry discharges and naturally occurring radioactive material NORMs. Active People for the Am. Way; mem. Biol. Stain Commn., 1948-80, trustee, 1971-80, emeritus trustee, 1981—, v.p., 1976-80; bd. dirs. Calif. Natural Areas Coord. Coun., 1981-90. Recipient Guggenheim fellowship, 1957-58 Fellow AAAS (coun. 1964-73, Sr. Scientists and Engrs. Nat. Network), So. Calif. Acad. Scis., Sigma Xi (exec. com. 1964-67, 68, 69, chpt.-at-large bd. 1968-69); mem. Am. Micros. Soc., Marine Biol. Assn. U.K. (life), Am. Soc. Parasitologists, Western Soc. Naturalists (pres. 1960-61), Soc. Protozoologists, Soc. Integrative and Comparative Biology, Ecol. Soc. Am., Calif. Native Plant Soc., Assn. Forest Svc. Employees Environ. Ethics, Common Cause, Huxleyan, Sierra Club, Phi Sigma, Theta Upsilon Omega. Home: 3819 Chanson Dr Los Angeles CA 90043-1601 E-mail: jmohr10000@aol.com.

MOHR, LAWRENCE CHARLES, physician; b. S.I., N.Y., July 8, 1947; s. Lawrence Charles Sr. and Mary Estelle (Dawsey) M.; m. Linda Johnson, June 14, 1970; 1 child, Andrea Marie. AB with highest honors, U. N.C., 1975, MD, 1979. Diplomate Am. Bd. Internal Medicine. Commd. 2d lt. U.S. Army, 1967, advanced through grades to col., 1989; med. intern Walter Reed Army Med. Ctr., Washington, 1979-80, resident in medicine, 1980-82, chief resident, 1982-83, attending physician, 1984-86, pulmonary fellow, 1986-87; command surgeon 9th Inf. Div., Ft. Lewis, Wash., 1983-84; med. cons. Madigan Army Med. Ctr., Tacoma, 1983-84; White House physician Washington, 1987-93; asst. prof. medicine Uniformed Svcs. U. of the Health Scis., Bethesda, Md., 1984-91; assoc. prof. medicine Uniformed Svcs. U. Health Scis., 1991-94; assoc. clin. prof. medicine George Washington U., Washington, 1990-94; prof. medicine Med. U. S.C., Charleston, 1994—, dir. environ. bioscis. program, 1995—. Attending physician Med. U. Hosp., Charleston, 1994—, Charleston Meml. Hosp., 1994—; mem. Working Group on Disability in U.S. Presidents, 1995—. Editor: International Case Studies in Risk Assessment and Magagement, 1997, Biomarkers, Medical and Workplace Applications, 1998; contbr. articles to profl. jours. and books. Bd. dirs. Internat. Lung Found., Washington; mem. adv. bd. Nat. Mus. Health and Medicine, Washington; mem. sci. adv. bd. Consortium in Environ. Risk Evaluation; prin. investigator Consortium in Molecular Epidemiology and Biomarker Rsch. Decorated Silver Star, Bronze Star with 2 V devices and 3 oak leaf clusters, Purple Heart, Meritorious Svc. medal with oak leaf cluster, Air medal, Army Commendation medal with oak leaf cluster, D.S.M.; recipient Erskine award Walter Reed Army Med. Ctr., 1982; named Outstanding Med. Resident, 1982. Fellow ACP, Am. Coll. Chest Physicians; mem. AMA, Army and Navy Club, Order Mil. Med. Merit, Harbour Club, Phi Beta Kappa. Episcopalian. Avocations: mountain climbing, skiing. Home: 673 Lake Francis Dr Charleston SC 29412-4345 Office: Med U S C Environ Bioscis Program 171 Ashley Ave Charleston SC 29425-0001

MOHR, ROGER JOHN, advertising agency executive; b. Milw., Sept. 8, 1931; s. Reinhold and Clara (Meissner) M.; m. Pauline Spicuzza, Oct. 18, 1958; children: Gregory, Mary Margaret, Kristin, Thomas, Kathleen. BS in Speech, Marquette U., 1953; postgrad. radio and TV, Northwestern U., 1955-56. Staff announcer radio sta. WBKB, West Bend, Wis., 1952, WCAN, Milw., 1952-54; with Arthur Meyerhoff Assos., Inc., Chgo., 1956-80, pres., 1965-80, BBDO, Chgo., 1980-82, chmn., 1982-90, vice chmn. internat., 1991-93; retired, 1993. Chmn. Lake Bluff (Ill.) Plan Commn., 1972-75; mem. Lake Forest (Ill.) Plan Commn., 1994-2000, chmn., 1999-2000; bd. dirs. Chgo. City Ballet, 1982-84, Off the Street Club, 1976-78; mem. adv. coun. Marquette U. Sch. Comm., 1993-99; alderman Lake Forest City Coun., 2000—. Served with AUS, 1954-55. Mem. Am. Assn. Advt. Agys. (chmn. Chgo. coun. 1966-67, sec., treas., nat. bd. dirs. 1976-77), Evans Scholars Alumni Assn. (pres. 1964-65), Western Golf Assn. (bd. dirs. 1980-2000, v.p. 1994-2000, trustee 2000—), Knollwood Club (bd. govs. 1980-85, 89-92), Tavern Club (bd. govs., v.p. 1988-94). Home: 2000 Knollwood Rd Lake Forest IL 60045-1137

MOHRAZ, JUDY JOLLEY, foundation administrator; b. Houston, Oct. 1, 1943; d. John Chesler and Mae (Jackson) Jolley; m. Bijan Mohraz; children: Andrew, Jonathan. BA, Baylor U., 1966, MA, 1968; PhD, U. Ill., 1974. Lectr. history Ill. Wesleyan U., 1972-74; asst. prof. history So. Meth. U., Dallas, 1974-80, coord. women's studies, 1977-81, assoc. prof. history, 1980-94, asst. provost, 1983-88, assoc. provost for student academics, 1988-94; pres. Goucher Coll., Towson, Md., 1994-2000, Virginia G. Piper Charitable Trust, Scottsdale, Ariz., 2000—. Cons. Ednl. Testing Svc., Princeton, N.J., 1984-93, Nat. Park Svcs., Seneca Falls, N.Y., 1992-93; bd. dirs. Balt. Equitable Soc., 1996-2000, The Assocs. First Capital, 1999-2000; bd. visitors U.S. Naval Acad., 1996-2001. Trustee The Lamplighter Sch., 1991-94, St. Mark's Sch. Tex., 1993-94; adv. bd. U. Tex. Southwestern Med. Sch., 1992-94; active Leadership Dallas, 1994; bd. dirs. Nat. Assn. Ind., The Balt. Cmty. Found. Recipient Disting. Alumni award Baylor U., 1993; named Woman of Merit, Omicron Delta Kappa, 1993. Office: Virgina G Piper Charitable Trust 6720 N Scottsdale Rd Ste 350 Scottsdale AZ 85253

MOHRFELD, RICHARD GENTEL, marketing professional; b. Camden, N.J., Dec. 30, 1945; s. Herbert Henry and Elizabeth Weldon (Gentel) M.; m. Ann Bacon, June 20, 1971 (div. 1975); m. Janice Lee Strickland, July 1, 1978; children: Kathryn Elizabeth, Christopher Hall. BSc in Geology, Dickinson Coll., 1971. Staff geologist Temple U., Phila., 1971-74; pres. Mohrfeld Inc., Collingswood, NJ, 1974—2002; sr. mktg. exec. Quest Environ. & Engring. Svcs., Inc., Clinton, 2002—. Bd. dirs. South Jersey Savs. & Loan Assn., Turnersville, N.J., 1984-2000. Bd. dirs. Boy Scouts Am., Camden County, N.J., 1985—; trustee Knight Park Trustees, Collingswood, 1986—, Health Care Support Found., Inc., 1994—. Sgt. USAF, 1969-71. Mem. ASHRAE, Air Conditioning Contractors Am. (pres. 1986-88), Fuel Mchts. Assn. N.J. (pres. 1992-94), Rotary (pres. Collingswood 1980-81). Episcopalian. Avocations: travel, photography. Home: 47 Treaty Elm Ln Haddonfield NJ 08033-3413 Office: PO Box 427 Collingswood NJ 08108-0427 E-mail: mfuel@comcast.net.

MOHRING, HERBERT, economics educator; b. Buffalo, Sept. 8, 1928; m. June 12, 1953. AB in Econs. and Maths. with honors, Williams Coll., 1950; PhD in Econs., MIT, 1959. Rsch. assoc. Willow Run Rsch. Ctr., U. Mich., Ann Arbor, 1951-52; teaching fellow dept. econs. MIT, Cambridge, 1952, 53-54; asst. study dir., study dir. Survey Rsch. Ctr. U. Mich., Ann Arbor, 1954-57; rsch. assoc. Resources for Future, 1957-58; rsch. economist Transp. Ctr., Northwestern U., Evanston, Ill., 1958-61; assoc. prof. U. Minn., Mpls., 1961-67, prof., 1967—95, prof. emeritus, 1995—. Cons. econ. survey Liberia Northwestern U., Evanston, Ill., 1961; adj. prof. law U. Minn., 1969—71; vis. prof. econ. U. Toronto, 1972—73, U. B.C., 1983, U. Calif., Irvine, 1990, Irvine, 1996—; vis. prof. polit. economy Johns Hopkins U., 1974; vis. prof. dept. econs. and stats. Nat. U., Singapore, 1982—83; dir. grad. studies dept. econs. U. Minn., 1977—81. Author: (with Mitchell Hartwitz) Highway Benefits: An Analytical Framework, 1962 (trans. into Japanese), Transportation Economics, 1976; (trans. into Japanese and Korean) The Economics of Transport, 1993; bd. editors Am. Econ. Rev., 1971-73, Jour. Urban Econs., 1979-90; contbr. articles to profl. jours., chpts. to books. 2d lt. USAF, 1953. Mem. Am. Econ. Assn., Royal Econ. Soc., Econometric Soc. Office: U Minn Dept Econs Minneapolis MN 55455-0430 Home (Winter): 9 Rustling Wind Irvine CA 92612-3210 E-mail: mohring@econ.umn.edu., mohring@uci.edu.

MOHRMAN, HENRY J(OE), JR. lawyer, investment manager; b. St. Louis, Jan. 28, 1948; s. Henry Joseph and Mavis Claire (Lynch) M.; m. Mary Beth Mohrman, Aug. 26, 1969; children: Aaron Henry, Anna Rose. BA, Yale U., 1969; JD, U. Chgo, 1973. Bar: Mo. 1973, Ill. 1974, U.S. Supreme Ct. 1997. Assoc. Greenfield & Davidson, St. Louis, 1973-76; asst. gen. counsel LaBarge, Inc., 1976-77; tax mgr. Ernst & Young, 1977-81; pvt. practice, 1982—. Gen. counsel Miss. Valley Equipment Co., St. Louis, 1982—, MKT Mfg., Inc., St. Louis, 1986—. Mem. ABA, U. Chicago Law Sch. Alumni Assn. (pres. St. Louis chpt. 1986—). Republican. Jewish. Avocations: horsemanship, literature, theater, mathematics. Office: 7751 Carondelet Ave Ste 805 Clayton MO 63105-3369

MOHRMAN-GILLIS, MARILYN, telecommunications specialist; b. St. Louis, Oct. 1, 1949; d. Raymond F. and Dolores M. Mohrman; m. John A. Gillis; children: Katharine, John, Brian, Brennan. BA, St. Mary's Coll., Notre Dame, Ind., 1972; MSW, Cath. U., Washington, 1975, JD, 1979. Assoc. Steptoe & Johnson, Washington, 1979-87; chief legal br., mass media FCC, 1987-90; v.p., policy and legal affairs America's Pub. TV, 1990—. E-mail: marilyn@apts.org.

MOHSEN, ZOHAIR HUSEIN, entomologist, research scientist; b. Baghdad, Iraq, Jan. 8, 1948; s. Husein Mohsen and Armouta Mousa Al-Kazzaz; m. Sawsan Mostafa El-Gamal, July 28, 1970; children Mohammad, Abeer, Ali. BSc, Al-Azhar U., Cairo, 1970; MSc, Baghdad U., 1973; PhD, U. Calif., Riverside, 1981. Dir. gen. Sci. Rsch. Coun., Baghdad, 1982-86, head sci. photographic unit, 1987-90; rsch. scientist Biol. Rsch. Ctr., 1981-87, sr. rsch. scientist, 1987-90; sr. entomologist Agrl. & Consultation Svc. Bur., Iraq, 1990-91; tech. cons. Arab Pest Control Ctr., Amman, Jordan, 1991-99; adj. lectr. dept. natural scis. U. Mich., Dearborn, 1999—. Contbr. numerous articles to profl. jours. Mem. Entomological Soc. Am., Soc. Invertebrate Pathology, Soc. Vector Ecology. Avocations: photography, music, reading, travel. Office: U Mich Dept Natural Scis 4901 Evergreen Rd Dearborn MI 48128-1491 Home: 2207 Hemlock Ct Ann Arbor MI 48108-2521 E-mail: zohair@umd.umich.edu.

MOINZADEH, KAMRAN, industrial engineer, educator; b. Tehran, Iran, Apr. 21, 1958; s. Tajeddin Moinzadeh and Gity Assly; children: Atoosa, Ashkaan. PhD in Indsl. Engring., Stanford U., 1985. Prof. U. of Wash., Seattle, 1984—. Prof. Burlington No. Found., 1996—2002.

MOISE, STEVEN KAHN, lawyer, rancher, merchant banker; b. Lubbock, Tex., July 28, 1944; s. Joseph J. and Marguerite K. M.; m. Beth Maxwell, June 2, 1968; children: Adam, Grant. BA, U. Colo., 1966, JD, 1969. Bar: Colo. 1969, N.Mex. 1971. Assoc. Rothgerber, Appel & Powers, Denver, 1969-71, Sutin, Thayer & Browne, Albuquerque, 1971-74, ptnr., 1974-94, pres., CEO, 1984-88, chmn., 1989-94, of counsel, 1995; pres. Moise & Co., 1995—. Bd. dirs. Wells Fargo Bank, N.Mex., N.A. Bd. dirs. U. Colo. Found., Boulder, 1969-79, 87-94; bd. dirs. U. Colo. Sch. Law Alumni, 1985-89, N.Mex. Amigos, 1987—; bd. dirs., exec. com. Albuquerque Cmty. Found., 1981-2001, pres. 1984-88; bd. dirs. Albuquerque Econ. Devel., 1982—, sec., 1984-86, v.p., 1986-88, pres., 1988-90, exec. com., 1984—; mem. Albuquerque Econ. Forum, 1989-98; chmn. Bingaman Circle, 1990-96; trustee Albuquerque Acad., 2001—, advisory dir. sr. discounts.com, 2001—; bd. dirs. N.Mex. Cancer Coalition, 2002—. Mem. N.Mex. Bar Assn., Colo. Bar Assn. Democrat. Jewish. Home: 6611 Guadalupe Trl NW Albuquerque NM 87107-6201 Office: Moise & Co PO Box 1705 Albuquerque NM 87103-1705 E-mail: steve@moiseco.biz.

MOISEYEV, ALEKSEY, software engineer; b. Moscow, Jan. 22, 1963; came to U.S., 1999; s. Anatoly Fridland and Ludmila Moiseyeva; m. Tatyana Goganskaja, Aug. 2, 1997. PhD, Moscow Railway Transp. Inst., 1992, MA, 1995. Asst. prof. Moscow Rlwy. Transp. Inst., 1991-96; sr. engr. Joint Stock HGS Ctr., Moscow, 1996-99; prin. software engr. Parametric Tech. Corp., Waltham, Mass., 1999—. Author: Macintosh in Computer Prepress, 1996; co-author: Computer Fonts: Creation and Using, 1997. Avocation: books. Home: 166 Ridgewood Dr Norwood MA 02062-5630 Office: Parametric Tech Corp 140 Kendrick St Needham MA 02494

MOIZE, JERRY DEE, lawyer, government official; b. Greensboro, N.C., Dec. 19, 1934; s. Dwight Moody and Thelma (Ozment) M.; m. Margaret Ann Wooten, Aug. 13, 1976; 1 child, Jerry Dee Jr. AB cum laude, Elon (N.C.) Coll., 1957; JD, Tulane U., New Orleans, 1960; diploma, Army Command & Gen. Staff Sch., USAR, 1981. Bar: Colo. 1961, U.S. Dist. Ct. Colo. 1961, U.S. Ct. Mil. Appeals 1962, U.S. Supreme Ct. 1965, N.C. 1965. Legal clk. Air Def. Commd., Colorado Springs, Colo., 1960-61, assistance officer, 1962-63; chief legal assistance divsn. 2nd Army, Ft. Meade, Md., 1964-65; staff JAG, Indiantown Gap Mil. Reservation, 1965; law clk. to hon. Eugen Gordon U.S. Dist. Ct. (mid. dist.) N.C., Winston-Salem, 1965-66; dir. Legal Aid Soc. Forsyth County, 1966-69; exec. dir. Forsyth Bail Project, 1968-69, Lawyer Referral Svc. of Bar of 21st Jud. Dist., Winston-Salem, 1968-69; staff atty. office of gen. counsel FAA, Washington, 1969-70, acting chief admin. & legal resources, 1970-71; staff atty. office of gen. counsel Dept. Housing & Urban Devel., 1971, counsel Jackson (Miss.) area office, 1971-83, chief counsel Jackson (Miss.) field office, 1983-94; chief counsel Office Gen. Counsel Miss., Jackson, 1994—; HUD del. Miss. Fed. Exec. Assn., 1997—. Lectr. U. W.Va. Conf. on Poverty Law, 1968; program svcs. adviser, 2000—. Editor N.C. Legal Aid Reporter, 1968-69, N.C. Legal Aid Directory, 1968, Avlex Legal Index (2nd supplement), 1971, developed Miss. low income housing financing mechanism 1975-76; contbr articles to profl. jours., articles to splty. mags. Dem. candidate N.C. Ho. of Reps., Guilford County, 1964; mem. mil. com. Forsyth County N.C. Red Cross, 1967-68; pack leader Andrew Jackson coun. Boy Scouts Am., 1986-92; active Project Adv. Group U.S. Office Econ. Opportunity Legal Svcs. Program, 1968-69, Adv. Com. on Housing & Urban Devel., Miss., Law Rsch. Inst., 1980-81, Pilot Mountain Preservation & Park Com., Winston-Salem, 1968-70; mem. Race Com. Whitworth Hunt Races, 1973-76; Am. Master of Foxhounds Assn., 1976-79; adv. Order DeMolay, 1997—; sec. Miss Scottish Games, 1999—; patron Miss. Church #366, 1999-2000. Capt. AUS, 1960-65; ret. lt. col. USAR, 1966-87. Decorated Meritorious Svc. medal, Army Commendation medal with oak leaf cluster, Army Res. Forces Achievement medal with three oak leaf clusters, Nat. Def. Svc. medal, Armed Forces Res. medal; named Hon. Knight Mason, 1999. Mem. NRA, Fed. Bar Assn., N.C. State Bar, Miss. Hist. Assn., Miss. Track Club, Iron Bridge Hunt (v.p. 1964-65), Whitworth Hunt (founder, master of foxhounds 1975-76), The Austin Hunt (joint master of foxhounds 1976-79), Caledonian Soc. Miss., Sons of Confederate Vets., Mason (sec. 1999—, 32 degree), KT, Order Eastern Star, Shriner, Rosicrucian, Capital Club (Jackson, Mo.), Pi Gamma Mu. Republican. Episcopal. Avocations: riding to hounds, running, book collecting. Home: 499 Pear Orchard Rd # 6-C Ridgeland MS 39157 Office: Miss State Dept Housing & Urban Devel Fed Bldg 100 W Capitol 9th Flr Jackson MS 39269

MOJICA, AGNES, academic administrator; Chancellor Inter Am. U. of PR, San German, P.R. Chair governing bd. Hispanic Assn. Colls. and Univs., 1995-96, co-chair leadership group; chair governing bd. Intercollegiate Athletic League, 2001-02. Pres., Consortium of Presidents and Chancellors for the Prevention of the Use and Abuse of Drugs and Alcohol, 1998-2002. Mem., Assn. Industrialists of P.R., Western C. of C., Am. Assn. Higher Edn., Assn. Profl. Women, Altrusa, Rotary (hon.), Alpha Delta Kappa, Phi Delta Kappa. Office: Inter Am U PO Box 5100 San German PR 00683-9801 E-mail: amojica@sg.inter.edu.

MOJTABAI, ANN GRACE, author, educator; b. N.Y.C., June 8, 1937; d. Robert and Naomi (Friedman) Alpher; m. Fathollah Mojtabai, Apr. 27, 1960 (div. 1966); children: Chitra, Ramin. BA in Philosophy, Antioch Coll., 1958; MA in Philosophy, Columbia U., 1968, MS in L.S., 1970. Lectr. philosophy Hunter Coll., CUNY, 1966-68; librarian CCNY, 1970-76; fellow Radcliffe Inst. Ind. Study, Cambridge, Mass., 1976-78; Briggs-Copeland lectr. on English Harvard U., 1978-83; writer-in-residence U. Tulsa, 1983—, Yaddo Found., Saratoga, N.Y., 1975, 76. Author: Mundome, 1974, The 400 Eels of Sigmund Freud, 1976, A Stopping Place, 1979, Autumn, 1982, Blessed Assurance, 1986, Ordinary Time, 1989, Called Out, 1994, Soon: Tales From Hospice, 1998. Recipient Richard and Hinda Rosenthal award Am. Acad. and Inst. Arts and Letters, 1983, Lillian Smith award So. Regional Council, 1986, Lit. Acad. award AAAL, 1993; Guggenheim fellow, 1981-82 Mem. PEN, Mark Twain Soc., Tex. Inst. Letters, Phi Beta Kappa Home: 2329 Woodside Drive Amarillo TX 79124-1036 Office: U Tulsa Dept English 600 S College Ave Tulsa OK 74104-3126 E-mail: ann_mojtabai@utulsa.edu., Agmojtabai@aol.com.

MOK, CARSON KWOK-CHI, structural engineer; b. Canton, China, Jan. 17, 1932; came to U.S., 1956, naturalized, 1962; s. King and Chi-Big (Lum) M.; m. Virginia Wai-Ching Cheng, Sept. 19, 1959. BSCE, Chu Hai U., Hong Kong, 1953; M.C.E., Cath. U. Am., 1968. Registered profl. engr., Md., D.C. Structural designer Wong Cho Tong, Hong Kong, 1954-56; bridge designer Michael Baker Jr., Inc., College Park, Md., 1957-60; structural engr., chief design engr., assoc. Milton A. Gurewitz Assocs., Washington, 1961-65; ptnr. Wright & Mok, Silver Spring, Md., 1966-75; owner Carson K.C. Mok, Cons. Engr., 1976-81, pres., 1982—. Facility engring. cons. Washington Met. Area Transit Authority, 1985-86; pres. Transp. Engring. and Mgmt. Assocs., P.C., Washington, 1986—; adj. asst. prof. Howard U., Washington, 1976-79, adj. assoc. prof., 1980-81. Contbr. articles to profl. jours. Bd. dirs. U.S. Pan Asian Am. C. of C. Sec.; N.Am. trustee China Grad. Sch. Theology, Wayne, Pa., 1972-74, pres., 1975-83, v.p., 1984-91; elder Chinese Bible Ch. Md., Rockville, 1978-80; chmn. Chinese Christian Ch. Greater Washington, 1958-61, 71, elder, 1972-76; dir. Evergreen Family Friendship Svc., Inc., A Pub. Benefit Corp., Colorado Springs, 1993—. Recipient Outstanding Std. of Tchg. award Howard U., 1980, Nat. Merit award U.S. Dept. Transp., 2000. Mem. ASCE, ASTM, Constrn. Specification Inst., Nat. Assn. Corrosion Engrs., Concrete Reinforcing Steel Inst., Am. Inst. Steel Constrn., Am. Concrete Inst., Am. Welding Soc., Prestressed Concrete Inst., Post-Tensioning Inst., Soc. Exptl. Mechanics, Internat. Assn. Bridge and Structural Engring., Pui Ching Mid. Sch. Alumni Assn. (pres. nation's capital chpt. 1991-97). Home: 4405 Bestor Dr Rockville MD 20853-2137 Office: 9001 Ottawa Pl Silver Spring MD 20910-2257 E-mail: ckm9001@aol.com.

MOK, SAMUEL T. federal agency administrator; Grad., Fordham U.; M Acctg., Cath. U., Washington. Chief fin. officer, comptroller U.S. Treasury Dept.; CEO GL Assocs.; mng. mem. Condor Cons., LLC; chief fin. officer U.S. Dept. Labor, Washington, 2002—. With U.S. Army. Decorated Meritorious Unit Citation, Meritorious Svc. medal; recipient James Saylor award Outstanding Svc., Assn. Goovt. Accts., Washington. Office: US Dept Labor 200 Constitution AVe NW Washington DC 20210*

MOK, YUE-PANG, anesthesiologist; b. China, May 6, 1948; MD, Taiwan U., Taipei, 1972. Diplomate Am. Bd. Anesthesia with added qualification in pain mgmt., Am. Bd. Pain Medicine. Intern Barberton Citizens Hosp., 1973-74, resident in gen. practice, 1974-76; resident in anesthesiology Aultman Hosp., Canton, Ohio, 1983-85; resident in pain mgmt. U. Va., 1985; staff Barberton Citizens Hosp., Wadsworth-Rittman Hosp., Wadsworth, Medina (Ohio) Gen. Hosp. Mem. AMA, Am. Acad. Med. Acupuncture, Am. Soc. Anesthesiologists, Am. Acad. Pain Mgmt. (bd. cert.), Ohio State Med. Assn. Office: 3593 S Arlington Rd Ste C Akron OH 44312-5271

MOKHTARZADEH, AHMAD AGHA, agronomist, consultant; b. Fassa, Fars, Iran, Oct. 23, 1933; came to U.S., 1989; s. Mohamad Hassan and Assieh (Kadivar) M.; m. Brigitte Becker, Nov. 12, 1960; 1 child, Mitra. BSc, BA, U. Tehran, Iran, 1956; MSc, U. Md., 1960; PhD, U. Paris, France, 1964. Assoc. prof. Shiraz U., Iran, 1964-80; cons. S. Pacifc regions Somalia, Vietnam, Namibia Food and Agrl. Orgn. U.N., Rome, 1981-89; cons. pvt. practice Leesburg, Va., 1990—. Mem. Pres. Program Com. Shiraz U., Iran, 1977-79; advisor German Remote Sensing in Agrl., Somalia, 1984; officer-in-charge Food Agrl. Orgn., U.N., Western Samoa, 1985. Co-author: Bibliography of Natural History of Iran, 1965; contbr. articles to profl. jours. including Crop Sci., Der Züchter, Nematologia Mediterranea. Recipient 4-yr. scholarship Govt. of Iran, 1958-62, 2-yr. scholarship Govt. of France, 1962-64, Fulbright fellowship N.D. State U., 1968-69, Rsch. fellowship, Energy Rsch. and Devel., Oak Ridge, Tenn., 1976-77. Mem. Am. Soc. Agronomy, Sigma Xi. Home and Office: 141 Davis Ave SW Leesburg VA 20175-3405 E-mail: gitteahmadagha@juno.com.

MOKODEAN, MICHAEL JOHN, lawyer, accountant; b. Canton, Ohio, Dec. 24, 1923; s. Michael and Elizabeth (Stroia) M.; m. Jean Cristea, Apr. 17, 1950 (dec.); children: Michael Dan, Christine Ann; m. Josephine Woodward, Jan. 28, 1995. BS in Edn, Kent (Ohio) State U., 1948; JD, William McKinley Sch. Law, Canton, 1955. Bar: Ohio 1955; C.P.A., Ohio. Agt. IRS, Canton, 1950-56; self-employed atty. C.P.A., 1957-69; tax accountant Elmer Fox & Co., Las Vegas, Nev., 1969; mgr. tax and ins. Diebold, Inc., Canton, 1969-74, sec., house counsel, 1974-78, v.p. legal, 1978-87, cons., 1987-89. Part-time instr. tax accounting Walsh Coll., N. Canton, 1963-64, bd. advisers, 1976— ;

bd. advisers Stark Tech. Coll., Canton, 1972-76 Bd. advisers Doctors' Hosp., Massillon, Ohio, 1986-93. With AUS, 1943-46. Mem. Brookside Country Club. Roman Catholic. Home: 2607 Charing Cross Rd NW Canton OH 44708-1588

MOKOTOFF, MICHAEL, pharmaceutical sciences educator; b. Bklyn., Jan. 23, 1939; s. Jack Israel and Pauline (Hochberg) M.; m. Bonnie Faith Arieff, Apr. 22, 1967; children: Jeffrey David, Naomi Joy, Jay Daniel. BS in Pharmacy, Columbia U., 1960; MS, U. Wis., 1963, PhD, 1966. Cert. pharmacist, N.Y. Fellow NIH, Bethesda, Md., 1966-68; asst. prof. U. Pitts., 1968-72; vis. scientist Weizmann Inst. Sci., Rehovot, Israel, 1978; assoc. prof. medicinal chemistry U. Pitts., 1972-85, assoc. prof. pharm. scis., 1985-95, prof. pharm. scis., 1995—. Mem. Pa. Drug, Device and Cosmetic Bd., Harrisburg, 1990-98. Editor, author: (with others) Pharmacokinetics and Pharmacodynamics Vol. 3: Peptides, Peptoids and Proteins, 1991; mem. editl. bd. Jour. Peptide Rsch.; contbr. articles to Jour. Protein Rsch., Jour. Medicinal Chemistry, Jour. Peptide Rsch.; contbr. chpt. to Principles of Medicinal Chemistry, 5th edit., 2002. Fellow Agy. Indsl. Sci. Tech., Tokyo, 1997. Mem. Am. Assn. Colls. Pharmacy, Am. Chem. Soc., Am. Assn. Cancer Rsch., Am. Assn. Pharm. Scientists. Achievements include patent for novel peptidyl amino steroids. Office: U Pitts 736 Salk Hl Pittsburgh PA 15261-0001 E-mail: moagie@pitt.edu.

MOKRASCH, LEWIS CARL, neurochemist, educator; b. St. Paul, May 9, 1930; s. Lewis and Anna (Dvorak) M.; m. Jane Carolyn Church, Apr. 20, 1974. BS magna cum laude, Coll. St. Thomas, 1952; PhD, U. Wis., 1955. Rsch. assoc. dept. psychiatry and neurology La. State U. Med. Center, New Orleans, 1956-57, assoc. prof. dept. biochemistry, 1971-76, prof., 1976-92, prof. emeritus, 1992—, acting head dept., 1978-79. Instr. medicine U. Kans. Med. Center, Kansas City, 1957-59, assoc. in medicine, dir. neurochemistry lab., 1959-62; asst. biochemist McLean Hosp., Belmont, Mass., 1960-64, assoc. biochemist, 1964-71; assoc. dept. biol. chemistry Harvard Med. Sch., Boston, 1964-67; asst. prof., 1967-71; adj. assoc. prof. biology Hellenic Coll., Brookline, Mass., 1969-71; staff scientist Neurosciences Research Programs, Brookline, 1970-71; vis. prof. neurology Duke U. Med. Center, 1981-82; lectr. in field Author book written on myelin; contbr. articles to profl. jours.; reviewer: jours. Sci., FASEB. Res. Belmont Preservation Soc., 1969; candidate Bd. Selectman, Belmont, 1969; active Forsyth County Adult Care Home Cmty. Adv. Com., Hospice, Sr. Fin. Care, Winston-Salem, Piedmont Opera Guild, Winston Salem Piedmont Triad Symphony Guild, Reynolda Ho. Mus. Am. Art, Reynolda Gardens, Sr. Svcs. Program, Winston Salem, Citizens Quality Nursing Home Care, 1991-92; sr. leader Duke Long Term Care Program. Grantee NIMH, 1973-74, Nat. Inst. Neurol. Disability and Blindness, 1957-90, Schlieder Found., 1971-72, 83-84, La. Bd. Regents, 1986-88. Fellow Am. Assn. Clin. Chemists; mem. AAUP, Am. Soc. Neurochemistry (local chmn. 1974), Am. Soc. Biol. Chemists, Soc. Neurosci. (founder, pres. local chpt. 1974-75), Soc. Rsch. Adminstrs. (membership chmn. New Eng. sect.), Nat. Citizens Coalition Nursing Home Reform, Am. Assn. Individual Investors (founder, past pres., sec. Piedmont chpt.), Peoples Med. Soc. Libertarian. Achievements include first demonstration of adaptive enzyme regulation in animals and allosteric control of fructose bisphosphatase, of incorporation of hydrouracil into transfer RNA, of thermogenic mechanism for arousing hibernators, of metabolic control in hibernation, of altered hydrophobic proteins in neurological disorders, of biosynthesis of hydrophobic proteins and mitochondrial proteins in brain in vitro, of altered transport processes in cells of neurological disease victims, of defective transport of acetylcholine precursors into cells of Alzheimer's victims and that such transport is modulatable; development of coestimation method for ketoses, aldoses, and pentoses; first isolation in pure form of receptor hydrophobic proteins from mammalian brain. Home: 2711 Pilgrim Ct Winston Salem NC 27106 E-mail: DrLewMokasch@cs.com. *Before I entered Science, I regarded it as a Priesthood of individuals dedicated to the service of humanity, whose common goal was the enhancement of human life and the remedying of its ills. After 30 years in Science, I hold this thesis more strongly and have found many colleagues who agree with it. I am certain now that the failures and abuses of Science derive from the use of it for the goals of wealth, fame and power.*

MOKRZECKI, LECH MARIAN, history of education educator; b. Warsaw, Poland, Apr. 5, 1935; s. Justyn and Irena (Druhowino) M.; m. Aleksandra Maria Horbowska, Aug. 20, 1983. MA, U. Toruń, Poland, 1956; dipl. cellist, Acad. Music, Gdańsk, Poland, 1962, MA, 1964; PhD, Higher Sch. Pedagogy, Gdańsk, Poland, 1967; DrHabil, U. Gdańsk, Poland, 1975; PhD (hon.), Linköping U., 1998. From asst. to prof. extraordinary Gdańsk U., Poland, 1966-92, prof. ordinary, 1993—. Author: Three Centuries of Gdansk Learning, 1969, 2d edit., 1976, The Study of the Teaching of History, 1973, In the Sphere of the Work of Gdansk Historians in XVII Century, 1974 (Min. of Edn. award 1976), The Beginning of the Knowledge of the Sea in the Former Kingdom of Poland, 1983, The Fortress Vistulamouth, 1978, Traditions of Teaching History to the Close of XVI Century-Selected Countries and Problems, 1992 (Min. of Edn. award 1993), From the Tradition of Teaching History to the End of 16th Century, 1992, Science and Education in Former Polish Republic, 2001; co-author, editor: In the Sphere of Culture, Music, Ballet, 1971 (Min. of Culture award 1972), Scientific Copy Books of Gdansk University, Pedagogy History of Education, 1993, 97; co-author: A Significant Social Revolution, 1994. Head, History of Social Sci. Commn., Policy Acad. Sci. Mem. Assn. Internat. pour History of Edn. Belgium, Com. Internat. Scis. History, Commn. History of Historiography Italy, Polish Acad. Scis. (History of Sci. and Tech. com.). Roman Catholic. Avocations: travel, reading poetry. Home: Biała 6-28 80-435 Gdańsk Poland Office: Gdansk U Inst Pedagogy B Krzywoustego 19 80-952 Gdańsk Poland

MOLAD, CLARISSE BEHAR, writer, consultant; b. Jerusalem, June 11, 1951; arrived in U.S., 1973; d. Israel and Draga Behar; m. Ofer Molad, Sept. 9, 1972 (div. May 1987); children: Leital, Danny, Shelley, Mickey. B, Ben Gurion U., Beer Sheva, Israel, 1973; M, U. North Tex., 1975; PhD, Union Inst. & U., Cin., 1996. Pres. Softex, Houston, 1983—85; gen. mgr. SAGA Mgmt. Info. Sys., 1986—88; bus. analyst MW Kellogg, 1988—90; R&D specialist Bechtel Corp., 1990—93; v.p. Plant STEP, Inc., 1993—95, Data Xchange Technologies, Houston, 1995—97; pres. CBM Cons., 1997—. Chair Houston Women in Tech. Forum, Houston, 1999—; bd. dirs. Women in Tech. Internat., Houston. Contbr. articles. Founder Technitude Competition for Girls; pres. Assn. Women in Computing, Houston, 1999—2000. With Israeli Navy, 1969—71. Named one of Top 20 Women in Tech., Assn. Women in Computing, 1999. Democrat. Jewish. Avocations: travel, reading, scuba diving, dancing. Home: 8106 Meadow Crest St Houston TX 77071-3633

MOLANDER, GLENN M. human resources executive; b. L.A., Feb. 26, 1940; s. Glenn M. and Ethel Louise (Reicherter) M.; m. Barbara H. Fanderlik, June 21, 1960 (div. Aug. 1964); 1 child, Lloyd Bryan Molander-Adams; m. Sara Rahauser, Apr. 18, 1974; 1 child, Leif Douglas. BA in Bus. Adminstrn., U. Hawaii, 1984; Cert. in Mgmt., Kauai C.C., 1978. Mgr. data processing Dyn Corp., Barking Sands, Hawaii, 1971-86, mgr. range ops., 1986-87, mgr. human resources Holloman AFB, N.Mex., 1987-92, mgr. adminstrv. svcs., 1992-94, mgr. human resources, 1994-97; mgr. timing sys. N.Mex. Tech. Group, LLC, White Sands Missile Range, 1997—. Mem. vocat. adv. bd. Kauai C.C., Lihue, 1984; mem. Hawaii Libr. Commn., 1985-87; mem. budget and allocations com. United Way of Otero County, N.Mex., 1990-91; pres. West Kauai Rotary, 1981-82. Recipient Bronze award United Way of Otero County, 1991. Mem. Nat. Contract Mgmt. Assn. (pres. 1995-96), So. N.Mex. Soc. Human Resources Mgmt. (Pinicle award 1995-96), Assn. of U.S. Army, Kiwanis. Avocations: skiing, camping, hiking, computers. Home: PO Box 1831 Alamogordo NM 88311-1831 Office: New Tec PO Box 398 White Sands Missile Range NM 88002 E-mail: molandeg@newtec.wsmr.army.mil.

MOLBEGOTT, LESTER PHILIP, anesthesiologist; b. N.Y.C., Sept. 28, 1949; MD, NYU, 1978. Diplomate Am. Bd. Anesthesiology, Am. Bd. Internal Medicine. Intern Albany Med. Ctr., 1978-79, resident internal medicine, 1979-81; resident anesthesiology U. Va. Med. Ctr., Charlottesville, 1983-85; anesthesiologist Monmouth Med. Ctr., Long Branch, N.J.; clin. asst. prof. Allegheny U. Health Scis., 1985—; pvt. practice Monmouth Beach, N.J., 1985—. Mem. Am. Soc. Anesthesiologists, Am. Soc. Critical Care Anesthesiologists, Internat. Anesthesia Rsch. Soc., N.J. State Soc. Anesthesiologists.

MOLDEN, A(NNA) JANE, counselor; b. Weeping Water, Nebr. BS, Schauffler Coll.; MA, Princeton (N.J.) Theol. Sem. Cert. adminstr., Iowa. Dir. outreach Chgo. City Union; dir. campus ministry Iowa State U., Ames; dir. Christian edn. 1st Congl. Ch.; dir. community outreach Congl. Chs., Kansas City, Mo.; ctrl. regional dir. Am. Friends Svc., Des Moines; dir. acad. support counseling Grand View Coll.; dir. Consortium of Higher Edn. Mem. Health Planing Coun. Ctrl. Iowa; mem. Gov.'s Vocat. Rehab. Adv. Coun., 1993—; mem. Protection and Adv. Pair Adv. Coun., 1993—; bd. dirs. Iowa Protection and Adv. Bd. Dir. Grand View Coll. Dems., 1971-93; active devel. com. for handicapped HUD, Des Moines; bd. dirs. Plymouth Pl.; mem. Dr. Martin Luther King Com., Des Moines, Internat. Black Children's Conf., Iowa Vocat. Rehab. Coun., Iowa Protection and Adv. Coun.; chair Des Moines Human Rights Commn.; mem. study com. LWV; past pres. Citizens Disability Coun.; mem. community adv. bd. McKinley Sch.; mem. George Washington Carver com. Simpson Coll.; bd. dirs. Bernie Lorenz House, Community Focus, Greater Des Moines YWCA, Christian Ednl. Plymouth Congl. Ch.; bd. dirs. Youth Incentives. Named Outstanding Educator Jack and Jill, Inc., Des Moines, Supporting Friend, Learning Disability Coun. Ctrl. Iowa. Mem. AACD, Torch Club Internat. (pres.), Delta Kappa Gamma. Democrat. Mem. United Ch. of Christ.

MOLDENHAUER, JUDITH A. graphic design educator; b. Oak Park, Ill., Feb. 28, 1951; d. Raymond L. and Jean Marie (Carqueville) M. BFA, U. Ill., 1973; MA, Stanford U., 1974; MFA, U. Wis., 1977. Design supr. N.E. Mo. State U., Kirksville, Mo., 1977-79; asst. prof. design, design dept. Kans. City Art Inst., 1979-83; asst. prof. art, graphic design Sch. Art U. Mich., Ann Arbor, 1983-92; vis. lectr. Wayne State U., 1990-92, asst. prof. graphic design, 1992-98, assoc. prof. graphic design, 1998—, area coord. graphic design, 1992—. Free-lance designer The Detroit Inst. Arts, Toledo (Ohio) Mus. Art, Burroughs Corp. (Unisys) Detroit, Detroit Focus Gallery; vis. designer N.S. Coll. Art and Design, 1986; juror Ohio Mus. Assn., 1986, Collaborator Presdl. Initiative "Healthy Start": prenatal and pre-conceptional booklets and ednl. modules designs, 1992—; presenter 8th Internat. Congress Women's Health Issues, U. Sask., 1997, 9th Internat. Congress on Women's Health Issues, Alexandria, Egypt, 1998, Internat. Inst. Info. Design, Schwarzenberg, Austria, 1998, Read Me exhbn., Bern, Switzerland, 1999, Expert Forum Manual Design, Malardalen U., Eskilstuna, Sweden, 2000; co-prin. investigator FIPSE grantee Dept. Edn., 2000; participant Read Me exhbn., Winterthur, Switzerland, 1999, 19th Biennale Graphic Design, Brno, Czech Rep., Nat. Inst. Design, Ahmenbad, India, 2000. Contbr. articles to profl. jours. Recipient award of distinction, merit award Am. Assn. Museums, 1985, 86, Excellence Design award Beckett Paper Co., 1991, gold award for softcover books Printing & Pub. Competition, 1994, Am. Graphic Design award, 1996, 98; Rackham grantee U. Mich., 1987, grantee Nat. Endowment for Arts, 1988. Mem. Am. Ctr. Design, Univ. and Coll. Designers Assn. (merit award 1979, gold award 1979), Coll. Art Assn. (chmn. panel 1991), Women's Caucus for Art (panel chmn. 1987), Amnesty Internat., Women in Design (excellence award Chgo. 1985, Sierra Club, Audubon Soc. Lutheran. Office: Wayne State U Dept Art and Art History 150 Art Bldg Detroit MI 48202 E-mail: FrogBoddg@aol.com.

MOLDENHAUER, NANCY A. social worker, consultant, educator; BSEd, Valparaiso U., 1976; MSW, cert. specialist in aging, U. Mich., 1984. Instr. Meiji Gakuin and Tokyo Med. and Dental U., 1977-81; corp. communication trainer Saito Internat., Inc., Tokyo, 1981-82; conf. coord. Ctr. for Japanese Studies U. Mich., Ann Arbor, 1982-84; gerontol. social worker Turner Geriatric Clinic U. Mich. Hosps., 1983-84; med. social worker Mo. Bapt. Med. Ctr., St Louis, 1985-88; geriatric social work specialist Program on Aging Jewish Hosp. Wash. U. Med. Ctr., St. Louis, 1988-92; dir. case mgmt. and corp. svcs. Aging Consult, 1993-95. Adj. prof. Wash. U., St. Louis, 1991-95; trainee in aging NIH, 1983-84; dir. Nat. Adult Day Svc. Assn., Nat. Coun. Aging, Washington, 1995-96; registration mgr. Landmark Edn. Corp., Alexandria, Va., 1997-98. Co-author: Positive Attitudes, Positive Aging: A Guide for Positive Actions in Later Life, NASDA Curriculum for Directors and Administrators, Adult Day Services - The Next Frontier, Handbook of Home Health Care Administration. Del. White House Conf. Aging, 1995. Named OWL Woman of Worth, 1993. Mem. Nat. Assn. Social Workers, Acad. Cert. Social Workers, Gerontol. Soc. Am., Am. Soc. Aging, Nat. Coun. on Aging, Alzheimer's Assn., Older Women's League (local bd. dirs., pres. 1991-95, nat. bd. dirs., v.p. 1993-96), Challenge Metro (bd. dirs., pres. 1986-90). Avocations: gourmet cooking, restaurants, wine, fishing, gardening. Office: 107 Kaye Ln Michigan City IN 46360-1730

MOLDENHAUER, WILLIAM CALVIN, soil scientist; b. New Underwood, S.D., Oct. 27, 1923; s. Calvin Fred and Ida (Killam) M.; m. Catherine Ann Maher, Nov. 26, 1947; children— Jean Ann, Patricia, Barbara, James, Thomas BS, S.D. State U., 1949; MS, U. Wis., 1951, PhD, 1956. Soil surveyor S.D. State U., Brookings, 1948-54; soil scientist U.S. Dept. Agr., Big Spring, Tex., 1954-57, soil. scientist Ames, Iowa, 1957-72, Morris, Minn., 1972-75; rsch. leader Nat. Soil Erosion Rsch. Lab., Agrl. Rsch. Svc. U.S. Dept. Agr., West Lafayette, Ind., 1975-85; prof. dept. agronomy Purdue U., 1975-85, prof. emeritus, 1985—. Contbr. articles to profl. jours. Served with U.S. Army, 1943-46 Fellow Am. Soc. Agronomy, Soil Sci. Soc., Soil Conservation Soc. Am. (pres. 1979), World Assn. Soil and Water Conservation (pres. 1983-85, exec. sec. 1985—). Home and Office: 317 Marvin Ave Volga SD 57071-2011

MOLDER, SYBIL AILENE, occupational health nurse; b. Djakarta, Indonesia, Nov. 27, 1945; came to U.S., 1960; d. Douglas Gordon and Frederika (Dykstra) Ebert; m. Enno Molder, June 24, 1967; children: Sonja, Ingrid. Student, Northeastern U., 1964-66; AS with honors, Tunxis Community Coll., 1980. RN, Conn.; cert. occupational hearing conservationist. Staff nurse Meriden-Wallingford (Conn.) Hosp., 1980-85; occupational health nurse The Napier Co., Meriden, 1985-88; clin. coord. Miller Meml. Community Ctr., 1988-90; clin. dir. Conn. Occupational Healthcenters, No. Haven, Milford, Conn., 1990-95; team leader State of Conn. Unit 2 Berkley Care, Farmington, 1996—2001; occupational health nurse Cytec Industries, Inc. , Wallingford, 2001—. Recipient Cert. of Recognition YWCA, 1987. Mem. Occupational Health Nurse's Orgn., Conn. Safety Soc. (v.p. 1987-88). Home: 136 Knob Hill Rd Meriden CT 06451-4930

MOLDOFF, WILLIAM MORRIS, retired lawyer; b. Phila., Jan. 1, 1921; s. David and Pauline (Arcusin) Moldoff; m. Doris Elaine Johnson (dec.); children: Phillip Douglas, Laura Ellen, Janet Susan Sayers, Allan William. BA, U. Iowa, 1943; JD cum laude, U. Miami, 1950; LLM, U. Mich., 1955. Law editor Lawyers Coop. Pub. Co., Rochester, N.Y., 1952-54, 57-60; instr. Ohio Northern U. Coll. of Law, 1955-57; proofreader N.Y. Codes, Rules and Regulations State of N.Y., 1960, adminstrv. asst. to exec. dep. Sec. of State, 1961-63; pvt. practice Nassau, N.Y., 1963-66; veterans claims examiner, rating bd. Vets. Adminstrn. Regional, N.Y.C., 1966-85; ret., 1985. Lt (jg) USNR, 1943—46. Republican. Jewish. Home: 2 Phillips St #151 Nassau NY 12123-0151

MOLDWIN, ROBERT, physician, urologist; BS, Adelphi U., Garden City, N.Y., 1980; MD, U. Chgo., 1984. Chief resident urology L.I. Jewish Med. Ctr., New Hyde Park, N.Y., 1984-90; urology fellow Thomas Jefferson Med. Coll., 1990-91; attending asst. prof. urology Albert Einstein Coll. Medicine, 1991—. Med. adv. bd. I. C. Assn., 1997—; cons. Med. Ctr., 1997—; reviewer jours. in field, Infectious/Inflammatory Urol. Diseases, Long Island Jewish Med. Ctr. Author: The Interstitial Cystitis Survival Guide, 2000; contbr. articles to profl. jours., chpts. to books; lectr. in field. Mem. AMA (Physician's Recognition award), Am. Microbiological SOc., Am. Urological Assn., Am. Assn. Clin. Urologists, Am. Urological Allied Assn., Am. Coll. Surgeons, Interstitial Cystitis Assn., Nassau Cty. Med. Soc., Nassau Cty. Acad. Medicine, Soc. Basic Urologic Rsch., N.Y. Acad. Medicine. Avocations: fishing, bicycling, boating, hiking. Office: L.I. Jewish Med. Ctr. Dept. Urology-260-05 76th New Hyde Park NY 11040

MOLE, RICHARD JAY, accounting company executive; b. Berea, Ohio, Aug. 10, 1951; s. Wells Warren Jr. and Helen Irene (Buse) M.; m. Kathleen Ann Brennan, Oct. 28, 1978; children: Kevin Michael, Eileen Anne. BBA, U. Notre Dame, 1973; MBA, U. Pitts., 1974. CPA, Ohio, Pa.; CMA, CFM. Staff acct. James P. Ross, CPA, Elyria, Ohio, 1974-75; mgr. acctg. Dean J. Benshoff, PA, Mogadore, 1975-77, John P. Hyland, CPA, Cleve., 1980; fin. adminstr. St. Joseph Ch. and Sts. Joseph and John Interparochial Sch., Strongsville, Ohio, 1977-80; v.p., contr. Citadel Alarm, Inc. div. Revco Drug Stores, Inc., Cleve., 1980-82; pres. Richard J. Mole, CPA, Inc., Andover, Ohio, 1982—. Instr. Lorain County Cmty. Coll., 1975. Chmn. bldg. com., v.p. Andover Pub. Libr., 1983—; mem. Ashtabula County Bd. Mental Retardation, Ashtabula, Ohio, 1987-89; chmn. fin. com. parish coun. Our Lady of Victory Cath. Ch., Andover, 1985-90; bd. dirs. Ashtabula County 503 Corp., 1986-92, pres., 1990-92; bd. dirs. Ashtabula County Revolving Loan Fund, 1986-92, pres., 1990-92; treas., bd. dirs. Civic Devel. Corp. Ashtabula County, 1994—; mem. Leadership Ashtabula County, 1989, grad. charter class; bd. dirs. Pymatuning Area Indsl. Devel. Corp., Andover, pres., 1986-88, 93-94; chmn. Andover Twp. Zoning Commn., 1989-94, mem., 1995, sec., 1996; treas. Andover Civic Improvement Corp., 1992-96, 97—, pres., 1996-97; treas. Andover Found., Inc., 1993—; coach, mgr. Pymatuning Area Youth Orgn., 1987-91, 95, 97-98, pres., 1991-92. Recipient leadership award Civic Devel. Corp., Ashtabula, 1985, Quality of Living award Pymatuning Area Indsl. Devel. Corp., 1986, Best of County award Ashtabula County Growth Partnership, 1992, Leadership award State of Ohio, 1993. Fellow AICPA, Ohio Soc. CPAs, Pa. Inst. CPAs; mem. Inst. Mgmt. Accts., Rotary Internat. (bd. dirs. Andover 1984—, pres. 1985-86, 96-97, treas. 1988-96, 98-99, 2000--, sec. 1987-88, 99-2000, Paul Harris fellow 1993, benefactor Rotary Found. 1999), Andover C. of C. (v.p. 1983-85, treas. 1985-87). Republican. Office: Richard J Mole CPA Inc PO Box 1270 124 S Main St Andover OH 44003-9601 E-mail: rmole@molecpa.com, numbersrus@molecpa.com.

MOLEN, JOHN KLAUMINZER, lawyer; b. Gary, Ind., June 13, 1952; s. Franklin B. and Jane Anne (Klauminzer) M.; m. Susan Wilson Blair, Aug. 10, 1985; children: Mary Wilson, Elisabeth Blair. AB with honors, U. N.C., 1974, MBA, JD with honors, U. N.C., 1978. Bar: Ala. 1978. Assoc. Bradley Arant Rose & White LLP, Birmingham, Ala., 1978-84, ptnr., 1984—. Mem. Rotary Club Birmingham-Sunrise. Presbyterian. Avocations: sailing, swimming. Office: Bradley Arant Rose & White LLP One Federal Pl 1819 5th Ave N Birmingham AL 35203-2104 E-mail: jmolen@bradleyarant.com.

MOLENBEEK, ROBERT GERRIT, accountant, realtor; b. Grand Rapids, Mich., Feb. 7, 1944; s. Gerrit John and Jean (Wierenga) M.; m. Marsha Lee Rockel, Mar. 23, 1966; children: Rebecca, Tammy, Brian, Brent. AS in Bus. Adminstrn. with honors, Davenport Coll., 1964; BBA in Acctg. with honors, Ferris State U., 1966; MBA, Grand Valley State U., 1976. CPA, Mich.; cert. comml. investment mem.; cert. exch. consular; cert. buyer broker; cert. internat. property specialist; accredited land consular. Staff acct. various firms, Grand Rapids, 1969-72; staff acct., ptnr. Tuori Jacobson, CPA, Muskegon, Mich., 1972-73; sr. internal auditor Wolverine Worldwide, Rockford, 1973-75; pvt. practice acctg. Grand Rapids, 1975—; controller Sq. Real Estate, 1976-87, real estate salesman, 1976—. Cons. Property Corp. Am., 1976-94, S & S Supplies, Grand Rapids, 1986—, Ea. Gardens, Inc., 1987-89. Active West Mich. R.R. Hist. Soc., Grand Rapids, 1986—, Muskegon R.R. Hist. Soc., 1985—, Trade exch. Am., 1985—; active Realtors Land Inst., 1987—, dir., 1990, sec.-treas., 1990-91, v.p. 1992, pres., 1993, 95, nat. gov.-at-large, 1991—, nat. market session com. chmn. 1995, nat. v.p. fin. 1996, 97; gov. Comml. Indsl. Group Mich. Assn. of Realtors, 1993, chmn.-elect, 1995, chmn. 1996. Mem. AICPA, Mich. Assn. CPAs, Nat. Assn. Realtors (internat. sect.), Mich. Assn. Realtors, Grand Rapids Assn. Realtors (mem. comm./indsl. com. 1989-92), Grand Rapids Exchangers and Traders, Comml. Investment Real Estate Inst. (Multimillion Sales award 1976—, Ten Million Sales award 1980, Top Ten Sales award 1980), Internat. Real Estate Fedn., Mich. Bus. Brokers Assn., Mich. Assn. Real Estate Exchangers (assoc., sec. 1989, pres. 1990), Ind. Real Estate Exchangers (affiliate), Chgo. Area Real Estate Exchangers (affiliate). Avocations: railroads, hunting, railroad antiques dealer. Home: 4440 7 Mile Rd NE Belmont MI 49306-9650 Office: SJ Wisinski & Co 2618 E Paris Ave SE Grand Rapids MI 49546-6137

MOLER, DONALD LEWIS, educational psychology educator; b. Wilsey, Kans., Jan. 12, 1918; s. Ralph Lee and Bessie Myrtle (Berry) M.; B.S., Kans. State Tchrs. Coll., Emporia, 1939; M.S., U. Kans., Lawrence, 1949, Ph.D., 1951; m. Alta Margaret Ansdell, Nov. 6, 1942; 1 son, Donald Lewis Jr. Tchr., Centralia (Kans.) High Sch., 1939-42, Carthage (Mo.) High Sch., 1946-48; asst. dir. Reading Clinic, U. Kans., 1948-51; dir. reading program Ea. Ill. U., 1951-70, prof. dept. ednl. psychology and guidance, 1963— , chmn. dept., 1963-84, dean Sch. Edn., 1980; vis. scholar U. Fla., 1965. Served with Signal Corps, U.S. Army, 1942-46. Recipient C.A. Michelman award, 1974; Disting Svc. award Ill. Assn. Counselor Educators, 1985. Mem. Ill. Guidance and Pers. Assn. (pres. 1968-69), Ill. Counselor Educators and Suprs., Ill. Coll. Pers. Assn., Am. Pers. and Guidance Assn. (senator 1970-71), Assn. Counselor Edn. and Supervision, Assn. Humanistic Edn. and Devel., Phi Delta Kappa, Xi Phi, Pi Omega Pi, Pi Kappa Delta, Sigma Tau Gamma. Methodist. Assoc. editor Ill. Guidance and Pers. Assn. Quar., 1970-84, mng. editor, 1984— . Home: 407 W Hayes Ave Charleston IL 61920-3303 Office: Ea Ill U Dept Ednl Psychology and Guidance Charleston IL 61920

MOLER, EDWARD HAROLD, lawyer; b. Oklahoma City, May 26, 1923; s. Harold Stanley and Rosemary (Callahan) M.; m. Donna Blocksom Cram, Sept. 12, 1964; children: John Frederick, Shelley Elizabeth, Christopher Bryan. BA, U. Okla., 1947, LLB, 1948. Bar: Okla. 1948, U.S. Supreme Ct. 1951. Pvt. practice law, Oklahoma City, 1948-52, 61—; asst. mcpl. counselor, 1952-59; mcpl. counselor, 1959-61; spl. justice Okla. Supreme Ct., 1977. Trustee Oklahoma City Mcpl. Improvement Authority, 1960-61; bd. dirs. Mummers Theatre, Inc., 1969—; bd. dirs. Greater Oklahoma City YMCA, 1981-91. 2d lt. USAAF, 1943-45. Mem. ABA, Okla. Bar Assn., Oklahoma County Bar Assn. (bd. dirs. 1963-67, pres. 1968), Rotary, Phi Delta Phi, Phi Gamma Delta (pres. local chpt. 1946, pres. Nu Omega Housing Assn. 1963-65). Home: 2540 NW Grand Blvd Oklahoma City OK 73116-4110 Office: 204 N Robinson Ste 2800 Oklahoma City OK 73102

MOLER, ELIZABETH ANNE, lawyer; b. Salt Lake City, Jan. 24, 1949; d. Murray McClure and Eleanor Lorraine (Barry) M.; m. Thomas Blake Williams, Oct. 19, 1979; children: Blake Martin Williams, Eleanor Bliss Williams. BA, Am. U., 1971; postgrad., Johns Hopkins U., 1972; JD, George Wash. U., 1977. Bar: D.C. 1978. Chief legis. asst. Senator Floyd Haskell, Washington, 1973-75; law clk. Sharon, Pierson, Semmes, Crolius & Finley, 1975-76; profl. staff mem. com. on energy and natural resources U.S. Senate, 1976-77, counsel, 1977-86, sr. counsel, 1987-88; commr. FERC, 1988-93, chair, 1993-97; dep. sec. Dept. of Energy, 1997-98, acting sec., 1998; ptnr. Vinson & Elkins, 1998-99; sr. v.p. Exelon Corp., 2000—. Mem. ABA, D.C. Bar Assn. Democrat. Office: Exelon Corp Suite 115 701 Pennsylvania Ave NW Washington DC 20004 Home: 1537 Forest Ln Mc Lean VA 22101-3317

MOLHO, LAURA, pathologist; b. Thessaloniki, Greece, Mar. 22, 1933; d. Mordecai and Bella (Counné) M.; m. Joseph Theodore Sard, June 24, 1960 (dec. July 1982); children: Mark, Bonnie. MD, U. of Thessaloniki, 1956. Diplomate Am. Bd. Pathology. Pathologist, assoc. dir. anatomic pathology Queens Hosp. Ctr., L.I. Jewish Med. Ctr., 1965-93; chief of surg. pathology L.I. Jewish Med. Ctr., New Hyde Park, N.Y., 1993-97; pathologist Mineola (N.Y.) Med. Lab., 1997-98, Mineola (N.Y.) Med. Lab. LLC, 1998—. Contbr. articles to profl. jours. Fellow Am. Coll. Pathologists; mem. Med. Soc. of State of N.Y., U.S.-Can. Acad. of Pathology, N.Y. Pathol. Soc. Avocations: music, theatre, reading, travel. Office: Mineola Med Lab LLC 110 Main St Mineola NY 11501-4014 E-mail: lmolho@aol.com.

MOLHOLM, KURT NELSON, federal agency administrator; b. Denver, June 24, 1937; s. Ervin Maurice and Helen Pauline (Nelson) M.; m. Sonja Dell Williams, Aug. 17, 1967; children: Kevin William, Paul Nelson. BS, U. Oreg., 1959; MS, George Washington U., 1974; grad., Indsl. Coll. Armed Forces, 1974. Computer specialist D.L.A. Adminstrv. Support Ctr., Alexandria, Va., 1963-65; with Hdqrs. Def. Logistics Agy., 1965-85, chief planning and policy office, 1975-76, chief ADP/T tech. div., 1984-85; adminstr. Def. Tech. Info. Ctr., 1985—. Pres. Nat. Fedn. Abstracting and Info. Svcs., Phila., 1993-94, treas., 1990-93; del. Va. Govs. Conf. Librs. Info. Svcs., 1990, Fed. Libr. Pre-White House Conf. On Librs. Info. Sci., 1990; vice chmn. Fed. Libr. and Info. Ctr. Com., 1992-93, 2002--; chmn. Commerce, Energy, NASA, NLM, Def. Info. Group, 1991-94, 99-2001; mem. NATO Agard Tech. Info. Panel, 1985-91, Internat. Coun. Sci. and Tech. Info., 1993—, treas., 1998-2001, chair editl. bd., 1999-2001, pres. 2001—; mem. Info. Infrastructure Task Force, 1993-97; chair panel 2 U.S. Nat. Commn. on Librs. and Info. Sci. Comprehensive Assessment of Pub. Info. Dissemination, 2000. 1st lt. U.S. Army,

1960-63. Recipient Meritorious award William A. Jump Meml. Found., 1973. Methodist. Office: Ctr 8725 John J Kingman Rd Fort Belvoir VA 22060-6218 E-mail: kmolholm@dtic.mil., kmolholm@aol.com.

MOLIERE, JEFFREY MICHAEL, cardiopulmonary administrator; b. San Pedro, Calif., Nov. 22, 1948; s. Dwight Hedrick and Geraldine Stabile. AA, L.A. Harbor Coll., 1968; postgrad., Calif. State U., Long Beach, 1968-69; cert. in respiratory care, Calif. Coll. for Health Sci., 1982, Biosystems Inst., 1984; assoc. degree, Ind. U., Indpls., 1987, B in Gen. Studies, 1990; MS in Cmty. Health Adminstrn., Calif. Coll. for Health Sci., 1994; postgrad., So. Calif. U. for Profl. Study. Registered respiratory therapist, respiratory care practitioner; cert. pulmonary tech. Nat. Inst. Occupl. Safety and Health; cert. advanced cardiac and basic life support instr., neonatal advanced life support; cert. disability analyst, diplomate Am. Bd. Disability Analysts. Alt. supr. Good Samaritan Hosp., Vincennes, Ind., 1976-79; critical care technician Winona Meml. Hosp., Indpls., 1979-80; neonatal ICU-critical care technician Mercy Hosp., Urbana, Ill., 1980-82; cardio-pulmonary supr. Winona Meml. Hosp., Indpls., 1982-92; dir. pulmonary svcs. MidWest Med. Ctr., 1992-93; mgr., bronchoscopy, pulmonary function testing, respiratory care VA Med. Ctr., 1993-96, ednl. coord., EEO counselor, 1993-96; mgr. cardiopulmonary, neurology, Sleep/Wake Ctr. Cmty. Hosps., 1996—, dir. Respiratory Care Tutorial Ctr. Mem. adj. faculty Ind. Vocat.-Tech. Coll., 1993—, Calif. Coll. Health Scis., Southern Calif. U. for Profl. Studies, 2001; adv. bd. Allied Health Ind. U., 1995—. Mem. adv. bd. Allied Health Ind. Vocat. Tech. Coll., 1987—. Mem. Nat. Bd. Respiratory Care (panel of cons. to exam. com.), Am. Assn. for Respiratory Care (clin. practice guideline rev. bd.), Ind. Soc. for Respiratory Care, Nat. Bd. for Respiratory Care, Am. Bd. Disability Analysts (charter, diplomate, sr. disability analyst), Alpha Sigma Lambda (charter, Membership award 1990).

MOLINA, MARIO JOSE, physical chemist, educator; b. Mexico City, Mexico, Mar. 19, 1943; arrived in U.S., 1968; s. Roberto Molina-Pasquel and Leonor Henríquez; m. Luisa Y. Tan, July 12, 1973; 1 child, Felipe. Bachillerato, Acad. Hispano Mexicana, Mexico City, 1959; Ingeniero Químico, U. Nacional Autónoma de México, 1965; postgrad., U. Freiburg, Fed. Republic Germany, 1966—67; PhD, U. Calif., Berkeley, 1972. Asst. prof. U. Nacional Autónoma de México, 1967—68; research assoc. U. Calif.-Berkeley, 1972—73, U. Calif.-Irvine, 1973—75, asst. prof. phys. chemistry, 1975—79, assoc. prof., 1979—82; sr. rsch. scientist Jet Propulsion Lab., 1983—89; prof. dept. earth, atom and planet sci., dept. chemistry MIT, Cambridge, 1989—96, Martin prof. atmospheric chemistry, 1997—, Inst. prof., 1997—. Recipient Tyler Ecology award, 1983, Esselen award for chemistry in pub. interest, 1987, Max-Planck-Forschungs-Preis, Alexander von Humboldt-Stiftung, 1994, Nobel Prize in Chemistry, 1995, Sasakawa prize, UNEP, 1999. Mem.: NAS, Inst. of Medicine, Am. Geophys. Union (Pres.'s Com. on Advisors on Sci. and Tech. 1994—2000), Am. Phys. Soc., Am. Chem. Soc. Achievements include discovery of the theory that fluorocarbons deplete ozone layer of stratosphere. Home: 8 Clematis Rd Lexington MA 02421-7117 Office: MIT Dept of EAPS 77 Mass Ave # 54-1814 Cambridge MA 02139-4307 E-mail: mmolina@mit.edu. *We have to understand our environment to find out if we are tampering with it. One of our accomplishments has been to call attention to society's potential altering of the atmosphere.**

MOLINA, RAFAEL EVENCIO, urologist; b. Havana, Cuba, July 6, 1923; came to U.S., 1961; s. Joseph M. and Maria H. Molina; m. Maria T. Rodriguez (div.); children: Louis R., Maria T., Manuel E., Rafael E. BA, BS, Colegio de Belen, Havana, 1941; MD, U. Havana, 1949. Bd. cert. Am. Bd. Urology. Resident U. Miami, Fla., 1963-66; physician Hoffman Urol., Huntington, W.Va., 1966—. Contbr. articles to med. jours. Mem. AMA, ACS, Am. Urodynamic Soc., Am. Urol. Assn., Am. Soc. Nephrology, Cuban Med. Soc. in Exile, Rotary Club, Elks Club, Huntington Area C. of C. Republican. Roman Catholic. Avocation: tennis. Home: 1695 Holderby Rd Huntington WV 25701-4127 Office: 601 20th St Huntington WV 25703-1512

MOLINAR, LUPE RODRIQUEZ, librarian, library director; b. Marathon, Tex., June 6, 1942; d. Luciano and Ignacia (Ramirez) Rodriquez; m. Victor O. Molinar, July 29, 1961; 1 child, Lynn Molinar Boutwell. AA, N.Mex. Jr. Coll., 1989. Cert. libr., Tex. Store clk., waitress Big Bend (Tex.) Nat. Pk., 1960-64; cafeteria worker Sul Ross State U., Alpine, Tex., 1964-65; nurse's aide Twilight Acres, Seminole, 1969-75; circulating clk. Gaines Co. Libr., 1975-76, processing clk., 1976-91, libr., 1991—. Vol. Voters Registration, Seminole, 1980—; chair St. James Fall Festival, Seminole, 1994; bd. trustees Seminole Ind. Sch. Dist., 1994—. Mem. Tex. Libr. Assn., Guadalupanas Soc. (pres. 1988-89). Democrat. Roman Catholic. Avocations: music, reading, handicrafts. Home: 400 NW H Seminole TX 79360 Office: Gaines County Libr 704 Hobbs Hwy Seminole TX 79360-3402

MOLINARI, ANA MARIA, salon owner; b. Lima, Peru, June 18, 1948; came to U.S., 1970; d. Jorge and Lucy Gonzales; children: Fabiola Guiliana Beckmann, Sergio Antonio Molinari. BA in Edn., Jorge Polar U., Lima, 1966; Cosmetology Degree, Helena Rubenstein, Lima, 1970. Hairstylist John Paul-Garfinkels, Washington, 1973-76; owner, designer Hide and Seek, Sarasota, Fla., 1976-80; co-owner, hairstylist Ambiance, 1980-85; owner, hairstylist Ana Molinari Inc., 1985—; owner LaMariee Bridal Salon, 2002—. Named Best of Best, Sarasota Mag., 1995—2000, Readers Choice, Sarasota Herald Tribune, 1995—2000, Small Bus. of Yr., Longboat Key C. of C., 2001; recipient award of excellence, Bus. Mag., 1993. Mem. Sarasota C. of C., Longboat Key C. of C. Avocations: exercise, beach, antique collecting.

MOLINARI, CAROL V. writer, investment company executive, educator; b. Bklyn., Oct. 14, 1931; d. Sabino and Anna (Mancusi) M. BS, Douglass Coll., 1953; MEd, Rutgers U., 1962; postgrad., U. Alaska, Anchorage, 1963—. Tchr. Bridgewater Twp. Schs., Bridgewater, N.J., 1953-56, Somerville (N.J.) H.S., 1956-59; tchr. phys. edn., guidance counselor Bridgewater H.S., Raritan, N.J., 1959-62; guidance counselor Anchorage Borough Sch. Dist., 1962-63, Air Force Dependent Sch., Tokyo, 1963-64, Arcturus Jr. H.S., Ft. Richardson, Alaska., 1965-67; asst. dir. student coll. ctr. Douglass Coll., Rutgers U., New Brunswick, N.J., 1967-69; cons., counselor Native Head Start program Alaska Meth. U., Anchorage, 1967-69; adminstr. asst., counselor U. Alaska, 1969-70; office sales mgr. Alcan Realty, 1971-74; dir. Ctr. for Alcohol and Addiction Studies U. Alaska, 1975-79; sales assoc. Century 21 Royal Realty, 1970-83; cons. in the devel. of Now Dimensions Holistic Health Ctr.; pres., dir. Molinari Investments Inc., Anchorage, 1982—. Developer fin. projects, 1978-82; seminar presenter on investing techniques. Author: The Magic of Financing and Investing, 1987, (cookbook) Mom's Italian Recipes, American's Wake Up We Can Heal Our Country, 1996; co-author: Out of Nowhere; contbr. articles to Alaska Tchr., This Alaska, Alcohol Health and Research World, others. Bd. dirs. Alaska region Nat. Coun. on Alcohol, Morning Song; mem. adv. bd. Salvation Army; mem. ch. coun. Holy Family Cathedral. Rutgers U. schoalr, 1975. Mem. NAFE, NEA, Alaska Edn. Assn., Bd. Realtors, Women of Vision and Action, Soroptimist. Avocations: hiking, reading, skiing, fishing, travel. Home: PO Box 101696 Anchorage AK 99510-1696 Office: Molinari Investment Inc 545 W 19th Ave Anchorage AK 99503-1830 E-mail: cmolin@webtv.net.

MOLINARI, JOSEPH FRANCIS, oculist; b. Worcester, Mass. s. Wallace F and Antoinette M (Tortora) Molinari. AA, Ctrl. New Eng. Coll., 1972; BS, New Eng. Coll., 1973, OD, 1974; MEd, Mercer U., 1979; postgrad., Air U., 1998. Diplomate Am Col Optometric Physicians (fellow). Staff optometrist Lahey Clin. Med. Ctr., 1977-79; asst. prof. U. Ala., 1979-82; gen. practice optometry Panama City Beach, Fla., 1982—. Consult USAF, Tyndall AFB, 1980—83; chief DS & M vet affairs, Tallahassee, 1994—. Contbr. articles to profl jours; item writer: Nat Bd Optometry, 1980—83. Pres Harbour Villas Asn, Inc, 1985—86, Gulf of Mex Optics Inc, Panama City Beach, 1984—96; chmn Bay Point Anterior Segment Symp, Inc, 1984—95. Col USAFR, 1974—. Recipient Spurgeon Eure Award, Am Optometric Found, 1978, 1981—82, Dallas Contact Lens Research Award, Brit Contact Lens Asn, 1984, Oustanding Serv and Recognition Award, Asn Mil Surgeons US, 1996, 25 Yr Recognition, Amred Forces Optometric Soc, 1996, Biomedical Sci Corps Individual Mobilization Augmentee of Yr, USAFR, 1996, Optometrist of the Yr Award, Armed Forces Optometric Soc, 1999. Fellow: Am Acad Optometry; mem.: Am Col Optometry Physicians, Neuro-Optometry Soc (chmn 1985—88), Fla Optometric Asn (del 1984—85), Am Legion. Office: 1607 St James Ct Tallahassee FL 32308 E-mail: Joseph.Molinari@med.va.gov.

MOLINARI, TODD MICHAEL, priest; b. Portland, Oreg., Oct. 29, 1968; s. Joseph Charles Molinari and Joan Marie Campbell. BA in Philosophy, Franciscan U., Steubenville, Ohio, 1990; Sacrae Theologiae Baccelaureate, Gregorian U., Rome, 1993, Sacrae Theoligiae Licentiate, 1996. Lic. moral theology. Parochial vicar St. John Bapt. Ch., Milw., 1995, St. Anne Ch., Grants Pass, Oreg., 1996-99; pastor St. Francis Ch., Roy, 1999—. Mem. Fellowship Cath. Scholars, Cath. League, KC (chaplain 1996—). Avocations: reading, golf, hiking, guitarist. Home and Office: Saint Francis Parish 39135 NW Harrington Rd Banks OR 97106-8210

MOLINARO-BLONIGAN, MARY ROBIN, corporate lawyer; BA in Econs., U. Iowa, 1991; JD, Ohio No. U., 1995. Bar: Iowa 1995, Fla. 1996, Colo. 1997. Corp. counsel Warren Transport, Inc., Waterloo, Iowa, 1995—. Mem. ABA, ATLA, Transp. Lawyers Assn., Assn. Transp. Law, Logistics & Policy. Office: Warren Transport Inc PO Box 420 Waterloo IA 50704-0420

MOLINA VILLACORTA, RAFAEL ANTONIO, technology management investment company executive; b. Sept. 5, 1963; s. Rafael Antonio and Rosa Isabel (Villacorta) M.; m. Maria Asuncion Cornejo, Sept. 28, 1985; children: Elisa Maria, Rafael Augusto, Cristian Adolfo, Leonardo Paolo. AA, Sacramento City Coll., 1983; BS, Golden Gate U., 1994. CFO MVM Investments, Sacramento, 1983-85; adminstr. State of Calif., 1985-93; CEO, mng. dir. C & T Investments, Dixon, Calif., 1988—; mng. dir. Data Systems, Los Altos, 1996—, DASA, S.A. de C.V., 1996—. Dir. MAM Co., Sacramento, 1985-96; CEO, dir. Del Sol Investments, Dixon, 1989-98. Mem. Calif. State Employees Assn., Sacramento, 1985, Am. Mgmt. Assn., Sacramento, 1991; pres. St. Peter's Ch., Dixon, 1992-94. Recipient Outstanding Achievement award Calif. Dept. Health Svcs., 1988, Primary Clinics, 1990. Mem. Am. Mgmt. Assn., Network Profl. Assn., Tele-Comms. Assn., Calif. Microcomputers Users. Roman Catholic. Avocations: travel, computers, reading. Office: C & T Investments Co Ste 013-76 1605-B Siempre Viva Rd San Diego CA 92154 E-mail: rafaelmolina@dasa.net.

MOLINDER, JOHN IRVING, engineering educator, consultant; b. Erie, Pa., June 14, 1941; s. Karl Oskar and Carin (Ecklund) M.; m. Janet Marie Ahlquist, June 16, 1962; children: Tim, Karen. BSEE, U. Nebr., 1963; MSEE, Air Force Inst. Tech., 1964; PhD EE, Calif. Inst. Tech., 1969. Registered profl. engr., Calif. Project officer Ballistic Systems Div., Norton AFB, Calif., 1964-67; sr. engr. Jet Propulsion Lab., Pasadena, 1969-70; prof. engring. Harvey Mudd Coll., Claremont, 1970—; prin. engr. Qualcomm Inc., 1996-97, part-time, 1997—; contractor Boeing Satellite Systems, 2000—. Part-time lectr. Calif. State U., L.A., 1970-74; mem. tech. adv. panel Kinemetrics, Pasadena, 1985-86; part-time mem. tech. staff Jet Propulsion Lab., Pasadena, 1974-97, rep. NASA Hdqrs., Washington, 1979-80; vis. prof. elec. engring. Calif. Inst. Tech., 1982-83. Contbr. articles to profl. jours. Served to capt. USAF, 1963-67. Mem. IEEE. Avocations: bicycling, reading, computers. Office: Harvey Mudd Coll Dept Engring 301 E 12th St Dept Of Claremont CA 91711-5901

MOLINE, JON NELSON, philosopher, educator, university administrator; b. Ft. Worth, May 12, 1937; s. Paul Ross and Elsie Virginia (Nelson) Moline; m. Sandra Lois Reininger, Aug. 13, 1960; children: Kevin, Eric. AB, Austin Coll., 1960, LHD, 1995; PhD, Duke U., 1964. Asst. prof. U. Wis., Madison, 1964-69, assoc. prof., 1969-73, prof. philosophy, 1973-86, prof. environ. studies, 1974-86, nat. humanities faculty advisor, 1976-82; v.p., dean St. Olaf Coll., Northfield, Minn., 1987-94; pres. Tex. Luth. U., Seguin, 1994—. Vis asst prof Univ Ill, Chicago, 1969; vis assoc prof Univ Tex, Austin, 1971—72; fellow Nat Humanities Ctr, 1979—80. Pres Madison Symphony Orchestra, 1975—77; mem Nat Coun Humanities, 1991—99, vice chair, 1993—99; dir Seguin Econ Develop Corp, 1999—, pres, 2001—; dir Jr Achievement S Tex, 1996—, Seguin Area C of C, 1999—; bd dirs Fund for Improvement Post-Secondary Educ, 1985—91. Fellow Vis, Inst Research Humanities, 1973, 1975—76, Spencer Found, 1974, Humanities, Rockefeller Found, 1975—76. Mem.: Seguin Area CofC (dir 2000—). Office: Texas Lutheran Univ 1000 W Court St Seguin TX 78155-5999 E-mail: jmoline@tlu.edu.

MOLINEAUX, CHARLES BORROMEO, lawyer, arbitrator, columnist, poet; b. N.Y.C., Sept. 27, 1930; s. Charles Borromeo and Marion Frances (Belter) M.; m. Patricia Leo Devereux, July 2, 1960; children: Charles, Stephen, Christopher, Patricia, Peter, Elizabeth. BS cum laude, Georgetown U., 1950; JD, St. Johns U., 1959. Bar: N.Y. 1959, Mass. 1981, D.C. 1988. From assoc. to ptnr. Nevius, Jarvis & Pilz and successor firms, N.Y.C., 1959-77; ptnr. Gadsby & Hannah, 1978-80; v.p., gen. counsel Perini Corp., Framingham, Mass., 1980-87; pvt. practice Washington, 1987—. Adj. faculty Internat. Law Inst., Washington, 1989—. Author numerous poems. Mem. adv. bd. Inst. for Transnat. Arbitration; committeeman, Rep. Party, Nassau County, NY, 1965—71, committeeman, mem. exec. com. Fairfax County, Va., 1969. 1st lt. U.S. Army, 1954—56. Fellow Am. Bar Found.; mem. ASCE, Am. Arbitration Assn. (constrn. ADR task force 1994—), Chartered Inst. Arbitrators, Fedn. Internat. Engrs.-Conseils (Assoc. Gen. Contractors del. constrn. contract com., Louis Prangey award for svc. to profession cons. engring. 1996), Del. Hist. Soc., London Ct. Internat. Arbitration, Fellowship Cath. Scholars. Roman Catholic. Home: 8321 Weller Ave Mc Lean VA 22102-1717 Office: 8201 Greensboro Dr Ste 1000 Mc Lean VA 22102 also: 46 Essex St London WC2R 3GH England E-mail: cmlnx@aol.com.

MOLINO, LORY JEAN, neurobiologist; b. Quezon, The Philippines, Mar. 1, 1964; came to U.S., 1967; d. Lorenzo Daban and Carmelita (Jason) M.; m. Anthony Francis Bonagura, Aug. 10, 1991 (div. 1998); children: Alexandra Grace, Michael Lorenzo. BS, SUNY, Brockport, 1986; MA, NYU, 1989. Rsch. asst. dept. psychology SUNY, Brockport, 1985-86, NYU, N.Y.C., 1986-87, rsch. asst. dept. biology, 1987-88; tech. rsch. specialist dept. psychiatry SUNY, Stony Brook, 1988-90; temp. regulatory affairs dept. Smithkline-Beecham, Phila., 1991-92; assoc. scientist cardiovascular biology dept. Rhone-Poulenc Rorer, Collegeville, Pa., 1992-93; sr. rsch. scientist Sterling-Winthrop PRD, 1993-94; rsch. assoc. RW Johnson PRI, Springhouse, Pa., 1995—. Presenter N.Y. Acad. Sci., 1989, Soc. for Neuroscience, 1989; contbr. articles to profl. jours. Mem. AAAS, Assn. for Women in Scis., N.Y. Acad. Scis., Soc. for Neurosci., Internat. Brain Orgn. Republican. Achievements include research in genetic predispositioning of learned helplessness in developmental neural circuitry; interactive capacity of monoaminerg system; vacillatory behavior in immature rats via a D-1 agonist; neurodegeneration from ischemia and head trauma; research in Alzheimer's neurodegeneration via the beta-amyloid protein apoptotic degeneration; research in molecular biology of neuropathic pain. Home: 2550 Railroad Ave Colmar PA 18915-9700 E-mail: lmolino@prius@jnj.com.

MOLINO, MICHAEL ROBERT, English educator; b. Washington, Sept. 17, 1956; s. Robert Anthony and Grace Marie (Smith) M.; m. Mary Louise Bogumil, Mar. 14, 1987. BA, U. South Fla., 1982, MA, 1984; PhD, Marquette U., 1991. Instr. Iowa State U., Ames, 1988-92, U. Mo., Rolla, 1992-94, Va. Commonwealth U., Richmond, 1994-95; asst. prof. Bradley U., Peoria, Ill., 1995-98; assoc. prof. So. Ill. Univ., Carbondale, 1998—. Author: Questioning Tradition, Language, and Myth, 1994; editor: Dictionary of Literary Biography; contbr. articles to profl. publs. including Modern Philology, Coll. English, Jour. of Irish Lit., Am. Jour. of Semiotics, The Comparatist, New Hibernia Rev. Sgt. USAF, 1975-79. Schmitt fellowship, 1989-90, Marquette Grad. fellowship, 1991; rsch. grant Bradley U., 1997. Mem. MLA, Am. Conf. for Irish Studies, Semiotic Soc. of Am. Democrat. Roman Catholic. Office: So Ill Univ Dept English Mail Code 4503 Carbondale IL 62901-4503 E-mail: mrmolino@aol.com.

MOLINO, MILDRED A. lawyer; b. N.Y.C., Sept. 24, 1951; d. Charles B. and Frances L. Molino; m. John B. Dunn, May 24, 1975; children: Casey Molino-Dunn, Roman Molino-Dunn. BA in Spanish and Polit. Sci., U. Dayton, 1973; JD, Drake U., Des Moines, 1976. Bar: Iowa Supreme Ct. 1976, Pa. Supreme Ct. 1976, U.S. Supreme Ct. 1992. Mem. staff, mng. atty. Lehigh Valley Legal Svcs., 1976—79; pvt. practice law Easton, 1979—. Bd. dirs. Children's Home of Easton, 1993—, Lehigh Valley Legal Svc., Easton, 1981-84. Mem. Pa. Bar Assn., Northampton Bar Assn. (bd. govs. 1999--). Office: 162 S Union St Easton PA 18042-4400

MOLINO, THOMAS MICHAEL, retired military officer; b. Bklyn., Feb. 16, 1947; s. Angelo Thomas and Jean (Tepedino) M.; m. Mary Ellen Thomas, June 3, 1973; children: T. Andrew, Sara Catherine. BA, St. Peter's Coll., 1968; MA, Loyola U., Chgo., 1979. Commd. 2d lt. U.S. Army, 1968, advanced through ranks to col., troop comdr. 2d Squadron, 11th Cavalry Regt. Vietnam, 1970-71, comdr. 2d Squadron 2d Cavalry Regiment Bamberg, Germany, 1983-85; spl. asst. to vice chmn. Joint Chiefs of Staff, Pentagon, 1987-89; exec. asst. to cmdr. in chief U.S. Army Europe, Heidelberg, Germany, 1990-92; cmdr. 2d Cavalry Regiment U.S. Army, Ft. Lewis, Wash. and Ft. Polk, La., 1992-94; chief strategic planning U.S. Army, Pentagon, Washington, 1995-96, ret., 1997; sr. def. analyst Sci. Applications Internat. Corp., 1997-98, v.p., regional security divsn. mgr., 1998-2001, corp. v.p., mgr. weapons proliferation and stategic planning, 2001—. Asst. prof. Loyola U. of Chgo., 1976-79. Decorated DSM, Def. Superior Svc. medal, 3 Legion of Merit awards, 2 bronze stars for combat, Republic of Vietnam Honor medal, Air medal, others; fellow-in-residence Harvard U., 1994-95; MIT Seminar XII fellow, 1996-97. Mem. Assn. U.S. Army, 2d Cavalry Assn., VFW, Army-Navy Country Club. Roman Catholic. Avocation: golf. Office: 1710 SAIC Dr Mc Lean VA 22102-3701 E-mail: molinot@saic.com.

MOLINS, MARCEL J. lawyer; b. Barcelona, Spain, Nov. 1, 1936; s. Pedro and Rosa (Viaplana) M.; m. Martina Molins, Aug. 5, 1963; children: Thomas, Nicole. JD, Barcelona U., 1958; LM, Northwestern U., 1964; JD, Loyola U., Chgo., 1966. Assoc. Baker & McKenzie, Chgo., 1964-70, ptnr., 1970—. Chmn. adv. bd. Instituto Cervantes, Chgo., 1996—. Recipient medalla merito civil Spanish Govt., Madrid, 1997. Office: Baker & McKenzie 130 E Randolph Dr 1 Prudential Plaza Chicago IL 60601 E-mail: marcel.j.molins@bakernet.com.

MOLINSKY, BERT, tax consultant; b. Bronx, N.Y., Feb. 25, 1938; s. Joseph and Ida G. (Rosenberg) M.; m. Donna L. Thurman, June 26, 1964; children: Avery, Lucy, Lois, Sarah. Student, U. Ariz., 1956-61, Diablo Valley Coll., 1986-88, Calif. State U., Hayward, 1988-92. CFP; CLU; ChFC; Enrolled Agt. Field supt. INA Life, Phoenix, 1968-72; regional life mgr. Sentry Life Ins. Co., Oklahoma City, 1972-73, Mpls., 1973-75, San Francisco, 1975-78; mgr. Acacia Mutual Life, Oakland, Calif., 1978-80; gen. agt. Am. United Life, Concord, 1980-82; owner East Bay Triple Check Tax Svcs., Walnut Creek, 1982—, Tax Tactics, LLC, Peoria, Ariz., 1993—. Instr. Golden Gate U. CPD, San Francisco, 1983-93, Mt. Diablo Sch. Dist., Concord, 1986-93; faculty Coll. for Fin. Planning, Denver, 1983-99; bd. dirs. Triple Check Licensee Coun. Contbr. articles to profl. jours. Nat. dir. U.S. Jaycees, Phoenix, 1967; pres. Bnai Brith Coun. of Lodges, San Francisco, 1986. With USNR, 1955-72. Named Jaycee of Yr. Ariz. Jaycees, 1967. Fellow Nat. Tax Practice Inst.; mem. Enrolled Agts., East Bay Assn Life Underwriters (pres. 1985-86), Peoria Sunset Lions (past pres.), Ariz. State Enrolled Agts. Assn. (past pres.), Nat. Assn. Enrolled Agents (mem. affiliates task force, 1997-99, bd. dirs. 1999—). Avocation: sports. Office: Plaza Del Rio Ctr 9401 W Thunderbird Rd Ste 140 Peoria AZ 85381-4817 also: PO Box 5129 Peoria AZ 85385-5129 E-mail: bertmol@aol.com.

MOLITOR, GARY WILLIAM, artist; b. Modesto, Calif., July 12, 1940; s. Milton William and Louise Emily (Kneppler) M. AA, San Francisco City Coll., 1961; BA, San Francisco State U., 1963, MA, 1965. Lectr. arts. U. Calif., Davis, 1967-69; asst. prof. Sonoma State U., Rohnert Park, Calif., 1970-73; assoc. prof. U. Nev., Las Vegas, 1972-73; sales supr. W.E. Mushet Co., San Francisco, 1973-84; exec. dir. Tifari, Sausalito, Calif., 1984-85; prodn. mgr. Ryan Paint Co., Oakland, Calif., 1985-87; mgr. mktg. svcs. Aervoe-Pacific, Gardnerville, Nev., 1987-90, Triangle Coatings, San Leandro, Calif., 1990—. Artist (sculpture) The Dilexi Years 1958-70; artist ceramic sculpture Cerama-Rama, 1977, Calif. Ceramics and Glass, 1974; artist mixed media sculpture Molitor, 1967, Funk Show, 1967. Recipient award Nat. Council Arts and Humanities, 1966 . Mem. Fedn. Socs. Coatings Tech., Golden Gate Soc. Coating Tech., Soc. for Advancement of Material and Process Engring., Am. Crafts Council, Archaeol. Inst. Am., U.S. Parachute Assn. Democrat. Home: 841 Saint Marys Ave San Leandro CA 94577-3853 Office: Triangle Coatings 1930 Fairway Dr San Leandro CA 94577-5631

MOLITOR, GRAHAM THOMAS TATE, lawyer; b. Seattle, Apr. 6, 1934; s. Robert Franklin and Louise Margaret (Graham) M.; m. Carlotta Jean Crate, July 30, 1960; children: Graham Thomas Tate, Anne Therese, Christopher Robert. BS, U. Wash., 1955; LLB, Am. U., 1963. Bar: D.C. 1963. Rsch. asst. U. Wash., Seattle, 1957; bailiff U.S. Criminal Ct. D.C., 1958-59; legis. counsel U.S. Ho. of Reps., Washington, 1961-63; dir. candidate rsch. Rockefeller for Pres. Com., 1963-64, 68; D.C. counsel, asst. dir. govt. rels. Nabisco, Inc., Washington, 1964-70; dir. govtl. rels. Gen. Mills, Inc., 1970-77; pres., CEO Pub. Policy Forecasting, Inc., Potomac, Md., 1977—; prin. ptnr. Pub. Policy Communicators, 1989-91. Prin., ptnr. Pub. Policy Action Inst., Potomac; adv. bd. Creative Bus. Strategies, Inc.; adj. prof. Grad. Sch. Bus. Am. U., Washington, 1969—75, Washington, 1979—85, Montgomer Coll., Rockville, Md., 1987—88; dir. rsch. White House Conf. on Indsl. World Ahead, 1971—72; mem. White House Adv. Com. on Social Indicators, 1975—76; chmn. Commn. on the Future of Montgomery County, 1986—88; guest lectr. numerous univs.; mem. White House Confs. on Food, Nutrition and Health, 1969—71, White House Conf. on Youth, 1970; bd. dirs. First Global Conf. on the Future, Inc., Can., 1980—; organizing com. Found. for the Future, 1997—, bd. advisors, 1999—, mem. scholar adv. bd., 2001—. Contbg. editor Food Tomorrow Newsletter, 1976-77; co-editor, chmn. editl. bd. Ency. of the Future, 1991-96; cons. editor Hist. Guide to Am. Govt., 1995-97, McMillan Compendium of the Twenty-First Century, 1998-99; editor Technological Forecasting and Social Change, 1999—chmn. editl. bd. Future Survey, 1995-97; mem. bd. editors Hudson Inst. Study of World Food Problems, 1975-77; mem. editl. bd. Bus. Tomorrow Newsletter, 1977-79; mem. bd. advisors New Mktg. Techs. Monitor, 1983-85; polit. editor On the Horizon, 1993-95; contbr. articles to profl. jours. Mem. Food Adv. Bd., N.Y.C., 1980-86. Served to 1st lt. U.S. Army, 1958-61. Recipient Disting. Service award Grocery Mfrs. Am., 1973-74, Disting. Service award Nat. Consumer Info. Center, 1974, Disting. Service award Am. Mgmt. Assn., 1975. Fellow: World Acad. Art and Sci. (mem. bd. trustees); mem.: World Future Soc. (gen. chmn. 2d Gen. Assembly 1975, v.p., dir. 1981—94, v.p., legal counsel 1994—, Disting. Svc. award 1975), E.D. Export Coun., Washington Indsl. Roundtable, Washington Bus.-Govt. Rels. Coun. (mem. exec. com. 2000—, chmn. commn. on Yr. 3000 2001—), Univ. Club, Phi Alpha Delta, Phi Kappa Sigma. Republican. Presbyterian. Home and Office: 9208 Wooden Bridge Rd Rockville MD 20854-2416

MOLITOR, MICHAEL A. entrepreneur, consultant; b. Bklyn., Nov. 7, 1965; s. Henry J. and Janet A. (Monti) M.; m. Michele A. Emery, July 8, 1995; 1 child, Michael. BS, Siena Coll., 1987; MBA, Columbia U., 2000. CFP. Fin, aid counselor Janet's Coll. Tuition Aid, Massapequa Park, N.Y., 1987-92; income tax acct. Michael A. Molitor, Massapequa, 1988—; owner, fin. aid counseling svc. Molitor Coll. Aid Counseling, 1992—; money mgr. Molitor Money Mgmt., 1992—. Cons. Alive-To-Thrive, Inc., Westchester, N.Y., 1992—, cons., adv. bd. Orphan's Aid Soc., Douglaston, N.Y., 1994—; cons. in field. Author: You Can Afford A College Education, 1992; contbr. articles to profl. jours., various TV talk shows. Con. to Guidance Dept. Massapequa Sch. Dist., Massapequa, 1995-98, mem. Long Island Assn., Hauppauge, N.Y., 1990-92. Recipient Top Producer-Pres. Club Transamerica Funds, Houston, 1993-94, mem. signature Club Oppenheimer Funds, Denver, 1995. Mem. Internat. Assn. Fin. Planning, N.Y. Fin. Air Adminstr. Assn., NAt. Assn. Fin. Aid Adminstr., BMW Car Club Am., Porsche Club Am. Mem. Christian Ch. Avocation: golf, drumming, track driving.

MOLITORIS, BRUCE ALBERT, nephrologist, educator; b. Springfield, Ill., June 26, 1951; s. Edward and Joyce (Tomasko) M.; m. Karen Lynn Wichterman, June 16, 1973; children: Jason, Jared, Julie. BS, U. Ill., 1973, MS in Nutrition, 1975; MD, Wash. U., 1979. Resident Sch. Medicine U. Colo., Denver, 1979-81, nephrology fellow, 1981-84, asst. prof. medicine, 1984-88, assoc. prof. medicine, 1988-93, prof., 1993; dir. nephrology Ind. U. Med. Sch., Indpls., 1993—; vis. scientist U. Colo., MCDB, Boulder, 1989-90, Max Planck Inst., Federal Republic of Germany, 1984-85. NIH reviewer, 1991-94; dir. home dialysis Denver VA Ctr., 1984-93; vis. scientist dept. molecular biology Colo. State U., Ft. Collins, 1998. Mem. editl. bd. Am. Jour. Physiology, 1989—, Am. Jour. Kidney Diseases, 1991, Am. Jour. Kidney Disease, 1996; assoc. editor Jour. Investigative Medicine, 1994-99; contbr. articles to profl. jours. Pres. Cherry Creek Village South Homeowners Assn., 1989-90, Pickwick Commons Home Owners Assn., 1999; v.p. Our Father Luth. Ch., Denver, 1989-90; coun. mem. King of Glory Luth. Ch., 1995-98, 1999-2002; coach Cherry Creek Soccer Assn., Greenwood Village, 1988-91,

Centennial Little League Titans Basketball; bd. dirs. CSSA, 1993. Recipient Upjohn Achievement award, 1979, Liberty Hyde Bailey award, 1973. Mem. Am. Assn. Physicians, Am. Soc. Nephrology (program chmn. 2003), Internat. Soc. Nephrology, N.Y. Acad. Sci., Am. Soc. Clin. Investigation, Am. Fedn. for Clin. Rsch. (nat. counselor 1991-94), Western Assn. Physicians. Avocations: bridge, fishing, antiques, hiking. Office: Indiana Univ Med Ctr Fesler Hall 115 1120 South Dr Indianapolis IN 46202-5135 E-mail: bmolitor@iupui.edu.

MOLL, CLARENCE RUSSEL, retired university president, consultant; b. Chalfont, Pa., Oct. 31, 1913; s. George A. and Anna A. (Schmidt) M.; m. Ruth E. Henderson, Nov. 19, 1941; children: Robert Henderson, Jonathan George. BS, Temple U., 1934, EdM, 1937; LHD, Pa. Mil. Coll., 1949; PhD, NYU, 1955; LLD, Temple U., 1963; ScD, Chungang U., Seoul, Korea, 1969; LLD, Swarthmore Coll., 1970, Gannon U., 1981; LittD, Delaware Valley Coll., 1976; Ped D, Widener U., 1981. Instr. physics and chemistry Conshohocken (Pa.) H.S., 1935-37; instr. sci. Freehold (N.J.) H.S., 1937-38; instr. physics, chemistry Meml. H.S., Haddonfield, N.J., 1938-42; instr. electronics and radar USN, Phila., 1942-43; assoc. prof. physics and elec. engring. Pa. Mil. Coll., Chester, Pa., 1943-45, registrar, coord. engring. program, 1945-47, dean admissions, student pers., prof. edn., 1947-56, v.p., dean pers. svcs., 1956-59, pres. coll., 1959-72; pres. Widener U. (formerly PMC Colls.), 1972-81, chancellor, 1981-88, pres. emeritus, 1988—; pres. RC Assocs., Inc., 1981—. Instr. electronics Temple U., 1944-46; headmaster Pa. Mil. Prep. Sch., 1945-47; trustee Ironworkers Bank., Project Mgrs. Edn. Found.; trustee emeritus Crozer Keystone Health Sys.; commr. Project Mgmt. Inst./Global Accreditation Commn. Author: History of PA Military College, 1955; contbr. numerous mag. articles. Chmn. Pa. Commn. Ind. Colls., 1969, Found. for Ind. Colls. Pa., 1970; chmn. Com. for Financing Higher Edn. in Pa., 1975; trustee Pa. Inst. Tech., 1985—; commr. Am. Assn. Homes for Aging Cont. Care Accrediting Commn., 1985-95. Recipient Horatio Alger award, 1962, Disting. Alumnus award Temple U., 1964, Cert. of Honor Temple U., 1997, B'nai B'rith Citizen Service award, 1966, Distinguished Citizen award, 1971, Themis award Del. County Bar, 1976, Good Citizenship award Phila. Bar, 1976, Exec. of Yr. award Soc. Advancement Mgmt., 1978, Gallery of Success award, Temple U., 1999. Mem. Assn. Mil. Colls. and Schs. (pres. 1969), Pa. Assn. Colls. and Univs. (chmn. 1970, Sheepskin award 1982), Am. Soc. Engring. Edn., Springhaven Club (Wallingford, Pa.), Tau Beta Pi, Phi Delta Kappa, Alpha Sigma Lambda, Phi Kappa Phi. Lutheran. Home: 1960 Dog Kennel Rd Media PA 19063-1008 Office: Widener U Pres Emeritus Office Chester PA 19013

MOLL, DAVID CARTER, civil engineer; b. Ames, Iowa, Aug. 5, 1948; s. Dale Curtis and Virginia (Carter) M.; m. Margaret E. Newman (div. 1989); 1 child, Megahn Elizabeth. BSCE, Iowa State U., 1971; cert. advanced study, Am. Grad. Sch. Internat. Mgmt., 1983; MBA with distinction, U. Mich., 1984. Cert. project mgmt. profl. Engr. in tng., Iowa; field engr. Chgo. Bridge & Iron Co., 1971; subcontract supr., field engr. Morrison-Knudsen Internat. Co., Inc., Surinam and Panama, 1976; site supt. engring., asst. supt. constrn. Fluor Corp., Saudi Arabia, 1977-82; group mgr. Cummins Engine Co., Columbus, Ind., 1984-85; mgr. spl. projects Kerr-McGee Coal Corp., Oklahoma City, 1985-88; project mgr. Kerr-McGee Corp., 1989, U.K., 1989-90, Saudi Arabia, 1990-92, Oklahoma City, 1993-98, Kerr-McGee Environ. Mgmt. Corp., Oklahoma City, 1998—. Lt. USN, 1971-75. Mem. ASCE, AGSIM (leadership circle), Civil Engr. Corps (Meritorious Svc. medal), Am. Soc. Quality Control (constrn. tech. com.), N.Y. Acad. Scis., Am. Legion, Order of the Knoll (Pres.' Cir.), Marston Club, Project Mgmt. Inst. (Red Earth chpt. dir. fin.), Chi Epsilon. Avocations: cross country skiing, jogging, golf, sailing, stamps.

MOLL, DEBORAH ADELAIDE, lawyer; b. Wilmington, Del., Jan. 19, 1946; BA, St. John's Coll., Annapolis, Md., 1969; MA, U. Tex., 1972, JD, 1975. Bar: N.Mex. 1977. Law clk. Tex. Ct. Criminal Appeals, Austin, 1975-76, U.S. Ct. Appeals (10th cir.), Santa Fe, 1977-78; asst. atty. gen. N.Mex. Atty. Gen., 1978-84; asst. appellate defender N.Mex. Pub. Defender Dept., 1984-87; staff atty. N.Mex. Taxation and Revenue Dept., 1987-92; shareholder Kemrer-Hayes & Moll, P.A., Albuquerque, 1992; gen. counsel N.Mex. Gen. Svcs. Dept., Santa Fe, 1993—. Mem. Supreme Ct. Bd. Legal Specialization Com. for Constrn. and Pub. Contracts, 2002—. Mem. N.Mex. State Bar (bd. dirs. pub. law sect. 1996—, chair pub. law sect. 1997-98, bd. dirs. bankruptcy sect. 1992, bd. dirs. employment law sect. 1999-2001, mem. adv. opinion com. 1993-96, chair ad hoc com. to rev. atty. and atty. hearing officer reclassifications 2001--). Avocation: photography. Office: NMex Gen Svcs Dept 715 Alta Vista St Santa Fe NM 87505-4108 E-mail: mollda@cs.com.

MOLL, GEORGE WILLIAM, pediatrician, educator; b. Milw., Nov. 23, 1947; s. George William, Sr. and Laverne Delores (Klein) M.; m. Susana Valdez Ramos, June 24, 1978; children: Christina, Teresa. BA in Chemistry cum laude, Carleton Coll., 1969; PhD in Biochemistry, U. Chgo., 1975, MD, 1977. Diplomate Nat. Bd. Med. Examiners; diplomate in pediatrics and pediat. endocrinology Am. Bd. Pediatrics; cert. PALS, CPR. Pediatric resident Mott Children's Hosp., U. Mich., Ann Arbor, 1977-79; pediatric endocrinology fellowship Wyler Children's Hosp., U. Chgo., 1979-81; asst. prof. pediatrics U. Chgo., 1981-85, Emory U. Sch. Medicine, Atlanta, 1985-87; assoc. prof. pediatrics U. Miss. Med. Ctr., Jackson, 1987-93, prof. pediatrics, 1993—; assoc. staff pediatric endocrinology Little Co. of Mary Hosp., Evergreen Park, Ill., 1981-85, The Meth. Hosps., Gary and Merrillville, Ind., 1981-85; staff pediatric endocrinologist The Emory Clinic, Atlanta, 1985-87, Henrietta Egleston Hosp. for Children, Atlanta, 1985-87, Grady Meml. Hosp., Atlanta, 1985-87; staff Emory Univ. Hosp., 1987, dir. pediatric endocrinology; staff U. Miss. Med. Ctr., Jackson, 1987—. Contbr. articles to profl. jours. Active Diabetes Found. of Miss., Inc., 1998, Juv. Diabetes Found. Internat., 1998, Filipino-Am. Assn. of Miss., 1990—, Chronic Disease Coalition of Miss., 1996—. Recipient med. scientist NIH scholarship/grant U. Chgo., 1970-77, Andrew Mellon Found. fellowship, 1981-82, Med. Excellence award So. Med. Assn., 1995; grantee Am. Lung Assn., 1987-89, Eli Lilly Co., Mobil Oil Co., 1991, Diabetes Rsch. and Edn. Found., Inct., 1992, Pharmacia & Upjohn, 1998, others. Fellow Am. Acad. Pediatrics, Am. Coll. Endocrinology; mem. AAAS, Nat. Bd. Med. Examiners (comprehensive task force for reprodn./endocrinology 1989-90), Chgo. Endocrine Club (sec. 1984-85), N.Y. Acad. of Sci., Am. Fedn. for Med. Rsch., Lawson Wilkins Soc. for Pediat. Endocrinology, Midwest and So. Soc. for Pediatric Rsch., Miss. State Med. Assn., Cen. Miss. Med. and Pediatric Soc., The Endocrine Soc. (regional rep. U.S. Pharmacopeia Quinquennial), Am. Diabetes Assn., Juv. Diabetes Found., Sigma Xi, others. Achievements include isolation of a bovine brain protein kinase and establishment of a protein kinase assay employing a novel PEI-cellulose thin-layer system as part of a PhD Biochemistry; established a novel modified flow-dialysis system for steady state hormone action studies, assisted the delineation of a LH-receptor defect related to precocious puberty and a novel genetic mutation in thyroid binding globulin in males. Avocations: carpentry, gen. handicrafts, electronics, computer repair work. Office: Univ Miss Med Ctr 2500 N State St Jackson MS 39216-4500 E-mail: gmoll@ped.umsmed.edu.

MOLL, JOHN LEWIS, electronics engineer, retired; b. Wauseon, Ohio, Dec. 21, 1921; s. Samuel Andrew and Esther (Studer) M.; m. Isabel Mary Sieber, Oct. 28, 1944; children: Nicolas Josef, Benjamin Alex, Diana Carolyn. B.Sc., Ohio State U., 1943, PhD, 1952; Dr. h.c., Faculty Engring., Katholieke U. Leuven, (Belgium), 1983. Elec. engr. RCA Labs., Lancaster, Pa., 1943-45; mem. tech. staff Bell Telephone Labs., Murray Hill, N.J., 1952-58; mem. faculty Stanford U., 1958-69, prof. elec. engring., 1959-69; tech. dir. optoelectronics Fairchild Camera and Instrument Corp., 1969-74; dir. integrated circuits labs. Hewlett-Packard Labs., Palo Alto, Calif., 1974-80, dir. IC structures research, sr. scientist, 1980-87, dir. Superconductivity Lab., 1987-90, mem. tech. staff, 1990-96; ret., 1996. Author: Physics of Semi Conductors, 1964; co-author Computer Aided Design and VLSI Device Development, 1985, rev. edit., 1988; inventor (with Ebers) first analytical transistor model, 1953, still valid and useful for circuit design. Recipient Howard N. Potts medal Franklin Inst., 1967, Disting. Alumnus award Coll. Engring., Ohio State U., 1970, Benjamin C. Lamme medal Coll. Engring., Ohio State U., 1988, Vladimir Karapetoff award Eta Kappa Nu, 1995; Guggenheim fellow, 1964, C&C Award, NEC Fund Integration Comm. and Computers, 1997. Fellow IEEE (Ebers award 1971, Thomas A. Edison medal 1991), Am. Acad. Arts and Scis.; mem. Am. Phys. Soc., Nat. Acad. Engring., Nat. Acad. Scis. Home: 1 W Edith Ave # A105 Los Altos CA 94022-2770 E-mail: John1Moll@aol.com.

MOLL, JOSEPH EUGENE, chemical engineer, chemical company executive; b. Evansville, Ind., Sept. 3, 1950; s. Jacob Eugene and Mary Ann (Zenthoefer) M., m. Karen Jean Pennington, Aug. 20. 1977; children: Laura, Angela, Jared. BS in Chem. Engring., Purdue U., 1972. Cert. ofcl. USS Swimming. Mem. mfg. mgmt. staff GE, Selkirk, Danville, N.Y., Ill, 1972-74, product devel. engr. Pittsfield, Mass., 1974-75; tech. specialist Betz Labs., Kokomo, Ind., 1975-78, account mgr. Evansville, 1978-88; account exec. GE Betz, 1988-90, area mgr., 1990—. Mem. Mayor's Tech. Adv. Com., Mt. Vernon, Ind., 1983— Instr. ARC, Evansville, 1971-73; ofcl. Ill. High Sch. Assn., Danville, 1972-73; min. of the word St. Matthew's Ch., Mt. Vernon, Ind., 1980—; amb. Promise Keepers Men's Ministry, 1994—, Sunday sch. tchr., 1996—; asst. cubmaster Boy Scouts Am., 1993-96, asst. scoutmaster, 1997—. Mem. AICE (v.p. 1971-72), Tech. Assn. of Pulp and Paper Industry, Am. Water Works Assn., Purdue Alumni Assn. (life), John Purdue Coaches Club, Elks, Omega Chi Epsilon, Triangle Fraternity. Roman Catholic. Avocations: golf, weight tng., swimming, bible study group. Home and Office: 28 Parkridge Dr Mount Vernon IN 47620-9405 E-mail: joseph.moll@gesm.ge.com.

MOLL, LLOYD HENRY, banker; b. Reading, Pa., June 26, 1925; s. Lewis J. and Katie (Rothermel) M.; m. Luise G. Keiper, Oct. 25, 1947; children: Lloyd E., Darryl M. BA, Albright Coll., Reading, 1952. Aircraft engine installer War Dept., 1942-47; tire inspector Firestone Tire & Rubber Co., Pottstown, Pa., 1947-48; asst. mgr. Household Fin. Corp., Reading, 1952-57; v.p. Meridian Asset Mgmt. Inc. and Meridian Trust Co. (formerly Am. Bank & Trust Co. of Pa.), 1957-94; v.p. sales and mktg. Investors Trust Co., Wyomissing, Pa., 1995—. Co-founder, past dir. Estate Planning Council of Berks County. Served with AUS, 1945-47. Mem. Am. Inst. Banking. (dir., chmn. bank relations Berks County chpt., pres. 1972-73), Toastmasters (pres. Reading club 1992), Optimists (pres. Reading club 1978-79). Democrat. Home: 213 W 39th St Crestwood Reading PA 19606 Office: Investors Trust Co 2201 Ridgewood Rd #180 Wyomissing PA 19610-1190 *Although it has been known to fail me on occasion I try to live by my understanding of the "Golden Rule". When it does fail me I'm usually able to discount such failure by recounting in my mind the many times it has been a two-way street or by convincing myself that I didn't try hard enough in this particular instance. All too often it comes to me much later that the other fellow's interpretation of the "Golden Rule" was far superior to mine. When this happens I have added to my learning. When it does not happen, it forces me to try that much harder to avoid "PERFECTION".*

MOLL, RICHARD (CHARLES RICHARD MOLL), actor; b. Pasadena, Calif., Jan. 13, 1943; s. Harry Findley and Violet Anita (Grill Yost) M. BA in History, U. Calif., Berkeley, 1964. Actor various film, TV, stage and comml. roles; actor TV series Night Court NBC, Burbank, Calif., 1983-92; actor TV series 100 Deeds for Eddie McDowd Nickelodeon, 1999—. Recipient Career Achievement award Acad. of Sci. Fiction, Fantasy, and Horror Films, 1986, Spl. Recognition award Alzheimer's Disease and Related Disorders Assn., 1987. Mem.: Friars (Calif.). Avocations: antique collecting, trout fishing.

MOLL, ROBERT HENDERSON, lawyer; b. Phila., May 25, 1946; s. Clarence Russel and Ruth Elizabeth (Henderson) M.; m. Victoria Lee Cousins, Feb. 16, 1974; 1 child, Timothy Courtlandt. AB, Washington & Lee U., 1968; JD, Temple U., 1971; LLM, George Washington U., 1979. Bar: Pa. 1971. Atty.-adviser U.S. CSC, Washington, 1971-74, sr. atty., 1974-78, U.S. Office Personnel Mgmt., Washington, 1978-80; atty.-adviser U.S. Dept. Interior, 1980-89, sr. atty., 1989-92, asst. solicitor, 1992—, acting asst. solicitor, 1993, 2001. Editor Fed. Bar News & Jour., 1980-81. Bd. dirs. Friends McLean (Va.) Cmty. Ctr., 1980-85; pres. Brookhaven-Forest Villa Civic Assn., McLean, 1985-86. Capt. USAR, 1968-76. Mem. McLean Racquet and Health Club. Lutheran. Avocations: antiques, travel, reading, camping. Office: US Dept Interior Office Solicitor 1849 C St NW Washington DC 20240-0001 E-mail: jasper1@erols.com.

MOLL, UTE MARTHA, pathologist, medical researcher; b. Deggingen, Baden, Germany, June 18, 1956; s. Hellmuth Jakob and Hildegard M.; m. Martin Rocek, Jan. 13, 1954; children: Thomas, Julian. MD, Ulm U., Germany, 1985. Cert. in Anatomical and Clin. Pathology. Rsch. assoc. Princeton (N.J.) U., 1990—92; asst. prof. SUNY, Stony Brook, 1992—97, assoc. prof., 1997—2001, prof., 2002—. Dir. Grad. Studies in Molecular and Cellular Biology, SUNY, 1999—. Contbr. articles to profl. jours. Rsch. grant Nat. Cancer Inst., 1992—, Am. Cancer Soc., 1999—, breast cancer rsch. grant U.S. Army, 1998—. Mem. Am. Soc. for the Advancement of Sci., Internat. Acad. of Pathology, Am. Soc. for Clin. Pathology, Coll. of Pathology. Office: SUNY at Stony Brook Level 9 Rooms 132-136 Basic Science Tower Stony Brook NY 11794-8691

MOLLAHAN, JOHN FRANCIS, JR. police officer; b. Queens, N.Y., Jan. 20, 1966; s. John F. Mollahan Sr. and Carol A. (Casazza) Mollahan; m. Margaret A. Sullivan, Oct. 15, 1989; children: Maureen, Katherine, John F. Mollahan III. BS in Criminal Justice, St. Thomas Aquinas Coll., Sparkhill, N.Y., 1991; MPA, Marist Coll., Poughkeepsie, N.Y., 1997. Cert. N.Y. State Correction Acad., Zone 3 N.Y. State Correction Acad., sch. resource officer N.Y. Nat. Assn. Sch. Resource Officers. Correction officer Putnam County Sheriff Dept., Carmel, N.Y., 1987-88; police officer White Plains (N.Y.) Police Dept., 1988-92; identification officer Rockland County Sheriff Dept., New City, N.Y., 1990-91; police officer Clarkstown Police Dept., 1992—. Vol. firefighter Vails Gate Fire Dept., Vails Gate, NY, 1993—. Mem.: Rockland County Police Emerald Soc. (pres.), Rockland County Shields, Orange County Ancient Order Hibernians (rec. sec. 1998—99), White Plains Police Benevolent Assn. (lifesaving award 1989), Rockland County Police Benevolent Assn. (Meritorious Svc. award 1996), Pipe and Drum Band. Roman Catholic. Avocation: golf. Home: 6 Franklin Dr Highland Mills NY 10930-3023 Office: Clarkstown Police Dept 20 Maple Ave New City NY 10956-5011

MOLLARD, JOHN DOUGLAS, engineering and geology executive; b. Regina, Sask., Can., Jan. 3, 1924; s. Robert Ashton and Nellie Louisa (McIntosh) M.; m. Mary Jean Lynn, Sept. 18, 1952; children: Catherine Lynn, Jacqueline Lee, Robert Clyde Patrick. BCE, U. Sask., 1945; MSCE, Purdue U., 1947; PhD, Cornell U., 1952; LLD (hon.), U. Regina, 1995. Registered profl. engr., profl. geologist Sask., Alta. and B.C., Can. Resident constrn. engr. Sask. Dept. Hwys and Transp., 1945; grad. asst. Purdue U., West Lafayette, Ind., 1946-47; rsch. engr. sch. civil engring. Cornell U., Ithaca, N.Y., 1950-52; air surveys engr., soil and water conservation and devel. Prairie Farm Rehab. Adminstrn., Govt. of Can., 1947-50, chief, airphoto analysis and engring. geology divsn., 1953-56; pres. J.D. Mollard and Assocs. Ltd., 1956—. Aerial resource mapping surveys tech. adv. Colombo plan, Govts. Ceylon and Pakistan, 1954-56; advisor Shaw Royal Commn. on Nfld. Agr.; Disting. lectr. series Ea. Can. Geotech. Soc., 1969; Cross Can. disting. lectr. Can. Geotech Soc., 1993; C.J. Mackenzie Disting. Grad. Meml. lectr. Coll. Engring. U. Sask., 1994; guest lectr., vis. lectr., instr. over 50 short courses on remote sensing interpretation aerial photos and satellite imagery numerous univs., cities and provinces in Can., also Cornell U., Ithaca, N.Y., Harvard U., Cambridge, Mass., U. Calif., Berkeley, U. Wis., Madison, U. Hawaii, 1952—. Author: Landforms and Surface Materials of Canada, 8 edits.; co-author: Airphoto Interpretation and the Canadian Landscape, 1986; contbr. over 100 articles to profl. pubs. Organizer, canvasser United Appeal campaigns; former bd. dirs. Regina Symphony Orch.; gov. gen. Can. Adrian Clarkson Rideau Hall. Fellow, Can. Acad. Engring., 2001, Engring. Group Inst. Can., 2002; Recipient Engring. Achievement award Assn. Profl. Engrs. Sask., 1984, Massey medal Royal Can. Geog. Soc., 1989, Allied Arts medal Royal Archtl. Inst. Can., 1998. Julian C. Smith medal, Engring. Inst. Can., 1999, U. Sask. Wall of Distinction, 2000, U. Sask. Alumni Wall of Distinction, The Sask. Geotech. Achievement award, Sask. Geotech. Group, 2002, Lt. Gov. Sask. Meritorious Achievement award, 2002; named Officer Order of Can., 2002. Fellow ASCE, Geol. Soc. Can., Geol. Soc. Am., Am. Soc. Photogrammetry and Remote Sensing (award for contbns. airphoto interpretation and remote sensing 1979), Can. Acad. Engring., Internat. Explorers Club, Engring. Inst. Can. (Keefer medal 1948, Julian C. Smith medal 1999); mem. Assn. Cons. Engrs. Can., Can. Geotech. Soc. (1st R.M. Hardy Meml. Keynote lectr. 1987, Thomas Roy award with engring. geology divsn. 1989, R.F. Legget award 1992), Regina Geotech. Soc., Geol. Soc. Sask., Can. Soc. Petroleum Engrs., Regina YMCA (former dir.), Rotary (former dir. Regina club). Mem. United Ch. of Can. Avocations: jogging, reading, golf, tennis, nature study. Home: 2900 McCallum Ave Regina SK Canada S4S OR2 Office: 810 Avord Tower 2002 Victoria Ave Regina SK Canada S4P 0R7 Fax: 306-352-8855. E-mail: mollard@jdmollard.com.

MOLLEMANS, FRANS, geologist, consultant, botanist, consultant; b. Mierlo, The Netherlands, July 17, 1956; arrived in U.S., 1994; s. Adrianus Alfonsus and Johanna Maria Mollemans; m. Marianila Presiados Mollemans, July 4, 1989; 1 child Marc Andrew. BS, U. Adelaide, Australia, 1981, BS with honors, 1982. Jackeroo, station hand various ranches, Australia, 1973, Australia, 1975—76, Australia, 1981; cons. botanist Dept. Environment, Australia, 1982—84; geologist, exploration mgr. Greenbushes, Australia, 1987—89; cons. botanist Dept. Conservation, Australia, 1990, Agr. Dept., Australia, 1991—93; pvt. practice Casual, Hawaii, 2001—. Co-author: Environmental Survey, 1984, Wildlife Management Plan, 1991; contbr. articles to profl. jours. Achievements include discovery of five new species of plants in Western Australia; two million dollars in tantalite in northern territory Australia. Avocation: art. Home and Office: PO Box 3055 Kailua Kona HI 96745

MOLLEN, EDWARD LEIGH, pediatrician, allergist and clinical immunologist; b. Richmond, Va., May 13, 1946; s. Irving Roth and Ruth (Damsky) M.; m. Mary Viola Jeffrey, Dec. 14, 1975; children: Shawn, Michael, Eric, Christopher. BS in Chemistry, Coll. William and Mary, 1968; MD, Med. Coll. Va., 1972. Diplomate Am. Bd. Pediatrics, Am. Bd. Allergy and Immunology. Resident in pediatrics Med. Coll. Va., Richmond, 1972-75, fellow in allergy and immunology, 1975-77; practice allergy and pediatric allergy and clin. immunology Allergy Assocs. of Richmond, 1977-85; pvt. practice allergy/pediatric allergy and clin. immunology Richmond, 1985—. Fellow Am. Acad. Allergy, Asthma and Immunology, Am. Acad. Pediatrics; mem. Med. Soc. Va., Richmond Acad. Medicine, Am. Thoracic Soc., Asthma & Allergy Soc. Va. Avocations: bicycling, running, gardening. Office: 5855 Bremo Rd Ste 702 Richmond VA 23226-1926 E-mail: elmollenmd@aol.com.

MOLLENAUER, LINN FREDERICK, physicist; b. Washington, Jan. 6, 1937; B of Engring. Physics, Cornell U., 1959; PhD in Physics, Stanford U., 1965. Asst. prof. physics U. Calif., Berkeley, 1965—72; rsch. staff Bell Labs./Lucent Techs., Holmdel, NJ, 1972—. Co-editor (with J.C. White): Tunable Lasers, 1987. Recipient Ballantine medal, Franklin Inst., 1986, Rank prize in Photonics, 1991; fellow, Bell Labs., 2000. Fellow: IEEE (LEOS Disting. Lectr. award 1991, LEOS Quantum Electronics award 2001), AAAS, Optical Soc. Am. (R.W. Wood prize 1982, Charles Hard Townes award 1997); mem.: NAE. Achievements include first to demonstrate optical soliton propagation, leading to the realization of soliton-based, ultra-high-capacity lightwave communication. Office: Bell Labs Lucent Technologies Rm 4C-306 Crawfords Corner Rd Holmdel NJ 07733 E-mail: linn@lucent.com.

MOLLENKOTT, VIRGINIA RAMEY, English literature and language educator, author, guest lecturer; b. Phila., Jan. 28, 1932; d. Robert Franklin and May (Lotz) Ramey; m. Frederick H. Mollenkott, June 17, 1954 (div. July 1973); 1 child, Paul F. BA, Bob Jones U., 1953; MA, Temple U., 1955; PhD, NYU, 1964; D in Ministries (hon.), Samaritan Coll., 1989. Chair English dept. Shelton Coll., Ringwood, N.J., 1955-63, Nyack (N.Y.) Coll., 1963-67; English dept. chair William Paterson U. of N.J., Wayne, 1972-76, prof. emeritus, 1997—, prof. English, 1967—97. Asst. editor Seventeenth Century News, N.Y.C., 1965-75; stylistic cons. New International Version of the Bible, Am. Bible Soc., 1970-78; translation com. An Inclusive Language Lectionary, Nat. Coun. Chs., 1980-88; bd. dirs. Pacem in Terris, Warwick, N.Y., 1980—, Kirkridge Conf. Ctr., Bangor, Pa., 1980-91, Upper Room AIDS Ministry, Harlem, N.Y.C., 1989-94; adv. bd. Program on gender and soc. Rochester (N.Y.) Divinity Sch., 1993—; manuscript evaluator Jour. of Feminist Studies in Religion, Cambridge, Mass., 1994—; contbg. editor The Witness, 1994-2000, 02-; lectr. in field. Author: Adamant and Stone Chips, 1967, In Search of Balance, 1969, Women, Men and the Bible, 1977 1st rev. edit. 1988, Korean translation, 1981, Speech, Silence, Action, 1980, (with others) Is the Homosexual My Neighbor? A Positive Christian Response, 1978, rev. edit. 1994 (Integrity award 1979), The Divine Feminine: Biblical Imagery of God as Female, 1983, in German 1985, French, 1990, Italian, 1993; (with others) Views from the Intersection, 1984, Godding: Human Responsibility and the Bible, 1987, Sensuous Spirituality: Out from Fundamentalism, 1992 (N.J. Lesbian and Gay Achievement award 1992), Omnigender: A Trans-Religious Approach, 2001 (Lambda Literary award 2002, Ben Franklin award 2002); editor: Women of Faith in Dialogue, 1987, Adam Among the Television Trees, 1971; editl. bd. Studies in Theology & Sexuality, 1997—. Recipient Lifetime Achievment award, Sr. Action in a Gay Environ., 1999. Mem. MLA (exec. com. religion and lit. 1976-80), Women's Inst. for Freedom of the Press (assoc.), Milton Soc. Am. (exec. com. 1974-76). Democrat. Episcopalian. Avocations: travel, gardening, grandmothering. Home and Office: 11 Yearling Trl Hewitt NJ 07421-2510 E-mail: jstvrm@warwick.net.

MOLLER, KARLIND THEODORE, dental educator, researcher; b. Stillwater, Minn., May 25, 1942; s. Theodore Lars and Mildred Marie (Lindquist) Moller; m. Susan Mary Moller, July 24, 1965; children: Kara Lynn, Kevin Jon. BS, U. Minn., 1964, MA, 1967; PhD, U. MInn., 1970. Dir. Cleft Palate and Craniofacial Anomolies Clins., U. Minn. Sch. Dentistry, Mpls. Cons. Minn. Dept. Health, St. Paul, 1970—85, VA, Mpls., 1972—80. Author: A Parent Guide to Cleft Lip and Palate, 1990; editor: Interdisciplinary Issues and Treatment, 1993; contbr. articles to profl. jours. Bd. dirs. Cleft Palate Found., Chapel Hill, NC, 1996—2000; com. mem. Shorevies-Roseville Jt. Water Study, Minn., 1978—80; vol. water monitor Pollution Control Agy., St. Paul, 1981—. Fellow: Am. Speech Lang. Hearing Assn. (Outstanding Clinical Achievement award 1985); mem.: Minn. Speech Lang. Hearing Assn. (pres. 1991—93), Omicron Kappa Upsilon. Avocations: racquetball, hiking, landscaping. Office: U Minn Sch Dentistry 515 Delaware St SE Minneapolis MN 55455 Business E-Mail: molle001@umn.edu.

MOLLER, MARY DENISE, psychiatric nurse practitioner; Cert. advanced registered nurse practitioner in psychiatry, CS, CPRP. Staff nurse Meth. Hosp., Omaha, 1971-76; instr. Meth. Sch. Nursing, 1976-82; asst. prof. nursing Midland Luth. Coll., Fremont, Nebr., 1982-89; asst. clin. prof. nursing Creighton U., Omaha, 1989-92; adj. instr. nursing Wash. State U. and Gonzaga U., 1993—; pres. Nurseminars, Inc., Spokane, Wash.; clin. dir. Suncrest Wellness Ctr.; CEO Psychiat. Resource Network, Inc. Keynote speaker Mayo Clinic Conf. on Mental Illness, 1995, 2d World Conf. on Schizophrenia, Vancouver, B.C., 8th Internat. Assn. for Psychocial Rehab. Svcs., others; chair Global Schizophrenia Forum, London, 1995; Dorothy Kent disting. lectr. Vanderbilt U., 1991; mem. NIMH Task Force on Families and Mental Illness; cons. Ministry of Health, State of Israel, 1999; vis. prof. NYU Sch. Nursing, 1999; presenter in field. Prodr. (video tape) Understanding and Communicating With...; contbr. over 40 articles and book chpts. Del. leader for People to People Amb. Program of Psychiat. Nurses to China, 1999, to Israel, 2000, to Cuba, 2001 Named Woman of Distinction, Omaha YWCA, 1989. Mem.: ANA (Washington State chpt. Leadership and Mgmt. award 2001), Nat. Alliance for the Mentally Ill (chair curriculum and tng. task force 2002—, Profl. of Yr. 1996), Soc. Edn. and Rsch. in Psychiat. Nursing, Am. Psychiat. Nurses Assn. (chair advanced practice com. 1999—2001, award for clin. excellence 1994), Sigma Theta Tau. E-mail: marymoller@aol.com.

MOLLES, EMILY DEMARTINO, artist, real estate broker; b. Norwalk, Conn., Mar. 20, 1938; d. Frank DeMartino and Mary Louise (Perriffo) DeMartino; m. Eugene Joseph Molles, Dec. 1, 1956 (div. 1976); children: Deborah Lynn Molles Boy'er, Eugene Scott; m. Robert DiNardo Sr., June 9, 2000. Student, Sacred Heart U., 1973, U. Conn., 1975; cert. in real estate law, Fairfield U., 1976; BFA, Ringling Sch. Art and Design, 1995; MA, NYU, 2001; student, Venice, 1999—2001. Grad. Realtors Inst.; cert. residential specialist. Pres. PRM, Inc., Norwalk, 1976—; realtor June Scott's Assocs., Beverly Hills, Calif., 1980-82, Len Hoff Realty, Marina Del Rey, 1982-84; founder, owner Country Homes, Milford, Conn., 1984-89, Country Homes of Saugatuck Shores, Westport, 1989-91. Mem. Nat. Mus. Women in Arts (assoc.). Avocations: sailing, music. Home: 2425 Gulf Of Mexico Dr Unit 2B Longboat Key FL 34228-3282 Studio: Artist Studio & Gallery 1373 Main St Sarasota FL 34236

MOLLET, CHRIS JOHN, lawyer; b. Bottineau, N.D., Jan. 31, 1954; s. Lyle Frank and Aileen Charlotte (Murdoch) M.; m. Lynne M. LaJone, Sept. 20, 1980; children: Ben C., Cory J., Jeff A. BA, U. Wis., 1976, JD, 1979. Bar: Wis. 1979, Ill. 1980. Staff counsel Michael Reese Hosp. and Med Ctr., Chgo., 1980-82; assoc. Gardner, Carton and Douglas, 1982-85; assoc. gen. counsel, asst. sec. Luth. Gen. Health Care System, Park Ridge, Ill., 1985-92; ptnr. Foley & Lardner, Chgo., 1992-96; co-chief exec. officer, sr. v.p., gen. counsel, asst. sec. Am. Pharm. Svcs., Inc., Naperville, Ill., 1996—. Chmn. bd., Dist. 64 Elem. Learning Found., 1999-2000, trustee. Contbr. chpts. to books and articles to profl. jours. Bd. dirs. Young Lawyers sect. Chgo. Bar Assn., 1984-86. Mem. Wis. Bar Assn., Am. Health Lawyers Assn., Ill. Assn. Hosp. Attys. (bd. dirs. 1988-91, sec.-treas. 1991). Home: 706 Wisner St Park Ridge IL 60068-2709 Office: Am Pharm Svcs Inc 1771 W Diehl Rd Ste 210 Naperville IL 60563-4843 E-mail: cmollet@mpan.com.

MOLLEUR, DENIS RICHARD, lawyer; b. Washington, Oct. 27, 1957; s. Richard Raymond and Rita Marie (Desaulniers) M.; m. Danielle Elizabeth Dugas, Sept. 30, 1984; children: Nicole, Colette, Madeleine, Elise. BA, Loyola Coll., 1980; JD, Georgetown U., 1983, LLM in Securities Regulation, 1988. Bar: D.C. 1983, Md. 1984, Mass. 1990, N.Y. 1992. Jud. clk. D.C. Superior Ct., Washington, 1983-84; atty. advisor U.S. Securities and Exch. Com., 1984-87; assoc. Goodwin, Procter & Hoar, Boston, 1987-89; asst. v.p., assoc. counsel Putnam Investments, 1989-90; v.p., sr. counsel Oppenheimer Funds, Inc., N.Y.C., 1991—. Office: OppenheimerFunds Inc 10th Fl South 498 7th Ave New York NY 10018

MOLLICA, SANTO, percussionist, songwriter, performer; b. Bronx, N.Y., Dec. 8, 1958; s. Salvatore and Vincenza Mollica. Student, Fordham, 1974, Hunter, N.Y., 1975-80. Pres., founder Source Unltd. Records, N.Y.C., 1981—. Prodr., writer, dir. (music LP records) American Way, 1985, Music from the Street, 1986, A Night in the Life, 1988, Self-Respect, 1989; dir. Desperate Times by Ed Peterson, 1994, Teaser by Dave Sasser and Mojo Conga Jam, 1996, Summer Heart by Jereme Lodeon, 1997, Home Grown by Tycoon Dog, 1998, Outskirts by Swivelchair, 1998. Office: Source Unltd Records 331 E 9th St New York NY 10003-7721

MOLLMAN, JOHN PETER, book publisher, consultant electronic publishing; b. Belleville, Ill., Feb. 8, 1931; s. Kenneth John and Maurine (Farrow) M.; m. Carol J. Piper, Apr. 4, 1998; children— Sarah Chase, Eric Cleburne BA, Washington U., St. Louis, 1952. Advt. specialist Gen. Electric Co., Schenectady and Boston, 1952-54; mgr. Enterprise Printing Co., Millstadt, Ill., 1956-66; gen. mgr. Monarch Pub. Co., N.Y.C., 1966-67; dir. prodn. Harper & Row Pubs., 1967-74; pub. Harper's Mag. Press, 1971-74; v.p. prodn. Random House Inc., 1974-81; sr. v.p. World Book-Childcraft Inc., Chgo., 1981-88; pres. World Book Pub., 1988-91; pub. cons., 1991-92; dir. intellectual property devel. Multimedia Publishing Microsoft, 1992-96; cons. in electronic pub. Carmel, Calif., 1996—. Mem. vis. com. Washington U.; mem. pub. com. Art Inst. Chgo.; bd. dirs. Yevba Buena Ctr. for the Arts, San Francisco; pres. Internat. ebook Award Found., N.Y. Mem. Golf Club at Quail Lodge, Phi Delta Theta, Sigma Delta Chi, Omicron Delta Kappa. Unitarian Universalist. Home: 25340 Vista Del Pinos Carmel CA 93923-8804 E-mail: pmollman@msn.com.

MOLLO, JOSEPH ANTHONY, university administrator; b. Binghamton, N.Y., Oct. 7, 1954; s. Joseph Anthony and Lena Lucy Mollo; m. Judith Moyer, May, 1995 (div. July 1998). BS, SUC, Buffalo, 1976; MSEd, SUNY, Buffalo, 1977. Mgr. recreational svcs. St. Joseph's Sch. Nursing, Elmira, 1978-83, dir. fin. aid, recruiting N.Y., 1984-86; residence dir. SUNY, Morrisville, 1986-88, assoc. dir. campus life Purchase, 1988-91; dir. student activities Ferrum Coll., Va., 1991-2000; dir. campus activities and events U. Maine, Orono, 2000—. Coord. blood drive ARC, SUNY, Purchase, 1988-91, vol., Roanoke, Va., 1991-2000; vol. Project Safe Kids, Roanoke, 1995-99; fund raising coord., We. Va. AIDS Coun., Roanoke, 1997, St. James Cmty. Ctr., Ferrum, Va., ARC, Roanoke, 1998, Franklin County Schs., Rocky Mountain, Va., 1999; vol. Toys for Tots, Roanoke, 1997-99 . With USNR, 1986. Recipient Hudson Valley Blood Bank, 1991, Meritorious Svc. award Area Eight Spl. Olympics, 1992. Mem. Nat. Assn. Campus Activities (unit regional leadership team 1992-2000, unit coord. Va. 1994-97, regional coop. buyer 1997-99, vol. devel. coord. 1999-2000, Outstanding Campus Activities Profls., 1999). E-mail: joseph.mollo@umit.maine.edu.

MOLLOFF, FLORENCE JEANINE, speech and language therapist; b. St. Louis, Aug. 28, 1959; d. Lawrence Allan and Rietta Gertrude (Fiegenbaum) M. BS, Fontbonne Coll., St. Louis, 1983; MEd summa cum laude, Nat. Louis U., St. Louis, 1989; student, Project ACCESS Inst., 1992, Judevine Ctr. Autistic Children Tng., 1992. Cert. speech correctionist, Mo. Intern St. Louis State Sch. for Profoundly Retarded, 1983-84; speech therapist St. Louis Pub. Schs., 1984—; Judvine Ctr. for Autistic Children Tng., 1992; speech/lang. therapist St. Louis Pub. Schs./Autism Program, 1992-93, 97—; speech/lang. therapist Michael Sch. Medically Fragile and Multiply Handicapped Michael Sch. Medically Fragile and Multiply Handicapped, 1993-96; speech and language therapist autism program Buder and Fanning, 1997—2002. Speech, lang. therapist St. Louis Pub. Schs./Michael Sch. for Medically Fragile and Multiply Handicapped, 1993—; ednl. cons. program devel. Mo. Coalition for Environ., St. Louis, Columbia, Kansas City, 1990—; cons., trainer in puppetry Kids on the Block, St. Louis Pub. Schs., 1988—; vol. grant writer West End Restoration Corp.; speech/lang. therapist Mid. Sch. for Medically Fragile and Multiply Handicapped, 1993-96. Author: (pseudonym F.J. Molotschnikov) 91 Seconds to Armageddon, 1999; author, creator transition curriculum: Consultative Resource Program, 1989; creator puppet program: Save Our Astonishing Planet, 1990; ednl. cons. program devel. young St. Louis audiences (adapted program for severe to profoundly handicapped children "Arabian Nights", 1994; editor: Strides Newsletter, St. Louis, 1996-98; contbr. artist St. Louis Internat. Jazz Mus.; vol. grant writer West End Restoration Corp. Educator, lobbyist Coalition for the Environ., St. Louis, 1990, newsletter editor, 2000-01; activist, lobbyist Housing Now, St. Louis, 1989; foster parent Christian Children's Fund, 1986—; activist Habitat for Humanity Internat., 1994—; mem., fundraiser Gateway I Have a Dream Found., 1995—; mem. nat. steering com. (hon.) Pres. Clinton's Re-election, 1995; contbg. mem. Dem. Nat. Com., 1995—; vol. grant writer West End Restoration Corp.; mem. Emily's List; participant Cross-Cultural Solutions Project, New Delhi, India, 1998. Mem. AAUW, ASCD, Coun. Exceptional Children (state rep. Mo. divsn. for children with communicative disorders 1988-89, presenter nat. conv. 1989), Internat. Platform Assn., Am. Fedn. Tchrs. (bldg. rep. 1992), Nat. Arbor Day Found., Nat. Parks and Conservation Assn., Nat. Women's Polit. Caucus, Mo. Assn. for Augmentative Comm. Systems, Met. St. Louis Women's Polit. Caucus, Emily's List, Am. Med. Writers Assn., Soc. for Tech. Com., NEA (editor Strides newsletter 1996—, grantee Internet project, sec. St. Louis 1997-99), Mo. NEA, Amnesty Internat. Democrat. Avocations: puppetry, profl. clowning, running track, film, debate, graphic arts. Home: 9823 Lullaby Ln Saint Louis MO 63114-2510

MOLLOHAN, ALAN B. congressman, lawyer; b. Fairmont, W.Va., May 14, 1943; s. Robert H. and Helen (Holt) M.; m. Barbara Whiting, Aug. 7, 1976; children: Alan, Robert, Andrew, Karl, Mary Kathryn. AB in Polit. Sci., Coll. William and Mary, 1966; JD, W.Va. U., 1970. Assoc. law firm, 1970-82; mem. U.S. Congresses from 1st W.Va. dist., 1983—; mem. appropriations com. With USAR, 1970—83. Mem. ABA, W.Va. Bar, Moose, Elks. Baptist. Office: US Ho of Reps 2346 Rayburn HOB Washington DC 20515-0001*

MOLLOY, ANGELA MARGARET, advertising, marketing, and public relations executive; b. July 16, 1948; d. John Robert and Angela Margaret (Culotta) Fanto; m. William Francis Molloy, June 24, 1970 (div. Oct. 1978); 1 child, Angela Margaret. BA, Duquesne U., 1970. cert. qualitative rsch. provider Burke Ins., 1995-96. Edtl. asst. Nat. Coun. Internat. Visitors, Washington, 1970-73; dir. devel. DeMatha H.S., Hyattsville, Md., 1973-75; mktg. officer Wash. Fed. Savs. & Loan, Washington, 1978-80; asst. v.p., dir. mktg. Md. Fed. Savs. & Loan, Hyattsville, 1980-83; asst. v.p., dir. mktg. and advt. B.F. Saul Co., Chevy Chase, Md., 1983-86; sr. v.p. Power House Comms. affiliate Gray & Co., pub. rels., 1986-87; exec. v.p. Susan Davis Advt., 1987-91; ptnr. Gardner, Keaton Molloy Advt., 1991-94; owner Molloy Mktg. Svcs., 1994—. Bd. dirs. YMCA Metro Washington, 1991-95. Mem. soc. Profl. Journalists, Women in Advt. and Mktg., Advt. Club Met. Washington, Mkt. Rsch. Assn., Women of Washington, Amer. Mktg. Assn. Democrat. Roman Catholic. E-mail: pmolloy@clark.net.

MOLLOY, CHRISTOPHER JOHN, molecular and cellular pharmacologist; b. N.Y.C., Feb. 18, 1954; s. James Francis and Dorothy Jean (Russell) M.; m. Geraldine McConville, July 5, 1992; children: Meaghan, Anne. BS in Pharmacy, Rutgers U., 1977, PhD in Pharmacology-Toxicology, 1987. Registered pharmacist, N.J. Pharmacist W.M. Weinstein Prescriptions, Livingston, N.J., 1977-81; tchg. asst. Rutgers Coll. Pharmacy, Piscataway, 1982-85; postdoctoral fellow Nat. Cancer Inst., NIH, Bethesda, Md., 1986-90; sr. rsch. investigator Bristol-Myers Squibb Pharm. Rsch. Inst., Princeton, N.J., 1990-98; exec. dir. discovery biology 3-Dimensional Pharm., Inc., Exton, Pa., 1998—; adj. asst. prof. Univ. Med. and Dentistry N.J.-Robert Wood Johnson Med. Sch., Piscataway, 1992—. Reviewer Molecular Pharmacology, Cardiovascular Rsch., Circulation, Hypertension, Jour. Molecular Cell Cardiology; contbr. articles to Nature, Molecular and Cellular Biology, Proc. NAS, Jour. Biol. Chemistry, Jour. Clin. Investigation, Cancer Rsch. Recipient Grad. fellowship award Soc. of Cosmetic Chemists, 1983, Biotech. fellowship Nat. Cancer Inst., Bethesda, Md., 1986, Visiting fellowship, Spanish Health Ministry, Madrid, 1990, Selected Reference (Hot Paper) The Scientist Newspaper, Phila., 1991. Mem. AAAS, Am. Soc. Biochem. and Molecular Biology, Am. Assn. Cancer Rsch., Sigma Xi. Office: 3-Dimensional Pharm Inc 665 Stockton Dr Ste 104 Exton PA 19341-1151 E-mail: chris.molloy@3dp.com.

MOLLOY, SYLVIA, Latin American literature educator, writer; b. Buenos Aires, Argentina, Aug. 29, 1938; came to U.S. 1967; d. Herbert Edward and Margarita Berta (Chasseing) M. Licence es Lettres, U. Paris, 1960, Diplome D'Etudes Superieures, 1961, Doctorat de U. Paris, 1967. Asst. prof. Spanish SUNY, Buffalo, 1967-69; asst. prof. Spanish Vassar Coll., Poughkeepsie, N.Y., 1969-70, Princeton U., Princeton, N.J., 1970-73, assoc. prof., 1973-81, Emory L. Ford prof., 1981-86; prof. Spanish Yale U., New Haven, 1986-90; Albert Schweitzer prof. of Humanities NYU, 1990—. Author: La Diffusion de la Litterature Hispanoamericaine en France, 1972, Las Letras de Borges, 1979, En Breve Carcel, 1981, At Face Value: Autobiographical Writing in Spanish America, 1991; co-author Women's Writing in Latin America, 1991, Hispanisms and Homosexualities, 1998; author short stories and contbr. articles to profl. jours.; cons., editorial bd. Revista Iberoamericana, 1979-81, 1985-89, Latin Am. Literary Rev., 1985—, Revista de Filología, Buenos Aires, 1985—. Fellow Am. Philos. Soc., 1970, NEH, 1976; Social Sci. Research Council grantee, 1983; Guggenheim Found. fellow, 1986-87 Mem. MLA (pres.), Asociacion Internacional de Hispanistas, Instituto Internacional de Literatura Iberoamericana

MOLMENTI, ERNESTO P. surgeon; b. Feb. 5, 1964; BA summa cum laude, Boston U., 1985, MD, 1989. Intern Barnes Hosp.-Washington U. Sch. Medicine, St. Louis, 1989-90, chief resident, 1995—96; instr. dept. anatomy and neurobiology Washington U. Sch. Medicine, 1992-96; fellow, instr., transplant surgeon U. Pitts., 1996-98; asst. prof. surgery S.W. Med. Ctr., U. Tex., Dallas, 1999—2001; transplant surgeon Children's Med. Ctr., Baylor U. Med. Ctr., 1999-2001; assoc. prof. surgery Johns Hopkins U., 2001—, surg. dir. kidney-pancreas transplantation, 2001—. Author: Atlas of Liver Transplantation, 2002; contbg. author Washington University Manual of Surgery, 1997, Laparoscopic Surgery: Principles and Procedures, Computed Body Tomography with MRI Correlation, 1997, Surgical Clnics of North America, 2000, Clnics in Liver Disease, 2000, Textbook of Critical Care, 2000; contbr. articles to profl. jours. Named Harold C. Case scholar, Boston U., 1984, Internat. scholar, 1984; recipient Avelino Gutierrez Biannual award, Nat. Acad. Medicine Argentina, 1987, Hist. Sci. award, Nat. Acad. Scis. Argentina, 1989, 1990, Excellence in Tchg. award, Washington U. Sch. Medicine, 1991, 1992, Hounsfield award, Soc. Computed Body Tomography Magnetic Resonance, 1995, Young Investigator award, Transplant Soc., 1998, Travel award, Internat. Assn. for the Study of Liver Disease, 1998, Young Investigator award, AST/Am. Soc. Transplant Surgeons, 2000; fellow Abbott Labs. and Crohns and Colitis Found., 1993—94, Faculty Rsch. fellow, ACS, 2002. Mem.: Mem. Argentine Med. Assn. (fgn. corr.), Phi Beta Kappa. Office: The Johns Hopkins Hosp 600 N Wolfe St # 402 Harvey 611 Baltimore MD 21287-8611 E-mail: emolmen1@jhmi.edu.

MOLNAR, BELA, school administrator; b. Elyria, Ohio, May 12, 1951; s. Bela and Olga Margaret (Strong) M.; m. Nancy Lynn Campbell, Aug. 9, 1975; children: Eric Bela, Melinda Renee. B.A., Heidelberg Coll., 1973; M.Ed., Cleve. State U., 1977; postgrad., Kent State U., Akron U. Cert. secondary tchr., Ohio. Health, phys. edn. tchr. Ford Jr. High Sch., Brook Park, Ohio, 1973-79, athletic coach, 1973-79, health, physical edn. dept. chair, 1977-79; unit prin. Berea High Sch., Ohio, 1979-82; asst. prin. Copley High Sch., Ohio, 1982-83, prin. 1984-90, Elyria High Sch., 1990—. Mem. Nat. Assn. Secondary Sch. Prins., Ohio Assn. Secondary Sch. Adminstrs., Summit County Prins. (pres. 1986-87), Heidelberg Alumni H Assn., Kiwanis. Avocations: jogging, golf, registered Ohio High Sch. Athletic Assn. baseball, softball official. Home: 108 Ashland Ave Elyria OH 44035-8284 Office: Elyria High Sch 311 6th St Elyria OH 44035-5792

MOLNAR, DONALD JOSEPH, landscape architecture educator; b. Springfield, Ill., Dec. 24, 1938; s. Joseph and Mabel Irene (Woods) M.; m. Carol Jeanette Smith, Aug. 22, 1958; children: Elaina Deanne, Amy Lynn, Holly Suzanne. BFA in Landscape Architecture, U. Ill., 1960, MFA in Landscape Architecture, 1964. Landscape architect Simonds and Simonds, Pitts., 1961-63; landscape architect campus planning U. Ill., Urbana, 1963-72, asst. dir., planner capital programs Urbana and Chgo., 1971-81; assoc. prof. landscape architecture Purdue U., West Lafayette, Ind., 1981-85, dir. landscape architecture coop. program, 1983—, prof. landscape architecture, 1985—, chair landscape architecture program, 1987—, dir. internat. exch. landscape architecture, 1988—. Cons. to architect, engrs., park agys., 1964—, Mobile Homes Mfrs. Assn., Chgo., 966-76; prin. Profl. Searches for Landscape Archs., employment cons., 2000—. Author: Anatomy of a Park, 2d edit., 1986; illustrator: Anatomy of a Park, 1971, Visual Approach to Park Design, 1980; developer software CompuPave, 1992, PaveCAD, 1996. Mem., program coord. Champaign (Ill.) Devel. Coun., 1966-78. Named Hon. Parks Commr., Champaign Park Dist., 1981. Fellow Am. Soc. Landscape Architects (licensing com. Ill. chpt. 1968-70, registration com. Ind. chpt. 1982-85, pres. 1991-92, award 1982). Avocations: travel, computers. Office: Purdue U Landscape Architecture Prog 1165 Horticulture Bldg West Lafayette IN 47907-1165

MOLNAR, LAWRENCE, lawyer; b. Czygand, Hungary, Apr. 14, 1927; came to U.S., 1954; s. Alexander and Marie (Vavra) M.; m. Virginia Hampton Broome, July 16, 1999. Juris Utriusque Candidatus, Charles U., Prague, Czechoslovakia, 1951; JD, NYU, 1962; LLM, LLD (hon.), Charles U., 1991. Bar: N.Y. 1962, U.S. Dist. Ct. (so. and ea. dists.) N.Y. 1970, Czech Republic, 1991. With U.S. Intelligence, Berlin, 1951-54, Lansen, Naeve Corp., N.Y., 1955-56; asst. mgr. export traffic Intra-Mar Shipping Corp., 1957-58; mgr. export traffic Melchior, Armstrong, Ridgefield, N.J., 1958-59; assoc. Hamburger, Weinschenk, N.Y.C., 1963-69; ptnr. Hamburger, Weinschenk, Molnar & Fisher, 1969—2001; counsel Hamburger, Weinschenk & Fisher, 2001—. Mem. ABA, Assn. of Bar of City of N.Y., Consular Law Soc. (v.p. 1980—), Fgn. Law Assn., Queens Bar Assn. Office: Hamburger Weinschenk Molnar & Fisher 36 W 44th St New York NY 10036-8102

MOLNAR, STEPHEN PAUL, research scientist; b. Toledo, July 8, 1935; s. Stephen C. and Ethel A. (Horvath) M.; divorced, 1989; children: Stephen, David; married 1992. BS, U. Toledo, 1957; MS, Purdue U., 1963; PhD, U. Cin., 1967. Asst. prof. Miami U., Oxford, Ohio, 1967-75; sr. rsch. chemist Armco, Middletown, 1975-82; sr. rsch. assoc. Franklin Internat., Columbus, 1984-85; mgr. chem. svcs. Nuclear Cons. Svcs., 1987-89; sr. researcher Edison Welding Inst., 1989-93; sr. project mgr. Triangle Labs. of Columbus, Inc., 1993-95, cons., 1995—; lab. dir. Lithchen Internat., 1999—2001; sr. rsch. scientist iMEDD, Inc., 2001—. Contbr. articles to profl. pubs. Col. U.S. Army Res., 1957-87; ret. Col. USAR, 1957—87. Mem. Am. Chem. Soc., Sigma Xi.

MOLO, STEVEN FRANCIS, lawyer; b. Chgo., June 30, 1957; s. Steven and Alice (Babinski) M.; m. Mary Wood, Dec. 31, 1986; children: Alexander, Madeline, Julia, Allison. BS, U. Ill., 1979, JD, 1982. Bar: Ill. 1982. Asst. atty. gen. criminal pros. and trial divsn., Chgo., 1982-86; assoc. Winston & Strawn, 1986-89, ptnr., 1989—, mem. exec. com., 2000—. Adj. prof. Loyola U. Law Sch., Chgo., 1988-93,. Northwestern U. Law Sch., Chgo., 1989—; mem. faculty Nat. Inst. Trial Advocacy, Chgo., 1989—; lectr. on trial advocacy, appellate advocacy, and evidence to various orgns. Co-author: Corporate Internal Investigations, 1993, updated annually, 1993—; bd. editors Bus. Crimes Bull: Litigation and Compliance, 1994—; contbr. articles to legal jours. Spl. counsel Ill. Jud. Inquiry Bd., 1986-90; spl. reapportionment counsel Cook County Judiciary, 1988-89, spl. reapportionment counsel to Rep. leadership Ill. Ho. of Reps. and Senate, 1991-92. Named World's Leading White Collar Crime Lawyers, Euromoney PLC, 1995, Leading Ill. Attys. Comml. Litigation and Criminal Law, 1996, Crain's Chicago Bus. "40 Under 40" Chicago Leaders, 1997, Best Lawyers in Am., 2000. Mem. ABA, FBA, Ill. Bar Assn., Chgo. Bar Assn., Theodore Roosevelt Assn., Chgo. Athletic Assn., Econ. Club Chgo., Tavern Club, Chgo. Inn of Ct. (master of bench, pres. 1997-98), Saddle & Cycle Club, Gilda's club Chgo. (presdl. gov. bd. 1999—). Office: Winston & Strawn 35 W Wacker Dr Ste 4200 Chicago IL 60601-1695

MOLOFF, ALAN LAWRENCE, army officer, physician; b. Bklyn., Sept. 29, 1954; s. Louis Rubin and Muriel (Trabeck) M. BS, U. Vt., 1976; DO, U. N.J., 1983; MPH, Harvard U., 1988; student, U.S. Army Command/Gen. Staff Course, 1994-95. Diplomate Am. Bd. Preventive Medicine; bd. cert. aerospace medicine, undersea medicine. Commd. platoon leader U.S. Army, 1976, advanced through grades to col., 1999; intern Fitzsimons Army Med. Ctr., Aurora, Colo., 1983-84; med. officer lst Battalion 10th Spl. Forces Group, Bad Tolz, Fed. Republic of Germany, 1984-87; resident in aerospace medicine Harvard U., Boston, 1987-89; chief spl. ops. forces divsn. Acad. Health Scis., San Antonio, 1989-92; command surgeon Spl. Forces Command, Ft. Bragg, N.C., 1992-93; dep. surgeon U.S. Army Spl. Ops. Command, 1993-94; with command and gen. staff coll. U.S. Army, 1994-95; dep. surgeon 30th Med. Brigade, Heidelberg, Germany, 1995-96; SETAF surgeon, 1995-97; dep. U.S. Army Europe Fwd Surgeon, Hungary, 1995-96; surgeon V Corps, Heidelberg, Germany, 1996-97; comdr. 212th M.A.S.H., Wiesbaden, Germany, 1997-99; fellow environ. policy inst. Army War Coll., 1999-2000; comdr. US Army Aviation Med. Ctr., 2000—. Lectr. advanced trauma life support Aerospace Med., Environ. Security, Undersea Medicine, Med. Support Contingency Ops. Contbr. articles to profl. jours. Active in civic activities. Decorated Meritorious Svc. medal with 4 oak leaf clusters, Joint Svc. Commendation medal, S.W. Asian Svc. medal, Army Commendation medal with oak leaf cluster, Joint Army Achievement medal, Armed Forces Svc. medal, Armed Forces Expeditionary medal, NATO medal, Kuwait Liberation medal, Kosovo Campaign medal, German Paratrooper badge, Pathfinder badge, Expert Field Med. badge, Order of Mil. Med. Merit, Master Parachutist award, Ranger Spl. Forces Qualified Master Flight Surgeon badge, Navy Dive Med. Officer badge. Fellow Am. Coll. Preventive Medicine, Aerospace Med. Assn.; mem. Am. Osteo. Assn., Aerospace Med. Assn., Assn. Mil. Surgeons U.S., Assn. Mil. Osteo Physicians and Surgeons, Soc. U.S. Army Flight Surgeons (life). Avocations: skiing, scuba diving, weightlifting, military history, rock climbing. E-mail: alan.moloff@se.amedd.army.mil.

MOLOKIE, MATTHEW JOSEPH (MATTHEW JEROME JOSEPH MOLOKIE), priest; b. Long Beach, Calif., Mar. 3, 1961; s. Richard G. and Dorothy Louise (Shuflitowski) Molokie, Dorothy Louise Molokie (nee) Shuflitowski. BM in Piano Performance, Oberlin Conservatory of Music, Ohio, 1983; BPh, U. of St. Thomas (Angelicum), Rome, 1989; STM, U. of St. Thomas (Angelicum), 1994. Music dir. St. Michael''s Abbey, Silverado , Calif., 1994—. Priest St. Justin Martyr Ch., Anaheim, Calif., 1995—; music cons., tutor Norbertine Sisters of St. Joseph, Tehachapi, Calif., 1995—. Mem.: Am. Guild of Organists (Orange County Chapter) (Member at Large 2001—03). Home and Office: 19292 El Toro Rd Silverado CA 92676 Personal E-mail: frjerome@juno.com. Business E-mail: frjerome@juno.com.

MOLONEY, STEPHEN MICHAEL, lawyer; b. L.A., July 1, 1949; s. Donald Joseph and Madeline Marie (Sartoris) M.; m. Nancy Paula Barile, Jan. 15, 1972; children: Michael, John, Kathleen. Student, St. John's Sem., Camarillo, Calif., 1967-69; BS, U. Santa Clara, 1971, JD, 1975. Bar: Calif. 1975, U.S. Dist. Ct. (cen. dist.) Calif. 1976, U.S. Supreme Ct. 1990. Assoc. Gilbert, Kelly, Crowley & Jennett, L.A., 1975-80, from ptnr. to sr. ptnr., 1980—. Arbitrator, settlement officer Los Angeles Superior Ct., 1985—. Contbr. articles to profl. jours. Dir. Calif. Def. Polit. Action Com., Sacramento, 1991—. With USAR. Recipient Svc. award to Pres. of So. Calif. Def. Counsel, Def. Rsch. Inst., Chgo., 1992. Mem. Assn. So. Calif. Def. Counsel (pres. 1992-93), Calif. Def. Counsel (dir. 1991—), L.A. County Bar Assn. (vols. in parole, 1976-77, exec. com. alternative dispute resolution com. 1992-96), Oakmont Country Club, La Quinta Resort and Club. Democrat. Roman Catholic. Avocations: politics, golf, reading, travel. Office: Gilbert Kelly Crowley & Jennett 1200 Wilshire Blvd Ste 6 Los Angeles CA 90017-1908 E-mail: smm@gilbertkelly.com.

MOLONEY, THOMAS E. lawyer; b. Rockville Ctr., N.Y., Jan. 9, 1949; BS, U. Dayton, 1971; JD, U. Notre Dame, 1974. Bar: Ohio 1974. Prin. Am. Energy Svcs., Inc., Columbus, Ohio. Office: Am Energy Svcs Inc 1105 Schrock Rd Ste 602 Columbus OH 43229-1174

MOLONEY, THOMAS JOSEPH, lawyer; b. Bklyn., Oct. 14, 1952; s. Thomas J. and Grace (Nelson) M.; m. Molly K. Heines, Dec. 26, 1976. AB, Columbia U., 1973; JD cum laude, NYU, 1976. Bar: N.Y. 1977, U.S. Dist. Ct. (so. dist.) N.Y. 1977, U.S. Dist. Ct. (ea. dist.) N.Y. 1978, U.S. Ct. Appeals (2d cir.) 1981. Assoc. Cleary, Gottlieb, Steen & Hamilton, N.Y.C., 1976-84, ptnr., 1984—. Bd. dirs. N.Y. Lawyers for Pub. Interest, N.Y.C., 1986-91; mediator U.S. Bankruptcy Ct. for So. Dist. N.Y., 1995. Asst. counsel Gov.'s Jud. Nominating Com., N.Y.C., 1981-85; chmn. bus. adv. coun. Washington Irving H.S., 1994—. Mem. ABA, Am. Bankruptcy Inst., Assn. of Bar of City of N.Y. (bankruptcy, corp. reorganization coms. 1983-86, chair com. legal assistance 1995-97), Order of Coif. Avocations: chess, golf, dance, travel, wine. Office: Cleary Gottlieb Steen & Hamilton 1 Liberty Plz Fl 38 New York NY 10006-1470

MOLONY, JOSEPH ANTHONY, retired editor; b. Charleston, Sc, Oct. 15, 1925; s. Henry Augustus and Margaret Hering Molony; m. Matrice Anderson Milstead, Apr. 19, 1980; children: Gayle Bridges, Greg Milstead; m. Sarah Lucille Kendall, Jan. 17, 1957 (div.); children: Mitchell Kendall, David Carlyle. AB Journalism, U. SC, Coumbia, SC, 1946—50. Editor Lake City Reporter, Lake City, Fla., 1956—58; wire editor Jacksonville Jour., Jacksonville, 1958—59, Panama City News-Herald, Panama City, 1959—61; info. specialist WRAMA, Robins AFB, Robins AFB, Ga., 1961—86; sports editor The Herald, Warner Robins, 1995—97; editor Tee Off in Ga., 1997—2001, Lions of Ga. State Newspaper, Eatontown, 1995—2002. Co-founder Charleston-Carolina Club, USC, Columbia, SC, Ga., 1947; comm. dir. Chpt. 296, AFA, Warner Robins, Ga., 1986—90; dist. gov. Dist. 18-E, Lions of Ga., 50 cities in southern GA, Ga., 1993—94. Editor: (newspaper) Lake City, FL Reporter (#1 in State, 1958), Warner Robins, GA Daily Sun (#1 in Ga. sports, 1968); contbr. (book) Pictorial History of Robins AFB, GA (SSP, 1982). Pres. Warner Robins Lions Club, Warner Robins, Ga., 1984—84; pub. rels. chmn. Ga. Lions Lighthouse, Decatur, 1995—2000. Signalman, 2nd class USN, 1943—46, Usa. Recipient Pulitzer Prize, Panama City News-Herald, 1962, Medal lof Merit, Chpt. 296, AFA, 1988, Top 10 Laymen in Ga., Ga. Recreation and Pk. Soc., 1968. Mem.: Air Force Assn. (life), Post 172, Am. Legion, Post 6605, VFW (life). Roman Catholic. Avocations: reading, baseball, golf. Home: 105 Tinker Blvd Warner Robins GA 31093

MOLONY, MICHAEL JANSSENS, JR. lawyer, arbitrator, mediator; b. New Orleans, Sept. 2, 1922; s. Michael Janssens and Marie (Perret)M.; m. Jane Leslie Waguespack, Oct. 21, 1951; children: Michael Janssens III (dec.), Leslie, Megan, Kevin, Sara, Brian, Ian, Duncan. JD, Tulane U., 1950. Bar: La. 1950, D.C. 1979, U.S. Dist. Ct. (ea. and mid. dists.) La. 1951, U.S. Ct. Appeals (5th cir.) 1953, U.S. Supreme Ct. 1972, U.S. Dist. Ct. (we. dist.) La. 1978, U.S. Ct. Appeals (11th and D.C. cirs.) 1981. Ptnr. Molony & Baldwin, New Orleans, 1950; assoc. Jones, Flanders, Waechter & Walker, 1951-56; ptnr. Jones, Walker, Waechter, Poitevent, Carrere & Denegre, 1956-75, Milling, Benson, Woodward, Hillyer, Pierson & Miller, New Orleans, 1975-91, Chaffe, McCall, Phillips, Toler & Sarpy, New Orleans, 1991-92, Sessions & Fishman, New Orleans, 1993-2000, Molony Law Firm, New Orleans, 2000—. Instr., lectr. Med. Sch. and Univ. Coll. Tulane U., 1953-59; mem. Eisenhower Legal Com., 1952. Bd. commrs. Port of New Orleans, 1976-81, pres., 1978; mem. bd. rev. Assoc. Br. Pilots, 1990—; bd. dirs. La. World Expn. Inc., 1974-84; bd. dirs., exec. com. New Orleans Tourist and Conv. Commn., 1971-74, 78, chmn.; family attractions com. 1973-75; chmn. La. Gov.'s Task Force on Space Industry, 1971-73; chmn. La. Gov.'s Citizens' Adv. Com. Met. New

Orleans Transp. and Planning Location of new Miss. River Bridge, 1971-77; mem. La. Gov.'s Task Force Natural Gas Requirements, 1971-72; mem. La. Gov.'s Proaction Commn. for Higher Edn., 1995; mem. Goals Found. Coun. and ex-officio mem. Goals Found., Met. New Orleans, 1969-73; vice chmn. Port of New Orleans Operation Impact, 1969-70, mem. Met. Area Com., New Orleans, 1970-84; trustee Pub. Affairs Rsch. Coun. La., 1970-73, mem. exec. com. Bus./Higher Edn. Coun., U. New Orleans, 1980-94, bd. dirs., 1980-2000, dir. emeritus, 2000—, v.p., 1986-88, pres., 1988-90, chmn. Task Force on Pub. Higher Edn. Funding, 1990-95, chmn. govtl. affairs, 1995-2000, Task Force on Edn./Econ. Devel. Alliances, 1993-95; mem. Mayor's Coun. on Internat. Trade and Econ. Devel., 1978; mem. Mayor's Transition Task Force Econ. Devel., 1994; bd. dirs. La. Partnership for Tech. and Innovation, 1989—, Acad. Sacred Heart, 1975-77, Internat. House, 1985-86, adv. coun., 1985—; bd. dirs. U. New Orleans Found., 1991—; mem. vis. com. Sch. Bus. Adminstrn., Loyola U., New Orleans, 1981-2001, trustee Loyola U., 1985-91, vice chmn. bd. trustees, 1990-91; mem. Dean's Coun. Tulane U. Law Sch., 1988-96, vice chmn. bldg. com., 1991-95; bd. dirs., mem. exec. com. Internat. Trade Mart, chmn. internat. bus. com., 1983-85, World Trade Ctr.-New Orleans (bd. dirs. 1983—, mem. Port Activity com. 1985-91, transp. com. 1991-95, 2000, 2001, govt. affairs com. 1996-99); chmn. Task Force on Internat. Banking, 1982; mem. Mayor's Task Force on Drug Abuse, 1989-90, vice comdr. La. Commandery, Mil. Order Fgn. Wars, 2000—. With U.S. Army Air Corp, 1942-46, PTO; capt. JAGDR, USAAF, 1950-. Recipient Leadership award AIAA, 1971, Yenni award Loyola U., New Orleans, 1979, New Orleans Times Picayune Loving Cup, 1986, First Citizen of the Learning Soc. Dean's award UNO Met. Coll., 1992; also various civic contbn. awards; co-recipient Silver Anvil award New Orleans chpt. Pub. Rels. Soc. Am., 1991. Fellow Coll. Labor and Employment Lawyers; mem. ABA (labor and employment law and litigation sects., com. equal opportunity law, chmn. regional com. liaison with equal opportunity commn., office of fed. contract compliance programs), D.C. Bar Assn., Fed. Bar Assn., La. Bar Assn. (past sec.-treas., bd. govs. 1957-60, editor jour. 1957-59, sec. spl. supreme ct. com. on drafting code jud. ethics), New Orleans Bar Assn. (dir legal aid bur. 1954, chmn. standing com. legis. 1968, vice chmn. standing com. pub. rels. 1970-71), Am. Judicature Soc., La. Law Inst. (asst. sec.-treas. 1958-70), Am. Arbitration Assn. (bd. dirs., 1995-98, chmn. reg. adv. coun., chmn. reg. adv. coun. employment law cases, mem. panels-employment, employee benefits, large complex employment and comml. arbitration/mediation cases, Whitney North Seymour Sr. award 1991), So. Inst. Mgmt. (founder), AIM, U.S. C. of C. (urban and regional affairs com. 1970-73), La. C. of C. (bd. dirs. 1963-66), New Orleans and River Region C. of C. (v.p. met. devel. and urban affairs 1969, past chmn. labor rels. coun., bd. dirs. 1970-78, pres.-elect 1970, pres. 1971, dir., exec. com. 1972, ex officio mem., bd. dirs. 1979—), Bienville Club, Pickwick Club, Plimsoll Club, Serra Club, So. Yacht Club, Sigma Chi (pres. alumni chpt. 1956). Roman Catholic. Home: 3039 Hudson Pl New Orleans LA 70131-5337 Office: Molony Law Firm 201 Saint Charles Ave Ste 3500 New Orleans LA 70170-3500 Fax: 504-582-1553. E-mail: mjm@mmolony-law.com.

MOLPUS, DICK H. management company executive; b. Philadelphia, Miss., Sept. 7, 1949; s. Richard and Frances (Blount) M.; m. Sally Nash, May 27, 1971; children— Helen Nash, Richard Gregory BBA, U. Miss., 1971. V.p. mfg. Molpus Co., Phila., 1971-80; exec. dir. Gov's Office Fed.-State Programs, Jackson, Miss., 1980-83; sec. of state State of Miss., 1984-96; pres., chmn. Molpus Co., Phila., 1996—; pres., dir. Molpus Woodlands Group, Jackson, Miss., 1996—; pres. Timberland Mgmt. Investment Orgn. Dir. Citizens Bank and Trust Co. Vice pres. Miss. Agr. and Forestry Mus., 1979; campaign dir., chmn. bd. United Givers Fund, Nehshoba County, Miss., 1979-80; bd. dirs. Miss. PTA, 1980—; founder Parents for Pub. Schs. orgn., 1989. Recipient Friends of Children award Miss. Assn. Elem. Sch. Adminstrs., 1984, Pub. Ofcl. of Yr. award Miss. chpt. Am. Soc. for Pub. Adminstrn., 1985 Mem. Miss. Forestry Assn. (bd. dirs. 1980-87), Nat. Assn. Secs. of State (pres. 1992), Nature Conservancy (bd. dirs. Miss. chpt.), Sigma Chi, Omicron Delta Kappa, Pi Sigma Alpha (Theta Beta chpt.). Avocations: hiking, tennis, running, reading. Office: 654 N State St Jackson MS 39202

MOLSON, ERIC H. beverage company executive; b. Montreal, Sept. 16, 1937; s. Thomas Henry Pentland and Celia Frances (Cantlie) M.; m. Jane Mitchell, Apr. 16, 1966; 3 children. AB, Princeton U., 1959. With Molson Inc., Montreal, chmn. bd., 1988—. Office: Molson Inc 1555 Notre Dame St E Montreal QC Canada H2L 2R5

MOLT, CYNTHIA MARYLEE, author, publisher; b. Sierra Madre, Calif., Nov. 1, 1957; d. Lawrence Edward and Evelyn Mary (Novak) Molt. BA in English Lit., Calif. State U., Long Beach, 1980. Mng. editor Assoc. Graphics, Arts and Letters, Monrovia, Calif., 1981—89, pub., sr. and mng. editor, 1987—; lectr., speaker, 1992—; author McFarland and Co., Inc., Pubs., Jefferson, 1988, Greenwood Press, Inc., Westport, Conn., 1989-93. Author pilot program Arcadia Unified Sch. Dist., Calif., 1992—; 5th and 6th grade tchr., 7th & 8th grade history tchr., 5th-8th grade girls' phys. edn. coach, El Monte Christian Sch., 1994; tchr. Arcadia Reading Clinic, 1994—; tutor all subjects and testing, 1995—. Author: Gone with the Wind on Film: A Complete Reference, 1990, (bio-bibliography) Vivien Leigh, 1992; author, editor: The Wind, 1981-89, Calif. Film, 1987-89; spl. corr.: Monrovia News-Post, 1985; corr.: Monrovia Rev., 1975, G.W.T.W. Collector's Club newsletter, 1979-82; editor: Iris Notes, 1992—. Vol. adminstrv. asst. student activities Monrovia High Sch., 1976; mem. Friends of Arcadia Pub. Libr., Friends of Monrovia Pub. Libr. Mem. Am. Biog. Inst. (mem. rsch. bd. advisors 1989—), Am. Iris Soc., Hist. Iris Preservation Soc., So. Calif. Iris Soc. (editor 1991—), Gone with the Wind Soc. (pres. 1985-89), Vivien Leigh Fan Club, Monrovia Garden Club (v.p. publicity programs 1992-93). Avocations: raising Yorkshire terriers, silkies and poodles, photography. Home and Office: 364 May Ave Monrovia CA 91016-2264 *Personal philosophy: Success is failure turned inside out, the silver tint of the clouds of doubt. So stick to the fight when you are hardest hit, it is when things seem worst that you must not quit.*

MOLTENI, AGOSTINO, pathology educator; b. Como, Lombardy, Italy, Nov. 12, 1933; came to U.S., 1963; s. Enrico and Antonia (Signorini) M.; m. Loredana Brizio, Sept. 5, 1963; children: Claudio Enrico, Ronald Stephen. MD, U. Milan, Italy, 1957; PhD in Pathology, SUNY, Buffalo, 1970. Intern and resident in internal medicine U. Milan (Italy), 1957-62; asst. prof. U. Milan, 1957-63; chief rsch. sect. Farmitalia Drug Co., Milan, 1963-65; rsch. assoc. SUNY, Buffalo, 1965-69, asst. prof., 1969-71; assoc. prof. U. Kans., Kansas City, 1971-76; prof. pathology Northwestern U., Chgo., 1976-96, prof. emeritus, 1996—; prof. pathology and pharmacology U. Mo., Kansas City, 1996—. Vis. prof. Harvard U., 1983-84. Editor, author: Endocrinology and Thermal Trauma, 1990; contbr. articles to profl. jours., chpts. to books. Recipient Sharer in Lasker award Lasker Found., N.Y.C., 1983, Rsch. Career Devel. award NIH, Washington, 1970, award Am. Heart Assn., Chgo., 1982. Fellow Am. Acad. Clin. Biochemistry; mem. Am. Acad. Pathology, Am. Soc. Investigative Pathology, Clin. Chemistry Soc. Achievements include patent for captopril as a cancer chemo-preventive agent; research on hypertension and hormonal regulation of cancer. Avocation: medieval history. Office: U Mo Truman Med Ctr 2301 Holmes St Kansas City MO 64108-2640

MOLTZ, JAMES EDWARD, investment brokerage company executive; b. Williamsport, Pa., July 25, 1932; s. George N. and Margaret L. (Abell) M.; m. Barbara Vance, Sept. 8, 1956; children: George Wilson, James Clay, John Thomas. BS, Williams Coll., 1954; MBA, Wharton Sch., U. Pa., 1956. Chartered fin. analyst. Fin. analyst Cyrus J. Lawrence Inc., N.Y.C., 1957-62, rsch. dir., 1962-64, gen. ptnr., 1964-71, mng. ptnr., 1971-73; chmn., pres. C.J. Lawrence/Deutsche Bank Securities Corp., 1973-95; chief investment officer Deutsche Bank Securities, 1996-99; vice chmn. ISI Inc., N.Y.C., 1999—. Mem. fin. com. Williams Coll.; trustee Sterling and Francine Clark Art Inst.; hon. trustee Williamsport-Lycoming Found.; chmn. Woods Hole Oceanographic Inst.; trustee Rockefeller Bros. Fund, Edna McConnell Clark Found. Mem. Fin. Analysts Fedn., N.Y. Soc. Security Analysts (former dir.), Union League Club (N.Y.C.), Wee Burn Country Club (dir.), Windsor Club (Vero Beach), The Links (N.Y.C.). Home: 29 Indian Spring Trl Darien CT 06820-2109 Also: ISI Inc 535 Madison Ave New York NY 10022-4212 E-mail: jmoltz@isimgt.com.

MOLTZ, KATHLEEN C. pediatric endocrinologist; b. Detroit, Dec. 6, 1964; d. Morton S. and Ruthann (Lang) M. BS in Chemistry with honors, Mich. State U., 1986, MD, 1990. Intern, resident Children's Hosp. of Mich., Detroit, 1990-93; fellow Yale U., New Haven, 1993-96; pediatric endocrinologist New Eng. Diabetes and Endocrinology Ctr., Waltham, Mass., 1996—. Gertrude Geindein Meml. scholar, 1987. Mem. AMA, Am. Diabetes Assn., Am. Acad. Pediatrics, Endocrine Soc., NOW. Avocations: needlework, photography, science fiction. Office: New Eng Diabetes and Endocrinology Ctr 40 2nd Ave Ste 170 Waltham MA 02451-1136

MOLTZ, MARTIN PAUL, lawyer; b. Chgo., Nov. 22, 1944; s. Joseph and Celia Moltz; m. Ann Kaplan, May 26, 1974; 1 child, Benjamin Harold. BA, U. Ill., Chgo., 1966; JD, U. Okla., 1969. Bar: Ill. 1971, Fla. 1976. Asst. states atty. Cook County States Atty.'s Office, Chgo., 1970-72; staff atty. States Atty.'s Appellate Prosecutor's Office, Elgin, Ill., 1972-98, dep. dir., 1997—. Instr. Roosevelt U., Chgo., 1987—. Contbr. articles to profl. jours. Mem. 49th Ward Dems., Chgo., 1970—. With U.S. Army, 1969-75. Mem. Chgo. Bar Assn. (bd. mgrs. 1997—; bd. dirs. pub. interest law initiative 1997—). Jewish. Avocations: amusement parks, roller coasters, tournament bridge. Home: 7306 N Winchester Ave Chicago IL 60626-5529 Office: States Attys Appellate Prosecutor 2032 Larkin Ave Elgin IL 60123-5845

MOLTZAU, HUGHITT GREGORY, retired management training specialist; b. Strum, Wis., Aug. 9, 1914; s. Herman Alfred and Goldie (Knudtson) M.; m. Orvetta Nellie Braker, Dec. 30, 1940; children: Paula Lou Moltzau Lepak, Ann Marie Moltzau Bosworth. BS in Edn., U. Wis., Stout, 1936; MS in Edn., Wayne State U., 1941. Tchr. Grosse Pointe Country Day Sch., Grosse Pointe Farms, Mich., 1938-41; tng. supr. Chrysler Corp., Detroit, 1941-46; tng. dir. Kaiser-Frazer Corp., Willow Run, Mich., 1946-49, Parke-Davis/Warner Lambert, Detroit, 1949-79; mgmt. cons. Warner Lambert, Morris Plains, N.J., 1979-89; ret., 1989. Conducted seminars in field. Author tng. materials. Pres. bd. dirs. Adult Psychiat. Clinic, Detroit, 1961-62; vice chmn. edn. com. Detroit Bd. Commerce, 1966-67. Mem. Am. Soc. Tng. and Devel. (pres. Greater Detroit chpt. 1962-63), Am. Mgmt. Assn., Epsilon Pi Tau, Phi Delta Kappa. Congregationalist. Avocations: golf, archery, photography, bridge.

MOLTZON, RICHARD FRANCIS, operations executive; b. Bklyn., Nov. 20, 1941; s. Arthur G. and Joan (Paladino) M.; m. Susan A. Anderson, Feb. 15, 1981; children: Paige, Kimberly, Michael, Keir. BS in Info. Systems Mgmt., U. Md., 1970. Various positions IBM Corp., various locations, 1965-70; plant mgr. Telex Terminal Communications, Inc., Raleigh, N.C., 1970-75, Carnes Co. div. Wehr Steel, Sanford, 1975-76; dir., gen. mgr. Modular Computer Systems, Inc., Ft. Lauderdale, Fla., 1980-87; v.p. ops. Profile Corp., Pompano Beach, 1987-88; dir. mfg. AMF, Inc., Herndon, Va., 1976-79, Documation, Inc., Melbourne, Fla., 1979-80, Concurrent Computer Corp., Oceanport, N.J., 1988-89; v.p. mfg. Internat. Tech. Corp., Clearwater, Fla., 1989-90; pres. The Realty Authority, Inc., 1990-92; v.p. ops. Combustion TEC, Divsn. of Eclipse Combustion, Inc., Orlando, Fla., 1992-99; sr. v.p. ops. Control Ctr. LLC, 1999—2001; v.p. product sourcing and mgmt. Environ.l Lighting Concepts, INc., Tampa, Fla., 2002—. With U.S. Army, 1961-64. Mem. KC, Omicron Delta Kappa. Roman Catholic. Avocations: golf, jogging, writing. Office: Envorn Lighting Concepts Inc 1214 W Cass St Tampa FL 33606 E-mail: rick_moltzon@terpalum.umd.edu.

MOLYNEAUX, DAVID GLENN, newspaper travel editor; b. Marion, Ind., Oct. 16, 1945; s. Glenn Ingersol and Barbara Wingate (Draudt) M.; children: Miles David, Rebecca Susan; m. Judi Dash, May 15, 1994. BS in Econs., Miami U., Oxford, Ohio, 1967. Reporter The Plain Dealer, Cleve., 1967-75, city editor, 1976-78, assoc. editor, 1979-80, editorial page editor, 1980-82, travel editor, 1982—. Editor: 75 Years-An Informal History of Shaker Heights, 1987. Trustee Shaker Heights Pub. Libr., 1987—. With U.S. Army, 1968-70. Mem. Cleve. Press Club. Office: Plain Dealer 1801 Superior Ave E Cleveland OH 44114-2198

MOLZ, PHILIP JACK, management consultant; b. N.Y.C., Jan. 28, 1929; s. Philip and Mary H. Molz; m. Margaret J. Ralph, July 29, 1978; 1 child, Philene M. BS in Math., CCNY, 1953; PhD in Internat. Bus. Adminstrn., Ky.-Western. Cert. quality auditor; cert. ISO/QS 9000 lead assessor; cert. MBTI instr.; cert. SYMLOG instr.; cert. team facilitator; cert. graphologist IGAS. Accountant, auditor GE, Schenectady, N.Y., 1953-61, treas. Rio, Brazil, 1961-65, CFO Wolfenbüttel, Germany, 1965-68; corp. fin. analyst ITT, N.Y.C., 1968-70; CFO, v.p. fin. adminstrn. Xerox Latin Am., Stamford, Conn., 1970-74; CFO Abbott Labs. Internat., N. Chicago, Ill., 1974-78; sr. CFO Macmillan Pub., N.Y.C., 1978-80; pres., owner TSI Co., Bridgeport, Conn., 1980-85; pres. IJ Cos., Knoxville, Tenn., 1985-89; pres., owner PMP Internat. Group, Kansas City, Kans., 1989—; sr. mgmt. cons. Co-author: Controller's Handbook, 1974, Treasurer's Handbook, 1976, Quality Manual Reference, 1988. With CIC U.S. Army, 1951-53, Korea. Republican. Roman Catholic. Avocations: skiing, racquetball, ranching, oil painting, foreign languages. Home and Office: 11930 Stearns St Overland Park KS 66213-1962 E-mail: molzpmpint@aol.com.

MOLZ, REDMOND KATHLEEN, public administration educator; b. Balt., Mar. 5, 1928; d. Joseph T. and Regina (Barry) M. BS, Johns Hopkins U., 1949, MA, 1950; MALS, U. Mich., 1953; DLS, Columbia U., 1976. Librarian I and II Enoch Pratt Free Library, Balt., 1953-56; pub. relations officer Free Library of Phila., 1958-62; editor Wilson Library Bull. H.W. Wilson Co., Bronx, N.Y., 1962-68; chief planning staff Bur. Libraries and Learning Resources U.S. Office Edn., Washington, 1968-73; prof. library sci. Sch. Library Service Columbia U., N.Y.C., 1976-80, Melvil Dewey prof., 1980-93; prof. pub. affairs Sch. Internat. and Pub. Affairs, Columbia U., 1993-99, prof. emeritus, 2000—. Cons. U.S. Nat. Commn. Libraries and Info. Sci., Washington, 1974-75, U.S. Adv. Commn. Intergovtl. Relations, Washington, 1979-80 Author: Federal Policy and Library Support, 1976 (Ralph R. Shaw award 1977), National Planning for Library Service, 1935-75, 1984, Library Planning and Policy Making: The Legacy of the Public and Private Sector, 1990, The Federal Roles in Support of Public Library Services, 1990, The Federal Roles in Support of Academic and Research Libraries, 1991; co-author (with Phyllis Dain) Civic Space/Cyberspace: The American Public Library in the Information Age, 1999; co-editor: The Metropolitan Library (anthology), 1972; author TV script Portraits in Print, 1959. Recipient Leadership Tng. award Fund for Adult Edn., 1956-57; recipient Disting. Alumnus award Sch. Library Sci. U. Mich., 1969, George Virgil Fuller award Columbia U., 1975, Johns Hopkins U. scholar, 1949-50, Horace H. Rackham fellow U. Mich., 1952-53, Columbia U. scholar, 1974-76, Tangley Oaks fellow, 1975-76; Council Library Resources Inc. Officers' grantee, 1974 Mem. ALA (councilor 1972-74, 76-80, exec. bd. 1976-80, chmn. legis. com. 1985-86), Freedom to Read Found. (dir. 1972-79, pres. 1977-79) Office: Columbia U Sch Internat & Pub Affairs New York NY 10027 E-mail: rkm2@columbia.edu.

MOLZ, ROBERT JOSEPH, manufacturing company executive; b. Yonkers, N.Y., Mar. 15, 1937; s. Philip and Maria Hilda (Geist) M.; m. Diane Ruth Horowitz, July 31, 1960 (dec. Feb. 2000); children— Jennifer Ann, Erica Beth BS, CCNY, 1960, MA, 1966; PhD, N.Y. Med. Coll., 1969. Tech. svcs. supr. E.I. DuPont de Neumours Co. Inc., Wilmington, Del., 1971-73, product mgr., 1973-75, quality assurance mgr. clin. sys. divsn., 1976, R&D mgr. clin. sys. divsn., 1976-84, asst. dir. R&D divsn. agrl. chem. dept., 1984-86, dir. departmental plans divsn., med. products dept., 1986-88, dir. med. scis. programs, cen. R&D, 1988-91, dir. new bus. devel., Cen. R&D, 1991-92, exec. dir. rsch. support, 1992-96, ret., 1996. Roman Catholic. Home: 306 Dove Dr Newark DE 19713-1212 E-mail: rmolz306@aol.com.

MOLZEN, DAYTON FRANK, consulting engineering executive; b. Newton, Kans., Jan. 6, 1926; s. Walter N. and Ionia Maude (Gordon) M.; m. Margaret Jean Hanna, Aug. 13, 1949; children: George Walter, Lucena Ann. BS, Kans. State U., 1950. Project engr. Kans. Hwy. Commn., Garden City, 1950-51; design engr. Wilson & Co., Engrs., Albuquerque and Salina, Kans., 1953-60; civil engr., pres. D.F. Molzen and Assocs., Inc., Albuquerque, 1960-74; pres. Molzen-Corbin & Assocs., 1974-96; founding prin., 1996-98; ret., 1998. Served with A.C. U.S. Army, 1942-45; Served with USAF, 1951-53. Fellow Am. Cons. Engrs. Coun. (nat. bd. dirs. 1982-85, exec. dir. N.Mex. 1985-93); mem. ASCE, Cons. Engrs. Coun. (past pres.), Am. Pub. Works Assn. Clubs: Masons, Shriners, Rotary, Appaloosa Horse (past pres. N.Mex., nat. dir.). Home: 3216 Calle De Estella NW Albuquerque NM 87104-3003 E-mail: dmolzen@rt66.com., dmolzen@landmarkphotos.com.

MOMAH, ETHEL CHUKWUEKWE, women's health nurse; b. Iyi-Enu, Ogidi, Nigeria, May 28, 1934; d. Zaccheus C. and Victoria U. (Orizu) Obi; m. Christian C. Momah, Nov. 21, 1959; children: Chukwudi, Adaora, Azuka. SRN, Harrow Hosp., Middlesex, U.K., 1956; SCM, Mothers Hosp., London, 1957; MTD, Midwife Tchrs. Coll., Surrey, U.K., 1964; BS, Upsala Coll., 1988. Cert. inpatient obstetric nurse Nat. Cert. Corp. Nurse-midwife Guy's Hosp., London, 1959; nursing sister, head nurse labor/delivery Univ. Coll. Hosp., Ibadan, Nigeria, 1960-62; midwife tutor Lagos (Nigeria) Island Maternity Hosp., 1963-66; nurse-midwife Brit. Hosp., Paris, 1966, Hosp. Cantonal, Geneva, Switzerland, 1967-78; patient care coord. St. Peter's Med. Ctr., New Brunswick, N.J., 1985-90, antenatal testing nurse, 1990—. Named Nurse of Yr. Women's Ambulatory Care Svc. St. Peters Univ. Hosp., 1997. Mem.: Assn. Women's Health, Obstetric and Neonatal Nurses, Nne-Egwu (dance mother), Women's Cultural Dance Group NJ. Office: St Peters Med Ctr New Brunswick NJ 08901 E-mail: chikem@aol.com.

MOMBAERTS, PETER, biology educator; b. Leuven, Belgium, Sept. 27, 1962; s. Leon Mombaerts and Daisy Kortleven. MD, Cath. U. of Leuven Belgium, 1987; PhD in Biology, MIT, 1992. Postdoctoral fellow Columbia U., NY, 1993—95; asst. prof. biology Rockefeller U., N.Y.C., 1995—2001, assoc. prof., 2001—. Recipient Presdl. early career award for scientists and engrs. Pres. of U.S., 1997, career scientist award Irma T. Hirschl Trust, 1997-2000, Takasago award for rsch. in olfaction Assn. for Chemoreception Scis., 2001, Firmerich Fragrance award, 2001; Searle scholar, 1996-99, Basil O'Connor starter scholar March of Dimes Birth Defects Found., 1997-99, scholar Rita Allen Found., 1998-2001; Alfred P. Sloan rsch. fellow, 1997-99, Klingenstein fellow in neurosci., 1997-2000, McKnight scholar in neurosci., 1997-2000, Guggenheim fellow, 1998-99. Office: Rockefeller U 1230 York Ave New York NY 10021 Fax: 212-327-7310. E-mail: peter@rockefeller.edu.

MOMCILOVIC, DRAGAN, veterinarian, medicated feed specialist; b. Maili Gradac, Croatia, Nov. 22, 1961; s. Milan and Zorka Momcilovic; m. Libuse Heinz, June 6, 1987; children: Petra, Nebojsa. DVM, Vet. Faculty, Zagreb, Croatia, 1987; MS, U. Zagreb, 1990; PhD, Va. Poly. Inst. and State U., 1995. Diplomate Am. Coll. Theriogenologists. Rsch./tng. asst. U. Zagreb, 1987-91; rsch. asst. Va. Poly. Inst. and State U., Blacksburg, 1992-95; theriogenology resident U. Fla., Coll. Vet. Medicine, Gainesville, 1995-97; vet. North Fla. Holsteins, Bell, 1997-99; medicated feed specialist FDA, Ctr. Vet. Medicine, Rockville, Md., 1999—. Cons. to FDA approval seeking clin. study North Fla. Holsteins, 1999; project officer FDA, Ctr. Vet. Medicine, 1999—. Contbr.: Current Veterinary Practice 4, Food Animal Practice, 1999; contbr. articles to profl. jours. Pres. Table Tennis Club, Zagreb, 1983-86. Recipient John Lee Pratt fellowship Va. Poly. Inst. and State U., 1992-95. Mem. AVMA, Am. Dairy Sci. Assn. Avocations: table tennis, classical music. Home: # 201 8860 Ashgrove House Ln Vienna VA 22182 Office: FDA 7500 Standish Pl Rockville MD 20855 Fax: 301-827-1484. E-mail: radiotesla@aol.com., dmomcilo@cvm.fda.gov.

MOMMSEN, KATHARINA, retired German language and literature educator; b. Berlin, Sept. 18, 1925; came to U.S., 1974, naturalized, 1980; d. Hermann and Anna (Johannsen) Zimmer; m. Momme Mommsen, Dec. 23, 1948. Dr.phil., U. Tübingen, 1956; Dr. habil., Berlin Free U., 1962. Collaborator Acad. Scis., Berlin, 1949-61; assoc. prof. Free U., 1962-70; prof. German Carleton U., Ottawa, Can., 1970-74; Albert Guerard prof. lit. Stanford U., 1974-94, ret., 1995. Vis. prof. U. Giessen, Tech. U. Berlin, 1965, State U. N.Y., Buffalo, 1966, U. Calif., San Diego, 1973 Author over 150 publs. on 18th-20th century German and comparative lit.; editor: Germanic Studies in America. Mem. Goethe Soc., Schiller Soc. Home: 980 Palo Alto Ave Palo Alto CA 94301-2223 E-mail: katmom@stanford.edu.

MONACELLI, GIANFRANCO, publishing executive; b. Milan; came to U.S., 1965; s. Rodolfo and Isabella (Paolillo) M.; m. Eugenia Hyman; children: Nurit, Fausto, Alexander. Dr., U. Turin, Italy, 1963, Acad. Santa Cecilia, 1964; BS, Mannes Coll., 1967; postgrad., Columbia U., 1969. Gen. mgr. Rizzoli Internat. Bookstore, N.Y.C., 1969-72, v.p., 1972-75; exec. v.p. Rizzoli Internat., Milan, 1975-78; pres., chief exec. officer Rizzoli Internat. Publs., Inc., N.Y.C., 1975-93, Rizzoli Internat. Bookstores, Inc., N.Y.C., 1975-92, Rizzoli Editore Corp., N.Y.C., 1975-89; sr. v.p. RCS Rizzoli Corp., 1989-93; pres. USITAL Ltd., 1993—, The Monacelli Press, Inc., N.Y.C., 1994—; v.p. Epikos Security Printing S.A., 1997—. Trustee Mannes Coll., N.Y.C., 1979-81; pres. Weathersfield Music Festival, Vert., 1993—; mem. vis. com. U. Miami, Coral Gables, Fla., 1988-89. Recipient Met. Home Design 100 award, 1997, collaborative achievement award AIA, 1999; named Pub. of Yr., AIA, 1996. Mem. Century Assn., Am.-Italy Soc. (pres. 1993-94).

MONACELLI, JEFFREY PAUL, elementary education educator; b. Ft. Dix, N.J., Aug. 14, 1970; s. Paul R. Monacelli and Elvira E. (Grattagliano) Hoskin; m. Erica Johnson, June 30, 1995. BA, Caldwell Coll., 1992. Tchr. grade 6 St. John Sch., Orange, N.J., 1992-94; tchr. social studies DePaul H.S., Wayne, 1994-95; program dir. Seton Hall Prep. Sch., West Orange, 1995-96; tchr. grade 3 Newark Pub. Schs., 1996-98; tchr. grade 5 H.B. Whitehorne Mid. Sch., Verona, N.J., 1998—. With Orange City Coun., 1992-2000, mem. planning bd., 1996-99. Democrat. Roman Catholic. Home: 11 Mount Vernon Sq Verona NJ 07044-2928

MONACO, ANTHONY PETER, surgery educator, medical institute administrator; b. Phila., Mar. 12, 1932; s. Donoto Charles and Rose (Consalvi) M.; m. Mary Louise Oudens, June 4, 1960; children: Anthony Peter, Marck Churchill, Christopher Donoto, Lisa Oudens. BA in Chemistry, U. Pa., 1952; MD magna cum laude, Harvard U., 1956. Diplomate Am. Bd. Surgery, Am. Bd. Thoracic Surgery. Prof. surgery Harvard Med. Sch., Boston, 1977-95, Peter Medawar prof. transplantation surgery, 1995—, mem. bd. acad. advisors, 1974-83; chief transplantation div. Sears Surg. Research Lab. Boston City Hosp., 1967-73; sci. dir. Cancer Research Inst., New Eng. Deaconess Hosp., Boston, 1980—, chief div. organ transplantation, 1975—; Peter Medacor prof. transplantation surgery Harvard Med. Sch., 1995. Mem. surgery study sect. NIH, 1973-77, mem. clin. sci. study sect., 1983— ; mem. adv. com. endstage renal disease Bur. Quality Assurance, HEW, 1975-76; mem. merit rev. bd. immunology VA, Washington, 1977-80; dir. Transplant Ctr. Beth Israel Deaconess Med. Ctr., Boston, 1998. Author: Biology of Tissue Transplantation, 1964; editor: Transplantation Procedures, 1970, 81; jour. Transplantation, 1969— . Trustee New Eng. Organ Bank, Boston, 1970— , chmn., 1981— ; bd. dirs. Kidney Found. Mass., 1978-81; mem. Harvard Med. Sch. Alumni Council, 1979-81. Recipient nat. scholar Harvard Med. Sch., 1952-56; recipient Henry Asbury Christian award Harvard Med. Sch., 1956, Lederle Med. Faculty award Harvard Med. Sch., 1968 Fellow Royal Coll. Surgeons, Eng. (hon., The Medowar prize 1998); mem. Transplantation Soc. (charter, v.p. 1971-74, pres. 1985, internat. pres. 1986), Am. Soc. Transplant Surgeons (charter, treas. 1982-85, pres. 1985—), Am. Surg. Assn., Soc. Univ. Surgeons, ACS (pres. Mass. chpt. 1985). Clubs: Harvard (Boston). Home: 25 Farlow Rd Newton MA 02458-2407 E-mail: amonaco@caregroup.harvard.edu.

MONACO, DANIEL JOSEPH, lawyer; b. Easton, Pa., May 12, 1922; s. Federico and Maria (Romano) M.; m. Marian P. Monaco, June 26, 1953 (div.); children: Denise E., Mimi D. AB with honors, Lafayette Coll., 1943; postgrad. studies, U. Mich., 1944-45; MA, U. Chgo., 1946; JD, Stanford U., 1950. Bar: Calif. 1951, U.S. Dist. Ct. (no. dist.) Calif. 1951, U.S. Supreme Ct. 1961. Mem. faculty U. Miami, Fla., 1946-47; founder, of counsel Monaco, Anderlini & Finkelstein, San Mateo, Calif., 1953—; probate judge State of Calif., 1963-67. Real estate broker, Calif., 1957-67; judge pro tem Calif. Mcpl and Superior Cts. Chmn. San Mateo County Dem. Ctrl. Com., 1960-61; mem. Calif. State Dem. Exec. Bd.; founder, pres. Circlon Internat., 1978-81; chmn. World Peace Through Law Ctr. com. to establish a Citizens' World Ct.; pres. peninsula com. UN Ednl. Sci. & Cultural Orgn., 1955-59; mem. No. Calif. Coun. Fgn. Affairs; San Mateo County Hosp. Found. Bd. With U.S. Army, 1943-46, lt. USAR, 1946-50. Mem. ABA, ATLA, UN Assn.-U.S.A. (pres. San Mateo County chpt. 1958-65), Calif. S ate Bar Assn., Calif. Trial Lawyers Assn. (bd. govs.) San Mateo County Trial Lawyers Assn. (pres.), World Jurist Assn. (pres. Ams., 1991-93, 2d v.p. 1995-97, 1st v.p. 1997-99, pres. 1999-2001, fin. chmn. 1995—), Am. Bd. Trial Advocates, Am. Soc. Internat. Law, Assn. World Citizens, Gorbachev Found., The Commonwealth Club, Peninsula Golf and Country Club. Democrat. Avocations: travel, internat. law, peace endeavors. Home: 295 Darrell Rd Hillsborough CA 94010-7109 Office: 400 S El Camino Real Ste 700 San Mateo CA 94402-1744 Fax: 650-348-0962. E-mail: dukemonaco@aol.com.

MONACO, ROBERT ANTHONY, radiologist; b. N.Y.C., July 5, 1945; s. Edmond V. and Jean M.; m. Susan Margaret Thompson; children: Kevin, Robert, Christopher, Sarah. BS, Siena Coll., 1967; MD, N.J. Coll. Medicine, 1971. Diplomate Am. Bd. Radiology, Am. Bd. Nuclear Medicine. Radiology resident N.J. Coll. Medicine, Newark, 1971-75; fellow in nuclear medicine med. ctr. NYU, N.Y.C., 1975-76; attending radiologist Med. Ctr. Ocean County, Point Pleasant, N.J., 1976-87, dir. dept. radiology, 1987—, sec. med. staff, 1998-2000. Gen. ptnr. Point Pleasant Radiology Group, 1987—; sec. bd. dirs. Found. Med. Ctr. Ocean County, Mid-Coastal IPA, 1997—. Capt. USAR, 1972-76. Mem. Am. Coll. Radiology, Am. Coll. Nuclear Medicine, Radiol. Soc. N.J. Roman Catholic. Avocations: tennis, fishing, swimming. Home: 2178 Lawrence Way Wall NJ 07719-9701 Office: Open MRI of Wall Rt 34 Wall NJ 07719 E-mail: rammdo1@aol.com.

MONAGAN, JOHN STEPHEN, retired congressman and lawyer, writer, lecturer; b. Waterbury, Conn., Dec. 31, 1911; s. Charles Andrew and Margaret Mary (Mulry) M.; children: Charles, Michael, Parthenia, Laura, Susan; m. Rosemary Ann Brady, May 23, 1949. AB, Dartmouth Coll., 1933; JD, Harvard U., 1937. Bar: Conn. 1938, D.C. 1973, U.S. Supreme Ct. 1973. Pvt. practice, Waterbury, 1938-59; mem. U.S. Ho. of Reps. 5th Dist. of Conn., Washington, 1959-73; ptnr. Whitman & Ransom, N.Y.C., 1973-80; writer, lectr. Washington, 1980—. Author: (biography) Horace, 1985, (memoir) Mellow Years-J. Holmes, 1988, (autobiography) Pleasant Institution, 2002; contbr. numerous revs., articles and commentaries to various publs. Pres. Civic Orch., Waterbury, 1938-42; alderman City of Waterbury, 1940-43, mayor, 1943-48; bd. dirs. Georgetown Ministry Ctr., Washington, 1986-88, Mattatuck Hist. Soc. Recipient nat. medal Sons of Lithuania, 1966, medal NCAA, 1972; named to Waterbury (Conn.) Hall of Fame, 1997. Mem. Former Mems. Congress (bd. dirs., pres. 1982—), Cosmos Club. Democrat. Roman Catholic. Avocations: group singing, piano playing. Home: 3043 W Lane Ky NW Washington DC 20007-3057 Fax: (202) 398-4598. E-mail: jsmonagan@aol.com.

MONAGHAN, ANNE, public relations consultant; b. L.A., Sept. 25, 1959; d. Barnett Mitchell Leland and Mary Anne Behrens; m. Kevin Thompson Monaghan, July 16, 1981 (div. Dec. 1991); 1 child, Kelly Anne. Student, Calif. Poly. State U., San Luis Obispo, 1982, U. Metaphysics, Encino, Calif., 1999. Editor Calif. Ctrs. Mag., Newport Beach, Calif., 1989-95; prin. Monaghan Communications, 1995—; exec. dir. Internat. Comm. Resources, 2001—, pres., CEO, 2001—. Mem. editl. adv. bd. Shopping Ctr. Bus. Mag., Atlanta, 1999—. Editor mag. Calif. Ctrs. Mag., 1989-95. Bd. dirs. City of Hope, Newport Beach, 1993-95, March of Dimes, Newport Beach, 1997. Mem. Internat. Coun. Shopping Ctrs. (mem. So. Calif. planning com. 1993—, chair 1999-2001), Assn. Corp. Real Estate Execs. Office: Monaghan Comms 3857 Birch St Ste 116 Newport Beach CA 92660-2616 E-mail: monacomm@pacbell.net.

MONAGHAN, CHARLES, writer, editor; b. Bklyn., Sept. 25, 1932; s. Andrew and Pauline (Dunlevy) M.; m. E. Jennifer Walker, Jan. 19, 1933; children: Leila, Anthony, Claire. BA, Manhattan Coll., 1954; MA, NYU, 1958. Copy editor Reuters News Agy., London, 1960-62, N.Y. Times, Paris and N.Y.C., 1962-67; editor Book World supplement to Washington Post and Chgo. Tribune, N.Y.C., 1972-75, Facts on File, N.Y.C., 1975-76; mng. editor Travel & Leisure Mag., 1977-83; food editor Bergen Record, Hackensack, N.J., 1990-92; Gilder Lehrman fellow Columbia U. Libr., 2002. Author: The Murrays of Murray Hill, 1998; editor: Zagat Survey of N.J. Restaurants, 1996-98; contbr. chpt. to book, more than 400 articles to various publs. including N.Y. Times, Wall St. Jour., Washington Post, Money Mag., Smithsonian Mag., Town and Country, Travel and Leisure, Food and Wine, Bon Appetit, Commonweal, Nat. Rev. Committeeman N.Y. State Dem. Com., 1972-74; dist. leader Kings County Dem. Com., Bklyn., 1972-74; Dem. candidate for state senate, Bklyn., 1976; vice chmn. N.Y. State Dem. Coalition, 1972-75; pres. Ctrl. Bklyn. Ind. Dems., 1970-72, 82-84; co-donor Charles and E. Jennifer Monaghan Collection of Literacy Textbooks, Kenneth Spencer Rsch. Libr., U. Kans., 2001. Mem. Century Club. Roman Catholic. Home: 534 3rd St Brooklyn NY 11215-3003

MONAGHAN, EILEEN See WHITAKER, EILEEN MONAGHAN

MONAGHAN, JESSINE ADRIENNE, lawyer; b. Floral Park, N.Y., May 5, 1953; d. Francis Adrian and Jessine Marion (Cordes) M. BA, Wellesley Coll., 1975; JD, Washington and Lee U., 1979. Bar: Va. 1979, D.C. 1980. Jud. clk. FTC, Washington, 1979-81; counsel Hunton & Williams, Richmond, Va., 1981-92, Environ. Health and Safety Progams GE Plastics, The Netherlands, 1992-95; with GE Corp. Environ. Programs Europe, 1995-98; dir. and European compliance officer Sotheby's, London, 1998-2000; mgr., counsel regulatory programs GE Plastics, Washington, 2000—. Chmn. subcom. magnet sch. task force Richmond Pub. Schs., 1989; lawyer Church Hill Pro Bono Office, Richmond, 1990-92. Mem. Omicron Delta Kappa. Avocation: violin. Office: GE Plastics 1299 Pennsylvania Ave NW Washington DC 20004-2407

MONAGHAN, M. PATRICIA PATRICIA, educator, writer, poet; b. Bklyn., Feb. 15, 1946; d. Edward Joseph and Mary Margaret (Gordon) M. BA in English, U. Minn., 1967, MA in English, 1970; MFA, U. Alaska, 1980; PhD, The Union Inst., 1995. News editor U. Alaska, Fairbanks, 1970-71; pub. rels. dir. Walker Art Ctr., Mpls., 1972; editor Minn. Monthly Minn. Pub. Radio, St. Paul, 1973-74; women's editor Daily News miner, Fairbanks, 1975; lectr., head English dept. Tana Valley C.C., 1976-87; instr. writing The Neighborhood Inst., Chgo., 1987-89; dir. cont. edn. St. Xavier U., 1990—; resident faculty DePaul U. Sch. for New Learning. Booklist reviewer ALA, Chgo., 1987—. Author: Book of Goddesses and Heroines, 1981, 90, Working Wisdom, 1994, O Mother Sun New View of Feminine, 1994, (poetry) Seasons of the Witch, 1992 (Friends of Lit. award 1992), Magical Gardens, 1997, The Goddess Path, 1999, The Goddess Companion, 2000, Meditation: The Complete Guide, 1999. Mem. South Shore Cultural Ctr., Chgo., 1989-92; bd. dirs. Athena Ctr. Recipient Rsch. award NUCEA, 1993, Univ. Alaska, 1987. Mem. Am. Conf. on Irish Studies, Soc. Midland Authors, Authors Guild. Democrat. Mem. Soc. Of Friends. Office: DePaul Univ Sch for New Learning 243 S Wabash Ave Fl 7 Chicago IL 60604-2302 E-mail: pmonagha@wppast.depaul.edu. *Women, who fill the churches each week, are awakening to the fact that we do not also lead the services. What will religion be like when we do?.*

MONAGHAN, PETER GERARD, lawyer; b. Belfast, Ireland, July 12, 1949; came to U.S., 1961; s. William Liam and Elizabeth (Eccles) M.; m. Barbara Marion Farrenkopf, Sept. 24, 1972; children: Brian Patrick, Kevin James, Allison Mary. BS, Fordham U., 1970; JD, St. John's U., Jamaica, N.Y., 1977. Bar: N.Y. 1978, U.S. Dist. Ct. (so. dist.) N.Y. 1978, U.S. Dist. Ct. (ea. dist.) N.Y. 1979, U.S. Supreme Ct. 1986. Claims examiner Royal Ins. Co., N.Y.C., 1970-76; assoc. Kroll, Edelman, Elser and Dicker, 1976, Bower and Gardner, N.Y.C., 1977-83, ptnr., 1984-91, Bartlett, McDonough, Bastone & Monaghan, LLP, Mineola, N.Y., 1992—. Cubmaster Boy Scouts Am., Bayside, N.Y., 1985-89. Capt. U.S. Army Res., 1970-78. Mem. ABA, Queens County Bar Assn., N.Y. State Bar Assn. (trial lawyers sect. com. on med. malpractice 1988—), Assn. of Trial Lawyers of Am., Nassau-Suffolk Trial Lawyers Assn., Nassau County Bar Assn. Office: Bartlett McDonough Bastone & Monaghan LLP 300 Old Country Rd Mineola NY 11501-4198

MONAGHAN, THOMAS JUSTIN, former prosecutor; JD, U. Nebr. Law School. Adjunct faculty College of St. Mary, Nebr., 1985—91; ptnr. Monaghan, Tiedman & Lynch, Omaha, 1978—93; U.S. atty. Dept. Justice, 1993—2001. Office: Monaghan Group 1321 Jones St Omaha NE 68102

MONAGHAN, THOMAS STEPHEN, retired restaurant chain executive; b. Ann Arbor, Mich., Mar. 25, 1937; m. Marjorie Zybach, Aug. 25, 1962; children— Mary, Susan, Margaret, Barbara Student, Ferris State Coll., U. Mich.; PhD (hon.), Cleary Coll., 1982, Madonna Coll., 1983, Eastern Mich. U., 1984, So. Fla. U., 1985. Ptnr. Dominick's Pizza, Ypsilanti, Mich., 1960-65; pres., chmn. bd., founder, CEO Domino's Pizza, Inc., Ann Arbor, 1960-98; ret., 1998. Owner Detroit Tigers, 1983-92. Author: (autobiography) Pizza Tiger. Bd. dirs. Cleary Coll., Ypsilanti, Henry Ford Hosp., Detroit, Detroit Renaissance, U. Steubinville, Ohio, St. Joseph's Hosp. Devel. Bd., Ann Arbor. Served with USMC, 1956-59 Named Entrepreneur of Yr. Harvard U. Bus. Sch., 1984, Pizzaman of Yr. Nat. Assn. Pizza Owners, 1984; recipient Golden Plate award Am. Acad. Achievement, 1984, Golden Chain award Multi Unit Franchise Svc. Orgn., 1986, Horatio Alger award, 1986, Restaurant Bus. Leadership award, 1986, Pope John Paul II Family Fidelity award 1988, Pine Mission's Knights of Charity award, 1990, Semper Fidelis award USMC, 1990. Mem. Internat. Franchise Assn. (Entrepreneur of Yr. 1986), Nat. Restaurant Assn. (Silver Plate award 1985), Mich. Restaurant Assn., Ypsilanti C. of C., U. Mich. Pres.'s Club, Ann Arbor Pres.'s Assn., Missionary Vehicle Assn. (bd. dirs.), AIA (hon.), Mich. Soc. Architects (hon.). Clubs: Barton Hills Country (Ann Arbor). Lodges: K.C. Avocations: collecting Frank Lloyd Wright furniture and memorabilia, classic cars.

MONAHAN, COURTNEY WILSON, lawyer; b. L.A., Sept. 14, 1963; d. Bruce and Joyce Wilson; m. Michael John U. Monahan, Oct. 22, 1994; children: Lauren Marie, Olivia Hannon. BA, U. Colo., 1985; JD, Suffolk U., 1989. Bar: N.Y. 1990, U.S. Dist. Ct. (ea. and so. dist.) N.Y. 1990. Assoc. atty. Colucci & Umans, N.Y.C., 1990-96, prnt., 1997—. Office: Colucci & Umans 101 E 52nd St New York NY 10022-6018 E-mail: cwilson@colucci-umans.com.

MONAHAN, DANIELLE JOAN, renal nutritionist; b. Tacoma, Feb. 22, 1952; d. Daniel Gustav and Bernice Elizabeth (Nordlund) Anderson; m. Jay Mitchell Littlefield, Nov. 13, 1976 (dec. 1997); children: David, Rachel, Paul; m. Aldrich B. Monahan, Jr., Oct. 30, 1999. BS, Va. Poly. Inst., 1974; MS, U. Md., 1975. Registered dietitian, Va. Therapeutic dietitian Samaritan Hosp., Troy, N.Y., 1976; renal dietitian BMA/Fresenius Med. Care (formerly Nat. Med. Care), Washington, 1977-85, Fairfax Dialysis (formerly BMA of Arlington), 1985—. Cons. Fairfax, 1985—; rep. network coordinating coun. Nat. Kidney Found., Chevy Chase, Md., 1980-84; chmn. BMA Dietitians Group, Washington, 1980-93. Contbr. articles to profl. jours., mags. Del. Va. Rep. Party, Vienna, 1982. Mem. Am. Dietetic Assn., No. Va. Dietetic Assn. Republican. Avocation: cooking. Office: Fairfax Dialysis 8316 Arlington Blvd #108 Fairfax VA 22031-5216

MONAHAN, EDWARD JAMES, geotechnical engineer; b. Bayonne, N.J., Sept. 18, 1931; s. John Joseph and Anna Monahan; m. Mary-Jean Thompson, Aug. 22, 1970. BSCE, Newark Coll. Engring., 1958, MSCE, 1961; PhD, Okla. State U., 1968. Registered profl. engr., N.J., N.Y. Instr. to prof. Newark Coll. Engring., 1958-84, prof. emeritus, 1984—; writer, cons. Bloomfield, N.J., 1984—. Advisor Tau Beta Pi, Newark, 1958-78, Chi Epsilon, Newark, 1958-81. Author: Construction of and on Compacted Fills, 1986, 2nd edit., 1994. Vol. performer, storyteller/singer at hosps., nursing homes, librs., schs. N.J. Storytellers Guild. Staff sgt. USAF, 1950-54. NSF summer grantee, Washington, 1960, NSF sci. faculty fellow, Washington, 1962. Mem. ASCE, Am. Soc. Engring. Edn. Baptist. Achievements include two patents on found. constrn. methodology. Home: 85 Newark Ave Bloomfield NJ 07003-4941

MONAHAN, JOHN T. law educator, psychologist; b. N.Y.C., Nov. 1, 1946; s. John Joseph and Dorothy (King) M.; m. Linda Costa, Aug. 24, 1969; children: Katherine, John. BA, SUNY, 1968; PhD, Ind. U., 1972. Asst. prof. U. Calif., Irvine, 1972-80; prof. U. Va., Charlottesville, 1980-84, Doherty prof., 1985—. Dir. mental health law MacArthur Found., Chgo., 1988-98. Author: Predicting Violent Behavior, 1981 (Guttmacher award 1981), Social Science in Law, 1998. Recipient Disting. Contbn. Pub. Policy award APA, Washington, 1990, Isaac Ray award, APA, N.Y., 1996. Mem. APA, Inst. of Medicine Office: U Va Sch Law 580 Massie Rd Charlottesville VA 22903-1738 E-mail: jmonahan@virginia.edu.

MONAHAN, LEONARD FRANCIS, musician, singer, composer, publisher; b. Toledo, Aug. 19, 1948; s. Leonard Francis and Theresa Margaret (Geraldo) M.; m. Elaine Ann Welling, Oct. 14, 1978. BS in Psychology and Philosophy, U. Toledo, 1980. Musician, writer Len Monahan Prodns., Toledo, 1971-75; musician, composer, pub. World Airwave Music, 1975—. Founder Red Dog Records Label. Author: If You Were Big and I Were Small, 1971, The Land of Echoing Fountains, 1972, Sending You My Thoughts, 1987, Another Road, 1987, Tapping at Your Window, 1988, Voice of the Guitar, 2000; composer numerous songs. Recipient Internat. Recognition of Christmas Music. Mem. Broadcast Music Inc., Internat. Platform Assn., Nat. Assn. Independent Recording Distbrs. E-mail: lfmwriter@hotmail.com.

MONAHAN, MARIE TERRY, lawyer; b. Milford, Mass., June 26, 1927; d. Francis V. and Marie I. (Casey) Terry; m. John Henry Monahan, Aug. 25, 1951; children: Thomas F., Kathleen J., Patricia M., John Terry, Moira M., Deirdre M. AB, Radcliffe Coll., 1949; JD, New Eng. Sch. Law, 1975. Bar: Mass. 1977, U.S. Dist. Ct. Mass. 1978, U.S. Supreme Ct. 1982. Tchr. French and Spanish Holliston (Mass.) High Sch., 1949-52; pvt. practice Newton, Mass., 1977—. Mem. Mass. Assn. Women Lawyers (pres. 1986). Avocations: reading, travel. Home and Office: 34 Foster St Newton MA 02460-1511

MONAHAN, THOMAS ANDREW, JR. accountant; b. Erie, Pa., Jan. 23, 1920; s. Thomas Andrew and Margaret (McEnery) M.; m. Patricia Tompkins, Sept. 4, 1948 (div. June 1983); children: Kathleen, Thomas P., Kevin, Margaret, Daniel; m. Rita Fargo, Sept. 3, 1985. BS, U. Pitts., 1942. CPA, Pa. Jr. acct. Price Waterhouse & Co., Pitts., 1942-43; sr. acct. Coopers & Lybrand, Phila., 1944-48; lectr. acctg. U. Pitts., 1948-49; pvt. practice acctg. Erie, 1949—. Lectr. Gannon U., Erie, 1965-78. Contbr. articles to profl. jours. Mem. AICPA (coun. mem. 1981-83), Pa. Inst. CPAs (v.p. 1971-72, coun. mem. 1968-71), Kahkwa Country Club (treas. Erie chpt. 1978-90). Home: 628 Delaware Ave Erie PA 16505-4602 Office: 100 State St Ste 500 Erie PA 16507-1457 E-mail: monahan@erie.net.

MONAHAN, THOMAS PAUL, accountant; b. Pitts., Feb. 27, 1951; s. Thomas Andrew and Patricia (Tompkins) M.; m. Ellen McKeithan Easterby, Aug. 2, 1975; children: Kelley Kathleen, Thomas Patrick, Kyle Easterby, Tessa Elizabeth. BS in Acctg., U. S.C., 1973. CPA, S.C. Staff acct. Rogers, Brigman, Peterson & Co., Columbia, S.C., 1972-75, ptnr., 1975-82; chmn., treas., prin. GMK Assocs., 1982—. Chmn., bd. dirs., treas. Devel. Properties, Inc.; trustee, pres. Town Theater Trust, 2000—. Mem. bus. coun. S. Dems., 1986—; bd. dirs. Cultural Coun. of Richland and Lexington Counties; pres. Town Theatre Trust; active Com. of 100. Mem. AICPA, S.C. Assn. CPAs, Columbia Stage Soc. (trustee, bd. dirs.), Spring Valley Country Club, Faculty House Club, Capital City Club, Sertoma, Zeta Beta Tau (trustee emeritus). Home: 1117 Adger Rd Columbia SC 29205-1942 Office: GMK Assoc Ste 2100 1201 Main St Columbia SC 29201-3263 E-mail: tmonahan@gmka.com.

MONAN, JAMES DONALD, university chancellor; b. Blasdell, N.Y., Dec. 31, 1924; s. Edward Roland and Mary Gertrude (Ward) M. AB, Woodstock Coll., 1948, PhL, 1949, STL, 1956; PhD, U. Louvain, 1959; post-doctoral research, Munich, Oxford, Paris; LHD (hon.), Le Moyne Coll., 1973, St. Joseph's Coll., 1973, New Eng. Sch. Law, 1975, Northeastern U., 1975, U. Mass., 1984; LLD (hon.), Harvard U., 1982, Loyola U., Chgo., 1987, Nat. U. Ireland, 1991, Boston Coll., 1996, U. Mass., 1997, Western New Eng. Coll., 2000, Xavier U., 2001. Prof. philosophy Le Moyne Coll., Syracuse, N.Y., 1960-68, v.p., acad. dean, 1968-72; pres. Boston Coll., Chestnut Hill, Mass., 1972-96, chancellor, 1996—. Cons. to N.Y. Jesuit Provincial for Higher Edn., 1966-72; dir. First Nat. Bank Boston, Bank of Boston Corp., 1976-96; interim pres. Assn. Jesuit Colls. and Univs., 1996-97. Author: The Philosophy of Human Knowing, 1952, A Prelude to Metaphysics, 1967, Moral Knowledge and Its Methodology in Aristotle, 1968. Chmn. edn. div. Boston United Way, 1974; chmn. steering com. of coll. pres. under phase II of ct.-ordered desegregation Boston Pub. Sch. System, 1974-76, Coun. for Aid to Edn., 1985-96, The Partnership, 1984-94, Sr. Thea Bowman Black Cath. Ednl. Found., 1989-96, Gov.'s Internat. Trade Adv. Bd., 1992; bd. dirs. Nat. Mentoring Partnership, 1991—, Naval Acad. Endowment Trust, 1998—; co-chair Mass. Mentoring Partnership, 1992-2001, bd. dirs., 1992—; co-chmn. Mass. Summit for Promise of Our Youth, 1997; trustee Le Moyne Coll., 1961-69, 1995—, Fordham U., 1969-75, Boston Coll., 1972-96, Canisius Coll., 1976-82, Georgetown U., 1979-84, Sta WGBH, 1972-96; exec. com. Boston Higher Edn. Ptnrship, 1988-96; mem. com. to Review and Implement Apostolic Constitution Ex Corde Ecclesiae, 1991-96. Mem. Assn. Jesuit Colls. and Univs. (dir., chmn. exec. com. 1983-86), Assn. Ind. Colls. and Univs. Mass. (exec. com. 1988-91, chmn. 1977-78), Nat. Assn. Ind. Colls. and Univs., Harvard Bd. Overseers (com. to visit grad. sch. bus. adminstrn., 1987-93), Nat. Collegiate Athletic Assn. (pres.'s commn. 1984-88), Metaphys. Soc. Am., Jesuit Philos. Assn., Soc. Phenomenology and Existential Philosophy, Soc. Ancient Greek Philosophy. Home: Boston Coll Chestnut Hill MA 02467

MONARCHI, DAVID EDWARD, management scientist, information scientist, educator; b. Miami Beach, Fla., July 31, 1944; s. Joseph Louis and Elizabeth Rose (Muller) M.; 1 child by previous marriage, David Edward. BS in Engring. Physics, Colo. Sch. Mines, 1966; PhD (NDEA fellow), U. Ariz., 1972. Asst. dir. bus. rsch. divsn. U. Colo., Boulder, 1972-75, asst. prof. mgmt. sci./info. sys., 1972-75, assoc. prof. mgmt. sci. and info. sys., 1975-97, prof. info. sys., 1997—, assoc. dir. divsn. info. sci. rsch., 1982-84, chair info. sys. divsn., 1999—. Chair, Information System Divn., 1999—, prin. investigator of socio-econ. environ. systems for govtl. agys., and local govt. orgns., State of Colo., also info. systems for pvt. firms, 1972-77, use of virtual reality in distance learning Colo. Commn. Higher Edn., 1996—. Contbr. numerous articles on socio-econ. modeling, object-oriented sys., info. sys. and artificial intelligence to profl. jours. Mem. Gov.'s Energy Task Force Com., 1974. Mem. IEEE, Inst. for Mgmt. Sci., Assn. Computing Machinery, Am. Assn. Artificial Intelligence. Home: 32 Benthaven Pl Boulder CO 80305-6210 Office: U Colo Grad Sch Bus Boulder CO 80309-0001

MONAT, WILLIAM ROBERT, university official; b. Biwabik, Minn., Oct. 9, 1924; s. William Stephen and Milda Aleta (Sundby) M.; m. Josephine Ann Sclafani, Sept. 9, 1951; children: Lise Ann, Kathryn, Margaret, William Michael, Eric. AA, Virginia (Minn.) Jr. Coll., 1947; BA magna cum laude, U. Minn., 1949, PhD, 1956; postgrad., Wayne U., 1949-50. Asst. prof. Wayne U., 1954-57; exec. asst. to Gov. Mich., 1957-60; asso. prof. Pa. State U., 1960-65, prof. polit. sci., 1965-69; asso. dir. Inst. Pub. Adminstrn., 1962-69; majority budget dir. Pa. Ho. of Reps., 1968-69; prof., chmn. dept. polit. sci. No. Ill. U., De Kalb, 1969-71, provost, 1976-78, Regency prof., 1986-92; Regency prof. emeritus, 1992—; pres. No. Ill. U., De Kalb, 1978-84; chancellor Ill. Bd. Regents, 1984-86; prof., dean faculties Baruch Coll., City U. N.Y., 1971-74, v.p. acad. affairs, 1974-76. Cons. USPHS, 1958, Office of Sec. Dept. Labor, 1963-64, Bur. Labor Stads., 1966, Office of Gov. Pa., 1968; bd. dirs. 1st Nat. Bank DeKalb, Castle Bancgroup, Inc. Author: Labor Goes to War, 1965, The Public Library and its Community, 1967, Politics, Poverty and Education, 1968; Editor: Public Adminstration in Era of Change, 1962, The Achieving Institution, 2000; contbr. articles to profl. jours. Mem. Gov.'s Commn. on Sci. and Tech., 1983-87; trustee Grad. Sch. Polit. Mgmt., N.Y., 1986-95; chmn. City of Dekalb Plan Commn. With AUS, 1943-46. Recipient Outstanding Achievement award U. Minn., 1981; decorated Bronze Star medal. Mem. Am. Polit. Sci. Assn., Am. Soc. Pub. Adminstrn., Phi Beta Kappa. Home: 1605 Mayflower Dr Dekalb IL 60115-1723 E-mail: wmonat@niu.edu.

MONATH, NORMAN, publishing company executive; b. Toronto, Ont., Can. came to U.S., naturalized, 1944; m. Pauline K. Farber, Aug. 30, 1952 (dec. Feb. 1972); children— Richard, Robert, Bruce. Dir. subsidiary rights Simon & Schuster, Inc., 1957-59; now cons.; founding pres. Cornerstone Library, Inc., N.Y.C., 1960—. Composer (with Walt Kelly) Songs of the Pogo; author: Know What You Want And Get It!; How To Play Popular Piano, 1984, How To Play Popular Guitar, 1994, (with William Cole) Folk Songs of England, Ireland, Scotland and Wales; editor (with Bobby Short) unpublished songs of Cole Porter; writer songs with Hal David, Sammy Cahn; recs. by Dionne Warwick, Supremes, Mitch Miller, Jerry Vale, Burns and Allen, Burl Ives. Served with Signal Corps AUS, 1942-45. Mem. ASCAP. Inventor Bali word game, 1954. Home: 3545 S Ocean Blvd Apt 101 Palm Beach FL 33480-5716 E-mail: nmonath@cs.com.

MONBO, DEAFUEH, accountant, researcher; b. Dec. 22, 1972; BS in Acctg., Morgan State U., 1995, MBA, 1998. CPA, Md. Auditing asst. Dept. Health and Mental Hygiene, Balt., 1994; student auditor/quality control officer Morgan State U., 1996-97; staff auditor Blue Cross & Blue Shield Md., Owings Mills, 1998; sr. auditor spl. program Mitchell & Titus, LLP, Washington, 1998—. Named Outstanding Acct. scholar Fin. Exec. Inst., 1993; grantee Senator Delores Kelly scholarship, 1996, Del. Emmett Burns Jr. scholarship. Mem. Morgan State MBA Assn. (organizer, pres. 1997, adv. bd. 1998—), Md. Assn. CPA (com. 1997—), Am. Soc. Women Accts. (chairperson 1995-96), Nat. Assn. Black Accts. Avocations: tennis, basketball, listening to music, meeting people. Home: 65 Fennington Cir Owings Mills MD 21117-1801

MONCLA, CAROLYN SUE, library director; b. Monroe, La., Nov. 4, 1947; d. Woodrow Wilson and Pauline May (Franklin) McBride; m. Stephen W. Moncla, Oct. 21, 1972; 1 child, Stephanie Sue. BS, La. Tech. U., 1969; MS, La. State U., 1972. Reference libr. Ouachita Parish Pub. Libr., Monroe, 1969-72, Cumberland County Pub. Libr., Fayetteville, N.C., 1972, Tex. City (Tex.) Pub. Libr., 1973-78; libr. dir. Moore Meml. Pub. Libr., Texas City, 1978—. Author: History of the Army Camp at Texas City, Texas, 1993; editor: (pictorial history book) Reflections: Texas City-LaMarque, 1996, Texas City Explosion 1947, 1997. Chmn. com. Texas City Sesquicentennial, 1986, All America City, 1995, 96; adv. bd. Galveston (Tex.) Hist. Found., 1996; chairperson Galveston Hist. Commn., 1996—. Scholar La. Libr. Assn. Mem. Tex. Libr. Assn. (dist. 8, chairperson 1995—), Rotary Club (sec. 1992-94), Delta Kappa Gamma (hon. mem.). Presbyterian. Avocations: genealogy, book discussion groups, book reviewing. Office: Moore Meml Pub Libr 1701 9th Ave N Texas City TX 77590-5469

MONCMAN, MICHAEL-GERARD JOSEPH, neurosurgeon; b. Allentown, Pa., Oct. 25, 1952; s. Anna Marie Moncman; m. Patricia A. Tribeck, Sept. 5, 1993; children: Alexis, Ryan. BS in Biology, Allentown Coll. St. Francis, 1974; MS in Biology, Cath. U. Am., 1977; DO, Phila. Coll. Osteo. Medicine, 1981, MS in Neurosurgery, 1987. Tchg. asst., tchg. fellow Cath. U. Am., Washington, 1974-77; intern, adminstrv. intern Allentown Osteo. Med. Ctr., 1981-82, mem. nursing insvc. staff, 1981-82; resident in gen. surgery Dr.'s Hosp., Columbus, Ohio, 1982-83; resident in neurologic surgery Met. Hosp., Phila., 1983-87, chief house officer, chief resident neurosurgery, 1986-87; dir. med. staff edn. Rehab. Hosp. of Altoona, Pa., 1988—. Chmn. adj. faculty mem. neurosurgery Ohio U. Coll. Osteo. Medicine, Athens, 1983-87; mem. utilization rev. com., Altoona Hosp., 1994, chmn., 1994—, mem. exec. com., 1994, chmn. utilization osteopathic concepts com. 1990-94; mem. courtesy staff HealthSouth Rehab. Hosp., Mercy Hosp., Clearfield Hosp., Nason Hosp., Meml. Hosp. of Bedford County. Contbr. articles to profl. publs. Fellow Am. Coll. Osteo. Surgeons (sec.-treas. neurologic seurgeons sect. 1990-92, mem. ethics com. 1990-91, mem. edl. com. 1992-93, chmn. neurologic surgeons sect. 1994); mem. AMA, Am. Osteo. Assn., Pa. Osteo. Med. Assn., Pa. Med. Soc., Cleve. Clinic Found. (affiliate physician), Blair County Med. Soc., Am. Acad. Pain Mgmt., Phila. Coll. Osteo. Medicine Alumni Assn. (life), Phi Sigma Gamma. Office: 1701 12th Ave Ste F Altoona PA 16601-3100

MONCREIFF, ROBERT P. lawyer; b. Evanston, Ill., Mar. 26, 1930; s. W. Philip and Maxine E. M.; m. Elisabeth M.; children: Anne, Philip, Jane. BA, Yale U., 1952; MA, Oxford U., Eng., 1954; LLB, Harvard U., 1957. Bar: Mass. 1957. Assoc. Palmer & Dodge, Boston, 1957-62, ptnr., 1963-95, of counsel, 1995—. City councillor, Cambridge, Mass., 1970-74. Office: Palmer & Dodge LLP 111 Huntington at Prudential Ctr Boston MA 02199-7613 E-mail: rmoncreiff@palmerdodge.com.

MONCRIEF, JACK WESLY, physician; b. Beaumont, Tex., Oct. 11, 1936; s. Carl Moncrief and Bess (Davis) Cropper; m. Betty Hale; children: Steve Hale, Ellen Hale, Blain Moncrief, Barrett Moncrief. BS, Lamar St. Coll., 1959; MD, U. Tex., 1962. Diplomate Am. Bd. Internal Medicine. Intern Detroit Receiving Hosp., 1962-63; resident in internal medicine U. Tex., Galveston, 1964-67; fellow in nephrology Georgetown U. Hosp., Washington, 1968; dir. internal medicine Brachenridge Hosp., Austin, Tex., 1971-74; prof. U. Tex. Med. Br., Galveston, 1973-83; pres., co-dir. Moncrief Popovich Rsch. Inst., Austin, 1977-97; CEO, chmn. Moncrief Mountain Ranch, Lake City, Colo., 1985-96; pres., chief med. examiner Jack Moncrief Group PA/Vidimedex, Austin, 1997-2000. Co-chmn. gov.'s com. to facilitate organ transplantation in the State of Tex., Austin, 1985. Capt. USAF, 1963-65. Named Tex. Rehab. Assn. Physician of the Yr., 1979-80; recipient Dialysis Pioneering award NKF, 1982, Disting. Physician award Austin Diagnostic Clinic, 1983. Fellow ACP; mem. AMA, NIH (mem. steering com.), ASAIO, Am. Bd. Internal Medicine, Alpha Omega Alpha. Republican. Baptist.

Achievements include inventor and patent in Method and Apparatus of CAPD, 1980; co-inventor and co-patent in Periodical Method of Implanting a Catheter, 1991. Avocations: wind surfing, sailing, fishing, travel. Office: Moncrief Dialysis Ctr 800 W 34th St Ste 101 Austin TX 78705-1144 E-mail: jbmoncrief@msn.com., jbmoncrief@hotmail.com.

MONCURE, JOHN LEWIS, lawyer; b. Houston, Nov. 4, 1930; s. Walter Raleigh Daniel and Margaret (Atkins) M.; m. Norma Steed, Dec. 29, 1954 (dec. June 1982); children: John Carter, Michael Lewis, Douglas Lee, Stuart Richard, Mary Margaret; m. Margaret Edmonston, Nov. 12, 1983. BBA, U. Houston, 1953; JD, U. Tex., 1956. Bar: Tex. 1956. Assoc. Butler, Binion, Rice, Cook & Knapp, Houston, 1956-68; ptnr. Prappas, Moncure & Eidman, 1969-86, John L. Moncure and Assocs., Houston, 1987—. Lectr. bus. law U. Houston, 1958-59, 68-69 Mem. sch. bd. St. Thomas Episcopal Sch., Houston, 1965-78; mem. vestry St. Thomas Episc. Ch., 1975-78. Named Distinguished Alumni Coll. Bus., U. Houston, 1968 Fellow Am. Coll. Probate Counsel; mem. Am., Tex., Houston bar assns., Assn. Christian Schs. (trustee), Coll. Bus. Alumni Assn. U. Houston (pres., dir.), U. Houston Alumni Fedn. (treas., dir.), Sigma Alpha Epsilon. Democrat. Home: 1220 W Clay Houston TX 77019 Office: 1200 River Oaks Tower 3730 Kirby Dr Houston TX 77098-3905

MONCZEWSKI, MAUREEN R. secondary art educator, visual artist; b. Scranton, Pa., Jan. 14, 1957; d. Walter Albert and Ann Hedwig (Sawicki) M. BA in Profl. Art, Marywood U., 1978, MFA in Painting, 1987. Cert. art educator K-12. Art instr. Internat. Corr. Sch., Scranton, Pa., 1983-98; grad. asst. Marywood U., 1985-86; art tchr. Moravian Acad., Bethlehem, Pa., 1989-90; adj. art instr. Penn State U., Lehman, 1990-91; art tchr. Notre Dame Jr./Sr. High Sch., East Stroudsburg, 1997—2001; secondary art tchr. Stroudsburg (Pa.) H.S., 2001—. Designer, painter of site specific murals Scranton Redevel. Authority, 1979, Scranton Sr. Activities Ctr., 1986, Carbondale (Pa.) Housing Authority, 1987, Teamsters Local 229, Scranton, 1990, Housing Authority of the County of Lackawanna-Dunmore (Pa.) Sr. Hi-Rise, 1994, The Artist's Studio, Scranton, 1995, Baird's County Kennel, Mehoopany, Pa., 1995, West Side Sr. Activities Ctr., Scranton, 1996, Wyo. Paint and Art Supply, Scranton, 1996, Suz's Marineland, Tunkhannock, Pa., 1996; represented in pvt. collections. Gen. Program grantee Boys & Girls Club, 1992, Housing Authority Mural grantee Lackawanna County, Dunmore, Pa., 1994, Arts to the People grantee Lackawanna County Commrs., Scranton, 1992, 95; recipient Cert. of Excellence award Dept. Labor, 1980. Mem. St. Luke's Art Soc., Kappa Pi. Democrat. Roman Catholic. Avocations: sculpture, metalworking, fabric design, travel. Home: 42 Brunswicke Dr Mount Pocono PA 18344-1144

MONDADORI, CESARE, neurobiologist, researcher; b. Zug, Switzerland, Jan. 2, 1946; s. Max and Dolores (Quadri) M.; m. Brigitte Joller, June 29, 1972; children: Patrick, Claudia. MSc, U. Zurich, 1971; PhD, Fed. Inst. Tech. (ETH), Zurich, 1977. Postdoctoral fellow U. Zurich, 1977-78; rschr. Ciba-Geigy, Switzerland, 1979-80; vis. prof. U. Toronto, 1981-82; head psychopharmacology Ciba-Geigy Basel, Switzerland, 1983-94; head pharmacology Marion Merell Dow, Strasbourg, France, 1994-96; head neuroscis. Hoechst-Marion-Roussel, Bridgewater, N.J., 1997-99; v.p., head neuroscis. Aventis, 1999-2000; head R&D Neuro3d, Mulhouse, France, 2000—. Vis. prof. McMaster U., Hamilton, Ont., Can., 1989—. Contbr. articles to profl. jours.; behavioral and neural biology rschr. Mem. AAAS, ACNP, European Neurosci. Assn., European Brain Behavior Soc. Home: Bodenmattstr 10 CH-4153 Reinach Switzerland Office: Neuro3d 12 Allee Nathan Katz 68086 Mulhouse France E-mail: cmondadori@neuro3d.fr.

MONDAL, KALYAN, engineering executive; b. Calcutta, India, Aug. 17, 1951; s. Dwijendra Nath and Bijali M.; m. Chitralekha Mandal; children: Indrani, Chandrani. M of Tech. in Computer Sci., U. Calcutta, 1974; PhD in Elec. Engring., U. Calif., Santa Barbara, 1978. Lectr. U. Calif., Santa Barbara, 1978-79; asst. prof. Lehigh U., Bethlehem, Pa., 1980-81; mem. tech. staff Bell Labs., Allentown, 1982-86, disting. mem. tech. staff Murray Hill, N.J., 1987-95; tech. mgr. Lucent Techs., 1996-2000; tech.mgr. Agere Sys., 2001—. Contbr. articles to profl. jours.; inventor equalizer filter configuration for processing real-valued and complex-valued signal samples, DVB frame synchronization, trellis decoder for real-time video rate decoding and deinterleaving. Mem. IEEE (Outstanding Paper award Internat. Solid State Cirs. Conf. 1984), C.A.S. (founding chmn. Lehigh Valley chpt. 1987-88), Eta Kappa Nu (life), Sigma Xi. Office: Agere Sys 4 Connell Dr Berkeley Heights NJ 07922 E-mail: kmondal@agere.com.

MONDALE, JOAN ADAMS, wife of former Vice President of United States; b. Eugene, Oreg., Aug. 8, 1930; d. John Maxwell and Eleanor Jane (Hall) Adams; m. Walter F. Mondale, Dec. 27, 1955; children— Theodore, Eleanor Jane, William Hall. BA, Macalester Coll., 1952. Asst. slide librarian Boston Mus. Fine Arts, 1952-53; asst. in edn. Mpls. Inst. of Arts, 1953-57; weekly tour guide Nat. Gallery of Art, Washington, 1965-74; hostess Washington Whirl-A-Round, 1975-76; ambassador to Japan, 1993-96. Author: Politics in Art, 1972, Letters from Japan, 1998. Mem. bd. govs. Women's Nat. Dem. Club; hon. chmn. Fed. Coun. on Arts and Humanities, 1978-80; bd. dirs. Associated Coun. of Arts, 1973-75, Reading Is Fundamental, Am. Craft Coun., N.Y.C., 1981-88, J.F.K. Ctr. Performing Arts, 1981-90, Walker Art Ctr., Mpls., 1987-93, Minn. Orch., Mpls., 1988-93, 97—, St. Paul Chamber Orch., 1988-90, Northern Clay Ctr., 1988-93, St. Paul, 1988-93, Nancy Hauser Dance Co., Mpls., 1989-93, Minn. Landmarks, 1991-93, Walker Art Ctr., Mpls., 1997—; trustee Macalester Coll., 1986—; mem. commn. Nat. Portrait Gallery, 1997—; chair Hiawatha Light Rail Transit Pub. Art and Design com., 2000—. Mem. Phi Beta Kappa Epsilon. Presbyterian. Home: 2116 Irving Ave S Minneapolis MN 55405-2541 E-mail: diggerkpr@aol.com.

MONDALE, WALTER FREDERICK, former Vice President of United States, diplomat, lawyer; b. Ceylon, Minn., Jan. 5, 1928; s. Theodore Sigvaard and Claribel Hope (Cowan) M.; m. Joan Adams, Dec. 27, 1955;children: Theodore, Eleanor, William. BA cum laude, U. Minn., 1951, LLB, 1956. Bar: Minn. 1956. Law clk. Minn. Supreme Ct.; pvt. practice law, 1956-60; atty. gen. State of Minn., 1960-64; U.S. senator from Minn., 1964-77; v.p. served under Pres. James Carter U.S., 1977-81; mem. Nat. Security Council, 1977-81; mem. firm Winston & Strawn, 1981-87; ptnr. Dorsey & Whitney, Mpls., 1987-93; U.S. amb. to Japan Tokyo, 1993-96. Author: The Accountability of Power*Toward a Responsible Presidency, 1975; mem. Minn. Law Rev. Dem. nominee for Pres. U.S., 1984. With U.S. Army, 1951-53. Presbyterian. Democrat.

MONDELLO, JOHN PAUL, financial consultant; b. N.Y.C., Aug. 9, 1948; s. Salvatore Carmelo and Mary (Monaco) M.; m. Catherine Mary Seyfried, Sept. 12, 1970; children: Lynn Marie, Timothy. BA in Econs., LeMoyne Coll., Syracuse, N.Y., 1971; MS in Fin. Svcs., Am. Coll., Bryn Mawr, Pa., 1986. CLU, Chartered Fin. Cons. Fin. cons. Signator Fin. Network, East Meadow, N.Y., 1972—. Instr. estate planning Am. Soc. CLU & ChFC, Garden City, 1990—, Empire State Coll., 1997—. 1st lt. U.S. Army N.G., 1971-77. Recipient Victor Goldberg Svc. award, Nassau Assn. of Ins. and Fin. Advisors, 1989. Mem. Nassau Assn. of Ins. and Fin. Advisors, Soc. of Fin. Svc. Profls., John Hancock Chmn.'s Coun., Million Dollar Round Table (life), John Hancock Pres.'s Cabinet. Avocations: golf, boating, water skiing. Office: Signator Fin Network 1900 Hempstead Tpke Ste 206 East Meadow NY 11554-1702 E-mail: jmondello@sfnonline.com.

MONDER, STEVEN I. orchestra executive; b. Newark, Mar. 12, 1945; B in Mus. Edn., Coll. Conservatory of Music, 1968, M in Mus. Edn., 1970. Tchr. orch., chorus, humanities McAuley H.S., Cin., 1970-71; prodn. mgr. Cin. Symphony Orch., 1971, asst. mgr., 1971-74, mgr., 1974-76, gen. mgr., 1976-89, exec. dir., 1989-98, pres., 1998—. Prodn. stage mgr. Cin. Opera Co., 1970, 71, adminstr., 1973. Office: Cin Symphony Orch Music Hall 1241 Elm St Cincinnati OH 45210-2231*

MONDLIN, MARVIN, retail executive, antiquarian book dealer; b. Bklyn., July 1, 1927; s. Samuel and Thelma (Schultz) M.; m. Phyllis Grossman, Oct. 23, 1962 (div. 1968); 1 child, Gerri; m. Irene Szmulewicz, Sept. 4, 1970. Student, Cornell U., 1945; student of Aesthetic Realism, with Eli Siegel, 1945—68; student, CCNY, 1948, Bklyn. Coll., 1969—71. Ptnr. Amory Books, N.Y.C., 1953-59; clk. Strand Book Store, 1951, estate book buyer, 1959-71, 74-76, sr. exec. v.p., 1976—. Bus. mgr. Definition Press., N.Y.C., 1957; cataloger U. Cath. de Louvain, Belgium, 1972. Author: Appraisals: A Guide for Bookmen, 1997; proofreader, copy editor Dover Publs., N.Y.C., 1958; editor Yearbook of Internat. Assocs., 1974. Mem. Antiquarian Booksellers Assn. Am., Appraisers Assn. Am., Bibliog. Soc. Am., Bibliog. Soc. London, Am. Photog. Hist. Soc., European Soc. History of Photography, The Ephemera Soc. Am., The Typophiles. Avocations: photography, non-silver processes lab. work, natural history, horticulture, music. Home: 889 Broadway Apt 3C New York NY 10003-1219 Office: Strand Book Store 828 Broadway New York NY 10003-4805 E-mail: marvinmondlin@erols.com., marv@strandbooks.com.

MONDORE, PATRICIA ANNE, health facility administrator, author, composer; b. Syracuse, N.Y., Feb. 8, 1956; d. George Gillis and Margaret Elaine (Lehmann) Wilson; m. Robert Jesse Mondore, May 20, 1989. BS in Music Edn., Houghton Coll., 1978; MA in Mus., Syracuse U., 1981. Cert. music tchr., N.Y. Choral music tchr. Fabius (N.Y.)-Pompey Cen. Schs., 1978-81; mgr. music dept. Sacred Melody Bookstore, Syracuse, N.Y., 1981-89; pediatric residency program coord. SUNY Upstate Med. U., 1989—. Dir. choral clinic Sacred Melody Bookstore, Syracuse, 1988; choir dir. LaFayette (N.Y.) Alliance Ch., 1988-89, ch. pianist/soloist, 1989—; singer various chs., meetings, coffeehouses, 1982—; talk show guest WMHR Radio, Syracuse, 1988, 89, WTVH Channel 5, Syracuse, 1987, Recumentary Video-Newschannels, TV, Syracuse, 1988. Author: Perennial Faith, 2001; author of poems; composer numerous songs; contbr. articles to profl. publs.; prodr. 5 CDs, 1 video. Organizer cmty. mall choir concerts, Syracuse, 1985-88, choral clinics, N.Y., 1982-89; singer, spkr. various prison ministries, 1983—, mus. mission concerts, Austria and Czeckoslovakia, 1988, 89; vol. crisis pregnancy counselor New Hope Family Svcs., Syracuse, N.Y., 1996—, website creator, web counselor, 2000—. Mem. Jorstadt Internat. Ministries (music leader 1983—), Nat. Right to Life. Republican. Avocations: singing, songwriting, jogging, fishing, reading. Home: PO Box 123 Jamesville NY 13078-0123 Office: SUNY Health Sci Ctr Pediats 750 E Adams St Syracuse NY 13210-2306 E-mail: patricia@gold-mountain.com.

MONDRY, PAUL MICHAEL, lawyer; b. Ludlow, Mass., June 15, 1953; BA, Western New Eng. Coll., 1975, JD, 1980. Bar: Mass. 1980, U.S. Dist. Ct. Mass. 1981. Pvt. practice, Ludlow, 1980—. Asst. treas. Hampden County, Springfield, Mass., 1982-83; legal counsel Hampden County Retirement Bd., Springfield, 1983—, City Springfield Retirement Bd., 1996—. Selectman Town of Ludlow, 1981—87, chmn. bd., 1983—84, 1986—87, mem. planning bd., 2001; mem. Ludlow Dem. Com., 1978—91, vice chmn., 1981—85; v.p. Polish Am. Citizens Club, Ind., Ludlow, 1985; bd. dirs. Ludlow Boys Club and Girls Club, Inc., 1990—93, charitable trust trustee, 1994—; dir. Ludlow Baseball Assn., Inc., 2002—. Mem. ABA, Mass. Bar Assn., Hampden County Bar Assn., Hampden County Bar Assn., Hampden County Estate Planning Coun., Nat. Acad. Elder Law Attys., Mass. Acad. Trial Attys., Unity Athletic Club. Avocation: golf. Office: 154 East St Ludlow MA 01056-3409

MONDSCHEAN, THOMAS HERBERT, economics educator; b. Chgo., Oct. 28, 1957; s. John Stephen and Caroline Diane Mondschean. BA, Northwestern U., 1979; MA, U. Wis., 1986, PhD, 1989. Rsch. asst. No. Trust Co., Chgo., 1979-81; rsch. analyst Dept. Devel., State of Wis., Madison, 1985-86; asst. prof. econs. DePaul U., Chgo., 1987-94, assoc. prof. econs., 1994—. Richter Internat. scholar Northwestern U., Evanston, Ill., 1978. Mem. Am. Econ. Assn., Midwest Econ. Assn., Fin. Mgmt. Assn., Beta Gamma Sigma (faculty). Avocations: travel, bridge, ethnic cooking. Office: DePaul Univ Dept Econs 1 E Jackson Blvd Dept Econs Chicago IL 60604-2287

MONDSCHEIN, LAWRENCE GEOFFREY, medical products executive; b. New Brunswick, N.J., Nov. 3, 1957; s. Harold and Florence (Kaplovsky) M.; m. Ellen Laurie Hirschhorn, Aug. 17, 1995. BS, Rutgers U., 1980, MLS, 1985, PhD, 1988. Regulatory asst. Janssen Pharmaceutica, Piscataway, N.J., 1983-84, database adminstr., 1984-86; rsch. adminstr. Janssen Rsch. Found., 1986-89; mgr. chem. info. Johnson & Johnson World Hdqrs., New Brunswick, N.J., 1989-98, mgr. worldwide environ. tng. and devel., 1999—. Contbr. articles to profl. jours. Trustee Essex Skating Club of N.J., sec., 1984-88, v.p., 1988-90, pres., 1990-93. Mem. U.S. Figure Skating Assn. (nat. judge 1992—, regional vice chmn. for judges 1993-95, sectional vice chmn. for judges 1995-98, chmn. singles and pairs com. 1998-2001, chmn. judges com. 2000—, bd. dirs. 1995—), Am. Soc. for Info. Sci. Avocations: figure skating (gold medalist in figures, free skating and ice dancing). Office: Johnson & Johnson 1 Johnson And Johnson Plz New Brunswick NJ 08933-0002

MONDSCHEIN, ROBERT H. surgeon; b. Hempstead, N.Y., Feb. 14, 1962; s. Gerald A. and Marcia R. Mondschein; m. Alyssa Chesler, Mar. 5, 1989; children: Erika, Jared, Ian. BS, Union Coll., 1983; MD, SUNY, Syracuse, 1987. Diplomate Am. Bd. Surgery. Resident Beth Israel Med. Ctr., N.Y.C., 1987-93; pvt. practice surgeon Massapequa, N.Y., 1994—. Fellow ACS. Office: 930 N Broadway Massapequa NY 11758-2303

MONDUL, DONALD DAVID, patent lawyer; b. Miami, Fla., Aug. 24, 1945; s. David Donald and Marian Wright (Heck) M.; children: Alison Marian, Ashley Megan; m. Anna Marie Towle, Oct. 12, 1996. BS in Physics, U.S. Naval Acad., 1967; MBA, Roosevelt U., 1976; JD, John Marshall Law Sch., 1979. Bar: Ill. 1979, Fla. 1980, Tex. 1998; U.S. Patent Office 1980; U.S. Ct. Appeals (fed. cir.) 1982; U.S. Supreme Ct. 1990. Commd. ensign USN, 1967, advanced through grades to comdr., 1977; mktg. rep. Control Data Corp., Chgo., 1977-79; patent atty. Square D Co., Palatine, Ill., 1979-81; group patent counsel Ill. Tool Works Inc., Chgo., 1981-87; assoc. Cook, Wetzel & Egan, 1987-89; ptnr. Foley & Lardner, Chgo. and Milw., 1989-95; sr. patent atty. IBM, East Fishkill, N.Y., 1995-96; gen. patent counsel Ericsson, Inc., Richardson, Tex., 1996-99; pvt. practice Dallas, 1999—. Patentee in methods and apparatus for multiplying plurality of numbers, N numbers, determining the product of two numbers, air baffle appartus, electrical encoding device. Commander, USNR, 1967-87. Office: 6631 Lovington Dr Dallas TX 75252-2519 E-mail: dmondul@aol.com.

MONEGRO, FRANCISCO, psychology educator, alternative medicine consultant; b. La Vega, Dominican Republic, Apr. 20, 1949; s. Francisco Monegro-Fdez and Ana A. (Pena) Monegro. Grad. cum laude, Pontifical U., Santiago, Dominican Republic, 1973; grad. psychology, Autonomous U. Santo Domingo, 1978, MD, 1986; MA in Ednl. Psychology, Tech. Inst. Santo Domingo, 1981; PhD in Nutrition, LaSalle U., Mandeville, La., 1993. Cert. natural health profl., hypnotherapist, profl. biofeedback profl.; diplomate in behavioral medicine, diplomate in pain mgmt.; lic. in psychology Autonomous U. Santo Domingo, 1978. Tchr. Peace H.S., Santo Domingo, Dominican Republic, 1975-76; dir. dept. psychology Holy Trinity Ednl. Ctr., 1978-80; prof. Sch. Medicine Tech. Inst. Santo Domingo, 1986-87; dir. dept. psychology Interam. U., Santo Domingo, 1988-89; prof. psychology and medicine Autonomous U. Santo Domingo, 1978-89, psychologist, counseling dept., 1979-84; staff mem. spl. edn. Bd. Edn. Dist. X, Bronx, N.Y., 1991-93; founder, chmn. N.Y. Inst. for Holistic Life, N.Y.C., 1991—; prof. psychology CUNY at HCC, Bronx, 1990—. Founder, pioneer in behavioral medicine Behavioral Medicine Clinic, Santo Domingo, 1987-94. Author: Biofeedback-Bio-retroalimentacion, 1988, Holistic Behavioral Medicine, 1993, Biomagnetic Medicine: Secrets and Power of Magnetic Energy, 1996, Psychology and Life Mind, Body and Society, 1997, (interactive CD-ROM) Psychology and Life, 2000; editor, pub.: BOEST, 1978, Dominican Bull. Behavioral Medicine, 1987, Holistic Life/Vida Holistica, 1991, others. Mem. Dominican Psychol. Assn. (treas. 1978-79), Soc. Behavioral Medicine, Assn. for Advancement of Behavior Therapy, Am. Acad. Pain Mgmt., Assn. for Applied Psychophysiology and Biofeedback. Democrat. Roman Catholic. Avocations: computers, golf, basketball, swimming, travel. Home: PO Box 302 Bronx NY 10458-0302 Office: NY Inst for Holistic Life 976 Mclean Ave Ste 370 Yonkers NY 10704-4105

MONEIM, MOHEB S. orthopaedic surgeon, educator; b. Cairo, May 14, 1941; came to U.S., 1970; m. Brigitte Moneim; children: Omar, Sonya. MD, Cairo U., 1963. Diplomate Am. Bd. Orthop. Surgery; lic. physician, N.Mex., Tex. Orthop. resident Duke U. Med. Ctr., Durham, N.C., 1972-75, Greenville (S.C.) Shriners Hosp., 1974-75; hand fellow, instr. surgery Hosp. for Spl. Surgery, Cornell Med. Coll., N.Y.C., 1975-76; pvt. practice Albuquerque, 1976—; attending orthop. surgeon U. N.Mex. Health Scis. Ctr., 1976—, chief of staff, 1991-93. Chief divsn. hand surgery dept. orthop. and rehab. U. N.Mex., Albuquerque, 1990—, prof. and chmn., 1991—. Contbr. articles to profl. jours., chpts. to books. Bd. trustees Univ. Hosp., Albuquerque, 1993-95. Fellow Royal Coll. Surgeons of Can.; mem. Am. Orthop. Assn., Am. Soc. for Surgery of the Hand (chmn. hand surgery fellowship com. 1992-94), Am. Acad. Orthop. Surgeons, Royal Coll. Physicians and Surgeons of Can., Alpha Omega Alpha. Office: Univ New Mex Health Sci Ctr Dept Orthop and Rehab 915 Camino De Salude NE Albuquerque NM 87131-0001

MONEK, DANIEL GLENN, music educator; b. NJ, Aug. 2, 1970; s. Glenn John and Christine (Norloff) Monek. AA, U. Fla., Gainesville, 1990; BS Music Edn., U.South Fla., Tampa, Florida, 1992; BM Vocal Performance, U. South Fla., Tampa, Florida, 1992; PhD, U. of Edinburgh, Edinburgh, Scotland, 1997. Dir. of choral activities Malone Coll., Canton, Ohio, 1998—2000; chmn., dept. of music Marietta Coll., Marietta, 2000—; music dir. Christ United Meth. Ch., 2001—. Chmn., Scottish divsn. Assn. Brit. Choral Dirs. (Scottish divsn.), Scotland, 1996—97; dir. New Edinburgh (Scotland) Orch., 1994—97. Mem.: Chorus Am., Coll. Music Soc., Music Educators Nat. Conf., Am. Choral Dirs. Assn. (ctrl. divsn. bd. mem. 1999—). Home: 105 Fort Sq Marietta OH 45750 Office: Marietta Coll 215 Fifth St Marietta OH 45750 E-mail: monekd@marietta.edu.

MONEY, JOHN WILLIAM, psychologist, educator; b. Morrinsville, New Zealand, July 8, 1921; came to U.S., 1947, naturalized, 1962; s. Frank and Ruth (Read) M. MA with honors, Victoria U. Coll., New Zealand, 1943; postgrad., U. Pitts., 1947; PhD, Harvard U., 1952; DHL (hon.), Hofstra U., 1992. Jr. lectr. philosophy and psychology U. Otago, New Zealand, 1945-47; part-time vis. lectr. Bryn Mawr Coll., Pa., 1952-53; mem. faculty Johns Hopkins U., Balt., 1951—, prof. med. psychology, 1972-86, assoc. prof. pediatrics, 1959-86, prof. emeritus med. psychology and pediatrics, 1986—; psychologist Johns Hopkins Hosp., 1955—, founder psychohormonal research unit, 1951. Vis. prof. pediats. Albert Einstein Coll. Medicine, 1969, U. Nebr. Coll. Medicine, 1972; vis. prof. endocrinology Harvard U., 1970; vis. prof. ob-gyn. U. Conn., 1975; Rachford lectr. Children's Hosp., Cin., 1969; bd. dirs. Sex Info. and Edn. Coun. U.S., 1965-68, Neighborhood Family Planning Ctr., 1970-82; mem. task force homosexuality NIMH, 1967-69; mem. study sect. devel. and behavioral scis. NIH, 1970-74; mem. task force on nomenclature Am. Psychiat. Assn., 1977-79, 85-87; pres. Am. Found. Gender and Genital Medicine and Sci., 1978—; bd. advisors Elysium Inst., 1980-2000; mem. external com. for rev. of Inst. for Sex Rsch., Ind. U., 1980; mem. sci. adv. bd. Kinsey Inst. for Rsch. in Sex, Gender and Reprodn., 1982-97; hon. chmn. internat. adv. bd. Nat. Inst. Rsch. in Sex Edn., Counseling and Therapy, 1991; Kan Tongpo vis. prof. dept. psychiatry U. Hong Kong, 1994. Mem. editl. bd. numerous jours.; field editor Medicine and Law: an Internat. Jour., 1982-95; subject of TV documentary Coming Home, 1999. Recipient Hofheimer prize Am. Psychiat. Assn., 1956, Gold medal Children's Hosp., Phila., 1966, citation Am. Urol. Assn., 1975, Harry Benjamin medal of honor Erickson Ednl. Found., 1976, Outstanding Contbn. award Md. Psychol. Assn., 1976, Lindemann lectr. pediatrics Cornell U., 1983, Bernadine Disting. lectr. U. Mo., 1985, Maurice W. Laufer Meml. lectr. Bradley Hosp. and Brown U., 1986, Disting. Scholar award Harry Benjamin Internat. Gender Dysphoria Assn., 1987, Outstanding Rsch. Accomplishments award Nat. Inst. Child Health and Human Devel., 1987, Gloria Scientae award, 1991, Lifetime Outstanding Sci. Contbn. award Internat. Cmty. Profls. for Treatment of Sex Offenders, 1991, Richard J. Cross award Robert Wood Johnson Med. Sch., 1992, Career Achievement award N.Y. Soc. Forensic Scis., 1994, Coun. of Sex Edn. and Parenthood Internat. award, 1994, gold medal for lifetime achievement World Assn. Sexology, 1995, sexology medal Am. Acad. Clin. Sexology, 1996; named Sexologist of Yr. Polish Acad. Sex. Sci., 1988; James McKeen Cattell fellow Am. Psychol. Soc., 1993; subject of book John Money: A Tribute (E. Coleman, editor), 1991. Fellow AAAS (life), Soc. Sci. Study Sex (charter, pres. 1974-76, award 1976, Past Pres. award 1987, Kinsey award western regional chpt. 1996), Harriet Lane Alumni Soc., Nat. Inst. Rsch. Sex Edn., Counseling and Therapy (hon.); mem. APA (master lectr. 1975, Disting. Sci. award 1985), Deutsche Gesellschaft für Sexualforschung, Internat. Orgn. Study Human Devel., Soc. Pediat. Psychology, Lawson Wilkins Pediat. Endocrine Soc. (founder), Am. Assn. Sex Educators, Counselors and Therapists (hon. mem., awards 1976, 85), European Soc. Pediat. Endocrinology (corr.), Internat. Acad. Sex Rsch. (charter, award 1991), Assn. Sexologists (life), Columbian Sexol. Soc. (hon.), Internat. Soc. Psychoneuroendocrinology, N.Y. Acad. Scis., Md. Soc. Med. Rsch., Internat. Coll. Pediats., Czechoslovak Sexology Soc. (hon., mem. internat. adv. bd. 1995), New Zealand Soc. on Sexology (hon., life), Sociedad Brasileira de Sexologia (hon.), Sociedad Andaluza de Sexologia (hon.), Can. Sex Rsch. Forum (hon.), Asian Fedn. for Sexology (hon.), Assn. de Especialistas en Sexologia (hon.), Nat. Assn. Sexology (chief patron). Home: 2104 E Madison St Baltimore MD 21205-2337 Office: Johns Hopkins Hosp Baltimore MD 21205 E-mail: jmoney@mail.jhmi.edu. *It has always been my policy to combine research with clinical care, academic teaching and public education. I have combined a lifelong interest in world travel and in research by lecturing on all continents except Antarctica.*

MONEY, MAX LEE, family nurse practitioner; b. Pineville, Ky., Apr. 17, 1949; s. Arthur Lee and Laura (Hendrickson) M. ASN, Lincoln Meml. U., 1991, BSN, 1993; MSN, U. Ky., 1997. RN, Ky., Tenn.; cert. family nurse practitioner. Staff nurse ICU Pineville Cmty. Hosp., 1991-93, med.-surg. flr. supr., 1993-94, med. surg. staff nurse, 1994-97; asst. prof. Sch. Nursing Lincoln Meml. U., Harrogate, Tenn., 1994—2001; family nurse practitioner Middlesboro Appalachian Regional Hosp., 1997—. Mem. profl. adv. bd. Comprehensive Home Health, Middlesboro, Ky., 1994; in-svc. educator Pineville Cmty. Hosp., 1994. Agent coll. fair Lincoln Meml. U., 1994, organizer breast cancer awareness seminar Schenck ctr., 1994, coord. Operation HealthCheck, 2001; tchr. Sunday sch. Harmony Bapt. Ch., Pineville, 1994. Recipient Bronze Good Citizenship award Nat. Soc. of Sons of Am. Revolution, 1991, Nursing Leadership award Tenn. Nurses Assn., 1991. Mem. ANA, Nat. League Nursing (adv. 1992—), Ky. Nurses Assn., Ky. Coalition Nurse Practitioners/Nurse Midwives, Sigma Theta Tau. Avocations: tea rose gardening, swimming, gospel music. Home: RR 1 Box 53 Pineville KY 40977-9706 Office: Middlesboro Appalachian Regl Hosp Middlesboro KY 40965 also: Middlesboro Appalachian Regional Hosp 3600 Cumberland Ave Middlesboro KY 40965-2614 E-mail: maxmoney@tcnet.net., mMaxmoney@arh.org.

MONEY, RUTH ROWNTREE, infant development and care specialist, consultant; b. Brownwood, Tex. m. Lloyd Jean Money; children: Jeffrey, Meredith, Jeannette. BA in Biology, Rice U., 1944; MA in Devel. Psychology, Calif. State U., Long Beach, 1971; BA in Early Childhood Edn., U. D.C., 1979. Rsch. psychologist Early Edn. Project, Capitol Heights, Md., 1971-73; lectr. No. Va. C.C., Anandale, 1973-74; tchr. preschs. Calif. and Va., 1979-81; dir. various preschs., Washington and Va., 1981-85; instr. guided studies Pacific Oaks Coll., Pasadena, Calif., 1986-88; cons. parent/infant programs Resources for Infant Educarers, L.A., 1986—; founder, dir. South Bay Infant Ctr., Redondo Beach, Calif., 1988-92; instr. child devel. Harbor Coll., L.A., 1992-93. Bd. dirs. Resources for Infant Educarers, 1986—; pres. bd. dirs. South Bay Infant Ctr., Redondo Beach, 1988-94, treas., 1994-98. Producer (ednl. videos) Caring for Infants, 1988—. Mem. League of Women Voters, 1956—, v.p., 1972-76. Mem. Nat. Assn. for Edn. of Young Children, Assn. for Childhood Edn. Internat., Infant Devel. Assn. Calif. Avocations: traveling, hiking. Home: 904 21st St Hermosa Beach CA 90254-3105 Office: Resources for Infant Educarers 1550 Murray Cir Los Angeles CA 90026-1644 E-mail: ruthmoney@earthlink.net.

MONEYPENNY, EDWARD WILLIAM, business executive; b. Long Branch, N.J., Jan. 28, 1942; s. Edward Henry and Eleanor Kathleen (O'Hagan) M.; m. Connie Wills, Feb. 19, 1966; children: Matthew, Jonathan, Christopher. BS in Acctg., St. Joseph's U., 1964; MS in Acctg. Sci., U. Ill., 1967. CPA, Tex. Audit mgr. Coopers & Lybrand, Phila., 1970-76; mgr. corp. acctg. Sun Co., Inc., Radnor, 1976-78; v.p. fin. adminstrn. Sun Prodn. Co., Dallas, 1978-81; v.p. fin., CFO Oryx Energy Co. (formerly Sun Exploration and Prodn. Co.), 1981-91; sr. v.p. fin., CFO Oryx Energy Co., 1992-94, exec. v.p. fin., CFO, bd. dirs., 1994-99; sr. v.p. fin., CFO Fla. Progress Corp., St. Petersburg, Fla., 1999-2000; exec. v.p. fin., CFO Covanta Energy Corp., Fairfield, NJ, 2001; sr. v.p. fin., CFO 7-Eleven, Inc., Dallas, 2002—. Chmn. bus. adv. coun. U. Ill. Sch. Bus., 2000-01, mem. exec. com., dean's bus. coun. 1st lt. U.S. Army, 1967-70. Mem. AICPA, Fin. Execs. Inst., Tex. Soc. CPAs. Home: 4712 Stonehollow Way Dallas TX 75287-7524 Office: 7-Eleven Inc City Place Ctr East N Haskill and N Central Dallas TX 75204 E-mail: emoneypenn@aol.com.

MONFERRATO, ANGELA MARIA, investor, writer, designer; b. Wissembourg, Alsace-Loraine, France, July 19, 1948; came to U.S., 1950; d. Albert Carmen and Anna Maria (Vieri) M. Diplomate, Pensionnat Florissant, Lausanne, Switzerland, 1966-67; BS in Consumer Related Studies, Mktg., Pa. State U., 1971, postgrad. in speech and comm., 1971-72. Simultaneous translator fgn. langs. Inst. for Achievement of Human Potential, Phila., 1976-78; art dir. The Artworks, Sumneytown, Pa., 1975-76; asst. productionist Film Space, State College, 1976; real property mgr. Pla. 15 Condominium, Ft. Lauderdale, Fla., 1979-80; legal asst., 1981-85; owner Rising Sun the Real Estate Corp. South Fla., 1986—. Pres. Kideos Video Prodns., 1985—; owner, designer Monferrato Designs, 1988-99; designer homes, interiors, furniture and landscapes. Avocations: writing, designing, yoga, faux painting, restoration of antiques. Office: Monferrato Designs Telluride 200 Front St Placerville CO 81430

MONFORT, RALPH DONALD, satellite operations director; b. Hartford City, Ind., Aug. 29, 1951; s. John William and Bertha Beatrice (Knecht) M.; m. Lonna Jean Hildebrand Handley, July 27, 1974 (dic. Mar. 1985); 1 child, Joseph. BS in Math., U. Notre Dame, 1974; MS in Phys. Scis., U. Houston, 1983. Satellite operator/planner Def. Meteorol. Satellite Program, Offutt AFB, Nebr., 1974-78; satellite operator Def. Satellite Program, Woomera, Australia, 1978-80; space shuttle mission contr. Johnson Space Ctr., Houston, 1980-85; inertial upper stage flight dir. Consolidated Space Test Ctr., Sunnyvale, Calif., 1985-91, Milstar divsn. chief Colorado Springs, 1991-96; dep. dir. Space and Missile Test and Evaluation Directorate, Albuquerque, 1996-97, chief space test and evaluation divsn., 1997-2000, dir., 2000—01. Col. USAF, 1974—. Home: # 162 11024 Montgomery Blvd NE Albuquerque NM 87111-3962

MONFORTE-MUÑOZ, HECTOR L. pathologist; b. San Diego, Feb. 17, 1959; s. Hector Monforte and Maria De La Luz Muñoz; m. Lana Jill Webster, Nov. 17, 1990; children: Laura, Mariana, Hector. MD, U. Autonoma de Guadalajara, 1984. Diplomate Am. Bd. Pathology, Am. Bd. Pediat. Pathology. Resident in pathology U. Miami - Jackson Meml. Hosp., Miami, Fla., 1985-89; fellow in pathology M.D. Anderson Cancer Ctr., Houston, 1989-90, U. So. Calif. Children's Hosp., L.A., 1990-91; pathologist All Children's Hosp., St. Petersburg, Fla., 1991-93, Children's Hosp. of L.A., 1993—, dir. autopsy program, 1998—, dir. insitu hybridization, 1996—. Contbr. articles to sci. and profl. jours. Recipient Clin. Fellow award Am. Cancer Soc., 1987-88. Fellow Coll. of Am. Pathologists; mem. Soc. for Pediat. Pathology. Roman Catholic. Avocation: model trains and ships. Office: Childrens Hosp of LA 4650 Sunset Blvd Box 43 Los Angeles CA 90027-6062

MONG, ROBERT WILLIAM, JR. media executive; b. Fremont, Ohio, Jan. 22, 1949; s. Robert William and Betty (Dwyer) M.; m. Carla Beth Sweet, July 25, 1975 (div. 1979); m. Diane Elizabeth Reischel, Jan. 23, 1988; children: Eric Robert, Elizabeth Diana. BA, Haverford (Pa.) Coll., 1971; graduate exec. bus. program, Stanford U., 1997. Reporter Cin. Post, 1973-75, Capital Times, Madison, Wis., 1975-77; city editor Madison Press Connection, 1977-79; asst. city editor Dallas Morning News, 1979-80, bus. editor, 1980-81, projects editor, 1981-83, asst. mng. editor, 1983-88, dep. mng. editor, 1988-90, mng. editor, 1990-96; pub. Owensboro Messenger-Inquirer, 1996-97; exec. v.p. A.H. Belo Corp., Dallas, 1997-98; pres., gen. mgr. The Dallas Morning News, 1998-2001, pres., editor, 2001—. Mem. Am. Soc. Newspaper Editors, Newspaper Assn. Am., Southern Newspaper Pubs. Assn., Am. Press Inst. (bd. dirs.). Office: The Dallas Morning News PO Box 655237 508 Young St Dallas TX 75202-4828 E-mail: bmong@tdmn.com.

MONGAN, JAMES JOHN, physician, hospital administrator; b. San Francisco, Apr. 10, 1942; s. Martin and Audrey Vera (Cunningham) M.; m. Jean Trotter Holmes, Apr. 22, 1972; children— John Holmes, Sarah Holmes. Student, U. Calif., Berkeley, 1959-62; BA, Stanford U., 1963, MD, 1967. Intern Kaiser Found. Hosp., San Francisco, 1967-68; med. officer USPHS, Denver, 1968-70; profl. staff mem. U.S. Senate Fin. Com., Washington, 1970-77; dep. asst. sec. for health HEW, 1977-79; assoc. dir. human resources Domestic Policy Staff, White House, 1979-81; asst. surgeon gen. USPHS, 1979-81; exec. dir. Truman Med. Center, U. Mo., Kansas City, 1981-96; dean sch. medicine U. Mo., 1987-96; pres. Mass. Gen. Hosp., 1996—. Prof. healthcare policy, prof. medicine Harvard Med. Sch.; mem. com. on consequences of unins. Inst. Medicine; chair adv. com. Commonwealth Fund Task Force; mem. Kaiser Commn. on Medicaid and the Unins. Trustee Kaiser Family Found., 1993—2001; med. officer USPHS, 1968—70; asst. surgeon gen., 1979—81. Med. officer USPHS, 1968—70, asst. surgeon gen. USPHS, 1979—81. Mem. NAS (Inst. Medicine), Am. Hosp. Assn. (trustee 1988-91), Am. Assn. Teaching Hosps. (bd. dirs. coun. teaching hosps. 1984-90), Inst. of Medicine. Home: 135 Crafts Rd Chestnut Hill MA 02467-1825 Office: Mass Gen Hosp 55 Fruit St Boston MA 02114-2696

MONGARELLA, GEORGENE HUGHES, interior designer; b. Yonkers, N.Y., May 28, 1951; d. George Victor Hughes and Joan Alicia (Smith) Dobransky; m. Joseph Andrew Mongarella, Nov. 18, 1973. A in Interior Design, N.Y. Sch. Design, 1978; BA in Bus. Adminstrn., Mercy Coll., Dobbs Ferry, N.Y., 1986. Hostess, bookkeeper Red Coach Grill, Yonkers, 1967-69; mgr. customer svc. Consol. Edison Co., White Plains, N.Y., 1969-86; chief exec. officer The Color Schemer Ltd., Scarsdale, 1983—. Advisor Jr. Achievement, Elmsford, 1981-83; cons. Yonkers Pub. Schs., 1986, Masked Ball, Am. Leukemia Soc., Elmsford, 1987; fundraiser Westchester Leukemia Soc., Elmsford, N.Y., 1987-88; fundraiser, tchr. design Yonkers Bd. Edn., 1988—; designer Gala Gourmet, March of Dimes, Rye, N.Y., 1989. Mem. Profl. Women in Constrn. (bd. dirs. 1986-87), Am. Soc. Interior Designers, Am. Womens Econ. Devel., Yonkers C. of C., Interior Design Soc., Illuminating Engring. Soc., Scarsdale Antiques Club. Republican. Roman Catholic. Avocations: jogging, aerobics, ballet, cooking. Home and Office: The Color Schemer Ltd 18 Coralyn Rd Scarsdale NY 10583-7404

MONGE, JAY PARRY, lawyer; b. N.Y.C., Mar. 15, 1943; s. Joseph Paul and Dorothy Emma (Oschmann) M.; m. Julia T. Burdick, 1966 (div. 1994); children: Justin Parry, Lindsay Newton; m. Elizabeth Ann Tracy, 1994. AB, Harvard U., 1966; LLB, U. Va., 1969. Bar: Ill. 1969, N.Y. 1981. Assoc. Mayer, Brown & Platt, Chgo., 1969-75, ptnr., 1976-79, N.Y.C., 1980-99, mng. ptnr., 1981-94, ptnr. Charlotte, NC, 2000—. Contbr. legal commentaries Ill. Inst. Continuing Legal Edn., 1974, 78, 81, 84, 87, 93, 96, 2002. Trustee Wagner Coll., 1996-2002. Mem. ABA, Assn. Bar City N.Y., Chgo. Club, Onwentsia Club, Sky Club, Westchester Country Club, Charlotte City Club, Carmel Country Club. Office: Mayer Brown Rowe & Maw 214 N Tryon St Ste 3800 Charlotte NC 28202 E-mail: jmonge@mayerbrownrowe.com.

MONGE, MARY T. graphic artist; b. Torrance, Calif., June 25, 1961; d. Del Raymond and Eva Mary Murphy. AA, Saddleback Coll., 1982; BA, Calif. State U., Fullerton, 1985; MA, Calif. State U., 1994. Graphic artist Lawrence Advt., Anaheim, Calif., 1986-88, Martin Graphics, Laguna Hills, 1988-89, Longendyke/Loreque, Inc., Santa Ana, 1989-90, Frames Data, Inc., Irvine, 1991-92, Sr. Highlights Mag., Laguna Hills, 1993-96, Crittenden Golf Inc. Mag., San Juan Capistrano, 1996-98, Duncan McIntosh Co., Irvine, 1999—. Artist Art Rental & Sales Gallery L.A., 1991—, Art Rental Gallery Laguna Art Mus., 1997—, nextmonet.com, San Francisco, 2000—, San Francisco Mus. Modern Art, 2000—. Artist: (books) The Best of Watercolor, 1995, People in Watercolor, 1996, The Best of Sketching and Drawing, 1999. Mem. L.A. Conservancy. Recipient cert. merit Watercolor Magic, 1998; Summer Arts scholar Calif. State U., Fullerton, 1994. Mwm. Watercolor West, Soc. Illustrators. Avocations: photography, tennis.

MONGELLI, THOMAS GUY, broadcast executive, radio personality; b. Jersey City, Sept. 14, 1952; s. Thomas A. and Margaret (Trevelise) M.; m. Sandra F. Castoro, Apr. 4, 1987; children: Thomas John, Jaclyn Amber. BA in Mass Communications, Rutgers U., 1974. Advt. salesman Sta. WNJR, Union, N.J., 1974-75; asst. sales mgr. Dispatch Pub. Co., Union City, 1975-78; N.Y. dist. sales mgr. Aquarian Pub. Co., Montclair, N.J., 1979-82; assoc. editor Bergen News Pub. Co., Palisades Park, 1982-84; producer, host Jazz 'n More Sta. WDHA-FM, Dover, 1981-95; program dir., entertainment editor, air talent Sta. WMTR, Morristown, 1984-91; reporter, nat. news audio coord. Metro/Shadow Broadcast Svcs., Rutherford, 1990—, N.J. news bur. chief, 2000—; air talent Sta. WKXW-FM, Trenton, 1991-95; audio producer MJI Broadcasting, N.Y.C., 1991-94; instr. North Bergen (N.J.) Bd. Edn., 1994-98. Instr. Conn. Sch. Broadcasting, Rochelle Park, N.J., 1993-96; account rep. Bergen Record, Hackensack, N.J., 1994-99; co-founder Maxx Comm. Ltd., 1989. Creator, prodr. Sound in Motion, Jazz Joint, Rock Formations broadcast series. Recipient Best Pub. Svc. Series award N.J. Broadcasters Assn., 1990, Recognition of Svc. award Big Bros./Big Sisters of Morris County, N.J., 1989-91. Home: 8302 2nd Ave North Bergen NJ 07047-6508 Office: Westwood One 201 State Rt 17 Rutherford NJ 07070-2574 E-mail: mongster1@aol.com., tom_mongelli@shadowtraffic.com.

MONGIN, ALEXANDER ANATOLIEVICH, neuroscientist, educator; b. Minsk, Belarus, Mar. 9, 1965; came to U.S., 1997; s. Anatoli I. and Tamara N. Mongin; m. Alena Rudkouskaya, July 22, 1987; children: Feodor, Anton, Katrine. MS, Belarussian State U., 1989; PhD, Acad. Scis. Belarus, 1995. Rsch. fellow Acad. Scis. Belarus, Minsk, 1995-97, sr. scientist, 1997; Fogarty fellow Albany (N.Y.) Med. Coll., 1997-99, asst. prof., 1999—. Contbr. chpts. to books, articles to profl. jours. Recipient award Fedn. European Societies Biochemistry, 1995, 1st prize European Soc. Neurochemistry, 1997, prize and medal European Acad., 1997. Mem. Am. Physio. Soc., Soc. Neuroscience, N.Y. Acad. Scis. Office: Albany Med Coll MC60 47 New Scotland Ave Albany NY 12208

MONGUIÓ, LUIS, Spanish language educator; b. Tarragona, Catalonia, Spain, June 25, 1908; came to U.S., 1939; s. Francisco and Matilde (Primatesta) M.; m. Helen Arnett, Mar. 7, 1933 (dec. Mar. 1976); m. Alicia de Colombi, Aug. 8, 1979. Licenciado en Derecho, U. Madrid, 1928; LLD (hon.), Mills Coll., 1963. Vice consul to 1st clas consul Spanish Fgn. Svc., 1930-39; from instr. to prof. Mills Coll., Oakland, Calif., 1942-43, 46-57; prof. Spanish U. Calif., Berkeley, 1954-75, prof. emeritus, 1975—. Vis. prof. dept. Hispanic and Italian SUNY, Albany, 1981-88, 93-94, hon. prof. Nat. U. of San Marcos, Lima, Peru, 1970—, U. Lima, 1992—. Author: Cesar Vallejo, 1952, es edit., 1960, Poesia postmodernista peruana, 1954, Don Jose Joaquin de Mora y el Peru del Ochocientos, 1967, Notas y estudios de literatura peruana, 1972; editor: Poesias de Don Felipe Pardo Y Aliaga, 1973, others. With AUS, 1944-46. Decorated Knight's Cross Civillian Merit, Spanish Govt., 1931; Teaching fellow Spanish U. Calif., Berkeley, 1940-42, Guggenheim Found. fellow, 1951. Mem. Internat. Inst. Ibero-Am. Literature (pres. 1951-53, mem. editl. bd. 1953-59), MLA (chmn. Spanish Am. lit. group 1951, 61, 66), Am. Soc. Aesthetics, Asociacion Internat. de Hispanistas, Peruvian Acad. Lang. (corr. mem.), others. Home and Office: 24 Berkshire Dr Clifton Park NY 12065-1711

MONHEIT, MOLLY JANE, artist, writer; b. Yakima, Wash., Aug. 5, 1922; d. Laurel LaVergne and Edna (Bracewell) Lugar; m. John Palmer Ruckel (dec. 1952); children: Gail Ruckel, Andrew Ruckel; m. George Monheit, Dec. 7, 1952; 1 child, William. Student, Art Ctr. Sch., Calif., 1942; BA magna cum laude, Wash. State U., 1944; MA, Mills Coll., 1947. Clk., artist, cons. Papyrus, Lafayette, Calif., 1976-97; ret., 1997. Exhibited paintings in Wash., Tex., and Calif.; prin. works represented in permanent collections in pvt. homes and museums in 38 countries; contbr. articles to Bird Watchers Digest. Precinct chmn. Reps., Lafayette, 1954-70; social chmn. Valley View Estates, Lafayette, 1954-80. Recipient fellowship Aurelia Reinhart, 1945-47. Mem. Soc. Western Artists, Am. Women Artists, East Bay Watercolor Soc., Audubon Soc., Am. Field Svc. (pres. 1970), Diablo Art Assn. (pres.), Alpha Gamma Delta. Presbyterian. Avocations: travel on birding trips, track and field (Calif. sr. champion 100m for age group 1980-92). Home: 1107 Magnolia Ln Lafayette CA 94549-3118

MONHOLLON, LELAND, lawyer; b. Corbin, Ky., Nov. 8, 1925; s. Lewis Tom and Thelma (Prewitt) M.; m. Gawinna Owens, 1946 (div. 1969); 1 child, Patricia Lynn; m. Alice Faye Burden, July 3, 1970. JD, U. Ky., 1952. Bar: Ky. 1952. Supervising adjustor Travelers Ins. Co., Louisville, 1955-69; pvt. practice law Madisonville, Ky., 1969-97; ret., 1997. With USN, 1943-46, PTO, USNR, 1963-69. Mem. Ky. Bar Assn., Hopkins County Bar Assn., Am. Legion, VFW. Republican. Methodist. Home: 185 Threadneedle Dr Madisonville KY 42431-6439 Office: 111 S Main St Madisonville KY 42431-2555

MONIA, JOAN, management consultant; b. Teaneck, N.J., Mar. 20, 1938; d. James Anthony and Anne Linden (Cairns) McCaffrey; m. Charles Anthony Monia, Dec. 30, 1961; 1 child, Clare Ann Woodman. BA, Ohio Dominican U., 1960. Info. specialist Battelle Meml. Inst., Columbus, Ohio, 1960-62; project leader Douglas Aircraft Corp., Huntington Beach, Calif., 1962-64; programmer analyst McDonnell Aircraft Corp., St. Louis, 1965-66; project mgr. Sanders Assocs., Nashua, N.H., 1968-70; database adminstrn. project leader Mass. Blue Cross, Boston, 1970-74; data strategist Factory Mut. Engring. Corp., Norwood, Mass., 1974-78; mgr. data resource planning Digital Equipment Corp., Maynard, 1978-84; sr. mem. tech. staff GTE Govt. Systems Corp., Needham, 1984-91; prin. DMR Group, Inc., Waltham, 1991-96; owner, mgr. Info-Driven Enterprise Structures, Marlborough, 1997, San Jose, Calif., 1998—. Recipient Sci. medal Bausch & Lomb, 1956. Avocation: painting. Home: 7553 Morevern Cir San Jose CA 95135-2106

MONICA, MARTIN J. law enforcement officer, educator; b. San Francisco; BA in Social Work, San Jose State U., 1980; postgrad., Golden Gate U., 1997—. Officer San Jose (Calif.) Police Dept., 1983—. Editor Am. Assn. for Pub. Adminstrs., San Jose; contbr. articles to Law and Order, Cmty. Policing Consortium. Bd. dirs. Housing Human Svcs., Sunnyvale, Calif. Mem. Latino Police Officers Assn., Hydrocephalaus Assn., Calif. Narcotics Officers Assn., No. Calif. Gang Investigators Assn. Democrat. Roman Catholic. Avocations: running, bicycling, camping, photography. Office: San Jose Police Dept 201 W Mission St San Jose CA 95110-1701 Address: 3061 Harding Ave Santa Clara CA 95051 E-mail: 4acinom@home.com.

MONICAL, ROBERT DUANE, consulting structural engineer; b. Morgan County, Ind., Apr. 30, 1925; s. William Blaine and Mary Elizabeth (Lang) M.; m. Carol Arnetha Dean, Aug. 10, 1947 (dec. 1979); children: Mary Christine, Stuart Dean, Dwight Lee; m. Sharon Kelly Eastwood, July 13, 1980; 1 stepson, Jeffrey David Eastwood. BSC.E., Purdue U., 1948, MSC.E., 1949. Engr. N.Y.C. R.R., Cin., 1949-51, So. Rwy., Cin., 1951; design engr. Pierce & Gruber (Cons. Engrs.), Indpls., 1952-54; founder, partner Monical & Wolverton (Cons. Engrs.), 1954-63, Monical Assocs., Indpls., 1963—, pres., 1975—; v.p. Zurwelle-Whittaker, Inc. (Engrs. and Land Surveyors), Miami Beach, Fla., 1975-90. Mem. Ind. Adminstrv. Bldg. Council, 1969-75; chmn., 1973-75; mem. Meridian St. Preservation Commn., 1971-75, Ind. State Bd. of Registration for Profl. Engrs. and Land Surveyors, 1976-84, chmn., 1979, 83 Served with USNR, 1943-46, USAR, 1948-53. Mem. ASCE (Outstanding Civil Engr. award Ind. sect. 1987), Cons. Engrs. Ind. (pres. 1969, Cons. Recognition award 1986), Am. Cons. Engrs. Council (pres. 1978-79), Ind. Soc. Profl. Engrs. (Engr. of Yr. 1980), Nat. Soc. Profl. Engrs., Am. Concrete Inst., Am. Inst. Steel Constrn., Indpls. Sci. and Engring. Found. (pres. 1992-93), Am. Legion, Lions, Masons, Shriners. Mem. Christian Ch. Home and Office: 18831 Whitcomb Pl Noblesville IN 46060-8130 E-mail: rduane@juno.com.

MONIF, GILLES R.G. physician; b. N.Y.C., May 7, 1936; s. Hassan Khan Monif and Henriette (Joseph) McQuade; m. Beatrice Laurence de la Peine, Sept. 5, 1967; children: Rex, William, Celine, Ashley. AB, Swarthmore Coll., 1957; MD cum laude, Boston U., 1961. Resident in internal medicine Bellevue Hosp., N.Y.C., 1961-63; research assoc. NIH, Bethesda, Md., 1963-65; resident in pathology NYU Sch. Medicine, 1965-68; asst. prof. ob-gyn U. Fla. Coll. of Medicine, Gainesville, 1968-71, assoc. prof. ob-gyn, 1971-84; prof. ob-gyn Creighton U. Sch. Medicine, Omaha, 1984-99, asst. dean, 1999-2000; adj. prof. ob-gyn. U. Mo., Columbia, 2000—. Pres. Infectious Diseases Inc., 1979—. Author 12 books, over 130 articles on infectious diseases to profl. jours. Served with USPHS, 1963-65. Democrat. E-mail: gmonif@aol.com.

MONIHAN, MARY ELIZABETH, lawyer; b. Cleve., Mar. 22, 1957; d. Michael Reilley and Donna (Warner) Monihan. BS in Econs., John Carroll U., 1979; JD, Cleve. State U., 1984. Bar: Ohio 1984, U.S. Dist. Ct. (no. dist.) Ohio 1985, U.S. Supreme Ct. 1989. Atty. in office of counsel Ameritrust Co. Nat. Assn., Cleve., 1984-85; assoc. Jones, Day, Reavis & Pogue, 1985-89, Squire, Sanders & Dempsey, Cleve., 1989-95; ptnr. Spieth, Bell, McCurdy & Newell, Co., L.P.A., 1995—. Pres. Estate Planning Coun. Cleve., 1994-95. Pres., vol. Coun. Cleve. Orch., 1998-2001; trustee Assn. Major Symphony Orch. Vols., 1997-99; trustee Women's Com. of the Cleveland Orch., 2000—. Mem.: ABA, Cleve. Cath. Lawyers Guild (exec. bd. 2001—), Cleve. Bar Assn., Ohio Bar Assn., Am. Coll. Trust and Estate Counsel, Jr. Com. Cleve. Orch. (pres. 1997—99). Office: Spieth Bell McCurdy & Newell Co LPA 925 Euclid Ave Ste 2000 Cleveland OH 44115-1407 E-mail: memonihan@spiethbell.com.

MONISMITH, CARL LEROY, civil engineering educator; b. Harrisburg, Pa., Oct. 23, 1926; s. Carl Samuel and Camilla Frances (Geidt) M. BSCE, U. Calif., Berkeley, 1950, MSCE, 1954. Registered civil engr., Calif. From instr. to prof. civil engring. U. Calif., Berkeley, 1951—, chmn. dept. civil engring., 1974-79, Robert Horonjeff prof. civil engring., 1986—, prof. emeritus, 1996. Cons. Chevron Rsch. Co., Richmond, Calif., 1957-93, U.S. Army CE Waterways Expt. Sta., Vicksburg, Miss., 1968—, B.A. Vallerga, Inc., Oakland, Calif., 1980-98, ARE, Austin, Tex. and Scotts Valley, Calif., 1978-92; cons. Bechtel Corp., San Francisco, 1982-86. Contbr. numerous articles to profl. jours. Served to 2d lt. C.E., U.S. Army, 1945-47. Recipient Rupert Myers medal U. NSW, 1976; named Henry M. Shaw Lectr. in Civil Engring., N.C. State U., 1993; sr. scholar Fulbright Found., U. NSW, 1971, Nat. Asphalt Pavelent Assn. Rsch. and Edn. Found. award, 2002, R.D. Kenyon Rsch. and Edn. award for Outstanding Contbns. for Hot Mix Asphalt Tech., 2002; named Disting. Engring. Alumnus, Coll. Engring., U. Calif., Berkeley, 1996. Fellow AAAS; mem. NAE, ASCE (hon. mem., pres. San Francisco sect. 1979-80, ednl. activities com. 1989-91, State of Art award 1977, James Laurie prize 1988), ASTM, Assn. Asphalt Paving Technologists (hon. mem., pres. 1968, W.J. Emmons award 1961, 65, 85), Transp. Rsch. Bd. (assoc., chmn. pavement design sect. 1973-79, K.B. Woods award 1972, 1st disting. lectureship 1992, Roy W. Crum award 1995), Am. Soc. Engring. Edn., Internat. Soc. for Asphalt Pavements (chmn. bd. dirs. 1988-90), Asphalt Inst. (roll of honor 1990), Nat. Asphalt Pavement Assn. Rsch. and Edn. Found., U. Calif. (Berkeley citation 1996). Avocations: swimming, stamp collecting. Office: U Calif Dept Civil Engring 215 Mclaughlin Hall Berkeley CA 94720-1721 E-mail: clm@newton.berkeley.edu.

MONITZ, THEODORE ALLAN, cardiologist; b. N.Y.C., Apr. 7, 1954; BS magna cum laude, SUNY, Stony Brook, 1975; MD, SUNY, Downstate, 1979. Diplomate Am. Bd. Internal Medicine, Am. Bd. Cardiovascular Diseases. Intern Nassau County Med. Ctr., East Meadow, N.Y., 1979-80, resident, 1980-82, chief resident, 1981-82; fellow in cardiovascular diseases Georgetown Affiliate Hosp., Washington, 1982-84; mem. staff Piedmont Hosp., Atlanta Med. Ctr., Kennestone Hosp., Atlanta, No. Ga. Med. Ctr., Ellijay, Mountainside Med. Ctr., Jasper, Ga.; clin. instr. medicine Sch. Medicine Georgetown U., Washington, 1982-84; asst. clin. prof. medicine Sch. Medicine Emory U., Atlanta, 1990—; pvt. practice, 1991—. Fellow ACC, AHA, Soc. of Cardiac Angiography and Interventions; mem. ACP, AMA, Am. Soc. Echocardiology, Med. Assn. Ga., Med. Assn. Atlanta. Address: 95 Collier Rd NW Atlanta GA 30309-1796 E-mail: tmonitz@aol.com.

MONJAN, ANDREW ARTHUR, health science administrator; b. N.Y.C., Feb. 9, 1938; s. Victor Momjian and Sonia (Sherinian) Dardarian; m. Susan Vollenweider, July 1961 (div. Nov. 1965); m. Usha Bose, Aug. 14, 1969; children: Matthew, Vanessa. BSc, Rensselaer Poly. Inst., 1960; PhD, U. Rochester, 1965; MPH, Johns Hopkins U., 1970. Rsch. asst. Sterling-Winthrop Rsch. Inst., Rensselaer, N.Y., 1960; USPHS rsch. fellow Ctr. for Brain Rsch. U. Rochester, 1964-66; asst. prof. depts. psychology and physiology U. Western Ont., London, Can., 1966-69; from asst. prof. to assoc. prof. dept. epidemiology Sch. Hygiene and Pub. Health Johns Hopkins U., Balt., 1971-83; expert epidemiology extramural programs br. NIH, Bethesda, Md., 1983-85, chief neurobiology/immunology programs physiology aging br., 1985-87, acting assoc. dir., 1987, chief neurobiology, acting chief neuropsychology brs., 1987—; exec. sec. Nat. Commn. on Sleep Disorders Rsch., 1990-92. Presenter in field. Contbr. articles to profl. jours. N.Y. State Regents scholar, 1955-59; N.Y. State Regents Grad. Tchg. fellow, 1960-62, USPHS rsch. fellow, 1962-64, 69-70. Mem. Soc. for Neurosci., Sigma Xi. Office: Nat Inst Aging Ste 3c307 7201 Wisconsin Ave Msc9205 Bethesda MD 20892-9205 E-mail: am39m@nih.gov.

MONK, ALLAN JAMES, baritone; b. Mission City, B.C., Can., Aug. 19, 1942; m. Marlene Folk; 3 children. Student, Elgar Higgin and Boris Goldovsky. Operatic debut in Old Maid and the Thief, San Francisco, 1967; joined touring co., later main co. San Francisco Opera; appeared with Tulsa Opera, Pitts. Opera, Edmonton Opera, Vancouver Opera, So. Alta. Opera, Chgo. Opera, Balt. Opera, Miami Opera, Colo. Opera, Mont real Opera, Hawaii Opera Theatre, Portland Opera.;, 1976. Met. Opera debut as Schaunard in La Boheme, 1976, sang title role in Wozzeck, Wolfram in Tannheuser, Dr. Malatesta in Don Pasquale, Rodrigo in Don Carlo, Sharpless in Madame Butterfly, Herald in Lohengrin; sang with Can. Opera Co. as Abelard in Heloise and Abelard, Macbeth, Rigoletto, Belcore in L'Elisir D'Amoure, Jago in Otello, as Ford in Falstaff, four villains in Les Contes d'Hoffman; with Nat. Arts Ctr. Opera Festival, Ottawa, Ont., Can., title role in Don Giovanni, Almaviva in Le Nozze Di Figaro, gulielmo in Cossi Fan Tutti, Tomsky in Pique Dame, Marcello in La Boheme; Carnegie Hall debut as Vladislav in Dalibor, 1977; European debut as Wozzeck, 1980; solo recitalist; toured with Nat. Arts Ctr. Orch. in USSR, Poland, Italy, 1973; movie debut as Baron Douphol in La Traviata, 1983. Named Artist of Yr. Can. Music Council, 1983, laureat Order of Can., 1985. Office: 14415 Parkland Blvd SE Calgary AB Canada T2J 4L5

MONK, ANTHONY JOHN, engineer; b. Coulsdon, Eng., Nov. 14, 1923; s. Frank Leonard and Barbara (Ashby) M.; m. Elizabeth Ann Samson, Apr. 14, 1951; children: Michael Frank, Anstace Elizabeth (dec.), Peter John Oliver, Andrew Anthony, Jonathan Patrick Bruce. BSc in Engring., London U., 1950; MSc, Cranfield U., 1972. Chartered engr. Engr. officer Royal Navy, 1941-78, rear admiral, 1974-78; dir. gen. Brick Devel. Assn., 1979-83; appeals organiser Royal Marsden Hosp., London, 1984-87; cons. Engring. Industry Tng. Bd., Watford, 1987-89. Recipient CBE Her Majesty the Queen, 1973. Fellow Royal Aeronautical Soc., Instn. of Mech. Engrs., Inst. of Marine Engrs., Royal Soc. of Arts; mem. Royal Instn., Worshipful Co. Engrs. (liveryman). Avocations: swimming, service pilot. Home: 1 Cissbury Windsor Rd Ascot SL5 7LF England

MONK, BRADLEY JAMES, gynecologic oncologist, researcher, educator; b. Provo, Utah, Apr. 10, 1961; children: Stephanie, Amanda. B of Zoology cum laude, Birgham Young U., 1984; MD, U. Ariz., 1988. Diplomate Am. Bd. Ob-Gyn., Am. Bd. Gynecologic Oncology. Resident UCLA, 1988-92; fellow, clin. instr. U. Calif., Irvine, 1992-95, asst. prof., 1998—; asst. prof Tex. Tech U., Lubbock, 1995-98. Investigator Gynecologi Oncology Group, 1995—. Recipient Acad. award Hewlett-Packard, 1988, Berlex Labs. award, 1991. Fellow ACS, ACOG; mem. Soc. Gynecologi Oncologists, Soc. Surg. Oncology. Achievements include patent on Vaginal Speculum for PDT & Method for Using. Office: U Calif Irvine Med Ctr 101 The City Dr S Bldg 23 Orange CA 92868-3201

MONK, CARL COLBURN, lawyer, academic administrator; b. Sept. 11, 1942; BA in Polit. Sci., Okla. State U., 1965; JD, Howard U., 1971. Bar: D.C. 1971, N.Y. 1973. Assoc. Simpson, Thacher & Bartlett, N.Y.C., 1971-74; from asst. prof. to assoc. prof. Washburn U., Topeka, 1974-78, from assoc. dean to dean, prof., 1976-88, disting. prof. law, 1988—. Dep. dir. Assn. Am. Law Schs., Washington, 1988-90, exec. dir., 1992—; vis. scholar Bklyn. Law Sch., 1985-86; vis. prof. law W.S. Richardson Sch. Law U. Hawaii Manao, 1990-91; lit. cons. Contbr. articles to profl. jours. Bd. dirs. Kans. Civil Liberties Union. Office: Assn Am Law Schs Ste 800 1201 Connecticut Ave NW Washington DC 20036-2605 E-mail: cmonk@aals.org.

MONK, DIANA CHARLA, artist, stable owner; b. Visalia, Calif., Feb. 25, 1927; d. Charles Edward and Viola Genevieve (Shea) Williams; m. James Alfred Monk, Aug. 11, 1951; children: Kiloran, Sydney, Geoffrey, Anne, Eric. Student, U. Pacific, 1946-47, Sacramento Coll., 1947-48, Calif. Coll. Fine Arts, San Francisco, 1948-51, Calif. Coll. Arts & Crafts, Oakland, 1972. Art tchr. Mt. Diablo Sch. Dist., Concord, Calif., 1958-63; pvt. art tchr. Lafayette, 1963-70; gallery dir. Jason Aver Gallery, San Francisco, 1970-72; owner, mgr. Monk & Lee Assocs., Lafayette, 1973-80; stable owner, mgr. Longacre Trg. Stables, Santa Rosa, Calif., 1989—. One-person shows include John F. Kennedy U., Orinda, Calif., Civic Arts Gallery, Walnut Creek, Calif., Vallery Art Gallery, Walnut Creek, Sea Ranch Gallery, Gualala, Calif., Jason Aver Gallery, San Francisco; exhibited in group shows at Oakland (Calif.) Art Mus., Crocker Nat. Art Gallery, Sacramento, Le Salon des Nations, Paris. Chair bd. dirs. Walnut Creek (Calif.) Civic Arts, 1972-74, advisor to dir., 1968-72;

exhibit chmn. Valley Art Gallery, Walnut Creek, 1977-78; juror Women's Art Show, Walnut Creek, 1970, Oakland Calif. Art. Home and Office: Longacre Tng Stables 1702 Willowside Rd Santa Rosa CA 95401-3922 E-mail: longacrestables@msn.com.

MONK, MEREDITH JANE, artistic director, composer, choreographer, filmmaker, director; b. N.Y.C., Nov. 20, 1942; d. Theodore G. and Audrey Lois (Zellman) Monk. BA, Sarah Lawrence Coll., 1964; ArtsD (hon.) , Bard Coll., 1988, U. of the Arts, 1989, Juilliard Sch. Music, 1997, San Francisco Art Inst., 1998, Boston Conservatory, 2001, Bennington Coll., 2002, Cornish Coll. Arts, 2002. Artistic dir., founder Ho. Found. Arts, N.Y.C., 1968—. Bd. dirs. Am. Music Ctr. Prin. works include 16 Millimeter Earrings, 1966, Vessel, 1971, Quarry, 1976, Recent Ruins, 1979, Turtle Dreams, 1983, The Games, 1983, Book of Days, 1988, Facing North, 1990, Atlas, 1991, Three Heavens and Hells, 1992, Volcano Songs, 1994, American Archeology, 1994, The Politics of Quiet, 1996, Magic Frequencies, 1998, Mercy, 2001, exhibitions include Libr. of Performing Arts, Lincoln Ctr., 1996, Walker Art Ctr., Mpls., 1998, Whitney Mus. Art, 2002, Exit Art, 2002. Recipient Obie award, Village Voice, 1972, 1976, 1985, Creative Arts award, Brandeis U., 1974, Villager award, 1980, 1983, Deutches Kritiker preis, 1981, 1986, Bessie award, 1985, Nat. Music Theatre award, 1986, Dance Mag. award, 1993, John D. and Catherine T. MacArthur award, 1995, Sarah Lawrence Disting. Alumna award, 1996, Samuel Scripps award, 1996, Sigma Phi Omega award, 1987; fellow Guggenheim, 1972, 1982, Norton Stevens, 1993—94, MacDowell Colony. Mem.: ASCAP (award 1980—2000). Office: House Found for Arts 131 Varick St New York NY 10013-1410

MONK, SUSAN MARIE, physician, pediatrician; b. York, Pa., May 7, 1945; d. John Spotz and Mary Elizabeth (Shelly) M.; m. Jaime Pacheco, June 5, 1971; children: Benjamin Joaquin, Maria Cristina. AB, Colby Coll., 1967; MD, Jefferson Med. Coll., 1971. Diplomate Am. Bd. Pediatrics. Pediatrician Children's Med. Ctr., Dayton, Ohio, 1975—; asst. clin. prof. pediat. Wright State U., 1976—83, 1983—2000, asst. prof., 2000—, assoc. clin. prof. pediat., 2000—. Mem. bd. dirs. Children's Med. Ctr., Dayton, 1991-96, chief-of-staff, 1992-94. Mem. Am. Acad. Pediatrics, We. Ohio Pediatric Soc., Pediatric Ambulatory Care Soc. Avocations: reading, gardening, travel, movies, theater. Office: Childrens Health Clinic 722 Valley St Dayton OH 45404-1845

MÖNKEMÜLLER, KLAUS ERIK, physician, researcher, clinician; b. Guatemala City, Guatemala, Apr. 10, 1965; came to U.S., 1992; s. Klaus Dieter and Julia Odily (Porras) M.; 1 child, Kirsten Odily. BS, U. Francisco Marroquin, Guatemala, 1987, MD, 1991. Diplomate Am. Bd. Internal Medicine; diplomate gastroenterology; cert. Ednl. Commn. for Fgn. Med. Grads. Intern in internal medicine U. Tenn., Memphis, 1992-93, resident in internal medicine, 1993-95, chief med. resident, 1995-96; assoc. fellow in gastroenterology U. Ala., Birmingham, 1996-99, asst. prof. medicine, 1999—; chief gastrointestinal endoscopy Vets. Hosp., 1999—. Attending physician Bapt. Meml. Hosp.-Monroe Clinic, Memphis, 1995-96, Vets. Hosp., Memphis, 1995-96, Vets. Hosp., Birmingham, 1997—; vis. lectr. U. Francisco Marroquin, 1996; vis. prof., L.Am. Congress Surgery, Guatemala City, 1997; invited prof., mem. adv. bd. Panamerican Congress of Gastroenterology, Peru, 2001; mem. internat. rels. com. Interamerican Assn. Gastroenterology; instr. dept. emergency medicine U. Ala., 1997-99. Inventor in field of gastrointestinal endoscopy; contbr. articles to profl. jours. and books. Mem., dir. med. activities Rotaract, Guatemala, 1986; pres. Med. Sch. Class, Guatemala, 1987-91; mem. exec. com. U. Tenn., 1992-95, ethics com., 1995-96. Recipient Young Investigator award DuPont and Am. Coll. Chest Physicians, 1995, Honor diploma Ministry of Health, Guatemala, 1996, Outstanding Vis. Scholar award U. Ala., 1998, ACG/ASTRA Pharms. award, 1998, othrs. Mem.: Internat. Assn. Pancreatology, Guatemalan Soc. Physicians and Surgeons (Best Clin. Investigation award 1989), Am. Coll. Physicians, Am. Soc. Gastrointestinal Endoscopy, Assn for Study of Liver Diseases, Am. Coll. Gastroenterology, Club Aleman Guatemala. Roman Catholic. Avocations: photography, reading, bicycling, travelling. Home: 546 Summit Place Birmingham AL 35243 Office: Univ Ala Dvsn Gastroenterology 633 Zrb Uab Sta Birmingham AL 35294-0001 E-mail: klaus1@uab.edu.

MONKS, JOHN GARVIE See LOUIS, WILLIAM JOSEPH

MONMONIER, MARK, geographer, graphics educator, essayist; b. Balt., Feb. 2, 1943; s. John Carroll and Martha Elizabeth (Mason) M.; m. Margaret Janet Kollner, Sept. 4, 1965; 1 child, Jo Kerry. BA, Johns Hopkins U., 1964; MS, Pa. State U., 1967, PhD, 1969. Asst. prof. U. Rhode Island, Kingston, 1969-70, SUNY, Albany, 1970-73; assoc. prof Syracuse U., N.Y., 1973-79, prof., 1979-98, Disting. prof. geography, 1998—. Cons. N.Y. State, Albany, 1974-93, Nat. Geog. Soc., 1987, Microsoft Corp., 1993-99, Belmont Rsch., 1995, AT&T Rsch., 1996-97, George Philip Ltd., England, 1996-97; rsch. geographer U.S. Geol. Survey, Reston, Va., 1979-84; dep. dir. N.Y. Ctr. for Geographic Info. and Analysis, 1989-90; Robinson vis. fellow George Mason U., 1985; Ida Beam Disting. vis. prof. U. Iowa, 1985; mem. adv. bd. GIS Law and Policy Inst., 1994-98; adv. bd. Philip Lee Philips Soc.; cons. and expert witness various law firms, 1995—; co-dir. History of Cartography in the Twentieth Century project, 1999--; mem. mapping sci. com. NRC, 2000—. Author: Maps, Distortion and Meaning, 1977, Computer-assisted Cartography, 1982, Technological Transition in Cartography, 1985, Maps with the News, 1989, How to Lie with Maps, 1991, 2d edit. 1996, French edit. 1993, Japanese edit. 1995, German edit. 1996, Korean edit. 1998, Czech edit., 2000, Mapping It Out, 1993, Drawing the Line, 1995, Cartographies of Danger, 1997, Air Apparent, 1999, Bushmanders and Bullwinkles, 2001; co-author: The Study of Population: Elements, Patterns, Processes, 1982, Map Appreciation, 1988; co-editor: History of Cartography Project, 1997—; assoc. editor: The American Cartographer, Falls Church, Va., 1977-82, editor, 1982-84; assoc. editor Mapping Scis. and Remote Sensing, 1987-97; contbg. editor Cartographica, 1984—; mem. editl. adv. bd. Mercator's World, 1997—. Statistician, Police Dept, Syracuse, 1978-80. Fellow John Simon Guggenheim Meml. Found., 1984, centennial fellow Pa. State U. Coll. Earth & Mineral Scis., 1996; recipient Chancellor's citation for Disting. Acad. Achievement, 1993, Disting. Geographer award Pa. Geog. Soc., 2000, O.M. Miller Cartographic medal, Am. Geog. Soc., 2001. Mem. Assn. Am. Geographers (Media Achievement award 2000), Am. Cartographic Assn. (pres. 1983-84), Authors Guild, Can. Cartographic Assn., N.Am. Cartographic Info. Soc. (editl. bd. 1998-2001), Pa. Acad. Sci. (editl. bd. 1979-2000), Philip Lee Phillips Soc., Soc. for History of Technology, Sigma Xi (pres. Syracuse chap. 2001-2002), Pi Tau Sigma, Tau Beta Pi. Roman Catholic. Home: 302 Waldorf Pky Syracuse NY 13224-2240 Office: Syracuse U Dept Of Geography Syracuse NY 13244-1020 E-mail: mon2ier@syr.edu.

MONOHAN, EDWARD SHEEHAN, IV, lawyer; b. Frankfort, Ky., Feb. 12, 1940; s. Edward Sheehan III and Mary (Lally) M.; m. Marilyn Louise Diebold, Aug. 31, 1963; children: Meredith, Edward, Patrick, Megan. BSChemE, Purdue U., 1962; JD, Georgetown U., 1965. Bar: D.C. 1966, Ky. 1966, Ohio 1990, U.S. Supreme Ct. 1975. Assoc. Vest & Ware, Covington, Ky., 1967-74; ptnr. Ware & Monohan, Florence, 1974-80, Monohan, Hertz & Blankenship, Florence, 1993-2000, Monohan & Blankenship, Florence, 2000—. Pres. Boone County Bar Assn., Florence, 1980-81. City councilman City of Crestview Hills, Ky., 1972-78. Mem. Ky. Bar Assn., Ky. Trial Lawyers Assn., No. Ky. Bar Assn., Louisville Bar Assn., Am. Inns of Ct. (master), Rotary (pres. 1981, 2001). Republican. Roman Catholic. Avocations: sailing, jogging, reading, French. Home: 21 Winding Way Crestview Hills KY 41017-2227 Office: Monohan & Blankenship 7711 Ewing Blvd Ste 100 Florence KY 41042-1814 Fax: 859-283-5155. E-mail: ed@kyattys.com.

MONOSSON, IRA HOWARD, physician; b. N.Y.C., Mar. 23, 1937; adopted s. Henry M.; s. I. Easer Rosenfield and Yetta Malvin; m. Aviva May Sokol, Sept. 20, 1970; children: Elana, Danielle, Ari. BA, Stanford U., 1959, MD, 1962. Diplomate Am. Bd. Preventive Medicine; cert. in occupational medicine. Intern Montefiore Hosp., Bronx, N.Y., 1962-63; resident L.A. County Gen. Hosp., 1963-64, Cedars of Lebanon Hosp., L.A., 1964-65; fellow Scripps Clinic and Rsch. Found., La Jolla, Calif., 1965-66; resident U. Calif., Irvine, 1976-77; pvt. practice San Diego, 1966-68, Southington, Conn., 1968-69, Ctrl. Med. Group, L.A., 1969-71; prin., owner Mid-City Med. Group, 1971-73; ptnr., physician Foley Med. Group, 1973-74; pub. health physician City of L.A., 1975; pub. health med. officer, chief Calif. State Divsn. Occupational Safety & Health, L.A., 1976-82; pvt. practice various, Calif., 1982—. Asst. clin. prof. medicine UCLA Sch. Medicine; asst. clin. prof. preventive medicine U. So. Calif. Sch. Medicine; com. mem. UCLA Inst. Biosafety Com., 1982—; adv. bd. Hazardous Substances Task Force, City of L.A., Calif. State Divsn. Indsl. Accidents, 1984-86, Occupl. Medicine Calif. Med. Assn., 1985-88; cons. in field; spkr. house of delegates Am. Coll. Occupl. & Environ Medicine, 1995. Mem. Environ. Occupl. Health com. Am. Lung. Assn. Calif., 1986-89; steering com. of L.A. 2000 project, 1980-81; adv. com. Del Amo/Montrose Superfund Site, 1995—, Permanent Disability Study, Calif. State Commn. Health and Safety and Workers Compensation; mem. L.A. Unified Sch. Dist. Bd. Edn. Ind. Commn. regarding The Belmont Learning Ctr., 1999, mem. Ind. Commn. for Belmont Learning Ctr., 1999—. Author: (with others) A Practical Approach to Occupational and Environmental Medicine, 1994; contbr. articles to profl. jours. Fellow Am. Coll. Preventive Medicine, Am. Coll. Occupl. Environ. Medicine (bd. dirs. 1993-95), Royal Soc. Medicine, Am. Acad. Occupl. Medicine; mem. AMA (Calif. chpt., L.A. chpt.), Calif. Soc. Indsl. Medicine and Surgery (pres. 1995, bd. dirs.), Calif. Indsl. Med. Coun. (mem. state regulatory bd. 1990—, chmn. 1990-93). Office: Ste 268W 2001 Santa Monica Blvd Santa Monica CA 90404-2102 Fax: 310-570-0110.

MONROE, CARL DEAN, III, lawyer; b. Birmingham, Ala., Sept. 15, 1960; s. Carl D. and Martha Jo M. BA, Birmingham-So. Coll., 1982; JD, Georgetown U., 1985. Bar: Ala. 1986, U.S. Ct. Appeals (11th cir.) 1988. Scheduler Siegelman for Atty. Gen., Montgomery, 1986; legal rsch. aide Office of Sec. of State State of Ala., 1986; asst. atty. gen., adminstrv. asst. Office of Atty. Gen., 1987-89; atty.-advisor Office Gen. Counsel, U.S. Dept. Energy, Washington, 1989—. Mem. panel of judges Georgetown Law Ctr. Moot Ct., 1991, 92, CIA Environ. Roundtable; lectr. waste mgmt. Johns Hopkins U., natural resources George Washington U. Mem. panel of judges Ala. YMCA Youth Legislature, Montgomery, 1979, 87, 88, 89; office coord. blood dr. ARC, Montgomery, 1987, 88; com. mem. Georgetown Alumni Admissions, Washington, 1986-91; mem. Nat. Trust for Hist. Preservationmem. Beahrs Environ. Leadership Seminar, Greater Smithsonian Devel., U. Calif.-Berkeley, 2001. Mem. ABA (author environ. law sect. newsletter Looking Ahead), Acad. Polit. Sci., Ala. Bar Assn., Birmingham-So. Alumni (alumni leader 1986—), Phi Beta Kappa. Democrat. Presbyterian. Avocations: water skiing, tennis, horseback riding. Home: 1200 N Nash St Apt 264 Arlington VA 22209-3620 E-mail: dean.monroe@hq.doe.gov.

MONROE, ERIN, psychiatric nurse practitioner; b. Topeka, Oct. 10, 1958; d. James Arthur and Virginia Marie Monroe. BA Psychology/Sociology magna cum laude, Bethany Coll., 1981; BSN magna cum laude, Washburn U., 1988; MSN summa cum laude, U. Kans., 1997. RN, Kans.; cert. addictions nurse; cert. advanced nurse practitioner; cert. group psychotherapist. Lic. mental health technician Topeka State Hosp., 1982-87; staff psychiat. nurse Menninger's, Topeka, 1988-98, advanced RN practitioner case mgr., 1998-99, primary clinician, 1999-2001, mem. quality assurance investigative com., 1999—, Stormont-Vail Regional Health Ctr., 2001—. Contbr. articles to profl. jours. Town rep. McPherson (Kans.) County Family Life Edn. Com., 1979. Mem. ANA, Am. Psychiat. Nurses Assn., Kans. State Nurses Assn., Psi Chi (pres., sec. 1979-81), Phi Kappa Phi, Sigma Theta Tau (Eta and Delta chpts.), Beta Tau Sigma. Democrat. Avocations: reading, films, psychoanalysis, art, walking. Office: Stormont Vail West Behavioral Health Ctr 3707 SW 6th Ave Topeka KS 66606

MONROE, HASKELL MOORMAN, JR. university educator; b. Dallas, Mar. 18, 1931; s. Haskell M. and Myrtle Marie (Jackson) M.; m. Margaret Joan Phillips, June 15, 1957; children: Stephen, Melanie, Mark, John. BA, Austin (Tex.) Coll., 1952, MA, 1954; PhD, Rice U., Houston, 1961; doctorate (hon.) , Austin Coll., 1984. From instr. to prof. Tex. A&M U., 1959-80; asst. dean Tex. A&M U. (Grad. Sch.), 1965-68, asst. v.p. acad. affairs, 1972-74, dean faculties, 1974-80, assoc. v.p. acad. affairs, 1977-80; pres. U. Tex., El Paso, 1980-87; chancellor U. Mo., Columbia, 1987-91, prof. history, 1987-97, chancellor emeritus, prof. history, 1997—; dean faculties emeritus, dir. Heritage Preservation Program Tex. A&M U., College Station, 1998. Instr. Schreiner Inst., Kerrville, Tex., summer 1959; vis. lectr. Emory U., summers 1967, 72; faculty lectr. Tex. A&M U., 1972; alumni lectr. Austin Coll., 1980; bd. dirs. Southwestern Bell Corp., Boone County Nat. Bank, SBC Comms., Inc.; history adv. com. Sec. Air Force, 1987-87; orientation com. Dept. Def.-Joint Chiefs, 1986; adv. bd. Army Command and Gen. Staff Sch., 1986-88; trustee Schreiner U., 2000—. Contbr. articles, revs.; editor: Papers of Jefferson Davis, 1964-69; adv. editor: Texana, 1964-71; bd. editorial advisers: Booker T. Washington Papers, 1965-85 . Bd. dirs. Brazos Valley Rehab. Ctr., 1975-77, Salvation Army, El Paso, 1984-87, Columbia, Mo., 1988-97, Crime Stoppers of El Paso, United Way Columbia, 1988-94, Keep Brazos Beautiful, 1999-, Washington-on-the-Brazos State Park Assn., 2002-; trustee Bryan Hosp., 1976-79, chmn., 1979; bd. ch. visitors Austin Coll., 1977-78; deacon First Presbyn. Ch., Bryan, 1961-63, elder, 1965-67, 69-71, 73-74, clk. of session, 1973-74, chmn. pulpit nominating com., 1971-72; mem. presbytery's coun. Presbytery of Brazos, 1969-71, mem. resources for the 80s steering com., 1978-80; elder 1st Presbyn. Ch., El Paso, 1984-87, 1st Presbyn. Ch., Columbia, 1994-96; mem. exec. bd. Great Rivers coun. Boy Scouts Am., 1990-97; mem. Pres. Coun. NCAA, 1986-87; chmn. Jefferson Davis award com. Confederate Mus., 1996-97; bd. dirs. Salvation Army, 1989-97. Recipient Citation of Appreciation, LULAC, 1982, Honor award Salvation Army, 1997, also numerous achievement awards; grantee Social Sci. Rsch. Coun., Tex. A&M U., Huntington Libr., Intrafraternity and Sorority Outstanding Tchr. award, 1997; named Ky. Col., 1967; named to Legends of Aggieland, 1998. Mem. Am. Hist. Assn., Orgn. Am. Historians, So. Hist. Assn. Hist. Found. Presbyn. and Reformed Chs. (pres. 1970-72), Coll. Football Assn. (chmn. bd. 1989-90, bd. dirs.), Truman Scholarship Panel, Soc. Conf. Deans Faculties and Acad. V.P.s (pres. 1978), Rotary (El Paso, hon. Columbia, Mo., Bryan, Tex., Paul Harris fellow 1986, 2000). Home: 1005 Sonoma Cir College Station TX 77845-7907 Office: Tex A&M U B615 Evans Libr College Station TX 77843 E-mail: monroehmm@aol.com.

MONROE, JAMES WALTER, retired organization executive; b. Fairfax, S.D., Feb. 13, 1936; s. Sherman William and Frances (Burnett) M.; m. Dorothy Lou Gillette, Apr. 1, 1961; children— Steven James, David Walter, Melody Anne, Andrew Scott. Student, Huron (S.D.) Coll., 1954-56, U. Nebr., 1956-57; BA, Nebr. Wesleyan U., 1960. Mgr. Belleville (Kans.) C. of C., 1960-61, Concordia (Kans.) C. of C., 1961-62; asst. chief Div. Nebr. Resources, 1962-65; dir. S.D. Indsl. Devel. Expansion Agy., 1965-67, Nebr. Dept. Econ. Devel., 1967-71; sec. Nebr. Resources Found., 1967-71; exec. dir. Omaha Econ. Devel. Council, 1971-76; pres. Kansas City (Mo.-Kans.) Area Devel. Council, 1976-90; pres., chief exec. officer New Orleans and the River Region C. of C., 1990-96, Metrovision Found., Econ. Devel. Coun. Metro, New Orleans; ret., 1996. Mem. Am. Indsl. Devel. Council, 1965— , chmn. certification bd., 1981-82; sec. labor mgmt. council Greater Kansas City, 1979-90; mem. exec. com. Gov.'s Econ. Devel. Adv. Council, 1979-81. Bd. dirs. Am. Econ. Devel. Coun., 1992—. Served with AUS, 1957-59. Republican. Presbyterian. Home: 413 12th Pl N Edmonds WA 98020-2970

MONROE, KENDYL KURTH, retired lawyer; b. Clayton, N.Mex., Sept. 6, 1936; s. Dottis Donald and Helen (Kurth) M.; m. Barbara Sayre, Sept. 12, 1956; children: Sidney, Dean, Loren. AB, Stanford U., 1958, LLB, 1960. Bar: N.Y. 1961, Calif. 1961. Assoc. Sullivan & Cromwell, N.Y.C., 1960-67, ptnr., 1968-94. Chmn. TEB Charter Svcs., Inc., Teterboro, NJ, El Valle Escondido Ranch Ltd. Co., Seneca, N.Mex., Higland Forests , Keeseville, NY, Eklund Assn. Clayton, N.Mex., N.Y. Chamber Soloists, N.Y.C.; bd. dirs. Clan Munro Assn., Great Falls, Va. Mem. bd. advisors N. Mex. Pilots' Assn.; chmn. adv. coun. The Mandala Ctr., Des Moines; mem. adv. com. Cornerstones Cmty Partnerships, Santa Fe; bd. dirs. N.Mex. First , Albuquerque, N.Mex. Water Dialogue, Gallup, Clayton (N.Mex.) Health Sys., Inc.; dir. emeritus Pub. Health Rsch. Inst., N.Y.C.; bd. dirs. N.Mex. Heritage Preservation Alliance, Santa Fe. Mem. State Bar Calif., Assn. of Bar of City of N.Y., N.Mex. Amigos, Met. Club (N.Y.C.). Home: 189 Sayre Rd Seneca NM 88437-9607 E-mail: kkmonroe@ptsi.net.

MONROE, KENNETH ANTHONY, facility and project management consultant; b. Chgo., June 16, 1951; s. Clarence Anthony and Edna Ruth (Waleski) M.; m. Cynthia Stearns, Mar. 26, 1988. BSME, Northwestern U., Evanston, Ill., 1975, M in Mgmt., 1983. Registered profl. engr., Ill. Staff engr. City of Chgo., 1975-77, Consoer, Townsend & Assocs., Chgo., 1977-78, FMC Corp., Itasca, Ill., 1978-80; project mgr. Michael Reese Hosp., Chgo., 1981-84; account mktg. rep. IBM, 1984-89; project mgr. St. Francis Hosp., Evanston, 1990-93; asst. dir. engring. Victory Meml. Hosp., Waukegan, Ill., 1993-94; pres. MC Enterprises, Evanston, 1994-99; hosp. cons. CA Buboltz, Inc., 1999—. Docent Chgo. Architecture Found., v.p., treas., 1991-92, pres., 1979-81, 90-91; Bus. Profl. Assn. Chgo. Symph. Orch., v.p. 1989-91, 93-94. Mem. ASME, ASHRAE (editor newsletter 1985-87), Internat. Facilities Mgrs. Assn. Roman Catholic. Avocations: photography, Corvettes, bicycling, trumpet, tennis. Home and Office: 904 Oakton St Apt 3 Evanston IL 60202-5339

MONROE, KEVIN JOEL, music educator; b. Wichita, Kans., Nov. 19, 1965; s. Leslie R. and Karen Monroe; m. Kathleen Slater; children: Lyndsee. MusB in Edn., U. of Kans., 1989. Cert. Tchr. Kans., 1989. Tchg. asst. Kans. Pub. Schools, Lawrence, Kans., 1988—89; dir. of orchestras Kans. Pub. Sch., El Dorado, 1989—. Dir. of music First United Meth. Ch., El Dorado, 1990—98; co-music dir., conductor El Dorado Mcpl. Band Assn., El Dorado, 1993—2002, music dir. and condr., 1989; asst. prin. violist Newton Mid-Kans. Symphony Orch., Newton, Kans., 1994—98; prin. violist Wichita State U. Met. Summer Orch., Wichita, Kans., 2000—01. Mem.: Am. String Teachers Assn. (kans. bd. mem. at-large 2000—02), Kans. Music Educators Assn. (dist. orch. chmn. 1992—94), Music Educators Nat. Conf., El Dorado Lions Club (pres. 1997—99). Methodist. Avocation: baseball. Office: USD 490 El Dorado KS Public Schools 401 McCollum Road El Dorado KS 67042 Business E-Mail: kmonroe@eldoradoschools.org.

MONROE, KRISTEN RENWICK, political scientist, educator; b. Princeton, Ill., May 17, 1946; d. James Oliver and Gertrude (Renwick) Monroe; m. R.G. Wilmot Lampros, Sept. 26, 1981; children: Alexander Hart Lampros, Nicholas Monroe Lampros, Chloe Lampros-Monroe. AB cum laude, Smith Coll., Northampton, Mass., 1968; MA, U. Chgo., 1970, PhD, 1974. Asst. prof. SUNY, Stony Brook, 1974-77; Killam fellow U. B.C., Vancouver, 1975-76; asst. prof. NYU, N.Y.C., 1977-83; vis. asst. prof. Princeton (N.J.) U., 1983-84; prof. dept. polit. sci. U. Calif., Irvine, 1984—. Vis. fellow, assoc. prof. Princeton U., 1990—93; dir. Informal Ctr. for Study of Morality, U. Calif. Irvine, assoc. dir. program in polit. psychology. Author: The Heart of Altruism, 1996 (Best Book award in polit. psychology Am. Polit. Sci. Assn.), Presidential Popularity and the Economy, 1984; editor: Economic Approach to Politics, 1991, Contemporary Empirical Political Theory, 1997, Political Psychology, 2001. Recipient Mentor of Distinction award Women's Caucus for Polit. Sci.; NEH grantee, NSF grantee; Earhart fellow, Lawrence Rockefeller fellow. Mem.: Midwest Polit. Sci. Assn. (v.p. 1999—2001), Internat. Soc. Polit. Psychology (mem. coun., program chair 1999—2001), Am. Polit. Sci. Assn. (v.p. 2002, pres. organized sect. in polit. psychology 2001—02). Democrat. Office: Univ of Calif-Irvine Dept Political Sci SSPA4103 Irvine CA 92697

MONROE, MELROSE, retired banker; b. Flowery Branch, Ga., Apr. 13, 1919; d. WillisIeptha and Leila Adell Cash; m. Lynn Austin, June 14, 1942. AB in Edn., Ga. State U., 1968. Negotiator Trust Co. Bank, Atlanta, 1962-89, ret., 1989. Mem. Nat. Women's C. of C. (pres. 1987-88), Atlanta Women's C. of C. (dir. 1965-66, pres. Fidelis SS class 1962-63), Nat. Am. Legion Aux. (so. divsn. chmn. aux. Americanism 1995-96, so. divsn. chmn. aux. emergency fund 1996-97, cmty. svc. com.), Am. Legion Aux. (pres. 5th dist. 1986-87, Ga. state chaplain 1989-90, state historian 1991-92, state 2d v.p. 1992-93, 1st v.p. 1993-94, pres. 1994-95, Americanism chmn. so. divsn. 1995-95, chmn. emergency fund 1996-97, mem. cmty. svc. com. 1997-98, nat. historian 1999-00, v. chmn. nat. poppy com. 2000-01), Order Ea. Star (worthy matron 1951-52). Democrat. Home and Office: 6243 Spout Springs Rd Flowery Branch GA 30542-5032

MONROE, MURRAY SHIPLEY, lawyer; b. Cin., Sept. 25, 1925; s. James and Martha (Shipley) M.; m. Sally Longstreth, May 11, 1963; children: Tracy, Murray, Courtney, David. BE, Yale U., 1946, BS, 1947; LLB, U. Pa., 1950. Bar: Ohio 1950, U.S. Dist. Ct. (so. dist.) Ohio 1954, U.S. Dist. Ct. (mid. dist.) Tenn. 1981, US. Dist. Ct. (mid. dist.) N.C. 1974, U.S. Dist. Ct. (mid. dist.) Pa. 1986, U.S. Dist. (ea. dist.) Pa. 1960, U.S. Dist. Ct. (we. dist.) Mo. 1974, U.S. Dist. Ct. Mass. 1978, U.S. Dist. Ct. (ea. dist.) La. 1979, U.S. Dist. Ct. (no. dist.) Ill. 1980, U.S. Ct. Appeals (4th cir.) 1984, U.S. Ct. Appeals (6th cir.) 1969, U.S. Supreme Ct. 1977, U.S. Ct. Appeals (3d cir.) 1990. Assoc. Taft, Stettinus & Hollister, Cin., 1950-58, ptnr., 1958-96; of counsel, 1997—. Mem. lawyers com. Nat. Ctr. for State Cts., 1985-96; faculty Ohio Legal Ctr. Inst., 1970-93. Contbr. articles to profl. jours. Trustee, treas. The Coll. Prep. Sch., 1972-76; trustee The Seven Hills Schs., 1982-88, chmn. bd., 1982-85. 2d lt. USNR, 1943-46. Recipient award Seven Hills Schs., 1985. Fellow Ohio Bar Found.; mem. ABA (speaker symposiums), Ohio Bar Assn. (coun. dels. 1977-82, bd. govs. antitrust sect. 1960-95, dir. emeritus 1995—, chmn. bd. govs. 1973-75, Merit award 1976, speaker symposiums), Bankers Club (Cin.), Cin. Country Club, Met. Club, Tau Beta Pi. Republican. Episcopalian. Avocations: sailing, tennis.

MONROE, ROBERT ALAN, music educator; b. Van Wert, Ohio, Dec. 4, 1950; s. Herbert Kimble and Dorothy Mildred Monroe; m. Marilyn Elizabeth May, July 27, 1974; children: Elizabeth, Katherine, Sarah. MusB, Miami U., Oxford, Ohio, 1973, PhD, 1994; MA in Edn., Ball State U., 1977. Instrumental music tchr. Marion (Ind.) Cmty. Schs., 1973—77; orch. dir. Princeton City Schs., Cin., 1977—, dist. music coord., 1995—. Condr., music dir. Seven Hills Sinfonietta, Cin., 1992—95. Alumni bd. mem. Acacia Fraternity, Miami U., 1981—92. Named Tchr. of the Yr., Ohio String Tchrs. Assn., 1994. Mem.: Ohio Sch. Orch. Assn. (sec.-treas. 1981—87), Ohio Music Edn. Assn. (adjudicator 1985—2002, all-state orch. chair 1993, 1994, adjudicated events chair 1995—97, orch. affairs chair 1999—2002, chair all-state ensembles 2002). Home: 767 Viewcrest Ct Cincinnati OH 45231 Office: Princeton HS 11080 Chester Rd Cincinnati OH 45246

MONROE, ROBERT RAWSON, engineering construction executive; b. Oakland, Calif., Sept. 25, 1927; s. Robert Ansley and Muriel Estelle (Burnham) M.; m. Charlotte Boies Anderson, Oct. 16, 1951; children: Robert Anderson, Nancy Lynn Monroe Sims, Susan Leslie Monroe Gordon. BS in Naval Sci., U.S. Naval Acad., 1950; MA in Internat. Rels., Stanford U., 1962. Commd. ensign USN, 1950, advanced through grades to vice-admiral, 1977; dir. Navy Systems Analysis, 1972-73; comdr. South Atlantic Force, 1973-74; comdr. Operational Test and Evaluation Force USN, 1974-77; dir. Def. Nuclear Agy., 1977-80; dir. Navy Rsch., Devel., Test and Evaluation, 1980-83; ret., 1983; joined Bechtel Nat., Inc., San Francisco, 1984, mgr. def. and space, 1984-89, v.p., 1985, sr. v.p., ptnr., 1987, mgr. mktg. and govt. ops., 1989-91, mgr. spl. projects, 1992-93, mgr. govt. ops. Washington, 1993—2002, sr. counselor, 2002—. Mem. nat. security adv. bd. Los Alamos (N.Mex.) Nat. Lab., 1983—88; mem. tech. evaluation panel U.S. Dept. Energy, 1983—88; mem. engring. adv. com. Oak Ridge (Tenn.) Nat. Lab., 1986—89, Rensselaer Poly. Inst., 1990—91; mem. bd. advisors Office Tech. Assessment, Washington, 1987—89, Nat. Contract Mgmt. Assn., 1986—91; mem. task forces Def. Sci. Bd., Washington, 1983—89; corp. mem. Charles Stark Draper Lab., Cambridge, Mass., 1983—; affiliate mem. Ctr. for Internat. Security and Cooperation, Stanford U., 1989—93; chmn. space transp. subcom. NASA's Adv. Coun., 1995—2001; mem. strategic adv. bd. Nev. Test Site, 1995—99; mem. Nat. Security adv. panel Sandia Nat. Labs., 1996—; mem. threat reduction adv. coun. (nuc. panel) Dept. Def., 1998—; mem. Enhanced Test Readiness External Rev. Group, 2002—. Decorated Def. D.S.M., USN D.S.M., Legion of Merit, Bronze Star medal with combat device, Joint Svcs. Commendation medal, USN Commendation medal with combat device; Legion of Honor (France). Mem. Nat. Def. Indsl. Assn., Soc. Am. Mil. Engrs. Avocations: tennis, golf, hiking, reading. Home: 2313 Sawdust Rd Vienna VA 22181-3044 Office: Bechtel Nat Inc 1015 15th St NW Ste 700 Washington DC 20005-2636

MONROE, STEPHEN A. educational administrator, financial consultant; b. N.Y.C., Aug. 23, 1947; s. Patrick and Anna (Nerney) M. MSc, London Sch. Econs., 1984; MS, St. John's U., Jamaica, N.Y., 1987; postgrad., NYU. Tchr. Nazareth Regional H.S., Bklyn., 1974-92; prof. actg. U. Md., College Park, 1992-94; asst. dir. office of occup. edn. N.Y.C. Bd. Edn., Bklyn., 1994-95; head tchr. Harvey Milk Sch., N.Y.C., 1995-97; asst. to the supr. Office of the Supt. of Bronx H.S., 1997-98; program supr. Ossining (N.Y.) Union Free Sch. Dist., 1998-99; tech. adminstr. NYC Bd. Edn., 1999—. Fin. cons., N.Y.C., 1970—. Mem. fund raising bd. Steps to End Family Violence, N.Y.C., 1993—.

Mem. Nat. Bus. Edn. Assn., East Bus. Edn. Assn., N.Y.C. Bus. Edn. Assn., Internat. Soc. Bus. Edn., Delta Pi Epsilon. Home: 7 Peter Cooper Rd Apt 4A New York NY 10010-6606 Office: NYC Bd Edn 47-14 94th St Elmhurst NY 11377-

MONROE, SUSAN MACGREGOR, chemist; b. Greenville, N.C., May 17, 1948; d. Calvin W. MacGregor and Lullah Cox Pringle; m. James Louie Monroe, Feb. 21, 1969; children: Matthew James, Michael Christopher. BS in Math., Chemistry and Physics, Mesa State U., 1987; PhD in Bioinorganic Chemistry, U. Denver, 1996. Quality control chemist Ricon Resins, Inc., Grand Junction, Colo., 1985-92; environ. chemist Quanterra, Inc., Arvada, 1992; rsch. chemist Matheson Gas Products, Longmont, 1996-98; sr. supr. analytical svc. and quality control Sulzer Biologics Inc., Wheat Ridge, 1998—. Contbr. articles to profl. jours. including Biochemistry, Biochim. Biophys. Acta, and Jour. Inst. Environ. Scis. and Tech. Named Richardson Leadership Found. scholar East Carolina U., 1968-69; recipient Chemistry award Dickinson State Coll., 1985. Mem. AAAS, Am. Chem. Soc. (alt. councilor 1998-99, councilor 1999—), Am. Soc. Quality (cert. quality mgr.).

MONROE, THOMAS EDWARD, industrial corporation executive; b. Ironton, MO, Nov. 19, 1947; s. Donald Mansfield and Edwina Frances (Carr) M.; children: Thomas Edward II, Katherine Jenna. BA, Drury Coll., 1969; postgrad., Washington U. Sch. Bus. Adminstrn., St. Louis, 1970. Acctg. mgr., asst. contr. Am. Transit Corp., St. Louis, 1970-74; mgr. corp. devel., asst. treas. Chromalloy Am. Corp., 1974-77, v.p. fin., 1977-78, exec. v.p., 1978-82; dir. Chromalloy Fin. Corp., 1976-82, Am. Universal Ins. Co., 1978-82; chmn. Capital Assocs. Corp., 1982—, Fed. Air Ambulance, The Safe Deposit Co., CompuVault, Inc., James Flying Svc., Inc., Lindbergh Leasing, Inc., Vault II, LLC. Trustee Kingsbury Place Assn. Mem. Algonquin Club. Presbyterian. Office: Capital Assocs Corp 515 S Lindbergh Blvd Saint Louis MO 63131-2731 E-mail: monroes@swbell.com.

MONROE, WILLIAM FREDERICK, marketing professional; b. Cin., Apr. 12, 1924; s. James and Martha Nixon (Shipley) M. Student, Williams Coll., Williamstown, Mass., 1942-44, U. Ariz., 1945, U. Pa. Sch. Medicine, 1945; BA, U. Pa., Phila., 1948. Salesman Wm. S. Merrell Co., Cin., 1948-49, asst. to advt. mgr., 1949-52, asst. advt. mgr., 1952-54; sales rep. IBM, 1954-59, mktg. profl., 1959-64; self-employed cons. evaluating businesses and techs., 1964—. Helped establish Cin. Elm Program, 1992—. Author: (collections of poems) Magic Coast of Maine, 1995-97, Struck by Wonder, 1995-97; sculptor stainless steel sculptures, 1988—. Avocations: tennis, golf. Home: 2200 Victory Pkwy Cincinnati OH 45206-2882

MONROE, WILLIAM LEWIS, human resources executive; b. Detroit, May 11, 1941; s. Lewis Stewart and Ada Jeanette (Williams) Monroe; m. Sharon Lynne Kahal, June 30, 1967; children: Andrea M. Dunk, William J. BA, Western Mich. U., 1963, MA, 1964. Rsch. analyst Chrysler Corp., Detroit, 1965-72, labor economist, 1972-77, mgr. retirement, savs. and unemployment benefit plans, 1977-81; dir. employee benefits W. R. Grace & Co., N.Y.C., 1981-87, v.p. human resources, 1987-2001, bd. trustee, v.p. coun. on employee benefits, 1989-2001, pres. coun. on employee benefits, 1995-96; cons. AON Cons./ASA, Boca Raton, 2001—02. Adj. prof. mgmt. FAU Univ., Boca Raton, 2001—; corp. bd. dirs. Internat. Found. Employee Benefits, 1986—88; mem. bus. rsch. adv. coun. U.S. Dept. Labor/Bur. Labor Stats., 1987—96; mem. Human Resources Policy Inst. Boston U., 1993—96. Co-chmn. closing com. PTSA Sch., Birmingham, Mich., 1977; chmn. pers. com. Wilton Presbyn. ch., Wilton, Conn., 1982—86; officer, bd. dirs. Forest Hills Property Owners Assn., Birmingham, 1974—80; mem. exec. bd. Gulf Stream coun. Boy Scouts Am., 1993—99. Served USAR, 1965—71. Mem.: Soc. for Human Resources & Mgmt., Princeton Club N.Y.C., Boca Raton Resort and Club. Republican. Presbyterian. Avocation: Avocations: tennis, golf. Office: PO Box 810851 Boca Raton FL 33481-0851

MONSARRAT, NICHOLAS, newspaper editor, writer, educator; b. Norwalk, Conn., Dec. 26, 1941; s. John and Margaret Jane (Cashatt) M.; m. Barbara Ann Curcio, Feb. 25, 1995; children: Sean, Andrea, J. Alexander. BA in Journalism, Washington and Lee U., 1963. Reporter, editor The Times Argus, Barre, Vt., 1969-85; mng. editor The Rutland (Vt.) Daily Herald, 1985-88; adj. prof. journalism St. Michael's Coll., Colchester, Vt., 1988-92, assoc. prof. journalism, 1992-95, writer, adj. prof. journalism, 1996—; editl. page editor Burlington (Vt.) Free Press, 1995-96. Writer/tchr. in field, 1996—; participant Am. Press Inst., Reston, Va., 1986, New Eng. Writers Workshop, Boston, 1989. Co-chmn. U.S.-Soviet Editors Exch. Program, New London, N.H., 1982, mem., Moscow, Leningrad, 1983, Middlebury, Vt., 1987. Staff sgt. USAF, 1963-67. Recipient Allan B. Rogers award for editl. writing UPI, 1981. Mem. New Eng. Soc. Newspaper Editors (pres. 1982-83), New Eng. Press Assn. (bd. dirs. 1986-91). Episcopalian. Home and Office: 3834 Mt Philo Rd Charlotte VT 05445-9366

MONSEN, ELAINE RANKER, nutritionist, educator, editor; b. Oakland, Calif., June 6, 1935; d. Emery R. and Irene Stewart (Thorley) Ranker; m. Raymond Joseph Monsen, Jr., Jan. 21, 1959; 1 dau., Maren Ranker. BA, U. Utah, 1956; MS (Mead Johnson grad. scholar), U. Calif., Berkeley, 1959, PhD (NSF fellow), 1961; postgrad. NSF sci. faculty fellow, Harvard U., 1968-69. Dietetic intern Mass. Gen. Hosp., Boston, 1956-57; asst. prof. nutrition, lectr. biochemistry Brigham Young U., Provo, Utah, 1960-63; mem. faculty U. Wash., 1963—, prof. nutrition and medicine, 1984—, prof. nutrition, adj. prof. medicine, 1976-84, chmn. div. human nutrition, dietetics and foods, 1977-82, dir. grad. nutritional scis. program, 1994-99, mem. Council of Coll. Arts and Scis., 1974-78, mem. U. Wash. Press com., 1981—; chmn. Nutrition Studies Commn., 1969-83. Vis. scholar Stanford U., 1971-72; mem. sci. adv. com. food fortification Pan-Am. Health Orgn., São Paulo, Brazil, 1972; tng. grant coordinator NIH, 1976-97. Editor-in-chief Jour. Am. Dietetic Assn., 1983—; mem. editorial bd. Coun. Biology Editors, 1992-96; author research papers on lipid metabolism, iron absorption. Bd. dirs. A Contemporary Theatre, Seattle, 1969-72; trustee, bd. dirs. Seattle Found., 1978-95, vice chmn., 1987-91, chmn., 1991-93; pres. Seattle bd. Santa Fe Chamber Music Festival, 1984-85; mem. Puget Sound Blood Ctr. Bd., 1996-99. Grantee Nutrition Found., 1965-68, Agrl. Rsch. Svc., 1969-84; recipient Disting. Alumnus award U. Utah, F. Fischer Meml. Nutrition Lectr. award, 1988, L.F. Cooper Meml. Lectr. award, 1991, L. Hatch Meml. Lectr. award, 1992, Goble Lectr. award Purdue U., 1997. Fellow: Am. Soc. Clin. Nutrition (sec. 1987—90), Am. Inst. Nutrition; mem.: Wash. Heart Assn. (nutrition coun. 1973—76), Am. Soc. Parenteral and Enteral Nutrition, Soc. Nutriton Edn., Am. Dietetic Assn. Office: U Wash PO Box 353410 Seattle WA 98195-3410

MONSEN, RONALD PETER, musician, music educator, artist; b. Milw., Sept. 20, 1940; s. Ray Thelmert and Eunice Irene (Friebl) M.; m. Joan Grace Williams, Dec. 21, 1963; children: Dirk Andrew (dec.), Peter Colin, Kirsten Jo. BSc, U. Wis., Milw., 1964; MMus, Northwestern U., Evanston, Ill., 1968; performer's diploma, Royal Acad. Music, London, 1971; D of Mus. Arts, U. Wis., Madison, 1978. Music tchr. Milw. pub. schs., 1964-67; prof. woodwinds Concordia Coll., Moorhead, Minn., 1968-73; prof. clarinet U. Ky., Lexington, 1980—. Clarinet clinican Selmer Co., Elkhart, Ind., 1986—. Clarinet recitalist appearances include Denver, 1983, London, 1984, Seattle, 1986, Cin., 1992; mem. Okla. Clarinet Symphony, 1985. Mem. Internat. Clarinet Assn. (mem. state chair, pres. 1992). Avocations: model railroading, photography, France. Office: Univ Ky Sch Music Coll Fine Arts Lexington KY 40506-0001

MONSKY, JOHN BERTRAND, investment banking executive; b. Montgomery, Ala., May 17, 1930; s. Harry and Belle (Golding) M.; m. Joan Gilbert, June 8, 1952; children: Leslie Joy, John Richard, Harry Robert. BA, Yale, 1952; MBA, Harvard, 1954. Sec. Devoe & Raynolds Co., Inc., Louisville, 1956-65; v.p., dir. Universal Marion Corp., Jacksonville, Fla., 1965-69, pres., chmn. bd., chief exec. officer, 1969-71, cons., 1971—; vice chmn. ServAmerica, Inc., 1972-74, co-chmn. bd. dirs., 1974-80, chmn. bd. dirs., 1980—; pres., chmn. bd. dirs. First Fla. Capital Corp., 1985—. Dir. Fla. Wire & Cable Co., Jacksonville, 1975-82 Past pres. bd. trustees Jacksonville Country Day Sch.; bd. dirs. Jacksonville Art Mus.; trustee Bolles Sch., Jacksonville, Jacksonville Symphony Assn. Served with USAF, 1954-56. Mem. Jacksonville Area C. of C. (com. of 100), Jackson County Citizen Involvement Clubs, Harvard Bus. Sch. Club of Ky. (exec. com. 1964-65), Phillips Acad. Andover Alumni Club of Ky. (pres. 1963-64), Epping Forest Cmty. Master Assn. (bd. dirs. 1994—), Yale Club N.E. Fla. (bd. dirs. 1987—), Yale Club of N.Y.C., Harvard Club (Jacksonville), Assn. Yale Alumni (del. 1996—), River Club, Ponte Vedra Club, Epping Forest Yacht Club. Home: Epping Forest 7015 Gaines Ct Jacksonville FL 32217-2672 Office: 300 Wharfside Way # B Jacksonville FL 32207-8153 E-mail: jbmonsky@aol.com.

MONSMA, JAMES EDWIN, retired consulting company executive; b. Grand Rapids, Mich., Aug. 11, 1929; s. Edwin Ype and Frieda (Van Wesep) M.; m. Janice Stravers; children: James Edwin, Frederick John, Sarah Marie. AB, Calvin Coll., Grand Rapids, 1951; MS, Mich. State U., 1953. Various positions IBM Corp., 1953-69; v.p. Interactive Sci. Inc., Brewster, N.Y., 1969-72, Decision Concepts Inc., N.Y.C., 1972-80, Fin. Pub. Co., Boston, 1980-85; pres. J.E. Monsma Cons. Inc., 1985-97; ret., 1997. Author: Executive's Guide to Computer Concepts, 1969. Home: 14 Rabbit Trail Rd Poughkeepsie NY 12603-6115

MONSMA, MARVIN EUGENE, library director; b. Prairie City, Iowa, May 14, 1933; s. John and Johanna Hester (Branderhorst) M.; m. Elaine Gross, Aug. 2, 1963; children: Kristy Lynne Monsma De Vos, Kimberly Sue Monsma Rottschafer, Michelle Eileen Monsma Haan. AB, Calvin Coll., 1957; AM in Secondary Edn., Mich. State U., 1961; AMLS in Librarianship, U. Mich., 1967. English tchr. Muskegon (Mich.) Christian Sch., 1957-60, Grand Rapids (Mich.) Christian H.S., 1960-63, Unity Christian H.S., Hudsonville, Mich., 1963-65; asst. libr. Calvin Coll. & Sem., Grand Rapids, 1965-67, head gen. svcs., 1967-68, asst. libr. dir., 1968-69, acting libr. dir., 1969-70, libr. dir., 1970-98, emeritus, 1998. Orthodox Presbyterian. Avocations: classical music, gardening, nature. Office: Calvin Coll and Sem Hekman Libr 3207 Burton St SE Grand Rapids MI 49546-4301

MONSMA, STEPHEN VOS, political scientist, educator; b. Pella, Iowa, Sept. 22, 1936; s. Martin and Marie Monsma; m. Mary Carlisle, Dec. 19, 1964; children: Martin S., Kristin J. AB, Calvin Coll., Grand Rapids, Mich., 1958; MA, Georgetown U., 1961; PhD, Mich. State U., 1965. Asst. prof. SUNY, Plattsburgh, 1964-67; prof. Calvin Coll., Grand Rapids, 1967-74; rep. State Legis., Lansing, Mich., 1974-78; senator State of Mich., 1978-82; dir. office quality rev. Dept. Social Svcs., 1985-87; prof. Pepperdine U., Malibu, Calif., 1987—, prof. and chair social sci. divsn., 1996-2000, Blanche E. Seaver chair in social sci., 1999—. Author: Pursuing Justice in a Sinful World, 1984, Positive Neutrality, 1993, When Sacred and Secular Mix, 1996; co-author: The Challenge of Pluralism: Church and State in Five Democracies, 1997; editor Church-State Relations in Crisis: Debating Neutrality, 2002; co-editor: Equal Treatment of Religion in a Pluralistic Society, 1998; corr. editor Christianity Today, 1993—. Mem. Natural Resources Commn., Lansing, 1983-85; bd. dirs. Ctr. for Pub. Justice, Annapolis, Md., 1996-2002, Bread for the World, Washington, 1991-93. Am. Polit. Sci. Assn. grantee, 1995, Earhart Found., 1985, Smith Richardson Found. grantee, 2000, Haynes Found. grantee 2000; Calvin Ctr. for Christian Scholarship vis. scholar, 1993-94. Mem. Am. Polit. Sci. Assn., Christians in Polit. Sci. (pres. 1994-96). Presbyterian. Office: Pepperdine University Social Science Divsn Malibu CA 90263 E-mail: smonsma@pepperdine.edu.

MONSON, DAVID CARL, school superintendent, farmer, state legislator, insurance agent; b. Langdon, N.D., July 30, 1950; s. Carl Arthur and Shirley Jean (Klai) M.; m. Mary Kathryn Greutman, July 8, 1972; children: Cordell Carl, Cale David, Jared Arthur. Cert. tchr., adminstr., N.D. Sci. tchr. Hankinson (N.D.) Pub. Sch., 1972-75; tchr. Nekoma (N.D.) Pub. Sch., 1975-76; tchr., prin. NeKoma (N.D.) Pub. Sch., 1976-79; tchr., supt. Nekoma (N.D.) Pub. Sch., 1979-80; tchr., prin. Milton (N.D.)-Osnabrock High Sch., 1981-84; supt. Adams (N.D.) Pub. Schs., 1984-88; ins. agt. N.Y. Life, Fargo, N.D., 1988-95; self-employed ins. agt., Osnabrock, 1988—; farmer, 1975—; mem. N.D. Ho. of Reps., Bismarck, 1993—, asst. majority leader, 1998—; supt. Edinburg (N.D.) Pub. Schs., 1995—. Dir. N.Am. Indsl. Hemp Coun., 1999—. Leader Bobcats 4-H Club, 1988—2001; mem. sch. bd. dirs. Osnobrock Sch. Bd., 1989—2001. Mem. N.D. Farm Bur., N.D. Coun. Sch. Adminstrs., Eagles, KP (grand sec. N.D. and Sask. 1985-93, award 1990). Republican. Lutheran. Avocations: skiing, gardening, hunting, coin collecting. E-mail: dmonson@state.nd.us.

MONSON, DIANNE LYNN, literacy educator; b. Minot, N.D., Nov. 24, 1934; d. Albert Rachie and Iona Cordelia (Kirk) M. BS, U. Minn., 1956, MA, 1962, PhD, 1966. Tchr. Rochester (Minn.) Pub. Schs., 1956-59, U.S. Dept. Def., Schweinfurt, West Germany, 1959-61, St. Louis Park (Minn.) Schs., 1961-62; instr. U. Minn., Mpls., 1962-66; prof. U. Wash., Seattle, 1966-82; prof. literacy edn. U. Minn., Mpls., 1982-97, prof. emeritus, 1997—. Chmn. curriculum and instrn. U. Minn., 1986-89. Co-author: (with Scott Foresman) Reading, 2000, New Horizons in the Language Arts, 1972, Children and Books, 6th edit., 1981, Experiencing Children's Literature, 1984, (monograph) Research in Children's Literature, 1976, Language Arts: Teaching and Learning Effective Use of Language, 1988, Reading Together: Helping Children Get A Good Start With Reading, 1991; assoc. editor: Dictionary of Literacy, 1995. Recipient Outstanding Educator award U. Minn. Alumni Assn., 1983, Alumni Faculty award U. Minn. Alumni Assn., 1991. Fellow Nat. Conf. Rsch. in English (pres. 1990-91); mem. ALA, Nat. Coun. Tchrs. English (exec. com. 1979-81), Internat. Reading Assn. (dir. 1980-83, Arbuthnot award 1993, Reading Hall of Fame 1997), U.S. Bd. Books for Young People (pres. 1988-90). Lutheran. Home: 515 S Lexington Pkwy # 604 Saint Paul MN 55116 E-mail: monso001@tc.umn.edu.

MONSON, JAMES EDWARD, electrical engineer, educator; b. Oakland, Calif., June 20, 1932; s. George Edward and Frances Eleanor (Fouche) M.; m. Julie Elizabeth Conzelman, June 25, 1954; children— John, Jamie, Jennifer. BSEE, Stanford U., 1954, MSEE, 1955, PhD in Elec. Engring., 1961. Mem. tech. staff Bell Telephone Labs., Murray Hill, N.J., 1955-56; devel. engr. Hewlett-Packard Co., Palo Alto, Calif., 1956-61; Robert C. Sabini prof. engring. emeritus Harvey Mudd Coll., 1961—. Mem. governing bd. Claremont Unified Sch. Dist., 1966-71, pres., 1969-70; pres. Claremont Civic Assn., 1974-75; bd. dirs. Claremont YMCA, 1978-82. Fellow NSF, 1954-55, Japan Soc. Promotion Sci., 1984; Fulbright Rsch. grantee, 1975-76; Fulbright sr. lectr., 1980. Fellow IEEE; mem. Phi Beta Kappa, Sigma Xi. E-mail: james. Home: PO Box 1029 Point Reyes Station CA 94956-1029 Office: Harvey Mudd Coll 301 E 12th St Claremont CA 91711-5901 E-mail: monson@hmc.edu.

MONSON, JOHN RUDOLPH, lawyer; b. Chgo., Feb. 4, 1941; s. Rudolph Agaton and Ellen Louise (Loeffler) M.; m. Susan Lee Brown, May 22, 1965; children: Elizabeth Louisa, Christina Lee, Donald Rudolph. BA with honors, Northwestern U., 1963; JD with distinction, U. Mich., 1966. Bar: Ill. 1966, N.H. 1970, Mass. 1985. Atty. assoc. Chapman & Cutler, Chgo., 1966-68, Levenfeld, Kanter, Baskes & Lippitz, Chgo., 1968-70, Nighswander, Martin & Mitchell, Laconia, N.H., 1970-71; mem., ptnr. Wiggin & Nourie, P.A., Manchester, 1972—, pres., 1991-94. Sec., gen. counsel Rock of Ages Corp., 1996-98. Mem. N.H. Fish and Game Commn., Concord, 1980-94, chmn., 1983-93; sr. bd. dirs. Brown-Monson Found., 1991—; incorporator Cath. Med. Ctr., 1988-95, Optima Health, 1994-99; commr. N.H. Land and Cmty. Heritage Commn., 1998-2000. Fellow Am. Coll. Trust and Estate Counsel, Safari Club Internat. (v.p. 1999-2001, dir.-at-large 1997-99, treas. 2001-02, pres. elect 2002—). Republican. Avocations: skiing, hunting, running. Home: 24 Wellesley Dr Bedford NH 03110-4531 Office: Wiggin & Nourie PA 20 Market St Manchester NH 03101-1931

MONSON, THOMAS SPENCER, religious organization administrator, former publishing company executive; b. Salt Lake City, Aug. 21, 1927; s. George Spencer and Gladys (Condie) M.; m. Frances Beverly Johnson, Oct. 7, 1948; children— Thomas L., Ann Frances, Clark Spencer. BS with honors in mktg, U. Utah, 1948; MBA, Brigham Young U., 1974, LLD (hon.), 1981. With Deseret News Press, Salt Lake City, 1948-64, mgr., 1962-64; mem. Council Twelve Apostles, Ch. of Jesus Christ of Latter Day Saints, 1963-85, bishop, 1950-55; pres. Canadian Mission, 1959-62; mem. first presidency Ch. of Jesus Christ of Latter-day Sts., 1985—; chmn. bd. Deseret News Pub. Co., 1977-96. Vice chmn. Deseret Mgmt. Corp.; pres. Printing Industry Utah, 1958; bd. dirs. Printing Industry Am., 1958-64; mem. Utah exec. bd. U.S. West Communications. Mem. Utah Bd. Regents; mem. nat. exec. bd. Boy Scouts Am.; trustee Brigham Young U.. With USNR, 1945-46. Recipient Recognition award, 1964, Disting. Alumnus award U. Utah, 1966; Silver Beaver award Boy Scouts Am., 1971; Silver Buffalo award, 1978; Bronze Wolf award World Orgn. of the Scout Movement, 1993. Mem. Utah Assn. Sales Execs., U. Utah Alumni Assn. (dir.), Salt Lake Advt. Club, Alpha Kappa Psi. Clubs: Exchange (Salt Lake City). Office: LDS Ch 47 E South Temple Salt Lake City UT 84150-9701

MONTAG, ANTHONY GERARD, pathologist, educator; b. Woodbine, Iowa, Aug. 21, 1954; s. Maurice Joseph Montag; m. Katherine Leslie Griem, Aug. 23, 1986; children: Hugh Graham, William Maurice, Caroline Elizabeth. BS, Iowa State U., 1975; MD, Med. Coll. of Wis., Milw., 1979. Diplomate Am. Bd. Pathology. Resident Med. Coll. of Wis., Milw., 1979-82, Brigham & Women's Hosp., Boston, 1982-84, fellow, 1984-85; asst. prof. U. Chgo., 1985-92, assoc. prof. pathology, 1992—. Contbr. articles to profl. jours. Mem. Internat. Acad. Pathology, Internat. Soc. Gynecologic Pathology, Arthur Purdy Stout Soc., Alpha Omega Alpha, Phi Beta Kappa. Avocations: gardening, natural science.

MONTAG, DAVID MOSES, telecommunications company executive; b. L.A., Apr. 30, 1939; s. Gustave and Esther (Kessler) M; children: Daniel Gershon, Esther Yael, Michael Menachem. Student, UCLA, 1957-61. Tech. writer L.H. Butcher Co., L.A., 1961; phys. sci. lab. technician East L.A. Coll., Monterey Park, 1961—. Pres., dir. Or Chadash, Inc., Monterey Park, 1968—; owner EDUCOMP, Monterey Park, Calif., 1980—; cons. David M. Montag & Assocs., Monterey Park, 1993—; pres. Aquinas Computer Corp.; v.p. Wireless Optical Networks, San Diego, 1996—, R & D Learnfast Corp., Downey, 2001—; ednl. cons. for computer-assisted instrn. V.p., bd. dirs. Coll. Religious Conf., 1968-92; rabbi Congregation Sha'arei Tshuvah, Santa Monica, Calif. Mem. AIAA, Assn. Orthodox Jewish Scientists, Laser Inst. Am., Internat. Sco. Tech. in Edn., Physics Instructional Resource Assn. E-mail: David M. Home and Office: PO Box 384 Monterey Park CA 91754-0384 E-mail: David_M._Montag@laccd.cc.ca.us.

MONTAG, JOHN JOSEPH, II, librarian; b. Omaha, Jan. 8, 1948; s. John Joseph and Ruth Helen (Johnston) M.; m. Linda Kay Lubanski, Apr. 8, 1971; children: Nicole Elizabeth, Megan Kristine. BA, Midland Luth. Coll., 1970; postgrad., Wash. State U., 1970-74; MA, U. Iowa, 1976; postgrad., U. Nebr., 1982-84. English tchr. pub. schs., Nebr., Iowa, 1972-75; reference librarian Concordia Coll., Moorhead, Minn., 1976-81; asst. prof. library sci. U. Nebr., Lincoln, 1981-84; dir. Office of Info. State Library Iowa, Des Moines, 1984-86, state librarian, 1986-87; dir. Thomas Library Wittenberg U., 1987-95, Cochrane-Woods Libr. Nebr. Wesleyan U., Lincoln, 1995-97, dir. libr. and computer svcs., 1997-99, univ. libr., 1999—. Trustee Bibliog. Ctr. for Research, Denver, 1986-87; adv. bd. No. Lights Library Network, Detroit Lakes, Minn., 1980-81; chair Southwest Ohio Consortium Higher Edn. Libr. Coun., 1991-94; mem. exec. com. Nebr. Inst., 1998—. Contbr. articles to profl. jours. Co-founder Nebr. Found. for Oral History, 2001—. Univ. Found. library improvement grantee, U. Nebr., 1983; Challenge grantee NEH, 1992. Mem. ALA, Assn. Coll. and Research Libraries, Nebr. Ind. Coll. Libr. Consortium (chmn. libr. dirs. 2000—). Office: Cochrane Woods Libr Nebr Wesleyan U 5000 Saint Paul Ave Lincoln NE 68504-2760

MONTAG, THOMAS WILLIAM, gynecologic oncologist; b. Denver, June 29, 1950; MD, U. Minn., 1978. Diplomate Am. Bd. Obstetricians and Gynecologists, Am. Bd. Gynecol. Oncology. Intern flex Hennepin County Med. Ctr., Mpls., 1978-79; resident ob-gyn. Med. Ctr. Hosp. Vt., Burlington, 1979-83; fellow gynecol. oncology U. So. Calif., Los Angeles, 1983-85; mem. staff Maryview Med Ctr, Portsmouth, Va., Chesapeake (Va.) Gen. Hosp., 1980—85; dir. gynecologic oncology U. Colo. H.S.C., 1985—87; pvt. prac. Denver, 1987—90, Burlingame, Calif., 1990—95, Asheville, NC, 1995—99, Cancer Treatment Ctr. of Am., Portsmouth, Va., 1999—; clin. asst. prof. Ea. Va. Med. Sch., Norfolk, 2000—. Fellow ACS, Am. Coll. Ob-Gyn.; mem. Am. Soc. Clin. Oncology, Soc. Gynecol. Oncologists, Western Assn. Gynecologic Oncologists, Internat. Gynecologic Cancer Soc., Mid Atlantic Gynecologic Oncology Soc. Office: Cancer Treatment Ctrs of Am Ctr 355 Crawford St Ste 300 Portsmouth VA 23704-2819

MONTAGNIER, LUC ANTOINE, virologist; b. Chabris, Indre, France, Aug. 18, 1932; 3 children. Cert. of Studies on Natural Scis., U. Poitiers, France, 1953, BS, 1955; MD, U. Paris, 1960. Asst. Faculté des Scis, Paris, 1955-60; attaché de recherche Nat. Ctr. Sci. Rsch., 1960-63, chargé de recherche, 1963-67, maitre de recherche, 1967-72, dir. research, 1974—, head lab. Orsay, France, 1965-72; head viral oncology unit Institut Pasteur, Paris, 1972—, head virology dept., 1982-85, prof., 1974—, head dept. AIDS and Retroviruses, 1990-96; disting. prof., dir. Ctr. for Molecular and Cellular Biology Queens Coll. of the CUNY, 1997-2001. Dir. virology course Institut Pasteur, 1980-85, head dept. AIDS and Retrovirus, 1991-97; mem. responsible research team CNRS; discovered HIV-1 virus, 1983 and HIV-2 virus, 1985; pres. adminstrv. coun. European Fed. for AIDS Rsch., 1988. Author: Vaincre le Sida, 1987, Des virus et des hommes, 1994, AIDS, Oxidative Stress and Cancer, 1997, Virus, in English, 2000. Pres. World Found. for AIDS Rsch. and Prevention, Paris, 1993—. Decorated comdr. Legion of Honor, comdr. Ordre Nat. du Mérite; recipient Lasker prize, 1986, Gairdner prize, 1987, Japan prize, 1988, Warrent Alpert Found. prize, 1998, Prince of Asturias prize, 2000, others. Mem. Acad. Nat. de Médecine, French Acad. Scis. Co-discoverer (with Robert Gallo) of AIDS virus. Office: Inst Pasteur 25-28 rue du Dr Roux 75015 Paris France

MONTAGUE, BRIAN JOHN, consulting company executive; b. Washington, Oct. 9, 1951; s. H.C. and Dorothy (Brand) M.; m. Kathryn Valente, Oct. 2, 1993. BA, Bridgewater Coll., 1973; student, St. Mary's (Md.) Coll., 1975, George Washington U., 1980, Miss. State U., 1981. Toxicology technician Hazelton Labs., Vienna, 1973-74; asst. mgr. Chesapeake Sea Farms, Ridge, Md., 1974-76; tng. instr., program coord. Natural Resources Dept., Annapolis, 1976-77; fishery biologist Nat. Aquarium, U.S. Fish and Wildlife Svc., Washington, 1977-82, curator aquarium, 1982-88; pres. Aquatic Images, Annapolis, 1989—. Lectr. local interest groups, 1990—; fisheries biologist, ecol. risk assessment specialist U.S. EPA, Washington. Office: Aquatic Images 3527 Jamestown Rd Davidsonville MD 21035-2009

MONTAGUE, DROGO K. urologist; b. Alpena, Mich., Dec. 11, 1942; s. Frank Wright and Susan Alice (Kidder) M.; m. Margaret Mary Barrett; children: Mark Andrew, Lisa Joy. Student, U. Mich., 1963, MD cum laude, 1968. Diplomate Am. Bd. Urology. Intern Cleve. Clinic Hosp., 1968-69, resident in gen. surgery, 1969-70, resident in urology, 1970-73; assoc. staff urologist Cleve. Clinic Found., 1973-75, staff urologist, 1975—, head sect. prosthetic surgery, 1981—, urology residence program dir., 1985—, dir. Ctr. for Sexual Function, 1987—; prof. surgery Ohio State U. Coll. Medicine, 1992—. Trainee cardiovascular rsch. tng. program NIH, 1962-68; trustee Am. Bd. Urology, 1989-95, mem. examination com., 1975-80, examiner cert. exam., 1980-88, rep. to Am. Bd. Med. Specialties, 1989-95. Reviewer various publs. in field; contbr. numerous articles to profl. publs., chpts. to books; editor: Disorders of Male Sexual Function, 1988, Surgical Treatment of Erectile Dysfunction, 1993; author audiovisual tapes in field; mem. editl. bd. Jour. Urology. James B. Angell scholar, 1961, 62, Nat. Found. scholar, 1963-68; recipient Russell and Mary Hugh Scott Edn. award, 1989, Iowa Rsch. award, 1967. Fellow ACS; mem. Am. Urolog. Assn. (chmn. sci. exhibits com. North Cen. sect. 1977, mem. residency edn. com. 1979-83, vice chmn. audio visual com. 1989-95, mem. various coms., editor Am. Urolog. Assn. Video Libr. 1995—, chmn. audio visual com. 1996—), Am. Assn. Genitourinary Surgeons, Cleve. Urolog. Soc. (sec.-treas. 1978-80, v.p. 1980-81, pres. 1981-82, 94-95), Soc. for Study of Impotence (pres. 1995). Office: Cleve Clinic Found Urol Inst 9500 Euclid Ave Cleveland OH 44195-0001

MONTAGUE, EDGAR BURWELL, III (MONTY MONTAGUE), industrial designer; b. Charlotte, N.C., Aug. 6, 1958; s. Edgar B. Jr. and Mary Sue (Calhoun) M.; m. Nancy Oliver Stallworth, Feb. 25, 1984; children: Nancy Lea, Edgar Eubank. B Environ. Design cum laude, N.C. State U., 1980. Indsl. design Design/Joe Sonderman, Inc., Charlotte, 1980-85; design prin. Bolt (formerly Machen Montague, Inc.), Charlotte, N.C., 1985—, BOLT, Charlotte, 1994—. Holder over 15 design and/or utility patents; work published in Product Design 1-6, Design for Humanity. Designer corp. identity program Habitat for Humanity, Charlotte, 1987 (logo design now used throughout world). Recipient ann. design award Internat. Design mag., 1988-93, ID-40 ID Mag., 1994, Disting. Alumni award N.C. State U., 1999. Mem. Indsl. Designer Soc. Am. (co-founder Carolina chpt., program chmn. 1981-83, vice chmn.

1984, 93, Kudo award for chpt. svc. 1982, Indsl. Design Excellence awards 1989-94). Avocations: travel, art, time with family, coaching soccer. Office: BOLT 1415 S Church St Ste S Charlotte NC 28203-4124 E-mail: monty@boltgroup.com.

MONTAGUE, JOEL GEDNEY, public health officer; b. N.Y.C., July 6, 1932; s. William Pepperrell and Jean Lois (Gedney) M.; m. Shahnaz Emami-Nikou, Dec. 16, 1963; children: Jahan, Maryam. BA, Oberlin Coll., 1956; MA, Johns Hopkins U., 1960; MS in Pub. Health, U. N.C., 1970; postgrad., U. Tehran, 1961. Field rep., mission chief CARE, Iran, Egypt, Tunisia, 1961-68, regional dir., 1968-69, The Population Coun., N.Y.C., 1971-76; dep. dir. Project for Strengthening Health Delivery Systems in Ctrl. and West Africa, Boston, also Ivory Coast, 1976-79; regional dir. Mgmt. Scis. for Health, Boston, 1979-80; head health and hosps. Secretariat of His Highness The Aga Khan, Aiglemont, France, 1980-85; v.p. John Snow Pub. Health, Boston, 1985-89; dir. Am. Friends of AICF, Washington, 1990-92; country rep. John Snow, Cambodia, Cambodia, 1994-97; pvt. pub. health cons., Wellesley, Mass., 1997—. Contbr. articles to profl. jours. Bd. dirs. Nat. Coun. for Internat. Health, 1993-96, Am. Coun. for Nationalities Svcs., 1992-95, U.S. Com. for Refugees, 1991-94; chmn. bd. Ptnrs. for Devel., 1996—. With signal corps U.S. Army, 1956-58. Decorated Medal of Honor, Iranian Red Cross, officer Order of the Republic (Tunisia) Fund; Fulbright grantee, 1961; Ford Found. fellow, 1970-71; Aspen Fund grantee, 1993; hon. fellow Inst. Advanced Study Humanities, U. Edinburgh, Scotland, 1997. Fellow Royal Soc. Tropical Medicine and Hygiene. Home: 24 Maugus Ave Wellesley MA 02481-7617

MONTAGUE, ROBERT LATANE, III, lawyer; b. Washington, Sept. 18, 1935; s. Robert Latane and Frances Breckinridge (Wilson) M.; m. Prudence Darnell, June 20, 1964; children: Anne Steele Mason Montague, Robert Latane IV. BA, U. Va., 1956, LLB, 1961. Bar: Va. 1961, D.C. 1966, U.S. Supreme Ct. 1966. Asst. atty. gen., Ky., 1961-64; pres. Historic Alexandria Found., 1968-70; chmn. Alexandria Environ. Policy Commn., 1970-74; pres. Conservation Coun. Va., 1978-80; chmn. Alexandria Commn. on Bicentennial of U.S. Constitution, 1987-91, Alexandria Historical Restoration and Preservation Commn., 1988—2001; trustee Assn. for Preservation of Va. Antiquities, 1990-96. Chmn. Bd. of Vis. of Gunston Hall, 1987-92; del. Moscow Conf. on Law and Econ. Coop., 1990. Comdr. USNR, 1956-79. Mem. Va. Bar Assn., Va. State Bar (chmn. environ. law sect. 1973-74), Alexandria Bar Assn. Office: 1007 King St Alexandria VA 22314-2922

MONTANA, ENRICO SAKAI, research scientist; b. Youngstown, Ohio, Aug. 2, 1977; s. Enrique C. and Corazon Montana. BS in Molecular Genetics magna cum laude, U. Rochester, 1999; postgrad., MIT, 1999—. DeKiewet Rsch. fellow U. Rochester, N.Y., 1998, ind. rschr., 1998-99. Bausch and Lomb scholar, 1995-99, Xerox scholar, 1995-99, Excellence scholar U. Rochester, 1995-99, Mary Agnes Brandewie scholar, 1995-96. Mem. Phi Beta Kappa. Office: Ctr Learning And Memory 50 Ames St Bldg E18605 Cambridge MA 02142-1308 E-mail: emontana@mit.edu.

MONTANA, PATRICK JOSEPH, management educator; b. N.Y.C. s. Joseph Paul and Constance (Frezza) M. BS cum laude, MS cum laude, L.I. U.; PhD, N.Y. U., 1966; MBA, U. Cin., 1974. Cert. golf tchg. profl. Asst. dean, asso. prof., dir. placement, chmn. mgmt. L.I. U., Bklyn., 1960-66; assoc. prof. Drexel U., Phila., 1966-67; asst. dean N.Y. U. Grad. Sch. Bus. Adminstrn., N.Y.C., 1967-69; asst. v.p., dir. planning and human resources devel. Sperry & Hutchinson Co. (trading stamps and subsidiaries), 1969-74; U.S. presdl. interchange exec., 1973; pres. Profl. Inst., Am. Mgmt. Assn., N.Y.C., 1974-76, Nat. Center Career Life Planning, 1975-80, 80—; prof. mgmt. Hofstra U. Sch. Bus. Adj. prof. mgmt. and mktg. Fordham U. Grad. Sch. Bus., N.Y.C., 1969-79; curriculum cons. U. P.R., 1968; guest lectr. Congress for Internat. Progress in Mgmt., 1965, IBM Corp. Mgmt. Sch., 1964-65, 76-77; mediator Pub. Employee Relations Bd., 1969; bd. dirs. Ednl. Systems and Publs., 1970-75. Author: The Marketing Executive of the Future, 1967, You Can Change Your Future, 1976, Managing Nonprofit Organizations, 1977, Marketing in Nonprofit Organizations, 1978, Career Life Planning for Americans, 1978, Overcoming Mid and Late Career Crises, 1978, Successful Teamwork—How Managers and Secretaries Achieve It, 1979, Managing Terrorism, 1982; Retirement Programs: How to Develop and Implement Them, 1985; Work Force Management in the Arabian Peninsula, 1986, Management, 1987, rev. 2d edit., 1993, rev. 3d edit., 2000, Preretirement Planning, 1988, Stepping Out, Starting Over, 1992, revised 2d edit. 1999, Managing Public and Nonprofit Organizations, 1994, Building Financial Security Through Retirement Planning, 1998, Conquering the Course, 2002; contbr. numerous articles to profl. publs. Recipient achievement award Wall Street Jour., 1959-60, U.S. Sec. Labor's recognition award 1974, Disting. Alumnus award L.I. U.; fellow Ford Found., 1963-64. Mem. Am. Assembly Collegiate Schs. Bus. (accreditation com. 1970-72, standards com. 1973-75, govt. relations com. 1976-78), Am. Mktg. Assn. (awards com., continuing edn. com.), Beta Gamma Sigma, Eta Mu Pi. Office: Hofstra U Sch Bus Hempstead NY 11550 Home: 279 River Rd Scarborough NY 10510

MONTANARI, FRANCO, classicist, educator; b. Sannazzaro de' Burgondi, PV, Italy, May 24, 1950; s. Renzo and Maria (Rastaldi) M.; m. Daniela Manetti, Sept. 21, 1978. Diploma liceale, Liceo Classico U. Foscolo, Pavia, Italy, 1969; laurea in lettere, U. Pisa, Italy, 1973; diploma, Scuola Normale Superiore, Pisa, 1973, perfezionamento, 1974. Contrattista quadriennale U. Pisa, Italy, 1975-77, prof. incaricato Italy, 1977-82, prof. associato Italy, 1982-86; prof. ordinario U. Genova, Italy, 1987—. Pres. XL and XLVIII Entretiens Fondation Hardt, Geneva, 1993, 2001; treas. Bur. of the Fedn. Internat. des Assn. des Etudes Classiques (FIEC), 1994—; mem. Conseil de Fondation and Conseil Scientifique of the Fondation Hardt (Geneva); dir. Centro Italiano dell'Année Philologique. Author: Studi di filologia omerica antica I, 1979, I frammenti dei grammatici Agathokles, Hellanikos, Ptolemaios, Epithetes, 1988, Introduzione a Omero, 1990, 92, Studi di filologia omerica antica II, 1995, GI. Vocabolario della lingua greca, 1995, Storia della Letteratura Greca, 1998; editor: Da Omero agli Alessandrini, 1988, La philologie grecque à l'époque hellénistique et romaine, 1994, Omero. Gli aedi, i poemi, gli interpreti, Firenze, 1998; mem. editl. bd. Corpus Papiri Filosofici, Florence. Mem. Soc. Internat. de Bibliographie Classique. Home: via Studiati 6 I-56127 Pisa Italy Office: Facoltà di Lettere U Genova Via Balbi 4 16126 Genova Italy E-mail: franco.montanar@unige.it.

MONTANE, FRAN L. poet, film producer; b. Manhasset, N.Y., Aug. 1966; d. John Montagnino and Christine Miller. BFA in Comm. Arts summa cum laude, NY Inst. Tech., 1990. Program coord. N.Y. Open Ctr., N.Y.C., 1990—92; asst. dir. Fireball Films, 1994; internat. segment prodr. In the Life Media, 1995; exptl. film/video dir. Sarasvati Prodns., 1996. Author: (collected poems) At the Grave's Mouth, 2001; prodr.: (stage play/video) The Owl Answers by Adrienne Kennedy, 1997. Scholar, U.S. Achievement Acad., 1987. Avocations: working out, reading, travel. Home: 502 Plandome Rd Manhasset NY 11030 Office: 502 Plandome Rd Manhasset NY 11030 Personal E-mail: sarasva@aol.com. E-mail: sarasva@aol.com.

MONTANEZ, MARY ANN CHAVEZ, counselor, consultant, writer; b. Pasadena, Calif., July 16, 1936; d. Vincent Chavez-Trujillo-Mendibles and Trinidad (Huerta-Molina) Chavez; m. R.E. Montanez, Nov. 17, 1956 (div. June 1976); children: Robert, Eric, (twins) Michael and Manuel. AA, Pasadena City Coll., 1980; BA, Pacific Oaks Coll., 1985, MA in Human Devel., 1988; cert. counseling, Calif. State U., L.A., 1994. Life cert. C.C. counseling and instrn. Placement officer Pasadena (Calif.) C.C. Dist., 1981-90, coll. instr., 1986-90; vocat. rehab. counselor Calif. Dept. Rehab., L.A., 1990—; exec. dir. Latins Writers & Film Makers, 1998—. Mem. outreach bd. Pasadena Mental Health Assn., 1976-79; field rep. El Centro De Accion Social, Inc., 1976-77; dir. program Pasadena Unified Sch. Dist., 1977-78; coord. outreach, crisis counselor Pasadena Mental Health, 1978-81; cons., field reader Women's Ednl. Equity Act, Washington, 1981; out-placement cood. PCC, 1984; staff recruitment program Pasadena C.C., 1987-88; acad. counselor Multi Cultural Ctr.-Cerritos Coll. Dist., 1990-91. Commr. Commn. on Disabilities, 1990—; adv. bd. mem. Fiesta Educativa, 1991-99; bd. mem. West Side Ctr. on Ind. Living, L.A., 1993-99; mem. credit com. Pasadena Employees Credit Union, 1996; active Huntington Libr.; mem. Christian Calvery Chapel. Recipient Golden Angel award, 1995. Mem. Soc. Hispanic Hist. Ancestral Rsch. Democrat. Roman Catholic. Avocations: writing, history, art. Home: 2533 Glenrose Ave Altadena CA 91001-5049 E-mail: documentary@earthlink.com.

MONTANO, ARTHUR, lawyer; b. Audubon, N.J., 1923; s. Domenick and Theresa (Grasso) M.; m. Ann B. Durkin; children: Sharon Adams, Sandra Bumgardner, Cheryl Ann Hughes, Arthur Jr., Bernadette, Michael. BME, Villanova U., 1950; LLB, Rutgers U., 1954. Bar: N.J. 1955, U.S. Dist. Ct. N.J. 1955, U.S. Ct. Appeals 1967, U.S. Supreme Ct. 1969. Assoc. Orlando, Devine & Tomlin, Camden, N.J., 1955-56, Orlando, Kisselman & Devine, Camden, 1956-58, Kisselman, Devine & Deighan, Camden, 1958-60; ptnr. Kisselman, Devine, Deighan & Montano, 1960-65, Kisselman, Devine, Deighan, Montano, King & Summers, Camden, 1965-71, Kisselman, Deighan, Montano & Summers, Cherry Hill, N.J., 1971-77; sr. ptnr. Montano, Summers, Mullen & Manuel, 1977-88; of counsel Montano, Summers, Mullen, Manuel & Owens, P.A., 1988-99; pvt. practice Audubon, N.J., 1998—. Adj. prof. law Rutgers Law Sch., Camden, N.J., 1984-93; arbitrator Am. Arbitration Assn., state and fed. cts. Navigator AC, U.S. Army, 1943-45. Recipient award for professionalism in law, 1997. Fellow Am. Coll. Trial Lawyers, Am. Bar Found.; mem. N.J. State Bar Assn. (trustee 1977-84), Trial Attys. N.J. (trial bar 1978), Camden County Bar Assn., Tavistock Country Club (Haddonfield, N.J.). Roman Catholic. Office: 1323 Mineo Dr Punta Gorda FL 33950-6637

MONTANO, LINDA, conceptual artist, educator; b. Kingston, N.Y., Jan. 18, 1942; d. Henry and Mildred (Kelly) M.; m. Mitchell Payne, June 6, 1970 (div. 1977). BA, Coll. New Rochelle, 1965; MA, Villa Schifanoia, Florence, Italy, 1965-66; MFA, U. Wis., 1969. Instr. sculpture Edgewood Coll., Madison, Wis., 1966-69, Nazareth Coll., Rochester, N.Y., 1969-71; instr. performance San Francisco Art Inst., 1977—, Chgo. Art Inst., 1977—, San Francisco State U., 1977—. Yoga therapist St. Mary's Hosp., 1972-75. Author: Art in Everyday Life, 1980. NEA grantee, 1977, 85. Fellow Ctr. Music Expt. Avocation: karate. Address: Art/Life Inst 85 Abeel St Kingston NY 12401-6009

MONTANYE, JAMES ALAN, economist, consultant; b. Saratoga Springs, N.Y., Dec. 20, 1946; s. Warren A. and Jean S. (Belensz) M. BS, Cornell U., 1972; MS, Syracuse U., 1973. Project mgr. Arbitron, Inc., Beltsville, Md., 1974-75; pvt. practice Washington, 1975-77; sr. cons. Transcomm, Inc., Falls Church, Va., 1977-85; pres. Cornell Cons. Group, Inc., 1985—. Guest Brookings Instn., Washington, 1975; presenter expert econ. testimony, more than 50 legal and adminstrv. procs. Contbr. articles to profl. jours. Ayer Found. fellow Syracuse U., 1973, Grad. fellow, 1974. Avocations: music, jazz guitar. Office: Cornell Cons Group Inc 7635 Trail Run Rd Falls Church VA 22042-3417

MONTE, BONNIE J. performing company executive, director, educator; b. Stamford, Ct., Nov. 27, 1954; d. Eugene N. and Ruth M. (Thompson) M. BA, Bethany Coll., 1976; diploma, Hartman Conservatory, Stamford, 1978. Assoc. artistic dir. Williamstown (Mass.) Theatre Festival, 1981-89; casting dir. Manhattan Theatre Club, N.Y.C., 1989-90; artistic dir. N.J. Shakespeare Festival, Madison, 1990—; mem. faculty Drew U., 1991—. Mem. faculty U. Notre Dame, The New Sch.-Eugene Lang. Coll. Recipient Nat. Soc. of Arts and Letters award, N.J., 1997, Alumni Achievement award for arts mgmt. Bethany Coll., 1999; grantee Lotte Crabtree Found., Boston, 1977. Democrat. Avocations: cycling, archery, writing, travel. Office: NJ Shakespeare Festival 36 Madison Ave Madison NJ 07940-1434

MONTE, JAY T. web site designer; b. Queens, N.Y., Feb. 14, 1976; AA, Mesa Coll., San Diego, 1998. Web designer Web 4 All, Baldwin, NY, 1998—. Personal E-mail: jason@webnbeyond.com.

MONTEAU, NORMAN KEITH, gemologist; b. Balt., Dec. 20, 1957; s. Milton Keith and Vieva Regina (Williams) M.; m. Sandra Lynn Staub, Dec. 7, 1987. Cert. diamond grading, Gemol. Inst., 1981, cert. colored stone grading, cert. gem identification, Gemol. Inst., 1982. Numerous certs. fro Gemol. Inst. Am. Owner, founder Monteau Gemol. Svcs., Woodland Hills, Calif., 1987-91, pres., 1992—; owner, pres. Am. Internat. Gemologists, Beverly Hills, 1993—; mng. ptnr. The William Staub Co., L.A., 1994—. V.p. bd. dirs. Lynn Meadows, 1999-2000, pres., 2000-2001; appraiser to Archdiocese of L.A., Cath. Ch., 1993—; arbitrator State Farm Ins. Co., 1993—, lectr. nat. retail jewelry stores, insurance cos. others on gemology and values, 1992—; advisor to ins. cos. in Calif. for earthquake property damage assessment, 1994, expert witness L.A. Mcpl. Ct., 1995; jewelry appraiser County of Los Angeles, 1996—; mem. Ptnrs. for Internat. Edn. and Tng./U.S. AID, 1996. Contbr. articles to profl. jours. Recipient Excellence award Aetna Ins. Co., 1992; honored guest of bd. govs. Gemol. Inst. Am., Carlsbad, Calif., 1996. Mem. Nat. Assn. Jewelry Appraisers, Am. Soc. Appraisers, Gemol. Inst. Am. (mem. Pres.'s Cir. 1992—), Calif. Jewelers Assn., Alumni Assn. Gemol. Inst. Am. (charter), Jewelers Bd. of Trade, Woodland Hills C. of C. Avocations: racquetball, mountain climbing, water skiing, jet car racing, white water rafting. Office: Monteau Gemol Svcs 21250 Califa St Ste 203 Woodland Hills CA 91367-5042

MONTEDONICO, JOSEPH, lawyer; b. Washington, May 30, 1937; s. Joseph and Linda (Love) M.; m. Lynne Morrell, Nov. 12, 1979; 1 child, Maria. BA, U. Md., 1962, JD, 1965. Bar: Md. 1965, D.C. 1965, U.S. Dist. Ct. D.C. 1965, U.S. Dist. Ct. Md. 1965. Law clk. to justice, Rockville, Md., 1965-66; assoc. Donahue, Ehrmantraut Mitchell, 1966-78; ptnr. Donahue, Ehrmantraut, Montedonico, Washington, 1978-88, Montedonico & Mason, Rockville, 1988-91, Montedonico, Hamilton & Altman, PC, Chevy Chase, Md., 1991—2001, Montedonico, Belcoure & Tazzara, Washington, 2001—. Cons., lectr. in field. Author: Medical Malpractice and Health Care Care, 1987; (with others) Anesthesia Clinics, 1987, Surgical Pathology, 1989. With U.S. Army, 1956-58. Named one of Best Lawyers in Am., Washingtonian Mag., 1989—96, Best 75 Lawyers in Washington, 2002. Mem.: D.C. Bar Assn., Md. Bar Assn., Internat. Acad. Trial Lawyers, Am. Bd. Trial Lawyers (pres. D.C. chpt.), Inns of Ct. Republican. Avocations: scuba, skiing, photography. Office: Montedonico Belcoure & Tazzara 1020 19th St NW Ste 420 Washington DC 20036 E-mail: jm@mbt-legal.com.

MONTEFERRANTE, JUDITH CATHERINE, cardiologist; b. N.Y., Jan. 27, 1949; d. Stanley and Monica (Vinckus) Sosaris; m. Ronald J. Monteferrante (div.); 1 child Jason Paul ; m. Roger E. Salisbury, Mar. 3, 1990. BS, Adelphi U., Garden City, 1970; MS, SUNY, Buffalo, 1973; MD, Mt. Sinai, N.Y.C., 1978. Diplomate Cert. Coun. Nuc. Cardiology. Attending N.Y. Med. Coll., Valhalla, N.Y., 1983—; pvt. practice Primary Care and Cardiovasc. Assocs., White Plains, 1984—; affiliate Cardiology Cons. of Westchester. Mem. med. bd. White Plains Med. Ctr., 1997—2000; spkr. on women and heart disease. Contbr. Past trustee Coll. Mt. St. Vincent, N.Y.C. Fellow: ACP, Am. Heart Assn. (past. pres. 1996—98), Am. Coll. Cardiology; mem.: Am. Soc. Nuc. Cardiology. Office: 15 N Broadway White Plains NY 10601-2225

MONTEFERRO, MOISES COSTAS, artist; b. Vigo, Pontevedra, Spain, Feb. 27, 1963; s. Moises and Regina Monteferro; m. Fabiola Velarde. BA, Santiago de Compostela U., Santiago, Spain, 1986. Mem. ARTEUTILE Project, 1999, BABELE ART Project, 1999. One-man shows include Madras Gallery Mexico DF Wrapped Dreams, 1993, one-man shows include Diciannove Galery Milano Walls, 1994, one-man shows include LOFT 9 Gallery NY Sketched Poetry, 2001, exhibited in group shows at Artesanos Gallery , Miami, Fla., 2001, New York Art Expo, N.Y.C., 2001. Founder, pres. Free Art Movement, N.Y.C., 1999. Mem.: N.Y. Artist Equity Assn. (assoc.), Art in Context Center for Communications (assoc.). Office: Monteferro Studio FDR Station POB 931 New York NY 10150 Business E-Mail: monteferro@aol.com.

MONTEIRO, GEORGE, English educator, writer; b. Cumberland, R.I., May 23, 1932; s. Francisco José and Augusta (Temudo) M.; m. Lois Ann Hodgins, Aug. 14, 1958 (div. 1992); children: Katherine, Stephen, Emily; m. Brenda Murphy, Mar. 25, 1995. AB, Brown U., 1954; AM, Columbia U., 1956; PhD, Brown U., 1964; DHL (hon.), U. Mass., Dartmouth, 1993. From instr. to assoc. prof. Brown U., Providence, 1961-72, prof. English, 1972-99, prof. Portuguese, 1984-99, adj. prof., 1999—. Vis. prof. Providence Coll., 1967-68; Fulbright prof. Am. lit. U. Sao Paulo, 1969-71. Author: Henry James and John Hay: The Record of a Friendship, 1965, The Coffee Exchange: Poems, 1982, Robert Frost and the New England Renaissance, 1988, Double Weaver's Knot: Selected Poems, 1989, The Presence of Camões, 1996, The Presence of Pessoa, 1998, Stephen Crane's Blue Badge of Courage, 2000, Fernando Pessoa and Nineteenth-Century Anglo-American Literature, 2000; editor: The Man Who Never Was: Essays on Fernando Pessoa, 1982, The Correspondence of Henry James and Henry Adams, 1877-1941, 1992, Conversations with Elizabeth Bishop, 1996; translator: In Crete with the Minotaur and Other Poems, 1980, Fernando Pessoa: Self Awareness and Thirty Other Poems, 1988, A Man Smiles at Death with Half a Face, 1991. Decorated Order of Prince Henry the Navigator (Portugal). Office: Brown U Portuguese & Brazil Studies Providence RI 02912-0001 E-mail: georgemonteiro@prodigy.net.

MONTEIRO, LOIS ANN, medical science educator; b. Central Falls, R.I., Mar. 22, 1934; d. William Henry and Martha Mae (Leach) Hodgins; m. George Monteiro, Aug. 14, 1958 (div. Feb. 1992); children: Katherine, Stephen, Emily. RN, Roger Williams Hosp., Providence, 1954; BA, Brown U., k1958, PhD, 1970; MS, Boston U., 1960. Asst. prof. Boston U., 1960-65, Brown U., Providence, 1971-77, assoc. prof., 1978-82, prof., 1983—, chmn. dept., 1985—, assoc. dean medicine, 1991—. Vis. prof. U. Va., 1990, U. Miss., 2002; bd. dirs. Harvard Cmty. Health Plan, 1990-95, Harvard Pilgrim Health Care Plan, New Eng., 1995—. Author: Montoring Health Status, 1976, Cardiac Rehabilitation, 1980; contbr. articles to profl. jours. Mem. Commn. State of R.I., Providence, 1989—. NSF grantee, 1969, Robert W. Johnson Found. grantee, Princeton, N.J., 1983, NIH grantee, 1987; Bunting Inst. fellow, Cambridge, Mass., 1981, Congrl. fellow House Vets. Affairs Commn., 1998; recipient Am. Sociol. Assn. Spivack award, 1998. Mem. Am. Sociol. Assn., R.I. State Nurses Assn. (pres. 1974-76), Women in Medicine/Assn. Am. Med. Colls. Democrat. Presbyterian. Avocation: collecting books on nursing history. Office: Brown U Dept Med Sci PO Box G-a413 Providence RI 02912-0001 E-mail: lois_monteiro@brown.edu.

MONTEITH, LARRY KING, chancellor emeritus; b. Bryson City, N.C., Aug. 17, 1933; s. Earl and Essie (King) M.; m. Nancy Alexander, Apr. 19, 1952; children: Larry, Carol, Steve. BSEE, N.C. State U., 1960; MSEE, Duke U., 1962, PhDEE, 1965. Registered profl. engr., N.C. Mem. tech. staff Bell Telephone Labs., Burlington, N.C., 1960-62, Resch. Triangle Inst., Raleigh, 1962-66, group leader rsch. sect., 1966-68; adj. asst. prof. elec. engring. N.C. State U., 1965-68, assoc. prof., 1968-72, prof., 1972—, head dept. elec. engring., 1974-78, dean of engring., 1978-89, interim chancellor, 1989-90, chancellor, 1990-98, chancellor emeritus, 1998—. Contbr. articles to profl. jours. With USN, 1952-56. Recipient Disting. Engring. Alumnus award Duke U., 1984, Outstanding Engring. Achievement award N.C. Soc. Engrs., 1990, Disting. Engring. Alumnus award N.C. State, 1999. Fellow IEEE, Am. Soc. for Engring. Edn.; mem. NSPE (edn. adv. group), Raleigh C. of C. (bd. dirs.), Rotary Internat. (Paul Harris fellow Rotary Found. 1991), Phi Beta Kappa, Sigma Xi, Sigma Iota Rho, Phi Kappa Phi, Eta Kappa Nu, Tau Beta Pi, Sigma Beta Delta.

MONTELEONE, PATRICIA, academic dean; MD, St. Louis Sch. of Med., 1961. Dean St. Louis U. Sch. Medicine, 1996—. Office: St Louis U Sch Medicine 1402 S Grand Blvd Saint Louis MO 63104-1004*

MONTELLARO, RANDELL, lawyer; b. Forest Hills, N.Y., Oct. 31, 1960; s. Lee and Bernadette (Shenton) M.; m. Lisa McCaffrey, Nov. 29, 1991. BBA, Hofstra U., 1982, JD, 1985. Bar: N.Y. 1986, D.C. 1987. Sr. tax cons. Deloitte, Haskins & Sells, N.Y.C., 1985-87; sr. cons. Price Waterhouse, 1988-89; assoc. Summit Soloman & Feldesman, 1989-93; ptnr. Epstein Becker & Green, 1993—. Mem. Hofstra Law Rev., 1984-85; contbg. author Employee Benefits Law, 1991. Mem. N.Y. State Bar Assn., D.C. Bar Assn. Democrat. Home: 81 N Kings Ave North Massapequa NY 11758-3402 Office: Epstein Becker & Green 250 Park Ave Fl 13 New York NY 10177-1211 E-mail: rmontell@ebg.law.com.

MONTELONGO, MICHAEL, federal agency administrator, career officer; b. N.Y.C. m. Debra Tenison; 1 child, Amanda. BS in Nat. Security and Pub. Affairs, U.S. Military Acad.; MBA in Corp. Strategy and Fin., Harvard U., 1988; grad., Command and Gen. Staff Coll., 1992. Commd. 2d lt. U.S. Army, 1977, advanced through grades to lt. col., platoon leader, 1980, staff officer, 1982, ops. officer, company comdr., 1986; admissions officer U.S. Military Acad., West Point, N.Y., 1991, asst. prof. social scis. dept., 1991; rsch. analyst office economic and manpower analysis U.S. Army, 1991; adviser, spl. asst. Comdr.-in-Chief U.S. Southern Command, 1991; bat. exec. officer, bat. and brigade ops. officer U.S. Army, 1993, special asst. to U.S. Army chief of staff, 1994; senate legis. asst., 1995; asst. secy. air force financial mgt. and comptroller U.S. Dept. Defense, Washington, 2001—. Sec. supervisory com. Ft. Bliss Fed. Credit Union, 1994; ch. music min., 1969—. Sec. Nat. Soc. Hispanic MBA, 1995; Mex.-Am. legal Def. and Ednl. Fund Advanced Legal Program, 1993, Leadership El Paso Program, 1993; trustee Unite El Paso, 1993. U.S. Army Advanced Civil Schooling fellow, 1986, Inter-Univ. Seminar on Armed Forces and Soc. fellow, 1990, Congl. Hispanic Caucus Inst. fellow, 1992, Army Congl. fellow, 1995. Office: US Dept Defense Financial Mgt and Comptroller 1130 Air Force Pentagon Washington DC 20330-1130 Office Fax: 703-693-1996.*

MONTEMAYOR, CARLOS RENE, advertising agency executive; b. San Antonio, Nov. 21, 1945; s. Raul Martin and Mary (Lyall) M.; m. Marina Cara Cook, Sep. 21, 1967 (div. Dec. 1978); m. Barbara Kay Volmer, Dec. 23, 1979; 1 child, Justin Norman. BBA in Mktg., U. Tex., 1967; MS in Journalism, Northwestern U., 1968. Account exec. Campbell-Ewald Co., Detroit and Cin., 1968-72, Ross Roy Inc., Detroit, 1972-74, Pitluk Group, San Antonio, 1974-76; v.p. GSD&M Advt., 1976-78; mktg. mgr. Church's Fried Chicken, 1978-81; v.p. Ed Yardang & Assocs., 1981-83; pres. Montemayor y Asociados, 1983—2002, vice chmn., 2002—, Global Hue, 2002—. Bd. dirs. USAA Fed. Savs. Bank, sec., San Antonio Zoo; past pres. Fiesta San Antonio, Ray Feo XLVII Fiesta, 1995; pres. Hispanic divsn. Global Hue. 2d Lt. USAR, 1968-74. Mem. S.W. Found. Biomed. Rsch. (bd. govs.), Club Giraud, Argyle Club, Friends of McNay Club, Govs. Club. Republican. Roman Catholic. Avocations: collecting classic cars, traveling, racquet ball. Home: 5 Bitterblue Ln San Antonio TX 78218-1790 Office: 8242 Vicar San Antonio TX 78218-1566

MONTENARO, REGINA LYNNE, secondary education educator; b. Huntington, W.Va., Sept. 17, 1947; d. Oscar Edward and Peggie Lee (Miser) Jeffers; m. Donald J. Montenaro, July 2, 1982; 1 child, Joshua Aaron. BA, Marshall U., 1971, MA, 1974; postgrad., Ashland U., Coll. of Mt. St. Joseph, Marshall U., Bowling Green State U., Ohio State U. Nat. Bd. Cert. Early Adolescent Lang. Arts, 2000. Reading tchr. Prichard (W.Va.) Elem. Sch., 1971-74; tchr. English, theater and speech, chair lang. arts dept. Buffalo H.S., Kenova, W.Va., 1974-83; tchr. English and theater Westerville (Ohio) South H.S., 1983-89; facilitator lang. arts dept. Heritage Mid. Sch., 1989—, Westerville City Schs. W.Va. state dir. All-Am. Drill Team and Flag Corps, 1978--; W.Va. state dir. Internat. Thespian Soc., 1978-81; mem. planning team Ctrl. Ohio Regional Profl. Devel. Ctr. Lang. Arts. Recipient Martha Holden Jennings scholar award, Time Warner Tchr. Adv. Bd., Columbus Educator award Time Warner Comms., 2001. Mem. ASCD, Nat. Coun. Tchrs. English (com. on media), Nat. Mid. Sch. Assn., Internat. Reading Assn., Assembly on Media Arts (exec. bd. dirs.), Nat. Telemedia Coun., Ohio Mid. Sch. Assn., Showcase Am. Aux. (judge), Ohio Coun. Tchrs. English Lang. Arts (coord. pre-K-8 writing awards). Home: 1826 Calico Ct Powell OH 43065-9518 E-mail: montenar@westerville.k12.oh.us.

MONTERO, CARLOS F. orthopedic surgeon; b. Buenos Aires, Argentina, Apr. 21, 1944; s. Aristides Carlos and Juana Beatriz (Chichisola) M. MD, U. Buenos Aires, 1968. Diplomate Am. Bd. Orthopedic Surgeons. Intern Nassau Hosp., Mineola, N.Y., 1968-69; resident in surgery Bronx VA Hosp., City Hosp., N.Y.C., 1969-70; resident in orthopedics Nassau County Med. Ctr., East Meadow, N.Y., 1970-73, fellow in hand surgery, 1973-74; pvt. practice hand surgery Levittown, 1974—; chief orthopedic surgery New Island Hosp., Bethpage. Asst. clin. prof. orthopedic surgery SUNY-Stony Brook. Office: Nassau Orthopedic Surgeons 2920 Hempstead Tpke Ste 1 Levittown NY 11756-1499

MONTERO, DARREL MARTIN, social worker, sociologist, educator; b. Sacramento, Mar. 4, 1946; s. Frank and Ann Naake; divorced; children: David Paul, Lynn Elizabeth, Laura Ann, Emily Kathryn. AB, Calif. State U., 1970; MA, UCLA, 1972, PhD, 1974. Postgrad. researcher Japanese-Am. Research Project UCLA, 1971-73, dir. research, 1973-75; assoc. head Program on

Comparative Ethnic Studies, Survey Research Ctr. UCLA, 1973-75; asst. prof. sociology Case Western Res. U., Cleve., 1975-76; asst. prof. urban studies, research sociologist Pub. Opinion Survey, dir. urban ethnic research program U. Md., College Park, 1976-79; assoc. prof. Ariz. State U., Tempe, 1979—. Cons. rsch. sect. Viewer Sponsored TV Found., Los Angeles, Berrien E. Moore Law Office, Inc., Gardena, Calif., 1973, Bur. for Social Sci. Research, Inc., Washington, Friends of the Family, Ltd., Nat. Sci. Found. Author: Japanese Americans: Changing Patterns of Ethnic Affiliation Over Three Generations, 1980, Urban Studies, 1978, Vietnamese Americans: Patterns of Resettlement and Socioeconomic Adaptation in the United States, 1979, Social Problems, 1988; mem. editorial bd. Humanity and Society, 1978-80; contbr. articles to profl. jours. Served with U.S. Army, 1966-72. Mem. Am. Sociol. Assn., Am. Assn. Pub. Opinion Research (exec. council, standards com.), Am. Ednl. Research Assn., Council on Social Work Edn., Soc. Study of Social Problems, D.C. Sociol. Soc., Am. Soc. Pub. Adminstrn., Nat. Assn. Social Workers, Pacific Sociol. Assn. Office: Ariz State Univ Sch Social Work Tempe AZ 85281

MONTERO, FERNAN GONZALO, retired advertising executive; b. Buenos Aires, May 22, 1948; came to U.S., 1952; s. Adolfo and Donne (Strang) M. BBA, U. Wis., 1971; M. Journalism in Advt., Northwestern U., 1972. With Young & Rubicam Inc., 1972-82; pres. Young & Rubicam Argentina, Buenos Aires, 1982-85; dep. area mgr. Young & Rubicam Latin Am., Sao Paulo, Brazil, 1985-87; sr. v.p., dir. bus. devel. Young & Rubicam Inc., N.Y.C., 1987-91, chmn., CEO Latin Am., 1991-92, chmn., CEO Europe, Middle East London, 1993-98.

MONTES, LEOPOLDO FELICIANO, dermatologist, educator; b. Buenos Aires, Nov. 22, 1929; came to U.S., 1955, naturalized, 1974; s. Leopoldo A. and Celia (Gaztambide) M.; m. Maria Mercedes Pfeiffer, Nov. 25, 1961; children— Carolina, Mercedes, Ana, Leopoldo, Teresa, William. MD, U. Buenos Aires, 1954; MS, U. Mich., 1959. Intern City of Buenos Aires Hosps., 1954-55; resident in dermatology Pa. Hosp., Phila., 1955-56; resident in dermatology, then instr. U. Mich. Med. Center, Ann Arbor, 1956-60; practice medicine specializing in dermatology Buenos Aires, 1960-63, 82—, Houston, 1963-66, Birmingham, Ala., 1966-81. Asst. prof. Baylor U. Coll. Medicine, Houston, 1963-66; mem. faculty U. Ala. Med. Center and Med. Coll. Ala., Birmingham, 1966—, prof. dermatology, 1969-81, asso. prof. microbiology, 1968-81, prof. emeritus, 1982—; adj. prof. anatomy Coll. Medicine, U. South Ala., Mobile, 1981-89; adj. prof. large animal surgery and medicine Auburn U. Sch. Veterinary Medicine, 1977—; dir. Dermatology Rsch. Structural Rsch. Ctr., Mobile, 1990—, Vitiligo Unit, 1990—. Author: Atlas of Skin Diseases of the Horse, 1983, Vitiligo-Nutritional Therapy, 1999. Recipient Research Career Devel. award USPHS, 1965-70; grantee USPHS; grantee NSF; grantee Kresge Found.; John A. Hartford Found. Fellow Am. Acad. Dermatology, Am. Acad. Microbiology, Royal Coll. Physicians and Surgeons Can.; mem. Am. Soc. Microbiology, Soc. Investigative Dermatology, Histochem. Soc., Am. Soc. Cell Biology, AAAS, Am. Fedn. Clin. Research, Electron Microscope Soc. Am., Internat. Soc. Tropical Dermatology (Asst. sec. gen. 1969-74), Am. Dermatol. Assn., Sigma Xi. Home: Suipacha 1308 1011 Buenos Aires Argentina Office: Paraguay 2302 1121 Buenos Aires Argentina also: Structural Rsch Ctr 120 Novatan Rd Mobile AL 36608 Fax: 5411.4314.4328. E-mail: leopoldo_montes@hotmail.com. *While taking care of a patient I always considered it indispensable to study and research as much as I could about the disease I was treating, to feel I was perhaps the only one in a position to help, to put myself-as Lord Lister said- in the patient's place.*

MONTFORD, CLAUDIAN HAMMOND, retired gifted and talented education educator; b. Bainbridge, Ga., Jan. 31, 1947; d. Eugene and Ruth Lee (Clark) Hammond; m. Redolphus Montford, Dec. 21, 1968; children: Randolph Eugene, Rudolph Levell. BA in Early Childhood and Elem. Edn., Newark State-Kean Coll., Union, N.J., 1969; MA in Scis. Edn., Fairleigh Dickinson U., 1996. Cert. tchr., N.J. Cashier Sears, Roebuck and Co., Watchung, N.J., 1965-68; tchr. sci. Camp Crusades, Plainfield, 1969; tchr. cons. Bank Street Coll., N.Y.C., 1973; tchr. gifted and talented edn. Plainfield Bd. Edn., 1969—72, 1974—2002, tchr. dir. Title I compensatory reading program, 1970-72, tchr. advisor instrnl. coun., 1981-83. Playground dir. Plainfield Recreation Dept., 1967-68. Fundraiser Black United Fund N.J., 1990, chmn., 1991-93; elem. coord. Sci. Fair, Plainfield, 1991-98; design-coach Am.'s Choice Sch. Design Reform, 1999-2002. Recipient 1st gov.'s tchr. recognition N.J. Dept. Edn., 1986, Excellence in Edn. award Frontiers Internat., 1988; grantee N.J. Dept. Edn., 1983, Tech. grantee AT&T, 1996, Union Carbide Corp., 1997-99, Evergreen Schs. N.J. Parent Participation Program grant, 2001; New Zealand Study Tour scholar Plainfield Bd. Edn., 1993. Mem. NEA, N.J. Edn. Assn., Union County Edn. Assn., Plainfield Edn. Assn., Evergreen Edn. Assn. Seeking Ednl. Equity and Diversity Project, Assn. Math. Tchrs. N.J. (exec. coun.), N.J. Systemic Sci. Initiative (adv. bd.). Democrat. Baptist. Avocations: reading, sewing and dress designing, macrame, horticulture, computer programming. Office: Evergreen Sch 1033 Evergreen Ave Plainfield NJ 07060-2698

MONTFORD, JOHN THOMAS, state legislator, academic administrator, lawyer; b. Ft. Worth, June 28, 1943; s. Thomas L. and Jewell F. (Coursey) M.; m. Pamela Jacobs, June 3, 1966 (div.); 1 child, Melinda; m. Debra Kay Mears, Dec. 24, 1975; children: Melonie, John Ross. BA, U. Tex., Austin, 1965, JD, 1968; LLD (hon.), Lubbock (Tex.) Christian U., 1989. Bar: Tex. 1968. Pvt. practice, Lubbock, 1971-78; criminal dist. atty. Lubbock County, 1979-82; state sen. Dist. 28, Lubbock, 1983-96; chancellor Health Scis. Ctr. Tex. Tech. U., 1996—. Adj. faculty Tex. TEch. Coll. of Edn., High Edn. Adminstrn. Program, 1999; founding pres. South Plains Pub. Sch. Found. Trustee S. Park Hosp., Lubbock, 1981-82; bd. dirs., trustee Tex. Boys Ranch, Lubbock, 1982—; chmn. profl. divsn. United Way, Lubbock, 1980; energy com. So. Legis. Conf., 1983; senate appointee So. Growth Policies Bd., 1983; chmn. adv. coun. Lubbock Substance Abuse Prevention Partnership; mem. bd. govs. West Tex. chpt. Multiple Sclerosis; mem. Dean's Roundtable U. Tex. Sch. Law, 1988; mem. Lubbock Symphony Orch. Bd., 1997—; v.p. Jaycees, 1974; adv. group Am. Heart Assn. Tex. affiliate, 1999; co-chmn., adv. coun. Tex. LWV Edn. Fund, 1999; bd. trustees The Nature Conservancy of Tex., 1999. Maj. USMC, 1968-71. Recipient Outstanding Young Man of Lubbock award Jaycees, 1973, Headliner of Yr. award Greater Lubbock Press Club, 1979, Man of Yr./Law Enforcement award Lubbock Optimist Club, 1979, Boss of Yr. award Legal Secs. Assn., 1980, Exec. of Yr., Lubbock Sales Exec. Assn., 1981; named Finest Freshman Tex. Bus. Mag., 1983, Outstanding State Sen. Tex. Youth Commn., 1988, Legislator of Yr. Tex. Pub. Health Assn., 1988, Legislator of Yr. Tex. Pub. Employees Assn. and State Employees, 1989, Outstanding Tex. Leader award John Ben Shepperd Pub. Leadership Forum, 1989, Best New Legislator award Tex. Monthly mag., 1983, Disting. Alumni, L.D. Bell H.S., 1984, Lubbock's Man of the Yr. LWV and Am. Diabetes Assn,. 1987, Disting. Svc. award Tex. C. of C., 1989, Outstanding Legislator in State of Tex., Epsilon Sigma Phi, 1989, Legislator of Yr. award Tex. Soc. Profl. Surveyors, 1989, Legislator of Yr. award 71st Legis., Tex. Mcpl. League, 1989, Tree of Life award Jewish Nat. Fund, 1989; named one of the Ten Best Legislators 71st Legis., Dallas Morning News, Tex. Monthly, 1989, 72d Legis., 1991, Tex. Monthly, 1989, 91, Outstanding Legislator Epsilon Sigma Phi, 1989, Tex. Mcpl. League, 1989; recipient Outstanding Svc. award Tex. Electric Coops., 1989, Pub. Ofcl. award Tex. Pub. Power Assn., 1990, George Woods award in politics NAACP, 1990, Legis. Leadership award 72d Legislator Tex. C. of C., 1992, One of the Seven Best Legislators 73d Legis. Dallas Morning News, 1993, 74th Legis. Dallas Morning News, 1995, One of the Ten Best Legislators 73d Legis. Tex. Monthly, 1993, 74th Legis. Tex. Monthly, 1995, Legislator of Yr. Tex. Pub. Employees Assn., 1993, award Lubbock arts Festival, 1994, award Tex. Mental Health Assn., 1994, honor award Tex. Commn. on the Arts, 1994, Cmty. Statesman award Heritage of Odessa Found., 1995, Legislator of Yr. award Tex. Game Warden's Assn., 1995, Judy coyle Tex. Liberty award Assn. Tex. Profl. Educators, 1995, Man of Yr. in Tex. Colls. & Univs., 1995, Outstanding Legislator award Tex. Police chiefs Assn., 1995, One of Top Ten, Harte-Hanks CComm., Inc., 1995, Newsmaker of 1995, Lubbock Avalanche Jour., One of Friends of Bus. 74th Legis., Tex. Bus. Mag., 1995, Outstanding Legislator, Tex. Jr. Coll. Tchrs Assn., 1995, Integrated Pest Mgmt. award in Excellence, Nat. Found. Integrated Pest Mgmt. Edn., 1996, Paul Harris fellow Rotary Internat., 1997, Founders award Ind. Coll. and Univ. Tex., 1997, Tex. most powerful citizen Lubbock Avalanche-Jour., 1999, Road Hand award Tex. Good Roads Assn., 1999, Declaration of Gratitude Tex. Tech. Sch. Pharmacy, 2000 and numerous others. Mem. State Bar Tex. (com. admissions), Tex. Criminal Def. Lawyers Assn., Tex. Dist. and County Attys. Assn. (life, legis. com.), Western State Water Coun., Tex. Assn. Cmty. Schs. (hon. life), Tex. Heart Inst. (nat. adv. coun. 1991), Lubbock C. of C. (Disting. Svcs. award 1996), Tex. Bar Found., Order of Coif (hon.), Rotary, Lions (Lubbock club), Omicron Delta Kappa, Delta Theta Phi, Phi Kappa Phi, Kappa Sigma (Pres. Commn. 2000), Phi Beta Delta. Office: PO Box 1709 Lubbock TX 79408-1709

MONTGOMERY, ANN D. federal judge, educator; b. Litchfield, Minn., May 9, 1949; m. Theodore Smetak; 2 children; 1 stepchild. BS, U. Kans., 1971; JD, U. Minn., 1974. Bar: Minn. 1974, U.S. Dist. Ct. Minn., U.S. Ct. Appeals (8th cir.), U.S. Supreme Ct. Law clk. D.C. Ct. Appeals, Washington, 1974-75; asst. U.S. atty. Dist. Minn., Mpls., 1976-83; mcpl. judge Hennepin County, 1983-85; judge Hennepin County Dist. Ct., 1985-94, U.S. Magistrate Ct., 1994-96; federal judge U.S. Dist. Ct., Mpls., 1996—. Adj. prof. U. Minn. Law Sch., Mpls., 1988—; steering com. mem., dir. criminal divsn. Minn. Jud. Coll., 1990-94. Recipient Trial Judge of Yr. award Am. Bd. Trial Advocates, 1996. Mem. FBA, Minn. Dist. Judges Assn., Minn. Bar Assn., Minn. Women Lawyers (Myra Bradwell award 2000), Hennepin County Bar Assn. (Professionalism award 1993). Office: US Dist Ct 300 S 4th St Minneapolis MN 55415-1320 Fax: 612-664-5097. E-mail: admontgomery@mnd.uscourts.gov.

MONTGOMERY, ANNA FRANCES, elementary school educator; b. Spokane, Wash., Nov. 5, 1945; d. Carl Jacob and Edna Frances (Evans) Kuipers; m. William Lee Montgomery Jr., Oct. 7, 1989. AA, Mid. Ga. Coll., 1965; BS in Elem. Edn., Woman's Coll. of Ga., 1966; MEd, Ga. Coll., 1969, specialist in edn., 1973. Cert. elem. tchr., Ga. Classroom tchr. Muscogee County Sch. Dist., Columbus, Ga., 1966—, reading tchr. Title 1 tutorial program, summer 1975, instr. staff devel. program, 1977-80; social sci. lead tchr. Wesley Heights Elem. Sch., 1992—, chmn. mgmt. team, 1997-98. Tennis and athletic instr. Camp Tegawitha, Tobyhanna, Pa., summer 1970; presenter workshop Chattahoochee Valley Coun. for Social Studies, 1977; mem. social studies textbook adoption com. Muscogee County Sch. Dist., 1977-78, 82-83, 98-99, mem. sick leave com., 1993-95; judge Columbus Regional Social Sci. Fair, 1977, 93-96; mem. basic skills program comprehensive planning task force Muscogee County Sch. Dist., 1995-96, mem. com. to revise the basic skills program in social studies, 1980; presenter in field. Editor: Muscogee County School District's Handbook for Beginning Teachers, 1979. Treas. Wesley Heights PTA, 1983-86; vol. Med. Ctr. Aux., Columbus, 1975-79; pres. pastor's Bible study class St. Luke United Meth. Ch., 1993-94, 96, 97, 98, mem. Sarah Cir. 11, sec., 1969-71, 78-80, co-chmn., 1974-76, chmn., 1976-78; mem. Bessie Howard Ward Handbells Choir; devel. chmn. Ga. state divsn. Centennial/fellowships com. AAUW, 1974-76. Recipient Valley Forge Tchrs. medal Freedoms Found. at Valley Forge, 1975, Outstanding Tchr. of Yr. award Wesley Hts. Elem. Sch., 1975, Muscogee County Sch. Dist., 1979; named Very Important Lady award Girl Scouts Am., Columbus, 1976, Outstanding Young Woman Am., 1982. Mem. AAUW (chmn. centennial fellowship com. Columbus br. 1973-75), Ga. PTA (hon. life), Profl. Assn. Ga. Educators (bldg. rep. Muscogee County chpt. 1983—, sec. 1992-94, treas. 1994-98, pres.-elect 1998-2000, Muscogee County's sys. rep. to the state 2000—), Nat. Coun. Social Studies (mem. hostess and registration coms. ann. meeting 1975), Ga. Coun. for Social Studies, Ga. Sci. Tchrs. Assn., Atlanta Alumni Club, Valley Area Sci. Tchrs. (corr. sec. 1996-98), Ga. Coll. Alumni Assn., Mid. Ga. Coll. Alumni Assn., Order of Amaranth (charity 1991-93, 95, truth 1994, assoc. conductress 1996, conductress 1997, assoc. matron 1998, royal matron 1999), Scottish Rite Ladies Aux., Alpha Delta Kappa (Rho chpt., sec. 1975-76, pres.-elect 1976-78, pres. 1978-80, chaplain, 1996-98), Delta Kappa Gamma (Beta Xi chpt., pres. 1980-82, chmn. pubs. and publicity 1976-78, chmn. profl. affairs 1978-80, nominations com. chair 1980-82, chmn. world fellowship and fund raising 1984-86, 96-2000, chmn. fin. 1990-92, chmn. membership 1994-96, 2000-02), Order Internat. Fellowship in Edn., Wesley Heights Elem. Sch. PTA, Phi Delta Kappa (Chattahoochee Valley Ga. chpt.). Avocations: reading, gardening, travel, fishing, playing clarinet and handbells. Home: 5134 Stone Gate Dr Columbus GA 31909-5573

MONTGOMERY, ANNE M. family practice physician, educator, consultant; b. Ft. Wayne, Ind., June 11, 1960; d. James L. and Iris M. Montgomery. BA, St. Olaf Coll., Northfield, Minn., 1981; MD, Mayo Med. Sch., 1986. Diplomate Am. Bd. Family Practice; cert. Internat. Bd. Lactation Cons. Resident in family practice St. John's unit U. Minn., 1986-89; pvt. practice, Northfield, Minn., 1989-94; mem. family practice residency faculty Providence-St. Peter Hosp., Olympia, Wash., 1994—. Clin. asst. prof. U. Minn. Med. Sch., Mpls., 1990-94; clin. assoc. prof. U. Wash. Sch. Medicine, Seattle, 1994—. Editor: Having Children, 1999; contbr. articles and revs. to med. jours., including Family Medicine, Family Practice Mgmt., Jour. Human Lactation, Birth, Western Jour. Medicine, Mothering mag., Primary Care Clinics N.Am. Fellow Am. Acad. Family Physicians (chmn. com. on women in family medicine 1992-94); mem. Internat. Lactation Cons. Assn., Wash. Acad. Family Physicians (chpt. pres. 1994—), La Leche League Med. Assocs., Acad. Breast Feeding Medicine (bd. dirs. 1998—). Office: Group Health Coop 700 Lilly Rd NE Olympia WA 98506-5101 E-mail: annemont@u.washington.edu.

MONTGOMERY, BETTY DEE, state attorney general, former state legislator; BA, Bowling Green State U.; JD, U. Toledo, 1976. Former criminal clk. Lucas County Common Pleas Ct.; asst. pros. atty. Wood County, Ohio, 1977—78, pros. atty., 1981—88, City of Perrysburg, 1978—81; mem. Ohio Senate, 1989—94; atty. gen. State of Ohio, Columbus, 1995—. Mem.: Wood County Bar Assn. Office: Attorney Generals Office State Office Tower 30 E Broad St Columbus OH 43215-3414*

MONTGOMERY, CHARLES HARVEY, lawyer; b. Spartanburg, S.C., Jan. 28, 1949; s. Dan Hugh and Ann Louise (Gasque) M.; m. Renée Jean Gubernot, Mar. 27, 1971; children: Charles Scott, Marie Renée. BA, Duke U., 1971; JD, Vanderbilt U., 1974. Bar: N.C. 1974, U.S. Dist. Ct. (ea. dist.) N.C. 1974, U.S. Supreme Ct. 1979, U.S. Dist. Ct. (mid. dist.) N.C. 1991; cert. family law specialist, N.C., 1995. Assoc. Jordan Morris & Hoke, Raleigh, N.C., 1974-75; atty. Wake County Legal Svcs., 1975-76; pvt. practice, 1977; ptnr. Montgomery & Montgomery, Cary, N.C., 1978-79, Sanford Adams McCullough & Beard, Raleigh, 1979-86, Adams McCullough & Beard, Raleigh, 1986-88, Toms Reagan & Montgomery, Cary, 1989-92, Toms & Montgomery, Cary, 1992-93; pvt. practice, 1993—. Bd. dirs. Br. Bank and Trust, Cary; pres. Family Law Mediation, Inc. Councilman Town of Cary, 1977-81, 83-87; vice-chmn. Wake County Dem. party, Raleigh, 1991-92; commr. Wake County, Raleigh, 1992; bd. dirs. East Cen. Cmty. Legal Svcs., Inc., 1997—, State Capitol Found., 1994—. Mem.: ABA, N.C. Acad. Trial Lawyers (chair family law sect. 1996—98), Wake County Bar Assn. (bd. dirs. 1999—2001), N.C. Bar Assn. (chmn. pub. info. com. 1994—96, dir. family law coun. 1994—97). Methodist. Avocation: sailing. Office: PO Box 1325 590 New Waverly Pl Ste 110 Cary NC 27512-1325 E-mail: charles@montylaw.com.

MONTGOMERY, CHARLES HOWARD, retired bank executive; b. Bloomington, Ill., Mar. 23, 1930; s. Dewey H. and Madeline (Wonderlin) M.; m. Diane Dickerson Cohen, Aug. 30, 1978 (dec. Oct. 1996); children: Alison, Douglas; m. Katharine Yang, Oct. 4, 1997. AB, Ill. Wesleyan U., 1951; MS, U. Ill., 1960. CPA, Ill. Auditor Lybrand Ross Bros. & Montgomery, Rockford, Ill., 1955-59; with Abbott Labs., North Chicago, 1959-67, controller, 1965-67; v.p. finance Anchor Coupling Co., Libertyville, 1967-69; v.p., comptroller First Nat. Bank Chgo., 1969-73, sr. v.p., 1973-75, exec. v.p., 1976-88, comptroller, 1973-88, First Chgo. Corp.; ret. Past chmn. Inter-Assn. Com. Bank Acctg. Served with AUS, 1952-53. Mem. Fin. Execs. Inst., AICPA, Ill. Soc. CPAs, Tau Kappa Epsilon, Phi Kappa Phi, Univ. Club (Chgo.) Home: 6321 N Avers Ave Chicago IL 60659-1001 also: 908B Frances St Key West FL 33040-3360 also: 6321 N Avers Ave Chicago IL 60659-1001 E-mail: chmontye@att.net.

MONTGOMERY, CLEOTHUS, minister; b. Henderson, Tex., Dec. 6, 1926; s. Lewis and Amanda (Waters) M.; m. Emma Agusta Tinch (dec. Aug. 23, 1987); children: Michael Dennis, Debra Marie, Pamela Key, Diane Renea, Anthony Cleothus (dec.). BS in Drafting, Calif. Coll., 1951; B in Theology, Union Bapt. Theol. Sem., 1962; M in Theology, Inter Bapt. Theol. Sem., 1965, DD, 1973; D in Sacred Theol. (hon.), Mt. Hope Bible Coll., 1973; M in Ministry, Trinity Theol. Sem., 1990, D in Ministry, 1993. Cert. christian counselor, Tex. Minister Northside Missionary Bapt. Ch., Houston, 1962—. Counselor Chemical Dependency, Houston, 1989-97, Internat. Christian Isnt., 1990-97; invited pastor by Campus for Christ to Israel, 1987, Africa, 1990, Russia, 1995-97. Pres. World Christian Tng. Ctr., Houston, 1985-90, Houston Minister Christian Fellowship, 1992-97; chmn. Minister Network Life Gift, Houston, 1988-90, Ministers Against Crime, Houston, 1989-97; treas. Life Investment for Tng., Houston, 1990-97; v.p. Ministerial Adv. to Mayor, Houston, 1995-97; trustee bd. of regency, adv. bd. Coll. of Biblical Studies. With U.S. Army, 1945-46. Mem. NAACP, Am. Assn. Christian Counselors (chemical dependency counselor 1993-97). Democrat. Baptist. Avocations: reading, devotional writings, bowling, traveling, jogging. Home: 1407 Laurentide St Houston TX 77029-3411 Office: Northside Missionary Bapt Ch 3202 Bennington St Houston TX 77093-9222

MONTGOMERY, CRANSTON PARKER, retired lawyer; b. Long Beach, Calif., June 16, 1922; s. Cranston Parker and Julia Louise Montgomery; m. Patricia Sutherland Austin, Feb. 17, 1947; children: Lynn Louise Weintraub, Joan Elizabeth Shutman, Edward Austin, Patricia Anne. AA, Pasadena (Calif.) Jr. Coll., 1942; AB, U. Calif., Berkeley, 1947, LLB, 1950. Bar: Calif., U.S. Ct. Appeals (9th cir.). Assoc. Ackerman & Mathews & E. Conrad Connella, San Francisco, 1951-53; with Union Carbide Corp., 1953-65, atty.-in-charge, 1965-66; staff atty. Hughes Aircraft Co., Culver City, 1966-75, group counsel, 1975-89; ptnr. Montgomery & Montgomery, Pasadena, 1989-98. 1st lt. USAF, 1943-45, ETO. Decorated Disting. Flying Cross. Mem. ABA, State Bar Calif., Pasadena Bar Assn., L.A. County Bar Assn., Altadena Town Country Club. Republican. Avocation: golf. Home: 1550 Meadowbrook Rd Altadena CA 91001

MONTGOMERY, DAVID BRUCE, marketing educator; b. Fargo, N.D., Apr. 30, 1938; s. David William and Iva Bernice (Trask) Montgomery; m. Toby Marie Franks, June 11, 1960; children: David Richard, Scott Bradford, Pamela Marie. BSEE, Stanford U., 1960, MBA, 1962, MS in Stats., 1964, PhD in Mgmt. Sci., 1966; D honoris causa, Limburgs U. Centrum, Belgium, 1998. Asst. prof. mgmt. MIT, 1966-69, assoc. prof., 1969-70; assoc. prof. mktg. and mgmt. sci. Stanford U., 1970-73, prof., 1973-78, Robert A. Magowan prof. mktg., 1978-92, Sebastian S. Kregge prof. mktg. strategy, 1992-99, prof. emeritus, 1999—. Prin. The MAC Group Inc., 1969-91; mem. adv. bd. LEK Partnership, London; mem. sci. adv. bd. Univ. Connection, Bonn, Germany; acad. trustee Mktg. Sci. Inst., 1994-2000, exec. dir., 1995-97. Author: (with Glen L. Urban) Management Science in Marketing, 1969, (with Massy and Morrison) Stochastic Models of Buying Behavior, 1970, (with Day et al) Planning: Cases in Computer and Model Assisted Marketing, 1973, (with others) Consumer Behavior: Theoretical Sources, 1973, (with G. J. Eskin) Data Analysis, 1975; editor 5 books; assoc. editor Jour. Internat. Mktg., 2000—; mem. editl. bd. Mgmt. Sci., Jour. Mktg. Rsch., Mktg. Sci., Jour. Internat. Mktg.; contbr. more than 90 articles and tech. reports to sci. and profl. jours. Trustee Family Service Assn. of Mid Peninsula, 1972-73. Recipient citation for outstanding contbns. to use of computers in mgmt. edn. Hewlett Packard, 1977, Best Paper award for outstanding contbn. to strategic mgmt. Strategic Mgmt. Soc., 1996, AMA Mahajan award for sustained contbns. to mktg. strategy, 2002. Fellow Royal Statis. Soc.; mem. Inst. Mgmt. Scis., Am. Mktg. Assn., Econometric Soc., Am. Inst. Decision Scis., Tau Beta Pi. Republican. Congregationalist. Home: 960 Wing Pl Stanford CA 94305-1028 Office: Stanford U Grad Sch Bus Stanford CA 94305 E-mail: montgomery_david@gsb.stanford.edu.

MONTGOMERY, DAVID CAMPBELL, physicist, educator; b. Milan, Mar. 5, 1936; s. Merrill Edward and Ruth E. (Campbell) M.; m. Shirley Arlene Imig, July 20, 1957; children: Kathleen Montgomery Sutton, Elizabeth. Student, U. Mo., 1953-55; BS, U. Wis., 1956; MA, Princeton, 1958, PhD, 1959; D honoris causa, Eindhoven U. of Tech., The Netherlands, 1996. Research assoc. Princeton U., 1959-60; instr. U. Wis., 1961-62; asst. prof. U. Md., 1962-65; assoc. prof. U. Iowa, Iowa City, 1965-70, prof., 1970-77; prof. physics Coll. William and Mary, Williamsburg, Va., 1977-84; prof. Dartmouth Coll., Hanover, N.H., 1984-88, Eleanor and A. Kelvin Smith prof. physics, 1988—. Vis. prof., rschr. U. Colo., 1966, U. Alaska, 1968, U. Calif.-Berkeley, 1969-70, Bell Labs., 1971, U. Wis., 1989; lectr. Internat. Summer Sch. Theoretical Physics, Les Houches, France, 1972, U. Wis., Madison, 1973; vis. prof. Hunter campus CUNY, 1973-74, U. Nagoya, Japan, 1983, Columbia U., N.Y.C., 1985, Tech. U., Eindhoven, The Netherlands, spring 1992; vis. scientist Nat. Ctr. Atmospheric Rsch., Boulder, Colo., summers 1975, 76, 79, 87, 2002, Riso Nat. Lab., Roskilde, Denmark, 2001; cons. NASA Hdqs., Washington, 1977-82, JET Joint Undertaking, Culham, U.K., fall 1991; vis. rsch. prof. U. Md., 1977-84; mem. vis. staff Los Alamos Sci. Lab., summers 1977, 78, 79, 80, 81, 86, 91, 92, 94; cons., collaborator, vis. staff mem. Los Alamos Sci. Lab.; former cons. Oak Ridge Nat. Lab., NASA; vis. rschr. Los Alamos Nat. Lab., 1987-88, cons., 1998-2000; J.M. Burgers prof. Eindhoven Tech. U., The Netherlands, 1995-96, 97, 98, 99, 2000, 01, U. Md., 1997; vis. rschr. Courant Inst. NYU, 1997. Former assoc. editor: Physics of Fluids, Internat. Jour. Engring. Sci.; contbr. more than 150 rsch. articles to profl. publs.; also monographs. Fellow Am. Phys. Soc.; mem. N.Y. Acad. Scis., Phi Beta Kappa, Sigma Xi, Pi Mu Epsilon, Phi Mu Alpha. Achievements include introduction of modern fluid turbulence methods into space and controlled fusion theory; developed maximum entropy, or "most probable" states, method of describing coherent structures achieved as a product of turbulent relaxation. Home: 46 River Rd PO Box 190 Hanover NH 03755-0190 Office: Dartmouth College Physics Dept Hanover NH 03755

MONTGOMERY, DAVID PAUL, professional baseball team executive; b. Phila. m. Lyn Sagendorph. BA in History, U. Pa., 1968; MBA, Wharton Sch., U. Pa., 1970. With Phila. Phillies, 1971—, successively mem. sales dept., dir. mktg., dir. sales, formerly exec. v.p., COO, pres., CEO, now mng. ptnr, pres., CEO.*

MONTGOMERY, DAVID RANDOLPH, aeronautical engineer; b. Altadena, Calif., Dec. 24, 1947; s. Randolph Briscoe Montgomery and Alma Leona Stewart; m. Clarice Marie Riggers, Sept. 16, 1972; children: Faith Faye, Aura Jane, Malia Janae. AA in Physics, Chabot Coll., 1968; BS in Physics, Santa Clara U., 1980. Test technician submarine launched ballistic missile program Lockheed Co., Sunnyvale, Calif., 1974-80; test engr. 767 comml. plane divsn. Boeing Co., Everett, Wash., 1980-84, test engr. B-2 stealth bomber, mil. airplanes divsn. Seattle, 1984-92, sys. adminstr. 777 comml. airplane divsn. Everett, 1992-96, test engr. F-22 fighter program mil. airplanes divsn. Seattle, 1996—. Author: The New World Government Exposed!, 2000, 2001. Candidate for U.S. Congress, 2d Congl. Dist., Wash., 1992, 94; pres. Vet. Meml. Day Com., Seattle, 1987-91; exec. dir. Freedom Internat., Edmonds, Wash., 1984-92. With USAF, 1970-74. Mem. AIAA. Avocation: oil painting. Office: Boeing Co F-22 Mil Airplane & Missile Sys Divsn M/S 4J-20 PO Box 3707 Seattle WA 98124-2207

MONTGOMERY, DAVID WILSON, music educator; b. Gastonia, NC, Apr. 29, 1976; s. Lydia Smith and Smith Michael; m. Annette Therese Peitzman. MusB, U. N.C., Greensboro, 1998. Band dir. East Gaston H.S., Mt. Holly, NC, 1998—2002. Mem.: N.C. Music Educators Assn., Music Educators Nat. Conf., Pi Kappa Lambda. Office: East Gaston HSl 1744 Lane Road Mount Holly NC 28120

MONTGOMERY, DILLARD BREWSTER, musician, educator; b. Memphis, Jan. 1, 1936; s. Mary Joyce Montgomery; m. Joyce Helena Beale, Dec. 9, 1965; 1 child, Lisa Jenean. BS, Tenn. State U., 1962, MA, 1968. Profl. musician Nashville Assn. Musicians, 1958—; band dir., keyboardist The New Imperials, Nashville, 1962—; tchr. Met. Nashville Schs., 1962-94, ret., 1994; asst. prin. W.A. Bass Middle Sch., 1984-93, prin., 1993-94. Choir dir. John Wesley United Meth. Ch., Nashville, 1958—, Dixon United Meth. Ch., 1970-71, Braden United Meth. Ch., 1985—; profl. model Terrance Hurd Agy., 1999—. Served with USAF, 1955-58. Mem. NEA, Tenn. Edn. Assn., Met. Nashville Edn. Assn., Nat. Musicians Union, Tenn. State U. Alumni Assn., Alpha Phi Alpha (life). Democrat. Methodist. Avocations: electronics, photography, traveling. Home: 638 W Nocturne Dr Nashville TN 37207 E-mail: dmontg1@bellsouth.net.

MONTGOMERY, EDWARD BRUCE, economics educator; b. N.Y.C., July 3, 1955; s. David and Martel Laneda (Wilcher) M.; m. Kari Lynn McPeck, Oct. 7, 1994; children: Elizabeth Joan, Lindsay Martel, Edward Julius. BS, Pa. State U., 1976; MA, Harvard U., 1980, PhD, 1982. Estimator, planner

Eastman Kodak Co., Rochester, N.Y., 1976-77; teaching fellow Harvard U., Cambridge, Mass., 1979-81; rsch. assoc. Bd. Govs. Fed. Res., Washington, 1980; asst. prof. Carnegie Mellon U., Pitts., 1981-86; assoc. prof. Mich. State U., East Lansing, 1986-90; assoc. prof. econs. U. Md., College Park, 1990-92, prof. econ., 1992—. Vis. scholar Bd. Govs. Fed. Res., 1983-84; Ameritech fellow Case Western Res. U., Cleve., 1988; Ford Found. scholar Nat. Bur. Econ. Rsch., Cambridge, 1989; cons. Fed. Res. Bank Cleve., 1985-86, Urban League Pa., Pitts., 1986, Friend of the Ct.-Mich., Lansing, 1988-89, Mich. Dept. Transp., Lansing, 1989; chief economist U.S. Dept. of Labor, 1997-98, asst. sec. for policy, 1999-2000, dep. sec. labor, 2000-2001. Contbr. articles to profl. publs. Mem. Am. Econ. Assn., Nat. Econ. Assn., Midwest Econ. Assn., Phi Kappa Phi. Avocations: scuba diving, rugby, squash, running, reading.

MONTGOMERY, GILLESPIE V. (SONNY MONTGOMERY), former congressman; b. Meridian, Miss., Aug. 5, 1920; s. Gillespie M. and Emily (Jones) M. BS, Miss. State U. Mem. Miss. Senate, 1956-66, 90th-104th Congresses from 3rd Miss. Dist., 1967-96; chmn. vets. affairs com., 1981-94; mem. vets. affairs com., chmn. spl. com. on S.E. Asia 90th-102d Congresses, 1978-96; ranking minority mem., 1994-96; mem. armed services. com. 90th-103d Congresses, chmn. select com. on missing persons in southeast Asia, 1975-96; mem. vets. affairs com.; mem. Woodcock Commn., 1977; CEO, pres. The Montgomery Group, Alexandria, Va., 1997—. Pres. Miss. N.G. Assn., 1959; pres. Miss. Heart Assn., 1967-68. Served with AUS, World War II, Korea, ret. maj. gen. Miss N.G. Decorated Bronze Star medal, Combat Inf. Badge; recipient Miss. Magnolia award, 1966, Lifetime Achievement award Mil. Educators & Counselors Assn., 1992. Mem. VFW, Am. Legion 40 and 8, Congl. Prayer Breakfast Group (pres. 1970) Lodges: Masons; Shriners; Scottish Rite. Episcopalian. Office: The Montgomery Group 11 Canal Center Plz Ste 104 Alexandria VA 22314-1595

MONTGOMERY, HENRY IRVING, financial planner; b. Dec. 18, 1924; s. Harry Biggs and Martha Grace (Wilkinson) M.; m. Barbara Louise Hook, Aug. 14, 1948; children: Barbara Ruth, Michael Henry, Kelly Ann, Andrew Stuart. Student, U. Iowa, 1942-43, 47-48; BBA, Tulane U., 1952; postgrad., U. Minn., 1976. CFP, Colo. Field agt. OSS, SSU, CIG, CIA, Cen. Europe, 1945-47; pres. Nehi Bottling Co., Decorah, Iowa, 1952-64; prin. Montgomery Assocs., Mktg. Cons., Trieste, Italy and Iowa, 1965-72; pres. Planners Fin. Svcs., Inc., Mpls., 1972-95, chmn., 1992—. Prin. Montgomery Investment Mgmt., 1992—. Author: Race Toward Berlin, 1945. With U.S. Army, 1943-46, ETO. Decorated Bronze Star; recipient P. Kemp Fain Profl. Svc. award, 1998; Montgomery scholarship awarded annually, 2001--. Mem. Inst. CFPs (bd. dirs. 1977-82, pres. 1980-81, chmn. 1981-82, CFP of Yr. 1984, chmn. fin. products stds. bd. 1984-88), Nat. Assn. Securities Dealers (mem. dist. 8 com. 1988-91, vice chmn. 1990), Internat. Assn. Fin. Planning Assn. (internat. dir. 1976-81, Minn. chpt. creation of scholarships in name of Henry & Andrew Montgomery Scholarships), Mpls. Estate Planning Coun., Met. Tax Planning Group (pres. 1984-87), Twin City Fin. Planners (pres. 1976-78), Twin Cities Soc. of Inst. CFPs, Am. Legion, Elks (Decorah), Beta Gamma Sigma. Avocations: Italian and German languages. Office: Planners Fin Svcs Inc 7710 Computer Ave Ste 100 Minneapolis MN 55435-5417

MONTGOMERY, HUGH EVERETT, JR. civilian military employee; b. Jackson, Miss., July 9, 1944; s. Hugh Everett and Clara (Neelly) M.; m. Liller Markel, May 19, 1966; children: Melinda Dawn, Michelle Elise. BS in Physics and Math., Miss. Coll., 1966; MS in Physics, U. Tenn., 1969, postgrad., 1969-70; diploma, Kennedy Sch. Govt. Harvard U., 1989. Rsch. physicist Naval Surface Warfare Ctr., Dahlgren, Va., 1966-72, dir. tech. br., 1972-79; dir. rsch. Naval Sea Systems Command, Washington, 1979-80; dir. planning and programming Office Naval Tech., 1980-81; industry ind. R&D mgr. Office Chief Naval Material, 1981-84; tech. dir. tech. assessment div. Office Chief Naval Ops., 1985-86, dep. dir. sci. and tech. div., 1986-90, dir. sci. and tech. divsn., 1990-98, dep. dir. test and evaluation and tech. requirements, 1999-2000; tech. dir. Marine Corps Warfighting Lab., 2001—; dir. Naval Rsch. Enterprise, 2001—. Exec. dir. Navy sci. and tech. requirements com. Office Chief Naval Ops., 1989-2000, chmn. Navy sci. and tech. working group, 1985-2000; chmn. Navy industry R & D bd. Office Chief Naval Material, 1982-84. Patentee in field; contbr. articles to profl. jours. Organizer, leader Sea Walker's Quartet, Fredericksburg, Va., 1979-99; spokesman Friends of the Rappahannock, Fredericksburg, 1986—, North Ferry Farm Civic Assn., Fredericksburg, 1972-80, Fredericksburg Environ. Group, 1974-78; deacon Ferry Farm Bapt. Ch., 1986—, deacon vice chmn., 2001, deacon chmn., 2002; tchr., 1974—; mem. devel. commn. Rappahannock Area, 1995—, mem. transp. adv. group, 1994—; mem. transp. adv. com. Spotsylvania County, 1994—; v.p. River Bluffs Owner's Assn., 1995-2000; chmn. Spotsylvania County Planning Commn., 1997, 2000, vice chmn., 1996. Recipient Navy Disting. Civilian Svc. award, 1992, 2001, Navy Superior Civilian Svc. award, 1987; named Presdl. Meritorious Exec., 1990. Mem. Fed. Exec. Inst. Alumni Assn., River Bluffs Civic Assn., Audubon Soc., Fredericksburg Sister City Assn., Miss. Soc. Washington, Harvard Kennedy Sch. Alumni Assn., Naval Acad. Alumni Assn., Sigma Pi Sigma, Omicron Delta Kappa. Avocations: boating, music, home construction, photography, church activities. Home: 3 River Oak Pl Fredericksburg VA 22407-2321 Office: Office of Chief of Naval Ops Code N911 2000 Navy Pentagon Washington DC 20350-2000

MONTGOMERY, JAMES HUEY, state government administrator, consultant; b. New Albany, Miss., Dec. 2, 1942; s. James Columbus and Ethel Louise (Todd) M.; children: Angela Lee, Leslie Louise; m. Sandra Jan Firnhaber, Apr. 25, 1998; stepchildren: Justine Firnhaber-Baker, Vanessa Firhaber-Baker. B degree, Wayne State U., 1991. Border patrol agt. U.S. Border Patrol, Calexico, Calif., 1964-66, Miami, Fla., 1967-71; spl. agt. U.S. Immigration and Naturalization, San Francisco, 1971-75, Chgo., 1975-76, Ft. Snelling, Minn., 1976-78, asst. regional commr., 1978-82, dist. dir. Detroit, 1982-93, ret., 1993; pres. Guard Well Inc., 1994—. Dir.. enforcement Bur. Comml. Svcs. Mich. Dept. Consumer and Industry Sv., Lansing, 1995-2001; dir. Tax Compliance Ctr., Mich. Dept. Treasury, Lansing, 2001—. Mem. Leadership Detroit, 1991—; mem. Mich. polit. leadership program Mich. State U., 1993—. 1st lt. U.S. Army, 1966-69. Recipient Appreciation award Korean Soc. Detroit, 1987, Chaldean Fedn. Am., 1988, Chaldean Kiwanis Club, 1988, Cmty. Appreciation award TV Orient, 1993, Appreciation award Arab Am. Chaldean Assn., 1993. Mem. Immigration Dirs. Assn. (chmn. 1988-91, dep. chmn. 1985-88), Internat. Border Assn. (pres. 1986, bd. dirs. 1982-93), Southeastern Mich. Chiefs of Police, Golden Key, Fed. Exec. Bd. (policy com. 1985-93, quality mgmt. com. 1992-93), Arab Am. C. of C. Detroit (bd. dirs. 1994), Internat. Inst. of Detroit (bd. dirs. 1995-96, adv. bd. 1996-97). Baptist. Avocations: photography, golf, computers. Home and Office: 3821 Thistlewood Rd Okemos MI 48864-3818

MONTGOMERY, JAMES ISSAC, JR. lawyer; b. Louisville, Apr. 18, 1956; s. James Isaac Sr. and Marie Ann M.; m. Charnette; children: Gwendolyn, Jennifer, James III. BA, Northwestern U.; JD, UCLA, 1981. With Gibbs, Giden Locher & Turner, L.A. Mem. ABA, Nat. Bar Assn., African-Am. Ins. Profls., Assn. So. Calif. Def. Coun., John M. Langston Bar Assn. (pres. 1996). Office: Gibbs Giden Locher & Turner 2029 Century Park E Fl 34 Los Angeles CA 90067-2901 E-mail: jimontgomery@gglt.com.

MONTGOMERY, JERRY LYNN, retired education educator; b. Owensville, Ind., Apr. 21, 1935; s. Philip Matthew and Lois Caroline (Anderson) M.; m. Murelyn Ann Rogers, Sept. 21, 1957 (div. Apr. 1976); stepchildren: Rebecca Williams Slominski, Matthew Williams; m. Gretchen Wendelroth Golzè, May 14, 1977; children: Robin Schneider, Lori Abbott, Vicki Randolph. BS, Purdue U., 1957; MA, Ball State U., 1964, EdD, 1969. Vocat. agrl. Milton (Ind.) Pub. Schs., 1957-58, Carthage (Ind.) Pub. Schs., 1958-61; sci. tchr. Angola (Ind.) City Schs., 1961-66; grad. asst. Ball State U., 1966-69, asst. prof. biology, 1969; edn. prof. Marietta (Ohio) Coll., 1969—2001; sci. educator Project Discovery, Athens, Ohio, 1994-99; Discovery dir. Dist. #11, 1997-98. Goal #4 com. Marietta (Ohio) City Schs., 1993-96, grade 4 profiency test content rev. and rangefinder coms. Ohio Dept. of Edn., Columbus, Ohio, 1994-2002; mem. young engrs. and scientists Marietta Telesis Group, Marietta, 1992-96; vis. prof. physics Ohio State U., 1994. Recipient Outstanding Educator Martha Holden Jennings Found., 1989. Mem. Assn. of Tchr. Educators (credentials com. 1991-2000), Nat. Sci. Tchrs. Assn., Sci. Edn. Coun. Ohio, Ohio Acad. of Sci., Phi Delta Kappa. Avocations: reading, canoeing, traveling, fishing, camping. Home: 105 Rathbone Ter Marietta OH 45750-1443 Office: Marietta Coll 215 5th St Marietta OH 45750-4033 E-mail: montgomj@marietta.edu.

MONTGOMERY, JOEL ROBERT, communications executive, consultant; b. Lexington, Ky., Sept. 9, 1946; s. Joseph Gwinn and Lucille O'Hair Montgomery. AA, U. Fla., 1966; BA, Fla. State U., 1968; MEd, EdD, Fla. Internat. U., 1992. Cert. group leader educator MATC, 1978, orgnl. develop. MATC, 1979. Commd. 2d lt. U.S. Army, 1969, advanced through grades to capt., ret., 1979; mgmt. cons. Coopers & Lybrand (now PriceWaterhouseCoopers), L.A., 1979—80; regional cons. interaction mgmt. Develop. Dimensions Internat., 1981—82; pres., cons. coach Resources Inst., Hollywood, Fla., 1982—93; mgr. learning arch. Andersen Cons. (now Accenture), St. Charles, Ill., 1993—98; sr. lead bus. cons. orgnl. change Origin Tech. in Bus. (now Atos-Origin), Dallas, 1999—2000; CEO, performance coach MetaLearning-.com, LLC, Geneva, 2000—. Pres. Internat. Inst. Develop. of Human Resources, Bogota, Colombia, 1982; adj. instr. Fla. Internat. U., Miami, 1989—91; performance coach, spkr., cons. Practical Bus. Assessments, Geneva, 2001—; adj. instr. Lake Forest (Ill.) Grad. Sch. Mgmt., 2002—. Author: (book) Catalog of Workshop-Seminar Materials for The Resources Institute and INDER-HU, 1983, Human Relations Workbook--The Human Side of Teaching, 1990, (Book) The Development, Application and Implications of a Strategy for Reflective Learning from Experience, 1992; contbr. articles. Men. Am. Red Cross, Washington, 1964—; chmn. bd. dirs. Am. Red Cross, Fox River chpt., St. Charles, 1993—96; bd. dirs. Am. Red Cross, Broward County chpt., Ft. Lauderdale, 1990—92. Captain United States Army, 1969—79, Global assignments. Recipient Joint Svc. Commendation medal, U.S. Army, 1975. Mem.: Ednl. Soc. Resource Mgmt., Am. Soc. Tng. & Develop., Orgnl. Develop Network, Internat. Found. Action Learning (leadership team U.S. chpt. 1995—2002), Acad. Human Resources Develop. (bd. dirs. 1997—99). Avocations: swimming, travel. Office: MetaLearning-.com LLC 717 Anderson Blvd Geneva IL 60134-1246 Office Fax: 630-626-7014. Personal E-mail: joelmonty@usa.net. Business E-Mail: joelmonty@MetaLearning.com.

MONTGOMERY, JOHN DICKEY, political science educator; b. Evanston, Ill., Feb. 15, 1920; s. Charles William and Lora Kathryn (Dickey) M.; m. Jane Ireland, Dec. 19, 1954; children— Faith, Patience, John. AB, Kalamazoo Coll., 1941, A.M., 1942, LL.D., 1962; A.M., Harvard, 1948, PhD, 1951. Dir. devel. research center African studies program Boston U., 1961-63; prof. pub. adminstrn. Harvard U., 1963-86, Ford Found. prof. internat. studies, 1987—90, chmn. dept. govt., 1980-84; dir. Pacific Basin Rsch. Ctr. Soka U. Am., L.A., 1991—, emeritus prof., 1990. Author: The Purge in Occupied Japan, 1953, Forced to be Free, 1957, The Politics of Foreign Aid, 1962, Foreign Aid in International Politics, 1967, Technology and Civic Life, 1974, Aftermath, Tarnished Outcomes of American Foreign Policy, 1986, Bureaucrats and People, 1988; editor: Values in Education, Social Capital Formation in Asia and the Pacific, 1997, Human Rights, Positive Policies in Asia and the Pacific Rim, 1998, (jours.) Pub. Policy, 1963-67, Policy Scis., 1999-01; co-editor: (with Dennis Rondinelli) Great Policies, Strategic Innovations in Asia and the Pacific Basin, 1995, (with Alex Inkeles) Social Capital as a Policy Resource, 2001; (with Nathan Glazer) Sovereignty Under Challenge, How Governments Respond, 2002. Home: 36 Hyde Ave Newton MA 02458-2311 Office: Harvard U 79 Jfk St Cambridge MA 02138-5801

MONTGOMERY, JOHN RICHARD, pediatrician, educator; b. Burnsville, Miss., Oct. 24, 1934; s. Guy Austin and Harriet Pauline (Owens) M.; m. Dottye Ann Newell, June 26, 1965; children: John Newell, Michelle Elizabeth. BS, U. Ala., 1955, MD, 1958. Intern U. Miss., Jackson, 1958-59, resident in pediat., 1959-60, Baylor Coll. Medicine, Houston, 1960-61, fellow in pediat. infectious diseases and immunoloty, 1964-66, asst. prof. pediat., 1966-70, assoc. prof., 1970-75; chief pediat. programs U. Ala. Sch. Medicine, Huntsville, 1975-95, prof., 1975-97, prof. emeritus, 1997—. Bd. dirs. State Bd. Health, Ala. Bd. Med. Examiners; adv. com. Ala. EMS for Children. Contbr. articles to books and profl. jours. Served with AUS, 1961-62, Korea, col. USAR ret. With AUS, 1961—62, col. USAR. Mem. Soc. Pediat. Rsch., Am. Assn. Immunologists, Infectious Diseases Soc., N.Y. Acad. Scis., Am. Acad. Pediats. (pres. Ala. chpt. 1991-93), Sigma Xi, Phi Beta Kappa. Achievements include assisting in development of germ-free invironmental bubble to protect patient with no natural immunity (patient later subject of movie The Boy in the Plastic Bubble, 1976). Personal E-mail: dnjrmont@bellsouth.net.

MONTGOMERY, JOHN WARWICK, law educator, theologian; b. Warsaw, Oct. 18, 1931; s. Maurice Warwick and Harriet (Smith) M.; m. Joyce Ann Bailer, Aug. 14, 1954; children: Elizabeth Ann, Catherine Ann; m. Lanalee de Kant, Aug. 26, 1988; 1 adopted child, Jean-Marie. Baron of Kiltartan and Lord of Morris. Comte de St. Germain de Montgommery. AB in Philosophy with distinction, Cornell U., 1952; BLS, U. Calif., Berkeley, 1954, MA, 1958; BD, Wittenberg U., 1958, MST, 1960; PhD, U. Chgo., 1962; Docteur de l'Université, mention Théologie Protestante, U. Strasbourg, France, 1964; LLB, LaSalle Extension U., 1977; diplôme cum laude, Internat. Inst. Human Rights, Strasbourg, 1978; MPhil in Law, U. Essex, Eng., 1983; D in Civil and Canon Law (hon.), Inst. Religion and Law, Moscow, 1999; LLM, Cardiff U., Wales, 2000. Bar: Va. 1978, Calif. 1979, D.C. 1985, Wash. 1990, U.S. Supreme Ct. 1981, Eng. 1984; lic. real estate broker Calif.; cert. law librarian; diplomate Med. Library Assn.; ordained to ministry Luth. Ch., 1958. Librarian, gen. reference service U. Calif. Library, Berkeley, 1954-55; instr. Bibl. Hebrew, Hellenistic Greek, Medieval Latin Wittenberg U., Springfield, Ohio, 1956-59; head librarian Swift Libr. div. and Philosophy, mem. federated theol. faculty U. Chgo., 1959-60; assoc. prof., chmn. dept. history Wilfred Laurier U. (formerly Waterloo Luth. U.), Ont., Can., 1960-64; prof., chmn. div. ch. history, history of Christian thought, dir. European Seminar program Trinity Evang. Div. Sch., Deerfield, Ill., 1964-74; prof. law and theology George Mason U. Sch. Law (formerly Internat. Sch. of Law), Arlington, Va., 1974-75; theol. cons. Christian Legal Soc., 1975-76; dir. studies Internat. Inst. Human Rights, Strasbourg, France, 1979-81; founding dean, prof. jurisprudence, dir. European program Simon Greenleaf U. Sch. Law, Anaheim, Calif., 1980-88; lic. disting. prof. theology and law, dir. European program Faith Evang. Luth. Sem., Tacoma, 1989-91; from prin. lectr. to reader in law Luton U., Eng., 1991-93, prof. law and humanities, dir. Ctr. Human Rights Eng., 1993-97, emeritus prof. Eng., 1997—; disting. prof. apologetics, law, and history of Christian thought, v.p. acad. affairs U.K. and Europe Trinity Coll. and Theol. Sem., Newburgh, Ind., 1997—; disting. prof. law Regent U., Va., 1997-99; sr. counsel European Ctr. Law and Justice, 1997-2001; founding dir. Internat. Acad. of Apologetics, Evangelism and Human Rights, Strasbourg, France, 1997—. Vis. prof. Concordia Theol. Sem., Springfield, Ill., 1964-67, DePaul U., Chgo., 1967-70; hon. fellow Revelle Coll., U. Calif., San Diego, 1970; rector Freie Fakultaten Hamburg, Fed. Republic Germany, 1981-82; lectr. Rsch. Scientists Christian Fellowship Conf. St. Catherines Coll., Oxford U., 1985, Internat. Anti-Corruption Conf., Beijing, China, 1995; Pascal lectr. on Christianity and the Univ., U. Waterloo, Ont., Can., 1987; A. Kurt Weiss lectr. biomed. ethics U. Okla., 1997; adj. prof. Puget Sound U. Sch. Law, Tacoma, 1990-91; founding dir. Internat. Acad. Apologetics, Evangelism and Human Rights, Strasbourg, France, 1997—; Worldwide Adv. Conf. lectr. Inns of Ct. Sch. Law, London, 1998; law and religion colloquium lectr. U. Coll. London, 2000; numerous other invitational functions. Author: The Writing of Research Papers in Theology, 1959, A Union List of Serial Publications in Chicago Area Protestant Theological Libraries, 1960, A Seventeenth-Century View of European Libraries, 1962, Chytraeus on Sacrifice: A Reformation Treatise in Biblical Theology, 1962, The Shape of the Past: An Introduction to Philosophical Historiography, 1962; author: (rev. edit.), 1975; author: The Is God Dead Controversy, 1966; author: (with Thomas J.J. Altizer) The Altizer-Montgomery Dialogue, 1967; author: Crisis in Lutheran Theology, 2 vols., 1967; author: (rev. edit.), 1973; author: Es confiable el Christianismo?, 1968, Ecumenicity, Evangelicals, and Rome, 1969, Where is History Going?, 1969, History and Christianity, 1970, Damned Through the Church, 1970, The Suicide of Christian Theology, 1970, Computers, Cultural Change and the Christ, 1970, In Defense of Martin Luther, 1970, La Mort de Dieu, 1971; author: (with Joseph Fletcher) Situation Ethics: True or False?, 1972; author: The Quest for Noah's Ark, 1972; author: (rev. edit.), 1974; author: Verdammt durch die Kirche, 1973, Christianity for the Toughminded, 1973, Cross and Crucible, 2 vols., 1973, Principalities and Powers: The World of the Occult, 1973; author: (rev. edit.), 1975; author: How Do We Know There is a God?, 1973, Myth, Allegory and Gospel, 1974, God's Inerrant Word, 1974, Jurisprudence: A Book of Readings, 1974; author: (4th edit.), 1992; author: The Law Above the Law, 1975, Cómo Sabemos Que Hay un Dios?, 1975, Demon Possession, 1975, The Shaping of America, 1976, Faith Founded on Fact, 1978, Law and Gospel: A Study for Integrating Faith and Practice, 1978; author: (3rd edit.), 1994; author: Slaughter of the Innocents, 1981, The Marxist Approach to Human Rights: Analysis & Critique, 1984, Human Rights and Human Dignity, 1987, Wohin marschiert China?, 1991, Evidence for Faith: Deciding the God Question, 1991, Giant in Chains: China Today and Tomorrow, 1994, Law and Morality: Friends or Foes?, 1994, Jésus: La Raison Rejoint L'Histoire, 1995; author: (with C.E.B. Cranfield and David Kilgour) Christians in the Public Square, 1996; author: Conflicts of Law, 1997, The Transcendent Holmes, 2000, The Repression of Evangelism in Greece, 2001, Tractatus Logico-Theologicus, 2002, Christ Our Advocate, 2002; editor: Lippincott's Evangelical Perspectives, 7 vols., 1970-72, 1970—72, International Scholars Directory, 1973, Simon Greenleaf Law Rev., 7 vols., 1981—88, Global Jour. Classical Theology, 1998—; contbg. editor: Christianity Today, 1965—84, New Oxford Review, 1993—95; films Is Christianity Credible, 1968, In Search of Noah's Ark, 1977, Defending the Biblical Gospel (11 videocassette series), 1985, writer Christianity on Trial, 1987—93; contbr. articles to acad., theol., legal encys. and jours., chapters to books. Nat. Luth. Ednl. Conf. fellow, 1959-60; Can. Council postdoctoral sr. research fellow, 1963-64; Am. Assn. Theol. Schs. faculty fellow, 1967-68; recipient Angel award Nat. Religious Broadcasters, 1989, 90, 92. Fellow Trinity Coll. (Newburgh, Ind.), Royal Soc. Arts (Eng.), Victoria Inst. (London), Acad. Internat. des Gourmets et des Traditions Gastronomiques (Paris), Am. Sci. Affiliation (nat. philosophy sci. and history sci. commn. 1966-70); mem. ALA, European Acad. Arts, Scis. and Humanities (corr. mem., Paris), Acad. Lit. France (titulary mem.), Lawyers' Christian Fellowship (hon. v.p. 1995—), Nat. Conf. U. Profs., Calif. bar Assn. (human rights commn. 1980-83), Internat. Bar Assn., World Assn. Law Profs., Mid. Temple and Lincoln's Inn (barrister mem.), Am. Soc. Internat. Law, Union Internat. des Avocats, Nat. Assn. Realtors, Tolkien Soc. Am., N.Y. C.S. Lewis Soc., Am. Hist. Assn., Soc. Reformation Rsch., Creation Rsch. Soc., Tyndale Fellowship (Eng.), Stair Soc. (Scotland), Presbyn. Hist. Soc. (North Ireland), Heraldry Soc., Soc. of Genealogists, Irish Geneaol. Soc., Am. Theol. Libr. Assn., Bibliog. Soc. U. Va., Evang. Theol. Soc., Internat. Wine and Food Soc., Soc. des Amis des Arts (Strasbourg), Chaîne des Rôtisseurs (commandeur), Athenaeum (London), Wig and Pen (London), Players' Theatre Club (London), Sherlock Holmes Soc. London, Soc. Sherlock Holmes de France (hon.), Club des Casseroles Lasserre (Paris), Ordre des chevaliers du Saint-Sepulcre Byzantin (commandeur), Heraldry Soc., Soc. Genealogists, Irish Geneal. Soc., Phi Beta Kappa, Phi Kappa Phi, Beta Phi Mu. Office: Church Lane Cottage 3-5 High St Lidlington Bedfordshire MK43 0RN England also: 2 rue de Rome 67000 Strasbourg France E-mail: 106612.1066@compuserve.com.

MONTGOMERY, JOSEPH WILLIAM, finance company executive; BBA, Coll. William and Mary, 1974. Cert. fin. planner; cert. portfolio mgr. Account exec. Wheat, First Securities, Inc., Lynchburg, Va., 1975-79, Williamsburg, 1979-81, v.p., investment officer, 1981-82, sr. v.p., investment officer, 1982-90; mng. dir. First Union Securities, 1990—. Mem. nat. nominating com. Outstanding Young Am. Program, 1998; bd. dirs. Future Hampton Roads, Inc., 1995—; mem. nat. campaign steering com. Campaign of 4th Century, William & Mary, 1992, bd. vis., 1995-99; mem. commn. tercentenary observanced Coll. William & Mary, 1992; mem. adv. coun. Peninsula White Sox, 1986; bd. dirs. Nat. Conf. Christians & Jews, peninsula chpt., 1986-91; mem. Williamsburg Cmty. Health Found., 1998; dir., treas. Franklin & Gladys Clark Found. Named Top 300 Fin. Advisors in Country, Worth Mag., 1998, The Chancellor's Circle, Coll. William and Mary, 1998, Broker Hall Fame, Rsch. mag., 1996, Top 250 Fin. Advisors, Worth Mag., 1999, Top 10 Ace Advisers, Ticker Mag., 2000. Mem. Internat. Assn. Fin. Planning, Inst. Cert. Fin. Planners, Investment Mgmt. Cons. Found., 1998, Soc. of Alumni William & Mary (pres. 1992, treas. 1991, sec. 1990, bd. dirs. 1989, Alumni Medallion 1996). Office: First Union Securities PO Box W Williamsburg VA 23187-3716

MONTGOMERY, KATHY MACLEAN, international business consultant; b. Burlington, N.C., Dec. 16, 1953; d. Herman Gilbert and Dorothy Jolene (Caldwell) MacLean; m. Loren Taylor Montgomery, Aug. 21, 1977. Student, London Sch. Econs., Cambridge (Eng.) Inst., Oxford (Eng.) U., U. Paris, U. Geneva, Switzerland, 1972-73; AA in Music, Peace Coll., 1974; BS in Psychology and Social Work, Western Carolina U., 1976. Casting dir., pres., CEO MacLean and Assocs., L.A. and Atlanta, 1978-86; dir. bus. devel. TSI-Bell Atlantic, Dallas, 1987-89; pres., CEO MacLean and Assocs., 1988—; mng. ptnr. RMH, Dallas, Beijing and Kuala Lumpur, Malaysia, Hong Kong and Taiwan, 1994-99. Cons. Omni Trade Group, Dallas, 1994—, DVX Golf and Sports Co., Denver, 1996-99; advisor/cons. MCI Connections Internat., Chgo., 1996-97; advisor Florinda Clothing, Dallas, 1997; pres. Tarastar Prodns., 1999—. Senate page State Pages, Raleigh, N.C., 1970; asst. to pres. Young Dems., Chapel Hill, N.C., 1971; personal page to lt. gov., N.C. State Pages, Raleigh, 1969-70. Mem. Am. Heart Assn., Muscular Dystrophy Assn., Tex. State Realtors Assn., Dallas Mus. Arts, Dallas Symphony Assn., Susan G. Komen Found. Democrat. Episcopalian. Avocations: writing and singing music, training quarter and Arabian horses, reading, traveling. Home and Office: RMH/MacLean and Assocs 210 N Hampton Rd Dallas TX 75208-5603

MONTGOMERY, LINDA STROUPE, county official; b. Havaco, W.Va., Feb. 12, 1943; d. James Allen Stroupe and Opal Marie (Daugherty) Leif; m. James R. Sutliff, Aug. 9, 1960 (div. Feb. 1982); children: Mark S., Debra Lynn, Amy Sutliff Sweckard; m. Paul L. Montgomery, Apr. 23, 1983. Student, S.W. Mo. State U., 1979-93. Sec. Va. Poly. Inst., Blacksburg, 1961-64; office mgr., paralegal William H. Wendt, Springfield, Mo., 1973-84; office adminstr. Greene County Commn., 1984-94; recorder of deeds Greene County, 1995—. Mem. legis. com. Local Area Govt. Employees Retirement Sys., State of Mo., 1993—; dist. dir. Mo. Assn. Counties, 1997—. Bd. dirs. Springfield-Greene County Libr. Dist., 1991-97, also past pres.; mem. allocations com., sect. chmn. United Way Ozarks, Springfield, 1990—; committeewoman, legis. chmn. Greene County Rep. Ctrl. Com., 1987—. Mem. Internat. Assn. Clks., Recorders, Election Ofcls. and Treas., Recorder's Assn. Mo., Springfield Area C. of C., Grand Order Pachyderms (past pres.), Phi Kappa Phi. Methodist. Avocations: reading, needlework, antiques. Home: 5209 S Shari Ln Rogersville MO 65742-9474 Office: Greene County Govt Recorder of Deeds 940 N Boonville Ave Springfield MO 65802-3804

MONTGOMERY, M. DARLENE, secondary education educator, English language educator; b. Muskogee, Okla., May 25, 1949; d. William Perry and Nemie Anne (Emery) Dunn; m. Rex Jay Montgomery, June 5, 1971; children: Emory Anne Lobb, April Marie. BA, Northeastern State U., 1971; M in Liberal Studies, U. Okla., 1994. Tchg. cert., Ark., Va., Okla. Journalism, speech, drama and English tchr. Virginia Beach (Va.) Pub. Schs., 1971-74; co-owner Taylor Rental Ctr., Ft. Smith, Ark., 1975-86; English tchr. Ft. Smith Pub. Sch., 1987—. Adj. English prof. Westark C.C., Ft. Smith, 1994-98. Editor (assn. newspaper) The Sounding Board, 1993-99. Choir/video technician Harvest Time Tabernacle, Ft. Smith, 1983-86. Recipient Lifetime PTA award Kimmons Jr. High, Ft. Smith, 1994, 1st place in state for assn. reporting Ark. Edn. Assn., Little Rock, 1996, 97. Mem. Ft. Smith Classroom Tchrs. Assn. (pres., 2000-02, faculty rep. 1992-93, bd. mem. 1993-99, publs. sec./editor 1993-99), Northside PTA, Phi Delta Kappa, Alpha Delta Kappa, Alpha Chi, Rho Theta. Avocations: reading, writing essays and short stories. Home: 3205 S 98th St Fort Smith AR 72903-5714 Office: Ft Smith Pub Schs 2301 N B St Fort Smith AR 72901-3433

MONTGOMERY, MARVIN, musical producer; Mem. band Light Crust Doughboys, from 1935; prodr., leader Light Crust Doughboys, mus. orgn., Mesquite, Tex., from 1947. Mem. touring act. State of Tex. Commn. on Arts. Originator western swing music. Nominee Grammy award, 1998, 1999, 2001, 2002, Dove award, 1999, 2002; named ofcl. music amb., Tex. Ho. of Reps.; named to Tex. Western Swing Hall of Fame, Rockabilly Hall of Fame. Home: Dallas, Tex. Died June 6, 2001.

MONTGOMERY, MICHAEL DAVIS, physics/astrophysics company executive, consultant , real estate company executive; b. San Luis Obispo, Calif., June 4, 1936; s. Herold Ray and Elva Dee (Davis) M.; m. Rita Martin, Dec. 28, 1957 (div. Sept. 1975); children: Jeanne, Gwen, Michele. MSEE, Stanford

U., 1959; PhD, U. N.Mex., 1967. Group leader Max Planck Inst. for Astrophysics, Munich, 1974-76; group leader advanced concepts Los Alamos (N.Mex.) Nat. Labs., 1976-83; program mgr. for simulation Maxwell Labs. Inc., San Diego, 1983-84, dep. for DNA programs, 1984-85, v.p. rsch. and devel., 1986-91, sr. v.p. applied tech., 1991-92; sr. cons., 1993-96; owner Casa Del Mar Inn, Santa Barbara, Calif., 1991-97; real estate investor Jamach Ctr. LLC, 1997—; cons., owner All Santa Fe Reservations. Assoc. editor Jour. Geophys. Research; contbr. articles to sci. jours. Served to lt. comdr. USN, 1959-62. Recipient (charter) Sr. Scientist award Alexander Von Humboldt Found., 1972. Mem. AAAS, Am. Phys. Soc., Phi Beta Kappa, Sigma Xi, Tau Beta Pi. Avocation: amateur radio, W5MGT. Home and Office: 8 San Juan Ranch Rd Santa Fe NM 87506-7539 E-mail: mikedmont@aol.com., mike@all-santafe.com.

MONTGOMERY, PAULA KAY, publisher; b. Omaha, Sept. 23, 1946; d. Floyd Woodrow and Adelyn Ann (Peterson) M. BA in English, Fla. State U., 1967, MLS in Libr. Sci., 1968; PhD in Reading Edn., 1989. Sch. libr. Montgomery County Pub. Sch., Rockville, Md., 1969-72, libr. specialist, 1972-79; chief sch. libr. Md. State Dept. Edn., Balt., 1979-88; pub. Crinkles Children's Mag./Sch. Libr. Media Activities Monthly, 1984—. Del. Gov.'s Conf. on Librs., Balt., 1990. Author: Teaching Library Media Skills, 1983, Thematic Approaches to Literature, 1991, Subject Approaches to Literature, 1991, Subject Approaches to Literature, 1991, Literary Forms Approach to Literature, 1995, The Bookmark Book, 1995; editor: (book series) Library Media Skills, 1982—. Mem. ALA, Nat. Assn. State Ednl. Media Profls. (pres. 1987), Assn. Edn. Communication and Tech. Lutheran. Office: 17 E Henrietta St Baltimore MD 21230-3910 E-mail: paulam@crinkles.com.

MONTGOMERY, PHILIP O'BRYAN, JR. pathologist; b. Dallas, Aug. 16, 1921; BS, So. Meth. U., 1942; MD, Columbia U., 1945. Diplomate Am. Bd. Pathology, Am. Bd. Clin. Pathology and Forensic Pathology. Intern Mary Imogene Bassett Hosp., Cooperstown, N.Y., 1945-46; fellow in pathology Southwestern Med. Sch., Dallas, 1950-51, asst. prof. pathology, 1953-55, assoc. prof., 1955-61, prof., 1961—, assoc. dean, 1968-70, Ashbel Smith prof. pathology, 1991—; rsch. asst. pathology and cancer rsch. Cancer Rsch. Inst. New Eng. Deaconess Hosp., Boston, 1951-52; spl. asst. to chancellor U. Tex. System, 1971-75. Exec. dir. Cancer Ctr. U. Tex. Health Sci. Ctr. Dallas, 1975-89; pathologist Parkland Meml. Hosp., Dallas, 1952—, Dallas City Zoo, 1955-68; med. examiner DallasCounty, 1955-58; cons. Navarro County Meml. Hosp., Corsicana, Tex., 1952-53, McKinney (Tex.) Vets. Hosp., 1952-65, Lisbons Vets. Hosp., Dallas, 1953—, St. Paul Hosp., Dallas, 1958—, Flow Meml. Hosp., Denton, Tex., 1958-65; pathologist Tex. Children's Hosp., Dallas, 1954-55. Contbr. numerous articles to profl. jours., sci. abstracts, jours. Bd. dirs. Planned Parenthood of Dallas, 1958-63, pres., 1958-60; trustee St. Mark's Sch. Tex., 1958—, v.p., chmn. exec. com. bd. trustee, 1966-68, v.p., 1968-69, pres. 1974-76; trustee Lamplighter Sch., 1967-70; chmn. Dallas Area Libr. Planning Coun., 1970-72, Goals for Dallas Health Task Force com., 1975-76, Fleet Adm. Nimitz Mus. commn., 1979-81; mem. adv. bd. Dallas Citizens coun., chmn. health com. 1988-89; bd. dirs. Met. YMCA, 1960-63, Dallas Coun. on World Affairs, 1962-65; pres., bd. dirs. Damon Runyon, Walter Winchell Cancer Fund, 1974-79; cord. Dallas Arts Dist., 1982-95. Fellow Am. Soc. Clin. Pathologists; mem. Am. Assn. Pathologists and Bacteriologists, Am. Assn. Cancer Rsch., Internat. Acad. Pathology, Am. Acad. Forensic Scis., Soc. Exptl. Biology and Medicine, Internat. Soc. Cell Biology, Biophys. Soc., Am. Soc. Cell Biology, Am. soc. Exptl. Pathology, Tissue Culture Assn., Internat. Fedn. Med. Electronics, Profl. Group Med. Electronics of Inst. Radio Engrs., AAAS, Optical Soc. Tex. (founding), Pan-Am. Med. Assn., AMA, So. Med. Assn., Tex. Med. Assn., AAUP. Home: 6343 Kalani Dallas TX 75368-0001 Office: 5323 Harry Hines Blvd Dallas TX 75390-7208

MONTGOMERY, R. LAWRENCE, department store chain executive; b. 1949; Pres., CEO Black's divsn. Allied Store Corp., 1985-87; sr. v.p., dir. stores, gen. mdse. mgr. Softlines L.S. Ayres divsn. May Dept. Stores, 1987-88; sr. v.p., dir. stores Kohl's Corp., Menomonee Falls, Wis., 1988-93, exec. v.p., 1993-96, vice chmn., 1996—, CEO, 1999—, also bd. dirs. Office: Kohn's Corp N56w17000 Ridgewood Dr Menomonee Falls WI 53051-5660*

MONTGOMERY, REX, biochemist, educator; b. Halesowen, Eng., Sept. 4, 1923; came to U.S., 1948, naturalized, 1963; s. Fred and Jane (Holloway) M.; m. Barbara Winifred Price, Aug. 9, 1948 (dec.); children: Ian, David, Jennifer, Christopher. BSc, U. Birmingham, Eng., 1943, PhD, 1946, DSc, 1963. Rsch. assoc. U. Minn., 1951-55; mem. faculty U. Iowa, Iowa City, 1955—, prof. biochemistry, 1963—, assoc. dean U. Iowa Coll. Medicine, 1974-95, v.p. rsch., 1989-90. Vis. prof. Nat. Australian U., 1969-70; mem. physiol. chemistry study sect. NIH, 1968-72; mem. drug devel. contract rev. com., 1975-87; chmn. com. biol. chemistry NAS, 1961-64; pesticide and fertilizer adv. bd. Iowa Dept. Agr., 1990-91; bd. dirs. Wallace Tech. Transfer Found., 1989-93; chmn. bd. dirs. Neurotron Inc., 1990-95; mem. rsch. com. Iowa Corn Promotion Bd., 1995—; rsch. dir. Biotech. Byproducts Consortium, 1989—; cons. in field. Author: Chemical Production of Lactic Acid, 1949, Chemistry of Plant Gums and Mucilages, 1959, Quantitative Problems in Biochemical Sciences, 2d edit., 1976, Biochemistry: A Case-Orientated Approach, 6th edit., 1996; mem. editl. adv. bd. Carbohydrate Rsch., 1968-80; mem. editl. bd. Molecular Biotherapy, 1988-92; contbr. articles to profl. jours. Postdoctoral fellow Ohio State U., 1948-49; fellow Sugar Research Found., Dept. Agr., 1949-51 Fellow: Royal Soc. Chemistry. Home: 701 Oaknoll Dr Iowa City IA 52246-5168 Office: U Iowa Coll Medicine Dept Biochemistry Iowa City IA 52242 E-mail: rex-montgomery@uiowa.edu.

MONTGOMERY, ROBERT LOUIS, chemical engineer; b. San Francisco, Nov. 20, 1935; s. Louis Clyde and Fay Elythe (Myers) M.; m. Patricia Helen Cook, Mar. 17, 1962; children: Cynthia Elaine, Jeanette Louise, Cecelia Irene, Howard Edwin. BS in Chemistry, U. Calif., Berkeley, 1956; PhD in Phys. Chemistry, Okla. State U., 1975. Registered profl. engr., Kans., Tex., Colo. Phys. chemist U.S. Bur. Mines, Reno, 1956-62; NSF predoctoral fellow Okla. State U., Stillwater, 1963-66; sr. engr. Boeing Co., Wichita, Kans., 1966-75; postdoctoral fellow Rice U., Houston, 1975-77, sr. research assoc., 1982-84; tech. data engr. M.W. Kellogg Co., 1977-82; staff engr. Martin Marietta, Denver, 1984-94. Contbr. articles to profl. jours. Mem. Am. Chem. Soc., Am. Soc. for Metals Internat., Kans. Soc. Profl. Engrs., Sigma Xi. Avocations: amateur radio, skiing. Home: P.O. Box 369 Wellington KS 67152-0369

MONTGOMERY, ROBERT MOREL, JR. lawyer; b. Birmingham, Ala., June 9, 1930; s. Robert Morel and Ella Bernice (Smith) M.; m. Mary Lemerle McKenzie, Mar. 6, 1953; 1 child, Courtnay Elizabeth. BS, U. Ala., 1952; LL.B., U. Fla., 1957. Bar: Fla. 1957; diplomate Acad. Fla. Trial Lawyers. With Howell & Kirby Attys at Law, Jacksonville, Fla., 1957-59; ptnr. Howell, Kirby, Montgomery, Sands & D'Aiuto, 1959-66, Howell, Kirby, Montgomery, D'Aiuto, Dean & Hallowes, West Palm Beach, 1966-75, Montgomery, Lytal, Reiter, Denny & Searcy, West Palm Beach, 1976-85, Montgomery Searcy & Denny, West Palm Beach, 1986-89; sr. ptnr. Montgomery & Larson, 1989—. Civil trial adv. Nat. Bd. Trial Advocacy. Chmn. Palm Beach Opera; chmn. emeritus Palm Beach Cultural Coun.; co-chmn. The Children's Place at Home Safe, Inc.; founder Armory Art Ctr., Palm Beach Inst. Contemporary Art; trustee Nat. Pub. Radio. 1st lt. AUS, 1952-54. Named Alumnus of Yr. U. Fla. Law Rev., 1983, Philanthropist of Yr. Nat. Assn. Fund Raising Execs., 1990, Honoree for Yr. City of Hope, 1991, Victim Adv. of Yr., Palm Beach County Sheriff's Office, 1997, Child Advocate of the Yr., 1996; recipient Learned Hand award Am. Jewish Com., 1985, Humanitarian award Albert Einstein Coll., 1990, Pub.'s award honor for contbg. most to improving quality of life in Broward and Palm Beach counties, 1992, Great Am. Traditions award B'nai B'rith, 1996, Humanitarian award Albert Einstein Coll. Medicine, 1999, Haym Solomon award Anti-Defamation League, 2000, Palm Beach C.C. Leadership award, 2002, Man of Yr. award Lake Worth Cultural Spotlight Com., 2002. Mem. ABA, Fla. Bar Assn. (lectr. continuing edn.), Palm Beach County Bar Assn., Trial Lawyers Assn. Am., Inner Circle Advs. Home: 1800 S Ocean Blvd Palm Beach FL 33480-5104 Office: PO Box 3086 West Palm Beach FL 33402-3086 E-mail: rmm@rmmjr.com.

MONTGOMERY, ROY DELBERT, retired gas utility company executive; b. Indpls., Apr. 24, 1926; s. Lloyd Sipes and Nona Mae (Brummett) M.; m. Barbara Ann Reno, Apr. 21, 1946; children: Stephanie, Rebecca, Jeffrey, Laura. Student, Purdue U., 1950-51; M.E., Internat. Corr. Schs., 1953; A.S. in Mgmt. and Adminstrn., Ind. U., 1973. Registered profl. engr. Ind. Engr. Citizens Gas & Coke Utility, Indpls., 1952-59, supt., 1959-60, dir., 1960-73, exec. dir., 1973-78, v.p., 1978-82, sr. v.p., 1982-86, cons., 1986-88. Contbr. articles to profl. jours. Vice pres. exploring Crossroads of Am. Coun. Boy Scouts Am., Ind., 1978; corp. rep. Jr. Achievement Ind., 1970-82; pres. Fairway Trace at Pendia I, 1994—, Fairway Trace Home Owners Assn., 1995—. Recipient Bronze Big Horn award Boy Scouts Am. Explorer Div., Ind., 1978 Mem. Am. Gas Assn. (merit award 1966), Ind. Gas Assn., Scientec Club Ind., Kiwanis. Republican. Avocations: oil painting, boating, golf, genealogy.

MONTGOMERY, SCOTT BRADFORD, art history educator; b. Stanford, Calif., July 27, 1963; s. David Bruce and Toby (Franks) M.; m. Alice Antoinette Bauer, June 14, 1991. BA in Art History, Pomona Coll., Claremont, Calif., 1985; MA in Art History, Syracuse U., 1988; PhD in Art History, Rutgers U., 1996. Adj. prof. Rutgers U., New Brunswick, N.J., 1992-96; vis. asst. prof. Oreg. State U., Corvallis, 1996-97, U. Iowa, Iowa City, 1997-98; asst. prof. art history U. N.Tex., Denton, 1998—. Mem. editl. bd. The Rutgers Art Rev., 1990, editor, 1991; contbr. articles to profl. jours. Florence fellow Syracuse U., 1986-87, Excellence fellow Rutgers U., 1989-92, U. N.Tex. Jr. Faculty Summer Rsch. fellow, 1999, 2000—; U. N.Tex. Faculty Rsch. Initiation grantee, 1999. Mem. Coll. Art Assn., Renaissance Soc. Am., Medieval Acad. Am., Italian Art Soc., Hagiography Soc., Soc. of Historians of E. European and Russian Art and Architecture. Avocations: songwriting, hiking, reading. Office: Univ of North Texas Sch Visual Arts PO Box 305100 Denton TX 76203-5100 E-mail: montgomery@unt.edu.

MONTGOMERY, TOMMIE SUE, political scientist, educator; b. Miami, Fla., Mar. 25, 1942; d. Clyde Waldron and Edith Elaine (Felton) M.; m. Carlos Francisco Gamba, July 11, 1987 (div. 1993); m. A. David Abrahams, June 23, 2001. AB, Wesleyan Coll., 1963; MA, Vanderbilt U., 1969; PhD, NYU, 1977. Instr. CUNY, 1973-75; asst. prof. Richmond Coll., S.I., N.Y., 1975-76, Bklyn. Coll., 1976-78, Ithaca (N.Y.) Coll., 1983-84; vis. asst. prof. Dickinson Coll., Carlisle, Pa., 1984-86; assoc. prof. Agnes Scott Coll., Decatur, Ga., 1986-93; vis. assoc. prof. Emory U, 1993; sr. rsch. fellow So. Ctr. for Internat. Studies, Atlanta, 1993-94; sr. rsch. assoc. North-South Ctr. U. Miami, Fla., 1994-96; rsch. cons. dept. telemedicine Ptnrs. Health Care Sys., 1998; grants mgr. telemedicine dept. Partners Healthcare Sys., Boston, 1998-99; contract sr. assoc. Abt Assocs., Inc., Cambridge, 1999-2000; contract assoc. Isaacson, Miller, Boston, 2000—. Cons. Calif. State U., Chico, 1986, Camino Film Projects, L.A., 1988—89, Ctrl. Am. Task Force Presbyn. Ch., 1982, 88, UN Higher Commr. for Refugees, Belize, 1991, UN Observer Mission, El Salvador, 1993—94; sr. scholar UN Inst. Disarmament Rsch. Project on Disarmament and Conflict Resolution, Geneva, 1994—95, U.S. Agy. Internat. Devel., El Salvador, 1996; vis. lectr. Tufts U., Medford, Mass., 1997; vis. prof. Trent U., Peterborough, Ont., 2002—. Author: Revolution in El Salvador: Origins and Evolution, 1982, Revolution in El Salvador: From Civil Strife to Civil Peace, 1994; editor: Mexico Today, 1982, Peacemaking and Democratization in the Western Hemisphere, 2000; contbr. articles to books and profl. jours. Deacon Old South Ch., Boston, 1998-2001; council St. Paul's Anglican Ch., Lindsay, Ont., 2002—. Recipient grants CUNY, 1978, Fulbright Found., 1986, 91, North-South Ctr., 1993-94, U.S. Inst. Peace and Ford Found., 1995-96. Mem. Latin Am. Studies Assn. Avocations: photography, travel. Home: RR 6 19 Bluewater Ave Lindsay ON Canada K9V 4R6 E-mail: tsmada@atteanada.ca.

MONTGOMERY, WILLIAM ADAM, lawyer; b. Chgo., May 22, 1933; s. John Rogerson and Helen (Fyke) Montgomery; m. Jane Fauver, July 28, 1956 (div. Dec. 1967); children: Elizabeth, William, Virginia; m. Deborah Stephens, July 29, 1972; children: Alex, Katherine. AB, Williams Coll., 1955; LLB, Harvard U., 1958. Bar: D.C. 1958, Ill. 1959, U.S. Ct. Appeals (7th cir.) 1959, U.S. Supreme Ct. 1977. Atty. civil divsn., appellate sect. Dept. Justice, Washington, 1958—60; assoc. Schiff Hardin & Waite, Chgo., 1960—68, ptnr., 1968—93; v.p., gen. counsel State Farm Ins. Cos., Bloomington, 1994—97, sr. v.p., gen. counsel, 1997—99; ptnr. Schiff Hardin & Waite, Chgo., 1999—. Author: (39 corp. practice series) Tying Arrangements, 1984; co-author: Insurance Antitrust and Unfair Trade Practices Law, 2002; contbr. articles to profl. jours. Fellow: Am. Coll. Trial Lawyers; mem.: ABA (coun. antitrust sect. 1989—92), Seventh Cir. Bar Assn. (pres. 1988—89), Chgo. Bar Assn., Econ. Club Chgo., Lawyers Club Chgo. Avocations: skiing, woodturning. Office: Schiff Hardin & Waite 6600 Sears Tower Chicago IL 60606 E-mail: wmontgomery@schiffhardin.com.

MONTGOMERY, WILLIAM D. ambassador; b. Carthage, Mo., Nov. 8, 1945; m. Lynne Germain Montgomery; children: Alexander, Amelia, Katarina. BA, Bucknell U.; MA, George Washington U.; student, Nat. War Coll., 1986-87. With Fgn. Svc., 1974, econ. officer Yugoslovia, 1975-78, comml. then polit. officer Moscow, 1979-81; line officer, secretariat staff then exec. asst. to under sec. polit. affairs Dept. State, 1981-84, exec. asst. to dep. sec., 1991-93; dep. chief mission Dar es Salaam, Tanzania, 1984-85, Sofia, Bulgaria, 1988-91; U.S. ambassador Bulgaria, 1993-96; spl. advisor to Pres. and sec. state for Bosnia peace implementation of the Bosnia peace plan, 1996-97; U.S. amb. to Republic of Croatia, 1998-2000; chief of mission U.S. Embassy, Belgrade, Yugoslavia, 2000—01; U.S. amb. to Yugoslavia, 2001—. With U.S. Army, 1967-1970. Decorated Bronze Star, Commendation medal with V device; decorated Order of the Horseman of the Madara, Order of the Stara Planina (Bulgaria), Order of Price Trpimir (Croatia); recipient ABA-CEELI award for promotions rule of law in Cen. and Ea. Europe. Mem. Am. Fgn. Svc. Assn. Office: Dept of State 5070 Belgrade Pl Washington DC 20521-5070

MONTGOMERY, WILLIAM WAYNE, surgeon; b. Proctor, Vt., Aug. 20, 1923; s. Charles Lynn and Ann (Jones) M. AB, Middlebury (Vt.) Coll., 1944; MD, U. Vt., 1947. Diplomate: Am. Bd. Otolaryngology. Intern Mary Fletcher Hosp., Burlington, Vt., 1947-48; gen. practice medicine W. Rutland, 1948-50; resident otolaryngology Mass. Eye and Ear Infirmary, 1952-55, mem. staff, 1956—, sr. surgeon in otolaryngology, 1966—; mem. staff Mass. Gen. Hosp., 1956—, surgeon otolaryngology, 1966-86. Prof. Harvard Med. Sch., 1986-94, John W. Merriam prof. otology and laryngology, 1994—, med. dir. voice lab., 1993. Author: Surgery of the Upper Respiratory System, vol. I, II, The Mustache that Walks Like a Man, 1995; contbr. articles to med. jours. Served as batallion surgeon USMCR, 1950-52, Korea. Decorated Purple Heart, Bronze Star, Commendation medal; recipient Disting. Alumni award U. Vt. Med. Sch., 1968, Alumni Achievement award Middleburg Coll., 1985. Fellow ACS; mem. AMA, Am. Acad. Ophthalmology and Otolaryngology (instr. 1963-67), Am. Broncho-Esophagological Assn., Am. Laryngol. Assn. (James E. Newcomb award 1990), Am. Otologic Soc., Am. Laryngol., Rhinol. and Otol. Soc. (Cert. of merit 1990), Pan Am. Med. Assn., Mass. Med. Soc. (program chmn. 1966—), Suffolk Med. Soc., Am. Triological Soc. (Mosher award 1963, v.p. 1987), New Eng. Otolaryngol. Soc. (pres. 1977-78), Am. Soc. Head and Neck Surgery, Am. Acad. Facial Plastic and Reconstructive Surgery. Achievements include spl. research paranasal sinuses and laryngeal surgery. Home: 20 Hilltop Rd Chestnut Hill MA 02467-1846 Office: 243 Charles St Boston MA 02114-3002

MONTGOMERY-DAVIS, JOSEPH, osteopathic physician; b. Annapolis, Md., Aug. 27, 1940; s. John and Flonila Alice (Sutphin) Swontek. Student, U. Wis., Milw., 1967-70; DO, Chgo. Coll. Osteo. Medicine, 1974. Diplomate Nat. Bd. Examiners for Osteo. Physicians and Surgeons; cert. family practice & osteo. manipulative treatment. Chief technologist nuclear medicine dept. Columbia Hosp., Milw., 1964-70; intern Richmond Heights (Ohio) Gen. Hosp., 1974-75; pvt. practice Raymondville, Tex., 1975—. Mem. med. care adv. com. Tex. Dept. Human Svcs., Austin, 1983—86, Austin, 1990—94, mem. physician payment adv. com., 1991—95, Austin, 2001—; cons. health care issues Tex. Osteo. Med. Assn., 1991—; health officer Willacy County Health Authority, Raymondville, 1984—; mem. med. care adv. com. Tex. Workers Compensation Commn., 1997—2001; clin. assoc. prof. dept. family medicine North Tex. Health Sci. Ctr., Ft. Worth, 2000—. Contbr. articles to profl. jours. With USAF, 1959-63. Mem. Am. Osteo. Assn., Am. Coll. Osteo. Family Physiaicns (spl. Recognition award 1995), Tex. Soc. Am. Coll. Osteo. Family Physicians (pres. 1985-86, Physician of Yr. award 1989, T.R. Sharp Meritorious Svc. award 1999), Tex. Med. Found., Tex. Osteo. Med. Assn. (pres. 1989-90), Tex. Coll. Osteo. Medicine Alumni Assn., Phi Eta Sigma, Sigma Sigma Phi. Office: Neighborhood Dr 525 S 10th St Raymondville TX 78580-2593

MONTI, LAURA ANNE, psychology researcher, educator; b. Evanston, Ill., Feb. 28, 1959; d. LeRoy John and Mary Alice (Foley) M. BA in Psychology, U. Ariz., 1981; MA in Cognitive Sci., Loyola U., Chgo., 1986, PhD, 1987; postgrad., Menninger Found., 1988. Mem. bd. dirs., co-owner Monti & Assocs. Inc., Arlington Heights, Ill., 1976—; v.p., co-owner MAM Imports and Creative Gifts, Kildeer, 1986-89; lectr. psychology Loyola U., Chgo., 1986-89; asst. prof. North Park Coll., 1989-91; instr. psychology Rush-Presbyn.-St. Luke's Med. Ctr., 1992-94, asst. prof., 1995-98. Vis. rsch. specialist U. Ill., Ill. Inst. Devel. Disabilities, 1989-90; cons. Walter H. Sobel FAIA & Assocs., Chgo., 1987—, Yate and Auberle, Oakbrook, Ill., 1987-88; postdoctoral fellow Northwestern U., Evanston, Ill., 1990-92. Contbr. articles to profl. jours.; co-author tech. reports to various orgns. Tuition scholar Loyola U., Chgo., 1983-84; NIH fellow, 1992-94; Loyola U. grad. asst., 1986. Mem. APA (divsn. psychology of women 1989-92, gen. psychology, exptl. psychology 1989—), Psi Chi (faculty rep. for North Park Coll. 1989-91), Sigma Alpha Iota. Roman Catholic. Avocations: tennis, piano. Home: 720 Cimarron Dr Cary IL 60013 E-mail: drlmonti@aol.com.

MONTIE, JAMES EDWARD, urologist, oncologist; b. Detroit, Aug. 13, 1946; m. Jeanne Lewis; children: Jeffrey Michael, Anne Elisa. BA, U. Notre Dame, 1967; MD, U. Mich. Med. Sch., 1971. Diplomate Am. Bd. Urology. Rotating intern Virginia Mason Hosp., Seattle, 1971-72; resident in urology Cleve. Clinic Found., 1973-76; staff urologist Wilford Hall USAF Med. Ctr., Lackland AFB, Tex., 1976-78, chief renal transplant svc., 1977-78; spl. fellow in urology Meml. Sloan-Kettering Cancer Ctr., 1978-79; head sect. urologic oncology Cleve. Clinic Found., 1979-83, chmn. dept. urology, 1983-85; chmn. Cleve. Clinic Cancer Ctr., 1982-84; asst. clin. prof. surgery/urology Case Western Reserve U. Sch. of Medicine, 1985-88; staff urologist Cleve. Clinic Fla., 1988-89, chmn. dept. urology, 1989-91, chmn. divsn. surgery, 1990-91; prof. urologic oncology Wayne State U. Sch. Medicine, Detroit, 1991-95; prof. dept. surgery U. Mich., Ann Arbor, 1995—, chmn. dept. urology, 1997—. Reviewer for Jour. Urology, Urology, Cancer, The Prostate; faculty urology dept. Cleve. Found., 1979-88, Wayne State U. Sch. of Medicine, 1991-95, U. Mich. Sch. Medicine Dept. Surgery, Sect. of Urology, 1995—. Author: (book) Clinical Management of Renal Adenocardinomas, 1989; mem. editorial bd. Jour. of Urologic Oncology, 1995; editor Seminars in Urologic Oncology, 1995; contbr. over 160 articles to profl. publs. and chpts. to books. Liaison mem. Am. Joint Com. on Cancer, 1991—; bladder cancer task force Coll. Am. Pathologists, 1994—. Recipient Outstanding Paper award Soc. Air Force Clin. Surgeons, 1977, Am. Cancer Soc. Clin. fellowship, 1978-79, Bruce Hubbard Stewart award Cleve. Clinic Found., 1986. Mem. AMA, ACS, Soc. Air Force Clin. Surgeons, Am. Soc. Clin. Oncology, Am. Urol. Assn., Internat. Soc. d'Urology, Soc. Surg. Oncology, Soc. Univ. Urologists, Soc. Urol. Oncology (treas. 1988-90, pres. elect 1990-91, pres. 1991-92, North Ctrl. Sect. Am. Urol. Assn., Cleve. Urol. Soc. (sec. treas. 1982-84, v.p. 1984-85, pres. 1985-86), Mich. Urol. Soc., Am. Cancer Soc. (chmn. profl. edn. com. Cuyahoga County Unit 1982-85, bd. dirs. 1985-88, profl. edn. com. Broward County 1990-91), Friends of Notre Dame Rowing Club, Friends of Detroit Boat Club Rowing. Avocations: competitive rowing, national masters champion 1990-93, 98. Office: 2916B Taubman Ctr PO Box 330 Ann Arbor MI 48106-0330

MONTO, ARNOLD SIMON, epidemiology educator; b. Bklyn., Mar. 22, 1933; s. Jacob and Mildred (Kaplan) M.; m. Ellyne Gay Polsky, June 15, 1958; children: Sarah D. Monto Maniaci, Jane E., Richard L., Stephen A. BA in Zoology, Cornell U., Ithaca, N.Y., 1954; MD, Cornell U., N.Y.C., 1958. Diplomate Am. Coll. Epidemiology. Intern, asst. resident in medicine Vanderbilt U. Hosp., Nashville, 1958—60; USPHS postdoctoral fellow in infectious disease Stanford U. Med. Ctr., Palo Alto, Calif., 1960—62; mem. staff virus diseases sect. mid. Am. rsch. unit Nat. Inst. Allergy and Infectious Disease, Panama, 1962—65; asst. prof. U. Mich. Sch. Pub. Health, Ann Arbor, 1965—76, chmn. dept. population planning and internat. health, 1993—97, dir. Ctr. for Population Planning, 1993—97, prof. epidemiology, 1996—, dir. Mich. Bioterrism and Health Preparedness Ctr., 1976—; dir. Mich. Bioterrorism and Health Preparednedd Rsch. and Tng. Ctr. Vis. scientist Clin. Rsch. Ctr., Northwick Park Hosp., Harrow, Eng., 1976; scholar-in-residence bd. on sci. and tech. for internat. devel. NAS and Inst. Medicine, Washington, 1983-84; vis. scientist div. communicable diseases WHO, Geneva, 1986-87; mem. pulmonary diseases adv. com. Nat. Heart, Lung and Blood Inst., Bethesda, Md., 1979-83; mem. nat. adv. coun. Nat. Inst. Allergy and Infectious Diseases, Bethesda, 1989-93. Contbr. articles to med. jours. Recipient career devel. award NIH. Fellow Am. Coll. Epidemiology, Infectious Diseases Soc. Am.; mem. APHA (governing coun. 1978-80), Am. Epidemiol. Soc. Achievements include research on respiratory viral infections in the community; demonstration of effectiveness of influenza vaccine in severe disease in the elderly; prevention of spread of influenza virus and treatment of illness, occurrence, causes and treatment of common cold. Office: U Mich Sch Pub Health I 109 Observatory St Ann Arbor MI 48109-2029

MONTONE, KENNETH ALAN, art director, creative director, consultant; b. Chgo., Aug. 30, 1938; s. George Joseph and Beatrice Mabel (Calcott) M.; m. Patricia Joan Klapperich, Feb. 1, 1964; children: James Paul, Ian Andrew, Paul Matthew, Anne Elizabeth. BFA with honors, U. Ill., 1963. Graphic designer U. Ill. Press, Champaign, 1962-63; staff graphic designer ABC-TV, Chgo., 1963-65; art dir. McCann-Erickson, Inc., Sydney, Australia, 1965-67; staff graphic designer CBS-TV, Chgo., 1967-69; syndicated cartoonist, "Kiwi" Chgo. Tribune-N.Y. News Syndicate; art dir. McCann-Erickson, Inc., Portland, Oreg., 1969-80; creative dir. Morton Advt., 1980-84, Ken Montone & Assocs., Portland, 1984—. Art dir.: "Celebrate" series, 1980. With USN, 1956-59. Recipient Reata Howard Trombley award Portland Ad Fedn., 1983, Art Dirs. Club award N.Y. Ad, 1983, Best in West award Am. Advt. Fedn., 1983. Mem. Advt. Industry Emergency Fund (bd. dirs.), Portland Ad Fedn., Advt. Museum. Avocations: walking, drawing, traveling. Home and Office: Ken Montone & Assocs 165 NW 95th Ave Portland OR 97229-6303 E-mail: kmontone@aracnet.com.

MONTOOTH, SHEILA CHRISTINE, state agency administrator; b. Pasadena, Calif., Mar. 12, 1952; d. Gerald Frank and Janet Laura (Ebert) M. BS, Calif. State U., L.A., 1974; MPA, Calif. State U., 1985. CPA, Calif. From auditor 1 to tax auditor IV State Bd. Equalization Calif. Bd. Equalization, Pasadena, 1974-81, supr. tax auditor 1 State Bd. of Equalization West Los Angeles, 1981-83, bus. taxes adminstr. III State Bd. of Equalization Lakewood, 1984-87, bus. taxes adminstr. IV State Bd. of Equalization Downey, 1987-92; bus. taxes adminstr. V State Bd. of Equalization, Hollywood, 1992-93, Arcadia, 1994, City of Industry, 1994-2000, V State Bd. Equalization, West Covina, Calif., 2000—. Active Futures for Children. Recipient Bronze award United Way, Los Angeles, 1984, Gold award, 1985. Mem. Nat. Mus. Am. Indian Smithsonian Instn. (charter). Democrat. Roman Catholic. Avocations: reading Native American history, classic and adventure movies, golf, travel. Office: State Bd Equalization 1521 W Cameron Ave Ste 300 West Covina CA 91790

MONTOYA, PATRICIA T. federal agency administrator; b. Albuquerque; BSN, U. N.Mex., 1975, MA in Pub. Health Adminstrn., 1983. Asst. dir. ANA, Washington, 1987-89; exec. dir. N.Mex. Health Resources, 1989-93; practice mgr. Presbyn. Family Healthcare, Albuquerque, 1993-94; regional dir. HHS, Dallas, 1994-98, commr. adminstrn. children, youth and families Washington, 1998—2001; mem., board of dir. New Mexico Voices for Children, Albuquerque. Office: New Mexico Voices for Children 801 Encino NE Ste F21 Albuquerque NM 87102*

MONTOYA, VELMA, economist, policy consultant; b. L.A., Apr. 9, 1938; d. Jose Gutierrez and Consuelo (Cavazos) Montoya; m. Earl A. Thompson; 1 child, Bret L. Thompson. BA in Diplomacy and World Affairs, Occidental Coll., 1959, MA in Internat. Rels., 1960; MS in Econs., Stanford U., 1965; PhD in Econs., UCLA, 1977. Asst. prof. econs. Calif. State U., L.A., 1965-68; vis. assoc. prof. U. So. Calif., 1979; instr. UCLA, 1981-82; staff economist The Rand Corp., Santa Monica, Calif., 1973-82; asst. dir. for strategy, White House Office of Policy Devel. Exec. Office of the Pres., 1982-83; expert economist Office Regulatory Analysis, OSHA, U.S. Dept. of Labor, 1983-85;

dir. of Studies in Pub. Policy and Assoc. Prof. of Political Economy, Sch. of Bus. Mgmt. Chapman U., 1985-87; adj. prof. Sch. Bus. Mgmt. Pepperdine U., 1987-88; pres. Hispanic-Am. Pub. Policy Inst., 1984-90; assoc. prof. fin. Sch. Bus. Adminstrn., Calif. State Poly. U., Pomona, 1988-90; mem. Occupl. Safety and Health Rev. Commn., 1990-97; cons. on regulatory and econ. policy, 1997—. Cons. Urban Inst., 1974, Mexican-Am. Study Project UCLA, 1966, Graduate and Profl. Fellowships to the Office of Post Secondary Education, U.S. Dept. of Edn.; editorial referee Contemporary Policy Issues, Economic Inquiry, Policy Analysis, The Journal of Economic Literature; discussion leader Am. Assembly on Rels. Between the U.S. and Mex.; pres. del. White House Conf. on Aging, 1981; reader of 1988 proposals for the U.S. Dept of Edn. for the Improvement and Reform of Schs. and Teaching; research participant U.S. Dept. of Edn. Delphi Assessment of Drug Policies for Use in Minority Neighborhoods, 1989; mem. hispanic adv. panel Nat. Commn. for Employment Policy, 1981-82; lectr. Brookings Inst. Seminars for U.S. Bus. Leaders; bd. adv. Close-Up Found., 1982-83; discussant Western Economic Assn. Meetings, 1985, 93; bd. adv. Nat. Rehab. Hosp., 1991-94; mem. nat. exec. adv. bd. Harvard Jour. of Hispanic Policy, 1993-95; reader of proposals for Hispanic Serving Instns., U.S. Dept. Edn., 2001; mem. regional panel to select White House Fellows, 2002. Mem. census adv. com. on hispanic population for 1990 census, 1988—93; mem. adv. com. Senate Rep. Conf. Task Force on Hispanic Affairs, Washington, 1991—; bd. regents U. Calif., 1994—; program rev. com. Los Alamos (N.Mex.) Nat. Lab.; mem. steering com. GetSmarter.org, 1998—99; mem. outreach adv. bd. U. Calif., 1998—; commr. Calif. Postsecondary Edn. Commn., 2000—01. Named One of the 100 U.S. Hispanic Influentials Hispanic Bus. Mag., 1982, 90, 97, Woman of the Yr. Mex.-Am. Oportunity Found., 1983, The East L.A. Com. Union, 1979, Marshall scholar, Fulbright scholar; recipient Freedom Found. at Valley Forge Honor Econ. Edn. Excellence Cert., 1986, Univ. fellow Stanford Univ., Internat. Rels. fellow Calif. PTA, John Hay Whitney Opportunity fellow; Calif. State Univ. Found. Faculty Rsch. grantee. Mem. ASTM (com. on rsch. and tech. planning 1985-87), Am. Econ. Assn. (session chair ann. meetings 1995), Nat. Coun. Hispanic Women (pres. 1997-2002—, rsch. dir., West Coast v.p. 2001--), State Bar of Calif., Calif. State Bar Ct. (exec. com. 1987-89, disciplinary bd. 1986-89), Western Econ. Assn., Indsl. Rsch. Inst. for Pacific Nations (adv. bd. 1988-89), Salesian Boys and Girls Club (bd. dirs. 1989—), Vets. in Com. Svc. (adv. com. 1989-94), Phi Beta Kappa, Omicron Delta Epsilon, Phi Alpha Theta. Home: 6970 Los Tilos Rd Los Angeles CA 90068-3107

MONTRONE, PAUL MICHAEL, scientific instruments company executive; b. Scranton, Pa., May 8, 1941; s. Angelo H. and Beatrice M. (Giancini) M.; m. Sandra G. Gaudenzi, May 30, 1963; children: Michele Marie Cogan, Angelo Henry, Jerome Lawrence. BS in Accounting magna cum laude, U. Scranton, 1962; PhD in Fin., Econs. and Ops. Research, Columbia U., 1965. Ops. analyst Office Sec. Def., Washington, 1965-67; exec. v.p., chief fin. officer Wheelabrator-Frye Inc., Hampton, N.H., 1970-83; exec. v.p. Signal Cos., Inc., La Jolla, Calif., 1983-85, pres. Engineered Products Group Hampton, N.H., 1983-85; exec. v.p. fin. and adminstrn. AlliedSignal Inc., Morristown, N.J., 1985-86; pres. The Henley Group Inc., Hampton, N.H., 1986-92, bd. dirs.; chmn., CEO Wheelabrator Techs. Inc., NH, 1987-90; pres., co-owner The Gen. Chem. Group Inc., 1989-94, chmn. bd., 1994-96; vice chmn. Abex Inc., Hampton, 1992-95; pres. Fisher Sci. Internat., Inc., 1997—98, chmn. bd., CEO, 1991—; chmn. bd. GenTex Inc. , 1999—. Bd. dirs. Waste Mgmt.; mem. adv. bd. Sintokogio, Ltd. Pres. Met. Opera Assn.; mem. bd. overseers The Bus. Roundtable, Bus. Sch. Columbia U., N.Y.C.; adv. com. Consumer Protection and Quality in the Health Care Industry, Washington. Capt. U.S. Army, 1965-67. Mem.: Brook, University (N.Y.C.); Bald Peak Colony (Melvin Village, N.H.); Lyford Cay (Nassau, Bahamas). Roman Catholic. Office: Gentek 1 Liberty Ln Hampton NH 03842-1808*

MONTS, RODD LYDELL, writer, journalist; b. Little Rock, June 15, 1965; BA in Advt. and Pub. Rels., Grand Valley State U., 1987; postgrad., Wayne State U., 1991-95. Pub. rels. asst. Mich. Coalition for Safety Belt Use, Waterford, Mich., 1991-92; intern/freelance writer Publs. Co., Blues Rev., Detroit, 1992-93; intern Automative News, 1994-95; reporter Monday Morning Newspapers, Warren, Mich., 1996-99, assoc. editor, sr. writer, 1999-2000; staff writer Detroiter Mag., 1996—; online news editor Internet Broadcast Sys., 2000—. Freelance writer Detroit Free Press, Health Care Weekly Rev., Network Jour., African Ams. on Wheels, Detroit, 1991—; adv. Pure Garbage mag., Detroit, 1998. Editor: Newspapers in Education, 1986; editor Bridge mag., 2001-. Bd. dirs., project coord. Vol. Impact, Southfield, Mich., 1999; mentor Focus: Hope Journalism Program, Detroit, 1997, 98, 99. Recipient award of merit for feature writing ACCE 1998, 99, award of excellence for feature writing, 1999, bronze medalion for newswriting Internat. Automotive Media Awards, 1999, APEX award 2000, IABC Renaissance award 2000. Mem. Soc. Profl. Journalists (del. nat. conf. 1998), Nat. Assn. Black Journalists, Omega Psi Phi (Southfield Alumni chpt. officer, charter mem.). Office: WDIV Channel 4 550 W Lafayette Blvd Detroit MI 48226-3123 Fax: (313) 223-2228. E-mail: rlmonts@aol.com.

MONTVILLE, THOMAS JOSEPH, food microbiologist, educator; b. Somerville, N.J., Jan. 10, 1953; s. Frank Vincent and Elisabeth (Para) M.; m. Nancy Helen Shiffner, June 6, 1976; children: Christopher, Rebecca, Matthew. BS cum laude, Rutgers U., 1975; PhD, MIT, 1979. Rsch. asst. food sci. dept. MIT, Cambridge, 1975-80; rsch. microbiologist USDA, Ea. Region Rsch. Ctr., Phila., 1980-84; assoc. prof. food sci. dept. Rutgers U., New Brunswick, N.J., 1984-91, prof., 1991—, dir. grad. program in food sci., 1991-94, chmn. food sci. dept., 1997-2000. Cons., lectr. in field, 1985—; panel mgr. USDA CSRS Food Safety Grants Program, 1992; mem. food adv. com. U.S. FDA, 1999—. Mem. editl. bd. Jour. Food Protection, 1985-98, Applied & Environ. Microbiology, 1980-83; bd. editors Food & Nutrition Press, 1988—, Process Biochemistry, 1993-98, Jour. Indsl. Microbiology, 1995—; editor: Food Microbiology, vols. 1, 2, 1987, Jour. Food Safety, 1993—, co-editor, 1989-93; contbr. articles to profl. jours. Recipient McGraff lectureship, Long Island U., 1991, Cert. Merit, USDA, 1983. Fellow Am. Acad. Microbiology, Inst. of Food Technologists; mem. AAAS, Internat. Assn. Milk Food and Environ. Sanitarians, Am. Soc. Microbiology, Inst. Food Technologists (chmn. biotech. div. 1991-92), Soc. Indsl. Microbiology, Soc. Applied Bacteriology, Phi Tau Sigma. Office: Rutgers U Food Sci Dept 65 Dudley Rd New Brunswick NJ 08901-8520 E-mail: montville@aesop.rutgers.edu.

MONTY, CHARLES EMBERT, utility company executive; b. Plainfield, Conn., Mar. 9, 1927; s. Arthur Ovila and Mary Louise (Bromley) M.; children: Charles E., Mary, Janice, Nathan, Marcia. BSEE, Northeastern U., 1950; MBA, U. Maine, 1969. Registered profl. engr., Maine. Chmn. bd. dirs. Maine Yankee Atomic Power Co., 1988-92; chief oper. officer Cen. Maine Power Co., 1984-89, also bd. dirs. Energy cons., 1989—; mem. mgmt. com. New Eng. Power Pool, 1982-86. Mem. IEEE, Maine Assn. Engrs. Republican. Mem. United Chs. of Christ.

MONTY, GLORIA, former television producer, film executive; b. Union City, N.J. d. Joseph and Concetta M. (Mango) Montemuro; m. Robert Thomas O'Byrne, Jan. 8, 1952 BA, NYU; MA, Columbia U. Dir. New Sch. Social Rsch., N.Y.C., 1952-53; dir. Old Towne Theatres, Smithtown, N.Y., 1952-56, Abbey Theatre Workshop, N.Y.C., 1952-56; chmn. N.J. Motion Picture & TV Commn., Newark. Cons. ABC Dir. numerous TV programs, including Secret Storm, 1956-72, Bright Promise, numerous episodes ABC Wide World Entertainment; exec. prodr. General Hospital, 1977-86, 90-92, The Hamptons, 1983-85; made-for-TV movies, including Confessions of a Married Man, 1982, The Imposter, 1984; exec. prodr. in devel. for primetime TV 20th Century Fox, 1987-90; head cons. daytime TV ABC, 1987-90; prin. Gloria Monty Prodns. for new ABC daytime drama devel.; co-exec. prodr. While My Pretty One Sleeps, 1994-95, CBS Remember Me, FAMILY CHANNEL, 1995-97, Let Me Call You Sweetheart, 1997—, Moonlight Becomes You, 1997—; made-for-TV movies in assn. with Grosso-Jacobson. Chair Film Commn., State of N.J. Recipient Emmy awards, 1982, 84, Am. Soc. Lighting Dirs. award, 1979, Most Successful TV Show in History of TV award ABC, 1982, Spl. Editors award Soap Opera Digest, 1984, numerous others; named Woman of Yr., Paulist Choristers So. Calif., 1986. Mem. Women in Film, Dirs. Guild Am. (mem. exec. com.), Stuntman's Assn. (hon.), Thunderbird Country Club (Rancho Mirage, Calif.), Bel Air Country Club (Calif.), Deal Country Club, Navesink Country Club. Office: NJ Motion Picture & TV Commn PO Box 47023 153 Halsey St 5th Fl Newark NJ 07101

MONYAK, WENDELL PETER, pharmacist; b. Chgo., Sept. 14, 1931; s. Wendell and Mary Elizabeth M.; m. Lorraine Mostek, Aug. 29, 1964. BS in Chemistry, Roosevelt U., 1957; BS in Pharmacy, St. Louis Coll. Pharmacy, 1961. Asst. chief pharmacist Little Co. of Mary Hosp., Chgo., 1961-66; chief pharmacist MacNeal Meml. Hosp., Berwyn, Ill., 1966-72; dir. pharmacy Ill. Masonic Med. Ctr., Chgo., 1972, dir. pharm. services, 1972-87; dir. pharmacy services St. Anne's Hosp., 1987-88, adminstr., 1989-97; v.p., chmn. bd. dirs. Tabor Hills Health Care Facility, 1989—. Tchg. assoc. U. Ill., 1972-87. Author: Hospital Formulary and Therapeutic Guide for Residents and Interns, 1974, 3d edit. 1986. Pres., chmn. bd. dirs. Bohemian Home for Aged, 1986-89. With M.C., AUS, 1955-57. Mem. Am. Pharm. Assn., Am. Soc. Hosp. Pharmacists, Ill. Pharm. Assn. (Spl. Recignition award), No. Ill. Soc. Hosp. Pharmacists, Chgo. Hosp. Coun. Clubs: Oakbrook Exec. Home: 8701 E Tether Trl Scottsdale AZ 85255-1492

MONYPENY, DAVID MURRAY, lawyer; b. Jackson, Tenn., Apr. 29, 1957; s. Kent Brooks Monypeny and Kathryn (Warner) Sadowski. BBA, U. Okla., 1980; JD, U. Memphis, 1983. Bar: Tenn. 1983; CPA, Tenn. Assoc. Glankler, Brown et al, Memphis, 1983-85; acct. Frazer, Thomas & Tate, 1985-87; ptnr. Diamond, Finklestein, Monypeny, 1987-88, Lowrance & Monypeny, Memphis, 1988-94, Monypeny, Simpson Walker & Schatz, Memphis, 1994-97; sole practice Law Offices of David Monypeny, PLLC, 1997—. Tax atty., cons. to nat. entertainers and celebrities. Author: (video) Wiping Out Tax Debt You Can't Afford To Pay, 1993. Mem. Bellevue Ch., Memphis, 1983—; campaign fin. chair Neil Small Chancellor, Memphis, 1990. Featured on TV, in mags. and newspapers for his client's tax settlements; named Bankruptcy Atty. of Yr., 1999, Tax Atty. of Yr., Memphis Bus. Rev., 2000. Republican. Baptist. Avocations: music, video. Office: Law Offices of David Monypeny M PLLC 5100 Poplar Ave Ste 2700 Memphis TN 38137-2701

MONZINGO, AGNES YVONNE, veterinary technician; b. Mangum, Okla., July 16, 1942; d. Ira Lee and Opal Alice (McAlexander) Mayfield; m. Monty Brent Monzingo, Dec. 19, 1959; children: Tara, Dawn, Michael, Kermit. AS, San Antonio Coll., 1969. Mgr. Tupperware Corp., Wichita Falls, Tex., 1966-69; with La Louisiane, San Antonio, 1974-79; counselor Diet Ctr., Duncanville, Tex., 1984-87; vet. technician DeSoto (Tex.) Animal Hosp., 1985-98, hosp. mgr., 1998—. Author: (weekly column) Happy Tracks, 1981. Commr. Boy Scouts Am., 1988—93, tng. chmn. Wisdom Trail Dist., 1991—98, dist. commr. Wisdom Trail commn., 1998—99; pres. Dallas Stake Primary, 1983—88. Recipient Wood badge Boy Scouts Am., 1987, Wisdom Trail Dist. award of merit, 1990, Silver Beaver award Boy Scouts Am., 1993. Mem. Tex. Assn. Registered Vet. Technicians (v.p. 1991), Tex. Assn. Animal Technicians (pres. 1988, com. chair 1990-92), Tex. Assn. Registered Technicians (pres. 1992), Am. Boxer Club, Dallas Boxers Club (sec. 1982-92), Metroplex Vet. Hosp. Mgrs. Assn. Mem. Lds Ch. Avocations: dog show exhibitor, dog breeder.

MOODY, DENMAN, business and insurance executive, periodicals editor; b. Houston, Apr. 27, 1942; s. Leroy Denman and Edna Kone (Lewis) M.; m. Mickey Bogess Reed, Nov. 28, 1963 (div. 1972); 1 child, Christy Lee; m. Marijo Lindsay, Aug. 7, 1976; 1 child, Lindsay Catherine. BA, U. Tex., 1965, JD, 1968. CLU; Chartered Fin. Cons. Briefing atty. Tex. Supreme Ct., Austin, 1968-69; assoc. McKay & Avery, 1969; travel aide Mr. Lloyd Bentsen, Houston, 1970; exec. asst. Senator Lloyd Bentsen, Washington, 1971-72; sr. v.p. Tex. Commerce Bank, Houston, 1972-81; v.p. Merrill Lynch, 1982-86; editor, publisher Moody's Wine Rev., 1978-83; contbg. editor Internat. Wine Rev., Ithaca, N.Y., 1984-90, Wine and Spriits, Princeton, N.J., 1990-91; v.p. Shearson Lehman Bros., Houston, 1986-91; pres. Nat. Compensation Plans, Inc., 1991-96; sr. v.p. The AFP Group, 1996—. Contbr. articles on wine to various publs.; co-host radio show Financially Speaking, Sta. KNWZ, Palm Desert, Calif., 1993-94. Mem. Houston Bus. and Estate Planning Coun.; mem. initial fund raising com. Neurosensory Ctr., Houston, 1978; mem. planned giving com. March of Dimes, Houston, 1978; chmn. men's major gift com. Houston Grand Opera, 1974-75; bd. dirs. St. Stephens Episcopal Sch., 1991-93; bd. dirs. Cystic Fibrosis Found., Houston, 1988-90, mem. dinner com., 1984-89; wine solicitation chmn. Houston Grand Opera Wine Classic, 1992, 94. Recipient Lifetime Achievement award Houston Grand Opera Wine Classic, 1996. Mem. Tex. Bar Assn., Houston Bar Assn., Internat. Wine and Food Soc. (host 1977), Commanderie de Bordeaux, Brotherhood Knights of Vine (founder Houston chpt., comdr. emeritus), Houston Country Club (wine com. 1987—). Republican. Baptist. Avocations: wine, ranching. Office: The AFP Group 1300 Post Oak Blvd Ste 1200 Houston TX 77056-3018

MOODY, ERIC JOHN, psychologist, researcher; b. Richland, Wash., Oct. 3, 1975; s. John Henry Moody, Melody Ann Moody; m. Makyla Marie Miller. BS, Pacific Luth. U., 1998—98. Psychol. rschr. Nat. Jewish Med. & Rsch. Ctr., Denver, 1998—; tchg. asst. U. Denver, 2001—. Author: (Journal article) Cyberpsychology and Behavior, 2001 (PLU Psychology Dept. Undergraduate Research Award, 1998); contbr. Presentation of research. Lutheran. Avocation: Avocations: travel, hiking, skiing, photography. Office: Nat Jewish Med and Rsch Ctr 1400 Jackson St Denver CO 80206 Personal E-mail: emoody@du.edu. Business E-mail: moodye@njc.org.

MOODY, FLORENCE ELIZABETH, education educator, retired college dean; b. Penn Yan, N.Y., Sept. 29, 1932; d. James William Southby and Rebecca (Worrall) M. BS, SUNY, Geneseo, 1954; MS, Syracuse (N.Y.) U., 1961; EdD, U. Rochester, N.Y., 1969. Elem. sch. tchr. N.Y. State, 1954-64, 66-68; coord. profl. devel. Eastern Regional Inst. Edn., Syracuse, 1969-71; mem. faculty SUNY, Oswego, 1971-92, prof. elem. edn., 1978-92, assoc. dean profl. studies, 1980-84, dean, 1985-92. Mem. N.Y. State Tchr. Edn. Cert. and Practice Bd., 1983-89; mem. Tchr. Edn. Conf. Bd., 1982-84. Nat. sec. Nat. Women's Party, 1974-76; bd. dirs. Oswego County Extension Svc., 1974-76. NDEA fellow, 1965-66; Danforth assoc., 1978—. Mem. ASCD, Am. Assn. Colls. Tchr. Edn. (pres. N.Y. State chpt. 1983-84), Assn. Tchr. Educators, Am. Ednl. Rsch. Assn., N.Y. State Assn. Tchr. Educators (sec., exec. bd. 1976-78), Order Eastern Star, Kappa Delta Pi, Pi Lambda Theta, Phi Delta Kappa, Delta Kappa Gamma. Home: 44 Franklin Ave Oswego NY 13126 also: 2008 New Bedford Dr Sun City Center FL 33573-6146

MOODY, FREDERICK JEROME, mechanical engineer, consultant; b. Apr. 2, 1935; s. Frederick J. and Ruth K. (King) M.; m. Phyllis Arlene Ivemeyer, Aug. 27, 1955; children: David, John, Paul, Daniel. BSME, U. Colo., 1958; MSME, Stanford U., 1965, PhD in Mech. Engring., 1971. Engr. GE, San Jose, Calif., 1958-78, prin. engr., 1978-81, cons. engr., 1981—99. Adj. prof. San Jose State U., 1971—; consulting engr. thermal-hydraulics GE, 1958-99. Author: Introduction to Unsteady Thermofluid Mechanics, 1990; co-author: The Thermal-Hydraulics of a Boiling Water Nuclear Reactor, 1977, 2d edit., 1993, The Day I Almost Quit-and Other Stretching Events, 1997. Chmn. bd. dirs. Med. Inst. Chaplains, San Jose, 1984. Named to Silicon Valley Engring. Hall of Fame, 2000. Fellow ASME (George Westinghouse Gold medal 1980, Pressure Vessels and Piping medal 1999); mem. Nat. Acad. Engring. Republican. Home and Office: 827 Larkspur Ln Murphys CA 95247-9694 E-mail: fmoody@goldrush.com.

MOODY, GENE BYRON, engineering executive, small business owner, minister; b. Calhoun, Ga., Aug. 29, 1933; s. Denzel Elwood and Mary Edna (Hughes) M.; m. Willie Earline Chauncey, Sept. 1, 1955; children: Byron Eugene, Iva Marie Levy. BSCE, U. Tenn., 1956. Registered profl. engr., Ala., Ark., Ga., La., Miss., Tex. V.p. S.I.P. Engring. Corp., Baton Rouge, 1968-70; project engr. S.I.P., Inc., Houston, 1970-73; dir. of engring. Jacus Assoc., Mpls., 1972-73; dir. of civil engring. Barnard & Burk, Baton Rouge, 1973-79; project mgr. Process Svcs., 1979-80, Salmon & Assoc., Baton Rouge, 1980-81; chief engr. Minton & Assoc., Lafayette, La., 1982; mgr. Assoc. Engr. Cons., Baton Rouge, 1982-86; owner Gene B. Moody, P.E., 1986—. Author: Deliverance Manual, 1989; contbr. articles to profl. jours. Tchr. Lake Hamilton Bible Camp, Hot Springs, Ark., 1981—. With U.S. Army, 1957. U. Chattanooga scholar, 1951, U. Tenn. scholar, 1953. Fellow ASCE; mem. Am. Soc. Safety Engrs., La. Soc. Profl. Surveyors, Soc. Automotive Engrs., Inst. Transp. Engrs., La. Engring. Soc., Transp. Res. Rsch. Bd., others. Home and Office: 14930 Jefferson Hwy Baton Rouge LA 70817-5217 E-mail: gbmoody@bellsouth.net.

MOODY, JOYCE HAMRICK, school system administrator; b. Thomaston, Ga., July 21, 1930; d. Henry and Mary (Cotton) Hamrick; m. Frank Foster Moody, Dec. 21, 1952 (dec. Apr. 1993); 1 child, Janice Elaine Moody. BA, Ga. State U., 1951; MEd, Mercer U., 1955. Tchr., libr. Yatesville (Ga.) H.S., 1951-52, Powers Sch., Macon, Ga., 1953-55; libr.-media adminstr. El Rancho Sch. Dist., Pico Rivera, Calif., 1955-74; owner, exec. dir. Bright-Bailey Schs., Whittier, 1974—. Mem. libr. adv. bd. Rio Hondo Coll., Whittier, 1963-74. Author: Hamricks of Upson County, 1998, Hamricks, Vol. II, 1998; contbr. articles to profl. jours. Mem. Thomaston-Upson Arts Coun., 1990—; spkr., contbr. Upson Hist. Soc., Thomaston, 1995-99. Mem. DAR (regent), AAUW, Am. Assn. Retired Persons, Ctrl. Ga. Genealogy Soc. Democrat. Baptist. Avocations: research, writing, quilting, oil painting, arts and crafts. Home: 14909 Los Lotes Ave Whittier CA 90605-1631 Office: Moody Woods Publs PO Box 5442 Whittier CA 90607-5442

MOODY, LIZABETH ANN, law educator; b. Johnson City, Tenn., July 11, 1934; d. Robert Alexander and Clara Pauline (Fine) M.; m. Alan Paul Buchmann, Sept. 5, 1959. AB, Columbia U., 1956; LLB, Yale U., 1959. Bar: Conn. 1959, Ohio 1960, U.S. Dist. Ct. Conn. 1960, U.S. Supreme Ct. 1977, U.S. Dist. Ct. (no. dist.) Ohio 1961. Assoc. Goldstein & Peck, Bridgeport, Conn., 1959-60, Slough & Slough, Cleve., 1960-61, 63-66, Ginsberg, Guren & Meritt, Cleve., 1962; ptnr. Metzenbaum, Gaines, Finley & Stern, 1967-71; assoc. prof. Cleve. State U., 1970-73, prof., 1973-94, interim dean and prof., 1987-88; vis. prof. U. Toledo, 1976-77; v.p., dean Coll. Law, prof. Stetson U., 1994-99, Disting. univ. prof., 1998—. Rev. authority on civil rights HEW, Washington, 1973—79; vis. prof. Nat. Law Ctr. George Washington U., 1981—82, U. Hawaii, Honolulu, 1988, Wallace S. Fugiama Disting. prof., 2002; CEO Law Sch. Admission Svcs., Newtown, Pa., 1991—93; dir., sec., mem. exec. com. Fla. Health Scis. Ctr., Tampa Gen. Hosp., Fla., 1998—. Author: (books) Smith's Review of Corps, 1987, Smith's Review of Estates, 1987; contbr. articles to profl. jours. Pres. Cuyahoga County Econ. and Community Devel., Cleve., 1984-88, Task Force on Violent Crime, Cleve., 1987-88; chmn. audit com. Law Sch. Admission Coun., New Town, Pa., 1988-89, bd. trustees Law Sch. Admission Coun., 1989-94, exec. dir., 1991-93, pres., CEO, dir. Law Sch. Admission Svc., 1991-93; commr. Ohio Ethics Commn., Columbus, Ohio, 1988-91, Ohio Pub. Defender Commn.; v.p., trustee Gt. Lakes Theatre Festival, Cleve., 1972-90; dir., sec. exec. com. Fla. Health Scis. Ctr., 1997—; dir. Cleve. Growth Assn., 1987-88; trustee Acad. Prep., St. Petersburg, Fla., 1999—. Recipient New Frontier award Ams. for Dem. Action, 1977, YWCA Women of Distinction award, 1988, Josephine Irwin award, 1990; Day named in her honor, May 8, 1990, Cleve. Mem.: AAUP, ABA (chair non-profit corp. com. 1987—91, house of dels. 1994—99, chair accreditation com. 1994—2000, sr. lawyers divsn. coun. 1997—2001, sect. legal edn. coun. 2000—, vice chmn. 2001—, bus. law sect., Glass Cutter award 1997), English Speaking Union (trustee 1986—89), Cleve. Bar Assn. (pres. 1987—88, meritorious svc. award 1987), Ohio State Bar Assn. (coun. of dels. 1981—91, Ohio Bar medal 1992), Am. Law Inst. (ALI-ABA com.), Assn. Am. Law Schs. (exec. com. 1977—81), Tampa Club, St. Petersburg Yacht Club. Office: 1401 61st St S Saint Petersburg FL 33707-3246 E-mail: moody@law.stetson.edu.

MOODY, MAXWELL, JR. retired physician; b. Tuscaloosa, Ala., Aug. 7, 1921; s. Maxwell and Jean Kilroy (Lahey) M.; m. Betty Alice Morrissey, May 10, 1946 (dec. Feb. 1994); children: Maxwell III, Susan, Elizabeth Sims; m. Barbara Loftis, Mar. 4, 1995. BA, U. Ala., 1941; MD, U. Pa., 1944. Diplomate Am. Bd. Internal Medicine. Intern Gorgas Hosp., Ancon, C.Z., 1944-45, 1944-45; resident Grad. Sch. Medicine, U. Pa., Phila., 1947-48, Univ. Hosp., Birmingham, Ala., 1948-50; jr. and sr. resident in medicine U. Ala. Hosp., 1948-50; pvt. practice Tuscaloosa, 1950-87; ret., 1987. Pres. Tuscaloosa County Med. Soc., Ala. Soc. Internal Medicine; pres., chn. bd. Ala. Heart Assn. Former state chmn., nat. trustee Ducks Unltd. Capt. U.S. Army, 1945-47. Fellow Am. Coll. Physicians. Republican. Episcopalian. Avocations: golf, hunting, fishing. Home: 7604 Mountbatten Rd NE Tuscaloosa AL 35406-1110

MOODY, NELSON LEON, protective services official, writer; b. Balt., Feb. 14, 1963; m. Lisa Maria Laws, July 29, 2001; children: Alexandria N., Alexia N.;1 child from previous marriage Nelson L. Jr. Aide Dept. Recreation, Balt., 1978—79; with U.S. Army, 1980—86; security officer Broadway Svcs., Balt., 1986—89; parking control agt., traffic officer Dept. of Transp., 1989—. Author: When a Judge Can't Judge, 2000, When a Judge Can't Judge Part Two (The Conclusion), 2002. Sgt. U.S. Army, 1980—86. Avocations: plants, fish, photography, travel, cooking.

MOODY, PATRICIA ANN, psychiatric nurse, artist, small business owner; b. Oceana County, Mich., Dec. 16, 1939; d. Herbert Ernest and Dorothy Marie (Allen) Baesch; m. Robert Edward Murray, Sept. 3, 1960 (div. Jan. 1992); children: Deanna Lee Cañas, Adam James Murray, Tara Michelle Murray, Danielle Marie Murray; m. Frank Alan Moody, Sept. 26, 1992. BSN, U. Mich., 1961; MSN, Washington U., St. Louis, 1966; student, Acad. of Art, San Francisco, 1975-78. RN; lic. coast guard, ocean operator. Psychiat. staff nurse U. Mich., Ann Arbor, 1961-62, Langley-Porter Neuro-Psychiat. Inst., San Francisco, 1962-63; instr. nursing Barnes Hosp. Sch. Nursing, St. Louis, 1963; psychiat. nursing instr. Washington U., 1966-68; psychiat. nurse instr. St. Francis Sch. Nursing, San Francisco, 1970-71; psychiat. staff nurse Calif. Pacific Med. Ctr., 1991-97. Psychiat. staff nurse Charter Heights Behavioral Health Sys., Albuquerque, 1996-97; owner, cruise cons. Cruise Holidays Albuquerque, 1995—. Oil and watercolors included in various group exhbns., 1982-93. V.p. Belles-Fundraising Orgn., St. Mary's Hosp., San Francisco, 1974; pres. PTO, Commodore Sloat Sch., 1982; docent Albuquerque Mus. Art and History, 1998—. Recipient Honor award Danforth Found., 1954, Freshman award Oreon Scott Found., 1958; merit scholar U. Mich., 1957. Mem. Nat. Alliance for Mental Illness (sec. bd. dirs. 2000), San Francisco Women Artists (Merit award for oil painting 1989), Artist's Equity (bd. dirs. No. Calif. chpt. 1987-89, pres. No. Calif. chpt. 1990), Met. Club. Republican. Lutheran. Avocations: cycling, hiking, sailing, photography, piano. Home: 219 Spring Creek Ln NE Albuquerque NM 87122-2013 Office: Cruise Holidays Albuquerque 11032 Montgomery Blvd NE Albuquerque NM 87111-3962 E-mail: patmoody@goodmoodcruises.com.

MOODY, R. BRUCE, writer; b. Flushing, N.Y., Sept. 22, 1933; s. Albert and Kathleen May Moody; 1 child. BA, Columbia Coll., 1958; MA, Hunter Coll., N.Y.C., 1978. Author: (novels) The Decline and Fall of Daphne Finn, Roadside: A Memoir, (short stories) The New Yorker, The Nat. Lampoon, others, (poetry) numerous lit. mags., (translations) various translations and adaptations of novels; actor: (plays) numerous, including Bay Area Theatre, N.Y. Theatre prodns. of Romeo and Juliet, Macbeth, Two Gentlemen of Verona, Saint Joan, Pygmalion, others. Cpl. U.S. Army, 1953—55. Recipient H.C. Brunner prize for Am. Literary Criticism, Columbia U., 1978.

MOODY, ROBERT ADAMS, neurosurgeon; b. Swampscott, Mass., Oct. 1, 1934; s. George F. and Florence P. M.; m. Claudia; children: Robert Adams, II, Cathy, Paul, Lisa, Sherri. BA, U. Chgo., 1955, BS, 1956, MD, 1960. Intern Royal Victoria Hosp., Montreal, Que., Can., 1960-61; resident in neurosurgery U. Vt. Affiliated Hosps., 1961-66; fellow Lahey Clinic, Boston, 1963-64; asst. prof. neurol. surgery U. Chgo. Med. Sch., 1966-71; sr. clin. instr., then asst. clin. prof. Tufts U. Med. Sch., 1972-74; prof. neurosurgery Abraham Lincoln Med. Sch., U. Ill., Chgo., 1975-81; chmn. div. neurosurgery Cook County Hosp., 1974-81, assoc. chmn. dept. surgery, 1976-81; clin. prof. neurosurgery SUNY-Binghamton, 1983—; chmn. neurosurgery Guthrie Clinic, Sayre, Pa., 1981-95; ret., 1995. Contbr. articles med. jours. USPHS fellow, 1957-58 Mem. ACS, Am. Assn. Neurol. Surgeons, Pa. Neurosurg. Soc. (councillor 1986-87, pres.-elect 1988, pres. 1989), Mid-Atlantic Neurosurg. Soc., Ctrl. Neurosurg. Soc. (pres. 1978-79), Alumni Assn. Lahey Clinic Found., Sigma Xi. Office: Guthrie Clinic Guthrie Sq Sayre PA 18840 E-mail: rcmoody@cyber-quest.com.

MOODY, RON, actor, writer; b. London, Jan. 8, 1924; s. Bernard and Kate (Ogus) Moodnick. BSc in Econs., U. London, 1953. Appeared in plays: 6 Years Revue, 1959, Candide, 1960, Oliver, as Shylock in Merchant of Venice, 1967, as Polinius in Hamlet, 1972, as Richard in Richard III, 1978, Iago in Othello, 1981, as Harpagon in Moliere's The Miser, Peter Pan, 2000, The Sunshine Boys, 2001, Comedians, 2001; (films) Oliver, 1967, Twelve Chairs, 1970, Dogpound Shuffle, 1973, Wrong is Right, 1981, Where is Parsifal?, 1983, Ghost in Monte Carlo, 1989, Kid at King Arthur's Court, 1995, The Three Kings, 1999, Paradise Grove, 1999, Chopsticks, 2000, Steps, 2000, Revelation, 2001; stage musicals: USA tour HMS Pinafore, 1987, Sherlock

Holmes, 1989, Streets of Dublin, 1992, Bertie, 1993, Peter Pan, 1995, The Canterville Ghost, 1998; on TV as Inspector Hart in Nobody's Perfect, ABC-TV, 1980, Dial M for Murder, 1981; dir. (play) Kafka In Love, 1991; author-composer musical comedies Joey, 1966, Saturnalia, 1970, Move Along Sideways, 1971, The Showman, 1976, Nine Lives, 1991; touring Move Along Sideways, 1991; author: (books) The Devil You Don't, 1980, Very Very Slightly Imperfect, Off the Cuff, 1987, The Soul of Leonardo, 1991, The Amazon Box, 1998. Served with RAF, 1943-48. Recipient Golden Globe award, 1968, Moscow Golden Bear award as best actor, 1970, Coco Trophy award, Clowns Internat., 1999; nominated Oscar, 1968. Mem. Am. Acad. Motion Picture Arts and Scis., Variety Club of Great Brit., Actors Equity, Screen Actors Guild, Clowns Internat. (pres. 1984), Performing Rights Soc. Writers, Soc. Authors. Home: Ingleside 41 The Green Southgate London N14 6EN England Office: Eric Glass Ltd 28 Berkeley Sq London W1 England also: care Barry Freed 2040 Ave Of Stars Ste 400 Los Angeles CA 90067-4703

MOODY, STANLEY ALTON, entrepreneur, financial consultant; b. Portland, Maine, Oct. 16, 1939; s. Alton Elwood and Mary Gwendolyn (Young) M.; m. Jo-Ann Newton Vercoe, Dec. 15, 1975 (dec. Apr. 1992); children: Karen Elizabeth, Kirt Edward, Leslie Ann; m. Barbara Marie Katkus, June 28, 1992; 1 child, Jonathan Edwards; foster child, Barbara Anne Lane. BSEE, U. Maine, 1962; postgrad., George Washington U., 1963-66; MA in Theol. Studies, Gordon-Conwell Theol. Sem., 1994; PhD in Theology, Trinity Theological Sem., 1999. Ordained to ministry Am. Bapt. Chs. U.S.A., 1996; registered Maine guide. Various positions Eastman Kodak Co., Kelsey-Hayes Co., Components, Inc., 1962-73; prin. Stan Moody Assoc., Augusta, Maine, 1973—; pres. Newton and Moody, Inc., Portland, 1980-84, Family Bookstores of New Eng., Portland, 1973—. Dir. bus. cons. Maine Devel. Found., 1984-86. Author: Entrepreneurship in Maine, 1985, Telecommunications Design Strategy for Maine, 1986, No Turning Back, 1989, I Will Walk Again, 1993, Crisis in Evangelical Scholarship, 2001. Selectman, Town of Manchester, 2001—; candidate for Gov. Maine, 1978; pastor North Manchester Meeting House, 1994—; chmn. Greater Portland C. of C. Energy Awareness Task Force, 1977; budget com. Town of Manchester, 1995—; chmn. Manchester Comm. awards Spirit of Am. Found., 1996. Mem. Safari Club Internat. Maine (v.p. 1993, pres. elect 1994), N. Am. Hunt Club (life). Republican. Avocations: hunting, fly fishing, writing. Home: PO Box 240 Manchester ME 04351-0240 Office: Stan Moody Assoc 98 Readfield Rd Manchester ME 04351-3213

MOODY, TENNEIL LEE, career services specialist; b. Reading, Pa., Dec. 20, 1975; d. Geraldine J. Daniels; m. Joshua R. Moody, Oct. 2001. BA, Lebanon Valley Coll., 1997; MS, Shippensburg U., 2000. Coord. alumni career devel. Shippensburg (Pa.) U., 1997-99; dir. alumni career svcs. Clemson (S.C.) U., 1999—. Mem. Southeastern Assn. Colls. & Employers (conf. co-chair 2000-01). Office: Clemson U 109 Daniel Dr Clemson SC 29631 E-mail: acs-l@clemson.edu.

MOODY, VIRGINIA LAREECE (VIRGINIA LAREECE GOODIN), realtor, small business owner; b. Oakland, Calif., Dec. 22, 1942; d. True Pete and Essie Mae (Lemons) Goodin; m. Robert Dean Walker, Sept. 15, 1962 (div. Sept. 1970); children: Kimberly, Kelly; m. William Francis Moody, Aug. 23, 1980 (div. 1988); stepchildren: Eric, Brandon. Student Orange County Jr. Coll., 1963-65, Midwestern U., 1961-62, Tarrant County Jr. Coll., 1975-83. Clk., agt., dispatcher Chgo. Rock Island R.R., Fort Worth, 1967-80; v.p., mgr. farms ops. Moody Farms, Inc., North Richland Hills, Tex., 1980— ; comml. realtor Roseberry Comml. Real Estate Co., North Richland Hills, 1985— ; owner Moody's Tex. Gifts. Mem. council City of North Richland Hills, 1984— ; mem. Women in Govt., Nat. League of Cities, 1984; bd. dirs. Indsl. Devel. Council, NE Tarrant County, 1984— , North East Fin Arts League, 1986— . Mem. Nat. Assn. Female Execs., Fort Worth Bd. Realtors, Comml. Real Estate Women, Haltom-Richland C. of C. Democrat. Episcopalian. Avocations: hist. areas, fine arts, video games. Home: 6313 Sunset Dr Fort Worth TX 76116-5506

MOODY, WILLARD JAMES, SR. lawyer; b. Franklin, Va., June 16, 1924; s. Willie James and Mary (Bryant) M.; m. Betty Glenn Covert, Aug. 21, 1948; children: Sharon Paige Moody Edwards, Willard J. Jr., Paul Glenn. AB, Old Dominion U., 1946; LLB, U. Richmond, 1952. Bar: Va. 1952. Pres. Moody, Strople Kloeppel & Basilone Inc., Portsmouth, Va., 1952—. Commr. Chancery, Portsmouth, 1960—, Accounts, 1960—. Del. Va. Ho. of Reps., Portsmouth, 1956-68; senator State of Va., 1968-83; chmn. Portsmouth Dems., 1983—. Recipient Friend of Edn. award Portsmouth Edn. Assn., 1981. Mem. ABA, Va. Bar Assn., Portsmouth Bar Assn. (pres. 1960-61, lectr. seminars), Va. Trial Lawyers Assn. (pres. 1968-69), Hampton Roads C. of C. (bd. dirs. 1983-86), Portsmouth C. of C. (bd. dirs. 1960-61), Inner Circle Advs., VFW, Cosmopolitan Club, Moose. Home: 120 River Point Cres Portsmouth VA 23707-1028 Office: Moody Strople Kloeppel & Basilone Inc 500 Crawford St Portsmouth VA 23705

MOOERS, CHRISTOPHER NORTHRUP KENNARD, physical oceanographer, educator; b. Hagerstown, Md., Nov. 11, 1935; s. Frank Burt and Helen (Miner) M.; m. Elizabeth Eva Fauntleroy, June 11, 1960; children: Blaine Hanson MacFee, Randall Walden Lincoln. BS, U.S. Naval Acad., 1957; MS, U. Conn., 1964; PhD, Oreg. State U., 1969. Postdoctoral fellow U. Liverpool, Eng., 1969-70; asst. prof. U. Miami, Fla., 1970-72, assoc. prof., 1972-76, U. Del., Newark, 1976-78, prof., 1978-79; prof., chmn. dept. oceanography Naval Postgrad. Sch., Monterey, Calif., 1979-86; dir. Inst. Naval Oceanography, Stennis Space Ctr., Miss., 1986-89; sci. advisor to dir. Inst. for Naval Oceanography, 1989; rsch. prof. U. N.H., Durham, 1989-91; prof., chmn. divsn. applied marine physics U. Miami, 1991-93, dir. Ocean Pollution Rsch. Ctr., 1992—2002, dir. Ocean Prediction Exptl. Lab., 1993—. Coord. Coastal Ocean Sci. Program, 1991—. Editor Jour. Phys. Oceanography, 1991-96; mng. editor Coastal and Estuarine Studies, 1978-99. With USN, 1957-64. NSF fellow, 1964-67; NATO fellow, 1969-70; Sr. Queen Elizabeth fellow, 1980 Mem.: AAAS, Estuarine Res. Fedn., Marine Tech. Soc., Am. Meteorol. Soc. (chmn. sci.& tech. com. on meterology & oceanography of Coastal Zone 1996—2002), U. Nat. Oceanog. Lab. Sys./Fleet Improvement Com. (chair 1994—97), U.S. Nat. Com. Internat. Union Geodesy and Geophysics (chmn. 1995—99), Ea. Pacific Oceanic Conf. (chmn. 1979—86), Am. Geophys. Union (pres. ocean sci. sect. 1982—84), The Oceanography Soc. (interim councilor 1987—88), Sigma Xi. Achievements include pioneering direct observation of transient coastal ocean currents and fronts plus mesoscale and coastal ocean prediction rsch. Home: 2521 Inagua Ave Coconut Grove FL 33133-3811 Office: U Miami Divsn Applied Marine Physics Opel/RSMAS 4600 Rickenbacker Causeway Miami FL 33149-1031 E-mail: cmooers@rsmas.miami.edu. *My central goal is to understand the ocean as a physical system by combining the interpretation of observations with dynamical theory and numerical models. Special emphasis has been on the dynamics of coastal oceans (continental shelf regions), now the scientific basis for practical mesoscale ocean prediction applied to marginal and semi-enclosed seas.*

MOOG, MARY ANN PIMLEY, lawyer; b. Havre, Mont., May 29, 1952; d. Orville Leonard and Della Mae (Cole) Pimley; m. Daren Russell Moog, Apr. 15, 1978; children: Eric John, Keith Cole, Trygg Orville. BS, Mont. State U., 1975; JD, U. Mont., 1981; LLM, NYU, 1983. Bar: Mont. Law clk. Mont. Supreme Ct., Helena, 1981-82; assoc., ptnr., staff atty. Bosch, Kuhr, Dugdale, Martin & Kaze, Havre, 1984—. Recipient Am. Jurisprudence Book award Lawyers Coop. Publ. Co., 1980-81, Tax award Prentice Hall, Inc., 1981, Northwestern Union Trust Co. award, 1981. Mem. ABA, Mont. Bar Assn., 12th Jud. Bar Assn. (pres. 1987-88), Phi Delta Phi. Democrat. Roman Catholic. Avocations: sports, arts and crafts, photography. Home: 925 Wilson Ave Havre MT 59501-4331 Office: Bosch Kuhr Dugdale Martin & Kaze PO Box 7152 Havre MT 59501-7152

MOOK, SARAH, retired chemist; b. Bklyn., Oct. 29, 1929; d. Wong and Lie Won (Woo) M. BA, Hunter Coll., 1952; postgrad., Columbia U., 1954-57, 62-65, U. Hartford, 1958-59. Cartographic aide U.S. Geol. Survey Dept. of Interior, Washington, 1952-54; rsch. asst. Mineral Beneficiation Lab. Columbia U., N.Y.C., 1954-57; analytical chemist nuclera divsn. Combustion Engring., Inc., Windsor, Conn., 1957-59; rsch. scientist Radiations Applications Inc., Long Island City, N.Y., 1959-62; chemist Marks Polarized Corp., Whitestone, 1962-64; sr. chemist NRA Inc. subs. Nuclear Rsch. Assoc., Inc., New Hyde Park, 1964-75; clin. chemist Coney Island Hosp., Bklyn., 1974-84, cmty. bd., 1978-80; assoc. chemist Bellevue Hosp. Ctr., 1984-89, prin. chemist, 1989-95; ret., 1995. Contbr. articles to profl. jours. Mem. adv. com. to state assemblyman State of N.Y., 1970-72; trustee park aVenue Christian Ch., 1973-82, sec., 1973-80, vice-chair, 1980-81, chair bd. trustees, 1981-82, pres. Christian Women's Fellowship, 1962-65, elder, 1982—; mem. Neighborhood Adv. Bd. for Cmty. Devel., 1996— (sec. 1996-99, chair 2000-02). Mem. Am. Assn. Clin. Chemistry (sec. N.Y. Met. sect. 1999—), AAAS, Am. Chem. Soc., N.Y. Acad. Scis., Van Slyke Soc. Republican. Home: 2042 E 14th St Brooklyn NY 11229-3314

MOOLLA, ZULKER NAIN, accountant; b. Johannesburg, South Africa, Dec. 2, 1961; s. Abdul Rashid and Aisa (Patel) M.; m. Najma Desai; children: Zaahida, Muhammad, Aslam, Zainab. BCompt, U. South Africa, Pretoria, 1985, BCompt with honors, cert. in theory of accountancy, U. South Africa, Pretoria, 1987; CFA, Inst. Comml. and Fin. Accts. of So. Africa, Johannesburg, 1992. Chartered acct., South Africa. Sr. credit contr. Nedfin Bank Ltd., Johannesburg, 1980-85; clk. Cajee & Takolia, 1986-87; chartered acct. Deloitte & Touche, 1987-92; mgmt. cons. M-Net TV, 1993-95; CEO Moolla Assocs. Chartered Accts., 1996—. Exec. cons. Deloitte & Touche, Johannesburg, 1993—, Goldclass Investments, Johannesburg, 1996—, Goldworths Investment Holdings, Johannesburg, 1997—, 786 Investment Holdings, Johannesburg, 1997—; group sec. Imperial Holdings, Ltd. Author: (manual) M-Net Internal Controls, 1995, (prospectus) Goldclass Profile, 1996, (books) Doing Business in South Africa, 1997, Small Business Handbook, 1997. Bd. dirs. Gauteng Tourism Bd., Johannesburg, 1997—, chmn. fin. com., 1997, chmn. audit com., 1997, mem. internat. exhbns. and trade shows com., 1997; spl. advisor to Dir. of Tourism Gauteng, Johannesburg, 1997. Mem. South African Inst. Chartered Accts. (chartered), Gauteng Soc. Chartered Accts., Ind. Mediation Svc. of South Africa (panelist 1994—, acctg. disclosure award 1994). Mem. African National Congress. Avocations: travel, game watching, squash, tennis, reading. Home: PO Box 2735 Houghton 2041 South Africa also: 111 Albatross St Johannesburg 1820 South Africa Office: Moolla Assocs Chartered Accts 28 Osborn Rd Houghton Johannesburg 2198 South Africa

MOOMAU, PAMELA HOOPER, economics educator; b. Chgo., Sept. 10, 1954; d. George Robert and Ruth (Reichmann) Hooper; m. Jerome Taylor Moomau, Apr. 3, 1982; children: James Tyler, Candace Carey, George Whittaker. BA, Harvard U., 1976, M.C.R.P., 1978; PhD, Tulane U., 1989. Urban policy specialist Office of the Mayor, New Orleans, 1978-80; dep. dir. Office of Fed. Programs, 1980-81, Office Econ. Analysis, New Orleans, 1981-82; instr. dept. econs. Tulane U., 1984-86; instr. dept. econs. and finance U. New Orleans, 1986-88, vis. asst. prof. dept. econs. and finance, 1989-90; vis. asst. prof. dept. econs. Tulane U., New Orleans, 1991—. Grad. fellow Tulane U., 1982-83. Mem. Am. Planning Assn., Am. Econs. Assn., Nat. Tax Assn.-Tax Inst. Am. Home: 10108 Crestwood Rd Kensington MD 20895-4244

MOOMAW, RONALD LEE, economics educator; b. Orkney Springs, Va., Aug. 1, 1943; s. Leo V. and Vivian (Fansler) M.; m. Juliana Pendleton, Dec. 27, 1971; children: Sara Christina, Kate Winston. BS with highest distinction, U. Va., 1964; PhD, Princeton (N.J.) U., 1976. Vis. asst. prof. U. Va., Charlottesville, 1968-72; asst. prof., assoc. prof. econs. Okla. State U., Stillwater, 1972-83, prof., 1983—, head dept., 1987-93; sr. rsch. assoc. Urban Inst., Washington, 1980-81; vis. assoc. prof. U. B.C., Vancouver, Can., 1983-84. Prof. bus. adminstrn. CBA Assocs., 1994—, Regents prof. 1998—. Co-author: Profile of Oklahoma, 1977, Economics and Contemporary Issues, 1996; asst. editor Jour. of Econs., 1991—, Jour. of Regional Sci., 1994—; editl. bd. Internat. Regional Sci. Rev., 1995—; contbr. articles to profl. jours. Vestryman St. Andrew's Episcopal Ch., Stillwater, 1979-80, treas., 1990—; mem. budget com. Diocese of Okla., 1994—. Woodrow Wilson fellow, 1964, NSF fellow, 1964-66. Mem. Am. Econ. Assn., So. Econ. Assn. (bd. trustees 1989-91, v.p. 1997—), Regional Sci. Assn., So. Regional Sci. Assn. (exec. com. 1985-87), Missouri Valley Econ. Assn. (pres.-elect 1995-96, pres. 1996-97). Office: Coll Bus Okla State U Stillwater OK 74078-0001

MOON, DAVID A. manufacturing executive; b. Washington, Aug. 2, 1956; d. Arthur Ray and Lillian (Baker) Moon. PhD in Comms., U.Ill., 1978. Owner,mgr. Indsl. Arts Svcs. Firm, Henderson, Nev., 1977; with N.L.R.B., 1977; industrialist I.C.R. Corp., Henderson, Nev., 1980; indusl. authority I.C.R. Corp. TM, Henserson, 1991—; pres., CEO Teledyne Inc., Center City, 1996. Baptist. Office: Indsl Arts Systems Firm 140 E. Rochell Rd Henderson NV 89015

MOON, DAVID C. information technology executive; Bachelors in Computer Sci., Brigham Young U. From software engr. to chief tech. officer, sr. v.p. devel. WordPerfect Corp. (acquired by Novell); chief info. officer, mem. gov.'s cabinet State of Utah; gen. ptnr. EsNet, Ltd., Provo; chmn. bd. dirs. Myfamily.com, Inc. Bd. dirs. Rappore Techs., Manzanita Holdings, Found, O2 Blue. Office: Myfamily.com 360 W 4800 N Provo UT 84604 Office Fax: 807-705-7001.*

MOON, HAROLD WARREN, JR. retired professional football player; b. L.A., Nov. 18, 1956; m. Felicia Hendricks; children: Joshua, Jeffrey, Chelsea, Blair. Degree in comm., U. Wash., 1978. With Edmonton Eskimos, 1978-84, Houston Oilers, 1984—93, Minn. Vikings, 1994—96, Seattle Seahawks, 1997-98, Kansas City Chiefs, 1999—2000. Named to Pro Bowl, 1988-93, Sporting News NFL All-Pro team, 1990. Achievements include AFC Passing Leader, 1992; holds NFL single-season records for most passes attempted-665, 1991; most passes completed-404, 1991, sheares NFL single game record for most times sacked-12, 1985; shares NFL single season records for most games with 300 or more yards passing-9, 1990, most fumbles-18, 1990; Played in Grey Cup CFL Championship Game 1978-82.*

MOON, JOHN HENRY, SR. banker; b. Van Buren, Ark., Aug. 19, 1937; s. B.R. and Alma (Witte) M.; m. Agnes Rose Dickens, Aug. 16, 1958; children: John Henry, Randall Allen. AA, Delmar Coll., Corpus Christi, Tex., 1956; BBA cum laude, Tex. A&M U., Kingsville, 1958. Sr. acct. Tex. Eastern Transp. Co. and subs., 1958-63; exec. v.p., dir. Houston Rsch. Inst., 1963-68; sr. v.p., asst. to chmn. bd., dir. Main Bank, 1968-; vice chmn. bd., dir. N.E. Bank, 1969; CEO, chmn. bd., dir. Pasadena (Tex.) Nat. Bank, 1970-81; gen. ptnr. Moon and Assocs., Ltd., 1977—. Chmn. bd., pres. Interservice Life Ins. Corp., Phoenix, Cmty. Bank, Houston, 1975-81, Interstate Bank, Houston, 1977-81; chmn. bd., pres. Moon Credit Corp., Pasadena, 1975—, Peoples Bank, Houston, 1983-93; chmn. bd. Cmty. Nat. Bank, Friendswood, Tex., 1981-93; chmn. bd. Peoples Nat. Bank, Pasadena, Tex., 1984-93; dir. San Jacinto River Authority, 1991-93; chmn., pres. Sam Houston Pky. Transp. Corp., 1991-93; bd. dirs. Harris County Indsl. Devel. Corp., 1996—, Pro Technologies, Inc., 1987-96, Quality Wire Rope Corp., chmn., 1999—. Past bd. dirs. Pasadena Heart Assn., Salvation Army, Tex. Assn. Prevention of Blindness; past chmn. City of Pasadena Bd. Devel.; past chmn. adv. bd. Pasadena Civic Ctr.; past dir. S.E. Econ. Devel., Inc.; bd. dirs. San Jacinto Coll. Found., 2000—, chmn., 2002--. Named Outstanding Young Man of Yr., Pasadena Jr. C. of C., 1973; named to Pasadena Hall of Fame, 1988. Mem. AICPA, Pasadena C. of C. (bd. dirs. S.E. Econ. Devel., Citizen of Yr. 1994), Tex. Soc. CPAs, Tex. Bankers Assn., Rotary. Home: 609 Bay Vista Seabrook TX 77586 Office: PO Box 910 Pasadena TX 77501-0910 E-mail: johnhmoonsr@aol.com.

MOON, M. JAE, political scientist, educator; b. Pusan, Rep. of Korea, Jan. 15, 1965; d. Pyungki Moon and Sooyeon Lee; m. Eunyi Kim Moon, May 31, 1992; 1 child Peter. BA in Polit. Sci., Yonsei U., 1989; MSc, Kyung hee U., 1991; MPA, U. Tex., Austin, 1993; PhD, Syracuse U., 1998. Tchg. asst. U. Tex., Austin, 1991, rsch. asst., 1992; from rsch. assoc. to adj. prof. Syracuse U., Syracuse, NY, 1993—98, adj. prof., 1998—99; prof. U. Colo., Denver, 1999—. Spkr. in field. Contbr. articles to profl. jours. Mem. exec. bd. Section for Environ. & Natural Resource Mgmt. ASPA, Washington, 2001. Fellow Chancellor's fellowship, Graduate Inst. Peace Studies, Korea, 1989—91, Armand Hammer fellow, U. Tex., 1991—93; grantee Roesco Martin grant, Syracuse U., 1997, Rsch. grant, PriceWaterhouseCoopers, USIA, 2001. Mem.: Am. Polit. Sci. Assn., Am. Soc. Pub. Adminstrn. (mem. exec. bd. 2001). Home: 10292 S Hunterwood Way Highlands Ranch CO Office: Univ Colorado at Denver GSPA Campus 142 PO Box 173364 Denver CO 80204

MOON, MARILYN LEE, economist; b. El Dorado, Kans., July 7, 1947; d. Jesse Morris and Shirley Lois M.; m. J. Douglas Gomery, Jan. 13, 1973. BA in Econs., Colo. Coll., 1969; MS in Econs., U. Wis., 1972, PhD in Econs., 1974. Rsch. assoc. Inst. for Rsch. on Poverty U. Wis., Madison, 1973-74, asst. prof. econs. Milw., 1974-80, assoc. prof. econs., 1980-81; sr. analyst human resources and cmty. devel. divsn. The Congl. Budget Office, Washington, 1981-83; sr. rsch. assoc. Health Policy Ctr. The Urban Inst., 1983-86; dir. pub. policy inst. AARP, 1986-89; sr. rsch. assoc. The Urban Inst., 1989-94, sr. fellow, 1994—. Cons. The Pepper Commn., 1989. Author: Medicare Now and in the Future, 1993, 2d edit., 1996, The Meaurement of Economic Welfare: Its Application to the Aged, 1977; co-author: Balancing Access, Cost and Politics: The American Context for Health System Reform, 1991, Entitlements and the Elderly: Protecting Promises, Recognizing Realities, 1995; editor: Economic Transfers in the United States, vol. 49, 1984; co-editor: Improving Measures of Economic Well-Being, 1977; columnist The Washington Post, 1993-2000; contbr. articles to profl. jours. Pub. trustee social security and Medicare trust funds, 1995-2000. Ford Found. fellow, 1971-73. Mem. Nat. Acad. Social Ins. (bd. dirs. 1993—), Assn. Pub. Policy & Mgmt. (policy coun. 1993—), Phi Beta Kappa. Avocations: photography, hiking, reading. Office: The Urban Inst 2100 M St NW Washington DC 20037 E-mail: mmoon@ui.urban.org.

MOON, MARLA LYNN, optometrist; b. Connellsville, Pa., July 31, 1956; BS, Pa. State U., 1978, Pa. Coll. Optometry, Phila., 1980; OD, Pa. Coll. Optometry, 1982. Cert. Nat. Bd. Examiners, Pa., N.J. Bds. of Optometric Examiners. Intern Gesell Inst. for Human Devel., New Haven, 1981, U.S. Mil. Acad., West Point, N.Y., 1981, Dr. William Moskowitz, Somerville, N.J., 1981-82, Elwyn Ins., Feinbloom Ctr., Phila., 1982; resident, pediatrics unit The Eye Inst., 1982-83; ptnr. Drs. Carlin and Moon, State College, Pa., 1983-96, Nittany Eye Assocs., Ltd., 1997—. Vis. lectr. Dominican Coll., Orangeburg, N.Y., 1985, Pa. State U., University Park, 1985-89, 91-92, 95; faculty Pa. Coun. Horseback Riding for Handicapped, State College, 1988-96; cons. JMS Mobility Assocs., Inc., Exton, Pa., 1983-89, Univ.Hosp. and Rehab. Ctr., Hershey, Pa., 1988-93, John Heinz Rehab. and Med. Ctr., Wilkes-Barre, Pa., 1990-98. Adv. bd., v.p. Learning Disabilities Assn., State College, 1983—92; com. chmn. Local Children's Team, 1985—89; pres., bd. dirs. Cen.-Clear Child Svcs., Philipsburg, Pa., 1984—96; active Task Force Project Self Sufficiency, Bellefonte, 1988—96; bd. dirs. Pa.-Del. Assn. for Educators and Rehab. Blind and Visually Impaired, Harrisburg, 1988—95. Recipient Phila. County Optometric Soc. award, 1982, Knight-Henry Meml. award Optometric Ext. Program, Phila., 1982, Disting. Svc. award Assn. Educators and Rehab. of Blind and Visually Impaired (Pa.-Del. chpt.), 1992, Woman of Distinction award Soroptimist Club of Centre County, 1996. Fellow: Am. Acad. Optometry (pres. 1987—); mem.: Pa. Coll. Optometry (bd. trustees 2002—04), Mid-Counties Optometric Soc. (pres. 1992—94, Optometrist of Yr. 2000), Pa. State Alumni Assn. (life), Pa. Optometric Assn. (chmn. 1989—91, bd. dirs. 1996—, pres.-elect 2001, pres. 2002, 2002, Optometrist of Yr. 2000), Am. Optometric Assn. (Optometric Recognition award 1985—96), Altrusa Club (sec., v.p.), Omega Epsilon Phi. Avocations: spectator sports, golf, tennis. Office: 428 Windmere Dr State College PA 16801-5308

MOON, MONA MCTAGGART, speaker, trainer, consultant, educator; b. Buffalo, Oct. 4, 1934; d. William Daniel and Helen Violet (Dubin) McTaggart; m. James McCallum Moon, July 14, 1957; children: Douglas, Melisa, Bruce. BA, UCLA, 1955; MA, San Diego State U., 1985. Lic. tchr., Calif., cert. adminstrn., supervision, Calif. Tchr. high sch. Acalanes High Sch., Lafayette, Calif., 1956-61, San Diego Unified Sch. Dist., 1967-82; pres. Motivation Dynamics, San Diego, 1982—. Contbr. articles to profl. jours. Dir. LWV San Diego, 1967-72. Recipient Outstanding Contbn. award Calif. Assn. Dirs. of Activities; named San Diego County Tchr. of Yr., 1980. Mem. ASTD, Nat. Speakers Assn., Phi Beta Kappa. Republican. Presbyterian. Office: 7910 Ivanhoe Ave # 29 La Jolla CA 92037-4511 E-mail: monammoon@aol.com.

MOON, NORMAN K. judge; BA, U. Va., 1959, JD, 1962, LLM, 1988. Judge U.S. Dist. Ct. (we. dist.) Va., 1997—. Office: PO Box 657 Lynchburg VA 24505-0657

MOON, PETER GEOFFREY, investment executive; b. Southampton, England, Nov. 4, 1949; s. Roland Charles and Constance Bernice (Fudge) M.; m. Susan Elizabeth Williams, May 31, 1975; children: Richard, Katherine, Simon. BS in Econs. with honors, U. Coll. London, 1972. Investment analyst Ctrl. Bd. Fin. Ch. of England, London, 1972-75, Slater Walker Securities, London, 1975-78; overseas equities mgr. Nat. Provident Instn., 1978-85; investment mgr. British Airways Pensions, 1985-92; chief investment officer Univ. Super-Annvation Scheme, 1992—. Investment advisor Teesside Super-Annvation Scheme, 1997—, Lincolnshire County Coun. Pension Fund, 1996—. Avocations: sailing, skiing, restaurant owner. Home: Hartnup House Smarden TN27 8QB England Office: USS Ltd 11th fl 1 Angel Ct London EC2R 7EQ England E-mail: pmoon@uss.co.uk.

MOON, RONALD T. Y. state supreme court chief justice; b. Sept. 4, 1940; m. Stella H. Moon. B in Psychology and Sociology, Coe Coll., 1962, LLD, 2001; LLB, U. Iowa, 1965; D Laws (hon.) , Coe Coll., 2001. Bailiff, law clk. to Chief Judge Martin Pence U.S. Dist. Ct., 1965-66; dep. prosecutor City and County of Honolulu, 1966-68; assoc. Libkuman, Ventura, Ayabe, Chong & Nishimoto (predecessor firm Libkuman, Ventura, Moon & Ayabe), Honolulu, 1968-72, ptnr., 1972-82; judge 9th div. 1st cir., Cir. Ct., State of Hawaii, 1982-90; assoc. justice Supreme Ct., State of Hawaii, 1990-93, chief justice, 1993—. Adj. prof. law U. Hawaii, 1986, 87, 88; lectr., guest spkr. numerous events. Mem. ABA, Hawaii Bar Assn., Assn. Trial Lawyers Am., Am. Bd. Trial Advocates (pres. 1986-93, nat. sec. 1989-91), Am. Inns of Cts. IV (bencher 1983—), Am. Judicature Soc., Hawaii Trial Judges' Assn., Conf. Chief Justices (bd. dirs.). Office: Supreme Ct Hawaii 417 S King St Honolulu HI 96813-2902 E-mail: cjrmoon@yahoo.com.

MOON, SPENCER, author, program consultant, educator; b. Talladega, Ala., May 11, 1948; s. Glascoe McCann and Florence Edna (Moon) Jackson. Baccalaureate in Filmmaking, Antioch Coll., 1977; MA in Film and Video Prodn., Columbia Pacific U., 1989. Film editor Sta. KPIX-TV, San Francisco, 1977-79, stage mgr., technician, 1979-91; prof. African-Am. studies dept. City Coll., 1995-2000, also cons.; office mgr. Nat. Writers Union/West, 2000—. Cons. Black Filmmakers Hall of Fame, Oakland, Calif., 1985-91, San Francisco Internat. Film Festival, 1986-90; cons. Castro-Valencia, Evans, S.E., and Phelan campuses City Coll.; artist in residence Calif. Arts Coun., San Bruno, 1986-89; program cons. KMTP-TV, 1991. Author: Reel Black Talk: A Sourcebook of 50 American Filmmakers, 1997; co-author: Blacks in Hollywood: Five Favorable Years, 1987-1991, 1992; producer, dir.: (film) Strivin' and Survivin', 1977, (videos) Interracialism: The National Denial, 1981, 5 Days In July, 1986, Art From Jail, 1989; contbr. articles to profl. jours. Mem. Nat. Writers Union, Bay Area Black Media Coalition (life, svc. award 1984, media award 1997), Internat. Alliance Theatrical Stage Employees (journeyman local 16). Home and Office: Realize Your Energy 766 1/2 Hayes St San Francisco CA 94102-4132 E-mail: moonrye@aol.com.

MOON, STEPHEN DOUGLAS, intern architect, songwriter; b. Marietta, Ga., Jan. 3, 1970; s. Douglas Ronald and Mary Cochran Moon; m. Victoria Austen, June 3, 1995. BS, Ga. Inst. of Tech., 1993. Intern architect Gardner, Spencer, Smith Sarden & Ptnrs., Architects, Atlanta, 1992-93, Potter & Cox Architects, Louisville, 1994-97; mem. staff K. Norman Berry Assocs. Architects, 1997-99; project mgr. Godsey Assocs. Architects, 1999—. Composer The Funeral of Mr. Disappointment, 1999. Bd. dirs. Highlands Cmty. Ministries, Louisville, 1997—, Highlands Ct. Apts., Louisville, 1997—, resource mgmt. com., Cmty. Coord. Child Care, 2001—, facilities com. chmn.; design com. Habitat for Humanity, Louisville, 1996-99; mem. Focus Louisville Alumni Group, 2002-. Mem. AIA (bd. dirs., assoc., program com. chair Ctrl. Ky. chpt. 1994—), Am. Soc. of Composers, Authors & Publs. Avocation: golf, travel. Office: PO Box 5044 Louisville KY 40255-0044

MOON, WILLIAM ARTHUR, JR. petroleum geologist, consultant; b. St. Louis, Oct. 20, 1932; s. William Arthur and Frances Anderson (Gannaway) M.; m. Marlene Joan Johnson, June 27, 1959 (dec. Mar. 1976) 1 adopted child, Arland David; m. Erika Cameron, Feb. 9, 1997. BSc in Geology, Va. Polytech. Inst., 1956, MSc in Geology, 1961. Field geologist Minerals Devel. Corp. subs. Norfolk and Western Rlwy., Pearisburg, Va., 1961-64; petroleum geologist offshore divsn. Texaco, New Orleans, 1964-70, staff geologist New Orleans divsn., 1970, asst. dist. geologist La., 1970-72; sr. geologist Texaco Ltd., London, 1972-75, advanced exploration geologist, 1975-77, sr. geol. supr., 1977-81, mgr. geol. ops., 1981-85, mgr. exploration ops., 1985-90, mgr. exploration, 1990-93, cons. geoscientist, 1993-97, ret., 1997. 1st lt. USAF,

1956-59. Decorated officer Order of the Brit. Empire. Mem. Am. Assn. Petroleum Geologists, Geol. Soc. Am., Petroleum Exploration Soc. Gt. Britain, Sigma Xi, Sigma Gamma Epsilon. Republican. Avocations: golf, walking, chess, pistols, sports cars. Home: 1602 Scott Dr Farmville VA 23901-2584

MOONA, NICKY, marketing professional; b. Bombay, July 26, 1970; d. Mahendra and Sandhya Moona. B in Bus. and Commerce, U. Bombay, 1990, M in Bus. and Commerce, 1992; MBA, Suffolk U., 1996. Account exec. Filmatt Prodns., Bombay, 1993—94, Grace & Rothschild Advt., N.Y.C., 1997—99; supr. branding and mktg. Frankfurt Balkind Comm., 1999—2000; supr. integrated mktg. and new bus. Ogilvy & Mather, 2000—01; mktg. cons., 2002—. Mem. Jericho Project, N.Y.C., 1999—2001. Mem.: Am. Advt. Assn. Home: 311 E 38th St Apt 4A New York NY 10016 Office: 309 W 49th St New York NY 10019-7316 Personal E-mail: nmoona@yahoo.com. Business E-Mail: nicky.moona@ogilvy.com.

MOONEY, BURTON LEE, secondary school educator, editor; b. Greenfield, Mass., Dec. 30, 1945; s. James Joseph Mooney and Dorthea Wilberta Atkins; m. Barbara Louise Vosburgh, Apr. 4, 1977 (div. Aug. 4, 1991); m. Lois Ann Hallet, May 30, 1997. BA in English, U. Calif., Chico, 1973; MA in Edn., Rollins Coll., 1981. Tchr. Polk County Sch. Bd., Lakeland, Fla., 1974—2002; ret., 2002. Head tchr. Elem. Polk Opportunity Ctr., Lakeland, 1987—94; adj. tchr. Polk C., Winter Haven, Fla., 1983—96; owner, pub. Writer's Helper, Lakeland, 1985—; editor-in-chief The Pride of Polk City newspaper, Auburndale Sun newspaper. Author: People, Places, Pets and Animals, 1989; freelance writer. With USAF, 1963-68. Decorated Bronze Star. Mem. VFW (life post 8002-Lakeland), Disabled Am. Vets. (life), Kung Fu Karate Assn. (black belt). Republican. Mem. Lds Ch. Avocations: coaching, music, swimming. Home: 1422 Creekwood Run Lakeland FL 33809 Office: PO Box 8172 Lakeland FL 33809 E-mail: bmoonwrite@aol.com.

MOONEY, CATHERINE LEE, real estate broker; b. Newark, Mar. 29, 1953; d. Robert Edward Lee and Catherine Mary (Sorrentino) Gosnell; m. Marvin Granville Coleman, May 20, 1972 (div. 1978); m. Jerome Henri Mooney, May 3, 1986 (div. 1995); 1 child, Stephen Lloyd Coleman. Student, Strayer Coll., 1972. Cert. residential specialist; lic. real estate agt., broker, Utah. Legal sec., 1976-82; mktg. asst. BSD Med. Corp., Salt Lake City, 1983; dir. investor rels. Kenman Corp., 1983-85; realtor, 1986-88; owner, broker Cathy Mooney Real Estate, Salt Lake City, 1988—. Del. Dem. Cen. Com., Salt Lake City, 1989. Mem. Women's Coun. Realtors (edn. chair 1991, Utah state treas. 1994), Residential Sales Coun., Nat. Assn. Realtors, Salt Lake Bd. Realtors (equal opportunity com. 1989, edn. com. 1989, realtor svcs. exec. com. 1992-94, grievance com. 1996—), Utah Assn. Realtors. Christian. Avocations: skiing, sailing, computers. Home and Office: 3672 Cove Point Dr Salt Lake City UT 84109 E-mail: cathy@cathymooney.com., cathy@cathymooneyhomes.com.

MOONEY, CHRISTOPHER ZIMMER, political science educator; b. Kewanee, Ill., June 20, 1958; s. Harris C. and Mary Lou Mooney; m. Laura Ann Zimmer, June 11, 1983; children: Allison Carmichael, Charles Zimmer. BA with honors, U. Wis., Milw., 1982; MPA, U. Wis., Madison, 1985, MA, 1987, PhD, 1990. Pres. Mootown Records, Madison, 1982-85; policy analyst Dept. Devel., State of Wis., 1985-86; instr. U. Wis., Milw., 1988-89, Madison, 1989-90; asst. prof. polit. sci. W.Va. U., Morgantown, 1990-96, assoc. prof., 1996-99, dir. grad. studies, 1997-99. Vis. lectr. U. Essex, Colchester, Eng., 1993-95, dir. Ill. Legis. Studies Ctr., U. Ill., Springield, 1999—. Co-author: Bootstrapping: . . ., 1993, West Virginia Politics and Government, 1996, Monte Carlo Simulation, 1997; mem. editl. bd. Am. Jour. Polit. Sci., 1994-97, Legis. Studies Quarterly, 1999—; editor: The Public Clash of Private Values, 2001; founding editor/pub. State Politics and Policy Quarterly; contbr. articles to profl. jours. Mem. Internat. Polit. Sci. Assn., So. Polit. Sci. Assn., Midwest Polit. Sci. Assn., Am. Polit. Sci. Assn. Avocations: jazz bass. Office: Ill Leg Studies Ctr Univ Ill Springfield IL 62794-9243

MOONEY, JAMES DAVID, JR. aerial photographer; b. Anderson, Ind., May 20, 1921; s. James David and Jane (Watson) M.; m. Christine Mott, Dec. 29, 1944 (div. 1957); children: Barbara, James II, Richard; m. Gloria van Bomel Schoninger, Dec. 8, 1972. Student, U.S. Naval Acad., 1940-43; naval aviator, USN Flight Sch., 1943; BS in Engring., Princeton U., 1947. Cert. protection profl. Am. Soc. for Indsl. Security; lic. comml. pilot FAA. Supply mgr. Willys-Overland Motors, Inc., Maywood, Calif., 1947-50; contr. F.L. Jacobs Co. Inc., Detroit, 1953-55; spl. rep. U.S. Steel Export Co., Washington, 1956-61; mgr. internat. ops. Armour Rsch. Found., Chgo., 1962-65; v.p. CDC Sys., Elizabeth, N.J., 1972-74; pres. Cash Control Corp., Mineola, N.Y., 1974-77; cons. J.D. Mooney Assoc., Oyster Bay, 1978-98; pres. Aerial Photos by JDM, Inc., 1998—. Author: Long Range Planning, 1967. Police commr. Village of Centre Island, Oyster Bay, 1979-83, mayor, 1983-89. Lt. USN, 1940-45, 51-53. Mem. Internat. Assn. Chiefs of Police, N.Y. State Conf. Mayors, Aircraft Owners and Pilots Assn., Cove Neck Tennis Club, Piping Rock Club. Roman Catholic. Avocations: tennis, sailing. Home: 527 Centre Island Rd Oyster Bay NY 11771-5015

MOONEY, JAMES HUGH, newspaper editor; b. Pitts., Aug. 18, 1929; s. James H. and Kathryn A. (Hall) M.; m. Eileen Jane Casey, July 30, 1960; children: Mark Hall, Sean Francis, Annina Marie, James Matthew, Lorelei Jane, Paul Adam, Kathryn Celeste. BA in Journalism, Duquesne U., Pitts., 1957. With advt. dept., then editorial dept. Pitts. Post-Gazette, 1953-61; writer-editor Nat. Observer, 1961-77, Nat. Geographic, 1977-79; editor Found. News mag., Washington, 1979-81; press sec. Congressman Mickey Edwards of Okla., 1982; asst. nat. editor Washington Times, 1982-83; editor Status Report, 1983-92; dir. info. resources Ins. Inst. for Hwy. Safety, 1992-93; editor Western Pa. Medicine, Johnstown, 1993-95, Embassy Flash, Aspen Hill, Md., 1995-96; pres. Mooney Comms., 1997—. Former mem. editl. adv. bd. Nat. Study Ctr. Trauma and Emergency Med. Systems. Served with AUS, 1951-53. Mem. European Assn. Sci. Editors, Washington Automotive Press Assn., Nat. Press Club. Home: 13820 N Gate Dr Silver Spring MD 20906-2215 E-mail: jekmooney@erols.com.

MOONEY, JAMES PIERCE, II, cable television executive; b. Fall River, Mass., May 28, 1943; s. James Pierce and Maria Anna (Antalek) Mooney Thompson; m. Louise Askew Rauscher, May 6, 1989; 1 child, James Pierce IV. JD, NYU, 1968. Congl. liaison officer EEOC, Washington, 1969-71; staff dir. U.S. Rep. John Brademas, 1971-77; chief of staff Office of Majority Whip, U.S. Ho. of Reps., 1977-81; v.p. govt. relations Nat. Cable TV Assn., 1981, exec. v.p., 1981-84; pres., CEO N000, 1984-93. Recipient Cable Pioneers award for leadership, 1986; named Exec. of Yr. Cable TV Bus. mag., 1986.

MOONEY, JEROME HENRI, lawyer; b. Salt Lake City, Aug. 7, 1944; s. Jerome Henri and Bonnie (Shepherd) M.; m. Carolyn Lasrich, Aug. 10, 1965 (div. Dec. 1978); 1 child, Dierdre Nicole; m. Kaitlyn Cardon, Sept. 23, 1995. BS, U. Utah, 1966, JD, 1972. Bar: Utah 1972, Calif. 1998, U.S. Ct. Appeals (10th cir.) 1974, U.S. Supreme 1984, U.S. Ct. Appeals (7th cir.) 1999, U.S. Ct. Appeals (9th cir.) 2001. Sole practice, Salt Lake City, 1972-75, 79-83; sr. ptnr. Mooney, Jorgenson & Nakamura, 1975-78, Mooney & Smith, Salt Lake City, 1983-87, Mooney & Assoc., Salt Lake City, 1987-94, Mooney Law Firm, Salt Lake City, 1995-98, Larsen & Mooney Law, Salt Lake City, 1999—. Bd. dirs. Mooney Real Estate, Salt Lake City; mem. Active Music, Calif. Copyright Conf. Mem. Gov.'s Coun. on Vet. Affiars, Salt Lake City, 1982-89; trustee Project Reality, Salt Lake City, 1976—, P.E.A.C.E.; SAMHSA sponsor Project Reality, 1994—; vice chair State Mil. Acad. Assoc. Served with U.S. Army N.G., 1992-93. Mem. ABA (criminal justice sect. U.S. Sentencing Commn. com.), Utah Bar Assn. (chmn. criminal bar sect. 1987-88), Beverly Hills Bar Assn., Nat. Assn. Rec. Industry Profls., Utah NG Assn. (trustee 1976), 1st Amendment Lawyers Assn. (v.p. 1986-88, pres. 1988-89), Nat. Assn. Criminal Def. Lawyers, Families Against Mandatory Minimums (adv. coun.), VFW. Democrat. Jewish. Avocations: sailng, computers. Home: 128 I St Salt Lake City UT 84103-3418 Office: 50 W Broadway Ste 100 Salt Lake City UT 84101-2066 E-mail: JerryM@MooneyLaw.com.

MOONEY, JUSTIN DAVID, motel executive; b. Kansas City, Mo., Feb. 21, 1932; s. J.L. and Phoebe (Lighton) M.; m. Alayne I. Kohn, June 15, 1958; children: Jo Ann, David Alan. BBA, U. Mich., 1954, MBA, 1957. Mgr. Woolf Bros., Kansas City, 1958-66, asst. to pres., 1967-70; pres. Mission Inn Motel, Inc., Overland Park, Kans., 1970-90, J & A Ventures, Inc., Shawnee Mission, 1990—. Bd. dirs. Nat. Fedn. of Ind. Bus., State of Kans., 1989-95, vice chmn., 1994-95; vice chmn. Small Properties Adv. Com., 1985-88, chmn. 1988-89, bd. dirs. 1979-90. Chmn. Hwy. 56 Bus. Dist., 1984-87, bd. dirs., 1984-90; bd. dirs. hospitality divsn. Johnson County C.C., 1982—, chmn. bd., 1986—; bd. dirs. Overland Park Conv. and Visitors Bur., 1983-90, v.p., 1987-90; bd. dirs. Temple B'nai Jehudah, 1972-81, 86-93, hon. bd. dirs., 1995—, pres. Men's Club, 1972-74; bd. dirs., pres. Catalina Bay, 1990-95, Heart Am. Jewish Hist. Soc., 1991-93, treas., 1991-93; bd. dirs., exec. com., pres. Spindrifter, 1990-95; bd. mem.-at-large Pavilions Property, 2002. Recipient Lifetime award Jewish Chatauqua, 1979, Temple Sisterhood, 1988; inductee Men's Club Hall of Fame, 1983. Mem. Am. Hotel and Motel Assn. (bd. dirs. 1983-88, exec. com. 1987-89, vice-chmn. small properties adv. coun. 1985-88, chmn. 1988-89), Kansas City C. of C. (Hall of Fame Man of Yr. 1971), Kans. Hotel Motel Assn. (bd. dirs. 1972-84, pres. 1982-84, Hotel Man of Yr. 1981), Greater Kansas City Hotel/Motel Assn. (bd. dirs. 1973—, pres. 1982-84, Life Time Achievement award 1997), Hotel Motel Assn. Kansas City Found. (bd. dirs. 2000), Kans. Lodging Assn. (bd. dirs. 1984, Hotel Man of Yr. 1983-84), Kansas City Athletic Club (treas. 1971-72, bd. dirs. 1969-72). Avocations: antique collecting, travel, sports. Home and Office: J&A Ventures Inc 14701 Delmar Shawnee Mission KS 66224-9545 E-mail: jdalayne@kc.rr.com.

MOONEY, LILLIAN HARNETT, social worker, consultant; b. N.Y.C., Jan. 20, 1926; d. James P. and Mary Ann (Sheehy) Harnett; m. Mills D. Mooney, Dec. 29, 1954; children: Jeanne Marie Hertzel, Joseph A. BA, Mt. St. Vincent, 1948; MSW, Fordham U., 1952; cert., N.Y. Sch. Interior Design, 1958. Lic. social worker, N.Y.; bd. cert. diplomate in clin. social work. Caseworker N.Y. Foundling Hosp., N.Y.C., 1948-50; program dir. Carroll Club, 1950-52; program cons. N.Y. Cath. Youth Orgn., 1952-55; sr. caseworker Nassau County Dept. Social Svcs., Mineola, N.Y., 1965-69; psychotherapist DePaul Clinic, Rochester, 1969-73; sch. social worker Fairport (N.Y.) Cen. Sch. Dist., 1973-88; cons. Bd. of Coop. Ednl. Svcs., Fairport, 1988-90. Mem. speaker's bur. Project Intervention, Rochester, 1989. Mem. mgmt. com. YMCA, Pittsford, N.Y., 1971-77. Mem. NASW, Acad. Cert. Social Workers, N.Y. State Sch. Social Workers, Rochester Community Players. Roman Catholic. Avocation: acting, interior decorating. Home: 14 Greylock Rdg Pittsford NY 14534-2318

MOONEY, MARILYN, lawyer; b. Pitts., July 29, 1952; d. James Russell and Mary Elizabeth (Cartwright) M. BA summa cum laude, U. Pa., 1973, JD, 1976. Bar: Mass. 1977, D.C. 1985, Pa. 1990, U.S. Dist. Ct. D.C. 1985, U.S. Ct. Appeals (D.C. cir.) 1985, U.S. Supreme Ct. 1986. Atty. E. I. du Pont de Nemours & Co., Wilmington, Del., 1976-84, Washington, 1985; assoc. Fulbright & Jaworski L.L.P., 1985-90, ptnr., 1990—. Contbr. articles to profl. jours. Mem. ABA (fed. regulation securities com.), Am. Soc. Corp. Secs. (securities law com.), Internat. Bar Assn. (issues and trading in securities com.). Office: Fulbright & Jaworski LLP 801 Pennsylvania Ave NW Washington DC 20004-2615 E-mail: mmooney@fulbright.com.

MOONEY, MICHAEL EDWARD, lawyer; b. Beloit, Wis., Jan. 21, 1945; s. William C. and Edith (Slothower) M. BA in Econs., St. Norbert Coll., 1966; JD, Boston Coll., 1969. Bar: Mass. 1969, Maine 1969, U.S. Tax Ct. 1975, U.S. Ct. Internat. Trade 1986. Assoc. Nutter, McClennen & Fish, LLP, Boston, 1969-77, sr. ptnr., 1978—, now mng. ptnr. V.p., exec. dir. Fed. Tax Inst. New Eng.; spkr., lectr. numerous seminars. Co-editor: Considerations in Buying or Selling a Business, 1985; mem. bd. editors Accounting for Law Firms, 1988—. Fellow Am. Coll. Tax Counsel; mem. Boston Bar Assn. (chmn. tax highlights com. 1986-95, mem. fin. com. 1990-92), Boston Tax Forum. Office: Nutter McClennen & Fish 1 International Pl Boston MA 02110-2699 E-mail: mem@nutter.com.

MOONEY, MICHAEL JOSEPH, college president; b. Evansville, Ind., Dec. 15, 1942; s. Joseph Thomas and Marie Louise (DeJean) Mooney; children: Susanne, Julia. AB summa cum laude, St. Meinrad Coll., 1964; STL magna cum laude, Univ. Innsbruck, Austria, 1968; M in Philosophy, Columbia U., 1973, PhD, 1982. Lectr. dept. religious studies, St. Mary's U., Halifax, N.S., Can., 1968-70, Union Theol. Sem., N.Y.C., 1972-74; project coord. Columbia U., 1973-74, preceptor dept. religion, 1975-76, spl. asst. to exec. v.p. for acad. affairs, 1976-77, asst. provost, 1977-79, assoc. provost, 1979-82, dep. provost, 1982-89; pres. Lewis and Clark Coll., Portland, Oreg., 1989—. Visitor Inst. for Advanced Study, Princeton, NJ, 1984; trustee Jour. Philosophy, 1982—; bd. dirs. Nat. Assn. Ind. Colls. and Univs., 1995—99, mem. exec. com., 1997, sec., 1998—99; mem. com. women in higher edn. Am. Coun. Edn., 1997, mem. commn. on internat. edn., 1993—95; bd. dirs. Reid Hall, Inc., N.Y.C. and Paris, 1977—89, v.p., 1983—89; mem. Truman Scholarship Finalists Selection Com., 2001—. Author: Vico in the Tradition of Rhetoric, 1985 (Gottschalk prize Am. Soc. 18th Century Studies 1985); editor: Renaissance Thought and Its Sources, 1979; co-editor: Toward a Theology of Christian Faith: Readings in Theology, 1968, Vico and Contemporary Thought, 1976, Small Comforts for Hard Times: Humanists on Public Policy, 1977. Bd. dirs. Roothbert Fund, 1980—92, Portland Opera Assn., 1992—93; trustee Oreg. Ballet Theater, 1992—, Lewis and Clark Bicentennial Oreg., 2001—, Scuola d'Italia, N.Y.C., 1986—89, World Affairs Coun., 1992—2001, pres., 1999—2000. Recipient Rome prize Am. Acad. in Rome, 1989; Roothbert Fund fellow, 1972, Kent fellow Danforth Found., 1972, Woodrow Wilson fellow, 1972, Presdl. fellow Columbia U., 1972, F.J.E. Woodbridge Disting. fellow Columbia U., 1973; NEH grantee, 1984; Cavaliere Ufficiale, Order Merit, Republic of Italy, 1991. Fellow Italian Acad. for Advanced Studies in Am. (sr.); mem. Soc. for Values in Higher Edn., Am. Soc. for Eighteenth-Century Studies, Internat. Soc. for History of Rhetoric, Renaissance Soc. Am., Am. Acad. Religion, Am. Philos. Assn., Phi Beta Kappa (hon.). Office: Lewis & Clark Coll Office Pres 0615 SW Palatine Hill Rd Portland OR 97219-7879 E-mail: pres@lclark.edu.

MOONEY, PATRICIA ANNE, educator, sales and service professional; b. Bronx, N.Y., June 6, 1948; d. Peter Joseph and Helen (Houlihan) M.; m. Anthony John Grasso, Nov. 21, 1970 (div. 1977); 1 child, A. Benjamin. BA, Coll. New Rochelle, N.Y., 1970, MS, 1975. Tchr. Archdiocese of N.Y., Harrison, 1970-78; salesperson N.Y. Telephone, N.Y.C., 1978-82; sales instr. AT&T, Aurora, Colo., 1983, sales mgr. N.Y.C., 1984, mgr. sales support dept., 1985, mgr. pricing and contract support dept. Morristown, N.J., 1986, mgr. new bus. support dept. Bridgewater, 1987, sales br. mgr. Englewood, Colo., 1988-92, sales change mgmt. orgn. Bridgewater, N.J., 1993, data networking customer svc. process mgmt. Bedminster, 1994, large bus. customer svc. strategy NJ, 1995-97; bus. process improvement Nextel, McLean, Va., 1997-98; operational process improvement, retention, after-market sales and ordering exec. Aerial (nowVoicestream), Tampa, Fla., 1998-2000; operational process improvement Intermedia (now Worldcom), 2000—01; tchr. Belleville (NJ) Sch. Dist., 2002—. Bd. dirs. Camp Rising Sun. Mem.: Coll. New Rochelle Alumni. Roman Catholic. Avocations: performing arts, travel, skiing. Home: 3 Tulip Ln Morristown NJ 07960-6768 E-mail: pamooney@att.net.

MOONEY, PATRICIA MAY, physicist; b. Bryn Mawr, Pa., July 12, 1945; d. William Henry and May (Howson) M. AB, Wilson Coll., 1967; MA, Bryn Mawr Coll., 1969, PhD, 1972. Asst. prof. physics Hiram (Ohio) Coll., 1972-74; research assoc. physics dept. SUNY, Albany, 1977-78; asst. prof. physics Vassar Coll., Poughkeepsie, N.Y., 1974-80; mem. research staff IBM T.J. Watson Research Ctr., Yorktown Heights, 1980—. Vis. scientist U. Paris VII, 1979-80, Fraunhofer IAF, Freiberg, Fed. Republic of Germany, 1987-88. Mem. editl. bd. Phys. Rev. B., 1998—, Applied Physics Letters/Jour. of Applied Physics, 1996-98, Jour. of Materials Sci., 1992—; author mongraphs; contbr. chpts. to books, articles to profl. jours. Juror Maria Mitchell Women in Sci. award 1998. Fellow AAAS (chair nom. com. indsl. sci. sect. (P) 2001-2002), Am. Phys. Soc. (various offices including vice-chair divsn. materials physics 1998-99, chair elect divsn. materials physics 1999-2000, chair divsn. materials physics 2000-01, past chair divsn. materials physics 2001-02); mem. Materials Rsch. Soc., N.Y. Acad. Sci. Avocation: gardening. Office: IBM J Watson Rsch Ctr PO Box 218 Yorktown Heights NY 10598-0218 E-mail: mooneyp@us.ibm.com.

MOONEY, RICHARD EMERSON, writer; b. Plainfield, N.J., Mar. 31, 1927; s. Wandell M. and Alice (Joy) M.; m. Elizabeth B. Coleman, Oct. 30, 1954; children: James C., Stephen E., John B. BA, Yale U., 1947; postgrad. (Nieman fellow), Harvard U., 1955-56. Writer United Press, N.Y.C., 1948-51, econ. reporter Washington, 1951-56, N.Y. Times, Washington, 1957-63, European econ. correspondent Paris, 1963-67, econ. reporter N.Y.C., 1967, asst. to exec. editor, 1968, asst. to mng. editor, 1969, dep. fgn. editor, 1970-72, asst. fin. editor, 1972-76, mem. editl. bd., 1982-95; contbg. editor, 1995-96; v.p. Hartford Courant, 1976-81, exec. editor, 1976-81, dir., 1977-81. Author: (with Edwin L. Dale, Jr.) Inflation and Recession, 1959. Trustee Hartford Courant Found., 1977-81. Served with USNR, 1944-48. Mem. Soc. Silurians (bd. govs. 1998—), Yale Club (N.Y.). Home: 130 E 67th St New York NY 10021-6136 Office: 1776 Broadway Ste 1000 New York NY 10019-2002 E-mail: remooney@aol.com.

MOONEY, RICHARD MICHAEL, martial artist, writer; b. Manhattan, NY, June 21, 1960; s. Frances H. Mooney, Theodore C. Mooney; m. Kathryn E. Gray; children: Simon Owen, Brittany Skeen, Alexandria Gray. Contbr. , articles to profl. jours. Mem. adv. bd. Fla. Crime Prevention Commn., Sarasota, 1994—98; Tex. state dir. Fedn. United Martial Artists, Wichita Falls, 1998, Fla. state dir. Sarasota, 1990—98, World Martial Arts Devel. Found., Sarasota, 1994—96. Named Master Instr. of Yr., World Martial Arts Hall of Fame, 2000, Grandmaster of Yr., N.Am. Blackbelt Hall of Fame, 2001. Mem.: 7th Inf. Divsn. Assn., 3rd Inf. Divsn. Assn., Am. Mil. Assn., Royal Air Force Martial Arts Assn. Independent. Avocations: martial arts, poetry, travel.

MOONEY, ROBERT MICHAEL, ophthalmologist; b. Mt. Vernon, N.Y., July 25, 1945; s. Robert Michael and Marie Evelyn (sabatini) M.; m. Dorothy May Kazmaier, Feb. 21, 1981. BS in Biology, Fordham U., 1966; MD, U. Bologna, Italy, 1972. Diplomate Am. Bd. Ophthalmology. Intern Grasslands Hosp., Valhalla, N.Y., 1972-73, resident in surgery, 1973-74; resident in ophthalmology N.Y. Med. Coll., Valhalla, 1974-76, chief resident ophthalmology, 1976-77; acting dir. dept. ophthalmology Westchester County Med. Ctr., Valhalla, 1980-86; pvt. practice Katonah-Mt. Kisco, N.Y., 1979—. Asst. clin. prof. ophthalmology N.Y. Med. Coll., Valhalla, 1982—. Fellow Am. Acad. Ophthalmology, Am. Coll. Surgeons; mem. Med. Soc. State of N.Y., Westchester County Med. Soc., Westchester Acad. Medicine (chmn. sect. ophthalmology 1987-89), MENSA. Republican. Roman Catholic. Avocations: travel, photography. Office: 185 Kisco Ave Mount Kisco NY 10549-3028

MOONEY, ROBERT THURSTON, health care educator; b. Bryan, Tex., Jan. 5, 1935; s. Archie T. and Eda Belle (Arrington) M.; m. Jean Russell, June 24, 1955; children: Cynthia Mooney Conyers, Sandra Mooney Cook. BS, Tex. A&M U., College Station, 1958, MEd, 1963. Cert. trainer. Tchr. Navasota (Tex.) Ind. Sch. Dist., 1958-61, Bay City (Tex.) Ind. Sch. Dist., 1961-65, dir. audio-visual instrn., 1965-66; ednl. media specialist Ednl. Media Labs., Austin, Tex., 1967-68; dir. edn. and tng. Bexar County Hosp. Dist., San Antonio, 1968-75; asst. prof. Southwest Tex. State U., San Marcos, 1974-80, assoc. prof., 1980—, chmn. allied health scis., 1976-81, dir. health svcs. mgmt., 1988-90, dir. Health Resource Ctr., 1981-82; mayor pro tem City of San Marcos, 1995-96. Dir. Sch. Paramed. Tng., Bexar County Hosp. Dist., San Antonio, 1970-72; cons. pvt. contractor, San Marcos, 1975—; mem. community/environ. task force Cen. Tex. Health Systems Agy., 1977; mem. health occupations edn. adv. com. Tex. Edn. Agy., 1989-91; mem. summer games organizing com. Tex. Spl. Olympics, 1990-91, security chmn., 1990; mem. health occupations projects adv. com. U. Tex., Austin, 1990-91. Author: Overhead Projection, 1968; (with Sister Rene Fisher and Beth Knox) Guidelines for the Development of a Hospital-Wide Education Service, 1979; contbr. articles to profl. jours. Chmn. disaster svc. Hays County Red Cross, San Marcos, 1988-89, bd. dirs., 1986-89; res. comdr. San Marcos Police Res., 1984-85; treas. Hays/Caldwell Counties Alcohol and Drug Abuse Coun., 1984-85, exec. bd. mem., 1984-85; res. dep. Hays County Sheriffs Dept., 1985-86, San Marcos Police Dept., 1986-87; zoning commr. City of San Marcos, 1991-93, city councilman, 1993-96; bd. dirs. Hays County Ctrl. Appraiser Dist., 1994-97; bd. pres. San Marcos/Hays County EMS; planning and zoning commr. City of San Marcos, 1997-2001; v.p. Hays County Appraisal Dist. Bd., 1996-98. Mem. ASTD, Am. Coll. Healthcare Execs., Soc. Human Resource Mgmt., Am. Soc. Healthcare Edn. and Tng. (bd. mem. 1971-72), Am. Hosp. Assn., Tex. Soc. Healthcare Educators (pres. 1971-72, pres. 1991-92, disting. svc. and achievement award 1989), Bay City Classroom Tchrs. Assn. (pres.), Navasota Classroom Tchrs. Assn. (pres.), Alamo Tng. and Insvc. Coun. Hosp. and Allied Health Educators (pres. 1969-71), Internat. Personnel Mgmt. Assn. (publs. adv. bd. 1988), Tex. Hosp. Assn., Assn. of Univ. Programs in Health Adminstrn., Soc. for Human Resource Mgmt. (reviewer HR magazine 1990-96), Kiwanis. Avocations: hunting, fishing. Home: 133 E Sierra Cir San Marcos TX 78666-2533 E-mail: rm02@swt.edu.

MOONEY, WILLIAM PIATT, actor; b. Bernie, Mo., May 2, 1936; s. Lowell E. and Louise S. M.; m. Valorie Shaw Goodall, Jan. 13, 1962; children: Sean Goodall, William Norvell. Student Am. theater wing, U. Colo. Pres. William Mooney Assocs., cons. to industry for exec. presentations Appeared in continuing role of Paul Martin on TV series All My Children, 1972-85 (2 Emmy nominations); one-man show Half Horse, Half Alligator & Damn Everything But the Circus; stage appearances: Brownsville Raid, We, A Man for All Seasons, Lolita; films: The Next Man, Network, A Flash of Green, Beer, Second Sight, C.A.T. Squad; author/star mus. play Banjo Reb and the Blue Ghost; co-author: ASAP-The Fastest Way to Create a Memorable Speech, 1992, Ready-to-Tell Tales, 1994, A Storyteller's Guide, 1995, Spiders in the Hairdo, 1999, (Grammy nominee 1998), (PBS) With a Dog's Eyes, 1997; recording artist: Why the Dog Chases the Cat, 1997 (ALA Notable Parent's Choice Gold and Naird awards), Spiders In The Hairdo, 1997, More Ready-To-Tell Tales From Around The World, 2000. Dir. jazz mus. Jam, 8 yrs. Colo. Univ. Opera Theater, others. Grammy nominee, 1995, 98. Address: 2879 Shadow Creek Dr #105 Boulder CO 80303

MOONIE, CLYDE WICKLIFFE, financial consultant; b. San Francisco, May 23, 1918; s. William B. and Vivienne (Selby) M.; m. Liana Maria Gabrielli, June 18, 1949; children: Gregory James, Barbara Marie. MBA, U. Chgo., 1941. C.P.A., Calif. C.P.A., N.Y. Mgr. Arthur Andersen & Co., C.P.A.s, 1941-58; adminstrv. mgr. Marcona Mining Co. S.A., 1958-62; controller Minerals & Chems. Philipp Corp., 1962-67; v.p., controller Engelhard Minerals & Chems. Corp. N.Y.C.; (merger Minerals & Chems. Philipp Corp. and Engelhard Industries, Inc.), 1967-73, sr. v.p., 1973-76, exec. v.p., 1976-80, Phibro-Salomon Inc. (formerly Engelhard Minerals & Chems. Corp.), 1981-82; exec. dir. Fin. Acctg. Standards Adv. Council, 1983-86; fin. cons., 1982—. Mem. panel arbitrators Am. Arbitration Assn. Served to capt. AUS, 1942-45. Recipient Forbes gold medal Calif. C.P.A. Soc., 1945 Mem. Am. Inst. C.P.A.s, Fin. Execs. Inst. Home and Office: 4 Lafayette Ct Ph Greenwich CT 06830-5320

MOONIE, LIANA MARIA, artist; b. Trieste, Italy, Mar. 22, 1922; came to U.S., 1947; d. Angelo and Maria (Canciani) Gabrielli; m. Clyde W. Moonie, June 18, 1949; children: Gregory J., Barbara M. Tchrs. cert., U. Trieste, 1945. Chair, editor Beaux Arts Mag., 1978-79; exhibited in group exhbns. at Nat. Acad. Design, N.Y.C., Salmagundi Club, N.Y.C., Hudson River Mus., N.Y., Gallery Hastings, N.Y., Stamford (Conn.) Mus., Discovery Mus., Conn., Islip (N.Y.) Art Mus., Bergen Mus. Art and Sci., N.J., Monmouth Art Mus. of South, Mobile, Ala., Chattanooga Ctr., Oklahoma City, others; represented in permanent collections Palm Beach Internat. Airport, Nat. Assn. Women Artists, Jane Voorhees Zimmerli Art Mus., N.J.; contbr. articles to profl. jours. Vol. Bruce Mus., Greenwich, Conn., 1997—; former pres. Mamaroneck Artists Guild, Hudson River Contemporary Artists; former bd. dirs. Am. Soc. Contemporary Artists, Scarsdale Art Assn.; former chmn. Beaux Arts Project in Westchester, N.Y. Recipient Emily Lowe award Allied Artists Am., 1985, Mary B. Hathaway award Scarsdale Art Assn., 1989, Therese Langhorne Duble award Hurlbutt Gallery, 1990, Quinn's award Greenwich Arts Ctr. Gallery, 1992, Jane Peterson Meml. award Allied Artists Am., 1992, Pres.' award Bush Holley Hist. House, 1995, F. Brooks award for graphic, Hurlbutt Gallery, 1998. Mem. Greenwich Art Soc. (bd. dirs. 1990—, pres. 1990-92, Pres.' award 1994, Mary B. Hathaway award 1993), Nat. Assn. Women Artists (pres. 1986-88, perm. adv. 1988—, chair Collection 1992-98, founder permanent collection 1992, founder Fla. chpt. 1995, Doris Kreindler award 1984, Elizabeth Morse Genius Found. award 1987, Ada Cecere Meml. award 1988, Myra Biggerstaff award 1995, Miriam E. Halpern Meml. award 1997). Home: 4 Lafayette Ct Ph Greenwich CT 06830-5320 Studio: 89 Maple Ave Greenwich CT 06830-5621 E-mail: cmoonie@aol.com.

MOOR, ROY EDWARD, finance educator; b. Riverside, Calif., Oct. 11, 1924; s. Hugh Erin and Clara Viola Moor; m. Beverly A. Colbroth, Aug. 29, 1959; children— Cynthia Ann, Sheryl Lynn BA, UCLA, 1949; PhD, Harvard U., 1958. Vice pres., chief economist Fidelity Bank, Phila., 1965-68; vice pres., chief economist Drexel Firestone, 1968-71, Warburg Paribas Becker, N.Y.C., 1971-81; sr. v.p., chief economist First Chgo. Corp., 1981-86; prof. fin. Ill. Inst. Tech., Chgo., 1986—. Dir. Nat. Bur. Econ. Research, Cambridge, Mass. Author: Federal Budget as an Economic Document, 1962 Fellow Nat. Assn. Bus. Economists (pres. 1973) Home: 1013 Woodrush Ct Westmont IL 60561-8823 Office: Ill Inst Tech 10 W 31st St Chicago IL 60616-3729 E-mail: rbmoor@kwom.com.

MOORADIAN, ARSHAG DERTAD, internist, educator; b. Aleppo, Syria, Aug. 20, 1953; arrived in U.S., 1981; s. Dertad and Araxi (Halajian) Mooradian; m. Deborah Lynn Miles, June 25, 1985; children: Arshag Dertad, Jr., Ariana Araxie. BS, Am. U., Beirut, 1976, MD, 1980. Diplomate Am. Bd. Internal Medicine. Asst. prof. medicine UCLA, 1985-88; assoc. prof. U. Ariz., Tucson, 1988-91; prof. St. Louis U., 1991. Contbr. articles to profl. jours. Grantee VA, 1985—97. Mem.: Am. Diabetes Assn. (chmn. task force micronutrients 1990—91, chmn. coun. nutrition and metabolism 2000—02), Endocrine Soc., Gerontol. Soc. Am., Am. Fedn. Clin. Rsch. Mem. Armenian Orthodox Ch. Achievements include identification of a potential biomarker of aging; research in on age-related changes in the blood-brain barrier; on age-related changes in thyroid hormone action; on diabetes related changes in the central nervous system. Office: Saint Louis U Med Sch 1402 S Grand Blvd Saint Louis MO 63104-1004

MOORE, ALBERT CUNNINGHAM, lawyer, insurance company executive; b. Miami, Fla., May 31, 1931; s. Elias Richard and Virginia Adelaide (Thompson) M.; m. Anne Cambreleng Bonynge, Aug. 24, 1957; children: Emily Robinson French, Barbara Raffield Moore, Catherine Anne Bonynge Wells. AB, U. N.C., 1953; JD, U. Va., 1959. Bar: N.Y. 1960. Atty. White & Case, N.Y.C., 1959-69; corporate sec. Studebaker-Worthington, Inc., 1969-72; sr. v.p., gen. counsel Crum & Forster, 1973-87. Former trustee N.J. Shakespeare Festival; former bd. dirs. DeBordieu Property Owners Assn., Debordieu Arch. Rev. Bd. With USNR, 1953-56. With USNR, 1953—56. Mem. ABA, Wilton Ctr. Tennis Club (N.H.), DeBordieu Club (S.C.), Phi Alpha Delta, Chi Phi. Home: 1318 Debordieu Blvd Georgetown SC 29440-7163

MOORE, ALBERT LAWRENCE, investment company executive, investment broker; b. Marion, Ind., Feb. 12, 1956; s. John Calvin and Alta Marie (Glandt) M.; m. Diane Kay Poe, Feb. 28, 1982; children: Wesley Calvin, Lisa Michelle. BA, Ind. U., Kokomo, 1978. Claims rep. Social Security Adminstrn., 1978-83; from investment broker to v.p. J.J.B. Hilliard W.L. Lyons, Inc., Greensburg, Ind., 1983-98, 1st v.p., 1998—. Pres. Decatur County Dem. Club, Greensburg, 1984-89, Decatur County United Fund, 1989-90; chmn. Greensburg Dem. Com., 1987; vice chmn. Decatur County Dem. Ctrl. Com., 1993-97; bd. dirs. Decatur County Meml. Hosp., chmn. bd., 1991-94, vice chair, 1996-2000; mem. Decatur County Election Bd., 1990—; mem. local coordinating com. Gov.'s Coun. for Drug Free Ind., 1991-93. Mem. Masons, Scottish Rite, York Rite, Indpls. Urban League, Interfaith Alliance. Presbyterian. Avocations: stamp collecting, politics, investments, European history. Home: 514 Baili Ct Greensburg IN 47240-8686 Office: JJB Hilliard WL Lyons Inc 101 E Main St Greensburg IN 47240-2031

MOORE, A(LVIN) C(RAWFORD), JR. investment analyst; b. Sylva, N.C., Sept. 14, 1943; s. Alvin Crawford and Breyl (Hooper) M.; m. Susan Bryson, Aug. 12, 1966 (div. 1970); m. Jo Ann Martha Lorberbaum, Dec. 29, 1971 (div. 1992); 1 child, Brett Crawford. B.B.A., Wake Forest U., 1964; J.D., U. N.C., 1967. Bar: N.C. 1967. Dir. instl. research Reynolds Securities, Inc., N.Y.C., 1968-75; pres. Dunvegan Assocs., Inc., N.Y.C., 1975-85; sr. v.p., dir. research Argus Research Corp., N.Y.C., 1985-90; sr. v.p. Argus Investment Mgmt., 1990—; dir. Dunvegan Assocs.; gen. ptnr. Sylva Ptnrs., 1979—; bd. visitors Wake Forest U. With USAF, 1966-70. Mem. ABA, N.Y. Soc. Security Analysts, Market Tech. Assn., Oil Analyst Group of N.Y., U.S. Tae Kwon Do Assn. Republican. Lutheran. Clubs: Union League, Metropolitan, N.Y. Stock Exchange Luncheon, Santa Barbara. Avocations: fitness, music, automobiles. Home: 4387 Del Mar Ave Santa Barbara CA 93108

MOORE, AMY NORWOOD, lawyer; b. Durham, N.C., Sept. 24, 1953; AB summa cum laude, Mt. Holyoke Coll., 1976; MA, U. Va., 1978, JD, 1983. Bar: D.C. 1984, U.S. Ct. Appeals (D.C. and 6th cirs.) 1985, U.S. Tax Ct., 1998. Law clk. to Frank M. Coffin, U.S. Ct. Appeals (1st cir.), 1983-84; ptnr. Covington & Burling, Washington. Articles editor Va. Law Rev., 1982-83. Mem. Phi Beta Kappa. Office: Covington & Burling 1201 Pennsylvania Ave NW Washington DC 20004-2401

MOORE, ANDREW GIVEN TOBIAS, II, investment banker, law educator; b. New Orleans, Nov. 25, 1935; m. Ann Elizabeth Dawson, June 5, 1965; children— Cecily Elizabeth, Marianne Dawson. BBA, Tulane U., 1958, JD, 1960. Bar: La. 1960, Del. 1963. Law clk. to chief justice Del., Dover, 1963; assoc. firm Killoran & Van Brunt, Wilmington, Del., 1964-70, partner, 1971-76; partner firm Connolly, Bove & Lodge, Wilmington, 1976-82; justice Del. Supreme Ct., 1982-94; sr. mng. dir. Wasserstein Perella & Co., Inc., N.Y.C., 1994—2001, Drsdner Kleinwort Wasserstein, Inc., N.Y.C., 2001—. Mem. Del. Bar Examiners, 1975-82; mem. Del. Gen. Corp. law com., 1969-83; chmn. joint com. Del. Bar Assn.-Del. Bankers Assn., 1978-79; chmn. Del. Jud. Proprieties Com., 1983-94, Del. Bench and Bar Conf., 1988-94; trustee Del. Bar Found., 1984-94; faculty Tulane Inst. European Legal Studies, Paris Inst., 1990-96, 99; adj. prof. law Georgetown U. Law Ctr., Widener U. Sch. Law, U. Iowa Coll. Law; guest lectr. law Columbia U., Tulane U., U. Toronto, Can., U. Tex., Villanova U., Washington U., St. Louis, U. Iowa, George Mason U., DeVrije U. van Brussel, Cath. U. Louvain La Neuve; mem. pres.'s coun. Tulane U., 1990-96; chmn. Tulane Corp. Law Inst., 1988-95; Lehmann disting. vis. prof. law Washington U., St. Louis, 1994, 96; Mason Ladd disting. vis. prof. U. Iowa, 1995; disting. vis. prof. law St. Louis U., 1995, 96, 99; bd. dirs. Am. Lawyer Media, Inc. Trustee Del. Home and Hosp. for Chronically Ill, Smyrna, 1966-70, chmn., 1966-69; mem. New Castle County Hist. Rev. Bd., Wilmington, 1974-82; mem. Del. Cts. Planning Com., 1982-94; dean's coun. Tulane U. Law Sch., 1988-96; bd. visitors Walter F. George Sch. Law, Mercer U., 1985-91, chmn., 1988-90. With JAGC, USAF, 1960-63. Mem. ABA, La. Bar Assn., Del. Bar Assn. (v.p. 1976-77, exec. com. 1982-83), Am. Judicature Soc. (bd. dirs. 1982-86), Order Barristers, Phi Delta Phi, Delta Theta Phi (hon.), Omicron Delta Kappa Democrat. Presbyterian. Office: Dresdner Kleinwort Wasserstein Inc 1301 Ave of the Americas New York NY 10019

MOORE, ANDREW TAYLOR, JR. banker; b. Tarboro, N.C., June 17, 1940; s. Andrew Taylor and Mary Dare (Allsbrook) M. BA in History, Duke U., 1962; LLB, U.Va., Charlottesville, 1965. Asst. sec. Signet Banking Corp., Richmond, 1965-71, asst. v.p., corporate sec., 1971-75, v.p., corporate sec., 1975-82, sr. v.p., corporate sec., 1982-94. Bd. dirs. Theatre IV, Richmond, Va., 1981-97, Va. State YMCA adv. coun., Lynchburg, 1988—; trustee Hist. Richmond Found., 1993-98; mem. presidents coun. Va. Hist. Soc., 1996—. Presbyterian (elder 1996—). Avocations: jogging; gardening; travel. Home: 2011 Hanover Ave Richmond VA 23220-3539

MOORE, ANNE, physician; b. N.Y.C., Apr. 28, 1944; d. John D.J. and Mary Foote Moore; m. Arnold L. Lisio, Sept. 6, 1969; children: Philip Moore, Mary Foote. BA, Smith Coll., 1965; MD, Columbia U., 1969. Diplomate Am. Bd. Internal Medicine, Am. Bd. Hematology (chmn. 1996), Am. Bd. Oncology. Intern dept. medicine N.Y. Hosp., N.Y.C., 1969-73, assoc. attending physician, 1981-95, attending physician, 1996—; postdoctoral fellow Rockefeller U., 1972-73, hematology-oncology fellow, 1973-75; asst. prof. medicine Cornell U. Med. Coll., N.Y.C., 1975-91, assoc. prof. clin. medicine, 1981-95, prof. clin. medicine, 1996—. Cons. Strang Cancer Prevention Ctr.; lectr., cons., in field. Author: Patient's Guide to Breast Cancer Treatment, 1992, rev. edit., 1997; ad hoc reviewer Am. Jour. Clin. Oncology, 1994, New Eng. Jour. Medicine, 1994, 96, 97; contbr. articles to profl. jours., chpts. to books. Trustee St. David's Sch., 1983-89, HealthCare Chaplaincy, Inc., 1991—; bd. dirs. Camilli Found., 1990—, Cure Myeloma Fund, 1988-98. Recipient award SHARE, 1992, Wholeness of Life award Hosp. Chaplaincy, 1992, Alumnae award Oak Knoll Sch., 1994, Eileen Dreyer Meml. Lectureship award Sass Found. for Med. Rsch., 1996, Commendation award Office of Exec. Nassau County, 1996, award Artists for Breast Cancer Survival, Inc., 2000. Mem. Am. Bd. Internal Medicine (bd. dirs. 1996—), Am. Soc. Hematology, Am. Soc. Clin. Oncology, N.Y. Acad. Scis., Soc. for Study of Blood (membership chmn. 1979-80), N.Y. Met. Breast Cancer Group (membership chmn. 1992-93, sec.-treas. 1993-95, v.p. 1995-96, pres. 1997—), Soc. for Study of Breast Disease, N.Y. Cancer Soc., N.Y. Acad. Medicine (trustee 1998—). Office: Weill-Cornell Med Ctr 428 E 72nd St New York NY 10021-4635

MOORE, ANNE, arts administrator, consultant, educator; b. Jackson, Tenn., Jan. 6, 1946; d. William Clifton and Frances (Woods) Moore; m. Michael Mezzatesta, Mar. 14, 1970 (div. July 1987); children: Philip Moore Mezzatesta, Alexander Woods Mezzatesta, Marya Frances Mezzatesta; m. Ernest Watson Hutton, Jr., Apr. 20, 1996. BA, Columbia U., 1969, MFA, 1971; MA in History of Art, Hunter Coll., 1982; Cert. in Mus .Mgmt., Am. Fedn. of the Arts, Berkeley, Calif., 1993. Lectr., rsch. assoc. Kimbell Art Mus., Ft. Worth, 1980-83; dir. outreach Dallas Mus. Art, 1986-88; curator edn. Allen Art Mus., Oberlin (Ohio) Coll., 1988-91, dir., 1991-96; lectr. NYU, N.Y.C., 1999—; project mgr. Peabody Essex Mus., Salem, Mass., 2000—. V.p. bd. trustees Intermus. Conservation Assn., Oberlin, 1994-96, trustee, 1991-94. Editor Bull. of the Allen Meml. Art Mus., 1991-93. Mem. Am. Assn. Museums. Home: 172 Pacific St Brooklyn NY 11201-6214

MOORE, BEATRICE, religious organization administrator; b. Somerville, Mass., Oct. 6, 1928; d. George and Christina Turner; m. Wendell Moore, May 9, 1953; children: Karl C., Linda Moore Flewelling, Diane Pearl, Larry. BA in Theology and English, Berkshire Christian Coll., Lenox, Mass., 1950. Pres. The Woman's Home and Foreign Mission Soc., Loudon, N.H., past nat. pres. Charlotte, NC, 1987—96; chmn. Nat. Spiritual Life. Sunday sch. tchr., deaconess Loudon Ridge Family Bible Ch.; chair Concord Christian Women's Club, 2002-03; active Women's Home and Fgn. Mission Soc., Loudon, past pres. N.H. Soc., past pres. ea. region; hostess, contact chmn., prayer adv., Bible club guide Stonecroft Ministries, Friendship Bible Study Guide; past leader 4-H Club. Mem.: Concord Christian Womens Club (chair). Office: Woman's Home & Foreign Mission 845 Loudon Ridge Rd Loudon NH 03307-1712

MOORE, BENJAMIN, theatrical producer; b. Boston, Oct. 25, 1945; s. Charles Frederick and Adeline Reeves (Nichols) Moore; m. Mary Bradford Paine, May 31, 1969 (div. Jan. 1982); m. Barbara Ann Dirickson, June 25, 1983 (div. May 1995); m. Marilyn McGuire, Oct. 9, 1999. BA, Dartmouth U., 1967; MFA, Yale U., 1970. Asst. mng. dir. Yale Repertory Theatre, New Haven, 1969-70; gen. mgr. Westport (Conn.) Country Playhouse, 1970; prodn. dir. Am. Conservatory Theatre, San Francisco, 1970-79, gen. mgr., 1979-81, mng. dir., 1981-85; mng. dir., bd. dirs. Seattle Repertory Theatre, 1985—. Mem. Seattle Arts Commn., 1986—90, chair, 1989; mem. Wash. State Arts Commn. Mem. Wash. State Arts Alliance, League Resident Theatres, Rainier Club. Office: Seattle Repertory Theatre 155 Mercer St Seattle WA 98109-4639

MOORE, BETTY JEAN, retired education educator; b. L.A., Apr. 4, 1927; d. Ralph Gard and Dora Mae (Shinn) Bowman; m. James H. Moore, Nov. 25, 1944 (div. 1968); children: Barbara, Suzanne, Sandra; m. George W. Nichols, Oct. 15, 1983. BA, Pasadena Coll., 1957; MA, U. Nev., 1963; PhD, U. Ill., 1973. Tchr. Calif. Elem. Schs., 1953-63; sec. tchr. Calif. pub. schs., 1963-68; asst. prof. Ea. Ill. U., Charleston, 1968-71; grad. teaching asst. U. Ill., Champaign, 1971-73; asst. prof. to assoc. prof. S.W. Tex. State U., San Marcos, 1973-83, prof. edn., 1983-89, ret., 1989, prof. emeritus, 1995—. Sch. evaluator; cons. in field; reading clinic dir. S.W. Tex. State U., 1974-85; cons. Min. Edn., Rep. of Singapore, 1980, 97; citizen ambassador People to People, China, 1998. Contbr. articles to profl. jours.; author: Teaching Reading, 1984; producer/dir. 5 ednl. videos. Active fund raising various charitable orgns.; vol. reading cons., Ariz. pub. schs., 2000—. Mem. Internat. Reading Assn. (chpt. pres. 1964-65), Nat. Council Tchrs. English, AAUP. Presbyterian. Avocations: reading, writing, swimming, cooking. Office: Southwest Tex State U C & I Dept San Marcos TX 78666 E-mail: bettynichols447@juno.com.

MOORE, BETTY JO, legal assistant; b. Medicine Lodge, Kans., July 10, 1921; d. Joseph Christy and Helen Blanche (Hubbell) Sims; m. Harold Frank Moore, June 19, 1941 (dec.); children: Terrance C., Harold Anthony, Trisha Jo. Cert., U. West L.A., 1978; student, Wichita (Kans.) U., 1940-41. Cert. legal asst./escrow officer. Sec. UCLA, 1949-59; escrow officer Security Pacific Nat. Bank, L.A., 1959-62, Empire Savs. & Loan Assn., Van Nuys, Calif., 1962-64; escrow supr. San Fernando Valley Bank, 1964; escrow officer Heritage Bank, Westwood, Calif., 1964-66; escrow coord. Land Sys. Corp., Woodland Hills, 1966-67; escrow officer/asst. mgr., real estate lending officer Security Pacific Nat. Bank, L.A., 1967-80; real estate paralegal Pub. Storage, Pasadena, 1980-81; asst. mgr. escrow dept. First Beverly Bank, Century City, Calif., 1982-84; escrow trainer/officer Moore's Tng. Temps Inc., Canoga Park, 1984—. Participant People to People Ambassador Program/Women in Mgmt. to USSR, 1989; observer Internat. Fedn. Bus. and Profl. Women's Congress, Washington, 1965, 81, Nassau, Bahamas, 1989, Narobi, Kenya, 1991. Adv. bd. escrow edn. Pierce Coll., Woodland Hills, Calif., 1968-80. Recipient Cert. of Appreciation, Pierce Coll., 1979, Calif. Fedn. Bus. and Profl. Women, 1989, Nat. Women's History Project, 1995. Mem. Nat. Fedn. Bus. and Prof. Women's Clubs, Calif. Fedn. Bus. and Profl. Women (pres. dist. 1987-88, Calif. Found. chmn. 1988-89, internat. concerns chmn. 1996—), Woodlands Hills Bus. and Profl. Women ((pres. 1991-92, 94-95), Tri Valley Dist. Bus. and Profl. Women (legis. chair 1992-93, exec./corr. sec. 1993-94, 94-95), Internat. Fedn. Bus. and Profl. Women, Nat. Women's Polit. Caucus (coord., sec. San Fernando Valley caucus 1986-87, sec. 1999-2000, legis. co-chair 1991-92, 92-93), Women's Orgn. Coalition San Fernando Valley (sec. 1992, mem. exec. com. L.A. Women's Equality Day 1995), San Fernando Valley Escrow Assn. (bd. dirs. 1962-64), Woodland Hills C. of C. (assoc.), San Fernando Valley Bd. Realtors, L.A. Women's Family Equity Coalition, U. West L.A. Alumni Assn. Democrat. Methodist. Avocations: reading, musical theater.

MOORE, BILLY DON, video scriptwriter, producer; b. Oklahoma City, Dec. 26, 1956; s. Orval L. and Mary E. (Perry) M.; m. Donna M. Lovelace; stepchildren: Derek, Ryan. BA in Journalism, U. Okla., 1979, MA in Journalism, 1993. Prodn. asst. FAA, Oklahoma City, 1979-81; media technician, supr. Oklahoma City C.C., 1981-85; video prodn. specialist Okla. Dept. Transportation, Oklahoma City, 1985-99; motion picture and broadcast archivist Okla. Hist. Soc., 1999—. Owner BVC Video. Editor, photographer (cable series) Connecting, 1983-85; prodr. pub. svc. announcements, (aviation video mag.) Okla. Approach, 1995-99; prodr. documentaries Okla. Pub. TV; prodr., editor, photographer: (TV show) Yesterday. Recipient Crystal award The Communicator, 1998, Telly award excellence, 1998, Aegis award, 1999, Videographer award excellence, 1999, 20th Anniversary Classic Telly award, 1999. Democrat. Baptist. Avocation: writing books on Oklahoma history. Office: Okla Hist Soc 2100 N Lincoln Blvd Oklahoma City OK 73105-4907 E-mail: bdmoore@ok-history.mus.ok.us.

MOORE, BLAINE AUGUSTA, lawyer; b. Greenwood, S.C., July 3, 1961; d. Blaine C. and Betty Springer Moore; m. Scott Kiefer, July 28, 1996. BS, Presbyn. Coll., 1983; JD, Cumberland Sch. of Law, 1987; LLM in Admiralty Law, Tulane U., 1988. Bar: La. 1987, U.S. Dist. Ct. (ea., mid. and we. dists.) La. 1987. Assoc. Ellefson, Pulver & Staines, New Orleans, 1989-94; pvt. practice, 1994-95; assoc. Duncan, ourington & Rydberg, 1995—. Vol. Big Bros./Big Sisters Am., New Orleans, 1994—. Mem. ABA, La. Bar Assn., New Orleans Bar Assn. Republican. Baptist. Avocations: travel, reading, refinishing furniture. Office: Duncan Courington & Rydberg 322 Lafayette St New Orleans LA 70130-3244

MOORE, BOB STAHLY, communications executive; b. Pasadena, Calif., July 3, 1936; s. Norman Hastings and Mary Augusta (Stahly) M. Student, U. Mo., 1954-58, MIT, 1958-62. News dir. WPEO, Peoria, Ill., 1958-60, KSST, Davenport, Iowa, 1960-62, WIRE, Indpls., 1962-64, WCFL, Chgo., 1964-67; White House corr. Metromedia, Inc., Washington, 1967-71; news dir. Gateway Communications, Altoona, Pa., 1972-74; Washington Bur. chief MBS, 1974-76, v.p. news Va., 1976-78, White House corr., 1978-81; dir. communications Fed. Home Loan Bank Bd., Washington, 1981-85; spl. asst. to bd. govs. Fed. Res. System, 1985—. Active ARC. Served with USAF, 1961-63. Recipient profl. awards Ind. News Broadcasters, 1963, Ill. News Broadcasters, 1965, UPI, 1960, 63, 65, AP, 1956, 58, 61, 65, 67, Mo. News Broadcasters, 1956, 61 Mem. Radio and Television News Dirs. Assn. (Profl. award), White House Corrs. Assn., State Dept. Corrs. Assn., Radio-Television Corrs. Gallery (U.S. Capitol), Chgo. Council on Fgn. Relations, Pub. Relations Soc. Am., Nat., Washington, Chgo. press clubs, U.S. Jr., Mo., Ill. chambers commerce, Sigma Delta Chi. Presbyterian. Home: 213 E Walsh Blvd Vandalia MO 63382 Office: 20th And Constitution NW Washington DC 20551-0001

MOORE, BONNIE LOU, biology educator, consultant; b. Hollister, Calif., June 12, 1960; d. John and Martha Helen Busch; m. Fritz Brinkman Moore, June 3, 1964. AS, Gavilan C.C.; BA, Calif. State U., Sacramento; PhD, U. Calif., Davis. Adj. instr. Napa (Calif.) Valley Coll., 1997—; lectr. U. Calif., Davis, 1999-2000; asst. prof. biology Ohlone Coll., Fremont, Calif., 2000—. Contbr. articles to profl. jours. Bank of Am. scholar, 1980, Achievement Rewards for Coll. Scholars scholar, 1994-96, Jastro Shields Rsch. scholar, 1991-93; Nestle Corp. fellow, 1989-93, NIH predoctoral fellow, 1994. Mem. Nat. Assn. Biology Tchrs., Phi Sigma. Office: Ohlone Coll 43600 Mission Blvd Office #8321 Fremont CA 94539 E-mail: bmoore@ohlone.cc.ca.us.

MOORE, BRADFORD L. lawyer; b. Brownfield, Tex., Feb. 9, 1952; s. Billie Buell and Jimmy (Green) M.; m. Carmelita Chaffin, June 20, 1971; children: April V., Ashli F. BA, Tex. Tech U., 1974, JD, 1977. Bar: Tex. 1978, U.S. Dist. Ct. (no. dist.) Tex. 1978, U.S. Dist. Ct. (we. dist.) Tex. 1987, U.S. Supreme Ct. 1987. V.p. McGowan & McGowan PC, Brownfield, 1978-90; pvt. practice, 1990—; mayor city of Brownfield, 1998-2000. Pres. Brownfield Little Girls Basketball, 1987-90. Recipient award for outstanding representation of abused children Tex. Dept. Human Svcs., 1984. Mem. Brownfield Bar Assn. (social chmn. 1980—), Rotary (sgt.-at-arms Brownfield 1980-81, pres. 1997-98), Kiwanis (pres. Brownfield 1984-86). Office: PO Box 352 Brownfield TX 79316-0352

MOORE, BRIAN CLIVE, actuary; b. Everett, Wash., Sept. 7, 1945; s. Frederic E. and Kathleen E. (Miller) M.; m. Lorraine Campbell, Feb. 11, 1946; children: Timothy, Jonathan. BA in Math., Yale U., 1970; MA in Math., U. Calif., 1971. Actuarial assoc. INA, Phila., 1971-73; asst. actuary Reliance Ins. Group, 1973-77, asst. sec., 1977-78, sec., 1978-80, asst. v.p., 1980-84, v.p., 1984-86, sr. v.p., 1986-99; asst. v.p. AIG Mktg., Wilmington, Del., 2000—. With U.S. Army, 1966-68. Fellow Casualty Actuarial Soc.; mem. Am. Acad. Actuaries. Office: AIG Mktg Inc 505 Carr Rd Wilmington DE 19809-2865

MOORE, BRUCE E. real estate company executive; CEO Brandywine Real Estate Mgmt. Svcs. Corp., Chedd Ford, Pa., 1989—. Office: Brandywine Real Estate Mgmt Svcs Corp 2 Ponds Edge Dr Chadds Ford PA 19317-9389

MOORE, BRUCE JOHN, psychologist; b. Sunnyside, Wash., Nov. 1, 1953; s. Ben Cook and Mary Louise Moore. BS, Wash. State U.; postgrad., Canyonview Bible Sem., Silverton, Oreg., Regent U., Vancouver, B.C., Can.; MBA, City U., Yakima, Wash. With U.S. Forest Svc., Packwood, Wash., Ukiah, Oreg., Wash.; info. specialist Wash. Coop. Ext., Pullman; interviewer asst. Bingon, Wash.; psychology tech. Yakima LWLMH. Staff reporter The Journalist, 1974, Yakama Watch, 1997. Home: PO Box 15 Yakima WA 98901-2918

MOORE, C. BRADLEY, chemistry educator; b. Boston, Dec. 7, 1939; s. Charles Walden and Dorothy (Lutz) Moore; m. Penelope Williamson Percival, Aug. 27, 1960; children: Megan Bradley, Scott Woodward. BA magna cum laude, Harvard U., 1960; PhD, U. Calif., Berkeley, 1963. Predoctoral fellow NSF, 1960-63; asst. prof. chemistry U. Calif., Berkeley, 1963-68, assoc. prof., 1968-72, prof., 1972-2000, vice chmn. dept., 1971-75, chmn. dept. chemistry, 1982-86, dean Coll. Chemistry, 1988-94, prof. grad. sch., 2000—; v.p. rsch. Ohio State U., Columbus, Disting. prof. math. and phys. sci., prof. chemistry, 2000—. Assoc. prof. Faculty Scis., Paris, 1970, 75; Miller Rsch. Prof. U. Calif., Berkeley, 1972-73, 87-88; vis. prof. Inst. for Molecular Sci., Okazaki, Japan, 1979, Fudan U., Shanghai, 1979, adv. prof., 1988—; vis. fellow Joint Inst. for Lab. Astrophysics, U. Colo., Boulder, 1981-82; faculty sr. scientist (Chemical Sci. Div.) Lawrence Berkeley Nat. Lab., 1974-2000, divsn. dir., 1998-2000: mem. editl. bd. Jour. Chem. Physics, 1973-75, Chem. Physics Letters, 1980-85, Jour. Phys. Chemistry, 1981-87, Laser Chemistry, 1982—; mem. Basic Energy Scis. adv. com. Office Sci. U.S. Dept. Energy. Editor: Chemical and Biochemical Applications of Lasers; assoc. editor Annual Review of Physical Chemistry, 1985-90; contbr. articles to profl. jours. Trustee Sci. Svc., 1995—, Sci. and Tech. Campus; mem. bd. govs. Ohio Supercomputer Centing Chair; rsch. officer Coun. of Ohio Bd. of Regents; pres. Ohio State U. Rsch. Found., chmn. bd. Recipient Coblentz award, 1973, E.O. Lawrence Meml. award U.S. Dept. Energy, 1986, Lippincott award, 1987, 1st award Inter-Am. Photochem. Soc., 1988; nat. scholar Harvard U., 1958-60; fellow Alfred P. Sloan Found., 1968, Guggenheim Found., 1969, Humboldt Rsch. award for Sr. U.S. Scientists, 1994. Fellow AAAS, Am. Acad. Arts and Scis., Am. Phys. Soc. (Plyler award 1994); mem. NSF adv. com. for education and human resources directorate, chair subcom. policy and planning 1997-99, NAS (chmn. com. undergrad. sci. edn. 1993-97, class I membership com., 1998-2000, 2002, 2000 nominating com.), Am. Chem. Soc. (past chmn. divsn. phys. chemistry, Calif. sect. award 1977). Avocation: cycling. Office: Ohio State U 208 Bricker Hall 190 N Oval Mall Columbus OH 43210-1321 E-mail: moore.1@osu.edu.

MOORE, CARL GORDON, chemist, educator; b. Zanesville, Ohio, Feb. 7, 1922; s. Henry Carl and Hilda Marie (Oberfield) M.; m. Sheila Marie O'Toole, Nov. 2, 1951; children: Carl, Patrick, Martina, Michael, Maureen, Regina, Madeleine, Terence. BS in Chem. Engring., Ga. Inst. Tech., 1947; MS in Chem. Engring., Carnegie Mellon U., 1948, postgrad., 1948-51, U. Newark, Del., 1973-74. Cert. tchr., Pa., Del. Chemist Manhattan Project, Oak Ridge, Tenn., 1944-46; chem. engr. Koppers Co., Pitts., 1946-47; rsch. chemist E.I. DuPont de Nemours & Co., Wilmington, Del., 1951-73; tchr. Chester (Pa.)-Upland Sch., 1974-78; tutor Del. Tutoring, Wilmington, 1981-88; instr. Del. Tech. and C.C., 1982-90, U. Del., Newark, 1984—. Author tech. reports on hydrogen over voltage of titanium and zirconium. Adult leader Wilmington area Boy Scouts Am., 1953-73; tchr. Sunday sch., Wilmington, 1962-67; group leader U.S. Census Bur., 1980. Sgt. U.S. Army, 1943-46. Mem. Am. Chem. Soc., Sigma Xi. Achievements include 13 patents, production of TiO_2 Rutile by chloride process, 100% oxygen oxidation of $TiCl_4$, 100% anatase by chloride process; research on turbulence and structure of water. Home and Office: 1913 Oak Lane Rd Wilmington DE 19803-5237 E-mail: cgsmmoore@aol.com.

MOORE, CARLETON BRYANT, geochemistry educator; b. N.Y.C., Sept. 1, 1932; s. Eldridge Carleton and Mabel Florence (Drake) M.; m. Jane Elizabeth Strouse, July 25, 1959; children: Barbara Jeanne, Robert Carleton; m. Diane Beets, Apr. 23, 2000. BS, Alfred U., 1954, DSc (hon.), 1977; PhD, Cal. Inst. Tech., 1960. Asst. prof. geology Wesleyan U., Middletown, Conn., 1959-61; mem. faculty Ariz. State U., Tempe, 1961—; nat. rsch. coun. rsch. assoc. NASA Ames Rsch. Ctr., 1974; prof., dir. Ctr. for Meteorite Studies Ariz. State U., Regents' prof., 1988—. Vis. prof. Stanford U., 1974; Prin. investigator Apollo 11-17; preliminary exam. team Lunar Receiving Lab., Apollo, 12-17. Author: Cosmic Debris, 1969, Meteorites, 1971, Principles of Geochemistry, 1982, Grundzügeder Geochemie, 1985; editor: Researches on Meteorites, 1961, Jour. Meteoritical Soc.; contbr. articles to profl. jours. Asteroid 5046 named Carletonmoore in his honor, 2000. Fellow Am. Geophys. Union, Ariz.-Nev. Acad. Sci. (pres. 1979-80), Meteoritical Soc. (life hon., pres. 1966-68), Geol. Soc. Am., Mineral. Soc. Am., AAAS (council 1967-70); mem. Geochem. Soc., Am. Chem. Soc., Am. Ceramic Soc., Sigma Xi. Home: 507 E Del Rio Dr Tempe AZ 85282-3764 Office: Ariz State U Ctr Meteorite Studies Tempe AZ 85287-2504 E-mail: cmoore@asu.edu.

MOORE, CAROLE IRENE, librarian; b. Berkeley, Calif., Aug. 15, 1944; AB, Stanford U., 1966; MLS, Columbia U., 1967. Reference libr. Columbia U., N.Y.C., 1967-68, U. Toronto, Can., 1968-80, head cataloging Can., 1980-85, assoc. libr. Can., 1985-86, chief libr. Can., 1986—. Mem. nat. adv. bd. Nat. Libr. Can., Ottawa, 1991-94; bd. dirs. Rsch. Librs. Group. 1994-2000, U. Toronto Press, 1994—. Recipient Disting. Alumni award Columbia U., 1989. Mem. ALA, Can. Libr. Assn., Can. Assn. Rsch. Librs. (pres. 1989-91, bd. dirs. 1996-98). Avocation: gardening. Office: U Toronto Libr 130 Saint George St Toronto ON Canada M5S 1A5

MOORE, CAROLYN OLSON, writer, educator; b. New River, Nc, Oct. 17, 1944; d. Gordon Hughes and Elaine Olson Moore. MA, U. of Mass., Amherst, Massachusetts, 1968; BA, Willamette U., Salem, Oregon, 1966. Writing educator Humboldt State U., Arcata, Calif., 1970—93; freelance writer and cons. self-employed, Portland, Oreg., 1993—2002. Lit. rep. Humboldt Arts

Coun., Eureka, Calif., 1982—84. Author: (book) The Hounded Heart, Death in the Darkroom. Recipient The Roberts Writing Award for Poetry, H.G. Roberts Found., 1988, Nat. League of Am. Pen Women's Marion Doyle Award, 1987, 1988, 1991, 1992, The Foley Poetry Award, Am. Mag., 1994, The Hart Crane Meml. Poetry Award, 1996, Golden Dozen Tchg. Award. Home: PO Box 230142 Portland OR 97281

MOORE, CASSANDRA CHRONES, real estate broker; b. Oneonta, N.Y., June 14, 1935; d. Constantine John and Antonia (Laskaris) Chrones; m. Thomas Gale Moore, Dec. 28, 1958; children: Charles Godwin, Antonia Laskaris. BA summa cum laude, Radcliffe Coll., Cambridge, Mass., 1956; MA, Harvard U., 1958; PhD, U. Mich., 1975. Lic. real estate broker, Calif. Lectr. Duquesne U., Pitts., 1962-65, Mich. State U., East Lansing, 1966-68; broker, owner Moore Assocs., Palo Alto, Calif., 1983-85; dir. state and mcpl. legislation Nat. Assn. Realtors, Washington, 1985-87; exec. dir. Fed. Interagy. Coun. on Homeless, 1987-89; adj. scholar Competitive Enterprise Inst., 1989—, mem. adv. bd., 1995—; adj. scholar Cato Inst., 1996—. Author: Haunted Housing, 1997. Co-chmn. Radcliffe Alumnae Lectureship Com., Palo Alto and San Francisco, 1984-2000; mem. nat. com. Radcliffe Alumnae Professorship Fund, 2001—. Recipient Fulbright fellowship U.S. Govt., Washington, 1956-57. Mem.: Palo Alto Bd. Realtors (dir. 1984, 1985), Tsintzinian Soc. (bd. mem. 1999—, alt. bd. mem. 2001—), Am. Assn. Small Property Owners (bd. mem. 1997—), Radcliffe Club Peninsula (pres. 1980—82), Phi Beta Kappa. Avocations: hiking, swimming, skiing. Office: 415 Cambridge Ave Palo Alto CA 94306 E-mail: ccmassoc@pacbell.net.

MOORE, CHARLES AUGUST, JR. psychologist; b. Medford, Oreg., Feb. 22, 1944; s. Charles August and Bernadine (Newlun) M. BS, Lewis and Clark Coll., 1965; MA, U. Colo., 1967, PhD, 1972. Lic. psychologist, Calif., Oreg. Teaching asst. U. Colo., Boulder, 1965-66, 70-71, rsch. asst., counselor, practicum supr., 1966-67, 71-72; asst. psychologist State Home and Tng. Sch., Grand Junction, Colo., 1967; intern in psychology Camarillo (Calif.) State Hosp., 1968-69; psychology assoc., program psychologist Camarillo Drug Abuse Program (The Family), 1969-70; intern in psychology Oxnard (Calif.) Mental Health Ctr., 1969; clin. psychologist, dir. intern tng. Rural Clinics, Reno, 1972; clin. psychologist Kern County Mental Health Svcs., Bakersfield, Calif., 1972-74; clin., cons. psychologist San Diego County Mental Health Svcs., 1974-88; pvt. practice La Jolla (Calif.) Clinic, 1976-78; August Ctr., Chula Vista, Calif., 1978-85; staff psychologist Dept. Vet.'s Affairs Domiciliary, White City, Oreg., 1988—. Guest lectr. Calif. State Coll., Bakersfield, 1973-74; mem. Health Systems Agy. Mental Health Task Force, 1979; mem. doctoral dissertation com. U.S. Internat. U., 1975-76; mem. mental health task force San Diego County Bd. Suprs., 1979. Contbr. articles to profl. jours. Mem. Univ. City Community Coun., San Diego, 1976-78; bd. dirs. Pub. Employees Assn., 1976-77. Recipient Experiment in Internat. Living European Study award Lewis and Clark Coll., 1962; USPHS fellow, 1967-68; U. Colo. Grad. Sch. Rsch. grantee, 1971; recipient Hands and Heart award Dept. Vets. Affairs, 1989-90, Domiciliary Spl. Contbn. and Outstanding Performance awards, 1990, 91. Mem. APA, Am. Psychology and Law Soc., Calif. Psychol. Assn., Western Psychol. Assn., San Diego County Psychol. Assn., Assn. County Clin. Psychologists San Diego, San Diego Psychology and Law Soc., San Diego Soc. Clin. Psychologists. Office: Dept VA Domiciliary Psychology Svc 8495 Crater Lake Hwy White City OR 97503-3011

MOORE, CHARLES E. engineer; b. Santa Fe, Mar. 30, 1941; s. Robert E. and Marianne E. (Tyler) M.; m. Frances A. Land, Feb. 13, 1963; children: Deborah, Sarah, Hugh, Guy, Roger. BS, U. Calif., Berkeley, 1966; MS, U. Rochester, 1978. Engr. Hewlett-Packard Co., Loveland, Colo., 1966-88, Ft. Collins, 1988—2000, Agilent Techs., Ft. Collins, 2000—. With U.S. Army, 1960-63. Mem. Optical Soc. Am. (past chpt. pres.). Achievements include patents in the areas of lens design, surveying instrument design and integrated circuit design. Home: 425 W 10th St Loveland CO 80537-4619 Office: Agilent Techs 4380 Ziegler Rd Fort Collins CO 80525

MOORE, CHARLES HEWES, JR. industrial and engineered products executive; b. Coatesville, Pa., Aug. 12, 1929; s. Charles Hewes and Jane Richards (Scott) M.; m. Judith L. McClellan, June 23, 1971; children: Charles Hewes III, James, David, Susan, Kevin, Christopher, Margery, Brian, Amanda. BME, Cornell U., 1952. With Lenape Forge Co. div. Gulf & Western Industries, West Chester, Pa., 1952-73; pres. Lapp div. Interpace Corp., Le Roy, N.Y., 1973-77; pres., chief exec. officer Allied Thermal Corp. subs. Interpace, 1978-79; sr. v.p., dir. Interpace, 1979-80; exec. v.p., dir. Interpace Corp., Parsippany, N.J., 1980-81; pres., chief exec. officer, dir. Clevepak Corp., 1981-83, 84-86, chief exec. officer, vice chmn. bd., dir., 1983-84; mng. dir. Peers & Co., 1987-88; chief exec. officer Peers Mgmt. Resources, Inc., 1987-88; pres., chief exec. officer Ransburg Corp., Indpls., 1988-92; pres. ITW Finishing Systems and Products, 1990-92; exec. v.p. Ill. Tool Works Inc., Glenview, 1991-92; vice-chmn. Advisory Capital Ptnrs., Inc., Greenwich, Conn., 1993-94; chmn. bd. dirs. Xpander Pak Inc., 1995-2000; dir. athletics Cornell U., 1994—99. Bd. dirs. The Sports Authority; dep. to chairs Com. to Encourage Corp. Philanthropy, NY, 1999—2000, exec. dir., NY, 2001—. Commr. Smithsonian Am. Art Mus.; chmn. audit com., pub. sector dir. U.S. Olympic Com., 1992—2000; mem. nat. bd. Smithsonian Instn., 1999—. Recipient Gold medal in 400 meter hurdles, 1952 Olympics, Herbert Adams Meml. award for advancement of Am. sculpture, Nat. Sculpture Soc., 1985. Mem. Pine Valley Golf Club (N.J.), Royal and Ancient Golf Club St. Andrews (Scotland), Cosmos Club (Washington), Blind Brook Golf Club (N.Y.). Republican. Episcopalian. Office: Com to Encourage Corp Philanthropy 140 E 45th St Fl 3D New York NY 10017-3144

MOORE, CHRISTOPHER BARRY, industrial engineer; b. Deal, Kent, Eng., Feb. 25, 1938; came to U.S., 1977; s. Ernest Stanley and Millicent Lillian (Harris) M.; m. Jill Irene Porter, July 6, 1963; children: Andrew, Stephen, Jeremy, Jennifer. Diploma mgmt. studies, Barking Regional Coll. Tech., Eng., 1966. Prodn. unit mgr. Plessey Co. Ltd., Ilford, Eng., 1968-70, productivity mgr. Upminster, 1970-72; regional indsl. engr. Ilford, 1972-74; mgr. mfg. devel. No. Telecom Ltd., Montreal, Que., Can., 1974-77, dir. mfg. engring. Nashville, 1977-88; dir. process devel. Nortel Networks, Atlanta, 1988-2000; rsch. advisor Ga. Inst. Tech., 2000—. With RAF, 1956-59. Mem. Inst. Elec. Engrs., Inst. Mgmt., Ravinia Club. Home: 5167 Killingsworth Trce Norcross GA 30092-1739 E-mail: Chris.Moore@marc.gatech.edu.

MOORE, CHRISTOPHER HUGH, writer; b. Stoke-on-Trent, Eng., June 9, 1950; arrived in Can., 1954; s. M. Vincent and Kathleen A. (Lennox) M.; m. Louise A. Brophy, May 7, 1977; children: Elizabeth, Kate. BA with honors, U. B.C., Vancouver, 1971; MA, U. Ottawa, Ont., Can., 1977. Staff historian Nat. Historic Pks. Svc., Louisbourg, N.S., Can., 1972-75; sec. to bd. Heritage Can. Found., Ottawa, 1977-78; writer, historian Toronto, Ont., 1979—; dir. Can-Copy Copyright Licensing Agy., 2001—. Author: Louisbourg Portraits, 1982, 2000, The Loyalists, 1984, 94, Eighteen Sixty-Seven, 1997; co-author: Illustrated History of Canada, 1987, The Story of Canada, 1992, Canada: Our Century, 1999. Recipient Gov. Gen.'s Lit. award Can., 1983, Sec. of State Prize Govt. Can., Ottawa, 1985, Mr. Christie's Prize Christie-Brown Ltd., Toronto, 1993. Mem. Writers' Union of Can. (chair contracts com. 1990-94, mem. nat. coun. 1995-97, nat. chair, 1999-00), Can. Hist. Assn. Office: 70 Woodside Ave Toronto ON Canada M6P 1M1 E-mail: cmed@interlog.com.

MOORE, CHRISTOPHER MINOR, lawyer; b. L.A., Oct. 12, 1938; s. Prentiss Elder and Josephine (French) M.; m. Gillian Reed, Sept. 29, 1965; children: Stephanie Kia Conn, Carrie Christine McKay. AB, Stanford U., 1961; JD, Harvard U., 1964. Dep. county counsel L.A. County Counsel, 1965-66; ptnr. Moore & Lindelof, L.A., 1966-69, Burkley & Moore, Torrance, Calif., 1969-74; pvt. practice Law Offices of Christopher Moore, 1974-81; ptnr. Burkley, Moore, Greenberg & Lyman, 1981-90; prin. Christopher M. Moore & Assoc., 1990-2000, Moore, Bryan & Schroff, Torrance, 2000—. Mem. bd. edn. Palos Verdes (Calif.) Peninsula Unified Sch. Dist., 1972-77. Fellow: Am. Acad. Matrimonial Lawyers, Am. Coll. Trust and Estate Counsel; mem.: Palos Verdes Golf Club, L.A. Yacht Club. Avocations: sailing, golf. Office: Moore Bryan & Schroff Ste 490 21515 Hawthorne Blvd Torrance CA 90503-6525 E-mail: chris@cmoorelaw.com.

MOORE, CHRISTOPHER ROBERTSON KINLEY, energy industry consultant; b. Manchester, Eng., Sept. 28, 1954; came to U.S., 1989; s. James Robertson Kinley and Irene (Mason) M.; m. Marian Isabel Pope, Sept. 3, 1977; children: Andrew Christopher, Scott David. BA, U. Cambridge, 1975, MA, 1979. Geologist Brit. Petroleum Co., Scotland, England, Tunisia, 1975-80; sr. geologist Tricentrol Oil Corp., London, 1980-88; planning mgr. ARCO Brit. Ltd., 1988-89; from exploration planning advisor to dir. exploration ARCO Internat. Oil & Gas Co., Plano, Tex., 1989-98; Bohai Bay asset mgr. ARCO China Inc., 1998-99, mgr. China ADT, 1999-2000; mng. dir. Moyes & Co., Inc., Dallas, 2000—. Fellow Geol. Soc. London; mem. Am. Assn. Petroleum Geologists, Soc. Petroleum Engrs., Internat. Assn. Petroleum Negotiators. Home: 2133 Country Club Dr Plano TX 75074-3638 Office: Moyes & Co Inc 8235 Douglas Ave Ste 1221 Dallas TX 75225-6012 E-mail: cmoore@moyesco.com.

MOORE, DAN STERLING, insurance executive, sales trainer; b. Lincoln, Nebr., June 27, 1956; s. Jack Leroy and Carolyn Marie (Bachman) M.; m. Marla Janine Collister, June 2, 1979; children: Tyler David, Anna Rose. Student, Red Rocks Coll., 1977. Lic. ins. exec. Asst. mgr. European Health Spa, Englewood, Colo., 1975-78; sales mgr. Colo. Nat. Homes, Westminster, 1979-80; sales assoc. Dale Carnegie, Denver, 1981; sales mgr. Paramount Fabrics, 1981-84; sales assoc. Mighty Distbg., Arvada, Colo., 1984-87; divsn. mgr. Nat. Assn. for Self Employed/United Group Assn., Englewood, 1987—. Divsn. mgr. Communicating for Agr. Assn., 1993-98, Am. Bus. Coalition, 1997-2000, Am. for Financial Security, 1999—. Leader, trainer Alpine Rescue Team, Evergreen, Colo., 1971-74; minister Jehovah's Witnesses, 1972—. Avocations: golf, skiing, backpacking, scuba diving, tennis. Home: 892 Nob Hill Trl Franktown CO 80116-7917 Office: Nat Assn Self Employed/United Group 10579 W Bradford Rd Ste 100 Littleton CO 80127-4247 E-mail: sterlingmoore@netscape.net.

MOORE, DANIEL EDMUND, psychologist, educator, retired educational administrator; b. Pitts., Dec. 31, 1926; s. John Daniel and Alma Helen (Goehring) M.; m. Rose Marie Blunkosky, Nov. 11, 1949; children: Catherine Chiodo, Claire Marie Moore Caveney, Mary Moore Brilmyer, Suzanne Moore Gray, Elizabeth Moore Sullivan. BSEd, Duquesne U., 1949, MEd, 1952; postgrad., California (Pa.) State Coll., 1954-56, U. Pitts., 1958-59, Mt. Mercy Coll., 1959-60, Cath. U. Am., 1966, W.Va. U., 1970-72. Lic. psychologist; cert. sch. psychologist. Tchr. math. Cecil Twp. Sch. Dist., McDonald, Pa., 1949-52, Pitts. Public Schs., 1952-53; with Mt. Lebanon Twp. (Pa.) Sch. Dist., 1953-88, psychologist, 1954-71, dir. pupil personnel svcs., 1988; psychol cons. Peters Twp. Sch. Dist., McMurray, Pa., 1961-88; psychol. cons. Blackhawk Sch. Dist., Beaver, 1989—98; psychol cons. Quaker Valley Sch. Dist., Sewickley, 1989-90; lectr., supr. Grad. and Undergrad. Sch. Edn. Duquesne U.; psychologist DePaul Inst., Pitts., 1992—98. Lectr. ednl. psychology Grad. Sch. Edn., Duquesne U., 1957-92, supr. student tchrs., 1989-92; ednl. cons. St. Francis Schs. Nursing, New Castle and Pitts., 1959-91; mem. test adv. bd. Ednl. Records Bur., 1976-86; hearing officer Right to Edn. Office, Dept. Edn., Harrisburg, Pa., 1975—; in-svc. adv. bd. Pa. Dept. Edn. Hearing Officers. Mem. Chartiers Valley Sch. Dist. Bd., 1963-94, pres., 1971, v.p., 1991; mem. Pkwy. West Tech. Sch. Bd. 1965-67; bd. dirs. secondary sch. rsch. program Ednl. Testing Svc., Princeton, 1971-85; bd. dirs. Robert E. Ward Home for Children, 1975-87, St. Agatha Parish Coun., 1988—, Pathfinder Sch., 1989, v.p., 1990-94, pres. sch. bd., 1991-92; vol. Bridgeville Area Food Bank, 1988—; chairperson Parish 100 Jubilee Ceremony, Goodwill Villa Bd., Goodwill Plaza, Inc., Goodwill Villa Bd. of Incorporators, 1992—; pres. bd. dirs. Goodwill Plaza, 1992—; jubilee chairperson St. Agatha's, Bridgeville, Pa. With USNR, 1945-48. Henry C. Frick grantee, 1970, 73; named Jaycee Educator of Yr. for South Hills Area, Ward Home Outstanding Community Leader, 1984, Outstanding Cmty. Leader, Chartiers Valley Human Rels. Coun., 1998; recipient Human Rels. award Chartiers Valley Inter-relationships Soc., 1998. Mem. Am., Pa. psychol. assns., Coun. Exceptional Children (pres. 1957), Phi Delta Kappa (pres. chpt. 1974-75, chmn. lay awards com. 1979-2001, Svc. Key award 1985). Roman Catholic. Home: 213 Station St Bridgeville PA 15017-1806

MOORE, DANIEL CHARLES, internist; b. Cin., Sept. 9, 1918; s. Daniel Clark and May (Strebel) M.; m. Betty Maxine Tobias, Aug. 5, 1945 (div. 1988); children: Barbara, Nancy, Daniel, Susan. Grad., Amherst (Mass.) Coll., 1940; MD, Northwestern U., 1944. Diplomate: Am. Bd. Anesthesiologists. Intern Wesley Meml. Hosp., Chgo., 1944, resident, 1945; dir. anesthesia Va. Mason Hosp., Seattle, 1947-72; anesthesiologist (Mason Clinic), 1947-72, sr. cons. in anesthesia, 1972-83. Clin. prof. U. Wash. Sch. Medicine, 1963—. Author: Regional Block, 1953, Stellate Ganglion Block, 1954, Complications of Regional Anesthesia, 1955, Anesthetic Techniques for Obstetrical Anesthesia and Analgesia, 1964, also papers. Served as capt. M.C. AUS, 1945-47. Recipient Ralph M. Waters award Ill. Soc. Anesthesiologists, Carl Koller Gold medal European Soc. Regional Anaesthesia, 1995. Mem. Am. Soc. Anesthesiologists (1st v.p. 1953-54, 2d v.p. 1954-55, pres. 1958-59, distinguished service award 1976), AMA (sec. anesthesiology sect. 1956-58), Am. Acad. Anesthesiology, Am. Soc. Regional Anesthesia (adv. bd., Gaston Labat award 1977), Wash. Soc. Anesthesiologists (pres. 1949-50), Wash. Med. Soc., King County Med. Soc., Faculty Anaesthetists Royal Coll. Surgeons (hon.), Northwest Forum, Beta Theta Pi, Nu Sigma Nu. Home: Madison Park Pl # 103 2000 43rd Ave E Seattle WA 98112-2704 Office: PO Box 900 Seattle WA 98111-0900

MOORE, DAVID ARTHUR, composer, music educator; b. Stillwater, Okla., Feb. 23, 1948; s. Gibbons Birmingham and Fern Augusta (Moyer) M.; m. Sheila Smart, May 15, 1982 (div. Dec. 1989); m. Susan Goldman, Dec. 27, 1992; 1 child, Hannah Fern. BA, U. Calif., Santa Barbara, 1970, MA, 1974; postgrad., Royal Music Acad., Aarhus, Denmark, 1974-75, Sibelius Acad., Helsinki, Finland, 1975-76; PhD, U. Rochester, 1986. Vis. instr. music SUNY, Potsdam, N.Y., 1981-82; music specialist Rochester (N.Y.) Pub. Libr., 1983-92; asst. prof. music SUNY, Cortland, 1992-96; adj. assoc. prof. music Roberts Wesleyan Coll., Rochester, 1997—; spl. collections asst. Sibley Music Libr. Eastman Sch. Music, 1997-98; adj. instr. U. Tulsa, 1998—. Music dir. Seneca United Meth. Ch., Rochester, 1984-89, United Ch. of Christ, Webster, N.Y., 1989-93; adj. instr. Tulsa C.C., 1999—; dir. music ministries First Christian Ch., Tulsa, 1999—; choir dir. Temple Israel, Tulsa, 2000—. Composer Vesper Symphony for Brass, 1993, composer numerous choral works, songs and chamber music; contbr. articles and revs. to profl. jours. Scholar Vaino Hoover Found., 1976-77. Mem. Am. Choral Dirs. Assn., Am. Music Ctr., Coll. Music Soc., Soc. Composers, Inc. Mem. Christian Ch. (Disciples Of Christ). Home: 1746 S Canton Ave Tulsa OK 74112-6938

MOORE, DAVID AUSTIN, pharmaceutical company executive, consultant; b. Phoenix, May 8, 1935; s. Harry Theodore and Helen Ann (Newport) M.; m. Emily J. McConnell, Jan. 26, 1991; children by previous marriage: Austin Newport, Cornelia Christina, Christopher Robinson. Grad. h.s., Glendale, Ariz.; study opera and voice with Joseph Lazzarini, 1954, 55, 57-64; studied opera and voice, Italy, 1955-56; study with Clarence Loomis, 1958-60; D Naturopathy, Clayton Sch. Natural Healing, Birmingham, Ala., 1994. Pres., owner David A. Moore, Inc., Phoenix, 1969-71, Biol. Labs. Ltd., Phoenix, 1972-78; pres., co-owner Am. Trace Mineral Rsch. Corp., 1979-83; pres., owner Biol. Mineral Scis., Ltd., 1979-82; rsch. dir., pres., owner Nutritional Biols. Inc., 1979-83; nutritional dir.-owner Nutritional Biol. Rsch. Co., 1984-85; rsch. dir., product formulator, owner Nutrition and Med. Rsch., Scottsdale, Ariz., 1986—. Biochem. cons. Nutripathic Formulas, Scottsdale, 1975-88; introduced di Calcium Phosphate free concept and 100 percent label disclosure, 1979-83. Pub. NMR Newsletter. Inventor first computerized comprehensive hair analysis interpretation, 1976. Recipient Plaque Am. Soc. Med. Techs., 1982, Mineralab Inc., 1976. Avocation: singing opera and Italian songs, teaching voice, coaching singers. Home and Office: PO Box 98 Barnesboro PA 15714-0098

MOORE, DAVID GRAHAM, sociologist, educator; b. Norwich, Conn., May 9, 1918; s. Royal Tolman and Alta Gladys (Jenkin) M.; children by previous marriage: Barbara E., Linda C. Turbyville; m. Margaret Louise Rider, Dec. 2, 1950; children: David G., Kathryn R. (Mrs. T.J. Miller). BA, U. Ill., 1940, MA, 1943; PhD, U. Chgo., 1954. Personnel research Western Electric Co., 1940-41; mem. personnel staff Sears, Roebuck and Co., 1941-43, 46-50; personnel dir. Am. Flange & Mfg. Co., 1943-46; asst. prof. sociology, indsl. relations U. Chgo., 1950-55, asso. prof. bus. adminstrn., sociology, dir. exec. program, 1955-56; prof. mgmt. Mich. State U., 1956-58, head dept. personnel and prodn. adminstrn., 1958-61, prof. mgmt., sociology, 1961-63; dean N.Y. State Sch. Indsl. and Labor Relations, Cornell U., 1963-71; sr. v.p. Conf. Bd., N.Y.C., 1971-73, exec. v.p., 1973-79; prof., chmn. dept. bus. adminstrn. U. North Fla., 1979-86, prof. bus. adminstrn., 1986-89, asst. to pres., 1983-84. Vis. Ford Found. prof. behavioral scis. U. Wis., fall 1962. Co-author: Human Relations in Industry, 4th edit, 1964, SRA Employee Inventory, 1951, The Enterprising Man, 1964. Mem. Am. Sociol. Assn., Soc. Applied Anthropology, Acad. Mgmt., Indsl. Relations Research Assn. Home: C205 1000 Vicar's Landing Way Ponte Vedra Beach FL 32082-1331 E-mail: dgmanew@cs.com.

MOORE, DAVID JOSEPH, design engineer; b. Fostoria, Ohio, July 9, 1941; s. Paul David and Gladys Lucille (Bennett) M.; m. Jacqueline Kay Marshall, Nov. 23, 1963; children: Nicole Marie, Danielle Renee. Student, Ohio State U., 1959-61; Assoc. in Machine Design, Chgo. Tech. Coll., 1967. Designer Excello Corp., Fostoria, 1967-72; owner Sportsman Shop, 1972-79; process engr. United Aircraft Products, Forest, Ohio, 1979-81; design engr. Autolite div. Allied Automotive, Fostoria, 1981-98; project engr. Bridgestone APM, Findlay, Ohio, 1998—. Co-inventor manufacture method of platinum spark plug (2); inventor manufacture method of platinum spark plug (2). Bd. dirs. Fostoria Athletic Boosters, 1973-79. Recipient Allied Signal Tech. Achievement award, 1991. Mem. Soc. Mfg. Engrs., Machine Vision Internat., Fostoria Area C. of C. (bd. dirs. 1976-79), Am. Soc. Quality Control (cert. quality engr.), Lions (youth com. 1965-75), Elks (trustee 1974-79). Republican. Methodist. Avocations: golf, boating, swimming, bowling. Office: Bridgestone APM Co 1800 Industrial Dr Findlay OH 45840-5439

MOORE, DENNIS, congressman; b. Anthony, Kans., 1945; m. Stephene; 7 children. BS, U. Kans., 1967; JD, Washburn U., 1970. Bar: Kans. 1970. Asst. atty. gen. State of Kans., 1971-73; pvt. practice, 1973-76; dist. atty. Johnson County, 1977-89; ptnr. Erker & Moore, LLC, 1991-98, Smith, Gill, Fisher & Butts, 1989-91; mem. U.S. Congress from 3d Kans. dist., 1999—. Mem. House Com. on Fin. Svcs. Sci. and the Budget. Elected to Johnson County C.C. bd. trustees, 1993; re-elected, 1997; bd. dirs. Johnson County Safehome, Coalition for Prevention of Child Abuse, Kans. Child Abuse Prevention Coun., CASA (Ct. Appointed Spl. Advocate), United Cmty. Svcs., Cmty. Corrections Adv. Bd.; unsuccessful Dem. candidate for state atty. gen., 1986. With U.S. Army, U.S. Army Res. Democrat. Achievements include personally prosecuting more than 25 felony jury trials; led Consumer Protection Divsn. in the investigation and successful prosecution of a nat. oil co. charged with rigging gas pumps to cheat consumers; established a victim assistance unit; was cited by an ind. cons. hired by the Johnson County Bd. Commrs. as running the most efficient office in Johnson County govt.; served as pres. Kans. County and Dist. Atty.'s Assn. Office: 431 Cannon Hob Washington DC 20515-0001

MOORE, DENNIS DUANE, English educator; b. Greenville, S.C., Oct. 25, 1949; s. Marvin R. Moore and Mildred E. Brown. BA, Clemson U., 1970; MA, U. N.C., 1971, PhD, 1990. Instr. English Greenville (S.C.) Tech. Coll., 1980-82, Clemson (S.C.) U., 1982-84; asst. prof. English U. Tex., El Paso, 1990-91, Fla. State U., Tallahassee, 1991-95, assoc. prof. English, 1995—. Dir. Bryan Hall Learning Cmty., 2000—. Editor: More Letters from the American Farmer: An Edition of Essays in English Left Unpublished by Crevecoeur, 1995; contbr. articles to profl. jours. V.p., program chair Friends of Fla. State U. Librs., 1995—; mem. Friends of Black History Archives, Fla. History Assocs., Mus. Fla. History, Tallahassee. C. Hugh Holman fellow U. N.C. Dept. English, 1989; Rsch. grantee NEH, 1991, 92; fellow in Early Am. History and Culture, Libr. Co. Phila. and Hist. Soc. Pa., jointly, 1988. Mem. Am. Studies Assn. (life mem.), Am. Soc. Eighteenth-Century Studies (life mem.), Soc. Early Americanists (exec. coord. 2001—), Toni Morrison Soc. (charter and life mem.), Internat. Iris Murdoch Soc. (founding mem., life mem., sec.), St. Marks Nat. Wildlife Refuge Assn. (life), Phi Theta Kappa (hon.). Democrat. Unitarian Universalist. Avocations: fly-fishing, birding, canoeing, traveling, films. Office: Dept English Fla State U Tallahassee FL 32306-1580 E-mail: dmoore@english.fsu.edu.

MOORE, DINTY WILLIAM, writer, educator; b. Erie, Pa., Aug. 11, 1955; s. William Patrick Moore and Mary Catherine Stearns; m. Renita Marie Romasco, May 22, 1984; 1 child, Maria Romasco-Moore. MFA, La. State U., 1990. Prof. Pa. State U., Altoona, 1990—. Author: The Emperor's Virtual Clothes, 1995, The Accidental Buddhist, 1997, Toothpick Men, 1999; editor Brevity, 1997—; non-fiction editor Pa. English, 1998—. Fiction fellow Nat. Endowment for the Arts, Washington, 1992. Office: Pa State Altoona Ivyside Park Altoona PA 16601 E-mail: dinty@psu.edu.

MOORE, DONALD EMERSON EMERSON, III, curator, wildlife biologist; b. Syracuse, N.Y., Jan. 9, 1954; s. Donald Emerson and Ruth Hodge (Steinhilber) M.; m. Adrienne Rose Whiteley (div.); children: Jessie Rose, Caitlin Grace; m. Suzanne L. Daley. BS in Environ. Sci. and Forestry, SUNY, Syracuse, 1976; MPA, Syracuse U., 1990; PhD, SUNY, Syracuse, 2001. Cert. biologist. Edn. asst. Burnet Park Zoo, Syracuse, 1976-77, technician animal care, 1977-79, zoologist, 1980-83, curator mammals, 1984-93; dir. Thompson Park Conservancy, 1993-95; curator Wildlife Conservation Soc., N.Y.C., 1997—. Sci. adviser Thompson Park Zoo, Watertown, N.Y., 1984—; mem. master plan team A New Breed of Zoo, 1980-86, Springdale Farm Park, 1985-88; exploring adviser, 1989—. Author: (mgmt. format) Species Mgmt. Plan, 1978; contbr. articles to sci. jours. Instr. ARC, Syracuse, 1978-87; mem. master plan team Millbrook Sch., 1988-89. Fellow Am. Assn. Zool. Pks. and Aquariums (prof.); mem. Am. Soc. Mammalogists, Wildlife Soc., Nat. Eagle Scout Assn., Internat. Union Conservation Nature and Natural Resources (deer specialist group, mustelid/viverrid specialist group), Soc. Conservation Biology, Internat. Soc. for Behavioral Ecology. Presbyterian. Avocations: skiing, hiking, canoeing, canning jams and jellies, photography. Office: Wildlife Conservation Soc 830 Fifth Ave New York NY 10021

MOORE, DONALD FRANCIS, lawyer; b. N.Y.C., Dec. 14, 1937; s. John F. and Helen A. (McLoughlin) M.; m. Alice L. Kalmar; children: Christina M., Marianne, Karen L., Alison A. AB, Fordham U., 1959; JD, St. John's U., Bklyn., 1962. Bar: N.Y. 1962, D.C. 1970, U.S. Supreme Ct. 1993. Assoc. Paul, Weiss, Rifkind, Wharton & Garrison, N.Y.C., 1962-70, ptnr., 1970-97, of counsel, 1998—. Editor in chief St. John's U. Law Rev., 1962. Served to 1st lt. U.S. Army, 1962-64. Mem. N.Y. State Bar Assn., Assn. of Bar of City of N.Y. Roman Catholic. Avocation: fishing. Home: 7 Wedgewood Ct Glen Head NY 11545-2229 Office: Paul Weiss Rifkind Wharton & Garrison Ste 4200 1285 Avenue Of The Americas Fl 21 New York NY 10019-6065

MOORE, DONALD WALTER, academic administrator, school librarian; b. Culver City, Calif., June 9, 1942; s. Raymond Owen and Jewel Elizabeth (Young) M.; m. Dagmar Ulbrich, Mar. 28, 1968; 1 child, Michael. AA, L.A. Valley Coll., 1967; BA in History, Calif. State U., Northridge, 1970; MA in Learning Disability, Calif. State U., 1973; MLS, U. So. Calif., 1974. Part time librarian L.A. Pierce Coll., Woodland Hills, Calif., 1974—; instr. reading L.A. Trade Tech. Coll., 1978-80, pres.'s staff asst., 1983-87; instr. learning skills L.A. City Coll., 1987-88, dir. amnesty edn., 1988-92, dir. Citizenship Ctr., 1992—. Adj. instr. computer sci. L.A. Trade-Tech. Coll., 1983—. Author: A Guidebook to U.S. Army Dress Helmets, 2000; contbr. fiction, articles, revs. to various publs. Mem. Ednl. Writers Am., Co. Mil. Historians, Edpress, Little Big Horn Assn., Planetary Soc. Republican. Roman Catholic. Avocations: writing, collecting U.S. frontier military memorabilia, computing. Office: LA City Coll Citizenship Program 855 N Vermont Ave Los Angeles CA 90029-3516 *Personal philosophy: To survive in this world you must believe in yourself and know what's worth fighting for and what's not. But never despair, despair is the greatest sin.*

MOORE, DORSEY JEROME, dentistry educator, maxillofacial prosthetist; b. Boonville, Mo., Feb. 8, 1935; s. Lloyd Elliott Moore and Mary Elizabeth (Day) Katemann; m. Mary Louise Foote, May 2, 1959; children: Elizabeth L., David J. DDS, U. Mo., Kansas City, 1959. Diplomate Am. Bd. Prosthodontics. Commd. ensign USN, 1955, advanced through grades to capt., 1973; gen. practice dentistry various naval stas., 1959-63; practice in prosthodontics USS Proteus AS-19, 1963-66; resident in prosthodontics and maxillofacial prosthetics Naval Dental Sch., Bethesda, Md., 1966-69, chief maxillofacial prosthetics divsn., 1969-70; sr. dental advisor Naval Adv. Group, Comdr. Naval Forces, Saigon, Vietnam, 1970-71; chief maxillofacial prosthetics div. Nat. Naval Dental Ctr., 1971-76; chief maxillofacial prosthetics br. Naval Regional Med. Ctr., Great Lakes, Ill., 1976-79, ret., 1979; vis. lectr. U. Mo. Sch. Dentistry, Kansas City, 1976-79, H.G.B. Robinson prof., chmn. dept. removable prosthodontics, 1979-2000, Hamilton G.B. Robinson emeritus prof. dentistry, 2000, ret., 2000; chief maxillofacial prosthetics Truman Med. Ctr., Kansas City, Mo., 2000—. Assoc. prof. U. Saigon Sch. Dentistry,

1970-71; advisor to Min. of Health, Saigon, 1970-71; profl. lectr. George Washington U., Washington, 1971-76; clin. assoc. prof. surgery U. Kans. City Sch. Medicine, 1987—; cons. maxillofacial prosthetics NIH Treatment Ctr., 1973—, Nat. Cancer Inst., 1973—, VA Hosp., North Chicago, Ill., 1976—, ADA Couns. Dental Edn., Hosp. Dental Svc. and Commn. on Accredition, 1978—; vice chancellor Devel. Adv. Com., 1983—; examiner Mo. Specialty Bd. Prosthodontics, 1982—; internat. cir. course lectr. Am. Prosthetics Soc., Indonesia, 1974, Guatelmala, 1975, N.Z., 1976, S.Africa, 1981, Japan, Taiwan, 1989, Mexico City, 1994, Beijing and Chengdu, China, 1996; nat. cons. U.S. Naval Dental Sch., Bethesda, 1991—; chief maxillofacial prosthetics Truman Med. Ctr., 2000-. Author: Practical Oral Rehabilitation of the Edentulous Patient, 8th edit., 1995; mem. editorial bd. Cancer of the Head and Neck: A Comprehensive Review of the Literature, 1982—; contbr. articles to profl. jours. Mem. adminstrv. ch. bd. Cen. Methodist Ch., 1981-88, pres. official ch. bd., 1983-85; bd. dirs. Ednl. Rsch. Found. Prosthodontics, 1982—, chmn. 1988—; bd. dirs. Penn Valley Fitness Trail Assn., 1982—. Decorated Legion of Merit with combat V, other awards; Navy Cross of Gallantry with palm (Republic of Vietnam); recipient Ackerman Meml. award outstanding contbns. to maxillofacial prosthetics, 1999. Fellow Am. Acad. Maxillofacial Prosthetics (bd. dirs. 1972-75, mem. exec. com. 1973-76, pres. 1978-79, mem. exec. coun. 1979-82), Am. Coll. Prosthodontics (charter), Am. Coll. Dentists, Acad. Prosthodontics, Internat. Coll. Dentist, Midwest Acad. Prosthodontics; mem. ADA. Avocations: jazz musician, string bassist. Office: Truman Med Ctrs 2301 Holmes Kansas City MO 64108 Office Fax: 816-855-6038. E-mail: mooredj@umkg.edu.

MOORE, DUNCAN THOMAS, optics educator; b. Biddeford, Maine, Dec. 7, 1946; s. Thomas Fogg Moore and Virginia Robinson Wing; m. Gunta Liders, July 1995. BA in Physics, U. Maine, 1969, DSc (hon.), 1995; MS in Optics, U. Rochester, 1970, PhD in Optics, 1974. Asst. prof. U. Rochester, N.Y., 1974-78, assoc. prof., 1978-86, prof., 1986—, Kingslake prof., 1993—, dean engring. and applied sci., 1995-97; pres., founder Gradient Lens Corp., Rochester, 1980; dir. N.Y. State Ctr. Advanced Optical Tech., 1987-94; assoc. dir. technology White House Office Sci. & Technology Policy, Washington, 1997-2000; spl. asst. to pres. Univ. Rochester, 2001—, prof. biomed. engring., 2001—. Vis. scientist Nippon Schlumberger, Tokyo, 1983; Congl. fellow Am. Phys. Soc., Washington, 1993—94; sci. advisor to Sen. John D. Rockefeller IV, W.Va., 1993—94; spl. asst. to pres. U. Rochester, 2001—; exec. dir. Univ., Industry and Govt. Partnership for Advanced Photonics, 2001—; mem. environ. and energy svc. rev. com. Idaho Nat. Engring. and Environ. Lab., 2001—02; mem. vis. com. NASA-Goddard Space Flight Ctr., 2002; mem. applied engring. and tech. directorate vis. com. Goddard Space Flight Ctr., 2002. Contbr. numerous articles to profl. jours.; patentee in field. Chmn. Hubble Indpendent Rev. Panel, 1990-91; mem. adv. bd. high tech. Rochester C. of C., 1988-93. Recipient Disting. Inventor of Yr. award Rochester Intellectual Property Law Assn., 1993, Grin Optics award Japanese Applied Physics Soc., 1993, Sci. and Tech. award Greater Rochester C. of C., 1992; named Engr. of Yr., Rochester Engring. Soc., 1999. Mem.: NRC, NAE, Am. Inst. Physics (state dept. fellowship selection com. 2001), Coalition for Photonics and Optics (chair 1996—97), Forum on Physics and Soc. (exec. com. 1996—97), Coun. Sci. Soc. (co-chair govt. affairs com. 1996—97), Materials Rsch. Soc., Am. Assn. Engring. Soc. (bd. govs. 1995—97, Nat. Engring. award 1999), Optical Soc. Am. (editor Applied Optics 1990—92, bd. dirs. 1987—89, 1992—97, v.p. 1994, pres. 1996, Leadership award 2001), Am. Soc. Precision Engring., Am. Ceramic Soc., Lasers and Electro-Optics Soc. IEEE. Home: 4 Claret Dr Fairport NY 14450-4610 Office: U Rochester Inst Optics PO Box 270186 Rochester NY 14627-0186 E-mail: moore@optics.rochester.edu.

MOORE, DWIGHT TERRY, lawyer; b. Nashville, Apr. 22, 1948; s. George Howard and Minnie Laura (Gregory) M.; m. Barbara Franklin, May 7, 1977; 1 child, Marian. BA, Vanderbilt U., 1970; MPA, U. Memphis, 1975, JD, 1983. Bar: Tenn. 1984, U.S. Dist. Ct. (we. dist.) Tenn. 1984, U.S. Ct. Appeals (6th cir.) 1991. With State of Tenn., Nashville, 1970-73, Shelby County, Memphis, 1974-79; asst. prof. U. Memphis, 1983-88; ptnr. Gardner & Moore, Memphis, 1984-91, Olsen, Kuhn & Moore, Memphis, 1991-93, Lowrance & Monypeny, Memphis, 1993-94; pvt. practice, 1994-99; with Olsen Kuhn & Moore, 1999—. Mem. ABA, Memphis Bar Assn. Libertarian. Unitarian Universalist. Avocations: tae kuk, fitness, reading. Office: 5100 Stage Rd Ste 4 Memphis TN 38134-3164 E-mail: dwightmoore1@aol.com.

MOORE, EDWARD RAYMOND, JR. pastor, chaplain, campaign consultant; b. Coos Bay, Oreg., Sept. 1, 1943; s. Edward Raymond Sr. and Daisy (Burnette) M.; m. Gail Pinckney, Aug. 23, 1969; children: E. Ray III, Richard P., Dorothy L., William R. BA in Polit. Sci., The Citadel, 1965; postgrad., Dallas Theol. Sem., 1965-68; MDiv cum laude, Grace Theol. Sem., 1974, ThM, 1979. Campus pastor at Purdue U. Trinity Fellowship, West Lafayette, Ind., 1977-85; so. regional dir. Freedom Coun., Virginia Beach, Va., 1985-86; state coord. Americans for Robertson (presdl. campaign), Columbia, S.C., 1986-88; v.p. for devel., pub. rels. Internat. Friendship Ministries, 1988-89; pres. Frontline Ministries, 1993—; dir. Exodus Mandate Project, 1997—. Chaplain USAR, Columbia, 1980—. Lt. Col., USAR, 1969-99, Persian Gulf. Decorated Bronze Star. Republican. Home: 2025 Cedar Springs Rd Blythewood SC 29016-8318

MOORE, EDWARD WARREN, lawyer; b. Odessa, Tex., July 21, 1959; s. Edward Warren and Gloria (Schroeter) M.; m. JoAnne Bisso; children: Peggy, Barbara. BA in Econs., Princeton U., 1981; JD, So. Meth. U., 1984. Bar: Tex. 1984, U.S. Dist. Ct. (no. dist.) Tex. 1984, U.S. Ct. Appeals (5th cir.) 1984, U.S. Ct. Appeals (10th cir.) 1985. Assoc. Ravkind, Kuehne & Biesel, Dallas, 1984-85; ptnr. Kuehne & Moore, 1984-96; pvt. practice, 1996-2000; mng. ptnr. Moore & Anderson. Dir. Rsch. Group Tex., Inc., Ascend Student Health Svcs., LLC. Vol. Park Cities YMCA, Ronald McDonald Ho. Mem. AAAS, ABA (litigation sect., trial practice sect. and com., product liability, antitrust, intellectual property sect.), ATLA (toxic, environ. and pharm. litigation sect., comml. litigation sect.), State Bar Tex., Dallas Bar Assn., Tex. Trial Lawyers Assn., Dallas Country Club, Safari Club Internat. (life), Dallas Safari Club. Methodist. Home: 7044 Turtle Creek Blvd Dallas TX 75205-1254 E-mail: eddymoor@sprynet.com.

MOORE, ELIZABETH ANN DAVIS, home fashion products specialist; b. Charleston, S.C., June 15, 1961; d. Victor M. and Ina Elizabeth (Anderson) Davis; m. William Scott Moore, June 21, 1986; children: David Scott, Daniel Paul, James Wesley. BS in Mktg. summa cum laude, U. Ala., 1983, MA in Elem. Edn., 1989. Dept. mgr. Parisian, Inc., Birmingham, Ala., 1983-84, Tuscaloosa, 1984-85; interior products specialist Phifer Wire Products, Inc., 1985—87; tchr. Walker Elem. Sch., Tuscaloosa County Schs., 1989—. Clin. master tchr. U. Ala., 1998—. Mem. Color Assn. of U.S. Methodist. Avocations: traveling, sewing, swimming, exercising, sports. Home: PO Box 152 Berry AL 35546-0152

MOORE, EMMA SIMS, educator; b. Branford, Fla., Oct. 27, 1937; d. Lawton Edward and Annie Ruth (Hewitt) Sims; m. H. Dean Moore, Sr., Sept. 30, 1961; 1 child, H. Dean Jr. Secretarial sci., Jones Coll., 1955; B., Butler U., 1984; MS, Ind. Wesleyan U., 1989; MA, The Fielding Inst., 1995, EdD, 1996. Cert. profl. sec.; cert. adminstrv. mgr. Sec. to svc. mgr. Buick Motor div. GM, Jacksonville, Fla., 1956-72, Charlotte, N.C., 1972-74; sec. to br. mgr. Motors Holding div. GM, Washington, 1974-78, Phila., 1978-82; exec. sec. to dir. product support Allison Gas Turbine div. GM, Indpls., 1982-92; ret., 1992. Mem. faculty Ind. Wesleyan U., 1993-94, So. Wesleyan U. Central, S.C., 1995-98, St. Leo U., Lake City, Fla., 1998—. Mem. exec. com. Boy Scouts Am., West Chester, Pa., 1981-82. Profl. Secs. Internat. (v.p. 1986-87, pres. 1987-89, 500 chpt., Sec. of Yr. 1986 500 chpt., 1989 Ind. divs.), CPS Acad., Inst. Certification. Baptist. Home: RR 13 Box 291 Lake City FL 32055-9007

MOORE, EMMETT BURRIS, JR. physical chemist, educator; b. Bozeman, Mont., June 14, 1929; s. Emmett Burris and Iris Marie (Brown) M.; m. Diane Elizabeth Girling, Oct. 1, 1960; children: Karen Elizabeth, Robin Diane. BS in Chemistry with honors, Wash. State U., 1951; PhD in Phys. Chemistry (Shell fellow), U. Minn., 1956. Teaching asst. U. Minn., Mpls., 1951-55, asst. prof. physics Duluth, 1957-59; mem. staff Boeing Sci. Research Labs., Seattle, 1959-73. Lectr. chemistry Seattle U., 1973; dir. power plant siting Minn. Environ. Quality Bd., St. Paul, 1973-76; gen. mgr. Richland (Wash.) Divsn. Olympic Engring. Corp., 1976-78; staff scientist Pacific N.W. Nat. Lab., 1978-96; mem. environ. engring. rev. panel EPA, 1989-95; alt. mem. Hanford Adv. Bd., 1995-2000; adj. prof. environ. sci. Wash. State U., 1990—. Author: (book) The Environmental Impact Statement Process and Environmental Law, 1997, 2d edit., 2000, An Introduction to the Management and Regulation of Hazardous Waste, 2000; contbr. articles to profl. jours. Trustee Mid-Columbia Symphony Soc., 1978-85, v.p., 1980-81, pres., 1981-83; trustee Richland Light Opera Co., 1984-88, bus. mgr., 1984-88. Recipient Land Grant Faculty Excellence award Wash. State U., 1999. Fellow AAAS; mem. Am. Phys. Soc., Am. Chem. Soc. (chmn. Pauling award com. 1971, sec. Puget Sound sect. 1971-73, mem. energy panel of com. on chemistry and pub. affairs 1983-86), Am. Assn. Physics Tchrs. (v.p. Wash. sect. 1965-66, pres. 1966-67), N.W. Sci. Assn., Phi Beta Kappa, Phi Kappa Phi, Phi Eta Sigma, Alpha Chi Sigma, Phi Lambda Upsilon, Sigma Alpha Epsilon (v.p. province 1972-73) Episcopalian (vestryman 1967-69, 76-79, 91, sr. warden 1969, del. diocesan conv. 1969-72). Home: 2323 Greenbrook Blvd Richland WA 99352-8427 Office: Wash State U 2710 University Dr Richland WA 99352-1671 E-mail: ebmoore@wsu.edu.

MOORE, ERNEST EUGENE, JR. surgeon, educator; b. Pitts., June 18, 1946; s. Ernest Eugene Sr. and Mary Ann (Burroughs) M.; m. Sarah Van Duzer, Sept. 2, 1978; children: Hunter Burroughs, Peter Kitrick. BS in Chemistry, Allegheny Coll., 1968; MD, U. Pitts., 1972. Surg. resident U. Vt., Burlington, 1972-76; chief of trauma Denver Health Med. Ctr., 1976—, chief dept. surgery, 1984—. Chief div. of trauma and EMS U. Colo., Denver, 1984—, prof. surgery, vice chmn. dept., 1985—; dir. facilities Colo. Trauma Inst., Denver, 1984-95. Editor: Critical Decisions in Trauma, 1987, Trauma, 1988, rev. edits., 1991, 96, 00, Early Care of the Injured, 1989; assoc. editor Jour. Trauma, Am. Jour. Surgery, Surgery-Problem Solving Approach, 2d edit., 1994, others; patentee retrohepatic vena cava shunt. Fellow ACS (com. on trauma, vice chair 1990), Soc. Univ. Surgeons (pres. 1989), Am. Assn. Surgery of Trauma (pres. 1993), Internat. Assn. Surgery of Trauma and Surg. Intensive Care (pres. 1998-99), Pan Am. Trauma Assn. (pres. 1991), Southwestern Surg. Congress (pres. 1998), Western Trauma Assn. (pres. 1989). Republican. Avocations: skiing, hockey, hunting, ultramarathons, fishing. Home: 2909 E 7th Avenue Pky Denver CO 80206-3839 Office: Denver Health Med Ctr Dept Surgery Denver CO 80204 E-mail: ernest.moore@dhha.org.

MOORE, ERNEST CARROLL, III, lawyer; b. Honolulu, Oct. 24, 1944; s. Ernest Carroll Jr. and Frances (Miller) M.; children: Tiffany Meredith, Alyssa Judi. BA, Dartmouth Coll., 1967; JD, So Meth. U., 1974. Bar: Hawaii 1974, U.S. Dist. Ct. Hawaii 1974, U.S. Ct. Appeals (9th cir.) 1974. Ptnr. Torkildson, Katz, Fonseca, Jaffe, Moore & Hetherington, Honolulu, 1974—. Trustee Hawaii Sch. Girls, 1998—. Bd. dirs. Hawaii chpt. ARC, Honolulu, 1979, trustee La Pietra-Hawaii Sch. for Girls, 1998—, Outrigger Duke Kahanamoku Found., 1999—. Mem. Am. Acad. Hosp. Attys., Nat. Health Lawyers Assn., Indsl. Relations Research Assn., Soc. for Human Resources Mgmt., Order of Coif, Pacific Club, Outrigger Canoe Club. Republican. Episcopalian. Avocations: tennis, photography. Office: Torkildson Katz Fonseca Jaffe Moore & Hetherington 700 Bishop St Fl 15 Honolulu HI 96813-4187

MOORE, EVERETT LEROY, library administrator; b. Eugene, Oreg., May 24, 1918; s. Clinton L. Moore and Elsie LaVerne (Crowder) Morgan; m. Fern Irene Owen, July 13, 1942; children: David LeRoy, Richard Eugene, Patricia Elaine. BA, Wheaton Coll., 1949; MA, Pasadena Coll., 1954; MA in Libr. Sci., Vanderbilt U., 1960; PhD, U. So. Calif., 1973. Cert. C.C. chief adminstrv. officer, Calif. Libr. Evangel Coll., Springfield, Mo., 1955-57; head tech. svcs. North Coastal Regional Libr., Tillamook, Oreg., 1957-60; head social sci. and bus. libr. Calif. State U., Chico, 1960-62; dir. libr. svcs. Coll. of the Desert, Palm Desert, Calif., 1962-75; dir. univ. libr. Am. U. Cairo, 1970-72; dir. libr. svcs. Woodbury U., L.A., 1976-87, dir. libr. svcs., prof. emeritus, 1987—. Pres. so. region Jr. Coll. Round Table, Calif. Libr. Assn., Sacramento, 1965-66; chair tech. svcs. com. Calif. C.C. Libr. Coop., 1968-70, chmn. Desert area, 1974-75. Contbr. to profl. jours. Avocations: reading, computers, politics. Home: 1395 W 12th Ave Chico CA 95926 Office: 1395 W 12th Ave Chico CA 95926

MOORE, FAY LINDA, systems engineer; b. Houston, Apr. 7, 1942; d. Charlie Louis and Esther Mable (Banks) Moore; m. Noel Patrick Walker, Jan. 5, 1963 (div. 1967); 1 child, Trina Nicole Moore. Student, Prairie View Agrl. and Mech. Coll., 1960-61, Tex. So. U., 1961, Our Lady Lake U.; capability maturity model assessor tng., Software Engring. Inst., 1995. Cert. ISO 9000 Internal Auditor, 1994-97. Instr. Internat. Bus. Coll., Houston, 1965; keypunch operator IBM Corp., 1965-67, sr. keypunch operator, 1967-70, programmer technician, 1970-72, asst. programmer, 1972-73, assoc. programmer, 1973-74, sr. assoc. programmer, 1984-87, staff programmer, 1987-92, staff sys. analyst, 1992-96; sr. software quality engr. Loral Space Info. Sys., 1996—; owner, pres. AFT Co., 1993—; sr. software quality engr. Lockheed Martin Corp., 1996-97; software quality engr. Motorola, Inc., Austin, 1998-2001, quality sys. rev. assessor, 1998-2001, info. tech. quality engr., 2000-2001; prin. sys. engr. Titan Sys. Corp., Houston, 2001—. Space shuttle flight support team IBM, 1985-92; mem. space sta. team IBM, 1992-93. Recipient Apollo Achievement award NASA, 1969, Quality and Productivity award NASA, 1986, 92. Mem. NAFE, Soc. Software Quality, Booker T. Washington Alumni Assn., Ms. Found. for Women, Inc. Democrat. Roman Catholic. Avocation: personal computing.

MOORE, FAYE ANNETTE, retired social services professional; b. Glasgow, Mont., Feb. 21, 1938; d. Chester Oliver and Viola Adelaide (Skalet) Baker; m. Russell Dale Guthrie, July 1, 1961 (div. Nov. 1975); children: Tamia Lee, Owen Bradley; m. William Bateman Moore, Jan. 6, 1979. BA Sociology, Mont. State U., 1959; MA Social Work, U. Chgo., 1961; MBA, N. Mex. State U., 1984, PhD Ednl. Adminstrn., 1989. Social worker Ill. Childrens Home and Aid Soc., Chgo., 1961-63, Divsn. Social Svcs., Fairbanks, Alaska, 1964-72, supr. social worker, 1972-74, staff mgr., 1974-75; regl. mgr. Divsn. Family and Youth Svcs., Anchorage, 1976-80, regl. adminstr., 1991-96; adminstr. Rsch. Ctr. N.Mex. State U. Coll. Bus., Las Cruces, 1984-86; instr. Golden Gate U., Holloman AFB/Alamogordo, N.Mex., 1989-91, Webster U., Ft. Bliss, El Paso, Tex., 1989-91; ret., 1996—. Presenter confs. in field. Contbr. articles to profl. jours. Recipient Supervisory Employee of the Year Commissioner's award Dept. of Health and Social Svcs., 1993. Mem. NASW, Realtor Assn. N.Mex. (state dir. 1990-91, chmn. state edn. com. 1991), Las Cruces Assn. Realtors (v.p. 1991), Am. Bus. Comm. Assn., Beta Gamma Sigma, Phi Kappa Phi. Avocations: gardening, walking, knitting, sewing. Home: PO Box 6162 Spring Hill FL 34611-6162

MOORE, FAYE L. MITCHELL, financial executive; b. Castalia, N.C., July 3, 1950; d. Frank and Mattie Jane Mitchell; m. Daniel Henry Moore, July 16, 1977; 1 child, Fenita LeSai. BS with honors, N.C. A&T State U., 1976. CPA, Md. Asst. acct. KPMG LLP, Balt., 1976-77, various positions to sr. mgr. Phila., 1977-86; dir. mergers and strategic planning Cigna, 1986-90; sr. mgr. Mitchell/Titus, N.Y.C., 1990-92; v.p. audit and acquisitions Providian Corp., Frazer, Pa., 1992-95; CFO, treas. Southeastern Pa. Transp. Authority, Phila., 1995—2002, gen. mgr., 2002—. Spkr. in field. Trustee Friends Select Sch., Phila., 1997—. Recipient Cmty. Svc. award INROADS/Phila., 1993. Mem. AICPA, NAFE, Md. Assn. CPAs, Nat. Assn. Black Accts., Inc. (life, pres. 1984-86, regional v.p. 1987-88, Profl. Achievement award 1986, chair ea. region student conf. 1997-98, Outstanding Mem. award 1990, Disting. Svc. award 2000), Beta Alpha Psi (Outstanding Alumni 2001, Nat. Achievement award 2002, Women's Transp. Sem. Phila. chpt. 1st Milestone award). Avocations: vacationing with family, crossword puzzles, dancing, spectator sports. Home: 5106 Wynnefield Ave Philadelphia PA 19131-2316 Office: Southeastern Pa Transp Authority 1234 Market St Ste 10 Philadelphia PA 19107-3721

MOORE, FLETCHER BROOKS, engineering company executive; b. Heiberger, Ala., June 15, 1926; s. Amzi Wallace and Mary Elizabeth (May) M.; m. Margaret Marian Foreman, Sept. 5, 1954; children— Larry Brooks, Ronald Howell. BS in Electronic Engring., Auburn U., 1948; MS in Electronic Engring., Ga. Inst. Tech., 1949. With U.S. Navy Mine Counter-Measures Sta., Panama City, Fla., 1949-52, Army Ballistic Missile Redstone Arsenal, Ala., 1952-60; with Marshall Space Flight Ctr., NASA, Huntsville, 1960-81; dir. Astrionics Lab. NASA Marshall Space Flight Ctr., 1968-81; chief missile system Teledyne Brown Engring., Huntsville, 1981-83; v.p. Control Dynamics Co., 1983-91; pres. Logicon Control Dynamics, Inc., 1991-94; dep. divsn. dir. Control Dynamics, a Divsn. of bd. Systems, 1996—. Past chmn. alumni engring. coun. Auburn U.; mem. Auburn U. rsch. coun.; vice chairman, Ala. Indsl. Coun. on Engring. Edn.; past mem. adminstrv. sci. adv. coun. U. Ala., Huntsville. Named to State of Ala. Engring. Hall of Fame, Ga. Tech. Engring. Hall of Fame. Mem. AIAA, NASA Alumni League (past pres. Marshall Space Flight Ctr. chpt.). Home: 119 Sherwood Dr SE Huntsville AL 35802-2430 E-mail: bmoore@cdy.bdsys.com.

MOORE, FLORIAN HOWARD, retired electronics engineer; b. Shelby, Ohio, Aug. 23, 1929; s. Carl Leslie and Mona Pearl (Dearth) M.; m. Dorothy Elizabeth Morse, Dec. 19, 1950. AA, Harvard U., 1974. Cert. indsl. maint. electrician; tchg. cert. indsl. electricity, indsl. electronics. With Diebold Inc., Boston, 1955-56; mem. electronics R & D staff Radio Corp. Am., Burlington, Mass., 1956-59; mem. electronics/mech. R & D staff MIT, Cambridge, 1959-74; mem. electricity/electronics/electromech. R & D staff Charles Stark Draper Labs., 1974-76; tchr. indsl. electronics Ashland County Joint Vocat. Sch., Ashland, Ohio, 1976-78; buyer Autocall divsn. Fed. Signal Corp., Shelby, 1978-79; journeyman electrician Excel Wire & Cable divsn. United Tech., Tiffin, Ohio, 1980-86; tchr. indsl. electricity Madison Comprehensive H.S., Mansfield, 1986-88; pres., CEO Florian H. Moore & Assocs., Shelby, 1988-2000, ret., 2000. Vol. Ohio Geneal. Libr., Mansfield; foster parent Commonwealth of Mass., 1962-82 (38 children). With USAF, 1948-52. Fellow Internat. Biog. Assn. (dep. dir. gen.); mem. Ohio Geneal. Soc. (v.p. Richland-Shelby gen. chpt. 1993-95, pres. 1995-97), Royal Lincolnshire Regtl. Assn. (life; Am. contingent, 10th Foot), DAV (life), Order Internat. Fellowship (charter, U.S. rep. 1995), Masons (32 degree), Kappa Delta Phi (life). Avocations: history, snow skiing, sky diving, computer programming. Home: 22A Commandery Ct Springfield OH 45504-5601

MOORE, FRANK JAMES, artist, educator; b. Columbus, Ohio, June 25, 1946; s. James F. and Constance (Chidester) M.; 1 child, Koala Bear. BA, Univ. N.M., 1972; MA in Psychology, Univ. Without Walls, Berkeley, Calif., 1976; MFA in Performanc, Video, San Francisco Art Inst., 1983. Tchr. univ. possibilities Inter-Rels., Inc., Berkeley, 1988—. Dir. Theater Human Melting, Berkeley, 1975-82; mgr. Blind Lemon Theatre, Berkeley, 1977-81; founder, dir. Internet News Svc. LUVer Alternative News, 2000—. Author: Cherotic Magic, 1990, Art of a Shaman, 1991, (poetry) Chapped Lap, 2000; co-author: Vision Theater, 1994; editor (mags.) The Cherotic (r)Evolutionary, 1991-1999; pub., editor Inter-Rels., Inc., Berkeley, 1993—; contbr. (anthologies) Range of Motion, 1993, Consider the Alternatives, 1996, Male Lust, 2000, Disability Culture Rap (video documentary), 2000, Beneath the Surface, 2000; contbr. articles to jours., periodicals, mags., newspapers; host of live weekly internet show, 1998—; creator of 3 large websites on the internet; founder, dir. award winning internet radio sta. Love Underground Vision Radio (Luver), 1999—, Frank Moore's Unlimited Possibilities, Pub. Access TV, Berkeley, Calif., 2001--; prodr., writer, dir.: Feisto, 2001. Performance Art fellow NEA, 1985; recipient Showcase award Cleve. Pub. Theatre Performance Art Festival, 1990, Honorable Mention, East Bay Video Festival, 1991, Second place, 1992, Best of Bay Performance Artist, Bay Guardian, San Francisco, 1992, Hon. Recognition Berkeley Video Festival, 1997. Avocations: computers, music, pop culture. Office: Inter Rels Inc PO Box 11445 Berkeley CA 94712-2445

MOORE, FRANK WILLIAM, computer science educator, pianist; b. Sault St. Marie, Mich., Aug. 3, 1962; Student, U. Cin., 1980-81; BS in Computer Engring., Wright State U., 1986, MS in Computer Engring, 1988, PhD in Computer Sci. and Engring., 1997. Tchg. asst. Wright State U., Dayton, Ohio, 1984-87; grad. rschr. Wright Patterson AFB, 1987; instr. Wright State U., 1987-89; mem. tech. staff I TRW Inc, Beavercreek, Ohio, 1989-92; mem. tech. staff II VEDA, Inc., Dayton, 1992-93; sr. sys. engr. Sumaria Sys., Inc., Fairborn, Ohio, 1993-95; rsch. asst. Wright State U., Dayton, 1995-96; vis. asst prof. U. Dayton, 1997-98; asst. prof. Miami U., Oxford, Ohio, 1998—. Profl. pianist, Dayton, 1977—; program com. mem. reviewer Midwest Artificial Intelligence and Cognitive Sci. Conf., 1998—, Genetic and Evolutionary Computation Conf., 1998—, Fla. Artificial Intelligence Soc., 1999—; chair Midwest Artificial Intelligence and Cognitive Sci. Conf., 2001. Author: Springer Verlag Lecture Notes in Computer Science, 1998, Evolutionary Computation Journal, 2002, IEEE Transactions on Control Systems Technology, 2002. Recipient competitive scholarship Dayton Area Grad. Studies Inst., 1995, 96, award for Outstanding PhD Workshop presentation Genetic Programming Conf., Stanford Calif., 1997, scholarship Officers Wives Club, 1980-81, Ohio Bd. Regents, 1980-85. Mem. IEEE, IEEE Computer Soc., Assn. for Computing Machinery, Wright State U. Alumni Assn. (life). Achievements include doctoral dissertation "A Methodology for Strategy Optimization.". Avocations: music, bicycling, skiing, travel. Office: Miami Univ Computer Sci Dept 230L Kreger Hall Oxford OH 45056 E-mail: moorefw@muohio.edu.

MOORE, FREDERICK APPEL, administrator; b. Boston, Apr. 25, 1925; s. Robert Webber and Josephine (Appel) M.; m. Cynthia Newton, June 17, 1950 (dec. June 2000); children: Lucinda Moore Hammett, Joanthan Newton, Stephanie Moore Schulz. AB, Bowdoin Coll., 1948. Chartered life underwriter. Agt. John Hancock Life Ins. Co., Boston, 1948-56; gen. agy. Mass. Indemnity & Life, Wellesley, 1956-69; 2d v.p. Chubb Life Ins. Co., Concord, N.H., 1969-87; owner Moore Ins. & Fin. Svcs., Enfield, 1987-90; dir. gift planning Dartmouth-Hitchcock Med. Ctr., Lebanon, 1990—. Pres. Disability Ins. Tng. Coun., Chgo., 1958-60; treas. Coll. Fin. Planning, Denver, 1973-77; mem. Conn. Valley Estate Planning Coun., Hanover, 1990—. Chmn. planning Bd., Orange, N.H., 1990-2000, Upper Valley Waste Mgmt. Dist., Lebanon, 1990-2000; sr. warden St. Thomas Episcopal. Ch., Hanover, N.H., 1993-95; bd. mem. Upper Valley Planned Giving Coun., 2002--; mem. Phillips Acad. Alumni Coun., Andover, N.H., 2002--. With USMC, 1943-45. Mem. Social Summit Lodge, Scottish Rite, Shriners. Republican. Episcopalian. Avocations: golf, sailing, tennis, theatre, symphony. Home: 365 N Main St #217 West Lebanon NH 03784 Office: Dartmouth-Hitchcock Med Ctr 1 Med Ctr Dr Lebanon NH 03756 E-mail: frederick.a.moore@Hitchcock.org.

MOORE, GEORGE CRAWFORD JACKSON, lawyer; b. Tenn. BA, U. Fla., 1963; PhB in Soviet Law, U. St. Andrews, Scotland, 1966; MA in English Law with honors, Cambridge U., Eng., 1968, LLM in Internat. Law, 1969. Bar: Eng. (Barrister, Inner Temple) 1970, Jamaica 1971, Fla. 1973, Turks & Caicos Islands 1974, U.S. Supreme Ct. 1976, Antigua and Barbuda, Brit. V.I., Grenada, Montserrat, St. Lucia 1977, Anguilla 1999. Legis. asst. to U.S. sen., Washington, 1970-72; asst. pub. defender Palm Beach County, Fla., 1973; pvt. practice West Palm Beach, 1973—. Founding pres. World Trade Coun. of Palm Beach County, 1981—; chmn. Fla. Coun. Internat. Devel., 1983—84, 2000—, Fla. Gov.'s Conf. on World Trade and Investment, 1989, Fla. Export Coun. of U.S. Dept. Commerce, 1991—92. Editor spl. issues Fla. Bar Jour., 1982, 87, chmn. editorial bd., 1988-89; mem. editorial bd. The Internat. Lawyer jour. of ABA, 1979-84; contbr. articles to profl. jours. Chmn. Fla. Econ. Growth and Internat. Devel. Commn., 1989-90. Fellow: Ctr. for Internat. Legal Studies, Soc. Internat. Bus. Fellows (v.p.); mem.: ABA, Fla. Bar (chmn. internat. law sect. 1994—95, mem. internat. law certification bd. 1998—, bd. cert. specialist in internat. law 1999—). Office: 105 S Narcissus Ave Ste 812 West Palm Beach FL 33401-5530

MOORE, GEORGE ELLIOTT, general contractor, management consultant; b. Pilot, N.C., Nov. 20, 1935; s. Woodrow Wilson and Kate Nell Moore; m. Barbara Jean Spivey, Aug. 29, 1958; children: Sharon Lynne, Todd Elliott. BA, U. N.C., 1962. Exec. dir. Sci. and Humanities Symposium, Duke U., Durham, N.C., 1962-66; dir. fed. programs Roanoke (Va.) City Schs., 1966-68; dir. devel. Hollins (Va.) Coll., 1968-80; assoc. vice chancellor N.C. State U., Raleigh, 1980-83; exec. v.p., chief exec. officer N.C. Med. Soc., 1983-93; sr. cons. Mgmt. Concepts, Inc., 1994-96; pres. Katewood Row, Builders, 1994—. Treas. Carolina Drs. Care, Inc., Raleigh, 1987-93, also bd. dirs.; bd. dirs. Med. Soc. Svcs., Inc., Raleigh, State Med. Jour. Advt. Bur., Inc., Chgo.; trustee, officer N.C. Med. Soc. Found., Inc., 1988-93; exec. v.p. Cmty. Assns. Inst. of the Carolinas, Raleigh, 1995-96. Contbg. author: Corporate Foundation Support for Public Institutions, 1985, Multiple Foundations: Advantages and Problems, 1986. Mem. adv. bd. Kate B. Reynolds Health Care Trust, Winston-Salem, N.C., 1983-93; committeeman N.C. Citizens for Bus. and Industry, Raleigh, 1984-94; bd. dirs. N.C. Forum for Rsch. and Econ. Edn., Raleigh, 1988-93; sec. bd. trustees Hollins Coll., 1968-80. Sgt. USMC, 1954-58. Recipient Grand award Alumni Programs, U.S. Steel Found., Pitts., 1978, Award for Excellence in Publs., Time Inc., N.Y.C., 1979, 80. Mem. Am.

Soc. Assn. Execs., Am. Assn. Med. Soc. Execs., N.C. Inst. Medicine, Assn. Execs. N.C. (bd. dirs. 1983-93), Capital City Club, Raleigh Country Club, Pine Valley Country Club, Univ. Club. Avocations: golf, carpentry and restoration, reading.

MOORE, GEORGE EMERSON, JR. geologist, educator; b. Lebanon, Mo., Jan. 2, 1914; s. George Emerson and Dorothea Louisa (Niewohner) M.; m. Wilma Corrine Leonard, May 20, 1939; children: George E. III, Dana Corinne, Craig G. AB, U. Mo., 1936, MA, 1938; PhD, Harvard U., 1947. Instr. U. Mo., 1938-39; teaching asst. Harvard U., 1940-42, 1946-47; geologist A.P. Green Fire Brick Co., Mexico, Mo., 1942-46; instr. Ohio State U. at Columbus, 1947-48, asst. prof., 1948-57, assoc. prof., 1957-64, prof., 1964-84, prof. emeritus, 1984—. Geologist U.S. Geol. Survey, 1952-83 Fellow Geol. Soc. Am.; mem. Phi Beta Kappa, Sigma Xi. Home: 58 Mulberry Dr Wakefield RI 02879-1416

MOORE, GEORGE EUGENE, surgeon; b. Minn., Feb. 22, 1920; s. Jesse and Elizabeth (MacRae) M.; m. Lorraine Hammell, Feb. 22, 1945; children—Allan, Laurie, Linda, Cathy, Donald. BA, U. Minn., 1942, MA, 1943, BS, 1944, B.M., 1946, MD, 1947, PhD in Surgery, 1950. Intern surgery U. Minn. Hosps., 1946-47; med. fellow gen. surgery, 1947; dir. tumor clinic, 1951-53; sr. research fellow USHPS, 1947-48; faculty U. Minn. Med. Sch., 1948-53, cancer coordinator, 1951-53; chief surgery Roswell Park Meml. Inst., Buffalo, 1953-72, dir., 1953-67; dir. pub. health research N.Y. State Health Dept., Albany, 1967-73; clin. prof. surgery State U. N.Y. at Buffalo, 1962-73, also prof. research biology, 1955-69; dir. surg. oncology Denver Gen. Hosp., 1973-97; prof. surgery U. Colo., 1973-97, prof. emeritus, 1997—. Author: Diagnosis and Localization of Brain Tumors, 1950, Cancerous Diseases, 1970; contbr. 660 articles to profl. jours. Recipient Outstanding Citizen award Buffalo Evening News, 1958, Outstanding Sci. Achievement award, 1959, Disting. Achievement award Modern Medicine mag., 1962, Chancellor's medal U. Buffalo, 1963, Charles Evans Hughes award pub. administrn. Albany, 1963, Bronfman prize Am. Pub. Health Assn., 1964, Tchr. of Yr. award Dept. Surgery, U. Colo., 1977, Disting. Svc. award U. Colo., 1990, Meritorious Svc. Regents award U. Colo., 1990. Mem. Soc. U. Surgs., Halsted Soc., Am. Surg. Assn., Colo. Oncology Found. (pres.). Home: 12048 Black Hawk Dr Conifer CO 80433-7137 Office: Denver Gen Hosp 645 Bannock St PO Box 1806 Denver CO 80201-1806 E-mail: moore@WCOX. *Individuals are miraculous temporal genetic patterns whose accomplishments will always transcend those of any committee, consensual group, or political assembly; society must provide special early educational opportunities for creative youngsters and those with genius. I hope to see the practical development of cell therapy for the infectious and cancerous diseases and genetic corrections of inherited disorders.*

MOORE, GEORGE W(ILLIAM), geologist; b. Palo Alto, Calif., June 7, 1928; s. George Raymond and Grace Amy (Hauch) M.; m. Ellen Louise James, Nov. 27, 1960; children: Leslie Ann, Geoffrey. BS, Stanford U., 1950, MS, 1951; PhD, Yale U., 1960. Geologist U.S. Geol. Survey, Menlo Park, Calif., 1951-94. Courtesy prof. geology, Oreg. State U., Corvallis, 1987—; geologist in charge La Jolla (Calif.) Marine Geology Lab., 1966-75; rsch. assoc. Scripps Instn. Oceanography, La Jolla, 1972-75; participant Deep Sea Drilling Project, Japan, 1977; chmn. arctic panel Circum-Pacific Map Project, 1979—; invited lectr. USSR Acad. Sci., 1980, Indonesian Marine Geol. Inst. and Nat. Petroleum Co., 1986, City of Corvallis Da Vinci Days, 1989-2001; rapporteur UN com. for coordination of offshore prospecting, Peoples Republic of China, 1985; advisor Calif. Coastal Commn., 1970-75; chmn. Earth and Space Scis. Awards, Internat. Sci. Fair, 1978. Author: Speleology—Caves and the Cave Environment, 1997; editor Geodynamic Map of the Circum-Pacific Region, 1990, Plate-Tectonic Map of the Circum-Pacific Region, 1992, Field Guide to the Geologic Processes in Cascadia, 2002. Exhibit com. mem. San Diego Natural History Mus., 1968-75. Fellow AAAS, Geol. Soc. Am., Nat. Speleol. Soc. (hon., pres. 1963); mem. Am. Assn. Petroleum Geologists (com. chmn. 1977), Am. Geophys. Union, Palo Alto Hist. Assn., Peninsula Geol. Soc. (pres. 1986). Democrat. Home: 3324 SW Chintimini Ave Corvallis OR 97333-1529 Office: Geosciences Oreg State U Corvallis OR 97331-5506 E-mail: mooreg@geo.orst.edu.

MOORE, GREG J. electrical engineer; b. L.A., Calif., Jan. 1, 1964; BSEE in Math., U. Calif., 1999. Engr. Arise Internat., Irvine, Calif., 1991—. Author: Controller Components, 2000. Business E-Mail: ai@ariseinternational.com.

MOORE, GREGORY L. editor; Reporter Dayton Journal Herald, 1976—80, Cleveland Plain Dealer, 1980—83, political editor, 1983—86; asst. metro editor Boston Globe, 1986—94, mng. editor, 1994—2002; editor Denver Post, 2002—. Office: The Denver Post 1560 Broadway Denver CO 80202-1577 E-mail: gmoore@denverpost.com.*

MOORE, GWEN LOVA, social sciences educator; b. Orange, N.J., Apr. 29, 1944; d. Milo H. and Sarah Helen (Wiley) M.; m. Richard D. Alba, Jan. 15, 1977; children: Michael, Sarah. AB, Bucknell U., Lewisburg, Pa., 1966; MA, NYU, 1971, PhD, 1977. Asst. field dir. Elmo Roper & Assocs., N.Y.C., 1966-68; rsch. asst. N.Y.C. Dept. Social Svcs., 1968-71, Russell Sage Found., N.Y.C., 1972; rschr. Bur. Applied Social Rsch., Columbia U., 1972-76; asst. prof. SUNY, Brockport, 1978-80, assoc. prof. Albany, 1988—. Assoc. prof. Russell Sage Coll., Troy, N.Y., 1982-88; adj. asst. prof. Cornell U., 1980; guest prof. Mannheim (Germany) U., 1993-94; dir. Inst. Rsch. on Women, SUNY, Albany, 1995-98. Co-editor (book series) Research in Politics and Society, 1985—, Gendering Elites: Economic and Political Leadership in 27 Industrialized Societies, 2000, 3 other books; mem. editl. bd. Sociol. Forum, Albany, 1995—, Gender and Soc., 1999—; contbr. numerous articles to profl. jours. Vis. fellow Australian Nat. U., Canberra, 1978, 79, Fulbright fellow Fed. Rep. Germany, 1986-87. Mem. Am. Sociological Assn., Sociologists for Women in Society, Ea. Sociological Soc. (sec. 1992-95), Internat. Network Social Network Analysis, Internat. Sociological Assn., Network East-West Women. Office: SUNY at Albany Dept Sociology 1400 Washington Ave Dept Albany NY 12222-1000 E-mail: g.moore@albany.edu.

MOORE, HAL G. mathematician, educator; b. Vernal, Utah, Aug. 14, 1929; s. Lewis Henry and Nora (Gillman) M.; m. D'On Empey, July 20, 1956; children: David, Nora (Mrs. Bret C. Hess), Alison (Mrs. Samuel M. Smith). BS, U. Utah, 1952, MS, 1957; PhD, U. Calif., Santa Barbara, 1967. Tchr. Salt Lake City Public Schs., 1952-53; instr. math. Carbon Jr. Coll., also Carbon High Sch., Price, Utah, 1953-55, Purdue U., Lafayette, Ind., 1957-61, adminstrv. asst. dept. math, 1960-61; from asst. prof. math. to assoc. prof. math. Brigham Young U., Provo, 1961-71, prof., 1971-95; prof. emeritus, 1995—; assoc. chmn. dept. Math. Brigham Young U., 1986-89. Author: Precalculus Mathematics, 2d edit, 1977, (with Adil Yaqub) Elementary Linear Algebra With Applications, 1980, College Algebra and Trigonometry, 1983, A First Course in Linear Algebra, 1992, 3d edit., 1998; contbr. articles to profl. jours. Mem. High Coun., Ch. of Jesus Christ of Latter Day Saints, 1985-91, MTC br. pres., 1991-94, Bishop, 1958-61, 78-82. NSF faculty fellow U. Calif., Santa Barbara, 1964-66. Mem. Am. Math Soc., Math Assn. Am. (bd. govs. 1989-92), Utah State Math. Coalition (planning dir. 1990, bd. dirs. 1991-92), Sigma Xi (dir. 1974-80, 82-85, com. chmn. 1982-90), Phi Kappa Phi. Home and Office: 631 W 650 S Orem UT 84058-6027 E-mail: mooreh@math.byu.edu. *Revelation and reason can work together to bring human beings closer to the truth of their existence and place in the universe. But charity and love and dedication are as necessary to the success of this union as they are to all others.*

MOORE, HELEN ELIZABETH, reporter; b. Rush County, Ind., Dec. 19, 1920; d. John Brackenridge and Mary Amelia (Custer) Johnson; m. John William Sheridan, July 6, 1942 (dec. Jan. 1944); m. Harry Evan Moore, May 15, 1954; 1 child, William Randolph. BS, Ind. U., 1972, MS, 1973. Ofcl. ct. reporter 37th Jud. Cir., Brookville, Ind., 1950-60; freelance reporter Rushville, 1960—. Conv. reporter various assns. With USMC, 1943. Recipient Sagamore of the Wabash award Gov. Ind., 1984, 99. Mem. Women Marines Assn. (charter, nat. pres. 1966-68), Am. Legion Aux. (various offices 1950—including Eight Forty nat. sec.-treas., pres. Ind. dept. 1966-67, conv. reporter), Bus and Profl. Women (dist. dir., various offices 1967—), Nat. Shorthand Reporters Assn. (registered profl. reporter), Ind. Shorthand Reporters Assn. (state treas., editor Hoosier Reporter, chmn. legal directory), Ind. German Heritage Soc. (state dir. 1984-92, pres. 1990-92), Ind. U. Alumni Assn., Benevolent and Protective Order Elks. Democrat. Methodist. Avocations: reading, genealogy, knitting, crocheting, gardening. Home and Office: PO Box 206 Rushville IN 46173-0206 E-mail: hem@comys.net.

MOORE, HELEN LUCILLE, adult education educator, consultant; b. Watseka, Ill., July 24, 1930; d. John Kenneth and Thelma Mae (Wollschlaeger) Weidert; m. Harold Junior Gossett, June 24, 1948 (div. May 1971); children: Steven, Joyce, Gary, Ricky, Kenny, Jane; m. Herff Leo Moore, Jr., Nov. 24, 1991. AS in Mgmt., Kankakee (Ill.) Jr. Coll., 1969. Sr. sec. Nimz Transp., Watseka, 1948-57; tchg. aide Glenn Raymond H.S., 1964-71; asst. pers. and safety mgr. Gt. Plains Bag Co., Jacksonville, Ark., 1971-81; sr. human resources rep. Maybelline Products Co., Inc. divsn. L'Oreal, North Little Rock, 1981-2000; recruiting dir. StaffMark, Little Rock, 2000—01; adult edn. cons. Dept. Workforce Edn., 2001—. Chmn. Ark. Human Resource Conf., Hot Springs, 1991-92. Contbr. articles to profl. publs. Bd. dirs. Ark. Urban League, Little Rock, 1985-93; co-founder, exec. bd. dirs. Workforce Alliance for Growth in Economy, 1993—; mem. Ark. Gov.'s Workforce Investment Bd. and Exec. Com., 1999—. Recipient Outstanding Ark. Human Resources Profl. award Ark. Human Resources Coun., 1994; named Sr. Inspirational Employee of Yr., ABLE (Ability Based on Long Experience), 1997. Mem.: Ctrl. Ark. Mfg. Pers. Assn. (chmn. 1990—99, co-founder), Ctrl. Ark. Human Resources Assn. (bd. dirs. 1988—90, profl.), Soc. for Human Resource Mgmt. (profl., Outstanding Profl. Mem. award 1989), Nat. Employer Coun. (Ark. chmn. local employer adv. couns. 1989—2000, sch.-to-work com., focus group 1998, Star Performer award 1999), Am. Legion Aux. (life). Office: Dept Workforce Edn Luther S Hardin Bldg Three Capitol Mall Rm 303 Little Rock AR 72034-3315

MOORE, HERFF LEO, JR. management educator; b. San Antonio, Jan. 24, 1937; s. Herff Leo Moore Sr. and Constance (Benesh) Wold; m. Helen Lucille Weidert, Nov. 1991; children by previous marriage: Terri Lynne, Christopher Scott, Kimberly Anne. BSBA, The Ohio State U., 1964; MBA, U. Tex., 1968; MS in Community Svcs., U. Rochester, 1976; PhD, U. Tex. at Arlington, 1980. Cert. sr. profl. in human resources (life). Prodn. mgmt., quality assurance officer Sacramento (Calif.) Air Logistics Ctr. USAF, 1964-67; personnel mgmt., adminstrv. cons. Aero. Systems Div. Wright-Patterson AFB, Dayton, Ohio, 1968-73; pers. mgmt. and quality assurance cons. Defense Contract Adminstrv. Svcs. Dist. Hdqrs., Rochester, N.Y., 1973-76; lectr. in mgmt. and doctoral student The Univ. of Tex. at Arlington, 1976-79; asst. prof. bus. adminstrn. Ea. Ky. U., Richmond, 1979-81; assoc. prof. mgmt. East Tex. State U. at Texarkana, 1981-83, Saint John Fisher Coll., Rochester, 1983-85, U. Cen. Ark., Conway, 1985-99, ret., 1999. Pres. H.M.C.C. Mgmt. Group, Conway, 1988—; participant Leadership Texarkana Leadership Tng., 1981-82; mgmt. cons., Calif., N.Y., Ark., Ohio, N.J., Fla., Ga., Tex., 1964—. Author: (with others) Language, Customs and Protocol: A Guidebook for International Students and Employees, 1992; contbr. numerous articles to profl. jours. Capt. USAF, 1964-76. Recipient Significant Performance Contbr. award Def. Supply Agy., 1975; Nat. scholar Phi Kappa Phi, 1968; named Honor Grad. USAF Officers Tng. Sch., 1964. Mem. Soc. for Human Resource Mgmt. (tng. and devel. com. 1989-94, select panel on edn. 1989-91, coll. rels. com. 1989-92, bd. dirs. area IV 1987-91, sec., treas. Ark. coun. 1986-87), Ark. Human Resources Assn. (pres. 1991-92, bd. dirs. 1991-93), Acad. Mgmt., Soc. Human Resource Mgmt. (superior merit awards student chpt. U. Ctrl. Ark. 1985-90, 93), Alpha Kappa Psi, Phi Kappa Phi, Sigma Iota Epsilon. Mem. Assembly of God Ch. Avocations: golf, chess, political buttons. Home: 1910 Amelia Dr Conway AR 72034-3315

MOORE, HERMAN JOSEPH, retired professional football player; b. Danville, Va., Oct. 20, 1969; BA in Rhetoric & Comm. Studies, U. Va., 1991. Wide receiver Detroit Lions, 1991—2001. Named to The Sporting News All-Am. 1st team, 1990; selected to Pro Bowl, 1994.*

MOORE, HONOR, writer, educator; b. N.Y.C., Oct. 28, 1945; d. Paul and Jenny (McKean) M. BA, Harvard U., 1967. Tchr. Young Writers Inst., Hartford, Conn., 1993—, Women Writing/Women Telling, Kent, 1994—, Poetry Workshops, Kent, 1994—. Vis. disting. writer in creative nonfiction U. Iowa, 1997. Author: Mourning Pictures, 1974 (Creative Artists Pub. Svc. grant 1975), Memoir (collection of poems), 1988, The White Blackbird, a life of the painter Margarett Sargent by her granddaughter, 1996; guest curator Margarett Sargent: A Modern Temperament, Davis Mus., Wellesley Coll., 1996. Mem. steering com. Women Writing Women's Lives seminar; vol. N.Y. Ctr. for Humanities, 1991-93, Ctr. for the Humanities, CUNY, 1993-95; bd. dirs. Jenny McKean Moore Fund for Writers, Washington, 1975—, Manhattan Theatre Club, N.Y.C., 1972-76, Music Theatre Group, N.Y.C., 1976-93. Artists grantee Conn. Commn. on Arts, 1992; Nat. Endowment for Arts Creative Writing fellow, 1981. Mem. Poets and Writers Inc. (bd. dirs. 1974-93), Poetry Soc. Am., PEN Am. Ctr. Avocation: hiking. Home and Office: Apt 8A 276 Riverside Dr New York NY 10025-5208

MOORE, HUGH JACOB, JR. lawyer; b. Norfolk, Va., June 29, 1944; s. Hugh Jacob and Ina Ruth (Hall) M.; m. Jean Garnett, June 10, 1972; children: Lela Miller, Sarah Garnett. BA, Vanderbilt U., 1966; LLB, Yale U., 1969. Bar: Tenn. 1970, U.S. Dist. Ct. (mid. dist.) Tenn. 1970, U.S. Dist. Ct. (ea. dist.) Tenn. 1973, U.S. Dist. Ct. (we. dist.) Tenn. 1982, U.S. Ct. Appeals (6th cir.) 1973, U.S. Ct. Appeals (fed. cir.) 1999, U.S. Supreme Ct. 1999. Law clk. U.S. Dist. Ct. (mid. dist.) Tenn., Nashville, 1969-70; trial atty. civil rights divsn. U.S. Dept. Justice, Washington, 1970-73; asst. U.S. atty. Eastern Dist. of Tenn., Chattanooga, 1973-76; assoc. Witt, Gaither & Whitaker, P.C., 1976-77, shareholder, 1977—, also bd. dirs. Mem. Commn. Women and Minorities Profession Law; mem. hearing com. Bd. Profl. Responsibility Supreme Ct. Tenn.; mem. mediation and arbitration panel U.S. Dist. Ct. (ea. dist.) Tenn.; cert. arbitrator, cert. mediator Tenn. Rule 31 Nat. Assn. Securities Dealers; cert. arbitrator N.Y. Stock Exch., Nat. Arbitration Forum; mem. adv. commn. on rules of civil and appellate procedure Tenn. Supreme Ct., chmn., 1999—. Contbr. articles to profl. jours. Bd. dirs. Adult Edn. Coun., Chattanooga, 1976-81, pres., 1977-79; bd. dirs. Chattanooga Symphony and Opera Assn., 1981-87, Riverbend Fesitval, 1983-85, 91—, pres., 1995-97, Landmarks Chattanooga, 1983-84, Cornerstones, 1995-98, Orange Grove Sch., 1996—; mem. alumni coun. McCallie Sch., 1980-85; trustee St. Nicholas Sch., 1983-89, chmn., 1986-88. Fellow Am. Coll. Trial Lawyers, Tenn. State Com., Tenn. Bar Found., Chattanooga Bar Found.(mem. hearing panel, Tenn. Bd. Profl. Responsibility, 1996-2002); mem. ABA (mem. bd. editors jour. Litigation News 1983-90), Tenn. Bar Assn., Am. Bar Found., Chattanooga Bar Assn. (mem. bd. govs. 1985-87), Mountain City Club, Rotary. Methodist. Home: 101 Ridgeside Rd Chattanooga TN 37411-1830 Office: Witt Gaither & Whitaker 1100 SunTrust Bank Bldg Chattanooga TN 37402 E-mail: hmoore@wgwlaw.com.

MOORE, IDA LAKE, special education educator, therapist; b. Pauls Valley, Okla., Dec. 15, 1950; d. Jimmie Lee and Alma Lake (Sullivan) Sparks; m. Dwight James Moore, Dec. 26, 1969 (dec. Dec. 1973); 1 child Cary Denise Moore Cuddeback. BS in Edn., Southwestern Okla. State U., 1977, MEd, 1981; cert. alphabetic phonics therapist, Kathryne B. Payne Edn. Ctr., Oklahoma City, 1994. Cert. psychometrist, edul. diagnostician, sch. counselor, elem. edn. tchr., phys. edn., health and safety tchr., learning disability tchr., mentally handicapped tchr., mid. sch. lang. arts and social studies tchr., psychology, Okla.; lic. profl. counselor, Okla. Tchr. spl. edn. Elk City (Okla.) Pub. Schs., 1988—, mem. crisis intervention team, 1995—, facilitator student assistance program, 1995—. Asst. test adminstr. Okla. cert. testing program with Nat. Evaluation Sys., Inc., Amherst, Mass., 1990—; tutor children with dyslexia, Elk City, 1992—; tchr. for ACT and SAT prep. classes Paula Stanford's Human Resources Network, Oklahoma City, 1996—; tchr. adults with dyslexia Okla. Dept. Rehab., Oklahoma City, 2000—; therapist Gt. Plains Regional Med. Ctr., Elk City, 2000—. Participant Gt. Expectations Summer Inst., Northeastern State U., Talequah, Okla., 1998-2001. Mem. ACA, NEA, Okla. Counseling Assn., Okla. Sch. Counselors Assn., Okla. Edn. Assn., Elk City Edn. Assn., Kappa Delta Pi. Republican. Avocations: reading, travel, sight-seeing, research, genealogy.

MOORE, J. SCOTT, advanced technology consultant; b. Detroit, Sept. 27, 1952; s. James Brown and Marguerite Louise (Loyselle) M.; m. Soon Ki Lee, Apr. 15, 1987; 1 child, Ross Lee. BS in Physics, Rensselaer Poly. Inst., 1974, MS in Materials Engring., 1977, PhD in Materials Engring., 1981. From engr. to sr. contracts adminstrn. IBM, East Fishkill, N.Y., 1982-88, Yorktown Heights, 1988-95; pvt. practice Mt. Kisco, 1995—. Mem. IEEE, IEEE Computer Soc., Soc. Chimie Industrielle, Sigma Xi. Avocations: Buddhism, vedanta, yoga, new media. Home and Office: 25 Barker St Apt 107 Mount Kisco NY 10549-1648

MOORE, J STROTHER, science educator, researcher; s. J. Strother and Jessie Louise Moore; m. Jo Anne O'Neil; children: Lisa, Jonathan, Chris. BS, MIT, 1970; PhD, U.Edinburgh, Scotland, 1973. Rsch. mathematician Xerox PARC, Palo Alto, Calif., 1974—76; sr. rsch. scientist SRI, Menlo Park; prof. U. Tex., Austin, 1981—87; chief scientist Computational Logic, Inc., 1987—97; Inman chair U. Tex., 1997—. Co-author: (software) Boyer-Moore Theorem Prover, 1971. Recipient Current prize in Automatic Theorem Proving, AMS, 1991, Herbrand award, CADE, 1999. Fellow: AAAI. Avocation: rock climbing.

MOORE, JACQUELYN, art educator, artist; b. Helena, Mont., July 31, 1949; d. John Winfield and Grace Genearl Oswalt Moore. BA in Art, Mont. State U., 1972, tchr. cert., 1980; MA in Art, U. Mont., 1979. Asst. claims adjuster Dept. Fish, Game and Wildlife, Helena, 1968; clk., auditor Dept. Revenue, 1972-79; instr. Carroll Coll., 1981-87, asst. dir. Guadalupe Hall, 1984-87; dispatcher Fire Tower Lookout Dept. State Lands, 1986; designer stained glass Shed Brand Studios, Charlotte, N.C., 1987; art tchr. Cedar Hill (Tex.) Ind. Sch. Dist., 1988—. Artist, co-planner Women's Commemorative Mural, Helena, 1979; artist, designer Carroll Coll., Helena, 1981-87; tchr. cmty. edn. Cedar Hill Ind. Sch. Dist., 1990-95, advisor/planner bldg. com., 1992-2001; asst. to Daniel Hillen, Carroll Coll. with various art exhbns./projects, 1981-2002. Numerous exhibits, including: Zula Bryant Wylie Libr., 1994, State Fair of Tex., 1992, Mont. Hist. Soc., Helena, 1982, Carroll Coll., Helena, 1984, Clay Gallery, Missoula, Mont., 1980, U. Mont., Missoula, 1978, others. Pres. libr. bd. Cedar Hill Zula Bryant Wylie Libr., Tex., 1999. Recipient 1st place watercolor award Zula Bryant Wylie Libr., 1994, hon. mention State Fair of Tex., 1992. Mem. Dallas Mus. Art, Dallas Symphony Soc., Kimball Mus./Ft. Worth. Avocations: painting, drawing, traveling, gardening, writing letters. Home: 707 Penn Pl Cedar Hill TX 75104-1747 Office: Beltline Intermediate Sch 504 Beltline Rd Cedar Hill TX 75104 E-mail: moorj@chisd.com.

MOORE, JACQUELYN CORNELIA, labor union official, editor; b. Dec. 25, 1929; d. James C. and Harriette I. Thomas; m. Clarence Carbin Moore, Jan. 19, 1947 (dec. Feb. 1970); children: Clarence Joseph, Janet Elizabeth Moore Marshall. Mail clk. U.S. P.O., Phila., 1966—93; editor Local 509 Newsletter Nat. Alliance of Postal and Fed. Employees, Washington, 1969—74, editl. newsletter chmn., 1969—74, sec. dist. 5, 1972—74, nat. editor Nat. Alliance, 1974—, mem. exec. bd., 1974—, union photographer, 1974—. Dir. 202 Housing for Elderly Corp. bds., Chattanooga, New Orleans, 1981—, Atlanta, 1988—; sec. supervisory com. Nat. Fed. Credit Union, 1977—82, 1984—94, chair, 1994—. Vol. D.C. Voting Rights Corp., Washington, 1979—; sustaining mem. Dem. Nat. Com., 1977—. Mem.: Nat. Press Club, Nat. Bus. and Profl. Women's Club. Roman Catholic. Home: 1102 R St NW Washington DC 20009-4364 Office: 1628 11th St NW Washington DC 20001-5086

MOORE, JAMES ALFRED, ski company executive, lawyer; b. Madisonville, Ky., Oct. 20, 1915; s. Virgil Yandell and Dorothy Ina (Price) M.; m. Lucile Carpenter, June 29, 1970; children by previous marriage: Marjorie M. Eickel, James Kelly, Kathleen M. Marozzi; m. Judith Gallen, June 10, 1995. AB, U. Ky., 1936; LL.B., Harvard U., 1939. Bar: Pa. 1940, D.C. 1969, Va. 1978. Assoc. firm Pepper, Hamilton & Scheetz, Phila., 1940-51, partner, 1951-69, partner firm, 1969-77; pres. Camelback Ski Corp., Tannersville, Pa., 1963-86, chmn., bd. dirs., 1986-93, chmn. emeritus, 1993—. Contbr. articles to various law revs. Bd. dirs. Phila. Soc. for Crippled Children and Adults, 1959-69. Served from ensign to lt. comdr. USNR, 1942-45. Mem. Am. Bar Assn., Am. Law Inst. Republican. Methodist. Office: Camelback Ski Corp PO Box 168 Tannersville PA 18372-0168 Home: PO Box 168 Tannersville PA 18372-0168

MOORE, JAMES CONKLIN, lawyer; b. Albany, N.Y., Dec. 20, 1939; s. James Alexander and Doris Virginia (Conklin) M.; m. Shirley Jean Mitchell, June 17, 1961; children: James, Jennifer, David, Eliza. BS, Cornell U., 1961, LLB, 1964. Bar: N.Y. 1964, U.S. Dist. Ct. (we. dist.) N.Y. 1966, U.S. Dist. Ct. (mid. dist.) Pa. 1981, U.S. Dist. Ct. (no. dist.) N.Y. 1980, U.S. Ct. Mil. Appeals 1965. Assoc. Wiser, Shaw, Freeman, VanGraafeiland, Harter & Secrest, Rochester, N.Y., 1966-74; ptnr. Harter, Secrest & Emery, 1974—. Author several articles, book chpts. and book revs. Trustee, pres. Friends of Rochester (N.Y.) Pub. Libr., 1993—98; bd. dirs., sec. Geva Theater, Inc.; pres.s. Legal Connection, Inc., 2002—; mem. Cornell U. Coun. , 1997—2002; chmn. bd. trustees N.Y. Lawyer Assistance Trust. Capt. U.S. Army, 1964—66, Vietnam. Mem. adv. bd. Rochester Area Ednl. TV, 1981-87; elder, trustee Third Presbyn. Ch., Rochester. Fellow ABA Found., Am. Coll. Trial Lawyers, N.Y. Bar Found. (bd. dirs. 1997-2000); mem. ABA (ho. of dels. 1998—, standing comm. on legal assistance to indigent defendants), Am. Law Inst. (elected), N.Y. State Bar Assn. (pres. 1998-99, mem. ho. dels. 1984-87, 89—, chmn. ins. sect. 1984-85, chmn. task force on liability ins. 1986-87, chmn. com. ins. programs 1988-94, mem. exec. com. 1992-00, v.p. 1994-97), Monroe County Bar Assn. (judiciary com. chmn. 1982-85), Nat. Conf. Bar Pres. (exec. coun. 1999-2002), Monroe County Bar Found. (bd. dirs. 2002—), Def. Rsch. Inst., Genesee Valley Club, Cornell Club N.Y.C. Republican. Avocations: U.S. history, refinishing old furniture. Home: 251 Windemere Rd Rochester NY 14610-1342 Office: Harter Secrest & Emery 1600 Bausch & Lomb Pl Rochester NY 14604-2711 E-mail: jmoore@hselaw.com.

MOORE, JAMES DANIEL, hydrogeologist; b. Fayette, Ala., July 7, 1946; s. James Everette and Norma Jean (Couch) M.; m. Sylvia Jean Black, Oct. 19, 1946; 1 child, Teresa Lynn. BS in Chemistry, U. Ala., Tuscaloosa, 1968, MS in Engring. Hydrology, 1970. Lic. profl. geologist, profl. hydrogeologist, Ala. Head surveying crew Owen-White Cons. Engrs., Baton Rouge, 1967; rschr. U. Ala., Tuscaloosa, 1969; geologist I, Geol. Survey Ala., 1970-75, hydraulic engr. II, 1975-79, dir. hydrogeology divsn., geol. survey mgr. II, 1979-96, acting state geologist, dir., 1996, dir. hydrogeology divsn., geol. survey mgr. II, 1996—; acting state oil and gas supr. State Oil and Gas Bd., 1996. Mem. water resources coun. Water Resources Rsch. Inst., Auburn, Ala., 1985—, water program adv. com. Ala. Dept. Environ. Mgmt., Montgomery, 1990—, tech. com. Nat. Resources Conservation Svc., Auburn, 1996—. Mem. Am. Water Resources Assn., Am. Inst. Hydrology (pres. Ala. sect.), Nat. Ground Water Assn., Assn. Ground Water Scientists and Engrs. Avocations: hunting, fishing. Office: Geol Survey Ala 420 Hackberry Ln Tuscaloosa AL 35486-9780

MOORE, JAMES E. state supreme court justice; b. Laurens, S.C., Mar. 13, 1936; s. Roy Ernest and Marie (Hill) M.; m. Mary Alicia Deadwyler, Jan. 27, 1963; children: Erin Alicia, Travis Warren. BA, Duke U., 1958, JD, 1961. Bar: S.C. 1961, U.S. Dist. Ct. S.C. 1961. Pvt. practice, Greenwood, S.C., 1961-76; cir. judge 8th Jud. Cir. S.C., 1976-91; assoc. justice S.C. Supreme Ct., 1992—. Mem. S.C. Ho. of Reps., Columbia, 1968-76. Mem. S.C. Bar Assn., ABA, Am. Judicature Soc. Baptist. Baptist. Home: 148 Amherst Dr Greenwood SC 29649-8901 Office: PO Box 277 Greenwood SC 29648-0277

MOORE, JAMES H. retired school system administrator; b. Iola, Kans., Oct. 26, 1915; s. Gerald Emmett Moore, Clara May Fowler; m. Roberta Evelyn Lee, Oct. 15, 1938; 1 child Gerald Edward. AA, Grand Junction (Colo.) Jr. Coll., 1936; MA, U. Wyo., 1946. 7th grade tchr. Clifton Pub. Schs., Colo., 1939—42; jr./sr. h.s. tchr. Riverton Pub. Schs., Wyo., 1942—43, prin., 1943—50, asst. supt. schs., 1958—59, supt. schs., 1959—74. Treas. Wyo. Sr. Citizens, Inc.; mem. cmty. coll. bd. Ctrl. Wyo. Coll. Mailing: PO Box 669 Riverton WY 82501

MOORE, JAMES R. lawyer; b. Longview, Wash., Sept. 14, 1944; s. James Carlton and Virginia (Rice) M.; m. Patricia Riley, Aug. 25, 1967 (div. 1978); 1 child, Katherine M.; m. Christine M. Monkman, July 14, 1979 (div. 1996); stepchildren: Amy McKenna, John McKenna; 1 foster child, Zia Sunseri; m. Kathryn Lindquist, Aug. 26, 1996; stepchildren: Matthew Elggren, Adam Elggren, Erin Elggren, David Heilner. BA, Whitman Coll., 1966; JD, Duke U., 1969. Bar: Wash. 1970, U.S. Ct. Appeals (4th cir.) 1972, U.S. Supreme Ct. 1973, U.S. Ct. Appeals (9th cir.) 1974, D.C., 1995. Law clk. to Hon. J. Barnes U.S. Ct. Appeals (9th cir.), L.A., 1969-70; trial atty. pollution control, land/natural resources div. U.S. Dept. Justice, Washington, 1970-74; asst. U.S.

atty. U.S. Atty.'s Office, Seattle, 1974-82; regional counsel U.S. EPA Region 10, 1982-87; counsel Perkins Coie, 1987-88, ptnr., 1989-98; sr. environ. counsel, v.p. Huntsman Corp., Salt Lake City, 1999—. Trainer, speaker on environ. litigation, negotiation and law. Contbr. articles to profl. jours. Bd. dirs. Environ. Law Inst., 1995-2000; chair audit com. Whitman Coll., 1994—; ethics com. Bd. Environ. Auditors Cert., 1998—. Mem. ABA (sect. natural resources 1987—), Wash. State Bar Assn. (environ. and land use sect. 1974—, spl. dist. coun. 1988-95). Democrat. Office: Huntsman Corp 500 Huntsman Way Salt Lake City UT 84108-1235 E-mail: jim_moore@huntsman.com.

MOORE, JANE NEWCOMB, economist, computer specialist; b. Oak Park, Ill., Mar. 15, 1924; d. Marion Watson and Harriet Jane (Morse) Newcomb; m. James Lincoln Turney, May 28, 1949 (div.); 1 child, Julia E. Turney. BA, Occidental Coll., 1946; MA, San Francisco State Coll., 1968; MPh, U. Hawaii, 1981. Asst. engr. Ill. Bell Telephone Co., Chgo., 1947-54; office auditor U.S IRS, San Francisco, 1962-65; systems analyst U.S. Army Engrs., 1965-72; computer supr. U.S. Forest Svc., Berkeley, Calif., 1973-76; economist Hawaii State Dept. Planning, Honolulu, 1978-80; computer clk. dept. land, natural resources aquatic divsn. State of Hawaii, 1980-83, program evaluation analyst dept. of transportation, 1983-90, computer specialist, 1990-87; retired, 1997. Author: (govt. publ.) Input Output Model Hawaii Integrated Energy Assessment, 1981. Vol. coord. Gregory House (AIDS housing), Honolulu, 1992—, Healing Touch Queens Med. Ctr., 1995—, St. Francis Hosp., 1996—. Mem. AAUW, Hawaii Stats. Assn., Univ. Hawaii Sch. Pub. Health Alumni, Phi Beta Kappa, Sigma Alpha Iota (life, v.p. 1944-46, Sword of Honor 1955), Sigma Alph Iota Alumnae (Evanston chpt.). Home: 25 Aulike St Apt 320 Kailua HI 96734-2748

MOORE, JANE ROSS, librarian, educator; b. Phila., Apr. 24, 1929; d. John William and Mary M. Ross; m. Cyril Howard Moore, Jr., June 1, 1956 (div. Mar. 1967). AB, Smith Coll., 1951; MS in Libr. Sci., Drexel U., 1952; postgrad., Columbia U.; MBA with distinction, NYU, 1965; PhD, Case Western Res. U., 1974. Cataloguer, Yale U. Library, 1952-54; chief tech. processes librarian Lederle Labs., Am. Cyanamid Co., Pearl River, N.Y., 1954-58; chief serials catalog librarian Bklyn. Coll. Library, 1958-65, asst. prof., chief catalog div., 1965-70, asso. prof., chief catalog div., 1971-73, asso. prof. asso. librarian adminstrv. services, 1973-76; prof., chief librarian Mina Rees Libr., Grad. Sch. and Univ. Center, CUNY, 1976-91, prof., chief libr. emerita, 1991—. Lectr. Syracuse U. Grad. Sch. Libr. Sci., summer 1967, 69, Queens Coll. Grad. Sch. Libr. and Info. Studies lectr., 1967-69; adj. assoc. prof., 1974-76, adj. prof., 1977-86; HEW Title IIB fellow Case Western Res. U. Sch. Library Sci., 1970-72; trustee N.Y. Met. Reference and Rsch. Libr. Agy., 1984-93, 2d v.p., 1985-88, v.p., 1988-90, treas. 1991-93; mem. chancellor's task force on librs. CUNY, 1979-81. Bd. dirs. Vis. Nurse Assn. of Bklyn., 1984—, mem. exec. com., 1987—, vice chmn., 2001-; elder, clk. of session, pres. of corp. Presbyn. Ch.; bd. dirs., exec. com., sec. Vis. Nurse Regional Health Care Sys., Inc., 2001–. Mem. AAUP, AAUW, N.Y. Libr. Assn. (pres. 1979-80, pres. resources and tech. svcs. sect. 1966-67, councilor 1966-67, 75-76, 78-81, sec.-treas. acad. and spl. librs. sect. 1973-75), ALA (membership com. 1967-71, chmn. coun. regional groups, resources and tech. services div. 1968-69, dir. div. 1968-70, 75-76, chmn. div. cataloging and classification sect. 1975-76), N.Y. Tech. Svcs. Librs. (pres. 1963-64, award 1976), Assn. Coll. and Rsch. Librs. (chmn. univ. librs. sect. 1983-84), N.Y. Libr. Club (sec. 1964-66, pres. 1980-81, coun. 1966-70, 73-77, 79-82), OCLC Users Coun. (SUNY del. 1981-85), Am. Printing History Assn., Archons of Colophon, Libr. Assn Gt. Britain., Spl. Librs. Assn., The Typophiles (sec.-treas. 1996—), NYU Grad. Sch. Bus. Adminstrn. Alumni Assn. (rec. sec. 1967-69, dir. 1969-70, 75-79), Smith Coll. Club Bklyn. (pres. 1966-67, 67-68, class treas. 1976-81), Smith Coll. Club N.Y., Princeton Club N.Y., Phi Kappa Phi. Home: 35 Schermerhorn St Brooklyn NY 11201-4826

MOORE, JANET MARIE, accountant, state official; b. Butler, Pa., Mar. 13, 1947; d. Jesse Robert and Katherine Mae (Pisor) Moore. A in Specialized Bus., New Castle Bus. Coll., 1972. Cost accountant Package Products Inc., Pitts., 1967-68; audit clk. Liberty Mut. Ins. Co., New Castle, Pa., 1968-71; acct. S.R. Snodgrass & Co., CPAs, New Castle, 1971-74; clerical supr. Pa. vital records Pa. Dept. Health, New Castle, 1974—; pvt. practice acctg., Volant, Pa., 1974—. Mem. NRA (life), Owner Handler Assn., Am. Numismatic Assn., Studebaker Family Nat. Assn. (life), New Castle Kennel Club (sec. 1978, dir. 1977-81, v.p. 1979-81). Democrat. Presbyterian. Home: RR 3 Box 101 Volant PA 16156-8815 Office: PO Box 1528 New Castle PA 16103-1528

MOORE, JEANNE, arts educator and administrator, retired; b. L.A., Aug. 28, 1932; d. George E. and Ellen Kearny (Patrick) Moore. AA, Pasadena (Calif.) City Coll., 1952; BA with honors, UCLA, 1954; MM, U. So. Calif., 1965, DMA, 1970. Music tchr. Arvin (Calif.) H.S., 1955-60, Santa Maria (Calif.) H.S., 1960-65, Arroyo H.S., El Monte, Calif., 1965-66; asst. prof. edn. U. Victoria, B.C., Can., 1968-70; asst. prof. music edn. Bowling Green (Ohio) State Coll., 1970-71; prof. music West Chester (Pa.) State Coll., 1971-72; lectr. music San Jose (Calif.) State U., 1972-73; asst. prof. music Madison Coll., Harrisonburg, Va., 1974-76; coord. fine arts W.Va. Dept. Edn., Charleston, 1977-98, ret., 1998. Choral dir. Santa Maria Choral Soc., 1963—64, Silver Lake Presbyn. Ch., L.A., 1966—67, Wesley United Meth. Ch., San Jose, 1972—74; cons./contbr. Nat. Study of Sch. Evaluation, Falls Church, Va., 1983—85, 1989. Co-author: Beyond the Classroom: Informing Others, 1987. Staff mem. Gov's Task Force on Arts Edn., W.Va., 1990—94. Grantee, Nat. Endowment for Arts, 1989—92. Mem.: W.Va. Art Edn. Assn. (bd. dirs., Outstanding Adminstr. award 1991, 1993, 1997, 1998), W.Va. Music Educators Assn. (bd. dirs., Presdl. award 1990, 1998, Disting. Svc. award 1998), Music Educators Nat. Conf., Nat. Coun. State Suprs. Music (pres. 1984—86), Nat. Art Edn. Assn., Mu Phi Epsilon, Pi Kappa Lambda, Phi Delta Kappa. Presbyterian. Home: 102 Brammer Dr Charleston WV 25311-1738

MOORE, JEANNETTE AILEEN, animal nutrition educator; b. Bellflower, Calif., Jan. 6, 1957; d. Harry Joseph Jr. and Alba Aurora (Celaya) M.; m. Matthew Henry Poore, Oct. 2, 1982. BS in Animal Scis., Calif. State Polytechnic U., 1980; MS in Animal Scis., U. Ariz., 1983, PhD in Nutritional Scis., 1987. Cert. nutrition specialist. Postdoctoral rsch. assoc. U. Ariz., Tucson, 1988-90, N.C. State U., Raleigh, 1990-92, coord. Spend-A-Day-At-State program, 1994-97, chair dept. info. tech. com., 1996-97, mem. coll. acad. computing adv. com., 1996—, undergrad. tchg. coord. dept. animal sci., 1997—, mem. coll. courses and curriculum com., 1998—, mem. univ. courses and curriculum com., 2000—, chair, 2002—. Vis. asst. prof. N.C. State U., Raleigh, 1992-98, asst. prof., 1998—, faculty advisor Animal Sci. Club, 1992—, advisor Acad. Quadrathlon Team, 1993-94, advisor Rodeo Club, 1994—, World Wide web coord. Dept. Animal Sci., 1994—. Author: (computer spreadsheet) Ruminant Animal Diet Evaluator, 1993; mem. editl. bd. Jour. Animal Sci., 1995—. Supt. jr. ewe show, N.C. State Fair, Raleigh, 1992-98; vol. N.C. Sci. and Math Partnership, Wake county, N.C., 1991—. Mem. Am. Soc. Nutritional Scis., Am. Soc. Animal Sci., Am. Coll. Nutrition, Nat. Assn. Colls. and Tchrs. Agr. (tchg. fellow 2001), Coun. Agrl. Sci. and Tech., Alpha Zeta, Gamma Sigma Delta. Avocations: horseback riding, aerobics, reading, travel. Office: NC State U Dept Animal Sci PO Box 7621 Raleigh NC 27695-7621

MOORE, JEANNIE MARIE, education educator, writer; b. Nowata, Okla., Sept. 11, 1952; d. Roy Hall and Ann N. Casper; m. Charles Arley Moore; children: Joanna. M, Northeastern State U., Tahlequah, Okla., 1994. Author: Character Lessons Plans, 2002; contbr. articles to profl. jours., mags. Home and Office: PO Box 802 Nowata OK 74048 E-mail: JeannieMoor@aol.com.

MOORE, JEFFREY A. municipal official; b. Savannah, Ga., Jan. 18, 1964; s. Charles David and Jane (Bolen) M.; m. Bobbi Farlow, July 12, 1986; children: Thomas Adam, Lyndsay Brooke. AA in Bus., Brevard Coll., 1984; BS in Acctg., U. N.C., Greensboro, 1986. CPA, N.C. In-charge acct. McGladrey & Pullen, CPAs, Greensboro, N.C., 1986-89; acctg. mgr. City of Salisbury, 1989-98; fin. dir. City of Shelby, 1998-99; fin. svcs. dir. City of High Point, NC, 1999—. Mem. N.C. Capital Mgmt. Trust Adv. Bd., 1995—97, 2000—02. Bd. dirs. Brevard Coll. Alumni Assn., 1997-99, 99-01; mem. allocation panels United Way of Rowan County, 1990-94, vice chair allocations com., 1995, v.p. allocations com., 1996, bd. dirs., 1996-98; adult vol. Pack 19 Old North State coun. Boy Scouts Am., den leader Pack 117 Piedmont Coun., den leader Pack 89 Old North State Coun., scoutmaster Troop 20; cmtys. in schs. vol. Marion Elem. Sch., Shelby, N.C.; adult choir Sun. sch. tchr. First United Meth. Ch., High Point, N.C.; basketball, t-ball coach High Point Parks and Recreation. Mem. AICPA, N.C. Local Govt. Investment Assn., N.C. Local Govt. Budget Assn., N.C. Assn. CPAs (chpt. rels. com. 1995-96, 97-98, pres. Ctrl. Piedmont chpt. 1996-97, pres.-elect 1995-96, CPE com. chair 1993-94, 97-98), N.C. Govt. Fin. Officers Assn. (investment adv. com. 1995, 96, govtl. acctg. stds. bd. rev. com. 1996, 97), Govt. Fin. Officers Assn. U.S. and Can. Republican. Methodist. Avocations: camping, hiking, fishing, golf. Office: City of High Point 211 S Hamilton St High Point NC 27260 E-mail: jeff.moore@ci.high-point.nc.us.

MOORE, JERRY JAY, sales executive, retired archaeologist; b. Ft. Sam Houston, Tex., Jan. 29, 1960; s. Richard Vernal and Irmgard Ludwiga Ottilia (Bennewitz) Moore. Student, Ea. Ill. U., 1980—83. Lab. asst. So. Ill. U., Carbondale, Ill., 1979; field/lab. technician Ill. State Mus. Soc., Springfield, 1980, asst. lab. supr. Havana, 1980—81, Am. Resources Group, Ltd., Carbondale, 1983—86; archaeol. technician Ill. State U., Normal, 1986—93; archaeol. asst. U. Ill., Urbana, 1993—94, U. S.C., Columbia, 1993—94; merchandising asst. J.C. Penney Co., Champaign, Ill., 1994—2000; sales profl. Bergner's/Saks Inc., Urbana, 2000—02, Dick's Sporting Goods, Inc., Champaign, 2002—. Contbr. articles to profl. jours. Scholar, State of Ill., 1978—82. Mem.: SAR, Iroquois County Hist. and Geneal. Soc., Sons of Union Vets of the Civil War (genealogist 1998—), Sons of the Revolution, Soc. of the War of 1812 (sgt. at arms 2000—), Phi Theta Kappa. Republican. Roman Catholic. Avocations: history, antiques, genealogy. Home: 590 S Park St Paxton IL 60957 Office: 2113 N Prospect Ave Champaign IL 61822

MOORE, JIMMIE LEE, accountant; b. Delbarton, W.Va., Jan. 27, 1935; s. Albert Mose and Thelma (Cooper) M.; m. Dianne Ruth Rowe, Jan. 7, 1962; children: James J., Kelly Jo Moore Wittry. BS, Marshall U., 1956. CPA, Ohio. Examining officer IRS, Columbus, Ohio, 1956-58; acct. Emmett C. Hurst, Acctg., Jackson, 1958-63, Eisnaugle & Moore, Jackson, 1963-67; pvt. practice, 1967—. Bd. dirs. Milton Banking Co., Wellston, Ohio, K.F.C. of Jackson, Inc., Payne's Chicken, Inc., Wellston. Mem. Ohio Soc. of CPAs, Fairgreens Country Club, Marshall Alumni Assn., Moose, Elks. Republican. Methodist. Avocations: fishing, hunting, golf. Home: 272 Missouri Dr Jackson OH 45640-2033 Office: PO Box 448 160 Main St Jackson OH 45640

MOORE, JOANNA ELIZABETH, real estate professional; b. Hot Springs, Ark., Dec. 2, 1937; d. Herbert A. and Jewel (Mosier) Casey; m. Merlin Richard Moore, July 13, 1956; children: Melanie Moore Sevcik, Rick Moore, Michelle Moore Folks. Student, Bethany Nazarene Coll., 1956-57, Houston C.C., 1978, U. St. Thomas, 1987-88, 90—. Cert. residential specialist, Residential Sales Coun. of Realtors Nat. Mktg. Inst., accredited buyer rep. Realtor Red Carpet Realtors, Temple, Tex., 1979-80, Century 21, Temple, 1981-85; broker-owner RE/MAX Realtors, 1986—. Spkr. Homebuilders Assn. seminars, 1985-88, 92. Fund chairwoman Bluebonnet coun. Girl Scouts U.S., 1987, mem. exec. bd., 1989; fund chairwoman March of Dimes, Temple, 1988; pres. Cen. Tex. chpt. Rep. Women's Club, 1983-84. Named Woman of Distinction, Girl Scouts U.S., 1992. Mem. Nat. Assn. Realtors, Tex. Assn. Realtors (mem. Polit. Action com. 1983-92), Temple-Belton Realtors (social chairwoman 1986, legis. chairwoman 1987, edn. chairwoman 1989, bd. dirs. 1998—), Temple Area Homebuilders (builder-realtor com. 1991, Realtor of Yr. 1993, 95, 96), Temple C. of C. (mem. govt. com. 1988, visitation com. 1989, tourist com. 1990, awards com., govt. affairs com. 1992). Home: 7112 Boutwell Dr Temple TX 76502-4204 Office: RE/MAX Realtors 4016 S 31st St Ste 200 Temple TX 76502-3348

MOORE, JOANNE IWEITA, pharmacologist, educator; b. Greenville, Ohio, July 23, 1928; d. Clarence Jacob and Mary Edna (Klepinger) M. AB, U. Cin., 1950; PhD, U. Mich., 1959. Rsch. asst. Christ Hosp. Inst. Med. Rsch., Cin., 1950-55, U. Mich., Ann Arbor, 1955-57, teaching fellow, 1957-59; postdoctoral fellow in pharmacology Emory U., Atlanta, 1959-61; asst. prof. pharmacology U. Okla. Coll. Medicine, Oklahoma City, 1961-66, assoc. prof., 1966-71, acting chmn., 1969-71, prof., interim chmn., 1971-73, prof., chmn. dept., 1973-93, David Ross Boyd prof., chair, 1993, David Ross Boyd prof. emeritus, 1999. Mem. gen. rsch. support rev. com. NIH, 1975-79, mem. biomed. scis. study sect., 1986-90; mem. adv. bd. Fogarty Internat. Ctr., 1992-94. Contbr. articles to profl. jours. USPHS grantee, 1963-69, 72-74, 79-87. Mem. AAAS, Am. Soc. Pharmacology and Exptl. Therapeutics, Assn. Med. Sch. Pharmacology, Am. Heart Assn. (bd. dirs. Okla. affiliate 1973-88, pres. 1979-80, chmn. bd. 1983-85, bd. dirs. Oklahoma City div. 1988-91, pres. 1989-90), Sigma Xi. Office: U Okla Coll Medicine Dept Cell Biology 728 BMSB OUHSC Oklahoma City OK 73190-0001 E-mail: joanne-moore@ouhsc.edu.

MOORE, JOHN LESLIE, lawyer; b. Gainesville, Fla., July 18, 1966; s. Robert Leslie and Janice (Appleby) M.; m. Kristie Marie Roenick, July 20, 1996; children: Collin Leslie, Ryan Patrick. BA in History, Stetson U., Deland, Fla., 1988; JD, U. Va., 1991. Bar: Fla. 1991. Assoc. Williams, Parker, Harrison, Dietz & Getzen, Sarasota, Fla., 1991-98, shareholder, 1998—. Harry S Truman scholar Truman found., 1985, George F. Hixon fellow Kiwanis Internat., 1997. Mem. Fla. Bar Assn., Am. Health Lawyers Assn., Kiwanis (pres. Sarasota chpt. 1993, 98). Office: Williams Parker et al 200 S Orange Ave Sarasota FL 34236-6802

MOORE, JOHN CORDELL, retired lawyer; b. Winchester, Ill., July 20, 1912; s. John Clayton and Winifred (Peak) M.; m. Pauline Ruyle, July 29, 1939 (dec. 1979); m. Wilma K. Smith Jackson, Aug. 1981. AB, Ill. Coll., 1936, LL.D., 1967; LL.B., Georgetown U., 1949, JD, 1967; postgrad. in geology, Am. U., 1955-57. Bar: Tenn., U.S. Supreme Ct. Rep. Universal Credit Co., St. Louis, 1937-39; tchr. Capitol Page Sch.; also clk. to mem. Ho. of Reps., 1939-41; examiner Metals Res. Co., 1941-42; exec. dir. Fgn. Liquidation Commn. for S. and C. Am., Balboa, C.Z., 1946-47; with Office Alien Property, Dept. Justice, 1947-50; asst. dir. property mgmt. Interior Dept., 1950-52, dir. security for dept., 1952-61; adminstr. Oil Import Adminstrn., 1961-65, asst. sec. for mineral resources, 1965-69; ret. U.S. rep. oil and energy com. OECD, Paris, 1965-69; former dir. Clark Oil, Milw. Served to comdr. USNR, 1942-46; capt. Res. Mem. Am. Legion, Scott County (Winchester, Ill.) Hist. Soc. (life), Delta Theta Phi, Elks, Army-Navy Club, Jacksonville Country Club.

MOORE, JOHN DAVID, management consultant; b. Mt. Pleasant, Iowa, Apr. 7, 1937; s. Burris P. and Esther I. (Copenhaver) M.; m. Karen K. Kriegel, June 19, 1957; children: Charles A., Michael J., Susan K., David J. AB, Muscatine (Iowa) C.C., 1961; BBA, Augustana Coll., 1966; postgrad., U. Iowa, 1966-88. Office mgr. Stanley Engring., Muscatine, 1956-64; pers. mgr. Oscar Mayer & Co., Davenport and Perry, Iowa, 1964-68; midwest regional mgr. A.S. Hansen, Lake Bluff, Ill., 1968-73; legal adminstr. Gardner, Carton & Douglas, Chgo., 1973-78, Heller Ehrman White & McAuliffe, San Francisco, 1978-84; v.p., dir. Hildebrandt, Inc., Walnut Creek, Calif., 1984-90; pres. Moore Cons. Inc., 1990—. Pres. Libertyville (Ill.) H.S. Bd., 1974, Libertyville Ecumenical Coun., 1975; bd. dirs. Libertyville YMCA, 1969-71. Recipient Muscatine Disting. Svc. award, 1963; named Outstanding State V.P., Iowa Jaycees, 1964, Outstanding Nat. Dir., U.S. Jaycees, 1965. Mem. Assn. Legal Adminstrs. (regional v.p. 1977-78, nat. v.p. 1979-81, nat. pres. 1982-83), Found. Assn. Legal Adminstrs. (pres. 1986-88), Golden Gate Assn. Legal Adminstrs. Republican. Methodist. Home and Office: 3205 Deerpark Dr Walnut Creek CA 94598-3637 E-mail: ktjdmoor@aol.com.

MOORE, JOHN EDWARD, marketing professional, freelance writer; b. Watertown, Wisc., Sept. 18, 1920; s. John Martin and Grace Marie (Dent) M.; m. Barbara J. Gates, Sept. 21, 1947 (div. 1957); m. Sally Elizabeth Bond, Oct. 18, 1958; children: Gerald Ian, Helen Louise, Jeffrey Craig, Tracy Patricia. U. Wisc., 1946. Mktg. rsch. mgr. Procter & Gamble (Manila) Phillippines, 1949-57; staff assignment Overseas Div. Procter Gamble, Cin., 1958-62; mkt. rsch. mgr. Procter & Gamble Scandinavia, Newcastle, Tyne, U.K., 1962-64, Export & Spl. Ops., Procter & Gamble A.G., Geneva, Switzerland, 1964-75; assoc. mgr. mkt. rsch. Procter & Gamble, Cin., 1976-79, internat. mktg. rsch. mgr., 1980-84; cons. J.E. Moore, 1984-95; freelance writer, 1990—. Pres. Philippine (Manila) Radio Broadcasting Corp., 1952-54, mem. European Opinion and Mktg. Congress, 1964-75. Contbr. articles to profl. jours. Chmn. Boy Scouts of Am. Geneva, 1975, pres. Cin. Youth Symphony Orch. 1980-82, Men's com. Cin. Art Mus. 1984-90, Duveneck Assn., 1990-99, fund raiser Art Acad., Cin. 1987; chmn. Duveneck Assn., 1999. With U.S. Army, ETO. Recipient Market Rsch. Pioneer award, Philippines, 1987. Mem. Am. Assn. Individual Investors, Smithsonian Assocs., Am. Assn. Retired Persons, Internat. Visitors Ctr. Episcopalian. Avocations: golf, freelance writing, travel. Home and Office: 6235 Nuevelle Ln Cincinnati OH 45243-2355

MOORE, JOHN FRANCIS, emergency physician; b. Pitts., Oct. 5, 1960; s. Francis Gerard Moore and Marilyn Martha Herzog. BS, Westminster Coll., 1982; DO, Midwestern U., Downers Grove, Ill., 1989; JD, U. Pitts., 1997. Diplomate Am. Bd. Managed Care Medicine, Am. Bd. Family Medicine, Am. Bd. Emergency Medicine. Rotating intern Metro Hosp., 1989; resident in family medicine Hamot Med. Ctr., 1990—92; staff physician VA Hosp. Erie, Pa., 1990-92; physician Acute Care Cons., Erie, 1991—94, Cleve. Urgent Care, 1991-92, Emergency Care Cons., Sharon, Pa., 1993—, physician, ptnr., 1996—. Fellow Am. Acad. Family Practice, Assn. Emergency Physicians; mem. AMA, Am. Osteopathic Assn., Am. Acad. Family Physicians. Home: 709 Churchill Ct Cranberry Township PA 16066-4211

MOORE, JOHN GEORGE, JR. medical educator; b. Berkeley, Calif., Sept. 17, 1917; s. John George and Mercedes (Sullivan) M.; m. Mary Louise Laffer, Feb. 8, 1946; children: Barbara Ann, Douglas Terence, Bruce MacDonald, Martha Christine. BA, U. Calif., Berkeley, 1939; MD, U. Calif., San Francisco, 1942. Diplomate: Am. Bd. Ob-Gyn (pres. 1974-78, chmn. 1978-82). Asst. prof. U. Iowa, 1950-51; assoc. prof. UCLA, 1951-65, prof., chmn. dept. ob-gyn, 1968-88, Columbia U. Coll. Physicians and Surgeons, N.Y.C., 1965-68; chief gynecology VA Hosp., Sepulveda, Calif., 1988-94. Contbr. articles to profl. jours. Served to maj. M.C. U.S. Army, 1942-46. Decorated Silver Star, Bronze Star, Purple Heart.; NIH grantee U. Copenhagen; Royal Postgrad. Sch. Medicine, London Mem. ACS, ACOG, Soc. Gynecol. Investigation (pres. 1967), Assn. Profs. Gynecology and Obstetrics (pres. 1975), Western Assn. Gynecol. Oncologists (pres. 1976), Am. Gynecol. Soc., Pacific Coast Ob-Gyn. Soc., L.A. Ob-Gyn. Soc., Pepperdine U. Assocs. Home: 5960 Paseo Canyon Dr Malibu CA 90265-2637

MOORE, JOHN HARTWELL, anthropology educator, consultant; b. Williston, Nd, Feb. 27, 1939; s. William Andrew and Mary Montgomery Moore; m. Shelley Ann Arlen, June 6, 1981; children: Jeremiah, Jessica, Alexandra. BAS, U. of Ark., Fayetteville, AK, 1962; Ph. D, NYU, New York, NY, 1974. Anthropology educator U. of Okla., Norman, Okla., 1977—93, U. of Fla., Gainesville, Fla., 1993. Cons. Native Am. Rights Fund, Boulder, Colo., 1979—, Sand Creek Massacre Descendants Trust, Anadarko, Okla., 1991—, Sawridge Indian Band, Slave Lake, Alberta, Canada, 1992—. Author: (book) The Cheyenne; editor: Political Economy of North American Indians. Del. to state conv. Dem. Party, Oklahoma City, 1991—91; chpt. pres. Vietnam Veterans Against the War, West Orange, NJ, 1969—69; state com. Rainbow Coalition, Oklahoma city, Okla., 1987—93. Second lt. U.S. Army, 1962—64, East Asia. Decorated Armed Forces Expeditionary Medal U.S. Army, UN Peacekeeping Medal UN; recipient Governor's Cmty. Svc. Award, State of Okla., 1990. Fellow: Ctr. for Advanced Study in the Behavioral Sciences, Am. Assn. for the Advancement of Scienceq (chair of anthropology sect. 1997—98); mem.: Human Genome Diversity Project (chair north am. cmty. 1998). D-Liberal. Ethical Culture. Achievements include research in Role of ethnogenesis in human evolution; Rates of gene flow from ethnic intermarriage. Home: 3328 North West 18 Avenue Gainesville FL 32605 Office: University of Florida 1112 Turlington Gainesville FL 32611 E-mail: moojohn@anthro.ufl.edu.

MOORE, JOHN HAYS, chemistry educator; b. Pitts., Nov. 6, 1941; s. John Hays and Mary (Welfer) M.; m. Judy Ann Williams, Aug. 10, 1963; children: John H. IV, Victoria Inez. BS, Carnegie Tech, 1963; MS, Johns Hopkins U., 1965, PhD, 1967. Rsch. assoc. Johns Hopkins U., Balt., 1967-69; program officer NSF, Washington, 1980-81, 85-86; asst. prof. U. Md., College Park, 1969-73, assoc. prof., 1973-78, prof., 1978—. Author: Building Scientific Apparatus, 1982, 2d edit., 1989; editor-in-chief: Encyclopedia of Chemical Physics and Physical Chemistry, 2001; contbr. 115 publs. to profl. jours. Named Joint Inst. for Lab. Astrophysics fellow, 1975, Am. Phys. Soc. fellow, 1990. Fellow: AAAS. Home: 3905 Commander Dr Hyattsville MD 20782-1025 Office: U of Maryland Chemistry Dept College Park MD 20742-0001

MOORE, JOHN JOSEPH, lawyer; b. West New York, N.J., Jan. 24, 1933; s. George Thomas and Dorothy (Zimmer) M.; m. Carmela Macrini, Mar. 10, 1957; children: Christine, John Joseph. BS, Jersey City State Coll., 1956; LLB, N.Y. Law Sch., 1961; LLM, NYU, 1970. Bar: N.Y. 1961. Since practiced in, N.Y.C.; assoc. with firm Dwyer & Lawler, after 1961; then mem. firm Reid, Devlin, Grubbs & Moore; chmn. bd. Leber Inc., 1983-93; mem. Barry McTierman and Moore, 1970—. Guest lectr. disclosure Fordham U.; tchr. social studies pub. schs., Union City, N.J.; Sponsor, coach local Biddy Basketball Team, 1972— Author: Discovery and Inspection, 1969, Legal Significance, 1975; editor: Defendant, 1969-73, 1987-92, 97-98. Trustee devel. fund Jersey City State Tchrs. Coll., 1973-81; trustee Jersey City State Coll., 1982, vice chmn. bd. trustees, 1983-87, chmn., 1989—; chmn. governing bds. Assn. State Colls. N.J., 1985-87; chair Civilian Rev. Complaint Bd., Teaneck, N.J., 1992—; mem. Bd. Higher Edn. State N.J., 1985-87, Coun. N.J. State Colls., 1984-85; mem. governing bds. Assn. State Colls. N.J., 1985-89. With AUS, 1956-58. Mem. ABA, Am. Arbitration Assn. (arbiter 1968—), N.Y. State Bar Assn., N.Y. County Bar Assn., Def. Assn. N.Y. (pres. 1973-74, chmn. bd. 1974-75, governing bd.), Assn. State Colls. N.Y. (gov. bd. 1985-93), Cath. Ins. Guild (pres. 1972-73, chmn. bd. 1973-74), Def. Rsch. Inst. (regional v.p. 1983-86). Roman Catholic (dir. mus. group). Home: 573 Standish Rd Teaneck NJ 07666-2605 Office: 25 Broadway New York NY 10004-1010 E-mail: jjm6160@aol.com.

MOORE, JOHN KENNETH, curator; b. La Plata, Md., Oct. 23, 1947; s. John Kenneth Moore and Miriam Elizabeth (McDowell) Smith; m. Judith Ann Smith, June 9, 1973 (separated 1990). BS in Music Edn., Concord Coll., 1970; MA in Ethnomusicology, Hunter Coll., 1976. Substitute tchr. Charles County Bd. of Edn., La Plata, Md., 1970; score libr. G. Schirmer's Inc., N.Y.C., 1970; security officer Met. Mus. of Art, 1970-75, asst. for slide orders, 1975-79, curatorial asst. mus. instruments, 1979-83, asst. curator mus. instruments, 1983-90, assoc. curator mus. instruments, 1990-97, assoc. curator and adminstr., 1997-99; quest curator Newark Mus., 1997; Frederick P. Rose assoc. curator-in-charge Met. Mus. Art, 1999, Frederick P. Rose curator-in-charge, 2000—. Creator, coord. model cross-cultural music program Met. Mus., 1989-92; panel mem. N.Y. State Coun. on the Arts, N.Y.C., 1990-92; advisor Lincoln Ctr. Libr. Gallery, 1986. Contbr. articles to profl. jours.; mus. arrangements: (off-Broadway show) The Wilde Spirit, 1996. Mem. Collegiate Chorale, 2000—. Travel grantee Met. Mus. of Art, 1983, 87, 93, 2000. Mem. Am. Musical Instrument Soc., Comite Internat. des Musee et Collections d'Instruments de Musique, Soc. for Ethnomusicology, Dramatist Guild. Avocations: composition, musical arrangements, lecturing, conducting Metropolitan Museum chorus. Office: Met Mus of Art 1000 5th Ave New York NY 10028-0113

MOORE, JOHN LEO, JR. journalist, writer, editor; b. Providence, June 24, 1927; s. John Leo and Annabelle Cecilia (Eastwood) M.; m. Dorothy Dolores Drankwicz, 1952; children: John Leo III, Christopher, Meredith Margaret Moore Poffenberger. AB, Brown U., 1950. Reporter Pawtucket (R.I.) Times, 1950-66, Providence (R.I.) Jour.-Bulletin, 1966; correspondent Carpenter News Svc., Washington, 1966-69; assoc. editor Nat. Jour., 1969-74; asst. mng. editor Congl. Quarterly, 1974-78, asst. dir. books, 1978-90; freelance writer, editor, 1990—. Cons. World Bank Internat. Monetary Fund, Washington, 1990—. Editor: Guide to U.S. Elections, 2d edit. 1985, 4th rev. edit. 2001, CQ's Washington Guidebook, 1990, Congressional Ethics, 1992; author: Speaking of Washington, 1993, Elections A to Z, 1999; contbr.: Encyclopedia of American Political History, 2001, Guide to the Presidency, 3d rev. edit., 2002. Committeeman Troop 15 Boy Scouts Am., Pawtucket, 1964-50, Troop 12, 1964-66; pres. Local 185 Newspaper Guild, Pawtucket, 1964-66; v.p. Community Assn., Severna Forest, Md., 1976-78. Recipient salute Pawtucket C. of C., 1965, resolution of praise Pawtucket City Coun., 1966; cited for disting. reporting pub. affairs Am. Polit. Sci. Assn., 1961. Mem. Soc. Profl. Journalists. Roman Catholic. Avocations: photography, home improvement, lawn and garden work, reading, walking. Home and Office: 807 Cottonwood Dr Severna Park MD 21146-2813

MOORE, JOHN NORTON, lawyer, diplomat, educator; b. N.Y.C., June 12, 1937; s. William Thomas and Lorena (Norton) M.; m. Barbara Schneider, Dec. 12, 1981; children: Victoria Norton, Elizabeth Norton. AB in Econs., Drew U.,

1959; LLB with honors, Duke U., 1962; LLM, U. Ill., 1965; postgrad., Yale U., 1965-66. Bar: Fla. 1962, Ill. 1963, Va. 1969, D.C. 1972, U.S. Supreme Ct. 1972. Walter L. Brown prof. law, dir. Ctr. Oceans Law and Policy Ctr. for Nat. Security Law, U. Va., 1965-72, 76—. Counselor on internat. law Dept. State, Washington, 1972-73; chmn. Nat. Security Coun. Task Force on Law of Sea and dep. spl. rep. of Pres. and amb. Law of Sea Conf., 1973-76; fellow Woodrow Wilson Internat. Ctr. for Scholars, Washington, 1976; adj. prof. Georgetown Law Ctr., 1978—; mem. Nat. Adv. Com. on Oceans and Atmosphere, 1984-85; mem. U.S. del. Conf. Security and Coop. in Europe, 1984; spl. counsel, dep. agt. for U.S. to World Ct.; former cons. to the Pres.'s Intelligence Oversight Bd., Arms Control and Disarmament Agy., U.S. Info. Agy.; chmn. bd. dirs. U.S. Inst. Peace; co-chmn. with the U.S. assoc. atty. gen. Moscow Seminar on the Rule of Law, 1990; legal advisor during Gulf crisis for Kuwait's Amb. to U.S., including legal adviser to the Kuwait Rep. to UN Boundary Commn., 1991-94. Author: Law and the Indo-China War, 1972 (Phi Beta Kappa award); editor: Law and Civil War in the Modern World, 1976, Readings in International Law, 1979, The Arab-Israeli Conflict, 3 vols., 1976, 4th vol., 1991, Nat. Security Law, 1990, Crisis in the Gulf, 1992, Nat. Security Law Documents, 1995, Treaty Interpretation, The Constitution and the Rule of Law, 2001, The National Law of Treaty Implementation, 2001; editor: The Real Lessons of the Vietnam War, 2002; bd. editors: Am. Jour. Internat. Law; contbr. articles on oceans policy, nat. security, internat. law, congl.-exec. rels. in fgn. policy, rule of law and democracy-bldg. to profl. jours. Sesquicentennial assoc. Ctr. Advanced Studies, U. Va., 1971-72; mem. adv. bd. on law of sea State Dept., 1977-80, mem. adv. bd. on internat. law, 1982; chmn. bd. dirs. U.S. Inst. Peace, 1986-89, 89-91; chmn. oceans policy com. Rep. Nat. Com.; mem. Consortium on Intelligence. Recipient Alumni award in arts Drew U., 1976; Compass Disting. Achievement award for significant contbns. to art and sci. of oceanography and marine tech., 1994; NIH fellow Yale U., 1965-66. Mem. ABA (past vice-chmn. sect. internat. law and past 5-term chmn. com. on law and nat. security), Am. Law Inst., Am. Oceanic Orgn. (exec. coun.), Marine Tech. Soc. (exec. coun.), Coun. Fgn. Rels., Order of Coif, Cosmos Club, N.Y. Yacht Club, Freedom House (bd. dirs.), Phi Beta Kappa. Republican. Episcopalian. Home: 824 Flordon Dr Charlottesville VA 22901-7810 *Life offers opportunity to pursue many worthwhile interests. In selecting among them it has seemed most useful to focus on those issues of sufficiently broad general significance as to justify the efforts of a lifetime. For me that has meant focus on promoting democracy and the rule of law, improving the functioning of government, controlling and reducing international conflict, and the policy choices of the ocean frontier.*

MOORE, JOHN PLUNKETT DENNIS, publisher; b. Mexico, Mo., Mar. 2, 1931; s. Dennis Talmage and Vona Mae (Vance) M.; m. Lydia Benz Ahern, Aug. 15, 1959; children: Alison Ahern, Lydia Benz, John Talmage, Maude Ahern, Meredith Coleman. Student, Princeton U., 1948-51, U.S. Naval Acad., 1951-53; BA, U. Mo., Columbia, 1953; postgrad., Harvard Law Sch., 1955-56. Coll. traveler The Dryden Press, Inc., N.Y.C., 1957-59; coll. traveler The Macmillan Co., 1959-60, editor, 1960-67; assoc. exec. editor Columbia U. Press, N.Y.C., 1968-74, editor in chief, 1974-80, pres., 1980-97, also bd. dirs. Bd. dirs., pres. Columbia U. Music Press; bd. dirs. Univ. Presses of Calif., Columbia and Princeton, Chichester, West Sussex, Eng., 1979-97, chmn., 1981-83, 85-87, 96-97; trustee Composer's Recordings, Inc., 1984-97. Author: Columbia University Press: A Historical Sketch, 1893-1993; mem. editl. bd. N.Y. Acad. Scis., 1993-01. Bd. dirs. Greenwich (Conn.) Health Assn., 1970-75; bd. dirs. assoc. Family Centers, Greenwich, Stamford, 1975—; trustee Princeton Libr. in N.Y.C., 1984—; mem. vestry St. Barnabas Ch., Greenwich, 1995-98. With U.S. Army, 1953-55. Mem. Assn. Am. Univ. Presses (chair internat. com. 1994-96, bd. dirs. 1996-97). Clubs: Publishers Lunch (N.Y.C., admissions com. 1996-99), Princeton (N.Y.C.), Faculty House Columbia U. (N.Y.C.), Century Assn. (N.Y.C.); Nassau (Princeton, N.J.), the Book Table (N.Y.C.). Episcopalian. Home: 321 Riversville Rd Greenwich CT 06831-3228 also: 1912 Kelton Ave Los Angeles CA 90025 E-mail: jdm123@aol.com.

MOORE, JOHN RONALD, manufacturing executive; b. Pueblo, Colo., July 12, 1935; s. John E. and Anna (Yesberger) M.; m. Judith Russelyn Bauman, Sept. 5, 1959; children: Leland, Roni, Timothy, Elaine. BS, U. Colo., 1959; grad. advanced mgmt. program, Harvard Grad. Sch. Bus., 1981. Mgmt. trainee Montgomery Ward & Co., Denver, 1960-65; distbn. mgr. Midas Internat. Corp., Chgo., 1965-71; v.p., gen. mgr. Midas, Can., Toronto, Ont., 1972-75; pres. Auto Group Midas Internat. Corp., Chgo., 1976-82, pres., chief exec. officer, 1982-98; ret., 1998. Bd. dirs. Lake Forest Grad. Sch. Mgmt.; mem. bus. adv. coun. U. Colo. Sch. Bus. Mem. Harvard Bus. Sch. Alumni Assn., U. Colo. Alumni Assn., Chgo. Coun. Fgn. Rels., Econ. Club Chgo., Comml. Club Chgo. Republican. *There is very little we accomplish in our lifetime that results from effort we alone expend. All of us should have the wisdom to express our appreciation to our families and associates who have helped us attain our goals and accomplishments— for failure to do so tarnishes our successes and breeds selfishness.*

MOORE, JOHN RUNYAN, agricultural and resource economics educator; b. Columbus, Ohio, Sept. 30, 1929; s. Lawrence Levi and Hazel Marie (Runyan) M.; m. Marjorie Ann Coy, June 14, 1953; children: Lee, Andrew. BSc in Agriculture, Ohio State U., 1951; MSc in Agrl. Econs., Cornell U., 1955; PhD in Agrl. Econs., U. Wis., Madison, 1959. County 4-H Club agt. Ohio Coop. Extension Svc., Steubenville, 1951; grad. rsch. asst. Cornell U., Ithaca, N.Y., 1953-55, U. Wis., Madison, 1955-58; asst. prof. Mich. State U., East Lansing, 1958-62; mktg. specialist, econ. cons. Ford Found., New Delhi, 1968-70; assoc. prof. U. Md., College Park, 1962-68, prof. in world food situation and food mktg., 1968-95, asst. dean internat. programs, 1979-94, prof. emeritus, 1995—. Econ. cons. FTC, Washington, 1963-64, World Bank, India and Nigeria, 1971-74, Kyrgyz Republic, 1997, U.S. AID, Indonesia, Malawi, Haiti, Liberia and Egypt, various dates, FAO, Beijing, 1990. Co-author: (book) Market Structure of Agriculture Industries, 1964, U.S. Investment In Latin American Food Processing, 1966, Indian Food Grain Market, 1972. Trustee S.E. Consortium for Internat. Devel., 1978-95; chmn. commrs. City College Park Housing Authority, 1996—. Lt. (j.g.) USNR, 1951-53. Recipient Internat. Honor award USDA, Washington, 1985, Cert. of Appreciation, 1986. Mem. Am. Agrl. Econ. Assn. (Thesis award 1960), Am. Econ. Assn., Internat. Agrl. Econ. Assn., Trees for the Future (chmn. bd. trustees 1997—), Rotary (pres. 1998-99). Avocations: photography, travel, gardening, golf. E-mail: JRM36162@cs.com.

MOORE, JOHN STERLING, JR. retired minister; b. Memphis, Aug. 25, 1918; s. John Sterling and Lorena (Bounds) M.; m. Martha Louise Paulette, July 6, 1944; children: Sterling Hale, John Marshall, Carolyn Paulette. Student, Auburn U., 1936-37; AB, Samford U., 1940; ThM, So. Bapt. Theol. Sem., 1944. Ordained to ministry So. Bapt. Conv., 1942. Pastor chs., Pamplin, Va., 1944-48, Amherst, 1949-57; pastor Manly Meml. Bapt. Ch., Lexington, 1957-84, pastor emeritus, 1984—. Mem. Hist. Commn., So. Bapt. Conv., 1968-75; pres. Va. Bapt. Pastor's Conf., 1963. Author: History of Broad Run Baptist Church, 1762-1987, 1987, The History of Second Baptist Church Richmond Virginia, 1998; co-author: Meaningful Moments in Virginia Baptist Life, 1715-1972, 1973; editor Va. Bapt. Register, 1972-2001; contbr. articles to profl. jours. Chmn. Lexington Mayor's Com. on Race Rels., 1962-65; bd. dirs. Stonewall Jackson Hosp., 1967-72, pres., 1969-71; treas. Rockbridge Mental Health Clinic, 1971-84. Recipient Disting. Svc. award Hist. Commn., So. Bapt. Conv., 1988. Mem. Am. Soc. Ch. History, So. Bapt. Hist. Soc. (bd. dirs. 1972-91, pres. 1975-76, sec. 1977-85), Va. Bapt. Hist. Soc. (exec. com. 1963—, pres. 1984-85), Va. Hist. Soc., Masons. Home: 1900 Lauderdale Dr Apt D-115 Richmond VA 23233-3918

MOORE, JOHN WARD, chemistry educator; b. Lancaster, Pa., July 17, 1939; s. Joseph D. and Lillian B. M.; m. Elizabeth Augustin, Aug. 26, 1961. AB, Franklin & Marshall Coll., 1961; PhD, Northwestern U., 1965. Asst. prof. Ind. U., Bloomington, 1965-71; assoc. prof. Eastern Mich. U., Ypsilanti, 1971-76, prof., 1976-89, U. Wis., Madison, 1989—. Cos. Ecology Ctr. of Ann Arbor, 1979-81; vis. prof. U. Wis., Madison, 1981-82; vis. assoc. prof. U. Nice, France, 1987—; dir. Project SERAPHIM, 1982—, Inst. for Chem. Edn., 1989—. Editor Jour. Chem. Edn.: Software, 1988-96, Jour. Chem. Edn., 1996—; contbr. articles to profl. jours. Recipient Disting. Faculty award for rsch., publ. and svc. Ea. Mich. U., 1977, sci. faculty profl. devel. award NSF, 1979, Disting. Faculty award Mich. Assn. Governing Bds., 1982, Catalyst award Chem. Mfg. Assn., 1982, silver medal CASE Prof. Yr., 1986, George C. Pimentel award in chem. edn. Am. Chem. Soc., 1991, James Flack Norris award in chem. edn., 1991, Upjohn award for excellence in tchg., 1993, Underkofler award for excellence in tchg. Wis. Power & Light Co., 1995. Home: 3995 Shawn Trl Middleton WI 53562-3521 Office: U Wis Dept Chemistry Dept Chemistry 1101 University Ave Madison WI 53706-1322 E-mail: jwmoore@chem.wisc.edu.

MOORE, JOHN WILSON, neurophysiologist, educator; b. Winston-Salem, N.C., Nov. 1, 1920; s. John Watson and Marjorie (MacAlpine) M.; m. Natalie Bayless, May 6, 1944 (div. 1977); children: John Reid, Marjorie Lee, Stephen Wilson; m. Ann E. Stuart, Apr. 2, 1978; 1 son, Jonathan Watson Stuart-Moore. BS in Physics, Davidson (N.C.) Coll., 1941; MS, U. Va., 1942, PhD in Physics, 1945. Asst. prof. physics Med. Coll. Va., 1946-50; biophysicist Naval Med. Research Inst., 1950-54, Lab. of Biophysics, Nat. Inst. Nervous Diseases and Blindness, NIH, 1954-61; mem. faculty Duke U., 1961—, prof. physiology and pharmacology, 1965-88, prof. neurobiology, 1988—. Vis. prof. dept. neurobiology Harvard U. Med. Sch., 1978-79 Trustee, mem. exec. com. Marine Biol. Lab., Woods Hole, Mass. DuPont fellow, 1941-46; Nat. Neurol. Research Found. scientist, 1961-66 Mem. IEEE, AAAS, Am. Physiol. Soc., Biophys. Soc. (coun., Cole award 1981), Soc. Neurosci., Marine Biol. Lab. Corp., Soc. Gen. Physiologists, Phi Beta Kappa, Omicron Delta Kappa. Office: Duke U Med Ctr Dept Neurobiology PO Box 3209 Durham NC 27710-0001 E-mail: moore@neuro.duke.edu.

MOORE, JOYCE KRISTINA, financial planner, director; b. Phila., June 19, 1955; d. Oscar Herbert Hariu and Virginia Wilson (Guss) Leas ; m. William Burns Moore, June 20, 1980 (div. 1990); children: William Patrick, Kristofer Sean. Student, Beloit Coll., 1973-74, U. Pa., 1974-75, Lafayette Coll., 1984-88, Am. Coll., 1991—. ChFC. Photographer Clair Pruett Studios, Drexel Hill, Pa., 1977-80; photographic cons. Dan's Camera City, Allentown, 1980-81; contr., co-founder BioService, Inc., Bethlehem, 1985-89; contr. Mega Video Inc., Easton, 1989-91; spl. rep. John Hancock Fin. Svcs., Allentown, 1990-93; prin. Joyce Moore Fin. Svcs., Macungie, 1993—. Co-editor: Estate Planning Success for Pennsylvania Residents, 2002. Former mem. Warren County Dem. Com., Phillipsburg, N.J., 1981-83; overseer Religious Soc. Friends, 1986-92; bd. dirs. Spring Garden Children's Sch., Easton, Pa.; den leader Cub Scout Pack 31, Williams Twp., Pa., 1991-95, scout leader, 1995-97; councilwoman Glendon Borough, 1992-97, coun. v.p. 1996-97; mem. Lehigh Valley Estate Planning Coun., 2001—. Mem. LWV (bd. dirs. Easton area 1987-91, pres. 1989-90), Am. Soc. Fin. Svc. Profls., Lehigh Valley Assn. Ins. Fin. Advisors (bd. dirs. 1995—, pres. 2000-01), Social Investment Forum, Progressive Asset Mgmt., First Affirmative Fin. Network, Pa. Assn. Ins. and Fin. Advisors (bd. dirs. 2002—). Avocations: needlework, folk music, canoeing. Office: Joyce Moore Fin Svc PO Box 175 Macungie PA 18062-0175 E-mail: jmoore@fwg.com.

MOORE, JULIANNE (JULIE ANNE SMITH), actress; b. Fayetteville, N.C., Dec. 3, 1960; BFA, Boston Univ. With The Guthrie Theater, 1988-89. Actress: (theatre) Serious Money, 1987, Bone-the-Fish, 1988, Ice Cream with Hot Fudge, 1990, Uncle Vanya, (TV soap operas) As the World Turns (Emmy award outstanding ingenue in daytime drama series 1988), The Edge of Night, (TV movies) Money, Power, Murder, 1989, Lovecraft, 1991, (feature films) The Hand That Rocks the Cradle, 1992, The Gun in Betty Lou's Handbag, 1992, Body of Evidence, 1993, Benny & Joon, 1993, The Fugitive, 1993, Short Cuts, 1993, Vanya on 42nd Street, 1994, Roommates, 1995, Nine Months, 1995, Safe, 1995, Assassins, 1995, Surviving Picasso, 1996, The Myth of Fingerprints, 1997, The Lost World: Jurassic Park, 1997, Hellcab, 1997, Boogie Nights, 1997, Chicago Cab, 1998, The Big Lebowski, 1998, Psycho, 1998, Map of the World, 1999, Magnolia, 1999, Cookie's Fortune, 1999, An Ideal Husband, 1999, The End of the Affair, 1999, Hannibal, 2001, Evolution, 2001, The Shipping News, 2001, Far From Heaven, 2002, The Hours, 2002. Office: CAA care Kevin Huvane 9830 Wilshire Blvd Beverly Hills CA 90212-1804*

MOORE, JUSTIN EDWARD, data processing executive; b. West Hartford, Conn., June 17, 1952; s. Walter Joseph and Victoria Mary (Calcagni) M. BS in Mgmt. Sci., Fla. Inst. Tech., 1974. Systems assoc. Travelers Ins., Hartford, Conn., 1974-77; data processing programmer R.J. Reynolds Inc., Winston-Salem, N.C., 1977-78; programmer/analyst Sea-Land Svc., Elizabeth, N.J., 1978-79, mgr. market analysis Oakland, Calif., 1979-82; asst. v.p., dir. application systems Fox Capital Mgmt. Corp., Foster City, 1982-86; mgr. bus. svcs. dept mktg. and pricing Am. Pres. Cos., Ltd., Oakland, 1987-88, dir. mktg. and pricing systems, 1988-89; dir. systems devel. The Office Club, Concord, Calif., 1989-91; dir. MIS Revo, Inc., Mountain View, 1992-93; account mgr. Imrex Computer Systems, Inc., South San Francisco, 1993-94; project mgr. Exigent Computer Group, Inc., San Ramon, Calif., 1994—. Democrat. Roman Catholic. Avocations: golf, personal computing, investment mgmt. Home: 5214 Jomar Dr Concord CA 94521-2343 Office: Exigent Computer Group Inc 4000 Executive Pky Ste 275 San Ramon CA 94583-4257 E-mail: jemoore@exigentinc.com., justin_moore@prodigy.net. *Personal philosophy: Strive always to do the right things, at the right time, the right way for the right reasons.*

MOORE, KAREN NELSON, judge; b. Washington, Nov. 19, 1948; d. Roger S. and Myrtle Nelson; m. Kenneth Cameron Moore, June 22, 1974; children: Roger C., Kenneth N., Kristin K. AB magna cum laude, Radcliffe Coll., 1970; JD magna cum laude, Harvard U., 1973. Bar: DC 1973, Ohio 1976, U.S. Ct. Appeals (DC cir.) 1974, U.S. Supreme Ct. 1980, U.S. Ct. Appeals (6th cir.) 1984. Law clk. to Hon. Harry A. Blackmun U.S. Supreme Ct., Washington, 1974—75; assoc. Jones, Day, Reavis & Pogue, Cleve., 1975—77; asst. prof. Case Western Res. Law Sch., 1977—80, assoc. prof., 1980—82, prof., 1982—95; judge U.S. Ct. Appeals (6th cir.), 1995—. Vis. prof. Harvard Law Sch., 1990—91. Mem. Harvard Law Rev., 1971—73; contbr. articles. Trustee Lakewood Hosp., Ohio, 1978—85, Radcliffe Coll., Cambridge, 1980—84. Fellow: Am. Bar Found.; mem.: Harvard U. Alumni Assn. (bd. dirs. 1984—87), Am. Law Inst., Phi Beta Kappa. Office: US Ct Appeals 6th Cir US Courthouse 801 W Superior Ave Cleveland OH 44113-1831

MOORE, KAREN CELYN, b. Waco, Tex., Jan. 7, 1964; d. Royce Kirby and Dorothy Ann (Schaefer) M. BBA, S.W. Tex. State U., 1986, MBA, 1993. Computer inventory assurance specialist Vogel Furniture Co., Lockhart, Tex., 1985-87; systems analyst III, programmer Tex. Dept. Transp., Austin, 1987-98; sys. analyst Coastal Oil and Gas, Houston, 1998-99; cons. analyst Dynamics/COAD Solutions, Austin, 1999, Epic Edge, Austin, 1999—2002; bus. /gen. edn. program dir. Virginia Coll. , Tex., 2001—. E-mail: kcmoore@texas.net., kmoore@vc.edu.

MOORE, KENNETH EDWIN, pharmacology educator; b. Edmonton, Alta., Can., Aug. 8, 1933; came to U.S., 1957, naturalized, 1966; s. Jack and Emily Elizabeth (Tarbox) M.; m. Barbara Anne Stafford, Sept. 19, 1953; children—Grant Kenneth, Sandra Anne, Lynn Susan. BS, U. Alta., 1955, MS, 1957; PhD, U. Mich., 1960. Instr. pharmacology Dartmouth Med. Sch., Hanover, N.H., 1960-61, asst. prof., 1962-66; assoc. prof. pharmacology Mich. State U., East Lansing, 1966-70, prof., 1970—, chmn. dept. pharmacology and toxicology, 1987—2001. Vis. scholar Cambridge (Eng.) U., 1974; instr. Lansing Community Coll., 1975-81; cons. NIH, also pharm. industry. Author 1 book; contbr. articles to profl. jours. Fellow Am. Coll. Neuropsychopharmacology; mem. Am. Soc. Pharmacology and Exptl. Therapeutics (chmn. bd. publs. trustees 1992-96, pres. 1998-2000), Soc. Exptl. Biology and Medicine, Soc. Neurosci. Home: 4790 Arapaho Trl Okemos MI 48864-1402 Office: Dept Pharmacology Mich State U East Lansing MI 48824 E-mail: moorek@pilot.msu.edu.

MOORE, KENNETH CAMERON, lawyer; b. Chgo., Oct. 25, 1947; s. Kenneth Edwards and Margaret Elizabeth (Cameron) M.; m. Karen M. Nelson, June 22, 1974; children: Roger Cameron, Kenneth Nelson, Kristin Karen. BA summa cum laude, Hiram Coll., 1969; JD cum laude, Harvard U., 1973. Bar: Ohio 1973, U.S. Dist. Ct. Md. 1974, U.S. Ct. Appeals (4th cir.) 1974, D.C. 1975, U.S. Dist. Ct. (no. dist.) Ohio 1976, U.S. Ct. Appeals (6th cir.) 1977, U.S. Ct. Appeals (D.C. cir.) 1979, U.S. Supreme Ct. 1980. Law clk. to judge Harrison L. Winter U.S. Ct. Appeals (4th cir.), Balt., 1973-74; assoc. Squire, Sanders & Dempsey, Washington, 1974-75, Cleve., 1975-82, ptnr., 1982—, mem. fin. com., 1990—, profl. ethics ptnr., 1996—. Chmn. Ohio Fin. Com. for Jimmy Carter presdl. campaign, 1976; del. Dem. Nat. Conv., 1976; chief legal counsel Ohio Carter-Mondale Campaign, 1976; trustee Hiram Coll., 1997—, mem. exec. com., 1999, chair audit com., 1999, vice chair bd. trustees, 2000—, chair faculty affairs subcom. of ednl. policy com., 2000—. With AUS, 1970-76. Mem. ABA, Fed. Bar Assn., Ohio Bar Assn., Cleve. Bar Assn., Cleve. City Club. Home: 15602 Edgewater Dr Cleveland OH 44107-1212 Office: Squire Sanders & Dempsey 4900 Society Ctr 127 Public Sq Ste 4900 Cleveland OH 44114-1304

MOORE, KENNETH E. anthropologist, educator, writer; b. Niagara Falls, N.Y., Sept. 19, 1930; s. Gordon Winslow and Marie Frances (Sinclair) M.; 1 child, Christopher T. BA, Mich. State U., 1954; MA, U. Ill., 1967, PhD, 1973. V.p. Wimble, Lane & Assocs., Flint, Mich., 1954-59; dir. pub. rels. Mus. Tent, Clio, 1956-65; editor McGraw Hill, N.Y.C., 1958-60; prof. anthropology U. Notre Dame (Ind.), 1970-00; prof. emeritus, 2000—; founding chmn. dept. anthropology, 1981-85. Univ. prof. U. Warsaw, 1992-93. Author: Those of the Street, 1976, Dublin Ghetto, 2000; editor, translator (with Anthony Kerrigan and Saul Bellow): Revolt of the Masses, 1985; editor, contbr. Waymarks, 1987; mem. editl. bd. U. Notre Dame Press, 1978-84. Spkr. opening panel Key West (Fla.) Literary Festival, 1986. Rsch. grantee NIH, 1968-71, Wilbur Found., 1990; recipient Faculty award Andrew Mellon Found., 1980. Fellow Am. Anthropol. Assn., Royal Anthropol. Inst.; mem. AAUP, Ctrl. States Anthropol. Soc., Soc. Urban Anthropology, Soc. Study Symbolic Interaction. Roman Catholic. Office: U Notre Dame Dept Anthropology 611 Flanner Hall Notre Dame IN 46556 E-mail: kmoore@nd.edu.

MOORE, KENNETH JAMES, agronomy educator; b. Phoenix, June 6, 1957; s. George Taylor and Barbara Joyce (Amy) M.; m. Gina Marie McCarthy Aug. 11, 1979; children: Ellyn Elizabeth, David Taylor, Mark Daniel. BS in Agr., Ariz. State U., 1979; MS in Agronomy, Purdue U., 1981, PhD in Agronomy, 1983. Asst. prof. agronomy U. Ill., Urbana, 1983-87; assoc. prof. N.Mex. State U., Las Cruces, 1988-89; rsch. agronomist Agrl. Rsch. Svc., USDA, Lincoln, Nebr., 1989-93; prof. Iowa State U., Ames, 1993—. Adj. assoc. prof. U. Nebr. Lincoln, 1989-93, prof., 1993-96; sr. rsch. fellow Ag Rsch. Grasslands, New Zealand, 1998. Author: Crop Science Laboratory Manual, 1988; editor Crop Mgmt., 2002--; assoc. editor Agronomy Jour., 1989-93, tech. editor, 1994-97; assoc. editor Crop Sci., 1994; contbr. chpts. to books. Bd. dirs. Lincoln Children's Mus., 1991-93, Children's Svcs. of Ctrl. Iowa, 1996-97; bd. dirs. Children's Mus. Ctrl. Iowa, 1997-2002, pres., 2000-01; mem. mgmt. com. N.E. YMCA, Lincoln, 1991-93; mem. youth policy forum Lincoln YMCA, 1991-92. Recipient Point of Light award USDA, 1991. Fellow Am. Soc. Agronomy, Crop Sci. Soc. Am. (divsn. chmn. 1990-92, Young Crop Scientist award 1993); mem. Am. Forage and Grassland Coun. (Outstanding Young Scientist award 1982, merit award 1991), Am. Soc. Animal Sci., Am. Dairy Sci. Assn. Republican. Presbyterian. Avocations: swimming, fishing, music. Office: Iowa State U Agronomy Dept 1567 Agronomy Hl Ames IA 50011-0001

MOORE, KENNETH LEE, executive; b. Oct. 26, 1959; BSBA, Shippensburg State coll., 1981. Sr. acct. Laventhol & Horwath, Harrisburg, Pa., 1981-86; v.p., controller, treas. Continental Med. Systems, Inc., Mechanicsburg, 1986-97; v.p mergers & acquisitions Select Med. Corp., 1997—. Home: 433 Gettysburg Pike Mechanicsburg PA 17055-5169

MOORE, KURT RICHARD, anthropologist, fundraiser, investor; b. Scott AFB, Ill., Oct. 9, 1955; s. Richard Vernal and Irmgard Ludwiga (Bennewitz) M.; m. Josée Lucille Bédard, May 20, 1989 (div. Jan. 1995); m. Gail Ann Smith, Aug. 25, 2001. AB, BFA, U. Ill., 1976; MA, So. Ill. U., 1981, postgrad., 1984-85; cert. fin. planner, 2001. Grad. tchg. asst. Field Sch. Archaeology So. Ill. U., Carbondale, 1977, grad. tchg. asst. Ctr. Continuing Edn., 1978, archaeol. field/lab. asst. Ctr. Archaeol. Investigations, 1978-79, grad. rsch. asst., 1979-80; archaeologist Ill. State Mus. Soc., Springfield, 1980-82; rsch. archaeologist Am. Resources Group, Ltd., Carbondale, 1982-85; mgr. tech. support TSG, Inc., 1985-86; dir. corp. and found. rels. Le Moyne Coll., Syracuse, N.Y., 1986-87; asst. dir. corp. devel. Cornell U., Ithaca, 1987-89, assoc. dir. major gifts, 1989-91; dir. major gifts and planned giving Crouse Irving Meml. Found., Syracuse, N.Y., 1991-93; dir. planned giving Fla. Inst. Tech., Melbourne, 1993-95; sr. dir. corp. and found. rels. Fla. State U., 1995-2001, dir. corp. R&D, 2001—. Contbr. articles to profl. jours.; author monographs. Bd. mem. Birdsong Nature Ctr., Thomasville, Ga., 1997—, v.p., 1998-99, pres., 1999—. Edmund J. James scholar U. Ill., Urbana, 1972-73, John T. Rusher Meml. scholar, 1975-76, So. Ill. U. scholar, 1981-87. Mem. Estate Planning Coun., Soc. Am. Archaeology, Fla. Anthrop. Soc., U.S. Racquetball Assn., Fla. Archaeological Coun., Phi Kappa Phi. Republican. Roman Catholic. Avocations: racquetball, art. Home: 1803 Folkstone Rd Tallahassee FL 32312-4002 Office: Fla State Univ Office Rsch 109 Westcott Bldg Tallahassee FL 32306-1330 E-mail: kmoore@mailer.fsu.edu.

MOORE, LAURENCE JOHN, business educator; b. Greeley, Colo., May 7, 1938; s. John Harold and Ruth Anderson M.; m. Nancy Kay Hibbert, Aug. 31, 1963 (div. Apr. 1996); children: Rebecca Ann, John Andrew, Stefani Ruth. BA in Econs., Monmouth Coll., Ill., 1962; MS in Econs., Ariz. State U., 1965, DBA in Mgmt. Sci., 1970. Dist. mktg. rep. Standard Oil Co. (Ind.), Chgo., 1962-63; sr. analyst long range and capital planning, 1964-66; head quantitative studies Continental Ill. Bank, Chgo., 1966-67; mem. faculty dept. mgmt. sci. Coll. Bus. Va. Poly. Inst. and State U., Blacksburg, 1970—, prof. Coll. Bus., 1977-85, C&P Disting. prof. bus., 1985-96, head dept. Coll. Bus., 1976-83, dir. univ. fin. planning and analysis, 1983-84, dir. univ. planning, 1988-89, Bell Atlantic-Va. prof. of bus., 1996—2002, Verizon prof. bus., 2002—. Cons. in field. Author: (with S.M. Lee, B.W. Taylor) Management Science, 1981, 4th edit., 1993, (with S.M. Lee) Introduction to Decision Sciences, 1975, (with E.R. Clayton) GERT Modeling and Simulation: Fundamentals and Applications, 1976. Served with U.S. Army, 1957-59. Recipient Disting. Service award SE region Am. Inst. Decision Scis., 1977 Fellow Am. Inst. Decision Scis. (pres. 1983-84, Disting. Svc. awrd 1986); mem. Inst. Mgmt. Sci. (Disting. Svc. award SE region), Inst. for Ops. Rsch. and Mgmt. Sci., Inst. Indsl. Engrs., Alpha Iota Delta, Beta Gamma Sigma, Omicron Delta Epsilon, Sigma Iota Epsilon. Presbyterian. Home: 1013 Chateau Ct Blacksburg VA 24060-3676 Office: Va Poly Inst and State U Dept Mgmt Sci 1007 Pamplin Hall Blacksburg VA 24061-5102 E-mail: ljmoore@vt.edu.

MOORE, LESTER LELAND, clergy, financial consultant; b. Troy, Iowa, May 9, 1926; s. Forest Allen and Ida May (Freeman) M.; m. Ruth Ellen Stremlow, Dec. 1, 1946 (dec. Jan. 31, 1990); children: David, Jeffrey, Jane, Randall. AB, Simpson Coll., 1949; STB, Boston U., 1952, STM, 1953; DD, Iowa Wesleyan Coll., 1988. Pastor Liberty (Iowa) Meth. Ch., 1946-49, South Middleboro-South Carver (Mass.) Meth. Ch., 1950-53, North Meth. Parish, Muscatine, Iowa, 1953-57, Manning (Iowa)-Dedham Parish, 1957-65; adminstrv. asst. U.S. Congress, Washington, 1965-66; pastor Corning (Iowa) Parish, 1966-72; pastor, dir. Collegiate/Wesley Found., Ames, Iowa, 1972-83; dist. supr. Muscatine (Iowa) Dist., 1983-89; pastor Perry (Iowa) Parish, 1989-91; interm pastor St. Luke's Parish, Dubuque, Iowa, 1995, 1st United Meth. Ch., Anchorage, 1996; ch. cons. Iowa United Meth. Found., Des Moines, 1997—. Trustee Iowa Wesleyan Coll., 1983—, mem. exec. com. Scriptwriter: Maybe We Can Do Something, 1979, How Are We Doing, 1987, Believe It or Not, 1992; contbr. articles to mags. Mem. Iowa Annual Conf. United Meth. Ch., 1952, mem. Gen. Conf., 1960-92; del. Dem. county and dist. and state convs., 1954-80; candidate State Legis., Iowa, 1954; chair people of faith com. State of Iowa, 1994; mem. exec. com. Child Safe, 1994-99; served on gov.'s com. for alcoholism, juvenile problems, UN and civil rights. Sgt. U.S. Army, 1944-46, ETO. Decorated Silver Star, Bronze Star, Purple Heart, French Croix de Guerre. Mem. Interfaith Alliance (chair organizing 1994), Democrat. Avocations: photography, stamps, postcards, travel. Home: 2003 Cessna St Ames IA 50014-7026

MOORE, LINDA KATHLEEN, personnel agency executive; b. San Antonio, Feb. 18, 1944; d. Frank Edward and Louise Marie (Powell) Horton; m. Mack B. Taplin, May 25, 1963 (div. Feb. 1967); 1 child, Mack B.; m. William J. Moore, Mar. 8, 1967 (div. Nov. 1973). Student, Tex. A&I Coll., 1962-63. Co-owner S.R.O. Internat., Dallas, 1967-70; mgr. Exec. Girls Pers. & Modeling Svcs., 1970-72, Gen. Employment Enterprises, Atlanta, 1972-88; owner, mgr. More Pers. Svcs., Inc., 1988-94, pres., chmn. bd., 1994—. Contbr. short story to Writer's Digest. Mem. NAFE, Nat. Fedn. Bus. and Profl. Women, Am. Soc. Profl. and Exec. Women, Women Bus. Owners, Nat. Assn. Women Cons., Nat. Assn. Personnel Svcs., Ga. Assn. Personnel Svcs.,

Women's Clubs, Atlanta C. of C. (speaker's bur.), Better Bus. Bur., Cobb County C. of C. Office: More Pers Svcs Inc 3016 Spring Hill Pkwy Ste D Smyrna GA 30080-4712 E-mail: monepersonnel@aol.com.

MOORE, LINDA PICARELLI, insurance executive; b. Bklyn., Jan. 13, 1943; d. Anthony Joseph and Alma Patricia (D'Angio) Picarelli; m. William H. Moore, Nov. 11, 1962 (div. 1974); 1 child, David A.; m. Spiro D. Demetriou, Dec. 9, 1977. Student, Wagner Coll., 1976, Coll. Ins., 1977-80. Licensed ins. broker. Ins. clk. Tchrs. Ins. and Annuity Assn., N.Y.C., 1959—61; claim examiner Aetna Life and Casualty Co., 1961—63; claim supr. Northeastern Life Ins. Co., 1963—66; corr. collector Dun and Bradstreet, S.I., NY, 1972—73; asst. underwriter Duncanson and Holt, Inc., N.Y.C., 1973—76; underwriting mgr. CNA Ins. Cos., 1976—85; account mgr. Marsh and McLennan Group Assn., 1985—87; asst. mgr. Home Ins. Co., 1987—89; dir. spl. risk underwriting Cigna Ins. Co., Phila., 1989—2002; prin. A&E Benefit Solutions, LLC, 2002—. Mem. Amnesty Internat., Am. Spl. Risk Assn. Democrat. Roman Catholic. Avocations: reading, swimming, travel. E-mail: lpjm. E-mail: @yahoo.com.

MOORE, LISA LYNN (LISA LYNN MARCEAU), geriatrics nurse; b. St. Johnsbury, Vt., Aug. 25, 1967; d. Glendon Paul and Ruth Aleta (Whitney) Marceau; m. Donald Moore Jr., May 18, 1991. ADN, U. Vt., 1987, BSN, 1990. RN, Vt. Charge nurse St. Johnsbury Health and Rehab. Ctr., 1987-91; inservice dir. St. Johnsbury Health & Rehab. Ctr., 1991-93, dir. nursing, 1993-2000, card plan coord., 2000—. Mem. Sigma Theta Tau (Kappa Tau chpt.). Home: 364 Old County Rd Barnet VT 05821-9585 Office: St Johnsbury Health & Rehab Ctr Hospital Drive Saint Johnsbury VT 05819

MOORE, LLOYD EVANS, retired lawyer; b. Feb. 10, 1931; s. Bascom Sturgill and Julia M. (Martin) M.; m. Marilyn Moore, June 12, 1955; children: William, Erik, Julia. BA, Ohio State U., 1957, JD, 1958. Bar: Ohio 1959, U.S. Dist. Ct. (so. dist.) Ohio 1962, U.S. Dist. Ct. (ea. dist.) Ky. 1965, U.S. Supreme Ct. 1963. County prosecutor Lawrence County, Ohio, 1973-76; assoc. Moore, Wolfe & Bentley, Ironton, 1989-95; ret., 1995. Author: The Jury, 1973, rev., 1988. Mem. Ironton Sch. Bd., 1966-69, pres., 1968-69; bd. dirs. Lawrence County Joint Vocat. Sch., 1966-69. With USMC, 1950-54. Fellow Royal Photog. Soc.

MOORE, LOIS JEAN, health science facility administrator; married; 1 child. Grad., Prairie View (Tex.) Sch. Nursing, 1957; BS in Nursing, Tex. Woman's U., 1970; MS in Edn., Tex. So. U., 1974. Nurse Harris County (Tex.) Hosp. Dist., 1957—; pres., chief exec. officer Harris County Hosp.; adminstr. Jefferson Davis Hosp., Houston, 1977-88, exec. v.p., chief ops. officer, 1988—2001; chief adminstr. U. Tex. Harris County Psychiat. Hosp., 2001—. Mem. adv. bd. Tex. Pub. Hosp. Assn. Contbr. articles to profl. jours. Mem. Mental Health Needs Council Houston and Harris County, Congressman Mickey Leland's Infant Mortality Task Force, Houston Crack-down Com., Gov.'s task force on health care policy, 1991; chairperson Tex. Assn. Pub. and Nonprofit Hosps., 1991, subcom. of Gov.'s task force to identify essential health care svc., 1992; bd. dirs. ARC, 1991—, Greater Houston Hosp. Coun., March of Dimes, United Way. Recipient Pacesetter award North-East C. of C., 1991; named Nurse of Yr. Houston Area League Nursing, 1976-77, Outstanding Black Achiever YMCA Century Club, 1974, Outstanding Women in Medicine YWCA, 1989. Mem. Am. Coll. Hosp. Adminstrs., Tex. Hosp. Assn. (chmn. pub. hosp. com.), Young Hosp. Adminstrs., Nat. Assn. Pub. Hosps. (bd. dirs., mem. exec. com. Tex. assn.), License Vocat. Nurses Assn., sigma Theta Tau. Home: 3730 S Macgregor Way Houston TX 77021-1506 Office: Univ Texas Harris County Psychiatric Ctr 2800 S Mar Briger Way Houston TX 77266

MOORE, LORI, information technology executive; BS in Polit. Sci., The Am. U. From mgr. to corp. v.p. Microsoft, Redmond, Wash., 1991—2000, corp. v.p. product support svc., 2000—. Office: One Microsoft Way Redmond WA 98052-6399*

MOORE, LYNDA JOYCE, religious studies educator; b. Winchester, Tenn., May 31, 1950; d. Willie Irene (Johnson) Taylor; m. Ronald Eugene Farley, 1972 (div. 1979); 1 child Ronald Eugene II Farley ; m. Wilbert James Moore, July 1985; 1 child Kenny Terrell. Student, Wayne C.C., Detroit, 1983—85; cert., Detroit Engring. Inst. Missionary Internat. Beginnings, Detroit, 1988—98, Bkbleway Pentecostal, Detroit, 1998—. Contbr. poetry to lit. publs. Recipient Celebration of Poets award, Poetry Guild, 1997, Editor's Choice award, Nat. Libr. Poetry, 1997. Avocations: cooking, reading, swimming, art. Home: 19929 Avon Detroit MI 48219

MOORE, MALCOLM FREDERICK, manufacturing executive; b. Kankakee, Ill., Sept. 19, 1950; s. Robert Dunham and Josephine Frances (Jones) M.; m. Patricia Claudine Bennert, June 13, 1971; children: Michael Dunham, Emily Suzanne, Marjorie Nicoll. BSBA, Am. U., 1972; M of Mgmt., Northwestern U., 1982. Internat. mktg. mgr., product mgr. FMC Corp., Chgo., 1973-84, mktg. and engring. mgr., 1985-90; cons. Frank Lynn & Assoc., 1984-85; v.p., gen. mgr. Lindberg unit of Gen. Signal, Watertown, Wis., 1990-93; pres. Abar Ipsen Industries, Inc., Bensalem, Pa., 1993-96, Centorr Vacuum Industries, Nashua, N.H., 1993-96, Linac Holdings, Inc., Rockford, Ill., 1994-96; pres., CEO Pangborn Corp., Hagerstown, Md., 1996-98; exec. v.p., COO Gehl Co., West Bend, Wis., 1999—. Inventor material handling equipment. Episcopalian.

MOORE, MARC ANTHONY, university administrator, writer, retired military officer; b. Dallas, July 15, 1928; s. Edward Clark and Mary Cathrine (Spake) M.; m. Mary Joan Donahue, Sept. 5, 1953; children— Daniel, Mary Ellen, Virginia, Andria. BA, So. Meth. U., 1951; MA, George Washington U., 1970; grad., Amphibious Warfare Sch., 1960, Nat. War Coll., 1974; LHD (hon.), Philippine Women's U., 1987. Enlisted man U.S. Marine Corps, 1946-48, commd. 2d lt., 1951, advanced through grades to maj. gen., 1978; regtl. comdr. Camp Pendleton, Calif., 1971; regtl. exec. officer, infantry bn. comdr. Vietnam, 1970; with Joint Chief Staff Ops., Washington, 1977-78; asst. dir. Marine Command and Staff Coll., 1972-73; dir. div. English and history U.S. Naval Acad., 1974-76; comdg. gen. 4th Marine Div., New Orleans, 1978-80; chief of staff U.S. Forces, Japan, from 1980, now ret.; former chancellor San Diego campus, v.p. for devel. Nat. U., 1990-91. Teaching asst. dept. psychology George Washington U., 1974; instr. dept. behavioral sci. U.S. Naval Acad., 1975-76; adj. faculty Nat. U., 1983 Co-founder Leadership 2000; mem. pres. council Calif. State U., San Marcos, 1993-96, 98-2000; mem. bd. advisors Marine Mil. Acad., 1983-95; founder and council advisors mem., Command Mus. and Warfare Leadership Ctr., Marine Recruit Depot, San Diego, 1984—. Decorated Def. Superior Svc. medal, Legion of Merit with combat V, Bronze Star with combat V with oak leaf cluster, Air medal, Def. Meritorious Svc. medal, Order Sacred Treasure (Japan); recipient Disting. Alumni award So. Meth. U., 1981. Mem. Marine Corps Assn., Phi Delta Theta. Roman Catholic. Home: 3611 Lago Sereno Escondido CA 92029-7902 E-mail: mmoore5692@aol.com.

MOORE, MARGARET BEAR, American literature educator; b. Zhenjiang, China, Mar. 14, 1925; came to U.S., 1929; d. James Edwin Jr. and Margaret Irvine (White) Bear; m. Rayburn S. Moore, Aug. 30, 1947; children: Margaret Elizabeth Moore Kopcinski, Robert Rayburn. BA, Agnes Scott Coll., 1946; MA, U. Ga., 1973. Book rev. editor East Ark. Record, Helena, Ark., 1948-50; bibliographer Perkins Libr. Duke U., Durham, N.C., 1950-52; instr. in English Hendrix Coll., Conway, Ark., 1955-56, U. Ctrl. Ark., Conway, 1958-59; editor Inst. Cmty. & Area Devel. U. Ga., Athens, 1974-79; tchr. Latin Athens Acad., 1980-81; ind. scholar Athens, 1981—. Author (book revs.) Am. Lit., 1989, 94, 2000, Nathaniel Hawthorne Rev., 1992, The Salem World of Nathaniel Hawthorne, 1998; contbr. articles to profl. jours. Tchr. Presbyn. Ch., Va., Ark., N.C. and Ga., 1945—; deacon, elder First Presbyn. Ch., Athens, 1974—. Mem.: MLA, Nathaniel Hawthorne Soc. (exec. com. 1987—90, sec. 1997—2000), South Atlantic MLA, Soc. for Study of So. Lit., Philol. Assn. Carolinas, Am. Lit. Assn., Va. Hist. Soc., House of Seven Gables, Peabody Essex Mus., Phi Beta Kappa, Mortar Board, Phi Kappa Phi. Avocations: reading, walking, travel. Home: 106 Saint James Dr Athens GA 30606-3926

MOORE, MARGARET RIVES, writer, financial manager; b. St. Louis, Jan. 22, 1939; d. Harold and Marian Vera (Zorn) Rives; m. Joseph Goodell Jr., Aug. 12, 1961 (div. 1978); children: Marian, Margaret, Martha, Maryellen; m. Daniel E. Moore, July 27, 1978. BA, Wellesley (Mass.) Coll., 1960; MA, Bowling Green (Ohio) State U., 1983. Adminstr. Am. Arbitration Com., N.Y.C., 1960-61, Adrian (Mich.) Coll., 1983-86; investment broker First of Mich., Battle Creek, 1986-88; prof. fin. Hillsdale (Mich.) Coll., 1987-92; trust and investments officer Hillside (Mich.) Coll., 1989-92. Fin. cons. Mardan Investments, Hillsdale, 1986—. Author: Americans in Bear Country, 2001. Bd. dirs. Domestic Harmony. Avocations: travel, reading, rose gardening.

MOORE, MARIANNA GAY, law librarian, consultant; b. La Grange, Ga., Sept. 12, 1939; d. James Henry and Avanelle (Gay) M. AB in French, English, U. Ga., 1961; MLS, Emory U., 1964; postgrad., U. Ga., 1965-66, U. Ill., 1967-68. Asst. law libr. U. Ga., Athens, 1964-66; asst. libr. Yavapai Coll. Libr., Prescott, Ariz., 1969-72; libr. U. Ill. Law Libr., Urbana, 1966-68; law libr. Leva, Hawes, Symington, Washington, 1972-75; libr. project coord. Wash. Occupational Info. Svc., Olympia, 1976-80, Wash. State Health Facilities Assn., Olympia, 1981-82; mgr. Wash. State Ret. Tchrs. Assn., 1982-83, exec. dir., 1984-89, Wash. State Retired Tchrs. Found., Olympia, 1986-89; law libr. Solano County Law Libr., Fairfield, Calif., 1989—. Libr. LIBRARY/USA N.Y. World's Fair, N.Y.C., 1965; consulting law libr. Dobbins, Weir, Thompson & Stephenson, Vacaville, Calif., 1989—; law libr. cons. Coconino County Law Libr., Flagstaff, Ariz., 1968-70. Author: Guide to Fin. Aid for Wash. State Students, 1979; tng. package to introduce librs. to Wash. State Info. Svc., 1980; indexer for Calif. Coun. of County Law Libr.'s publ. For Your Information, 1999—; contbg. author Solano County Bar Assn. pub. VOIR DIRE. Bd. dirs. Thurston County Sr. Ctr., Olympia, 1976-84, Thurston-Mason Nutrition Program, Olympia, 1977-79, Wash. Soc. Assn. Execs., Edmonds, 1987-89. Mem. Am. Assn. Law Librs., No. Calif. Assn. Law Librs., Calif. Coun. of County Law Librs. Avocations: reading, tatting, travel, music, calligraphy, cats. Office: Solano County Law Libr Hall of Justice 600 Union Ave Fairfield CA 94533-6324 E-mail: mmoore@solanocounty.com.

MOORE, MARK HARRISON, criminal justice and public policy educator; b. Oak Park, Ill., Mar. 19, 1947; s. Charles Eugene and Jean (McFeely) M.; m. Martha Mansfield Church, June 15, 1968; children— Phoebe Sylvina, Tobias McFeely, Gaylen Williams. Student, Phillips Acad., 1962-65; BA, Yale U., 1969; M.Public Policy, Harvard U., 1971, PhD, 1973. Teaching fellow, instr. public policy J.F. Kennedy Sch. Govt., Harvard U., Boston, 1971-73, asst. prof., 1973-74, 75-76, assoc. prof., 1976-79, Guggenheim prof. criminal justice policy and mgmt., 1979—; dir. Hauser Ctr. Non-Profit Orgns. Harvard U., 1998—. Spl. asst. to adminstr., chief planning officer Drug Enforcement Adminstrn., U.S. Dept. Justice, Washington, 1974-75; cons. U.S. Dept. Justice, 1975-76, 81 Author: Buy and Bust: The Effective Regulation of an Illicit Market in Heroin, 1977, Creating Public Value: Strategic Management in Government, 1995, (with others) Dangerous Offenders, 1985, From Children to Citizens: Vol. 1, The Mandate for Juvenile Justice, 1987, (with Malcolm K. Sparrow) Ethics in Government, 1990, (with Malcolm K. Sparrow and David Kennedy) Beyond 911: A New Era for Policing, 1991; editor: (with Joel Fleishman and Lance Leibman) Public Duties, 1980, (with Dean Gerstein) Alcohol and Public Policy, 1981. Dir. Hauser Ctr. for Non Profit Orgns. Mem. Assn. Schs. Public Policy and Mgmt., Phi Beta Kappa Home: 331 Waverley St Belmont MA 02478-2418 Office: JF Kennedy Sch Govt Harvard U 79 Jfk St Cambridge MA 02138-5801

MOORE, MARK TOBIN, museum curator, art educator, artist; b. Washington, Jan. 19, 1954; s. Selden George and Dorothy May (Tobin) M.; m. Denise Annette Poole, Oct. 20, 1987 (div. Jan. 1995); 1 child, James Tobin; m. Lisa Ann Yates, Feb. 1, 2002. BA in Art, U. Charleston, 1983; MA in Art, Marshall U., 1985; MFA in Painting, W.Va. U., 2000. Art instr. Ohio U., Ironton, Ohio, 1985-87, Ashland (Ky.) C.C., 1985-87, U. Charleston, W.Va., 1985-87; art specialist U.S. Army Europe/Giessen Arts and Crafts, 1987-91; exhibits coord. W.Va. State Mus., Charleston, 1992-93, exhibits dir., 1993-98; grad. tchg. asst. art dept. W.Va. U., Morgantown, 1999-2000, vis. adj. prof., 2001; asst. prof. art W. Va. State Coll., Institute, 2001—. Art instr. U. Charleston, 1995-98, W.Va. State Coll. Inst., 1995-98; adj. instr. art dept. Marshall U., Huntington, W.Va., 1998; gallery adv. bd. U. Charleston, 1997. One-person shows include Sunrise Art Mus., 1996, Sleeth Gallery, W.Va. Wesleyan Coll., 1995, Perspective Galerie, Giessen, 1990, Alderson-Broadus Coll., Phillipi, W.Va., 2001, Cultural Ctr. of Fine Arts, Parkersburg, W.Va., 2002; group shows include Salon of French and Allied Forces, The Palace of Luxemburg, Paris, Ariel Gallery, N.Y.C., 1989, Huntington (W.Va.) Mus. Art, 1992, 94, 97, Gov.'s Mansion W.Va., 1997, Omaha Ctr. for Contemporary Art, 1999, The Dairy Barn Cultural Arts Ctr., Athens, Ohio, 2000, Paul Mesaros Gallery, W.Va. U., Morgantown, 2000, OCAF, Athens, Ga., 2002, W.Va. State Mus., 2002. With USN, 1972-83. Recipient Arthur Carpenter award for excellence in art, 1985, Merit award Nat. Collage Soc. Juried Exhbn., Cleve., 1998, award of excellence Allied Artists W.Va. Juried Exhbn., Sunrise Mus., Charleston, 1998. Office: Mesaros Gallery WVa Univ Morgantown WV 26505 also: WVa State Coll Dept Art Institute WV 25112 Home: # A 628 Beech Ave Charleston WV 25302-2730

MOORE, MARSHA LYNN, elementary school educator, counseling administrator; b. Washington, May 19, 1946; d. Marshall Alexander and Doris Virginia (Diggs) Moore. BA, Howard U., 1967; MEd, U. Md., 1973. Sch. counseling K-12, cert. tchr. grades 1-6, sci. resource tchr. grades 1-6. 1st grade demonstration tchr. Anne M. Goding Sch. D.C. Pub. Schs., 1967-72; counselor Balt. County Schs., Towson, Md., 1972-77; fashion coord., mgr. Wallach's Ladies' Store, Nanuet, NY, 1977-80, Livingston, NJ, 1977-80; adult edn. cons., counselor East Orange (N.J.) Adult High Sch., 1980-83; minority counselor Essex County Community Coll., Newark, 1984-85; equal opportunity fund counselor, instr. Kean Coll., Union, 1985-87; tchr. Washington Pub. Schs., 1987—. Coord. counselor Summer Youth Program, East Orange, 1982; career fair coord. East Orange Adult H.S., 1981, Essex County C.C., 1985; tchr. Randle Highlands Elem. Sch., Washington, 1987—90; math. tutor coord., sch. newspaper coord. Brookland Sch., Washington, 1990—92, readers/writers club coord., 1992—93, chairperson restructuring team, student coun. coord., 1993—94, Washington, 1996—98, 5th grade chairperson, 1996—98; mem. discipline com. PTA, 1996—98, liaison, exec. bd., hospitality com., multicultural com., 2000—, Shepherd Elem. Sch., D.C., 1998—, sci. fair. coord., 1999—, African-Am. history com., hands on sci. leader, sch. restructuring team, 1999, 2000—, co-writer, 1999—2000, 2001—02, sch. plan, 1999, math. resource tchr., 1999—2000, coord. math bee, Math. 24 Challenge program; math.-a-thon coord. St. Jude's, 2000, coord. Parent Math. workshop, 00, sci. resource tchr., 2000—; coord. Sci. Careers Expo and 1st Sci. Bee, 2001; math. tutor, 2000—01; coord. Sci. Club, 2000—; asst. to cheerleading coach, 2001—02; co-sponsor Student Coun., 2001—02; facilitator DCACTS, 2001—02. Editor: Sci. newsletter. Chmn. Teen Lift, NJ, Delteens, Washington; 2d v.p. Washington Pan-Hellenic Coun., 1994—96, fin. sec., 1996—98, co-chair Greek Forum, 1996—98. Mem.: AFT, Washington Tchrs. Union, Friends of Andrew Rankin Chapel (adj. sec. 1994—97, newsletter co-chair), Howard U. Alumni Assn. (life mem. Washington chpt., N.J. coord. 1980—87, v.p. Washington 1989—91, pres. 1991—93, reunion planning com. 1967, parliamentarian Washington chpt. 1999—2001, editor, mem. fundraising com.), Delta Sigma Theta (Diamond Life mem.). Episcopalian. Avocations: tennis, gardening, landscaping designing, swimming, travel. Office: Washington Pub Schs 825 N Capitol St NE Washington DC 20002-4210

MOORE, MARTIN, educator; b. Wilson, Ark., June 16, 1934; s. Martin Williams and Grace Watson (Adams) M. BA, U. Miss., 1958. Tchr. Latin Peekskill (N.Y.) Mil. Acad., 1959-65; tchr. Latin, French The Browning Sch. for Boys, N.Y.C., 1965-66; tchr. English, Latin Hobbs (N.Mex.) High Sch., 1966-67; tchr. Latin, ancient history Bklyn. Friends Sch., 1967—. Poll watcher South Bklyn. Dem. Club, 1974; mem. Met. Coun. Housing, Bklyn., 1986—; tour dir. Ch. of St. Mary the Virgin, N.Y.C., 1978-82. Mem. Classical Assn. of the Empire State, Classical Assn. of the Atlantic States, N.Y. Classical Club (pres. 1991-92, scholar 1987). Democrat. Episcopalian. Avocations: music, theater, running, tennis, reading. Home: 80 Livingston St Brooklyn NY 11201-5004 Office: Bklyn Friends Sch 375 Pearl St Brooklyn NY 11201-3760

MOORE, MARY ELLEN, community health, hospice nurse; b. New Milford, Conn., May 16, 1949; d. Robert J. and Josephine (Parylak) Moore; widowed. BSN, Russell Sage Coll., 1971; postgrad., Boston U. Head nurse Faulkner Hosp., Jamaica Plain, Mass., Hebrew Rehab. Ctr., Roslindale; nurse Hospice of Wilkes Inc./Wilkes Regional Med. Ctr., North Wilkesboro, N.C., 1982-90; charge nurse inpatient unit Caldwell County Hospice, Lenoir, 1990-94; cons., insvc. instr. HomeCare Mgmt. Corp., 1994-95, supr. health svcs. N.C., 1995-97, lead supr., 1997-98, program supr., 1998—. Bd. dirs. Alexander County Cmty. Alternative Program; mem. ethics com. Wilkes Regional Med. Ctr., 1990—92; com. mem. Alzheimer's Support Group, Burke County, NC; mem. profl. adv. bd. Hospice of Wilkes, Inc.; adv. com. Area Health Edn. Com., 1997—, Cmty. Alternative Program for Disabled Adults, 1997—; home care bd., divsn. aging, epidemiology and social svcs. Caldwell Interagy. Network Facilitator, 1988—, sec., 1999; safety com. HomeCare Mgmt. Corp., 2001—; mem. Catawba County Interagy. Network; instr. Ctr. on Aging, Raleigh, NC. Sec. 1st Responders of Boomer; treas., bd. dirs. Ctr. for Awakening; active United Way, other cmty. projects; head class agt. Russell Sage Alumnae Assn., 1996. Boston U. scholar. Home: PO Box 3204 Lenoir NC 28645-3204 Office: 315 Wilkesboro Blvd NE Ste 2A Lenoir NC 28645-4498

MOORE, SISTER MARY FRANCIS, parochial school educator; b. Bklyn., Aug. 17, 1928; d. Daniel and Mary Frances (Downing) M. B in Social Studies, St. Francis Coll., Bklyn., 1971; M in Elem. Edn., L.I. U., Bklyn., 1976; cert. in adminstrn. and supervision, Manhattan Coll., Riverdale, N.Y., 1988. Joined Sisters of Mercy, Roman Cath. Ch., 1957. Acct. N.Y. Tel. Co., Bklyn., 1945-57; tchr. 2nd grade St. Mary's Sch., Roslyn Heights, N.Y., 1960-62; tchr. 1st grade St. Brigid's Sch., Bklyn., 1962-68; tchr. 2nd and 6th grades St. Jerome's Sch., 1968-74; tchr. 3rd grade St. Bernard's Sch., 1974-81, tchr., prin., 1981-82, prin., 1982-85; tchr. 1st grade Maria Regina Sch., Seaford, L.I., N.Y., 1985—. Cooperating tchr. for tchr. tng. program St. Joseph's Coll., Brentwood, L.I., N.Y., 1968-70. Recipient Appreciation award Bergen Beach Civic Assn., Bklyn., 1985, The Thomas Cuite Meml. award Ancient Order of Hibernians, 1993. Mem. Nat. Cath. Edn. Assn. (tchr. assoc.). Roman Catholic. Avocations: reading, walking, baseball, movies, enjoying friends. Office: Maria Regina Sch 4045 Jerusalem Ave Seaford NY 11783-1627

MOORE, MARY FRENCH (MUFFY MOORE), potter, community activist; b. N.Y.C., Feb. 25, 1938; d. John and Rhoda Walker French; m. Alan Baird10091982 Minier; children: Jonathan Corbet, Jennifer Corbet, Michael Corbet. BA cum laude, Colo. U., 1964. Ceramics mfg., Wilson, Wyo., 1969-82, Cheyenne, 1982—. Commr. County Teton (Wyo.), 1976-83, chmn. bd. commrs., 1981, 83, mem. dept. pub. assistance and social svc., 1976-82, mem. recreation bd., 1978-81, water quality adv. bd., 1976-82. Bd. dirs. Teton Sci. Sch., 1968-83, vice chmn., 1979-81, chmn., 1982; bd. dirs. Grand Teton Music Festival, 1963-68, Teton Energy Coun., 1978-83, Whitney Gallery of Western Art, Cody, Wyo., 1995—, Opera Colo., 1998—; mem. water quality adv. bd. Wyo. Dept. Environ. Quality, 1979-83; Dem. precinct committeewoman, 1978-81; mem. Wyo. Dem. Ctrl. Com., 1981-83; vice chmn. Laramie County Dem. Ctrl. Com., 1983-84, Wyo. Dem. nat. committeewoman, 1984-87; chmn. Wyo. Dem. Party, 1987-89; del. Dem. Nat. Conv., 1984, 88, mem. fairness commn. Dem. Nat. Com., 1985, vice-chairwoman western caucus, 1986-89; chmn. platform com. Wyo. Dem. Conv., 1982; mem. Wyo. Dept. Environ. Quality Land Quality Adv. Bd., 1983-86; mem. Gov.'s Steering Com. on Troubled Youth, 1982, dem. nat. com. Compliance Assistance Commn., 1986-87; exec. com. Assn. of State Dem. Chairs, 1989; mem. Wyo. Coun. on the Arts, 1989-95, chmn., 1994-95, Dem. Nat. Com. Jud. Coun., 1989—; legis. aide for Gov. Wyo., 1985, 86; project coord. Gov.'s Com. on Childrens' Svcs., 1985-86; bd. dirs. Wyo. Outdoor Coun., 1984-85; polit. dir., dep. mgr. Schuster for Congress, 1994-95; pres.' adv. com. on the performing arts John F. Kennedy Ctr. for the Performing Arts, 1999-2001. Recipient Woman of Yr. award Jackson Hole Bus. and Profl. Women, 1981, Dem. of Yr. Nellie Tayloe Ross award Wyo. Dems., 1990. Mem. Alden Kindred of Am., Jackson Hole Art Assn. (bd. dirs., vice chmn. 1981, chmn. 1982), Assn. State Dem. Chairs, Soc. Mayflower Descendents, Pi Sigma Alpha. Home: 8907 Cowpoke Rd Cheyenne WY 82009-1234 E-mail: marym6@aol.com.

MOORE, MARY JOHNSON, nurse; b. West Point, N.Y., Feb. 8, 1940; d. Robert Phillip and Edith Virginia (Carr) Johnson; m. Prentis Monroe Moore, Dec. 28, 1960 (dec. Jan. 1990); children: Carol Edith, Tracey Marie. Diploma, Boston City Hosp. Sch. Nursing, 1960. RN. Clinic nurse in pediatrics and obstetrics Harris County Health Dept./Lyons Clinic, Houston, 1982-85; clinic nurse Tex. Sch. for the Deaf, Austin, 1986-87; staff nurse pediatrics Ben Taub Hosp., Houston, 1989-92; telephone triage nurse, ob-gyn. McGregor Clinic, 1992-93; staff nurse pediatrics Grant Hosp., Chgo., 1994-96; clinic nurse Columbus-Maryville Hosp., 1996—. Mem. vol. choir St. Chrysostoms Episcopal Ch., 1997—. George Monks Meml. scholar, 1960. Mem. Assn. Rehab. Nurses (state sec. 1982-83), Soc. Pediatric Nurses, ARC. Democrat. Avocations: art, music, history, collecting unicorns, angels and lighthouses. Home: 732 W Bittersweet Pl Apt 1008 Chicago IL 60613-2351 Office: Columbus-Maryville Children's Reception Ctr 810 W Montrose Ave Chicago IL 60613-1409

MOORE, MARY JULIA, educator; b. Pitts., Oct. 10, 1949; d. Edward Henry and Julia Ann (Polkabla) Sauer; 1 child, Jason Michael Sauer; m. John Harold Moore, Oct. 27, 1990; 1 adopted child, Jocelyn Quan. BS in Art Edn., Edinboro State Coll., 1971; MS in Spl. Edn., Clarion State Coll., 1980; postgrad, U. Pitts., 1988—. Cert. art tchr., spl. edn. tchr. for mentally retarded. Tchr. Polk (Pa.) State Sch. & Hosp., 1971-72; vol. VISTA, Bath, N.Y., 1972-73; tchr. Polk Ctr., 1973-80, program specialist, 1980-92; residential svc. supr., qualified mental retardation profl. Polk (Pa.) Ctr., 1992—. Lectr., speaker, video on local TV on history of Polk Ctr., 1987. Patentee beer bottle shaped cake pan; cakes displayed in TV videos and in various mags.; creator history video Polk Ctr., Some Leaky Boot Statues, Polk Center--100 Years. Past vol. Big Bros./Big Sisters. Democrat. Roman Catholic. Avocations: cake decorating, reading, maintaining 5 rental houses. Home: 657 Keely Rd Franklin PA 16323-9803

MOORE, MATTHEW SCOTT, publisher, deaf advocate, author; b. Indpls., Dec. 31, 1958; s. Scott Moore and JoNelle (Painter) Giegerich. BA in Social Work, Rochester Inst. Tech., 1983. Founder, pres. MSM Prodns., Ltd., Rochester, N.Y., 1984—; pub., co-editor-in-chief Deaf Life, 1986—. Flying Words Project, Rochester, 1989—; lectr., spkr. in field; organizer confs. Co-author: For Hearing People Only, 1992, Great Deaf Americans, 2nd edit., 1996; launched several websites; lectr., spkr. in field; conf. organizer. Founder Deaf Rochesterians' Cmty. Ctr. Core Team, 1992; chmn. Third N.Y. State Conf. for Sign-Lang. Instrs., Rochester, 1992; coord. Am. Sign-Lang. Tchrs. Assn. 1st Nat. Profl. Devel. Conf., Rochester, N.Y., 1999. Recipient Recognition cert. World Recreation Assn. of Deaf, 1990, Humanitarian award Delta Sigma Phi, 1991, Pres. award Am. Sign Lang. Tchrs. Assn. Lilac chpt., 1993, Outstanding Alumni award NTID, 1993, Tex. Deaf Caucus award, 1993, Alice Cogswell award Gallaudet U., 1994, Printing Week award, 1995, Disting. Alumni Modern Era award Ind. Sch. Deaf, 1997, Georgianna Elliott award Dallas Deaf Celebration, 1998. Avocations: writing, performing, theater, collecting birdhouses. Office: MSM Prodns Ltd PO Box 23380 Rochester NY 14692-3380

MOORE, MCPHERSON DORSETT, lawyer; b. Pine Bluff, Ark., Mar. 1, 1947; s. Arl Van and Jesse (Dorsett) M. BS, U. Miss., 1970; JD, U. Ark., 1974. Bar: Ark. 1974, Mo. 1975, U.S. Patent and Trademark Office 1977, U.S. Dist. Ct. (ea. dist.) Mo. 1977, U.S. Ct. Appeals (8th, 10th and fed. cirs.). Design engr. Tenneco, Newport News, Va., 1970-71; assoc. Rogers, Eilers & Howell, St. Louis, 1974-80; ptnr. Rogers, Howell, Moore & Haferkamp, 1981-89, Armstrong, Teasdale, Schlafly & Davis, St. Louis, 1989-95, Polster, Lieder, Woodruff & Lucchesi, St. Louis, 1995—. Engr. City of Ladue, Mo., 1998-2000. Bd. dirs. Legal Svcs. Ea. Mo.; mem. Ladue Zoning and Planning Commn., 1998—. With USAR, 1970-76. Mem. ABA, Bar Assn. Met. St. Louis (chmn. young lawyers sect. 1981-82, sec. 1984-85, v.p. 1985-86, chmn. trial sect. 1986-87, pres. 1988-89), Ark. Bar Assn., St. Louis Bar Found. (sec. 1984-85, v.p. 1988-89, pres. 1989-90), The Mo. Bar (chmn. patent, trademark and copyright law com. 1992-94, co-chmn. 1994-95), St. Louis County Bar Assn., Women Lawyers Assn., Am. Intellectual Property Law Assn., Mound City Bar Assn., Phi Delta Theta Alumni (treas. St. Louis chpt. 1987-88, sec. 1988-89, v.p. 1989-90), Racquet Club (St. Louis). Home: 33 Deerfield Rd Saint Louis MO 63124-1412 Office: Polster Lieder Woodruff & Lucchesi 763 S New Ballas Rd Ste 160 Saint Louis MO 63141-8750

MOORE, MECHLIN DONGAN, communications executive, marketing consultant; b. N.Y.C., May 21, 1930; s. Albere Ethier and Pamela (Robinson) M.; m. Elizabeth Ann Tonkin, Feb. 11, 1956 (dec. 1992); children: Lansing,

Pamela; m. Valery Ann Shields, July 14, 1995. AB, Harvard U., 1952. Reporter Washington Post, 1955-59; dir. build Am. better com. Nat. Assn. Real Estate Bds., D.C., 1960-64; dir. info. Urban Land Inst., 1964-66; exec. v.p. Ctrl. Assn. Seattle, 1966-70; asst. to pres. United Airlines, Inc., Chgo., 1971-72, sr. v.p. external affairs, 1972-74, group v.p. mktg., 1975-76, sr. v.p. pub. affairs, 1976-79; pres. Ins. Info. Inst., N.Y.C., 1979-91; chmn., CEO Informatrix Worldwide SuperSite Devel., 1996-98; pvt. practice Naples, Fla., 1991—; advisor Vertical Net, Inc., 1998-2001. Pres. Eagles Mere Water Co., 1993-96; bd. electors Ins. Hall of Fame; bd. govs. Internat. Ins. Seminars. Contbg. author publs. Nat. Assn. Real Estate Bds.; assoc. editor Jour. Property Mgmt. Adv. bd. mem. Traffic Inst. Northwestern U.; past mem. St. George's Vestry, N.Y.C. 1st lt. U.S. Army, 1952-54. Recipient Disting. Service award Central Assn. Seattle, 1972 Mem. Univ. Club, Pelican Marsh Golf Club, Shenorock Shore Club. Republican. Episcopalian. Home: 8711 Spikerush Ln Naples FL 34109 Fax: 941-594-8575. E-mail: mmoore7412@aol.com.

MOORE, MELANIE, sociology educator; b. Norfolk, Va., Mar. 23, 1960; d. James and Jane (Juengst) M. BA, Pa. State U., 1981; MA, U. Ga., 1983; PhD, U. Wash., 1991. Instr. U. Wash., Seattle, 1984-91; postdoctoral fellow Ind. U., Bloomington, 1991-93; assoc. prof. sociology U. No. Colo., Greeley, 1993—. Mem. faculty rsch. and publs. bd., U. No. Colo., 1999—, chair acad. policies com., 1998-99, faculty senator, 1996-99, mem. exec. com., 1998-99. Contbr. Ency. Criminology, 2000; contbr. articles to profl. jours. Bd. mem. Boulder (Colo.) Pride, 1999—; cmty. resource connection Gay and Lesbian Ctr., Denver, 1998-99, support staff Denver Women's Chorus, 1994-97; domestic violence advocate Middle Way Ho., Bloomington, 1991-93. Mem. Am. Sociol. Assn. (membership com. 1986—), Nat. Women's Studies Assn., Am. Ednlo. Rsch. Assn. Democrat. Avocations: photography, running, writing, tennis. Office: U No Colo Dept Sociology Greeley CO 80639-0001 E-mail: mmoore@bentley.unco.edu.

MOORE, MELANIE RUTH, veterinary technician; b. San Jose, Calif., Nov. 21, 1955; d. Alan Claude and M. Laverne (Galeener) M. BS in Biol. Sci., U. Calif., Davis, 1977. Registered vet. technician; registered x-ray technician; registered vet. dermatologist. Head registered vet. technician Berryessa Animal Hosp., San Jose, Calif., 1977—. Cons. CARE, Animal Res. Orgn., San Jose, 1994-2000; behavioral study participant Primate Ctr., U. Calif., Davis, 1976-77. Editor, cons. (humor book) Collecting Dead Relatives, 1987, Further Undertakings, 1989. Mem. Human Soc.; petition circulator Three Strikes and You're Out Campaign, San Jose. Mem. ASPCA, Archaeol. Inst. Am., Soc. Expdns. Democrat. Avocations: archaeology, evolutionary biology, world travel, horticulture, reading. Office: Berryessa Animal Hosp 940 Berryessa Rd San Jose CA 95133-1001

MOORE, MICHAEL WATSON, musician, educator; b. Cin., May 16, 1945; s. Clarence Watson and Jeannette Elizabeth (Gardner) M.; m. Renee Allyn White, Oct. 23, 1993; children: Benjamin Butler, Matthew Satyavan. Attended, Cin. Coll. Conservatory of Music, 1964-65. Bass instr. Summer Stage Bank Clinic, 1969, Eastman Sch. of Music, Rochester, N.Y., 1974-87, U. Bridgeport, Bridgeport, Conn., 1981-83, L.I. U., Bklyn., 1993-96, William Patterson U., Wayne, N.J., 1994-95. String bass player with Cal Collins Trio, Cin., 1965, Woody Evans Trio, Cin., 1965, Woody Herman Band, USO, Africa, Ea. Europe, 1966-67, Marion McPartland Trio, N.Y.C., 1968, Freddie Hubbard Quintet, N.Y.C., 1969-70, Jack Wilkins Trio, N.Y.C., 1971, Chet Baker Quartet, N.Y.C., 1972-73, Phil Woods Quartet, N.Y.C., 1972, Gene Bertoncini Duo, N.Y.C., 1972—, Stan Getz Quartet, N.Y.C., 1973, Tony Bennett, N.Y.C., 1973, Ruby Braff, George Barnes Quartet, N.Y.C., 1973-75, Gerry Mulligan Quartet, N.Y.C., 1974, Benny Goodman Sextet, N.Y.C., 1974-76, Lee Konitz Quartet, N.Y.C., 1975, Teddy Wilson Duo, N.Y.C., 1977, Jim Hall Trio, N.Y.C., 1977, Bill Evans Trio, N.Y.C., 1978, Bob Brookmeyer Quintet, N.Y.C., 1978, Mike Abene, Michael Moore Quintet, N.Y.C., 1978, Zoot Sims Quartet, N.Y.C., 1979, Gary Burton Quartet, N.Y.C., 1981-82, Louis Belson Quartet, N.Y.C., 1982, Roger Kellaway Duo and Trio, N.Y.C., 1980s, Jimmy Rowles Duo, N.Y.C., 1980s, Jon Scoffield Duo and Quartet, N.Y.C., 1980s, Lew Tabackin Trio, N.Y.C., 1980s, Hank Jones Trio, N.Y.C., 1980s, Shelly Mann Trio, N.Y.C., 1980s, Pepper Adams Quartet, N.Y.C., 1980s, Lou Levy Duo, N.Y.C., 1980s, Al Cohen Trio, N.Y.C., 1980s, Jake Hanna Quartet, N.Y.C., 1980s, Rosemary Clooney, N.Y.C., 1987-88, Louis Stewart Trio, Ireland and U.K., 1990, Howard Alden Trio, N.Y.C., 1990s, Warren Vache Trio, N.Y.C., 1990s, Harry Allen Trio, N.Y.C., 1990s, Ken Peplowski Trio, N.Y.C., 1990s, Charlie Byrd Quartet, N.Y.C., 1990s, Dave Brubeck Quartet, 2001; co-leader duo with Rufus Reid, 1995, with Chris Potter, 1995; leader duo with Bill Charlap, 1995; tour Japan with Harry Allen, 1997; leader trio with Ken Peplowski and Tom Melito, 1998-, Dave Brubeck Quartet, 2001—; composer: Rio Pindare, 1986, Wake Me When It's Over, 1988, The Lilter, 1989, The Old New Waltz, 1992, Zoot's Suite, 1995, Just Me, Just Me, 1995, When I Wage Battle Next, 1999, Moon Dog, 1999; recs. Michael Moore Trio Plays Gershwin, 1993, Michael Moore/Bill Charlap, 1995 (One of the Best Jazz CDs of 95, The New Yorker, 1996), Michael Moore/Rufus Reid Doublebass Delights, 1996 (One of the Best Jazz CDs of 96, The New Yorker, 1997), Michael Moore/Rufus Reid The Intimacy of the Bass, 1999, Michael Moore and His Trio The History of Jazz: Vol. 1, 2000, The Michael Moore Trio The History of Jazz Vol. 2 Dedication, 2002, Video with Rufus Reid, 1998; author: Melodic Improvising in the Thumb Position: Method for Improvisation for the String Bass, 1986; performer: (with Weslia Whitfield) The White House, 1996. Councilman Borough of Bangor, Pa., 1987-88. Mem. ASCAP. Avocation: piano. Home and Office: 5 E 22d St Apt 15M New York NY 10010-5325

MOORE, MICHAEL KEITH, political science educator; b. Leavenworth, Kans., Mar. 3, 1965; s. Harold E. and Carol J. Moore. BA, Washburn U., 1987; MA, U. Nebr., Lincoln, 1989, PhD, 1993. Assoc. prof. polit. sci. U. Tex., Arlington, 1992-98, assoc. prof., 1998—, asst. v.p. acad. affairs, 2000—. Contbr. articles to profl. jours. Mem. com. on legal svcs. to the bar in criminal matters State Bar Tex., Austin, 1995—. Mem. Am. Polit. Sci. Assn., Midwest Polit. Sci. Assn., So. Polit. Sci. Assn. (exec. bd. 1999—). Office: U Tex Office of Provost Box 19918 Arlington TX 76019

MOORE, MICHAEL PATRICK, artist; b. Oceanside, Calif., July 15, 1964; s. William Thomas Jr. and Lela Irene (Lowe) Moore. BFA, U. Kans., 2000. Dir. tech. mkt. Oldukai Corp., Miami, Fla., 1989—94; pres. Nebalae Creation Inc., Boca Raton, 1992—95; product mgr. Quantum Leap Inc., 1994—95; artist Kansas City, Kans., 1989—. Mem., activist HEMP Awareness Coun., U. Miami, 1993—95; lectr. Drug and Alcohol Svcs., Mission, Kans., 1993—. Sgt. USMC, 1983—87. Recipient Amsden Book award, Kress Found., Lawrence, Kans., 1998, Gwendolyn Hawley award, Kansas City Blind All Stars, 1998, 2000; grantee Pollock Krasner Found. grantee, 2001—. Libertarian. Roman Catholic. Avocations: drumming, banjo, juggling. Mailing: 6816 Weld Merriam KS 66203

MOORE, MICHAL CHARLES, land economist, educator; b. L.A., Mar. 30, 1947; s. Robert John and Elizabeth (Bagwell) M.; m. Candace Craig Long, Sept. 6, 1969 (div. May 1977). BS, Humboldt State U., Arcata, Calif., 1972; MS, U. Calif., Davis, 1974. Prin. Bainbridge, Behrens & Moore Inc., Monterey, Calif., 1974-77; county supr. Monterey County, Salinas, 1977-85; dep. dir. Gov.'s Office, State of Calif., Sacramento, 1985-90; v.p. Chas. Clyde & Co. Inc., 1985-90; prin. Walp and Moore, San Francisco, 1990—. Adj. prof. Monterey Inst. Internat. Studies, 1976—; chief econ. cons. Landmark Land Co., Rocklin, Calif., 1990—. Mem. Calif. Seismic Safety Commn., Sacramento, 1977-85. With U.S. Army, 1967-69. Named Man of Yr., Monterey Peninsula Jaycees, 1981. Mem. Internat. Inst. Forecasters, Atlantic Econ. Soc., Calif. State Bd. Landscape Architects, Sports Car Club Am. Republican. Avocations: backcountry skiing, automobiles. Home: 32281 Albion Ridge Rd Albion CA 95410-9708 Office: 400 Montgomery St Ste 300 San Francisco CA 94104-1211

MOORE, MIKE, state attorney general; m. Tisha Moore; 1 child Kyle. Grad., Jackson County Jr. Coll., 1972; BA, U. Miss., 1974, JD, 1976. Asst. dist. atty. State of Miss., 1977—78, dist. atty., 1979, atty. gen., 1988—. Office: Office of Atty Gen PO Box 220 Jackson MS 39205-0220*

MOORE, MILDRED THORPE, dietician; b. St. Louis, July 11, 1924; d. Walter Proctor and Rose Frances (Fiala) Thorpe; m. John Austin Moore, June 7, 1947; children: John A. Jr., Frances Ann, Thomas Thorpe, Lynn Brownell. BS in Dietetics, U. Ala., 1945; postgrad., St. Louis U. Hosps., 1945-46. Registered dietitian. Clin. dietitian Jefferson-Hillman Hosp., Birmingham, Ala., 1946-47, VA Hosp., Tuscaloosa, 1947-48; teaching dietitian Riverside Hosp. Sch. Nursing, Newport News, Va., 1963-82; cons. registered dietitian Va. Bapt. Retirement Cmty., 1975-90, Sarah Bonwell Hudgins Assn. Retarded Citizens, Hampton, 1980—. Sec.-treas. Nutritionists in Nursing Edn., 1979—81; mem. Peninsula Nutrition Coun., 1983—, Gerontol. Nutrition Practice, 1982—. Spkr. in field. Den mother Boy Scouts Am., Newport News, 1963—64; vol. Am. Heart Assn., Am. Cancer Soc., Leukemia Assn., 1959—; pres. PTA, Newport News., 1965, 1968; vol. reading tutor 2d-4th grades, 1994—; elder Presbyn. Ch., 1986—89, 1999—2002, pres., hon. life mem. Presbyn. Women, 1999—2002. Mem.: AAUW, Cons. dietitians Health Care (pres. Hampton br. 1961—63), Tidewater Dietetic Assn. (pres. 1956, 1968), Va. Dietetic Assn. (pres. 1972—74, del. 1976—79, Dietitian of the Yr. 1978), Am. Dietetic Assn. (mem. by-laws com. 1977—79), Va. Peninsula Alumni Zeta Tau Alpha (sec. 1994), Zeta Tau Alpha (alumni pres. 1983, Cert. Merit award 1985, Order of the Shield 1992). Republican. Avocations: travel, walking, antiques, bridge. Home and Office: 152 Milstead Rd Newport News VA 23606-1118 E-mail: mtmjam@aol.com.

MOORE, MILES DAVID, journalist; b. Lancaster, Ohio, Mar. 8, 1955; s. Russell Emerson and Dorothy Louise (Camp) M. BS in Journalism, Ohio U., 1977. Asst. editor Rubber and Plastics News, Akron, Ohio, 1977-80; Washington corrs. Rubber and Plastics News/Tire Bus., Washington, 1980—. Adminstr. Word Works Washington Prize, 1995—. Founder, host Iota Poetry Series, Arlington, Va., 1994—; publs. editor: The Federal Poets, Washington, 1992-95; co-editor: Winners: A Retrospective of the Washington Prize, 1999; mem. editl. bd. Word Works, 1995—; author: The Bears of Paris, 1995, Buddha Isn't Laughing, 1999, Fatslug Unbound, 2000. Recipient Sidney Sulkin prize Poet Lore, 1998, Poetry prize Potomac Rev., Port Tobacco, Md., 1996, Rose Lefcowitz prize, Poet Lore, Bethesda, Md., 1994, Crain award Crain Comms., Inc., Chgo., 1991, 2000. Mem. Nat. Press Club, The Writer's Ctr., The Fed. Poets. Lutheran. Avocations: reading, walking, theater, movies. Office: Crain Comms Inc 814 National Press Building Washington DC 20045-1801

MOORE, MILO ANDERSON, banker; b. Orange, N.J., Aug. 26, 1942; s. Milo H. and Helen (Wiley) M.; m. Judith J. Colosimo, May 4, 1968; children: Milo Robert, Matthew Wiley, Marykate Bartlett. BS, Ithaca Coll., 1964; MBA, Rutgers U., 1971. Traffic supt. N.Y. Tel. Co., N.Y.C., 1964-71; trust officer Midlantic Nat. Bank, Newark, 1971-76; v.p. Shearson Loeb Rhoades, N.Y.C., 1976-80; sr. v.p. Donaldson Lufkin & Jenrette, 1980-85; sr. mng. dir. Bear, Stearns & Co., 1985-92; v.p. JP Morgan Pvt. Bank, Morristown, N.J., 1992—. Advisor Jr. Achievement, Bronx, N.Y., 1967-68; pres. Chatham Jaycees, N.J., 1974; big bros. Morris County Big Bros., Morristown, 1971-81; pres. Stanley Congl. Ch., Chatham, N.J., 1995-97; trustee SAGE Solutions, 1994—, pres., 2002. Mem. Securities Industry Assn. (tax shelter com. 1982-85), Glenburnie Club (pres. 1989—), Canoe Brook Country Club (Summit, N.J.), Beta Gamma Sigma. Office: JP Morgan Chase Pvt Banking 225 South St Morristown NJ 07960-5336 E-mail: milo.moore@jpmorgan.com.

MOORE, MITCHELL JAY, lawyer, law educator; b. Lincoln, Nebr., Aug. 29, 1954; s. Earl J. and Betty Marie (Zimmerlin) M.; m. Sharon Lea Campbell, Sept. 5, 1987. BS in Edn., U. Mo., Columbia, 1977, JD, 1981. Bar: Mo. 1981, U.S. Dist. Ct. (we. dist.) Mo. 1981, Tex. 1982, U.S. Ct. Appeals (8th cir.) 1998. Sole practice, Columbia, Mo., 1981—. Coordinating atty. student legal svcs. ctr. U. Mo., Columbia, 1983-89. Mem. Columbia Substance Abuse Adv. Commn., 1989—; bd. dirs. Planned Parenthood of Ctrl. Mo., Columbia, 1984-86, Opportunities Unltd., Columbia, 1984-86, ACLU of Mid-Mo., 1991-98; Libertarian candidate for Atty. Gen. of Mo., 1992, 2000, for 9th congl. dist. U.S. Ho. of Reps., 1994, 96, for Mo. State Rep. 23d dist., 1998, for Atty. Gen. Mo., 2000; mem. Probation and Parole Citizens Adv. Bd., 1997-99. Mem. Boone County Bar Assn., Assn. Trial Lawyers Am., Phi Delta Phi. Libertarian. Unitarian Universalist. Avocations: softball, camping, Tae Kwon Do. Office: 1210 W Broadway Columbia MO 65203-2126 E-mail: mmoore259@mchsi.com.

MOORE, NANCY ANN, director, writer; b. Salem, Okla., Oct. 4, 1971; m. Justin A. Moore, Aug. 1, 1996; 1 child Mackenzie Ann. BS in Acctg., Okla. State U., 1994; MBA, U. Tulsa, 2000. Staff auditor Ernst and Young, LLP, Dallas, 1994—95; divsn. dir. Robert Half Internat., Tulsa, 1996—98; terr. mgr., admissions U. Tulsa, 1998—99, budget mgr., enrollment and student svcs., 1999—; adj. instr. Tulsa C.C., 2000—. Pub. spkr. Moore House Pub., Jenks, Okla., 1999—. Author (children's book): P.S. Eddie Takes a Trip, 1999. Bd. dirs. Safe and Drug Free Youth, Tulsa, 1999—; mem. adv. bd. Chi Omega, U. Tulsa1, 0999—. Mem.: Gt. Plains Assn. Coll. Admissions Counselors, Assn. Coll. Pers. Adminstrs., Okla. Soc. Coll. Pers. Adminstrs. E-mail: NancyM3237@aol.com.

MOORE, NANCY ANNE GARDNER, retired counselor; b. Altoona, Pa., June 10, 1941; d. Willard A. and Helen Catherine (Zeek) Gardner; m. Thomas I. Moore, June 1, 1963; children: James T., Melissa A. BS in Edn., Ind. State Coll., 1963; MEd, Indiana U. of Pa., 1965, cert. in guidance, 1967. Cert. counselor, dir. vocat. edn., Pa. Bus. edn. tchr., guidance counselor Altoona Area Sch. Dist., 1963-76; guidance counselor, supr. vocat. evaluation ctr. Altoona Area Vocat.-Tech. Sch., 1976-97; ret., 1997. Mem. planning com. Pa. Vocat. Edn. Conf.; chmn. Pa. Adv. Coun. for Vocat. Edn., 1984-85; mem. Pa. Adv. Commn. for Career Devel. Mem. behavioral health and mental retardation adv. bd. Blair County; bd. govs. Scottish Rite Masonic Learning Ctr. for Dyslexic Children, Altoona Center, Pa. Mem. NEA, ACA, Pa. Sch. Counselors Assn. (chair membership com., Secondary Counselor of Yr. 1994), Am. Vocat. Assn. (life, guidance divsn. policy com. 1993-99), Pa. Career and Tech. Edn. Assn., (life, exec. bd. dirs., Vocat. Educator of Yr. 1992), Pa. State Edn. Assn. (ret.), Blair County Assn. of Ret. Sch. Employers. Avocations: golf, reading, sewing.

MOORE, NEVALYN, music educator; b. Laurel, Miss., Mar. 12, 1948; d. Shelby Milburn Price Sr. and Neva Trapp; m. James W. Moore, Aug. 29, 1970; children: Christopher, Brian, Bonnie, Jenny K., Matthew. BA in Music, Judson Coll., 1969; MusM in Organ Perf., U. Miss., 1971. Music therapist Dyer County (Tenn.) Sch. System, 1979-80; instr. music Dyersburg (Tenn.) State C.C., 1975-80; asst. prof. music Campbellsville (Ky.) U., 1980—; staff organist Lexington Ave. Bapt., Danville, 1989-96; staff accompanist Danville (Ky.) Children's Choir, 1993-98; asst. music dir. Louisville Youth Choir, 1998-2000; staff organist St. Matthews Bapt. Ch., Louisville, 1998-2000. Keyboard specialist Ky. Bapt. Conv., Louisville, 1989-93; organ cons. Pleasant Hill Bapt. Ch., Campbellsville, 1984-85. Co-compiler: Organ Registration, 1991, Organ Techniques, 1992, Let's Get Back to Basics, 1992; co-compiler, author: The Expressive Organist, 1993. Mem. h.s. restructuring com. Campbellsville H.S., 1993-94, sch. improvement com., 1994-95. Nevalyn Moore scholarship Danville Children's Choir, 1998. Mem. Music Educators Nat. Conf., Ky. Music Educators Assn. (4th dist. Coll./U. Tchr. of Yr., 2000, 02, Coll./U. Tchr. of Yr. 2002), Music Tchrs. Nat. Assn. (cert.), Ky. Music Tchrs. Assn. (master tchr. 1988—), Am. Guild of Organists, Am. Guild of English Handbell Ringers. Baptist. Avocations: sewing and design, bicycle riding, hiking, folk music. Home: 316 N Columbia Ave Campbellsville KY 42718-2267 Office: Campbellsville U 1 University Dr Campbellsville KY 42718-2799

MOORE, NORMA JEAN, real estate broker; b. Keota, Iowa, Mar. 23, 1935; d. George E. and Eula Margaret (Martin) Dillon; m. Gordon George Moore, Sep. 1, 1956; children: Steven, Ronald, Cynthia Wojcik. BS, Iowa State U., 1957. Tchr. N. Haven H.S., North Haven, Conn., 1957-60, Hicksville (N.Y.) Jr. High, 1960-61; real estate assoc. Brucker Real Estate, Hatboro, Pa., 1978-82; assoc. broker Prudential Felte Real Estate, Willow Grove, 1982—. Mem. Ea. Montgomory County Bd. of Realtors, Pa. Assoc. of Realtors, Nat. Assoc. of Realtors. Presbyterian. Avocations: sewing, cooking, investing. com. Home: 163 Greyhorse Rd Willow Grove PA 19090-1646 E-mail: resold@comcast.net.

MOORE, OLIVER SEMON, III, publishing executive, consultant; b. Jersey City, July 26, 1942; s. Oliver S. and Ann Loy (Spies) M.; m. Dina Downing DuBois, Feb. 23, 1961 (div. 1974); 1 child, Deborah; m. Christine Laine Meyers, May 12, 1990; 1 child, Kathryn Laine. BA, U. Va., 1964. Chief bur. Richmond (Va.) Times-Dispatch, 1964-66; corr. Time mag., N.Y.C., 1966-67, contbg. editor, 1967-68; assoc. editor Newsweek, 1969-71; freelance writer, 1972-75; mng. editor Motor Boating and Sailing, N.Y.C., 1976-78, editor, 1980-82; exec. editor US Mag., N.Y. Times Co., 1978-80; dep. editor Town & Country Mag., N.Y.C., 1982-84; editor Sci. Digest Mag., 1984-86; pub. dir. Yachting Mag., 1986-95; editorial dir. Outdoor Life, 1993-95; v.p. The Outdoor Co., 1994-95; editor-at-large Motor Boating & Sailing, 1995—2001; pres. Alamo Pub. Svcs., Inc., Detroit, 1995—. Co-founder, chmn. bd. Corp! (Mag.), 1998. Author: (poems) Voices International, 1969; contbg. editor Sports Afield, 1996—; photographer (mags.) Motor Boating and Sailing, Yachting, Working Woman, (books) Lines to a Little Girl, Rancho Paradiso. Recipient Merit award Art Dirs. Club, 1981, award of merit Soc. Publ. Designers, 1981, Excellence in Media award Nat. Arbor Day Found., 1985. Mem. Am. Soc. Mag. Editors, Mag. Pubs. Assn. (nat. mag. award 1995), N.Y. Yacht Club, Grosse Pointe (Mich.) Club, Bayview (Mich.) Yacht Club, The Huntsman (Mich.), Wyndeme Club (Fla.). Republican. Episcopalian. Avocations: sailing, antique cars. Office: Corp! 3645 Crooks Rd Troy MI 48084-1642

MOORE, OMAR KHAYYAM, experimental sociologist; b. Helper, Utah, Feb. 11, 1920; s. John Gustav and Mary Jo (Crowley) M.; m. Ruth Garnand, Nov. 19, 1942; 1 child, Venn. BA, Doane Coll., 1942; MA, Washington U., St. Louis, 1946, PhD, 1949. Instr. Washington U., St. Louis, 1949-52; teaching assoc. Northwestern U., Evanston, Ill., 1950-51; rsch. asst., prof. sociology Tufts Coll., Medford, Mass., 1952-53; researcher Naval Rsch. Lab., Washington, 1953-54; asst. prof. sociology Yale U., New Haven, 1954-57, assoc. prof. sociology, 1957-63; prof. psychology Rutgers U., New Brunswick, N.J., 1963-65; prof. social psychology, sociology U. Pitts., 1965-71, prof. sociology, 1971-89, prof. emeritus, 1989—; scholar-in-residence Nat. Learning Ctr.'s Capital Children's Mus., Washington, 1989-90. Pres. Responsive Environ. Found., Inc., Estes Park, Colo., 1962—; assessor of rsch. projects The Social Scis. and Humanities Rsch. Coun. Can., 1982—; adj. prof. U. Colo., Boulder, 1992—. Contbg. editor Educational Technology; contbr. numerous articles to profl. jours.; patentee in field; motion picture producer and director. Recipient Award The Nat. Soc. for Programmed Instruction, 1965, Award Doane Coll Builder Award, 1967, Ednl. Award Urban Youth Action, Inc., 1969, Award House of Culture, 1975, Cert. of Appreciation, 1986, Cert. of Appreciation D.C. Pub. Schs., 1987, da Vinci Award Inst. for the Achievement of Human Potential, 1988, Cert. of Appreciation Capital Children's Museum, 1988, award Jack & Jill of America Found., 1988, Cert. of Appreciation U.S. Dept. of Edn., 1988, Cert. of Appreciation D.C. Pub. Schs., 1990, Person of Yr. in Ednl. Tech. award Ednl. Tech. mag., 1990. Mem. AAAS, Am. Math. Soc., Am. Psychol. Assn., Internat. Sociol. Assn., Am. Sociol. Assn., Assn. for Symbolic Logic, Assn. for Anthrop. Study of Play, Philosophy Sci. Assn., Psychonomics Soc., Soc. for Applied Sociology, Soc. for Exact Philosophy, Math. Assn. Am. Republican. Avocation: mountaineering. Home and Office: 2341 Upper High Dr PO Box 1673 Estes Park CO 80517-1673 E-mail: okmoore@aol.com.

MOORE, PAT HOWARD, engineering and construction company executive; b. Laredo, Tex., Sept. 16, 1930; s. Howard Warren and Odette Evelyn (Bunn) M.; m. Elsie Mae Crossman, Mar. 23, 1954; children: Linda Marie Ford, Margaret Ann, Andrew Patrick. BA, Rice U., 1952, BS in Civil Engring., 1953; postgrad., Tulane U., 1956-58. Registered profl. engr., Tex., La. Spl. investigator Army Counter Intelligence Corps., Houston, 1954-56; div. engr. McDermott Inc., Morgan City, La., 1956-58; pres., dir. Navasota Tel. Co., Tex., 1958-63; project mgr. Brown & Root, Inc., Houston, 1963-67, exec. v.p., chief fin. officer, dir., 1990-95; pres., dir. Fluor Ocean Svcs., 1968-80; sr. v.p. Raymond Internat., Inc., 1980-86; pres., dir. Martin Moore Inc., Bellaire, Tex., 1986-90; dir. Charter Builders, Inc., Dallas, 1988-90; mgmt. cons. Bellaire, 1996—. Adv. dir. Tex. Commerce Bank, Houston, 1979-86; lectr. ethics Rice U., 1996—; bd. dirs. Versar, Inc., Springfield, Va., 1997-2001, XServ, Inc., Houston, 1997-. Bd. govs. Rice U., 1984-88. With U.S. Army, 1954-56. Fellow ASCE; mem. Chi Epsilon. Lodges: Kiwanis (pres. 1960). Home: 5251 Birdwood Rd Houston TX 77096-2503 Office: PO Box 1156 Bellaire TX 77402-1156

MOORE, PATRICIA ANN, medical technology investor, consultant; b. Huntington, N.Y., July 16, 1954; d. Joseph Nicholas and Dorothy Patricia (Olszewski) Mamola; m. William Martin Moore, Feb. 15, 1986; children: William Eric, Kyle Martin. BS, U. Santa Clara, 1976. Ops. mgr. Laguna Fed. Savs. & Loan, Orange, Calif., 1977-79; customer svc. rep. Bentley Labs., Irvine, 1979-80, mgr. custom products, 1980-82, internat. custom product specialist, 1981-82; dist. sales mgr. Am. Bentley Labs., San Francisco, 1982-83, Nellcor, Inc., San Francisco, 1983-84, product mgr. Hayward, Calif., 1984-85, nat. accounts mgr., 1986-88, internat. distbn. mgr., 1985-88; dir. internat. mktg. and sales NATUS Med., Inc., Foster City, 1989-92; mng. ptnr.seed investment proprietary med. tech. Alpine Ptnrs., Incline Village, 1992—; bd. dirs. Responsive Med. Applications, 1996—. Bd. dirs. Alpine Med. Concepts Incline Village. Designer, patent holder skin-mounted surg. drain holder "Comfort Hold", 1998. Avocations: bicycling, hiking, traveling. Office: Alpine Ptnrs 153 Country Club Dr Ste 8 Incline Village NV 89451-9348

MOORE, PATRICIA KAY, investor, public relations director; b. Peoria, Ill., Jan. 20, 1947; d. David Harold and Mary Jane (Gregoryk) Jenkins. BBA, U. Mo., 1978; MBA, 1981. Planning analyst Emerson Electric Corp., St. Louis, 1972-79; mgr. mktg. adminstrn. Emerson Electric WED, Houston, 1979; dir. mktg. adminstrn. HBE Corp., St. Louis, 1979-82; mgr. market rsch. Emerson Electric ESD, 1982-92; dir., investor rels. ESCO Techs. Inc., 1992—. Mem. Nat. Investor Rels. Inst. (past pres. St. Louis chpt.), U. Mo. Alumni Assn. Home: 10335 Cable Ave Saint Louis MO 63131-2710 Office: ESCO Techs Inc 8888 Ladue Rd Ste 200 Saint Louis MO 63124-2056

MOORE, PATRICK J. paper company executive; Asst. treas. Jefferson Smurfit Corp., St. Louis, 1987-90, treas., 1990-93, v.p., treas., 1993-94; v.p., gen. mgr. Indsl. Packaging divsn., 1994-96; v.p., CFO Smurfit-Stone Container Corp., Chgo., 1996—. Office: Smurfit-Stone Container Corp 150 N Michigan Ave Chicago IL 60601-7568*

MOORE, PATRICK NEILL, lawyer; b. Fort Smith, Ark., Apr. 4, 1946; s. George Hugh and Mildred (Troy) M.; m. Janice Beth Barker De Bauge, Aug. 21, 1967 (div. June 1990); children: Shawn Patrick, Colin Hugh. BA magna cum laude, Harding Coll., 1967; JD, So. Meth. U., 1970. Bar: Ark. 1970, Tex. 1970. Ptnr. Warner Smith & Harris, Fort Smith, 1970—. Bd. dirs. We. C.C. Found., Fort Smith. Trustee Fort Smith Employees Pension Plan, 1982-88; bd. dirs. Holt Krock Clinic Instl. Rev. Bd. Fellow Am. Coll. Trust and Estate Coun.; mem. ABA, Ark. Bar Assn., State Bar Tex., Phi Alpha Theta, Alpha Chi. Mem. Christian Ch. (Disciples Of Christ). Home: 418 S 25th St Fort Smith AR 72901-7703 Office: Warner Smith & Harris PLC 214 N 6th St Fort Smith AR 72901-2106

MOORE, PATSY SITES, food service consultant; b. San Marcos, Tex., Mar. 29, 1939; d. Sam W. and Hilda (Wiede) Sites. BS in Home Econs. Edn., S.W. Tex. State U., 1970. Owner, operator Westoner Kindergarten and Nursery Sch., San Marcos, 1965-68; food svc. dir. San Marcos Consol. Ind. Sch. Dist., 1975-97; cons. to food svc. industry, San Marcos, 1997—. Cons. in field., 1997—. Mem. steering com. Play Scape/Children's Park, San Marcos, 1992; mem. Hays County Pks. Adv. Bd., City of San Marco Sr. Citizens Adv. Coun.; sr. adv. bd. City of San Marcos, 2000—; adv. bd. Hays County Parks, 1998—. Mem. Am. Sch. Food Svc. Assn., Tex. Sch. Food Svc. Assn., Ctrl. Tex. Sch. Food Svc. Dirs. Assn. (founder, past pres.), Order Eastern Star, San Marcos Fedn. Rep. Women (pres.), Spring Lake Garden Club (sec. 1999, 2000, pres. 2002--). Lutheran. Avocations: gardening, oil painting, lapadary. Home and Office: 285 Hilliard Rd San Marcos TX 78666-8905

MOORE, PAUL, JR. bishop; b. Morristown, N.J., Nov. 15, 1919; s. Paul and Fanny Weber (Hanna) M.; m. Jenny McKean, Nov. 26, 1944 (dec.); children: Honor, Paul III, Adelia, Rosemary, George Mead, Marian Shaw, Daniel Sargent, Susanna McKean, Patience; m. Brenda Hughes Eagle, May 16, 1975 (dec.). Grad., St. Paul's Sch., Concord, N.H., 1937; BA, Yale U., 1941; S.T.B., Gen. Theol. Sem., N.Y.C., 1949, S.T.D. (hon.), 1960; D.D. (hon.), Va. Theol. Sem., 1964, Berkeley Divinity Sch., 1971; PhD (hon.), City Coll. N.Y. Ordained to ministry Episcopal Ch., 1949. Mem. team ministry Grace Ch., Jersey City, 1949-57; dean Christ Ch. Cathedral, Indpls., 1957-64; suffragan bishop Washington, 1964-70; bishop coadjutor Diocese, N.Y., 1970-72, bishop, 1972-89. Lectr. St. Augustine's Coll., Canterbury, Eng., 1960; chmn.

commn. Delta ministry Nat. Coun. Chgs., 1964-67; mem. urban divsn., nat. exec. coun. Episcopal Ch., 1952-68; dep. to Gen. Conv., 1961, Anglican Congress, 1963; chmn. com. 100; legal def. fund NAACP. Author: The Church Reclaims the City, 2d edit, 1970, Take A Bishop Like Me, 1979, Presences, 1997. Trustee Bard Coll.; former trustee Gen. Theol. Sem., Trinity Sch., Berkeley Div. Sch. at Yale U., N.Y.C.; mem. Human Rights Watch; mem. adv. coun. Gov.'s Com. on AIDS, 1983-87; chmn. The Timor Project, Project on Religion and Human Rights; adv. coun. Anglican Office, UN. Capt. USMCR, 1941-45, PTO. Decorated Navy Cross, Silver Star, Purple Heart.; recipient Margaret Sanger award Planned Parenthood, 1984, Frederick Douglas award North Star Fund, 1989, Freedom of Worship medal Franklin and Eleanor Roosevelt Inst., 1991, Gen. John Russell Leadership award USMC Found., Patrick Moynihan medal Citizens Com. of N.Y.C.; Yale Corp. sr. fellow, 1964-90, St. Paul's School Alumni Assn. award. Mem.: Anglers Club (N.Y.C.), Century Club (N.Y.C.). Home and Office: 55 Bank St New York NY 10014-2146 E-mail: bishpaulmoore@aol.com.

MOORE, PAULA RUTH, writer; b. Portales, N.Mex., Dec. 3, 1942; d. Howard Paul and Ora Belle Edmonds; m. Leon Hugh Moore, Dec. 25, 1961; children: Scott Leon, John Howard. B.Ind. Studies, N.Mex. State U., 1985, MA, 1989; MFA, Warren Wilson Coll., Asheville, N.C., 1991. Exec. asst. to exec. v.p. N.Mex. State U., Las Cruces, 1985—97, exec. asst. to the pres., 1997—. Co-author (with Jesse Lydick): One Man's Word, 1990 (winner Nightjar Press Book award, 1989); contbr. ; assoc. fiction editor Puerto del Sol, 1981—2000. Policy manual com. N.Mex. State U., 2000, Ralph Crouch Meml. award com., 1996—99; sec., mem. exec. com. Doña Ana Arts Coun., 2000—. Recipient Resolution, N.Mex. State U. Bd. Regents, 2000, Pres.'s award, 1995, Frank Waters Fiction award, N.Mex. State U., 1987. Mem.: Phi Kappa Phi. Avocations: reading, golf. Home: 3340 Karen Dr Las Cruces NM 88001

MOORE, PEARL B. nurse; b. Pitts., Aug. 25, 1936; d. Hyman and Ethel (Antis) Friedman; 1 child, Cheryl. BS in Nursing, U. Pitts., 1968, M Nursing, 1974. Staff nurse Allegheny Gen. Hosp., Pitts., 1957-60; instr. Liliane S. Kaufman Sch. Nursing, 1960-70, asst. dir., 1970, dir., 1970-72; cancer nurse specialist Montefiore Hosp., 1974-75; coord. Brain Tumor Study Group, 1975-83; adj. asst. prof. U. Pitts., 1983—. Contbr. articles in field to profl. publs. Fellow Am. Acad. Nursing; mem. ANA, Oncology Nursing Soc. (exec. dir. 1983—, CEO 1999, Disting. Svc. award 1995), Am. Soc. Clin. Oncology, Am. Soc. Assn. Execs., Nurses Alumnae U. Pitts., Sigma Theta Tau. Home: 4221 Winterburn Ave Pittsburgh PA 15207-1101 Office: 501 Holiday Dr Pittsburgh PA 15220-2749 E-mail: pearl@ons.org.

MOORE, PEGGY SUE, corporation executive; b. Wichita, Kans., June 16, 1942; d. George Alvin and Marie Aileene (Hoskinson) M. Student, Wichita State U., 1961-63, Wichita Bus. Coll., 1963-64. Contr. Mears Electric Co., Wichita, 1965-69; pres., CEO CPI Corp., 1969—2001, also bd. dirs., pres., CEO, 1999—; dir. food svc. Bethel Coll., 2001—. Trustee Fringe Benefits Co., Kansas City, Mo., 1984-85. Active Rep. Nat. Com., Washington, 1985-86, task force, 1986—; treas., bd. dirs. Good Shepherd Luth. Ch., Wichita, 1980-85, mem., 1977—; active Wichita Commn. on Status of Women, 1988. CPI Corp. recipient of Blue Chip Enterprise prize U.S. C. of C., 1996. Mem. NAFE, DAR, Nat. Assn. of Women Bus. Owners, Wichita C. of C., Women's Nat. Bowling Assn. (bd. dirs., pub. com. 1969-76), Internat. Platform Assn., Kans. Purveyors Assn. (bd. dirs. 1988-89), Women's Speakers Bur. Avocations: bowling, golf, fishing. Office: CPI Corp 816 E Funston St Wichita KS 67211-4398

MOORE, PETER BARTLETT, biochemist, educator; b. Boston, Oct. 15, 1939; s. Francis Daniels and Laura Benton (Bartlett) M.; m. Margaret Sue Murphy, Jan. 30, 1966; children: Catherine, Philip. BS, Yale U., 1961, MA (hon.); PhD, Harvard U., 1966. Postdoctoral fellow U. Geneva, 1966-67, MRC Lab. of Molecular Biology, Cambridge, Eng., 1967-69; asst. prof., then assoc. prof. dept. molecular biophysics Yale U., New Haven, 1969-76, assoc. prof. dept. of chemistry, 1976-79, prof., 1979—, chmn. dept. chemistry, 1987-90. Contbr. numerous articles to profl. publs. Guggenheim Found. fellow, 1979-80. Fellow AAAS; mem. Am. Chem. Soc., Am. Soc. Biol. Chemists and Molecular Biologists, Nat. Acad. Scis., Biophys. Soc. (editor Biophys. Jour.) Office: Yale U Dept of Chemistry 225 Prospect Ave New Haven CT 06512-1958

MOORE, PHILIP JOHN, organist, artistic director, conductor, composer; b. London, Sept. 30, 1943; s. Cecil and Marjorie (Brewer) M.; divorced; children: Sophie, Bianca, Thomas. BMus, Durham U. Music master Eton Coll., 1966-68; asst. organist Canterbury Cathedral, 1968-74; organist, master of the choristers Guildford Cathedral, 1974-82; organist, master of music York Minster, 1983—. Fellow Royal Coll. Music, Royal Coll. Organists. Anglican. Home: 1 Minster Ct York YO1 7JJ England E-mail: info@yorkminster.org.

MOORE, PHILIP NICHOLAS, author; b. Atlanta, Nov. 29, 1957; s. Nicholas George and Addy Marie (Todd) M. DDiv, Immanuel Bapt Theol. Sem., 1998. Pres. Rams Head Press Inc., Atlanta, 1995—. Author: The End of History—Messiah Conspiracy, 1996, Nightmare of the Apocalypse, 1997, Eternal Security for True Believers, 1997, A Liberal Interpretation of the Prophecy of Israel-Disproved, 1997, What if Hitler Won the War, 1998. Avocations: reading, writing, researching, travel to Israel, study of Hebrew. Home: 2995 Slaton Dr NW Atlanta GA 30305-2005 Fax: 1-404-816-9994.

MOORE, POWELL ALLEN, federal agency administrator; b. Milledgeville, Ga., Jan. 5, 1938; s. Jere N. and Sarah (Allen) Moore; m. Pamla Hill Prochnow, Sept. 29, 2001; 1 child Frances Moore Preston ;1 child Powell Allen Jr. BA in Jounalism, U. Ga., 1959. Press sec. to Richard Russell, U.S. Senate, Washington, 1966-71; dep. dir. pub. info. Dept. Justice, 1971-72; dep. spl. asst. to Pres. for legis. affairs The White House, 1973-75, dep. asst. to Pres. for legis. affairs, 1981-82; cons. pub. affairs, 1975-81; asst. sec. for congl. rels. Dept. State, 1982-83; v.p. legis. affairs Lockheed Corp., 1983-85, Ginn, Edington, Moore and Wade, Washington, 1985-90; pres. ASL Internat., 1990-93; sr. prin., mng. dir. Capitoline, MS&L, 1993-98; chief of staff Office of Sen. Fred Thompson, 1998-2001; asst. secy. for legis. affairs U.S. Dept. Defense , 2001—. Dir. press Com. to Re-elect the Pres., Washington, 1972; cons. Pres. Ford Com., 1976, Reagan-Bush Com., 1980. Served to capt., inf. U.S. Army, 1959-62. Mem. Belle Haven Country Club, Met. Club. Republican. Episcopalian. Office: US Dept Defense Legislative Affairs 1300 Defense Pentagon Washington DC 20301-1300 Office Fax: 703-693-5530.

MOORE, RAYBURN SABATZKY, American literature educator; b. Helena, Ark., May 26, 1920; s. Max Sabatzky and Sammie Lou (Rayburn) M.; m. Margaret Elizabeth Bear, Aug. 30, 1947; children: Margaret Elizabeth Moore Kopcinski, Robert Rayburn. AB, Vanderbilt U., 1942, MA, 1947; PhD, Duke U., 1956. Script writer King Biscuit Time, Interstate Grocer Co., KFFA, 1947-50; Vice pres. Interstate Grocer Co., Helena, 1947-50; research and grad. asst. Duke U., 1952-54; asst. prof. English, Hendrix Coll., Conway, Ark., 1954-55, asso. prof., 1955-58, prof., 1958-59; asso. prof. U. Ga., Athens, 1959-65, prof., 1965-90, prof. emeritus, 1990—, chmn. Am. studies program, 1968-90, chmn. div. lang and lit., 1975-90. Vis. scholar Duke U., 1958, 64 Author: Constance Fenimore Woolson, 1963, For the Major and Selected Short Stories of Constance Fenimore Woolson, 1967, Paul Hamilton Hayne, 1972, A Man of Letters in the Nineteenth-Century South: Selected Letters of Paul Hamilton Hayne, 1982; sr. editor: History of Southern Literature, 1985, Selected Letters of Henry James to Edmund Gosse (1882-1915): A Literary Friendship, 1988, The Correspondence of Henry James and the House of Macmillan, 1877-1914: All the Links in the Chain, 1993, The Letters of Alice James to Anne Ashburner, 1873-1878, Resources for American Literary Study, vol. 27 numbers 1 and 2, 2001; mem. editorial bd. U. Ga. Press, 1972-74, Ga. Rev., 1974-82, chmn., 1980-82; contbr. articles, revs. to profl. jours. Adv. bd. mem. Letters of Henry James complete edit., 1995—, editl. bd., 1997—; mem. troop com. Boy Scouts Am., Athens, 1973-75; deacon, elder Presbyterian Ch., 1962—; mem. Lamar Meml. Lectures com. Mercer U., 1984-91. Served to capt. U.S. Army, 1942-46, PTO. Recipient John Hurt Fisher award for disting. svc. to the profession South Atlantic Assn. Depts. English, 2000, honoree English Language and Lit., Philoological Assn. of Carolina, 1990. Mem. MLA (exec. com. Gen. Topics VI 1972-75), Soc. Study So. Lit. (exec. com. 1968-69, 74-79, 85-88, 91-94, v.p. 1981-82, pres. 1983-84), South Atlantic Grad. English Coop. Group (exec. com. 1969-79, chmn. 1971-72), South Atlantic Modern Lang. Assn. (exec. com. 1975-77, nominating com. 1985-87), Am. Lit. Assn., Am. Lang. and Lit. Assn. (hon.), Va. Historical Soc., Philological Assn. Carolinas, Edgar Allan Poe Soc., William Gilmore Simms Soc. (exec. com. 1993—, pres.-elect 1993-95), Blue Key, Phi Beta Kappa, Sigma Chi. Office: U Ga Dept English Park Hall Athens GA 30602-6205

MOORE, RAYMOND EDWARD, retired physician; b. Groveland, Mass., Sept. 9, 1912; s. Edward Bishop and Louise Maud (Fowler) M.; m. Christine Isobel Vaughan, June 18, 1938; children: Susan, Stephen. BA, Weslyan U., 1933; MD, Tufts U., 1937. Diplomate Am. Bd. Family Practice. Intern R.I. Hosp., Providence, 1937-39; pvt. practice Hampstead, N.H., 1939-97; ret., 1997. Chief of staff Hale Muni Hosp., Haverhill, Mass., 1968-70. Fellow Am. Acad. Family Physicians (pres. N.H. chpt. 1970-72), Phi Beta Kappa. Office: PO Box 865 Hampstead NH 03841-0865 E-mail: raymondmoore@attbi.com.

MOORE, RHONDA J. epidemiologist, consultant; b. Chgo. S.B, Northwestern U., 1988; student in anthropology, Stanford U., 1990—97, PhD, 1997; M. in Stats., Rice U., 2002. Fellow in psychiatry and behavioral scis. Stanford U. Med. Sch., 1996—97; fellow in epidemiology UT M.D. Anderson Cancer Ctr., Houston, 1998—. Grantee Mellon Foundation, Mellon Foundation/Stanford U., 1995-1996. Office: Ut MD Anderson Cancer Ctr Box 189 1515 Holcombe Blvd Houston TX 77030

MOORE, RICHARD, former academic administrator, educator; m. Susan Moore; children: Betsy, Parker. BS in Econs., Claremont Men's Coll., 1955, PhD, 1965; MBA, U. Calif., 1956. Asst. prof. mktg. San Jose (Calif.) State U., 1959-61; instr., divsn. dir. San Bernardino Valley (Calif.) Coll., 1961-66; dean instrn. Moorpark Coll., Calif., 1966-74; pres., supt. Santa Monica (Calif.) Coll., 1974-94; pres. C.C. So. Nev., Las Vegas, 1994-99, Nev. State Coll. Henderson, 2000—02, prof., 2002—. Active C.C. H.S. program Clark County Sch. Dist., Boys & Girls Clubs, Learning and Earning Program, Weekend Coll., Silver Sage Coll., Peace Officers Acad., Video Distance Edn., other acad. programs. Lt. U.S. Army, 1957-59. Office: Nev State Coll 1125 Dawson Ave Henderson NV 89015*

MOORE, RICHARD THOMAS, writer, poet; b. Stamford, Conn., Sept. 25, 1927; s. James Howard and Gertrude Ann (Ehrhardt) M.; m. Janet Elizabeth Packer, May 12, 1961 (div. 1985); children: Stephanie, Tania, Claudia. BA, Yale U., 1950; MA, Trinity Coll., 1956. Lectr. New Eng. Conservatory Music, Boston, 1965-88. Lectr. Clark U., 1997, 2000, Framingham State Coll., 1997, 98; Fannie Hurst vis. prof. Brandeis U., Waltham, Mass., 1976. Author: (poems) A Question of Survival, 1971, Word from the Hills, 1972, Empires, 1981, The Education of a Mouse, 1983, No More Bottom, 1991, Bottom Is Back, 1994, The Mouse Whole: An Epic, 1996, Pygmies and Pyramids, 1998, The Naked Scarecrow, 2000, (essays) The Rule That Liberates, 1994, (novel) The Investigator, 1991; transl.: Captivi of Plautus, 1995, Hippolytus of Euripides, 1998; contbr. over 500 articles to profl. publs, also essays, opera librettos, sonnets. With USAF, 1950—53. Mem. PEN, New England Poetry Club. Avocations: mathematics, yoga meditation, found art. Home: 81 Clark St Belmont MA 02478-2450 E-mail: richardmoorepoet@att.net.

MOORE, RICHARD ALAN, optometrist; b. La Harpe, Ill., Jan. 6, 1948; s. Emory Royal and Betty Jane (Baldwin) M.; divorced; children: Shannon Louise, David Matthew; m. Karina Beth Martin, Apr. 4, 1998. BA in Philosophy, Drake U., 1970; BS in Optometry, Pacific U., 1972, OD, 1974. Lic. optometrist Ill., Oreg., Calif. Pvt. practice optometry, Portland, Oreg., 1974-79, Carthage, Ill., 1980-99, Macomb, 1998—2001, Monmouth, 2001—. Mem. clin. faculty Pacific U., Forest Grove, Oreg., 1978-79; lectr. Ill. Paraoptometric Soc. State Seminar, 1984. Editor: (newsletter) Southwester (Service Above Self award 1978-79). Mem. planning commn. City of Carthage, 1982-90; bd. dirs. Hancock Ctrl. Sch. Dist., Carthage, 1985-90, pres., 1987-90; v.p. Coll. Edn. Found., Inc., 1989—, Carthage Pk. Dist., 1982-88; organizer, pres. Hancock Transp. Coalition, 1990-92; organizer, pres. protem Hancock County Sch. Bd. Assn., 1990; Rep. candidate for state rep. from 95th dist., 1990, Hancock County Bd., 1990-94, chmn. legis. com., 1993; mem. Hancock County Rep. Ctrl. Com., 1990-92; precinct committeeman Hancock Twp., 1990-92; pres. Carthage chpt. Kiwanis, 1981-82. Mem. Am. Optometric Assn. (Best Non-Tech. Article award 1988, Recognition award 1989, Best Guest Editorial award 1991), Ill. Optometric Assn. (exec. coun. 1985-91, organizer, 1st chmn. soc. pres.'s coun. 1987, v.p. govtl. rels. 1987-91, chmn. polit. action com. 1987-91, mem. pres.'s cabinet 1987-91, chmn. resolutions com. 1991), West Ctrl. Ill. Optometric Soc. (pres. 1985-87), Carthage C. of C. (pres. 1983-84). Republican. Avocations: music, travel, genealogy, history of religion. Home: 137 Doe Run Macomb IL 61455-9703 Office: 1190 N 6th St Monmouth IL 61462

MOORE, RICHARD ALAN, landscape architect; b. St. Louis, Jan. 17, 1930; s. Ira Mack and Helen Adoline (Fakes) M.; m. Patricia Ruth Burke, Mar. 15, 1952 (div. 1967); children: Sheryl Louise, Richard Dennis, Sara Lynn, Sandra Lee. BS, U. Mo., 1951; MLA, U. Oreg., 1957. Registered landscape architect, Calif., Hawaii. Asst. prof. landscape architecture Calif. State Poly. Coll., Pomona, 1957-61; assoc. prof., head dept. landscape architecture N.C. State U., Raleigh, 1962-67; pvt. practice landscape architecture Pomona, Calif., 1957-61; dir. land devel. and planning Oceanic Properties Inc., Honolulu, 1967-69; pvt. practice, 1969-70, 79—; dir. ops. Eckbo, Dean, Austin & Williams, 1970-71, v.p. ops., 1971-73; pres. EDAW, Inc., San Francisco, 1973-76, chmn. bd., 1976-78; prof. landscape architecture Tex. A&M U., Bryan, 1977-79. Prin. works include Whispering Pines Motor Lodge, N.C., 1964 (award of merit N.C. chpt. AIA 1964), North Shore Devel. Plan, Kauai, Hawaii, 1973, Comprehensive Zoning Ordinance, County of Kauai, 1973 (Am. Soc. Landscape Architects honor award 1973, HUD honor award 1974), Lihue Devel. Plan, Kauai, 1975, Koloa, Poipu, Kalaheo Devel. Plan, Kauai, 1978, Gen. Plan Update, Kauai, 1982, Mililani Town Devel. Plan, 1967-69 (Am. Soc. Landscape Architects merit award 1970), Lanai Land Mgmt. and Devel. Study, 1969 (Am. Soc. Landscape Architects merit award 1970), Wailea Master Devel. Plan, 1971, Kukuiula Devel. Plan, 1983, Lanai Project Dist. Master Plan, 1983-89, Maliu Ridge Devel. Plan, North Kohala, 1985, Mililani Mauka Devel. Plan, 1988, Devel. Plan, Lanai City Comml. Dist., 1990, Dandan Golf Course, Guam, 1991. Lst lt. U.S. Army, 1951-53, Korea. Fellow Am. Soc. Landscape Architects; mem. Masons. Avocations: sports, drawing, painting.

MOORE, RICHARD CARROLL, JR. family physician; b. Balt., Nov. 24, 1946; s. Richard Carroll and Virginia Mae (Clark) M.; m. Jeremy Pierson, Jan. 27, 1973; children: Peter Gregory, Laura Alexandra. BA, Johns Hopkins U., 1968, MPH, 1981; MD, UCLA, 1972. Diplomate Am. Bd. Family Practice. Intern South Balt. Gen. Hosp., 1972-73; commd. med. officer USPHS, 1976, ret., 1997; chief med. div. USCG Aviation Tng. Ctr., Mobile, Ala., 1976-80; chief med. ops. USCG, Washington, 1981-86; sr. med. officer USCG Yard, Curtis Bay, Md., 1986-88; dir. Health Unit # 1, USPHS, 1988-97; staff physician Piedmont Prime Care, Danville, Va., 1997-98; med. dir. Carilion Occupl. Medicin, Roanoke-Salem Ctr., 1999—2001, Roanoke Elec. Steel, 2000—; clin. asst. prof. family medicine U. Va., 1999—; med. dir. occpl. health svcs. Valley Health System, 2001—. Mem. exec. bd. Emergency Med. Svcs. Coun., Mobile County, 1979, Med. and Chirurg. Faculty Md. Mem. editl. bd. MD Med. Jour., 1995-97. Bd. dirs. Midway Fed. Credit Union, 1989-96, pres., 1991-96. With USN, 1973-76. Mem. Aerospace Med. Assn., So. Med. Assn, Soc. U.S. Naval Flight Surgeons, Johns Hopkins U. Alumni Assn., Commd. Officers Assn. USPHS, UCLA Alumni Assn., Alpha Omega Alpha, Sigma Phi Epsilon, Republican. Office: Occupational Health Svcs 607 E Jubal Early Dr Winchester VA 22601 Home: Hobby Horse Hill 3223 Browntown Rd Front Royal VA 22630-7647

MOORE, RICHARD GEORGE, lawyer; b. Indpls., July 15, 1957; s. E. James and Joyce Judith (Dobeck) M.; m. Alison Ann Holladay, Feb. 25, 1984; children: Richard George Jr., Stephanie Ellen, Ryan James. BBA magna cum laude, Baylor U., 1979, JD, 1982. Bar: Tex. 1982. Briefing atty. U.S. Dist. Ct. (no. dist.) Tex., Dallas, 1982-84; assoc. Worsham, Forsythe, Sampels & Wooldridge, 1984-87; supervising atty. Fed. Asset Disposition Assn., 1987-89; asst. gen. counsel NationsBank, 1989-95; pvt. practice, 1995—. Mng. editor, contbr. Baylor U. Law Rev., 1981-82. Mem. Tex. Bar Assn., Dallas Bar Assn., Tex. State Bd. Pub. Accountancy, Sigma Alpha Epsilon. Republican. Roman Catholic. Avocations: fishing, basketball, softball. Home and Office: 6955 Lakeshore Dr Dallas TX 75214-3551

MOORE, RICHARD KERR, electrical engineering educator; b. St. Louis, Nov. 13, 1923; s. Louis D. and Nina (Megown) M.; m. Wilma Lois Schallau, Dec. 10, 1944; children: John Richard, Daniel Charles. BS, Washington U. at St. Louis, 1943; PhD, Cornell U., 1951. Test equipment engr. RCA, Camden, N.J., 1943-44; instr. and rsch. engr. Washington U., St. Louis, 1947-49; rsch. assoc. Cornell U., 1949-51; rsch. engr., sect. supr. Sandia Corp., Albuquerque, 1951-55; prof., chmn. elec. engring. U. N.Mex., 1955-62; Black and Veatch prof. U. Kans., Lawrence, 1962-94; prof. emeritus, 1994—; dir. remote sensing lab. U. Kans., 1964-74, 84-93. Pres. Cadre Corp., Lawrence, 1968-87; cons. cos., govt. agys. Author: Traveling Wave Engineering, 1960; co-author: (with Ulaby and Fung) Microwave Remote Sensing, Vol. I, 1981, Vol. II, 1982, Vol. III, 1986; contbr. to profl. jours. and handbooks. Lt. (j.g.) USNR, 1944-46. Recipient Achievement award Washington U. Engring. Alumni Assn., 1978, Outstanding Tech. Achievement award IEEE Geosci. and Remote Sensing Soc., 1982, Louise E. Byrd Grad. Educator award U. Kans., 1984, Irving Youngberg Rsch. award U. Kans., 1989, Australia prize, 1995. Fellow AAAS, IEEE (sect. chmn. 1960-61, Outstanding Tech. Achievement award coun. oceanic engring. 1978); mem., NAE, AAUP, Am. Soc. Engring. Edn., Am. Geophys. Union, Internat. Sci. Radio Union (chmn. U.S. commn. F 1984-87, internat. vice chmn. commn. F 1990-93, chmn. 1993-96), Kiwanis, Sigma Xi, Tau Beta Pi. Presbyterian (past elder). Achievements include research in submarine communications, radar altimetry, radar as a remote sensor, radar oceanography; patent for polypanchromatic radar. Home: 1712 Carmel Dr Lawrence KS 66047-1840 Office: U Kans R S & Remote Sensing Lab 2335 Irving Hill Rd Lawrence KS 66045-7612 E-mail: rmoore@sunflower.com.

MOORE, RICHARD LAWRENCE, structural engineer, consultant; b. Rocky Ford, Colo., Feb. 7, 1934; s. Lawrence and Margaret Kathryn (Bolling) M.; m. Donna St. Clair, Mar. 26, 1972 (div. 1983); 1 child, Andrew Trousdale; m. Margaret Ann Guthrie, May 4, 1984. BSCE, U. Colo., 1957; MS, Princeton U., 1963; PhD, Calif. Western U., Santa Ana, 1975. Registered profl. engr., Mass., Maine, Colo., Pa., Iowa, Nebr., N.Mex., Wyo., Ill., Ark., Mo., N.D., Mich., Okla., Mont. Structural engr. Cameron Engrs., Denver, 1964-66; v.p. Moore Internat., Jeddah, Saudi Arabia, 1967-78; asst. to pres. C.H. Guernsey Co., Oklahoma City, 1979-82; pres. R.L. Moore Co., Boston, 1983—; v.p., dir. Isolink Ing., Basel, Switzerland, 1990—. Nat. chmn. Roof Cons. Inst., Raleigh, N.C., 1988-92; prof. Episcopal Sch. Theology, Denver, 1967-71. Patentee in field. Member Mound City (Mo.) Libr. Bd., 1963-64; pres. Dist. Rep. Party, Boston, 1988—; sr. warden St. John Chrysostom Epis. Ch., Denver, 1966-71. Danforth Found. scholar, 1962. Mem. ASCE, NSPE, Am. Concrete Inst., Nat. Forensic Ctr. Avocations: golf, travel, antique pocket watch collecting. Home and Office: RL Moore Co 534 E Broadway Boston MA 02127-4407

MOORE, RICHARD THOMAS, state legislator; b. Milford, Mass., Aug. 7, 1943; s. Thomas James and Helen Eliza (Andrew) M.; m. Joanne Bednarz, May 26, 1979. BA in History, Clark U., 1966; MA in Student Pers., Colgate U., 1967; postgrad., Clark U., 1967-70, U. Mass., 1981-85. Cert. tchr. secondary level social studies. Assoc. dean students Assumption Coll., Worcester, Mass., 1967-69; asst. to pres. Bentley Coll., Waltham, 1969-77; mem. Mass. Ho. of Reps., Boston, 1977-94; assoc. dir. mitigation Fed. Emergency Mgmt. Agy., Washington, 1994-96; mem. Mass. Senate, Boston, 1996—, chmn. senate com. on pub. svc., 1997-98, chmn. senate com. healthcare, 1999—. Pres. Mass. Selectmen's Assn., Boston, 1975-76; chmn. House Com. on Election Laws, Boston, 1992-94, House Com. on Taxation, Boston, 1983-85, House Com. on State Adminstrn., Boston, 1983. Chmn. Blackstone Nat. Heritage Corridor Commn., Uxbridge, Mass., 1988-90, 2000—; presdl. elector Mass. Electoral Coll., Boston, 1992; chmn. Mass. Dem. Leadership Coun., Boston, 1990-93; trustee Nichols Coll., 1997—, Named Outstanding Legislator Mass. Town Clks. Assn., Boston, 1993, New Dem. of Yr. Mass. Dem. Leadership Coun., Boston, 1994; recipient Disting. Svc. award Fed. Emergency Mgmt. Agy., 1996. Mem. ASPA (bd. dirs. Mass. chpt. 1981-85, chpt. v.p. 1999-2000, pres.-elect 2000-2001, pres. 2001—, Disting. Pub. Adminstrn. award 1997, Coun. State Govt.'s 2000 Toll fellow), Nat. Conf. State Legislatures (exec. com.), Nat. Emergency Mgmt. Assn., Knights Holy Sepulchre. Roman Catholic. Avocations: politics, collecting political items. Office: State House Rm 312D Boston MA 02133 E-mail: rmoore@senate.state.ma.us.

MOORE, ROBERT HENRY, financial services executive; b. Madisonville, Ky., Sept. 16, 1940; s. William Lee Moore and Robbie (Pritchett) Ruby; m. Diana Churchill, Aug. 17, 1963 (div. 1978); children: Randall Lee, Robin Churchill; m. Patricia Mary George, Oct. 4, 1981; 1 child, Christopher Robert. BA, Davidson (N.C.) Coll., 1962; MA, U. N.C., 1964; PhD, U. Wis., 1972. Asst. dir. admissions Davidson Coll., 1963-64; teaching asst. U. Wis., Madison, 1965-68; staff and faculty U.S. Mil. Acad., West Point, N.Y., 1968-70; lectr., asst. prof. U. Md., College Park, 1970-76, assoc. prof., 1976; cons. U.S. Congress, Washington, 1976-77; emerging issues coordinator The Conf. Bd., N.Y.C., 1977-79; dir. govt. relations Beneficial Corp., Washington, 1977-78; v.p. Alexander & Alexander, Inc., 1978-81, Alexander & Alexander Svcs. Inc., N.Y.C., Washington, 1981-85, sr. v.p. corp. rels., 1985-95, sr. v.p. (inactive), 1995-97; chmn., pres. A & A Govt. and Industry Affairs Inc., Washington, 1990-94, Aon Corp., Vienna, 1997—. Del. Nat. Security Affairs Conf., Washington, 1978-82; mem. adv. bd. Career Opportunities Inst., U. Va., Charlottesville, 1982-86, Ctr. for New Am. Work Force, 1992-96; mem. corp. adv. bd. Queens Coll., CUNY, 1985-96; mem. V.P.'s Forum, 1989-94; mem. coun. Conf. Bd. Corp. Comm. Execs., 1990-94; mem. Pub. Rels. Sem., 1993-97; editl. advisor Ctr. for Mind-Body Medicine, Washington, 1998-2000; adv. coun. Mindfulness Practice Ctr. of Fairfax, 1998—; lectr. Shepherd's Ctr., 1999—; bd. visitors Dictionary of Am. Regional English, 1999—; adv. to chmn. NEH, 1999-2001. Co-author: (with others) School for Soldiers: West Point and the Profession of Arms, 1974 (NYT award 1974); contbr. articles to profl. jours.; contbr. interviews to nat. mags., newspapers, radio and TV. Mem. kitchen cabinet Points of Light Found., 1991-95. With U.S. Army, 1968-70, capt. USAR, 1970-72. Ops. Crossroads Africa fellow, 1960; U. Md. rsch. grantee, 1972, 76. Mem. Nat. Assn. Ins. Brokers (exec. com., bd. dirs., pres. 1985-86, chmn. past presidents adv. coun. 1989-93).

MOORE, ROBERT MADISON, food industry executive, lawyer; b. New Orleans, June 21, 1925; s. Clarence Greer and Anna Omega (Odendahl) M.; m. Evelyn Eileen Varva, Apr. 11, 1953; children: Eileen Alexandria Moore Wynne, John Greer. BBA, Tulane U., 1947; JD, U. Va., 1952; LLM (Food Law Inst. fellow), NYU, 1953. Bar: La. 1956, Calif. 1972. Asst. to pres., gen. counsel Underwear Inst., N.Y.C., 1953-55; pvt. practice law New Orleans, 1955-56; asst. gen. atty., dir. Legal services, sec. and gen. atty. Standard Fruit & Steamship Co., 1957-72; v.p., gen. counsel Castle & Cooke Foods, 1972-81, Castle & Cooke, Inc., 1973-81, sr. v.p. law and govt., 1981-82; pres. Internat. Banana Assn., 1983-98; acting exec. dir. Pan Am. Devel. Found., 1999. Dir. Ferson Optics of Del., Inc., 1958-69, Baltime Securities Corp., Pan American Devel. Found. Asst. atty. gen., La., 1960-66. Served with AUS, 1943-46. Mem. ABA, Calif. Bar Assn., La. Bar Assn., SAR (sec. 1960-61), KM, Cosmos Club, Phi Delta Phi, Alpha Tau Omega. Democrat. Roman Catholic. Home: 3323 R St NW Washington DC 20007-2310 E-mail: rmevmoore@aol.com.

MOORE, ROBERT WILLIAM, professional organization executive; b. Claysburg, Pa., June 4, 1924; s. Frank B. and Sarah A. (Edelbute) M.; m. Helen Lingenfelter, July 17, 1948; children: Thomas R., Priscilla Jane. BA, Pa. State U., 1948. With Price Waterhouse & Co., Pitts., 1948-62, mgr., 1955-62; asst. contr. Con-Gas Svc. Corp., Pitts., 1962-65, Consol. Natural Gas Svc. Co., Inc., Pitts., 1966-72, contr., 1972-78, Consol. Natural Gas Co., Pitts., 1972-78; pres. Fin. Execs. Inst., Morristown, N.J., 1978-89, pres. emeritus, 1989—. Mem. Fin. Acctg. Standards Adv. Coun., 1978-89. Bd. dirs. Central Blood Bank, Pitts., 1960-78, treas. corp., 1962-68, chmn. finance com., 1962-68, chmn. bd., 1969-72; mem. exec. bd. Pa. State U. Alumni Council, 1975-83; mem. exec. com. Campaign for Pa. State U., bd. vis.; pres. Pa. State Coll. Bus. Adminstrn. Soc., 1981-83. Served with AUS, 1943-45. Mem. Am., Pa. insts. C.P.A.s, Nat. Assn. Accountants, Fin. Execs. Inst., Pa. State U. Alumni Assn., Pa. Soc., Beta Alpha Psi (nat. forum), Delta Tau Delta. Clubs: University (dir., pres. 1975-76), Valley Brook Country (dir. 1968-70, v.p. bd. 1970), Duquesne (Pitts.), University, St. Clair Country, Morris County Golf, Morristown (N.J.). Episcopalian. E-mail: rmoorepgh@msn.com.

MOORE, ROBERT YATES, neuroscience educator; b. Harvey, Ill., Dec. 5, 1931; s. Raymon Irwin and Marie Louise (Fischer) M.; children: Elizabeth Allen, Matthew McCormick, Joshua Gilbert, Thomas Douglas. BA magna cum laude, Lawrence U., 1953; MD with honors, U. Chgo., 1957, PhD, 1962; MD (hon.), Lund (Sweden) U., 1974. Diplomate: Am. Bd. Psychiatry and Neurology. Intern Univ. Hosp., Ann Arbor, Mich., 1958-59; resident U. Chgo., 1959-64, asst. prof. neurology and anatomy, 1964-66, assoc. prof., 1966-70, prof., 1970-74; prof. neurosci. U. Calif., San Diego, 1974-79; prof., chmn. dept. neurology SUNY, Stony Brook, 1979-90; prof. psychiatry, neurology and neurosci. U. Pitts., 1990—, chmn. dept. neurology, 1992-2000. Cons. Contbr. numerous articles to profl. jours. Recipient numerous grants. Fellow Am. Acad. Neurology; mem. Am. Neurol. Assn., Soc. Neurosci., Internat. Brain Research Orgn., Am. Assn. Anatomists. Office: U Pitts Dept Neurology 3471 5th Ave Ste 811 Pittsburgh PA 15213-3232

MOORE, ROBIN RAGSDALE, management analyst; b. Astoria, Oreg., Jan. 28, 1955; d. John O'Neill and JoAnn Lindsay Ragsdale; m. David Kevin Gandolfo, Apr. 16, 1983 (div. May 1996); m. Pete Dean. Moore, July 6, 2002. children: Ashley Brooke, Gia Marie. BBA, U. Tex., 1978; MS, Naval Postgrad. Sch., 1987. Commd. ens. USN, 1980, advanced through grades to comdr., 1996; occupl. analyst Navy Occupl. Devel. and Analysis Ctr., Washington, 1987-90; adminstrv. officer Nuclear Field A Sch., Orlando, Fla., 1990-93; exec. officer Navy Recruiting Dist., Memphis, 1993-95; mgmt. analyst Naval Edn. and Tng. Profl. Devel. and Tech. Ctr., Pensacola, Fla., 1995-98; ret. USN, 1998; mgmt. analyst Alpha Solutions Corp., Pensacola, 1998-99; program mgr. Anteon Corp., Orlando, 2000—; sales rep. Rexall Showcase Internat., Pensacola and Orlando, 1999—. Mem. Ret. Officer's Assn. Republican. Avocations: aerobics, quilting. Home: 313 Celtic Ct Oviedo FL 32765-6599 Office: Anteon Corp 12605 Challenger Pkwy Orlando FL 32826 E-mail: robinr63@cs.com., rrmoore@anteon.com.

MOORE, ROGER ALBERT, JR. archaeologist; b. Tampa, Fla., Dec. 18, 1946; s. Roger Albert Moore and Frieda E. (Heil) Hutchison; m. Susan Kay Waters, Sept. 8, 1978; children: Tabitha Rose, Roxie Ann. BA in Anthropology, Ohio State U., 1972; student, U. Tenn., 1974-75; MA in Anthropology, Ea. N.Mex. U., 1981. Lic. archael. surveyor, N.Mex., Colo., Utah, Wyo., Ariz. Crew chief, field foreman U. Tenn., Knoxville, 1973-74, excavator, lab. asst., 1974-75, Cahokia Mounds State Park, Collinsville, Ill., 1974; lithic analyst Ea. N.Mex. U., Portales, 1975-78; lab. dir. U. Colo., Cortez, 1978-79; field dir. ESCA-Tech, Inc., Ridgeway, Colo., 1980; lab. dir. Navajo Nat. Archaeology Dept., Farmington, N.Mex., 1980-82; supervisory archaeologist San Juan County Mus. Assn., Bloomfield, 1982-88; owner, prin. investigator Moore Anthropol. Rsch., Aztec, 1988—; owner Southwest Archaeol. Svcs., 1996-99; v.p., prin. investigator 4 Rivers Archaeology, Inc., 1999-2000. Instr. San Juan Coll., Farmington, 1983; mem. strategic action team Aztec Mcpl. Sch. Dist., 1995. Co-author: Old Dallas Historical Archaeology Project, 1987; contbr. articles to profl. jours. Vol. Portales (N.Mex.) Food Coopr., 1976-78, Salmon Ruin Mus., Bloomfield, 1982-88, Bonds for Books Plus Com., Aztec, 1994; mem. lithic dictionary com. N.Mex. Archaeol. Coun., 1989—; chmn. com. B.L.M. Cultural Adv. Group, Farmington, 1991—; mem. Aztec H.S. parent adv. com., 1996-97. Mem.: San Juan Archaeol. Soc., Nat. Trust for Hist. Preservation, San Juan County Mus. Assn. (bd. dirs. 1993—95), Ariz. Archaeol. and Hist. Soc., Archaeol. Soc. N.Mex. (cert., bd. trustees 1998—, Archaeol. Achievement award 1994), N.Mex. Archaeol. Coun., Tenn. Anthropol. Assn. (life), Soc. Am. Archaeology (life), Aztec Main St. Assn. (bd. dirs. 1997—), Aztec C. of C. (bd. dirs. 1995—97), Clan Muir (convener S.W. Territory-USA 2001—), Phi Kappa Phi. Republican. Presbyterian. Avocations: running, hiking, tennis, reading. Office: Moore Anthropol Rsch PO Box 1156 Aztec NM 87410-1156

MOORE, RONALD BRUCE, visual effects producer; b. Lindsay, Calif., Sept. 11, 1945; s. Louis Clay and Mary Viola (Gates) M.; m. Barbara Doral Wesling. BPA, Brooks Inst., 1972; diplomas, Nat. Radio Inst., 1973-76. With Universal Title, North Hollywood, Calif., 1983-84; visual effects editor Boss Film Corp., Marina del Rey, 1984-86; optical supr. Robert Abel and Assocs., Hollywood, 1986-87; visual effects supr. Paramount Pictures, L.A., 1987—. Optical camera Ghostbusters, 1984, 2010, 1985; visual effects editor Poltergeist II, 1985, Boy Who Could Fly, 1985, Big Trouble in Little China, 1986, Solarbabies, 1986; optical supr. Moonstruck, 1986; visual effects supr. Star Trek: The Next Generation, 1987-94 (Emmy nominee 1989, 90, Emmy Winner 1992, 99, 2000), Star Trek Generations, 1994, Star Trek Voyager, 1994-2001, Star Trek Enterprise, 2001—. With USNR, 1965-67. Mem. NATAS, Internat. Cinematographers Guild, Motion Picture Editors Guild. Avocations: computers, videos, music, photography, bicycles. Office: Paramount Pictures Cooper Bldg 201 5555 Melrose Ave Los Angeles CA 90038-3197 E-mail: Ron@TrekVFX.com.

MOORE, ROY DEAN, retired judge; b. Chickasha, Okla., Jan. 15, 1940; s. Frank B. and Delia Pauline (Morgan) M.; m. Carolyn Kaye Wood, Aug. 10, 1962; children— Darla Kaye, Jared Dean, Amy Darise. BA, Central State U., 1962, M. Teaching, 1966; JD, Oklahoma City U., 1970; grad., Nat. Coll. State Trial Judges, 1972. Bar: Okla. 1970. Coach debate, instr. dramatics Kingfisher (Okla.) High Sch., 1962-67; instr. English and journalism, head dept. lang. arts. Jarman Jr. High Sch., Midwest City, Okla., 1967-70; pros. atty. City of Lawton, 1970; spl. dist. judge 5th Jud. Dist. Okla., 1971-72; pvt. practice law Lawton, 1973-90; dist. judge 5th Jud. Dist. Okla., 1990—2002. Pres. Swinney PTA, 1975-76; Editor: Problems in Teaching in the Secondary School, 1966. Pres. Comanche County Mental Health Assn., 1973-74, bd. dirs., 1972-76; co-chmn. Kingfisher County Reps. for Congressman James V. Smith, 1966; mem. state exec. com. Okla. Republican Com., 1973-74, chmn. auditing com., 1977-78; del. Rep. Nat. Conv., 1976; chmn. cts. com. Assn. South Central Okla. Govts. Crime Commn.; chmn. Comanche County Reps. for Reagan for Pres., 1973-83; mem. adv. bd. Jim Taliferro Mental Health Center, 1977-78; del. Nat. Mental Health Assn. Conv., 1975; bd. dirs. Lawton Campfire Girls; elder N.W. Ch. of Christ, 1977—; dir. Back to Bible Campaigns, 1976-2002. Named Outstanding Dist. Judge in State of Okla., Okla. Trial Lawyers Assn., 1999. Mem. Am., Okla., Comanche County bar assns., Okla. Trial Lawyers Assn., Lawton Antique Auto Club, Ford Retractible Club Am., Alpha Psi Omega, Delta Theta Phi. Republican. Mem. Ch. of Christ (elder). Clubs: Fraternal Order of Police, Lion. Home: 2114 NW Atlanta Ave Lawton OK 73505-3923

MOORE, ROY S. state supreme court chief justice; m. Kayla Moore; children: Heather, Roy, Caleb, Micah. BS, U.S. Mil. Acad., 1969; JD, U. Ala., 1977. Dep. dist. atty. Etowah County, Ala., 1977—82; pvt. practice Gadsden, 1982—92; cir. judge 16th Judicial Cir., 1992—2001; chief justice Ala. Supreme Ct., 2001—. Republican. Baptist. Office: Ala Supreme Ct 300 Dexter Ave Montgomery AL 36104-3741*

MOORE, SANDRA KAY, counselor, administrator; b. Sellersville, Pa., June 28, 1943; d. Sheldon Ellsworth and Olive (Moyer) McElroy; m. Thomas Van Moore, June 8, 1963; children: Thomas Shawn, Tara Quinn, Tammy Colleen, Thador Shelby. Student, East Stroudsburg (Pa.) U., 1961-63; BA, Gwynedd-Mercy Coll., 1986; MS, Chestnut Hill Coll., 1990. Cert. in student assistance program. Crisis counselor Archbishop Ryan H.S., Phila., 1989-90; guidance counselor Mt. St. Joseph Acad., Flourtown, Pa., 1990-93, dir. guidance, 1993—. Lectr. Gwynedd-Mercy Coll., Gwynedd, Pa., 1995—; lectr. in field. Author: So You Want to Go to College, 1994. Bd. dirs. Today, Inc., Hilltown, Pa., 1976-80; mem. Hilltown (Pa.) Civic Assn., 1975-85; pres. Bux-Mont Neighbors, Souderton, Pa., 1985, John M. Grasse Home and Sch. Assn., Perkasie, Pa., 1981; chairwoman Christian Edn. Com., Perkasie, 1994. Mem. APA, Ind. Counselors Assn., Nat. Assn. for Coll. Admissions Counselors, Specialists in Schs., Pa. Assn. Secondary Sch. and Coll. Admission Counselors. Democrat. Lutheran. Avocations: horseback riding, reading, writing, travel, collecting antique Santa Claus'. Office: Mount Saint Joseph Academy 120 W Wissahickon Ave Flourtown PA 19031-1802

MOORE, SCOTT, state official; b. York, Nebr., 1960; m. Danene Tushar, 1989. BA in Polit Sci., U. Nebr. Legis. aide Nebr. Legislature, 1981-86, mem., 1986-94, chair appropriations com., 1991-94; sec. of state State of Nebr., 1995—2000; dir. gov. affairs United Pacific R.R., 2000—. With Moore & Sons. Office: 1416 Dodge St Room 801 Omaha NE 68179 Address: 615 N 62nd St Omaha NE 68132-1958*

MOORE, SCOTT MICHAEL, lawyer; b. Grand Rapids, Mich., July 3, 1958; s. Bruce Friend and Sharon Diane (Eister) M.; m. Marilisa Mannisto, June 21, 1995. BS, Ea. Mich. U., 1983, MA in Econs., 1985; JD, Wayne State U., 1989. Bar: Mich. 1990, N.Y. 2002, U.S. Dist. Ct. (we. dist.) Mich. 1991, U.S. Ct. Appeals (6th cir.) 1991, U.S. Ct. Internat. Trade 1991, U.S. Ct. Appeals (fed. cir.) 1992, U.S. Supreme Ct. 1995, U.S. Dist. Ct. (we. dist.) N.Y. 1997. Pvt. practice, Houghton, 1990-91, Mohawk, 1992-98, San Francisco, 1998—. Forum panelist: Perspectives on War in the Middle East-International Law and the War Mich. Tech. U., 1991. Mem. ABA (internat. law sect.), Am. Econ. Assn., Mich. Bar Assn. (coun. mem. internat. law sect. 1999), Internat. Bar Assn., Omicron Delta Epsilon. Office: 388 Market St Ste 500 San Francisco CA 94111-5313 E-mail: smm@milopc.com.

MOORE, SHIRLEY THROCKMORTON (MRS. ELMER LEE MOORE), accountant; b. Des Moines, July 4, 1918; d. John Carder and Jessie (Wright) Throckmorton; m. Elmer Lee Moore, Dec. 19, 1946; children: Fay, Lynn Dallas. Student, Iowa State Tchrs. Coll., 1937-38, Madison Coll., 1939-41; MCS, Benjamin Franklin U., 1944. CPA. Asst. bookkeeper Sibley Hosp., Washington, 1941-42, Alvord & Alvord, 1942-46, bookkeeper, 1946-49, chief acct., 1950-64, fin. advisor to sr. ptnr., 1957-64; dir. Allen Oil Co., 1958-74; pvt. practice acctg., 1964—. Contbr. articles to profl. jours. Mem. sch. bd. Takoma Acad., Takoma Park, Md., 1970—; mem. hosp. bd. Washington Adventist Hosp., 1974-85; chmn. worthy student fund Takoma Park Seven Day Adventist Ch., 1987-88; trustee Benson Found., 1963-99; vol. Am. Women's Vol. Svc., 1942-45. Recipient Disting. Grad. award Benjamin Franklin U., 1961. Mem. AICPA, D.C. Inst. CPAs (pub. rels. com. 1976—), Am. Women's Soc. CPAs, Am. Soc. Women Accts. (legis. chmn. 1960-62, nat. dir. 1952-53, nat. treas. 1953-54), Bus. and Profl. Women's Club (treas. D.C. 1967-68), Benjamin Franklin U. Alumni Assn. (Disting. Alumni award 1964, charter, past dir.), DAR, Md. Assn. CPAs (charter chmn. membership com. Montgomery Prince George County 1963-64, chmn. student rels. com. 1964-67, pres. 1968-69, mem. fed. tax com. 1971-73). Mem. Seventh Day Adventist Ch. Home and Office: 2401 Pine Lake Dr West Columbia SC 29169-3737

MOORE, SPENCER RONEAL, retired business owner, accounts receivable funder; b. Levelland, Tex., Apr. 3, 1934; s. Joe Bailey and Ida Maye (Williams) M.; m. Valeria a., Dec. 28, 1966. Student, Hartnell Coll., 1952-53. Sales asst. Dick Bruhns, A Man's Store, Salinas, Calif., 1951-52; salesman Pauson's Men's Store, San Francisco, 1953-54; mdse. buyer Hart's Dept. Store, San Jose, Calif., 1954-64; buyer men's, boys Demery's Wurzbergs, Detroit and Grand Rapids, Mich., 1966-70; opers. mgr. Saks Fifth Ave., Woodland Hills, Calif., 1971-74; mdse. mgr. Vornado, Inc., Whittier, 1974-75; self employed The Mole Hole, La Jolla, 1976-93; ret., 1994. Mem. Am. Cash Flow Industry, La Jolla Profl. Men's Soc., Kiwanis (Torrey Pines). Democrat. Avocations: golf, travel, reading, family, fitness excercise. Home: 24440 Woodsage Dr Bonita Springs FL 34134-7959 Office: Express Small Bus Funding 17595 S Tamiami Trl Fort Myers FL 33908-4570

MOORE, STEPHANIE ALLEN, gifted and talented educator, consultant; b. Kansas City, Mo., May 11, 1955; d. Arthur Kenneth and Barbara Allen; 1 child Jamie Allen Mitchell. BA, Lincoln U., 1977. Tchr. gifted and talented Kansas City (Mo.) Sch. Dist., 1989—98; curriculum coord. Crispus Attucks Elem., 1998—2000; national urban coach cons. Westport Edison Mid. Sch., 2001—. Urban coach Cons. Bus., Kansas City, 2001—02; dir. Learning Acad., Kansas City, 1985—88. Author: Urban Coach Resource Manual, 2002; contbr. articles to mags. Mem.: NAACP, Twin Citians. Democrat. Avocations: travel, writing, inventing. Home: 7909 E 162nd Pl Belton MO 64012 Personal E-mail: sam493@earthlink.net.

MOORE, STEPHEN EDWARD, county judge; b. Tacoma, Mar. 23, 1946; s. Edward Chauncey and Jean Teresa (Fuller) M.; m. Pamela Louise Reynolds, Feb. 14, 1970 (dec. 1998); children: Matthew Stephen, Heather Anne. BA, Wash. State U., 1973, MA, 1974; JD, U. Wash., 1977. Bar: Wash. 1977, U.S. Dist. Ct. (we. dist.) Wash. 1977, U.S. Ct. Appeals (9th cir.) 1978, U.S. Supreme Ct. 1987. Dep. pros. atty. King County, Seattle, 1977-88; judge pro tem King and Shohomish County Dist. Cts., 1989-2000; judge Lynnwood Mcpl. Ct., 2000—. Lectr. Nat. Coll. Dist. Attys., Houston, 1981-88; ct. commr. Federal Way Dist. Ct., 1990—. With USN, 1967-71. Mem. ABA, Wash. State Bar Assn., Seattle-King County Bar Assn. Republican. Episcopalian.

MOORE, STEPHEN JAMES, lawyer; b. Kansas City, Mo., Aug. 9, 1947; s. James Andrew and Frances Clare (Kennedy) M. BSBA, Rockhurst Coll., 1969, BA, 1975; JD, U. Mo., Kansas City, 1977, LLM, 1997. Bar: Mo. 1978, U.S. Dist. Ct. (we. dist.) Mo. 1978, U.S. Ct. Appeals (8th cir.) 1980, U.S. Ct. Appeals (10th cir.) 1981, U.S. Ct. Fed. Claims 1991, U.S. Ct. Appeals (6th cir.) 1997. Law intern Mo. Atty. Gen.'s Office, Kansas City, 1976-77, asst., 1978; assoc. Popham, Conway, Sweeny, Fremont & Bundschu PC, 1978-84, Freilich, Leitner & Carlisle, PC, Kansas City, 1985, Herrick, Feinstein, Kansas City, 1985-86, Freilich, Leitner, Carlisle & Shortlidge, Kansas City, 1986-90; ptnr. Freilich, Leitner & Carlisle, Kansas City, Dallas, L.A., 1987-2000, Aspen, Colo., 1997-2000, Peters, Moore & Jones, LLC, Kansas City, Mo., 2001—. Adj. prof. law U. Mo., Kansas City, 1995—. Mem. Friends of Art, Nelson-Atkins Mus. Art, Kansas City, 1988—, Smithsonian Inst., Washington, 1985—, Nat. Trust for Historic Preservation, Washington, 1988—, Libr. of Congress Assocs., The Federalist Soc., Nat. Audubon Soc. Mem. ABA, Assn. Trial Lawyers Am., Kansas City Metro Bar Assn., Sports Car Club Am., Am. Mus. Nat. History, Porsche Club Am., Lake Ozarks Yacht Assn., Boat Owners Assn. U.S., Ancient Order of Hibernians, Delta Theta Phi, Tau Kappa Epsilon. Roman Catholic. Avocations: vintage sportscars, boating. Home: 5840 McGee St Kansas City MO 64113-2132 Office: Peters Moore & Jones LLC 916 Traders on Grand Bldg 1125 Grand Ave Kansas City MO 64106 E-mail: moore@pmj-law.com.

MOORE, STEVEN WOODROW, lawyer; b. Norfolk, Va., Sept. 7, 1967; s. Woodrow Wilson and Helena (Sorzano) M.; m. Erin Torda, May 22, 1993; children: Madeline Lois, Robert Lewis. BA in English, Old Dominion U., 1989; JD, U. Denver, 1993. Bar: Colo. 1993, Calif. 1997, U.S. Dist. Ct. Colo. 1993, U.S. Ct. Appeals (10th cir.) 1993. Assoc. atty. Nathan Davidovich and Assocs., Denver, 1993-95; ptnr. Lindquist-Kleissler, Cooper and Moore, LLC, 1995-98; sr. asst. city atty. Denver City Atty.'s Office, 1998—2001, asst. city. atty.-specialist, 2001—. Mem. ABA, Colo. Bar Assn., Denver Bar Assn., State Bar Calif., Faculty Fed. Advocates. Avocations: skiing, golf, hiking. Home: 2765 S Gaylord St Denver CO 80210-6073 Office: Denver City Attys Office 1437 Bannock St Rm 353 Denver CO 80202 E-mail: pacificmarlin@msn.com.

MOORE, TERESA MARGARET, artist; b. St. Paul, Aug. 26, 1963; d. Leo J. and Dorothy Moore. AA in Theater, Fine Arts, Scottsdale Coll., 1985. Set designer Exit Theatre, San Francisco, 1998. One-woman shows include Visual Arts Ctr., Phoenix, 1989, Trojanowska Gallery, San Francisco, 1992, 93, 94, Greenwood Gallery, Seattle, 1995, Bastoky Gallery, Seattle, 1996, Sixteen, N.Y.C., 1997, Old Fed. Res. Bank, San Francisco Enrico's, 1998, L'espace Richelieu, Paris, 1999; group exhibits include Galleria Paolucci, Rome, 1988, Galleria Bianco Oro, Rome, 1988, Fina Cocina, Phoenix, 1989, 90, Galaxy Gallery, Miami Beach, Fla., 1989, 93, 94, Ariz. Mus. for Youth, Mesa, 1989, 90, Phoenix Union Gallery, 1990, Gallery Genesis, Chgo., 1990, Bay Area Discovery Mus., Sausalito, Calif., 1994, Nat. Mus. on Women in the Arts Libr. and Archives, Washington, 1996—, Objects and Images Gallery, Bronxville, N.Y., 1998, Phoenix Hotel, San Francisco, 1998, Liss Gallery, Toronto, Can., 1998. Avocations: theatre, bat watching and conservation, collecting pulp paperback books.

MOORE, TERRY WAYNE, high technology venture management consultant; b. North Kingston, R.I., Feb. 26, 1957; s. Robert Wendell and Marilyn (Rose) M. BS in Engring., U. Fla., 1981; MBA, U. San Diego, 1993; postgrad., U. Calif., San Diego, 1994. Sr. materials engr. U.S. Dept. Def., Alameda, Calif., 1981-85, program mgr., 1985-87; staff engr., scientist Gen. Atomics, La Jolla, 1987-89, project mgr., 1989-92, mktg. program mgr., 1992-93; owner Moore Consulting Co., San Diego, 1994—. Entrepreneur Venture Mgmt., Moore Cons. Co., San Diego, 1990—; new high tech. ventures cons. for emerging growth and start up cos., 1991—; mem. dirs. database com. Internat. Forum Corp. Dirs., 1995—, program com., 1995—, membership com., 1996—, improving dir. effectiveness cert.; mem. San Diego Regional Tech. Alliance, Calif. State Office Strategic Tech. Devel. Trade and Commerce; mem. Team Dennis Conner's Am.'s Cup Syndicate, 1995, crew mem. Stars and Stripes, winner Pacific Class Nat. Championships, 1995. Judge San Diego Sci. Fair, 1989—; rep. Neighborhood Watch, La Costa, Calif., 1989—; vol. fund raiser Am. Cancer Soc., Epilepsy Soc., United Way, U. Calif. San Diego Cancer Ctr. Found. Mem. Am. Soc. for Materials Internat. (sec.-treas. 1990-92, vice chmn. 1993-94, chmn. 1994-95, past chmn. 1995-96, bd. dirs. 1989—, nat. chpt ops. com., chmn. computer subcom. 1991—, chmn. 1994-95), Project Mgmt. Inst. (sec. 1993-94, treas. 1994-95, bd. dirs. 1993—), Nat. Bd. Cert. Project Mgmt. Profl. (cert.), San Diego Engring. Soc. (program chmn. bd. dirs. 1995-96), Soc. Advancement of Material and Process Engring., San Diego Venture Mgmt. Group, MIT Enterprise Forum (mem. panel selection com.), Found. for Enterprise Devel., San Diego Yacht Club. Republican. Presbyterian. Avocations: financial investments, ocean yacht racing, reading, triathlons, private pilot. Home and Office: 905 Orchid Way Carlsbad CA 92009-4830

MOORE, THELMA WYATT, judge; b. Amarillo, Tex., July 6, 1945; d. James Odis and Annie LaVernia (Lott) Wyatt; m. Luke C. Moore (dec. Nov. 1994); children: Khari Cummings, Ayanna Cummings. BA, UCLA, 1965; JD, Emory U., 1971. Bar: Ga. 1971. Atty. Ward and Wyatt, Atlanta, 1974-77; judge Mcpl. Ct., 1977-80, City Ct., Atlanta, 1980-85, State Ct., Fulton County, 1985-90; judge, chief judge Superior Ct., 1990—92. Mem. exec. com. Nat. Jud. Coun., 1987—, chmn., 1986-87; spkr. in field. Assoc. editor Jour. Pub. Law, 1969-71; contbr. articles to profl. jours. Former chair adminstrv. bd. Cascade United Meth. Ch.; bd. trustees Emory U.; bd. dirs. Joint Ctr. for Polit. and Econ. Studies. Recipient WSB TV Living Legend award, 1991, 92, Disting. Alumni award Emory U., 1986, Essence award, 1982, Wiley Branton award NBA, 1999, Rehnquist award for Jud. Excellence, 2001, numerous others; John Hay Whitney fellow; Nat. Urban League fellow; Emory Law scholar; State of Ill. fellow. Mem. ABA, Nat. Bar Assn., Ga State Bar Assn., Atlanta Bar Assn., Gate City Bar Assn. (historian 1990-93), World Peace Through Law Ctr., Am. Judges Assn., Ga. Assn. Black Women Attys., Nat. Assn. Women Judges, Mo-So Lit. Circle, The Links, Inc., Order of Coif, Bryan Soc., Alpha Kappa Alpha, Phi Delta Phi. Office: 185 Central Ave SW Ste T4905 Atlanta GA 30303-3691

MOORE, THOMAS JOSEPH, financial company executive; b. Kalamazoo, Jan. 5, 1943; s. John Joseph and Bernita (Ryan) M.; m. Laura Leigh Johnson, Aug. 1, 1975; children: Ryan Michael, Janelle Marie, Darcie Kathleen. BBA, Western Mich. U., 1965; MBA, So. Meth. U., 1990. Various sales and mktg. positions IBM Corp., Southfield, Mich., 1968-79; exec. v.p., owner Carsonville (Mich.) Metal Products Corp., 1976-79; assoc. prof. Oakland Coll., Farmington Hills, Mich., 1977-78; group mgr. industry mktg. Recognition Equipment Inc., Dallas, 1979-81; mgmt. cons. APC Skills div. Alexander Proudfoot Co., Palm Beach, Fla., 1982-83; pres., chief exec. officer Lumentech of Am., Inc., Dallas, 1983-85; v.p., prin. Capital Alliance Corp., 1985-2001; ptnr. EquiCap Ptnrs., LLC, 2001—. Chmn., CEO, Laura Leigh Stores, Inc., Plano, Tex., 1993—; vis. lectr. Baylor U., Waco, Tex., 1986-89, sponsor, CEO roundtable, 1989-93; bd. dirs. MJ Designs, Inc., Coppell, Tex., 1997-98. Pres. Bent Tree Homeowners Assn., Dallas, 1981-83; co-chair Jesuit Coll. Prep. Sch. Challenge Dr., 1992-95; chair car raffle Ursuline Acad. of Dallas, chmn. maj. donor campaign, 1994-95, co-chair bridge the gap campaign, 1995-96, chair underwriting, 1996. Mem. M&A Internat., So. Meth. U. Exec. MBA Alumni Assn. (bd. dirs. 1990-92). Republican. Roman Catholic. Avocations: running, reading, racquetball. Home: 4402 Cobblers Ln Dallas TX 75287-6732 Office: EquiCap Ptnrs LLC Park Central III Ste 514 12700 Park Central Dr Dallas TX 75251 E-mail: tjmpersonal@hotmail.com., tmoore@equicappartners.com.

MOORE, THOMAS CARROL, botanist, retired educator; b. Sanger, Tex., Sept. 22, 1936; s. Thomas M. and Willie Mae M.; m. Arvida Inmon DePriest, Sept. 1, 1956; children— Cynthia, Linda, Alan. BA in Biology, U. N. Tex., Denton, 1956; MA in Botany, U. Colo., 1958, PhD (Outstanding Grad. Student in Biology award 1960, USPHS predoctoral fellow 1960-61), 1961. Instr. biology, then part-time instr. U. Colo., 1958-60; asst. prof. Ariz. State Coll., Flagstaff, 1961-63; mem. faculty Oreg. State U., Corvallis, 1963-93, prof. botany, 1971-93, prof. emeritus, 1993—, chmn. dept. botany and plant pathology, 1973-86, asst. to v.p. for rsch. and grad. studies, 1972-73. Vis. prof. Colo. State Coll., 1963. Mem. editorial bd. Plant Physiology, 1981-86; editor in chief Jour. Plant Growth Regulation, 1982-99; contbr. articles to profl. jours. Recipient Mosser award outstanding undergrad. teaching Oreg. State U., 1966 Mem.: Internat. Plant Growth Substances Assn., Am. Soc. Plant Physiologists. Democrat. Home: 560 NW Merrie Dr Corvallis OR 97330-6524

MOORE, THOMAS DAVID, academic administrator; b. Rochester, N.Y., July 26, 1937; s. Robert Franklin and Hilda (Kennedy) M.; m. Virginia Muller, June 13, 1959; children: Kathleen Mary, Michael David, Thomas David. BSS, St. John Fisher Coll., 1959; MS, SUNY, Brockport, 1962; EdD, Rutgers U., 1966. Tchr. Rochester City Schs., 1959-62; grad. asst. Rutgers U., New Brunswick, N.J., 1963-65; from asst. to full prof. Kent (Ohio) State U., 1965-93, asst. v.p. acad. affairs, 1976-83, v.p. faculty affairs and personnel, 1984-86, provost, v.p. acad. and student affairs, 1987-91, prof. emeritus ednl. philosophy, 1991—; provost, v.p. acad. affairs Ctrl. Washington U., 1993-97, prof. edn. and philosophy, 1997—. Roman Catholic. Avocations: sports, film, public affairs, music.

MOORE, THOMAS EDWIN, biology educator, museum director; b. Champaign, Ill. s. Gerald E. and Velma (Lewis) M.; m. E. Eleanor Sifferd, Feb. 4, 1951; children: Deborah S., Melinda S. BS, U. Ill., 1951, MS, 1952, PhD, 1956. Tech. asst. Ill. Natural History Survey, Urbana, 1950-56; instr. zoology U. Mich., Ann Arbor, 1956-59, asst. prof. zoology, 1959-63, assoc. prof. zoology, 1963-66, prof. biology, 1966—, curator insects, 1956—, dir. exhibit mus., 1988-93. Vis. prof. Orgn. for Tropical Studies, San Jose, Costa Rica, 1970, 72; bd. dirs. Orgn. Tropical Studies, San Jose, 1968-79; mem. steering com. tropical biome U.S. Internat. Biol. Program, 1969-72; mem. conf. planning com. Nat. Inst. for Environment, 1991-92; mem. steering com. Univ. Colloquium on Environ. Rsch. and Edn., 1991-93, grievance com. U. Mich., 1997-98, faculty handbook com., 1997-98. Co-editor: Lectures on Science Education, 1991-1992, 1993; Cricket Behavior and Neurobiology, 1989; author movie 17-Year Cicadas, 1975, tv, 1998. County rep. Huron River Watershed Coun., Ann Arbor, 1987-95; mem. Mich. H.S. Accreditation Adv. Com., Ann Arbor, 1988-92; mem. U. Mich. Senate Adv. Com. on Univ. Affairs, 1993-96, vice chair, 1995-96; bd. mem. U. Mich. Acad. Freedom Lecture Fund, 1995—, treas., 1995-98; cons. NSF Visual Tech. in Environ. Curricula, 1994-97. Rsch. grantee NSF, 1963-66, 66-69, 96-97, rsch. equipment grantee, 1984-86, rsch. grantee Def. Advanced Rsch. Project Agy./Office of Naval Rsch. 1998—. Fellow AAAS, AAUP (pres. U. Mich. chpt. 1996—, exec. bd. Mich. conf. 1996-98), Royal Entomol. Soc. London, Linnaen Soc. London; mem. Assn. Tropical Biology (pres. 1973-75), Sigma Xi (pres. U. Mich. chpt. 1994-96, coun. 1993-98). Home: 4243 N Delhi Rd Ann Arbor MI 48103-9485 Office: Mus of Zoology U Mich Ann Arbor MI 48109-1079 E-mail: temoore@umich.edu.

MOORE, THOMAS GALE, economist, educator; b. Washington, Nov. 6, 1930; s. Charles Godwin and Beatrice (McLean) M.; m. Cassandra Chrones, Dec. 28, 1958; children: Charles G., Antonia L. BA, Geroge Washington U., 1957; MA, U. Chgo., 1959, PhD, 1961. Fgn. research analyst Chase Manhattan Bank, N.Y.C., 1960-61; asst. prof. econs. Carnegie Inst. Tech., 1961-65; assoc. prof., then prof. econs. Mich. State U., East Lansing, 1965-74; sr. staff economist Council Econ. Advisers, 1968-70; hon. research fellow Univ. Coll., London, 1973-74; adj. scholar Am. Enterprise Inst., 1971—, CATO Inst., 1982—; sr. fellow Hoover Inst. on War, Revolution and Peace-Stanford U., 1974—, dir. domestic studies program, 1974-85; mem. Council Econ. Advisers, Washington, 1985-89. Mem. Nat. Critical Materials Council, 1985-89; mem. econ. adv. bd. Dept. Commerce, 1971-73; mem. adv. com. RANN, 1975-77, NSF, 1975-77; cons. Dept. Transp., 1973-74, 81-83; mem. adv. panel Synthetic Fuels Corp., 1982; mem. adv. bd. Reason Found., 1982—; dir. Stanford Savs. & Loan, 1979-82, chmn., 1982. Author: The Economics of American Theater, 1968, Freight Transportation Regulation, 1972, Trucking Regulation: Lessons from Europe, 1976, Uranium Enrichment and Public Policy, 1978; co-author: Public Claims on U.S. Output, 1973; contbr. articles to profl. jours. Served with USN, 1951-55, Korea. Fellow

Earhart Found., 1958-59; fellow Walgreen Found., 1959-60, Hoover Instn., 1973-74 Mem. Am. Econ. Assn., Mont. Pelerin Soc., Chevy Chase Club. Home: 3766 La Donna Ave Palo Alto CA 94306-3150 Office: Stanford U Hoover Instn Stanford CA 94305

MOORE, THOMAS J. media coordinator; b. Waukon, Iowa, Mar. 7, 1958; s. James Patrick and Virginia May M.; m. Pamela Sue Hall, May 28, 1988; children: Matthew, Sarah and Suzanne. BA in journalism, BA in broadcasting and film, Univ. Iowa, Iowa City, IA, 1980, MA in journalism, 1984. Grad. asst. Univ. Iowa News, Iowa City, 1980-84; journalist KCRG-TV, Cedar Rapids, 1980-89; media coord. Univ. Iowa Hosps. and Clins., Iowa City, 1989—. Media trainer, Wixted, Popa, Nora & Assoc., Des Moines, IA, 1997—, narrator, Audio Internatl., North Liberty, IA, 1998—. Prodr., Video Health Reports (awd. IABC, 1992) 1989—. Soccer coach Iowa City Kickers, Iowa City, 1998—; basketball coach North Dodge Athletic Club, 1999—; Lector & Chldrns Ch. Leader St. Mary's , 1989—. Mem., Alliance for Health Care Mktg., 1998—. Independent. Catholic. Avocations: basketball, camping, reading, fitness, weight training. Office: Univ of Iowa Health Care 200 Hawkins Dr Rm 8798 Iowa City IA 52242-1009 E-mail: thomas-moore@uiowa.edu.

MOORE, THOMAS KAIL, district court judge; b. Idaho Falls, Idaho, Jan. 15, 1938; s. Burton L. and Clara E. (Kail) Moore; m. Judith Diane Gilman, July 30, 1966; children: David T., Jonathan G. AB in Phys. Scis., Harvard U., 1961; JD, Georgetown U., 1967. Bar: D.C., V.I., Va. Law clk. to Hon. John A. Danaher U.S. Ct. Appeals (D.C. Cir.), 1967-68; staff atty. Office Gen. Coun., Office Sec. Dept. Transp., Washington, 1968-69; assoc. Stanford, Reed & Gelenian, 1969-70; asst. U.S. Atty. U.S. Attys. Office, 1970-71, U.S. Attys. Office (ea. dist.), Va., 1971-76, prin. asst. Alexandria office, 1974-76; asst. U.S. Atty. U.S. Attys. Office (V.I. dist.), 1976-78; pvt. practice St. Thomas, V.I., 1978-81; shareholder Hoffman & Moore, P.C., 1981-87; ptnr. Grunert, Stout, Moore & Bruch, 1987-92; dist. judge U.S. Dist. Ct. (V.I. dist.), 1992—. Editor-in-chief Georgetown Law Journal, 1966-67. Scoutmaster Antilles Sch. Troop; trustee V.I. Montessori Sch. Capt. USAF, 1961-64, USAFR. Mem.: ABA, Va. Bar Assn., V.I. Bar Assn. (judicial), St. Thomas Yacht Club. Avocations: tennis, swimming, sailing. Office: Dist Ct of VI 5500 Veterans Dr Ste 310 Saint Thomas VI 00802-6424

MOORE, THOMAS LLOYD, librarian; b. Springfield, Ill., Oct. 4, 1942; s. Edward Joseph and Dorothy A. (Menezes) M.; m. Ann Mary Walsh, Aug. 29, 1971; children: Sean Christopher, Martin Thomas, Kathleen Adele. AA, Springfield Coll., 1963; BA, Cardinal Glennon Coll., St. Louis, 1968; MA in Library Sci., Rosary Coll., 1973. Tchr. Little Flower Grade Sch., Springfield, 1963-66; head of adult services Elk Grove Village (Ill.) Pub. Library, 1973-74; dir. Northlake (Ill.) Pub. Library Dist., 1974-75, Danville (Ill.) Pub. Library, 1975-78; adminstrv. librarian Palatine (Ill.) Pub. Library Dist., 1978-81; dir. Wake County Dept. of the Pub. Library, Raleigh, N.C., 1981—; trainer Roger Schwarz & Assocs., Chapel Hill, 1997—. Bd. dirs. Commit to a Healthier Region, 1991-93, Planned Parenthood of the Capital & Coast, 1993-97, sec., 1994; bd. dirs. Pirates Cove Homeowners Assn., 1992-97, v.p., 1993-94, pres., 1995-96; mem. Libr. Power Adv. Com., 1993-95, Facilitatators Orgnl. Devel. Group, 1995—, ASSIST Wake to Health Coalition, 1992-94. Mem. ALA, N.C. Library Assn. Democrat. Roman Catholic. Office: Wake County Pub Libr 4020 Carya Dr Raleigh NC 27610-2913

MOORE, THOMAS PAUL, retired broadcast executive; b. Danville, Ill., Feb. 29, 1928; s. Lester Rufus and Mabel Ellen (Jackson) M.; m. Jean LaVonne Sather, Aug. 31, 1952; children: Randyl Ellen, Patricia Kay, Gregory Sather. BA, North Cen. Coll., Naperville, Ill., 1952; postgrad., Denver U., 1952-53. Newscaster Sta. KFEL-AM-FM-TV, Denver, 1952-54; sales rep. Sta. KGMC, Englewood, Colo., 1954-56; sales mgr. Sta. KDEN-AM-FM, Denver, 1956-62; pres. Stas. WBCO, WQEL, Bucyrus, Ohio, 1962-98; ret., 1998. Hon. dir. First Fed. Cmty. Bank, 2001—. Lay leader, mem. program council Ohio Sandusky Conf., United Methodist Ch., 1966-69 (pres. gen. laity bd. and laymen's found. 1968-72); mem. Gen Council on Ministries, 1980-84, N.W. Ohio Water Devel. Adv. Com., 1967-69, Sandusky River Basin Water Pollution Study Com., 1968-69; v.p., bd. mgrs. EUB Men, Evang. United Brethren Ch., 1958-68; pres. Rocky Mountain Conf., 1957-61; mem. gen. bd. Nat. Council Christian Chs. Am., 1968-72; charter pres. Bucyrus Bratwurst Festival, Inc., 1968; adv. bd. Bucyrus Salvation Army, 1964-68; mem. planning com. East Ohio Conf., 1972-76 (chmn. commn. on minimum salaries, 1968-72, lay leader, 1972-76); vice chmn. council ministries, mem. episcopal com., 1972-76, head. del. to gen. conf., Portland, Oreg., 1976, Balt., 1984; head del. to Jurisdictional Conf., Sioux Falls, 1976, Duluth, Minn., 1984; pres. United Meth. Communications, 1972-76, mem. gen. council fin. and adminstrn., 1976-80; mem. communications comm. Nat. Council Chs., 1972-76; mem. communications con. Ohio Council Chs.; mem. Episc. com., chmn. New Vision Task Group, both East Ohio Conf., North Cen. Jurisdiction, United Meth. Ch.; mem. exec. com. Council on Ministries, 1980-86; mem. World Meth. Council, 1986-91, World Meth. Conf., 1996; trustee United Theol. Sem., 1972-80; trustee Ohio Northern U., 1986—, mem. exec. com., 1991—, chair student affairs com., 1991-95, chair, 1995—; mem. exec. com. East Ohio del. to United Meth. Gen. Conf. and Jurisdictional Conf., 1987-91; sec. Community Improvement Corp., Bucyrus, 1989-91; mem. Overall Econ. Devel. Com. of Crawford County, 1992-96; chmn. Crawford County Traffic Safety Council, 1979-89, 96-98; pres. Crawford County Econ. Devel. Adv. Coun., 1992-96; mem., sec. Crawford County Devel. Bd., Inc., 1997-2000; mem. exec. com. of del. to 1988 Gen. Conf. United Meth. Ch., St. Louis; bd. dirs. Bucyrus Community Hosp., 1992, mem. fin. com., 1993-96, chair nominating com., 1993-96, campaign dir., chair fundraising com., 1993-96, v.p. bd. dirs., 1994-96; chmn. N. Ctrl. Ohio Health Sys., 1996-98; mem. Crawford County Rep. Ctrl. Com., 1998-2001; mem. City of Bucyrus Bd. of Zoning Appeals, 1998-2001; pres. Crawford County Devel. Bd., 20002001; chmn. City of Bodyrus Bd. Zoning Appeals, 2000—. Served with USN, 1946-48. Named a Civic Leader of Am., 1968. Mem. Nat. Assn. Broadcasters (legis. liaison 1984-91, mem. small market radio com.), Ohio Assn. Broadcasters (pres. 1982-85), North Ctrl. Ohio Broadcasters Assn. (pres. 1983-84, 96-98, v.p. 1985-96), Bucyrus Area C. of C. (chmn. airport study com. 1967-68, bd. dirs. 1964-67, pres. 1989-91), Rotary (pres. Bucyrus chpt. 1992-93). E-mail: tommoore@cybrtown.com., ccdbinc@cybrtown.com.

MOORE, THOMAS RONALD (LORD BRIDESTOWE), lawyer; b. Duluth, Minn., Mar. 27, 1932; s. Ralph Henry and Estelle Marguerite (Hero) M.; m. Margaret C. King, Sept. 10, 1955; children: Willard S., Clarissa, Charles R.H. BA magna cum laude, Yale U., 1954; JD, Harvard U., 1957. Bar: N.Y. 1958, U.S. Supreme Ct. 1965. Instr. Harvard Law Sch., 1956-57; with Dewey Ballantine, N.Y.C.; ptnr. Breed, Abbott & Morgan, Finley Kumble & Wagner, N.Y.C., Law Offices of Thomas R. Moore, N.Y.C. Lectr. on law Cornell Law Sch., NYU, Practising Law Inst., N.Y.C., Las Vegas, New Orleans; lectr. Oxford, N.Y.C., San Antonio, Tampa, LA, Moscow, Charlottesville, Washington, Kansas City. Author: Plantagenet Descent, 31 Generations from William the Conqueror to Today, 1995; co-author: Estate Planning and the Close Corporation; editor-in-chief: Gastronome, bd. editors: The Tax Lawyer; contbr. articles to profl. jours.; often in popular press and TV commentaries, including 12 media interviews Jan. 24, 2002. Bd. dirs. exec. com. Citymeals on Wheels; pres. bd. dirs. Nat. Soc. to Prevent Blindness, 1973-81, chmn., 1981-83, now hon. pres.; sec.-treas., trustee A.D. Henderson Found., Del.; trustee, Fla.; bd. dirs. Phoenix Theatre Inc., Inst. Aegean Prehistory, Found. Future of Man, Am. and Internat. Friends of Victoria and Albert Mus., London; conservator N.Y. Pub. Libr.; trustee Found. for Renaissance of St. Petersburg (Russia), Malcolm Wiener Found., Lawrence W. Levine Found.; bd. dirs. Gov.'s Commn. on Scholastic Achievement, 2002--; constl. advisor to Pres. George Bush; advisor to King Michael of Romania. Recipient Coat of Arms and created Knight of St. John, Queen Elizabeth II, Order of Crown of Charlemagne, Order of Plantagenet, Order of Barons of Magna Charta, Order of Descendants Knights of the Garter, Thomas R. Moore Disting. Pub. Servant award, Nat. Soc. to Prevent Blindness; scholar of House, Class Marshall, Yale. Mem.: St. Andrews Soc., St. George Soc., Confrerie de la Chaine des Rotisseurs (nat. pres., dir., exec. com. world coun. Paris), Robert Burns Soc., Nat. Wine Coalition (bd. dirs. 1989—), Chevalier du Tastevin, The Pilgrims, Church Club, Univ. Club, Delta Sigma Rho. Republican. Presbyterian. Office: 730 5th Ave Ste 900 New York NY 10019-4105

MOORE, THURSTON ROACH, lawyer; b. Memphis, Dec. 10, 1946; s. Richard Charlton Moore and Halcyon Hall (Roach) Lynn; m. Corell Luckhardt Halsey, Sept. 26, 1998. BA with distinction, U. Va., 1968, JD, 1974. Bar: Va. 1974. Rsch. analyst Scudder, Stevens & Clark, N.Y.C., 1968—71; ptnr. Hunton & Williams, Richmond, Va., 1974—. Bd. dirs. Met. Advantage Corp., Richmond. Trustee Va. Aerospace Bus. Roundtable, Hampton, 1989—, Va. Ea. Shore Sustainable Devel. Corp., 1995—2000; bd. dirs. Mary Morton Parsons Found., Charlottesville, The Nature Conservancy, Charlottesville, chmn. Va. chpt. Mem.: ABA (bus. law sect., chmn. ptnrs. com. 1992—96, mem. fed. regulation security com., bus. law coun.), Va. State Bar, Va. Bar Assn. Office: Hunton & Williams Riverfront Plz E Tower 951 E Byrd St Richmond VA 23219-4074

MOORE, TIMOTHY JOEL, health and fitness consultant; b. Washington, Feb. 2, 1959; s. Durrell Daniel and Betty Jane (Middlesworth) M. BA, U. Md., 1981, MA, 1984, PhD, 1994. Track/strength coach U. Md., College Park, 1982-88; program dir. Inst. Human Performance, Langley Park, Md., 1984-85; pres. Exercise Sci., Inc., Greenbelt, Md., 1985-95; dir. Prince George's C.C., Largo, Md., 1989-93, Nat. Hosp. Orthopaedics and Rehab., Landover, 1993-95; fitness editor Shape & Living Fit Mag., Woodland Hills, Calif., 1996-98; pvt. cons., 1998—. Presenter in field; TV and internet contbr. Contbr. articles to profl. publs., books. Mem. Am. Coun. Exercise (cert.), Nat. Commn. Health Edn., Am. Coll. Sports Medicine, Nat. Strength and Conditioning Assn., Omicron Delta Kappa. Avocations: art, music. Home: 913 Euclid St Apt 6 Santa Monica CA 90403-3090

MOORE, TODD ALLEN, poet; b. Freeport, Ill., Nov. 14, 1937; s. John Earl and Helen Marie (Babcock) M.; m. Barbara Diane Mayfield, Dec. 21, 1963. BS in Edn., No. Ill. U., 1962, MA in L.S., 1968. Cert. tchr. English secondary level, Ill. English tchr. Forreston (Ill.) Schs., 1962-63, Freeport (Ill.) Schs., 1963-68; Libr. No. Ill. U., DeKalb, 1968-70; English tchr. Belvidere (Ill.) Schs., 1970-93. Author: Working on my Duende, 1999, The Corpse Is Dreaming, 2000; contbr. poetry to numerous publs. and anthologies, including Poets on Photography, 1981, Prairie Smoke, 1990, Gildzen at 50: A Celebration, 1990, A New Geography of Poets, 1992, A Gathering of Poets, 1992, The Outlaw Bible of American Poetry, 1999; also critical studies. Mem. Great Plains Writers Assn. Home: 3216 San Pedro Dr NE Albuquerque NM 87110-2634 E-mail: moorebt@spinn.net.

MOORE, VERNA, county official; b. Belleville, Ill., June 26, 1926; d. Walter William and Stella Blomenkamp; m. Jay H. Moore, Apr. 5, 1952 (wid.); 1 child, Gail Moore Elmore. High sch. dipl., H.S., Belleville. Classified advt. mgr., sales rep. The Item, Sumter, S.C., 1966-91; dep. coroner Sumter County, 1975-92, coroner, 1993—. Bd. mem. S.C. Child Fatality, Columbia, S.C. Elected Ofcls., Columbia. Active S.C. Dem. Party, Sumter, 1966—. Avocations: bowling, golfing. Home: 1814 W Oakland Ave Sumter SC 29150-5539 Office: Courthouse 141 N Main St Sumter SC 29150-4965

MOORE, VERNON JOHN, JR. pediatrician, lawyer, medical consultant; b. Chgo., Mar. 18, 1942; s. Vernon John Moore; m. Rutheva deVera Dizon, Feb. 27, 1979; children: Christopher, Joseph. BS, Loyola U., Chgo., 1964, JD, 1986; MD, U. Ill.-Chgo., 1968. Bar: Ill. 1986, U.S. Dist. Ct. (no. dist.) Ill. 1986. Intern St. Joseph Health Care Ctrs. and Hosp., Chgo., 1968-69, resident in pediats., 1971-74, chief resident, 1972-74, mem. med. staff, 1974-76, 78-86; pvt. practice, 1974-76, 97—; mem. med. staff Naval Hosp. Great Lakes, 1976-78; med. officer Chgo. Mil. Entrance Processing Sta., 1996—2002, Midwest Ctr. for Youth and Families, Kouts, Ind., 1997—; mem. med. staff Ill. Masonic Med. Ctr., Chgo., 1997—, Swedish Covenant Hosp., Chgo., 1998—, Luth. Gen. Hosp., Park Ridge, 1998—, Alexian Bros. Med. Ctr., Elk Grove Village, 2000—. Asst. dir. pediat. edn. St. Joseph Health Care Ctrs. and Hosp., 1974-76, co-dir., 1978-86, acting chmn. dept. pediats., 1985-86; clin. assoc. prof. pediat. Loyola U., Maywood, Ill., 1981-87; med. cons. CNA Ins. Cos., Chgo., 1987-94; pediatric med. cons. Hartgrove Hosp., Chgo., 1996—, Alexian Bros. Behavioral Health Hosp., Hoffman Estates, Ill., 1999-2001. Part-time staff Chgo. office Sen. Everett M. Dirksen, 1961-64. With USN, 1969-71, 76-78; capt. USNR, to 2002. Fellow Am. Acad. Pediat.; mem. Ill. Bar Assn. (chmn. standing com. on interprofl. coop. 1991-92, mem. health law sect. coun. 1997-98), U. Ill. Alumni Assn. (bd. dirs. 1983-89), Alumni Assn. Coll. Medicine U. Ill. (alumni councillor 1989-99), U. Ill. Pres. Coun. Republican. Roman Catholic. Home: 146 Park Ave River Forest IL 60305-2040 Office: 5758 N California Ave Chicago IL 60659-4726

MOORE, VERNON LEE, agricultural consultant, retired food products company executive; b. Creston, Iowa, Mar. 29, 1928; s. Newton and Eulalia Pearl (Lewis) M.; m. Lorene Shirley Burns, Jan. 29, 1949; children: Dianne, Nancy, Jack. BS in Agr., Iowa State U., 1951. Instr. vocat. agrl. Gowrie (Iowa) Sch. Dist., 1951-55; with Land O'Lakes, Inc., Mpls., 1955-88, sr. v.p., 1988, ret., 1988; pvt. practice agrl. cons., 1989—. Bd. dirs. exec. com. Agrl. Coop. Devel. Internat., Washington, 1972-89, Am. Inst. Coop., Washington, 1975-88, Minn. 4-H Found., Washington, 1980-91; bd. dirs. Vols. in OVerseas Coop. Devel., Washington, 1980-88, The Coop. Found., St. Paul, 1978-88; commr. Civil Svc. Commn., Columbia Hts., Minn., 1974-98; mem. U. Minn. Adv. Com., St. Paul, 1984-91; various leadership positions Fridley United Meth. Ch., Minn., 1971—; dir. adminstrn. Russian Farm Cmty., 1993—. Recipient Internat. Coop. award Coop. Coordinating Group, 1987. Mem.: Rotary, Masons, Shriners. Avocations: photography, woodworking, gardening.

MOORE, VIRGINIA BRADLEY, librarian; b. Laurens, S.C., May 13, 1932; d. Robert Otis Brown and Queen Esther (Smith) Bradley; m. David Lee Moore, Dec. 27, 1957 (div. 1973). BS, Winston-Salem State U., 1954; MLS, U. Md., 1970. Cert. in libr. sci. edn. Tchr. John R. Hawkins H.S., Warrenton, N.C., 1954-55, Happy Plains H.S., Taylorsville, 1955-58, Young and Carver elem. schs., Washington, 1958-65; libr. Davis and Minor elem. schs., 1965-72, Ballou Sr. H.S., Kramer Jr. H.S., Washington, 1972-75, 78-80, Anacostia Sr. H.S., Washington, 1975-77, 80-95; libr. I, adult svcs. Greenbelt (Md.) Br. Libr., 1997—. Dir. ch. libr. workshops Asbury United Meth. Ch., Washington, 1972—74, 1976; speaker, presenter Ch. and Synagogue Libr. Assn., 1975, 80, 83, speaker spring workshop, 99, presenter, 2000; mem. serials com. Prince George's County Meml. Libr. Sys., 2000—; chair-competency based curriculum D.C. pub. schs., 1978—93; chair local arrangements launching Nat. Sch. Libr. Media Month U.S. Capitol, 1985; mem. 1st libr. and info. sci. del. to People's Republic China, 1985; mem. faculty 1st established pub. svc. acad. in nation Anacostia Sr. H.S., 1990—95; presenter in field. Author: (bibliography) The Negro in American History, 1619-1968, 1968; (with Helen E. Williams) Books By African-American Authors and Illustrators for Children and Young Adults, 1991; TV script for vacation reading program, 1971, sound/slide presentation D.C. Church Librs.' Bicentennial Celebration, 1976; video script and tchr.'s guide for Nat. Libr. Week Balloon Launch Day, 1983; bibliography Black Literature/Materials, 1987; contbr. articles to profl. jours. Co-chmn. nat. libr. involvement com. Martin Luther King, Jr. Fed. Holiday Commn., 1990—99, chmn., 1996—99; trustee Humanitarian Merritt Fund, 2002—; libr. Mt. Carmel Bapt. Ch., Washington, 1984, chair ch. libr. com., 2000—, member ad hoc com. for churchwide programs, 2001—, libr. Sunday Sch. Mother's Day coord., 1990—94, jr. ch. pianist, 1994—97, Sunday Sch. adult dept. pianist, 1984—, co-chmn. African-Am. History Mo. commn., 1996—, chmn. publicity com., 1996—99, mem. com. renovation of Rev. Arthur H. Pace Libr. Multipurpose Rm., 1999—, vice-chair publicity liaison com., 1999—, soprano sanctuary choir, 1995—, soprano soloist women's day and tribute commemoration, 1998, music com., 1998—; chmn. Am. Libr. Assn. Social Responsibilities Roundtable Martin Luther King Jr. Holiday Task Force, 1999—; rec. sec. Washington Pan-Hellenic Coun., 1975. Named outstanding educator, Mt. Carmel Bapt. Ch., 1984; recipient Outstanding Congl. Libr., Ch. and Synagogue Libr. Assn., 2001, certs. of award, D.C. Pub. Libr., 1980, D.C. Pub. Schs., 1983; fellow Grad. fellow, U. Md., 1969; scholar NDEA scholar, Central State Coll., Edmond, Okla., 1969, U. Ky., 1969, Ball State U., 1969. Mem. ALA (councilor-at-large 1983-91; 96—, Freedom to Read Honor Roll, 1999, chmn.), LWV (sec. Prince George's County, Md. 1997-99, v.p. 1999-2000, pres. 2000—), AARP, Internat. Assn. Sch. Librs., NEA (life), Am. Assn. Sch. Librs. (coms. 1973-83, 1987—), D.C. Assn. Sch. Librs. (pres. 1971-73, citation 1973, newsletter editor 1971-75, 83), Intellectual Freedom Com. (chmn. 1983—), Freedom to Read Found., Soc. Sch. Librs. Internat. (charter), Intellectual Freedom Roundtable (bd. dirs. exec. com. 1989-91), D.C. Libr. Assn., Md. Libr. Assn., Md. Ednl. Media Orgn., Internat. Platform Assn., S.E. Neighbors Club, Am. First Day Cover Soc., Nat. Coun. of Negro Women, Zeta Phi Beta (v.p. chpt. 1972-74), Delta Kappa Gamma (v.p. Alpha chpt. 1990-92, pres. 1992-95, Nu State D.C. membership chmn. 1991-92, rec. sec. 1994-95, v.p. 1995-97, liaison U.S. Forum 1995-97, 99—, spkr., state pres. 1997-99, steering com. speaker Soc. Internat. Legislative seminar 1998). Democrat. Home: 2100 Brooks Dr Apt 721 Forestville MD 20747-1016 Office: Prince Georges County Meml Libr Sys Greenbelt Br Libr 11 Crescent Rd Greenbelt MD 20770-1891

MOORE, VIRGINIA LEE SMITH, elementary education educator; b. Middletown, N.Y., May 13, 1943; d. James William and Anna Van Alst (Suydam) Smith; m. Thomas J. Moore, Oct. 16, 1965 (div. Apr. 1980); 1 child, Christian Thomas. AA in Liberal Arts, Orange County C.C., 1963; BA in Sociology magna cum laude, SUNY, Buffalo, 1965; MS in Edn., SUNY, New Paltz, 1980; MS in Edn. of Gifted, Coll. New Rochelle, 1990, cert. elem. edn., staff devel., 1994; cert. sch. adminstrn., 1994. Cert. elem. tchr., N.Y. Spl. edn. tchr. The Devereux Found., Glen Loch, Pa., 1965-66; elem. tchr. Harris Sch., Coatesville, 1967, Pine Bush (N.Y.) Cen. Schs., 1967-70, 78-00, substitute tchr., 1970-71; nursery sch. tchr. Olivet Meth. Nursery Sch., Coatesville, Pa., 1976-78; profl. devel. coord. Pine Bush Sch. Dist., 1998. Presenter ednl. workshops Pine Bus Sch. Dist., Haldane Sch. Dist., Cold Spring, NY, Eldred Sch. Dist., Marlboro, NY, Middletown (N.Y.) Tchr. Ctr., N.Y. State Tech. Edn. Assn., Brookhaven Nat. Lab., NY, 1994, Nevele Conference Ctr., Ellenville, NY, 1995, Rochester (N.Y.) Inst. Tech., 1996, SUNY, Oswego, 1996, Rensselaer Poly. Inst., Troy, NY, 1997, Marriot Conf. Ctr., Syracuse, NY, 1999, Sci. Tchrs. Assn. N.Y. State, Nevele Conf. Ctr., Ellenville, , 1995, Internat. Tech. Edn. Assn., Indpls., 1999; participant math., sci. and tech. on elem. level program NSF, 1997—2000. Contbr. articles to profl. jours., sci. and tech. articles to profl. publs. Pres. Redtown Residents' Assn., Middletown, 1988—. Recipient Dean's Acad. Excellence award Coll. of New Rochelle, 1991, Orange County Conservation Tchr. of Yr., 1993, N.Y.S. Conservation Tchr. of Yr., 1993, Presdl. award for excellence in math. and sci. tchg. N.Y. State, 1997; Partnership in Edn. grantee Area Fund Orange County, N.Y., 1991, Energy grantee Orange and Rockland Utilities, 1995, Tech. grantee Mid-Hudson Tchr. Ctr., 1997, 98, Energy grantee N.Y. State Electric and Gas, 1998. Mem. NSTA, Internat. Tech. Edn. Assn. (N.Y. State Elem. Sch. Tchr. Excellence award 1998-99), N.Y. State United Tchrs., Sci. Tchrs. Assn. N.Y. State (Outstanding Sci. Tchr. award 1992, Excellence in Sci. Tchg. award 1995), N.Y. State Tech. Edn. Assn. (Tech. grantee 1999), Phi Beta Kappa. Baptist. Avocations: piano, reading, local environmental issues, development of interactive science museum exhibits. Home: 1672 Route 211 E Middletown NY 10941-3718

MOORE, W. DARIN, minister; b. Mt. Vernon, N.Y., Mar. 25, 1960; s. William David Moore and Constance Louise Farrow; m. Devieta Chevette, June 9, 1984; children: W. Daron, Dana M., Dion B. Student, Livingstone Coll., 1980-84; BS, Purchase Coll., 1995; postgrad., Yale U., 2000—. Ordained elder AME Zion Ch. Pastor Clarksville AME Zion Ch., Monroe, N.C., 1983-84, Morning Star AME Zion Ch., Monroe, 1983-84, Mt. Olivet AME Zion Ch., Greensboro, N.C., 1984-89, Jones Tabernacle, Indpls., 1989-93, Greater Centennial AME Zion Ch., Mt. Vernon, N.Y., 1993—. Presiding elder Indpls. Dist. AME Zion Ch., 1991-93; nat. dir. young adult ministries AME Zion Ch., founding chmn. young adults in Christian ministries. Mem. Guilford County (N.C.) Commn. on Youth, 1988-89; pres. Ch. Fedn., Indpls., 1992-93; founder, chmn. Save Our Seed Ministries, Mt. Vernon, 1994—; trustee Mt. Vernon Bd. Edn., 1998—. Mem. NAACP, Nat. Alliance Black Sch. Educators, Nat. Sch. Bds. Assn., United Black Clergy of Westchester (v.p.), Interdenomination Mins. Assn., Alpha Phi Alpha. African Meth. Episcopal Zion. Avocations: travel, reading, golf. Office: Greater Centennial AME Zion Ch 100 W 4th St Mount Vernon NY 10550-4044

MOORE, W. DAVID, charitable foundation executive, minister; b. Andalusia, Ala., June 2, 1949; s. Manning Lamar and Jeanette Floyd M.; m. Rebecca H. Moore, Jan. 1, 1972; children: Holly, Joy. BA, Samford U., 1970; MDiv, Southwestern Bapt. Seminary, Ft. Worth, Tex., 1972; PhD, Baylor U., 1978. CFP. Pastor Deer Park Bapt. Ch., Newport News, Va., 1975-81, Souths de Bapt. Ch., Dothan, Ark., 1981-87; pres. TV 65, Pine Bluff, 1987-94; pastor Immanuel Bapt. Ch., 1987-94; pres., treas. Ark. Bapt. Found., Little Rock, 1994—. Sec. Ark. chpt. IAFP, Little Rock, 1997-98. Mem. Fin. Planning Assn., Nat. Com. on Planned Giving. Baptist. Avocations: golf, computer, boating. Office: Ark Bapt Found 10117 Kanis Little Rock AR 72205

MOORE, WALTER CALVIN, retired chemical engineer; b. Oklahoma City, Oct. 21, 1910; s. Walter Arthur and Mary Helen (Hingeley) M. Student, U. Okla., 1927-31; diploma in nuc. tech., Capitol Radio Engr. Inst., 1963, diploma in electronics tech., 1967; BS in Chemistry, Regents Coll. U., Albany, 1986. Sanitary engr. U.S. Army C.E., Tallahassee, 1942-44; chem. engr. gaseous diffusion plant Union Carbide Corp., Oak Ridge, Tenn., 1944-50, asst. chief engr., 1950-52; project mgr. Oak Ridge Nat. Lab., 1953, asst. supt. tech. divsn. plant Y-12, 1954-58; rsch. mgr. plastics in packaging Union Carbide Devel. Co., N.Y.C., 1958-59; Exptl. Beryllium Oxide Reactor nuc. reactor project mgr. Gen. Atomic, San Diego, 1959-62; v.p. engring. and rsch. York (Pa.) divsn. Borg-Warner Corp., 1962-76, cons., 1976-81. Cons. mgmt. and rsch., 1981—. Author: (with others) Our Western World's Most Beautiful Poems, 1985; contbr. articles to Supervisory Mgmt. Am. Mgmt. Assn. Asst. gen. chmn. corp. contbns. fund campaign York United Way, 1969-71; bd. dirs. Sheltered Workshop, 1971, York County Solid Waste and Refuse Authority, 1983. Mem. AIChE, ASHRAE, Am. Chem. Soc., Am. Nuc. Soc. (charter), Internat. Inst. Refrigeration (mem. E-1 air conditioning commn. 1972-75), N.Y. Acad. Scis., York Area C. of C. (chmn. nat. govtl. affairs com. 1967-69), Rotary (dist. chmn. group study exch. 1974). Republican. Achievements include patents for control circuit and oil separator. Home: 2204 Bernays Dr York PA 17404 E-mail: moorewc@supernet.com.

MOORE, WALTER DENGEL, rapid transit system professional; b. Chgo., Sept. 16, 1936; s. Walter D. and Velma Louise (Rhode) M.; m. Sandra M. Stetzel, Jan. 23, 1965 (div. 1980); children: Thomas, Timothy; m. Janice Masilun, Nov. 30, 1996. BA in Liberal Arts and Scis., U. Ill., 1958; BSEE, Ill. Inst. Tech., 1972. Cert. keel boat sailor. Supt. maintenance of way Chgo. Transit Authority, 1963-89; supr. track and rail tech. support Met. Transp. Assn. Los Angeles County, L.A., 1989-99, ret., 1999; cons. in rapid transit maintenance and tech. support, 1999—. With U.S. Army, 1958-60. Mem. Am. Pub. Transp. Assn. (vice chmn. power com. 1974-75), Am. Ry. Engring. Assn. (vice chmn. subcom. on power signals and comm. 1990-99), Underwater Soc. Am. (N.Am. record in spear-fishing 1988), Calif. Pub. Utilities Commn. (gen. order 1995), Nat. Rsch. Coun., NAS (transp. rsch. bd.), Nat. Acad. Engrs. (project C3 and D6 light rail track manual), Morro Bay Art Assn. (exhibitor), Morro Bay Yacht Club (chmn. summer sailing, portfin. officer), Baywood Navy Retirees. Avocations: free diving, theater, sailing. Home: 1180 9th St Los Osos CA 93402-1325

MOORE, WALTER LEON, civil engineer, educator; b. Estrella, Calif., Mar. 12, 1916; s. Leon Wallace and Nellie (Munson) M.; m. Reta Mae Nunn, Nov. 28, 1942; children— Claire Louise, Catherine Adele, Geneva Elaine, James Walter. BS in Engring, Calif. Inst. Tech., 1937, MS in Civil Engring, 1938; PhD, State U. Iowa, 1951. Registered profl. engr., Tex. Jr. engr. Soil Conservation Service coop. lab. Calif. Inst. Tech., 1939-40; research analyst, research engr. Lockheed Aircraft Corp., 1940- 47; faculty U. Tex., 1947—, prof. civil engring., 1953-85, prof. emeritus, 1985—, chmn. dept., 1958-65, mem. grad. faculty, 1958—; pres. Waveguard Internat., 1975—; chmn. Moore and Sethness Inc., 1982—. Author, co-author papers, articles. Mem. ASCE (pres. Tex. 1957, chmn. coms., Collingwood prize for juniors, water resources coordinator hydrology div.), Am. Soc. Engring. Edn. (dir. civil engring. div., chmn. com.), Am. Geophys. Union, Internat. Assn. Hydraulic Research, Nat. Soc. Profl. Engrs., Tex. Soc. Profl. Engrs. (chmn. water edn. com.), Nat. Commn. Fluid Mechanics Films, Internat. Hydrological Decade Commn. Edn. and Tng. Assocs Calif. Inst. Tech., Sigma Xi, Tau Beta Pi, Chi Epsilon. Presbyterian (elder). Club: Rotarian (pres. N. Austin club). Research hydraulics, hydrology, fluid mechanics. Home: PO Box 81398 Austin TX 78708-1398

MOORE, WARD WILFRED, medical educator; b. Cowden, Ill., Feb. 12, 1924; s. Cecil Leverett and Velma Leona (Frye) M.; m. Frances Laura Campbell, Jan. 29, 1949; children— Scott Thomas, Ann Gail, Brian Dean, Kevin Lee. AB, U. Ill., 1948, MS, 1951, PhD, 1952; DSc (hon.), Mahidol U.,

Bangkok, 2001. Instr., rsch. assoc. U. Ill., 1952-54; asst. prof. Okla. State U., Stillwater, 1954-55, Ind. U., Bloomington, 1955-59, assoc. prof., 1959-66, prof. physiology, 1966-89, prof. physiology and biophysics emeritus, 1989—, acting chmn. dept. anatomy, 1971-73, assoc. dean basic med. scis., 1971-89, assoc. dean, dir. med. scis. program, 1976-89. Vis. prof. Postgrad. Med. Center, Karachi, Pakistan, 1963-64; staff mem. Rockefeller Found., 1968-71; vis. prof., chmn. dept. physiology, faculty sci. Mahidol U., Bangkok, Thailand, 1968-71 Served with U.S. Army, 1943-46. Mem. Am. Physiol. Soc., Endocrine Soc., Am. Soc. Nephrology, Soc. Study Reproduction, Am. Assn. Anatomists, Soc. Exptl. Biology and Medicine, Am. Assn. Med. Colls., AAAS, Am. Inst. Biol. Scis., AAUP, Ind. Acad. Sci., Ind. Hist. Soc., Soc. Sons of Am. Revolution, Sigma Xi, Phi Sigma. Home: 3500 E Bradley St Bloomington IN 47401-4201 Office: Indiana U Jordan Hall # 105 Bloomington IN 47405 E-mail: moorew@indiana.edu.

MOORE, WESLEY BOYD, occupational physician; b. Nashville, Nov. 2, 1953; s. Jesse Perry and Anna Lou Moore; m. Regina G. Moore, Sept. 25, 1976; children: Daniel Trent, Amy Leigh, Emily Annette. BS in Chemistry, Middle Tenn. State U., 1975; MD, U. Tenn., 1978. Bd. cert. family medicine and occupl. medicine. Intern, resident family practice U. Pa., Jackson (Tenn.) Madison County Gen. Hosp., 1979-81; emergency physician William Gaw, M.D., Nashville, 1982-85; family physician LaVergne (Tenn.) Med. Clin., 1985-86, Family Med. Ctr., Inc., Antioch, Tenn., 1986-91; staff physician Miller Med. Group, 1991-93; co. physician Nissan Motor Mfg., Inc., Smyrna, Tenn., 1989—. Pres. Andrew Jackson chpt. Tenn. Acad. Family Physicians, Nashville, 1983-84; bd. mem. Tenn. Acad. Family Physicians, 1987-93. Founding editor Tenn. Family Physician, 1989, assoc. editor, 1990-99. Fellow Am. Acad. Family Practice; mem. AMA, Am. Coll. Occupl. and Environ. Medicine, Tenn. Coll. Occupl. and Environ. Medicine (bd. mem. 1998-99), LaVergne Men's Club (Man of Yr. award 1989). Office: Nissan Motor Mfg Inc 983 Nissan Dr Smyrna TN 37167-4405

MOORE, WILL H. political science educator; b. Balt., Mar. 9, 1962; s. William H. Jr. and Roberta (Lord) M.; m. Kathleen Berger, Dec. 28, 1985; children: Kristopher, Chelsea, Kevy. BA in Econs., U. Colo., 1984, PhD in Polit. Sci., 1991. Sales assoc. Kroy, Inc., Chgo., 1984-85; account exec. Beco, Inc., Park Ridge, Ill., 1995-96; asst. prof. U. Calif., Riverside, 1991-97; assoc. prof. polit. sci. Fla. State U., Tallahassee, 1997—. Mem. editl. bd. Polit. Rsch. Quar., 1996-2000, Internat. Studies Quar., 1999—, Comparative Polit. Studies, 2000—; contbr. articles to profl. jours., including Jour. Conflict Resolution, Am. Jour. Polit. Sci., Comparative Polit. Studies, Internat. Interactions, Polit. Rsch. Quar. Mem. adv. bd. Minorities at Risk Project, College Park, Md., 1999—, Polity Project, College Park, 2000—. Rsch. grantee NSF, 1994, 95, 2001. Mem. Am. Polit. Sci. Assn. (exec. com. conflict processes sect. 1996-99), Peace Sci. Soc. (councilor 1999-2001), Internat. Studies Assn., Midwest Polit. Sci. Assn. Office: Fla State U Dept Polit Sci Tallahassee FL 32306-2230 E-mail: will.moore@fsu.edu.

MOORE, WILLIAM BLACK, JR. retired aluminum company executive; b. Jackson, Miss., Sept. 18, 1924; s. William Black and May Isom (Whitten) M.; m. Lillian Wells, Sept. 14, 1946; children: Kathryn Ramsey Moore Dannels, William Black III, Bethany Moore Richmond. BSChemE, U. Louisville, 1945, MSChemE, 1947. Registered profl. engr., Ky. Chem. engr. U. Louisville Rsch. Inst., 1947-49; mktg. mgr. Reynolds Metals, Louisville, 1949-58, dir. mktg. Richmond, Va., 1958-61, regional gen. mgr. St. Louis, 1961-69, v.p. Richmond, 1969-80; ret. Mem. adv. bd. Bay Trust Co. Author: Letters to Rebecca; contbr. articles to profl. jours. Pres. bd. dirs. Rappahannock Found.; pres. Lagniappe Found.; dir. adv. bd. Bay Trust Co., Kilmarnock, Va. Served to Lt. USNR, 1943-47. Mem. AIA (hon.), Indian Creek Club (Kilmarnock, Va.), Country Club of Va. (Richmond). Baptist. Avocations: fishing, farming, genealogy. Home: PO Box 1300 Kilmarnock VA 22482-1300 E-mail: wbmoore@crosslink.net.

MOORE, WILLIAM GROVER, JR. management consultant, former air freight executive, former air force officer; b. Waco, Tex. s. William Grover and Annie Elizabeth (Pickens) Moore; m. Marjorie Y. Gardella, Jan. 18, 1943; 1 child Allyson. Student, Kilgore (Tex.) Coll., 1937—39, Sacramento State Coll., 1951, George Washington U., 1962; grad., Air War Coll., Air U., 1957, Nat. War Coll., 1962. Enlisted U.S. Army Air Force, 1940, commd. 2d lt., 1941, advanced through grades to gen., 1977; comdr. 777th Squadron, 15th AF, Italy, 1944—45, 3535th Maintenance and Supply Group, Mather AFB, Calif., 3d Bomb Group, Korea, 1952; chief bases and units divsn. Hdqrs. USAF, 1952—56; asst. dep. chief of staff ops. Hdqrs. USAF Europe, 1957—61; comdr. 314th Troop Carrier Wing, Stewart AFB, Tenn., 1962—63, 839th Air Divsn., 1963—65; asst. J3 U.S. Strike Command, 1965—66; comdr. 834th Air Divsn., Vietnam, 1966—67; dir. operational requirements Hdqrs. USAF, 1967—70; comdr. 22d AF, 1970—73, 13th AF, 1973; chief of staff Pacific Command, 1973—76; asst. vice chief of staff Hdqrs. USAF, 1976—77; comdr. in chief Mil. Air Lift Command, 1977—79; ret., 1979; pres., COO Emery Air Freight Corp., Wilton, Conn., 1981—83; bus. cons., 1983—. Pres. Met. Nashville Airport Authority, 1984—. Decorated Def. D.S.M., Air Force D.S.M. with 2 oak leaf clusters, Legion of Merit with 4 oak leaf clusters, Silver Star, D.F.C. with oak leaf cluster, Air Medal with 9 oak leaf clusters, Air Force Commendation medal with 10 oak leaf clusters (U.S.), Croix de Guerre with palm France, Armed Forces Honor medal 1st class Vietnam, Republic of China Cloud and Banner, Legion of Honor Republic of the Philippines; named to Minuteman Hall of Fame, 1979; recipient L. Mendel Rivers award of excellence; fellow Jimmy Doolittle fellow in aerospace edn., 1978. Mem.: Am. Ordnance Assn., Nat. Def. Transp. Assn., Air Force Assn. Home: 932 W Main St Franklin TN 37064-2730 Office: Nashville Internat Airport 1 Terminal Dr Ste 501 Nashville TN 37214-4110

MOORE, WILLIAM JOHN MYLES, electrical engineer, researcher; b. Edinburgh, Scotland, May 3, 1924; arrived in Can., 1928; s. William Harold and Doris Kate (Paddon) M.; m. Ruth Elizabeth Duffy, Aug. 21, 1948; children: Roberta Louise, Marilyn Elizabeth. B in Applied Sci., U. B.C., Can., 1946; postgrad., NRC, Ottawa, Can., summer 1947; M in Engring., McGill U., 1948. Rsch. officer NRC Can., Ottawa, Ont., 1948-51, 55-88, sect. head power engring sect. elec. engring. div., 1988-90, ret., 1990; rsch. officer Can. Armament R&D Establishment, Valcartier, Que., 1951-52, head analysis sect., 1952-54, group leader analysis, control and simulation sects., 1954-55. Cons. prof. Huazhong U. Sci. and Tech., Wuhan, Peoples Republic of China., 1988. Author: The Current Comparator, 1987; holder 10 patents. Fellow IEEE (chmn. Ottawa sect. 1966-67, chmn. Elec. and Electronic Measurement and Test Instrumentation Conf. and Instrumentation and Measurement Symposium 1969, pres. Group on Instrumentation and Measurement 1974, chmn. power systems instrumentation and measurement com. Power Engring. Soc. 1981-82, Morris E. Leeds award, 1987, Centennial medal 1984, A.G.L. McNaughton medal 1991), Assn. Prof. Engrs. Ont. Avocations: downhill skiing, personal computing. Home: 797 Dunloe Ave Ottawa ON Canada K1K 0K3 E-mail: af266@freenet.carleton.ca.

MOORE, WILLIAM LEROY, JR. career officer, physician; b. Savannah, Ga., June 1, 1934; s. William Leroy Sr. and Helen Louise (Robbins) M.; m. Anna Elizabeth Ballard, Mar. 15, 1958; children: William L., Christopher A., Mary Beth. Student, Ga. Inst. Tech., 1951-52; AB, Emory U., 1955; MD, Med. Coll. Ga., 1959; postgrad. mil. tng. courses, 1962-94. Diplomate Am. Bd. Internal Medicine, Am. Bd. Infectious Diseases. Commd. capt. U.S. Army, 1962, advanced through grades to maj. gen., 1991; intern Floyd Hosp., Rome, 1959-60; pvt. practice Italy, 1960-61; resident in internal medicine Brooke Gen. Hosp., Ft. Sam Houston, Tex., 1965-68; rsch. fellow in infectious diseases U. Tex. Southwestern Med. Sch., Dallas, 1968-70; resident in internal medicine Parkland Meml. Hosp., 1968-70; gen. med. officer Martin Army Hosp., Ft. Benning, Ga., 1962, 5th Spl. Forces Group, Spl. Warfare Ctr., Ft. Bragg, N.C., 1962-63; gen. internist, group surgeon, commdg. officer 1st Spl. Forces Group, Spl. Action Force, Okinawa, Japan, 1963-65; asst. chief to chief infectious disease svc. Brooke Gen. Hosp., Ft. Sam Houston, Tex., 1970-74; chief internal medicine svc., chief dept. medicine, chief profl. svcs. Eisenhower Army Med. Ctr., Ft. Gordon, Ga., 1978-83; comdr. Frankfurt (Germany) Army Regional Med. Ct., 97th Gen. Hosp., 1983-86; project mgr. Office of Surgeon Gen., Washington, 1986-88; adj. faculty Nat. Def. U., Ft. Lesley J. McNair, Washington, 1986-88; vice comdr. Joint Mil. Med. Command, Randolph AFB, Tex., 1988-91; comdr. Brooke Army Med. Ctr., Ft. Sam Houston, 1988-91, U.S. Army Med. Dept. Ctr. & Sch., Ft. Sam Houston, 1991-94; state epidemiologist, dir. communicable & environ. disease Tenn. Dept. Health, 1995-2001; prof. medicine divsn. infectious diseases Vanderbilt U. Sch. Medicine, Nashville, 1994—; cheif of staff VA Med. Ctr., 2001—. Clin. assoc. in medicine U. Tex. Southwestern Med. Sch., 1969-70; clin. assoc. prof. medicine U. Tex. Med. Sch., 1970-74; chief. sect. of infectious diseases Med. Coll. Ga., 1974-75, assoc. prof., 1974-78, clin. prof., 1978-83; prin. investigator infectious disease rsch. VA Hosp., Augusta, Ga., 1974-78, asst. chief med. svc., 1974-75, dir. clin . microbiology lab., 1974-78, epidemiologist, 1974-78; head intenal medicine infectious disease 97th gen. Hosp., Frankfurt, 1983-86, Walter Reed Army Med. Ctr., 1986-88; clin. prof. medicine U. Tex. Health Sci. Ctr., San Antonio, 1989-94; mem. ref. panel on Am. Hosp. Formulary Svc. of Am. Soc. Hosp. Pharmacists, 1974-78; faculty Advisor Lane-Walker AMSA Free Clinic, Augusta, 1975-78; mem. various coms. and bds., VA Hosp., Augusta, 1974-78. Contbr. articles to profl. jours. Mem. Army Comty. Coun. San Antonio, 1988-94; dir., bd. dirs. Army Med. Dept. Mus. Found. Inc., 1989-94; bd. dirs. San Antonio Area chpt. ARC, 1989. Decorated Army Commendation medal, Meritorious Svc. medal (3), Legion of Merit with three oak leaf clusters, Disting. Svc. medal Army Med. Dept. Regiment, 1994, Order of Mil. Med. Merit; recipient Scholastic Excellence award C.V. Mosby Co., 1959, Laureate award, Am. Coll. Physician, 1996, Dirs. Commendation VA Hosp., Augusta, 1978, Surgeon Gen.'s A Profl. Designer for Internal Med., 1982. Fellow ACP, Infectious Diseases Soc. Am.; mem. NAS (nat. rsch. coun. 1995-96), Assn. Mil. Surgeons U.S. (mem.-at-large exec. coun. Alamo chpt. 1989), Soc. Med. Cons. to Armed Forces (chmn. com. on cons. activities 1977-79), Am. Heart Assn. (bd. dirs. San Antonio divsn. 1988-89), San Antonio Rsch. Club (sec., pres. 1970-74), Tenn. Med. Assn., Nashville Acad. Medicine, Tenn. Pub. Health Assn., Coun.State and Territorial Epidemiologists. *Strict adherence to moral and ethical principles, willingness to work hard, use all of one's talents to benefit others and take advantage of all of the opportunities one finds to improve one's self while serving others are the elements of success in this life.*

MOORE, WILLIAM THEODORE, JR. judge; b. Bainbridge, Ga., May 7, 1940; s. William T. and Mary (Talbert) M.; m. Jane Hodges, July 18, 1964; children: Sarah S., Mary T. William T III. AA, Ga. Military Coll., 1960; JD, U. Ga., 1964; Law (hon.), Ga. Mil. Coll., 1978; LLM, U. Va., 2001. Bar: Ga. 1964, U.S. Dist. Ct. (so. dist.) Ga. 1964, U.S. Ct. Appeals (5th and 11th cirs.) 1979, U.S. Supreme Ct. 1980. U.S. atty. So. Dist. Ga. U.S. Dept. of Justice, Savannah, 1977-81; ptnr. Corish, Smith, Remler & Moore, 1967-77, Sparkman, Harris & Moore, Savannah, 1981-87, Oliver Maner & Gray, Savannah, 1988-94; judge U.S. Dist. Ct. for So. Dist. Ga., 1994. Atty. Savannah-Chatham County Bd. Pub. Edn., 1975-77, mem. U.S. Atty. Gen's. Adv. com. D.C. 1978-81. Recipient Spl. Appreciation award Ga. Bur. of Investigation, 1980, U.S. Dept. Treasury Bur. of Alcohol, Tobacco & Firearms, D.C., 1980; Extraordinary Svc. award Savannah Chapt. Fed. Bar Assn., 1980. Fellow Am. Bd. Criminal Lawyers (pres. 1993); mem. NACDL, Nat. Assn. Former U.S. Attys. (bd. dirs. 1984—), Jud. Conf. U.S. (com. on criminal law), Ga. Assn. Criminal Def. Lawyers (v.p. 1986—), Ga. Bar Assn. Democrat. Episcopalian. Avocations: jogging, weight training, golf, reading. Office: US Dist Courthouse 125 Bull St PO Box 10245 Savannah GA 31412-0445

MOORE, WILLIAM VINCENT, political science educator; b. Columbia, Mo., Apr. 13, 1944; s. Willis and Mabelle (Rogers) M.; m. Suzanne Shelton, July 14, 1967 (div. Feb. 1984); children: Mark, Laura. BA, So. Ill. U., 1966, MA, 1968; PhD, Tulane U., 1975. Instr. Fla. Meml. Coll., Miami, 1968-69, Xavier U., New Orleans, 1970-72; asst. prof. to assoc. prof. polit. sci. Coll. of Charleston, S.C., 1972-83, prof., 1983-99, disting. prof., 1999—, scholar-in-residence S.C., 1976, dir. summer sessions, 1984-87, chmn. dept., 1987-93, dir., masters in pub. adminstrn. dept., 1993-99. Chmn. S.C. Interagy. Merit Coun., Columbia, 1987-99; instr. jr. statesmen program Northwestern U., Evanston, Ill., 1996. Author: Political Extremism in the U.S.A., 1983; co-author: Politics and Government in South Carolina, 1994; contbr. articles to profl. jours. Recipient Disting. Tchg. award Coll. of Charleston, 1981, 2000, Disting. Advising award, 2001, Disting. Tchr. scholar award, 2001; grantee U. N.C., 1980; rsch. fellow U. S.C., 1983; NEH seminar Harvard U., 1995; named S.C. Gov.'s Prof. of Yr. 1997. Mem. Am. Polit. Sci. Assn., So. Polit. Sci. Assn., S.C. Polit. Sci. Assn. (pres. 1983-84), Phi Kappa Phi (chpt. pres. 1982-84), Pi Sigma Alpha (chpt. pres. 1987-93), Pi Alpha Alpha. Avocations: tennis, racquetball. Home: 389 Cross St Charleston SC 29407-6977 Office: Coll of Charleston Polit Sci Dept Charleston SC 29424

MOORE, WISTAR, cardiovascular surgeon; b. Feb. 16, 1959; BA, U. N.C., 1981, MD, 1985. Bd. cert. gen. surgery, thoracic surgery. Gen. surgery resident Mass. Gen. Hosp., 1985-90; cardiothoracic resident The Emory Clinic, 1990-93; cardiovasc. surgeon Watson Clinic, Lakeland, Fla., 1993-2000; chief divsn. cardiovasc. thoracic surgery Lakeland Regional Med. Ctr., 1996-2000; cardiovasc. surgeon Cardiovasc. Surgeons, Orlando, Fla., 2000—. Fellow ACS, Am. Coll. Chest Physicians; mem. Fla. Soc. Thoracic and Cardiovasc. Surgeons, So. Thoracic Surg. Assn., Soc. Thoracic Surgeons. Office: 217 Hillcrest St Orlando FL 32801-1211

MOORHEAD, GERALD LEE, architect; b. Davenport, Iowa, Feb. 18, 1947; s. Wayne Lee and Marilou (George) M. BA, Rice U., 1969, BArch, 1971. Arch. Middleton & Statton, El Paso, Tex., 1967, MA Floyd Assocs., Houston, 1968, CRS Design Inc., Houston, 1969-70, Phillips & Peterson AIA, Houston, 1969-73; arch., v.p. Charles Tapley Assocs., 1973-83; prop. Lloyd Jones Fillpot Assocs., 1986-87, Gerald Moorhead, Arch., 1983-98; arch. Ray Bailey Archs., Inc., 1998—. Photography exhibited in group shows at Galveston Arts Coun., Tex., 1976, Jewish Cmty. Ctr., Houston, 1977, Cronin Gallery, Houston, 1977; one-man photog. exhbns. include Autry Ho. Gallery, Houston, 1979; editor, photographer: Houston Architectural Guide, 1999, Buildings of Texas; editor: Houston Architectural Ballade, 2000; contbg. editor Tex. Arch., Arthtl. Record; contbr. articles on architecture to profl. publs.; exhbn. curator Houston Mus. Natural Sci., 1990, Mus. Fine Arts, Houston, 1991, FotoFest, Houston, 1996. Treas. Houston Ctr. for Photography, 1985-87. Recipient Spl. award Houston AIA/Houston Home & Garden, 1979, Internat. prize Union Archs. Kazakstan, 1991; named Arch. Laureate of Kazakstan, 1992. Fellow AIA (Honor award Houston chpt. 1979, Young Arch. award Houston chpt. 1985); mem. Soc. Archtl. Historians, Nat. Trust for Hist. Preservation, Tex. Soc. Archs. (1st Honor award 1976, Interiors award 1986, Flowers Journalism award 1995), Rice Design Alliance. Home: 1755 W Main Ave Houston TX 77098-3607

MOORHEAD, PATRICK HENRY, secondary school administrator; b. Chgo., Feb. 2, 1943; s. Louis David and Ann Patricia (Dorsey) M.; m. Mary Elizabeth Burch, Dec. 28, 1966; children: Susan Patricia, Laura Ann, James Patrick, David John, Kathleen Dorsey. BA in Philosophy, Regis Coll., Colo., 1964; MEd in Counseling, Loyola U., Chgo., 1968, EdD in Student Per., 1983. Jr. high tchr. St. Vitus Sch., Chgo., 1965-66; dir. student svcs. St. Patrick H.S., 1966-71; coll. counselor Loyola Acad., Wilmette, Ill., 1971-84, asst. headmaster, 1984-90; chmn. counseling svcs. Deerfield (Ill.) H.S., 1990—. Trustee Sacred Heart Schs., Chgo., 1985-95, past chmn. trustee, 1992-95, hon. trustee, 1995—; trustee Woodlands Acad., Lake Forest, Ill., 1995—, chair trustees, 1999—; dist. leadership acad., asst. prin. Highland Park (Ill.) H.S., 2001—. Author: The Shimer College Presidency 1930-1980, 1983. Past pres., v.p. parish coun. Holy Cross Parish, Deerfield, 1980-83, vol. career renewal program, 1994-95; co-chairperson, co-founder Parent U., Deerfield, 1997, co-chairperson fund raising, 1998. Mem. Alpha Sigma Nu. Roman Catholic. Avocations: skiing, railroad enthusiast.

MOORHEAD, ROLANDE ANNETTE REVERDY, artist, educator; b. Périgueux, France; d. RémyJean and Andrée Marcelle (Lavollée) Reverdy; m. Elliott Swift Moorhead, III, Sept. 30, 1960; children: Edward Marc, Roland Elliott, Rémy Bruce. Degree in liberal arts, Coll. Technique, Nice, France, 1954. Bi-lingual sec., France, 1957-58, French Embassy, Washington, 1959-60, 68-70; chmn. exhibit com. Lauderdale-By-The-Sea Art Guild, Ft. Lauderdale, Fla., 1972-75, v.p., 1972-74, founder group 5 Women Artists; exhibit com. Broward Art Guild, 1976; treas., dir. Alliance Francaise, Miami, 1973-75. Juror, lectr. in field; invited guest artist Franco-Am. Art Show, Curemonte, France, 1996-97. One-woman shows include numerous galleries, Ft. Lauderdale area, 1971—, Ocean Club Art Gallery, Ft. Lauderdale, 1971-74, Pier 66 Gallery, Ft. Lauderdale, 1973, 75, 76, Ft. Lauderdale City Hall, 1974, 77-78, 81-88, 91-94, 95-2000, St. Basil Orthodox Ch., North Miami Beach, 1977, Galerie Vallombreuse, Biarritz, France, 1977, Gallerie du Palais des Fêtes, Périgueux, 1978, 88, Le Club Internat., Ft. Lauderdale, 1979, Leonard Gallery, Ft. Lauderdale, 1990-92, Tallahassee (Fla.) Capitol Bldg., 1990, Lighthouse Pt. (Fla.) Gallery, 1990, Hollywood (Fla.) Art and Cultural Ctr., 1987, 89, 90, 91, 93, 95, Ft. Lauderdale Arts Inst., 1991, 93-95, Dover Gallery, Boca Raton, Fla., 1992; exhibited in group shows: Broward Art Guild, 1971, 73, 74, Point of Am. Gallery, Ft. Lauderdale, 1971, 73, Internat. Festival, Miami, 1976, Internat. Salon, Biarritz, 1977, Internat. Summer Salon, Paris, 1977, Fine Art Gallery Show and Competition, Long Galleries, Ft. Lauderdale, 1979, Pembroke Pines (Fla.) City Hall, 1982, Hollywood City Libr., 1982, also area banks, chs. and librs., numerous local art festivals, Schacknow Mus. Plantation, Fla., 2000, Ft. Lauderdale Mus. Art, 2000; represented in permanent collections: Fr. Lauderdale City Hall, DAV Hdqrs., Washington, Associated Aircraft Co., March of Dimes Bldg. (both Ft. Lauderdale), Oakland Park Libr., Fla., St. Josephs Convent, St. Augustine, Fla., U.S. Air Force Mus., Ohio, Main Line Fleets, Inc., Palm Beach, Fla., Creditreform, Dusseldorf, Germany, St. Front Cathedral, Périgueux, St. Sacerdoce, Sarlat, France, Club Med, Fla. and Caribbean, also numerous pvt. collections U.S. and Europe; author art manual for Broward Arts Coun., Fla., 1986. Recipient Best in Show award Internat. Salon, Biarritz, 1977; named artist in residence Broward County Sch., 1985. Mem. Am. Soc. Portrait Artists, Nat. Assn. Women Artists, Fla. Watercolor Soc., Palm Beach Watercolor Soc., Nat. League Am. Penwomen, Art 24, Périgueux, Internat. Soc. Marine Painters, Am. Watercolor Soc., Nat. Mus. Women in Arts, Nat. Mus. Am. Indian, Gold Coast Water Color Soc. (pres. 1984-87), 2+3 The Artist's Orgn., Union des Francais de l'Etranger. Office: PO Box 8692 Fort Lauderdale FL 33310-8692

MOORHEAD, SYLVESTER ANDREW, education educator retired; b. Denver, Feb. 23, 1920; s. Ray Rodney and Cora Margaret (Payne) M.; m. Katherine May Schlessman, July 21, 1945; children: Rodney A., Sylvia Kay, Kent A., Pamela Ann. BA, U. No. Colo., 1942; PhD, Stanford U., 1950. Tchr. secondary sch., Redwood City, Calif., 1947-48, Sunnyvale, 1948-49; mem. faculty U. Miss., 1949—, prof. edn., 1955—, dean U. Sch. Edn., 1961-85, dean emeritus, 1985—. Contbr. articles profl. jours. Served with USAAF, 1942-45. Mem. NEA (life), Kappa Delta Pi, Phi Delta Kappa. Lodges: Rotary. Baptist. Home: 211 Vivian St Oxford MS 38655-2719

MOORHEAD, THOMAS BURCH, lawyer, corporation and government executive; b. Evanston, Ill., May 3, 1934; s. John William and Jane (Hendrich) M.; m. Christie Barnard, Dec. 31, 1966 (div. June 1992); children: Merrell Hendrich, Hannah Christie, Rachel McGill; m. Elizabeth Howard, May 3, 2002. BA, Yale U, 1956; postgrad., The Hague Acad. Internat. Law, 1958; JD, U. Pa., 1959; LLM, NYU, 1964. Bar: N.Y. 1960, Conn. 1971, U.S. Supreme Ct. 1965. Assoc. Milbank, Tweed, Hadley & McCloy, N.Y.C., 1959-63; assoc. counsel, asst. sec. Hooker Chem. Corp., 1963-68, dir. indsl. rels., 1968-69, v.p. indsl. rels., 1969-72; v.p. employee rels. Champion Internat. Corp., 1972-74; v.p. adminstrn. Beker Industries Corp., Greenwich, Conn., 1974-76; v.p. corp. affairs Estée Lauder, Inc., N.Y.C., 1976-84, sr. v.p., 1984-87; v.p. human resources Carter-Wallace, Inc., 1987—2001; dep. undersec. for internat. affairs U.S. Dept. Labor, 2001—. Bd. dirs., vice chmn. Transaction Billing Resources, Inc., 1991-97; elected mem. Corp. Culinary Inst. of Am., 1993-2000. Mem. New Canaan (Conn.) Rep. Town Com., 1980-85; elected mem. New Canaan Town Coun., 1985-2001, vice chmn., 1989-98, chmn. 1998—; justice of the peace State of Conn., 2001—; bd. dirs. Employment Policy Found., 1993-2001, Les Amis d'Escoffier Soc., 1990-2001, Les Amis d'Escoffier Found., 1990-2001, Yale U. Alumni Fund, 1987-92, Nat. Choral Coun., 1988-93, United Way Tri-State, Inc., 1986-89, United Way New Canaan, 1983-89, pres., 1986-87; mem. Conn. Oversight Commn., Metro-North Commuter R.R., 1985-89; U.S. del. ILO, 1985, 93, 94, 95, 96, 2000, 01, head U.S. employer del., 1994, 95, 96, 2000 and to ILO Asian Regional Meeting, 1997, ILO Ams. regional meeting, 1999, elected v.p. ILO conf., Geneva, 2000, elected mem. governing body ILO, 2001—. Mem. ABA, Assn. of Bar of City of N.Y., Am. Soc. Internat. Law, Met. Club, New Canaan Country Club, Gridiron Club of New Canaan (pres. 1990-2001), Yale Club. Home: 800 25th St NW Apt 501 Washington DC 20037 Office: 200 Constitution Ave NW Washington DC 20210

MOORHOUSE, MARY FRANCES, rehabilitation nurse; b. Seattle, Sept. 13, 1947; d. Francis E. and Frances L. (Ranus) McGlothlin; m. Jan G. Moorhouse, Feb. 3, 1968; children: Paul, Jason. Diploma, Beth El Sch. Nursing, Colorado Springs, Colo., 1968; BSN, U. Colo., Colorado Springs, 2001. CRRN; cert. legal nurse cons. Med.-Legal Cons. Inst.; cert. forensic nursing U. Colo. Patient care coord. critical care Penrose Cmty. Hosp., Colorado Springs, 1974-79; dir. nursing Nurses PRN of Denver, Inc., 1985; owner, cons. TNT-RN Enterprises, 1985—; nurse cons. Fortis Corp., 1989-92. Mem. adj. nursing faculty Pikes Peak CC. Author: Nursing Care Plans: Nursing Diagnosis in Planning Patient Care, 6th edit., 2002, The Nurses' Pocket Guide: Nursing Diagnosis with Interventions, 8th edit., 2002, Care Plans for Critical Care, 1987. Recipient Outstanding Book of Yr. award Nursing, 1984, AJN Book of Yr. award, 1989; named Nurse of Yr., Colo. Nurses Assn., 1987, So. Colo. Woman of Yr. in Health Field So. Colo. Womens Life Festival and Sta. KOAA-TV, 1988. Mem. AACN, Colo. Nurses Assn. (Sustained Contbn. to Nursing Profession honor 1992, Improvement of Health Status and Well-being of Citizens of Colo. honor 1994), N.Am. Nursing Diagnosis Assn., Nursing Found. Colo. Assn. Rehab. Nurses. Home and Office: 1219 E Bijou St Colorado Springs CO 80909-5515

MOORING, F. PAUL, physics editor; b. Pitt County, N.C., Feb. 6, 1921; s. Benjamin Arthur and Amanda Elizabeth (Congleton) M.; m. Jean Louise Carpenter, Aug. 28, 1948; children: Cecily Hamm, Carol Larson, Margaret. BA, Duke U., 1944; PhD, U. Wis., 1951. Instr. Duke U., Durham, N.C., 1943-46; teaching asst. U. Wis., Madison, 1946-50, rsch. asst., 1950-51; physicist Argonne (Ill.) Nat. Lab., 1951-83; editor, cons. Am. Inst. Physics, Argonne, 1983—. Adj. prof. St. Louis U., 1966-83. Contbr. articles to profl. jours. Pres. The Ill. Prairie Path, Wheaton, Ill., 1971-93, Ill. Audubon Soc., Wayne, Ill., 1978-81. Fulbright Rsch. fellow U. Helsinki, 1962-63. Mem. AAAS, Am. Phys. Soc. Democrat. Home: 295 Abbotsford Ct Glen Ellyn IL 60137-4803 E-mail: fmooring@aol.com.

MOORMAN, JOHN A. librarian; b. Humboldt, Nebr., Sept. 15, 1947; m. Ileen Mary Geiger, Dec. 20, 1968; children: Johanna, Jessica, John A. AB, Guilford Coll., Greensboro, N.C., 1969; MSLS, U. N.C., 1972; postgrad., U. N.C., Greensboro, 1974-75; PhD, U. Ill., 2002. Pub. svcs. and circulation libr. Guilford Coll., 1972-75; dir. Elbert Ivey Meml. Libr., Hickory, N.C., 1975-80, Brazoria County Libr. System, Angleton, Tex., 1980-86, Oak Lawn (Ill.) Pub. Libr., 1986-88; exec. dir. Cumberland Trail Libr. System, Flora, Ill., 1989-92; city libr. Decatur (Ill.) Pub. Libr., 1992-2000; dir. Williamsburg (Va.) Regional Libr., 2000—. Author: Managing Small Library Collections in Businesses and Community Organizations: Advice for Non-Librarians, 1989. Grad. Decatur Leadership Inst., 1993. Mem. ALA (com., chair 2002), Va. Libr. Assn. (legis. com.). Mem. Soc. Of Friends. Avocations: travel, reading, woodworking, sports. Home: 8216 Old Mill Ln Williamsburg VA 23188-1135 Office: Williamsburg Regional Libr 7770 Croaker RD Williamsburg VA 23188 E-mail: jmoorman@mail.wrl.org.

MOORMAN, JOYCE SOLOMON, music educator; b. Tuskegee, Ala., May 11, 1946; d. Walker Emanuel and Mary Willie (Winkfield) Solomon; m. Wilson Moorman, Nov. 28, 1980. BA, Vassar Coll., 1968; MFA, Sarah Lawrence Coll., 1975; EdD, Columbia U., 1982. Tchr. Harlem Sch. of the Arts, N.Y.C., 1979-80, Manna House Workshops, N.Y.C., 1981-83, LEGAM Music Sch., Bklyn., 1982-90, Bklyn. Music Sch., 1982-93; adj. asst. prof. LaGuardia C.C., L.I., N.Y., 1992—. Adj. asst. prof. Borough of Manhattan C.C., N.Y.C., 1983-88, York Coll., Jamaica, N.Y., 1991-92; panelist N.Y. State Coun. on Arts, N.Y.C., 1997-99; judge Nat. NAACP ACISO Competition, 1996-99. Composer: (mus. compositions) The Soul of Nature, 1975 (Detroit Symphony Forum award 1990), Sing My People, 1980, In Time of Silver Rain, 1990 (commn. 1990), Cygnus Chamber Ensemble Commn., 1991: Trio for Guitar, Flute, Drumset, A Tone Poem for Victims of Racism and Hatred, 1998 (Vienna M. M. commn. 1997). Sec. Logan Condominium Assn., Bklyn., 1996-98. Mem. ASCAP. Avocations: tennis, current events, reading, gardening. Home: # 1E 104 Saint Marks Pl Apt 1E Brooklyn NY 11217-2065

MOORMAN, ROBERT LAWSON, real estate appraiser and broker; b. Waco, Tex., Sept. 2, 1951; s. George Robertson and Gladys Lee Billie (Scoggin) M.; m. Rebecca Ann Averitt, Sept. 9, 1983; children: Jason, Benjamin, Kate, William, Bethany, John. BBA, So. Meth. U., 1973; MS in Fin., Tex. A&M U., 1990. Cert. real estate appraiser; lic. real estate broker. Self-employed musician, Austin, N.Mex., 1973-83; asst. v.p. Brenham (Tex.) Nat. Bank, 1983-85, First Nat. Bank, Navasota, Tex., 1985-87, First Savs. Assn., Brenham, 1987-89; lectr. fin. Tex. A&M U., College Station, 1990—; pres. RLM Fin. Group, Inc., Brenham, 1990—. Editor: (book) Goals for Washington County, 1984. Bd. dirs. Brenham Opportunity Ctr., 1983-85, Greater Brenham-Bellville Bd. of Realtors, 1998—, Washington County Bros. Keepers, 1997-99; mem. Downtown Parking Com., Brenham, 1985; chmn. Parks Adv. Bd., Brenham, 1988-93; pres. Washington County Coalition, Brenham, 1993; pres. bd. trustees Brenham Ind. Sch. Dist., 1998—. Recipient Bookman Peters Banking fellowship Tex. A&M Grad. Sch. Bus., 1989, 90. Mem. SAR, Am. Soc. Appraisers, Appraisal Inst. (assoc.), Soc. Tex. A&M Real Estate Profls., Nat. Assn. Realtors, Tex. Assn. Realtors, Greater Brenham-Bellville Assn. Realtors. Avocations: guitar, jogging, scripture study. Office: Ste 415 221 S Day St Brenham TX 77833-5578 E-mail: rlm@rlmfinancial.com.

MOOS, H. WARREN, physicist, astronomer, educator, administrator; b. N.Y.C., Mar. 26, 1936; s. Henry H. and Dorothy E. (Warren) M.; m. Doris Elaine McClure, July 13, 1957; children: Janet, Paul, Daniel, David. BS, Brown U., 1957; MA, U. Mich., 1959, PhD, 1962. Rsch. assoc. Stanford (Calif.) U., 1961-63; acting asst. prof. Johns Hopkins U., Balt., 1963-64, asst. prof., 1964-68, assoc. prof., 1968-71, prof., 1971—, dir. Ctr. for Astrophys. Scis., 1988-93, chmn. Physics & Astronomy, 1993-96. Cons. in field; mem. com. on planetary and lunar exploration NRC/Nat. Acad. Sci., Washington, 1982-86; mem. space and earth sci. adv. com. NASA, Washington, 1984-87; vis. fellow Joint Inst. for Lab. Astrophysics, 1972-73, 80-81. Editor: Optical Properties of Ions in Crystals, 1967; contbr. over 300 articles to profl. jours. Trustee Assoc. Univs., 2001—. Sloan Found. fellow, 1965-69. Fellow Am. Phys. Soc.; mem. Am. Astron. Soc., Internat. Astron. Union. Achievements include prin. investigatorof far ultraviolet spectroscopic explorer; co-investigator of Apollo 17 ultraviolet spectrometer, of Hopkins Ultraviolet Telescope, of Voyager ultraviolet spectrometer, of space telescope imaging spectograph; research on ultraviolet astronomy and fusion plasma diagnostics. Office: Johns Hopkins U Dept Physics & Astronomy 34th & Charles Sts Baltimore MD 21218

MOOS, RUDOLF H. psychologist, researcher; b. Berlin, Sept. 10, 1934; s. Henry R. and Herta M. (Ehrlich) M.; m. Bernice Schradski, June 9, 1963; children: Karen, Kevin. BA in Psychology, U. Calif. at Berkeley, 1956; PhD, U. Calif.-Berkeley, 1960. Mem. faculty psychiatry Stanford (Calif.) U., 1962—, dir. psychiatry research tng. program, 1967-92, prof. psychiatry, 1972—, dir. social ecology lab., 1967-92; chief research, research career scientist VA Med. Center, Palo Alto, Calif., 1975—, dir. Ctr. for Health Care Evaluation, 1984—, dir. Program Evaluation and Resource Ctr., 1990-99. Vis. prof. Inst. Psychiatry, also Maudsley and Royal Bethlem Hosp., London, 1969-70 Author: Issues in Social Ecology, 1974, Evaluating Treatment Environments, 1974, Health and the Social Environment, 1974, Evaluating Correctional and Community Settings, 1975, Human Adaptation Coping with Life Crises, 1976, The Human Context, 1976, Environment and Utopia, 1977, Coping with Physical Illness, 1977, Evaluating Educational Environments, 1979, Coping with Physical Illness: New Perspectives, 1984, Coping with Life Crises: An Integrated Approach, 1986, Alcoholism Treatment: Content, Process and Outcome, 1990, Group Residential Facilities for Older Adults, 1994, Evaluating Residential Facilities, 1996, The Quality of Psychiatric and Substance Abuse Programs, 1997; mem. editl. bd. Jour. Behavioral Medicine, Internat. Jour. Therapeutic Comtys., Prevention in Human Svcs., Psychosomatic Medicine, Jour. Personality and Social Psychology, 1985-91, Health Psychology: An Internat. Jour., Violence, Agression, and Terrorism, Jour. Substance Abuse, Jour. Applied Gerontology, Jour. Cmty. and Applied Social Psychology, Psychology and Aging, 1986-91, Evaluation and Program Planning, Environment and Behavior, 1987-91, Indian Jour. Clin. Psychology, 1996—, Jour. Studies on Alcohol, 1997. Fellow APA, Acad. Behavioral Medicine, Soc. Behavioral Medicine, Am. Orthopsychiat. Assn., Nat. Inst. on Alcohol Abuse and Alcoholism (mem. coun.); mem. Am. Sociol. Assn., Am. Psychosomatic Assn. (mem. coun.). Home: 25661 W Fremont Rd Los Altos CA 94022-1600 Office: Stanford U Dept Psychiatry MC 5550 Palo Alto CA 94305

MOOSBRUKER, JANE BARBARA, organization development consultant; b. Jamaica, N.Y., Oct. 29; d. Raymond Andrew and Evelyne (Ross) M. BA in Psychology, Adelphi U., 1960; MA, Radcliffe Coll., 1962; PhD in Social Psychology, Harvard U., 1965. Asst. prof. Tufts U. Sch. Dental Medicine, Boston, 1964-66, Boston Coll., Chestnut Hill, Mass., 1966-70; cons. orgn. devel. Bolton, 1970—. Mem. Nat. Tng. Labs., 1975—, bd. dirs., 1992-96; rsch. assoc. Harvard Sch. Dental Medicine, Boston, 1967-70, lectr., 1970-82; cons. Honeywell, Inc., Mpls. and Lexington, Mass., 1973-89, Harvard Cmty. Health Plan, Cambridge, Mass., 1983-85, So. N.H. Med. Ctr., 1980-86, 91-94, Digital Equipment Corp., Maynard, Mass., 1984-92, Biogen, Inc., 1993-97, Ma Doer, 1998-2000; adj. prof. Sch. Pub. Affairs, Am. U., 2002—. Contbr. articles to profl. jours. and books. Mem. Bolton Conservation Commn., 1987-95, chmn., 1990-94; bd. dirs. Walden Earthnet, 1991-93. Mem. Soc. for Psychol. Study of Social Issues, Orgn. Devel. Network, Nat. Audubon Soc., Union Concerned Scientists, Zero Population Growth. Avocations: skiing, hiking, gardening, birding. E-mail: jamoos@ziplink.net.

MOOSSA, A. R. surgery educator; b. Port Louis, Mauritius, Oct. 10, 1939; s. Yacoob and Maude (Rochecoute) M.; m. Denise Willoughby, Dec. 28, 1973; children: Pierre, Noel, Claude, Valentine. BS, U. Liverpool, Eng., 1962, MD (hon.), 1965; postgrad., Johns Hopkins U., 1972-73, U. Chgo., 1973-74. Intern Liverpool Royal Infirmary, 1965-66; resident United Liverpool Hosps. and Alder Hey Children's Hosp., 1966-72; from asst. prof. surgery to assoc. prof. U. Chgo., 1975-77, prof., dir. surg. rsch., chief gen. surgery svc., vice chmn. dept., 1977-83; chmn. dept. surgery U. Calif.-San Diego Med. Ctr., 1983—. Litchfield lectr. U., Oxford, Eng., 1978; praelector in surgery U. Dundee, Scotland, 1979; Hampson Trust vis. prof. U. Liverpool, Eng., 1992, G.B. Ong. vis. prof. U. Hong Kong, 1993, Philip Sandblon vis. prof. U. Lund, Sweden. Editor: Tumors of the Pancreas, 1982, Essential Surgical Practice, 1983, 4th edit., 2000, Comprehensive Textbook of Oncology, 1985, 2d edit., 1991, Gastrointestinal Emergencies, 1985, Problems in General Surgery, 1989, Operative Colorectal Surgery, 1993. Fellow Royal Coll. Surgeons (Hunterian prof. 1977); mem. ACS, Am. Surg. Assn., Soc. Univ. Surgeons, Am. Soc. Clin. Oncology. Office: U Calif San Diego Med Ctr 200 W Arbor Dr San Diego CA 92103-9000

MOOSSY, JOHN, neuropathologist, neurologist, consultant; b. Shreveport, La., Aug. 24, 1925; s. John Yazbeck and Rose (Ferris) M.; m. Yvonne Reese, Mar. 15, 1951; children: John Jefferson, Joan Marie. MD, Tulane U., 1950. Intern Charity Hosp. of New Orleans, 1950-51, neurology resident, 1951-53; neuropathology fellow Columbia U. Coll. of Physicians and Surgeons, N.Y.C., 1953-54; assoc., lectr. in neuropathology Tulane U. Sch. Medicine, New Orleans, 1954-57; asst. to prof. in pathology, neurology La. State U., 1957-65; prof. pathology, grad. faculty U. Pitts., 1965-67; prof. pathology neuropathology Bowman Gray Sch. of Medicine, Winston-Salem, N.C., 1967-72; prof. pathology and neurology, dir. div. neuropathology U. Pitts., 1972-93, emeritus prof., 1993—. Dir. Cerebrovascular Disease Study, World Fedn. of Neurology, Antwerp, Belgium, 1960-61; cons. Armed Forces Inst. of Pathology, Washington, 1977—, mem. sci. adv. bd., Washington, 1984-86. Editor: Cerebral Vascular Disease Seventh Conference, 1970, Cerebrovascular Diseases 12th Research Conference, 1981; editor-in-chief Jour. Neuropathology and Exptl. Neurology, 1981-91; mem. editorial bd. Archives Neurology, 1982-92. Recipient Excellence in Teaching award U. Pitts. Sch. of Medicine, 1987-88; named Commencement Speaker U. Pitts. Sch. of Medicine, 1989. Mem. Am. Acad. Neurology (sec.-treas. 1963-655), Am. Neurol. Assn. (v.p. 1977-78), Am. Assn. Neuropathologists (pres. 1974-75, Neuropathology award 1992), Internat. Soc. Neuropathology, Coun. Biology Editors.

MOOTE, A. LLOYD, history educator; b. Hamilton, Ont., Can., Mar. 22, 1931; s. Stanley Alanson and Esther Grace (Wood) M.; m. Barbara Brown, Dec. 27, 1956 (div. 1982); children: Karen, Peter, Daphne, Robert; m. Dorothy Carter May, May 30, 1986. BA, U. Toronto, 1954; MA, U. Minn., Mpls., 1956, PhD, 1958. Tchg. asst. U. Minn., Mpls., 1955-58; lectr. U. Toronto, 1958-61; asst. prof. U. Cin., 1961-62; from asst. prof. to prof. history U. So. Calif., L.A., 1962-92, prof emeritus, 1993—. Vis. prof. Queen's U., Kingston, Ont., 1965-66; chmn. gen. edn. program U. So. Calif., 1978-81; mem. Inst. Advanced Study, Princeton, 1988-89; affiliated prof. Rutgers U., 1994—. Author: The Seventeenth Century, 1970, The Revolt of the Judges, 1971, The World of Europe: The Seventeenth Century, 1973, 2d edit., 1979, Louis XIII: The Just, 1989, paperback edit., 1991; co-editor, contbr. issue of French hist. studies on biography, 1996; mem. editl. bd. French Hist. Studies, 1971-74; internat. adv. bd. European History Quar., 1983— . Founder, convener So. Calif. Early Modern French Studies Group, 1980-93, Rutgers, Princeton and Phila. Early Modern History Group, 1994—. Recipient William Koren prize Soc. French Hist. Studies, 1962, creative scholarship award U. So. Calif. Assocs., 1973, faculty book award U. So. Calif. chpt. Phi Kappa Phi, 1990; younger scholar NEH, 1969; grantee Am. Philos. Soc., 1962, Haynes Found., 1973, Wellcome Inst. for History Medicine, 1993-94, Burroughs-Wellcome Fund, 1996; Guggenheim fellow, 1976, fellow U. Essex, Eng., 1993-94, Rutgers Ctr. for Hist. Analysis, 1995-97. Mem. Am. Hist. Assn., Past and Present Soc., Soc. French Hist. Studies (pres. 1984-85), Western Soc. for French History, Soc. for Study French History (U.K.), Sixteenth-Century Studies Conf. Home: 149 Meadowbrook Dr Princeton NJ 08540-3664 E-mail: dmoote@erols.com.

MOOTS, PHILIP ROY, lawyer; b. Bellefontaine, Ohio, June 10, 1940; s. Philip King and Margaret Frances Moots; children from previous marriage: Rachel Margaret, Rebecca Jane; m. Marilyn June Perrin, Nov. 20, 1993. BA, Ohio State U., 1962; JD, Harvard U., 1965; LLD (hon.), W.Va. Wesleyan U., 1978. Ptnr. Dunbar, Kienzle & Murphy, Columbus, Ohio, 1965-71; legal advisor State of Ohio, Dept. Indsl. Rels., 1971-72; dep. dir. State of Ohio, Dept. Commerce, 1972; exec. asst. Office of Gov., State of Ohio, 1972-75; dir. Ctr. for Constitutional Studies, South Bend, Ind., 1977-81; ptnr., pres. Moots, Cope & Carter, LPA, Columbus, 1975—. Adj. prof. Ohio State U. Coll. Law, Columbus, 1972-77; bd. dirs. Cmty. Mut. Ins., Ohio. Co-author: Church and Campus, 1979, Government and Campus, 1982; contbr. articles to profl. jours. Trustee, chmn. bd. dirs., Meth. Theol. Sch. in Ohio, 1985-2000. Mem Nat. Assn. Ind. Colls. and Univs. (chair legal svcs. rev. panel 1990—), Clintonville C. of C. (bd. dirs. 2000—), Phi Beta Kappa, Phi Alpha Theta. Democrat. United Methodist. Office: Moots Cope & Carter LPA 3600 Olentangy River Rd Columbus OH 43214

MOOTY, JOHN WILLIAM, lawyer; b. Adrian, Minn., Nov. 27, 1922; s. John Wilson and Genevieve (Brown) M.; m. Virginia Nelson, June 6, 1952 (dec. 1964); children: David N., Bruce W., Charles W.; m. Jane Nelson, Jan. 15, 1972. BSL, U. Minn., 1943, LLB, 1944. Bar: Minn. 1944. Ptnr. Gray, Plant, Mooty & Bennett, Mpls., 1945—. Bd. dirs. Internat. Dairy Queen, Inc., Bur. of Engraving, Inc., Riverway Co. and subs., Rio Verde Svcs., Inc., Ariz. Author: (with others) Minnesota Practice Methods, 1956. Chmn. Gov.'s Task Force on Edn., 1981; pres. Citizens League Mpls., 1970; acting chmn. Republican Party of Minn., 1958. Mem. ABA, Minn. Bar Assn., Hennepin County Bar Assn., U. Minn. Alumni Assn. (pres. 1982), Tonto Verde Country Club, Minikahda (Mpls.) Club, Mpls. Club. Home: 6601 Dovre Dr Minneapolis MN 55436-1711

MORA, ALBERTO, federal agency administrator; Grad. with honors, Swarthmore Coll.; grad., U. Miami. Bar: Fla., Washington. Gen. counsel Navy Dept. Def., Washington, 2001—; fgn. svc. officer U.S. State Dept., 1975—78; gen. counsel of U.S. Info. Bush Adminstrn., 1989—93; pres., Senate-apptd. seat Broadcasting Bd. Govs.; counsel Greenberg Traurig, Washington. Bd. dirs. Nat. Coun. for Internat. Visitors, Radio Free Asia, Radio Free Europe/Radio Liberty. Editor-in-chief: Law of the Ams.: U. Miami Jour. of Internat. Law. Fellow, Orgn. of Am. States. Mem.: Coun. Fgn. Rels. Office: Dept Def Gen Counsel Navy 1000 Navy Pentagon Washington DC 20350-1000

MORA, ANTONIO GONZALEZ, III, broadcast journalist; b. Havana, Cuba, Dec. 14, 1957; came to U.S., 1960; s. Antonio Gonzalez Jr. and Natalia (Sandoval) M.; m. Julie Good, Aug. 27, 1994; children: Clara, Antonio Daniel. JD, U. Catolica Andres Bello, Caracas, Venezuela, 1980; LLM, Harvard U., Cambridge, Mass., 1981; DHL, Our Lady of Holy Cross, New Orleans, 2000; PhD (hon.) , Ursinus Coll., 2001. Assoc. Debevoise & Plimpton, N.Y.C., 1981-88; anchor Sta. WXTV, Secaucus, N.J., 1990-91, Sta. WNJU, Teterboro, 1991; anchor Nightside NBC, Charlotte, N.C., 1992; reporter, anchor Sta. WTVJ-TV, Miami, 1992-93; host Good Day LA Tv Sta. KTTV, L.A., 1993—94; host Good Morning America Sunday ABC, N.Y.C., 1994-95, correspondent, 1995-99, news anchor Good Morning America, 1999—2002; evening news anchor TV Sta. WBBM, Chgo., 2002—. Recipient Emmy award, 2000, Peabody award, 2000-01, Edward R. Murrow award, 2000. Mem.: Coun. Fgn. Rels.

MORA, ENRIQUE TRINIDAD, musician, vocational rehabilitation counselor; b. El Paso, Tex., Mar. 28, 1943; s. Trinidad and Catalina Mora; m. Sherrin Mora; m. Vicki Gail Mora (div.); children: Stacey Jane, Eric Christian. MA, Calif. State U., Los Angeles, California, 1995, BA, 1978. Cert. Independent Vocational Educator State of Calif. Bandleader Henry Mora Orch., Los Angeles, Calif., 2002; vocat. counselor Intracorp, 2002, VIP Rehab., Los Angeles, 2002, Rehab. Associates, Montclair, 2002. Author: (book) The Redcatcher Express. E-4 US Army, 1969—70, Vietnam. Recipient Spl. Recognition Grad. Studies, Calif. State U., 1995, Excellence in Jazz Studies, 1994. Roman Catholic. Avocations: golf, tennis. Home: 4307 Granada Street Montclair CA 91763 Home Fax: 909-624-1124. Personal E-mail: etmora@cs.com.

MORA, FEDERICO, neurosurgeon; b. Guatemala, Guatemala, Jan. 11, 1926; came to the U.S., 1945; s. Carlos Federico and Rosa (Castaneda) M.; m. Natalie Viriginia Ramin, June 30, 1951; children: Federico, Clara Luz, Ana Maria, Claudia Ines, Juan Rafael. Student, Harvard Coll., 1945-46, MD, 1950. Diplomate Am. Bd. Neurol. Surgery. Pvt. practice neurol. surgery, Guatemala, 1958-59, Albuquerque, 1959-95; asst. prof. surgery and anatomy U. N.Mex. Sch. Medicine, 1969-70. Capt. USAFR, 1954-56. Mem. Alpha Omega Alpha. Democrat. Avocations: scuba diving, nature studies. Home: 1809 Avenida Alturas NE Albuquerque NM 87110-4956 E-mail: locomora1@aol.com.

MORA, FRANCISCO, artist, printmaker; b. Uruapan, Mexico, May 7, 1922; s. Jose Maria and Clotilde (Perez) Mora; m. Elizabeth Catlett Mora, Oct. 31, 1946; children: Francisco, Juan, David. Student, Escuela de Pintura y Escultura La Esmeralda, 1941-46. Tchr. drawing Sch. Pub. Edn. Mexico, 1949-54; art adviser Mexican Acad. Edn., 1956—2002. Mem.: Mex. Acad. Edn. (founder), Salon de la Plastica Mexicana (founder). Died 2002.

MORA, GABRIELA, language educator, researcher; b. Santiago, Chile; d. Carlos Mora and Rosario Cruz; m. Harold Fruchtbaum, June 20, 1972. PhD in Hispanic Lit., Smith Coll., 1971. Prof. de Castellano Santiago Coll., 1957—60; asst. prof. Spanish CUNY, N.Y.C., 1971—76; instr. Spanish U. Mass., Amherst, Mass., 1963—69; asst. prof. Spanish Columbia U., N.Y.C., 1977—80; assoc. prof. Spanish Rutgers U., New Brunswick, NJ, 1989—98, prof. II of Spanish, 1998—. Book evaluator U. Tex., Austin, Duke U., Durham, NC, 1996; cons. reader PMLA. Author: Hostos intimista: Introduccion a su Diario, 1976, Theory and Practice of Feminist Literary Criticism, 1982, Diario de Hostos Introduction, 1990, En Torno al Cuento, 1994, El Cuento Modernista, 1996, Clemente Palma: El Modernismo, 2000. Mem.: MLA (chair divsn. L.Am. 1995—96), L.Am. Studies Assn. (Juror prize 1998). Home: 560 Riverside Dr 7K New York NY 10027 Office: Rutgers U 105 George St New Brunswick NJ 08901-1414

MORA, JAMES ERNEST, former professional football coach; b. Glendale, Calif., May 24, 1935; s. Mario Joseph and Helen Laverne (Thompson) M.; m. Connie Beatrice Saunders, Dec. 18, 1959; children— James L., Michael J., Stephen P. BS, Occidental Coll., 1957; MA, U. So. Calif., 1967. Asst. coach U. Washington, Seattle, 1975-78, Seattle Seahawks, Seattle, 1978-82, New England Patriots, Foxboro, MA, 1982-83; head coach Philadelphia Stars (name changed to Baltimore Stars), Baltimore, MD, 1983-86, New Orleans Saints, New Orleans, 1986-96, head coach, v.p. L.A., 1994-96; commentator NFC Football, 1997; head coach Indianapolis Colts, Ind., 1998—2002. Served to capt. USMCR, 1957-60 Mem. Am. Football Coaches Assn. Republican. Lutheran. Avocations: working out; golf; skiing; reading; biking.*

MORA, PHILIPPE, screenwriter, producer, director, painter; b. Paris, Aug. 8, 1949; s. Georges and Mirka Madeleine (Zelik) M.; m. Pamela Mai Krause, Aug. 1, 1980; children: Madeleine Mai, Georges Ritchie Maximillian, Dominic Marceau. Student, La Trobe U., Melbourne, Australia, 1967. Screenwriter, dir., producer, 1969—. Founder Cinema Papers mag., Melbourne, 1967. Dir., writer, prodr. (films) Trouble in Molopolis, 1969, The Howling III: The Marsupials, 1987, Snide and Prejudice, 1997, According to Occam's Razor, 1999, Project 65, 2002; co-writer (film) Double Headed Eagle, 1971; dir., writer: (films) Swastika, 1972 (Blue Ribbon award 1974), Brother Can You Spare a Dime, 1975, Mad Dog, 1976 (John Ford Meml. award 1976), According to Occam's Razor, 2000; dir.: (films) The Beast Within, 1980, The Return of Captain Invincible, 1981, A Breed Apart, 1983, The Howling II, 1984, Death of a Soldier, 1985, Back in Business, 1996; dir. prodr.: Communion, 1990, Art Deco Detective, 1994, Pterodactyl Woman from Beverly Hills, 1994, Precious Find, 1995, Burning Down the House, 1996, Thick and Thin, 1997, Joseph's Gift, 1999; dir., prodr.: (film) Hamlet, 2001; painter exhibited in group shows at Argys Gallery, Melbourne, 1967, Clytie Jessop Gallery, London, 1968-71, Sigi Kraus Gallery, London, 1970-71, Camden Arts Centre, London, 1970, Richard Demarco Gallery, Edinburgh, 1971, Tolarno Gallery, Melbourne, 1971, Watters Gallery, Sydney, Australia, 1972, William Mora Gallery, Melbourne, 1987, Caz Gallery, L.A., 1990; represented in permanent collection Nat. Gallery Collection, Canberra, Australia, 1982, Mus. Modern Art Australia; English Lit. exhibition Victorian Edn. Authority, Victoria, Australia, 1966. Mem. Dirs. Guild Am., Acad. Motion Picture Arts and Scis., Australian Film Dirs. Assn. Office: Michael Blaha Esq 2530 Wilshire Blvd Santa Monica CA 90403-4616

MORABITO, BRUNO PAUL, machinery manufacturing executive; b. Motticella, Italy, Feb. 10, 1922; s. Paul and Maria Antoinetta (Tedesco) M.; m. Therese Riccelli, June 29, 1946; 1 dau., Paula. B.C.E., Syracuse U., 1945. Application engr. Machinery and Systems div. Carrier Corp., Syracuse, N.Y., 1945-55, engring. mgr., 1955-66, mgr. centrifugal sales, 1966-69, mgr. machinery mktg., 1970-73, mgr. mktg., 1973-81; group v.p., gen. mgr. Environ. Systems Group Aeronca, Inc., Pineville, N.C., 1981-84; cons. Syracuse/Onondaga County Planning Agy., 1985-93; pres. BPM Planning and Cons., 1988-93. Adv. bd. Syracuse U. Energy Sys., 1998—. Chmn. sewage disposal dist. com. and street lighting dist. com. of Syracuse Gardens Tract, 1951-52; mem. Onondaga County Citizens Energy Com., 1993-96, vice chmn., 1996-98, chmn., 1998—. Recipient ASHRAE Wolverine Diamond Key award, 1961, Silver Knight of Mgmt. award Nat. Mgmt. Assn., 1978. Fellow ASHRAE (presdl. mem., bd. dirs. 1970-78, v.p. 1974-76, pres. 1977-78); mem. Beaver Meadows Golf and Recreational Club (bd. dirs. 1973-80, 84-89). Roman Catholic. Home and Office: 720 Henry Clay Blvd Apt 23B Liverpool NY 13088-6229 E-mail: BPMorabito@cs.com.

MORABITO, ROCCO ANTHONY, urologist; b. Huntington, W.Va., Nov. 23, 1950; s. Nicola F. and Theresa M. (Lobaldo) M.; m. Deborah Gayle Hall, 1973 (div. 1986); m. Brenda Kay Lyons, June 14, 1991; children: Shawn, Chris, Rocco Jr., Justin. BA, W.Va. U., 1972, MD, 1976. Diplomate Am. Bd. Urology, Nat. Bd. Med. Examiners. Surg. residency W.Va. U. Hosp., Morgantown, 1976-78, urol. residency, 1978-81; pres. Huntington (W.Va.) Urol. Assn., 1981—, Midwest Mobile Lithotripsy, Huntington, 1989-96, Tri-State Health Ptnrs., Huntington, 1994-96; pres. med. staff Cabell Huntington Hosp., 1991-93, St. Mary's Hosp., 1997-99. Clin. assoc. prof. urology, W.Va. U. Sch. Medicine, 1981—, Marshall U. Sch. Medicine, Huntington, 1981—. Fellow ACS; mem. AMA, Am. Urol. Assn., So. Med. Assn., W.Va. State Med. Assn., Cabell County Med. Soc., W.Va. U. Sch. Medicine Alumni Assn. (chmn. 1989-94). Republican. Roman Catholic. Avocations: tennis, boating, skiing, music, cooking. Home: 20 Kensington Ln Huntington WV 25705-3860 Office: Huntington Urological Assn 2860 3rd Ave Ste 230 Huntington WV 25702-1453 E-mail: wvu2@home.com.

MORACZEWSKI, ROBERT LEO, publisher; b. Saint Paul, Nebr., May 13, 1942; s. Leo and Florence (Wadas) M.; m. Virginia Kay Rohman, July 26, 1960; children— Mark, Matthew, Monika, Michael BS in Agrl. Journalism, U. Nebr., 1964. Assoc. editor Farmer Mag. Webb Co., St. Paul, 1964-72; mng. editor Farm Industry News Webb Co., 1972-74; editor Big Farmer Mag., Chgo., 1974-75; editorial dir. Webb Agrl. Services, St. Paul, 1976; editor The Farmer, The Dakota Farmer Webb Co., 1983-89; group pub. Webb Co., 1989-90, sr. v.p., 1990—. Chmn. Minn. Agri-Growth Coun. Contbr. articles to profl. jours. Mem. sponsors bd. Nat. FFA. Recipient numerous media awards. Mem. Am. Agrl. Editors Assn., Nat. Agrl. Mktg. Assn. Roman Catholic. Home: 32993 Kale Ave Chisago City MN 55013-2644 Office: Primedia Bus Media 7900 Internat Dr Minneapolis MN 55425 E-mail: bmoraczewski@primediabusiness.com.

MORADI, AHMAD F. software company executive, consultant; b. Tehran, Persia, Mar. 21, 1955; came to U.S., 1973; s. Akbar and Afsar (Mokaram) M.; m. Lourdes Pernas; l child, Aimee. AS, Broward Community Coll., 1978; BA, Fla. Atlantic U., 1980, MBA, 1982; PhD, LaSalle U., 1989. Advisor restaurant industries, Miami, Fla., 1974-78; pres. Octa-8, Inc., Ft. Lauderdale, 1980-82; mgmt. cons. MGI-MCG, Boca Raton, 1982-83; dir. ops. Datamation, Hollywood, 1983-85; pres. Software Intelligence Corp., Ft. Lauderdale, 1985—; with ARM Financial Corp., 1987-89; MIS dir., CIO Churchill Tech., Inc., Davie, Fla., 1992—; MIS dir. Westmack Group Holding Co., Delray Beach, 1995—; prin. G4, Inc., Ft. Lauderdale, 1992—; CEO Futuretrak Internat. OTC BB:FTRK, 1998-99, Worldcast Interactive Inc.; with Biomed. Rsch. Techs., 1997—, Interchange Med., Inc., 1999—, Maxwell Rand Inc., 1999—, Netstairs.com , 2000—. Lectr. South Fla. Bus. Jour., 1984-85, Victoria Hosp., Miami, Fla., 1985, Mt. Sinai Hosp., Miami, Fla., 1985, U. Miami, Fla., 1986, Chiropractic Today, 1989; cons., bus., mktg., internat. mktg. and telemarketing mgmt. Software Intelligence Corp., 1985—; systems analyst Softway, Inc., Ft. Lauderdale, 1986—. Mem. Data Processing Mgmt. Assn., Small Bus. Inst. E-mail: g4@ix.netcom.com., g41@bellsouth.net., g4med@yahoo.com.

MORAHAN-MARTIN, JANET MAY, psychologist, educator; b. N.Y.C., Jan. 13, 1944; d. William Timothy and May Rosalind (Tarangelo) Morahan; m. Curtis Harmon Martin, June 2, 1979; 1 child, Gwendolyn May. AB, Rosemont (Pa.) Coll., 1965; MEd, Tufts U., 1968; PhD, Boston Coll., 1978. Asst. mkt. rsch. analyst Compton Advt. Co., N.Y.C., 1965-67; mkt. rsch. analyst Ogilvy & Mather Advt., 1967; edn!. rsch. asst. Tufts U., Medford, Mass., 1968-69; counselor Psychol. Inst. Bentley Coll., Waltham, 1971-72; dir. counseling svcs. Bryant Coll., Smithfield, R.I., 1972-75, psychology instr., 1972-76, asst. prof. psychology, 1976-81, assoc. prof. psychology, 1981-91, prof. psychology, 1991—. Bd. dirs. Multi-Svc. Ctr., Newton, Mass., 1980-82. Contbr. articles to profl. jours., chpts. to books; reviewer APA Conv., 1985—, Teaching of Psychology Jour., 1988—, Collegiate Micro-Computer Jour., 1991, 93, Nat. Soc. Sci. Jour., 1991; mem. editl. bd., spl. edit. editor Cyber Psychology and Behavior. Bd. dirs. Wellesley (Mass.) Community Children's Ctr., 1986-90, Coun. for Children, Newton, Mass., 1984-86. NIMH fellow, 1967-68; NSF grantee, 1974-76, U.S. Office Edn. grantee, 1980. Mem. APA, Mass. Audubon Soc., Internat. Soc. for Online Mental Health (founding mem.), Soc. for Tchg. of Psychology, Soc. Computers in Psychology. Avocations: photography, antiques, gardening, literature. Home: 17 Fuller Brook Rd Wellesley MA 02482-7108 Office: Bryant Coll 1150 Douglas Pike Smithfield RI 02917-1291 E-mail: jmorahan@bryant.edu.

MORAITIS, KAREN KARL, real estate broker; b. Orange, Tex., Sept. 28, 1943; d. Richard Louis and Betty (Crandall) Karl; m. George Reynold Moraitis, Aug. 14, 1965; children: George Reynold Jr., Alexandra. BS in Advt., U. Fla., 1965; MEd, Fla. Atlantic U., 1968, EdS, 1974. Cert. real estate broker. Welfare worker State of Fla., Ft. Lauderdale, 1967; guidance counselor Broward County Pub. Schs., 1968-70; adj. faculty Fla. Atlantic U., Boca Raton, 1971-74; real estate assoc. Blackwell Realty, Ft. Lauderdale, 1976-77; real estate broker Karen Moraitis Realty, Inc., 1978—. Editor: Official Florida Publications, 1966. Mem. Pres.'s Council U. Fla., 1980—, scholarship ptnr. Gator Boosters, 1983—; pres. Harborside at Hillsboro Beach (Fla.) Condominium Assn., 1982, Parent Tchr. Student Orgn. Ft. Lauderdale High Sch., 1985-91. pres., 1986-88, Parent Tchr. Student Assn. Sunrise Middle Sch., Ft. Lauderdale, 1981-87. pres., 1982-84; v.p. PTA Bayview Elem. Sch., Ft.

Lauderdale, 1980; chmn. Winter Cotillion, Ft. Lauderdale, 1986-88; bd. dirs. Sunrise Intracoastal Homeowners Assn., 1977, 96—, Broward County Zoning Bd., 1980-81, Imperial Village Condominium Assn., Ft. Lauderdale, 1983; ambassador edn. City of Ft. Lauderdale, 1986-88. Served with USN, 1965. Mem. Nat. Assn. Realtors, Fla. Assn. Realtors, Ft. Lauderdale Bd. Realtors, Humane Soc. Broward County (life), Navy League (life), Ft. Lauderdale H.S. Boosters (pres. 1984-85, 87-88), Broward County Athletic Assn. (waiver rev. com. 1992-96), Nat. Football Found. and Coll. Hall of Fame (bd. dirs. Brian Piccolo chpt. 1992-96). Democrat. Avocation: travel. Office: Karen Moraitis Realty Inc 631 Middle River Dr Fort Lauderdale FL 33304-3509

MORALES, DIANE K. federal agency administrator; b. Houston, July 11, 1946; d. Arthur Clement and Helen Mary (Araiza) M. BA, U. Tex.-Austin, 1968. Account exec. Goodwin, Dannenbaum, Littman & Wingfield, Houston, 1968-70; pub. relations rep. Gittings, Inc., Dallas, 1970-71; asst. buyer, mgr. Neiman-Marcus, 1971-80; sr. assoc., mktg. mgr. 3/D Internat., Houston, 1980-81; dep. asst. sec. policy U.S. Dept. Interior, Washington, 1981-83; bd. dirs. CAB, 1983-86; v.p. Earth Tech. Corp., 1986-88; pvt. practice cons., 1988-90; dep. asst. sec. def. for logistics Dep. Def., 1990—; dep. under secy. logistics material readiness U.S. Dept. Defense, 2001—. Mem. Def. Depot Maintenance Coun.; chmn. Def. Material Mgmt. Bd, Def Transp. Polic Coun., Def. Energy Policy Coun. Pres. Downtown Rep. Women's Club, Dallas, 1979-80, bd. dirs. Dallas County Men's Rep. Club, 1980, Dallas County Women's Rep. Club, 1980; mem. Rep. Women's Fed. Forum, Rep. Nat. Hispanic Assembly. Presbyterian. Office: US Dept Defense Logistics Material Readiness 3500 Defense Pentagon Washington DC 20301-3500 Office Fax: 703-693-0555.*

MORALES, EMMITT, mechanical engineer; s. Emilio and Alice Morales; m. Virginia Eilene Lopez, Nov. 27, 1951; children: David, Michael. Grad. h.s., Port Arthur, Tex. Co-owner Tool Tech, Beaumont, Tex., 1999—, Indsl. Techs., Beaumont. With U.S. Army, 1969—71. Conservative. Church Of Christ. Achievements include patents for stud removal and fastening tool. Avocation: golf. Home: 5260 Stardust Beaumont TX 77706 Office: Tool Tech 5420 Gorman Rd Beaumont TX 77705

MORALES, JOHN RUEDA, corporate accounting executive; b. Chgo., Oct. 16, 1956; s. Juan Santa Maria and Elena (Rueda) M.; m. Carla Ann Cosentino, Apr. 19, 1980; 1 child, Samantha. BA, St. Xavier U., 1979. CPA, Ill. Mgmt. analyst Chgo. Water Reclamation Dist., 1980-85; sr. auditor Ernst & Young, Chgo., 1985-87; prin. auditor Am. Nat. Can Co., 1987-90; supr. internal audit Square D Co., Palatine, Ill., 1990-93, contr. corp. acctg., 1993-95, sr. fin. analyst mktg. group, 1996—. Sponsor Chgo. Tng. Alliance, 1992, 93, 94, 95, 96. Mem. AICPA, Ill. Soc. CPAs, Inst. Internal Auditors. Avocations: golf, swimming, billiards, reading, travel. Office: Square D Co Executive Pla Palatine IL 60067

MORALES, JOSE, psychotherapist, writer; b. Hatillo, P.R., May 27, 1930; s. Polonio and Marciala (Dorta) M.; m. Ramona Velez, Oct. 24, 1954 (div. Mar. 1976); 1 child, Jose R. Jr.; m. Carmen Iris Lopez, Apr. 12, 1976; 1 child, Delia. BA in Edn., U. P.R., 1960; MSW, NYU, 1968; PhD, U. Calif., Santa Barbara, 1985. Cert. social studies tchr., P.R., N.Y.; cert. social worker, N.Y. Tchr. P.R. Bd. Edn., Arecibo, 1960-63; ednl. counselor Puerto Rican Migration Dept., N.Y.C., 1964; case worker Lincoln Hall, 1964-66, social worker, 1968-70; social worker, supr. Greenpoint Hosp., Bklyn., 1970-76; social worker VA Hosp., Phila., 1977-80; social work supr. Kings County Hosp., Bklyn., 1981-93; psychotherapist CCM, 1993—. Cons./supr. N.Y. PCC, Bklyn. Author: Puerto Rican Spiritism, 1977 (Meritorious award 1981), Pepito, 1998, El Morro, 1998, Galeria de Heroes de Puerto Rico, 1997 (Meritorious award 1999); freelance journalist Eco Latino, 1993, El Latino Americano, 1997. Co-founder CILI, Bklyn., 1973, ACCEPIA, Bklyn., 1993. Mem. NASW, Am. Psychology Soc., Latin Am. Assn. Poets and Writers (co-founder, sec. 1997—, leadership com. 1998), N.Y. Acad. Scis. Avocations: reading, writing, researching geneology. Home: Bay Ridge Sta PO Box 234 Brooklyn NY 11220-0234 Office: CCM 185 Montague St Fl 9 Brooklyn NY 11201-3608 E-mail: JMora52825@aol.com.

MORALES, JULIO K. lawyer; b. Havana, Cuba, Jan. 17, 1948; came to U.S., 1960; s. Julio E. and Josephine (Holsters) M.; m. Suzette M. Dussault, May 31, 1970 (div. 1978); children: Julio E., Karel A.; m. Barbara A. Miller, July 14, 1979 (div. 1988); 1 child, Nicolas W. BA, Carroll Coll., 1969; JD, U. Mont., 1972. Bar: Mont. 1972, U.S. Dist. Ct. Mont. 1972, U.S. Ct. Mil. Appeals 1972, U.S. Ct. Appeals (9th cir.) 1980. Law clk. to presiding justice Mont. Supreme Ct., Helena, 1972; sole practice Missoula, Mont., 1973-78, 88—; sr. ptnr. Morales & Volinkaty, 1978-88; pvt. practice law Morales Law Office, 1988—. Author: Estate Planning for the Handicapped, 1975. Pres. Rockmont, Inc., Missoula, 1985-2001. Served to 2d lt. U.S. Army, 1972. Named Boss of the Yr., Missoula chpt. Mont. Assn. Legal Secs., 1988. Mem. ABA (dist. rep. 1975-79, exec. coun. young lawyer divsn. 1977-79), Mont. Bar Assn. (chmn. law day 1974, 75, 77), Am. Judicature Soc., Assn. Trial Lawyers Am., World Assn. Lawyers, Missoula Soccer Assn. (pres. 1983-85), Mont. Sailing Assn. (bd. dirs. 1994—), Nat. Exch. Club (bd. dirs. Yellowstone dist. 1987-88, pres. 1990-91), Missoula Exch. Club, Elks (officer 1999-2001, exalted ruler 2001—), Phi Delta Phi. Roman Catholic. Avocations: sports, coaching youth, boating, skiing, golf. Office: PO Box 9311 430 Ryman St Missoula MT 59802-4249 E-mail: jmorales@dsnetworks.net.

MORALES, REYNALDO, physicist; BS in Physics, St. Mary's U., San Antonio, 1959; MA in Physics, U. Tex., 1962, PhD in Physics, 1967. Physicist Los Alamos Nat. Lab., N.Mex., 1966—85, 1987—95, 1997—; sci. counselor State Dept., Washington, 1987—95; fgn. affairs specialist ACDA, 1995—96; physicist Dept. of Def./ATSD/NCB, 1996—97. Mem. Army Sci. Bd. Mem.: AAAS, Soc. of Hispanic Profl. Engrs., Soc. for Advancement of Chicanos and Native Ams. in Sci., Am. Phys. Soc. Office: Los Alamos National Lab PO Box 1663 MSM719 Los Alamos NM 87545*

MORALES, STEVEN ROQUE, social worker; b. San Jose, Calif., Jan. 19, 1954; s. Roque Joseph and Mary Ellen Morales; m. Mary Alice Rios, May 29, 1976 (div. Dec. 31, 1989); m. Ana Gil Moran, Apr. 1, 2000; children: Melissa Moran, Matthew, Ben Moran, Michael, Leslie. AA in Bus. Adminstrn., San Jose City Coll., 1976; BA in Psychology, San Jose State U., 1985, MSW, 1993. Pupil pers. svc. credential. Crisis counselor Suicide and Crisis Svcs. Santa Clara County, San Jose, 1990—91; mental health counselor San Jose Care and Guidance Ctr., 1990—91; crisis counselor Emergency Treatment Ctr., Santa Clara, 1991—93; mental health therapist Centro de Bienestar Gardner Health Ctr., San Jose, 1993—95; psychiat. social worker II Mental Health Dept. Santa Clara County, 1995—; mental health technician Santa Clara Valley chpt. ARC. Part-time lectr. BASW program Coll. Social Work San Jose State U., 1997—2001. Mem.: NASW. Democrat. Evang. Christian. Avocation: white-water rafting. Office: Mental Health Clinic at Juvenile Hall 840 Guadalupe Pky Ste 238 San Jose CA 95110 Fax: 408-971-2651. Personal E-mail: s.r.morales@worldnet.att.net.

MORALES-GALARRETA, JULIO, psychiatrist, child psychoanalyst; b. Trujillo, Peru, Dec. 1, 1936; came to U.S., 1973; s. Julio Morales-Fernandez and Lidia (Galarreta) Morales; (div.); children: Lourdes Lydia, Julio Fernando. MD, U. Trujillo, 1966; grad., St. Louis Psychoanalytic Inst., 1984, grad. in child psychoanalysis, 1985. Diplomate Am. Bd. Psychiatry and Neurology; cert. psychoanalyst.; cert. child psychoanalyst. Resident in psychiatry Ministry of Pub. Health, Peru, 1965-68; supr. psychiat. tng. program Ministry Pub. Health, Peru, 1970-72; physician and surgeon U. Trujillo, 1966; instr. pschaitry St. Marcos U., Peru, 1968-72; resident in psychiatry Fairfield Hills Hosp., Newtown, Conn., 1972-74; fellow in child psychiatry Washington U., St. Louis, 1974-76, instr. child psychiatry, 1976-82; dir. child devel. project St. Louis Psychoanalytic Inst., 1982-94, dir. child and adolescent psychotherapy program, 1993—, dir. child psychoanalysis, 1996—; assoc. clin. prof. psychiatry and pediatrics St. Louis U., 1983-96, clin. prof. psychiatry and pediatrics, 1996—. Faculty psychoanalysis and child analysis St. Louis Psychoanalytic Inst., 1984—, supervising analyst in child analyst, 1988, tng. and supervising analyst in adult and child psychoanalysis, 1991—. Fellow Peruvian Psychiat. Assn., Am. Psychiat. Assn. (mem. cert. com. bd. on profl. stds. 1996—), Am. Psychol. Assn.; mem. St. Louis Met. Med. Soc., Am. Acad. Child Psychiatry, Am. Psychoanalytic Assn. (mem. of cert. com. in psychoanalysis 1996—), Am. Soc. Adolescent Psychiatry, Assn. Child Psychoanalysis, St. Louis Psychiat. Soc. (pres. 1997-99). Avocations: classical music, biking, tennis, golf. Home: 665 S Skinker Blvd Saint Louis MO 63105-2300 Office: 8820 Ladue Rd Ste 314 Saint Louis MO 63124

MORAN, ANN, education educator; b. Joliet, Ill., Nov. 30, 1945; d. William and Ann Agnes (Ahern) Grinton; m. Thomas Lee Moran, Aug. 17, 1968; 1 child, Cristi Ann. BS, Murray State U., 1968; MA, U. Ky., 1977. Tchr. Trigg County Sch. System, Cadiz, Ky., 1968-70, Diocese of Covington, Versailles, 1976-83, Diocese of Lexington, 1984—, resource tchr. for intern tchrs., 1986, 89, 91. Mentor acad. support tchr., 1997-99.

MORAN, BARBARA BURNS, librarian, educator; b. Columbus, Miss., July 8, 1944; d. Robert Theron and Joan (Brown) Burns; m. Joseph J. Moran, Sept. 4, 1965; children: Joseph Michael, Brian Matthew. AB, Mount Holyoke Coll., S. Hadley, Mass., 1966; M in Librarianship, Emory U., Atlanta, 1973; PhD, SUNY, Buffalo, 1982. Head libr. The Park Sch. of Buffalo, Snyder, NY, 1974-78; prof. Sch. Info. and Libr. Sci. U. N.C., Chapel Hill, 1981—, asst. dean, 1987-90, dean, 1990-98, prof., 1999—. Participant various seminars; evaluator various edn. progs.; cons. in field; bd. govs. UNC Press, 1998—. Author: Academic Libraries, 1984; co-author: (with Robert D. Stueart) Library Management, 6th edit., 2002; contbr. articles to profl. jours., chpts. to books; mem. editl. bd. Jour. Acad. Librarianship, 1992-94, Coll. and Rsch. Libraries, 1996—. Coun. Libr. Resources grantee, 1985, Univ. Rsch. Coun. grantee, 1983, 89, others. Mem. ALA, Assn. for Libr. and Info. Sci. Edn., Popular Culture Assn., N.C. Libr. Assn., Beta Phi Mu. Home: 1307 Leclair St Chapel Hill NC 27517-3034 Office: Univ NC Sch Info & Libr Sci Chapel Hill NC 27599-0001 E-mail: moran@ils.unc.edu.

MORAN, CHARLES A. securities executive; b. Chgo., Feb. 7, 1943; s. Charles W. and Rose B. (Sutcher) M.; m. Donna L. Orbach, Sept. 3, 1967; children: Scott Alan, Erin Elizabeth. AB, Princeton U., 1964; JD, U. Mich., 1967; postgrad. advanced mgmt., Harvard U., 1982. CFP. With Chase Manhattan Bank, N.Y.C., 1967-70; pension trust officer, adminstrv. officer, officer in charge new bus. devel., pension div. Mfrs. Hanover Trust Co., 1970-87, sr. v.p., officer-in-charge employee benefit trust div., 1979-80; chmn. bd., pres., CEO MH/Edie Investment Counsel (formerly Lionel D. Edie & Co.), 1980-82, officer-in-charge corp. trust div., 1982-83, officer in charge-global securities group, 1983-87; pres. Govt. Securities Clearing Corp., 1987-96; asst. prof., faculty fellow The Coll. of N.J., Trenton, 1996-99; pres. Strategic Financial Adv., Montclair, N.J., 1996—; prof. Harvard U., Cambridge, summer 1997—, Bucknell U., 1999—. Former bd. dirs. Mfrs. Hanover Trust Co. Calif., Mfrs. Hanover Data Svcs. Corp., Mortgage Backed Securities Clearing Corp., Nat. Securities Clearing Corp.; chmn. bd. dirs. Inform, Inc.; former lectr. bus. and econs. Bloomfield Coll.; former lectr. sociology and fin. employee benefits C.W. Post Coll., L.I. U.; cons. Urban Vol. Cons. Group, Inc.; mem. adv. coun. U.S. Dept. Labor; mem. adv. bd. BNA Pension Reporter; mem. Employees Retirement Income Security Act of 1974 Roundtable; mem. industry adv. com. Future Electronic Funds Payments Svcs. Fed. Res. Contbr. articles to profl. jours. Mem. Am. Inst. Banking, Am. Employee Benefits Inst. (treas. 1976-79), N.Y. State Bankers Assn. (employees trust com.), Assn. Pvt. Pension and Welfare Plans (dir., mem. exec. com.), ERISA Industry Com. (pres., dir., mem. exec. com., treas.), Am. Bankers Assn. (chmn. employee benefit trust com. 1977-82), Internat. Found. Pension and Welfare Plans, Bank Adminstrn. Inst. (mem. tech. commn.), N.Y. C. of C. (task force on pub. pensions), Fin. Planning Assn. (dir.), The Inst. of Cert. Fin. Planners (bd. dirs., com. on career devel.), N.J. Soc. Inst. Cert. Fin. Planners (bd. dirs., sec., treas.), World Future Soc., Internat. Soc. Cert. Employee Benefit Specialists, Am. Acad. Mgmt., Am. Soc. Fin. Svcs. Profls., Princeton Club, Harvard Bus. Sch. Club of N.Y. E-mail: cmoransfa@yahoo.com.

MORAN, DANIEL AUSTIN, mathematician, educator; b. Chgo., Feb. 17, 1936; s. Austin Thomas and Violet Lillian (Johnson) M.; m. Karen Krull, Sept. 14, 1963; children: Alexander, Claudia. BS summa cum laude, St. Mary's of Tex., 1957; MS, U. Ill., 1958, PhD, 1962. Research instr. U. Chgo., 1962-64; asst. prof. Mich. State U., 1964-68, assoc. prof., 1968-76, prof. math., 1976—. Vis. scholar U. Cambridge, 1970-71, U. North Wales, 1978 Contbr. articles to profl. jours. Mem. Math. Assn. Am., Sigma Xi, Pi Mu Epsilon, Delta Epsilon Sigma, Kappa Mu Alpha. Roman Catholic. Home: 2633 Roseland Ave East Lansing MI 48823-3870 Office: Dept Math Michigan State Univ East Lansing MI 48824

MORAN, DANIEL THOMAS, dentist, poet; b. N.Y.C., Mar. 9, 1957; s. Thomas Daniel and Jean Elizabeth Moran; m. Karen Kay; children: Lindsay Alison, Ashley Zurl, Gregory Riordan. AS, Nassau Coll., 1977; BS, SUNY, Stony Brook, 1979; D in Dental Sci., Howard U., 1983. Staff assoc. Southhampton (N.Y.) Hosp., 1988-94; host L.I. Radio mag., Southampton, NY, 1994—99; literary corr. L.I. Pub. Radio, 1994—2001; pvt. practice Shelter Island, N.Y., 1987—. Author: Dancing for Victoria, 1991, Gone to Innisfree, 1993, Sheltered by Islands, 1995, In Praise of August, 1999, From Hilo to Willow Pond, 2002; contbr. poetry to profl. publs. Shared decision com. Shelter Island Sch., 1993-97; dir. Gardiner's Bay Country Club, 1993-98, historian 1993—, tournament chmn., 1993-96); v.p. Walt Whitman Birthplace Assn., Huntington, N.Y., 1997—, v.p., 2001—; hon. dir. Wildlife Rescue Ctr. of the Hamptons. Grantee Poets and Writers, Inc., 1996-99. Mem. Poetry Soc. of Am. Avocations: golf, harmonica, drums. Home: PO Box 2008 Shelter Island NY 11964-2008 Office: 51A North Ferry Rd Shelter Island NY 11964

MORAN, ELIZABETH AMES, library director; b. Camden, Maine, June 22, 1940; d. Robie Frank and Dorothy Dyer Ames; m. Andrew Jackson Moran, Dec. 3, 1966; children: Heather Elizabeth, Melissa Ames. BA, U. Maine, 1962; MA in Law & Diplomacy, Fletcher Sch. Law & Diplomacy, 1964; MLS, U. S.C., 1997. Intelligence officer CIA, Washington, 1964-68; sch. libr. Fairfax (Va.) County Schs., 1981-87; libr. Camden (Maine) Pub. Libr., 1988-90, libr. dir., 1990—. Bd. dirs. Camden Tech. Conf., 1997-98; chair Maine Libr. Commn., 2000—. Mem. ALA, Maine Libr. Assn. (pres. 1998-2000), Pub. Libr. Assn. Small Pub. Libr. Assn., Camden Garden Club, Phi Beta Kappa. Republican. Episcopalian. Avocations: sailing, needlework. Home: 32 Atlantic Hwy Northport ME 04849-3010 Office: Camden Pub Libr 55 Main St Camden ME 04843-1794 E-mail: emoran@camden.lib.me.us.

MORAN, EMILIO FEDERICO, anthropology and ecology educator; b. Habana, Cuba, July 21, 1946; s. Emilio F. Sr. and Caridad B. (Corrales) M.; m. Maria del Carmen Mendez, (div. 1970); m. Millicent Fleming, Dec. 15, 1972; 1 child, Emily Victoria. BA, Springhill Coll., 1968; MA, U. Fla., 1969, PhD, 1975. Asst. prof. Ind. U., Bloomington, 1975-79, assoc. prof., 1979-84, chmn. dept. anthropology, 1980-87, prof. dept. anthropology, 1984—. Rudy prof. anthropology, 1996—, dir. Anthrop. Ctr. Tng. and Rsch. on Global Environ. Change, 1992—. Co-dir. Ctr. for Study of Instns., Population and Environ. Change, 1996—; leader Focus 1, Land-Use/Cover Change Program, 1999—; vis. prof. soil sci. N.C. State U., Raleigh, 1984; adv. panelist NSF, Washington, 1987-88, 90. Author: Developing the Amazon, 1981, Human Adaptability, 1982, The Human Ecology of Amazonian Populations, 1993; editor: The Dilemma of Amazonian Development, 1983, The Ecosystem Concept in Anthropology, 1984, The Ecosystem Approach in Anthropology, 1990, The Comparative Study of Human Societies, 1995, Transforming Societies, Transforming Anthropology, 1996; mem. editl. bd. Jour. Latin Am. Studies (Japan), 1992—, Jour. Forest and Conservation History, 1986-95, Anthropol. Linguistics, 1982-87, World Cultures, 1987-97, Human Ecology, 1993—. Grantee Fulbright Found., 1973, 76, 89, NIMH, 1974, NSF, 1991-93, 93—, Dept. of Energy, 1991-95, Wenner-Gren, 1989, NICHD, 1997-2001, NASA, 1998-2001, NOAA, 2000—; recipient A.J. Hanna Disting. Lectr. Rollins Coll., 1985, ERDAN award for best sci. paper, 2000, Robert McNetting award Assn. Am. Geographics, 2002; postdoctoral fellow Tinker Found., 1983-84; Guggenheim Meml. Found. fellow, 1989; named Disting. Ecologist Colo. State U., 1987. Fellow AAAS (nominations com. 1987—, coun. rep. to AAAS bd.), Am. Anthrop. Assn. (chmn. panel on devel., chmn. task force on environment, pres. anthropology and environ. sect. 1995-98), Linnean Soc. London. Home: 3005 Forrester S Bloomington IN 47401-4494 Office: Ind U Student Bldg 240 Bloomington IN 47405

MORAN, GREGORY ALLAN, real estate developer and consultant; b. Oklahoma City, Oct. 23, 1962; s. Emet Allan and Joyce (Ladon) M.; m. Bridget Ellen Moran, Aug. 11, 1991; children: Ian Anderson, Conor Alexander, Kathlyn Maeve. BSBA in Fin. and Real Estate, U. Denver, 1985. Rsch. analyst Boettcher & Co., Denver, 1983-85; broker assoc. Del E. Webb Co., 1985-87, Grubb & Ellis Co., Denver, 1987-90; sr. broker assoc. The Colfax Group, Austin, Tex., 1990-96, Frederick Ross Co., Denver, 1996-98; v.p. leasing Miller Weingarten Realty, LLC, Englewood, 1998—. Burns fellow U. Denver-Burns Sch. Real Estate, 1999—. SEc., Kappa Sigma-Beta Omicron Housing Corp., Denver, 1996—. Mem. Internat. Coun. Shopping Ctrs. (assoc., state dir. 1997-2000, state govt. rels. dir. 2000—), Urban Land Inst., Denver Univ. Club. Republican. Roman Catholic. Avocations: alpine skiing, running. Office: Miller Weingarten Realty LLC 850 Englwood Pkwy Ste 200 Englewood CO 80110-2304

MORAN, GREGORY JOHN, emergency medicine physician, educator; b. Kansas City, Mo., July 30, 1961; MD, U. Kans., 1987. Cert. in emergency medicine; cert. in internal medicine; bd. cert. in infectious disease. Intern UCLA, 1987-88, resident in internal medicine, 1988-90, resident in emergency medicine, 1990-92, fellow in infectious diseases, 1993-96; emergency medicine physician Olive View-UCLA Med. Ctr. Assoc. prof. medicine UCLA, 1993—. Mem. Am. Coll. Emergency Physicians, Infectious Diseases Soc. Am., Alpha Omega Alpha. E-mail: gmoran@ucla.edu.

MORAN, JAMES JOSEPH, JR. insurance executive; s. James J. and Marilyn A. (Sullivan) M.; m. Mary Therese Stevens, Oct. 6, 1979; children: Sean M., James E., Matthew S. AB cum laude, Boston Coll., 1975, JD, 1978. Bar: Mass. 1978, U.S. Ct. Appeals (1st cir.) 1979, U.S. Dist Ct. Mass. 1979, U.S. Tax Ct. 1979, U.S. Supreme Ct. 1982; CPCU; Assoc. in Reins. Assoc. Haussermann, Davison & Shattuck, Boston, 1978-84, Morrison, Mahoney & Miller, Boston, 1984-87, ptnr., 1988-98; pres. Eastern Casualty Ins. Co., Marlborough, 1998—2001; v.p, gen. counsel Quincy (Mass.) Mutual Fire Ins. Co., 2001—. V.p., gen. counsel Ind. Property-Casualty Insurers Mass. Inc., 1991-98; counsel Mass. Assn. Ins. Agts., 1985-96; ins. broker, Mass.; New Eng. regional regulatory counsel Alliance of Am. Insurers, 1994-98; trustee New Eng. Coll. Fin., 1998-2000; speaker in field. Contbr. articles to profl. jours. Bd. dirs. (gubernatorial appointee) Mass. Pollution Liability Reinsurance Corp., 1988-90. Recipient Econ. Leadership award Orgn. New Equality, 1997. Mem. Internat. Assn. Def. Coun., Mass. Bar Assn., CPCU Soc. (pres. Boston chpt. 1993-94), Fedn. Ins. Corp. Coun., Ins. Libr. Assn. Boston (trustee 1983—, pres. 1989-90). Roman Catholic. Home: 15 Bramel Cir Walpole MA 02081-2043 Office: Quincy Mutual Fire Ins Co 57 Washington St Quincy MA 02169-9155

MORAN, JAMES MICHAEL, JR. astronomer, educator; b. Plainfield, N.J., Jan. 3, 1943; s. James Michael and Martha (Algermissen) M.; m. Barbara Putney Smith, Nov. 30, 1974; children: Susan Harrison, Michael Putney. BS, U. Notre Dame, 1963; SM, MIT, 1965, PhD, 1968. Mem. staff MIT Lincoln Lab., Lexington, Mass., 1968-70; sr. radio astronomer Smithsonian Astrophys. Obs., Cambridge, 1970—; prof. practice of astronomy Harvard U., 1979-89, Donald H. Menzel prof. astrophysics, 2001—; assoc. dir. Harvard-Smithsonian Ctr. Astrophysics, 1987-92, dir. Submillimeter Array Project, 1996—. Jansky lectr. Nat. Radio Astronomy Obs., 1996; trustee N.E. Radio Obs. Corp., Cambridge, 1983—. Contbr. numerous articles on radio astronomy to profl. publs. Co-recipient Rumford prize Am. Acad. Arts and Scis., 1971; recipient Sr. awrd Alexander von Humboldt Soc., 1993. Fellow AAAS; mem. IEEE (sr.), NAS, Am. Astron. Soc. (Pierce prize 1978), Explorers Club. Achievements include development of technique of very long baseline interferrrometry; research in study of black holes. Home: 93 Anson Rd Concord MA 01742-5704 Office: Harvard-Smithsonian Center for Astrophysics 60 Garden St Cambridge MA 02138-1516

MORAN, JAMES BYRON, federal judge; b. Evanston, Ill., June 20, 1930; s. James Edward and Kathryn (Horton) M.; children: John, Jennifer, Sarah, Polly; stepchildren: Katie, Cynthia, Laura, Michael. AB, U. Mich., 1952; LLB magna cum laude, Harvard U., 1957. Bar: Ill. 1958. Law clk. to judge U.S. Ct. of Appeals (2d cir.), 1957-58; assoc. Bell, Boyd, Lloyd, Haddad & Burns, Chgo, 1958-66, ptnr., 1966-79; judge U.S. Dist. Ct. (no. dist.) Ill., Chgo., 1979—. Dir. Com. on Ill. Govt., 1960-78, chmn., 1968-70; vice chmn., sec. Ill. Dangerous Drug Adv. Coun., 1967-74; dir. Gateway Found., 1969— ; mem. Ill. Ho. of Reps., 1965-67; mem. Evanston City Council, 1971-75. Served with AUS, 1952-54. Mem. Chgo. Bar Assn., Chgo. Council Lawyers, Lawyers Club, Phi Beta Kappa. Home: 117 Kedzie St Evanston IL 60202-2509 Office: US Dist Ct 219 S Dearborn St Chambers 1946 Chicago IL 60604-1800 E-mail: jbm117@aol.com.

MORAN, JAMES D., III, psychologist, child development educator; b. Bklyn., Mar. 2, 1951; s. James D. and Monica (Scherzinger) M.; m. Laurette Virginia Miller, Aug. 11, 1973; children: Ryan, Mollie. BA magna cum laude, Duke U., 1973; MS, U. Okla., 1975; PhD, Okla. State U., 1978. Asst. prof. U. Okla., Norman, 1978-80, Va. Poly. Inst. and State U., Blacksburg, 1980-83, assoc. prof., asst. head dept. famly and child devel., 1983-85; prof., head dept. family rels. and child devel. Okla. State U., Stillwater, 1985-89; assoc. dean coll. human ecology U. Tenn., 1989-98, dean, 1998—2002, assoc. vice provost, accreditation and state relations, 2002—. V.p. U. Tenn. Rsch. Corp.; mng. dir. Tande Tech. Licensing. Mem. editl. bd. Home Econs. Rsch. Jour., 1983-85, Family Rels., 1985-91, Creativity Rsch. Jour., 1988-90, Home Econs. Forum, 1990-91, Jour. Family and Consumer Scis., 1993-95. Recipient Outstanding Rsch. award, Va. Home Econs. Assn., 1982, Disting. Alumnus award, Coll. Human Environ. Scis., Okla. State U., 2001. Mem.: Nat. Assn. for Edn. Young Children, Am. Assn. Family and Consumer Scis. (vice chmn. family rels. and child devel. sect. 1985—86, chmn. nominating com. 1987, chair coun. for accreditation 1989, 1991, chair strategic planning com. 1989, chair collegiate assembly 1995—97, vice chair bd. on human scis. 1999—2001, named among New Faces to Watch 1984, Leadership award 1986), Phi Kappa Phi, Kappa Omicron Nu. Democrat. Roman Catholic. Avocation: golf. Home: 824 Andover Blvd Knoxville TN 37922-1532 Office: 413 AHT U Tenn Knoxville TN 37996-0184 E-mail: jmoran@utk.edu., jdmoran3@aol.com.

MORAN, JAMES PATRICK, JR. congressman, stockbroker; b. Buffalo, May 16, 1945; s. James Patrick and Dorothy (Dwyer) M.; m. Mary Craig, Dec. 27, 1967 (div. 1974); children: Jimmy, Mary; m. Mary Howard; children: Michael, Patrick, Dorothy. BA in Econs., Coll. of Holy Cross, Worcester, Mass., 1967; postgrad., CUNY, 1967-68; MA in Pub. Adminstrn., U. Pitts., 1970. Budget analyst HEW, Washington, 1969-74; budget and fiscal policy specialist, Congl. rsch. Libr. of Congress, 1974-76; sr. staff appropriations com. U.S. Senate, 1976-79; city councilman City of Alexandria, Va., 1979—84, vice-mayor, 1982-84, mayor, 1985-91; investment broker A.G. Edwards & Sons, Alexandria, 1979—; mem. U.S. Congress from 8th Va. dist., Washington, 1991—; mem. appropriations com., budget com. Councilman, City of Alexandria, 1979-82, vice-mayor, 1982-84, mayor, 1985—; chmn. No. Va. Transportation Bd., 1988—, United Way, 1977-79; vice chmn. Mental Health Retard and Substance Abuse Bd., 1976-78, vice chmn. D.E.O., 1976-78;dir., Met. Area Council Govts., dir. No. Va. Transp. Commn., 1985—. Recipient Outstanding Citizenship award YMCA, 1983. Mem. C. of C. (dir. 1985-86). Democrat. Roman Catholic. Home: 205 Uhler Ter Alexandria VA 22301-1551 Office: US Ho of Reps 2239 Rayburn Ho Office Bldg Washington DC 20515-4608*

MORAN, JERRY, congressman; m. Robba A. Moran. Senator dist. 37 State of Kans.; mem., asst. majority whip U.S. Congress from 1st Kans dist., 1997—, mem. agr., transp., infrastructure, vets. affairs coms., steering com.; chmn. Rural Caucus Task Force on Telecommunications; co-chmn. Congressional Beef Caucus. Republican. Home: 2758 Thunderbird Dr Hays KS 67601-1403 Office: US Ho of Reps 1519 Longworth Hob Washington DC 20515-1601*

MORAN, JOAN JENSEN, physical education and health educator; b. Chgo., Sept. 25, 1952; d. Axel Fred and Mary J. (Maes) J.; m. Gregory Keith Moran. BS in Edn., Western Ill. U., 1974; MS in Edn., No. Ill. U., 1978. Cert. tchr., Ill. Tchr., coach East Coloma Sch., Rock Falls, Ill., 1974—. Part-time recreation specialist Woodhaven Lakes, Sublette, Ill., 1975-79; cons. Ill. State Bd. Edn., Springfield, 1984—; instr. NDEITA, Ill., 1988—; facilitator Project Wild, Ill., 1990—. Instr. ARC, Rock Falls, 1978—, Am. Heart Assn., Rock Falls, 1978—; exec. bd. East Coloma Cmty. Club; fitness del. to Russia and Hungary, 1992; cons. Alcohol Awareness & Occupant Restraint Ill. State Bd. Edn., Substance Abuse Guidance Edn. Com., Rock Falls Drug Free Cmty. Grant com., Whiteside County CPR Coord. com. Recipient Western Ill. U. Alumni Achievement award, 1993, Western Ill. Master Tchr. award, 1993, Svc.

award Ill. Assn. Health, Phys. Edn., Recreation and Dance, 1991, 92, Outstanding Young Woman award, 1986, Phys. Educator of Yr. award, 1988; named Mid. Sch. Phys. Edn. Tchr. of Yr. Midwest AAHPERD, 1993, Ill. Assn. Health, Phys. Edn., Recreation and Dance, 1992, Gov.'s Coun. Health and Phys. Edn. award, 1991, Am. Tchr. of Yr. award Walt Disney Co., 1993, Excel award Ill. State Bd. Edn., 1995, finalist Ill. Tchr. of Yr., 1996, Milkin Nat. Educator award, 1997, Health Edn. award and Quarter Century award Ill. Assn. Health, Phys. Edn., Recreation and Dance, 1999, Presidential citation, 1998; named to USA Today Tchr. Team, 2000. Mem.: AAHPERD (Health Tchr. of Yr. midwest chpt. 2001), Environ. Edn. Assn. Ill., East Coloma Edn. Assn. (pres., pub. rels., v.p. 1993—94), Ill. Edn. Assn., No. Dist. Ill. Assn. Health, Phys. Edn., Recreation and Dance (newsletter editor 1984—85, exec. bd. 1985—90, treas. 1985—90), Ill. Assn. Health, Phys. Edn., Recreation and Dance (v.p. teenage youth 1988—90, pres. 1994, past pres., conv. coord. 1995, Honor Fellow award 1996). Democrat. Lutheran. Avocations: skiing, hiking, biking, reading, traveling. Home: 1903 E 41st St Sterling IL 61081-9449

MORAN, JOHN BERNARD, government official, retired; b. Saginaw, Mich., Nov. 26, 1936; s. Leo Lewis and Marie Katherine (Langley) M.; m. Diann Marie Markey, May 20, 1963 (div.); m. Barbara Jane Livingston, Aug. 18, 1978; children— Leslie Marie, Leanne Rene, Jeffrey John BS in Metall. Engring., Ill. Inst. Tech., 1959. Sr. automotive specialist Dow Chem. Co., Midland, Mich., 1962-71; program dir. research EPA, Research Triangle Park, N.C., 1971-75, dir. monitoring tech. div. Washington, 1975-76; dir. div. safety research Nat. Inst. for Occupational Safety and Health, Ctrs. for Disease Control, USPHS, HHS, Morgantown, W.Va., 1976-77, 83-88; dir. research and devel. safety products div. Am. Optical Corp., Southbridge, Mass., 1977-80; v.p., dir. ops. Geomet, Inc., Rockville, Md., 1980-83; program dir. Hartford Engring. Tech., Inc., Windsor, Conn., 1988; assoc. dir. health and safety laborers Associated Gen. Contractors, 1988-89; dir. safety and health Laborers Health and Safety Fund, 1989-95; spl. asst. to dep. asst. sec. Worker Health and Safety U.S. Dept. Energy, Washington, 1995; dir. policy OSHA, U.S. Dept. Labor, 1996; expert cons. to asst. sec. OSHA, 1996—; expert cons. to CDC Chem./Bioagts., 1996-99, ret.; now cons. in field. Mem. Nat. Mine Health Rsch. Adv. Com., Atlanta, 1980-84; govt. del. ILO, Geneva, 1985; mem. Nat. Adv. Com. on Constrn. Safety and Health, 1985-88, 92-95, Bur. Labor Stats. Rsch., 1991-95, hazardous material transp. info. com. NAS, 1991-93, Hazardous Materials Control Rsch. Inst.; chmn. lead subcom. Bldg. Constrn. Trades Dept., 1991-95; adj. asst. prof. mech. engring. W.Va. U., 1985-88; vis. ext. prof. U. Conn., Storrs, 1988-90; mem. Fed. Facilities Environ. Restoration Com., constrn. com. A 10 Am. Nat. Stds. Inst.; co-chair EPA-Labor Superfund Task Force, 1990-95, 96—; mem. nat. lead task force HUD, 1993-95; cons., expert witness. Patentee; contbr. articles to profl. jours, chpts. to books. Mem. Task Force on Hazardous Materials, Rockville, Md., 1983. chmn. Nat. Tech. Workshops on Safety and Health Issues. Served to capt. USMC, 1959-65 Recipient Bronze medal for commendable service EPA, 1974, Commitment to Life award Nat. Safe Workplace Inst., 1988. Mem. Internat. Soc. Respiratory Protection (pres. 1985-87, bd. dirs. 1987-89), Am. Conf. Govtl. Indsl. Hygienists. Roman Catholic. Home: PO Box 267 Franklinton NC 27525-0267

MORAN, JOHN THOMAS, JR. lawyer; b. Oak Park, Ill., Mar. 15, 1943; s. John T. and Corinne Louise (Dire) M.; m. Catherine Casey Pyne, May 16, 1981; 1 child, Sean Michael Pyne-Moran. AB cum laude, U. Notre Dame, 1965; JD, Georgetown U., 1968. Bar: Ill. 1969, Colo. 1976, U.S. Supreme Ct. 1973. Chief appeals div. Pub. Defender Cook County, Ill., 1970-82, gen. counsel, 1984-86; chief litigation atty. Frank & Flaherty, 1982; cons. ABA, 1982-83; sole practice, 1986-93; founder Law Offices of John Thomas Moran, 1993-97, John T. Moran & Assocs., 1993—. Editor: Gideon Revisited, 1983. Bd. dirs. Lawyers for the Creative Arts, 1973-97. Ford Found. grantee Internat. Common Law Colloquium, London, 1976, NEH grantee, Harvard Law Sch., 1977. Mem. Ill. State Bar Assn., Appellate Lawyers Assn., Nat. Legal Aid and Defenders Assn., Am. Soc. Internat. Law, Georgetown U. Law Ctr. Alumni Soc., Sorin Soc. U. Notre Dame. Avocation: sailing. Home: 930 Oakwood Ave Wilmette IL 60091-3320 Office: John T Moran & Assocs 309 W Washington St Ste 900 Chicago IL 60606-3209

MORAN, MARTIN JOSEPH, fundraising company executive; b. Bklyn., Nov. 3, 1930; s. Dominick and Mary (Lydon) Moran; m. Mary Therese Schofield, June 5, 1954; children: Martin Joseph, John P., Maureen M., Thomas S., Robert P., William M., Maria M. BA, St. John's U., 1952. Profl. fundraising cons., 1956—; founder Martin J. Moran Co., Inc., N.Y.C., 1964, pres., 1964—74, chmn. bd., 1974—. Mem. Am. Revolution Bicentennial Commn., Oyster Bay, NY, Massapequa Park Ethics Commn., 1969—72; trustee Notre Dame Coll., S.I, 1969—72, La Salle Acad., N.Y.C., 1971—87; mem. pres.'s coun. Cath. U. P.R., Ponce, 1966—71; mem. Cardinal's Com. for Edn., N.Y.C., 1970—79, Cardinal's Com. for Laity Archdiocese N.Y., 1979—98, Massapequa Park (NY) Bd. Zoning Appeals, 1972—84, chmn., 1978—84; bd. councilors, sec., treas. Equestrian Order Holy Sepulchre of Jerusalem, 1990—, sec.-treas., 1990—93, pres., 1993—. Served as aviator USNR, 1952—56. Decorated knight Order Holy Sepulchre, Pope Paul VI, Knight of Malta Pope Paul VI, papal Knight of Order of St. Gregory the Gt. Pope John Paul II, knight comdr.; recipient Pietas medal, St. John's U., N.Y., 1988. Mem.: Am. Assn. Fundraising Counsel (bd. dirs. 1970—75), Navy Hist. Assn., Navy League, Friendly Sons of St. Patrick, Nassau County Hist. Soc., St. John's U. Alumni Assn. (pres. 1987—94), Old Port Yacht Club, Lost Tree Club (N. Palm Beach, Fla.), Madison Sq. Garden Club (N.Y.C.), KC. Home: 1300 Lakeshore Dr Massapequa Park NY 11762-1764 also: 677 Village Rd North Palm Beach FL 33408-3329 Office: Martin J Moran Co 1 Penn Plz Ste 1626 New York NY 10119-1626 E-mail: mjmmarty@aol.com.

MORAN, MARY SHANKS, hydrogeologist; b. Biloxi, Miss., Feb. 8, 1950; d. John William and Sara Lillie (Kirklin) Shanks; m. William Madison Moran, June 5, 1971; 1 child, Alice Janette. BS in geology, Tenn. Tech. Univ., 1973; MS in geology, Vanderbilt Univ., 1977; postgrad., Ohio Univ., 1979. Cert. and lic. profl. geologist. Hydrologist U.S. Geological Survey, Nashville, 1974-77; hydrogeologist, rsch. assoc. Oak Ridge Nat. Lab., Oak Ridge, Tenn., 1977-80; sr. hydrogeologist Henningson, Durham & Richardson, Knoxville, 1980-81; hydrogeologist rsch. staff Oak Ridge Nat. Lab., 1981-85; hydrogeologist Birmingham, Ala., 1985-87; sr. hydrogeologist Sci. Applications Internat., 1987-89; environmental svcs. mgr. Atec Assocs., 1989; chief scientist & prin. Gallet & Assocs., Inc., 1989—. Cons. Geotech and environmental cons. , 1989—; mem. Ala. Bd. Licensure Profl. Geologists, 1996—; adv. bd. Geoenviron. Cons., 1995—, Ala. State Drinking Water Act, 1998—; mem. Ala. Onsite Sewage Mgmt. Com., 1999—. Co-author: Sourcebook of Hydrologic/Ecological Features Water Resource Regions of the Conterminous U.S., 1980, Water Resources Investigations U.S. Geological Survey, 1977; contbr. articles to profl. jours. Recipient Svc. award Am. Inst. Profl. Geologists; named Outstanding Young Woman of Am. Mem. ASCE (mem. geoinst. mem. com. 1999—), Assn. of Groundwater Scientists & Engrs. (dir. 1995-97, Svc. award, 1995), Geological Soc. Am., Am. Inst. of Profl. Geologists (sect. pres. 1993-95), ASFE Profl. Firms Practicing in the Geoscis. (Geoenviron. Com. Svc. award, 1998), Rotary Club (pres. 1994-95), Sigma Xi. Avocations: flying, needlework, field geology, drawing. Home: 913 Masters Ln Birmingham AL 35244-3262 Office: Gallet & Assocs Inc 320 Beacon Pkwy W Birmingham AL 35209-3171 E-mail: mmoran@gallet.com.

MORAN, MELVIN ROBERT, oil industry executive; b. St. Joseph, Mo., Sept. 18, 1930; s. Meyer Moran and Elsie Fine; m. Jasmine Dolores Lindsay, Nov. 22, 1953; children: Marilyn Townsend, Elisa, David. BS in Bus. Adminstrn., U. Mo., 1951. Asst. to supt. Moran Oil Co., Seminole, Okla., 1953-55; mgr., corp. sec. Moran Pipe & Supply Co., Inc., 1955-81; mng. ptnr. Moran K Oil, 1979—, Moran Oil Enterprises, Seminole, 1979—. Dir. Banc First, Oklahoma City, 1983—. Pres. BNai Brith, 1960—; mayor, councilman City of Seminole, 1965-79; bd. dirs. Seminole Industries Found., 1977—; chmn. state campaign U.S. Senator David Boren, 1982-94; regent, chmn. Seminole State Coll., 1983-97; trustee Okla. Found. Excellence, 1986—; founder Jasmine Moran Children's Mus., Seminole, 1993; elected bd. dirs. Okla. Heritage Assn., 1999—. Lt. USAF, 1951-53, Eng. Recipient Philanthropist of Yr. award Okla. Fundraising Execs., 1995; named to Hall of Fame, Okla. Heritage Assn., 1997, Oilman of Yr. Seminole Hist. Soc., 2002. Mem. Okla. Ind. Petroleum Assn. (dir., pres.), Seminole C. of C. (pres. dir. 1975—, Citizen of Yr. 1975, Hall of Fame 1980), Rotary (pres. 1960, apptd. blue ribbon jud. com. 1998—, apptd. bus. cir. for arts 1998—, apptd. Okla. Arts Coun. 1999, Mem. of Yr. 1997). Democrat. Jewish. Avocations: golfing. Office: Moran Oil Enterprises PO Box 1295 Seminole OK 74818-1295 E-mail: melvinmoran@webtv.net., moe@renet.com.

MORAN, MICHAEL LEE, physical therapist, computer consultant; b. Batavia, N.Y., Sept. 26, 1955; s. John Henry and Jane Miriam (Daly) M.; m. Jeanne Marie Grunau, Oct. 14, 1978; children: Katie, Michael L. BS, SUNY, Stony Brook, 1978; MS, U. Scranton, Pa., 1983; ScD, Nova U., Ft. Lauderdale, 1990; Cert. in Gerontology, Coll. Misericordia, 1997. Staff/chief phys. therapist Allied Svcs. for the Handicapped, Scranton, Pa., 1978-81; chief phys. therapist Mercy Hosp., Wilkes-Barre, 1981-83; staff phys. therapist Spinks & Violand, Monticello, N.Y., 1983-84; dir. phys. therapy Moran Phys. Therapy, Scranton, 1984-88, Manor Health Care, Inc., Kingston, Pa., 1988-92, Coll. Misericordia, Dallas, 1992, asst. prof., 1992-98, assoc. prof., 1998—. Cons. Phys. Therapy Online Network, Shawnee Mission, Kans., 1989-92; article abstractor Jour. Am. Phys. Therapy Assn., 1983-97; cons. geriatrics and phys. therapy malpractice cases. Assoc. editor Issues on Aging, 1992-94, editor, 1994-96; contbr. articles to profl. jours. Mem. Nat. Eagle Scout Assn. Avocations: computers, fishing. Office: Coll Misericordia Dept Phys Therapy 301 Lake St Dallas PA 18612-1098 E-mail: mmoran@epix.net.

MORAN, PAUL JAMES, journalist, columnist; b. Buffalo, July 20, 1947; s. Paul James and Frances (Sciortino) M.; m. Kim Maldiner, Mar. 17, 1975 (div. July 1979); m. Colette Stass (div. Jan. 1997); 1 child, Heather. Student, SUNY, Buffalo, 1965-67, Millard Fillmore Coll., 1971-73. Sports editor Tonawanda News, North Tonawanda, N.Y., 1972-75; writer/columnist Fort Lauderdale (Fla.) News/Sun Sentinel, 1975-85, N.Y. Newsday, Melville, 1985—. Cons. Green Country Racing Assn., Tulsa, 1983-85. Author: (with others) Crown Jewels of Thoroughbred Racing; contbr. articles to mags. and newspapers. Sgt. USAF, 1967-71. Recipient Eclipse award Thoroughbred Racing Assn., 1985, 90, Disting. Writing award Am. Soc. Newspaper Editors, 1990, Deadline Writing award Soc. Silurians, 1990, Deadline Reporting award L.I. Press Club, 1991, Disting. Sports Writing award N.Y. Newspaper Pubs. Assn., 1992, (with others) Journalism collection Best Newspaper Writing 1991, Media award L.I. Vet. Med. Assn., 1997, excellence in continuing feature Fla. Mag. Assn., 1999. Mem. N.Y. Turf Writers' Assn. (pres. 1990-92, sec.-treas. 1992-94), Nat. Turf Writers' Assn. (bd. dirs. 1987-90). Republican. Avocations: photography, art collecting. Home: 40 Carnation Ave Floral Park NY 11001-1730 Office: Newsday 235 Pinelawn Rd Melville NY 11747-4250

MORAN, PHILIP DAVID, lawyer; b. Lynn, Mass., June 3, 1937; s. J. Francis and Margaret M. (Shanahan) M.; m. Carole A. Regan, May 12, 1962; children: Maura F., Philip David. AB, Holy Cross Coll., 1958; EdM, Salem State Coll., 1961; JD, Suffolk U., 1968. Bar: Mass., 1968, U.S. Dist. Ct. Mass., 1972, U.S. Supreme Ct., 1988, U.S. Ct. Appeals (1st cir.), 1993. House counsel Viatron Computer Systems Corp., Burlington, Mass., 1968-71; ptnr. Kane & Moran, Lynn, 1972-78; pvt. practice law Salem, 1978—; propr. Law Offices of Philip D. Moran P.C., 1993—. Asst. dist. atty. Essex County (Mass.), 1974-78; mem. pres.'s coun. Holy Cross Coll., 1985—, Nat. Inst. Trial Advocacy U. Colo., 1973; gen. chmn. bicentenary com. Maynooth Coll., Boston, 1994-96. Contbg. author: Encyclopedia of Biomedical Policy, 1995. Bd. dirs. Nat. Right to Life Inc., 1977-83, 87—, treas., 1981-83; bd. dirs. Mass. Citizens for Life, 1973—, pres. 1979-80, chmn. 1991-93; mem. Salem Conservation Commn., 1980-89, chmn., 1982-89. With U.S. Army, 1960-66. Recipient Ignatius O'Connor Pro Life award, 1994, Gold medatl St. Patrick Maynooth Coll., Irelnd, 1996, Knight of Malta, 1997, Family, Faith and Freedom award Family Rsch. Coun., 1997, Citizenship award Mass. Family Inst., 1997. Mem. Mass. Bar Assn., Salem Bar Assn., Lynn Bar Assn., Am. Trial Lawyers Assn., Nat. Acad. Elder Law Attys., Murray Inn of Ct., Pro Life Legal Def. Fund (pres. 1997), Hibernian Civil Rights Coalition (bd. dirs. 1997, pres. 1997), Irish Am. Partnership, Nat. Coalition of Pro Life Dems. (bd. dirs., treas. 1999—), Dem State Com., Catholic Alliance (bd. dirs., gen. coun. 1999—). Roman Catholic. Avocations: swimming, reading, gardening, boating, photography. Home: 415 Lafayette St Salem MA 01970-5337 Office: 265 Essex St Salem MA 01970-3419

MORAN, RACHEL, lawyer, educator; b. Kansas City, Mo., June 27, 1956; d. Thomas Albert and Josephine (Portillo) Moran. AB, Stanford U., 1978; JD, Yale U., 1981, UCLA, 2002. Bar: Calif. 1984. Assoc Heller, Ehrman, White & McAuliffe, San Francisco, 1982-83; prof. law U. Calif., Berkeley, 1984—, Robert D. and Leslie-Kay Raven prof. law, 1998—. Vis. prof. UCLA Sch. Law, 1988, 2002, Stanford (Calif.) U. Law Sch., 1989, N.Y.U. Sch. of Law, 1996, U. Miami Sch. Law, 1997, U. Tex. Law Sch., 2000, UCLA Sch. Law, 2002; chair Chicano/Latino Policy Project, 1993-96. Contbr. numerous articles to profl. jours. Recipient Disting. Tchg. award, U. Calif. Mem. ABA, Am. Law Inst., Calif. Bar Assn., Phi Beta Kappa. Democrat. Unitarian Universalist. Avocations: jogging, aerobics, reading, listening to music. Office: U Calif Sch Law Boalt Hall Berkeley CA 94720

MORAN, RICARDO JULIO, economist; b. Havana, Cuba, Sept. 4, 1939; came to U.S., 1960; s. Jose Ricardo and Maria Luisa (Forcade) M.; m. Mayra Buvinic, Dec. 24, 1973 (div. 1981); m. Mary Louise Fox, Apr. 25, 1987. BA, Tulane U., 1963; MA in Econs., U. Calif., Berkeley, 1966, postgrad., 1968. Prof., sr. rsch. assoc. Universidad Catolica de Chile, Santiago, 1967-70; pvt. practice Washington, 1970-73; v.p. Moran Equities, Inc., Miami, Fla., 1973; economist The World Bank, Washington, 1973-90; prin. Moran Internat., 1990-92; sr. economist Interam. Devel. Bank, 1992—. Co-author: Declining Births in Chile, 1972, Brazil, 1981; contbr. articles to profl. jours. Fellow Latin Am. Teaching Program Tufts U., 1957, Ford Found., 1965, OAS, 1963-65. Mem. Am. Econ. Assn. Avocation: literature, music, travel, tennis. Home: 2910 Cortland Pl NW Washington DC 20008-3429 Office: Interam Devel Bank Washington DC 20577-0001

MORAN, RONALD WESSON, retired English educator, dean, writer; b. Phila., Sept. 9, 1936; s. Ronald Wesson and Julia Marie (Hagymasi) M.; m. Jane Edith Hetzler, Jan. 31, 1959; (twins) Sally and Ronald Wesson III. BA, Colby Coll., 1958; MA, La. State U., 1962, PhD, 1966. Instr. English La. State U., Baton Rouge, 1963-66; asst. prof. English U. N.C., Chapel Hill, 1966-69, assoc. prof., 1969-75; prof. English Clemson (S.C.) U., 1975-99, head dept. English, 1975-80, asst. dean, 1986-91, assoc. dean, 1991-99, interim dean Coll. Arch., Arts and Humanities, 1999-2000; ret., 2000. Arts and scis. adv. bd. Greenville (S.C.) Tech. Coll., 1986-89; Fulbright lectr., Würzburg, Germany, 1969-70; bd. dirs. Clemson Area Retirement Ctr., Inc. Author: So Simply Means the Rain, 1965, Louis Simpson, 1972, Life on the Rim, 1988, Sudden Fictions, 1994, Getting the Body to Dance Again, 1995, Fish Out of Water, 2000, Ronald Moran: Greatest Hits, 1965-2000, 2001; co-author: Four Poets and the Emotive Imagination, 1976; assoc. editor: South Atlantic Bull., 1975—77, adv. bd. : S.C. Rev., 1980—. Recipient Nat. Looking Glass Poetry Chapbook award, 1994. Mem. Assn. Acad. Affairs Adminstrs.-Southeastern Region (bd. officers 1989-93). Methodist. Home: 114 Princess Ln Clemson SC 29631-2120 E-mail: rmoran@statecom.net.

MORAN, SHARYN LEE, financial consulting company executive; b. Savannah, Ga., May 19, 1946; d. John J. and Sara Helen (Pritchett) M.; m. John Weisner, Feb. 28, 1973 (div. Aug. 1979). Grad. high sch., Marietta, Ga. Procider liaison, supr. Blue Cross/Blue Shield, Atlanta, 1970-77; acct. exec. Sta. WEEL Radio, Fairfax, Va., 1977-78; adminstrv. asst. Vis. Nurse Assn., Atlanta, 1978-80; ins. coord, supr. Ambulatory Svcs. Am. Inc., 1980-83; retail mgr. Interior Design Store, 1983-90; mgr. accounts receivable Robert H. Pogue & Assocs., 1990-92; mgr., ins. specialist So. Orthopedic Clinic PC, 1992-94; owner, mgr. Barrington Fin. Group, Inc., Atlanta and Lawrenceville, Ga., 1994—. Designer, writer procedure manuals related to ins., personal tng. and renal dialysis. Vice pres. Crown Park Homeowners Assn., 1996-97. Winner nat. contest Supervisory Mgmt. publ., 1973; featured in Atlanta Jour., 1973. Mem. NAFE. Democrat. Baptist. Avocations: interior design, antiques, snow skiing, publishing cookbook decared to her grandmother. Home: 102 Knotts Landing Dr Woodstock GA 30188-4559 Office: Barrington Fin Group Inc PO Box 1853 Lawrenceville GA 30046-1853

MORAN, THOMAS HARRY, university administrator; b. Milw., Oct. 21, 1937; s. Harry Edward and Edna Agnes Moran; m. Barbara Ellen Saklad, June 10, 1969; children: David Thomas, Karen Ellen. BS, U. Wis., 1964, MA, 1972, PhD, 1974. Dir. capital budgeting Wis. Dept. Adminstrn., 1962-64; exec. dir. Wis. Higher Ednl. Aids Bd., 1964-69; spl. cons. tax policy Wis. Dept. Revenue, 1973-74; dep. dir. Wis. Manpower Coun., Office of Gov., 1974-76; v.p. bus. and fin., treas. U. Detroit, 1976-78; exec. assoc. v.p. health affairs U. So. Calif., L.A., 1979-87, v.p. bus. affairs, 1988—. USN fellow, 1957-59, U.S. Office Edn. rsch. fellow, 1973. Mem. Am. Assn. Higher Edn., Phi Kappa Phi. Office: U So Calif 200 Town & Gown University Park Los Angeles CA 90089-1122 E-mail: tmoran@busaff.usc.edu.

MORAN, WILLIAM EDWARD, academic administrator; b. White Plains, N.Y., May 28, 1932; s. Frank Joseph and Margaret Mary (Farrell) M.; m. Barbara Carol Baillet, Apr. 20, 1963; children: Kathryn, Kevin, Colin, Christian. AB, Princeton U., 1954; MBA, Harvard U., 1959; PhD, U. Mich., 1967. Mgmt. cons. Booz, Allen & Hamilton, N.Y.C., 1959-61; mem. adminstrv. staff Harvard U., Boston, 1961-63; asst. exec. v.p. SUNY-Stony Brook, 1966-71; chancellor Flint Campus U. Mich., 1971-79, U. N.C., Greensboro, 1979-94; sr. v.p. Connors Investor Svcs., Inc., 1994—. Bd. dirs. Greensboro, N.C. Connors Investor Services, Reading, Pa., Cross Engring. & Sales Co., 2001—, Piedmont Land Conservancy, 2001—, U. N.C. at Greensboro Investment Fund, 2001—. Contbr. articles to profl. jours. Pres. So. Univ. Conf., 1987. Served with USN, 1954-57. Mem. N.C. Assn. Colls. and Univs. (pres. 1992), Princeton Club (N.Y.), Rotary. Home: 5206 Barnfield Rd Greensboro NC 27455-2136

MORAN, WILLIAM MADISON, fundraising executive; b. Albany, Ky., Apr. 15, 1948; s. Marvin Madison and Eula Pickens (Duvall) M.; m. Mary Ruth Shanks, June 5, 1971; 1 child, Alice Janette. Student, U. Ky., 1966-68; BS, Tenn. Technol. U., 1971. Field rep. March of Dimes, Nashville, 1972-77; state dir. Nat. Found. March of Dimes, 1977; dir. devel. East Tenn. Children's Hosp., Knoxville, 1977-84; exec. dir. St. Vincent's Found. Ala., Birmingham, 1984—. Founding participant, Children's Miracle Network Telethon, 1982-84. Co-founder, bd. dirs. Ronald McDonald House, Knoxville, 1982-84; bd. dirs. Tanasi coun. Girl Scouts U.S.A., Knoxville, 1981-84, Cahaba coun. Girl Scouts U.S.A., Birmingham, 1986-94; bd. dirs. Cath. Housing Authority, Birmingham, 1989—, pres., 2000—, Seton Inst. for Internat. Devel., 1994-2000. Recipient Thanks badge Girl Scouts Am., 1992, 94. Fellow Assn. Healthcare Philanthropy (regional dir. 1986-88, bd. dirs. 1987-88, chmn. 1992 internat. conf.); mem. Assn. Fundraising Profls. (advanced cert., pres. Tenn. chpt. 1983, pres. Ala. chpt. 1989, 1990, bd. dirs. 1989-94, 2000, 01, asst. treas. 1990, exec. com. 1990-94, 2000, 01, chmn. fin. com. 1991, 92, 93, 2000, 01, treas. 1992, 93, 2000, vice chair 1994, mem. ACFRE advanced certification bd. 1995-2001, chair, 1999, 2000, Outstanding Fundraising Exec. Ala. 1988), Optimists (Knoxville), Kiwanis (Birmingham), Newcomer Soc. U.S., Phi Delta Theta. Methodist. Avocations: photography, flying, history of sci. and technology. Home: 913 Masters Ln Birmingham AL 35244-3262 Office: St Vincent's Found 2800 University Blvd Ste 304 Birmingham AL 35233-2847

MORAND, PETER, investment company executive; b. Montreal, Que., Can., Feb. 11, 1935; s. Frank and Rose Alice (Fortier) M.; m. Dawn McKell, Oct. 10, 1957; children: Clifford, Tanya. BSc with honors, Bishop's U., Lennoxville, Que., 1956, DCL (hon.), 1991; PhD, McGill U., Montreal, 1959; hon. Doctorate (hon.) , U. Ottawa, 2001. NATO postdoctoral fellow Imperial Coll., London, 1959-61; sr. rsch. chemist Ayerst Labs., Montreal, 1961-63; asst. prof. chemistry U. Ottawa, Can., 1963-67, acad. asst. vice rector Can., 1968-71, dean sci.and engring. Can., 1976-81, prof. chemistry, dir. rsch. svcs. Can., 1981-87, vice rector univ. R&D, 1987—90; pres. Natural Scis. and Engring. Rsch. Coun., Ottawa, 1990-95; pres., CEO Can. Sci. and Tech. Growth Fund, 1996—; chmn. Adherex Techs. Inc., Ottawa, 1998—, Liponex Inc., Ottawa, 2001—, Inno-centre Ottawa, 2000—. Bd. dirs. Ottawa Life Scis. Coun., Can. Swedish Bus. Assn. Contbr. articles to profl. jours.; patentee in field. Trustee Royal Ottawa Health Care Group, 1992-2000. Natural Scis. and Engring. Rsch. Coun. grantee, 1964-90. Fellow Chem. Inst. Can. Office: Adherex Techs Inc 600 Peter Morand Cres # 340 Ottawa ON Canada K1G 5Z3

MORANG, DIANE JUDY, writer, television producer, business entrepreneur; b. Chgo., Apr. 28, 1942; d. Anthony Thomas Morang and Laura Ann Andrzejczak. Student, Stevens Finishing Sch., Chgo., 1956, Fox Bus. Coll., 1959-60, UCLA, 1967-69. Mem. staff Chgo. Sun Times, Daily News, 1957, Drury Ln. Theatre, Chgo., 1961-62, AM Show ABC-TV, Hollywood, Calif., 1970-71. Judge 2 categories regional Emmy Awards, 1985, chair, mem. judging panel, 89. Author: How to Get into the Movies, 1978; author, creator: The Rainbow Keyboard, 1991, The Translation of the Code of Music into Mathematics; creator: The Best Kids' Show in the World; contbr. numerous articles to newspapers, mags. Bd. dirs., mem. scholarship com. Ariz. Bruins, UCLA Alumni Assn.; mem. Nat. Mus. Women in the Arts, Washington, D.C.; mem. Nat. Women's Hall of Fame, Seneca Falls, N.Y. Mem. NATAS (mem. Hollywood Emmy Award-winning team Hollywood, Calif. 1971), Ariz. Authors Assn. (bd. dirs.), Women of the West Mus. Roman Catholic.

MORANO, ALISON BERKE, Internet development consultant; b. Whitestone, N.Y., May 11, 1964; d. Michael I. and Monica M. B.; m. Alexander G. Morano, Sept. 26, 1999. BS, Antioch Coll., 1986. Trader Nash Weiss & Co., Jersey City, 1986-89; v.p., dir. mktg. Quotabusters, Great Neck, N.Y., 1989-94; pres. bworks.com, 1994—. Instr. Great Neck Adult Edn.; chair ednl. event "Families on the Net", 1998; founder Small Office/Home Office Group of Wesley Chapel, 2001.. Editor: (book) Cybergrrl Guide to Going Online, 1997; host: (radio show) Tales from the Internet, 1997. Hon. mayor Wesley Chapel, 2002; bd. dir. Greater Wesley Chapel C. of C. Recipient Sml. Bus. Person of Yr. award Nassau Coun. of Chambers, L.I., 1998. Mem. Webgrrls (founder, pres. 1995—), Great Neck C. of C. (v.p. 1998-99), L.I.org (bd. dirs. 1997-2000), Wesley Chapel C. of C. (bd. dirs. 2001), Internet Bus. Assn. Internat., Inc. (chair polit. action com. 2000—). Avocations: writing, music. Office: bworks dot com 26720 Affirmed Dr Wesley Chapel FL 33544-1510 E-mail: alison@bworks.com.

MORANO, GERARD JOHN, marketing executive; b. Mount Vernon, N.Y., Oct. 23, 1944; s. Gerard Anthony and Pauline (Ungaro) M.; m. Allison Lenore Folz, June 28, 1975; 1 child, Steven Christopher. BS in Fin., CUNY, 1974; BA in Mktg., Pace U., Pleasantville, N.Y., 1981; MBA, Pace U., White Plains, N.Y., 1982. Fin. planner ITT Continental, Rye, N.Y., 1968-74, product mgr., 1974-80, mgr. sales promotion, 1980-84; dir. mktg. Quality Bakers Am., Greenwich, Conn., 1984-88, v.p. mktg. and sales, 1988-96, sr. v.p. mktg. and comm., 1996-2000; exec. v.p. QBA, Advt., Inc., 1992-2000; sr. v.p. Solutions Mktg. LLC, Darien, Conn., 2001—. Alumni mentor Pace U., 1988—; fund raiser Vietnam Vets. Meml. Com., Washington, 1980-82. With U.S. Army, 1966-68, Vietnam. Decorated Bronze Star; decorated Conspicious Silver Svc. Star and Order of Merit, State of N.Y., 2001. Mem.: ABA (mem. mktg. com.), Promotional Mktg. Assn., Am. Film Inst., 199th Inf. Assn., Vets. Bus. Network, Ellis Island Found., Vietnam Vets. Am., Wildlife Conservation Soc. Avocations: photography, videography. Office: Solutions Mktg LLC 800 Post Rd Darien CT 06820 E-mail: jmorano2000@aol.com.

MORANT, RICARDO BERNARDINO, psychology educator; b. New Britain, Conn., Feb. 13, 1926; s. J. Ramon and Rosario (Ciscar) M.; m. G. Francisca Giner, Dec. 26, 1955; children— Ramon, Francisca, Dolores, Ricardo. AB, Harvard, 1948; postgrad., Wesleyan Coll., Middletown, Conn., 1948-49; MA, Clark U., 1950, PhD, 1952. From faculty to prof. Brandeis U., Waltham, Mass., 1952—91, Minnie and Harold L. Fierman prof. psychology, 1991—, prof. Volen Nat. Ctr. for Complex Sys., 1994—. Prin. investigator NIMH, Spencer Found., Rothman Found. 1960— ; spl. research space perception, body orientation. Bd. dirs. Coun. Pub. Schs., 1970-73; mem. steering com. Sensory Aid Eval. and Devel. Ctr., MIT, 1963-67; chmn. bd. trustees Hiatt Ednl. Programs, 1982-94. Served with USNR, 1946-48. Fellow APA; mem. Psychonomic Soc. Home: 35 Cliff Rd Wellesley MA 02481-3001 E-mail: morant@brandeis.edu.

MORANTZ, PAUL ROBERT, lawyer, writer; b. Los Angeles, Aug. 16, 1945; s. Nathan and Jeannette (Kates) M. B.A. in Journalism, U. So. Calif., 1968, J.D., 1971. Bar: Calif. Los Angeles pub. defender, 1972; atty. Office of Donald Cohen, Los Angeles, 1977-80; freelance writer, 1972— ; cons. state, fed. agys. on cults, brainwashing, psychol. malpractice, 1977— ; lectr., 1977— ; lobbyist. Author TV Movie of Week: Deadman's Curve, 1978. Contbr. articles to mags.

MORARI, MANFRED, chemical engineer, educator; b. Graz, Austria, May 13, 1951; came to U.S., 1975; s. Manfred and Hilde (Florian) M.; m. Marina Korchynsky, May 12, 1984. Diploma Chem. Engring., Eidgenoessische Technische Hochschule, Zurich, Switzerland, 1974; PhD in Chem. Engring.,

U. Minn., 1977. Asst. prof. U. Wis., Madison, 1977-81, assoc. prof., 1981-83; prof. chem. engring. Calif. Inst. Tech., Pasadena, 1983-94, McCollum-Corcoran prof., 1991-94, exec. officer, 1990-93, prof. control and dynamical sys., 1993-94; exec. officer, 1993-94; head automatic control lab. ETH. Gulf vis. prof. chem. engring. Carnegie Mellon U., 1987. Contbr. articles to profl. jours. Recipient D.P. Eckman award Am. Automatic Control Coun., 1980. Mem. IEEE (George S. Axelby Outstanding Paper award 1990), NAE, AIChE (A. P. Colburn award 1984, Profl. Progress award 1995), Am. Soc. for Engring. Edn. (Curtis W. McGraw rsch. award 1989), Am. Chem. Soc. Home: Laerchentobelstrasse 22 CH-8700 Kuesnacht Switzerland Office: Automatic Control Lab ETH-Z ETL I 29 CH-8092 Zurich Switzerland

MORATH, MAX EDWARD, entertainer, composer, writer; b. Colorado Springs, Colo., Oct. 1, 1926; s. Frederic Palmer and Gladys Hester Nancy (Ramsell) M.; m. Norma Loy Tackitt, Oct. 23, 1953 (div. 1992); children: Kathryn, Christine, Frederic; m. Diane Fay Skomars, May 24, 1993. BA in English, Colo. Coll., 1948; postgrad., Stanford NBC-Radio-TV Inst., Palo Alto, Calif., 1951; MA in Am. Studies, Columbia U., 1996. Touring nationally in concerts and theater The Ragtime Man, 1997—; recordings on Epic, RCA, Vanguard, SoloArt, Omega, Premier; author: The Road to Ragtime, 2002, The NPR Curious Listener's Guide to Popular Standards, 2002. Mem. Broadcast Music, Inc., Am. Fedn. Musicians, AFTRA, Screen Actors Guild, Actors Equity Assn. Home and Office: Ste 700 850 7th Ave New York NY 10019-5230 E-mail: rathmo@aol.com.

MORAVCSIK, JULIUS MATTHEW, philosophy educator; b. Budapest, Hungary, Apr. 26, 1931; came to U.S., 1949; s. Julius and Edith (Fleissig) M.; m. Marguerite Germain Truninger, Sept. 14, 1954; children: Adrian Clay, Peter Matthew. BA, Harvard U., 1953, PhD, 1959. Asst. prof. U. Mich., Ann Arbor, 1960-66, assoc. prof., 1966-68; prof. Stanford (Calif.) U., 1968—. Author: Understanding Language, 1975, Thought and Language, 1990, Plato and Platonism, 1992, Meaning, creativity, and the Partial Inscrutability of the Human Mind, 1998. Recipient Sr. Humanist prize Humboldt Found., 1983; fellow Ctr. Advanced Studies Behavioral Scis., 1986-87, Inst. Advanced Studies, 1988. Fellow Inst. Advanced Studies Budapest; mem. Am. Philos. Assn. (pres. Pacific divsn. 1987-88), Am. Soc. Aesthetics (trustee 1988-92), Soc. Ancient Greek Philosophy (pres. 1989-91, bd. dirs. Jour. History Philosophy, James Wilbur Award Value Theory 2000), Hungarian Acad. Arts and Scis. (external mem.). Avocations: golf, tennis. Office: Stanford U Dept Of Philosophy Stanford CA 94305 E-mail: julius@csli.stanford.edu.

MORAWETZ, CATHLEEN SYNGE, mathematician; b. Toronto, Ont., Can., May 5, 1923; arrived in U.S., 1945, naturalized, 1950; d. John Lighton and Elizabeth Eleanor Mabel (Allen) Synge; m. Herbert Morawetz, Oct. 28, 1945; children: Pegeen Morawetz Rubinstein, John Synge, Lida Morawetz Jeck, Nancy. BA, U. Toronto, 1945; SM, MIT, 1946; PhD, NYU, 1951; degree (hon.), Ea. Mich. U., 1980, Smith Coll., 1982, Brown U., 1982, Princeton U., 1986, Duke U., 1988, N.J. Inst. Tech., 1988, U. Waterloo, 1993, U. Dublin, 1996, U. Toronto, 1996. Research assoc. Courant Inst., NYU, 1952—57, asst. prof. math., 1957—60, assoc. prof., 1960—65, prof., 1965—, assoc. dir., 1978—84, dir., 1984—88. Chmn. bd. Sch. Theoretical Physics Dublin Inst. for Advanced Studies, 1995—2000. Former editor various math. jours., author articles in applications of partial differential equations, especially transonic flow and scattering theory. Trustee Princeton U., 1973—78, Sloan Found., 1980—94. Recipient Nat. medal of Sci., NSF, 1998; fellow Guggenheim, 1967, 1979; grantee Office of Naval Rsch., 1990. Fellow: AAAS, Royal Soc. Can.; mem.: NAS, London Math. Soc., Royal Irish Acad., Soc. Indsl. and Applied Math., Am. Philos. Soc., Am. Acad. Arts and Scis., Am. Math. Soc. (term trustee 1975—85, pres. 1995—97). Office: CIMS 251 Mercer St New York NY 10012-1110

MORAWETZ, HERBERT, chemistry educator; b. Prague, Czechoslovakia, Oct. 16, 1915; came to U.S., 1945, naturalized, 1951; s. Richard and Frida (Glaser) M.; m. Cathleen Synge, Oct. 28, 1945; children: Pegeen Morawetz Rubinstein, John S., Lida Morawetz Jeck, Nancy B. BASc, U. Toronto, 1943, MASc, 1944; PhD, Poly Inst. Bklyn., 1951. With Bakelite Co., 1945-49; mem. faculty Poly. U. (formerly Poly. Inst. Bklyn.), 1951-81, prof. polymer chemistry, dir. Inst. Polymer Research, 1971-81; Inst. prof., 1981-86; Inst. prof. emeritus, 1986—; mem. materials research adv. com. NSF, 1977-80. Author: Macromolecules in Solution, 1965, rev. edit., 1975; Polymers: The Origins and Growth of a Science, 1985, Dover paperback edit., 1995; mem. editorial bd. Jour. Polymer Sci., 1969-89; contbr. articles to profl. jours. Recipient Heyrovsky medal Czechoslovakia Acad. Sci., 1990; Case Centenary scholar, 1980; Whitby Meml. lectr. U. Akron, 1984. Fellow AAAS; mem. Am. Chem. Soc. (award in polymer chemistry 1986, assoc. editor Macromolecules 1991—). Home: 246 W 12th St New York NY 10014-1912 Office: 6 Metrotech Ctr Brooklyn NY 11201-3840

MORBY, JACQUELINE, venture capitalist; b. Sacramento, June 19, 1937; d. Junior Jennings and Bertha (Backer) Collins; m. Jeffrey L. Morby, June 21, 1959; children: Andrew Jennings, Michelle Lorraine. BA in Psychology, Stanford U., 1959; M in Mgmt., Simmons Grad. Mgmt. Sch., Boston, 1978. Assoc. TA Assocs., Boston, 1978-81, gen. ptnr., 1982-89, mng. dir., 1989—. Bd. dirs. HVL, Inc., Pitts., Softmed Sys. Inc., Bethesda, Md., Ansys, Inc., Houston, Pacific Life Corp., Newport Beach, Calif., J&B Software, Inc., Bluebell, Pa. Trustee Simmons Coll., Pitts. Pub. Theater, Pitts. Symphony. Mem. Nat. Venture Capital Orgn. Avocations: theatre, reading, art, skiing, travel. Office: TA Assocs 125 High St Boston MA 02110-2704 E-mail: jmorby@ta.com.

MORDECAI, BENJAMIN, theatrical producer, drama educator; b. N.Y.C., Dec. 10, 1944; s. Allen Lewis Mordecai and Florence Doris (Goldman) Holl; m. Sherry Lynn Morley, July 20, 1974; 1 child, Rachel Elizabeth. BA, Buena Vista Coll., 1967; MA, Eastern Mich. U., 1968; postgrad., Ind. U., 1968-70. Founder, producing dir. Ind. Repertory Theatre, Indpls., 1971-82; mng. dir. Yale Repertory Theatre, New Haven, 1982-93; assoc. dean Yale Sch. Drama, 1992—; mng. ptnr. Benjamin Mordecai and Assocs., New York, 1992—; ptnr. Producers' Mgmt. Group, 1999—. Cons. Found. for the Extension and Devel. of the Am. Profl. Theatre, N.Y.C., 1974; adj. prof. Yale Sch. of Drama, 1982—; ind. cons., New Haven, 1984—. Dir.: (plays) Fables Here and Then, 1972, Dracula, 1973, Bird in the Hand, 1975; assoc. prodr. (plays) Fences, 1987 (Tony award, 1987), Joe Turner's Come & Gone, 1988 (N.Y. Drama Critics Cir. award, 1988), A Walk in the Woods, 1988, gen. mgr. A Walk in the Woods (USSR), 1989; exec. prodr.: (plays) The Piano Lesson, 1990 (N.Y. Drama Critics Cir. award, 1990, Drama Desk award, 1990), Two Trains Running, 1992, Angels in America (N.Y. Drama Critics award, 1993, Tony award, 1993, Tony award, 1994); prodr.: Redwood Curtain, 1993, Twilight: Los Angeles, 1992, 1994; assoc. prodr. The Kentucky Cycle, 1993; prodr.: Gate of Heaven (U.S. Holocaust Mus.), 1995, August Wilson's Seven Guitars, 1996 (N.Y. Drama Critics award, 1996), Golden Child (Kennedy Ctr.), 1997, (Singapore, N.Y.), 1998, Jitney, 2000 (N.Y. Drama Critics award, 2000), August Wilson's King Hedley II, 2001, August Wilson's Jitney (Nat. Theatre, London), 2001 (Olivier award for best play); exec. prodr.: Harlem Nutcracker, 1997—99, Moscow Art Theatre's Three Sisters, 1998; prodr.: Thunder Knocking on The Door, 2002, Enid Papers, 2002, Flower Dram Song, 2002. Recipient Disting. Svc. award Indpls. Jaycees, Indpls., 1979, spl. commendation City-County Coun., Inpls., 1982, Robert Whitehead award for outstanding comml. producing, 1993, Special Achievement award New England Theatre Conf., 1998, Outstanding Producing award Hollywood NAACP, 1990, 92; named Outstanding Young Alumnus, Buena Vista Coll., 1987. Mem. League of Resident Theatres (exec. com. 1981-91), Assn. Arts Adminstrn. Educators (sec.-treas. 1984-88), Am. Theatre Exchange Initative (bd. dirs. 1987—, pres. 1994—), Writers Theatre (bd. advisors 1983—), Stage Dirs. and Choreographers Found. (bd. dirs. 1990—), League Am. Theatres & Prodrs., Nat. Theatre Conf.

MORDECAI, DAVID K.A. financial economist, journal editor; b. N.Y.C., Oct. 18, 1961; s. Kenneth and Vinette Mordecai; m. Samantha Kappagoda, July 18, 1996. BA, Kings Coll., Briarcliff Manor, N.Y., 1983; MBA in Fin., NYU, N.Y.C., 1987; PhD in Fin. Econs., U. Chgo., 2002. Dir. comml. asset backed group Fitch IBCA, N.Y.C., 1997-98; v.p. fin. engring. AIG Risk Fin., 1998-2000; v.p. fin. engring. and prin. fin. AIG Global Investments, 2000-01; v.p. fin. engring. AIG Structured Products, 2001; mng. dir. structured products Clinton Group, 2001—. Mem. instnl. investment mgmt. adv. com. N.Y. Mercantile Exch., N.Y.C., 1998—. Editor in chief Jour. Risk Fin., 1999—. Mem.: Am. Fin. Assn., Am. Econ. Assn., Internat. Assn. Fin. Engrs. Home: #14 K 30 W 63rd Street New York NY 10023-7114 E-mail: dkmordecai@aol.com.

MORDEN, JOHN REID, security-business intelligence company executive; b. Hamilton, Ont., Canada, June 17, 1941; s. Warren Wilbert and Isabelle Gemmell (Reid) M.; m. Margaret Keens, June 27, 1964; children: Michael, Geoffrey. BA, Dalhousie U., 1962; postgrad., Dalhousie Law Sch., 1962-63. With Can. Dept. External Affairs, various worldwide cities, 1963-84; asst. dep. min. dept. native claims Dept. Indian & Northern Devel., Can., 1984-85; trade and econ. policy Can. Dept. External Affairs, 1985-86; asst. sec. to cabinet Fgn. and Def. Affairs, Can., 1986-87; dir. Can. Security Intelligence Svc., 1987-91; dep. min. fgn. affairs Govt. Can., 1991-94; pres, CEO, Atomic Energy of Can., Ltd., Ottawa, Canada, 1994-98; mng. dir. Kroll Asocs. Can., Toronto, 1999-2000; chmn. KPMG Corp. Intelligence Inc., 2000—02; pres. RM & A, Inc., 2002—. Bd. dirs. CDN Inst. Internat. Affairs; mem. adv. bd. Imagis Tech., Inst. for Study Violence and Terrorism; chair bd. govs. Trent U. Mem. internat. adv. coun. York U.; mem. Can. com. Coun. for Security and Cooperation in Asia and Pacific. Recipient Ian L. Macrae award, 1998. Mem. Toronto Hunt Club, Order of Can., Order of the So. Cross (Brazil). Avocations: photography, music, ballet, reading. E-mail: r.mordenassoc@aol.com.

MORDES, MARVIN, neurologist; b. Balt., Nov. 2, 1943; s. Irvin and Minnie (Riback) M.; m. Elayne Jayne Rubenstein, Aug. 19, 1967; 1 child, Stephanie Martine. BS, U. Md., 1965; MD, U. Ghent, Belgium, 1972. Intern Union Meml. Hosp., Balt., 1972-73; resident Pa. Hosp., Phila., 1973-76; attending neurologist Johns Hopkins Hosp., Balt., 1978—; chief of neurology St. Joseph Med. Ctr., Towson, Md., 1984—. Trustee Hirshhorn Mus. and Sculpture Garden, Smithsonian Instn., Washington, 1997—. Jewish. Avocation: art collecting. Home: 3701 Breton Way Baltimore MD 21208-1708 Office: 120 Sister Pierre Dr Ste 109 Towson MD 21204-7521 E-mail: emm3701@comcast.net.

MORDY, JAMES CALVIN, lawyer; b. Ashland, Kans., Jan. 3, 1927; s. Thomas Robson and Ruth (Floyd) M.; m. Marjory Ellen Nelson, Nov. 17, 1951; children: Jean Claire Mordy Jongeling, Rebecca Jane Mordy King, James Nelson. AB in Chemistry, U. Kans., 1947; JD, U. Mich., 1950; postgrad., George Washington U., 1950-51. Bar: Kans. 1950, Mo. 1950; cert. in bus. bankruptcy law, Am. Bankruptcy Bd. Cert. Assoc. Morrison, Hecker, Buck, Cozad & Rogers, Kansas City, Mo., 1950-59; ptnr. Morrison & Hecker LLP, 1959-96, sr. counsel, 1996-97, of counsel, 1997-2000. Contbg. author: Missouri Bar Insurance Handbook, 1968, Missouri Bar Bankruptcy Handbook, 1991, also supplements; contbr. articles to profl. jours. Chmn. bd. Broadway United Meth. Ch., Kansas City, 1964-70, chmn. bd. trustees, chmn. fin. com., 1988-90, 94, 2000-2002; bd. dirs. Broadway Child Enrichment Ctr., 1980—; bd. dirs., exec. com. Della C. Lamb Neighborhood House, Kansas City, 1973-80; bd. dirs., treas. Friends of Sacred Structures, Kansas City, 2000—; coun. mem. St. Paul Sch. Theology, Kansas City, 1986—; del. 17th World Meth. Conf., Rio de Janeiro, 1996. With USN, 1845-46, 51-53, comdr. USNR, ret. Summerfield scholar, 1943-47; recipient Shepherd of the Lamb award Della Lamb Neighborhood House, 1980. Fellow Am. Coll. Bankruptcy, Am. Bar Found. (life); mem. ABA, Am. Judicature Soc., Am. Bankruptcy Inst., Mo. Bar Assn., Kansas City Met. Bar Assn., Lawyers Assn. Kansas City, Workout Profs. Assn. Kansas City, Univ. Club (v.p., bd. dirs. 1983, 86), Barristers Soc., Phi Beta Kappa, Delta Tau Delta (pres. Kansas City alumni chpt. 1965-72, pres. U. Kans. House Corp. 1966-72), Alpha Chi Sigma, Phi Alpha Delta. Avocations: travel, geography (maps), history, music, theology. Home: 8741 Ensley Ln Leawood KS 66206-1615 Office: Stinson Morrison Hecker LLP 2600 Grand Ave Kansas City MO 64108-4606

MORE, DOUGLAS MCLOCHLAN, lawyer; b. N.Y.C., Apr. 21, 1926; s. Morgan Berkeley and Lucinda (Bateson) M.; m. Pamela Bennett Marr, Aug. 6, 1954; children— Robin Maclachlan More Eddy, Alison Marr More Davies. Grad., Phillips Exeter Acad., 1943; BA, Harvard U., 1947; LL.B., Columbia U., 1950. Bar: N.Y. State bar 1950, Conn. bar 1981, Fla. bar 1983. With N.Y. Trust Co., 1950-51; asso. firm Bigham, Englar, Jones & Houston, N.Y.C., 1951-53; fin. analyst Johns-Manville Corp., 1953-54; assoc. firm Kissam & Halpin, N.Y.C., 1954-59; assoc. counsel Hooker Chem. Corp., 1959-63, gen. counsel, 1963-72, v.p., 1967-72; v.p. law Airco, Inc., 1972-75; gen. counsel Beker Industries Corp., 1975-81, v.p., 1975-78, sr. v.p., 1978-81; ptnr. firm More Phillips & Duncan, P.C., Greenwich, Conn., 1981-88, of counsel, 1988—. Served to lt. (j.g.) USNR, 1943-46. Mem. ABA, Conn. Bar Assn., Greenwich Bar Assn., Phi Delta Phi, Phoenix S-K Club, Hasty Pudding Inst. 1770 (Harvard). Home and Office: 27 Skylark Rd Greenwich CT 06830-4624

MORE, JAY, neurosurgeon; b. Newark, May 19, 1960; BSc, McGill U., 1982; MD, N.Y. Med. Coll., 1987. Diplomate Am. Bd. Neurol. Surgeons. Attending surgeon JFK Med. Ctr., Edison, N.J., 1994—; dir. spine surgery N.J. Neuroscience Inst., 1994—; chief divsn. neurosurgery Muhlenberg Hosp., Plainfield, N.J., 2000—. Asst. prof. Seton Hall U., S. Orange, N.J., 1994—. Mem.: Am. Coll. Physician Execs., N.J. State Neurol. Soc., Joint Sect. Spine and Peripheral Nerve Surgery, Congress Neurol. Surgeons, Am. Assn. Neurol. Surgeons (mem. Think First 1994—).

MORE, PHILIP HARVEY BIRNBAUM, business administration educator; b. San Diego, Jan. 21, 1944; s. Louis and Ruth Laureen (Bay) B.; m. Marlin Sue Van Every, Dec. 26, 1964; 1 child, Brian Philip. BA, U. Calif., Berkeley, 1965; PhD, U. Wash., 1975. Internal cons./analyst Los Angeles County Civil Svc. Commn., 1965-67; tchg. assoc. U. Wash., Seattle, 1972-74; asst. prof. bus. adminstrn. Ind. U., Bloomington, 1975-80, assoc. prof., 1980-85, prof., 1986—. Resident dir. J.F.K. Int., Tiburg U., The Netherlands; vis. scholar Polish Aca. Scis., Tokyo U., SDA Bocconi, Milan, Italy, Seoul Nat. U., Korea, Dartmouth Coll. Co-author: Organization Theory: Structural and Behavioral Analysis, Modern Management Techniques for Engineers and Scientists, International Research Management: Studies in Interdisciplinary Methods From Business, Government and Academics, 1990; assoc. editor IEEE Transaction on Engring. Mgmt. jour.; contbr. articles to profl. jours., book revs., sects. to books, invited papers Germany, Poland, Eng., Can., Thailand, Hong Kong, Korea. With USAF, 1967-71. NSF fellow, 1974-75, N.Y. Acad. Scis. fellow, 1981; U. Hong Kong Sr. Fulbright scholar, 1981-82. Mem. Acad. Mgmt. (pres. tech. and innovation mgmt. divsn. 1989-90), Engring. Mgmt. Soc., Inst. Ops. Rsch. and Mgmt. Scis., Internat. Assn. for Study of Interdisciplinary Rsch., Beta Gamma Sigma, Beta Alpha Psi, Sigma Iota Epsilon, Sigma Chi. Methodist. Office: Univ So Calif Marshall Sch Bus Los Angeles CA 90089-0808 E-mail: phbmore@marshall.usc.edu.

MOREAU, JAMES WILLIAM, stuntman; b. Old Town, Maine, May 2, 1948; s. Clement Joseph and Madilene Daisy (Trask) M.; m. Peggy Louis Hatch, Feb. 2, 1974 (div. 1975); 1 child, Tina Marie; m. Sherrie Ray Bentley Gates; 1 child, Shasta Ann. Student, Mattanawcook Acad., Lincoln, Maine, 1963-64. Prop. person Joie Chitwood Thrill Show, Tampa, Fla., 1965; stuntman/clown, motorcyclist Buddy Wagner's Lucky Hell Drivers, Phila., 1966—69, 1971; stuntman King Kovas Auto Daredevils, Fort Lauderdale, Fla., 1970; stuntman, stunt coord. The Death Riders Motorcycle Thrill Show, Danville, Ill., 1972-75, Dan Fleenor's Hurricane Hell Drivers, Tampa, Fla., 1973; stuntman Crash Prodns., Bangor, Maine, 1976-77, Ray Boyea's Auto Daredevils, 1977, Johnny Olson's Daredevils, Poughkeepsie, NY, 1978; producer, owner Internat. Danger Angels, Bangor, Maine, 1978; stuntman, thrill show clown Bill Siros Thrill-A-Rama, Houston, 1979, 1981—84; dynamite act John Anderson's World Series of Thrills, Bellefontaine, Ohio, 1980; stuntman Gordie Allen's Internat. Hell Drivers, Tampa, Fla., 1983, Jake Plumstead/Tonni Petersen's Fantasy on Wheels, Jack Kochman Hell Drivers, Winston-Salem, NC, 1985; stuntman, human torch Jake Plumstead's All Am. Stunt Team, Mt. Holly, NJ, 1986; stuntman Hollywood Stunt Show, Tampa, Fla., 1987-88; stuntman, coord., cons. Can. Auto Circus, Montreal, 1989-90; prin., stuntman Crash Prodns. Death Drivers, Bangor, Maine, 1990. Stuntman Am. unit Can. Auto Circus, Renfrew, Pa., 1991, Am. Motor Sports, Milw., 1991—92, DBR Motorsports Promotions, St. Paul, 1992, St. Paul, 95, Jake Plumstead/Joe Barbagallo's Thrill show, Branchville, NJ, 1993—94, Paul Riddell's Imperial Hell Drivers, Yarmouth, N.S., Canada, 1995—97, 2000—01; prodr. stunt coord. C.M. Motorsports Internat. Thrill Masters Stunt Show, Bangor, Maine, 1994—97, 2000—01, Mike Foster's Daredevil Enterprise, Elverson, Pa., 1994—95, Tricky Travelstead's Hot Stunt Show, Louisville, 1995, Toyota's Hollywood Stunt Show ' 98, Tampa, Fla., Stuntman Crash Prodns., 1998—2001, Stuntman Extreme Stunt Show, Louisville, 1999—2000, Stuntman Doug Dangers Stunt Spectacular, Palmer, Mass., 1999—2002; prodr. Thrillmaster "2000" Stunt Show, Bangor, Maine, 2000; stunt advisor Wildman's Auto Daredevils, Whitefield, NH, 2002. Stuntman (TV series documentary), Thrill Seekers, 1972, (documentary film) Death Riders, 1974, (film) Death Driver, 1975, TNN's Magic Mountain Jamboree, 1993, (video) Big Bubba's Motorcycle Night of Thrills, 1995, Fox Family Channel's AXN-TV (Action TV), 1998. Named Rookie Stuntman of Yr., Internat. Stuntman's Assn., Phila., 1966. Mem. World Fedn. Internat. Daredevils, New Eng.'s Showman's Assn., Pinetree Showman's Assn., Circus Fans of Am. Democrat. Roman Catholic. Avocations: snowmobiling, cooking, attending circuses and thrill shows, collecting stunt memorabilia. Home: 7 Railroad St Lincoln ME 04457-1411 Office: Crash Prodns PO Box 40 Bangor ME 04402-0040 E-mail: crashmoreau@yahoo.com.

MOREAU, LARRY WAYNE, JR. purchasing agent, poet; b. New Orleans, July 29, 1960; s. Larry Wayne Moreau, Chrysta Lou Finnan; m. Wanda Louise Deal, Sept. 2, 1989; children: Rodney Wimpy, James Wimpy, Shawna Wimpy. Crane operator Poet Ship Svc., Arabi, La., 1975—78; dockland crewboat Port Ship Svc., 1978—79; electronic assembler Semans, New Orleans, 1984—86; elec. tractor assembler Tug Mfg., Marietta, Ga., 1987—88, foreman elec. tractor, 1988—91, floor supr. Kennesaw, 1991—94, purchasing agt., 1994—2001, S/S Tug Mfg., Marietta, 2001—. Author: Poetic Pictures, 1996. Bd. dirs. Riverside Bapt. Ch., McCaysville, Ga., 2000—, Sunday sch. tchr., 2000—. With USMC, 1979—83. Named one of Outstanding Poets of 20th Century, Nat. Poetic Soc., 2001. Republican. Baptist. Avocations: cooking, horseback riding, writing, public speaking. Mailing: 279 Deal Hollow Rd Copperhill TN 37317 Office: Stewart/Stevenson Tug 815 Allgood Rd Marietta GA 30062

MOREFIELD, MICHAEL THOMAS, financial executive; b. Chgo., Aug. 13, 1956; s. Preston Thomas and Geraldine Judith (Kasmierski) M. BA in Acctg., Lewis U., 1978; M in Fin., Loyola U., Chgo., 1987. Gen. acctg. mgr. Gen. Binding Corp., Northbrook, Ill., 1980, dir. corp. acctg., 1981-83, dir. corp. fin. planning, 1983, asst. corp. contr., 1984-86, corp. contr., 1986-88; sr. v.p. fin. and adminstrn., CFO Toyoda Machinery USA, Inc., Arlington Heights, Ill., 1988-93; v.p. fin., CFO Schmalbach-Lubeca Holdings, Inc., Downers Grove, 1993-99; v.p., CFO United Plastics Group, Inc., Westmont, 1999—2001; v.p. fin. Exelon Svcs. Inc., 2002—. Bd. dirs. White Cap de Venezuela, Valencia, White Cap do Brasil, San Paulo; gen. mgr. White Cap Mex. S.A. de C.V., Cuatitlan, 1996-99. Active Friars Civic Orgn., Romeoville, Ill., 1976-78. Mem. Nat. Machine Tool Builders Assn. (fin. com. 1988-90), Arlington Heights C. of C. Avocations: scuba diving, music, skiing, basketball, baseball. Home: 6836 Bantry Ct Darien IL 60561-3688 Office: 2315 Enterprise Dr Westchester IL 60154

MOREHEAD, ANNETTE MARIE, disabled children's facility administrator, child advocate; b. San Diego; d. Michael Peter and Katherine Helen (Keegan) Russomondo; m. Peter James Morehead; children: Bradley Michael Caloca, Katherine Dana. AS in Acctg., Normandale C.C., Bloomington, Minn., 2000. Dir. Rayito Day Care Ctr., San Diego, 1981-85; instrnl. asst. for children with disabilities San Diego City Schools, 1985-88; owner, operator Scripps Ranch Childcare Ctr. for Disabled Children, San Diego, 1990—. Child advocate; speaker San Diego Bd. Edn., 1986, News Eight Local TV News, 1989, Miramar Coll., 1991, Scottish Rite Charities, 1992, U. Calif., San Diego, 1992, Exceptional Parents Found., 1993. Vol. Schweitzer Ctr. for Disabled Children, San Diego, 1985, Stein Edn. Ctr. for Autistic Children, San Diego, 1987-88; bd. dirs. San Diego Autism Soc., 1989. Mem. Mensa. Democrat. Avocations: home, fine architecture. E-mail: pandamorehead@hotmail.com.

MOREHEAD, FREDERICK FERGUSON, retired physical chemist; b. Roanoke, Va., July 30, 1929; s. Frederick Ferguson and Laura Hilda (Fox) M.; m. Nancy Jane Taylor, July 18, 1954 (div. Oct. 1997); children: Laura Helen Gleeson, James Frederick, Elizabeth Ann Bella, John Taylor, Sarah Jane Barden; m. Joyce Haskel, May 17, 1998. BA in Chemistry, Swarthmore Coll., 1950; MS in Phys. Chemistry, U. Wis., 1951, PhD in Phys. Chemistry, 1953. Asst. prof. chemistry Union Coll., Schenectady, N.Y., 1953-54; staff rsch. lamp divsn. GE, Cleve., 1954-59; staff group leader rsch. divsn. IBM, Yorktown Heights, N.Y., 1959-88; adv. engr. Semiconductor R&D Ctr., IBM, East Fishkill, 1988-96; ret. Temp. lectr. chemistry U. Conn., Waterbury, 1999—. Contbr. chpt. to book and over 60 articles to profl. jours. Bd. mem., chair Aunt Bessies Open Door, Peekskill, N.Y., 1965-75, Yorktown (N.Y.) Outdoor Edn., 1966-85; cubmaster, asst. scout master Boy Scouts Am., Yorktown, 1967-70; dist. leader Dem. Party, Yorktown, 1971-75; active Heritage Village Ambulance Assn., 1997—; mem. Southbury (Conn.) Zoning Commn., 1999—. Avocations: computer imaging, photography, video, golf, tennis. Home: 771B Heritage Village Southbury CT 06488-1306

MOREHEAD, KRISTOPHER R. secondary school educator; b. Wichita, Kans., Mar. 24, 1973; s. Dwight A. Morehead and Colleen G. Cameron. BA in Edn., Wayne (Nebr.) State Coll., 1997. Cert. edn. K-12 Instrumental & 7-12 French 1997. Instr./counselor Mid-America Jr. High Music Camp, Lincoln, Nebr., 1991—; mdse. host Walt Disney World Co., Orlando, Fla., 1996; guest rels. AmFac Parks and Resorts, Zion Nat. Pk., Sprindale, Utah, 1998—98; dir. of bands Seward (Nebr.) H.S., 1998—. Mem.: NEA, Heartland Color Guard Assn. (pres. 2002—), Nebr. State Educators Assn., Nebr. Music Educators Assn., Music Educators Nat. Conf., Nebr. State Bandmasters Assn., Alpha Mu Gamma, Kappa Kappa Psi (pres. 1992—93). Roman Catholic. Avocations: bouldering, bicycling, sailing.

MOREHOUSE, DAVID FRANK, geologist; b. Charles City, Iowa, Dec. 8, 1943; s. Neal Francis and Florence E. (Schwendener) M. BS in Gen. Scis., State U. Iowa, 1967; MS in Geology, Iowa State U., 1970; postgrad., Pa. State U., 1970-74. Staff geologist Nat. Gas Survey and Planning and Spl. Projects Div., FPC, Washington, 1974-78; dir. Info. Processing and Interpretation and Analysis Divs. Oil and Gas Info. System, Energy Info. Adminstrn., 1978-80, sr. supervisory geologist, 1980-95, sr. petroleum geologist, 1996—. Advisor petroleum data sys. U. Okla., Norman, 1975-86; Energy Info. Adminstrn. rep. Am. Gas Assn. Com. on Natural Gas Res., Washington, 1991-95, Potential Gas Com., Boulder, Colo., 1991—; Dept. of Energy rep. Fed. Geog. Data Com. Coordination Group, 1997—; Nat. Critical Infrastructure Task Force Energy Group, 1998—. V.p. Iowa Jr. Acad. Scis., 1961. Recipient awards for outstanding performance Fed. Govt., Washington, 1974—. Fellow Nat. Speleological Soc.; mem. AAAS, AIME, AGI, Am. Geophys. Union, Internat. Assn. Math. Geology, N.Y. Acad. Scis. Congregationalist. Achievements include first evidence that sulfuric acid can be important to speleogenesis; exercising the prin. responsibility for design and establishment of fed. govts. domestic oil and gas reserves estimation and analysis program. Office: Energy Info Adminstrn EI-46 1000 Independence Ave SW Washington DC 20585-0644 E-mail: david.morehouse@eia.doe.gov.

MOREHOUSE, LAWRENCE GLEN, veterinarian, educator; b. Manchester, Kans., July 21, 1925; s. Edwy Owen and Ethel Merle (Glenn) M.; m. Georgia Ann Lewis, Oct. 6, 1956; children: Timothy Lawrence, Glenn Ellen. BS in Biol. Sci., DVM, Kans. State U., 1952; MS in Animal Pathology, Purdue U., 1956, PhD, 1960. Lic. vet. medicine. Veterinarian County Animal Hosp., Des Peres, Mo., 1952-53; supr. Brucellosis labs. Purdue U., West Lafayette, Ind., 1953-60; staff veterinarian lab. svcs. USDA, Washington, 1960-61; discipline leader in pathology and toxicology, animal health divsn. USDA Nat. Animal Disease Lab., Ames, Iowa, 1961-64; prof., chmn. dept. veterinary pathology U. Mo. Coll. Vet. Medicine, Columbia, 1964-69, 84-86, dir. Vet. Med. Diagnostic Lab., 1968-88, prof. emeritus, 1986—. Cons. USDA, to comdg. gen. U.S. Army R & D Command, Am. Inst. Biol. Scis., NAS, Miss. State U., St. Louis Zoo Residency Tng. Program, Miss. Vet. Med. Assn., Okla. State U., Pa. Dept. Agr., Ohio Dept. Agr. Co-editor: Mycotoxic Fungi, Mycotoxins, Mycotoxicoses: An Encyclopedic Handbook, 3 vols., 1977; contbr. numerous articles on diseases of animals to profl. jours. Active Trinity Presbyn. Ch., Columbia, 1989-92; bd. dirs. Mo. Symphony Soc., Columbia, 1989-92. Pharmacists mate second class USNR, 1943-46, PTO; 2d. lt. U.S. Army, 1952-56. Recipient Outstanding Svc. award USDA, 1959, merit cert., 1963, 64, Disting. Svc. award U. Mo. Coll. Vet. Medicine, 1987, Dean's Impact award, 1996. Fellow Royal Soc. Health London; mem. Am. Assn. Vet. Lab. Diagnosticians (E.P. Pope award 1976, chmn. lab. accreditation bd.

1972-79, 87-90, pres. 1979-80, sec.-treas. 1983-87), World Assn. Vet. Lab. Diagnosticians (bd. dirs. 1984-94, dir. emeritus 1994—), N.Y. Acad. Sci., U. S. Animal Health Assn., Am. Assn. Lab. Animal Sci., Mo. Soc. Microbiology, Am. Assn. Avian Pathologists, N.Am. Conf. Rsch. Workers in Animal Diseases, Mo. Univ. Retirees Assn. (v.p. 1996-98, pres. 1998-99). Presbyterian. Avocations: classic cars, boating, genealogy. Home: 916 Danforth Dr Columbia MO 65201-6164 Office: U Mo Vet Med Diagnostic Lab PO Box 6023 Columbia MO 65205-6023

MOREHOUSE, RICHARD EDWARD, psychology educator; b. LaCrosse, Wis., May 21, 1941; s. Ervin Lenard and Anna Martha (Weiland) Morehouse; m. Rita Spangler, Aug. 20, 1966; 1 child Lyda Ann. BS, U. Wis., 1971, MST, 1973; PhD, The Union Inst., 1979. Teaching asst. U. Wis., LaCrosse, 1971-72; ednl. cons. Coop. Ednl. Svcs. Agy., 1972-80; dir. coop. edn. Viterbo U., 1980-85; from asst. to prof. psychology Viterbo Coll., 1985—. Dept. chmn. Viterbo U., LaCrosse, 1986—93, chair, 1995—; vis. scholar Tex. Wesleyan U., Ft. Worth, 1993—94. Co-author: Student Study Guide for Human Development Across the Lifespan, 1991, 1994, Beginning Qualitative Research, 1994; co-editor: Analytic Teaching, 1991—96; editor, 1996—; author: Five Year Longitudinal Study of Healthy Families, 2001. Grantee Gifted Edn., Elem. and Secondary Edn. Act, 1976—79, Tchr. Tng., Cmty. Awareness, Wis. Humanities, 1982, Coll., Cmty. Symposium, 1983. Mem.: Am. Psychol. soc. (charter), N.Am. Assn. for Cmty. Inquiry (founder, 1st pres. 1994). Democrat. Unitarian Universalist. Home: 1131 Charles St La Crosse WI 54603-2508 Office: Viterbo Coll 815 9th St S La Crosse WI 54601-4777 E-mail: remorehouse@viterbo.edu.

MOREHOUSE, SARAH MCCALLY, retired political science educator; b. Boston, Jan. 15, 1927; d. Ralph Dewey and Eugenia Whitehead (Norris) Powell; m. W. Bradley Morehouse, Nov. 8, 1969 (div. Nov. 1986); children: Richard, John, Catherine, David; m. Malcolm Edwin Jewell, Dec. 28, 1991. BA in Polit. Sci., Wellesley Coll., 1948; PhD in Polit. Sci., Yale U., 1964. Instr. Conn. Coll., New London, 1964-66; lectr. Hunter Coll., Bronx, N.Y., 1966-69; assoc. prof. Manhattanville Coll., Purchase, 1969-75; prof. U. Conn., Stamford, 1976-92, prof. emerita, 1992—. Univ. senator U. Conn., 1982-85, assoc. dir., 1990-91. Author: State Politics, Parties and Policy, 1981, The Governor as Party Leader, 1998; contbr. various articles to profl. jours. Sec. Charter Revision Commn. Fairfield, Conn., 1960; chmn. Ethics Commn., Fairfield, 1984-88; pres. LWV, 1996-98; state LWV sec. bd. dirs. 1998-2001; political parties/elections, 2001. Vis. professorship for women NSF, 1991; fellow Danforth Found., 1960; rsch. grantee Russell Sage Found., 1983; vis. scholar U. Calif, Berkeley, 1991-92. Mem. Wellesley Club. Home: 242 Somerset Ave Fairfield CT 06430-4935

MOREHOUSE, VALERIE JEANNE, librarian; b. Taft, Calif., Jan. 30, 1947; d. Gordon Stanley and Cloe Ozelle (Reed) Hogue; m. Keith Herbert Morehouse, Aug. 22, 1968 (div. 1994); 1 child, Gordon. AA, Taft Coll., 1966; AB in English, U. Calif., Berkeley, 1968; MSLS, Simmons Grad. Sch. Libr. Sci., 1977. Cert. profl. librarian, Mass. Asst. libr. dir. Plymouth (Mass.) Pub. Librs., 1977—82; asst. exec. dir. Southeastern Librs. Coop., Rochester, Minn., 1982—84; libr. automation cons. N.D. State Libr., Bismarck, 1984—89; dist. libr. media dir. Bismarck Pub. Sch. Dist., 1989—97; sys. adminstr. MARINet, San Rafael, Calif., 1997—2000; libr. Temple Isaiah of Contra Costa County, Lafayette, 2001—. Adv. panelist for literature Mass. Coun. on Arts and Humanities, Boston, 1980-82. Editor, writer Libr. A Word to the Wise, 1995-97; author: Anthology: A Collection of Cape Cod Poets, 1974. Legis. chair, membership chair N.D. Libr. Assn., 1987-93; mem. N.D. Gov.'s Adv. Libr. Vision 2004 Com., Bismarck, 1995-96; mem. Ctrl. Dakota Libr. Network Bd., Bismarck, 1992—. Recipient Capewide 1st prize for poetry Provincetown Assn. for Living Arts, 1972, Spl. Recognition award COSMEP, 1977, Pres.' award for svc. to librs. N.D. Libr. Assn., 1994. Mem. ALA (chair publs. com. 1985-87, columnist, reviewer The Book List 1977-79), Calif. Libr. Assn., Beta Phi Mu. Avocations: gardening, travel. Office: MARInet 3501 Civic Center Dr Rm 414 San Rafael CA 94903-4189

MOREHOUSE, WARD, human rights organization executive, publisher; b. Evanston, Ill., Mar. 26, 1929; s. Edward Ward and Anna (Ely) M.; m. Cynthia Thomas, Oct. 3, 1953; children: John T., Andrew E. AB in History and Anthropology, Yale U., 1950; AM, Asia Inst., 1953; postgrad., NYU, 1953-59. Exec. sec. Internat. Conf. on Asian Problems, N.Y.C., 1952-54, Conf. on Asian Affairs, Inc., N.Y.C., 1954-57; instr. dept. govt. NYU, 1956-57; ednl. dir. Asia Soc., N.Y.C., 1957-62; UNESCO fellow in South and Southeast Asia, 1962-63; dir. Ctr. for Internat. Programs and Comparative Studies Univ. of the State of N.Y., 1963-76; pres. Coun. on Internat. and Pub. Affairs, N.Y.C., 1976—. Chmn. Intermediate Tech. Devel. Group N.Am., 1979—; pub. The Apex Press, 1988—; rsch. assoc. So. Asia Inst., Soc. Internat. Affairs, Columbia U., 1977—; cons. in field; vis. prof. U. Lund, Sweden, 1976-77, Adminstrv. Staff Coll. of India, Hyderabad, 1969-70. Author: (with M. Arun Subrasanias) The Bhopal Tragedy: What Really Happened and What It Means for American Workers and Communities at Risk, 1986, Building Sustainable Communities: Tools and Concepts for Self Reliant Economic Change, 1989, Abuse of Power: The Social Performance of Multinational Corporations, 1990, (with Lucinda Wykel and David Dembo) Worker Empowerment in a Changing Economy, 1991, others; contr. articles to profl. jours., chpts. to books. Trustee Coun. on Internat. and Pub. Affairs, 1954—, Ctr. for Devel. Policy, Washington, 1979-82; mem. steering com. Ctr. for Study of Expanded Capital Ownership, Washington, 1984-87; mem. Citizens Comn. on Bhopal, 1985-87, Corod. Com. on Toxics and Drugs, 1981-86; mem. adv bd. Croton Housing Task Force, Croton-on-Hudson, N.Y., 1988-90; bd. dirs. Croton Community Land Conservancy, Inc., 1990—; mem. state com. Liberal Party of N.Y. State, 1973—, mem. policy com., 1990—, others. Mem. Assn. for Asian Studies, Internat. Group for Grass Roots Initiatives (bd. dirs. 1986—), Oil Chem. and Atomic Workers (chief steward Local 8-149 1991—). Unitarian Universalist. Home: RR 1 Box 348 Croton On Hudson NY 10520-9747 Office: 777 United Nations Plz # 3C New York NY 10017-3521

MOREIRA, MARCIO MARTINS, advertising executive; b. Sao Paulo, Brazil, Nov. 20, 1947; came to U.S. 1980; naturalized, 1990; s. Guido Martins and Maria Rosa (Macrine) M.; children from previous marriage: Joaquim Pedro Rezende Martins Moreira; m. Maria Auxiliadora Godinho, Oct. 18, 1981; children: Eliana Maria Godinho Martins Moreira. Ed., U. Sao Paulo, Brazil, 1970. TV producer-copywriter McCann-Erickson, Sao Paulo, Brazil, 1967-71, creative dir., 1974-77, group creative dir. London, Lisbon and Frankfurt, 1971-74, executive creative dir. Latin America, 1977-80, internat. creative dir., 1980-88; vice chmn., chief creative officer McCann Erickson Worldwide, 1988—; vice chmn., regional dir. Asia-Pacific McCann-Erickson Worldwide, 1995-99, chief creative officer, dir. global brands, 1999—. Lectr. various univs. Author: Terraplenagem, 1968 Liquidacao, 1979; lyricist, 1968—; contbr. articles to profl. jours. U.S. judge, pres. jury Cannes Film Festival, 1989; chmn. bd. judges The New York Festivals. Recipient 5 Clio awards, 1976-89, Gold Lion, Silver Lion, Bronze Lion awards, Cannes, France, H.K. McCann award, Brazil, 1977, Paul Foley award Interpub. Group of Cos., 1983, Terence Cardinal Cooke medal for Disting. Svc. in Health Care, N.Y. Med. Coll., 1994. Mem. Brazilian-Am. C. of C. (bd. dir.). Republican. Roman Catholic. Avocations: cinema, songwriting, cars, speedwalking. Office: McCann-Erickson Worldwide 750 3rd Ave Fl 21 New York NY 10017-2703

MOREIRA-CAUNEDO, DEBRA, agricultural products executive; b. N.Y.C., July 2, 1966; d. Alfredo and Myrteline Moreira; m. Carlos Caunedo Jr., Nov. 25, 1995; children: Robert Carlos, Jessica Allie. BA, Iona Coll., New Rochelle, N.Y., 1988, MS, 1991. Analyst, market rsch. Am. Tobacco Co., Stamford, Conn., 1990-92, assoc. trade program mgr., 1992-94, trade sys. mgr., 1994-95; sales promotion mgr. Brown & Williamson, Louisville, 1995-97, mgr. logistics and planning, 1997-99, mgr. program com., 1999; program mgr., merchandising U.S. Tobacco, Greenwich, Conn., 1999—. Roman Catholic. Avocations: acting, singing, dancing, scuba diving, horseback riding. Home: 17 Fair Way Poughkeepsie NY 12603-5033 Office: US Tobacco Corp 100 W Putnam Ave Greenwich CT 06830-5316

MOREL, JIM E. nuclear engineer, researcher; BS in Math., La. State U., Baton Rouge, 1972; MS in Nuclear Engring., La. State U., 1974; PhD in Nuclear Engring., U. N.Mex., Albuquerque, 1979. Nuclear rsch. officer Air Force Weapons Lab., Albuquerque, 1974—76; tech. staff mem. Sandia Nat. Labs., 1976—84, Los Alamos Nat. Lab., Los Alamos, 1984—. Adj. prof. U. N.Mex., Albuquerque, 1980—; vis. mem. grad. faculty Tex. A&M U., College Sta., 1997—; affiliate mem. grad faculty La. State U., Baton Rouge, 1995—97. Contbr. articles. 1st lt. USAF, 1974—76, Kirtland AFB, NM. Recipient Disting. Performance award, Los Alamos Nat. Lab., 1992, Weapons Program award of Excellence, Dept. of Energy, 1994. Mem.: Soc. Indsl. and Applied Math. Office: Los Alamos Nat Lab PO Box 1663 MS D409 Los Alamos NM 87545 Office Fax: 505-665-5782. Business E-Mail: jim@lanl.gov.

MOREL, JORGE (JORGE SCIBONA), music educator, composer; b. Buenos Aires, May 9, 1931; arrived in U.S., 1961; s. Domingo Scibona and Angela Romeo-Scibona; widowed; children: Jorge Scibona, Francesca Scibona. BA in Music, Buenos Aires U., 1950; studied with, N.Y.C., 1974—76. Adj. prof. music and classical guitar Lehman Coll., Bronx, NY, 1979—. Composer: over 120 titles for guitar, 1945—. Home: 109-20 Queens Blvd Forest Hills NY 11375 E-mail: moreljs@aol.com.

MORELAND, DONALD EDWIN, plant physiologist; b. Enfield, Conn., Oct. 12, 1919; s. Albert Sinclair and Ruth (Cowan) M.; m. Verdie Brown Stallings, Nov. 6, 1954; 1 child, Donna Faye; stepchildren: Frank C., Paul Ziglar. BS in Forestry, N.C. State U., 1949, MS in Plant Physiology, 1950, PhD in Plant Physiology, 1953. Plant physiologist SUNY Coll. Forestry, Syracuse, 1952-53, USDA-Agrl. Rsch. Svc., Raleigh, N.C., 1953-71, rsch. leader, 1972-78, sr. exec., 1979-95, collaborator, 1996—; asst. prof. to prof. N.C. State U., 1953-95, prof. emeritus, 1996—. Mem. toxicology study sect. NIH, USPHS, Bethesda, Md., 1963-67. Editor: Biochemical Responses Induced by Herbicides, 1982; mem. editorial bd. Pesticide Biochemistry and Physiology, 1971-97, Pesticide Sci., 1987-96; contbr. articles to profl. jours. 1st lt. U.S. Army, 1941-46. AEC predoctoral fellow, 1950-52. Fellow AAAS, Weed Sci. Soc. Am. (outstanding rsch. award 1973); mem. Am. Chem. Soc., Plant Growth Regulator Soc. Am., Am. Soc. Plant Physiologists, So. Weed Sci. Soc., Sigma Xi. Avocations: woodworking, surf fishing, square dancing. Home: 1508 Pineview Dr Raleigh NC 27606-2562 Office: NC State U USDA-Agrl Rsch Svc Dept Crop Sci 3127 Ligon St Raleigh NC 27607-5376

MORELL, WILLIAM NELSON, JR. foreign trade association executive, government agency administrator; b. July 13, 1920; s. William N. and Louise (Cox) M.; m. Patricia Leonhard, Apr. 3, 1943; 1 child, Lynn Noble. Student, Coll. William and Mary, 1938-40; AB, George Washington U., 1942; MA, U. Pa., 1948; postgrad., Am. U., 1950-51; grad., Nat. War Coll., 1956. Jr. economist Bur. Labor Stats., 1941; asst. to prof. fin. George Washington U., 1941; naval mem. U.S. mil. mission to Moscow, 1944-46; asst. prof. Drexel Inst. Tech., 1946-48; instr. U. Pa., 1947-48; with CIA, 1949-68, staff mem. Office Nat. Est., 1950-52, mng. dir. U.S. econ. intelligence com., 1955-65, chmn., 1966-67; chmn. spl. study group NSC Planning Bd., 1960; econ. counselor Am. Embassy, Moscow, 1960-61; dep. dir. office rsch. and reports CIA, 1962-66, dir. Office Econ. Rsch., 1966-67, mem. U.S. econ. def. adv. com., adv. com. export policy, 1966-67; lectr. on Communist econs., 1960-68; faculty Nat. War Coll., 1968; econ. counselor Am. Embassy, Tapei, Taiwan, 1968-73, spl. asst. to sec. treasury, 1973-77; treasury mem. U.S. Nat. Intelligence Bd., 1973-77; mng. dir. USA-ROC Econ. Coun., Crystal Lake, Ill., 1977-78, pres., 1979-90; cons. U.S. Taiwan Trade, 1979-94, ret., 1994. Author, lectr. on Taiwan economy. Eucharistic min. Episc. ch. Lt. USNR, 1942-46. Decorated Order Brilliant Star Taiwan, Order Brilliant Star with Violet Grand Cordon; recipient Superior Achievement award, medal of merit CIA, Exceptional Svc. medal Treasury Dept., U.S. Nat. Intelligence Disting. Svc. award, Taiwan Econ. Ministry medal. Mem. Artus. Home: 340 S Berkshire Dr Lake Forest IL 60045-4823

MORELLA, CONSTANCE ALBANESE, congresswoman; b. Somerville, Mass., Feb. 12, 1931; d. Salvatore and Mary Christine (Fallette) Albanese; m. Anthony C. Morella, Aug. 21, 1954; children: Paul, Mark, Laura; guardians of: Christine, Catherine, Louise, Rachel, Paul, Ursula. AA, Boston U., 1950, AB, 1954; MA, Am. U., 1967, D of Pub. Svc. (hon.), 1988, Norwich U. and Dickinson Coll., 1989, Mt. Vernon Coll., 1995, U. Md. U. Coll., 1996, USUHS, 1997, U. Md., 1997, Elizabethtown Coll., 1999. Tchr. Montgomery County (Md.) Pub. Schs., 1956-60; instr. Am. U., 1968-70; prof. Montgomery Coll., Rockville, Md., 1970-86; mem. Md. Ho. Dels., Annapolis, 1979-86, U.S. Congress from 8th Md. dist., 1987—; mem. sci. com., tech. subcom., basic rsch. subcom., govt. reform com., chair D.C. subcom., mem. civil svc. subcom. Mem. civil svc., adv. bd. Am. Univ., Washington. Mem. adv. coun. Montgomery County Hospice Soc.; hon. bd. mem. Nat. Kidney Found; active Human Rights Caucus; Congressional Women's Caucus, Older Ams. Caucus, Population and Devel. Caucus; mem. Bd. Cafritz Found. Named Glamour Woman of Yr. Glamour mag. 1995, Washingtonian of Yr. 1991; named to Md. Women's Hall of Fame, Md. Women's Hall of Fame, 1994. Avocations: theatre, tennis, reading. Office: US Ho of Reps 2228 Rayburn Bldg Washington DC 20515-2008 also: 51 Monroe St Rockville MD 20850-2421*

MORELLI, PETER RICHARD, electronic executive; b. Chgo., May 11, 1945; s. Frank and Jennie (Bellocchio) M.; m. Kathleen Alice Stasek, Nov. 6, 1971; children: Trisha Lynn, Cheryl Ann. BS, Ill. Inst. Tech., 1975; MBA, Northwestern U., Evanston, Ill., 1993. Engr. Extel Corp., Northbrook, Ill., 1975-78; engring. mgr. AM Internat., Mt. Prospect, 1978-81, Northrop-Grumman, Rolling Meadows, 1981-98; mgr. electronic commerce devel. Verifone divsn. Hewlett Packard, Mililani, Hawaii, 1998-2000, Roseville, Calif., 2000-2001; global program mgr. bus. customer sales orgn. bus. ops. Hewlett Packard, 2001—. Sgt. U.S. Army, 1965-67, Vietnam. Avocations: golf, skiing. E-mail: peter_morelli@hp.com.

MORELLO, CELESTE ANNE, historian, criminologist; b. Norristown, Pa., July 22, 1958; d. Ann M. Morello. Student, Loyola U., Rome, 1978; BA in Classics cum laude, BA in Art History magna cum laude, Chestnut Hill Coll., 1980; MS in Criminology, St. Joseph's U., Phila., 1994; MA in History, Villanova U., 2000; grad., Civilian Police Acad., Phila., 2000. Tchr. history, social studies, sci. Archdiocese of Phila., Phila., 1977-84; lectr. on ancient history of Sicily, 1982—; cons. criminologist in Mafia and LCN history Phila. Police and U.S. Atty.'s Office, 1993—. Pioneer in criminal and Mafia history; petitioner, originator over 20 hist. sites in Phila. for Pa. Hist. and Mus. Commn. Hist. Marker Program, 1993—; lectr. Villanova U., Immaculata U. Author: Beyond History: The Times and Peoples of St. Paul's R.C. Church, 1843-1993, 1992; writer, dir. History of the Mafia and LCN in Philadelphia 1880-1959 for Dept. of Justice, FBI, Phila., 1997, History of South Philadelphia, Introduction, Institute for Service Learning, 1996, Survey of Illicit Narcotics Use in Philadelphia 1900-45 for Dept. of Justice, High Intensity Drug Traffic Area, Philadelphia/Camden, The Phenomenon of the Mafia, 1997, Oral Histories of Three Men: All Mafiosi Before 1930, 1998, The Early Sicilian American Mafia Before 1930, 1998, Case Study of A Western Sicilian Colony in Suburban Philadelphia, 1998, The Philadelphia Italian Market Cookbook, 1999, Before Bruno: The History of Philadelphia's Mafia, Book I 1880-1931, 1999, Before Bruno: The History of Philadelphia's Mafia, Book II 1931-46, 2001; contbr. articles to profl. jours. Founder Sicilian Culture Collection Balch Inst. for Ethnic Studies, Phila.; adv. bd. 3d Dist. Phila. Police. Mem. Moyamensing Hist. Soc. (founder), Pa. Hist. Assn., Arba Sicula, Sicilian Lang./Lit. Jour., Internat. Assn. for the Study of Organized Crime. Roman Catholic. Office: 1234 S Sheridan St Philadelphia PA 19147-4820

MORELLO, JOSEPH ALBERT, musician, educator; b. Springfield, Mass., July 17, 1928; s. Joseph Charles and Lilia (LaPalme) M.; m. Jean Ann Mehnert. Grad. high sch., Springfield. Ind. drummer, Springfield, 1945-49; drummer Gil Melé, Stan Kenton, Tal Farlow, Johnny Smith, N.Y.C., 1953-55, Dave Brubeck Quartet, touring worldwide, 1955-68; clinician Selmer Ludwig Drum Co., Elkhart, Ind., 1957-92; leader Joe Morello Quartet, 1979—; clinician DW Drums, Oxnard, Calif., 1993—; rec. artist Digital Music Products Inc., 1993—. Rec. artist Savoy, Capitol, Norgran, Blue Note, Columbia, RCA labels; innovator finger control in jazz drumming; author: Joe Morello Drum Method, The Natural Approach to Technique, 1993, Joe Morello Drum Method 2, 1994, also New Directions in Rhythm, Rudimental Jazz, Off the Record, Master Studies; releases include (with Joe Morello Quartet) Going Places, 1993, Morello's Standard Time, 1994, Marion Mc Partland's Hickory House Trio, 1999, Marion McPartland Trio with Joe Morello, 2002, Rufus Reid Live at Shanghai Jazz, 2002. Named to Hall of Fame, Modern Drummer mag., 1988, Percussive Arts Soc. Hall of Fame, 1993, Am. Jazz Hall of Fame, 2001, Trumpets Jazz Hall of Fame, 2002; recipient New Star award, Downbeat mag., 1955, Melody Maker mag. award, 1963—67, Jazz mag. award, 1964—67, Thomas A. Edison Lifetime Achievement award, 1990, Lifetime Achievement award, Jersey Shore Jazz and Blues Found., 1996, poll winner, Downbeat mag., 1963—65, Playboy mag., 1963—67, Recognition of Outstanding Leadership award, Kosa Internat. Percussion Workshops, 2002. Mem.: N.J. Jazz Soc. Avocation: photography.

MORELLO, JOSEPHINE A. microbiology and pathology educator; b. Boston, May 2, 1936; married, 1971. BS, Simmons Coll., 1957; AM, Boston U., 1960, PhD in Microbiology, 1962. Diplomate Am. Bd. Med. Microbiology. Inst. microbiology Boston U., 1962-64; rsch. assoc. Rockefeller U., 1964-66; resident in med. microbiology Columbia U. Coll. Physicians & Surgeons, N.Y.C., 1966-68; asst. prof. microbiology Columbia U., 1968-69; dir. microbiology Harlem Hosp. Ctr., 1968-69; from asst. prof. to assoc. prof. pathology and medicine U. Chgo., 1973-78, prof. pathology and medicine, 1978-2001, emerita prof. pathology, 2001, dir. clinical microbiology, 1970—2001. Vice-chair pathology, dir. hosp. lab. U. Chgo., 1994-2001. Editor Clin. Microbiology Revs., 1988-97, Clin. Microbiology Newsletter, 1979—. Recipient Profl. Recognition award Am. Bd. Med. Microbiology, 1998. Fellow Am. Acad. Microbiology; mem. Acad. Clin. Lab. Physicians and Scientists, Am. Soc. Microbiology (Sonnenwirth Meml. award 1991, Disting. Svc. award 1992), Am. Soc. Clin. Pathologists, Ill. Soc. Microbiology (Pasteur award 1988), Sigma Xi. Achievements include rsch. in improved methods clin. microbiology; epidemiology and characteristics pathogenic neisseria. Home: 4255 Pebble Pointe Dr Lakeland FL 33813-1946

MORELLO, ROBERT FRANK, ophthalmologist; b. New Rochelle, N.Y., May 8, 1947; s. Joseph Frank and Felicia (Gargiulo) M.; m. Nordeen Michelle Squilla, July 31, 1976; children: Samantha, Scott, Sabrina. BS in Biology, St. John's U., 1969; MD, Autonomous U., Guadalajara, Mex., 1976. Diplomate Am. Bd. Ophthalmology. Resident in internal medicine Bronx Lebanon Hosp. Ctr./Albert Einstein Coll. Medicine, 1977-78, resident in ophthalmology, 1978-81; attending ophthalmologist Sound Shore Med. Ctr. Westchester, New Rochelle, N.Y., 1981—. Cons. ophthalmologist Calvary Hosp., Bronx, N.Y., 1983—. Participating physician Vol. Health Program. Fellow Am. Coll. Surgeons, Internat. Coll. Surgeons, Am. Acad. Ophthalmology. Avocation: computers. Office: 120 Warren St New Rochelle NY 10801-5403 E-mail: ophthobob@aol.com.

MORELLO, STEVEN J. federal agency administrator, lawyer; b. Saginaw, Mich., Sept. 17, 1952; m. Francia S. Morello, Apr. 8, 1978; children: Steven Jr., Rebecca. BS in Fgn. Studies, Georgetown U., 1974; JD, U. Detroit, 1977; MBA, Boston U., Heidelberg, Fed. Republic Germany, 1980. Bar: Mich. 1977, Ill. 1984. Atty. contract Northrop Co., Rollings Meadows, Ill., 1982-84; atty., mgr. Digital Equipment Corp., Arlington Heights, 1984—; army gen. counsel U.S. Dept. Defense, Washington, 2001—. Served to capt. JAGC, U.S. Army, 1978-82. Fellow Nat. Contract Mgmt. Assn. (pres. Chgo. chpt. 1985-86). Office: US Dept Defense Army General Counsel 104 Army Pentagon Washington DC 20310-0104 Office Fax: 703-693-9254.*

MOREL-SEYTOUX, HUBERT JEAN, civil engineer, educator; b. Calais, Artois, France, Oct. 6, 1932; came to U.S., 1956; s. Aimé and Suzanne Claire (Rousseau) M.-S.; m. Margery K. Keyes, Apr. 16, 1960; children: Aimée, Claire, Sylvie, Marie-Jeanne. BS, Ecole St. Genevieve, Versailles, France, 1953; MS, Ecole Nationale des Ponts et Chaussées, Paris, 1956; PhD, Stanford U., 1962. Research engr. Chevron Oil Field Research Co., La Habra, Calif., 1962-66; prof. Colo. State U., Ft. Collins, 1966-91, prof. emeritus, 1991—; chargé de recherches U. Grenoble, France, 1972-73; maitre de recherches Ecole des Mines de Paris, Fontainebleau, France, 1982; directeur de recherches ORSTOM, Montpellier, France, 1991—; cons. hydrology Atherton, Calif., 1992—. Cons. AID, Dakar, Senegal, 1985-86, 88, Ministry of Agriculture and Water, Riyadh, Saudi Arabia, 1978-83, City of Thornton, Colo., 1986-88, King Abdulaziz U., Jeddah, Saudi Arabia, 1987, 89—, Ford Found., India, 1976, 79, South Fla. Water Mgmt. Dist., West Palm Beach, 1991—, Battelle Pacific Northwest Labs., Richland, Wash., 1991—, City of Paris, France, 1992—, Agence de l'Eau Seine-Normandie, 1992—, Utah State U., Logan, 1994-95, Reservoir Engring. Rsch. Inst., Palo Alto, 1994-95, Bay Delta Modeling forum, 1997—, U.S. Bur. Reclamation, 1998—; vis. prof. Ecole Polytechnique Federale de Lausanne, 1987; vis. scholar Stanford U., 1992—; adj. prof. U. Colo., Boulder, 1992—; lectr. U. Calif., Berkley, 1993. Editor: Hydrology Days, 1981—, 3d Internat. Hydrology Symposium, 1977, Unsaturated Flow in Hydrologic Modeling, 1989. Pres. Internat. Ctr., Ft. Collins, 1984-86. Served to lt. French Army Marine Corps Engrs., 1959-62. Sr. Fulbright scholar, France, 1972-73; recipient Abell Faculty Rsch. award Colo. State U. Coll. Engring., 1985. Mem. Am. Geophys. Union, ASCE, Soc. Petroleum Engrs., Am. Meteorol. Soc., Am. Soc. Agrl. Engrs. Home: 57 Selby Ln Atherton CA 94027-3926 Office: Hydrology Days Publs 57 Selby Ln Atherton CA 94027-3926

MORENCY, PAULA J. lawyer; b. Oak Park, Ill., Mar. 13, 1955; AB magna cum laude, Princeton U., 1977; JD, U. Va., 1980. Bar: Ill. 1980, U.S. Dist. Ct. (no. dist.) Ill. 1980, U.S. Ct. Appeals (7th cir.) 1981, U.S. Ct. Appeals (5th cir.) 1990, U.S. Dist. Ct. (ctrl. dist.) Ill. 1999, U.S. Dist. Ct. (ea. dist.) Wis. 2000. Assoc. Mayer, Brown & Platt, Chgo., 1980-86, ptnr., 1987-94, Schiff Hardin & Waite, Chgo., 1994—. Adj. prof. trial advocacy Northwestern U. Sch. Law, Chgo., 1997--; faculty Midwest Regional, Nat. Inst. for Trial Advocacy, 1988—; mem. pres.'s council Dominican U., 1998—. Author: Cross-Examination of a Franchise Executive, 1995, Insurance Coverage Issues in Franchise and Intellectual Property Litigation, 1996, Re-Emergence of Franchise Class Actions, 1997, Judicial and Legislative Update: ABA Forum on Franchising, 1999, How to Find, Use and Defend Against the Expert Witness, 2000, Dealing With System Change in a High-Tech World, 2001. Mem. ABA (forum franchising, governing com., litigation sect., intellectual property sect.), Chgo. Coun. of Lawyers (bd. govs. 1989-93), Constnl. Rights Found. Chgo. (chair 2001). Office: Schiff Hardin & Waite 7300 Sears Tower Chicago IL 60606

MORENO, BARRY, historian, writer; b. L.A. s. Rafael S. and Eva Maria Moreno. BA in History, Calif. State U., L.A., 1985. Libr., historian Statue of Liberty and Ellis Island, N.Y.C., 1988—. EEO counselor Nat. Park Svc., N.Y.C., 1988-96. Author: The Statue of Liberty Encyclopedia, 2000; (foreword) Ellis Island Interviews, 1997, (bibliography) Statue of Liberty Revisited; cons. for, appeared on numerous film, TV and radio documentaries including Ellis Island: Everyman's Monument, 1991, Ont the Inside: The Statue of Liberty, 1999, Building a Colossus: The Statue of Liberty, 2001, The Sweetest Sound., 2001; contbr. chpts. to books, articles to profl. jours. Recipient EEO Counseling award Statue of Liberty Nat. Monument, 1994. Mem. Mus. Coun. N.Y., Am. Immigration and Ethnic History Soc., Calif. Hist. Soc., Monarchist League, Vaudeville History Soc., English-Speaking Union. Roman Catholic. Avocations: writing, studying languages, reading. Office: Statue of Liberty Nat Monument and Ellis Island Liberty Island New York NY 10004 Office Fax: 212 363 6302. E-mail: barry_moreno@nps.gov.

MORENO, CARLOS R. state supreme court justice; b. L.A., Nov. 4, 1948; m. Christine Moreno; children: Keiko, Nicholas. BA in Polit. Sci., Yale U., 1970; JD, Stanford U., 1975. Dep. city atty. L.A. City Atty.'s Office; atty. with Mori & Ota (now known as Kelley, Drye & Warren), 1979; apptd. justice Mncpl. Ct., 1986—93; justice L.A. County Superior Ct., 1993—97, US Dist. Ct. (ctrl. dist.) Calif., 1998—2001; assoc. justice Supreme Ct. Calif., 2001—. Bd. visitors Stanford Law Sch.; bd. govs. Assn. Yale Alumni; dir. Arroyo Vista Family Health Ctr. Recipient Criminal Justice Superior Ct. Judge of Yr. award, L.A. County Bar Assn., 1997, For God, For Country and For Yale award, Yale U., 2001. Avocations: theater , opera, crossword puzzles. Office: Calif Supreme Ct 350 McAllister St San Francisco CA 94102-4783*

MORENO, CHRISTINE MARGARET, lawyer; b. Miami, Fla., Sept. 7, 1960; d. Arthur and Christine Moreno. BS magna cum laude, Barry U., 1981; JD cum laude, U. Miami, Coral Gables, Fla., 1984. CPA Fla.; bar: Fla. 1984, D.C. 1985, U.S. Dist. Ct. (so. dist.) Fla. 1985, U.S. Dist. Ct. (mid. dist.) Fla. 1987, U.S. Tax Ct. 1987, U.S. Supreme Ct. 1988, U.S. Ct. Appeals (11th cir.) 1988. Law intern U.S. Securities Exch. Commn., Miami, Fla., 1984; assoc. atty. Ruden, Barnett, McCloskey, Ft. Lauderdale, 1984-85, Koppen, Watkins, Ptnrs. & Assocs., Miami, 1985-89; mayor City of North Miami, 1989-91; owner, atty., CPA Law Offices of Christine M. Moreno, North Miami, Stuart, Fla., 1989—; commr. Jensen Beach (Fla.) Cmty. Redevelopment Agy., 1994-98, Martin County Environ. Control Bd., 1999—; legal counsel to

Ambassador Ray Cantillo, rep. to U.N. Miccosukee Nation, 1998—. Bd. dirs. North Miami Energy Adv. Bd.; life time dir. Mayor's Econ. Task Force, North Miami, 1989—. Co-author: Senior Citizens Handbook, 1990. Bd. dirs. Nat. League of Cities, Washington, 1990—91; v.p. polit. action Miami Dade C.C. Alumni, 1991—98, sec., 1998—. Mem.: AICPA, North Dade Bar Assn. (bd. dirs. Gold Coast chpt.), Fla. Inst. CPA (treas. Gold Coast chpt.), North Miami Jaycees (Jaycee of Yr. 1993), Dade County Rep. (com. woman 1990—94), Martin County Rep. Club (exec. com.), Phi Alpha Delta, Internat. Law Fraternity (Miami alumni chpt. justice 1985—). Office: 4450 SE Federal Hwy Stuart FL 34997-

MORENO, DONNA MARIE, communications executive; b. Amesbury, Mass., July 25, 1957; d. Robert and Marie Doris (Lucier) Menzigian; m. Carlos Moreno, Nov. 17, 1999. BS in Math., U. Lowell, 1979, MBA in Ops., 1983. Material control analyst AVCO Corp., Wilmington, Mass., 1979-81; ops. analyst Blue Cross & Blue Shield, Boston, 1981-83, risk analyst, 1983-84; systems analyst Bell Atlantic Corp., Bethesda, Md., 1984-86, cons. internal, 1986-89, project mgr., 1989-91, new tech. strategic planning mgr., 1992-97, sr mgr. sales channel devel., 1997—2001; sr. mgr. mktg. Verizon, 2001—. Speaker FUSE Nat. and Regional Confs., 1988, 91 Inventor (software) User-assisted Adhoc Reporting, 1988, Natural English Report Access, 1988. Vol. Montgomery County Vol. Assn., Montgomery, Md., 1983—, PALS Montgomery County, 1984—; chair spl. events New Mem. Svcs. John F. Kennedy Ctr. Performing Arts, Washington, 1985—, mem. vol. adv. com., 1991, 92; chair vol. adv. com. Kennedy Ctr., 1992—; bd. dirs. Sister City Corp., Rockville, 1992—, v.p., 1993-95, pres.-elect, 1994-95, pres., 1995—; Geissenbier mem. Jr. Chamber Internat. Found., 1996—; Geissenbier mem. U.S. Jr. C. of C. Found., 1997—. Recipient Internat Tng. Fellow, JCI, 2001—. Mem. NAFE, Ops. Rsch. Soc., Intelligent Computer Rsch. Inst., Focus User Group (co-chmn. artificial intelligence group 1989, leader, coord. spl. interest groups for Nat. Com., 1989, nat., regional spkr. 1988, 91), Rockville Jr. C. of C. (sec. 1992-93), Md. Jr. C. of C. (program mgr. internat. involvement 1992-93, dist. dir. 1993-94, cmty. devel. v.p. 1994-95, U.S. Jr. C. of C. internat. affairs commn. 1995-98, JCI individual devel. commn. 1996, spl. asst. to world pres. 1997—), Internat. Spkrs. Platform, Jr. C. of C. Republican. Roman Catholic. Avocations: photography, travel. Office: Verizon 13100 Columbia Pike Silver Spring MD 20902

MORENO, JEANNE SIMONNE, cardiac nurse; b. Fall River, Mass., July 5, 1968; d. Theodore J. and Simonne Bernier; m. Gabriel Moreno; children: Christopher Michael, Elora Jeanne, Alyssa Paige, Gabriel Matthew. BSN, Southeastern Mass. U., North Dartmouth, 1990. RN, Mass. Nurse Vis. Nurses Assn. Southeastern Mass., Inc., Fall River, 1999—. Clin. nursing instr. Diman Regional Sch. Practical Nursing, 1999—.

MORENO, NANCY PEARSON, botanist, educator; b. Mpls., Aug. 10, 1953; d. Marvin Wallace and Geraldine Gould P.; m. Felix R. Moreno, 1974; children: Helena, Felix. BA, U. Wis., 1974; MS, Inst. Nacional Investigaciones Bioticas, Xalapa, Veracruz, Mex., 1982; PhD, Rice U., 1993. Investigator Inst. Nacional de Investigationes sobre Recursos Bioticos, Xalapa, 1978-85; instr. Baylor Coll. Medicine, Houston, 1993-94, assoc. prof. family and cmty. medicine, 1995—2001, assoc. dir. Ctr. Ednl. Outreach, 1997—. Author: Glosario Botanico Ilustrado, 1984; co-author: Sleep and Daily Rhythms: Guide to Activities to Teachers, 2000, Muscles and Bones: Activities Guide for Teachers, 2000, My Home Planet Earth: Activities Guide for Teachers, 1999. Recipient Sci. Edn. Partnership award Nat. Inst. Environ. Health Scis., 1994-97, 97-2000, Sci. Edn. Partnership award Nat. Ctr. Rsch. Resources, NIH, 1998-2001. Office: Baylor Coll Medicine 1709 Dryden Ste 545 Houston TX 77030

MORENO, ROSA-MARIA, modern languages educator; b. Guatemala City, Guatemala, Sept. 4, 1946; d. Armando and Lily (Cordon) Moreno; children: Liza Maria, Angie Michele, David William. Diploma, Liceo Bilingue, Guatemala, 1964; BA, Ohio State U., 1982, MA in Policy and Leadership, 1995; MA in Spanish Lit., Ohio U., 2000. Fgn. dept. asst. Banco del Agro, Guatemala, 1964-66; regional mgr. asst. gen. food div. Incasa, 1966-68; translator/asst. human rsch. ctr. Ohio State U., Columbus, 1968-69, dirs. asst. internat. program, 1969-71, acad. program coord. dept. Slavic and East European langs., 1971-97, mem. adminstrv. resources mgmt. sys. liaison team, 1996-97; asst. chmn. modern langs. Ohio U., Athens, Lancaster and Ea. campuses, 1997-99, grad. tchr. assoc. Spanish Athens, 1998-2000, instr. modern langs., 2000—. V.p./treas. St. Anthony Sch. Bd., Columbus, 1982-86; bd. dirs. St. Francis DeSales Sch., Columbus, 1991-95; liaison on the comms. and edn. team Adminstrv. Resource Mgmt. Sys. Project, 1996-97. Mem. Dobro Slovo Slavic Honor Soc., Phi Kappa Phi, Sigma Delta Pi. Avocations: reading, traveling. Office: Ohio U Dept Modern Langs Gordy Hall 259 Athens OH 45701 E-mail: moreno@ohio.edu.

MORENO, ZERKA TOEMAN, psychodrama educator; b. Amsterdam, The Netherlands, June 13, 1917; d. Joseph and Rosalia (Gutwirth) Toeman; m. Jacob L. Moreno (dec. Aug. 1949); 1 child, Jonathan D.; 1 stepchild, Regina. Student, Willesden Tech. Coll., 1937-38, NYU, 1948-49. Cert. trainer, educator, practitioner of psychodrama and group psychotherapy Am. Bd. Examiners. Rsch. asst. Psychodramatic and Sociometric Insts., N.Y.C., 1942-51; pres. Moreno Inst., N.Y.C. and Beacon, N.Y., 1951-82; trainer in psychodrama Studiefrämjandet, Stockholm, 1976-83, Finnish Psychodrama Assn., Lahti, Finland, 1976-83. Lectr., trainer, Gt. Britain, Australia, New Zealand, Norway, Sweden, Italy, Germany, Japan, 1976-96, Argentina, Brazil, Greece, The Netherlands, Denmark, Belgium, Spain, Israel, Korea and Taiwan, 1977—; hon. pres. Chinese Zerka Moreno Inst., Nanjing, China; acad. advisor mental health Nanjing Brain Hosp., China, 1997. Co-author: Psychodrama, Surplus Reality, and the Art of Healing, (book of poetry) Love Songs to Life, 1971, 93; co-author: Psychodrama, Vol. II, 1967, Vol. III, 1969, The First Psychodramatic Family, 1964. Named hon. citizen Comune di Roma, Assessorato Alla Cultura, 1983, Municipalidad de la Ciudad de Buenos Aires, 1984, Hon. Mem. Federacao Brasiliero de Psicodrama, Sao Paulo, 1996; first recipient of prize from Astrid Badina Stiftung (Baden-Baden), 1999; nominated for Sigmund Freud award psychotherapy City of Vienna, 1999. Fellow Am. Soc. Group Psychotherapy and Psychodrama (pres. 1967-69, hon. pres. 1988—, sec.-treas. 1955-66); hon. mem. Internat. Assn. Group Psychotherapy (treas. 1974-76, bd. dirs. 1976-80), Soc. Psicodrama Sao Paulo (hon.), Sociedad Argentina Psicodrama (hon.). Home: The Colonnades C24 2600 Barracks Rd Charlottesville VA 22901-2198 Fax: 434-245-4007.

MORENO-CABRAL, CARLOS EDUARDO, cardiac surgeon; b. Zacatecas, Mex., Nov. 4, 1951; s. Manuel Julio Moreno and Dominga Cabral; m. Elaine Moreno-Cabral; children: Rodrigo, Iza, Daniel. MD, Nat. U. Mex., 1976. Diplomate Am. Bd. Thoracic Surgery. Resident in gen. surgery U. Hawaii, 1977-80, Mich. State U., 1980-82; fellow in cardiac surgery Stanford (Calif.) U., 1982-84, 86-88; tng. in thoracic surgery SUNY, Bklyn., 1984-86; dir. cardiac transplant program St. Francis Hosp., Honolulu, 1989—. Author: Postoperative Management in Adult Cardiac Surgery, 1988. Fellow ACS; mem. Soc. Thoracic Surgeons. Avocation: photography. Office: 1380 Lusitana St Ste 912 Honolulu HI 96813-2448 E-mail: cemoreno@aol.com.

MORENO-RIANO, GERSON, political science educator; b. Bogota, May 15, 1971; s. Hector Moreno Castro and Ruby Esperanza Riano; m. Ellen Anna Gaddy, Dec. 21, 1991; children: Isaac, Victoria, Abraham, Emma, Abigail. BA, Cedarville (Ohio) Coll., 1994; MA, U. Cin., 1998; PhD, 1999. Charles P. Taft doctoral fellow U. Cin., 1998-99; assoc. fellow Ctr. Study Dem. Citizenship, Cin., 1999—; asst. prof. polit. sci. Cedarville U., 1999—. Polit. analyst 90.3 FM WCDR Radio, Cedarville, 2000—; guest spkr. Men in the Marketplace, Springfield, Ohio, 1999-2000. Contbr. articles to profl. peer-reviewed jours. Mem. Am. Polit. Sci. Assn., Medieval Acad. Am. Office: Cedarville U 251 N Main St Cedarville OH 45314 Fax: (937) 766-7583. E-mail: morenog@cedarville.edu.

MOREST, DONALD KENT, neuroscientist, educator; b. Kansas City, Mo., Oct. 4, 1934; s. F. Stanley and Clara Josephine (Riley) M.; m. Rosemary Richtmyer, July 13, 1963; children: Lydia, Claude. BA, U. Chgo., 1955; MD, Yale U., 1960. Sr. asst. surgeon USPHS, Bethesda, Md., 1960-63; asst. prof. U. Chgo., 1963-65; asst. to assoc. prof. Harvard Med. Sch., Boston, 1965-77; prof., dir. Ctr. for Neurol. Scis. U. Conn. Health Ctr., Farmington, 1977—. Cons. NIH, Bethesda, 1975—, European Commn. Contbr. articles to profl. jours. and books. Recipient Loeser award U. Conn. Health Ctr., Farmington, 1982; Career Devel. awardee NIH, 1971; named Javits neurosci. investigator NIH, 1984, Claude Pepper awardee, 1990. Mem. Am. Assn. Anatomists (C. Judson Herrick award 1966), Soc. for Neurosci., Assn. for Rsch. in Otolaryngology, Conn. Acad. Sci. and Engring. (elected), Cajal Club (pres. 1980). Avocations: flute, badminton. Home: 18 Shady Ln West Simsbury CT 06092-2232 E-mail: kent@neuron.uchc.edu.

MORETON, THOMAS HUGH, minister; b. Shanghai, China, Dec. 2, 1917; came to U.S., 1946; s. Hugh and Tsuru M; m. Olive Mae Rives, Apr. 1, 1947 (dec. Apr. 1986); children: Ann Rives Moreton Smith, Andrew Hugh, Margaret Evelyn Moreton Hamar; m. Selma Littig, June 7, 1986. LLB, 1939, BD, 1942, PhD, 1946; ThD, Trinity Sem., 1948; LittD, 1949. Ordained to ministry Bapt. Ch., Glasgow, Scotland, 1942. Min. various chs., also tchr. Seaford Coll., Eng., 1945-46; tchr. coll. and sem. level. divsn. courses various schs., Atlanta, Oklahoma City, 1946-51; founder Tokyo Gospel Mission, Inc., House of Hope, Inc., Tokyo, from 1951; also World Gospel Fellowship, Inc., Norman, Okla., from 1967. Pastor chs., Moore, Okla., Shawnee, Okla., Ada., Okla., Del City, Okla., Tahlequah, Okla. and Oklahoma City, 1968—; preacher numerous fgn. countries; internat. tour dir., radio broadcaster. Contbr. articles to religious jours. Charter mem. Am.-Japan Com. for Assisting Japanese-Am. Orphans. Chaplain AUS, 1952-63. Recipient various awards Japanese govt. Fellow Royal Geog. Soc., Philos. Soc.; mem. Royal Soc. Lit., Am.-Japan Soc., Israel-Japan Soc. Died Sept. 22, 2001.

MORETTI, EDWARD CHARLES, environmental engineer, consultant; b. Pitts., Feb. 8, 1962; s. Raymond and Mary Nancy (Corvari) M.; m. Deborah Benson, May 6, 1989; 1 child, Matthew. BSChE, U. Pitts., 1984; M Pub. Mgmt., Carnegie Mellon U., 2001, M Pub. Mgmt., 2001. Engr., prototype ops. GE, Schenectady, N.Y., 1985-86; sr. engr. Radian Corp., Research Triangle Park, N.C., 1986-90, SAIC, Monroeville, Pa., 1990-92; mgr. environ. compliance Michael Baker Corp., Coraopolis, 1992—. Course instr. AIChE Continuing Edn. Program, Ctr. for Profl. Advancement, Inst. Gas Tech. Author: Current and Potential Future Industrial Practices for Reducing and Controlling Volatile Organic Compounds, 1993, Practical Solutions for Reducing Volatile Organic Compounds and Hazardous Air Pollutants, 2001; contbr. Environ. Analysis and Remediation, 1997; contbr. articles to profl. jours., including Chem. Engring. Progress. Mem. AIChE, Air and Waste Mgmt. Assn., Assn. Iron & Steel Engrs. Avocations: tennis, theater. Office: Baker Environmental 420 Rouser Rd Coraopolis PA 15108-2722 E-mail: ecmoretti@yahoo.com ., emoretti@mbakercorp.com.

MORETTI, JAY DONALD, lawyer; b. Waukesha, Wis., May 20, 1947; s. Orest and Jeanne A. (Charlevoix) M.; m. Joann Senn, Nov. 8, 1975; children: Angela, Rocco, Luciano. BA in History, U. Wis., 1969, JD, 1971. Bar: Wis. 1972, U.S. Dist. Ct. (we. dist.) Wis. 1972, U.S. Dist. Ct. (ea. dist.) Wis. 1973. Atty. Reigel Law Office, Madison, Wis., 1971-72; pvt. practice, 1973-76, Cross Plains, Wis., 1975—. Supr. Dane County, Madison, 1990-96, chmn. pub.protection and judiciary com., chmn. planning structure com., vice chmn. ways and means com., mem. EXPO expansion com.; mem. Bd. Health; mem. exec. bd. Dane County Rep. Com., 1988-90; mem. Wis. Citizens com. AODA, 1987-91. Recipient William Campbell award Wis. Rep. Com., 1989, svc. award, 1991; community svc. award Cross Plains Jaycees, 1980, Columbian of the Yr. award 1999, Excellence award Dane County Dep. Sheriff's Assn., 1995. Mem. State Bar Wis., Dane County Bar Assn., Cross Plains Bus. Assn. (pres. 1979,99, v.p.), Am. Legion, Italian Workmen's Club (pres. 1976), Lions (pres. Cross Plains 1985, dist. parliamentarian 1986-2001, zone chmn. 1988-91). Roman Catholic. Avocations: canoeing, gardening. Office: 2305 Main St Cross Plains WI 53528-9529 E-mail: moretti@chorus.net.

MORETTI, ROBERT JAMES, psychologist, educator; b. Chgo., Aug. 28, 1949; s. James John and Elva Eve (Bonini) M.; m. Carol L. Curt, Dec. 6, 1986. BS in Psychology, Loyola U., Chgo., 1971, PhD in Clin. Psychology, 1982; MA in Behavioral Sci., U. Chgo., 1976; diploma in analytical psychology, Jung Inst., Chgo., 1997. Lic. clin. psychologist, Ill. Rsch. fellow Ill. State Psychiat. Inst., Chgo., 1974-76; clin. asst. prof. Loyola U. Sch. Dentistry, 1976-81; asst. prof. behavioral scis. Northwestern U. Dental Sch., 1981-91, assoc. prof., 1991—2000. Asst. dir. clin. tng., dir. health psychology Northwestern U. Med. Sch., 1988-93; asst. prof. Grad. Sch., Northwestern U., 1986-91, assoc. prof., 1991—; faculty mem. C.G. Jung Inst., Chgo., 1993—, mem. tng. com., 1999-2000; staff Northwestern Meml. Hosp.; sr. faculty AIDS Mental Health Edn. and Evaluation Project, 1986-89, dir. relaxation and epilepsy project, 1991—; pvt. practice clin. psychology, 1983—; Jungian analysis, 1997—. Mem. editl. bd. Jour. of Am. Analgesia Soc., 1987-93; contbr. articles to profl. jours., chpts. to books. Served with Ill. Army Nat. Guard, 1971-77. Kellogg fellow Am. Fund Dental Health, 1981. Mem. APA, Ill. Psychol. Assn., Assn. Applied Psychophysiology and Biofeedback, Soc. Personality Assessment, Internat. Stress Mgmt. Assn., Chgo. Soc. Jungian Analysts (sec. 1999-2000, v.p. 2000—), Internat. Assn. for Analytical Psychology, Inst. Noetic Scis. Home: 3458 N Normandy Ave Chicago IL 60634-3717 Office: 151 N Michigan Ave Apt 801 Chicago IL 60601-7543 E-mail: r-moretti@northwestern.edu.

MORETTO, JANE ANN, nurse, public health officer; b. Belgium, Ill., Apr. 9, 1934; d. Bernard James and Mildred Bertha (Sutton) Moretto; RN, Mercy Hosp. Sch. Nursing, Urbana, Ill., 1955; B.S. in Nursing, St. Joseph Coll., Emmitsburg, Md., 1969. Relief head nurse, staff nurse Mercy Hosp., Urbana, Ill., 1955-57; staff nurse in psychiatry VA Hosp., Danville, Ill., 1957-59; staff nurse pulmonary disease VA Hosp., Long Beach, Calif., 1959-60, staff nurse surg. unit, L.A., 1960-61, staff nurse oper. rm., 1961-64; commd. lt. comdr. USPHS, 1969, advanced through grades to capt., 1975—; staff nurse USPHS Hosp., Galveston, Tex., 1964-66, staff nurse tumor ICU, Balt., 1967, asst. oper. rm. supr., New Orleans, 1969-71, oper. rm. supr., Brighton, Mass., 1971-78, dep. dir. nursing, dir. insvc. edn. Carville, La., 1978-80, dir. nurses Gillis W. Long Hansen's Disease Ctr., 1980-91, clin. nurse cons. lower extremity amputation prevention program Carville Diabetic Foot Program, 1991-95; cons. in field; lectr. in field. Inventor teaching foot model. Recipient Superior Performance award, USPHS Hosp., Galveston, 1966, Outstanding Svc. medal for exemplary performance of duty Dept. Health Human Svcs.-Pub. Health Svc., 1986 (citation, 1990, Unit Commendation award USPHS, 1981, Isolated Hardship award USPHS, 1981, Hazardous Duty award USPHS, 1992, Commendation medal USPHS, 1993); named Nurse of Yr., Baton Rouge Dist. Nurses Assn., 1991. Mem. Am. Nurses Assn., La. Nurses Assn., La. Hosp. Assn., La. Soc. Nursing Svc. Adminstrs., Nat. Assn. for Uniformed Svcs., Assn. Mil. Surgeons of U.S., Assn. Oper. Rm. Nurses, Alumnae Assn. of Schlarman High Sch., Alumnae Assn. of St. Joseph Coll., Commd. Officers Assn. USPHS. Roman Catholic. Home: 1741 Cobble Ln Mount Dora FL 32757-6251

MORETZ, CHERYL ANN, educational administrator; b. Bound Brook, N.J., May 27, 1950; d. Joseph Gerard and Claire Mae (Blume) Neach; 1 child, Christin Ann Moretz. BS in Secondary Edn., Bucknell U., 1972; EdM in Elem. Edn., Rutgers U., 1980, EdD in Adminstrn. and Supervision, 1995. Cert. supr., elem. tchr., N.J. Tchr. Monmouth Junction (N.J.) Elem. Sch., 1980-87, asst. prin., 1987-91; prin. Brayton Sch., Summit, N.J., 1991—. Author: (simulation game) Stock Market, 1988, Who Am I? series, 1990. Mem. ASCD, N.J. Math. Tchrs. Assn. Avocations: skiing, tennis, reading, cooking. Office: Brayton Sch Tulip St Summit NJ 07901 E-mail: cmoretz@summit.k12.nj.us.

MOREWITZ, STEPHEN JOHN, behavioral scientist, consultant, educator; b. Newport News, Va., May 14, 1954; s. Burt M. and Ruth (August) M., Lora Friedman (stepmother). BA, Coll. William and Mary, 1975, MA, 1978; PhD, U. Chgo., 1983. Rsch. asst. Michael Reese Hosp., Chgo., 1979-84; asst. social scientist Argonne (Ill.) Nat. Lab., 1984-85; asst. to dean, asst. prof. U. Ill., Chgo., 1988-92, sr. rsch. splst., 1991-92; vol. rsch. staff San Francisco Gen. Hosp., 1993-97; pres. S. Morewitz, PhD & Assocs., Chgo. and Buffalo Grove, Ill., 1988—, San Francisco, 1992—. Part-time sociology faculty DePaul U., Chgo., 1985—; mem. faculty St. Elizabeth's Hosp., 1987—88; assoc. prof. Calif. Coll. Podiatric Medicine, 1997—2000, prof., rsch. dean, 2000—; cons. in field. Author: (monograph) Sexual Harassment, 1996, Stalking & Violence, 2002; co-author: Medical Malpractice, 1996; contbr. articles, chapters to books. Vol. docent Garfield Farm Mus., LaFox, Ill., 1979—; curator The Saving of S.S. Quanza, Chgo., 1991—. Mem. Am. Pub. Health Assn., Am. Diabetes Assn. (profl. sect.), Assn. for Behavioral Scis. and Med. Edn., Am. Sociol. Assn. (cert., nat. finalist med. sociology), Soc. Behavioral Medicine, Generalist in Med. Edn., Sociol. Practice Assn. Avocations: theatre, museum design, swimming, environmental preservation. Office: S Morewitz PhD & Assocs PMB M858 28 E Jackson Blvd 10 Fl Chicago IL 60604

MOREY, ANN-JANINE, English educator; b. Atlanta, Oct. 31, 1951; d. Donald Franklin and Martha Ann (Ballew) M.; m. Todd Hedinger, July 19, 1986; children: Lucia Rose Hamilton Morey, Gabriel Todd Morey. BA, Grinnell Coll., 1973; MA, U. So. Calif., L.A., 1977, PhD, 1979. Prof. So. Ill. U., Carbondale, 1979-99, dir. Univ. Core Curriculum, 1993-99; assoc. dean for interdisciplinary programs James Madison Univ., 1999—. Author: Apples and Ashes, 1982, Religion and Sexuality in American Literature, 1992, What Happened to Christopher: An American Family's Story of Shaken Baby Syndrome, 1998; contbr. articles to profl. jours. Recipient SIUC Woman of Distinction award, 1999, 20th Annual Student Affairs award for svc. to students, 1999; listed in Contemporary Authors, 1994; named Outstanding Tchr., Coll. Liberal Arts. Mem. MLA, Am. Acad. Religion (panel judge awards for excellence 1989-91), Soc. for Values in Higher Edn., Am. Lit. Assn., Am. Religion and Lit. Soc. (pres. 1997-2001). Office: James Madison Univ Coll of the Arts & Letters Msc 2105 Harrisonburg VA 22807-0001

MOREY, CARL REGINALD, musicologist; b. Toronto, Ont., Can., July 14, 1934; s. Reginald Donald and Julia Beatrice (Mabey) M.; m. Lorna Ann Dalton, June 2, 1960 (dec.); 1 child, Rachel Adriana MusB, U. Toronto, 1957; MusM, Ind. U., 1961, PhD, 1965. Asst. prof. Wayne State U., Detroit, 1962-63; assoc. prof. U. Windsor, Ont., 1964-70; prof. music U. Toronto, 1970-2000, dean faculty of music, 1984-90, Jean A. Chalmers prof., dir. Inst. for Can. Music, 1991-2000. Author: Music in Canada: A Research and Information Guide, 1997; MacMillan On Music, 1997, An Opera Sampler, 1998; editor: (musical) Works of Glenn Gould (Schott), 1995, 96, 97, 99, Opera Viva, 2000. Avocation: swimming. Home: 540 Palmerston Blvd Toronto ON Canada M6G 2P5 Office: U Toronto Faculty of Music Toronto ON Canada M5S 2C5 E-mail: carl.morey@utoronto.ca.

MOREY, CHARLES LEONARD, III, theatrical director; b. Oakland, Calif., June 23, 1947; s. Charles Leonard Jr. and Mozelle Kathleen (Milliken) M.; m. Mary Carolyn Donnet, June 10, 1973 (div. 1975); m. Joyce Miriam Schilke, May 29, 1982; 1 child, William. AB, Dartmouth Coll., 1969; MFA, Columbia U., 1971. Artistic dir. Peterborough (N.H.) Players, 1977-88, Pioneer Theatre Co., Salt Lake City, 1984—. Actor: N.Y. Shakespeare Festival, Playwrights Horizons, New Dramatists, ARK Theatre Co., Ensemble Studio Theatre, Cubiculo, Folger Theatre, Syracuse Repertory Theatre, Theatre by Sea, others; over 150 plays acted in or directed; guest dir. Ensemble Studio Theatre, ArK Theatre, Am. Stage Festivel, McCarter Theatre, Pioneer Theatre Co., PCPA Theatrefest, The Repertory Theater of St. Louis, Meadow Brook Theatre, Utah Shakespearean Festival; author Laughing Stock and new adaptations Alexander Dumas' The Three Musketeers, Bram Stoker's Dracula, Charles Dickens' A Tale of Two Cities, Victor Hugo's The Hunchback of Notre Dame, Alexandre Dumas' The Count of Monte Cristo. Trustee Utah Arts Endowment, Inc., Nat. Theatre Conf.; panelist Nat. Endowment for Arts. Mem. Soc. Stage Dirs. and Choreographers, AEA, SAG, AFTRA, Salt Lake City C. of C. (Honors in the Arts award 1991), Utah Assn. Gifted Children (Community Svc. award 1991), Peterborough Players (Edith Bond Stearns award 1990). Democrat. Episcopalian. Office: Pioneer Theatre Co 300 S 1400 E Salt Lake City UT 84112-0660 E-mail: chuck@ptc.utah.edu.

MOREY, JEAN W. artist; d. Carl Adolf Wuerfel and Lillian Florence Brown; m. William Joseph Morey., June 19, 1948; children: Susan, Nancy, Kenneth, David, Peter. Student, Art Inst. Chgo., DePauw U. Artist, illustrator Consolidated Publ. Co., Chgo., The Fair Store, Chgo. Co-founder Sci. Hall and Jr. Mus., Bradenton, Fla.; illustrator children's books Rand McNally, Children's Press, Ency. Britannica, Bonific Press; guest instr. Wheaton (Ill.) Coll.; lectr. in field. Illustrator 19 books, 6 readers, 3 childrens books. Deaconess Fox Valley Presbyn. Ch., Geneva, Ill., 1969-76. Mem. Nat. Women's Book Assn., Fla. Watercolor Soc., Citrus Water Color Club, Citrus County Art League, Nature Coast Painters. Avocations: archaeology, painting, softsculpture, boating, swimming. Home: 3590 N Wagon Pt Beverly Hills FL 34465-4484

MOREY, PHILIP STOCKTON, JR. mathematics educator; b. Houston, July 11, 1937; s. Philip Stockton and Helen Holmes (Wolcott) M.; m. Jeri Lynn Snyder, Sept. 5, 1964; children: William Philip, Christopher Jerome. BA, U. Tex., 1959, Ma, 1961, PhD, 1967. Asst. prof. math. U. Nebr., Omaha, 1967-68; assoc. prof. Tex. A&I U., Kingsville, 1968-76; prof. Tex. A&M U., 1976—. Lectr. U. Tokyo, 1976, U. Hokkaido, 1977, 88. Contbr. articles to Tensor N.S., Internat. Jour. Engring. Sci, Tex. Jour. Sci. Recipient Researcher of Yr. awrd Tex. A&I Alumni Assn., 1985. Mem. Tex. Acad. Sci. (chmn. math. sect. 1982, 85, 99), Am. Math. Soc., Tensor Soc., (Japan). Achievements include research in extensor analysis, tensor analysis, differential geometry, mathematical physics. Home: 1514 Lackey St Kingsville TX 78363-3199 Office: Tex A&M Univ Dept Math Kingsville TX 78362 E-mail: kfpsm00@tamuk.edu.

MOREY, ROBERT HARDY, communications executive; b. Milw., Sept. 5, 1956; s. Lloyd W. and Ruby C. (McElhaney) M. AA, Ricks Coll., 1978; BA, Brigham Young U., 1983. Program dir. Sta. KABE-FM, Orem, Utah, 1982-83, sales mgr., 1983; nat. mgr. ops. Tiffany Prodns. Internat., Salt Lake City, 1983-84; account exec. Osmond Media Corp., Orem, 1984; corp. sec., bd. dirs. Positive Communications, Inc., 1984—87, chief exec. officer, 1987—; gen. mgr. Sta. KSRR, 1985—; pres. K-Star Satellite Network, 1986—89, Broadcast Media Svcs., Orem, 1987—; gen. mgr. Sta. KMGR, Salt Lake City, 1993; ops. mgr. KQMB-FM, 1994-95, gen. mgr., 1995-98; gen. mgr. KCFM, 1998—. Guest lectr. various colls. and univs., 1981—. Chmn. Rep. voting dist., Orem, 1984. Recipient Community Service award Utah Valley Community Coll., 1983; named one of Outstanding Young Men in Am. U.S. Jaycees, 1983. Avocations: reading, collecting stamps. Home: PO Box 828 Orem UT 84059-0828 Office: Sta KSRR Ventura Media Ctr 1240 E 800 N Orem UT 84097-4318

MOREYRA, ABEL E. physician, medical educator; b. Mar del Plata, Argentina, Dec. 2, 1941; came to U.S., 1972; s. Genaro and Emilia (Basso) M.; m. Maria Elena Moreyra; children: Maria Eugenia, Maria Evelina, Fernando Abel. MD, U. Nacional de La Plata, Argentina, 1967. Fellow Cleve. Clinic Found., 1972-75; asst. prof. medicine UMDNJ-Robert Wood Johnson Med. Sch., New Brunswick, N.J., 1975-83, assoc. prof., 1983-95, prof., 1995—. Fellow ACP, Am. Coll. Cardiology; mem. Am. Coll. Angiology. Office: UMDNJ-RW Johnson Med Sch CN-19 Rm 582A New Brunswick NJ 08903 E-mail: moreyrae@umdnj.edu.

MORFOPOULOS, V. metallurgical engineer, materials engineer; b. Athens, Greece, Oct. 22, 1937; BS, Purdue U., 1958; MS, Columbia U., 1961, ScD in Engring. Sci., 1964. Rsch. assoc. metall. engring. Purdue U., 1957-60; rsch. engr. U.S. Steel Corp., 1961; instr. chem. CUNY, 1961-63; rsch. engr. Argonne Nat. Lab., 1963, Am. Iron & Steel, Columbia U., 1964-65, sr. metall. sci., 1965-66; tech. dir. R&D testing Am. Standards Testing Bur., 1966—. Cons. govt. and industry, 1966—; mem. Int. Commn. Chem. Thermodyn. & Kinetics; mem. Transp. Rsch. Bd., Nat. Rsch. Coun. Mem. AAAS, Am. Inst. Mining, Metall. Petroleum Engrs., Am. Soc. Engr. Edn., Assn. Cons. Chemists and Chem. Engrs., N.Y. Acad. Sci. Achievements include research and consulting in fields of corrosion and oxidation phenomena. low and high temperature thermodynamics, liquid metals and compounds, surface phenomena, electrometallurgy and electrode phenomena, electrical and magnetic properties of matter, failure and stress analysis, metal finishing, joining and working. Office: Am Standards Testing Bur Inc 40 Water St New York NY 10004-2626 E-mail: worldteck@aol.com .

MORFORD, JOANN (JOANN MORFORD-BURG), state senator, investment company executive; b. Miller, S.D., Nov. 26, 1956; d. Darrell Keith Morford and Eleanor May (Fawcett) Morford-Steptoe. BS in Agrl.-Bus., Comml. Econs., S.D. State U., 1979; cert. in personal fin. planning, Am. Coll., 1992. Chartered fin. cons. Agrl. loan officer 1st Bank System, Presho, S.D., 1980-82, Wessington Springs, 1982-86, Am. State Bank, Wessington Springs, 1986; registered investment rep. ARM Fin. Svcs. Inc., 1986-96; Miller, 1997—; mem. S.D. State Senate, Wessington Springs, 1990-96, majority whip, 1993-94, minority whip, 1995-96, mem., 1990-97, Miller, 1997-98; ins. agt. Western Fraternal Life Assn., 2001—. Mem. senate appropriations com. 1993-98; chair senate ops. and audit com. 1993, 94; mem. ops. and audit com., 1995-98; mem. Nat. Conf. State Legislators' Assembly of Fed. Issues Environ.

Com., 1994-98, vice chair, 1996-97. Mem. Midwestern-Can. task force Midwest Conf., 1990-94; mem. transp. com., commerce com., taxation com. S.D. State Senate, Pierre, 1990-92; treas. twp. bd. Wessington Springs, 1990-92; mem. Wessington Springs Sch. Improvement Coun., 1992-95. Fleming fellow Ctr. Policy Alternatives, 1996. Mem.: S.D. Farmers Union, Bus. and Profl. Women, Alumni Coun. Young Polit. Leaders (China delegation 1996, host El Salvador delegation 1999), Future Farmers Am. (adv. bd. Wessington Springs chpt. 1984—96), S.D. State U. 4-H Alumni Assn., Order Ea. Star (various offices 1980—). Democrat. Methodist. Home and Office: PO Box 21 Miller SD 57362-0021

MORFORD, LYNN ELLEN, state official; b. Peoria, Ill., June 17, 1953; d. Raymond Scott Jr. and Georgiana (Woodhall) M. BA, Millikin U., 1975; MA, U. Ill. was Sangamon State U., Springfield, Ill., 1984. News reporter Stas. WJBC-WBNQ, Bloomington, Ill., 1975-76, Sta. WSOY-AM-FM, Decatur, 1976-78, Stas. WXCL-WZRO-FM, Peoria, 1978, Sta. KACY-AM-FM, Ventura, Calif., 1978, Sta. WKAN, Kankakee, Ill., 1979-82; freelance news reporter Sta. WMAQ, Chgo., 1982; news dir. Stas. WXCL-WKQA-FM, Peoria, 1983; press sec. Ill. Ho. of Reps. Rep. Press Office, Springfield, 1984-85; chief Press Office, Ill. Dept. Commerce and Community Affairs, 1986-95, comms. coord., 1995—. Mem. adv. bd. Ill. AP, 1983; radio news contest judge Okla. AP, 1983; bd. dirs. Ill. News Broadcasters Assn., 1980-84; mem. Gov.'s Conf. on Mgmt. of Illinois River, 1997—. Mem. adv. bd. Leadership Ill., 1992—, spring conf. chair, 1994; Springfield St. Patrick's Day Parade Com., 1991-99; chmn. pub. rels. film fund raiser Vachel Linds ay Assn., Springfield, 1989; mem. Springfield Jr. League, 1990-91; mem. Samaritans St. John's Hosp., Springfield, 1995—, Ill. River Econ. Devel. Action Team, 1996-97, Orlene Moore Scholarship Com., 1996—, Student of Yr. Selection Com., 1996; pres., bd. trustees Sherman Pub. Libr. Dist., 1995—; elder Buffalo Hart Presbyn. ch., 1998—; pres. Buffalo Hart Women's Assn., 1997—; mem. Town and Country Women's Assn., 1998—. Recipient Best Contbr. award Ill. AP, 1983; Robert Howard scholar Sangamon State U., 1983; named to Hon. Order of Ky. Cols., 1992. Mem. Order of Ea. Star. Presbyterian. Avocations: golf, competitive sewing and baking (state fair champion), vocal music, gardening, decorating. Home: 2 Willow Hill Dr Sherman IL 62684-9769 Office: Ill Dept Commerce and Community Affairs 620 E Adams St Springfield IL 62701-1615 E-mail: lmorford@commerce.state.il.us.

MORFORD, MARIE ARLENE, insurance company executive; b. Wichita, Oct. 21, 1929; d. George and Bertha (Wear) Bachman; divorced; children: Stephen, Cheryl, Phillip. Clk. McKesson Robbin Drug, Wichita, 1948-49, Safeway Offices, Wichita, 1952-55; ins. sec. Benfer Ins., Newton, Kans., 1955-70, Ctrl. Agy., Newton, 1970-87; patient admitting operator Halstead (Kans.) Hosp., 1988-90; ins. rep., office mgr., lic. rep. State Farm, Newton, Kans., 1990—. Dir. religious edn. St. Mary's Ch., Newton, 1988, advisor adult religious edn., 1996, eucharistic minister, 1982; rep. Mother to Mother Ministry, Newton, 1988, Harvey County Citizens for Life, Newton, 1989; regent Daughters of Isabella St. Joseph's Cir., Kans., 1993-97, treas., 1995—, state vice regent, 1999—; pres. Wichita Diocesan Coun. of Cath. Women, 1993-95; adv. bd. Wichita Diocesan Religious Edn. Mem. Daus. of Isabella (state vice regent 1999-2001, state auditor 2001, regent 2001—, state trustee, 2000—). Home: 1206 Harrison PO Box 135 Newton KS 67114-0135

MORGALI, DIANE, retired non-profit corporation administrator; b. Chgo., Aug. 30, 1937; d. Ellsworth Frederick and Hazel Marie Flesch; m. James Rollin Morgali, Sept. 22, 1957; children: Catherine, David, Daniel. BA with distinction, Stanford U., 1957, MA, 1959. Adminstrv. dir. Women's Ctr. of San Joaquin County, Stockton, Calif., 1976-84; exec. dir. Sunflower Presents..., 1990-97, ret., 1997. Chair tng. adv. com. CETA, Stockton, 1979-80; chair inmate svcs. com., mem. San Joaquin County Jail Adv. Task Force, Stockton, 1984-86. Commr. San Joaquin County Housing Authority, Stockton, 1988—, chair commn., 1990-92, 98-99; pres. non-profit housing devel. agy. Villa Real, Stockton, 1999&; bd. dirs. Hmong Artisans, Stockton, 1994-97. Named Woman of Achievement, San Joaquin Commn. on Status of Women, 1981. Methodist. Avocations: travel, hiking, reading.

MORGAN, ALAN VIVIAN, geologist, educator; b. Barry, Glamorgan, Wales, Jan. 29, 1943; emigrated to Can., 1964, naturalized, 1977; s. George Vivian Williams and Sylvia Nesta (Atkinson) M.; m. Marion Anne Medhurst, June 14, 1966; children: Siân Kristina, Alexis John. B.Sc. with honors in Geology and Geography, U. Leicester, Eng., 1964; M.Sc. in Geography, U. Alta., Calgary, Can., 1966; PhD in Geology, U. Birmingham, Eng., 1970. Postdoctoral fellow U. Western Ont. and U. Waterloo, Ont., Can., 1970-71; asst. prof. earth scis. and man-environ. studies U. Waterloo, 1971-78, assoc. prof. earth scis., 1978-85, prof., 1985—, assoc. dir. Quaternary Scis. Inst. Ont., Can., 1992-97, dir. Quaternary Scis. Inst. Canada, 1997—2002. Mem. Brit. Schs. Exploring Soc. Ctrl. Iceland Expdn., 1960; rep. Can. Geosci. Coun., 1977-83, exec. dir., 1988-94, adminstrv. dir., 1996-2001; mem. com. on global change Royal Soc. Can., 1988-91, mem. com. on pub. awareness of sci., 1989-94; coord. global change Geol. Survey Can., 1990-92; sr. officer Internat. Geosci. Edn. Orgn., 2000—, nat.; dir. Can. Prize Awards Found., 2000—. Author 6 field guides; editor newsletter OYEZ, 1990-94; contbr. articles to numerous profl. publs.; dir., prodr. documentary film The Heimaey Eruption, 1974. Recipient award for MS thesis Can. Assn. Petroleum Geologists, 1967, Bancroft award Royal Soc. Can., 1994, John H. Moss award Nat. Assn. Geology Tchrs., 1995, J. Willis Ambrose medal Geol. Assn. Can., 1997. E.R.W. Neale medal Geol. Assn. Canada, 1998; Charles Lapworth scholar, 1970; Nat. Scis. and Engring. Rsch. Coun. Can. grantee, 1971— Fellow Geol. Assn. Can. (hon. life, sec.-treas. 1975-83, disting. fellow), Geol. Soc. Am.; mem. Am. Quaternary Assn. (pres. 1990-92), Can. Quaternary Assn. (pres. 1987-89), Brit. Quaternary Research Assn., Internat. Union Quaternary Research (sec. gen. XII congress 1983-87). Office: U Waterloo Dept Earth Scis Waterloo ON Canada N2L 3G1

MORGAN, ALBERT GEORGE LEONARD, retired airline pilot, writer; b. West Terre Haute, Ind., Mar. 23, 1922; s. Kingsley John and Juliet Freda (Gardner) M.; m. Margaret Clark May, Nov. 27, 1943; children: Terry Len, Juliet Kathryn. Student, U. Louisville, 1948. Lic. airline transport pilot FAA. Photogrammetrist Park Aerial Surveys, Inc., Louisville, 1945-46; capt. Braniff Internat., Dallas, 1949-82; owner Morgan Aviation Books, 1955-75; writer, pub., 1955-99. Investor, Palm Harbor, Fla., 1993-99; cons. U.S. Dept. Justice, Washington, 1988. Author: Crackup!, 1968, Aviation Hall of Fame, 1970, View From the Cockpit, 1985, Vectors, 1992, others; prodr.: Fasten Seat Belts, 1969, Aircraft of the Vietnam War, 1971, The Lady Be Good, 1982, others; co-author: (with G. Bradford) 50 Famous Tanks, 1967, (with T.L. Morgan) The Boeing Scrapbook, 1978; contbr. articles on aviation to profl. jours. With Royal Can. Air Force, 1941-42, U.S. Army Air Forces, 1942-45, Ky. Air N.G., 1946-49. Recipient writing awards Aviation and Space Writers Assn., 1977, 78. Mem. Am. Aviation Hist. Soc., Air Line Pilots Assn., Braniff Internat. Silver Eagles. Presbyterian. Avocations: aviation history research, accident research, collecting rare books. Office: PO Box 6190 Palm Harbor FL 34684-0790 E-mail: bnf747@aol.com.

MORGAN, ANDREW LANE, urologist, educator; b. May 13, 1920; s. James Albert and Elsie Edna (Johnson) M.; m. Miriam Cleary, June 9, 1951; children: Andrew Lane, Christine, Martha, James. Exch. fellowship, St. John's U., Shanghai, China, 1939—40; BA, Dartmouth Coll., 1942; MD, Cornell U., 1945. Diplomate Am. Bd. Urology. Intern Lenox Hill Hosp., N.Y.C., 1945-46; resident Queen's Med. Ctr., Honolulu, 1948-50, Yale U., 1950-52; practice medicine, specializing in urology Honolulu, 1952-87; ret., 1987. Chmn. dept. surgery Queen's Med. Ctr., 1979; clin. prof. urology John Burns Sch. Medicine, U. Hawaii; mem. renal transplant team St. Francis Med. Ctr. Past pres. Hawaii Med. Libr., 1957-58. Served to capt., AUS, 1946-48. Fellow ACS; mem. AMA, AM. Urol. Assn. (past pres. Western sect.), Hawaii Med. Assn., Societe Internationale d'Urologie, Honolulu County Med. Soc. (bd. govs. 1970-76, treas. 1978-79), Pacific Club (Honolulu). Episcopalian. Home: 44 Puako Beach Dr Kamuela HI 96743-9707

MORGAN, ANN LEE, art historian, writer; b. Mpls., Jan. 12, 1941; d. Joe Warner and Jeanne (Murray) M.; m. Charles William Gear, Nov. 19, 1976; stepchildren: Kathlyn Jo Gear, Christopher Gear. BA, Knox Coll., 1962; MA, Fla. State U., 1963; PhD, U. Iowa, 1973. Instr., asst. prof. U. Ill., Urbana-Champaign, 1968-73, 73-78; asst. editor, Chgo. and Midwest editor New Art Examiner, Chgo., 1979-81, 81-82; art ref. books editor St. James Press, 1982-85; vis. asst. prof. U. Ill., 1985-86; vis. lectr. Sch. of Art Inst. Chgo., 1985-86; editor Twenty One/Art and Culture, Chgo., 1987-90; ind. scholar Princeton, N.J., 1990—. Lectr. Columbia Coll., Chgo., 1981-82; revs. editor Art Jour., N.Y.C., 1992-93; mem. planning and program coms. Nat. Coalition Ind. Scholars Convention, 1996. Author: Arthur Dove: Life and Work, 1984; editor: Contemporary Designers, 1984, International Contemporary Arts Directory, 1985, Dear Stieglitz, Dear Dove, 1988; co-editor: Contemporary Architects, 1987. Rev. panelist NEH, Washington, 1979-80, 2000, 01. Rsch. grantee Kress Found., 1972, U. Ill. Rsch. Bd., 1976; Fla. State U. grad. fellow, 1962. Mem. Princeton Rsch. Forum (v.p. 1993-95, pres. 1995-99), Coll. Art Assn., Am. Studies Assn., Soc. Archtl. Historians. Avocations: travel, reading. Fax: (609)737-7023. E-mail: ALM@research.nj.nec.com.

MORGAN, ANNE MARGARET BARCLAY, artist, author, psychologist; b. Washington, June 20, 1952; d. George A. and Margaret R. (Taylor) Morgan; m. Harper Brent Mashburn, Aug. 3, 2001. PhD in Psychology, U. Vienna, Austria, 1977; MA in Art History, U. Fla., 1990. Lectr. on contemporary art; design cons. for serene environments, spiritual healing. Prodr.(dir., writer): (art documentaries including) Video Art to Virtual Reality, 1992; exhibitions include , U.S. and Eruope; contbr. articles and revs. to profl. jours. and books; contbg. editor: Sculpture Mag. Mem. APA, Coll. Art Assn., Internat. Assn. Art Critics (southeastern rep.). Office: 1119 NW 36th Dr Gainesville FL 32605-4944

MORGAN, ANNE MARIE G. broadcast journalist, educator; b. Paducah, Ky., Apr. 23, 1955; d. Ralph Edward and Vera Christine Gill; m. Michael William Morgan, Nov. 19, 1977; children: Deborah, Jon, James. BA in Govt. and Psychology, Coll. William and Mary, 1976; MA in Polit. Sci., U. Richmond, 1997; postgrad. in Pub. Policy, Va. Commonwealth U., 1998. H.S. tchr. Williamsburg (Va.)/James-City County Schs., 1977, Colonial Hgts. (Va.) Schs., 1977-79; TV and radio journalist Va. Pub. Broadcasting/Capital News Va. News Network, Sta. WRIC-TV, WTVR-TV, Richmond, Va., 1984—; asst. prof. polit. sci. U. Richmond, 1998—; broadcast news anchor Va. News Network, Richmond, 2000—02; broadcast journalist WVTF Va. Pub. Radio, Roanoke, 2002—. Author: (with others) Controversies in American Public Polity, 1999, Opposing Viewpoints Series, 1991. Sec. Parents' Guidance/Pupil Pers. Guidance Com., Powhatan, Va., 1996—98; bd. dirs. Va. Pub. Broadcasting, Richmond, 2000—02, Va. Adv. Coun. Adult Edn. and Literacy, Richmond, 1999—2002, Coun. Child Care and Early Childhood Devel., Richmond, 1995—96; chair bd. dirs. State Bd. for Cmty. Colls., 1997—2002, Va. Coun. Status of Women, Richmond, 1994—2002. Recipient Gov.'s proclamation Anne Marie Morgan Day in Commonwealth Va., Gov. Va., 1997; Meritorious award Va. Associated Press Broadcasters, 2002. Mem. Am. Polit. Sci. Assn., Capitol Corrs. Assn., Va. Press Women, Nat. Fedn. Press Women, Soc. Profl. Journalists, Va. Press Women, Soc. Profl. Journalists (Va. Profl. chpt.), Pi Sigma Alpha. Avocations: music, singing, mentoring.

MORGAN, ANNIE HUTCHINSON, medical association administrator, consultant; b. New York, Ny, May 6, 1950; d. Mac Rogers and Helen Neilly Morgan; m. James Francis Kelley, Sept. 8, 2002; children: Andrew Morgan Baker, Curtis Bonds Baker. Attended, Simon's Rock Coll., Massachusetts, 1970—70, Boston U., 1970—71. Exec. dir. Ovarian Cancer Inst., Atlanta, 2001—, consulting, 1999—2000; dir. External Affairs High Mus. of Art, 1993—99; dir. od devel. Goizueta Bus. Sch. Emory U., 1990—93; pres. St. Joseph's Hosp. Found., 1982—90; dir. of devel. The Atlanta Opera, 1980—82. Cons. Simon's Rock Coll. of Bard, Barrington, Mass., 2000—00, Intelitix, Atlanta, 2001—01. Trustee/dir. Brandon Hall Sch., Atlanta, 1997—2002, Tech Corps, Atlanta, 1995—2002, Ovarian Cancer Inst., Atlanta, 2000—01. Mem.: Angler's Club NYC, Piedmont Driving Club Atlanta. Avocations: tennis, skiing, reading, cooking, piano. Office: Ovarian Cancer Institute 1100 Johnson Ferry Road # 510 Atlanta GA 30342

MORGAN, ARDYS NORD, school improvement consultant; b. South Bend, Ind., Nov. 1, 1946; d. Arthur August and Janet Ardis (Eide) Nord; children: Elizabeth Elayne, Matthew Richard. BS in Elem. Edn., Ind. U., Bloomington, 1968; MS in Elem. Edn., Ind. U., Indpls., 1972; reading cert., Ind. U., South Bend, 1982; EDS, Ind. U., Bloomington, 1992; adminstr. lic., Ind. U.-Purdue U., Indpls., 1989; EdD in Curriculum and Sch. Adminstrn., Ind. U., 1994. Tchr., South Bend, 1968-69, 73-87; adminstr. dept. instrn. and curriculum, 1987-90; tchr. Indpls., 1969-70; resident lectr. Ind. U./Purdue U., 1970-73, adminstr., 1989; mem. adj. faculty Ind. U., South Bend, 1985-90, acting program dir. elem. and secondary edn., 1990-92; asst. supt. schs. Michigan City (Ind.) Area Schs., 1992-94; supt. Union North United Schs. Corp., 1994-96; ednl. cons., tech. and staff devel. in curriculum Lightspan Partnership, San Diego, 1997-99; pres. Sch. Improvement Partnership, Inc., Granger, Ind., 1999—. Cons. on implementation of tech., mid. grades and effective teaching strategies, elem. curriculum, reading and lang. arts, fed. and state projects, staff devel. Recipient Disting. Alumni award div. edn. Ind. U., South Bend, 1990. Lilly Endowment fellow, 1987. Home: 51550 Stratton Ct Granger IN 46530-8342 Office: Sch Improvement Partnership 51550 Stratton Ct Ste 300 Granger IN 46530-8342

MORGAN, ARLENE NOTORO, university administrator; b. Phila., July 27, 1945; d. James Vincent and Mary Rose (Actis-Grande) Notoro; m. David J. Morgan, Mar. 3, 1948; children: Elizabeth, Lauren. BS in Journalism, Temple U., 1967. Reporter Delaware County Daily Times, Chester, Pa., 1967-69, Phila. Inquirer, 1969—, dep. metro editor, 1990-91, sr. editor, asst. mng. editor, 1991-2000, reader advocate columnist, 1998-2000; asst. dean Columbia U. Grad. Sch. Journalism, N.Y.C., 2000—. Bd. dirs. Friends Hosp., Phila., 1978—; mem. adv. bd. Temple U., La. State U.; mem. Am. Soc. Newspaper Editors Journalism Credibility Project; dir. Columbia Race Project. Recipient Phila. Newspapers Inc. Employee Recognition award, 1987, Excellence in Diversity award Knight Ridder, 1995; Media Studies Ctr. fellow Freedom Forum, 1996-97. Mem. Soc. Profl. Journalists., Newspaper Assn. Am. (diversity com.). Roman Catholic. Avocations: ballet, travel, opera and art appreciation, advocate to the mentally ill. Office: Columbia Univ 2960 Broadway New York NY 10027-6900 E-mail: amorg@aol.com.

MORGAN, BARBARA JOAN, real estate broker; b. Mattoon, Ill., July 5, 1940; d. Wendel Lewis and Helen Irene (Adkins) Huddleston; m. David A. Morgan, Aug. 22, 1958; children— Wendy A., Eric W., D. Gregory. B.S. in Ed., Ea. Ill. U., 1962. Tchr. Lincoln Sch., Mattoon, Ill., 1962-66; real estate broker, Paris, Ill. 1974— ; real estate broker, owner Paris Realty, 1978— ; real estate tchr. Lakeland Jr. Coll., Mattoon, 1980—. Served on Region 23 Pvt. Industry Council, 1987-90. Pres. Paris Newcomers club, 1974-75; chair United Way of Edgar County, 1988; bd. dirs. YMCA. Named Paris BPW Woman of Yr., 1985. Mem. Ill. Assn. Realtors (inst. grad. 1977, cert. residential specialist 1979), East Central Ill. Bd. Realtors (pres. 1978-79, 88-89), Bus. and Profl. Women Paris (pres. 1983-84), Paris C. of C. (v.p. 1984-86). Republican. Clubs: Altrusa (pres. 1990-92), Prairies Edge Toastmaster's (charter, pres. 1989). Lodge: Order Eastern Star. Office: Paris Realty 207 N Central Ave Paris IL 61944-1701

MORGAN, BARBARA R. astronaut; b. Fresno, Calif., Nov. 28, 1951; m. Clay Morgan; 2 children. BA in Human Biology with distinction, Stanford U., 1973; tchg. credential, Coll. Notre Dame, 1974. Tchr. remedial reading and math Flathead Indian Reservation Arlee (Mont.) Elem. Sch., 1974; tchr. reading, math McCall-Donnelly Elem. Sch., Idaho, 1975—78, tchr., 1979—98; tchr. elem. English and sci. Colegio Americano de Quito, Ecuador, 1978—79; astronaut, educator mission specialist candidate NASA, Johnson Space Ctr., Houston, 1998—. Backup candidate for Tchr. in Space Program NASA, 1985; mem. fed. task force for women and minorities in sci. and engring. NSF. Recipient Citizen of Yr. award, USA Today, 1986, Edn. award, Women in Aerospace, 1991, Wright Bros. "Kitty Hawk" Sands of Time Edn. award, L.A. C. of C., 1991, Space Pioneer award for edn., Nat. Space Soc., 1992, Pres.'s Medallion award, U. Idaho, 1998, Idaho Fellowship award, 1998. Mem.: Challenger Ctr. for Space Sci. Edn. (Challenger 7 award 1995), Internat. Tech. Edn. Assn. (Lawrence Prakken Profl. Cooperation award 1996), Internat. Reading Assn., Nat. Sci. Tchrs. Assn., Nat. Coun. Tchrs. Math., Idaho Edn. Assn., Nat. PTA (hon.; life), Phi Beta Kappa. Office: Astronaut Office/CB NASA Johnson Space Ctr Houston TX 77058*

MORGAN, BEVERLY CARVER, pediatrician, educator; b. N.Y.C., May 29, 1927; d. Jay and Florence (Newkamp) Carver; children— Nancy, Thomas E. III, John E. MD cum laude (Mosby Scholar), Duke U., 1955. Diplomate Am. Bd. Pediatrics (oral examiner 1984-90, mem. written examination com. 1990—), Nat. Bd. Med. Examiners. Intern, asst. resident Stanford U. Hosp., San Francisco, 1955-56; clin. fellow pediatrics, trainee pediatric cardiology Babies Hosp.-Columbia Presbyn. Med. Center, N.Y.C., 1956-59; research fellow cardiovascular diagnostic lab. Columbia-Presbyn. Med. Center, 1959-60; instr. pediatrics Coll. Physicians and Surgeons, Columbia U., 1960; dir. heart sta. Robert B. Green Meml. Hosp., San Antonio, 1960-62; lectr. pediatrics U. Tex., 1960-62; spl. research fellow in pediatric cardiology Sch. Medicine, U. Wash., Seattle, 1962-64, from instr. to prof. pediatrics, 1962-73, chmn. dept. pediatrics, 1973-80; mem. staff U. Wash. Hosp., chief of staff, 1975-77; mem. staff Harborview Med. Ctr., Children's Orthopedic Hosp. and Med. Ctr., dir. dept. medicine, 1974-80; prof., chmn. dept. pediatrics U. Calif., Irvine, 1980-88, prof. pediat. and pediat. cardiology, 1980—; pediatrician in chief Children's Hosp. Orange County, 1988. Mem. pulmonary acad. awards panel Nat. Heart and Lung Inst., 1972-75; mem. grad. med. edn. nat. advisory com. to sec. HEW, 1977-80; mem. Coun. on Pediatric Practice; chmn. Task Force on Opportunities for Women in Pediatrics, 1982; mem. nursing rev. com. NIH, 1987-88. Contbr. articles to profl. jours.; mem. editorial bd. Clin. Pediatrics, Am. Jour. Diseases of Children, Jour. of Orange County Pediatric Soc., Jour. Am. Acad. Pediatrics, Los Angeles Pediatric Soc. Recipient Women of Achievement award Matrix Table, Seattle, 1974; Distinguished Alumnus award Duke U. Med. Sch., 1974; Ann. award Nat. Bd. Med. Coll. Pa., 1977; USPHS career devel. awardee, 1966-71 Mem. Am. Acad. Pediat. (chmn. com. on pediat. manpower 1984-86), Am. Coll. Cardiology, Soc. for Pediat. Rsch., Am. Fedn. Clin. Rsch., Am. Pediat. Soc., Assn. Med. Sch. Pediat. Dept. Chmn. (sec.-treas. 1981-87), Western Soc. for Pediat. Rsch., Alpha Omega Alpha. Office: U Calif Irvine Med Ctr Dept Pediatrics 101 The City Dr S Orange CA 92868-3201 E-mail: bcmorgan@vci.edu.

MORGAN, BEVERLY HAMMERSLEY, middle school educator, artist; b. Wichita Falls, Tex. d. Vernon C. and Melba Marie (Whited) Hammersley; m. Robert Lewis Morgan, Sept. 21, 1957 (div. 1972); children: Janet Claire, Robert David. BA, So. Meth. U.; MA, U. Ala., 1980, AA certification, 1982; postgrad., U. Tex., 1991—. Cert. art tchr., Tex., Ala.; cert. elem. tchr., Ala. Tchr. art Ft. Worth Pub. Schs., 1955-60; tchr. English, Lincoln County Schs., Fayetteville, Tenn., 1961-62; elem. tchr. Huntsville (Ala.) Pub. Schs., 1960-61, 62-68, tchr. art, 1972-92, 93-94. One-woman shows include U. Ala., 1980, Huntsville Art League, 1981, and various other art gallerys, art shows and exhbns. Mem. HAL Gallery, Huntsville, Madison County Sr. Art Gallery. Mem. Huntsville Mus. Art, Am. Contract Bridge League. Republican. Avocations: bridge, travel, collector of Hammersley English bone china. Home: 12027 Chicamauga Trl SE Huntsville AL 35803-1544

MORGAN, BRONWYN JORDAN, human resources specialist, consultant; b. Easton, Md., Mar. 12, 1949; d. Joseph Stevens and Ethel (Brown) Jordan; m. John Fox Morgan, July 25, 1968; children: Matthew Stevens, Jonathan Brett, Jason Travis. BA in English and History with honors, U. N.C., Wilmington, 1980; postgrad., LSIS. Program dir. secondary edn. and adult studies Learning Founds. Inc., Wilmington, 1970-78; libr. Area Health Edn. Ctr., 1981; trade broker Nat. Commerce Exch., 1982-84; instrnl. developer Tng. Systems Inc., 1984-86, project mgr., 1987-91; v.p. organizational devel., 1991—. Com. mem. Parent, Student, Tchr. Assns., New Hanover County, N.C., 1976-89; bd. dirs. Lower Cape Fear Hist. Soc., Wilmington, 1987-90, newsletter editor, 1987-91. Recipient Most Valuable Staffer award Raleigh News and Observer, 1967, Outstanding Achievement award N.C. Hist. Soc., 1989. Mem. ASTD (v.p. communications 1988-89, pres.-elect 1990, pres. 1991, forest products steering com. 1988-89, sec. industry group 1990, Nat. Chpt. award for communications 1988, 89), Paper Industry Mgmt. Assn. (affiliate, nat. conf. com. 1991). Avocations: travel, photography, needlework. Home: 5032 Clear Run Dr Wilmington NC 28403-1932 Office: Tng Systems Inc PO Box 2131 404 N 3rd St Wilmington NC 28401-4006

MORGAN, BRUCE RAY, international consultant; b. Los Angeles, Oct. 28, 1932; s. Francis Raymond and Rose Hall (Black) M.; m. Bette Jeanne Moore, Oct. 7, 1957; children: Michael John, Brian Leo, Jeanne Anne. AA, Sacramento Jr. Coll., 1952; BS, U. Calif.-Berkeley, 1954, LL.B., 1957. Bar: Calif. 1957. Judge adv. USAF, Saudi Arabia and Morocco, 1958-61; atty. firm Thelen, Marrin, Johnson & Bridges, San Francisco, 1961-67; dep. dir. Peace Corps, Nepal, 1967-68, dir Nepal, 1968-70; exec. dir. Center Research and Edn., Denver, 1971-75; dir. U.S. representation to Saudi Arabia-U.S. Joint Commn. on Econ. Coop., Riyadh, 1975-76; pres. Bruce Morgan Assocs., Inc., Washington, 1976—. Editor: Calif. State Bar Jour. Legis. Rev, 1957. Served with USAF, 1958-61. Mem. U.S., Calif. bars. Office: Bruce Morgan Assocs 3014 New Mexico Ave NW Washington DC 20016-3519 E-mail: bmorgan@bmainc.com.

MORGAN, CATHERINE MARIE, psychologist, writer; b. Duluth, Minn., Mar. 27, 1947; m. Ralph Morgan, 1967; 1 child, Andrew. BS, U. Nebr., 1968; MEd, U. Okla., 1973; PhD, Okla. State U., 1987; postgrad. Menninger Found., Psychotherapy Tng. Program, 1987-89. Child devel. specialist Southwest Guidance Ctr., Wheatland, Okla., 1973-74; pvt. practice Family Counseling Assocs., San Antonio, 1974-75; psychol. asst. Edmond Guidance Ctr., Okla., 1975-82; psychol. asst. supr. Southeast Guidance Ctr., Del City, 1982-86; psychol. intern Cleve. County Health Dept., Moore, 1986-87; psychologist Cen. State Hosp., Norman, 1987-89; pvt. practice assocs. in psychology Edmond; vice chair bd. mgrs. Integris Mental Health; pres. Assocs. in Psychology, 1988—. Mem. AAUW, APA, Okla. Psychol. Assn., Am. Bus. Women's Assn., P.E.O., Kappa Delta Pi. Avocations: writing, reading, knitting, racquetball. Office: 3545 NW 58th St Ste 220 Oklahoma City OK 73112-4725

MORGAN, CHRISTOPHER DONALD, engineer, consultant; b. South Bend, Ind., June 4, 1965; s. George Henry and Janis Sue M.; m. Catherine Elizabeth Diane Foley-Morgan, Nov. 21, 1991; 1 child, Caitlin Elizabeth Barbra Morgan. BS in Mech. Engring., Purdue U., West Lafayette, Ind., 1988, MS in Mech. Engring., 1991; PhD, U. Akron, Ohio, 1996. Registered profl. engr., Ohio, Mich. Engring. intern AC Rochester, Flint, Mich., 1985-91; advanced tire engr. Bridgestone/Firestone, Inc., Akron, Ohio, 1992-96; rsch. engr. Kumho Tires, 1996-2000, SuperTrapp Industries, Inc., Cleve., 2000-01; noise/vibration/harshness specialist Breed Techs., Inc., Sterling Heights, Mich., 2001—. Proprietor, cons. H&P Engring., Akron, Ohio, 1996—. Mem.: IEEE, ASME, Assn. Computing Machinery, Acoustical Soc. Am., Soc. Indsl. Applied Math., Soc. Exptl. Mechanics, Soc. Auto. Engrs. Avocations: software development, playing soccer. E-mail: nvh_engr@ieee.org.

MORGAN, CLARA MCMAHON, publishing consultant; b. Ironton, Ohio, Nov. 10, 1955; d. Nicholas G. McMahon and Barbara Ann Jarrett; m. Richard D. Brown, June 18, 1977 (div.); m. George Pidcock Morgan, Oct. 8, 1983; children: David Christopher, Sean Jarrett. BS, Miami U., Oxford, Ohio, 1977. Health ministries coord. Synod the Covenant Presbyn. Ch., Columbus, Ohio, 1977-82; dir. Nat. Abortion Rights Action League of Ohio, 1982-84; orgnl. devel. cons. PC (USA), 1988—92, Cmty. Involvement Coun., Tarpon Springs, Fla., 1992—95; substitute tchr. Tarpon Springs Elem. Sch., 1992—95; ednl. cons. Houghton Mifflin Co., Boston, 1995—. Co-author: Responsibility and Respect, 1992. Sec., treas. Harbor Woods Homeowners Assn., Palm Harbor, Fla., 1992—94; cmty. involvement coord. Tarpon Springs Elem. Sch., 1993—95, chair sch. adv. coun., 1992—95; founder, bd. dirs. Presbyn. Affirming Reproductive Options, Louisville, 1991—; bd. dirs. Presbyn. Health, Edn. and Welfare Assn., 1978—86, 1997—2000; elder Presbyn. Ch. USA, 1993—. Mem.: ASCD, AAUW, Nat. Sci. Tchrs. Assn., Nat. Coun. Tchrs. Math., Fla. Reading Assn., Internat. Reading Assn. Democrat. Avocations: photography, travel, gourmet cooking, piano.

MORGAN, CLYDE NATHANIEL, dermatologist; b. Bell County, Tex., Nov. 2, 1923; s. Xenophen William and Rhoda Ella (Deck) M.; m. Birdie Joyce Rich, Mar. 3, 1951; children: Clyde Nathaniel Jr., Reinette Jean, Nancy Elaine. BS, Abilene Christian Coll., 1948; MD, U. Tex. Galveston, 1953. Assoc. prof. biology Abilene (Tex.) Christian Coll., 1954-56; pvt. practice Abilene, 1954-67; dermatologist, 1969—. Contbr. articles to profl. jours. Mem. AMA, SAR (chpt. pres. 1997-99, award 1995), Am. Coll. Cryosurgery, Internat. Soc. Cryosurgery, Tex. Med. Assn., Tex. Dermatologic Soc., Taylor-

Jones-Haskell County Med. Soc. Republican. Mem. Ch. of Christ. Avocations: golf, fishing, hunting, cryogenics research. Home: 1718 Cedar Crest Dr Abilene TX 79601-3228 Office: 1166 Merchant St Abilene TX 79603-5014 E-mail: clybird@juno.com.

MORGAN, CONSTANCE LOUISE, real estate executive; b. Denver, July 24, 1941; d. Willis Stephen and Evelyn (Rutar) Claus; m. Robert M. Morgan, Jan. 3, 1963; children: Stephen, Melayne. BS, U. N. Mex., 1963. Lic. real estate broker; Fla. master gardener, 1996. Realtor, assoc. Investors Realty, Tallahassee, 1980-82, br. mgr., 1982-83; pres., broker Connie Morgan Realty, Inc., 1983-96, Constance L. Morgan, Broker, Tallahassee, 1996—; founder Network for Ind. Brokers, 1989-93. Chmn. docents Fla. Gov.'s Mansion, Tallahassee, 1979-80; pres. Newcomers-Univ. Women, Tallahassee, 1968, Hunters Crossing Homeowners Assn., 1998-99; bd. dirs. Tallahassee Symphony Orch., 1990-96; bd. dirs. Rotary Youth Camp, Inc., 1995—, Tallahassee United Way. Mem. Nat. Assn. Realtors, Fla. Assn. Realtors, Tallahassee Bd. Realtors (chmn. Multiple Listing Svc. 1984, 94), Tallahassee Cmty. Realty Group, Tallahassee C. of C. (bd. dirs. 1984-86, 89-92), Rotary, Chi Omega (treas. 1962), Phi Gamma Nu (pres. 1962). Home and Office: 3322 Remington Run Tallahassee FL 32312-1462

MORGAN, CRAIG DOUGLAS, orthopaedic surgeon; b. Olean, N.Y., Oct. 2, 1950; s. James Franklin Jr. and Helen Aileen (Dawson) M.; m. Natalie Jean Holt, July 9, 1975; children: Craig Drewry, Holt Franklin. BA in Chemistry and Biology cum laude, Hope Coll., Holland, Mich., 1972; MD cum laude, Emory U., 1977. Diplomate Am. Bd. Orthopaedic Surgery. Intern U. Hosp. Mich. Affiliated Hosps., Ann Arbor, 1977-78; resident U. Mich., 1982; pres., founding mem. Del. Orthopaedic Ctr., Wilmington, 1986-97; pres. Morgan Kalman Clinic, 1997—. Dir. sports medicine Alfred I. duPont Inst., Wilmington, 1988—; clin. instr. orthopaedic surgery Thomas Jefferson U., Phila., 1989—94, assoc. prof., 1994—97; bd. dirs., cons. Arthrex, Inc., Naples, Fla.; clin. prof. dept. orthop. surgery Allegheny U., Phila., 1997—98, U. Pa., Phila., 1999—; cons. Bowen, Inc., Rockville, Md., 1982—; cons. Oratec, Inc., Palo Alto, Calif., Arthrex, Inc., Naples, Fla., Bowen & Co., Rockville, Md., Stryker Endoscopy, Palo Alto, Calif. Assoc. editor Jour. Arthroscopy, 1990-97; contbr. chpts. to books and articles to profl. jours.; patentee in field. Mem. Am. Orthopaedic Soc. Sports Medicine, Am. Acad. Orthopaedic Surgeons, Internat. Arthroscopy Assn. (bd. dirs. 1990-95, sec.), Internant. Knee Soc. (bd. dirs. 1993-95, sec.), Internat. Arthroscopy, Knee and Sport Medicine Soc. (bd. dirs. 1995-97, sec.), Alpha Omega Alpha. Avocation: fly fishing. Office: Morgan Kalman Clinic 2501 Silverside Rd Wilmington DE 19810-3726 E-mail: scopeshop@aol.com.

MORGAN, CRYSTAL FAYE, health services administrator; b. Amarillo, Tex., Jan. 31, 1967; d. Larry Cleveland Bowerman and Loretta Faye (Blackburn) Jordan; m. David James Morgan, Sept. 1, 1986; children: David James Jr., Andrea Faye. AS in Aerospace Group Equipment Tech., C.C. of Air Force, Ft. Lauderdale, Fla., 1989, AS in Health Svcs. Adminstrn., 1995; BS in Bus. Mgmt., Nova U., 1992; MS in Human Resources Mgmt., Wilmington Coll., 1995. Receptionist, ins. clk. Atoka (Okla.) Chiropractic, 1984-85; enlisted woman USAF, 1985, advanced through grades to staff sgt., 1993, aerospace ground equipment mechanic Panama, from 1985, Cannon AFB, N.Mex., until 1991, supr. med. records 27th med. group, 1991-92, asst. supr. managed care, 1992-93, supr. med. records 436th med. group Dover AB, Del., 1993, supr. quality improvement, quality cons., 1994-95, supr. managed care, 1995—. Examiner Del. Quality Award, Dover, 1994-95. Mem. Am. Soc. Quality Control, Nat. Assn. for Healthcare Quality. Republican. Baptist. Avocations: reading, exercise. Office: 436th Med Group/SGST 307 Tuskegee Blvd Dover Air Force Base DE 19902

MORGAN, DAHLIA, museum director; BA, McGill U., Montreal, 1958; postgrad., Sir George Williams U., Montreal, 1968-69, U. Miami, Fla., 1974. Lectr. Mus. of Fine Arts, Montreal, 1965-70; lectr./rschr. Sir George Williams U., 1968-70; grad. asst. dept. art and art history U. Miami, Fla., 1971-74; adj. prof. visual arts dept. Fla. Internat. U., Miami, 1975-77, vis. rof. visual arts dept., 1978-79, faculty visual arts dept., 1979—, dir. Art in State Bldgs. Program, 1984—, dir. Art Mus., 1980—. Lectr. in field; curator numerous exhbns.; panelist NEA Mus. Grants, 1993, Cultural Advancement Grants, 1992, 90; cons. Fed. Gen. Svcs. Adminstrn., 1992, Metro-Dade Art in Pub. Places Program, 1992. Prodr. numerous catalogues to exhbns. Juror South Miami Art Fair Photo Group; bd. dirs. Nat. Found. for Advancement in the Arts, 1984—; founder Friends of the Art Mus. Support Group at Fla. Internat. U., 1984—; chmn. State of Fla. Art in Bldgs., 1984—; chmn. Art in Pub. Places, Dade County, Fla., 1980-84. Recipient 3d Ann. MAXIE award Miami Arts Exchange, 1990; grantee Fla. Endowment for Humanities, 1986, Metro Dade County Cultural Affairs Coun., 1986, Fla. Internat. U., 1990, 91; U. Miami-Coral Gables merit scholar, fed. scholar. Mem. Assn. Coll. and Univ. Mus. and Galleries, Am. Assn. Mus., Coll. Art Assn. Am., Fla. Mus. Dirs. Assn., Fla. Higher Edn. Arts Network, Internat. Coun. Mus. (fine arts com.), Miami Cultural execs. Coun., Southeastern Mus. Assn., Fla. Cultural Action Alliance, Phi Kappa Phi. Office: Art Mus Fla Internat U University Park Pc # 110 Miami FL 33199-0001

MORGAN, DAVID A. art history educator; b. Ogden, Iowa, Dec. 21, 1957; BA, Concordia Coll., 1980; MA, U. Ariz., 1984; PhD, U. Chgo., 1990. Prof. Valparaiso (Ind.) U., 1990—, Duesenberg prof. Christianity and the arts, 2001—. Chair Internat. Study Commn. on Media, Religion and Culture. Author: Icons of American Protestantism, 1996, Visual Piety, 1998, Protestants and Pictures, 1999, Visual Culture of American Religions, 2001. Recipient CHOICE Outstanding Book award, 1996, PSP award Assn. Am. Pubs., 1999-2000, Franklin Rsch. award Am. Philosophical Soc., 2001-03 ; fellow Yale U., 1994-95, Getty Grant Program, 1996-97, Am. Antiquari an Assn., 1997-98, NEH, 2001-02. Lutheran. Office: Valparaiso Univ 651 College Ave Valparaiso IN 46383 E-mail: david.morgan@valpo.edu.

MORGAN, DAVID ALLEN, electronic engineer; b. Sidney, Nebr., June 1, 1962; s. Richard Dennis and Gerda Dorene (Foged) M.; m. Ann Marie Zollman, June 7, 1987; children: Olivia, Delaney. BS in Elec. Engring., Colo. State U., 1984; MSEE, U. Colo., 1992. Engr. NCR VLSI Processor Products, Colo. Springs, Colo., 1984-85, NCR Digital Signal Processing, Fort Collins, 1985-87; engr., project leader NCR Computer Aided Design, 1987-93, AT&T GIS Software Devel., Ft. Collins, 1993-95, Symbios Logic Inc., ASIC Design & Phys. Design Kits., Ft. Collins, 1995-97; corp. phys. design tech. leader Symbios Inc., 1997-98; phys. design sys. architect LSI Logic Phys. Design Automation Group, 1998—2001; disting. engr. LSI Logic Design Tech. Sys. Architecture, 2001—. Mem. IEEE, Assn. for Computing Machinery. Avocations: golf, tennis, skiing. Office: LSI Logic 2001 Danfield Ct Fort Collins CO 80525-2905

MORGAN, DAVID J. tool & die maker, writer; s. John Morgan and Carol Lee Reid; 1 child from previous marriage Kylie. Student, Niagara County C.C., Sanborn, N.Y., 1985—87, Niagara U., 1987; grad. Mil. Sci., Empire State Mil. Acad., Peekskill, N.Y., 1989. Tool & Die Pre-Apprenticeship 1995, Cnc Programming (Turning) 1999. With Swagelok Mfg. Co., Solon, Ohio. Author: (novels) Nighted Colours: Legends of Celdor, 1996, Wolves of the Moor: Legends of Celdor, 1997, Dream Dragons: Legends of Celdor, 1997, Forgetmenots: Legends of Celdor, 1998, Darkfire: Witchlore, 2001. 1st lt. USAR, 1985—93. Master: Masons (senior decon 1994); mem.: PAVAS Internat. (hon.). Avocations: swimming, biking, hiking, camping, drawing. Personal E-mail: nightedcolors@aol.com.

MORGAN, DENNIS ALAN, federal official; b. St. Joseph, Mo., Feb. 1, 1947; s. John Frederick and Eunice L. (Seiter) M.; m. Linda Terrell James, June 22, 1968 (div. 1983); 1 child, Tracey Melinda. BA, U. Mo., 1969; MS, U. So. Calif., 1973; PhD, Pacific Western U., 1991. With Dept. of Navy, Washington, 1969—, dir. joint programs and acquisition reform, 1984—, also chmn. mgmt. com., dir. acquisition reform joint program. Lectr. in field. Author: The Pechora Intercept, 1988, Act of Contrition, 1991. Curators scholar U. Mo., 1965. Mem. SAR, Mensa, East Barcroft Assn. (bd. dirs. 1985—), Nat. Geog. Soc., Earthwatch, Nat. Parks and Conservation Assn., Lambda Chi Alpha. Republican. Avocations: reading, writing, travel, geneology. Home: 21625 Weatherby Ln Lexington Park MD 20653-2539

MORGAN, DENNIS RAYMOND, electrical engineer; b. Cin. children: Darby L. Melnik, Raymond S. PhDEE, Syracuse U., 1970. Sr. engr. electronics lab. GE, Syracuse, NY, 1965—84; disting. mem. tech. staff Bell Labs., Lucent Techs., Murray Hill, NJ, 1984—. Author: (book) Active Noise Control Systems: Algorithms andDSP Implementations, 1996. Mem.: IEEE. Home: 4 Sycamore Ln Morristown NJ 07960 Office: Bell Labs Lucent Techs 700 Mountain Ave 2d-537 New Providence NJ 07974-0636

MORGAN, DENNIS RICHARD, lawyer; b. Jan. 3, 1942; s. Richard and Gladys Belle (Brown) Morgan. BA, Washington and Lee U., 1964; JD, U. Va., 1967; LLM in Labor Law, NYU, 1971. Bar: Ohio 1967, Va. 1967, U.S. Ct. Appeals (4th cir.) 1968, U.S. Ct. Appeals (6th cir.) 1971, U.S. Supreme Ct. 1972. Law clk. to chief judge U.S. dit. Ct. (ea. dist.) Va., 1967—68; mem. Marshman, Snyder & Seeley, Cleve., 1971—72; dir. labor rels. Ohio Dept. Adminstrv. Svcs., 1972—75; asst. city atty. Columbus, Ohio, 1975—77; dir. Ohio Legis. Reference Bur., 1979—81; assoc. Clemans, Nelson & Assocs., 1981; pvt. practice, 1978—92. Lectr. in field; guest lectr. Cen. Mich. U., 1975; judge moot ct. Ohio State U. Sch. Law, 1981, 83, grad. divsn., 73, 74, 76; guest lectr. Baldwin-Wallace Coll., 1973; legal counsel Dist. IV Comms. Workers Am., 1982—88; pers. dir. Pub. Utilities Commn., Ohio, 1989—91; asst. atty. gen. State of Ohio, 1991—. Negotiator Franklin County United Way, 1977—81; regional chmn. ann. alumni fund-raising program U. Va. Sch. Law; mem. Greater Hilltop Area Commn., 1989—; pres. Woodbrook Village Condominium Assn., 1985—; trustee Hilltop Civic Coun., Inc., 1997—99; vice-chmn. Franklin County Dem. Party, 1976—82; dem. com. person Ward 58, Columbus, 1973—95; chmn. rules com. Ohio State Dem. Conv., 1974; co-founder, trustee Greater West Side Dem. Club; bd. dir. Hilltop Civic Coun., Inc., 1997—99. Capt. U.S. Army, 1968—70. Recipient Am. Jurisprudence award, 1967; scholar Robert E. Lee Rsch., 1965. Mem.: ABA, Am. Judicature Soc., Fed. Bar Assn., Indsl. Rels. Rsch. Assn., Columbus Metropolitan club (charter), Pi Sigma Alpha. Roman Catholic. Home: 1261 Woodbrook Ln # G Columbus OH 43223-3243

MORGAN, DIRCK, broadcast journalist; b. L.A., Feb. 3, 1954; s. Phillip Barton and Katherine (Ramirez) Segall; m. Ellen Tomoye Matsumoto, Dec. 1, 1993; 1 child, Makena Sunao. AA, Pierce Coll., 1973. Assignment editor KFWB/Group W. Westinghouse, L.A., 1972-74; corp. comm. specialist Northrop Corp., 1975-78; news dir. Stas. KARM, KFIG, Fresno, Calif., 1978-84; editor, anchor Sta. KGIL, L.A., 1984-85; fin. anchor Sta. KWHY-TV, 1985-87; cmty. resources specialist Optimist Boys Home, 1985-87; reporter Sta. KFWB, CBS, 1988—. Media crisis mgmt. instr. L.A. County Fire Dept., 1990—, L.A. Police Dept., 1991—, LAUSD, 1996, Calif. State Mil. Res., L.A., 1990-95. Helicopter airborne reporter Sta. KFWB, 1988-91, broadcast series on L.A. riots, 1992 (L.A. Press Club award), L.A. Police Dept. Ballistics, 1994 (L.A. Press Club award), Radio TV News Assn. Instr., announcer Kenkojuku World Karate, L.A., 1984-92; host Nissei Week, L.A., 1990-98. Recipient 19 Golden Mike awards Radio and TV News Assn. Mem. L.A. Police Protective League (hon. life). Avocations: karate, Japanese koi fish, firearms, classic cars. Office: KFWB/CBS 6230 Yucca St Los Angeles CA 90028-5295

MORGAN, DONALD CRANE, lawyer; b. Detroit, Sept. 17, 1940; s. Donald Nye and Nancy Morgan; m. Judith Munro, June 23, 1962; children: Wendy, Donald. BA, Ohio Wesleyan U., 1962; JD, U. Mich., 1965. Bar: Mich. 1966, U.S. Dist. Ct. (ea. dist.) Mich. 1966, U.S. Ct. Appeals (6th cir.) 1967, U.S. Supreme Ct. 1971. Ptnr. Kerr, Russell and Weber, Detroit, 1965-87; of counsel Draugelis & Ashton, Plymouth, Mich., 1988-93; pvt. practice, 1993—. Twp. atty. Plymouth Twp., 1970-85, Northville Twp., 1972-85; city atty. City of Plymouth, 1995-98; mediator Wayne County Mediation Tribunal, Detroit, 1981—, Oakland County Mediation Tribunal, Pontiac, Mich., 1992—; hearing panelist Mich. Atty. Discipline Bd., 1981—. Chmn. Wayne County II congl. Dist. Rep. Party, 1979-81; bd. dirs. Growth Works, Inc., treas., 1992-95, pres. 1995-99; ruling elder 1st Presbyn. Ch., Plymouth, 1976-79, 90-93; local bd. 222 mem. U.S. Selective Svc. Sys.; mem. spl. grants and agy. admissions com. United Way Cmty. Svcs.; elder commr. Detroit Presbytery. Paul Harris fellow, 1980. Mem. ABA, Mich. Def. Trial Counsel, State Bar of Mich. (rep. assembly 1979-85, 89-95, chmn. medicolegal problems com. 1995-96), Oakland County Bar Assn., Detroit Assn. Def. Trial Counsel, Plymouth Rotary (pres. 1985-86), Plymouth Rotary Found., Inc. (sec. 1996-98, dir. 1995, 99-2002), Phi Alpha Delta, Sigma Alpha Epsilon, Pi Sigma Alpha. Republican. Presbyterian. Avocations: reading, travel, sports. Home: 1440 Woodland Pl Plymouth MI 48170-1569 Office: 134 N Main St Plymouth MI 48170-1236 E-mail: morganlaw48170@aol.com.

MORGAN, DONNA JEAN, psychotherapist; b. Edgerton, Wis., Nov. 16, 1955; d. Donald Edward and Pearl Elizabeth (Robinson) Garey. BA, U. Wis., Whitewater, 1983, MS, 1985. Cert. psychotherapist, Wis.; cert. mental health and alcohol and drug counselor; nat. cert. alcohol and drug abuse counselor; lic. marriage and family therapist, Wis.; lic. ind. social worker; lic. clin. ind. social worker; nat. cert. counselor; lic. profl. counselor; lic. advanced practice social worker. Clin. supr. Stoughton (Wis.) Hosp., 1985-88; pvt. practice Janesville, Wis., 1988-91; prin. Morgan and Assocs., 1991-96; pvt. practice New Focus, Waukesha and Mukwonago, 1996-97, William N. Watson & Assocs., MD, S.C., Oconomowoc, Waukesha, 1997-98, Morgan Counseling, LLC, Janesville, 1998—. Mem. underaged drinking violation alternative program Rock County, 1986—96; co-chmn. task force on child sexual abuse, 1989—91; mem. Rock County Multi-disciplinary Team on Child Abuse, 1990—96; mem. spkrs. bur. Rock County C.A.R.E. House, 1990—; adv. bd. Parents Place, Waukesha County, Wis., 1997—99; active ARC, 2001—; vol. Red Cross, 2001—. Mem. APA, ACA., Am. Profl. Soc. on Abuse of Children, Wis. Profl. Soc. on Abuse of Children (bd. dirs. 1994-98, v.p. 1997-98), Am. Assn. Mental Health Counselors, Wis. Assn. Mental Health Counselors, Am. Assn. Marriage and Family Therapy (clin. mem.), Am. Assn. Christian Counselors, Wis. Counseling Assn., Am. Psycotherapy Assn.

MORGAN, EDMUND SEARS, history educator; b. Mpls., Jan. 17, 1916; s. Edmund Morris and Elsie Sears (Smith) M.; m. Helen Theresa Mayer, June 7, 1939; children: Penelope, Pamela; m. Marie Caskey, June 22, 1983. AB, Harvard U., 1937, PhD, 1942. Instrument maker Radiation Lab., MIT, 1942-45; instr. U. Chgo., 1945-46; asst. prof. Brown U., 1946-49, asso. prof., 1949-51, prof., 1951-55, acting dean grad. sch., 1951-52; prof. Yale U., 1955-65, Sterling prof., 1965-86, prof. emeritus, 1986—. Rsch. fellow Huntington Libr., 1952-53; Johnson rsch. prof. U. Wis., 1968-69 Author: The Puritan Family, 1944, Virginians at Home, 1953; author: (with Helen M. Morgan) The Stamp Act Crisis, 1953; author: The Birth of the Republic, 1956, The Puritan Dilemma, 1958, The Gentle Puritan, 1962, Visible Saints, 1963, Roger Williams, 1967, So What About History, 1969, American Slavery American Freedom, 1975, The Challenge of the American Revolution, 1976, The Meaning of Independence, 1976, The Genius of George Washington, 1980, Inventing the People, 1988, Benjamin Franklin, 2002; mem. editl. bd.: N.E. Quar.; contbr. articles and revs. to hist. jours. Trustee Smith Coll., 1984-89. Recipient Nat. Humanities medal, 2000. Mem.: Am. Acad. Arts and Scis., Orgn. Am. Historians (pres. 1971—72), Royal Hist. Soc., Brit. Acad., Conn. Acad. Arts and Scis., Am. Philos. Soc., Am. Antiquarian Soc., Mass. Hist. Soc., Colonial Soc. Mass.

MORGAN, ELIZABETH, plastic and reconstructive surgeon; b. Washington, July 9, 1947; d. William James and Antonia (Bell) Morgan; 1 child Elena. BA magna cum laude, Harvard U., 1967; postgrad. (fellow), Oxford U., 1967, 70; MD, Yale U., 1971; PhD in Psychology, U. Canterbury, Christchurch, New Zealand, 1995. Diplomate Am. Bd. Surgery, Am. Bd. Plastic Surgery. Intern Yale-New Haven Hosp., 1971-72, resident, 1972-73, 76-77, Tufts-New Eng. Med. Center, Boston, 1973-76, Harvard-Cambridge (Mass.) Hosp., 1977-78; columnist Cosmopolitan mag., 1973-80; pvt. practice specializing in cosmetic surgery Washington, 1978-87; pvt. practice specializing in cosmetic plastic surgery McLean, Va., 1998—, Chevy Chase, Md., 1998—. Assoc. faculty Am. U. Dept. Law, Justice and Soc., 1998. Author: (book) The Making of A Woman Surgeon, 1980, Solo Practice, 1982, Custody, A True Story, 1986, The Complete ok of Cosmetic Surgery for Men, Women and Teens, 1988. Fellow: ACS, Am. Soc. Plastic Surgeons; mem.: APSCA, APA, Am. Profl. Soc. Abused Children, Internat. Soc. Study Dissociation. Episcopalian. Office: Chevy Chase Bldg 5530 Wisconsin Ave Ste 1414 Chevy Chase MD 20815-4302 Fax: (301) 951-8128. E-mail: mail@drelizabethmorgan.com.

MORGAN, ELIZABETH SEYDEL, writer, speaker; b. Atlanta, Feb. 19, 1939; d. John Rutherford and Jane Reynolds Seydel; children: Matthew, John, Elizabeth Borkey. BA, Hollins College, Roanoke, Va, 1956—60; MFA, Virginia Commonwealth University, Richmond, Va, 1983—86. Teacher, english and creative writing St. Catherine's School, Richmond, Va. Author: (,poet,book,) Parties, 1988, (book) The Governor of Desire, 1993, On Long Mountain, 1998; translator: (part of penn greek drama series) "Electra" by Euripides, 1998; author: (short fiction) "Economics", 1991 (Emily Clark Balch Prize, 1992); contbr. essay; author: (screenplay) Queen Esther, 1993. Board member Richmond Public Library Foundation, Richmond, Va, 1999—2003. Mem.: Fellows Council, Virginia Center for the Creative Arts. Home: 504 Honaker Avenue Richmond VA 23226

MORGAN, EMMA, poet, essayist, educator; b. Bristol, Pa. d. Donald L. and Ann Ellen Shapiro. BA in Writing, Vt. Coll., 1995. Freelance writer, 1981—; presch. tchr. Horace Man Sch. for Nursery Yrs., N.Y.C., 1987, Common Sch., Amherst, Mass., 1988-90. Puppet artist, Northampton, Mass., 1995—; camp dir., curriculum designer Friends and Lovers Cmty., Mass., 1996-99; vis. writer SUNY, Farmingdale, 1999; poet-in-the-schs. Crocker Farm Elem. Sch., Amherst, 1995; vis. lectr. on disability Smith Coll. Sch. Social Work, Northampton, 1998, 99; presenter in field. Author: (poetry) Gooseflesh, 1993, A Stillness Build of Motion: Living with Tourette's, 1996; contbg. poet: Staring Back: The Disability Experience from the Inside Out, 1997; contbr. numerous other works; contbg. essayist to Nat. writers UNion Freelance Writers' Guide, 2000. Hebrew sch. tchr. Congregation B'nai Israel, Northampton, 1989-91. Mem. Nat. Writers Union (chmn. nat. diversity campaign 1998-2001, past mem. local steering com., past trustee, nat. del.), Tourette Syndrome Assn., Co-Op Am, Jewish Cmty. Amherst (chmn. critical issues com. 1997-2000, bd. dirs. 1997-99, mem. various coms.). Mem. Green Party. Avocations: puppetry, soft sculpture, herbal medicine, hiking, beach combing. Home and Office: 491 Bridge Rd Apt 724 Northampton MA 01062

MORGAN, EVAN, retired chemist; b. Spokane, Wash., Feb. 26, 1930; s. Evan and Emma Anne (Klobucher) M.; m. Johnnie Lu Dickson, Feb. 14, 1959; 1 child, James. BS, Gonzaga U., 1952; MS, U. Wash., 1954, PhD, 1956. Staff chemist IBM Corp., Poughkeepsie, N.Y., 1956-60; group supr. Olin Mathieson Co., New Haven, 1960-64; assoc. prof. chemistry High Point (N.C.) Coll., 1964-65; sr. rsch. chemist Reynolds Metals Co., Richmond, Va., 1965-72; chemist Babcock & Wilcox, Lynchburg, 1972-95, Lynchburg Tree Steward, Lynchburg, 1995—; ret., 2002—. Mem. Am. Chem. Soc. Home: 5128 Wedgewood Rd Lynchburg VA 24503-4208

MORGAN, FLORENCE MURDINA, nurse; b. Northern Manchester, Jamaica, Mar. 1, 1936; came to U.S., 1967; d. James William and Juanita Agatha (Lorraine) M. RN, Wanstead Hosp., Hermon Hill London, 1962; State Cert. Midwife, Rochford Hosp., Essex, Eng., 1963; Queens Nurse, Queens Inst. Dist. Nursing, Eng., 1965; BSN cum laude, CUNY, 1989, MSN, 1992. Cert. Childbirth Educator. Staff nurse Toronto Gen. Hosp., 1964-65; jr. supr., queens nurse/midwife Surrey County Coun., Kingston-on-Thames, Eng., 1965-66; staff midwife St. Luke's Hosp., Guildford, Surrey, 1966-67; staff nurse No. Westchester Hosp., Mt. Kisco, N.Y., 1967-70, Vis. Nurse Svc., N.Y.C., 1970-71; pvt. duty med. surg. nurse, 1971-76; staff nurse divsn. substance abuse Beth Israel Med. Ctr., 1976—. Tb coord., tchr. health, tb. prevention, AIDS prevention Beth Israel Med. Ctr., N.Y.C., 1993—; vol. nursing Spalding Hosp., Jamaica, 1955-57. Vol. Luth. Ch., N.Y.C., 1967-76; vol. 1199 Polit. Action., N.Y.C., 1989-95. Mem. N.Y. Acad. Scis., Hunter-Bellevue Alumni Assn., Sigma Theta Tau. Democrat. Avocations: swimming, tennis, arts and crafts, dance, unpublished poems. Home: 445 E 14th St Apt 3D New York NY 10009-2805

MORGAN, FRANK EDWARD, II, lawyer; b. Burlington, Vt., May 16, 1952; s. Robert Griggs and Ruth (Jepson) M. First Class Cert. Merit, U. Edinburgh, Scotland, 1973; AB with honors, Brown U., 1974; LLM, Cambridge U., Eng., 1976; JD, U. Va., 1978. Bar: Mass. 1978, N.Y. 1990. Assoc. Gaston & Snow, Boston, 1978-82; v.p., gen. counsel Madison Fund, Inc. and Adobe Resources Corp., N.Y.C., 1982-87; ptnr. Gaston & Snow, 1987-91, Mayer, Brown & Platt, N.Y.C., 1991-96, Dewey Ballantine, N.Y.C., 1996—. Mem. ABA, N.Y. State Bar Assn., Am. Soc. Internat. Law. Republican. Congregationalist. Home: 14 Sutton Pl S New York NY 10022-3071 Office: Dewey Ballantine LLP 1301 Avenue Of The Americas New York NY 10019-6022 Business E-Mail: fmorgan@dbllp.com.

MORGAN, FRANK T. business educator, consultant; b. Shamokin, Pa., July 8, 1944; s. Burgess Sherman and Marion Regina (Lewis) M.; m. Nancy Ida Bishop, May 30, 1970; children: Elizabeth Marion, Douglas Bishop. AB, Princeton U., 1966; MS, Pa. State U., 1967; postgrad., Stevens Inst. Tech., Hoboken, N.J., 1976-79; PhD, Calif. Coast U., 1983. Cert. sr. profl. in human resources. Plant pers. mgr. Gen. Foods, Jacksonville, Fla., 1967-69, assoc. placement mgr. White Plains, N.Y., 1969-70, mgr. sales devel., 1970-71; mgr. orgn. devel. Berol Corp., Daubury, Conn., 1971-73, v.p. human resources, 1973-78, sr. grop v.p. internat., 1978-87; prof., dir. exec. edn. U. Va. Darden Grad. Sch. Bus., Charlottesville, 1987-94; global dir. exec. edn. U. N.C., Chapel Hill, 1994-99; dir. exec. devel. The Dow Chem. Co., Midland, Mich., 1999—. Bd. dirs. Danbury Med. Ctr., 1977-85; chmn. Danbury Edn. Adv. Coun., 1978-86; pres. Morgan Assocs., Charlottesville, 1987—. Contbr. articles to publs. Mem. Am. Psychol. Assn., Am. Soc. for Tng. and Devel., Soc. for Pers. and Human Resources (chair), Consortium for Exec. Edn. Republican. Episcopalian. Avocations: sailing, tennis, history. Office: The Dow Chem Co Edc Midland MI 48674-0001

MORGAN, FREDERICK, poet, editor; b. N.Y.C., Apr. 25, 1922; s. John Williams and Marion Haviland (Burt) M.; m. Constance Canfield, Dec. 20, 1942 (div. Aug. 1957); children: Gaylen, Veronica, George F.; m. Rose Fillmore, Aug. 14, 1957 (div. Aug. 1969); m. Paula Deitz, Nov. 30, 1969. AB magna cum laude, Princeton U., 1943. Founder, editor The Hudson Rev., N.Y.C., 1947, editor, pres., 1947-97; chmn. adv. council dept. Romance langs. and lits. Princeton U., N.J., 1973-91. Author: A Book of Change, 1972, Poems of the Two Worlds, 1977, The Tarot of Cornelius Agrippa, 1978, Death Mother and Other Poems, 1979, The River, 1980, Refractions, 1981, Northbook, 1982, Eleven Poems, 1983, The Fountain and Other Fables, 1985, Poems: New and Selected, 1987, Poems for Paula, 1995, The Night Sky, 2002, The One Abiding, 2002. Served with U.S. Army, 1943-45. Decorated chevalier de l'Ordre des Arts et des Lettres (France); recipient Aiken Taylor award for poetry, 2001. Mem.: Knickerbocker (N.Y.C.) (gov. 1981-89), University (N.Y.C.), Somerset (Boston). Office: The Hudson Review 684 Park Ave New York NY 10021-5043

MORGAN, FREEMAN LOUIS, JR. engineer, consultant; b. Farrell, Miss., Aug. 23, 1931; s. Freeman Louis Sr. and Florence (McCloud) M.; m. Billie Delores Mason, June 20, 1954; children: Deborah Lee, Randall Douglas. BS, La. State U., Baton Rouge, 1954. Registered profl. engr., Tex., La. Process supr. Humble Oil and Refining Co., Houston, 1956-65; pvt. practice cons. engr. Houston, Chandler, Tyler, Tex., 1965—. Contbr. articles to profl. jours. Served to lt. U.S. Army, 1954-56. Republican. Avocation: golf. Home and Office: 3310 Greenoak Pl Tyler TX 75701-7805 E-mail: morgans@cox-internet.com.

MORGAN, G. KENNETH, association executive; b. Farmville, Va., Dec. 2, 1947; s. Raymond Henry and Evelyn (Healy) M.; m. Winnie Williams, Mar. 17, 1989; 1 child, Rebecca. BA, U. Richmond, 1974; MEd, Va. Commonwealth U., 1978. Cert. fundraising exec.; cert. assn. exec. Program dir. Va. affiliate Am. Heart Assn., Richmond, 1970-79, mgmt. cons. nat. office Dallas, 1979-82, exec. v.p. N.C. Chapel Hill, 1982-93; nonprofit cons. Morgan & Assocs., 1993—98. Mem. bd. advisors U. N.C. Sch. Pub. Health, Chapel Hill, 1984-93. Vol. Orange County chpt. ARC; bd. dirs. Orange County United Way, Triangle United Way. Mem. Nat. Health Agy. (pres. 1989-90), Am. Soc. Assn. Execs., Va. Assn. Rescue Squads (life, past pres.), N.C. Assn. Life Underwriters (exec. dir. 1995—), Rotary (Service Above Self award). Presbyterian. Home: PO Box 16067 Chapel Hill NC 27516-6067

MORGAN, GARY LORIN, biophysicist, inventor, researcher; b. Balt., Oct. 23, 1948; s. Lorin C. and Pearl C. (Dise) M.; m. Kathleen Marie Lamm Morgan, Dec. 6, 1986; children: Ashley, Lauren. BS in Engring. Sci., Johns Hopkins U., 1975. Rsch. assoc. Johns Hopkins U., Balt., 1966-75; sr. rsch. scientist Pfizer Med. Systems, Columbia, Md., 1976-84; quality assurance mgr. U.S. Design Corps., Lanham, 1984-88; dir. R&D Pacific Sci. Co., Silver Spring, 1988-93; chief rsch. scientist Triton Thalassic Tech., Elkridge, 1994—. Contbr. articles to profl. jours. Pres., dir. Marshallee Civic Assn. Mem. Water Environment Fedn. Achievements include patents for particle detecting instrument with sapphire detecting cell, particle measurement system with sonically measured flow rate, sterilization of opaque liquids with ultraviolet radiation, lamp for generating high power ultraviolet radiation. Avocations: boating, marine sci. Office: Ship Point Rsch Lab 5821 Bellanca Dr Elkridge MD 21075 E-mail: gmorg@erols.com.

MORGAN, GAYLIN F. public relations consultant; b. Cedar Falls, Iowa, Nov. 3, 1938; BS in Journ., Bus., Iowa State U., 1962. Creative dir. Reiman Assocs., 1965-75; pres. Morgan & Myers, Jefferson, Wis., 1976-97, cons., 1997—. Address: 304 E Linden Dr Jefferson WI 53549-2146 E-mail: gfmorgan@charter.net.

MORGAN, GEORGE EMIR, III, financial economics educator; b. Carmel, Calif., Jan. 2, 1953; s. George Emir Jr. and Dolores (Przydzial) M.; m. Donna Batts Vail, Dec. 31, 1977; 1 child, Abbie Vail. BS in Math., Georgetown U., 1973; MS in Stats., U. N.C., 1975, PhD in Fin., 1977. Sr. fin. economist Office of the Compt. of the Currency, Washington, 1978-79; asst. prof. U. Tex., Austin, 1979-84; assoc. prof. Va. Poly. Inst., Blacksburg, 1984-89, dir. PhD program, 1985-89, prof., 1989—, Suntrust prof. fin., 1995—, head dept. fin., 1995-96, acting head dept. fin., 1999-2000; assoc. dir. bus. rsch. Ctr. Comml. Space Comms., 1990-92; assoc. dir. Ctr. for Wireless Telecomms., 1992-94; exec. dir. Ctr. for Wireless Telecom., 2001—, Space and Wireless Bus. Ctr., 1994-2001; pres. Robert Properties Investment Advising, Cin., 1996-2000. Editor (newsletter) 90 Day Notes, 1986-90. Mem. Am. Econ. Assn., Am. Fin. Assn., Am. Statis. Assn., So. Fin. Assn., Fin. Mgmt. Assn., Macintosh Blacksburg Users Group (faculty advisor 1989-92), Beta Gamma Sigma. Avocation: Macintosh personal computers. Office: Va Poly Inst Dept Fin 1016 Pamplin Hall Blacksburg VA 24061

MORGAN, GEORGE WESLEY, minister; b. Hagerstown, Md., Mar. 6, 1941; s. George Willis and Bessie Mildred (Valentine) M.; m. Peggy Kathryne Lumm, Sept. 1, 1963; children: Lizanne Noelle, David Edwin. AA, Hagerstown (Md.) Jr. Coll., 1963; AB, Bethany Coll., 1971; D of Ministry, Lexington (Ky.) Theol., Seminary, 1976. Ordained to ministry Christian Ch. (Disciples of Christ), 1972. Minister First Christian Ch., Pineville, Ky., 1973-78; exec. assoc., regional minister Christian Ch. in N.C., Wilson, 1978-83; dir. Christian Ch. Div. Homeland Ministries, Indpls., 1983-85; minister First Christian Ch., Texas City, Tex., 1985—. Mem. com. on ministry Christian Ch. in Southwest, Ft. Worth, 1986—, chair, 1990—; mem. So. Acad. of Teaching, Indpls., 1966—, chair, 1981-84; chair Leader Devel. Dept., Coastal Plains Area, Houston, 1990—, Dept. of Ministry, 1986-90. Author: Teacher As Learner As Teacher, 1976, Christian Stress Management, 1984; editor: Design Manual, 1983, Trainer Development, 1984. Chmn. Pineville Community Ctr., 1975-78, Pineville InterFaith Housing Assn., 1977-78, Texas City New Focus, 1990—, steering com. CASA of Galveston County, Texas City, 1990—; pres. Tex. City Day Nursery Bd., 1997—; v.p. Tex. City Chpt. Habitat for Humanity, 1998—; mem. Habitat Steering Com., 1998—. Recipient Leadership award Hagerstown Jr. Coll., 1963, Masonic Cmty. Builders award, 1998; named Minister of Yr. Conservation Club of W.Va., 1969, Community Leaders and Noteworthy Ams., 1978. Mem. Cameron Ministers Assn. (pres. 1966-69), Ohio Valley Ministers Assn. (pres. 1968-69), Pineville Ministers Assn. (pres. 1974-77), Texas City Ministers Fellowship (pres. 1986—), Kiwanis (bd. dirs. Pineville chpt. 1976-78, bd. dirs. Texas City chpt. 1990-91), Tex. City Chpt. (pres. 1995-96). Ordained by Christian Ch. Disciples of Christ, 1972. Office: First Christian Church PO Drawer B Texas City TX 77592 Home: Apt 709 2201 Montgomery Park Blvd Conroe TX 77304-3551 *I believe that everything is curriculum! We can learn from every experience. I also believe that life is a choice. God has given us the ability and the freedom to choose our response to every event in life.*

MORGAN, GERALD LEE, artist; b. Nashville, Dec. 4, 1946; s. Charles Lee and Modine (Nash) M.; m. Judith Ann Andrews, Feb. 13, 1975; 1 child, Tisha Claire Morgan Vaden; 1 child by previous marriage, Timothy Lee. Student, Austin-Peay State U., 1975-76, Western Ky. U., 1976-77. Graphic artist Jim Johnson Illustration & Design, Nashville, 1973-75; art dir. Nicoll & Assocs. Pub. Rels. & Advt., Hendersonville, Tenn., 1977-86; artist pvt. practice, 1986—. Selected solo exhibits include: Pickering Galleries, Nashville, 1982, Bethune Arts Ctr., Charleston, S.C., 1987, Best of Tenn. Art Exhbns., Watkins Inst., Nashville, 1990, Fine Arts Ctr., Madisonville, Ky., 1992, Folon-Rigsby Gallery, Nashville, 1995, Galerie Vanhove, Quimper, France, 1997, 99, Parthenon Mus., Nashville, 1998, Yvonne Rapp Gallery, 1999, 2001; group or invitational shows; Volunteer State Coll., Gallatin, Tenn., 1987, Highland Gallery, Atlanta, Capitol Arts Ctr., Bowling Green, Ky., Belmont U. Leu Gallery, Nashville, (2-person exhbn.), 1993; juried shows: Bluegrass Regional Painting Exhbn. Louisville, 1977 (monetary award), 1987 (purchase award), Eight State Ann., 1982, J.B. Speed Art Mus., (purchase award), Mid-Am. Biennial-Nat., Owensboro Mus. Fine Art, 1979 (purchase award), 88, Tenn. All-State Exhbn., 1977-86, 88-91, 95, (7 hon. mentions, 2 first pl. awards); works in corp. collections include: First Union Bank, Nashville, Found. for Ky. Women, Louisville, Opryland Hotel, Chez Jacky, Riec sur Bélon, France, Bell South Telecomm., Nashville; also in pvt. collections in U.S. and France. Mem. gallery com. Hendersonville (Tenn.) Arts Coun., 1984-85, chmn. 1986, bd. dirs. 1987-91. With U.S. Army, 1965-68, Vietnam. Avocations: philately, art history, jogging. Home: 118 Donna Dr Hendersonville TN 37075-3630

MORGAN, GLENN L. lawyer, photography; b. New Orleans, Dec. 1943; m. S.E. and S.T. Morgan. BA, U. La., Lafayette, 1965; JD, Loyola U., 1972. Bar: La. 1972, U.S. Dist. Ct. (all dists.) La. 1972, U.S. Ct. Appeals (5th cir.) 1972, U.S. Supreme Ct. 1975, U.S. Ct. Appeals (fed. cir.) 1982, U.S. Claims Ct. 1982, U.S. Internat. Trade Ct. 1982, U.S. Mil. Appeals Ct. 1986. Adj. faculty U. Phoenix South La. C.C. Republican. Home: PO Box 354 Breaux Bridge LA 70517-0354 Office: PO Box 5006 Lafayette LA 70502-5006 Fax: 337-332-0584. E-mail: morgancaw@juno.com.

MORGAN, GRETNA FAYE, retired automotive executive; b. Galveston, Ind., Aug. 24, 1927; d. Fred Monroe and Vera Arnetha (Oakley) Goodier; m. Marvin L. Morgan, Mar. 30, 1946; children: Gary Lynn, Vonna Annette, Marvin Richard, Darla Sue, Janice Arnetha. Diploma in cosmetology, Approved U., Indpls., 1946. Sales distributor Kirby Co., Ft. Wayne, Ind., 1955-62; with Dana Corp., Churubusco, 1962—, plant mgr. Athens, Ga., 1978-81, Churubusco, Ind., 1981-90; ret., 1990; with Lee Meml. Hosp. Sys., Ft. Myers, Fla., 1997—. Bd. dirs. Passages, Inc., Whitley County. Chmn. mayor's com. Employment Handicapped, Athens, Ga., 1980-81; mem. interview bd. selection com. Congressman Dan Coats Mil. Acad., Ft. Wayne, 1985-88, bus. adv. bd. Whitley County Opportunity Ctr., Columbia City, Ind., 1986-90, Chem. Dependency Task Force Whitley County, Ind. Gov.'s Task Force on Drunk Driving, budget com. Whitley County United Way; bd. regents Dana U., Toledo, 1978-82; bd. dirs., pres. Whitley County Jr. Achievement, 1977-78; bd. dirs. Passages, Inc., Columbia City, Ind., 1989—, Whitley County Meml. Hosp. Found., Columbia City, 1989—; mem. Noble County Friends of the Libr., 1990—; mem. First Assembly of God, Ft. Myers, Fla., Churubusco C. of C. (pres. 1975-76), Dana Retirees of Fla. Club (pres. 1993—). Mem. Churubusco C. of C. (pres. 1975-76), Dana Retirees of Fla. Club (pres. 1993—), Calvary Temple Worship Ctr. Avocations: power boating, reading, fishing. Home: 1981 Carbonata Dr Alva FL 33920-3647 Office: Dana Corp PO Box 245 Churubusco IN 46723-0245

MORGAN, GWYN, oil and gas executive; b. Carstairs, Alta., Can., Nov. 4, 1945; s. Ian and Margaret (Hergenhein) M. BSc in Mech. Engring., U. Alta., 1967; postgrad., Cornell U. Petroleum engr. Alta. Energy Resources Conservation Bd.; mgr. ops. and engring. Consolidated Natural Gas Ltd., Consolidated Pipelines Ltd., Norlands Petroleums Ltd.; with Alta. Energy Co., Ltd., Calgary, 1975—2002; pres., CEO En Cana Corp., 2002—. Bd. dirs. HSBC-Bank N.Am.; dir. LaFarge N.Am. Trustee Fraser Inst.; dir. Inst. of the Ams., Can. Coun. Chief Execs.; gov. Coun. for Can. Unity. Mem. Can. Assn. Petroleum Prodrs., Can. Coun. Chief Execs. Avocations: sailing, hiking, skiing, physical fitness, cycling. Office: EnCana Corp 1800-855 2d St SW Calgary AB Canada T2P 2S5

MORGAN, HARRY NEW, education educator; b. Blenheim, Va., June 6, 1926; s. John Alexander and Cheyney (Lewis) M.; children: Parris Mitchell, Lawrence Milan. BS, NYU, 1949; MSW, U. Wis., 1969; EdD, U. Mass., 1970. Cert. social worker, N.Y. Dir. N.E. region Head Start, N.Y.C., 1965-67; program coord. Bank St. Coll., 1967-70; prof. and chmn. African-Am. Studies Ohio U., Athens, 1970-72, Syracuse (N.Y.) U., 1972-84; prof. and chmn. earl chldhood edn. West Ga. Coll., Carrollton, 1984—. Conducted rsch. studies on cmty. and classroom issues, 1984-95. Author: Affective Education for Cognitive Development, 1967, The Learning Community, 1970, Historical Perspectives on the Education of Black Children, 1995, Cognitive Styles and Classroom Learning, 1997, The Imagination of Early Childhood Education, 1999. Bd. dirs. Marcy Settlement House, Bklyn., 1962-65; pres., co-founder bd. Met. Sch. for Arts, Syracuse, 1975; founder housing cooperative, Syracuse, trustee Davis-Putter Scholarship Fund. Mem. APA, Am. Ednl. Rsch. Assn. Avocation: antiques. Home: 2284 Lakeview Pky Villa Rica GA 30180-8082 Office: State U West Ga Maple St Carrollton GA 30118-0001 E-mail: hmorgan@westga.edu.

MORGAN, HENRY COKE, JR. judge; b. Norfolk, Va., Feb. 8, 1935; s. Henry Coke and Dorothy Lea (Pebworth) M.; m. Margaret John McGrail, Aug. 18, 1965; children: A. Robertson Hanckel Jr., Catherine Morgan Stockwell, Coke Morgan Stewart. BS, Washington and Lee U., 1957, JD, 1960; LLM in Jud. Process, U. Va., 1998. Bar: Va. 1960, U.S. Dist. Ct. (ea. dist.) Va. 1961, U.S. Ct. Appeals (4th cir.) 1964. Asst. city atty. City of Norfolk, 1960-63; ptnr. Pender & Coward, Virginia Beach, Va., 1963-92; vice chmn., gen. counsel Princess Anne Bank, 1986-92; judge U.S. Dist. Ct. (ea. dist.) Va., 1992—. Served with U.S. Army, 1958-59. Episcopalian. Office: US Dist Ct Eastern Dist Va Walter E Hoffman US Courthouse 600 Granby St Ste 183 Norfolk VA 23510-1915 E-mail: henry_morgan@vaed.uscourts.gov.

MORGAN, HICKS BERNARD, lawyer, treasurer; b. Beaumont, Tex., Sept. 29, 1947; s. Guy H. Sr. and Amy Zella (Hebert) M.; m. Vicki Carol Null, Mar. 27, 1971; children: Hope Layne, Michelle Amy, Heather Elizabeth, Nathan Pollard, Andrew Thomas. AB, Dartmouth Coll., 1970; JD, Georgetown U., 1977. Gen. counsel Morgan Bldgs. & Spas, Dallas, 1977—, sec., 1978—, treas., 1983—. Bd. dirs. officer ATMC Investments, Las Vegas, Nev., AM Investment Co. Pres. St. Rita Sch. Bd., Dallas, 1985; chair Dallas-Riga USSR Ptnr. Cities Exchange, 1990-91; pres. Dallas-Riga Sister City Commn., 1999, Montserrat Retreat Ho. bd. trustees, 2001. Sgt. USAF, 1971-75. Mem. Tex. Bar Assn., Dallas County Bar Assn., Dartmouth Lawyers Assn., St. Rita Men's Club, Dallas-Riga Sister Cities (v.p.). Roman Catholic. Avocation: travel. Office: Morgan Bldgs Spas Pools & RVs 2800 Mccree Rd Garland TX 75041-3998

MORGAN, HUGH JACKSON, JR. bank executive; b. Nashville, Aug. 10, 1928; s. Hugh Jackson and Robert Ray (Porter) M.; m. Ann Moulton Ward, Aug. 28, 1954; children— Ann, Grace, Caroline, Hugh AB, Princeton U., N.J., 1950; LL.B., Vanderbilt U., Nashville, 1956; A.M.P., Harvard Bus. Sch., 1976. Bar: Tenn. 1956. Practice law Miller & Martin, Chattanooga, 1956-60; atty. So. Natural Gas Co., Birmingham, Ala., 1961-65, gen. atty., 1966-70, v.p., 1971-78, pres., 1982-84, chmn. bd., 1984-87; v.p. Sonat Inc., 1973-78, sr. v.p., 1979-84, exec. v.p., 1984, vice chmn. bd., 1984-87; vice chmn. Nat. Bank of Commerce, 1987-90; chmn. Nat. Bank Commerce, 1990—, also bd. dirs. Bd. dirs. Atrion Corp. Chmn. Birmingham Airport Authority, 1986-2000; trustee Children's Hosp. Ala., Birmingham, 1974— . Served to lt. (j.g.) USN, 1950-53. Recipient Bennett Douglas Bell Meml. prize Vanderbilt Law Sch., 1956 Mem. Order of the Coif. Clubs: Mountain Brook (pres. 1972), Redstone, (Birmingham); Belle Meade (Nashville); Linville Golf (N.C.). Lodges: Rotary. Home: 3121 Brookwood Rd Birmingham AL 35223-2016 Office: Nat Bank of Commerce 1927 1st Ave N Ste 100 Birmingham AL 35203-4058

MORGAN, JACK M. lawyer; b. Portales, N.Mex., Jan. 15, 1924; s. George Albert and Mary Rosana (Baker) M.; m. Peggy Flynn Cummings, 1947; children: Marilyn, Rebecca, Claudia, Jack. BBA, U. Tex., 1948, LLB, 1950. Bar: N.Mex. 1950. Sole practice law, Farmington, N.Mex., 1956—. Mem. cmty. bd. dirs. Wells Fargo, Farmington, N.Mex. Mem. N.Mex. State Senate, 1973-88. Served with USN, 1942-46. Mem. N.Mex. Bar Assn., S.W. Regional Energy Coun. (past chmn.), Kiwanis, Elks. Republican. Office: PO Box 2151 Farmington NM 87499-2151 E-mail: jmorgansr@fisi.net.

MORGAN, JACOB RICHARD, cardiologist; b. East St. Louis, Ill., Oct. 10, 1925; s. Clyde Adolphus and Jennie Ella Henrietta (Van Ramshorst) M.; m. Alta Eloise Ruthruff, Aug. 1, 1953; children: Elaine, Stephen Richard. BA in Physics, BBA, U. Tex., 1953; MD, U. Tex., Galveston, 1957. Diplomate Am. Bd. Internal Medicine, Am. Bd. Cardiology. Ensign USN, 1944, advanced through grades to capt., 1969; intern U.S. Naval Hosp., Oakland, Calif., 1957-58, chief medicine Taipei, Republic of China, 1962-64; internal medicine staff San Diego, 1964-67, chief cardiology, 1969-73; ret., 1973; dir. medicine R.E. Thomas Gen. Hosp., El Paso, Tex., 1973-75; asst. clin. prof. medicine U. Calif., San Diego, 1970-73; prof. medicine, assoc. chmn. dep. Tex. Tech U. Sch. Medicine, Lubbock and El Paso, 1973-75; pvt. practice National City, Calif., 1976—; dir. cardiology Paradise Valley Hosp., 1976-88. Presenter in field. Contbr. articles on cardiology to sci. jours. Recipient Casmir Funk award, 1972. Fellow ACP, Am. Coll. Cardiology, Am. Coll. Chest Physicians, Am. Heart Assn. (coun. on clin. cardiology). Avocation: golf. Home: 9881 Edgar Pl La Mesa CA 91941-6833 Office: 2409 E Plaza Blvd National City CA 91950-5101

MORGAN, JACQUI, illustrator, painter, educator, writer; b. N.Y.C., Feb. 22, 1939; d. Henry and Emily (Cook) Morganstern; m. Onnig Kalfayan, Apr. 23, 1967 (div. 1972); m. Tomás Gonda, Jan. 1983 (dec. 1988). BFA with honors, Pratt Inst., Bklyn., 1960; MA, CCNY, 1978. Textile designer M. Lowenstein & Sons, N.Y.C., 1961-62, Fruit of the Loom, N.Y.C., 1962; stylist-design dir. Au Courant, Inc., 1966—; assoc. prof. Pratt Inst., Bklyn., 1977—. Guest lectr. U. Que., Syracuse U., Warsaw TV & Radio, Poland, NYU, Parsons Sch. Design, N.Y.C., Sch. Visual Arts, N.Y.C., Va. Commonwealth U., Fashion Inst. of Tech., others; mem. profl. juries; curator Tomás Gonda retrospective exhbn.; condr. workshops. One-person shows include Soc. Illustrators, N.Y.C., 1977, Art Dirs. Club, N.Y.C., 1978, Gallerie Nowe Miasto, Warsaw, 1978, Gallerie Baumeister, Munich, W.Ger., 1978, Hansen-Feuerman Gallery, N.Y.C., 1980, Krannert Mus./U. Ill., 1998, Art Gallery at Marywood U., Scranton, Pa., 1998; group shows include Mus. Contemporary Crafts, N.Y.C., 1975, Smithsonian Instn., Washington, 1976, Mus. Warsaw, 1976, 78, Mus. Tokyo, 1979, Nat. Watercolor Soc., 1989, Salmagundi Club, 1990, New Eng. Watercolor Soc. Open, 1990, Miss. Watercolor Grand Nat., 1990, Illustration West 29, 1990, Adirondack Nat., 1990, Die Verlassenen Schuhe, 1993, N.Y. restaurant Sch., 1994, Lizan-Tops Gallery, 1996, The Art Club, 2000; represented in permanent collections: Smithsonian Instn., Mus. Warsaw; author, illustrator: Watercolor for Illustration; produced 3 instrnl. watercolor videos; series of prints pub., 1995; series of plates publ., 1995; co-curator Tomas Gonda Retrospective, Va. Commonwealth U., Rutgers U., Carnegie Mellon U., others in U.S., Museo Del Arte Moderno, Buenos Aires, Ulmer Mus., Ulm, Germany; illustrator Lights Along the Path, 1999, The Healing Garden, 1999; contbr. articles to profl. jours. Recipient more than 150 awards from various orgns. including Soc. Illustrators, Fed. Design Coun., Comm. Arts Mag., Am. Inst. Graphic Arts, N.Y. Art Dirs. Club, Print Design Ann. Mem. Graphic Artists Guild (dir. 1975-79), Soc. Illustrators, Women Artists of the West, Pa. Watercolor Soc. Studio: 176 E 77th St Apt 11C New York NY 10021-1910 *Finally, I understand that it's the pleasure of the process and the internal knowledge of improvement that gives the greatest satisfaction.*

MORGAN, JAMES C. computer equipment company executive; b. 1938; BSME, MBA, Cornell U.; DEng (hon.), De Anza Coll., 1994. Mem. corp. staff Textron Inc., 1963-72; sr. ptnr. West Ven Mgmt., San Francisco, 1972-76; chmn. bd., pres., CEO Applied Materials, Inc., Santa Clara, Calif., 1976-87, chmn. bd., CEO, 1987—. Co-author Cracking the Japanese Market: Strategies for Success in the New Global Economy. Apptd. by Pres. Clinton to Commn. U.S.-Pacific Trade and Investment Policy, 1996; past mem. Nat. Adv. Com. Semiconductors. Recipient Cmty. Svc. award NCCJ, 1995, Nat. Medal of Tech., Pres. Clinton, 1996; named to Jr. Achievement Hall of Fame, 1991; named Internat. Citizen of Yr., World Forum of Silicon Valley, 1995. Mem. Am. Electronics Assn. (past bd. dirs.), SEMI/SEMATECH (past bd. dirs.), World Presidents Orgn., Congrl. Econ. Leadership Inst. (bd. dirs.), Nat. Ctr. Asia-Pacific Econ. Cooperation (bd. dirs.), Coun. Competitiveness, Pacific Basin Econ. Coun. (chmn.'s circle), Semiconductor Equipment and Materials Internat. (dir. emeritus, past pres.). Office: Applied Materials Inc 3050 Bowers Ave Santa Clara CA 95054-3298*

MORGAN, JAMES DURWARD, retired computer company executive; b. N.Y.C., Sept. 10, 1936; s. Durward Field and Harriet (Airey) M.; m. Ruth Ann Dobson, Jan. 14, 1967; children: Jennifer, Andrew. BEE, Yale U., 1961, MEE, 1962. Systems engr. Calspan Corp., Buffalo, 1962-68; v.p. Comptek Rsch. Inc., 1968—83, 1990—2001, also bd. dirs.; v.p. Barrister Info. Systems Corp., 1983-90, also bd. dirs., 1983—2001. Mem. adv. coun. Erie C.C., Amherst, N.Y., 1985-2000, past chmn.; bd. dirs. Yale Alumni Bd., Buffalo, 1987-2001. Served with USN, 1959-61. Mem.: IEEE, ACM.

MORGAN, JAMES EARL, librarian, administrator; b. Wheeling, W.Va., June 30, 1941; s. James H. L. and Ethel Irene (Goodwin) M.; m. Carman H. Head, Dec. 23, 1966; 1 child, Scott Andrew BS in Edn., Ariz. State Coll., 1965; MSLS, Fla. State U., 1966. Reference asst. social scis. Fla. State U., Tallahassee, 1965-66; head pub. services Ga. Coll., Milledgeville, 1967-69; dir. pub. services U. Tex. Med. Br., Galveston, 1969-73; dir. libraries U. Conn. Health Ctr., Farmington, 1973-76, Oreg. Health Sci. U., Portland, 1976—. Contbr. articles to profl. jours. Grantee Nat. Library Medicine, 1974-76, 78-81 Mem. ALA (life), Med. Libr. Assn. (chmn. Pacific N.W. chpt. 1981), Oreg. Health Scis. Librs. Assn., Pacific N.W. Libr. Assn., Spl. Libr. Assn., Oreg. Libr. Assn., Portland Area Spl. Librarians Assn., Assn. Coll. and Rsch. Librs., Am. Med. Informatics Assn., Nat. Rural Health Assn. Democrat. Office: Oreg Health & Sci U 3181 SW Sam Jackson Park Rd Portland OR 97201-3098 E-mail: morgan@ohsu.edu.

MORGAN, JAMES JOHN, environmental engineering educator; b. N.Y.C., June 23, 1932; s. James and Anna (Treanor) M.; m. Jean Laurie McIntosh, June 15, 1957; children— Jenny, Johanna, Eve, Michael, Martha, Sarah BCE, Manhattan Coll., 1954; MSCE, U. Mich., 1956; postgrad., U. Ill., 1956-60; PhD, Harvard U., 1964; ScD (hon.), Manhattan Coll., 1989. Instr. civil engring. U. Ill., Urbana, 1956-60; assoc. prof. U. Fla., Gainesville, 1963-65, Calif. Inst. Tech., Pasadena, 1965-69, prof. environ. engring., 1969-87, Marvin L. Goldberger prof. environ. engring. sci., 1987—, dean of students, 1972-75, dean grad. studies, 1981-84, v.p. student affairs, 1980-89; exec. officer environ. engring. sci., 1993-96. Mem. environ. studies bd., NRC, 1974-80; chmn. Acid Deposition Sci. Adv. Com., Calif., 1983-98; chmn. Gordon Rsch. Conf. on Environ. Sci.; Water, 1970. Author: (with Werner Stumm) Aquatic Chemistry, 1970, 2d edit., 1981, 3rd edit. 1996; editor Environ. Sci. and Tech., 1966-74; contbr. articles to profl. jours. Recipient Stockholm Water prize, 1999, Clarke Water prize, 1999. Mem. ASCE (award 1997), Am. Chem. Soc. (award 1980), AAAS, Am. Soc. Limnology and Oceanography (editorial bd. 1977-80), Nat. Acad. Engring., Assn. Environ. Engring. Profs. (award 1981, 83, 94), Am. Water Works Assn. (award 1963), Sigma Xi, Chi Epsilon. Clubs: Athenaeum. Democrat. Roman Catholic. Avocations: tennis; folk music. E-mail: morgan. E-mail: morgan_j@caltech.edu.

MORGAN, JAMES PHILIP, pharmacologist, cardiologist, educator; b. Cin., Jan. 13, 1948; s. James Weldon and Dorcas Adele (Meyer) M.; m. Kathleen Greive, Dec. 22, 1973; children: James Patrick, Jonathan Michael. BS, U. Cin., 1970, PhD, 1974, MD, 1976. Diplomate Am. Bd. Internal Medicine, Am. Bd. Cardiovascular Disease. Fellow in internal medicine Mayo Clinic, Rochester, Minn., 1976-79, fellow in cardiovascular disease, 1979-83; asst. in medicine Beth Israel Hosp., Boston, 1983—. Instr. pharmacology U. Cin., 1975—76; asst. prof. pharmacology, instr. medicine Mayo Clinic, 1981—83; asst. prof. medicine Harvard U., Boston, 1983, assoc. prof., 1988—96, Herman Dana prof. medicine, 1996—; affiliate faculty, dept. pharmacology Harvard Med. Sch., 1986—; chief and prgram dir. cardiovascular divsn. Beth Israel Hosp., 1994—2001, vice chmn. medicine, 2000—. Contbr. articles to profl. jours. Recipient Young Investigators award Am. Coll. Cardiology, 1982, Balfour award Mayo Clinic, 1983, Advanced Cardiac Life Support Spl. Recognition award Mayo Clinic, 1983, Rsch. Career Devel. award NIH, 1985-90. Mem. AMA, Am. Heart Assn., Biophys. Soc. Am. Soc. Pharmacology and Exptl. Therapeutics, Masons. Avocation: philatelics. Office: Beth Israel Deaconess Med Ctr 330 Brookline Ave Boston MA 02215-5400 E-mail: jmorgan@caregroup.harvard.edu.

MORGAN, JANE HALE, retired library director; b. Dines, Wyo., May 11, 1926; d. Arthur Hale and Billie (Wood) Hale; m. Joseph Charles Morgan, Aug. 12, 1955; children: Joseph Hale, Jane Frances, Ann Michele. BA, Howard U., 1947; MA, U. Denver, 1954. Staff Detroit Pub. Libr., 1954-87, exec. asst. dir., 1973-75, dep. dir., 1975-78, dir., 1978-87; ret., 1987. Mem. Mich. Libr. Consortium Bd.; exec. bd. Southeastern Mich. Regional Film Libr.; vis. prof. Wayne State U., 1989—. Trustee New Detroit, Inc., Delta Dental Plan of Mich., v.p. Delta Dental Fund, Delta Dental Plan of Ohio; v.p. United Southwestern Mich.; pres. Univ.-Cultural Ctr. Assn.; bd. dirs. Rehab. Inst., YWCA, Met. Affairs Corp., Literacy Vols. Am., Detroit, Mich. Ctr. for the Book, Interfaith Coun.; bd. dirs., v.p. United Comty. Svcs. Met. Detroit; chmn. Detroiters for Adult Reading Excellence; chmn. adv. coun. libr. sci. U. Mich.; mem. adv. coun. libr. sci. U. Mich., mem. adv. coun. libr. sci. Wayne State U.; dir. Met. Detroit Youth Found.; chmn. Mich. LSCA adv. coun.; mem. UWA Literacy Com., Attys. Grievance Com., Women's Commn., Mich. Civil Svc. Rev. Com.; vice-chair Mich. Coun. for Humanities; v.p. Commn. for the Greening of Detroit; adv. com. Headstart; mem. Detroit Women's Com., Detroit Women's Forum, Detroit Exec. Svc. Corps.; sec., treas. Delta Dental Fund, pres., 1999. Recipient Anthony Wayne award Wayne State U., 1981, Summit award Greater Detroit C. of C.; named Detroit Howardite of Year, 1983 Mem. ALA, AAUW, Mich. Library Assn., Women's Nat. Book Assn., Assn. Mcpl. Profl. Women, NAACP, LWV, Women's Econ. Club, Sorosis Club (v.p.), Alpha Kappa Alpha. Democrat. Episcopalian.

MORGAN, JEFF SCOTT, research engineer; b. Salt Lake City, Sept. 3, 1954; s. David Nyle and Dene Huber (Olsen) M.; m. Linda Mae Marquez, May 28, 1982 (div.); m. Stephanie Sugamura, Oct. 25, 1998. BS, U. Calif., San Diego, 1976; MS, U. Hawaii, 1978, PhD, 1982. Rsch. assoc. U. Hawaii, Honolulu, 1982-85; sr. rsch. assoc. Stanford U., Palo Alto, Calif., 1985—90; rsch. engr. U. Wash., Seattle, 1990—. Mem. Am. Astron. Soc. Office: U Wash Dept Astronomy PO Box 351580 Seattle WA 98195-1580

MORGAN, JOAN, financial planner; b. Key West, Fla., Dec. 4, 1953; d. Henry Sturgis Morgan and Fanny Gray Little Pratt. BA, Barnard Coll., 1975; MBA, Columbia U., 1977; postgrad., Adelphi U., 1983. CFP. Assoc., syndicate dept. Morgan Stanley & Co., N.Y.C., 1977-80; fin. planner, asst. v.p. Bankers Trust, 1983-86; prin. Joan Morgan Adminstrv. Svcs., 1986-93; fin. planner Am. Express Fin. Advisors, Inc., Washington, 1993-95, Dondero & Assocs., Ltd., Alexandria, Va., 1997-2000; prin. Joan Morgan Adminstrv. Svcs., 2001—. Bd. dirs. The Madeira Sch., McLean, Va., 1993—, pres., bd. dirs., 2000—; bd. dirs. Ind. Sch. Chairpersons Assn. Mem.: Fin. Planning Assn. Avocations: skiing, rowing. Home: 3133 Connecticut Ave NW Washington DC 20008-5147

MORGAN, JOHN BRUCE, hospital care consultant; b. Youngstown, Ohio, Oct. 25, 1919; s. John Benjamin and Ida May (Lane) M.; m. Marian Frampton, July 11, 1969; children: John B., Carolyn, Leonard, Suzanne (dec.). BS, Miami U., 1941; MBA, Harvard U., 1946. Field rep. Gen. Motors Acceptance Corp., Youngstown, 1941; pres. Asso. Hosp. Service, Inc., 1947-74, Hosp. Care Corp. (Blue Cross), Cin., 1974-83, cons., 1983—; pres. Health Maintenance Plan, 1974-83, Health Care Mutual, Cin., 1974-83. Chmn. bd. govs., chmn. exec. com. Blue Cross Assn., Chgo., 1981-82; chmn. bd. Community Life Ins. Co., Worthington, Ohio, 1979-83; mem. joint exec. com. Blue Cross-Blue Shield Assns., mem. joint bds., Chgo.; mem. bus. adv. com. Miami U., Oxford, Ohio. Gen. chmn. United Fund campaign, Youngstown, 1965; pres. Cancer Soc., 1965; chmn. bd. trustees Ch. of the Palms, 1996. Served with AUS, 1942-46. Mem. Am. Hosp. Assn. (Justin Ford Kimball award 1983), Ohio Hosp. Assn., Ohio C. of C. (bd. dirs.), Youngstown Area C. of C. (pres. 1966-67), Delray Beach, Fla. C. of C., Delray Dunes Golf and Country Club (bd. dirs., v.p.), Rotary (bd. dirs. Delray Beach club, pres. 1992, Paul Harris fellow), Masons, Elks, Sigma Alpha Epsilon, Delta Sigma Pi. Mem. United Ch. of Christ. Home: 9 Slash Pine Dr Boynton Beach FL 33436-5524 Office: 1351 William Howard Taft Rd Cincinnati OH 45206-1721

MORGAN, JOHN DAVID, middle school educator; b. Wilmington, Del., June 7, 1937; s. Eberlin Starr and Elizabeth M. (McKelvie) M. BS, West Chester U., 1960, MEd, 1966. Tchr. Chichester Jr. High Sch., Boothwyn, Pa., 1960-71, Beverly Hills Jr. High Sch., Upper Darby, 1971-80, Beverly Hills Mid. Sch., Upper Darby, 1980-92; sec. membership First Presbyn.Ch., West Chester, Pa., 1997—. Vol. AARP, Meals on Wheals, 1992-, Habitat for Humanity of Chester County, 1999-. Presbyterian. Avocations: collectibles, stamps, travel. Home: 9 S Brandywine St West Chester PA 19382-2826

MORGAN, JOHN DAVIS, consultant; b. Newark, Feb. 14, 1921; s. John Davis and Caroline Frommel (Schaller) M.; m. Leta Maude Bretzinger, June 27, 1953; children: John Davis III, Bret Zinger. BS, Pa. State U., 1942, MS, 1947, PhD, 1948, E.M., 1950; grad. extension course, Indsl. Coll. of Armed Forces, Washington, 1953. Asst. for materials and stockpile policies Nat. Security Resources Bd., Washington, 1948-51; dir. materials rev. div. DPA, 1951-53; materials expert ODM, 1953-56; mem. staff President's Cabinet Com. on Mineral Policy, 1953-54; cons. bus. and def. problems in metals, minerals and fuels Washington, 1956-71; mem. nat. def. exec. res. for ODM, 1956-58, OCDM, 1958-61, Office Emergency Planning, 1961-71, Emergency Minerals Adminstrn., 1972-95; mem. spl. stockpile advisory com. to ODM, 1957-58; com. on scope and conduct of materials research NAS, 1959-60, then, mem. com. on mineral sci. and tech., 1966-70; mem. Interagy. Adv. Com. on Mining and Mineral Research, 1977-95. Head dept. sci. and math. Daytona Beach C.C., Fla., 1961-71; asst. dir. mineral position analysis U.S. Bur. Mines, Dept. Interior, Washington, 1971-74, acting dir. bur., 1973-74, 77-78, assoc. dir. mineral and materials supply/demand analysis, 1974-79, chief staff officer, 1979-95, Interior Dept. liaison to Com. Internat. Econ. Policy Staff, 1973-77, to Econ. Policy Bd. Staff, 1974-77, to Dept. Def. Materials Steering Group, 1975-78, to FPA-FEMA Stockpile Com., 1975-88, to Winter Energy Emergency Planning Group of Dept. of Energy, 1977-81; alt. Interior rep. Trade Policy Rev. Group, 1975-81; chmn. minerals rev. com. Non-Fuel Minerals Policy Study, 1978; chmn. materials supply task force NSC Stockpile Study, 1983-87; liaison to Dept. Def. Stockpile Com., 1988-95; mem. Def. Logistics Agy. Market Impact Com., 1988-95; mem. Def. Dept. Adv. Com. Operation and Modernization of Stockpile, 1993-95; U.S. rep. UN Sci. Conf. on Resources, 1949; lectr. numerous univs. including Nat. Def. U., War Coll., Indsl. Coll., Def. Intelligence Coll., Army War Coll., 1949—; hon. prof. Indsl. Coll., 1983—; invited spkr. nat. meetings sci. and engrng. socs., 1949—. Author: Domestic Mining Industry of the U.S. in World War II, 1949; corr.: Mining Ann. Rev., London, 1958-95; contbr. articles to profl. jours. Served from 2d lt. to maj. Corps Engrs. AUS, 1942-46. Decorated Bronze Star; recipient Distinguished Service gold medal Interior Dept., 1976; named Meritorious Exec. Sr. Exec. Service, 1983 Fellow Soc. Am. Mil. Engrs.; mem. Sci. Research Soc. Am., Soc. Mining Engrs. (Disting. mem.), AIME (nat. Krumb lectr. 1973, Legion of Honor 1989), Sigma Xi, Tau Beta Pi, Sigma Tau, Pi Mu Epsilon, Phi Lambda Upsilon, Phi Kappa Phi, Phi Eta Sigma, Sigma Gamma Epsilon. Clubs: Cosmos (Washington). Home: 5013 Worthington Dr Bethesda MD 20816-2748

MORGAN, JOHN DERALD, electrical engineer; b. Hays, Kans., Mar. 15, 1939; s. John Baber and Avis Ruth (Wolf) M.; m. Elizabeth June McKneely, June 23, 1962; children: Laura Elizabeth, Kimberly Ann, Rebecca Ruth, John Derald. BSEE, La. Tech. U., 1962; MS, U. Mo., Rolla, 1965, Degree in Elec. Engrng. (hon.), 1987; PhD, Ariz. State U., 1968. Registered profl. engr., forensic engr., Mo., N.Mex. Elec. engr. Tex. Eastman div. Eastman Kodak Co., 1962-63; instr. U. Mo., Rolla, 1963-65, Ariz. State U., 1965-68; asso. prof. elec. engring. U. Mo., Rolla, 1968-72, Alcoa Found. prof. elec. engring., 1972-75, chmn. elec. engring., 1978-85, assoc. dir. Ctr. Internat. Programs, 1970-78, Emerson Electric prof., 1975-85; dean engring. N.Mex. State U., 1985-99; v.p. univ. advancement U. Ala. in Huntsville, 1999—; exec. sec. U. Ala. Huntsville Found., 1999—. Nat. adv. com. Engring. Exploring; cons. to industry. Author: Power Apparatus Testing Techniques, 1969, Computer Monitoring and Control of Electric Utility Systems, 1972, Control and Distribution of Megawatts Through Man-Machine Interaction, 1973, Electromechanical and Electromagnetic Machines and Devices, 1986; also articles. Pres. bd. trustees First United Meth. Ch., Rolla, 1971-73, pres. adminstrv. bd., 1978-79; v.p., mem. bd. adminstrn. People to People, 1976; bd. dirs., cubmaster Ozarks dist. Boy Scouts Am., 1968-79, asst. dist. commr., 1971-73, cubmaster Yucca coun., 1986-90, coun. commr., 1989-90, asst. scout master, 1990-99, dist. com. Sunshine Dist., dist. chmn. Meramec dist., 1978-80, engring. exploring nat. com.; chmn. Creek Dist., 2000—, bd. mem., Greater Ala. Cornell No. Svc. Dist., 2000—; bd. dirs. Mo. Partners of the Americas. Recipient Scouters Key award and Scouter Tng. award Ozarks coun., Boy Scouts Am., 1971, Dist. award of merit 1977, Silver Beaver award, 1982, Cub Leader award, Webelos Leader award, James West Soc. award, Sunshine Dist. Yucca coun.; T.H. Harris scholar, 1959-61; John H. Horton scholar, 1961-62. Fellow IEEE (chmn. internat. practices subcom. 1972-79, sec. PSE com., vice chmn., chmn. 1979-85, chmn. ednl. resources subcom. 1973-78, selected award of Merit St. Louis sect., Educators award St. Louis sect., honor award St. Louis sect., Centennial award 1984), Nat. Acad. Forensic Engrs., ASTM; mem. NSPE (bd. govs., nat. dir., vice chmn., S.W. chmn. Profl. Engrs. in Edn.. v.p., mem. Steinman Coun.), N.Mex. Soc. Profl. Engrs. (N.Mex. Engr. of Yr. 1993), Am. Soc. Engring. Edn. (chair bylaws com. 1999-2001), Sigma Xi, Tau Beta Pi, Eta Kappa Nu, Omicron Delta Kappa, Phi Kappa Phi, Kappa Sigma (faculty and alumni advisor), Epsilon Gamma (grand master, grand procurator, PSI exec. of yr. 1993), SAR, Rotary Internat. (Paul Harris fellow 1997). Home: 113 Lansdowne Dr Madison AL 35758-7613 Office: U Ala in Huntsville Alumni House 102 Huntsville AL 35899-0001

MORGAN, JOHN RONALD, pediatric cardiologist; b. Ft. Payne, Ala., Mar. 29, 1940; s. Ronald R. and Miriam Josephine (Johnson) M.; m. Donna Louise Gardner, Dec. 26, 1961; children: Susan E., John David, Michael A., Stephen G. BA, David Lipscomb U., 1962; MD, Vanderbilt U., 1966. Diplomate Am. Bd. Pediatrics. Dir. pediatric cardiology T.C. Thompson Children's Hosp., Chattanooga, 1973—; prof. pediatrics U. Tenn. Coll. Medicine. Bd. dirs. Boyd-Buchanan Sch., Chattanooga, 1980—. Capt. USAF, 1968-70. Fellow Am. Acad. of Pediatrics, Am. Coll. Cardiology; mem. Alpha Omega Alpha. Mem. Ch. of Christ. Avocations: scouting, computer. Office: Children's Hosp 910 Blackford St Chattanooga TN 37403-1499

MORGAN, JOHN WALTER, research geochemist; b. Walsall, Eng., Jan. 27, 1932; s. Harold Waldo and Annie (Homer) M.; m. Juliet Wall, Feb. 28, 1959 (div. 1989); children: Susan, Alan. BSc in Pure Scis., Birmingham (Eng.) U., 1955; PhD in Geochemistry, Australian Nat. U., Canberra, 1966. Exptl. officer Australian Atomic Energy Commn., Lucas Heights, NSW, Australia, 1959-61; rsch. asst. Australian Nat. U., Canberra, ACT, Australia, 1961-66, rsch. fellow Australia, 1966; sr. rsch. scientist Australian Atomic Energy Commn., Lucas Heights, 1966-68; rsch. assoc. U. Ky., Lexington, 1968-70; sr. rsch. assoc. U. Chgo., 1970-76; assoc. prof. U. Tex., San Antonio, 1976-78; rsch. chemist U.S. Geol. Survey, Reston, Va., 1977-80, chief chemist, 1980-85, rsch. chemist, 1985-95, Gilbert fellow, 1986-87, Isotope br. rep., 1987-94; sci. advisor U.S. Nat. Park Svc., Washington, 1985-86; sr. rsch scientist U. Md., College Park, 1995—2002, Colo. State U., Fort Collins, 1995—2001. Mem. radio-isotope applications com. Australian Atomic Energy Commn., Lucas Heights, 1966-68; prin. U.S. del. Internat. Assn. Volcanology and Chemistry of Earth's Interior, 1979; mem. lunar and planetary panel NASA, Houston, 1981-82, mem. spl. meteorite working group, 1982-83, mem. rev. panel for planetary instrument definition and devel. program, 1997; mem. internat. coordinating com. U.S. Geol. Survey, Reston, 1982-83, mem. reactor ops. com., 1980-95. Contbr. articles to profl. jours., chpts. to books. Recipient traveling fellowship Australian Nat. U., Canberra, 1966, Gilbert fellowship U.S. Geol. Survey, Reston, 1986-87, meritorious svc. award U.S. Geol. Survey, 1991; grantee Welch Found., San Antonio, 1976, NASA, San Antonio, 1976, Reston, 1977-81, 90-95, College Park, 1995-2002, NSF, Fort Collins, 1996-98, 97-99, College Park, 1998-2002. Mem. Internat. Assn. for Volcanology and Chemistry of Earth's Interior (mem. internat. nominating com. 1983, prin. U.S. del. 1983, mem. U.S. nat. com. 1982-87), Internat. Union Geodesy and Geophysics, Am. Geophys. Union, Meteoritical Soc. Avocations: fair-to-middling ragtime and jazz pianist, running, reading. E-mail: csmium186@earthlink.net.

MORGAN, JOYCE KAYE, social worker; b. Acme, Pa., July 17, 1941; d. Jesse Gray and Lillian (Kubick) Hoyman; m. James Edward Morgan, Oct. 13, 1967. BS in Secondary Edn., Calif. State Coll., 1963; MSW, W.Va. U., 1967. Cert. social worker; lic. social worker, Pa.; bd. cert. diplomate social work. Tchr. Scottdale (Pa.) Jr.-Sr. High Sch., 1963-64, Hempfield Jr. High, Greensburg, Pa., 1966; social worker, supr. Rosewood State Hosp., Owings Mills, Md., 1967-72, Latrobe (Pa.) Area Hosp., 1974-79; pvt. practice Mt. Pleasant, Pa., 1987-2000. Mem. Multi Disciplinary Team Child Abuse, Greensburg, Pa., 1978-79; sec. adv. bd. Westmoreland County Children's Bur., Greensburg, 1979-83. Avocations: gardening, crafts, painting. Home: RR 5 Box 484 Mount Pleasant PA 15666-8927

MORGAN, KATE TARLOW, artist; b. N.Y.C., Mar. 15, 1954; d. Thomas Bruce and Joan Zuckerman Morgan. M in Cultural History, NYU, 1986; cert., Sch. for Body-Mind Centering, 1989. Urban archaeologist, N.Y.C., 1979-89; dance tchr. N.Y.C., Alstead, N.H., 1986—; movement therapist, 1991—; curriculum cons., 1996-99. Organizer, founder Pinkster Festival, Bklyn., 1990-91; writer archaeology curriculum South St. Seaport Mus., N.Y.C., 1999; trustee Orchard Sch., Alstead, 1998—. Exhibited works at Grand Monadnock Arts, Keene, N.H., 1998, 99; dancer, dir. (multi-media performance video) Red Train/Blue Brain, 1997, The El, 1999, In Transit, 2000. Grantee Arts Internat., Washington, 1994, Coun. for Basic Edn., Washington, 1995. Mem. Body-Mind Centering (editl. bd.). Jewish. Avocations: swimming, traveling, oral history, movies, salsa dancing. Home: 55 Bley Rd Alstead NH 03602

MORGAN, KATHRYN GRACE, health facility administrator, community caregiver; b. Phila., June 12, 1963; d. Guido Gary and Eleanor Patterson Inforzato; children: Ashley Marie, Joseph Capasso. Student, Temple U., 2001—. Sr. claims examiner John Hancock/TPL, Devon, Pa., 1989—96; sr. operator, asst. supr. Healthphone, Upper Darby, 1997—99; customer svc. rep. Keystone Mercy PS/RMU, Phila., 1999—. Mem. editl. bd. On Que-Keystone Mercy Health Plan, Phila., 2000, ERP bd. mem., 00. Cmty. caregiver CYS, Upper Darby, 2000—; team leader mission partnership Keystone Mercy Health Plan, Phila., 2000—. Democrat. Baptist. Avocations: reading, helping children, drawing, jazz. Office: Keystone Mercy Health Plan 200 Stevens Dr Philadelphia PA 19113

MORGAN, KERMIT JOHNSON, lawyer; b. Henderson, Iowa, Feb. 13, 1914; s. Samuel Jr. and Jennie Amelia Morgan; m. Georgina R. Morgan, Oct. 12, 1940 (dec. 1958); children: Georgina Morgan Street, Wilson S.; m. Ortrud Impol, Dec. 9, 1960. BA, U. Iowa, 1935; JD, U. So. Calif., 1937. Bar: Calif. 1939. Pvt. practice, L.A., 1940—45; ptnr. McBain & Morgan, 1945-65, McBain, Morgan & Roper, L.A., 1965-71, Morgan & Armbrister, L.A., 1980-91; pvt. practice, Santa Monica, Calif., 1991—. Mem. ABA, Am. Bd. Trial Advs. (diplomate, nat. pres. 1973, pres. L.A. 1972, 77), Assn. Def. Trial Attys. (bd. dirs. 1982-85), Internat. Assn. Ins. Counsel, Hon. Order of Blue Goose, Calif. State Bar, Assn. So. Calif. Def. Counsel (bd. dirs. 1966-67), L.A. Bar Assn., Wilshire Bar Assn. Republican. Congregationalist. Avocation: golf. Home: 2108 Stradella Rd Los Angeles CA 90077-2325 Office: 3420 Ocean Pk Blvd Santa Monica CA 90405

MORGAN, LARRY RONALD, minister; b. Springhill, La., Mar. 12, 1936; s. Woodrow Wilson Morgan and Alma Elizabeth (Dunn) Burch; m. Elizabeth Dianne Baker, May 24, 1958; children: Elizabeth Denise Morgan Davis, Dennis Kevin. ADiv, Bapt. Missionary Assn. Theol. Sem., Jacksonville, Tex., 1990. Ordained to ministry Bapt. Ch., 1971. Clk., carrier U.S. P.O., Springhill, La., 1956-71; assoc. pastor Webb Chapel Bapt. Ch., Dallas, 1971-72, pastor, 1972-99, First Bapt. Ch., Springhill, La., 1999—. Clk., trustee Bapt. Missionary Assn. Sem., Jacksonville, 1983-86; chmn. bd. trustees Bapt. Progress, Dallas, 1984-87. Pres. PTA Browning Elem. Sch., Springhill, 1969-70. With USAR, 1959-66. Mem. Bapt. Missionary Assn. Am. (v.p. hdqrs. Little Rock 1985-86, pres. 1986-88, v.p. Am. 1996-98, pres. 1998-2000), Dallas County Bapt. Assn. (moderator 1982-84), Bapt. Missionary Assn. of La. (moderator 2000—)., Springhill Baptist Assn. (moderator 2001-). Home: 611 Butler St Springhill LA 71075-2519 E-mail: ronaldmorgan1@juno.com.

MORGAN, LEON ALFORD, retired utility executive; b. Washington, Dec. 29, 1934; s. Albert Lewis and Alice Viets (Alford) M.; children: David Richard, Sherry Alice; m. Jacqueline Jamieson, Feb. 14, 1993. BSEE, Worcester (Mass.) Poly. Inst., 1957. Registered profl. engr., Conn. With United Illuminating Co., New Haven, 1957-94, gen. ops. mgr., then v.p. ops., 1973-76, exec. v.p., 1976-83, sr. v.p. fin., 1984-94. Republican. Episcopalian. Home: 43 Forest Brook Rd Guilford CT 06437-2245 E-mail: lamorgan@cshore.com.

MORGAN, LESLIE TALBOT, English language educator; b. Radford, Va., Nov. 2, 1968; d. David Conrad and Wilna Faye (Buckingham) M. BA, U. Mich., 1991; MA, U. Tex., 1994. Vice-chief instr. GEOS, Shiki, Japan, 1994-97; instr. Bunkyo Univ. Women's Coll., Chigasaki, Japan, 1997-2000, The Internat. Sch. Choueifat, Cairo, 2000—. Mem. Phi Kappa Phi. Avocations: hiking, art. Home: 204 Rockingham Dr Columbia MO 65203-1645 Office: Internat Sch Choueifat-Cairo PO Box 2760 Al Horreya Heliopolis Egypt

MORGAN, LINDA GAIL, b. Tallahassee, May 14, 1952; d. Thomas Mitchell Morgan Sr. and Helen Frances (Rives) Stokes. BS, Fla. State U., 1974. Prodn. mgr. Valley Forge Ballet-5th World Peace Youth Culture Festival, Honolulu, 1985, Salute to Lady Liberty, Madison Square Gardens, 1986, U.S. Constn. 200 Yr. Anniversary Parade, Phila., 1986-89, Columbus Day Parade, N.Y.C., 1988, Gift of the White Bird Parade-Landmark Entertainment, Oita, Japan, 1990-91, 1996 Olympic Opening and Closing Ceremonies-Centenniel Events, Inc., Olympic Stadium, Atlanta, 1996, Super Bowl XXXI Half Time Show, New Orleans, 1997, N.Y. Jets Halftime Show, Meadowlands Stadium, N.J., 1997; prodn. state mgr. Walt Disney Bus. Prodns., 1998; coordinating prodr. (musical) This Is America, The New World, Freedom Music, Santa Monica, Calif., 1989, California Traditional Music Festival, Human Rights Lectr. Series, Soka U. Am., L.A., 1992-95, The Genius and the Great, L.A., 1993, Every Child Deserves a Chance, L.A., 1994, A Tribute to Burt Reynolds, L.A., 1994, Celebrate the Garnet and Gold IV Honoring Charles Nelson Reilly, L.A., 1995, Leisure Quest Internat./Entertainment Devel. Group, Burbank, Calif., 1997; artist agt., co. gen. mgr. Zoli Mgmt., Inc., N.Y.C., 1986-89; orch. prodn. mgr. All Am. Gen. Meeting, Spectrum, Phila., 1987; asst. prodn. mgr. 8th World Peace Culture Festival, Fukuoka, Japan, 1987, This Is America, Madison Square Gardens, 1988, 1991 Olympic Festival Opening Ceremonies Radio City Spl. Events, Dodger Stadium, L.A., 1991; prodn. staff Inauguration Mayor of Atlanta, Civic Ctr., Atlanta, 1998; event mgr. Coke on Ice World of Coca Cola, Atlanta, 1997-98, Disney Events Productions, 1998-2001; prodr. Anheuser-Bush Creative Svcs., 2001-. Mem. Soka Gakkai Internat. (arts divsn. culture dept. 1995-99), Fla. State U. So. Calif. Alumni Assn. (bd. dirs. 1991-95, Garnet/Gold award 1995), Internat. Spl. Event Soc., Alpha Chi Omega. Democrat. Buddhist. Avocations: arts, needlepoint, antiques, piano, gardening.

MORGAN, LINDA JOAN, federal agency administrator; b. Chester County, Pa., May 19, 1952; m. Michael E. Karam; 1 child, Meredith Lyn. AB in Hispanic Studies, Vassar Coll., 1973; JD, Georgetown U., 1976; postgrad., Harvard U., 1991. Assoc. Welch & Morgan, Washington, 1976-78; staff counsel U.S. Senate Com. on Commerce, Sci. and Transp., 1978-86, gen. counsel, 1987-94; mem. ICC, Washington, 1994-96, chmn., 1995-96, Surface Transp. Bd., Washington, 1996—. Mem. D.C. Bar Assn., Bar of Supreme Ct. of U.S., Women's Bar Assn., Women's Transp. Seminar. Office: Surface Transp Bd 1925 K St NW Mercury Bldg Washington DC 20423-0001

MORGAN, LINDA RICE, secondary education educator; b. Troy, Ohio, Feb. 14, 1949; d. George William and Eileen Dolores (Sines) R.; m. Thomas Buford Morgan, Nov. 25, 1978; 1 child, Malory Sue. BA, Marshall U., 1971, MS, 1974. Cert. profl. tchr., W.Va. Tchr. Marshall U. Community Coll., Huntington, W.Va., part-time 1977-79, Fairfield Sch., Cabell County Pub. Schs., Huntington, 1971-80; tchr. bus. edn. Huntington High Sch., 1980—, chmn. dept. bus., 1989—. Bd. dirs. Tri-State Montessori Pre-Sch., 1988-89. Mem. NEA, W.Va. Edn. Assn., Nat. Bus. Edn. Assn., Cabell County Edn. Assn., Phi Delta Kappa. Democrat. Avocations: reading, raising Chinese SharPeis, movies. Home: 2224 Pleasant Valley Dr Huntington WV 25701-9304 E-mail: lsmorgan@access.k12.wv.us.

MORGAN, LUCY WARE, journalist; b. Memphis, Oct. 11, 1940; d. Thomas Allin and Lucile (Sanders) Keen; m. Alton F. Ware, June 26, 1958 (div. Sept. 1967); children: Mary Kathleen, Andrew Allin; m. Richard Alan Morgan, Aug. 9, 1968; children: Lynn Elwell, Kent Morgan AA, Pasco Hernando C.C., New Port Richey, Fla., 1975; student, U. South Fla., 1976-80. Reporter Ocala Star Banner, Fla., 1965-68, St. Petersburg Times, 1968-, capitol bur. chief, 1986—. Assoc. editor and bd. dirs. Times Pub. Co. Recipient Paul Hansel award Fla. Soc. Newspaper Editors, 1981, First in Pub. Service award Fla. Soc. Newspaper Editors, 1982, First Place award in pub. service Fla. Press Club, 1982, Pulitzer award for investigative reporting Columbia U., 1985, First Place award in investigative reporting Sigma Delta Chi, 1985; named to Kappa Tau Alpha Hall of Fame, 1992. Home: 7030 Spencer Dr Tallahassee FL 32312-3548 Office: St Petersburg Times 336 E College Ave Tallahassee FL 32301-1551

MORGAN, M. JANE, computer systems consultant; b. Washington, July 21, 1945; d. Edmond John and Roberta (Livingstone) Dolphin (dec.); 1 child, Sheena Anne. Student, U. Md., 1963-66, Montgomery Coll., 1966-70; BA in Applied Behavioral Sci with honors, Nat.-Louis Univ., 1987, MS in Mgmt., 1991; postgrad. diploma in info. resource mgmt, Am. U., 1995; cert., USDA Grad. Sch., 2000; postgrad. diploma, State U. Calif., Northridge, 2002. With HUD, Washington, 1965-84, computer specialist, 1978-84; pres., CEO Systems and Mgmt. Assocs., 1983-91; dir. systems engring. Advanced Tech. Systems, Inc., Vienna, 1984-86, sr. cons., 1989; chief tech. staff Tech. and Mgmt. Svcs., Inc., 1986-89; sr. computer scientist Integrated Systems divsn. Computer Scis. Corp., 1989-90; computer systems specialist gen. svcs. adminstrn. U.S. Govt., 1991—2001; divsn. dir. U.S. Gen. Svcs. Adminstrn., 2001—. Mgmt. cons. Author: Radid Identification of Critical Staff, 1991. Bd. dirs. PL Active. Mem. Federally Employed Women (life, nat. exec. v.p. 1998-2000), Order Eastern Star. Episcopalian.

MORGAN, MARABEL, author; b. Crestline, Ohio, June 25, 1937; d. Howard and Delsa (Smith) Hawk; m. Charles O. Morgan, Jr., June 25, 1964; children— Laura Lynn, Michelle Rene. Ed., Ohio State U. Pres. Total Woman, Inc., Miami, Fla., 1970—. Pub. speaker. Author: The Total Woman, 1973, Total Joy, 1976, The Total Woman Cookbook, 1980, The Electric Woman, 1985. Office: c/o Total Woman Inc 1300 NW 167th St Ste 3 Miami FL 33169-5738

MORGAN, MARIANNE, corporate professional; b. Muncie, Ind., Oct. 13, 1940; d. Clarence Wilson and Mary Estle (Shafer) M. BA, Calif. State U., Long Beach, 1962; MS, U. So. Calif., 1968. Lic. real estate salesperson, Fla. Lab. technician Ball Meml. Hosp. Pathology Lab, Muncie, 1956-61; sr. libr. asst. Anaheim (Calif.) Pub. Libr., 1963-68; coll. libr. Orange Coast Coll., Costa Mesa, Calif., 1968-73; exec. v.p. Brady Products, Inc., Clearwater, Fla., 1973—. Bd. dirs. Brady Products, Inc., Clearwater, Suncoast Fluid Power, Inc., Clearwater. Fiction book reviewer, Libr. Jour., 1969-73; photography pub. in Irvine mag., 1973. Named Alice Miriam Kitselman Scholar, Kitselman Estate, Muncie, 1958. Mem. Nat. Water Well Assn., Boat Owners of the U.S., U.S. Tennis Assn., Sea Ray Boat Owners Club, RVing Women, Carefree Club, Sapphire Lakes Country Club, The Cliffs Country Club. Republican. Avocations: boating, tennis, photography, travel, raising AKC Bulldogs.

MORGAN, MARK QUENTEN, astrophysics educator; b. Topeka, Dec. 27, 1950; s. Walter Quenten and Barbara Gene (Haynes) M. BA in Astronomy, San Diego State U., 1972; PhD in Astronomy, U. Addison, Ont., Can., 1976. Jet engine and power plant engr. N.Am. Aviation, Palmdale, Calif., 1966-68; astron. observer San Diego State U., 1970-74; engr., solar observer U. Md.-Clark Lake Radio Obs., Borrego Springs, Calif., 1978-82; engr., lectr. Sci. Atlanta, San Diego, 1979-97; adv. rsch. engr. Intel Corp., 1998—. Inventor continuous wave laser, 1965, high intensity sound acoustic screening system, 1979. Mem. Inst. Environ. Scis., Acoustic Soc. Am., Astrophys. Soc. Am., Union Concerned Scientists, Planetary Soc. Office: Sci Atlanta PO Box 4254 San Diego CA 92164-4254

MORGAN, MARY DAN, librarian; b. Tallulah, La., Nov. 30, 1943; d. Daniel Boone and Mary Louise (McLeod) M.; m. William Jefferson Day (div. Dec. 1995); 1 child, Forrest Jefferson Day. BA, La. Coll., 1965; MS in Libr. Sci., La. State U., 1968; MA in Edn., Murray State U., 1976; MS in Social Work, U. Louisville, 1992. Cert. social worker, Ky., Ind. Libr. Ascension Parish Schs., Donaldsonville, La., 1966-68, Jefferson County Schs., Louisville, 1968-75; tchr. Webster County Schs., Dixon, 1975-79, Hardin County Schs., Elizabethtown, 1979-82, dir. media ctr., 1982-87, tchr. day and residential juvenile facilities, 1987-91, tchr. mid. and sr. high alt. schs., 1991-93; social worker Hospice of Ctrl. Ky., 1993-2000, Gentiva Health Svcs., Louisville, 1995, Lincoln Trail Dist. Home Health, Elizabethtown, 1997-98; libr. Luther Luckett Correctional Complex, La Grange, Ky., 2000—. Pres. Webster County Tchrs. Assn., Dixon, Ky., 1977-78; sec. Ky. Libr. Network Bd., Frankfort, 1986-87. Mem. NEA (life), NASW, AAUW, Filson Club, Am. Libr. Assn. Office: Luther Luckett Correctional Complex PO Box 6 La Grange KY 40031

MORGAN, MARY ANN, lawyer; b. Orlando, Fla., Mar. 12, 1955; d. Charles Clayburn and Eileen Louise (Mutzbauer) M.; m. Patrick Thomas Burke, Dec. 12, 1992. BS in Criminology, Fla. State U., 1978, JD, 1986. Bar: Fla. 1986, U.S. Dist. Ct. (mid. dist.) Fla. 1986, U.S. Supreme Ct. Investigator Auditor Gen.'s Office State of Fla., Orlando, 1979-83; staff analyst criminal justice com. Fla. Ho. of Reps., Tallahassee, 1985-86; ptnr. Billings, Cunningham, Morgan & Boatwright, Orlando, 1986—. Chmn. renovation com. Orange County Hist. Mus., Orlando, 1995—; spkr. Physician/Lawyer Drug Awareness Program, Orange County Schs., Orlando, 1997. Mem. ABA, ATLA, Fla. Bar Assn. (spkrs. bur. 1997, chair grievance com. 1993-96, vice chair 9th jud. cir. fee arbitration com.), Orange County Bar Assn. (exec. coun. 1991—, chmn. renovation com. 1995—, del. ABA 1989, 90, pres. young lawyers sect. 1990-91, pres. 2001—), Acad. Fla. Trial Lawyers, Ctrl. Fla. Assn. for Women Lawyers (bd. dirs. 1990-92), Fla. State U. Alumni Assn. (bd. dirs. 1996—), Orange County Legal Aid Soc. (bd. dirs. 1997—, pres.-elect 1998-99, pres. 1999—), Nat. Assn. Women Lawyers, Am. Inns of Ct., Tiger Bay Club, Million Dollar Advs. Club. Avocations: waterskiing, golf, boating. Office: Billings Cunningham Morgan & Boatwright 330 E Central Blvd Orlando FL 32801-1921

MORGAN, MARY LOU, retired education educator, civic worker; b. Chgo., Mar. 5, 1938; d. William Nicholas and Esther Lucille (Galbraith) Wanmer; m. James Edward Morgan, May 30, 1963. *Mary Lou's father, Dr. William Wanmer, AB, DC, class president, descended from Daniel Olmstead, New York, a son of the American Revolution. Her mother, Esther Galbraith, Emmons regional manager, Missouri/California, was daughter of Dr. Amos, DC; principal, Illinois. Her sister, Dr. Sally Thomas, RN, PhD, was a nationally prominent researcher, fellow of American Academy of Nursing and was UCLA department head and Associate Professor. Her brother, William, AB, MS, was Executive director of a treatment center, a boys ranch director, principal, and mentor teacher in California. Her spouse, James is a 35-year Boeing, Wichita employee, a WWII veteran, and an American Political Dynasties descendant of Israel Washburn, DAR #55527, in Missouri.* BA in Bus. Edn. and Econs., Wichita State U., 1971, MEd in Student Pers. and Guidance, 1974; postgrad., Kans. State U., 1986. Cert. bus. tchr., Kans. Reservationist Braniff, Wichita, Kans., 1961-62; stenographer, fin. analyst, clk.-typist Boeing Co., 1962-68, tng., pers. and records positions, 1979-93; pers. cons. Rita Pers. Svc., 1974-75; adminstrv. aide, manpower specialist, job developer City of Wichita, 1975-76; account exec., employment counselor Mgmt. Recruiters, 1976-77; pers. mgr., patient cons. Women's Clinic, 1977; vocat. rehab. counselor State of Kans., Parsons, 1977-79; pvt. detective Investigation Svcs., Wichita, 1981-84; instr. career devel. Wichita State U., 1988-90. Paralegal asst. Turner & Hensley, Wichita, 1975. Coord. funding Women's Crisis Ctr., Wichita, 1975; docent Carver Mus., Hoover Mus.; vice chmn. Hist. Preservation Commn.; founder, coord. Am. Women's Chautauqua; Precinct committeewoman Wichita Dem. Com., 1992—94; pres. Jasper County-Newton County Dems., 1998; mem. Grover Beach Dems., 2001—; bd. dirs. City of Wichita, Wichita Commn. on Status of Women, 1988—91. Mem.: NOW (founder, 1st pres., v.p. program chmn. Wichita chpt. 1969—93, asst. state coord. polit. action com. Wichita chpt. 1993—95, at-large state bd. Joplin com. 1994—95, 1997—98, 1999—2000, at-large state mem. Grover Beach chpt. 2001—), AARP, LWV (v.p. issues study Joplin area chpt. 1998—2000, Grover Beach chpt. 2001—, off board dir. 2002—), AAUW (bd. dirs. edn., equity, women's issues Joplin br. 1999—2000, Grover Beach br. 2001—, pres.-elect Grover Beach br. 2002—). Avocations: water skiing, boating, collecting Victorian clothing, travel.

MORGAN, MARY LOUISE FITZSIMMONS, fund raising executive, lobbyist; b. N.Y.C., July 22, 1946; d. Robert John and Mary Louise (Gordon) Fitzsimmons; m. David William Morgan, Aug. 7, 1971; children: Mallory Siobhan, David William. BA, Marquette U., 1964; MA, Catholic U., Wash., 1966. Asst. prof. Monmouth U., West Long Branch, N.J., 1966-69; campaign dir. United Way, N.Y.C., 1969-80; pres. Morgan Communications, 1980-82; capital campaign dir. YMCA of Greater N.Y., 1982-85; dir. devel. N.Y. Med. Coll., Valhalla, 1985-88; counsel Challenger Ctr., Va., 1988-89; v.p. Ctr. Molecular Medicine & Immunology, Newark, 1989-92, Garden State Cancer Ctr., Newark, 1989-92; chief devel. and pub. affairs officer Mental Health Assn., White Plains, N.Y., 1993-95; dir. external affairs St. Vincents Svcs., 1996—. Adj. prof. Iona Coll., New Rochelle, N.Y., 1994-95; dir. Meth Ch. Home for Aged, Riverdale, N.Y., Casita Maria Inc., N.Y.C., 1975-95; pres., founding dir. Achievement Rewards for Coll. Scientists Inc., 1978-80. Sec. Darien (Conn.) Dem. Town Com., 1984—, vice chmn. Darien nominating com. 1986—. Recipient 50th Anniversary award Casita Maria Inc., N.Y.C., 1984, Iris award Bus. Communicators of Am., 1991, Nat. Depression Awareness Campaign award NMHA, 1994.Am. Graphic Design Awd., 2002. Mem. Nat. Soc. Fund Raising Execs., Nat. Soc. Hosp. Adminstrn., Spring Lake (N.J.) Bath and Tennis Club. Democrat. Roman Catholic. Avocations: golf, gardening, tennis. Office: 66 Boerum Pl Brooklyn NY 11201-5705 E-mail: MaryL.Morgan@svs.org.

MORGAN, MICHAEL VINCENT, lawyer; b. July 31, 1947; s. Stanley William and Alice (Michalski) M.; m. Susan Wanda Staub, Aug. 21, 1970; children: Jason, Allison. BA, U. Detroit, 1969, JD, 1972. Bar: Mich. 1972, U.S. Dist. Ct. (ea. dist.) Mich. 1972. Chmn. Lic. Appeal Bd. Mich. Dept. State, Detroit, 1972-73; pvt. practice, 1973-75, Troy, Mich., 1975—. Lectr. in field. Editor: Michigan Drunk Driving Law & Practice, 1986, 3rd edit. 1999; contbr. articles to profl. publs. Bd. dirs. U. Detroit Nat. Alumni Bd., 1974-77. Recipient Athletic Dirs. award U. Detroit, 1983. Mem. Mich. Bar Assn., U. Detroit Law Alumni Assn. (bd. dirs. 1996—), Titan Club (bd. dirs. 1982-86), Advocates Club (Detroit). Roman Catholic. Office: 3155 W Big Beaver Rd Ste 100 Troy MI 48084-3006

MORGAN, MONROE, retired savings and loan executive; b. Long Beach, Calif., Sept. 4, 1921; s. Karle Barett and Ethel (Monroe) M.; m. Ann Betts, Sept. 30, 1949; children: Sarah Nell, Daniel, Margaret Jane BA, Pomona Coll., 1942. Cert. vol. counselor Health Ins. Counseling and Advocacy Program, Calif. Acctg. exec. Coast Fed. Savs. and Loan Assn., Los Angeles, 1945-50; sec., treas. Am. Savs. and Loan Assn., Whittier, Calif., 1952-56; sr. v.p. Gt. Western Fin. Corp., Beverly Hills, 1956-87. Also officer subs. savs. and loan assns.; trustee Depositors Investment Trust, 1984-85; mem. investment mgmt. com. Internat. Found. Employees Plans, 1970-76; chmn. Thrift Industry Acctg. Com., 1976-78 Active Los Angeles County Art Mus.; chmn. Ethnic Arts Coun., 1977-80; dir. non-profit food distbn. orgn. Love Is Feeding Everyone, 1986-90, treas., 1981-94; bd. dirs. Amberjack, Ltd., Bloomington, Ill., 1985-98; mem. alumni coun. Pomona Coll., 1989-92, chmn. edn. com., 1992-94. Maj. USMCR, 1942-45, 50-51. Mem. Savs. and Loan Instns. (bd. govs. 1957-62), Fin. Mgrs. Soc. for Savs. Instns., Calif. Savs. and Loan League, Savs. Assns. Fin. Execs. (pres. 1968-75), Fin. Analysts Fedn. Home: 922 San Vicente Blvd Santa Monica CA 90402-2004

MORGAN, NEIL, writer, newspaper editor, lecturer, columnist; b. Smithfield, N.C., Feb. 27, 1924; s. Samuel Lewis and Isabelle (Robeson) M.; m. Caryl Lawrence, 1945 (div. 1954); m. Katharine Starkey, 1955 (div. 1962); m. Judith Blakely, 1964; 1 child, Jill. AB, Wake Forest Coll., 1943. Columnist San Diego Daily Jour., 1946-50; columnist San Diego Evening Tribune, 1950-92, assoc. editor, 1977-81, editor, 1981-92; assoc. editor, sr. columnist San Diego Union-Tribune, 1992—. Syndicated columnist Morgan Jour., Copley News Service, 1958— ; lectr.; cons. on Calif. affairs Bank of Am., Sunset mag. Author: My San Diego, 1951, It Began With a Roar, 1953, Know Your Doctor, 1954, Crosstown, 1955, My San Diego 1960, 1959, Westward Tilt, 1963, Neil Morgan's San Diego, 1964, The Pacific States, 1967, The California Syndrome, 1969, (with Robert Witty) Marines of Margarita, 1970, The Unconventional City, 1972, (with Tom Blair) Yesterday's San Diego, 1976, This Great Land, 1983, Above San Diego, 1990, (with Judith Morgan) Dr. Seuss & Mr. Geisel, 1995, (with Judith Morgan) Roger: The Biography of Roger Revelle, 1997; conbr. non-fiction articles to Nat. Geog., Esquire, Redbook, Reader's Digest, Holiday, Harper's, Travel and Leisure, Ency. Brit. Lt. USNR, 1943-46. Recipient Ernie Pyle Meml. award, 1957, Bill Corum Meml. award, 1961, Disting. Svc. citation Wake Forest U., 1966, Grand award for travel writing Pacific Area Travel Assn., 1972, 78, Fourth Estate award San Diego State U., 1988, The Morgan award Leadership Edn. Awareness Devel. San Diego, 1993; co-recipient Ellen and Roger Revelle award, 1986; named Outstanding Young Man of Yr. San Diego, 1959, 1st place news commentary, Calif. News Pub. Assn., 1993, Harold Keen award, 1996, Chancellors medal, U. Calif., San Diego, 2000; named Mr. San Diego, Rotary, 1999. Mem. Authors Guild, Soc. Profl. Journalists (award for best column 1999), Soc. of Am. Travel Writers, Bohemian Club, Phi Beta Kappa. Home: 7930 Prospect Pl La Jolla CA 92037-3721 Office: PO Box 191 San Diego CA 92112-4106 E-mail: neil.morgan@uniontrib.com.

MORGAN, PAUL WILLIAM, engineer, researcher; b. Highland Park, Mich., June 29, 1952; s. Kenneth Hayden and Margaret Anne (Rourk) M.; children: Paul James, Thomas Edward, Anna Florence. BSEE, Wayne State U., 1975. Design engr. Marposs Gauges, Madison Heights, 1977-79, Lebow Assocs., Troy, Mich., 1979-80, quality mgr., 1980-81; project engr. Eaton-Lebow, 1981-83, sr. project engr., 1983-92; chief engr. Key Transducers, Sterling Heights, Mich., 1992-98; pres. Engineered Measurement Syss., Redford, 1998—. Inventor and patentee in field. Achievements include inventions, patents, and the manufacturing of unique, high precision, torquemeters for NASA, Nat. Lab., aerospace and automotive applications. Home: 5976 Dwight Ave Waterford MI 48327-1329 Fax: 313-255-0487. E-mail: EMSTorque@aol.com.

MORGAN, RAYMOND F. plastic surgeon; b. Pitts., Apr. 24, 1948; s. Edwin J. and Alberta (Hirt) M.; m. Sue Ann; children: Ryan Frederic, Alexander Evan, Elizabeth Anne. BS, U. Pitts., 1969, MEd, DMD, U. Pitts., 1972; MD, W.Va. U., 1976. Diplomate Am. Bd. Plastic Surgery, Am. Bd. Hand Surgery. Intern Johns Hopkins U. Hosp., Balt., 1976-77, resident surgery, 1977-80, resident plastic surgery, 1980-82; resident hand surgery Union Meml. Hosp.; staff U. Va. Health Scis. Ctr., Charlottesville, M.T. Edgerton prof., chmn. dept. plastic surgery, 1988—. Mem. ACS, Soc. Univ. Surgeons, So. Surg. Assn., Am. Soc. for Surgery of the Hand, Am. Assn. Plastic Surgeons. Office: U of Va Dept Of Plastic Surgery Charlottesville VA 22908-0001

MORGAN, RAYMOND FRANKLIN, education educator; b. Crisfield, Md., Dec. 19, 1943; s. Raymond Franklin and Anna Marie (Evans) M.; m. Susan Morgan, July 1, 1978; children: Jonathan, Christopher. BA, Randoph-Macon Coll., 1966; MEd, U. Va., 1970, EdD, 1974. Tchr. English and reading Chesterfield Pub. Schs.; English tchr. York Acad. and Miller Sch. of Albemarle; asst./assoc. prof. grad. program dir. in reading, then prof. edn. Old Dominion U., Norfolk, Va., 1974—. Presenter, cons. in field. Co-author: Reading for Success, 1996, Reading to Learn in the Content Areas, 4th edit., 2000, others; co-author: The Psychology of Human Development, 2nd edit., 1985, 3rd edit., 1993, Critical Reading-Thinking Skills for the College Student, 1st edit., 1985, 2nd edit., 1986; mem. editl. bd. Reading in Va., editl. rev. bd. Reading Improvement; contbr. over 60 books, articles and monographs to profl. pubs. Recipient Tonelson award Darden Coll. Edn., over 3.5 million dollars in grants for svc. and rsch. Mem.: Nat. Soc. for the Study of Edn., Coll. Reading Assn., Va. Beach Couns. of Internat. Reading Assn., Va. State Reading Assn., Assn. Lit. Scholars Critics, Internat. Reading Assn., Phi Kappa Phi. Avocation: golf. Home: 5298 W Valleyside Ct Virginia Beach VA 23464-2606 E-mail: rmorgprof@cox.net., rmorgan@odu.edu.

MORGAN, RAYMOND VICTOR, JR. university administrator, mathematics educator; b. Brownwood, Tex., May 10, 1942; s. Raymond Victor and Lovey Lucile (Tate) M.; m. Mary Jane Folks, Aug. 13, 1967; children: Jason Wesley (dec.), Jeremy Victor. BA, Howard Payne U., 1965; MA, Vanderbilt U., 1966; PhD, U. Mo., 1969. Asst. prof. So. Meth. U., Dallas, 1969-75; assoc. prof. Sul Ross State U., Alpine, Tex., 1975-82, math. dept. chmn., 1976-85, prof., 1982—, dean of scis., 1979-86, exec. asst. pres., 1985-90, pres., 1990—. Bd. dirs. Tex. Internat. Edn. Consortium. Author textbook: Agricultural Mathematics, 1978; author articles. Bd. dirs. Texas Rural Communities, 1998—; founder regional commr. Alpine Soccer League, 1984; v.p. coach Alpine Baseball League, 1983; pres. Alpine PTA, 1982-83; founder, pres. So. Meth. U. Faculty Club, 1973-75; mem. exec. com. Tex. Assn. Coll. and Univ. Student Personnel Adminstrs., 1990-92; mem. commn. on colls. class of 2003 So. Assn. of Colls. and Schs. NSF grantee, 1979. Mem. Am. Assn. Higher Edn., Tex. Assn. Coll. Tchrs. (chpt. v.p. 1978-79), Math. Assn. Am. (chmn. Tex. sect. 1985-86), So. Assn. Colls. and Schs. (mem. commn. on colls. 1999—), Lions Club (pres. 1979-80, Lion of Yr. 1980, 83), Alpine Country Club. Republican. Mem. Ch. of Christ. Avocations: motocycling, golf, shooting. Home: PO Box 1341 Alpine TX 79831-1341 Office: Sul Ross State U E Highway 90 PO Box C114 Alpine TX 79831-0114 E-mail: rvmorgan@sulross.edu.

MORGAN, REBECCA SUSAN, psychologist; b. Oakland, Calif., Oct. 7, 1949; d. Theodore B. Wilmoth and Colleen (Schell) Groesbeck; m. Dan Morgan, June 13, 1970. AB in Psychology, Stanford U., 1971; PhD, U. Minn., 1976. Lic. psychologist Ill., Iowa. Clin. psychologist Robert Young Mental Health Ctr., Rock Island, Ill., 1975-78, staff coord. Day Hosp., 1978-82, coord. psychol. svcs., 1982-86; clin. psychologist Moline, 1986—. Cons. psychologist Robert Young Mental Health Ctr., 1986—; cons. Home Start East Moline. NIMH fellow, U. Minn., 1971; VA traineeship, St. Paul, Minn., 1972-75. Mem. APA, Ill. Psychol. Assn., River Bend Psychol. Assn. Luth. Office: 2101 47th St Moline IL 61265-3663

MORGAN, RICHARD ERNEST, political scientist, educator; b. Centre County, Pa., May 17, 1937; s. James Ernest and Helen Estelle (Hogge) M.; m. Jean Mary Yarbrough, 1996. AB, Bowdoin Coll., Brunswick, Maine, 1959; A.M., Columbia U., 1961, PhD, 1967. Instr. in govt. Columbia U., 1962-63, 65-67, asst. prof. govt., 1967-68; assoc. prof. govt. Bowdoin Coll., 1969-75, William Nelson Cromwell prof. constl. law and govt., 1975—. Fellow in law and govt. Harvard U. Law Sch., 1968-69; research dir. Twentieth Century Fund Project on Polit. Surveillance in Am., 1975-79 Author: The Politics of Religious Conflict, 1968, The Supreme Court and Religion, 1972, (with others) American Politics: Directions of Change, Dynamics of Choice, 1979, Domestic Intelligence: Monitoring Dissent in America, 1980, Disabling America: The Rights Industry in Our Time, 1984, People, Power and Politics, 1994; contbg. editor, City Journal, 1998—; contbr. articles to profl. publs.; editor: (with James E. Connor) The American Political System: Introductory Readings, 1971. Chmn. Spl. Commn. on Legis. Compensation, State of Maine, 1973-74; chmn. Maine adv. com. U.S. Commn. on Civil Rights, 1985-87. Served to 1st lt. U.S. Army, 1963-65. Mem. Am. Polit. Sci. Assn., New. Eng. Polit. Sci. Assn. (pres. 1988-89). Republican. Episcopalian. Home: 55 Otter Brook Rd South Harpswell ME 04079-9802 Office: Bowdoin Coll Brunswick ME 04011

MORGAN, RICHARD GREER, lawyer; b. Houston, Dec. 23, 1943; s. John Benjamin (stepfather) and Audrey Valley (Brickwede) Haus; children: Richard Greer, Jonathan Roberts. AB in History, Princeton U., 1966; JD, U. Tex., 1969. Bar: Tex. 1969, D.C. 1970, Minn. 1976, U.S. Ct. Appeals (D.C. cir.) 1970, U.S. Ct. Appeals (5th and 9th cirs., temporary emergency ct. appeals) 1976. Atty., advisor to commr. Lawrence J. O'Connor, Jr. Fed. Power Commn., Washington, 1969-71; assoc. Morgan, Lewis & Bockius, 1971-75; ptnr. O'Connor & Hannan, 1975-89, Lane & Mittendorf, Washington, 1989-97; mng. ptnr. Shook, Hardy & Bacon, L.L.P., Houston, 1997—. Bd. dirs. Hexagon, Inc.; instr. law seminars; lectr. in field. Author: Gas Lease and Royalty Issues, Natural Gas Yearbook, 1989, 90, 91, 92, 2002; contbr. articles on energy law to profl. jours. Bd. dirs. Mighty Spl. Music Makers, U. Tex. Law Sch. Found. Mem. ABA, Fed. Bar Assn., Energy Bar Assn. (bd. dirs.), D.C. Bar Assn., Princeton Alumni Coun., Princeton Alumni Assn. Houston, Energy Law Found. (pres.). Office: Shook Hardy and Bacon LLP 600 Travis St Ste 1600 Houston TX 77002-2911

MORGAN, ROBERT ARTHUR, accountant; b. Decatur, Ill., Oct. 23, 1918; s. Robert Howard and Katherine (Massey) M.; m. Julia Ann Franklin, June 28, 1941; children: Robert A., Susan Ruth. BS, U. Ill., 1941. Acct. Pure Oil Co., 1941, Caterpillar Tractor Co., Peoria, Ill., 1945-56, controller, 1956-78; mem. Fin. Acct. Standards Bd., Stamford, Conn., 1978-82; cons. Morton, Ill., 1982—. Contbr. articles to acctg. periodicals. Past mem. fin. acctg. standards adv. coun. Fin. Acctg. Found.; pres. bd. edn. Morton Twp. High Sch., 1960-61. Civilian auditor AUS, 1942-44. Mem. Nat. Assn. Accts. (nat. dir., nat. v.p. 1965-66, chmn. mng. practices 1974-75), Machinery and Allied Products Inst. (fin. coun. II 1956-78), Fin. Execs. Inst. (mem. com. corp. reporting 1977-78), Internat. Fedn. Accts. (chmn. com. fin. and mgmt. acctg. 1983).

MORGAN, ROBERT ASHTON, minister, ethics and world religions educator; b. Mpls., May 5, 1929; s. Thomas Ashton and Kathryn (Roberts) M.; m. Honoria Wilson, Jan. 15, 1955 (dec. Mar. 1995); 1 child, Emily Kathryn. BA, Macalester Coll., 1950, DD, 1978; MDiv, Yale U., 1954. Ordained to ministry Presbyn. Ch., 1954. Min. First Presbyn. Ch., Eveleth, Minn., 1954-58; asst. min. Westminster Presbyn. Ch., Mpls., 1958-67, min. Austin, Minn., 1967-92; instr. Riverland C.C., 1992-99. Bd. dirs. Austin (Minn.) Med. Ctr. Author: Advent Recollections, 1985, Stories Around the Baby, 1991. Bd. dirs. ARC, Mower County, 1967-92, bd. chmn., 1991-92. Mem. Rotary (pres. 1972-73). Presbyterian. Avocations: reading, gardening, travel. Home: The Oaks (130) 1200 18th Ave NW Austin MN 55912-1891

MORGAN, ROBERT MARION, educational research educator; b. Ponca City, Okla., Feb. 5, 1930; s. Perry Harrison and Velma Beatrice (Stowe) M.; m. Constance Louise Claus, Jan. 3, 1963; children— Stephen, Melayne. BS, Okla. State U., 1955, MS, 1956; PhD, Ohio State U., 1958; LLD, Dongah U., Pusan, Korea. Asst. prof. U. N.M., 1958-62; pres. Gen. Programmed Tchg. Corp., Palo Alto, Calif., 1961-64; v.p. Ranchers Corp., Albuquerque, 1962-64; dir. edni. systems Litton Industries, College Park, Md., 1964-66; dep. dir. divsn. vocational rsch. U.S. Office Edn., Washington, 1966-68; prof., head dept. ednl. rsch. Fla. State U., Tallahassee, 1968-74; dir. Center for Ednl. Tech., 1968-75, Learning Systems Inst., 1975—. Lectr. Catholic U. Am., 1966-68, Seoul (Korea) Nat. U., 1970-71; cons. AID, Republic of Brazil, Korea, Italian Air Force, Navy Dept., U.S. Naval Acad.; Chmn. Fla. R & D, Council, 1969—; sch. bd. U. Sch., Tallahassee, 1969-74. Author: Programmed Instruction-A Concept of Learning, 1963, An Educational Systems Analysis for the Republic of Korea, 1970; contbr. articles to profl. jours. Bd. dirs. U.S. Coalition for Edn. for All, 1992—; trustee Aerospace Ednl. Found. With AUS, 1949-52. Fellow Royal Soc. Arts; mem. Am. Ednl. Research Assn., Am. Psychol. Assn., Nat. Soc. for Programmed Instrn., Am. Mgmt. Assn., Rotary, Sigma Xi. Republican. Presbyterian. Home: 3322 Remington Run Tallahassee FL 32312-1462 Office: Fla State Univ C4605 University Ctr Tallahassee FL 32306 E-mail: rmorgan@lsi.fsu.edu.

MORGAN, ROBERT MILES, paramedic, educator; b. Memphis, Oct. 5, 1971; s. Charles Oscar Morgan and Maria T. (Tartaglia) Parton. Tech. Cert. Paramedicine, Shelby State Coll., Memphis; Tech. Cert. CCEMT-P, U. Md., Balt. EMS Southaven (Miss.) Emergency Med. Svc., 1991-92; EMT Mid-South Emergency Med. Svc., Southaven, 1992; EMT - intermediate Desoto County Emergency Med. Svc., Walls, Miss., 1992-95, paramedic, 1995—2002; critical care paramedic Air Care Team, Orlando, Fla., 2002—. Named EMT of the Yr., Desoto County Emergency Med. Svc., 1993, 94, Paramedic of the Yr., 1995. Mem. Nat. Registry EMTs. (cert.), Nat. Flight Paramedics Assn., Miss. EMT Assn. Baptist. Avocations: scuba diving, travel, water sports. Home: #13107 2470 Lake Debra Dr Orlando FL 32835 Office: Air Care Team 1414 S Orange Ave Orlando FL 32806-2095

MORGAN, ROBERT PETER, engineering educator, consultant; b. Bklyn., Feb. 26, 1934; s. Jack and Minna (Cohen) M.; m. Nancy Beverly Hutchins, Dec. 20, 1958; children: Thomas Albert, Jonathan Andrew. BChE, Cooper Union, 1956; SM, MIT, 1959, NuclE, 1961; PhD, Rensselaer Poly. Inst., 1965. Asst. dir. MIT Practice Sch., Oak Ridge, 1958-59; instr. chem. engring. Rensselaer Poly. Inst., 1960-64; asst. prof. nuclear and chem. engring. U. Mo., 1964-68; assoc. prof. engring. Washington U., St. Louis, 1968-74, prof. tech. and human affairs, 1974-87, Elvera and William Stuckenberg prof. tech. and human affairs, 1987-99, prof. emeritus tech. and human affairs, 1999—, dir. Ctr. for Tech. Assessment and Policy, 1968-98, chmn. dept. tech. and human affairs, 1976-83; sci. and pub. policy fellow Brookings Instn., 1982-83. Chmn. adv. subcom. NASA Tech. Transfer Program, 1978-80; mem. nat. adv. bd. program on ethics and values in sci. and tech. NSF, 1977-79; mem. com. on research grants NRC, 1983-86; Sigma Xi nat. lectr., 1981-83; vis. sr. analyst Office of Tech. Assessment of U.S. Congress, 1989-90; NAE fellow, sr. analyst, 1997-98; sr. Am. Ednl. Rsch. Assn. fellow NSF-Sci. Resources Studies, 1999-00; vis. rsch. prof. Sch. Pub. Policy, George Mason U., 2001-02. Author: The Role of U.S. Universities in Science and Technology for Development, 1979, Renewable Resource Utilization for Development, 1981; Science and Technology for International Development: An Assessment of U.S. Policies and Programs, 1984; contbr. numerous articles to profl. publs.; mem. editorial bd. Telecommunications Policy, 1976-80, Sci., Tech. and Human Values, 1977-79, 81-88 . Recipient Disting. Faculty award Washington U., 1989; AEC fellow, 1959-60. Fellow: AAAS (com. on sci., engring. and pub. policy 1977—80, program com. 1992—98); mem.: Am. Soc. Engring. Edn. (Chester F. Carlson award 1978), Fed. Am. Scientists, Sigma Xi (bd. dirs. 1997—99), Tau Beta Pi. E-mail: rpm@cec.wustl.edu.

MORGAN, ROBIN EVONNE, poet, author, journalist, activist, editor; b. Lake Worth, Fla., Jan. 29, 1941; 1 child, Blake Ariel. Grad. with honors, The Wetter Sch., 1956; student, pvt. tutors, 1956-59, Columbia U.; DHL (hon.), U. Conn., 1992. Free-lance book editor, 1961-69; editor Grove Press, 1967-70; editor, columnist World column Ms. Mag., N.Y.C., 1974-87, editor in chief, 1989-93, internat. cons. editor, 1993—. Vis. chair and guest prof. women's studies New Coll., Sarasota, Fla., 1973; disting. vis. scholar, lectr. Ctr. Critical Analysis of Contemporary Culture, Rutgers U., 1987, U. Canterbury, Christchurch, New Zealand, 1989, U. Denver Grad. Sch. Internat. Affairs, 1996-97; invited spl. cons. UN com. UN Conv. to End All Forms Discrimination Against Women, Sao Paulo and Brasilia, Brazil, 1987; mem. adv. bd. ISIS (internat. network women's internat. cross-cultural exch.); spl. advisor gen. assembly conf. on Gender UN Internat. Sch., 1985-86; free-lance journalist, lectr. cons., editor, 1969—; invited speaker numerous confs., orgns., acad. meetings, U.S. and abroad. Author, compiler, editor: Sisterhood Is Powerful: An Anthology of Writings from the Women's Liberation Movement, 1970, Swedish edit., 1972, Sisterhood Is Global: The International Women's Movement Anthology, 1984, U.K. edit., 1985, Spanish edit., 1994, Feminist Press edit., 1996; author: (nonfiction) Going Too Far: The Personal Chronicle of a Feminist, 1978, German edit., 1978, The Anatomy of Freedom: Feminism, Physics and Global Politics, 1982, 2d edit., 1994, fgn. edits. U.K., 1984, Germany, 1985, Argentina, 1986, Brazil, 1992, The Demon Lover: On the Sexuality of Terrorism, 1989, U.K. edit., 1989, Japanese edit., 1992, Italian edit., 1998, revised U.S. edit., 2002, The Word of a Woman: Feminist Dispatches 1968-91, 1992, 2d edit., 1994, U.K. edit., 1992, Chinese edit., 1996, A Woman's Creed, English, Arabic, French, Italian, Sanskrit, Hindi, Russian, Spanish, Portuguese, Chinese and Persian edits., 1995, Saturday's Child: A Memoir, 2000, (fiction) Dry Your Smile: A Novel, 1987, U.K. edit., 1988, The Mer-Child: A New Legend, 1991, German edit., 1995, Korean edit., 2000, (poetry) Monster: Poems, 1972, Lady of the Beasts: Poems, 1976, Death Benefits: Poems, 1981, Depth Perception: New Poems and a Masque, 1982, Upstairs in the Garden: Selected and New Poems, 1968-88, 1990, A Hot January: Poems 1996-1999, 1999, (plays) In Another Country, 1960, The Duel, 1979; co-editor: The New Woman: Anthology, 1969; contbr. numerous articles, essays, book revs., poems to various publs.; presenter poetry readings, univs., poetry ctrs., radio, TV, others, 1970—. Mem. 1st women's liberation caucus CORE, 1965, Student Nonviolent Coordinating Com., 1966; organizer 1st feminist demonstration against Miss Am. Pageant, 1968; founder, pres. The Sisterhood Fund, 1970; founder, pres. N.Y. Women's Law Ctr., 1970; founder N.Y. Women's Ctr., 1969; co-founder, bd. dirs. Feminist Women's Health Network, Nat. Battered Women's Refuge Network, Nat. Network Rape Crisis Ctrs.; bd. dirs. Women's Fgn. Policy Coun.; adv. trustee Nat. Women's Inst. for Freedom of Press; founding mem. Nat. Mus. Women in Arts; founder Sisterhood is Global Inst. (internat. think-tank), 1984, officer, 1989-97, chair adv. bd., 1997—; co-organizer, U.S. mem. official visit Coalition of Philippines Women's Movement, 1988; chair N.Y. state com. Hands Across Am. Com. for Justice and Empowerment, 1988; mem. adv. bd. Global Fund for Women, Equality Now. Recipient Front Page award for disting. journalism, Wonder Woman award for internat. peace and understanding, 1982, Feminist of Yr. award Fund for Feminist Majority, 1990; writer-in-residence grantee Yaddo, 1980; grantee Nat. Endowment for Arts, 1979-80, Ford Found., 1982, 83, 84. Mem. Nat. Mus. Women in Arts, Feminist Writers' Guild, Media Women, N.Am. Feminist Coalition, Pan Arab Feminist Solidarity Assn. (hon.), Israeli Feminists Against Occupation (hon.). Office: c/o Edite Kroll Literary Agency 12 Grayhurst Park Portland ME 04102-3601

MORGAN, ROSE MARIE, retired biology educator; b. Minot, N.D., Nov. 17, 1935; d. Clinton Edward and Clara Adlyn (Fedje) Morgan. BS, Minot (N.D.) State U., 1963; MS, N.D. State U., 1968; PhD, Tex. Woman's U., 1981; postgrad., Oxford (Eng.) U., 1985. Rsch. microbiologist N.D. State U., Fargo, 1965-75; teaching asst. Tex. Woman's U., Denton, 1977-81; prof. biology Minot State U., 1983-99, prof. emerita, 1999—, program dir. clin. lab. sci., 1996-99. Bench med. technologist Trinity Med. Ctr., 1960-65, adj. prof. clin. lab. sci., 1989-99; extension lectr. in anatomy, physiology, microbiology and biochemistry Minot State U., 1981-83; adj. prof. clin. lab. sci. St. Josephs Hosp., Minot, 1989-99, Trinity Med. Ctr., Minot, 1989-99; invited judge Nat. Native Am. Sci. Found; reviewer NSF, N.D. Sci. and Engring. Fair; textbook reviewer Times Miror Mosby, West Pub. Co., Prentice-Hall, William C. Brown, Macmillan, Saunders, Harper-Collins, McGraw-Hill; presenter numerous sci. meetings. Contbr. articles to profl. jours. including Jour. Environ. Sci. Health, Tex. Jour. Sci., Am. Jour. Med. Tech., Jour. Am. Sci. Pollution (London), Am. Biology Tchr. Mem. Mayor's Coun. for traffic safety; active various cmty. coms. Bush Found. grantee, Oxford (Eng.) U., Smithsonian Instn., Washington, 1985; also numerous other grants. Mem. AAUW (internat. fellowship panel Washington 1993-95), NEA, Am. Soc. Clin. Pathologists (assoc.), Am. Soc. Med. Technologists (nat. membership chmn.), N.W. Dakota Sci. Tchrs. Assn., N.D. Acad. Sci. (chairperson Dennison com. 1988-89), N.Y. Acad. Sci., N.D. Higher Edn. Assn., N.D. Edn. Assn., Minot State U. Edn. Assn., Sigma Xi, Phi Delta Kappa, Phi Delta Gamma (Alpha Theta chpt.), Delta Kappa Gamma (Gamma chpt.). Lutheran. Achievements include research in co-insult effects on physiological mechanisms, physiological changes in vital organ systems following interactions of cadmium and gamma radiation; pioneer in effects on interactions of environmental pollutants; comparison and report of differential effects of three different radiations on seed germination and cadmium lethalities. Home: 823 6th St SW Minot ND 58701-4581 E-mail: morgan@minot.com.

MORGAN, RUTH PROUSE, academic administrator, educator; b. Berkeley, Calif., Mar. 30, 1934; d. Ervin Joseph and Thelma Ruth (Prcesang) Prouse; m. Vernon Edward Morgan, June 3, 1956; children: Glenn Edward, Renée Ruth. BA summa cum laude, U. Tex., 1956; MA, La. State U., 1961, PhD, 1966. Asst. prof. Am. govt., politics and theory So. Meth. U., Dallas, 1966-70, assoc. prof., 1970-74, prof., 1974-95; prof. emeritus, 1995—; asst. provost So. Meth. U., Dallas, 1978-82, assoc. provost, 1982-86, provost ad interim, 1986-87, provost, 1987-93, provost emerita, 1993—; pres. RPM Assocs., 1993—; v.p. ABATECH, Inc., 1995—. Tex. state polit. analyst ABC, N.Y.C., 1972-84. Author: The President and Civil Rights, 1970; mem. editorial bd. Jour. of Politics, 1975-82, Presdl. Studies Quar., 1980—; contbr. articles to profl. jours. Active Internat. Women's Forum, 1987—, City of Dallas Redistricting Commn., 2001; trustee Hockaday Sch., 1988-94, The Kilby Awards Found., 1993-95; bd. dirs. United Way, Met. Dallas, 1993-99; adv. com. U.S. Army Command and Gen. Staff. Coll., 1994-97; founder Archives of Women of the Southwest, 1992, chmn. adv. com. 1995-99; charter mem. Girls, Inc. Aux; mem. Women's Ctr. Dallas, Dallas Women's Found. Mem. Am. Polit. Sci. Assn., So. Polit. Sci. Assn. (mem. exec. coun. 1979-84), Southwestern Polit. Sci. Assn. (pres. 1982-83, mem. exec. coun. 1981-84), The Dallas Forum of Internat. Women's Forum (pres. 1996-97), Charter 100 Club (pres. 1991-92), Nat. Mus. for Women in the Arts (charter), The Women's Mus. (charter), Ctr. for the Study of the Presidency, Acad. Polit. Sci., Dallas Summit Club (pres. 1992-93), Phi Beta Kappa, Pi Sigma Alpha, Phi Kappa Phi, Theta Sigma Phi. Avocations: photography, travel.

MORGAN, SAMUEL P(OPE), physicist, applied mathematician; b. San Diego, July 14, 1923; s. Samuel Pope and Beatrice Marie (Summers) M.; m. Mary Caroline Annin, Jan. 23, 1948; children: Caroline Gail, Lesley Anne, Alison Lee, Diane Elizabeth. BS, Calif. Inst. Tech., 1943, MS, 1944, PhD in Physics, 1947. Mem. tech. staff AT&T Bell Labs., Murray Hill, N.J., 1947-59, head dept. math. physics, 1959-67, dir. computing tech., 1969-70, dir.

computing sci. research center, 1967-82, disting. mem. tech. staff, 1982-95, Lucent Tech./Bell Labs., 1996-98, ret., 1998. Research, publs. on electromagnetic theory, applied math., queueing theory; patentee in field. Fellow IEEE (life); mem. AAAS, Am. Phys. Soc., Sigma Xi. Home: 9 Raleigh Ct Morristown NJ 07960-2535

MORGAN, SHARON DENISE, engineering-technical support company executive; b. Arab, Ala., July 13, 1964; d. Ralph Junior King and Erma Dean (Smith) Norris; m. Timothy Dee Morgan, June 4, 1988. AS in Bus. Adminstrn., Snead State Jr. Coll., Boaz, Ala., 1984; BSBA in MIS and Math., U. Ala., Huntsville, 1986; MBA, U. Ala., 1992. Patient svcs. rep. Arab Hosp., 1981-84, coord. patient accounts, 1984; customer svc. rep. DeltaCom, Arab, 1984-86; exec. asst. v.p.'s Brindlee Mountain Telephone Co., 1986-87; mktg. mgr. DeltaCom, Birmingham, Ala., 1987-88, MIS mgr. Huntsville, 1988-90; pres., chmn. bd. dirs. Morgan Rsch. Corp., 1990—. Baptist. Avocations: piano, organ, reading, golf. Office: 4811A Bradford Dr NW Huntsville AL 35805-1948 E-mail: smorgan@morganres.com.

MORGAN, SHIRLEY ANN, information systems executive; b. Farmington, Mich., Mar. 13, 1940; d. Clyde Elmer and Callie Mae (Morgan) Card; children: Cindy Jeanne, Dennis Carl, Vicki Anne. BBA, Orlando (Fla.) Coll., 1992. Cert. prodn. and inventory mgmt., Am. Prodn. and Inventory Control Soc. With Anchor Coupling Co., Plymouth, Mich., 1959-74; data processing supt. Photon Sources, Livonia, 1976-80; data processing mgr. S&H Fabricating, Sanford, Fla., 1980-85; MIS mgr. ABB Power Distbn., 1985-92, Wheeled Coach, Inc., Winter Park, Fla., 1992-94; dir. info. systems Crane Tech. Group Inc., Daytona Beach, 1994-97; bus. sys. cons. MCS Bus. Techs., Sarasota, 1997—2002; mfg. cons. Exact Software, Deltona, 2002—. Independent. Avocations: swimming, sports. Office: Exact Software 1067 Gaucho Cir Deltona FL 32725 E-mail: shirley.morgan@exactsoftware.com.

MORGAN, STEPHEN CHARLES, academic administrator; b. Upland, Calif., June 2, 1946; s. Thomas Andrew and Ruth Elizabeth (Miller) M.; m. Ann Marie McMurray, Sept. 6, 1969; 1 child, Kesley Suzanne. BA, U. La Verne, 1968; MS, U. So. Calif., 1971; EdD, U. No. Colo., 1979. Devel. officer U. La Verne, Calif., 1968-71, asst. to pres., 1971-73, dir. devel., 1973-75, v.p. devel., 1975-76, pres., 1985—; dir. devel. U. So. Calif., L.A., 1976-79; exec. dir. Ind. Colls. No. Calif., San Francisco, 1979-85. Bd. dirs. PFF Bank and Trust; dir. Ind. Colls. So. Calif., L.A., 1985—. Bd. dirs. Mt. Baldy United Way, Ontario, Calif., 1988-98, McKinley Children's Ctr., San Dimas, Calif., 1989-99, LeRoy Haynes Ctr. for Family and Children's Svcs., 2000—; chair nat. com. on higher edn. Ch. of Brethren, Elgin, Ill., 1988-90; dir. Pomona Valley Hosp. Med. Ctr., 1992-98, 99—, Inter Valley Health Plan, 1992-97, PFF Bank and Trust, 2001—. Mem. Assn. Ind. Calif. Colls. and Univs. (exec. com. 1989—, vice-chmn. 1996-2000, chmn. 2000-2002), L.A. County Fair Assn. (bd. dirs.), Western Coll. Assn. (exec. com. 1992-98, pres. 1996-98), Western Assn. Schs. and Colls. (sr. accrediting commn. 1996-2001), Pi Gamma Mu. Avocations: orchid culture, fly fishing, golf. Home: 2518 N Mountain Ave Claremont CA 91711-1579 Office: U LaVerne Office Pres 1950 3rd St La Verne CA 91750-4401 E-mail: morgans@ulv.edu.

MORGAN, STEPHEN R. land surveyor; b. Washington, Jan. 1, 1944; s. Mary E. Morgan; children: Stephanie, Travis, Sandra. BS in Math., Ft. Hays State U., 1968. Cert. land surveyor Kans. State Bd. Tech. Professions. Asst. survey engr. Union Pacific R.R. Co., Kansas City, 1973—90; farm worker Hanover, Kans., 1990—93; engrng. technician Platte City Pub. Works, Mo., 1993—94, Torres Consulting Engr. Inc., Kansas City, 1994—95; party chief Rhodes Surveying, P.A., Kans., 1995—96; engr. technician III, Douglas County Pub. Works, Lawrence, 1996—. Instr. Johnson County C.C., Overland Park, Kans., 1995—96. Recipient 3 Yr. Svc. award, Cub Scouts Am., 1988. Mem.: Kansas City Met. Surveying Assn., Kans. Soc. Land Surveyors. Avocations: golf, tennis, fishing. Home: 501 S 4th St Apt A-6 Edwardsville KS 66111

MORGAN, SYLVIA DENISE (MRS. HAROLD MORGAN), school administrator, poet; b. Rome, Sept. 1, 1952; d. Herman Hamilton and Garnette Lucille (Strickland) Haynes; m. Harold Morgan, Feb. 22, 1980; 1 child, Amber. BS in English, Knoxville Coll., 1974; MEd, Ga. State U., 1977; EdS, Jacksonville State U., 1989. From tchr. to ednl. supr. Ga. Sch. for the Deaf, Cave Spring, 1974—96, ednl. supr., 1996—2002, coord. family and student svcs., 2002—. Co-owner Uncle John's BBQ. Grad. Ga. Leadership Program. Mem. NAACP, NEA, Ga. Assn. Educators, Ga. Educators for the Hearing Impaired, Am. Assn. Persons with Disabilities, Coun. Exceptional Children (recognized as preferred spl. edn. tchr.), Floyd County and Tng. Svc. Ctr., Ga. Sch. for Deaf Alumni Assn., Ga. Assn. of the Deaf, Caregivers Assn. Avocations: speaking, writing poetry. Home: 8 Tasso Cir Rome GA 30161-5776 E-mail: sylvia@bellsouth.net.

MORGAN, THEODORE, economist; b. Middletown, Ohio, May 31, 1910; s. Ben and Anna Louella (Knecht) M.; m. Catharine Moomaw, June 30, 1943; children: Stephanie H., Marian, Laura S. AB, Ohio State U., 1930, AM, BSE, 1931; MA, Harvard U., 1940, PhD, 1941. Asst. prof. Randolph-Macon Women's Coll., Lynchburg, Va., 1941-42; teaching fellow, tutor, instr. Harvard U., Cambridge, Mass., 1940-41, 42-47; advisor, dep. gov. Cen. Bank of Ceylon, Colombo, 1951-53; assoc. prof. to prof. U. Wis., Madison, 1947-80, prof. emeritus, 1980—. Vis. prof. U. Singapore, 1967-69, Gadjah Mada U., Yogjakarta, Indonesia, 1959-60, Nankai U., Tianjin, China, 1990, U. Manchester, Eng., 1980-82, Sussex U., Brighton, Eng., 1975-76; sr. staff Coun. Econ. Advisors, Washington, 1964-65; advisor Ministry of Econ. Affairs. Govt. Thailand, Bangkok, 1970; rsch. fellow Resource Systems Inst. East-West Ctr., Honolulu, 1985-86. Author: Hawaii, A Century of Economic Change, 1948, Income and Employment, 1947, Introduction to Economics, 1950, 56, Economic Development, 1975, and others. Mem. Royal Econ. Soc. (life), Am. Econ. Assn. Mem. Unitarian Ch. Avocations: tennis, bicycling, skiing, hiking. Home: 3534 Topping Rd Madison WI 53705-1441 Office: U Wis Social Sci # 7313 Madison WI 53706

MORGAN, THOMAS ROWLAND, retired marine corps officer; b. Allentown, Pa., Jan. 6, 1930; s. Harry Campbell and Olwen (Pierce) M.; m. Barbara A. Croze, June 29, 1957; children— Lynn A., Susan E., Beth E. BA in History, Colgate U., 1952; student, Marine Corps Command and Staff Coll., 1965-66; MA in Edn., U. Va., 1973. Commd. 2d lt. USMC, 1952, advanced through grades to gen., 1986; naval aviator Naval Air Sta., Pensacola, Fla., 1953-54; asst. maintenance officer 3d Marine Aircraft Wing, El Toro, Calif., 1954-55; personnel officer Marine Aircraft Group Western Pacific, 1954-55; aide to comdg. gen. 1st Marine Aircraft Wing, Pacific, 1955; asst. ops. officer Marine Aircraft Group, Kaneohe Bay, Hawaii, 1956-57; squadron pilot, ground tng. officer Marine Attack Squadron, 1957-59; flight instr. Naval Air Sta., Olathe, Kans., 1959; personnel officer, aircraft maintenance officer Marine Fighter Squadron, Beaufort, S.C., 1959-61; exec. officer Hdqrs. and Maintenance Squadron, Atsugi, Japan, 1961-62; fleet liaison officer Marine Corps Air Sta., Yuma, Ariz., 1962-65; comdr. Marine Fighter Attack Squadron, Beaufort, 1966-67; group ops. officer, officer-in-charge DaNang DASC, Vietnam, 1968-69; exec. officer Marine Corps Air Sta., Quantico, Va., 1969-71; exec. officer Naval ROTC unit U. Va., 1971-73; chief war plans br. J-5 U.S. European Command Hdqrs., Stuttgart, Fed. Republic Germany, 1973-76; asst. to dep. chief of staff requirements and programs Hdqrs. U.S. Marine Corps, Washington, 1976-77; asst. div. comdr. 3d Marine Div., Okinawa, Japan, 1977-78; asst. chief of staff C-5 Combined Forces Command, Seoul, 1978-80; dep. comdr. FMF Pacific, Camp Smith, Hawaii, 1980-81; dep. chief of staff for requirements and programs Hdqrs. Marine Corps, Washington, 1981-85, dep. chief staff for plans, policies and ops., acting Chief of Staff, 1985-86, asst. commandant, 1986-88, ret. Decorated D.S.M., Def. Superior Service medal, Legion of Merit, Bronze Star medal, Meritorious Service medal, Air medal; Order of Nat. Security medal, Cheonsu medal (Korea) Mem. Am. Legion Avocations: golf, skiing, water sports.

MORGAN, TIMI SUE, lawyer; b. Parsons, Kans., June 16, 1953; d. James Daniel and Iris Mae (Wilson) Baumgardner; m. Rex Michael Morgan, Oct. 28, 1983; children: Tessa Anne, Camma Elizabeth. BS, U. Kans., 1974; JD, So. Meth. U., 1977. Bar: Tex. 1977, U.S. Dist. Ct. (no. dist.) Tex. 1978, U.S. Ct. Appeals (5th cir.) 1979, U.S. Tax Ct. 1980; cert. tax law specialist. Assoc. Gardere & Wynne, Dallas, 1977-79, Akin, Gump, Strauss, Hauer & Feld, Dallas, 1979-83, ptnr., 1984-86; of counsel Stinson, Mag & Fizzell, 1986-88; sole practice, 1988—. Adj. lectr. law So. Meth. U., 1989-90, 92-98. Bd. dirs. Dallas Urban League Inc., 1987-91. Mem. State Bar Tex. (mem. taxation sect.), Dallas Bar Assn., So. Meth. U. Law Alumni Coun. (sec. 1985-86), Order of Coif, Beta Gamma Sigma. Republican. Episcopalian.

MORGAN, TODD BYERS, financial and management consultant; b. Pitts., Jan. 16, 1956; s. Robert Arthur and Betty (Byers) M.; m. Maria Michelon; children: Lauren Elizabeth, Andrew Robert, Megan Marie. BS in Bus. Administrn., Susquehanna U., 1978; MBA, Marshall U., 1979. Assoc. Booz Allen & Hamilton, Inc., Lexington Park, Md., 1979-85; v.p. Eagan, McAllister Assocs., Inc., 1985-94, exec. v.p., 1995—. Instr. St. Mary's C.C., Lexington Park, Md., 1980—95, U. Coll. U. Md. , Lexington Park, 1984—94; assoc. prof. Embry-Riddle Aero U., 1991—. V.p. Wildewood Home Owners Assn., California, Md., 1985—86, pres., 1986—91; com. mem. Boy Scouts Am., Lexington Park , 1988—, asst. cub scoutmaster, 1999—; Active Com. to Elect Ronald Regan, 1979—80, fund raiser, 1983—84; active Bush for Pres. Campaign, 1988; treas Egan for County Commr. Campaign, 1987, 1990; vestry mem. Ch. of Ascension (Epsicopalian), Lexington Park. Mem.: Eagle Scout Assn., Masons. Republican. Avocations: stamp and coin collecting, basketball. Home: 20740 Chestnut Ridge Dr Leonardtown MD 20650-4522 Office: Eagan McAllister Assocs Inc PO Box 986 Lexington Park MD 20653-0986

MORGAN, VICTORIA, performing company executive, choreographer; BFA, U. Utah, 1973, MFA magna cum laude, 1976. Prin. dancer Ballet West, 1969-78, San Francisco Ballet, 1978-87; resident choreographer San Francisco Opera; artistic dir. Cin. Ballet, 1997—. Lead dancer with roles in numerous classical, neoclassical and modern ballets including works by George Balanchine, Forsythe, and Kudelka; dancer in lead roles for TV and film; choreographer, creating over 40 works for 20 ballet and opera cos. across U.S. including Utah Ballet, Pacific Northwest Ballet, Glimmerglass Opera and Cin. Opera; creator, prodr. ballet CD-ROM; choreography featured in documentary: The Creation of O.M.O. Office: Cincinnati Ballet 1555 Central Pkwy Cincinnati OH 45214-2863 E-mail: vmorga@cincinnatiballet.com.*

MORGAN, VIRGINIA DEAPO, business owner; b. Syracuse, N.Y., Oct. 28, 1934; d. William John and Mary (Sojewicz) Deapo; m. Robert Lee Morgan Jr., Sept. 1, 1962; 1 child, Robert Lee III. BS, SUNY, Cortland, 1956, MS, 1961; EdD, Nova U., 1979. Tchr. math. Camillus (N.Y.) Sch. Dist. # 1, 1956-61, Dept. Def. Dependent Sch., Clark AFB, The Philippines, 1961-63, Charles County Bd. Edn., La Plata, Md., 1966-68; asst. prof. math. Charles Community Coll., 1968-72; instr. Anson Tech. Coll., Ansonville, N.C., 1972-74, dean students, 1974-79; prin. Southview Acad., Wadesboro, 1979-82; funeral dir. Morgan & Son. Funeral Home, Marshville, 1982—. Dept. chair arts and scis., math. instrn. Montgomery Community Coll., Troy, N.C., 1985—; part time instr. Gardner-Webb Coll., Boiling Springs, N.C., 1988—. Chmn. Union County Bd. Edn., Monroe, N.C., 1977-85; mayor Marshville, N.C., 1997—. Mem. Am. Math. Assn. Two Yr. Colls., N.C. Assn. Tchrs., N.C. Funeral Dirs. Assn., Women Adminstrs. N.C. Higher Edn., N.C. State Sch. Bd. Assn. (bd. dirs. 1981-85). Avocations: knitting, crafts, sea shell collecting, traveling, porcelain doll making. Office: Montgomery C C PO Box 787 Troy NC 27371-0787

MORGAN, VIRGINIA MATTISON, magistrate judge; b. 1946; BS, Univ. of Mich., 1968; JD, Univ. of Toledo, 1975. Bar: Mich. 1975, Federal 1975, U.S. Ct. Appeals (6th cir.) 1979. Tchr. Dept. of Interior, Bur. of Indian Affairs, 1968-70, San Diego Unified Schs., 1970-72, Oregon, Ohio, 1972-74; asst. prosecutor Washtenaw County Prosecutor's Office, 1976-79; asst. U.S. atty. Detroit, 1979-85; magistrate judge U.S. Dist. Ct. (Mich. ea. dist.), 6th circuit, 1985—. Mem. bd. Fed. Jud. Ctr., 1997-2001; mem. jud. conf. U.S. Com. on Long Range Planning, 1993-96. Recipient Spl. Achievement award Dept. of Justice, Disting. Alumni award U. Toledo, 1993. Fellow Mich. State Bar Found.; mem. FBA (chpt. pres. 1996-97), Fed. Magistrate Judges Assn. (pres. 1995-96). Office: US Courthouse 231 W Lafayette Blvd Detroit MI 48226-2700

MORGAN, WILLIAM, art historian, educator; b. Princeton, N.J., June 13, 1944; s. Minot Canfield and Kate Merriam (Davis) M.; m. Carolyn Johnson, Dec. 28, 1978; children: Whitney, James, Joel, Lindsay. AB, Dartmouth Coll., 1966; MA, cert. architecture, Columbia U., 1968; PhD, U. Del., 1971. Lectr. Princeton U., 1971-74; prof. U. Louisville, 1974—. Guest lectr. Åbo Akademi, Turku, Finland, 1989. Architecture critic Courier-Jour., Louisville, 1975-80; author: Almighty Wall, 1983, Collegiate Gothic, 1989. Chmn. Ky. Hist. Preservation Rev. Bd., Frankfort, 1975-90. Mem. Soc. Architecture Historians, Dublin Hist. Soc. Office: Hite Art Inst U Louisville Louisville KY 40292-0001

MORGAN, WILLIAM J. accounting company executive; b. Bklyn., Jan. 12, 1947; s. William J. and Emma T. (Kraft) M.; m. Patricia A. Maltz, Mar. 23, 1968; children: Michele, Jennifer. BS, St. John's U., 1968. CPA, N.Y. Conn., N.J. Mng. ptnr. Stamford office, audit staff KPMG Peat Marwick, N.Y.C., 1968-72, audit supr., 1972-74, audit mgr., 1974-77, ptnr.-in-charge pvt. bus. adv. service, 1977-79, nat. office, ptnr.-in-charge recruiting, 1979-82, ptnr. comml. health care practice, 1982-91, ptnr.-in-charge N.J. audit practice, 1989-91, mng. ptnr. Fairfield/Westchester counties practice, 1991-94, ptnr. in charge met. N.Y. area mfg., retail and distbn. practice, 1993-96, ptnr. in charge global accts., 1996-98. Mem. Bus. Unit Planning Task Force, 1987-90, mem. compensation com., 1990-91, bd. dirs., 1991—, chmn. profit distbn. com., 1991-95, mem. future direction com., 1991-93, pension task force, 1991-92, chmn. compensation com., mem. bd. process com., 1997—. Acctg. adv. bd. Grad. Sch. Bus. Fordham U., 1979-82, mem. standardization com. Nat. Retail Mchts. Assn., 1979; trustee Tri County Sholarship Fund, 1984-91; v.p., exec. com., adv. bd. Fairfield coun. Boy Scouts Am., 1993-95; bd. dirs. Stamford Symphony, 1995-99; bd. dirs., chmn. bus. ops. com. heritage affiliate Am. Heart Assn., 1997-2000; chmn. Fairfield County Info. Exch., 1992-94; chmn. SACIA, the Bus. Coun. of Fairfield, 2001--; chmn. bd. dirs. S.W. Area Commerce and Industry Assn., 1994—, Inroads Fairfield and Westchester County chpt., 1992-95; with Bus. Execs. for Nat. Security, 1995-99, Ambs. Roundtable, 1995-99; exec. com. Conn. Policy and Econs Coun., 1998—. Recipient Stamford Good Scout award, 1999, Walter H. Wheeler Disting. Leadership award, 2000. Mem. Am. Inst. CPA's (small bus. devel. com. 1979-81, acctg. lit. awards com. 1983-86), N.J. Soc. CPA's (chmn. acctg. and auditing stds. com. 1988-90, trustee 1990-92, pub. rels. task force, 1987, subcom. health care acctg. 1983-86), N.Y. State CPA's (retail acctg. com. 1975-78, com. on edn. in coll. and univs. 1978-82), Nat. Assn. Accts. (dir. manuscripts 1975-77, v.p. N.Y. chpt. 1977-81, pres. N.Y. chpt. 1981-82, nat. publs. com. 1982-83, com. acad. relations 1983-84, nat. dir. 1983-86, Disting. Service award 1975), Health Care Fin. Mgmt. Assn. (N.J. chpt. chmn. auditing com. 1982-83, legis. task force com. 1985-86, chmn. joint ventures com., 1987-88), Swedish Am. C. of C. (bd. dirs. 1995—), Fairmount Country Club (bd. govs., treas. 1987-90), Woodway Country Club, Conn. Golf Club, Landmark Club. Roman Catholic. Office: KPMG LLP 3001 Summer St Stamford CT 06905-4317

MORGAN, WILLIAM BRUCE, naval architect; b. Fairfield, Iowa, Dec. 20, 1926; s. Orville Burns and Mary Verle (Balderson) M.; m. Mary Maxine Gillam, June 21, 1950; children: Margaret Ann, Ann Elise. BS in Marine Engrng., U.S. Mcht. Marine Acad., 1950; MS in Hydraulic Engrng., U. Iowa, 1951; DEng in Naval Architecture, U. Calif., 1961. Hydraulic engr. David Taylor Model Basin, Bethesda, Md., 1951-52, naval architect, 1952-58, naval architect supr., 1958-62, head propeller br., 1962-70; head hydromechanics div. David Taylor Naval Ship Research & Devel. Ctr. (formerly David Taylor Model Basin), Md., 1970-79; head hydromechanics directorate David Taylor Model Basin, 1979—2001; ret. Chmn. exec. com. Am. Towing Tank Conf., 1983-86; mem. exec. com. Internat. Towing Tank Conf., 1984-90. Co-inventor ventilated propeller, supercavitating propeller with air ventilation; contbr. articles to profl. jours. Recipient Navy Disting. Civilian Svc. award USN, 2000, Navy Superior Civilian Svc. award, 1974, Navy Meritorious Svc. award, 1967, Meritorious Exec. award Office of Pres., 1987, William Froude medal Royal Instn. Naval Architects, 1989, Capt. Robert Dexter Conrad award USN, 1993, Gibbs Bros. medal NAS, 1997; named to U. of Iowa Disting. Engrng. Alumni Acad., 1999. Fellow Soc. Naval Architects and Marine Engrs. (hon. life; exec. com. 1985—, Davidson medal 1986), ASME (chmn. fluids engring. div. 1981-82); mem. NAE, Schiffbautechnische Gesellschaft, Am. Soc. Naval Engrs. (Gold Medal award 1993), Chinese Soc. Naval Architects and Marine Engrs. (hon.), Sigma Xi. Mem. Ch. of Brethren. Home: 110 Upton St Rockville MD 20850-1836 E-mail: wbmorgan@erols.com.

MORGAN, WILLIAM FRANCIS, JR. police chief; b. Hartford, Conn. s. William Francis and Nancy M.; m. Kathleen Buckley, Oct. 12, 1985. B.Criminal Justice, U. New Haven, 1982; JD, Quinnipiac Coll., Hamden, Conn., 1998; Cert., FBI Nat. Acad., Quantico, Va., 1999. Bar: Conn. 1998. Police officer Conn. State Capitol Police, Hartford, 1985-89, sr. police officer, 1989-97, sgt., 1997-99, lt., 1999-2000, chief of police, 2000—. Mem. consumer adv. network Nat. Criminal Justice Ref. Svc., Rockville, Md., 2000. Recipient Samuel J. Lucian award Police Officer Tng. Coun., 1986, Trooper Allen Tuskowski award, 1986, Legis. Staff Achievment award Nat. Conf. State Legislators, 2002, John Everhardt Trooper award Nat. Legis. Svcs. and Security Assn., 2002. Mem. Nat. Legis. Svc. and Security Assn. (regional 3 chair 1997-98, 3d trustee 1998-99, 1st trustee 1999-2002). Office: Conn State Capitol Police 210 Capitol Ave Hartford CT 06106

MORGAN, WILLIAM JAY, minister, educator; b. Huntington, W.Va., Dec. 15, 1929; s. Fred Joseph and Mabel Clare Morgan; m. Dorothy Clay Morgan, Mar. 16, 1931; children: William David, Dennis James, Beverly Jean Haak. BA, Ky. Christian Coll., Grayson, KY, 1950; MA, U. Tex. El Paso, El Paso, TX, 1973. Founding dir. Spanish Am. Evangelism, El Paso, Tex., 1964—75; pres. and founder El Paso Christian Coll., 1974—81; prof. gen. studies Dallas Christian Coll., Dallas, 1983—; prof. english North Lake Coll., Irving, 1985—; founding dir. Spanish Am. Evangelism, El Paso, 1998—. Mem.: Delta Epsilon Chi. Home: 3060 Coombs Creek Drive Dallas TX 75233 Office: Dallas Christian College 2700 Christian Parkway Dallas TX 75234 E-mail: bmorgan@dallas.edu.

MORGAN, WILLIAM LIONEL, JR. physician, educator; b. Honolulu, Nov. 18, 1927; s. William Lionel and Lucy Salisbury (Grimes) M.; m. Joan Brunjes, Apr. 10, 1954; children: Nancy Salisbury, Linda Pittman. BA cum laude, Yale U., 1948; MD magna cum laude, Harvard U., 1952. Diplomate: Am. Bd. Internal Medicine. (mem. bd. 1973-80, mem. residency review com. 1975-80, chmn. residency rev. com. 1979-80). Intern Mass. Gen. Hosp., Boston, 1952-53, resident in medicine, 1953-54, 56-57, fellow in cardiology, 1957-58; asso. physician div. cardiovascular disease Henry Ford Hosp., Detroit, 1958-62; asso. prof. medicine U. Rochester (N.Y.) Sch. Medicine and Dentistry, 1962-65, prof., 1966-89, prof. medicine emeritus, 1989—, asso. chmn. dept. medicine, 1966-89. Author: (with G.L. Engel) The Clinical Approach to the Patient, 1969. Served with USPHS, 1954-56. Mem. ACP (Master), Am. Clin. and Climatol. Assn., Phi Beta Kappa, Alpha Omega Alpha Home: 160 Collingsworth Dr Rochester NY 14625-2024 Office: Strong Meml Hosp Dept Medicine 601 Elmwood Ave Rochester NY 14642-0002

MORGAN, WILLIAM NEWTON, architect, educator; b. Jacksonville, Fla., Dec. 14, 1930; s. Thomas and Kathleen (Fiske) M.; m. Bernice E. Leimback, July 31, 1954; children: William Newton, Dylan Thomas. AB magna cum laude, Harvard Coll., 1952, MArch Grad. Sch. of Design, 1958. Pres. William Morgan Architects, P.A., Jacksonville, Fla., 1961—. Critic various archtl. schs.; lectr. in field; adj. prof. of art history, Jacksonville U., 1995-96, U. North Fla., 1997; Beinecke-Reeves Disting. Prof. Architecture, U. Fla., 1998-99. Prin. works include Fla. State Mus., Jacksonville Police Meml. Bldg., Pyramid Condominium, Ocean City, Md., Fed. Cts. and Offices, Ft. Lauderdale, Fla., Westinghouse World Hdqs., Orlando, Fla., Neiman-Marcus store, Ft. Lauderdale, 1st Dist. Ct. Appeal, Tallahassee, Fla., Conf. Ctr., Tallahassee, U.S. Embassy, Khartoum, Sudan, U.S. Courthouse, Tallahassee; author; Prehistoric Architecture in the Eastern United States, 1980, Prehistoric Architecture in Micronesia, 1988, Ancient Architecture of the Southwest, 1994, Precolumbian Architecture in Eastern North America, 1999. Subject of The Architecture of William Morgan (Paul Spreiregen) 1987, Images Master Architect Series: William Morgan (Robert McCarter), 2002; Fulbright grantee to Italy, 1958-59; grantee Graham Found. Advanced Studies Arts, 1973; Lehman fellow Harvard U., 1957, Wheelwright fellow 1964-65, fellow NEA, 1991; Sam Gibbons Eminent scholar Fla. A&M U. and U. South Fla. Fellow AIA (past chmn. com. design) AIA Inst. honor for rsch. into the beginnings of archtl. creativity 1998, Fla. 2000 Millenium award honor for design 2000). Office: William Morgan Architects 220 E Forsyth St Jacksonville FL 32202-3328 E-mail: wnmorgan@aol.com.

MORGAN, WILLIAM RICHARD, mechanical engineer; b. Cambridge, Ohio, Mar. 27, 1922; s. Wilbur Alfred and Treva Beatrice (Minto) M.; m. Marjorie Eleanor Stevens, Feb. 17, 1946; children: Carol M. Morgan Dingledy, William R., Jr. BSME, The Ohio State U., 1944; MSME, Purdue U., 1950, PhD in Mech. Engring., 1951. Lic. profl. engr., Ohio. Power plant design engr. Curtiss Wright Corp., Columbus, Ohio, 1946-47; instr., rsch. fellow Purdue U., West Lafayette, Ind., 1947-51; supr. exptl. mech. engring. GE, Cin., 1951-55, mgr. controls analysis, devel. Aircraft Gas Turbine Divsn., 1955-59, mgr. XV5A vertical take-off and landing aircraft program, 1959-65, mgr. acoustic engring. Flight Propulsion Divsn., 1965-69, mgr. quiet engine program Flight Propulsion Divsn., 1969-71; pres. Cin. Rsch. Corp., 1971-73; v.p., COO SDRC Internat., Cin., 1973-79; engring. and mgmt. cons., 1979—. Author of papers presented at Brookhaven Nat. Lab., AEC Heat Transfer Symposium, 1954, ASME Fall Meeting, Thermal Conductivity of Insulation Material for Use in Nuclear Reactors, 1957, Am. Inst. Aero. Engrs. Ten-Ton V/STOL Lift Fan Transport, 1961, Dynamics Loads Symposium, XV5A Dynamic Load Characteristics, 1963, Joint Meeting of AGARD-Nato on Aircraft Engine Noise and Sonic Boom, 1969, ASME Meeting, Analytical Prediction of Fan/Compressor Noise, 1969. Lt. j.g. USNR, WWII. Westinghouse Rsch. fellow. Mem. ASME, Masons, Sigma Xi, Pi Tau Sigma, Pi Mu Epsilon. Achievements include patents in Humidity Detection and Indicating Instrument, Stall Prevention/Acoustic Tip Treatment, Acoustic Treatment, Inlet Noise Reduction Configuration. Home and Office: 312 Ardon Ln Cincinnati OH 45215-4102

MORGAN, WILLIAM W. language educator; b. Atlanta, Aug. 19, 1940; s. William Woodrow and Frances Elizabeth (Coffee) Morgan; m. Mary Gaston Melton, Dec. 21, 1963 (div. June 1973); children: William Eric, Jason Francis; m. Deborah Sue Moore, May 15, 1998. AB, North Ga. Coll., 1962; MA, U. Tenn., Knoxville, 1963; PhD, U. Tenn., 1969. Instr. English U.S. Mil. Acad., West Point, NY, 1966—69; prof. English Ill. State U., Normal, 1969—. Exec. prodr. Poetry Radio, WGLT-FM, Normal, Ill., 1990—; dir. Thomas Hardy Poetry Page. Author: (chapbook of poems) Trackings: The Body's Memory..., 1998; editl. bd. (journal) Victorian Poetry, 1980—, Victorians Inst. Jour., 1992; co-author: (essays) Voices in Tragic Harmony, 2000; co-editor: Thomas Hardy's Emma Poems, 2001; contbr. Capt. U.S. Army, 1966—69. Recipient Sow's Ear Poetry prize, Sow's Ear Poetry Rev., 1993, Dead Metaphor prize, Dead Metaphor Press, 1996. Mem.: MLA, Acad. of Am. Poets, Poetry Soc. Am., Thomas Hardy Assn. (exec. v.p. 1988—). Home: 603 N School St Normal IL 61761 Office: Illinois State Univ Dept English 4240 Normal IL 61790

MORGANROTH, FRED, lawyer; b. Detroit, Mar. 26, 1938; s. Ben and Grace (Greenfield) M.; m. Janice Marilyn Cohn, June 23, 1963; children: Greg, Candi, Erik. BA, Wayne State U., 1959, JD with distinction, 1961. Bar: Mich. 1961, U.S. Dist. Ct. (ea. dist.) Mich. 1961, U.S. Ct. Claims 1967, U.S. Supreme Ct. 1966; trained matrimonial arbitrator. Ptnr. Greenbaum, Greenbaum & Morganroth, Detroit, 1963-68, Lebenbom, Handler, Brody & Morganroth, Detroit, 1968-70, Lebenbom, Morganroth & Stern, Southfield, Mich., 1971-78; pvt. practice, 1979-83; ptnr. Morganroth & Morganroth P.C., 1983-94, Morganroth, Morganroth, Alexander & Nye, P.C., Birmingham, Mich., 1994-98, Morganroth, Morganroth, Jackman & Kasody, PC, Bloomfield Hills, 1999—. Mem. ABA (family law sect. 1987—), Mich. Bar Assn. (hearing panelist grievance bd. 1975—, Oakland County family law com. 1988—, vice chmn. 1992-93, chair 1993—), State Bar Mich. (mem. family law coun. of family law sect. 1990—, treas. 1993-94, chmn.-elect 1994-95, chmn. 1995-96), Detroit Bar Assn., Oakland Bar Assn. (cir. ct. mediator 1984—), Am. Arbitration Assn. (Oakland County family law com. 1985—, vice chmn. 1992-93, chmn. 1993-94, trained matrimonial arbitrator), Detroit Tennis Club (Farmington, Mich., pres. 1978-82), Charlevoix Country Club, Tam-O-Shanter Country Club. Jewish. Avocations: commercial pilot, golfing. Home: 30920 Woodcrest Ct Franklin MI 48025-1435 Office: 40701 Woodward Ave Ste 250 Bloomfield Hills MI 48304 E-mail: fmmman1@aol.com.

MORGANROTH, MAYER, lawyer; b. Detroit, Mar. 20, 1931; s. Maurice Jack Morganroth and Sophie (Reisman) Blum; m. Sheila Rubinstein, Aug. 16, 1958; children: Lauri, Jeffrey, Cherie. JD, Detroit Coll. Law, 1954. Bar: Mich. 1955, U.S. Dist. Ct. Mich. 1955, Ohio 1958, U.S. Dist. Ct. (no. dist.) Ohio 1958, U.S. Ct. Appeals (6th cir.) 1968, U.S. Supreme Ct. 1971, N.Y. 1983, U.S. Dist. Ct. N.Y. 1985, U.S. Tax Ct. 1985, U.S. Ct. Appeals (4th cir.) 1985, U.S. Ct. Claims 1986, U.S. Ct. Appeals (2d cir.) 1986, U.S. Ct. Appeals (fed. cir.), U.S. Ct. Appeals (8th cir.) 1994. Sole practice, Detroit, 1955—, N.Y.C., 1983—; ptnr. Morganroth & Morganroth, 1989—. Cons. to lending instns.; lectr. on real estate NYU, 1980—, bus. entities and structures Wayne State U., 1981—; trial atty. in fed. and state jurisdictions, nationwide. Served with USN, 1948-50. Mem. ABA, FBA, N.Y. State Bar Assn., Southfield Bar Assn., Oakland Bar Assn., Assn. Trial Lawyers Am., Assn. Trial Lawyers Mich., Am. Judicature Soc., U.S. Supreme Ct. Hist. Soc., Nat. Criminal Def. Assn., West Bloomfield (Mich.) Club, Fairlane Club (Dearborn, Mich.), Knollwood Country Club, Edgewood Athletic Club (pres. 1963-65). Democrat. Jewish. Office: 3000 Town Ctr Ste 1500 Southfield MI 48075-1186 also: 156 W 56th St Ste 1101 New York NY 10019-3800

MORGANS, SUSAN FLEMING, editor; b. Pitts., Dec. 11, 1947; d. William Emmett and Ruthe (Motts) Fleming; m. Arthur Heister Stroyd Jr., July 21, 1973 (div. 2001); 1 child, Elizabeth; m. Harold G. Morgans, June 16, 2001. AB in English, Miami U., Oxford, Ohi, 1969; MAT, U. Pitts., 1971, postgrad., 1981-82; cert. pub. procedures course, Radcliffe Coll. Gen. assignment reporter, photographer coord. Pitts. Suburban Community Newspapers, 1969; news aide Washington Post/Internat. Herald Tribune, 1969-70; tchr. English and journalism Mt. Lebanon (Pa.) H.S., 1971-75, 80; reporter Spenley Newspapers, 1975-77; contbg. editor Mt. Lebanon Mag., 1981-85, sr. editor, 1985-97, editor-in-chief, pub. info. officer, 1997—. Instr. C.C. of Allegheny County, 1990-91. Editor Jr. League Mag. Dir. Parent and Child Guidance Ctr., Performing Arts for Children, Ctr. for Theater Arts, Jr. League Pitts., South Hills Interfaith Ministries; chmn. Women's Press Club Scholarship Competition, Pitts. Children's Mus. Discovery Rm., Designer's Show House Program Com., Pitts. Symphony Fashion Gala Publicity Com.; mem., vol. Pitts. Symphony Assn., Pitts. Opera Aux., Pitts. Pub. Theater. Recipient Golden Triangle awards Internat. Assn. Bus. Communicators, 1984, 86, 87, 91, 94, 95, 99, Golden Quill Press Club of Western Pa., 1995, 99, 2001, Matrix award Women in Comm., 1987, 90, 95, 96, 98, 99, 2001, 1st place award ea. region Soc. Facial Plastic and Reconstructive Surgery, 1991. Mem. Internat. Assn. Bus. Communicators, City County Comms. Mgrs. Assn., Women's Press Club of Pitts., Press Club of Western Pa. E-mail: smorgans@mtlebanon.org.

MORGANSTERN, GERALD H. lawyer; b. N.Y.C., Dec. 19, 1942; s. Jack and Mildred M.; m. Karen Gibbs, Apr. 28, 1968; children: Jeffrey, Bradley. BS in Econs., U. Pa., 1963; LLB, Columbia U., 1966. Bar: N.Y. 1967, U.S. Dist. Ct. (ea. dist.) N.Y. 1967. Atty. Hofheimer Gartlit & Gross LLP, N.Y.C., 1967—, mgn. ptnr., 2000—. Mayor Village Hewlett Harbor (N.Y.), 1990-2000, trustee, 1982-90. Home: 207 Richards Ln Hewlett NY 11557-2629 Office: Hofheimer Gartlir & Gross LLP 530 5th Ave New York NY 10036-5101 E-mail: gmorganstern@hgg.com.

MORGANTE, JOHN-PAUL, human resources specialist; b. Yonkers, N.Y., June 26, 1962; s. Enzo and Teresa (DellaToffola) M.; m. Ellen Rothberger, May 26, 1984; children: Camden Anne, Bethany Nicole, Hailee Marie. BA, U. So. Calif., L.A., 1984. Ordained to ministry Christian Ch., 1987; cert. profl. in human resources; sr. profl. human resources. Adminstrv. dir. MCM Internat., Lomita, Calif., 1984-87; dir. human resources, 1987-91; exec. dir. Champions for Christ, Austin, Tex., 1991-93; pres. Annimar Assocs., 1993-95; tng. officer Tex. Dept. Health, 1995-97; mgr. human resources The TFE Group, Augusta, Ga., 1997-99, sr. mgr., 2000; corp. human resources mgr. Morris Comms. Corp., 2000—. Contbr. to profl. jours. Mem. ctrl. com. Orange County (Calif.) Reps., 1988-89; intern U.S. Rep. Robert Badham, Washington, 1983, campaign worker, 1984; intern Assemblyman Curt Pringle, Garden Grove, Calif., 1988; campaign worker U.S. Senator Chic Hecht, 1982, U.S. Rep. Robert Dornan, 1984, Reagan-Bush, 1984, Tex. State rep. Terry Keel, Austin, 1996; mem. solicitation bd. City of Austin, 1996-97; del. Dist. 14 Rep. Conv., Austin, 1996; bd. dirs. Area II Soc. for Human Resource Mgmt.; mem. nat. nominating com. Outstanding Young Ams., 1996-2001; peer moderator Nat. Issues Conv., Phila., 1996; campaign work George W. Bush, 2000. Recipient Rep. Presdl. Legion of Merit, Presdl. Commemorative Honor Roll, 1991, Staff Mem. of Yr., 1987; commd. Hon. Texan by Gov. George Bush, 1995. Mem. ASTD, Soc. for Human Resource Mgmt., Augusta-Aiken Soc. for Human Resource Mgmt. (sec. 2000, pres. elect, 2001, pres. 2002). Avocations: golf, travel, music. Office: Morris Communications Corp 725 Broad St Augusta GA 30901 Fax: 706-828-3830. E-mail: jpmorgante@comcast.net.

MORGANTHALER, MARY ELIZABETH, foundation executive; b. Ravenna, Mich., Dec. 3, 1906; d. Ferdinand Ambrose and Bessie Lynn (Hudson) Portzline; m. Otis Philip Morganthaler, Jan. 28, 1948 (dec. Dec. 1975); 1 child, Philip David. R.N., Presbyterian Hosp. Sch. Nursing, Chgo., 1930; B.S., U. Chgo., 1932; M.A., Columbia U., 1933; postgrad. U. Mich., 1939. Supt. nurses Methodist Hosp., Indpls., 1934-36; spl. nurse Dr. Henshaw, dean of dental sch., Indpls., 1936-38; pub. health nurse State Bd. Health, Carroll, Iowa, 1939-41; pres. O. P. Morganthaler Found., Inc., 1964— ; dir. Open Door Sch. for Retarded and Handicapped, New Port Richey, Fla., 1977— . Avocations: bridge; bowling; reading. Office: Open Door Sch Open Door Sch 330 E Ve St New Port Richey FL 34652

MORGAN-WHITE, STEPHANIE LYNN, lawyer; b. Elizabethtown, Ky., Sept. 3, 1970; d. James Carrol and Evelyn Jeanette Morgan. BA cum laude, Wittenberg U., 1992; JD, Samford U., 1995. Bar: Ky. 1995, Ala. 1996, U.S. Dist. Ct. (mid. dist.) Ala. 1996, U.S. Dist. Ct. (we. dist.) Ky. 1997, U.S. Dist. Ct. (ea. dist.) Ky. 1998, U.S. Ct. Appeals (6th cir.) 1998. Staff atty. Ky. Ct. Appeals, Bowling Green, 1995-97; assoc. Goldberg & Simpson, Louisville, 1997—. Mem. Jr. League Louisville, Bus. and Profl. Women, Alpha Delta Pi. Avocation: scuba diving. Office: Goldberg & Simpson 3000 National City Tower Louisville KY 40202 E-mail: stephanie@gsatty.com.

MORGENROTH, EARL EUGENE, entrepreneur; b. Sidney, Mont., May 7, 1936; s. Frank and Leona (Ellison) M.; m. Noella Nichols, Aug. 2, 1958; children: Dolores Roxanna, David Jonathan, Denise Christine. BS, U. Mont., 1961. From salesman to gen. mgr. Sta. KGVO-AM Radio, Missoula, Mont., 1958-65; sales mgr. Stas. KGVO-TV, KTVM-TV and KCFW-TV, Missoula, Butte, Kalispell, 1965-66, gen. mgr., 1966-68, Sta. KCOY-TV, Santa Maria, Calif., 1968-69; v.p., gen. mgr. Western Broadcasting Co., Missoula, 1966-69, gen. mgr., pres., 1969-81, numerous cos., Mont., Calif. Idaho, P.R., Ga., 1966-84; pres., chmn. Western Broadcasting Co., Missoula, 1981-84, Western Communications, Inc., Reno, 1984-90; prin. Western Investments, 1984—. Chmn. Western Fin., Inc., Morgenroth Music Ctrs. Inc., Mont. Band Instruments, Inc., E&B Music Inc., Times Square, Inc., Rio Plumas Ranches, LLC; mem. presdl. adv. coun. U. Mont., 1996—, mem. biol. scis. adv. coun., 2001—. Mem. Mont. Bank Bd., Helena; commencement spkr. U. Mont., 1988, mem. pres.' adv. coun., 1992--, mem. biol. scis. adv. coun., 2001--; bd. dirs. U. Mont. Found., 1985-95. With U.S. Army, 1954-57. Named Boss of Yr. Santa Maria Valley J.C.s, 1968, Alumnus of the Yr., U. Mont. Bus. Sch., 1998. Mem. U. Mont. Century Club (pres.), Missoula C. of C. (pres.), Rocky Mountain Broadcasters Assn. (pres.), Craighead Wildlife-Wildlands Inst. (bd. dirs. 1991-97), Boone and Crockett Club (pres. 2001—), Grizzly Riders Internat. (bd. dirs., v.p.), Bldg. A Scholastic Heritage (bd. dirs. 1987-97). Republican. Methodist.

MORGENSON, GRETCHEN C. reporter; b. State College, Pa., Jan. 2, 1956; BA in English and History, Saint Olaf Coll., 1976. Asst. editor Vogue Mag., 1976—81; stock broker Dean Witter Reynolds, N.Y.C., 1981—84; staff writer Money Mag., 1984—86; editor, investigative bus. writer Forbes Mag., 1986—93; exec. editor Worth Mag., 1993—95; mng. editor Forbes Mag., 1996—98; asst. bus. and fin. editor NY Times, 1998—. Author: Forbes Great Minds of Business, 1997; co-author: The Woman's Guide to the Stock Market, 1981. Recipient Gerald Loeb award, 1998. Office: NY Times 229 W 43d St New York NY 10036*

MORGENSTEIN, WILLIAM, shoe company executive; b. Bklyn., Jan. 11, 1933; s. Samuel and Jeanne Marie (Mittentag) M.; m. Sylvia Dove, June 8, 1952; children: Lee Brian, David Barry. BS in Fin., U. Ala., 1955. Salesman Greenwald Shoe Co., Birmingham, Ala., 1954-56; sr. buyer Melville Shoe Corp., N.Y.C., 1958-67; pres. Kitty Kelly Shoe Co., 1967-70; exec. v.p. A.S. Beck Shoes, 1970-71, Sandia Internat., Englewood Cliffs, N.J., 1971-75; pres., chief exec. officer Marquesa Internat. Corp., Englewood, 1975-95; sr. acct. mgr. Signature Group divsn. Montgomery Ward, 1995-99; regional dir. Advanceme.com Inc., 1999—. Internat. cons. footwear exporting, 1965—. Served with U.S. Army, 1956-58. Mem. Footwear Distbrs. and Retailers Am. (vice chmn., bd. dirs., exec. com.), Internat. Footwear Assn. (chmn. 1989—, vice chmn. 1986—, exec. com. 1986—), 210 Assn. (Pres.' Circle 1987), Toastmasters (past pres. Teaneck, N.J. chpt.). Republican. Jewish. Avocations: history, golf. E-mail: bmorgens@aol.com., bmorgenstein@advanceme.com.

MORGENSTERN, HANS GEORGE, consulting engineer; b. Berlin, Germany, May 29, 1936; came to U.S., 1949; s. Oskar Adolph and Wally Marie (Prothmann) M. SB in Chem. Engring., MIT, 1958. Cert. safety mgr., safety and security dir. Project engr. Bethlehem Steel Corp., Sparrows Point, Md., 1958-66, Edgewood (Md.) Arsenal GS-11, 1966-69; cons. engr. Md. Equities, Ltd., Towson, 1969-75; pres. HGM Assocs Profl. Engring. Cons., Joppa, Md., 1975—. Mem. Rep. Nat. Com., Washington, 1960—; mem. Am. Security Coun., Boston, Va., 1963—; mem. Nat. Com. to Preserve Social Security and Medicare, Washington, 1970—; mem. Ideas for America's Future, Wilmington, Del.; mem. Transit Now, Washington, 1995—. Maj. U.S. Army, ret. Mem. AIChE, KC (3d degree), NRHS, World Safety Assn., Nat. Assn. Self Employed, Internat. Airline Passenger Assn., Res. Officers Assn. (treas. chapt. 28). Roman Catholic. Avocations: photography, model railroading, coin collecting, railfan. Office: 301 Trimble Rd B3 Joppa MD 21085-3817

MORGENSTERN, LEON, surgeon; b. Pitts., July 14, 1919; s. Max Samuel and Sarah (Master) M.; m. Laurie Mattlin, Nov. 27, 1967; 1 son, David Ethan. Student, CCNY, 1936-37; BA magna cum laude, Bklyn. Coll., 1940; MD, N.Y. U., 1943. Diplomate: Am. Bd. Surgery. Intern Queens Gen. Hosp., Jamaica, N.Y., 1943-44, fellow, asst. resident in pathology, 1947-48, resident in surgery, 1948-52; practice medicine, specializing in surgery Los Angeles, 1953-59, 60—, Bronx, N.Y., 1959-60; dir. surgery Cedars of Lebanon Hosp., Los Angeles, 1960-73, Cedars-Sinai Med. Center, Los Angeles, 1973-88, emeritus dir. surgery, 1989—; dir. Bioethics Program Cedars-Sinai Med. Ctr., L.A., 1995—; prof. surgery UCLA Sch. Medicine, 1973-90, prof. in residence, 1985—, prof. emeritus, 1990—. Asst. prof. surgery Albert Einstein Coll. Medicine, N.Y.C., 1959-60; adj. prof. bioethics U. Judaism, L.A., 1996—; dir. Ctr. Health Care Ethics Cedars-Sinai Med. Ctr., 1998—. Assoc. editor Mount Sinai Jour. Medicine, 1984-88; contbr. articles to profl. publs. Served to capt. M.C. U.S. Army, 1944-46. Mem. Soc. for Surgery Alimentary Tract, Soc. Am. Gastrointestinal Endoscopic Surgeons (hon.), Am. Gastroent. Assn., L.A. Surg. Soc. (pres. 1977), ACS (sec.-treas. 1976-77, pres. 1978, bd. dirs. So. Calif. chpt. 1976-84, gov.-at-large), Internat. Soc. Surgery, Western Surg. Assn., Pacific Coast Surg. Assn., AMA, Calif. Med. Assn., L.A. County Med. Assn., Am. Surg. Assn., others. Home: 5694 Calpine Dr Malibu CA 90265-3812 E-mail: morgenstern@cshs.org.

MORGENSTERN, LEWIS B. medical educator; Grad., U. Mich.; postgrad., U. Tex. Resident in neurology Johns Hopkins Hosp., Balt.; assoc. prof. neurology U. Tex. Med. Sch., Houston, 1994—2002. Recipient Clinician Scientist award Am. Heart Assn., 1996. Mem. Alpha Omega Alpha. Office: U Mich Health Sys TC 1920/0316 1500 E Medical Center Dr Ann Arbor MI 48109

MORGENSTERN, MATTHEW, computer scientist; b. N.Y.C. BSEE, Columbia U., 1968, MSEE and Computer Sci., 1970; MS in Computer Sci. and Mgmt., MIT, 1975, PhD in Computer Sci., 1976. Asst. prof. computer sci. Rutgers U., New Brunswick, N.J., 1976-82; research computer scientist Info. Scis. Inst., U. So. Calif., Los Angeles, 1982-84; sr. computer scientist SRI Internat., Menlo Park, Calif., 1984-90; dir. R & D programs advt. info. tech. divsn. Xerox, Cambridge, Mass., 1990-92; prin. scientist Xerox Design Rsch. Inst./Cornell U., Ithaca, N.Y., 1992—. Cons. Hewlett-Packard Corp., Palo Alto, Calif., 1990, Cornell U., 1996—; prin. investigator U.S. Govt. DARPA projects on heterogeneous databases and metadata repositories, 1992—. Co-author: Database Security VIII, 1994; contbr. articles to profl. jours. Mem. IEEE, Am. Assn. Artificial Intelligence, Assn. Computing Machinery, Sigma Xi, Tau Beta Pi, Eta Kappa Nu. Office: Xerox Design Research Inst Cornell Univ 603 Rhodes Hall Theory Ctr Ithaca NY 14853-3801 E-mail: mmorgen@alum.mit.edu.

MORGENSTERN, NORBERT RUBIN, civil engineering educator; b. Toronto, Ont., Can., May 25, 1935; s. Joel and Bella (Skornik) M.; m. Patricia Elizabeth Gooderham, Dec. 28, 1960; children: Sarah Alexandra, Katherine Victoria, David Michael Gooderham. BASc, U. Toronto, 1956, DEng h.c., 1983; DIC, Imperial Coll. Sci., 1964; PhD, U. London, 1964; DSc h.c., Queen's U., 1989. Rsch. asst., lectr. civil engring. Imperial Coll. Sci. and Tech., London, 1958-68; prof. civil engring. U. Alta., Edmonton, Can., 1968-83, Univ. prof. Can., 1983—, chmn. dept. civil engring. Can., 1994-97. Cons. engr., 1961— Contbr. articles to profl. jours. Bd. dirs. Young Naturalists Found., 1977-82, Edmonton Symphony Soc., 1978-85. Decorated Order of Can.; recipient prize Brit. Geotech. Soc., 1961, 66, Huber prize ASCE, 1971, Legget award Can. Geotech. Soc., 1979, Alta. order of Excellence, 1991; Athlone fellow, 1956. Fellow Royal Soc. Can., Can. Acad. Engring., Indian Nat. Acad. Engring. (fgn.); mem. U.S. Nat. Acad. Engring. (fgn. assoc.), Royal Acad. Engring. (fgn. mem.), Cancian Geosci. Coun. (pres. 1983), Order Can., Can. Geotechnical Soc. (pres. 1989-91), Internat. Soc. for Soil Mechanics and Found. Engring. (pres. 1989-94), Royal Glenora Club, Athenaeum (London), various other profl. assns. Home: 106 Laurier Dr Edmonton AB Canada T5R 5P6 Office: U Alta Dept Civil Engring Edmonton AB Canada T6G 2G7

MORGENSTERN, SHELDON JON, symphony orchestra conductor; b. Cleve., July 1, 1939; s. Irwin Arthur and Harriet Sue Morgenstern; m. Patricia Lou Bradshaw; 1 child, Sali Sharpe Hagan. BMus, Northwestern U., 1961; MMus, New Eng. Conservatory, 1966; DMA (hon.), Greensboro (N.C.) Coll., 1986. Mem. conducting staff New Eng. Conservatory, 1965-66; music dir. Greensboro Symphony Orch., 1967-74; prin. guest conductor Betica Philharmonic, Seville, Spain, 1978-82, Polish Radio Orch., Warsaw, Poland, 1990—. Music advisor Miss. Symphony Orch., 1985-86; bd. mem. Istanbul (Turkey) Internat. Festival, 1975—, Company for Televised Theatre; mus. cons. U.S. Dept. Interior for Wolf Trap Farm Park, 1972; mem. adv. bd. Avery Fisher Award, 1978—; music dir. Ea. Music Festival, Greensboro, 1962-98, music dir. emeritus, 1998—. Author: No Vivaldi in the Garage, 2001. Recipient O'Henry award City of Greensboro, 1980, Long Leaf Pine award State N.C., 1989, Nat. Alumni award Northwestern U., 1990. Home: Airans/Farges Ch des Charmys 01550 Collonges France

MORGENSTERN-CLARREN, PAT, federal judge; b. 1952; AB in Polit. Sci., U. Mich., 1974; JD, Case Western Res. U., 1977; LLM, London Sch. Econs./Polit. Sci., 1979. Law clk. to Hon. Jack Grant Day Ohio Ct. Appeals (8th dist.), 1977-78; assoc. to ptnr. Hahn Loeser & Parks, Cleve., 1979-87, 87-95; bankruptcy judge U.S. Bankruptcy Ct., 1995—. Mem. bankruptcy appellate panel U.S. Ct. Appeals (6th cir.), 1999—. Assoc. editor Case Western Res. U. Law Rev. Mem. Order of Coif, Soc. of Benches. Office: US Bankruptcy Ct 3201 Key Tower 127 Public Sq Ste 3001 Cleveland OH 44114-1309

MORGENTHALER, JOHN HERBERT, chemical engineer; b. Cleve., Jan. 5, 1929; s. Frederick Herman and Anna Margarethe (Welke) M.; m. Kathleen Ann Merriman, June 23, 1956 (dec. Oct. 1986); children: John David, Jennifer Ann, Jeffrey Paul; m. Susan Kay Braaten, Dec. 27, 1988. SB, MIT, 1951, SM, 1952; PhD, U. Md., 1965. Group leader Procter & Gamble Co., Cin., 1954-58; project mgr. Atlantic Rsch. Corp., Alexandria, Va., 1958-62; sr. staff engr. applied physics lab. Johns Hopkins U., Silver Spring, Md., 1962-65; project scientist Marquardt's Gen. Applied Sci. Labs., Westbury, N.Y., 1965-67; rsch. dir. Textron's Bell Aerospace Co., Buffalo, 1967-74; sect. mgr. Stauffer Chem. Co., Richmond, Calif., 1974-77; mgr. comml. ventures Bechtel Corp., San Francisco, 1977-78; pres. JHM Assocs., Tacoma, 1978—, Penn Valley, Calif., 1978—. Cons. Moore Rsch. Labs., Inc., Bethesda, Md., 1959-65; mem. adv. bd. U. Tenn. Space Inst., Tullahoma, 1967-68, Assn. Bay Area Govts., Oakland, Calif., 1976-77; chmn. membership com. Nat. Capitol sect. Am. Inst. Chem. Engrs., 1959-61; treas. Buffalo sect. AIAA, 1974. Contbr. articles to Internat. Jour. Heat and Mass Transfer, Jour. Fluids Engring., Jour. Spacecraft and Rockets; patentee in field. Chmn. Joe Berg Sci. Soc., Niagara Falls, N.Y., 1967-71, com. chair Lewiston (N.Y.) Cub Scouts, 1970-71, Walnut Creek (Calif.) Boy Scouts, 1980-82; v.p. Homeowners Assn., Walnut Creek, 1983-85. 1st lt. chem. corps U.S. Army, 1952-54. Scholar Westinghouse Corp., 1947, MIT, 1947-51. Mem. AAAS, Elks, Sigma Xi, Kappa Kappa Sigma (hon.). Republican. Unitarian Universalist. Home and Office: 17646 Long Branch Ct Penn Valley CA 95946-9523 E-mail: jhm6@juno.com.

MORGENTHALER-LEVER, ALISA, lawyer; b. St. Louis, June 3, 1960; d. Gerald Thomas and Mary Louise (Neece) M. BA, S.W. Mo. State U., 1982; JD, Cornell U., 1985. Bar: N.Y. 1986, D.C. 1988, Calif. 1990. Law clk. City of Springfield, Mo., 1981; atty. bd. govs. Fed. Res. Sys., Washington, 1984, staff atty., 1985-86; assoc. Kirkpatrick & Lockhart, 1986-88, Stroock & Stroock & Lavan, Washington, 1988-89; ptnr. Christensen, Miller, Fink, Jacobs, Glaser, Weil & Shapiro, L.A., 1989—. Sec., bd. dirs. L.A. Retarded Citizens Found. Mem. ABA, Calif. Bar Assn. (del. to com. on adminstrn. justice), D.C. Bar Assn., N.Y. Bar Assn., L.A. County Bar Assn. (judicial appts. com.), Beverly Hills Bar Assn., Century City Bar Assn., Women Lawyers Assn. of L.A. (bd. dirs.), 3019 Third St. Owners Assn. (bd. dirs.), Order of Omega, Phi Alpha Delta, Rho Lambda, Phi Kappa Phi, Pi Sigma Alpha, Gamma Phi Beta. Office: Christensen Miller Fink Jacobs Glaser Weil & Shapiro 2121 Ave Of Stars Fl 18 Los Angeles CA 90067-5010 E-mail: amorgenthaler@chrismill.com.

MORGENTHAU, ROBERT MORRIS, prosecutor; b. N.Y.C., July 31, 1919; s. Henry Jr. and Elinor (Fatman) M.; m. Martha Pattridge (dec.); children: Joan, Anne, Elinor, Robert P., Barbara; m. Lucinda Franks, Nov. 19, 1977; children: Joshua, Amy. Grad., Deerfield (Mass.) Acad., 1937; BA, Amherst Coll., 1941, LLD (hon.), 1966; LLB, Yale U., 1948; LLD (hon.), N.Y. Law Sch., 1968, Syracuse Law Sch., 1976, Albany Law Sch., 1982, Colgate U., 1988. Bar: N.Y. 1949. Assoc. firm Patterson Belknap & Webb, N.Y.C., 1948-53, ptnr., 1954-61; U.S. atty. So. Dist. N.Y., 1961-62, 62-70; dist. atty. New York County, 1975—. Former pres. N.Y. State Dist. Attys. Assn.; lectr. London Sch. Econs., 1993. Chmn. Police Athletic League; trustee Baron de Hirsch Fund, Federated Jewish Philanthropies; chmn. Gov.'s Adv. Com. on Sentencing, 1979; counsel N.Y. State Law Enforcement Coun.; chmn. A Living Meml. to the Holocaust-Mus. of Jewish Heritage; Dem. candidate for Gov. of N.Y., 1962; trustee Temple Emanu-El, N.Y.C.; bd. dirs. P.R. Legal Def. and Edn. Fund. Lt. comdr. USNR, 1940—45. Recipient Emory Buckner award Fed. Bar Coun., 1983, Yale Citation of Merit, 1982, Fordham-Stein prize, 1988, Thomas Jefferson award in law U. Va., 1991, Brandeis medal U. Louisville, 1995, Omanut award Yeshiva U., 1995, Trumpeter award Nat. Consumers League, 1995, Frank S. Hogan award N.Y. State Dist. Atty's. Assn., 2000, Lone Sailor award USN Meml. Found., 2000; Matheson-Morgenthau Disting. Professorship in Law named in his honor, Va. Law Sch. Fellow Am. Bar Found.; mem. ABA, N.Y. State Bar Assn. (award for Excellence in Pub. Svc. 2001), Assn. of the Bar of the City of N.Y., N.Y. County Lawyers Assn. (Disting. Pub. Svc. award 1993), Amherst Alumni Assn. (hon. pres. 2001), Phi Beta Kappa. Office: Office Dist Atty 1 Hogan Pl New York NY 10013-4311

MORGERA, VINCENT D. lawyer; b. Providence, Aug. 7, 1935; s. Frank and Elena (Andreoli) M. BA, U. R.I., 1960; JD, St. John's U., 1963. Bar: N.Y. 1963, U.S. Dist. Ct. (so. dist.) N.Y. 1965, R.I. 1977, U.S. Ct. Appeals (1st cir.) 1979, U.S. Supreme Ct., Mass. 1996. Ptnr. Kourakos & Morgera, N.Y.C., 1964-69; mgr. Legal Svc. Clinic, Bronx, N.Y., 1969; ptnr. Ruderman & Morgera, N.Y.C., 1970-73, Kuzmier & Morgera, N.Y.C., 1973-76; assoc. Kirshenbaum & Kirshenbaum, Providence, 1977-81; ptnr. Lovett & Morgera, 1981-82; pvt. practice, 1982-97; ptnr. Lang & Morgera, LLP, Boston, 1997—. With USAF, 1954-58. Mem. ABA, Am. Trial Lawyers Assn. (bd. govs. 1985-87), R.I. Bar Assn. (spkr., chmn. Bench Bar 1981-85), R.I. Trial Lawyers Assn. (spkr.). Avocation: race car driver. Address: Lang And MorgeraLLP 6 Beacon St Ste 615 Boston MA 02108-3801

MORGISON, F. EDWARD, investment broker; b. Clay Center, Kans., Oct. 4, 1940; s. Fred and Lena Edna (Chaput) M.; m. Karen Lorene Herdman, Nov. 21, 1964; 1 child, Diana Michelle. BA in Math., Emporia State U., 1963; MSBA, U. Mo., Columbia, 1964; postgrad., U. Mo., Kansas City. Cert. purchasing mgr.; registered securities agt., Mo., Kans., Ill., 2001. Computer programmer U. Mo. Med. Ctr., Columbia, 1964-65; adminstrv. and budget analyst Urban Renewal Project, Independence, Mo., 1965-66; acct. exec., bank broker Stifel Nicolaus & Co., Kansas City, 1966-73; pres., CEO Will-Mor Investment Sys., 1973-75; br. mgr. Edward Jones & Co., 1975; editl. and exec. asst. to Morgan Maxfield for U.S. Congress, 1976; sr. acct. exec., merger and acquisitions specialist Rowland & Co., 1976-77; chmn. bd., pres., CEO Mo. Securities, Inc., 1977-78; v.p., regional mgr. Charles Schwab & Co., 1978-79; v.p. Profl. Assistance, 1979-81; exec. v.p. J. Penner & Assocs., 1981-82; pres. J. Penner & Co., 1982-83; acct. exec., registered broker Lowell H. Listrom & Co., 1981-84; pres., CEO First Allen Securities, Inc., 1983-89, Venture House, Kansas City, 1989—. Agt. Offerman & Co., Kansas City, 1979-81, CEO Morgison & Assoc., Kansas City, 1979-81; fiscal dir. Housing Authority of Kansas City, 1981; dir., sec. Hubach Group, Inc., 1987-88; treas. Skytrader Corp., 1986-89, Emergency Sys. Svcs., 1986-87, Internat. Tex. Industries, Inc., San Antonio, 1986-88; chmn. bd. , treas. Masters Mark, Inc., 1986-89; CFO Am. Utilicraft Corp., 1992-97, v.p. purchasing, 1997--; acct. exec. N.Y. Stock Exch., Am. Exch., 1965-89. Recipient Bausch and Lomb Sci. award, 1959, Sci. award Lambda Delta Lambda, 1962. Mem. NRA (life), U. Mo. Alumni Assn. (life), Emporia State U. Alumni Assn. (life), U.S. Chess Fedn. (life), Mensa (life). Home: 1000 NE 96th Ter Kansas City MO 64155-2145 Office: Venture House PO Box 28100 Kansas City MO 64188-0100

MORGNER, AURELIUS, economist, educator; b. N.Y.C., May 23, 1917; s. Oscar A. and Anna G. (Hoffmeister) M. BS in Bus. Adminstrn., U. Mo., 1938, MA in Econs., 1940; PhD, U. Minn., 1955. Investigator Dept. Labor, 1941; project dir. Employment Stblzn. Research Inst., 1941-42; instr. bus. adminstrn. U. Minn., 1942-46; lectr. Northwestern U., 1946-47; assoc. prof. Tex. A&M U., 1947-56, prof., 1956-58; vis. prof. U. São Paulo, Brazil, 1958-60, dir. grad. social studies, 1959-60; prof. econs. U. So. Calif., L.A., 1960—, chmn. dept., 1962-69; prof. internat. econs. Sch. Internat. Relations, 1960—. Pub. panel mem. Chgo. Regional War Labor Bd., 1943-45; pub. rep. minimum wage com. Dept. Labor, 1942,43; cons. Govt. Eucador, 1965-68, Govt. Guyana, 1968, state Nev., 1970, Philippines, 1971-72, Yemen Arab Republic, 1974-75; U.S. State Dept. vis. lectr., Brazil, summer 1966 Co-author: Local Labor Markets, 1948, Problems in Economic Analysis, 1948, Problems in the Theory of Price, 1954 (trans. Spanish 1965, Portuguese 1967). Ford faculty fellow Columbia U., 1954-55 Mem. So. Calif. Econ. Assn. (pres. 1965-66), Am. Econs. Assn., Western Econ. Assn., Am. Arbitration Assn., Internat. Studies Assn. Office: U So Calif Dept Econs Los Angeles CA 90089-0001

MORI, ALLEN ANTHONY, university dean, consultant, researcher; b. Hazleton, Pa., Nov. 1, 1947; s. Primo Philip and Carmella (DeNoia) M.; m. Barbara Epoca, June 26, 1971; 1 child, Kirsten Lynn. BA, Franklin and Marshall Coll., Lancaster, Pa., 1969; MEd, Bloomsburg U. Pa., 1971; PhD, U. Pitts., 1975. Spl. edn. tchr. White Haven (Pa.) State Sch. and Hosp., 1969-70, Hazleton Area Sch. Dist., 1970-71, Pitts. Pub. Schs., 1971-74; supr. student tchrs. U. Pitts., 1974-75; prof. spl. edn. U. Nev., Las Vegas, 1975-84; dean coll edn. Marshall U., Huntington, W.Va., 1984-87; dean coll. edn. Calif. State U., L.A., 1987—. Hearing officer pub. law 94-142 Nev. Dept. Edn., Carson City, 1978—; mem. Nev. Gov.'s Com. on Mental Health and Mental Retardation, 1983-84; cons. Ministry Edn., Manitoba, Can., 1980-82; pres. Tchr. Edn. Coun. State Colls. and Univs., 1993-94. Author: Families of Children with Special Needs, 1983; co-author: Teaching the Severely Retarded, 1980, Handbook of Preschool, Special Education, 1980, Adapted Physical Education, 1983, A Vocational Training Continuum for the Mentally and Physically Disabled, 1985, Teaching Secondary Students with Mild Learning and Behavior Problems, 1986, 93, 99; author numerous articles, book revs. and monographs. Bd. dirs. Assn. Retarded Citizens San Gabriel Valley, ElMonte, 1989-94. Recipient grants U.S. Dept. Edn., 1976-91, Nev. Dept. Edn., W.Va. Dept. Edn., Calif. State U. Chancellor's Office. Mem. Assn. Tchr. Educators, Coun. for Exceptional Children (div. on Career Devel. exec. com. 1981-83), Nat. Soc. for Study of Edn., Phi Beta Delta, Phi Delta Kappa, Pi Lambda Theta. Avocations: jogging, travel. Office: Calif State U 5151 State University Dr Los Angeles CA 90032-4226

MORI, MARIKO, artist; b. Tokyo; Student, Bunka Fashion Coll., Tokyo, 1986-88, Byam Shaw Sch. Art, London, 1988-89, Chelsea Coll. Art, 1989-92, Whitney Mus. Am. Art, 1992-93. One-woman shows include Geneva Project Room, N.Y.C., 1993, Shiseido Gallery, Tokyo, 1995, Am. Fine Arts Co., N.Y., 1995, Galerie Emmanuel Perrotin, Paris, 1996, Ctr. Nat. D'Art Contemporain de Grenoble, 1996, Deitch Projects, N.Y., 1996, Gallery Koyanagi, Tokyo, 1997, Dallas Mus. Art, 1997, Ctr. Nat. d'art Contemporain de Grenoble, Venice, Biennale, Italy-Nordic Pavilion, 1997, L.A. County Mus. Art, 1998, Mus. Contemporary Art, Chgo., 1998, Serpentine Gallery, London, 1998, Andy Warhol Mus., Pitts., 1998, Bklyn. Mus. Art, Kunstmuseum Wolfsburg, 1999, Fondazione Prada, Milan, 1999, Ctr. Pompidou, Paris, Ctr. Nat. Photography, Paris, 2000, Mus. Contemporary Art, 2002. Office: c/o Deitch Projects 76 Grand St New York NY 10013-2220 E-mail: mariko@mariko.net.

MORI, MARYELLEN TOMAN, language educator, translator, literature educator; b. Chgo., July 10, 1950; d. John Charles and Helen Veronica (Kelley) Toman; m. Shozo Mori, Feb. 18, 1978; 1 child, Jonathan Masami. BA in English, Yale U., 1972; student, Tokyo Sch. Japanese Lang., 1973-76; MA, Harvard U., 1978, PhD, 1988. Instr. English Kansai Lang. Group, Ito and Tokyo, Japan, 1972-76; instr. Japanese studies, modern Japanese lit. in translation Harvard U., Cambridge, Mass., 1982-83; assoc. prof. Japanese, head Japanese sect. Santa Clara (Calif.) U., 1988—. Contbr. chpt. to book The Woman's Hand: Gender and Theory in Japanese Women's Writing, 1996; contbr. articles and book revs. to profl. jours. and books; translator (book) Kangaroo Notebook, 1996 (PEN USA West Translation award, 1997), numerous short stories. Fellow Harvard U., 1976-77, Stanford U., 1978; scholar Nat. Def. Fgn. Lang., 1977-78; grantee NEH, summer 1997; rsch. fellow Japan Soc. for Promotion Sci., 1999. Mem. AAUW (Dissertation fellow 1987-88), Am. Literary Translators Assn., Assn. Asian Studies, Assn. Tchrs. Japanese, Assn. Japanese Literary Studies, The Japan Soc., MLA, So. Comparative Lit. Assn., PEN Am. Soc., PEN Ctr. USA West, Phi Sigma Iota. Democrat. Avocations: reading, skiing, music, aerobics, cooking. Office: Santa Clara U Dept Modern Langs and Lit 500 The Alameda Santa Clara CA 95053-0001 E-mail: themoris@aol.com.

MORIARTY, DONALD WILLIAM, JR. bank executive; b. Amarillo, Tex., Sept. 15, 1939; s. Donald William and Lorraine Julia (Walck) Moriarty; m. Rita Ann Giller, Nov. 28, 1964; children: Mary Kathleen, Jennifer Ann, Anne Marie, Kerry Lee, Erin Teresa. Student, St. Benedict's Coll., 1957-59, 60-61; BSc, Washington U., 1962; MSc, St. Louis U., 1965, PhD, 1970. Cost acct. Emerson Electric, St. Louis, 1959-63; grad. fellow in econs. St. Louis U., 1963-65, instr., 1965-68; asst. prof. U. Mo., 1968-70; with Fed. Res. Bank of St. Louis, 1968-83, v.p., 1971-74, sr. v.p., controller, 1974-77, 1st v.p., 1977-83; sr. v.p. Gen. Bancshares Corp., 1983-86; exec. v.p. Commerce Bancshares, Inc., 1986-87; bank cons., 1987-89; pres., CEO, bd. dirs. Duchesne Bank, St. Peters, Mo., 1989-95; sr. cons. Universal Fin. Group, Inc., 1996—; assoc. prof. bus. Fontbonne U., St. Louis, 1998—. Vis. instr. Webster Coll., 1975—82; adviser City of Des Peres, Mo., chmn. fin. com., Mo., 1976—78, chmn. mgmt. com., Mo., 1978—81, mem. pers. commn., Mo., 1978—81, mem. planning and zoning com., Mo., 1981—83; bd. dirs. Mid-Am. Payments Exch., Duchesne Bank. Mem. parent's coun. Creighton U., Omaha, 1995—97; mem. adv. bd. St. Joseph Acad., 1982—86; mem. pres.'s coun. St. Louis U., 1983—; dist. chmn. Boy Scouts Am., 1991—93, vice chmn., 1994—2001; trustee, chmn. St. Joseph Hosp., 1982—93; bd. dirs. ea. Mo. region NCCJ, 1987—93. Recipient Alumni Merit award, St. Louis U., 1979. Mem.: Am. Mgmt. Assn., Am. Fin. Assn., Am. Econ. Assn., St. Peters C. of C., Alhpa Kappa Psi, Beta Gamma Sigma.

MORIARTY, GEORGE MARSHALL, lawyer; b. Youngstown, Ohio, Sept. 16, 1942; s. George Albert Moriarty and Caroline (Jones) Bass; m. Elizabeth Bradley Moore, Sept. 11, 1965 (div. 1986); children: Bradley Marshall, Caroline Walden, Sarah Cameron; m. Phyllis A.N. Thompson, May 2, 1998. BA magna cum laude, Harvard U., 1964, LLB magna cum laude, 1968. Bar: Mass. 1969, U.S. Dist. Ct. Mass. 1973, U.S. Ct. Appeals (1st cir.) 1976, U.S. Ct. Appeals (D.C. cir.) 1984, U.S. Claims Ct. 1983, U.S. Supreme Ct. 1976, U.S. Ct. Appeals (2d cir.) 1997. Law clk. to Hon. Bailey Aldrich U.S. Ct. Appeals (1st cir.), Boston, 1968-69; law clk. to Hon. Warren Burger, Hon. Hugo Black, Hon. Potter Stewart, Hon. Byron White U.S. Supreme Ct., Washington, 1969-70; spl. asst. to Hon. Elliot L. Richardson, Dept. Health, Edn. & Welfare, 1970-71, exec. asst., 1971-72; assoc. Ropes & Gray, Boston, 1972-77, ptnr., 1977—. Pres. Boston Athenaeum; trustee Brigham and Women's Hosp., Ptnrs. Cmty. HealthCare, Inc. Mem. ABA, Am. Law Inst., Boston Bar Assn., Somerset Club, Tavern Club, Met. Club. Office: Ropes & Gray 1 Internat Pl Boston MA 02110

MORIARTY, JOHN, opera administrator, artistic director; b. Fall River, Mass., Sept. 30, 1930; s. John J. and Fabiola Marie (Ripeau) M. MusB summa cum laude, New Eng. Conservatory, 1952, DM, 1992. Artistic adminstr. Opera Soc. of Washington, 1960-62, Santa Fe Opera, 1962-65; dir. Wolf Trap Co., Vienna, 1972-77; chmn. opera dept. Boston Conservatory, 1973-89, New Eng. Conservatory, 1989—. Prin. condr. Central City Opera, Denver, 1978—, artistic dir., 1982-98, artistic dir. emeritus, 1998—; panelist Nat. Inst. Music Theater, 1985, 86, 87, Conn. Arts Coun., 1982, 84; adjudicator various contests including Met. Opera auditions, 1965—. Author: Diction, 1975. Bd. dirs. Wm. Matheus Sullivan Found.; trustee Boston Concert Opera; recs. on Cambridge Records and Newport Classics; adv. bd. Shoshana Found. Recipient Frank Huntington Beebe award, Boston, 1954, Disting. Alumni award New Eng. Conservatory Alumni Assn., 1982, Gold Chair award Central City Opera House Assn., 1988. Mem. Nat. Opera Assn., Sigma Alpha Iota, Delta Omicron, Pi Kappa Lambda. Office: New Eng Conservatory 290 Huntington Ave Boston MA 02115-5018 also: Cen City Opera House Assn 621 17th St Ste 1601 Denver CO 80293-1601

MORIARTY, JOHN KLINGE, electronics engineer, consultant; b. Washington, Feb. 6, 1956; s. John Klinge and Mary (Cozart) M.; m. Elizabeth Rouse, Dec. 31, 1987; children: Maire Elizabeth, John Lank, Harris James. BS in Physics, Va. Poly. Inst. and State U., 1981; M of Engring. in Elec. Engring., Clemson U., 1996. Project engr. Delco Electronics divsn. G.M.C., Kokomo, Ind., 1981-84; staff engr. Hekimian Labs., Gaithersburg, Md., 1984-85; sr. LSI design engr. Case Comms., Inc., Columbia, 1985-86; ind. electronics cons. Gaithersburg, 1986-88; mem. tech. staff Bell Labs., Reading, Pa., 1988-97; ind. electronics cons., 1997—. Cons. Squire Comms., Miami, Fla., 1986, Delco Electronics Corp., Kokomo, 1986—88, Mfg. Networks Inc., San Francisco, CPClaie Corp., Beverly, Mass., Wireless Sys. Techs., Inc., San Jose, Calif.; tutorial presenter West Med. Design and Mfg. Conf., Anaheim, Calif., East Med. Design and Mfg. Conf., N.Y.C., 1991; mem. tech. adv. bd. SOMA Networks, Inc., San Francisco; cons. Squire Comms., Miami, Fla., 1986, Delco Electronics Corp., Kokomo, 1986—88, Mfg. Networks Inc., San Francisco, CPClare Corp., Beverly, Mass., Wireless Sys. Techs., Inc., San Jose, Calif.; mem. tech. adv. bd. SOMA Networks, Inc., San Francisco; tutorial presenter West Med. Design and Mfg. Conf., Anaheim, Calif., 1991, East Med. Design and Mfg. Conf., N.Y.C., 1991. Contbr. articles to profl. jours. including IEEE Jour. Solid State Cirs., Procs. IEEE Custom Integrated Cirs., Cancer Treatment Reports. Recipient Supplier Recognition award Hughes Aircraft Corp., 1992. Mem. IEEE, IEEE Electron Device Soc., IEEE Solid State Cirs. Soc., IEEE Cirs. and Sys. Soc. Achievements include patents in field. Home: 2557 River Rd Reading PA 19605-2840 E-mail: jmoriarty@ieee.org.

MORIARTY, JOHN TIMOTHY, writer, transportation consultant; b. Cleve., Jan. 23, 1939; s. James Joseph and Margaret (Healy) M.; m. Angela Marie Veneziano, June 29, 1968; children: Patrick J., Sean Gerald. Student, John Carroll U., 1957, Cleve. State U., 1964-67. Traffic analyst, Cleve., 1957-82; transp. cons. Norfolk So. R.R., 1982—. Author: One Square Mile of Mayhem, 1998, Honest John, 1998, The Phantom Employee, 1998, Sister Mommy, 1999, Thin Ice, 2001, Streets of Gold, 2001. With U.S. Army, 1961-63. Mem. Ill. Internat. Freight Coun. Roman Catholic. Avocations: basketball, billiards, reading. Home: Apt 2615 1111 Independence Ave Akron OH 44310-1896

MORIARTY, KAREN, state agency administrator; b. Mesa, Ariz., June 15, 1957; d. Glenn Federick and Rosalee Mae (Russell) Bowers; m. Brian Logan Moriarty, Aug. 15, 1981; children: Lisa Louise, Kimberly Ann. Cert. pub. mgr. Clk. typist State of Ariz. Indsl. Commn., Phoenix, 1978, acctg. clk., 1978-85, fiscal specialist svcs. I, 1985-96, fiscal speicalist svcs. II, 1996—. Leader, trainer Ariz. Cactus Pine coun. Girl Scouts U.S., 1994—; active United Way, Phoenix, 1996, Big Bros./Big Sisters, Phoenix, 1987-91. Named Vol. of Yr., City of Chandler, 1995. Mem. NAFE, Nat. Assn. of the Deaf, Girl Scouts U.S. (life). Avocations: cross-stitch, swimming. Office: State of Ariz Indsl Commn 800 W Washington St Phoenix AZ 85007-2934

MORIARTY, MICHAEL EUGENE, retired humanities educator; b. Goshen, Ind., Feb. 7, 1941; s. Frank B. and LaVon Edith M. BA, St. Francis Coll., 1965; MA, Western Mich. U., 1968; PhD, Ind. U., 1971. Ouiseau de passage litéraire, Passim, 1971-85; assoc. prof. lang. arts Valley City (Md.) State U., 1986-96; adj. assoc. prof. humanities U. Phoenix, Maitland, Fla., 1998-2000. Interim chair comms. arts and social scis. Valley City State U., 1995-96. Author: Semiotics of World Literature, 1996; contbr. articles to profl. jours. Mem. MLA, Masons, Linguistic Cir. of Manitoba and N.D. (life). Buddhist. Avocations: gardening, hiking, human rights activism. Home: 1417 Illinois St Orlando FL 32803-4155 E-mail: mmoriar2@bellsouth.net.

MORICE, WILLIAM DANIEL, business and tax counselor; b. May 6, 1946; s. John Lowry and Evelyn Mae (Brown) M.; m. Kay Iris Mason, June 14, 1975; children: Elizabeth Anne, Charlotte Katherine, Michelle Alexandra. BSEE, U. Md., 1973; MBA, Emory U., 1976. CPA, Md. Tech. rep. Xerox Corp., Washington, 1965-66, So. Ry., Atlanta, 1973; cons. Mantech of N.J., Washington, 1975, Peat Marwick Mitchell & Co., Washington, 1976-82; prin. Booz Allen & Hamilton, Inc., Bethesda, Md., 1982-84; owner Gen. Bus. Services, 1985-98; CEO Gen. Tax Svcs., Inc., 1996-98; v.p. Century Small Bus. Solutions, Inc., 1998-2000; ea. region mgr. Fiducial, Inc., 2000—. Pres. Apple Limousine Inc., 1988—. Morice and Blohm LLC, 1995-98. Bd. dirs., treas. Nat. Pbt. Bus. Polit. Fund. With U.S. Army, 1966-69. Mem. Md. Assn. Accts., Capital Area Franchise Assn. (bd. dirs.), Beta Gamma Sigma, Tau Kappa Epsilon, Terrapin Club, Friends of Kennedy Ctr. (founding mem.), River Hill Music Boosters (founder). Republican. Episcopalian. Office: Fiducial Inc 10480 Little Patuxent Pkwy Ste 300 Columbia MD 21044 E-mail: william.morice@fiducial.com., bill@moriceclan.com.

MORIE, MARY ANN, non-profit administrator; b. Lee's Summit, Mo., Apr. 10, 1939; d. Philip Edson and Erma Lee (Gibson) Whiting; m. Gerald Prescott Morie, June 3, 1961; children: Christopher Scott, Gregory Vaughn, Bradley Ryan. BS in Edn., Cen. Mo. State U., 1961; postgrad., Ohio State U., 1961-65, Presbyn. Sch. of Christian Edn., 1981-82. Cert. dir. of Christian edn.; elementary sch. tchr. Tchr. elem. Columbus Ohio Sch. System, 1961-65; dir. Christian edn. First Presbyn. Ch., Kingsport, Tenn.; 1981-85; exec. dir. Vol. Kingsport, 1987—. Program dir. Dirs. of Vols. in Agys., Tenn., 1987—, Kingsport Social Services, 1987—, Vol.: The Nat. Ctr., Arlington, Va., 1987—; elder Waverly Rd. Presbyn. Ch., Kingsport, 1986—; pres. Kingsport PTA, 1980-87; cons. Serving People in Need, Church Hill, Tenn., 1987; bd. dirs. Waverly Rd. Day Care Ctr., adv. bd. Link House, 1987—; treas. Families and Community Together, 1985-87. Mem. Kingsport Jr. League. Democrat. Avocations: tennis, needlework, gardening, travel. Home: 4522 Mitchell Rd Kingsport TN 37664-2124 Office: Vol Kingsport 1501 Mccoy St Kingsport TN 37664

MORILLO, VIRGINIA LYNN, hotel executive; b. Silver Spring, Md., Nov. 20, 1967; d. Petronio E. and Wendy A. Morillo. Student, Trinity Coll., 1990-93. Asst. contr. Sheraton Nat. Hotel, Arlington, Va., 1989-98; chief acct. Sheraton Crystal City Hotel, 1998—. Mem. Nat. Soc. Pub. Accts. Avocations: reading, environmental issues, swimming, scuba diving, travelling. Office: Sheraton Crystal City Hotel 1800 Jefferson Davis Hwy Arlington VA 22202-4597

MORIMASA, YOSHIHIKO, educational psychology educator, dean; b. Hijemi City, Hyogo, Japan, Mar. 21, 1936; s. Moriji and Mieko (Suzuki) M.; m. Masako Funayama, Apr. 2, 1963; children: Yumiko, Hiromichi, Risako. BEd, Tokyo U., 1960, MEd, 1962. Asst. Faculty of Edn., Okayama (Japan) U., 1965-67, lectr., 1967-70, assoc. prof., 1970-80, prof., 1980-94, Faculty of Edn., Soka U., Hachiouji, Japan, 1994—, dean Japan, 1996—. Vis. rschr. dept. psychiatry London U., 1976-77. Editor, author: Educational Psychology, 1986, Psychology of Teaching Methods--A Theoretical Approach, 1993. Mem. Japan Soc. Theoretical Psychology (bd. dirs. 1997—, pres. 1998—), Japanese Psychol. Assn., Japan Soc. Ednl. Psychology. Avocation: Go. Office: Soka U Faculty of Edn Tangi-cho 1-236 192-0003 Hachiouji, Tokyo Japan

MORIMOTO, CARL NOBORU, computer system engineer, crystallographer; b. Hiroshima, Japan, Mar. 31, 1942; came to U.S., 1957, naturalized, 1965; s. Toshiyuki and Teruko (Hirano) M.; m. Helen Kiyomi Yoshizaki, June 28, 1969; children: Matthew Ken, Justin Ray. BA, U. Hawaii, 1965; PhD, U. Wash., 1970. Research assoc. dept. chemistry Mich. State U., East Lansing, 1970-72; postdoctoral fellow dept. biochemistry and biophysics Tex. A&M U., College Station, 1972-75; sr. sci. programmer Syntex Analytical Instruments Inc., Cupertino, Calif., 1975-78; prin. programmer analyst, software engring. mgr. Control Data Corp., Sunnyvale, 1978-83; mem. profl. staff GE Aerospace, San Jose, 1983-93; prin. engr. GE Nuclear Energy, 1993-97; mem. tech. staff Silicon Graphics, Inc., Mountain View, Calif., 1997-98; contractor GE Nuclear Energy, San Jose, 1998-2000; project dir. ReachIn, Inc., Mountain View, 2001; editor, Golden Statements Golden State Bonsai Fedn., Inc. Mem. Am. Crytallographic Assn., Assn. Computing Machinery, Am. Chem. Soc., Sigma Xi Am. Baptist. Home: 4003 Hamilton Park Dr San Jose CA 95130-1223 E-mail: cmorimoto@msn.com.

MORIN, EDWARD ARTHUR, writer, English educator, translator; b. Chgo., Feb. 25, 1934; s. Edward Arthur Sr. and Katherine Ann Mindock M.; m. Patricia Elizabeth Rile, Aug. 13, 1960 (div. June 23, 1970); children: Rachel Beatrice, Jocelyn Louise Morin Theophylactou, Leonard Thomas; m. Camille Louise Orso, Sept. 4, 1983; 1 child: Anthony Jasper. AB in philosophy, Maryknoll Coll., 1956; AM in English lang. and lit., Univ. Chgo., 1958; PhD in English, Loyola Univ., 1967. Instr. English, U. Ky., Lexington, 1961-63, U. Cin., 1963-66; asst. prof., lectr. Wayne State U., Detroit, 1966-70, 71-84, 91; comm. expert, rsch. analyst Blue Cross and Blue Shield, 1972-83; product info. analyst Unisys Corp., Plymouth, Mich., 1984-90; lectr. English, U. Mich., Ann Arbor, 1991, Coll. Creative Studies, Detroit, 2000—. Proofreader, Poetry Mag., Chgo., 1957-59. Author: The Dust of our City, 1978, Labor Day at Walden Pond, 1997; editor: Mich. State Univ. Press, 1970-71; editor/co-translator: The Red Azalea: Chinese Poetry since the Cultural Revolution, 1990; assoc. editor: Literary Olympians, San Diego, 1991-92; assoc. and mng. editor: Chgo. Review, 1956-57. Mem. dist. com. Great Sauk Trail coun. Boy Scouts Am., 1996-99, asst. scoutmaster troop 1, Ann Arbor, 1997—. Recipient 2nd prize Internat. Order Narrative Poets, 1983, hon. mention, 1986, 87. Mem. MLA, Am. Literary Translators Assn. Avocations: acting, singing, tennis, baseball, fishing.

MORIN, GARY EDWARD, personal trainer, educator; b. Brockton, Mass., 1963; s. Gary Francis and June Agnes Morin; m. Holly Ann Voill; children: Ally Madelon. P.H.D. Sport Sciences, U. of Conn., Storrs, CT, 1998; MS . Exercise Sci., U. of Mass., Anherst, MA, 1987; BSEHE,Health Edn., Slippery Rock U., Slippery Rock , PA, 1985. Assoc/asst prof./ athletic So. Conn. State Univ., New Haven, 1990; athletic trainer Am. Internat. Coll., Springfield, Mass., 1987—90. Author: (articles) Journal of Athletic Training, Journal of Sport Rehabilitation. Recipient CT. Athletic trainer of the yr., Conn. Athletic Trainers Assoc, 2000. Mem.: Conneuticut Athletic Trainer Assoc. (honors/awards 1990), Ea. Athletic Trainers Assn., Nat. athletic trainers assoc. Office: Southern Connecticut State University 501 Crescent Street New Haven CT 06515

MORIN, LEE MILLER EMILE, astronaut; b. Manchester, N.H., Sept. 9, 1952; married; 2 children. BS in Math./Elec. Sci., U. N.H., 1974; MS in Biochemistry, NYU, 1978, MD, 1981, PhD in Microbiology, 1982; MPH, U. Ala., Birmingham, 1988. With Media Lab., MIT, 1974; resident in gen. surgery Bronx Mcpl. Hosp. Ctr., Montefiore Hosp. Med. Ctr., N.Y.C.; commd. lt. USN, 1982, advanced through grades to capt., 1998; undersea med. officer Naval Undersea Med. Inst., Groton, Conn., 1983; med. officer, diving med. officer, submarine med. officer USS Henry M. Jackson; naval flight surgeon, diving med. officer Naval Aerospace Med. Inst., Pensacola, Fla.; pvt. practice in occupl. medicine Jacksonville; flight surgeon Operation Desert Shield, 1990; spl. project officer Naval Aerospace Med. Inst.; dir. warfare specialty programs Naval Aerospace and Operational Med. Inst., resident in aerospace medicine; astronaut NASA, 1996, mission specialist. Decorated Navy Commendation medal, Navy Achievement medal, Nat. Def. medal; recipient Excellence in Mil. Medicine award, Chmn. Joint Chiefs of Staff, 1994, Sustaining Membership Lecture award, Assn. Mil. Surgeons of U.S., 1996. Mem.: Soc. U.S. Naval Flight Surgeons, Undersea and Hyperbaric Med. Soc., Force Recon Assn., Aerospace Med. Assn. Avocations: amateur machinist, math, jogging. Office: Astronaut Office/CB NASA Johnson Space Ctr Houston TX 77058

MORIN, LOUIS, judge; b. Que., Can., Sept. 29, 1941; s. Paul-Emile and Jeanne Dechene) M.; m. Marthe Champoux, Sept. 12, 1970; children: Francois, Antoine, Brigitte. BA, Coll. Jesuites, 1962; LLL, U. Laval, 1965. Atty. Grondin LeBel Morin, Que., Can., 1966-77; judge Que. Labor Ct., 1977—, chief judge, 1990-98. Mem. Que. Jud. Coun., Montreal, 1992-96; tchr. labor law U. Laval, Que., 1989. Mem. Can. Bar Assn., Que. Bar Assn., Que. Young Bar Assn. (pres. 1975-76), Que. Judge's Assn. (pres. 1989-90). Avocations: skiing, cycling. Office: Que Labor Ct 700 Rene Levesque E St 31 e Etage Quebec QC Canada G1R 5Z2 E-mail: morinls@quebectel.com.

MORIN, PAULA MARIE YVETTE (MARYAN MORIN), photographer, artist, wild horse researcher; b. Hollywood, Calif., Feb. 4, 1945; d. Charles Eugene Robert Anthony Joseph and Mary Elsa (Hoffmann) M.; m. Robert C. McCamey, 1970 (div. 1974); children: Mark Richard McCamey, Ian Eugene McCamey. BA in Fine Art magna cum laude, So. Oreg. Univ., Ashland, 1978; cert. secondary tchr., So. Oreg. Univ./U. Wash., Ashland and Seattle, 1990. Photographer, oral historian Circle Sky Prodns., Talent, Oreg., 1979-81; photographer U. Mont., Missoula, 1981-82; owner, photographer Heritage Photo Works LLC, Prescott, Ariz., 1991-96, Hamilton, Mont., 1991-96; artist, photographer Paula Morin Photo Art and Looking Glass Images, Missoula, 1997—. Field rschr. Oreg. Folk Arts, Oreg. Art Commn., Salem, 1979; mem. adj. faculty Prescott (Ariz.) Coll., 1993; founding dir. N.W. Exposure Photography Inc., Ashland, Oreg., 1979; arts pro cons. Mont. Arts Coun., 1999. Represented in permanent collections Casa Grande (Ariz.) Mus., Mt. Angel Abbey, Oreg., Buffalo Bill Hist. Ctr., Wyo., 1999, Monastery of the Ascension (Idaho), 1999; nat. traveling exhibit Honest Horses: A Profile of the Wild Horse in Nev., 2000-. Profl. devel. grantee Ariz. Commn. on Arts, Phoenix, 1993, Nat. Endowment Arts/U.S. Forest Svc. Ptnrship. grantee, 1999. Roman Catholic.

MORIN, PIERRE JEAN, retired management consultant; b. Quebec City, Que., Can., Aug. 5, 1931; s. Augustin Norbert and Yvonne (Gaudry) M.; m. Colette Poulin, Apr. 3, 1954; children: Anne, Gilles, Louis. BS, Concordia U., Montreal, 1964; MS, Laval U., Que., 1970, D.Sc., 1973. Quality control technician Dow Brevery, Montreal, Que., 1952-56; research assoc. Royal Victoria Hosp., 1957-67; coordinator of research Que. Heart Inst., 1967-73; dir. research labs. Laval Hosp., Que., 1973-80, lectr. dept. medicine, 1973-77; dir. gen. Community Service Ctr., 1980-88; mgmt. cons., 1988-91; ret., 1991. Cons. Que. Minister of Environ., 1975-84. Contbr. articles to profl. jours. and news media. Schering Travelling fellow, 1971 Mem. AAAS Roman Catholic. Home: 336 Rg Castor Leclercville QC Canada G0S 2K0 *Well assumed failure may be a must towards later success.*

MORIN, WILLIAM RAYMOND, bookstore chain executive; b. Escanaba, Mich., Apr. 19, 1949; s. Raymond Louis and Naomi Rita (Flynn) M.; m. Yvonne Catherine Singleton, Aug. 7, 1971; children: Timothy Raymond, Kathryn Naomi. BS in Bus. summa cum laude, No. Mich. U., 1974; MBA, Mich. State U., 1979. Grad. teaching assoc. Mich. State U., East Lansing, 1977-79; instr. U. Wash., Seattle, 1979-80; regional franchise rep. Taco John's, Cheyenne, Wyo., 1981-87; dir. franchising Dawn Donut Systems, Inc., Flint, 1987-91; sr. rep. leasing and rsch. Family Christian Stores, Grand Rapids, Mich., 1991-93; dir. real estate and legal Family Bookstores, 1993—. Contbr.: (book) Principles of Modern Management, 1980. Staff sgt. U.S. Army, 1967-70. Office: 5300 Patterson Ave SE Grand Rapids MI 49512-9512

MORIN, YVES-CHARLES, linguistics educator, researcher; b. St. Germain, Yvelines, France, Nov. 7, 1944; arrived in Can. 1972; s. Georges and Denise (Montaudouin) M.; 1 child, Yannig Lic., U. Paris, 1967; Diploma in Engring., Ecole Centrale, 1967; MA in Linguistics, U. Mich., 1970, PhD in Computer Sci., 1971. Engr. Mil. Radar Estab., Pontoise, France, 1971-72; asst. prof. U. Montreal, Montreal, Que., Can., 1972-76, assoc. prof. Can., 1967-82, prof. Can., 1982—, mem. exec. com. Faculty of Arts and Scis. Can., 1984-86. Invited prof. Bourguiba Inst., Tunis, Tunisia, 1977; mem. cons. bd. Humanities and Social Scis. Research Council of Canada, Ottawa, 1980-83; vis. scholar Centre d'Etudes Metriques de Nantes (France), 1994. Contbr. articles to profl. jours. Served to lt. Logistics-Radar, 1971-72; France Harkness fellow Commonwealth Fund, 1967; Camargo Found. fellow, 2002. Mem. Linguistic Soc. Am., Can. Linguistic Soc., Can. Jour. Linguistics, Société Asiatique, Sigma Xi, Phi Kappa Phi Office: U Montreal Dept Linguistics CP 6128 Montreal QC Canada H3C 3J7

MORING, JOHN FREDERICK, lawyer; b. Farmville, Va., Oct. 30, 1935; s. Scott O'Ferrall and Margaret Macon (Mitchell) M.; m. Margaret Ann Clarke, Mar. 30, 1959; children: Martha, Elizabeth, Scott, Lee. BS, Va. Poly. Inst., 1957; JD, George Washington U., 1961. Bar: Va. 1961, D.C. 1962, U.S. Supreme Ct. 1964. Assoc. Morgan, Lewis & Bockius, Washington, 1961-68, ptnr., 1969-78, Jones, Day, Reavis & Pogue, Washington, 1978-79; founding ptnr. Crowell & Moring, Washington, Irvine, London, Brussels, 1979-2000. Sec. Associated Gas Distbrs., Inc., 1977-2000. Local gas utility columnist: Nat. Gas Jour., 1989—2000; mem. editl. bd. Natural Gas Contracts, 1994—2001. Chmn. bd. dirs. Washington Legal Counsel for Elderly, 2000—01; Rep. candidate 23d Dist./Va. Gen. Assembly, Alexandria, 1973; mem. bd. govs. St. Stephen's and St. Agnes Sch., 1989—95; pres. St. Stephen's Found., Inc., 1990—93; sr. warden Immanuel Ch. on the Hill, Alexandria, 1988, 1989; trustee Ch. Schs. of Diocese of Va., 1996—. 2d lt. U.S. Army, 1958. Mem.: ABA (natural resources law sect. 1982—86, coun.), Fed. Energy Bar Assn. (sec. 1963—66, pres. 1982—83), Indian Creek Yacht and Country Club (Kilmarnock, Va.). Episcopalian. Avocations: golf, fishing, canoeing. Office: Crowell & Moring 1001 Pennsylvania Ave NW Fl 10 Washington DC 20004-2595 also: 2010 Main St Irvine CA 92614-7203 also: 180 Fleet St London ECAA2 HD England Home: PO Box 224 White Stone VA 22578 E-mail: fmoring@cromor.com.

MORIS, LAMBERTO GIULIANO, architect; b. Siena, Tuscany, Italy, Mar. 29, 1944; came to U.S., 1972; s. Gualtiero Luigi and Giovanna (Avanzati) M.; m. Tracy P. Schilling, 1970 (div. 1985); children: Giacomo, Stefano; m. Beverly Chiang, Mar. 28, 1986; 1 child, Christopher. MA in Arch., U. Florence, Italy, 1970. Assoc. Marquis Assocs., San Francisco, 1972-78, prin., 1978-85, Simon Martin-Vegue Winkelstein Moris, San Francisco, 1985—. Tchr. San Francisco City Coll.; juror DuPont Antron Design Awards, 1989; mem. adv. com. Acad. of Art-Coll., San Francisco, 1991—; lectr. Aircraft Interior Expo, Cannes, France, 2000; lectr. aircraft interiors, Long Beach, Calif. Mem. San Francisco Opera Guild; San Francisco Heritage Assn., 1977; mem. design com. Clairmont Pines Task Force, 1991; charter mem. Forecast 21 Principals Roundtable, 1993; mem. Bldg. Industry Conf. Bd. Fellow AIA (mem. Coll. Fellows, mem. interior arch. sect., juror Honor Award for interiors 1996); mem. Italingua Inst. (bd. dirs.), Oakland Met. C. of C., The Engrs. Club, Il Cenacolo Club. Roman Catholic. Avocations: coin collecting, skiing, travel. Office: SMWM 989 Market St 3d Fl San Francisco CA 94103 Fax: (415) 88207098. E-mail: lmoris@smwm.com.

MORISATO, SUSAN CAY, actuary; b. Chgo., Feb. 11, 1955; d. George and Jessie (Fujita) M.; m. Thomas Michael Remec, Mar. 6, 1981. BS, U. Ill., 1975, MS, 1977. Actuarial student Aetna Life & Casualty, Hartford, Conn., 1977-79; actuarial asst. Bankers Life & Casualty Co., Chgo., 1979-80, asst. actuary, 1980-83, assoc. actuary, 1983-85, health product actuary, 1985-86, v.p., 1986-95, sr. v.p., 1996—, also bd. dirs. Participant individual forum Health Ins. Assn. Am., 1983; spkr. in field. Adv. panel on long term care financing Brookings' Inst. Fellow Soc. Actuaries (workshop leader 1990, 93, news editor health sect. news 1988-90, conf. spkr. 2001,02); mem. Am. Acad. Actuaries, Health Ins. Assn. Am. (long term care task force 1988—, chair 1993-95, tech. adv. com. 1991-93, legis. policy com. 1996-99, nominating com. 1996-98, other coms., policy coord. coun. 1999—, sr. mkt. task force chair 2000-01, Founders award 1996), Health Ins. Assn. Am. (conf. spkr. 2000), Life Ins. Mgmt. Rsch. Assn. (strategic mktg. ins. com. 2001-), Urban Inst. long-term care conf. Sharing the Burden, 1994, Nat. Assn. Ins. Commrs. (ad hoc actuarial working group for long term care nonforfeiture benefits

1992), Am. Coun. Life Ins. (accelerated benefits/long term care com. 1997-2001), Chgo. Actuarial Assn. (sec. 1983-85, program com. 1987-89), Health Ins. Assn. Am. (Founders award 1996), Phi Beta Kappa, Kappa Delta Pi, Phi Kappa Phi. Office: Bankers Life & Casualty Co 222 Merchandise Mart Plz 19th Fl Chicago IL 60654 E-mail: s.morisato@banklife.com.

MORISHITA, AKIHIKO, trading company executive; b. Osaka, Japan, Oct. 14, 1941; came to U.S., 1981; s. Sueyoshi and Toshiko Morishita; m. Fumiko Okamura; children: Shizuko, Kumiko, Okamura. BA in Econs., Wakayama U., Wakayama, Japan, 1965. Mgr. Hanwa & Co. Ltd., Osaka, 1965-80; cons. oil dept. Pacific Southwest Trading Co., San Diego, 1981-82; exec. Pacific Marine Bunkering, Inc., L.A., 1982—. Mem. Woodland Hills Country Club. Home: 4610 Don Pio Dr Woodland Hills CA 91364-4205

MORISON, JOHN HOPKINS, casting manufacturing company executive; b. Milw., June 29, 1913; s. George Abbot and Amelia (Elmore) M. m. Olga de Souza Dantas, July 29, 1944; children: Maria de Souza Dantas, John Hopkins III. AB, Harvard U., 1935; LLD, New Eng. Coll., 1973. Various positions Bucyrus-Erie Co., South Milwaukee, Wis., U.S. and Latin Am., 1935-49; pres., dir. Hitchiner Mfg. Co., Inc., Milford, N.H., 1949-93, chmn. bd., 1973-93, chmn. emeritus, 1994—. Pres., treas. Upland Farm Inc., Peterborough, N.H., 1986-98, sec., 1967—; chmn. RiverMead Retirement Community, Peterborough, N.H., 1991-96, trustee 1991—. Commr. N.H. Commn. on Arts, 1967-77; mem. regional exec. com. Boy Scouts Am., Framingham, Mass., 1970-76; mem. exec. com., pres., N.H. Coun. on World Affairs, 1955-76; trustee Canterbury Shaker Village, 1982-96; trustee Land Use Found. N.H., 1970-75, World Peace Found., 1962-90, Currier Gallery Art; pres. bd. dirs. Matthew Thornton Health Plan, 1972-82; bd. dirs. Forum on N.H.'s Future, 1979-81; pres., distbg. dir. N.H. Charitable Fund, 1968-79; mem. corp. MacDowell Colony; v.p. bd. govs. N.H. Public TV, 1979-89. Lt. (j.g.) USNR, 1943-46. Recipient Lifetime Achievement award N.H. Bus. and Industry Assn., 1993, N.H. High Tech. Coun., 1996, Granite State award U. N.H., 1994. Mem. Somerset Club. Unitarian Universalist. Home: PO Box 2001 Milford NH 03055-2001

MORISON, NIALL MACLAINE, business executive; b. Oakham, Rutland, Eng., May 3, 1944; s. Niel and Dorothy Marion Symington (Smith) M.; m. Alison Linda Hill, Feb. 22, 1948; children: Ruairiadh, Ludovic, Madeleine, Lachlan. Student, Edinburgh (Scotland) Acad., 1957-63. Articled clk. Bird & Bird, London, 1963-66; exec. Kidsons, 1967-70; asst. sec. Retail Distbrs. Assn., 1970-74, Gen. Coun. of the Bar, London, 1974-85, dep. sec., 1985-86, dep. chief exec., 1986-94, chief exec., 1994—. Gov. Stonegate (Eng.) Primary Sch., 1995-2000. Home: Bramdean Cottage Stonegate TN5 7EP England Office: Gen Coun of the Bar 3 Bedford Row London WC1R 4DB England E-mail: chiefexec@barcouncil.org.uk.

MORISON, WARWICK LINDSAY, dermatologist, educator, consultant; b. Sydney, Australia, Mar. 31, 1941; came to U.S., 1975; s. Frank and Jean M.; m. Browyn Jones, Mar. 27, 1971. MB, BS, U. Sydney, 1963, MD, 1975. Diplomate Am. Bd. Dermatology. Asst. prof. dermatology Harvard Med. Sch., Boston, 1980-81, Johns Hopkins U., Balt., 1981-85, assoc. prof., 1984-95, prof., 1995—. Sr. rsch. scientist Nat. Cancer Inst., Frederick, Md., 1981-85. Adv. com. Skin Cancer Found., N.Y.C., 1983—, Nat. Psoriasis Found., Portland, Oreg., 1994—. Assoc. editor Jour. Photodermatology, 1999—. Fellow Royal Coll. Physicians, Am. Acad. Dermatology; mem. Photomedicine Soc. (pres. 1999—), Am. Soc. Photobiology, Soc. Invesigative Dermatology, British Assn. Dermatology, Wine and Food Soc. Md. (bd. govs.). Avocations: travelling, gardening, wine and food appreciation. Office: Johns Hopkins Greenspring 10753 Falls Rd S-355 Lutherville MD 21093 E-mail: wmorison@jhmi.edu.

MORISSEAU, NAN KRUGER, television personality; b. Oklahoma City; d. Albert William and Lillie Mae (Kubala) K.; m. Fay Edwin Morisseau Esq., III, June 8, 1974; children: Katherine, Paul. BS, U. Okla., 1972; postgrad., U. Houston, 1986-90. Fashion designer Charm of Hollywood, L.A., 1972-74, Jackson Sq., New Orleans, 1974-75; buyer Federated Dept. Stores Foleys Houston, 1975-80; stockbroker Prudential Securities, Houston, 1980-86; pres. The Newport Beach (Calif.) Recital Series, 1995-99, also bd. dirs.; pres. Cachet' Prodns. Internatl., Newport Beach, 1994—, Golden Girl Jewelry, Newport Beach, 1997—; TV talk show host Rise & Shine with Nancy Morgan Pacific Family Entertainment, Fountain Valley, Calif., 1997—, also bd. dirs., 1996-97. Author (plays) White Russian, 1988, Meyerhold, 1990, (screenplay) Triumph of The Spirit, 1992; actor (situation comedy) Student Union, 1992, (play) Charon Unleashed, 1993. Hostess Chamber Music Salons, 1995-99; pres. Friends of Newport Beach Recital Series, 1995—; bd. dirs. Orange County Philharm. Soc., Big Canyon, Calif., 1996-97. Vol. Ctr. devel. grantee, 1996; recipient Bronze medal Nastar Downhill Skiing, 1996. Mem. AAUW (chair classical music sect. 1997), Womens Diversity Forum, North Orange County Computer Club, Arts Orange County. Avocations: skiing, surfing, computer graphics, music, ballet. Home and Office: Cachet Prodns Internatl 77 Montecito Dr Corona Del Mar CA 92625-1018

MORITA, RICHARD YUKIO, microbiology and oceanography educator; b. Pasadena, Calif., Mar. 27, 1923; s. Jiro and Reiko (Yamamoto) M.; m. Toshiko Nishihara, May 29, 1926; children— Sally Jean, Ellen Jane, Peter Wayne BS, U. Nebr., 1947; MS, U. So. Calif., 1949; PhD, U. Calif., 1954. Microbiologist Mid-Pacific Expdn., 1950, Danish Galathea Deep-Sea Expdn., 1952, Trans-Pacific Expdn.; Postdoctoral fellow U. Calif., Scripps Inst. Oceanography, 1954-55; asst. prof. U. Houston, 1955-58; asst. prof., assoc. prof. U. Neb., 1958-62; prof. microbiology and oceanography Oreg. State U., Corvallis, 1962-89, prof. emeritus microbiology and oceanography, 1989—. Prog. dir. biochemistry NSF, 1968-69; Disting. vis. prof. Kyoto Univ.; cons. NIH, 1968-70; researcher in field. Contbr. articles to sci. lit. Patentee in field. Served with U.S. Army, 1944-46 Grantee NSF, 1962—, NIH, 1960-68, NASA, 1967-72, Office Naval Research, 1966-70, Dept. Interior, 1968-72, NOAA, 1975-82, Bur. Land Mgmt., 1982, EPA, 1986—; recipient awards including King Fredericus IX Medal and Ribbon, 1954, Sr. Queen Elizabeth II Fellowship, 1973-74, Hotpack lectr. and award Can. Soc. Fellow Japan Soc. for Promotion Sci.; mem. Am. Soc. Microbiology (Fisher award). Office: Oreg State U Dept Microbiology Corvallis OR 97331

MORITA, TOSHIYASU, technology professional; b. Tokyo, Feb. 8, 1967; s. Hiroshi and Fusako (Ishikawa) M. Grad. high sch., 1985. Programmer Origin Systems, Inc., Austin, Tex., 1987; engr. Cyclops Electronics, Boerne, 1988-90; programmer Taito R&D, Bothell, Wash., 1990; mgr. new tech. LucasArts Entertainment, San Rafael, Calif., 1990-93; tech. dir. Sega Tech. Inst., Redwood City, 1993-94, Sega of Am., Redwood City, 1994-96, SegaSoft, Redwood City, 1996-97; dir. tech. Sega Am., 1997—. Mem. IEEE Computer Soc. (affiliate), Mensa.

MORITSUGU, KENNETH PAUL, physician, government official; b. Honolulu, Mar. 5, 1945; s. Richard Yutaka and Hisayo Joan (Nishikawa) M.; children: Erika Lizabeth, Vikki Lianne (deceased). Student, Chaminade Coll. Honolulu, 1963-65; BA in Classical Langs. with honors, U. Hawaii, 1967; MD, George Washington U., 1971; MPH, U. Calif., Berkeley, 1975; DSc (hon.), Coll. Osteopathic Medicine, U. New Eng., 1988, Midwestern U., 1993; D Pub. Svc. (hon.), U. North Tex., 1994; LHD (hon.), Western Univ. of Health Sciences, 2002, Alliant Internat. Univ., 2002. Diplomate Am. Bd. Preventive Medicine (fellow); cert. correctional health profl. Intern USPHS Hosp., San Francisco, 1971-72, resident, 1972-75; commd. USPHS, 1968, advanced through grades to med. dir., 1979; promoted to rank of rear adm., asst. surgeon gen., 1988; staff med. officer USPHS Hosp., San Francisco, 1972-73; regional cons. med. manpower planning and devel. HEW, 1976-78, chief internat. edn. programs br. Washington, 1978, dep. dir. div. medicine, 1978; dir. Bur. Health Professions, div. medicine HHS, Rockville, Md., 1978-83, dir. Nat. Health Service Corps, 1983-87, dep. dir. Bur. Health Professions, 1987; med. dir. Fed. Bur. Prisons Dept. Justice, Washington, 1987-98; dep. surgeon gen. USPHS, Rockville, Md., 1998—, acting surgeon gen., 2002—. Decorated D.S.M.; recipient Commendation medal, Meritorious Svc. medal, Outstanding Svc. medal, Surgeon Gen.'s medallion, Surgeon Gen.'s medal, Dirs. award U.S. Marshal's Svcs., John D. Chase award AMSUS, Nathan Davies award AMA, Disting. Svc. award ACHSA, DSM award U.S. Dept. Justice, Fed. Bur. Prisons, Knight Grand Cross of Mil. and Hospitaller Order St. Lazarus of Jerusalem, Disting. Alumus, George Washington Univ., 2002. Fellow Am. Coll. Preventive Medicine, Royal Soc. Health, Royal Soc. Medicine; mem. APHA, Assn. Tchrs. Preventive Medicine, Assn. Mil. Surgeons U.S., Res. Officers Assn., Mensa, Am. Guild Organists, Am. Acad. Physicians Assn. (hon.), Delta Omega, Omicron Delta Kappa. Office: USPHS Office of Surgeon Gen 5600 Fishers Ln Ste 18-67 Rockville MD 20857-0001

MORITZ, BETTY ANN, retired editor; b. Quincy, Ill., Sept. 26, 1935; d. Walter Henry and Esther Johannes (Brandes) Bunte; m. Gary Lee Moritz, Apr. 25, 1959; 1 child, Randal Alan. BS in Journalism, U. Ill., 1957. Reporter Quincy (Ill.) Herald-Whig, 1957-58, women's news editor, 1958-68, living sect. editor, 1970-95, ret., 1995. Home: 3905 Evergreen Dr N Quincy IL 62305-5815

MORITZ, CHARLES FREDRIC, book editor; b. Cleve., Jan. 23, 1917; s. Frederic and Alberta (Hartwig) M. BA, Ohio State U., 1942; student, Harvard U., 1946-47, Columbia U., 1947-48; BS in L.S. Middlebury (Vt.) Coll., 1948, MA, 1950. Asst. librarian rare book room and reference dept. Yale Library, 1948-50; mem. staff N.Y. Pub. Library, 1950-52; asst. prof. Grad. Sch. Library Service, Rutgers U., 1955-58; editor of Current Biography, 1958-92. Cons. editor Current Biography, 1993—; contbr. book revs. for Booklist, 1952-55; also articles. Served with AUS, 1942-45. Mem. ALA, Bibliog. Soc. Am. Democrat. Lutheran. Home: 3210 Arlington Ave Bronx NY 10463-3338 Office: Current Biography 950 University Ave Bronx NY 10452-4224

MORITZ, DONALD BROOKS, mechanical engineer, consultant; b. Mpls., June 17, 1927; s. Donald B. and Frances W. (Whalen) M.; m. Joan Claire Betzenderfer, June 17, 1950; children: Craig, Pamela, Brian. BS in Mech. Engring., U. Minn., 1950; postgrad., Western Res. U., 1956-58. Registered profl. engr., Ill. Minn., Ohio. V.p., gen. mgr. Waco Scaffold Shoring Co., Addison, Ill., 1950-72; group v.p. Bliss and Laughlin Industries, Oak Brook, 1972-83; sr. v.p. AXIA Inc. (formerly Bliss and Laughlin Industries, 1983-84, exec. v.p., chief operating officer, 1984-88; cons. Exec. Svc. Corps Chgo., 1988—; pres. Image-A-Nation, Unltd., 1988—. Bd. dirs. Am. Photographic Acad. Patentee in field. Served with USN, 1945-46. Mem. ASME, Scaffold and Shoring Inst. (founder, past pres.), Mensa, Meadow Club. Office: Moritz and Assocs PO Box 305 Clarendon Hills IL 60514-0305

MORITZ, MILTON EDWARD, security consultant; b. Reading, Pa., Sept. 5, 1931; s. Edward Raymond and Anna May M.; m. Elizabeth Ann Walls, June 6, 1952; children: Betsy Ann Moritz Koppenhaver, Stephen Edward, Sandra E. Student, U. Md., 1950-51, Fla. State U., 1959-60. Enlisted U.S. Army, 1949, chief warrant officer 3, 1968, spl. agt. M.I.; ret., 1970; safety and security dir. Harrisburg (Pa.) Hosp., 1970-72; security mgr. Sprint, Carlisle, Pa., 1972-94; prin. Moritz Assocs., Harrisburg, 1994—. Lectr., instr. Harrisburg Area Community Coll.; mem. Indsl. Security Adv. Coun. Assoc. editor: Protection of Assets Manual. Pres. Greater Harrisburg Crime Clinic, 1974. Decorated Bronze Star with oak leaf cluster. Mem. Am. Soc. Indsl. Security (past pres., chmn. bd. dirs.), Assn. Former Intelligence Officers, Internat. Narcotic Enforcement Officers Assn., Pa. Crime Prevention Assn. (bd. dirs.), Internat. Fraud Tng. Inst. (bd. dirs.). Republican. Lutheran. Home and Office: 7723 Avondale Ter Harrisburg PA 17112-3805 E-mail: 76231.1131@compuserve.com.

MORITZ, TIMOTHY BOVIE, psychiatrist; b. Portsmouth, Ohio, July 26, 1936; s. Charles Raymond and Elisabeth Bovie (Morgan) M.; m. Joyce Elizabeth Rasmussen, Oct. 13, 1962 (div. Sept. 1969); children: Elizabeth Wynne, Laura Morgan; m. Antoinette Tanasichuk, Oct. 31, 1981; children: David Michael, Stephanie Lysbeth. *Wife Antoinette, a teacher, with a master's degree from Ohio State and additional graduate work at University of Georgia, has subsequently devoted herself to raising her children. Son David is a National Merit Scholar attending Barrett Honors College, Arizona State University. Daughter Stephanie is a student in Las Vegas. Daughter Laura Tresca, a teacher with a master's degree from Boston College, is mother of Thomas John, Katherine Elizabeth, and Phillip Timothy Tresca. Daughter Elizabeth Moss, Business and Scientific Administrator, MRC Centre for Developmental Neurobiology, King's College London, is mother of James Frederick Moss.* BA, Ohio State U., 1959; MD, Cornell U., 1963. Diplomate Am. Bd. Psychiatry and Neurology. Intern in medicine N.Y. Hosp., N.Y.C., 1963-64, resident in psychiatry, 1964-67; spl. asst. to dir. NIMH, Bethesda, Md., 1967-69; dir. Community Mental Health Ctr., Rockland County, N.Y., 1970-74, Ohio Dept. Mental Health, Columbus, Ohio, 1975-81; med. dir. psychiatry Miami Valley Hosp., Dayton, 1981-82; med. dir. N.E. Ga. Community Mental Health Ctr., Athens, Ga., 1982-83, Charter Vista Hosp., Fayetteville, Ark., 1983-87; clin. dir. adult psychiatry Charter Hosp., Las Vegas, Nev., 1987-94; pvt. practice psychiatry, 1987—; med. dir. Problem Gambling Cons., 2000—. Prof. Wright State U., Dayton, Ohio, 1981-82; asst. prof. Cornell U., N.Y.C., 1970-73; mem. human subjects biomed. scis. rev. com. U. Nev., Las Vegas, 2000—; cons. NIMH, Rockville, Md., 1973-83. *After he provided 6 years of leadership improving its state and community mental health, mental retardation, and drug abuse services, the State of Ohio recognized his contributions by renaming its Central Ohio Forensic Psychiatric Hospital as "The Timothy B. Moritz Forensic Psychiatric Hospital". During his 16 years of fulltime public service as a psychiatrist at the federal, state, and community levels, he received recognition for leadership in developing comprehensive community services and improved state services. Since 1983 he has been fulltime in the private practice of psychiatry devoted to providing the best possible quality treatment to individual patients.* Author: (chpt.) Rehabilitation Medicine and Psychiatry, 1976; mem. editorial bd. Directions in Psychiatry, 1981— Dir. dept. mental health and mental retardation Gov.'s Cabinet, State of Ohio, Columbus, 1975-81. Recipient Svc. award Ohio Senate, 1981, Svc. Achievement award Ohio Gov., 1981. Fellow Am. Psychiat. Assn. (Disting. Svc. award 1981); mem. AMA, Nev. Assn. Psychiat. Physicians, Nev. State Med. Assn., Am. Assn. Chronic Fatigue Syndrome, Clark County Med. Soc., Cornell U. Med. Coll. Alumni Assn. Office: 1640 Alta Dr Ste 11 Las Vegas NV 89106-4165 E-mail: TBMoritz@msn.com.

MORIYAMA, IWAO MILTON, statistician, consultant; b. San Francisco, Jan. 26, 1909; s. Saburo and Reki Moriyama; m. Toshiko Kako Moriyama; children: Halley Isao, Ken. BS, U. Calif., Berkeley, 1931; MPH, Yale U., 1934, PhD, 1937. Chief mortality analysis Nat. Office of Vital Stats. USPHS, Washington, 1946—61, dir. Office of Health Stats., Nat. Ctr. for Health Stats. Rockville, Md., 1961—74, assoc. dir. internat. stats. Nat. Ctr. Health Stats., 1974—75; chief epidemiology and stats. dept. Radiation Effects Rsch. Found., Hiroshima, Japan, 1975—78; dep. exec. dir. Internat. Inst. for Vital Registration and Stats., Bethesda, Md., 1978—86, pres. and exec. dir., 1986—; chief epidemiology and stats. dept. Atomic Bomb Casualty Commn., Hiroshima, 1971—73. Vis. prof. faculty of medicine U. Tokyo, Japan, 1988; collaborator program for accelerated improvement of civil registration and vital stats. in developing countries UN/WHO; mem. expert panel on health stats. WHO, Geneva, 1950—75, head U.S. delegation Internat. Conf. for 9th Decennial Revision of Internat. Classivication of Diseases, 1975; lectr. Am. U., Washington, 1965; vis. lectr. biostats. U. Calif., Berkeley, 1967; project officer Longitudinal Study of Survival and Outcome of a Birth Cohort, Safdarjung Hosp., New Delhi, 1969—89, Longitudinal Studies in Human Reprodn., Christian Med. Coll., Vellore, India, 1973—89; lectr. in field; biostatistician vital stats. divsn. Bur. of Census, U.S. Dept. Commerce, 1940—46; exec. sec. U.S. Nat. Com. on Vital and Health Stats., 1949—75; editl. cons. Demography, 1966—75; cons. in field. Recipient Disting. Svc. award, U.S. Dept. HEW, Halbert L. Dunn award, Nat. Assn. Pub. Health Stats. and Info. Systems. Fellow: APHA, Population Assn. Am., AAAS, Am. Statis. Assn.; mem.: Internat. Epidemiol. Assn., Am. Epidemiol. Soc., Cosmos Club, Sigma Xi, Delta Omega. Home: 7120 Darby Rd Bethesda MD 20817-2914

MORK, GORDON ROBERT, historian, educator; b. St. Cloud, Minn., May 6, 1938; s. Gordon Matthew and Agnes (Gibb) M.; m. Dianne Jeannette Muetzel, Aug. 11, 1963; children: Robert, Kristiana, Elizabeth. Instr. history U. Minn., Mpls., 1966; lectr., asst. prof. U. Calif., Davis, 1966-70; mem. faculty Purdue U., West Lafayette, Ind., 1970—, assoc. prof., 1973-94, prof. history, 1994—, dir. honors program in the humanities, 1985-87, dir grad. studies in history, Am. studies, 1987-93, mem. Jewish studies com., 1980—, head dept. history, 1998—; resident dir. Purdue U.-Ind. U. Program, Hamburg, Fed. Republic Germany, 1975-76; rsch. fellow in humanities U. Wis., Madison, 1969-70. Mem. test devel. com., advanced placement European history Ednl. Testing Svc., 1993-99, chair, 1995-99. Author: Modern Western Civilization: A Concise History, 3d edit., 1994; editor: The Homes of Ober-Ammergau, 2000; mem. adv. bd. Teaching History, 1983—, History Tchr., 1986—. Mem. citizens task force Lafayette Sch. Corp., 1978-79; bd. dirs. Ind. Humanities Coun., 1986-89; bd. dirs., sec. Murdock-Sunnyside Bldg. Corp., 1980—; elder Cen. Presbyn. Ch., Lafayette, 1973-75, deacon, 1996-99, trustee, 2001—. Mem. Internat. Soc. History Didactics (v.p. 1991-95, 96-00), Am. Hist. Assn., German Studies Assn., Soc. History Edn., Com. for History in the Classroom (treas. 1990-93), Phi Beta Kappa. Home: 1521 Cason St Lafayette IN 47904-2642 Office: Purdue U Dept of History West Lafayette IN 47907-1358 E-mail: gmork@purdue.edu.

MORKIN, CLAIRE D. singer, actress; b. Waukesha, Wis., Nov. 1, 1959; d. Killian Thomas Morkin and Diane Sue Genrich. Writer, performer, prodr. one-woman show Hildgarde, 2000; appeared in Off Broadway musical Zombies From the Beyond, 1995.

MORKOVIN, MARK VLADIMIR, aerospace and mechanical engineer; b. Prague, Czech Republic, July 28, 1917; came to U.S., 1935; m. Alva Heup, 1940; children: Michael, Gregory. AB, U. So. Calif., 1937; MA, Syracuse U., 1938; PhD in Applied Math., U. Wis., 1942. Instr. Mich. State U., 1941-42; Rockefeller fellow Brown U., 1942-43, instr. civil engring., 1943; rsch. aerodynamicist Bell Aircraft Corp., N.Y., 1943-46, Office Naval Rsch., Washington, 1946-47; asst., assoc. prof. aero. engring. U. Mich., Ann Arbor, 1947-51; rsch. scientist Johns Hopkins U., Balt., 1951-58; prin. staff scientist Rsch. Dept. Balt. Divsn. Martin-Marietta Corp., 1958-67; prof. Ill. Inst. Tech., 1967-82, emeritus prof. mech. & aero. engring., 1982—. Lectr. Johns Hopkins U., Balt., 1951-67; cons. in field; mem. subcom. high-speed aerodynamics Nat. Adv. Com. Aeronautics, 1946-49; mem. adv. rsch. com. fluid dynamics NASA, 1968-70; mem. U.S. Transition Study Group, 1975-94; sr. exch. scientist with Soviet Acad. Sci., 1979; guest lectr. Czechoslovak Acad. Sci., 1976, Polish Acad. Sci., 1979. Recipient Alexander von Humboldt Sr. award, 1977, 78, ICASE/NASA Theodorsen lectr. award, 1998; elected to NAE, 1987. Fellow ASME (Fluids Engring. award 1987), AIAA (First Fluid & Plasmadynamics award 1976, tech. com. fluid dynamics 1973-74), Am. Phys. Soc.; mem. Sigma Xi. Home: Apt 209 1116 Washington Blvd Oak Park IL 60302-3650

MORLAND, JOHN KENNETH, sociology and anthropology educator; b. Huntsville, Ala., July 4, 1916; s. Howard Cannon and Ethel Mae (Cowan) M.; m. Margaret Louise Ward, Feb. 26, 1949; children: Carol, Katherine, Evelyn. BS, Birmingham So. Coll., 1938; B.D., Yale U., 1943; PhD, U. N.C., 1950. Instr. Yale in China Middle Sch., Changsha, Hunan, 1943-46; exec. sec. Yale in China Assn., New Haven, 1946-47; asst. prof. Coll. William and Mary, Williamsburg, Va., 1949-53; Charles A. Dana prof., chmn. dept. sociology and anthropology Randolph Macon Woman's Coll., Lynchburg, 1953-87; rsch. analyst City of Lynchburg, 1989-94. Cons. U.S. Dept. Edn., Dept. Commerce, NEH, So. Regional Coun. NSF, Ednl. and Rsch. Found., Lynchburg, Va. Author: Social Problems in the United States, 1975, Millways of Kent, 1958, (with John Williams) Race, Color and the Young Child, 1976, (with Jack Balswick) Social Problems: A Christian Understanding and Response, 1990; contbr., editor: The Not So Solid South, 1971. Pres. bd. nat. ministries Am. Bapt. Chs., USA, 1973-79. Named Eminent Laureate of Va., 1981; recipient Disting. Alumnus award Birmingham-So. Coll., 1985, Nat. Conf. Christians and Jews Humanitarian award, 1994; Fulbright scholar Chinese U., Hong Kong, 1966-67; grantee NSF, Taiwan, 1975, U.S. Dept. Edn., 1972, Liberty Bell award Lynchburg Bar Assn., 1997. Fellow Am. Anthropol. Assn.; mem. Am. Sociol. Assn., So. Sociol. Soc., Va. Social Sci. Assn. (pres. 1963), AAUP (pres. 1962) Home: 1619 Dogwood Ln Lynchburg VA 24503-1923 Office: Randolph Macon Woman's Coll Lynchburg VA 24503-1526

MORLAND, RICHARD BOYD, retired educator; b. June 27, 1919; s. Howard Cannon and Ethel May (Cowan) M.; m. Jessie May Parrish, Mar. 17, 1949; 1 child, Laura. AB, Brimingham-So. Coll., 1940; MEd, Springfield Coll., 1947; PhD, N.Y. Univ., 1958. Phys. dir. YMCA, Frankfort, Ky., 1940-41; dir. athletics, head basketball coach Fla. So. Coll., 1947-50; lectr. in edn. N.Y. Univ., 1950-51; from chmn. dept. phys. edn. to sr. active prof. Stetson U., Deland, Fla., 1952-89, sr. active prof., 1989-90. Chmn. grad. coun, 1962-69, chmn. dept. edn., 1969-75; head basketball coach Stetson U., Deland, Fla., 1952-57. Contbr. articles to profl. jours. Lt. USNR, 1941-45. Decorated 11 battle stars, USS Lexington; named to Stetson U. Sports Hall of Fame; recipient McEniry award for Excellence in tchg., 1983, Richard B. Morland Disting. Alumni award named in his honor; bronze bust by Harry Messersmith dedicated, 1992; So. Fellowships Fund fellow 1957-58. Mem. Philosophy of Edn. Soc. (pres. region 1963-64), Fla. Coun. Deans and Dirs. Tchr. Edn. (pres. 1974-75), Fla. Founds. Edn. and Policy Studies Soc. (exec. bd. 1987-90), DeLand Country Club, Omicron Delta Kappa, Phi Alpha Theta, Kappa Delta Pi, Phi Delta Kappa (pres. region 1977-78, editl. bd. 1978-83, named Regional Educator of Yr. 1991, panel gallup poll on edn., 1995). Home: 524 N Mcdonald Ave Deland FL 32724-3643

MORLEY, GEORGE WILLIAM, gynecologist; b. Toledo, June 6, 1923; s. Francis Wayland and Florence (Sneider) M.; m. Constance J. Morley, July 27, 1946 (dec. 1960); children: Beverly, Kathryn, George W. Jr.; m. Marcheta F. Morley, June 14, 1963. BS, U. Mich, 1944, MD, 1949, MS, 1955; cert. in Gynecologic Oncology, Am. Bd. Ob-Gyn., 1974. Diplomate Am. Bd. Ob-Gyn. Intern U. Mich. Hosp., 1949-50, asst. resident, 1950-51, resident, 1951-52, jr. clin. instr., 1952-53, sr. clin. instr., 1953-54; mem. faculty Sch. Medicine U. Mich., Ann Arbor, 1956—, prof. ob.-gyn., 1970-97, dir. gynecology svc., 1973-85, dir. gynecologic oncology svc., 1964-86, 94-95, Norman F. Miller prof. dept. ob.-gyn., 1987-98, assoc. chmn., 1987-91, prof. emeritus, 1997—. Chmn. Mich. Jud. Commn., Lansing, 1988-92. Contbr. to med. publs. George W. Morley professorship established U. Mich., 1995. Fellow, ACS (bd. govs. 1986-91), Am. Coll. Ob.-Gyn. (pres. 1987); mem. Rotary. Republican. Presbyterian. Avocations: golf, music. Home: 1120 Chestnut St Ann Arbor MI 48104-2826 Office: U Mich Med Ctr 1500 E Medical Center Dr Ann Arbor MI 48109-0005 E-mail: gwmorley@umich.edu.

MORLEY, HARRY THOMAS, JR. real estate executive; b. St. Louis, Aug. 13, 1930; s. Harry Thomas and Celeste Elizabeth (Davies) M.; m. Nelda Lee Mulholland, Sept. 3, 1960; children: Lisa, Mark, Marci. BA, U. Mo., 1955; MA, U. Denver, 1959. Dir. men's student activities Iowa State Tchrs. Coll., 1955-57; dir. student housing U. Denver, 1957-60; pvt. practice psychol. consulting St. Louis, 1960-63; dir. adminstrn. County of St. Louis, Mo., 1963-70; regional dir. HUD, Kansas City, 1970-71, asst. sec. adminstrn., 1971-73; pres. St. Louis Regional Commerce and Growth Assn., 1973-78, Taylor, Morley, Inc., St. Louis, 1978—. Teaching cons.-lectr. Washington U., St. Louis, 1962-70; bd. dirs. Mid-Am. Alliance Corp. and Life Ins. Co. Bd. dirs., mem. exec. com. St. Louis Coll. Pharmacy; past chmn. Better Bus. Bur.; chmn. Mo. Indsl. Devel. Bd., Mo. State Hwy. Commn.; bd. dirs. St. Luke's Hosps., St. Johns Hosp., Downtown St. Louis, Inc., Laclede's Landing Redevel. Corp. Served with USN, 1951-53. Mem. Am. Nat. Assn. Homebuilders, St. Louis Homebuilders Assn. (pres.), St. Louis Advt. Club, Mo. Athletic Club, St. Louis Club, Noonday Club, Castle Oak Country Club, Round Table Club, Sunset Country Club. Republican. Methodist. Home: 14238 Forest Crest Dr Chesterfield MO 63017-2818 Office: 17107 Chesterfield Airport Chesterfield MO 63005 E-mail: harrym@taylormorley.com.

MORLEY, JOHN EDWARD, physician; b. Eshowe, Zululand, South Africa, June 13, 1946; came to U.S., 1977; s. Peter and Vera Rose (Phipson) M.; m. Patricia Morley, Apr. 4, 1970; children: Robert, Susan, Jacqueline. MB, BCh, U. Witwatersrand, Johannesburg, South Africa, 1972. Diplomate Am. Bd. Internal Medicine, subspecialty cert. endocrinology and geriatrics. Asst. prof. Mpls. VA Med. Ctr. and U. Minn., 1979-81; assoc. prof. U. Minn., Mpls., 1981-84; prof. UCLA San Fernando Valley, 1985-89; dir. GRECC Sepulveda (Calif.) VA Med. Ctr., 1985-89; Dammert prof. gerontology, dir. div. geriatric medicine St. Louis U. Med. Ctr., 1989—; dir. geriatric rsch., edn. and clin. ctr. St. Louis VA Med. Ctr., 1989—. Author: (with others) Nutritional Modulation of Neuronal Function, 1988, Neuropeptides and Stress, 1988, Geriatric Nutrition, 1990, 2d edit., 1995, Medical Care in the Nursing Home, 1991, 2d edit., 1997, Endocrinology and Metabolism in the Elderly, 1992, Memory Function and Aging Related Disorders, 1992, Aging and Musculoskeletal Disorders, 1993, Aging, Immunity and Infection, 1994, Sleep Disorders and Insomnia in the Elderly, 1993, Quality Improvement in Geriatric Care, 1995, Focus on Nutrition, 1995, Applying Health Services Research to Long-Term Care, 1996, Cardiovascular Disease in Older People, 1997, Hydration and

Aging, 1997, Advances in Care of Older People with Diabetes, 1999, Endocrinology of Aging, 1999, Science of Geriatrics, 2000, Subacute Care, 2000; mem. editl. bd. Peptides, 1983—, Internat. Jour. Obesity, 1986-89, Jour. Nutritional Medicine, 1990—, Clinics in Applied Nutrition, 1990-92; editor geriatrics sect. Yearbook of Endocrinology, 1987—, Nursing Home Medicine, 1992-97, Clin. Geriatrics, 1992-97, Sandwich Generation, 1997, others; editor Jour. Gerontology: Med. Scis., 2000—. Mem. adv. bd. Alzheimer's Assn., St. Louis, 1990-92; mem. adv. com. for physicians Mo. Divsn. Aging, Jefferson City, 1990—; bd. dirs. Mo. Assn. Long Term Care Physicians, 1991—, Long Term Care Ombudsman Program, St. Louis, 1992, Fund for Psychoneuroimmunology, 1990—, Hamilton Hts. Health Resource Ctr., 1992—. Recipient Mead Johnson award, Am. Inst. Nutrition, 1985, Cmty. Svc. award, BREM, 1997, Robert H. Bollinger Disting. Acad. award, U. Kans., 1997, Longevity prize, Ispen Found., 1999, Circle award, Am. Dietetics Assn., 2001, Nasher/Manning award, Am. Geriatric Soc., 2002. Mem. ACP (geriatrics subcom. 1991-92), Am. Soc. Clin. Investigation, Endocrine Soc., Am. Fedn. Clin. Rsch., Am. Acad. Behavioral Sci., Gerontology Soc. Am., Am. Diabetes Assn., Am. Soc. Pharmacy and Therapeutics, Soc. for Neurosci., La Asociacion de Gerontologica y Geriatrica, A.C. (hon.), Assn. Dirs. Geriatric Acad. Programs. Office: Saint Louis U Sch Medicine 1402 S Grand Blvd Rm M238 Saint Louis MO 63104-1004

MORLEY, LAWRENCE WHITAKER, geophysicist, remote sensing consultant; b. Toronto, Feb. 19, 1920; s. George Whitaker and Mary Olive (Boyd) M.; divorced; children; Lawrence, Patricia, Chris, David; m. Beverly Anne Beckworth; step-children: Sandra Wellman, Stephen Burdett, Richard Burdett. BA, U. Toronto, 1946, MA, 1949, PhD, 1952; DSc (hon.) (hon.) , York U., Toronto, 1974; Dr Environ. Studies (hon.) , U. Waterloo, 2001. Dir. geophysics div. Geol. Survey Can., Ottawa, 1952-71; founding dir. gen. Can. Centre for Remote Sensing, 1971-80; founding exec. dir. Inst. for Space and Terrestrial Sci., Toronto, 1987-91; pres. Teledetection Internat., 1991—. Lt. Can. Navy, 1941-45. Decorated Order of Can. Fellow Royal Soc. Can., Can. Aeronautics and Space Inst., Royal Can. Geog. Soc.; mem. Can. Soc. Remote Sensing (founding pres. 1971-74), Am. Geophys. Union, Am. Soc. Photogrammetry and Remote Sensing, Soc. Exploration Geophysicists, Can. Geophys. Union, Can. Geomatics Inst. Home and Office: 795 2d Ave W Owen Sound ON Canada N4K 4M2 E-mail: morleys2@sympatico.ca.

MORLEY, LLOYD ALBERT, electrical engineering educator; b. Provo, Utah, Oct. 28, 1940; s. John Jr. and Dorothea (Nielsen) M.; m. Jo Ann Bryant, Feb. 22, 1975; 1 child, Paul Loring. BS in Mining Engring., U. Utah, 1968, PhD in Mining Engring., 1972. Tchg. asst., rsch. assoc. U. Utah, Salt Lake City, 1968-71; asst. prof. mining engring. Pa. State U., University Park, 1971-75, assoc. prof., 1975-80, prof., 1980-85; prof., head dept. mineral engring. U. Ala., Tuscaloosa, 1985-93, endowed chair mining engring., 1993-99, prof. elec. engring., 1996—, assoc. dept. head elec. and computer engring., 1997-99, interim head, 1999-2000, head, 2000—. Cons. Jim Walter Resources, Inc., Brookwood, Ala., 1987-98, Pitts. and Midway Coal Mining Co., Englewood, Colo., 1990-98, Drummond Co., Inc., Birmingham, Ala., 1991-98. Author: Mine Power Systems, 1990; contbr. articles to profl. jours. Staff sgt. USNG, 1958-66. Recipient Wilson Outstanding Teaching award Pa. State U., 1980; Outstanding Rsch. Report awards U.S. Bur. Mines, 1983-84, grantee, 1971-87. Fellow IEEE (bd. dirs. 1991-92, 94, 97-99, v.p. publs. 1994, 99, v.p. tech. activities 1997, 98); mem. Industry Applications Soc. IEEE (Mining Best Paper awards 1984, 88, 90, pres. 1988, Disting. lectr. 1991, Disting. Svc. award 1995), Power Engr. Soc., Computer Soc. Standards Assn. Avocations: high-fidelity systems, classic sports cars, rose growing, music. Office: U Ala Dept Electrical and Computer Engring PO Box 870286 Tuscaloosa AL 35487-0286 E-mail: l.morley@ieee.org.

MORLEY, ROBERT, JR. electrical engineer, educator; b. St. Louis, Apr. 20, 1951; s. Robert E. Morley, Mary Jane Morley; m. Deborah Lee Horsfall; children: Jonathan, Merinda, Kerstin. BSEE, Washington U., 1973, MSEE, 1975, DSc in Elec. Engring., 1977. V.p. engring. Micro-Term, Inc., St. Louis, 1976—81; asst. prof. Washington U., 1981—87, assoc. prof., 1987—. Expert witness in patent infringement litigation, 1983—. Mem.: IEEE (sr. Young Profl. award 1981). Achievements include invention of digital hearing aid. Office: Washington Univ Box 1127 One Brookings Dr Saint Louis MO 63130 Office Fax: 314-935-7500. Business E-Mail: rem@ee.wustl.edu.

MORLEY, WILLIAM GEORGE, retired military officer, educator; b. Stockton, Calif., June 4, 1924; s. George Irwin and Helen Geers M.; m. Marian Elise Morley, Nov. 24, 1945; children: Susan Elise, John Philip, Kristina, Kevin James. BS in Polit. Sci., Georgetown U., 1956. Commd. 2d lt. USAF, 1943, advanced through grades to lt. col., dir. combat aircraft ops. 815th Air Divsn. Vietnam, 1969—70, ret., 1973; exec. administr. Arnold Air Soc., Washington, 1973-90. Mo. valley liaison officer USAF Acad., St. Louis, 1960-63. V.p. Greater Lake Palstine Coun., Chandler, Tex., 1997-2002. Decorated Air medal, USAF, 1991. Mem. AF Assn. (advisor 1976-90, Citation 1990), Arnold Air Soc. (trustee Silver Wings 1990—). Republican. Roman Catholic. Avocations: golf, real property development, writing. Home: Emerald Bay 134 Marina Dr Bullard TX 75757 Office: Blue Heron Publs Emerald Bay Profl Ctr Bullard TX 75757 E-mail: blueheronpub@yahoo.com.

MORLOK, EDWARD KARL, engineering educator, consultant; b. Phila., Nov. 3, 1940; s. Edward Karl and Anna Marie (Kurtz) M.; m. Ottilia Angela Husz, Dec. 14, 1968 (div. July 1983); 1 child, Jessica Angela; m. Patricia Campbell Conboy, Mar. 23, 1991. BE, Yale U., 1962; PhD, Northwestern U., 1967; MA (hon.), U. Pa., 1973. Civil engr., transp. U.S. Dept. Commerce, Washington, 1966-67; from asst. prof. civil engring. to assoc. prof. Northwestern U., Evanston, Ill., 1967-73, asst. dir. rsch., transp. ctr., 1969-73; 1907 Found. assoc. prof. U. Pa., Phila., 1973-75, chmn., transp. grad. group, 1983-86, 91-95, UPS found. prof. transp., 1975—, prof. systems engring., 1986—, chair systems grad. program, 1988-91. Cons. nat. transp. policy study commn., Washington, 1978-79. Author: Analysis Transportation Technology and Network Structure, 1969, Introduction to Transportation Engineering and Planning, 1978; assoc. editor Transp. Rsch. Jour., 1975—; consulting editor series in transp. for McGraw-Hill Publ. Co., 1980-98; contbr. more than 80 articles to profl. jours. Mem. Nat. Assembly Engring. panel on innovation in transp., Washington, 1979-80, panel on hazardous material transp., Washington, 1980-81. Recipient U.S. Sr. Scientist award Alexander von Humboldt Found., 1980-81; rsch. grantee Commonwealth of Pa., Consol. Rail Corp., K-Line Am., U.S. Dept. Transp., NASA, NSF. Mem. Inst. Ops. Rsch. and Mgmt., Transp. Rsch. Forum (v.p. 1974-75, pres. 1975-76, bd. disting. mems. 1983—, Disting. Transp. Rsch. award 1998), Transp. Rsch. Bd. (rev. com. of coun. of univ. transp. ctrs. 1985-88, coun. mem. 1988-90, chair freight transp. planning and logistics com. 1994-99, chair com. on policy options for intermodal freight trans. 1996-98). Lutheran. Office: U Pa Dept Elec and Systems Engring 220 S 33rd St Philadelphia PA 19104-6315 E-mail: morlok@seas.upenn.edu.

MORNEAU, BILL, financial consultant; Pres., CEO Morneau Sobeco, Toronto, Canada. Office: Morneau Sobeco 1500 Don Mills Rd Ste 50 Toronto ON Canada M3B 3K4

MORNER, SVEIN OLAV, mechanical engineer, researcher; b. Oslo, Norway, Aug. 23, 1966; s. Bjorn H. Ruud, AAse Morner. PhD, Norwegian Inst. Tech., Trondheim, Norway, 1995. Registered profl. engr., Wis. Project engr. ABB Environ., Oslo, 1995—96; postdoctoral staff U. Wis., Madison, 1997—98; sr. engr. Farnsworth Group, Inc., 1999—. Contbr. articles to profl. jours. Sgt. Norwegian Army, 1990—91. Mem.: ASHRAE, Rotary. Home: 6908 Tottenham Rd Madison WI 53711 Office: Farnsworth Group Inc 7601 Ganser Way Madison WI 53719 Office Fax: 608-827-6886. Business E-Mail: smorner@f-w.com.

MORNHINWEG, CLAUDIA BETH JONES, music educator; b. Edmond, Okla., Nov. 27, 1951; d. Claude George and Dorothy Gwyn (Frederick) Jones; m. Steve Pierson Mornhinweg, Feb. 15, 1975; children: Jeffrey, Paul, Gary. B in Music Edn., U. Ctrl. Okla., 1974; BS in Elem. Edn., East Ctrl. U., 1979. Elem. music tchr. Whitesboro (Okla.) Elem. Sch., 1976-77; pvt. piano tchr., 1975—; elem. music tchr. Byng (Okla.) Elem. Sch., 1988—; ch. organist, pianist Asbury Meth. Ch., Ada, Okla., 1991—. Mem. Okla. Music Tchrs. Assn. (judge 1985—, membership com. 1992-94), Music Edn. Nat. Assn., Nat. Fedn. of Music Clubs, Beta Sigma Phi (all offices, City Girl of Yr. 1985). Republican. Methodist. Avocations: reading, music, piano, snow skiing, travel. Home: RR 6 Box 860 Ada OK 74820-9262 Office: Byng Elem Sch RR 3 Box 215 Ada OK 74820-9517

MORNING, JOHN, graphic designer; b. Cleve., Jan. 8, 1932; s. John Frew and Juanita Kathryn (Brannan) M.; m. Carole Ann Coleman, Jan. 24, 1964 (div. July 1984); children: Ann Juanita, John Floyd. BFA, Pratt Inst., 1955. Art dir. McCann-Erickson, Inc., N.Y.C., 1958-60; pvt. practice design, 1960—. Bd. dirs. Dime Savings Bank N.Y. Trustee Wilberforce U., 1986-, CUNY, 1997-, Rockefeller BRos. Fund, 1999-, Charles Stewart Mott Found., 2000-; trustee com. on edn. Mus. Modern Art; chmn. bd .trustees Pratt Inst., Bklyn., 1988—92; vice chmn. N.Y.C. Cultural Affairs Adv. Commn., 1994—2000; dir. N.Y. Coun. for Humanities, 1999—; Bd. dirs. N.Y. Landmarks Conservancy, Charles E. Culpepper Found., 1990-, Henry St. Settlement, chmn., 1979-86, Bklyn. Acad. Music, 1993, Lincoln Ctr. Inst., 1993, Vivian Beaumont Theater, 1995-; bd. dirs. Mus. African Art, N.Y.C., co-chair, 1991-94. With U.S. Army, 1956—58. Recipient Alumni medal Pratt Inst., 1972, Presdl. Recognition award Pres. of U.S., 1984, Lillian D. Wald Humanitarian award, 1992. Mem.: Assn. Governing Bds. Colls. and Univs. (bd. dirs., chmn. 1998—2000), Am. Acad. Dramatic Arts (trustee 1988—95). Republican. E-mail: 110733.3622@compuserve.com .

MOROCHNIK, PAUL J. lawyer; b. New Britain, Conn., Dec. 19, 1967; s. Sidney A. and Phyllis P. Morochnik; m. Halley Steele, Aug. 14, 1993; children: Rachel, Zachary. BA in Econs., Hofstra U., 1990; JD, Emory U., 1993. Bar: Ga. 1993, U.S. Dist. Ct. (no. dist.) Ga. 1993, U.S. Ct. Appeals (11th cir. 1993), U.S. Dist. Ct. (mid. dist.) Ga. 1998, U.S. Supreme Ct. 1998. Assoc. Alexander and Oliver, Atlanta, 1993, Alexander & Assocs., Atlanta, 1993-95, Thompson, O'Brien, Kemp & Nasuti, P.C., Norcross, Ga., 1995—. Office: Thompson O'Brien Kemp & Nasuti PC 4845 Jimmy Carter Blvd Norcross GA 30093-3614

MORONEY, JAMES M. publishing executive, broadcast executive; m. Barbara Moroney; 5 children. BA in Am. Studies, Stanford U., 1978; MBA, U. Tex., 1983. With Petry TV, NY; acct. exec. Belo stas. WFAA, KFDM-TV, Beaumont, Tex., 1978—84; local sales mgr. WFAA, 1985; controller Belo, Dallas, 1989, asst. to pres. co.'s broadcast divsn., 1990—92, exec. v.p., 1998; founding pres. Belo Interactive (subs. of Belo), 1999; promoted to gen. sales mgr. KOTV, pres., gen. mgr., 1992, promoted to pres., gen. mgr., 1993, v.p. broadcast divsn., 1993; exec. v.p. TV Group, 1995, promoted to pres., 1997; pub., CEO The Dallas Morning News, 2001—. Mem. Dallas Citizens Coun.; mem. bd. dirs. TV Bur. Adv., Goodwill Industries, Dallas, Tulsa, United Way Tulsa, Cath. Charities Tulsa, Jr. Achievement Tulsa, Gilcrease Mus. Tulsa, Cistercian Perp. Sch. Dallas, Greater Dallas Chamber, State Fair Tex.; mem. bd. dirs. Coll. Comm. U. Tex. Austin. Office: Dallas Morning News PO Box 655237 Dallas TX 75265-5237 Address: 508 Young St Dallas TX 75202-4808*

MORONEY, LINDA L.S. (MUFFIE), lawyer, educator; b. Washington, May 27, 1943; d. Robert Emmet and Jessie (Robinson) M.; m. Clarence Renshaw II, Mar. 28, 1967 (div. 1977); children: Robert Milnor, Justin W.R. BA, Randolph-Macon Woman's Coll., 1965; JD cum laude, U. Houston, 1982. Bar: Tex. 1982, U.S. Ct. Appeals (5th cir.) 1982, U.S. Dist. Ct. (so. dist.) Tex. 1982, U.S. Supreme Ct. 1988. Law clk. to assoc. justice 14th Ct. Appeals, Houston, 1982-83; assoc. Pannill and Reynolds, 1983-85, Gilpin, Pohl & Bennett, Houston, 1985-89, Vinson & Elkins, Houston, 1989-92. Adj. prof. law U. Houston, 1986-91, dir. legal rsch. and writing, 1992-96, civil trial and appellate litigation and mediation, 1996—. Mem. ABA, State Bar Tex., Houston Bar Assn., Assn. of Women Attys., Tex. Women Lawyers, Order of the Barons, Phi Delta Phi. Episcopalian. Home and Office: 4010 Whitman St Houston TX 77027-6334

MORONEY, MICHAEL JOHN, lawyer; b. Jamaica, N.Y., Nov. 8, 1940; s. Everard Vincent and Margaret Olga (Olson) M.; children: Sean, Megan, Matthew. BS in Polit. Sci., Villanova U., 1962; JD, Fordham U., 1965; Police Sci. (hon.), U. Guam, 1976. Bar: Hawaii 1974, U.S. Dist. Ct. Hawaii 1974, U.S. Ct. Appeals (9th cir.) 1974, Guam 1976, U.S. Dist. Ct. (Guam dist.) 1976, U.S. Ct. Claims 1976, U.S. Tax Ct. 1976, U.S. Ct. Mil. Appeals 1977, U.S. Supreme Ct. 1977, High Ct. Trust Ters. 1977, U.S. Dist. Ct. (No. Mariana Islands) 1983. Spl. agt. FBI, Memphis and Nashville, 1965-67, Cleve. and Elyria, Ohio, 1967-71; spl. agt., prin. legal advisor FBI, U.S. Dept. Justice, Honolulu, 1971-97; v.p. Merrill Corp., 1997-2000; mgr. Investigative Svcs. Worldwide, 2000—; mng. dir. Paradise Meml. Park, LLC, Honolulu, 2000—; pres., mgr. ISW, LLC, 2000—. Bar examiner and applications rev. com. Supreme Ct. Hawaii, 1980—; pres. Hawaii State Law Enforcement Assn., 1985-86; mem. and del. to congress Gov.'s Task Force on Hawaii's Internat. Role, 1988; mem. Charter Commn., City and County of Honolulu, 1998-2000; mem. Consular Corps of Hawaii, 1997-2000; regent Harris Manchester Coll., Oxford U., 2000—. Gov.'s task force, del. gov.'s congress on Hawaii's Internat. Role, 1988—; apptd. hon. consul gen. Republic of Palau, Pres. Kunio Nakamura, 1999. Recipient Govs. Award for outstanding contbns. to law enforcement Govt. of Guam, 1974, 76, cert. of appreciation Supreme Ct. Hawaii, 1981, Honolulu Police Commn., 1984, 86; named Fed. Law Enforcement Officer of Yr., State of Hawaii, 1992, Outstanding Career award in law enforcement and commitment to Hawaii State Law Enforcement Ofcls. Assn., 1998. Mem. ABA, Hawaii Bar Assn., Guam Bar Assn., Inst. Jud. Adminstrn., Hawaii State Law Enforcement Ofcls. Assn., Hilo Yacht Club, Oahu Country Club, Plaza Club, Rotary Club Honolulu. Address: 7858 Makaaoa Pl Honolulu HI 96825-2848 Office: Paradise Meml Park LLC 1154 Fort Street Mall Ste 300 Honolulu HI 96813-2712 Fax: 808-599-5004. E-mail: mmoro007@aol.com.

MOROOKA, HIROSHI, neurosurgeon; b. Kurashiki, Okayama, Japan, Aug. 28, 1946; s. Shigeru and Akiko (Kobayashi) M.; m. Michiko Ninomiya, June 6, 1976; children: Takatoshi, Hanako, Teruko. MD, U. Okayama, 1971, D Med. Sci., 1978. Diplomate Japanese Bd. Neurol. Surgery. Clin. asst. neurosurgery U. Okayama Med. Sch., 1972-77, instr. neurosurgery, 1980-83, asst. prof. neurosurgery, 1984-86; rsch. assoc. neurology U. Miami (Fla.) Med. Sch., 1977-79; chief neurosurgery Okayama Rousai Hosp., 1987-92, Bizen City Hosp., 1993-95, Okayama Saidaiji Hosp., 1996—. Author: Cytoprotection & Cytobiology, 1995-97, Medical Biochemical & Chemical Aspects of Free Radicals, 1989, Intracranial Pressure VII, 1989, Brain Edema IX, 1993. Recipient Nat. Rsch. grant, 1981. Mem. Japan Neurol. Soc., Societas Neurologica Japonica, N.Y. Acad. Scis., Am. Heart Assn. Liberal Dem. Christian. Avocation: golf, Go (7th degree). Home: 880-165 Minato 703 8266 Okayama Japan Office: Okayama Saidaiji Hosp 8-41 Saidaiji Nakano Honmachi Okayama 704-8192 Japan E-mail: morooka@okym.enjoy.ne.jp.

MOROSANI, GEORGE WARRINGTON, real estate developer, realtor; b. Cin., July 20, 1941; s. Remy Edmond and Virginia Caroline (Warrington) M.; m. Judith Clontz, July 3, 1980; children by previous marriage: Katherine Carmichael, Elizabeth Warrington. BA, Rollins Coll., 1964, MBA, 1965. Fin. mgr. Lunar Orbitor and Minuteman Programs, Boeing Co., Cape Canaveral, Fla., 1965-68; controller Equitable Leasing Co., Asheville, N.C., 1968-69; founder, pres., treas. Western Carolina Warehousing Co., Asheville, 1969-87; co-founder, pres. Asheville Jaycee Housing, Inc., 1971-77; founder, pres., treas. A Mini Storage Co. (dba George's Stor-Mor), Asheville, N.C., 1976—; co-founder, treas. Accent on Living Co., Asheville, 1978-81; founder, pres., treas. G.M. Leasing, Asheville, N.C. 1986—, The Kingswood Co., Fletcher, N.C., 1986—; gen. partner Pine Needle Apts., Arden, N.C., 1978—, Pine Ridge Apts., Skyland, N.C., 1980—, Morganton Heights Apts., Morganton, N.C., 1981—, Maiden (N.C.) Apts., 1981—, Valley View Shopping Ctr., Candler, N.C., 1982-86, Meadow Garden Apts., Hendersonville, N.C., 1983—, Drexel Apts., N.C., 1983—, Heritage Hill Apts., Marion, N.C., 1983—, Cavalier Arms Apts., Waynesville, N.C., 1986—, Gwenmont Arms Apts., Murphy, N.C., 1986—, Nicol Arms Apts., Sylva, N.C., 1986—, Meadowwood Arms Apts., Gray, Tenn., 1986—, 4 Seasons Apts., Erwin, Tenn., 1986—, M. Realty LP, Asheville, 1986—, Woods Edge Apts., North Wilksboro, N.C., 1987—, Pond and Assocs., Asheville, 1992-94, Deer Park Apts., Cleve., N.C., 1987—; ptnr. Laurel Ridge Realty, Litchfield, Conn., 1973—, Laurel Properties, Rochester, Vt., 1978-94, Ashland Assocs., Asheville, N.C., 1985-88, Airport Assocs., Asheville, 1986-87; founder, owner George W. Morosani & Assocs., Asheville, 1981—, George's Rent-All, Asheville, N.C., 1988—; mgr. FI Realty I LLC, 1993—, Western Realty LLC, Asheville, 1994—, M Realty I LLC, 1994—, Sweeten Creek Realty LLC, 1994—, FI Realty I, LLC, 1994—, Patton Ave, LLC, 1995—, 3M Realty, LLC, 1995—, 3883 Sweeten Creek, LLC, 1997—. Bd. dirs. Jr. Achievement Greater Asheville Area, 1977—; mem. Regional Housing Adv. Com., 1981-86, Land-of-Sky Regional Coun., 1981-86, bd. dirs, 1990—; mem. Council Rural Housing and Devel., 1982-86, N.C. Real Estate Licensing Bd., S.C. Real Estate Commn., Tenn. Real Estate Commn., Ga. Real Estate Licensing Bd., Asheville Multiple Listing Svc., Hendersonville Multiple Listing Svc.; co-founder, treas. N.C. Council Rural Rental Housing, 1985—, sec., 1986-91; mem. Buncombe County Bd. Adjustment, 1988—, vice chmn., 1991—. Named Man of Yr., Asheville Jaycees, 1976. Mem. Sales and Mktg. Execs. Asheville (dir. 1974-76, 1982-84. chmn. membership com. 1976-77), Asheville Bd. Realtors, Hendersonville Bd. Realtors, Nat. Assn. Realtors, N.C. Assn. Realtors (property mgmt. div.). Mem. Asheville Comml. and Investment Realty Assn. (v.p. programs 1986-87, sec.-treas. 1987-92, 94—, pres., 1993), Nat. Mini-Storage Inst., W.N.C. Exchangers, Greater Asheville Apt. Assn. (chmn. membership com. 1988-89), Council Ind. Bus. Owners, Better Bus. Bur. Asheville/Western N.C. (dir. 1987—, second vice chmn. 1990, first vice chmn. 1991, chmn., 1992, chmn. nominating com., 1993), Econ. Devel. Assn. Western N.C., Self-Service Storage Assn., Asheville Area C. of C. (chmn. indsl. relations 1978-79), Hendersonville C. of C. Episcopalian. Clubs: Biltmore Forest Country. Lodge: Civitan (dir. 1975-77). Office: 932 Hendersonville Rd Asheville NC 28803-1733

MOROSO, MICHAEL JOSEPH, aerospace engineer; b. Centerville, Iowa, Jan. 26, 1923; s. John and Antonietta (Sartor) M.; m. Jody Mary Scripter, June 16, 1951; children— Barbara, Michael, Robert, Philip. B.S.M.E., U. Wis., 1952. Naval aviator, Pensacola, Fla.; designer Douglas Aircraft Co., Santa Monica, Calif., 1952-65; engr., scientist McDonnell Douglas launch ctr. Vandenberg AFB, Calif., 1965-70; engr., sci. specialist McDonnell Douglas Astronautics Co., Huntington Beach, Calif., 1970-76; sr. propulsion engr. Northrop Corp., Hawthorne, Calif., 1976-79; staff engr. Douglas Aircraft Co., Long Beach, Calif., 1979— . Served to lt. USN, 1943-47. Mem. advancement com. Boy Scouts Am., Santa Maria, Calif., 1966-69; Little League mgr., coach, Santa Maria, 1967-69. Assoc. fellow AIAA; mem. So. Calif. Profl. Engrs. Assn., Am. Legion (adjutant, fin. officer 1950-65), Douglas Mgmt. Club. Democrat. Roman Catholic. Home: 964 Lansing Ln Costa Mesa CA 92626-2821 Office: 3855 N Lakewood Blvd Long Beach CA 90846-0003

MOROTE, ELSA-SOFIA, humanities educator, business consultant; b. Lima, Peru, Apr. 3, 1967; came to U.S., 1995; d. Fernando Agustin and Elsa Jacinta (Canales de) M.; m. Victor R. Cordova, Mar. 26, 1994; 1 child, Isabella Fernanda. BS in Indsl. Engring., U. Lima, 1987; MPA, Ctr. Rsch. and Econ. Tchg., Mexico, 1992; MS in Computational Fin., Carnegie Mellon U., 1996; EdD in Edn. Adminstrn., U. Pitts., 2001. Bus. mgr. Women Clothes Factory, Lima, 1989-90; divsn. head programming and budget evaluation Mex. Dept. Labor, Mexico City, 1992; prof. divsn. mgmt. and econs. Monterey Inst. of Tech. and Higher Edn., 1993-96; full prof. grad bus. Tech. Inst. and U. Monterrey, 1996-97; instr. grad sch. indsl. engring. Carnegie Mellon U., Pitts., 1996-97; fellow Latin Am. studies, social and pub. policy U. Pitts., 1999—2001; postdoctoral fellow rsch. in sci. edn. MIT, Cambridge, Mass., 2001—. Rsch. in physics edn./tech., MIT, 2001—. Contbr. articles to profl. jours., chpt. to book. Mem. Coun. Grad. Students in Edn., Lat. Am. Cultural Union (webmaster 1995-01), Colegio de Ingenieros del Peru. Avocation: dance. Office: 77 Massachusetts Ave 26-227 Cambridge MA 02139

MOROWITZ, HAROLD JOSEPH, biophysicist, educator; b. Poughkeepsie, N.Y., Dec. 4, 1927; s. Philip Frank and Anna (Levine) M.; m. Lucille Rita Stein, Jan. 30, 1949; children: Joanna Lynn, Eli David, Joshua Alan, Zachary Adam, Noah Daniel. BS, Yale U., 1947, MS, 1950, PhD, 1951. Physicist Nat. Bur. Stds., 1951-53, Nat. Heart Inst., Bethesda, Md., 1953-55; mem. faculty Yale U., 1955-88, assoc. prof. biophysics, 1960-68, prof. molecular biophysics and biochemistry, 1968-88, master Pierson Coll., 1981-86; mem. faculty George Mason U., Fairfax, Va., 1988—, Robinson prof. biology and natural philosophy, 1988—; dir. Krasnow Inst. for Advanced Study, 1993-98. Chmn. com. on models for biomed. rsch. NRC, 1983-85, mem. bd. on basic biology, 1986-92. Author: Life and the Physical Sciences, 1964, (with Waterman) Theoretical and Mathematical Biology, 1965, Energy Flow in Biology, 1968, Entropy for Biologists, 1970, (with Lucille Morowitz) Life On The Planet Earth, 1974, Ego Niches, 1977, Foundations of Bioenergetics, 1978, The Wine of Life, 1979, Mayonnaise and the Origin of Life, 1985, Cosmic Joy and Local Pain, 1987, The Thermodynamics of Pizza, 1991, Beginnings of Cellular Life, 1992, (with James Trefil) The Facts of Life, 1992, Entropy and the Magic Flute, 1993, The Kindly Dr. Guillotin, 1997; editor Complexity, 1994—; contbr. articles to profl. jours. Mem. sci. adv. bd. Santa Fe Inst., 1991-97, co-chmn. sci. adv. bd., 2000—. Mem. Biophys. Soc. (mem. exec. com. 1965), Nat. Ctr. for Rsch. Resources (mem. coun. 1987-92). Office: George Mason U Krasnow Inst Advanced Study Fairfax VA 22030

MOROWITZ, NOAH DANIEL, film director, television director; b. Orange, Conn., Feb. 17, 1960; s. Harold Joseph and Lucille Stein M. BA in Film, Yale U., 1983. Prodr., dir., writer programs various networks including NBC, CBC, TLC, Discovery, others, 1988-99; dir. Walden Films, Santa Monica, Calif., 1999—; pres. Morowitz Media, 2002—. Dir. (film) Master of the Manor, 1989 (CINE Golden Eagle 1989); prodr. (TV spl.) The Truth About Lies, 1990 (Peabody award 1990); dir., writer, prodr. (TV series) Civil War Journal, 1994, Biography, 1997, (TV spl.) The Napoleon Murder Mystery, 1999, The White House: 200th Anniversary, 2000; prodr. (TV series) Crime & Punishment, 2001. Mem. Dir. Guild Am. E-mail: noahmz@aol.com.

MOROZ, JOHN ANTHONY, sales and marketing professional; b. Mpls., Feb. 19, 1962; m. Janyce Marie Moroz, Aug. 17, 1991; children: Marianna Elena, James Mykol. BA, U. Minn., 1984; MBA, Monterey Inst., 1987. Dir. European ops. Anagram Internat. Inc., Eden Prairie, Minn., 1989-95; pres., CEO Miram Internat. Inc., Plymouth, 1995-97; dir. bus. devel. Mobility Electronics, Scottsdale, Ariz., 1997-99; v.p. sales and mktg. CrossWorks, Inc., Hopkins, Minn., 1999-2000; v.p. sales Datakey, Inc., Burnsville, 2000—. Bd. dirs. Axial Tech., Inc., New Hope, Minn. Patentee in field. Named Disting. Alumni U. Minn., 1997. Avocations: music, athletics, travel, reading.

MOROZ, PAVEL EMANUEL, research scientist; b. Leningrad, Russia, 1928; came to U.S., 1976. Degree in Medicine, Pavlov Med. Inst., Leningrad, 1952, MD in Cytology and Biophysics, 1960. Rsch. scientist various insts., Leningrad, 1952-75. Contbr. articles to profl. jours. Mem. N.Y. Acad. Scis. Achievements include research in the effects of the force of gravity and centrifugal force on the cell and development of centrifuge microscope; analysis of the physical limits of biological evolution. Home: 15-17 Willet St Apt 3K New York NY 10002

MORPHEW, DOROTHY RICHARDS-BASSETT, artist, real estate broker; b. Cambridge, Mass., Aug. 4, 1918; d. George and Evangeline Booth (Richards) Richards; children: Jon Eric Richards, Marc Alan Richards, Dana Kimball Richards. Grad., Boston Art Inst., 1949. Draftsman United Shoe Machinery Co., 1937—42; blueprinter, advt. artist A.C. Lawrence Leather Co. , Peabody, Mass., 1949—51; propr. Studio Shop and Studio Potters, Beverly, 1951—53; tchr. ceramics and art Kingston, NH, 1953—; real estate broker, 1965—81; two-man exhbn. Topsfield (Mass.) Libr., 1960; owner, operator Ceramic Shop, West Stewartstown, NH. With USNR, 1942—44. Recipient Profl. award, New Eng. Ceramic Show, 1975, also numerous certs. in ceramics. Mem.: York (Maine) Art Assn., Englewood (Fla.) Art Guild. Home: 557 Palomino Trl Englewood FL 34223-3951 Studio: 24 Wanaque Rd Cape Neddick ME 00002-7130

MORPHONIOS, DEAN B. lawyer; b. Miami, Fla., Apr. 27, 1956; s. Alexander George and Ellen (James) M.; m. Joan Julien, Aug 7, 1982; children: Kimberly Anne, Matthew James. BA, Fla. Internat. U., Miami, 1979; JD, Fla. State U., 1983. Bar: Fla. 1983, U.S. Dist. Ct. (so. dist.) Fla. 1985, U.S. Dist. Ct. (mid. and no. dists.) 1988, U.S. Ct. Appeals, U.S. Supreme Ct. 1989. Assoc. gen. counsel Fla. Police Benevolent Assn., Tallahassee, 1983-84; pvt. practice Miami, 1984-86; asst. state atty. State Attys. Office/2d Jud. Cir., Tallahassee, 1986-88; assoc. Kitchen Judkins Simpson & High, 1988-97; pvt. practice, 1997—. Mem. Bench Bar Com., Tallahassee, 1996—, Conflict Rev.

Com., Tallahassee, 1996—. Mem. Fla. Assn. Criminal Defendant Attys. (pres. Tallahassee chpt. 1994-95). Republican. Office: 610 N Duval St Tallahassee FL 32301-1135 E-mail: dmorphon@yahoo.com.

MORPHY, JAMES CALVIN, lawyer; b. Pitts., Jan. 16, 1954; s. Robert Samson and Autumn (Phillips) M.; m. Priscilla Winslow Plimpton, July 11, 1981; children: Calvin, Katherine, Victoria. BA, Harvard U., 1976, JD, 1979. Bar: N.Y. 1980. Assoc. Sullivan & Cromwell, N.Y.C., 1979-86, ptnr., 1986—, mng. ptnr. com., 1992—, mng. ptnr. M&A group, 1995—. Author (contbg.): (treatise) New York and Delaware Business Entities: Choice Formation, Operation, Financing, and Acquisition, 1997, Transactional Lawyer's Deskbook, 2001. Trustee Greenwich Acad. Mem. ABA (com. on fed. securities law 1992—), Assn. Bar of City of N.Y., Wianno Club (bd. govs.), Greenwich Country Club, Harvard Club N.Y., Wianno Yacht Club, Phi Beta Kappa. Office: Sullivan & Cromwell 125 Broad St Fl 28 New York NY 10004-2489

MORRA, PABLO HERNÁN, economist; b. Buenos Aires, May 26, 1974; s. Eduardo Héctor Morra and Noemí Alicia Armagno; m. Flavia Beatriz Ferreiro. Degree in econs., Argentine Cath. U., Buenos Aires, 1997. Cert. master in fin. Econ. and fin. analyst Ricardo Arriazu and Assocs., Buenos Aires, 1996—99; assoc. economist Goldman Sachs, N.Y.C., 2000—. Roman Catholic. Avocations: travel, reading, sports.

MORREALE, BEN, retired history educator, novelist; b. N.Y.C., Apr. 10, 1924; s. Marco Morreale and Teresa Melluzo. BA, Bklyn. Coll., 1950; PhD, U. Paris, 1957. Prof. history Goddard Coll., Vt., 1960-63, SUNY, Plattsburgh, 1963-90; ret., 1990. Author: The Seventh Saracen, 1959, A Few Virtuous Men, 1973, Never Come Sunday, 1975, Down and Out in Academia, 1980, La Storia, 1992, The Loss of Miraculous, 1997, Sicily the Hallowed Land, A Memoir, 2001. With USAF, 1942-45. Roman Catholic. Avocations: writing, painting.

MORREALE, JOSEPH CONSTANTINO, higher education administrator, public administration educator, economic and financial consultant; b. Bronx, N.Y., Oct. 26, 1944; s. Joseph Vincent Morreale and Grace (Soricelli); m. Barbara McAdorey; children: Gwenn F., Margaret I., Adam J. BA, Queens Coll. CUNY, 1967; MA, SUNY, Buffalo, 1969, PhD in Econs., 1972; MS in Higher Ednl. Adminstrn., SUNY, Albany, 1989. Asst. prof. econs. Western Mich. U., Kalamazoo, 1970-74; rsch. assoc. U. Wis., Madison, 1974-75; asst. to assoc. prof. health svcs. adminstrn., econs. Grad. Sch. Pub. Health U. Pitts., 1975-79; assoc. to prof. econs., environ. studies Bard Coll., Annandale-On-Hudson, N.Y., 1979-88; vis. rsch. fellow Grad. Sch. Edn., H.E. Adminstrn. SUNY, Albany, 1988-89; prof., chmn. dept. pub. adminstrn. Grad. Sch. Pace U., White Plains, N.Y., 1989-96; vice provost for planning assessment and instnl. rsch. Pace U., N.Y.C., Westchester, 1996-98, v.p. planning, assessment, rsch. and acad. support, 1998—. Health care and govt. fin. cons. to fed. agencies, state and local govts., pvt. firms, 1979—; adj. prof. law Pace U., 1990-96; adj. prof. pub. adminstrn. Grad. Sch. Pub. Affairs, SUNY-Albany, 1990-96; vis. prof. U. Lancaster, Eng., 1984-85; rsch. assoc., bd. dirs. Hudsonia Environ. Rsch., Annandale, 1985-95; fin. planner Prudential Fin. Svcs., Newburgh, N.Y., 1987-89. Author: Health Care Economics, 1977, Policies, Practices, Precautions, 1997; editor: The U.S. Medical Care Industry, 1974; contbr. articles to profl. jours. Appoint pub. rep. Westchester County Deferred Compensation Bd. Recipient NDEA fellowship, 1967-70, Pharm. Mfg. Assn. fellowship, 1969-70, post-doctoral fellowship Health Econ. Rsch. Ctr. U. Wis., 1974-75, rsch. fellowship Grad. Sch. Edn. SUNY-Albany, 1988-89, ACE fellowship UNC, Charlotte, 1995-96, sr. rsch. fellow Harvard IEM Inst., 2000. Mem. Am. Soc. for Pub. Adminstrn., Am. Econ. Assn., Am. Ednl. Fin. Assn., Assn. Instl. Rsch., Am. Assn. Higher Edn., Am. Coun. Edn. (fellow 1995-96), N.Y. State Govt. Fin. Officers Assn. (bd. dirs. 1990-95). Mem. Soc. Of Friends. Avocations: photography, tennis, music, environ. concerns. Office: Pace U VP 1 Pace Plz New York NY 10038-1598

MORREALE, PATRICIA ANDERSON, computer scientist, educator; b. Evanston, Ill., June 3, 1962; d. Thomas Patrick and Elizabeth Toof Anderson; m. James Joseph Morreale, Mar. 21, 1987; children: Joseph Patrick, Thomas James. BS in Computer Sci., Northwestern U., Evanston, Ill., 1983; MS in Computer Sci., U. Mo., Rolla, 1986; PhD in Computer Sci., Ill. Inst. Tech., 1991. Sr. telecom. engr. McDonnell Douglas Corp., St. Louis, 1983-86; project mgr. Sears Comm. Network, Arlington Heights, Ill., 1986-89; asst. prof. Northeastern Ill. U., Chgo., 1991-97; rsch. assoc. prof. Stevens Inst. Tech., Hoboken, N.J., 1995-98, assoc. dean R&D, 1999-2000, assoc. prof., 1999—. Editor: The Telecommunications Handbook, 2000, The CRC Handbook of Modern Telecommunications, 2001; contbr. articles to profl. jours.; patentee in field. Mem. IEEE, Assn. Computing Machinery. Home: 1527 Lewis Rd Edwardsville IL 62025 Office: Stevens Inst Tech Castle Point on Hudson Hoboken NJ 07030

MORREIM, E. HAAVI, medical ethics educator; b. Austin, Minn., July 21, 1950; d. Paul Eugene and Florence Adeline Morreim. BA in Philosophy, St. Olaf Coll., 1972; MA in Philosophy, U. Va., 1976, PhD, 1980. Med. philosopher program in human biology and soc. U. Va. Sch. Medicine, Charlottesville, 1980-82, asst. prof. philosophy in medicine, 1982-84; from asst. to assoc. prof. dept. human values and ethics U. Tenn. Coll. Medicine, Memphis, 1984-93, prof. dept. human values and ethics, 1993—. Adj. prof. philosophy Va. Commonwealth U., Richmond, 1980; vis. prof. philosophy St. Olaf Coll., Northfield, Minn., 1982; Andrew Mellon vis. asst. prof. humanities and medicine Georgetown U. Sch. Medicine, Washington, 1983; sr. vis. rsch. scholar Kennedy Inst. Ethics, Georgetown U., 1983; manuscript reviewer; presenter and lectr. in field. Author: Balancing Act: The New Medical Ethics of Medicine's New Economics, 1991, Holding Health Care Accountable: Law and the New Medical Marketplace, 2001; mem. editl. adv. bd. Jour. Medicine and Philosophy, bd. editors, Jour. Law, Medicine and Ethics; contbr. articles to profl. jours. Active Hastings Ctr. Mem. Am. Health Lawyers Assn., Am. Soc. Law, Medicine, and Ethics, Am. Soc. for Bioethics and Humanities, Phi Beta Kappa. Avocations: running, high-performance automobile driving, photography, skiing. Home: 8343 Stavanger Cv Cordova TN 38018-7246 Office: Univ Tenn Coll Medicine 956 Court Ave Ste B328 Memphis TN 38163-2814 E-mail: hmorreim@utmem.edu.

MORREL, WILLIAM GRIFFIN, JR. banker; b. Lynchburg, Va., Aug 25, 1933; s. William Griffin and Virginia Louise (Baldwin) M.; m. Sandra Virginia Coats, Jan. 31, 1959; children: William Griffin, John Coats, Elisabeth White, Jere Coleman. BS, Yale U., 1955; postgrad. Rutgers U., 1965-67. With Md. Nat. Bank, Balt., 1955-84, asst. v.p., 1959, v.p., 1964, sr. v.p., 1975-84, mgmt. com. 1979-84, chmn. three lending coms., others; pres., bd. dirs. Md. Nat. Overseas Investment Corp.; chmn. bd. London Interstate Bank Ltd.; chmn. bd. dirs. Md. Internat. Bank; sr. v.p., chief operating officer Abu Dhabi Internat. Bank, Inc., 1984-86, pres., chief exec. officer Heritage Internat. Bank, 1986-89; dir., pres., CEO Madison Fin. Group, 1989-97, chmn., 1997—; CEO, chmn. The Valley Fin. Group, Balt., 1989—; pres., chief exec. officer Summit Bancorp, Balt., 1990-92; consul of the Netherlands at Balt., 1978-84. Mem. Balt. Consular Corps, 1978-84; chmn. Md. World Trade Efforts Commn., 1983-84; mem. Md. Trade Policy Council, 1985-88; vice chmn. Dist. Export Council, 1983—. Contbr. articles to profl. jours. Sr. fellow Ctr. for Internat. Banking Studies, Darden Grad. Bus. Sch. U. Va., 1978-91. Served with U.S. Army, 1956-58. Mem. Bankers Assn. for Fgn. Trade (bd. dirs. 1975-78), Robert Morris Assocs. (nat. bd. dirs. 1984-88), Internat. Lending Council (bd. dirs., chmn., 1978-80), Md. Hist. Soc. (trustee), Balt. Council Fgn. Relations (trustee), Econ. Devel. Council. Republican. Presbyterian. Clubs: Yale, Farmington Country, Elkridge, Md. Club. Home: 6 Beechdale Rd Baltimore MD 21210-2207 Office: 6 Beechdale Rd Baltimore MD 21210-2207

MORRELL, CHARLES FRANCIS, surgeon; b. Cambridge, Mass., Feb. 25, 1921; AB, Boston U., 1942; MD, Harvard U., 1945. Intern U.S. Naval Hosp., San Diego, 1945-46; resident Long Beach (Calif.) VA Hosp., 1948-52; fellow in cancer surgery Westfield (Mass.) State Hosp., 1952-53; with Cmty. Hosp., Long Beach, Harbor/UCLA Med. Ctr., Torrance, Calif., Meml. Hosp., Long Beach. Asst. clin. prof. surgery UCLA. Mem. Am. Coll. Surgeons. Office: 1760 Termino Ave Long Beach CA 90804-2105

MORRELL, GENE PAUL, liquid terminal company executive, consultant; b. Ardmore, Okla., Oct. 4, 1932; s. Paul T. and Etta L. (Weaver) M.; m. Jan A. Foster, Aug. 20, 1954; children: Jeffrey T., Kelly Ann, Rob Redman. BS in Geology, U. Okla., 1954, LLB, 1962. Bar: D.C. 1973. Geologist Gilmer Oil Co., Ardmore, Okla., 1957-59, atty.-geologist, 1962-63; pvt. practice, 1963-69; ofcl. Dept. Interior, Washington, 1969-72; v.p. Lone Star Gas Co., 1972-76; sr. v.p. United Energy Resources, Inc., Houston, 1976-86; vice chmn. Petro United Terminals, Inc., 1986-98; cons. on investments, 1998—. Contbr. articles to profl. jours. Commr. City of Ardmore, 1967-69, vice-mayor, 1968. Mem. ABA, D.C. Bar Assn., Am. Assn. Petroleum Geologists, Galveston Country Club, The Yacht Club (Galveston), River Oaks Country Club (Houston), Phi Alpha Delta, Sigma Alpha Epsilon. Episcopalian. Fax: (713) 522-5343.

MORRELL, WAYNE BEAM, JR. artist; b. Clementon, N.J., Dec. 24, 1923; s. Wayne Beam and Martha L. (Plack) M.; student Drexel Inst., Phila. Sch. Indsl. Art.; grad. Famous Artist Sch., Westport, Conn.; m. Lillian Eunice Major, July 14, 1952 (dec. 1994); children: David Wayne (dec.), Lisa Anne. Exhibited one-man show Washington County Art Mus., Hagerstown, Md., 1973, Drexel U., 1992; exhibited nat. group shows including NAD, Conn. Acad. Fine Arts, Butler Inst. Am. Art, Am. Artists Profl. League, Knickerbocker Artists, N.Y.C., Newman Gallery, Phila., Houston, Palm Beach, Fla., Carmel, Calif., Guild Boston Artists, Wadsworth Atheneum, Addison Gallery Am. Art, Mus. Fine Arts, Columbus, Ga., New Britain Mus., Smithsonian Inst., Expn. Intercontinental, Monaco, France, Gateway Art Gallery, Palm Beach, Fla., Bleich Galleries, Carmel, Calif., Mus., Bombay, India, 1967, City Hall, Hong Kong, 1975-76; indsl. exhibitor, designer John Oldham Studios, 1955-58, art dir., 1958-61; designer Paris and Brussells Worlds Fairs, other maj. exhibits; designer cover Reader's Digest, 1967, Yankee mag., 1980. Served with AUS, 1949-52. Recipient Louis Seley purchase award; Gold medal Rockport Art Assn., 1969; Gold medal Jordan Marsh, Boston; award Council Am. Art Socs., 1971; Canelli Gold Medal award Academic Artists Assn., 1974; others. Mem. Allied Artists Am. (Jane Peterson award 1969, 74), Am. Artists Profl. League, Am. Vet. Soc. Artists, Springfield Acad. Artists (past council), Rockport Art Assn. (William Mariboe award, Harriet Mattson award, award for Winter Marshes 1980, Meyerowitz Meml. award 1989, William Meyerwith award 1989), North Shore Art Assn., Americana Gallery, Golden Web, Santa Fe, Montcrest Gallery, Chattanooga (Tenn.) 210 Gallery, Grand Central Art Galleries, Newman Galleries Phila. and Bryn Mawr, Pa., Dassin Gallery, L.A., Salmagundi Club (Louis Seley Purchase award 1969, Gwynne Lennon prize 1971, Phillip J. Ross award 1971, 1st hon. mention 1971). Home and Office: 1 Squam Holw Rockport MA 01966-2164

MORRILL, JOYCE MARIE, social worker, educator; b. Rockland, Maine, Dec. 27, 1939; d. Henry Higgins and Julia Ellen (Philbrook) Thompson; m. Edward Morrill, Sept. 7, 1972; 1 son, Gregory Hodgman; 1 stepchild, Shawn Morrill. BA, U. Hartford, 1964; MSW, Hunter Coll., 1972. Co-host Today in Conn. Program Sta. WHNB-TV, Hartford, 1964—65; clin. social worker, field instr. Rehab. inst., N.Y., 1972—78; dir., founder Wellness Svcs., Jamaica Estates, NY, 1979—95; pres. Morrill Support, 1996—. Photographer-artist. Mem.: NASW, Inst. Noetic Scis., Alliance of Queens Artists, Profl. Woman Photographers. Home and Office: 181-38 Midland Pky Jamaica Est NY 11432 E-mail: Joyce@morrillsupport.com.

MORRILL, PENNY CHITTIM, art historian; b. San Antonio, Feb. 4, 1947; d. Jack Robert and Dorothy Born (Sutherland) Chittim; m. James Agrippa Morrill, July 12, 1969; children: Jackson Forrest, Julia Chiltipin. BA with honors, Tulane U., 1969; MA, U. Pa., 1971; PhD, U. Md., 2001. Program coord. Cancer Rsch. Found. Am., Alexandria, Va., 1990-95; intern Nat. Gallery Art, Washington, 1997; adj. prof. Md. Inst. Coll. Art, Balt., 2000, U. Md., College Park, 2001. Curator & catalogue author for traveling exhbn. on Mex. silver San Antonio Mus. of Art., 1998—. Author: Silver Masters of Mexico, 1996, Mexican Silver, 1994; contbr. articles to profl. jours. Vol. teen pregnancy prevention Nat. ARC, Washington, 1986-98; participant Coro Women in Leadership, Washington, 1988; adv. com. Betty Ford Breast Health Ctr., Washington, 1997-98; adv. com. Nat. Rehab. Hosp., Washington, 1991—; mem., v.p. Newcomb Coll./Tulane U. Alumnae Bd., 1990-94; mem., pres. Lyceum Mus., Alexandria, 1992-97; mem., editor, pres. Hist. Alexandria Found., 1980-89; curator exhbn. Carlyle House Mus., Alexandria, 1980. Recipient Achievement award Jr. League of Phila., 1985, Award for RAP and AMAZE, Nat. ARC, 1988, Spirit of Volunteerism award Jr. League of Washington, 1992, Recognition award Nat. Rehab. Hosp., 1997. Mem. Coll. Art Assn., Am. Soc. Jewelry Historians. Episcopalian. Avocations: knitting, gardening.

MORRILL, RICHARD LELAND, geographer, educator; b. L.A., Feb. 15, 1934; s. Robert W. and Lillian M. (Riffo) M.; m. Joanne L. Cooper, 1965; children: Lee, Andrew, Jean. BA, Dartmouth Coll., 1955; MA, U. Wash., 1957, PhD, 1959. Asst. prof. geography Northwestern U., 1959-60; NSF research fellow U. Lund, Sweden, 1960-61; asst. prof. U. Wash., Seattle, 1961-65, asso. prof., 1965-69, prof., 1969—, chmn. dept. geography, 1974-83, asso. dir. environ. studies, 1974-98; chmn. urban planning PhD program, 1992-98. Vis. asso. prof. U. Chgo., dir. Chgo. Regional Hosp. Study, 1966-67; cons. population, regional and urban planning. Author: Geography of Poverty, 1970, Spatial Organization of Society, 1973, Political Redistricting and Geographic Theory, 1981, Spatial Diffusion, 1987. Mem. King County Boundary Rev. Bd. Guggenheim fellow, 1983-84 Mem. Assn. Am. Geographers (Meritorious Contbn. award 1970, mem. coun. 1970-73, sec. 1979-81, pres. 1981-82), Regional Sci. Assn., Wash. Regional Sch. Assn. (pres. 1993-94), Population Assn. Am., Lambda Alpha. Office: U Wash Dept Geography Seattle WA 98195-0001

MORRILL, THOMAS CLYDE, insurance company executive; b. Chgo., July 1, 1909; s. Walter and Lena Elpha (Haney) M.; m. Hazel Janet Thompson, Oct. 18, 1930; children: Dorothy Mae (Mrs. Gerald L. Kelly), Charles T. Student, Cen. Coll. Arts and Scis., Chgo., 1928-29, Northwestern U., 1929-30. With Alfred M. Best Co., Inc., 1929-45, assoc. editor, 1940-45; with N.Y. State Ins. Dept., 1945-50, dep. supt. ins., 1947-50; with State Farm Mut. Automobile Ins. Co., Bloomington, Ill., 1950-77, v.p., 1952-77; chmn. bd. State Farm Fire and Casualty Co., 1970-86, State Farm Gen. Ins. Co., Bloomington, 1970-91; cons. State Farm Ins. Cos., 1991—. Founder, chmn. dir. Ins. Inst. for Hwy. Safety; co-founder, dir. Hwy. Loss Data Ins. Chmn. exec. subcom. Nat. Hwy. Safety Adv. Com., 1971-73; chmn. tech. com. on transp. White House Conf. on Aging, 1971; mem. Pres.'s Task Force on Hwy. Safety. Mem.: Union Hills Country Club, Union League Club (Chgo.).

MORRILL-CUMMINS, CAROLYN, social worker, consultant; b. Alexandria, Va., June 29, 1957; d. William Ashley and Lois (Birrell) Morrill; m. Joseph Paul Cummins, June 4, 1983; children: Katharine Jean, Cody William. BS in Psychology cum laude, Union Coll., Schenectady, N.Y., 1979; MSW, U. Albany, 1983. Cert. social worker, N.Y. Ptnr. Marion River Restaurant, Blue Mountain Lake, N.Y., 1979-82; home visitor Warren-Hamilton Counties Head Start, Indian Lake, 1983-84; social worker, case mgr. Sunmount Devel. Disabilities Svc. Office, Tupper Lake, 1984-86; social worker Wilton Devel. Disabilities Svc. Office, Indian Lake, 1986-93; tchr. asst. Indian Lake Ctrl. Sch., 1993-94; social worker Cmty. Workshop, Inc., Glens Falls, N.Y., 1994-95; clin. social worker Hamilton County Cmty. Svcs. Office, Indian Lake, 1995—. Social work cons. Mercy Healthcare Ctr., Tupper Lake, 1985-86, Warren-Washington ARC, Glens Falls, 1993, Eddy Home Care, Troy, N.Y., 1993-97. Bd. dirs. Hamilton County Cmty. Svcs. Bd., Indian Lake, 1983-84, Warren-Hamilton Counties Head Start, 1984-85, Hudson Headwaters Health Network, Warrensburg, N.Y., 1993-99, Indian Lake Ctrl. Sch. Bd. Edn., 1999—, pres. 2002; co-pres. Indian Lake Ctrl. Sch. PTA, 1994-99, pastor parish rels. com. Blue Mountain Lake United Meth. Ch., 1993—. Mem.: NASW. Home: PO Box 993 Sabael NY 12864-0993

MORRIN, PETER PATRICK, museum director; b. St. Louis, Oct. 31, 1945; s. Kevin Charles and Helen Louise (Clanton) M.; m. Carolyn Brooks, Oct. 5, 1974; children: Matthew, Rebecca. AB, Harvard U., 1968; MFA, Princeton U., 1972. Asst. prof., dir. art gallery Vassar Coll., Poughkeepsie, N.Y., 1974-78; curator 20th century art High Mus. Art, Atlanta, 1979-86; dir. Speed Art Mus., Louisville, 1986—. Panelist Nat. Endowment Arts. Contbr. articles to profl. publs. Served with USAR, 1968-74. Office: Speed Art Mus 2035 S 3rd St Louisville KY 40208-1812 E-mail: pmorrin@speedmuseum.org.

MORRIONE, MELCHIOR S. management consultant, accountant; b. Bklyn., Dec. 31, 1937; m. Joan Finnerty, June 22, 1968; children: Karyn Morrione Frick, Nicole. BBA magna cum laude, St. John's U., 1959. CPA, N.J., N.Y. Tax ptnr. Arthur Andersen, N.Y.C., 1959-91; mng. dir. MSM Consulting LLC, Woodcliff Lake, N.J., 1992—. Lectr. in field. Contbr. articles to profl. jours. With U.S. Army, 1960-61. Mem. CPAs, N.Y. State Soc. CPAs, N.J. Soc. CPAs, Internat. Fiscal Assn., Internat. Tax Assn., Ridgewood Country Club. Republican. Roman Catholic. Avocations: golf, tennis. Office: MSM Consulting LLC 11 Ginny Dr Woodcliff Lake NJ 07677-8115 E-mail: morrione@att.net.

MORRIS, ALBERT JEROME, medical company executive; b. N.Y.C., Jan. 3, 1919; s. Peter and Minnie (Miller) M.; Barbara McLeod, Feb 6, 1943; children: Peter A., Lee Ellen Morris Guenther, Lisa Ann Morris Rasche. BS in Electronics, U. Calif., Berkeley, 1941; MS in Electronics, Stanford U., 1948, Degree of Engr., 1950. Registered profl. engr., Calif. Sr. v.p., co-founder Levinthal Elec. Products, Palo Alto, Calif., 1953-60; pres., dir. Radiation at Stanford, 1960-63; pres., chief exec. officer Energy Systems Inc., 1963-66, Genesys Systems Inc., Palo Alto, 1967-84, Biosys, Palo Alto, 1983-88, chmn. bd., 1989; also chmn. bd. TurboEnergy Systems, Phoenix, 1989-90; chmn. bd., chief exec. officer Neural Systems Corp., Palo Alto, 1991—. Cons. to schs. of engring., Stanford U. and 18 other major univs.; chmn. San Francisco coun. Western Electronics Mfrs. Assn., 1965; chmn. bd. Western Electronics Show and Conv., Calif., 1961, Neural Sys. Corp. Author over 50 papers on ship stabilization, high power electronics, med. electronics and continuing edn. Recipient Best Paper award IEEE/ASEE Frontiers in Edn. Conf., 1978. Fellow IEEE, Sigma Chi Iota; mem. AAAS. Avocations: tennis, golf.

MORRIS, ANN HASELTINE JONES, social welfare administrator; b. Springfield, Mo., Feb. 3, 1941; d. Mansur King and Adelaide (Haseltine) Jones; m. Ronald D. Morris, Nov. 29, 1963 (div. 1990); children: David, Christopher. BA in Edn. and Art, Drury Coll., 1963. Art instr. Ash Grove (Mo.)/Bois D'Arc Pub. Sch. Dist., 1963-64; instr. Drury Coll., Springfield, 1966-67; tchr. Springfield R-12 Sch. Dist., 1974-86; exec. dir. S.W. Ctr. for Ind. Living, Springfield, 1986—. Adv. com. Springfield R-12 Spl. Edn., 1993—; tech. cons. and alternative dispute resolution mediator Ams. with Disabilities Act EEOC, Dept. of Justice Network, 1993—; peer reviewer Office Spl. Edn. and Rehabilitative Svcs. Bd. dirs. Ozark Greenways, 1991-93, Springfield Deaf Relay, 1988-90; adv. task force Allied Health Program Devel. S.W. Bapt Univ., 1988; mem. Drury Coll. Women's Aux., 1984-96, conservator of the peace, handicap parking enforcement action team, 1991—; bd. treas. Mo. Parent Act, 1989-91, Diversity Network of the Ozarks, 1990—; svc. coord. Youthnet, 1990—; community adv. bd. Rehab. Svcs., St. John's Regional Health Care Ctr., 1988-91; mem. Springfield Homeless Network, 1989—, others; apptd. to Mo. Gov.'s Coun. on Disability; pres. Statewide Ind. Living Coun; mem. Gov.'s Commn. on Home and Cmty. Based Svcs., 2000—. Mem. NOW (sec. 1991), P.E.O., Mo. Assn. of Ctrs. for Ind. Living (v.p. 1990-97), Mo. Assn. for Social Welfare (bd. treas. 1989-95), Nat. Assn. of Ind. Living Ctrs. (AIDS task force 1993-96), Assn. of Programs for Rural Ind. Living, Nat. Soc. of Fund Raising Execs., Mo. Rehab. Assn., C. of C. (healthcare divsn.), Zeta Tau Alpha. Home: 1748 E Arlington Rd Springfield MO 65804-7742

MORRIS, ASHLEY, information scientist, educator; b. DeFuniak Springs, Fla., Oct. 20, 1963; s. Kenneth Eugene and Dorothy Morris; m. Hana Žižková. BS, U. So. Miss., 1985, MS, 1995; PhD, Tulane U., 1999. Software specialist Digital Equipment Corp., Culver City, Calif., 1987—89; cons. Ashley Morris Cons., L.A., 1989—93, AT&T, Seattle, 1993—94; instr. Oracle, Redwood Shores, Calif., 1997—98; prof. U. Idaho, Moscow, 1998—2000, DePaul U., Chgo., 2000—. Cons. H.A. Morris, Inc., New Orleans, 1994—, Oracle, Atlanta, 1997—98; rschr. Naval Rsch. Lab., Stennis Space Ctr., Miss., 1997—98. Contbr. articles. Grantee Nat. Leadership grant, Inst. Mus. & Libr. Svcs., 1998, Rsch. grant, U. Idaho, 1999, Oracle, 1999, U. Idaho, 1999. Mem.: IEEE Computer Soc., Assn. Computing Machinery, Internat. Fuzzy Sets Assn., N.Am. Fuzzy Info. Processing Soc., Upsilon Pi Epsilon. Avocations: music, hockey, travel. Office: DePaul Univ 243 S Wabash Ave Chicago IL 60604 Office Fax: 312-362-6116. Personal E-mail: ashley@ashleymorris.com. Business E-Mail: amorris@acm.org.

MORRIS, AUDREY M. lawyer; b. Annapolis, Md., Dec. 6, 1963; d. Thomas M. and Audrey M. (Kunzinger) Burton; m. Michael S. Morris, Apr. 20, 1985; children: Matthew L., Andrew S. AA in Bus., Manatee Jr. Coll., Bradenton, Fla., 1983; BA in Acctg., U. West Fla., 1984; JD, U. Miami, Fla., 1990. Bar: Tex. 1991, U.S. Tax Ct. 1991, U.S. Dist. Ct. (no. dist.) Tex. 1992, U.S. Supreme Ct. 1998. Revenue agt. IRS, Miami, 1986-88, Dallas, 1988-91, tax atty., 1991—. Mem. ABA. Roman Catholic. Office: IRS District Counsel 4050 Alpha Rd 13th Fl MC 2000 NWSAT Dallas TX 75244

MORRIS, BOSHER BLYTH, poet; b. Muskogee, Okla., Sept. 4, 1960; widowed. Student, U. Okla. Agt. Warrent/Gorham Lamont, Versailles, N.Y. Contbr. poetry to Internat. Soc. of Poets, (Editor's Choice award 1999). With U.S. Army, 1982-84. Vol. Vet. award VA Hosp., Muskogee, Okla., 1986. Mem. Am. Legion. Democrat. Presbyterian. Avocation: photography. Office: Soc Internat Poetry 1 Poetry Plz Owings Mills MD 21117-6282

MORRIS, BRUCE D. technical writer, test engineer, educator, literary historian; b. San Francisco, July 10, 1947; s. William and Helen S. (Jorgensen) M. AA, Coll. San Mateo, Calif., 1968; BA in English and Linguistics, San Francisco State Coll., 1969; MA in English Lit., San Francisco State U., 1972; PhD, U. Denver, 1977. Grad. teaching fellow dept. English U. Denver, 1973-77; asst. instr. Pacific Crest Outward Bound Sch., Portland, Oreg., 1978; jr. tech. writer Harris-Farinon, San Carlos, Calif., 1979-82; sr. tech. writer Verilink Corp., San Jose, 1985-88, Tektronix Corp., Mountain View, 1988-90, MorComm Tech. Writing Svcs., Belmont, 1991—, MorComm Press, Belmont, 1992—; sr. tech writer Alpha Lab Telco Sysss., Fremont, 1994-96; sr. tech. writer Carrier Access Corp., Boulder, Colo., 1996-97; ind. contractor Fujitsu Ltd. Network Tech. Group Profl. Svcs. Divsn., Campbell, Calif., 1998-2000, DCM Industries, Inc., Union City, 2000—. Author: DCM Model 555A Full Duplex DS1/DSO Analyzer Operating Manual and User's Guide , 1994, Work Instructions for V.54 Fractional Loopback Testing T1/FT1 Multiport Channel Svc. Units/DSUs, 1995, Access Bank II Dual T1 Voice & Data Multiplexer Installation and User's Manual, 1996, Net 2 Desk Model 150 Remote Access Router User Guide, 1999, Rock Climber's Guide to Skyline Boulevard, 2000, CMS-2000 Computerized Automatic Cable Measuring System Operating Instructions , 2001, Bouldering Guide to the Castle Rock Area, 2002; editor: Arthur Symons: Letters to Yeats, 1989. Calif. State grad. fellow. Mem.: IEEE, IEEE Stds. Orgn., Irish-Am. Cultural Inst., IEEE Commns. Soc., Commonwealth Club Calif., Access Fund, Alpha Gamma Sigma. Avocations: rock climbing, bicycle racing, distance running. Home and Office: MorComm Press Tech Writing Svcs 2221 Thurm Ave Belmont CA 94002-1547 E-mail: morcomm@attbi.com.

MORRIS, CARLOSS (WILLIAM MORRIS), lawyer, insurance company executive; b. Galveston, Tex., June 7, 1915; s. William Carloss and Willie (Stewart) M.; m. Doris Poole, Dec. 2, 1939; children: Marietta (Mrs. Morgan Maxfield), William Carloss III, Malcolm Stewart, Melinda Louise (Mrs. Glen Ginter). BA with distinction, Rice Inst., 1936; JD with highest honors, U. Tex., 1939. Bar: Tex. 1938. With Stewart Title Guaranty Co., Houston, 1939—, pres., 1951-75, chmn. bd. dirs., chief exec. officer, 1975-91; chmn. bd. dirs., co-chief exec. officer Stewart Info. Services Inc., 1975-2000; chmn. exec. com. Stewart Title Guaranty Co., 1975—. Stockholder Morris, Lendais, Hollrah and Snowden, Houston. Chmn. Interdisciplinary Commn. on Housing and Urban Growth, 1974-77; chmn. Star Hope Mission, 1951-90, hon., 1991—; pres. Tex. Safety Assn., 1950-51; bd. dirs. Goodwill Industries; bd. dirs., mem. exec. com. Billy Graham Evangelistic Assn., 1956-2000, adv. dir., 2000—; chmn. Baylor Coll. Medicine, 1968, trustee, 1952—; trustee, deacon 1st Bapt. Ch., Houston, chmn. bd. deacons, 1987-89; trustee Baylor U., 1952-72, past vice chmn. bd. dirs.; trustee Oldham Little Ch. Found., B.M. Woltman Found. Recipient Book of Golden Deeds award Exch. Club of Houston, 1974, Disting. Svc. awrad Tex. Soc. Sons Am. Revolution, 1988, Gen. Maurice Hirsch award Soc. for Fund Raising Execs., 1988, George Washington Honor medal Freedoms Found. at Valley Forge, 1990; inducted into Tex. Bus. Hall of Fame, 1995. Fellow Am. Bar Found., State Bar Tex. Found.; mem. ABA (past chmn. younger lawyers sect.), Tex. Bar Assn., Tex. Young Lawyers Assn. (past pres.), Chancellors, Order of Coif, Phi Delta Phi, Alpha Tau Omega. Clubs: River Oaks Country, University. Lodges: Kiwanis. Office: 1980 Post Oak Blvd Ste 800 Houston TX 77056-3826

MORRIS, CYNTHIA TAFT, economics educator; b. Cin., Apr. 28, 1928; d. Charles Phelps and Eleanor Kellogg (Chase) Taft; m. Donald Richard Morris, Sept. 18, 1955 (div. 1984); children: David Taft Morris, Michele Taft Morris. BA, Vassar Coll., 1949; MSc in Econs., London Sch. Econs., 1951; PhD, Yale U., 1959. Econ. analyst Info. Sect. Mutual Security Agy., Paris, 1951-53; tutor, fellow Kirkland Ho., Harvard U., Cambridge, 1955-57; rsch. fellow AAUW, Washington, 1958-59; asst. prof. econs. Am. U., Beirut, 1961-62, assoc. prof. econs. Washington, 1964-69, prof. econs., 1969-83; Charles N. Clark profl. econs. Smith Coll., Northampton, Mass., 1983—. Coord. Washington Area Econ. History Seminar, 1981—; cons. Office of Program and Policy Coordination Agy. for Internat. Devel., Washington, 1962-69; cons. electricity power com. Econ. Commn. of Europe, Geneva, 1960. Co-author: The Evolution of Wage Structure, 1956, Society, Politics and Economic Development, 1967, Economic Growth and Social Equity, 1973, Comparative Patterns of Economic Development, 1850-1914, 1988. Rsch. grantee NSF, 1965-73, 80-82. Fellow AAAS; mem. Econ. History Assn. (v.p. 1984-85, pres. 1993-94), Cliometric Soc., Am. Econ. Assn. Democrat. Avocations: languages, literature, travel. Home: Apt 6008 4301 Massachusetts Ave NW Washington DC 20016-5570

MORRIS, DAVID, retired electrical engineer; b. N.Y.C., July 18, 1924; s. Morris Elia and Esther (Kohn) M.; m. Minnie Kramer, Feb. 2, 1957. BEE, CCNY, 1947, MEE, 1954. Elec. engr. Magnetic Amplifiers Inc., L.I., N.Y., 1951-53; chief engr. Square Root Mfg. Corp., Yonkers, 1953-56; sect. head Poly. R&D, Bklyn., 1956-58; chief engr. Brach div. Gen. Bronze Corp., Newark, 1958-62; unit head Kearfott div. Singer Corp., Little Falls, 1962-70; group leader Monroe div. Litton Industries, Orange, 1970-72; sr. mem. tech. staff Lepel High Frequency Labs., Maspeth, N.Y., 1972-80, I.T.T. Avionics, Nutley, N.J., 1980-89; ret., 1989. Contbr. articles to profl. jours.; 7 patents in field. Mem. IEEE (life). Achievements include development of off line transistor switching regulator; radiation hardened hybrid electro-magnetic device for protection of semiconductor circuits; multi-winding power inductor; design of magnetic amplifiers for servo mechanisms used in the Ballistic Missile early warning system; power systems for N.Y. Fire Dept., T.F.X. fighter aircraft, AH64 Apaache helicopter. Avocations: experimental physics, classical music, chess. Home: 806 Maple Hill Dr Woodbridge NJ 07095-4109

MORRIS, DAVID JOHN, mining engineer, consultant, mining executive; b. Seattle, May 6, 1945; s. Jack Abraham and Alice Jean (Hanson) M.; m. Melania F. Kearney, July 28, 1978; children: Whitney Elizabeth, Benton James, Sienna Elise. BA in Math. and Physics, Whitman Coll., 1968; BS in Mining Engring., Columbia U., 1968. Registered profl. engr., Colo., Utah, Wash. Mining engr. Union Oil of Calif., Los Angeles, 1968-69, John T. Boyd Co., Denver, 1974-76, sr. mining engr., 1976-78, v.p., mgr., 1978-87; sr. cons., 1998—; mng. ptnr. Palmer Coaking Coal Co., Black Diamond, Wash., 1976-82, 90—; pres. Pacific Coast Coal Co., 1982—, Pacific Hydropower Devel., Inc., Seattle, 1995—. Mem. Bd. Overseers Whitman Coll., Walla Walla, Wash., 1986—, vice chair, 1993-95, chmn. Rep. campaign for Whitman, Denver, 1985; coach youth athletics. Served as lt. USN, 1969-74, Vietnam. Henry Krumb scholar Columbia U., N.Y.C., 1967-68. Mem. NSPE, Soc. Mining Engrs. (admissions com. 1985-88, Howard Eavenson award com. 1984-87, Woomer award com. 1990-93, chair 1993—, Ramsay award com. 1992-95, 99—, chair 1995—), Nat. Coal Assn. (bd. dirs. 1990-98, exec. com. 1993-94, 96-98), Nat. Coal Coun. (appointed by Sec. of Energy 1992, 94, 96, 98, 2000), Nat. Mining Assn. (bd. dirs. 1995-98), Seattle C. of C. (chmn. energy com. 1991-94), Western Rugby Football Union (sec. 1980), Broadmoor Golf Club, Rotary. Republican. Avocations: golf, hunting, fishing, gardening, handball. Home: 3711 E Madison St Seattle WA 98112-3838 Office: Pacific Coast Coal Co Inc PO Box 450 Black Diamond WA 98010-0450 E-mail: djmorris@aol.com.

MORRIS, DAVID JOSEPH, communications systems consultant, educator; b. Jerusalem, Israel, June 3, 1931; s. Isaac and Ray (Goldberg) M.; m. Rina Juz, Mar. 30, 1966; children: Guy, Yael. BSEE, Technion-Israel Inst. Tech., Haifa, 1956, diploma in engring., 1960; MSc in Rsch., U. Nottingham, Eng., 1961. Rsch. engr. Ericson Telephones Ltd., Beeston, Eng., 1957-61; computer memory rsch. sect. head English Electric Computers Ltd., Kidsgrove, Eng., 1961-67; command and ctrl. project leader Israel Def. Forces, Tel-Aviv, 1967-77; mgmt. cons. Elbit Computers Ltd., Haifa, 1977-83; projects coord. Israel Aircraft Industries Ltd., Lod Airfield, 1983-93; comm. systems cons. Holon, 1993—. Sr. lectr. Ben-Gurion U. of the Negev, Beer-Sheva, 1972-83, 93—, Feinberg Grad. Sch. of Weisman Inst. Sci., Rihovot, 1978-79, Technion Further Edn. Sch., Tel-Aviv, 1969-77; lectr. Nottingham Tech. Coll., 1958-60. Author: Introduction to Command Control Systems, 1977, Pulse Code Formats for Fiber Optical Data Communication, 1983, Communication for Command and Control Systems, 1983; contbr. articles to profl. jours.; inventor in field. Fellow IEE Eng. (Horseason prize 1958, hon. sec. grad. com. for East Midland, Eng. 1959-60; com. Israel sect. 1990—, Israel internat. conf. organizer 1995). Office: PO Box 578 Holon Israel E-mail: dmorris@zahar.net.il.

MORRIS, DAVID MICHAEL, insurance executive, lawyer; b. San Juan, P.R., Dec. 8, 1948; s. Edwin Thaddeus and Winifred Isabel (Walsh) M.; m. Carol Anderson Worden, Aug. 7, 1971; children: Laura H., John C. BA, U. Md., 1971; JD, U. Balt., 1975. Bar: Md. 1976, U.S. Dist. Ct. Md. 1976; CLU. Owner Franklin/Morris Assocs., LLC, Balt., 1976—. Columnist legal newspaper Daily Record, 1985-87. Pres., trustee 2d Presbyn. Ch., Balt., 1980-86, elder, 1988—; vice chmn. Balt. div. United Way, 1981-84; fund raiser Johns Hopkins Children's Ctr., Balt., 1984-88; trustee Roland Park Country Sch., 1988-89, 90-98; mem. exec. com. Gilman Sch. Parents Assn., 1989-91; grad. Leadership Md., 1998. Mem. ABA, Md. Bar Assn., Balt. Bar Assn., Assn. Advanced Life Underwriting, Balt. Life Underwriters Assn. (chmn. ethics 1977-80, bd. dirs. 1982-85, bd. dirs. Charitable Found., 1998—), Balt. Soc. CLUs and Chartered Fin. Cons. (chmn. ethical guidance com., bd. dirs.), Million Dollar Round Table (life), Md. Club, Balt. Country Club, Leadership Maryland. Avocations: tennis, golf, wine. Home: 205 Paddington Rd Baltimore MD 21212-3438 Office: Franklin/Morris Assocs LLC 7 E Redwood St Ste 1900 Baltimore MD 21202-1113

MORRIS, DESMOND (JOHN) (DESMOND JOHN MORRIS), zoologist, author, artist; s. Harry Howe Morris and Dorothy Marjorie (Hunt) Fuller; m. Ramona Joy Baulch, July 30, 1952; 1 son, Jason. BSc, Birmingham (Eng.) U.; PhD, Oxford (Eng.) U.; DSc (hon.), Reading (Eng.) U., 1998. Rsch. worker zoology U. Oxford, Eng., 1954-56; head Granada T.V. and Film Unit, Zool. Soc. London, 1956-59, curator mammals, 1959-67; dir. Inst. Contemporary Arts, London, 1967-68; rsch. fellow Wolfson Coll., Oxford, 1973-81. Author: Biology of Art, 1962, Apes and Monkeys, 1965, Big Cats, 1965, Mammals: A Guide to the Living Species, 1966, The Naked Ape, 1968, The Human Zoo, 1969, Intimate Behavior, 1971, Manwatching: A Field Guide to Human Behavior, 1977, The Soccer Tribe, 1981, The Book of Ages, 1983, The Art of Ancient Cyprus, 1985, Bodywatching: A Field Guide to the Human Species, 1985, The Illustrated Naked Ape, 1986, Catwatching, 1986, Dogwatching, 1986, The Secret Surrealist, 1987, Catlore, 1987, The Animals Roadshow, 1988, The Human Nestbuilders, 1988, Horsewatching, 1988, The Animal Contract, 1990, Animalwatching, 1990, Babywatching, 1991, Christmas Watching, 1992, The World of Animals, 1993, The Human Animal, 1994, Body Talk, A World Guide to Gestures, 1994, The Naked Ape Trilogy, 1994, Illustrated Cat Watching, 1994, Illustrated Babywatching, 1995, Illustrated Dogwatching, 1996, Catworld: A Feline Encyclopedia, 1996, The Human Sexes, 1997, Illustrated Horsewatching, 1998, Cool Cats: The 100 Cat Breeds of the World, 1999, Body Guards, 1999, Dogs: A Dictionary of Dog Breeds, 2001, Peoplewatching, 2002, others; co-author: (with Ramona Morris) Men and Snakes, 1965, Men and Apes, 1966, Men and Pandas, 1966, The Giant Panda, 1981, Gestures: Their Origins and Distribution, 1979; autobiography Animal Days, 1979, The Naked Eye, 2000; editor: Primate Ethology, 1969, (fiction) Inrock, 1983; contbr. numerous articles to zool. jours.; one-man shows include Mayor Gallery, London, 1997, Pub. Art Gallery, Buxton, 1997, Keitelman Gallery, Brussels, 1998, Rossaert Gallery, Antwerp, 1998, Witteveen Gallery, Amsterdam, 1999, Mus. Modern Art, 2002, others. Address: care Jonathan Cape RandomCH 20 Vauxhall Bridge Rd London SWIV 2SA England E-mail: dmorris@patrol.i-way.co.uk.

MORRIS, DIANE BAKER, nurse; b. Houston, Sept. 24, 1945; d. Ray Vernon and Eleanor (Perry) Gillispie; m. John M. Baker, June 2, 1966 (dec. July 1982); children: Brian C. Baker, Angela L. Baker Frey; m. J. Wayne Morris, Sept. 3, 1994. Diploma, Hermann Hosp. Sch. Nursing, Houston, 1967; BSN, U. Tex., Tyler, 1992; MSN, Tex. Tech U. Health Sci. Ctr., Lubbock, 1998. RN, Tex.; cert. diabetes educator; cert. family nurse practitioner. Nurse Shrine Crippled Children's Hosp., Houston, 1967, Meth. Hosp., Houston, 1968-70, Hermann Hosp., Houston, 1970-71; dir. nurses Doctors Hosp., Conroe, 1974-79; dir. ICU Mother Frances Hosp., Tyler, 1979-82; clin. coord. day surgery East Tex. Med. Ctr., 1983-91; paralegal Potter Law Firm, 1991-92; diabetes educator Good Shepherd Hosp., Longview, Tex., 1992-94; dir. diabetes edn. Titus Regional Med. Ctr., Mt. Pleasant, 1994-97, diabetes educator, 1993-98; family nurse practitioner women's clinic Titus County Meml. Health Dist., Health Essentials NP-C, 1999—; family nurse practitioner Sulpher Springs Family Health Clinic, 2000—. Mem. Tex. Nurses Assn., Am. Assn. Diabetes Educators, Tex. Nurse Practitioners, Sigma Theta Tau. Republican. Roman Catholic. Avocations: horses, gardening, music, cooking. Home: 110 Keith St Mount Vernon TX 75457

MORRIS, DOLORES ORINSKIA, psychologist, psychoanalyst; PhD, Yeshiva U., N.Y.C., 1974; cert. psychoanalysis and psychotherapy, NYU, 1980. Pvt. practice psychologist, N.Y.C., 1980—. Supr. psychotherapy and psychoanalysis program NYU, 1990—2001. E-mail: domorris@worldnet.att.net.

MORRIS, DONALD, tax specialist; b. Chgo., Oct. 13, 1945; s. Donald Charles and Cathleen (Lautner) M.; children: Keith, Sarah. BA, Calif. State U., L.A., 1968; MA, De Paul U., 1972, MS in Taxation, 1987; PhD, So. Ill. U., 1978. CPA, Ill., N.Mex.; CFP. Prof. philosophy John A. Logan Coll., Carterville, Ill., 1972-79; tax mgr. Evans-Gries & Co. CPAs, Addison, 1980-83; sr. tax advisor Alexander Grant, CPA, Chgo., 1983-84; tax mgr. Evans & Co., Itasca, Ill., 1984-87; pvt. practice CPA Addison, 1987-88, Bloomingdale, 1988-93; Roselle, Ill., 1993-97; assoc. prof. acctg. E. N.Mex. U., Portales, 1997—, dept. chmn. divsn. advanced bus. studies. Author: Dewey and the Behavioristic Context of Ethics, 1995; contbr. chpt. to book. Libertarian candidate for comptroller State of Ill., 1986. Mem. AICPA, N.Mex. Soc. CPAs, Am. Philos. Assn., Am. Acctg. Assn., Assn. Cert. Fraud Examiners, Assn. Informal Logic and Critical Thinking, Delta Mu Delta. Avocations: distance running (4 marathons), tennis, woodworking. Home: 269 Oklahoma Dr Portales NM 88130-7089 Office: Coll Bus East NMex U Portales NM 88130 E-mail: don.morris@enmu.edu.

MORRIS, DONALD ARTHUR ADAMS, college president; b. Detroit, Aug. 31, 1934; s. Robert Park and Margaret Lymburn (Adams) M.; m. Zella Mae Stormer, June 21, 1958; children: Dwight Joseph, Julie Adams. BA, Wayne State U., 1961; M.P.A., U. Mich., 1966, PhD, 1970; LLD (hon.), Olivet Coll., 1987. Copy boy Detroit Times, 1952-55, reporter, 1955-57, edn. writer, 1957-60; adminstrv. asst. Wayne State U., Detroit, 1960-62; mng. editor news service U. Mich., 1962-64, mgr. spl. programs, 1964-68; mgr. Met. Detroit Devel. Program, 1968-71; v.p. for devel. Hobart and William Smith Colls., Geneva & N.Y., 1971-76, exec. v.p., 1976-77; pres., prof. polit. sci. Olivet (Mich.) Coll., 1977-92; pres. emeritus Olivet Coll., Mich., 1992—, cons., 1992-93. Trustee Mich. Intercollegiate Athletic Assn., 1977-92, chair, 1978-79, 85-86, 90-91; trustee Assn. Ind. Colls. and Univs. Mich., 1977-92, chair, 1984-85; cons. evaluator North Ctrl. Assn. Colls. and Schs., 1986-92; mem. Mich. Jud. Tenure Commn., 1991-94; mem. Newspaper Guild of Detroit, 1952-60, exec. bd., 1958-60. Contbr. articles to profl. jours. Trustee Olivet Coll., 1977-92, Mich. Coll. Found., 1977-92, exec. com., 1989-92; trustee Ecumenical Inst. Jewish-Christian Studies, 1988-89; mem. Mich. Higher Edn. Assistance and Student Loan Authorities, 1986—2002, chair, 1989-94; bd. dirs. Planned Parenthood of Finger Lakes, N.Y., 1973-77, pres., 1975-77; bd. dirs., treas. Genesee Regional Family Planning Program N.Y., 1975-77; trustee Coun. Higher Edn., United Ch. of Christ, 1977-92, mem. exec. com., 1982-92, chair, 1986-88; trustee Glen Lake Cmty. Libr. Bd., 1993—, pres., 1994-99; mem. Sleeping Bear Noontiders, 1993—, sec., 1995, v.p. 1996-97, pres., 1997-98, South Manitou Meml. Soc., 1980—, chair nominating com., 1996-97, pres., 1997—; dir. Dorado # 4 Assn., 1998—, pres., 2000—; mem. So. Ariz. Scottish Soc., 1998—, Chris-Craft Antique Boat Club, 1999—, Mayo Smith Soc., 1985—. Mem. Am. Assn. for Higher Edn., Leelanau Athletic Club, U. Mich. Alumni Assn. (life), U. Mich. Alumni Club Grand Traverse, U. Mich. Alumni Club Tucson, Friends of Tucson-Pima Pub. Libr., Sigma Delta Chi, Omicron Delta Kappa, Alpha Lambda Epsilon, Kappa Sigma Alpha, Gamma Iota Sigma, Alpha Mu Gamma, Phi Mu Alpha Sinfonia, Rotary (local pres. 1987-88, Paul Harris fellow). Congregationalist. Home: 8330 S Dunns Farm Rd Maple City MI 49664-8721 also: 6551 E Dorado Blvd Tucson AZ 85715-4705

MORRIS, DONALD CHARLES, commercial real estate mergers and acquisitions; b. Iowa City, Nov. 15, 1951; s. Lucien Ellis and Jean (Pinder) M.; m. Barbara Louise Small, Apr. 28, 1973 (div. Apr. 1980); m. Jana Susan Moyer, Aug. 28, 1982; children: Alexander Charles, Elisa Jean. Student, Cantab Coll., Toronto, Can., 1970-71; BSC, U. Guelph, Can., 1974; MSC, U. Guelph, 1975; PhD, U. B.C., Vancouver, 1978. Instr. U. B.C., Vancouver, 1975-77; pres. Morley Internat., Inc., Seattle, 1976-81; self-employed Comml. Investment Real Estate, 1981-83; v.p., regional mgr. DKB Corp., 1983-86; pres. Morris Devel. Svcs., Inc., 1986—, Washington Group, Inc., Seattle, 1986—; sec.-treas., exec. v.p. Interactive Imagination Corp., 2000—. Bd.dirs., sec., treas., exec. v.p. Interactive Imagination Corp., Seattle, 2000—. Bd. dirs. Perservation Action, Washington, 1985-90; mem. Nat. Trust for Historic Preservation. Mem. Nat. Assn. Realtors, Wash. Assn. Realtors. Avocations: skiing, sailing, boating. Office: Wash Group Morris Devel PO Box 4584 Rollingbay WA 98061-0584

MORRIS, DONALD G. b. Santa Barbara, Calif., Nov. 19, 1943; BSBA, North Ga. Coll. and State U., 2000, MPA, 2001. Various to mfg. engr. Goetze Corp. of Am., LaGrange, Ga., 1986—89; plant mgr. Jakes Mfg., Greenwood, Miss., 1989—92; CEO Morris & Assocs., Gainesville, Ga., 1992—. Contbr. articles. Recipient Leadership award, Wall Street Jour., 2000. Mem.: Fabricators and Mfrs. Assn., Soc. Die Cast Engrs.

MORRIS, DOROTHEA LOUISE, nurse midwife, retired; b. Emporia, Kans., Oct. 30, 1944; d. Clarence Earl and Dorothy Ann (Draper) Richardson; m. David B. DeKalb, May 1, 1966 (div. Dec. 1981); children: Michele E. DeKalb, Cheryl L. Lines, David B. DeKalb Jr.; m. James Henry Morris, July 4, 1984. Diploma, Beth-El Sch. Nursing, Colorado Springs, Colo., 1966; BSN, Alaska Meth. U., 1975; MPA, Troy State U., 1988; MSN, U. N.Mex., 1990. RN Colo., N. Mex. Commd. 1st lt. USAF, 1977, advanced through grades to lt. col., 1992; staff nurse Meml. Hosp., Colorado Springs, 1966-67; staff nurse, supr. Albany (Oreg.) Gen. Hosp., 1969; staff nurse, obstetrics Harrisonville (Mo.) Hosp., 1970, USAF Hosp., Anchorage, 1970-75; staff nurse, instr. BOCES, Verona, N.Y., 1976-77; staff nurse, instr. ADN program Mohawk Valley C.C., Utica, 1976-77; staff nurse obstetrics Chanute AFB, Rantoul, Ill., 1977-79; nurse-midwife Homestead AFB (Fla.) Hosp., 1980-85, Weisbaden (Germany) Regional Med. Ctr., 1985-88; nurse-midwife, instr. Midwifery Sch., Andrews AFB, Md., 1990-97; nurse-midwife OB/GYN Assocs. of Farmville, AC, Farmville, VA, 1998, ret., 1998. Asst. dir. Air Force Nurse-Midwifery Program, Andrews AFB, 1991-97, dir., 1997; pres. CNM Svc. Dirs., Inc., 1995-97. Lt. col. USAF, 1977-97. Mem.: Uniformed Nurse Practitioner assn., NANP in Reproductive Health, Nurses Assn. Obstetrics and Gynecology, Am. Coll. Nurse Midwives (cert.), Women of the Loyal Order of the Moose, Order Ea. Star. Baptist. Avocations: painting, knitting, crocheting. Home: RR 2 Box 609-b Appomattox VA 24522-8706

MORRIS, DOROTHY KAY, writer; b. Charleston, S.C., Dec. 25, 1935; d. Robert Oliver and Desma Lee (Rudd) M.; m. Andre Marechal, Aug. 20, 1955 (div. July 1965); children: Désirée Katherine Araeipour, Suzette Maréchal. Pvt. coach competitive horseback riding, 1972-92; credit professional Internat. Credit Unocal Corp., Brea, Calif., 1985-99; ret., 1999. Author: Secret Sins of the Mothers, 1999; contbr. articles to horsemanship mags. Vol. English tchr., tutor Thai Cmty., L.A., 1986-91; vol. book writing Allexperts.com. Mem.: NSDAR (Gen. Richard Gridley chpt.). Republican. Buddhist. Avocations: geneaology, languages. E-mail: dkm2001@msn.com.

MORRIS, EARLE ELIAS, JR. retired state official, business executive; b. Greenville, S.C., July 14, 1928; s. Earle Elias and Bernice (Carey) M.; m. Jane L. Boroughs, Apr. 12, 1958; children: Lynda Lewis, Carey Mauldin, Elizabeth McDaniel, Earle Elias III; m. Carol Telford, Oct. 4, 1972; 1 son, David Earle. BS, Clemson Coll., 1949, LLD; D.Pub. Svc. (hon.), U. S.C., 1980, S.C. State Coll., 1990; Dr. Med. Sci., U. S.C.; LLD (hon.), The Citadel, Cen. Wesleyan Coll.; HHD (hon.), Lander Coll., Francis Marion Coll., 1984, U. Charleston, 1992; DHL, Winthrop U., 1996. Pres., chmn. bd. Morris & Co., Inc. (wholesale grocers), Pickens, S.C.; v.p., dir. Pickens Bank, 1956-69, Bankers Trust S.C., Pickens, 1968-75; pres. Gen. Ins. Agy., 1970—; chmn. bd. dirs. Carolina Investors, Inc., chmn., 1993—; ptnr. Morris Realty Co., Pickens; mem. S.C. Ho. of Reps., 1950-54, S.C. Senate, 1954-70; lt. gov. State of S.C., 1971-75, comptr. gen., 1976-99. Chmn. bd. Santee Cooper Fisheries (Far East) Ltd., Hong Kong, Tai Pan Technologies, Ltd., Hong Kong; dir. Brunswick Worsted Mills, S.C. Devel. Corp., Pickens Savs. & Loan Assn.; hon. consul Republic of Korea. Pres. Clemson U. Found., 1984-85; state dir. Selective Svc. Sys. Served to brig. gen. S.C. N.G., maj. gen. S.C. S.G. Decorated Legion of Merit, Meritorious Svc. medals; recipient Algernon Sydney Sullivan award, 1980, Donald L. Scantlebury award, 1985, Nations Most Valuable Pub. Ofcl. award, 1993, Pub. Svc. award Am. Legion, 1993, Living Legend award S.C. Hist. Found., 1997, Clemson Medallion award 1997; named Disting. Alumnus, Clemson Coll. Mem. Nat. Assn. State Comptrollers (pres. 1982), Nat. Assn. State Auditors, Comptrollers and Treasurers (pres. 1988-89), S.C. Nat. Guard Assn. (pres. 1980-81), S.C. Jr. C. of C., S.C. Rehab. Assn. (v.p.), Govtl. Acctg. Standards Adv. Coun. (chmn. 1989-96), Fin. Acctg. Found. (trustee 1985-88, 96—, v.p. 2000-01), S.C. Retirees Assn. (pres.), Blue Key, Palmetto Club, Faculty Club (Columbia), Poinsett Club (Greenville), Masons, Shriners, Lions, Order of Saint Stanislas (grand chancellor, Knight Grand Cross), Order of white Eagle of Saint Stanislas, Sovereign Mil. Order Swabia, Order of Polonia Restituta (knight comdr., 2d class), Knights of Malta. Presbyterian (elder, former deacon, synod trustee). Home: 159 Lake Murray Ter Lexington SC 29072-9103 *In my personal, public and professional life I have tried to follow the Biblical admonition of "loving mercy, doing justly, and walking humbly.".*

MORRIS, EDITH HENDERSON, lawyer; b. Birmingham, Ala., Mar. 25, 1944; d. William and Roberta (Sterrett) H.; m. Joseph M. Morris Jr., Nov. 29, 1963; children: Robert Joseph, Edith L. BA, Our Lady of Holy Cross Coll., New Orleans, 1974; JD, Loyola U., New Orleans, 1985. Bar: La. 1985, U.S. Dist. Ct. (ea. dist.) La. 1985. Assoc. Sessions & Fishman, New Orleans, 1985-87, Lowe, Stein, Hoffman & Allweis, New Orleans, 1987-89; pvt. practice, 1989—. Instr. family skills course Law Sch. Loyola U., 1989—; spkr. on divorce, mediation and adoption. Bd. dirs. La. Mediation Coun., 1991-94. Fellow Am. Acad. Matrimonial Lawyers; mem. ABA, Am. Acad. Adoption Attys. (trustee 1999-2001), Assn. Women Attys., Acad. Family Mediators (practitioner), La. State Bar Assn. Avocation: walking. Home: 241 Rosa Ave Metairie LA 70005-3415 Office: 1515 Poydras St Ste 1870 New Orleans LA 70112-3770 E-mail: ehmorris@bellsouth.net.

MORRIS, EDWARD WILLIAM, JR. lawyer; b. Medford, Oreg., Apr. 12, 1943; s. Edward William and Julia Loretta (Sullivan) M.; m. Margaret Ellen McKenna, 1976; children: John McKenna, Elizabeth Anne. BS, Fordham Coll., 1965, JD, 1971. Bar: N.Y. 1973. Dir. Drug Products Co., Inc., Union City, N.J., 1968-71; asst. arbitration dir. N.Y. Stock Exch., N.Y.C., 1971-73, arbitration dir., 1973-74, asst. sec., arbitration dir., 1974-89, v.p. arbitration, 1989-91, chief hearing officer, 1991—. Dir. Stock Clearing Corp., N.Y.C.; mem. Securities Industry Conf. on Arbitration, N.Y.C., 1977— ; lectr. in field. Served to sgt. U.S. Army, 1965-68, Vietnam. Mem. ABA, Am. Arbitration Assn. (comml. law com. 1983—), Assn. Bar City N.Y. (retail fin. svcs. com. 1989—), N.Y. County Lawyers Assn. (sec. com. on arbitration 1983—), High Mountain Golf Club, N.Y. Roadrunners Club. Home: 67 Arlton Ave Allendale NJ 07401-1331 Office: NY Stock Exch Inc 20 Broad St New York NY 10005-1974 E-mail: emorris@nyse.com.

MORRIS, EUGENE JEROME, retired lawyer; b. N.Y.C., Oct. 14, 1910; s. Max and Regina (Cohn) M.; m. Terry Lesser, Mar. 28, 1934 (dec. Sept. 1993); 1 child, Richard S.; m. Blanche Bier Funke, June 22, 1994. BSS., CCNY, 1931; LL.B., St. John's U., 1934. Bar: N.Y. 1935. Practiced, N.Y.C., 1935-99; sr. and founding partner firm Demov, Morris & Hammerling, 1946-87; v.p., sr. counsel Ea. region Am. Title Ins. Co., N.Y.C., 1990-93; of counsel Spector & Feldman, 1991-99; ret., 1999. Adj. prof. land use regulation NYU Grad. Sch. Pub. Adminstrn., 1978-81; adj. prof. legal issues in real estate, Real Estate Inst. NYU, 1988—; spl. master Supreme Ct. State of N.Y., 1979-99; arbitrator Civil Ct. N.Y., 1994-99. Editor weekly column N.Y. Law Jour., 1965-87, It's the Law, Real Estate Forum, 1982-87; editor-in-chief N.Y. Practice Guide: Real Estate, 4 vols., 1986, Real Estate Development, 4 vols., 1987; contbr. articles to profl. jours. Mem. N.Y. State Tax Revision Commn., 1977-80, N.Y.C. Rent Guidelines Bd., 1983-85. Served with AUS, 1943-45. Recipient Justice award N.Y. sect. Am. Jewish Congress, 1996. Mem. ABA (chmn. spl. com. housing and urban devel. 1970-73, coun. sect. real property, probate and trust law 1971-74, assoc. editor Real Property, Probate and Trust Jour. 1979-86, editor Real Property, Probate and Property mag., articles editor 1986-94), Am. Judges Assn., Assn. Bar City N.Y. (chmn. com. housing and urban devel. 1971-74, com. on lectures and continuing edn. 1980-83, coun. on jud. adminstrn. 1989-92), N.Y. State Bar Assn. (exec. com. 1980-97, chmn. com. meetings and lectures 1982-92, CLE com. 1984-90, ho. of dels. 1986-95, co-editor Real Property Jour. 1995-97), Citizens Union, Lambda Alpha (bd. dirs. 1990-98, pres. N.Y. chpt. 1990-93, sec. 1993-95, treas. 1996-97). E-mial. Home: 200 Central Park S New York NY 10019-1415 Fax: 212-983-0874. E-mail: specfeld@aol.com. *After 66 years of marriage and 65 years of practicing law, I have retired. However, like the old fire horse when the bell rings I run; thus I am still teaching real estate law as an Adjunct Professor at the New York Universitsy Real Estate Institute, am counsel to my firm and stay active in bar associations, civic groups and fraternities. I am always an optimist at work, with friends, and with my family.*

MORRIS, FLORENCE HENDERSON, auditor; b. Mobile, Ala., Sept. 8, 1964; d. Thomas Gordan Henderson and Joanne Elizabeth (Pfleger) Martin; m. Fred S. Morris, July 28, 1995; 1 son, David Patrick. BS in Fin., U. Ala., 1986. Payment and receipt rep. SouthTrust Bank of Mobile, 1988-89; internal bank auditor SouthTrust Corp., Birmingham, 1989-90, compliance audit officer, 1990-92; prin. compliance auditor, asst. v.p. SouthTrust Corp. and SouthTrust Bank of Ga., Atlanta, 1992-95; compliance audit supr., v.p. SouthTrust Corp., Birmingham, 1995-98; retail audit mgr., v.p. SouthTrust Bank, 1998—. Mem. Inst. Internal Auditors, Bankers Adminstrn. Inst. (cert. regulatory compliance mgr.), Am. Bankers Assn., Ala. Fin. Assn., U. Ala. Alumna, Delta Sigma Pi. Office: SouthTrust Bank Audit Dept 210 Wildwood Pkwy 4th Fl A-001-WB-0402 Birmingham AL 35209-7154

MORRIS, FRANK CHARLES, JR. lawyer, educator; b. Pitts., May 11, 1948; s. Frank Charles and Mary Louise Morris; m. Kathleen Williams; children: Frank Charles III, Alexander Greg. BS with distinction, Northwestern U., 1970; JD, U. Va., 1973. Bar: Pa. 1973, U.S. Ct. Appeals (4th and 7th cirs.) 1974, D.C. 1975, U.S. Ct. Appeals (1st, 2d and 9th cirs.) 1975, (U.S. Ct. Appeals (10th cir.)) 1976, U.S. Supreme Ct. 1976, U.S. Ct. Appeals (5th and D.C. cirs.) 1977, U.S. Dist. Ct. D.C. 1977, U.S. Dist. Ct. (ea. dist.) Wis. 1980, U.S. Dist. Ct. (ea. dist.) Pa. 1993, U.S. Ct. Appeals (6th, 7th and 8th cirs.) 1987, U.S. Ct. Appeals (11th cir.) 1981, U.S. Dist. Ct. Md. 1985, U.S. Ct. Appeals (3d cir.) 1991. Rsch. asst. Bernard Dunau, Washington, 1972—73; appellate ct. br. atty. NLRB, 1973—76; assoc. McGuiness & Williams, 1976—78, Epstein Becker & Green, P.C., Washington, 1978—80, ptnr., 1981—88, sr. ptnr., 1988—. Mem. adj. faculty Law Sch. Cath. U. Am., Washington, 1979—80, adj. prof. law, 1984—; adj. prof. law, Law Sch. George Washington U., Washington; mem. faculty Sch. Indsl. and Labor Rels. EEO study program, Cornell U., N.Y.C., 1979—, ALI-ABA course Employment Discrimination and Civil Rights Actions, 1988, Trial Evidence, Civil Practice, and Effective Litigation Techniques in Fed. and State Cts.; co-chair ALI-ABA Fed. Jud. Ctr., Video Law Rev., Ams. with Disabilities Act, 1992; co-chair video law rev. ALI-ABA How to Present and Challenge Experts in Employment Cases, 1994; co-chair Current Devels. in Employment Law, 1994—; faculty Litigating Employment Cases: Views from the Bench Georgetown U., 1998—; spkr., lectr. in field. Author: Current Trends in the Use (and Misuse) of Statistics in Employment Discrimination Litigation, 1977, 2d edit., 1978; editor-in-chief The Equal Employer Newsletter, 1981—86, editl. adv. bd. ADA Policy & Law, 1992—, Corp. Counsel's Guide to ADA, 1993—. Dir. Northwestern U. Alumni Admissions Coun., Washington Area Coun., 1978—81. Named to Outstanding Young Men of Am., U.S. Jaycees, 1982;

recipient Sustained Superior Performance award, NLRB Gen. Counsel, 1974, cert. commendation for outstanding performance, 1975, commendation for collective bargaining, Social Security Adminstrn. Commr., 1988. Mem.: ABA (labor and employment law, adminstrv. and litigation sects.), Fed. Bar Assn., D.C. Bar Assn. (adminstrv. law, labor rels. and litigation divsns.), Pa. Bar Assn., Northwestern U. Alumni Club (bd. govs. 1975—), John Evans Club of Northwestern U., D.C. Rd. Runners Club.

MORRIS, G. RONALD, industrial executive; b. East St. Louis, Ill., Aug. 30, 1936; s. George H. and Mildred C. M.; m. Margaret Heino, June 20, 1959; children: David, Michele, James. BS in Metall. Engring, U. Ill., 1959. Metall. engr. Delco-Remy div. Gen. Motors Corp., 1959-60; factory metallurgist Dubuque Tractor Works, John Deere Co., Iowa, 1960-66; with Fed.-Mogul Corp., 1966-79, v.p., group mgr. ball and roller bearing group, 1979; pres. Tenneco Automotive div. Tenneco, Inc., Deerfield, Ill., 1979-82; pres., chief exec. officer PT Components, Inc., Indpls., 1982-88; vice-chmn. Rexnord Corp., 1988-89; chmn., pres., chief exec. officer CTP Holdings Inc., 1986-88; chmn. Integrated Technologies, Inc., Indpls., 1990-92, also bd. dirs.; pres., chief exec. officer Western Industries, Inc., Milw., 1991-99. Chmn. bd. dirs. Milnot Holding Corp., St. Louis, NN, Inc., Erwin, Tenn.; bd. dirs. Dalco Metals, Inc., Walworth, Wis., Hines Hort., Inc., Irvine, Calif. Mem. Pres.'s Coun., U. Ill., mem. adv. bd. Coll. Engring., mem. sr. adv. bd. Sch. Materials Sci. and Engring; mem. U. Ill. Found. Mem. ASM, SAE, Exmoor Country Club (Highland Park, Ill.), The Landings Club (Savannah, Ga.), Masons, Scottish Rite Consistory, Kiwanis Internat. Republican. Presbyterian.

MORRIS, GERALD DOUGLAS, newspaper editor; b. Boston, May 7, 1937; s. George Christopher and Lucy Bell (MacPhee) M.; m. Elaine Louise Owen, Nov. 13, 1964 (div. 1976); children: Laura Louise, Douglas Owen; m. Mary Elizabeth Simpson Stevens, Apr. 15, 1977; children: Jeffrey David Stevens Morris, Wendy Elizabeth Stevens Morris. Student, Boston U., 1959. Reporter Patriot Ledger, Quincy, Mass., 1961-66; copy editor Boston Globe, 1966—, travel editor, 1989—. Syndicated columnist Globe-Trotting, 1970—. Author: Boston Globe Guide to Boston, 1989, New England under Sail, 1993, Guide to Cape Cod, 1999. Chmn. Canton (Mass.) Cable Adv. Bd., 1990-92; bd. dirs. Lowell Thomas Found., 1997. With U.S. Army, 1959-61. Mem. Soc. Am. Travel Writers (chmn. N.E. chpt. 2000—), Skal Club Boston, Lions (pres. Canton 1969-70, 80-81). Avocations: photography, travel. Home: 873 Harris Ave Woonsocket RI 02895-1824 Office: Globe Newspaper Co 135 Morrissey Blvd Boston MA 02125-3310

MORRIS, GORDON JAMES, financial company executive, consultant; b. Mt. Vernon, Ohio, Oct. 6, 1942; s. R. Hugh and Betty Jane (Roberts) M.; m. Janet Ann Swanson, Aug. 28, 1965 (div. 1971); m. Nancy Joan Meyfarth, July 26, 1975 (div. Oct. 1998); 1 child, Lawrence Hugh; m. Phyllis J. Hersha, Jan. 1, 2000. Student, Ohio State U., 1960-61; BA, Otterbein Coll., 1966; postgrad. in law, Capital U., Bexley, Ohio, 1967-68; postgrad., Coll. Fin. Planning, Denver, 1983-90, Inst. Cert. Fund Specialists, 1991. Registered investment advisor; cert. fin. planner; cert. fund specialist; lic. loving trust advisor; cert. divorce planner. Asst. to pres. Jaeger Machine Co., Columbus, Ohio, 1968-73; rep. Equitable Fin. Svcs., Sarasota, Fla., 1974-81; pres. Beacon Wealth Mgmt. Inc. (formerly Morris & Assocs., P.A.), 1981—; co-gen. ptnr. Beacon Bridge Loan Pool, Ltd., 1994-97. Chmn. bd. dirs. MAP Fin. Group, Inc., Sarasota, 1985-89; co-owner U.S.I.S.L. West Fla. Fury Soccer Team, 1996-98; bd. dirs., v.p. Soccer Resource Group, Sarasota, 1997-99, Radyx Capital Ptnr., Tampa, 1999—. Columnist The Creative News. Past chmn. West Coast chpt. March of Dimes, Bradenton, Fla., bd. dirs., 1986-88; v.p. All Sch. Kids, Inc., 1998-99; pres. Epilepsy Found. S.W. Fla., Inc., 1986-87. Mem. Inst. Cert. Fin. Planners, Million Dollar Roundtable, Sertoma (pres. local club 1979-80). Republican. Methodist. Home and Office: 2822 Countryside Ln Sarasota FL 34233-2122 Fax: 775-258-5570. E-mail: striker.five@comcast.net.

MORRIS, GRANT HAROLD, law educator; b. Syracuse, N.Y., Dec. 10, 1940; s. Benjamin and Caroline Grace (Judelson) Morris; m. Phyllis Silberstein, July 4, 1967; children: Joshua, Sara. AB, Syracuse U., 1962, JD, 1964; LLM, Harvard U., 1971. Bar: N.Y. 1964. Atty. N.Y. Mental Hygiene Law Recodification Project, Inst. Public Adminstrn., N.Y.C., 1964-66; faculty Wayne State U. Law Sch., 1967-70, prof., 1970-73, dean acad. affairs, 1971-73; prof. U. San Diego Law Sch., 1973—, Univ. prof., 1996-97, acting dean, 1977-78, 88-89, assoc. dean grad. legal edn., 1978-81, interim dean, 1997-98; prof. law in psychiatry Wayne State U. Med. Sch., 1970-73; adj. prof. U. Calif. Med. Sch., San Diego, 1974-84, clin. prof. dept. psychiatry, 1984—. Legal counsel Mich. Legis. Com. to Revise Mental Health Statutes, 1970-73; organizer law and psychiatry sect. Assn. Am. Law Schs., 1973, chmn., 1973-74; patients advocate, San Diego County, 1977-78; cons. Criminal Code Commn., Ariz. Legis., 1974; reporter task force on guidelines governing roles of mental health profls. in criminal process Am. Bar Assn. standing com. on assn. standards for criminal justice, 1981-84; cert. rev. hearing officer San Diego Superior Ct., 1984-90, ct. commr./judge pro tem, 1990-92, mental health hearing officer, 1992-97; hearing officer San Diego Housing Commn., 1988-92; mem. exec. com. sect. law and mental disability Assn. Am. Law Schs., 1990-97. Author: The Insanity Defense: A Blueprint for Legislative Reform, 1975; co-author: Mental Disorder in the Criminal Process: Stan Stress and the Vietnam/Sports Conspiracy, 1993; editor, contbr.: The Mentally Ill and the Right to Treatment, 1970. Mem. Atascadero State Hosp. adv. bd., 2000—. Mem. Phi Alpha Delta (faculty adv. 1970-73, 75-92). Home: 8515 Nottingham Pl La Jolla CA 92037-2125 Office: U San Diego Law Sch 5998 Alcala Park San Diego CA 92110-2492 E-mail: gmorris@sandiego.edu.

MORRIS, GREGORY W, music educator; b. West Plains, Mo., Feb. 9, 1962; s. Charles Morris, Irma Morris; m. Sheila Hayes; children: Sarah, Nicholas. B Music Edn., Evangel U., 1984; MusM, Tex. Christian U., 1985; D Musical Arts, U. North Tex., 1990. Asst. prof. music Brevard Coll., Brevard, NC, 1990—98; assoc. prof. music Evangel U., Springfield, Mo., 1999—. Mem.: Music Tchrs. Nat. Assn. (pres. Springfield chpt. 2001—). Home: 227 Sunshine Rd Rogersville MO 65742 Office: Evangel U 1111 N Glenstone Springfield MO 65802

MORRIS, HARRIET R. elementary school educator; b. Springfield, Mass., July 4, 1923; d. Walter Dewitt and Ida Ann (Rome) Bearg; m. Samuel Morris, Oct. 14, 1945 (dec. 1993); children: Robert, Julia, Jonathan, Daniel. BS, Am. Internat. Coll., 1944; MS, Butler U., 1973, EdS, 1985. Cert. tchr. K-12 Ind., mentally retarded, emotionally disturbed, LD/neurol. impaired, reading tchr. Ind., lic. sch. psychologist INd. Tchr. lang. arts, grades 1-6 Children's Ho., Indpls., 1971-72; tchr. Indpls. Pub. Schs., 1972-89; sch. psychologist Avon (Ind.) Sch. Sys., 1990. Leader cub scouts Boy Scouts Am., Schenectady, NY, 1955—56; leader brownies Girl Scouts U.S., 1957—58; Sunday sch. tchr. Indpls. Hebrew Congregation, 1964—66; bd. dirs. Indpls. chpt. Hadassah, 1990—; guardian ad litem Ind. Advs. for Children, 1994—95; docent Indpls. Children's Mus., 1996—97; vol. Older Adult Svc. and Info. Sys., 1996—98. Mem.: Mensa.

MORRIS, HELEN DELORES, b. Florence, S.C., Dec. 16, 1964; d. Levern and Helen Mae Morris; 1 child Alexius Sade Johnson. Home: Apt 4-G 2909 Campbellton Rd Atlanta GA 30311

MORRIS, HELEN JULIA, artist; b. Wilmette, Ill. d. William Neville and Marjorie (Raiguel) M. BFA, Sch. Art Inst. Chgo., 1969. Exhibitions include Orlando Ctrl. Libr., 1990-91, Mount Dora Ctr. for the Arts, 1992, 97. Mem. Mt. Dora Ctr. for Arts. Mem. South Lake Art League (pres. 1998-99). Avocations: sailing, reading, native plant rescue, travel. Home: PO Box 121401 Clermont FL 34712-1401

MORRIS, HENRY ALLEN, JR. retired publisher; b. Moncks Corner, S.C., Feb. 9, 1940; s. Henry Allen Sr. and Edith Luther (Wall) M.; divorced; 1 child, Anthony Duane Allen. A in Acctg., Palmer Jr. Coll., Charleston, S.C., 1959; BA in English cum laude, Belmont Abbey Coll., N.C., 1974. Office mgr. Gas Engine and Electric Co., Charleston, 1959; cargo coord. S.C. State Ports Authority, 1959-70; headmaster St. Stephen Acad., S.C., 1973-77; gen. mgr. The Berkeley Democrat, Moncks Corner, 1977-86, owner, 1989—; pub., editor Berkeley Ind., 1987—2002; pres. Berkeley Pub. Inc., 1987—2002. Author: (short story) The Easter Gift, 1973. Bd. dirs. Council of Govts. Regional Forum, Charleston, 1987, Winthrop Coll., 1983, Moncks Corner Downtown, Inc., 1986-87; mem. Moncks Corner City Council, 1983-88; mayor pro tem, 1986-88; commr. S.C. Vocat. Rehab. Agy.; treas. bd. dirs. Berkeley County YMCA; founder Charleston Opera Corp.; past pres., bd. mem. Berkeley County Vol. Action Com.; former mem. parents' and cmty. leaders' focus group Berkeley County Sch. Dists. Strategic Planning Com.; founder, bd. mem. Lord Berkeley Conservation Trust; bd. mem., chmn. pub. rels. com. Berkeley H.S. Acad. Booster Club; bd. mem. Berkeley Trident United Way Adv. Bd.; active Moncks Corner Planning and Zoning Commn.; bd. mem., spl. events chmn., exec. bd. sec. Moncks Corner Merchants Assn. Recipient Pres. award Berkeley Arts Council, 1985, Charleston Jaycees, 1971, Friend of Edn. award Berkeley County Sch. System, 1991; named Handicapped Man of Yr., Moncks Corner's Mayor's Com., 1990. Mem. Trident C. of C. (bd. dirs.), Rotary (past pres.), Moncks Corner Rotary Club (chmn. pub. rels. com.). Episcopalian. Avocations: reading, painting, collecting art. E-mails. Home: 1328 Southwood St Alice TX 78332 E-mail: amorrisman@webtv.net., amorrisman@aol.com.

MORRIS, HENRY MADISON, III, minister, speaker, writer, consultant; b. El Paso, Tex., May 15, 1942; s. Henry Madison and Mry Louis (Beach) M.; m. Janet Deckman, July 25, 1965; children: Henry M., Scotta Marie. BA summa cum laude, Christian Heritage Coll., 1976; MDiv, Luther Rice Sem., 1977; DMin, 1978; MBA, Pepperdine U., 1989. Ordained to ministry Bapt. Ch., 1968. Regional mgr. Integon Ins. Co., Greenville, S.C., 1969-75; pastor Hallmark Bapt. Ch., 1969-75; assoc. prof. Bible Christian Heritage Coll., El Cajon, Calif., 1977-78; adminstrv. v.p., 1978-80; pastor First Bapt. Ch., Canoga Park, Calif., 1980-86; chief adminstrv. officer, CFO SunGard Fin. Sys. Inc., 1986-94; v.p. sales and mktg., 1994-96; adminstrv. pastor Ch. at Rocky Peak, Chatsworth, Calif., 1996-99; regional sales mgr. SunGard Ins. Sys., 2000—01; exec. v.p. Inst. for Creation Rsch., Santee, Calif., 2002—. Lectr. in field; cons. World Pubs., 1995. Author: Baptism: What is It?, 1977, Explore the Word, 1978, Churches: History and Doctrine, 1980; co-author: Many Infallible Proofs, 1996, Sampling the Psalms, 1999; contbg. editor: The Defenders Bible, 1995. Served with U.S. Army, 1959-66. Republican. Office: Inst for Creation Rsch 10996 Woodside Ave N Santee CA 92091

MORRIS, HENRY MADISON , JR. education educator; b. Dallas, Oct. 6, 1918; s. Henry Madison and Ida (Hunter) M.; m. Mary Louise Beach, Jan. 24, 1940; children: Henry Madison III, Kathleen Louise, John David, Andrew Hunter, Mary Ruth, Rebecca Jean. BS with distinction, Rice Inst., 1939; MS, U. Minn., 1948, PhD, 1950; LLD, Bob Jones U., 1966; LittD, Liberty U., 1989. Registered profl. engr., Tex. Jr. engr. Tex. Hwy. Dept., 1938-39; from jr. engr. to asst. engr. Internat. Boundary Commn., El Paso, 1939-42; instr. civil engring. Rice Inst., 1942-46; from instr. to asst. prof. U. Minn., Mpls., also research project leader St. Anthony Falls Hydraulics Lab., 1946-51; prof., head dept. civil engring. Southwestern La. Inst., Lafayette, 1951-57, Va. Poly. Inst., Blacksburg, 1957-70; v.p. acad. affairs Christian Heritage Coll., San Diego, 1970-78, pres., 1978-80; dir. Inst. for Creation Rsch., 1970-80, pres., 1980-96, pres. emeritus, 1996—. Author (with Richard Stephens): (report) Report on Rio Grande Cosnervation Investigation, 1942; author: 2d edit That You Might Believe, 1946; author: (with Curtis Larson) (book) Hydraulics of Flow in Culverts , 1948; author: The Bible and Modern Science, 1951, rev. edit, 1968; author: (with John C. Whitcomb) The Genesis Flood, 1961; author: Applied Hydraulics in Engineering, 1963, The Twilight of Evolution , 1964, Science, Scripture and Salvation, 1965, 2d edit, 1971, Studies in The Bible and Science, 1966, Evolution and the Modern Christian, 1967, Biblical Cosmology and Modern Science , 1970, The Bible has the Answer, 1971, Science and Creation: A Handbook for Teachers, 1971; author: (with J.M. Wiggert) Applied Hydraulics, 1972; author: A Biblical Manual on Science and Creation, 1972, The Remarkable Birth of Planet Earth, 1973, Many Infallible Proofs , 1974, Scientific Creationism, 1974; : 2d edit , 1985, Troubled Waters of Evolution, 1975, The Genesis Record , 1976, Education for the Real World , 1977, (songs) 3d edit , 1991, The Scientific Case for Creation, 1977, The Beginning of the World, 1977, 2d edit , 1991, Sampling the Psalms, 1978, King of Creation , 1980, Men of Science, Men of God, 1982, 2d edit, 1988, Evolution in Turmoil, 1982, The Revelation Record, 1983, History of Modern Creationism, 1984, 2d edit, 1993, The Biblical Basis for Modern Science, 1984, Creation and the Modern Christian , 1985, Science and the Bible , 1986, Days of Praise, 1986, The God Who is Real, 1988, 2d edit., 2000, The Remarkable Record of Job, 1987; author: (with Martin Clark) The Bible Has the Answer; author: (with Gary E. Parker) What is Creation Science?, 1982; author: 2d edit., 1988, The Long War Against God, 1989; author: (with John D. Morris) Science, Scripture and the Young Earth, 1989; author: The Bible Science and Creation , 1991, Creation and the Second Coming , 1991, Biblical Creationism, 1993, The Defender's Bible, 1995, The Modern Creation Trilogy , 1996, The Heavens Declare the Glory of God, 1997, That Their Woods May be Used Against Them, 1998, The Origin of Earth and its People, 1999, Defending the Faith, 1999, Treasures in the Psalms, 2000, Solomon and His Remarkable Wisdom, 2001. Fellow AAAS, ASCE, Am. Sci. Affiliation; mem. Am. Soc. Engring. Edn. (sec.-editor civil engring. divsn. 1967-70), Trans-Nat. Assn. Christian Schs. (pres. 1983-95), Creation Rsch. Soc. (pres. 1967-73), Am. Geophys. Union, Geol. Soc. Am., Am. Assn. Petroleum Geologists, Geochem. Soc., Gideons (pres. La. 1954-56), Phi Beta Kappa, Sigma Xi, Chi Epsilon, Tau Beta Pi. Baptist. Home: 6733 El Banquero Pl San Diego CA 92119-1129 *The Bible is the inerrant word of God and thus should be believed and obeyed in all things.*

MORRIS, HOWARD EUGENE, construction company executive, retired; b. Nashville, May 2, 1934; s. Harry Howard and Mary Sue (Biggers) M.; m. Martha Lou Hayes, June 28, 1952; chldren: Sadricia Anne Morris Wilson, Karen Dyanne Morris Leupold. Student, U. Ala., 1959-61, Ga. State U., 1973, Chattanooga State Tech. U., 1980. Mem. design devel. staff Monsanto Chem. Co., Decatur, Ala., 1954-62; project engr. Brown Engring. Co., Inc., Huntsville, 1962-70; chief exec. officer, bd. dirs. Tech. Svcs., Inc., Florence, 1970-96, ret., 1996. Patentee electro-mechanical devices. Chmn. bd. dirs. Internat. Bible Coll., Florence, 1980-82; panelist Nat. Housing for the Elderly Conf. Mem. Nat. Mgmt. Assn., So. Bldg. Code Conf., Ala. Inventors Assn., Shoals C. of C. Republican. Mem. Ch. of Christ.

MORRIS, JAMES BRUCE, internist; b. Rochester, N.Y., May 13, 1943; s. Max G. and Beatrice Ruth (Becker) M.; m. Susan Carol Shencup, July 31, 1966; children: Carrie, Douglas, Deborah, Rebecca. BA, U. Rochester, 1964; MD, Yale U., 1968. Diplomate Am. Bd. Internal Medicine, Am. Bd. Infectious Diseases. Intern SUNY, Buffalo, 1968-69, resident, 1969-70, 72-73, chief resident, 1973; pvt. practice medicine & infectious diseases Plantation, Fla., 1974—. Chmn. infection control com. Lauderdale Lakes Gen. Hosp., 1974-76; chmn. infection control com. Plantation Gen. Hosp., 1976-80, 83-85, chmn. pharmacy com., 1980-81, chmn. tissue com., 1982; sec., program chmn. dept. medicine Bennett Community Hosp., 1978-80, chmn. dept. medicine, 1980-81, vice chief staff, 1981-83; chmn. infection control com. Fla. Med. Center, 1980-82; chief staff Humana Hosp. Bennett, 1983-85, trustee, 1983-88, chmn. infection control com., 1985-87; clin. assoc. prof. U. Miami Med. Sch., 1975—. With USAR, 1970-72. Named one of Top Docs in South Fla., Miami Metro; recipient Recognition, Town & Country Guide to Primary Care Physicians; fellow, U. Miami, 1974. Fellow ACP; mem. AMA, Am. Soc. Microbiology, Infectious Diseases Soc. Am., Am. Soc. Internal Medicine, Fla. Med. Assn., Broward County Med. Assn. Office: Morris Sklaver Mestre & Denney MD PA 7353 NW 4th St Plantation FL 33317-2202

MORRIS, JAMES CARL, architect; b. Richmond, Va., Sept. 2, 1930; s. James Carl and Florence Virginia (Hey) M.; m. Frances Parrott Wooten, June 9, 1952; children: James Carl Jr., David Palmer. Student, N.C. State U., 1948-50; BS in Bldg. Constrn., Va. Polytechnic Inst., 1952. Cert. Nat. Coun. Archtl. Registration Bds. Archtl. draftsman Va. Electric & Power Co., Richmond, Va., 1955-56, Marcellus, Wright & Son, Richmond, 1956-57; architect C.W. Huff, Jr., 1957; ptnr. to prin./owner Huff-Morris Architects, 1966—. Pres. Point of Rocks Devel. Corp., Chesterfield, Va., 1986—; ptnr. Rivermont Assocs., Chesterfield, 1987—, JCM Partnership, Chesterfield, 1988—. Contbr. articles to profl. jours. Bd. dirs. Chesterfield Preservation Commn.; deacon Branch's Ch., Richmond, 1986-90; chmn. Va. Bapt. Extension Bd., Richmond, 1991—; mem. 250th anniversary com. Chesterfield County, 1999. With U.S. Army, 1953-54. Recipient award of Merit S.S. Bd. of So. Bapt., Nashville, Excellence in Masonry Design award Va. Masonry Coun., Richmond. Mem. AIA (past pres. Richmond chpt.), Constrn. Specifications Inst., Interfaith Forum on Religion, Art & Architecture, Commonwealth Club of Va. Avocations: woodworking, fishing, hunting. Office: Huff-Morris Arch PC 8 N 1st St Richmond VA 23219-2102 E-mail: huffmorris@aol.com.

MORRIS, JAMES E. lawyer, judge, educator; b. Rochester, N.Y., Nov. 20, 1942; s. Ira H. and Hortense Morris; m. Ruth J. Myers, June 15, 1965 (div. Oct. 1977); children: Kim I., Deborah M. Field; m. Virginia B. Morris, Aug. 22, 1983; children: Katelyn E., Eric W. BS, Syracuse U., 1964, LLB, 1967. Bar: N.Y. 1967. Ptnr. Morris and Morris, Rochester, N.Y., 1967—; asst. dist. atty. County of Monroe, 1968-72; Brighton Town justice Town of Brighton, 1972—. Adj. prof. Monroe C.C., Rochester, 1975—; mem. criminal procedure law adv. bd. N.Y. State Office Ct. Adminstrn., 1980-86. Author: You Can Win Big in Small Claims Court, 1981, 2002, Victim Aftershock, 1983; co-author: New York Village, Town and District Courts Guide, 1995. Mem., past pres. Med. Motor Svc. at Al Sigl Ctr., Rochester, N.Y., 1971—, Brighton Fire Dept., 1985—; mem. Convalescent Hosp. for Children, Rochester, 1980s. Mem. N.Y. State Bar Assn., N.Y. State Trial Lawyers Ass., N.Y. State Magistrates Assn. (past pres.), Am. Soc. Writers on Legal Subjects, Monroe County Bar Assn.; fellow Am. Coll. Civil Trial Mediators. Republican. Office: Morris and Morris 30 Corporate Woods Ste 120 Rochester NY 14623

MORRIS, JAMES MALACHY, lawyer; b. Champaign, Ill., June 5, 1952; s. Walter Michael and Ellen Frances (Solon) M.; m. Mary Delilah Baker, Oct. 17, 1987; children: James Malachy Jr., Elliot Rice Baker, Walter Michael, Nicholas Aidan. Student, Oxford U. (Eng.), 1972; BA, Brown U., 1974; JD, U. Pa., 1977. Bar: N.Y. 1978, U.S. Dist. Ct. (so. and ea. dists.) N.Y. 1978, Ill. 1980, U.S. Tax Ct. 1982, U.S. Supreme Ct. 1983; admitted to Barristers Chambers, Manchester, Eng., 1987. Assoc. Reid & Priest, N.Y.C., 1977-80; sr. law clk. Supreme Ct. Ill., Springfield, 1980-81; assoc. Carter, Ledyard & Milburn, N.Y.C., 1981-83; sole practice, 1983-87; counsel FCA, Washington, 1987—; acting sec., gen. counsel FCS Ins. Corp., McLean, Va., 1990-98. Cons. Internat. Awards Found., Zurich, 1981—, Pritzker Architecture Prize Found., N.Y.C., 1981—, Herbert Oppenheimer, Nathan & VanDyck, London, 1985—. Contbr. articles to profl. jours. Mem. ABA, Ill. Bar Assn., N.Y. State Bar Assn., N.Y. County Lawyers Assn., Assn. Bar City N.Y., Brit. Inst. Internat. and Comparative Law, Lansdowne Club (London), Casanova (Va.) Hunt Club. Office: PO Box 1407 Mc Lean VA 22101-1407

MORRIS, JAMES W. retired metallurgist; b. Lafayette, Ky., June 2, 1934; s. Bouldin and Irene M.; m. Thelma Roberta, Nov. 26, 1959 (dec. Apr. 1996); children: James, Jr., Jennifer. BS, U. Ky., 1957. Jr. metallurgist NASA, Cleve., 1957; 2d lt. USAR, Aberdeen, Md., 1958, ret.; metallurgist, supr. design metallurgy Pratt & Whitney Aircraft, West Palm Beach, Fla., 1958-92. Lutheran. Avocations: choir, teaching Bible class, travel.

MORRIS, JANE ELIZABETH, home economics educator; b. Marietta, Ohio, Nov. 28, 1940; d. Harold Watson and LaRue (Graham) M. Student, U. Ky., 1960; BS, Marietta Coll., 1962, postgrad., 1963; MA, Kent State U., 1970, postgrad., 1985-87, Coll. Mt. St. Joseph, 1984-86, John Carroll U., 1986, Ashland Coll., 1987. Cert. high sch. tchr., Ohio. Tchr. home econs. Chagrin Falls (Ohio) Mid. and High Sch., 1963-95; pres. JEM Creations, Inc. Head cheerleading advisor Chagrin Falls H.S., 1970-80, freshman class advisor, 1981-82, head fine and practical arts dept., 1982-84, sophomore class advisor, 1982-85, 87-89, mem. prin.'s cabinet, 1987-88, tchr., adminstr. adv. coun., 1990-93. Vice chmn. The Elec. Women's Round Table, Inc., Cleve., 1968, chmn., 1969-71; treas. Trees Condominium Assn., 1981-83, pres., 1991-94; active Chagrin Falls chpt. Am. Heart Assn., Am. Cancer Soc., Geauga County Humane Soc., Valley Save a Pet; pres. Eagles Nest Condo Assn., 1999. Mem. AAUW, NEA, PEO, Career Edn. Assn., Ohio Edn. Assn., Ohio Retired Tchrs. Assn., Chagrin Falls Edn. Assn. (bldg. rep. 1986-95, negotiating team 1990, negotiating com. 1993, commendation State of Ohio rep. assembly 1995), Nat. Soc. Arts and Letters (treas.), Marietta Coll. Alumni Assn. (mem. Mid Ohio Valley chpt.), Washington County Hist. Soc., Marietta Photographic Soc., Friends of the Mus. Campus Martius Mus., Order Ea. Star (mem. Marietta chpt. no. 59), Alpha Xi Delta (treas. alumni bd.). Methodist. Avocations: swimming, interior design, sewing, gourmet cooking.

MORRIS, JANET ELOISE, web designer, poet; b. Lincoln, Nebr., May 10, 1952; d. Robert D. and Jessie E. (Hillhouse) M.; m. John W. Tucker, Aug. 1, 1973 (div. Mar. 1, 1979); 1 child, Jon W. Tucker. Grad., So. H.S., Wymore, Nebr., 1970. Contr. Ideus Constrn. Co., Lincoln, 1976-82; acct. Coopers & Lybrand, 1984-94; CEO Cinetropic, Toluca Lake, Calif., 1995—. Author: (poetry poster) A New Epitaph for Pere Lachaise, 1993 (33d best seller in world 1995); contbg. author The Doors Collectors Mag., 1993-99. Office: Cinetropic 10707 Camarillo St Toluca Lake CA 91602-1402 E-mail: jempoet@aol.com.

MORRIS, JEFFREY BRANDON, law educator; b. N.Y.C., Jan. 8, 1941; s. Richard B. and Berenice (Robinson) M.; m. Dona Gene Baron, July 9, 1972; children: David Brandon, Deborah Helaine. AB, Princeton U., 1962; JD, Columbia U., 1965, PhD in Polit. Sci., 1972. Bar: N.Y. 1967, U.S. Supreme Ct. 1970, D.C. 1978, U.S. Dist. Ct. D.C. 1978. Lectr., instr., asst. prof. CUNY, N.Y.C., 1968-74; spl. asst. to provost Columbia U., 1974-76; jud. fellow U.S. Supreme Ct., Washington, 1976-77, rsch. assoc. adminstrv. asst. chief justice, 1977-81; asst. prof. polit. sci. U. Pa., Phila., 1981-88; vis. assoc. prof. Bklyn. Law Sch., N.Y.C., 1988-90; from assoc. prof. to prof. law Touro Law Sch., Huntington, N.Y., 1990—. Rapporteur Nat. Conf. on Causes Population Dissatisfaction, with Popular Dissatisfaction Adminstrn. of Justice, St. Paul, 1976; cons. bicentennial exhibitions Independence Nat. Hist. Park, 1986. Author: Federal Justice in the Second Circuit, 1988, U.S. District Court Eastern District N.Y., 1965-90, 1992, Making Sure We are True to Our Founders, 1997, Brooklyn Law School: The First Hundred Years, 2001, Calmly to Poise the Scales of Justice, 2001; co-author: A Pocket History of the United States, 9th rev. edit., 1992; editor: Encyclopedia of American History, 1982, 7th edit., 1996; assoc. editor Yearbook, Supreme Ct. Hist. Soc., 1979-83. Mem. Brookings Conf. on Interbr. Rels., Williamsburg, Va., 1980, 81. Jewish. Avocations: opera, dance, theater. Home: 234 Forest Rd Flushing NY 11363-1303 Office: Touro Law Sch 300 Nassau Rd Huntington NY 11743-4346 E-mail: jeffreym@tourolaw.edu.

MORRIS, JEFFREY SELMAN, orthopedic surgeon; b. Johannesburg, South Africa, June 26, 1948; arrived in Can., 1979; came to U.S., 1990; s. Israel and Anna Riva (Belikoff) M.; m. Carol Parker, Jan. 21, 1973 (div. 1986); children: Amit, Leora; m. Cheryl Tyler, Aug. 16, 1997; 1 stepchild, Jennifer Tyler. BSc, U. Witwatersrand, Johannesburg, 1970, B of Medicine, B of Surgery, 1973. Cert. pvt. pilot, FAA. Rotating intern Natalspruit Hosp., South Africa, 1974, surg. resident South Africa, 1975-76; resident in orthopedic surgery Cen. Emek Hosp., Afula, Israel, 1977-79, Queen's U., Kingston, Ont., Can., 1979-82; orthopedic surgeon Port Arthur Clinic, Thunder Bay, 1983-86, Joseph Brant Meml. Hosp., Burlington, 1986-90, Beachwood (Ohio) Orthopedic Assocs., 1990-98; sole practitioner Twinsburg, Cuyahoga Falls, Ohio, 1998—. Mem. active staff South Pointe Hosp., Cleve.; assoc. staff Hillcrest Hosp., Cleve., Cuyahoga Falls Gen. Hosp.; provisional staff Summa Health Sys., Akron, Ohio. Contbr. articles to profl. jours., chpt. to book. Med. advisor Arthritis Soc., Thunder Bay, 1983-86. Mem. ACS, Am. Bd. Independent Med. Examiners, Am. Bd. Forensic Medicine, Can. Med. Assn., Ont. Med. Assn., Can. Orthopedic Assn., Ont. Orthopedic Assn., Ohio Orthopedic Soc., Cleve. Orthopedic Soc., Royal Coll. Physicians and Surgeons (Can.), Can. Soc. Surgery of the Hand, Ohio Med. Assn. Jewish. Avocations: music, tennis, theatre, aviation. Office: PO Box 1027 Hudson OH 44236-6227 also: Falls Group Bldg Ste 104 3033 State Rd Cuyahoga Falls OH 44223-2545

MORRIS, JIMMY HUDSON, musician, educator; b. Philadelphia, Pa., 1942; s. Royal Ferdinand and Ethel Ftancis Morris; m. Phyllis Elaine Morris; children: Brian C. MusB, Eastman Sshool of Music, Rochester, NY, 1964; MusM, U. of Miami, FL, Miami, FL, 1970. Musician US mil. acos band, Westpoint, NY, 1964—67, Miami Philharman Orch, Miami, Fla., 1970—73; tchr. miami (dade co.) Sch., 1968—74, New Hope-Solebury sch. dist., New Hope, Pa., 1974—2002. Musician Lehigh Valley Chamber Orch, Leheigh Valley, Pa., 1983—97, Allentown Orch, Allentown, Pa., 1993—94. Adjudicator/chmn. Bucks County Music Educators, Bucks co., Pa., 1974—2002. Specialist 5 U.S. Army, 1964—67, West Point, New York. Recipient Hon. Edn. Soc., Kappa Delta pI,. U. of Miami, 1970. Mem.: Am.

String Teachers Assoc. (assoc.; mem. 2000—02), PA Music Educators (assoc.; mem. 1974—02), Am. Fed. of Musicians (assoc.; mem. 1983—2002). Home: Bunker Hill Road Revere PA 18953 Personal E-mail: forstrings@fost.net.

MORRIS, JOHN, composer, conductor, arranger; b. Elizabeth, N.J. s. Thomas Arthur and Helen (Sherratt) M.; m. Francesca Bosetti; children: Evan Bosetti, Bronwen Helen. Student, Julliard Sch. Music, 1946-48, U. Wash., 1947, New Sch. Social Research, 1946-49. Composer mus. scores for (films) The Producers, The Twelve Chairs, The Gamblers, Blazing Saddles (nominated Acad. award 1976), The Bank Shot, Young Frankenstein, Sherlock Holmes Smarter Brother, Silent Movie, The Last Remake of Beau Geste, The In-Laws, The World's Greatest Lover, In God We Trust, High Anxiety, The Elephant Man (nominated Acad. award 1981), Table for Five, History of the World Part I, Yellowbeard, The Doctor and the Devils, Clue, To Be or Not To Be, Woman in Red, Johnny Dangerously, Haunted Honeymoon, Dirty Dancing, Spaceballs, Ironweed, The Wash, Stella, Life Stinks; (Broadway stage plays) My Mother, My Father and Me, Doll's House, Camino Real; (mus.) A Time for Singing; (off-Broadway) Take One Step, Young Andy Jackson, N.Y. Shakespeare Festival Much Ado About Nothing, Peer Gynt, Richard III, Love's Labor's Lost, Electra, As You Like It, Comedy of Errors, Titus Andronicus, Henry IV Parts 1 and 2, Romeo and Juliet, Hamlet, The Cherry Orchard, Stratford Connecticut Shakespeare Festival The Tempest, Julius Caesar, Antony and Cleopatra, Measure for Measure, Twelfth Night, Lincoln Ctr. King Lear; (TV shows) Fresno, Katherine Anne Porter, Ghost Dancing, The Firm, The Mating Season, Splendor in the Grass, The Electric Grandmother, The Scarlet Letter, The Adams Chronicles, Georgia O'Keeffe, The Franken Project, The Tap Dance Kid (Emmy award 1986), Make Believe Marriage, ABC After Sch. Spl. Theme, Making Things Grow Theme, The French Chef Theme, The Desperate Hours, The Skirts of Happy Chance, Infancy and Childhood, The Fig Tree, The Little Match Girl, Our Sons, The Last to Go, The Last Best Year, The Sunset Gang, Coach Theme, Favorite Son, Journey Into Genius, When Lions Roared, Scarlett Mini Series, With God On Our Side, Ellen Foster, Murder in a Small Town, The Lady in Question, several documentary films; mus. supr., conductor, arranger numerous TV spls., Broadway and off-Broadway shows and recordings including Anne Bancroft Spl. #1 (Emmy award), 'S Lemmon 'S Gershwin 'S Wonderful (Emmy award), Hallmark Christmas Spls., (Broadway) Peter Pan, Bells Are Ringing, Bye-Bye Birdie, All-American, Wild Cat, Kwanmina, Baker Street, Mack and Mabel, Much Ado About Nothing, (off-Broadway) Hair, (records) Wildcat, All-American, Bells Are Ringing, First Impressions, Bye-Bye Birdie, Kwamina, Baker Street, Rodgers and Hart, George Gershwin vols. I and II, Jerome Kern, Lyrics of Ira Gershwin, Cole Porter, others. Mem. ASCAP, Acad. Motion Picture Arts and Scis., Soc. Composers and Lyricists, Am. Fedn. Musicians. Avocations: computers, humorous poetry, cooking. Office: Alan Stein 270 Madison Ave New York NY 10016-0601 E-mail: baldor@computer.net.

MORRIS, JOHN ALLEN, JR. state government administrator, educator; b. Charleston, S.C., Nov. 22, 1946; s. John Allen and Margaret Mary (Kelly) M.; m. Jennie Farquhar Holmes, Nov. 11, 1972; children: Daniel Holmes, Paul McCarrel. BA, St. Mary's Seminary and Univ., Balt., 1968; MSW, Washington U., St. Louis, 1978. Lic. ind. social worker. Child welfare caseworker Fulton County Dept. Family and Children Svcs., Atlanta, 1968-69; psychiat. nursing asst. S.C. State Hosp. S.C. Dept. Mental Health, Columbia, 1969-71, family svcs. coord. div. alcohol and drug addiction svcs., 1971-72, group therapy coord. div. alcohol and drug addiction svcs., 1972-76, dir. spl. programs office div. alcohol and drug addiction svcs., 1978-86, dir. child and adolescent svc. S.C. State Hosp., 1986; dir. ancillary svcs. William S. Hall Psychiat. Inst. child and adolescent svcs. S.C. State Hosp., 1986-88; exec. asst. to state commr. S.C. Dept. Mental Health, 1988-90, dep. dir., 1990—, interim state dir. mental health, 1995-97; clin. prof. dept. neuropsychiatry and behavioral sci. U. S.C. Sch. Medicine, 1988-94, clin. assoc. prof., 1994-97, prof. neuropsychiatry and behavioral scis., 1997—; dir. nterdisciplinary affairs S.C. Dept. Mental Health, 1997—. Vis. prof. George Warren Brown Sch. Social Work, Washington U., St. Louis; adj. prof. U. S.C. Coll. Social work, 1997—; mem. vis. faculty U. S.C., 1972-76, 80, 82, 91; dir. youth substance abuse treatment unit St. Louis State Hosp., 1977-78; chair treatment resources subcom. Gov. Children's Coordinating Cabinet, 1985; mentor Nat. Assn. State Mental Health Program Dirs. Rsch. Inst., 1993—; mem., chair sub-com. S.C. Pub. Acad. Mental Health Consortium, 1991—; mem. state adv. coun. S.C. Prochild, 1989-91; mem. spl. grant review panels, 1987-89; regional clin. supr. S.C. Alcohol and Drug Abuse Commn., 1986-87; mem. steering com. Children's Advocacy Ctr., 1987; vis. lectr. mental health policy Washington U., St. Louis, 1991—; cons. in field. Author: (chpt.) Managing Finances, Personnel and Information in Human Services, 1985; contbr. articles to profl. jours. Vol. counselor Camp Kemo, 1987—, chmn. programs coun., 1989—; mem. steering com. Columbia Youth-The Year 2000, 1986-88; chartered orgn. rep. Post 295 Boy Scouts Am.; v.p. Columbia Choral Soc., 1987-88, sec., 1986-87; mem. Palmetto Leadershi Soc. Recipient Outstanding Vol. award Mental Health Assn. Mid-Carolina, 1988, Pres.'s award S.C. Youth Worker's Assn., 1986, Disting. Alumnus award Washington U., 1996, Excellence award S.C. Pub. Mental Health Acad. Consortium, 1997, Corbitt Leadership award S.C. Action Coun. for Cross Cultural Mental Health, 1997. Fellow Am. Coll. Mental Health Adminstrn. (pres.-elect 1997—); mem. Am. Coll. Healthcare Execs. (diplomate), Mental Health Assn. Mid-Carolina (co-chair, chair 1986-88, steering com. parent support project 1988), Rock Hill Alliance for Mentally Ill, S.C. State Employees Assn., Washington U. Alumni Assn. Home: 1001 Barton St Columbia SC 29203-4207 Office: USC-SC Dept Mental Health Clin Edn Bldg 3555 Harden Street Ext Columbia SC 29203-6894

MORRIS, JOHN DAVID, research institute administrator, geology educator; b. Mpls., Dec. 7, 1946; s. Henry Madison and Mary Louise (Beach) M.; m. Dalta Jan Eads, Sept. 3, 1977; children: Chara Mischelle, Timothy Adam, Beth Anna. BSCE, Va. Tech., 1969; MS in Geol. Engring., U. Okla., 1977, PhD in Geol. Engring., 1980. Civil engr. City of L.A. Pub. Works, 1969-73; adj. rsch. scientist Inst. for Creation Rsch., Santee, Calif., 1972-84, prof. geology, 1984-95, pres., 1995—; asst. prof. geol. engr. U. Okla., 1980-84. Author: Adventure on Ararat, 1973, The Ark on Ararat, 1976, Tracking Those Incredible Dinosaurs, 1980, Noah's Ark and the Lost World, 1988, Science, Scripture and the Young Earth, 1989, Grand Canyon: Monument to Catastrophe, 1994, The Young Earth, 1994, Noah's Ark and Ararat Adventure, 1994 (Gold Medal 1994), Daddy, Is There Really a God?, 1997, Noah's Ark, Noah's Flood, 1998, Dinosaurs, The Lost World and You, 1999, How Firm a Foundation in Scripture and Song, 1999, Abraham's Family, 1998, The Creation, 1998, A Trip to the Ocean, 2000, The Geology Book, 2000, others; co-author: Science, Scripture and the Young Earth, 1989, What Really Happened to the Dinosaurs?, 1990, Scopes: Creation on Trial, 1995, Weapons of our Warfare, 1998, When Christians Roamed the Earth, 2002, Modern Creation Trilogy, 1996, others; contbr. articles to profl. jours. Republican. Mem. Bible Ch. Office: Inst for Creation Rsch 10946 Woodside Ave N Santee CA 92071-2833

MORRIS, JOHN SELWYN, philosophy educator, college president emeritus; b. Tonypandy, Wales, July 2, 1925; came to U.S., 1954, naturalized, 1993; s. Jenkin and Hannah M. (Williams) M.; m. Enid Elry Walters, Apr. 10, 1954; 1 child, Paul John. BA, Univ. Coll. South Wales and Monmouthshire, 1951; MA, Cambridge (Eng.) U., 1953; student, Union Theol. Sem., 1957-60; MA, Colgate U., 1961; PhD, Columbia U., 1961; LL.D. (hon.), Hartwick Coll., 1979; LHD (hon.), Elmyra Coll., 1990; DLitt, Skidmore Coll., 1991. Ordained to ministry Presbyterian Ch., 1954; minister Vernon (N.Y.) and Vernon Center Presbyn. chs., 1954-57; instr. Colgate U., Hamilton, N.Y., 1960-63, asst. prof., 1963-66, asso. prof., 1966-70, prof. philosophy and religion, 1970-79, dir. div. humanities, 1970-72, dir. div. univ. studies, 1972-73, provost, dean of faculty, 1973-79, acting pres., 1977; prof. philosophy Union Coll., Schenectady, 1979-90, pres., chancellor Union U., 1979-90, pres. emeritus, rsch. prof. philosophy, 1990—. Leverhulme vis. fellow U. Exeter, Eng., 1968-69; chmn. Commn. Ind. Colls. and Univs., 1984-86; bd. dirs. Trustco N.Y.; trustee Cazenovia Coll., N.Y. Trustee Skidmore Coll.; chancellor New England Coll., N.H. With RAF, 1943-47. Recipient Disting. Svc. award Colgate U. Alumni Corp., 1978, Schenectady Patroon award, 1989, Union Coll. Founders Medal, 1990. Mem. AAUP, Am. Philos. Assn., Am. Acad. Religion, Royal Inst. Philosophy, Soc. for Study Theology, Nat. Welsh Am. Found. (bd. advisors). Office: Union Coll Humanities Ctr Schenectady NY 12308

MORRIS, JOHN THEODORE, planning official; b. Denver, Jan. 18, 1929; s. Theodore Ora and Daisy Allison (McDonald) M.; BFA, Denver U., 1955; m. Dolores Irene Seaman, June 21, 1951; children: Holly Lee, Heather Ann, Heidi Jo, Douglas Fraser. Apprentice landscape architect S.R. DeBoer & Co., Denver, summer 1949, planning technician (part-time), 1954-55; sr. planner and assoc. Trafton Bean & Assocs., Boulder, Colo., 1955-62; prin. Land Planning Assocs., planning cons., Boulder, 1962-65; planning dir. and park coord. Boulder County, 1965-67; sch. planner Boulder Valley Sch. Dist., 1967-84, also dir. planning and engring., 1967-84, supr. facility improvement program, 1969-84; pvt. sch. planning cons., 1984—; cons. U. Colo. Bur. Ednl. Field Svcs., 1974. Bd. dirs. Historic Boulder, 1974-76; mem. parks and recreation adv. com. Denver Regional Coun. Govts., 1975-84. Served with USCG, 1950-53. Mem. Am. Inst. Cert. Planners, Am. Planning Assn., Longmont Artist Guild. Home and Office: 7647 32nd St Boulder CO 80302-9327

MORRIS, JOHN WOODLAND, II, businessman, former army officer; b. Princess Anne, Md., Sept. 10, 1921; s. John Earl and Allice (Cropper) M.; m. Geraldine Moore King, May 12, 1947; children: Susan K., John Woodland III. BS, U.S. Mil. Acad., 1943; MS, U. Iowa, 1947; postgrad., Army War Coll., 1961-62, U. Pitts., 1966. Commd. 2d lt. U.S. Army, 1943, advanced through grades to lt. gen., 1976; dep. dist. engr. Savannah, Ga., 1952-54; resident engr. Goose Bay, Labrador, 1955-57; staff officer Office Chief Engrs., 1957-60; comdg. officer 8th Engr. Bn., Korea, 1960-61; dist. engr. Tulsa, 1962-65; dep. comdt. U.S. Mil. Acad., 1965-67; dep. chief legis. liaison Office Sec. Army, Washington, 1967-69; comdg. gen. 18th Engr. Brigade, Vietnam, 1969-70; div. engr. Missouri River Div., Omaha, 1970-72; dir. civil works Office C.E., Washington, 1972-75; dep. chief engr. U.S. Army, 1975-76, chief engr., 1976-80; ret., 1980; exec. dir. Royal Volker Stevin, 1980-84; pres. J.W. Morris Ltd., 1981—; prof. U. Md., 1983-86; chmn. bd., CEO, cons. PRC Engring., 1986-88. Engr. advisor, cons. Zorc, Rissetto, Weaver & Rosen, 1988-92; engr. advisor Seltzer & Rosen, 1992-98; bd. dirs. Air Water Tech., Morganti Constrn. Co., Search Techs. Inc., Thaco Rsch. Inc., Dutra Corp. Mem. Indian Nations coun. Boy Scouts Am., 1962-65; chmn. Water Resources Congress, 1988-90; trustee U.S. Mil. Acad. Assn. Grads, 1986—; advisor dean engring. and math. U. Vt., 1990-96. Decorated Legion of Merit with three oak leaf clusters, Army D.S.M., Def. D.S.M.; recipient Merit award Am. Cons. Engrs. Council; Palladium medal Audubon Soc.; award of excellence Constrn. Industry Inst., 1997. Fellow ASCE (Disting. Constructor award 2000); mem. AIA (hon.), Internat. Navigation Congress (v.p.), U.S. Soc. Mil. Engrs. (pres.), Nat. Acad. Engrs. (Founders award 1996), U.S. Com. on Large Dams (past chmn. environ. effect com., named Constrn. Man of Yr. 1977, Navigation Hall of Fame 1990, Golden Beaver award for engring. 1995, Golden Eagle award, 1998, Acad. of Dist. Eng. U. Iowa, 1998, Dist. Grad. of U.S. Mil. Acad., 1998). Episcopalian. Home: 1329 N Lynnbrook Dr Arlington VA 22201-4918 Office: 3800 Fairfax Dr Apt 5 Arlington VA 22203-1703 E-mail: morrisJ@aol.com.

MORRIS, JOSEPH ALLAN, lawyer; b. Gary, Ind., Oct. 24, 1951; s. Herbert J. and Marian Louise (Washam) M. AB, U. Chgo., 1973, JD, 1976. Bar: U.S. Dist. Ct. (no. dist.) Ill. 1976, Ill. Supreme Ct. 1976, U.S. Dist. Ct. (no. dist.) Ind. 1979, U.S. Ct. Apls. (7th cir.) 1980, U.S. Supreme Ct. 1981, U.S. Ct. Appeals (5th cir.) 1982, U.S. Ct. Appeals (D.C. cir.) 1984. Assoc., Rothschild, Barry & Myers, Chgo., 1976-81; gen. counsel U.S. Office Personnel Mgmt., Washington, 1981-85; U.S. del. UN Commn. on Human Rights, Geneva, 1986; chief staff, gen. counsel U.S. Info. Agy., Washington, 1986-87; dir. office liaison svcs. Dept. Justice, Washington, 1987-88; gen. counsel, chief exec. officer Mid-Am. Legal Found., Chgo., 1988-89; ptnr. Morris, Rathnau & De La Rosa, Chgo., 1989—; pres. Lincoln Legal Found., Chgo., 1989—; mem. Bd. Fgn. Svc. U.S., Washington, 1981-84, Adminstrv. Conf. U.S., Washington, 1981—, Fed. Legal Coun., Washington, 1981-86; chmn. Gen. Counsels Com., Washington, 1983-85; mem. Fed., State, Local Adv. Commn. on Prosecutorial Rels., 1987-88. Co-author: Congressional Cowardice, 1986, Steering the Elephant, 1986, Man and State, 1988, Mandate III, 1988; mng. editor The Am. Spectator, 1973. Chmn. Young Rep. Orgn. Cook County, Ill., 1976-77, vice chmn., 1977-79; pres. United Rep. Fund Ill., 1995—; v.p. pub. policy Lake-Porter (Ind.) Leadership Coun., 1981—; mem. sch. of law ctr. for law and nat. security U. Va., 1985—. Trustee scholar U. Chgo., 1969-73; recipient Edmund Randolph award Dept. Justice, Washington, 1988. Mem. ABA (standing commn. on law and nat. security 1985—), Fed. Bar Assn. (chmn. gen. counsels com. 1984, 85), Ill. Bar Assn., Fed. Communications Bar Assn., Chgo. Bar Assn., Federalist Soc. (bd. advisers 1988—), Thomas More Soc. Am. (bd. dir. 1986—), Phila. Soc. (trusee 1987-94), Am. Prosecutors Rsch. Inst. (bd. dirs. 1988—), Quadrangle Club (Chgo.), B'nai B'rith (nat. pres. capital legal coun. 1986-88, chmn. com. internat. govt. and Israel affairs 1992-94). Republican. Jewish. Office: Morris Rathnau & De La Rosa 100 W Monroe St Ste 1600 Chicago IL 60603-1967

MORRIS, JOSEPH ANTHONY, health science association administrator; b. Marboro, Md., Mar. 6, 1918; s. Charles Lafayette and Essie (Stokes) M.; m. Ruth Savoy, Nov. 1, 1942; children: Carol Ann, Marilyn T., Joseph A., Larry A. BS, Cath. U. Am., 1940, MS, 1942, PhD, 1947. Asst. scientist Josiah Macy, Jr. Found., N.Y.C., 1943-44; virologist Depts. Agr., Interior, Laurel, Md., 1944-47; virologist, chief hepatitis virus rsch. Walter Reed Army Inst. Rsch., Washington, 1947-56; virologist, asst. chief, dept. virus and rickettsial dis. U.S. Army Med. Command, Japan, 1956-59; virologist chief sect. respiratory diseases divsn. biologics stds. NIH, Bethesda, Md., 1959—. Dir. slow, latent and temperate virus br. FDA, Bethesda, 1972-76; lectr. dept. microbiology U. Md., College Park, 1977-79; vice-chmn. Bell of Atri, Inc., College Park, 1979-82, chmn., 1983; cons. Commn. on Influenza, Armed Forces Epidemiologic Bd., 1960—, Nat. Inst. Neurol. Diseases and Blindness, 1962—. Mem. Soc. Tropical Medicine and Hygiene, Soc. Am. Microbiologists, Soc. Exptl. Biology and Medicine, Am. Assn. Immunologists, N.Y. Acad. Scis. Achievements include discovery of respiratory sycytial virus; research on infectious hepatitis, respiratory diseases of virus etiology and zoonosis. Home: 23E Ridge Rd Greenbelt MD 20770-0714 Office: PO Box 40 College Park MD 20741-0040

MORRIS, JOSEPH RAYMOND, business and economics educator; b. Stuckey, Ga., May 29, 1939; s. Joseph Alton and Ora Lou (Hinson) M.; m. Joyce Marilyn Speiller, Mar. 17, 1984; children from previous marriage: Theresa, Marianne, Jennifer. BA, Nova U., 1986, M of Internat. Bus. Adminstrn., 1988. Sales profl. Dixie Pllywood Corp. Inc., Miami, Fla., 1964-68; sales mgr. Bradley Plywood Corp. Inc., Savannah, Ga., 1968-73; mgr. City Motel Inc., Franklin, N.C., 1973-78; pres., owner Coweee Gem Shop, 1973-78; with Eastern Airlines Inc., Miami, 1978-90; adj. prof., then full-time/part-time prof. Broward C.C., Ft. Lauderdale, Fla., 1989—. Adj. prof. Palm Beach C.C., Boca Raton, Fla., 1995, Fla. Internat. U., Miami,1990—, Lynn U., Boca Raton, 1998—; instr. part-time Nova Southeastern U., Ft. Lauderdale, 1996—, Johnson & Wales U., 2000—. With USN, 1956-64. Recipient Enterpreneurship Inst. Svc. award, 1998, Fla. Inernat. U. Cmty. Svc. award, 1997. Mem. Am. Inst. Econ. Rsch., Acad. Internat. Bus., Franklin Gem and Mineral Soc., , Lions (pres. Franklin chpt. 1976-77, v.p. 1973-75, chmn. western counties 1977-78), Civitans (treas. 1982-83), Toastmasters, Masons, Shriners. Republican. Baptist. Avocations: golf, swimming, community service, time with students. Home and Office: PO Box 292104 Davie FL 33329-2104

MORRIS, JUDY, artist; b. Calif., 1944; m. Tom Morris; 1 child, Sarah. BS, So. Oreg. State Coll., 1967, MS, 1976. Exhibited in group shows Water Color Soc. of Oreg., N.W. Watercolor Soc., Midwest Watercolor Soc., La. Watercolor Soc., Tex. Watercolor Soc., Nat. Watercolor Soc., Art-USA, Watercolor Art Soc. Houston, Salmagundi Club, N.Y.C., Ariz. Aqueous; works featured in publs. including The Artist's Mag., The Best of Watercolor, In Watercolor: People, The Artist's Guide, Splash 4, Splash 5, The Artistic Touch, The Best of Floral Painting 2, Watercolor Highlights 2, others; author: Watercolor Basics, LIGHT. Finalist in portrait, still life and landscape categories The Artist's Mag., 1991, all media competition, 1994, 96. Mem. Nat. Watercolor Soc. (signature, regional rep.), Watercolor Soc. Oreg., N.W. Watercolor Soc. (signature), West Coast Watercolor Soc., Midwest Watercolor Soc. (signature), Rogue Valley Art Assn. Address: 2404 E Main St Medford OR 97504-6919 E-mail: jmorrisnws@aol.com.

MORRIS, JUSTIN ROY, food scientist, consultant, enologist, research director; b. Nashville, Feb. 20, 1937; s. Roy Morris; m. Ruby Lee Blackwood, Sept. 5, 1956; children: Linda Lee, Michael Justin. BS, U. Ark., 1957, MS, 1961; PhD, Rutgers U., 1964. Instr. Rutgers U., New Brunswick, N.J., 1964-67; extension horticulturist U. Ark., Fayetteville, 1964-67, from asst. to assoc. prof., 1967-75, prof., 1975-85, univ. prof., 1985-97, disting. prof., 1997—; dir. Inst. Food Sci. and Engring. Ctr. for Food Processing and Engring., 1995—; Disting. prof. U. Ark., Fayetteville, 1997—. Cons. viticulture sci. program Fla. A&M U., Tallahassee, 1979-81; cons. viticulture and enology program Grayson City Coll., Denison, Tex., 1987-97; cons. J. M. Smucker Co., 1982-91. Co-author: Small Fruit Crop Management, 1990, Quality and Preservation of Fruits, 1991, Modern Fruit Science Text Book, 1995; assoc. editor: Am. Jour. Enology and Viticulture, 1985; contbr. more than 337 articles to sci. jours. Recipient rsch. award Nat. Food Processors Assn., 1982, Faculty Disting. Svc. award for rsch. and pub. svcs. U. Ark., 1993, Disting. Achievement award ea. sect. Am. Soc. Enology and Viticulture, 1995, Nat. Merit award Am. Soc. Enology & Viticulture, 1996, Spitze Land-grant U. Faculty award for excellence, 1997, Food Processors 49er Leadership award, 1998, award of merit Am. Wine Soc., 1999. Fellow Am. Soc. for Hort. Sci. (assoc. editor 1985, Gourley award 1979, Outstanding Rsch. award 1983), Inst. Food Technologists (co-organizer fruit and vegetable divsn. 1987—); mem. Food Processors Guard Soc. (life), Ozark Food Processors Assn. (exec. v.p. 1988—), Coun. for Agrl. Sci. and Tech. (bd. dirs. 1987-93, chmn. nat. concerns 1987-91, pres.-elect 1993, pres. 1994, 95), Am. Soc. Enology and Viticulture/ES (chairperson 1996-97), Gamma Sigma Delta. Achievements include development of mechanical cane fruit harvester, of mechanical strawberry harvester, of modified grape harvester for wine grapes, of mechanical shoot positioner for grapes; development of systems for the production, harvesting, handling and utilization of grape juice and wine. Office: U Ark Inst Food Sci and Engring 2650 N Young Ave Fayetteville AR 72704-5690 E-mail: jumorris@comp.uark.edu.

MORRIS, LEAH CURTIS, lawyer; b. Greenville, Tex., Nov. 21, 1961; d. Harold F. Jr. and Carol (Fischer) Curtis; m. Allen McCullouch, Nov. 6, 1993. BA in Art History, Newcomb Coll., 1984; JD, St. Mary's U., 1987. Bar: Tex. 1987. Asst. criminal dist. atty. Bexar County Criminal Dist. Atty.'s Office, San Antonio, 1988-95; ptnr. Curtis, Alexander, McCampbell & Morris, Greenville, Tex., 1995—. Mem. adminstrv. bd. Kavanaugh Meth. Ch., 1997—; pres. Boys and Girls Club of Hunt County, 1997-98. Named one of Outstanding Young Women of Am., YMCA, 1997, Hidalgo de San Antonio de Bexar, Bexar County Commr.'s Ct., 1995. Mem. Hunt County Bar Assn., Rotary (pres.-elect Greenville chpt. 1998-99, pres. 1999—, Rotarian of Yr. 1998). Office: PO Box 1256 2708 Washington Greenville TX 75403-1256 E-mail: leahcmorris@hotmail.com.

MORRIS, LEAH MCGARRY, lawyer; b. Boston, Mar. 27, 1951; d. A. Louis and Shirley L. (Pustilnick) McGarry; m. Justin T. Loughry, May 19, 1990; children: Benjamin, Lindsay, Nora. AB, Bryn Mawr Coll., 1972; JD, Temple U., 1975. Bar: Pa. 1975, N.J. 1976. Staff atty. Camden (N.J.) County Pub. Defender's Office, 1976-96, first asst. dep., 1996—2000; asst. pub. defender N.J. Office Pub. Defender, Trenton, NJ, 2001—, N.J. Supreme Ct. com. on minority concerns, 2001—. Bd. trustees Camden Regional Legal Svcs., 1996-2000; mem. com. on women, N.J. Supreme Ct., 2002—. Mem. Camden County Youth Svcs. Commn., 1984-2000, Camden County Vicinage Com. Minority Concerns, 1997-2000, Camden County Human Rels. Commn., 1997-2000; vice chair Haddonfield (N.J.) Human Rels. Commn., 1994—; chair Haddonfield Neighborhood Disputes Mediation Commn., 1997—; mem. Camden County Citizens Adv. Bd. Named one of the Women Who Have Made a Difference Camden County Bd. Freeholders and Camden County Commn. Women, 1996; fellow Leadership N.J. (Partnership for N.J.), 1998; recipient N.J. 15th Anniv. Leadership Justice award, 2001. Mem. Assn. Criminal Def. Lawyers N.J. (bd. trustees 1994—), N.J. Network Drug Ct. Profls., Camden County Bar Assn. (co-chair criminal practice com. 1997-2000, bd. trustees 1998-2000). Democrat. Avocations: mediation, advocacy for youth, writing. Home: 106 Prospect Rd Haddonfield NJ 08033-1314 Office: Box 850 Hughes Justice Complex Trenton NJ 08625

MORRIS, LEIGH EDWARD, retired hospital executive officer; b. Hartford City, Ind., Dec. 26, 1934; s. Fredus Orlando and Martha (Malott) M.; m. Marcia Renee Meredith, Oct. 7, 1967; children: Meredith Anne, Curtis Paul. BS in Commerce, Internat. Coll., 1954; BSBA, Ball State U., 1958; M in Health Adminstrn., U. Minn., 1972. Mem. labor relations staff Borg-Warner Corp., Muncie, Ind., 1961-64; various positions then personnel mgr. Internat. Harvester Co., Ft. Wayne, 1964-70; pres. Huntington (Ind.) Meml. Hosp., 1972-78, La Porte (Ind.) Hosp., 1978-2000; ret. Bd. dirs. First of Am. Bank of Ind., Am. Hosp. Svcs., Inc., Health Forum, Inc.; chmn., bd. dirs. Am. Hosp. Pub. Co.; chmn. La Porte Devel. Corp., 1980-81. Chmn. La Porte chpt. ARC, 1984-86; bd. dirs. John G. Blank Ctr. for the Arts. With U.S. Army, 1958-60. Recipient Disting. Alumni award Ball State U., Muncie, Ind., 1968, James A. Hamilton award U. Minn., Mpls., 1972, Trustees award Am. Hosp. Assn., 1996. Fellow Am. Coll. Healthcare Adminstrn. (life), Health Care Fin. Mgmt. Assn.; mem. APHA, Am. Hosp. Assn. (trustee, regional chmn. 1985-89), Soc. for Healthcare Planning and Mktg. (bd. dirs.), Soc. Ind. Pioneers (bd. dirs.), Ind. Hosp. Assn. (chmn. 1980-81), La Porte C. of C. (chmn. 1981-82). Republican. Presbyterian. Avocations: classic cars, civic affairs. Home: 424 Lake Shore Dr La Porte IN 46350-2917 E-mail: lmorris@csinet.net.

MORRIS, LOIS LAWSON, education educator; b. Antoine, Ark., Nov. 27, 1914; d. Oscar Moran and Dona Alice (Ward) Lawson; m. William D. Morris, July 2, 1932 (dec.); 1 child, Lavonne Morris Howell (dec.). BA, Henderson U., 1948; MS, U. Ark., 1951, MA, 1966; postgrad., U. Colo., 1954, Am. U., 1958, U. N.C., 1968. History tchr. Delight H.S., Ark., 1942-47; counselor Huntsville Vocat. Sch., 1947-48; guidance dir. Russellville Pub. Sch. Sys., Ark., 1948-55; asst. prof. edn. U. Ark., Fayetteville, 1955-82, prof. emeritus, 1982—. Ednl. cons. Ark. Pub. Schs., 1965-78. Author: Biographical Essays, 2000; contbr. articles to profl. jours. Mem. Hist. Preservation Alliance Ark.; pres. Washington County Hist. Soc., 1983-85, Pope County Hist. Assn.; mem. Ark. Symphony Guild; charter mem. Nat. Mus. in Arts; bd. dirs. Potts Inn Mus. Found. Named Ark. Coll. Tchr. of Yr., 1972; recipient Plaque for Outstanding Svcs. to Washington County Hist. Soc., 1984. Mem. LWV, AAUW, NEA, Washington County Hist., Soc. (exec. bd. 1977-80), Ark. Edn. Assn., Ark. Hist. Assn., Pope County Hist. Assn. (pres. 1991-92), The Ga. Hist. Soc., U. Ark. Alumni Assn., Sierra Club, Nature Conservancy, Ark. River Valley Arts Assn., Phi Delta Kappa, Kappa Delta Pi, Phi Alpha Theta. Democrat. Episcopalian. Address: 1601 W 3d St Russellville AR 72801-4725

MORRIS, MAC GLENN, advertising bureau executive; b. Bessemer City, N.C., Jan. 24, 1922; s. Manly T. and Erin C. (Cline) M.; m. Janelle Connevey, July 27, 1946; children— Robert S., Janelle C., Patricia A., John Logan. AB, Davidson Coll., 1942. Space salesman Progressive Farmer mag., N.Y.C., 1946-52; exec. v.p., advt. dir. This Week mag., 1952-68; pres. Newspaper One, N.Y.C., 1968-71; sr. v.p. nat. sales Newspaper Advt. Bur., 1972-87; proprietor MGM Assocs., Princeton, N.J., 1987—. Bd. dirs. Princeton Bank & Trust Co. divsn. Chem. Bank N.J., N.A., now owned by P.N.C. Bank, N.Y.C. Served to 1st lt., pilot USMCR, World War II. Decorated D.F.C. (2), Air medal (7). Mem. Newcomen Soc. in N. Am., Pi Kappa Phi. Presbyn. (deacon). Club: Springdale Golf (Princeton, N.J.) (bd. govs.). Home and Office: 383 Herrontown Rd Princeton NJ 08540 *I am always an optimist at my work, with friends, and with my family.*

MORRIS, MARGARET ELIZABETH, marketing professional; b. N.Y.C., Nov. 1, 1962; d. John Daniel and Jean Bingham (MacCollom) M. BA in English, Georgetown U., 1984. Cert. Rubenfeld Synergy Method, 1997. Mem. staff mktg. programs AT&T Nat. Fed. Mktg., Arlington, Va., 1985; mktg. tech. cons. AT&T Nat. Fed. Systems, Washington, 1985-87; tech. cons. computer mktg. Cin. Bell Tel. Co., 1987-89, mktg. tech. cons., 1989-95; sr. acct. exec.-strategic accts., 1995—. Tutor (vol.) Ptnrs. in Edn. Editor: (newsletter) District Action Project RAP, 1981-82; contbr. chpt. to book. Intern Citizen's Complaint Ctr., Washington, 1981-82; asst. coach River City Volleyball Club; coach CYO Girls Volleyball; vol. tech. amb. Corryville Cath. Sch.; vol. coord. SPCA Cin.; participant Leukemia and Lymphoma Soc. Am. Team in Tng., Suzuki Rock n Roll Marathon, San Diego, 2000, Walt Disney World Marathon, Orlando, 2001, Flying Pig Marathon, Cin., 2001. Named Salesperson of Yr., 1997, Corp. Vol. of Yr., SPCA Cin., 2001. Mem.: Telephone Pioneers Am. (Pioneer Vol. of Yr. 2000). Office: Cin Bell Tel Co 201 E 4th St Rm 102-1136 Cincinnati OH 45202-4122

MORRIS, MARGRETTA ELIZABETH, conservationist; b. Oakland, Calif., Sept. 14, 1950; d. Joseph Francis and Mildred Ruth Madeo; m. Dennis W. Morris, July 22, 1972; children: Matthew B., Roseanna A. BA in Geography, Radford U., 1972. Paralegal Law Office of Henry F. Zwack, Stephentown, N.Y., 1980-91; exec. dir. Ea. Rensselaer County Waste Mgmt. Authority, 1991-97; v.p., founder ERC Cmty. Warehouse, 1996—; mgr. govt. and cmty. rels. EnergyAnswers, Albany, N.Y., 1997—. Co-founder MDM Prodns., Stephentown, 1986—. Councilperson Town of Stephentown, 1987-92; treas. Stephentown Meml. Libr., 2002-. Mem.: Fedn. N.Y. Solid Waste Assns. (chmn. 1997—), N.Y. State Assn. for Reduction, Reuse and Recycling (treas. 1992—), N.Y. State Assn. for Solid Waste Mgmt. (rec. sec. 1992—94), Nat. Recycling Coalition (bd. dirs. 1999—, pres.), Antilles H.S. Alumni Assn. (treas. 2002), Gamma Theta Upsilon. Republican. Roman Catholic. Avocations: cross-country skiing, hiking, biking. Office: EnergyAnswers 79 N Pearl St Albany NY 12207-2294

MORRIS, MARILYN ANN, social worker; b. Chgo., Feb. 18, 1945; d. Jack and Melba Lea Hakan. BA, Roosevelt U., 1967; MA, U. Chgo., 1969. Lic. clin. social worker, Ill.; bd. cert. diplomate clin. social work. Social worker III Chgo. Read Mental Health Ctr.; dir. intake Roscoe House, Chgo.; pvt. practice clin. social work Chgo. and Northbrook, Ill. Mem. NASW, Ill. Soc. Clin. Social Workers, Acad. Cert. Social Workers, Ill. Group Psychotherapy Soc., Employee Assistance Profls. Assn. Home: 2005 Valencia Dr Apt 203D Northbrook IL 60062-7050

MORRIS, MARK WILLIAM, choreographer; b. Seattle, Aug. 29, 1956; s. William and Maxine (Crittenden) M. Studied with, Verla Flowers and Perry Brunson. Artistic dir. Mark Morris Dance Group, N.Y.C., 1980—, Théâtre Royal de la Monnaie, Brussels, 1988-91; co-founder White Oak Dance Project, 1990. Performed with Lar Lubovitch Dance Co., Hannah Kahn Dance Co., Laura Dean Dancers and Musicians, Eliot Feld Ballet, Koleda Balkan Dance Ensemble. Choreographer for Mark Morris Dance Group of more than 100 works including L'Allegro, il Penseroso ed il Moderato, 1988, Dido and Aeneas, 1989, The Hard Nut, 1991, Lucky Charms, 1994, The Office, 1994, Sang-Froid, 2000, Four Saints in Three Acts, 2000, others; choreographer: Mort Subite, Boston Ballet, 1986, Esteemed Guests, Joffrey Ballet, 1986, Drink to Me Only With Thine Eyes, Am. Ballet Theatre, 1988, Ein Herz, Paris Opera Ballet, 1990, Nixon in China, Houston Grand Opera, 1987, Orfée et Euridice, Seattle Opera, 1988, The Death of Klinghoffer, Théâtre de la Monnaie, 1991, Platée, Royal Opera, Covent Garden, 1997, Maelstrom, San Francisco Ballet, 1994, Pacific, San Francisco Ballet, 1995, Sandpaper Ballet, San Francisco Ballet, 1999, A Garden, San Francisco Ballet, 2001, Gong, Am. Ballet Theatre, 2001; (television) Great Performances/Dance in America The Hard Nut, 1992; dir. Die Fledermaus, Seattle Opera, 1988, Falling Down Stairs, 1994, Dido and Aeneas, 1995; dir. (Broadway) The Capeman. Recipient N.Y. Dance and Performance award, 1984, 90; Guggenheim fellow, 1986, MacArthur Found. fellow. Office: Mark Morris Dance Group 3 Lafayette Ave Brooklyn NY 11217

MORRIS, MARK EDWIN, osteopathic physician; b. Houston, Oct. 14, 1956; s. James Ellis and Odessa T. (Waddell) M.; m. Lorna Lynn Fields, Apr. 1983; 1 child, Stephen Mark. BS in Biology, U. Houston, 1980; DO, Tex. Coll. Osteo. Medicine, 1989. Jr. clk. Tex. Ea. Transmission Co., Houston, 1975; docking and loading worker Am. Warehouses, 1977; libr. asst. U. Houston, 1979-80; medication technician I, M.D. Anderson Hosp. and Tumor Inst., Houston, 1981-85; pvt. practice, Dallas, 1990—. Sr. pastor Mt. Calvary Missionary Bapt. Ch. Lead guitar, vocalist Servants Of Principles Reviving Our Christ Oneness Spirit singers, Houston, 1971—; motivational speaker adopt-a-sch. Ft. Worth Ind. Sch. Dist., 1990—, actor, head sound and spl. effects New Macedonia Bapt. Ch. Community Players, Houston, 1980—; dir., founder Restoration Singers, Ft. Worth, 1986—, Mt. Calvary Community Players, Ft. Worth, 1990—. Recipient Houston Gospel award, 1982; Johns scholar Houston Endowment Corp., 1975. Mem. Am. Osteo. Assn., Am. Coll. Gen. Practtioners, Tex. Osteo Med. Assn., Tex. Med. Assn., Sigma Sigma Phi. Baptist. Avocations: guitar, chess, aerobics, acting, Biblical research. Home: 6567 Curzon Ave Fort Worth TX 76116-4320

MORRIS, MARTHA JOSEPHINE, information services administrator; b. LaPorte, Ind., Jan. 16, 1951; d. John J. and Pearl L. Gorski; m. Richard Dale Morris, Sept. 5, 1970; children: Valerie A., Marlene N. ASN, Purdue U., Westville, Ind., 1977; BSN, Nazareth (Mich.) Coll., 1989. Charge nurse alcoholism/med. surg. unit Borgess Med. Ctr., Kalamazoo, 1977-81, asst. clin. mgr. substance abuse, 1981-88, asst. clin. nurse mgr. nephrology, 1988-90, contingency and patient intensity coord., 1990-93, mgr. patient info. tech., 1993-98, clin. analyst, project leader info. svcs., 1998—2002, info. tech. dir. clin. sys. and web devel., 2002—. Test devel. com. for informatics nursing Am. Nurses Credentialing Ctr., Washington, 1994—. Mem. ANA, Mich. Nurses Assn. Roman Catholic. Avocations: painting, flower gardening. Office: Borgess Medical Ctr 1521 Gull Rd Kalamazoo MI 49048-1666 E-mail: mmorris@borgess.com.

MORRIS, MARY ANN, bookkeeper; b. Great Falls, Mont., Feb. 16, 1946; d. Francis Leonard and Dorothy Irene (Howe) De Lacey; m. Donald Edward Wermuth, June 29, 1968 (div. Jan. 1974); 1 child, Deborah Ann; m. Larry Dallas Morris, Apr. 23, 1977; stepchildren: Serena Jo, Bradley Dwayne, Brian Dale, Bruce Dean. Student, North Idaho Coll., 1985. Sales clk. Dundas Office Supply, Great Falls, 1964-68, Stationer's Office Supply, Tacoma, 1969-70; bookkeeper Miller's Office Supply, Puyallup, Wash., 1971-72, Judge Moving & Storage (Allied), Great Falls, 1973-74; bookkeeper, credit mgr. Meadow Gold Dairy, 1974; pro-rate clk. Builders Transport, 1975-77; bookkeeper C&S Glass, Coeur d'Alene, Idaho, 1978-81, Morris Trucking, Coeur d'Alene, 1977-82, LDM Transport, Hayden Lake, Idaho, 1982—, profl. truck driver (class A vehicle), 1988—. Mem. Women's Retail Credit Mgrs. Assn. Republican. Home and Office: PO Box 2350 Hayden ID 83835-2350

MORRIS, MAX KING, foundation executive, former naval officer; b. Springfield, Mo., Oct. 23, 1924; s. Lee Howard and Aldyth (King) M.; m. Mary Jane Bull, June 19, 1952; children: Jane, William, Mary. BS, U.S. Naval Acad., 1947; MA in Internat. Law, Tufts U., 1960, MA in Internat. Econs., 1961, PhD, 1967. Commd. ensign U.S. Navy, 1947, advanced through grades to rear adm., 1972; carrier pilot with combat duty in Korea and Vietnam, 1947-71; comdr. jet squadron U.S.S. America, 1965-67; maj. command at sea, 1969-70; comdt. U.S. Naval Acad., 1971-73; Joint Chiefs of Staff rep. UN Law of Sea Conf., 1973-77; ret., 1977. Pres. Thalassa Rsch. Co., Jacksonville, Fla., 1977—; trustee Arthur Vining Davis Founds., Fla. Author: Politico-Military Coordination in the Armed Forces, 1968; Contbr. numerous articles to naval and legal journs. Served with arty. U.S. Army, 1942-44. Decorated D.S.M., Legion of Merit (2), Air medal (5) Mem. Internat. Inst. Strategic Studies (London), Council on Fgn. Relations, Middle East Inst., U.S. Naval Inst. Clubs: N.Y. Yacht, Fla. Yacht; Belfry (London); Ponte Vedra (Fla.). Home: 4123 Duval Dr Jacksonville Beach FL 32250-5813

MORRIS, MELANIE MARIE, nurse; b. Lima, Ohio, Aug. 3, 1963; d. Andrew J. and Helen (Kaniclides) Menegos. BSN, U. Akron, 1986, MBA in Mgmt., 1993. RN, Ohio. Home health aid Nurses' Ho. Calls, Akron, Ohio, 1985, Portamedic, Akron, 1985; intravenous technician Akron City Hosp., 1985-86, nurse, 1987-88, Vis. Nurse Svc., Akron, 1988-89, Akron Gen. Med. Ctr., 1989—, clin. mgr. SICU/MICU, 1994-2001. Co-owner, cert. legal nurse cons. Profl. Med. Legal Svcs., 2001—. Mem. Annunciation Ch. Choir, Akron, sec. 1989-90 , 92-94, pres. 1995-97, v.p. 1998-99. Mem. Daus. of Penelope (treas. 1988-90). Republican. Greek Orthodox. Avocations: reading, skiing, counted cross-stitching. E-mail: melanie803@aol.com.

MORRIS, MICHAEL DALE, athletic director, educator; b. Pocahontas, Ark., Aug. 8, 1952; s. Murl Daniel and Willa Dean (Hawkins) M.; children: Heather E., Holly A. BS/BSE, U. ctrl. Ark., 1975; MS, Kans. State U., 1977, U. Ill., 1980; EdS, Ball State U., 1985; PhD, U. Miss., 1991. Cert. phys. edn. tchr., mid-mgmt. adminstr., Tex.; cert. gen. sci. and phys. edn. tchr., Ark. Athletic dir., educator Ranger (Tex.) Coll. Adj. prof. Am. U. of Hawaii. Capt. U.S. Army, 1976-84. U. Ill. grad. assistantship, 1978-79; U. Miss. doctoral fellow, 1988-91. Mem. Am. Legion, Hon. Order Ky. Cols., Kappa Delta Pi, Phi Delta Kappa, Pi Kappa Alpha. Republican. Mem. Lds Ch. Avocations: camping, hiking, outdoor family-related activities. Home: PO Box 102 Ranger TX 76470

MORRIS, MICHAEL G. utilities executive; b. Fremont, Ohio, Nov. 11, 1946; married; two children. BS, Ea. Mich. U., MS, 1973; JD cum laude, Detroit Coll. Law. With environ. dept. Commonwealth Assocs., Jackson, Mich.; pres. ANR Gathering Co.; exec. v.p. mktg., transp. and gas supply ANR Pipeline Co.; pres. Colo. Interstate Gas Co.; with Consumers Energy subsidiary of CMS Energy Corp., 1988—, COO, exec. v.p., pres., CEO; chmn., pres., CEO Northeast Utilities. Exec. com., trustee Inst. Gas Tech.; trustee Ea. Mich. U. Found.; trustee Detroit Coll. Law, Delta Sigma Phi Found.; mem. Olivet Coll. Leadership Adv. Coun.; bd. dirs. Libr. Mich. Found.; bd. regents Ea. Mich. U., 1997—. Recipeint Disting. Alumnus award Ea. Mich. U., 1995. Mem. Mich. Bar Assn., Delta Sigma Phi (pres.). Address: PO Box 270 Hartford CT 06141-0270 Office: Northeast Utilities 174 Brush Hill Ave West Springfield MA 01089-1204*

MORRIS, NAOMI CAROLYN MINNER, medical educator, administrator, researcher, consultant; b. Chgo., June 8, 1931; d. Morris George and Carrie Ruth (Auslender) Minner; m. Charles Elliot Morris, June 28, 1951; children: Jonathan Edward, David Carlton. BA magna cum laude, U. Colo., 1952, MD, 1955; MPH magna cum laude, Harvard U., 1959. Diplomate Am. Bd. Preventive Medicine. Rotating intern L.A. County Gen. Hosp., 1955-56; clin. fellow in pediats. Mass. Gen. Hosp., Boston, 1957; pub. health physician Mass. Dept. Health, 1957-58; clin. pediatrician Norfolk (Va.) King's Daus. Hosp., 1959-61; from rsch. assoc. to prof. dept. maternal/child health Sch. Pub. Health, U. N.C., Chapel Hill, 1962-70, 71-74, chair dept., 1975-77; prof., dir. cmty. pediats. U. Health Scis., Chgo. Med. Sch., 1977-80; prof. Sch. Pub. Health, U. Ill., Chgo., 1980—, dir. cmty. health scis. divsn., 1980-95. Advisor to chief pub.health officer, Guam, 1970-71; mem. liaison com. with Lake County Med. Soc. 1978-80; nursing divsn. adv. com. Lake County Health Dept., 1978-98; resource person Ill. 1980 White Ho. Conf. on Children, 1979-80; participant Enrich-A-Life series Chgo. Dept. Health, 1984-85, Ill. Health and Hazardous Substance Registry Pregnancy Outcome Task Force, 1984-86; mem. profl. adv. bd. Beethoven Project Ctr. Child Devel., 1986-96; mem. planning com. for action to reduce infant mortality Chgo. Inst. Medicine, 1986-89; founding mem. Westside Infant Mortality Network, 1986; mem. Ill. vital stats. supplement Ill. Dept. Pub. Health, 1987; investigator and team leader Rev. Mo. Families Maternal and Child Health State Svcs., 1989; mem. children and youth 2000 task force MacArthur Found., 1992—; active Ill. Caucus on Teenage Pregnancies, 1978—. Chgo. Dept. Health Child Health Task Force, 1982-83, HSC Interprofessional Edn. Com., 1983-84, Med. Task Force Project Life, 1983-88, Women's Studies Curriculum Com., 1985-90, Com. Rsch. on Women, 1985-90, Mayor's Adv. Com. on Infant Mortality, 1986-2002, Gov. Adv. Coun. on Infant Mortality, 1988-96, Ctr. for Rsch. on Women Fellowship Com., 1993-98; cons. pediat. nursing resources group Ill. Dept. Pub. Health, 1983-84; cons. Cook County Hosp. Study of Preventive Childhood Obesity, 1983-84, Chgo. Dept. Pub. Health Coun. for an Integrated Svc. Sys., 2001—. Contbr. chapters to books, articles to profl. jours. Mem. Ill. MCH Coalition, 1994—, Voices for Ill. Children, 1993—, Children and Youth 2000, 1992—. Fellow APHA (task force on adolescence maternal and child health sect. 1977-85, sec. 1979-80, cons. manpower project 1982-83, publ. bd. 1985-87, coun. pediat. rsch. to Am. Acad. Pediats. 1985-92, Martha May Eliot award outstanding contbns. to field of maternal and child health 1999), Am. Coll. Preventive Medicine, Am. Acad. Pediats. (Ill. chpt. com. on sch. health, 1992-94, and com. adolescent health 1993—); mem. Ambulatory Pediat. Assn., Assn. Tchrs. Maternal and Child Health (exec. com. 1981-87, com. on tng. and continuing edn. needs of MCH/CCS dirs. 1982-83, liaison com. to fed. DCMH office 1983-87, pres. 1983-85), Chgo. Pediat. Soc. (Disting. Svc. award 2002), Phi Beta Kappa, Alpha Omega Alpha, Delta Omega, Sigma Xi. Avocations: photography, swimming, reading, classical music, travel. Office: U Ill Chgo Sch Pub Health 1603 W Taylor St Chicago IL 60612-4246 E-mail: numi@uic.edu.

MORRIS, NORVAL, criminologist, educator; b. Auckland, New Zealand, Oct. 1, 1923; s. Louis and Vera (Burke) M.; m. Elaine Richardson, Mar. 18, 1947; children: Gareth, Malcolm, Christopher. LLB, U. Melbourne, Australia, 1946, LLM, 1947; PhD in Criminology (Hutchinson Silver medal 1950), London Sch. Econs., 1949. Bar: called to Australian bar 1953. Asst. lectr. London Sch. Econs., 1949-50; sr. lectr. law U. Melbourne, 1950-58, prof. criminology, 1955-58; Ezra Ripley Thayer teaching fellow Harvard Law Sch., 1955-56, vis. prof., 1961-62; Boynthon prof., dean faculty law U. Adelaide, Australia, 1958-62; dir. UN Inst. Prevention Crime and Treatment of Offenders, Tokyo, Japan, 1962-64; Julius Kreeger prof. law and criminology U. Chgo., 1964—, dean Law Sch., 1975-79. Chmn. Commn. Inquiry Capital Punishment in Ceylon, 1958-59; mem. Social Sci. Rsch. Coun. Australia, 1958-59; Australian del. confs. div. human rights and sect. social def. UN, 1955-66; mem. standing adv. com. experts prevention crime and treatment offenders. Author: The Habitual Criminal, 1951, Report of the Commission of Inquiry on Capital Punishment, 1959, (with W. Morison and R. Sharwood) Cases in Torts, 1962, (with Colon Howard) Studies in Criminal Law, 1964, (with G. Hawkins) The Honest Politicians Guide to Crime Control, 1970, The Future of Imprisonment, 1974, Letter to the President on Crime Control, 1977, Madness and the Criminal Law, 1983, Between Prison and Probation, 1990, The Brothel Boy and Other Parables of the Law, 1992, The Oxford History of the Prison, 1995, Maconochie's Gentlemen, 2001. Served with Australian Army, World War II, PTO. Decorated Japanese Order Sacred Treasure 3d Class. Fellow Am. Acad. Arts and Scis. Home: 1207 E 50th St Chicago IL 60615-2908 Office: U Chgo Law Sch 1111 E 60th St Chicago IL 60637-2776 E-mail: norval_morris@law.uchicago.edu.

MORRIS, OWEN GLENN, engineering corporation executive; b. Shawnee, Okla., Feb. 3, 1927; s. Vestus and Myrtle (Lindsey) M.; m. Joyce Gast; children: Deborah Moree, Janine Inez. BS in Mech. Engring, U. Okla., 1947, M.Aero. Engring., 1948; postgrad., U. Va., 1952-53, Va. Poly. Inst., 1955-56, Coll. William and Mary, 1957-58. Aero., research scientist NASA, Langley Field, Va., 1948-61; mgr. mission engring. NASA (Apollo), Houston, 1961-64, mgr. reliability and quality assurance, 1964-66, chief project engr. lunar module, 1966-69, mgr. lunar module, 1969-72; mgr. NASA (Apollo Spacecraft Program), 1972-73; dep. mgr. NASA (Space Shuttle Orbiter), 1973-80; mgr. systems integration NASA (Space Shuttle), 1974-80; pres. Eagle Engring., 1980-86; pres., chief exec. officer Eagle Aerospace, Houston, 1987-90, chmn., chief exec. officer, 1990-93, chmn. bd., 1992—. Served with USNR, 1943-46. Recipient U.S. Medal of Freedom, 1972, NASA Distinguished Service medal, 1973, NASA Exceptional Service medal, 1969, Outstanding Leadership medal NASA, 1979. Asso. fellow Am. Inst. Aeros. and Astronautics; mem. Am. Astronautical Soc., Am. Aviation Hist. Soc., Acad. Model Aeros., Tau Beta Pi, Tau Omega. Presbyterian (elder 1964—). Club: Rotary. Home: 14914 Timberland Ct Houston TX 77062-2922

MORRIS, RALPH WILLIAM, chronopharmacologist; b. Cleveland Heights, Ohio, July 30, 1928; s. Earl Douglas and Viola Minnie (Mau) M.; m. Carmen R. Mueller; children: Christopher Lynn, Kirk Stephen, Timothy Allen and Todd Andrew (twins), Melissa Mary. BA, Ohio U., Athens, 1950, MS, 1953; PhD, U. Iowa, 1955; postgrad., Seabury-Western Theol. Sem., 1979-81, McHenry County Coll., 1986-88. Research fellow in pharmacology, then teaching fellow U. Iowa, 1952-55; instr. dept. pharmacology Coll. Medicine, 1955-56; asst. prof. dept. pharmacognosy and pharmacology Coll. Pharmacy, 1956-62, assoc. prof., 1962-69; prof. Med. Center, U. Ill., 1969-98, prof. emeritus, 1998, adj. prof. dept. pharmacodynamics, 1998-2000. Mem. adv. com. 1st aid and safety Midwest chpt. ARC, 1972-83; cons. in drug edn. to Dangerous Drug Commn., Ill. Dept. Pub. Aid, Chgo., Ill. Dept. Profl. Regulataions, Ill. Dept. Corrections and suburban sch. dists.; adj. prof. edn. Coll. Edn., U. Ill., Chgo., 1976-85; vis. scientist San Jose State U., Calif., 1982-83, St. George Med. Sch., Grenada, 1994. Referee and contbr. articles to profl. and sci. jours., lay mags., radio and TV appearances. Trustee Palatine (Ill.) Pub. Libr., 1967-72, pres., 1969-70; trustee North Suburban Libr. System, 1968-72, pres. 1970-72, mem. long-range planning com., 1975-81; chmn. Ill. Libr. Trustees, 1970-72, intellectual freedom com.; mem. Title XX Ill. Citizens Adv. Coun., 1981-83; trustee McHenry (Ill.) Pub. Libr. Dist., 1987-89, pres., 1987-89; trustee St. Gregory's Abbey, Three Rivers, Mich., 1989-96; bd. dirs. North Suburban Libr. Found., Wheeling, Ill., 1998-99; bd. dirs. United Campus Ministry U. Ill. at Chgo., 1983-87; pres. R.W. Morris & Assocs., 1988—; v.p. Lake Barrington Shores Condo X Assn., bd. dirs., 1999—; mem. archtl. commn. Lake Barrington Shores Master Bd., 1999—. Recipient Golden Apple Teaching award U. Ill. Coll. Pharmacy, 1966; cert. of merit Town of Palatine, 1972 Mem. AAAS, Am. Assn. Coll. Pharmacists, Internat. Soc. Chronobiology, European Soc. Chronbiology, Am. Soc. Pharmacology and Exptl. Therapeutics, Am. Library Trustee Assn., Ill. Library Trustee Assn. (v.p. 1970-72, dir. 1969-72), Sigma Xi, Rho Chi, Gamma Alpha. Episcopalian. Home and Office: 584 Shoreline Dr Lake Barrington IL 60010-3883 Fax: 847 304-5314. E-mail: raphaelmor@aol.com.

MORRIS, REBECCA ANN BRITTAIN, accountant; b. Alexandria, La., June 26, 1959; d. Jack Oliver and Ann Marie (Williams) Brittain; m. Wallace Eugene Morris, Sept. 26, 1981; children: Winfield Hancock, Wade Hampton. BS in Acctg., La. State U., 1981. CPA, La. Staff acct. Arthur Anderson, New Orleans, 1981-84, Payne, Moore & Herrington, LLP, Alexandria, La., 1984-91, ptnr., 1991—. Asst. treas., treas. Jr. League of Alexandria, 1992, 93, com. chair, 1991, 94-98; Sunday sch. tchr., staff parish rels., mem. children's coun., mem. family life team, mem. fin. com. First United Meth. Ch., Alexandria, 1989-98; treas. City Park Players Cmty. Theater, Alexandria, 1992-95; mem. Cabrini Found., 1997—; coach Crossroads Soccer, Alexandria, 1997-98. Mem. AICPAs, La. Soc. CPAs (Alexandria chpt. treas., bd. dirs. 1987-90), rotary (bd. dirs. 1998, sec.-treas. 1999—). Avocations: roller hockey, water skiing. Office: Payne Moore & Herrington LLP 1419 Metro Dr Alexandria LA 71301-3425

MORRIS, ROBERT, reinsurance analyst; b. Cambridge, Mass., Apr. 20, 1923; s. Henry Winthrop and Alice May (Bartlett) M.; m. Sigrid Margarete Henker, June 18, 1948; children: Elaine Antoinette, Susan Jeanette, Steven Walter. Diploma, Dalhousie Comml. Coll., Can., 1942; BA, MA, U. Pa., 1964. CPCU. Enlisted U.S. Army, 1942, advanced through grades to sgt. maj., 1949, ret., 1962; ins. adjustor Ins. Co. N.Am., Phila., 1962-65, asst. underwriter, 1965-71; asst. v.p. Am. Mut. Reinsurance Co., Chgo., 1971-73, v.p. regional sales, 1973-80, v.p. underwriting, 1980-83, sr. v.p. underwriting, 1983-85; v.p. U.S. Reinsurance Corp., Boston, 1985-89; reins. analyst, advisor, 1989—. Instr. Ins. Soc. Phila., 1966-71; reinsurance cons., Chgo., 1985. Contbr. articles to profl. and tech. jours. Dir. Gulph Mills (Pa.) Civic Assn., 1971-76, v.p., 1972-73. Mem. Soc. CPCU (chmn. edn. com. Phila. chpt. 1966-80, mem. reinsurance sect. Boston chpt. 1982-89), Retired Officers Assn. (life), Am. Legion. Clubs: Chgo. Athletic Assn., Princeton of N.Y. , Ambassadors (Kansas City, Mo.) (life). Lodges: Masons, Shriners. Republican. Avocations: world travel, mountain hiking, genealogy, cycling. Home and Office: 3 Laurelwood Cir Haverhill MA 01832-1512

MORRIS, ROBERT, educator; b. Akron, Ohio, Nov. 21, 1910; s. Joseph and Katherine (Spielberger) Schmaltz; m. Sara Goldman, Dec. 20, 1940. AB, U. Akron, 1931; MSc, Western Res. U., 1935; DSW, Columbia U. Sch. Social Work, 1959; D of Humane Letters (hon.), Brandeis U., 1984. Prin. welfare officer UNRRA, 1945; regional dir. social services VA, Chgo., 1946-48; social planning cons. Council Jewish Fedns. and Welfare Funds, N.Y.C., 1948-58; prof. social planning Brandeis U., Waltham, Mass., 1959-68, Kirstein prof. social planning, 1968-83, Kirstein prof. social planning emeritus, 1983—. Cardinal Medeiros lectr. U. Mass., Boston, 1983—, lectr. Harvard U. Sch. Pub Health, 1974-88; prof. Inst. Health Professions, Mass. Gen. Hosp., 1980-83, U. Md. cons. adj. prof., 1999—; mem. adv. com. Aging Rsch., U.S. Dept. Health, Edn. and Welfare, 1971, Helen Keller Internat. Found. on the Overseas Blind, 1971-74; mem. spl. med. adv. group VA, Washington, 1969-71; cons. on Geriatric Rsch., Nat. VA, 1974-78, U.S. Office of Human Devel. Svcs., 1978-79; v.p. Vis. Nurses Assn., Boston, 1979-92; mem. Fed. Adv. Coun. on Aging Rsch., Mass. State Health Coord. Coun., 1984-85; vice chmn. Mass. Health Data Consortium, 1979-89; chmn. Internat. Rev. Com. Brookdale Inst. for Gerontology and Adult Human Devel., Israel, 1982-83, cons., 1984-85; chmn. Am. Found. for the Blind Com. on Geriatric Blindness, 1969-74; adv. com. Md. Dept. Health and Mental Health, 1993-95; pub. policy com. Nat. Coun. on the Aging, 1993-95, Ctr. for Health Planning, Program and Devel., U. Md. Baltimore County, 2000—. Author: Feasible Planning for Social Change, 1966, Urban Planning and Social Policy, 1968, Centrally Planned Change, 1964, Trends and Issues in Jewish Social Welfare in the U.S., 1966, Encyclopedia Social Work and Social Welfare, 1971, Toward a Caring Society, 1974, Centrally Planned Change: A Re-Examination of Theories and Concepts, 1974, Social Policy of the American Welfare State, 1979, 2d edit., 1985, Allocating Resources for the Aged and Disabled, 1981, Rethinking Social Welfare: Why Care for the Stranger, 1986, Retirement Reconsidered, 1988, Economic Roles for the Elderly, 1987, Testing the Limits of Social Welfare; International Perspectives on Policy Changes in Nine Countries, 1988, International Perspectives on State and Family Support for the Elderly, 1993, The National Government and Social Welfare, 1997, Personal Assistance: The Future of Home Care, 1998, Welfare Reform 1996-2000: Is There a Safety Net, 1999, Social Work at the Millenum, 2000; editor Jour. of Social Work, 1960-72, Jour. Aging and Social Policy, 1983—. Cons. NIMH, 1964-70; chmn. adv. bd. Mass. Dept. Welfare, 1968-69; profl. adv. com. Easter Seal Soc., 1971-80; mem. Mass. Gov.'s Commn. on Nursing Homes, 1962-67, on Aging, 1962-67, on Hosp. Costs, 1967, Mass. Soc. Prevention Blindness, 1971-75; organizer Odyssey Forum on Federal Social Policy, 1995—. With AUS, 1943-44. Fulbright award, Italy, 1965-66, 68, Ford Found. fellow U.K., 1969-70; recipient rsch. awards Ford Found., 1960-65, Treuhaft Found., 1964, 72, Max and Anna Levinson Fund, 1970, 72, U.S. Pub. Health Svcs., 1957, 59, 65, NSF, 1975-78, W.K. Kellog Found., 1997, Retirement Rsch. Found., 1998, Louis Lowy award Mass. Gerontology Soc., 1994. Fellow AAAS, APHA, Gerontol. Soc. Am. (Kent award 1988, Maxwell Pollack award 1992, pres. 1966-67), Mass. Pub. Health Assn. (Lemuel Shattuck medal 1976), Ctr. for Applied Gerontology (Heritage award 1987), Commonwealth of Mass. and Assn. for Gerontology in Higher Edn. (Spl. Recognition award 1987), Columbia U. Sch. Social Wor (centennial award for leadership in edn.). Home: 830 W 40th St Apt 604 Baltimore MD 21211-2164 Office: Univ Mass Boston MA 02125

MORRIS, ROBERT BARRETT, city manager; b. Mankato, Minn., Mar. 1, 1922; s. Albert Barrett and Della Elma (Mathews) M.; m. Louise Spaeth, Oct. 10, 1948; children: Sandra Lockwood, Rolf Barrett, Paul Spaeth, Jane Louise. BS, U. Minn., 1942, MAPA, 1948; LLD (hon.), No. Ill. U., 1997. Rsch. asst. Mcpl. Ref. Bur. U. Minn., Mpls., 1946-47; asst. to city mgr. City of Albert Lea, 1947-48; field rep. League of Minn. Cities, Mpls., 1947-48; staff mem. Internat. City/County Mgmt. Assn., Chgo., 1948-49, ICMA Range rider Glencoe, 1991—; asst. village mgr. Village of Glencoe, Ill., 1949-51, village mgr., 1951-82; midwest mgr. ICMA Retirement Corp., Evanston, 1982-86, dir. tng. and devel., 1986-91. Lectr., adj. prof. Roosevelt U., Chgo., 1965-94; adj. prof. No. Ill. U., DeKalb, Ill., 1982-84; cmty. svc./continuing edn. coun. State Bd. of Higher Edn., Springfield, Ill., 1968-72; lectr. Northwestern U. Traffic Inst., Evanston, 1953-56; bus. adv. coun. Sch. of Profl. Studies U. of Wis., Green Bay, 1969-72; tech. assistance team grad. study in public adminstrn. U. Kans., Lawrence, 1975; site visit team, MPA program Sangamon State U., Springfield, 1987, Memphis State U., 1988, U. Mo. Kansas City, 1992, U. Ark., Little Rock, 1993, Southern Ill. U., Edwardsville, 1998; bd. trustees No. Ill. Police Crime Lab., Highland Park, Ill., 1980-82; Ill. local govt. law enforcement officers tng. bd. State of Ill., Springfield, 1974-82; presdl. mgmt. intern program U.S. Govt., Washington, 1980-82. Mem. exec. bd. N.E. Ill. Boy Scout Coun., Glencoe, 1961-64, Family Counseling Svc., Glencoe, 1961-66; pres. Glencoe Rotary Club, 1962-63, 91-92. Sgt. USAAF, 1943-46. Mem. Internat. City/County Mgmt. Assn. (v.p. 1965-67, Disting. Svc. award 1991, Life time Achievement award 1994), Ill. City Mgmt. Assn. (pres. 1964-65), Metro Chgo. City Mgmt. Assn. (pres. 1957), Am. Soc. for Public Adminstrn. (pres. Chgo. chpt. 1966-67). Avocation: golf. Home and Office: 250 Park Ave Glencoe IL 60022-1350

MORRIS, ROBERT CRANE, management training executive; b. El Centro, Calif., July 22, 1937; s. George Howser Morris and Lillian Cauthen Barnhouse; m. Susanne Rockne, Feb. 17, 1968. BS, U. Calif., Davis, 1961, MS, 1972; PhD, Mich. State U., 1984. Vol. U.S. Peace Corps, Lyallpur, Pakistan, 1961-63, asst. dir. Lahore, Pakistan, 1963-64; cons. Swedish Internat. Devel. Agy., Stockholm, 1965; dir. overseas ops. sch. partnership program U.S. Peace Corps, Washington, 1966-68; dir. info. ctr. Internat. Secretariate Vol. Svc., 1968-69; fellow Social Sci. Rsch. Coun., Colombia, 1972-74; faculty dept. comm. Mich. State U., 1974-78; exec. dir. Mgmt. Tng. and Devel. Inst.,

Washington, 1978—. Chmn. Mgmt. Tng. & Devel. Inst., Singapore, 1995-97. Author: Overseas Volunteer Programs; guest editor Rural Africana, 1977; editor, mgmt. comm. series SUNY Press, Albany, 1994—. Adv. com. Indus Found., 1997—. Mem. ASTD, Soc. Internat. Devel., Assn. Internat. Educators. Avocation: guitar. Home: 1230 4th St SW Washington DC 20024-2302 Office: Mgmt Tng & Devel Inst 6204-B Old Franconia Rd Alexandria VA 22310 E-mail: randsmorris@mindspring.com.

MORRIS, ROBERT DARRELL, reading education educator; b. Durham, N.C., Nov. 25, 1947; s. Robert James and Lily B. (O'Kelly) M.; m. Verda Wilson Ingle, July 20, 1978; children: Joseph, Katherine. BA in Psychology, Randolph-Macon Coll., 1972; MA in Psychology, U. Richmond, 1976; EdD in Reading Edn., U. Va., 1980. Spl. edn. tchr. Culpeper (Va.) County Schs., 1974-76; assoc. prof. edn. Nat. Coll. Edn., Evanston, Ill., 1979-89; prof. edn. Appalachian State U., Boone, N.C., 1989—. Dir. reading clinic Nat. Coll. Edn., 1981-87, Appalachian State U., 1989—; dir. Howard St. Tutoring Program, Chgo., 1979-85; creator, cons. Early Steps Reading Intervention Program, Ill., N.Y., N.C., Mont., 1987—. Author: Howard Street Tutoring Manual, 1999; contbr. articles to profl. jours. Mem. Nat. Reading Conf., Internat. Reading Assn. (Exemplary Reading Program award 1987), Am. Ednl. Rsch. Assn., Internat. Dyslexia Assn. Avocations: basketball, football, baseball, fishing, blues music. Office: Appalachian State U Reading Clinic Boone NC 28608-0001

MORRIS, ROBERT G(EMMILL), retired foreign service officer; b. Des Moines, July 20, 1929; s. Robert William and Iva May (Gemmill) M.; m. Beverly Schupfer, July 3, 1955; children: Robert William II, John Schupfer, Richard Edward. BS, Iowa State U., 1951; postgrad., Charles Francis U., Graz, 1951-52; MS, Calif. Inst. Tech., 1954; PhD, Iowa State U., 1957. Asst. prof. S.D. Sch. Mines and Tech., Rapid City, 1958-59, assoc. prof., 1959-62, prof., head dept. physics, 1962-68; phys. sci. officer Office of Naval Research, Washington, 1968-73, dir. electronics program, 1973-74; U.S. fgn. service officer U.S. Dept. State, 1974-78; counselor for sci. and technol. affairs U.S. Mission to OECD, Paris, 1978-82, U.S. Embassy, Bonn, Fed. Republic Germany, 1982-85; dep. asst. sec. of state for sci. and tech. affairs Washington, 1985-87; fgn. svc. officer U.S. Embassy, Buenos Aires, 1987-90, Madrid, 1990-92. Author: Diplomatic Relations, 2000; contbr. articles to profl. jours. Fulbright scholar, Austria, 1951; Swiss govt. fellow, Zurich, 1957. Fellow APS; mem. Am. Fgn. Service Assn.

MORRIS, ROBERT LOUIS, management consultant, consultant; b. Phila., Aug. 24, 1932; s. Joseph Aloysius and Philomena Mary Ellen (Clauser) M.; m. Elizabeth Marie Smyth, Sept. 10, 1955; children: Robert L., Thomas J., Lawrence F., Elizabeth M., Mary Ellen, Richard B. BS, Drexel U., 1955; MS, U. Pa., 1957; postgrad., U. Cin., 1965-66, U. Chgo., 1969-71. Group leader Proctor & Gamble Co., Miami Valley Labs., 1958-68; dir. computing svcs. rsch. & devel. divsn. Kraft, Inc., Glenview, Ill., 1968-71; dir. rsch. and process devel. Continental Baking Co., St. Louis and Rye, N.Y., 1971-77, v.p. tech. affairs, 1978-92; tech. dir. food and chem. products ITT, Inc., N.Y.C., 1977-78; pres. Mng. Tech., Inc., Williamsburg, Va., 1992—, Regu-Tech. Assocs., Inc., Lightfoot, 1997—. Patentee in field. Bd. dirs. Fundacion Chile, Santiago, 1978-79, 83-85; mem. Greenwich Rep. Town Meeting, 1977. With AUS, 1957. NSF fellow, 1955-56, Wilson S. Yerger fellow, 1956-57. Fellow Am. Inst. Chem. Engrs.; mem. Assn. Rsch. Dirs., Indsl. Rsch. Inst. (bd. dirs. 1988-91), Am. Assn. Cereal Chemists, Ford's Colony Golf Club. Roman Catholic. Office: The MTI Group PO Box 679 Lightfoot VA 23090-0679 E-mail: rlmatmti@tni.net.

MORRIS, ROBERT RENLY, minister, clinical pastoral education supervisor; b. Jacksonville, Fla., Feb. 15, 1938; s. Joseph Renly and Sybil (Stephens) M.; m. Lenda Smith, Dec. 7, 1963; children: Christopher Renly, Jennifer Kelly. BA, U. Fla., 1959; MDiv, Columbia Theol. Sem., Atlanta, 1962, ThM, 1967, D Ministry, 1990. Ordained to ministry Presbyn. Ch. (U.S.A.), 1962. Min. to students Ga. State Coll., Atlanta, 1959-60; asst. min. Trinity Presbyn. Ch., 1960-62; min. Clanton (Ala.) Presbyn. Ch., 1963-65, Kelly Presbyn. Ch., McDonough, Ga., 1965-67; pastoral counselor Ga. Assn. for Pastoral Care, Atlanta, 1966-68; coord. pastoral svcs. Winter Haven (Fla.) Hosp. and Community Health Ctr., 1969-79; min. Presbytery of Greater Atlanta, mem. div. pastoral care, 1984-86; dir. clin. pastoral edn. Emory Ct. for Pastoral Svcs., Atlanta, 1979-98; dir. pastoral svcs. Emory U. Hosp., 1998—, The Emory Clinic, Atlanta, 1998—, Crawford Long Hosp., 2000—. Adj. faculty Candler Sch. Theology, 1979-88. Contbr. book chpts., articles to profl. jours. Mem. AIDS Task Force, Atlanta, 1988-95, Task Force on Chem. Dependency, 1988; pres. bd. dirs. Atlanta Hosps. Hospitality Ho., 1998-2000. Mem. Am. Assn. Pastoral Counselors, Profl. Chaplains Assn., Am. Assn. Marriage and Family Therapists (clin.), Assn. for Clin. Pastoral Edn. (cert. supr., gen. assembly nominating com. 1984, chmn. 1985, coord. ann. conf. 1986, long range planning com. of C com., standards com. S.E. region 1990-93), Am. Assn. Adult and Continuing Edn., Beta Theta Pi. Democrat. Avocations: antique key collecting, canoeing, fishing, sailing. Home: 11 Westchester Sq Decatur GA 30030-2370 Office: Emory U Hosp Dept Pastoral Svcs 1364 Clifton Rd NE Dept Pastoral Atlanta GA 30322-1061 E-mail: Robert_Morris@emoryhealthcare.org.

MORRIS, RONALD ANTHONY, county official; b. Wilmington, Del., Nov. 8, 1946; s. Elwood and Sophia (Ptak) M.; m. Barbara Marie Szostkowski, July 16, 1976. BS, U. Balt., 1970; MBA, Widener U., 1975. Cert. govt. fin. mgr. Cost acct. Atlas Chem. Industries, New Castle, Del., 1966-67; sr. cost acct. Bethlehem Steel Corp., Balt., 1967-70; sr. acct. J.K. Lasser & Co., CPAs, Wilmington, 1970-71; dep. dir. fin. City of Wilmington, 1971-74; acctg. supr. New Castle County, 1974-75, controller, 1975-80, budget and acctg. mgr., 1980-97, CFO, 1997—. Recipient Achievement award Nat. Assn. Counties, 1990, 92, 94, EXSL award Nat. Ctr. for Pub. Productivity, 1990, Award of Excellence, Nat. Assns. County Info. Officers, 1989. Mem. Del. Assn. Govtl. Fin. Officers (v.p. 1990-94), Am. Soc. Pub. Adminstrn., Del. Assn. for Pub. Adminstrn. (councilman 1980-82), Govt. Fin. Officers Assn., U.S. and Can. (com. mem. 1989—, Fin. Reporting Achievement award 1981-2002, Disting. Budget Presentation award 1991-2002), Am. Acctg. Assn., Nat. Assn. Accts. Avocations: classic cars, coins, currency. Home: 904 Wawaset St Wilmington DE 19806-3244 E-mail: rmorris@co.new-castle.de.us.

MORRIS, RONALD LEW, oil and gas company executive; b. Jacksonville, Fla., Feb. 17, 1946; s. Joel and Lillian M.; m. Yan Wang, Feb., 2001; m. Lynda Lea Johnson, Jan., 1967 (div. Oct. 2000); children: Adria Jenny, Adam Poff. BSc in Aero. Engring., U. Okla., 1970; MSc in Mech. Engring., Colo. State U., 1972. Project coord. Danish Undergrounds Consortium, Copenhagen, 1979-83; mgr. planning and econs. Texaco Ltd., London, 1983-84; drilling mgr., dist. engr. Texaco North Sea UK, Aberdeen, Scotland, 1984-89; portfolio evaluations mgr. Texaco USA, Midland, Tex., 1989-91; asst. gen. mgr. Texaco-Angola, Luanda, 1991-96; v.p., mng. dir. Texaco Exploration Myanmar Inc., Yangon, 1996-98; mng. dir. CACT-Ops. Group, Shekou, China, 1998—2001; gen. mgr. Ori Ox Energy Assocs. Ltd., Hong Kong, Beijing, China, 2001—. Chmn. bus. mgmt. seminar 7th Oil & Gas Conf., Beijing, 2000. Contbr. Instr. Jr. Achievement and Young Astronauts, Midland, 1990-93; cub scout leader Boy Scouts Am., Aberdeen, 1986-88. Recipient Fgn. Friendship award, Guangdong, China, 2001. Mem. Am. C. of C., Soc. Petroleum Engrs. Avocations: golf, travel, pilot. Home: Dong Run Feng Jing Yuan 2-901 Beijing 100016 China Mailing: c/o Adria Morris 281 41st St Apt 31 Oakland CA 94611

MORRIS, ROY LESLIE, lawyer, electrical engineer, venture capitalist; b. N.Y.C. BE, SUNY, Stony Brook, 1975; EE, SM, MIT, 1978; JD, George Washington U., 1984; MBA, Wharton U., 1995. Bar: D.C. 1984, U.S. Patent Office. Mem. tech. staff Bell Telephone Labs., Holmdel, N.J., 1978-80; sr. staff engr. FCC, Washington, 1981-83; assoc. regulatory counsel MCI Communications, 1983-87; dep. gen. counsel Allnet Comms., 1988-95; dir. pub. policy and regulatory affairs Allnet/Frontier Comms., 1989-96; mng. ptnr. RoyLyn L.L.C., Arlington, Va., 1996—; v.p. govt. affairs and revenue devel. US ONE Comms., McLean, 1996-97; mng. ptnr. Strategic Tech. Investors LLC, Arlington, 1998—; pres. MIT Enterprise Forum, Washington/Balt., 1998—. Ednl. counselor MIT; adj. prof. Capitol Coll., Laurel, Md., 1998—. Contbr. numerous articles to profl. publs. Mem. ABA, IEEE, MIT Enterprise Forum, Sigma Xi, Tau Beta Pi. Address: Strategic Tech Investors LLC 4001 9th St N Ste 306 Arlington VA 22203-1957

MORRIS, SANDRA JOAN, lawyer; b. Chgo., Oct. 13, 1944; d. Bernard and Helene (Davies) Aronson; m. Richard William Morris, May 30, 1965 (div. Jan. 1974); children: Tracy Michelle, Bretton Todd; m. William Mark Bandt, July 12, 1981; 1 child, Victoria Elizabeth. BA, U. Ariz., 1965; JD, Calif. Western U., 1969. Bar: Calif. 1970, U.S. Dist. Ct. (so. dist.) Calif. 1970; diplomate Am. Coll. Family Trial Lawyers. Ptnr. Morris & Morris, APC, San Diego, 1970-74; sole practice, 1974—. Mem. Adv. Commn. on Family Law, Calif. Senate, 1978-79. Contbr. articles to profl. jours. Pres. San Diego Community Child Abuse Coordinating Coun., 1977; mem. human rsch. rev. bd. Children's Hosp., San Diego, 1977-92. Fellow: Internat. Acad. Matrimonial Lawyers, Am. Acad. Matrimonial Lawyers (chpt. pres. 1987—88, nat. bd. govs. 1987—89, 1993—94, parliamentarian 1989—91, treas. 1994—97, v.p. 1997—2000, 1st v.p. 2000—01, pres.-elect 2001—); mem.: San Diego Cert. Family Law Specialists (chair 1995—96), State Bar Calif. (cert. family law specialist 1980—), ABA (family law sect. exec. com. marital property 1982—83, 1987—94, faculty mem. Trial Advocacy Inst. 2001—), Lawyers Club San Diego (bd. dirs. 1973). Republican. Jewish. Avocations: art, travel, skiing. Office: 3200 4th Ave Ste 101 San Diego CA 92103-5716

MORRIS, SHARON LOUISE STEWART, emergency medical technician, paramedic; b. Washington, Feb. 9, 1956; d. George Arthur Jr. and Shirley Ann (Dickinson) S. (dec.); m. Brian Stanley Morris, Feb. 9, 1979; children: Jessica Kristin, Krystle Maria. BS, Atlantic Christian Coll., Wilson, N.C., 1978; student, Wilson County Tech. Coll., 1998; paramedic stud., Nash Community Coll. Cert. tchr. elem. edn. and math., N.C., EMT paramedic, ACLS, Pediatric Advanced Life Support, pediat. edn. prehosp. profls., AHA CPR/BLS instr.; cert. pre-hosp. trauma life support (PHTLS); automatic external defibrilator (AED) instr.; basic trauma life support (BTLS); farm medic. Cashier Safeway Fin., Wilson, 1980-81, Provident Fin., Wilson, 1981-85; mktg. svc. mgr. Beneficial of N.C. Inc., 1985-91; ind. carrier Wilson Daily Times, 1991-94; child care provider Crestview Day Sch., Wilson, 1994-95; EMT vol. Elm City, N.C., 1996—; EMT paramedic Wilson County Emergency Med. Svcs., 1998—. Agt. Cen. Nat. Life Ins., Wilson, 1988-91, Olde Republic, 1990; EMT Elm City Emergency Svcs., 1996, attendant, driver Am. Med. Response, 1997; paramedic Sch. Nash Tech. C.C. Notary pub. State of N.C., 1986—; bd. dirs. Elm City, 1997, 2nd, 1999; paramedic for Johnston Ambulance Svc., 2002—. Democrat. Methodist. Avocations: crocheting, cross-stitch, needlepoint, plants, baking. Home: PO Box 1028 Elm City NC 27822-1028

MORRIS, STEPHANIE ANN, chemist, educator; b. Norfolk, Va., Oct. 5, 1958; d. Billy Charles and Barbara Ann Howard; m. David Glenn Morris, Dec. 28, 1979 (dec. Aug. 2000); children: Ian Charles, Piper Ann. BS in Chemistry, Fla. State U., 1979; MS in Chemistry, U. Tenn., Knoxville, 1981. Rsch. asst. U. Tenn., Knoxville, 1980-81, Oak Ridge (Tenn.) Nat. Lab., 1981-82; instr. to asst. prof. Roane State C.C., Harriman, Tenn., 1983-88; asst. prof. to assoc. prof. chemistry Pellissippi State Tech. C.C., Knoxville, 1988—, instr. "Chemistry Magic" Knoxville Talented and Gifted, 1994-95, 98—, organizer, instr. Coll. for a Day, 1995, 97. Author, editor: (lab notebooks/manuals) Chemistry 1110 Laboratory Manual, 2002, Chemistry 1120 Laboratory Manual, 2002. Recipient Sarah Ellen Benroth Outstanding Faculty award Roane State C.C., 1987-88, Excellence in Tchg. award Pellissippi State Tech. C.C., 1997-98, Catalyst award Regional award for Excellence in Sci. Tchg., Chem. Mfrs. Assn., 1998; named Tenn. Prof. of the Yr., Carnegie Found. for Advancement of Tchg. and Coun. for Advancement and Support of Edn., 1998. Mem. AAUP, Am. Chem. Soc. (chmn. edn. divsn.), Alpha Chi Sigma. Republican. Methodist. Avocation: tennis. Home: 716 Lago Cir Knoxville TN 37922-4100 Office: Pellissippi State Tech Cmty Coll 10915 Hardin Valley Rd Knoxville TN 37932-1412 E-mail: smorris@pstcc.cc.tn.us.

MORRIS, STEPHEN BRENT, association executive; b. Dallas, Mar. 28, 1950; s. Jack Brent and Maxene (Peek) M.; m. Nancy Marie Turner, May 22, 1971 (div.); children: Terrance Brent, Mary Patricia; m. Jacquelynn Lee Bost, Dec. 30, 2000. BS, So. Meth. U., 1971; AM, Duke U., 1973, PhD, 1974; MS, Johns Hopkins U., 1980. Instr. math. Duke U., Durham, N.C., 1972-75; mathematician Dept. Def., Washington, 1975—2000; dir. membership devel. Supreme Coun. 33 degree Scottish Rite Masons, 2000—. Lectr. elec. engring. and computer sci. Johns Hopkins U., Balt., 1979-85. Mem. editl. bd. Scottish Rite Jour., 1989-98; editor Heredom, transactions of Scottish Rite Rsch. Soc., 1992—; contbr. articles to profl. jours.; co-inventor method for accessing in dynamic memories, fast parallel sorting processor; Author: Magic Tricks, Card Shuffling, and Dynamic Computer Memories, 1998. Chmn. edn. com. Scottish Rite Charitable Found. Inc., Balt., 1983-95. Fellow Philalethes Soc. (exec. sec. 1975-85); mem. Am. Math Soc. (joint com. on employment opportunities 1988-97, chmn. 1992-93, data com. 1995-97), Math. Assn. Am. (com. on mathematicians outside academia 1990-96, chmn. 1994-96, bd. govs. 1991-94, vis. lectr. 1991-98, membership com. 1995-2000, vis. lectr. com. chmn. 1996-98, com. on cons. 1996-2000, task force grad. students 1996-2000, dept. liaisons com. 1996-2000), Assn. Computing Machinery (disting. lectr. 1990-2001), Soc Indsl. and Applied Math. (vis. lectr. 1993-2001), Masons (33d degree, grand dir. ceremonies Md. 1980-81), Pi Mu Epsilon (nat. coun. 1996-2000). Methodist. Office: Supreme Coun 33 degree Scottish Rite Masons 1733 16 St NW Washington DC 20009-3103 E-mail: bmorris@srmason-sj.org.

MORRIS, STEPHEN BURRITT, marketing information executive; b. Morristown, N.J., Aug. 13, 1943; s. Grinnell and Cornelia Rogers (Kellogg) M.; m. Victoria Ann French, Feb. 18, 1967; children: Christopher Jackson, Robin Taylor BA, Yale U., 1965; MBA, Harvard U., 1969. With product mgmt. Gen. Foods Corp., White Plains, N.Y., 1969-83, gen. mgr. Maxwell House Coffee div., 1983-85, v.p., 1983-87, pres. Maxwell House div., 1986-87; founder, dir. Spectra Mktg. Systems Inc., Chgo., 1987-90; pres., CEO Vid Code Inc., Waltham, Mass., 1990-92; pres., CEO, Arbitron Inc., N.Y.C., 1992—. Bd. dirs. John B. Stetson Co. Trustee N.Y. Theatre Workshop, 1995; bd. dirs. Advt. Rsch. Found. Served to 2d lt. USMCR, 1965-66. Avocations: tennis, gardening. Home: 300 Mt Holly Rd Katonah NY 10536-3546 Office: Arbitron Inc 142 W 57th St Fl 11 New York NY 10019-3397

MORRIS, STEVEN LYNN, engineering consultant, retired career officer; b. Dallas, Dec. 7, 1952; s. William Ira and Alta Faye (McCarley) M.; m. Jacqueline Ann Fenter, July 30, 1977; children: Steven Sean, Michael Wayne. BS in Engring. Scis., USAF Acad., 1975; MS in Aero. Engring, Air Force Inst. Tech., 1980; PhD in Aerospace Engring., Tex. A&M U., 1989. Commd. 2d lt. USAF, 1975, advanced through grades to lt. col., 1991, ret., 1999; assoc. prof., dep. head dept. aeronautics USAF Acad., Colo., 1989-99; engring. specialist SRS Techs., Colorado Springs, 1999-2000; sr. staff cons. Engring. Systems, Inc., 2000—. Named Outstanding Young Man Am., Jaycees, 1981. Fellow AIAA (assoc., sr. flight mechanics tech. com. 1991-94, 98-2001, dep. dir. for edn. region V 1992-94, dep. dir. for precoll. outreach region V 1998-2002); mem. USAF Acad. Assn. Grads., Soc. Automotive Engrs., Air Force Assn., Tex. A&M U. Assn. Former Students, Tau Beta Pi, Sigma Gamma Tau. Baptist. Avocations: running, photography, hiking. Home: 5331 Wells Fargo Dr Colorado Springs CO 80918 Office: Engring Systems Inc Ste 106 4775 Centennial Blvd Colorado Springs CO 80919

MORRIS, THOMAS QUINLAN, hospital administrator, physician; b. Yonkers, N.Y., Jan. 3, 1933; s. William Thomas and Mary Berenice (Quinlan) M.; m. Jacqueline Ingram, Sept. 12, 1959; children: Thomas, Amy, MaryAnne. BS, U. Notre Dame, 1954; MD, Columbia U., 1958. Diplomate Am. Bd. Internal Medicine. From instr. to assoc. prof. clin. medicine Coll. Physicians and Surgeons, Columbia U., N.Y.C., 1964-79, prof., 1979—, acting chmn. dept. medicine, 1978-82, assoc. dean academic affairs, 1979-82, vice dean faculty of medicine, 1982-84, vice chmn. dept. medicine, 1993-94, sr. assoc. v.p. for health scis., vice dean faculty medicine, 1994—, alumni prof., 2000—; acting dir. Med. Services, Presbyn. Hosp., 1978-82, pres., 1985-90. V.p. for programs N.Y. Acad. Medicine, 1990-94, advisor 1994—. Med. editor Complete Home Medical Guide, 1985. Trustee Mary Imogene Bassett Hosp., Cooperstown, N.Y., 1980—, chmn. 1994—; trustee Am. Univ. of Beirut, N.Y.C., 1985—. Served to capt. USAF, 1962-64. Fellow ACP; mem. Greater N.Y. Hosp. Assn. (bd. govs. 1985-90), League of Voluntary Hosps. and Homes (chmn. bd. dirs. 1985-89). Clubs: The Century, Harvey Soc. (N.Y.C.). Office: Coll Physicians and Surgeons 630 W 168th St New York NY 10032-3702 also: New York Acad Medicine 2 E 103rd St New York NY 10029-5207

MORRIS, THOMAS WILLIAM, symphony orchestra administrator; b. Rochester, N.Y., Feb. 7, 1944; s. William H. and Eleanor E. M.; m. Jane Allison, Aug. 7, 1965; children: Elisa L., Charles A., William H. AB, Princeton U., 1965; MBA, Wharton Sch. U. Pa., 1969. Adminstrv. asst., Ford Found. fellow for adminstrv. interns in arts Cin. Symphony, 1965-67; payroll clk. bus. office Boston Symphony Orch., 1969-71, asst. mgr. bus. affairs, 1971-73, mgr., 1973-78, gen. mgr., 1978-86, v.p. spl. projects and planning, 1986; pres. Thomas W. Morris and Co., Inc., Boston, 1986-87; exec. dir. Cleve. Orch., 1987—. Chmn. policy com. Maj. Orch. Mgrs., 1977-79; chmn. orch. panel Nat. Endowment for Arts, 1979-80. Chmn. Cleve. Cultural Coalition, 1992-95; mem. Cleve. Bicentennial Commn., 1993-97; mem. bd. overseers Curtis Inst. Music, 1998—. Mem. Am. Symphony Orch. League (dir. 1977-79) Office: Cleve Orch Severance Hall 11001 Euclid Ave Cleveland OH 44106-1713

MORRIS, VALERIE BONITA, performing arts administrator; b. Beverly, Mass., May 22, 1947; d. Glen Franklin and Helen (Benjamin) M.; m. Boris Bohun-Chudyniv, Jan. 7, 1975; children: Alexander, Anya. BA, Am. U., 1968; MA, U. Mich., 1972. Promotions dir. McCarter Theatre, Princeton, N.J., 1972-73; assoc. mgr. Jorgensen Auditorium, Storrs, Conn., 1973-74; dir. art mgmt., chair performing arts Am. U., Washington, 1974-98, chair faculty senate, 1989-91; dean Sch. Arts Coll. of Charleston, S.C., 1998—. Exec. editor Jour. Arts Mgmt., Law and Soc., 1982-88, 90—; co-editor: Future of the Arts, 1990, The Arts in an New Millennium, 2002. Bd. dirs. Everyday Theatre, Washington, 1990-93, The Support Ctr., 1980-98, The Theatre Lab, 1994—, Charleston Symphony, 1998—, ABC Project, 1999—, Scaae, 2000-. Named one of Outstanding Women of Am., 1983. Mem. Assn. Arts. Adminstrv. Edn. (sec. treas. 1989-91, pres. 1997-98), Am. Coun. for Arts (rsch. adv. coun.), Assn. Performing Arts Presenters, Omicron Delta Kappa. Home: 710 Willow Lake Rd Charleston SC 29412-9164 Office: Coll of Charleston 66 George St Charleston SC 29424-1407 E-mail: morrisv@cofc.edu.

MORRIS, VICTOR FRANKLIN, JR. meteorology educator; b. Hyannis, Mass., Mar. 1, 1947; s. Victor Franklin and Florence Muriel (Rund) M. Student, MIT, 1965-66; BS in Atmospheric Scis., U. Wash., 1969; MS in Meteorology, U. Hawaii, 1975; MA in Environ. Geography, San Diego State U., 1979. Cert. community coll. instr. earth scis., Calif.; cert. advanced and instrument ground instr. FAA. Rsch. asst. U. Hawaii, Honolulu, 1973-75; teaching asst., lectr. San Diego State U., 1976-80; instr. San Diego Community Colls., 1976-80; prof. aero. sci. in meteorology Embry-Riddle Aero. U., Daytona Beach, Fla., 1981-94; pres. Caribbean Weather Svc., Rincon, Puerto Rico, 1994—. Cons. meteorologist Surfer Publs., Dana Point, Calif., 1980—; chief East Coast meteorologist Surf Line, Huntington Beach, Calif., 1987—. Author: The Weather Surfer, 1977, Meteorology: A Study Guide, 1985; writer monthly newsletter Sea Watch, 1980—; contbr. articles to profl. jours. and mags. Lt. USN, 1970-72. Mem. Am. Meteorol. Soc., Phi Kappa Phi. Avocations: surfing, distance running, gardening, beachcombing, amateur radio. Home: PO Box 384874 Waikoloa HI 96738-4874

MORRIS, WILLIAM CHARLES, investor; b. St. Louis, Apr. 15, 1938; s. Barney Lockhart and Kathryn (Evers) M.; m. Susan VanAvery Follett, Aug. 26, 1961; children: Edward F., David L., Kenneth V. SB in Chem. Engring., MIT, 1960; MBA, Harvard U., 1963. Assoc. Mobil Chem. Co., N.Y.C., 1963-66, Lehman Bros., N.Y.C., 1967-72; mng. dir. Lehman Bros. Kuhn Loeb Inc. (and predecessor), 1973-84; sr. advisor Shearson Lehman Bros., 1985-87; chmn. Carbo Ceramics Inc., Dallas, 1987—, J&W Seligman & Co., Inc., N.Y.C., 1988—. Chmn. Tri-Continental Corp., N.Y.C., 1988—, The Seligman Group of Investment Cos., N.Y.C., 1988—; bd. dirs. Kerr-McGee Corp., Oklahoma City, 1977—. Mng. dir. Metro. Opera Assn., N.Y., 1995—. Ensign USCGR, 1961. Office: J & W Seligman & Co Inc 100 Park Ave New York NY 10017-5598

MORRIS, WILLIAM LEWIS, mathematician; b. Hamilton, Ohio, Aug. 19, 1931; s. Harmon Edward and Loretta Margaret Morris; m. Rosemary Ann Heyob, Aug. 25, 1956; children: Mary, John, Matthew, Enid, Francis, Charlotte. AB in Math., U. Cin., 1958, AM in Math., 1960; PhD in Math., U. Tenn., 1967. Rsch. engr. Honeywell, Duarte, Calif., 1962—64; staff scientist Oak Ridge (Tenn.) Nat. Lab., 1964—66; lectr. U. Tenn., Knoxville, 1965—68; cons. NASA, Houston, 1973—75; prof. U. Houston, 1968—77; dir. Numerical Analysis Group, Center, Tex., 1978—. Author: Differential Equations, 1975; contbr. Fellow Taft tchg. fellow, U. Cin., 1959—60. Avocation: farming. Home: 7034 FM-711 Center TX 75935

MORRIS, WILLIAM OTIS, JR. lawyer, educator, writer; b. Fairmont, W.Va., Dec. 2, 1922; s. William Otis and Flora Helois (Preston) M.; m. Hazel Irene Kolbus, May 28, 1948; children: Barbara Ann, Melinda Lou. Student, Fairmont State Coll., 1940-41; AB, Coll. William and Mary, 1944; LLB, U. Ill., 1946, JD, 1968; DHC, Nicholas Copernicus U., Torun, Poland, 1992. Bar: Va. 1945, Ill. 1946, U.S. Supreme Ct. 1949. Prof. bus. law U. Ill., 1947-55; assoc. prof. law Stetson U., 1955-58; prof. law W.Va. U., Morgantown, 1958-94, prof. emeritus law, 1994—. Vis. U. Vienna, Austria, Nat. U., Singapore, Nat. U., Seoul, Korea, U. Sydney, Australia, East China Inst. of Law and Politics, U. Thessaloniki, Greece. Author: Dental Litigation, 1972, 2d edit., 1977, The Law of Domestic Relations in West Virginia, 1975, Veterinarian in Litigation, 1976, Revocation of Professional License, 1985, Handbook of Dental Law, 1994, The Dentist's Legal Advisor, 1994; mem. bd. editors Jour. Law and Ethics in Dentistry, Med. Malpractice Prevention, Clin. Jour.; contbr. articles to profl. jours. Decorated Merit medal (Poland); recipient Spl. award Nat. U. Seoul, Old Guard Medallion Coll. William and Mary, 1994, Lifetime Achievement Award Dentistry, 1994. Fellow Cleve. Clinic Med. Inst.; mem. ATLA, Va. Bar, Ill. Bar, W.Va. Trial Lawyers Assn., Order of Coif, Order of White Jackets, Sir Robert Boyle Soc. Republican. Lutheran. Home: 644 Bellaire Dr Morgantown WV 26505-2421 E-mail: bajrmig@webtv.net.

MORRISEY, MARENA GRANT, art museum administrator; b. Newport News, Va., May 28, 1945; BFA in Interior Design, Va. Commonwealth U., 1967, MA Art History, 1970. With Orlando (Fla.) Mus. Art, 1970—, exec. dir., 1976—. Former v.p., chmn. mus. svcs. com., mem. ad hoc com. on collections sharing and long range planning com., past chmn. exhbns. and edn. com. Am. Fedn. Arts; former mem. nat. adv. coun. George Washington U. Clearinghouse on Mus. Edn.; former mem. accreditation com. Nat. Found. for Interior Design Edn. Rsch. Former mem. strategic planning adv. coun. Orange County Sch. Dist.; former mem. advt. rev. bd. BBB; former mem. Orlando Pub. Art Adv. Bd., Orlando Leadership Coun., Orlando Hist. Bldg. Commn.; mem. art selection com. Orlando Internat. Airport, former chmn.; former mem. bd. dirs. Sta. WMFE-TV; bd. dirs. New World Sch. of Arts; vol. Sister Cities of Orlando; mem. internat. arts and culture com. Metro Orlando Internat. Affairs Commn. Named Orlando's Outstanding Woman of Yr. in Field of Art; recipient Fla. State of Arts award. Mem. Am. Assn. Mus. (former mem. governing bd., accreditation commn., profl. stds. and practices com., internat. coun. of mus.), Assn. Art Mus. Dirs. (comm. and publs. com.), Southeastern Mus. Conf. (past pres.), Fla. Art Mus. Dirs. Assn. (past pres.), Fla. Assn. Mus. (former bd. dirs.), Greater Orlando C. of C. (past mem. steering com. Leadership Orlando), Jr. League Orlando-Winter Park, Rotary Club Orlando (program com. Orlando, membership com., chmn. found. com., Paul Harris fellow). Office: Orlando Museum of Art 2416 N Mills Ave Orlando FL 32803-1483 E-mail: mgmorrisey@omart.org.

MORRISEY, MICHAEL A. health economics educator; b. Crookston, Minn., Mar. 20, 1952; s. Charles Arthur and Eleanor E. (LaFleur) M.; m. Elaine M. Mardian, Aug. 26, 1972; children: Michelle Ann, David Michael. BA, No. State U., Aberdeen, S.D., 1974; MA in Econs., U. Wash., 1975, PhD in Econs., 1979. Rsch. asst., specialist Battelle HARC, Seattle, 1976-79; sr. economist Am. Hosp. Assn., Chgo., 1979-85; sr. economist, asst. dir. Hosp. Rsch. & Ednl. Trust, 1983-85; vis. scholar Northwestern U., Evanston, Ill., 1984-85; assoc. prof. U. Ala., Birmingham, 1985-88, prof., 1988—, disting. faculty investigator, 1999-2000; dir. Lister Hill Ctr. for Health Policy, 1990—. Dep. editor Med. Care, Cleve., 1987—96; mem. Pa. Mandates Benefits Rev. Panel, Harrisburg, 1987—, Ala. Task Force on Rural Health Care Crisis, 1989; cons. NIH, VA, U.S. HHS, Washington, 1980—, pvtl industry; mem. health svcs. devel. grants rev. com. Agy. for Health Care Rsch. and Quality, Rockville, Md., 1992—96. Author: Price Sensitivity in Health Care, 1992, Cost Shifting in Health Care, 1994, Managed Care and Changing Health Care Markets, 1998; mem. editl. bd. Health Affairs, 1998—, Jour. Gerontology, 1998-2001, Health Svcs. and Outcomes Rsch. Methodology, 1999—, Health

Adminstrn. Press, 1999—, Med. Care Rsch. and Rev., 2000—; contbr. more than 110 articles to profl. jours. Recipient John D. Thompson prize in health svc. rsch., Assn. Univ. Programs in Health Adminstrn., 1991; fellow, Employee Benefits Rsch. Inst.; grantee, Nat. Ctr. Health Svcs. Rsch., NIH, Agy. for Health Care Rsch. and Quality, Robert Wood Johnson Found. Mem.: APHA (com. chmn. 2000), Internat. Health Econs. Assn. (treas. 1994—2000, sec.-treas. 2000—), Acad. for Health Svcs. Rsch. and Health Policy, Am. Econ. Assn. Republican. Roman Catholic. Office: UAB Sch Pub Health Birmingham AL 35294-0022 E-mail: morrisey@uab.edu.

MORRISH, ALLAN HENRY, electrical engineering educator; b. Winnipeg, Man., Can., Apr. 18, 1924; s. Stanley and Agnes (Payne) M.; children: John Stanley, Allan Richard. B.Sc. with Honors, U. Man., 1943; MA, U. Toronto, 1946; PhD, U. Chgo., 1949. Mem. faculty U. B.C., Vancouver, Can., 1949-52; research asst. Radiation Lab., McGill U., Montreal, Que., Can., 1952-53; with dept. elec. engring. U. Minn., Mpls., 1953-64, prof. dept. elec. engring., 1959-64; prof. U. Man., Winnipeg, 1964—, head dept. physics, 1966-87, disting. prof., 1984—. Vis. prof. Monash U., Clayton, Victoria, Australia, 1971-72, U. Calif., Davis, 1978, Ariz. State U., Tempe, 1984, U. Wash., Seattle, 1984, Tex. A&M U., College Station, 1989, Iowa State U., Ames, 1991; cons. Honeywell, Inc., Hopkins, Minn., 1956-57, 59-63 Author: The Physical Principles of Magnetism, 1965, reprint, 2001, Canted Antiferromagnetism: Hematite, 1994; also numerous articles. NRC Can. postdoctoral fellow U. Bristol, Eng., 1950-51; Guggenheim fellow U. Oxford, Eng., 1957-58 Fellow Royal Soc. Can., Inst. of Physics (Eng.); mem. Can. Assn. Physicists (pres. 1974-75, medal for achievement in physics 1977), Sigma Xi. Achievements include research on magnetic materials using superconducting solenoids. Home: 71 Agassiz Dr Winnipeg MB Canada R3T 2K9

MORRISH, THOMAS JAY, golf course architect; b. Grand Junction, Colo., July 6, 1936; s. Wilbur Merle and Margaret Beula (Cronk) M.; m. Louise Ann Dunn, Apr. 2, 1965; children: Carter J., Kimberly L. Coder. AA, Mesa Coll., Grand Junction, 1956; BS in Landscape and Nursery Mgmt., Colo. State U., 1964. Golf course arch. Robert Trent Jones, Montclaire, N.J., 1964-67, George Fazio, Jupiter, Fla., 1967-69, Desmond Muirhead, Newport Beach, Calif., 1969-72, Jack Nicklaus, North Palm Beach, Fla., 1972-83; prin. Jay Morrish & Assocs. Ltd., Flower Mound, Tex., 1983—. Prin. golf course designs include: Troon Golf & Country Club, Scottsdale, Ariz., Las Colinas Sports Club, Irving, Tex., Mira Vista, Ft. Worth, Foothills Golf Course, Phoenix, Forest Highlands, Flagstaff, Ariz. (One of 100 Top Golf Courses in World, Golf mag., Golf Digest), Bentwater on Lake Conroe, Houston, Shadow Glen Golf Club, Olathe, Kans. (Best New Private Course, Golf Digest 1989), Troon North Golf & Country Club, Scottsdale (One of 100 Top Courses in U.S., Golf mag.), Harbor Club on Lake Oconee, Greensboro, Ga., Loch Lomond, Scotland, The Country Club of St. Albans, Mo., Broken Top, Bend, Oreg., Dauble Eagle Club, Galena, Ohio (one of Top 100 Courses in World, Golf Mag.), Buffalo Creek Golf Course, Rockwall, Tex., La Cantera, San Antonio (Best New Pub. Course of 1995, Golf Digest Mag.), numerous others. Edn. grantee State of Colo., 1961-64; Trans-Miss. golf scholar, 1962-64; named Architect of Yr. Golf World Mag., 1996. Mem. Am. Soc. Golf Course Archs. (pres. 2002), Dallas Safari Club. Republican. Avocation: hunting. Office: 3700 Forums Dr Ste 207 Flower Mound TX 75028-1847

MORRISON, ANN HESS, information technology specialist; b. Grants Pass, Oreg., Mar. 29, 1944; d. Wilbur Lill and Esther Elaine Groner; m. Robert Thornton Morrison, Apr. 14, 1996; children: David William Hess, William Albert Hess. BSEE, BS in Math., Oreg. State U., 1968; MBA in Info. Tech., Maryville U., St. Louis, 2001. Engr. Lawrence Livermore Lab., Livermore, Calif., 1968-69; mgr., owner RBR Scales, Inc., Anaheim, 1969-84; lead engr. Rockwell Internat., Seal Beach, 1984-86, '87-88; software engr. Hughes Aircraft Co., Fullerton, 1986-87; sr. engr. Logican Eagle Tech., Inc., Eatontown, N.J., 1988-91; owner Holistic Eclectic Software Svc., Orange, Calif., 1991—92; sys. specialist Jacobs Engring Group, 1993—2001; owner Homeland Def. 4U Inc., Clayton, Mo., 2002—. Active Calif. Master Chorale, Santa Ana, 1990-92. Mem. Am. Soc. Quality Control, Phi Kappa Phi, Eta Kappa Nu, Tau Beta Pi, Sigma Beta Delta. Lutheran. Avocations: singing, art, gardening. E-mail: ann@homeland_defense4u.com.

MORRISON, ASHTON BYROM, pathologist, medical school official; b. Northern Ireland, Oct. 13, 1922; came to U.S., 1955; s. Samuel and Henrietta (Good) M.; m. Claire Morris, M.D.; 1 dau., Mary Claire. MB, Queen's U, Belfast, No. Ireland, 1946; PhD, Queens U., Belfast, No. Ireland, 1950, MD (hon.), 1988; MD, Duke U., 1946. Intern Royal Victoria Hosp., Belfast, 1947; asst. lectr. Queens U., 1947-52; registrar dept. exptl. medicine Cambridge U., 1952-55, dir. med. studies Corpus Christi Coll., 1954-55; assoc. Duke U., N.C., 1955-58; asst. prof. pathology U. Pa. Sch. Medicine, 1958-61; assoc. prof. U. Rochester Sch. Medicine, 1961-65; prof. pathology, chmn. dept. Rutgers U. Med. Sch., 1965-80; v.p. acad. affairs Eastern Va. Med. Authority, 1980-83; dean Eastern Va. Med. Sch., 1980-83; prof. pathology Robert Wood Johnson Med. Sch.-U. Medicine and Dentistry N.J., Camden, 1983-93; assoc. dean in charge Robert Wood Johnson Med Sch.-U. Medicine and Dentistry N.J., 1983-89, prof. pathology emeritus, 1993-96, prof. pathology and lab. medicine emeritus, 1997—; prof. pathology Ea. Va. Med. Sch., 1994—. 22nd Scott Heron lectr. Royal Victoria Hosp., Belfast, No. Ireland, 1978. Recipient Disting. Alumnus award Duke U. Med. Sch., 1987. Mem. Am. Assn. Investigative Pathologists (emeritus), Am. Physiol. Soc. (emeritus), Soc. Exptl. Biology and Medicine (emeritus), Am. Soc. Nephrology (emeritus). Home: 3518 Rue Delfeur Columbus OH 43221 Office: Eastern Va Med Sch 358 Mowbray Arch Ste 108 Norfolk VA 23507-2219

MORRISON, BARBARA HANEY, educational administrator; b. Ft. Campbell, Ky., June 27, 1953; d. Charles L. and Rosemary (Blakeman) Haney; m. J.D. Morrison; 1 child, Carol Marie. BA, U. Ala., 1978; MS, Troy State U., 1985. Cert. profl. healthcare quality, healthcare quality and risk mgmt. cons. Dir. quality improvement and edn. Charter Med. Corp., Dothan, Ala., 1992-96, dir. edn., 1987-96, student assistance program dir.; classroom tchr. Ozark; dir. Westgate Learning Ctr., Albany, Ga., 1993-96. Mem. drug adv. bd. Houston County Schs. Mem. ASCD, NEA, Ala. Edn. Assn., Coun. for Children with Behaviour Disorders, Assn. for Healthcare Quality, Dothan-Houstan C. of C. (edn. com.), Alpha Delta Kappa.

MORRISON, BARTON DOUGLAS, minister; b. Westminster, Calif., Dec. 3, 1965; s. Willis Carrol and Elva Adelee (Cashman) M.; m. Becky Lynn Goodin, June 3, 1988; children: Christopher Barton, Hayley Diane-Maree. B in Music Edn., Okla. Bapt. U., 1988; MusM, Southwestern Bapt. Theol. Sem., 1991; postgrad., Oberlin Coll., 1997, U. Tenn., 1999. Cert. gen. and vocal music tchr., Okla., Orff-Schulwerk Level I and II. Organist Birchman Bapt. Ch., Ft. Worth, 1988-90, min. music, 1990-92, Concord Bapt. Ch., St. Louis, 1992-2000; min. music and worship First Bapt. Ch., Corinth, Tex., 2000—. Adj. prof. music Mo. Bapt. Coll., 1997-2000; ch. accompanist Trinity Bapt. Ch., Westminster, 1979-83, Southwestern Bapt. Theol. Sem., Ft. Worth, 1988-91; vocalist, pianist Continental Singers, Thousand Oaks, Calif., 1982-83; chapel pianist Okla. Bapt. U., Shawnee, 1983-88; music asst. 1st So. Bapt. Ch., Del City, 1984-85; organist Univ. Bapt. Ch., Shawnee, 1985-88; organist, pianist Falls Creek Bapt. Assembly, Davis, Okla., 1985-86, 88-89; pianist Tex. Bapt. Pastor's Conf., 1990; judge Mo. Bapt. State Keyboard Festival, 1994-2000; organist Mo. Bapt. State Conv., 1995, 98; symposium Voice Care Assocs. and the Univ. of Tenn. Voice Inst., Memphis, 1999; combined adult choir and orch. condr. St. Louis Bapt. Assn., 1997; accompanist, singer Ft. Worth Oratorio Chorus tour of Israel, 1999. Solo/ensemble judge CSAMSL, 1998, 99. Mem. Am. Choral Dirs. Assn. (life, student adv. com. 1990-92, judge Mo. All-Dist. All-State Choirs 1995-98), So. Bapt. Ch. Music Conf. (life), Phi Mu Alpha Sinfonia (sec. 1985-88), Zeta Pi Lambda (svc. com. 1985-88). Avocations: reading, golf, walking, running. Office: 3033 Meadowview Dr Corinth TX 76210-2789

MORRISON, BRUCE ANDREW, government executive, public affairs consultant; b. N.Y.C., Oct. 8, 1944; s. George and Dorothea A. (Meyer) M.; m. Nancy A. Wanat, Sept. 22, 1991; 1 child, Drew. S.B., MIT, 1965; MS, U. Ill., 1970; JD, Yale U., 1973; Litt.D. (hon.), Quinnipac Coll. Staff atty. New Haven Legal Assistance Assn., 1973-74, mng. atty., 1974-76, exec. dir., 1976-82; mem. 98th-101st Congresses from 3d Conn. dist., 1983-91; chmn. L.I. Sound Caucus, chmn. Third World Debt Caucus. Chmn. judiciary subcom. on immigration, refugees, and internat. law U.S. Ho. of Reps.; chmn. Fed. Housing Fin. Bd., 1995-2000 ; co-chmn. ad hoc com. on Irish affairs; mem. U.S. commn. on immigration reform, 1991-97; chair Irish Ams. for Clinton-Gore, 1992, 96; chair Ams. for a New Irish Agenda, 1993-95; vice chmn. GPC Internat., 2000-2001; chmn. Morrison Pub. Affairs Group, 2001--. Mem. Nat. Dem. Ethnic Coordinating Com.; bd. dirs. Rock Mountain Mut. Housing Assn., Alliance for Responsible Cuba Policy. Mem. ABA, Conn. Bar Assn., New Haven County Bar Assn., Am. Immigration Lawyers Assn. Lutheran. Office: 6004 Onondaga Rd Bethesda MD 20816 E-mail: b.a.m@att.net.

MORRISON, CHARLES E. think-tank executive; b. Billings, Mont., 1944; m. Chieko Hayashi; children: Karen, Erica, Kenneth, Douglas. BA in Internat. Studies, MA, PhD, Johns Hopkins U. Legis. asst. U.S. Senate, 1972-80; part-time sr. rsch. assoc. Japan Ctr. for Internat. Exch., 1980-92; asst. to pres. East-West Ctr., 1986-92, dir. program on internat. econs. and politics, 1992-95, pres., 1998—; dir. Asia Pacific Econ. Coun. Study Ctr., 1996-98; chair U.S. Consortium of APEC Study Ctrs., 1996-98. Editor: Asia-Pacific Security Outlook books, 1996—; author: wide range of books, papers and analyses; widely quoted by major news media on issues of regional cooperation, internat. rels., U.S. Asia policy and trade policies, U.S.-Japan rels. and the Asian economic crisis. Office: East West Ctr 1601 E West Rd Honolulu HI 96848-1601

MORRISON, CHERYL LYNN, petroleum engineer, project manager; b. Galveston, Tex., Mar. 12, 1953; d. John Lipuscek and Dorothy Eloise (Weed) Morrison. BS in Biology, U. Ala., Tuscaloosa, 1975, BS in Petroleum Engring., 1979. Assoc. ops. engr. Getty Oil Co., Mobile, Ala., 1979—82, prodn. engr. Kilgore, Tex., 1982—85; drilling engr. Mobil Oil Co., Lafayette, La., 1985—87, Houston, drilling supr., 1987—89; drilling rep. Chevron USA, Lafayette, 1989—90, Bakersfield, Calif., 1990—96, petroleum engr., 1996—99, project mgr., 1999—2000, Chevron Texaco, San Ramon, 2000—. Mem. Soc. Petroleum Engrs. (sec., treas., bd. dirs. 1979-), Tex. State Profl. Engrs. Methodist. Home: PO Box 2568 San Ramon CA 94583-7568 Office: Chevron Texaco Co 60901 Bollinger Canyon Rd San Ramon CA

MORRISON, CLINTON, banker; b. Mpls., Mar. 26, 1915; s. Angus Washburn and Helen (Truesdale) M.; m. Mary K. Morrison. BA, Yale U., 1937; MBA, Harvard U., 1939. With Shell Oil Co., N.Y.C., St. Louis, 1939-41; with Vassar Co., Chgo., 1946-48, Holding Co., Mpls., 1948, First Nat. Bank, Mpls., 1955-80, former vice chmn. bd., chmn. trust com. Former dir. Gt. No. Ins. Co., Minn. Title Fin. Corp., Munsingwear, Inc.; Dep. regional dir. Far East Fgn. Operations Adminstrn. for U.S. Govt., 1953- 55; mem. Internat. Pvt. Investment Adv. Council to AID, Dept. State, 1967-68, Nat. Adv. Council on Minority Bus. Enterprise, 1968-72 Life trustee Mpls. Art Inst., Mpls. Coll. Art and Design; former trustee Lakewood Cemetery Assn. Served to maj. Q.M.C. AUS, 1942-46. Mem. U.S. C. of C. (chmn. 1975-76), Bankers Assn. (exec. com. trust div. 1969-72), Twin Cities Soc. Security Analysts, Mpls. Econ. Roundtable. Home: 2400 Cedar Point Dr Wayzata MN 55391-2618 Office: 730 Second Ave South Ste 1350 Minneapolis MN 55402

MORRISON, DARREL GENE, landscape architecture educator; b. Orient, Iowa, June 20, 1937; s. Raymond Delbert and Rosy Christina (Mensing) M.; m. Dawna Lee Hauptman, June 29, 1963 (div. Sept. 1987); children: Jon David, Scott Darrel. BS in Landscape Architecture, Iowa State U., 1959; MS in Landscape Architecture, U. Wis., 1969. Landscape arch. Md. Nat. Capital Park and Plan Commn., Silver Spring, 1962-64, T.D. Donovan & Assocs., Silver Spring, 1964-66, City Washington, 1966-67; rsch. asst. U. Wis., Madison, 1967-69, mem. faculty, 1969-83, John Bascom prof., 1978; dean environ. design U. Ga., Athens, 1983-92, prof. environ. design, 1992—. Co-editor: Landscape Jour., 1981-88. With U.S. Army, 1960-62. Recipient Disting. Tchg. award U. Wis., 1976, Bracken medal Pa. State U., 1996, Tchg. award Am. Hort. Soc., 1998, Hutchinson medal Chgo. Hort. Soc., 1998; named Outstanding Educator, Coun. Educators in Landscape Architecture, 1977, 94. Fellow Am. Soc. Landscape Architects (v.p. 1987-89). Office: Sch of Environtl Design Univ Ga Athens GA 30602 Address: 3501 S Barnett Shoals Rd Watkinsville GA 30677-2240 E-mail: darrelmo@arches.uga.edu.

MORRISON, DAVID EUGENE, lawyer; b. York, Nebr., May 6, 1952; s. Louis Eugene and Eleanor (Curry) M. BA, U. Nebr., 1974; JD, Duke U., 1977. Bar: Tex. 1977. Sr. ptnr. Thompson & Knight LLP, Dallas, 1977-2000; ptnr. Fulbright & Jaworski LLP, 2000—. Mem. bd. govs. Dallas Symphony Assn., Inc., 1990-2001, mem. exec. bd., 1993-2001, sec., 1993-98; trustee Tex. Internat. Festivals, Inc., Dallas, 1997-98, mem. exec. com., 1997-98, sec., 1997-98; mem. bd. mgmt. Town North Family YMCA, Dallas, 1997-2000. Methodist. Avocations: spectator sports, gardening, woodworking. Home: 4738 San Gabriel Dr Dallas TX 75229-4233 Office: Fulbright & Jaworski LLP 2200 Ross Ave Ste 2800 Dallas TX 75201 E-mail: dmorrison@fulbright.com.

MORRISON, DEBORAH JEAN, lawyer; b. Johnstown, Pa., Feb. 18, 1955; d. Ralph Wesley and Norma Jean (Kinsey) Morrison; m. Ricardo Daniel Kamenetzky, Sept. 6, 1978 (div. Nov. 1991); children: Elena Raquel, Julia Rebecca. BA in Polit. Sci., Chatham Coll., 1977; postgrad., U. Miami, Fla., 1977-78; JD, U. Pitts., 1981. Bar: Pa. 1981, Ill. 1985. Legal asst. Klein Y Mairal, Buenos Aires, Argentina, 1978-79; legal intern Neighborhood Legal Svcs., Aliquippa, Pa., 1980-81; law clk. Pa. Superior Ct., Pitts., 1981-84; atty. John Deere Credit Co., Moline, Ill., 1985-89; sr. atty. Deere & Co., 1989-96, sr. counsel, 1996—. Mem. ABA, Pa. Bar Assn., Phi Beta Kappa, Order of the Coif. Democrat. Mem. United Church of Christ. Office: Deere & Co 1 John Deere Pl Moline IL 61265-8098

MORRISON, DONALD FRANKLIN, statistician, educator; b. Stoneham, Mass., Feb. 10, 1931; s. Daniel Norman and Agnes Beatrice (Packard) M.; m. Phyllis Ann Hazen, Aug. 19, 1967; children: Norman Hazen, Stephen Donald. BS in Bus. Adminstrn, Boston U., 1953, AM, 1954; MS, U. N.C., 1957; PhD, Va. Poly. Inst. and State U., 1960; MA (hon.), U. Pa., 1971. Mem. staff Lincoln Lab., M.I.T., 1956; cons. math. statistician NIMH, Bethesda, Md., 1956-63; mem. tech. staff Bell Labs., Holmdel, N.J., 1967; mem. faculty, dept. stats. Wharton Sch., U. Pa., 1963-99, prof. stats., 1973-99, chmn. dept., 1978-85, prof. emeritus, 2000—. Author: Multivariate Statistical Methods, 3d edit., 1990, Applied Linear Statistical Methods, 1983; editor: The American Statistician, 1972-75; assoc. editor: Biometrics, 1972-74; contbr. articles to profl. jours. Served with USPHS, 1956-58. NSF grantee, 1966 Fellow Am. Stats. Assn., Inst. Math. Stats.; mem. Internat. Statis. Inst., Royal Statis. Soc., B&M R.R. Hist. Soc., Nat. R.R. Hist. Soc., R.R. and Locomotive Hist. Soc., N&W Hist. Soc., Bridge Line Hist. Soc., N.E. Elec. Rwy. Hist. Soc. Democrat. Lutheran. Home: 118 E Brookhaven Rd Wallingford PA 19086-6327 E-mail: donaldm@wharton.upenn.edu.

MORRISON, DONALD GRAHAM, business educator, consultant; b. Detroit, Feb. 26, 1939; s. Roderick and Ethelyne (Murray) M.; m. Sherie Leaver, Sept. 12, 1964; children: Heather Margaret Cloonan, Tracey Michelle Oliva. BSM.E., MIT, 1961; PhD in Ops. Research, Stanford U., 1965. Instr. Stanford U., Calif., 1965-66, vis. prof., 1982-97; mem. faculty Columbia U., N.Y.C., 1966-87, prof., 1973-87, Armand G. Erpf prof. bus., 1985-87; William E. Leonard prof. Anderson Grad. Sch. Mgmt., UCLA, 1987—. Vis. prof. U. Calif., Berkeley, 1970-71; cons. in field, UCLA faculty athletic rep. to NCAA. Editor in chief Mgmt. Sci., 1983-90; founding editor Mktg. Sci., 1980-82. Elder Hitchcock Presbyn. Ch., Scarsdale, N.Y., 1978-84, Westwood Presbyn. Ch., L.A., 1991-94, 95-98; treas. Scarsdale Jr. H.S. PTA, 1977-78; acad. trustee Mktg. Sci. Inst., 1986-92; mem. Decision, Risk and Mgmt. Sci. rev. bd. NSF, 1989-91. Mem. Inst. Mgmt. Sci. (pres. 1990-92), Ops. Rsch. Soc. Am., Am. Statis. Assn. Presbyterian. Avocations: golf; jogging; bridge. Office: UCLA Anderson Grad Sch Mgmt 110 Westwood Plz Los Angeles CA 90095-0001

MORRISON, DONALD WILLIAM, lawyer; b. Portland, Oreg., Mar. 31, 1926; s. Robert Angus and Laura Calista (Hodgson) M.; m. Elizabeth Margaret Perry, July 25, 1953; children: Elizabeth Laura, Carol Margaret. BSE.E., U. Wash., 1946; LL.B., Stanford U., 1950. Bar: Oreg. 1950, Calif. 1950, N.Y. 1967, Ill. 1968, Ohio 1974. Assoc. Pendergrass, Spackman, Bullivant & Wright, Portland, 1950-57, ptnr., 1957-60; gen. atty. Pacific N.W. Bell, Portland, 1960-66; atty. AT&T, N.Y.C., 1966-68; counsel Ill. Bell Telephone Co., Chgo., 1968-74; v.p., gen. counsel Ohio Bell Telephone Co., Cleve., 1974-91; of counsel Arter & Hadden, 1991—. Trustee Citizens League Rsch. Inst., Cleve. Chamber Music Soc.; trustee, mem. exec. com. Cleve. Coun. on World Affairs; mem. adv. com. Cleve. Play House; mem. adv. com., trustee Cleve. Bot. Garden; trustee Cleve. Archaeol. Soc. With USN, 1943—50. Recipient various bar and civic appreciation awards. Mem. ABA, Ohio State Bar Assn., Bar Assn. Greater Cleve., Oreg. State Bar Assn., Calif. Bar Assn., The Country Club, Rowfant Club. Office: Arter & Hadden 1100 Huntington Bldg Cleveland OH 44115

MORRISON, ELLEN M. writer, researcher; b. Marysville, Calif., Apr. 17, 1954; d. Louis Arch and Mildred Claire (Hansen) Morrison; m. Kenneth William Lann, Jun. 26, 1976; 1 child, Mallory. BA, UCLA, 1977; MA, U. Chgo., 1982, PhD, 1979-87. Rsch. asst. U. Chgo., 1980-82, rsch. analyst, 1982-84; project dir. Northwestern U., Evanston, Ill., 1984-87; fellow U. Calif., San Francisco, 1988-90; program dir. Inst. for the Future, Menlo Park, Calif., 1990-95; author, editor, lit. cons. San Carlos, 1995-01; sr. rschr. U. Calif., San Francisco, 01—. Co-author: Strategic Choices For America's Hospitals, 1990 (Book of Yr.); contbr. articles to profl. jours. Mem. NOW, Amnesty Internat., Greenpeace. Democrat. Avocations: education, human rights and enviromental activism, foreign language study, travel, gardening. Home and Office: UCSF Ctr for Hlth Profls 3333 California St Ste 410 San Francisco CA 94118 E-mail: emm@itsa.ucsf.edu.

MORRISON, GARY RAY, instructional technology educator, researcher; b. Bedford, Ind., Nov. 17, 1948; s. Glenn Molar and Betty Ann Morrison. BS in Edn., Ind. U., 1971, EdD, 1977. Instrnl. designer U. Mid-Am., Lincoln, Nebr., 1976-78, Solar Turbines Internat., San Diego, 1978-80, GE Corp. Consulting Group, Bridgeport, Conn., 1980, Tenneco Oil Co. E&P, Houston, 1980-84; prof. U. Memphis, 1984-98, Wayne State U., Detroit, 1998—. Author: Designing Effective Instruction, 3d edit., 2000 (L.C. Larson award 1995), Integrating Computer Technology in the Classroom. Mem. Assn. Ednl. Comm. and Tech. (pres. rsch. and theory div. and div. instrnl. design), Am. Ednl. Rsch. Orgn. Office: Wayne State Univ 399 Edn Detroit MI 48202 E-mail: Gary_Morrison@wayne.edu.

MORRISON, GLENN, neurosurgeon; b. Phila., June 16, 1940; married, 3 children. AB, Colgate U., 1962; MD, Case Western Reserve U., 1967; postgrad., Nat. Comm. Disease Ctr., 1968. Diplomate Am. Bd. Neurological Surgery, Am. Bd. Pediatric Neurological Surgery. Intern Cleve. Met. Hosp., 1968; resident in neurosurgery Univ. Hosps. Cleve., 1970-74; with Neurosurg. Assocs., Coral Gables, Fla., 1974-85, Baptist Hosp., Miami, 1974—; pvt. prac. Coral Gables, 1985—2000; chief pediatric neurological surgery Miami Children's Hosp., 1986—. Prof. dept. neurological surgery, U. Miami Sch. Med., dir. pediat. neurosurg. alliance; cons. divsn. children's med. svcs. state of Fla. Lt. Cmdr. USPHS, 1968-70. Recipient Nat. Found. Rsch. award, 1967. Fellow ACS (sec., treas. greater Miami chpt. 1979-83, pres. 1983-85, interview com. 1980—); mem. AMA, Am. Assn. Neurol. Surgeons, Congress Neurol. Surgeons, Am. Acad. Pediats., Am. Heart Assn., Neurol. Soc. Am., Internat. Soc. Pediat. Neurosurgery, So. Neurosurg. Soc. (v.p. 1989-90, treas. 1992-95, pres. 1996-97), Fla. Neurosurg. Soc. (pres. 1982), Greater Miami Neurosurg. Soc. (pres. 1978), numerous others. Office: Miami Children's Hosp 3200 SW 60th Ct Ste 301 Miami FL 33155-4071

MORRISON, GLENN LESLIE, minister; b. Cortez, Colo., Feb. 26, 1929; s. Ward Carl Morrison and Alma Irene (Butler) Anderson; m. Beverely Joanne Buck, Aug. 26, 1949; children: David Mark, Betty Jo Morrison Mullen, Gary Alan, Judith Lynn Morrison Oltmann, Stephen Scott. Student, San Diego State U., 1948-49, Chabot Coll., 1968-69. Ordained to ministry Evang. Ch. Alliance, 1961. Dir. counseling and follow-up Oakland (Calif.) Youth for Christ, 1954-56; pres. Follow Up Ministries, Inc., Castro Valley, Calif., 1956—. Assoc. pastor 1st Covenant Ch., Oakland, 1956-58; exec. dir. East Bay Youth for Christ, Oakland, 1960-66; supervising chaplain Alameda County (Calif.) Probation Dept., 1971-90; vol. chaplain Alameda County Sheriff's Dept., 1971—; seminar leader Calif. Dept. Corrections, Sacramento, 1978—, mem. chaplains coordinating com., 1988—; founder, dir. God Squad Vol. Program for Prison Workers, 1972—. Author: Scripture Investigation Course, 1956. Mem. Am. Correctional Assn., Am. Protestant Correctional Chaplains Assn. (regional pres., sec. 1980-86, nat. sec. 1986-88, nat. 2nd v.p. 1996-98). Office: Follow Up Ministries Inc PO Box 2514 Castro Valley CA 94546-0514 E-mail: fumi2000@email.msn.com.

MORRISON, GORDON MACKAY, JR. investment company executive; b. Boston, Jan. 18, 1930; s. Gordon Mackay and Alice (Blodgett) M.; m. Barbara J. Lee (deceased), June 15, 1954; children: Lee, Leighton, Faith. AB, Harvard U., 1952, MBA, 1954. Regional mgr. Bankers Leasing Corp., Boston, 1965-68; portfolio mgr. Loomis, Sayles and Co., 1969-71; sr. v.p. Ft. Hill Investors Mgmt., 1972-75; chmn. bd. Bradford Gordon Ptnrs., 1977—2001, gen. ptnr., 1977—, emeritus, 2001—. Trustee East Boston Savs. Bank, 1962-91; trustee Meridian Fin. Svcs., Inc., 1991-2002, hon. trustee, 2002--. Bd. dirs. The New Eng. Hosp., 1961-96, emeritus, 1996—. Republican. Congl. Club: Harvard. Lodge: Masons. Home: 5 Neptune Ln Biddeford ME 04005-9594 Office: Bradford Gordon Ptnrs 50 Congress St Boston MA 02109-4027

MORRISON, GREGG SCOTT, minister, college administrator; b. Rome, Mar. 9, 1964; s. Glen Warren and Joyce (Lannom) M.; m. Laura Edge, Jan. 21, 1995. BS in Acctg., U. Ala., 1986; MDiv, Samford U., 1996; postgrad., Emory U., 1998-2000, Catholic U. Tax assoc. Coopers & Lybrand, Atlanta, 1986, tax specialist, 1987-88, tax supr. Birmingham, Ala., 1988-89, sr. tax assoc., 1990-91, tax mgr., 1991-93; min. outreach Shades Mountain Bapt. Ch., 1993-96; dir. external rels. Beeson Div. Sch., Samford U., Birmingham, Ala., 1996—2001; interim pastor New Prospect Bapt. Ch., Jasper, 1998, Bluff Park Bapt. Ch., Birmingham, 1999. Adj. faculty Bethel Sem. of the East, John Leland Ctr. for Theol. Studies. Active United Way Ctrl. Ala., Inc., Birmingham, 1989; pres. student govt. assn. Beeson Div. Sch. of Samford U., 1995-96; bd. dirs. Ctr. for Urban Missions, Inc., Birmingham, chmn. fin. com., 1991-94, 96-2001; bd. dirs. Univ. Cmty. Coop., Inc., Tuscaloosa; sec.-treas., pres. ACCESS; treas. Martin Luther King Unity Breakfast Planning Com.; southside campaign capt. Boy Scouts Am.; mem. planned giving adv. group Bapt. Hosp. Found., Inc.; deacon Shades Mt. Bapt. Ch., 1992-94, 96-99, mem. strategic planning com. chmn. Innercity Ministry Partnership Task Force, 1996-2001; adv. bd. Baptist Ctr. Leadership Devel; mem. long range planning com. City of Vestavia Hills, Ala. Named one of Outstanding Young Men Am., 1996. Mem. Soc. Bibl. Lit., Am. Acad. Religion, Evang. Theol. Soc., Inst. Bibl. Rsch., Birmingham Hist. Soc. (planning com. 1990-91), PGA (fin. com.), Vestavia Country Club, Theta Chi (treas. Alpha Phi house corp. 1992-94). Republican. Bapt. Avocations: golf, tennis, reading, politics. Home: 6942 Spruce St Falls Church VA 22046

MORRISON, GUS (ANGUS HUGH MORRISON), mayor, engineer; b. Buffalo, Sept. 13, 1935; s. John Weir and Mary (Norton) Morrison; m. Joy Rita Hallenbarter, Feb. 7, 1959; children: Frank, Gloria, Heather. Technician Bell Aircraft Corp., Niagara Falls, N.Y., 1956-58, Lockheed Missiles and Space Corp., Sunnyvale, Calif., 1958-63, test engr., 1963-78, group engr., 1978-86, dept. mgr., 1986-94; ret., 1994. Mayor Fremont, Calif., 1985-99, 94—, council mem., 1978-85, 91-94, planning commr., 1977-78; bd. dirs. Tri City Ecology Ctr., 1976—. Served with USN, 1953-56. Democrat. Roman Catholic. Avocations: computers, photography, seriography. Office: Office Mayor PO Box 5006 Fremont CA 94537-5006*

MORRISON, HARRIET BARBARA, retired education educator; b. Boston, Feb. 23, 1934; d. Harry and Harriet (Hanrahan) M. BS, Mass. State Coll., 1956, MEd, 1958; EdD, Boston U., 1967. Elem. tchr. Arlington (Mass.) Pub. Schs., 1956-67; instr. U. Mass., 1967; asst. prof. edn. No. Ill. U., Dekalb, 1967-71, assoc. prof., 1971-85, prof., 1985-97; ret., 1997. Author: The Seven Gifts, 1988; editor Vitae Scholasticae. Mem. ASCD, Am. Ednl. Studies Assn., Philosophy of Edn. Soc., Midwest Philosophy Edn. Soc., Ill. ASCD, Pi Lambda Theta. Home: 834 S 8th St Dekalb IL 60115-4551

MORRISON, HARRY, chemistry educator, university dean; b. Bklyn., Apr. 25, 1937; s. Edward and Pauline (Sommers) M.; m. Harriet Thurman, Aug. 23, 1958; children: Howard, David, Daniel. BA, Brandeis U., 1957; PhD, Harvard U., 1961. NATO-NSF postdoctoral fellow Swiss Fed. Inst., Zurich, 1961-62; rsch. assoc. U. Wis., Madison, 1962-63; asst. prof. chemistry Purdue U., West Lafayette, Ind., 1963-69, assoc. prof., 1969-76, prof., 1976—, dept. head, 1987-92, dean Sch. Sci., 1992—2002. Acad. adv. com. Indsl. Rsch. Inst., 1993-96; mem. sci. adv. bd. Photogen, Inc. Contbr. numerous articles to profl.

jours. Bd. fellows Brandeis U. Mem. Am. Chem. Soc., Am. Soc. Photobiology, Inter-Am. Photochem. Soc., Coun. for Chem. Rsch. (chmn. 1995), Phi Beta Kappa, Sigma Xi. Office: Purdue U Sci Adminstrn Math Bldg West Lafayette IN 47907-1390

MORRISON, JACQUELINE ANN, social worker, psychologist; b. Chattanooga, June 1, 1943; d. Curtis Matthew and Jacqueline Ann (Hurley) Hinsley; m. Randal Charles Morrison, Sept. 16, 1967; 1 child, Laura Jo. BS, Ohio State U., 1965, MSW, 1968, PhD, 1995. Cert. clin. social worker, lic., Ohio; lic. psychologist. Recreation dir., case worker United Meth. Children's Home, Worthington, Ohio, 1968-70; casefinding coord. The Nisonger Ctr./Ohio State, Columbus, 1972-74, social work faculty, 1978-79; project coord. cancer rehab. project Ohio State U. Cancer Ctr., 1974-77; social worker Cen. Ohio Dialysis Ctr., Columbus, 1978; asst. prof. Coll. of Social Work Ohio State U., 1979-81, grad. rsch. assoc., 1987-88; clinician, cons. Netcare, Inc., Columbus, 1986-87; social worker, pvt. practice Cancer and Chronic Illness Counseling, 1980—. Adj. faculty Ohio State U., 1976-77, 84-85; cons. Harding Hosp., Columbus, 1994—, psychologist, 1998—; cons. Kids n' Kamp, Columbus, 1988—, Hospice of Columbus, 1983-85, Multiple Sclerosis Arthritis Prog., Columbus, 1982-85, Family Counseling/Crittenden Svcs., Columbus, 1982, Cystic Fibrosis Cen. Ohio, 1983. Author: To Find the Invisible Child; author/editor: Franklin County Community Cancer Resource Guide, 1975; designer/editor: (pamphlet) Make Today Count, 1979; developer breast cancer therapy support group prog., Woman to Woman, 1982-86. Chmn. unit mem. LWV, Columbus, 1972, 73; adv. com. Franklin County Unit Am. Cancer Soc., 1976-84; steering com. Make Today Count (cancer patient group), Columbus, 1977-83, others. Nominated for Jefferson award J.C. Penney, 1982; recipient Outstanding Human Svc. award Ohio State U., 1987. Diplomate Am. Bd. Examiners in Social Work; mem. NASW, Cen. Ohio Psychol. Assn. (membership chairperson), Ohio Psychological Assn., Golden Key. Democrat. Methodist. Avocations: tennis, swimming, cooking, reading, travel, writing poetry. Home and Office: 1260 Clubview Blvd S Columbus OH 43235-1632

MORRISON, JAMES FREDERICK, management consultant; b. Evanston, Ill., Aug. 12, 1933; s. Paul Leslie and Carolyn Lola (Rosemeier) M.; m. Myra Val Wokoun, June 22, 1957; children: Myra Hollie Morrison Nielsen, Cynthia Leslie Morrison. BA, Northwestern U., 1955, MBA, 1958. CPA, Wis. Accounting mgr. Froedtert Malt Corp., Milw., 1958-61; asst. controller, asst. v.p. Northwestern Nat. Ins. Co., 1961-65; controller Eutectic Welding Alloys Corp., Flushing, N.Y., 1965-68; internal auditor Sterling Drug, N.Y.C., 1968-69; controller Internat. Flavors and Fragrances, 1970-76, mng. dir., v.p. Europe London, 1977-80, v.p. new bus. group U.S. N.Y.C., 1981-84, v.p. export and communications U.S. Hazlet, N.J., 1984-96, cons., 1996—. Instr. fin. Marquette U., 1960-65. Co-chmn. Milw. Festival of Arts, 1965; treas. Manhasset Student Aid Assn., 1970—71; mem. Manhasset (N.Y.) Bd. Edn., 1970—75, v.p., 1975, United Fund Manhasset, 1971—72; chmn. priorities com. United Way Monmouth County, 1992, 1993, strategic planning com., 1995—97; elder First Presbyn. Ch., Red Bank, NJ, 1996—2000, sec., treas., 2000—; bd. dirs. United Way Monmouth County, 1991—99, Monmouth Ocean Found. for Ednl. Enhancement, 1996—. Lt. USAF, 1955—57, lt. USAFR, 1958—68. Mem. AICPA, Fin. Execs. Inst. (pres. L.I. chpt. 1975-76), Internat. Trade Facilitation Coun. (vice-chmn. 1991-92), Wis. Soc. CPA's, Internat. Commerce Club N.J., Systems and Procedures Assn. (pres. Milw. chpt. 1965), Culver Acad. Alumni Club Milw. (pres. 1965), Internat. Srs. Amateur Golf Soc. (treas. 1998—), Eastern Sr. Golf Assn. (treas. 1994-98, 2d v.p. 1999-2000, 1st v.p. 2000—, internat. team capt. 1994-99), Rumson Country Club (bd. dirs. 1996—), Beta Gamma Sigma. Presbyterian. Avocation: golf. Home and Office: 124 Silvermist Ct Little Silver NJ 07739-1813

MORRISON, JAMES KENT, higher education administrator; b. Mpls., Sept. 1, 1940; s. James L. and Elsie L. (Tasher) M.; m. Dorothy Jeanne Darke, Dec. 29, 1977; children: Michael L., Mark T., Malcolm A. BA, U. Va., 1962; MA, Ea. N.Mex. U., 1965, U. Wash., 1966, PhD, 1970. Prof., assoc. grad. dean U. Utah, Salt Lake City, 1970-89; dean Grad. Sch. U. R.I., Kingston, 1989-95; v.p. for acad. affairs Walden U., Mpls., 1995-99, pres., 1999—2002, chancellor, 2002—. Bd. govs. U. Press of New Eng., Hanover, N.H., 1991-95; mem. exec. com. Coun. for Rsch. Policy & Grad. Edn., Nat. Assn. State Univs. and Land Grant Colls., Washington, 1992-95. Pres. Com. on Fg. Rels., Salt Lake City, 1985-89; bd. dirs. Coun. Grad. Schs., Washington, 1993-96. 1st lt. USAF, 1962-65. NSF fellow, 1968-70, David P. Gardner fellow U. Utah Bd. Regents, 1977; Fulbright-Hays scholar Coun. for Internat. Exch. of Scholars, 1983-84. Mem. Pi Kappa Alpha. Home: 2420 Lee Ave N Minneapolis MN 55422 Office: Walden U 155 5th Ave S Ste 200 Minneapolis MN 55401-2511 E-mail: jkm@waldenu.edu.

MORRISON, JAMES R. retired banker; b. Duluth, Minn., May 1, 1924; s. Earl Angus and Jessie (McLean) M.; m. Clarice Mae Wolf, June 5, 1949; children— Kenneth, Alan, Jane, Richard MBA, U. Chgo., 1976. Br. mgr. Parkersburg State Bank, Iowa, 1947-49; asst. cashier Bank of Sparta, Wis., 1949-50; cashier Tobacco Exchange Bank, Edgerton, 1950-53; sr. v.p. Fed. Res. Bank Chgo., 1953-89, ret. Bd. dirs. Bank of Tokyo-Mitsubishi Chgo., 1994-98; chmn. subcom. on credits and discounts Fed. Res. Sys., Chgo., 1984-86; mem. Mt. Prospect Fin. Commn., 1989-2001. Served with U.S. Army, 1943-46, ETO

MORRISON, JAMES WILLIAM, JR. lobbyist, government relations consultant; b. Bluefield, W.Va., Jan. 14, 1936; s. James William and Winnie Ella (Hendricks) M.; m. Marva Elizabeth Tillman, Aug. 8, 1957 (div.); children: Traquita Renee, James William III; m. Jean Murray Barber, May 15, 2001; 1 stepchild, Susannah Claire. BA, W.Va. State Coll., 1957; MPA, U. Dayton, 1970. Inventory mgr. Dayton Air Force Depot/Def. Electronics Supply Ctr., 1959-63; mgmt. specialist Air Force Logistics Command, Dayton, 1963-72; exec. asst. to dir. mgmt. sys. NASA, Washington, 1972-74; sr. mgmt. assoc. Exec. Office of Pres. Office Mgmt. and Budget, 1974-79; asst. dir. econ. and govt. U.S. Office of Pers. Mgmt., 1979, dir. congl. rels., 1979-81, assoc. dir. compensation, 1981-87; sr. mgt. CNA Ins. Co., 1987-88; pres. Morrison Assocs., 1988—. Vis. lectr. pub. exec. project SUNY Albany, 1974-76. Contbr. articles to profl. jours. Mem. adv. com. Dayton Bd. Edn., 1971. With U.S. Army, 1957-59. Recipient Presdl. Rank award of Disting. Exec., 1985. Mem. Alpha Phi Alpha, Pi Delta Phi, Pi Alpha Alpha. Republican. Presbyterian. Home: 35056 N 80th Way Scottsdale AZ 85262

MORRISON, JEANNINE R. concert pianist, teacher of piano; b. Atlanta, Mar. 26, 1930; d. George Elliott and Maggie S. Romer; m. Don T. Morrison, Oct. 27, 1967; children: George, Julie, Alan. BMusic, Rollins Coll., Winter Park, Fla., 1951; MA, Columbia U., 1953; Licentiate in Piano Performance, Royal Acad. Music, London, 1979. Master level cert. Music Tchrs. Nat. Assn. Organist, dir. music Episcopal Ch. of the Epiphany, Atlanta, 1953-58, Emory Presbyn. Ch., Atlanta, 1966-69; instr. music Ga. State U., 1970-72; prof. music Clayton Coll. and State U., Morrow, Ga., 1972-92, prof. emerita of music, 1992—; pvt. piano studio Decatur, 1953—. Mem. piano selection com. Fulbright Scholarships, N.Y.C., 1996, 97, 98; adjudicator Nat. Guild Piano Tchrs., Austin, Tex., 1955—; adjudicator for numerous piano tchr. orgns., 1967—; lecture, recitals, workshops, masterclasses in various locations. CD recs. include A Virtuoso Duo Piano Showcase, 1991, Duo-Piano Favorties, 1996, Festive Duo, 1996; piano debut recitals at Town Hall, N.Y.C., 1958, Nat. Gallery Art, Washington, 1959. Mem. DeKalb County Hist. Soc., Decatur, 1992—, DeKalb County Arts Coun., Decatur, 1997—. Mem. Music Tchrs. Nat. Assn., Nat. Guild Piano Tchrs., Leschetizsky Assn. Am., Liszt Soc. Am., Decatur Music Tchrs. Assn., Atlanta Music Club (pres. 1996-98, Outstanding Svc. award 1994). Republican. Episcopalian. Avocations: reading, bicycling, walking. Home: 609 E Ponce De Leon Ave Decatur GA 30030-1944

MORRISON, JOHN M. hospital administrator, bank executive; Owner, CEO Ctrl. Bank Group, Golden Valley, Minn.; chmn., CEO (interim) Allina Health Sys., 2001—. Mem. Fairview U. Med. Ctr. Bd., Fairview Health Sys. Corp. Bd.; chmn. exec. com. bd. trustees U. St. Thomas; former mem. bd. govs., chmn. bd.'s fin. com. U. Minn. Acad. Health Ctr.; former mem. Johns Hopkins Medicine bd. visitors Johns Hopkins U. Mem.: U. St. Thomas Sch. Law (mem. bd. govs. , founder John. M. Morrison Ctr. Entrepreneurship). Office: Allina Hosps and Clinics 710 E 24th St Minneapolis MN 55404*

MORRISON, JOHN HADDOW, JR. engineering company executive; b. Bozeman, Mont., Aug. 24, 1933; s. John Haddow Sr. and Rosalie (Lehrkind) M.; m. Shirley Easbey, Sept. 11, 1954; children: Robert, Richard; m. Minh Le, Apr. 25, 2001. BS, Mont. State U., 1955. Registered profl. engr., Mont., Nev., Utah, Ariz., Calif.; registered land surveyor, Mont. Project engr. Morrison-Maierle, Inc., Helena, Mont., 1957—64, chief airport design, 1964—73, chief exec. officer, 1973—88, chmn., 1998—2000, dir. emeritus, 2000—, pres., 2000—02. Bd. dirs. Mont. State U. Found., Inc., 1983—, chmn. 1992-94; sec.-treas. Helena YMCA, 1977-80. With U.S. Army 1955-57. Mem. ASCE, NSPE (pres. Helena chpt. 1968-69, Outstanding Young Engr., Helena chpt. 1965), Cons. Engrs. Council Mont. (past sec., past v.p., pres. 1986-87). Lodges: Kiwanis, Masons. Methodist. Avocations: golf, photography. Home: 2415 E Windsong Dr Phoenix AZ 85048 Office: Morrison Maierle Inc 120 N 44th St Ste 410 Phoenix AZ 85034-1822 E-mail: jmorrison@m-m.net.

MORRISON, JOHN HORTON, lawyer; b. Sept. 15, 1933; BBA, U. N.Mex., 1955; BA, U. Oxford, 1957; JD, Harvard U., 1962. Bar: Ill. 1962, U.S. Supreme Ct. 1966. Assoc. Kirkland & Ellis, Chgo., 1962-67, ptnr., 1968-99. Named Hon. Officer Most Excellent Order Brit. Empire, 1994; Rhodes scholar. Mem. ABA, Internat. Arbitration (arbitrator, mediator London Ct.), Internat. Bar Assn., Am. Arbitration Assn. (internat., large complex case and Chgo. panels), Assn. Am. Rhodes Scholars (pres. 1998—), Chgo. Bar Assn., Chgo. Internat. Dispute Resolution Assn. (dir.). Home: 2717 Lincoln St Evanston IL 60201-2042 Business E-Mail: john_morrison@kirkland.com. E-mail: jhmobe@aol.com.

MORRISON, JOSEPH YOUNG, transportation consultant; b. Flushing, N.Y., Jan. 4, 1951; s. William Barrier and Barbara Helen (Lowe) M.; children: Susan Parker, Travis Barrier. AS, Montreat (N.C.)-Anderson Coll., 1971; BA, Oglethorpe U., 1989. Dept. head J.C. Penny & Co., Atlanta, 1971-74; uniform patrol officer City of Atlanta, 1974-80; spl. agt. U.S. Dept. Transp., Atlanta, 1980-82; group dir. safety and ins. Western Express, 1982-85; dir. safety Taylor Maid Transp., Albany, 1985-86; v.p. risk mgmt. Burlington Motor Carriers, Inc., Daleville, Ind., 1986-96; pres. Motor Carrier Safety Cons. Inc., Noblesville, 1996-97; v.p. safety & risk mgmt. LinkAmerica Corp., Tulsa, Okla., 1997—; pres. Nat. Transp. Cons., Inc., Noblesville, Ind., 1997—. Contbg. author: Guide to Handling Hazardous Material, 1986. Mem. Am. Trucking Assn. (hazardous materials com. 1982-86, chmn. injury control com. 1984-88, safety mgmt. coun. 1982—, interstate carrier conf. 1985—, nat. freight claims and security coun. 1985—, Safety Improvement awards, Accident Reduction awards, Injury Reduction awards), Kenilworth Civic Club (treas. Stone Mountain Ga. chpt. 1981-83, pres. 1983-84), Am. Soc. Safety Engrs., Sertoma Club, Sigma Alpha Epsilon. Methodist. Avocations: home remodeling, restoring old cars. Home: 7111 Oakview Cir Noblesville IN 46060-9419 Office: Nat Transp Cons 1109 S 10th St PO Box 2067 Noblesville IN 46061-2067 E-mail: jmorrison@ntconsult.com.

MORRISON, KAREN MARGARET, family practice physician; b. Columbus, Ohio, Jan. 7, 1963; d. Gilbert and Margaret (DeVictor) Raines; m. Scott William Morrison, Oct. 26, 1991; children: Jonathan Scott, Eleanor Margaret, Jennifer Marie. BS in Edn., Ohio State U., 1986, MD, 1992. Diplomate Am. Bd. Family Practice. Resident in family practice Mt. Carmel Health Sys., Columbus, 1992-95; family practice physician Hilliard (Ohio) Family Health, 1995-97; assoc. dir. residency Mt. Carmel Health Sys., 1997—. Website developer www.fphandheld.com : The Family Physician's Guide to Handheld Computers; author: The Handheld Computer Medical Software Craze: MD NEt Guide, 2001; co-author: Family Medicine, 2000, Book 1 and Book 2, 2000. Mem. Am. Acad. Family Physician, Christian Med. & Dental Soc., Ohio Acad. Family Physicians, Soc. of Tchrs. of Family Medicine, Ctrl. Ohio Acad. Family Physicians (pres.-elect 2002). Avocations: piano, drumming, golf, basketball, Bible study.

MORRISON, KENNETH DOUGLAS, author, columnist; b. Mpls., Apr. 1, 1918; s. Kenneth Mortimore and Florence Myrtle (Sutton) M.; m. Helen Curtis, Feb. 25, 1943; children: Kenneth D., Sally, Steven C., Mary. AB, Carleton Coll., 1940; grad. study, U. Miami, 1940-41, U. Minn., 1941. Free lance writer, Mpls., 1941; editor publs. Minn. Dept. Conservation, 1942-47; Minn. rep. to Nat. Audubon Soc., 1947-49, dir. pub relations, editor Audubon mag., 1949-56, v.p., 1955-56; dir. Mountain Lake Sanctuary and Singing Tower Am. Found., 1956-80, dir. environ. concerns, 1980-82, fellow, 1982-83; syndicated nature-conservation newspaper columnist 4 papers, 1985—. Audubon tour lectr., 1958-63; interviewer naturalists Wildlife Unltd., TV sta. WOR-TV, N.Y.C., 1951- 52; Mem. Minn. Bird Commn., 1951-54; trustee emeritus Fla. Nature Conservancy; trustee Fla. Conservation Found.; v.p., trustee Conservation 70's; mem. Gov. Fla. Natural Resources Com., State Parks Adv. Council, 1971-79 Author: Favorite Birds of America, 1951, Favorite Animals of America, 1951, Mountain Lake Almanac, 1984; Compiler: (with Mrs. M. E. Herz) Where to Find Birds In Minnesota, 1950. Bd. dirs. Defenders Wildlife; adv. bd. Webber Coll., 1969— . Recipient Gov. Fla. Wildlife Conservation award, 1960, Gulf Oil Conservation award, 1982, Feinstone Environ. award SUNY, 1987, Carleton Coll. Disting. Achievement award, 1990, Grassroots Leadership award Fla. Nature Conservancy, 1996. Mem. Wilson Ornithol. Soc., Wilderness Soc., Greenpeace, Native Plant Soc., Fla. Audubon Soc. (pres., Award of Merit 1964, Cruickshank Conservation award 1993), Hawk Mountain Sanctuary Assn. (bd. sponsors), Nature Conservancy, Sierra Club, Friends of Earth, Green Horizon Land Trust (bd. dirs. 1999—), Pi Delta Epsilon. Methodist. Home: 1351 Hollister Rd Babson Park FL 33827-9684 *We ought to keep in mind that we are mammals and that we need to renew regularly our contact with the basic, simple life of soil, sun, water, animals and trees.*

MORRISON, L. WARREN, computer engineer; BSEE, CCNY, 1951; MS in Med. and Indsl. Electronics, Bklyn. Poly. Inst., 1951—52; PhD in Elec. Engring., U. So. Calif., 1969. Pres. Direct Data Corp., 1971—83; asst. v.p. BDM Internat., Inc., 1984—89; chief scientist Info. Technologies Group, 1990—; vis. scientist Software Engring. Inst., Carnegie Mellon U., Pitts., 1994—. Mem. Army Sci. Bd., 1978—87, 1996—. Contbr. Recipient Cert. of Appreciation for Patriotic Civilian Svc., 1987, Recognition for Outstanding Performance, Office of Dep. Chief of Staff for Ops. and Plans, Dept. of Army, 1987. Mem.: IEEE, N.Y. Acad. Scis., Eta Kappa Nu. Office: Software Engineering Inst Carnegie Mellon Univ 4500 Fifth Ave Pittsburgh PA 15213-3890*

MORRISON, LISA ANN, clinical nurse specialist; b. Mar. 20, 1952; M in Nursing, U. Ks., Kansas City, 1980. Psychiat. clin. nurse specialist pvt. practice, Leawood, Kans. Office: 8014 State Line Rd Leawood KS 66208

MORRISON, MALCOLM HAROLD, health care executive; b. Cambridge, Mass., Aug. 5, 1943; s. Theodore and Elizabeth (Shelman) M.; m. Judith Louise Parker, Aug. 20, 1967 (div. May 1995); children: Andrew David, Seth Gabriel; m. Jacquelyn Larson Kelley, May 7, 1995. BSc, McGill U., Montreal, Can., 1965; MA, Boston U., 1967; MPA, U. Mich., 1968; PhD, Brandeis U., 1974. Social sci. rsch. analyst, economist U.S. Social Security Adminstrn., Balt., 1973-77, grant/contract officer Washington, 1977-79, dir. disability studies Washington, Balt., 1986-90; chief rsch. support staff U.S. Dept. Labor, Washington, 1979-83; faculty rsch. assoc. Wharton Sch., Phila., 1983-85; dir. rsch. Nat. Assn. Rehab. Facilities, Washington, 1990-92; v.p. Continental Med. Systems, Mechanicsburg, Pa., 1993-95; pres. Morrison Informatics, Harrisburg, 1996—. Bd. dirs. Am. Soc. Aging, San Francisco, Com. Accreditation Rehab. Facilities, Tucson, Fedn. Am. Health Systems, Washington. Author: Economics of Aging: The Future of Retirement, 1982; contbr. articles to profl. jours. Co-chair Aging Disability and Rehab. Network Am. Soc. Aging, San Francisco, 1993-95; mem. sci. adv. bd. Henry H. Kessler Found., West Orange, N.J., 1995—; bd. dirs. Recreation and Revitalization Connection, Inc., Chevy Chase, Md., 1989—. Mary E. Switzer fellow Nat. Rehab. Assn., 1986, 91, Interovernmental fellow U. Pa., 1983-85; Comp Health scholar Kenan-Flagler Bus. Sch. U. N.C., 1995. Fellow Gerontol. Soc. Am. Home and Office: Morrison Informatics Inc 1150 Lancaster Blvd Ste 101 Mechanicsburg PA 17055-4495 E-mail: informatic@informaticinc.com.

MORRISON, MANLEY GLENN, real estate investor, former army officer; b. Weston, W.Va., July 29, 1915; s. Henry Frank and Alice (Riffle) M.; m. Ida Lerlene Johnson, Dec. 12, 1942 (dec. 1982); children: Manley James (dec.), Richard Glenn, Sandra Lynn.; m. Samma Annette Muffley, July 30, 1983. BS, U. Md., 1958; MA, Am. U., 1960; postgrad., U. Pitts., 1961, Ind. U., 1968; grad., Command and Gen. Staff Coll., Ft. Leavenworth, Kans., 1956, Army War Coll., Carlisle Barracks, Pa., 1960, DeVry Inst. Tech., 1974; D.H.L., Mass. Coll. Optometry, 1973. Table waiter Mills Cafeteria, Columbus, Ohio, 1935-36; mgr. Speer's Cafe, Twin Falls, Idaho, 1937-38; exec. chef steward U.P. R.R., Sun Valley, 1939-42; commd. 2d lt. U.S. Army, 1942, advanced through grades to brig. gen., 1969; chief statis. analysis Hdqrs. EUCOM and USAREUR, Berlin, Nurnberg, Heidelberg, 1948-52; chief Manpower Div., Office Surgeon Gen., Washington, 1952-55; comptroller Walter Reed Army Med. Center, 1956-59; dir. adminstrn. and asst. exec. officer Office Surgeon Gen., 1960-62; chief of systems analysis Office of Mgmt., dep. chief of staff for logistics Dept. Army Gen. Staff, 1962-64; exec. officer, dir. personnel and adminstrn. Office of Surgeon, Hdqrs. U.S. Army Europe, Heidelberg, 1964-67; exec. officer Office of Comptroller, Office Army Surgeon Gen., Washington, 1967-69; chief of Army Med. Service Corps, 1969-73; ret., 1973; self-employed as real estate investor, 1973—. Community Scout leader, Heidelberg, 1948-52; bd. dirs. Teen Clubs, Am. Youth Assocs., Heidelberg, 1967; chmn. Residents' Coun. Freedom Pla., Peoria, Ariz. Decorated D.S.M., Legion of Merit, Bronze Star, Commendation medal with oak leaf cluster; recipient Wisdon award of Honor, Wisdon Soc.; named to Wisdon Hall of Fame. Mem. Assn. Mil. Surgeons U.S., Alumni Assn. Army War Coll., Fed. Health Care Execs. Inst. Alumni Assn., Baylor U. Alumni Assn., Phi Kappa Phi, Pi Sigma Alpha. Clubs: Union Hills Country (Sun City, Ariz.) (bd. dirs. 1985-86, pres.). Lodges: Masons. Republican. Home: Unit 113 13373 N Plaza Del Rio Blvd # 7764 Peoria AZ 85381-4873 *I have sincerely tried to assess each problem and challenge in a positive manner. Once the decision has been made and an objective plan established, I have attempted to achieve the objectives while avoiding what I consider the most Common Mistakes of Man: (1) the delusion that individual advancement is made by crushing others, (2) the tendency to worry about things that cannot be changed or corrected, (3) insisting that a thing is impossible because we cannot accomplish it, (4) neglecting development and refinement of the mind and not acquiring the habit of reading and studying, (5) refusing to set aside trivial preference, (6) attempting to compel other persons to believe and live as we do, (7) attempting to quantify in mathematical terms the depth of human experience.*

MORRISON, MARGARET L. artist, educator, consultant; b. Atlanta, Oct. 06; d. Watson Russell Sr and Eva D. Morrison. BS in Edn., U. Ga., 1970. Cert. tchr., Ga. Supr. KPMG Peat Marwick, Atlanta, 1971-97; art tchr. Decatur (Ga.) City Schs., Decatur, 1997-99; pvt. instr. in art and edn., 2000—. Pvt. practice cons. interior design, 1998—. Exhbns. include Coastal Ctr. for the Arts, St. Simons Island, Ga., Gallery One, St. Simons Island, Decatur Arts Alliance, Acad. Midi, Paris, The Glynn County Art Assn., Jekyll Island, Ga., L'Orangerie Mus., Paris. Royal patron Hutt River Province, Queensland, Australia, 1995; active High Mus. Art, Atlanta, 1989—; bd. govs. Internat. Biog. Ctr.; adv. bd. Am. Biog. Inst. Fellow Acad. Midi (hon.); mem. DAR, NAFE, AAUW, Internat. Platform Assn., Nat. Mus. Women in Arts, Allied Artists of Ga., Pen and Ink, U. Ga. Alumni Soc. Home and Office: PO Box 2590 Decatur GA 30031-2590

MORRISON, MARTHA KAYE, photolithography engineer, executive; b. San Jose, Calif., Oct. 5, 1955; d. Myrle K. and Arthena R. Morrison; 1 child, Katherine A. AA, West Valley Coll., Saratoga, Calif., 1978. Prodn. worker Signetics Co., Sunnyvale, Calif., 1973-75, equipment engr., 1976-78, 79-80, prodn. supr., 1978-79; expediter Monolithic Memories, 1975-76; photolithography engr. KTI Chems., 1980-81; founder, chief engr., CEO, pres. Optalign, Inc., Livermore, Forest Ranch, Calif., 1981—. Participant West Valley Coll. Tennis Team # 1 Singles and Doubles, 1976-78; regional profl. ranking NCTA Opens Singles/Doubles, 1982-85, 93, 94, 95, 96, 97, 98, rankings 15-20 singles/#2-#8 doubles, Culiacan, Mex., 1998, ITF 10 K satellite ; instr. tennis Chico Racquet Club, 1994, Butte Creek Country Club, 1995—; participant exhbn. tennis match with Rosie Cosals and Billie Jean King, 1994, 95; USPTA tchg. profl., 1992—. Dir. benefit Boys & Girls Club of Chico. Named Champion Chico Open Finalist Woodridge Open, 1994, 1993 #2 NCTA Women's Open Doubles, Doubles #3, 1994, Tracy Open, 1996, Vacaville Open, 1998, Winner 3 pts WTA circuit; WTA world ranking women's doubles, 1999. Mem. USPTA (cert.), Tennis Profl. Chico Racquet Club, Butte Creek Country Club. Office: PO Box 718 Forest Ranch CA 95942-0718

MORRISON, MARTIN, computer systems analyst; b. Oakland, Calif., Mar. 28, 1947; s. Raymond Earl and June (Cabral) M. AB with distinction, U. Calif., Berkeley, 1967, MA, 1969, postgrad., 1969-73. Certified (life) nat. tournament dir.; cert. jr./community coll. tchr. (life), Calif. Instr. classics and English composition U. Calif. at Berkeley, 1967-73; instr. legal argument Boalt Hall Law Sch., 1972; with exec. office CF Air Freight, Inc., 1979-83, asst. to traffic mgr. for spl. projects, 1982-83, computer systems mgr., 1982-83; computer systems analyst Qantel Bus. Computers, 1983-86, sr. computer systems analyst, 1986-92; sr. tech. writer Shared Med. Systems, 1992-96, supr. tech. writing, 1996-98, mgr. tech. writing, 1998—. Mem. Amateur Chamber Music Players, 1978—. Author: Writing Argument, 1972, USCF Yearbooks, 1974-76, Official Rules of Chess, 1975, 77, Chess Competitor's Handbook, 1980, Latin Works for Transparent Language Computer Program, 1992-93; editor: Chess Voice, 1968-73, Keeping Ancient Rome Alive, 1987-89; contbg. author: Fundamentals of Management, 3d edit., 2000; chess editor: Oakland Tribune, 1965-66; columnist Via Lorenzo, 1987-88, Metric Today, 1985—; pub., bus. mgr. Chess Life & Rev., 1977-78, Bancroft Music Sch., 1958-60. Asst. concertmaster Berkeley Chamber Chorus and Orch., 1980-83; concertmaster Oakland Philharm., 1987-90, bd. dirs., corp. sec., 1988-90; 1st violin Albany Trio, 1987-91, Mostly Baroque Ensemble, 1999-2000; vol. staff Chabot Sci. Ctr., 1981-84, chmn. computer system mgmt. staff; sec., treas. AstroSoft, 1983-87. Schola Gregoriana San Francisco, 1989-92, Schola Cantemus, 1992-95; dir. St. John Schola, 1995—. Fellow U.S. Metric Assn. (chmn. consumer edn. com. 1984—, Spl. Citation 1986, cert. advanced metrication specialist 1987); mem. Am. Philol. Assn., Am. Classical League, Eastbay Astron. Soc. (bd. dirs. 1981-84, v.p. 1983-84), Internat. Assn. Chess Press (v.p. 1973-77), Soc. for Tech. Comm. (sr.), Chess Journalists Assn. (pres. 1972-75), World Chess Fedn. (internat. life arbiter, mem. rules com. 1973-78, chmn. 1976-78), U.S. Chess Fedn. (bd. dels. 1968-78, 1st v.p. Pacific Region 1972-73, nat. sec. 1972-75, tech. dir. 1973-76, exec. dir. 1976-78, Disting. Vol. award, 1982, Spl. citation, 1984, Disting. Svc. award 1995), Calif. Alumni Assn. (life, scholarship com., chmn. 1987-93, Disting. Chmn. award 1990), San Lorenzo Garden Homes Assn. (v.p./sec. 1985-86, pres. 1986-92), Mensa, Phi Beta Kappa.

MORRISON, MICHAEL DEAN, lawyer, law educator; BA with high honors, Okla. U., 1971, JD, 1974. Bar: Okla. 1975, Kans. 1975, Tex. 1981, U.S. Ct. Appeals (5th cir.) 1980, U.S. Dist. Ct. (ea., no. and so. dists.) Tex. 1983, U.S. Dist. Ct. (we. dist.) Tex. 1980, U.S. Dist. Ct. (we. dist.) Okla. 1975, U.S. Supreme Ct. 1979. Pvt. practice, Wichita, Kans., 1974-75; asst. dir. Law Ctr. Okla. U., 1975-77, asst. prof., 1977-80, assoc. prof., 1980-82, prof. law, 1982-90. William J. Boswell chair of law, 1990—. Mayor City of Waco, 1996—2000; ordained elder 1st Presbyn. Ch. Waco, stated clk. of session, 1996—98. Mem. Order of Coif, Phi Beta Kappa. Office: PO Box 97288 Waco TX 76798-7288

MORRISON, MURDO DONALD, architect; b. Feb. 21, 1919; s. Alexander and Johanna (Macaulay) M.; m. Judy D. Morrison (dec. May 1999); children from previous marriage: Paula L., Reed A., Anne H. BArch, Lawrence Tech. U., 1943. Individual practice arch., Detroit, 1949, Klamath Falls, Oreg., 1949-65, Oakland, Calif., 1965-78; ptnr. Morrison Assocs., San Francisco, 1978-85, Burlingame, Calif., 1985-89, Redwood City, 1989—. V.p. Lakeridge Corp., 1968—, Oreg. Bd. Archtl. Examiners, 1961-65, chmn., 1964. Architect: Gilliam County Courthouse, 1955 (Progressive Arch. Design award), Chiloquin (Oreg.) Elem. Sch., 1963, Lakeridge Office Bldg., Reno, 1984, Provident Cen. Credit Union Bldg., Monterey, Calif., 1986, Embarcadero Fed. Credit Union, San Francisco, 1991, Warrick Residence, The Sea Ranch, Calif., 1996, Spectre Industries Office Bldg., Milpitas, Calif., 1997, Rosenbaum Residency, Los Altos Hills, Calif., 1998, McCabe Residence, Los Altos Hills, 2001, others; master planner, Lakeridge, a 945-acre cmty. in Reno, v.p. devel., 1963—. Mem. Town Coun. Klamath Falls, 1955-57; co-chmn. Oakland Pride Com., 1968-77; mem. Redwood City Gen. Plan Com., 1986, Emerald Hills Design Rev. Bd., 1990-97; vice chmn. Redwood City Design Rev. Com., 1991—. With USN, 1943-46. Recipient Progressive Arch. award, 1955, Alumni of Yr. award Lawrence Inst., 1965. Mem. AIA (Archtl. fellow 2002, treas. East Bay, chmn. Oakland chpt., dir. San Mateo County chpt. 1996—, v.p.-elect 2001, pres. 2002-). Presbyterian. Home and Office: 3645 Jefferson Ave Redwood City CA 94062-3149 E-mail: mdmfaia@aziz.com.

MORRISON, PATRICE B. lawyer; b. St. Louis, July 8, 1948; d. Frank J. and Loretta (S.) Burgert; m. William Brian Morrison, Aug. 12, 1969; 1 child, W. Brett. AB, U. Miami, 1971, MA, 1972; JD, Am. U., 1975; LLM in Taxation, Georgetown U., 1978. Bar: Fla. 1975, D.C. 1977, N.Y. 1983. Atty. U.S. Dept. Treas., Washington, 1975-79; atty., ptnr. Nixon Hargrave Devans & Doyle, LLP, Palm Beach County, Fla., 1980-89, Nixon Peabody LLP (formerly Nixon, Hargrave, Devans & Doyle), Rochester, N.Y., 1989—. Bd. dirs. Rochester Friendly Sr. Svcs., Inc., 1996—. Contbr. articles to The Practical Lawyer. Bd. dirs. Alzheimer's Assn., Rochester, 1990-95, Nat. Women's Hall of Fame, 1990-92; mem. Rochester Women's Network; mem. exec. com. Estate Planning Coun. Rochester, 1992-95; dir. Cloverwood Sr. Living, Inc., 2000—. Mem. Am. Immigration Lawyers Assn. Republican. Office: Nixon Peabody LLP PO Box 31051 Rochester NY 14603-1051

MORRISON, PATRICIA KENNEALY, author; b. N.Y.C., Mar. 4, 1946; d. Joseph Gerard and Genevieve Mary (McDonald) Kennely; m. James Douglas Morrison, June 24, 1970 (dec. July 3, 1971). Student, St. Bonaventure U., 1963-65; BA, Harpur Coll., 1967. Editor Jazz & Pop Mag., N.Y.C., 1968-71; sr. copywriter RCA Records, 1971-73; copy dir. CBS Records, 1973-79, New Sch., N.Y.C., 1979-81; author, pres., CEO Lizard Queen Prodns., Inc., 1984—. Author: The Copper Crown, 1984, The Throne of Scone, 1986, The Silver Branch, 1988, The Hawk's Gray Feather, 1990, The Oak Above the Kings, 1994, The Hedge of Mist, 1996, Blackmantle, 1997, The Deer's Cry, 1998, Strange Days: My Life With and Without Jim Morrison, 1992; contbr.: Rock She Wrote, 1995; tech. advisor, actress The Doors, 1990-91. Mem.: Sovereign Mil. Order of Temple of Jerusalem (dame comdr.), Mensa. Democrat. Avocation: Celtic studies. Office: Lizard Queen Prodns Inc 151 1st Ave Ste 120 New York NY 10003-2965 also: Henry Morrison Inc PO Box 235 Bedford Hills NY 10507-0235 E-mail: lizard_queen@angelfire.com.

MORRISON, PORTIA OWEN, lawyer; b. Charlotte, N.C., Apr. 1, 1944; d. Robert Hall Jr. and Josephine Currier (Hutchison) M.; m. Alan Peter Richmond, June 19, 1976; 1 child, Anne Morrison. BA in English, Agnes Scott Coll., 1966; MA, U. Wis., 1967; JD, U. Chgo., 1978. Bar: Ill. 1978. Ptnr., mem. exec. com. Piper Rudnick, Chgo., 1978—. Lectr. in field. Pres. Girl Scouts of Chgo. Mem.: ABA, Comml. Real Estate Women, Chgo. Fin. Exch., Pension Real Estate Assn., Chgo. Bar Assn. (real property com., subcom. real property fin., alliance for women), Am. Coll. Real Estate Lawyers (treas., bd. govs.). Office: Piper Rudnick 203 N La Salle St Ste 1800 Chicago IL 60601-1210 E-mail: portia.morrison@piperrudnick.com.

MORRISON, RICHARD ALEX, software engineer; b. Phila., Aug. 13, 1940; s. Alexander and Victoria (Hochstein) M.; m. Jeanne Iverson, Nov. 7, 1971; m. Elly Von Scharnberg, May 17, 1994; children: Steve, Gary Vasiloff, Richard Wagner. BA, Coll. of Wooster, 1962; MS, U. Chgo., 1964, PhD, 1969. Prof. Talladega (Ala.) Coll., 1969-86; vis. scientist Nat. Inst. Stds./Tech., Gaithersburg, Md., 1986-89; software engr. Syntek, Bethesda, 1989-94, Naval Rsch. Lab., Washington, 1994, AT&T, Herndon, Va., 1995—. Cons., inventor Micro Tech. Unltd., Raleigh, N.C., 1984-86. Mem. AAAS, IEEE. Avocations: Hungarian music & dance. Home: 135 Eagle View Dr Charleston SC 29414-5761 E-mail: ellyandrich@knology.net.

MORRISON, ROBERT ELIOT, ophthalmologist; b. Bklyn., Apr. 6, 1962; s. Alan N. and Judy M. (Fenichel) M.; m. Amy Ellen Bardasch, June 23, 1985; children: Abby, Rachel. BA, U. Rochester, 1984; MD, Chgo. Med. Sch., 1988. Diplomate Am. Bd. Ophthalmology. Intern Evanston (Ill.) Hosp., 1988-89; resident Cook County Hosp., Chgo., 1991-94; pvt. practice Bethlehem, Pa., 1995—. Mem. Am. Acad. Ophthalmology, AMA, Pa. Med. Soc., Pa. Acad. Ophthalmology, Alpha Omega Alpha. Home: 1493 Buck Trail Rd Allentown PA 18104-2058 Office: 5325 Northgate Dr Ste 206 Bethlehem PA 18017 Fax: 610-882-9885.

MORRISON, ROBERT HAYWOOD, real estate developer; b. Hickory, N.C., Mar. 27, 1927; s. Charles Tyson and Rebecca Grace (Tuttle) M. AB, U. N.C., 1947, MA, 1948. Pres. Dialectic Soc., Chapel Hill, N.C., 1945; editor Daily Tar Heel, 1945-46; pres. Publs. Bd., 1946-47; asst. instr. U. Ill., Urbana, 1948-49; chmn. bus. communication dept. U. Kans., Lawrence, 1949-51; editor Daily News-Enterprise, Newton, N.C., 1952-54; prof. Winthrop Coll., Rock Hill, S.C., 1955-59; pres., gen. ptnr. Morrison and Co., Charlotte, N.C., 1955—; pres. Catawba Captial Corp., 1961—. Pres. Investors Corp. S.C., Columbia. Author: A Guide to Bank Correspondence, 1949, Problems and Cases in Business Writing, 1951, Better Letters, 1952, Profit-Making Letters for Hotels and Restaurants, 1959, (with others) Modern Journalism, 1962, Bank Correspondence Handbook, 1964; contbr. articles to profl. jours. Chmn. 1st Rep. precinct, Charlotte, 1970's. Mem. Charlotte Region Bd. Realtors, Phi Beta Kappa, Delta Sigma Pi. Lodges: Rotary (Charlotte) (Paul Harris fellow). Methodist. Office: Catawba Capital Corp 1373 E Morehead St Ste 2 Charlotte NC 28204-2900 E-mail: morrisonrh@hotmail.com.

MORRISON, ROBERT LEE, physical scientist; b. Omaha, Nov. 22, 1932; s. Robert Alton and Lulu Irene (Ross) M.; m. Sharon Faith Galliher, Feb. 19, 1966; children: Dennis, Karyn, Cheryl, Tamara, Traci. BA, U. Pacific, Stockton, Calif., 1957, MS, 1960. Chief chemist Gallo Winery, Modesto, Calif., 1957-66; rsch. scientist Lawrence Livermore Nat. Lab., Livermore, 1966-69, sr. rsch. scientist, 1973-93; pres. Poolinator, Inc., Gardena, 1970-72; owner R.L. Morrison Techs., Modesto, 1993—. Cons., speaker, presenter in field. Contbr. numerous articles to profl. jours.; patentee in field. Recipinet Excellence in Nuclear Weapons award U.S. Dept. Energy, 1990, others. Mem. Am. Chem. Soc. Avocations: flying, skiing, scuba diving, photography. Home: 1117 Springcreek Dr Modesto CA 95355-4820

MORRISON, ROBERT REID, retired language educator; b. Gainesville, Fla., Aug. 1, 1929; s. Robert Reid Morrison and Florrie O. Ergle; m. Patricia Ann Carey, Aug. 16, 1951; children: Gary, Karen. BA, George Washington U., 1950; MA, Middlebury Coll., 1954; PhD, U. Fla., 1963. Asst. prof. East Carolina U., Greenville, NC, 1958—64, assoc. prof., 1964—67; prof., chmn. modern langs. So. Adventist U., Collegedale, Tenn., 1967—87; assoc. prof. Presbyn. Coll., Clinton, SC, 1988—94; ret., 1994. Dir. NDEA Insts. for Tchrs. Spanish East Carolina U., Greenville, 1965, Greenville, 67. Author: Lope de Vega and the Comedia de Santos, 2000; contbr. articles to profl. jours. Mem.: MLA, South Atlantic MLA, Am. Assn. Tchrs. Spanish and Portuguese, The Comedlantes, Nat. Rlwy. Hist. Soc. Avocations: music, travel.

MORRISON, ROBERT THOMAS, aerospace engineering and marketing consultant; b. Manson, Iowa, June 4, 1918; s. Charles Henry and Ida Magdeline (Fuessley) M.; m. Callie Louise Warren, July, 25, 1942; children: Linda Ann, Allan Charles, Janis Lou. BS in Mech. Engring., Iowa State U., 1942; MS in Engring., U. Calif., Los Angeles, 1961. Engr. Gen. Electric Co., Schenectady, N.Y., 1942-45; sales engr., inventory supr. Gen. Electric Supply Corp., Omaha, 1945-50; pres. Morrison Mfg. Co., 1950-52; elec. system designer Douglas Aircraft, Long Beach and Santa Monica, Calif., 1952-58; system engr., proposal mgr. Rockwell Internat., Downey, Seal Beach, Anaheim, 1958-81; freelance cons. Garden Grove/Palm Desert, 1981—2000. Originator, coord. system engring. program West Coast U., L.A., 1963-71, assoc. dir. devel., 1972; moderator Rockwell System Engring. Seminar, 1964. Author: Proposal Manager's Guide, 1972, Proposal Style Guide, 1988, Proposal Publications Guide, 1988. Lay minister Crystal Cathedral, Garden Grove, 1980-97, dir. New Hope Telephone Counseling Ctr., 1990-95; Garden Grove Energy Commn., 1982-85, Garden Grove Planning Commn., 1960-61; com. chmn. March of Dimes, Orange County, 1973-75; pres. Meth. Men, Garden Grove, 1964, 65. Recipient Apollo Achievement award NASA, 1970, Apollo-Soyuz Test Project award NASA, 1975, Space Shuttle Approach and Landing Test award NASA, 1978, Profl. Achievement citation in Engring. Iowa State U., 1984. Mem. World Future Soc., Inst. Mgmt. Scis., Ops. Rsch. Soc. Am., Assn. Proposal Mgmt. Profls., Tech. Mktg. Soc. Am., Masons, Toastmasters, Palm Springs Tennis Club, Sun City Computer Club, Photography Club. Republican. Avocations: travel, photography, gardening, computer systems, writing. Home and Office: 78580 Platinum Dr Sun City Palm Desert CA 92211-1858

MORRISON, ROGER BARRON, geologist; b. Madison, Wis., Mar. 26, 1914; s. Frank Barron and Elsie Rhea (Bullard) M.; m. Harriet Louise Williams, Apr. 7, 1941 (dec. Feb. 1991); children: John Christopher, Peter Hallock and Craig Brewster (twins). BA, Cornell U., 1933, MS, 1934; postgrad., U. Calif., Berkeley, 1934—35, Stanford U., 1935—38; PhD, U. Nev., 1964. Registered profl. geologist, Wyo. Geologist U.S. Geol. Survey, 1939-76; vis. adj. prof. dept. geoscis. U. Ariz., 1976-81, Mackay Sch. Mines, U. Nev., Reno, 1984-86; cons. geologist; pres. Morrison and Assocs., Morrison Cons. Corp., 1978—. Prin. investigator 2 Landsat-1 and 2 Skylab earth resources investigation projects NASA, 1972-75. Author 3 books; co-author 1 book; co-editor 2 books; editor Quaternary Nonglacial Geology, Conterminous U.S., Geol. Soc. Am. Centennial Series, vol. K-2, 1991; mem. editl. bd. Catena, 1973-88; contbr. over 250 articles to profl. jours. Fellow Geol. Soc. Am.; mem. AAAS, Internat. Union Quaternary Rsch. (mem. Holocene and paleopedology commns., chmn. work group on pedostratigraphy), Am. Soc. Photogrammetry and Remote Sensing, Internat. Soil Sci. Soc., Am. Quaternary Assn., Colo. Sci. Soc., Geol. Soc. Nev. Achievements include research in on Quaternary geology and geomorphology, hydrogeology, environmental geology, neotectonics, remote sensing of Earth resources, paleoclimatology, pedostratigraphy; technology for converting waste wood, garbage, municipal solid waste, natural gas, landfill gas, etc. to mixed-alcohol motor fuel; development of of forest and range land and a new town in western Paraguay. Home and Office: 13150 W 9th Ave Golden CO 80401-4201 E-mail: rbmorrison@earthlink.net.

MORRISON, SAMUEL F. library administrator, chief librarian; b. Flagstaff, Ariz., Dec. 19, 1936; s. Travis B. and Esther (Polk) M. AA, Compton Jr. Coll., 1955; BA in English, Calif. State U., 1971; MLS, U. Ill., 1972; DHL (hon.), St. Thomas U., 1998. Dir. Frostproof (Fla.) Living/Learning Library, 1972-74; adminstrv. asst. Broward County Library System, Ft. Lauderdale, Fla., 1974-76, dep. dir., 1976-87; first dep. commr., chief librarian Chgo. Pub. Library/Chgo. Library System, 1987-90; dir. Broward County Libr. System, Ft. Lauderdale, Fla., 1990—. Asst. libr. USAF, Morocco, 1956—58; instr. Inst. Multicultural Librarianship, U. Mich.; bd. trustees Fla. Meml. Coll., 2002—. Bd. dirs. Fla. Humanities Coun., United Way, Urban League, Ft. Lauderdale (Diversity Champion award 1998), Bonnet House, Ft. Lauderdale, Nat. Conf. Cmty. and Justice, Youth Orch. Fla., Tower Forum, Solinet, Broward County Special Olympics, Broward Partnership for Homeless, Broward Pub. Libr. Found., Kids Voting Broward, Old Dillard Found., SEFLIN, Sickle Cell Assn., Broward, S. Fla. Annenberg Challenge, Trejo Foster Found.; parliamentarian Area Agy. on Aging of Broward County, Ft. Lauderdale; pres. Gold Coast Jazz Soc., Ft. Lauderdale. Recipient HEW Title II fellowship U. Ill. Library Sch., Champaign, Faculty award U. Ill. Library Sch., Champaign, Freeman Bradley award NAACP, Silver Medallion Brotherhood award Nat. Conf., Pillar award The Links, Inc., 1998; named Advocate of Yr., Broward County Adv. Bd. for Persons with Disabilities, Achiever Emeritus, In Focus mag., 1998. Mem. ALA, NAACP, Fla. Libr. Assn., Nat. Assn. Black Pub. Adminstrs., Urban Librs. Coun., S.E. Libr. Assn., Pub. Libr. Assn., Broward County Libr. Assn. Office: Broward County Divsn Librs 100 S Andrews Ave Fort Lauderdale FL 33301-1830 E-mail: morrison@browardlibrary.org.

MORRISON, SARAH LYDDON, author; b. Rochester, N.Y., May 19, 1939; d. Paul William and Winifred (Cowles) Lyddon. BA, U. Vt., 1961. Sec. asst. Glamour mag., N.Y.C., 1961-63, Vogue mag., N.Y.C., 1963-65; asst. editor Venture mag., 1966-71; dir. pub. rels. for tourism Commonwealth of P.R., 1971-75; asst. Am. Legion, Washington, 1988-98; owner Sarah Lyddon Morrison Pub. Rels., 1999—. Author: The Modern Witch's Spellbook, 1971, Book II, 1983, The Modern Witch's Dream Book, 1985, The Modern Witch's Book of Home Remedies, 1988, The Modern Witch's Book of Healing, 1991, The Modern Witch's Book of Symbols, 1997, Modern Witch's Guide to Magic and Spells, 1998. Mem. Washington Club, Nat. Press Club. Mem. Univ. Club, DAR (dir. pub. rels. Emily Nelson chpt. 1999, 2000), Colonial Dames XVII. Avocations: travel, reading, swimming, rock music, cooking. E-mail: sarahlyd@aol.com.

MORRISON, SCOT RAYMOND, military officer, writer; b. Sharon, Pa., Sept. 22, 1964; s. John Raymond and Judith Ann Morrison. BA Psychology, Chapman Univ., Orange, CA, 2002. Missile maintenance chief USAF, Ellsworth, SD, 1982—94, team leader Vandenberg, 1994—99, team chief, 1999—2001. Pers. adv. coun. 576 Flight Test, Vandenberg, Calif., 1995—96. Mem.: Am. Psychol. Assn., Western Psychol. Assn. Home: 120 South M Street Apt A Lompoc CA 93436 Personal E-mail: srmorrison1@yahoo.com.

MORRISON, SCOTT DAVID, senior consultant; b. Duluth, Minn., May 8, 1952; s. Robert Henry and Shirley Elaine (Tester) M. (dec. 1990); m. Jana Louise Bergeron, May 29, 1976; chilren: Robert Scott (dec. 1999), Matthew John. Cert. in welding, Duluth Area Inst. Tech., 1971; student, U. Wis.-Superior, 1976-77; A in Mfg. Mgmt., N. Hennepin C.C., 1985; BA, Concordia Coll., St. Paul, 1988; MBA, St. Thomas U., St. Paul, 1991. Cert. in quality tech., Am. Soc. Quality, 1985; lic. vocat. instr., Minn. Cert. welder Litton Ship Systems, Pascagoula, Miss., 1971-72, Barko Hydraulics, Superior, Wis., 1972-76, Am. Hoist and Derrick Co., Mpls., 1977-79, cert. level II nondestructive exam. insp., 1979-80; quality supr. Colight Inc., 1980, Tol-O-Matic, Inc., Mpls., 1980-82; quality assurance engr. ADC Telecommunications, 1982-84, design assurance engr., 1985-86, product assurance engr., 1986-87, sr. product assurance engr., quality improvement facilitator, 1987-88, product engr. supr., 1988-90, mgr. design assurance, quality assurance, component engring., 1990-92; dir. quality and reg. affairs Waters Instruments, Inc., 1992-96, sr. quality engr., 1996, corp. quality sys. mgr., 1996-98; corp. mfg. and quality Compaq Computer Corp., Houston, 1996-98; sys. engr., sr. cons. Dimension Product Group, 1998-99, Dell Computer Corp., Austin, Tex., 1998—, quality engr., sr. cons. Transactional Line of Bus., 1999—, mgr. quality syss. application team project, 2000, supplier quality engr., sr. cons., 2000—01; sr. cons. ABS Cons. Mgmt. Sys. divsns., Houston, 2001—; mgr. Mgmt. Systems Cons., 2002—. Judge U.S. Amateur Boxing Fedn., Mpls., 1978-87, 95-97; examiner Minn. Quality Award Minn. Coun. for Quality, 1993, 95, Tex. Quality Award, 1997; mem. quality coun. Am. Electronics Assn., 1994-95; mem. bd. dirs. Rochester Quality Coun., 1994-95; examiner Malcolm Baldridge Nat. Quality award Nat. Inst. Standards and Technology, 1994-95, sr. examiner, 1996-97, alumni examiner, 1999-2000; site visit evaluation broad prize edn., 2002-; reviewer fellowship grant applications ASQ, 1996; adj. instr. Riverland Technical Coll., Rochester, Minn., 1995; lic. profl. boxing judge Tex. Dept. Licensing and Regulation, 1996—; cert. lead quality auditor British Standards Internat., 1996; facilitator Malcolm Bridge Nat. Quality Award Regional Conf., 1997; ind. quality cons.; owner Dimensions in Quality. Recipient Technical Excellence award ADC Telecoms., 1987, 88. Mem. ASTM, Am. Soc. Quality (cert. quality engr. cert. quality auditor, cert. quality mgr., chmn. host and attendance subcom. 1986-87), Am. Welding Soc., Soc. Mfg. Engrs., Internat. Platform Assn. Roman Catholic. Office: Am Bur Shipping 16855 Northchase Dr Houston TX 77060

MORRISON, SHELLEY, actress; b. N.Y.C., Oct. 26, 1936; d. Maurice Nissim and Hortense Mitrani; m. Walter R. Dominguez, Aug. 11, 1973. Student, L.A. City Coll., 1954-56. Presenter Alma awards, 2002, Nosotros Golden Eagle awards, 2002. Actress: (films) Interns, 1962, The Greatest Story Ever Told, 1964, Castle of Evil, 1965, Divorce, American Style, 1965, How to Save a Marriage, 1966, Funny Girl, 1967, Three Guns for Texas, 1969, Man & Boy, 1971, Blume in Love, 1972, McKenna's Gold, 1967, Breezy, 1973, People Toys, 1973, Rabbit Test, 1975, Max Dugan Returns, 1982, Troop Beverly Hills, 1988, Fools Rush In, 1996, (TV movies) Three's a Crowd, 1969, Once an Eagle, 1974, The Night That Panicked America, 1975, Kids Don't Tell, 1984, Cries From the Heart, 1994, (TV series) Laredo, 1965-67, The Flying Nun, 1966-70, First and Ten, 1987, I'm Home, 1990, The Fanelli Boys, 1990, Love, Lies and Murder, 1990, Playhouse 90, Dr. Kildare, The Fugitive, Gunsmoke, Marcus Welby, and many others, 1960-70, Man of the People, Sisters, 1991, 92, Murder She Wrote, 1992, Johnny Bago, 1993, Columbo, 1993, L.A. Law, 1994, Live Shot, 1995, Courthouse, Home Improvement, 1997, Nothing Sacred, 1997, Prey, 1997, Nearly Yours, 1998, (recurring role) Will & Grace, 1998—, series regular 1999—, numerous others, (stage prodns.) Pal Joey, 1956, Bus Stop, 1956, Only in America, 1960, Orpheus Descending, 1960, Spring's Awakening, 1962, over 65 other prodns., 1956-1970; prodr., writer live shots, 1975—. Condr. seminars (with husband Walter Dominguez) about Native Americans to keep traditions and ceremonies flourishing. Honored (with husband Walter Dominguez) for work with homeless City of L.A., 1985, for work during L.A. riots, 1992. Mem. SAG, AFTRA, Actors Equity Assn. Democrat. Presenter ALMA Awards, 2001, Imagan Awards, 2001.

MORRISON, SHIRLEY MARIE, nursing educator; b. Stuttgart, Ark., June 13, 1927; d. Jack Vade Wimberly and Mabel Claire (Dennison) George; m. Dana Jennings, Mar. 12, 1951 (dec. Dec. 1995); children: Stephen Leslie, Dana Randall, William Lee, Martha Ann Morrison Smith. Diploma, Bapt. Hosp. Sch. Nursing, Nashville, 1949; BSN, Calif. U., Fullerton, 1977; MSN, Calif. U., L.A., 1980; EdD, Nova Southeastern U., 1987. RN, Tex., Calif.; cert. pub. health nurse, Calif.; cert. secondary tchr., Calif. Staff nurse perinatal svcs. Martin Luther Hosp., Anaheim, Calif., 1960-77, relief 11-7 house supr., 1960-77; dir. vocat. nursing program Inst. Med. Studies, 1978-81; mem. faculty BSN program Abilene (Tex.) Intercollegiate Sch. Nursing, 1981-92, dir. ADN program, 1992-97; nursing educator Cisco Jr. Coll., Abilene, Tex., 1997—. Mem. profl. adv. bd. Nurse Care, Inc., Abilene, 1988—. Mem. adv. bd. parent edn. program Abilene Ind. Sch. Dist., 1985—; active Mar. Dimes, Abilene, 1990—, Ednl. Coalition for Bob Hunter, Abilene, 1994; bd. dirs. Hospice Big Country, Abilene, 1987—, The House That Kerry Built, 2000—. Grantee NIH, 1992; recipient Nat. Humor Project award Jour. Nursing Jocularity, 1996. Mem. Nat. Orgn. Assn. Degree Nurses (mem. program com. 10th anniversary nat. conv.), Tex. Orgn. Assoc. Degree Nurses, So. Nursing Rsch. Soc. (rsch. presenter), Health Edn. Resource Network Abilene (founding mem., pres. elect, pres. 1995-96), Sigma Theta Tau (bd. dirs. Internat. Omicron Zeta chpt. 1999—). Democrat. Methodist. Avocations: traveling, reading. Home: PO Box 2583 Abilene TX 79604-2583 Office: Cisco Jr Coll Dept Nursing PO Box 2583 Abilene TX 79604-2583 E-mail: shirleyfromtx@webtv.net.

MORRISON, STEPHEN GEORGE, lawyer; b. Pasadena, Calif., Aug. 10, 1949; s. Ira George and Virginia Lee (Zimmer) M.; m. Gail Louise Moore, June 10, 1972; 1 child, Gregory Stephen. BBA, U. Mich., 1971; JD, U. S.C., 1975. Ptnr. Nelson, Mullins, Riley & Scarborough, Columbia, S.C., 1975—. Adj. prof. U. S.C., Columbia, 1973-75, 82—; pres. Defense Rsch. Inst., 1995-96; exec. v.p., gen. counsel, sec., chief adminstrv. officer Policy Mgmt. Sys. Corp.; presenter in field. Author/editor: Products Liability Pretrial Notebook, 1989, South Carolina Appellate Practice Handbook, 1986. Bd. dirs. S.C. Com. Humanities, Columbia, 1986—, S.C. Gov. Sch. Arts, Columbia, 1988-95; pres., bd. dirs. Richland County Pub. Defender Assn., Columbia, 1991-95. Fellow S.C. Bar Found.; mem. Internat. Assn. Defense Coun., Lawyers for Civil. Justice (bd. dirs. 1995—, pres. elect 1997—). Democrat. Episcopalian. Avocations: fishing, country music, chamber music, physics, history. Home: 2626 Stratford Rd Columbia SC 29204-2342 Office: Nelson Mullins Riley & Morrison 1330 Lady St Fl 3 Columbia SC 29201-3300

MORRISON, TONI (CHLOE ANTHONY MORRISON), novelist; b. Lorain, Ohio, Feb. 18, 1931; d. George and Ella Ramah (Willis) Wofford; m. Harold Morrison, 1958 (div. 1964); children: Harold Ford, Slade Kevin. BA in English, Howard U., 1953; MA, Cornell U., 1955. Tchr. English and humanities Tex. So. U., 1955-57, Howard U., 1957-64; editor Random House, N.Y.C., 1965—; assoc. prof. English SUNY, Purchase, NY, 1971-72, Schweitzer Prof. of the Humanities Albany, 1984-89; Robert F. Goheen Prof. of the Humanities Princeton Univ., Princeton, NJ, 1989—; chair, creative writing pgm. Princeton U. Visiting prof., Yale Univ., 1976-77, Bard Coll., 1986-88. Author: The Bluest Eye, 1969, Sula, 1973 (National Book award nomination 1975, Ohioana Book award 1975), Song of Solomon, 1977 (National Book Critics Circle award 1977, American Acad. and Inst. of Arts and Letters award 1977), Tar Baby, 1981, (play) Dreaming Emmett, 1986, Beloved, 1988 (Pulitzer Prize for fiction 1988, Robert F. Kennedy Book award 1988, Melcher Book award Unitarian Universalist Assn. 1988, National Book award nomination 1987, National Book Critics Circle award nomination 1987), Jazz, 1992, Playing in the Dark: Whiteness and the Literary Imagination, 1992, Nobel Prize Speech, 1994, Birth of a Nation'hood: Gaze, Script & Spectacle in the O.J. Simpson Trial, 1997; editor: The Black Book, 1974, Race-ing Justice, En-Gendering Power: Essays on Anita Hill, Clarence Thomas, and the Construction of Social Reality, 1992; lyricist: Honey and Rue, 1992. Recipient New York State Governor's Art award, 1986; Washington College Literary award, 1987; Elizabeth Cady Stanton award National Organization for Women; Nobel prize in Literature Nobel Foundation, 1993. Mem. Author's Guild (council) Office: Princeton U Writing Program 185 Nassau St Princeton NJ 08544-2003 also: Internat Creative Mgmt 40 W 57th St New York NY 10019-4001*

MORRISON, WILLIAM DAVID, lawyer; b. Aug. 19, 1940; s. Maxey Neal and Mary Fuller (Chase) M.; m. Barbara Heath, Aug. 25, 1962 (div.); children: David Conrow, Stephen Munro, John Pomeroy; m. Sandra Elizabeth Butter, Mar. 16, 1983; children: Charles, Nicholas, Sophie Natasha. BA, Princeton U., 1962; LLB, Yale U., 1965. Bar: N.Y. 1966, Calif. 1975. Assoc. Winthrop, Stimson, Putnam & Robert, N.Y.C., 1965-74; ptnr. Erickson & Morrison, and predecessor firms, L.A., 1974—79, LeBoeuf, Lamb, Leiby & Macrae, N.Y.C., 1979-88, Bryan Cave, St. Louis, 1988-97, Sidley, Austin, Brown & Wood, N.Y.C., 1997—. Lectr. on Saudi Arabian law. Active Internat. Inst. for Strategic Studies, Royal Geog. Soc. Mem. ABA, Assn. of Bar of City of N.Y., Calif. Bar Assn., Internat. Bar Assn., The Pilgrims, Brooks, City of London Club, Marks Club, Annabel's, RAC Club, Princeton Club (N.Y.C.). Home: 34 Norland Sq London WII4PU England Office: Sidley Austin Brown & Wood 7 Princes St London EC2R 8AQ England Business E-Mail: wmorrison@sidley.com.

MORRIS-ROGERS, CHERYL-ANN, daycare provider, director, educator; b. Chgo., Feb. 26, 1958; d. Richard Lee and Ruth Hortence (Davis) M. AA, Cen. YMCA Coll., 1979; BA, DePaul U., 1982. Cert. in child devel. Supr. C.E.T.A. Program, Chgo., 1979; asst. dir. WLS AM/FM Radio Pub. Affairs, 1981-82; educator Auburn Pk. Day Care, Kindergarten, 1982-83, pres., dir., 1983—; educator, pres., dir. Lakefront Children's Acad., 1999—. Cons. in field. Mem. NAACP, Chgo., 1988—, United Negro Coll. Fund, Chgo., 1988—; com. mem. Election Judge Loretta Hall Morgan, Chgo., 1989; vol. Election Mayor Harold Washington, Chgo., 1987. Recipient Child Devel. award Love Drops Mag., 1987; named to Dean's List, 1980. Mem. Nat. Assn. Women-Bus. Owners, League Black Women, Preschool Owners Assn., Nat. Assn. for Edn. Young Children, Chgo. Assn. for Edn. Young Children. Avocations: reading, writing, swimming, camping, travel. Office: Auburn Pk Day Care 741 W 79th St Chicago IL 60620-2423 also: Ladefront Childrens Acad 400 E Randolph St Chicago IL 60601-7329

MORRISS, FRANK, writer, educator; b. Pasadena, Calif., Mar. 28, 1923; s. B. Gerard Morriss and Regina Spann; m. Mary Rita Moynihan, Feb. 11, 1950 (dec. Oct. 23, 1996); children: Patricia, Mary Ellen Hill, Regina, Gerard. BS (philosophy magna cum laude), Regis Coll., Denver, CO, 1943; JD, Georgetown U. of Law, Washington, DC, 1948. Editor Register Newspapers, Denver, 1949—61; assoc. editor Vt. Cath. Tribune, Burlington, Vt., 1961—63; editor Register Newspapers, Denver, 1961—67; contbg editor The Wanderer, St. Paul, 1967—; educator Coloradko Cath. Acad., Wheat Ridge, Colo., 1973—. Bd. Wanderer Forum Found., St. Paul, 1969—; dir. Colo. League in Def. of Teens, Wheat Ridge, Colo., 1995—; policy expert Heritage Found., 1995—. Author: (book) Saints In Verse, Two Chapels. Founder Colo. Cath. Acad., Wheat Ridge, Colo., 1970—2002. S/sgt. US Army, 1943—45, Pacific. Mem.: Fellowship of Cath. Scholars, VFW. R-Consevative. Roman Catholic. Home: 3505 Owens Street Wheat Ridge CO 80033 Home Fax: 303-422-1475.

MORRISS, FRANK HOWARD, JR. pediatrics educator; b. Birmingham, Ala., Apr. 20, 1940; s. Frank Howard Sr. and Rochelle (Snow) M.; m. Mary J. Hagan, June 29, 1968; children: John Hagan, Matthew Snow. BA, U. Va., 1962; MD, Duke U., 1966. Diplomate Am. Bd. Pediatrics, Am. Bd. Perinatal and Neonatal Medicine. Intern Duke U. Med. Ctr., Durham, N.C., 1966-67, resident in pediatrics, 1967-68, fellow in neonatology, 1970-71, U. Colo., Denver, 1971-73; asst. prof. to prof. U. Tex. Med. Sch., Houston, 1973-86; prof. U. Iowa Coll. Medicine, Iowa City, 1987—, chmn. dept., 1987—. Editor: Role of Human Milk in Infant Nutrition and Health, 1986; contbr. numerous articles to profl. jours, chpts. to books. Lt. comdr. USN, 1968-70. NIH grantee, 77-87, 90—. Mem. Am. Pediatric Soc., Soc. Pediatric Rsch., Am. Acad. Pediatrics, Soc. Gynecol. Investigation, Midwest Soc. Pediatric Rsch., Assn. Med. Sch. Pediatric Dept. Chmn. Methodist. Avocation: tennis. Office: U Iowa Hosps & Clinics Dept Pediatrics Iowa City IA 52242

MORRISS, MARY JEANNETTE HAGAN, pediatric cardiologist, educator; b. Youngstown, Ohio, Aug. 6, 1943; m. Frank H. Morriss Jr. BS in Biology, Bucknell U., 1965; MD, Duke U., 1969. Diplomate Am. Bd. Pediat.,

Am. Bd. Pediatric Cardiology. Asst. prof. pediatrics Baylor Coll. Medicine, Houston, 1975-87, U. Iowa, Iowa City, 1987-95, asoc. prof. pediatrics, 1995-99. Office: U Iowa Hosps & Clins Pediat Card 2849 JPP 200 Hawkins Dr Iowa City IA 52242-1009

MORRISSEY, CHARLES THOMAS, historian, educator; b. Newton, Mass., Nov. 11, 1933; s. Leonard Eugene and Margaret (McCarthy) M. AB, Dartmouth Coll., 1956; MA, U. Calif., Berkeley, 1957. Instr. Dartmouth Coll., Hanover, N.H., 1961-62; oral historian Harry S. Truman Library, Independence, Mo., 1962-64; chief oral history project John F. Kennedy Libr., Washington, 1965-66; dir. Vt. Hist. Soc., Montpelier, 1966-71, 73-75; dir. oral history project Ford Found., 1971-73; adj. prof. history U. Vt., Burlington, 1969-73, 75-85; dir. Oral History and Archives Office, cons. Baylor Coll. Medicine, Houston, 1985—. Vis. instr. oral and pub. history Portland State U., 1979-82, 84-2001, Vt. Coll., Montpelier, 1985-2000, 02--; lectr. in field. Author: Vermont: A Bicentennial History, 1981, (with others) Vermont, 1985; editor: Oral History Assn. Newsletter, 1968-71, Vermont History, 1967-71, 73-76, Internat. Jour. Oral History, 1985-89; contbg. editor: Vermont Life mag., 1969-81, editor, 1982-83; also articles; radio commentator Sta. WDEV, Waterbury, Vt., 1982—; columnist Hardwick (Vt.) Gazette, 1997—. Recipient Harvey Kantor award New England Assn. Oral Historians, 1980. Fellow Ctr. for Rsch. on Vt.; mem. Soc. Am. Archivists, Oral History Assn. (pres. 1971-72), Am. Assn. for History of Medicine, Nat. Coun. on Pub. History (coun. 1980-82), Assn. Oral History Educators, Sharpshooters Club (North Fayston, Vt.), Cosmos Club (Washington).

MORRISSEY, DOLORES JOSEPHINE, investment executive; b. N.Y.C., July 22; d. Joseph Lawrence and Madeleine Catherine (Curran) M. BS, NYU, 1963, MBA, 1968. Sr. v.p., treas. Bowery Savs. Bank, N.Y.C., 1958-87; exec. v.p. Mut. of Am., 1987-94; pres., CEO Mut. of Am. Capital Mgmt., 1994-96; CEO, chair Mut. of Am. Securities Corp., 1996—. Pres., CEO, chair Mut. of Am. Investment Corp., 1989—; pres., CEO Mut. of Am. Instnl. Fund, 1996—; adv. commn. N.Y. State Comptroller Investment Adv. Com., N.Y.C., 1979-87. Past pres. Soroptimist Internat. N.Y., N.Y.C.; dir. Yorkville Common Pantry, Yorkville Christian-Jewish Coun., N.Y.C., 1978—. Mem. Money Marketeers of NYU, NYU Bus. Forum, Women's Bond Club, Women's Econ. Round Table, Alpha Kappa Delta Roman Catholic. Avocations: travel, photography, opera. Home: 180 East End Ave New York NY 10128-7763 Office: Mutual of America 320 Park Ave Fl 9 New York NY 10022-6839

MORRISSEY, EDMOND JOSEPH, classical philologist; b. N.Y.C., June 5, 1943; s. William J. and Anne K. (Gaffney) M.; m. Patricia M. Hanlon, Oct. 11, 1987; children: William, Edmond, Kathleen, Patrick, Jennifer, Lisa, Paula. AB summa cum laude, Boston Coll., 1965; BA, U. Oxford, 1967, MA, 1971, Harvard U., 1969, PhD, 1974. Seminarian Pope John XXIII Nat. Sem., Weston, Mass., 1974-77; collaborator prof. Sterling Dow Harvard U., Cambridge, 1977-95. Cons. in pub. and photoreprodn. Author: Studies in Inscriptions Listing the Agonistic Festivals, 1974, A Quinquagesimal History of the Church of St. Bernadette, 1987; contbr. articles to profl. jours. Pres., chmn. adminstrn. fin., St. Bernadette's Ch., Archdiocese of Boston, 1980—; founding dir. Theol. Lectures Series, Randolph, Mass., 1978—, Randolph Hist. Commn., 1988—; staff vol. Cardinal Medeiros Program for Handicapped, 1980-82; treas., bd. dirs. Randolph Community Food Pantry, 1994—. Marshall scholar, 1965-67; Wilson scholar, 1965— ; Gen. Motors scholar, 1962-65; Ford Found. fellow, 1967-69; Harvard U. fellow, 1969-71 Mem. Am. Inst. Archaeology, Am. Philol. Assn., Alumni Assn. Harvard, Oxford U. Alumni Assn., Boston Coll. Alumni Assn. Democrat. Roman Catholic. Home: 4 Bennington St Randolph MA 02368-2106

MORRISSEY, ELIZABETH R. investment company executive; b. Springfield, Mass., Dec. 18, 1961; d. Robert M. and Nancy (Rennet) M. BA, Mount Holyoke Coll., 1984; MA, NYU, 1986. Rsch. assoc. Middle East Inst., Washington, 1984; acct. exec. Walker & Co., N.Y.C., 1985-86, Hoxter, Inc., N.Y.C., 1986-87; mng. ptnr. Kleiman Internat. Cons., Inc., N.Y.C., Washington, 1987—. Screening com. USAID/AAAS, Washington, 1994-95. Co-author: Securities Market Development in Transition & Emerging Markets, 1997; editor Emerging Bond & Money Market Guide, 1993-96. Mem. Mt. Holyoke Alumnae Club (co-pres. 1995—). Episcopalian. Office: Kleiman Internat Cons Inc 1825 I St NW Ste 400 Washington DC 20006-5415

MORRISSEY, GEORGE MICHAEL, judge; b. Chgo., Aug. 12, 1941; s. Joseph Edward and Mary Bernice (Shields) M.; m. Mary Kay McCarthy, Jan. 3, 1976; children: Meghan Catherine, Colleen Mary. BS, Ill. Inst. Tech., 1963; JD, De Paul U., 1971. Bar: Ill. 1972, U.S. Dist. Ct. (no. dist.) Ill. 1978, U.S. Supreme Ct. 1981. Auditor Touche Ross & Co., Chgo., 1963-68; pvt. practice Evergreen Park and Worth, Ill., 1972-77; chief 5th Mcpl. Dist. Cook County Pub. Defender, Chgo., 1978-90; assoc. judge Cook County Cir. Ct., 1991—. Mem. spl. commn. on adminstrn. of justice in Cook County, Chgo., 1984-91. Mem. commn. on future of Ill. Inst. Tech., Chgo., 1976-77; bd. trustees Oak Lawn (Ill.) Library, 1979-85; bd. dirs. Crisis Ctr. for South Suburbia, Worth, 1979—. Served with U.S. Army, 1963-69. Mem. Chgo. Bar Assn. (jud. retention com., bar pres. com.), S.W. Bar Assn. (past pres.), Coalition of Suburban Bar Assn. (past pres.), Alpha Sigma Phi. Clubs: Columbia Yacht (commodore 1976-78) (Chgo.), Chgo. Yachting (commodore 1982). Lodges: Elks. Roman Catholic. Office: Cir Ct of Cook County 2600 Richard J Daley Ctr Chicago IL 60602

MORRISSEY, JOHN CARROLL, SR. lawyer; b. N.Y.C., Sept. 2, 1914; s. Edward Joseph and Estelle (Caine) M.; m. Eileen Colligan, Oct. 14, 1950; children: Jonathan Edward, Ellen (Mrs. James A. Jenkins), Katherine, John, Patricia, Richard, Brian, Peter. BA magna cum laude, Yale U., 1937, LLB, 1940; JSD, N.Y. U., 1951; grad., Command and Gen. Staff Sch., 1944. Bar: N.Y. State 1940, D.C. 1953, Calif. 1954, U.S. Supreme Ct. 1944. Asso. firm Dorsey and Adams, 1940-41, Dorsey, Adams and Walker, 1946-50; counsel Office of Sec. of Def., Dept. Def., Washington, 1950-52; acting gen. counsel def. Electric Power Adminstrn., 1952-53; atty. Pacific Gas and Electric Co., San Francisco, 1953-70, assoc. gen. counsel, 1970-74, v.p., gen. counsel, 1975-80; individual practice law San Francisco, 1980-2000. Dir. Gas Lines, Inc. Bd. dirs. Legal Aid Soc., San Francisco; chmn. Golden Gate dist. Boy Scouts Am., 1973-75; commr. Human Rights Commn. of San Francisco, 1976-89, chmn., 1980-82; chmn. Cath. Social Svc. of San Francisco, 1966-68; adv. com. Archdiocesean Legal Affairs, 1981—; regent Archdiocesan Sch. of Theology, St. Patrick's Sem., 1994-99; dir. Presidio Preservation Assn., 1995-99. Served to col. F.A. U.S. Army, 1941-46. Decorated Bronze star, Army Commendation medal. Mem. NAS, AAAS, ABA, Calif. State Bar Assn., Fed. Power Bar Assn., N.Y. Acad. Scis., Calif. Conf. Pub. Utility Counsel, Pacific Coast Electric Assn., Pacific Coast Gas Assn., Econ. Round Table of San Francisco, World Affairs Council, San Francisco C. of C., Calif. State C. of C., Harold Brunn Soc. Med. Rsch., Electric Club, Serra Club, Commonwealth Club, Yale Club of San Francisco (pres. 1989-90), Pacific-Union Club, Sometimes Tuesday Club, Sovereign Mil. Order Malta, Phi Beta Kappa. Roman Catholic. Home: 2030 Jackson St San Francisco CA 94109-2840 Office: PO Box 77000 123 Mission St Ste 1709 San Francisco CA 94105-1590 E-mail: dadjcm@aol.com.

MORRISSEY, KAREN MARY, credit manager; b. Jamestown, N.D., Nov. 28, 1937; d. Joseph Patrick and Adeline (McCully) Morrissey. BA, Coll. St. Catherine, 1960; MA, U. Wis., 1976. Cert. credit counselor, foreclosure prevention specialist. Tchr. Archdiocese St. Paul, 1960—66, St. Paul Pub. Schs., 1969—81; mgr. oncology pvt. practice, Mpls., 1989—92; credit counselor MFM, Roseville, 1996—99, Luth. Social Svc. Minn., St. Paul, 1999—. Author numerous poems. Pres. Fest. Chamber Chorale, St. Paul; chair worship bd. St. Williams, Fridley, 2001—02. Recipient Silver Poet award, 1986. Democrat. Roman Catholic. Avocations: writing, singing, cooking, reading. Home: 5710 Squire Ln Saint Paul MN 55112 Office: Luth Social Svc 590 Park St Ste 310 Saint Paul MN 55112 E-mail: marytighekm@msn.com.

MORRISSEY, LEE, language educator; b. Boston, Aug. 21, 1964; s. Leo Joseph and Margaret Mary (Harney) M. Student, Oxford U., 1984-85; AB in Philosophy and English, Boston Coll., 1986; MA in English, Columbia U., 1988, MA in History, 1990, PhD in English and Comparative Lit., 1995. Print archivist The Kitchen Ctr. for the Arts, N.Y.C., 1988-95; instr. logic rhetoric Columbia U., 1991-93, preceptor lit. humanities, 1993-95; asst. prof. English Clemson (S.C.) U., 1995-99, assoc. prof., 1999—. Author: From the Temple to the Castle: An Architectural History of British Literature 1660-1760, 1999; editor, contbr.: The Kitchen Turns 20, 1992; contbr. articles to profl. jours. Presdl. fellow Columbia U., 1990-91, Summer Dissertation fellow Mellon Found., 1993; Quarterly grantee S.C. Arts Commn., 1996-99. Mem. Am. Soc. 18th Century Studies (Grad. Student Essay prize 1994), MLA. Office: Clemson U Dept English 801 Strode Tower PO Box 340523 Clemson SC 29634-0523 E-mail: lmorris@clemson.edu.

MORRISSEY, MICHAEL JOSEPH, investment banker; b. Mount Holly, N.J., June 26, 1947; s. Edward Francis and Winifred (Monahan) M.; m. Joanne Stone, June 5, 1982; children: Scott Christopher, Nathanial Joseph Cake. AB, Boston Coll., 1969; MBA, Dartmouth Coll., 1971. Security analyst Philo Smith & Co., Inc., Stamford, Conn., 1971-73, Kidder Peabody & Co., Inc., N.Y.C., 1973-74, asst. v.p., 1974-76, v.p., 1976-77, Dean Witter Reynolds, Inc., N.Y.C., 1977-78, Crum and Forster, Morristown, N.J., 1978-80, sr. v.p., 1980-83; pres. Firemark Cons., Inc., 1983-85, chmn. bd., 1985—; exec. v.p. Manhattan Nat. Corp., N.Y.C., 1985, pres., chief operating officer, 1985-86. Recipient CFA award, 1977. Fellow Fin. Analysts Fedn.; mem. Young Pres.' Orgn. Clubs: World Trade Ctr., Dartmouth (N.Y.C.). Republican. Presbyterian. Home: 45 Headley Rd Morristown NJ 07960-5913 Office: FireMark Cons 1 Gatehall Dr Parsippany NJ 07054-4514 *A successful career is something one has; a successful person is something one is. A man or woman cannot be considered a true success in my judgement unless he or she fulfills that very special obligation to parents, spouse, and children along the way. The world is made better by good people, not just efficient career machines.*

MORRISSEY, PATRICIA A. commissioner; PhD Spl. Edn., Pa. State U. Sr. assoc. Booz Allen Hamilton , McLean, Va.; commr. adminstrn. and devel. disabilities U.S. Health and Human Svcs. (HHS) , 2001—. With Senate, Ho. of Reps., Pres. Ronald Regan; with Senate Ticket to Work and Work Incentives Improvement Act Wis. Gov. Thomson's Office; with Pres. George W. Bush's New Freedom Initiative. Office: 200 Independence Ave SW Washington DC 20201 Business E-Mail: pmorrissey@acf.dhhs.gov.*

MORRISSEY, RONALD JAMES, chemical company executive, chemist; b. S.I., N.Y., Sept. 25, 1934; s. Francis Joseph and Dolores Florence (Kane) M.; m. Elizabeth Ann Schwimer, Sept. 18, 1965; children: Ronald P., Patrick F., James E., Maria G. BS, St. Peter's Coll., 1956; MS, Fordham U., 1959, PhD, 1961. Rsch. assoc. AMP, Inc., Harrisburg, Pa., 1962-72; tech. rep. Technic Inc., Cranston, R.I., 1972-73, tech. dir., 1973-84, v.p., 1984—. Cons. Northland Chem., Providence, 1977-78, Davis, Joseph & Negley, Austin, 1998—. Contbr. articles to profl. jours.; patentee in field. Capt. U.S. Army, 1961-62. Fellow Inst. of Metal Finishing; mem. Am. Chem. Soc., Electrochem. Soc. (chmn. Boston sect.), Am. Electroplaters and Surface Finishers Soc. Republican. Roman Catholic. Avocations: photography, rifle and pistol markmanship. Home: 82 Woodstock Ln Cranston RI 02920-4639 Office: Technic Inc 1 Spectacle St Cranston RI 02910-1058

MORRISSEY RIZZUTO, HELEN, language educator; b. N.Y.C. BA, St. Joseph's Coll. for Women, 1966; MA, Hunter Coll., 1973; postgrad., Columbia U. Cert. regularly apptd. tchr. h.s. English, lic. permanent lic. N.Y.C., cert. permanent cert. N.Y. state. Tchr. English Newtown H.S., N.Y.C., 1966—73; tchr. English as secondary lang. Newton H.S. Evening Sch., 1973—77; co-founder, dir. Scholastic Achievement Tutoring, Inc., 1975—78; resident poet, fiction writer N.Y. State Coun. on Arts, Poets in Pub. Svc.; pvt. tutor PSAT, SAT, SSAT, CCOP, GRE, others, 1966—; pvt. cons., freelance editor, 1981—; instr. creative writing liberal arts divsn. Univ. Coll., Hofstra U., N.Y.C., 1981—2001; tchr. English humanities dept. Townsend Harris H.S. at Queens Coll., 1990—; adj. prof. English Queens Coll., 1990—. Contbg. editor: Poetry Forum; contbr. ; author: (poetry) Evening Sky on a Japanese Screen; actor: (poetry) A Bird in Flight. Mem.: Poetry Soc. Am., Poets and Writers.

MORRIS-YAMBA, TRISH, educational and social service association director; b. Binghamton, N.Y. d. Maurice and Lillian (Flippen) Walker; 1 child, Lae D.; m. A. Zachary Yamba. BA, Livingston Coll., 1972; MEd, Rutgers U., 1973. Exec. dir. Newark Day Ctr., 1981—. CEO Salon Par Excellence, Newark, 1993—; pres. TRZ Assocs., Inc.; chair Mayor's Commn. on Status of Women, 1992—; bd. dirs. Newark Pub. Libr., 1996—. Mem. Women's Bd., N.J. Performing Arts Ctr.; mem. adv. bd. Thirteen-Wnet, 1999—; sec. Our Children's Found. N.J.; chair Early Childhood Coalition Newark, 2001. Named one of 100 Most Influential award City News Pub. Co., 1998; recipient Outstanding Contb. to Children award N.J. Black Child Devel. Inst., 2000, Meritorious Svc. award Nat. Assn. Negro Bus. and Profl. Women's Clubs, 2000. Mem.: Nat. Polit. Congress Black Women (1st vice chair). Baptist. Office: Newark Day Ctr 43 Hill St Newark NJ 07102-2697

MORRONE, FRANK, electronic manufacturing executive; b. Marano Marchesato, Cosenza, Italy, May 13, 1949; s. Luigi and Emma (Molinaro) M.; m. Katherine Ann Kuehn, Feb. 1, 1975; children: Louis H., Cecilia E., Joseph V. BSEE, U. Wis., 1972; MBA, Northwestern U., 1993. Project engr. 3M Co., St. Paul, 1972—73; product engr., mgr. Eaton Corp., Kenosha, Wis., 1973—79; chief elec. engr. Tree Machine Tool, Racine, 1979—80; v.p. engring. MacPower divsn. Manu-Tronics, Inc., Kenosha, 1980—84, exec. v.p., 1984—99, bd. dirs., sec., 1988—99; v.p. ops. Sanmina Corp., 1999—2001, sr. v.p., 2001—. Mem. exec. bd. southeast coun. Boy Scouts Am., Racine, 1987—; bd. dirs. Kenosha Libr., 1987-98, U. Wis.-Parkside Benevolent Found., 2000—; mem. mgmt. coun. Lakeview Tech. Acad., 1997-99. Mem. IEEE, Kenosha County Club (bd. dirs.). Office: Sanmina Corp 8701 100th St Pleasant Prairie WI 53158-2202

MORROW, ANDREW NESBIT, interior designer, business owner; b. Fremont, Nebr., Feb. 22, 1929; s. Hamilton N. and May (Oberg) M.; m. Margaret M. Stoltinberg; children: Megan Beth, Molly Jean, Andrew C. BFA, U. Nebr., 1950. Interior designer Hardy Furniture, Lincoln, Nebr., 1950-61, Morrow Interiors, Lincoln, 1961—. Bd. visitors Found. for Interior Design Edn. and Rsch., 1976-84; mem. standards com. Found. for Interior Design Edn. and Research, N.Y.C. Exhibitor Fremont Art Gallery, 1986, Haymarket Art Gallery, 1984. Pres. First Luth. Ch., Lincoln, 1987-90; bd. dirs. Lincoln Symphony, 1988-91, Nebr. Republicans for Choice, 1992, Luth. Family Svcs. of Nebr., 1994, Luth. Family Svc. Nebr. Found., 1995—; treas. NCID, 1992—. Fellow Am. Soc. Interior Designers (bd. dirs. Nebr.-Iowa chpt. 1974-78, pres. 1986-88); mem. Interior Design Educators Council (hon.). Republican. Avocations: gardening, horseback riding, cross-country skiing. Home: 301 Park Vista Lincoln NE 68510 Office: Morrow Interiors Inc 1010 K St Lincoln NE 68508-2880

MORROW, ARDYTHE LUXION, adult education educator, researcher; b. Elgin, Ill., Aug. 30, 1955; d. Walter William and Edith Lenora (Moffatt) Luxion; m. Robert Clegg Morrow, June 5, 1976; children: Winona, Justin. PhD, U. Tex., Houston, 1991. Prof. Eastern Va. Med. Sch., Norfolk, 1992—2001; assoc. dir. Ctr. for Pediatric Rsch., 1998—2001; prof. U. Cin. Coll. Medicine, 2001—; dir. Ctr. for Epidemiology and Biostats., Cin. Children's Hosp. Med. Ctr., 2001—. Contbr. articles to profl. jours. Recipient Faculty Rsch. award Eastern Va. Med. Sch., 1999; fellow Exec. Leadership in Acad. Medicine program MCP Hahnemann U., 2000-01; named Jackie Schnell Meml. scholar Rice U., Brown Coll., 1974. Mem. Am Coll. Epidemiology. Avocations: travel, piano, music. Home: 6234 Orchard Ln Cincinnati OH 45213 Office: Ctr Epidemiology and Biostats Cin Children's Hosp 3333 Burnet Ave Cincinnati OH 45229

MORROW, BARRY NELSON, screenwriter, producer; b. Austin, Minn., June 12, 1948; s. Robert Clayton and Rose Nell (Nelson) M.; m. Beverly Lee McKenzie, Mar. 3, 1969; children: Clayton McKenzie, ZoeAnna Rachel. BA, St. Olaf Coll., 1970; DHL (hon.), U. La Verne, Calif., 1990. Media specialist U. Iowa, Iowa City, 1974-81; freelance screenwriter Los Angeles, 1981-90; pres. Morrow-Heus Prodns., 1990-00. Storywriter (TV film) Bill, 1981 (Emmy award 1982); screenwriter: (TV films) Bill: On His Own, 1983, Conspiracy of Love, 1987, Silent Victory, 1988, The Karen Carpenter Story, 1989, (feature film) Rain Man, 1988 (co-recipient Acad. award Best Original Screenplay 1989); screenwriter, exec. prodr.: Christmas on Division Street, 1991; exec. prodr.: Switched at Birth, 1991 (Emmy nomination), Gospa, 1995, The Fifties, 1997, Behind the Mask, 1999; screenwriter, prodr. Race the Sun, 1996; monologist: Bill for Short, 1992. Recipient Pres.'s award Am. Acad. for Devel. Medicine, 1978, Outstanding Contbn. award Mid-Am. Congress on Aging, 1983, SI award NASW, 1991, Pope John XXIII award Viterbo Coll., 1992. Mem. Writers Guild Am. West, Acad. TV Arts and Scis., Acad. Motion Picture Arts and Scis., Motion Picture Screen Cartoonists Guild.

MORROW, BRUCE WILLIAM, educational administrator, business executive, consultant, author; b. Rochester, Minn., May 20, 1946; s. J. Robert and Frances P. Morrow; m. Jenny Lea Morrow. BA, U. Notre Dame, 1968, MBA in Mgmt. with honors, 1974, MA in Comparative Lit., 1975; grad., U.S. Army Command and Gen. Staff Coll., 1979. Chmn. elem. German U. Notre Dame, 1973-75; co-mgr. Wendy's Old Fashioned Hamburgers, South Bend, Ind., 1976-77; adminstrn. mgr. Eastern States Devel. Corp., Richmond, Va., 1977; v.p. JDB Assocs., Inc., Alexandria, 1976-78; sr. cons. Data Base Mgmt., Inc., Springfield, 1979-80; owner Aardvark Prodns., Alexandria, 1980-82; sys. analyst/staff officer Hdqrs., Dept. Army, Washington, 1980-84; chmn. bd. Commonwealth Dominion Corp., Sierra Vista, Ariz., 1982—. Strategic planner, dep. comdr. Fort Pickett, Blackstone, Va., 1986-89; dir. continuing edn. Southside Va. C.C., Alberta, 1989-91; co-founder S.W. Bus. Group, Tucson, 1995-99; pres. Sierra Vista Golf, Inc., Ariz., 1994-95; Cochise County team leader Ariz. Coun. Econ. Conversion, 1994-95; mem. com. Ariz. Small Bus. Initiative, 1994-99; internet webmaster, 1996—; exec. dir. Southeastern Ariz. Contrs. Assn., 1997-98; corp. adminstr., Garcia Cos., Sierra Vista, Tucson, Phoenix, Ariz., 1997-99; property adminstr. Brown & Root Svcs., Ft. Huachuca, Ariz. and Land Between the Lakes, Ky., 1999-2001; logistics coord. Brown & Root Svcs., Land Between the Lakes, 2001—. Author (radio series) Survival in the Computer Jungle, 1986, (classroom text) Introduction to Computers, 1988, 2d edit., 1993, Defense Conversion Handbook, 1995, business Assessment Manual, 1996, Employee Manual Guide, 1996, Business Plan Guide, 1996, Marketing Plan Guide, 1996, (screenplay) Gray Rock, 2000; contbg. columnist Notre Dame mag., 1974-86; exec. prodr. (motion picture) Beneath the Law, 1995-96; composer songs. Active Boy Scouts Am., 1960-69; firefighter Roanoke Wildwood Vol. Fire Dept., 1991-93. Lt. col. USAR, ret. Decorated Bronze Star, Army commendation medals, Army Achievement medal, Meritorious Svc. medals, Parachutist's badge, Army Gen. Staff badge. Mem. VFW (life), Nat. Eagle Scout Assn., Lake Gaston C. of C. (bd. dirs.), Am. Legion, Sierra Vista Area C. of C., Lions (v.p. local club), Friends Internat. (Am. v.p. 1969-71, Boeblingen, Germany), Order of DeMolay, Beta Gamma Sigma, Delta Phi Alpha. Office: Commonwealth Dominion Corp 334 Landing Strip Rd Hardin KY 42048-9413 E-mail: cdc@theriver.com.

MORROW, CAROL LYNN, lawyer; b. Chambersburg, Pa., May 7, 1943; d. Erwin C. and Amanda (Graeber) Kline; children: Quinn A., Bill E. BA, S.W. Tex. State U., 1966, JD, 1977. Bar: Tex. 1977. Assoc. gen. counsel GPM Life Ins. Co., San Antonio, 1977—. Pres. GPM Credit Union, San Antonio, 1990-92. Mem. Am. Corp. Counsel Assn. (pres. San Antonio chpt. 1999, treas. 1996-98). Avocations: drama, theater. Office: GPM Life 800 NW Loop 410 Ste 600S San Antonio TX 78216-5623

MORROW, CHERYLLE ANN, accountant, bankruptcy consultant; b. Sydney, Australia, July 3, 1950; came to U.S., 1973; d. Norman H. and Esther A. E. (Jarrett) Wilson. Student, U. Hawaii, 1975; diploma Granville Tech. Coll., Sydney, 1967. Acct., asst. treas. Bus. Investment, Ltd., Honolulu, 1975-77; owner Lanikai Musical Instruments, Honolulu, 1980-86, Cherylle A. Morrow Profl. Svcs., Honolulu, 1981—; fin. managerial cons. E.A. Buck Co., Inc., Honolulu, 1981-84; contr., asst. trustee THC Fin. Corp., Honolulu, 1977-84, bankruptcy trustee, 1984-92; v.p., sec., treas. Innervation, Inc., 1989—; panel mem. Chpt. 7 Trustees dist. Hawaii U.S. Depart. Justice, 1988-91; co-chair Small Bus. Hawaii Legis. Action Com., 1990-92; dir./treas. Women's Fin. Resource Ctr., 1997—. Mem. Small Bus. Hawaii PAC, Lanikai Community Assn., Arts Coun. Hawaii; vol., mem. Therapeutic Horsemanship for Handicapped, program chair, 1990-92, vice chair, 1990-95, chair, 1995—; vol., mem. Small Bus. Adminstrn. Women in Bus. Com. 1987—; vol. tax preparer IRS VITA, 1990—, site coord., 1993—; mem. Bus. Task Force Regulatory Reform, Hawaii, 1996—; mem. working group Task Force Econ. Revitalization, Hawaii, 1997 acct. exec. U.S. Small Bus. Adminstrn., 1997. Recipient City and County of Honolulu award, State of Hawaii award, 1996, 97, Women in Bus. Advocate award U.S. Small Bus. Adminstrn., 1996, Small Bus. Booster award Small Bus. Hawaii, 1996, City and County of Honolulu award U.S. Small Bus. Adminstrn., 1997, Acct. Adv. award. Mem. AARP (vol. tax preparer TCE 1991—), NAFE, Australian-Am. C. of C. (bd. dir. 1985-92, corp. sec. 1986-92, v.p. 1988-92), Pacific Islands Assn. Women (corp. sec./treas. 1988-90), Pacific Islands Assn. (asst. treas. 1988—), Associated Builders and Contractors (Hawaii chptr., mem. vol. com. 1997—), Soc. Fire Protection Engrs. (Hawaii chptr.), Instrumentation Soc. Am., Nat. Fedn. Ind. Bus. Avocations: reading, music, dancing, sailing, gardening. Office: Innervation, Inc 424 Iliwahi Loop Kailua HI 96734-1836

MORROW, CRAIG M. music educator; b. Seattle, Oct. 9, 1947; s. Raymond and Beverley May Morrow; m. Eva Kristina Morrow. PhD, NYU, New York, New York, 1993; MA, Queens Coll., Flushing, Queens, New York, 1973; BA, Yale Univeristy, New Haven, Connecticut, 1973. Music educator Bay Shore H.S., Bay Shore, NY, 1989—; organist Patchogue Congl. Ch., Patchogue, 1997—; choir dir. St. Ann's Episcopal Ch., Sayville, 1982—97; piano instr. Taubman Piano Inst., Amherst, Mass., 1982—87; music educator South Haven Pub. Sch., South Haven, NY, 1979—85. Pvt. piano tchr., Bellport, NY, 1976—. Composer: Franliszt the Passions of a Virtuoso. Recipient First Pl. Bach Tricentennial Competition, Am. Coll. of Musicians, 1985, First Pl. Seattle Symphony Concerto Competition, Seattle Symphony, 1963. Mem.: Suffolk County Music Edn. Assn., Am. Coll. of Musicians (judge 1989—2002). Episcopalian. Avocations: tennis, swimming. Office: Bay Shore High School 115 Third Avenue Bayshore NY 11706

MORROW, DAVID AUSTIN, III, veterinary medical educator; b. Arch Spring, Pa., Jan. 14, 1935; s. David Austin and Mary Harnish (Burket) M.; m. Sarah Linda MacDonough, Aug. 28, 1965; children: David Austin IV, Laurie Elizabeth, Melanie MacDonough. BS, Pa. State U., 1956; DVM, Cornell U., 1960, PhD, 1967. Postdoctoral fellow Cornell U., Ithaca, N.Y., 1965-68; assoc. prof. Mich. State U., East Lansing, 1968-81, prof. Coll. Vet. Medicine, 1981-90, prof. emeritus, 1990—; vet. cons., 1990—. Vis. scientist Colo. State U., Ft. Collins, 1975-76. Editor: Current Therapy in Theriogenology, 1980, 2d edit., 1986. Elder Presbyn. Ch.; trustee Pa. State U., 1987-2002, chmn. bd. trustees phys. plant com., 1994-96, presdl. selection com., 1995. Recipient Norden Disting. Teaching award Mich. State U., 1975, Outstanding Teaching award, 1979-80, 84-86, Dairy Sci. Disting. Alumnus award Pa. State U., 1992, Hon. Lion Ambassador award Pa. State U., 1993, Hon. Alumnus award Mich. State U. Coll. Veterinary Medicine, 1993; coach 1st place team SAVMA Nat. Intercollegiate Bovine Reproduction Contest, 1986, 88-90; named Industry Person of Yr. World Dairy Expo, 1997, Alumni fellow Pa. State U., 1998. Mem. AVMA (Borden award 1980, Am. Feed Mfg. award 1992), Am. Coll. Theriogenologists (charter diplomate), Pa. State U. Coll. Agr. Alumni Soc. (pres.-elect 1985-86, pres. 1987-89, past pres. 1989-91), Greek Alumni Interest Group (pres. 1995-2000), Pa. State U. Alumni Coun. (exec. bd. 1983-95, pres.-elect 1989-91, pres. 1991-93, past pres. 1993-95, Lions Paw award 2002), Phi Zeta (pres. 1977-79), Phi Kappa Phi (exec. bd.), Golden Key (hon.), Alpha Zeta (life, bd. dirs., Centennial Honor Roll 1997, chpt. Centennial Disting. Alumnus 1998), Sigma Xi. Republican. Avocations: skiing; gardening. Home and Office: 1060 Haymaker Rd State College PA 16801-6900 E-mail: dmorrow@psu.edu.

MORROW, DAVID CARL, plant supervisor, writer; b. Corpus Christi, Tex., Jan. 7, 1945; s. Harvey Carl Morrow and Mary Sue Richardson; m. Nancy Lee Bennett, Dec. 26, 1965 (div. June 1967); 1 child, Monika Joy. AA, Del Mar Coll., 1965; BA, U. Tex., 1971. Attendant Austin State Hosp., 1966-68; surveyor Enging. Dept., Dallas, 1972-74; lab. asst. Wastewater Dept., Corpus Christi, 1974-76, U. Tex. Health Sci. Ctr., Dallas, 1976-77, Water Dept., Arlington, 1977-83, plant supr. Corpus Christi, 1983—2002. Author essays and short stories; contbr. articles to profl. jours. Active, editor Men's Rights Assn., Forest Lake, Minn., 1975—; active Coalition of Free Men, Manhasset, N.Y., 1975—. With U.S. Army, 1969-71. Avocations: science, social science, history, language.

MORROW, ELIZABETH HOSTETTER, sculptress, museum administrator, farmer, educator; b. Sibley, Mo., Feb. 28, 1947; d. Elman A. and Lorine H. Morrow; married, 1970 (div. 1979); children: Jan Pawel, Lorentz Arthur.

Student, William Jewell Coll., 1958-59, Colo. Coll., 1959-60, U. Okla., 1960-62; BFA, U. Kans., 1964, MFA, 1967; postgrad., U. Minn., 1965, U. Kans., 1968. Pres. E. Morrow Co., Kansas City, Mo., 1966-67; head dept. art U. Hawaii, Honolulu, 1968-69, Tarkio (Mo.) Coll., 1970-74; exec. dir. Pensacola (Fla.) Mus. Art, 1974-76; pres., owner Blair-Murrah Exhbns., Sibley, Mo., 1980—. Pres. bd. trustees, CEO Blair-Murrah Inc., 1991—; sec.-treas. Coun. for Cultural Resources, 1995—. Del. White House Conf. on Small Bus., 1986. Lew Wentz scholar U. Okla., 1960-62. Mem. Internat. Coun. of Mus., Internat. Coun. Exhbn. Exch., Internat. Soc. Appraisers, Am. Assn. Mus., Internat. Trade Club of Greater Kansas City, Nat. Assn. Mus. Exhibitions, Ft. Osage Hist. Soc., Friends Art, Internat. Com. Fine Arts, Internat. Com. Conservation, Internat. Sculpture Ctr., DAR (regent Ft. Osage chpt.), Delta Phi Delta. Republican. Avocations: historical and cultural activities, antique cars, midwest farm auctions, genealogy. Home: RR # 1 Sibley MO 64088 Office: Blair-Murrah Vintage Hill Orch Sibley MO 64088 also: 7 rue Muzy PO Box Nr 554 1211 Geneva 6 Switzerland E-mail: elizabethmorrow@blair-murrah.org., exhibits@blair-murrah.org.

MORROW, GEORGE LESTER, retired oil and gas executive; b. New Haven, Apr. 27, 1922; s. Lester W.W. and Esther (Morrow) M.; m. Mary L. Evenburg, Dec. 28, 1946; children: Susan Morrow Donaldson, William, John, Thomas. BS, Rutgers U., 1943; MBA, U. Chgo., 1954. Registered profl. engr., Ill. With Peoples Gas Light and Coke Co., Chgo., 1947-77, v.p. ops., 1966-71, pres., 1971-77; also dir.; pres. Natural Gas Pipeline Co. Am., 1977-83; vice chmn., dir. Midcon Corp., 1983-87. Capt. AUS, 1943-46. Mem. Sarasota Yacht Club, Lake Zurich Golf Club. Presbyterian.

MORROW, GRANT, III, medical research director, physician; b. Pitts., Mar. 18, 1933; married, 1960; 2 children. BA, Haverford Coll., 1955; MD, U. Pa., 1959. Intern U. Colo., 1959-60; resident in pediat. U. Pa., 1960-62, fellow neonatology, asst. instr., 1962-63, instr., 1963-66, assoc., 1966-68, asst. prof., 1968-70, assoc. prof., 1970-72, U. Ariz., 1972-74, prof., 1974-78, assoc. chmn. dept., 1976-78; med. dir. Columbus (Ohio) Children's Hosp., 1978-94; prof. neonatology and metabolism, chmn. dept. Ohio State U., 1978-94; med. dir., dir. divsn. molecular and human genetics Children's Hosp. Rsch. Found., Columbus, 1994-98. Med. dir. Children's Rsch. Inst., Columbus, Ohio, 1978—. Mem. Am. Pediat. Soc., Am. Soc. Clin. Nutrition, Soc. Pediat. Rsch. Achievements include research on children suffering inborn errors of metabolism, mainly amino and organic acids. Office: Children's Rsch Inst 700 Childrens Dr Columbus OH 43205-2696 Fax: (614) 722-2716. E-mail: morrowg@pediatrics.ohio-state.edu.

MORROW, JAMES THOMAS, investment banker, financial executive; b. Seattle, Apr. 24, 1941; s. James Elroy and Helen Margaret (Helzer) M.; m. Gwendolyn Fay Peck Switzer, Feb. 28, 1987; 1 child, Shannon F. BSEE, BS in Gen. Sci., Oreg. State U., 1964; MBA, U. Santa Clara, 1966, PhD, 1973. Registered profl. engr.; registered investment advisor. Engr. Gen. Electric Co., San Jose, Calif., 1964-66; engring. mgr. Beckman Instruments, Inc., Palo Alto, 1966-69; pres. MSA Cons., Inc., Portland, Oreg., 1969-75; asst. prof. U. Portland, 1969-75; mgr. A.T. Kearney, Inc., San Francisco, 1975-78; v.p. mktg. Pierce Pacific Mfg., Portland, 1978-79; chmn., chief exec. officer Lanco Internat., Inc., Clackamas, Oreg., 1979-81; regional mgr., v.p. Case & Co., Portland, 1981-82; chmn. bd., exec. v.p. Morley Fin. Svcs. Inc., 1982-94; exec. v.p., chmn. bd. Biojet, Med. Systems Ltd., 1985-94; ptnr. WAM Partnership, 1987-96; sec.-treas. Environ. Waste of Am., Inc., Seattle, 1992-94; chmn., pres., CEO Capital Devel. Group, Inc., Portland, 1994-96; chmn., CEO USA/China Design and Mfg. Inc., Tianjing, China, 1994-95, The Apollo Fin. Group, N.Y.C., 1996-98; pres., chmn., CEO G.I.C. Acceptance Corp., Portland, 1992—; pres., CEO Turtle Cove Resort, Cabo San Lucas, Mex., 1998-2000; chmn., CEO Olympic Healthcare Tech., Inc., Portland, N.Y.C., 1998—. Chmn. bd. dirs. Ship Harbor Resort and Marina, Inc., 1998—, Turtle Cove Resort, Inc., 1998-2000, Olympic Capital, Inc., 1998—; bd. dirs. Accucom Data Network, Inc., Pierce Pacific Mfg., Lanco Internat., Energy Guard, Inc., G&R Devel. Co., Inc., MSA Cons., Inc.; sec.-treas. Everybody's Record Co., Inc. Contbr. articles to profl. jours., chpts. to textbooks; patentee Biojector Needleless Syringe. Bd. dirs. Found. for Oreg. Rsch. and Edn., Jr. Achievement, First August Fin., Inc., Met. Youth Symphony; chmn. steering com. R.S. Dow Neurol. Scis. Inst.; mem. Russian ANT-25 Aviation Com. Mem. Oreg. Pilots Assn. (pres. Beaverton chpt.). Republican. Congregationalist. Home: 2616 NW 81st Pl Portland OR 97229-4104 E-mail: olympicpdx@aol.com.

MORROW, JAMES FRANKLIN, lawyer; b. Shenandoah, Iowa, Oct. 23, 1944; s. Warren Ralph and Margaret Glee (Palm) M. BS, Kans. State U., 1967; JD, U. Ariz., 1973. Bar: Ariz. 1973, U.S. Dist. Ct. Ariz. 1973. Ptnr. Bilby, Shoenhair, Warnock & Dolph, Tucson, 1973-83, Quarles & Brady Streich Lang LLP, Tucson, 1984—. Mng. editor U. Ariz. Law Rev., 1972-73. Past chmn. bd. trustees Palo Verde Mental Health Svcs.; past pres. U. Ariz. Alumni Assn.; past chmn. bd. Palo Verde Hosp., Ariz. Tech. Devel. Corp.; past pres. bd. Cath. Cmty. Svcs.; past chmn. bd. dirs. U. Ariz. Found. Capt. U.S. Army, 1967-70. Mem. Am. Coll. Real Estate Lawyers, Am. Coll. Mortgage Attys., State Bar Ariz. (cert. real estate specialist, adv. com. real estate specialists, past chmn. real estate property sect.), Pima County Bar Assn., Calif. Bar Assn. Democrat. Roman Catholic. Avocation: golf. Office: Quarles & Brady Streich Lang LLP Ste 1700 One South Church Ave Tucson AZ 85701

MORROW, JASON DREW, medical and pharmacology educator; b. St. Louis, Mar. 30, 1957; s. Ralph Ernest and Vera Rowena (Cummings) M.; m. Lisa Lee Hyman, Mar. 26, 1983; children: Jeremy Nash, Stephanie Rose. BA magna cum laude, Vanderbilt U., 1979; MD, Washington U., St. Louis, 1983. Diplomate Am. Bd. Internal Medicine, Am. Bd. Infectious Diseases. Med. intern, resident Vanderbilt U. Hosp., Nashville, 1983-86, Hugh J. Morgan chief med. resident, 1987-88, rsch. fellow in clin. pharmacology, 1988-91; sr. rsch. fellow dept. pharmacology Vanderbilt U., Sch. Medicine, 1991-94, asst. prof. pharmacology and medicine, 1994-95; assoc. prof. Vanderbilt U., 1995-99, F. Tremaine Billings prof. medicine, 1999—, dir. Eicosanoid Core Lab. dept. pharmacology, 1992—; clin. fellow in infectious diseases Barnes Hosp./Washington U., 1986-87; staff physician in medicine and infectious diseases VA Med. Ctr., Nashville, 1991—; dir. med. scholars program Vanderbilt Med. Sch., 1997—. Mem. internat. adv. com. 9th Internat. Conf. on Prostglandins and Related Compounds, Florence, Italy, 1994, 10th Conf., Vienna, Austria, 1996. Ad hoc reviewer Jour. Biol. Chemistry, Prostglandins, numerous other sci. publs.; contbr. over 290 articles, revs. and papers to sci. jours., chpts. to books. Physician Nashville Union Rescue Mission, 1988-00. Recipient Physician-Scientist award NIH, 1990-91, grantee; recipient Rsch. Found. Devel. award Internat. Life Scis. Inst., 1992-96, Burroughs Wellcome Fund award in Transitional Rsch., 1999—; Centennial Clin. Pharmacology fellow Boehringer-Ingelheim, 1990-91, Howard Hughes Med. Inst. Physician rsch. fellow, 1991-94; grantee Liddle Med. Rsch., 1996. Mem. AMA, ACP, AAAS, Am. Fedn. Clin. Rsch., Am. Soc. Clin. Investigation, So. Soc. Clin. Investigation, Infectious Diseases Soc. Am., Am. Soc. Pharmacology Exptl. Therapeutics, Am. Soc. Biochemistry and Molecular Biology, Phi Beta Kappa. Avocations: running, fishing, outdoors. Home: 6408 Eastbourne Dr Brentwood TN 37027-4802 Office: Vanderbilt U Dept Pharmacology 23rd And Pierce Ave Nashville TN 37232-0001

MORROW, LEE, communications executive; b. Balt., Mar. 16, 1946; d. Kenneth Richard and Betty Jane (Hampson) Lee; m. Phillip Buddemeyer, May 29, 1965 (div. July 1970); children: Christopher, Gwenda Lee Bond; m. Harry Lee Morrow, Oct. 1, 1994. Student, U. Balt., Catonsville C.C. Asst. mgr. market rsch. Noxell Corp., Balt., 1963-66; media buyer W.B. Doner, 1970-73; account exec. WXYZ-TV, Detroit, 1973, Balt. Sunpapers, 1973-79, Media Networks Inc., Balt., 1979-80; mktg. info. mgr. Sweetheart Brands, 1980-84; sr. v.p. med. dir. Ehrlich-Manes Assoc., Washington, 1985-90; sr. account exec. WKRZ Radio, Harrisburg, Pa., 1992-93; dir. Media Buying Acad., Taneytown, Md., 1993—. Author: (book) How to Sell Radio Time to a Savvy Media Buyer , 1990, if You Think It's Tough to Sell, Try Buying, 1994, Bootcamp Workbooks 101, 102, 103, and 104, 1993, How to Get the Most Out of your Advertising Agency , If You Think it's Tough to Sell, Try Buying , How To Get The Most Out of Your Advertising Agency, 2000. Mem. Soc. to Advance Media Professionalism (cert. media generalist, pres. 1995-96). Democrat. Methodist. Avocations: reading, skeet shooting, bridge. Office: Media Buying Acad 57 W Baltimore St Taneytown MD 21787-2015 E-mail: mba@netstorm.net.

MORROW, MARILEE M. media consultant; b. New Castle, Pa., July 18, 1969; m. William Thomas Hampton; children: Erin Morrow Hampton, Tucker Morrow Hampton, Oscar Morrow Hampton. BSC, Ohio U., Athens, 1991; MA, W.Va. U., Wheeling, 2001. Continuity and prodn. dir. Tschudy Broadcasting Co., WEYQ-FM and WBRJ-AM, Marietta, Ohio, 1991; prodr. and announcer Reams Broadcasting Co., WZRZ-FM, Cin., 1991—92, Jacor Broadcasting Corp., WCKY-AM, Cin., 1992—95; sr. prodr. Benedek Comm. Corp., WTAP-TV, Parkersburg, W.Va., 1995—98; adj. prof. Marietta Coll., Mass Media Dept., Marietta, Ohio, 1998—; pres. Morton Media and Mktg., 2000—. Prodr.: (documentary) Storm of the Decade, 1999 (AP Best Documentary, 1999). Mem.: Ea. Communication Assn. Office: Morton Media and Marketing 501 Foster Lane Marietta OH 45750

MORROW, MAUREEN JANE, interior designer; b. Clinton, Iowa; d. Joseph Kenneth and Rosena Viola (Henricksen) Melvin; m. James Richard Morrow, June 15, 1963; children: Colleen Renée, Kent Richard. AA, Mount Saint Clare, Clinton, Iowa, 1959; BA, U. Iowa, 1961; MS, Calif. Poly. U., 1983. Instr. art Santa Maria (Calif.) Elem Sch. Dist., 1961-63, tchr., 1963-67; cons. interior design Design Collaboration, Santa Maria, 1980-88; instr. design Allan Hancock Coll., 1983-85, Calif. Polytech. State U., San Luis Obispo, 1984-86; designer, owner Coastal Design Assocs., Santa Maria, 1988—. Coordinator hist. preservation Hart Home, Santa Maria Valley Hist. Soc., 1983-93; sec. Notables of Santa Maria; pres. Dames of Authentic Californiales. Mem. Santa Maria Valley Geneal. Soc. (pres. 1999-2000), Sisquoc Genealogy Soc. (pres.). Avocation: genealogy.

MORROW, PATRICK DAVID, English educator; b. L.A., Oct. 1, 1940; s. Patrick Francis and Mary Lillian (Keefe) M.; m. Joyce Mae Rothschild, June 14, 1984; children: Milan Elizabeth, Christopher Patrick, Paul Issac Hotchkiss, Judith Spenceley, Mary Vehrs. Student, Sacramento State Coll., 1958-61; BA, U. So. Calif., 1963; MA, U. Wash., 1965, PhD, 1969. Asst. prof. English U. So. Calif., 1969-75; assoc. prof. English, prof. Auburn (Ala.) U., 1975—. Vis. assoc. prof. Am. studies U. N.Mex. and Idaho State U., summers, 1972, 73; cns. Ctr. Western Studies, Augustana Coll. Author: The Popular and the Serious in Select Twentieth Century American Novels, 1991, Katherine Mansfield's Fiction, 1993, Post-Colonial Essays on South Pacific Literature, 1998, others. Mem. Local Multiple Sclerosis Support Group. Fulbright grantee U. Canterbury, Christchurch, New Zealand, 1981, U. South Pacific, Suva, Fiji, 1989, rsch. grantee Auburn U., 1993, 95. Mem. MLA, Assn. Am. Australian Lit. Studies. Democrat. Jewish. Avocations: music, sports. Office: Auburn U Dept English Auburn AL 36849-0002 E-mail: morrpd@mail.auburn.edu.

MORROW, PAUL EDWARD, toxicology educator; b. Fairmont, W.Va., Dec. 27, 1922; s. Paul Reed and Imogene (Tench) M.; m. Anne Kelly, June 14, 1947; children— Robert Randolph, William David. BS in Chemistry, U. Ga., 1942, MS in Chemistry, 1947; PhD in Pharmacology, U. Rochester, N.Y., 1951. Diplomate Am. Bd. Indsl. Hygiene. Indsl. hygienist Tenn. Eastman Corp., Kingsport, 1942-43; instr. pharmacology and toxicology U. Rochester, 1952-56, asst. prof. radiation biology and pharmacology, 1956-60, assoc. prof. radiation biology and pharmacology, 1960-66, prof. radiation biology and pharmacology, 1967-85, assoc. prof. pharmacology and toxicology, 1967-69, prof. pharmacology and toxicology, 1969-85, emeritus prof. toxicology, 1985—, acting chmn. dept. radiation biology and biophysics, 1975-77. NIH-USPHS fellow U. Göttingen, Germany, 1959-60, U. Zurich, Switzerland, 1960-61; mem. Internat. Commn. for Radiol. Protection Com., 1967-77; space sci. bd. Nat. Acad. Scis., 1967; adv. com. NRC, 1968, toxicology info. program com., 1979-82; mem. Nat. Coun. for Radiation Protection, 1977-87; primary reviewer Oxides of Nitrogen Criteria Document, Health Effects, U.S. EPA, 1989, contbr., reviewer Air Quality Criteria Document on Particulate Matter, 1995-97; peer reviewer Toxicol. Profile for Uranium, Agy. for Toxic Substances and Disease Registry, USDHHS, 1996-99, A Rev. of Sci. Lit. as It Pertains to Gulf War Illnesses, vol. V, Rand Corp. for Office of Sec. Def., 1998, Depleted Uranium-Human Exposure Assessment Consultation #26-MF-7666-OOC Report, 2001. Contbg. author: Inhalation Carcinogenesis, 1970, Environmental Factors in Respiratory Disease, 1972, Respiratory Defense Mechanisms, 1978, Pulmonary Diseases and Disorders, 1978; editor: Assessment of Airborne Particles, 1972, Polluted Rain, 1980, Occupational and Industrial Medicine: Concepts and Methods, 1984, Aerosols in Medicine, 1985, 93, others; contbr. numerous articles to profl. jours. Advisor particulate matter control criteria Nat. Air Pollution Control Adminstrn., Nat. Acad. Scis. Health Effects of Fossil Fuel Combustion Products, 1968-69; cons. Comitato Nazionale Per L'Energia Nucleare, Casaccia Center, Rome, Italy, 1968-69; mem. temporary staff Med. Research Council, Carshalton, Eng., 1968-69; chmn. com. air pollution Rochester Com. Sci. Info., 1972— ; chmn. com. environ. health planning Genesee Region Health Planning Council, 1970-74. Served with USNR, 1943-45. Recipient Aerosol Rsch. award Internat. Soc. Aerosols Med., 1988, Founders award Chem. Industry Inst. Toxicology, 1989, Mercer award Am. Assn. Aerosol Rsch. and Internat. Soc. of Aerosols in Medicine, 1995. Fellow AAAS, N.Y. Acad. Scis., Acad. Toxicology Scis.; mem. Am. Indsl. Hygiene Assn., Am. Inst. Biol. Scis., Radiation Research Soc., Am. Coll. Toxicology, Health Physics Soc., Soc. Toxicology (Inhalation Toxicology Speciality Sect. Achievement award 1985), Am. Thoracic Soc., Am. Assn. Aerosol Research, Gesellschaft für Aerosolforschung, Soc. of Leukocyte Biology, Internat. Soc. Aerosols in Med., Am. Acad. Hygiene, Internat. Soc. Study Xenobiotics. Home: 200 Laney Rd Rochester NY 14620-3018 Office: U Rochester Dept Environ Medicine Box EHSC Rochester NY 14642

MORROW, PAUL LOWELL, forensic pathologist; b. N.Y.C., Mar. 30, 1949; s. Rufus Clegg and Dorothy Bell (Jackson) M.; m. Emily G. Rubenstein, Jan. 13, 1978; 1 child, Lillian Elaine. BA, Haverford Coll., 1971; MD, U. Vt., 1976. Diplomate Am. Bd. Pathology. Resident in pathology SUNY, Syracuse, 1976-78, Evanston (Ill.) Hosp., 1978-80; asst. chief med. examiner N.C. Office of Chief Med. Examiner, Chapel Hill, 1980-81; dep. chief med. examiner Vt. Office Chief Med. Examiner, Burlington, 1981-90, chief med. examiner, 1990—. Asst. clin. prof. pathology U. of Vt., Burlington, 1981-92, assoc. clin. prof. pathology, 1992—. Contbr. articles to profl. jours. Fellow Am. Acad. Forensic Scis.; mem. Nat. Assn. Med. Examiners. Mem. Soc. Of Friends. Office: Office of Chief Med Examin 111 Colchester Ave # 1 Burlington VT 05401-1473

MORROW, RICHARD MARTIN, retired oil company executive; b. Wheeling, W.Va., Feb. 27, 1926; married. B.M.E., Ohio State U., 1948. With Amoco Corp., 1948-91; v.p. Amoco Prodn. Co., 1964-66; exec. v.p. Amoco Internat. Oil Co., 1966-70, Amoco Chem. Corp., 1970-74, pres., 1974-78, Amoco Corp., 1978-83, chmn. chief exec. officer, 1983-91; ret., 1991. Trustee U. Chgo. and Rush-Presbyn. St. Luke's Med. Ctr. Office: 200 E Randolph Dr Ste 7909 Chicago IL 60601-7704

MORROW, SANDRA KAY, librarian; b. Levelland, Tex., Jan. 6, 1944; d. Oran Eiland and Martha Jane Johnson; m. Troy Leon Morrow; children: Paul, Kile. AA, Lubbock Christian U., 1964; BS in Edn., Abilene Christian U., 1966. Cert. libr. sci. Tex., 1973. Tchr. Andrews Sch. Dist., Andrews, Tex., 1966—68, New Deal Sch. Dist., New Deal, 1970—71, Ector County Sch., Odessa, 1971—72; libr. Austin Sch. Dist., Austin, 1974—77; tchr. Brentwood Christian Sch., 1984—. Originator Christian Librarians' Conf., Searcy, Tex., 1996—2002; presenter in field; dir. Yearly Booklist for primary, intermediate and Jr. H.S., 1992—. Ministry leader Westover Hills Ch. of Christ, Austin, 1977—2002, nursery dir., 1975—85. Recipient Lamplighter award, 2001, Children's Crown Gallery award, 2001, Disting. Alumni Award, Lubbock Christian U., 2002. Mem.: Nat. Christian Sch. Assn. (awards dir. 1996—, Christian Educator of Yr. award 2001), Tex. Christian Schools Assn. (Tchr. of Yr. award 2001), Tex. Libr. Assn. Republican. Mem.Church Of Christ. Avocations: reading, gardening, jogging, music. Home: 8308 Grayledge Drive Austin TX 78753 Office: National Christian School Association 11908 North Lamar Boulevard Austin TX 78753 Home Fax: 512-836-9247; Office Fax: 512-835-2184. Business E-mail: smorrow@brentwoodchristian.org.

MORROW, SCOTT DOUGLAS, choreographer, educator; b. N.Y.C., Jan. 29, 1954; s. Alfred Lionel and Lorraine (Power) M. BFA in Dance, SUNY, Purchase, 1976; MA in Choreography, UCLA, 1986. Prin. instr. Phil Black Dance Studio, N.Y.C., 1969-77; dir. dance divsn. No. Ill. U., DeKalb, 1976-78; artistic dir., resident choreographer No. Ill. Repertory Dance co., 1976-78; artistic dir. Scott Morrow Dance Theatre Co. and Sch., L.A., 1978-85; prin. instr. Mary Tyler Moore Los Angeles Dance Ctr., 1979-80; resident dance master South Coast Repertory Acting Conservatory, Calif., 1979-82; vis. prof. Wright State U., Ohio, 1981; ballet master, resident choreographer Empire State Ballet, Buffalo, 1984-85; asst. prof. U. Kans., Lawrence, 1985-88. Choreographer Morrow Dance Theatre-in-Residence, U. Kans., 1985-88, 92d St. Dancer Ctr., YMHA and YWHA, N.Y.C., 1989; founder, dir. Jazz Dance Ministry for Racial Reconciliation, Peace and Healing, N.Y.C., 1988—; assoc. dir., dir. edn. pub. sch. dance programs K-12, Bronx Dance Theatre Performing Arts Ctr., N.Y.C., 1990-93; faculty Internat. Summer Sch. Royal Acad. Dancing, N.Y.C., 1991-92, Calif. State U. Sys. Summer Inst. for Tchg. and Learning, 1994; sr. faculty Lilly Conf. on Coll. Tchg., Miami U., Ohio, 1991—; dance specialist State Edn. Dept. Summer Inst. on Assessment in Arts, N.Y., 1992; founder, dir. in chief Inst. Advancement Edn. Dance, N.Y.C., 1992—; adv. bd. Internat. Found. for Performing Arts Medicine, 1992—; advisor Performing Arts Medicine Ctr., Kessler Inst. Rehab., N.J., 1995—; Walter H. Annenberg disting. vis. artist-scholar The Renaissance Sch., N.Y.C., 1995-96; cons. presenting and commissioning program Nat. Endowment for Arts, 1993-95; peer rev. panel Fund for Innovation in Edn. U.S. Edn. Dept., 1993-94; co-chmn. dance edn. com. World Dance Allliance: Americas Ctr., 1993-97; internat. artistic advisor Noyam Exptl. Dance Co. and Rsch. Project, Ghana, 1998—; founder, min. in chief Embassy of Sekyere Kwamang Traditional Area, Ghana, 1998—; internat. adv. bd. Ctr. for Nat. Culture, Kumasi, Asante, Ghana, 2001—. Choreographer: (mus. theater) Broadway Musical Classics on International Tour, (film musicals) Chestnuts, Rainbows Edn., (teleseries) Adventures of Hans Christen Andersen, (telespecial) Rapsodia Afrikiko: A Celebration in Dance, (indsl. show) Le Parfum Salvador Dali; film dir. Of One Blood: Returning Home to Africa, 1999 (Best Documentary Film award Black Internat. Cinema Festival); world premieres presented at festivals including Morningside Dance Festival, N.Y.C., Mid Am. Dance Festival, L.A. Dance Kaleidoscope Festival, Middfest Internat., Ohio, Smithsonian Instn's Duke Ellington Festival, Washington, Marche Internat. de Disque et de l'Edition Musicale, Cannes, France, Anokyekrome Festival, Kumasi, Ghana, Royal Performance King Nana Barimah Abeyie Ntori Nimpah II, Sekyere Kwamang, Asante Nation, Ghana, Black Internat. Cinema Festival, Berlin; creator over 40 ballets. Nat. Festival for the Performing Arts Choreographers fellow, 1989; Josephine & Randolph Stewart African Heritage Fund Edn. and Rsch. grantee, 1997; named Choreographer of the Yr., Kaymore Found. for Arts, 1984, Master Educator and Disting. Fellow, Am. Bd. Master Educators, 1987; Alvin Ailey scholar, Sch. Am. Ballet scholar, Harkness House for Ballet Arts scholar; recipient Grand Prize for Choreography, Ann. Internat. Artistic Impression Competition, 1991, citation U.S. Edn. Dept., 1993, contbns. to growth and advancement of performing arts award, U.S. Arts Coun. Co-op, 1993, instrnl. approach recognized as an ednl. innovation Internat. Bur. Edn., UNESCO, 1996; named Traditional Chief and Spl. Advisor in Edn. and Human Devel. to King, Sekyere Kwamang, Asante Nation, Ghana, 1997, Pan-African and Humanitarian Vision award African Profiles USA mag., 2001. Office: Lorraine Prodns Ste 8 28-04 33d St Astoria NY 11102

MORROW, STEVEN ROGER, computer scientist; b. Sioux Falls, S.D., Sept. 20, 1963; s. Roger Lee and Rose Mary (Cooper) M.; m. Kerri Rene Verburg, Dec. 28, 1991; children: Melody Rene, Stephany Rose. BS, U. S.D., 1986, MA, 1988; MBA, Mankato State U., 1993. From programmer analyst to sr. software developer Firepond, Mankato, Minn., 1988-98; data repository specialist Immanuel-St. Joseph's-Mayo Health Sys., 1999—2001; sr. programmer analyst Mayo Health Sys., 2001—. County conv. del. Rep. County Conv., Mankato, 1996—; baritone player Mankato State U. Cmty. Symphonic Band, 1989—; mem. Hope Bapt. Ch., Mankato, 1990—, mem. leadership team, 1998—. Mem. IEEE, Assn. Computing Machinery. Baptist. Avocations: running, Bible study, collecting stamps & coins, sports. Home: 213 James Ct Eagle Lake MN 56024-9600 Office: Immanuel-St Josephs Mayo Health Sys 1025 Marsh St Mankato MN 56001-4752

MORROW, SUSAN DAGMAR, psychic, medium educator, writer, consultant; b. Harrisburg, Pa., July 10, 1932; d. William Lime and Margaret Louise (Deckard) Brubaker; m. Henry Taylor Morrow, June 9, 1952 (div. Mar. 1984); children: Quenby Anne, Christopher Brian. Student, Carnegie Inst. Tech., 1950-52, U. Ariz., 1952-54, U. Calif., Berkeley Ext., 1960-72, Foothill Coll., 1980-81. Self-employed psychic, psychic tchr., Palo Alto, Calif., 1976-80, Mountain View, 1980—; medium, psychic, tchr Seekers Quest Profl. Ctr., San Jose, 1983—. Tchr. Sunnyvale Community Ctr., 1977-87; tchr. San Andreas Health Coun., Palo Alto, 1981-83; lectr. U. Calif., Berkeley, 1978, Foothill Coll., Los Altos, Calif., 1980; lectr. in field; medium, cons. in cases of mental disorientation to psychologists, Palo Alto and Mountain View, 1978—, to detectives and police in cases of missing persons, animals or property, 1983—, pvt. tutor, medium, cons. past lives, archeological information, 1990—. Contbr. articles on psychic awareness to various publs. Mem. Assn. Psychic Practitioners (co-founder, v.p. 1982-83, editor and writer newsletter 1982-83), Mountain View C. of C., Mind Being Found., Assn. Rsch. and Enlightenment, Inst. Noetic Sci., Friends of the Animals. Democrat. Episcopalian. Avocations: physical mediumship, painting, swimming, sailing.

MORROW, TIMOTHY WILLIAM, urologist; b. Lawrenceburg, Tenn., June 1, 1950; s. William Herman and Elize Marie (Holt) M.; m. Linda Lee Branham, June 23, 1973; children: Melinda Lee, Michael Edward. BS, U. Tenn., Knoxville, 1972; MD, U. Tenn., Memphis, 1975. Diplomate Am. Bd. Urology. Intern St. Thomas Hosp., Nashville, 1975-77; resident in urology U. Tenn. Ctr. for Health Scis., Memphis, 1977-80; pvt. practice, Montgomery, Ala., 1980—. Active med. staff Bapt. Med. Cr., Montgomery, 1980—, sec.-treas., 1984-85, 95-97; courtesy med. staff Jackson Hosp., Montgomery, 1980—; mem. staff East Montgomery Med. Ctr., 1980—. Mem. bd. ventures Bapt. Hosp., Montgomery, 1989-91. Fellow ACS, Internat. Coll. Surgeons; mem. Am. Urol. Assn. (alt. del. bd. dirs.. S.E. sect. 1995—), Montgomery Surg. Soc. (sec.-treas. 1993-96), World Tang Soo Do Assn. (1st degree black belt). Baptist. Avocations: tennis, weight lifting. Home: 307 Foxhall Rd Pike Road AL 36064-3405 Office: 2055 E South Blvd Ste 802 Montgomery AL 36116-2007

MORROW, WALTER EDWIN, JR. electrical engineer, university laboratory administrator; b. Springfield, Mass., July 24, 1928; s. Walter Edwin and Mary Elizabeth (Ganley) M.; m. Janice Lila Lombard, Feb. 25, 1951; children: Clifford E., Gregory A., Carolyn F. S.B., M.I.T., 1949, S.M., 1951. Mem. staff Lincoln Lab., MIT, Lexington, Mass., 1951-55, group leader, 1956-65; head div. communications MIT Lincoln Lab., 1966-68, asst. dir., 1968-71, asso. dir., 1972-77, dir., 1977-98, dir. emeritus, 1998—. Contbr. articles to profl. publs. Recipient award for outstanding achievement Pres. M.I.T., 1963, Edwin Howard Armstrong Achievement award IEEE Communications Soc., 1976 Fellow IEEE, Nat. Acad. Engring. Achievements include patent for synchronous satellite, electric power plant using electrolytic cell-fuel cell combination. Office: MIT Lincoln Lab PO Box 73 Lexington MA 02420-9108

MORROW, WILLIAM EARL, retired government official; b. Perryopolis, Pa., Oct. 22, 1923; s. Robert Ferguson and Daisy (Johnson) M.; m. Danna Katunaric, Apr. 26, 1958; children: Jamie Johnson, Tammara Marie, Kim Ina, William Joseph, Geoffrey Sean. BS in Psychology, Waynesburg Coll., 1948; MA, U. Pitts., 1953; LLD (hon.), U. Zagreb, 1958; postgrad., U. Md., 1969, Indsl. Coll. Armed Forces, 1969-70. With Survey Rsch. Ct. U. Mich., 1947; auditor, employment interviewer, then asst. dir. personnel Jones & Laughlin Steel Corp., 1948-54; exec. coord. Peoples Cab Co., 1954; labor-mgmt. adviser, policy coord. Arabian Am. Oil Co., Saudi Arabia, 1954-57; personnel expert UN/ILO, 1957-58; cons., 1958-59; tng./program officer AID U.S. Dept. State, Eastern Caribbean, 1959-65; adminstrv. officer Bur. Internat. Labor Affairs Labor Dept., 1965-68, dep. divsn. chief, 1968-72, projects dir. L.Am., Caribbean, 1973-80; asst. dir. Office Fgn. Rels., 1980-86; exec. sec. Employee Retirement Income Security Act Office of Sec. Labor U.S. Dept. Labor, 1986—95; ret., 1995. Guest prof. U. Coll. W.I., 1960-64; lectr. Prince George's Community Coll., 1965-97; lectr. U. Md., 1967-97; adj. prof. U. Md., 1997—. Mem. Tantallon (Md.) Citizens Assn. With USAF, 1942-44. Mem. Indsl. Rels. Rsch. Assn., Prince George's County Bd. Realtors, Am. Fedn. Govt. Employees, Am. Soc. Tng. Dirs., Am. Legion, D.A.V., Masons, Scottish Rite, Shriners, Tantallon Country Club (control com.), U. Md. Faculty Club, Psi Chi Iota, Phi Alpha Theta, Delta Sigma Phi. Methodist. Home: 1220 Swan Harbour Cir Fort Washington MD 20744-7027 E-mail: willmorrow@aol.com.

MORROW, WINSTON VAUGHAN, financial executive; b. Grand Rapids, Mich., Mar. 22, 1924; s. Winston V. and Selma (von Egloffstein) M.; m. Margaret Ellen Staples, June 25, 1948 (div.); children: Thomas Christopher, Mark Staples; m. Edith Burrows Ulrich, Mar. 2, 1990. AB cum laude, Williams Coll., 1947; JD, Harvard U., 1950. Bar: R.I. 1950, U.S. Dist. Ct., U.S. Supreme Ct. Assoc. atty. Edwards & Angell, Providence, 1950-57; exec. v.p., asst. treas., gen. counsel, bd. dirs. Avis, Inc. and subs., 1957-61; v.p., gen. mgr. Rent A Car div. Avis, Inc., 1962-64, pres., bd. dirs., 1964-75; chmn., chief exec. officer, bd. dirs. Avis, Inc. and Avis Rent A Car System, Inc., 1965-77; chmn., pres., bd. dirs. Teleflorists Inc. and subs., 1978-80; pres. Westwood Equities Corp., L.A., 1981-95, CEO, 1984-95, also bd. dirs.; chmn., pres., chief exec. officer Ticor Title Ins. Co., 1982-91, also bd. dirs.; chmn. TRTS Data Svcs. Inc., 1985-91; bd. dirs. AECOM Tech. Corp., L.A., 1990-99. Mem. Pres.'s Industry and Govt. Spl. Travel Task Force, 1968, travel adv. bd. U.S. Travel Svcs., 1968-76, L.A. City-wide Airport Adv. Com., 1983-85; co-chmn. L.A. Transp. Coalition, 1985-91. Mem. juvenile delinquency task force Nat. Coun. Crime and Delinquency, 1985-86, L.A. Mayor's Bus. Coun., 1983-86, Housing Roundtable, Washington, 1983-85; chmn., pres. Spring St. Found., 1991—; bd. dirs. Police Found., Washington, 1983-91; trustee Com. for Econ. Devel., Washington, 1987-91; trustee Adelphi U., 1970-75. Decorated Stella Della Solidarieta Italy, Gold Tourism medal Austria). Mem. R.I. Bar Assn., Car and Truck Rental Leasing Assn. (nat. pres. 1961-63), Am. Land Title Assn. (bd. govs. 1989-90), L.A. Area C. of C. (bd. dirs. 1983-90), Williams Club, L.A. Tennis Club, Phi Beta Kappa, Kappa Alpha. Home: 4056 Farmouth Dr Los Angeles CA 90027-1314 also: Meadowview Farm 286 Clubhouse Corner Rd Freedom NH 03836-0221

MORROW BORDEN, DEBBIE MARIE, secondary education educator; b. Schenectady, N.Y., July 12, 1962; d. James Donald and Marcia Marie (Petricca) M.; m. Daniel M. Borden, 1 child, Danielle Morrow Borden AAS, SUNY, Morrisville, 1982; BA, SUNY, Albany, 1984; cert. in broadcasting, New Sch. Contemporary Radio, Albany, 1985; MEd, Coll. St. Rose, Albany, N.Y., 1994. Lic. gen. class radio broadcaster, N.Y. Announcer, disc jockey Sta. WMVQ-FM, Amsterdam, N.Y., 1985-86; sec., asst. radio bd. operator Sta. WMHT-FM, Schenectady, 1986; sec. Sta. WXXA-TV, Albany, 1985—97, broadcast engr., 1985—87, cameraperson, 1987-94, continuity dir., 1987—94, 1996—97; sec. St. Clare's Hosp., Schenectady, 1994-99; tchr. Burnt Hills-Ballston Lake Schs., Scotia, 1994—99. Tutor, tchr. WSWHE BOCES, Saratoga Springs, N.Y., 1999-2001; summer sch. tchr. Regents Ballston Spa (N.Y.) H.S., 2000—, Schenectady City Schs., 2001- Editor various campus pubs., 1980-82. Roman Catholic. Avocations: photography, piano, writing, reading. Home: 1137 Outer Dr Schenectady NY 12303 Office: 108 Education Dr Schenectady NY 12303

MORSCH, THOMAS HARVEY, lawyer; b. Oak Park, Ill., Sept. 5, 1931; s. Harvey William and Gwenodyne (Maun) M.; m. Jacquelyn Casey, Dec. 27, 1954; children: Thomas H. Jr., Margaret, Mary Susan, James, Kathryn, Julia. BA, Notre Dame U., 1953; BSL., Northwestern U., 1953, JD, 1955. Bar: Ill. 1955, D.C. 1955. Assoc. Crowell & Leibman, Chgo., 1955-62; ptnr. Leibman, Williams, Bennett, Baird & Minow, 1962-72, Sidley & Austin, Chgo., 1972-97, counsel, 1998-2000. Bd. dirs. Chgo. Lawyers Com. for Civil Rights Under Law, chmn., 1982-83; bd. dirs. Pub. Interest Law Initiative, pres., 1993-95; No. Dist. Ill. Civil Justice Reform Com., 1991-95, Ill. Equal Justice Commn., 1999—; mem. vis. com. Law Sch. Northwestern U., 1989-90, dir. Small Bus. Opportunity Ctr., 1998—, assoc. clin. prof., 1998—. Pres. Republican Workshops of Ill., 1970; gen. counsel Ill. Com. to Re-elect the Pres., 1972; mem. LaGrange Plan Commn., Ill., 1972-80, LaGrange Fire and Police Commn., 1968-72; trustee LaGrange Meml. Hosp., 1983-89; adv. bd. Catholic Charities of Chgo., 1985— Fellow Am. Coll. Trial Lawyers; mem. ABA, Ill. State Bar Assn., Chgo. Bar Assn. (bd. mgrs. 1979-81), DC Bar Assn., Northwestern Law Sch. Alumni Assn. (pres . 1988-89), Chgo. Bar Found. (bd. dirs., pres. 1995-97), 7th Cir. Bar Assn. Clubs: Univ. (Chgo.),, LaGrange Country, Palisades Park Country (Mich.), Point O'Woods Country (Mich.). Roman Catholic. Home: 301 S Edgewood Ave La Grange IL 60525-2153 Office: Northwestern U Sch Law 357 E Chicago Ave Chicago IL 60611 E-mail: tmorsch@law.northwestern.edu.

MORSE, ANNE BERNADETTE, educational consultant; b. Bklyn., May 7, 1925; d. Salvatore and Lucia (Romano) Somma; m. George Morse, Oct. 14, 1951; children: Jonathan, David. BBA in Acctg., CCNY, 1950. Office mgr. Chesterfield Hat Corp., N.Y.C., 1947-54; spl. asst. edn. Office Borough Pres. Queens, 1975-90; cons. Queensborough C.C. Fund, 1991-95. Pres. PTA P.S. 188Q, Bayside, N.Y., 1967-69; founding mem., 1st chair Sch. Dist. 26 Pres. Coun., Queens, 1968-69; mem., v.p. Cmty. Sch. Bd. 26, 1969-75; apptd. mem. N.Y. State Task Force Edn., Albany, 1974-75; founding mem. Alley Pond Environ. Ctr., 1975—; mem. Queens Com. Childrens Svcs., 1976—; bd. dirs. Queens Child Guidance Ctr., 1982—, outreach com. chair; charter mem. Ams. Italian Heritage, 1982—; mem. adv. bd. Queensborough C.C. Holocaust Rsch. Ctr., 1983—, chair, 1999—. Recipient Girl Scouts Am. Cert. of Appreciation, 1975, Sonia Strumpf Humanitarian award, 2000. Mem. Coun. Suprs. and Adminstrs. (spl. edn. awards com.). Avocations: travel, opera, reading, walking, theatre.

MORSE, BURNHAM SPOTTSWOOD, broadcast executive; b. Washington, Mar. 16, 1948; d. Augustin DeMouy and Mildred (Burnham) Spottswood; m. Jerome Samuel Morse, Oct. 25, 1970; children: Jordana Eve, Alexander Lewis. BA in Internat. Rels., Clark U., 1970; cert. in editing publs., George Washington U., 1974; cert. in project mgmt., Wharton Bus. Sch., 1980; M.Tech. Mgmt., U. Md., 1998. Asst. to dir. legis. affairs Corp. Pub. Broadcasting, Washington, 1972-74, radio projects adminstr., 1974-76; freelance broadcasting cons. Arlington, Va., 1976-78; dir. policy and planning representation divsn. Nat. Pub. Radio, Washington, 1978-85, dir. future interconnection sys. project office, 1987-96; telecomms. policy analyst Nat. Telecomms. and Info. Adminstrn., U.S. Dept. Commerce, 1985-87; dir. technology projects WETA-TV/FM, Arlington, Va., 1996-98; dir. DTV, Pub. Broadcasting Svc., Alexandria, 1998-2001; sr. dir. broadcast ops. Pub. Broadcasting Svc., 2001—. Democrat. Jewish. Office: Pub Broadcasting Svc 1330 Braddock Pl Alexandria VA 22314-1650

MORSE, CARL ROBERT, writer, editor; b. Skowhegan, Maine, Dec. 3, 1934; s. Roland Delmont and Blanche Roselma (Grignon) M. BA, Yale U., 1956; postgrad., U. Aix-Marseilles, 1956-57, U. Clermont-Ferrand, 1957-58. Editor Doubleday & Co., Inc., N.Y.C., 1958-62, Crowell-Collier & Macmillan, Inc., N.Y.C., 1963-66; mng. editor Western Pub. Co., Inc., 1966-69, Mus. Modern Art, N.Y.C., 1970-72, editor-in-chief, 1972-76, dir. pubs., 1976-77. Vis. poet Sarah Lawrence Coll., Martin-Hetrick H.S., CUNY, NYU; creator, organizer, dir. Open Lines, N.Y.C.; Fulbright lectr. Le Centre Paul Valery, U. Aix-Marseilles, Nice, Faculte de Lettres, U. Clermont-Ferrand. Author: (poetry) Dive, 1970, Turtleflow, 1973, The Curse of the Future Fairy, 1982, Three New York Poets, 1987, (plays) Annunciation, 1993, Fruit of Your Loins: Four Comedies, 1995, The Sunshine State, 2000; author poetry in mags. and anthologies; translator: (from French) The Art of Paul Verlaine, 1963, From Proust to Camus, 1966, Walt Disney's Snow White, 1967; anthology editor: Gay & Lesbian Poetry in Our Times: An Anthology, 1988; contbr. articles, essays, and book revs. to N.Y. Times, N.Y. Native, Poets and Writers, Gay Cmty. News, Village Voice, among others. Fellow N.Y. Found. for the Arts, 1989; recipient Playwright Devel. award La Ma Ma. E.T.C., 1993, Acad. Am. Poets prize Acad. Am. Poets, 1956. Mem. Elizabethan Club, Yale GALA (Gay and Lesbian Alumni). Home: Apt 17B 460 W 24th St New York NY 10011

MORSE, DARLENE M. medical/surgical nurse; b. Lebanon, N.H., Mar. 13, 1956; d. George Alfred Grace, Jr. and Barbara Jean Grace; m. Edward Charles Morse, May 28, 1977; children: Marcia Marie, George (Skip) Edward. Diploma in nursing, Cheshire Hosp. Sch. Nursing, Keene, N.H., 1977; BS in Behavioral Sci., Coll. Lifelong Learning, 2000. RN N.H., 1977. RN Alice Peck Day Hosp., Lebanon, 1977—78, Dartmouth Hitchcock Hosp., Lebanon, 1978—80, Mascoma-Visiting Nurses, Canaan, 1981—84, Valley Regional Hosp., Claremont, 1984—85, Dr. David Kroner, Lebanon, 1985—. Leader Weight Watcher N.H., Lebanon, 1986—97. Avocations: writing, crocheting.

MORSE, EDMOND NORTHROP, investment management executive; b. Balt., Dec. 31, 1922; s. Edmond Harris and Ethel (Dannenberg) M.; m. Sidney Harvey Phillips, June 5, 1948; children: Edmond H., David F., Judith B., Anne S., John B. BA, Brown U., 1944; MBA, Harvard U., 1947. With Smith, Barney & Co. (investment bankers), N.Y.C., 1947-81, gen. partner, 1961-64, v.p., dir., 1964-68, sr. v.p., dir., 1968-70, exec. v.p., dir., 1970-76; with Smith Barney Venture Corp., 1972-96; exec. v.p., dir. Smith Barney, Harris Upham, 1976-81; exec. v.p. First Manhattan Co., 1981-89; gen. ptnr. Morse Equity Ptnrs., Darien, Conn., 1989—. Mem. Darien Pension Rev. Bd., 1989—. Capt. USMCR, 1943-50. Mem.: Harvard Club N.Y., Wee Burn Country Club. Home: 166 Ridge Acres Rd Darien CT 06820-2616 Office: 36 Old Kings Hwy S Darien CT 06820-4523

MORSE, EDWARD LEWIS, petroleum industry executive; b. N.Y.C., Jan. 5, 1942; s. Jonah Benjamin and Rebecca (Freiberg) M.; m. Linda Kasle Jones, Aug. 15, 1965; children: Michael Ari, Molly Rachel. BA, Johns Hopkins U., Balt., 1963; MA, Johns Hopkins U., Washington, 1966; PhD, Princeton U., 1969. Asst. prof. internat. politics Woodrow Wilson Sch. Princeton (N.J.) U., 1969-75; sr. rsch. fellow Coun. on Fgn. Rels., N.Y.C., 1975-78; exec. asst. to undersec. econ. affairs U.S. Dept. State, Washington, 1978-79, dep. asst. sec. for internat. energy policy, 1979-81; dir. internat. affairs Phillips Petroleum Co., Bartlesville, Okla., 1981-84; mng. dir. Petroleum Fin. Co., Ltd., Washington, 1984-96; pres., publisher Petroleum Intelligence Weekly, N.Y.C., 1988-99, The Oil Daily Co., N.Y.C., 1996-99; exec. Hess Energy Trading Co., 1999—. Author: Foreign Policy and Interdependence in Gaullist France, 1973, Modernization and the Transformation of International Relations, 1976; contbr. articles to various publs. Home: 117 E 57th St # 30B New York NY 10022-2009 Office: HETCO 1185 Avenue Of The Americas New York NY 10036-2601 E-mail: elmorse@hess.com., edmorse@aol.com.

MORSE, F. D., JR. dentist; b. Glen Lyn, Va., Apr. 5, 1928; s. Frank D. and Ida Estell (Davis) M.; m. Patsy Lee Apple, Feb. 4, 1967; 1 child, Fortis Davis; m. Nancy Zink; 1 child, Pamela Marie. Student, U. Va., 1945; BS, Concord Coll., 1951; DDS, Med. Coll. Va., 1955. Freelance photographer, 1950-56; practice dentistry Pearisburg, Va., 1958—; mem. staff Giles Hosp., 1958-86. Served from asst. dental surgeon to sr. asst. dental surgeon USPHS, 1955-57; assigned to USCG, 1957-58. Honors scholar U. Va. Mem. AAAS, ADA, S.W. Va. Dental Assn., Assn. Mil. Surgeons, Nat. Assn. Advancement Sci., Fedn. Dentaire Internat., Internat. Platform Assn., W.Va. Collegiate Acad. Sci., Kiwanis, Beta Phi. Achievements include research in dental ceramics and roof coatings. Home: Bicuspid Acr Pearisburg VA 24134 Office: Giles Profl Bldg Pearisburg VA 24134

MORSE, FLO, writer; m. Joseph Morse; children: Joel N., Jonathan. BA, Barnard Coll., 1943. Author: Yankee Communes: Another American Way, 1971, How Does It Feel to Be a Tree?, 1976, The Shakers and the World's People, 1980, rev. edit., 1987, The Story of the Shakers, 1986, A Young Shaker's Guide to Good Manners, 1998; contbr. poetry to various books, jours, mags., articles to newspapers. Trustee Friends of Shakers, New Gloucester, Maine, 1976—; corporator United Soc. of Shakers, New Gloucester. Mem. Authors Guild.

MORSE, HELVISE GLESSNER, physical and life sciences educator; b. Frederick, Md., Sept. 17, 1925; d. George Edward and Rosa May (Durphy) Glessner; m. Melvin Laurance Morse, Jan. 25, 1949; children: Margaret Louise, Laurance Clinton. BA, Yale U., 1946; MS, U. Ky., 1949, U. Colo., Denver, 1963, PhD, 1966. Supr. cytogenetics lab. Children's Hosp., Denver, 1978-79; postdoctoral fellow U. Colo. Med. Ctr., 1966-67, rsch. assoc., 1968-73, rsch. cytogeneticist, 1974-78, asst. prof. biochemistry, biophysics and genetics, 1979-88, assoc. prof. biochemistry, 1988—; dir. cytogenetics CORE for Cancer Ctr. U. Colo. Cancer Ctr., 1988—; Eleanor Roosevelt Inst. Cancer Rsch. fellow U. Colo., 1979—. Mem. cytogenetics subcom. Nat. Children's Cancer Study Group, U.S.A. and Can., 1980-87. Contbr. articles on gene mapping, cytogenetics and Leukemia research to profl. publs., 1970—. Active So. Poverty Law Ctr. Mem. NAACP, Mortar Bd., Sigma Xi. Democrat. Avocations: photography of wild flowers, attending local symphony orchestra concerts and opera. Home: 254 S Jasmine St Denver CO 80224-1033 Office: Univ Colo Health Scis Ctr Dept Biochem/Biophys/Genet 4200 E 9th Ave Dept Biochem Denver CO 80220-3706

MORSE, JACK HATTON, management consultant; b. San Diego, June 4, 1923; s. John Henderson and Alberta (Peterson) M.; m. Kathleen Clark (div.); children: David Eugene, Steven Allen; m. Jean Larson. BA, San Diego State U., 1956, M in Bus. Sci., 1971. Exec. San Diego Gas & Electric, 1947-89; pres. S.D. Pub. Safety Com., 1981-82; chmn. mil. affairs San Diego C. of C., 1982-84; pres. Project Handclasp, 1991—. Cons. Pub., contbr. Sea Power mag., 1987-89. Pres. Cystic Fibrosis Found., San Diego, 1980-83; pres. Oceans Found., 1992-94, chmn., 1996-99. Comdr. USNR, 1943-46, 52-54. Recipient Dr. Frederick Patterson award, United Negro Coll. Fund., San Diego, 1989, Essence of Life award, San Diego Elders Help, 2002. Mem. IEEE, Pacific Coast Elec. Assn., Pacific Coast Gas Assn. (Silver medal 1981), Navy League U.S. (hat. pres., chmn. adv. com. 1987-89, Disting. Svc. award 1979, 88, 89, Hoover Hi Hall of Fame 1998), Essence of Life Award, Elder Help, 2002, La Jolla Beach and Tennis Club, Masons (Knight Comdr. Ct. of Honor), Rotary. Republican. Mem. Lds Ch. Avocations: traveling, public speaking. Home and Office: 6125 Terryhill Dr La Jolla CA 92037-6837

MORSE, JAMES L. state supreme court justice; b. N.Y.C., Sept. 11, 1940; m. Gretchen B, June 19, 1965; children: Rebecca Penfield, Rachel Lasell. AB, Dartmouth Coll., 1962; JD magna cum laude, Boston U., 1969. Bar: Vt. 1970, U.S. Dist Ct. Vt. 1970, U.S. Ct. Appeals (2d cir.) 1970, U.S. Supreme Ct. 1973. Law clk. to Judge Sterry R. Waterman U.S. Ct. Appeals (2nd cir.), 1969-70; pvt. practice Burlington, Vt., 1970-73, 75-76; asst. atty. gen. State of Vt., Montpelier, 1973-75, defender gen., 1976-81; judge Vt. Superior Ct., 1981-88; assoc. justice Vt. Supreme Ct., 1988—. Editor in chief Boston U. Law Rev., 1967-69. Lt. USNR, 1963-66. Mem. Vt. Bar Assn. Office: Vt Supreme Ct 109 State St Montpelier VT 05609-0001*

MORSE, JEAN AVNET, higher education administrator, lawyer; b. N.Y.C., Jan. 2, 1947; d. Samuel and Helen (Hershfield) Avnet; m. Stephen John Morse, Dec. 26, 1966; 1 child, Elisabeth Avnet Morse. BA in History with high honors, Wellesley Coll., 1968; JD cum laude, Harvard U., 1971. Bar: Mass. 1971, Calif. 1974, U.S. Dist. Ct. Mass. 1972, U.S. Dist. Ct. (ctrl. dist.) Calif. 1974. Law clk. Superior Ct. Commonwealth of Mass., Boston, 1971-72; atty. Palmer & Dodge, 1972-74; assoc. to ptnr. Kaplan, Livingston, Goodwin, Berkowitz & Selvin, Beverly Hills, Calif., 1974-81; ptnr. Hufstedler & Kaus, L.A., 1981-87, of counsel, 1988; dep. assoc. dean, dir. coll. office, Sch. Arts and Scis. U. Pa., Phila., 1989-93; lectr. sociology, ind. study supr. U. Pa. Sch. Arts and Scis., 1991; acting asst. provost U. Pa., 1991-92, dean's acad. planning cons., 1992-93; assoc. dean for adminstrn. NYU Sch. Law, N.Y.C., 1993-94; dep. to pres. U. Pa., 1994-95; exec. dir. Commn. on Higher Edn. Middle States Assn. of Colls. and Schs., Phila., 1996—. Bd. govs. Greater Phila. Philosophy Consortium, 1990-93; bd. dirs. Women in Bus., 1985-88, The Women's Bldg., 1985-86; chair individual rights sect. L.A. County Bar Assn., 1985-86, vice-chair, 1986-88, exec. com. mem., 1985-88.

MORSE, JEROME SAMUEL, government administrator, trade specialist; b. Worcester, Mass., Feb. 25, 1947; s. Manuel and Bernice Morse; m. Burnham Marie Spottswood, Oct. 25, 1970; children: Jordana Eve, Alexander Lewis. BA in Internat. Rels., Clark U., 1969; MA in Internat. Affairs, George Washington U., 1971. Internat. trade specialist U.S. Dept. Commerce, Washington, 1970-78, dep. dir. export awareness divsn., 1978-82, dep. dir. World's Fair staff, 1982-84, project mgr. trade devel., 1984-92, dir. planning and mgmt. divsn., 1992—2002, dir. office of machinery, 2002—. Author: The Complete Guide to Operating An Import/Export Business, 1989. Mem. fundraising com. McLean (Va.) H.S. Choral Parents Assn., 1997-2001; mem. McLean Theater Alliance, 1998—, treas., 2000—. Recipient Congl. fellowship Am. Polit. Sci. Assn., 1979. Mem. Multinational Mktg. Assocs. (v.p. 1986-90), Phi Beta Kappa. Democrat. Jewish. E-mail: Jerry_Morse@ita.doc.gov. Avocation: collecting Boston Red Sox memorabilia. Home: 1935 Rockingham St Mc Lean VA 22101-4923 Office: US Dept Commerce ITA TD/TM/OM Rm 4310 Washington DC 20230-0001 E-mail: morsefamily4@aol.com.

MORSE, JOHN HARLEIGH, lawyer, director; b. Estherville, Iowa, Sept. 22, 1910; s. James W. and Winifred E. (Williams) M.; m. Marie A. Forrest, Nov. 11, 1936 (div. June 1962); children: James W. II, Bruce F.; m. Ann U. Stanton, May 23, 1964. BA, State U. Iowa, 1930; MBA, Harvard U., 1932; JD, Yale U., 1935. Bar: N.Y. 1936. Since practiced in, N.Y.C.; with firm Carter, Ledyard & Milburn, 1935, Cravath, Swaine & Moore, 1936-76, ptnr., 1946-76; vice chair Nat. Forge Co., 1977-91. Pres. Forest Property Owners Assn., 1992-94. Mem. ABA (chmn. labor rels. law sect. 1961-62), Phi Beta Kappa, Phi Gamma Delta. Address: Shell Point 5807 Turban Ct Fort Myers FL 33908-1668

MORSE, LEWIS DAVID, microencapsulation polymer chemist, consultant; b. N.Y.C., Oct. 29, 1924; s. Simon and Mary Tillie Morse; m. Vivian Mirell, Oct. 20, 1945; 1 child, Marjorie. BS, NYU, 1948; MS, Bklyn. Coll., 1952; postgrad., Polytechnic Inst. Bklyn., 1952-54. Rschr. in enzymology Coll. Physicians and Surgeons, Columbia U., N.Y.C., 1950-64; mgr. product rsch. Ionac Chem. Co., Birmingham, N.J., 1964-67; product devel. fellow Merck & Co., Rahway, 1967-79; sr. rsch. assoc. Calgon Corp. divsn. Merck & Co., Pitts., 1979-89; cons. chemist, 1989—. Patentee in field. Sgt. U.S. Army, 1942-45, Europe. Mem. Am. Chem. Soc. (former chmn. polymer sect.), Inst. Food Technologists, Pitts. Chemists Club (chmn.). Home and Office: 307 S Dithridge St Apt 705 Pittsburgh PA 15213-3519 E-mail: lewmorse@cs.com.

MORSE, M. HOWARD, lawyer; b. Louisville, May 30, 1959; s. Marvin Henry and Betty Anne (Hess) M.; m. Laura E. Loeb, Apr. 17, 1988; children: Elizabeth Loeb, Marni Loeb. AB summa cum laude, Dartmouth Coll., 1981; JD cum laude, Harvard U., 1984. Bar: D.C. 1984, U.S. Ct. of Internat. Trade 1985, U.S. Ct. Appeals (fed. cir.) 1985, U.S. Dist. Ct. D.C. 1986, U.S. Ct. Appeals (D.C. cir.) 1986, U.S. Ct. Appeals (4th cir.) 1987. Assoc. Arnold & Porter, Washington, 1984-88; atty. FTC Bur. Competition, 1988-91, dep. asst. dir. for policy, 1991-93, asst. dir. for merger litigation, 1993-97; ptnr. Drinker, Biddle & Reath, Washington, 1998—. Adj. prof. law Georgetown Law Ctr., Washington, 1995—2000. Mem. ABA (mem. antitrust sect., chair computer industry com. 1996-99, chair antitrust issues in high-tech industries program 1999, chair intellectual property com. 1999-2002, coun. 2002-), FBA, D.C. Bar Assn., Phi Beta Kappa. Office: Drinker Biddle & Reath 1500 K St NW Ste 1100 Washington DC 20005-1209 E-mail: morsemh@howard.morse.com.

MORSE, MARTIN A. plastic surgeon; b. Louisville, June 25, 1957; s. Marvin Henry and Betty Anne (Hess) M. BS in Zoology with distinction, Duke U., 1979, MD, 1983. Diplomate Nat. Bd. Med. Examiners, Am. Bd. Plastic Surgery. Intern, jr. resident in surgery Barnes Hosp./Washington U., St. Louis, 1983-85; rsch. fellow dept. pediat. surgery Children's Hosp./Harvard Med. Sch., Boston, 1985-87; sr. resident in surgery U. Rochester, N.Y., 1987-89, chief resident, 1989-90; rsch./clin. fellow in transplantation dept. pediatric surg. Children's Hosp. Med. Ctr., Cin., 1990-92; clin. fellow hand and upper extremity surgery dept. orthopedic surgery U. Pitts. Med. Ctr., 1992-93; fellow in plastic and reconstructive surgery, dept. surgery U. Fla. Coll. Medicine, Gainesville, 1993-95; clin. staff Georgetown U., Washington, 1995—; pvt. practice plastic and reconstructive surgery McLean and Reston, Va., 1995-98; prin., owner The Great Falls (Va.) Plastic Surgery Ctr., 1999—. Lab. investigator Lab. Exptl. Pathology divsn. cancer cause and prevention Nat. Cancer Inst./NIH, Rockville, Md., summer 1974-80; invited prof. dept. grad. nursing Simmons Coll., Boston, 1986-87; NASA flight surgeon, 1994—. Contbr. articles to profl. jours. Vol. Cystic Fibrosis, Am. Cancer Soc., Am. Heart Assn., March of Dimes, Am. Lung Assn.; founding mem. Statue of Liberty/Ellis Isle Found., N.Y.C., 1985, JFK Libr. Found., Boston, 1987, Challenger Ctr. for Space Sci. Edn., Washington, 1987, U.S. Naval Meml. Found., Washington, 1990; active Friends Nat. Libr. Medicine, Col. Williamsburg Found., Met. Mus. Art, Boston Mus. Fine Arts, Carnegie Mellon Mus.; patron The John F. Kennedy Ctr. for the Performing Arts, Wolf Trap, Friends of the Nat. Zoo, Nat. Audobon Soc., World Wildlife Fund, U.S. Holocaust Mus.; vol. surgeons overseas medical Missions, 1998—; vol. physician Wolf Trap Farm Park, Nat Park Svc., Vienna, Va., 1998—. Farley Found. fellow Children's Hosp., Harvard Med. Sch., 1986; recipient Outstanding Svc. award Nat. Cancer Inst., NIH, 1977, Nat. Def. medal. Fellow ACS (assoc.); mem. AMA (Physician's Recognition award 1984, 87, 90, 93, 96, 99), AAAS, Am. Soc. Plastic Surgeons (candidate), Soc. Laparoendoscopic Surgeons, Am. Soc. Artificial Internal Organs, Am. Trauma Soc., Fla. State Med. Soc., Assn. for Acad. Surgery, Surg. Infection Soc., Aerospace Med. Assn., Assn. Mil. Surgeons U.S., Am. Soc. Cell Biology and Tissue Culture Assn., Southeastern Soc. Plastic and Reconstructive Surgeons (candidate), So. Med. Assn., Physicians for Social Responsibility, Rochester Surg. Soc., N.Y. Acad. Scis., Fairfax County Med. Soc., Fla. State Med. Soc., Fla. Hand Soc., Va. State Med. Soc., Am. Legion, Naval Res. Assn., Res. Officers Assn., Phi Beta Kappa, Alpha Omega Alpha, Phi Lambda Epsilon. Achievements include patent for Controlled Cellular Implantation Using Artificial Matrices; first to describe long-term growth of established human extrahepatic biliary epithelial cells in culture; first to describe a specific chemoattractant neutral proteinase in whole human skin, fibroblasts, lymphocytes, and granulocytes.

MORSE, MARVIN HENRY, judge; b. Mt. Vernon, N.Y., July 19, 1929; s. Frank Irving and Lillian (Seeger) M.; m. Betty Anne Hess, Dec. 27, 1953; children: Martin Albert, Michael Howard, Lee Anne. AB, Colgate U., 1949; LLB, Yale U., 1952. Bar: N.Y. 1952, Ky. 1956, Md. 1964, U.S. Supreme Ct. 1960, U.S. Ct. Appeals (6th cir.), U.S. Dist. Ct. (we. dist.) Ky., U.S. Ct. Mil. Appeals, U.S. Ct. Claims, U.S. Ct. Appeals (D.C. cir.), U.S. Ct. Appeals (fed. cir.), U.S. Dist. Ct. (no. dist.) Tex., U.S. Dist. Ct. Hawaii. Pvt. practice, Louisville, 1956-62; asst. advisor Office of Gen. Counsel Dept. Navy, Washington, 1962-65; asst. counsel Office of Gen. Counsel Office Sec. Def., 1965-68; asst. gen. counsel GSA, 1968-70, U.S. Postal Svc., Washington, 1970-73; adminstrv. law judge Fed. Energy Regulatory Commn., 1973-75, Postal Rate Commn., Washington, 1975-77, CAB, Washington, 1977-80; dir. adminstrv. law judges Office Pers. Mgmt., 1980-82; chief adminstrv. law judge SBA, 1982-87, asst. adminstr. hearings and appeals, 1985-87; adminstrv. law judge Exec. Office of Immigration Rev. Dept. Justice, 1987—2002; mem. Bd. of Immigration Appeals, 1998—2002. Mem. Adminstrv. Conf. of U.S., 1980-84, govt. mem., 1985-86, 87-95, liaison mem.; faculty and faculty coord. The Nat. Jud. Coll., 1977, 79-80. Author: (with S. Groner) ABA Handbook chpt. on adminstrv. law, 1981, (with Lvey Moran) Troubling the Waters 33 J1 of Maritime Law and Commerce, 2002. Trustee Washington area chpt. Am. Digestive Disease Soc., 1976-87. With JAGC, USAF, 1952-56, to col. USAFR, ret. 1979. Decorated USAF Legion of Merit; recipient Disting. Svc. award Am. Digestive Disease Soc., 1980. Mem. ABA (exec. com. 1977-82, 84-87, chmn. 1980-81, conf. adminstrv. law judges, del. ho. of dels. 1984-87, lawyers in govt. com. 1985-86, jud. selection, tenure and compensation com. 1987-93, govt. pub. sect. lawyers divsn., coun. 1996-02), Fed. Bar Assn. (nat. coun. 1976—, chmn. career svc. sect. 1983-86, chmn. judiciary sect. 1986-88, sect. coord. 1988-90, sec. 1991-92, del. to ABA ho. of dels. 1992-93, 97-99, v.p. 1993-94, pres.-elect 1994-95, pres. 1995-96), Am. Law Inst., Fed. Adminstrv. Law Judges Conf. (exec. com. 1975-77, 82-96, 2000-01), Nat. Assn. Adminstrv. Law Judges (hon.), Fed. Am. Inn of Ct. (coun. 1990-92, pres. 1992-94). Home: 11221 Potomac Crest Dr Potomac MD 20854-2743 Office: US Dept Justice 5107 Leesburg Pike Falls Church VA 22041-3234 E-mail: marvin.morse@usdoj.gov.

MORSE, PETER HODGES, ophthalmologist, educator; b. Chgo., Mar. 1, 1935; s. Emerson Glover and Carol Elizabeth (Rolph) M. AB, Harvard U., 1957; MD, U. Chgo., 1963. Diplomate: Am. Bd. Ophthalmology. Intern U. Chgo. Hosp., 1963-64; resident Wilmer Inst. Johns Hopkins Hosp., Balt., 1966-69; fellow, retina service Mass. Eye and Ear Infirmary, Boston, 1969-70; asst. prof. ophthalmology, chief retina service U. Pa., 1971-75, assoc. prof., 1975, U. Chgo., 1975-77; prof. ophthalmology, 1979-93; sec. dept. ophthalmology, 1976-77; chief retina service, prof., 1979-93; clin. prof. ophthalmology U. S.D. Sch. Medicine, Sioux Falls, 1993—. Prof. La. State U., 1978; chmn. dept. ophthalmology, chief retina service Ochsner Clinic and Found. Hosp., New Orleans, 1977-78; clin. prof. Tulane U., 1978 Author: Vitreoretinal Disease: A Manual for Diagnosis and Treatment, 1979, 2d edit., 1989, Practical Management of Diabetic Retinopathy, 1985; co-editor: Disorders of the Vitreous, Retina, and Choroid; bd. editors Perspectives in Ophthalmology, 1976— , Retina, 1980— ; contbr. articles to profl. jours. Served with USNR, 1964-66. Fellow ACS, Coll. Ophthalmologists Eng., Am. Acad. Ophthalmology, Royal Soc. Health (Eng.), Royal Coll. Ophthalmologists (Eng.); mem. AMA, La. Med. Soc., Orleans Parrish Med. Soc., New Orleans Acad. Ophthalmology, La. Ophthalmol. and Otolaryngol. Soc., Miss. Ophthalmol. and Otolaryngol. Soc., Assn. Rsch. Vision and Ophthalmology, Retina Soc., Soc. Heed Fellows, Ophthalmol. Soc. U.K., Pan Am. Assn. Ophthalmology, Oxford Ophthalmol. Congress, All-India Ophthalmol. Soc., Soc. Eye Surgeons, Vitreoretinal Soc. (India), Sigma Xi. Republican. Episcopalian. Home: 1307 S Holly Dr Sioux Falls SD 57105-0221 Office: Sioux Valley Clin Dept Ophthalmology 1100 E 21st St Sioux Falls SD 57105-1002

MORSE, RICHARD ALAN, accountant; b. Newburgh, N.Y., Mar. 2, 1954; s. Wesley Benjamin and Louise Barbara (Spinner) M. BS, Ill. State U., 1977. CPA, N.Y. Pvt. practice acctg., Met. N.Y. area, 1977—. Actor in various plays, films and TV shows; musician performing in various clubs and recordings. Mem. N.Y. State Soc. CPAs, AFTRA, Screen Actor's Guild, Actor's Equity Assn.

MORSE, RICHARD JAY, human resources and organizational development consultant, manufacturers' representative company executive; b. Detroit, Aug. 2, 1933; s. Maurice and Belle Rosalyn (Jacobson) M. BA, U. Va., 1955; MA in Clin. Psychology, Calif. State U., L.A., 1967. Area pers. adminstr. Gen. Tel. Co. of Calif., Santa Monica, 1957-67; sr. v.p. human resources The Bekins Co., Glendale, Calif., 1967-83; pvt. cons. human resources and orgn. devel. Cambria, 1983—. Contbr. articles to profl. jours. Fund raiser various orgns., So. Calif., 1970—. Mem. Internat. Soc. Performance Improvement (founding mem. 1958—). Republican. Jewish. Avocations: travel, tennis, walking, swimming. Home and Office: 6410 Cambria Pines Rd Cambria CA 93428-2009 E-mail: dickmorse@earthlink.net.

MORSE, RICHARD VAN TUYL, manufacturing executive, consultant; b. N.Y.C., May 7, 1931; s. Norvell V. and Julie M. (Lamisha) M.; m. Florence Denby, June 21, 1953 (div. June 1983); children: Stuart V., Andrew D.; m. Emilie Atolli, Sept. 14, 1983. BS in Econs., U. Pa., 1953; MBA, NYU, 1958. Account supr. various advt. agys., N.Y.C., 1956-66; v.p., account supr. Wells, Rich, Greene, Inc., 1960-70, Norman, Craig & Kummell, Inc., N.Y.C., 1970-74; sr. v.p., mgmt. supr. William Free & Co., 1974-80; v.p. mktg. Canada Dry, Inc., 1980-87; v.p. mktg. comm. Lithonia Lighting, Conyers, Ga., from 1987. Dir. Pop Warner Football, N.Y.C., 1967-69. Contbr. articles to profl. jours. Elected Rep. rep. Union County, N.J., 1970-76; chmn. bd. Atlanta Shakespeare Co., 1986-92. Capt. USAR. Mem. Am. Mktg. Assn., Nat. Lighting Bur. (chmn. bd. 1995—), Bus. and Profl. Advt. and Mktg. Assn. Republican. Episcopalian. Avocations: trap and skeet shooting, travel, Brit. Victorian mil. history. Home: Springfield, Pa. Died Jan. 15, 2002.

MORSE, ROBERT HARRY, lawyer; b. Bklyn., May 25, 1941; s. Soll and Rachel Morse; m. Sandra Goldstein, July 22, 1967; children: Lisa Jennifer, Eric Jeffrey. BSEE with honors, MIT, 1963, MSEE with honors, 1964; JD, Harvard U., 1967. Bar: N.Y. 1968, D.C. 1978, Md. 1985. Assoc. Kenyon & Kenyon, Reilly, Carr & Chapin, N.Y.C., 1967-71; trial atty. antitrust divsn. Dept. Justice, Washington, 1971-74, sr. trial atty., 1974-78; ptnr. Peabody, Lambert & Meyers, 1978-82, Galland, Kharasch, Morse & Garfinkle, Washington, 1982-96, Ropes and Gray, Washington, 1997-2000; pres., CEO Esrom Consulting LLC, Rockville, Md., 2000—. Dir. Earle Palmer Brown Cos., 1984-98. Mem. nat. capital area coun. Boy Scouts Am., gen. counsel, 1991-94, exec. bd. dirs., 1990—, pres. 2001-02, chmn., 2002—. Recipient Spl. Achievement award Dept. Justice, 1973, Meritorious award Dept. Justice, 1976, Silver Beaver award Boy Scouts Am., 1999. Mem. ABA, D.C. Bar Assn., Patent Bar, MIT Club Washington (sec. 1981-82, pres. 1983-84), Nat. Alumni Assn. MIT (bd. dirs. 1986-88), Sigma Xi, Tau Beta Pi, Eta Kappa Nu. E-mail: esrom4consulting@aol.com.

MORSE, ROBERT PARKER, investment company executive; b. Nyack, N.Y., May 8, 1945; s. Robert Willard Parker and Julia (Larson) M.; m. Sarah Morgan Cumings, Sept. 23, 1978; children: Robert Bradley St. Clair, Parker Morgan, Sarah Spencer. BS in Econs., U. Pa., 1967; student in advanced currency theory, Adelphi Suffolk U., 1970-71. V.p. Am. Express/W.H. Morton Divsn., N.Y.C., 1970-74; sr. v.p., ptnr. William G. Campbell & Co., Inc., 1975-80; chmn., CEO Morse, Williams & Co., Inc., 1981—. Bd. dirs. Optix Networks, Inc. Gov. Soc. Mayflower Descs., N.Y., 1993-98; trustee Plimoth Plantation, Mass., 1994-2000, Bermuda Biol. Sta. Rsch., 1983-2000, Gen. Svc. Bd., N.Y., 1981-93, trustee, chmn. fin. English Spkg. Union, 1998—, U.S. del. internat. coun., English Spkg. Union, London, 2002; bd. assocs. The Whitehead Inst., MIT, 1996—; bd. dirs. Arlington Inst., 1995-2001; chmn. bd. The Wall Street Fund, 1984—. Lt. USNR, 1967-78. Mem. Am. Def. Preparedness Assn., Pilgrims of U.S., River Club, Bond Club N.Y., U.S. Naval Inst., Pilgrims of the U.S., Union Club, N.Y. Yacht Club, Links Club, River Club. Episcopalian. Avocations: sailing, skiing, reading, golf, tennis, squash. Office: Morse Williams & Co Inc 230 Park Ave Rm 1635 New York NY 10169-1602 E-mail: rpm@morsewilliams.com.

MORSE, SAUL JULIAN, lawyer; b. Jan. 17, 1948; s. Leon William and Goldie (Kohn) M.; m. Anne Bruce Morgan, Aug. 21, 1982; children: John Samuel, Elizabeth Miriam. BA, U. Ill., 1969, JD, 1972. Bar: Ill. 1973, U.S. Dist. Ct. (so. dist.) Ill. 1976, U.S. Ct. Appeals (7th cir.) 1983, U.S. Supreme Ct. 1979, U.S. Tax Ct. 1982. Law clk. State of Ill. EPA, 1971-72, Ill. Commerce Commn., 1972, hearing examiner, 1972-73; trial atty. ICC, 1973-75; asst. minority legal counsel Ill. Senate, 1975, minority legal counsel, 1975-77; mem. Ill. Human Rights Commn., 1985-91; dir., treas., chair grievance com. Ill. Comprehensive Health Ins. Plan; gen. counsel Ill. Legis. Space Needs Commn., 1978-92; pvt. practice Springfield, Ill., 1977-79; ptnr. Gramlich & Morse, 1980-85; prin. Saul J. Morse and Assocs., 1985-87; ptnr. Morse, Giganti and Appleton, 1987-92; v.p., gen. counsel Ill. State Med. Soc., 1992—. Lectr. in continuing med. edn., 1986-90; counsel symposia; adj. asst. prof. med. humanities So. Ill. Sch. Medicine; pres. Springfield Profl. Baseball, LLC. Bd. dirs. Springfield Ctr. for Ind. Living, 1984-89, Ill. Comprehensive Health Ins. Plan Bd., United Cerebral Palsy Land of Lincoln, v.p. adminstrn., 2002; bd. dirs. United Way Cen. Ill., Inc., 1991-97, G.I.N.I. Inst., 2002; dir. Hope Sch.; mem., bd. dirs. Springfield Jewish Fedn., 1992-95, mem. bd. dirs. Hope Sch., Springfield; mem. task force on transp. Rep. Nat. Com., 1979-80, Springfield Jewish Comty. Rels. Coun., 1976-79, 82; mem. spl. com. on zoning and land use planning Sangamon County Bd., 1978; treas. City of Leland Grove, 1999—, vice-chmn., 2002; exec. com. AMA and State Med. Socs. Litigation Ctr., 1999—; commr. Ill. Guardianship and Advocacy Commn., 2002; mem. chancellor's cmty. adv. bd. U. Ill.-Springfield, 2002. Named Disabled Adv. of Yr., Ill. Dept. Rehab. Svcs., 1985; recipient Chmn.'s Spl. award Ill. State Med. Soc., 1987, Susan S. Suter award as outstanding disabled citizen of Ill., 1990. Mem. ABA (vice-chmn. medicine and law com. 1988-90, tort and ins. practice sect., forum com. on health law), Am. Assn. Health Lawyers, Am. Soc. Law and Medicine, Ill. State Bar Assn. (spl. com. on reform of legis. process 1976-82, spl. com. on the disabled lawyer 1978-82, young lawyers sect. com. on role of govt. atty. 1977-80, chmn. 1982, sect. coun. adminstrv. law, vice-chmn. 1981-82), Sangamon County Bar Assn., Am. Soc. Med. Assn. Counsel, Phi Delta Phi. Home: 1701 S Illini Rd Springfield IL 62704-3301 Office: Ill State Med Soc 600 S 2nd St Ste 200 Springfield IL 62704-2578 E-mail: morse@ismie.com.

MORSE, STACEY ANN, art studio owner; b. Arcadia, Calif., Jan. 18, 1964; d. Lewis Richard and Phyllis Juanita (Verdugo) Corbet; m. Stuart Hopkins Morse, June 6, 1987; children: Merill Leann, True Corbet. BFA, Maryville U., St. Louis, 1989. With William Tao & Assocs., St. Louis, 1984-87; comml. photographer Voyles Photography, 1988-94; fine art photographer Stacey A. Morse Photography, 1987—; cons. Chesterfield Arts Inc., Chesterfield, Mo., 1996—; co-owner, v.p. Morse Fine Art Studios, Inc., 1994—. Exec. dir. Chesterfield Arts, Inc., Chesterfield, Mo., 2002—. Mem. Reg. Commerce and Growth Assn., St. Louis, 1997. Recipient Young Alumni award Maryville U., 1992, Byron lee Fine Arts award, 1988. Mem. Nat. Soc. Arts & Letters, Art St. Louis. Avocations: tennis, skiing, backpacking. Office: Morse Fine Art Studios Inc PO Box 74 Chesterfield MO 63006-0074 E-mail: mfas@morsefineart.com.

MORSE, STEPHEN SCOTT, virologist, immunologist, epidemiologist; b. N.Y.C., Nov. 22, 1951; s. Murray H. and Phyllis Morse; m. Marilyn Gewirtz, Feb. 1991. BS, CCNY, 1971; MS, U. Wis., 1974, PhD, 1977. NSF trainee dept. bacteriology U. Wis., Madison, 1971-72, rsch. asst., 1972-77; Nat. Cancer Inst. rsch. fellow Med. Coll. Va./Va. Commonwealth U., Richmond, 1977-80, instr. microbiology, 1980-81; asst. prof. microbiology Rutgers U., New Brunswick, N.J., 1981-85; rsch. assoc. Rockefeller U., N.Y.C., 1985-88, asst. prof., 1988-96, adj. faculty, 1996—; asst. prof. epidemiology Mailman Sch. Pub. Health, Columbia U., 1996—, assoc. prof.; dir., assoc. prof. epidemiology Ctr. for Pub. Health Preparedness; dir. Mailman Sch. Pub. Health, Columbia U., 2000—; program mgr. Def. Advanced Rsch. Projects Agy., 1996-2000. Cons. U.S. Congress Office Tech. Assessment, Washington, 1989; chair conf. on emerging viruses NIH, 1989; mem. com. microbial threats to health, chair subcom. on viruses, 1990-92, steering com., Forum on Emerging Infections, 1996—, Inst. Medicine-NAS; chair Fedn. Am. Scientists (FAS) program for monitoring emerging diseases (ProMED), 1993—. Author: Emerging Viruses, 1993, Evolutionary Biology of Viruses, 1994; sect. editor Ctr. for Disease Control and Prevention Jour. "Emerging Infectious Diseases"; editor-in-chief Pasteur Inst. Jour. "Research in Virology," 1996-99. Fellow N.Y. Acad. Scis. (vice chair microbiology sect. 1994-96, chair 1996-98); mem. Am. Soc. Microbiology, Am. Assn. Immunologists, Marine Biology Lab., Sigma Xi. Office: Columbia U Mailman Sch Pub Health Divsn Epidemiology 722 W 168th St New York NY 10032-3722 E-mail: ssm20@columbia.edu.

MORSE, TERRI FRASER, engineering administrator; d. James Howard and Bonnie Lou Fraser; m. Mark Harry Morse, Oct. 19, 1990. BA in Edn./Math. and Music, Ctrl. Wash. U., Ellensburg, 1978. Youth/Christian edn. dir. Kelso (Wash.) Presbyn. Ch., 1978-80; stability and flight controls engr. The Boeing Co., Seattle, 1980-82, avionics computer engr., 1982-85, flight sys. lab. engr. lead, 1985-86, engr. supr., 1986-89, rsch. engring. supr., 1989-90, mech./elec. supr., 1990-95, elec. processes/computing mgr., 1995—. Vol. mission team mem. Africa U., Zimbabwe, 1996; bd. dirs. Multifaith Works, Seattle, 1998—; mem. bishops coun. on children and poverty United Meth. Ch., Seattle, 1998—; loaned exec. Corp. Coun. for the Arts, Seattle, 1993-95, Leadership Tomorrow--Seattle Commerce/United Way, 1997-98. Mem. AIAA (sr.), Soc. Women Engrs. (life; bylaws chair, program chair). Avocations: hiking, camping, skiing, kite-flying, home improvement.

MORSE, WILLIAM SENTENNE, investment company executive; b. Hartford, Conn., May 3, 1946; s. Nathaniel Berwin and Alice Claire (Kilpatrick) M.; m. Carolyn Bliss Wheeler, May 17, 1975; children: Christopher William, Leigh Elizabeth. BA in Econs., Middlebury Coll., 1968. Registered investment advisor. Credit analyst Conn. Bank and Trust, Hartford, 1969-70, investment analyst, 1971-72, asst. treas., 1972-75, asst. v.p., 1976-79, v.p., 1980-85, sr. v.p., 1986-90; pres. Morse Investment Mgmt. Co., 1991—. Trustee, investment com. Stowe-Day Found., Hartford, 1992—. Sponsor, advisor Jr. Achievement, Hartford, 1976-81; coun. mem. Capitol Region Coun. on Govt., Hartford, 1982-85. Mem. Asn. Investment Mgmt. and Rsch., Country Club Farmington (dir. and treas. 1992—, trustee employee pension plan 1993—). Avocations: reading, golfing, skiing, camping. Office: Morse Investment Mgmt Co 15 Lewis St Hartford CT 06103-2502

MORSE-MCNEELY, PATRICIA, poet, writer, retired middle school educator; b. Galveston, Tex., Apr. 2, 1923; d. Bleecker Lansing Sr. and Annie Maud (Pillow) Morse; m. Chalmers Rankin McNeely, Mar. 22, 1949 (div. Aug. 1959); children: David Lansing McNeely, Timothy Ann McNeely Caldwell, Patricia Grace McNeely Dragon, Abigail Rankin McNeely. BS in Edn., U. Tex., 1972; MA in Ednl. Psychology, Spl. Edn. LLD, U. Tex., San Antonio, 1976, MA in Ednl. Psychology-Spl. Edn. Counseling, 1981. Cert. tchr. Tex., profl. counselor. Sec./adminstrv. sec. various cos., Galveston & Austin, Tex., 1945-49, 60-70; dep. clk. Ct. of Civil Appeals, Galveston, 1947-48; police stenographer Austin Police Dept., 1970-74; history and spl. edn. tchr. N.E. Ind. Sch. Dist., San Antonio, 1974-76; spl. edn. tchr. S.W. Ind. Sch. Dist., 1978-81; vocat. adjustment coord. East Ctrl. Ind. Sch. Dist., 1981-82; counselor, tchr. Stockdale (Tex.) Ind. Sch. Dist., 1982-84; clinic sec. Humana Hosp., Dallas, 1985-87; tchr. history and spl. edn. Dallas Ind. Sch. Dist., 1987-2000; ret., 2000. TSTA/NEA assn. rep. Hill Mid. Sch., Dallas, 1988—89, E.B. Comstock Mid. Sch., Dallas, 1991—2000. Author: (poetry) Texas City, 1947, A Gift of Love, 1978, The Key, 1991, The House, The Gull's Quill, 2001; contbr. , articles to prof. newspapers and profl. jours. V.p. zone, sec., libr., com. mem. Parents Without Ptnrs., Inc., Austin, 1965—72, chmn. internat. ad hoc com. for writing leadership tng. program, 1968, newsletter editor, 1967—72. Mem.: NAFE, AARP, NEA (life), Nat. Trust for Edn. (trustee), Tex. Writers' League, U. Tex. Austin Alumni Assn. (First Bernice Milburn Moore scholarship award 1972), Tex. State Tchrs. Assn., Classroom Tchrs. Dallas (del. to Tex. State Tchrs. Assn. Conf. 1978—81, 1991—97), Internat. Soc. Poets, Internat. Libr. Poetry (Hall of Fame 1997), Assn. Am. Poets. Episcopalian. Avocations: writing, reading, music, sewing/handcrafts, book collecting. E-mail: pmmcneely@prodigy.net.

MORSHED, MD MOQBUL, civil and environmental engineer; b. Rajshahi, Bangladesh, July 17, 1962; came to U.S., 1986; s. M. Rahman and Khojesta Fasiha (Akhter) Sarkar; m. Tahmina Rahman, Jan. 3, 1991. BSCE, Bangladesh U., 1984; MSCE, Wayne State U., 1987. Registered profl. engr., Pa., Oreg. Asst. engr. Bur. Cons. Engrs. Ltd., Dhaka, Bangladesh, 1984-86; civil/environ. engr. CH2M Hill, Phila., 1987-92; sr. environ. engr. Oreg. Dept. of Environ. Quality, Portland, 1992—. Recipient 1st grade Merit scholarship Rajshahi, Bangladesh Bd. Edn., 1977-84. Mem. ASCE (assoc.), APWA, Assn. of State and Territorial Solid Waste Mgmt. Officials, Solid Waste Assn. N.Am., Chi Epsilon. Home: Apt 203 5605 Legacy Crescent Pl Riverview FL 33569-2803

MORSI, ABD EL WAHAB, artist; b. Fakos, Egypt, Feb. 23, 1931; s. Abdulwahab Mursi; married; 2 children. BA in Fine Arts, Cairo U., 1957; diploma, High Inst. Art Edn., 1958; spl. studies in graphic field, San Vernando, Spain, 1971. Staff Documentary Ctr. Egyptian Monuments, 1958-74; gen. dir. exhbns. Ministry of Egyptian Culture, 1974-80, gen. dir. art museums, 1980-90. Min. of Edn., 1977. Exhbns. include Biennial of Alexandria, Egypt, 1957, 59, 61, 68, 70, 96, Internat. Exhbn. Belgrade, 1961, Internat. Biennial Young Artists, Paris, 1965, Palette Bleue Gallery, Paris, 1965, Internat. Exhbn. African Art, Dakar, 1966, Biennial of Venice, 1968, Sport Biennial, Madrid, 1969, Toison Gallery, Spain, 1972, Nika Exhbn., Japan, 1973, Biennial of Rabat, Morocco, 1975, Kany Carmer Exhbn., Nice, France, 1975, Gallery Contemporain, Geneva, Holland Biennial of Venice, 1975, Internat. Exhbn. African Art, Lagos, Nigeria, 1976, Exhbn. Egyptian Graphic Art, West Germany, 1979, numerous galleries in Cairo, exhbns. in Paris, 1999, Mus. Modern Art Cairo, 1969, Ekhnaton Gallery, Cairo, 1964, Goethe Inst., Cairo, 1970, 1979, exhbns. Frankfurt, Prais, Austria, Finland, Paris, 1981-82, Khan El Magraby, Cairo, 1996-98, others; represented in collections Roil Mus., Madrid, White House, U.S., Mus. Barcelona, Nat. Mus. Jordan, Mus. Modern Art, Cairo, Mus. Alexandria, Mus. Port Said, Egypt, Mus. Teito Grade, Yugoslavia. Recipient 2d prize Biennale Exhbn. at Alexandria, 1970, prize Biennale Exhbn. at Barcelona, Spain, 1971, prize Biennale Exhbns., Paris, Madrid. Mem. Fine Arts Grads. Assn. Avocation: creative art. Address: 7 Sharia Dr Mustafa al-Nagdi al-Sirkh Quarter Shubra Cairo Egypt E-mail: fhs@menanet.net.

MORT, JOHN, librarian, writer; b. Warsaw, Nov. 24, 1947; s. Louis Byron and Nora Mae Mort; m. Sarah Louise Mort, 1972 (div. 1984); 1 child, Nathan; m. Patricia Eileen Hogan, Feb. 14, 1994. BA in English and Secondary Edn., U. Iowa, 1972, MFA in Writing, 1974, MLS, 1976. Libr. Southwest Mo. State U., Springfield, 1982-86, St. Petersburg (Fla.) Times, 1987-88; book reviewer Kirkus Revs., N.Y.C., 1992—; adult svcs. specialist River Bluffs Regional Libr., St. Joseph, Mo., 1997—2001; librarian Kansas City (Mo.) Pub. Libr., 1988-92, 94-96; columnist, reviewer Booklist, Chgo., 1996—; reference libr. Maple Woods C.C., Kansas City, Mo., 2001—. Author: Tanks, 1986, The Walnut King, 1990, Soldier in Paradise, 1999, Christian Fiction: A Guide to the Genre, 2002; contbr. articles to profl. jours., newspapers and mags. Sgt. U.S. Army, 1968-70, Vietnam. Recipient Bill Boyd Lit. Novel prize, 2000; NEA fellow, 1992. Mem. ALA, Mo. Libr. Assn. (Mo. Author of Yr. 2000), Sci. Fiction Writers of Am. Avocations: gardening, travel, reading, carpentry. Home: 5695 NW State Hwy 92 Smithville MO 64089 Office: Maple Woods Cmty Coll Libr 2601 NE Barry Rd Kansas City MO 64156 E-mail: johnmort@juno.com.

MORTAZAVIAN, HAROLD, electrical engineer, researcher; b. Isfahan, Iran, Dec. 12, 1953; s. Kamal and Mariam Mortazavian; m. Joelle Anne-Marie Urien. MA, PhD, Case Western Res. U., 1980. Rschr. computer sci. and control French Nat. Rsch. Inst., Rocquencourt and Versailles, 1980—82; vis. rsch. assoc. U. Toronto, Canada, 1982—83; sr. rsch. assoc. Systems Applications Inc., Beachwood, Ohio, 1986—90; asst. prof. Wayne State U., Detroit, 1990—93; asst. rsch. elec. engr. UCLA, L.A., 1993—99, assoc. rsch. engr. computer sci., 1999—. Cons. NSF, N..Y U., N.Y.C., 1980—81; resident prof., acad. advisor Ford Eng. Engring. Rsch. & Develop. Ctr., Basildon, Essex, 1992; sr. rsch. assoc. NASA Ames Rsch. Ctr., Moffet Field, Calif., 1992; project dir. NASA-UCLA Ctr. for Flight Systems Rsch., 1994—99; project dir. computer sci. dept. UCLA, 1999—. Charter mem. Rep. Nat. Com., Washington, 2002—; co-chmn. The President's Dinner, 2002, hon. sponsor, 2001—01; mem. exec. com. Rep. Presdl. Roundtable, 1998—2000. Recipient Rep. Senatorial Medal of Freedom, Nat. Rep. Senatorial Com. Office: UCLA Computer Sci Dept 4532J Boelter Hall Los Angeles CA 90095-1594 Office Fax: 310-794-5057. Personal E-mail: hmorucla93@aol.com. Business E-Mail: mor@cs.ucla.edu.

MORTEN, RALPH EDWARD, protective services official; b. Yankton, S.D., Aug. 23, 1950; s. Claude Leslie and Evelyn Madeline (Steele) M.; m. Alison Joan Squire, Apr. 3, 1982; children: Joshua, Lauren, Sarah, Erin. BS in Criminal Justice Adminstrn., Calif. State U., 1983. Cert. tchr. C.C. level, Calif. Police officer Phoenix Police Dept., 1974-79, L.A. Police, 1979—; pres. The Morten Group, Upland, Calif., 1995—. Firearms cons. Nat. Tactical Officers Assn., LaMirada, Calif., 1986-90, Internat. Assn. Chiefs Police, Washington, 1986-91; firearms, security cons. R.M. Consulting, Upland, Calif., 1989—; del., union rep., LA Police Protective League, 1994-99. Inventor: Robotic Forklift (remote control), 1995. Baseball coach Little League, Upland, Calif., 1994-96. With USMC, 1971-73. Recipient medal of valor L.A. Police Dept., 1990; named Officer of Yr. Internat. Footprint Assn., L.A., 1990. Mem. Internat. Assn. Bomb Technicians and Investigations, Peace Officers Assn. L.A. County. Republican. Methodist. Avocations: running, weight trraining, coaching baseball, softball, shooting. Office: LA Police Dept 150 N Los Angeles St Los Angeles CA 90012-3302

MORTENSEN, ARVID LEGRANDE, lawyer; b. July 11, 1941; s. George Andrew and Mary Louise (Myers) M.; m. Elaine Marie Mains, Aug. 2, 1968; children: Marie Louise, Anne Catherine, Joseph Duncan, Susan Kumari. BS in English and Psychology, Brigham Young U., 1965, MBA in Mktg. and Fin., 1967; JD cum laude, Ind. U., 1980. Bar: Ind. 1980, U.S. Supreme Ct. 1983, Mo. 1985, D.C. 1985; CLU; accredited estate planner; cert. dive master Profl. Assn. Diving Instrs.; lic. amateur radio operator FCC, amateur extra class. Agt. Conn. Mut. Life Ins. Co., Salt Lake City, 1967-68, agt., br. mgr. Idaho Falls, Idaho, 1968-74; with Rsch. and Rev. Svc. Am., Inc./Newkirk Assocs., Inc., Indpls, 1974-83, sr. editor, 1975-79, mgr. advanced products and seminars, 1979-80, sr. mktg. exec., 1980-83; tax and fin. planner Indpls., 1980-85, St. Louis and Chesterfied, Mo., 1985-90, Tampa Bay, Fla., 1990-91, Orange County, Calif., 1991—. Mem. sr. mgmt. com., v.p. Allied Fidelity Corp., 1983-85, Allied Fidelity Ins. Co., 1983-85, Tex. Fire and Casualty Ins. Co., 1983-85; v.p., bd. dirs. Gen. Am. Ins. Co., St. Louis, 1985-86, v.p., 1985-90; pvt. practice law, Indpls., 1980-85, St. Louis, Chesterfield and Bridgeton, Mo., 1985-90, Tampa Bay, 1990-91, Orange County, 1991—. Author: Employee Stock Ownership Plans, 1975, Fundamentals of Corporate Qualified Retirement Plans, 1975, 78, 80, Buy-Sell Agreements, 1988, The Key Executive Sale, 1989, (with Norman H. Tarver) The IRA Manual, 1975-87 edits., The Keogh Manual, 1975, 77, 78, 80 edits., The Section 403 (b) Manual, 1975, 77, 78, 80, 84, 85, 87 edits., sole author, 1991, 93, 94, edits., (with Leo C. Hodges) The Life Insurance Trust Handbook, 1980; contbr. articles to profl. jours.; editor-in-chief various tax and fin. planning courses; bd. editors Ind. Law Rev., 1977-78. Active Ch. Jesus Christ of Latter-day Saints, Denver, Idaho Falls, Indpls., St. Louis, Chesterfield, Tampa Bay Area and Orange County, Calif. Mem. Assn. Advanced Life Underwriting, Mo. Bar Assn., Bar Assn. Met. St. Louis, D.C. Bar Assn., Ind. Bar Assn., Am. Soc. CLUs, Nat. Assn. Life Underwriters, Orange County. Office: 620 Newport Center Dr Ste 1100 Newport Beach CA 92660-8011 also: PO Box 6362 Laguna Niguel CA 92607-6362

MORTENSEN, DALE THOMAS, economics educator; b. Enterprise, Oreg., Feb. 2, 1939; s. Thomas Peter and Verna Bernice Mortensen; m. Beverly Patton, July 13, 1963; children: Karl, Lia Osborne, Julie Glanville. BA, Willamette U., 1961; PhD, Carnegie-Mellon U., 1967. From asst. prof. to assoc. prof. Northwestern U., Evanston, Ill., 1965-75, prof. econs., 1975-85, Ida C. Cook prof. econs., 1985—. Fellow Inst. for Advanced Study, Hebrew U., Jerusalem, 1979; vis. Morgenstern prof. econs. NYU, N.Y.C., 1985; vis. economist Cen. Inst. Math.-Econ., Moscow, 1989, Australian Nat. U., Canberra, 1996. Contbr. articles to profl. jours. Fellow Econometric Soc., Am. Acad. Arts and Scis. Office: Northwestern U Dept Econs Evanston IL 60201 E-mail: d-mortensen@northwestern.edu.

MORTENSEN, GORDON LOUIS, artist, printmaker; b. Arnegard, N.D., Apr. 27, 1938; s. Gunner and Otillia Ernestine (Reiner) M.; m. Phoebe Hollis Hansen, Apr. 10, 1965 (div. 1968); m. Linda Johanna Sisson, Dec. 7, 1969. BFA, Mpls. Coll. Art and Design, 1964; postgrad., U. Minn., 1969-72. One-man shows include Minn. Mus., St. Paul, 1967, Concept Art Gallery Pitts., 1981, 83, 85, 87, 89, 91, 93, C.G. Rein Galleries, Mpls., 1978, 80, 85, 89, 91, 93, others; exhibited in group shows Miami U., Oxford, Ohio (1st place award 1977), Phila. Print Club (George Bunker award 1977), 12th Nat. Silvermine Guild Print Exhbn., New Canaan, Comm., 1976, 78, 80, 83, 86, 94, 96 (Hearsch Mag. award 1978, Purchase award 1983, 86), 4th Miami Internat. Print Biennial (4th place award 1980), Rockford Internat., 1981, 85 (Juror's award 1981), Boston Printmakers Nat. Exhbn., 1977, 79, 80, 81, 83, 97 (Purchase award 1977, 79, 83, Juror's Accomodation), others; represented permanent collections, Achenbach Found. Graphic Arts at Palace Legion of Honor, San Francisco, Bklyn. Mus., Phila. Mus. Art, Libr. of Congress, Minn. Mus. Art, Met. Mus. and Art Ctr., Miami, Fla., Mus. Am. Art, Washington, Art Inst. Chgo., Mus. Art at Carnegie-Mellon Inst., Pitts., Walker Art Ctr., Mpls., Dulin Gallery Art, Knoxville, Tenn., numerous corp. collections; profiled in numerous art jours. Served with USMC, 1957-60. Mem. Boston Printmakers, Phila. Print Club, L.A. Printmaking Soc., Albany Print Club, Am. Print Alliance. Home and Office: 4153 Crest Rd Pebble Beach CA 93953-3052

MORTENSEN, JOSEPH IDE, clergy member, educator; b. Cheyenne, Wyo., May 28, 1936; s. Axel Christian Mortensen and Mabel G. Ide; m. Linda Ann Larsen, Aug. 7, 1959 (dec. Aug. 1974); m. Kathleen N. Nummy, Dec. 27, 1975; children: Andrew, Anne, Peter, Charles, John. BA, Wheaton Coll., 1958; BD, Gordon-Conwell Theol. Sem., 1961; D in Theology, Boston U., 1966. Ordained to ministry Bapt. Ch., 1961. Assoc. pastor First United Bapt. Ch., Lowell, Mass., 1961-63; pastor Dudley St. Bapt. Ch., Boston, 1963-66, Univ. Bapt. Ch., Mt. Pleasant, Mich., 1966-69; sr. pastor First Bapt. Ch., Midland, 1969-93; area min. Am. Bapt. Chs. Mich., East Lansing, 1997—2001. Adj. prof. ch. history No. Bapt. Theol. Sem., Lombard, Ill., 1984-98; vis. prof. New Testament, Moscow Theol. Sem., 1996—. Editor (newsletter) Lighten Up, 1995--; contbr. articles to profl. jours. Pres. Pardee Cancer Treatment Fund, Midland, 1997--; trustee Elsa U. Pardee Found., Midland, 1998--; bd. dirs. MidMichigan Med. Ctr., Midland, 1999--; treas. Neighborhood Clinic, Midland, 1997--. Named Clergyman of Yr., Civitan Club, 1993; Paul Harris fellow Rotary Internat., 1993. Mem. Am. Bapt. Chs. Mich. (pres. 1973-74, pres. min. coun. 1993-95), Phi Alpha Chi. Avocations: computers, travel. Home: 4214 Chelsea Ct Midland MI 48640 E-mail: jmortensen@chartermi.net.

MORTENSEN, PETER, banker; b. Ellwood City, Pa., Dec. 4, 1935; s. Norman Peter and Mary Letitia (Brown) M.; m. Collette; children: Linda V. Hill, Kelly J. Hebble, Nancy Sarah Patton, Karen Sue Harris. BA, Coll. of Wooster, Ohio, 1956. With First Nat. Bank of Pa., Hermitage, Pa., 1959—; chmn. F.N.B. Corp., 1973—. Mem. United Church of Christ Avocation: hunting.

MORTENSEN, PETER LESLIE, English language educator; b. Glendale, Calif., Feb. 9, 1961; s. Fred Leslie and Elizabeth Mary (Haymaker) M. BA, U. Calif., San Diego, 1983, PhD, 1989. Asst prof. dept. English U. Ky., Lexington, 1989-95, assoc. prof., 1995-99; assoc. prof. dept. English U. Ill., Urbana, 1999—. Mem. Nat. Coun. Tchrs. of English, Modern Lang. Assn., Conf. on Coll. Composition and Comm. Office: U Ill Dept English 608 S Wright St Urbana IL 61801-3630 E-mail: pmortens@uiuc.edu.

MORTENSEN, ROBERT HENRY, landscape architect, golf course architect; b. Jackson, Mich., June 9, 1939; s. Henry and Charlotte Marie (Brown) M.; divorced; children: Phillip, Paul, Susan, Julia; m. Meta Jane Hearne Blakely, Nov. 1975; stepchildren: Laura, Kathryn. B in Landscape Architecture, Ohio State U., 1961; M in Landscape Architecture, U. Mich., 1965. Registered landscape arch., Va., Md. Landscape arch. various firms, Louisville, 1960, 61-63; with Ohio Divsn. Pks., Columbus, 1960-61; landscape arch. various firms, Toledo, 1963, 65-67; pvt. practice Ann Arbor, Mich., 1963-65; ptnr. firms Toledo, 1967-78; pres. Harvey Jones and Assocs., Clearwater, Fla., 1979-81; owner Mortensen Assocs., Toledo and Falls

Church, Va., 1979-85; prin. Mortensen, Lewis & Scully, Inc., Vienna, 1985-93; owner Mortensen Assocs., 1993—. Assoc. prof. U. Mich. Grad. Sch., 1973; vis. lectr. Ohio State U., 1965—, Bowling Green (Ohio) State U., 1969—, U. Mich., 1971, Purdue U., 1971, Mich. State U., 1973—, U. Mass., 1986—; mem. archtl. environ. rev. com. Ohio Arts Coun., 1974-78; adj. prof. Dept. Landscape Architecture, U. Md., 1992—; chmn. Merrifield Master Plan Task Force, 1998-2001. Editor: Handbook of Professional Practice, 1972, Marketing Landscape Architectural Services to the Federal Government, 1974. Mem. Ohio Bd. Unreclaimed Strip Mined Lands, 1973-76; mem. Lucas County facilities rev. com. Health Planning Assn. N.W. Ohio, 1972-76, chmn. maternal and child health subcom., 1972-74; bd. dirs. No. Va. Cmty. Appearance Alliance, 1988—, chair, 1991, pres., 1994. Recipient Disting. Svc. award Health Planning Assn. N.W. Ohio, 1973, Disting. Alumni award U. Mich. Sch. Natural Resources, 1985, Disting. Alumnus award Ohio State U. Coll. Engring., 1985. Fellow Am. Soc. Landscape Architects (trustee 1977-82, v.p. 1982-83, pres.-elect 1983-84, nat. pres. 1984-85, del. to Internat. Fedn. Landscape Architects 1987-92, del. Internat. Landscape Alliance 1994-2000); mem. Ohio Soc. Landscape Architects (pres. 1969-74), Landscape Inst. U.K. (hon. corr.), Toledo C. of C. (chmn. sts. and hwys. transit com. 1972-73), Greater Merrifield Bus. and Profl. Assn. (bd. dirs. 1993, chmn. bd. dirs. 1998, pres. 1997), Washington Golf and Country Club (officer, bd. mem. 1999—), Sigma Phi Epsilon. Home: 6843 Churchill Rd Mc Lean VA 22101-2822 Office: Mortensen Assocs 2787 Hartland Rd Falls Church VA 22043-3529 E-mail: rhmort@aol.com. *One of the best continuing educational experiences for a practising professional is to teach students what you have learned. They respond in a critical and ever-so-fresh "so what" atmosphere, and demand more of you sometimes than you demand of yourself. Thus, there is learning on both sides of the lectern.*

MORTENSEN-SAY, MARLYS, school system administrator; b. Yankton, S.D., Mar. 11, 1924; d. Melvin A. and Edith L. (Fargo) Mortensen; m. John Theodore Say, June 21, 1951; children: Mary Louise, James Kenneth, John Melvin, Margaret Ann. BA, U. Colo., 1949, MEd, 1953; Adminstrv. Specialist, U. Nebr., 1973. Tchr. Huron (S.D.) Jr. H.S., 1944-48, Lamar (Colo.) Jr. H.S., 1950-52, Norfolk Pub. Sch., 1962-63; sch. supr. Madison County, Madison, Nebr., 1963-79. Mem. ASCD, NEA (life) AAUW, Am. Assn. Sch. Adminstrs., Dept. Rural Edn., Nebr. Assn. County Supts., N.E. Nebr. County Supts. Assn. Assn. Sch. Bus. Ofcls., Nat. Orgn. Legal Problems in Edn., Nebr. Edn. Assn., Nebr. Sch. Adminstrs. Assn. Republican. Methodist. Home: 1222 W S Airport Rd Norfolk NE 68701-1349

MORTENSON, ERIK K. private school educator; b. Haverhill, Mass., Sept. 9, 1972; s. Byron H. and Maria D. Mortenson; m. Staci L. Strauss, June 22, 2001. Diploma, Tabor Acad., Marion, Mass., 1990; BA, Colby Coll., 1994; MA, NYU, 2000. English tchr. Blue Ridge Sch., Dyke, Va., 1994-96, Portsmouth (R.I.) Abbey Sch., 1996-98, Rye (N.Y.) Country Day Sch., 1999-2001, King and Low-Heywood Thomas Sch., Stamford, Conn., 2001—. Online Poetry Classroom fellow, Acad. Am. Poets, N.Y.C., 2000—. Mem. U.S. Lacrosse, 1987—. Office: King and Low-Heywood Thomas Sch Newfield Ave Stamford CT 06905 E-mail: emortenson@worldnett.att.net.

MORTENSON, KRISTIN OPPENHEIM, real estate broker, violinist; b. San Antonio, July 14, 1964; d. Russell E. and Martha Kunkel Oppenheim; m. Gary Curtiss Mortenson; children: Caitlan Reese, Sarah Reese. Attended, U. Tex., 1984; MusB, La. State U., 1987, MusM, 1988. Violinist Austin Symphony Orch., Austin, Tex., 1981—84, Baton Rouge Symphony, Baton Rouge, 1985—89; violin/viola tchr. Pvt. Music Studio, Manhattan, Kans., 1989—; violinist Wichita Symphony Orch., Wichita, 1991—93, Des Moines Symphony, Des Moines, 1993—2001; assoc. concertmaster Topeka Symphony Orch., Topeka, 2001—; broker/owner Mortenson Homes, Manhattan, 2001—. Bd. dirs. Manhattan Assn. Realtors, Manhattan, Kans., 2001—; violinist/violist Pernambuco String Quartet, Manhattan, Kans., 2001—. Assistant editor The International Trumpet Guild Jour., 2001. violinist (live performances with) Ray Charles, Dionne Warwick, Hope, Shirley Jones, Marvin Hamlisch, Rich Little, La., Kans., Nebr. Mem. Lee Sch. Site Coun., Manhattan, Kans., 2000—02; pres. Lee Sch. PTO, 2000—01; sec. Grandview Hills Neighborhood Assn., 2000—02. Mem.: Am. String Tchrs. Assn. (state pres. La. 1988—89), Pilot Club of Manhattan (editor Pilot Times 2001), Sigma Alpha Iota (pres. U. Tex. 1983—84, Coll. Honor award, Sword of Honor 1984). Home: 522 Westview Dr Manhattan KS 66502 Personal E-mail: kristin@flinthills.com.*

MORTENSON, R. STAN, lawyer; b. Columbia, S.C., Feb. 14, 1945; s. Edwin M. and Marie E.M. Mortenson; m. Roselane Mortenson; 1 child J. Charisse. BA, Ohio U., 1967; JD, U. Mich., 1970. Bar: U.S. Dist. Ct. D.C. 1972, U.S. Dist. Ct. (ea. dist.) Mich. 1987, U.S. Ct. Appeals (D.C. cir.), 1972, U.S. Supreme Ct. 1975. Law clk. U.S. Ct. Appeals (9th cir.), La., 1970-71; assoc. Paul, Weiss, Rifkind, Wharton & Garrison, Washington, 1971-75; ptnr. Miller, Cassidy, Larroca & Lewin, 1975-2000, Baker Botts, LLP, Washington, 2001—. Fellow Am. Coll. Trial Lawyers (Fed. Criminal Procedures com.); mem. Edward Bennett Williams Am. Inn Ct., NACDL, D.C. Assn. Criminal Def. Lawyers (R. Kenneth Mundy Lawyer Yr. award 1995). Office: Baker Botts, LLP 1299 Pennsylvania Ave NW 13th Fl Washington DC 20004

MORTENSON, THOMAS THEODORE, medical products executive, management consultant; b. Hallock, Minn., Dec. 18, 1934; s. Theodore William and Esther (Hanson) M.; m. Alice L. Girdvain, June 27, 1958; children: Kim M., Laura Dee Mortenson Pavlides. BSBA, U. N.D., 1956, postgrad., 1957-58. Sales rep. Johnson & Johnson, Detroit, 1960-66, tng. and product dir. New Brunswick, N.J., 1967-72; dir. market devel. C.R. Bard, Murray Hill, 1973-75; gen. mgr. MacBick, 1976-78; dir. mktg. Bard Med. Systems, 1979-81, dir. sales, 1982; dir. sales/mktg., bd. dirs. Bac-Data Med. Info. Systems, Totowa, N.J., 1983-84; v.p. mktg. and sales United Med. Corp., Haddenfield, 1985-86; exec. v.p. Daltex Med. Scis., West Orange, 1987-92; assoc. ConMed Corp., Utica, N.Y., 1993—. Guest lectr. Am. Mgmt. Assn., 1971, Mktg. Scis. Inc., N.Y.C., 1978, Internat. Novel Drug Delivery Techs., Tustin, Calif., 1987. *Thomas Mortenson has held increasingly responsible positions in sales, marketing, product/market development and general management in the domestic and international medical device industry. Notable new concept designs/developments were developed, manufactured & sold with vacuum formed trays and packaging for sterile procedural kits, melamine and thermoplastic orthopedic casting/bracing materials, operating room drape systems (Johnson & Johnson), non-woven dressings, and procedure packs, electrosurgical electrodes and grounding systems, ECG electrode mechanized manufacturing, unit dose packaging, surgical instruments (C.R. Bard/Macbick), software based operating room scheduling and physicians communications systems (Nursystem/Phycom), anti-infective implantable devices (Daltex/Columbia University/Arrow Intl./ Gore Medical) and new design laparoscopic surgical instruments (Conmed Endoscopy).* With USMR and U.S. Army, 1953-58. Mem. Am. Mgmt. Assn. (instr. 1971), Berkeley Swim Club (Berkeley Heights, N.J.) (pres. 1979-82, bd. dirs. 1974-84). Avocations: woodworking, gardening, WWII history. Home: 44 Ironwood Rd New Hartford NY 13413-3906 Office: 525 French Rd Utica NY 13502 E-mail: tom_mortenson@mail.conmed.com.

MORTHAM, SANDRA BARRINGER, former state official; b. Erie, Pa., Jan. 4, 1951; d. Norman Lyell and Ruth (Harer) Barringer; m. Allen Mortham, Aug. 21, 1950; children: Allen Jr., Jeffrey. AS, St. Petersburg Jr. Coll., 1971; BA, Eckerd Coll. Cons. Capital Formation Counselors, Inc., Bellair Bluffs, Fla., 1972-74; commr. City of Largo, 1982-86, vice mayor, 1985-86; mem. Fla. Ho. of Reps., 1986-94, Rep. leader pro tempore, 1990-92, Rep. leader, 1992-94; Sec. of State State of Fla., 1995-98; pub. affairs dir., CEO, exec. v.p. Fla. Med. Assn., 1999—. Bd. dirs. Performing Arts Ctr. & Theatre, Clearwater, Fla.; exec. com. Pinellas County Rep. Com., Rep. Nat. Com. Named Citizen of Yr., 1990; recipient Tax Watch Competitive Govt. award, 1994, Bus. and Profl. Women "Break the Glass Ceiling" award, 1995, Fla. League of Cities Quality Floridian award, 1995, also numerous outstanding legislator awards, achievement among women awards from civic and profl. orgns. Mem. Am. Legis. Exch. Coun., Nat. Rep. Legislators Assn., Largo C. of C. (bd. dirs. 1987—, pres.), Largo Jr. Woman's Club (pres., Woman of Yr. award 1979), Suncoast Community Woman's Club (pres., Outstanding Svc. award 1981, Woman of Yr. award 1986), Suncoast Tiger Bay, Greater Largo Rep., Belleair Rep. Woman's, Clearwater Rep. Woman's, Tallahassee Rep. Woman's Club (pres. 1999-2000), Fla. Fedn. Rep. Women (2d v.p.). Presbyterian. Home: 6675 Weeping Willow Way Tallahassee FL 32311-8795

MORTIER, JEFFREY JAMES, lawyer; b. Ottawa, Ill., May 15, 1965; s. James G. and K. Ann M.; m. Lisa A., Mar. 9, 1991; children: Logan A., Graham E. BA, Northwestern U., 1987; JD, Valparaiso U., 1991. Bar: Ind. 1991, U.S. Dist. Ct. (no. and so. dists.) Ind. 1991, U.S. Ct. Appeals (7th cir.) 1991. Assoc. Locke Reynolds, Indpls., 1991-98, ptnr., 1999—. Mem. ABA, Defense Trial Counsel Ind., Ind. State Bar Assn., Indpls. Bar Assn., Defense Rsch. Inst. Democrat. Avocations: tennis, gardening, wine, travel. Office: Locke Reynolds 1000 Capital Ctr S 201 N Illinois St Ste 1000 Indianapolis IN 46204-4210

MORTILLARO, LOUIS FRANCIS, psychologist; b. Ft. Dodge, Iowa, Dec. 8, 1944; s. Louis and Catherine (Perri) M.; m. Linda Vivian Tapp Johnson, Sept. 18, 1982 (div. July 1994); children: Ross, Darren. BS, Loyola U. L.A., 1966; MS, MPA, U. So. Calif., 1974; PhD, U.S. Internat. U., San Diego, 1978; cert. in neuropsychology, Fielding Inst., Santa Barbara, Calif., 1998. Lic. psychologist, Nev.; lic. MFT, Nev. Chief psychologist Clark County Juvenile Ct., Las Vegas, Nev., 1971-78, JHC Rehab. Ctr., Las Vegas, 1978-89; pvt. practice, 1989—; psychology dir. Nev. Pain and Rehab. Ctr., 1990-95; chief psychologist Novacare Pain and Rehab. Ctr., 1995—; evaluator Las Vegas Metro Police Dept., 1995-98. Mem. Bd. Psychol. Examiners, Nev., 1992-2000, pres., 1998-2000. Co-author: (chpt.) Field Events and Theory for Counselors, 1975; contbr. articles to profl. jours. Pres., bd. dirs. Big Bros./Big Sisters, Las Vegas, 1984-86; bd. dirs. Boys and Girls Club, Las Vegas, 1986—, Youth Charities of So. Nev. Recipient Outstanding Svc. award Big Bros./Big Sisters, 1978, 83, Outstanding Svc. award Boys and Girls Club, 1992, 97. Mem. APA, AAMFT, Nat. Acad. Neuropsychology, Nev. State Psychol. Assn. (past treas. 1975-76, 91-92, pres. elect 2001), Phi Kappa Phi. Avocations: golf, structured exercise, traveling. Office: 501 S Rancho Dr Ste F-37 Las Vegas NV 89106-4834 E-mail: lfmort@aol.com.

MORTIMER, DAVID WILLIAM, communications engineer; b. Redding, Calif., June 8, 1962; s. Walter L. and Phyllis B. (Winters) M.; m. Jenene McGhie, Sept. 20, 1997. BSEE, Brigham Young U., 1988; MBA, Syracuse U., 1997. Devel. engr. Scala Electronics, Medford, Oreg., 1988-89; asst. sta. mgr. Holzkirchen Radio Free Europe/Radio Liberty, Munich, 1989-90, asst. sta. mgr. Spain Playa de Pals, 1990-93, ops. dir. Portugal Lisbon, 1993-95, tech. asst. Prague, Czech Republic, 1995; project mgr. Siemens Transp. Sys., Sacramento, 1999—; acting mng. dir. Portugal Radio Free Europe/Radio Liberty, Lisbon, 1995. Mem. IEEE, Aircraft Owners and Pilots Assn., Nat. Eagle Scout Assn. (life.), Project Mgmt. Inst. (cert. project mgmt. profl.).

MORTIMER, JAMES WINSLOW, analytical chemist; b. Mt. Kisco, N.Y., Mar. 11, 1955; s. James Winslow and Eileen Ruth (Cutting) M.; m. Dawn Romay Kania, Apr. 30, 1977. BA, Washington and Jefferson U., 1976. Tech. sales rep. Waters Assocs., Milford, Mass., 1978-82; dir. nat. accounts Zymark Corp., Hopkinton, 1982-89; v.p. Microflex Tech., Triadelphia, W.Va., 1989-90; mgr. mktg. Berthold Systems, Inc., Aliquippa, Pa., 1990-95; dir. life sci. and chems. Fisher Sci., Pitts., 1995—. Speaker at profl. confs. Author: Laboratory Robotics, 1987; cons. editor Lab. Robotics Jour., Hershey, Pa., 1990—; assoc. editor Lab. Robotics and Automation, 1988, 90; contbr. articles to tech. publs. Mem. TAPPI, Soc. Analytical Chemists (speaker 1978, 87), Masons. Achievements include development of cleavastat surgical instrument, beaker that will not cause vortexing action. Home: 113 Little John Dr Mc Murray PA 15317-2542 Office: Fisher Scientific 2000 Park Lane Dr Ste 2 Pittsburgh PA 15275-1104

MORTIMER, KENNETH P. retired academic administrator; Pres. Western Wash. U., Bellingham, 1988-93, U. Hawaii Sys., Honolulu, 1993—2001. Office: U Hawaii Sys Bachmann Hall 202 2444 Dole St Honolulu HI 96822-2302*

MORTIMER, MARY R. counselor; b. Muskegon, Mich., Oct. 22, 1945; d. Frederick A. Moldenauer and Margaret Olive Murray; m. Colin J. Casey, 1979 (dec. 1990); m. Eugene C. Mortimer, Dec. 30, 1994; stepchildren: stepchildren: Peter C. Casey, Harold E. Mortimer, Margaret H. Cinnella. BS in Criminology, Coll. of Santa Fe, 1986; MA in Counseling, Webster U., 1991. Nat. cert. counselor; lic. counselor, N.Mex. Mktg. rep. U.S. West, Albuquerque, 1963-72, disbursing agt., 1972-78, benefit adminstr., 1978-86, purchasing agt., 1986-90; mental health counselor Cottonwood Treatment Ctr., Los Lunas, N.Mex., 1990-94; vol. mental health counselor Taos Ski Valley (N.Mex.) EMS, 2000—. Vol. breast helpline Am. Cancer Soc., Albuquerque, 1991-98, Reach to Recovery, Albuquerque, 1994-2001, Taos, 1999—, Early Support, Albuquerque, 1998-2000, Taos, 1999—, Breast Self Exams in Sch. Edn., Albuquerque, 1991-98, N.Mex. Breast Cancer Core Team, Albuquerque, 1994-2000, People Living Through Cancer, Albuquerque, 1996-2000, Nat. Breast Cancer Coalition, Albuquerque, 1998—, LEAD, Albuquerque, 1998—, Rio Grande Coalition, Albuquerque, 1995-99; cert. vol. firefighter Taos Ski Valley Vol. Fire Dept., 1991—; vol. wilderness 1st responder Taos Ski Valley Emergency Med. Sys., 2000—; vol. critical incident stress counselor N.Mex. Critical Incident Stress Mgmt. Team, Taos Ski Valley, 2000—; vol. peer reviewer Dept. Def. Rev. Panel for Breast Cancer Rsch., Washington, 2000; vol. spkr., fundraiser United Way of Ctrl. N.Mex., Albuquerque, 1991-2000. Recipient Nat. Jefferson award Am. Inst. Pub. Svc., 1991, vol. recognition award Albuquerque chpt. ARC, 2000, recognition in Celebrating Life, S.W. divsn. ARC, 2000, named Vol. of Yr., 1997, featured vol. annual report cover, 1997, Am. Cancer Soc. Avocations: backpacking, hiking, whitewater canoeing, skiing.

MORTIMER, RICHARD WALTER, mechanical engineer, educator; b. Phila., Dec. 7, 1936; s. Horace and Almira Duffield (Matthews) M.; m. Doris Claire Ridler, June 29, 1957; children: Patrick Lee, David Walter, James Matthew, Daniel Scott. BSME, Drexel U., 1962, MSME, 1964, PhD, 1967. Prof. Drexel U., Phila., 1967—, assoc. dean grad. sch., 1974-76, head dept. mech. engring., 1976-85, assoc. v.p. acad. affairs, 1985-89. Mem. exec. com. Engring. Accreditation Com., N.Y.C., 1986-91. Contbr. over 40 articles to profl. jours. Pres. Haverford (Pa.) Twp. Sch. Dist., 1980-83. With U.S. Army, 1958-60. With U.S. Army, 1958—60. Recipient Achievement award Am. Soc. Nondestructive Testing, 1973, Best Tech. Paper award, 1973; fellow NASA, 1967, 68; grantee numerous orgns. including NASA, USAF, NSF, 1967-87; Fellow Members awd., Am. Soc. for Engineering Education, 1992. Fellow Am. Soc. Engring. Educators; mem. ASME (mem. numerous coms., bds. and chairs 1976-92). Republican. Episcopalian. Achievements include research in fields of structural dynamics and composite materials.

MORTIMER, ROBERT AMSDEN, political science educator; b. N.Y.C., Oct. 16, 1938; s. James Sinclair and Ivy (Amsden) M.; m. Mildred Palmer, June 9, 1962; children: Anne-Michele, Janine, Sylvie, Denise. BA, Wesleyan U., Middletown, Conn., 1960; MA, Columbia U., N.Y.C., 1963, PhD, 1968. Asst. prof. Haverford (Pa.) Coll., 1966-72, assoc. prof., 1972-80, prof. polit. sci., 1980—. Fulbright prof. U. Algiers, Algeria, 1974-75, U. Dakar, Senegal, 1991-92; Aspinall lectr. Mesa Coll., Grand Junction, Colo., 1986; dir. West African Rsch. Ctr. Dakar, 1998. Author: The Third World Coalition in International Politics, 1980, 84, Politics and Society in Contemporary Africa, 1988, 92, 99 (Best Book award 1988); contbr. articles to profl. jours. Mem. bd. trustees Wesleyan U., 1999—. Fulbright scholar, France, Senegal, 1960, 69, Woodrow Wilson fellow, 1961, 64. Mem. Internat. Studies Assn., Am. Polit. Sci. Assn., African Studies Assn. Democrat. Avocations: running, skiing, tennis. E-mail: rmortime@haverford.edu.

MORTIMER, WENDELL REED, JR. judge; b. Alhambra, Calif., Apr. 7, 1937; s. Wendell Reed and Blanche (Wilson) M.; m. Cecilia Vick, Aug. 11, 1962; children: Michelle Dawn, Kimberly Grace. AB, Occidental Coll., 1958; JD, U. So. Calif., L.A., 1965. Bar: Calif. 1966. Trial atty. Legal div. State of Calif., L.A., 1965-73; assoc. Thelen, Marrin, Johnson & Bridges, 1973-76, ptnr., 1976-93; pvt. practice San Marino, Calif., 1994-95; judge L.A. Superior Ct., 1995—, mem. complex litigation panel, 2000—. With U.S. Army, 1960-62. Mem. ABA, Internat. Acad. Trial Judges, Los Angeles County Bar Assn., Calif. Judges Assn., Am. Judicature Soc., Am. Judges Assn., Legion Lex., ABOTA, San Marino City Club, Pasadena Bar Assn., Balboa Yacht Club. Home: 1420 San Marino Ave San Marino CA 91108-2042

MORTIMER-SZYMCZAK, HALINA BARBARA, economics educator; b. Katowice, Silesia, Poland, Sept. 4, 1926; d. Fryderyk Mortimer and Stanisława Jadwiga (Szubińska) Bursa; m. Tadeusz Szymczak, May 28, 1955. MA, Jagiellonien U., Cracow, Poland, 1950; PhD, Inst. Nat. Economy, Moscow, 1954; postgrad., H.S. of Commerce, Warsaw, Poland, 1963. Asst. Jagiellonien U., 1948-50; rsch. fellow Plechanov Inst. Economy, Moscow, 1951-54; asst. prof. U. Łódź, Poland, 1954-62, assoc. prof. Poland, 1963-70, extraordinary prof. Poland, 1971-77, prof. econs. Poland, 1978—, vice dean faculty commerce Poland, 1957-59, vice rector Poland, 1978-81, head dept. econ. policy Poland, 1954-96. Mem. Ctr. Urban and Regional Study, U. Birmingham, Eng., 1985-90. Author: Territorial Balance of Money, 1964, Economic Policy, 1974, 2d edit. 80, Problems of Demography and Employment, 1978, 2d edit., 1985; contbr. articles to profl. publs. Mem. Mcpl. Coun. of City of Łódź, 1965-73; pres. Women Provincial Com. of Łódź, 1971-80; cons. Sci. Coun. Inst. of Work, Warsaw, 1970-95. Recipient Chivalrous Cross of Polish Revival State, Coun. Polish Republic, 1973, medal of commn. of nat. edn. Ministry of Edn., Poland, 1981, Meritorious Tchr. award Polish People Republik, Ministry of Edn., 1984. Mem. Polish Acad. Sci. (mem. demography com. 1984-92, mem. com. of work and social policy 1975—), Lodz Soc. Sci., London Sch. Econs. Soc. Avocations: theater, museums, sightseeing, gardening. Home: Boya Żelenskiego 12 m 6 91-704 Łódź Poland Office: U Lodz Dept Econs POW Str nr 39 90-214 Lodz Poland

MORTLOCK, ROBERT PAUL, microbiologist, educator; b. Bronxville, N.Y., May 12, 1931; s. Donald Robert and Florance Mary (Bellaby) M.; m. Florita Mary Welling, Sept., 1954; children: Florita M., Jeffrey R., Douglas P. BS, Rensselaer Poly. Inst., N.Y., 1953; PhD, U. Ill., Urbana, 1958. Asst. prof. microbiology U. Mass., Amherst, 1963-68, assoc. prof. microbiology, 1968-73, prof. microbiology, 1973-78, Cornell U., Ithaca, N.Y., 1978-99, prof. emeritus, 2000. Editor: Microorganisms as Model Systems for Studying Evolution, 1984, The Evolution of Metabolic Function, 1992. Served to 1st lt. U.S. Army, 1959-61 Fellow Am. Acad. Microbiology; mem. AAAS, Am. Soc. Microbiology, Northeastern Microbiologists, Physiology, Ecology and Taxonomy (pres. 1984-91). Office: Cornell U Dept Microbiology Wing Hall Ithaca NY 14852 E-mail: rpm2@cornell.edu.

MORTOLA, EDWARD JOSEPH, academic administrator emeritus; b. N.Y.C., Feb. 5, 1917; s. John and Letitia (Pellarano) M.; m. Doris Slater, May 3, 1941; children: Doreen Mortola LeMoult, Elaine Mortola Clark. BA, Fordham U., 1938, MA, 1941, PhD, 1946, L.H.D. (hon.), 1964; postgrad., Columbia U., 1946; L.H.D. (hon.), Medaille Coll., 1980; LL.D. (hon.), Bryant Coll., 1965, Syracuse U., 1967, N.Y. Law Sch., 1968; Litt.D. (hon.), Manhattan Coll., 1967, Coll. St. Rose, 1971; LL.D. (hon.), Western State U., 1985; L.H.D. (hon.), Pace U., 1987. Grad. fellow, sch. edn. Fordham U., 1938-39, asst. registrar, 1939-41, asst. registrar, city hall div., lectr. grad. faculty, sch. edn., 1946-47; instr. math. Cooper Union and Townsend Harris High Sch., N.Y.C., 1941-42; mem. faculty St. Peter's Coll., Jersey City, part time 1946-47; with Pace U., N.Y.C., 1947—, asst. dean, 1947-49, dean, 1949-50, provost, 1950-54, v.p., 1954-60, pres., 1960-84, chancellor, 1984-90, chancellor emeritus, 1990—. Mem. Community Planning Bd. 1, Borough Manhattan, 1954-66, chmn., 1956-58; mem., chmn. legis. com. Assn. Colls. and Univs. State N.Y., v.p., 1965-66, pres., 1967-68; mem. adv. council on higher edn. State Edn. Dept.; trustee, past pres. Com. on Ind. Colls. and Univs.; mem. Middle States Assn. Colls. and Schs., N.Y. Gov.'s Commn. on Quality, Cost and Finance of N.Y. State Elementary and Secondary Edn., 1969-71, Westchester Planning Commn., 1966-73, Westchester County Assn., N.Y.C. Council on Econ. Edn., Commn. on Ind. Colls. and Univs. State N.Y., chmn., 1961-63; mem. council Fordham U.; mem. Mayor's Com. on Long-Term Fin. of N.Y.C.; former mem. adv. bd. Elizabeth Seton Coll.; past dir. and sec. Greater N.Y. Council Fgn. Students; chmn. bd. govs. Fordham U. Alumni Fedn., 1958-60; formerly trustee Rosemont Coll., St. Joseph's Sem., Yonkers, N.Y.; co-chmn. N.Y. State Edn. Dept. Task Force on Teaching Profession, 1987-88; chmn. Lincoln Ctr. Inst., 1987; bd. dirs. Lincoln Ctr., 1987—; hon. dir. N.Y.C. Partnership, 1987—; bd. dirs. N.Y. Telephone Co., Bank of N.Y., J.C. Penney Co., Nat. Reins. Co., Continental Ins. Co. Bd. govs. New Rochelle Hosp.; hon. bd. govs. White Plains Hosp.; Downtown-Lower Manhattan Assn., Econ. Devel. Council; former trustee Instructional TV. Served with USNR, 1942-46; lt. comdr. Res. Decorated Knight of Malta, Knight Comdr. Order of Merit of Republic of Italy; recipient Ann. Achievement award in edn. Fordham Coll., 1960, William O'Brien award Cardinal Newman Found., 1964, Ednl. award Westchester chpt. Am. Com. Italian-Immigration, 1969, James E. Allen Jr. Meml. award Disting. Svc. to Edn. Bd. Regents N.Y. State, 1977, Leadership in Edn. award Assn. Colls. and Univs. State of N.Y., 1986, Outstanding Achievement award 100 Yr. Assn. of N.Y., 1983, Big Bros. of N.Y. Achievement award, 1987, Distinguished Alumni award Fordham U. Sch. Edn. Alumni Assn., 1970, Outstanding Achievement award One Hundred Yr. Assn., 1983, Achievement award in edn. Big Bros. N.Y., 1987, Starr award Good Counsel Acad., 1991, Family of Yr. award Family Svc. of Westchester, 1990; named Man of Yr. B'nai B'rith Youth Services, 1975 Mem. N.Y. Acad. Pub. Edn. (pres. 1962-64, dir.), N.Y. C. of C. (chmn. edn. com. 1966-68, mem. exec. com.), Nat. Office Mgmt. Assn., NEA, N.Y. Adult Edn. Coun., Knights of Malta. Clubs: Metropolitan (N.Y.C.), Univ. (N.Y.C.); Larchmont Yacht Club.

MORTON, BRIAN, writer, editor; b. N.Y.C., July 8, 1955; s. Richard Paul and Tasha (Brisman) Morton. BA, Sarah Lawrence Coll., 1978. Instr. grad. dept. English, NYU, N.Y.C., 1992-94, 98—; tchr. 92d St. YMCA, 1993-98; instr. New Sch. Social Rsch., 1995-97; exec. editor Dissent Mag., 1994-99; instr. Sarah Lawrence Coll., Bronxville, 1998—. Author: (novels) The Dylanist, 1991, Starting Out in the Evening, 1998; book rev. editor: Dissent Mag., 1988—2000. Finalist PEN/Faulkner award, 1999; recipient Koret Jewish Book award for fiction, 1998, Acad. Lit. award, Am. Acad. Arts and Letters, 2000; fellow Guggenheim, 2001. Office: Sarah Lawrence Coll One Mead Way Bronxville NY 10708

MORTON, CRAIG RICHARD, real estate investor; b. Mpls., Dec. 8, 1942; s. William Charles and Patricia Louise (Hare) M.; m. Barbara Jean Larsen, 1998; children: Kelly McCall, Bradley Winslow; step-son Thomas Paul Caspers. Student, U. Philippines, Quezon City, 1961-62; BA in Geography of Southeast Asia, U. Minn., 1966; postgrad., St. John's Coll., Annapolis, 1966. Vol. U.S. Peace Corps, Philippines, 1966-68; v.p. Rent Mgmt., Inc., Mpls., 1970-80; pres. Diversified Hawaiian Investments, Inc., 1981-99, Craig R. Morton & Assoc., Inc., Mpls., 1980-2000, N. Am. Land Corp., 2002—. Founder 49 real estate ltd. partnerships, Minn., N.Mex., Hawaii, Tex.; real estate developer Enchanted Lakes, Minn., 1990; pres. Am. Forex Corp., 1995-98, Sweet Magnolia HOA, 2001. Am. Field Svc. scholar to Pakistan, 1960. Mem. Soc. Mayflower Descs., Jaguar Club Minn., Country Classics Car Club, Rotary (Paul Harris fellow), Order of DeMolay, Boy Scouts Order of Arrow, Loyal Order of Moose, Internat. Arabian Horse Assn. Republican. Avocations: tree farming, reading, stamp collecting, woodsmanship, raising Arabian horses. Home: 40305 303rd Lane Aitkin MN 56431-8723

MORTON, CYNTHIA MAUREEN, molecular biologist, educator; d. William Morton and Anne H. Hardy. PhD, CUNY, 1993. NATO fellow Kew (Eng.) Gardens; NERC advanced fellowship Reading (Eng.) U., 1995—98; asst. prof. Auburn (Ala.) U., 1998—. Dir. herbarium Auburn U., 1998—; internal/external referee NSF. Editor: Pollen and Spores: Morphology and Biology, 2000. Grantee, Royal Soc., 1997—98, Stanley Smith Hort. Trust, 1997—98, NSF, 2000—, ADECA, 2000—02. Mem.: Bot. Soc. of Am., Am. Soc. of Plant Taxonomists, Systematics Assn. (coun. mem. 1996—98), Fellow of the Linnean Society Society. Democrat. Avocations: running, field work, photography, gardening, working for Habitat for Humanity. Office: Auburn U 101 Life Science Auburn AL

MORTON, DAVID RAY, sales and marketing executive; b. Rockford, Ill., Dec. 7, 1948; s. Raymond Thomas and Nathalie Ilene (Hendricks) M.; m. Carol Lynn Pott, Apr. 1, 1972; children: Rebecca Lynn, Eric David. BS in Forestry, U. Ill., 1971; MBA, Ohio State U., 1983. Field svc. rep. So. Forest Products Assn., New Orleans, 1972-73; sales rep. chem. divsn. Ga. Pacific Corp., Columbus, Ohio, 1973-76; lumber broker Fireside Forest Industries, 1976-77; sr. tech. sales & svc. rep. chem. divsn. Ga. Pacific Corp., 1977-84; dir. mktg. Monitronix Corp., 1984-85; dir. mktg. & sales Freeman Mfg. & Supply Co., Cleve., 1985-88; nat. sales and mktg. mgr. Hexcel Corp.-Resins Group, L.A., 1988-95; sales mgr. Hapco, Inc., Hanover, Mass., 1995-96; nat.

sales mgr. Conap, Olean, N.Y., 1996-99; sr. market devel. mgr. H.B. Fuller Co., N.Am. ASC Group, Assembly Group, St. Paul, 1999—. Del.-at-large Rep. Platform Planning Com., Avon Lake, Ohio, 1992. Sgt. maj. U.S. Army N.G., 1971-99. Mem. Soc. Mfg. Engrs. (treas. 1982-84), Am. Foundrymen's Soc. (publ. chmn. 1992-99), Ohio State Alumni Assn., U. Ill. Alumni Assn., Polyurethane Mfrs. Assn. (del. 1990-95), Ohio N.G. Enlisted Assn., Enlisted Assn. N.G. U.S., Phi Kappa Sigma. Avocations: sailing, handball, tennis, woodworking. Home: 296 Chestnut Ct Avon Lake OH 44012-2141 E-mail: david.morton@hbfuller.com.

MORTON, DEBORAH BURWELL, lawyer; b. Midwest City, Okla., June 15, 1953; d. Thornton Allen and Dona (Morine) Burwell; 1 child, Stephen Chase. BS in Edn., Tex. Christian U., 1973; JD, So. Meth. U., 1978. Bar: Md. 1979, Tex. 1984, U.S. Dist. Ct. (no. dist.) Tex. 1985. Ptnr. Neubauer & DeLuca, Balt., 1979-84; assoc. Simon, Anisman, Doby, Wilson & Skillern, Ft. Worth, 1985-88; prin. Law Offices Deborah B. Morton, 1988-98; assoc. Law, Snakard & Gambill, 1998—. Mem. Tarrant County Bar Assn. Office: Law Snakard & Gambill 1600 W 7th St Ste 500 Fort Worth TX 76102-3859 E-mail: dmorton@lawsnakard.com.

MORTON, DONALD CHARLES, astronomer; b. Kapuskasing, Ont., Can., June 12, 1933; s. Charles Orr and Irene Mary (Wightman) M.; m. Winifred May Austin, Dec. 12, 1970; children: Keith James, Christine Elizabeth. BA, U. Toronto, 1956; PhD, Princeton U., 1959. Astronomer U.S. Naval Rsch. Lab., Washington, 1959-61; from rsch. assoc. to sr. rsch. astronomer with rank of prof. Princeton (N.J.) U., 1961-76; dir. Anglo-Australian Obs., Epping and Coonabarabran, Australia, 1976-86; dir. gen. Herzberg Inst. Astrophysics, NRC of Can., Ottawa and Victoria, 1986—2000; rschr. emeritus NRC of Can., 2000—. Contbr. numerous articles to profl. jours. Fellow Australian Acad. Sci.; mem. Internat. Astron. Union, Royal Astron. Soc. (assoc. 1980), Astron. Soc. Australia (pres. 1981-83, hon. mem. 1986), Royal Astron. Soc. Can., Am. Astron. Soc. (councilor 1970-73), Can. Astron. Soc. Australian Inst. Physics (Pawsey Meml. lectr. 1985), Can. Assn. Physicists, U.K. Alpine Club, Am. Alpine Club, Alpine Club Can. Avocations: mountaineering, rock climbing, ice climbing, marathon running. Office: Herzberg Inst Astrophysics NRC Can 5071 W Saanich Rd Victoria BC Canada V9E 2E7

MORTON, DONALD JOHN, librarian; b. Bklyn., Jan. 11, 1931; s. Ellwood Stokes and Gladys (Hassler) M.; m. Ann Mayo Tilden, Aug. 16, 1958; children— Saundra Kay, Donald John, Mary Ann. BS, U. Del., 1952; MS, La. State U., 1954; PhD, U. Calif. at Berkeley, 1958; MS in Libr. Sci., Simmons Coll., 1969, Dr. Arts in Library Sci, 1976. Asst. prof. botany N.M. State U., Las Cruces, 1957-58; asst. prof. plant pathology N.D. State U., Fargo, 1959-61; plant pathologist Agr. Dept., Tifton, Ga., 1961-65; asso. prof. plant pathology U. Del., Newark, 1965-68; librarian Northeastern U., Boston, 1968-70; head librarian, asst. prof. history of medicine U. Mass. Med. Sch., Worcester, 1970-74, dir. libr., assoc. prof. libr. sci., 1974-94, libr. cons., 1994—; tchr. med. librarianship Worcester State Coll., 1974-94; libr. cons., 1994—; computer cons. Hampton Hist. Soc., 1995—; libr. advisor Exeter (N.H.) Hosp., 1996—. Cons. in field; mem. adv. com. med. librarianship Simmons Coll., 1972-94; mem. task force com. New Eng. Regional Libr. Svc., 1971-94; mem. cooperating staff Worcester Found. Exptl. Biology, 1972-94; chmn. Coun. Developing Med. Librs., 1974; pres. North Atlantic Health Scis. Librs., 1974-75, Worcester Area Coop. Librs., 1974-75. Contbr. articles to profl. jours. Mem. Oliver Wendell Holmes endowment com. Boston Med. Libr., 1973-74, U. Mass. Bicentennial Com., 1973-75. Mem. Am. Assn. Univ. Adminstrs., Simmons Coll. Libr. Sch. Alumni Assn. (pres. 1975-76), Worcester Art Mus., Worcester Hist. Soc., Northboro Hist. Soc., Hampton Hist. Soc., N.H. Hist. Soc., Am. Soc. Info. Sci., ALA, Mass. Libr. Assn., Med. Libr. Assn. (chmn. New Eng. group 1974-75), Mycol. Soc. Am., Spl. Librs. Assn., New Eng. Coll. Librarians, Piscataqua Pioneers Hereditary Soc., Sigma Xi, Phi Kappa Phi, Phi Sigma, Delta Tau Delta, Alpha Zeta. Home: 314 High St Hampton NH 03842-4004

MORTON, EDWARD JAMES, insurance company executive; b. Ft. Wayne, Ind., Nov. 8, 1926; s. Clifford Leroy and Clara Marie (Merklein) M.; m. Jean Ann McClernon, Apr. 30, 1949; children: Marcia Lynn, Anne; m. Matthild Schneider, Sept. 19, 1986; 1 child, Katherine. BA, Yale U., 1949. With John Hancock Mut. Life Ins. Co., Boston, 1949—, v.p., then sr. v.p., 1967-74, exec. v.p., 1974-82, pres., chief operating officer, 1982-86, chmn., chief exec. officer, 1987-92, also bd. dirs. Trustee Gettysburg Coll. 1990-2002; hon. life overseer Children's Hosp. Fellow Soc. Actuaries; mem. Actuaries Club Boston, Comml. Club Boston, Algonquin Club Boston, Phi Beta Kappa. Office: John Hancock Life Ins Co PO Box 111 C-01-03 Boston MA 02117-0111

MORTON, ERIC, liberal arts educator; b. Detroit, Feb. 24, 1934; s. Lee Jack and Theresa Magdalen (Leonard) M.; children: Tracey Lynn, Theresa Dallas; m. Virgie Tillman, Sept. 27, 1997. AA, Merritt Coll., 1992; BA, U. Calif., Berkeley, 1992; M of Profl. Studies, Cornell U., 1994; MA, SUNY, Binghamton, 1998, PhD, 1999. Internat. organizer Am. Fedn. of State, County, Mcpl. Employees, Calif., 1970-73; field rep. State Senator Nicholas Petris, Oakland, 1973-75; mktg. adminstr. Safegate Aviation Systems, 1975-80; asst. to dir. recreational sports U. Calif., 1980-92; grad. tchg. asst. Africana Studies and Rsch. Ctr., Cornell U., 1992-94; adj. lectr., rschr., tchr. SUNY, Binghamton, 1994-2000; assoc. prof. philosophy Fort Valley (Ga.) State U., 2000—. Mem., multicultural core group Cornell U., 1992-94; lectr., rschr., tchr. SUNY Binghamton, 1994-2000; assoc. prof. philosophy Fort Valley State U., Ga., 2000—. Compiler (book) Mississippi Black Paper, 1965; contbr. articles to profl. jours. Active polit. campaigns; project mgr. Ctr. for Ind. Living, Berkeley, 1975-77. With U.S. Army, 1951-54. Recipient Award Met. Trans. Commn., 1973. Avocations: photography, reading. Home: 119 Red Oak Rd Byron GA 31008-6326 E-mail: be83464@binghamton.edu., mortone@mail.fusu.edu.

MORTON, FREDERIC, author; b. Vienna, Austria, Oct. 5, 1924; s. Frank and Rose (Ungvary) M.; m. Marcia Colman, Mar. 28, 1957; 1 dau., Rebecca. BS, Coll. City N.Y., 1947; MA, New Sch. Social Research, 1949. Author: The Hound, 1947, The Darkness Below, 1949, Asphalt and Desire, 1952, The Witching Ship, 1960, The Schatten Affair, 1965, Snow Gods, 1969, An Unknown Woman, 1976, The Forever Street, 1984, Crosstown Sabbath, 1987, (biography) The Rothschilds, 1962 (nominated for Nat. Book award), A Nervous Splendor-Vienna 1888/9, 1979 (nominated for Nat. Book award), Thunder at Twilight-Vienna 1913/14, 1989; books translated into 14 langs.; actor (documentary made in English and German) Crosstown Sabbath, 1995 (broadcast in Austria, Germany, Switzerland, P.B.S. Stas., U.S.); contbg. editor: Vanity Fair; contbr. to publs. including Martha Foley's Best Am. Short Stories and other anthologies, N.Y. Times, Harper's mag., Atlantic mag., Nation, Playboy, Esquire, N.Y. Mag., Hudson Rev., Wall Street Jour., Vanity Fair, L.A. Times, others; columnist Village Voice, Conde-Nast Traveler, Wall Street Jour. Recipient Author of Year award Nat. Anti-Defamation League, B'nai B'rith; Hon. Professorship award Republic of Austria, 1980, Tom Osborne Disting. lectureship U. Nebr., 1989; Dodd, Mead Intercollegiate Lit. fellow, 1947; Yaddo residence fellow, 1948, 50; Breadloaf Writers' Conf. fellow, 1947; Columbia U. fellow, 1953; recipient Golden Merit award City of Vienna, 1986, City of Vienna medal of honor in gold, 2001. Mem. Author's Guild (exec. council), P.E.N. Home: 110 Riverside Dr New York NY 10024-3715 Office: The Lantz Office 200 W 57th St New York NY 10019 *As a writer I'm trying to tell the truth interestingly.*

MORTON, GEORGE THOMAS, reporter; b. Cin., Jan. 25, 1954; s. George Thomas and Marian Elizabeth (Wilt) Morton. BA in English, Miami U., Oxford, Ohio, 1976; MDiv, Gordon-Conwell Theol. Sem., South Hamilton, Mass., 1983. Reporter Beaumont (Tex.) Enterprise, 1983-88, Colorado Springs (Colo.) Gazette Telegraph, 1988-90; freelance writer, 1991-92; reporter Casper (Wyo.) Star-Tribune, 1992—. Fgn. corr. Hearst News Svcs., N.Y.C., 1986; instr. sociology of religion U. Colo., Colorado Springs, 1989, Colorado Springs, 90. Author: (book) The Survivor's Guide to Unemployment, 1992; ghostwriter: book Parenting Teen with Love and Logic, 1992, freelance reporter: Religion News Svc., 1989—93, freelance reporter: Christianity Today, 1991—93; actor: Casper Coll. Theatre, 1996, Stage III Theatre, 1996, 1998, 2001. Recipient Comm. award, Bapt. Gen. Conv. Tex., 1986, Thomas Stokes award, Washington Journalism Ctr., 1968, Media award, Am. Acad. Nursing, 1994, Pacemaker award, Wyo. Press Assn., 1993, 1996, 1999, 2001; fellow, Inst. Journalism and Natural Resources, 1998. Mem.: Investigative Reporters and Editors, Soc. Environ. Journalists, Soc. Am. Bus. Editors and Writers, Soc. Profl. Journalists. E-mail: morton@trib.com.

MORTON, HUGH WESLEY, producer, director; b. Pasadena, Calif., Dec. 8, 1931; s. Hugh Wesley Morton and Timey Delacey Hopper; m. Paula Dozois, Nov. 30, 1951 (dec. May 1954); m. Norma Antonia Daloisio, Apr. 22, 1965 (div.); 1 adopted child, Wil Guido. BA, Northwestern U., 1954; BS, U. Mont., 1959; MA, U. Oreg., 1961. Mailboy, prodn. office clk. Paramount Prodns., Hollywood, Calif., 1962-64; dir., tchr. Profl. Theatre Workshop, Desilu Studios, 1964-66; asst. to contr. Columbia Pictures TV, 1966-68, asst. to exec. v.p. TV prodn., 1968-75; asst. to studio pres. The Burbank (Calif.) Studios, 1975-78; dir. Hollywood Central, Glendale, Calif., 1978-82; spl. events prodr., dir. studio facilities Fox Studios/News Corp., L.A., 1982-97; vol. oncology, sr. peer counseling Providence St. Joseph Hosp., Burbank, Calif., 1997—; cons. on call IV Prodns., L.A., 1997—. Prodr. 400 TV episodes, 50 films; author: Assistant Director's Handbook, 1973. Mem. Mus. of Arts, City of Hope, L.A.; libr. assoc. Coll. Canyons; prodr. Ciba Geigy, L.A.; prodr. various spl. events. Named Vol. of Yr. Providence St. Joseph Hosp., 1998; recipient Outstanding Support award White House Comms. Agy., 1994, Outstanding Svc. award C. of C., 1983, Award of Merit Media Workshop Found. Mass Comm. and Educating Am. Youth; Fulbright scholarship Alternate Royal Acad. Mem. Acad. of TV Arts and Scis., Screen Actors Guild, Am. Fedn. of TV and Radio Artists, Internat. Alliance of Theatrical State Employees Artists and Allied Crafts of the U.S., Calif. State Sheriff's Assn., Canyon Theatre Guild, Met. Mus. of Art (assoc.), Wildlife Sta., Calif. State Parks Assn., L.A. County Mus. of Arts, L.A. Natural History Mus., The Colony Playhouse. Avocations: hiking, gardening, singing, reading. Office: IV Prodns PO Box 2517 Toluca Lake CA 91610

MORTON, JAMES CARNES, JR. automotive company executive; b. Duncan, Okla., May 8, 1945; s. James Carnes and Syble Lyda (Looney) M.; m. Susan Phillips, May 25, 1968; children: James III, Terrissa Anne, Scott Thomas. BA, Westminster Coll., 1967; JD, U. Mo., 1972. Bar: Mo. 1972. Tax acct. Arthur Andersen Co., St. Louis, 1972-74; tax atty. Gen. Dynamics Corp., 1974-76; asst. gen. counsel Michelin Tire Corp., Greenville, S.C., 1976-86; gen. counsel Michelin Tire Corp. and Michelin Tires (Can.) Ltd., 1990-92; dir. pub. rels. and govt. affairs Michelin Tire Corp., 1986-92; exec. dir. external rels. Michelin N.Am., 1992-96; v.p. pub. rels. and govt. rels. Michelin N.Am., Inc., 1996-2000; sr. v.p. fin. & adminstrn. Nissan North Am., Inc., Gardena, Calif., 2000—. Bd. dirs. Greenville Symphony Orch., 1986-89, United Way Greenville, 1987-88, Greenville YMCA, 1988-89; mem. S.C. Reorganization Commn., 1986-98; trustee S.C. Gov.'s Sch. for Sci. and Math., 1996-99; mem. sch. bd. Christ Ch. Episcopal Sch., Greenville, 1997-2000; vice chmn. S.C. Ports Authority, 1999-2000. Lt. U.S. Army, 1967-70, Vietnam; capt. Mo. N.G., 1971-72. Mem. ABA, Assn. Internat. Automobile Mfrs. (bd. dirs., exec. com. 2000—), Rubber Mfrs. Assn. (bd. dirs. 1995-2000, govt. affairs com., tire mgmt. com.), Alliance of Auto. Mfrs. (bd. dirs. 2000—), Mo. Bar Assn. (nonresident), S.C. C. of C. (bd. dirs., pres. 1993-94, chmn. 1994-95, exec. com. 1981-84, 86-95, Svc. Recognition award 1982), Greater Greenville C. of C. (chmn. govt. affairs com. 1990, chmn. legis. affairs com. 1996-98, bd. dirs. 1990-93), Calif. C. of C., L.A. Urban League (bd. dirs. 2001--), Greenville Country Club, Rolling Hills Country Club, Manhattan Country Club. Presbyterian. Avocation: golf. Office: Nissan NAm Inc PO Box 191 Gardena CA 90248-0191 E-mail: jim.morton@nissan-usa.com.

MORTON, JEFFREY BRUCE, aerospace engineering educator; b. Chgo., Apr. 25, 1941; s. Max E. and Tillie (Forman) M.; m. Judy Gail Moss, June 14, 1964; children: Jonathan, Amy, Michael. BS, Mass. Inst. Tech., 1963; PhD, Johns Hopkins U., 1967. Sr. scientist U. Va., Charlottesville, 1967-68, asst. prof., 1968-72, assoc. prof., 1972-80, prof., 1980—2001, prof. emeritus, 2001. Lectr. U. Va., 1967-68; pres. M.J. Systems Inc., Charlottesville, 1976-96, chmn. bd., 1996-97. Contbr. articles to profl. jours. Assoc. Fellow AIAA; mem. Am. Soc. Engring. Edn. (southeast sect. rsch. award 1981), Am. Physical Soc., Sigma Xi. Office: U Va Dept Mech Aerospace Engring Charlottesville VA 22901

MORTON, JERRY LEE, journalist; b. South Bend, Ind., May 7, 1943; s. Wade Donovan and Regina Helen (Hosinski) M. AA, Lake Michigan Coll., 1963; BA in Journalism with high honors, Mich. State U., 1965, PhD in Higher Edn., 1991; MS in Journalism, Northwestern U., 1966. Reporter Hammond (Ind.) Times, 1969-71; free-lance writer in the Middle East, 1971-72; columnist The Enquirer, Battle Creek, Mich., 1973-78; reporter Akron (Ohio) Beacon Jour., 1979-80; prof. journalism Mich. State U., East Lansing, 1981-86, 89-93, Western Mich. U., Kalamazoo, 1987-88; v.p., ptnr. ComServ Internat., East Lansing, 1991—. Cons. writer, photographer W.K. Kellogg Found., Battle Creek; pres. The Jerry Lee Press, East Lansing, 1985—. Author, photographer: Yesterday in Hodunk, 1985, Footprints and Friends, 1988, Back to Algansee, 1993, Romania, 1996, The Sound of Words, 2001; photographs exhibited in various art shows. VISTA vol. Cmty. Action Agy., Balt., 1966-68; writer, editor Nat. Violence Commn., Chgo., 1968; dist. dir. McGovern Campaign, Mich., 1972—; writer and lectr. on history of capital punishment. Recipient Juror's award Our Town Art Show, Birmingham, Mich., 1996; McCormick scholar Northwestern U., Evanston, Ill., 1965; NEH Journalism fellow U. Mich., Ann Arbor, 1976; Fulbright prof. journalism, Timisoara, Romania, 1993. Mem. Barry County Hist. Soc., Fulbright Assn., Sigma Delta Chi, Kappa Tau Alpha, Phi Kappa Phi. Roman Catholic. Avocations: sports, travel. Home and Office: ComServ Internat 6120 Gossard Ave East Lansing MI 48823-1534 E-mail: jlm.csi@usa.net., jerryleetiger@aol.com.

MORTON, LINDA P. journalism educator; b. Nashville, Oct. 3, 1946; d. Clerence Augustus and Wanda Lou (Greenleigh) King; m. Truman F. Patterson, Aug. 14, 1964 (dec.); m. Gail Morton, Feb. 14, 1976 (dec.); children: Jene C., John D., Erica T.; m. James H. Sullivan, June 2, 2000. BA in English Edn., Northeastern State U., Tahlequah, Okla., 1971; MA in English, Ark. State U., 1972; EdD in Higher Edn., Okla. State U., 1984. Prof. lang. arts Bacone Coll., Muskogee, Okla., 1972-76; dir. pub. rels. Carl Albert Jr. Coll., Poteau, 1976-80; pub. info. officer Coll. Bus. Adminstrn., Okla. State U., Stillwater, 1980-83; asst. prof. pub. rels./advt. N.E. Mo. State U., Kirksville, 1983-84; coord. and lang. arts, coord. journalism Carl Albert Jr. Coll. Extension Office, Sallisaw, Okla., 1985-88; dir. pub. rels., assoc. prof. pub. rels. Miss. U. for Women, Columbus, 1988-90; asst. prof. journalism U. So. Miss., Hattiesburg, 1990-92; prof. journalism U. Okla., Norman, 1992—. Owner Sultan Comms.; lectr. in field. Mem. rev. bd. Pub. Rels. Rev., 1994—, Pub. Rels. Rsch., 2000—; submissions editor Tchg. Pub. Rels., 2000—; contbr. articles to scholarly and profl. jours. Recipient Grad award for comm. programs CASE, 1983, Silver Addy for vision poster Ctrl. Miss. Advt. Assn., 1989. Mem. Pub. Rels. Soc. Am. (accredited, dir. ednl. sect. 1993-94, dir. at large ednl. sect. 1994-95, sec.-treas. ednl. sect. 1995, ednl. affairs com. 1994-96, editor ednl. sect. newsletter 1996), Okla. Coll. Pub. Rels. Assn. (pres. 1980-81), Assn. for Educators in Schs. of Journalism and Mass Comm. Methodist. Home: 2401 Larkhaven St Norman OK 73071-4326 Office: U Okla Gaylord Coll 860 Van Vleet Oval Norman OK 73019-2050 E-mail: lmorton@ou.edu.

MORTON, MARILYN MILLER, retired genealogy and history educator, lecturer, researcher, travel executive, director; b. Water Valley, Miss., Dec. 2, 1929; d. Julius Brunner and Irma Faye (Magee) Miller; m. Perry Wilkes Morton Jr., July 2, 1958; children: Dent Miller Morton, Nancy Marilyn Morton Driggers, E. Perian Morton Dyar. BA in English, Miss. U. for Women, 1952; MS in History, Miss. State U., 1955. Cert. secondary tchr. Tchr. English, speech and history Starkville (Miss.) H.S., 1952-58; part-time instr. Miss. State U., 1953-55; spl. collection staff Samford U. Libr., Birmingham, Ala., 1984-92; lectr. genealogy and history, instr. Inst. Genealogy & Hist. Rsch., Samford U., 1985-93, assoc. dir., 1985-88, exec. dir., 1988-93; founding dir. SU British and Irish Inst. Genealogy & Hist. Rsch. Samford U., Birmingham and British Isles, 1986-93; owner, dir. Marilyn Miller Morton Brit-Ire-U.S. Genealogy, Birmingham, also British Isles, 1994—. Instr. genealogy classes Samford U. Metro Coll., 1986-94; lectr. nat. conf. Fedn. of Geneal. Socs. Contbr. articles profl. jours. Miss. state pres. Future Homemakers Am., 1947-48; active Birmingham chpt. Salvation Army Aux., 1982—. Named to Miss. U. for Women Hall of Fame, 1952. Fellow Irish Geneal. Rsch. Soc. London; mem. Internat. Soc. for Brit. Genealogy and Family History (trustee 1999), Nat. Geneal. Soc. (mem. nat. program com. 1988—, lectr. nat. mtgs.), Assn. Profl. Genealogists, Soc. Genealogists London, Antiquarian Soc. Birmingham (sec., 2d v.p. 1982-84), DAR (regent Cheaha chpt. 1977-78), Daus. Am. Colonists (regent Edward Waters chpt. 1978-79), Nat. League of Am. Penwomen, Phi Kappa Phi (charter mem. Samford U. chpt. 1972). Avocations: reading, research, travel, bridge, public speaking. Home and Office: 3508 Clayton Pl Birmingham AL 35216-3810

MORTON, MARSHALL NAY, finance executive; b. Chgo., Oct. 3, 1945; s. Frederick Samuel and Margaret Elizabeth (Burke) M.; m. Caroline Sanders, Sept. 13, 1969; children— Marshall Burke, Margaret Elizabeth. BA, U. Va., 1970, MBA, 1972. Fin. analyst West Point Pepperell Inc., Ga., 1972-73, budget dir., 1973-74, fin. mgr., 1974-75, asst. treas., 1975-81, treas., 1981-86, v.p., contr., 1986-89, sr. v.p., CFO, Media Gen., Inc., Richmond, Va., 1989—. Pres., Valley United Fund, West Point, 1982, Am. Cancer Soc., West Point chpt., 1985-87; v.p. fin. Lanier Council Boys Scouts Am., 1986-87; former bd. dirs. Commonwealth Girl Scout Coun. of Va.; bd. govs. St. Catherine's Sch.; past pres. Metro Bus. Fond.; pres. The Robert E. Lee Coun. Boys Scouts Am. Served with USN, 1966-68, Vietnam. Episcopalian. Mem. Richmond Metro C. of C. (former bd. dirs.), Union League Club (N.Y.C.), Country Club of Va., The Commonwealth Club. Avocations: tennis, sailing. Office: Media Gen Inc 333 E Grace St Richmond VA 23293-1000

MORTON, MARY MADELINE, family nurse practitioner; b. Bronx, N.Y., Aug. 7, 1952; d. David E. and Frances P. (Perrone) Bennett; children: Anthony, Kathryn; m. Robert B. Morton, May 25, 1991. AAS in Nursing-RN with distinction, Pace U., 1989, BSN summa cum laude, 1994, MSN, 1996. Cert. LPN; RN, N.Y.; cert. family nurse practitioner. Med. asst. C.A. Vera, MD, Bronx, 1970-79; staff nurse med.-surg., pediatric, orthopedic and cardiac units Hudson Valley Hosp. Ctr., Peekskill, N.Y., 1986-96; office nurse William Higgins, MD, Mohegan Lake, 1993-95; pvt. practice, 1998—; dir. Med. Clinic St. Vincent's Hosp, Westchester, N.Y., 1997-98; nurse practitioner Skyview Health Care Ctr., Croton, 1996-97. Camp nurse Summer Trails Day Camp, Somers, N.Y., summer, 1992; clin. instr./lectr. LPN program Bd. Cooperative Ednl. Svcs. Tech. Ctr., Yorktown Height, N.Y., 1994-95; adj. prof. Pace U. Leinhard Sch. Nursing, Pleasantville, N.Y., 1995. Tchr. religious edn. St. Mary's Ch., Katonah, N.Y., 1988, 89. Mem. ANA, N.Y. State Coalition of Nurse Practitioners, Sigma Theta Tau, Alpha Chi. Democrat. Roman Catholic. Home: PO Box 455 Lincolndale NY 10540-0455

MORTON, MICHAEL JAMES, software engineer; b. Long Beach, Calif., Apr. 15, 1969; s. Thomas James and Carol Ann Morton. B in Computer Sci., U. Calif., Irvine, 1994. Photo finisher One Hour Moto Photo, Lake Forest, Calif., 1988-94; software engr. Quarterdeck Corp., Marina Del Rey, 1994-96, Connect-3, Los Alamitos, 1996-97, Beckman Instruments, Fullerton, 1997—. Co-founder Tru Justice LLC, Claremont, Calif., 1996—. Mem. Phi Beta Kappa (sponsor, contbr.). Libertarian. Avocations: automobiles, electronics/circuit design, photography, aviation, horology. Home: 6260 E Via Ribazo Anaheim CA 92807-2334 Office: 4300 N Harbor Blvd Fullerton CA 92835-1091 E-mail: morton555@worldnet.att.net.

MORTON, MICHAEL RAY, retail company consultant; b. Memphis, Nov. 10, 1952; s. James Ray and Margaret Regina (Stevens) M.; m. Mary Elizabeth Harkness; children: Mary Harkness, Margaret Jeanne, Molly Ray. BBA, U. Miss., 1973; MBA, U. Denver, 1975. Cost acct. Dover Corp., Memphis, 1975-76; internal auditor W.R. Grace and Co., 1976-78, sr. fin. analyst N.Y.C., 1979-80, v.p. Handy Dan div. San Antonio, 1981-82; chief fin. officer, sec., treas. Home Ctrs. Am., 1983; sr. v.p. Builders Square K-Mart Corp., 1984-89; pres. Orion Strategic Solutions, Inc., 1989-95; mng. ptnr. Critical Path Strategies, Boerne, Tex., 1996—. Bd. dirs. Builders Design Inc., Dania, Fla., 1989-91, treas., 1985-87, Materials Evolution Devel. USA. CEO, bd. dirs., 2001—; bd. dirs., v.p. Tex. Ind. Newspapers, Inc., San Antonio; mem. exec. com. Home Ctr. Industry Conf.; bd. dirs., Critical Path Strategies, 1995—. Bd. dirs. Friends of Cibolo Wilderness, pres., 2001—, Cibolo Land Trust Conservancy. Mem. Boerne C. of C. (amb. 1981), Home Ctr. Leadership Coun. Republican. Roman Catholic. Avocations: running, golf, reading. Home: 8060 Pimlico Ln Boerne TX 78015-4705 Office: 33 FM 474 Boerne TX 78006

MORTON, RICHARD, lawyer, financial consultant; b. Jamaica, N.Y., Sept. 25, 1925; s. Lawrence and Irma (Gross) M.; m. Helen Malone, May 9, 1965; children: Bruce, Greg, Terri L. Sloan. BSBA, U. Denver, 1949; postgrad., Stetson Coll. Law, 1961; JD, U. Miss., 1963; LLM, Yale U., 1964. Bar: Miss. 1963, Fla. 1971. Builder, developer, N.Y., Fla., 1962-60; prof. law U. Ga., Athens, 1965-68; pvt. practice law Miami, 1971—; mng. ptnr. Morton Towers, 1988-97. Pres. S. Fla. Savs. & Loan, Miami, 1980-84; bd. dirs. Bank of Fla., Founders Nat. Mortgage Corp.; of counsel Katz, Barron, Squitero & Faust, 1998—; adv. com. Apt. Investment & Mgmt. Co., Denver. Contbr. articles to profl. jours. Served to 1st. lt. U.S. Army. Decorated Bronze Star. Office: 2699 S Bayshore Dr Fl 7 Miami FL 33133-5408 Home: 17215 Courtland Ln Boca Raton FL 33496 E-mail: richardmorton@msn.com.

MORTON, ROBERT, producer; b. Long Beach, N.Y., May 20, 1953; s. Gilbert and Sally (Dalven) M. BA, Am. U., Washington, 1975. Producer, program exec. Warner QUBE, Columbus, Ohio, 1976-78; assoc. producer Sta. WCVB-TV, Boston, 1978, Sta. ABC-TV, N.Y.C., 1978-79, NBC Tomorrow Show, N.Y.C., 1979-81; writer, assoc. producer Good Morning America ABC, 1981; creative dir. MTV, 1981-82; producer Late Night With David Letterman NBC, 1982—. Mem. Writers Guild Am., AFTRA. Office: NBC 30 Rockefeller Plz Fl 2 New York NY 10112-0036

MORTON, ROBERT ALLEN, small business owner; b. Boston, Oct. 18, 1954; s. Ralph A. and A. Louise (Dibblee) M.; m. Cynthia Walpole, Apr. 19, 1980; children: Angela Walpole, Jared Walpole. Grad. high sch., Walpole, 1972. Machinist Foxboro (Mass.) Co., 1972-73, Bird Machine Co., South Walpole, 1973-75; v.p., treas. A&W Instruments, Inc., Walpole, 1976-88, pres., 1988—. Member Nat. Arbor Day Found., 1985—, Mass. Audubon Soc., 1988—, Nat. Parks & Conservation Assn., 1990—; life mem. Rep. Nat. Com., 1991—, Eisenhower Commn., 1995. Mem. Nat. Tooling and Machining Assn., Nat. Fedn. of Ind. Bus. (guardian mem. 1981—), U.S. C. of C., Neponset Valley C. of C. Roman Catholic. Avocations: golf, skiing, sports, boating, gardening. E-mail: awmachine@aol.com.

MORTON, STEPHEN DANA, chemist, consultant; b. Madison, Wis., Sept. 7, 1932; s. Walter Albert and Rosalie (Amlie) M. BS, U. Wis., 1954, PhD, 1962. Asst. prof. chemistry Otterbein Coll., Westerville, Ohio, 1962-66; postdoctoral fellow water chemistry, pollution control U. Wis., Madison, 1966-67; water pollution rsch. chemist WARF Inst., 1967-73, head environ. quality dept., 1973-76; mgr. quality assurance Raltech Sci. Svcs., 1977-82; pres. SDM Cons., 1982—. Author: Water Pollution-Causes and Cures, 1976. 1st lt. Chem. Corps, AUS, 1954-56. Mem. AAAS, Am. Chem. Soc. Home and Office: 1126 Sherman Ave Madison WI 53703-1620

MORTON, WILLIAM ALEXANDER, JR. insurance agency executive; b. Wilmington, Del., Nov. 19, 1946; s. William Alexander and Bertha (Talley) M.; m. Sandra Waters Jorgensen, Feb. 12, 1972; children: Cassandra L., W. Alexander III, Ian A. BS, U. Del., 1968, MBA, 1970. CPCU. Asst. v.p. Union Trust Bank, Balt., 1973-80; sr. v.p. mktg. Riggs, Counselman, Michaels & Downes, 1981—. Devel. com. mem. Maryvale Prep. Sch., Brooklandville, Md., 1992-93; class phonathon chair Friends Sch. of Balt., 1993; mem. alumni assn. coll. bus. and econs. U. Del., Newark. 1st Lt. U.S. Army, 1970-72. Episcopalian. Avocations: fishing, music, reading. Home: 101 Longwood Rd Baltimore MD 21210-2119

MORTON, WILLIAM GILBERT, JR. stock exchange executive; b. Syracuse, N.Y., Mar. 13, 1937; s. William Gilbert and Barbara (Link) M.; m. Margaret Halleron, Nov. 26, 1982; children: Andrew Baker, William Gilbert III, Sarah Ellsworth, Kate Spencer. BA, Dartmouth Coll., 1959; MBA, NYU, 1965. Asst. v.p. Discount Corp. N.Y., 1960-67; co-mgr. trading, sr. v.p., dir. Mitchell Hutchins Inc., 1967-79; mng. stock exch. floors, sr. v.p., dir. Dean Witter Reynolds Inc., 1979-85; chmn., CEO Boston Stock Exch. Inc., 1985-2001, chmn. emeritus, 2001—. Chmn. allocation com. NY Stock Exch., floor ofcl., 1976—81, com. mem.; 1970—85; bd. dirs. Radio Shack Corp., Ft. Worth, Griswold & Co., N.Y.C., Morgan Stanley Instnl. Funds, NY, The Griswold Co., NY. Bd. dirs. Vt. Acad., Saxton's River, 1984-90, Boston 2000 Commn., 1998-2001, Nat. Football Found. and Coll. Hall of Fame, N.Y.;

trustee search com. Dartmouth Alumni Coun., 1988-91; trustee Berklee Coll. Music, Stratton Mountain Sch., Stratton, Vt. With USMC, 1959-65. Mem. Boston Econ. Club, Mass. Bus. Roundtable, Nat. Orgn. Investment Profls., Racquet and Tennis Club N.Y.C., Stratton Mt. Country Club (Vt.), Colo. Arlberg Club (Winter Park), Brae Burn Country Club (Newton), Ekwanok Country Club (Vt.), Royal Poinciana Club (Fla.), Stock Exch. Luncheon Club N.Y.C., Theta Delta Chi. Republican. Presbyterian. Office: Boston Stock Exch 100 Franklin St Boston MA 02110-1401

MORTVEDT, JOHN JACOB, soil scientist, researcher; b. Dell Rapids, S.D., Jan. 25, 1932; s. Ernest R. and Clara (Halvorson) M.; m. Marlene L. Fodness, Jan. 23, 1955; children: Sheryl Mortvedt Jarratt, Lori Mortvedt Klopf, Julie Mortvedt Stride. BS, S.D. State U., 1953, MS, 1959; PhD, U. Wis., 1962. Soil chemist TVA, Muscle Shoals, Ala., 1962-87, sr. scientist, 1987-92, regional mgr. field programs dept., 1992-93; ext. soils specialist Colo. State U., Ft. Collins, 1994-95, ext. environ. and pesticide edn. specialist, 1996. Agr. cons. U.S. Borax, 1997—. Co-author: Fertilizer Technology and Application, 1999; editor: Micronutrients in Agriculture, 1972, 2d edit., 1991; contbr. articles to profl. jours. 1st lt. U.S. Army, 1953-57. Fellow AAAS, Soil Sci. Soc. Am. (pres. 1988-89, editor-in-chief 1982-87, Profl. Svc. award 1991, Disting. Svc. award 1996), Am. Soc. Agronomy (exec. com. 1987-90); mem. Internat. Soil Sci. Soc., Colombian Soil Sci. Soc. (hon.), Exch. Club (pres. Florence, Ala. chpt. 1987-88), Toastmasters (pres. Florence chpt. 1964-65), Phi Kappa Phi. Avocations: photography, golf. Office: Colo State U Dept Soil And Crop Scis Fort Collins CO 80523-1170

MOSBAUGH, PHILLIP GEORGE, urologist, educator; b. Noblesville, Ind., Jan. 15, 1938; s.Ward C. and Frances J. Mosbaugh; m. Vera A. Deganutti Green, Jan. 21, 1963 (dec. May 2000); children: Anne R. Mosbaugh Knapp, Virginia G. AB, Ind. U., Bloomington, 1959; MD, Ind. U., Indpls., 1963. Diplomate Am. Bd. Urology. Intern Orange County Hosp., Orange, Calif., 1963-64; resident in gen. surgery and urology Ind. U. Med. Ctr., Indpls., 1964-68; pvt. practice, 1970—. Asst. clin. prof. urology Ind. U. Sch. Medicine, 1975—; mem. med. adv. bd. on interstitial cystitis ALZA Pharms., 1988—, mem. spkr.'s bur., 1998—. Contbr. articles to med. jours., including Jour. Urology. Capt. M.C., USNR, 1968-70. Fellow ACS; mem. Interstitial Cystitis Assn. (med. advisor Ind. chpt. 1987—). Republican. Roman Catholic. Avocations: golf, travel, reading, crosswords. Home: 623 Round Hill Rd Indianapolis IN 46260-2915 Office: Urology of Ind LLC 1801 Senate Blvd Ste 655 Indianapolis IN 46202-1259

MOSBO, JOHN ALVIN, dean; b. Davenport, Iowa, June 11, 1947; s. Alvin Oswald and Marie Lindeen Mosbo; m. Anna Marie Mosbo, Dec. 14, 1968; children: Kristina, Julie. BA, U. No. Colo., 1969; PhD, Iowa State U., 1973. Faculty mem. Ball State U., Muncie, Ind., 1973-86; dept. head James Madison U., Harrisburg, Va., 1986-94; coll. dean U. Ctrl. Ark., Conway, 1994-98, provost, 1998—2001; dean faculty, v.p. for acad. affairs Gustavus Adolphus Coll., St. Peter, Minn., 2002—. Cons. Merck Co., 1991-94, AMP, Inc., 1988, Anchor-Hocking, 1985-86. Author: (with others) Inorganic Reactions and Methods, 1991; contbr. articles to profl. publs. Bd. dirs. Staunton (Va.) Civic Dance Co., 1991-94, Faulkner County (Ark.) United Way, 2000-01.. Student Rsch. grant NSF, 1993-95, Equipment grant Hewlett-Packard, 1992, Merck Co., 1991-92, NSF, 1991. Mem. AAAS, Am. Assn. of Higher Edn., Am. Chem. Soc., Am. Conf. of Acad. Deans, Coun. of Undergrad. Rsch., Sigma Xi. Avocations: softball, jogging, bicycling, in-line skating. Office: Gustavus Adolphus Coll 800 W College Ave Saint Peter MN 56082

MOSBY, DOROTHEA SUSAN, municipal official; b. Sacramento, May 13, 1948; d. William Laurence and Esther Ida (Lux) M. AA in Sociology, Bakersfield (Calif.) Coll., 1966-69; BS in Recreation, San Jose State U., 1969-72; MPA, Calif. State U. Dominguez Hills, Carson, 1980-82. Asst. dept. pers. officer San Jose Pks. and Recreation Dept., 1972-73, neighborhood ctr. dir., 1973-74; sr. recreation leader Santa Monica Recreation and Pks. Dept., 1974-76, recreation supr., 1976-83; head bus. divsn. Santa Monica Recreation and Parks Dept., 1983-88; bus. adminstr. Santa Monica Cultural & Recreation Svcs., 1988-91; dir. pks. and recreation City of South Gate, Calif., 1991—. Bd. dirs., officer Santa Monica City Employees Fed. Credit Union, 1980-89, pres. 1986-87; mem. citizens adv. com. L.A. Olympic Organizing Com., 1982-84. Mem. choir, flute soloist Pilgrim Luth. Ch., Santa Monica, 1974-98, treas. Luth. ch. coun., 1984-86; mem. choir, flute soloist Christ Luth. Ch., Downey, Calif., 1999—; vol. driver XXIII Olympiad, L.A., 1984; contbr. local housing assistance U.S. Olympic Com., L.A., 1984; mem. adv. com. Windsor Sq. Hancock Park Hist. Soc., L.A., 1983, dir. Christmas carolling, 1980—, chmn. Olympic com., 1984, trustee, 1984-90, chmn. pub. programs, 1985, co-chmn. pub. programs, 1986, co-vice chair, 1987, chmn., 1988, 89; Downey Symphony Guild; bd. dirs. Downey Symphony; mem. Samuel C. May Grad. Student Rsch. Paper Judging Com., Western Govt. Rsch. Assn., 1994; trustee Calif. Found. for Parks and Recreation. Recipient Outstanding Profl. of Yr. award Los Angeles Basin Pk. and Recreation Commrs. and Bd. Mems., 1993. Mem. Calif. Pk. and Recreation Soc. (bd. dirs. 1979-82, 86, mem. Calif bd. pk. and recreation cert. 1990—, Scholarship Found. Bd. 1992—, chair 1996, 97, 98—, dist. 10 v.p. 1994, 95, 96, Dist. 10 Spl. Recognition award 1998, State CPRS Citation award 1999), Nat. Recreation and Pk. Assn., Calif. Found. Pks. Recreation (trustee), Mgmt. Team Assocs. (sec., treas. 1979-83), Western Govtl. Rsch. Assn., Nat. Assn. Univ. Women, South Gate C. of C., Kiwanis Club (past pres.), Chi Kappa Rho (pres. 1986), Pi Alpha Alpha. Avocations: flute, piano, reading, bicycling, tennis. Home: 9329 Elm Vista Dr Apt 103 Downey CA 90242-2992 Office: City of South Gate Dept Pks & Recreation 4900 Southern Ave South Gate CA 90280-3462

MOSBY, HOWARD ALAN, finance director; b. Atlanta, June 20, 1961; s. Nathaniel and Gwendolyn (Mizell) M. BBA, Ga. State U., 1992. CPA, Ga. Internal auditor Grady Health Sys., Atlanta, 1994-95, mgr. spl. projects, 1995-96, dir. fin. med. affairs, 1998—. Advisor ARC, DeKalb-Rockdale chpt., Atlanta. Avocations: guitar, piano. Home: 2101 Sugar Creek Falls Dr SE Atlanta GA 30316-4959 Office: Grady Health Sys 80 Butler St SE Atlanta GA 30303-3031 Fax: (404) 616-3066. E-mail: mosb7101@aol.com.

MOSBY, JOHN SINGLETON, JR. chiropractor, educator, consultant; b. Memphis, Aug. 15, 1950; s. John Singleton Sr. and Corinne (Mellard) M.; m. Donna Marie Redding, June 15, 1978; 1 child, John Singleton III. BA, Hendrix Coll., 1972; BS, Palmer Coll. Chiropractic, Davenport, Iowa, 1976; DC, Palmer Coll. Chiropractic, 1976; MD, Am. U./Caribbean Sch. Medicine, B.W.I., 1984. Pvt. practice, Osceola, Ark., 1976-79; educator Tex. Chiropractic Coll., Pasadena, 1979-80; educator, clin. cons. diagnosis pathology dept. Palmer Coll. Chiropractic, Davenport, 1985-89, faculty mem. spl. programs, 1988—, clin. cons. staff, educator continuing edn., coord. clinic acad. curriculum, 1989-92, spl. care unit coord., 1991—; clinician Palmer Cmty. Outreach Clinic, 1998—. Co-author, co-editor: (text) Chiropractic Secrets, 2000. Vol. Ark. Children's Colony, Conway, Ark., 1971. With USMC, 1972. Named to Outstanding Young Men Am. 1977, 88, Outstanding Faculty of Yr. Palmer Cmty. Outreach Clinics, 1999. Mem. Ark. Chiropractic Assn. (bd. dirs. 1977-80), SAR, Am. Chiropractic Assn., Osceola C. of C., Palmer Internat. Alumni Assn., Rotary, Phi Lambda Kappa (nat. soc.), Delta Delta Pi. Methodist. Home: 2303 Salem Ct Bettendorf IA 52722-3136

MOSBY, REBEKAH PRESSON, audio producer; b. Fresno, Calif., Oct. 7, 1952; d. Donald Ray Presson and Jacqueline Louise Evenson; m. Fred Tarverdi, Jan. 26, 1989 (div. Mar. 1991); m. Dewey Franklin Mosby, Feb. 3, 1996; stepchildren: Christophe, Veronique. AB, U. Calif., Berkeley, 1975; MA, U. Mo., Kansas City, 1987. Prodr., host New Letters on the Air, Kansas City, Mo., 1983-95; cultural reporter NPR, Washington, 1987—; freelance poetry anthologist Rhino Records, L.A., 1992—, Sourcebooks, Inc., Naperville, Ill., 2000—. Mem. adv. bd. Helicon Nine, Kansas City, 2000—. Editor, prodr. (audio anthology) In Their Own Voices: A Century, 1996, Our Souls Have Grown Deep Like the Rivers, 2000, (audio documentary) Healing the Wounds of War With Words, 1993, Poetry Speaks: Hear the Voices, 2001. Vol. prodr. Vets. Voices Audio, Kansas City, 1991-95. Recipient 1st prize features, Kans. Broadcasters Assn., 1988, Earphones award, Audio File mag., 1992, 2001, 2002, 1st prize, Pres.'s Coun. for People with Disabilities, 1993, Audie award for poetry, 2001. Roman Catholic. Avocations: horseback riding, private pilot, swimming, water and snow skiing, weight lifting. Home: 1738 Preston Hill Rd Hamilton NY 13346 E-mail: rpmosby@dreamscape.com.

MOSBY, ROBERT J. psychologist; b. Granite City, Ill. s. Joseph T. and Dorothy L. (Propes) M.; m. Bess M., June 10, 1950; children: Donna, Dan, Dean, Bob, Robin, David. BS, Washington U., 1950, MA, 1958, PhD, 1975; MS, Purdue U., 1964. Lic. psychologist State Mo.; bd. cert. diplomate, fellow psychomaracology Prescribing Psychologists Register, Inc. Tchr. Ferguson-Florrisant (Mo.) Pub. Schs., 1950-62, h.s. counselor, 1964-68; dir. student personnel & rsch. Kirkwood (Mo.) Schs., 1969-75; dir. Franklin County Co-op. Union (Mo.) Schs., 1975-79; psychologist R.J. Mosby & Assocs., Inc., Kirkwood, 1979—. Cons. U.S. Dept. Edn., 1977-79, St. Louis Regional Conf., 1979-85; chair spl. need adv. com. Meramec Jr. Coll., Kirkwood, 1980-92; founder Gateway chpt. Assn. Couples in Marriage Enrichment. Author: Dynamic Marriage for Companionship Living Through Dynamic Dialogue Training, 2001. Mem. Am. Marriage & Family Therapist Assn. (Mo. Therapist of Yr. 1997), APA, Kirkwood C. of C., Rotary. Presbyterian. Home: 315 Dickson St Kirkwood MO 63122-4631

MOSCA, VIRGINIA, retired language educator; b. Bklyn., Oct. 26, 1934; d. Edward Paul and Margaret Mary (Phant) M. BA, St. Joseph Coll., 1957; MA, NYU, 1960. Cert. English tchr., N.Y., N.J. Tchr. English Bklyn. Tech. H.S., 1957-59; rschr. Sheed & Ward Pub., Manhattan, N.Y., 1959-60; chmn. English Angela Hall Acad., Bklyn., 1960-75; tchr. English, acad. counselor St. Joseph H.S., 1977-98. Adj. instr. St. Joseph Coll., Bklyn., 1981-83. Mem. Mystery Writers Am. Roman Catholic.

MOSCHELLA, SAMUEL L. dermatology educator; b. East Boston, Mass., Apr. 22, 1921; BS, Tufts U., 1943, MD cum laude, 1946. Diplomate Am. Bd. Dermatology. Intern in medicine Boston City Hosp., 1946-47; resident in dermatology U.S. Naval Hosp., Phila., 1948, St. Albans, 1951; postgrad. in skin and cancer Bellevue Hosp., N.Y.C., 1952-53; chief dermatology U.S. Naval Hosp., Phila., 1953-54, chief dermatology, asst. chief medicine, Guantanamo Bay, Cuba, 1948-51, chief dermatology, Chelsea, Mass., 1956-62, chmn. dept. dermatology, Phila., 1962-67; chmn. dept. dermatology Lahey Clinic Med. Ctr., Burlington, Mass., 1969-82; clin. prof. dermatology Harvard U. Med. Sch., Boston, 1980-91, prof. emeritus, 1991—. Cons. U.S. Naval Hosp., Phila., 1967-72, U. Pa. Grad. Sch., 1962-67, Harvard Sch. Tropical Medicine, 1975—, Nat. Hansen's Disease Ctr., Baton Rouge, 2002—. Author/editor: (with otherw) Dermatology, 3d edit., 1992; contbr. articles to profl. jours.; also papers, book chpts. Fellow ACP; mem. AMA, Am. Acad. Dermatology, Am. Dermatol. Assn., Am. Soc. Dermapathology, Internat. Leprosy Assn., Internat. Soc. Dermatology, New Eng. Dermatologic Soc., Mass. Acad. Dermatology, Mass. Med. Soc., soc. Investigative Dermatology Home: 887 Commonwealth Ave Newton MA 02459-1036 Office: Lahey Clinic Med Ctr 41 Mall Rd Burlington MA 01805-0002 E-mail: samuel.l.moschella@lahey.org.

MOSCHOS, DEMITRIOS MINA, lawyer; b. Jan. 8, 1941; s. Constantine Mina and Vasiliky (Strates) Moschos; m. Celeste Thomaris, Sept. 28, 1975; children: Kristin M, Thomas W. BA magna cum laude, U. Mass., 1962; JD magna cum laude, Boston U., 1965; grad. basic courses, U.S. Army JAG Sch., Charlottesville, va., 1966. Bar: Mass 1965, US Dist Ct Mass 1975, US Ct Mil Appeals 1966. Exec. asst. to city mgr., spl. legal counsel City of Worcester, 1968-75, asst. city mgr., spl. legal counsel, 1975-80; assoc. Mirick, O'Connell, Worcester, 1980-81, ptnr., 1982—. Lectr labor relations Worcester State Col, 1975—88, Clark Univ, 1978—; chmn Worcester Housing Comt, 1968—78, Worcester Energy Comt, 1978—80; mem Mass Joint Labor Mgt Comt, 1978—80. Drafter admin codes: ; contbr. articles to profl jours. Past pre.s archiocesan coun. Greek Orthodox Archdiocese Am.; bd. dirs. Worcester Regional Rsch. Bur., Worcester Regional C. of C. Capt JAGC U.S. Army, 1966—68. Decorated Army Commendation Medal; named Outstanding Young Man of Worcester County, Worcester County Jaycees, 1969, in resolution of commendation, Worcester City Coun, 1980; recipient Alumni Acad Achievement Award, Boston Univ Law Sch, 1965. Fellow: Coll. Labor and Employment Lawyers; mem.: ABA, Worcester Bar Assn (former chmn labor sect), Mass Bar Asn (Comty Serv Award 1987), Tatnuck Country Club. Office: Mirick O'Connell 100 Front St Ste 1700 Worcester MA 01608-1426

MOSCHOS, MICHAEL CHRISTOS, lawyer; b. Worcester, Mass., Jan. 8, 1941; s. Constantine Mina and Vassiliky (Strates) M.; m. Mary Patricia Dermody, Feb. 20, 1977 (div. Dec. 1991); children: Charles, Michael Patrick; m. Susan Smith Harrington, June 6, 1998; 1 stepchild, Katherine L. BBA cum laude, U. Mass., 1962; JD, Boston U., 1965. Bar: Mass. 1965, N.Y. 1970, U.S. Dist. Ct. Mass. 1982, U.S. Supreme Ct. 1982. Lawyer Investors Group, N.Y.C., 1968-72; assoc., spl. counsel Cabot, Cabot, Forbes, Boston, 1972; pvt. practice, 1973, Worcester, 1979—. Spl. counsel Esso-Pappas, S.A., Athens, Greece, 1969-70; investment banker, counsel Worcester Bancorp., 1974-79; cons. atty. Baskins-Sears Esq., N.Y.C., 1979; counsel Downtown Worcester Bus. Devel. Corp., 1974-76. Legal officer Worcester Heritage Soc., 1975-82; mems. coun. Worcester Art Mus., 1975-83; incorporator Worcester Natural History Soc., 1977-98; spl. counsel, acting mng. dir. Hellenic Bottling Co., S.A., Hellenic Canning Industries, S.A., Internat. Canning Industry, S.A., Athens, Greece, 1973. Capt. U.S. Army, 1965-67. Mem. Worcester County Bar Assn. Greek Orthodox. Home: 4004 Brompton Cir Worcester MA 01609-1160 Office: 250 Commercial St Ste 210 Worcester MA 01608

MOSEBY, LEBARON CLARENCE, JR. mathematics and computer science educator; b. Phila., Oct. 8, 1944; s. LeBaron Clarence and Louise (Walker) M. BA in math., Harvard U., 1966, MA in math., 1967, D in edn., 1972. Asst. dean admissions and studies Harvard Grad. Sch. Edn., 1971-73; faculty Nat. Sci. Found. Project Simmons Coll., Boston, 1974; asst. prof. edn. and dir. student teaching Simmons Coll., 1973-76; acting chmn. edn. dept. Trinity Coll., Hartford, 1977-78, asst. prof. edn. and dir. student teaching, 1976-81; dir. social context teaching and learning program U. Tex., Austin, 1981-83; asst. prof. math. and computer sci. South West Tex. State U., 1983-86; tech. edn. con. and tech. edn. specialist Wang Labs., Lowell, Mass., 1987—. Cons., writer Southern Assn. Colls. and Schs., 1968-69; dir., coord. Miles Coll., 1968-69. Contbr. articles to profl. jours. Cons. Capitol Region Edn. Coun., Hartford, 1979, Nat. Inst. Edn., Washington, 1979-83, Hartford Pub. Schs., 1980, New Eng. Ctr. Urban Rsch., Hartford, 1978-80, Ct. State Dept. Edn., 1980; reviewer Am. Edn. Rsch. Assn., 1979-83; co-founder, bd. dirs. New Eng. Cmty. Rsch. Initiative, 1989-92; proposal reviewer Boston Dept. Health, 1989—, Mass. Dept. Pub. Health, 1989—; cons. Haitian Am. Cultural Ctr., 1989, Haitian Am. Pub. Health Initiative, 1990, Boston Living Ctr., 1990, Cambridge Cares about AIDS, 1991, Archdiocese of Boston, Cath. Charities, Office AIDS Ministry, 1991; bd. dirs. SPIN, Boston AIDS Consortium, 1991; mem. client adv. bd. AIDS Action Com. Mass., 1992-98; mem. sci. adv. bd. Mass. Dept. Pub. Health, 1995—; mem. off-label drug adv. panel Mass. Inst. Commn., 1997—. Recipient cmty. recognition award AIDS Action Cmty. Mass., 1998; fellow in edn. Harvard U., 1970-71. Mem. IEEE, Math. Assn. Am., Phi Delta Kappa. Home: 89 Union Park St Apt 407 Boston MA 02118-2470 E-mail: lebaronm@post.harvard.edu., LeBaronm@USA.com.

MOSEKILDE, LEIF, endocrinologist, educator; b. Aarhus, Denmark, Sept. 24, 1942; Eyvind and Vibeke (Freund) M.; m. Eydna Joensen, Nov. 12, 1971; children: Rune, Anna-Maria, Jacob. GCE sci., Aarhus (Denmark) Kathedral Sch., 1961; MD, Aarhus U., 1968, DMS, 1979; specialist in internal medicine and endocrinology. Cert. specialist in internal medicine and endocrinology. Registrar Aarhus County Hosp., 1968-72, spl. edn. positions, 1972-73, registrar, sr. registrar, 1973-77, chief physician, 1980—, med. dir., 1990-95, prof. osteoporosis and metabolic bone disease, 1995—, mem. rsch. coun.; sr. registrar Randers (Denmark) Ctrl. Sys., 1977-79; chief physician King Fahd Ctrl. Hosp., Gizan, Saudi Arabia, 1985-86. Chmn. Med. Soc. Jutland, Aarhus, 1984-90, 93—, Internat. Congress XXIVth symposium, 1995, Baltic Bone and Cartilage Conf., 1997, 98, 99, 2002; bd. dirs. European Soc. Calcified Tissues, 1987-97, European Osteoporosis Found., 1991-94, Danish Nutritional Bd., Copenhagen, 1995-98; chmn. Danish Osteoporosis Study, 1999—; mem. bibliometry group Danish Rsch. Agy., 2000—. Lt. Navy, Faroe Islands, 1979-80. Recipient Hagedorn prize Danish Med. Soc., 1990, Gert Espersens prize Jutland Soc. Medicine, 1991; Queen Ingrid's Festival lectr., 2002. Mem. Danish Bone and Tooth Soc. (chmn. 1986-92), Danish Soc. Internal Medicine, Danish Med. Soc. Rsch. Coun. Avocations: sailing, photography, diving, skiing, traveling. Home: Skolebakken 11th DK 8000 Aarhus Denmark Office: Aarhus Amtssygehus Tage Hansensgade 2 DK 8000 Århus Denmark

MOSELEY, CARLOS DUPRE, music executive, musician; b. Laurens, S.C., Sept. 21, 1914; s. Carlos Roland and Helen Allston (DuPre) M. BA magna cum laude, Duke, 1935; postgrad., Phila. Conservatory Music, 1941-44; student piano with Harold Morris, Olga Samaroff, Sophia Rosoff; LHD (hon.), Wofford Coll., 1966, Duke U., 1985; MusD (hon.), Converse Coll., 1971; DFA (hon.), U. S.C., 1989; LHD (hon.), The Juilliard Sch., 1995. Head fgn. information research div. OWI, N.Y.C., 1944-45; chief music sect. State Dept., Washington, 1946-48; music officer Office Mil. Govt. for Bavaria, Munich, Germany, 1948-49; chief fine arts and exhibits sect. reorientation br. Army Dept., N.Y.C., 1949-50; dir. Sch. Music, prof. music U. Okla., 1950-55; dir. press and pub. relations N.Y. Philharmonic Symphony Soc., N.Y.C., 1955-59, assoc. mng. dir., 1959-61, mng. dir., 1961-70, pres., 1970-78, vice chmn., 1978-83, chmn., 1983-85, chmn. emeritus, 1985—. U.S. del. to UNESCO Music Conf., Paris, 1948; U.S. del Internat. Music Coun., Paris, 1953; mem. music panel Nat. Endowment for Arts, 1967-69, N.Y. State Coun. on Arts, 1973-77, Nat. Coun. on Arts, 1985-91; life trustee Converse Coll., 1998—. Soloist, N.Y. Philharmonic Orch., N.Y.C. Symphony, Berkshire Music Center Orch., San Diego Symphony, Portuguese Nat. Symphony, Lisbon, Vt. Symphony, others. Dir. Fan Fox and Leslie R. Samuels Found., Eleanor Naylor Dana Charitable Trust; hon. dir. Charles A. Dana Found.; mem. Lincoln Ctr. coun. Lincoln Ctr. for Performing Arts, 1961-78; chmn. performing arts adv. com. Asia Soc., 1970-91; mem. Met. Opera Assn.; dir. N.Y. Philharm. Winner MacDowell Nat. Young Artists Competition, 1939; recipient N.Y.C. Mayor's medal of honor for arts and culture, 1978, Disting. Svc. citation U. Okla., 1989, Order of the Palmetto, State of S.C., Nat. citation Nat. Fedn. Music Clubs, 1991, Lifetime Achievement award S.C. Gov.'s Sch. of the Arts, 1995, Lotus award Young Coun. Artists, N.Y.C., 1999. Mem. Met. Opera Assn., Century Assn. (N.Y.C.), Piedmont Club (S.C.), Phi Beta Kappa, Mu Phi Epsilon, Pi Kappa Lambda, Phi Eta Sigma. Office: care Samuels Found 350 Fifth Ave New York NY 10118

MOSELEY, CAROL JUNE, security supervisor, small business owner; b. Portland, Oreg., Apr. 20, 1952; d. David Palmore Moseley and Patricia Ann (Goar) Craig. AS in Criminal Justice, Portland C.C., 1985; degree in psychology, Portland State U., 1985-88. Cert. in pvt. security Oreg. Bd. on Pub. Safety Stds. and Tng. Security supr. Burns Internat. Security Svcs., Portland, 1991—; owner Tomorrows Star Natural Health. Cons. on security Bethlehem Ch., Lake Oswego, 1993-94, Tech. Design and Constrn., Portland, 1996. Vol. case asst. Clackamas (Oreg.) Parole & Probation, 1984, State of Oreg. Parole & Probation, Portland, 1985-88; lifeguard, swim instr. City of Portland Pks. and Recreation, 1990-95; chief of peace officers Bethlehem Ch.-Coffeehouse, Lake Oswego, Oreg., 1992; deaconess Bethlehem Ch., Lake Oswego, 1990-94; supporter Right to Life, Portland, 1994—; 1st lt. CAP Aux., USAF, 1986-88. Named Outstanding Security Officer, Portland Trailblazers NBA, 1988. Mem. Internat. Platform Assn., Internat. Soc. of Poets (disting. mem., life mem.), Ofcl. Centennial Olympic Games Club, Elks (ladies aux.), Fraternal Order of Eagles (patron, ladies aux.). Avocations: swimming, crocheting, oil painting, beachcombing.

MOSELEY, CHRIS ROSSER, marketing executive; b. Balt., Apr. 13, 1950; d. Thomas Earl and Fern Elaine (Coleman) Rosser; m. Thomas Kenneth Moseley. BA with honors, The Coll. of Wooster, 1972. Asst. dir. advt. and promotion Sta. WBAL-TV, Balt., 1972-74; dir. pub. rels. Mintz & Hoke Advt. Inc., Hartford, Conn., 1974-75; promotion mgr. Sta. WFSB-TV, 1975-77; audience promotion mgr. Sta. WTVJ-TV, Miami, Fla., 1977-78; pres. CMA Mktg. Cons., Hyde Park, N.Y., 1979-82; promotion mgr. Ind. Network News-Sta. WPIX-TV, N.Y.C., 1982-84; sr. v.p., mgmt. supr. Christopher Thomas Muller Jordan Weiss, 1984-89, Earle Palmer Brown/N.Y., N.Y.C., 1989-90; sr. v.p. advt., promotion Discovery Networks, U.S., Bethesda, Md., 1990-99; exec. v.p. mktg. ABC, Inc., N.Y.C., 1999—. Recipient Best Bus.-to-Bus. award Art Direction mag., 1984, award of achievement in media rels. and edn. Nat. Resources Coun. Am., 1991, Best Editorial Excellence award Mag. Age, 1992, Best Overall Mktg. Campaign award MIP/MIPCOM, 1994, 1st Place Print award: Media Promotion, London Internat. Advt. awards, 1993, Gold award Broadcast Designers, 1993, Mktg. 100 award Ad Age, 1995, Cable Marketer of Yr. award Ad Age, 1995. Mem. CTAM (chair, Mark award 1995, 96, co-chair 1997, bd. dirs. 1997), NCTA (conv. com. 1995, 96, Vanguard award for mktg. 1996), WIC, AWNY, PROMAX Internat. (chair 1996-97), CTPAA. Democrat. Avocations: horticulture, travel. Home: 5224 Los Encantos Way Riderwood MD 90027-0418 Office: ABC Inc 12700 Ventura Blvd Ste 100 Studio City CA 91604-6201

MOSELEY, CLIFFORD WAYNE, writer, poet; b. Odessa, Tex., Aug. 10, 1947; s. Leylon Ivan and Josephine Opal Moseley; m. Cathryn Lualice Brotherton, Oct. 11, 1968; children: Clifford Wayne Jr., Patrick Lee. AAS, Odessa Coll., 1989; B in Bus. Mgmt., U. Tex. Permian Basin, Odessa, 1994. Enlisted U.S. Army, 1968, rose through grades to sfc., 1982; with Ready Reserves, 1985—89; writer tech. manuals Dover, NJ, 1971-75; ret. Contbr. poems to Tomorrow's Dreams, 1995. Decorated Bronze Star, 1971; nominee Tex. Scout of Yr., Boy Scouts Am., 1966. Mem. Order of Arrow, Boy Scouts Am., 1963-66. Republican. Avocation: collecting military paraphernalia. Home and Office: 4280 Bonham Ave Odessa TX 79762 Fax: (915) 362-1475. E-mail: Cliff_Moseley@yahoo.com.

MOSELEY, JAMES FRANCIS, lawyer; b. Charleston, S.C., Dec. 6, 1936; s. John Olin and Kathryn (Moran) M.; m. Anne McGehee, June 10, 1961; children: James Francis Jr., John McGehee. AB, The Citadel, 1958; JD, U. Fla., 1961. Bar: Fla. 1961, U.S. Supreme Ct. 1970. Pres. Moseley, Warren, Prichard & Parrish, Jacksonville, Fla., 1963—. Chmn. jud. nominating com. 4th Jud. Cir., 1978-80 Assoc. editor: American Maritime Cases; contbr. articles on admiralty, transp. and ins. law to legal jours. Pres. Jacksonville United Way, 1979; chmn. bd. dirs. United Way Fla., 1992-93, S.E. regional coun. United Way, 1992-96; trustee Jacksonville Cmty. Found.; chmn. bd. trustees Jacksonville Pub. Libr.; trustee Libr. Found., sec., 1987-91; trustee CMI Am. Found.; chmn. Jacksonville Human Svcs. Coun., 1989-91; chmn. bd. trustees United Way N.E. Fla., 1995-97; bd. govs. United Way Am., 1996—. Recipient Meritorious Pub. Svc. award/medal U.S. Dept. Transp./USCG, 1998. Fellow Am. Coll. Trial Lawyers, Am. Bar Found.; mem. Jacksonville Bar Assn. (pres. 1975), Fla. Coun. Bar Pres. (chmn. 1979), Maritime Law Assn. U.S. (exec. com. 1978-81, chmn. navigation com. 1981-88, v.p. 1992-96, pres. 1996-98), Comm. Maritime Internat. (titulary), Com. on Collision (Lisbon Rules), Fed. Ins. Corp. Counsel (chmn. maritime law sect.), Internat. Assn. Def. Counsel (chmn. maritime com. 1989-91), Am. Inns of Ct. (master of bench), Assn. of Citadel Men (bd. mem. 1989-93, exec. com. 1994, Man Yr. award 1992, Palmetto award/medal 2001), Citadel Inn of Ct. (sr. bencher), Deerwood Club, River Club, India House (N.Y.C.), Army Navy Club (Washington), St. John's Dinner Club (pres. 1988). Home: 7780 Hollyridge Rd Jacksonville FL 32256-7134 Office: Moseley Warren Prichard & Parrish 1887 West Rd Bay St Jacksonville FL 32216-4542

MOSELEY, JAMES R. federal agency administrator, farmer; b. Peru, Ind. BS in horticulture, Purdue U. Owner Ag Ridge Farms, Clarks Hill, Ind.; mng. ptnr. Infinity Pork LLC; asst. sec. agr. natural resources and environ. USDA, 1990—92; dir. agrl. svcs. and regulations. State of Ind., Purdue U., West Lafayette, 1992—95; dep. sec. agr. USDA, Washington, 2001—. Agrl. advisor to adminstr. U.S. Environ. Protection Agy., 1989—90; chmn. industry negotiating team Am. Clean Water Found. Nat. Environ. Dialogue on Pork Prodn., 1997; cons. Nat. Assn. State Depts. Agr., 1995. Past. mem. editl. bd. Farm Jour. Pub., past polit. analyst. Office: USDA Office of the Sec 1400 Independence Ave SW Washington DC 20250*

MOSELEY, JULIA W. music teacher, historic preservationist; b. Tampa, Fla., Mar. 21, 1919; d. Hallock Preston and Ruby Winifred Moseley. BA, Agnes Scott Coll., Decatur, Ga., 1940. Nat. cert. music tchr. Asst. food and fashion editor Atlanta Constn., 1940-41; credit report typist, publicist, fund raiser Mchts. Assn. Tampa, 1942-43; teletype operator, writer/editor, commodities marketer USDA, Atlanta, 1943-47; self-employed music tchr., 1945-47; hist. rschr. New Orleans, 1947-48; self-employed music tchr. Fla., 1948—; also cattle raiser, citrus grower; preservationist Moseley Homestead, Brandon, Fla., 1948—. Author, editor: Come to My Sunland, 1997; co-author: Internet Lake Atlas, 1999, Recipes and Remembrances, 1999; composer song Brandon, Brandon. Mem. Brandon Citizens Adv. Com.; established Timberly Trust, Inc., 1994; worked with Historic Tampa/Hillsborough County Preservation Bd., 1983-92; spokesperson to Hillsborough County Bd. Commrs. on land use and preservation, 1966-99; mem. Brandon Task Force involved with county devel. issues; mem. hist. com. Brandon Centennial Celebration, 1990. Elizabeth Ordaway Dunn Found. grantee, 1998. Mem.: Fla. State Music Tchrs. Assn. (past officer), Limona Acad. Arts, Letters and Scis. (past officer and dir.), Art Publ. Soc. (Guild tchr.), Nat. Fedn. Music Clubs, Nat. Guild Piano Tchrs., Music Tchrs. Nat. Assn., Tampa Music Tchrs. Assn. (officer), Fla. Breeding Bird Atlas, Tampa Preservation, Inc., Nature Conservancy, Fla. Trust for Historic Preservation, Nat. Trust for Historic Preservation, Friday Morning Musicale Club. Avocations: bird watching, reading, walking, photography, star gazing. E-mail: ttland@hotmail.com.

MOSELEY, KAREN FRANCES FLANIGAN, retired school system administrator, educator; b. Oneonta, N.Y., Sept. 18, 1944; d. Albert Francis and Dorothy (Brown) Flanigan; m. David Michael McLaud, Sept. 8, 1962 (div. Dec. 1966); m. Harry R. Lasalle, Dec. 24, 1970 (dec. Feb. 1990); 1 child, Christopher Michael; m. Kel Moseley, Jan. 22, 1994. BA, SUNY, Oneonta, 1969; MS, SUNY and Hockerill Coll., Eng., 1970. Cert. secondary edn. tchr., Fla., Mass., N.Y. Tchr. Hanover (Mass.) Pub. Schs., 1970-80; lobbyist Mass. Fed. Nursing Homes, Boston, 1980-84; tchr., dept. chair Palm Beach County Schs., Jupiter, Fla., 1985-95; ret., 1996; chair of accredidation Jupiter H.S., 1990-91. Fulbright tchr., Denmark, 1994-95. Author: How to Teach About King, 1978, 10 Year Study, 1991. Del. Dem. Conv., Mass., 1976-84; campaign mgr. Kennedy for Senate, N.Y., 1966, Tsongas for Senate, Boston, 1978; dir. Plymouth County Dems., Marshfield, Mass., 1978-84; Sch. Accountability Com., 1991-95; polit. cons. Paul Tsongas U.S. Senate, Boston, 1978-84, Michael Dukakis for Gov., Boston, 1978-84; mem., spkr. PBC chpt. ARC; disaster team vol. Palm Beach County Red Cross. Mem. AAUW (No. Palm Beach county, officer), NEA (lifetime mem.), Nat. Honor Soc. Polit. Scientists, Classroom Tchrs. Assn., Palm Beach County Classroom Tchrs. Assn., Mass. Coun. Social Studies (bd. dirs. Boston chpt. 1970-80), Mass. Tchrs. Assn. (chair human rels. com. Boston chpt. 1976-80), Plymouth County Social Studies (bd. dirs. 1970-80), Mass. Hosp. Assn. (bd. dirs. Boston chpt. 1980-84), Nat. Coun. for Social Studies, Fulbright Alumni Assn., Prologue Soc., Lyceum Soc., Fla. History Ctr., Marine Life Ctr., Norton Mus. Art. Roman Catholic. Avocations: reading, fishing, traveling, art collector, snorkeling. Home: 369 River Edge Rd Jupiter FL 33477-9350

MOSELEY, MARC ROBARDS, sales executive; b. L.A., July 14, 1954; s. Thomas Robards and Doris Cecile (Tye) M.; m. Laura Hoon Hamilton, 1999. Student, U. Ky., 1972-74, U. Ga., 1977-78; BA, La. Tech. U., 1985; postgrad., Western Mich. U., 1986. Svc. rep. Ky. Mortgage Co., Lexington, 1973; loan rep. Termplan Fin. Co., Atlanta, 1975-77; sr. cons. Co-Ordinated Planning Assocs., 1979-80; sales rep. Nat. Starch & Chem. Corp., Monroe, La., 1980-84; v.p. sales Ednl. Funding Svc., 1984-85; tech. sales rep. polymer divsn. Ralston Purina, St. Louis, 1985-87; account mgr. Protein Techs. Internat. Polymer Group subs. Ralston Purina, 1988-90, sr. account mgr., 1990-92, area dir. market ops., 1992-96; dir. industry mgmt. and bus. devel. Polymer Group subs. Dupont Ag Enterprise, 1996-98; dir. strategic accounts Polymer Group Dupont Soy Polymers, 1999—. V.p. sales and mktg. RANA Enterprises, Inc., Atlanta, 1991-98; dir. Radiant Chem., Atlanta, 1992—; v.p., dir. Bishop Pharm. Co., Inc., West Monroe, La., 1994-96. Mem. TAPPI Greater Atlanta, U. Ky. Alumni Assn. (bd. dirs. 1991-97, exec. v.p. Ga. sect. 1992-94). Avocations: water and snow skiing, basketball, music, golf. Home: 12220 Brookfield Club Dr Roswell GA 30075-1265 Office: DuPont Soy Polymers 1034 Danforth Dr Saint Louis MO 63102-1008 E-mail: mrmosley@mindspring.com.

MOSELEY, THERESA A. guidance counselor, actress; b. Ft. Bragg, N.C., Feb. 27, 1958; d. Clarence B. and Hazel Mae (Stinney) M. BA, Ga. State U., 1988; MEd, Bowie State U., 1994; PhD, Am. U., Washington, 1998. Receptionist Brannell Coll., Atlanta, 1981-84; red coat Continental Airlines, Newark, 1988-93; counselor U. Md., College Park, 1994; counselor, tchr. Prince Georges County Sch., Upper Marlboro, 1995—. Mem. Assn. for Multi-cult. counseling and devel., 1993—, Md. Assn. for Counseling and Devel., 1993—, v.p. Montgomery County Parent Policy Coun., Rockville, Md., 1994-95; founder, pres. TereSerenity Place Inc., 1998—. Vol. Dem. Convention, Atlanta, 1988. With U.S. Army, 1976-80. Recipient Outstanding Educator Prince George's County C. of C. Mem. ACA, Am. Sch. Counseling Assn., Nat. Assn. for the Edn. of Young Children, Md. State Tchrs. Assn. (del. 1998), Md. Assn. for Counseling and Devel., Prince Georges County Edn. Assn., AFTRA, SAG, Chi Sigma Iota. Democrat. Baptist. Avocation: acting, singing, dancing, photography, travel. Home: 12223 Castlewall Ct Bowie MD 20720

MOSELEY, WILLIAM EARL, career officer; b. Kinston, N.C., Dec. 10, 1948; s. Emanuel and Mamie Lee Moseley; divorced; children: Timothy, Anthony; m. Chung Hee Lee, June 14, 1995. BS in Math., Elizabeth City (N.C.) State U., 1971; MA in Mgmt., Webster U., St. Louis, 1978; postgrad., Air War Coll., Maxwell AFB, Ala., 1994-95. Commd. 2d lt. USAF, 1975, advanced through grades to col., 1998; comdr. McGuire AFB, N.J., 1988-91, dep. dir. Joint U.S. Mil. Affairs Group Korea, 1991-94; dep. comdr. 97th logistics group Altus AFB, Okla., 1995-97; dep. comdr. 18th logistics group Kadena AB, Japan, 1997-98; comdr. 82d tng. group Sheppard AFB, Tex., 1998-2000; chief aircraft ops. divsn. Ogden Air Logistics Ctr. Hill AFB, Utah, 2000—02; insp. gen. Ogden Air Logistics Ctr., Hill AFB, 2002—. Assoc. prof. Ala. State U., Montgomery, 1979-81; sr. advisor Air Force Cadet Officer Mentoring Action program, Kadena, AB, Japan, 1997-98. Mem. VFW, Air Force Assn., Airlift/Tanker Assn., Logistics Officer's Assn., Omega Psi Phi. Avocations: high school basketball officiating, golf, traveling. E-mail: william.moseley@hill.af.mil.

MOSELY, JACK MEREDITH, thoracic surgeon; b. Hodge, La., July 20, 1917; s. Charles Hodge and Lucille (Hays) M.; m. Kathryn L. Stephenson, Apr. 30, 1954 (div. May 1972); children: Kathryn S. Mosely-Bennett, Jack Meredith Jr.; m. Elberta Pate, Sept. 23, 1995. BS, La. State U., Baton Rouge, 1939; MD, La. State U., New Orleans, 1943. Diplomate Am. Bd. Surgery, Am. Bd. Thoracic Surgery. Intern Univ. Hosp., Mpls., 1943-48, resident in surgery, head resident, instr. Syracuse, N.Y., 1946-48, 49-50; fellow in surgery Lahey Clinic, Boston, 1948-49; resident in thoracic surgery Herman Kiefer Hosp., Detroit, 1952-53; instr. thoracic surgery Tulane U. Med. Sch., New Orleans, 1953; pvt. practice thoracic surgery, 1953, Santa Barbara, Calif., 1953—. Chmn. health sect. Welfare Planing Coun., Santa Barbara, 1955-57; mem. Atty. Gen.'s Vol. Adv. Coun., State of Calif., 1974-75; chmn. dept. thoracic and cardiovascular surgery Cottage Hosp., Santa Barbara, 1995—. Pres. bd. dirs. Wood Glen Hall, Santa Barbara, 1971-73. Capt. M.C., U.S. Army, 1944-46. Fellow ACS, Am. Thoracic Soc., Pan Am. Med. Assn., Southeastern surg. Congress; mem. Valley Club of Montecito. Avocations: golf, travel, reading, gardening. Home: 134 Coronada Cir Santa Barbara CA 93108-1825 E-mail: drmose@aol.com.

MOSELY, TEED M. career officer; BA in Polit. Sci., Tex. A&M, 1971, MA in Polit. Sci., 1972. Commd. 2d lt. USAF, 1971, advanced through grades to brig. gen., 1996; various assignments 338th Flying Tng. Squadron, 78th Flying Tng. Wing, Webb AFB, Tex.; mission comdr., instr. pilot, flight lead 7th Tactical Figher Squadron, 49th Tactical Fighter Wing, Holloman AFB, N.Mex., 1977-79; weapons and tactics officer, F-15 mission comdr. 18th Tactical Fighter Wing, Kadena AB, Japan, 1979-83, flight examiner, instr. pilot Japan, 1979-83; course officer Air Command and Staff Coll., Maxwell AFB, Ala., 1983-84; chief tactical fighter br. Hdqrs. USAF, the Pentagon, Washington, 1984-87; comdr. F-15 divsn., instr. pilot USAF Fighter Weapons Sch., Nellis AFB, Nev., 1987-89; course officer Nat. War Coll., Washington, 1989-90, chief of staff of the AF chair, 1990-92; comdr. 33rd Ops. Group, 33rd Fighter Wing, Eglin AFB, Fla., 1992-94; chief AF Gen. Officer Matters Office Hdqrs. USAF, The Pentagon, Washington, 1994-96; comdr. 57th Wing, Nellis AFB, Nev., 1996-97; dep. dir. for politico-mil. affairs Asia/Pacific and Middle East, the Joint Staff, Washington, 1997—. Decorated Air medal, Legion of Merit with oak leaf cluster, Air Force Achievement medal. Office: Office Sec of Air Force 1160 Air Force Pentagon Washington DC 20330-1160

MOSEMANN, LLOYD KENNETH, II, business executive; b. Lancaster, Pa., May 16, 1936; s. Lloyd Kreider and Beatrice Elizabeth (Frey) M.; m. Arlene K. White, Sept. 6, 1957; children— Gigi Renee Mosemann Falke, Lloyd Kenneth III, Douglas Lamar, Holly Joy AB in Social Sci., U. Chgo., 1957, AM in Internat. Rels., 1959. Gen. supply officer Navy Electronics Supply Office, Great Lakes, Ill., 1958-62; inventory mgmt. specialist Def. Electronics Supply Ctr., Dayton, Ohio, 1962-63; head integrated-retail supply and support br. Naval Supply Systems Command, Washington, 1963-69; dep. chief logistics support analysis office Def. Logistics Agy., Alexandria, Va., 1969-71; dep. for supply and maintenance Office Sec. of Air Force, Washington, 1971-74; dep. asst. sec. for logistics and communications Dept. Air Force, 1974-91, dep. asst. sec. for comm., computers and logistics, 1991-93, dep. asst. sec. for comm., computers and support systems, 1993-96; software and acquisition cons., 1996-97; sr. v.p. corp. devel. Sci. Applications Internat. Corp., McLean, Va., 1997—. Mem. Air Force Exec. Resources Bd., 1981—95. Decorated DSM; recipient Meritorious Svc. medal Sec. Air Force, 1977, Exceptional Civilian Svc. medal sec. Air Force, 1979, 81, 82, 87, 96, Meritorious Sr. Exec. award Pres. of U.S., 1982, 87, Def. Meritorious Civilian Svc. medal, 1985. Mem. Soc. Logistics Engrs. (bd. advisers 1983— , Founders medal 1983, H. Mark Grove award for excellence in software mgmt. 1996, Govt. Computer News Hall of Fame 1996, Fed. Computer Week "100" award 1996), Am. Def. Preparedness Assn. (bd. dirs. 1974-83), Nat. Inst. for Urban Search and Rescue (exec. bd. dirs. 1990—). Home: 10013 Blake Ln Oakton VA 22124

MOSENSON, STEVEN HARRIS, lawyer; b. Phila., Dec. 3, 1956; BS, NYU, 1978, M of Pub. Adminstrn., 1979; JD, Yeshiva U., 1982. Bar: N.Y. 1983, U.S. Ct. Appeals (2d cir.) 1983, U.S. Dist. Ct. (so. and ea. dists.) N.Y. 1983, U.S. Ct. Internat. Trade 1985, U.S. Supreme Ct. 1986. Assoc. Baden Kramer Huffman & Brodsky, N.Y.C., 1982-85; asst. corp. counsel N.Y.C. Law Dept., 1985-89; gen. counsel United Cerebral Palsy Assns. of N.Y. State, Inc., N.Y.C., 1989—. Pres. bd. dirs. Bklyn. Heights Ctr. for Counseling, Inc., 1992—; bd. dirs. Walden, N.Y. Local Devel. Corp., 1998—; mem. Walden Cmty. Coun., 1998—. Mem. N.Y. State Bar Assn. (chmn. com. on issues affecting people 1997—), Guardianship Assn. of N.Y. State, Inc. (v.p. 1995—). Office: United Cerebral Palsy Assns of NY 330 W 34th St Fl 13 New York NY 10001-2488 Fax: 212-356-0746. E-mail: mosenson@aol.com.

MOSER, C. THOMAS, lawyer; b. Seattle, Aug. 10, 1947; s. Carl Thomas and Helen Louise (Felton) M.; m. Deborah J. St. Clair, Sept. 25, 1976; children: Nicole, Lauren. BA, Cen. Wash. U., 1972; M in Pub. Adminstrn., George Washington U., 1974; JD, Gonzaga U., 1976. Bar: Wash. 1977; U.S. Dist. Ct. (we. dist.) Wash. 1977, U.S. Dist. Ct. (ea. dist.) Wash. 1980, U.S. Ct. Appeals (9th cir.) 1980, U. S. Supreme Ct. 1981. Dep. pros. atty. Skagit County Pros. Atty., Mount Vernon, Wash., 1976-77, chief civil dep., 1979-80, pros. atty., 1980-86, San Juan County Pros. Atty., Friday Harbor, 1977-79; pvt. practice Mount Vernon, 1987—. Hearing examiner pro tem Skagit County, 1992—. Author: Gonzaga Law Review, 1975. Bd. dirs. Wash. Environ. Coun., Seattle, 1971-72, Padilla Bay Found., Skagit County, Wash., 1988; bd. trustees Wash. Assn. County Ofcls., Olympia, 1983; exec. bd. North Pacific Conf. Evang. Covenant Ch., vice sec. 1991-96; bd. trustees Skagit Valley Coll., 2000—. Sgt. U.S. Army, 1967-69, Korea. Recipient Silver Key award ABA Student Law Div., 1976, Legion of Honor award Internat. Order DeMolay, Kansas City, Mo., 1982, Chevalier award 1982. Mem. ATLA, Nat. Coll. Advocacy (advocate), Wash. State Trial Lawyers Assn. (bd. govs. 1990-92, 96-97), Wash. Assn. Pros. Attys. (bd. dirs. 1983-85), Skagit County Bar Assn. (pres. 1995-96), Kiwanis Club Mt. Vernon, Affiliated Health Svc. (ethics com.), Christian Legal Soc. Democrat. Evangelical. Avocations: skiing, golf, jogging, woodworking. Office: 411 Main St Mount Vernon WA 98273-3837

MOSER, DAVID JOHN, management consultant; b. Leavittsburg, Ohio, Dec. 15, 1921; s. Elmer Noble and Della Loretta (Dorland) M.; m. Wilma Grace McManus, May 3, 1944; children: David Martin, Bruce John, James Ralph (dec.). Degree in applied scis., Syracuse (N.Y.) U., 1954. Contract mgmt. LTV-Kennedy Space Ctr., Fla., 1966-67; sr. indsl. engr. Eastern Airlines, Miami, 1967-70, Mobil Oil Co., Macedon, N.Y., 1971; cons. Rockwell Internat., Syracuse, 1972, Crucible Steel Co., Syracuse, 1974, Harley-Davidson Co., York, Pa., 1975; dir., indsl. engr. Stow Mfg., Binghamton, N.Y., 1977-78; cost mgr., indsl. engr. Boeing Co., Seattle, 1978-84; ptnr., owner, mgmt. cons. TSD, Inc., 1983; disaster cons. Fed. Emergency Mgmt. Agy. (FEMA), Washington, 1991—. Election insp. Onon Co., Syracuse, N.Y., 1984—; supv. 1990 census, U.S. Commerce Dept., Washington, 1988-90; 2000 census, U.S. Commerce Dept., Washington, 1998—. Flight Engr. USAF, 1942-45. Decorated Air Medal, ETO medal USAF, 1944; named Hon. Lt. Col. Ala. Militia/Gov. Jim Folsom, 1994. Mem. Hist. Soc. (dir. 1984—), Air Force Assn., Am. Legion, Inst. Indsl. Engrs. (life, pres, v.p., dir. 1957—), Am. Legion, Masons (master lodge # 524, 1993, OES patron 1995), Order Ea. Star (patron chpt. # 289 1995). Republican. Episcopalian. Avocations: golf, reading, gardening. Home: 45 South St Marcellus NY 10318-1327

MOSER, DONALD SCOTT, investment broker; b. Woodbury, N.J., Mar. 19, 1967; s. Carl Donald and Linda Kay (Lampkin) M.; 1 child, Rebecca Anne; m. Karen Ann Downs, Oct. 17, 1999. Clk. Phila. Exch. Fgn. Options, 1989-90; fgn. divsn. Janney, Montgomery, Scott, Phila., 1990-95, opers. mgr., investment broker Mt. Laurel, N.J., 1995—. Hunter safety instr. State of N.J., 1998—. Mem. OES, Masons (steward 1994-98, trustee 1999-2000). Methodist. Avocations: skiing, golf, archery, unicycling, shooting. Office: Janney Montgomery Scott PO Box 6600 Mount Laurel NJ 08054-0660

MOSER, FRANKLIN GEORGE, neuroradiologist, researcher; b. N.Y.C., Jan. 17, 1956; s. Alexander Sander and Belle (Herz) M.; m. Caroline Labiner, Aug. 25, 1984; children: Claire Irene, Julia Hannah. BS, Yale U., 1977; MD, McGill U., Montreal, Can., 1981. Diplomate Am. Bd. Radiology, Am. Bd. Neuroradiology. Intern in surgery and medicine Sir Mortimer Davis Hosp., Montreal, 1981-82; resident in radiology Mt. Sinai Med. Ctr., N.Y.C., 1982-85; fellow in radiology Neurologic Inst. N.Y. Columbia U., 1985-86, asst. prof. radiology, 1986-87; asst. prof. radiology, dir. neuroradiology Montefiore Med. Ctr., 1987-90; chief neuroradiology Lenox Hill Hosp., 1990-92; dir. clin. & intervtnl. neuroradiology, dir. outpatient radiology Cedars-Sinai Med. Ctr., L.A., 1992—. Contbr. articles to profl. jours. Mem. Am. Soc. Neuroradiology (sr.), Am. Soc. Theraputic and Interventional Neuroradiology, Radiol. Soc. N.Am., Am. Coll. Radiology, Soc. Rsch. Nervous and Mental Disease, Am. Roentgen Ray Soc., Am. Soc. Spine Radiology, Calif. Radiol. Soc., N.Y. Radiol. Soc., N.Y. Neurosurgical Soc. (hon.), L.A. Radiol. Soc., Yale Club. Avocations: arts & crafts, furniture, pottery. Office: Cedars Sinai Med Ctr 8700 Gracie Allen Dr Los Angeles CA 90048-3811 E-mail: moser@cshs.org.

MOSER, GREGG ANTHONY, retired career officer; b. Holton, Kans., Aug. 6, 1954; s. Paul Robert and Ila Rose (Jenkins) M.; m. Shari Ann Larson, Nov. 3, 1984 (div. Apr. 1999). BS in Constrn. Sci., Kans. State U., 1979; MS in Safety, Ctrl. Mo. State U., 1984. Commd. 2d lt. USAF, 1980, advanced through grades to maj., 1991; ret., 2000. Mem. Air Force Assn. (pres. Lt. Erwin R. Bleckley chpt. 1992-93, v.p. Sate of Kans. 2001-, Medal of Merit 1994), Lions (pres. Wichita Flying Lions chpt. 1992-93, zone 1 chmn. dist. 17-SE region II 1993-94, dir. Scott Comty. Lions Club 1994-95, v.p. Scott Comty. Lions Club 1995-96), Air Force Assn. (pres. Gen. Fry chpt. 2001), Lions Club (dir. Holton chpt. 2001—, sec. Kans. dist. K-6, 2001-02, vice dist. gov. 2002-). Republican. Methodist. Avocations: photography, reading. Home: 617 West Fifth St Holton KS 66436-1406 E-mail: GreggAMoser@aol.com.

MOSER, HAROLD DEAN, historian; b. Kannapolis, N.C., Oct. 31, 1938; s. Walter Glenn and Angie Elizabeth (Allen) M.; m. Carolyn Irene French, Mar. 28, 1964; children: Andrew Paul, Anna Elizabeth. AA, Wingate Coll., 1959; BA cum laude, Wake Forest U., 1961, MA Univ. fellow, 1963; PhD Ford fellow, U. Wis., 1977. Tchr. Robert B. Glenn High Sch., Winston-Salem, N.C., 1961-62; instr. history Chowan Coll., Murfreesboro, 1963-65; teaching asst dept. history U. Wis., Madison, 1967-69; Nat. Hist. Publ. Commn. fellow The Papers of Daniel Webster (Dartmouth Coll.), Hanover, N.H., 1971-72, asst. editor, 1972-73, assoc. editor, 1973-76, co-editor, 1976-77, editor corr. series, 1978-79; editor dir. The Papers of Andrew Jackson, 1979—; adv. bd. The Papers of Albert Gallatin, Baruch Coll., CCNY, 1987—; rsch. prof. history U. Tenn., Knoxville, 1987—. Contbr. articles to profl. jours. Mem. Am. Hist. Assn., So. Hist. Assn., Orgn. Am. Historians, Soc. Historians of Early Am. Republic, Assn. for Documentary Editing, Tenn. Hist. Soc., Phi Alpha Theta, Eta Sigma Phi, Phi Theta Kappa Democrat. Episcopalian. Home: 9605 Tallahassee Ln Knoxville TN 37923-2737 Office: U Tenn Hoskins Library Knoxville TN 37996-0001

MOSER, HUGO WOLFGANG, physician; b. Switzerland, Oct. 4, 1924; came to U.S., 1940, naturalized, 1943; s. Hugo L. and Maria (Werner) M.; m. Ann Boody, Dec. 28, 1963; children— Tracey, Peter, Karen, Lauren. MD, Columbia U., 1948; A.M. in Med. Sci, Harvard U., 1956. Intern Columbia-Presbyn. Med. Center, N.Y.C., 1948-50; asst. in medicine Peter Bent Brigham Hosp., Boston, 1950-52; research fellow dept. biol. chemistry Harvard U., 1955-57; asst. resident, resident in neurology Mass. Gen. Hosp., 1957-59, asst. neurologist, 1960-67, assoc. neurologist, 1967-69, neurologist, 1969-76. Teaching fellow neuropathology Harvard Med. Sch., 1959-60, instr. neurology, 1960-64, assoc. in neurology, 1964-67, asst. prof., 1967-69, asso. prof., 1969-72, prof., 1972-76; dir. research and tng. Walter E. Fernald State Sch., 1963-68, asst. supt., 1968-73, acting supt., 1973-74, supt., 1974-76; dir. Center for Research on Mental Retardation and Related Aspects of Human Devel., dir. univ. affiliated facilities for mentally retarded, 1965-74; co-dir. Eunice Kennedy Shriver Center for Mental Retardation, Inc., 1969-74; pres. John F. Kennedy Inst., Balt., 1976-88; prof. neurology and pediatrics Johns Hopkins U., 1976—. Author: (with others) Mental Retardation: An Atlas of Diseases with Associated Physical Abnormalities, 1972; Contbr. (with others) articles to med. jours. Served with AUS, 1943-44; to capt. U.S. Army, 1952-54. Recipient Hower award Child Neurology Soc., 1994, Becker award German Soc. for Neuropediats., 1999. Mem. Am. Acad. Neurology, Am. Assn. Mental Deficiency, Am. Assn. Neuropathologists, Am. Neurol. Assn., Internat. Soc. Neurochemistry, Am. Pediatrics Soc., Sigma Xi, Alpha Omega Alpha. Home: 100 Beechdale Rd Baltimore MD 21210-2209 Office: Kennedy Inst Inc 707 N Broadway Baltimore MD 21205-1832 E-mail: moser@KennedyKrieger.org.

MOSER, JEFFERY RICHARD, state agency administrator, public affairs and public management executive, artist, writer, former state official; b. Miller, S.D., Feb. 8, 1961; s. Richard and Ardessa Joan (Yost) M. Student, U. Minn., 1979-84, Duke U., 1995, Northwestern U., 1997. Cert. lay minister; cert. in pub. policy and pub. fin.; cert. CPR, Am. Red Cross. Lab asst., intern U. Minn. Dept. Limnology, Mpls., 1980-81; exec. intern pub. affairs dept. Target Corp., 1982; Nat. Farmers Union, Nat. Youth Adv. Coun., Denver, 1980-81; intern/asst. for legis. and policy Minn. Agri-Growth Coun., Bloomington, 1984-85; field office asst. U.S. Congressman Thomas A. Daschle, Aberdeen, S.D., 1986; pvt. cons. to non-profit orgns., 1986-89; notary pub. State of S.D., 1986-99; acting camp dir. S.D. Farmers Union Edn. Program, 1987-88; small bus. owner, 1986—; exec. dir. S.D. Assn. Towns and Twps., 1990-95; dep. state treas. to treas. Richard D. Butler State of S.D., Pierre, 1995-99; dir. econ. & co-op devel. Nat. Farmer's Union, Aurora, Colo., 1999—. Participant 4-H/UN/USAID Presdl. young adult exch. program to Kenya and Botswana, Africa, summer 1985. Vol. U. Minn. Hosps., 1979-83, U. Minn. Dept. Minn. Unions, Mpls., 1983-84; gen. election poll watcher Hand County Rural precincts, 1988; past mem. Beadle County Dems., Hand County Dems., Brown County Dems., Hughes County Dems., v.p., 1997-98, Arapahoe County Dems., 1999—; del. State Dem. Conv., 1990, 92, 94; alt. del. Nat. Dem. Conv., Chgo., 1996, Clinton for Pres., 1992; nom. Dem. candidate State Auditor, 1994, U.S. House, 1998; donor S.D. Dems., Dem. Nat. Com.; Dem. Nat. Senate Task Force; Dem. Congl. Campaign Com.; chair, del. Selection/Affirmative Action Com., 1996; Clinton-Gore, mem. State Adv. Com., 1996; at. del. Dem. Nat. Conv., 1996; mem. Hughes County Steering Com. to Re-Elect Senator Tom Daschle, 1997-98; dem. candidate S.D. at-large dist. U.S. Ho. of Rep., 1998; vol. leader, advisor, and state fair judge S.D. 4-H Program, 1981-94; bd. dirs. S.D. Rural Devel. Coun., 1993-95, S.D. State Adv. Com. for Green Thumb, Inc., 1993-95; mem. task force Nat. Urban Comparative Risk Environ., 1994, Common Cause S.D., 1991-94; dist. edn. dir. S.D. Farmers Union, 1988-93; dir. Minn. Union Coordinating Bd., U. Minn., 1982-84; bd. dirs. Golden Razor Hair Salon, Inc., Mpls., 1983-84, bd. dirs. Internat. Study & Travel Assn., Mpls., 1982-83; mem. Rose Hill Presbyn. Ch., Clan Campbell Soc. (N.Am.), E. River Sierra Club, Rocky Mountains/Hi Plains Group Sierra Club, S.D. AG Heritage Mus., S.D. Com. for World Food Day, S.D. Bread for the World, Dakota Rural Action, S.D. Project Prosperity Coalition, S.D. Farmers Union, S.D. Horticulture Soc., Dakota Rural Action, South Dakotans For the Arts, Wilson Ctr., Am. Mus. Nat. Hist., Smithsonian Assocs., Lib. Congress, Oscar Howe Art Ctr., Siouxland chpt. Alzheimer's Assn., S.D. Health Care Reform Coalition, S.D. Artists Network, S.D. Hist. Soc., Colo. Pub. Radio (donor), 9th Jud. Circuit Ct. Soc., Nat. Resource Defense Coun., Nat. Audubon Soc., Internat. 4-H Programs; host family Botswana Agr. Exch. Program, 1992; Presbytery of S.D., sec. Congl. Devel. Ministry, 1988-91, Advocacy Devel. Ministry unit, 1992-93, ch. camp dean, moderator Soc. Witness and Action Com., 1995-99, mem. com. representation, 1995-99, mem. com. Self-Devel. People, 1995-99; exec. Presbytery Search com., 1995-96, active Am. Heart Assn. Pierre Area Heart Walk, 1995, 97; vol. coord. Bread for the World Hunger Awareness event, Huron, 1993; mem. planning com. 1993 Regional 4-H Leaders Forum, Sioux Falls; past del. rep. S.D. Nat. 4-H Congress, 1981; past del. rep. Nat. Farmers Union Nat. conf., Presbyn. Ch. USA Gen. Assembly, Presbyn. Ch. USA Consultation on Sustainable Devel., 1995, Nat. 4-H Coun. Master Communicators Conf., Albuquerque, Presbyn. Ch. USA Synod Lakes and Prairies Workshop on Representation and Nominations, Rochester, Minn., 1997, Common Cause Nat. Leadership conf., Washington, 1993, Sharing Global Harvests Nat. Tng., Nat. Assn. Towns and Twps. Am.'s Town Meeting, Washington, 1992, strategic leadership for state execs. course Duke U., 1995, Inst. Pub. Fin. Northwestern U., 1997; bd. co-chair Huron Postal Customer Adv. Bd., 1993-95; bd. dirs. S.D. Peace and Justice Ctr., sec.-treas., 1994, v.p., 1995, dir. 1994-97; copywriter Minn. Ag. Manual, 1985; active Fed. Credit Union. Mem. Nat. Audubon Soc., S.D. Hort. Soc., Phi Beta Kappa, Omicron Delta Kappa, Mortar Bd., Golden Key. Democrat. Address: PO Box 1682 Aurora CO 80040-1682

MOSER, KATHLEEN ANNE, systems analyst and data modeling educator, consultant; b. Sept. 18, 1957; BSc, DeVry Inst. Tech., Phoenix, 1985; MSc, Ariz. State U., 1989, PhD, 1991. Instr. Ariz. State U., Tempe, 1988-90; asst. prof. Iowa State U., Ames, 1991-98; assoc. prof. No. Ariz. U., Flagstaff, 1998—. Cons. Heartland, Ft. Dodge, Iowa. Contbr. articles to profl. jours. Mem. Assn. Info. Sys., Decision Scis. Inst. Office: No Ariz U PO Box 15066 Flagstaff AZ 86011-0001 Fax: 520-523-7331. E-mail: kam@nau.edu.

MOSER, KENNETH SANDERS, information services executive; b. St. Charles, Ill., Apr. 8, 1960; s. Gerald Lee and Marcia (Davis) M. BS, U. Conn., 1982; M.Liberal Sci., Ea. Mich. U., 1997. Cert. Novell adminstr.; cert. network security auditor, cert. Internet Webmaster. Sys. analyst Abbott Sys., Norwalk, Conn., 1982-84; sys. mgr. Cognitive Sys., New Haven, 1984-86; ops. mgr. Data Broadcasting, Vienna, 1986-88, Info. Data Resources, Vienna, 1989; network adminstr. Telos, Washington, 1990; facility mgr. Hughes/STX, 1991-92; dir. info. svcs. APICS, Falls Church, Va., 1992—. Author mo. col. The Performance Advantage, 1996-99; contbr. articles to profl. jours. Pres. Village Park Homeowners Assn., Fairfax, Va., 1992—. Republican. Methodist. Avocations: canoeing, hiking, dogs. Home: 5553 Winford Ct Fairfax VA 22032-4017 Address: APICS Amer Product & Inventory 5301 Shawnee Rd Alexandria VA 22312-2317 E-mail: k_moser@ix.netcom.com, k_moser@apicshq.org.

MOSER, LARRY EDWARD, marketing professional; b. Chgo., Oct. 29, 1952; s. Paul Edward and Catherine Molly (Sittner) M.; m. Michelle Ann Lorden, Sept. 21, 1974 (div. Jan. 1984); children: Jennifer, Jacqueline. BS in Mktg., No. Ill. U., 1974, MBA, 1976. CLU, CPCU. Statis. analyst Addressograph-Multigraph, Mt. Prospect, Ill., 1974-75; grad. asst., mktg. instr. No. Ill. U., DeKalb, 1975-76, 77; mktg. asst. Allstate Ins. Co., Northbrook, Ill., 1977-78, project coord., 1978-80, agt. West Dundee, 1980, mktg. project mgr. to sr. product mgr. Northbrook, 1981—, prin. coord. Allstate WYO flood ins. program, 1994—, mem. nat. flood ins. program mktg. com., 1995—. V.p. Flood Ins. Svc. Cos. Am., 1997—; chmn. Allstate Share (United Way) Campaign, Northbrook, 1982-83, Allstate Helping Hands Com., Northbrook, 1985-86, Allstate Family Day Sports, Northbrook, 1991-94; pres. Allstate Men's Softball League, 1984—; mem. flood com. Inst. for Bus. and Home Safety; vice chairperson flood com. IBSH, 2002- . Active Twinbrook YMCA parent/child prog., Schaumburg, Ill., 1983-90; commr. Schaumburg Athletic Assn. Girls Softball, 1990-92. Recipient Am. Mktg. Assn. Scholastic Achievement award No. Ill. Univ., DeKalb, 1974, James E. Bell Superior Promise & Scholarship in Mktg. Mgmt. No. Ill. Univ. Dept. Mktg., DeKalb, 1976, William J. Hendrickson award for Outstanding Contbn. From An Alumni, DeKalb, 1988. Mem. Am. Soc. CLU, CPCU Soc., Pi Sigma Epsilon (pres.

1975-76), Phi Kappa Sigma, Beta Gamma Sigma, Omicron Delta Kappa. Roman Catholic. Avocations: travel, golf, tennis, skiing, snorkeling. Home: 611 W Burning Tree Ln Arlington Heights IL 60004-2034 Office: 2775 Sanders Rd Ste Co9 Northbrook IL 60062-6110

MOSER, MARTIN, retired music educator; s. Abraham and Ethel (Isaacs) Moser; children: Jennifer, Lynne. BA, CCNY, 1951; MA, Queens Coll., 1953. Cert. tchr. NY, asst. prin. NY, sch. prin., supr. NJ, intermediate adminstr., supr. Conn. Condr. and assoc. condr. All-City H.S. Band, N.Y.C., 1966—85; asst. prin., chmn. music dept. N.Y.C. Pub. High Schs., 1972—85; dist. dir. of music Leonia (NJ) Pub. Schools, 1985—86; tchr., grad. program in edn. Manhattan Sch. of Music, N.Y.C., 1987—89; adj. prof. of music St. John's U., Jamaica, 1987—. Seminar/workshop leader New Sch. of Am. Music, NY, 1993—. With USAF, 1953—57. Mem.: NY State Sch. Music Assn. (zone rep.). Office: St John's U 8000 Utopia Pkwy Jamaica NY 11439

MOSER, M(ARTIN) PETER, lawyer; b. Balt., Jan. 16, 1928; s. Herman and Henrietta (Lehmayer) M.; m. Elizabeth Kohn, June 14, 1949; children—Mike, Moriah, Jeremy AB, The Citadel, Charleston, S.C., 1947; LLB, Harvard U., 1950. Bar: Md. 1950, U.S. Supreme Ct., U.S. Ct. Appeals (4th cir.). Asst. states atty. City of Balt., 1951, 53-54; assoc. Blades Rosenfeld, Balt., 1950, 53-54; ptnr. Frank, Bernstein, Conaway & Goldman and predecessor firms, 1955-90, co-chmn. firm, 1983-86; counsel, 1991-92; of counsel Piper Marbury Rudnick & Wolfe LLP, 1992—. Instr. U. Balt. Law Sch., 1954-56, 86, U. Md. Law Sch., 1986-87. Contbr. articles to profl. jours. Del., chmn. local govt. com. Md. Constl. Conv., 1967-68; mem. Balt. City Planning Commn., 1961-66, Balt. Regional Planning Council, 1963-66, Md. Commn. to Study Narcotics Laws, 1965-67, Mayor's Task Force on EEO, 1966-67, Met. Transit Authority Adv. Council, 1962, Com. to Revise Balt. City Planning Laws, 1962, Com. to Revise Balt. City Charter Provision on Conflicts of Interest, 1969-70; mem. Citizens Adv. Com. on Dist. Ct., chmn., 1971, Dist. Adv. Bd. for Pub. Defender System for Dist. 1, 1973-85; mem. Atty. Grievance Commn. of Md., 1975-78, chmn. 82-86; chmn. Md. State Ethics Commn., 1987-89; bd. dirs. Sinai Hosp., 1983—, Lifebridge Health Sys., 1998—, Ct. of Appeals Comm. to Study the Model Rules, 1983-86, 2002–. Served with JAGC, U.S. Army, 1951-53 Fellow: Balt. Bar Found., Md. Bar Found. (pres. 1979—80), Am. Bar Found. (pres. 2002—); mem.: Lawyers' Round Table Club (pres. 1970—71), Wednesday Law Club, Balt. Bar Assn. (pres. 1970—71), Md. State Bar Assn. (pres. 1979—80), ABA (treas. 1993—96). Democrat. Jewish. Office: Piper Rudnick LLP 6225 Smith Ave Baltimore MD 21209-3600

MOSER, MARVIN, physician, educator, author; b. Newark, Jan. 24, 1924; s. Sol and Sophia (Markowitz) M.; m. Joy Diane Lipez, July 1, 1954; children: Jill, Stephen, John. AB, Cornell U., 1943; MD, Downstate Coll. Medicine, N.Y.C., 1947. Diplomate: Am. Bd. Internal Medicine, subbd. cardiovascular disease; cert. specialist in hypertension Am. Soc. Hypertension. Intern univ. div. Kings County Hosp., N.Y.C., 1947-48, resident in medicine, 1948-49, Montefiore Hosp., N.Y.C., 1949-50; Nat. Heart Assn. fellow Mt. Sinai Hosp., 1950-51; charge vascular service Walter Reed Army Hosp. Med. Centre, Washington, 1951-53; practice medicine specializing in cardiology White Plains, N.Y., 1953-95; assoc. physician cardiology Montefiore Hosp., 1953-75, in charge hypertension sect., 1960-71. Attending physician cardiology White Plains Hosp., 1968-95, chief cardiology, 1969-78; adj. physician in cardiology Grasslands Hosp., Valhalla, N.Y., 1953-60; attending physician in medicine in charge Hypertension Clinic, Westchester County Med. Center, Valhalla, 1974-84; asst. clin. prof. medicine Albert Einstein Coll. Medicine, 1965-75; clin. prof. medicine N.Y. Med. Coll., 1974-84, Yale U. Sch. Medicine, 1984—; sr. med. cons. nat. high blood pressure program NIH, 1975-2002, mem. nat. high blood pressure coordinating com., 1976—; chmn. Joint Nat. Com. Hypertension, 1975-76, vice-chmn., 1979, mem., 1984-88, 92, 96; mem. exec. com. Nat. Citizens for Treatment High Blood Pressure, 1976-78, vice chmn., 1978-88; mem. N.Y. State Adv. Com. on Hypertension, 1977-84; chmn. Nat. Conf. on High Blood Pressure Control, 1979; mem. select panel on hypertension in Am. Congl. Subcom. on Aging, 1978-79; cons. cardiology N.Y. State Dept. Health, Gen. Hosp., Saranac Lake, N.Y., 1980-90; med. dir. Westchester County Hypertension Program, N.Y., 1979-88. Author: (with A.M. Master, M. Moser. H. Jaffee) Cardiac Emergencies and Heart Failure, 2d edit., 1955, (with A. Goldman) Hypertensive Vascular Disease, 1967, Hypertension, A Practical Approach, 1975, Lower Your Blood Pressure and Live Longer, 1988; co-editor, contbr. Yale University School of Medicine Heart Book, 1992, Week by Week to a Strong Heart, 1992, Heart Healthy Cooking for all Seasons, 1996, Clinical Management of Hypertension, 1996, 5th edit., 2001, 6th edit., 2002, Myths, Misconceptions and Heroics, the Story of the Treatment of Hypertension, 1997, 2002, (with J. Sowers) Management of Cardiovascular Risk Factors in Diabetes, 2001; editl. bd. Preventive Cardiology, 1998—, Jour. Medicine and Sports, 1999—; ; assoc. editor Angiology, 1976-85; bd. editors Primary Cardiology, 1975-78, assoc. editor-in-chief, 1978-96; editor-in-chief Jour. of Clin. Hypertension, 1999—. Chmn. Narcotics Guidance Coun., Scarsdale, 1968-72; trustee Scarsdale Bd. Edn., 1970-73, Trudeau Inst., Nat. Hypertension Found., 1992-2001, Third Ave. Value and Sml. Cap Funds, 1994—, Nutrition 21, 1997—; exec. dir. Hypertension Edn. Found., 1977—. Served U.S. Army, 1941-46; capt. M.C. USAF, 1951-53. Nat. Heart Inst. grantee, 1958-62; recipient Achievement awards for contbns. to hypertension control Nat. High Blood Pressure Edn. Program, 1985, 97. Fellow: Am. Heart Assn. ((various offices: pres. coun. geriatric cardiology 1996-97, others)), Am. Coll. Cardiology, ACP; mem.: Century Country Club, N.Y. Cardiol. Soc. Home and Office: 13 Murray Hill Rd Scarsdale NY 10583 E-mail: moserbp@aol.com.

MOSER, MICHAEL R. newspaper editor; b. Shelby, Ohio, May 27, 1952; s. Roger and Patricia (Welch) M.; m. Gayle Overby, Aug. 20, 1985 (div. Nov. 1997); children: Maggie, Amber, Skye, Tess. Assoc. of Fire Sci., Shelton State Coll. Editor Ctrl. Ala. Advertiser, Clanton, 1972-75, Englewood (Ohio) Independent, 1975-78, St. Clair News-Aegis, Pell City, Ala., 1978-83, Crossville (Tenn.) Chronicle, 1984—. City planner Crossville Regional Planning Commn., 1989—. Actor Cumberland County Playhouse, 1989—; author: The Beauty of Riverside, 1992. Bd. dirs. Cumberland Teen Ranch, Crossville, 1988-90, Cumberland County Playhouse, 1992—. Recipient Helen Byrd award Cumberland County Playhouse, 1992. Mem. Nat. Newspaper Assn. (numerous awards 1985—), Tenn. Press Assn., Kiwanis, soc. Profl. Journalists. Office: Crossville Chronicle PO Box 449 Crossville TN 38557-0449 Home: 81 Rhodendrum Cir Crossville TN 38555-5355

MOSER, RICHARD PETER, neurosurgeon; b. Fort Wayne, Ind., Dec. 4, 1948; s. Virgil and M. (Lynch) M.; m. Pliree Madoo; children: Sunil, Risha, Erik. BS, Loyola U., Chgo., 1971, MD, 1974. Resident neurosurgery U. Minn., Mpls., 1975-81; fellow neurosurgery Karolinska Inst., Stockholm, 1981-82; assoc. prof. U. Tex., Houston, 1982-92; neurosurgeon Surg. Neurology Assocs., Elk Grove Village, Ill., 1992—; chmn. dept. surgery HCH, Arlington Heights. Bd. dirs. Am. Cancer Soc., Arlington Heights, Ill.; council Chgo. Med. Soc., 1994-95. Author: Pineal Region Tumors, 1984, Prognosis in Neurological Diseases, 1993; contbr. articles to profl. jours. Grantee Dunn Found., 1988; recipient Saul Korcy award Am. Artery Neurology, 1974. Fellow ACS; mem. AMA, Am. Assn. Neurol. Surgeons, Am. Soc. Clin. Oncology, Ill. State Med. Soc. (del.), Chgo. Med. Soc. (councilor), Congress Neurol. Surgeons. Roman Catholic. Home: 1530 Rfd Long Grove IL 60047-9507 Office: Surg Neurology Assocs 810 Biesterfield Rd Ste 403 Elk Grove Village IL 60007-7312

MOSER, ROBERT HARLAN, physician, educator, writer; b. Trenton, N.J., June 16, 1923; s. Simon and Helena (Silvers) Moser; m. Linda Mae Salsinger, Mar. 18, 1989; children from previous marriage: Steven Michael, Jonathan Evan. BS, Loyola U., Balt., 1944; MD, Georgetown U., 1948. Diplomate Am. Bd. Internal Medicine. Commd. 1st lt. U.S. Army, 1948, advanced through grades to col., 1966, intern D.C. Gen. Hosp., 1948—49, fellow pulmonary disease D.C. Gen. Hosp., 1949—50, bn. surgeon Republic of Korea, 1950—51; asst. resident Georgetown U. Hosp., 1951—52; chief resident Georgetown U. Hosp. U.S. Army, 1952—53, chief med. service U.S. Army Hosp. Austria, 1953—55, Wurzburg, Germany, 1955—56, resident in cardiology Brooke Gen. Hosp., 1956—57, asst. chief dept. medicine Brooke Gen. Hosp., 1957—59, chief Brooke Gen. Hosp., 1967—68, fellow hematology U. Utah Coll. Medicine, 1959—60, asst. chief U.S. Army Tripler Gen. Hosp., 1960—64, chief William Beaumont Gen. Hosp., 1965—67, chief Walter Reed Gen. Hosp., 1968—69, ret., 1969; chief of staff Maui (Hawaii) Meml. Hosp., 1969—73, chief dept. medicine, 1975—77; exec. v.p. Am. Coll. Physicians, Phila., 1976—86; v.p. med. affairs The NutraSweet Co., Deerfield, Ill., 1986—91. Assoc. prof. medicine Baylor U., 1958—59; clin. prof. medicine Hawaii U., 1969—77, Washington U., 1970—77, Abraham Lincoln Sch. Medicine, 1974—75; adj. prof. medicine U. Pa., 1977—86, Northwestern U., 1987—91; adj. prof. Uniformed Svcs. U. Health Scis., 1979—97; clin. prof. medicine U. N.Mex. Coll. Medicine, 1992—96, emeritus, 1996—; flight contr. Project Mercury, 1959—62; cons. mem. med. evaluation team Project Gemini, 1962—66; cons. Project Apollo, 1967—73, Tripler Gen. Hosp., 1970—77, Walter Reed Army Med. Ctr., 1974—86; sr. med. cons. Canyon Cons. Corp., 1991—; mem. cardiovascular and renal adv. com. FDA, 1978—82; chmn. life scis. adv. com. NASA, 1984—87, mem. adv. coun., 1983—88; chmn. gen. med. panel Hosp. Satellite Network, 1984—86; mem. adv. com. NASA Space Sta., 1988—93; mem. Dept. Def. Com. on Grad. Med. Edn., 1986—87, Life Scis. Strategic Planning Study Group, 1986—88; mem. space studies bd. NRC, 1988—93, space exploration initiation study, 1990; mem. NASA Space Sta. Commn., 1992—93, mem. com. adv. tech. human supp. space, 1996—97. Rev. edit., 1969, House Officer Training, 1970; editor, chief divsn. sci. publs. Jour. AMA, Chgo., 1973—75; author, co-author: Adventures in Medical Writing, 1970; contbg. editor: Med. Opinion and Rev., 1966—75; chmn. editorial bd.: Diagnosis mag., 1986—89; mem. editorial bd. Hawaii Med. Jour., Family Physicians, Archives of Internal Medicine, 1967—73, Western Jour. Medicine, 1975—87, Chest, 1975—80, Med. Times, 1977—84, Quality Rev. Bull., 1979—91, The Pharos, 1991—, Travel Medicine, 1994—96, Emergency Med., 1993—, book rev. editor, 2000—; contbr. over 200 articles to med. sci. jours. and med. books; author: Diseases of Medical Progress, 1955, 1969, House Office Training, 1970; co-author: Decade of Decision, 1992; ; editor (chief divsn. sci. publs.): Jour. AMA, 1973—75; contbg. editor Med. Opinion and Rev., 1966—75, chmn. editl. bd. Diagnosis mag., 1986—89, mem. editl. bd. Hawaii Med. Jour., Family Physicians, Archives of Internal Medicine, 1967—73, Western Jour. Medicine, 1975—87, Chest, 1975—80, Med. Times, 1977—84, Quality Rev. Bull., 1979—91, The Pharos, 1991—, Emergency Medicine, 1993—, Travel Medicine, 1994—96; contbr. articles. Master: ACP (exec. v.p. 1977—86); fellow: Am. Clin. and Climatol. Assn., Am. Coll. Cardiology, Royal Coll. Physicians and Surgeons Can. (hon.); mem.: AMA (adv. panel registry of adverse drug reactions 1960—67, coun. on drugs 1967—73), Soc. Med. Cons. to Armed Forces, Coll. Physicians Phila., Chgo. Soc. Internal Medicine, Nat. Assn. Physician Broadcasters, Inst. Medicine-NAS, Am. Osler Soc., Am. Therapeutic Soc., Am. Med. Writers Assn., Alpha Omega Alpha, Alpha Sigma Nu. Democrat. Jewish. Avocations: hiking, international travel, white water rafting. Home and Office: 943 E Sawmill Canyon Pl Green Valley AZ 85614

MOSER, ROBERT LAWRENCE, pathologist, health facility administrator; b. Passaic, N.J., Mar. 22, 1952; s. Robert George and Marjorie Ann (Frankenberger) M.; m. Rosemarie Scolaro, June 16, 1978; children: Rachel Ann, Alexander Robert. BA in Biology magna cum laude, Lafayette Coll., 1974; MD Microbiol./Internal Med. with honors, Hahnemann Med. Coll., 1978. Diplomate Am. Bd. Pathology, Am. Bd. Anatomic Pathology, Am. Bd. Clin. Pathology, Am. Bd. Forensic Medicine. Intern, fellow dept. Pathology The Johns Hopkins Hosp., Balt., 1978-79, resident, fellow dept. Pathology, 1979-81, chief resident, fellow dept. Pathology, 1981-82, resident, fellow dept. lab. medicine, 1982-84; cons. pathologist Perry Point (Md.) VA Med. Ctr., 1983-84; pathologist Helene Fuld Med. Ctr., Trenton, N.J., 1984-88; med. dir. St. Francis Med. Ctr., 1988—; dir. clin. info. sys. Franciscan Health Sys., 1995-96, Cath. Health Initiatives, 1996—2000. Pres. Pathology Assocs., Lawrenceville, N.J., 1981—. Contbr. articles to profl. jours. Fellow Coll. Am. Pathologists, Coll. Physicians of Phila.; mem. Am. Med. Informatics Assn., Med. Soc. N.J., Mercer County Med. Soc., Ctrl. Jersey Ind. Physician Assn. (v.p. 1994-95, sec.-treas. 1995-96, exec. v.p. 1997—), Ea. Pathology Assocs. (v.p. 1996—), Phi Beta Kappa. Avocations: golf, gardening, skiing.

MOSER, ROYCE, JR. physician, medical educator; b. Versailles, Mo., Aug. 21, 1935; s. Royce and Russie Frances (Stringer) M.; m. Lois Anne Hunter, June 14, 1958; children: Beth Anne Moser McLean, Donald Royce. BA, Harvard U., 1957, MD, 1961; MPH, Harvard Sch. Pub. Health, Boston, 1965. Diplomate Am. Bd. Preventive Medicine (trustee 1989-98). Commd. officer USAF, 1962, advanced through grades to col., 1974; resident in aerospace medicine USAF Sch. Aerospace Medicine, Brooks AFB, Tex., 1965-67; chief aerospace medicine Aerospace Def. Command, Colorado Springs, Colo., 1967-70; comdr. 35th USAF Dispensary Phan Rang, Vietnam, 1970-71; chief aerospace medicine br. USAF Sch. Aerospace Medicine, Brooks AFB, 1971-77; comdr. USAF Hosp., Tyndall AFB, Fla., 1977-79; chief clin. scis. div. USAF Sch. Aerospace Medicine, Brooks AFB, 1979-81, chief edn. div., 1981-83, sch. comdr., 1983-85, ret., 1985; prof. dept. family and preventive medicine U. Utah Sch. Medicine, Salt Lake City, 1985—, vice chmn. dept., 1985-95; dir. Rocky Mountain Ctr. for Occupl. and Environ. Health, 1987—. Cons. in occupational, environ. and aerospace medicine, Salt Lake City, 1985—; presenter nat. and internat. med. meetings. Author: Effective Management of Occupational and Environmental Health and Safety Programs, 1992, 2d edit. 1999; contbr. book chpts. and articles to profl. jours. Mem., past pres. 1st Bapt. Ch. Found., Salt Lake City, 1987-89; mem., chmn. numerous univ. coms., Salt Lake City, 1985—; bd. dirs. Hanford Environ. Health Found., 1990-92; mem. preventive medicine residency rev. com. Accreditation Coun. Grad. Med. Edn., 1991-97; mem. ednl. adv. bd. USAF Human Sys. Ctr., 1991-96; chmn. long-range planning com. Am. Bd. Preventive Medicine, 1992-95. Decorated Legion of Merit (2); recipient Harriet Hardy award New England Coll. Occupl. and Environ. Medicine, 1998. Fellow Aerospace Med. Assn. (pres. 1989-90, chair fellows group 1994-97, Harry G. Mosely award 1981, Theodore C. Lyster award 1988, Eric Liljencrantz award 2001), Am. Coll. Preventive Medicine (regent 1981-82), Am. Coll. Occupl. and Environ. Medicine (v.p. med. affairs 1995-97, Robert A. Kehoe award 1996); mem. Internat. Acad. Aviation and Space Medicine (selector 1989-94, chancellor 1994-98), Soc. of USAF Flight Surgeons (pres. 1978-79, George E. Schafer award 1982), Phi Beta Kappa. Avocations: photography, fishing. Home: 664 Aloha Rd Salt Lake City UT 84103-3329 Office: Rocky Mountain Ctr Occupl & Environ Health 75 S 2000 E Salt Lake City UT 84112-8930 E-mail: rmoser@rmcoeh.utah.edu.

MOSER, SANDRA JEAN, piano teacher; b. Ft. Wayne, Ind., Oct. 11, 1952; d. Earl Laverne and Julia Anne Hetzel; m. Richard Lee Moser, Mar. 19, 1977; children: Joel Martin, Alicia Marie, Jeanette Grace. BS in Biol. Scis., Purdue U., 1975, MS, 1985. Clin. lab. technician Ft. Wayne State Hosp., 1976-78; piano tchr. Ft. Wayne, 1994—. Ch. organist Bible Bapt. Ch., Ft. Wayne, 1982—. Mem. N.E. Ind. Music Tchrs. Assn. (sec. 1999—), Ind. Music Tchrs. Assn., Music Tchrs. Nat. Assn. Baptist. Avocation: classic literature. E-mail: dmoser@fwi.com.

MOSER, VIRGINIA CLAYTON, neurotoxicologist; b. Charlotte, N.C., Apr. 23, 1954; d. Overton Wilson and Margaret Belle (McCauley) Clayton; m. Roy Darrel Moser, May 10, 1980; children: Sara Virginia, Lauren Melissa. BS in Pharmacy, U. N.C., 1977; PhD in Pharmacology and Toxicology, Med. Coll. Va., 1983. Diplomate Am. Bd. Toxicology; registered pharmacist, N.C. Postdoctoral assoc. NRC, U.S. EPA, Research Triangle Park, N.C., 1983-85; rsch. scientist ManTech Environ. Tech., 1985-93, EPA, Research Triangle Park, 1993—. Study dir. collaborative study WHO, 1989—; cons., 1988—. Contbr. articles to sci. jours. A.D. Williams fellow Med. Coll. Va., 1979. Mem. AAAS, Am. Soc. Pharmacology and Exptl. Therapeutics, Soc. Toxicology, Soc. Neurosci., Behavioral Pharmacology Soc., Behavioral Toxicology Soc. Home: 1012 N Wellonsburg Pl Apex NC 27502-7127

MOSER, WILLIAM OSCAR JULES, mathematics educator; b. Winnipeg, Can., Sept. 5, 1927; s. Robert and Laura (Fenson) M.; m. Beryl Rita Pearlman, Sept. 2, 1953; children— Marla, Lionel, Paula. B.Sc., U. Man., 1949; MA, U. Minn., 1951; PhD, U. Toronto, 1957. Lectr. U. Sask., 1955-57, asst. prof., 1957-59; asso. prof. U. Man., 1959-64, McGill U., 1964-66, prof., 1966-97, prof. emeritus, 1997—. Author: (with H.S.M. Coxeter) Generators and Relations for Discrete Groups, 1957, 4th edit., 1980, (with E. Barbeau, M. Klamkin) 500 Mathematical Challenges, 1995; also research papers.; Editor: Can. Math. Bull, 1962-70, Can. Jour. Math., 1982-85. NRC fellow, 1951-53; Can. Council leave fellow, 1971 Mem. Am. Math. Soc., Can. Math. Soc. (pres. 1975-77), Math. Assn. Am. Office: McGill U Dept Math 805 Sherbrooke St W Montreal QC Canada H3A 2K6 E-mail: moser@math.mcgill.ca.

MOSES, ABE JOSEPH, international financial consultant; b. Springfield, Mass., July 15, 1931; s. Mohammed Mustapha and Fatima (Merriam) M.; m. Donna C. Moses (dec. 1987); children: James Douglas, John C., Peter J.; m. Mary Jo Morris, Aug. 25, 2001. BA, Amherst Coll., 1955; MA in Internat. Affairs, Johns Hopkins U., 1957. Legis. aide Sen. J.F. Kennedy, 1955-57; fgn. service officer Dept. State, 1960-65; v.p., gen. mgr. Libyan Desert Oil Co., Texfel Petroleum Corp., Tripoli, Libya, 1965-67; v.p. adminstrn., fin. Occidental Petroleum Corp., Libya, 1967-70; v.p. fin., dir. Northrop Corp., 1970-74; chmn. Transworld Trade Ltd., Washington, 1971—; v.p., mng. dir. world adv. group Chase Manhattan Bank, 1974-80; pres. Berkshire Properties, 1976-95; pres., COO, Grolier Internat., Inc., Danbury, Conn., 1980-82; CEO, dir. Galadari Bros., Dubai, United Arab Emirates, 1982-86; internat. bus. and fin. cons. Traxol, 1986—; fin. cons. Govt. Costa Rica, 1986-89. Chmn. Aviation Sys. Corp., Northampton, Mass., 1974, Dillon Internat., Akron, Ohio, 1986—; mng. dir. Sheraton Suites Akron, Cuyahoga Falls, Ohio, 1990—; owner's rep. Monarch Sheraton Hotel, Springfield, Mass., 1993-95; bd. dirs., v.p. Morgan Freeport Co., Hudson, Ohio; bd. dirs. Seeds of Peace, Washington; gen. ptnr. BPM Ltd. Partnership, 1995—. Pres., bd. dirs. Riverside Comty. Urban Redevel. Corp.; mem. exec. com., bd. dirs. Near East Found., N.Y.C., 1978—; pres. Riverfront Ctr. Assn., Cuyahoga Falls, 1992-95; bd. dirs. Gulfcoast Radio Ptnrs., 1997-99, Capitol City Radio Ptnrs., 1998-2000, Ind. Radio Ptnrs., Commonwealth Opera Co., Northampton, Mass. Capt. USAF, 1957-60. Ford Found. fellow Johns Hopkins U., 1955, Barr Found. fellow, 1955-57. Democrat. Home: 16 Highmeadow Rd Northampton MA 01062-2625 Office: Riverside CURC 1989 Front St Cuyahoga Falls OH 44221-3811 E-mail: abejmoses@aol.com.

MOSES, ALFRED HENRY, lawyer, writer, retired diplomat; b. Balt., July 24, 1929; s. Leslei William and Helene Amelia (Lobe) Moses; m. Carol Whitehill, Nov. 24, 1955; children: Barbara, Jennifer, David, Amalie. BA, Dartmouth, 1951; postgrad., Woodrow Wilson Sch., Princeton U., 1951-52; JD, Georgetown U., 1956. Bar: D.C. 1956. Assoc. Covington & Burling, Washington, 1956-65, ptnr., 1965-94, 97—; spl. advisor, spl. counsel Pres. Jimmy Carter, 1980-81; amb. to Romania Am. Embassy, Bucharest, 1994-97; Pres. spl. emissary for Cyprus, 1999-2001. Legal advisor minority rights Dem. Nat. Com., Washington, D.C. Commn. Urban Renewal; lectr. Am. Law Inst., ABA, New Orleans, Washington, AICPA, Georgetown U Law Ctr., Tex. Exec. Inst., Washington, Tulane Tax Inst. , New Orleans; guest lectr. non-legal subjects Coun. of Europe, Yale U., Princeton (N.J.) U., Dartmouth Coll.; commr. Pub. Housing, Fairfax County, Va., 1971—72; chmn. UN Watch, Geneva, 2001—; chmn. nat. bd. Hebrew Coll., Newton Centre, Mass., 2002—. Contbr. articles to profl. jours. Pres. Am. Jewish Com., 1991—94; bd. dirs. Paralysis Cure Rsch. Found., 1978—81; trustee Phelps Stokes Fund, N.Y.C., 1978—84, Jewish Publ. Soc., 1989—94, Haifa U., 1988—90; chair nat. bd. Hebrew Coll., Newtown Centre, Mass., 2002—; co-chmn. legal divsn. United Givers Fund, Washington, 1975—76; mem. Coun. Fgn. Rels., N.Y.C., 1977—; pres. Nat. Children's Island, Washington, 1975—76, Golda Meir Assn., 1986—88, nat. chmn., 1988—93; mem. bd. regents Georgetown U., 1986—92. Mem.: ABA, D.C. Bar Assn., Met. Club. Democrat. Jewish. Home: 7710 Georgetown Pike Mc Lean VA 22102-1431 Office: 1201 Pennsylvania Ave NW Washington DC 20004-2401

MOSES, CLAIRE GOLDBERG, history and womens studies educator; b. Hartford, Conn., June 22, 1941; d. Abraham Raymond and Pauline Hurwich Goldberg; m. Arnold Moses, Sept. 11, 1966; children: Lisa Moses Leff, Leslie. AB, Smith Coll., 1963; MPhil, George Washington U., 1972, PhD, 1978. Prof. U. Md., College Park, 1977—. Author: French Feminism in the 19th Century, 1984 (Joan Kelly Meml. prize), Feminism, Socialism & French Romanticism, 1993; editor: U.S. Women in Struggle, 1994, Feminist Studies. Named honorée Women Legislators of the State Md., 1986. Mem. Am. Hist. Assn. (profl. divsn. 1997-98, program com. chair 2000), Nat. Women's Studies Assn. (program adminstrs. adv. com. 1999—), Conf. Group for Women in History (pres. 1987-90), World Wide Orgn. for Women's Studies (exec. com. 1995-99), Soc. for French Hist. Studies, Phi Beta Kappa (pres. Gamma chpt. 1985-86). Office: U Md Dept Womens Studies Univ Md College Park MD 20742-0001

MOSES, DANIEL, writer, singer; b. Hartsville, S.C., Dec. 4, 1954; s. Paul Henry and Maggie (James) M.; m. Burlean Smith, May 10, 1980; 1 child, Brian Ashley. BS in Bus. Mgmt., Coker Coll., 1978; M in Human Resources, Kennedy We. U., 1997; PhD, Kennedy Western U., 1999; studied with Amelia Smith, U. S.C., 1974-84, studied with Richard Conant; studied with Shirley Goins, studied with Laurence Siegel, studied with Betty Swenson; studied with William Vessels, Kennedy Western U., 1999. Mgr. Jewel Cos., Jacksonville, Fla., 1981-85, Pharmor Drug Store, Columbia, S.C., 1985-88; agent Lincoln Benefit Life, Columbia and Lincoln, Nebr., 1989-97; cons. Bridge Counseling Ctr. Benedict Coll., Columbia, 1989-92; recruiter Edward Waters Coll., Jacksonville, Fla., 1995-96; publ., researcher, genealogist Daniel Moses Inc., Delaware, S.C., 1994—; co-founder Project Heritage Quest Inc. Former prof. Jones Coll., Jacksonville; prof. Phoenix U., Jacksonville; bd. dirs. Theatre Works. Author: (poems) Poetic Living: The Mind of Young America, 1980, The James Family: A Historical Perspective 1770-1980s, 1989, A Descroptive Study of Issues Associated with Sexual Harassment in the Workplace, 2001; co-author 2 books; contbr. poems to anthologies; operatic debut Othello Opera A'La Carte, Jacksonville, Fla., 1981; appeared in Samson and Delilah, Barber of Seville, Pagliacci, Cavalleria Rusticana, Carmen, Arpad Darazs; with S.C. Philharmonic Chorus, Columbia Choral Soc., Town Theatre's Show Stoppers; performances (with Butler H.S. Chorus) Concerts Abroad, Graz, Austria, for HM Queen Elizabeth the Queen Mother, Montreal, Can., Maria Isabel Sheraton, Mexico City, Internat. Platform Assn. Conv. Capitol Hill, Washington, Jerusalem 3000, 1996, Rahasee Hiten, Cairo, 2000. Recipient Towney award Town Theater, Columbia, S.C., 1987, Merit award Internat. Music Festival, 1993, Jr. Achievement, Carolina Music Acad., 1992-94. Mem. SHRM, Am. Parliamentary Assn., Internat. Platform Assn. (chmn. poetry program 1977—, Disting. Mem. 1985, mem. bd. govs.), Am. Inst. Parliamentarians, S.C. Philharmonic Orch., WWII Tank Destroyer Soc., Southside Businessmen's Club, Fort Mose Hist. Soc., African-Am. Cmty. of Freedom, Inc., Congredd Word Poets, World Acad. Arts and Scis., Honorable Order of Ky. Col., Columbia (S.C.) C. of C. (amb. 1992—), Jacksonville (Fla.) C. of C., Southside Bus. Mens Club. Avocations: writing, horticulture, travel, photography. Home: PO Box 2403 Jacksonville FL 32203-2403

MOSES, DANIEL DAVID, civil engineer; b. Courtois, Mo., May 28, 1949; s. Jewell Artie and Genevieve Alice (Wilson) M.; married, 1970 (div. 1984); 1 child, Daniel David Jr.; m. Delores Clara Leslie, June 29, 1985; 1 child, Christopher Daniel. AAS, Mineral Area Coll., Flat River, Mo., 1969. Registered profl. engr., Mo., Ill. Highway designer Mo. Highway and Transp. Dept., Kirkwood, 1969-79; civil engr. Harland Bartholomew & Assoc., St. Louis, 1979-83; sr. project engr. Booker Assoc., Inc., 1983-94, v.p., Ill. divsn. mgr., sr. project engr., 1994—, also bd. dirs.; pres. Booker Assoc., Inc. of Ill., Fairview Heights, 1996—. Bd. dirs. Nat. Kidney Found., St. Louis, 1994-97, Leadership Coun. of Southwestern Ill., 1997—; active Belleville (Ill.) Econ. Progress, 1993—. Mem. NSPE, Am. Pub. Works Assn., Soc. Am. Mil. Engrs. (1st v.p., pres. 1990-95, bd. dirs. 1995—), Cons. Engrs. Coun. Ill. Presbyterian. Avocation: pedal steel guitar. Home: 998 Tree Trails Ln Fenton MO 63026-3640 Office: Booker Assoc Inc 6701 N Illinois St Fairview Heights IL 62208-2019

MOSES, EDWARD JOEL, physicist, consultant; b. Newark, Oct. 9, 1938; s. Hans and Ruth Moses; m. Karen Ruth Wright, May 2, 1965; children: Arikha, Michael. PhD, Johns Hopkins U., 1967. Rsch. assoc. Vanderbilt U., Nashville, 1967—71; sr. scientist Raff Assoc., Silver Spring, Md., 1971—75; exec. scientist ORI, Inc, 1975—91; head, application devel. sect. Johns Hopkins Applied Physics Lab., Laurel, 1991—2001, prin. staff, 2001—; instr. elect. engring. Cath. U. Am., Washington, 2001—. Contbr. articles to profl. jours. Home: 14506 Woodcrest Dr Rockville MD 20853 Office: Johns Hopkins Applied Physics Laboratory 11100 Johns Hopkins Rd Laurel MD 20707

MOSES, FRANKLIN L. psychologist; b. Newark, 1943; m. Janice L. Ryshavy, Dec. 27, 1971; children: Deborah, Steven. BA, U. Pa., 1965; MS, Tufts U., 1967, PhD, 1971. NIH postdoc. fellow NYU, N.Y.C., 1970—71; assoc. prof. Trinity Coll., Washington, 1971—73; rsch. psychologist U.S. Army Rsch. Inst., Alexandria, Va., 1973—97, supervisory rsch. psychologist, 1997—. Contbr. articles to profl. jours. Mem.: Mil. Ops. Rsch. Soc., Human

Factors Soc. Avocations: classical music, photography, travel. Office: US Army Rsch Inst for Beh & Soc Scis 5001 Eisenhower Ave Alexandria VA 22333-5600 Office Fax: 703-617-3573. Business E-Mail: moses@ari.army.mil.

MOSES, GLORIA, nurse; b. Balt., Aug. 26, 1952; d. Isiah Rhinehart and Doris Saundrs; m. Robert Lee Moses, May 12, 1973 (div. Aug. 1990); children: Alicia Reneé, Timothy Tyvan. AS, C.C. of Balt., 1974; BS, Coppin State Coll., Balt., 1995; MS, U. Md., 1999. Cert. oncology nurse. Nurse clinician I U. Md. Med. System, Balt., 1974-80, nurse clinican II, 1980-85, ptnr., 1985-89, sr. ptnr., 1989-99, nurse practitioner, 1999—. Recipient Excellence in Clin. Nursing Black Womens Assn. of Balt., 1994. Office: U Md Med System 2105 W Redwood St Rm 202 Baltimore MD 21201 E-mail: gmoses@umm.edu.

MOSES, HAMILTON, III, medical educator, hospital executive, management consultant; b. Hamilton Jr. and Betty Anne (Theurer) M.; m. Elizabeth Lawrence Hormel, 1977 (dec. 1988); m. Alexandra McCullough Gibson, 1992. BA in Psychology, U. Pa., 1972; MD, Rush Med. Coll., Chgo., 1975. Clk. Nat. Hosp. for Nervous Diseases, London, 1974; intern in medicine Johns Hopkins Hosp., Balt., 1976-77, resident in neurology, 1977-79, chief resident, 1979-80, assoc. prof. neurology, 1986-94, vice chmn. neurology and neurosurgery, 1980-88, v.p., 1988-94, dir. Parkinson's Ctr., 1984-94; dir. neurol. inst., prof. neurology and neurosurgery and mgmt. U. Va., Charlottesville, 1994-97; sr. advisor Boston Cons. Group, 1995—; prof. Darden Sch. Bus. U. Va., Charlottesville, 1994-98; cons. neurologist Mass. Gen. Hosp., Boston, 1997—; vis. prof. neurology and psychiatry Harvard U. Sch. Medicine, 1997-99. Sr. advisor Ptnrs. Healthcare, Boston; spl. advisor Nat. Health Svc., Eng., 1988-91. Editor, major author: Principles of Medicine, 1985-96; editor newsletter Johns Hopkins Health, 1988-94; contbr. numerous articles to med. jours. Mem. com. on med. ministries Episcopal Diocese Md., Balt., 1987; bd. dirs. Valleys Planning Ct.; trustee McLean Hosp., Belmont, Mass., 1997—. Fellow Am. Acad. Neurology (sec. 1989-91), Royal Soc. Medicine (U.K.) (overseas fellow 2000—); mem. Am. Neurol. Assn., Md. Neurol. Soc. (pres. 1984-86), Movement Disorders Soc. Republican. Avocations: landscape photography, sailing. Office: PO Box 150 North Garden VA 22959-0150 also: 4800 Hampden Ln Bethesda MD 20814-2930

MOSES, HOWARD, neurologist; b. Oct. 5, 1930; MD, MS, U. Ill., 1954. Intern U. Ill. R&E Hosp., Chgo., 1954-55; submarine med. U.S. Navy, New London, 1955-57; resident in neurology Johns Hopkins Hosp., Balt., 1958-61, fellow in neurology, 1961-65; head divsn. neurology GBMC, Towson, Md., 1988—; assoc. prof. neurology Johns Hopkins U., Balt., 1995—. Home: 1560 Blue Mount Rd Monkton MD 21111-1226 Office: 1205 York Rd Lutherville MD 21093-6210

MOSES, JOEL, computer scientist, educator; b. Petach Tikvah, Israel, Nov. 25, 1941; came to U.S., 1954, naturalized, 1960; s. Bernhard and Golda (Losner) M.; m. Margaret A. Garvey, Dec. 27, 1970; children: Jesse, David. BA, Columbia U., 1962, MA, 1963; PhD, MIT, 1967. Asst. prof. dept. elec. engrng. and computer sci. M.I.T., 1967-71, assoc. prof., 1971-77, prof., 1977—, assoc. dir. Lab for Computer Sci., 1974-78, assoc. head computer sci. and engrng., dept. elec. engrng. and computer sci., 1978-81, head dept., 1981-89, D.C. Jackson prof., 1989-99, dean Sch. Engrng., 1991-95, provost, 1995-98, prof. engrng. sys. divsn., 1999—, Inst. prof., 1999—. Vis. prof. Harvard Grad. Sch. Bus. Adminstrn., 1989-90; vis. adj. sr. rsch. scientist Columbia U. FU Found. Sch. Engrng. and Applied Sci., 1998; bd. dirs. Analog Devices, Inc. Editor: The Computer Age: A Twenty Year View, 1979; co-originator Knowledge Based System Concept; developer MACSYMA system for formula manipulation. Recipient Achievement award MIT Lab. for Computer Sci., 1985. Fellow IEEE, AAAS, Am. Acad. Arts and Scis.; mem. Nat. Acad. Engrng., Assn. for Computing Machinery, Am. Soc. Engrng. Edn. (Centennial Cert.). Office: MIT Lab Computer Sci NE43-407 Cambridge MA 02139 E-mail: moses@mit.edu.

MOSES, LINCOLN E. statistician, educator; b. Kansas City, Mo., Dec. 21, 1921; s. Edward Walter and Virginia (Holmes) Moses; m. Jean Runnels, Dec. 26, 1942; children: Katherine, James O'D., William C., Margaret, Elizabeth; m. Mary Louise Coale, 1968. AB, Stanford, 1941, PhD, 1950. Asst. prof. edn. Columbia Tchrs. Coll., 1950—52; faculty Stanford U., 1952—, prof. stats., 1959—, exec. head dept., 1964—68; assoc. dean Stanford U. (Sch. Humanities and Scis.), 1965—68, 1985—86, dean grad. studies, 1969—75; faculty Stanford U. (Med. Sch.), 1952—; adminstr. Energy Info. Adminstrn., Dept. of Energy, 1978—80. L.L. Thurstone disting. fellow U. N.C., 1968—69; com. mem., intermittently Am. Friends Svc. Com., 1954—, chmn. No. Calif. chpt., 1972—76, 1984—88. Bd. dirs. Am. Found. for AIDS Rsch., 1992—97. Fellow Guggenheim, 1960—61, Ctr. for Advanced Study in Behavioral Scis., 1975. Fellow: Inst. Math. Stats. (coun. 1969—72), Am. Acad. Arts and Scis.; mem.: Internat. Statis. Inst., Biometric Soc. (pres. Western N.Am. region 1969), Am. Statis .Assn. (coun. 1966—67), Inst. Medicine of NAS. Office: Stanford U Med Ctr Divsn Biostats Stanford CA 94305

MOSES, MICHAEL JAMES, insurance company executive; b. Roaring Spring, Pa., Apr. 13, 1956; s. William E. and Carol J. (Berkey) M.; m. Laura L. Bishop, June 7, 1980 (div. 1990); children: J'aime Lee, Justin Michael. AS, Williamson Trade Sch. Salesman 84 Lumber, Cresson, Pa., 1977-78; area mgr. Nat. Home Life Ins. Co., Valley Forge, 1978-80; regional v.p. A.L. Williams Agy. (name changed to Primerica), Duluth, Ga., 1981—. Republican. Mem. Pentecostal Ch. Avocations: basketball, golf, tennis.

MOSES, RAPHAEL JACOB, lawyer; b. Girard, Ala., Nov. 6, 1913; s. William Moultrie and Anna (Green) M.; m. Marian Eva Beck, Aug. 22, 1938 (dec. Feb. 1976); 1 child, Marcia (Mrs. William S. Johnson); m. Fletcher Lee Westgaard, Jan. 20, 1979. AB, U. Colo., 1935, JD, 1937. Bar: Colo. 1938. Practiced in, Alamosa, 1938-62, Boulder, 1962—; pres. Moses, Wittemyer, Harrison & Woodruff (P.C.), from 1970, now of counsel. Spl. asst. atty. gen. Rio Grande Compact, 1957-58; mem. Colo. Water Conservation Bd., 1952-58, chmn., counsel, 1958-76, cons., 1976-77; research asso., faculty law U. Colo., 1962-66, vis. lectr., 1966-76, resident counsel, 1964-66, regent, 1973-74; grad. faculty Colo. State U., 1963-67; mem. Western States Water Council, 1965-77, chmn., 1966-70. Trustee Rocky Mountain Mineral Law Inst., 1964-66; bd. dirs. U. Colo. Found., 1977-97, chmn., 1977-79, mem. chancellor's adv. coun., 1981-97; bd. dirs. Colo. Open Lands, 1983-91, U. Colo. Improvement Corp., 1980-90, Colo. Endowment for Humanities, 1986-89; mem. adv. bd. Natural Resources Ctr., U. Colo. Sch. Law, 1983-92, chmn., 1986-88. Served to lt. (s.g.) USNR, 1942-45. Recipient William E. Knous award U. Colo. Sch. Law, 1971, Norlin award U. Colo., 1972; Raphael J. Moses Disting. Natural Resources professorship established U. Colo., 1994. Fellow Am. Bar Found. (life), Colo. Bar Found. (trustee 1977-90), Am. Coll. Trial Lawyers; mem. ABA (chmn. water rights com. sect. natural resources 1959-60), Colo. Bar Assn. (pres. 1959-60, Award of Merit 1972), San Luis Valley Bar Assn. (pres. 1942), Am. Counsel Assn., Order of Coif (hon.) Presbyterian (elder). Clubs: Boulder Country; Garden of the Gods (Colorado Springs). Home: 4913 Clubhouse Cir Boulder CO 80301-3715 E-mail: RayMoise@aol.com.

MOSES-FOLEY, JUDITH ANN, special education educator; b. Steubenville, Ohio, Sept. 1, 1936; d. Joseph and Katherine Ann (Pavich) Moses; m. John P. Foley, 1958 (div. 1986); children: Katherine Ann Foley, John Joseph Foley, Sean Michael Foley, Judith Kristina Foley; m. John H. Murphy, 1986 (dec. 1992). BS in Edn., Ohio U., 1958; MA in Ednl. Adminstrn., Fresno Pacific U., 1981; postgrad., Brigham Young U., 1982-84, U. San Francisco, 1985-86, U. N.Mex., 1993-98, Western N.Mex. U., 1997-98. Cert. in ednl. adminstrn., Calif.; tchr., N.Mex., Ohio; spl. edn., bilingual/TESOL, and as transition resource specialist, N.Mex.; notary pub., N.Mex. Adminstr., tchr. health and social sci., coach Madera (Calif.) Unified Schs., 1958-81; chair dept. phys. edn. Dos Palos (Calif.) H.S., 1963-64; prin. Chowchilla (Calif.) Elem. Schs., 1981-85; instr. phys. edn. Merced (Calif.) C.C., 1981-85; supt., prin. St. Luke's Sch., Merced, 1985-86; instr. polit. sci. and bus. adminstrn. West Hills C.C., Lemore, Calif., 1985-86; instr. phys. edn. Mohave C.C., Kingman, Ariz., 1989-90; transition resource specialist Silver Consol. Sch., Silver City, N.Mex., 1993—. Adj. prof. early childhood edn. Western N.Mex. U., Silver City; spl. edn. resource specialist Silver H.S., Silver City, 1990—, coach U.S. acad. decathlon, 1991-99; grant writer Circle of Life, 1994-97; coord., grant writer R.E.: Learning; mem. North Ctrl. Accreditation Steering Com., 1992-95; v.p. divsn. transition and curriculum devel. State of N.Mex., sch. to work grant writer, 1997—; mem. N.Mex. State Bd. com. U.S. Acad. Decathlon, 1993—; developer lang. arts, social studies transition curriculum 9-12 Silver Consolidated Schs., N.Mex.; tchr. Acad. N.Mex. Goals 2000; coord. Southwest Regional Cooperative Ctr. Sch. to Work; mem. profl. std. commn. N.Mex. State Licensure and Competencies, 1999-2000; mem. State N.M. Dept. Edn. State Licensing Competency Revision Com., 1999; instr. English 9-12, 2001-. Pres. Bobby Sox Softball League, Madera, 1975-78; head coach track and field Jr. Olympics, Madera County, 1970-81; coord. Gathering of War Birds Airshow, Madera, 1976-79. Recipient Master Tchr. award Calif. State U., Fresno, 1978-79; recipient scholarships and grants. Mem. AAHPER, AAUW, Nat. Notary Assn., Am. Assn. Ret. Persons, Coun. for Exceptional Children. Mem. ASCD. Avocations: flying, jewelry design, painting, water skiing, fishing. Home: PO Box 2 Buckhorn NM 88025-0002 Office: Silver Consol Schs 3200 N Silver St Silver City NM 88061-7283 Fax: (505) 535-2929.

MOSETTIG, MICHAEL DAVID, television producer, writer; b. Washington, July 21, 1942; s. Erich and Ann (Nelson) M.; m. Anne L. Groer. Student, Ind. U., 1960-61; BA in Polit. Sci., George Washington U., 1964; MA in European History, Georgetown U., 1968. Reporter Leslie E. Carpenter News Bur., Washington, 1961-65, Newhouse Nat. News Svc., Washington, 1965-69, UPI, London and Brussels, 1969-70; editor, reporter Nat. Jour., Washington, 1970-71; producer NBC News, Washington and N.Y.C., 1971-79; assoc. Grad. Sch. Journalism Columbia U., N.Y.C., 1979-83; prodr. MacNeil/Lehrer News Hour, 1983-85, sr. prodr. fgn. affairs and def., 1985-95, News Hour with Jim Lehrer, 1995—. Mem. Internat. Inst. for Strategic Studies, London, Coun. Fgn. Rels., N.Y. Author: DeGaulle and His Anglo-Saxon Allies, 1968, (with Ronald Müller) Revitalizing America, 1980. With USCGR, 1966-68, USNR, 1968-78. Herman Lowe Meml. scholar Washington chpt. Sigma Delta Chi; Joan Barone award Radio-TV Corrs. Assn., Nat. Emmy award, 1997. Mem. Overseas Writers, Cosmos Club. Home: 3340 Northampton St NW Washington DC 20015-1653

MOSHEA, KEVIN JAMES, communications executive; b. Milw., Aug. 15, 1952; s. Herbert and Betty M. AD in Visual Comm., 1974; B in Tech. Comm., U. Wis., Menomonie, 1977, M in Media Tech., 1978. Media specialist Milw. Area Tech. Coll., 1972-73; photographer West Allis (Wis.) Post, 1973-76; media prodn. coord. Anstro Prodn., Inc., Milw., 1973-74; audio visual specialist Brown Deer (Wis.) Mid. Sch., 1974-75; audio visual tech. Nicolet High Sch., Glendale, Wis., 1975-76; instructional television. audio grad. asst. WHWC-TV Channel 28, Menomonie, 1978-79; sr. audio visual design producer Kimberly Clark Corp., Neenah, 1980-97, mgr. audio visual svcs., 1997—. Hospice vol. Vis. Nurse Assn., Appleton, Wis., 1995—. Staff sgt. USAFR, 1971-77. Recipient Gold Reel award Internat. Television Assn., 1987, Silver Reel award, 1986. Home: 3300 Blueberry Ln Appleton WI 54915-7209 Office: Kimberly-Clark Corp 401 N Lake St Neenah WI 54956-2072

MOSHEGOV, NIKOLAY, engineer; b. Kebezen Village, Altaiskiy Region, Russia, May 18, 1960; arrived in U.S., 1999; s. Timofei Moshegov and Solomeya Moshegova; m. Tatyana Kichigina; children: Sofya Moshegova, Lyudmila Moshegova. BS in Phys. Engring., Novosibirsk (Russia) Elec. Engring. Inst., 1982; PhD in Solid State Physics , Inst. Semiconductor Physics, Novosibirsk, 1997. Cert. phys. engring. Engr., sr. engr., leading engr.-tech., assoc. rsch. scientist Inst. Semiconductor Physics, Novosibirsk, 1983—97; assoc. rschr. Instituto de Fisica de Sao Carlos, Brazil, 1998—99; postdoctoral rschr., rsch. assoc. Pa. State U., University Park, 1999—2001; sr. Epitaxial engr. Lasertel Inc., Tucson, 2001—01; sr. scientist IPG Photonics Corp., Oxford, Mass., 2001—. Mem.: IEEE, Am. Phys. Soc. Office: IPG Photonics Corp 50 Old Webster Rd Oxford MA 01540 Personal E-mail: moshegov@hotmail.com.

MOSHER, CHARLES D. mayor, real estate manager; b. Portland, Oreg., Dec. 14, 1941; s. Harold Clarke and Leona (Hostetler) M.; m. Betty C. Mosher, June 12, 1965; ch ildren: Jeffrey, Jason, Janelle. BS, Oreg. State U., 1965; MBA, Portland State U., 1972. Audit mgr. U.S. Gen. Acctg. Office, Seattle, 1965-93; prin. EXECURENT, Bellevue, Wash., 1976—; mem. City Coun., City of Bellevue, 1996—, dep. mayor, 1998-99, mayor, 2000—. Exec. sec. Pacific N.W. Intergovtl. Audit Forum, Seattle, 1977-79; bd. dir. Sound Transit, Washington State Mcpl. Rsch. Coun. Chmn. Cascade Water Alliance, Bellevue, 1999-2000; mem. energy, environment and natural resources steering com. Nat. League of Cities, Washington, 1999-2001; chair Bellevue Planning Commn., 1994-95, Wash. State citizen's adv. com. on pipeline safety, Olympia, 2000-; pres. Whispering Heights and Collingwood Cmty. Assn., 1991-92; chmn. Newport Covenant Ch., 1986-87; exec. com. Rep. Mayors and Local Govt. Ofcls., 2000-01, sec.-treas., 2001-02. U.S. Nat. Bank scholar, Portland, 1959-65. Fellow Am. Water Resources Assn. (nat. pres. 1993); mem. Assn. Wash. Cities (dist. 7 dir. 1997-2001, sec. 2000-01, v.p. 2001-02), Advance Bellevue (bd. dirs. 1998-2001, Best of Bellevue award 1998). Republican. Avocations: dahlias, gardening, skiing, running, geneology. Home: 4730 154th Pl SE Bellevue WA 98006 Office: City of Bellevue PO Box 90012 11511 Main St Bellevue WA 98009-9012 E-mail: chuck@mosher.net.

MOSHER, D. RUSSELL, physical therapist, cancer therapist; b. Dunkirk, N.Y., Dec. 29, 1964; s. David Stuart and Linda Sue (Hayes) M. AAS with honors in Radiation Therapy, Erie C.C., 1987; BS in Kinesiology, SUNY, Buffalo, 1998, BS in Phys. Therapy, 2000. Lic. radiation therapist, Fla., N.Y., Pa., Ky., La.; lic. phys. therapist, Va. Staff therapist Mt. Sinai Hosp., Miami Beach, Fla., 1987-88, Kendall (Fla.) Therapy, 1988-89; staff therapist, clin. educator North Shore Hosp., Miami, Fla., 1989-96, RT Temps, Devon, Pa., 1996-99; phys. therapist Newport News, Va., 2000—. Tumor registry com. chair Griffith Cancer Ctr., Miami, 1994-96; cert. rape prevention instr., Miami, 1995-96, Buffalo, 1996-97; martial arts instr. Cons. Kendall Therapy Treatment Policy Manual, 1988. Math. and sci. tutor Buffalo Traditional Sch., 1996-98; phys. therapy vol. U. Sports Medicine Clinic, Buffalo, 1997. Mem. Assn. Registered Radiation Therapists, Am. Soc. Radiation Therapists, Am. Phys. Therapists Assn., Phi Theta Kappa, Golden Key Nat. Honor Soc. Achievements include research in biomechanics/comuterized goneometrics. Avocations: martial arts, manufacturing hand made medieval armor and jewelry, Renaisance reenactor, sailing.

MOSHER, DONALD ALLEN, artist; b. Malden, Mass., Oct. 11, 1945; s. Allen M. and Florence C. (Post) M.; m. Christine Ann Crivello, Feb. 15, 1969; 1 child, Heather Ann. Cert., Vesper George Sch. Art, Boston. Comml. artist Stop & Shop Corp., Boston, 1971-75, Rich's Dept. Store, Salem, Mass., 1975-81; profl. artist Rockport, 1972—. Exhibited Am. Watercolor Soc. and NAD, Butler Inst., Chgo., Cleve. Meml. Gallery, SUNY, Mystic Seaport Mus., New Bedford Whaling Mus., Mint Mus. Fine Arts, Tuskegee Inst., numerous others. Recipient more than 150 awards from various art assns. Mem. Rockport Art Assn. (v.p. 1988-92, curator 1988-94), New Eng. Watercolor Soc., Guild of Boston Artists, Copley Soc., Salmagundi Club, Am. Artists Profl. League, North Shore Art Assn., Whiskey Painters Am., Am. Soc. Marine Artists, Acad. Artists Assn., Hudson Valley Arts Assn. Home: 13 Main St Rockport MA 01966-1512

MOSHER, EDWARD BLAKE, investment company executive, consultant; b. San Antonio, Apr. 9, 1969; s. Stephen Edward and Suzanne (Wolters) M. BA, U. Tex., 1992. Intern Jenswold, King and Assocs., Houston, summer 1989, Merrill Lynch, Austin, spring 1990; pvt. practice investor Houston, 1992-93; CEO Mosher Internat., Inc., 1993—. Bd. advisors Mars Hill Prodns., Houston, 1989—, Mosher Inst. for Internat. Policy Studies, College Station, Tex., 1991—, Ctr. for Internat. Studies, U. St. Thomas, Houston, 1994—; bd. trustees Francis A. Schaeffer Found., Briar Cliff Manor, N.Y., 1992—; bd. dirs. U.S. Baltic Found., Camp RedCloud, Inc., 1994—. Editorial columnist: The Daily Texan, 1991; editor-in-chief: (quarterly publs.) Footnotes, 1992—. Youth leader Bethel Ind. Presbyn. Ch., Houston, 1992—. Mem. Am. Enterprise Inst. (sponsor), The Wilson Ctr. (assoc.), Univ. Club Houston. Avocations: playing guitar, writing songs, mountain climbing, basketball, tennis. Office: Mosher Internat Inc PO Box 26914 Austin TX 78755-0914 Address: MOSHER INTERNATIONAL PO Box 26914 Austin TX 78755-0914

MOSHER, FREDERICK KENNETH, engineering consultant; b. Middletown, N.Y., Aug. 25, 1943; s. Fred J. and Ruth M. (Werlau) M.; student N.Y.U., 1970-72, Lafayette U., 1973-74; m. Gail J. Berry, Jan. 24, 1968; children— Scott, Kerri, Dean. With Mayo, Lynch & Assos., Architect & Engrs., Hoboken, N.J., 1962-64, designer, 1964-69; mech. designer Louis Goldberg & Assos., Metuchen, N.J., 1969-74, assoc., 1975; partner Brownworth, Mosher & Doran, Piscataway, N.J., 1976-90, Mosher & Doran, Edison, N.J., 1990—. Pres., St. Luke's Luth. Ch., Washington, N.J., 1975-81; mem. Warren County Uniform Constrn. Code Bd. Appeals. Served with Security Agy., U.S. Army, 1965-71. Recipient Mem. Recognition award Cons. Engrs. Coun. N.J., 1990. Fellow Am. Soc. Cert. Engring. Technicians, Am. Cons. Engring. Coun. (Nat. Award for Engring. Excellence 1979); mem. N.J. Cons. Engrs. Coun. (chmn. engring. excellence com.), Am. Soc. Mil. Engrs., IEEE, ASHRAE (3d pl. award for alternative or renewable energy utilization 1982), Nat. Soc. Profl. Engrs., Constrn. Specification Inst. Lutheran. Home: 21 Oak Ridge Rd Washington NJ 07882-1503 Office: 3090 Woodbridge Ave Ste 300 Edison NJ 08837-3255

MOSHER, STEVEN AKER, health educator; b. Newton, Mass., Sept. 23, 1952; s. James Clayton and Effie Marie (Farrenkopf) M.; m. Sandra Delores Seals, Jan. 1, 1975 (div. Mar. 1999); children: Kerrie Ann, Jaime Melissa. BA in Polit. Sci. cum laude, U. S.C., 1973, MA in Internat. Studies, 1977, PhD in Govt./Internat. Studies, 1980. Asst. prof. pub. adminstrn. and polit. sci. Ferrum (Va.) Coll., 1978-81, assoc. prof., 1981, dir. pub. affairs and adminstrv. program, 1978-81; asst. prof. pub. adminstrn./polit. sci. Avila Coll., Kansas City, Mo., 1982-85, assoc. prof., 1985-89, coord. pub. adminstrn. program, 1982-89; assoc. prof. health care adminstrn. and polit. sci. Mary Baldwin Coll., Staunton, Va., 1989-96, prof. health care adminstrn., 1996—, dir. health care adminstrn. program, 1989—. Cons. Bath County Cmty. Hosp., Hot Springs, Va., 1993-95, Kuley, Ryan & Assocs., Staunton, 1994-97, Va. Vets. Care Ctr., 1996—; lectr. in field. Contbr. articles to profl. jours. Mem. planning com. Augusta Health Care, Inc., Fishersville, Va., 1991—; adv. bd. Dr. Jarnette Children's Psychiat. Hosp., Staunton, 1989-96; bd. trustees Humana Hosp.-Overland Park, Kans., 1986-88; mem. Valley Health Coun., N.W. Health Sys. Agy., Va., 1989-96; mem. Mayor's Com. on UN Day, Kansas City, 1986; vol. Am. Heart Assn., 1990-93. Named to Outstanding Young Men of Am., 1985; Province of Que. grantee, 1990, 93. Mem. APHA, Va. Rural Health Assn. (bd. dirs. 1995-97), Assn. Univ. Programs of Health Adminstrn., Am. Coun. for Que. Studies, Internat. Assn. Housing and Svcs. Aged, Assn. Can. Studies in the U.S., Am. Coll. Healthcare Execs., Omicron Delta Kappa. Roman Catholic. Avocations: weightlifting, jogging. Office: Mary Baldwin College Health Care Adminstrn Prog Staunton VA 24401

MOSHER, SUE A. computer consultant; b. Havre, Mont., Aug. 21, 1953; d. Richard B. and Malinda Grace (Simpson) Billingsley; m. Robert Allen Mosher, June 21, 1986; 1 child, Ann Maura. BA in Sociology, Coll. of William & Mary, Williamsburg, Va., 1974. Asst. music dir. Sta. WOWI-FM, Norfolk, Va., 1974-75; news dir. Sta. WNOR-AM/FM, 1976-77; reporter, editor, writer Sta. WSOC-AM/FM, Charlotte, N.C., 1977-79; editor, writer AP Broadcast Svcs., N.Y.C., 1979-82, asst. broadcast editor, 1982-83, gen. broadcast editor N.Y.C. and Washington, 1983-85, asst. dir. adminstrn. Washington, 1985-87, asst. dir. tech. devel., 1989-94; prin. Slipstick Sys., Arlington, Va., 1994—2001; pres. Turtle Flock, LLC, 2001—. Author: AP NewsDesk User's Manual, 1991, Microsoft Exchange User's Handbook, 1997, Microsoft Outlook E-mail and Fax Guide, 1998, Teach Yourself Microsoft Outlook 2000 Programming in 24 Hours, 1999, Microsoft Outlook 2000 E-mail and Fax Guide, 2000; outlook editor Windows NT Mag. Exch. Adminstr., 1998-; contbg. editor: Inside Windows: Networking Edition, 1994; contbr.: Spl. Edition Using Windows NT Workstation 3.51, 1996, Spl. Edition Using Windows NT Workstation 4.0, 1996, Microsoft Office Expert Solutions, 1996. Trustee, Universalist Nat. Meml. Ch., Washington, 1990-91, 2001-. Mem. Radio-TV News Dirs. (data transmission guidelines com. 1986-96), Soc. Tech. Comm., Computer Press Assn.

MOSHFEGH, MOUSSA, surgeon; b. Tehran, Iran, Jan. 17, 1947; MD, U. Tehran, 1972. Diplomate Am. Bd. Surgery. Intern Kern Med. Ctr., Bakersfield, Calif., 1980-81, resident in gen. surgery, 1981-85, Sinai Med. Ctr., Tehran, 1974-78; pvt. practice L.A. Mem. staff Cedars-Sinai Med. Ctr., L.A., Midway Hosp., L.A., Greater El Monte Hosp., Whittier Med. Ctr., Brotman Med. Ctr., L.A., Suburban Hosp., L.A.; chmn. dept. surgery Greater El Monte Cmty. Hosp., 1993—94, 1997—98, chmn. emergency svcs., 1995—96, chmn. credential com., 1998—2002. Fellow ACS; mem. AMA, Am. Soc. Gen. Surgeons, Internat. Coll. Surgeons. Office: 6221 Wilshire Blvd Ste 616 Los Angeles CA 90048-5201 E-mail: drmoussa2000@aol.com.

MOSHMAN, JACK, statistical consultant; b. Richmond Hill, N.Y., Aug. 12, 1924; s. Morris and Sadye (Posner) M.; m. Annette Gordon, Aug. 10, 1947; children: Gordon, Marc, Sherri, Ira. BA, NYU, 1946; MA, Columbia U., 1947; PhD, U. Tenn., 1953. Instr. Queens Coll., Flushing, N.Y., 1946-47, U. Tenn., Knoxville, 1947-53; statistician AEC, Oak Ridge, Tenn., 1948-50; sr. statistician Oak Ridge (Tenn.) Nat. Labs., 1950-54; mem. tech. staff Bell Tel. Labs., Murray Hill, N.J., 1954-57; v.p. C-E-I-R Inc., Washington, 1957-66; mng. dir. EBS Mgmt. Cons., 1966-68; sr. v.p. Leasco Systems & Rsch., Bethesda, Md., 1968-69; pres. Moshman Assocs. Inc., 1970—. Adj. prof. Rutgers U., 1963-66; professorial lectr. George Washington U., 1959-62; chmn. Inst. for Safety Analysis, Rockville, Md., 1975-89. Editor: Faith, Hope & Parity, 1967; author Ency. sect. Computers & Politics, 1985, 90, 93; contbr. articles to profl. jours. Trustee Babbage Found., St. Paul, 1983-87; pres. Moshman Charitable Found., Bethesda, 1996—; v.p. Eleanor & George Kokiko Sr. Found., Bethesda, 1997—. With U.S. Army, 1943-46, ETO. Fellow Am. Statis. Assn. (coun. 1956, 58); mem. Am. Fedn. Info. Processing Soc. Am. (bd. dirs., pres. 1986-87), Assn. for Computing Machinery (sec. 1956-64, v.p 1964), Inst. for Math. Stats., Inst. for Mgmt. Scis., Ops. Rsch. Soc. Am., Biometrics Soc. Avocation: psephology. Office: Moshman Assocs Inc 4340 East West Hwy Bethesda MD 20814-4411 E-mail: jmoshman@aol.com.

MOSHOYANNIS, PHILLIP DEMETRI ALEXANDER, educator; b. Manhattan, N.Y., Mar. 30, 1968; s. Demetri S. M. and Susan Elizabeth Perry. BS, Cornell U., 1990; MA, Columbia U., 1992, MPhil, 1999. Tchr. 4th grade A. Fantis Parochial Sch., Bklyn., 1990-91; substitute tchr. Oyster Bay, East Norwich, N.Y., 1992-93; social studies specialist Sch. of Transfiguration, Corona, 1993-94; tchr. 5th grade Lee Ave. Sch., Hicksville, 1995—. Adj. asst. prof. Nassau C.C., Garden City, N.Y., 1994—. Capt. U.S. Army N.G., 1990—. Decorated Army Commendation medal, Army Achievement medal, Nat. Def. Svc. medal. Mem. Am. Sociol. Assn., Hicksville Congress Tchrs., Am. Hellenic Ednl. Progressive Assn., Am. Legion, Kappa Delta Pi. Home: 1 Cortelyou St W Huntington Manor NY 11746-3306 Office: Lee Ave Sch 1 7th St Hicksville NY 11801-5421

MOSICH, ANELIS NICK, accountant, writer, educator, consultant; b. Croatia, Aug. 30, 1928; came to U.S., 1939, naturalized, 1951; s. Dinko and Josephine (Ursich) M.; m. Dorothy V. Rasich, June 15, 1958; children: Lori, Lisa, Jeffrey. BS, UCLA, 1951, MBA, 1953, PhD (fellow), 1963. CPA, Calif. Mem. faculty UCLA, 1955-63, Calif. State U., Northridge, 1963-64; examiner for Calif. State Bd. Accountancy, 1964-70; prof. acctg. U. So. Calif., Los Angeles, 1964-74, William C. Hallett prof. acctg., 1974-81, Ernst & Young prof., 1981-90, chmn. acctg. dept., 1970-74, 77-78, prof. emeritus, 1993. Cons. various bus. orgns., 1953—; expert witness; guest spkr. various profl. and bus. groups in Calif., Oreg., NY, Tex., Fla. and Hawaii, 1963—93. Author: Intermediate Accounting, rev. 6th edit., 1989, Financial Accounting, 1970, 75, Accounting: A Basis for Business Decision, 1972, Modern Advanced Accounting, 4th edit., 1988, The CPA Examination: Text, Problems and Solutions, 1978; editor: Education column Calif. CPA Quar., 1965-66; contbg. editor: Education and Professional Training column Jour. Accountancy, 1971-77; contbr. numerous articles to jours. and acctg. Mem. productivity commn. City of L.A., 1993—94; bd. dirs. Bill Hannon Found. With U.S. Army, 1953—55. Recipient Dean's award Sch. Bus. Adminstrn., U. So. Calif., 1973, 78, Fred B. Olds Support Group award U. So. Calif., 1994, Disting. Svc. award for Leventhal Sch. Acctg., 1999. Office: U So Calif Leventhal Sch Acctg University Park Los Angeles CA 90089-0001

MOSIER, ARVIN RAY, chemist, researcher; b. Olney Springs, Colo., June 11, 1945; s. Isaac James Ellen Rena (Ross) M.; m. Susan Minnick, Dec. 30, 1965; children: Andrew, Katherine. BS, Colo. State U., 1967, MS, 1967-68, PhD, 1974. Chemist agr. research services USDA, Ft. Collins, 1967—. Contbr. papers and book chpt. to profl. jours. Mem. AAAS, Am. Soc. Agronomy, Soil Sci. Soc. Am., Internat. Soil Sci. Sco., Council Agrl. Sci. Tech., Phi Kappa Phi, Sigma XI, Gamma Sigma Delta. Republican. Methodist. Avocations: tennis, soccer. Home: Unit 40 950 Southridge Greens Blvd Fort Collins CO 80525-6728 Office: USDA Agrl Rsch Svc PO Box E Fort Collins CO 80522-0470 E-mail: amosier@lamar.colostate.edu.

MOSIER, HARRY DAVID, JR. physician, educator; b. Topeka, May 22, 1925; s. Harry David and Josephine Morrow (Johnson) M.; m. Nadine Oclea Merilatt, Aug. 24, 1949; children: Carolyn Josephine Mosier Pohlmeyer, William David, Daniel Thomas, Christine Elizabeth Mosier Mahoney; m. Marjorie Knight Armstrong, Sept. 26, 1963. BS magna cum laude, U. Notre Dame, 1948; MD, Johns Hopkins U., 1952. Diplomate Am. Bd. Pediatrics, Am. Bd. Pediatric Endocrinology. Intern Johns Hopkins Hosp., Balt., 1952-53; resident in pediat. Los Angeles Children's Hosp., 1953-54, resident pediatric pathology, 1954-55; fellow pediatric endocrinology Johns Hopkins U., 1955-57; asst. prof. pediat. UCLA, 1957-61, assoc. prof., 1961-63; dir. rsch. Ill. State Pediatric Inst., Chgo., 1963-67; assoc. prof. U. Ill., 1963-67; prof. pediat. U. Calif.-Irvine, 1967—2002, emeritus, 2002—, head divsn. pediat. endocrinology, 1967-2000; staff Children's Hosp. Med. Ctr., Long Beach, Calif., 1970—, U. Calif. Irvine Med. Ctr., Orange, 1979—; dist. cons. Med. Bd. Calif., 1995—. Contbr. articles to med. jours. With AUS, 1943-46, col. U.S. Army Med. Corps, 1990-91, Persian Gulf War. USAR Med. Corps. 1952-62, 83-93 (ret.). Office: U Calif Dept Pediat 101 City Dr S Orange CA 92868-3201

MOSIER, JO ANN, mathematics educator; b. Louisville, Dec. 3, 1942; d. Melvin R. and LaVerne (Yates) Mudd; m. Rudy W. Mosier, June 12, 1971; children: Holly Leigh, Kristi Ann. BA in Math. Edn., Spalding U., 1964; MAT in Math., U. Louisville, 1971, postgrad., 1977. Tchr. math. Ind. U. Southeast, Spalding U., Bellarmine Coll., Louisville, 1975-85, U. Louisville, 1975-85, Jefferson County (Ky.) Pub. Schs., Louisville, 1964-74, 85-91, 1997-98; dir. Ky. Math. Portfolio Program Ky. Dept. Edn., Frankfort, 1991-97; with Ky. Dept. Edn. Highly Skilled Educator, 1997-2000; ednl. cons. Ky. Dept. Edn., 2001-2001; resource tchr. Jefferson County Schs.; Ky. project mgr. Dwok Mid. Grades Rsch. Project, 2001—. Cons. in field. Mem. sch. bd. St. Agnes Sch., Louisville, 1982-85. Mem. ASCD, Nat. Coun. Tchrs. Math., Coun. Presdl. Awardees for Excellence in Tchg. Math., Nat. Suprs. of Math. Home: 1426 Rosewood Ave Louisville KY 40204-1548 Office: Collaborative for Tchg & Learning/ Galef Inst 2303 River Rd Ste 100 Louisville KY 40206-1010 E-mail: jmosier@ctlonline.org.

MOSIER, MARY C. (CATHY MOSIER), business owner; b. Dayton, Ohio, June 3, 1954; d. Herman Ullery and Cecilia Agnes (Mc Cluskey) Chrowl; m. Ronald Eugene Swank Jr., Jun. 7, 1975 (div. Oct. 1982); children: Angela, Ronald III, Samantha; m. David Michael Neufeld, Aug. 18, 1983 (div. 1991); children: Michael Brent Neufeld, Andrew Jonathan Neufeld; m. Steven Lynn Mosier, Nov. 6, 1992. Mgmt. asst. Air Force Maintenance, Supply and Munitions Mgmt. Engring. Team, Wright-Patterson AFB, Ohio, 1977-82, Air Force Svc. Info. and News Ctr., Kelly AFB, Tex., 1982-88; owner Cat's Crafts, San Antonio, 1988—; pres. Perfect Presentations, 1993—; stock fund mgr., resource advisor 76th Logistics Group, Kelly AFB, 1988—. Leader Webelos and Bear Dens Boy Scouts, 1994—. Recipient Dan Berkant award Air Force Assn., 1985. Mem. NAFE, Fed. Mgrs. Assn., Nat. Assn. Military Comptrollers. Republican. Avocations: crafts, reading, sports. Home and Office: Perfect Presentations 152 High Ridge Trl SE Rio Rancho NM 87124-3973

MOSIER, WILLIAM ARTHUR, psychologist, physician assistant, medical educator, administrator, researcher; b. Richmond, Calif., Oct. 21, 1946; s. William Nathaniel and Violet Olga (Luzum) M.; m. Virginia Rondero (div. Apr. 1992); children: Robert Carlos, Cristina Dominique; m. Gloria Sifuentes (div. 1998); 1 child, William Nathaniel; m. Gabriela Pickett; 1 chld, Gabriela. BA, Webster U., 1971, MA in Tchg., 1973; MD, U. Ctrl. del Este, Dominican Republic, 1986; EdD, U. So. Calif., 1987; BS with distinction, U. Okla., 1991; MPAS in Psychiatry, U. Nebr., 1997. Diplomate Am. Bd. Forensic Medicine, Am. Bd. Med. Psychotherapists, Am. Bd. Psychol. Specialties, lic. physician asst. Tex., Fla., N.Y., Va.; lic. marriage and family therapist and chem. dependency counselor Tex. Tchr. St. Louis Pub. Schs., 1971—74; tchr., ctr. dir. Project Head Start, Vallejo, Calif., 1975—77; dir. rsch. Ctr. for Study of Child Devel., Sacramento, 1977—95; physician asst. U.S. Army, Ft. Hood/Ft. Sam Houston, Tex., 1989—91; assoc. prof. U. Mary Hardin-Baylor, Belton, 1991—92; psychotherapist pvt. practice, 1993—95; mem. adj. faculty dept. psychiatry Barry U., Miami Shores, Fla., 1997—2000; med. dir. Fla. Inst. Neuro Devel., Vero Beach, 1995—2000; clin. assoc. prof. psychiatry Nova Southeastern U., Ft. Lauderdale, 1997—99; asst. prof. medicine, assoc. dir. acad. curriculum George Washington U., 2000—01; assoc. prof. psychiatry Kettering Coll. med. Arts Kettering (Ohio) Med. Ctr., 2001—02; child devel. cons., marriage and family therapist, 2001—; asst. prof., child devel. Wright State U., Dayton, Ohio, 2002—. Mem. test writing com. Nat. Assn. for Cert. Nat. Bd. Med. Examiners, 1995—. Contbr. ; newspaper columnist: , mem. editl. adv. bd.: Advance for PAs. With USA, 1967-68, Vietnam, maj. USAFR, 1987—. Decorated Bronze Star, Air medal. Fellow: Am. Assn. Surg. PAs, Am. Acad. Physician Assts., APA (mem. adv. bd. 1997—, editl. adv. bd. Annals of Am. Psychotherapy Assn.), Am. Coll. Forensic Examners (life), Aerospace Med. Assn. (life), Assn. Mil. Surgeons U.S. (life); mem.: Assn. of Psychiat. PAs (founding mem., pres.), Soc. PAs in the Addiction Medicine (exec. bd., pres.-elect). Democrat. Mem. Soc. Of Friends. Avocations: musical composition, piano, guitar, swimming, yoga. Office: 649 Greenlawn Ave Dayton OH 45403-3356 E-mail: drwillmosier@yahoo.com.

MOSK, RICHARD MITCHELL, judge; b. L.A., May 18, 1939; s. Stanley and Edna M.; m. Sandra Lee Budnitz, Mar. 21, 1964; children: Julie, Matthew. AB with great distinction, Stanford U., 1960; JD cum laude, Harvard U., 1963. Bar: Calif. 1964, U.S. Supreme Ct. 1970, U.S. Ct. Mil. Appeals 1970, U.S. Dist. Ct. (no., so., ea., and cen. dists.) Calif 1964, U.S. Ct. Appeals (9th dist.) 1964. Staff Pres.'s Commn. on Assassination Pres. Kennedy, 1964; rsch. clk. Calif. Supreme Ct., 1964-65; ptnr. Mitchell, Silberberg & Knupp, L.A., 1965-87; prin. Sanders, Barnet, Goldman, Simons & Mosk, PC, 1987-2000; justice Calif. Ct. Appeal, 2nd Dist., 2001—. Spl. dep. Fed. Pub. Defender , L.A., 1975—76; instr. U. So. Calif. Law Sch., 1978; judge Iran-U.S. Claims Tribunal, 1981—84, 1997—2001, substitute arbitrator, 1984—97; mem. L.A. County Jud. Procedures Commn., 1973—82, chmn., 1978; co-chmn. Motion Picture Assn. Classification and Rating Adminstrn., 1994—2000; mem. panel Ct. Arbitration for Sport-Geneva, 1998—2001. Contbr. articles to profl. jours. Mem. L.A. City-County Inquiry on Brush Fires, 1970; bd. dirs. Calif. Mus. Sci. and Industry, 1979-82, Vista Del Mar Child Ctr., 1979-82; trustee L.A. County Law Libr., 1985-86; bd. govs. Town Hall Calif., 1986-91; mem. Christopher Commn. on L.A. Police Dept., 1991; mem. Stanford U. Athletic Bd., 1991-95. With USNR, 1964-75. Hon. Woodrow Wilson fellow, 1960; recipient Roscoe Pound prize, 1961. Fellow: Am. Bar Found.; mem.: FBA (pres. L.A. chpt. 1972), ABA (coun. internat. law sect. 1986—90), L.A. County Bar Assn., Beverly Hills Bar Assn., Internat. Bar Assn., Phi Beta Kappa. Office: Ct Appeal 300 S Spring St Los Angeles CA 90013

MOSKAL, ANTHONY JOHN, former dean, professor, management and education consultant; b. South Amboy, N.J., May 31, 1946; s. Anthony Joseph and Jennie (Salamon) M.; m. Kathryn Jean Coakley, July 8, 1978; 1 child, Nicole Elizabeth. AB, Villanova (Pa.) U., 1968, MA, 1972; MEd, Ga. State U., 1974; PhD, Columbia Pacific U., San Rafael, Calif., 1987. Prin. instr. U.S. Army, Ft. Benning, Ga., 1969-71; research mgr. Blue Cross and Blue Shield, Columbus, 1972-74; sales rep. J.C. Penney Co., Parlin, N.J., 1974-76; dean of students Alliance Coll., Cambridge Springs, Pa., 1976-77; tchr. Sayreville (N.J.) pub. schs., 1977-79; county 4-H agt. Rutgers U., New Brunswick, 1979-86; pres. Eagle Assocs., South Amboy, N.J., 1985—. Adj. faculty Georgian Ct. Coll., Lakewood, NJ, 1987—, U.S. Army Command and Gen. Staff Coll., Ft. Leavenworth, Kans., 1989—2000, Nat. Def. U., Washington, 1991—2000; cons. dir. Union County Ednl. Svcs. Commn., 2000—; cons. in mgmt., leadership, edn., volunteerism, youth programs, career planning; spl. liaison to Mercer Cty. Bd. Edn., Sayreville, 1991—95, Sayreville, 2000—; area admissions rep. U.S. Mil. Acad., 1984—91. Contbr. articles to profl. jours. Mem. Boy Scouts Am.; counselor, mem. dist. com. Ctrl. N.J. Coun. Boy Scouts Am., 1982—; pres., bd. dirs. Vol. Action Ctr., Middlesex County, 1979—87; pres. Sayreville War Meml. H.S. Band Parents Assn., 1994—96; county committeeman Middlesex County, 1990—94, 2000—; dir. religious edn. Sacred Heart Parish, South Amboy, 1988—91. With U.S. Army, 1969—71, with U.S. Army, 1990—92, lt. col. USAR. Decorated Meritorious Svc. medal, Army Commendation medal (2), Mil. Outstanding Vol. Svc. medal; recipient Order of the Arrow award Boy Scouts Am., 1960, 20th Century award of Achievement, Nat. Assn. Chiefs of Police, Desert Shield/Desert Storm medal State of N.J., Disting. Svc. medal State of N.J.; United Way of Ctrl. Jersey grantee, 1984, others. Mem.: ASCD, Holy Name Soc., U.S. Army Officer Candidate Alumni Assn., Am. Fedn. Police (award of merit 1989, legion of honor 1990, J. Edgar Hoover Meml. medal 1991, St. Michael the Archangel award 1992, patriotism award 1993), Nat. Assn. Ext. 4-H Agts. (regional contact 1981—83, cert. appreciation 1983), Res. Officers Assn., Mil. Police Regtl. Assn., N.J. Assn. 4-H Agts. (pres. 1985—86, outstanding svc. citation 1981, 1987), Vietnam Vets. of Am. (life; rec. sec., honor guard), Nat. Infantry Assn. (life), Nat. Eagle Scout Assn., Am. Legion, K. of C. (3d degree officer, cmty. activities dir., vol. coord. fife and drums corps, degree team co-capt., 4th degree officer, color corps comdr., diocesan degree team, Family of Mo., 4th degree Family of Yr., Dist. Color Corps Man of Yr., Assembly Color Corps Man of Yr., Knight of Mo. (3), 3d degree Family of Yr.), Kiwanis, Pi Gamma Mu, Epsilon Sigma Phi, Alpha Phi Omega. Republican. Roman Catholic. Avocations: reading, music, recreational camping, travel, woodworking. Office: Eagle Assocs 166 Luke St South Amboy NJ 08879-2231

MOSKALENKO, IGOR VLADIMIROVICH, physicist, astrophysicist; b. Moscow, May 4, 1962; s. Vladimir Anatolievich and Galina Petrovna (Kuznetsova) M.; m. Irina Viktorovna Surikova, July 12, 1984 (div. May 1992); 1 child, Maria; m. Irina Vladimirovna Malkova, June 10, 1994. MS, M.V. Lomonosov Moscow State U., 1985, PhD in Physics, 1990. Rschr. Moscow State U. Inst. Nuc. Physics, 1985-93, sr. scientist, 1993—; sr. rsch. assoc. Lab. for High Energy Astrophysics NASA/Goddard Space Flight Ctr., Greenbelt, Md., 1999—2001; assoc. rsch. scientist NASA/Goddard Space Flight Ctr. and Joint Ctr. for Astrophysics/U. Md. Baltimore County, 2002—. Guest scientist Łodz (Poland) Inst. Physics, 1990-91, Ctr. d'Etude Spatiale des Rayonnements, CNRS, Toulouse, France, 1994-95, Max-Planck-Inst. für Extraterrestrische Physik, Garching, Germany, 1996-99. Contbr. numerous articles to profl. jours., chpts. to books, and conf. procs. Grantee Am. Astron. Soc., 1992, Am. Phys. Soc., 1992, Soros Found., Moscow, 1993; Max Planck fellowship Max Planck Soc., 1996-99; sr. associateship NRC/NASA/GSFC, 1999-2001. Russian Orthodox. Avocations: tennis, skiing, swimming, travel. Home: 8150 Lakecrest Dr Apt 803 Greenbelt MD 20770 Office: NASA/Goddard Space Flight Ctr Code 660 Greenbelt MD 20771-0001 E-mail: imos@milkyway.gsfc.nasa.gov.

MOSKALEWICZ, JACEK, sociologist, educator; b. Starachowice, Kieleckie, Poland, Aug. 19, 1948; s. Władysław and Helena Maria (Turketti) M.; m. Danuta Beata Postnikoff, Feb. 21, 1974; children: Paweł Jakub, Olga. MA, Warsaw (Poland) U., 1972, PhD, 1997. Cert. in sociology and philosophy. Rschr. Inst. of Orgn. of Machine Industry, Warsaw, 1973-77, Inst. of Psychiatry and Neurology, Warsaw, 1978-96, asst. prof., 1997—. Sci. sec. of team of experts Commn. on Counteracting Alcoholism at Coun. of Mins., Warsaw, 1980-82; cons. WHO, Copenhagen, 1992; nat. coord. Phare Program on Fight Against Drugs, Warsaw, 1994-95. Co-author: (book) Alcohol and the Community, 1995 (award of Sci. Coun. of Inst. of Psychiatry and Neurology 1996). Recipient La Médaille de la Ville de Paris, Le Maire, 1995. Mem. Kettil Bruun Soc. (mem. coord. com. 1988-90). Avocations: traveling, gardening, photography. Office: Inst Psychiatry/Neurology 1/9 Sobieskiego Str 02-957 Warsaw Poland

MOSKIN, JOHN ROBERT, editor, writer; b. N.Y.C., May 9, 1923; s. Morris and Irma (Rosenfeld) M.; m. Doris Marianne Bloch, Oct. 7, 1948 (div. 1978, dec. 2002); children: Mark Douglas, David Scott, Nancy Irma; m. Lynn Carole Goldberg, Apr. 10, 1986. Grad., Horace Mann Sch., 1940; BS, Harvard U., 1944; MA, Columbia U., 1947. Reporter Boston Post, 1941-42, Newark News, 1947-48; asst. to gen. mgr. N.Y. Star, 1948-49; editor Westport (Conn.) Town Crier, 1949; med. editor Look mag., N.Y.C., 1950-51, articles editor, 1951-53, sr. editor, 1956-66, fgn. editor, 1966-71; mng. editor Woman's Home Companion, 1953-56; sr. editor Collier's, 1956; editor at large Saturday Rev., 1972-75; sr. editor World Press Rev., 1976-87, contbg. editor, 1987-93; editorial dir. Aspen Inst., 1977-83. Editorial dir. Commonwealth Fund, 1984-87, sr. editorial advisor, 1987-93. Author: (with others) The Decline of the American Male, 1958, Morality in America, 1966, Turncoat, 1968, The U.S. Marine Corps Story, 1977, 82, 87, 92, Among Lions, 1982, (with Julia Vitullo-Martin) The Executive's Book of Quotations, 1994, Mr. Truman's War, 1996, 2002; editor: The Marines, 1998; mem. editl. adv. com. Dimensions mag, 1970-71, Present Tense, 1973-90. Trustee Scarsdale Adult Sch., 1965-72, chmn., 1969-70; mem. Dana Reed Prize com. Harvard, 1947-2000; mem. com. Class of 1944, 1943—; mem. communications screening com. Council Internat. Exchange of Scholars, 1974-77, President's Coun. Heritage Coll., 1995—; bd. dirs. SIECUS, 1972-80, Jerusalem Found., 1977—, Marine Corps Hist. Found., 1979-82, 89-95, Faculty for Continuing Med. Edn., 1983-86, Authors Guild Found., 2000—, Lotos Club Found., 2000-. Served with AUS, 1943-46. Recipient Benjamin Franklin gold medal for pub. service Woman's Home Companion, 1955, Page One award Newspaper Guild N.Y., 1965, Sidney Hillman Found. award, 1965, National Headliners award, 1967, Overseas Press Club award, 1969, citation for excellence, 1971, Disting. Svc. award Marine Corps Combat Corrs. Assn., 1978, 99, Nat. Jewish Book award, 1983, Disting. Svc. award Marine Corps Hist. Found., 1996, Gen. O.P. Smith award Marine Corps Heritage Found., 1999. Mem. Am. Hist. Assn., Soc. Mil. History, Authors Guild, Fgn. Editors Group (chmn. 1970-71), Nat. Press Club (Washington), Overseas Press Club (gov. 1975-79), The Century Assn., Harvard Club (N.Y.C.), Lotos Club, (bd. dirs. 1988-90, 94-2002, pres. 1991-94), Sigma Delta Chi (mem. nat. freedom of info. com. 1964, 71) Home: 945 5th Ave New York NY 10021-2655 also: 157 Jerusalem Rd Tyringham MA 01264 E-mail: jrmedit@worldnet.att.net.

MOSKIN, MORTON, lawyer, director; b. N.Y.C., Mar. 28, 1927; s. Barnett and Sonia (Burr) M.; m. Rita Lee Goldberg, June 15, 1952; children: Tina, Ilene, Jonathan. BA, Pa. State Coll., 1947; LL.B., Cornell U., 1950. Assoc. White & Case, N.Y.C., 1950-61, ptnr., 1962-94, cons., 1995—. Chmn. exec. com. Mallinckrodt, Inc. (formerly IMCERA, previously Internat. Minerals & Chem. Corp.), St. Louis, 1988-91, chmn. corp. governance com., 1993-97; sec. BT Mortgage Investors, Garden City, N.J., 1975-82. Editor (with Field): New York and Delaware Business Entities: Choice, Formation, Operation, Financing, Acquisitions, 1997; editor: Transactional Lawyer's Deskbook: Advising Business Entities, 2001, Commercial Contracts: Strategies for Drafting and Negotiating, 2002. Bd. dirs. Fedn. Employment and Guidance Svcs.; bd. dirs., pres. Henry M. Blackmer Found., N.Y.C.; bd. dirs. Achievement Found., Stamford, Conn., pres., 1988-94; bd. dirs. Jewish Cmty. Svcs. L.I., 1974-93, pres., 1984-87. Fellow Am. Bar Found.; mem. ABA, N.Y. State Bar Assn., N.Y. County Lawyers Assn. (dir. 1981-86, 99-02), Norfolk (Conn.) Country Club, Cornell Club N.Y. Home: 1160 Park Ave Apt 15B New York NY 10128-1212 Office: White & Case 1155 Ave of Americas New York NY 10036-2711 E-mail: mmoskin@whitecase.com.

MOSKO, SIGMUND WEINER, electrical engineer, researcher; b. Phila., June 9, 1936; m. Brenda C. Krauss, Aug. 25, 1963; children: Joel, Tammy, Beth. BSEE, Drexel U., 1958; postgrad., U. Tenn., Knoxville, 1958-61. Registered profl. engr., Tenn. Rsch. assoc. Oak Ridge (Tenn.) Nat. Lab., 1958-61, rsch. staff mem., 1961-78, sr. rsch. staff mem., 1978—. Contbr. articles on nuclear sci., nuclear instruments and methods to IEEE Transactions on Nuclear Sci. Contbr. articles on nuclear sci., nuclear instruments and methods to IEEE Transactions on Nuclear Sci., 1962—. Bd. dirs. Clinch Valley Coun. of Camp Fire Boys and Girls, Oak Ridge, 1985-91. Mem. IEEE (sr.), Nat. Soc. Profl. Engrs. Home: 104 Windgate Rd Oak Ridge TN 37830-8625 Office: Oak Ridge Nat Lab PO Box 2008 Oak Ridge TN 37831-2008 E-mail: moskosw@ornl.gov.

MOSKOS, CHARLES C. sociology educator; b. Chgo., May 20, 1934; s. Charles and Rita (Shukas) M.; m. Ilca Hohn, July 3, 1966; children— Andrew, Peter. BA cum laude, Princeton, 1956; MA, UCLA, 1961, PhD, 1963; LHD (hon.) , Norwich U., 1992, Towson U., 2002. Asst. prof. U. Mich., Ann Arbor, 1964-66; assoc. prof. sociology Northwestern U., Evanston, Ill., 1966-70, prof., 1970—. Fellow Progressive Policy Inst., 1992—; mem. Presdl. Commn. on Women in the Mil., 1992. Author: The Sociology of Political Independence, 1967, The American Enlisted Man, 1970, Public Opinion and the Military Establishment, 1971, Peace Soldiers, 1976, Fuerzas Armadas y Sociedad, 1984, The Military--More Than Just A Job?, 1988, A Call to Civic Service, 1988, Greek Americans, 1989, Soldiers and Sociology, 1989, New Directions in Greek American Studies, 1991, The New Conscientious Objection, 1993, All That We Can Be, 1996, Reporting War When There Is No War, 1996, The Media and the Military, 2000, The Postmodern Military, 2000. Chmn. Theodore Saloutos Meml. Fund; mem. Archdiocesan Commn. Third Millenium, 1982-88; mem adv. bd. Vets. for Am., 1997—; mem. Congl. Commn. on Mil. Tng. and Gender-Related Issues, 1998-99, Nat. Security Study Group, 1998-2001. Served with AUS, 1956-58. Decorated D.S.M., Fondation pour les Etudes de Def. Nat. (France), S.M.K. (The Netherlands); named to Marshall rsch. chair ARI, 1987-88, 95-96; Ford. Found. faculty fellow, 1969-70; fellow Wilson Ctr., 1980-81, guest scholar, 1991; fellow Rockefeller Found. Humanities, 1983-84, Guggenheim fellow, 1992-93, fellow Annenberg Washington Program, 1995; grantee 20th Century Fund, 1983-87, 92-94, Ford Found., 1989-90; recipient Nat. Educator Leadership award Todd Found., 1997, Book award Washington Monthly, 1997, Honored Patriot award Selective Svc. Sys., 1998; Pub. Policy fellow Wilson Ctr., 2002; Eisenhower chair Royal Mil. Acad. Netherlands, 2002. Mem. Am. Sociol. Assn., Internat. Sociol. Assn. (pres. rsch. com. on armed forces and conflict resolution 1982-86), Am. Polit. Sci. Assn., Inter-Univ. Seminar on Armed Forces and Soc. (chmn. 1987-99), Am. Acad. Arts and Scis. Greek Orthodox. Home: 2440 Asbury Ave Evanston IL 60201-2307

MOSKOS, HARRY, writer, former newspaper editor; b. Chgo., Oct. 8, 1936; m. Victoria Marie Poulos; 3 children. BA, U. N.Mex., Albuquerque, 1958. With Albuquerque Tribune, 1953-59; editor Grants (N.Mex.) Daily Beacon, 1959-60; newsman AP, Albuquerque, 1960, state editor, 1961-63, chief of bur. Honolulu, 1963-69; city editor Albuquerque Tribune, 1969-73, mng. editor, 1973-81; editor El Paso Herald-Post, 1981-84, Knoxville News-Sentinel, 1984—2001; staff writer Albuquerque Jour., 2001—. Office: 7777 Jefferson St NE Albuquerque NM 87109 E-mail: hmoskos@abqjournal.com.*

MOSKOVITZ, JIM, radio, television and film producer, writer; b. L.A., Aug. 14, 1958; s. Mayer and Charlotte (Creamer) M.; m. Joyce Ferro, Nov. 25, 1989. BA in Pol. Sci., Stanford U., 1980. Pres. JMJ Films, Inc., N.Y.C., 1991—, Marathon Sports Group, Inc., 1998—. Writer/prodr. Pat Summerall's Sports in Am., N.Y.C., 1990-97, Instant Replay with R. MacLean, Toronto, 1992-97, Talking Sports with Tim McCarver, 1998-2000, The Tim McCarver Show, 2000—. Author: Pat Summerall's Sports in America, 1997, The 12 Greatest Rounds of Boxing: The Untold Stories, Sports Illustrated, 2000; developer (motion picture) The Boys of Summer, 1999; writer, dir., prodr. (television special) Grand Slam!, 1989; writer, prodr. (TV show) Tim McCarver Show, 1998—, (Showtime) The 12 Greatest Rounds of Boxing: The Untold Stories, 2000 Recipient Sports Video of Yr. award Video Magazine, N.Y.C., 1989, Video Review, N.Y.C., 1990, silver medal Internat. Radio Awards, N.Y.C., 1996; named finalist Internat. Radio Awards, N.Y.C., 1994. Mem. Assn. Composers, Authors, Producers, Israel Policy Forum, Peace Now, Stanford Alumni Assn. Avocations: baseball, history, politics. Office: JMJ Films Inc 11 W 84th St Apt 4 New York NY 10024-4761 Fax: 212-724-7712.

MOSKOVITZ, STUART JEFFREY, lawyer; b. Phila., Jan. 21, 1949; s. Martin and Jean (Sandler) M.; m. Toni Cheryl Gans, June 1, 1980; children: Lauren Michelle, Leanne Meredith, Lisa Morgan. BA, Hofstra U., 1970; JD, Boston U., 1973. Bar: Pa. 1973, U.S. Dist. Ct. (mid. dist.) Pa. 1974, U.S. Claims Ct. 1975, U.S. Supreme Ct. 1979, N.Y. 1981, U.S. Dist. Ct. (so. dist.) N.Y. 1982, U.S. Ct. Appeals (2d cir.) 1983, N.J. 1993, U.S. Dist. Ct. N.J. 1993. Asst. atty. gen. Pa. Dept. Transp., Harrisburg, 1973-79; atty. Westinghouse Electric Corp., Pitts., 1980-81; ptnr. Berman, Paley, Goldstein & Berman, N.Y.C., 1981-90, Tanner, Propp & Farber, N.Y.C., 1991-94, Stadtmauer Bailkin, L.L.P., N.Y.C., 1995-98, McGowan & Moskovitz, L.L.P., N.Y.C. & South Amboy, NJ, 1999—2000; pvt. practice, 2001—. Pres. Ivanhoe Village Homeowner's Assn., 1984; mem. Coun. Excellence in Govt., Washington, 1991-93, N.Y. Bldg. Congress, 1991-94; elected Manalapan Twp. Com., 1999; mem. Manalapan Twp. Com., 1999, mayor, 2000. Mem. ABA (forum com. on constrn. industry), N.Y. State Bar Assn. (comml. fed. litigation sect. com. on constrn.), Assn. of Bar of City of N.Y., Pa. Bar Assn., N.J. State Bar Assn. Office: Ste B 509 Stillwells Corner Rd Freehold NJ 07728-5303

MOSKOWITZ, ARNOLD X. economist, strategist, educator; b. N.Y.C., Jan. 27, 1944; s. Morris and Millie (Kozichovsky) M.; m. Sandra Moskowitz; children: Nicole, Alex Michael Archangel. BS in Elec. Engring., CCNY, 1966; MS in Indsl. Mgmt., Poly. Inst. N.Y., 1970; MPhil, NYU, 1979, PhD in Econs. and Fin., 1985. Analyst Grumman Corp., N.Y.C., 1968-70; assoc. economist Dean Witter Reynolds, Inc., 1970-74, first v.p., economist, 1975-82, sr. v.p., economist, 1983-89; sr. v.p., dir. investment strategy County NatWest U.S.A., 1989-90; chmn. Moskowitz Capital Cons. Inc., 1990—. Lectr. New Sch. Social Research, 1978— ; adj. assoc. prof. fin. Pace U., N.Y.C., 1980-82; pres. Money Marketers NYU, 1988-89. Contbr. articles to profl. jours.; chpts. to books, including Security Selection and Active Portfolio Management; contbr. to Ency. of Economics, How to Beat Wall Street Mem. Am. Econ. Assn., Nat. Econ. Club, Nat. Assn. Bus. Economists, Atlantic Soc., Beta Gamma Sigma Jewish. Office: Moskowitz Capital Cons 109 Puritan Ave Forest Hills NY 11375-6027 *Our guidelines for success starts with our principles to provide the highest level of service to our customers and treat our employees as partners in the business. Our goal is to maintain the highest level of integrity in dealing with clients and workers in order to maximize our performances.*

MOSKOWITZ, HAROLD, radiologist; b. N.Y.C., Jan. 21, 1936; s. Sol and Ruth (Gutman) M.; m. Janet Ann Greenberg, June 27, 1957; children: Ellen, Robert. AB, NYU, 1955; MD, SUNY, N.Y.C., 1959. Resident in radiology Jefferson Med. Coll., Phila., 1960-63, instr. in radiology, 1963-64; asst. prof. SUNY, N.Y.C., 1966-69; dir. dept. radiology Mt. Sinai Hosp., 1969—. Assoc. prof. U. Conn., Hartford, 1969, clin. prof. radiology, 1996; clin. assoc. prof. Yale U., New Haven, 1969; pres. med. staff Mt. Sinai Hosp., Hartford, 1982-83; nat. dir. radiology svc. Allied Health Group. Contbr. articles to profl. jours. Mem. Soc. Breast Imaging (founder), Hartford Med. Soc. (Meritorious Svc. medal 1992), RAD Soc. N.Am. (Gold medal for exhibit 1969) Avocations: golf, fishing. Office: U Conn Health Ctr Dept Radiology Farmington CT 06032

MOSKOWITZ, HERBERT, management educator; b. Paterson, NJ, May 26, 1935; s. David and Ruth (Abrams) M.; m. Heather Mary Lesgnier, Feb. 25, 1968; children: Tobias, Rebecca, Jonas. BS in Mech. Engring., Newark Coll. Engring., 1956; MBA, U.S. Internat. U., 1964; PhD, UCLA, 1970. Rsch. engr. GE, 1956-60; systems design engr. Gen. Dynamics Convair, San Diego, 1960-65; asst. prof. Purdue U., West Lafayette, Ind., 1970-75, assoc. prof., 1975-79, prof., 1979-85, Disting. prof., 1985-87, James B. Henderson Disting. prof., 1987-91, Lewis B. Cullman Disting. prof. mfg. mgmt., 1991—, dir. Dauch Ctr. Mgmt. Mfg. Enterprises. Cons. AT&T, Inland Steel Co., Abbott Labs., others; adv. panelist NSF, 1990—. Author: Management Science and Statistics Texts, 1975-90; assoc. editor Decision Scis. Jour., 1984-90, Jour. Behavioral Decision Making, 1986-90; contbr. articles to jours. in field. Bd. dirs. Sons of Abraham Synagogue, Lafayette, Ind., 1970—; mem. Lafayette Klezmorem, 1973—. Capt. USAF, 1956-60. Recipient Disting. Doctoral Student award UCLA Alumni Assn., 1969-70; Fulbright Rsch. scholar, 1985-86. Fellow Decision Scis. Inst. (sec. 1985-87, v.p. 1978-80); mem. Ops. Rsch. Soc. Am./Inst. Mgmt. Sci. (liaison officer 1977—, panel mem., advisor NSF and Fulbright Scholar program 1993—), Tau Beta Pi, Pi Tau Sigma. Jewish. Avocations: Jewish music, tennis. Home: 1430 N Salisbury St West Lafayette IN 47906-2420 Office: Purdue U Krannert Grad Sch Mgmt Ctr Mgmt Mfg Enterprises West Lafayette IN 47907-1310

MOSKOWITZ, JAY, public health sciences educator; b. N.Y.C., Jan. 9, 1943; s. Murray and Helene Moskowitz; m. Joanne Cathy Schindelheim, Dec. 27, 1970; children: Michael Bradley, Andrew Cory. BS, Queens Coll., 1964; postgrad., CUNY, 1965; PhD, Brown U., 1969. From research assoc. in pharmacology to dep. dir. NIH, 1969—93, dep. dir. for sci. policy & tech. transfer, prin. dep. dir., 1993; various positions Nat. Heart, Lung and Blood Inst., 1976-86; acting dir. Nat. Inst. on Deafness and Other Communication Disorders, 1988-90, dep. dir., 1993-95; sr. assoc. dean for rsch. devel., prof. pub. health scis. Wake Forest U. Sch. Medicine, Winston-Salem, NC, 1995—2001, sr. assoc. dean, 1997—2001; assoc. v.p. health sci. rsch. Pa. State U., 2002—, vice dean rsch. coll. medicine, 2002—. Contbr. articles to profl. jours. Served to lt. comdr. USPHS. Recipient Meritorious award William A. Jump Meml. Found., 1977, Dir.'s award NIH, 1978, Superior Svc. award USPHS, 1980, performance awards Sr. Exec. Svc., Presdl. Meritorious Exch.

Rank award 1989, Disting. Svc. award HHS, 1991, Disting. Svc. award Nat. Inst. on Deafness and Other Comm. Disorders, 1994. Mem. AAAS, Soc. Exptl. Biology and Medicine, N.C. Inst. Medicine. Jewish. Home: 7908 Lasley Forest Dr Lewisville NC 27023-8244 Office: Penn State College Medicine 500 Univ Drive Hershey PA 17033 E-mail: jmoskowitz@psu.edu.

MOSKOWITZ, JOEL STEVEN, lawyer; b. N.Y.C., Jan. 14, 1947; s. Jack I. and Myra (Shor) M.; m. Anna Boucher; children: David, Michael, Ellen. BA, UCLA, 1967, JD, 1970. Bar: Calif. 1971, U.S. Ct. Appeals (9th cir.) 1971, U.S. Ct. Appeals (D.C. cir.) 1975, U.S. Supreme Ct. 1975, U.S. Ct. Appeals (2d cir.) 1979. Dep. atty. gen. Calif. Dept. Justice, Sacramento, 1970-83; dep. dir. Calif. Dept. Health Svcs., 1983-85; of counsel Gibson, Dunn & Crutcher, L.A., 1985-88, ptnr., 1988-96, Moskowitz, Brestoff, Winston & Blinderman LLP, 1996—. Author: Environmental Liability in Real Property Transactions, 1995; contbr. articles to legal publs. Mem. Phi Beta Kappa. Office: 1880 Century Park E Ste 350 Los Angeles CA 90067-1603 E-mail: jsm6@ix.netcom.com.

MOSKOWITZ, MICHAEL ARTHUR, neuroscientist, neurologist; b. N.Y.C., May 26, 1942; s. Irving Lawrence and Clara (Dranoff) M.; m. Mary Henderson, May 18, 1991; 1 child, Jenna Rachel. AB, Johns Hopkins U., 1964; MD, Tufts U., 1968; MSc (hon.), Harvard U., 1992. Diplomate Am. Bd. Psychiaty and Neurology, Am. Bd. Internal Medicine. Intern Yale U. Dept. Medicine, 1968-69, resident, 1969-71; resident in neurology Peter Bent Brigham Children Hosp., 1971-74; asst. prof. Med. Sch., Harvard U., Boston, 1975-79, assoc. prof., 1979-92; prof. divsn. health sci. and tech. Harvard-MIT, 1992—. Established investigator Am. Heart Assn., 1980-85; neurophysiologist and assoc. neurologist Mass. Gen. Hosp., Boston, 1981—; H.J. Barnett lectr. Canadian Heart Assn., Queens U., Kingston, Ont., 1993—, Witter lectr. U. Calif., San Francisco, 1994—, Barraquer-LaFora lectr. Spanish Neurol. Soc., Barcelona, Spain, 1994—, Decade of the Brain lectr. Am. Acad. Neurology, 1995, Briggs lecture dept. pharmacology U. Tex., San Antonio, 1995, Richardson lectr. Canadian Neurol. Assn., 1998, John Graham lectr. Am. Assn. Study Headache, Merck Sharpe Dohme Neurosci. lectr. Birmingham, Eng., 2000; chmn. sci. adv. bd. Max Plank Inst., Kön; program project dir. stroke and migraine NIH program projects, NIH rev. study sect. mem. 1982-85, 88-91, 97—; 2nd internat. hon. lectureship European Stroke Conf., 1997; cons. pharm. industry; chmn. sci. adv. bd. Max Planck Inst., U. of Ottawa, Can., Queen's Neuroscience Inst.; scientific adv. bd. Queen's Med. Ctr., Honolulu, U. Ottawa. Editl. bd. Stroke, Acta Neurol. Scandinavica Cephalalgia, Jour. Cerebral Blood Flow & Metabolism, Cerebrovascular Disease; editor: Animal Models of Headache, 1996; basic sci. editor Stroke (AHA jour.); contbr. numerous articles to profl. jours; patentee in field. MIT postdoctoral fellow, 1974-76, Alfred Sloan Found. fellow, 1978-80; recipient Enrico Greppi award Italian Neurology Soc., 1986, 88, Tchr.-Investigator award Nat. Inst. Neurol. Disease and Stroke, 1975-80, Zülch prize Max-Planck Soc./Inst., 1996, John Graham award AASH, 1998; rsch. grantee Bristol-Myers Squibb, 1993—, MGH Interdepartmental Stroke Ctr. Mem. Am. Heart Assn. (nat. rsch. com. 1991-96, exec. com. stroke coun. 1991-96), Am. Neurol. Assn., Am. Heart and Stroke Assn. (co-chair program com. 2001—), Am. Acad. Neurology, Am. Pain Soc., Soc. Neurosci., Internat. Soc. for Cerebral Blood Flow and Metabolism (bd. dirs., pres. 2001—), Internat. Symposium Pharm. of Cerebral Ischemia, Can. Neurol. Soc. (hon.). Achievements include research in neuro-scientific, neurology literature including stroke and migraine. Office: Mass Gen Hosp Charleston Navy Yard 149 13th St Charlestown MA 02129-2020

MOSKOWITZ, ROLAND WALLACE, internist; b. Shamokin, Pa., Nov. 3, 1929; MD, Temple U., 1953. Intern Temple U. Hosp., Phila., 1953-54; fellow in internal medicine Mayo Clinic, Rochester, Minn., 1954-55, 57-60; mem. staff U. Hosps. Cleve.; prof. medicine Case Western Res. U. Sch. Medicine, Cleve. Mem.: ACR, Alpha Omega Alpha. Office: Parkway Med Ctr Ste 307 3609 Park East Dr Beachwood OH 44122 E-mail: rolliemoskowitz@aol.com.

MOSKOWITZ, STANLEY ALAN, financial executive; b. N.Y.C., June 8, 1956; s. Sol and Kate (Mermelstein) M.; m. Eve Kronenberger, Sept. 20, 1981; children: Alana, Kate. BA, Queens Coll., 1978; MBA in Fin., St. John's U., 1980. Sr. credit analyst Mfrs. Hanover Leasing Corp., N.Y.C., 1979-81; gen. ptnr. Exec. Leasing Co., 1981-83; pres. Execulease Corp., Elmont, N.Y., 1983-97; pres., CEO QuestTech Fin. LLC, Danbury, Conn., 1997—. Bd. dirs. UFA/Fedn. of Greenwich, Conn., 1995—, treas., 1997—. Mem. Ea. Assn. Equipment Lessors (chmn. pub. rels. 1985-90, bd. dirs. 1988-92, Meretorious Svc. award 1986-87, chmn. ethics com. 1991-92), Omicron Delta Epsilon. Republican. Jewish. Avocations: reading, cycling. Office: QuesTech Fin LLC 98 Mill Plain Rd Danbury CT 06811-6101 E-mail: sammy@qtfc.com.

MOSKOWITZ, STUART STANLEY, lawyer; b. N.Y.C., Aug. 27, 1955; s. Arthur Appel and Rebecca (Gordon) M. BS magna cum laude, SUNY, Albany, 1977; JD with honors, Union U., Albany, 1981; LLM, NYU, 1990. Bar: N.Y. 1982, U.S. Tax Ct. 1983, U.S. Dist. Ct. (so. dist.) N.Y. 1985. Law clk. to presiding judge U.S. Tax Ct., Washington, 1981-83, U.S. Ct. Appeals for 2d cir., N.Y.C., 1983-84; sr. counsel IBM, Armonk, N.Y., 1984—. Research asst. fin. SUNY Sch. of Bus., Albany, 1976-77, corp. law Albany Law Sch., 1980-81; instr. acctg. Ednl. Opportunities Program SUNY, Albany, 1977-78. Tax counselor for elderly Am. Assn. Ret. Persons, Westchester County, N.Y., Corp. Lawyers of Svc. to the Elderly, Westchester County Legal Svcs., N.Y. Mem. ABA, Order of Justinian. Home: 153 Princeton Dr Hartsdale NY 10530-2010 Office: IBM New Orchard Rd Armonk NY 10504 E-mail: smoskowi@us.ibm.com.

MOSLER, JOHN, retired financial planner; b. N.Y.C., Sept. 24, 1922; s. Edwin H. and Irma M.; children: Bruce Elliot, John Edwin, Michele Andree. Student, Philips Exeter Acad., 1938-41, Princeton U., 1941-43; L.H.D., Fordham U., 1965; D.C.S., Duquesne U., 1968. With Mosler Safe Co., 1945-67, exec. v.p., 1948-61, pres., 1961-66, chmn., 1966-67; pres., dir. Mosler Lock Co., 1953-67, Mosler de Mexico S.A., 1953-67; exec. v.p., dir. Mosler Research Products, Inc., 1956-67; dir. 1st Caribbean Mainland Capital Co., Inc., 1962-68, chmn. bd., 1963-68, pres., 1966-68; v.p., dir. Am. Standard Inc., 1967-68; chmn. bd., dir., chief exec. officer Holmes Protection, Inc., 1968-73, Holmes Protection Services Corp., 1968-73; chmn. bd. Hidromex, S.A. de C.V., Mex., 1968—, Mosler N.V., Europe, 1973—, Internat. Controls Corp., 1973-87, resigned, 1987. Past chmn. bd. Royal Bus. Funds Inc.; pres. Mosler Investments. Mem. Mayor's Com. on Judiciary; pres. Am.-Romanian Flood Relief Com.; past dir. Jr. Achievement N.Y.; spl. U.S. amb. to Mauritius, to Zambia's Indpendence ceremony; vice chmn. N.Y. Rep. County Com.; chmn. John Mosler Found.; trustee, dir. Nat. Urban League; trustee Appeal of Conscience Found., Linden Hall Sch. for Girls, Lititz, Pa.; hon. trustee, past pres. N.Y. Urban League; founder Harlem Prep. Sch. With CIC, AUS, 1943-46. Decorated knight comdr. Ordo Supremus Militaris A. Lilio Regni Navarrae; Sovereign Order Hospitallers St. John of Jerusalem, Knights of Malta; comdt. L'Ordre Senegal; recipient Man of Conscience award Appeal of Conscience Found., 1969 Mem. Young Pres.'s Orgn. (past pres.), U.S. C. of C., N.Y. World Bus. Coun., Bankers of Mex. Club (Mex.)., Princeton U. (N.Y.), Confrerie des Chevaliers du Tastevin, Manhattan, Real Nautico de Barcelona (Spain), Sag Harbor Yacht, Univ. Club, Wall St. Club.

MOSLEY, ALISA GALE, legal administrator; b. Spartanburg, S.C., Dec. 16, 1956; d. J.L. and Evelyn (Edwards) M.; m. Thomas Joseph Kosmata, Apr. 8, 1989; 1 child, Lane marie Mosley Kosmata. BA, U. S.C., Columbia, 1977, MEd, 1980. Career svcs. dir. Coastal Carolina U., Conway, S.C., 1981-85; placement dir. U. S.C., Columbia, 1985-99; exec. dir. S.C. Law Enforcement Officers Assn., 1999—. Cons. U. S.C. Daniel Mgmt. Ctr., Columbia, 1995—; dir. S.C. law Enforcement Hall of Fame, Columbia, 1999—, S.C. Safe Kids, Columbia, 1999—, Operation Lifesaver, Columbia, 1999—. Author: (weekly column) The State Newspaper; contbr. articles to local papers. Champion Palmetto-Richland Childrens Hosp., Columbia, S.C., 2000. Recipient Star award Southeastern Assn. Coll. Employers, 2000, Legis. award Mothers Against Drunk Driving, Columbia, S.C., 2000. Mem. ASAE, S.C. Soc. Assn. Execs., Internat. Chiefs of Police, Toastmasters. Episcopalian. Office: 7339 Broad River Rd Irmo SC 29063 E-mail: scleoa@scleoa.org.

MOSLEY, EVERETT L. federal agency administrator; m. Alice Mosley; 1 child Damian. B Acctg., Crambling State U. From entry level to asst. inspector gen. audit USDA, Washington, 1969—80, regional inspector gen. audit, 1980—88; deputy asst. inspector gen. audit USDA/OIG, 1988—94; deputy inspector gen. USAID, 1994—2000, inspector gen., 2000—. Office: USAID RRB 1300 Pennsylvania Ave NW Washington DC 20523-2901*

MOSLEY, GLENN RICHARD, religious organization administrator, minister; b. Akron, Ohio, May 23, 1935; s. James Garfield and Viola Mildred (Wiseman) M.; m. Martha Lorella Mitchell, July 17, 1952; children: Glenn R. Jr., Tracey, Susan, Kristin, Robert. BA, MA, Wayne State U., 1974; PhD, Walden U., 1976; MS in Adminstrn., Cen. Mich. U., 1991; DD (hon.), Unity Sch. Christianity, Kansas City, Mo., 1976. Ordained to ministry Unity Ch., 1961. Letter writer, student min. Silent Unity Prayer Soc., Kansas City, Mo., 1957-59; min. Unity Ch., Flushing, N.Y., 1959-64, Des Moines, 1964-65, co-min. N.Y.C., 1965-68; min. Unity Temple, Detroit, 1968-75, Unity Ch., Akron, 1975-85; pres., CEO Assn. Unity Chs., Lee's Summit, Mo., 1985—. Author, co-author of nine books; mem. editl. staff Jour. Thanatology, 1966-76; contbr. numerous articles and monographs to profl. jours. Mem. AAAS, John Templeton Found. (Sewanee, Tenn., judge for Templeton prize for progress in religion), Rep. Presdl. Coun. Office: Assn Unity Chs 401 SW Oldham Pkwy Lees Summit MO 64081-2747 *The Religious Truth message we teach is eternal, and the techniques for teaching it work best for me when I develope new ways to teach which meet a great diversity of learning styles. There are almost zero days left in the current millennium; what an exciting period in which to live and teach.*

MOSLEY, JESSIE BRYANT, retired science educator; b. Houston, Nov. 30, 1903; d. William and Emma Bryant; m. Charles Clint Mosley (dec.); children: Charles Mosley, Jr., Gene Lavell, Wilma Emma Clopton. LHD, BS, Jarvis Christian Coll.; LHD (hon.) , Tougaloo Coll.; lifetime tchr.'s cert. Cert. libr. sci. Teen cons. YWCA, Jackson, Miss., 1950—60; bank teller State Mut. Fed. Savs. and Loan, 1960—65; tchr. Jackson Pub. Schs., 1965—70; founder Smith Robertson Mus. and Cultural Ctr., 1970, dir., 1970—90, mus. dir., 1970—90. Author: The Negro In Mississippi History, 1950, The History of the Women's Movement in Mississippi, 1978. State convener Nat. Coun. Negro Women, Jackson, 1977—2001; mem. LeFleur's Bluff Links, 1970, 100 Black Women, Jackson, 1990, Miss. Humanities Coun., Jackson, 1990; founder Farish St. Dist. Neighborhood Found., 1980; mem. Jackson Urban League, 1967, Nat. Bus. League, Jackson, 1968, Integrated Ch. Women United, Jackson, 1960, Fedn. of Colored Women's Clubs, Jackson, 1950; chmn. Iwy, 1977; chaperone Y-Teens, 1950. Named Dr. Jessie B. Mosley Health and Human Services Bldg., Hinds County, 1990, Dr.Jessie B. Mosley St., City of Jackson, 1990, Disting. Black Citizen, U. Miss., 1990, Mary McCleod Bethune Living Legend, NCNW, 1998; recipient Carter G. Woodson award, NEA, Outstanding and Dedicated Svc. award, NCNW, 1978, Disting. Svc. to Religious and Civic Orgn. award, United Christian Ch., 1984, Outsanding Leadership award, NCNW, 1996, Outstanding Achievement-Civics, Arts and Culture award, NOBW, 1998-1999, Years of Endearing and Committed Svc. award, Nat. Coun. of Negro Women, 2000, Resolution for Life-Long Svc. award, NCNW, 2000, Cmty. Partners award, State Instns. Higher Learning bd. trustees, 2000. Mem.: AAUW, Alpha Kappa Alpha (hon. Dedicated Svc. to Cmty. 1986). Home: 1968 Wingfield Cir Jackson MS 39209-7101*

MOSLEY, MARY ALMA KREHBIEL, freelance writer/editor, lobbyist; b. Nampa, Idaho, Sept. 29, 1943; d. Benjamin Jacob and Mary Emma (Smith) Krehbiel; m. Jack B. Mosley, Sept. 4, 1965; 1 child, Benjamin Carson. BA, U. Puget Sound, 1964; MA, U. Mo., 1969, PhD, 1976. Instr. Westminster Coll., Fulton, Mo., 1966-68; prof. Shimer Coll., Mt. Carroll, Ill., 1975-77; instr. Ohio State U., Columbus, 1977-80; editor Scott, Foresman & Co., Glenview, Ill., 1981-84; freelance editor and writer Fulton, 1984—; lobbyist Mo. NOW, Jefferson City, 1993—2002. Adj. prof. Spanish Lincoln U., Jefferson City, 2001, William Woods U., Fulton, Mo., 2002; legis. dir. Mo. Equal Rights Amendment Campaign, Jefferson City,, 1999—; bd. dirs. Mo. Family Health Coun., Jefferson city, 1990—, treas., 1996-98. Author: (textbook) Paso a Paso 3, 1996. Mem. Mo. Women's Coun., Jefferson City, 1994-2000; chair Mo. Alliance for Choice, Kirksville, 1997-98. Recipient Leadership award, Mo. Women's Network, 1992, Annual award, 1998, Individual Non-Educator Equity award St. Louis Ednl. Equity Consortium, 1995. Mem. NOW (state coord. 1990-93, nat. bd. dirs. 1994-98, regional dir. 1996-98), Mo. Women's Network (legis. chair), Women's Polit. Caucus, Learning Disabilities Assn. (pres. Columbia affiliate 1995-96). Democrat. Avocations: tatting, sewing, knitting. Home: 1010 Vine St Fulton MO 65251-2305 E-mail: mmosley@coin.org.

MOSLEY, MARY MAC, retired librarian; b. Rome, Nov. 11, 1926; d. William McKinley and Mary (Caldwell) H.; m. Samuel A. Mosley, June 12, 1946 (div. 1964); children: Samuel A. Jr., Pamela Ann, James Irwin. Student, Ga. State Coll. for Women, 1943-45; BS, Auburn U., 1947; cert. in teaching, Athens Coll., 1963; M in Library, Emory U., 1968. Tchr. sci. Rome City Schs., 1964-66; extension libr. Tri-County Regional Libr., 1966-67; libr. Shorter Coll., 1967-68, assoc. prof. libr. sci., 1968-76, dir. libr. svcs., 1968-93. Corr. sec. Rome Symphony Women's Guild; pres., ch. historian, v.p. Christian Women's Fellowship, 1st Christian Ch., 1998—; corr. sec. Rome Symphony Women's Assn., v.p., 1996-99, pres., 1999—; vol. Good Neighbor Ministry, ARC, Rome Floyd County Libr. Mem. ALA, AAUW (pres. Rome br.), N. Ga. Assn. Librs., Ga. Libr. Assn., Christian Women's Fellowship, Coosa Country Club, Delta Kappa Gamma. Democrat. Mem. Christian Ch. Avocations: piano, reading, gardening. Home: 205 Benton Dr Rome GA 30165-1703

MOSLEY, RAYMOND A. federal agency administrator; b. Greenville, Miss., July 27, 1947; s. Raymond Clay and Grace Elizabeth (Correro) M.; m. Julia A. Fisk. BA, Miss. State U., 1969; postgrad., Georgetown U. Dir. Records Appraisal Disposition Divsn., Nat. Archives, 1981-84; dep. asst. archivist Fed. Records Ctrs., 1984-89, chief of staff, 1989-94; asst. archivist Spl. and Regional Archives, 1994-96; dir. Fed. Register, 1996—. Office: Nat Archives and Records Adminstrn 800 N Capitol St NW Washington DC 20408-0001 E-mail: raymondamosley@hotmail.com., ray.mosley@fedreg.nara.gov.

MOSLEY, SHELLEY ELIZABETH, library administrator; b. Baxter Springs, Kans., Sept. 8, 1950; d. Billy Ralph and Jennie Naomi Burrell; m. David Ray Mosley, Mar. 26, 1971; children: Andrew Scott, Jessica Rae. BS in Edn., Grand Canyon U., 1971; MLS, U. Ariz., 1977. Instr. Grad. Libr. Sch. U. Ariz., Tucson, 1976-78, 92; sch. libr. Tucson Unified, 1977-78, Glendale (Ariz.) Elem. Sch., 1978-79; libr. Glendale Pub. Libr., 1979-85, libr. mgr., 1985—. Author: (novels) Talk About Love, 1999, It's in His Kiss, 1999, One Starry Night, 2000, My Favorite Flavor, 2000, What Do I Read Next?, 1999, What Do I Read Next? Vol. 1-2, 2000, 2001, What Do I Read Next? Vol. 1, 2002, Romancing the Holidays, 2001; columnist: newspaper Glendale Star, 1999—2000, reviewer: Booklist, reviewer: Library Jour.; editor (tech.): Selecting Library Furniture, 1989; contbr. articles to profl. jours. Chair benchmarking team City of Glendale, 1993-95, co-chair diversity task force, 1999—, mem. diversity task force, 1996—, visionary Magnetic Mile Project, 1990; co-founder Show Them a Better Way, Glendale, 1993-95; bd. dirs. Mayor's Alliance for Youth, Glendale, 1994-2000; adult participant Youth Town Hall, Glendale, 1994—; mem. gifted edn. task force Glendale Elem. Schs., 1991-93, mem. textbook adoption com., 1989; soprano First United Meth. Ch., 1997—; mem. Friends of the Glendale Libr., 1985—. Mem.: Soc. Children's Book Writers and Illustrators, Romance Writers Am. (program chair Valley of the Sun chpt. 1998—2001, v.p. 2002, Librarian of Yr. award 2001), Maricopa Assn. Govts. (prevention/intervention task force 1996—), Ariz. State Libr. Assn. (sec.-treas. pub. libr. divsn. 1980—, conf. co-chair 1988), Beta Phi Mu, Alpha Chi Omega, Alpha Lambda Delta. Democrat. Methodist. Avocations: writing lyrics, writing limericks, playing the piano, singing, reading. Home: 8619 N 53rd Dr Glendale AZ 85302-4847 Office: Velma Teague Libr 7010 N 58th Ave Glendale AZ 85301-2425 E-mail: smosley@ci.glendale.az.us.

MOSLEY, WILLIAM HARRY, JR. public affairs specialist; b. Richmond, Va., Dec. 29, 1955; s. William Harry Sr. and Amy Thompson Mosley; m. Lisa Gaye Dowden, Apr. 1, 1990. BA in Polit. Sci. and Russian Area Studies, U. Richmond, 1978; MA in Journalism, U. Md., 1983. Audio technician Va. Voice, Richmond, 1978-79; gen. mgr. N.E. Ind. Radio Reading Svc., Ft. Wayne, 1979-80; pub. affairs clk. U.S. Dept. Transp., Washington, 1982-87, pub. affairs specialist, 1987—. Columnist: Prince George's Jour., 2001—; contbr. articles to polit. jours.; mem. editl. com.: Dem. Left Mag., 1997—. Chair D.C./Md./N.E. Va. Dem. Socialists of Am., Washington, 1984-86, 88-90, 93-95; adv. neighborhood commr. D.C. Govt., 1999-2001, chair adv. neighborhood commn., 1999-2001. Avocations: travel, reading, theater. Office: US Dept Transp 400 7th St SW Washington DC 20590 E-mail: billmosley@starpower.net.

MOSORA-STAN, FLORENTINA IOANA, physics educator; b. Cluj, Romania, Jan. 7, 1940; arrived in Belgium, 1968; d. Oprea and Cornelia (Stanescu) M.; m. Stephan Stan, Jan. 22, 1977; 1 child, Guy Bart. B in Biol. Sci. with highest distinction, U. Bucharest, Romania, 1961, B in Phys. Sci. with highest distinction, 1967, PhD in Biophysics cum laude, 1971. Cert. biologist and physicist. Rsch. fellow U. Bucharest, 1967-71, U. Liege, Belgium, 1971-74, maitre de conferences Belgium, 1974-75; head rsch. fellow Inst. Physics, U. Liege, Belgium, 1975-79, lectr. Belgium, 1979-88, prof. Belgium, 1988—. Author: Elements of General Physics and Biophysics, vol. 1, 1974, vol. 2, 1975, Introduction to the Mechanics of Physiologic Fluids, 1984-85, Mechanics of Microcirculation, 1990: Editor: Biomechanical Transport Processes, 1991. Mem. European Med. Rsch. Coun. Devel. of Resch. in Nutrition and Stable Isotopes, 1991—. Decorated officer Ordre of Leopold II, (Belgium), 1981, comdr. Ordre de la Couronne (Belgium, 1992; recipient Agathon de Potter prize Royal Acad. Belgium, 1982. Mem. Stareso Oceanographic Rsch. Calvi (sci. coun. 1987—), Isotopes Stables (v.p. 1987—), Inst. Recherches Marines et Interactions Air-Mer (pres. 1989—), Hemo Liege (founder), Belgian Soc. Biophysics, Internat. Soc. Rsch. Circulation and Environ. Diseases, N.Y. Acad. Scis. Roman Catholic. Avocations: swimming, gymnastics. Home: Residence Verdi Av Blonden 7 4000 Liège Belgium Office: U Liege Inst Physics B5 4000 Liège Belgium

MOSQUEIRA, CHARLOTTE MARIANNE, dietitian; b. L.A., July 26, 1937; d. Leo and Magdalene Tollefson; children: Mark, Michael. BA, St. Olaf Coll., 1959; postgrad., U. Oreg. Med. Sch., 1959-60; MA, Ctrl. Mich. U., 1980. Registered dietitian. Dir. dietetics Riverside Meth. Hosp., Columbus, Ohio, 1977-79; dir. nutrition and food svcs. Fresno (Calif.) Cmty. Hosp. and Med. Ctr., 1980-91; mem. faculty Dept. Enology and Food Sci. Calif. State U., Fresno, 1984-93; dir. nutritional svcs. Emanuel Med. Ctr., Turlock, Calif., 1991-97, Bapt. Health Med. Ctr., Little Rock. Mem. Am. Dietetic Assn., Calif. Dietetic Assn. Lutheran. E-mail: charlotte500@msn.com.

MOSS, AMBLER HOLMES, JR. lawyer, former ambassador; b. Balt., Sept. 1, 1937; s. Ambler Holmes and Dorothea Dandridge (Williams) M.; m. Serena Welles, May 6, 1972; children: Ambler H., Benjamin Sumner, Serena Montserrat, Nicholas George Oliver. BA, Yale U., 1960; JD, George Washington U., 1970. Bar: D.C., Fla. Joined Fgn. Svc., Dept. State, 1964; vice consul Barcelona, 1964-66; adviser U.S. del. to OAS, 1966-69; Spanish desk officer Dept. State, Washington, 1968-70; assoc. Coudert Bros., 1971-73, resident atty. Brussels, 1973-76; mem. U.S. Negotiating Team for Panama Canal treaties, 1977; dep. asst. Sec. of State, Washington, 1977-78; amb. to Panama, Am. Embassy, Panama City, 1978-82; of counsel Greenberg, Traurig, LLP, Miami, 1982-87, 95—; prof., dir. North-South Ctr. U. Miami, Fla., 1984—, dean Grad. Sch. Internat. Studies, 1984-94. Bd. dirs. Espirito Santo Bank of Fla. Mem. Panama Canal Consultative Com., 1995-2000. With USN, 1960-64. Mem. ABA, Am. Soc. Internat. Law, Inter-Am. Bar Assn., Am. Fgn. Svc. Assn., Coun. Fgn. Rels., Am. Legion, Inter-Am. Dialogue (Washington), Navy League, Greater Miami C. of C. (gov. 1983-86), Royal Inst. Internat. Affairs (London), Internat. Inst. Strategic Studies (London), Army and Navy Club, Order of the Coif. Address: 5711 San Vicente St Coral Gables FL 33146-2724 E-mail: ahmoss@miami.edu.

MOSS, ANDREA, fundraiser, community service volunteer; b. Balt., Feb. 19, 1943; d. Manuel and Sylvia (Fox) Schwartz; m. Paul Moss, Oct. 23, 1966; Danielle Lea, Kevin Scott, Shara Alyse. BS, U. Md., 1965. N.E. regional charge de presse Chaine des Rotisseurs, 1993—96; com. mem. Women's Campaign Fund Party of Your Choice, 2001—02. Restaurant critic and writer: Gastronome, 1987; bd. advisors Insider's Guide to Florida Restaurants. Pres. Svc. League, Monmouth Med. Ctr., Long Branch, N.J., 1971-73; corr. sec., ball chmn. Ruth Newman Shapiro Cancer and Heart Fund, Atlantic City, N.J., 1977—, com. mem. The Faberge Collection with Resorts, Atlantic City, 2000; bd. dirs., mem. fine arts com. Congregation Beth Israel, Northfield, N.J., 1977—; mem. Atlantic City Med. Ctr. Aus.; co-chmn. Shore chpt. World Affairs Coun., Phila. and Atlantic City, 1985—; nat. bd. dirs., founder, chmn. Atlantic City chpt. Am. Assocs. Ben Gurion U. of Negev, 1986-2002; co-chmn. Pro-Am LPGA Atlantic City Classic Golf Tournament, 1985—; mem. nat. hostess com. Miss Am. Pageant, Atlantic City, 1989-96; mem. hostess com. Miss Am. Pagent, 1989--2002; mem. nat. gastronome advt. com. Chaine des Rotisseurs, 1990—; mem. com. Save Our Strength, 1988; mem. spl. gifts com. United Way Atlantic County, 1989-90; host Dine for Dimes event March of Dimes; mem. devel. com. Noyes Mus.; mem. Jewish Agy. Com. Atlantic County, Breast Health Inst., Phila., Hadassah and Nat. Coun. Jewish Women, Asbury Park, N.J., 1971-75; chmn. gala for RNS designer showhouse, 1992-99; mem. inspection team Dirona Award, Am. Express; mem. com. on wine/jazz festival Sta. WJHU, Nat. Pub. Radio, 1994; mem. com. on Asian tour luncheon Balt. Symphony Orch., 1994; mem. Beaux Art Ball com. Balt. Mus. Art, 1995; mem. treasure chest com. Mt. Washington Pediat. Found., 1995; angel Balt. Sch. Arts Found., 1995; mem. bd. govs. Israel Bonds, Balt., 1995-97; com. mem. Women's Campaign Fund, N.Y.C., 1998; mem. com. LPGA's Taste of the LPGA, 1999, 2000. Named Showstopper of Yr., The Sun Newspaper, Atlantic City, 1985; officer chargé de presse La Chaine des Rotisseurs, 1991, N.E. Region, 1994—, L'Ordre Mondial, Dirona inspector Am. Express, 1994—; recipient Negev award Ben Gurion U., 1997, Recognition of Achievement award Chaine des Rolisseure, 1999. Mem. AAUW, Am. Acad. Restaurant and Hospitality Scis. (founding trustee), Sigma Delta Tau (chpt. historian, Most Outstanding Mem. 1965). Republican. Home: 204 Arbor Ct E Linwood NJ 08221-2152

MOSS, ARTHUR HENSHEY, lawyer; b. Reading, Pa., July 26, 1930; s. John Arthur and Christine Bracken (Henshey) M.; m. E. Leslie Fritz, Feb. 1982; 1 child by previous marriage, John Arthur. AB, Williams Coll., 1952; JD, U. Pa., 1955. Bar: Pa. 1956. Assoc. Montgomery, McCracken, Walker & Rhoads, Phila., 1960-69, ptnr., 1969-2000, of counsel, 2000—. Editor U. Pa. Law Rev., 1953-55; contbr. articles to profl. jours. Chmn. Radnor-Haverford-Marple Sewer Authority, 1968-83; pres. Wayne Civic Assn., 1964-65; steward, deacon Wayne Presbyn. Ch., 1963-66, ruling elder, 1966-72, 79-84, 89-95, clk. of session, 1973-74, 78-79, trustee, 1987-93; commr. Gen. Assembly Presbyn. Ch. (U.S.A.), 1983; bd. dirs. John Bartram Assn., 1987-2002, treas., 1989—, emeritus dir., 2002-; trustee Presbytery of Phila., 1984, 94-2001, treas., 1996-2001; trustee Radnor Twp. Meml. Libr., 2001—. Lt. USN, 1955-60. Mem. Radnor Hist. Soc. (dir., sec. 1978-90), Broadacres Trouting Assn., Athenaeum of Phila., Merion Golf Club, Edgemere Club. Home: 200 Walnut Ave Wayne PA 19087-3423 Office: Montgomery McCracken Walker & Rhoads 123 S Broad St Philadelphia PA 19109-1099 E-mail: wwwwesq@aol.com.

MOSS, ARTHUR JAY, physician; b. White Plains, N.Y., June 21, 1931; s. Abraham Loeb and Ida (Bank) M.; m. Joy Folkman, June 23, 1957; children: Katherine, Deborah, David. BA, Yale U., 1953; MD, Harvard U., 1957. Resident Mass. Gen. Hosp., 1957-58, 60-61; fellow in cardiology med. ctr. U. Rochester, N.Y., 1961-65, from asst. to assoc. prof. sch. medicine and dentistry, 1966-71, clin. assoc. prof., 1971-82, clin. prof., 1982-91, prof. medicine, 1991—, dir. heart rsch. follow-up program med. ctr., 1971—. Mem. cardiology adv. com. Nat. Heart, Lung, and Blood Inst., NIH, 1980-82, chmn., 1982-84, mem. epidemiology and disease control study sect., 1998—. Author: Antiarrhythmic Agents, 1973; editor: Clinical Aspects of Life-threatening Arrhythmias, 1984, QT Prolongation and Ventricular Arrhythmias, 1992, Noninvasive Electrocardiology, 1995; editor-in-chief Ann. Noninvasive Electrocardiology, 1996—; mem. editl. bd. Am. Jour. Cardiology, 1988—, Jour. Am. Coll. Cardiology, 1997-2001. Lt. USNR, 1958-60. Mem. Assn. Am. Physicians, Alpha Omega Alpha. Home: 581 Claybourne Rd Rochester NY 14618-1224 Office: Univ Rochester Med Ctr PO Box 653 Rochester NY 14642-8653 E-mail: heartajm@heart.rochester.edu.

MOSS, BARBARA GAE, education educator; b. Akron, Ohio, Apr. 7, 1950; d. Bruce E. and Gae C. (Caldren) Kesselring; m. Patrick L. Moss, June 25, 1988; 1 child, Brian Singleton. BEd, Ohio State U., 1971; MEd, Kent State U., 1975, PhD, 1988. Cert. educator, Ohio. Tchr. Crestwood Schs., Mantua, Ohio,

1971-81; elem. cons. Portage County Bd. Edn., Ravenna, 1981-88; asst. prof. U. Akron, 1988-94, assoc. prof., 1994-99, prof., 1999—2001; rsch. assoc. Comprehensive Assessment Sys. for Adult Students San Diego State U., 2001—. Profl. devel. editor; reading tchr.; cons. Barbara Moss Cons., Stow, Ohio, 1988—. Assoc. editor Reading Tchr., 1992-94; contbr. articles to profl. jours. Co-pres. Literacy Educators and Advocates, Columbus, Ohio. Recipient scholarship Delta Kappa Gamma, 1987. Mem. Nat. Coun. on Rsch. in English, Internat. Reading Assn., Coll. Reading Assn., Nat. Coun. Tchrs. English, Phi Delta Kappa (co-editor newsletter 1994). Avocations: reading, travel. Home: 4327 Goldfinch St San Diego CA 92103-1315 E-mail: bmoss4327@cox.net.

MOSS, BEN FRANK, III, art educator, painter; b. Phila., Feb. 28, 1936; s. B. Frank Jr. and Helen Charlotte (Figge) M.; m. Jean Marilyn Russel, Aug. 26, 1960; children: Jennifer Kathleen, Benjamin Franklin IV. BA, Whitworth Coll., 1959; postgrad., Princeton Theol. Seminary, 1959-60; MFA, Boston U., 1963; MA (hon.), Dartmouth Coll., 1993; studied with Walter Murch, Karl Fortess and Herman Keys. Instr. Gonzaga U., Spokane, Wash., 1964-65; assoc. prof., dir. MFA and vis. artist program Fort Wright Coll., 1965-72; acting dean, co-founder Spokane Studio Sch., 1972-74; prof. painting and drawing Sch. Art and Art History U. Iowa, Iowa City, 1975-88; George Frederick Jewett prof. art Dartmouth Coll., Hanover, N.H., 1993—. Chmn. studio art dept. Dartmouth Coll., Hanover, 1988-94, Vt. Studio Ctr., Johnson, 1990; area head painting U. Iowa, 1985; artist-in-residence Queens Coll., U. Melbourne, Australia, 1993-94; vis. artist, lectr. Northwest Mo. State U., Maryville, 1996, Houghton (N.Y.) Coll., 1996, Gordon Coll., Wenham, Mass., 1996, Northwestern U., Evanston, Ill., 1997, Colo. State U., Ft. Collins, 1997, Ravenscroft Sch., Raleigh, N.C., 1997, Coe Coll., Cedar Rapids, Iowa, 1998, numerous others. Represented by Pepper Gallery, Boston, Francine Seders Gallery, Ltd., Seattle, Susan Conway Galleries, Washington; one-man shows include Susan Conway Galleries, 1990, Dartmouth Coll., 1989, 94, Kraushaar Galleries, 1981, 83, 87, Swarthmore Coll., Pa., 1984, Stony Brook (N.Y.) Sch., 1982, Saint-Gaudens, Picture Gallery, Cornish, N.H., 1981, Kans. State U., 1980, Francine Seders Gallery, Seattle, 1979, 82, 99, Hudson D. Walker Gallery, Fine Arts Work Ctr., Provincetown, Mass., 1978, Arnot Art Mus., Elmira, N.Y., 1977, Kirkland Coll., Clinton, N.Y., 1977, Juniper Tree Gallery, Spokane, 1975, Middlebury (Vt.) Coll., 1971, Seligman Gallery, Seattle, 1967, 69, Cheney Cowels Meml. Mus., Spokane, 1967, Loomis Chaffee Sch., 1995, Tasis England Am. Sch., 1994, Queens Coll., U. Melbourne, 1994, Houghton Coll., 1996, Gordon Coll., 1996, N. W. Mo. State U., 1996, Brattleboro Mus. and Art Ctr., 1995, Nat. Acad. and Design, 1995, Messiah Coll., 1995, Phillips Exeter Acad., 1995, Susan Conway Galleries, 1993, 96, Chase Gallery City Hall, Spokane, 1993, Colby-Sawyer Coll., New London, N.H., 1992, Idaho State U., Pocatello, 1972, Kraushaar Galleries, 1978—, exhibited in group shows at Blair Acad., Blairstown, N.J., 1996, Albright Knox Gallery, Buffalo, N.Y., 1995-96, Smith Coll., North Hampton, Pa., 1996, Nat. Acad. Design, N.Y.C., 1995, Boston U., 1995, Brattleboro (Vt.) Mus. and Art Ctr., 1995, Susan Conway Galleries, 1989—, Middlebury Coll. Mus. Art, Babcock Galleries, N.Y.C., Albany Inst. History and Art, Owensboro (Ky.) Mus. Fine Art, Westmoreland Mus. Art, Greenburg, Pa., Md. Inst. & Coll. Art, 1993-94, Gallery 68, 1992, Vt. Studio Ctr. Visiting Critics, Vergennes, 1992, 79th Ann. Maier Mus. Art, Randolph, Macon Women's Coll., Lynchburg, Va., 1990, Del. Ctr. Contemporary Arts, Wilmington, 1988, U. Iowa, 1976, 78, 80, 82, 84, 86, 88, Bladen Meml. Mus., Fort Dodge, Iowa, 1987, Phila. Mus. Art, 1986, Union League Club, N.Y.C., 1986, Blackfish Gallery, Portland, 1986, Columbia (S.C.) Mus. Art, 1985, Columbus Mus. Art, 1982-86, Paine Art Ctr., Oshkosh, Wis., 1985, Burpee Art Ctr., Rockford, Ill., 1985, Ill. State U., Normal, 1985, Wilkes Coll., Wilkes-Barre, Pa., 1985, Albright-Knox Mus., Buffalo, N.Y., 1984, Ark. Art Ctr., Little Rock, 1984, Millersville (Pa.) U., 1983, Fairfield (Conn.) U., 1983, Marion Koogler McKay Inst., San Antonio, 1983, Boston City Hall Gallery, 1983, Cedar Rapids (Iowa) Mus. Art, 1982, Montclair (N.J.) Jr. League, 1981, Iowa Arts Coun., Des Moines, 1980-81, Pepper Gallery, Boston, 1997-98, Spheris Gallery Fine Art, 1997, The Art Spirit Gallery of Fine Art, Walpole, N.H., 1997, Coeur d' Alene, Ind., 1998, numerous others. Sr. Faculty fellow Va. Ctr. for Creative Arts, 1996, Dartmouth Coll., 1993, MacDowell Colony, 1992, Devel. grant U. Iowa, 1980, 86; Summer fellowship U. Iowa, 1979, Rsch. and Travel grantee Ford Found., 1979-80, Yaddo Found., 1965, 72, Travel grantee U. Iowa Found., 1986,; recipient Disting. Alumni award Boston U., 1988 Mem. NAD (academician mem.), Coll. Art Assn. Independent. Presbyterian. Avocations: music, poetry, travel, tennis. Office: Dartmouth Coll Hb 6081 Studio Art Hanover NH 03755

MOSS, BERNARD, virologist, researcher; b. N.Y.C., July 26, 1937; s. Jack and Goldie (Altman) M.; m. Toby Frima Lieberman, Dec. 25, 1960; children: Robert, Jennifer, David. BA, NYU, 1957, MD, 1961; PhD, MIT, 1967. Diplomate Am. Bd. Med. Examiners. Intern Children's Hosp., Boston, 1961-62; investigator, sect. head NIH, Bethesda, Md., 1966—, lab. chief, 1984—. Mem. adv. bd. Virus Res., 1984—, Current Opinion Biotech., 1989—. Assoc. editor Virology Jour., 1976-92, editor., 1992—; mem. editorial bd. Jour. of Virology, 1972—, Antimicrobial Agts. and Chemotherapy, 1973-79, Jour. Biol. Chemistry, 1982-87; AIDS rsch. Human Retroviruses, 1989—; contbr. more than 600 articles to profl. jours. Mem. adv. com. Am. Cancer Soc., N.Y.C., 1983-86; bd. dirs. Found. Advanced Edn. in Scis., Bethesda, 1985-91; mem. NIH AIDS vaccine selection com., 1989—. Served as med. dir. USPHS, 1966-98. Named one of 100 Most Innovative Scientists of 1986, Sci. Digest; recipient Solomon A. Berson Alumni Achievement award Sch. Medicine, NYU, Meritorious Svc. medal USPHS, Disting. Svc. medal USPHS, Dickson prize in medicine, Invitrogen award for eukaryotic gene expression, ICN Internat. prize in Virology, Taylor Internat. prize in medicine., Bristol-Myers Squibb Award, Distinguished Achievement in Infectious Disease Research, 2000. Fellow AAAS; mem. Am. Soc. for Biochemistry and Molecular Biology, Am. Acad. Microbiology, Am. Soc. Microbiology, Am. Soc. Virology (pres. 1995), Nat. Acad. Sci., Phi Beta Kappa, Sigma Xi, Alpha Omega Alpha. Office: NIH 4 Center Dr Bethesda MD 20892-0445 E-mail: bmoss@nih.gov.

MOSS, BETTY SMITH, social worker; b. Fairfield, Ala., Dec. 8, 1931; d. James William Clarke and Helen Sarah (McKelduff) Smith; m. Cameron Gresham, Nov. 1, 1952; children: James Michael, David Patrick, Catherine Alice Moss Hodges, Nancy Carol Moss Weaks. BSSW, U. Ala., Birmingham, 1983. Lic. social worker, Ala.; cert. AIDS counselor, Fla. Staff Cooper Green Hosp., Birmingham, Ala., 1983-86; vol. Medicare, Medicaid Advocacy prog. counselor AARP, Panama City, Fla., 1987; vol. chmn. of hosp. vols. ARC, Tyndall AFB, 1987-88; case mgr. Bay County Coun. on Aging, 1988; discharge planner Bay Med. Ctr., Panama City, Fla., 1988-94; ret., 1994. Bd. dirs. Western Mental Health Clinic; com. mem. AIDS Task Force, Birmingham, 1985-86. Mem. Nat. Assn. Social Workers, Acad. of Cert. Baccalarate Social Workers, Omicron Delta Kappa, Phi Kappa Phi, Alpha Lambda Delta. Home: 3007 Whispering Pines Ln Fultondale AL 35068-1029

MOSS, BILL RALPH, lawyer; b. Amarillo, Tex., Sept. 27, 1950; s. Ralph Voniver and Virginia May (Atkins) M.; 1 child, Brandon Price. BS with honors, West Tex. A&M U., 1972, MA, 1974; JD, Baylor U., 1976; cert. regulatory studies program, Mich. State U., 1981. Bar: Tex. 1976, U.S. Dist. Ct. (no. dist.) 1976, U.S. Tax Ct. 1979, U.S. Ct. Appeals (5th cir.) 1983. Briefing atty. Ct. Appeals 7th Supreme Jud. Dist. Tex., Amarillo, 1976-77; assoc. Culton, Morgan, Britain & White, 1977-80; hearings examiner Pub. Utility Commn. Tex., Austin, 1981-83; asst. gen. counsel State Bar Tex., 1983-87; founder, owner Price & Co. Publs., 1987-97; asst. gen. counsel Tex. Ethics Commn., 1997—. Instr., lectr. West Tex. State U., Canyon, Ea. N.Mex. U., Portales, 1977-80; spkr. in field. Active St. Matthew's Episcopal Ch.; election inspector State of Tex., 1998—. Mem. ABA, Tex. Bar Assn., Nat. Orgn. Bar Counsel, Internat. Platform Assn., Alpha Chi, Lambda Chi Alpha, Omicron Delta Epsilon, Phi Alpha Delta, Sigma Tau Delta, Pi Gamma Mu. Home: 506 Explorer St Lakeway TX 78734-3447 Office: Sam Houston Bldg 201 E 14th St Fl 10 Austin TX 78701 E-mail: bill.moss@ethics.state.tx.us.

MOSS, CARL ARTHUR, psychologist; b. Port Huron, Mich., Aug. 12, 1940; s. August Carl and Frances Elizabeth Moss; m. Patricia Elizabeth Howe, Feb. 13, 1965; children: Miriam, Anne Elizabeth. AA, Port Huron Jr. Coll., Mich., 1960; BS, Ea. Mich. U., 1966, MS, 1973. Cert. sch. psychologist Mich. Psychologist Port Huron Area Schs., 1967—. Trustee Port Huron Mus., 1970—76, bd. pres., 1974—76; founding mem. Riverside Heritage Assn., 1972—78; active Olde Town Dist. Com., 2000—. With U.S. Army, 1963—69. Recipient Spirit of Port Huron award for civic involvement, 2002. Mem.: Mich. Assn. Sch. Psychologists, Macomb/St. Clair Psychol. Assn. Episcopalian. Avocations: civil war history, antiques. Home: 1617 Military St Port Huron MI 48060

MOSS, CHARLES, advertising agency executive; b. Bklyn., Sept. 7, 1938; s. Samuel and Celia (Liebes) Moskowitz; m. Margo Jean Schekman, July 3, 1963 (div.); 1 child, Robert Evan; m. Susan Dukes Calhoun, Mar. 18, 1977; children: Mary Calhoun, Samuel Calhoun. BA cum laude, Ithaca Coll., 1961. Copywriter Doyle, Dane, Bernbach, N.Y.C., 1962-65; group copy supr. J. Tinker & Partners, 1965-66; creative dir. Wells, Rich, Greene, Inc., 1968-74, pres., chief operating officer, 1971-76, vice chmn., corp. creative dir., 1976—, also bd. dirs.; now chmn. Moss/Dragoti (ptnr. co. DDB Worldwide), N.Y.C. Author (with Stan Dragoti); film Dirty Little Billy, 1971. Mem. adv. bd. NYU Sch. Continuing Edn.; mem. creative rev. bd. Com. for Drug Free Am. Served with AUS, 1962-68. Recipient Gold Key Copy Club, 1968, 1st prize Clio award, 1968, 1st prize Art Dirs. Club, 1968; Andy award N.Y. Advt. Club, 1968, spl. Tony award, Golden Apple award for I Love New York advt. campaign 1978, Clio Classic Hall of Fame award 1983, 86, Gold medal for Hertz Corp., Internat. Film Festival, 1995. Mem. Writers Guild Am., Screen Authors Guild. Avocations: golf, tennis. Office: Moss Dragoti 437 Madison Ave New York NY 10022-7001

MOSS, CHARLOTTE ANN, interior design and decorative accessories executive; b. Jan. 24, 1951; d. Edward Joseph and Martha Clare (Skinner) M.; m. James Brian Hotze, Dec. 29, 1973 (div. May 1979); m. Barry Sewell Friedberg, Oct. 10, 1985; stepchildren— Benjamin, James. B.A., Va. Commonwealth U., 1973. Asst. dir. admissions Va. Commonwealth U., Richmond, 1973; ins. underwriter Frank B. Hall Co., Atlanta, 1975-77; freelance writer, 1978; v.p. mktg. Becker Paribas, N.Y.C., 1979-84, Merrill Lynch, N.Y.C., 1984-85; pres. Charlotte Moss & Co., Ltd., N.Y.C., since 1985— . Bd. trustees Stepfamily Assn. Am., Balt., 1985, fundraising chairperson N.Y. chpt., 1983-85 ; patron Met. Mus. Art, N.Y.C., 1986—; bd. dirs. Benefit com. Irvington House for Med. Research. Mem. N.Y. Hort. Soc., Victorian Soc. Am., Brit. Am. C. of C. (corp. mem.), Royal Oak Found. (corp. mem.). Home: 555 Park Ave New York NY 10021-8166 Office: Charlotte Moss & Co Ltd 16 E 65th St # 1 New York NY 10021-7030

MOSS, CLIFTON MICHAEL, factory laborer, small business owner; b. Chardon, Ohio, Sept. 17, 1947; s. Clifton Cleveland and Millicent Grace (Magee) M.; 1 child from prior marriage, Alyson Dahn Moss; m. Suzanne Jo Bechtel, Nov. 25, 2000. Grad., Cardinal H.S., Middlefield, Ohio. Insp., packer Heinz U.S., Fremont, Ohio, 1998—; ind. distbr. Cell Tech. Super Blue Green Products; inspector, packer Heinz U.S.a., Fremont, 1998—. Ward rep. Seneca County Rep. Party, Tiffin, Ohio, 1978. Named Jaycee of Yr., Tiffin Jaycees, 1979. Republican. Methodist. Home: 375 County Rd # 50 Helena OH 43435

MOSS, DAN, JR. stockbroker; b. Greensboro, N.C., Aug. 11, 1948; s. Dan and Caroline (Callaway) M.; m. Gail Summers, Sept. 11, 1976; 1 child, Morgan Callaway. BA, U. N.C., 1970. Mgr. Edison Bros. Stores, Syracuse, N.Y., 1970-72; acct. exec. duPont Walston, Atlanta, 1972-74; v.p. E.F. Hutton & Co., 1974-88; sr. v.p. investments Prudential Securities, Inc., 1988—. Adj. instr. Emory U., Atlanta, 1975—. Bd. dirs. Lady Tara Golf Classic, Atlanta, 1981-82. Mem. Internat. Assn. Fin. Planners (cert.), Rotary (local pres. 1981-82, pres. Altanta Coun. of Club Pres. 1981-82). Avocations: antiques, art, collecting antique stocks and bonds. Home: 251 W Paces Ferry Rd NW Atlanta GA 30305-1163 Office: Prudential Securities 14 Piedmont Ctr NE Ste 200 Atlanta GA 30305-4607 E-mail: danmossjr@aol.com.

MOSS, DAVE JEROME, music educator; b. Miami, Fla., Apr. 26, 1956; s. Osborne Charles and Dorothy Moss; m. Shirley Ann Daniels, Mar. 27, 1982; children: Danielle, Simone. B in Music Edn., Fla. State U., 1978. Band dir. Sunrise Mid. Sch., Ft. Lauderdale, Fla., 1979—81; music tchr. Edison Park Elem. , Miami, 1981—84; band dir. Madison Jr. High, 1984—89; music tchr. Royal Palm Elem., Ft. Lauderdale, 1989—98; music cons. Condit Elem. and Sycamore Elem., Claremont, Calif., 1998—99; band dir. Fremont Mid. Sch., Pomona, 1999—. Mem.: APT (sch. rep.), SCSBOA, Music Educators Nat. Conf. Avocations: bowling, golf, sports, singing, ensemble playing. Home: 1729 W Phillips Dr Pomona CA 91766 Office: Fremont Mid Sch 725 W Franklin Ave Pomona CA 91767 Fax: 909-620-6009. E-mail: daveinca_2000@yahoo.com.

MOSS, DOUGLAS MABBETT, military officer, airline pilot, test pilot; b. Washington, Mar. 21, 1954; s. Lon Harold and Mildred (Mabbett) M. BS in Nuclear Engring., Ga. Inst. Tech., 1976, MS in Mech. Engring., 1981; MBA, U. Phoenix, 1994. Commd. 2d lt. USAF, 1976, advanced through grades to lt. col., 1997, T-37 instr. pilot, F-15 figher pilot and exptl. test pilot Calif., 1977-90; sr. exptl. test pilot, instr., program mgr. MD-80/MD-90/MD-11 Douglas Aircraft Co., Long Beach, 1990-97; pilot and project mgr. B-727/A-320 United Airlines, L.A., 1997—. Mem. Soc. Exptl. test Pilots, Martin-Baker Tie Club. USAF, 2002. Avocations: flying, skiing, scuba diving. Home: 25935 Rolling Hills Rd Apt 318 Torrance CA 90505-7251 Office: United Airlines LA Internat Airport LAXFO Los Angeles CA 90009 *Personal philosophy: Always aim for the stars, but be content with who you are and what you have.*

MOSS, ELIZABETH LUCILLE (BETTY MOSS), transportation company executive; b. Ironton, Mo., Feb. 13, 1939; d. James Leon and Dorothy Lucille (Russell) Rollen; m. Elliott Theodore Moss, Nov. 10, 1963 (div. Jan. 1984); children: Robert Belmont, Wendy Rollen. BA in Econs. and Bus. Adminstrn., Drury Coll., 1960. Registrar, transp. mgr. Cheley Colo. Camps, Inc., Denver and Estes Park, 1960-61; office mgr. Washington Nat. Ins. Co., Denver, 1960-61; sec. White House Decorating, 1961-62; with Ringsby Truck Lines, Denver, Oakland, Calif., and L.A., 1962-67, System 99 Freight Lines, L.A., 1967-69, terminal mgr. Stockton, Calif., 1981-84; with Yellow Freight System, L.A., 1969-74, Hayward, Calif., 1974-77, ops. mgr. Urbana, Ill., 1977-80; sales rep. Calif. Motor Express, San Jose, 1981; regional sales mgr. Schneider Nat. Carriers, Inc., No. Calif., 1984-86; account exec. TNT-Can., Nev. and Cen. Calif., 1986-88; mgr. Interstate-Intermodal Divs. HVH Transp., Denver, 1988-89; regional sales mgr. MNX, Inc., Northern Calif., 1989-91; sales dir., nat. accts. mgr., terminal mgr. Mountain Valley Express, Manteca, Calif., 1992—. Chmn. op. coun. for San Joaquin and Stanislaus Counties Calif. Trucking Assn., 1983-84, Truck Accident Reduction Projects, San Joaquin County, 1987-88. Mem. Econ. Devel. Coun. Stockton C. of C., 1985-86; active Edison High Sch. Boosters, 1982-88. Mem.: Calif. Trucking Assn. (tri county unit steering com. 2001—), So. Calif. Round Table (bd. dirs. 1993—2001), Coun. Logistics Mgmt., Oakland Traffic Club, Ctrl. Valley Traffic Club, Stockton Traffic Club (bd. dirs. 1982—84, Trucker of Yr.), Nat. Def. Transp. Assn. (bd. dirs. 1986—87), Delta Nu Alpha (bd. dirs. Region 1 1982—84, v.p. chpt. 1984—85, pres. chpt. 1985—86, chmn. bd. 1985—87, regional sec. 1987—88, Outstanding Achievement award 1986, 1988). Methodist. Avocations: reading. Home: 949 Salisbury Santa Maria CA 93454 E-mail: MossBetty@aol.com., bmoss@mtnviy.com.

MOSS, FRANCES ELAINE, retired secondary school educator; b. Horse Cave, Ky., Mar. 22, 1922; d. Henry C. and Denta Bunnell Moss. BS, Western State Tchrs. Coll., 1943. Cert. tchr., Ky. Tchr. Glendale (Ky.) H.S., 1942-43, Meml. H.S., Hardyville, Ky., 1943-53, So. H.S., Okolona, 1953-54, Valley H.S., Valley Station, 1954-72, Caverna H.S., Horse Cave, 1972-77; ret., 1977. Author: Eyes of Brown, Eyes of Blue, 1979, The Spirit of Memorial, 1980, History of Hart RTA, 1998, Hardyville: A Big Little Town, 2000. Mem. Ky. Ret. Tchrs. Assn., Hart County Ret. Tchrs. Assn. (pres. 1982-86), 4th Dist. Ret. Tchrs. Assn. (pres.). Democrat. Mem. Ch. of Christ. Avocations: needlework, piano playing, singing, writing.

MOSS, GENE RICHARD, psychiatrist; b. Buffalo, Nov. 3, 1938; BS, U. Chgo., 1960; MD, SUNY, Syracuse, 1964. Diplomate Am. Bd. Psychiatry and Neurology. Asst. prof. UCLA Sch. Medicine, 1971-72; pres. Behavioral Med. Assocs., Inc., San Diego, 1972—, LifeMAX, San Diego, 1994—. Clin. assoc. prof. U. So. Calif. Sch. Medicine, L.A., 1978-85. Author: Healthcare Reform: D.O.A., 1994. Mem. Am. Psychiat. Assn., Sigma Xi. Office: PO Box 90507 San Diego CA 92169-2507 E-mail: lifemax@compuserve.com.

MOSS, GERALD S. dean, medical educator; b. Cleve., Mar. 4, 1935; s. Harry and Lillian (Alter) M.; m. Wilma Jabak, Sept. 1, 1957; children: William Alan, Robert Daniel, Sharon Lynn. BA, Ohio State U., 1956, MD cum laude, 1960. Diplomate Am. Bd. Surgery (apptd. assoc. examiner com. 1989); lic. Ill. Intern Mass. Gen. Hosp., Boston, 1960-61, resident, 1961-65; from asst. prof. to assoc. prof. dept. surgery Coll. Medicine U. Ill., Chgo., 1968-72, prof., 1973-77, 89—, head dept. surgery, 1989, dean, 1989—; prof. dept. surgery Pritzker Sch. Medicine U. Chgo., 1977-89. Tutor in surgery Manchester (Eng.) Royal Infirmary, 1964; asst. chief surgical svcs. VA West Side Hosp., Chgo., 1968-70; attending surgeon dept. surgery Cook County Hosp., Chgo. 1970-72, chmn. 1972-77; dir. surgical rsch. Hektoen Inst. for Med. Rsch., Cook County Hosp., 1972-77, Michael Reese Hosp. and Med. Ctr., Chgo., 1977-89, chmn. dept. surgery, 1977-89, chief svc. 1989, trustee, 1981, and numerou coms.; appointed to Nat. Rsch. Coun., NAS, 1966-68, Ad Hoc Subcom., NAE, 1970, Ad Hoc Study Sect., 1970, del. to Third Joint U.S-USSR Symposium, 1983, Blood Diseases and Resources Adv. Com., 1984-88, Planning Com. for discussing key blood problems, Nat. Heart and Lung Inst., 1987, chmn. Plasma and Plasma Products Com., 1979, bd. dirs., 1983, v.p., 1985, Ad Hoc Transition Com., Am. Blood Commn., 1989, Panel on Rsch. Opportunities, Office Naval Rsch. Program, 1987, exec. com., coord. com., Nat. Blood Edn. Program, 1988, Tech. Adv. Task Force Am. Hosp. Assn., 1988, chmn. review panel contract proposals, NIH, 1975, program project site visit, 1976, chmn. site-visit review group, 1977, adv. com. Blood Resources Work group, 1978, Planning Com. for Consensus, 1987, Small Bus. Innovation Rsch., 1988, Med. Rsch. Scv. Merit Review Bd. VA, 1978-81, Liaison Com. Graduate Med. Edn. AMA, 1979, and numerous other coms. for various med. organizations; cons. Nat. Heart and Lung Inst., Transfusion Medicine Acad. Awardees Program; vis. prof. Montefiore Med. Ctr. Bronx, N.Y., 1986, Ohio State U., 1988, U. N.Mex., Albuquerque, 1989, Seton Med. Ctr., Austin, Tex., 1990, U. Ill. Coll. Medicine, Peoria, 1991; guest lectr., participant numerous meetings, symposiums; cons. in field. Contbr. numerous articles to profl. jours., chpts. to books.. With USN, 1965—68, Vietnam. Teaching fellow Harvard Med. Sch., 1962; recipient Stitt Lectr. award Assn. Mil. Surgeons U.S.A., 1981; grantee U.S. Navy, 1969-84, U.S. Army, 1971-74, 75-78, NIH, 1969, 83-84, Dept. Pub. Health, 1973, HEW, 1974-77, UpJohn, 1974, Northfield Labs. 1985-89. Fellow ACS (pre and postoperative care com. 1975-83, rep. Am. blood commn. 1977—, mem. various coms., speaker various symposiums), Am. Soc. Surgery Trauma; mem. Am. Surgical Assn. (rep. Nat. Soc. Med. Rsch. 1984-88), Am. Trauma Soc., Am. Physicians Fellowship (rep. Israel Med. Assn.), Assn. Acad. Surgery (chmn. membership selection com. 1973-75, pres. elect 1974-75, pres. 1975-76, exec. coun. 1977-79), Soc. Univ. Surgeons (rep. Nat. Soc. Med. Rsch. 1973-77, com. Surgical Edn. 1979-81), Ctrl. Surgical Soc. (rep. Nat. Soc. Med. Rsch. 1973-77), Shock Soc. (chmn. planning com. 1986, chmn. program com. 1986, pres. elect 1986-87, pres. 1987-88), Soc. for Surgery Alimentary Tract (mem. com. west north ctrl. region 1978-82), Internat. Soc. Blood Transfusion, Surgical Biology Club II, Nat. Soc. for Med. Rsch., Collegium Internationale Chirugiae Digestivae, Societe Internationale de Chirugie, Sigma XI, Alpha Omega Alpha (faculty advisor 1972-73). Office: U Ill Coll Medicine Chgo 1853 W Polk St # M/C 784 Chicago IL 60612-4316

MOSS, JACK GIBSON, lawyer; b. Jackson, Miss., Sept. 1, 1956; s. Joe G. and Permelia (Williams) M. AA, Hinds Jr. Coll., Raymond, Miss., 1975; BS, Miss. State U., 1977; JD, U. Miss., 1980. Bar: Miss. 1980, U.S. Dist. Ct. (no. and so. dists.) Miss. 1980. Assoc. Keyes, Moss & Piazza, Jackson, 1980-82; pvt. practice Raymond, 1982—. Mem. ABA, Miss. Bar Assn., Hinds County Bar Assn., Hinds Community Coll. Alumni Assn. (pres. Hinds chpt. 1987-88), Ducks Unltd. (regional v.p.). Baptist. Avocation: sports. Office: PO Box 49 Raymond MS 39154-0049

MOSS, KIRK D. music educator; b. St. Joseph, Mich., Dec. 29, 1964; s. Clarence and Dona A. Moss; m. Deborah A. Schultz, May 9, 1987; children: Bethany, Luke. B in Music Edn., U. of Mich., 1987; M in Music, Cin. Coll.-Conservatory of Music, 1991. Orch. dir. Fern Creek H.S., Louisville, Ky., 1987—89; grad. tchg. asst. Cin. Coll.-Conservatory of Music, 1989—91; orch. dir. Davidson Fine Arts Magnet Sch., Augusta, Ga., 1991—93, Walton H.S., Marietta, 1993—2001; asst. prof. music edn. Valdosta (Ga.) State U., 2001—. Recipient Outstanding Tchr. Recognition Program, U. of Calif., San Diego, 2001; fellow alumni fellow, U. Fla., 2002; scholar Kirk D. Moss Coll. scholar, Walton H.S., (Awarded annually - named in my honor). Mem.: Coll. Music Soc., Ga. Music Educators Assn., Music Educators Nat. Conf., Am. String Tchrs. Assn. (nat. exec. bd. 2002—, pres. Ga. chpt. 1994—96). Home: 5351 Golf Dr Lake Park GA 31636 Office: Valdosta State U Dept Music Valdosta GA 31698 Office Fax: 229-259-5578. E-mail: kdmoss@valdosta.edu.

MOSS, LARRY W. nursing administrator, quality management consultant; b. Pierre, S.D., Feb. 26, 1946; m. Harriett E. Rew, June 28, 1967; children: Ronald, Dana. BSN, S.D. State U., 1969; M in Nursing Adminstrn., U. S.C., 1981. Comd. 2d lt. U.S. Army, 1967, advanced through grades to lt. col., ret., 1988; nursing methods analyst Fitzsimons Army Med. Ctr., Aurora, Colo., 1982-85; asst. and acting dir. nursing Irwin Army Community Hosp., Ft. Riley, Kans., 1985—88; field. rep. Joint Commn. on Accreditation of Healthcare Orgns., Chgo., 1988—; chief quality improvement, utilization mgmt. U.S. Army Hosp., Ft. Riley, Kans., 1991-94. Decorated Legion of Merit; recipient Clara Barton gold medal. Mem. Am. Orgn. Nurse Execs., Nat. Assn. Healthcare Quality, Sigma Theta Tau, Phi Kappa Phi. Home: 3029 Arbor Dr Manhattan KS 66503-3128

MOSS, LESLIE OTHA, protective services official; b. Detroit, Mar. 8, 1952; s. Lonnie and Emma (Robinson) M. BA, U. Mich., 1982, postgrad., 1990—. Cert. protection officer, security supr., protection profl. Technician oper. rm. Sinai Hosp., Detroit, 1972-75; nurses' technician Detroit Osteo. Hosp., 1976-83; supr. Southfield (Mich.) Placement Ctr., 1983-85; rsch. asst. Wayne County Commr.'s Office, Detroit, 1985-86; fin. aid counselor Wayne State U., 1986-87; probation officer Dept. Corrections State of Mich., 1988—; exec. asst. Human Rights Dept., City of Detroit; rsch. asst. Law Dept. City of Detroit, 1990; asst. pers. mgr. Detroit Osteo. Hosp., 1991-93, Highland Pk. C.C., 1991-93; mental health worker Mich. Health Ctr.-Adult Mental Health and New Ctr. Hosp., Detroit, 1992-94; legal technician Ptnrs. Against Crime, 1994; social work technician, 1994. Sgt. of arms Detroit Police Res., 1987—; intern, assoc. prodr. local TV sta., Detroit, 1993; mem. bd. advisors, mem. bd. govs. Am. Biog. Rsch. Inst., dep. gov., 1994; exec. cons. in field., 1993—; asst. pers. mgr., 1993—. Bd. advisors Am. Biog. Inst., 1994; active re-election com. Mayor Coleman A. Young, Detroit, 1989-93; patient care counselor; adv. various causes, including industrialized Am., higher edn., automotive quality. Recipient Twentieth Century Achievement award Biog. Centre, 1994, Spl. Recognition award Detroit Pub. Sch. Sys., 1992, Internat. Man of Yr. award, 1992-93; award for mass media svc. participation Barden Cable Vision, Detorit, 1991, Man of the Yr. award, 1996, Disting. Alumni Award Mumford H.S. Detroit, 1996, Most Outstanding Men of the Twentieth Century award, 1999; named Most Admired Man of Decade, 1994, Disting. Alumnus, Detroit Pub. Schs. Mich., 1995, Most Admired Man of the Yr., State of Mich., 1995; named to Internat. Honors Hall of Fame, 1998, Millenium Hall of Fame, 1998; inducted 500 Leaders of Influence Pub., 2000. Mem. NAFE, NAACP (advisor 1989), Internat. Order of Merit, Assn. Pre-Med Students (cons. 1988—), Assn. Psychologists, Am. Biog. Rsch. Inst. Assn. (mem. bd. govs. 1993, dep. gov.), Internat. Platform Assn., U. Mich. Alumni Assn., Golden Key Internat. Honor Soc. (life), Kappa Alpha Psi, Phi Theta Kappa. Home and Office: 1190 Seward St Apt 306 Detroit MI 48202-2336

MOSS, LOGAN VANSEN, lawyer; b. Atlanta, Apr. 17, 1957; s. Joseph Henry Moss and Elsie Louise (McCown) Daniels. BA, Bates Coll., 1979; JD, U. Tulsa, 1982. Bar: Okla. 1982, U.S. Dist. Ct. Okla. 1982, Maine 1984, U.S. Dist. Ct. Maine 1984, U.S. Supreme Ct. 1986. Law clk. to presiding justice Okla. Ct. Appeals, Tulsa, 1982-84; assoc. Strout, Payson et al, Rockland, Maine, 1984-87, Joseph M. Cloutier & Assocs., Camden, 1987-88, Armstrong & Assocs., Tulsa, Okla., 1988-91; asst. gen. counsel Temple-Island Forest Products Corp., Diboll, Tex., 1991—. Mem. Assn. Trial Lawyers Am. Republican. Roman Catholic. Avocation: Catholic studies. Office: Temple Inland Forest Products Corp 303 S Temple Dr Diboll TX 75941-2419 E-mail: lmoss@TempleInland.com.

MOSS, MADISON SCOTT, editor; b. Charlotte, N.C., May 23, 1948; s. James Madison and Nellie Lee (Jenkins) M. BA in English, U. N.C., 1970. Editl. aide NASW, Inc., Washington, 1974, promotions specialist, 1974-79, assoc. editor, 1979-80, editor, 1980-90, mng. editor, 1990—. Creator numerous videos. Campaign coord. Eugene McCarthy for Pres., Rutherford County,

N.C., 1968. Recipient award for Pub. Excellence Comms. Concepts, 1993, 94, 95, 96, 97, 98, Bronze award newspaper gen. excellence Soc. Nat. Assn. Publs., 1996, Silver award, 1997. Mem. ACLU, U. N.C. Gen. Alumni Assn., Am. Found. AIDS Rsch. Democrat. Avocations: video producing, creating digital art and animations, reading. Office: NASW Inc 750 1st St NE Ste 700 Washington DC 20002-8011 E-mail: Smoss@naswdc.org.

MOSS, MELVIN LIONEL, anatomist, educator; b. N.Y.C., Jan. 3, 1923; s. Maurice and Ethel (Lander) M.; m. Letty Salentijn, Apr. 1970; children (by previous marriage)— Noel Morrow, James Andrew. AB, N.Y. U., 1942; D.D.S., Columbia, 1946, PhD, 1954. Mem. faculty Columbia, 1954—, prof., 1967-93; prof. emeritus, 1993; also dean Columbia (Sch. Dental and Oral Surgery.). Recipient Lederle Med. Faculty award, 1954-56 Fellow AAAS, Royal Anthrop. Soc. Gt. Britain; mem. Am. Assn. Anatomists, Am. Assn. Phys. Anthropologists, Internat. Assn. Dental Research (craniofacial biology award), Am. Soc. Zoologists, Sigma Xi, Omicron Kappa Upsilon. Achievements include research, numerous publs. on skeletal growth and application of computer-assisted methods of numerical and graphic analysis of growth. edu. Home: 560 Riverside Dr New York NY 10027-3202 E-mail: MLM7@columbia.

MOSS, MICHAEL, economist; b. N.Y.C., Feb. 6, 1943; s. Murray and Rose M.; m. Sally Schneider, Dec. 12, 1984. Student, Miami Dade Coll., 1961-62, U. Miami, 1963-64. CLU. Div. mgr. Nat. Cash Register, Miami, Fla., 1964-69; asst. gen. agt. Mass Mutual Corp., 1969-74; mgr. Home Life Ins. Co. of N.Y., Coral Gables, Fla., 1974-80; pres. Moss Group, San Diego, 1982—. V.p. Physicians Planning Service, 1975-81. Author: White Torpedo, 1980. Mem. Young Pres. of Mt. Sinai Hosp., Miami Beach, 1977-82, charter mem. Research Council Scripps Clinic and Research Found., La Jolla, Calif., 1985—, Balboa Park Mus. Art, San Diego, 1986—. Mem. Gen. Agts. and Mgrs. Assn. (pres. 1978-79, Nat. Mgmt. award 1976, 77, 78, State of Fla. Ram award 1979), Mkt. Technicians Assn., San Diego Computer Soc., Soc. Investigation of Recurring Events, Optimist Club Internat., Masons, Shriners, Order of the Nail (Brotherhood award 1981), Elks. Avocation: golf. Home: 12851 Camino Ramilotte San Diego CA 92037

MOSS, MYRA ELLEN (MYRA MOSS ROLLE), philosophy educator; b. L.A., Mar. 22, 1937; m. Andrew Rolle, Nov. 5, 1983. BA, Pomona Coll., 1958; PhD, The Johns Hopkins U., 1965. Asst. prof. Santa Clara (Calif.) U., 1968-74; prof. Claremont McKenna Coll., 1975—, chmn. Dept. of Philosophy, 1992-95. Assoc. dir. Gould Ctr. for Humanities, Claremont, Calif., 1993-94; adv. coun. Milton S. Eisenhower Libr./Johns Hopkins U., 1994-96, 2001--. Author: Benedetto Croce Reconsidered, 1987; translator: Benedetto Croce's Essays on Literature & Literary Criticism, 1990; co-author: Values and Education, 1998; assoc. editor Special Issues; Journal of Value Inquiry, 1990-95 (Honorable Mention, Phoenix award); cons. editor Jour. Social Philosophy, 1988—; assoc. editor: Value Enquiry Book Series, 1990-95; editor: The Philosophy of José Gaos, by Pio Colonnello, Value Inquiry Book Series, 1997. Dir. Flintridge (Calif.) Riding Club, 1991. Bogliasco fellow, Liguria, Italy, 2000. Mem. Am. Philos. Assn., Am. and Internat. Soc. for Value Inquiry, Soc. for Aesthetics, Collingwood Soc. (life), Phi Beta Kappa (hon.). Avocations: gardening, horseback riding. Office: Claremont McKenna Coll 850 Columbia Ave Claremont CA 91711-3901

MOSS, RANDY, professional football player; b. Feb. 13, 1977; , Marshall U. Wide receiver Minn. Vikings, 1998—. First round draft pick NFL, 1998; named Rookie of Yr. NFL, 1998. Achievements include Marshall U. record holder for touchdowns in a career. Ranks second in total yards and third in total receptions. Office: MN Vikings 9520 Viking Dr Eden Prairie MN 55344-3898*

MOSS, RICHARD LUDLOW, newspaper official; b. San Diego, Jan. 1, 1959; s. William W. and Madeleine S. Moss; m. Patricia Wertman. BA, Washington and Lee U., 1980. Chief copy desk Rochester (N.Y.) Dem. and Chronicle. Office: Rochester Dem and Chronicle 55 Exchange Blvd Rochester NY 14614

MOSS, RICHARD SPENCER, communications executive; b. Portland, Oreg., May 26, 1949; s. Harry and Mary Louise (Ruckdeschel) M.; divorced; children: Emily Anne, Paul Spencer, Kathryn Elizabeth, Brian Richard. AA, Mount Hood C.C., 1975; BA in Comm., U. Portland, 1977. Publs. mgr. First Nat. Bank Oreg., Portland, 1977; mgr. employee comm. Ga.-Pacific Corp., Portland, 1977-80; dir. alumni and cmty. rels. U. Portland, 1980-84; dir. employee comm. NERCO Inc., Portland, 1984-87; pres. R.S. Moss & Assocs., Corp. Comms, Portland, 1987—. With USN, 1969-73; Vietnam. Recipient Arnold's Admirables award The Ragan Report, 1982, Award of Excellence Annual Reports, Comm. Arts mag., Design Annual, 1989-90, Excellence award Soc. for Tech. Comms., 1989. Mem. Pub. Rels. Soc. Am., Internat. Assn. Bus. Communicators (chpt. dir., chpt. pres. 1985-86, Gold Quill award 1979, 83), Portland Advt. Fedn., Vietnam Vets. Am. (chpt. dir., state coun. dir.). Republican. Anglican. Home and Office: 9625 SW Inglewood St Portland OR 97225-4924

MOSS, ROBERT WILLIAMS, real estate developer; b. Balt., May 16, 1942; s. Ambler Holmes and Dorothea (Williams) M.; m. Marguerite McKee, Jan. 30, 1971; children: Dorothy Williams, Lucile Aycock. BA, MCP, Yale U., 1967. V.p. Howard R&D Corp. subs. The Rouse Co., Balt., 1967-73; dir. devel. Flower Mound New Town Raymond D. Nasher Co., Dallas, 1973-76; regional dir. Campaign for Yale Yale U., 1976-78; dir. devel. Tecon Realty (Murchison Interests), 1978-85; exec. v.p. Cityplace Devel. Corp. subs. The Southland Corp., 1985-91; prin. Moss & Assocs., 1991-96; pres., CEO City of Dallas Bus. Devel. Corp., 1996—. Dir. Historic Landmarks, Inc. Mem. Urban Land Inst., Yale Club Dallas (pres. 1984-86). Episcopalian. Avocations: reading, tennis, skiing, jogging. (e). Home: 4319 Allencrest Ln Dallas TX 75244-7406 Office: Bishop Arts Bldg 408 W Eighth St Ste 206 Dallas TX 75208 E-mail: mossdbdc@airmail.net.

MOSS, ROGER WILLIAM, historian, writer, administrator; b. Zanesville, Ohio, Jan. 31, 1940; s. Roger William and Dorothy Elizabeth (Martin) M.; m. Gail Caskey Winkler, 1981; children by previous marriage: Elizabeth Moss McQuiston, Victoria Stiles Moss. BS in Edn., Ohio U., 1963, MA, 1964; postgrad., Attingham, Eng., summer 1966; PhD, U. Del., 1972. Staff Peace Corps, Cameroon, 1962-63; Curator of rare books Ohio U., 1962-64; lectr., dept. history U. Del., 1966-68, U. Md., 1967-68; exec. dir. Athenaeum of Phila., 1968—. Lectr. to adj. prof. architecture U. Pa., Phila., 1981—. Publs. include Morgan Collection, 1965, Master Builders, 1972, Century of Color, 1981, Biographical Dictionary of Philadelphia Architects, 1985, Philadelphia, 1986, Victorian Interior Decoration, 1986, Victorian Exterior Decoration, 1987, Lighting for Historic Buildings, 1988 (Joel Polsky prize 1989), The American Country House, 1990, Philadelphia Victorian, 1998, Historic Houses of Philadelphia, 1998; gen. editor Athenaeum Libr. of Nineteenth-Century Am. series, 1975—; editor: Paint in America, 1994; contbr. to profl. jours. Bd. dirs. Conservation Ctr. for Art and Hist. Artifacts, 1984-96, chmn., 1993-95, Woodlands Cemetery Co., 1990-99, Rsch. Librs. Group, 1993-96; exec. com., Phila. Area Consortium Spl. Coll., Librs., 1988-93; sec. Christopher Ludwick Found., 1969—; bd. dirs. Brit. Cathedrals and Historic Chs. Found., sec.-treas., 1996-2001, pres., 2002—, bd. dirs. Abraham Lincoln Found., 1996—; bd. dirs., sec., treas. Victorian Soc. in Am., 1969-88; assoc. Nat. Preservation Inst., 1982-93; bd. dirs. Hist. House Assn. Am., 1978-83, Com. for Preservation of Archtl. Records, 1978-80, Phila. Area Cultural Consortium, 1977-82, also treas., Mus. Coun. Phila., 1976-78; sec. Hopkinson House Council, 1982-93, Clivden Coun., Nat. Trust for Hist. Preservation, 1974-81, 84-86, Harriton House, 1969-81, Friends of Laurel Hill, 1978-83, Franklin Inn Club, 1976-79. NEH grantee, 1983-85. Fellow Royal Soc. Arts; mem. Soc. Archtl. Historians, Soc. Preservation New Eng. Antiquities, Hist. Soc. Pa., Libr. Co., Rushlight Club. Office: Athenaeum of Phila 219 S 6th St Philadelphia PA 19106-3794 E-mail: rmoss@philaathenaeum.org.

MOSS, SANDRA HUGHES, legal administrator; b. Atlanta, Dec. 24, 1945; d. Harold Melvin and Velma Aileen (Norton) H.; m. Marshall L. Moss, May 1, 1965 (dec. Aug. 2000); children: Tara Celise, Justin Hughes. Student, West Ga. Coll., 1964-65, Ga. State U. Legal sec. Smith, Cohen, Ringel, Kohler & Martin, Atlanta, 1965-78; real estate sales Century 21-Phoenix, College Park, Ga., 1978-80; office mgr./pers. dir. Smith, Cohen, Ringel, Kohler & Martin, Atlanta, 1980-85; dir. adminstrn. Smith, Gambrell & Russell LLP, 1985—. Bd. dirs., sec. North Clayton Athletic Assn., Riverdale, Ga., 1981-83; sec. E.W. Oliver PTA, Riverdale, 1981; exec. com. E.W. Oliver and N. Clayton Jr. PTA, Riverdale, 1980, 81, 82; den leader Cub Scouts, Pack 959, Riverdale, 1984. Mem. Soc. Human Resource Mgmt., Assn. Legal Adminstrs. (sec. Atlanta chpt. 1988, v.p., pres. 1990-91). Home: 405 Pendleton Trail Tyrone GA 30290 Office: Smith Gambrell & Russell LLP 1230 Peachtree St NE Ste 3100 Atlanta GA 30309-3592 E-mail: smoss@sgrlaw.com.

MOSS, STEPHEN B. lawyer; b. Jacksonville, Fla., July 14, 1943; s. Rudy and Betty (Sobel) M.; m. Rhoda Goodman, Nov. 24, 1984; children: Kurt, Shannon. BA, Tulane U., 1964; JD, Samford U., 1968. Bar: Fla. 1968, U.S. Dist. Ct. (so. dist.) Fla., U.S. Tax Ct. From assoc. to ptnr. Heiman & Crary, Miami, Fla., 1971-74; pvt. practice law So. Miami, 1974-75; ptnr. Glass, Schultz, Weinstein & Moss P.A., Coral Gables, 1975-78, Ft. Lauderdale, 1978-80, Holland & Knight, LLP, Ft. Lauderdale, 1980—. Mem. pro bono com. 17th Jud. Cir., 2000; co-founder, co-chair Broward County Child Welfare Initiative, 2001. Capt. U.S. Army, 1968-70, Vietnam. Named Outstanding Kiwanian, Miami, 1974; Olympic torchbearer, 1996. Fellow ABA, Fla. Bar Found.; mem. Fla. Bar Assn., Legal Aid Svc. of Broward County (bd. dirs. 2000), Greater Ft. Lauderdale C. of C. (gen. counsel 1991-92, chmn. bd. dirs., bd. govs. 1995, Chmn.'s award 1991, 2000), Tower Club, Tower Forum (pres. 1993-94, bd. dirs. 2001—). Democrat. Jewish. Avocations: running, softball, hiking. Office: Holland & Knight LLP 1 E Broward Blvd Fl 13 Fort Lauderdale FL 33301-1845 E-mail: smoss@hklaw.com.

MOSS, STEPHEN EDWARD, lawyer; b. Washington, Nov. 22, 1940; s. Morris and Jean (Sober); m. Sharon S. Moss; children: Aubrey, Hilary. BBA, Baldwin-Wallace Coll., 1962; JD with honors, George Washington U., 1965, LLM, 1968. Bar: D.C. 1966, Md. 1971. Assoc. Cole & Groner, Washington, 1965-70; pvt. practice law Bethesda, Md., 1971-80; pres. Stephen E. Moss, P.A., 1981-89, Moss, Strickler & Weaver, Bethesda, 1990-94, Moss, Strickler & Sachitano, P.A., Bethesda, 1995—. Lectr. in family law and trial practice. Fellow Am. Acad. Matrimonial Lawyers (cert.), Internat. Acad. Matrimonial Lawyers; mem. Montgomery County Bar Assn. Inc. (chmn. family law sect. 1980), Md. Bar Found., Inc. (cert. mediator). Office: Moss Strickler & Sachitano PA 4550 Montgomery Ave Ste 700 Bethesda MD 20814-3304 E-mail: smoss@mss-law.com.

MOSS, THOMAS HENRY, science association administrator; b. Cleve., June 27, 1939; s. Joseph Harold and Elsa Margaret (Lemkau) M.; m. Kathleen Goddard, May 31, 1966; children: Ellen, Joseph, Cheryl, David. AB, Harvard U., 1961; PhD, Cornell U., 1965. Cons. analyst govtl. sci. policy U.S. Govt. Office Mgmt. and Budget, Washington, 1963-67; research physicist IBM Corp., Yorktown, N.Y., 1967-74, 75-76; staff dir., sci. advisor Office of Congressman George E. Brown, Washington, 1976-79; staff dir. subcom. sci., research and tech. Ho. of Reps., 1979-82; prof. physics, dean grad. studies and research Case Western Res. U., Cleve., 1982-96; exec. dir. Govt.-Univ.-Industry Roundtable, 1996—2001; with Nat. Acad. Scis, Washington; dir. Univ. relations Ohio Aerospace Inst., 2001—. Adj. prof. physics Columbia U., N.Y.C., 1966-76; mem. nat rev. com. Office of Nuclear Waste Isolation, Columbus, 1983-87; bd. dirs. Univ. Tech. Inc., Cleve.; bd. dirs. Ctr. Great Lakes, Chgo., 1985-89; v.p. Edison Poymer Innovation Corp., Independence, Ohio, 1986-90. Editor: The Three Mile Island Nuclear Accident-Lessons, 1981; asst. editor Environ. Profl. mag.; cons. editor Sci, Tech. and Human Values Environ. mag.; contbr. articles to profl. jours. Treas. Lake Bancroft Cmty. Assn., Falls Church, Va., 1980; mem. adv. bd. Small Bus. SBIR Program, Cleve., 1983-85; mem., v.p. Shaker Heights (Ohio) Bd. Edn., 1989-96; chmn. N.E. Region Ohio Systemic Statewide Initiative in Sci. and Math. Edn., 1992-95. ASME fellow, 1995-96, NSF fellow Nobel Instn., 1966-67. Fellow Am. Phys. Soc. (chmn. forum on physics and soc. 1990-91), Nat. Coun. Univ. Rsch. Adminstrs. (Nat. Innovation Program award 1987), Scientists Inst. Pub. Info. (Disting. Svc. award Harlem Prep. Sch. 1971), AAAS (chmn. com. on sci., engring. and pub. policy 1989-91, chmn. sect. X 1998-99). Avocations: gardening, camping.

MOSSAD, SHERIF BENIAMEEN, physician; b. Cairo, Egypt, Apr. 2, 1964; came to U.S., 1990; Diplomate Am. Bd. Internal Medicine, Am. Bd. Infectious Diseases. Resident Cleve. Clinic Found., 1990-93, fellow, 1993-96, clin. assoc. staff, 1996-98, assoc. staff, 1998-2000, staff, 2000—. Contbr. articles to profl. jours. Mem. AMA, ACP, Infectious Disease Soc. Am. Avocations: jogging, history of medicine. Office: Cleve Clinic Found 9500 Euclid Ave Cleveland OH 44195-0001

MOSSAVAR-RAHMANI, BIJAN, oil and gas company executive; b. Tehran, Iran, June 14, 1952; arrived in U.S., 1978; s. Morteza and Fatemeh (Mohtashem-Nouri) Mossavar-R.; m. Sharmin Batmanghelidj, Oct., 1980. BA, Princeton U., 1974; MS, U. Pa., 1975; MPA, Harvard U., 1982. Oil and energy columnist Kayhan Group of Newspapers, Iran, 1975-78; energy policy analyst Govt. of Iran, 1976-78; vis. rsch. fellow The Rockefeller Found., N.Y., 1978-80; rsch. coord. internat. natural gas study Harvard U., Mass., 1982-85, asst. dir. internat. energy studies, 1985-87; pres. Apache Internat., Inc., Houston, 1988-96; bd. dirs., treas. Am.-Iranian Coun., N.J., 1998-2000; sr. exec. cons., dir. oil and gas studies Temple, Barker & Sloane, Inc., Mass., 1983-87; chmn. bd. Mondoil Corp., N.Y.C., 1996—. Author: Energy Policy in Iran, 1981; co-author: OPEC and the World Oil Outlook, 1983, World Natural Gas Outlook, 1984, The OPEC Natural Gas Dilemma, 1986, Energy Security Revisited, 1987, Natural Gas in Western Europe, 1987, Lower Oil Prices: Mapping the Impact, 1988, Competition and Realignment in Global Energy Markets, 1997, Energy Policies and Markets: New Trends or Old Cycles, 2001, Energy Liberalization and Regulation Revisited, 2002; mem. editl. adv. bd. Offshore mag., 1992-94. Bd. dirs. U.S.-Angola C. of C., 1990-92, Persepolis Found.; mem. coun. Internat. Exec. Svc. Corps, 1991-96. Decorated Comdr. de l'Ordre Nat. de Cote d'Ivoire. Mem. Denver U. Club, Nassau Club, Harvard Club of N.Y. Address: 953 Fifth Ave New York NY 10021

MOSSAWIR, HARVE H., JR. retired lawyer; b. Morton, Miss., Aug. 9, 1942; s. Harve H. and Madeline (Price) M.; children: Anna Christine, Karen Elyse; m. Judy S. Bardugo, Aug. 5, 1985; 1 child, Leigh Sarah. BA with honors, U. Ala., 1964; MA in Econs., U. Manchester, 1965; JD with honors, U. Chgo., 1968. Bar: Calif. 1970. Asst. prof. U. Ala. Law Sch., Tuscaloosa, 1968-69; assoc. Irell & Manella, L.A., 1969-74, ptnr., 1974-94, of counsel, 1994-96. Mem. bd. editors U. Chgo. Law Rev., 1966-68; contbr. articles to profl. jours. Fulbright scholar, 1964-65, Floyd Russell Mecham scholar, 1965-68. Republican. E-mail: labard1@yahoo.com.

MOSS BOWER, PHYLIS DAWN, medical researcher; b. Waco, Tex., Oct. 27, 1959; d. Phillip Carroll and Teloiv Anita (Marrs) Eddins; m. W. Taylor Moss, Mar. 22, 1980 (div. Aug. 1990); children: Amber Nikkole Moss, Beau Christian Moss; m. Kevin Eugene Bower, May 27, 1992 (div. Sept. 1994). Student, Tex. Tech. U., 1977-78, 4-C Bus. Coll., 1989-90. Tumor registry Scott & White Hosp., Waco, 1988-92; clin. rsch. in oncology LaGrange (Ill.) Hosp., 1992-93; clin. rsch. asst. pharm. Christie Clinic, Champaign, Ill., 1993-96; data entry, bill clk., office mgr. Restaurant Equipment & Supply Co., 1996—. Spirit of Scott & White com. mem. Scott & White Hosp., Temple, Tex., 1992. Leader Girl Scouts USA, Waco, 1983; com. mem. Children's Miracle Network, Temple, 1988-92; breast cancer prevention team Nat. Surg. Adjuvant Bowel and Breast Protocol, LaGrange, 1992-93. Mem. Nat. Tumor Registrars Assn., Tex. Tumor Registrars Assn. (fin. com. mem. 1988-92, membership com. 1989-90), Soc. Clin. Rsch. Assn. (fin. com. mem. 1992—). Methodist. Avocations: calligraphy, embroidery, bowling, cooking, crafts. Home: 2125 Hermanson Dr Waco TX 76710-2619

MOSSEL, PATRICIA L. retired opera executive; b. N.Y.C., Nov. 19, 1933; d. Burnet Thomas and Martha Camille (Leigh) Kraut; m. Allan A Fleischer, Dec. 30,. 1956 (div. 1987); children: Hillary Lee Fleischer, Jason Allan; m. John W. Mossel, Sept. 4, 1993. BA, U. Rochester, 1955; MA, Yale U., 1956. Cert. fund raising exec. Tchr. Colby Coll., New London, N.H., 1956-57; editor Far Eastern Pub.-Yale U., New Haven, 1957-60; dir. devel. San Francisco Opera, 1979-84; dir. devel., mktg. and pub. relations The Wash. Opera, 1984-95, exec. dir., 1995—. Mem. bd. San Francisco Symphony and Opera; bd. chmn., exec. dir. Mt. Diablo Rehabilitation Ctr.; co-founder Medi-Physics, Inc.; cons. D.C. Humanities Council, 1989—. Editor: Western Lit. on China, 1959. Mem. adv. council Fund Raising Sch., Indpls.; v.p. Nat. Soc. Fund Raising Exec. Found. bd. dirs., Washington, 1985-87. Named Fund Raising Exec. of Yr., Nat. Soc. Fund Raising Execs., 1986. Mem. Assocs. of Yale Alumni (del. 1988-91), Yale Club, Order of Rio Branco (officer), Phi Beta Kappa. Republican. Presbyterian. Avocations: painting, writing, piano. E-mail: patlm@aol.com.

MOSSELMANS, CAREL MAURITS, investment banker; b. East Knoyle, Wiltshire, Eng., Mar. 9, 1929; s. Adriaan Willem and Nancy Henriette (Van der Wyck) M.; m. Prudence Fiona McCorquodale, Jan. 4, 1962; children: Michael Lodowick Stewart, Julian Frederick Willem. MA, Trinity Coll., Cambridge, Eng., 1952. With Sedgwick Collins & Co., 1952-63; dir. Sedgwick Collins & Co. Ltd., 1963-71; dir., mng. dir. Sedgwick Collins (Underwriting) Ltd., 1971, 72-73; chmn. Sedgwick Lloyd's Underwriting Agts., 1974-89, Sedgwick Forbes Marine Ltd., 1974-78, Sedgwick Forbes Svcs. Ltd., 1978-81, Sedgwick Ltd., 1981-84, Sedgwick Group Plc., 1984-89, The Sumitomo Marine & Fire Ins. Co. (Europe) Ltd., 1981-90; Coutts & Co., 1981-95; chmn. Rothschild Asset Mgmt. Ltd., 1989-99, Rothschild Int. Asset Mgmt., 1989-96. Chmn. Exco Plc, 1991-96, Janson Green Holdings Spl. Trust Ltd., 1993-96, Rothschild Fund Mgmt. Ltd., 1990-96; chmn. Janson Green Ltd., 1993-96, non-exec. dir., 1997-98. Avocations: shooting, fishing, music, golf. Home: 15 Chelsea Sq London SW3 6LF England

MOSSINGHOFF, GERALD JOSEPH, patent law expert; b. St. Louis, Sept. 30, 1935; m. Jeanne Carole Jack, Dec. 29, 1958; children: Pamela Ann Jennings, Gregory Joseph, Melissa M. Ronayne. BSEE, St. Louis U., 1957; JD with honors, George Washington U., 1961. Bar: Mo. 1961, D.C. 1965, Va. 1981. Project engr. Sachs Electric Corp., 1954-57; dir. congl. liaison NASA, Washington, 1967-73, dep. gen. counsel, 1976-81; asst. Sec. Commerce, commr. patents and trademarks U.S. Patent Office, 1981-85; pres. Pharm. Rsch. and Mfrs. Am., Washington, 1985-96; Cifelli prof. intellectual property law George Washington U., 1996—; sr. counsel Oblon, Spivak, McClelland, Maier & Neustadt, Arlington, Va., 1997—. Amb. Paris Conv. Diplomatic Conf.; adj. prof. George Mason U. Law Sch. Recipient Exceptional Svc. medal NASA, 1971, Disting. Svc. medal, 1980, Outstanding Leadership medal, 1981, Jefferson medal, 2000; Disting. Alumnus George Washington U., 1996; granted presdl. rank of meritorious exec., 1980; Disting. Pub. Svc. award Sec. of Commerce, 1983 Fellow Am. Acad. Pub. Adminstrn.; mem. Reagan Alumni Assn. (bd. dirs.), Cosmos Club, Knights of Malta, Order of Coif, Eta Kappa Nu, Pi Mu Epsilon. Home: 1530 Key Blvd Penthouse 28 Arlington VA 22209-1532 Office: Oblon Spivak McClelland Maier & Neustadt 1755 Jefferson Davis Hwy Fl 4 Arlington VA 22202-3509

MOSSMAN, ROBERT GILLIS, IV, civil and environmental engineer; b. Youngstown, Ohio, Jan. 28, 1960; s. Robert Gillis III and Carol (Hoyt) M. B Engring., Youngstown State U., 1984. Engr. Lynn, Kittenger & Noble, Inc., Warren, Ohio, 1984-85, Thomas Fok & Assocs., Ltd., Youngstown, 1985-86, Daniel C. Baker Assocs., Inc., Beaver, Pa., 1986-87; cons. Youngstown, 1987—. Avocations: photography, poetry, dancing, art, nature study. Home and Office: 58 Norwick Dr Youngstown OH 44505-1626 E-mail: mossydork@prodigy.net.

MOSSMAN, THOMAS MELLISH, JR. broadcasting consultant; b. Honolulu, Nov. 20, 1938; s. Thomas Mellish and Marian (Ledwith) M.; children: Thomas Mellish III, James Michael; m. Jan Carla MacAlister, Dec. 31, 1989. Student, U. Hawaii, 1954-57; BA, U. Denver, 1958, MA, 1965. Producer-dir. KRMA-TV, Denver, 1960-64, KCET-TV, L.A., 1964-72; pres. Mosaic Films, 1972-73; prodn. and operations dir. KLCS-TV, 1973-78, sta. mgr., 1978—87, 1996-2000; dept. dir. Archdiocese of L.A., 1987-96. Instr. Calif. State U., Northridge, 1981-94; chairperson, founder L.A. Community TV, 1987-95. Chmn. exec. bd. Regional Ednl. TV Adv. Coun., 1989—93; chmn., founding mem. Alliance Distance Edn. in Calif., 1991—95; bd. dirs. L.A. Cable TV Access Corp., 1995—2001. Mem.: Alliance for Cmty. Media, Dirs. Guild Am., ATAS. Episcopalian. Office: 10701 Commerce Ave Tujunga CA 91042 E-mail: tmossman1@juno.com.

MOSSO, LYLE DAVID, financial executive; b. Pasadena, Calif., Aug. 13, 1926; s. Joseph Ernest and Marian (Ure) M.; m. Lee McVoy Pierce, June 11, 1955; children: Janet, Andrew, Jocelyn. BBA magna cum laude, Washburn U., 1950, D in Commerce (hon.), 1982; MA in Econs, U. Minn., 1951. CPA, Va. With Santa Fe Ry., 1942-44; instr. econs. and acctg. Washburn U., 1954-55; with U.S. Treasury Dept., 1955-77, commr. accounts, 1971-73, dep. asst. sec. treasury, 1973-75, asst. sec., 1975-77; with Fin. Acctg. Stds. Bd., 1978-96; vice chmn. Fin. Acctg. Standards Bd., 1986-87; adj. prof. acctg. Fordham U., 1996—; chmn. Fed. Acctg. Stds. Adv. Bd., 1997—. Arbitrator Am. Arbitration Assn., 1997—. Contbr. articles to profl. jours. Mem. Comptr. Gen.'s Acctg. Stds. Adv. Coun., 1987-90; mem. charter revision commn. City of Stamford, 1986-87, Can.-U.S. Adv. Group on Fed. Reporting, 1984-86; alt. trustee Nat. Gallery Art, 1975-77; dir. Stamford Emergency Med. Svc., 1993-94. 1st lt. AUS, 1944-46, 51-53. Recipient Alexander Hamilton award Treasury Dept., 1977 Mem. AICPA (Elijah Watt Sells award 1962), Va. Soc. CPAs (Gold medal 1962), Am. Acctg. Assn., Assn. Govt Accts. (dir. Washington chpt. 1972-73, Disting. Leadership award 1977, Elmer Staats award 1990), Treasury Hist. Assn. (pres. 1978), Tau Delta Pi, Pi Gamma Mu, Phi Kappa Phi. Home: 111 Saddle Hill Rd Stamford CT 06903-2307 Office: 441 G St NW Ste 6814 Washington DC 20548-0001

MOSSOP, GRANT DILWORTH, geologist, researcher; b. Calgary, Alta., Can., Apr. 15, 1948; s. Cyril S. and Freida E. (Dilworth) Mossop; m. Ruth Shaver, May 24, 1969; children: Jenny, Jonathan, David. BSc in Geology, U. Calgary, 1970, MSc in Geology, 1971; PhD, DIC in Geology, Imperial Coll., U. London, 1973. Postdoctoral fellow U. Calgary, Canada, 1974; asst. rsch. officer Alta. Rsch. Coun., Edmonton, 1975—77, assoc. rsch. officer, 1977—80, head geol. survey dept., 1980—84, sr. rsch. officer, 1985—91; dir. Geol. Survey of Can., Calgary, 1991—2001, rsch. scientist, 2001—. Acad. visitor dept. earth sci. Oxford U., England, 1984—85. Project mgr., editor: Geological Atlas of Western Canada Sedimentary Basin. Fellow: Geol. Assn. Can. (pres. 1986—87); mem.: Can. Soc. Petroleum Geologists. Home: 68 Colleen Cres SW Calgary AB Canada T2V 2R3 Office: Geol Survey Can 3303 33d St NW Calgary AB Canada T2L 2A7 E-mail: gmossop@nrcan.gc.ca.

MOSS-SALENTIJN, LETTY (ALEIDA MOSS-SALENTIJN), anatomist, educator; b. Amsterdam, The Netherlands, Apr. 14, 1943; came to U.S., 1968; d. Ewoud and Johanna Maria (Schoonhoven) Salentijn; m. Melvin Lionel Moss, Apr. 17, 1970. DDS, State U., Utrecht, The Netherlands, 1967, PhD, 1976. Asst. prof. histology State U., Utrecht, 1967-68; asst. prof. Columbia U., N.Y.C., 1968-74, assoc. prof., 1974-86, prof., 1986—, Edwin S. Robinson prof., 1999—, dir. dental radiology, 1980-86, dir. grad. program dental sci., 1986—, dir. postdoctoral affairs, 1987-90, asst. dean postdoctoral programs, 1990-94, assoc. dean acad. affairs, 1994—. Author: Orofacial Histology & Embryology, 1972; Dental and Oral Tissues, 1980, 2d edit., 1984, 3d edit., 1990; contbr. chpts. to books, articles to profl. jours. Fellow Royal Microscopical Soc., Am. Coll. Dentists; mem. Am. Assn. Anatomists, Internat. Assn. Dental Rsch., Am. Soc. Biomechs., Sigma Xi (chpt. sec. 1980-87, pres. 1987-89, 98-99), Omicron Kappa Upsilon (pres. local chpt. 1987). Avocation: stained glass art. Home: 560 Riverside Dr Apt 20K New York NY 10027-3242 Office: Columbia U/SDOS Assoc Dean Academic Affairs 630 W 168th St New York NY 10032-3702 E-mail: lm23@columbia.edu.

MOST, JACK LAWRENCE, lawyer, consultant; b. N.Y.C., Sept. 24, 1935; s. Meyer Milton and Henrietta (Meyer) M.; children: Jeffrey, Peter; m. Irma Freedman Robbins, Aug. 8, 1968; children: Ann, Jane. BA cum laude, Syracuse U., 1956; JD, Columbia U., 1960. Bar: N.Y. 1960, U.S. Dist. Ct. (so. and ea. dists.) N.Y. 1963. Assoc. Hale, Grant, Meyerson and O'Brien, N.Y.C., 1960-66; dep. assoc. dir. OEO, Exec. Office of The Pres., Washington, 1965-67; asst. to gen. counsel C.I.T. Fin. Corp., N.Y.C., 1968-70; corp. counsel PepsiCo, Inc., Purchase, N.Y., 1970-71; v.p. legal affairs Revlon, Inc., N.Y.C., 1971-76; asst. gen. counsel Norton Simon, Inc., 1976-79; ptnr. Rogers Hoge and Hills, 1979-86, Finkelstein Bruckman Wohl Most & Rothman LLP, N.Y.C., 1986-97, mng. ptnr., 1990-93, Ferster Bruckman Wohl Most & Rothman LLP, 1997-98; ptnr. Goetz, Fitzpatrick, Most & Bruckman LLP, 1999—. Corp. sec. Requa, Inc., Flowery Beauty Products, Inc., 1987—. Contbr. articles to profl. jour. and mags. Bd. dirs. Haym Salomon Home for the Aged, 1978-91, pres., 1981-91; bd. dirs. The Jaffa Inst. for Advancement Edn., 1994-95; bd. dirs. Jewish Fellowship of Hemlock Farms, 1995-2001, treas., 1996-98, sec. 1998-99; bd. dirs., 1992—, pres. Haym Salomon Found., 1992-99; mem. bd. advisors Touro Coll. Health Scis., 1989-90. Mem. ABA (food, drug and cosmetic law com., trademark and unfair competition com.), N.Y. State Bar Assn. (food, drug and cosmetics sect.), YRH Owners Corp. (bd. dirs., pres. 1989-92), Lords Valley Country Club (bd. govs. 1984-90, 1st v.p. 1987-88, 2d v.p. 1989-90), Zeta Beta Tau, Omicron (trustee Syracuse chpt. 1988-91). Jewish. Home: 429 E 52nd St New York NY 10022-6430 Office: Goetz Fitzpatrick Most & Bruckman LLP One Penn Plz New York NY 10119 E-mail: jmost@goetzfitz.com.

MOST, NATHAN, mutual fund executive; b. L.A., Mar. 22, 1914; s. Bernard and Bertha (Saltzman) M.; m. Evelyn Rosenthal, July 10, 1964; children—Stephen, John, Robert, Barbara. BA, UCLA, 1935. Exec. v.p. Getz Bros. & Co., San Francisco, 1945-60; pres. Carad Corp., Palo Alto, 1961-64; exec. v.p. James S. Baker Co., San Francisco, 1964-65, Pacific Vegetable Oil Corp., San Francisco, 1965-70, Am. Import Co., San Francisco, 1970-74; pres. Pacific Commodities Exchange, 1974-76; spl. asst. to chmn. Commodity Futures Trading Commn., Washington, May-Dec. 1976; pres. Amex Commodities Exch., N.Y.C., 1977-80; v.p. new products devel. Am. Stock Exch., 1980—96, sr. v.p., 1996—2002; pres., chmn., CEO iShares Inc., Wilmington, Del., 1990—92; pres., chmn. bd., CEO iShares Trust, 2000—; chmn. emeritus, bd. dirs. iShares Inc. and iShares Trust, Wilmington, 1992—. Pres. Amex Commodities Corp., Inc., N.Y.C., 1982-96; v.p. Calif. Council Internat. Trade, 1966-67; pres. Commodity Club San Francisco, 1970— ; bd. dirs. San Francisco-Pacific Commodity Exch., 1970— , San Francisco World Trade Assn., 1970— , World Affairs Council No. Calif., 1953-65; pres. San Francisco World Trade Assn., 1956-58; pres., chmn. bd. IShares Trust, San Francisco, 2000—. Councilman Atherton, Calif., 1959-64. Named one of 30 most influential people in the world of investing, Smart Money. Mem. Export Mgmt. Assn. No. Calif. (pres. 1972—), San Francisco Commodity Club (dir.). Home: PO Box 193 Burlingame CA 94011-0193 E-mail: natemost@aol.com.

MOSTAFA, JAVED, information scientist, educator; b. Chittagong, Bangladesh, July 31, 1966; came to U.S., 1984; s. Ghulam Mustafa and Jobeda Khatun; m. Sigma Salahuddin, June 7, 1991. BSc magna cum laude, N.W. Okla. State U., 1987; MA, Ohio State U., 1990; PhD, U. Tex., 1994. Dir. info. processing lab U. Tex., Austin, 1991-92; asst. prof. Ind. U., Bloomington, 1994—, Victor Yngve asst. prof., 1998-2000, Victor Yngve assoc. prof. info. sci., 2000—, assoc. prof. Sch. Informatics, 2000—. Adj. asst. prof. computer sci. dept. Ind. U., Inpls., 1996—, adj. assoc. prof. 2001-, rschr. web lab., 1996-97; vis. scholar sys. engrng. dept. Chinese U. Hong Kong, 1998. Author: Easy Internet Handbook, 1994; contbr. articles to profl. jours. Grantee NSF, 1999, 2000, Eli Lilly & Co., 1999, IMLS, 2001, NIH, 2002. Fellow Ctr. Social Informatics; mem. Am. Soc. Info. Sci., Assn. Computing Machinery, Am. Assn. for the Advancement of Sci., IEEE Computer Soc., bd. dir. ACM Trans. on Info. Sys., Phi Kappa Phi. Avocations: reading, traveling, jogging, racquetball. Home: 6456 Deerwood Ct Greenwood IN 46143 Office: Ind U SLIS # 025 10th & Jordan Ave Bloomington IN 47405-1801

MOSTELLER, FREDERICK, mathematical statistician, educator; b. Clarksburg, W.Va., Dec. 24, 1916; s. William Roy and Helen (Kelley) M.; m. Virginia Gilroy, May 17, 1941; children: William, Gale. ScB, Carnegie Inst. Tech. (now Carnegie-Mellon U.), 1938, MSc, 1939, DSc (hon.), 1974; AM, Princeton U., 1942, PhD, 1946; DSc (hon.), U. Chgo., 1973, Wesleyan U., 1983; D. of Social Scis. (hon.), Yale U., 1981; LLD (hon.), Harvard U., 1991. Research assoc. Office Pub. Opinion Research, 1942-44; spl. cons. research br. War Dept., 1942-43; research mathematician Statis. Research Group, Princeton, applied math. panel Nat. Devel. and Research Council, 1944-46; mem. faculty Harvard U., 1946—, prof. math. stats., 1951-87, Roger I. Lee prof., 1978-87, prof. emeritus, 1987—, chmn. dept. stats., 1957-69, 75-77, chmn. dept. biostats., 1977-81, chmn. dept. health policy and mgmt., 1981-87; dir. Tech. Assessment Group, 1987—; dir. Ctr. for Evaluation Am. Acad. Arts and Scis., 1994—. Vice chmn. Pres.'s Commn. on Fed. Stats., 1970-71; mem. Nat. Adv. Council Equality of Ednl. Opportunity, 1973-78, Nat. Sci. Bd. Commn. on Pre-coll. Edn. in Math., Sci. and Tech., 1982-83; Fund for Advancement of Edn. fellow, 1954-55; nat. tchr. NBC's Continental Class-room TV course in probability and stats., 1960-61; fellow Center Advanced Study Behavioral Sciences, 1962-63, bd. dirs., 1980-86; Guggenheim fellow, 1969-70; Miller research prof. U. Calif. at Berkeley, 1974-75; Hitchcock Found. lectr. U. Calif., 1985. Co-author: Gauging Public Opinion (editor Hadley Cantril), 1944, Sampling Inspection, 1948, The Pre-election Polls, 1948, 49, Stochastic Models for Learning, 1955, Probability with Statistical Applications, 1961, Inference and Disputed Authorship, The Federalist, 1964, The National Halothane Study, 1969, Statistics: A Guide to the Unknown, 3d edit., 1988, On Equality of Educational Opportunity, 1972, Sturdy Statistics, 1973, Statistics By Example, 1973, Cost, Risks and Benefits of Surgery, 1977, Data Analysis and Regression, 1977, Statistics and Public Policy, 1977, Data for Decisions, 1982, Understanding Robust and Exploratory Data Analysis, 1983, Biostatistics in Clinical Medicine, 1983, 3d edit., 1994, Beginning Statistics with Data Analysis, 1983, Exploring Data Tables, Trends and Shapes, 1985, Medical Uses of Statistics, 1986, 2d edit., 1992, Quality of Life and Technology Assessment, 1989, Fundamentals of Exploratory Analysis of Variance, 1992, Meta-analysis for Explanation, 1992, Doing More Good Than Harm, 1993, Medicine Worth Paying For, 1995; author articles in field. Trustee Russell Sage Found.; mem. bd. Nat. Opinion Research Center, 1962-66. Recipient Outstanding Statistician award Chgo. chpt. Am. Statis. Assn., 1971, Boston chpt., 1989, named Sports Statistician of 1996; recipient Myrdal prize Evaluation Research Soc., 1978, Paul F. Lazarsfeld prize Council Applied Social Research, 1979, R.A. Fisher award Com. of Pres.'s of Statis. Socs., 1987, Medallion of Ctrs. for Disease Control, 1988. Fellow AAAS (chmn. sect. U 1973, dir. 1974-78, pres. 1980, chmn. bd. 1981), Inst. Math. Statistics (pres. 1974-75), Am. Statis. Assn. (v.p. 1962-64, pres. 1967, Samuel S. Wilks medal 1986), Social Sci. Research Council (chmn. bd. dirs. 1966-68), Math. Social Sci. Bd. (acad. governing bd. 1962-67), Am. Acad. Arts and Scis. (council 1986-88), Royal Statis. Soc. (hon.); mem. Am. Philos. Soc. (council 1986-88), Internat. Statis. Inst. (v.p. 1986-88, pres.-elect 1989, pres. 1991-93), Math. Assn. Am., Psychometric Soc. (pres. 1957-58), Inst. Medicine of Nat. Acad. Scis. (council 1978), Nat. Acad. Scis., Biometric Soc. Office: 1 Oxford St Cambridge MA 02138-2901

MOSTELLER, HENRY W. retired electrical engineer; b. Detroit, Nov. 6, 1932; s. Walter A. and Elberta H. Mosteller; m. Louise Blanchard, July 11, 1955; children: Elaine, Janice. BS in Math., U.Mich., Ann Arbor, 1955; BSEE, U.Mich., 1955; MEE, Cornell U., Ithaca, N.Y., 1959; PhD, Cornell U., 1963. R&D engr. GE, Schenectady, NY, 1957—64, analytical engr., 1964—68, systems engr. Binghamton, NY, 1968—70, sr. engr. Schenectady, 1972—94. Adj. asst. prof. Union Coll., Schenectady, NY, 1964—68; adj. asst. prof. SUNY, Binghamton, 1968—70; dir. GE Computerization, Schenectady, NY, 1972—94; reviewer Assn. for Computing Machinery, N.Y.C., 1972—94. Contbr. Dir. Spiritual Frontiers Fellowship, Albany, NY, 1988—2001. 1st lt. U.S. Army, 1955—57. Mem.: IEEE (sr.), Sigma Xi, Eta Kappa Nu. Achievements include development of new design procedure for subsynchronous modal frequency protective relays, and transient performance models for boiling water (nuclear) reactors. Avocations: tchr. gardening classes, investing (computerized). Home: 24 Cedar Ln Scotia NY 12302

MOSTELLER, JAMES WILBUR, III, data processing executive; b. Ft. Riley, Kans., June 21, 1940; s. James Wilbur Jr. and Ruth Renfro (Thompson) M.; m. Sandra Josephine Stevenson, Oct. 13, 1962; children: Margaret, Steven, Michael. BS in Econs., Rensselaer Poly. Inst., 1962; MBA, Temple U., 1971. Cert. in data processing. Data processing sys. analyst Philco-Ford, Ft. Washington, Pa., 1966-69; data processing analyst and supr. Merck Sharp & Dohme, West Point, 1969-75; dir. mgmt. info. sys. KELCO divsn. Merck and Co., San Diego, 1975-87; dir. info. mgmt. Advanced Sys. divsn. United Technologies, 1987-88; computer scientist Navy Personnel Research and Devel. Ctr., 1988-97; head prodn. sys. Navy SPAWAR Sys. Ctr., 1997—. Bd. dirs. New Horizons Montessori Sch., Ft. Washington, 1974-75; leader youth programs North County YMCA, 1977-81; mem. San Diego Rsch. Park Com., 1978-86; 1st v.p., mem. exec. com. San Diego Space and Sci. Found., 1985-92. With USN, 1962-66, capt. res., 1966-93. Mem. Data Processing Mgmt. Assn., Assn. Sys. Mgmt., Naval Res. Assn. (life), U.S. Naval Inst. (life), Royal Scottish Country Dance Soc. (chmn. San Diego br. 2001—), La Playa Yacht Club, Beta Gamma Sigma, Sigma Alpha Epsilon (chpt. pres. 1961-62). Office: Navy SPAWAR Sys Ctr D0294 San Diego CA 92152-5001

MOSTELLER, ROBERT P. law educator; b. 1948; BA, U. N.C., 1970; MA, Harvard U., 1975; JD, Yale U., 1975. Bar: N.C. 1975, D.C. 1976. Law clk. to Hon. Braxton Craven U.S. Ct. Appeals (4th cir.), Asheville, NC, 1975-76; atty., chmn. trial div., tng. dir. D.C. Pub. Defender Svc., 1976-83; assoc. prof. Duke U., Durham, NC, 1983-87, prof., 1987-2001, Harry R. Chadwick, Sr. prof., 2001—, sr. assoc. dean, 1989-91, chair acad. counsel, 1998-2000. Mem. Phi Beta Kappa (pres. 1969-70). Office: Sch Law Duke U Durham NC 27708

MOSTER, MARY CLARE, public relations executive; b. Morristown, N.J., Apr. 7, 1950; d. Clarence R. and Ruth M. (Duffy) M.; m. Louis C. Williams, Jr., Oct. 4, 1987. BA in English with honors, Douglass Coll., 1972; MA in English Lit., Univ. Chgo., 1973. Accredited pub. rels. counselor. Editor No. Trust Bank, Chgo., 1973-75, advt. supr., 1975-77, communications officer, 1977-78; account exec. Hill & Knowlton, Inc., 1978-80, v.p., 1980-83, sr. v.p., 1983-87, sr. v.p., mng. dir., 1987-88; staff v.p. comms. Navistar Internat. Corp., 1988-93; v.p. corp. comms. Comdisco, Inc., Rosemont, Ill., 1993—. Bd. dirs. The Pegasus Players, 1993-2000. Author poetry, poetry translation. Bd. govs. Met. Planning Coun., Chgo., 1988-94; fellow Leadership Greater Chgo., 1989-90; bd. dirs. New City YMCA, Chgo., 1986-92; corp. devel. bd. Steppenwolf Theatre Co., Chgo., 1988-90; mem. The Chgo. Network, 1994—, bd. dirs., 1996-99. Mem. Nat. Investor Rels. Inst. (bd. dirs. 1988-89, 90-99, pres. Chgo. chpt. 1998-99), Arthur W. Page Soc., Pub. Rels. Soc. Am., Internat. Women's Forum. Avocations: sailing, cross-country skiing. Office: Comdisco Inc 6111 N River Rd Rosemont IL 60018-5158

MOSTILLO, RALPH, medical association administrator; s. Joseph and Antoinette Mostillo. BA in Chemistry magna cum laude, Rutgers U., Newark, 1972; MA in Biochemistry, Princeton U., 1974, PhD in Biochemistry, 1978. NIH rsch. fellow Princeton (N.J.) U., 1972-78; sr. scientist drug regulatory affairs Hoffmann-La Roche, Inc., Nutley, N.J., 1979-85; founder, chmn., chief exec. officer Am. Cancer Assn., 1986—. With USN, 1962—66, Vietnam. Mem.: N.Y. Acad. Scis., Am. Mktg. Assn., Am. Mgmt. Assn., Am. Chem. Soc., Vietnam Vets. Am., Am. Legion, Phi Beta Kappa, Sigma Xi. Achievements include research in on molecular transport systems in E. coli as general models for drug delivery into cells. Home: PO Box 505 Nutley NJ 07110-0505 Office: Am Cancer Assn PO Box 87 Nutley NJ 07110-0087 E-mail: ralphmost@hotmail.com.

MOST-LEVIN, CAROL LYNN, physician, geriatrician; b. Long Island, N.Y., Sept. 1, 1959; d. Herbert Jules and Jean (Friedman) Most; m. Ronald Mitchell Levin, June 17, 1979; children: Jay Samuel, Marc Andrew, Eric Brian. BA magna cum laude, La Salle Coll., Phila., 1981; MD, Med. Coll. Pa., 1985. Diplomate Nat. Bd. Med. Examiners; diplomate in internal medicine and geriatric medicine Am. Bd. Internal Medicine. Intern and resident Abington (Pa.) Meml. Hosp., 1985-88; pvt. practice, 1988-95, 2001—; internist Abington Meml. Hosp., 1995-2001, mem.-at-large med. exec. com., 1999—. Med. dir. U.S. Homecare, Phila., 1991-94; clin. instr. Temple U., Phila., 1995-96; instr. Jefferson U., 1996—; med. sch. interviewer Alleghany U., 1995-97; spkr. in field. Contbr. articles to mag., jours. Recipient First prize Eleanor Dixon Writing/Rsch. Competition, 1988. Fellow ACP; mem. AMA (Physician's Recognition award 1991, 94, 97, 2000), Am. Geriatrics Soc., Pa. Med. Soc., Montgomery County Med. Soc., Delaware Valley Geriatrics Soc. Avocations: traveling, cooking, decorating. Office: Levin and Most-Levin Med Assocs LLC 6921 B Frankford Ave Philadelphia PA 19135 E-mail: cmlmdfacp@aol.com.

MOSTOFF, ALLAN SAMUEL, lawyer, consultant; b. N.Y.C., Oct. 19, 1932; s. Morris and Ida (Goldman) M.; m. Alice Tamara Popelowsky, July 31, 1955; children: Peter Alexander, Nina Valerie. BS, Cornell U., 1953; MBA, NYU, 1954; LLB, N.Y. Law Sch., 1957. Bar: N.Y. 1958, D.C. 1964. Assoc. Olwine Connelly Chase O'Donnell & Weyher, N.Y.C., 1958-61; atty. SEC, Washington, 1962-66, asst. dir., 1966-69, assoc. dir., 1969-72, dir. divsn. investment mgmt. regulation, 1972-76; ptnr. Dechert Price & Rhoads, 1976-2000, Dechert, Washington, 2000—. Adj. prof. Georgetown U. Law Ctr., 1972-82; mem. Fin. Acctg. Standards Adv. Bd., 1982-86; adv. bd. Investment Lawyer; pres. Mutual Fund Dirs. Forum. Mem. ABA, Assn. of Bar of City of N.Y., Fed. Bar Assn. (past chmn. exec. coun. securities regulation com. 1990-92), Am. Law Inst. Home: 6417 Waterway Dr Falls Church VA 22044-1325 Office: Dechert 1775 I St NW Washington DC 20006-2402 E-mail: allan.mostoff@dechert.com.

MOSTOFI, FATHOLLAH KESHVAR, pathologist, educator, consultant; b. Teheran, Iran, Aug. 10, 1911; came to U.S., 1931; s. Farajullah Khan and Kursum (Khanum) M.; m. Dorothy Ida Krock, June 20, 1940; 1 child, Keith. AB, BSc, U. Nebr., 1935; MD, Harvard U., 1939, grad. Kennedy Sch. Govt., 1982. Diplomate Am. Bd. Pathology. Intern St. Luke's Hosp., Bethlehem, Pa., 1939-40; house officer Peter Bent Brigham Hosp., Boston, 1940-41; resident in pathology Boston Lying-In Hosp. and Free Hosp. for Women, 1941-42, Children's Hosp., Boston, 1942-43; asst. pathologist Mass. Gen. Hosp., 1943-44; rsch. fellow Nat. Cancer Inst., Bethesda, Md., 1947-48; pathologist, spl. asst. VA Cen. Lab. Anat. Pathology Armed Forces Inst. Path., Washington, 1948-62; chmn. dept. genitourinary pathology Armed Forces Inst. Pathology, 1948—. Sci. dir. Am. Registry Pathology, 1957-59; clin. assoc. prof. pathology Johns Hopkins U., Balt., 1960—; clin. prof. pathology Georgetown U., 1961—, U. Md., 1968—, Uniformed Svcs. U. Health Scis., Bethesda, Md., 1970—; head Collaborating Ctr. for Histological Classification of Tumors in Urinary Tract and Male Genital Sys., WHO, Geneva, 1963—; hon. prof. Chinese Peoples Liberation Army Gen. Hosp. Postgrad. Med. Sch., Beijing, 1988—; registrar Am. Urol. Assn., Washington, 1949—. Co-author: Tumors of the Male Genital System, 1973, International Histological Classification of Bladder Tumors, 1974, of Testes Tumors, 1977, of Prostatic Tumors, 1980, of Kidney Tumors, 1981, (four books transl. into Russian, French, Spanish) Atlas of Kidney Biopsies, 1980; editor: Bilharziasis Proc., 1976; co-editor: The Kidney, 1966, The Skin, 1971, The Platelet, 1972, The Liver, 1973, Striated Muscle, 1973, Kidney Disease: Present Status, 1979. Maj. M.C., U.S. Army, 1944-47. Recipient Presdl. Rank of Disting. Exec. Svc., 1982, Ferdinand C. Valentine award N.Y. Acad. Medicine, John Shaw Billings Lifetime Achievement award DOD-AFIP, ARP, 1995; 2 books dedicated to him. Fellow Royal Coll. Pathologists Australasia (hon.), Royal Coll. Pathologists U.K. (hon.); mem. Internat. Acad. Pathology (sec.-treas. 1952-70, pres. 1972-76), Internat. Soc. Pathology, U.S.-Can. Acad. Pathology (pres. 1972-73, gold medal 1974, ann. F.K. Mostofi award for disting. svc. to pathology established in his name), Internat. Coun. Socs. Pathology (sec.-treas. 1970—), Acad. Medicine (pres. 1992—), Cosmos Club, Harvard Club. Republican. Moslem. Avocation: photography. Home: 7001 Georgia St Chevy Chase MD 20815-4135 Office: Armed Forces Inst Pathology 14th And Alaska Ave NW Washington DC 20306-0001 E-mail: mostofi@afip.osd.mil.

MOSTOVOY, MARC SANDERS, conductor, music director; b. Phila., July 1, 1942; s. Ira and Floretta (Schiff) M. MusB, Temple U., 1963; postgrad., U. Pa., 1964-66; pvt. study in U.S.A., France, 1950-66; MusD (hon.), Combs Coll. Music, 1980; diploma, Acad. Music, Nice, France. Conductr, music dir. Concerto Soloists of Phila., 1964—; also bd. dirs., 1964—. Cultural advisor to gov. Commonwealth of Pa., Harrisburg, 1971—77; music dir. Mozart on the Sq., Phila., 1980—91; music advisor Walnut St. Theater, Phila., 1970—75; mem. music adv. panel Pa. Coun. on the Arts, 1991—92. Condr.: numerous nat. and internat. concert tours with Concerto Soloists Chamber Orch. of Phila., artistic dir.: Laurel Festival of the Arts, 1990—95; editor: various music compositions. Program adv. com. Nat. Mus. Am. Jewish History, 1985-86; bd. dirs. Citizens for the Arts in Pa., 1984-86. Recipient Orpheus Club award, 1958, Govs. citation Commonwealth of Pa., 1976, Mayors citation City of Phila., 1984; Temple U. scholar, 1960-63. Mem. Mus. Fund Soc. Phila., Greater Phila. C. of C. (adv. com. arts and cultural com. 1984-88). Jewish. Office: The Chamber Orch Phila 5th Fl 1520 Locust St Philadelphia PA 19102 E-mail: csoloists@aol.com.

MOSTOW, GEORGE DANIEL, mathematics educator; b. Boston, July 4, 1923; s. Isaac J. and Ida (Rotman) M.; m. Evelyn Davidoff, Sept. 1, 1947; children: Mark Alan, David Jechiel, Carol Held, Jonathan Carl. BA, Harvard U., 1943, MA, 1946, PhD, 1948; DSc (hon.), U. Ill., Chgo., 1989. Instr. math. Princeton U., 1947-48; mem. Inst. Advanced Study, 1947-49, 56-57, 75, mem. bd. of trustees, 1982-92; asst. prof. Syracuse U., 1949-52; asst. prof. math. Johns Hopkins U., 1952-53, assoc. prof., 1954-56, prof., 1957-61; prof. math. Yale U., 1961-66, James E. English prof. math., 1966-81, Henry Ford II prof. math., 1981-98, chmn., 1971-74, prof. emeritus, 1998—. Vis. prof. Conselho Nat. des Pesquisas, Inst. de Matematica, Rio de Janiero, Brazil, 1953-54, 91, U. Paris, 1966-67, Hebrew U., Jerusalem, 1967, Tata Inst. Fundamental Rsch., Bombay, 1970, Inst. des Hautes Etudes Scientifiques, Bures-Sur-Yvette, 1966, 71, 75, Japan Soc. for Promotion of Sci., 1985, Eidgenossische Technische Hochschule, Switzerland, 1986; chmn. U.S. Nat. Com. for Math , 1971-73, 83-85, Office Math. Scis., NRC, 1975-78; mem. sci. adv. coun. Math. Scis. Rsch. Inst., Berkeley, Calif., 1988-91; mem. sci. adv. com., bd. govs. Weizmann Inst., Israel, 1987—; bd. govs. Tel Aviv U., 1990-2000; mem. Harvard Grad. Coun., 1988-91; mem. vis. com. dept. math. Harvard U., 1975-81, MIT, 1981-94; Ritt lectr. Columbia U., 1982, Bergman lectr. Stanford U., 1983, Sachar lectr. Tel Aviv U., 1985, Karcher lectr. U. Okla., 1986, Markert lectr. Pa. State U., 1993. Assoc. editor Annals of Math, 1957-64, Trans. Am. Math. Soc, 1958-65, Am. Scientist, 1970-82, Geometrica Dedicata, 1985-90; bd. cons. Jour. D'Analyse Mathématique, 1994—; editor Am. Jour. Math, 1965-69, assoc. editor, 1969-79; author rsch. articles. Fulbright rsch. scholar, Utrecht U., The Netherlands; Guggenheim fellow, 1957-58 Mem. AAAS, NAS (chmn. sect. math. 1982-84), Am. Math. Soc. (pres. 1987-88, Steele prize for Paper of Lasting Importance 1993), Internat. Math. Union (chmn. U.S. del. to Gen. Assembly Warsaw 1982, exec. com. 1983-86), Phi Beta Kappa, Sigma Xi. Home: 25 Beechwood Rd Woodbridge CT 06525-1309 Office: Yale Univ Dept Mathematics New Haven CT 06520 E-mail: george.mostow@yale.edu.

MOSTOWYCZ, LEONIDAS, radiologist; b. Ukraine, Oct. 4, 1919; came to U.S., 1957; MD, U. Innsbruck, 1951. Intern Sts. Mary & Elizabeth Hosp., Louisville, 1957-58; resident U. Clinics, Innsbruck, 1952-55, U. Hosps., Innsbruck, 1955-57, U. Louisville Hosp., 1961-64; prof. emeritus U. Ky. Coll. Medicine, 1994—. Cons. in radiology for new ind. East European states. Mem. AMA, Am. Coll. Radiology, Radiol. Soc. N.Am., Urkanian Med. Assn. N.Am., Ky. Med. Assn.

MOSZKOWICZ, VIRGINIA MARIE, quality administrator; b. Uniontown, Pa., July 6, 1952; d. Edward Louis and Theresa Elizabeth (Congelio) Olsavicky; m. Michael John Moszkowicz, Sept. 29, 1979. BA in Chemistry, Thiel Coll., 1974; MS in Organic Chemistry, Duquesne U., 1978; MS in Mgmt. Tech., MIT, 1987. Devel. chemist PPG Inds., Pitts., 1974-75; analytical chemist Bayer/Mobay Chem. Corp., 1975-78; chem testing leader sensitized goods mfg. divsn. Eastman Kodak Co., Rochester, 1978-80, devel. engr. sensitized goods mfg. divsn., 1980-84, product mgr. motion picture film, 1984-86, unit dir., quality assurance orgn. mfg. supply & distbn., 1987-91; mid. mgr. quality and indsl. engring. Equipment Mfg. Divsn., Ro, 1991-94, quality leader mechanical products, 1995-96; project mgr. consumer cameras Eastman Kodak Co., Rochester, 1996; quality mgr. mfg. Xerox Corp., 1996-2000; quality dir. logistics R.R. Donnelly & Sons, Chgo., 2000—. Past bd. dirs. Lifetime Assistance Inc. Mme. Am. Soc. Quality Control, Toastmasters Internat. (dist. gov. 1991, club pres. 1994, Toastmaster of Yr. 1981, Disting. Toastmaster 1987). Avocations: skiing, golf, travel, French and German langs. E-mail: ginng.moszkowicz@rrd.com.

MOTAMED, THOMAS FIROUZ, insurance company executive; BA, Adelphi U., 1971; JD, Delaware Law Sch., 1975. Sci. faculty Malvern Prep. Sch., Pa., 1975-76; field underwriter New York Life, Carle Place, NY, 1976-77; exec. v.p. Chubb & Son Inc. (subs. of Chubb Corp.), Warren, N.J., 1977—. Office: Chubb Corp 15 Mountain View Rd Warren NJ 07059 E-mail: tmotamed@chubb.com.

MOTE, CLAYTON DANIEL, JR. university president, mechanical engineer, educator; b. San Francisco, Feb. 5, 1937; s. Clayton Daniel and Eugenia (Isnardi) M.; m. Patricia Jane Lewis, Aug. 18, 1962; children: Melissa Michelle, Adam Jonathan. BSc, U. Calif., Berkeley, 1959, MS, 1960, PhD, 1963; Doctorate (hon.), Tashkent State Tech. U., 2001; DSc, Ohio State U., 2001. Registered profl. engr., Calif. Asst. specialist U. Calif. Forest Products Labs., 1961-62; asst. mech. engr., 1962-63; lectr. mech. engring. U. Calif., Berkeley, 1962-63, asst. prof., 1967-69, asst. research engr., 1968-69, assoc. prof., assoc. research engr., 1969-73, prof., 1973-98, vice chmn. mech. engring. dept., 1976-80, 83-86, chmn. mech. engring. dept., 1987-91, vice chancellor univ. rels., FANUC chair mech. systems, 1991-98; research fellow U. Birmingham, Eng., 1963-64; asst. prof. Carnegie Inst. Tech., 1964-67; pres., Glen L. Martin Inst. prof. engring. U. Md., College Park, 1998—, pres., 1998—. Vis. prof. Norwegian Inst. Wood Tech., 1972—73, vis. sr. scientist, 1976, 78, 80, 84, 85; cons. in engring., design and analysis; sr. scientist Alexander Von Humboldt Found., Germany, 1988, Japan Soc. for Promotion of Sci., Japan, 1991. Mem. editl. bd. Soma Jour. Sound and Vibration, Machine Vibration; contbr. articles to profl. jours.; patentee in field. NSF fellow, 1963-64, Sr. Scientist fellowship Japan Soc. Promotion Sci., 1991, Berkeley fellow, 2001; recipient Disting. Teaching award, U. Calif., 1971, Pi Tau Sigma Excellence in Teaching award, U. Calif., 1975, Humboldt Prize, Fed. Republic Germany, 1988, Disting. Engring. Alumnus award U. Calif., 2001, Frederick W. Taylor Rsch. medal. Soc. Mfg. Engrs., 1991, Hetenyi award Soc. Exptl. Mechanics, 1992, Eagle award Met. Washington chpt. ARCS, 2000. Fellow: AAAS, NAE, ASME (hon.; v.p. environ. and transp. 1986—90, nat. chmn. noise control and acoustics 1980—84, chmn. San Francisco sect. 1978—79, Blackall award 1975, Disting. Svc. award 1991, Charles Russ Richards award 1994, Rauleigh lectr. 1994), Acoustical Soc. Am., Internat. Acad. Wood Sci.; mem.: ASTM (com. on snow skiing F-27 1984—87), Orthopaedic Rsch. Soc., Am. Soc. Biomechanics, Am. Acad. Mechanics, Am. Soc. Engring. Edn. (Ralph Coast Roe award 1997), Internat. Soc. Skiing Safety (v.p., sec. 1977—85, bd.dirs. 1977—, chmn. sci. com. 1985—), Nat. Soc. Collegiate Scholars, Golden Key Nat. Honor Soc., Phi Kappa Phi, Omicron Delta Kappa, Tau Beta Pi, Pi Tau Sigma, Sigma Xi. Home: Pres' Residence One Presidential Dr College Park MD 20740 Office: Office of the President University of Maryland Main Administration Building College Park MD 20742-5025 E-mail: dmote@deans.umd.edu.

MOTE, MARIE THERESE, reference librarian; b. Madisonville, Ky., May 5, 1948; d. John H. and Mary Cecelia (Sullivan) M. BA, Lincoln Meml. U., 1973; MLS, Vanderbilt U., 1974. Children's libr. Harris County Libr. System, Houston, 1975-76; learning resource ctr. coord. Aldine Sch. Dist., 1976-81; reference libr. Bellaire (Tex.) City Libr., 1983—. Poetry columnist Tazewell-New Tazewell Observer, 1969-74. Mem. ALA (social responsibility roundtable, intellectual freedom roundtable), Pub. Libr. Assn., Tex. Libr. Assn., Alpha Chi, Phi Alpha Theta. Avocations: art, writing fiction, Mulan ch'uan, Tai chi ch'uan, Tai chi sword, Tai chi broadsword. Home: PO Box 1752 Bellaire TX 77402-1752 Office: Bellaire City Libr 5111 Jessamine St Bellaire TX 77401-4424 E-mail: mmote@pdq.net.

MOTEJUNAS, GERALD WILLIAM, lawyer; b. Boston, Jan. 18, 1950; s. Peter and Eva C. (Jankus) M.; m. Patricia A. McKeon, June 23, 1984; children: Scott Peterson, Mark Whitney. BA, Northeastern U., 1972; JD, Suffolk U., 1976. Bar: Mass. 1976, U.S. Dist. Ct. Mass., 1977, U.S. Supreme Ct. 1983. Assoc. Lecomte, Emanuelson, Motejunas & Doyle, Boston, 1976-85, ptnr., 1985—2002; shareholder Smith & Brink, 2002—. Author: Suffolk U. Law Rev., 1975; editor, 1976. Mem. ABA (chmn., editor, vice chmn. property ins. law com.), ATLA, Def. Rsch. Inst., Mass. Bar Assn., Boston Bar Assn., Loss Execs. Assn., Boston Athenaeum, Appalachian Mountain Club (exec. com. 1980-81). Avocations: skiing, golf. Office: Smith & Brink 122 Quincy Shore Dr Quincy MA 02171

MOTES, JOSEPH MARK, cruise and convention promotion company executive; b. Leesburg, Fla., Oct. 12, 1948; s. Lewis Jackson and Yolanda (Fernandez) M. AA in Computer Sci., Miami-Dade Community Coll., 1976. Promoter Trekruise & Seatrek, 1975—; conv. promoter Trekon & Vulkon, Fla., 1977—; v.p. Seatrek Ent., Inc., Cooper City. Pres. Genesis Prodns., Inc., 1992—. Sgt. USMC, 1967-74, Vietnam. Mem. SAR, SCV. Republican. Roman Catholic. Avocations: water sports, travel, boating, photography. Home and Office: 2133 NW 208th Ter Pembroke Pines FL 33029-2320

MOTES, MICHAEL ALLEN, psychologist; b. Yuma, Ariz., Aug. 21, 1970; s. Larry Franklin and Cecilia Mary (Langford) M.; m. Kendra Rose Hensley-Motes, Jan. 1, 1997. AA, Fla. C.C., Jacksonville, 1993; BA in Psychology, U. N.Fla., 1995, MA in Gen. Psychology, 1996. Grad. student tchg. asst. U. N. Fla., Jacksonville, 1995-96, Tex. Christian U., Ft. Worth, 1998—. Vis. instr. dept. psychology, U. N. Fla., Jacksonville, 1996-98. Contbr. articles to profl. jours. Mem. Fla. Coun. of Sexual Abuse Svcs., Inc., 1994-96. Recipient scholarship Humana Found., 1990-94. Mem. Am. Psychol. Soc., Southwestern Psychol. Assn., Southeastern Psychol. Assn. Libertarian. Avocations: computer programming, skiing, surfing. Office: Tex Christian U/Dept Psyc PO Box 298920 Fort Worth TX 76129-0001 E-mail: mmotes@netzero.net.

MOTHERSBAUGH, ROBERT LEW, fundraising executive; b. Bellefonte, Pa., May 5, 1965; s. Robert Charles and Kathy Lee (Meyer) M.; m. Lori Anne Marchese, Mar. 9, 1991;children: Leah Rhian, Cameron Robert. BS, Pa. State U., 1987. Cert. fundraising exec. Asst. dir. fundraising Pa. State U., University Park, 1987-90; assoc. dir. fundraising Gettysburg (Pa.) Coll., 1990-91, dir. devel., 1991-93; dir. devel. fundraising Lycoming Coll., Williamsport, 1993-94, chief devel. officer, 1994—. Republican. Lutheran. Home: RR 2 Box 181F Centre Hall PA 16828-9760 Office: Lycoming Coll 700 College Pl Williamsport PA 17701-5157

MOTHKUR, SRIDHAR RAO, radiologist; b. Mothkur, India, Oct. 5, 1950; came to U.S., 1975; naturalized. s. Venkat Rao and Laxmi Bai (Gundepally) M.; m. Sheila Rama Rao Paga, Nov. 30, 1973; children: Swathi, Preethi, Venkat Krishna. Student, Coll. Arts and Sci. Osmania U., Siddipet, India, 1966; MB, BS, Osmania U., Hyderabad, India, 1972, DPH, 1974; MPA, Ind. U. N.W., 2000. Diplomate Am. Bd. Radiology. Rotating intern Osmania Gen. Hosp., Hyderabad, 1972-73, internal medicine intern, 1973, resident in surgery, 1974-75; resident Resurrection Hosp., Chgo., 1975-76; resident in radiology Luth. Gen. Hosp., Park Ridge, 1976-79, chief resident radiology, 1978-79; with rotations in nuclear medicine, angiography and neuroradiology Rush-Presbyn. St. Luke's Med. Ctr., Chgo., 1978; chmn. and med. dir. dept. radiology Louise Burg Hosp., 1979-85, Shriner's Hosp., Chgo., 1986-88; fellow in ultrasound and computered tomography U. Ill., 1988-89, fellow in magnetic resonance imaging, 1988-89; staff radiologist St. Anthony Hosp., Michigan City, Ind., 1989—, med. dir. MRI Ctr., 1989—; pvt. practice, 1989—; staff radiologist Kingwood Hosp., 1989-94, Charter Hosp., Behavioral Health Sys. Ind., Michigan City, 1994-96; pres. Michigan City Radiologists, Inc., 1998—. Cons., radiologist Med. Group Michigan City, 1989—98, Franklin Clin. and Med. Watch, Michigan City, 1989—; spl. staff radiologist Christ hosp. Med. Ctr., Oak Lawn, Ill., 1988—89, Jasper County Meml. Hosp., Rensselaer, Ind., 1994—, United Diagnostic Svcs., Westchester, Ill., 1979—2000; med. dir. interventional radiology St. Anthony and Meml. Hosp., Michigan City, 1989—93; dir. MRI Ctr. Meml. Hosp., 1989—97; med. dir. interventional radiology St. Anthony and Meml. Hosp., Michigan City, 1989—93; clin. asst. prof. radiology U. Ill., Chgo., 1990—; others in field. Mem. Chinmaya Mission, Vishva Hindu Parishad. Fellow: Internat. Coll. Angiology, Am. Coll. Angiology, Am. Coll. Internat. Physicians; mem.: AmAm. Assn. Therapeutic and Interventional Neuroradiology, La Porte County Med. Soc., Telugu Assn. Greater Chgo., Chgo. Med. Soc., Ind. Med. Soc., Ill. Med. Soc., Ind. Assn. Physicians Indian Origin, India Med. Assn. N.W. Ind. (bd. dirs. 1999—2001), Am. Assn. Radiologists Indian Origins, Ind. Interventional Radiol. Assn., Tristate Telugu Assn., Indian Radiol. and Imaging Assn., Ind. Assn. Physicians from India, Soc. Magnetic Resonance in Medicine, Soc. Cardiovascular and Interventional Radiology, Soc. Magnetic Resonance Imaging, Am. Coll. Healthcare Execs., Am. Telugu Assn., Am. Soc. Head and Neck Radiology, Am. Coll. Emergency Physicians, Am. Diabetes Assn., Am. Assn. Physicians of Indian Origin, Am. Roentgen Ray Soc., Telugu Assn., Radiol. Soc. N.Am., AMA, Am. Assn. Andhra Brahmins, Internat. Soc. Krishna Consciousness, Pi Alpha Alpha. Republican. Home: 1457 Sand Creek Dr Chesterton IN 46304-3393 Office: Michigan City Radiologists Inc 8865 W 400 N Ste 115 Michigan City IN 46360-9223

MOTIN, REVELL JUDITH, retired data processing executive; b. Bayonne, N.J., July 24, 1941; d. Charles and Belle (Laks) Motin; children from a previous marriage: Laura Mantell, Deborah Mantell. BS in Psychology cum laude, Bklyn. Coll. CUNY, 1969. Systems analyst Univac div. Sperry Corp., N.Y.C., 1961-66; programmer, analyst J.C. Penney Co., 1966-67; systems and programming cons. Automated Concepts, Inc., 1968-72; ind. systems and programming cons., 1972-76; mgr. systems and programming Citibank, NA, 1976-83; v.p. data processing Columbia Savs. Bank, Fair Lawn, N.J., 1983-96; ret., 1996. Mem. Fin. Mgrs. Soc., Mensa. Jewish. Home: 43 Riverside Ave Haverstraw NY 10927-2009 E-mail: revnorm@aol.com.

MOTLEY, CONSTANCE BAKER (MRS. JOEL WILSON MOTLEY), federal judge, former city official; b. New Haven, Sept. 14, 1921; d. Willoughby Alvha and Rachel (Huggins) Baker; m. Joel Wilson Motley, Aug. 18, 1946; 1 son, Joel Wilson, III. AB, NYU, 1943; LLB, Columbia U., 1946. Bar: N.Y. bar 1948. Mem. Legal Def. and Ednl. Fund, NAACP, 1945-65; mem. N.Y. State Senate, 1964-65; pres. Manhattan Borough, 1965-66; U.S. dist. judge So. Dist. N.Y., 1966-82, chief judge, 1982-86, sr. judge, 1986—. Author: Equal Justice Under Law, 1998. Mem. N.Y. State Adv. Council Employment and Unemployment Ins., 1958-64. Mem. Assn. Bar City N.Y. Office: US Dist Ct US Courthouse 500 Pearl St New York NY 10007-1316 E-mail: constance_motley@nysd.uscourts.gov.

MOTLEY, MICHAEL TILDEN, communication educator; b. Salt Lake City, Jan. 4, 1945; s. Henry Lee and Lyda Edyth (Simpson) M.; m. Deirdre Mary Sullivan, Dec. 15, 1973; children: Shannon, Shane. BA, U. Tex., 1965, MA, 1967; PhD, Pa. State U., 1970. Asst. prof. Calif. State U., Fresno, 1970-71, asst. prof., assoc. prof. L.A., 1971-77; assoc. prof. Ohio State U., Columbus, Ohio, 1977-82; prof. U. Calif., Davis, 1982—. Author: Orientations to Language and Communication, 1978, Overcoming Your Fear of Public Speaking: A Proven Method, 1995; contbr. articles to profl. jours. Mem. Western Speech Communication Assn. (chair lang. behavior divsn. 1974-76), Speech Communication Assn. (chairlang. sci. divsn. 1976-77). Avocations: jazz saxophone, skiing, Bonsai art. Office: U Calif Dept Communication Davis CA 95616

MOTOLA, JAY A. urologist; b. Bklyn., Aug. 9, 1960; s. Charles and Florence (Negrin) M.; m. Sue R. Mandel, June 20, 1982; children: Hillary, Allison, Craig. BA summa cum laude, Boston U., 1982; MD, SUNY, Stony Brook, 1986. Diplomate Am. Bd. Urology. Intern in surgery L.I. Jewish Med. Ctr., 1986-87, resident in surgery, 1987-88, resident in urology, 1988-91, chief resident in urology, 1991-92, physician, urologist N.Y., 1986-92; pvt. practice Carmel, 2000—; physician, urologist East Hudson Urology Group, 1992-2000; chmn. dept. surgery Putnam Hosp., 1999—. Attending physician No. Westchester Hosp. Ctr., Putnam Hosp., Hudson Valley Hosp.; asst. attending physician Columbia Presbyn. Hosp.; presenter in field. Contbr. articles to profl. jours. Recipient award Am. Coll. Surgeons, 1989, Rsch. grant El DuPont De Nemours & Co., Inc., 1989, Rsch. grant Haemonetics Corp., 1989. Fellow ACS; mem. AMA, Am. Urol. Assn., Endourology Soc., N.Y. State Med. Soc., Putnam County Med. Soc. (pres. 1997, v.p. 1996, sec. 1995), Phi Beta Kappa, Alpha Epsilon Delta, Psi Chi, Pi Sigma Alpha. Home: 7 Lawrence Farms Crossway Chappaqua NY 10514-1209 Office: The Barns Office Ctr 667 Stoneleigh Ave Carmel NY 10512-2454 E-mail: jaymotola@worldnet.att.net.

MOTRONI, HECTOR JOHN, manufacturing executive; b. Havana, Cuba, Dec. 2, 1943; came to U.S., 1956; s. Marco Antonio and Lilia Ines (Suarez) M.; m. Myra Helene Egan, Aug. 9, 1969; children: Marcus Alan, Melissa Aimee. BA, Dartmouth Coll., 1966, BE, 1967, ME, 1968. Engr. USPHS, Bethesda, Md., 1969-71; various positions Xerox Corp., Stamford, Conn., 1971-99, corp. sr. v.p., chief staff officer, 1999—. Bd. dirs. Prep for Prep. Trustee Temple Israel, Westport, Conn., 1981-84; bd. adv. Outward Bound USA, 1998; bd. dirs. Nat. Action Coun. for Minorities in Engring. Named Hispanic Achiever of Yr., Hispanic Corp. Achievers, 1997; recipient Eagle award Nat. Eagle Inst., 1997. Mem. Nat. Policy Assn. (bd. dirs., chmn. com. new Am. realities 1996—), Dartmouth Soc. Engrs. (pres. 1977-85), Dartmouth Coll. Alumni Coun. (chmn. communications 1983-88), Coun. of the Ams. (adv. bd. 1983-89), Forum for World Affairs (bd. dirs. 1996—). Avocation: running. Office: Xerox Corp PO Box 1600 Stamford CT 06904-1600

MOTSENBOCKER, REX ALAN, construction company executive; b. Norman, Okla., Dec. 14, 1962; s. Rex Albert and Nondace Nadine (Bonner) M.; m. Karla Doreen Miller, Nov. 14, 1992. BS in BA, Calif. State U., Sacramento, 1984; BS in Constrn. Engring., Ariz. State U., 1986; MBA in Fin. magna cum laude, Western Internat. U., Phoenix, 1994; postgrad., So. Calif. U., Newport, 1994—. Cert. fin. cons. Project coord. Tibshraeny Bros., Mesa, Ariz., 1986; project mgr. Joe E. Woods, Tempe, 1986-87; project engr. Sundt Corp., Phoenix, 1987—; pres. Master Investments, 1994—; CFO Master Builders Devel., LLC, Las Vegas, Nev., 1994—; mgr., CFO Remington Estates Devel., L.L.C., Phoenix, 1995—. Bd. dirs. bullion Recovery Sys., Inc., Phoenix. Author: Financial Aspects of Investing in Mexico, 1994. Team leader Senator McCain Re-election Campaign, Phoenix, 1992-94; project dir. Christmas in April, Phoenix, 1989-93. Mem. Project Mgrs. Inst. (v.p. membership 1990—), Am. Mgrs. Assn., Constrn. Mgmt. Assn., Phoenix C. of C., Nat. Asbestos Council, Ariz. State U. Alumni Assn. (v.p. bd. 1994—), Delta Mu Delta (v.p. 1993—). Republican. Avocations: triathlons, singing. Home: 15833 N 7th Dr Phoenix AZ 85023-4435

MOTSETT, CHARLES BOURKE, sales and marketing executive; b. Peoria, Ill., Jan. 13, 1949; s. William James and Matilda (Robb) M.; m. Mary T. Werner, Aug. 26, 1972; children: Jon Bourke, Jill Suzanne, Brian Werner. BA in Polit. Sci., Econs. and Mktg., U. So. Fla., 1974. Product support mktg. analyst Caterpillar Tractor Co., 1974-75; parts and service sales rep. Caterpillar Ams. Co., Mexico City, 1976-79; product support rep. Caterpillar Tractor Co., Vancouver, B.C., Can., 1979-80, group prodr. mgr. remanufactured products Peoria, 1981-84, dist. mgr. parts and service sales Jacksonville, Fla., 1984-85; v.p. sales, customer svc. and mktg. Multi Media Productions of Am., Inc., 1985-86; v.p. sales and mktg. Consol. Indsl. Skills Corp., 1987—, corp. officer, 1988-92; v.p., gen. mgr. Ogden CISCO Inc., 1992-94; v.p. sales and mktg. CompuTower Technologies Corp., Miami, 1994—, Shred All, 1995; pres., CEO, Bus. Devel. Specialists, Inc., Jacksonville, 1996—. Author: If It Wasn't for the People...This Job Would Be Fun (Coaching for Buy-in and Results, 1998; contbr. ; co-author: How To Find a Qualified Corporate or Executive Coach, 2001. V.p. PTO, Dunlap, Ill., 1981—82; mem. adv. coun. Sch. Bd. Vocat. Edn., 1991—92; pres. bd. dirs. N.E. Fla. Jr. Achievement, Jr. Achievement Fla. First Coast, Inc.; vice chmn. St. Anthony's Ch., Vancouver, 1979—80; chmn. St. Jude Ch., Dunlap, 1982—83, Bishop Kenny H.S. PTO Polit. Action Com., 1989; pres. bd. dirs. Cath. Charities Housing Assn. Decorated Silver Star, Air medal with V device, Bronze Star with V device, Purple Heart with oak leaf cluster, Army Commendation medal with V device, Good Conduct medal, Combat Infantryman's badge. Mem. ASTD, Internat. Coach Fedn., Soc. Automotive Engrs., Am. Soc. Naval Engrs., Soc. Naval Architects and Marine Engrs., Am. Inst. Plant Engrs. (bd. dirs., conf. presenter), Am. Nuclear Soc., Assn. Plant Engrs., U.S. Army Forces Assn., Nat. Assn. Bus. Coaches (bd. dirs., chmn. credentialing com.), Spl. Internat. Coach Fedn., Assn. Facilities Engrs., Propellor Club. Republican. Roman Catholic. Avocations: scuba diving, sailing, reading, golf. Home: 4457 Barrington Oaks Dr Jacksonville FL 32257-5092 E-mail: cork@bdspec.com.

MOTSINGER, JOHN KINGS, lawyer, mediator, arbitrator; b. Winston-Salem, N.C., Aug. 13, 1947; s. Madison Eugene and Margaret Mary (Kings) M.; m. Elisabeth Sykes, June 18, 1989; children: Christian Sykes, Lissa Sykes, John, Jr. BA, Washington & Lee U., 1970; MS, Georgetown U., 1972; JD, Wake Forest U., 1983. Bar: N.C. 1983, U.S. Dist. Ct. (mid. dist.) N.C. 1984. Consumer affairs assoc. U.S Postal Svc., Washington, 1972-73; pres., gen. mgr. Sta. WIPS-Radio, Ticonderoga, N.Y., 1973-79; staff atty. United Guaranty Corp., Greensboro, N.C., 1983-86, Republic Mortgage Ins. Co., Winston-Salem, 1986-91; v.p. law RMIC Corp., 1988-91; exec. dir. Carolina Conciliation Svcs. Corp., 1992—. Past pres. Unitarian-Universalist Fellowship of Winston-Salem, 1993-94. Mem. ABA, N.C. Bar Assn. (corp. counsel sect. councilor 1989-93), N.C. State Bar, Am. Arbitration Assn., N.C. Assn. Profl. Family Mediators (past pres.), Assn. Conflict Resolution (mem. family sect.). Democrat. Unitarian-Universalist. Avocations: jogging, music, reading. Home: 204 Cascade Ave Winston Salem NC 27127-2029 Office: Carolina Conciliation Svcs Corp PO Box 10328 Old Salem Sta Winston Salem NC 27108-0328 E-mail: johnmot@conciliation.com.

MOTT, CHARLES DAVIS, civil engineer; b. Phila., Aug. 30, 1914; s. Charles Hillard and Emma (Davis) M.; m. Ellen Mary Hooge, Aug. 13, 1938 (dec.); children: Ellen H., Charles H., Joseph W. H.; m. Helen M. Michaels, 1993. BSc in Civil Engring., U. Pa., Phila., 1932; grad., Army-Navy Guided Missile Sch., Ft. Bliss, Tex., 1951; M Engring. Adminstrn., George Washington U., 1967. Engr. Cruse Kemper Co., Ambler, Pa., 1936-37; flight leader Am. Vol. Group, Burma, China, 1941-45; tech. staff/mgr. Analytic Svcs., Arlington, Va., 1963—. Mem. staff Rsch. and Devel. Bd., Office Sec. of Def., Washington, 1952-55. Pres. Lakevale Ct. Citizens Assn., Vienna, Va., 1972, 87. Capt. USN (aviator), 1937-41, 1946-63. Decorated DFC; recipient Cloud and Banner medal Chinese Air Force, 1958, POW medal USN, 1990. Mem. AIAA (mem. coun. Nat. Capitol sect. 1984-86), Am. Def. Preparedness Assn. Baptist. Achievments include membership in concept formulation team, F-15, Navy Torpedo Programs Review Group and participant in Project Forecast: rsearch in air to surface guided weapons. Home: 2522 Rocky Branch Rd Vienna VA 22181-4068 Office: 2522 Rocky Branch Rd Vienna VA 22181-4068

MOTT, EARL, artist; b. San Augustine, Tex., May 9, 1949; s. J.B. and Lillie Mae M.; m. Frances Katherene Mott, Oct. 30, 1975 (dec. Apr. 1993); children: Amber Katherene Fanning; stepchildren: Ricky Lynn Plunk, Gary Lee Plunk, Jamey Leon Plunk. Student, Art Instrn. Schs., 1968—71, Virginia Blackmon, 1973—74, Foster Caddell's Art Sch., 1977. Author, artist: Secrets From an Oil Painting Diary, 1988; artist The Best of Portrait Painting, 1998; contbr. articles to profl. publs.; one man shows at Angelina Coll., 1975, 82, 83, 87, Kurth Meml. Libr., 2001; group shows at Mus. East Tex., 1995, others. With USN, 1968-70. Recipient numerous awards for paintings. Mem. Oil Painters of Am. Baptist. Avocations: poetry, reading, hiking, writing, photography. Home: 304 Paul Ave Lufkin TX 75901

MOTT, FREDERICK B., JR. publishing executive; Pub. Post-Tribune , Gary, Ind., 1991—95; pres., publ. The State, Columbia, SC, 1995—. Office: The State 1401 Shop Rd Columbia SC 29201-4814*

MOTT, JUNE MARJORIE, school system administrator; b. Faribault, Minn., Mar. 8, 1920; d. David C. and Tillie W. (Nelson) Shifflett; m. Elwood Knight Mott, Oct. 18, 1958. BS, U. Minn., 1943, MA, 1948. Tchr. high schs. in Minn., 1943-46, 48-53, 54-57; script writer Hollywood, Calif., 1953-54; tchr. English, creative writing and journalism Mt. Miguel H.S., Spring Valley, 1957-86, chmn. English dept., 1964-71, chmn. dist. English coun., 1967-68; elected mem. Grossmont Union H.S. Governing Bd., 1986—, clk. sch. bd., 1989, v.p. governing bd., 1989-90, 93, pres. sch. bd., 1991-92, v.p., 1992-93, pres. governing bd., 1993-94, v.p., 1998. Mem. Press Bur., Grossmont (Calif.) H.S. Dist., 1958-86. Author, editor in field; scriptwriter TV prodn. Lamp Unto My Feet, Jam Dandy Corp.; free-lance writer, cons. travel writer, photographer; editor, publ. Listening Heart, 1989. Vice chmn. polit. action San Diego County Regional Resource Ctr., 1980-81; mem. S.D. Bd. of Alcohol and Drug Abuse Prevention, 1990—, Curriculum Com. Grossmont Dist., 1990—, Site Facilities Com., Master Planning Com., 1992—, East County Issues and Mgmt. Com., 1990—, East County Women in Edn.; apptd. del. Calif. Sch. Bds. Assn., 1992—, del. assembly, 1992—, apptd. to Race/Human Rels. Com., 1992—, elected to region 17 del. assembly, 1993—; v.p., pub. rels. chmn. Lemon Grove Luth. Ch., 1962-78, 89—, v.p., 1993, pres., 1994, chair concert series, 1997—. Writing project fellow U. Calif., San Diego, 1978; named Outstanding Journalism Tchr., State of Calif., Outstanding Humanities Tchr., San Diego County, Tchr. of Yr. for San Diego County, 1978, Woman of Yr., Lemon Grove Soroptimists, 1990; U. Cambridge scholar, 1982. Mem. ASCD, NEA, AAUW, Nat. Coun. Tchrs. English, Nat. Journalism Assn., Calif. Assn. Tchrs. English, Calif. Tchrs. Assn., So. Calif. Journalism Assn., Calif. Sch. Bds. Assn. (elected del. region 17, del. assembly 1993—), Calif. Elected Women's Assn. for Edn. Rsch. (ednl. cons. 1990), Lemon Grove C. of C., San Diego County Journalism Educators Assn. (pres. 1975-76), Grossmont Edn. Assn. (pres. 1978-80), Greater San Diego Coun. Tchrs. English, Nat. Writers Club, Am. Guild Theatre Organists, Am. Guild Organists (Palomar chpt.), Am. Poets, L.G. Friends of the Libr., Libr. Congress, Palomar chpt. Organ Soc., San Diego Mus. Art, Lemon Grove Hist. Soc., Lemon Grove Friends of Libr., Spreckels Organ Soc., Calif. Ret. Tchrs. Assn. (membeship chairwoman 1986-89, pres. chpt. #69 1989-94, parlimentarian 1992-93, chair bylaws 1996—), Lemon Grove C. of C. (mem. econ. devel. com. 1994—), Nat. Sch. Bds. Assn., Order Ea. Star, Kiwanis (pres. elect Lemon Grove chpt. 1992, program chmn., pres. 1993-94), Sigma Delta Chi, Delta Kappa Gamma (pres. Theta Gamma chpt. 1993—).. Democrat. Home and Office: 2885 New Jersey Ave Lemon Grove CA 91945-2826 *Personal philosophy: Christian principles have sustained me all my life; my topmost priority is to love others and promote peace.*

MOTT, MARY ELIZABETH, retired educational administrator; b. West Hartford, Conn., July 10, 1931; d. Marshall Amos and Mary Herman Mott. BA, Conn. Coll. for Women, 1953; MA, Western Res. U., 1963. Cert. tchr., Ohio; cert. computer tchr., Ohio. Mgr. sales promotion Cleve. Electric Illuminating Co., 1953-60; tchr. Newbury Bd. Edn., Ohio, 1960-67, West Geauga Bd. Edn., Chesterland, 1967-69, ret., 1997. Chmn. state certification com. in computers ECCO, Mayfield, Ohio, 1983—, exec. bd., 1980—. Asst. dir. West Geauga Day Camp, Chesterland, 1968. Mem. Ednl. Computer Consortium Ohio, West Geauga Edn. Assn. (exec. bd. 1975-97), Delta Kappa Gamma. E-mail: pci238@aol.com.

MOTT, PEGGY LAVERNE, sociologist, educator; b. Stephenville, Tex., Mar. 23, 1930; d. Artemis Victor Dorris and Tempie Pearl (Price) Hickman; m. J.D. Mott, Sept. 11, 1947 (dec. Apr. 1988); children: Kelly A. Wilcoxson, Kimberly S. Minesinger. BA, Southwest Tex. State U., 1980, MA, 1982. Cert. instr. ceramic arts Nat. Ceramic Art Inst., 1972. Instr. ceramics Arts & Crafts Ctr. Lackland AFB, San Antonio, 1969-72, dir. sales Arts & Crafts Ctr., 1972-77; asst. instr. S.W. Tex. State U., San Marcos, 1980-82; instr. sociology Palo Alto Coll., San Antonio, 1991—. Author: Screaming Silences, 1994, (poem) Concho River Rev., 1993, Inkwell Echos, 1989-95, Lucidity, The T.O.P. Hwupp, 1994-95, Hwap, Patchwork Poems, 1995; co-author: Activities Field Studies and Other Fun Stuff. Vol. coord. Fisher Houses, Inc., Lackland AFB, 1992—; parliamentarian Artistic Expressions, 1996—. Named Vol. of Month, USAF, 1976, 77, 78, Vol. of Quarter, 1976, 77, 78, 84, Vol. of Yr., 1980. Mem. Internat. Soc. Poets, Clipper Ship Poets, San Antonio Poets Assn. (v.p. 1991-92, pres. 1992-93, Poet Laureate 1994-95), San Antonio Ethnic Arts. Avocations: reading, writing, needlework. Home: 1307 Canyon Ridge Dr San Antonio TX 78227-1727 E-mail: profpurple@delwet.com.

MOTT, ROBERT LEWIS, writer, sound effects artist; b. Nyack, N.Y. s. Morgan Edward and Grace (Groben) M.; m. Catherine O'Keefe, June 28, 1947 (div. 1974); children: Susan Patricia, Gail Ann, Cathee Caron, Nancy Jean; m. Cinda M. Yank, Dec. 28, 1985. Grad., NYU, 1947-50. Freelance writer, 1951—; sound effects artist CBS, N.Y.C., 1951-69, NBC, Burbank, Calif., 1970-89. Writer (children's record) Rocket to Mars, 1954, (cartoon series) Cool McCool, 1956, (Broadway mus.) Girls Against the Boys, 1958; comedy writer The Ed Sullivan Show, Garry Moore Show, Andy Williams Show, Dick Van Dyke Show, Red Skelton Show; author: Sound Effects: Radio, TV and Film, 1988, Sound Effects: Who Did It and How, in the Era of Live Broadcasting, 1993 (Best Lit. List, Choice Mag. 1993), Radio Live! Television Live! When Horses Were Coconuts!, 2000. Served with USMC, 1943-45, ETO. Decorated 4 campaign battle stars; recipient 3 Emmy award nominations Acad. TV Arts and Scis., 1986, 87, Byron Kane award, Lifetime achievement award Soc. to Preserve and Encourage Radio Drama, Variety and Comedy. Mem. Writers Guild Am., Pacific Pioneer Broadcasters. Home: 396 Miller Way Arroyo Grande CA 93420-2004

MOTT, STEWART RAWLINGS, business executive, political activist; b. Flint, Mich., Dec. 4, 1937; s. Charles Stewart and Ruth (Rawlings) M.; m. Kappy Wells, Oct. 13, 1979 (div. Mar. 1999); 1 child, Samuel Apple Axle. Grad., Deerfield (Mass.) Acad., 1955; BS in Bus. Adminstrn, BA in Comparative Lit, Columbia, 1961, postgrad. English lit., 1961-62. Exec. trainee various cos., 1956-63; English instr. Eastern Mich. U., 1963-64; corp. dir. U.S. Sugar Corp., Clewiston, Fla., 1965—. Investor various diversified cos., 1968—. Founder Flint Community Planned Parenthood, 1963; pres. S.R. Mott Charitable Trust, 1968—; pres., founder Spectemur Agendo (merged with S.R. Mott Charitable Trust 1989), N.Y.C. and Flint, 1965—; bd. dirs. Fund For Peace, N.Y.C., 1967— , Nat. Com. for Effective Congress, N.Y.C., 1968— , Planned Parenthood Fedn. Am., 1964-81, Am. Commn. on U.S.-Soviet Rels., 1977-92, Citizens Research Found., 1977— , Ams. for Dem. Action, 1978-90, Friends of Family Planning, 1979-84, Voters for Choice, 1979-89; bd. dirs., founder Fund Constl. Govt., 1974— ; bd. dirs. Population Action Council, 1978-82; maj. donor McCarthy, McGovern, Anderson campaigns. Mem. Phi Beta Kappa. *At age 18 I realized that two problems confront planet earth that dwarf and aggravate all conventional problems: namely the threat of nuclear war and the continuing worldwide population explosion. Coming to grips with these realities, I decided to dedicate my life to help find solutions to these two problems through public service in philanthropy and politics.*

MOTTE, SISTER MARY MARGARET, missionary; b. Providence, Dec. 4, 1936; d. Edwin Gerard and Emma Veronica (O'Donnell) M. BA, St. Joseph's Coll., Bklyn., 1962; MA, Boston Coll., 1963, MEd, 1967, PhD, 1972. Mem. Mission Resource Office Franciscan Missionaries of Mary, Rome, 1974-81; dir. Nat. Mission Conf. U.S. Cath. Mission Assn., Washington, 1982-83; asst. provincial U.S. Province-Franciscan Missionaries of Mary, N.Y.C., 1984-87, 91-95, provincial, 1999—; coord. Nat. Ecumenical Mission Consultation U.S. Cath. Mission Assn., 1985-87, also bd. dirs., 1990-93; dir. Mission Resource Ctr. Franciscan Missionaries of Mary, North Providence, 1988-99; mem. internat. mission rsch. team Franciscan Missionaries of Mary, 1993-96, govt. study, 1997—99, sending and receiving in mission, 1999—2001. Trustee Maryknoll Sch. Theology, 1990-95, Overseas Ministries Study Ctr., 1991-2000; mem. rev. and selection com. Rsch. Enablement Program, 1992-99; mem. core com. Missiology of Western Culture Rsch. Program, 1993-97; mem. exec com., bd. dirs. Agrl. Missions/NCCC-USA, N.Y.C., 1984-96; bd. dirs. Gospel and Culture Network Project, 1996-2000; cons. U.S. Cath. Mission Assn., 1997-98; mem. adv. com. Maryknoll Ctr. for Mission Rsch. and Study, 2001—; mem. Cath. Mission Forum. Co-editor: Mission in Dialogue, 1982; contbg. editor Internat. Bull. of Missionary Rsch., New Haven, 1980—; contbr. articles to profl. jours. Doctoral fellowship Boston Coll., 1966; Walsh-Price fellowship Maryknoll Fathers & Bros., 1979. Mem. Am. Soc. Missiology (bd. dirs., v.p. 1991-93, pres. 1993-94), Am. Profs. of Mission (v.p. 1990-91, pres. 1991-92), Leadership Conf. Women Religions (liaison to US Cath. Bishops Com. on Mission 2000—), Religious Formation Conf. Home and Office: 3305 Wallace Ave Bronx NY 10467-6519 E-mail: mmotte@aol.com.

MOTTER, THOMAS FRANKLIN, medical products executive; b. Modesto, Calif., June 27, 1948; s. Thomas Dean and Beverley June (Mosier) M.; m. Wanda Lenice Parker, Feb. 9, 1968 (div. Jan. 1972); children: Eric Franklin (dec.), Katrina Lenice; m. Jerry Ann Averill, Oct. 24, 1976; children: Heidi Marika, Courtney Averill. AA, Cabrillo Jr. Coll., Santa Cruz, Calif., 1968; BA, Stephens Coll., 1970; MBA, Pepperdine U., 1975. Social worker County of Santa Cruz and Amador, 1970-77; nat. dir. mktg. Humphrey Instruments/SmithKline, San Leandro, Calif., 1978-88; internat. gen. mgr. HGM Med. Lasers, Salt Lake City, 1988-89; pres., CEO Paradigm Med. Industries Inc., 1989—. Mem. Nat. Ski Patrol, Stockton, 1973-79; v.p. Sandy (Utah) Pony Baseball, 1994-95; coach Kearns (Utah) Am. Legion Baseball, 1995-96. Capt. U.S. Army, 1970-76. Named Mem. Nat. Adult Baseball Assn. (mem. Nat. Championship team), Am. Legion, Sons of the Am. Revolution Utah State Chpt., Knight Orthodox Order of the Knights of the Hosp. of St. John of Jerusalem. Episcopalian. Avocations: skiing, hardball baseball, coaching, fly fishing, hunting. Office: Paradigm Med Industries Inc 2355 S 1070 W Salt Lake City UT 84119-1552

MOTTET, NORMAN KARLE, pathologist, educator; b. Renton, Wash., Jan. 8, 1924; s. Louis John and Amalia (Lentzner) M.; M. Nancy Noble, June 21, 1952; children: Gretchen, Kurt, Mark. BS summa cum laude, Wash. State U., 1947; MD, Yale U., 1952. Diplomate: Am. bd. Pathology. Postdoctoral fellow Strangeways Research Lab., Cambridge, Eng., 1952-53, vis. scientist Eng., 1969-70; rotating intern, then intern in pathology Yale Med. Ctr., 1953-55, resident in pathology, 1955-56, mem. faculty med. Sch., 1951-52, 55-59; pathologist, dir. labs. Griffin Hosp., Derby, Conn., 1955-59; mem. faculty U. Wash. Med. Sch., Seattle, 1959—, prof. pathology, 1966—. Dir. hosp. pathology Univ. Hosp. U. Wash. Med. Sch., Seattle, 1959-74; mem. extramural program council Fred Hutchinson Carcer Research Ctr., 1975 Contbr. articles to med. jours.; mem. editorial bds. Served with AUS, 1942-45. James Hudson Brown fellow, 1949-50; fellow nat. Found. Infantile Paralysis, 1952-53; recipient Keese prize Yale U., 1952; trainee pathology USPHS, 1954-55; spl. rsch. fellow USPHS, 1969-70. Fellow Am. Soc. Clin. Pathology, AAAS; mem. Am. Soc. Pathology, Tetatology Soc., Internat. Soc. Trace Element Research, Internat. Com. Occupational Health, Internat. Com. Trace Metals, Sigma Xi, Alpha Omega Alpha Home: 360 E Old Olson Rd Shelton WA 98584-8447 Office: U Wash Sch Medicine Dept Path Seattle WA 98195-0001

MOTTO, GERALYN, multi-media artist; b. Chgo., May 6, 1957; d. Ralph J. and Dorothy A. (Casaletto) M. AA in Liberal Arts, Triton Coll., 1979; BA in Social Sci., Northea. Ill. U., 1979. High fashion model, comml. actress, Chgo., N.Y.C., L.A., Paris and Milan, 1980-87; smoking and weight control therapist, dir. Schick Ctrs., L.A., 1987-90; promoter, salesperson Eco Expo, Topango, Calif., 1990-91; sales mgr. Birkenstock, L.A., 1991-96; CEO Gallery of Environ. Renewal Arts Unltd., Malibu, Calif., 1997—, Gera Unltd., Malibu, 1997—. Cultural activities cons. Miramonte Hotel, Indian Wells, 1999—; wholistic practitioner, 1999—; co-curator Spring St. Gallery; pub. rels. person Lakota Ednl. and Bldg. Found., 1997—, Cal Earth, Hesperia, Calif., 1997—. Work featured in The Book of Los Angeles, 1990-95, Brentwood Bla-Bla, 1990, Artisans Gallery of Sedona, Ariz., 1994-95, Moonshadows of Redondo Beach, Calif., 1994-95, P.L.A.N., Los Angeles County Museum of Art, 1995; exhibits T. Heritage Gallery, Westwood, Calif., 1998; active mem. and recipient award in juried shows. Active Green Party, L.A., 1992—. Mem.: Malibu Art Assn. (v.p. 1993, hon. mention 1990, 1992, 2d place 1992), Amnesty Internat., Habitat for Humanity, Sierra Club. Avocations: long distance bike-a-thons, photography, trekking. Mailing: PO Box 2744 Malibu CA 90265-7744

MOTTO, JEROME ARTHUR, psychiatry educator; b. Kansas City, Mo., Oct. 16, 1921; MD, U. Calif., San Francisco, 1951. Diplomate Am. Bd. Neurology and Psychiatry. Intern San Francisco Gen. Hosp., 1951-52; resident Johns Hopkins Hosp., Balt., 1952-55; sr. resident U. Calif., San Francisco, 1955-56, from instr. to prof. emeritus., 1956—. Contbr. articles to profl. jours. With AUS, 1942-46; ETO. Fellow Am. Psychiatric Assn. (life).

MOTTOLA, THOMAS, entertainment company executive; Pres., CEO Sony Music Entertainment Inc, N.Y.C., now chmn., CEO, 1998-. Office: Sony Music Entertainment Inc 550 Madison Ave Fl 32 New York NY 10022-3211*

MOTTUS, JANE E. college administrator, historian; b. Passaic, N.J., Aug. 13, 1948; d. Milton F. and Selma (Geller) M. BA in History, Am. U., 1970; MA in History, NYU, 1973, PhD in History, 1980. Rsch. asst. dean divsn. humanities Lehman Coll. of CUNY, Bronx, 1980-83, asst. to assoc. provost, 1983-87, exec. asst. to dean, divsn. Natural and Social Scis., 1987—. Author: New York Nightingales: Emergence of Nursing Profession and Bellevue and New York Hospital, 1850-1920, 1981; contbr. Ency. of N.Y.C., 1995. Mem. Orgn. of Am. Historians, Am. Hist. Assn. Home: 3 Washington Square Vlg # 17-0 New York NY 10012-1836 Office: CUNY Lehman Coll 250 Bedford Park Blvd W Bronx NY 10468-1527 E-mail: jemlc@cunyvm.cuny.edu.

MOTULSKY, ARNO GUNTHER, geneticist, physician, educator; b. Fischhausen, Germany, July 5, 1923; arrived in U.S., 1941; s. Herman and Rena (Sass) Molton; m. Gretel C. Stern, Mar. 22, 1945; children: Judy, Harvey, Arlene. Student, Cen. YMCA Coll., Chgo., 1941—43, Yale U., 1943—44; BS, U. Ill., 1945, MD, 1947, DSc (hon.) , 1982, MD (hon.) , 1991. Diplomate Am. Bd. Internal Medicine, Am. Bd. Med. Genetics. Intern, fellow, resident Michael Reese Hosp., Chgo., 1947-51; staff mem. charge clin. investigation dept. hematology Army Med. Service Grad. Sch., Walter Reed Army Med. Ctr., Washington, 1952-53; research assoc. internal medicine George Washington U. Sch. Medicine, 1952-53; from instr. to assoc. prof. dept. medicine U. Wash. Sch. Medicine, Seattle, 1953-61, prof. medicine, prof. genetics, 1961—; head div. med. genetics, dir. genetics clinic Univ. Hosp., 1959-89; dir. Ctr. for Inherited Diseases, 1972-90. Attending physician Univ. Hosp., Seattle; cons. Pres.'s Commn. for Study of Ethical Problems in Medicine and Biomed. and Behavioral Rsch., 1979—83; cons. various coms. NRC, NIH, WHO, and others. Editor: Am. Jour. Human Genetics, 1969—75, Human Genetics, 1969—97. Fellow Commonwealth Fund in human genetics, Univ. Coll., London, 1957—58, Ctr. Advanced Study in Behavorial Scis., Stanford U., 1976—77, Inst. Advanced Study, Berlin, 1984; scholar John and Mary Markle in med. sci., 1957—62. Fellow: AAAS, ACP; mem.: Am. Acad. Arts & Scis., Inst. of Medicine, Am. Assn. Physicians, Am. Soc. Clin. Investigation, Am. Soc. Human Genetics, Western Soc. Clin. Rsch., Genetics Soc. Am., Am. Fedn. Clin. Rsch., Internat. Soc. Hematology, NAS. Home: 4347 53rd Ave NE Seattle WA 98105-4938 Office: U Wash Medicine and Genome Scis PO Box 357730 Seattle WA 98195-7730 E-mail: agmot@u.washington.edu.

MOTYL, ALEXANDER JOHN, political science educator; b. N.Y.C., Oct. 21, 1953; s. Alexander and Maria Victoria (Bojczuk) M.; m. Irene Helene Mudretzkyj, June 30, 1979; 1 child, Katherina. BA summa cum laude, Columbia Coll., 1975; MIA, Sch. Internat. Affairs, 1979; M of Philosophy, Columbia U., 1983, PhD, 1984. Asst. prof. Columbia U., N.Y.C., 1985-90, assoc. prof., 1990-92, dir. nationality and siberian studies program, 1988-92; assoc. dir. Harriman Inst., 1992-98; assoc. prof. Rutgers U., Newark, 1999—, dir. Ctr. Global Change and Governance, 1999—. Cons. RFE-RL, Inc., Washington, 1989-90. Author: The Turn to the Right, 1980, Will the Non-Russians Rebel?, 1987, Sovietology, Rationality, Nationality, 1990, Dilemmas of Independence, 1993; editor: Thinking Theoretically about Soviet Nationalities, 1992, The Post-Soviet Nations, 1992, Revolutions, Nations, Empires, 1999; editor Westview Press Series on Post-Soviet Republics, 1990—, The Encyclopedia of Nationalism, 1997—. Mem. Am. Assn. for the Advancement of Slavic Studies, Am. Polit. Sci. Assn., Phi Beta Kappa. Greek Catholic. Avocation: painting.

MOTZ, DIANA GRIBBON, federal judge; b. Washington, July 15, 1943; d. Daniel McNamara and Jane (Retzler) Gribbon; m. John Frederick Motz, Sept. 20, 1968; children: Catherine Jane, Daniel Gribbon. BA, Vassar Coll., 1965; LLB, U. Va., 1968. Bar: U.S. Dist. Ct. Md. 1969, U.S. Ct. Appeals (4th cir.) 1969, U.S. Supreme Ct. 1980. Assoc. Piper & Marbury, Balt., 1968—71; asst. atty. gen. State of Md., 1972—81, chief of litigation, 1981—86; ptnr. Frank, Bernstein, Conaway & Goldman, 1986—91; judge Md. Ct. of Special Appeals, 1991—94, U.S. Ct. Appeals (4th Cir.), 1994—. Mem.: ABA, Fed. Cts. Study Com., Lawyers Round Table, Md. Bar Found., Am. Bar Found., Am. Law Inst., Balt. City Bar Assn. (exec. com. 1988), Md. Bar Assn., Wranglers Law Club. Roman Catholic. Office: 101 W Lombard St Ste 920 Baltimore MD 21201-2611

MOTZ, JOHN FREDERICK, federal judge; b. Balt., Dec. 30, 1942; s. John Eldered and Catherine (Grauel) M.; m. Diana Jane Gribbon, Sept. 20, 1968; children: Catherine Jane, Daniel Gribbon AB, Wesleyan U., Conn., 1964; LLB, U. Va., 1967. Bar: Md. 1967, U.S. Ct. Appeals (4th cir.) 1968, U.S. Dist. Ct. Md. 1968. Law clk. to Hon. Harrison L. Winter U.S. Ct. Appeals (4th cir.), 1967-68; Assoc. Venable, Baetjer & Howard, Balt., 1968-69; asst. U.S. atty. U.S. Atty.'s Office, 1969-71; assoc. Venable, Baetjer & Howard, 1971-75, ptnr., 1976-81; U.S. atty. U.S. Atty.'s Office, 1981-85; judge U.S. Dist. Ct. Md., 1985—, chief judge, 1994—2001. Trustees Friends Sch., Balt., 1970-77, 1981-88, Sheppard Pratt Hosp., 1987-97, 99—. Mem.: ABA, Am. Coll. Trial Lawyers (mem. bd. editors. Manual of Complex Litigation (4th), mem. Judicial Panel on Multidist. Litigation), Am. Law Inst., Am. Bar Found., Md. State Bar Assn. Republican. Mem. Soc. Of Friends. Office: US Dist Ct 101 W Lombard St Rm 510 Baltimore MD 21201-2605

MOTZ, JULIE ANN, energy healer, author; b. N.Y.C., Jan. 12, 1943; d. Lloyd and Mimme (Rosenbaum) Motz. Student, Bryn Mawr (Pa.) Coll., 1959-61, U. Coll. London, 1961-62; BS, Columbia U., 1964, MFA, 1971, MPH, 1975. Co-founder, prodr. Hudson River Film & Video Co., Garrison, N.Y., 1970-92; self-employed energy healer N.Y.C. and San Francisco, 1992—. Vis. prof. Inst. Health and Healing, Calif. Pacific Med. Ctr., 1997. Prodr.: (TV documentary) Christina's World, 1973 (Emmy 1976), Henry Hudsons River, 1979 (Emmy 1980); author: Rescue 911 Family Emergency and First Aid Book, 1996, Hands of Life, 1998. Home: PO Box 75 Lake Peekskill NY 10537-0075 E-mail: jamtoday@bestweb.net.

MOTZ, KENNETH LEE, former farm organization official; b. Grand Junction, Colo., Mar. 6, 1922; s. Harold I. and Acquila (Ulmer) M.; m. Margaret Florence Mitchell, Oct. 9, 1948; children: Gwendolyn Ann, Stephen Mitchell. AA, Mesa Jr. Coll., 1942; BSBA, Denver U., 1947. Bookkeeper Farmers Union Mktg. Assn., Denver, 1942-43; asst. sec. Nat. Farmers Union, 1947-50, 59-66, sec.-treas., 1966-72, 85-86, treas., asst. sec., 1972-85, retired, 1987; treas. Green Thumb, Inc., 1980-85, sec.-treas., 1985-86, retired, 1987. Ins. acct. Nat. Farmers Union Ins. Cos., Denver, 1952-59. Sec. uniform pension com. Nat. Farmers Union, 1959-93; Dem. precinct committeeman, 1960-68; elder Calvary Presbyn. Ch. Maj. USMCR, ret. 1982. Recipient Svc. award Farmers Union, 1991. Mem. Nat. Presby. Mariners, Masons, Delta Sigma Pi. Presbyterian. Home: 2018 Fairway Hills Dr Huntsville AL 35802-4329

MOTZER, ROBERT JOHN, oncologist, educator; b. Paterson, N.J., Nov. 20, 1954; s. John William and Muriel M.; m. Sara Evelyn Gaylord, June 30, 1979; children: Katherine, Rachel, Andrew. BA, Hope Coll., Holland, Mich., 1977; MD, U. Mich. Med. Sch., 1981. Assoc. chmn. Meml. Sloan Kettering Cancer Ctr., New York, 1996—, attending physician, 2000—; prof. Cornell U. Med. Coll., 1998—. Contbr. over 65 articles to profl. jours.; lectr. in field. Recipient Career devel. award, Am. Cancer Soc., Mid-career Devel. award, NIH, 1999—. Mem. Am. Soc. Clin. Oncology, Am. Assn. Cancer Rsch., Kidney Cancer Assn. (exec. bd.). Office: Meml Sloan Kettering Cancer Ctr 1275 York Ave New York NY 10021-6094 E-mail: motzerr@mskcc.org.

MOU, THOMAS WILLIAM, physician, medical educator and consultant; b. Phila., May 17, 1920; s. Thomas Simonsen and Ellen Marie (Mathiesen) M.; m. Marie Elizabeth Hartmann, Dec. 29, 1945 (div. Oct., 1976); children: Susan, Roberta; m. M. Delma Jane Schreiber, Nov. 11, 1976. BSc in Bacteriology, Phila. Coll. Pharm & Sci., 1941; MD, U. Rochester, 1950. Diplomate Nat. Bd. Med. Examiners. Instr. medicine and bacteriology U. Rochester (N.Y.) Sch. of Medicine, 1954-56; asst. prof. preventive medicine to prof. cmty. medicine SUNY at Syracuse, 1956-70; exec. dean to assoc chancellor health sci. SUNY Ctrl. Adminstrn., Albany, 1970-77; dean clin. campus W. Va. U., Charleston, 1977-85; pres. Ednl. Commn. for Fgn. Med. Grads., Phila., 1986-88; dean emeritus W. Va. U. Med. Ctr., Morgantown, 1986—; geriatric practice Adult Medicine Specialists, Pueblo, Colo., 1990-2000. Cons. Carnegie Commn. for Advancement of Tchg., Princeton, N.J., 1987-88, Charles A. Dana Found., N.Y.C., 1988, Geriatric Pharmacy Inst. of Phila. Coll. of Pharmacy and Sci., 1988. Contbr. 36 article or presentations to profl. jours or sci. confs. Trustee Phila. Coll. Pharmacy and Sci., 1972-81. Capt. Sanitary Corps, 1941-45 Recipient Disting. Alumnus award Phila. Coll. Pharmacy and Sci., 1975, award of distinction and honor Ben Franklin Soc. SUNY, N.Y.C., 1975, Koch medal Am. Optometric Soc., N.Y.C., 1976; T.W. Mou Endowed Lectureship W. Va. U., Charleston, 1985. Fellow Am. Coll. Physicians, Am. Coll. Preventive Medicine, Phila. Coll. Physicians, Infectious Diseases Soc. Am. (founding fellow). Avocations: violin, travel. Home: 3050 Valleybrook Ln Colorado Springs CO 80904-1154 Office: Adult Medicine Specialists 314 W 16th St Pueblo CO 81003-2728

MOUBARAK, CHUKRI A. financial analyst, consultant; b. Kuwait City, Kuwait, July 4, 1976; s. Nada A. Moubarak. BA, U. Calif., San Diego. Fin. mgmt. cons. and adviser Goldman Sachs, N.Y.C., 1999—; legal adviser Brown & Wood LLP. Dir. Herriott Found., N.Y.C. Campaign mgr. Gore Campaign for Pres., N.Y.C.

MOUBRAY, JOHN MITCHELL, engineering company executive; b. Harare, Zimbabwe, Feb. 2, 1949; arrived in U.K., 1986; s. James W. and Dorothy May (Robinson) M.; m. Edith I. Dashorst, Jan. 4, 1976; children: Alastair, Donovan, Cameron. BSc in ME, U. Cape Town, South Africa, 1971. Engr. Metal Box Co., Cape Town, 1971-73; field engr. Mobil Oil, Johannesburg, South Africa, 1973-74; dir. P-E Cons. Svcs., 1974-86; CEO Aladon LLC, Asheville, N.C., 1986—. Author: Reliability-Centered Maintenance, 1991, 2nd edit. 1997. Mem. Soc. Maintenance and Reliability Profls. Avocation: reading. Office: 6 Deerfield Rd Asheville NC 28803-3012

MOUCHATY, SUZETTE KAY, biologist; b. Morenci, Mich., Jan. 7, 1965; d. Ray Allen Durall and Janet Sue (Gould) Fretz; m. Georges Mouchaty, Mar. 16, 1994. AS, San Juan Coll., 1986; BS, U. Alaska, 1990, MS in Biology, 1993; PhD in Genetics, Lund (Sweden) U., 1999. Fire patrol officer U.S. Forest Svc.-Sawtooth Nat. Forest, 1989; vol. interpreter U.S. Nat. Park Svc.-Tusayan Mus., Grand Canyon Nat. Park, winter 1989-90; curatorial asst. U. Alaska Mus., Fairbanks, 1990; tchg. asst. U. Alaska, 1991-92, Tex. A&M U., College Station, 1993-95; Fulbright fellow Genetics Inst., U. Lund, Sweden, 1996-97; sr. projects coord. Baylor Coll. Medicine Human Genome Sequencing Ctr., Houston, 2000; edn. program mgr. Mus. Health and Med. Sci., 2001; adj. lectr. U. Houston, 2002—. Planner, author (mus. exhibit) Systematics Rsch., U. Alaska Mus., 1993. Mem. AAAS, Sigma Xi. Office: 1515 Herman Dr Houston TX 77004-7126 Home: 1815 Tuam Ave Houston TX 77004-1254 E-mail: smouchaty@mhms.org.

MOUDUD, JAMEE K. economist, economics educator, researcher; BS, Cornell U., 1986, M in Engring., 1987; postgrad., Ecole Ctrl. de Lyon, France, 1987-88; MA, New Sch. for Social Rsch., 1994, PhD with honors, 1998. Engring. cons., Karachi, Pakistan, 1988-90; grad. rsch. intern World Policy Inst. New Sch. for Social Rsch., 1993, rsch. asst. Ctr. for Econ. Policy Analysis, 1997; asst. economist The N.Y.C. Office of the Comptr., 1998; resident scholar The Jerome Levy Econs. Inst. Bard Coll., 1998-2000, rsch. assoc., 2001—; econ. educator Sarah Lawrence Coll., Bronxville, N.Y., 2000—. Adj. instr. dept. econs. New Sch. for Social Rsch., 1993, 96, NYU, 1995, 96, 97, Bard Coll., 1998, 2000; adj. instr. Borough of Manhattan C.C., 1995; adj. instr. dept. liberal studies New Sch. for Social Rsch., 1996, 97; presenter in field. Contbr. articles to profl. jours. Scholar Cornell U., 1982-86, full exch. student scholar Ecole Ctrl. de Lyon, 1987-88; Polit. Economy Dissertation fellow New Sch. for Social Rsch., 1994-96, Dean's fellow Eugene Lang Coll., New Sch. for Social Rsch., 1995-96, MacArthur Dissertation fellow MacArthur Program on Global Change and Liberalism, New Sch. for Social Rsch., 1996-97, Ctr. for Econ. Policy Analysis Dissertation fellow New Sch. for Social Rsch., 1997-98. Home: 19 Tulip Tree Ln Brookfield CT 06804 Office: Sarah Lawrence Coll Dept of Econ 1 Mead Way Bronxville NY 10708 E-mail: moudud@aol.com., jmoudud@slc.edu.

MOUGHAN, PETER RICHARD, JR. lawyer; b. Phila., July 29, 1951; s. Peter Richard and Catherine L. (Gavin) M.; m. Janice Billick, Aug. 3, 1974 (div. Aug. 2000); children: Peter Richard III, Gavin Patrick, Jacob Daniel. BA, Wheeling Coll., 1973; MS, Gonzaga U., 1975, MBA, JD, Gonzaga U., 1977. Bar: Pa. 1973, N.Mex. 1980. Legal rschr. Am. Law Inst.-ABA, Phila., 1977-78; claim rep. Allstate Ins., 1978-79; assoc. Larry D. Beall, P.A., Albuquerque, 1979-81; pvt. practice law Moughan Law Firm , 1981—. Mem.: K.C., Albuquerque Aardvarks Rugby Football Club (chmn. 1980—84), Ancient Order of Hibernians (Albuquerque) (pres. 1984—85, 1992—), Phi Alpha Delta. Office: PO Box 715 Albuquerque NM 87103-0715 Home: 623 San Pedro Dr SE Albuquerque NM 87108 E-mail: moughan2@lawyer.com., moughan2@yahoo.com.

MOUL, JUDD WENDELL, urologist, surgeon; b. York, Pa., Feb. 8, 1957; s. George William and Dorothy Dodd (Firebaugh) M.; m. Ellen R. Jablonski, Oct. 3, 1981. BS summa cum laude, Pa. State U., 1979; MD, Jefferson Med. Coll. of Phila., 1982. Diplomate Am. Bd. Urology. Commd. 2d lt. Med. Corps U.S. Army, 1982, advanced through grades to col., 2000; intern, resident Walter Reed Army Med. Ctr., Washington, 1982-87, attending urologist Army Med. Corps, 1987—; urologic oncology fellow Duke U., Durham, N.C., 1988-89; asst. prof. surgery Uniformed Svcs. U. of Health Scis., Bethesda, Md., 1989-93, assoc. prof. surgery, 1993-99, prof., 1999—. Dir. Dept. of Def. Ctr. for Prostate Disease Rsch., H.M. Jackson Found., Rockville, Md., 1992—; nat. cons. "Us-Too" Prostate Cancer Support Group Hinsdale, Ill., and Nat. Assn. for Continence, Union, S.C., 1992—. Contbr. over 250 articles to profl. jours.; mem. editl. bd. numerous profl. jours. U.S. Army Med. Rsch. and Material Comd. Rsch. grantee, 1992—. Fellow ACS; mem. AMA (Cmty. Svc. award 1995), Am. Urol. Assn. (prostate cancer guidelines com., meeting essay prizes 1986, 89, Gold Cystoscope award 1997), Soc. Urologic Oncology, Am. Assn. Cancer Rsch. (Meeting prize 1995), Soc. Univ. Urologists, Assn. Mil. Surgeons of the U.S. (History of Med. Mil. History award 1992, Sir Henry Wellcome medal and prize 1996), Uniformed Svcs. Urology Rsch. Group (Pres. award 2000), Phi Beta Kappa, Alpha Omega Alpha, Phi Kappa Phi, Alpha Epsilon Delta. Home: 8917 Holly Leaf Ln Bethesda MD 20817-2654 Office: CPDR 1530 E Jefferson St Rockville MD 20852-1501 E-mail: jmoul@cpdr.org.

MOUL, MARLIN EUGENE, real estate broker; b. York, Pa., Apr. 22, 1947; s. Carl E. and Beulah M. Moul; divorced; 1 child, Danielle. Lic. broker Commonwealth of Pa.; cert. commercial investment member Commercial Investment Real Estate Inst. Structural draftsman Buchart-Horn Engring., York, 1969-72, Noonan Engring., York, 1972-77; salesman Brandt Real Estate, 1977-81; gen. ptnr. Watkins Assocs., 1981-83, Baughman Assocs., York, 1983-86; treas. The Real Estate People, 1986-90; salesman Bennett Williams Realty, 1990-95; owner, record broker Blue Marlin Real Estate, Inc., 1995—. Cons. Young Mens Christian Assn., York, 1997—. Co-author: Method to Our Madness, 1984; author column York Daily Record, 1986-90; co-contbr. articles to Real Estate Today. Bd. dirs. York Co. Econ. Devel. Authority, 1999-2002, YorkArts, 1999-2002. 1st. Lt. U.S. Army, 1966-69. Mem. Nat. Assn. Realtors, Pa. Assn. Realtors (PAR Excellence Gold award 1997, 98), Realtors Assn. York & Adams Counties (treas. 1996-98, Realtor of Yr. 1998), Rotary. Avocations: golf, hunting, fitness, travel. Home: 2380 Grandview Rd York PA 17403-5109 Office: Blue Marlin Real Estate Inc 2020 S Queen St York PA 17403-4829 Fax: (717) 845-7247. E-mail: mmoul@netrax.net.

MOUL, WILLIAM CHARLES, lawyer; b. Columbus, Ohio, Jan. 12, 1940; s. Charles Emerson and Lillian Ann (Mackenbach) M.; m. Margine Ann Tessendorf, June 10, 1962; children: Gregory, Geoffrey. BA, Miami U., Oxford, Ohio, 1961; JD, Ohio State U., 1964. Bar: Ohio 1964, U.S. Dist. Ct. (so. dist.) Ohio 1965, U.S. Ct. Appeals (2d cir.) 1982, U.S. Ct. Appeals (6th cir.) 1984, U.S. Ct. Appeals (3d cir.) 1985. Assoc., ptnr. George, Greek, King, McMahon & McConnaughey, Columbus, 1964-79; ptnr. McConnaughey, Stradley, Mone & Moul, 1979-81; ptnr.-in-charge Thompson, Hine & Flory, 1981-89, exec. com., 1989-98. Chmn. Upper Arlington Civil Svc. Commn., Ohio, 1981-86. Mem. ABA, Ohio State Bar Assn. (labor sect. bd. dirs. 1983—), Columbus Bar Assn. (chmn. ethics com. 1980-82), Lawyers Club Columbus (pres. 1976-77), Athletic Club, Scioto Country Club, Wedgewood Country Club, Masons. Lutheran. Home: 2512 Danvers Ct Columbus OH 43220-2822 Office: Thompson Hine & Flory 10 W Broad St Ste 700 Columbus OH 43215-3435

MOULDER, T. EARLINE, musician; b. Buffalo, Oct. 11; d. Earl Young and Ruby M. (Phillipot) M.; m. R. David Plank, Dec. 21, 1980; children: Jeannine Stanton, Jon Stanton, Timothy Stanton. AB in Biology and French, Drury Coll., 1973; studied piano with Soulima Stravinsky, 1961; M in Music, Ind. U., 1963; D in Musical Arts, U. Kansas, 1991; pvt. organ study, Andre Marchal, Paris, France, 1971. Concert organist, 1964—; exec. editor Drury Coll. Mirror, Springfield, Mo., 1971-73; rschr. Am. U., Beirut, 1973; journalist U.S. Naval Res., Springfield and Treasure Island, Calif., 1975-77; organist King's Way Meth. Ch., Springfield, Mo., 1983-93; chair organ dept. Drury U., 1968—, univ. organist, 1991—. Lectr. recitals on Jewish music, 1991—; translator, Profl. documents, 1990—. Author: Organ Works of Elsa Barraine, 1995, Music of Alice Jordan, 1998; composer organ composition The Crucifixion, 1995; contbr. articles to profl. jours. Charter mem. Nat. Mus. Am. Indian, 1994—. Recipient Teaching fellow U. Kans., Drury Mirror award Rank I Mo. Coll. Newspaper Assn. Mem. Mortar Bd., Sigma Alpha Iota, Alpha Lambda Delta, Pi Delta Phi, Beta Beta Beta, Pi Kappa Lambda, Organ Hist. Soc., Am. Guild Organist. Home: 3563 E Linwood Dr Springfield MO 65809-2131 Office: Drury Univ 900 N Benton Ave Springfield MO 65802-3712 E-mail: emoulder@drury.edu., dplank@msn.com.

MOULDER, WILLIAM H. chief of police; b. Kansas City, Mo., Feb. 19, 1938; s. Roscoe B. and Charleen M. (Flye) M.; m. Louise M. Pollaro, Aug. 2, 1957; children: Deborah, Ralph, Robert. BA, U. Mo., Kansas City, 1971, MA, 1976. Cert. police officer, Mo., Iowa. From police officer to maj. Kansas City (Mo.) Police Dept., 1959-84; chief of police City of Des Moines, 1984—. Mem. Internat. Assn. Chiefs of Police, Police Exec. Rsch. Forum, Iowa Police Exec. Forum. Avocations: racquetball, travel. Office: Office of Police Chief 25 E 1st St Des Moines IA 50309-4800

MOULDER, WILTON ARLYN, financial management consultant; b. Atlanta, July 1, 1931; s. Ottis Arrell and Eula Mae (Whitlock) M.; m. Margie Nell Harrington, Mar. 12, 1955; children: W. Arlyn Jr., Carol Elaine. Student, Ga. Inst. Tech., Atlanta, 1949-50; BA, Emory U., Atlanta, 1953, MDiv, 1956, D Ministry, 1977. Ordained to ministry Meth. Ch. as deacon, 1954, as elder, 1956; cert. fin. planner, cert. fund raising exec.; lic. real estate salesperson. Pastor St. Luke Meth. Ch., Atlanta, 1956-57, St. Matthew Meth. Ch., East Point, Ga., 1957-62; assoc. pastor Druid Hills Meth. Ch., Atlanta, 1962-64; pastor Duluth (Ga.) United Meth. Ch., 1964-69; devel. dir. United Meth. Children's Home, Decatur, Ga., 1969-95. Self-employed cons.; trustee United Meth. Found., Atlanta, 1984-2001; del. Jurisdictional Conf., Lake Junaluska, N.C., 1984; sect. chmn. United Meth. Assn. Health and Welfare Ministries Pub. Rels. and Devel., 1978-80. Author: Financial Planning for Clergy Families, 1987. Judge Ga. Occupational Award of Leadership Program, Decatur, 1985-90; bd. dirs. DeKalb Coll. Found., Decatur, 1990-97; trustee United Meth. Children's Home, Decatur, 1997—. Mem. Rotary (bd. dirs. Decatur club 1988-90). Home and Office: 117 Augusta Dr Peachtree City GA 30269-3813 E-mail: wmoulder@aol.com.

MOULDS, ERIC SHANNON, professional football player; b. Lucedale, Miss., July 17, 1973; , Miss. State U. Wide receiver, kickoff return Buffalo Bills, 1996—. First round draft pick NFL, 1996. Office: Buffalo Bills 1 Bills Dr Orchard Park NY 14127-2296*

MOULDS, JOHN F. federal judge; m. Elizabeth Fry, Aug. 29, 1964; children: Donald B., Gerald B. Student, Stanford U., 1955-58; BA with honors, Calif. State U., Sacramento, 1960; JD, U. Calif, Berkeley, 1963. Bar: U.S. Supreme Ct., U.S. Dist. Ct. (no. dist.) Calif., U.S. Dist. Ct. (ea. dist.) Calif. 1968, U.S. Ct. Claims 1982, U.S. Ct. Appeals (9th cir.) 1967, Calif. Rsch. analyst Calif. State Senate Fact-Finding Com. on Edn., 1960-61; adminstrv. asst. Senator Albert S. Rodda, Calif., 1961-63; staff atty. Calif. Rural Legal Assistance, Marysville, 1966-68, dir. atty. Marysville field office and Sacramento legis. adv. office, 1968-69; staff atty. Sacramento Legal Aid, 1968-69; ptnr. Blackmon, Isenberg & Moulds, 1969-85, Isenberg, Moulds & Hemmer, 1985; magistrate judge U.S. Dist. Ct. (ea. dist.) Calif., 1985—, chief magistrate jduge, 1988-97. Moot ct. and trial practice judge U. Calif. Davis Law Sch., 1975—, U. of Pacific McGeorge Coll. Law, 1985—; part-time U.S. magistrate judge U.S. Dist. Ct. (ea. dist.) Calif., 1983-85; mem. 9th Cir. Capital Case Com., 1992—, U.S. Jud. Conf. Com. on the Magistrate Judge Sys., 1992—, Adv. Com. to the Magistrate Judges' Divsn. Adminstv. Office of U.S. Jud. Conf., 1989—. Author: (with others) Review of California Code Legislation, 1965, Welfare Recipients' Handbook, 1967; editor: Ninth Circuit Capital Punishment Handbook, 1991. Atty. Sacramento Singlemen's Self-Help Ctr., 1969-74; active Sacramento Human Relations Commn., 1969-75, chair, 1974-75; active community support orgn. U. Calif. at Davis Law Sch., 1971—; mem., atty. Sacramento Community Coalition for Media Change, 1972-75; bd. dirs. Sacramento Country Day Sch., 1982-90, Sacramento Pub. Libr. Found., 1985-87; active various polit. orgns. and campaigns, 1960-82. Mem. ABA, Fed. Bar Assn., Nat. Coun. Magistrates (cir. dir. 1986-88, treas. 1988-89, 2d v.p. 1989-90, 1st v.p. 1990-91), Fed. Magistrate Judges Assn. (pres.-elect 1991, pres. 1992-93), Calif. State-Fed. Jud. Coun. Conf. (panelist capital habeas corpus litigation 1992), Fed. Jud. Ctr. Training Conf. for U.S. Magistrate Judges (panel leader 1993), Milton L. Schwartz Inns of Ct. Office: 8240 US Courthouse 501 I St Ste 8-240 Sacramento CA 95814-7300

MOULDS, WILLIAM J. retired aeronautical engineer; b. Newton, Kans., Mar. 7, 1933; s. William J. and Edith M. (Cox) Moulds; m. Myra Teresa Cummins, Dec. 28, 1955; children: Michael J., Robert W., Barbara L., Anne T. Moulds-Laughlin, Patrick L., Margaret L. Moulds-Vittitow. BSME, U. N.Mex., 1957; MSME, N.Mex. State U., 1970. Registered profl. engr., N.Mex. Rsch. engr. rsch. lab. Allis-Chalmers, Cin., 1956—57; supr. aero. engr. Air Force Spl. Weapons Ctr., Albuquerque, 1958—63; sr. aero. rsch. engr. Air Force Weapons Lab., 1963—72, theoretical rsch. engr., 1972—79, chief tech. svcs. divsn., staff rsch. engr. to comdr., 1979—89; ret., 1989. Contbr. articles to profl. jours.; patentee in field. Vol. Barrett House; founder, 1st pres. U. N.Mex. Sch. Engring Alumni Assn.; bd. dirs. N.Mex. State Bd. Registration for Profl. Engrs. and Land Surveyors, 1990—95, chmn. com. on rules, regulations and statues, 1992; com. mem. Barrett Found. Recipient Honor award, U. N.Mex. Sch. Engring., 2000. Republican. Roman Catholic. Home: 1401 Cardenas NE Albuquerque NM 87110-6623

MOULE, WILLIAM NELSON, electrical engineer, consultant; b. Highland Park, Mich., Sept. 13, 1924; s. Hollis Creager and Kate DeEtte (Hill) Moule; m. Barbara Ann Bagley, June 27, 1953; children: Janice Louise, Robert Hollis(dec.) , Linda Anne, Nancy Lynn Moule Moles. BSEE, Mich. State U., 1949; MSEE, U. Pa., 1957. Reg. profl. engr., N.J. Design engr. Radio Corp. of

Am., Camden, NJ, 1949—59, sr. design engr. Moorestown, 1959—67; sr. engr. Emerson Elec. Co., St. Louis, 1967—70, Emerson Elec. Rantec Divsn., Calabasas, Calif., 1970; sr. staff engr. Raytheon Co., Santa Barbara, 1970—73, ITT Gilfillan, Van Nuys, 1973, Jet Propulsion Lab., Pasadena, 1973—79; sr. rsch devel. engr. Lockheed Advanced Devel. Co., Burbank, 1979—2000, cons. engr., 2000—. Patentee numerous inventions, 1956—. Dir. nat. alumni bd. Mich. State U., East Lansing, 1984-87; pres. Big Ten Club of So. Calif., L.A., 1992. Staff sgt. USAAF, 1943-46. Mem. IEEE (sr., L.A. chpt. sec., treas. Antennas and Propagation soc. 1987-89, vice chmn. 1989-90, chmn. 1990-91), 305th Bombardment Group Meml. Assn. (life; pres. 2000-2001). Democrat. Presbyterian. Avocations: travel, photography, genealogy. Home: 5831 Fitzpatrick Rd Calabasas CA 91302-1104 Office: 5831 Fitzpatrick Rd Calabasas CA 91302-1104 E-mail: wmoule@qnet.com.

MOULIN, JANE ANN FREEMAN, ethnomusicology educator, researcher; b. Oak Park, Ill., Mar. 4, 1946; d. James Frederic and Georgia Charlotte (Rahn) Freeman; m. Jacques Edouard Moulin, Apr. 26, 1975; children: Jean-Philippe Keala, Marie-Chantal Mahala. BA in Music cum laude, U. Hawaii, 1969; MA in Music, UCLA, 1971; PhD in Music, U. Calif., Santa Barbara, 1991. Libr. Music Libr UCLA, 1970-71; tchr. English Companions, Osaka, Japan, 1972; dancer Te Maeva and Tahiti Nui, Papeete, Tahiti, 1973-76; rsch. fellow U. Auckland, New Zealand, 1989; fellow East-West Ctr., Honolulu, 1984-85, 91; assoc. prof. Hawaii Loa Coll., Kaneohe, 1980-92; prof. U. Hawaii, Honolulu, 1992—. Dir. Europa Early Music Consort, Honolulu, 1981-2000; primary rschr. field work in French Polynesia, 1973-77, 85, 89, 95, 98, 2000, Territorial Survey Oceanic Music, Marquesas Islands, 1989; cons. Video series Dancing, WNET Channel 13, N.Y.C., 1989-92. Author: The Dance of Tahiti, 1979, Music of the Southern Marquesas Islands, 1994, (audio catalog) Music of the Southern Marquesas Islands, 1991, ency. and jour. articles on Tahitian and Marquesan performing arts, field recordings of Tahitian and Marquesan music; editl. bd. Jour. Perfect Beat, 1993—, Pacific Islands Monograph Series, 1997—; bd. dirs. Hawaii Assn. Music Socs., Honolulu, 1983-88. Bd. dirs. Tahiti-USA Assn., Honolulu, 1997-2000; mem. adv. bd. folk arts State Found. Culture and Arts, Honolulu, 1985-87. Recipient Regents' fellowship U. Calif., 1970-71, 88-89, rsch. grant UNESCO/Archives of Maori and Pacific Music, Auckland, 1989, Regents' award for excellence in tchg. U. Hawaii, Honolulu, 1997, First Prize Thèse-Pac Assn. Competition, New Caledonia, 1994. Mem. Soc. Ethomusicology (mem. coun. 1995-97), Internat. Coun. Traditional Music, Polynesia Soc., Pacific Arts Assn., Viola da Gamba Soc. Am. Avocations: Tahitian dance, hula, consort playing. Office: U Hawaii Music Dept 2411 Dole St Honolulu HI 96822-2329

MOULLETTE, JOHN BRINKLEY, retired corporate trainer, consultant; b. Camden, N.J., Jan. 23, 1927; s. Clarence Earle Moullette and Margaret Dorothea Philipsen; m. Lillian Marie Laye, Jan. 30, 1954 (div. 1979); children: John, Bruce, Jeanne, Edward, Jennifer. BEd, Trenton (N.J.) State Coll., 1957; MEd, Rutgers U., 1966, EdD, 1970. Cert. vocat.-tech. inst. adminstr., N.J. Instr. tech. writing Salem County Tech. Inst., Penns Grove, N.J., 1961-65; supr. vocat. edn. N.J. State Dept. Edn., Trenton, 1965-66; lectr. in edn. Rutgers U., New Brunswick, N.J., 1966-70; assoc. prof. Wash. State U., Pullman, 1970-71; rsch. prof. Ohio State U., Columbus, 1971-75; mgr. proposal devel. Telemedia, Inc., Chgo., 1975-77; mgr. edn. and tng. Royal Saudi Naval Forces, Dammam, 1977-79; mgmt. and profl. trainer Saudi Aramco, Dhahran, Saudi Arabia, 1980-89, ret. Saudi Arabia, 1989. Cons. Royal Saudi Naval Forces naval tech. tng. facilities, Dammam, Saudi Arabia, 1990-91, tng. ship Tarpon Springs, Fla., 1991-93, UN Devel. Program, Internat. Labor Orgn. Nat. Tng. Secretariat, Phnom Penh, Kingdom of Cambodia, 1993-94, Mil. Sea Lift Command USNS Comfort, 1996. Author: Technical Writing, 1969, Training Start-Up and Planning Guide, 1989, International Relations, 1993. Sgt. USMC, 1944-46, PTO, 1950-52, Korea; quartermaster/boatswain U.S. Mcht. Marine, 1946-49. Recipient Disting. Svc. award Grad. Sch. Edn., Rutgers U., New Brunswick, 1992. Mem.: Am. Legion (comdr. China Post #1, Dhahran 1986, 1988), Phi Delta Kappa, Epsilon Pi Tau. Avocations: scuba diving, offshore sailing, pioneer trekking, camping. Office: Internat Tng Consultants 3937 Winding Rd Fort Garland CO 81133

MOULTHROP, EDWARD ALLEN, architect, artist; b. Rochester, N.Y., May 22, 1916; s. Ray Josiah and Jetta (McDonald) M.; m. Mae Elizabeth Crotser, Jan 31, 1942; children: Mark, Philip, Samuel, Timothy. B.Arch., Western Res. U., 1939; M.F.A., Princeton, 1941. Asst. prof. architecture Ga. Inst. Tech., 1943-46, asst. prof. physics, 1944-46; chief designer Robert and Co. Asso. Architects and Engrs., Atlanta, 1948-72; prin. Edward Allen Moulthrop (architect and cons.), 1972—. 1st chmn. Ga. Art Commn., 1954-65 Exhibited in Watercolor U.S.A., 1962, USIA crafts traveling show to Russia, 1970., 1970, to Europe, 1990-93, Wichita Nat. Decorative Arts and Ceramics Exhbn., 1972, Ga. artists exhibit, High Mus. Art, Atlanta, 1971, 72, 74, Vatican Mus., Italy, 1978, Art of Woodturning show, Smithsonian Renwick Gallery, Washington, 1993—; represented in permanent collections Mus. Modern Art, N.Y., Met. Mus. Art, N.Y., Phila. Mus. Art, Chgo. Art Inst., The White House, Mint Mus. Art, Charlotte, N.C., High Mus. of Art, Atlanta, Boston Mus. Fine Arts, Ariz. State U. and Mus., Chgo. Art Inst., Copenhagen Mus. Art, Detroit Inst. Arts, Arkansas Arts Ctr. Decorative Arts Mus., Am. Craft Mus., N.Y., Renwick Gallery Mus. Am. Art, Smithsonian Inst., Mobile Mus. Art, Columbus Mus., Ga.; pvt. collections include Met. Mus. Art; instnl. collections include a. Gov.'s Office, Ga. Inst. Tech., Ga. State U., Atlanta Hist. Soc., Shepard Spinal Clinic, (permanent trophy and ann. trophies) Vintage Invitational Golf Tournament, White Ho. Collection Am. Crafts; corp. collections include So. Bell Hdqs., Atlanta, First Am. Bank, Nashville, Charlotte, Coca-Cola Co. World Hdqrs., St. Louis, Columbia Pictures, M.C.I., Hallmark, Phillip Morris, Cox Communication Co., IBM, Fuqua Inds., Atlanta, Rockefeller Ctr. Rainbow Room; spl. invited exhbts. Artists in Ga. High Mus. Art, Atlanta, 1971, 72, 74, The Vatican Mus., Rome, Internat. Exhbn.,Smithsonian Instn., 1978, Renwick Gallery Smithsonian Instn., 1978, XII Olympics Art Exhbn., Lake Placid, N.Y., 1980, Art for Use Nat. Crafts Exhbn. Am. Craft Mus., N.Y., 1980, Twenty-Fifth Anniversary Exhbn. Am. Craft Exhbn., 1981, Am. Craft Mus., N.Y., 1986, U.S. Info Agy. Ea. Europe, 1986-89; one man exhbn. High Mus. Art, 1987, U.S Info. Agy. European exhbn., overseas exhbn., 1992-95, 95-98; pubs. include Wall St. Jour., N.Y. Times, Village Voice, Atlanta Jour., Ariz. Republic, So. Accents, Creative Ideas, Home Mechanics, Fine Woodworking, American Craft, The Woodworker (with cover Great Britain), Holz und Elfenbein (with cover German), World of Wood, Popular Woodworking, Woodturning, Great Britain, Forbes Mag. Recipient Nat. Design award Am. Inst. Steel Constrn. 1959, 67, 1st purchase award for crafts Atlanta Arts Festival 1963, 64, 67, 72, 74, 77, 78, Atlanta Arts Festival First awards in crafts, 1963, 65, 67, 69, 73, 74, 77, 78, Craftsman U.S. award of merit 1966, Judges Choice award Western Colo. Center for Arts 1973, Purchase award 1975, Prize award, 1975, prize Marietta Coll. Crafts Nat. 1974, 76, prize awards Marietta Crafts Nat. Exhbn., Ohio, 1974, 75, 76, selected for exhibited 1973, 77, 78, N.C. prize awards Piedmont Regional Biennial Crafts Exhbns. Mint Mus. Art, Charlotte, 1974, 76, 78, Craftwork prize Am. Crafts Council 1976, 78, Prize awards, Am. Crafts Coun. S.E. Regional Biennial Crafts Exhbns., 1976, 78, Craftsmanship medal Atlanta chpt. Am. Instn. Archs., 1978, Ga. Assn. Am. Instn. Archs., 1980, Ga. State Gov's. award in Arts, 1981, Ga. Gov.'s Award in Arts 1981, Disting. Achievement award Ariz. State U., 1999. Fellow AIA (pres. Ga. chpt. 1953), Am. Craft Coun., Am. Craft Coun., 1987; mem. Ga. Engring. Soc. (pres. 1958, spl. hon. mem. 1969), Am. Craftsmens Coun. (Ga. rep. 1973-75), Ga. Designer Craftsmen (pres. 1975-76). Achievements include providing gifts for President Clinton, Queen Margrethe of Denmark and President Earnesto of Mexico. Home and Office: 4260 Carmain Dr NE Atlanta GA 30342-3504

MOULTON, DAVID AUBIN, library director; b. Portsmouth, N.H., Nov. 20, 1952; s. Howard Turner and Dorothy Margaret (McLaughlin) M. BA in History, U. N.H., 1974; MLS, Simmons Coll., 1976. Asst. libr. Strayer Coll., Washington, 1976-83, dir. LRC Arlington, Va., 1983-86; dir. librs. Strayer U., Washington, 1987—. Chair libr. networking com. Consortium for Continuing Higher Edn. in No. Va., 1987. Mem. covenants com. Parc East Condominium, Alexandria, Va, 1987-90. Mem. ALA, Va. Libr. Assn. Avocation: collecting children's and boy's books, 1820-1940. Office: Strayer Univ 1133 15th St NW Washington DC 20005-2710 E-mail: dam@strayer.edu.

MOULTON, EDWARD QUENTIN, civil engineer, educator; b. Kalamazoo, Nov. 16, 1926; s. Burt Frederick and Esther (Fairchild) M.; m. Joy Wade, Jan. 2, 1954; children: Jennifer Fairchild, Charles Wade, David Frederick II, Alison Joy. BS, Mich. State U., 1947; MS, La. State U., 1948; PhD, U. Calif., Berkeley, 1956; DSc (hon.), Wittenberg U., 1980; LLD (hon.), Xavier U., 1983, Wilmington Coll., 1983. Registered profl. engr., Ohio. Instr. civil engring Mich. State U., 1947; hydraulic engring. fellow La. State U., 1947-48; engr. U.S. Waterways Expt. Sta., Vicksburg, Miss., 1948; rsch. fellow U. Wis., 1948-49; asst. prof. civil engring. Auburn U., 1949-50; lectr. civil engring. U. Calif., Berkeley, 1950-54; asst. prof. civil engring. Ohio State U., 1954-58, assoc. prof., 1958-64; asst. dean Ohio State U. (Grad. Sch.), 1958-62, assoc. dean Grad. Sch., Coll. Arts and Scis., chmn. geodetic sci., 1962-64; dean off-campus edn., assoc. dean faculties for personnel budget, prof. engring. mechanics Ohio State U. Grad. Sch., Columbus, 1964-66; dir. Coll. Sci. and Engring. Dayton campus Miami U.-Ohio State U., 1963-66; pres. U. S.D., 1966-68; exec. asst. to pres. Ohio State U., 1968-69, sec. bd. trustees Ohio Agr. Devel. Ctr., 1968-79, prof. civil engring., 1968-79, v.p. adminstrv. ops., 1969-70, exec. v.p. adminstrv. ops., 1970-71, exec. v.p., 1971-73, v.p. bus. and adminstrn., 1973-79, v.p., sec. emeritus, 1984—; chancellor Ohio Bd. Regents, 1979-84, chancellor emeritus, 1984—; exec. v.p. Cranston Securities Co., 1984; pres. Lake Erie Coll., 1985-86; pres., gen. mgr. Columbus Symphony Orchestra, 1986-88, mem. trustees cir., 2000—. Cons. civil engring. 1954—. Author articles, reports, bulls. on environ. engring. and edn. Trustee Blue Cross Ctrl. Ohio, 1971-77, 80-82, Columbus Symphony Orch., 1980-85, Riverside Meth. Hosp., 1979-95, chmn. fin. and assets com., 1983-94, treas., 1988-94, vice-chmn., 1994-95; nat. adv. coun. for small bus. to U.S. Sec. Treasury, 1975-76; steering com. Devel. Com. Greater Columbus, 1970-1980, chmn., 1978-79; nat. adv. coun. SBA, 1973-76; bd. dirs. Columbus Safety Coun., 1970-79; bd. mem. Greater Columbus Arts Coun., 1970-78, Mid-Ohio Health Planning Commn., 1973-74, Am. Univs. for Rsch. in Astronomy, 1972-79, Ohio Transp. Rsch. Ctr., 1979-83, U.S. Health Corp. (now Ohio Health), 1995-97; chmn. Grant/Riverside Meth. Hosps., 1995-97, mem. trustees' coun., 1998—, trustee emeritus, 1999—; vice-chmn. Ohio Higher Edn. facilities Commn., 1979-83; bd. mem. Ohio Sch. and Coll. Bd. Registration, 1979-83, Ohio Ednl. TV Commn., 1979-83, Midwest Edn. Commn., 1979-85; chmn. Columbus Symphony Grand Ball, 1983; chmn. judging Internat. Sci. and Engring. Fair, 1984. With USN, 1945-46, PTO. Fellow ASCE; mem. Ohio Hist. Soc. (bd. dirs. 1979-83), State Higher Edn. Exec. Officers (exec. com. 1981-83), Meml. Soc. Columbus Area (pres. 1999-2000, bd. mem.), Ohio Commodore, Scioto Country Club, Faculty Club (Columbus), Athletic Club Columbus, Sigma Xi, Tau Beta Pi, Pi Mu Epsilon, Chi Epsilon, Delta Omega, Romophos, Sigma Alpha Epsilon. Congregationalist. Home: 1303 London Dr Columbus OH 43221-1541

MOULTON, FRANK RAY, JR. retired oil company executive; b. Winthrop, Mass., June 17, 1924; s. Frank Ray and Mildred Pauline (Hendrickson) M.; m. Louise Pearl Kiser, May 10, 1952 (div. June 1982); children: Catherine Moulton Olde, Thaddeus Ray (dec.); m. Barbara Julie Shearer, Aug. 1, 1983. BS in Naval Sci., Brown U., 1945; Geophys. Engr., Colo. Sch. Mines, 1951; BA in Classical Studies, Ursinus Coll., 1989; MA in Classical Studies, Villanova U., 1993. Field geologist, seismologist Superior Oil Co., Bakersfield, Calif., 1951-52; geophysicist Carter Oil Co., Tulsa, and Miles City, Mont., 1952, Internat. Petroleum (Colombia) Ltd., Bogota, 1953-56; staff geophysicist Petroleo Brasileiro (Petrobras), Rio De Janeiro, 1956-60; geophysicist Texasgulf Sulphur Co., Houston, 1961-65, regional mgr. exploration, 1965-68, asst. gen. mgr. oil & gas, 1969-71; v.p., gen. mgr. oil & gas divsn. Texasgulf Inc., 1972-82; pres. Texasgulf Oil & Gas Co., 1978-82; ret., 1982. Pres., COO Omni Exploration Inc., Radnor, Pa., 1983-84. Lt. (j.g.) USN, 1943-48, PTO. Medalist Colo. Sch. Mines, 1974. Mem. Am. Assn. Petroleum Geologists, Geol. Soc. Am., East India Club London (overseas mem.), Petroleum Club of Houston. Mem. United Ch. of Christ. Avocation: Classical and philosophical studies. Home: 69 Saint Andrews Ln Glenmoore PA 19343-9559

MOULTON, GRACE CHARBONNET, physics educator; b. New Orleans, Nov. 1, 1923; d. Wilfred J. and Louise A. (Hellmers) Charbonnet; m. William Gates Moulton, June 1, 1947; children: Paul Charbonnet Moulton, Nancy Gates Moulton. BA, Tulane U., 1944; MS, U. Ill., 1948; PhD, U. Ala., 1962. Asst. prof. physics U. Ala., Tuscaloosa, mem. 1962-65; asst. prof. physics Fla. State U., Tallahassee, 1965-74, assoc. prof. physics, 1974-80, prof. physics, 1980-91, prof. emerita, 1991. Cons. State Bd. Regents, Fla., 1985-90, Fla. Univ. System, 1985, 90. Referee jour. articles Jour. Chem. Physics, Radiation Rsch.; contbr. many sci. rsch. articles to profl. jours. Four Yr. Undergrad. scholar Tulane U., scholar U. Ill.; rsch. grantee NIH. Mem. Am. Phys. Soc., (mem. coun. southeastern sect. 1988-92). Avocations: gardening, music (classical and folk), birding. Office: Fla State U Dept Physics Tallahassee FL 32306

MOULTON, HUGH GEOFFREY, lawyer, retired business executive; b. Boston, Sept. 18, 1933; s. Robert Selden and Florence (Bracq) M.; m. Catherine Anne Clark, Mar. 24, 1956; children: H. Geoffrey, Cynthia C. Moulton Bassett. BA, Amherst Coll., 1955; LL.B., Yale U., 1958; postgrad. Advanced Mgmt. Program, Harvard U., 1984. Bar: Pa. 1959. Assoc. Montgomery, McCracken, Walker-Rhoads, Phila., 1958-66, ptnr., 1967-69; v.p., counsel Dolly Madison Industries, Inc., 1969-70; sec. Alco Std. Corp., Valley Forge, Pa., 1970-72, v.p. law, 1973-79, v.p., sec., gen. counsel, 1979-83, sr. v.p., gen. counsel, 1983-92, exec. v.p., chief adminstrv. officer, gen. counsel, 1992-94; exec. v.p. Alco Std. Corp. now IKON Office Solutions Inc., 1994-96, Unisource Worldwide, Inc., 1997-99; ret., 1999. Pres. Wissahickon Valley Watershed Assn., Ambler, Pa., 1975-78, treas., 1978—; mem. Pa. Coun. for Econ. Edn., bd. dirs., 1985-95; trustee Arcadia U., 1991—, chair, 1998-02; Montgomery Co. Lands Trust (trustee 2000—), Whitemarsh Found. (trustee, pres. 2002—). Mem. Am. Corp. Counsel Assn. (bd. dirs. Delaware Valley chpt. 1984-88, pres. 1986-87), Nature Conservancy (trustee Pa. chpt. 1991—, chmn. 1993-97), Sunnybrook Golf Club (Plymouth Meeting, Pa.), Cape Cod Nat. Golf Club (Harwich, Mass.), Lemon Bay Golf Club (Englewood, Fla.). Home: 300 Williams Rd Fort Washington PA 19034-2015 E-mail: hgmoulton@att.net.

MOULTON, IAN FREDERICK, English educator; b. London, May 30, 1964; s. Edward Calvin and Alice Moulton; m. Wendy Rae Williams, Mar. 11, 2000. BA in English and French, U. Man., Winnipeg, Can., 1986; MA in English, U. We. Ont., London, Can., 1988; PhD in English, Columbia U., 1995. Asst. prof. English Ariz. State U. West, Phoenix, 1995-2001, assoc. prof. English, 2001—. Author: Before Pornography, 2000; contbr. articles to profl. jours. Mem. MLA, Renaissance Soc. Am., Shakespeare Assn. Am. Office: Ariz State U West 4701 W Thunderbird Rd Phoenix AZ 85069-7100

MOULTON, JAMES ROGER, small business owner; b. Washington, Dec. 9, 1950; s. Roger Daniels and Vivian (Marshall) M.; m. Lynne Fellman, Feb. 5, 1977 (div. Aug. 12, 1984); m. Diane Marthe Allard, Jan. 6, 1986; children: Melissa Jane, Justin Roger. BS in Computer Sci., N.C. State U., 1972; MS in Computer Sci, U. Md., 1981. Computer specialist U.S. Naval Acad., Annapolis, Md., 1973-75; mem. tech. staff Computer Scis. Corp., Arlington, Va., 1975-78; sytem developer System Devel. Corp., McLean, 1978-81; computer specialist Nat. Bur. of Standards, Gaithersburg, Md., 1981-86; dist. mgrg. Bell Comm. Rsch. Inc., Red Bank, N.J., 1989-90; pres. Open Network Solutions, Inc., Sterling, Va., 1981—, ATN Software Ltd., Sterling, 1998—. Cons. Protocol Stds. and Comm., Ottawa, Can., 1986-88, ORS Assocs., McLean, Va., 1989-93, Open Network Solutions, Inc., Sterling, Va. Co-author (with others) Internat. Computer Standards, 1980-88; contbr. numerous articles to profl. jours. Recipient Dept. of Commerce Bronze medal, 1981. Democrat. Avocations: flying, mountaineering. Office: Open Network Solutions Inc 22636 Glenn Dr Ste 305 Sterling VA 20164-4443

MOULTON, PATRICIA L. experimental psychologist, researcher; b. Denver; d. Ralph and Richardine Moulton; m. May 21, 1994. MA, U. N.D., 1999, postgrad., 2001—. Grad. asst. dept. psychology U. N.D., Grand Forks, 1997—. Mem. APA (dissertation fellow 2001). Avocation: martial arts. Office: PO Box 8380 Grand Forks ND 58202-8380 E-mail: patricia_moulton@und.nodak.edu.

MOULTON, PAUL DOUGLAS (PETE MOULTON), infosystems engineering consultant; b. Binghamton, N.Y., Sept. 1, 1944; s. Fredrick Douglas and Helene Marjorie (Cole) M.; children: Susan Jennifer, Jeremy Matthew. BS in Math., Clarkson Coll. Tech., 1966, MS in Indsl. Mgmt., 1968. Instr. indsl. mgmt. Clarkson Coll., Potsdam, N.Y., 1967-68; tech. staff Sanders Data Systems, Inc., Nashua, N.H., 1968-71; grad. asst. Pa. State U., University Park, 1971-72; computer specialist Nat. Weather Svc., Silver Spring, Md., 1972; mgr. Info. & Communication Applications, Inc., Rockville, 1972-75, Rehab. Group, Inc., Arlington, Va., 1975-77; supr. spl. projects U.S. Senate, Washington, 1977-80; sr. cons. specialist telecommunications policies and programs Gen. Electric Info. Svcs. Co., Rockville, 1980; dir. Moulton, Minasi & Co., 1981—. Internat. lectr., cons. in microcomputers and telecommunications. Author: Hard Disk Quick Reference, 1989, Que Corporation, 1989, A+ Certification and Repair Guide, 2000, 02, The Telecommunications Survival Guide, 2001, Small Office/Home Office LANS, 2002; host DialANerd radio show WIFK and WCBM, Balt., 1998-2001; exec. prodr., host Technically Correct TV show WMAR ABC-TV2, Balt.; contbr. chpts. to books, articles to profl. jours. N.Y. Regent scholar. Mem. IEEE, Am. Inst. Indsl. Engrs. (sr.). Home and Office: 7146 Rivers Edge Rd Columbia MD 21044-4235

MOULTON, PAUL RUSH, ophthalmologist; b. Bangor, Maine, May 30, 1958; s. Gardner Nelson and Bonnie Dale (Rush) M.; m. Gabrielle Helen Strunc, May 26, 1984; children: Amanda, Alexander, Julianna. BS in Engring., Duke U., 1980; MD, Tufts U., 1984. Diplomate Am. Bd. Ophthalmology. Intern Meml. Med. Ctr., Corpus Christi, Tex., 1984-85; resident in ophthalmology Greater Balt. Med. Ctr., 1985-88; pvt. practice, Bangor, 1988—; chief ophthalmology Ea. Maine Med. Ctr., 1996—. Fellow Am. Acad. Ophthalmology; mem. AMA, New England Ophthal. Soc., Maine Med. Assn., Maine Soc. Eye Physicians and Surgeons, Penobscot County Med. Soc. Office: 5 Grove St Bangor ME 04401-5309

MOULTON, WILBUR WRIGHT, JR. lawyer; b. Pensacola, Fla., Dec. 3, 1935; s. Wilbur Wright and Evelyn (Nobles) M.; m. Ann Arnow, Nov. 10, 1978; 1 child, Kelly Arnow. BA, Duke U., 1957; LLB, U. Va., 1959; LLM in Taxation, NYU, 1964. Bar: Fla. 1959; cert. tax lawyer, Fla. Assoc. Beggs & Lane, Pensacola, 1964-69; gen. counsel The Moulton Trust, 1970-74; pvt. practice, 1974-83; ptnr. Carlton, Fields, Ward, Emmanuel, Smith & Cutler, P.A., 1983-2000, Moulton, McEachern & Walker (formerly Carlton, Fields et al), Pensacola, 2000—. Pres. Pensacola Heritage Found., 1971-72, Lakeview Ctr., Inc., Pensacola, 1975-77, dir. emeritus, 1984; chmn. bd. Lakeview Found., Inc., Pensacola; bd. trustees Pensacola Mus. Art. Lt. USNR, 1960-64. Mem. ABA, Fla. Bar Assn., Estate Planning Coun. N.W. Fla. (pres. 1978), Escambia-Santa Rosa Bar Assn. (pres. 1988-89), Rotary, Pensacola Country Club, Pensacola Yacht Club. Republican. Episcopalian. Avocations: reading, travel. Office: Bank of Am Bldg 5041 Bayou Blvd Ste 300 Pensacola FL 32503 Fax: 850-969-0566.

MOULTRIE, FRED, geneticist, researcher; b. Albertville, Ala., Apr. 18, 1923; s. Walter Louis and Minnie Alma (Bodine) M.; m. Frances Grace Aldridge, May 28, 1947; children: Marilyn R. Moultrie Phillips, Elizabeth Anne Moultrie Becker, Janet Carol Moultrie Gauger. BS, Auburn U., 1948, MS, 1949; PhD in Genetics, Kan State U., 1953. Asso. prof. Auburn U., 1951-55, prof., 1955-56; geneticist Arbor Acres Farm, Inc., Glastonbury, Conn., 1956-59, research coordinator, 1959-62, v.p., dir. research, 1962-64, exec. v.p., 1964-72, pres. domestic div., 1972-73; pres. Corbett Breeders, Westover, Md., 1973-81; v.p., dir. research Corbett Enterprises, Inc., 1973-81, Kennebec Internat., 1981-84; geneticist Perdue Farms, Salisbury, Md., 1984-88; genetics cons., 1988—. Served with USCGR, 1942-46. Mem. World's Poultry Sci. Assn., Am. Poultry Sci. Assn., Poultry Breeders Am. (pres. 1967-68), Sigma Xi, Phi Kappa Phi, Alpha Zeta, Gamma Sigma Delta. Clubs: Masons. Home and Office: 30390 Southampton Bridge Rd Salisbury MD 21804-2497

MOULY, EILEEN LOUISE, financial planner; b. Milw., Apr. 18, 1955; d. George Joseph and Gertrude Mary (DuBois) M. BBA in Acctg. summa cum laude, U. Miami, Coral Gables, Fla., 1977, MBA, 1978. CPA, Fla.; cert. fin. planner, personal fin. specialist. Acct. Main Hurdman, CPA's, Miami, Fla., 1979-82, Coopers & Lybrand, CPA's, West Palm Beach, 1982-83, Pannell Kerr Forster CPA's, Miami, 1983-84; cert. fin. planner Consortium Group, 1984-86; ptnr., fin. planner Evensky & Brown, 1986-91; pres. Mouly Fin. Mgmt. Inc., 1991—. Instr. U. Miami, 1987-90, Fla. Internat. U., 1987-90; speaker in field. Mem. AICPA, Fla. Inst. CPAs (bd. dirs. 1991-93, bd. govs. 2000-01, sec. South Dade chpt. 1993-94, treas. 1994-95, v.p. 1995-96, pres. 1997-98, 99-2000), Fin. Planning Assn., Registry Fin. Planning Practitioners, Inst. CFPs (cert., v.p. greater Miami chpt. 1987-91), Leadership South Dade. Office: Mouly Fin Mgmt Inc 290 NW 165th St Plz 300 Miami FL 33169-6457

MOUNSEY, JOSEPH BACKHOUSE, investment consultant; b. Lisburn, Northern Ireland, Mar. 27, 1949; arrived in Can., 1994; s. Colin Anthony and Helen (Roake) M.; m. Josephine Jennifer Gough, July 6, 1995; 1 child, Elizabeth Helen. MA with honors, Oxford (Eng.) U., 1970. Sr. v.p. Internat. Investments Manulife Fin., 1991-94; chmn. Western Trust and Savings Ltd., 1991-94; sr. v.p. investments Manulife Fin., Toronto, Ont., Can., 1994-97; cons., 1998—. Mem. Caribbean Investment Fund (investment com. 2000—). Home: 218 Blythwood Rd Toronto ON Canada M4N 1A6 E-mail: mounsey@sympatico.ca.

MOUNT, WILLIE LANDRY, state legislator; b. Lake Charles, La., Aug. 25, 1949; d. Lee Robert and Willie Veatrice (McCullor) Landry; m. Benjamin Wakefield Mount, Aug. 19, 1976. BS, McNeese State U., 1971. Geophys. asst. La. Land and Exploration, Lake Charles, La., 1971-76; pharm. rep. Lederle, 1976-80; realtor Mary Kay Hopkins, 1976-87; co-owner Paper Place, 1991-95; mayor City of Lake Charles, 1993-99; senate La. State, 2000—, vice-chair edn. com., mem. select com. on consumer protection, mem. jud. B, health and welfare, legis. audit adv. commn., mem. state tech. adv. commn.; joint juvenile justice commn.; millennium port com.; sch. fin. rev. commn. Gov. Violent Crime & Homicide Task Force, Baton Rouge, 1993—95; mem. steering com. La. conf. Mayors bd. pres. La. Asset Mgmt. Pool Bd., 1997. Guest condr. Lake Charles Symphony, 1992; active La. Mcpl. Assn., Baton Rouge, 1995-98; pres. Jr. League of Lake Charles; mem. state interagy. coordinating coun. Dyslexia Study Com.; mem. adv. bd. S.W. La. Literacy Coalition; mem. adv. coun. Pet Overpopulation; active First United Meth. Ch., La. Meth. Conf., McNeese State U. Found., Prevent Child Abuse bd. Micro-Enterprise Devel. Alliance of La. Bd., United Way, Children's Miracle Network; exec. com. Coun. for a Better La. Recipient Spiritual Aims award Kiwanis Club, 1991, Cmty. Svc. award, 1995, Citizen of Yr. 1996-97, Dorthea Combre award NAACP, 1994, Patron Architecture, 2000; named Woman of Yr., Quota Club, 1991, Citizen of Yr., Women's com. S.W. La., 1992, Woman of Yr., Pub. Ofcl. of Yr. Msgr. Cramers KC, Pub. Ofcl. of Yr., NASW, 1997, La. Mcpl. Assn. Cmty. Achievement award, 1995-97, Disting. Citizen award Boy Scouts Am., 1999; Disting. Alumni award McNeese State U., 2000, Golden Apple award Delta Kappa Gamma, 2002, Spl. Friend of La. Mcpl. Assn. award, 2002, Disting. Svc. award La. Restaurant Assn., 2002. Mem. LWV, S.W. La. Mayor's Assn. (chmn. 1993-94). Home: 205 Shell Beach Dr Lake Charles LA 70601-5933 Office: PO Box 3004 Lake Charles LA 70602-3004 E-mail: lasen27@legis.state.la.us.

MOUNTAIN, CLIFTON FLETCHER, surgeon, educator; b. Toledo, Apr. 15, 1924; s. Ira Fletcher and Mary (Stone) M.; children: Karen Lockerby, Clifton Fletcher, Jeffrey Richardson. AB, Harvard U., 1946; MD, Boston U., 1954. Diplomate Am. Bd. Surgery. Dir. dept. statis. rsch. Boston U., 1947-50; cons. rsch. analyst Mass. Dept. Pub. Health, 1951-53; intern U. Chgo. Clinics, 1954, resident, 1955-58, instr. surgery, 1958-59; sr. fellow thoracic surgery Houston, 1959. Mem. staff U. Tex. Anderson Cancer Ctr.; asst. prof. thoracic surgery U. Tex., 1960-73, assoc. prof surgery, 1973-76, prof., 1976-94, prof. emeritus, 1995—, prof. surgery Sch. Medicine, 1987—, chief sect. thoracic surgery, 1970-79, chmn. thoracic oncology, 1979-84, chmn. dept. thoracic surgery, 1980-85, cons. dept. thoracic and cardiovascular surgery, 1996—, chmn. program in biomath. and computer sci., 1962-64, Mike Hogg vis. lectr. in S. Am., 1967; prof. surgery U. Calif., San Diego, 1996—; mem. sci. mission on cancer USSR, 1970-78, and Japan, 1976-84; mem. com. health, rsch. and edn. facilities Houston Cmty. Coun., 1964-78; cons. Am. Joint Com. on Cancer Staging and End Result Reporting, 1964-74, Tex. Heart Inst., 1994-96; mem. Am. Joint Com. on Cancer, 1974-86, chmn. lung and esophagus task force; mem. working party on lung cancer and chmn. com. on surgery Nat. Clin. Trials Lung Cancer Study Group, NIH, 1971-76; mem. plans and scope com. cancer therapy Nat. Cancer Inst., 1972-75, mem. lung cancer study group, 1977-89, chmn. steering com., 1973-75, mem. bd. sci. counselors divsn. cancer treatment, 1972-75; hon. cons. Shanghai Chest Hosp. and Lung

Cancer Ctr., Nat. Cancer Inst. of Brazil; sr. cons. Houston Thorax Inst., 1994-96. Editor The New Physician, 1955-59; mem. editl. bd. Yearbook of Cancer, 1960-88, Internat. Trends in Gen. Thoracic Surgery, 1984-91; contbr. articles to profl. jours., chpts. to textbooks. Chmn. profl. adv. com. Harris County Mental Health Assn.; bd. dirs. Harris County Chpt. Am. Cancer Soc. Lt. USNR, 1942-46. Recipient award Soviet Acad. Sci., 1977, Garcia Meml. medal Philippine Coll. Surgeons, 1982, Disting. Alumni award Boston U., 1988, Disting. Achievement U. Tex. M.D. Anderson Cancer Ctr., 1990, Disting. Svc. award Internat. Assn. for the Study of Lung Cancer, 1991, Disting. Alumnus award Boston U. Sch. of Medicine, 1992, ALCASE Internat. award for excellence, 1997, Rudolf Nissen medal German Soc. Cardiovascular and Thoracic Surgery, 1998, named hon. pres. First Internat. Congress on Thoracic Surgery, 1997; Fellow ACS Am. Coll. Chest Physicians (chmn. com. cancer 1967-75), Am. Assn. Thoracic Surgery, Inst. Environ. Scis., N.Y. Acad. Sci., Assn. Thoracic and Cardiovascular Surgeons of Asia (hon.), Hellenic Cancer Soc. (hon.), Chilean Soc. Respiratory Diseases (hon., hon. pres. 1982). Mem. AAAS, Am. Assn. Cancer Rsch., AMA, So. Med. Assn., Am. Thoracic Soc., Soc. Thoracic Surgeons, Soc. Biomed. Computing, Am. Fedn. Clin. Rsch., Internat. Assn. Study Lung Cancer (pres. 1976-78), Am. Radium Soc., European Soc. Thoracic Surgeons, Pan-Am Med. Assn., Houston Surg. Soc., Soc. Surg. Oncology, James Ewing Soc., Sigma Xi. Achievements include conception and development of program for application of mathematics and computers to the life sciences, of resource for experimental designs, applied statistics and computational support; concept and implementation of multidisciplinary, site specific cancer mgmt. clinics; first clinical use of physiological adhesives in thoracic surgery; demonstration of clinical behavior of undifferentiated small cell lung cancer; first laser resection of lung tissue at thoracotomy; development of international system for staging of lung cancer. E-mail: cmountain@ucsd.edu.

MOUNTCASTLE, KENNETH FRANKLIN, JR. retired stockbroker; b. Winston-Salem, N.C., Oct. 8, 1928; s. Kenneth Franklin and May M.; m. Mary Katharine Babcock, Sept. 1, 1951; children: Mary Babcock, Laura Lewis, Kenneth Franklin, Katharine Reynolds. BS in Commerce, U. N.C., 1950. With Mountcastle Knitting Co., Lexington, N.C., 1952-55, Reynolds & Co., N.Y.C., 1955-71, Reynolds Securities Inc. (formerly Reynolds and Co.), N.Y.C., 1971-95; sr. v.p. Reynolds Securities Inc., 1974-78, Dean Witter Reynolds (formerly Reynolds Securities Inc.), N.Y.C., 1978-95; ret., 1995. Trustee New Canaan (Conn.) Country Sch., 1962-68, Ethel Walker Sch., Simsbury, Conn., 1973-85, Coro Found., 1980—, nat. chmn., 1986-89; past bd. dirs., past pres. Mary Reynolds Babcock Found., Winston-Salem; former bd. visitors U. N.C., Chapel Hill,; bd. dirs. Inform, N.Y.C., Fresh Air Fund, N.Y.C., The Giraffe Project, Friends of 13, Bus. Execs. Nat. Security. Served with U.S. Army, 1950-52. Mem. Country Club of New Canaan, Wee Burn Country Club (Darien, Conn.), Old Town Club (Winston-Salem), Racquet and Tennis Club, Ocean Forest Golf Club (Sea Island, Ga.), Sea Island Club, Pine Valley Golf Club, Bond Club, Stock Exch. Luncheon Club, The Down Town Assn. (N.Y.C.). Office: 49 Locust Ave Ste 104 New Canaan CT 06840-4764

MOUNTCASTLE, VERNON BENJAMIN, neurophysiologist; b. Shelbyville, Ky., July 15, 1918; s. Vernon and Anne-Francis Marguerite (Waugh) Mountcastle; m. Nancy Clayton Pierpont, Sept. 6, 1945; children: Vernon Benjamin III, Anne Clayton, George Earle Pierpont. BS in Chemistry, Roanoke Coll., Salem, Va., 1938, DSc (hon.) , 1968; MD, Johns Hopkins U., 1942; DSc (hon.) , U. Pa., 1976; DSc (hon.) , U. Minn., 1995; MD (hon.) , U. Zurich, 1983, U. Siena, 1984, U. Santiago, Spain, 1990; DSc, Northwestern U., 1985. House officer surgery Johns Hopkins Hosp., 1942—43; mem. faculty Johns Hopkins Sch. Medicine, 1946—, prof. physiology, 1959, dir. dept., 1964—80, Univ. prof. neurosci., 1980—92, prof. emeritus, 1992—; dir. Neurosci. Research Program, Rockefeller U., 1981—84; dir. Bard Labs. Neurophysiology Johns Hopkins U., Balt., 1981—91; pres. Neurosci. Research Found., 1981—85. Spl. rsch. physiology brain; chmn. physiology study sect., mem. physiology tng. com. NIH, 1958—61; adv. coun. Nat. Eye Inst., 1971—74; vis. prof. Coll. de France, Paris, 1980. Editor-in-chief: Jour. Neurophysiology, 1961—64, assoc. editor: Bull. Johns Hopkins Hosp., 1954—62, mem. editl. bd.: Physiol. Revs., 1957—59, mem. editl. bd.: Exptl. Brain Rsch., 1966—85, editor, contbr.: Med. Physiology, 12th edit., 1968, editor, contbr.: Med. Physiology, 13th edit., 1974, editor, contbr.: Med. Physiology, 14th edit., 1980, with G.M. Edelman: The Mindful Brain, 1978, : Perceptual Neuroscience: The Cerebral Cortex, 1998, author articles in field. Lt. (s.g.) M.C. USNR, 1943—46. Recipient Lashley prize, Am. Philos. Soc., 1974, F.O. Schmitt prize and medal, MIT, 1975, Sherrington prize and gold medal, Royal Acad. Medicine, London, 1977, Horowitz prize, Columbia U., 1978, Helmholtz prize, 1982, Fyssen Internat. prize, Paris, 1983, Lasker award, 1983, Nat. Medal Sci., 1986, Zotterman prize and medal, Swedish Physiol. Soc., 1989, McGovern prize and medal, AAAS, 1990, award in neurosci., Fidia Fedn., 1990, Australia prize, 1993. Mem.: AAAS, NAS (chmn. sect. on physiology 1971—74, award in neurosci. 1998), Acad. Sci. (Finland, fgn.), Royal Soc. London (fgn.), Acad. Scis. (France, fgn.), Nat. Inst. Medicine, Am. Philos. Soc. (councillor 1979—82), Soc. Neurosci. (pres. 1970—72, Gerard prize 1980), Harvey Cushing Soc., Am. Acad. Arts and Scis., Am. Physiol. Soc., Physiol. Soc. (hon.; London), Am. Neurol. Assn. (hon. Bennett lectr. 1978), Sigma Xi, Phi Chi, Alpha Omega Alpha, Phi Beta Kappa. Home: 15601 Carroll Rd Monkton MD 21111-2009 E-mail: vernon@fastfire.mb.jhu.edu.

MOUNTS, WILLARD, retired comptroller; b. Cedar, W.Va., Mar. 30, 1915; s. Kimble Anderson Mounts and Nancy Margaret Marcum; m. Faith Mallory, May 25, 1935 (div. Apr. 1957); children: Beatrice J., Faith D., Linda S.; m. Virginia Mariem Grambill, Jan. 10, 1958 (dec.). Student, Mountain State Coll., 1934—37; degree in bus., Regis Coll., 1960; postgrad., Hamilton Night Sch., 1980. Bookkeeper, acct. Kolbe Fisheries, Erie, Pa., 1937—39, Protane Corp., Erie, 1939—42; asst. office mgr. Lord Mfg. Corp., 1942—44; comptroller, bus. mgr. Goodyear Tire & Rubber, Denver, 1944—48, Luby Chevrolet Co., Denver, 1948—69, Jack Kent Cadillac Co., Denver, 1969—80; ret. Author: The Pioneer and the Prairie Lawyer, 1991, The Rugged Southern Appalachia, 1995. Pres. People to People Sister City, Nairobi, Kenya, 1974—75; scoutmaster Boy Scouts Am., Erie, 1939—44, Denver, 1956—; chmn. pastor/paris rels. com., lay leader Meth. Ch. Mem.: Denver Consistory (class pres. 1996—), Eastern Star, Shriners, Masons (sr. steward 2000—02). Republican. Methodist. Avocations: writing, lecturing, skiing, golf, travel. Office: Ginwill Pub Co 10973 Chinook Tr Parker CO 80138

MOUNTZ, LOUISE CARSON SMITH, retired librarian; b. Fond Du Lac, Wis., Oct. 20, 1911; d. Roy Carson and Charlotte Louise (Scheurs) Smith; m. George Edward Mountz, May 4, 1935 (dec. Oct. 3 1951); children: Peter Carson, Pamela Teeters Mountz McDonald. Student, Western Coll. for Women, 1929-31; AB, The Ohio State U., 1933; MA, Ball State U., 1962; postgrad., Manchester Coll., 1954, Ind. U., 1960-61. Cert. tchr., Ind. Tchr. Monroeville (Ind.) H.S., 1953-54, Riverdale H.S., St. Joe, Ind., 1954-55; libr. High Sch., Avilla, 1955-58; head libr. Penn H.S., Mishawaka, 1958-67, Northwood Jr. H.S., Ft. Wayne, 1967-69, McIntosh Jr. H.S., Auburn, 1969-74; dir. Media Ctr. DeKalb Jr. H.S., 1974-78; ret., 1978; cons. media ctr. planning Penn-Harris-Madison Sch. Corp., Mishawaka, 1966-67. Author: Biographies for Junior High Schools and Correlated Audio-Visual Materials, 1970; contbr. articles to profl. jours. Bd. dirs. DeKalb County chpt. ARC, 1938-42, 51-53, DeKalb County Heart Assn., 1946-52, DeKalb County Cmty. Concert Assn., 1946-58, Am. Field Svc. Mishawaka chpt., 1960-67; mem. Ft. Wayne Philharmonic Orch. Assn., Ft. Wayne Art Mus., DeKalb County Hist. Soc., Garrett Hist. Soc., DeKalb County Genealogy Soc., Acres Landtrust, Preservation of DeKalb County Heritage Assn., DeKalb Meml. Hosp. Women's Guild, also life mem. Mem. Ind. Sch. Librarians Assn. (dir. 1963-67), Internat. Assn. Sch. Librarianship, Ind. Assn. Ednl. Communication and Tech., Assn. Ind. Media Educators, Nat. Ret. Tchrs. Assns., Nat. Trust Hist. Preservation, Hist. Landmarks Found. Ind., Delta Kappa Gamma (charter mem., Beta Beta chpt.), Kappa Kappa Kappa (pr. officer 1941-45, pres. Alpha Chi chpt. 1938-40, organizer Garrett Assoc. chpt. pres. Garrett Assoc. chpt. 1971-73), Greenhurst Country Club, Ft. Wayne's Women's Club, Athena Lit. Club (hon.), Ladies Lit. Club of Auburn (hon.), Delta Delta Delta (house pres.). Methodist.

MOUNTZ, WADE, retired health service management executive; b. Winona, Ohio, Nov. 19, 1924; s. Lowell J. and Ethel M. (Coppock) M.; m. Betty G. Wilson, June 3, 1946; children: David John, Timothy Wilson. BA, Baldwin-Wallace Coll., 1948; MHA, U. Minn., 1951; LHD (hon.), Ky. Wesleyan Coll., 1991. With Norton Meml. Infirmary, Louisville, 1951-69, adminstr., 1958-69; pres. Norton-Children's Hosps., Inc., Louisville, 1969-81, NKC, Inc., Louisville, 1981-85, vice chmn., 1985-87; pres. emeritus Norton Healthcare, 1987—. Vice chmn. Comprehensive Health Planning Council Ky., 1968-73, chmn., 1973-79; bd. dirs. Louisville chpt. ARC, 1961-74; trustee Blue Cross Hosp. Plan, 1959-72; trustee Am. Hosp. Assn., 1971-76, chmn. bd., 1975. Served with A.C., USNR, 1943-45. Recipient Disting. Service award Ky. Hosp. Assn.; Disting. Layman award Ky. Med. Assn. Fellow Am. Coll. Hosp. Healthcare Execs. (life, gold medal), Masons. Home: 9 Muirfield Pl Louisville KY 40222-5074 Office: 4350 Brownsboro Rd Ste 110 Louisville KY 40207-1681

MOUNTZOURES, HARRY LOUIS, writer; b. Fishers Island, N.Y., July 9, 1934; s. Louis Philip and Sophia Pappas Mountzoures; m. Mary Ann Cawley, Oct. 8, 1964; 1 child, John. BA in English, Wesleyan U., 1956. Author: (book of short stories) The Empire of Things, 1968, (novel) The Bridge, 1972; contbr. short stories to mags. and publs. (O Henry award 1969). With U.S. Army, 1956-58. Mem. PEN Internat. Home: 29 Old Black Point Rd Niantic CT 06357-2815

MOURA, JOSE, wine consultant; b. Ponce, P.R., Dec. 6, 1961; s. Santiago Moura and Juana Castellar; children: Sharon, José E., José F. BBA in Mktg., U. P.R., 1985; M Direct Mktg., NYU, 1992. Wine cons. Banfi Vintner's, N.Y., 1988-97, Czaznove Opici Wine Corp., 1999—; wine columnist, restaurant critic El Diario, La Prensa, 1994-99; food and wine editor El Puente Latino.com, 2000—; sales mgr. Codorniu Internat. U.S.A., 2000—. Mem. tasting panel Wine & Spirits Mag., N.Y., 1997-99; cons. N.Y. City TV Sta., 1993, Indian TV Network, N.Y., 1993; lectr. in field. Author: Al Pan Pan y al Vino Vino, 1997; editor Food and Wine, 2000; columnist Hablando de Vinos, 1994-99. Mem. adv. bd. Pub. Sch. 1987, 1997; vol. Hispanic Commn. on AIDS, 1996; baseball coach West Side League, N.Y.C.; basketball coach Save Heaven League, N.Y.c. Home: Urbanizacion San Antonio Cll 2 U5 Ponce PR 00731

MOURA, JOSÉ MANUEL FONSECA, electrical engineer, educator; b. Beira, Mozambique, Portugal, Jan. 9, 1946; s. Josè Saraiva and Maria José (Fonseca) M.; m. Maria Tereza Fernandes, 1969 (div. 1981); 1 child, Barbara Fernandes; m. Maria Manuela Veloso, 1981; children: Andrè Veloso, Pedro Veloso. Engenheiro Electrotecnico, Instituto Superior Tecnico, Lisbon, 1969; MS in Elec. Engring., MIT, 1973, ScD in Elec. Engring. and Computer Sci., 1975. Prof. auxiliar Instituto Superior Tècnico, Lisbon, 1975-78, prof. aggregado, 1978, prof. catedrático, 1979-86; prof. Carnegie Mellon U., Pitts., 1986—. Vis. assoc. prof. elec. engring. and computer sci. MIT, Cambridge, 1984-86, vis. prof. elec. engring., 1999-2000; vis. scholar U. So. Calif., Los Angeles, summers 1978, 79, 80, 81. Editor: (with others) Nonlinear Stochastic Problems, 1983, Acoustic Signal Processing for Ocean Exploration, 1993; contbr. articles to profl. jours. Fellow IEEE (editor-in-chief trans. on Signal Processing 1995-99, v.p. publs. Signal Processing Soc. 2000-02, mem. govs. 1998—, v.p. publs. Sensors Coun. 2000-02, editl. bd. Proc. 1999-2001); mem. NAS Portugal (corr. mem.), Am. Math. Soc., Soc. Indsl. and Applied Math., Ordem dos Engenheiros. Office: Carnegie-Mellon U Dept Elec & Computer Engring 5000 Forbes Ave Pittsburgh PA 15213-3890 E-mail: moura@ece.cmu.edu.

MOURA-RELVAS, JOAQUIM M.M.A. electrical engineer, educator; b. Aveiro, Portugal, May 9, 1926; s. Joaquim Moura and Maria Emilia Albuquerque (Branco de Melo) Relvas; m. Maria Alice Barata Portugal, May 9, 1953; children: Jose Pedro, Joao Paulo, Luis Filipe, Joaquim Jose, Francisco Manuel, Maria Isabel. Degree in Elec. Engr., U. Porto, Portugal, 1951. Asst. engr. CTT (State Telecomms.), Lisbon, Portugal, 1951-53; design engr. UEP (Elec. Power Co.), Porto, 1953-73; prof. U. Coimbra, Portugal, 1973-81; chief engr. EDP (Electricidade de Portugal), Lisbon, 1981-88; prof. Poly. Inst. of Gaya, Vila Nova de Gaia, Portugal, 1988—. Author: Introduction to Digital Electronics, 1971, Introduction to Microcomputers, 1981, Digital Electronics, 1986. Mem. AASS, N.Y. Acad. Scis., Ordem dos Engenheiros, Planetary Soc. Avocations: swimming, walking, photography, home movies, historical books. Home: Av da Republica 1815 Vila Nova de Gaia 4430-206 Portugal Office: ISP Gaya R Antonio R da Rocha 341 Vila Nova de Gaia 4430-206 Portugal

MOURASHKIN, BORIS V. composer, sound therapist, poet, performer, producer; b. Kemerovo, Siberia, Feb. 27, 1949; BA in Musical Theory and Composition, Novosibirsk Mus. Coll., 1976; MA in Music Theory and Composition, M.I. Glinka Conservatory, 1980. Head rsch. lab. (Bio-Energetic Music) for Bio-Energetic and Ecology of Consciousness Russian Fedn., Inst. Human Ecology, Acad. Tech. Scis., Moscow, 1993—. Prof., composer various styles of music including choir music, piano composition, compositions for string orchs., incidental music, musical scores for films and plays;compositions include Jungle Passion, Odd & Even, Two-Step for Lovers, The Stirrings of Love, Blizzard Dance, Without End..., Dedicated to Alfred Schnittke (a musical poetry and dialogue), 1987, others; music editor Novosibirsk-Telefilm, 1980-83; rec. engr., composer, film actor TV, 1980-90; composer: This Is Us, O Lord!, 1991, Kama Sutra, 1991, Points of Light, 1994, Healing Music, 1994, Bio-Energetic Psychotropic Music, Touching the Mystical of Outer Space (dedicated to Steven Spielberg, Jeffrey Katzenberg and David Geffen), Night of Open Doors, 1995, author: (poetry and prose) The Existence of Man Begins with Protest (a tribute to V.M. Schukschin), The Broom's Solo, God Loves the Righteous; Cds include Howl of the Siberian Wolf, 2000, Tribute to the East, 2000; inventor, founder Bio-Enegetic Psychotropic Music, Healing Power of Music, 1983; founder, dir., prodr. Golden Fund of Documentary Films (extraordinary Russian-Americans); contbr. various articles to newspapers and mags. Vol. Siberian Orphanage, 1972-89, Siberian Prison, 1976-89, St. Christopher-Ottilie Home, Bio-Energetic Psychotropic Music Therapy Workshops for mentally and retarded children, Sea Cliff, N.Y., 1992-94, Gift of Life, Inc., 1993, Manhattan Psychiat. Ctr. workshops with Bio-Energetic, Psychotropic Music with mentally disordered people, Wards Island, N.Y., 1997; bd. dirs., mem. adv. bd. Tchertkoff Meml. & Cultural Found.; hon. mem. operation kids program Nat. Police Def. Found., 1999. Named Famous Poet, Famous Poets Soc., 1998, One of Best Poets of 2000 Internat. Libr. Poetry, 2000; recipient award of recognition Famous Poets Soc., 1998, Poet of the Yr. medallion Famous Poets Soc., 1999, Diamond Homer trophy Famous Poets Soc., 1999, Internat. Poet of Merit award medallion Internat. Soc. Poets, 1999, Pres. Recognition Lit. Excellence The Drifting Sands, Nat. Libr. Poetry, 1999. Fellow Internat. Informatization Acad. UN (academician, prof., SciD Art of Music Alternative Music Therapy, PhD Art of Science Practical Elaboration and Expertise BioSound Therapy Tech. and Soundpsycho-neuro-reflective immunotherapy); mem. Internat. Union Info., World Assn. Edn. Worlddidac, Nat. Acad. Rec. Art & Scis. Inc., Internat. Soc. Poets (disting.; Internat. Poet of Merit award medallion 1999, Poet of Yr. 1999, Prometheus Muse of Fire trophy 2000), Broadcast Music, Inc., Cinematographer's Union of Russian Fedn., Nat. Authors Registry. Home: 165 Brown St Sea Cliff NY 11579-1601 E-mail: bmourashkin@yahoo.com.

MOURSUND, KENNETH CARROLL, grocery chain executive; b. Austin, Oct. 21, 1937; s. Leif Erickson and Ethel Alberta Moursund; m. Claudia Frances Moursund, Dec. 21, 1963; 1 sond, Kenneth Carroll. BBA, U. Tex., Austin, 1963. Mgmt. trainee Am. Warehouses, Inc., 1963-64; with Kroger Co., Houston, 1964—, transp. supr., 1964, distbn. mgr. charge all warehousing and transp. Houston div., 1969-83, dir. distbn. Houston, S. Tex. and S. La., 1983-86, dir. distbn. Tex., 1986—. Profl. baseball player N.Y. Yankees and Detroit Tigers, 1957-61. Vestryman Trinity Episcopal Ch., 1977-79, jr. warden, 1978, sr. warden, 1979, mem. endowment bd., 1980-82; bd. dirs. Bill Williams Ann. Capon Charity Dinner, Inc. Served with USAR, 1960-66. Mem. NRA, Tex. Long Horn Breeders Assn., Cattlemen's Tex. Longhorn Registry, Houston Livestock and Rodeo Assn. (life, bd. dirs., chmn. group ticket com., v.p. 1996-98), Ex-Student Assn. U. Tex., Delta Nu Alpha (life). Office: PO Box 1309 Houston TX 77251-1309

MOUSEL, CRAIG LAWRENCE, lawyer; b. St. Louis, July 22, 1947; s. George William and Charlotte (Howard) M.; m. Polly Deane Burkett, Dec. 21, 1974; children: Donna, Dennis, D'Arcy. AB, U. So. Calif., 1969; JD, Ariz. State U., 1972. Bar: Ariz. 1973, U.S. Dist. Ct. Ariz. 1973, U.S. Ct. Appeals (9th cir.) 1973, U.S. Dist. Ct. (cen. dist.) Calif. 1984, Colo. 1993; registered lobbyist, Ariz. Adminstrv. asst. to Hon. Sandra O'Connor Ariz. State Senate, Phoenix, 1971-72; asst. atty. gen. Ariz. Atty. Gen.'s Office, 1973-75; ptnr. Sundberg & Mousel, 1975—. Spl. counsel City of Chandler, 1991 Hearing officer Ariz. State Personnel Bd., 1976-80, spl. appeals counsel, 1978—; hearing officer Ariz. Outdoor Recreation Coordinating Commn., 1975; dep. state land commr. Ariz. State Land Dept., 1978; precinct capt. Rep. Com.; mem. Ariz. Kidney Found., Orpheum Theatre Found., Phoenix Zoo Curators Club; sponsor Phoenix Art Mus.; varsity baseball coach Valley Luth. H.S., 1995-97, St. Mary's H.S., 2000; asst. baseball coach St. Mary's H.S., 1997-99. Fellow Ariz. Bar Found.; mem. ABA, ATLA, Ariz. Bar Assn., Maricopa County Bar Assn., Sports Lawyers Assn., Internat. Platform Assn., Ariz. Club, Am. Baseball Coaches Assn., Nat. High Sch. Baseball Coaches Assn., Ariz. Baseball Coaches Assn., USC Ptnrs. Alumni Group, U. So. Calif. Alumni Assn., Ariz. State U. Alumni Assn., Ariz. State Coll. Law Alumni Assn. Office: Sundberg & Mousel 934 W Mcdowell Rd Phoenix AZ 85007-1730 E-mail: mousel@mindspring.com.

MOUSER, ROBERT WINSTON, physician; b. Indpls., Oct. 21, 1931; s. Sylvan Leslie Mouser and Evelyn Mae Shipman; m. Patricia Ann Monser, June 6, 1958 (div. Feb. 1986); children: Cynthia, Laura, Phillip Bradley; m. Donna Jane, Feb. 28, 1986; children: Duane Elliott, Shawn Nguyen. BS, Ind. U., 1951, MD, 1954. Diplomate Am. Bd. Family Practice. Intern Indpls. Meth. Hosp.; physician, 1957—. Contbr. articles to profl. jours. Fellow Am. Coll. Med. Quality, Am. Acad. Family Practice; mem. Am. Coll. Legal Medicine. Presbyterian. Home: 406 Bent Tree Ln Indianapolis IN 46260 Office: Cornerstone Family Physicians Ste 110 9011 N Meridian St Indianapolis IN 46260

MOUSSEAU, DORIS NAOMI BARTON, retired elementary school principal; b. Alpena, Mich., May 6, 1934; d. Merritt Benjamin and Naomi Dora Josephine (Pieper) Barton; m. Bernard Joseph Mousseau, July 31, 1954. AA, Alpena Community Coll., 1954; BS, Wayne State U., 1959; MA, U. Mich., 1961, postgrad., 1972-75. Profl. cert. ednl. adminstr., tchr. Elem. tchr. Clarkston (Mich.) Community Schs., 1954-66; elem. sch. prin. Andersonville Sch., Clarkston, 1966-79, Bailey Lake Sch., Clarkston, 1979-94; ret., 1994. Oakland County rep. Mich. Elem. and Mid. Schs. Prins. Assn. Retirees Task Force, 1996. Cons., rsch. com. Youth Assistance Oakland County Ct. Svcs., 1968-88; leader Clarkston PTA, 1967-94; chair Clarkston Sch. Dist. campaign, United Way, 1985, 86; mem. allocations com. Oakland County United Way, 1987-88. Recipient Outstanding Svc. award Davisburg Jaycees, Springfield Twp., 1977, Vol. Recognition award Oakland County (Mich.) Cts., 1984, Heritage Chair for 40 yrs. svc. with Clarkston (Mich.) Cmty. Schs., 1994. Fellow ASCD, MACUL (State Assn. Ednl. Computer Users); mem. NEA (del. 1964), Mich. Elem. and Middle Sch. Prins. Assn. (treas., regional del. 1982—, pres.-elect Region 7 1988-89, program planner, pres. 1989-90, sr. advisor 1990-91, Honor award Region # 7 1991), Mich. Edn. Assn. (pres. 1960-66, del. 1966), Clarkston Edn. Assn. (author, editor 1st directory 1963), Women's Bowling Assn., Elks, Spring Meadows Golf Club (Sr. Ladies Net Champion 1999), Phi Delta Kappa, Delta Kappa Gamma (pres. 1972-74, past state and nat. chmn., Woman of Distinction 1982). Republican. Avocations: golf, gardening, reading, cross country skiing, clarinet. Home: 6825 Rattalee Lake Rd Clarkston MI 48348-1955

MOUSSEUX, RENATE, language educator; b. Stuttgart, Germany, Oct. 27, 1942; came to U.S., 1964; d. Emile and Gertrud Muller; m. Patrick Mousseux, Dec. 12, 1974; 1 child, Marc. BA, Padagogische Hochschule, Germany; MA, Grand Canyon U.; BL French, German, ESL, Phoenix U. Cert. French, German, psychology, bilingual French, ESL, secondary grades 7-12, Ariz., Calif. Prof. German Berlitz Sch. Lang., Sherman Oaks, Calif., 1966-67, Thunderbird Grad. Sch. Internat. Mgmt., Glendale, Ariz., 1968-72; prof. German and French Scottsdale Dist. H.S., 1980—; prof. French and German Rio Salado C.C., 1976-86; prof. French Scottsdale C.C., 1990-96, U. Phoenix, 1991—, 1991—; lit. and talent agt., co-prodr. for film and lit., 1991—; editor, pub. poetry books, 1991—. Distbr. Native Am. Music; bus. lang. trainer, course developer various corps.; trainer student tchrs. Ariz. State U., Ottawa U. Author: Accellerated French (Vive le Francais), 1989, Accellerated German (Willkommen Deutsch), 1990, Accellerated Spanish (Viva el Espanol), 1991, Accellerated Japanese (Moshi Moshi), 1991, Accellerated English (Hello English), 1992. With Essential Skills Com. Ariz. State Bd. Edn. Recipient Ariz. Fgn. Lang. Tchr. of Yr. award Ariz. Assn. Fgn. Lang. Tchrs., 1986, Exceptional Mentorship Skills award Ariz. State U., 1994, Excellence in Mentorship cert. Ariz. State U., 1995; named Tchr. of Yr., U.S. West Outstanding Tchr. Program, 1989, Nat. Day of Excellence award 1996, award in leadership and quality in edn. ASCD, 1990. Mem. NEA, Nat. Geographic Soc., Am. Assn. Tchrs. German, Alliance Francaise, French Tchrs. Assn., Cultural Heritage Alliance, Ariz. Fgn. Lang. Assn., Scottsdale Edn. Assn. Avocation: reading, writing, psychology, anthropology. Home: 15611 N Boulder Dr Fountain Hills AZ 85268-1814 Office: Chaparral HS 6935 E Gold Dust Ave Scottsdale AZ 85253-1484

MOUTON, ANDRE PAUL, artist; b. Baton Rouge, Jan. 11, 1958; s. Chester Paul and Dolores Fournet M. AA, C.C. of Denver, 1992. Pres., founder Vegas Artist Guild, Las Vegas, 1993—, The Art Guild, Denver, 1998—. Exhibitions include Las Vegas Art Mus., Mouton Gallery, TaGallery, Ctr. for Creative Devel. Roman Catholic. Avocations: travel, bicycling, teaching artist marketing skills. Home: 846 Kalamath St Denver CO 80204 Office: Ctr for Creative Devel 622 W Sixth Ave Denver CO 80204-5030 E-mail: artdenver@aol.com.

MOUTON, CHARLES PETER, physician, educator; b. New Orleans, Jan. 9, 1960; m. Yvette Mouton. BS, Howard U., 1981, MD, 1986; MS, Harvard U., 1997. Diplomate Am. Bd. Family Practice. Resident Prince George's Hosp. Ctr., Cheverly, Md., 1987-90; fellow George Washington U. Med. Ctr., D.C., 1990-92; asst. prof. Sch. Medicine U. Medicine and Dentistry N.J., Newark, 1992-97; asst. prof. Health and Sci. Ctr. U. Tex., San Antonio, 1997—. Adv. bd. Guardianship Svcs., San Antonio, 1997—. Contbr. articles to profl. jours., chpts. to books. Fellow Am. Acad. Family Physicians, Assn. Am. Med. Colls.; mem. AMA, Am. Geriatrics Soc., Nat. Med. Assn., Gerontol. Soc. Am., Soc. Tchrs. Family Medicine, Knights Peter Claver. Avocations: reading, sports, judo, music. Home: 20915 El Suelo Bueno San Antonio TX 78258-2923 Office: U Tex Health Sci Ctr 7703 Floyd Curl Dr San Antonio TX 78284-6200 E-mail: mouton@uthscsa.edu.

MOUTTET, JANE ELIZABETH, librarian; b. Grand Rapids, Mich., Mar. 23, 1961; d. Roger Willis and Celia Driesens; m. David Frederick Mouttet, June 4, 1988; 3 children. BA, Calvin Coll., 1983. Cert. elem. tchr. ACSI. Tchr., libr. Hilltop Christian Sch., Window Rock, Ariz., 1983—. Contbr. column. Mem.: Taa Dine Libr. Assn., N.Mex. Libr. Assn., ALA. Office: Hilltop Christian School 02A Deerfield Gallup NM 87301

MOVSAS, BENJAMIN, radiation oncologist, researcher; b. Apr. 14, 1963; m. Tammy Movsas; children: Shoshana, Avielle, Shira, Aviva. BA, Harvard U., 1986; MD, Washington U., St. Louis, 1990. Diplomate Am. Bd. Radiology. Intern Sinai Hosp., Balt., 1990-91; resident physician Nat. Cancer Inst., Bethesda, Md., 1992-95; vice chmn. radiation oncology Fox Chase Cancer Ctr., Phila., 1995—. Prin. investigator Radiation Therapy Oncology Group, 1997—. Contbr. articles to med. jours. Mem. Phi Beta Kappa, Alpha Omega Alpha. Office: Fox Chase Cancer Ctr Dept RadOnc 7701 Burholme Ave Ste 2 Philadelphia PA 19111-2497 E-mail: b_movsas@fccc.edu.

MOW, ROBERT HENRY, JR. lawyer; b. Cape Girardeau, Mo., Dec. 10, 1938; s. Robert H. Sr. and Ann Elise (Beck) M.; m. Jody K. Boggs, Aug. 29, 1987; children: Robert M., Brynn A., W. Brett, Rebecca M., W. Kirk, Allison M. Student, Westminster Coll., 1956-57; AB with distinction, U. Mo., 1960; LLB magna cum laude, So. Meth. U., 1963. Bar: Tex. 1963, U.S. Dist. Ct. (no. dist.) Tex. 1965, U.S. Dist. Ct. (so. dist.) Tex. 1969, U.S. Dist. Ct. (ea. and we. dists.) Tex. 1976, U.S. Ct. Claims 1973, U.S. Ct. Appeals (5th cir.) 1972, U.S. Ct. Appeals (11th cir.) 1981, U.S. Ct. Appeals (fed. cir.) 1994, U.S. Supreme Ct. 1978. Assoc. Carrington, Johnson & Stephens, Dallas, 1963-69; ptnr. Carrington, Coleman, Sloman & Blumenthal, 1970-85, Hughes & Luce, LLP, Dallas, 1985—. Editor-in-chief Southwestern Law Jour., 1962-63. Trustee First Bapt. Acad., chair, 1999-2002. Served to 1st lt. U.S. Army, 1963-65. Fellow Am. Coll. Trial Lawyers; mem. Dallas Assn. Def. Counsel (chmn. 1976-77), Tex. Assn. Def. Counsel (v.p. 1981-82), Am. Bd. Trial Advocates (pres. Dallas chpt. 1983-84). Republican. Baptist. Office: Hughes & Luce LLP 1717 Main St Ste 2800 Dallas TX 75201-4685 E-mail: mowb@hughesluce.com.

MOW, VAN C. engineering educator, researcher; b. Chengdu, China, Jan. 10, 1939; B. Aero. Engring., Rensselaer Poly. Inst., 1962, PhD, 1966. Mem. tech. staff Bell Telephone Labs., Whippany, N.J., 1968-69; assoc. prof. mechanics Rensselaer Poly. Inst., Troy, N.Y., 1969-76, prof. mechanics and biomed. engring., 1976-82, John A. Clark and Edward T. Crossan prof. engring., 1982-86; prof. mechanical engring. and orthopedic bioengring. Columbia U., N.Y.C., 1986—; dir. Orthopedic Research Lab., Columbia-Presbyn. Med. Ctr., 1986—, Stanley Dicker prof. of biomed. engring., 1998—. Vis. mem. Courant Inst. Math. Sci., NYU, 1967-68; vis. prof. Harvard U., Boston, 1976-77; chmn. orthopaedics and musculoskeletal study sect. NIH, Bethesda, Md., 1982-84; hon. prof. Chengdu U. Sci. Tech., 1981, Shanghai Jiao Tong U., 1987; mem. grants rev. bd. Orthopaedic Rsch. Edn. Found., 1992-96; bd. dirs. Hoar Rsch. Found., 1993—; chmn. adv. com. divsn. Med. Engring. Rsch. Nat. Health Rsch. Inst., Taiwan, 1999—; cons. in field. Assoc. editor Jour. Biomechanics, 1981—, Jour. Biomech. Engring., 1979-86; chmn. editorial adv. bd. Jour. Orthopedic Rsch., 1983-90; adv. editor Clin. Orthopedic Rel. Rsch., 1993—; contbr. numerous articles to profl. jours. Founder Gordon Research Conf. on Bioengring. and Orthopedic Sci., 1980. NATO sr. fellow, 1978; recipient William H. Wiley Disting. Faculty award Rensselaer Poly. Inst., 1981; Japan Soc. for Promotion Sci. Fellow, 1986, Fogarty Sr. Internat. fellow, 1987; Alza disting. lectr. Biomed. Engring. Soc., 1987; H.R. Lissner award ASME, 1987, Kappa Delta award AAOS, 1980, Giovani Borelli award, 1991. Fellow ASME (chmn. biomechanics divsn. 1984-85, Melville medal 1982), Am. Inst. Med. Biol. Engring.; mem. NAE, Orthopaedic Rsch. Soc. (pres. 1982-83), Am. Soc. Biomechanics (founding), Internat. Soc. Biorheology, U.S. Nat. Com. on Biomechanics (sec.-treas. 1985-90, chmn. 1991-94), Inst. of Medicine, Nat. Acad. Sci. Office: Dept Biomed Engring Columbia U 351 Engring Terr MC 8904 1210 Amsterdam Ave New York NY 10027 E-mail: vcm1@columbia.edu.

MOWATT, E. ANN, women's voluntary leader, lawyer; BA in History, Dalhousie U., Halifax, Nova Scotia, 1982, LLB, 1985. Barrister, solicitor Patterson Palmer, 1986—2001; small claims adjudicator Patterson Palmer Hunt Murphy, 1999-2001; dir. gen. survivors and high performance Income Security br. Human Resources Devel. Can., 2001—. Bd. dirs. YMCA-YWCA of Saint John N.B., Can., 1987-93; also mem. exec., fin., social action, and camp coms., pres., 1991; bd. dirs. YWCA of Can., 1989-98, chair constn. task force, mem.-at-large, treas., v.p., pres., 1995-97, past pres., 1997-98; bd. dirs. Coalition of Nat. Vol. Orgns., 1994-2001, chair; pres. Saint John chpt. Multiple Sclerosis Soc. Con., 1987-88, bd. dirs. Atlantic divsn., 1988-97, mem. nat. bd. dirs., 1992-95, 97-2001, pres. Atlantic divsn., 1993-95. Mem. Can. Bar Assn. (mem. N.B. coun. 1986-89), Law Soc. N.B. (mem. legal aid com. 1989-92), Eclectic Reading Club Avocations: reading, films, camping, canoeing, theatre. Home: 114 Orange St Saint John NB Canada E2L 1M4 also: Apt 1416 160 Chapel St Ottawa ON Canada K1N 8P5 Office: PO Box 1324 Saint John NB Canada E2L 4H8 E-mail: ann.mowatt@hrdc-drhc.gc.ca.

MOWBRAY, CAROL BEATRICE THIESSEN, social worker, educator, mental health services professional, researcher; b. Boston, Aug. 20, 1948; d. Peter Isaac and Jessamine Beatrice (Olpin) Thiessen; m. Charles Sherman Mowbray, June 1, 1970; children: Orion, Nicholas. BS, Tufts U., 1970, MS, 1971; PhD, U. Mich., 1975. Lectr. dept. psychology Mich. State U., East Lansing, 1974-75; social rsch. analyst Mich. Dept. Mental Health, Lansing, 1975-76, dir. spl. analytical studies, 1976-77, exec. asst. to dir., 1977-78, dir., program and grants coord., 1978-80, dir. rsch., evaluation and demonstration, 1980-90; assoc. prof. social work Wayne State U., Detroit, 1990-94; assoc. prof. U. Mich., Ann Arbor, 1994-2000, prof., 2000—, faculty assoc. Poverty Risk and Mental Health Rsch. Ctr., 1995—2002, assoc. dean rsch., 1996—2001, dir. Poverty Risk and Mental Health Rsch. Ctr., 2002—. Cons. grant rev. substance abuse mental health svcs. adminstrn. Ctr. for Mental Health Svcs. and NIMH, Rockville, Md., 1981—. Author: Women and Mental Health, 1984; co-editor: Consumers as Providers in Psychiatric Rehabilitation, 1997, Supported Education: Models & Methods, 2002; mem editl. bd.: Evaluation and Program Planning, mem editl. bd.: Rsch. in Social Work Practice, mem editl. bd.: Am. Jour. Evaluation, mem editl. bd.: Psychiat. Rehab. Jour., cons. editor: Social Work Rsch.; contbr. articles. Rsch. grantee dual diagnosis NIMH, 1989-95, supported edn. grantee Ctr. for Mental Health Svcs., Substance Abuse-Mental Health Svcs. Adminstrn., 1992-97, mentally ill mothers grantee NIMH, 1994-2001, cmty. action grantee Ctr. for Mental Health Svcs./Substance Abuse Mental Health Svcs. Adminstrn., 1997-2001, Fund for the Improvement of Post-Secondary Edn., U.S. Dept. Edn., 2000—, Assessing consumer-operated svcs. grantee NIMH, 2000—. Fellow: APA (sect. chmn. 1990—92, Divsn. 18 Disting. Svc. award 1988); mem.: CSWE, NASW, Soc. Social Work Rsch. (Outstanding Rsch. Article award 2000, 2002), Midwest Psychol. Assn., Am. Evaluation Assn., Internat. Assn. Psychosocial Rehab. Svcs. (rsch. com. 1994—, chair rsch. com. 1998—2001, Armin Loeb award 1998). Avocations: needlework, gardening, piano, jazz/blues music. Home: 5460 Prairie Vw Brighton MI 48116-7715 Office: U Mich Sch Social Work 1080 S University Ann Arbor MI 48109-1106 E-mail: cmowbray@umich.edu.

MOWBRAY, ROBERT NORMAN, natural resource management consultant, ecologist; b. Warren, Pa., Feb. 26, 1935; s. Leonard Kelly and Jean Elizabeth (Lowes) M.; m. Sonia de los Angeles Baquerizo, June 7, 1969; children: Norma Mercedes, Elizabeth Laning. BA, Dartmouth Coll., 1957; M of Forestry, Yale U., 1963; postgrad., Duke U., 1966-70. Rsch. asst. forest ecology Duke U., Panama, 1967, Ecuador, 1968-70, U. Tenn., Knoxville, 1970-71; rsch. asst. ecology Oak Ridge (Tenn.) Nat. Labs., 1971-72; reclamation crew chief Tenn. Mountain Mgmt., Knoxville, 1972; assoc. dir. Peace Corps, Asunción, Paraguay, 1972-78; agrl. devel. officer U.S. Agy. for Internat. Devel., San Jose, Costa Rica, 1978-80, U.S. AID, Kingston, Jamaica, 1980-83, Washington, 1983-88, 90-91, forestry devel. officer Quito, Ecuador, 1988-90, sr. forest ecologist, natural resource mgmt. specialist Washington, 1991-94; internat. natural resource mgmt. cons., Reston, Va., 1994—. Forestry vol. Peace Corps, Ecuador, 1963-66, editor tech. newsletter, 1964-66; botany vol. The Nature Conservancy, 1997-98. Author: (with others) Natural Resource Management and Conservation of Biodiversity and Tropical Forests in Ecuador-A Strategy for USAID, 1989; editor (spl. issues) NicAvance, 1995-96; contbr. articles to profl. jours. Vol. Reston Assn. Environ. Adv. Com., chmn. Recycling Subcom., mem. Watershed Subcom., 2000—. Recipient U.S. Forest Svc. Chief's Internat. Forestry award, 1994. Mem. World Wildlife Fund, Nature Conservancy, Assn. for Tropical Biology, Internat. Soc. Tropical Foresters, Friends of the Nat. Zoo, Nat. Coun. Returned Peace Corps Vols., Soc. Conservation Biology. Avocations: gardening, photography. Home and Office: 2218 Wheelwright Ct Reston VA 20191-2313 E-mail: rnmowbray@worldnet.att.net.

MOWE, GREGORY ROBERT, lawyer; b. Aberdeen, Wash., Feb. 23, 1946; s. Robert Eden and Jeannette Effie (Deyoung) M.; m. Rebecca Louise Nobles, June 14, 1969; children: Emily, Tom. BA, U. Oreg., 1968, MA, 1969; JD magna cum laude, Harvard Law Sch., 1974. Bar: Oreg. 1974, U.S. Dist. Ct. Oreg. 1974, U.S. Ct. Appeals (9th cir.) 1974. Assoc. atty. Stoel Rives Boley Jones & Grey, Portland, Oreg., 1974-79; ptnr. Stoel Rivis Boley Jones & Grey, 1979—. Pres. bd. dirs. Planned Parenthood of Columbia/Willamette, Portland, 1989-90. 1st lt. U.S. Army, 1969-71, Vietnam. Mem. ABA, Phi Beta Kappa. Office: Stoel Rives Boley Jones & Grey 900 SW 5th Ave Ste 2300 Portland OR 97204-1229

MOWELL, GEORGE MITCHELL, lawyer; b. Balt., July 31, 1951; s. George Robert and Polly (Sattler) M.; m. Patricia Edith Forbes, Sept. 23, 1978; children: Rachel Elizabeth, George Robert. BA, Washington Coll., Chestertown, Md., 1973; JD, U. Balt., 1977. Bar: Md. 1978, U.S. Dist. Ct. Md. 1981, U.S. Bankruptcy Ct. 1982. Claims authorizer Social Security Adminstrn., Balt., 1973-79; law clk. to presiding justice Kent County Cir. Ct., Chestertown, 1979-81; ptnr. Boyer & Mowell, 1981-87, Mowell, Nunn & Wadkorsky, Chestertown, 1987-98, Wadkovsky & Mowell, Chestertown, 1998—. Atty. Kent County Planning Commn., Chestertown, 1982—, Betterton Planning Commn., 1987—, Town of Rock Hall, 1987—; panel atty Public Defenders Office, 1981—, Md. Vol. Lawyers, 1981—; mem. adv. bd. Farmers Bank of Md., 1994-99. Bd. dirs. Kent County Heart Assn., Chestertown, 1983-84; atty. Galena Planning Commn., 1997—. Mem. ABA, Md. Bar Assn. (com. on laws 1984-87), Kent County Bar Assn. (sec. 1985-86, treas. 1987-88, v.p. 1988-89, pres. 1990-93), Balt. Bar Assn., Md. Trial Lawyers Assn., Elks. Democrat. Episcopalian. Home: 140 Deer Field Dr Chestertown MD 21620-2482 Office: Wadkovsky & Mowell 107 Court St Chestertown MD 21620-1507 Fax: 410-778-9325.

MOWEN, JOHN C. business educator; b. Charlottesville, Va., Nov. 13, 1943; s. John Calvin and Hope Hopkins Mowen; m. Maryanne Myers, June 12, 1971; children: Katherine, Cara. BA, William & Mary U., 1969; PhD, Ariz. State U., 1977. Prof. in bus. Okla. State U., Stillwater, 1978—. Cons. in field; bd. dirs. Consumer Credit Counseling Svc., Oklahoma City. Pres. Payne County United Way, Stillwater, 1996; co-chair House Campaign for Dem. Legislator, Stillwater, 1976; founder, bd. dirs. Mission of Hope Shelter for Homeless, Stillwater, 1987-98. Capt. U.S. Army, 1969-73, Vietnam. Decorated Bronze Star; recipient Best Article award Jour. Personal Selling, 1992. Mem. APA, Am. Mktg. Assn. (Best Article award 1998), Soc. for Consumer Psychology, Assn. for Consumer Rsch., Stillwater C. of C. (bd. dirs. 1997—), CCCS Ctrl. Okla. (bd. dirs. 1998-99). Avocations: golf, water gardening. Office: Okla State U Coll Bus Stillwater OK 74078-0001 E-mail: jcmmkt@okstate.okway.edu.

MOWER, MORTON MAIMON, cardiologist; b. Balt., Jan. 31, 1933; MD, U. Md. Sch. Medicine, 1959. Diplomate Am. Bd. Internal Medicine. Intern U. Md. Hosp., Balt., 1959-60; resident Sinai Hosp., 1960-63, fellow in cardiology, 1965-66. Fellow Am. Coll. Cardiology, Am. Coll. Chest Physicians, Am. Coll. Physicians; mem. Am. Fedn. Clin. Rsch., Am. Soc. Internal Medicine. Home: 3908 N Charles St Apt 1001 Baltimore MD 21218-1753*

MOWERY, GERALD EUGENE, publisher, writer; b. Buena, Wash., Mar. 7, 1927; s. Jennings Bryan and Opal Mae Mowery; children: Colleen, Theresa, Rhonda, Laura, Victoria, Charles, Peggy. Degree in bus., Kinmen's U. Lic. pub. acct., Wash. Supr. Boeing Airplane Co., Seattle, 1968-78; owner Jerry's Coin, Book and Frame Shops, Puyallup, Wash., 1978-85, Rudolph Maurer Pub., Puyallup, Wash., Tampa, Fla., 1985—. Author and pub. more than 152 books including All Matter Originates from Electrons, Positrons and Neutrinos, 1981, E=GM Squared, 1994, The Revised Periodic Table of Elements, The Four Unacknowledged Elements, 1999; co-author with Gene Buck: The Entrepreneurs Favorite Short Stories, Favorite Poems, Favorite Facts and Stuff; author, publ. Adjusted Periodic Table of Elements, 1982, 93, 97, 98, 2001; author children's books The Adventures of Alexander Smiriotes series including Alexander Smiriotes Rides his Alligator Through Tampa, Alexander Visits Athens, Greece. Achievements include defining the atomic mass make up of sub atomic particles and their relationship to carbon 12; prepared (atomic mass) sub atomic particle table from the equation atomic mass squared x 938.27231 equals measured MeV Values. Avocations: philosophical thinking, bridge, stamp collecting, writing stories and poems. Address: 203 South G St #217 Tacoma WA 98405 E-mail: GEMowery@msn.com.

MOWERY, J. RONALD, geologist, physicist, educator; b. Princeton, N.J., Nov. 2, 1939; s. J. Harry and Dorothy E. (Miller) M.; m. Nancy J. Bricker, Aug. 10, 1963 (div. Jan. 10, 1990); children: Stephen A., Karen L.; m. Judy A. Bauer, Dec. 27, 1992. BS, Shippensburg State U., 1964; MS, U. S.D., 1969. Tchr., dept. chmn. Pen Argyl (Pa.) Area H.S., 1964-68; prof. geology and physics Harrisburg (Pa.) Area C.C., 1969—; cons. Personal Profl. Svc., Harrisburg, 1980—. Cons. Dunn Geosci., Harrisburg, 1977, R.E. Wright & Assocs., Harrisburg, 1980-82. Author: Physical Science Laboratory Manual, 1973; editor: Geology & Hydrology of Delaware River Basin, 1982, (field guidebook) Susquehanna River Valley, 1983; developer/producer phys. sci. video course for coll. freshman, 1996. Cubmaster Boy Scouts Am., 1973-76; commr. Susquehanna Twp. Bd. Commn., 1984-89. With USN, 1958-63. NSF rsch. grantee, 1973, 92; recipient NISOD award 1996. Mem. AAAS, Harrisburg Area Geol. Soc. (pres. 1970), Nat. Assn. Geology Tchrs. Republican. Avocation: mineral and fossil collecting. Home: 273 W Main St Hummelstown PA 17036-1425 Office: Harrisburg Area CC 1 Hacc Dr Harrisburg PA 17110-2903 E-mail: rmowery@epix.net.

MOWERY, WARD FRANKLIN, retired music educator; s. Walter James and Mary Elizabeth Mowery; m. Anita Mae Hitchcock, June 12, 1960; children: Dale Richard, Angela Denise Mowery-Bemus. Bachelor Sci., Ohio State U., Columbus, Ohia, 1958—62; Master Sci., Master Art, U. Ill., Champagn, Illinois, 1962—68. Cert. nationally registered music educator, 1991, Teachers Certificate Ohio, ASCI teachers certificate Assn. Christian Schools Internat. Tchr. River View local schools, Warsaw, 1962—63, Lima Shawnee local schools, Lima, 1963—65; instr. Wilkes Coll., Wilkes-Barre, Pa., 1968—69; tchr. Lincolnview local sch., Van Wert, Ohio, 1969—74; music ministry Mowerys, Lima, 1974—85; assoc. prof. Bluffton Coll., Bluffton, 1976—90; tchr. Lima city schools, Lima, 1989—99; adj. prof. Bluffton Coll., Bluffton, 1990—99; tchr. Christian Acad. Louisville, Louisville, 1999—2002. Pricipal bassist Lima Symphony Orch., Lima, Ohio, 1977—99; ch. musician Lydon Christian Ch., Louisville, 1999—, SE Christian Ch., Louisville, 1997—. Composer musical compositions. Mu2 USN, 1955—58, Hawaii. Mem.: MENC (adjudicator 1978—95). R-Conservative. Protestant. Achievements include Mowery's music ministry performed over 1600 concerts 1974-1985; Numerous Former Students Now Major Teachers. Avocations: music performance, church music, physical conditioning. Home: 7215 Quail Ridge Road Louisville KY 40291-1878 Personal E-mail: wamowery@aol.com.

MOWLANA, HAMID, international relations and communication educator; b. Tabriz, Iran, Feb. 25, 1937; came to U.S., 1958; s. Karim Seyyed Agha Mowlana and Robab Ibrahimi; m. Bonnie J. Byrnes. BA equivalent, U. Tehran and Northwestern U., 1959; MS, Northwestern U., 1960, PhD, 1963. Asst. prof. U. Tenn., Knoxville, 1965-68; assoc. prof. Am. U., Washington, 1968-71, prof., 1971—, dir. internat. comm. studies, 1968—. Vis. prof. various univs., 1968-2000. Author: Global Information and World Communication, 1986, 96, The Passing of Modernity, 1992, Global Communication in Transition, 1997, others. Mem. Internat. Assn. Media and Comm. Rsch. (pres. 1994-98). Avocations: walking, photography, gardening, tennis. Office: Am U Sch Internat Svc Washington DC 20016 E-mail: mowlana@american.edu.

MOWRER, ROBERT RANCK, educator; b. Bryn Mawr, Pa., Sept. 8, 1956; s. Albert O. and Bettie M. M.; m. Gail Lynn Puckett, Apr. 12, 1985; children; Chelsea, Shawna. BA, Susquehanna U., 1978; MA, U. N.Mex., 1982, PhD, 1984. Asst. prof. psychology Ft. Hays (Kans.) State U., 1984-88; assoc. prof. psychology Angelo State U., San Angelo, Tex., 1988—. Emer. coord. San Angelo Amateur Radio Club, 1998-2001. Mem. APS, AAAS, Animal Behavior Soc. Avocations: amateur radio, southwestern history, skywarn. Home: 2307 Carlton Way San Angelo TX 76901 Office: Angelo State U 2601 W Ave N San Angelo TX 76909 Fax: 915-942-2290. E-mail: robert.mowrer@angelo.edu.

MOWREY, TIMOTHY JAMES, information technology executive, financial planner; b. Lewiston, N.Y., Oct. 18, 1958; s. William Ronald and Joan (Cupp) M.; children: Christin R., Andrea M., Ryan T. B of Profl. Studies in Mgmt., Empire State Coll., Buffalo, 1982. Registered investment advisor; cert. accredited asset mgmt. specialist. Rsch. technician Carborundum Co., Niagara Falls, N.Y., 1978-79; programmer KVS Info. Sys., Kenmore, 1979-80; sys. analyst Moore Bus. Forms Inc., Niagara Falls, 1980-83; coord. telecom. project Marine Midland Bank, N.A., Buffalo, 1983-85; pres., owner Micro-Tec, Niagara Falls, 1982-86; telecom. specialist Electronic Data Sys., Lockport, N.Y., 1985-86; from mng. cons. to practice dir. mgmt. cons. Computer Task Group Inc., Buffalo, 1986-93; owner Mowrey Investment Mgmt., 1992—; pres. The Odysseus Group, 1993—; sr. dir. bus. devel. Infoseek Corp., 1997-98; v.p. bus. devel. News Real Inc., 1998-99. Scholarship N.Y. State Bd. of Regents, 1976. Roman Catholic. Avocations: hiking, reading, running, martial arts, tennis. Office: Mowrey Investment Mgmt 3333 Clandon Park Dr Raleigh NC 27613-8841

MOWRY, ELIZABETH, artist; b. N.Y., Mar. 8, 1940; d. Joseph Hudela and Veronica Byczek; children: Jennifer, Albert, Andrew. BA, Alliance Coll., 1961; postgrad., Carnegie Inst., 1972-74; MA, SUNY, New Paltz, 1983. Instr. Woodstock (N.Y.) Sch. Art, 1986—. One-person shows include Albany Inst. History Art-Rice Gallery, 1986; exhibited in group shows Nat. Arts Club, N.Y.C., 1989-02, Pastel Soc. West Coast, Sacramento, 1988, 91, 94, 97, 99, 2000-02, Degas Pastel Soc., New Orleans, 1990, 91, (Excellence award, Landscape award), Knickerbocker Artists USA, Washington, 1993 (Gold medal, Most Innovative Use of Color), Pastel Soc. Am. (7 awards), Pastel Soc. West Coast (7 awards), Allied Artists of Am. (2 awards), Hermitage Mus., Norfolk, Va., Xi'an Acad. Fine Art, China, Knickerbocker USA (Gold medal for pastel), Pastel en France (Prix d'Art du Pastel en France award, award Conseil Gen. de la Seine Maritime 2002); author: Paint the Changing Seasons in Pastel, 1994, The Pastelists' Year, 2001, The Poetic Landscape, 2001; contbg. author: Pastel Interpretations; work included in Best of Flower Painting I, 1993, II, 1996. Mem. Nat. Assn. Women Artists, Pastel Soc. Am., Pastel Soc. West Coast, Pastel Painters Soc. Cape Cod. Avocations: gardening, travel, hiking.

MOWRY, FRANK HENRY, journalist, photojournalist; b. Oak Ridge, Tenn., Sept. 11, 1952; s. Ralph Lenord Mowry and Estella Elise Dietz. Student, U. Kans., 1972-77. Journalist, pub. affairs specialist USN Comdr. 6th Fleet, Gaeta, Italy, 1985-89, USN, Yokosuka, Japan, 1990-92, Naval Support Facility, Diego Garcia, Brit. Indian Ocean Terr., 1990-98; journalist, copy editor Pacific Stars & Stripes, Tokyo, 1992-94; journalist, photojournalist, broadcaster radio & TV Am. Forces Network, Sigonella, Italy, 1994-97; journalist, photojournalist, webmaster USN Comdr. in Chief Pacific Fleet, Pearl Harbor, Hawaii, 1999—. Contbr. pub. affairs Y2K, 1999. Instr., ARC, Yokosuka, 1992-94. Journalist 1st class, USN, Hawaii, 1996-2002. Petty officer 1st class USN, 1996. Mem. VFW (life), Nat. Press Photographers Assn., Soc. Profl. Journalists, Nat. Profl. Photoshop Assn. Democrat. Buddhist. Avocation: experiencing world cultures. Fax: (808) 422-0771. E-mail: fhmowry@hotmail.com., mowryfh@worldnet.att.net.

MOWRY, ROBERT WILBUR, pathologist, educator; b. Griffin, Ga., Jan. 10, 1923; s. Roy Burnell and Mary Frances (Swilling) M.; m. Margaret Neilson Black, June 11, 1949; children: Janet Lee, Robert Gordon, Barbara Ann. BS, Birmingham So. Coll., 1944; MD, Johns Hopkins U., 1946. Rotating intern U. Ala. Med. Coll., 1946-47, resident pathology, 1947-48; sr. asst. surgeon USPHS-NIH, Bethesda, Md., 1948-52; fellow pathology Boston City Hosp., 1949-50; asst. prof. pathology Washington U., St. Louis, 1952-53, U. Ala. Med. Ctr., Birmingham, 1953-54, assoc. prof. pathology, 1954-57; prof. U. Ala. Med. Center, 1958-89, prof. emeritus, 1989—, prof. health svcs. adminstrn., 1976-84, dir. Anat. Pathology Lab., 1960-64, dir. grad. programs in pathology, 1964-72. Sr. scientist U. Ala. Inst. Dental Research, 1967-72, dir. autopsy services, 1975-79; vis. scholar dept. pathology U. Cambridge, Eng., 1972-73; cons. FDA, 1975-81 Author: (with J.F.A. McManus) Staining Methods: Histologic and Histochemical, 1960; mem. editorial bd. Jour. Histochemistry and Cytochemistry, 1960-75, Stain Tech., 1965-90, AMA Archives of Pathology, 1967-76, Biotechnics and Histochemistry, 1991—. Served with USPHS, 1948-52. Mem. Am. Soc. Investigative Pathology, Internat. Acad. Pathology, Biol. Stain Commn. (v.p. 1974-76, pres. 1976-81, trustee 1966—), Soc. for Glycobiology, Am. Assn. Univ. Profs. Pathology, Phi Beta Kappa, Sigma Xi, Delta Sigma Phi, Alpha Kappa Kappa. Presbyterian. Achievements include perfection of staining methods for complex carbohydrates (Alcian blue and colloidal iron) and insulin (Alcian blue-aldehyde fuchsin); showed the utility of these in diagnostic histopathology. Home: 4165 Sharpsburg Dr Birmingham AL 35213-3234

MOXLEY, JOHN HOWARD, III, internist; b. Elizabeth, N.J., Jan. 10, 1935; s. John Howard Jr. and Cleopatra (Mundy) Moxley; m. Doris Banchik; children: John Howard IV, Brook, Mark. BA, Williams Coll., 1957; MD, U. Colo., 1961; DSc (hon.) , Sch. Medicine Hannemann U. Diplomate Am. Bd. Internal Medicine. Intern Peter Bent Brigham Hosp., Boston, 1961—62, resident in internal medicine, 1962—66; with Nat. Cancer Inst., USPHS, 1963—65; asst. to dean, instr. medicine Harvard Med. Sch., Boston, 1966—69; dean Sch. Medicine, U. Md., 1969—73; vice chancellor health scis., dean Med. Sch., U. Calif.-San Diego, 1973—79; asst. sec. for health affairs Dept. Def., Washington, 1979—81; sr. v.p. Am. Med. Internat., Beverly Hills, Calif., 1981—87; pres. MetaMed. Inc., Playa Del Rey, 1987—89; mgr. dir. Korn/Ferry Internat., L.A., 1989—. Cons. FDA, NIH; dir. Nat. Fund for Med. Edn., 1986—, chmn., 1993—; dir. Henry M. Jackson Found. for Adv. Mil. Medicine. Contbr. articles to profl. jours. Dir. Polyclinic Health Svcs. Games of XXIII Olympiad. Recipient Gold and Silver award, U. Colo. Med. Sch., 1974, commr.'s citation for outstanding svc. to over-the-counter drug study, FDA, 1977, spl. achievement citation, Am. Hosp. Assn., 1983, Sec. of Def. medal for disting. pub. svc., 1981. Fellow: ACP, Am. Coll. Physician Execs. (disting.); mem.: AMA (chmn. coun. sci. affairs 1985), Am. Hosp. Assn. (trustee 1979—81), Soc. Med. Adminstrs., Calif. Med. Assn. (chmn. sci. bd. 1978—83, councilor), Inst. Medicine NAS, San Diego C. of C., Rotary, Alpha Omega Alpha. Office: Korn Ferry Internat 1800 Century Park E Ste 900 Los Angeles CA 90067-1512 E-mail: moxleyj@kornferry.com.

MOXON, BARBARA WISCHAN, volunteer; b. Phila., May 2, 1921; d. Ernst and Helen Legget (Boggs) W.; m. Robert Kerwin Moxon, Mar. 4, 1944; children: Peter, Christopher, Laurel Suggs. BA, U. Pa., 1942; MS in Edn., 1943; LLD (hon.) , Newberry Coll., 1990. Family case worker Main Line Fedn. Chs., Ardmore, Pa., 1943-47. Past pres., chair fin. devel., pub. affairs, edn., vol. counselors, spkrs. bur. Planned Parenthood, S.C.; state v.p. Common Cause, state action alert coord.; state chair ERA S.C., editor newsletter; pres., v.p. bd. Killingsworth Home; precinct chair Dem. Party; pres. PTA; bd. dirs. S.C. Christian Action Coun., dir. citizenship, pub. affairs; mem. state bd., sec., membership chair, fundraising com. S.C. Coalition Choice; mem. choir St. Paul's Luth. Ch., Columbia, S.C.; mem. various coms., past pres. Luth. Ch. women; chair, sec., chair Women's History Week project S.C. Commn. on Women; organizer, state chair, legis. chair S.C. Advocates for Women on Bds. and Commns. Recipient Legis. award Nat. Assn. Social Workers, 1988, Advocacy awrd S.C. Assn. Health, Phys. Edn., Recreation and Dance, 1988, Outstanding Contbns. to Health Edn. award, 1988, Pres.'s award S.C. Primary Prevention Coun., 1989, award S.C. Christian Action Coun., 1990, Dedicated Svc. and Commitment to Family Planning award Planned Parenthood S.C., 1991, Pub. Citizen of Yr. award Nat. Assn. Social Workers, 1992, Pub. Svc. award Common Cause, 1996, Retird Disting. Svc. award for svc. to edn. by a non-member S.C. Edn. Assn., 1999, S.C. Order of the Palmetto, Gov. James Hodges, 1999. Mem. AAUW (pres. Annapolis, Md. br., Portsmouth, Va. br., Greater Columbia, S.C. br., pub. policy chair local and state, v.p. local and state program, chair women's issues, budget, Ednl. Found. honoree 1984, 88, B. Moxon Ednl. Endowment named after her), LWV (state and local pres., chair mem., fin. devel. state and local, sec., chair orgn., 50th ann. com., Making Democracy Work comm., Barbara W. Moxon award named in her honor, one of 25 women featured in exhibit Women in Action: Rebels and Reformers 1995-96), Phi Beta Kappa. Democrat. Lutheran. Avocations: needlework, music, swimming. Home: 31 Joseph Walker Dr West Columbia SC 29169-6961

MOY, AUDREY, retired retail buyer; b. Bronx, N.Y., May 6, 1942; d. Ferdinand Walter Melkert and Stella (Factorow) Schroff; m. Edward Moy, Aug. 16, 1974. BA in Biology, Hunter Coll., 1964, MA in Biology, 1966. Asst. buyer Bonwit Teller, N.Y.C., 1961-68; dept. mgr. Franklin Simon, 1968; asst. buyer Saks Fifth Ave, 1968-73; buyer Martins, Bklyn., 1973, Belk Store Svcs, N.Y.C., 1974-97. Avocations: cooking, antique collecting, gardening.

MOY, GWENDOLYN C.I. home health nurse, educator; b. Honolulu, Aug. 29, 1946; d. Git Lum and Florence (Look) M. BSN, Calif. State U., Chico, 1969. RN, Calif.; cert. BCLS instr. Clin. instr., pharmacology, anatomy and physiology instr. Berkeley Sch. Nursing Arts, Santa Monica, Calif.; emergency room and relief staff coord. Kaiser Permanente, West L.A.; clin. nurse I, II, head nurse oncology unit, grad. preceptor UCLA; clin. instr. St. Joseph Med. Ctr., Burbank, Calif.; staff nurse, computer user rep. St. John's Hosp. and Health Ctr., Santa Monica, 1984-87; adminstrv. supr. oncology dept. Torrance (Calif.) Meml. Hosp. Med. Ctr.; field nurse Visiting Nurse Assn. of L.A., Inc., Santa Monica, 1988-91; dir. staff devel. Hallmark Nursing Ctr., Playa Del Rey, Calif., 1992-93; edn.-orientation coord. Angeles Home Health Care, Inc., L.A., 1993-95; educator, field nurse, relief team leader UCLA Home Health, 1996—2002, acting dir., 2000-01, edn. compliance coord., 2001—02. Office: UCLA Home Health West Med Bldg Ste 2212 1010 Veteran Ave Los Angeles CA 90095

MOY, RONALD LEONARD, dermatologist, surgeon; b. Stuttgart, Germany, June 10, 1957; s. Howard Leonard Stephen and Jenny (Yee) M.; m. Lisa Wing Lan Lin, Aug. 10, 1986; children: Lauren, Erin. Grad., Rensselaer Poly. Inst., 1977, Albany Med. Coll., 1981. Dir. Mohs micrographic surgery div.

dermatology UCLA, 1988-93, dir. dermatologic surgery div. dermatology, 1988-93, co-chief div. dermatology, 1992-93; chief dermatologic surgery VA-West Los Angeles Med. Ctr., 1988—. Gov. apptd. Med. Bd. Calif., 2000-. Author: Atlas of Cutaneous Flaps and Grafts, 1990, Facial Rejuvenation, 1999; editor: Principle and Practice of Dermatologic Surgery, 1993, Facial Rejuenation, 2000; editor-in-chief: Dermatologic Surgery, 1997—; contbr. articles to profl. jours. Bd. dirs. L.A. Costal unit Am. Cancer Soc., 1988. Recipient J. Lewis Pipkin award in dermatology Nat. Student Rsch. Forum, 1981, Henry Christian award Am. Fedn. Clin. Rsch., T-cell and Cytokine Patterns in Skin Cancer award NIH, 1992. Fellow: Am. Acad. Dermatology (Gold award 1986); mem.: L.A. County Med. Assn. (pres. Bay dist. 1997—98), Assn. Acad. Dermatologic Surgeons (bd. dirs. 1992—95), Am. Coll. Mohs Micrographic Surgery and Cutaneous Oncology (bd. dirs. 1992—95), Am. Soc. Dermatologic Surgery (bd. dirs. 1993—96, v.p. 2001—02, pres. elect 2002—). Roman Catholic. Office: 100 UCLA Med Plz Ste 590 Los Angeles CA 90024-6992

MOYA, PATRICK ROBERT, lawyer; b. Belen, N.Mex., Nov. 7, 1944; s. Adelicio E. and Eva (Sanchez) Moya; m. Sara Dreier, May 30, 1966; children: Jeremy Brill, Joshua Dreier. AB, Princeton U., 1966; JD, Stanford U., 1969. Bar: Calif. 1970, Ariz. 1970, D.C. 1970, U.S. Dist. Ct. (no. dist.) Calif. 1970, U.S. Ct. Claims 1970, U.S. Tax Ct. 1970, U.S. Ct. Appeals (D.C. cir.) 1970, U.S. Supreme Ct. 1973. Assoc. Lewis and Roca, Phoenix, 1969—73, ptnr., 1973—83; sr. ptnr. Moya, Bailey, Bowers & Jones, P.C., 1983—84; ptnr., mem. nat. exec. com. Gaston & Snow, 1985—91; ptnr. Quarles & Brady LLP, 1991—; mem. nat. exec. com. Quarles & Brady, LLP, 2000—02. Instr. sch. of law Ariz. State U., 1972; bd. dirs. homebid.com, inc., 1999-2000; BIGE Real Estate, Inc., 2000-. Mem. Paradise Valley Bd. Adjustment, 1976-80, chmn., 1978-80; mem. Paradise Valley Town Coun., 1980-82; bd. dirs. Phoenix Men's Arts Coun., 1973-81, pres., 1979-80; bd. dirs. The Silent Witness, Inc., 1979-84, pres., 1981-83; bd. dirs. Enterprise Network, Inc., 1989-94, pres., 1991-92; bd. dirs. Phoenix Little Theatre, 1973-75, Interfaith Counseling Svc., 1973-75; precinct committeeman Phoenix Rep. Com., 1975-77; dep. voter registrar Maricopa County, 1975-76; mem. exec. bd. dirs. Gov.'s Strategic Partnership for Econ. Devel.; pres. GSPED, Inc.; mem. of Steering Com. for Sonora-Ariz. Joint Econ. Plan; mem. Gov.'s Adv. Com., Ariz. and Mex., Ariz. Corp. Commn. Stock Exch. Adv. Coun., Ariz. Town Hall. Mem. ABA, Nat. Hispanic Bar Assn., Los Abogados Hispanic Lawyers Assn., Nat. Assn. Bond Lawyers, Ariz. Bar Assn., Maricopa County Bar Assn., Paradise Valley Country Club, Univ. Club. Office: Quarles & Brady LLP One Renaissance Sq Two North Central Ave Phoenix AZ 85004-2391

MOYA, ROSEMARY MERCEDES, mental health administrator; b. Santa Fe, Aug. 11, 1957; d. Willie and Mercedes Sadie Ramona (Rivera) Padilla; m. Raymond Anthony Moya, Aug. 9, 1980; children: Joslyn Monique, Alyssa Nichole. BS in Edn., U. N.Mex., 1979, MPA, 1990. Adminstrv. asst. Hubbard Broadcasting, Albuquerque, 1980; staff asst. N.Mex. Mcpl. League, Santa Fe, 1980-81, Div. Mental Health/Dept. of Health, Santa Fe, 1981-82, pers. adminstr., 1982-84, planner, 1981-88, health program mgr., 1988-91, chief community programs bur., 1991—97, chief enhancement bur., 1997—. Parent vol. St. Francis Cath. Sch., 1990-2000; vol. Am. Cancer Soc., 1993, Easter Seals, Santa Fe, 1991; sec. liturgy com. Santa Maria de la Paz Cath. Com., 1991-94, chair liturgy com., 1994-97, mem. bldg. com., 1991-94, mem. art selection com., 1992-94, mem. fin. coun., 2000-; chmn. acad. com. St. Michael's H.S., mem. parent coun. exec. com., 2001-, mem. alumni assn., 2000-. N.Mex. Mcpl. League scholar, 1987-90; named Woman of Yr., Girls Club, Santa Fe, 1987. Mem. NAFE, Nat. Orgn. for Victim Assistance, Pi Alpha Alpha, Phi Kappa Phi. Democrat. Roman Catholic. Avocations: volleyball, skiing, tennis, camping, reading. Office: Dept Health/Behavioral Health Scis. Divsn 1190 S Saint Francis Dr Santa Fe NM 87505-4182

MOYA, SARA DREIER, educator; b. N.Y.C., June 9, 1945; d. Stuart Samuel and Hortense (Brill) Dreier; m. P. Robert Moya, May 30, 1966; children: J. Brill, Joshua D. BA, Wheaton Coll., Norton, Mass., 1967; postgrad., Mills Coll., Oakland, Calif., 1967-68; MPA, Ariz. State U., 1995, PhD, 2002. Mem. Paradise Valley (Ariz.) Town Coun., 1986-98, vice mayor, 1990-92; instr. advanced pub. exec. programs Ariz. State U. Adj. prof. Sch. Planning and Landscapte Architecture, Ariz. State U.; chmn. Gov.'s Homeless Trust Fund Oversight Com., 1991—; pres. Ctr. for Acad. Precosity, Ariz. State U., Tempe, 1987-95; bd. dirs. Ariz. Assn. Gifted and Talented; participant 3d session Leadership Am., 1990; mem. steering com. Maricopa County Homeless Continuum of Care, 1999—, mem. planning subcom., 2000—; mem. planning com. N.E. Valley Family Advocacy Ctr., 2001—; adj. prof. planning and landscape arch. Ariz. State U. Mem. Citizens Adv. Bd. Paradise Valley Police Dept., 1984-86, Valley Citizens League Task Force on Edn.; bd. dirs. Valley Leadership Inc., 1988-94; chair Maricopa Assn. Govts. Task Force on Homeless, 1989-92, 95-98; mem. Emergency Food and Shelter Program, FEMA bd. Maricopa County and Ariz., 1989—, chmn., 1996—; dir. Valley Youth Theater, 1990-93, Maricopa County Homeless Accomodation Sch., 1991—. Mem. ASPA (bd. dirs. 1996-98, pres. 1999-2000), Ariz. Women in Mcpl. Govt. (sec. 1988-89, bd. dirs. 1986—, pres. 1989-90), Western Social Sci. Assn., Ariz. State U. Students of Pub. Affairs Network (sec./treas. 1996-98), Data Network for Human Svcs. (bd. dirs. 1990-93), Maricopa Assn. Govts. (regional coun. 1988-98, vice-chmn. mag. regional devel. policy com. 1989-91, chair 1992-98, mag. joint econ. devel./human resources subcom. 1990-94, mag. youth policy adv. com. 1994-98, blue ribbon com. 1995-97, vision 2025 com. 1997-2000, chair urban features subcom. 1998-2000, valley vision 2025 steering com. 1999-2000), Maricopa Assn. Govts. (air quality policy com. 1994-96), Ariz. Acad., Ariz. Planning Assn. (bd. dirs., citizen planner, 1996-98), Paradise Valley Country Club, Phi Kappa Phi, Pi Alpha Alpha. Republican. Avocations: traveling, golfing, reading. Home: 5119 E Desert Park Ln Paradise Valley AZ 85253

MOYÉ, DEAN, lighting design professional; b. Phila., Jan. 7, 1969; Tech. dir. Stratford Playhouse, Houston, 1984-90, Country Playhouse Theatre, Houston, 1986-91, Aloha Showroom, 1991; asst. lighting designer Theatre Under The Stars, 1989-92; lighting dir., asst. prodn. mgr. Neil Diamond World Tour, 1991-93; lighting dir. Tom Collins Tour of World Figure Skating Champions, 1992—. Lighting designer Lido de Paris Tour of South America, 1995, Lido de Paris, 1994; asst. lighting designer Ann Margret Tour, Phantom Tour, 1991; lighting dir. George Lucas Superlive Adventure Japan Tour; resident lighting designer Cleve. Ballet, San Jose Ballet; asst. lighting designer Blue Suede Shoes Nat. Tour. Asst. lighting designer (mus. theatre) Mame (nat. tour), 1990, The Unsinkable Molly Brown, 1989, Ain't Misbehavin', 1989-90; lighting designer/prodn. mgr. Kalapana (Calif. tour), 1988; lighting designer (musical) Merrily We Roll Along, 1985, Barnum, 1986, Company, 1988 (Best Lighting Design award), Little Shop of Horrors, 1987-88 (Best Lighting Design award), Side By Side by Sondheim, 1988, A...My Name Is Alice, 1988, Peter Pan, 1989, Annie, 1989, Into The Woods, 1991. Recipient Orchid award Country Playhouse, 1987-90, Ruby award Country Playhouse, 1987-90, Dean Moyé Honor award Stratford Playhouse, 1987, Gov. of Hawaii Clothing Design award, 1991, Best Lighting Design award for stage mus. Best Little Whorehouse in Tex. Avocations: photography, film, computers, video. Office: Empire State Bldg 350 5th Ave Ste 3304 New York NY 10118-3399

MOYE, JOHN EDWARD, lawyer; b. Deadwood, S.D., Aug. 15, 1944; s. Francis Joseph and Margaret C. (Roberts) M.; children: Kelly M., Mary S., Megan J. BBA, U. Notre Dame, 1965; JD with distinction, Cornell U., 1968; LLD, U. Denver, 1999. Bar: N.Y. 1968, Colo. 1971. Prof. law U. Denver, 1972-78, assoc. dean Coll. Law, 1974-78; prof. law So. Meth. U., Dallas, 1973; ptnr. Moye, Giles, O'Keefe, Vermeire & Gorrell, Denver, 1976—. Lectr. Harcourt Brace Jovanovich, Chgo., 1972-95, Profl. Edn. Group, Minnetonka, Minn., 1982-95, West Profl. Tng. Program, 1995-98; chmn. Bd. Law Examiners, Denver, 1988-92. Chmn. Denver Urban Renewal Authority, 1988-93, Colo. Hist. Found., Denver, 1987—; pres. Downtown Denver, Inc., 1986-88; mem. Consumer Credit Commn., 1985-99; chmn. Stapleton Devel. Corp., 1995—; bd. dirs. Denver Bot. Gardens, 1996—, Colo. Pub. Radio, 1998-99. Named Prof. of Yr., U. Denver, 1972-74, 76-78, Outstanding Faculty Mem., 1997. Fellow Am. Bar Found.; mem. ABA, Colo. Bar Assn. (chmn. corp., banking and bus. sect. 1982-84, Young Lawyer of Yr. award 1980, pres. 2002), N.Y. State Bar Assn., Denver Bar Assn. (Young Lawyer of Yr. award 1980), Law Club (pres. 1982-84). Republican. Roman Catholic. Office: 1225 17th St Denver CO 80202-5534

MOYER, ALAN DEAN, retired newspaper editor; b. Galva, Iowa, Sept. 4, 1928; s. Clifford Lee and Harriet (Jacques) M.; m. Patricia Helen Krecker, July 15, 1950; children: Virginia, Stanley, Glenn. BS in Journalism, U. Iowa, 1950. Reporter, copy editor Wis. State Jour., Madison, 1950-53; reporter, photographer Bartlesville (Okla.) Examiner-Enterprise, 1953; telegraph editor Abilene (Tex.) Reporter-News, 1954-55; makeup editor Cleve. Plain Dealer, 1955-63; mng. editor Wichita (Kans.) Eagle, 1963-70; exec. editor Wichita Eagle and Beacon, 1970-73; mng. editor Phoenix Gazette, 1973-82, Ariz. Republic, 1982-89; ret., 1989. Pres., dir. Wichita Profl. Baseball, Inc., 1969-75; mem. jury Pulitzer Prizes, 1973-74, 85, 86, 88. Mem. AP Mng. Editors Assn. (dir. 1973-78), Am. Soc. Newspaper Editors, Wichita Area C. of C. (dir. 1970-72), Sigma Delta Chi. Office: Phoenix Newspaper Inc 200 E Van Buren St Phoenix AZ 85004-2238 E-mail: patmoyusa@netscape.net.

MOYER, BERNADETTE ANN, writer, publisher, business owner; b. Hazelton, Pa., Oct. 7, 1959; d. Bernard M. and Inez S. (Totani) O'Connell; m. Randall H. Moyer, Dec. 2, 1978 (dec. Feb. 1983); 1 child, Ariane M.; m. Brian T. Sahm, Aug. 1, 1998; children: (twins) Briana, Brandon. Student, Bryn Mawr U., 1977-79; BS in Bus., Towson U., 1988. Lic. real estate broker, Md. Realtor O'Conor, Piper & Flynn, Lutherville, Md., 1986-96; pub. Two Bee..., Hunt Valley, 1997—, retail store owner, 1997—; events mgr. The Children's Guide, Balt., 2000—. Author: Two Bee..., 1997, Angel Stacey, 1998, Caesar Salad, 1999, But...We Are Twins, 1998, Bare Breasted Heart, 1999; contbg. author: Surviving Ophelia, 2001. Active Bush Campaign Rep. Orgn., Towson, Md., 2000; pub. spkr. Young Widowed, Balt., 1999; rm. mother Hampton Elem. Sch., Lutherville, Md., 2000-01; vol. Boyu Scouts Am., Hunt Valley, Md., 1998—. Mem. Nat. Pubs. Network, Md. Pubs. Assn., Toastmasters, Internat. Poets (hon.). Republican. Roman Catholic. Avocations: travel, reading, cooking, writing, speaking. Home: 1210 Malbay Dr Lutherville MD 21093

MOYER, CHERYL LYNN, non-profit administrator; b. St. Petersburg, Fla., Apr. 4, 1953; d. Joseph Paul Safko and Doris Marie (Wolf) Sniegocki; m. John Arthur Weber (div. 1982); m. Ross Allen Moyer, June 21, 1983; children: Deborah, Martin, Brian, Spencer. BS, Lock Haven U., 1986; MPA, Pa. State U., 1987. Lic. realtor, N.J. Office mgr. Piper Aircraft Corp., Lock Haven, Pa., 1974-76; radio rep. Sta. WTGC Radio, Lewisburg, 1976-77; sales rep. Sears, Lycoming Mall, 1977-83; ptnr., dir. The Trading Post, Williamsport, 1983-85; mgr., founder Lock Haven U. Day Care, 1985-86; field mgr. Pa. Pub. Interest Coalition, State Coll., Pa., 1987-88; exec. dir. Pa. Assn. Families, Harrisburg, 1988-91; unit dir.-residential Resources for Human Devel., Phila., 1989-93; mgr. ob-gyn. clinic Meth. Hosp., 1993-94, bus. analyst, 1994; owner Family Fin. Svcs., 1994-95; chair bd. dirs., fin. dir. Matchmaker Internat. Midlantic; owner/ptnr. Remax Connection, 2000—. Nat. reg. lobbyist. Recipient Million Dollar Sales Club Gold award, 1999, 2000; grantee Family Planning Svcs., 1994. Mem. Nat. Assn. Dual Diagnosis, Pa. State Alumni Assn., Interfaith Assn., Mensa. Home: 50 Wentwood Ct Medford NJ 08055-9327 E-mail: ReMaxxclm@aol.com.

MOYER, CHRISTINA BETH, elementary education educator, reading specialist; b. Titusville, Pa., Sept. 24, 1947; d. Clayton Eugene Moyer and Elizabeth Ruth (Morse) Vogt. BS in Edn., Clarion State Coll., 1969; MS in Edn., Duquesne U., 1973, postgrad., 1991-93. Cert. elem. educator, reading specialist, reading supr., Pa. Tchr. Seneca Valley Sch. Dist., Harmony, Pa., 1969-75, reading specialist, 1975—. Vol. ARC, 1985; active Baby Boomers Workshop, 1992; instr. adult ch. sch., 1994-98. Mem. NEA, Pa. Edn. Assn., Internat. Reading Assn., Nat. Coun. Tchrs. English, Nat. Woodcarvers Assn., Chisels and Chips Carvers, Keystone State Reading Assn., Seneca Valley Edn. Assn. (del. 1987-93, chmn. instrn. and profl. devel. 1985-88, co-chmn. negotiations 1987-89, chmn. negotiations 1989-92, mem. instrnl. support team 1992—, site based mgmt. team 1999-2000, summer sch. curriculum com. 2000instrn. and profl. devel. com. 2000—), Butler County Reading Coun. Democrat. Home: 226 N Clay St Zelienople PA 16063-1125 Office: Connoquenessing Valley Elem Sch Pittsburgh and Beaver Sts Zelienople PA 16063 E-mail: moyerc@seneca.k12.miu4.pa.us.

MOYER, CRAIG ALAN, lawyer; b. Bethlehem, Pa., Oct. 17, 1955; s. Charles Alvin and Doris Mae (Schantz) M.; m. Candace Darrow Brigham, May 3, 1986; 1 stepchild, Jason; 1 child, Chelsea A. BA, U. So. Calif., 1977; JD, U. Calif., L.A., 1980. Bar: Calif. 1980, U.S. Dist. Ct. (cen. dist.) Calif. 1980. Assoc. Nossaman, Krueger et al, L.A., 1980-83, Finley, Kumble et al, Beverly Hills, Calif., 1983-85; ptnr. Demetriou, Del Guercio, Springer & Moyer, L.A., 1985—, Manatt, Phelps, & Phillips, LLP, L.A. Instr. Air Resources Bd. Symposium, Sacramento, 1985—, U. Calif., Santa Barbara, 1989—; lectr. Hazmat Conf., Long Beach, Calif., 1986—, Pacific Automotive Show, Reno, Nev., 1989—; lectr. hazardous materials, environ. law UCLA; lectr. environ. law U. Calif., Santa Barbara; lectr. hazardous materials regulatory framework U. Calif., Santa Barbara. Co-author: Hazard Communication Handbook: A Right to Know Compliance Guide, 1990, Clean Air Act Handbook, 1991, Brownfields: A Practical Guide to the Cleanup, Transfer and Redevelopment of Contaminated Property, 1997; contbr. articles to profl. jours. Pres. Calif. Pub. Interest Rsch. Group, L.A., 1978-80. Mem. ABA (natural resources sect.), Calif. Bar Assn., L.A. County Bar Assn. (environ. law sect., chmn. legis. rev. com., mem. exec. com.), Tau Kappa Epsilon (pres. L.A. chpt. 1975-76, Outstanding Alumnus 1983). Republican. Avocation: bicycling. Fax: 310-312-4224. E-mail: cmoyer@manatt.com.

MOYER, DAVID S. executive search consultant; b. Balt., May 21, 1952; BA in History, SUNY, Purchase, 1975. Spl. asst. for pub. affairs Grumman Corp., Bethpage, N.Y., 1975-76; instr. R.T.Y., Inc., N.Y.C. and Miami, Fla., 1976-77; exec. v.p. Wesley-Brown, Ltd., N.Y.C. and L.A., 1977-83; v.p. Paul Stafford Assocs. Ltd., N.Y.C., 1983-90, Fenwick Ptnrs., Inc., N.Y.C., 1990-91, Moyer, Sherwood Assocs., Inc., Stamford, Conn., 1991-97, N.Y.C., 1997—. Contbr. articles to profl. publs. Bd. dirs. The Helicon Found., N.Y.C., 1999—. Mem. Stamford (Conn.) Yacht Club (chmn. membership com. 1993-97). Office: 1285 Ave Americas 35th Fl New York NY 10019

MOYER, F. STANTON, financial executive, advisor; b. Phila., June 7, 1929; s. Edward T. and Beatrice (Stanton) M.; m. Ann P. Stovell, May 16, 1953; 1 child, Alice E. BS in Econs., U. Pa., 1951. Registered rep. Smith, Barney & Co., Phila., 1951-54, Kidder, Peabody & Co., Phila., 1954-60; mgr. corp. dept. Blyth Eastman Dillon & Co., Inc. (formerly Eastman Dillon, Union Securities & Co.), 1960-65, instl. sales mgr., 1965-67, gen. partner, 1967-71, 1st v.p., 1971-74, sr. v.p., 1974-80; v.p., resident officer Kidder, Peabody & Co. Inc., Phila., 1980-86; chmn. Pa. Mcht. Group Ltd., Radnor, 1987-88; exec. v.p. Rorer Asset Mgmt., Phila., 1990-92; chmn. Mercer Capital Mgmt., 1992-93, Global Mgmt. Group, Inc., 1993-95; mng. dir. Avonwood Capital Corp., 1995-97; chmn. Main Line Capital Ptnrs. Inc., 1997—. Trustee U. Pa., 1978-83, Hosp. of U. Pa., 1978-87; bd. dirs. Atwater Kent Mus., Phila., 1983—. Mem. Racquet Club (Phila.), St. Anthony Club (Phila.), Merion Cricket Club (Haverford, Pa.), Gulph Mills Golf Club (King of Prussia, Pa.), Gulf Stream Golf Club (Fla.), Gulf Stream Bath and Tennis Club, The Little Club (Gulf Stream), Delta Psi. Republican. Episcopalian. Home: 445 Caversham Rd Bryn Mawr PA 19010-2901 also: 3 Little Club Rd Gulf Stream FL 33483 E-mail: growthguy@aol.com.

MOYER, H. WAYNE, political science educator; b. Phila., Aug. 18, 1939; s. H. Wayne and Ruth Stevens Moyer; m. Helen Johnson, June 29, 1963. BA with honors, U. Va., 1961; MA in Internat. Rels., Yale U., 1969, MPhil in Polit. Sci., 1972, PhD in Polit. Sci., 1976. Instr. polit. sci. Grinnell (Iowa) Coll., 1972-76, asst. prof., 1976-79, assoc. prof., 1979-86, prof. polit. sci., 1986—, Rosenfield prof., 1985—. Author: Agricultural Policy Reform: Politics and Process in the USA and EC, 1990. Lt. USN, 1961-67. Mem. Am. Polit. Sci. Assn., Internat. Studies Assn., Iowa Conf. Polit. Sci. (pres.), European Cmty. Studies Assn. Democrat. Avocations: sailing, gardening. Home: 890 Juniper Ave Kellogg IA 50135 Office: Grinnell Coll 1131 Park St Grinnell IA 50112 E-mail: moyer@grinnell.edu.

MOYER, HOMER EDWARD, JR. lawyer; b. Atlanta, Nov. 20, 1942; s. Homer Edward and Mildred Joye (Wilkerson) M.; m. Beret Butter, July 6, 1974; children: Bronwen, Homer, Eli, Kaia Joye. BA, Emory U., 1964; LLB, Yale Law Sch., 1967. Bar: Ga. 1967, D.C. 1973. Assoc. Covington & Burling, Washington, 1973-76; from dep. gen. counsel to gen. counsel U.S. Dept. of Commerce, 1976-81; ptnr. Miller & Chevalier, 1981—. Co-author: Export Controls as Instruments of Foreign Policy, 1988, Justice and the Military, 1972. Bd. visitors Emory U., Atlanta, 1987-91. Mem. ABA (chmn. internat. law and practice sect. 1990-91, chmn. trade com. 1984-86, chmn. Cen. and East European Law Initiative 1990—, chmn. Moscow conf. on law and bilateral econ. rels. 1990). Episcopalian. Office: Miller & Chevalier 655 15th St NW Ste 900 Washington DC 20005-5799

MOYER, JERRY MILLS, financial services company executive; b. Oklahoma City, Mar. 19, 1940; s. Charles and Dorothy M.; m. Cecilia L. Clark, Aug. 28, 1960; children: Jerry, James. BS, Okla. State U., 1962. Salesman Jamco, Inc., 1965; salesman P&G, Cin., 1966; from salesman to credit mgr. B.F. Goodrich Co., N.Y.C., 1967-71; staff UCC Comm. Systems, Inc., Dallas, 1971-73; mgr. funds control Dr. Pepper Co., 1973-80; pres. Cash Cons. Inc., 1985—. V.p. Interfirst Svcs. Corp., Houston, 1981-85; v.p. fin. Med. Acceptance Corp., Houston, 1986; internat. treas. Yemen Hunt Oil Co., 1987-90; owner, pres. ASI Embroidery, Dallas, 1997-98; pres., CEO 88 Petroleum Co., Inc., Oklahoma City, 2000—; gen. ptnr. Moyer O-G&I Ltd. Partnership, 2001 Contbr. articles to profl. jours. Active United Fund, Interfirst Polit. Action Com. With U.S. Army, 1962-65. Decorated Air medal, Purple Heart; various profl. awards. Mem. Tex. Cash Mgmt. Assn. (founder, past pres.), Nat. Corp. Cash Mgmt. Assn. (co-founder), Masons, Shriners. Baptist.

MOYER, JUNE FAYE, retired critical care nurse; b. Lansdale, Pa., Mar. 14, 1939; d. Marvin D. and Mildred K. M. BS in Bible, Phila. Biblical U., 1961; diploma, Presbyn. Hosp., 1964; BSN, La Salle U., 1985. Staff nurse Presbyn. Hosp. Med. Ctr., Phila., 1964-65; dept. mgr. Grandview Hosp., Sellersville, 1966—2001, ret., 2001—. Mem. AACN, Pa. Orgn. Nurse Leaders, Sigma Theta Tau. Home: 110 Lawn Ave Apt B Souderton PA 18964-1870

MOYER, LINDA LEE, artist, educator; b. Niles, Mich., Feb. 11, 1942; d. Roy Delbert and Estelle Leona (Beaty) Moyer; m. Brock David Williams Dec. 3, 1994; 1 child from previous marriage, Metin Ata Gunsay. Student, Occidental Coll., 1959-61; BA, UCLA, 1964; MA, Calif. State U., Long Beach, 1977, MFA, 1980. Cert. tchr. secondary edn., cert. computer graphics, Calif. Instr. art. Huntington Beach (Calif.) Union High Sch., 1967-81, Calif. State U., Long Beach, 1981-85, Saddleback Coll., Mission Viejo, Calif., 1986-88, Fullerton (Calif.) Coll., 1990, 94, Goldenwest Coll., Huntington Beach, 1990. Artist-in-residence St. Margaret's Episc. Sch., San Juan Capistrano, 1993; lectr., workshop presenter Santa Barbara (Calif.) C.C., 1992; series lectr. Rancho Santiago Coll., 1985, 90; lectr. Cypress Coll., 1986, Watercolor West, 1987, others; methods and materials show instr. Am. Artist Mag., 1996, 97, 98, 99, 99, 2000, 01; juror fine art exhbns; presenter workshops in field; website co-founder watercolor-online.com. One-woman shows include Laguna Beach (Calif.) Mus. Art, 1982, Orlando Gallery, Sherman Oaks, Calif., 1983, Orange County Ctr. Contemp. Art, 1982, 1985, Cerritos Coll., Norwalk, Calif., 1986, Louis Newman Galleries, Beverly Hills, 1986, 1988, 1990, Westmont Coll., Santa Barbara, 1992, Maturango Mus., Ridgecrest, Calif., 1996, exhibited in group shows at Owensboro (Ky.) Mus. Fine Arts, 1979, Burpee Art Mus., Rockford, Ill., 1981, Newport Harbor Art Mus., Newport Beach, Calif., 1981, Nat. Acad. Galleries, N.Y.C., 1982, exhibited in group shows at Leslie Levy Gallery, Scottsdale, Ariz., 1983, Art Inst. So. Calif., 1984, Saddleback Coll., Mission Viejo, Calif., 1988, Riverside (Calif.) Art Mus., 1989, Ch. of Jesus Christ of LDS Mus. Art and History, Salt Lake City, 1988, 1991, Mt. San Antonio Coll., Calif., 1996, Springville (Utah) Art Mus., 1999, 2000, others. Represented in permanent collections Springville Mus. Art, Home Savs. Bank of Am., Nat. Bank of La Jolla, Greenburg Deposit Bank, Ashland, Ky., INMA Gallery, Saudi Arabia, pvt. collectors. Recipient Gold Medal of Honor, Am. Watercolor Soc., 1982, Walser S. Greathouse medal, 1988, Gold Medal of Honor for watercolor Allied Artists Am., 1982, cash merit award Ch. of Jesus Christ Latter Day Saints Mus. Art and History, 1991, Best of Show award Utah Watercolor Soc., 2000, 2d award, Religious and Spiritual Art of Utah Exhbn., 2d award, 1998, 3d award, 1999. Signature mem. Nat. Watercolor Soc., Watercolor West (1st award 1984, N.W.S. award 1999, pres. 1999-2001), Watercolor West (life), Utah Watercolor Soc. Mem. Lds Ch. Avocations: reading, dancing, playing piano. Home and Office: 22 Lakeview Stansbury Park UT 84074 E-mail: lindamoyer@watercolor-online.com.

MOYER, R. CHARLES, finance educator, consultant; b. Reading, Pa., July 11, 1945; s. Ralph Charles and Jane Anne (Huls) M.; m. Sally Louise Prizer, May 19, 1973; children: Laura Prizer, Craig Prizer. BA in Econs., Howard U., 1967; MBA, U. Pitts., 1968, PhD in Fin., 1971. Asst. prof. fin. U. Houston, 1971-76; fin. economist U.S. Maritime Adminstrn., Washington, 1973-74; assoc. prof. Lehigh U., Bethlehem, Pa., 1976-77; from assoc. prof. to prof. U. N.Mex., Albuquerque, 1977-80; prof., chmn. fin. dept. Tex. Tech U., Lubbock, 1980-87; CMAC ins. chair in fin., Babcock Grad. Sch. Wake Forest U., Winston-Salem, NC, 1988—, dean Babcock Grad. Sch. of Mgmt., 1996—; dir. King Pharmaceutical, Inc., Bristol, Tenn., 2000—. Pres., founder R.O.E. Cons. Group, Lubbock, 1978; cons. Pub. Svc. Co. N.Mex., 1978—, KN Energy, Denver, 1979—, Gas Co. N.Mex., 1985—, San Diego Gas Electric Co., 1986—; bd. dirs. Inst. Banking Fin. Studies, 1982-86. Author: Managerial Economics, 9th edit., 2002, Contemporary Financial Management, 9th edit., 2003, Financial Management with Lotus 1-2-3, 1986; contbr. articles to profl. jours. Vice-chmn. Lubbock Gen. Hosp. Found., 1985-88. Capt. U.S. Army, 1969-71. Fed. Res. Bank Cleve. fellow, 1970-71. Mem.: We. Fin. Assn., Ea. Fin. Assn., So. Fin. Assn. (v.p. 1990—93, pres. 1993), Am. Econs. Assn., Am. Fin. Assn., Fin. Mgmt. Assn. (bd. dir. ombudsman 1985—87, v.p. 1988—, sec.-treas. 1994—), Twin City Track Club, Old Town Club, Bermuda Run Country Club, Beta Gamma Sigma, Phi Beta Kappa. Avocations: tennis, golf, swimming. Office: Wake Forest U Babcock Grad Sch PO Box 7659 Winston Salem NC 27109-7659

MOYER, THOMAS J. state supreme court chief justice; b. Sandusky, Ohio, Apr. 18, 1939; s. Clarence and Idamae (Hessler) M.; m. Mary Francis Moyer, Dec. 15, 1984; 1 child, Drew; stepchildren: Anne, Jack, Alaine, Elizabeth. BA, Ohio State U., 1961, JD, 1964. Asst. atty. gen. State of Ohio, Columbus, 1964-66; pvt. practice law, 1966-69; dep. asst. Office Gov. State of Ohio, 1969-71, exec. asst., 1975-79; assoc. Crabbe, Brown, Jones, Potts & Schmidt, 1972-75; judge U.S. Ct. Appeals (10th cir.), 1979-86; chief justice Ohio Supreme Ct., 1987—. Sec. bd. trustees Franklin U., Columbus, 1986-87; trustee Univ. Club, Columbus, 1986; mem. nat. council adv. com. Ohio State U. Coll. Law, Columbus. Recipient Award of Merit, Ohio Legal Ctr. Inst.; named Outstanding Young Man of Columbus, Columbus Jaycees, 1969. Mem. Ohio State Bar Assn. (exec. com., council dels.), Columbus Bar Assn. (pres. 1980-81), Critchon Club, Columbus Maennerchor Club. Republican. Avocations: sailing, tennis. Office: Ohio Supreme Ct 30 E Broad St Fl 3 Columbus OH 43215*

MOYERS, ERNEST EVERETT S. retired computer research scientist; b. Gadsden, Ala., Sept. 4, 1933; s. Ernest Everett S. Moyers and Lena Mae (Goode) Grigsby; m. Mary Violet Roden, Oct. 25, 1952; children: Mary N., Ernest E.S. III, Nora E., Karl H., Barton V., Troy W. BS, Midwestern U., 1954; MS, U. Miss., 1957; PhD, Rice U., 1963, Pacific West U., 1988. Mathematician various cos., 1963-76; rsch. scientist other def. contractors, Huntsville, Ala., 1976-82; missile scientist Delta Rsch., Inc., 1982—, v.p., 1989-95; nat. missile def. testbed scientist Aegis Rsch., Inc., 1997-2000. Dir. Evangel Christian Sch., Huntsville, 1977-80; assoc. prof. computer sci. Ala. A&M U., 1999-2002. Designer anti-tank missile system, 1985; contbr. articles to tech. publs. Pastor Grace Bapt. Ch., Huntsville, 1977-79, Parkview Bapt. Ch., Ardmore, Ala., 1984-89. Lawrence Livermore Nat. Lab. Summer Rsch. fellow, 2001. Mem. IEEE, Math. Assn. Am., Soc. Computer Simulation (chmn. 1983-94), Soc. for Indsl. and Applied Math., Am. Math. Soc., Toastmasters (founder High Noon club). Republican.

MOYERS, JUDITH DAVIDSON, television producer; b. Dallas, May 12, 1935; d. Henry Joseph and Eula E. (Dendy) Davidson; m. Bill D. Moyers; children: William Cope, Suzanne, John. BS, U. Tex., 1956; LittD (hon.), L.I. U., 1989, SUNY, 1990. Pres., exec. prodr. Pub. Affairs TV, N.Y.C., 1987—. Bd. dirs. Ogden Corp. Exec. prodr. T.V. documentaries (Emmy 1980, 93, 98, DuPont 1999, Christopher 1990, Parker 1992, Gold Hugo 1991, Humanitas prize 1995); contbr. articles to profl. jours., newspapers, mags. Trustee SUNY, 1976-90; commr. U.S. Commn. UNESCO, Washington, 1977-80, White House commn. Internat. Yr. of Child, Washington, 1978-80; mem. jud.

selection com. State N.Y., 1992-93; dir. Pub. Agenda Found. Mem. Acad. TV Arts and Scis., Century Club. Mem. Congregational Ch. Office: Pub Affairs TV Inc 450 W 33rd St Fl 7 New York NY 10001-2603

MOYERS, ROBERT CHARLES, systems analyst, state official, microcomputer consultant, government systems developer; b. San Angelo, Tex., Mar. 15, 1951; s. Robert Eugene and Florence (Sprinkles) M.; m. V. Jean Wiggermann, June 30, 1984. BA, U. Tex., 1975. Cons. programming Xerox Ctr. Health Care Research, Houston, 1973-74; systems analyst, mgr. software support Baylor U. Coll. Medicine, 1974-79; systems analyst Tex. Dept. Transp., Austin, 1980-87, dir. ADP systems, 1987-94; client/server cons., 1994—. Cons. microcomputer, 1988—; freelance writer, 1987—; internet programmer, 1998—; system developer RFD and Assocs., 1994—. Creator computer programs Loan Analyzer, 1987, BASIC Line Number Generator, 1987, Capital Gains Calculator, 1987, Loan Officer, 1988, PARD Office Program, 1990, Round Rock PARD System, 1992, PARDner, 1994; contbr. articles to profl. jours. Mem.: Assn. Systems Mgmt. Roman Catholic. Avocations: golf, guitar. Home: 1605 Drop Tine Dr Cedar Park TX 78613-4902 Office: RFD & Assocs 401 Camp Craft Rd Austin TX 78746-6507 E-mail: robertmoyers@hotmail.com.

MOYERS, SYLVIA DEAN, retired medical record librarian; b. Independence, W.Va., Oct. 22, 1936; d. Wilkie Russell and Ina Laura (Watkins) Collins; m. Paul Franklin Moyers, June 29, 1957; children: Tammy Jeanne, Thomas Paul, Tara Sue. Student, Am. Med. Record Assn., 1977-79. Sec. Teets Lumber Co., Terra Alta, W.Va., 1954-58, Preston County News, Terra Alta, 1958-60; med. record clk. med. record dept. Hopemont (W.Va.) Hosp., 1960-75, dir., 1975-88; sec. The Terra Alta Bank, W.Va., 1990-95; ret., 1995. Charter mem., past mother advisor Terra Alta Assembly No. 26, Order of Rainbow for Girls, past grand editor Mountain Echoes; vol. Preston Meml. Hosp., ARC, Salvation Army, Am. Cancer Soc.; mem. Kingwood Fire Dept. Aux. Mem. Kingwood Civic Club. Republican. Methodist. Home: 120 Miller Rd Kingwood WV 26537-1321

MOYES, NORMAN BARR, journalism educator, writer, photographer; b. Fairmont, W.Va., Aug. 26, 1931; s. Roland Dare and Lillian T. (Barr) M.; div. 1980; children: Christine, Mark, Elizabeth. AB in English/Spanish, West Liberty State Coll., 1963; MA in English, W.Va. U., 1956; PhD in Comm., Syracuse (N.Y.) U., 1968. Instr. West Liberty (W.Va.) State Coll., 1955-58; prof. Syracuse U., 1958-63; prof. journalism Boston U., 1963—. Author: Journalism in the Mass Media, 1970, Mass Media Journalism, 1975, Journalism, 1984, Journalism Resource Book, 1985, Battle Eye, 1995. With U.S. Army, 1953-55. Named Outstanding Alumnus West Liberty State Coll., 1992. Avocation: photography. Home: 1629 Commonwealth Ave Brighton MA 02135-4942 Office: Boston U 640 Commonwealth Ave Boston MA 02215-2422 E-mail: nmoyes@bu.edu.

MOYLAN, JAMES HAROLD, lawyer; b. Omaha, Oct. 17, 1930; s. Harold Thomas and Margaret Ellen (Emery) M.; m. Lila Marie Fitzgerald, July 9, 1960; children: James P., Michael T., Patrick W., Jean M., Mary M., Molly C. BS, Creighton U., 1952, JD, 1957. Bar: Nebr. 1957, Iowa 1957, U.S. Dist. Ct. Nebr. 1957, U.S. Dist. Ct. (so. dist.) Iowa 1957. Assoc. Richling, Shrout & Brown, Omaha, 1957-60; dep. atty. Douglas County, 1960-67; ptnr. Garvey, Nye, Crawford, Kirchner & Moylan, 1967-87, Fellman, Moylan, Omaha, 1987-99, 1999—. Chmn. Douglas County Dem. Com., 1966-68; mem. Christ and King Sch. Bd., Omaha, 1967-71, Archbishop's Com. on Ednl. Devel., Omaha, 1975—; assoc. bd. regents St. Mary's Coll., Omaha, 1968-72; bd. regents U. Nebr., 1971-89. Mem. Nebr. Bar Assn. (exec. coun. 1975-81), Iowa Bar ASsn., Nat. Lawyers Assn., Sokol Club, Regency Lake and Tennis Club, Westroads Racquet Club, Eagles, Elks, Am. Legion. Avocation: politics. Home: 2245 S 86th St Omaha NE 68124-2131 Office: Fellman Moylan Natvig Wilke & Wik 100 Continental Bldg Omaha NE 68046 E-mail: jameshmoylan@aol.com.

MOYLAN, JAMES JOSEPH, lawyer; b. Forest Hills, N.Y., Feb. 3, 1948; s. James Gerard and Jessie Cora (Geary) M.; m. Barbara Chesrow, Aug. 29, 1970; children: James C., Joseph O., Alicia G. BSBA, U. Denver, 1969, JD, 1971. Bar: Colo. 1972, D.C. 1972, Ill. 1975, U.S. Dist. Ct. Colo. 1972, U.S. Supreme Ct. 1975. Trial atty. SEC, Washington, 1972-75; assoc. gen. counsel Chgo. Bd. Options Exch., Ill., 1975-77; assoc. Abramson & Fox, Chgo., 1977-80; ptnr. Bowen, Knepper & Moylan Ltd., 1980-82, Moylan & Early, Ltd., Chgo., 1983-84; prin. James J. Moylan and Assocs., Ltd., 1984-95; ptnr. Arnstein & Lehr, 1995-2000, Tressler, Soderstrom, Maloney & Priess, Chgo., 2000—. Adj. prof. law IIT Chgo. Kent Coll. Law, 1976—; former pub. dir. MidAm. Commodity Exch. divsn. Chgo. Bd. Trade, Chgo. Contbr. articles to profl. jours. Mem.: ABA (sect. corp., banking and bus. law, sect. litigation), D.C. Bar Assn., Chgo. Bar Assn., Ill. State Bar Assn. (sect. coun. mem.), Theta Chi (grand chpt. 1993—2000, funds bd. 2000—). Republican. Roman Catholic. Fax: 312-627-1717. E-mail: jmoylan@mail.tsmp.com.

MOYLAN, STEVE, publishing executive; BA, Boston Univ.; MA, Univ. of San Francisco. Pres, CEO Infoworld, San Mateo, 2000—. Office: 28 E 28th St New York NY 10016*

MOYLE, PETER BRIGGS, fisheries and biology educator; b. May 29, 1942; s. John Briggs and Evelyn (Wood) M.; m. Marilyn Arneson, June 11, 1966; children: Petrea Ruth, John Noah. BA, U. Minn., 1964, PhD, 1969; MS, Cornell U., 1966. Asst. prof. Calif. State U., Fresno, 1969-72; from asst. prof. to prof. U. Calif., Davis, 1972—, chmn. dept. wildlife and fisheries, 1982-87. Head, Delta Native Fishes Recovery Team, 1993-95. Author: Inland Fishes of California, 1976, 2d edit., 2002, Fishes: An Introduction to Ichthyology, 4th edit., 2000, Distribution and Ecology of Stream Fishes of Sacramento San Joaquin Drainage, 1982, Fish: An Enthusiast's Guide, 1993. Fellow Calif. Acad. Sci.; mem. Am. Fisheries Soc. (life, award of excellence West divsn. 1991, Outstanding Educator award 1995), Ecol. Soc. Am., Am. Soc. Ichthyologists and Herpetologists, Soc. Conservation Biology, Natural Heritage Inst. (v.p. 1994—). Home: 612 Eisenhower St Davis CA 95616-3031 Office: Dept Wildlife Fish & Conservation Biology U Calif Davis CA 95616 E-mail: pbmoyle@ucdavis.edu.

MOYLES, PHILIP VINCENT, JR. financial services company executive; b. N.Y.C., July 14, 1964; s. Philip Vincent and Anne Kane Moyles; m. Beth O'Connor. BA in History, Kenyon Coll., 1986; postgrad., Dartmouth Coll., 2000. Mgmt. trainee Rollins Burdick Hunter Co., Chgo., 1986-87; assoc. Johnson & Higgins, N.Y.C., 1987-90; sr. acct. rep. Marsh & McLennan Inc., 1990-91, asst. v.p., 1991-93, v.p., 1993-95, sr. v.p., 1995-96; mng. dir., practice leader mergers and acquisitions Marsh Inc., 1996—. Mem. Union League Club N.Y., Allegheny Country Club (Sewickley, Pa.). Republican. Roman Catholic. Office: Marsh Inc 1166 Ave of Americas New York NY 10036

MOYNAHAN, JOHN DANIEL, JR. retired insurance executive; b. Chgo., Dec. 10, 1935; s. John Daniel and Helen (Hurley) M.; m. Virginia Thomas, Oct. 10, 1959; children: Laura, Mark, Tricia, Kate. BA cum laude, U. Notre Dame, 1957. With Met. Life Ins. Co., N.Y.C., 1957—, regional v.p., from 1971, with nat. div. group nat. accounts, 1979-80, sr. v.p. group life and health ops., 1980-86, exec. v.p., 1986-97.

MOYNAHAN, JULIAN LANE, English language educator, author; b. Cambridge, Mass., May 21, 1925; s. Joseph Leo and Mary (Shea) M.; m. Elizabeth Rose Reilly, Aug. 6, 1945; children: Catherine (dec.), Brigid, Mary Ellen. AB, Harvard U., 1946, A.M., 1951, PhD, 1957. Cataloguer, rare books asst. Boston Pub. Library, 1948-49, 51; teaching fellow Harvard U., 1951-53; instr. English Amherst Coll., 1953-55; instr., asst. prof. English Princeton, 1955-63; Fulbright lectr. Am. and English lit. Univ. Coll., Dublin, 1963-64; assoc. prof. English Rutgers U., 1964-66, prof., 1966-93, disting. prof., 1976-93, prof. emeritus, 1993—. Vis. prof. U. Wyo., summer 1965, Harvard U., summer 1967, Bread Loaf Sch., 1969, NYU, 1997; NEH vis. prof. Manhattanville Coll., 1972; Gauss lectr. Princeton U., 1975; vis. scholar English dept. U. Utah, spring 1980; lectr. N.J. Coun. for Humanities, 1998, 99. Author: Sisters and Brothers, 1960, The Deed of Life, A Critical Study of D.H. Lawrence, 1963, Pairing Off, 1969, Vladimir Nabokov, 1971, Garden State, 1973, Where the Land and Water Meet, 1979, Anglo-Irish: The Literary Imagination in a Hyphenated Culture, 1995; editor: (D.H. Lawrence) Sons and Lovers: Text, Criticism, Backgrounds, 1968, 77, The Viking Portable Thomas Hardy, 1977; contbr. revs. and criticism to N.Y. Times Book Rev., T.L.S., Washington Post Book World, N.Y. Rev. Books; contbr., mem. editl. bd. The Recorder, Jour. Am. Irish Hist. Soc., 1994—. Bicentennial preceptorship Princeton, 1960-63, grants-in-aid Am. Council Learned Socs., Am. Philos. Soc.; mem. Pulitzer Prize Fiction Jury, 1981, chmn., 1987. Served with AUS, 1943-44. 7500 creative writing award Nat. Found. Arts, 1966; Ingram-Merrill award, 1967; NEH fellow, 1975; Guggenheim fellow, 1983-84. Mem. MLA, AAUP, PEN, Harvard Club of Princeton. Democrat. Home: 136 Bayard Ln Princeton NJ 08540-3041 Address: Apt 9B London Ter 405 W 23d St New York NY 10011 also: Chatham Lodge Oldcastle Kells Ireland E-mail: moy@nji.com.

MOYNE, JOHN ABEL, computer scientist, linguist, educator; b. Yezd, Iran, July 6, 1920; came to U.S., 1956, naturalized, 1965; s. Abul Kasim and Sogra (Afshar) M.; m. Claudia Wienert, July 4, 1963; children: David, Nicholas, Parvin. BA, Georgetown U., 1959, MA, 1960; PhD, Harvard U., 1970. With Brit. Govt., Iran and India, 1943-52, market rsch. officer Tehran, 1952; linguist U.S. Govt., Cyprus, 1953-56; rsch. assoc. Georgetown U., Washington, 1960-63; mgr. applied linguistics dept. IBM Corp., Cambridge, Mass., 1963-71; prof., chmn. computer sci. dept. Queens Coll. CUNY, Flushing, 1971-81, chmn. divsn. math. and natural scis., 1978-81, chmn. univ. faculty for PhD in Computer Sci., 1978-82, exec. officer Grad. Sch. PhD Program in Linguistics, 1983-88, prof. linguistics and computer sci., 1971—91, prof. emeritus linguistics and computer sci., 1991—. Author, co-author: Hafiz of Shiraz, 1946, Life in India, 1949, Open Secret, 1984, Understanding Language: Man or Machine, 1985, Unseen Rain, 1986, Rumi: These Branching Moments, 1988, This Longing Poetry, Teaching Stories, and Letters of Rumi, 1988, LISP: A First Language for Computing, 1991, Say I Am You, 1994, The Essential Rumi, 1995, Rumi and the Sufic Tradition: Essays on the Mowlavi Order and Mysticism, 1998; contbr. articles to profl. jours., chpts. to books. Grantee EURATOM, AEC, NSF, CUNY. Mem. Linguistics Soc. Am., Am. Brit. Inst. Engring. Tech., The Acad. Am. Poets. Democrat. Home: 40 Prospect Ave Sea Cliff NY 11579-1029 Office: CUNY PhD Program Linguistics Grad Ctr 365 5th Ave New York NY 10016-4334 E-mail: jmoyne@post.harvard.edu., jmoyne@gc.cuny-edu.

MOYNIHAN, CAROLYN JEAN, clinical social worker; b. San Diego, Aug. 17, 1943; d. Donald Eugene and Katherine Elaine (Wright) Johnson; m. Jack Oldham Bradt, Aug. 17, 1974; children: Mitchell M., Ann Elise, Margaret; stepchildren: Elizabeth Hickman, Katherine McVey. BS in Sociology, Immaculate Heart Coll., 1965; MSW, CUA, 1967; postgrad., Harvard Coll., 1978, Georgetown U. Med. Ctr. Child psychiatry-family social worker, 1966-69; faculty dept. psychiatry Georgetown U. Med. Ctr., 1967-79; family therapist Overbrook Children's Ctr., 1968-70; co-founder, clin. dir. tng. dept. The Groome Ctr. for Families, 1969-78; founding faculty dept. psychiatry postgrad. program in family sys. psychotherapy Georgetown U., 1969-74; pvt. practice Washington, 1978-88. Mem. faculty Georgetown U. Med. Ctr., Washington; lectr. dept. sociology Georgetown U. Coll. Arts and Sci., Washington; dir., family therapist The Family Place, Verona, Wis., 1987—; family psychotherapist The Healing Collective, Madison, 1990—; lectr. U. Wis. Sch. Social Work. Co-editor, pub. (with J. Bradt, MD) Systems Therapy, 1971, The Nuclear Family-Life in a Vacuum, 1976, Specialized Techniques Used in Family Therapy Practice, 1978, Dual Career Marriage, 1982; author: (with others) Resources for Remarriage, 1985. Mem. NASW, AAUW, Am. Family Therapy Acad., Commn. on Women, Wis. Assn. Outpatient Mental Health, Women Bus. Owners of Wis., Call to Action. Roman Catholic. Office: The Family Place 8283 N Riley Rd Verona WI 53593-9081

MOYNIHAN, DANIEL PATRICK, former senator, educator; b. Tulsa, Mar. 16, 1927; s. John Henry and Margaret Ann (Phipps) M.; m. Elizabeth Therese Brennan, May 29, 1955; children: Timothy Patrick, Maura Russell, John McCloskey. Student, CCNY, 1943; BA cum laude, Tufts U., 1948; MA, Fletcher Sch. Law and Diplomacy, 1949, PhD, 1961, LLD (hon.), 1968; Fulbright fellow, London (Eng.) Sch. Econs. and Polit. Sci., 1950-51; LLD (hon.), Cath. U. Am., 1968, New Sch. Social Rsch., 1968, U. Notre Dame, 1969, Fordham U., 1970, St. Bonaventure U., 1972, Boston Coll., 1976, Yeshiva U., 1978, Rensselaer Polytech. Inst., 1983, Syracuse U. Sch. Law, 1984, Columbia U., 1987, U. Rochester, 1994; LLD (hon.) , Yale U., 2000, Harvard U., 2002; D in Pub. Adminstrn. (hon.), Hamilton Coll., 1968; DSI (hon.), Defense Intelligence Coll., 1984; numerous other hon. degrees. With Internat. Rescue Com., 1954; successively asst. to sec., asst. sec., acting sec. to gov. State of N.Y., 1955-58, dir. Syracuse U. govt. rsch. project, 1959-61, spl. asst. to sec. labor, 1961-62, exec. asst. to sec., 1962-63, asst. sec. labor, 1963-65; dir. Joint Ctr. for Urban Studies MIT and Harvard U., 1966-69; prof. edn. and urban politics Kennedy Sch. Govt., Harvard U., 1966-73, sr. mem., 1966-77, prof. govt., 1973-77; asst. for urban affairs to Pres. U.S., 1969-70; counsellor to Pres. U.S., mem. Cabinet, 1969-70, cons. to Pres. U.S., 1971-73; mem. U.S. del. 26th Gen. Assembly, UN, 1971, Pres.'s Sci. Adv. Com., 1971-73; ambassador to India New Delhi, 1973-75; U.S. permanent rep. to UN, N.Y.C., 1975-76; U.S. senator from N.Y., 1977-2001; chmn. senate fin. com., 1993-94; ranking mem., senate fin. com., 1995-2001; prof. Syracuse U. Maxwell Sch. Citizenship/Pub. Affairs, 2001—. Chmn. commn. on Reducing and Protecting Govt. Secrecy, 1994-97,vice chmn. Pres.'s Temp. Commn. on Pennsylvania Avenue, 1964-73; chmn. adv. com. traffic safety dept. HEW; fellow Ctr. Advanced Studies, Wesleyan U., 1965-66; hon. fellow London Sch. Econs. and Polit. Sci., 1970—; sec. pub. affairs com. N.Y. State Dem. Com., 1958-60; alt. del. Dem. Nat. Conv., 1960, 76; sr. pub. policy scholar Woodrow Wilson Policy Ctr., 2001. Author: Maximum Feasible Misunderstanding, 1969, The Politics of a Guaranteed Income, 1973, Coping: On the Practice of Government, 1974, A Dangerous Place, 1978, Counting Our Blessings, 1980, Loyalties, 1984, Family and Nation, 1986, Came the Revolution: Argument in the Reagan Era, 1988, On the Law of Nations, 1990, Pandaemonium: Ethnicity in International Politics, 1993, Miles To Go: A Personal History Of Social Policy, 1996, Secrecy: The American Experience, 1998; co-author: Beyond the Melting Pot, 1963; editor: The Defenses of Freedom, 1966, On Understanding Poverty, 1969, Ethnicity: Theory and Experience, 1975, others; editorial bd. Pub. Interest; contbr. articles to profl. jours. Vice chmn. Woodrow Wilson Internat. Ctr. for Scholars, 1971-76; chmn. bd. trustees Joseph H. Hirshhorn Mus. and Sculpture Garden, 1971-85; mem. bd. regents Smithsonian Instn., 1987—. With USN, 1944-47. Recipient Meritorious Svc. award U.S. Dept. Labor, 1965, Centennial medal Syracuse U., 1969, Internat. League for Human Rights award, 1975, John LaFarge award for Interracial Justice, 1980, Medallion SUNY Albany, 1984, Henry medal Smithsonian Instn., 1985, SEAL Medallion, CIA, 1986, Meml. Sloan-Kettering Cancer Ctr. medal, 1986, Britannica award, 1986, Notre Dame U. Laetare medal, 1992, Thomas Jefferson award AIA, 1993. Mem. AAAS (vice chmn. 1971, dir. 1972-73), Am. Philos. Soc. (Hubert Humphrey award 1983, Thomas Jefferson medal 1993), Nat. Acad. Pub. Adminstrn., Am. Acad. Arts and Scis. (chmn. seminar on poverty), Century Club, Harvard Club. Home: 801 Pennsylvania Ave NW LBBY 1 Washington DC 20004

MOYNIHAN, GARY PETER, industrial engineering educator; b. Little Falls, N.Y., Mar. 5, 1956; s. Peter H. and Frances S. (Ferjanec) M.; m. Eleanor T. McCusker, Mar. 10, 1984; children: Andrew Ross, Keith Patrick. BS in Chemistry, Rensselaer Polytech. Inst., 1978, MBA in Opsl. Mgmt., 1980; PhD in Indsl. Engring., U. Ctrl. Fla., 1990. Prodn. supr. Am. Cyanamid, Bound Brook, N.J., 1978-79, Nat. Micronetics, Kingston, N.Y., 1980-81; assoc. mfg. engr. Martin Marietta Aerospace, Orlando, Fla., 1981-82, indsl. engr., 1982-85, sr. indsl. engr., 1985-87, group indsl. engr., 1987-90; asst. prof. indsl. engring. U. Ala., Tuscaloosa, 1990-96, assoc. prof., 1996—2001, prof., 2001—. Cons. in field. Contbr. articles to profl. jours. Regents scholar N.Y. State Bd. Regents, 1974-78; rsch. fellow NASA, 1992-93, 98-99; rsch. grant BellSouth Telecomm., 1994-96; recipient Outstanding Tchg. award AMOCO Found., 1993-94, Ralph R. Teetor Engring. Educator award Soc. Automotive Engrs, 2000. Mem. IEEE, Inst. Indsl. Engrs. (sr. mem., chpt. dir. 1991-95, chpt. pres. 1996-97), Aerospace & Def. Soc. (v.p. fin. and adminstrn. 1994-97). Achievements include design and development of information systems applications for the aerospace and foundry industries; 2 software copyrights in field of measurement and prediction of on-line information system failure costs. Office: U Ala Dept Indsl Engring Tuscaloosa AL 35487-0001

MOYNIHAN, JOHN BIGNELL, retired lawyer; b. N.Y.C., July 25, 1933; s. Jerome J. and Stephanie (Bignell) M.; m. Odilia Marie Jacques, Nov. 13, 1965; children: Blair, Dana. BS, Fordham U., 1955; JD, St. John's U., N.Y.C., 1958. Bar: Tex. 1961, U.S. Supreme Ct. 1965, U.S. Dist. Ct. (we. dist.) Tex. 1968, U.S. Ct. Appeals (5th cir.) 1973. Sole practice, Brownsville, Tex., 1961-62; asst. city atty. City of San Antonio, 1962-63; sole practice San Antonio, 1963-65; estate tax atty. IRS, 1965-73; dist. counsel EEOC, 1974-79; asst. U.S. atty. Office U.S. Atty., 1980-87, sr. litigation counsel, 1987-94; sole practice, 1995-98; ret., 1998. Chmn. reform and renewal com., San Antonio Roman Cath. Archdiocese, 1968. Served with U.S. Army, 1958-60; lt. col. USAFR (ret.), 1986. Mem. San Antonio Bar Assn. (chmn. state and nat. legis. com. 1972-73, Meritorious Svc. award 1968), Fed. Bar Assn. (bd. dirs. San Antonio chpt. 1983—, pres. elect 1986, pres. 1987), KC (pres. 1967). Home: 11011 Whispering Wind St San Antonio TX 78230-3746 E-mail: djmoynihan@aol.com.

MOYNIHAN, WILLIAM J. museum executive; b. Little Falls, N.Y., Apr. 8, 1942; s. Bernard J. and Mary A. (Flynn) M.; m. Irene A. Sheilds, July 2, 1966; children: Patricia, Erin, Sean. BA, SUNY, Binghamton, 1964; MA, Colgate U., 1966; PhD, Syracuse U., 1973. From asst. to assoc. prof. Colgate U., Hamilton, NY, 1973—77, from asst. to assoc. dean faculty, 1977—80, dean students, 1980—83, dean coll., 1983—88; v.p.m. dir. Am. Mus. Natural History, NYC, 1988—95; pres., CEO Milw. Pub. Mus., 1995—2002; ret., 2002. Bd. dirs. N.Y. State Mus.; adv. com. arts and culture Congressman J. Nadler, N.Y.C., 1993-95. Adv. editor Curator jour., 1991-95. Mem. Am. Mus. Assn., Am. Assn. Museums (mem. ethics com., bd. dirs.), Wis. Acad. of Scis., Arts and Letters (councillor-at-large 1995—), Univ. Club. Home: RD 1 84 Eaton St Hamilton NY 13346 Address: 1626 N Prospect Ave Apt 1707 Milwaukee WI 53202-2422

MOZENA, JOHN DANIEL, podiatrist; b. Salem, Oreg., June 9, 1956; s. Joseph Iner and Mary Teresa (Delaney) M.; m. Elizabeth Ann Hintz, June 2, 1979; children: Christine Hintz, Michelle Delaney. Student, U. Oreg., 1974-79; B in Basic Med. Scis., Calif. Coll. Podiatric Medicine, D in Podiatric Medicine, 1983. Diplomate Am. Bd. Podiatric Surgery. Resident in surg. podiatry Hillside Hosp., San Diego, 1983-84; pvt. practice podiatry Portland, Oreg., 1984—; dir. residency Med. Ctr. Hosp., 1985-91. Lectr. Nat. Podiatric Assn. Seminar, 1990, Am. Coll. Gen. Practitioners, 1991, Am. Coll. Family Physician, 1995; adj. faculty health profl. sect. Portland C.C., 1999. Cons. editor Podiatry Today Mag., 1999—, Podiatry Today, 1999—; contbr. articles to profl. jours.; patentee sports shoe cleat design, 1985. Podiatric adv. coun. Oreg. Bd. Med. Examiners, 1994-97. Named Clinician of the Yr., Eastmoreland Hosp., 2000-01. Fellow Am Coll. Ambulatory Foot Surgeons, Am. Coll. Foot Surgeons. Republican. Roman Catholic. Avocations: softball, basketball, piano, jogging, electric bass guitar, coaching children's sports programs. Office: Town Ctr Foot Clinic 8305 SE Monterey Ave Ste 101 Portland OR 97266-7728

MOZILO, ANGELO R. diversified financial services company executive; BS, Fordham U., 1960; LLD with hon. , Pepperdine U. Ptnr., co-founder Countrywide Credit Industries, Inc., Calabasas, Calif., 1969—, CEO, 2000—, also vice chmn.; chmn., CEO Countrywide Home Loans, Inc. subs., chmn., CEO, pres. Vice chmn. Office: Countrywide Credit Industries Inc 4500 Park Granada Calabasas CA 91302-1613*

MOZLEY, PAUL DAVID, retired obstetrics and gynecology educator; b. Decatur, Ala., Oct. 27, 1928; s. James Howard and Ruth Dianne (Brindely) M.; m. Mary Dale Goss, Aug. 30, 1983; children from previous marriage: Susan Ruth, Paul David Jr., Sally Robin. BA, U. Ala., 1950; MD, Med. Coll. Ala., 1955. Diplomate Am. Bd. Ob-Gyn, Am. Bd. Psychiatry and Neurology. Commd. lt. USN, 1955, advanced through grades to capt., 1970; resident ob-gyn Corona (Calif.) and San Diego Naval Hosp., 1956-59; resident in psychiatry Bethesda, Md., 1964-66, Phila. Naval Hosp., 1969-70; staff gynecologist U.S. Naval Hosp., Yokosuku, Japan, 1959-62, chief gynecologist Memphis, 1962-64, dir. med. services Naples, Italy, 1966-68, comdg. officer Italy, 1969; chmn. neuropsychiatry Naval Regional Med. Ctr., Portsmouth, Va., 1970-75; ret., 1975; assoc. prof. psychiatry Eastern Va. Med. Sch., Norfolk, 1975-77, prof., interim chmn. dept., 1977-78, vice chmn. psychiatry, 1978-79; prof., dir. undergrad. edn. Dept. Ob-Gyn Sch. Medicine, East Carolina U., Greenville, 1979-84; prof. ob-gyn, chmn. dept., Coll. Community Health Scis. U. Ala., Tuscaloosa, 1984-99, prof. ob-gyn, assoc. chmn. dept. Sch. Medicine, 1984-99, prof., chmn. emeritus Sch. Medicine, prof. emeritus obstetrics, 1999—; ret., 2002. Dir. psychiat. services Norfolk Gen. Hosp., 1975-79; chmn. dept. ob-gyn DCH Regional Med. Ctr., Tuscaloosa, 1986—; cons. med. liability law legal firms., Ala., Tenn., 1980—. Contbr. numerous articles to profl. jours. Mem. Regional Parental Adv. Council, Montgomery, Ala., 1986-87; sponsor Tuscaloosa Symphony Assn. Recipient Meritorious Service medal Pres. U.S., 1975, Surgeon Gen.'s Merit award, 1975, Attending of Yr. award Residents in Psychiatry, 1979, Clin. Sci. Course award Dept. Ob-Gyn grad. class, 1982, Eastern Va. Sch. Medicine; named one of Outstanding Young Men in Am., Jaycees, 1964 Fellow ACS, Am. Coll. Ob-Gyn (chmn. various programs 1974, 76, 77, Chmn.'s award clin. research 1969, life), Am. Psychiat. Assn. (Continuing Med. Edn. Standards award 1977, life); mem. AMA (Physician's Recognition award 1986), Am. Soc. Psychosomatic Ob-Gyn (founding mem., pres. 1979-80, chmn. nominating com. 1981, permanent steering com. 1982), Va. Ob-Gyn Soc., Assn. Acad. Psychiatry, Va. Med. Soc., N.C. Neuropsychiat. Assn., Pitt County Med. Soc., Med. Assn. Ala., Ala. Psychiat. Assn., LWV, Torch Club (Portsmouth), Alpha Epsilon Delta. Democrat. Mem. Ch. of Christ. Avocations: cabinetry, goldsmithing. Home: 563 N Mobile St Fairhope AL 36532-2609

MOZZOCHI, DEANNA JEAN, interior designer, business owner; b. North Platte, Nebr., Sept. 30, 1938; d. Francis Whitford and Nancy Elizabeth (Hale) Donnell; m. Michael Joseph Mozzochi Jr., Sept. 8, 1962; children: Susan Elizabeth, Michael Joseph III. BA, U. Nebr., 1960; A in Fine Arts, Cottey Coll., 1958; cert. interior design, Paier Coll. Art, 1977. Cert. Nat. Coun. for Interior Design Qualification. Owner DM Interiors, Clinton, Conn., 1978—. Mem. Am. Soc. Interior Designers, Fedn. Garden Clubs Conn., Inc. (chmn. judges coun. 1989-93, membership chmn., 2d v.p. 1993-95, 1st v.p. 1995—), Nat. Coun. State Garden Clubs, Inc. (master flower show judge 1982—), Arbor Garden Club (pres. 1985-88). Avocations: skiing, floral design, bridge (Am. Contract Bridge League bronze life master). Home and Office: 189 Salt Island Rd Westbrook CT 06498-1919

MRACHEK, LORIN LOUIS, lawyer; b. Fairmont, Minn., Jan. 5, 1946; s. Louis L. and Kathleen (Loring) M.; m. Elizabeth Moss, Aug. 31, 1968; children: Kathleen Elizabeth, Louis Moss. BA with honors, Fla. State U., 1968; MBA, JD, Columbia U., 1974. Bar: Fla. 1974, Va. 1977, U.S. Ct. Mil. Appeals 1977, U.S. Supreme Ct. 1978; cert. in civil trial law and bus. litigation Fla. Bar Bd. Certification; cert. in bus. bankruptcy law Am. Bd. Bankruptcy Certification; cert. in civil trial advocacy Nat. Bd. Trial Advocacy. Commd. 2d lt. USMC, 1969, advanced through grades to capt., 1974, chief def. counsel Marine Corps. Recruit Depoit, 1975-77, resigned, 1977; spl. asst. to gen. counsel U.S. Ry. Assn., Washington, 1977-78; shareholder Gunster, Yoakley, Valdes-Fauli & Stewart, P.A., West Palm Beach, Fla., 1978-2000; founding shareholder Page, Mrachek, Fitzgerald & Rose, 2000—. Mem. leadership coun. Fla. State U. Coll. Arts. and Scis. Editor-in-chief Columbia Jour. Law and Social Problems, 1973-74; contbr. articles to profl. jours. Fellow Am. Coll. Trial Attys.; mem. ABA, Am. Bankruptcy Inst., So. Fla. Bankruptcy Bar Assn. Avocations: running, tennis, golf. Office: 505 S Flagler Dr Ste 600 West Palm Beach FL 33401-5941 E-mail: lmrachek@pm-law.com.

MRACKY, RONALD SYDNEY, marketing and promotion executive, travel consultant; b. Sydney, Australia, Oct. 22, 1932; came to U.S., 1947, naturalized, 1957; s. Joseph and Anna (Janousek) M.; m. Sylvia Frommer, Jan. 1, 1960; children: Enid Hillevi, Jason Adam. Student, English Inst., Prague, Czechoslovakia, 1943-47; grad., Parsons Sch. Design, N.Y.C., 1950-53; postgrad., NYU, 1953-54. Designer D. Deskey Assocs., N.Y.C., 1952-53; art dir., designer ABC-TV, Hollywood, Calif., 1956-57; creative dir. Neal Advt. Assocs., L.A., 1957-59; pres. Richter & Mracky Design Assocs., 1959-68; pres., CEO Richter & Mracky-Bates divsn. Ted Bates & Co., 1968-73, Regency Fin., Internat. Fin. Svcs., Beverly Hills, Calif., 1974-76; sr. ptnr. Sylron Internat., L.A., 1973—, mgmt. dir. for N.Am. Standard Advt.-Tokyo, 1978-91. CEO Standard/Worldwide Cons. Group, L.A., Tokyo, 1981-87; officer, bd. dirs. Theme Resorts, Inc., Denver, 1979—; prin., officer Prodn. Travel & Tours, Universal City, 1981—, Eques Ltd., L.A., 1988—; mng. ptnr. GO! Pubs., 1993—; cons. in field; exec. dir. Inst. for Internat. Studies and

Devel. L.A., 1976-77; mng. ptnr. Africa Consult Group, 1998—. Contbr. articles to profl. jours.; mem. editl. bd., mktg. dir. The African Times and Africa Quar., 1990—. With U.S. Army, 1954-56. Recipient nat. and internat. awards design and mktg. Mem. Am. Mktg. Assn., African Travel Assn. (amb.-at-large, internat. secretariat), L.A. Publicity Club, Pacific Asia Travel Assn., S.Am. Travel Assn., Am. Soc. Travel Agents. Office: Ste 115 6363 Wilshire Blvd Los Angeles CA 90048

MRAK, ROBERT EMIL, neuropathologist, educator, electron microscopist; b. Oakland, Calif., Dec. 18, 1948; s. Emil Marcel and Vera Dudley (Greaves) M.; m. Paula Elizabeth North, Oct. 18, 1980; children: Lara North, Eric North, Ian North. BS in Math., U. Calif., Davis, 1970, MD, 1975, PhD in Zoology, 1976. Diplomate Am. Bd. Pathology, Am. Bd. Neuropathology. Resident in pathology Vanderbilt U. Hosp., Nashville, 1976-78, fellow in molecular biology, 1978-80; asst. prof. pathology Vanderbilt U., 1980-84, U. Ark. for Med. Scis., Little Rock, 1984-87, assoc. prof. pathology and anatomy, 1987-93, prof. pathology and anatomy, 1993—, chief neuropathology, 1999—, dir. neuropathology core, Alzheimer Disease Core Ctr., 2001—. Chief electron microscopy VA Hosp., Little Rock, 1984-98; cons. in neuropathology Ark. Children's Hosp., Little Rock, 1984—. Editl. bd. mem. Jour. Neuropathy & Explt. Neurology, 1996-99, Human Pathology, 1996—; contbr. articles and abstracts to profl. jours. Rsch. grantee VA, 1980-83, Muscular Dystrophy Assn., 1981-85, NIH, 1986-90, 95—. Mem. Am. Assn. Neuropathologists, Soc. for Neurosci., U.S. and Can. Acad. Pathology. Avocations: running, skiing. Office: U Ark for Med Scis 4301 W Markham St Little Rock AR 72205-7101 E-mail: mrakroberte@uams.edu.

MRAMOR, JAMES PLUMMER, security consultant; b. Cleve., Feb. 10, 1943; s. Frank James and Lucille (Cannon) M.; m. Dolores Dergane, Oct. 17, 1964 (div. June 1974); m. Patricia Ann Taddeo, June 12, 1976; children: Michael, Wendy, Allison. B in Criminal Justice, Youngstown State U., 1999; postgrad., Cleve. State U., 1999—. Police lt. East Cleve. (Ohio) Police Dept., 1964-79; v.p., security Centran Corp./ Central Bank, Cleve., 1979-86, Soc. Nat. Bank, Cleve., 1986; security dir. Cleve. Mus. Art, 1987—. Cons. Topwatch Corp., Cleve., 1986; adj. instr. Case Western Reserve U., Cleve., 1979. With U.S. Army, 1961-64. Mem. Ohio State Bar Assn. (student mem.), Cugahoya County Bar Assn. (student mem.), Cleve. Bar Assn. (student mem.). Democrat. Avocations: gourmet cooking, travel, sports. Home: 3070 Nantucket Dr Willoughby OH 44094-7679 E-mail: mramorsd@hotmail.com.

MRAZEK, DAVID ALLEN, pediatric psychiatrist; b. Ft. Riley, Kans., Oct. 1, 1947; s. Rudolph George and Hazel Ruth (Schayes) M.; m. Patricia Jean, Sept. 2, 1978; children: Nicola, Matthew, Michael, Alissa. AB in Genetics, Cornell U., 1969; MD, Wake Forest U., 1973. Lic. psychiatrist, child psychiatrist, N.C., Ohio, Colo., D.C., Va., Md., Minn.; med. lic. N.C., Ohio, D.C., Va., Md., Minn. Lectr. child psychiatry Inst. of Psychiatry, London, 1977-79; dir. pediatric psychiatry Nat. Jewish Ctr. for Immunology and Respiratory Medicine, Denver, 1979-91; chmn. psychiatry Children's Nat. Med. Ctr., Washington, 1991-98; chair psychiatry and behavioral scis. George Washington U. Sch. Medicine, 1996-2000; dir. Children's Rsch. Inst. Neurosci., 1995-98; chair psychiatry and psychology Mayo Clinic, Rochester, Minn., 2000—; prof. psychiatry, psychology and pediat. Mayo Sch. Medicine, 2000—. Asst. prof. psychiatry U. Colo. Sch. Medicine, 1979-83, assoc. prof. psychiatry and pediatrics, 1984-89, prof., 1990-91; prof. psychiatry and pediatrics George Washington U. Sch. Medicine, 1991-2000, Leon Yochelson prof. psychiatry and behavioral scis. Contbr. articles and book chpts. on child devel. and asthma to profl. publs. Recipient Rsch. Scientist Devel. awards NIMH, 1983-88, 88-91, Irving Phillips Meml. award for outstanding rsch. in prevention Acad. Child and Adolescent Psychiatry, 2000. Fellow Am. Acad. Child Psychiatry, Royal Soc. Medicine, Am. Psychiat. Assn. (Blanche F. Ittleson award 1996, Agnes Purcell McGavin award 1999), Royal Coll. Psychiatrists; mem. Am. Coll. Psychiatrists, Group for the Advancement of Psychiatry, Colo. Child and Adolescent Psychiatry Soc. (pres. 1984), Benjamin Rush Soc. Office: Mayo Clinic Dept Psychiatry/Pschology 200 1st St SW Rochester MN 55905 Fax: (507) 266-3319. E-mail: mrazek.david@mayo.edu.

MRKVICKA, EDWARD FRANCIS, JR. financial writer, publisher, consultant; b. Aurora, Ill., Oct. 17, 1944; s. Edward Francis Sr. and Ruth Caroline (Phillips) M.; m. Madelyn Helen Rimnac, July 1, 1972; children: Edward Francis III, Kelly Helen. Cert. comml. pilot, U. Ill., 1965; diploma, Dept. Def., 1967, Bank Mktg. Assn., 1972, grad. cert., 1973. Mktg. officer Downers Grove (Ill.) Nat. Bank, 1964-72; asst. v.p., mktg. officer Bank of Westmont, Ill., 1972-73; v.p., cashier 1st State Bank Hanover Park, 1973-76; pres. 1st Nat. Bank Marengo, 1976-81, Reliance Enterprises, Inc., Fin. News Syndicate, Omni, Fin. Group, Eagle Publishing, Marengo, 1981—. Adv. coun. Am. Monetary Found., Fullerton, Calif., 1987; mem. panel of experts Boardroom Reports, 1990—. Pub.: (newletter) Money Insider; author: Battle Your Bank-And Win!, 1984, Moving Up, 1985; (with others) The Complete Book of Personal Finance, 1987, The Bank Book, 1989, 91, 94, 1,037 Ways to Make or Save Up to $100,000 This Year Alone, 1991, The Rational Investor, 1992, Your Bank is Ripping You Off, 1997, 99, J.K. Lasser's Pick Winning Stocks, 2000; contbr. articles to profl. jours. and newspapers; fin. columnist Nat. Enquirer, 1996—. Bd. dirs. DuPage County Lung Assn., Downers Grove, 1970, Western Suburbs Combined Com. Appeal, Downers Grove, 1971, McHenry County Easter Seals Clinic, Woodstock, Ill., 1979; v.p., treas. Marengo/Union Chamber, 1980; Am. rep. Cans. for Constitutional Money, 1990—. Sgt. USAF, 1965-69. Mem. Nat. Writers Union. Republican. Avocations: bowling, fishing. Office: Reliance Enterprises Inc PO Box 413 Marengo IL 60152-0413

MROSZCZYK, ROSE VICTORIA, guidance counselor, educator; b. Waltham, Mass., Dec. 20, 1945; d. Henry Edward and Nandina Louise Mroszczyk; m. William J. McDonald, Dec. 29, 1976 (div. 1993); children: Dylan, Alex, William Henry. BA in French, Brandeis U., 1967; MS in Edn., Bank St. Coll. Edn., 1969; MA in Counseling Psychology, Antioch U., 1978. Tchr. Newton (Mass.) Pub. Schs., 1968-70, Lab. Kindergarten Nursery Brandeis U., Waltham, 1970-73, Shady Hill Sch., Cambridge, Mass., 1973-75; therapist alcohol and individual therapy Mental Health Svcs. of Southeastern Vt., White River Junction, 1976-77; child and family therapist United Counseling Svc., Bennington, Vt., 1977-78; family therapist Alternatives for Human Growth and Devel., West Lebanon, N.H., 1979-81; mid. sch. counsel Hartford (Vt.) Sch. Dist., 1989-92; elem. counselor Ottauquechee Sch., Quechee, Vt., 1992—. Mem. NEA, Am. Sch. Counselor Assn., Vt. Sch. Counselor Assn. (bd. dirs. 1989-91)., Vt. Assn. Counseling and Devel. (bd. dirs. 1989-91). Avocations: reading, cooking, swimming, astronomy, writing. Office: Ottauquechee Sch Dody Ln Quechee VT 05059

MROZ, RICHARD S. lawyer; b. Camden, N.J., June 16, 1961; s. Stanley and Jeanette Mroz; m. Lynne Mroz, Sept. 9, 1995; 1 child, Julia Jeanette. BA, U. Del., 1983; JD, Villanova U., 1986. Bar: N.J., Pa., D.C., U.S. Ct. Appeals (3d cir.), U.S. Supreme Ct. Law sec. Judge I.V. DiMentino, Camden, N.J., 1986-87; assoc. Cahill, Wilinski & Cahill, Haddonfield, 1987-91; asst. county counsel County of Camden, 1991, county counsel, 1991-94; dir. state authorities Office of Gov., Trenton, 1994-98, spl. counsel, 1998-2000, chief counsel, 1999-2000; of counsel Strodley, Ronon, Stevens & Young, Phila. and N.J., 2000—. Mem. NY. bd. dirs. Fed. Home Loan Bank, 2002—. Campaign atty. County Rep. Comm., Camden County, 1990-91, Rep. committeeman, 1989-91. Mem. N.J. Bar Assn., Camden County Bar Assn., Copernicus Soc. So. N.J. (sec., treas., pres.), N.J. Alliance for Action (bd. dirs.). Roman Catholic. Avocations: sport, running, skiing, golf, wine tasting. Home: 331 Knolltop Ln Haddonfield NJ 08033-3718 Office: Office of Gov PO Box 1-stateh Trenton NJ 08625-0001

MRUK, CHARLES KARZIMER, agronomist; b. Providence, Sept. 23, 1926; s. Charles and Anna (Pisarek) M. BS in Agr., U. R.I., 1951, MS in Agronomy, 1957. Soil scientist soil conservation svc. Dept. Agr., Sunbury, Pa., 1951; insp. Charles A. McGuire Co., Providence, 1952; claims insp. R.R. Perishable Inspection Agy., Boston, 1953-55; asst. in agronomy U. R.I., 1955-57; agronomist Hercules Inc., 1957-79, tech. salesman, 1957-79; sr. tech. sales rep. BFC Chems., Inc., 1981-82; are devel. supr. Ea. States, 1982-84, ret., 1984. Cons. turf maintenance Olympic Stadium and Grounds, Mexico City, 1968, Fenway Park, Boston, 1963-70; bd. mem. L. Troll/G.C.S.A.N.E. Turf Rsch. Fund; advisor Mass. TurfGrass Conf. and Trade Show, Chicopee. Author and editor articles on turf culture and fertilizers, 1960-81. Mem. Rep. Ward Com., Providence, 1963-76. With USN, 1944-46. U.S. Golf Assn. Green Sect. grantee, 1955-57. Mem. Am. Soc. Agronomy, New Eng. Sports Turf Mgrs. Assn. (life), R.I. Golf Course Supts. Assn., Mass. Turf and Lawn Grass Coun. (dir., mem. planning com., chmn. fin. com., 1987, pres., 1987-89), VFW, Am. Registry Cert. Profls. in Agronomy (cert. agronomist), Sigma Xi, Alpha Zeta. Mem. Polish National Ch. Home: 75 Burdick Dr Cranston RI 02920-1517

MRUK, EUGENE ROBERT, retired marketing professional, urban planner; b. Buffalo, Sept. 12, 1927; s. Stanley and Lucy Ann (Wolanski) M.; m. Florence Helen Guzy, Apr. 15, 1950; children: Linda, Lawrence, Edith, Ginny. AA in Engring., U. Buffalo, 1966, BA in Sociology, 1970; cert. sys. analysis & application admin., U. Wis., 1971; MA in Econs., U. Buffalo, 1974; cert. sys. analysis & application admin., U. Wis., 1971. Asst. dir. planning City of Buffalo, 1958-70; commr. planning Erie County, N.Y., Buffalo, 1970-74; dir. socioecon. studies Ecology and Environment, Inc., 1974-79, dir. transp. system studies, 1979-81, dir. bus. devel., 1981-86, v.p. sales and mktg., 1986-90, sr. v.p. sales and mktg. nat. and internat., 1990-94, cons., 1994-96; ret., 1996. Pvt. practice planning cons. Buffalo area, 1950-64; v.p. rsch. and planning coun. WNY, 1971-74; mem. indsl. adv. bd. dept. chem. engring. SUNY, Buffalo. Author various mcpl. govt. plans. Coord. Econ. Devel. program, Buffalo, 1966; exam. cons. Civil Svc. Commn. City of Buffalo, 1974; grand marshal Gen. Pulaski Parade com., Buffalo, 1972; trustee Villa Maria Coll. Buffalo, 1992-93. Named Man of Yr. in Govt. Am-Pole Eagle newspaper, 1970; gold medal sr. olympics, N.H., silver medal, N.Y. Mem. Am. Assn. Cert. Planners, Am. Planning Assn. (Disting. Leadership award N.Y. upstate chpt. 1992), Profl. Businessmen's Assn., Fr. Kolbe Soc./Polish Union of Am. (pres. 1995-2000). Democrat. Roman Catholic. Avocations: tennis, senior olympic basketball, photography, oil and acrylic painting. Home: 3 Dennis Ln Cheektowaga NY 14227-1301

MRUTHYUNJAYA, G.T. pediatrician; b. Mar. 8, 1956; Degree, Mysore (India) Med. Coll., 1962. Intern Griffin Hosp., Derby, Conn., 1973-74; resident U. Ky., Lexington, 1974-76; fellow U. Calif., Irvine; practice medicine specializing in pediatrics Mission Viejo, Calif., 1972—. Mem. Am. Acad. Pediatrics, Indian Doctors Assn. So. Calif. (past pres., past trustee). Office: Ste 300 27800 Medical Center Rd Mission Viejo CA 92691-6410

MSEZANE, ALFRED ZAKELE, physics educator; b. Springs, Transvaal, South Africa, Dec. 31, 1938; came to US, 1978; s. Albert and Esther (Mbuli) M.; m. Gail Patrick, Nov. 30, 1969; children: Temba, Lambda. BSc, U. South Africa, 1962; BSc (hon), 1964; MSc, U. Sask. (Can.), 1968; PhD, We. Ont., 1973; DSc (hon.), U. Fort Hare, South Africa, 1998. Rsch. assoc. U. Witwatersrand, Johannesburg, South Africa, 1968-69, Ga. State U., Atlanta, 1974-76; instr. U. New Brunswick, Fredericton, Can., 1976-78; vis. prof. La. State U., Baton Rouge, 1978-80; from asst. prof. to assoc. prof. physics Morehouse Coll., Atlanta, 1980-83; prof. physics Atlanta U., 1983-89; chmn. physics dept., 1986-89; prof. Clark Atlanta U., 1989—; chmn. physics dept., 1991-92. Dir. NSF Ctr. Theoret. Studies of Phys. sys., 1991—; bd. dirs. Nat. alliance Rsch. Ctrs. Excellence, acting chmn., 1998—; chmn. physics and astronomy group U. Ctr. Ga., 1983-84; rev. NSF Dept. Edn., NASA, Dept. Energy; vis. prof. Inst. Theoret. Atomic and Molecular Physics, Harvard Ctr. Astrophysics, 1994; Martin Luther King, Jr. Meml. vis. prof. Wayne State U., 1998; presenter in field. Contbr. articles to profl. jours.; referee Phys. Rev. A, Jour. Phys. B., others Trustee Marist Sch., Atlanta, 1998—; del. to China People to People, Spokane, Wash., 1990; soccer coach YMCA, Decatur, Ga., 1980-90, Baton Rouge, 1978-80; treas. East Lake Cmty. Assn., 1983-89; mem. J. Erkine Love Fellowship Com. World Univ. Svc. scholar, 1965-67, Witwatersrand U. scholar, 1968-69; rsch. grantee NSF, 1983—, DOE, Acad. Applied Sci., 1981—, USAF Office Sci., 1994-97, edn. grantee NASA, 1998—; recipient Bursary Rotary Club, 1962, Bursary City Coun. Springs, 1960-62, Sir Oppenheimer Meml. Bursary Anglo am. Corp., 1965, 69, Bouchet award Am. Phys. Soc., 1999; recognized as exemplary immigrant Atlanta Jour.-Constitution, 1993. Fellow Am. Phys. Soc.; mem. AAAS, Nat. Phys. Sci. Consortium (bd. dirs. 1989-91, 97—, fellowship com.), Am. Phys. Soc. (mem. subcommittee on internat. sci. affairs), Black Physicists, Sigma Pi Sigma. Office: Clark Atlanta U Dept Physics 223 James P Brawley Dr SW Atlanta GA 30314-4358 E-mail: amsezane@ctsps.cau.edu.

MU, YAOMING, physicist, researcher; b. Shanghai, Jan. 6, 1965; s. Xiantang Mu and Aizhu Lin; m. Weiqun Mao; children: Chaoqi. BS, Sichuan Normal U., Chengdu, China, 1985; MS, Sichuan Normal U., 1988; PhD, Fudan U., Shanghai, 1991. Postdoctoral fellow Nat. Lab. Infrared Physics, Shanghai Inst. Tech. Physics, 1991—93, asst. prof., 1993, assoc. prof., 1994—98; postdoctoral fellow SVEC, U. Houston, 1998—. Vis. scholar Linköping (Sweden) U., 1995—96. Contbr. articles to profl. jours. Recipient Nat. Natural Sci. prizes of China, Nat. Sci. and Tech. Com., 1995, Shanghai Sci. and Tech. Progress award, Shanghai Sci. and Tech. Com., 1998. Mem.: Sigma Xi. Office: SVEC U Houston 724 Sci & Rsch Bldg 1 Houston TX 77204-5004 Office Fax: 713-747-7724.

MUBASHIR, BASHAR AHMAD, internist, oncologist, hematologist; b. Pakistan, June 12, 1944; MBBS, Nishtar Med. Coll., Multan, Pakistan, 1967. Diplomate Am. Bd. Internal Medicine, Am. Bd. Oncology, Am. Bd. Hematology. Intern Toledo Hosp., 1968-69; resident in internal medicine Univ. Medicine and Dentistry of N.J., Newark, 1969-71; fellow in hematol. oncology U. Tex.-Md Anderson Hosp., Houston, 1971-73; fellow in med. hematology Case Western Res. U. Hosp., Cleve., 1973-74; pvt. practice Akron. Mem. staff St. Thomas Hosp. Med. Ctr., Akron; assoc. prof. medicine Northeastern Ohio U., Akron. Fellow ACP. Office: 444 N Main St Akron OH 44310-3110

MUCCI, GARY LOUIS, lawyer; b. Buffalo, Nov. 12, 1946; s. Guy Charles and Sally Rose (Battaglia) M.; m. Carolyn Belle Taylor, May 4, 1991. BA cum laude, St. John Fisher Coll., 1968; JD, Cath. U., 1972. Bar: N.Y. 1972. Law clk. to Hon. John T. Curtin U.S. Dist. Ct., Buffalo, 1972-74; assoc. atty. Donovan Leisure Newton & Irvine, N.Y.C., 1974-75, Saperston & Day P.C., Buffalo, 1975-80, sr. ptnr., 1980—2001; ptnr. Hiscock Barclay Saperston & Day, 2001—. Chmn. bd. Buffalo Philharm. Orch., 1985-86; pres. Hospice Buffalo, 1986-87; mem. N.Y. State Coun. on the Arts, 1987-2000; chmn. Citizens Com. on Cultural Aid, Buffalo, 1992-98; trustee St. John Fisher Coll., Hardin Acad.; mem. City of Buffalo Bd. Ethics. Recipient Brotherhood award NCCJ, Buffalo, 1983; named Man of Yr. William Paca Soc., 1984. Mem. Erie County Bar Assn., N.Y. State Bar Assn. Home: 27 Tudor Pl Buffalo NY 14222-1615 Office: Hiscock Barclay Saperston & Day PC 3 Fountain Plz Ste 1100 Buffalo NY 14203-1486

MUCCI, PATRICK JOHN, financial consultant, realtor, commercial loan broker; b. Albany, N.Y., July 5, 1947; s. Philip and Angelina (Patrella) M.; m. Beverly Ann Scully, June 8, 1968; children: Philip Michael, Angelina Maria. AAS, Hudson Valley Community Coll., Troy, N.Y., 1967; BS, SUNY, Albany, 1977; MBA, Fairleigh Dickinson U., 1979. Cert. review appraiser, comml. investment mgr., real estate broker, internat. financier; registered mortgage underwriter; lic. ins. broker for life and accident ins. Adminstrv. asst. Nat. Savs. Bank, Albany, 1973-76; asst. v.p. Heritage Savs. Bank, Kingston, N.Y., 1976-78, Home Savs. Bank, Albany, 1978-81, v.p., 1981, Home & City Savs. Bank, Albany, 1981-83, sr. v.p. lending, 1983-90; pres., chmn. bd., founder Greenbush Assocs., Inc., East Greenbush, N.Y., 1990—. Chmn. bd., founder, pres. Patrician Funding, Inc., 1997—, East Greenbush; bd. dirs. Vec Tech., Inc., Philangie Corp.; v.p., sr. comml. loan officer 2d Provantage Funding Corp., 2000—. Active Italian-Am. Community Ctr.; mem. City of Albany Strategic Planning Com., 1986; treas., bd. dirs. Theater Voices, 1990; bd. dirs. Albany League Arts, Discovery Ctr. Capital Region, 1990, N.Y. State Mus. Inst., Capital Affordable Housing Funding Com., Albany County Affordable Housing Corp.; mem. Rensselaer County Com. Sewer & Water Authority, 1993-94. Staff sgt. USAF, 1969-72. Mem. Nat. Assn. Mortgage Brokers, N.Y. State Mortgage Brokers Assn., N.Y. State Assn. Comml. and Indsl. Brokers, Soc. Internat. Financiers, Worldwide Network, N.E. Assn. Mtge. Bankers. Avocations: bicyclist, travel, reading, photography, computers. Home: 296 Luther Rd East Greenbush NY 12061-4312

MUCCIA, JOSEPH WILLIAM, lawyer; b. N.Y.C., May 31, 1948; s. Joseph Anthony and Charlotte (Mohring) M.; m. Margaret M. Reynolds, June 29, 1985. BA magna cum laude, Fordham U., 1970, JD, 1973. Bar: N.Y. 1974, U.S. Dist. Ct. (so. dist.) N.Y. 1974, U.S. Dist. Ct. (ea. dist.) N.Y. 1980, U.S. Ct. Appeals (2d cir.) 1974, U.S. Ct. Appeals (D.C. cir.) 1980, U.S. Supreme Ct. 1980. Assoc. Cahill Gordon & Reindel, N.Y.C., 1973-82; ptnr. Corbin Silverman & Sanseverino, 1983—2001, Brown Raysman Millstein Felder & Steiner LLP, N.Y.C., 2002—. Assoc. editor Fordham Law Rev., 1972-73. Mem. ABA (litigation sect.), N.Y. County Lawyers Assn., Fed. Bar Coun., N.Y. State Bar Assn. (com. litigation sect.), Phi Beta Kappa, Pi Sigma Alpha. Office: Brown Raysman et al 900 3d Ave New York NY 10022 E-mail: jmuccia@brownraysman.com.

MUCHA, JOHN, III, lawyer; b. Flint, Mich., Jan. 28, 1955; s. John Jr. and Mary M.; m. Patricia Brautigan, 1981. AB cum laude, U. Mich., 1977, M in Pub. Policy, 1979, JD, 1987. Bar: Mich. 1987 (coun. litigation sect. 1995-99, chair 1998-99), U.S. Dist. Ct. (ea. dist.) Mich. 1987, U.S. Ct. Appeals (6th cir.) 1990. Assoc./clk. Lord Bissell & Brook, Chgo., summer 1986; assoc. Pepper, Hamilton & Scheetz, Detroit, 1987-95; ptnr. Dawda, Mann, Mulcahy & Sadler, Bloomfield Hills, Mich., 1995—. Contbg. author: Business Opportunities in the United States, 1992. Bd. dirs. Families for Adoption, Canton, Mich., 1994-96. Recipient Disting. Vol. Legal Svcs. award Detroit Bar Assn., 1994. Office: Dawda Mann Mulcahy & Sadler 39533 Woodward Ave Ste 200 Bloomfield Hills MI 48304-2815 E-mail: jmucha@dmms.com.

MUCHA, JOHN AARON, physical chemist; b. Pitts., Jan. 29, 1944; s. John and Agnes (Manko) M.; m. Linda Marie Adams, Sept. 11, 1976; children: Jason, Alex. BA, Washington and Jefferson Coll., 1965; PhD, U. Pitts., 1974. Rsch. chemist Nuclear Materials and Equipment Corp., Apollo, Pa., 1967-69; NRC postdoctoral rsch. fellow Nat. Inst. of Sci. and Tech., Boulder, Colo., 1975-77; mem. tech. staff AT&T, Lucent Bell Labs., Murray Hill, N.J., 1977-2000; Lucent assignee, project mgr. Sematech, Austin, Tex., 1996-99; sr. scientist for process applications Inficon, Inc., Syracuse, N.Y., 2000—. Sci. tech. adv. bd. Semiconductor Rsch. Corp., Research Triangle Park, N.C., 1992—, chmn. interconnect sci. tech. adv. bd., 1999-2000; process tech. adv. bd. Sematech, Austin, 1993-95; adv. panel on plasma processing rsch. Nat. Rsch. Coun., Washington, 1990. Contbr. articles to profl. jours. including Jour. of Phys. Chemistry, Analytical Chemistry, Jour. of Applied Physics, Applied Physics Letters, Applied Spectroscopy, Jour. of Chem. Physics, Chem. Physics Letters; contbr. 3 books. Pres. Madison Jaycees, 1982. NRC postdoctoral fellow NRC, NAS, 1975, 76. Mem. AAAS, Am. Chem. Soc., Am. Vacuum Soc., Soc. for Applied Spectroscopy. Achievements include developed lasers and spectroscopic analyses for monitoring kinetics of stratospheric free radicals, semiconductor process reaction mechanisms; patents for novel dielectric materials and semiconductor etching systems, analytical methods of measuring trace moisture in gases and entrapped in electronic components; novel interconnect strategies for copper metallization in advanced semiconductor devices; development of sensor and advanced process control strategies for semiconductor processing. E-mail: Jay.Mucha@inficon.com.

MUCHA, JOHN FRANK, information systems professional; b. Ludlow, Mass., Sept. 12, 1950; s. Joseph Walter and Sophie (Chrusciel) M.; m. Anne Virginia Casey, Sept. 1, 1973 (div. Feb. 1989); m. Anna C. Isaacs, Sept. 17, 1994. BA in Polit. Sci., U. Mass., 1972; MBA in Tech. and Profl. Comm., Frostburg State U., 1985. Computer programmer IRS, Washington, 1974-79, computer sys. programmer, 1979-81, Martinsburg, W.Va., 1981-86; staff sys. programmer fed. systems divsn. IBM, Gaithersburg, Md., 1986-87; chief tech. support IRS Martinsburg Computing Ctr., 1987-91; staff asst. to projects dir. info. sys. devel. IRS, Washington, 1991-92, computer specialist transition mgmt. office, 1992-95, sect. chief, 1995-97; team leader oversight team Govt. Program Mgmt. Office, New Carrollton, Md., 1997; sect. chief operating systems software ACS/ICS, 1997-2000; program mgr. Nat. Transmittal Ctr., 2000-2001; acting chief sys. support divsn. Systems Software br. IBM, 2001, chief capacity mgmt., 2001—. Contbr. articles to profl. jours. Team mem., bd. dirs. Beginning Experience of Balt., 1989-96; pres. Cath. Single Again Coun. of Balt., Inc., 1991-95, bd. dirs. Mem. Nat. Assn. for Tech. Profls., Inst., Inst. for Certification of Computer Profls. (cert. computing profl.), Profl. Mgrs. Assn., Moose, Fed. Mgrs. Assn. Libertarian. Methodist. Avocations: reading, instrumental music, travel, single again ministry. Home: 2482 Warm Spring Way Odenton MD 21113-1542 E-mail: john.f.mucha@irs.gov., jfmucha@aol.com.

MUCHANT, DIANNE GAIL, pediatric nephrologist; b. Waynesburg, Pa., Dec. 13, 1954; d. Robert William Muchant and Marion Marie Gussoff; m. Robert Warren Hazard, Sept. 11, 1999. BS, Alderson Broaddus, 1976; MD, W.Va. U., 1986. Bd. cert. internal medicine, pediat., pediat. nephrology. Intern and resident in internal medicine and pediats. W.Va. U., 1986—90; fellow U. Va. Med. Sch., Charlottesville, 1990-94; assoc. prof. W.Va. U. Med. Sch., Morgantown, 1994—. Mem. Internat. Soc. Pediat. Nephrology, Am. Soc. Pediat. Nephrology, Am. Soc. Nephrology, Physician's for Social Responsibility. Office: WV Univ Dept Pediats PO Box 9214 Morgantown WV 26506-9214 E-mail: dmuchant@hsc.wvu.edu.

MUCHMORE, DON MONCRIEF, museum, foundation, educational, financial fund raising and public opinion consulting firm administrator, banker; b. Wichita, Kans., Dec. 26, 1922; s. Floyd Stephen and Ivy Fay (Campbell) Muchmore; m. Virginia Gunn, June 18, 1949 (div. Dec. 1978); children: Melinda, Marcia. BA, Occidental Coll., Los Angeles, 1945; postgrad., U. So. Calif. Law Sch., 1945, UCLA. Intern Nat. Inst. Pub. Affairs, Washington, 1944; exec. asst. to congressman, 1946-48; teaching asst. UCLA, 1949-50; mem. faculty San Diego State U., 1950-51; asst. prof., adminstr. Calif. State U., Long Beach, 1951-56; pres., chief exec. officer The Campbell Found., L.A., 1956—; spl. asst. to supt. pub. instrn. Calif. Dept. Edn., Sacramento, 1956-57; exec. mus. dir. Calif. Mus. Sci. and Industry, L.A., 1957-62, 82-89; exec. v.p., chief exec. officer Calif. Mus. Found., 1957-62, 82-89; dep. dir. (on loan from mus.) Calif. Dept. Fin., Sacramento, 1960; exec. vice chancellor Calif. State Colls. and Univs. System, Long Beach, 1962-64; first exec. asst. to chmn. and chief exec. officer Calif. Fed. Savs. and Loan Assn., L.A., 1964-66; sr. v.p. Calif. Fed. Savs. and Loan Assn, 1966-82; pres., CEO PE Conservation Svcs., Inc., 1990-94. Chmn. bd. dirs., CEO Opinion Rsch. of Calif. Opinion Surveyors, The State Poll and Mktg. Surveys, Inc., Long Beach, 1948—71; syndicated by L.A. Times, 1961—70; also M-R Assocs. Campaigns; cons. in pub. opinion mus. mgmt. and fund raising, 1948—71; chmn., CEO, cons. DMM & Assocs., Long Beach, 1961—; sec., treas. EVENUP for the Homeless, 1994—97; mem. Inst. Mus. Svcs., 1983—88. Contbr. Participant in pub. opinion work Dem. and Rep. Campaigns, 1954—72; mem., chmn. 4 presdl. commns., 1970—82, Just Say No Internat., 1989—91, Reading is Fundamental, 1989—, The Buckley Sch., 1989—90; cons. overseas traveling sci. exhibit, planning mus., 1984—96; sr. adminstr., advisor, cons. PCS (South Ctrl. L.A.) Sr. Citizens, 1995—96; cons. Long Beach com. Improvement League, 1995—96; lead cons. New Solution to Homeless, 1993—98; prin. officer Peruvians Cultural Exhibit, 1988—96; prin. cons. cultural exhibit Wonders of World, 1992—95, Queensway Bay, Long Beach, 1992—98; bd. dirs. Bus. Tele Network, 1995—97; active Even up for the Homeless, 1996—98; cons. Christian Outreach Agy., 1998—99; pres. Harborplace Tower Home Owners Assn., 1999—; pres. bd. trustees East Village Cmty. Ch., 1998—, pres., 1998—2001. Named Chpt. Advisor of Yr., Sigma Alpha Epsilon, 1999, Pollster of Yr., Newsweek, 1968; recipient Highest Mus. Edn. award, Sigma Alpha Epsilon, 1992, Citizen of Yr. award and numerous other awards from nat., state and local groups; scholar Elks Nat. scholar. Mem.: AAAS, Calif. Mus. Assn. (pres. 1960, bd. dirs. 1982—88), Am. Polit. Sci. Assn., Am. Assn. Pub. Opinion Rsch., Assn. Sci. and Tech. Ctrs. (bd. dirs. 1982—88), Am. Assn. Mus. Office: The Campbell Found DMM & Associates 525 E Seaside Way Unit 209 Long Beach CA 90802-8001 Fax: 562-983-1143.

MUCHMORE, JOHN STEPHEN, endocrinologist; b. L.A., Jan. 1, 1945; s. Allan Winner and Lyntha Carol (Weed) M.; m. Susan Jill Crawford, June 13, 1968; children: Adam Ian, Rachel Kathleen. AB, Knox Coll., 1967; MD, U. Okla., 1975; PhD in Pharm. and Toxicology, U. Rochester, 1976. Diplomate AM. Bd. Internal Medicine in endocrinology and metabolism. Intern U. Okla. Health Sci. Ctr., 1975-76, resident in medicine, 1976-78, fellow endocrinology, metabolism and hypertension, 1978-80; Pvt. practice Oklahoma City, 1980—. Cardiac transplant physician Okla. Transplantation Inst. Bapt. Med. Ctr. of Okla., Oklahoma City, 1989—93; med. dir. Info. Sys. Integris Health, Oklahoma City, 1993—99; med. dir. clin. analysis svcs., med. divsn. inpatient mgmt. and utilization rev. Integris-Health, Oklahoma City. Recipient Nat.

Rsch. Svc. award Nat. Heart, Lung and Blood Inst., Bethesda, Md., 1978. Mem. AMA, AAAS, Am. Coll. Physicians, Alpha Omega Alpha. Office: Ste 350 3366 Northwest Expy Oklahoma City OK 73112-4462

MUCHMORE, ROBERT BOYER, engineering consultant executive; b. Augusta, Kans., July 8, 1917; s. Ray Boyer and Charlotte (McPherron) M.; m. Betty Vaughan, Jan. 29, 1944; children: Andrew Vaughan, Douglas Boyer. BS, U. Calif., Berkeley, 1939; degree in Elec. Engring., Stanford U., 1942. Project engr. Sperry Gyroscope Co., Garden City, N.Y., 1942-46; sr. mem. tech. staff Hughes Aircraft, Culver City, Calif., 1946-54; v.p., chief scientist TRW Systems, Redondo Beach, 1954-73, cons. Sonoma, 1973—. Lectr. in engring. UCLA, 1954-58. Author: Essentials of Microwaves, 1952. Fellow IEEE; mem. AAAS, Assn. Computing Machinery, Sierra Club. Home: 4311 Grove St Sonoma CA 95476-6046

MUCHMORE, WILLIAM BREULEUX, zoologist, educator; b. Cin., July 7, 1920; s. Oliver Charles and Ruby (Breuleux) M.; m. Marjorie Murrin, Aug. 15, 1943; children— Susan Jane, Patricia Ann. BA, Oberlin Coll., 1942; PhD in Zoology, Washington U., St. Louis, 1950. Instr. biology U. Rochester, N.Y., 1950-52, asst. prof., 1952-58, asso. prof., 1958-70, prof., 1970-85, prof. emeritus, 1985—, asst. chmn. dept. biology, 1964-66, assoc. chmn., 1974-78; vis. prof. U. Hull, Eng., 1963-64. Research assoc. Fla. State Collection Arthopods, 1974— Contbr. articles to profl. jours. Served with U.S. Army, 1943-46. NSF grantee, 1958-69, 73-76; Fulbright travel grantee, 1963-64; Office Naval Research grantee, 1979-81 Fellow Rochester Acad. Sci., Nat. Speleological Soc.; mem. Am. Arachnological Soc., Brit. Arachnological Soc., Internat. Soc. Arachnology. Office: Dept Biology Univ of Rochester Rochester NY 14627-0211

MUCHNICK, RICHARD STUART, ophthalmologist; b. Bklyn., June 21, 1942; s. Max and Rae (Kozinsky) M.; BA with honors. Cornell U., 1963, MD, 1967; m. Felice Dee Greenberg, Oct. 29, 1978; 1 child, Amanda Michelle. Intern in medicine N.Y. Hosp., N.Y.C., 1967-68, now assoc. attending ophthalmologist, chief Pediatric Ophthalmology Clinic; resident in ophthalmology, 1970-73; practice medicine, specializing in ophthalmology, notably strabismus and ophthalmic plastic surgery N.Y.C., 1974— ; attending surgeon, chief Ocular Motility Clinic, Manhattan Eye, Ear and Throat Hosp., N.Y.C.; clin. assoc. prof. ophthalmology Cornell U., N.Y.C., 1984— . Served with USPHS, 1968-70. Recipient Coryell Prize Surgery Cornell U. Med. Coll., 1967. Diplomate Am. Bd. Ophthalmology, Nat. Bd. Med. Examiners. Fellow A.C.S., Am. Acad. Ophthalmology; mem. Am. Soc. Ophthalmic Plastic and Reconstructive Surgery, Am. Assn. Pediatric Ophthalmology and Strabismus, Internat. Strabismological Assn., N.Y. Soc. Clin. Ophthalmology, AMA, N.Y. Acad. Medicine, Greater N.Y. Soc. for Pediat. Ophthalmology and Strabismus (pres.), Manhattan Ophthal. Soc., Alpha Omega Alpha, Alpha Epsilon Delta. Clubs: Lotos, 7th Regt. Tennis. Clin. researcher strabismus, ophthalmic plastic surgery, 1973— . Office: 69 E 71st St New York NY 10021-4213

MUCHOVEJ, JAMES JOHN, educator; b. Elizabeth, NJ, June 3, 1953; s. Stephen Mucha and Shirley Holder; m. Angela Purchio Muchovej, Aug. 27, 1993; children: Sarah, Stephen, John Edward. BSc, Purdue U., 1975, MSc, 1976; PhD, Va. Tech. Inst., 1984. Assoc. prof. Universidade Fed. de Vicosa, Brazil, 1978—91, Fla. A&M U., Tallahassee, 1992—. Author: (book) Basic Notions of Mycology, 1989; contbr. numerous articles to profl. jours. Mem.: Rotary (asst. gov. dist. 2001—, pres. Monticello club 1999—2001). Home: PO Box 25 Lloyd FL 32337-0025 Office: Fla A&M University 306 Perry Paige Bldg Tallahassee FL 32307 Home Fax: 850-997-2070; Office Fax: 850-561-2613. Personal E-mail: muchovej@quixnet.net.

MUCHOW, DAVID JOHN, lawyer; b. Holliston, Mass., Aug. 25, 1944; s. Albert J. and Mildred E. (Gerni) M.; m. Marilee Nietmann, July 10, 1971; children: Heather, Scott. BS, Sch. Fgn. Svc., Georgetown U., 1966, JD, 1971; postgrad., Cornell U. Law Sch., 1966-68. Bar: Fla. 1972, U.S. Supreme Ct. 1977, D.C. 1979, Va. 1988. Staff asst. to Congressman James Haley, Washington, 1962-66; with Office Mgmt. and Budget, 1968-69; staff Nat. Security Coun., 1969-70; assoc. Smathers & Herlong, 1970-73; trial atty., spl. asst. to asst. atty. gen. U.S. Dept. Justice, 1973-76; gen. counsel, corp. sec. Am. Gas Assn., Arlington, Va., 1976-98, counsel, 1998—; gen. counsel Bus. Coun. for Sustainable Energy; pres., CEO SkyBuilt, LLC, 2001—. Co-editor: Energy Law and Transactions; co-author: Regulation of the Gas Industry. Recipient Spl. Achievement award Dept. Justice, 1975. Mem. ABA (vice-chmn. gas com. pub. utility law sect.). Home and Office: 4449 N 38th St Arlington VA 22207-4551

MUCI KÜCHLER, KARIM HEINZ, mechanical engineering educator; b. Valencia, Carabobo, Venezuela, May 22, 1964; came to Mexico, 1981; s. Moussa and Luise Gertrud (Küchler) Muci Abraham; m. Alejandra Castañeda González, June 25, 1983; children: Karim Ibrahim, Moses Alejandro, Claudia María. BS, Inst. Tech. y Estudios Superiores Monterrey, Mexico, 1985; MS, Inst. Tech. y Estudios Superiores Monterrey, 1988; PhD, Iowa State U., 1992. Mech. maintenance Altos Hornos de Mexico, Monclova, 1986; teaching asst. Iowa State U., Ames, 1989, rsch. asst., 1989-92; prof. mech. engring. Inst. Tech. y Estudios Superiores Monterrey, 1993—. Mem. ASME (assoc.), Internat. Soc. Boundary Elements, Sigma Xi (assoc.), Tau Beta Pi, Phi Kappa Phi. Achievements include development of higher order boundary elements for three dimensional problems.

MUCINO-QUINTERO, VICTOR HUGO, mechanical engineering educator, consultant; b. Mexico City, Jan. 2, 1952; arrived in U.S., 1985; s. Alfonso Mucino-Reyes and Marcelina Quintero-Elizondo; m. Elisabeth Sanchez, Jan. 26, 1990; children: Andrea, Veronique. BSME, Poly. Inst. Mex., Mexico City, 1974; M Engring., U. Wis., Milw., 1977, DEng, 1981. Registered profl. engr., Wis., W.Va. Rsch. assoc. J. I. Case Co., Racine, Wis., 1977-80; prof. Nat. U. Mex., Mexico City, 1981-85; prof. mech. engring. W.Va. U., Morgantown, 1985—. Dir. indsl. outreach program in Mex. W.Va. U.; indsl. cons. *Dr. Victor H. Mucino is an expert on mechanical engineering design and dynamics of mechanical systems, including I.C. engines, automotive transmissions, and heavy-duty tanker truck stability and crashworthiness. In addition, he developed the "Industrial Outreach Program in Mexico" at WVU, teaming up engineering students from the U.S. and Mexico to solve practical industrial problems for Mexico and the U.S. industries.* Contbr. articles to profl. jours., including ASME Jour. Mech. Design, Indsl. Tribology, SAE Trans., Jour. Sound and Vibrations, others. Mem.: ASME, Am. Soc. Engring. Educators, Acad. Engring. Mex., Soc. Automotive Engrs. (Ralph Teetor award 1995). Avocations: music, poetry. Office: WVa U PO Box 6106 Morgantown WV 26506 E-mail: vmucino@wvu.edu.

MUCK, RUTH EVELYN SLACER (MRS. GORDON E. MUCK), education educator; b. Buffalo, July 17, 1910; d. Robert A. and Hattie E. (Sheridan) Slacer; B.S., State U. Coll. at Buffalo, 1938, M.S., 1952; Ed.D., State U. N.Y. at Buffalo, 1966; m. Gordon E. Muck, Dec. 27, 1934; 1 child, Linda Mae McGuire. Tchr. pub. schs., Lockport, N.Y., 1931-42; tchr. primary level campus sch. State U. Coll., Buffalo, 1942-66, prof. edn. div. elem., from 1966, now emeritus; cons. tchr. edn. workshops, Minn., Fla. Dir. youth edn. United Meth. Ch., 1960-69; pres. United Meth. Women, Grand Island, N.Y.; bd. dirs. United Meth. Found., West N.Y., 1986-92, N.Y. Dist. United Meth. Extension Soc., Buffalo, 1988-94; pres. Town of Lockport N.Y. Hist. Soc., 1987—; vol. community svc.; dir. children's used clothing shop. Recipient Mission Recognition award United Meth. Women, 1994, ecumenical cmty. svc. award, 1998. Mem. Assn. Tchr. Educators (state pres. 1972-73), Internat. Reading Assn. (chmn. 1969-71), Delta Kappa Gamma, Pi Lambda Theta. Home: 1091 Stony Point Rd Grand Island NY 14072-2712

MUCKENFUSS, CANTWELL FAULKNER, III, lawyer; b. Montgomery, Ala., Apr. 25, 1945; s. Cantwell F. and Dorothy (Dauphine) M.; m. A. Angela Lancaster, June 25, 1978; children: Alice Paran Lancaster, Cantwell F. IV. BA, Vanderbilt U., 1967; JD, Yale U., 1971. Bar: N.Y. 1973, D.C. 1976. Law clk. to presiding justice U.S. Ct. Appeals (6th cir.), 1971-72; atty., project developer Bedford Stuyvesant D and S Corp., Bklyn., 1972-73; spl. asst. to the dir. FDIC, Washington, 1974-77, counsel to the chmn., 1977-78; sr. dep. comptroller for policy Office of the Comptroller of the Currency, 1978-81; ptnr. Gibson, Dunn & Crutcher LLP, 1981—. Mem. editorial adv. bd. Issues in Bank Regulation, Rolling Meadows, Ill., 1977-91, Electronic Banking Law and Commerce Report, 1996—; mem. bd. advisors Rev. Banking and Fin. Svcs., N.Y.C., 1985—; bd. dis. Fair Tax Edn. Fund, Washington, 1987-90. Served with USNG, 1968-70, USAR, 1970-74. Recipient Spl. Achievement award U.S. Dept. Treasury, 1979, Presdl. Rank award U.S. Govt., 1980. Mem. ABA, Fed. Bar Assn. Clubs: Kenwood Country (Bethesda, Md.); Yale (N.Y.C.). Democrat. Episcopalian. Office: Gibson Dunn & Crutcher LLP 1050 Connecticut Ave NW Ste 900 Washington DC 20036-5306

MUCKENHOUPT, BENJAMIN, retired mathematics educator; b. Newton, Mass., Dec. 22, 1933; s. Carl Frederick and Sarah Joanna (Boell) M.; m. Mary Kathryn Heath, Aug. 29, 1964; children: Margaret, Carl Edward. AB, Harvard U., 1954; MS, U. Chgo., 1955, PhD, 1958. Instr. DePaul U., Chgo., 1958-59, asst. prof. math., 1959-60; faculty Rutgers U., New Brunswick, N.J., 1960-91, prof. math., 1970-91. Vis. assoc. prof. Mt. Holyoke Coll., 1963-65; visitor Inst. Advanced Study, Princeton, N.J., 1968-69, 75-76; vis. prof. SUNY-Albany, 1970-71 Contbr. articles to profl. jours. NSF rsch. grantee, 1965-88; Rutgers Rsch. Coun. fellow, 1968-69. Mem. Am. Math. Soc., Math. Assn. Am., Phi Beta Kappa, Sigma Xi. Home: 196 Woodfern Rd Neshanic Station NJ 08853-4054 E-mail: muckenho@post.harvard.edu.

MUCKERMAN, NORMAN JAMES, priest, writer; b. Webster Groves, Mo., Feb. 1, 1917; s. Oliver Christopher and Edna Gertrude (Hartman) M. BA, Immaculate Conception Coll., 1940, M. in Religious Edn., 1942. Ordained priest Roman Catholic Ch., 1942. Missionary Redemptorist Missions, Amazonas, Para, Brazil, 1943-53, procurator missions St. Louis, 1953-58; pastor, adminstr. St. Alphonsus Ch., Chgo., 1958-67, St. Gerard, Kirkwood, Mo., 1967-71; mktg. mgr. circulation Liguori Pubs., Liguori, 1971-76; editor Liguorian Mag., 1977-89. Author: How to Face Death Without Fear, 1976, Redemptorists on the Amazon, 1992, Preparation for Death, 1998, Into Your Hands, 2001, From the Heart of St. Alphonsus, 2002; contbg. editor: Liguorian, 1989—95. Recipient Nota Dez award Caixa Fed. Do Para, Brazil, 1958 Mem. Cath. Press Assn. (cons. 1971-95, bd. dirs. 1976-85, pres. 1981-84, St. Francis De Sales award 1985). Avocations: golf; travel; reading. E-mail: nmuckerman@compuserve.com.

MUCKLESTONE, PETER JOHN, lawyer; b. Seattle, Aug. 21, 1955; s. Robert Stanley and Susan (Quilliam) M. BA in History, U. Wash., 1977; JD, Columbia U., 1981. Bar: Wash. 1981, U.S. Dist. Ct. (we. and ea. dist.) Wash. Assoc. Bogle & Gates, Seattle, 1981-83; counsel Rainier Nat. Bank, 1983-89, Security Pacific Bank, Seattle, 1989-92; sr. counsel Seattle First Nat. Bank, 1992; counsel West One Bank, Seattle, 1992-95, U.S. Bancorp, Seattle, 1995-97; ptnr. Davis Wright Tremaine LLP, 1997—. Office: Davis Wright Tremaine LLP 1501 4th Ave Seattle WA 98101-1688 E-mail: petermucklestone@dwt.com.

MUDAVANHU, BLESSING, research scientist; b. Harare, Mashonaland, Zimbabwe, May 26, 1971; s. Jackson and Gladys Mudavanhu; m. Mutsa Tongoona, July 22, 1996. BS in Gen. Math. and Stats., U. Zimbabwe, Harare, 1993, BS in Math., 1995; M in Fin. Engring., U. Calif., Berkeley, 2002; MS, U. Wash., 1998, PhD, 2002. Rsch. asst. U. Wash., Seattle, 1996—2001; derivatives quantitative analyst Am. Internat. Group, N.Y.C., 2002—. Fellow U. of Zimbabwe Math. fellow, 1995; scholar Fulbright scholar, U.S. Govt., 1996—98. Mem.: Internat. Assn. for Fin. Engrs., Soc. for Indsl. and Applied Math., Am. Math. Soc., Fulbright Assn. (bd. dirs. Puget Sound chpt. 2000—02).

MUDD, ANNE CHESTNEY, attorney at law, mathematics educator, real estate agent; b. Macon, Ga., June 30, 1944; d. Bard Sherman Chestney and Betty (Bartow) Houston; children: Charles Lee Jr., Richard Chestney, Robert Jason. BA, U. Louisville, 1966, MA, 1976; postgrad., John Marshall Law Sch., 1995—98. Math statistician U.S. Bur. Census, Jeffersonville, Ind., 1966-70; instr. math. U. Louisville, 1975-77, Coll. DuPage, Glen Ellyn, Ill., 1978-85, 92; tchr. math and substitute tchr. Lyons Twp. High Sch., La Grange, 1986-91; realtor First United Realtors, Western Springs, 1989-92; owner, mgr. retail bus., 1992—. Math tutor Louisville 1969-77, Western Springs, Ill. 1977—. Editor: Mathematics Textbook, 1991-92. Mem. steering com. Village Western Springs, 1986-87; bd. dirs. Children's Theater, 1987-91; mem. Dupage County bar assn. legal aid, committee. Mem. NAFE, LWV (pres. 1983-85, bd. dirs.), Western Springs Hist. Soc. Avocations: local govt., theater, gardening. Home: 3958 Hampton Ave Western Springs IL 60558-1011

MUDD, JOHN O. lawyer; b. 1943; BA, Cath. U., 1965, MA, 1966; JD, U. Mont., 1973; LLM, Columbia U., 1986; JSD of Law, 1994. Bar: Mont. 1973. Pntr. Mulroney, Delaney, Dalby & Mudd, Missoula, Mont., 1973-79; lectr. U. Mont., 1973-74, 75-76, prof. law, dean, 1979-88; ptnr. Garlington, Lohn & Robinson, 1988-1999; sr. v.p. Providence Svcs., 2000—, also bd. dirs. Pres. Mid-Continent Assn. Law Schs., 1982—83; bd. dirs. Ascension Health. Editor: Mont. Law Rev., 1972—73. Chmn. Mont. Commn. Future of Higher Edn.; elected Dem. candidate U.S. Senate, 1994; bd. dirs. St. Patrick Hosp., 1985—90. With U.S. Army, 1967—73. Mem.: State Bar Mont., Am. Judicature Soc. (bd. dirs. 1985—89).

MUDD, JOHN PHILIP, lawyer; b. Washington, Aug. 22, 1932; s. Thomas Paul and Frances Mary (Finotti) M.; m. Barbara Eve Sweeney, Aug. 10, 1957; children: Laura, Ellen, Philip, Clare, David. BSS, Georgetown U., 1954; JD, Georgetown Law Center, 1956. Bar: Md. 1956, D.C. 1963, Fla. 1964, Calif. 1973. Pvt. practice, Upper Marlboro, Md., 1956-66; v.p., sec., gen. counsel Deltona Corp., Miami, Fla., 1966-72; sec., gen. counsel Nat. Community Builders, San Diego, 1972-73; gen. counsel Continental Advisers (adviser to Continental Mortgage Investors), 1973-75, sr. v.p., gen. counsel, 1975-80, Am. Hosp. Mgmt. Corp., Miami, 1980-89; legal coord. Amerifirst Bank, 1989-92; v.p., legal counsel Cartaret Savs. Bank, Morristown, N.J., 1991-93, cons., 1991-92; gen. counsel Golden Glades Hosp., Miami, 1992-93, Bank of N.Am., Miami, 1994—. Gen. counsel Golden Glades Hosp., Miami, 1992-93; cons. FSLIC, 1988-89, J.E. Robert Cos., Alexandria, Va., 1988-89, Real Estate Recovery, Inc., Boca Raton, Fla., 1991-92, Bank N.Am., Ft. Lauderdale, Fla., 1992; dir. Unitower Mortgage Corp., Miami, Fla.; dir. Unitower Mortgage Corp., Miami; pres. Marquette Realty Corp., Miami. Former mem. Land Devel. Adv. Com. N.Y. State; chmn. student interview com. Georgetown U.; bd. dirs. Lasalle High Sch., Miami; corp. counsel Com. of Dade County, Fla.; trustee Golden Glades Gen. Hosp., Miami, Fla., 1992—, gen. counsel, 1991—, Bank of North Am., Miami, 1992—. Mem. Fla. Bar Assn., Calif. Bar Assn., Md. Bar Assn., D.C. Bar Assn., Fla. State Bar (exec. com. on corp. counsel com.). Democrat. Roman Catholic. Home: 607 Velarde Ave Coral Gables FL 33134-7044 Office: Bank of North Am Golden Glades Med Plz 8701 SW 137th Ave Ste 301 Miami FL 33183-4498

MUDD, ROGER HARRISON, news broadcaster, educator; b. Washington, Feb. 9, 1928; s. Kostka and Irma Iris (Harrison) M.; m. Emma Jeanne Spears, Oct. 26, 1957; children: Daniel H., Maria M., Jonathan, Matthew M. AB, Washington and Lee U., 1950; MA, U. N.C., 1953. Tchr. Darlington Sch., Rome, 1951-52; reporter Richmond News Leader, Va., 1953; news dir. Sta. WRNL, Richmond, 1953-56; reporter radio and TV Sta. WTOP, Washington, 1956-61; corr. CBS, 1961-80; chief Washington corr. NBC, 1980-87; Congl. corr. MacNeil/Lehrer News Hour, 1987-92; prof. journalism Princeton U., 1992-94, Washington & Lee U., 1995-96. Host The History Channel, 1995—. Trustee Randolph-Macon Women's Coll., Lynchburg, Va., 1971-78, Robert F. Kennedy Journalism Awards Com., 1971-78, Blue Ridge Sch., Dyke, Va., 1978-84; bd. dirs. Fund for Investigative Journalism, PEN/Faulkner, 1985-92, Va. Found. for Humanities, Va. Hist. Soc., 1988-94, RIAS Berlin Commn., 1996-99, Va. Found. for Ind. Colls., 1997—, Nat. Portrait Gallery Commn., 1997—, Civil War Trust, 1999-01; mem. adv. com. Mt. Vernon Ladies Assn., Eudora Welty Found., 2002—; bd. dirs. Media Gen., 1998-01. With AUS, 1945-47. Mem. Radio-TV Corr. Assn. (chmn. exec. com. 1969-70).

MUDD, SIDNEY PETER, former beverage company executive; b. St. Louis, Jan. 21, 1917; s. Urban Sidney and Hallie Newell (Perry) M.; m. Ada Marie Herbermann, Oct. 22, 1942; children: Sidney Peter, Ada Marie, Peter, Michael, Mary, Elizabeth, Catherine. AB magna cum laude, St. Louis U., 1938; L.H.D., Coll. New Rochelle, N.Y., 1974; LHD, Iona Coll., 1985. Distr. Joyce Seven-Up, Chgo., 1938, sales mgr., 1939, coordinator N.Y. ops., 1941, v.p. charge ops., 1949-51; exec. v.p. N.Y. Seven-Up Bottling Co., Inc., New Rochelle, 1951-63, pres., 1963-73, dir., 1952-84, chmn. bd., 1973-84; pres. Joyce Beverages, Inc. (Joyce Advt.), 1973-84; past chmn. bd. Joyce Beverages/N.Y., N.J., Conn., Ill., Wis. Past dir. Joyce Beverages Inc., Joyce Advt., Joyce Beverages/N.Y., N.J., Conn., Chgo., Washington, Wis., Ill., Joyce Assocs.; dir., vice-chmn. Westchester Fed. Savs. Bank; bd. dirs. Marine Midland Bank Regional Bd., chmn. 1987-88. Past pres., bd. trustees St. Joseph's Hosp., N.Y.C., St. Francis Hosp.; chmn. Westchester County Assn.; past bd. lay advisers St. Agnes Hosp., White Plains; past chmn. bd. trustees Coll. of New Rochelle; past bd. dirs. U.S. Cath. Hist. Soc.; former trustee St. Louis U.; bd. dirs., v.p. John M. and Mary A. Joyce Found.; chmn. N.Y. Industry-Labor Com. for Resource Recovery; bd. dirs. Am. Alliance Resource Recovery Interests, Westchester Pub. Issues Inst., 2001-; pres. New Rochelle Devel. Council; bd. dirs. Keep Am. Beautiful, Inc.; chmn. Westchester 2000, 1984-2000. Served with USNR. Decorated Knight of Malta, knight Equestrian Order of Holy Sepulchre; recipient St. Louis U. Alumni award, 1967, Dr. Martin Luther King, Jr. award New Rochelle Community Action Agy., 1978, New Rochelle K.C. Civic award, 1978, Outstanding Citizen award New Rochelle YMCA, 1979, Disting. Service award Westchester region NCCJ, 1980, Medallion award Westchester Community Coll. Found., 1981; honoring resolution N.Y. State Senate, 1982; honoring resolution N.Y. State Assembly, 1982; honoring proclamation County of Westchester, City of Yonkers, City of White Plains, 1982; ARC award of excellence, 1983, Man of Yr. award Beverage Industry, 1974, Disting. Service award Sr. Personnel Employment Council, 1986, Disting. Achievement award Mental Health Assn., 1987, Disting. Citizen award New Rochelle Hosp. Med. Ctr., 1990; named to St. Louis U. Sports Hall of Fame, 1976, Beverage World Hall of Fame, 1984. Mem. Nat. Soft Drink Assn. (dir., pres. 1974-76, Disting. Achievement award 1980), N.Y. State Soft Drink Assn. (pres. 1966-67, Disting. Service award 1985, 86), Theta Kappa Phi, Crown and Anchor Soc. (St. Louis U.), Westchester County Assn. (Chmn.'s award 2002). Clubs: Winged Foot Golf (Westchester) (founder, past v.p., dir.); Sales and Mktg. Execs. *A happy life, a successful life is a life lived in love; love of God; love of self, love of others. To love and be loved is life's greatest reward on earth.*

MUDER, ROBERT RICHARD, physician, epidemiologist; b. Pitts., June 11, 1951; s. Richard Edward and Gemma (Lombardi) M.; m. Janet D. Vlha, June 4, 1977 (div. 1993); children: Jane Elizabeth, Michael Richard. BA, Oberlin (Ohio) Coll., 1973; MD, U. Pitts., 1977. Diplomate Am. Bd. Internal Medicine. Intern, then resident in medicine Mercy Hosp., Pitts., 1977-81, asst. coord. med. edn., 1983-84, coord. med. edn., 1984-86, assoc. program dir., 1986-89, fellow in infectious disease, 1981-83; asst. prof. medicine U. Pitts., 1989-94, assoc. prof., 1994—2001, prof., 2002—; chief infection control Pitts. VA Med. Ctr., 1986—. Sect. editor Infectious Disease Alert; contbr. articles to profl. jours. Mem. ACP, Am. Soc. for Microbiology, Infectious Diseases Soc. Am., Soc. for Healthcare Epidemiology Am., Phi Beta Kappa, Alpha Omega Alpha. Office: VA Pitts Healthcare Sys University Dr # C Pittsburgh PA 15240 E-mail: robert.muder@med.va.gov.

MUDGE, LEWIS SEYMOUR, theologian, educator, university dean; b. Phila., Oct. 22, 1929; s. Lewis Seymour and Anne Evelyn (Bolton) M.; m. Jean Bruce McClure, June 15, 1957; children: Robert Seymour, William McClure, Anne Evelyn. BA, Princeton U., 1951, M Div, 1955, PhD (Kent fellow), 1961; BA with honors in Theology, Oxford (Eng.) U., 1954, MA (Rhodes scholar), 1958. Ordained to ministry Presbyn. Ch., 1955. Presbyn. univ. pastor Princeton, 1955-56; sec. dept. theology World Alliance Ref. Chs., Geneva, 1957-62; minister to coll. Amherst Coll., 1962-68, asst. prof. philosophy and religion, 1962-64, assoc. prof., 1964-70, prof. philosophy and religion, 1970-76, chmn. dept. philosophy and religion, 1968-69, 75-76; dean faculty, prof. theology McCormick Theol. Sem., Chgo., 1976-87, San Francisco Theol. Sem., 1987—; prof. Grad. Theol. Union, Berkeley, Calif., 1987-95; dir. Ctr. for Hermeneutical Studies, Grad. Theol. Union/U. Calif., 1990-97; Stuart prof. theology Grad. Theol. Union, Calif., 1995—. Mem. commn. on faith and order Nat. Council Chs., 1965-70; sec. spl. com. on confession faith United Presbyn Ch., 1965-67, chmn. spl. com. on theology of the call, 1968-71; chmn. theol. commn. U.S. Consultation on Ch. Union, 1977-89; co-chmn. Internat. Ref.-Roman Cath. Dialogue Commn., 1983-90; observer Extraordinary Synod Bishops, 1985. Author: One Church: Catholic and Reformed, 1963, Is God Alive?, 1963, Why is the Church in the World?, 1967, The Crumbling Walls, 1970, The Sense of a People: Toward a Church for the Human Future, 1992, The Church as Moral Community, 1998, Rethinking the Beloved Community, 2001; also numerous articles and revs.; editor: Essays on Biblical Interpretation (Paul Ricoeur), 1980, (with James Poling) Formation and Reflection: the Promise of Practical Theology, 1987, (with Thomas Wieser) Democratic Contracts for Sustainable and Caring Societies, 2000. Pres. Westminster Found. in New Eng., 1963-67; chmn. bd. Nat. Vocation Agy., 1972-75; mem. com. selection Rhodes Scholars, Vt., 1966, Wis., 1983-85, Iowa, 1986. Mem. Phi Beta Kappa. Democrat. Home: 2444 Hillside Ave Berkeley CA 94704-2529 Office: Grad Theol Union 2905 Dwight Way Berkeley CA 94704-2514 E-mail: lewismudge@aol.com.

MUDGIL, LALTA RANI, internist, geriatrician; b. Sialkot, Punjab, India, Jan. 30, 1940; came to U.S., 1969; d. Dina Nath and Krishna Rani (Alagh) Dewan; m. Virat Mudgil, June 3, 1967 (div. Sept. 1977); children: Ananth Vijay, Adarsh Vijay. MD, All India Inst. Med. Scis., New Delhi, 1967; BSc, Isabella Thoburn Coll., Lucknow, India, 1957; MBBS, Christian Med. Coll., Ludhiana, India, 1962. Diplomate Am. Bd. Family Practice; diplomate in internal medicine and geriatrics Am. Bd. Internal Medicine. Intern Edgewater Hosp., Chgo., 1970; fellow in clin. pharmacology Hahnemann Med. Ctr., Phila., 1971, NYU, N.Y.C., 1972-73; attending, emergency room, primary care, internal medicine Kings County Hosp., Bklyn., 1973-78; resident Maimonides Hosp., 1978-79, Coney Island Hosp., Bklyn., 1979-80; attending and staff physician VA Hosp., 1980—. Instr. medicine Downstate Med. Ctr., Bklyn., 1985-2000, asst. prof., 2000—; tchg. fellow in pharmacology, lectr. All India Inst. Med. Scis., New Delhi, 1965-69, Bangalore (India) Med. Coll., 1968-69, St. Johns Med. Coll., Bangalore. Contbr. articles to profl. jours. Active Radha Swami Meetings, N.Y.C., 1977—, Rama Krishna Ashram of India, Calcutta, 1968—. Col. Army, 1981—. Fellow ACP. Republican. Hindu. Home: 151 S Kensington Ave Rockville Centre NY 11570-5616 E-mail: mudgil.lalta_R@new_york.va.gov.

MUDROCH, KIMBERLY ANN, veterinarian; b. Jonesboro, Ark., Mar. 7, 1969; d. Jackie Harold and Marcia Gail (Fuller) M.; m. Vance Andrew Aldridge, Aug. 30, 1997; 1 child, Gregory Dean Aldridge. BS in Agrl. Scis. and Natural Resources, Okla. State U., 1992, DVM, 1995. Veterinarian Garvin County Vet. Hosp., Elmore City, Okla., 1995-97, Profl. Animal Health Ctr., Newcastle, 1997—. Mem. Am. Vet. Med. Assn., Okla. Vet. Med. Assn. Avocations: outdoor activities, show pigs, exercise. Office: Profl Animal Health Ctr 2005 S Main St Newcastle OK 73065-5342

MUDRY, MICHAEL, pension and benefit consultant; b. Lucina, Czechoslovakia, Dec. 5, 1926; (parents Am. citizens); s. John Zaleta and Helen (Molchan) M.; m. Kendall Archer, June 17, 1960; children: F. Goodrich Archer, Benjamin Kendall. BA, U. Conn., 1951. Sr. v.p. Hay/Huggins Co. Inc., Phila., 1956-93; self-employed pension and benefit cons. Wayne, Pa., 1994—. Former actuary Ch. Pensions Conf. Contbr. articles to profl. jours. Bd. mem., actuary Am. Coun. on Gift Annuities, Indpls., 1978—. Served with U.S. Army, 1945-46. Fellow: Conf. Cons. Actuaries, Soc. Actuaries; mem.: Internat. Assn. Cons. Actuaries, Internat. Actuarial Assn., Am. Acad. Actuaries, Tri-State Jazz Soc. (bd. dirs. 2001—, treas. 2001—).

MUECHLER, EBERHARD KARL, physician; b. Radebuel, Germany, Mar. 6, 1939; came to U.S., 1966; s. Hans Karl Wilhelm and Dorothea (Knorn) M.; m. Deirdre Margaret Lagone, Oct. 23, 1971; children: Christian, Danielle, Brittany. MD, U. Tuebingen, Germany, 1964. Intern Monmouth Med. Ctr., Long Branch, N.J., 1966-67; resident Downstate U., Bklyn., 1967-71; fellow in reproductive endocrinology U. Pa., Phila., 1971-73; asst. prof. U. Miss., Jackson, 1973-74, U. Rochester, N.Y., 1974-80, assoc. prof., 1980-87; pvt. practice Inst. Reproductive Health and Infertility, Rochester, 1987—. Dir. dept. gynecology Park-Ridge Hosp., Rochester, 1991—. Author chpt. to book. Fellow Ford Found., 1971-73. Mem. AAAS, Am. Soc. Reproductive Medicine, Am. Coll. Ob-Gyn., Am. Assn. Gynecology Laproscopy, Endocrine Soc., Soc. Reproductive Endocrinology. Republican. Avocations: windsurfing, skiing, swimming, camping. Office: Inst Reproductive Health and Infertility 1561 Long Pond Rd Rochester NY 14626-4117 E-mail: e.k.muechler@aol.com.

MUEHL, LOIS BAKER, freelance/self-employed writer, retired secondary school educator; b. Oak Park, Ill., Apr. 29, 1920; d. Arthur Franklin and Mary Hull Baker; m. Siegmar Muehl, Apr. 15, 1944; children: Erika, Sigrid, Torsten, Brian. BA in English, Oberlin Coll., 1941; MA in English Edn., U. Iowa, 1966.

English tchr., drama coach Upper Sandusky (Ohio) H.S., 1941—42; TV sta. camera operator, actress WZXBK, Chgo., 1942—43; news anchor WIS Radio Sta., Columbia, SC, 1944; freelance writer, 1959—; dir. reading lab., assoc. prof. rhetoric U. Iowa, Iowa City, 1964—66, 1968—85; reading specialist Johnson C. Smith U., Charlotte, NC, 1966—68; English tchr. Hohei U., Nanjing, China, 1987—88. Tchr. creative writing, adult edn. Iowa City Pub. Schs., 1961—63; tchr. ESL adult edn. Merced (Calif.) Pub. Schs., 1984, 86, Kyungnam U., Masan, Republic of Korea, 1985. Author: My Name is ______, 1959 (Jr. Lit. Guild choice), Worst Room in the School, 1961 (N.Y. Times 100 Best List, 1961), The Hidden Year of Devlin Bates, 1967, Winter Holiday Brainteasers, 1979, A Reading Approach to Rhetoric, 1983, Talkable Tales, 1993; co-author: Trading Cultures in the Classroom, 1993; : New Adventures of Mother Goose, 1993, contbr. poetry to: Golf, It's Just a Game, 1996, : Phonics Through Poetry, 1998; contbr. Vol. tchr. writing Sr. Ctr., Iowa City, 1991—93; co-founder, sustainer wild flower pk. Neighborhood Assn., 1998—. Recipient Cmty. Svc. commendation, Merced County, Calif., 1984, award, Lucidity, Midwest Poetry Rev., Grand prize, The Poetry Guild, 1997; fellow Old Gold Creative fellowship, U. Iowa, 1980. Mem.: Univ. Club Writers' Group, Iowa Poetry Assn. (area rep. 1990—, poetry prize), Nat. League Am. PEN Women (treas. 1990—, poetry prize, prizes for craft work), Phi Beta Kappa. Avocations: folk art, gardening, swimming, beachcombing, yoga.

MUEHLBAUER, JAMES HERMAN, manufacturing executive; b. Evansville, Ind., Nov. 13, 1940; s. Herman Joseph and Anna Louise (Overfield) M.; m. Mary Kay Koch, June 26, 1965; children: Stacey, Brad, Glen, Beth, Katy. BSME, Purdue U., 1963, MS Indsl. Adminstrn., 1964. Registered profl. engr. Engr. George Koch Sons, Inc., Evansville, 1966-67, chief estimator, 1968-72, chief engr., 1973-74, v.p., 1975-81, dir., 1978—, exec. v.p., 1982-98, Koch Ent., Inc., 1999—; pres. George Koch Sons LLC, 1999—. V.p., bd. dirs. Brake Supply Co., Evansville, Gibbs Die Casting Corp., Henderson, Ky., Uniseal, Inc., Evansville; bd. dirs. Fifth Third Bank Indiana, George Koch Sons (Europe) Ltd., Lichfield, Eng., Red Spot Paint & Varnish Co., Inc., Evansville, Koch Air LLC, Evansville, George Koch Sons de Mex., Monterrey, George Koch Sons GmbH, Cologne. Co-author: Tool & Manufacturing Engineering Handbook, 1976; patentee in paint finishing equipment. Bd. dirs., past pres. Evansville Indsl. Found., 1980—; bd. dirs., past pres., past campaign chmn. United Way S.W. Ind., Evansville, 1983—; bd. dirs., past vice-chmn. Univ. So. Ind. Found., Evansville, 1988-2001; bd. dirs. Deaconess Hosp., Evansville, 1986—, treas., 1991-96, vice-chmn., 1999—; bd. dirs. Cath. Found. Southwestern Ind., 1998—; dir. bd. visitors U. So. Ind. Sch. Bus., 1997—, chmn., 2001-02; bd. dirs. Ind. Assn. United Ways, 2000—, Alliance Indpls., 1997-99, pres. 1999; mem. Brute Soc., Cath. Diocese Evansville, 1997, Equestrian Order of the Holy Sepulchre of Jerusalem, 1996—. Named Engr. of Yr. S.W. chpt. Ind. Soc. Profl. Engrs., 1983; recipient Tech. Achievement award Tri-State Coun. for Sci. and Engring., Evansville, 1984, Purdue U. Alumni Citizenship award, 1991. [e]m. Soc. Mfg. Engrs. (past nat. chmn. finishing and coating tech. divsn.), ASME, NSPE, Evansville Country Club, Evansville Petroleum Club, Evansville Kennel Club (bd. dirs. 1997-2001). Republican. Roman Catholic. Home: 2300 E Gum St Evansville IN 47714-2338 Office: Koch Enterprises 14 S 11th Ave Evansville IN 47744-0001 E-mail: jhm@kochllc.com.

MUEHLEISEN, GENE, retired protective services administrator, state official; b. San Diego, Dec. 28, 1915; s. Adolph and Vesta C. (Gates) M.; m. Elsie Jane Conover, Sept. 14, 1940 (dec. Mar. 17, 1999); 1 son, John Robert. Student, San Diego State Coll., 1935-39, San Diego Jr. Coll., 1957. U.S. park ranger Yosemite Nat. Park, summers 1936-39, 79-84; with San Diego Police Dept., 1940-60, dir. tng., 1957-59, comdg. officer patrol div., capt., 1958-60; exec. dir. Commn. on Peace Officer Standards and Tng., Calif. Dept. Justice, Sacramento, 1960-65, 67-76; assoc. dir. Pres.'s Commn. on Law Enforcement and Adminstrn. of Justice, Nat. Crime Commn., 1965-67; chmn. police sci. adv. com. San Diego Jr. Coll., 1957-60, police sci. faculty, 1957-60; staff instr. San Diego Police Acad., 1954-60; guest instr. police adminstrn. Sacramento State Coll., 1964; grad. FBI Nat. Acad. 51st Session, 1953, pres. of class, guest faculty, 1963-66; cons. Ford Found. Internat. Assn. Chiefs of Police Project, 1964-67. Cons. U.S. Nat. Park Svc., 1965-84, spl. asst. to regional dir. Western region, 1977-79; adviser Royal Can. Mounted Police, 1961—; guest lectr., 1960—. Composer music. U.S. rep. Interpol Symposium on Police Edn. and Tng., Paris, 1965; mem. adv. com. FBI, 1972—; vice-chmn. Calif. Commn. Peace Officer Stds. and Tng., 1959—60; chmn. police svcs. task force Calif. Coun. Criminal Justice, 1968—78; mem. Atty. Gen.'s Commn. Police and Cmty. Rels., 1971—, Gov.'s Pub. Safety Planning Coun., 1974—; bd. dirs. San Diego Hist. Soc.; chmn. Atty. Gen.'s Com. on Law Enforcement Stds., 1957—59; mem. adv. com. on police tng. Ford Found., 1964—. Active duty USN, 1940—45, WWII, capt. USNR, 1940—75. The Gene Muehleisen Nature Area, Valley Oak Park, Sacramento dedicated, 1992. Mem. Nat. Conf. Police Assns. (com. chmn.), Calif. Peace Officers Assn. (com. chmn.), Peace Officers Research Assn. Calif. (pres. 1959-60, com. chmn.), Am. Soc. Pub. Adminstrn. (dir. San Diego County chpt.), Nat. Assn. State Dirs. Law Enforcement Tng. (pres. 1972-73), Am. Corrections Assn., Calif. Assn. Adminstrn. of Justice Educators, Park Rangers Assn. of Calif., Internat. Police Assn. (life, v.p. region 29 USA), Internat. Assn. Chiefs of Police (life), Calif. Parks and Recreation Soc. (Citizen of Yr. 1992), Sacramento Tree Found. (tech. adv. com. 1983—). Clubs: Kiwanis, San Diego Ski (pres.). Home and Office: 4221 Corona Way Sacramento CA 95864-5301

MUELLEMAN, ROBERT LEO, physician, researcher medical educator; b. Omaha, July 4, 1957; s. Joseph John and Virginia Lee (Fromm) M.; m. Diane Marie Schekirke, June 18, 1982; children: Therese, Thomas, Daniel, Robert. BS cum laude, U. Nebr., Omaha, 1979, MD with honors, 1984. Diplomate Am. Bd. Emergency Medicine. Emergency medicine resident Truman Med. Ctr., Kansas City, Mo., 1984-87, rsch. fellowship, 1987-88; asst. prof. U. Nebr. Med. Ctr., Omaha, 1988-93; assoc. prof. U. Mo., Kansas City, 1993-98; med. dir. Dept. Emergency Medicine Nebr. Health Sys., 1998—; sect. chief emergency medicine U. Nebr. Med. Ctr., Omaha, 1998—, assoc. prof., 1998-2000, prof., 2000—. Mem. injury control adv. com. Mo. Dept. Health, Jefferson City, 1994-98, co-dir. rsch. Dept. Emergency Medicine, 1993-98. Contbr. chpt. to book and articles to profl. jours. Fellow Am. Coll. Emergency Physicians (trauma care and injury control com. 1996-98); mem. Soc. Acad. Emergency Medicine, Alpha Omega Alpha. Democrat. Roman Catholic. Avocations: family, reading, outdoors. Office: Nebr Med Ctr Emergency Dept 981150 Nebr Med Ctr Omaha NE 68198-0001

MUELLER, BARBARA STEWART (BOBBIE MUELLER), youth drug use prevention specialist, volunteer; b. Weslaco, Tex., Oct. 5, 1934; d. Roy Wesley Stewart and Marjorie Eleanor (Crossley) Willis; m. Charles Paul Mueller, Sept. 5, 1957 (div. 1985); children: Kathryn Anne Bencomo, John Stewart. BA, U. Tex., 1957. Owner Kid Puppets and Co., San Antonio. Cons. Parent Music Resource Ctr., Washington, 1986; drug edn. prevention chmn. U.S. Attys. Office, San Antonio, 1989-90; prevention chmn. Mayor's Alcohol and Drug Task Force, San Antonio, 1986-88. Author: (childrens TV): Henry Blue Shoe KONO-TV San Antonio, 1957; contbr. articles to profl. publs. Sec. Alamo Heights (Tex.) Recreation Coun., 1977-78; pres. San Antonio Petroleum Aux., 1978-79; founder, pres. Community Families in Action, 1980-89; trustee Youth Alternatives, Inc., 1983-85; mem. allocation panel United Way, 1988-90; mem. alcolol and drug adv. com. N.E. Ind. Sch. Dist., 1986-91; mem. drug free schs. com. S.W. Ind. Sch. Dist., 1991-92; regional coord. Texans War on Drugs, 1988-92; vol. U.S. Dept. Justice, San Antonio, 1984-88; mem. proclamation com. Stop Tex. Epidemic, 1982 Recipient Yr. award Drug Awareness Ctr., San Antonio, 1984, Bexar Co. Med. Soc. Aux., San Antonio, 1984, Gov.'s Cert., Texans War on Drugs, Austin, 1982, Commendation U.S. Pres. Child Safety Partnership, Washington, 1986. Mem. Women in Communications, Inc. (hon.) (Pub. Awareness award 1984), Zeta Tau Alpha (sec., v.p., pres. San Antonio chpt. 1969-77, Nat. Merit award 1980). Avocations: genealogy, puppetry, hand embroidery, creative writing.

MUELLER, BETTY JEANNE, social work educator; b. Wichita, Kans., July 7, 1925; d. Bert C. and Clara A. (Pelton) Judkins; children— Michael J., Madelynn J. MSSW, U. Wis., Madison, 1964, PhD, 1969. Asst. prof. U. Wis., Madison, 1969-72; vis. asso. prof. Bryn Mawr (Pa.) Coll., 1971-72; asso. prof., dir. social work Cornell U., Ithaca, N.Y., 1972-78, prof. human svcs. studies, 1979-96, prof. policy and mgmt., 1996-98, prof. emeritus, 1998—. Nat. cons. Head Start, Follow Through, Appalachian Regional Commn., N.Y. State Office Planning Svcs., N.Y. State Dept. Social Svcs., N.Y. State Divsn. Mental Hygiene, Nat. Congress PTA, ILO; mem. internat. adv. com. Family Resources Tng. Ctr., Singapore, 1999—. Author: (with H. Morgan) Social Services in Early Education, 1974, (with R. Reinoehl) Computers in Human Service Education, 1989, Determinants of Human Behavior, 1995; contbr. articles to profl. jours. Recipient Fulbright Rsch. award, 1990; grantee, HEW, 1974—76, 1979—80, State of N.Y., 1975—95, Israeli Jewish Agy., 1985—87. Mem. Leadership Am., Chi Omega. Democrat. Unitarian Universalist. Home: 412 Highland Rd Ithaca NY 14850-2216 Office: Cornell U Policy and Mgmt 108 MVR Hall Ithaca NY 14853 E-mail: bjm5@cornell.edu.

MUELLER, CARL RICHARD, theater arts educator, author; b. St. Louis, Oct. 7, 1931; s. Anton John and Bonita Blanche (Lacy) M. BS, Northwestern U., 1954; MA, UCLA, 1960, PhD, 1967; cert., Freie U., Berlin, 1961. Prof. theater dept. Sch. Theater, Film and Television UCLA, 1967—; dramaturg New Theatre, Inc., L.A., 1975-2000. Cons. U. Calif. Press, 1972—. Translator plays published include Buechner: Complete Plays and Prose, 1963, Brecht: The Visions of Simone Machard, 1965, Brecht: The Measures Taken, 1977, Hauptmann: The Weavers, 1965, Hebbel: Maria Magdalena, 1962, Strindberg: A Dream Play and The Ghost Sonata, 1966, Strindberg: Five Major Plays, 2000, Schnitzler: La Ronde and Game of Love, 1964, Hofmannsthal: Electra, 1964, Wedekind: The Marquis of Keith, 1964, Wedekind: The Lulu Plays, 1967, Wedekind: Four Major Plays, 2000, Zuckmayer: The Captain of Koepenick, 1972, Horváth: Tales from the Vienna Woods, 1998, Schnitzler: Four Major Plays, 1999, Sophocles: The Complete Plays, 2000, Pirandello: Three Major Plays, 2000, Kleist: Three Major Plays, 2000, Wedekind: Four Plays, vol. 2, 2002, Strindberg: Five Major Plays, vol. 2, 2002; translator plays produced include Anon: The Puppet Play of Dr. Johannes Faustus, Hauptmann: The Beaver Coat, Schnitzler: Dr. Bernhardi, Schnitzler: Anatol, Sternheim: The Underpants, Brecht: Mother Courage, Brecht: Caucasian Chalk Circle, Brecht: The Trial of Joan of Arc, Brecht: In the Jungle of Cities, Brecht: Man is Man, Brecht: He Who Says Yes, Brecht: He Who Says No, Brecht: The Exception and the Rule, Brecht: Round Heads, Peaked Heads, Brecht: Schweyk in the Second World War, Kleist: The Broken Jug, 1992, Lessing: Nathan the Wise, 1993, Toller, The Blind Goddess, 1993, Sophokles, Elektra, 1994, Zweig, Volpone, 1995, Sternheim, The Snob, 1996; gen. editor Visual Resources, Inc., 1976-2000; theater editor Mankind mag., 1975-82; editor New Theater/Teatro Nuevo, 1985-87; author catalogue and slides A Visual History of European Theater Arts, 1978, A Visual History of European Experimental Theater, 1983, Greek and Roman Classical Theatre Structures and Performance Iconography, 1991, Medieval Theater and Performance Iconography, 1991, The Theater of Meyerhold, 1992, Stanislavsky and the Moscow Art Theater, 1992, The Commedia dell'Arte, 1992, Russian Scene and Costume Design, vols. 1 and 2, 1993, The Baroque Stage, 1993, 18th and 19th Cen. European Theater Structures, Performance Iconography and Costume Designs, 1994, Renaissance Theater Structures, Performance Iconography and Costume Designs, 1994, The Genius of the Russian Theatre 1900-1990, 1995, 20th Century World Theater, From Appia to Dali, 1900-50, vol. 1, 1996, 20th Century World Theater, From Mother Courage to Hair, 1951-68, vol. 2, 1996, 20th Century World Theater, From Svoboda to Hockney, 1968-91, vol. 3, 1996, The Genius of the Russian Theater, From Meyerhold to the Present, 1996, Contemporary European Experimental Theater, vol. 1, Italy and Germany, 1996, The Classical Experience: The Greek Theater and Its World, 1996, The Classical Experience: The Roman Theater and Its World, 1996; dir.: (plays) Spring's Awakening, Endangered Species, Hedda Gabler, My Body, Frankly Yours, Hamlet, Macbeth, Dionysos. Served with U.S. Army, 1954-56. Recipient Samuel Goldwyn Creative Writing award Goldwyn Found., 1959; Fulbright exchange grantee Berlin, 1960-61 Mem. Internat. Arthur Schnitzler Research Assn., UCLA Center for Medieval and Renaissance Studies (mem. adv. com. 1980-83) Democrat. Office: UCLA Dept Theater Sch Theater Film TV 102 E Melnitz Box 951622 Los Angeles CA 90095-1622 E-mail: cmueller@tft.ucla.edu. *Communication has always been the primary goal of my life. The challenge of passing on to generations of new students the life sustaining ideas of human culture is formidable; the joy of searching out new ideas and methods of thought and action is a privilege of which far too few of us take proper advantage.*

MUELLER, CHARLES BARBER, surgeon, educator; b. Carlinville, Ill., Jan. 22, 1917; s. Gustav Henry and Myrtle May (Barber) M.; m. Jean Mahaffey, Sept. 7, 1940; children: Frances Ann, John Barber, Richard Carl, William Gustav. AB, U. Ill., 1938; MD, Washington U., St. Louis, 1942; LHD (honoris causa), Blackburn Coll., 1987; BSc (hon.) , SUNY, 2002. Intern, then resident in surgery Barnes Hosp., St. Louis, 1942-43, 46-51; asst. prof. Washington U. Med. Sch., 1951-56; prof. surgery, chmn. dept. State U. N.Y. Med. Sch., Syracuse, 1956-67; prof. surgery McMaster U. Med. Sch., Hamilton, Ont., Can., 1967—, chmn. dept., 1967-72. Contbr. articles to med. jours. Served with USNR, 1943-46. Decorated Purple Heart with 2 oak leaf clusters, Bronze Star; recipient Favorite Son award So. Ill. Med. Soc., 1996; Jackson Johnson fellow, 1938-42; Rockefeller postwar asst., 1946-49; Markle scholar, 1949-54. Mem. ACS (v.p. 1987-88, Disting. Svc. award 1984), Am. Surg. Assn., Ctrl. Surg. Assn., Soc. Univ. Surgeons, Assn. Acad. Surgery, Royal Coll. Physicians and Surgeons (Duncan Graham Disting. Svc. award 1992), Phi Beta Kappa, Sigma Xi, Alpha Omega Alpha, Phi Kappa Phi. Home: 139 Dalewood Crescent Hamilton ON Canada L8S 4B8 Office: McMaster U 1200 Main St W Hamilton ON Canada L8N 3Z5

MUELLER, CHARLES FREDERICK, radiologist, educator; b. Dayton, Ohio, May 26, 1936; s. Susan Elizabeth (Wine) W.; m. Kathe Louise Lutterbei, May 28, 1966; children: Charles Jeffrey, Theodore Martin, Kathryn Suzanne. BA in English, U. Cin., 1958, MD, 1962. Diplomate Am. Bd. Radiology, Am. Bd. Nuclear Medicine. Asst. prof. radiology U. N.Mex., Albuquerque, 1968-72, assoc. prof. radiology, 1972-74, Ohio State U., Columbus, 1974-79, acting chmn. dept. radiology, 1975, prof. radiology, 1979—, prof. radiology, dir. post grad. program radiology, 1980-2000, acting chmn. dept. radiology, 1990—93, prof. emeritus, 2002—. Bd. dirs. Univ. Radiologists, Inc., Columbus, v.p., 1980-86; pres., founder Ambulatory Imaging, Inc., Columbus, 1985—. Author: Emergency Radiology, 1982; contbr. articles to profl. jours.; editl. bd. Emergency radiology, 1995—; editor Internat. Trauma, Am. Jour. Roentgenology, 1997—. Com. chmn. Boy Scouts of Am., Columbus, 1980-84. Served to capt. USAF, 1966-68. Research grantee Ohio State U. 1975, Gen. Electric Co., 1986-88; Gold medalist ASER, 2001. Fellow Am. Coll. Radiologists; mem. AMA, Assn. Univ. Radiologists, Am. Roentgen Ray Soc., Am. Soc. Emergency Radiology (founder 1988, pres. 1993-94, Gold medal 2001), Radiol. Soc. N.Am., N.Mex. Soc. Radiologists (pres. 1973-74), Ohio State Radiol. Soc. (pres. 1986-87). Lodges: Commandery #6, Consistory. Republican. Presbyterian. Avocations: flying, fly fishing, hiking. Office: Ohio State Univ Hosps Dept Radiology 410 W 10th Ave Columbus OH 43210-1240

MUELLER, DIANE MAYNE, lawyer; b. Milw., Aug. 8, 1934; d. George and Ann (Matuszewski) Markussen; widowed; 1 child, Paul Wilhite; m. Milton W. Mueller, Jan. 1, 1990. AB, Valparaiso U., 1956; MSW, Fla. State U., 1963; JD summa cum laude, DePaul U., 1974. Bar: Ill. 1974, U.S. Dist. Ct. (no. dist.) Ill. 1974, U.S. Dist. Ct. (ea. dist.) Wis. 1977, N. Mex., 1996. Assoc. Seyfarth, Shaw, Fairweather & Geraldson, Chgo., 1974-82, ptnr., 1982-86; asst. group counsel LTV Steel Co., Cleve., 1986-93, sr. atty., 1993-95. Adj. prof. Northwestern U. Sch. Law, 1984-86. Mem. Exec. Club of Chgo. (chmn. bd. 1984-85, mem. adv. bd. 1986-96), Econ. Club Chgo., Albuquerque Petroleum Club. Home: 1216 Rock Rose Rd Albuquerque NM 87122-1115

MUELLER, EDWARD ALBERT, retired transportation engineer executive; b. Madison, Wis., May 12, 1923; s. Edward F. and Lulu (Wittl) M.; m. Margaret Wetzel, Sept. 12, 1953; children: Lynn, Karen. Student, U. Wis., 1941-43; BCE, Notre Dame U., 1947; cert. in traffic, Yale U., 1953; postgrad., Fla. State U., 1955-62; MCE, Catholic U. Am., 1967. Registered profl. engr., Fla. Project engr. Carl C. Crane, Inc., 1947-50; engr. Ammann & Whitney, Inc., Milw., 1950-52; rsch. asst. Yale U., 1953-55; asst. dir., dir. traffic and planning div. Fla. State Rd. Dept., Tallahassee, 1955-63; engr. traffic and ops. Transp. Rsch. Bd., Washington, 1963-70; sec. Fla. Dept. Transp., Tallahassee, 1970-72; exec. dir. Jacksonville (Fla.) Transp. Authority, 1972-80; mgr. transp. div. Reynolds, Smith & Hills, 1980-83; v.p. Morales and Shumer Engrs., Inc., 1983-95. Occasional lectr. U. Fla., 1971-76, U. N.Fla., 1974-76 Author: Steamboating on the St. Johns, 1979, Ocklawaha River Steamboats, 1983, St. Johns River Steamboats, 1986, Perilous Journeys, 1990, Upper Mississippi River Ratting Steamboats, 1995, Steamships of the Two Henrys, 1996, Along the St. Johns and Ocklawaha River, 1999, Queen of Sea Routes, 2000, The Savannah Line, 2001; contbr. engring. articles to profl. jours. Mem. Fla. Com. of 100, 1970-72; bd. dirs. Luth. Social Svcs., Jacksonville, 1982-94, v.p., 1981-91; regional v.p. Fla.-Ga. dist. Luth. Laymen's League, 1982-92; curator Jacksonville Maritime Mus., 1990-99, mem. exec. com., 1989-95, pres., 1993-95, exec. dir., 1995-99. Recipient Disting. Svc. award Coll. Engring., U. Fla., 1975, Samuel Ward Stanton award for lite achievement Steamship Hist. Soc. Am., 2001; named one of top 10 pub. works ofcls. in U.S., 1978. Mem. Southeastern Assn. State Hwy. Ofcls. (pres., v.p. 1971-72), Engrs. in Govt. (chmn., vice-chmn. sec.), Fla. Engring. Soc. (pres. Northeast chpt. 1982-83, Engr. of Yr. Tallahassee chpt. 1972, Jacksonville chpt. 1974, award for outstanding tech. achievement 1976, outstanding svc. to engring. profession 1989, James Shivler award 1993), Inst. Transp. Engrs. (pres. 1977, disting. svc. award Fla. sect. 1976), Fla. Transit Assn. (pres. 1974-75), Fla. Engring. Found. (sec. 1986-95). Lutheran. Home: 4734 Empire Ave Jacksonville FL 32207-2136 E-mail: eam27@juno.com.

MUELLER, GERHARD G(OTTLOB), retired financial accounting standard setter, retired educator; b. Eineborn, Germany, Dec. 4, 1930; came to U.S., 1952, naturalized, 1957; s. Gottlob Karl and Elisabeth Charlotte (Hossack) M.; m. Coralie George, June 7, 1958; children: Kent, Elisabeth, Jeffrey. AA, Coll. of Sequoias, 1954; BS with honors, U. Calif.-Berkeley, 1956, MBA, 1957, PhD, 1962; D Econs. (hon.), Swedish Sch. Econs. and Bus. Adminstrn., 1994; D Laws (hon.), Kwansei Gakuin U., 2000. CPA, Wash. Staff accountant FMC Corp., San Jose, Calif., 1957-58; faculty dept. accounting U. Wash., Seattle, 1960-96, assoc. prof., 1963-67, prof., 1967-96, chmn. dept., 1969-78, dir. grad. profl. acctg. program, 1979-90, sr. assoc. dean, 1990-95, acting dean, 1994, Hughes M. Blake prof. internat. bus. mgmt., 1992-95, Julius A. Roller prof. acctg., 1995-96, mem. fin. acctg. stds. bd., 1996—2001; ret., 2001. Dir. U. Wash. Acctg. Devel. Fund, Overlake Hosp. Med. Ctr., Bellevue, 1984-96, chmn. bd. trustees, 1991-93; cons. internat. tax matters U.S. Treasury Dept., 1963-68; cons. Internat. Acctg. Rsch., 1964-96; vis. prof. Cranfield Sch. Mgmt., Eng., 1973-74, U. Zurich, Switzerland, 1973-74; lectr. in field. Author: International Accounting, 1967; co-author: Introductory Financial Accounting, 3d edit., 1991, A Brief Introduction to Managerial and Social Uses of Accounting, 1975, International Accounting, 1978, 2nd edit., 1992, Accounting: An International Perspective, 1987, 4th edit., 1997; editor: Readings in International Accounting, 1969, Accounting-A Book of Readings, 2d edit., 1976, A New Introduction to Accounting, 1971, A Bibliography of Internat. Accounting, 3d edit., 1973, Essentials of Multinational Accounting— An Anthology, 1979, Frontiers of International Accounting, 1986, AACSB Curriculum Internationalization Resource Guide, 1988; contbr. chpts. to books, numerous articles to profl. jours. Expert legal witness, IRS, 1991-93. Recipient U. wash. Disting. Tchg. award, 1983, Disting. Svc. award, U. Wash., 1984; fellow Price Waterhouse Internat. Acctg. Rsch. fellow, 1962—64, Ford Found. fellow, 1958—59. Fellow Acad. Internat. Bus.; mem. AICPA (internat. practice exec. com. 1972-75, exec. coun. 1987-89, Disting. Achievement in Acctg. Edn. award 2000), Am. Acctg. Assn. (pres. 1988-89, acad. v.p. 1970-71, chmn. adv. bd. internat. acctg. sect. 1977-79, Wildman medal 1986, Nat. Outstanding Educator 1981, Disting. Internat. Lectr. in Black Africa 1987, Outstanding Internat. Acctg. Educator 1991), Fin. Execs. Inst., Wash. Soc. CPAs (pres. 1988-89, Outstanding Educator award 1985, Pub. Svc. award 1995), Acctg. Edn. Change Commn. (chmn. 1994-96), Beta Alpha Psi (Acad. Acct. of Yr. 1987), Beta Gamma Sigma (Disting. scholar 1978-79), Alpha Gamma Sigma. Home: 15794 Dovewood Ct Poway CA 92064-2282 Business E-Mail: gmueller@u.washington.edu. *It has always been important to me to associate with people and tangible and intangible things of the highest quality. I make it a practice to set clear goals and then pursue them actively. A broad world view on all aspects of life engenders more success and happiness than special interest perspectives. I welcome change in professional matters, but seek constancy in personal and family affairs. Fate has played a role in my successes. I believe in God, Protestant ethics, and the merits of classical academic scholarship.*

MUELLER, GERRY, retired computer company executive; b. N.Y.C., Mar. 17, 1944; s. John and Mary (Choisy) M.; m. Debra Pritt, Sept. 17, 2000. BA, St. Johns U., 1965; MBA, Adelphi U., 1970. Mktg. exec. IBM, White Plains, N.Y., 1967-84; pres., gen. mgr. Prodigy Network, 1985-97; ret. Avocations: wine collecting, golf. Home: 6738 N Ocean Blvd Ocean Ridge FL 33435

MUELLER, HELGA WILFRIEDE, economist; b. Esens, Germany, Jan. 12, 1960; came to U.S., 1990; d. Eilt Friedrich and Ida Magda (Eilts) M. Master's, U. Goettingen (Germany), 1985, PhD in Econs., 1990. Rsch. asst. U. Goettingen, Goettingen, 1985-90; economist World Bank, Washington, 1990—. Author: Internationale Kapitalbewegungen, 1992. Mem. Am. Econ. Assn. Avocations: theater, movies, books. Home: 1505 Crystal Dr Apt 404 Arlington VA 22202-4177

MUELLER, I. LYNN, strategic planning and communications consultant; b. Cin., Feb. 2, 1941; s. Irwin Ludwig and Helen Marie (Bloomfield) Mueller; m. Maria Rose Cavallino; children: Adria Whitney, Shallah Whitney, Geoffrey Koskinen. BBA, U. Cin., 1964, MBA, 1966; postgrad., George Washington U., 1966-68. V.p., founder Robert-Lynn Assocs., Ltd., Washington, 1968-72; spl. asst. N.Y. State Assembly Spkr., Albany, 1971-74; v.p. adminstrn. and fin. Epsilon Data Mgmt., Boston, 1974-75; founder, sr. v.p. First Tuesday Comms., Buffalo, 1974-78; v.p. cmty. affairs Gardenway Mgmt., Troy, 1976; pres. ILM Enterprises, Old Chatham, 1977-91; exec. dir. Minority Leader, N.Y. State Assembly, Albany, 1983-91; founder Decision Strategies Group, 1991—. Contbr. chpt. to book. Trustee Chatham (N.Y.) Meth. Ch., 1992-94; mem. Chatham Sch. Bd., 1990-93; Cons. to Gov. George Pataki Transition Com., 1994; advisor Morris Meml. Bd., Chatham, 1984-98; alumni rep. George Washington U., Albany, 1993—. Mem. Nat. Space Soc., Planetary Soc., Cin. Soc. (pres. 1961-62), McMicken Soc., Sigma Sigma, Omicron Delta Kappa, Alpha Kappa Psi, Beta Alpha Psi. Republican. Presbyterian. Avocations: basketball, tennis, sailing, bridge, reading non-fiction. Office: Decision Strategies Group Ste 2001 One Commerce Plz Albany NY 12210 E-mail: lynnmueller@decisionstrategiesgroup.com.

MUELLER, JAMES H. priest; b. Buffalo, Mar. 24, 1944; s. Henry Frank Mueller and Veronica Caroline Gorski. BA, St. John Vainney Sem., 1968, MDiv, 1969, MA, 1972; DMin, Fuller Theol. Sem., 1997. Parochial min. Roman Cath. Diocese of Buffalo, 1969—81, Archidioceses of Newark , Newark, Archidioceses of L.A., 1981—86, Roman Catholic Diocese of Phoenix, 1994—2000; asst. prof. philosophy and religious studies, campus min. Villa Maria Coll. of Buffalo, 1981—86; retreat dir., spl. dir. Carmelite Spiritual Ctr., Darien, Ill., 1986—88; exec. dir., prof. theology Kino Inst., Phoenix, 1988—94; chaplain Our Lady of Grace Carmelite Monastery, Christoval, Tex., 2001—. Mem.: Coun. Socs. for Study of Religion, Coll. Theol. Soc. Home: 6200 CR 339 # 2 Christoval TX 76935 Office: Our Lady of Grace Carmelite Monastery 62oo CR 339 # 2 Christoval TX 76935

MUELLER, JEAN MARGARET, nursing consultant; b. Huntington, N.Y., June 3, 1951; Diploma in Nursing, Pilgrim State Hosp., 1973; BSN, SUNY, Stony Brook, 1979; M in Profl. Studies, New Sch. for Social Rsch., 1986. RN, N.Y. Nurses aide Huntington Hosp., N.Y., 1971, LPN, 1972, RN, charge ICU/CCU, MICU/SICU, telemetry, 1973-77; charge nurse, MICU North Shore U. Hosp, Manhasset, 1977-78; private duty cases, Holter monitor scanning, 1978-84; dir. nursing svcs., assoc. dir. nursing svcs. Nesconset (N.Y.) Nursing Ctr., 1984-86; nursing edn. instr. St. Charles Hosp., Port Jefferson, N.Y.; labor and delivery nurse SUNY, Stony Brook; teaching and rsch. nurse II Diabetes Ctr., SUNY; tchg. hosp. insvc. educator I SUNY, 1990-94; hosp. nursing svcs. cons. Office Health Sys. Mgmt., N.Y. State Dept. Health, Hauppauge, N.Y., 1994—; team leader cross functional team pub. health edn. and info. N.Y. State Commr. Health, 1998—. Mem. adj. faculty Sch. of Nursing SUNY, Stony Brook, 1992—, St. Joseph's Coll., 1994; rsch. com. dept. family medicine with E. Stark, E.A.P.; hosp. nursing svcs. cons. office health sys. mgmt. N.Y. State Dept. Health, 1994—; lectr. Med., Emotional and Psychol. Indicators of Family Violence. Contbr. articles to profl. jours. Active Mothers Against Drunk Driving; mem. Suffolk County Family Violence Task Force. Recipient President's award for leadership tng. programs SUNY, 1993, for spl. needs of elderly tng. programs and humanistic approach to health care tng. programs, 1994. Mem. Nat. Nurses Assn., Sigma Theta Tau. Home: 234 Hallock Rd Stony Brook NY 11790-3026

MUELLER, JOHN ERNEST, political science educator, dance critic and historian; b. St. Paul, June 21, 1937; s. Ernst A. and Elsie E. (Schleh) M.; m. Judy A. Reader, Sept. 6, 1960; children: Karl, Karen, Susan AB, U. Chgo., 1960; MA, UCLA, 1963, PhD, 1965. Asst. prof. polit. sci. U. Rochester, N.Y., 1965-69, assoc. prof., 1969-72, prof., 1972-2000, prof. film studies, 1983-2000, founder, dir. Dance Film Archive, 1973—; prof. polit. sci., Wood Hayes chair of nat. security studies Ohio State U., 2000—. Lectr. on dance in U.S., Europe, Australia, 1973—; OP-ED columnist Wall St. Jour., 1984—, L.A. Times, 1988—, N.Y. Times, 1990—; mem. dance panel NEA, 1983-85; columnist Dance Mag., 1974-82; dance critic Rochester Dem. and Chronicle, 1974-82; mem. adv. bd. Dance in Am., PBS, 1975; chmn. Nat. Security Studies Ohio State U. Author: War, Presidents and Public Opinion, 1973 (book selected as one of Fifty Books That Significantly Shaped Public Opinion Rsch. 1946-95 Am. Assn. Pub. Opinion Rsch. 1995), Dance Film Directory, 1979, Astaire Dancing: The Musical Films, 1985 (de la Torre Bueno prize 1983), Retreat From Doomsday: The Obsolescence of Major War, 1989, Policy and Opinion in the Gulf War, 1994, Quiet Cataclysm: Reflections on the Recent Transformation of World Politics, 1995, Capitalism, Democracy, and Ralph's Pretty Good Grocery, 1999; co-author: Trends in Public Opinion: A Compendium of Survey Data, 1989; editor: Approaches to Measurement, 1969, Peace, Prosperity, and Politics, 2000; co-editor Jour. Policy Analysis and Mgmt., 1985-89; mem. editl. bd. Pub. Opinion Quar., 1988-91, Jour. Cold War Studies, 1999—, Ohio State U. press, 2001—; prodr. 12 dance films/recorded commentator on 2nd soundtrack of laser disc edit. Swing Time, 1986; co-adapter (musical) A Foggy Day, 1998; prodr. Shaw Festival Niagara-on-the-Lake, Ont., 1998, 99. Grantee NSF, 1967-70, 74-75, NEH, 1972-73, 74-75, 77-78, 79-81; Guggenheim fellow, 1988. Mem. Am. Acad. Arts and Scis., Am. Polit. Sci. Assn., Dance Critics Assn. (bd. dirs. 1983-85). Home: 420 W 5th Ave Columbus OH 43201-3159 Office: Ohio State U Polit Sci Dept Columbus OH 43210-1373

MUELLER, KATHRYN LUCILE, occupational and emergency medicine educator; b. Lincoln, Nebr., Feb. 14, 1951; d. Roland Fredrick and Elizabeth (Brown) M.; m. Rex A. Logemann, Apr. 27, 1978; children: Elizabeth C., Alexander F. BA, U. Nebr., 1973, MD, 1977; MPH, Med. Coll. Wis., 1994. Diplomate Am. Bd. Emergency Medicine, Am. Bd. Preventive Medicine in Occupational Medicine. Instr. Rush Med. Sch., Chgo., 1981-87; asst. prof. U. Colo. Health Scis. Ctr., Denver, 1987-98, dir. student and occupational health svcs., 1989-96, assoc. prof. surgery and preventive medicine, 1998—; med. dir. Colo. Divsn. Worker's Compensation, 1991—. Project med. dir. Christ Hosp. EMS program, Chgo., 1983-87; physician advisor Emergency Med. Svcs. State of Colo., Denver, 1991-92; peer reviewer Tomes Plus, 1991—; oral bd. examiner Am. Bd. Emergency Medicine, Ill., 1992-95; chair first test com. Am. Bd. Ind. Med. Examiners, 1994-95. Mem. editl. bd., contbr. The Guides Newsletter AMA, 1996—. Am. Coll. Emergency Medicine fellow, 1983; Robert Wood Johnson grantee, 1998-2000. Fellow Am. Coll. Occupational and Environ. Medicine (chair com. state legis. affairs 1996—, bd. dirs. 2000—); mem. Rocky Mountain Acad. Occupational and Environ. Medicine (bd. dirs. 1992-94, pres. 1997). Avocations: cross country skiing, travel, reading. Office: U Colo Health Scis Ctr 4200 E 9th Ave B 211 Denver CO 80262-0001

MUELLER, KEITH J. education educator; b. Milw., May 12, 1951; s. Milton A. and Marie T. Mueller; m. Gloria D. Mueller, Jan. 2, 1982; 1 child Amy ; m. Kathyrne Mueller, 1973. BA, U. Wis., 1973, MA, 1975; PhD, U. Ariz., 1979. Dir. Rural Policy Rsch. Inst. Ctr. Mem. Nat. Adv. Commn. on Rural Hea, Washington, 2001—. Author: Zero Base Budgeting in Local Government, 1981, Health Care in the U.S., 1993. Pres. Nat. Rural Hea Assn., Kansas City, Mo., 1997. Named Disting. Rschr., Nat. Rural Hea Assn., 1998, Vol. of Yr., 1999. Office: Dept PSM 984350 NE Med Ctr Omaha NE 68198-4350 E-mail: kmueller@unmc.edu.

MUELLER, LISA MARIA, chemical engineer; b. Macedonia, Ohio, Aug. 29, 1966; d. Dieter Hermann and Hannelore (Habeck) M. BSChemE, U. Akron, Ohio, 1988, postgrad., 1988-89, Kent State U., 1993; MEChemE, Lamar U., 1999. Newspaper delivery The Bull./Newsleader, 1979—80; dry cleaner Nordonia Dry Cleaners & Coin Laundromat, 1980—87; sys. adminstr. Engring. and Computer Graphics Facility, 1985—87; rschr. Process Engring. Computer Catalyst Controls, Akron, 1986-88; devel. engr. chem. divsn. Goodyear, 1988-90; engr. AcroMed Corp., Cleve., 1990; process design engr. NorPro, Akron, 1991-93; contract and assoc. engr. BF Goodrich Co., 1994-95; contract engr. BASF, Taco Bell, Kingfish Restaurant, Louisville, 1996; sr. process engr. Mobil, Beaumont, Tex., 1996-97; contract engr. Matrix Engring., 1998. Co-author paper Food Engring. Ann. Nat. Meeting, Chgo., 1993. Mem.: Nat. Assn. Women in Sci., Soc. Women Engrs., Tau Beta Pi, Nat. Honor Soc. Avocations: music, stamps, computers, Tae Kwon Do.

MUELLER, LISEL, writer, poet; b. Hamburg, Germany, 1924; Vis. faculty Goddard Coll., 1977-80, Warren Wilson Coll., 1983, 85-86; vis. lectr. U. Chgo., 1984; disting. writer-in-residence Wichita State U. Author: Dependencies, 1965, 2d edit. 1998, Life of a Queen, 1970, The Private Life, 1976, Voices from the Forest, 1977, The Need to Hold Still, 1980, Waving fro Shore, 1989, Second Language, 1986, Learning to Play by Ear, Alive Together: New & Selected Poems, 1996 (Pulitzer prize). Recipient Pulitzer prize for poetry, Nat. Book award for poetry, Carl Sandburg award, Ruth Lilly Poetry prize; NEA fellow. Office: La State U Press PO Box 25053 Baton Rouge LA 10894-5053

MUELLER, LOIS M. psychologist; b. Milw., Nov. 30, 1943; d. Herman Gregor and Ora Emma (Dettmann) M. BS, U. Wis., Milw., 1965; MA, U. Tex., 1966, PhD, 1969. Cert. family mediator; lic. psychologist, Ill., Fla. Postdoctoral intern VA Hosp., Wood, Wis., 1969-71; counselor, asst. prof. So. Ill. U. Counseling Ctr. and dept. psychology, Carbondale, 1971-72, coord. personal counseling, asst. prof., 1972-74, counselor, asst. prof., 1974-76; individual practice clin. psychology, 1972-76, Clearwater, Fla., 1977-90, Port Richey, 1990—. Family mediator, 1995—; mem. profl. adv. com. Mental Health Assn. Pinellas County, 1978, Alt. Human Services, 1979-80; cons. Face Learning Center, Hotline Crisis Phone Service, 1977-87; advice columnist Clearwater Sun newspaper, 1983-90; pub. speaker local TV and radio stas., 1978, 79; talk show host WPLP Radio Sta., Clearwater, 1980-83, WTKN Radio Sta., Tampa Bay, 1988-89, WPSO Radio Sta., New Port Richey, 1991. Contbr. articles to profl. jours. Campaign worker for Sen. George McGovern presdl. race, 1972; sec. bd. dirs. PACE Ctr. for Girls of Pasco; bd. dirs. Suncoast Girl Scout Coun. Mem. APA, Fla. Psychol. Assn., Pinellas Psychol. Assn. (founder, pres. 1978), Am. Soc. Clin. Hypnosis, Fla. Soc. Clin. Hypnosis, Calusa Bus. & Profl. Women (pres., Woman of Yr. 1999), West Pasco C. of C., Cmty. Svc. Coun.. Office: 9501 US Highway 19 Ste 212 Port Richey FL 34668-4658

MUELLER, MARGARET S. musician, educator; b. Creston, Iowa, Dec. 3, 1924; d. Homer Cowan and Pearl Callahan Snodgrass; m. John Storm Mueller, June 10, 1958; 1 child, Laura Marjorie Mueller Woods. Student, Kans. U., 1943-46; MusB, Oberlin Conservatory, 1950, MusM, 1958. Instr. piano N.D. State Tchrs. Coll., Minot, 1950-51; instr. piano and organ Iowa State U., Ames, 1951-55, Randolph-Macon Woman's Coll., Lynchburg, Va., 1957-58; prof. organ and theory Salem Coll., Winston-Salem, N.C., 1958-95, prof. emerita, 1995—. Performing artist organ various concerts throughout the U.S. and Europe, 1953—; organist St. Paul's Episcopal Ch., Winston-Salem, 1963—2001; judge André Marchal Internat. Competition, Biarritz, France, 2001. Grantee Fulbright Assn., Frankfurt, Germany, 1955-56, Aeolian grantee, Paris, 1956-57. Mem.: Nat. Guild Piano Tchrs. (judge piano and organ), Winston-Salem Profl. Piano Tchrs. Assn., Music Tchrs. Nat. Assn. (judge piano and organ), Organ Hist. Soc., Am. Guild Organists (judge state, regional and nat. competitions 1965—, performing artist organ nat. and regional convs. 1973, 1976, 1987, 1993), Pi Kappa Lambda, Mu Phi Epsilon. Democrat. Episcopalian. Home: 1524 Sharon Rd Winston Salem NC 27103-4816 Office: Salem Coll Salem Square Winston Salem NC 27108

MUELLER, MARK CHRISTOPHER, lawyer; b. Dallas, June 19, 1945; s. Herman August and Hazel Deane (Hatzenbuehler) M.; m. Linda Jane Reed. BA in Econs., So. Meth. U., 1967; MBA in Acctg., 1969, JD, 1971. Bar: Tex. 1971, U.S. Dist. Ct. (no. dist.) Tex. 1974, U.S. Tax Ct. 1974; CPA, Tex. Acct. Arthur Young & Co., Dallas, 1967-68, A.E. Krutilek, Dallas, 1968-71; pvt. practice law, 1971—; assoc. L. Vance Stanton, 1971-72. Instr. legal writing and rsch. So. Meth. U., Dallas, 1970-71, instr. legal acctg., 1975; mem. unauthorized practice of law com. Supreme Ct. Tex. Leading articles editor Southwestern Law Jour., 1970-71. Mem. NRA, Tex. Bar Assn., Tex. State Rifle Assn., Tex. Soc. CPA's, Dallas Bar Assn., SAR, Sons Republic Tex., Sons of Union Vets. of Civil War, Sons Confederate Vets., Mil. Orer Stars and Bars, Order of Coif, Dallas Hist. Soc., Dallas County Pioneer Assn., Rock Creek Barbeque Club, Masons, Shriners, York Rite, Grotto, Scottish Rite (32 degree Knight Commdr. Ct. of Honor), Beta Alpha Psi, Phi Delta Phi, Sigma Chi. Home: 7310 Brennans Dr Dallas TX 75214-2804 Office: 6510 Abrams Rd Ste 565 Dallas TX 75231-7292

MUELLER, O. THOMAS, molecular geneticist, pediatrics educator; b. Berlin, Germany, Aug. 17, 1950; arrived in U.S., 1955; s. Heinz Carl and Gertrud (Jung) M.; m. Mary Gail Craig, April 24, 1976; children: Cara Lynne, Kyle Thomas, Eric Andreas. BA, Lehigh U., 1972; PhD in biol. chemistry, Pa. State U., 1978. Diplomate: Am. Bd. Med. Genetics in Molecular and Biochemical Genetics. Postdoctoral fellow U. Colo. Med. Ctr., Denver, 1978-80; rsch. asst. Roswell Park Meml. Inst., Buffalo, 1980-84, rsch. affiliate, 1984-87; assoc. prof. pediats. U. So. Fla., Tampa, 1987—; dir. molecular genetics All Children's Hosp., St. Petersburg, Fla., 1994—. Contbr. numerous articles to scientific jours. including Human Genetics, Am. Jour. Med. Genetics, Am. Jour. Human Genetics, Jour. Biol. Chemistry, and others. Avocations: triathlons, sailing. Home: 2001 Point Overlook Dr NE Saint Petersburg FL 33703-3435 Office: Dept Pathology All Children's Hosp 801 6th St S Saint Petersburg FL 33701-4816 E-mail: otmuelle@hsc.usf.edu.

MUELLER, PAUL HENRY, retired banker; b. N.Y.C., June 24, 1917; s. Paul Herbert and Helen (Cantwell) M.; m. Jean Bonnel Vreeland, Sept. 10, 1949; 1 child, Donald Vreeland. BS, NYU, 1940; AB, Princeton U., 1941; LittD (hon.), Heriot-Watt U., Edinburgh, Scotland, 1981; LHD (hon.), Bloomfield Coll., 1991. Page Citibank N.A., 1934; on leave, 1939-46; asst. cashier, 1947-52; asst. v.p., 1952-58; v.p., 1958-65; sr. v.p., 1965-74; chmn. credit policy com., 1974-82; chmn. Saab-Scania Am. Inc., 1982-90, Atlas Copco N.Am. Inc., 1975-93; ret., 1993. Dir. Atlas Copco AB, Stockholm, 1982-91, Skandinaviska Enskilda Banken Corp., 1983-93, Ericsson N.Am., Inc., 1986-91; entered U.S. Fgn. Svc., served in Panama, Cairo, Washington, 1941-43; asst. adminstrv. sec. UN Montary and Fin. Conf., Bretton Woods, N.H., 1944; divisional asst. Dept. State, 1946; sec. West Indian Conf., 2d session, St. Thomas, V.I., 1946; vis. lectr. U. Va., 1980-2001; founding chmn., sr. fellow Ctr. Internat. Banking Studies, 1977-91. Author (contbg.): Offshore Lending by U.S. Commercial Banks, 1975, 2d edit., 1981, Bank Credit, 1981, Classics in Commercial Bank Lending, 1981, Vol. II, 1985, Loan Portfolio Management, 1988, Credit Culture, 1994, Credit Risk Management, 1995; author: (with Leif H. Olsen) Credit and the Business Cycle, 1979; author: Learning from Lending, 1979, Credit Doctrine for Lending Officers, 1976, 1981, 2d edit., 1997, Credit Endpapers, 1982, Perspective on Credit Risk, 1988, In a Nutshell, 2002; contbr. articles to profl. jours. Trustee Bloomfield Coll., N.J., 1983-91, vice chmn., 1987-88, chmn., 1988-91, trustee emeritus; treas. Marcus Wallenberg Found. (U.S.), 1984—. Served from 2d lt. to capt. USMCR, 1944-45. Decorated Order Polar Star (Sweden); recipient Alumni award Grad. Sch. Credit and Fin. Mgmt., Dartmouth Coll., Disting. Svc. award Robert Morris Assocs., award for journalistic excellence, 1991. Mem. Bankers Assn. Fgn. Trade (hon., v.p. 1976), Pilgrims, SAR, Swedish-Am. C. of C. USA (chmn. 1989-90, hon. dir.), Royal Econ. Soc. (U.K.), Univ. Club (N.Y.C.), Beta Gamma Sigma. Republican. Presbyterian. Home: 75 Rotary Dr Summit NJ 07901-3131

MUELLER, PEGGY JEAN, dance educator, choreographer, rancher; b. Austin, Tex., June 14, 1952; d. Rudolph George Jr. and Margaret Jean (Locke) M.; m. John Yerby Tarlton, June 24, 1972 (div. June 1983). BS in Home Econs., Child Devel., U. Tex., Austin, 1974. Dance tchr. Shirley McPhail Sch. Dance, Austin, 1972-75, Jean Tarlton Sch. Dance, Alpine, Tex., 1975-77, College Station, 1977-80, Sul Ross State U., Alpine, 1975-77, Tex. A&M U., College Station, 1977-80, A&M Consol. Community Edn., Coll. Station, 1977-78, Jean Mueller Sch. Dance, Austin, 1980—, U. Tex., Austin, 1980—. Dancer, contest judge Gt. Tex. Dance-Off, Austin, 1985—86; mem. equestrian com. Austin Travis County Livestock Show and Rodeo, 1980—92, chmn. trail ride, 1986—, Star Tex. Fair and PRCA Rodeo, 2000—; trial boss, pres. Austin Founders Trail Ride, 1986—; trail boss Bandera Longhorn Cattle Dr. and Trail Ride, 1990, 91; choreographer, head cheerleader Austin Texans Pro Football Team, 1981; dance tchr. Austin Ballroom Dancers, 1988, the Austin Club, 1997, 98; dancer, agt. George Strait/Bud Light Comml. Auditions, 1990; head contest judge Am.'s Ultimate Dance Contest, Austin, 1994; contest judge Two-Stepping Across Am., Austin, 1994; hon. trail boss Dream Catcher Ranch Trail Ride, Franklin, Tex., 1995, 96, Grapevine/Housgon Country Donkey, Mule and Horse Trail Ride, 1997, 2000. Dancer Oklahoma, Austin, 1969, Kiss Me Kate, Austin, 1970; choreographer, lead role Cabaret, Alpine, 1976, (mini-series) True Women, 1997. Active Women's Symphony League Austin, 1972—, Settlement Club, Austin, 1987—; recreation chmn. St. Martin's Evang. Luth. Ch., Austin, 1972—; hon. trail boss St. Jude Children's Rsch. Hosp. Trail Ride, Austin and Kyle, Tex., 1991. Recipient Outstanding Trail Rider of Yr. award Wild Horse Trail Ride, Okla., 1984; named Tex. First Lady Trail Boss, Gov. Mark White, Mayor Frank Cooksey, Austin City Coun., 1986, Judge Bill Aleshire, Travis County Commrs., 1989, Outstanding Intramural Sports Team Mgr.-Player, Tex. A&M U., 1978-79. Mem. Tex Assn. Tchrs. of Dancing, Inc., U.S. Twirling and Gymnastics Assn., Univ. Tex. Ex-Students Assn., Tex. Execs. in Home Econs., Am. Vet. Med. Assn. Aux. (v.p. 1978-79, pres. 1979-80), Am. Horse Shows Assn., Internat. Arabian Horse Assn., Austin Women's Tennis Assn. (v.p. 1985-86, pres. 1986-90, spl. events chmn. 1990-92, advisor 1990—, winner 2d ann. Harriet Crosson Outstanding Player & Community Svc. award), Women's Team Tennis of Austin Assn. (pres.-elect 1992-93, pres. 1993-94), Capital Area Tennis Assn. (membership com. 1991, 92), Houston Salt Grass Trail Ride Assn., San Antonio Alamo Trail Ride Assn., Ft. Worth Chisholm Trail Ride Assn., U. Tex. Longhorn Alumni Band, Austin C. of C., Am. Bus. Women's Assn., Austin Alumnae Panhellenic Assn. (1st v.p. 1989-90, rush forum chmn. 1990, pres. 1990-91, parliamentarian 1991-92), Lone Grove Cmty. Club (treas. 199697, v.p. 1997-99, pres. 1999—, exec. trustee 1997-99, exec. dir. 1999-2000), Omicron Nu (v.p. 1973-74), Jr. Austin Woman's Club (historian 1990-91), Austin Country Club (team tennis captain 1994-95, player 1994—, dance tchr. 1993-96), Zeta Tau Alpha (Austin Alumnae Chpt., alumnae photographer, social advisor 1982-87, treas. 1987-89, publicity chmn. 1989, Easter Seals fundraiser, Honor Cup winner 1990, pres. 1991-92, internat. convention official del. 1988, 92, nominating chmn. 1992-93, mem. yearbook com. 1992-94, 2d v.p. 1993-94). Clubs: Cen. Tex. Arabian Horse, Capitol Area Quarter Horse Assn., Jr. Austin Woman's, Austin Country. Republican. Avocations: theatre, piano, drums, sports, travel. Home and Office: PO Box 5868 Austin TX 78763-5868 E-mail: aftr@USATrailRides.com.

MUELLER, PETER STERLING, psychiatrist, educator; b. N.Y.C., Dec. 28, 1930; s. Reginald Sterling and Edith Louise (Welleck) M.; m. Ruth Antonia Shipman, Aug. 9, 1958; children: Anne Louise, Peter Sterling, Paul Shipman, Elizabeth Ruth. AB, Princeton U., 1952; MD, U. Rochester, 1956. Am. Cancer Soc. student fellow Francis Delafield Hosp., N.Y.C., summer 1955; intern Bellevue Hosp., Columbia U., 1956-57; asst. resident in psychiatry Henry Phipps Psychiat. Clinic, Johns Hopkins Hosp., Balt., 1963-66; asst. prof. psychiatry Sch. Medicine, Yale U., New Haven, 1966-72; asso. prof. psychiatry Coll. Medicine and Dentistry of N.J., Rutgers Med. Sch., Piscataway, 1972-76, clin. prof. psychiatry, 1976-82; cons. for Rehab. Unit and Center for Indsl. Human Resources, Community Mental Health Center, 1973—; mem. courtesy staff dept. psychiatry Princeton Med. Center, 1976—. Cons. in psychotherapy Conn. Valley Hosp., Middletown, 1966-72; cons. in psychiatry Carrier Clinic, Belle Mead, N.J., 1973-82, VA Hosp., Lyons, N.J., 1975-78 Contbr. writings in field to profl. publs. U.S. and Brit., papers to profl. confs. on the use patents in U.S. and fgn. countries for direct dopamine agonists in the treatment of tobacco addiction. Served with USPHS, 1957-63. Recipient Exemplary Psychiatrist award Nat. Alliance for the Mentally Ill, 1994. Mem. Am. Psychosomatic Soc., Am. Psychiat. Assn., AAAS, Amyotrophic Lateral Sclerosis Found. (adv. bd.), Sigma Xi. Episcopalian. Home: 182 Snowden Ln Princeton NJ 08540-3915 Office: 601 Ewing St Princeton NJ 08540-2757 *For some, a hyperactive learning disorder is a curse that hobbles them throughout life; but for others, including myself, this disorder has become a somewhat uncomfortable and bewildering spur for lifelong compulsive puzzle-solving. This bittersweet mandate has produced the original, serendipitous, and occasionally disconcerting ideas which have marked my life.*

MUELLER, PHILIP WINFIELD, lawyer; b. Little Falls, N.Y., Oct. 8, 1953; s. Allen William and Phyllis Jane (Whitaker) M. BA, Union Coll., Schenectady, N.Y., 1975; JD, Cornell U., 1979. Bar: Oreg. 1980, Mass. 1981, D.C. 1991, N.Y. 1991. Law clk. U.S. Dist. Ct., Portland, Oreg., 1979-80; atty. Foley Hoag and Eliot, Boston, 1981-83, 85-89; dep. chief asst. dist. atty. Schenectady County, N.Y., 1990—. Editor-in-chief Cornell Law Rev., 1978-79. Named Lawyer of Yr. Schenectady County Bar Assn., 1998. Avocations: bicycling, reading. Office: 612 State St Schenectady NY 12305-2112

MUELLER, RENEE ANN, lawyer; b. Brenham, Tex., May 18, 1962; d. Johnnie Dewayne and Shirley Mueller. AA, Blinn Jr. Coll., 1981; BA, Tex. Luth. Coll., 1983; JD, South Tex. Coll. Law, 1986. Bar: Tex. 1986. Asst. dist. atty. 21st Jud. Dist. Attys. Office, Brenham, 1987-96; county atty. Washington County, 1997-00; dist. atty. 21st Judicial dist. Washington & Burleson Co., 2001—. Chmn. legal assts. adv. com. Blinn Coll., Brenham, 1995-98; panel chair Dist. 8A Grievance Com., Brenham, 1994-97; part-time criminal justice instr., Blinn Coll., 1998—. Mem. ethics com. Trinity Hosp., Brenham, 1990—. Mem. Washington County Bar Assn. (pres. 1990-92), Tex. Dist. and County Attys. Assn., Nat. Dist. Attys. Assn., Rotary, Washington County C. of C. (bd. dirs. 1995-97). Democrat. Lutheran. Avocations: tennis, beadwork. Office: Dist Atty 100 E Main St Ste 303 Brenham TX 77833-3701

MUELLER, RICHARD WALTER, foreign service officer; b. Washington, Dec. 1, 1944; s. Walter Julius and Eleanor (Maack) M.; m. Claire McCormick, Mar. 15, 1975; children: Jonathan R., Eric R. AB, Coll. William and Mary, 1966. Joined Fgn. Svc., Dept. State, 1966; assigned Am. Embassy, Canberra, Australia, 1967-68, polit. officer Saigon, Vietnam, 1969-71; staff officer Office Sec. State, Washington, 1971-74; econ. officer U.S. Liaison Office, Beijing, Peoples Republic China, 1976-78; dep. dir. Office East-West Trade Dept. State, Washington, 1978-81, dep. dir. Office Chinese Affairs, 1981-83; chief econ. sect. Am. Consulate Gen., Hong Kong, 1983-86; dep. exec. sec. Office Sec. of State Dept. State, Washington, 1986-89, dep. asst. sec. Office Legis. Affairs, 1989-92; consul gen. Am. Consulate Gen., Hong Kong, 1993—. Office: Am Consulate General 26 Garden Rd Hong Kong Hong Kong

MUELLER, ROBERT LOUIS, business executive; b. Denver, Aug. 25, 1927; s. George Winchester and Ruth Mabel (Cole) M.; m. Sue McCoy, July 3, 1949; children: Robert, Richard, Edward, Mark; m. Susan Galbraith, June 23, 1985. BSMechE, Yale U., 1948. Chief computer Western Geophys. Co., Mont., Wyo., Colo., Tex., 1949-50; dist. mgr. Armco Steel Corp., Colo., Ohio, N.Y., 1950-63, L.B. Foster Co., N.Y.C., 1963-66; v.p. Wheeeling Pitts. Steel Co., W.Va. and Pa., 1966-75; chmn., pres., chief exec. officer Connors Steel Co., Ala., 1975-82; pres., chief exec. officer Judson Steel Co., Calif., 1982-87; pres., COO Proler Internat., Houston, 1987-94, also bd. dirs., 1987-94, cons., 1994—; dir. Employee Solutions, Inc., 1995—; pres. Mueller Resources, Inc., Sedona, Ariz., 1993—. Co-author: Handbook of Drainage and Construction Products, 1954. With USN, 1945-46. Mem. ASCE, Assn. Iron and Steel Engrs., Duquesne Club (Pitts.), Houston City Club, Sedona Racquet Club, The Sedona 30.

MUELLER, ROBERT SWAN, III, Federal Agency Administrator, Lawyer; b. N.Y.C., Aug. 7, 1944; s. Robert Swan Jr. and Alice (Truesdale) M.; m. Ann Standish, Sept. 3, 1966; children: Cynthia, Melissa. BA, Princeton U., 1966; MA, NYU, 1967; JD, U. Va., 1973. Bar: Mass., U.S. Dist. Ct. Mass., U.S. Ct. Appeals (1st cir.), Calif., U.S. Dist. Ct. (no. dist.) Calif., U.S. Ct Appeals (9th cir.). Assoc. Pillsbury, Madison & Sutro, San Francisco, 1973-76; asst. U.S. atty. U.S. Atty.'s Office, No. Dist. Calif., 1976-80; chief unit spl. prosecutions, Calif. no. dist. U.S. Atty.'s Office, 1980-81, chief criminal div., 1981-82, chief criminal div. Mass. dist. Boston, 1982-85, 1st asst. U.S. atty. in Boston, 1985, U.S. atty. for Mass. dist., 1986-87, dep. U.S. atty. for Mass. dist., 1987-88; ptnr. Hill and Barlow, 1988-89; asst. to atty. gen. for criminal matters U.S. Dept. Justice, Washington, 1989-90, asst. atty. gen. for criminal div., 1990-93; lawyer Hale & Dorr, 1993—95; US atty, Calif no. dist U.S. Dept of Justice , 1998—2001, acting dep. U.S. Atty. Gen., 2001; dir. F.B.I. U.S. Dept. Justice, Washington, 2001—. Capt. USMC, 1967-70; Vietnam. Decorated Bronze Star, Purple Heart, Vietnamese Cross of Gallantry. Office: FBI J Edgar Hoover Bldg 935 Pennsylvania Ave NW Washington DC 20535-3404 Office Fax: 202-324-4705.*

MUELLER, ROBIN SUE, biologist; b. Dubuque, Iowa, June 24, 1959; d. Louis Edward Hanson and Patricia Catherine Mills; m. Philip Wayne Clarkson, Jr., Apr. 21, 1979 (div. 1989); children: Tyler Louis Clarkson, Timothy Patrick Clarkson; m. Matthew James Mueller, Aug. 2, 1990. AAS, Hawkeye C.C., 1988; BS in Allied Health, U. Ala.-Birmingham, 1995, MEd, 1999. Cert. med. lab. technician Assn. Soc. Clin. Pathologists; profl. educator Ala., clin. lab. scientist Nat. Cert. Agy. Med. lab. technician ARC, Dubuque, Iowa, 1988—90; overnight technologist United Clin. Labs., 1990—91; med. technologist Lab. Corp. Am., Birmingham, 1991—96; rsch. asst. U. Ala., 1997—99; tchr. biology and marine biology Erwin H.S. Jefferson City Bd. Edn., 1999—. Com. mem. Textbook Com. Adv. Bd., Birmingham, 2001—02; sponsor Student Govt. Assn., Erwin H.S., Birmingham, 2000—02. Mem. Parent-Tchr. Assn., Birmingham, 1991—. Grantee grantee, Nat. Energy Coun., Erwin H.S., 2001. Avocations: travel, reading, music. Home: 5508 Spanish Trace Pinson AL 35126 Office: Erwin H S 532 23d Ave NW Birmingham AL 35215 E-mail: birdie0624@yahoo.com.

MUELLER, SHARON LEE (SHERRY MUELLER), educational organization executive; b. Chgo., Aug. 17, 1943; d. LeRoy Elmer Arthur and Lucille Viola (Armborst) M. BA, Am. U., 1965; MA in Law and Diplomacy, Tufts U., 1966, PhD, 1977. Group leader Experiment in Internat. Living, 1969; cross-cultural trainer Nat. F-H Found., 1970-71; cons. U.S. Dept. State, 1972, contract escort officer, 1970-77; cons. Fletcher Sch. Law and Diplomacy, 1976-81; lectr. dept. polit. sci. U. R.I., Kingston, 1975-77; adj. prof. Sch. Internat. Svc. Am. U., Washington, 1981-87; program officer Inst. Internat. Edn., 1978-82, dir. prof. exch. programs, 1982-96; exec. dir. Nat. Coun. for Internat. Visitors, 1996—2001, pres., 2001—. Mem. editl. adv. bd. Internat. Educator, 1991—; bd. dirs. Nat. Coun. for Internat. Visitors, 1983-88; bd. dirs., trustee World Learning. Author: Careers in International Education, Exchange, and Development, 1998; contbr. chpts. to books; guest editor, contbr. Internat. Educator, 1992. Mem. exec. com. Internat. Student House, Washington, 1992-95; usher Foundry Meth. Ch., Washington, 1990—; mem. The Pres.'s Cir. Coun., Am. U., Washington, 1988-98, chair, 1996-98. Recipient Alumni Recognition award Am. U., 1990, award of appreciation Nat. Coun. for Internat. Visitors, 1988, award of appreciation World Ctr. for Tng. and Devel., 1988, Disting. Alumni award Lake Park High Sch., 1995, Outstanding Svc. award U.S.I.A., 1996. Mem. Nat. Press Club (assoc.), Sch. Internat. Svc. Alumni Assn. The Am. U. (founding pres. 1981-83), Sigma Iota Rho (hon.), Cosmos Club. Home: 1317 N Lynnbrook Dr Arlington VA 22201-4918 Office: NCIV 1420 K St NW Ste 800 Washington DC 20005-2500

MUELLER, SHIRLEY ANNE, lawyer, real estate broker; b. Miami, Fla., Aug. 25, 1950; d. Robert Peter and Arvella Gertrude (Feldkamp) M.; divorced; children: Peter, Tybe, Samantha. AA in Journalism, Miami Dade Jr. Coll., 1970; BA in Philosophy, U. Calif., Berkeley, 1972; JD, Benjamin Cardozo Sch. Law, N.Y.C., 1982. Dir. children's advt. div. Coun. Better Bus. Bur., N.Y.C., 1973-79; assoc. Cutner & Rathkopf, 1983-87; pres. Uncommon Properties, Inc., 1990-94; pvt. practice, 1994—. Fundraising com. Children's Air Ctr., N.Y. Hosp., N.Y.C., 1988—, Nightingale Bamford Sch., N.Y.C., 1987-98. Roman Catholic. Avocations: reading, music, travel, dancing. Home and Office: Ste 18A 275 Central Park West New York NY 10024

MUELLER, SUZANNE, secondary school educator; b. Pueblo, Colo., Nov. 9, 1944; d. William Carl and Helen Anna (Hoffmann) Shontz; m. James Walter Mueller, Dec. 18, 1993; children: William Glenn Pickrel, Bryan Neil Pickrel. BA, U. Colo., 1966. Cert. English tchr., Nebr. 7th and 8th grade tchr. Christ the King Sch., Omaha, 1981-85; tchr. Millard South H.S., 1985-2000. Civilian blue and gold officer U.S. Naval Acad., 1985-89. Mem. NEA, Nebr. State Edn. Assn., Millard Edn. Assn. (bldg. rep. 1993-95), Nat. Coun. Tchrs. English. Republican. Lutheran. Avocations: reading, jazzercize, embroidery. Home: 2103 Eagle Crest Plz Papillion NE 68133-2461

MUELLER, THOMAS JAMES, engineering educator, researcher; b. Chgo., May 25, 1934; s. John Anthony and Margaret Mary (Staudenmaier) M.; m. Sarah Ann Holthaus, Nov. 18, 1961; children: Mark, Monica, Annmarie, Matthew, James. BSME, Ill. Inst. Tech., 1956; MSME, U. Ill., 1958, PhD in Gas Dynamics, 1961. Asst. prof. U. Ill., Urbana, 1961-63; sr. rsch. scientist United Tech., East Hartford, Conn., 1963-65; assoc. prof. U. Notre Dame, Ind., 1965-69, prof. aero. engring., 1969-88, assoc. dean engring., 1985-88, dept. chair, 1988-96, Roth-Gibson prof., 1988—. Vis. scientist Von Karman Inst., Brussels, 1973-74; cons. ARO, Inc., Tullahoma, Tenn., 1966-70, Lockheed-Ga. Co., 1980-82, AGARD, NATO, paris, 1983-84, Office Naval Rsch., Arlington, Va., 1999—. Co-author: Fr. T. Hesburg Commitment, Compassion, Consecration, 1989; editor: Low Reynolds Number Aerodynamic, 1989; contbr. over 180 articles to profl. publs. in aerodynamics, propulsion, flow visualization and acoustics. Mem. Fellow ASME, AIAA (assoc., edn. achievement award 1980-81), Royal Aero. Soc.; mem. Supersonic Tunnel Assn. (pres. 1994-95). Avocations: music, reading, investing. Home: 1535 Hoover Ave South Bend IN 46615 Office: U Notre Dame 112 Hessert Ctr Notre Dame IN 46556

MUELLER, VIOLET HUBBARD HOLSINGER, designer, educator; b. Belleville, Ill., Mar. 16, 1907; d. Jacob Wilson and Violet Eldro (Hubbard) Holsinger; m. Harry Edgar Mueller, Aug. 25, 1932. Student McKendree Coll., 1924-26, Parsons Sch. Design, 1926-28; B.S., U. Ill., 1937. Tchr., Granite City Schs., Ill., 1929-32, Salem Schs., Ill., 1941-42, 46-50; designer Stix Baer & Fullar, St. Louis, 1952-79; interior designer Cons. in Design and Color, Belleville, Ill., 1979— . Design works include: interior Grace United Methodist Ch., Salem, 1970. Republican. Methodist. Avocation: designing. Office: Cons in Design and Color 2920 W Main St Belleville IL 62226-6614

MUELLER, VIRGINIA SCHWARTZ, lawyer; b. Palo Alto, Calif., Apr. 27, 1924; d. William Leonard and Anstrice (Bryant) S.; m. Paul F.C. Mueller, Sept. 24, 1945; children: Christian William, Lisa Turcotte. AB in Polit. Sci. and Law, Stanford U., 1944; JD, Cornell U., 1946; LLD, U. Paris, 1950. Bar: Calif. 1946, Wash. 1952, U.S. Supreme Ct. 1966. Research atty. Calif. Dist. Ct. Appeals, San Francisco, 1946-49; atty.-at-law Karr and Combelic, Seattle, 1952-53; dep. pros. atty. King County Pros. Atty., 1953-56; dep. supr. Inheritance Tax div. Wash. State Tax Commn., Olympia, 1956-58; asst. atty. counsel Calif. Bd. of Equalization, Sacramento, 1959; dep. dist. atty. Sacramento County Dist. Atty., 1959-66; legal counsel Legal Aid Soc. of Sacramento, 1966-71; pvt. practice Sacramento, 1971—. Chmn. Port of Sacramento, 1988-90, commr., 1983-91; mem. adv. bd. Alternative Sentencing Program, Sacramento, 1976—. Contbr. articles to profl. jours. Pres. No. Calif. chpt. Sister Cities Internat., 1990-93, state rep., Alexandria, Va., 1987-89, coord. for No. Calif., 1993-2000; counselor Soc. Mayflower Descs. inCalif., 1981-2001; chmn. bd. visitors spl. com. on status of women in law Stanfrd U., 1973-75; pres. World Affairs Coun. Sacramento, 1971-72, chmn. by-laws com., 1976-77; No. Calif. rep. nat. com. UNICEF, 1972-75. Named Outstanding Woman YMCA Sacramento, 1985, Disting. Businesswoman Sacramento C. of C., 1980. Mem. ABA (mem. standing com. World Order under Law 1979-86, coun. mem. sect. of internat. law 1976-80, sr. lawyers divsn. liaison to sect. internat. law, co-chair membership com., sr. lawyers divsn. council 2001—), Sacramento County Bar Assn. (chair sr. lawyers sect. 2000—, Lawyer of Yr. 1995), Nat. Assn. Women Lawyers (pres. 1985-86, liaison sect.of internat. law and practice), Fedn. Internat. des Femmes des Carrieres Juridiques (bd. dirs. 1972-88, 97—, v.p. 2000—), State Bar Calif. (sec. exec. com. sr. lawyer sect. 1998—), Union Internat. des Avocats, Women Lawyers of Sacramento (pres. 1964, 65, Frances Newell Carr Achievement award 1995), Fedn. Internat. de Abogadas (v.p. 2000—), AAUW (pres. 1978-79, Centennial award 1981), Soroptimist (pres. 1975-76), Internat. Fedn. Women Lawyers (v.p. 2000—). Avocation: internat. travel. Home: 4310 Moss Dr Sacramento CA 95822-1662 Office: 106 L St Sacramento CA 95814-3227 E-mail: vsmueller@webtv.net.

MUELLER, WAYNE DENNIS, music educator; b. Scottsbluff, Nebr., Apr. 20, 1947; s. Roger Wayne Mueller and Lorraine Rose Marie Eisenach; m. Mitzi Marie Hummel, Aug. 22, 1969; children: Robert. Bachelors in Music Edn., U. of Nebr., Lincoln, NE, 1970. Cert. Teaching Certificate, K-12 Music Nebr. 6-12 vocal / instrumental music Thedford Pub. Schools, Thedford, Nebr., 1970—70; 7-12 vocal / instrumental music Morrill Pub. Schools, Morrill, 1970—72; 7-21 vocal music Mitchell Pub. Schools, Mitchell, 1972—73; sales and instrumental repair Jay's Music, Scottsbluff, 1973; 6-12 instrumental music North Platte Pub. Schools, North Platte, 1974—. Musician Mcpl. Band, North Platte, Nebr., 1975—, Sandhills Symphony, North Platte, Nebr., 1975—; condr. Sandhill Symphony, North Platte, Nebr., 1994—2000; musical dir. Cmty. Playhouse, North Platte, Nebr., 1995. Pres., sec., elder, choir dir. Beautiful Savior Luth. Ch., North Platte, Nebr., 1980—2002; soccer referee Am. Youth Soccer Orgn., 1985—90. Recipient Art Beat Award, North Platte Chamber of Commerce, 1996; grantee Music Grant for Accelerated Program, North Platte Pub. Sch. Found., 2000-2001. Mem.: Nebr. Music Edn. Assn., North Platte Edn. Assn. (pres. 1974—2002), Optimist Club. Lutheran. Avocations: golfing, coaching football and baseball, coaching football and baseball, coaching football and baseball, community musical events. Home: 2607 West Philip Avenue North Platte NE 69101 Office: North Platte Public Schools 1000 West Second Street North Platte NE 69101

MUELLER, WERNER HEINRICH, chemical company executive; b. Aldersbach, Germany, Apr. 7, 1939; came to U.S., 1984; s. August and Rosina (Schned) M.; m. Janice Williams, Aug. 14, 1968; children: Carolyn, Alexander. BS, Tech. U. Munich, 1963, MS in Organic Chemistry, 1965, PhD in Organic Chemistry, 1967; postgrad., Temple U., 1967-68. Rsch. specialist Monsanto Co., Pensacola, Fla., 1968-72; group leader spl. chemistry Hoechst AG, Frankfurt, Germany, 1972-80, asst. to mem. bd. Germany, 1980-83, rsch. specialist div. electronic products Wiesbaden, Germany, 1983-84, asst. ops. mgr. Knapsack Works, 1984-85; mgr. indsl. chemistry Am. Hoechst Corp., Coventry, R.I., 1985-88; assoc. dir. R&D adv. tech. group Hoechst Celanese, Corpus Christi, Tex., 1988-89, tech. dir. chems. group, 1989-93, dir. tech. devel. group engring., spl. chems. group Charlotte, N.C., 1993-97; pres. CHD Techs. Inc., 1997—. Mem. indsl. vis. com. dept. chemistry and biochem. U. Tex., Austin, 1990-93. Contbr. articles to profl. jours. Mem. AAAS, Am. Chem. Soc., N.Y. Acad. Scis., Indsl. Rsch. Inst., Inc., Coun. for Chem. Rsch. Achievements include 80 patents in field of specialty chemicals, polymers, nylon intermediates, pharmaceuticals and agricultural chemicals. Office: CHD Technologies Inc 4725 Wyndfield Ln Charlotte NC 28270-0460

MUELLER, WILLARD FRITZ, economics educator; b. Ortonville, Minn., Jan. 23, 1925; s. Fritz and Adele C. (Thormaehlen) M.; m. Shirley I. Liesch, June 26, 1948; children: Keith, Scott, Kay. BS, U. Wis., 1950, MS, 1951; PhD, Vanderbilt U., 1955. Asst. prof. U. Calif., Davis, 1954-57; prof. U. Wis., 1957-61; chief economist small bus. com. U.S. Ho. of Reps., 1961; chief economist, dir. bur. econs. FTC, 1961-68; exec. dir. President's Cabinet Com. on Price Stability, 1968-69; William F. Vilas rsch. prof. econs., agrl. and applied econs., Law Sch. emeritus U. Wis., Madison, 1969—. Past bd. editors Rev. Ind. Orgn., Antitrust Law and Econ. Rev., Antitrust Bull., Jour. Reprints for Antitrust Law and Econs. Served with USN, 1943-46. Recipient Distinguished Service award FTC, 1969 Fellow Am. Agrl. Econs. Assn.; mem. Am. Econ. Assn., Am. Agr. Econ. Assn. (profl. excellence awards in policy contbn. 1980, in communications 1985, in rsch. discovery 1988). Assn. Evolutionary Econs. (pres. 1974-75), Indsl. Orgn. Soc. (pres. 1989-90), Argus Econ. Svcs. (pres.). Unitarian Universalist. Home: 121 Bascom Pl Madison WI 53705-3975 Office: U Wis 427 Lorch St Madison WI 53706-1513 E-mail: wfritzmueller@aol.com.

MUELLER, WILLYS FRANCIS, JR. retired pathologist; b. Detroit, July 15, 1934; s. Willys Francis and Antoinette Frances (Stimac) M.; m. Dolores Mae Vella, Aug. 25, 1956; children: Renee Ann, Willys Francis, Paul E., Mark A., Maria D., Beth M., Matthew P. MD, U. Mich., 1959. Intern Providence Hosp, Detroit, 1959-60, resident, 1960-62, Wayne County Gen. Hosp., Eloise, MIch., 1962-64; asst. pathologist Grace Hosp., Detroit, 1964; assoc. pathologist Hurley Hosp., Flint, Mich., 1964-66, Hurley Med. Ctr., Flint, 1968-97, dir. lab., 1981-97; chief dep. med. examiner Genesee County, Mich., 1971-79, ret., 1979—. Pres. Pathology Assocs. Inc.; assoc. clin. prof. Coll. Human Medicine, Mich. State U.; med. dir. blood svcs. Wolverine region/ Great Lakes region ARC, 1981-96. Editor Bull. of Genesee County Med. Soc. Served with U.S. Army, 1966-68. Fellow Am. Soc. Clin. Pathologists, Coll. Am. Pathologists, Am. Acad. Forensic Scis.; mem. AMA (Physicians Recognition awards), Mich. State Med. Soc., Mich. Soc. Pathologists (sec.-treas. 1981-83, pres. 1985), Genesee County Med. Soc. (pres. 1987), Mich. Assn. Blood Banks (bd. dirs., pres. 1992), Nat. Assn. Med. Examiners, K.C. Republican. Roman Catholic. Home: 1096 Berkshire Ln Tarpon Springs FL 34688-7624

MUELLER-HEUBACH, EBERHARD, medical educator; b. Berlin, Germany, Feb. 24, 1942; came to U.S., 1968; s. Heinrich Gustav and Elisabeth (Heubach) M.; m. Cornelia Rosemarie Uffmann, Sept. 6, 1941; 1 child, Oliver Maximilian. MD, U. Koeln, 1966. Intern U. Koeln (Germany) Women's Hosp., 1967-68, Middlesex Gen. Hosp., New Brunswick, N.J., 1968-69; rsch. fellow Columbia U., 1969-71; resident Columbia-Presbyn. Med. Ctr., N.Y.C., 1971-74, chief resident, 1974-75; asst. prof. Magee-Women's Hosp. U. Pitts., 1975-81, assoc. prof. Magee-Women's Hosp., 1981-89; prof., chmn. ob-gyn. Sch. Medicine Wake Forest U., Winston-Salem, 1989—2002, prof., 2002—. Mem. editl. bd.: Ob-Gyn, 1999—2002. Mem. Am. Gyn.-Ob Soc. (asst. sec. 1999-2001, sec. 2002—), Soc. Gynecol. Investigation, The Perinatal Rsch. Soc., Coun. Univ. Chairs Ob-Gyn. (pres. 1998-2000). Avocations: horses, travel, arts. Office: Wake Forest U Bapt Med Ctr Medical Center Blvd Winston Salem NC 27157-0001 E-mail: emueller@wfubmc.edu.

MUELLNER, GEORGE, aerospace transportation executive; Commd. USAF, advanced through grades to lt. gen.; prin. dep. Asst. Sec. of Air Force for Acquisition; chief info. officer USAF; dir. requirements Air Combat Comand, USAF, program mgr., program exec. officer Joint Strike Fighter Program; v.p., gen. mgr. Boeing Phantom Wks., Seal Beach, Calif. Mem. Aero. and Space Engring. Bd., Nat. Acad. Scis. Office: boeing Phantom Wks PO Box 2515 Seal Beach CA 90740*

MUENCH, KARL HUGO, clinical geneticist; b. St. Louis, May 3, 1934; MD, Wash. U., St. Louis, 1960. Diplomate Am. Bd. Med. Genetics. Intern Barnes Hosp., St. Louis, 1960-61; fellow in biological chemistry Stanford U. Sch. Medicine, 1961-65; staff mem. Jackson Meml. Hosp., Miami, Fla.; prof. medicine U. Miami Sch. Medicine. Mem. AMA, Am. Coll. Med. Genetics, Am. Coll. Physicians. Office: U Miami Sch Med Div Genetic Med PO Box 16960 Miami FL 33101-6960 E-mail: karlmuench@aol.com.

MUERTH, CHERIE ANNE, social worker; b. Atlanta, July 22, 1946; d. Albert Martin and Ruth (Wheeler) M. BS in Edn., U. Tenn., 1968; MSW, Va. Commonwealth U., 1973. Lic. clin. social worker, Ga.; diplomate NASW (acad. cert. social workers). Sch. social worker Walker County Dept. Edn., Lafayette, Ga., 1983; med. social cons. Team Evaluation Ctr., Chattanooga, 1973-78; caseworker Family and Children Svcs., 1978-83. Mem.: Sch. Social Workers Ga., Profl. Assn. Ga. Educators. Democrat. Presbyterian. Home: 617 Debbie Ln Ringgold GA 30736-5560 Office: Walker County Dept Edn PO Box 29 La Fayette GA 30728-0029

MUETH, JOSEPH EDWARD, lawyer; b. St. Louis, Aug. 8, 1935; s. Joseph and Marie Clare (Reher) M.; m. Ellen Agnes O'Heron, Dec. 24, 1973; children: Erin R., Patricia A. B.Chem. Engring., U. Dayton, 1957; LL.B., Georgetown U., 1960, LL.M., 1961. Bar: Calif. 1964. Practice law, L.A.; ptnr. Wills, Green & Mueth, 1974-83; pvt. practice law Calif., 1983-94; of counsel Sheldon & Mak, Pasadena, 1994—. Adj. prof. law U. Calif. Hastings Coll. Law, San Francisco, 1972-75; lectr. Claremont Grad. Sch., 1982—. Author: Copyrights Patents and Trademarks, 1974. Chmn. bd. Rio Hondo council Camp Fire Girls Inc., 1967-72. Mem. AAAS, Am., Los Angeles County bar assns., State Bar Calif., N.Y. Acad. Scis., L.A. Athletic Club. Home: PO Box 3369 1217 Seal Way Seal Beach CA 90740-6419 Office: 225 S Lake Ave Ste 800 Pasadena CA 91101-4858

MUETHER, CHARLES ALEXANDER, writer, educator; b. Port Jefferson, Ny, Nov. 14, 1964; s. Herbert Robert and Anne Muether; m. Kristie Jo Muether, Aug. 27, 1988. MA Curriculum and Devel., Dordt Coll., Sioux Center, Iowa, 1997, BA English and Secondary Edn., 1987. English and drama educator Pella Christian, Pella, Iowa, 1989—2001; prinicipal and educator Volga Christian, Volga, SD, 1988—89. Writer Wioarey Press, Des Moines, 2000—02. Author: (book) Theatre in the Middle; editor: Assessing the Whole Child. Deacon and v.p. Covenant Ref. Ch., Pella, Iowa, 2002. Recipient Walmart Tchr. of the Yr. Award, Walmart, 2000, Golden Apple Award, Who-TV, 1995. Mem.: Nat. Coun. of Teachers of English, Iowa H.S. Press Assn. Independent. Covenant Reformed Church. Avocations: reading, photography, model railroading. Home: 310 Prairie Street Pella IA 50219

MUFFOLETTO, MARY LU, retired school program director, consultant, editor; b. Chgo., May 25, 1932; d. Anthony Joseph and Lucile (Di Giacomo) M. PhB in Philosophy, DePaul U., 1959; ME, U. Ill., 1967. Tchr. elem. edn. Community Cons., Palatine, Ill., 1959-65; tchr. gifted children Sch. Dist. 15, 1965-67, curriculum supr., 1967-75, dir. gifted edn. program Ill., 1972-95, coord. state and fed. programs, 1975-95, asst. prin. Ill., 1975-95, retired, 1995; assoc. prof. Nat. Coll. Edn., Evanston, 1979-95; editor Tchg. Ink, Inc., 1995—. Chairperson State Bd. of Edn. Adv. Com. on Gifted Edn., Springfield, Ill., 1977-85; pres. No. Ill. Planning Commn. for Gifted, 1978-80. Editor: (tchr. activity books) Teaching Ink, 1995—. Mem. Nat. Coun. for Social Studies, Assn. for Curriculum and Supervision, Coun. for Exceptional Children, U. Ill. Alumni Assn. (pres. Champaign chpt. 1982-85, Loyalty award), Kiwanis, Phi Delta Kappa (sec. 1985-87). Home: 21302 W Brandon Rd Lake Zurich IL 60047-8618

MUFSON, MAURICE ALBERT, physician, educator; b. N.Y.C., July 7, 1932; s. Max and Faye M.; m. Diane Cecile Weiss, Apr. 1, 1962; children: Michael Jeffrey, Karen Andrea, Pamela Beth. AB, Bucknell U., 1953; MD, NYU, 1957. Intern Bellevue Hosp., N.Y.C., 1957-58, resident, 1958-59; chief resident Cook County Hosp., Chgo., 1965-66; sr. surgeon USPHS Lab. Infectious Diseases, NIH, 1961-65; from asst. prof. medicine to prof. U. Ill., 1965-76; prof. Marshall U., 1976—, chmn. dept. medicine, 1976-2000, chmn. emeritus, 2000—. Vis. scientist Karolinska Inst., 1984-85 Contbr. articles to profl. jours. Served with U.S. Navy, 1959-61. WHO grantee, 1967; recipient Meet-the-Scholar award Marshall U., 1986, Rschr. of Yr. award Sigma Xi, Marshall U., 1989, Solomon A. Berson Alumni Achievement award in health sci. NYU Sch Medicine, 1997; co-recipient Louis Weinstein award Jour. Clin. Infectious Diseases, 1994. Master ACP (traveling scholar 1987, Laureate award W.Va. chpt.), Infectious Diseases Soc. Am.; mem. AMA, Soc. Exptl. Biology and Medicine, Ctrl. Soc. Clin. Rsch., So. Soc. Clin. Investigation, W.Va. State Med. Assn., Assn. Profs. Medicine (counselor 1992-95, pres.-elect 1995-96, pres. 1996-97, past pres. 1997-98), Alpha Omega Alpha. Office: Marshall U Sch Medicine 1600 Med Ctr Dr Ste G500 Huntington WV 25701 E-mail: maurice@ezwv.com., mufson@marshall.edu.

MUFTI, AFTAB A. civil engineering educator; b. Sukkur, Sind, Pakistan, Apr. 24, 1940; arrived in Can., 1963; s. Abdul Wahid D. and Shah Jahan M.; children: Javed, Alex; m. Zehra Mehdi, Sept. 22, 2000. BCE, NED Engring. U., Karachi, Sind, 1962; MCE, McGill U., Montreal, 1965, PhD, 1969. Registered profl. engr., Man., B.C. Asst. prof. McGill U., 1969-72; assoc. prof., head dept. comp. sci. Acadia U., Wolfville, Nova Scotia, 1972-76, prof., dir. Sch. Comp. Sci., 1976-80; prof. civil engring. Dalhousie U., Halifax, 1980-2000; pres. ISIS Can. Network of Ctrs. of Excellence U. Man., Winnipeg, Can., 2000—, prof. structural engring. Can., 2000—. Pres. Advanced Composite Materials in Bridges and Structures Network of Can.; judge Can. Cons. Engring. Awards, 1987; earthquake cons. Lepereau Nuclear Power Plant and Confedn. Bridge. Author: Elementary Computer Graphics, 1982, Bridge Engineering, 1994; editor: Advanced Composite Materials in Bridges and Structures, 1972, Finite Element Method in Civil Engineering, 1993, Developments in Short and Medium Span Bridge Engineering, 1994, Bridge Superstructures New Developments, 1996; contbr. numerous articles to refereed jours., also conf. papers. Vol. fireman Wolfville Fire Dept., 1976-77. Recipient award for Distinction in Engring., Assn. Profl. Engrs. of Nova Scotia, 1996. Fellow Can. Acad. Engring., Engring. Inst. Can. (Phelp Johnson prize 1969), Can. Soc. Civil Engring. (Whitman Wright award 1990, Pratley award 1993), ASCE (Lt. Govs. award Engring. Excellence in Nova Scotia 1996, IRF award 1997, ACI design award 1998, Nova award 2000). Achievements include patents for Bridge Deck and Steel Free Bridge Deck. Office: ISIS Can Admin Ctr U Man Rm 227 Engring Bldg Winnipeg MB Canada R3T 5V6 E-mail: muftia@cc.umanitoba.can.

MUFTIC, FELICIA ANNE BOILLOT, consumer relations professional; b. Muskogee, Okla., Feb. 27, 1938; d. Lowell Francois and Geneva Margaret (Halstead) Boillot; m. Michael Muftic, Sept. 6, 1961; children: Tanya Muftic-Stretcher, Theodore B., Mariana C. BA, Northwestern U., 1960. Exec. dir. Metro Dist. Atty.'s Consumer Office, Denver, 1973-79; talk show host KNUS, 1981-83; clk., recorder City and County of Denver, Colo., 1984-91; spl. projects dir. Consumer Credit Counseling, Denver, 1991-95; cons. consumer affairs pvt. practice, 1995—. Pres. Muftic and Assocs., Denver, 1980-83; commr. Uniform Consumer Credit Code, Colo., 1991—. Author: Colorado Consumer Handbook, 1982. Candidate for mayor, Denver, 1979. Named Media person of Yr., NASW, Colo., 1982; recipient Outstanding Contbrn. in Consumer Affairs award Denver (Colo.) Fed. Exec. Bd., 1982. Mem. Inst. Internat. Edn. (bd. mem. 1980—), Rotary Internat. Democrat. Avocation: showing horses in dressage.

MUGGENBURG, BRUCE AL, veterinary physiologist; b. May 2, 1937; s. Elmer Carl and Gladys O. (Bakke) M.; m. Marianne Nordgren, June 18, 1960 (dec. 1976); m. Carolyn Seale, July 16, 1977; children: Katherine Ann, Carl Thor, Virginia Hope. BS, U. Minn., St. Paul, 1959, DVM, 1961; MS, U. Wis., 1964, PhD, 1966. Asst. prof. U. Wis., Madison, 1966-69; sr. scientist Lovelace Inhalation Toxicology Rsch. Inst., Albuquerque, 1969—. Vis. prof. Universidade do Rio Grande dul Sol, Porto Alegre, Brasil, 1966-68; clin. rsch. prof. dept. medicine U. N.Mex., Albuquerque, 1988—, clin. prof. coll. pharmacy, 1993—. Contbr. articles to profl. jours. Mem. AVMA, Am. Thoracic Soc., Am. Physiol. Soc., Health Physics Soc., Radiation Rsch. Soc., Scandinavian Club of Albuquerque (pres. 1983, 87, 88). Lutheran. Home: 2805 Calle Del Rio NW Albuquerque NM 87104-3141 Office: Lovelace Respiratory Rsch Inst 2425 Ridgecrest Dr SE Albuquerque NM 87108 E-mail: bmuggenb@lrri.org.

MUGGERIDGE, DEREK BRIAN, dean, engineering consultant; b. Godalming, Surrey, U.K., Oct. 10, 1943; arrived in Can., 1956; s. Donald William and Vera Elvina (Jackson) M.; m. Hanny Meta Buurman, Dec. 4, 1965; children: Karen Julie, Michael Brent. BS in Aero. Engring., Calif. State Polytech. U., 1965; MASc in Aerospace Engring., U. Toronto, 1966, PhD in Aerospace Engring., 1970. Spl. lectr. U. Toronto, Ont., Can., 1971; indsl. post-doctoral fellow Fleet Mfg. Co., Fort Erie, 1970-72; from asst. prof. to prof. Meml. U. of Nfld., St. John's, 1972-93, univ. rsch. prof., 1990-93; dir. Ocean Engring. Rsch. Ctr., 1982-93; dean Okanagan U. Coll., Kelowna, B.C., Can., 1993—, assoc. v.p. rsch. Can., 1998—. Pres. Offshore Design Assocs. Ltd., Portugal Cove, Nfld., 1980—; sec., ptnr. Nfld. Ocean Cons., St. John's, 1981-93; ptnr. LNF Joint Venture Ltd., St. John's, 1984-90; vis. prof. U. Victoria, B.C., 1988-89. Co-author: Ice Interaction with Offshore Structures, 1988; contbr. articles to profl. jours.; contbr. conf. articles, reports. U. Toronto Grad. fellow, 1965, Nat. Rsch. Coun. Can. Grad. fellow U. Toronto, 1966-70. Mem. Assn. Profl. Engrs. & Geoscis. of Province of B.C. Marine and Naval. Avocations: windsurfing, sailing, rock collecting. Home: 16438 Carr's Landing Rd Lake Country BC Canada V4V 1C3 Office: Okanagan Univ Coll 3333 College Way Kelowna BC Canada V1V 1V7

MUGGLI, DARRIN SCOT, engineering educator; b. Grand Forks, N.D., Sept. 23, 1969; married. PhD, U. Colo., 1998. Asst. prof. chem. engring. U. N.D., Grand Forks, 1999—. Mem.: AIChE. Home: 5198 W Maple Ave Grand Forks ND 58202 Personal E-mail: darrin_muggli@yahoo.com.

MUGLIA, BOB, information technology executive; B in Computer Sci., U. Mich. Devel. mgr. ROLM Co.; with Microsoft, Redmond, Wash., 1988, v.p. Enterprise Storage Svcs. Group. Mem. Sr. Leadership Team, Bus. Leadship Team, Microsoft. Office: Microsoft One Microsoft Way Redmond WA 98052-6399*

MUGNAINI, ENRICO, neuroscience educator; b. Colle Val d'Elsa, Italy, Dec. 10, 1937; came to U.S., 1969. children: Karin E., Emiliano N.G. MD summa cum laude, U. Pisa, Italy, 1962. Microscopy lab. rsch. fellow dept. anatomy U. Oslo Med. Sch., 1963, asst. prof., head of electron microscopy lab., 1964-66, assoc. prof., 1967-69; prof. biobehavioral scis. and psychology, head lab. of neuromorphology U. Conn., Storrs, 1969-95; E.C. Stuntz prof. cell biology, dir. Inst. for Neurosci., Northwestern U., Chgo., 1995—. Vis. prof. Dept. Anatomy Harvard U., Boston, 1969-70; traveling lectr. Grass Found., spring 1986, fall 1990. Mng. editor USA Anatomy and Embryology Jour., 1989—; contbr. more than 150 articles to books and jours. Recipient Decennial Camillo Golgi award Acad. Nat. dei Lincei, 1981, Sen. Javits Neurosci. Rsch. Investigator award NIH, 1985-92. Mem. AAAS, Am. Assn. Anatomists, Am. Soc. Cell Biology, Internat. Brain Rsch. Orgn., Internat. Soc. Developmental Neurosci., Norwegian Nat. Acad. Scis. and Letters, Soc. Neurosci., Cajal Club (pres. 1987-88). Office: U Northwestern Inst Neurosci 5-474 Searle Bldg 320 E Superior St Chicago IL 60611-3010

MUGRIDGE, DAVID RAYMOND, lawyer, educator, writer; b. Detroit, Aug. 6, 1949; s. Harry Raymond and Elizabeth Lou (Aldrich) M.; m. Sandra Lee Jackson, June 25, 1988; children: James Raymond, Sarah Lorraine. BA, U. of Ams., Puebla, Mex., 1970; MA, Santa Clara U., 1973; JD, San Joaquin Coll. of Law, 1985. Bar: Calif. 1986, U.S. Dist. Ct. (ea. dist.) Calif. 1986, U.S. Ct. Appeals (9th cir.) 1987, U.S. Supreme Ct. 1996; cert. specialist in criminal law. Staff atty. to presiding justice 5th Dist. Ct. Appeals, Fresno, Calif., 1985-87; assoc. Law Office of Nuttall, Berman, Magill, 1987-88; pvt. practice, 1988—. Tchr. Fresno City Coll., 1988-96; tchr. Spanish for legal profession, Fresno, 1994; tchr. Fresno Pacific U., 1997—; arbitrator Fresno County Bar Assn., 1988—; judge pro-tem juvenile, traffic and small claims Fresno County Superior Ct., 1988—. Contbg. author: Practical Real Estate Law, 1995,99. Mem. Calif. Attys. for Criminal Justice, Calif. State Bar Assn. (cert. specialist in criminal law). Republican. Roman Catholic. Avocations: fishing, travel, photography, hiking. E-mail: mugridge@juno.com.

MUHAMMAD, MUHSIN, II, football player; b. Lansing, Mich. m. Christa; children: Jordan Taylor, Chase Soen. Student, Mich. State U. Wide receiver Carolina Panthers, 1996—. Founder M2 Found.; spokesperson Men For Change group that generates money and awareness for a battered women's shelter. Named to Pro Bowl, 1999; named Panther's Man of Yr. for his cmty. efforts, 1999. Office: Carolina Panthers 800 S Mint St Ste 2 Charlotte NC 28202-1502*

MÜHLANGER, ERICH, ski manufacturing company executive; b. Liezen, Austria, Aug. 26, 1941; came to U.S., 1971, naturalized, 1975; s. Alois and Maria (Stückelschweiger) M.; m. Gilda V. Oliver, July 13, 1973; 1 child, Erich. Assoc. Engring., Murau Berufsschule Spl. Trade, Austria, 1959; student Inst. Tech. and Engring., Weiler Im Allgau, Germany, 1963-65. Salesman, Olin Ski Co. (Olin-Authier), Switzerland, 1965-67, mem. mktg. dept., 1967-69, svc. and mfg., 1969-71, quality control insp., Middletown, Conn., 1971-77, supr., 1977-78, gen. foreman, 1978-83, process control mgr., 1983-88; dir. mfg. Entech Corp., 1988-89; prodn. mgr. Metallizing div. Risden Corp., Thomaston, Conn., 1989-94, quality process engr., 1994— ; pres. Bus. Consolidating Svcs. Internat., Rocky Hill, Conn., 1989—, quality control technician, 1990—; quality process request divsn., fragrance divsn., 1993—; pres. Consulting Svcs. Internat. Charter mem. Presdl. Task Force, trustee; preferred mem. of U.S. Senatorial Club. Served to cpl. Austrian Air Force, 1959-60. Mem. Screenprinting Assn. Am., Am. Mgmt. Assn., Am. Soc. for Qualtiy Control, Mgmt. Club. Roman Catholic. Home: 13 Clemens Ct Rocky Hill CT 06067-3218 Office: 60 Electric Ave Thomaston CT 06787-1617 also: Bus Consolidating Svcs Internat Rocky Hill CT 06067

MUHLBACH, ROBERT ARTHUR, lawyer; b. Los Angeles, Apr. 13, 1946; s. Richard and Jeanette (Marcus) M.; m. Kerry Eldene Mahoney, July 26, 1986. BSME, U. Calif., Berkeley, 1967; JD, U. Calif., San Francisco, 1976; MME, Calif. State U., 1969; M in Pub. Adminstrn., U. So. Calif., 1978. Bar: Calif. 1976. Pub. defender County of Los Angeles, 1977-79; assoc. Kirtland & Packard, Los Angeles, 1979-85, ptnr., 1986—2001, sr. ptnr., 2001—. Chmn. Santa Monica Airport Commn., Calif., 1984-87, chmn., bd. dirs. Hawthorne Airport Cmty. Assn. Inc. Served to capt. USAF, 1969-73. Mem. ABA, AIAA, Internat. Assn. Def. Counsel, Am. Bd. Trial Advs. Office: Kirtland & Packard Ste 2600 1900 Avenue Of The Stars Los Angeles CA 90067-4507 E-mail: ram@kirtland-packard.com.

MUHLBERGER, RICHARD CHARLES, former museum administrator, writer, educator; b. Engelwood, N.J., Jan. 20, 1938; s. George Albert and Margaret Bertha (Heins) M. AA, Calif. Concordia Coll., 1958; BA, Wayne

State U., 1964; MA in Art History, Johns Hopkins U., 1967. Curator mus. edn. Worcester Art Mus., Mass., 1966-72; chmn. edn. Detroit Inst. Arts, 1972-75; dir. Mus. Fine Arts and George Walter Vincent Smith Art Mus., Springfield, Mass., 1976-87; vice dir. for edn. Met. Mus. Art, N.Y.C., 1987-89; dir. Knoxville (Tenn.) Mus. Art, 1990-91; adj. prof. art history Western New England Coll., Springfield, Mass., 1991—. Guest curator Mus. Am. Folk Art, 1997-98; mem. adv. panel NEH, 1976-78, Mass. Coun. on Arts and Humanities, 1979-81; mem. policy panel, mus. program Nat. Endowment Arts, 1981-83. Author: The Bible in Art, The New Testament, 1990, The Bible in Art, The Old Testament, 1990, The Christmas Story, 1990, What Makes a Raphael a Raphael, 1993, What Make a Bruegel a Bruegel, 1993, What Makes a Rembrandt a Rembrandt, 1993, What Makes a Monet a Monet, 1993, What Makes a Degas a Degas, 1993, What Make a Van Gogh a Van Gogh, 1993, What Makes a Leonardo a Leonardo, 1994, What Makes a Goya a Goya, 1994, What Makes a Cassatt a Cassatt, 1994, What Makes a Picasso a Picasso, 1994, The Unseen Van Gogh, 1998, American Folk Marquetry, 1998, Charles Webster Hawthorne: Paintings and Watercolors, 1999. Woodrow Wilson fellow, 1965-66; recipient Outstanding Young Man award Greater Worcester Jaycees, 1970 Mem. Am. Assn. Museums (chmn. com. on edn. 1974-76, councilor 1988-91), New England Mus. Assn. (pres. 1985-87), Phi Beta Kappa. Home: 41 Smithfield Ct Springfield MA 01108-3129

MUHLENBRUCH, CARL W. civil engineer; b. Decatur, Ill., Nov. 21, 1915; s. Carl William and Clara (Theobald) M.; m. Agnes M. Kringel, Nov. 22, 1939; children: Phyllis Elaine (Mrs. Richard B. Wallace), Joan Carol (Mrs. Frederick W. Wenk). BCE, U. Ill., 1937, CE, 1945; MCE, Carnegie Inst. Tech., 1943; LLD, Concordia U., River Forest, Ill., 1995. Research engineer Aluminum Research Labs., Pitts., 1937-39; cons. engring., 1939-50; mem. faculty Carnegie Inst. Tech., 1939-48; assoc. prof. civil engring. Northwestern U., 1948-54; pres. TEC-SEARCH, Inc. (formerly Ednl. and Tech. Consultants Inc.), 1954-67, chmn. bd., 1967—; lect. in Civil Engring. Northwestern U., 1998—. Pres. Profl. Centers Bldg. Corp., 1961-77; lectr. civil engring., 1997—. Author: Experimental Mechanics and Properties of Materials; Contbr. articles engring. publs. Treas., bd. dirs. Concordia Coll. Found.; dir. Mo. Lutheran Synod, 1965-77, vice chmn. 1977-79. Recipient Stanford E. Thompson award, 1945 Mem. Am. Econ. Devel. Coun. (cert. econ. developer), Am. Soc. Engring. Edn. (editor Ednl. Aids in Engring.), NSPE, ASCE, Sigma Xi, Tau Beta Phi, Omicron Delta Kappa. Clubs: University (Evanston). Lodges: Rotary (dist. gov. 1980-81, dir. service projects Ghana and the Bahamas). Home and Office: Tec-Search Inc 4071 Fairway Dr Wilmette IL 60091-1005

MUHLERT, JAN KEENE, art museum director; b. Oak Park, Ill., Oct. 4, 1942; d. William Henry and Isabel Janette (Cole) Keene; m. Christopher Layton Muhlert, Jan. 1, 1966; 1 son, Michael Keene. BA in Art and French, Albion (Mich.) Coll., 1964; MA in Art History, Oberlin (Ohio) Coll., 1967; student, Neuchatel (Switzerland) U., Inst. European Studies, Paris, Inst. de Phonetique, Acad. Grande Chaumiere. Asst. curator Allen Meml. Art Mus., Oberlin, 1967-68; asst. curator 20th Century painting and sculpture Nat. Collection Fine Arts, Smithsonian Instn., Washington, 1968-73, assoc. curator, 1974-75; dir. U. Iowa Mus. Art, 1975-79, Amon Carter Mus., Ft. Worth, 1980-95, Palmer Museum of Art, University Park, Pa., 1996—. Author museum brochures, catalogues. Mem. Nat. Mus. Act. Adv. Coun., 1980—83; vis. com. Allen Meml. Art Mus. Oberlin Coll., Ohio, 1987—2000; chair adv. com. North Tex. Inst. Educators on the Visual Arts, U. North Tex., 1992—95. Grantee Nat. Endowment Arts-Donner Found., 1979; recipient Friend of Art Edn. award Tex. Art Edn. Assn., 1994. Mem. Assn. Art Mus. Dirs. (trustee 1981-82, 84-86, 92-93, chmn. govt. and art com. 1982-84, chmn. profl. practices com. 1990-92), Western Assn. Art Mus. (regional rep. 1978-79), Am. Assn. Mus. (commn. for new century 1981-84, gen. co-chair 1993 ann. meeting), Am. Arts Alliance (dir. 1980-86, vice-chmn. 1982-84). Office: Palmer Museum of Art Pa State U Curtin Rd University Park PA 16802-2507

MUI, JIMMY KUN, architect, network marketing executive; b. Hong Kong, Sept. 1, 1958; came to U.S., 1971; s. Yuk-on and Kum-Ngor (Yuen) M.; m. Susan Yew, Sept. 23, 1989; 1 child, Deborah Yoke-Kit, Peter Wai-Loon BArch, SUNY, Buffalo, 1982, postgrad., 1982-84. Registered architect N.Y. Constrn. mgr. Ctrl. Bklyn. Fedayeen Constrn. Co., LLC, 1998—; architecture aide City of N.Y. Dept. of Health, 1978; intern architect Niagara Frontier Transp. Authority, Buffalo, 1983; architect, drafter Bradley Corp. Park, Blauvelt, N.Y., 1984-85; asst. architect City of N.Y. Dept. of Housing Preservation and Devel., 1985-87, N.Y.C. Bd. Edn., 1987-91; design cons. J.K. Mui Design, Bronx, N.Y., 1989—; project coord. N.Y.C. Pub. Schs., 1991-98; pres. Mui Enterprises Internat., Bronx, 1994—. Vice chmn. bd. dirs. Hong Kong Students Assn. N.Y. Inc., 1989-91, chmn., 1987-89, pres., 1986; sec. Moy Shee Family Assn., N.Y.C., 1999—. Recipient N.Y. State Regent Scholarship award, 1977-81, Husted Award Scholarship award SUNY, 1980. Roman Catholic. Home: 2237 Haviland Ave Bronx NY 10462-5202 Office: Ctrl Bklyn Fedayeen Constrn Co LLC 2381 Dean St Brooklyn NY 11233-4329

MUICO-MERCURIO, LUISA, critical care nurse; b. Caloocan, Manila, Philippines, Nov. 17, 1955; d. Amado B. and Eustaquia (Buenavista) Muico; m. Wilfred Tongson Mercurio, Dec. 28, 1974; children: Elyjah Matthew, Kristoffer Ross, Mercurio. ADN, Harbor City Coll., 1978; BSN, Calif. State U., 1990, postgrad., 1992—. Cert. ACLS instr., BLS instr; CCRN; cert. pub. health nurse. Staff nurse ICU Long Beach (Calif.) Meml. Med. Ctr., 1978-80; staff nurse CVT/ICU Cedar Sinai Med. Ctr., L.A., 1980-84; staff nurse ICU, CCU, emergency rm., cath. lab. Long Beach Cmty. Hosp., 1982-86; ICU, CCU coord. Pioneer Hosp., Artesia, Calif., 1986-87; staff nurse CSU Kaiser-Permanente, L.A., 1988-90, pub. health nurse, 1990, asst. dept. adminstr., 1990-92, Sunset and Bellflower, Calif.; cardiovascular/thoracic surgery nurse coord. Kay Med. Group/Hosp. Good Samaritan, L.A., 1992—; adminstrv. supr. Barlow Respiratory Hosp., 1993; staff nurse critical care unit UCLA, 1994—, staff nurse liver transplant unit, 1996—; nursing faculty Pacific Coast Coll., 1994—, ICU-Kaweah Delta Dist. Hosp., Visalia, Calif., 1996—; adminstr., cons. Welco Guest Homes, Porterville, 1996—. Named to Dean's list Harbor City Coll., 1976-78, Dean's list Calif. State U., 1987-89. Mem. AACN (cert.), Nat. Golden Key Honor Soc., Nursing Honor Soc., Sigma Theta Tau (Nu Mu chpt.). Republican. Avocations: small arms competition, Hapkido, racquetball competition, singing.

MUIR, HELEN, journalist, author; b. Yonkers, N.Y., Feb. 9, 1911; d. Emmet A. and Helen T. (Flaherty) Lennehan; m. William Whalley Muir, Jan. 23, 1936; children: Mary Muir Burrell, William Torbert. With Yonkers Herald Statesman, 1929-30, 31-33, N.Y. Evening Post, 1930-31, N.Y. Evening Jour., 1933-34, Carl Byoir & Assocs., N.Y.C., Miami, 1934-35; syndicated columnist Universal Svc., Miami, 1935-38; columnist Miami Herald, 1941-42; children's book editor, 1949-56; women's editor Miami Daily News, 1943-44; freelance mag. writer numerous nat. mags., 1944—. Drama critic Miami News, 1960-65. Author: Miami, U.S.A., 1953, expanded edit., 2000, Biltmore: Beacon for Miami, 1987, 3d rev. edit., 1998, Frost in Florida: A Memoir, 1995. Trustee Coconut Grove Libr. Assn., Friends U. Miami Libr., Friends Miami-Dade Pub. Libr.; vis. com. U. Miami Librs.; bd. dirs. Miami-Dade County Pub. Libr. Sys., chmn. emeritus, 1999. Recipient award Delta Kappa Gamma, 1960, trustees and friends award Fla. Libr. Assn., 1973, award Coun. Fla. Librs., 1990, trustee citation ALA, 1984, spirit of excellence award, 1988; named to Fla. Women's Hall of Fame, 1984, Miami Centennial '96 Women's Hall of Fame; named chmn. emeritus Metro-Dade Libr. Sys., 1999. Mem. ALA (named leading libr. advocate of 20th Century), Women in Communications (cmty. headliner award 1973), Soc. Women Geographers (meritorious svc. award 1996, Authors Guild, Fla. Groups First Woman of World award 2000), Author's Guild, Fla. Women's Press Club (award 1963, Cosmopolitan Club (N.Y.C.), Biscayne Bay Yacht Club. Home: 3855 Stewart Ave Miami FL 33133-6734

MUIR, J. DAPRAY, lawyer; b. Washington, Nov. 9, 1936; s. Brockett and Helen Cassin (Dapray) M.; m. Louise Rutherfurd Pierrepont, July 16, 1966. AB, Williams Coll., 1958; JD, U. Va., 1964. Bar: Md., Va., D.C. 1964, U.S. Supreme Ct. 1967. Asst. legal advisor for econ. and bus. affairs U.S. Dept. State, 1971-73; ptnr. Ruddy & Muir, LLP, Washington. Mem. U.S. del. to Joint U.S./USSR Comml. Commn., 1972; chmn. D.C. Securities Adv. Com., 1981-84, mem. 1985-88. Bd. editors Va. Law Rev, 1963-64; contbr. articles to profl. jours. Bd. dirs. Trust Mus. Exhbns., 1997—, Internat. Fedn. Insts. Advanced Study, 1992—97. Lt. (j.g.) USNR, 1958—61. Mem. D.C. Bar (chmn. internat. law div. 1977-78, chmn. environ., energy and natural resources div. 1982-83, Met. Club (Washington), Chevy Chase (Md.) Club, Am. Arbitration Assn. (panel of comml. arbitrators 1997—). Home: 3104 Q St NW Washington DC 20007-3027 Office: 1730 K St NW Ste 304 Washington DC 20006

MUIR, JOHN DOUGLASS, physician; b. Toronto, Ontario, Can., Sept. 11, 1947; BSc with honors, U. Toronto, 1970, MD, 1973. Diplomate Am. Bd. Internal Medicine, Am. Bd. Pulmonary Disease, Am. Bd. Critical Care. Intern N. York Gen. Hosp., Toronto, Can., 1973-74; resident U. Toronto, 1974-79; fellowship Royal Coll. Physicians Can., 1979; cons. in pulmonary and critical care medicine, 1979-95; pulmonary, critical care physician Naples (Fla.) Cmty. Hosp., 1995—. Fellow ACP, Am. Coll. Chest Physicians, Royal Coll. Physicians (diplomate). Office: 11181 Health Park Blvd Ste 2260 Naples FL 34110-5734

MUIR, KAREN LYNN, cultural anthropolgy educator, consultant; d. Palmer Blain and Esther Milton Stickney; m. John Rowland Muir, Sept. 7, 1975; children: Justin Reilly, Ian Nathaniel, Ross Remington, Shaina MacKenzie. Phd, Ohio State U., Columbus, Ohio, 1972—84. Assoc. prof. Columbus State CC, Columbus, Ohio, 1989—. Muticultural cons. freelance, Columbus, Ohio, 1984—. Co-director Dublin charity cup soccer tournament, Dublin, 2000—02; cons. Laotian Mut. Assistance Assn., Columbus, 1983—2002. Recipient Distinguished Tchg., Columbus State CC, 2001; grantee Internat. Student Experience, Coulumbus State CC, 2001. Mem.: Nat. Ctr. Sci. Edn., Am. Anthropology Assn., Soc. Anthropology. Office: Columbus State Community College 550 East Sprint Street Columbus OH 43216 Home Fax: 614-287-5301. E-mail: kmuir@cscc.edu.

MUIR, MALCOLM, federal judge; b. Englewood, N.J., Oct. 20, 1914; s. John Merton and Sarah Elizabeth Muir; m. Alma M. Brohard, Sept. 6, 1940 (dec. 1985); children: Malcolm, Thomas, Ann Muir, Barbara (dec.), David Clay. BA, Lehigh U., 1935; LL.B., Harvard U., 1938. Sole practice, Williamsport, Pa., 1938-42, 45-49, 68-70; mem. firm, 1949-68; judge U.S. Dist. Ct. (mid. dist.) Pa., 1970—. Active charitable orgns., Williamsport, 1939-70 Mem. ABA, Pa. Bar Assn. (pres.-elect 1970) Avocation: reading. Office: US Dist Ct Ste 401 240 W 3rd St Williamsport PA 17701-6461

MUIR, PATRICIA ALLEN, professional association administrator; b. Dallas, Nov. 4, 1929; d. Jack Charleton Allen and Anna Patricia (Hovis) Allen Atchison; m. Lester Doyle Rader, Jr., Aug. 4, 1950 (dec. Sept. 1950); 1 child, Lester Doyle III; m. Perren James Muir, June 2, 1956 (div.); children: Edward John, Patricia Jane. Grad., Our Lady of Victory Coll., 1948; student, George Washington U., 1948-49, Washington Sch. for Secs., 1949-50. Traffic mgr. Am. Storage Co., Washington, 1960-69; asst. sec. Ind. Telephone Pioneer Assn., 1969-76; adminstrv. asst. ALA, 1977-98, staff liaison to Fed. Librs. Round Table, 1991-98, staff liaison to Armed Forces Librs. Round Table, 1991-98, staff liaison to Govt. Documents Round Table, 1991-98; office mgr. Fed. Documents Clearing House, 1998-2000, cons., 2000—. Columnist, contbr. The Ind. Pioneer, 1969-76. V.p. Friendship House Child Devel. Ctr. Parents, Washington, 1978, pres., 1979—83; mem. parish coun. St. Peter's Cath. Ch., 1987—91, mem. edn. and spiritual devel. com., 1986—, chair, 1988—91, coord. Bible study, 1999—; vol. St. Peter's Interparish Sch. Reading Program, 2001—02. Mem. Ladies Ancient Order of Hibernians (state pres. 1991-97, nat. budget com. 1996-98, nat. elections com. 1998—, nat. constn. com. 1998-02, nat. rules of order com. 2000-02). Avocations: travel, genealogy, reading, writing. Home: 343 11th St SE Washington DC 20003-2105

MUIR, WARREN ROGER, chemist, executive; b. N.Y., 1945; s. Ernest Roger and Phyllis (Stirn) M.; m. Jo-Ann McNally; children: Amy, Douglas, Michael, Gregory, Daniel. AB in Chemistry cum laude, Amherst Coll., 1967; MS in Chemistry, Northwestern U., Evanston, Ill., 1968, PhD in Chemistry, 1971; postgrad. in epidemiology, Johns Hopkins U., 1975-77. Sr. staff mem. environ. health Council on Environ. Quality, EPA, Washington, 1971-78; dir. Office of Toxic Substances, EPA, 1978-81; pres. Hampshire Rsch. Assocs., Inc., 1981-99, Hampshire Rsch. Inst., 1987-99; exec. dir. divsn. earth and life studies NRC/Nat. Acad. Scis., 1999—. Assoc. environ. health scis. Johns Hopkins U., 1981-99; rsch. prof. biology Am. U., 1985; sr. fellow INFORM, 1982-95; mem. Nat. Conf. Lawyers and Scientists, 1987-89; bd. environ. scis. & toxicology Nat. Rsch. Coun., 1997-99. Contbr. articles on environ. quality to profl. jours. Mem., chair several Nat. Rsch. Coun. coms.; pres. Children's Friendship Project for No. Ireland, 1997-99, bd. dirs. 1995—, chair 1997—. Recpient NSF Acad. award, 1966, Howard Waters Doughty prize Amherst Coll., 1967, Forris Jewett Moore fellow, 1967; comdr., 1996, officer brother Most Venerable Order of St. John, 1992; co-recipient Adminstrs.' award U.S. EPA, 1992. Mem.: AAAS, Am. Chem. Soc. Home: 9426 Forest Haven Dr Alexandria VA 22309-3151

MUIR, WILLIAM KER, JR. political science educator; b. Detroit, Oct. 30, 1931; s. William Ker and Florence Taylor (Bodman) M.; m. Paulette Irene Wauters, Jan. 16, 1960; children: Kerry Macaire, Harriet Bodman. BA, Yale U., 1954, PhD, 1965; JD, U. Mich., 1958. Bar: N.Y. 1960, Conn. 1965. Instr. U. Mich. Law Sch., 1958-59; assoc. firm Davis Polk & Wardwell, N.Y.C., 1959-60; lectr. in polit. sci. Yale U., 1960-64, 65-67; from assoc. to ptnr. Tyler Cooper Grant Bowerman & Keefe, New Haven, 1964-68; prof. emeritus polit. sci. U. Calif.-Berkeley, 1968-98, dept. chmn., 1980-83; speechwriter v.p. U.S., 1983-85; columnist Oakland (Calif.) Tribune, 1992-93; writer Gov. of Calif., Sacramento, 1994. Sr. cons. Calif. State Assembly, Sacramento, 1975-76; cons. Oakland (Calif.) Police Dept., 1969-74; vis. prof. polit. sci. Harvard U., summers 1976, 79; vis. prof. Hawaii Pacific U., 2000, U. Ariz., 2002; vis. disting. scholar Hawaii Pacific U., 2000; vis. lectr. U. Ariz., 2002. Author: Prayer in the Public Schools, 1967, later republished as Law and Attitude Change, 1974, Police: Streetcorner Politicians, 1977, Legislature: California's School for Politics, 1982, The Bully Pulpit: The Presidential Leadership of Ronald Reagan, 1993. Mem. Berkeley (Calif.) Police Rev. Commn., 1981-83; chmn. New Haven Civil Liberties Coun., 1965-68; bd. visitors Found. for Cmty. and Faith Ctr. Enterprise, 2002; Rep. candidate Calif. State Assembly, 1996. Recipient Hadley B. Cantril Meml. award, 1979, Disting. teaching award U. Calif., Berkeley, 1974, Phi Beta Kappa No. Calif. Assoc. Excellence In Teaching award, 1994. Mem. Am. Polit. Sci. Assn. (Edward S. Corwin award 1966) Republican. Presbyterian. Home: 59 Parkside Dr Berkeley CA 94705-2409 Office: Dept Polit Sci U Calif Berkeley CA 94720-1950 E-mail: sandymuir@aol.com.

MUIR, WILLIAM LLOYD , III, academic administrator; b. Norton, Kans., Mar. 20, 1948; s. John Thomas and Rosalie June (Benton) M. BBA, Kans. State U., 1977. Asst. sec. of state State of Kans., Topeka, 1971-72, fin. adminstr. atty. gen. office, 1972-79, comptr. Office of Gov., 1979-87, sec. of cabinet, 1979-87, asst. sec. adminstrn., 1986-87; dir. econ. devel. Kans. State U., Manhattan, 1987-91, asst. to v.p., dir. cmty. rels., 1991—2002, faculty rep., senator Student Governing Assn., 1992—, mem. union governing bd., 1997—, asst. v.p. for cmty. rels., 2002—. Chmn. housing appeals bd. City of Manhattan, 1996—, mem., vice chmn. econ. devel. adv. bd., 1999—2002; trustee Kans. State U. Found., 1993—; mem. Leadership Kans., 1989; state officer Native Sons and Daus., 1997—2002, pres., 2001; bd. dirs. United Way Riley County, 1989—99, chmn., 1992, treas., 2001—. Mem. Friends of Cedar Crest Assn., Nat. Geog. Soc., Sierra Club, Masons (Scottish rite), Blue Key, Alpha Tau Omega (nat. officer), Alpha Kappa Psi. Episcopalian. Avocations: travel, volunteer work, advising. Home: 2040 Shirley Ln Manhattan KS 66502-2059 Office: Kansas State U 122 Anderson Hall Manhattan KS 66506-0100 E-mail: billmuir@ksu.edu.

MUIRHEAD, JAMES RUSSELL, federal judge; b. 1941; BS, Cornell U., 1963, LLB, 1966. Bar: N.H. 1966. Pvt. practice, Manchester, N.H., 1966-95; magistrate judge for N.H., U.S. Fed. Ct., Concord, 1995—. Office: WB Rudman US Courthouse 55 Pleasant St Concord NH 03301-3954

MUIRHEAD, VINCENT URIEL, retired aerospace engineer; b. Dresden, Kans., Feb. 6, 1919; s. John Hadsell and Lily Irene (McKinney) M.; m. Bobby Jo Thompson, Nov. 5, 1943; children: Rosalind, Jean, Juleigh. BS, U.S. Naval Acad., 1941; BS in Aero. Engring, U.S. Naval Postgrad. Sch., 1948; Aero. Engr., Calif. Inst. Tech., 1949; postgrad., U. Ariz., 1962, 64, Okla. State U., 1963. Midshipman U.S. Navy, 1937, commd. ensign, 1941, advanced through grades to comdr., 1951; nav. officer U.S.S. White Plains, 1945-46; comdr. Fleet Aircraft Service Squad, 1951-52; with Bur. Aeros., Ft. Worth, 1953-54; comdr. Helicopter Utility Squadron I, Pacific Fleet, 1955-56; chief staff officer Comdr. Fleet Air, Philippines, 1956-58; exec. officer Naval Air Tng. Center, Memphis, 1958-61; ret., 1961; asst. prof. U. Kans., Lawrence, 1961-63, assoc. prof. aerospace engring., 1964-76, prof., 1976-89, prof. emeritus, 1989—, chmn. dept., 1976-88. Cons. Black & Veatch (cons. engrs.), Kansas City, Mo., 1964— Author: Introduction to Aerospace, 1972, 5th edit., 1994, Thunderstorms, Tornadoes and Building Damage, 1975. Decorated Air medal. Fellow AIAA (assoc.); mem. Am. Acad. Mechanics, Am. Soc. Engring. Edn., Tau Beta Pi, Sigma Gamma Tau. Mem. Ch. of Christ (elder 1972-96). Achievements include research on aircraft, tornado vortices, shock tubes and waves. Home: 503 Park Hill Ter Lawrence KS 66046-4841 Office: Dept Aerospace Engring Univ Kans Lawrence KS 66045-0001 E-mail: vmuirhead@aol.com.

MUJICA, MAURO E. architect; b. Antofagasta, Chile, Apr. 20, 1941; came to U.S., 1965, naturalized, 1970; s. Mauro Raul and Graciela (Parodi-Blayfus) M.; m. Barbara Louise Kaminar, Dec. 26, 1966; children: Lillian Louise, Mariana Ximena, Mauro Eduardo Ignacio III. BArch, MArch, Columbia U., 1971. Head designer Columbia U. Office Archtl. Planning, N.Y.C., 1966-71; project mgr. Walker, Sander, Ford & Kerr, Architects, Princeton, N.J., 1971-72; prin. Mauro E. Mujica, Architect, N.Y.C., 1972-74; dir. internat. divsn. Greenhorne & O'Mara, Inc., Riverdale, Md., 1974-78; ptnr. Mujica & Reddy Architects, Washington, 1978-80; prin. Mauro E. Mujica, Architect, 1980-81; ptnr. Mujica & Berlin Investment Bankers, 1982-85, Mujica Keppie Henderson Internat., Washington and Glasgow, Scotland, 1981-83, Mujica-Seifert Architects, Washington and London, 1983-87; pres., DEO, The Pace Group, Washington, 1987-91; ptnr. Pace/Walsh Internat., London and Washington. Chmn. bd., CEO, U.S. English Found., Washington, 1993—; hon. mem. Emmanuel Coll. Cambridge (Eng.) U., 1995; mem. adv. bd. U.S.-U.K. Fulbright Commn., 1995-2000.

MUJUMDAR, VILAS SITARAM, structural engineer, management executive; b. Indore, India, June 26, 1941; s. Sitaram and Kamala (Kulkarni) M.; m. Ingrid M. Dietrich, Mar. 1, 1969. BScin Civil Engring., Vikram U., India, 1961; MS, U. Roorkee, India, 1962; MBA, U. Santa Clara, Calif., 1980; D in Pub. Adminstrn., U. So. Calif., 2000. Registered profl. engr., U.S., Can., U.K.; registered structural engr., Calif. Design engr. U.S.D. & Co., India, 1962-65, Donovan H. Lee & Ptnrs., London, 1965-66; asst. chief engr. Francon & Spancrete Ltd., Montreal, Can., 1966-68; gen. mgr., dir. engring. Modular Constructors, Woburn, Mass., 1968-70; sr. project engr., tech. mgr. LeMessurier Assocs., Cambridge, 1970-74; v.p. Precast Systems Cons., Woburn, 1974-77; prin. structural engr. Ecodyne Corp., Santa Rosa, Calif., 1977-79; v.p. Foster Engring., Inc., San Francisco, 1979-81, 3D/Internat. Inc., Houston, 1981-85; pres. VSM Assocs., Santa Rosa, Calif., 1985-88; v.p. BSHA, Inc., San Diego, 1988-90; pres. McNamara, Salvia, Mujumdar, Inc., 1990-92; chief of ops. Div. State Architect Dept. Gen. Svcs., Calif., 1992-2000; exec. dir. Concrete Masonry Assn. Calif., Nev., 2000—. Mem. steering con. U.S.-Japan Seismic Rsch. Author: Concrete Design Manual, Structural Engineer Review Course; inventor pre-cast concrete bldg. systems; contbr. articles to profl. jours. Merit scholar Govt. India, 1957-62, Gold medal; recipient numerous awards. Fellow: ASCE, Am. Concrete Inst., Inst. Structural Engrs. U.K.; mem.: Structural Engrs. Assn. Calif. (chmn. seismology com. 1992—93), Prestressed Concrete Inst. (chmn. several earthquake engring coms.), Beta Gamma Sigma (hon. bus. soc.). Home: 7739 Oakshore Dr Sacramento CA 95831-5795 E-mail: vilasm@jps.net.

MUKAMAL, DAVID SAMIER, sign manufacturing company executive; b. Baghdad, Iraq, Oct. 6, 1944; came to U.S., 1950; s. Abraham Sassoon and Mary (Murad) M.; m. Anitamarie Costa, July 31, 1970; children: Adam Scott, Rebecca Kate. BBA in Econs. with honors, Bryant Coll., 1970; MBA in Fin. Mgmt., Iona Coll., 1975. Budget analyst USV Pharm./Revlon, Inc., Tuckahoe, N.Y., 1970-72; sr. budget officer Met. Transp. Authority, N.Y.C., 1972-74; sr. fin. analyst Am. Airlines, Inc., Dallas, 1974-82; chmn. DSM Industries Inc.; pres. All State Signs, Richardson, Tex., 1982—, Framed Enterprises, Inc., Irving, 1995-99. With USN, 1965-66. Recipient Jerremiah Clarke Barber award Bryant Coll., 1970. Mem. Dallas Apt. Assn., Tex. Sign Mfrs. Assn., Internat. Sign Assn., La Cima Club (bd. dirs.), Omicron Delta Epsilon. Republican. Jewish.

MUKASYAN, ALEXANDER SERGEEVICH, scientist; b. Samara, Russia, Jan. 17, 1956; came to U.S., 1995; s. Sergey Papchanovich Mukasyan and Victorina Alexandrovna Bessonova; m. Alla Gennadievna Klimova, Aug. 12, 1976; children: Vasiliy, Alexander. MS, Phys. Engring. Inst., Moscow, 1980; PhD, Russian Acad. Scis., Moscow, 1986; DSc, Russian Acad. Scis., Chernogolovka, Russia, 1994. Scientist Russian Acad. Scis., Inst. Chem. Physics, Moscow, 1980-88; sr. scientist Russian Acad. Scis., Inst. Structural Macrokinetics, Chernogolovka, 1989-93, head lab., 1993-96; mgr. lab. dept. chem. engring. U. Notre Dame, Ind., 1996-2000, prof., 2000—. Mem. sci. bd. Inst. Structural Macrokinetics, Chernogolovka; vice-chmn. Internat. Symposium, Wuhan, China, 1995. Mem. editl. bd. Internat. Jour. Self-Propagating High-Temperature Synthesis. Recipient medal Exhbn. Inds. Achievements, Moscow, 1986. Mem. AIChE, Am. Chem. Soc., Internat. Combustion Inst., Acad. Internat. Info. (academician). Achievements include invention of methods for production of ceramics. Avocations: soccer, volleyball, history. Home: 4005 Parkwood Cir Mishawaka IN 46545-2648 Office: Dept Chem Engring Univ Notre Dame Notre Dame IN 46556-7878 Fax: 574-631-8366. E-mail: amoukasi@nd.edu.

MUKAWA, AKIO, pathology educator; b. Kanazawa, Ishikawa, Japan, June 10, 1928; s. Tatsuchiyo and Moto (Ohtsuka) M.; m. Hiroko Matsuo, May 5, 1968; children: Chisui, Yasutake. MD, U. Kanazawa, Japan, 1954, PhD, 1959. Diplomate Am. Bd. Pathology. Resident pathology Queens Hosp. Ctr., N.Y.C., 1959-63; lectr. pathology U. Kanazawa Med. Sch., 1963-67; neuropathology fellow Albert Einstein Coll. Medicine, N.Y.C., 1966-67; dir. pathology Nat. Hosp. Kanazawa, 1967-72; prof. pathology Kanazawa Med. U., Uchinada, Japan, 1972-96, emeritus prof. pathology Japan, 1996—; cons. Mukawa Inst. Pathology, 1996—. Author: Autopsy Technique, 1988. Fellow Coll. Am. Pathologists, Japanese Path. Soc., Am. Soc. Clin. Pathologists (fgn. fellow 1989—). Avocation: gardening. Home and Office: Taiseidai 55 Uchinada Ishikawa 920-0267 Japan E-mail: mukawa@po.sphere.ne.jp.

MUKERJEE, DEBDAS, environmental health scientist, educator; b. Darjeeling, India; came to U.S., 1959. s. Suresh Chandra and Bidyutlata Mukerjee; m. Bhaisa Freny Dee, July 15, 1959; 1 child Shaibal. BSc with honors, Calcutta (India) U., 1954, MSc, 1957; PhD, U. Ky., 1962. Rsch. prof. pathology Jefferson Med. Coll., Thomas Jefferson U., Phila., 1974-80; sr. sci. advisor, environ. health scientist U.S. EPA Environ. Criteria Assessment Office, Cin., 1980-91; environ. health scientist U.S. EPA Nat. Ctr. for Environtl. Assessment, 1991—; adj. prof. toxicology Inst. Toxicology, U. Kiel (Germany) Med. Sch., 1990—. Adj. prof. environ. toxicology Ohio No. U., Ada, 1998—; assoc. prof. pathology, dir. divsn. basic rsch. U. Tex. Med. Br., Galveston, 1969-74; asst. prof. biology M.D. Anderson Hosp. & Tumor Inst., U. Tex. Cancer Ctr., Houston, 1966-69; mem. NATO/Com. Challenges of Modern Soc. Study on Internat. Info. Exch. of Dioxins and Related Compounds, 1985-88. Contbr. articles to profl. jours., chpts. to books. Sir J.C. Bose rsch. scholar Bose Inst., Calcutta, 1958; recipient cert. of appreciation for contbn. to devel. of guidelines for health risk chem. mixtures, 1996; recipient medal for commendable svc. to EPA, 1980, medal USEPA, 2002. Mem. AAAS, World Affairs Coun. Greater Cin., N.Y. Acad. Scis. Achievements include pioneering in risk assessment of dioxins, pcbs, children's risk from aggregate exposures to environmental pollutants; methodology of risk assessment, xenoestrogen related feminization of males in human, in vitro transformation of cells from cancer genetic susceptible persons; human secondary trisomy chromosome, transclocation between sex and somatic chromosomes, sex chromosome abnormalities. Avocations: comparative religion, philosophy of life, reading, writing. Office: US EPA Nat Ctr Environ Assessment Cincinnati OH 45268-0001 E-mail: mukerjee.debdas@epa.gov.

MUKERJEE, PASUPATI, chemistry educator; b. Calcutta, India, Feb. 13, 1932; s. Nani Gopal and Probhabati (Ghosal) M.; m. Lalita Sarkar, Feb. 29, 1964 (dec.); m. Mina Maitra, Nov. 14, 1998. B.Sc., Calcutta U., 1949, M.Sc., 1951; PhD, U. So. Calif., 1957. Lectr., vis. asst. prof. U. So. Calif., 1956-57; rsch. assoc. Brookhaven Nat. Lab., L.I., 1957-59; reader in phys. chemistry Indian Assn. Cultivation of Sci., Calcutta, 1959-64; guest scientist U. Utrecht,

Holland, 1964; sr. scientist chemistry dept. U. So. Calif., 1964-66; vis. assoc. prof. U. Wis., Madison, 1966-67, prof. Sch. Pharmacy, 1967-94, emeritus prof., 1994—. Vis. prof. Indian Inst. Tech., Kharagpur, 1971-72; mem. commn. on colloid and surface chemistry Internat. Union Pure and Applied Chemistry Contbr. articles to profl. jours.; mem. editl. bd. Jour. Colloid and Interface Sci., 1978-80, Asian Jour. Pharm. Scis., 1978-85, Colloids and Surfaces, 1980-86. Grantee USPHS, NSF, Nat. Bur. Stds., Petroleum Rsch. Fund. Fellow AAAS, Acad. Pharm. Scis., Am. Inst. Chemistry; mem. Am. Chem. Soc. (editorial bd. Langmuir 1985-86), Am. Pharm. Assn., Acad. Pharm. Scis., Rho Chi. Home: 5526 Varsity Hl Madison WI 53705-4652 Office: 777 Highland Ave Madison WI 53705-2222

MUKHERJEE, AMIYA K, metallurgy and materials science educator; PhD, Oxford (Eng.) U., 1962. Prof. U. Calif., Davis. Recipient Alexander von Humboldt award Fed. Republic Germany, 1988, Albert Easton White Disting. Tchr. award Am. Soc. Materials, 1992, Pfeil medal and prize Inst. Materials, 1993, U. Calif. prize and citation, 1993, Anatoly Bochvar medal U. Moscow, 1996, Inst. medal Max Planck Inst. for Metallforschung, 1997. Office: U Calif Davis Dept Chem Engring & Material Sci Davis CA 95616 E-mail: akmukherjee@ucdavis.edu.

MUKHERJEE, ASIT BARAN, geneticist, educator; b. Suri, India; came to U.S., 1963; s. Shyama Pada and Sabasana (Chatterjee) M.; m. Tapani Ghoshal; 1 child, Deepro. BS, U. Utah, 1965, MS, 1966, PhD, 1968. Rsch. assoc. Upstate Med. Ctr., Syracuse, N.Y., 1968-69, Columbia U. Med. Ctr., N.Y.C., 1969-70; instr. Albert Einstein Coll. Medicine, 1970-72; from asst. prof. to prof. Fordham U., 1972-83, prof., 1983—. Author, co-author monographs, book chpts.; contbr. over 50 articles to profl. jours. Tchg. fellow U. Utah, 1965-67, Presl. fellow, 1967-68, NIH fellow, 1969-70; grantee W. Alton Jones Found., 1973-83, Whitehall Found., 1977-83, NIH, Minority Access to Rsch. Career, 1984-89. Mem. Gerentol. Soc. Am., Am. Soc. Human Genetics. Office: Fordham U 441 E Fordham Rd Bronx NY 10458-9993 E-mail: mukherjee@fordham.edu.

MUKHERJEE, SANDIP KUMAR, cardiologist; b. India, Oct. 28, 1961; came to U.S, 1965; s. Tridib and Debdasi (Chatterjee) M.; m. Sholeh Moghaddam, Dec. 21, 1985; children: Mina, Alexander. BS, Tex. A&M U., 1982; MD, Tex. Tech U., 1988. Diplomate Am. Bd. Internal Medicine, Am. Bd. Cardiovascular Disease. Intern and resident in internal medicine Yale U. Sch. Medicine, New Haven, 1988-91, chief med. resident, 1991-92, fellow in cardiovascular medicine, 1992-95, asst. clin. prof. medicine, 1996—; ptnr. pvt. practice Cardiology Assocs. of New Haven, P.C. Co-dir. NIH/NHLBI study, 1996—; dir. cardiovascular workshop Yale Med. Sch.; presenter in field. Editl. fellow Med. Letter, 1997—; contbr. articles to profl. jours. Fellow Am. Coll. Cardiology; mem. AMA, ACP, Am. Heart Assn. Clin. Cardiology Coun., Beta Beta Beta. Office: Cardiology Assn New Haven 40 Temple St Ste 6A New Haven CT 06510-2715

MUKHERJEE, SIDDHARTHA, application developer; b. Calcutta, W. Bengal, India, Sept. 27, 1967; s. Birendra Bijoy and Sadhana Mukherjee; m. Indrani Halder, May 7, 1974. BS, Jadavpur U., India, 1990; MS, Jdadvpur U., India, 1992; PhD, Indian Inst. Tech., India, 1997. Sr. rsch. engr. Inst. High Performance Computing, Singapore, 1998—99; postdoctoral rsch. assoc. Tex. A&M U., College Station, 1999—2000; devel. engr. Ansys Inc., Canonsburg, Pa., 2000—. Developer (software for design optimization) DesignXplorer, 2002 (Best of Show award NDES, 2002); contbr. articles to profl. jours. Fellow, U. Grants Commn., Govt. of India, 1990—92, Ministry of Human Resource and Devel., Govt. of India., 1992—97. Mem.: U.S. Assn. Computational Mechanics. Home: 3520 Washington Pike Apt 1302 Bridgeville PA 15017 Office: Ansys Inc 275 Technology Dr Canonsburg PA 15317 Home Fax: 724-514-3114; Office Fax: 724-514-3114. Personal E-mail: siddhartha.mukherjee@ansys.com. E-mail: siddhartha.mukherjee@ansys.com.

MUKHTAR, ABDU SARKINBAI, physician, researcher, molecular biologist, entrepreneur; b. Dambatta, Kano, Nigeria; came to U.S., 1993; s. Sarkinbai and Habiba Mukhtar; m. fatima Farouk Labaran, 1996. MBBS, Ahmadu Bello U., Zaria, Nigeria, 1991; PhD in Pathology and Lab. Medicine, Boston U., 1999; postgrad., Harvard U., 1999—. Diplomate Nat. Bd. Med. Examiners; lic. physician, Nigeria. House officer Murtala Gen. Hosp., Kano, 1991-92; med. officer Aso Rock Clinic, Abuja, Nigeria, 1992-93; rsch. asst. dept. pathology Boston U., 1993-96, postdoctoral fellow Pulmonary Ctr., 1996-99. NHLBI/NIH fellow, 1996, Free U. Amsterdan surg. rsch. fellow, 1991, Commonwealth med. Found. fellow, 1991. Mem. AAAS, N.Y. Acad. Sci., Mass. Med. Soc., Boston Cancer Rsch. Assn., Nigerian Med. Assn., Internat. Aids Soc., Interntа. Fedn. Med. Students Assns. (hon. life; Nigerial profl. exch. chair 1989-91), Am. Assn. Immunologists, Am. Soc. Gene Therapy, Am. Soc. Investigative Pathology, Alpha Epsilon Lambda. Achievements include cloning of a human gene. Avocations: politics, reading, basketball. Office: Boston Univ sch Medicine Pulmonary Ctr 80 E Concord St Boston MA 02118-2307

MUKUNDAN, GOPALAN, information technologist; b. Karaikudi, India, Mar. 15, 1960; came to U.S., 1984; s. Srinivasan and Lakshmi (Chakravarthi) Gopalan; m. Subhashini Mukundan, Oct. 31, 1988; children: Ananya, Aditya. BTech in Mech. Engring., Indian Inst. Tech., Kharagpur, 1982; MEng, Asian Inst. Tech., Bangkok, 1984; MS in Computer Sci., Ariz. State U., 1986; PhD in Systems Engring., Oakland U., Rochester, Mich., 1995. Sr. engr. Auto-Trol Tech., Denver, 1986-89, Electronic Data Systems, Troy, Mich., 1989-96; advanced tech. specialist Product Design Office, Auburn Hills, 1996—. Author: Automotive Exterior Surface Deesign, 1996. Mem. Soc. Mfg. Engrs., Soc. Indsl. and Applied Math. Home: 6508 Shoreline Dr Troy MI 48085-1056 Office: Product Design Office 800 Chrysler Dr Auburn Hills MI 48326-2757

MULAC, PAMELA ANN, priest, pastoral counselor; b. Salem, Ohio, Dec. 6, 1944; d. Elmer John and Dorothy Adelaide (McGee) M.; m. George Robert Larsen, Aug. 8, 1987. Student, Bryn Mawr Coll., 1962-64; AB, U. Chgo., 1966; MDiv, Seabury-Western Theol. Sem., 1974; PhD, Garrett Evang. Theol. Sem., Northwestern U., 1988. Ordained to ministry Episcopal Ch. as priest, 1978. Asst. deacon, priest St. Luke's Ch., Evanston, Ill., 1974-84; asst. priest St. Mark's Ch., Upland, Calif., 1984-88, St. Ambrose Ch., Claremont, 1988-90; assoc. priest for pastoral care All Saints Ch., Pasadena, 1991-93; asst. interim pastor St. George's, La Canada, 1994-95; chaplain Foothill Presbyn. Hosp., Glendon, 1994-95; interim pastor St. Timothy's Ch., Apple Valley, 1995-96; interim rector St. Michael's Ch., Riverside, 1996—. Pastoral counselor Swedish Covenant Hosp., Chgo., 1975-84; adj. lectr. Seabury-Western Theol. Sem., Evanston, 1981-82, trustee, 1981-84; pastoral counselor Walnut (Calif.) Valley Counseling Ctr., 1984-89; adj. lectr. marriage and family therapy program Azusa Pacific U., 1988-89, adj. lectr. operation impact, 1991-92; adj. prof. Sch. of Theology at Claremont, 1994-95; adj. prof. Episc. Theology Sch., Claremont, 1994-96. Bd. dirs. Cathedral Shelter Chgo., 1980-84; co-chairperson Leader's Sch. Cursillo, Chgo., 1981-83; mem. Commn. on Alcoholism, Diocese of L.A., 1985-87 Episcopal Ch. Found. fellow, 1978-81. Mem. Am. Assn. Pastoral Counselors (sec. Pacific region 1984-85, treas. 1984-91, fin. chair 1988-91), Assn. Clin. Pastoral Edn. Home and Office: 1439 Bonnie Jean Ln La Habra Heights CA 90631-8665

MULARZ, THEODORE LEONARD, architect; b. Chgo., Nov. 6, 1933; s. Stanley A. and Frances (Baycar) M.; m. Ruth L. Larson, Nov. 9, 1963; children: Anne Catherine, Mark Andrew. BArch, U. Ill., 1959. Registered arch., Colo., Oreg. Prin. Theodore L. Mularz, AIA Architects, Aspen, Colo., 1981-90; v.p. Benedict-Mularz Assocs., Inc., 1978-81; pvt. practice Ashland, Oreg., 1990—. Designer numerous archtl. projects, including comml., indsl., religious, recreational, residential and hist. restoration. Vice-chmn. Pitkin County Bd. Appeals, 1972-90, City of Aspen Bd. Appeals, 1985-90; adv. com. City of Aspen Planning/Building Dept., 1989; mem. Colo. Bd. Examiners of Archs., 1975-85, pres., 1976-80, v.p., 1978; mem. Oreg. Bd. Examiners of Archs., 1996-2000; bd. dirs. Rogue Valley Symphony, Ashland, 1990-92, treas., 1991-92, chmn. fin. com., 1991-92. Served with USCGR, 1953-55. Fellow AIA; mem. Nat. Coun. Archtl. Registration Bds. (profl. conduct com. 1977-78, procedures/documents com. 1978-82, chmn. 1983-84, chmn. edn. com. 1982-83, dir. 1982-84, internat. rels. com. 1984-89, exec. com. 1984-87, mem. interprofl. coun. on registration 1984-85, pres. 1985, internat. oral exam com. 1984-89, broadly experienced arch. interview com. 1987-2001), Colo. Soc. Archs. (Cmty. Svc. award 1975), Aspen C. of C. (past dir., pres., v.p.), Aspen Hist. Soc. (com. chmn. 1963-64), Rotary (dir. Ashland found. 2001-, pres. 2001-). Roman Catholic. Studio: 793 Elkader St Ashland OR 97520-3307 E-mail: tmularz@aol.com.

MULASE, MOTOHICO, mathematics educator; b. Kanazawa, Japan, Oct. 11, 1954; came to U.S., 1982; s. Ken-Ichi and Mieko (Yamamoto) M.; m. Sayuri Kamiya, Sept. 10, 1982; children: Kimihico Chris, Paul Norihico, Yurika. BS, U. Tokyo, 1978; MS, Kyoto U., 1980, DSc, 1985. Rsch. assoc. Nagoya (Japan) U., 1980-85; JMS fellow Harvard U., Cambridge, Mass., 1982-83; vis. asst. prof. SUNY, Stony Brook, 1984-85; Hedrick asst. prof. UCLA, 1985-88; asst. prof. Temple U., Phila., 1988-89; assoc. prof. U. Calif., Davis, 1989-91, prof., 1991—, vice chair dept. math., 1995-96, chair dept. math., 1998—2001. Mem. Math. Scis. Rsch. Inst., Berkeley, Calif., 1982-84, Inst. for Advanced Study, Princeton, N.J., 1988-89; vis. prof. Max-Planck Inst. for Math., Bonn, Germany, 1991-92, Kyoto U., 1993, 94, Humboldt U., Berlin, Germany, 1995, 1996, 2002. Contbr. articles to profl. jours. Treas. Port of Sacramento Japanese Sch., 1990-91. Mem. Am. Math. Soc. (com. on internat. affairs 1993-96). Avocation: music. Office: U Calif Dept Math Davis CA 95616 E-mail: mulase@math.ucdavis.edu.

MULCAHY, GABRIEL M. pathologist; b. Jersey City, Feb. 16, 1929; s. Joseph Alphonsus and Anna Elizabeth Mulcahy; m. Vesna Maria Mulcahy, May 24, 1958; children: Mary, Michael, Robert, Richard, Thomas, John, Gabriel Jr. AB, St. Peter's Coll., Jersey City, 1950; MD, Georgetown U., 1954. Diplomate Nat. Bd. Med. Examiners, Am. Bd. Pathology. Intern St. Michaels Hosp., Newark, 1954-55; med. officer U.S. Pub. Health Svc., Crownpoint, N.Mex., 1955-57, resident in pathology Seattle, 1957-59, Staten Island, N.Y., 1959-61, chief pathology svc. Detroit, 1961-62; with pathology faculty Creighton U., Omaha, 1962-69; dir. pathology Jersey City Med. Ctr., 1969-78; mem. pathology faculty Univ. Medicine and Dentistry N.J., Newark, 1978-2001; chief lab. med. Univ. Hosp., 1978-2001. Mem. editl bd.: Annals of Clin. and Lab. Sci., 2000—; contbr. articles to profl. jours. Mem. adv. bd. St. Ann's Home for the Aged, Jersey City, 1973-89, sec., 1973-83; pres. bd. edn. St. Paul's Parish Sch., Jersey City, 1973-78. Mem. AAAS, Am. Soc. Human Genetics, Am. Assn. Blood Banks, Assn. Clin. Scientists (sci. coun. 1999—), Coll. Am. Pathologists, Soc. Med. Decision Making. Roman Catholic. Avocations: history, philosophy, philology, photography. E-mail: mulcahy@comapp.org.

MULCAHY, KATHLEEN LYNN, neonatal and pediatric nurse practitioner; b. Syracuse, N.Y., Jan. 3, 1956; d. Richard F. and Kathleen (Clark) M. Diploma in Nursing, Crouse Irving Meml. Hosp., 1976; BSN, SUNY, Utica-Rome, 1984; Neonatal Nurse Practitioner, Georgetown U., 1988; MSN, PNP, Syracuse U., 1994. RN, N.Y.; cert. neonatal nurse practitioner, adult, pediat. and infant CPR instr., pediatric advanced life support. Staff nurse adult ICU Crouse-Irving Meml. Hosp., Syracuse, 1977-79, staff nurse emergency dept., 1979-83, staff nurse neonatal ICU, 1983-87; neonatal nurse practitioner SUNY Health Sci. Ctr., 1987-95; PNP Brighton Hill Pediat., 1995—. Regional instr. CPR, Am. Acad. Pediat., 1989—; transport nurse Crouse Irving meml. Hosp., 1985-95; lectr. in field. Mem. NAACOG, Nat. Assn. Neonatal Nurses, Coalition Nurse Practitioners (pres. Syracuse chpt. 1997-98), N.Y. State Nurse Practitioner Coalition, N.Y. State Nurses Assn. Avocations: boating, water skiing, camping. Home: 213 East Ave East Syracuse NY 13057-2105 Office: Brighton Hill Pediatrics 151 Intrepid Ln Ste 1 Syracuse NY 13205-2571 E-mail: klmulcahy@aol.com.

MULCAHY, RICHARD PATRICK, history educator, consultant; b. Greensburg, Pa., Mar. 18, 1958; s. Patrick Francis and Frances Catherine (Bell) M. BA, St. Vincent Coll., 1980; MA, Duquesne U., 1982, U. Pitts., 1985; PhD, W.Va. U., 1988. Tchg. asst. Duquesne U., Pitts., 1980-82; instr. history La Roche Coll., 1982-83; lectr. history W.Va. U., Morgantown, 1988-89; asst. prof. U. Pitts., Titusville, Pa., 1989-95, assoc. prof., 1995—, dir. social sci. divsn., 1997—. Reader, referee Okla. U. Press, Norman, 1990, U. Tenn. Press, Knoxville, 2000; archival cons. W.Va. U., Morgantown, 1992; summer faculty Chautauqua Inst. Spl. Schs., 1996-99. Mem. editl. adv. bd. Collegiate Press., 1993; author: A Social Contract for the Coal Fields: The Rise and Fall of the UMWA Welfare and Retirement Fund, 1946-78, 2000; author chpt. to book; contbr. articles to profl. jours. Woods scholar W.Va. U., 1987; fellow Ctr. for No. Appalachian Studies, Saint Vincent Coll., Latrobe, Pa., 1996—. Mem. AAUP (mem. Pitt. exec. coun. 1991—, elected sec. Pa. conf.), Chautaugua Lit. and Sci. Cir. (class of 1999), Soc. of the Hall in the Grove, Appalachian Studies Assn., Am. Fedn. Tchrs., Phi Alpha Theta. Democrat. Roman Catholic. Avocations: computer programming, ham radio. Office: U Pitts 504 E Main St Titusville PA 16354-2010

MULCAHY, ROBERT EDWARD, management consultant; b. Cambridge, Mass., Mar. 2, 1932; s. George Frances and Hazel (Douglas) M.; m. Ethel Walworth, Nov. 14, 1953; children: Linda, Scott, Steven, Susan. BS, Lowell Textile Inst., 1953. With Allied Chem. Corp., Morristown, N.J., 1953—; from engr. to mktg. mgr. Nat. Aniline div. Allied Corp., 1953-63, from dir. indsl. mktg. to v.p.-mktg. Fibers div., 1963-69, asst. to group v.p., corporate office, 1969, v.p. and gen. mgr.-consumer group Fabricated Products div., 1969-71, pres. Fibers div., 1971-74, group v.p., 1974-75, pres., dir., 1975-79, asst. to chmn. and dir., 1979-80; sr. assoc. The Corp. Dir., Inc., N.Y.C., 1981-83; pres. Counselors to Mgmt. Inc., 1984—.

MULCAHY, ROBERT JOSEPH, lawyer; b. Evergreen Park, Ill., Jan. 22, 1942; s. Robert J. and Mary J. Mulcahy. BS, U. Ill., 1964; JD, Calif. Western Law Sch., 1972. Bar: Calif. 1973, Ill. 1973; cert. legal specialist in work compensation, Calif. Pvt. practice, Chgo., 1973-81, San Diego, 1981-85; dep. city atty. criminal divsn. City of San Diego, 1986-91, dep. city atty. work compensation divsn., 1991—, dep. city atty. civil divsn., 1991—. Capt. USMC, 1964-67, Vietnam. Decorated Purple Heart. Office: City of San Diego 1200 3d Ave Ste 1200 San Diego CA 92101 E-mail: rum@cityatty.sannet.gov.

MULCAHY, ROBERT WILLIAM, lawyer; b. Milw., Jan. 11, 1951; s. T. Larry and Mary Margaret (Chambers) M.; m. Mary M. Andrews, Aug. 3, 1974; children: Molly, Kathleen, Margaret, Michael. BS, Marquette U., 1973, JD, 1976. Staff atty. NLRB, Milw., 1976-79; ptnr. Mulcahy & Wherry, S.C., 1979-90, Michael, Best & Friedrich, Milw., 1990—. Bd. dirs. WERC Coun. on Mcpl. Collective Bargaining, 1990-93. Co-author: Strike Prevention and Control Handbook, 1983, Comparable Worth: A Negotiator's Guide, 1985, Public Sector Labor Relations in Wisconsin, 1994. Bd. dirs. Milw. Repertory Theater, 1993-97; chmn. Charles Allis/Villa Terrace, 1991—; mem. St. Monica Parish Coun., 1988-96; chmn. Whitefish Bay Police Commn.; divsn. chmn. United Performing Arts Fund, 1993-94; co-chair Villa Terrace Garden Renaissance Project, 2000—. Mem. ABA, State Bar Wis. (chair labor sect. 1986-87), Milw. Bar Assn. (co-chair labor sect. 1988-95), Nat. Assn. Counties, Nat. Pub. Employers Labor Rels. Assn., Nat. Assn. Coll. & Univ. Attys., Wis. Counties Assn., Indsl. Rels. Rsch. Assn., Mgmt. Resources Assn., Wis. Sch. Attys. Assn., Milw. Area Mcpl. Employers Assn. Office: Michael Best & Friedrich 100 E Wisconsin Ave Ste 3300 Milwaukee WI 53202-4108 E-mail: rwmulcahy@mbf-law.com.

MULCH, ROBERT F., JR. physician; b. Quincy, Ill., June 21, 1951; s. Robert Franklin and Martha Jo (Nisi) M.; m. Barbara Ann Best, Apr. 5, 1975; children: Matthew, Luke. BS, U. Ill., 1973; MD, Rush Med. Coll., Chgo., 1977. Diplomate Am. Bd. Family Practice; cert. in geriatrics. Intern Riverside Meth. Hosp., Columbus, Ohio, 1977-78, resident in family practice, 1978-80; family physician Hillsboro (Ill.) Med. Ctr., Hillsboro, Ill., 1980—; ptnr., assoc. med. dir. Springfield Clin., 1998—. Asst. clin. prof. family medicine So. Ill. U., Springfield, 1981—; advisor Montgomery County Counseling Ctr.; reviewer Ctrl. Ill. Peer Rev. Orgn. Fellow Am. Acad. Family Practice; mem. AAFP, Am. Cancer Soc., Am. Coll. Physician Execs. Lutheran. Avocations: computers, boating, swimming. Office: Hillsboro Med Ctr SC 1250 E Tremont St Hillsboro IL 62049-1912 E-mail: rmulch@mcleodusa.net., rmulch@springfieldclinic.com.

MULCHAHEY, TERRY S. human resources executive, management consultant; b. Laurium, Mich., May 3, 1948; s. Raymond G. and Lila Mulchahey; m. Patricia Brooks Mulchahey. BA with honors, Mich. State U., 1970; degree in Indsl. and Labor Rels. Studies, Cornell U., 1973. Various human resources positions Mobil Corp., Princeton, NJ, 1976—85; mgr. employee rels. Rubbermaid, Inc., Wooster, Ohio, 1984—89; dir. human resources and labor rels. KLM Royal Dutch Airlines, Elmsford, NY, 1989—95; v.p. human resources Alper Holdings USA, N.Y.C., 1995—98, Uniscribe Profl. Services, Inc., Norwalk, Conn., 1998—99; prin. The Hyde Hazen Group, Ridgefield, 1999—. Mem.: Am. Arbitration Assn. (labor mgmt. edn. com. 1991—94), Internat. Assn. Corp. and Profl. Recruiters (nat. bd. mem., chmn. Fairfield/Westchester chpt. 1994—96), Embry Riddle Aero. U., US Squash Racquets Assn. (life). Episcopalian. Office: The Hyde Hazen Group 406 North Street Ridgefield CT 06877

MULCHANDANI, ASHOK KIMATRAI, chemical engineer, educator; b. Ajmer, India, Oct. 21, 1956; s. Kimatrai C. and Kalawanti M.; m. Priti Vadhva, Nov. 18, 1990; children: Anjali, Divya. B of Tech., Nagpur U., India, 1976; M of Tech., Indian Inst. Tech., Bombay, 1978; PhD, McGill U., Montreal, Can., 1985. Design engr. Vulcan-Laval Ltd., Pune, India, 1978-80; rsch. assoc. Laval U., St. Foy, Can., 1985-87, Biotech. Rsch. Inst., Nat. Rsch. Coun. Can., Montreal, 1987-90; asst. prof. dept. chem. U. Western, London, Can., 1990-91; asst. prof. dept. chem. & biochem. engring. U. Calif., Riverside, 1991-95, assoc. prof. dept. chem. & environ. engring., 1995-99, prof. dept. chem. & environ. engring., 1999—, chair dept. chem. & environ. engring., 2000—. Faculty rsch. participant U.S. Dept. Energy, Oak Ridge Nat. Lab, 1999-2000; cons. in field. Editor: Biosensors for Process Monitoring and Control, 1995, Protocols and Techniques in Enzyme and Microbial Biosensors, 1998, Protocols and Techniques in Affinity Biosensors, 1998, Chemical and Biological Sensors for Environmental Monitoring, 2000. Recipient Rsch. Intiation award NSF, 1993-96, Rsch. Participation award Dept. Energy Faculty, 1999-2000; grad. fellow U. Grants Commn., New Delhi, India, 1976-78. Mem. AIChE, Am. Chem. Soc. Avocations: music, tennis, squash, badminton. Office: U Calif Dept Chem & Environ Engring Bourns Hall Riverside CA 92521

MULCKHUYSE, JACOB JOHN, retired energy conservation consultant; b. Utrecht, The Netherlands, July 21, 1922; arrived in U.S., 1982; s. Lambertus D. and Aagje (Van Geyn) Mulckhuyse; m. Cornelia Jacoba Wentink, Jan. 17, 1953; children: Jacobien, Hans, Dieuwke, Linda, Marloes. MSc, U. Amsterdam (the Netherlands), 1952, PhD, 1960. Dir. Chemisch-Farmaceutische Fabriek Hamu, the Netherlands, 1951-57; tech. asst. mgr. Polak & Schwarz (now IFF), the Netherlands, 1957-60; asst. tech. mgr. Albatros Superphosphate Fabrieken, the Netherlands, 1960-61; tech. mgr. for overseas subsidiaries Verenigde Kunstmestfabrieken, the Netherlands, 1961-64, gen. mgr. process engring. dept. the Netherlands, 1964-70; dept. head process engring. dept. Unie van Kunstmestfabrieken, the Netherlands, 1970-82; sr. chem. engr. World Bank, Washington, 1982-83, sr. cons. chem. engr., 1983-87; ind. cons. environ. engring. World Bank and several cons. firms, 1987-97; ret., 1999. Author (with Heath and Venkataraman): (book) The Potential for Energy Efficiency in the Fertilizer Industry, 1985; author: (with Gamba and Caplin) Industrial Energy Rationalization in Developing Countries and Constraints in Energy Conservation, 1990, Process Safety Analysis: Incenvtive for the Identification of Inherent Process Hazards, 1985, Energy Efficiency and Conservation in the Developing World, 1992; editor: Environmental Balance of the Netherlands, 1972. Mem.: AIChE, N.Y. Acad. Scis., Internat. Inst. for Energy Conservation (bd. dirs. 1990—93), Fertilizer Soc. (pres. 1969—70), Royal Dutch Chem. Soc., Rotary. Avocations: philosophy, tennis, advising developing countries. Home: 21 Broken Island Rd Palmyra VA 22963-2064 E-mail: Mulckhuyse@aol.com.

MULDAUR, DIANA CHARLTON, actress; b. N.Y.C., Aug. 19, 1938; d. Charles Edward Arrowsmith and Alice Patricia (Jones) M.; m. James Mitchell Vickery, July 26, 1969 (dec. 1979); m. Robert J. Dozier, Oct. 11, 1981. BA, Sweet Briar Coll., 1960. Actress appearing in: Off-Broadway theatrical prodns., summer stock, Broadway plays including A Very Rich Woman, 1963-68; guest appearances on TV in maj. dramatic shows; appeared on: TV series Survivors, 1970-71, McCloud, 1971-73, Tony Randall Show, 1976, Black Beauty, 1978; star: TV series Born Free, 1974, Hizzoner, 1979, Fitz & Bones, 1980, Star Trek: The Next Generation, 1988-89; NBC miniseries and TV series A Year in the Life, 1986; TV movie Murder in Three Acts, The Return of Sam McCloud, 1989; TV series L.A. Law, 1989-91; motion picture credits include McQ, The Lawyer, The Other, One More Train to Rob, Mati, etc. Bd. dirs. Los Angeles chpt. Asthma and Allergy Found. Am.; bd. advisors Nat. Ctr. Film and Video Preservation, John F. Kennedy Ctr. Performing Arts, 1986. Recipient 13th Ann. Commendation award Am. Women in Radio and TV, 1988, Disting. Alumnae award Sweet Briar Coll., 1988. Mem. Acad. Motion Picture Arts and Scis., Screen Actors Guild (dir. 1978), Acad. TV Arts and Scis. (exec. bd., dir., pres. 1983-85), Conservation Soc. Martha's Vineyard Island. Office: Bauman Bedanty & Shaul 5757 Wilshire Blvd Ste 473 90036

MULDER, DAVID S. cardiovascular surgeon; b. Eston, Sask., Can., July 28, 1938; s. Peter and Laura (Lovie) M.; m. Norma D. Johnston, Aug. 19, 1961; children— Scott D., Lizabeth J., John C. MD, U. Sask., 1962; M.Sc., McGill U., 1964. Intern, resident in surgery Montreal Gen. Hosp., McGill U., 1963-67; resident in cardiac surgery U. Iowa, 1967-69; surgeon-in-chief Montreal Gen. Hosp., 1977-98; prof. surgery McGill U., 1979—; chmn. dept. surgery, 1993-98. Contbr. articles to med. jours. Fellow: ACS, Royal Coll. Surgeons Can.; mem.: Soc. Thoracic Surgeons (named Order Can. 1997), Am. Assn Thoracic Surgery, Am. Assn. Trauma, Nat. Hockey League Team Physicians Assn., Soc. Univ. Surgeons. Conservative. Home: 76 Sunnyside Ave Westmount QC Canada H34 1C2 Office: Montreal Gen Hosp Room D-6-136 Montreal QC Canada H3G 1A4 E-mail: David.Mulder@muhc.mcgill.ca., dsmulder@sympatico.ca.

MULDER, EDWIN GEORGE, retired minister, church official; b. Raymond, Minn., Mar. 25, 1929; s. Gerrit and Etta (Dresselhuis) M.; m. Luella Rozeboom, June 14, 1952; children: Timothy, Mary, Mark, Elizabeth. BA, Cen. Coll., Pella, Iowa, 1951, DD (hon.), 1979; BD, Western Theol. Sem., Holland, Mich., 1954. Ordained to ministry Ref. Ch. in Am., 1954. Pastor Reformed Ch. in Am., 1954-83, v.p. particular N.J. Synod, 1975-76, pres. particular N.J. Synod, 1976-77, v.p., then pres. Gen. Synod, 1978-80, gen. sec., 1983-94; chmn. bd. dirs. Relgion in Am. Life, 1995—. Chair U.S. Ch. Leaders, 1989-94; mem. exec. com. World Alliance Reformed Chs., 1990-97, Nat. Coun. Chs., 1991; mem. cen. com. World Coun. Chs., 1991-94; gen. sec. Reformed Ch. in Am., 1983-94. Trustee Cen. Coll., 1968-94; assoc. min. Marble Collegiate Ch., N.Y.C., 1995—.

MULDER, PATRICIA MARIE, education educator; b. South Bend, Ind., Dec. 28, 1944; d. Ervin James and Carmen Virginia (Sheeley) Anderson; m. James R. Mulder, Dec. 27, 1964; children: Todd Alan, Scott Robert. BA, Western Mich. U., 1967. Freelance writer, photographer, Berrien Springs, Mich., 1980—; tchr. Eau Claire (Mich.) Pub. Schs., 1969-70; staff writer, sales rep. Jour. Era, Berrien Springs, 1979-81; sales rep. Berrien County Record, Buchana, Mich., 1981-82; account exec. WHFB Radio Palladium Pub. Co., St. Joseph, 1982-86; substitute tchr. Berrien County Intermediate Dist., 1986-89; instr. Southwestern Mich. Coll., Dowagiac, 1989-96, cons. Writing Ctr., 1996—; corp. trainer, 2000—. Editor The Positive Image newsletter, 1980—, The F Stop, 1982-90; author: Poetry Anthologies, 1989—; staff writer Decision Point, 1988-89; newsletter editor Fernwood Nature Photographers, 1980—. Ofcl. photographer Ind. and Internat. Spl. Olympics, Notre Dame, 1986. Named Emerging Artist Ind. Coun. for the Arts, 1989, Honor award Southwestern Coun. of Camera Clubs, 1988, Photographer of the Yr. Berrien County Photographic Artists, 1987, 90. Mem. AAUW, Nat. Authors Registry, Meth. Profl. Women (sec. 1990—), Berrien County Artists (v.p. 1986), Berrien County Photographic Artists (v.p. 1984), Southwestern Mich. Coun. Camera Clubs, Berrien Springs Camrea Club (v.p. 1980—). Methodist. Avocations: writing, photography, oil painting, watercolor painting. Home: 10252 Castner Dr Berrien Springs MI 49103-9602 Office: Southwestern Mich Coll 58900 Cherry Grove Rd # 316L Dowagiac MI 49047-9726

MULDOON, PAUL, creative writing educator, poet; b. Portadown, No. Ireland, 1951; came to U.S., 1987; BA in English Lang. and Lit., Queen's U., Belfast, No. Ireland, 1973. Prodr. arts programs radio BBC No. Ireland, 1973-78, sr. prodr. arts programs radio, 1978-85, TV prodr., 1985-86; Judith E. Wilson vis. fellow Cambridge U., 1986-87; creative writing fellow U. East Anglia, 1987; writer-in-residence 92d St. Y, N.Y.C., 198; Roberta Holloway lectr. U. Calif., Berkeley, 1989; lectr. Princeton (N.J.) U., 1990—, prof., 1995—, dir. creative writing program, 1993—2002, Howard G.B. Clark '21 prof., 1998—; prof. poetry U. Oxford, Eng., 1999—. Part-time tchr. writing divsn. Sch. of Arts, Columbia U., 1987-88; part-time tchr. creative writing program Princeton U., 1987-88; vis. prof. U. Mass., Amherst, 1989-90. Author: (poetry) Knowing My Place, 1971, New Weather, 1973, Spirit of Dawn, 1975, Mules, 1977, Immram, 1980, Why Brownlee Left, 1980, Out of Siberia, 1982, Quoof, 1983, Selected Poems 1968-83, 1986, Meeting the British, 1987, Madoc: A Mystery, 1990, Incantata, 1994, The Prince of the Quotidian, 1994, The Annals of Chile, 1994, Hay, 1998, Moy Sand and Gravel, 2002, others, (criticism) To Ireland, I, 2000, (opera libretto) Shining Brow, 1993, Bandanna, 1999, (TV play) Monkeys, 1989, (translation from Irish) The Astrakhan Cloak, 1993, (children's book) The O-O's Party, 1981, The Noctuary of Narcissus Batt, 1997; editor: (poetry) The Scrake of Dawn, 1979, The Faber Book of Contemporary Irish Poetry, 1986, The Essential Byron, 1989, The Faber Book of Beasts, 1997; contbr. to anthologies. Recipient Eric Gregory award, 1972, Sir Geoffrey Faber Meml. award, 1980, 91, T.S. Eliot prize, 1994, Acad. award in lit. Am. Acad. Arts and Letters, 1996, Irish Times prize for poetry, 1997; John Simon Guggenheim Meml. fellow, 1990. Fellow Royal Soc. Lit.; mem. Am. Acad. Arts and Scis., Aosdana. Office: Princeton Univ Creative Writing Program Princeton NJ 08544-0001

MULDOON, ROBERT JOSEPH, JR. lawyer; b. Somerville, Mass., Nov. 16, 1936; s. Robert Joseph and Catherine Eileen (Hurley) M.; m. Barbara Joyce Mooney, Aug. 24, 1968; children: Andrew Robert, Catherine Lane, Timothy John. AB, Boston Coll., 1960, MA, 1961, LLB, 1965. Bar: Mass. 1965, U.S. Tax Ct. 1966, U.S. Supreme Ct. 1970. Law clk. Supreme Jud. Ct. Mass., 1965-66; assoc. Withington, Cross, Park & Groden, Boston, 1966-71, ptnr., 1972-82, Sherin and Lodgen, LLP, Boston, 1982—. Mem. Bd. Bar Examiners Mass.; chmn. Nat. Conf. Bar Examiners, 1985-86; pres. Mass. Continuing Legal Edn., Inc., 1992-94. Trustee Boston Coll. H.S., 1990-96, chmn. bd. trustees, 1995-96. Fellow Am. Coll. Trial Lawyers; mem. Am. Law Inst., Boston Bar Assn., Curtis Club, Nisi Prius Club, Tavern Club. Office: Sherin and Lodgen LLP 100 Summer St Ste 2800 Boston MA 02110-2109 E-mail: rjmuldoon@sherin.com.

MULDOON, THOMAS LYMAN, writer; b. Sioux Falls, S.D., Apr. 23, 1945; s. Lyman Thomas and Margaret Mary (Wallace) M.; m. Kathryn Lee Harmon, June 30, 1973; m. Kathryn Muldoon. B in Polit. Sci., Merrimack Coll., 1967; MS in Mass Comm., Fla. State U., 1973, MA in English, 1994. Bur. chief Palm Beach Post, 1970; gen. reporter Daytona Beach News-Jour., 1973; contract editor Frankfurt, Germany, 1973-74; reporter North Dade County bur. Miami Herald, 1977-78; journalist Nat. Enquirer, 1978-89; travel editor Petite Mag., 1992; media cons., 1996—. Tchr. journalism, TV journalism, cinema, TV prodn. Fla. State U., 1971-73. Author: (novel) An Execution of Honor, 2002; contract writer: Football Little Big Leaguers, 1990, More Baseball Little Big Leagues, 1991; freelance writer newspapers and mags.; appearances on local TV shows; interviewee nat. programs; producer TV programs for local ednl. TV; scriptwriter Future Shock; screenwriter 8 movie scripts. Polit. press sec. Mayor Kevin White, Boston, 1974-75; pub. affairs dir. Boston Community Schs., 1975; campaign pres sec. State Rep. Joseph Timilty, 1975; pub. affairs dir. Barry U., Miami, 1976-77; sports info. dir. Quantico Marines football and basketball programs, 1968. With USMC, 1968-70, Vietnam.

MULDOWNEY, MICHAEL PATRICK, finance executive; b. Chgo., Oct. 8, 1963; s. James Joseph and Clare (Sexton) M.; m. Daniela Nicoletta Pernis, Apr. 25, 1992; children: Michael James, Patrick Nicholas. BA, St. Ambrose U., 1985. CPA, Ill., Mass. Acctg. mgr. Fletcher Engring., Des Plaines, Ill., 1985; asst. auditor Marsh & McLennan Cos., Chgo., 1986, auditor London, 1987, sr. auditor N.Y.C., 1988; asst. corp. contr. Temple, Barker & Sloane, Lexington, Mass., 1989; regional contr. Temple, Barker & Sloane/Strategic Planning Assocs., 1990; dir. fin. and adminstrn. Mercer Mgmt. Consulting, 1991, corp. contr. N.Y.C., 1992-97; v.p. fin. Nextera Enterprises, Lexington, 1997-98, CFO, 1998—. Mem. Boston mgmt. com. Mercer Mgmt., Lexington, 1994-96; chmn. Fin. Execs. Mgmt. Consulting Firm, Boston, 1995. Chmn. United Way fundraiser Mercer Mgmt. Consulting, Lexington, 1992, chmn. co. fundraiser, 1993; trustee Meadowbrook Water Trust, Dover, Mass., 1993-97. Mem. AICPA, Ill. Soc. CPA's, Mass. Soc. CPA's, Fin. Execs. Inst., Wellesley Country Club (Tennis champion 1995-98). Avocation: tennis. Office: Nextera Enterprises LLC 1 Cranberry Hl Ste 9 Lexington MA 02421-7321

MULDROW, TRESSIE WRIGHT, psychologist; b. Marietta, Ga., Mar. 1, 1941; d. Festus Blanton and Louise Williams Wright Summers; 1 child DeJuan Denise. BA, Bennett Coll., 1962; MS, Howard U., 1965, PhD, 1976. Rsch. asst. W.C. Allen Corp., Washington, 1966-68; pers. rsch. psychologist Dept. Navy, 1968-73, Office Pers. Mgmt., CSC, 1973-79; chief adv. coun. on alternative selections procedures Office Pers. Mgmt., Washington, 1979-86, chief consultative svcs., 1986-91, chief multidimensional assessment br., 1992-94; spl. advisor Office of Diversity, 1994-95; leader Bus. Re-engring. Task Force, 1995-96, acting divsn. dir. Assessment Svcs. Divsn., 1996-97; dir. Performance Am., 1998-2000, sr. scientist, 2000—, exec. advisor, 2002—. Lectr. Howard U., 1979, guest lectr., 1999—. Contbr. articles to profl. publs. Mem. Washington Inter-Alumni coun. United Negro Coll. Fund, 1970—, pres., 1988—92; trustee Bennett Coll., vice chmn., 1985—90; v.p. Family Life Ctr. br. Boys and Girls Club of Washington, 1984—90; loaned exec. Combined Fed. Campaign, 2001—02; nat. fundraising chair Bennett Coll. Alumnae, 2001—, sr. advisor employment svcs., 2001—. Named Alumna of Yr., United Negro Coll. Fund, 1971, Outstanding Alumna, Morehouse Coll., 1978, Bennett Coll., 1993, Outstanding Woman, Am. Bus. Women's Assn., 1994, Outstanding Loaned Exec. to Combined Fed. Campaign, 2001; recipient Individual Achievement award, United Negro Coll. Fund, 1984, Exemplary Performance award, 1995, Outstanding Leadership award, Washington Inter-Alumni Coun., Dirs. award for excellence, 2000, Outstanding Alumnus award, United Negro Coll. Fund, 2001. Mem.: APA, Bennett Coll. Alumnae Assn. (nat. pres. 1978—85, 1993—97), Delta Sigma Theta. Presbyterian. Office: 1900 E St NW Washington DC 20415-0001 E-mail: muldro@starpower.net.

MULFORD, RAND PERRY, business executive; b. Denver, Sept. 30, 1943; s. Roger Wayne and Ann Louise (Perry) M.; 1 child, Conrad Perry; m. Paula Marie Skelley, 1987. BS in Basic Engring., Princeton U., 1965; MBA, Harvard U., 1972. Mgmt. cons. McKinsey & Co. Inc., Chgo., 1972-80; v.p. planning and control splty. chem. group Occidental Chem. Co., Houston, 1980-82; pres. Technivest Inc., 1982-85; exec. dir. corp. planning Merck & Co., Inc., Rahway, N.J., 1985-88; v.p. fin. Advanced Tissue Scis., Inc., La Jolla, Calif., 1989-90; CEO Chiron Mimotopes Peptide Systems, San Diego, 1991-94; COO Xytronyx, Inc., 1994-95; chmn. of bd. Medication Delivery Devices, 1991-95; CEO World Blood, Inc., 1997-99; mng. dir. bus strategy Spencer Trask, Inc. Bd. dirs. ZymeTx, Inc., Oklahoma City, Diamonex Inc., Allentown, Pa. Lt. USN, 1965-70. Home: 2178 Caminito Del Barco Del Mar CA 92014-3619 Office: The Immune Response Corp 6935 Darwin Ct Carlsbad CA 92008

MULFORD, RICHARD ALBERT, mechanical engineer, professional society administrator; b. Phila., Dec. 13, 1930; s. William Abernathy and Jeanne Ann (Roy) Mulford. BSME, U. Pa., 1952, MS in Mech. Engring., 1957; Diploma in Bus., Dartmouth Coll., 1985. Registered profl. engr., Pa. Engr. Phila. Elec. Co., 1952-64, sr. engr., 1964-67, project mgr., 1967-85, staff engr., 1985-91; exec. dir. Engrs. Club of Phila., 1991—. Vol. Paoli Meml. Hosp., Pa., 1991—; donor Phila. Orch. Assn., 1980—; treas., donor Phila. Engring. Found., 1991—. Recipient Disting. Svc. award, Pa. Soc. Profl. Engrs., 1991, 1998, D. Robert Yarnall award (Outstanding Engring. Alumnus), U. Pa., 1981, Alumni award of merit, 1993, Presdl. award, Phila. sect. Am. Soc. Civil Engrs., 2002. Fellow: Engrs. Club Phila. (sec.-treas. 1953—, George Washington medal 1998); mem.: NSPE, Union League Phila. (scholarship trustee 1963—), Racquet Club Phila. Republican. Achievements include patents in field. Avocations: classical music, antique cars, home and lawn maintenance. Home: 1231 Wisteria Dr Malvern PA 19355-9736 Office: Engrs Club of Phila 215 S 16th St Ste 36 Philadelphia PA 19102-3349 E-mail: info@engrclub.org.

MULGAONKAR, PRASANNA G. computer scientist; B.Tech. in Elec. Engring., Indian Inst. Tech., Kanpur, 1979; MS in Computer Sci., Va. Poly. Inst. and State U., 1981, PhD in Computer Sci., 1984. Computer scientist robotics lab. SRI Internat., Menlo Park, Calif., 1984—90, dir. machine vision and robotics program, 1990—93, dir. advanced automation tech. ctr., 1993—. Sci. adv. com. Def. Sci. Bd.; bd. visitors NSF; mem. Army Sci. Bd., 2002—; bd. dirs. AddressFree Corp. Contbr. Mem.: ASME (emeritus chair exec. com. for material handling engring. divsn.), IEEE Computer Soc. Office: SRI International 333 Ravenswood Ave Menlo Park CA 94025-3493*

MULHAUSER, LYNDA CAHAN, clinical social worker, educator, administrator; b. Phila. m. Joel C. Mulhauser, Apr. 11, 1970; children: Scott, Dana. BA, U. Pitts.; M in Social Work, Catholic U.; postgrad., Cath. U.; PhD in Social Work, Catholic U., 2002. Lic. clin. social worker, Md., D.C. Clin. social worker George Washington U. Med. Ctr., Washington, Children's Hosp., Washington, 1978-87, sr. supr., asst. dir. dept. social work, 1988-93, clin. mgr., 1993-94; dir. social work dept. Columbia Hosp. for Women, Wash., 1996-99; clin. social worker Children's Nat. Med. Ctr., 2002—. Adj. faculty Cath. U., 1994-95, U. Md., 1995. Contbr. articles to profl. mags. Chmn. profl. health adv. com. March of Dimes, Arlington, Va., 1985—91, bd. dirs. nat. capital chpt., 1988—; 1st v.p. Variety Club, Washington, 1988—90; bd. dirs. Spina Bifida Assn., 1984—, Down Syndrome Assn., Washington, 1986—90. Mem. Soc. Hosp. Social Work Adminstrs. (pres. D.C. metro chpt. 1995), Spina Bifida Assn. Am. (profl. adv. com.). Office: 4550 Montgomery Ave Ste 733N Bethesda MD 20814-3342

MULHEM, DOMINIQUE WILLIAM, painter, holographer, computer painter; b. Neuilly-sur-Seine, France, June 13, 1952; s. André G. and Micheline O. (Laroche) M.; m. Doria L. Camacho-Ayala, Oct. 28, 1993; 1 child, Sophia. Student, Art Sch. Paris, 1970-73, Archtl. and Graphic Rsch. Group, Paris, 1973-74, Nat. Superior Sch. Art, 1975-79, Mus. Holography, 1979-81. Author: Galerie l'orangeraie, 1982, Anne-Marie Christakis, 1982, Editions SOS, 1984, Georges Blache, 1984, Edition Cogèpar, 1988, Claude Fayette, 1988, Editions Galerie Eterso, 1993, Pierre Restany, 1993, Aero Graphic, 1997; author: (with Bernard Peigneux) Technique of Airbrush, 1981; over 112 exhbns., 33 one-man shows; represented in pub. collections French Mus. Holography Paris, Palais des Arts Acropolis, City of Nice, City of Asnières, City of Cannes, Mus. Holography USA; represented in co. collections Galerie Art Concorde, Galerie Ferrero, Galerie des Trois Ormeaux, Galerie Liliane Francois, Galerie Hermès, Galerie Arc-en-Ciel, Galerie de l'Orangeraie, Musèe et Centre d'Art Contemporain Prince Murat, Galerie Jade, Galerie Eterso, Le Mariè Tranier Gallery USA, Hors Cadre Galerie, U.G.C., Co. Gè. Par., C.S.P. Mècènat, Holographia Gallery, Switzerland, Cristal Relexion, USA. Recipient Spl. award Art Jonction, City of Cannes, France, 1993, award City of Asnieres, France, 1994. Avocations: friendship, books, travel, science, art. Home: 1 residence les Camelias 7 rue du 18 Juin 1940 F-92600 Asnieres France

MULHERN, EDWIN JOSEPH, lawyer; b. Bklyn., Mar. 8, 1927; s. Edward Thomas and Jennie (Keenan) M.; m. Maureen P. Purcell, Oct. 2, 1964; children: Edwin T., Deborah J., Kevin T. BBA, St. John's U., 1950, LLB, 1954. Bar: N.Y. 1954, U.S. Dist. Ct. (ea. and so. dists.) N.Y. 1954, U.S. Supreme Ct. 1960. Sr. acct. Susquehanna Mills Inc., N.Y.C., 1947-53; chief acct. Rockwood Chocolate Co., Bklyn., 1953-54; trial atty. Allstate Ins. Co., Freeport, N.Y., 1954-57; claims rep. State Farm Ins. Co., Hempstead, N.Y., 1957-58; sole practice, Bellmore, N.Y., 1958-70, Mineola, N.Y., Carle Place, N.Y., 1970—; mem. joint grievance com. for 10th jud. dist. (N.Y.), 1981-89. Pres. Christian Bros. Boys' Assn., 1975-82; bd. dirs. Legal Aid Soc. of Nassau County, 1980—. Served with USAAF, 1945-46. Mem. ABA, N.Y. State Bar Assn., Nassau Bar Assn. (bd. dirs. 1981-83, chmn. admissions com. 1979, chmn. grievance com. 1980-82), Suffolk County Bar Assn., Nassau Lawyers Assn. (pres. 1975, exec. dir. 1993—, Man of Yr. 1981), Criminal Cts. Bar Assn. of Nassau County (pres. 1976), Criminal Cts. Bar Assn. of Suffolk County, Am. Assn. Trial Lawyers. Clubs: University of L.I. (Hempstead), K.C. (new Hyde Park, N.Y.). Office: 1 Old Country Rd Ste 145 Carle Place NY 11514-1801

MULHERN, JEAN K. academic library director, consultant; b. Tiffin, Ohio, 1947; d. George P. and Frieda V. Graumlich; m. Raymond A. Mulhern, 1972; 1 child, Kathryn Brandt. BA, Heidelberg Coll., 1969; MLS, Kent Stat U., 1970. Reference libr. Fairfield County Dist. Libr., Lancaster, Ohio, 1970-72; educator Caldwell (Ohio) Exempted Village Schs., 1972-74; libr. dir. Wilberforce (Ohio) U., 1982—. Assessment facilitator Wilberforce U., 1999—, institutional accreditatin coord., writer, writer, 1997-99, CLIMB rsch. advisor, 1992; rep. Southwestern Ohio Coun. on Higher Edn. Libr. Coun., Ohio Pvt. Acad. Librs., Ohio LINK; libr. cons. Payne Thol. Sem., Wilberforce. Mem. Acad. Libr. Assn. of Ohio. Office: Wilberforce U 1055 N Bickett Rd Wilberforce OH 45384-1003

MULHERN, MARTIN ROBERT, engineer; b. New Brunswick, N.J., June 12, 1946; s. Thomas Desmond and Helen Casserly M. BS in Civil Engring., U. Calif., Berkeley, 1968; MS in Civil Engring., U. Wash., 1982. Cert. inshore/offshore hydographer Am. Congress of Surveying and Mapping; unltd. master merchant marine lic. USCG. Structures weights engr. The Boeing Co., Everett, Wash., 1968; capt. NOAA Corps., Silver Spring, Md., 1969-98; cons. Boulder, Colo., 1998-2001. NOAA rep. U. Nat. Oceanographic Lab. System, Silver Spring, 1992-96; comdg. officer NOAA ship Whiting. Recipient H. Arnold Karo award Soc. of Am. Mil. Engrs., 1980, 88. Mem. The Oceanography Soc. (charter, life mem.), Soc. Am. Mil. Engrs. (life), Am. Geophys. Union (life), The Hydrographic Soc. Achievements include conducting geodetic and hydrographic surveys with the Nat. Ocean Survey, extensive duty with labs. and hdqtrs. of the Office of Atmospheric and Oceanographic Rsch. Avocations: hiking, one-design sailing, skiing, music. Office: PO Box 19545 Boulder CO 80308-2545 E-mail: mmulhern@attglobal.net.

MULHOLLAN, DANIEL PATRICK, research director; b. Louisville, July 12, 1944; s. Daniel Paul and Martha Nell (McClain) M.; m. Julianne Finlayson, June 3, 1967; children: Willa Joanna Mulhollan Neale, Erin Finlayson, Julianne Gertrude. BA with honors, Coll. of St. Thomas, St. Paul, 1966; PhD comprehensives passed, Georgetown U., 1969. Sr. specialist Am. nat. govt., chief govt. divsn. Congrl. Rsch. Svc., Libr. of Congress, Washington, 1991, dir., 1994—; acting dep. libr. Libr. of Congress, 1992-94. Cons. Georgetown U., Washington, 1990-92; bd. visitors Sch. Info. Scis., U. Pitts., 1995; mem. adv. bd. Ind. U. Libr. Contbr. essay to book and articles to profl. jours. GE scholar, 1962; NDEA fellow, 1966. Mem. ALA, Am. Polit. Sci. Assn. (mem. centennial exec. com.), Midwest Polit. Sci. Assn. Roman Catholic. Office: Library of Congress Congressional Rsch Svc 1st & Independence Ave SE Washington DC 20540-0001

MULHOLLAND, JANE E. management consultant; b. Iowa City, Apr. 20, 1942; d. Ryland W. and Augusta H. (Eiben) Crary; divorced; children: Stephen Thompson, Nathan Thompson; m. James J. Mulholland, Jan. 23, 1986. BA, U. Pitts., 1964, MEd, 1975. Human resources profl. Gulf Oil Corp., Houston and Phila.; underwriter N.Y. Life Ins. Co., Houston; v.p. key exec. svcs. Right Assocs.; pres. JEM Consulting, 1997—. Former mem. Pa. Commn. for Women. Home: 3003 Freshmeadows Dr Houston TX 77063-4805 Office: JEM Consulting 6750 West Loop S Ste 740 Bellaire TX 77401-4108

MULHOLLAND, KENNETH LEO, JR. health care facility administrator; b. Chgo., July 16, 1943; s. Kenneth Leo Sr. and Virginia May (Groble) M.; m. Betty Lou Bledsoe, Feb. 18, 1978; children: Arthur G. Pope (dec.), Michelle Rae Pope Nobles. BS, Loyola U., 1969; M in Mgmt., Northwestern U., 1974. RN. Nurse VA Med. Ctr., Chgo., 1970-72, health care adminstr. tng., 1972-74, assoc. dir. tng. Lexington, Ky., 1976-77, assoc. dir. Muskogee, Okla., 1977-79, Knoxville, Iowa, 1979-81, acting dir., 1981, assoc. dir. Richmond, Va., 1981-83, dir. Bronx, N.Y., 1983-85, Memphis, 1985—. Pres. Memphis Area Fed. Exec. Assn., 1988—; bd. dirs. Memphis chpt. ARC, 1985—, Health Sys. Agy., Memphis, 1985-87; mem. citizen's adv. bd. St. Joseph's Hosp., 1993—; mem. dean's adv. bd. Grad. Sch. Bus., Christian Brothers U., 1996—. Recipient Presdl. Rank award for meritorious executive, 1989. Mem. Memphis Area Fed. Exec. Assn. Lodges: Rotary. Home: 2024 Thorncroft Dr Germantown TN 38138-4017 Office: VA Med Ctr 1030 Jefferson Ave Memphis TN 38104-2127

MULHOLLAND, S. GRANT, urologist; b. Springfield, Ohio, Sept. 1, 1936; s. Stanford Wallace and Florence Kathryn (Grant) M.; m. Ruth Fritz, Aug. 21, 1961; children: David, Michael, Mark, John. BS, Dickinson Coll., Carlisle, Pa., 1958; MD, Temple U., 1962; MS, U. Va., 1966. Intern Reading (Pa.) Hosp., 1962-63; resident in surgery Tampa (Fla.) Gen. Hosp., 1963-64; resident in urology U. Va., Charlottesville, 1964-68; urologist U.S. Naval Hosp., St. Albans, N.Y., 1968-70; epidemiologist Grad. Hosp. of U. Pa., Phila., 1971-74, asst. urologist, 1970-77; chief urologist Phila. Gen. Hosp., 1972-77; asst. surgeon Children's Hosp. Phila., 1974-77; urologist Hosp. U. Pa., Phila., 1974-77; chmn. dept. urology Thomas Jefferson U. Hosp., 1977—. Cons. VA Ctr., Phila., 1974-77, Bryn Mawr Hosp., VA Hosp., Wilmington, Del., 1977—. Author: Antibiotic Treatment, 1996, Urinary Tract Infections, 1999—2001, Prostate Cancer, 1999—2000, Bladder Defense Mechanisms, 2000—02. Lt. comdr. USN, 1968-70. Grantee NIH, Jefferson U., 1989. Fellow ACS; mem. Am. Urol. Assn. (pres. 1988-89), Phila. Urol. Assn. (pres. 1988-89), Internat. Soc. Urology, AMA, Phila. Country Club (Gladwyne, Pa.). Republican. Avocations: golf, fishing, skiing. Home: 1783 Sheedermill Rd Birchrunville PA 19421 Office: Jefferson Med Coll 1025 Walnut St # 1112 Philadelphia PA 19107-5001 E-mail: grant.mulholland@mail.tju.edu.

MULHOLLEN, MICHAEL EDWARD, education director; b. Franfurt, Germany, May 22, 1960; came to U.S., 1966; s. James Lawrence and Margie Ruth (Joslin) M. AA, Ctrl. Tex. Coll., Killeen, 1985; BA, Columbia Pacific U., 1987, MA, 1988; PhD, La Salle Univ., 1993. Instr. foreign lang. Def. Lang. Inst., Monterey, Calif., 1979-81; prof. criminal justice Nat. Training Ctr., Ft. Irwin, 1982-84; tchr. Russian Def. lang. Inst., Monterey, 1984-86; edn. adminstr. Mil. Intelligence Acad., Augsburg, Germany, 1986-89; dir. edn. Computer Processing Institute, East Hartford, Conn., 1989-92; pres. M.E.M. & Assocs., Manchester, 1992—. Author: Criminal Justice, 1989, Criminal Law, 1989, Russian Review Grammar Text Book, 1993. With U.S. Army, 1978-89. Fellow Conn. Soc. CPAs; mem. ABA, Am. Trial Lawyers Assn. Avocations: foreign languages, financial planning, law. Home: 66 Cushman Dr Manchester CT 06040-2314

MULJADI, PAULUS BENJAMIN, electrical engineer, webmaster; b. Jakarta, Indonesia, Mar. 28, 1964; came to U.S., 1977; s. Daniel and Emelia Muljadi. BS, U. Tex., San Antonio, 1987; postgrad., U. Tex., Austin, 1987-89, So. Meth. U., 1991. Registered profl. engr., Tex.; cert. computing profl. Grad. rsch. asst. U. Tex., San Antonio and Austin, 1987-89, tech. asst. Austin, 1989; devel. engr. Motorola, Inc., Ft. Worth, 1990-93; elec. engr. K.M. Ng & Assocs., San Antonio, 1993—. Co-founder 4JavaWeb, Austin, 1996, Giftware, Etc., San Antonio, 1995; founder GiftLite, San Antonio, 1995, PBM, Ft. Worth, 1990. Webmaster, coord. ednl. website, 1995; author, pub.: (computer software) Giftware, 1995; contbr. articles to profl. jours. Mentor San Antonio BEST, 1995-98; computer cons. Youth Orch., San Antonio, 1994; vol. Compumentor, Ft. Worth, 1992. Rsch. grantee MBRS, San Antonio, 1987-88. Mem. IEEE, NSPE, Tex. Soc. Profl. Engrs., Lightning Protection Inst. Unitarian Universalist. Achievements include development of novel peak-to-peak detection using DSPs. Address: PO Box 100393 San Antonio TX 78201-1693 E-mail: paul@muljadi.com.

MULKEY, DAVID ALLEN, pathologist, educator; b. Bonne Terre, Mo., Mar. 17, 1939; s. James Robert and Helen Elizabeth (Eydmann) M.; m. Laura Taylor Mulkey, Sept. 3, 1997; children: John David, Christopher Lee. BS, MD, U. Ark., 1964. Diplomate Am. Bd. Pathology. Intern U. Ark. Med. Ctr., Little Rock, 1964-65; resident pathology U. Colo. Med. Ctr., Denver, 1965-69; cons. pathology Webb-Waring Inst. Pulmonary Rsch., 1965-69; assoc. pathologist Hosp. of the Good Samaritan, L.A., 1969-72; assoc., dep. dir. Valley Clin. Lab., Palm Desert, Calif., 1972-74; assoc. Associated Pathologists Lab., Las Vegas, Nev., 1974—. Asst. clin. prof. U. So. Calif. Sch. Medicine, L.A., 1970-80; dir. sci. adv. com. Cmty. Blood Bank, Palm Springs, Calif., 1973-74; co-investigator, exec. mem. pathology com., chmn. lung pathology subcom. S.W. Oncology Group, 1976-77; chmn. Las Vegas Com. for Fluoride, 1976—; med. dir. Nev. Blood Services, 1979-91; chmn. dept. pathology, dir. labs. U. Med. Ctr., Las Vegas, 1998—; clin. prof. pathology U. Nev. Sch. Medicine, 1999—. With USAR, 1956. Mem. Nev. Med. Assn. (chmn. allied health commn. 1979—), Am. Soc. Clin. Pathologists, Coll. Am. Pathologists, Am. Soc. Cytopathology, Nev. Soc. Pathologists, Nev. Lung Soc., Clark County Med. Soc. (coun. 1979-85, sec. 1984-85). Home: 2839 Queens Courtyard Dr Las Vegas NV 89109-1562 Office: 4230 Burnham Ave Las Vegas NV 89119-5408

MULKEY, JACK CLARENDON, library director; b. Shreveport, La., Oct. 31, 1939; s. Jack Youmans and Hilda Lillian (Beatty) M.; m. Mary Lynn Shepherd, Jan. 30, 1971; 1 child, Mary Clarendon. BA, Centenary Coll., 1961; postgrad. (Rotary scholar), U. Dijon, France, 1961-62, Duke U. Law Sch., 1962-63; MS, La. State U., 1969. Jr. exec. Lykes Bros. S.S. Co., 1964-66; asst. dir. admissions Centenary Coll. of La., 1966-67; head reference services and acquisitions Shreveport Pub. Library, 1968-71; dir. Green Gold Library System of N.W. La., 1971-73; mgmt. cons. Miss. Library Commn., 1973-74, asst. dir., 1974-76, dir., 1976-78, Jackson Met. Library System, 1978-85; assoc. dir. Ark. State Library, 1986-2000; State Librarian of Ark., 2000—. Adj. prof. U. So. Miss. Grad. Sch. Libr. Sci., 1979—; treas., bd. dirs. Southeastern Library Network (SOLINET), 1985-86; cons. in field; mem. White House Conf. Taskforce on Libraries and Info. Services, 1980—. Chmn. Miss. Govs. Conf. on Libraries, 1979; chmn. Miss. delegation White House Conf. on Libraries, 1979; hon. del. White House Conf. on Librs., 1991. Served with USAF, 1963-64. Mem. ALA (chmn. state libr. agy. sect. 1995-97), Southeastern Libr. Assn. (bd. dirs. 1994—), Miss. Libr. Assn. (pres. 1981-82), Ark. Libr. Assn. (exec. bd. dirs. 1994—), Chief Officers of State Libr. Agys., Phi Alpha Delta, Beta Phi Mu, Omicron Delta Kappa, Phi Kappa Phi. Episcopalian. Home: 1805 Martha Dr Little Rock AR 72212-3840 Office: 1 Capitol Mall Little Rock AR 72201-1049 E-mail: jmulkey@webtv.net.

MULKEY, SHARON RENEE, gerontology nurse; b. Miles City, Mont., Apr. 14, 1954; d. Otto and Elvera Marie (Haglof) Neuhardt; m. Monty W. Mulkey, Oct. 9, 1976; children: Levi, Candice, Shane. BS in Nursing, Mont. State U., 1976. RN, Calif.; nat. cert. gerontol. nursing. Staff nurse, charge nurse VA Hosp., Miles City, Mont., 1976-77; staff nurse obstetrics labor and delivery Munster (Ind.) Cmty. Hosp., 1982-83; nurse mgr. Thousand Oaks Health Care, 1986-88; unit mgr. rehab. Semi Valley (Calif.) Adventist Hosp., 1988-89, DON TCU, 1989-91; DON Pleasant Valley Hosp. Extended Care Vacility and Neuro Ctr., 1991-93, Victoria Care Ctr., Ventura, Calif., 1993—; clin. supr. Procare Home Health, Oxnard, 1996-97; staff nurse acute rehab. Los Robles East Campus Rehab. Unit, Westlake, 1998, clin. coord., 1998—2002; founder, CEO Internat. Womens Conf. Spkr. for Spiritual Growth and Devel., 2000—. Internat. conf. spkr. WCCD, 1991—. Mem. ANA, Nat. Gerontol. Nursing Assn., Internat. Platform Assn., Alpha Tau Delta (pres. 1973-75), Phi Kappa Phi. Home: 3461 Pembridge St Thousand Oaks CA 91360-4565

MULL, CHARLES LEROY, II, retired naval officer and travel agency executive; b. Reading, Pa., Dec. 30, 1927; s. Charles Leroy and Harriet Jane (MacMullen) M.; m. Sara Louise Tooke, July 19, 1952; children: Deborah Louise, Carolyn Tooke Mull, Charles Wesley. BS in Marine Engring., U.S. Naval Acad., 1950; BS in Engring. Electronics, U.S. Naval Postgrad. Sch., 1957. Commd. ensign USN, 1950; advanced through grades to capt., 1970; shore electronics engring. officer U.S. Naval Ship Repair Facility, Yokosuka, Japan, 1964-67; nuclear guided missile cruiser combat system project officer U.S. Naval Ship Engring. Ctr., Washington, 1967-70; comdg. officer U.S. Naval Electronics Engring. Ctr., Charleston, S.C., 1970-73; tech. dir. U.S. Naval Guided Missile Frigate Project, Washington, 1973-76; supr. shipbldg., overhaul and repair USN, Bath, Maine, 1976-81; ret., 1981; pres. Stowe Travel Internat., Inc./Am. Express, Brunswick, Maine, 1981-99. Monthly travel columnist Pejepscot Cryer, Brunswick, 1985-94. Corporator Mid Coast Hosp., Brunswick, 1986—; campaign chmn. Bath-Brunswick Area United Way, 1986; pres. United Way Mid Coast Maine, 1989-91; chair rector search com. St. Paul's Episcopal Ch., Brunswick, Maine, 1996-97; pres. Appletree Homeowners Assn., 1998-99. Decorated Legion of Merit, Meritorious Svc. medal with oak leaf cluster; recipient Joshua Chamberlain award Bath-Brunswick Mil. Community Coun., 1981; named (with wife Sally) Co-Citizens of Yr., Brunswick Area C. of C., 1992. Mem. U.S. Naval Inst., Navy League U.S. (pres. Casco Bay, Maine coun. 1988-96), Brunswick Area C. of C. (chmn. 1993-94), Nat. Trust Hist. Preservation, Pejepscot Hist. Soc., Ret. Officers Assn., Brunswick Downtown Bus. Assocs. (chmn. 1994-96, coord. downtown master devel. plan steering com. 1995-98), Brunswick-Topsham-Bath Milit. Cmty. Coun. (chmn. 1994-95), U.S. Naval Acad. Alumni Assn., Brunswick Rotary (Pres.'s award Bath chpt. 1978), Masons, Shriners. Republican. Episcopalian. Avocations: tennis, sports fan, theater, community activities, travel.

MULL, DAWN KATHLEEN, accountant, auditor; b. Harrisburg, Pa., Sept. 23, 1973; d. John Stephen and Sandra Ann (Cavanaugh) Sellers. BS in Profl. Accountancy, Pa. State U.-Harrisburg, Middletown, 1997. Mg., asst. mgr. Dairy Queen, Camp Hill, Pa., 1990-96; bookkeeper, cons. Best's Ultra Svc. Ctr., Mechanicsburg, 1996-97; intern/auditor Profit Recovery Group, Internat., Camp Hill, 1997-98; acctg. mgr. Valley Supply, Inc., Mechanicsburg, Pa., 1998—. Hall honors scholar, 1992-93, others. Mem. Inst. Mgmt. Accts. Avocations: boating, hiking.

MULL, GALE W. lawyer; b. Hillsdale, Mich., Sept. 8, 1945; s. Wayne E. and Vivian M. (Bavin) M.; m. Holly Ann Allen, Aug. 2, 1969 (div. Nov. 1983); 1 child, Carter B.; m. Jeanne Anne Haughey, Aug. 18, 1985. BA, Mich. State U., 1967; MA in Sociology, Ind. U., 1969; JD, Emory U., 1972. Bar: Ga. 1972, U.S. Dist. Ct. (no. dist.) Ga. 1972, U.S. Ct. Appeals (5th cir.) 1973, U.S. Ct. Appeals (11th cir.) 1981. Instr. sociology Clemson (S.C.) U., 1968-69, Spelman Coll., Atlanta, 1969-70; pvt. practice, 1972-75; ptnr. Mull & Sweet, 1975-81; pres. Gale W. Mull, P.C., 1981—. Bd. dirs. BOND Community Fed. Credit Union, Atlanta, 1975-81; directing atty. Emory Student Legal Services, Atlanta, 1975-91; Sociology instr. Clemson U., Clemson, S.C., 1968-69, Spelman Coll., Atlanta, Ga., 1969-70. Pres. Inman Park Restoration, Inc., Atlanta, 1972-74, BASS Orgn. for Neighborhood Devel., Inc., 1974-78; mem. Housing Appeals Bd., Atlanta, 1982-88; mem. Mayor's Task Force on Prostitution, 1984-86; bd. dirs. ACLU Ga., 1981-92, sec. bd. dirs., 1983-85, cooperating atty., 1972—; vestry St. John's Episcopal Ch., 1992-99, sr. warden, 1998-99; bd. dirs. St. John's Episcopal Day Sch., 1992-97, Bethlehem Ministries, 1997—. Trinity Towers, Inc., 1999-2000. Mem. ABA, Ga. Bar Assn., Atlanta Bar Assn., Lawyers Club Atlanta. Clubs: Quail Unltd. (bd. dirs., sec. 1984-86). Office: 990 Edgewood Ave NE Atlanta GA 30307-2581

MULLADY, JOHN PATRICK, poet, educator; b. Roslyn, N.Y., July 20, 1949; s. Robert Emmet and Nan Teresa Mullady; m. Kathleen Eleanor Kruger, Jan. 18, 1992; 1 child Michael Robert. BA in English, Niagara U., 1971. Sr. group acct. corr. N.Y. Life Ins. Co., N.Y.C., 1972—78; asst. tchr. AHRC, 1987—88. Mem.: K.C. Avocation: writing poetry and plays. Home: 42 Baxter St Rutland VT 05701

MULLAN, DONALD WILLIAM, archbishop; b. Galt, Ont., Apr. 26, 1937; s. William James and Lillian Maude (Sachs) M.; m. Cathy Templeman. Presiding bishop Christ Cath. Ch. Internat.; pastor Cathedral of St. Luke, Niagara Falls, Ont. Editor (mag.) The St. Luke Mag. Trustee Bd. Edn., Preston, Ont., 1962-68, Waterloo County, Ont., 1969-70, Wellington County, Ont., 1971-72. Mem. Order of Noble Companions of the Swan (grand prelate), Moose, Scouts of Can. E-mail: dmullan1@cogeco.ca.

MULLAN, JOHN FRANCIS (SEAN MULLAN), neurosurgeon, educator; b. County Derry, Northern Ireland, May 17, 1925; came to U.S., 1955; naturalized, 1962; s. John and Mary Catharine Ann (Gilmartin) M.; m. Vivian C. Dunn, June 3, 1959; children: Joan Claire, John Charles, Brian Francis. MB, BCh, BAO, Queen's U., Belfast, Northern Ireland, 1947, DSc (hon.), 1976; postgrad., McGill U., 1953-55. Diplomate Am. Bd. Neurol. Surgery. Trainee gen. surgery Royal Victoria Hosp., Belfast, 1947-50, trainee in neurosurgery, 1951-53; trainee gen. surgery Guy's Hosp. and Middlesex Hosp., London, 1950-51, Montreal Neurosurg. Inst., Que., Can., 1955; asst. prof. neurol. surgery U. Chgo., 1955-61, assoc. prof., 1961-63, prof., 1963—, John Harper Seeley prof., chmn. dept., 1967-93, emeritus, 1993—, dir. Brain Rsch. Inst., 1970-84. Author: Neurosurgery for Students, 1961; contbr. over 150 articles to profl. jours.; mem. editorial bd. Jour. Neurosurgery, 1974-84, Archives of Neurology, 1976-87. Recipient Olivecrona medal Karolinska Inst., 1976, Wilder Penfield medal Can. Neurosurg. Soc., 1979, Jamieson medal Australian and New Zealand Neurosurg. Soc., 1980. Fellow ACS, Royal Coll. Surgeons; mem. Soc. Neurol. Surgeons (past pres.), Acad. Neurol. Surgery, Am. Assn. Neurol. Surgeons, Am. Neurol. Assn., Cen. Neurosurg. Soc., Chgo. Neurol. Soc., World Fedn. of Neurosurg. Socs. (sec. 1989-93, hon. pres. 1993—). Roman Catholic. Achievements include conducting research on vascular diseases of the brain, pain, head injury. Avocations: walnut tree farming, gardening. Office: U Chgo Med Ctr 5841 S Maryland Ave Chicago IL 60637-1463

MULLANE, DENIS FRANCIS, insurance executive; b. Astoria, N.Y., Aug. 28, 1930; s. Patrick F. and Margaret (O'Neill) M.; m. Kathryn Mullman, June 28, 1952; children: Gerard, Kevin, Denise. BS in Mil. Engring, U.S. Mil. Acad., 1952; LHD (hon.), U. Conn., 1988, St. Joseph's Coll., 1990; LLD (hon.), U. Hartford, 1993, Trinity Coll., Hartford, Conn., 1995; MS in Fin. Svcs., The Am. Coll., Bryn Mawr, Pa., 1995. CLU. With Conn. Mut. Life Ins. Co., Hartford, 1956—, v.p., 1969-72, sr. v.p., 1972-74, exec. v.p., 1974-76, pres., 1977—, chief exec. officer, 1983-85, chmn., chief exec. officer, 1985-90, chief exec. officer, pres., 1990-93; chmn. Mulane Enterprises, Inc., Hartford, Conn., 1994—; with Mullane Enterprises, West Hartford, 1994—. Bd. dirs. Conn. Natural Gas Co.; chmn. The Am. Coll., Bryn Mawr, Pa., 1993-96; chmn. joint planning com. Am. Coll. and Soc. Fin. Svcs. Profls., 1996-99. Dir. U.S. Chamber, 1991-95. 1st lt. C.E., U.S. Army, 1952-56. Recipient John Newton Russell award, 1987, Knight of St. Gregory award. Mem.: Assn. Grads. U.S. Mil. Acad. (pres. 1989—93), Nat. Assn. Ins. and Fin. Advisors, Am. Soc. Corp. Execs. Republican. Roman Catholic. Office: Mullane Enterprises Inc 29 S Main St Hartford CT 06107-2449

MULLANE, JOHN FRANCIS, pharmaceutical company executive; b. N.Y.C., Mar. 10, 1937; s. John Gerard and Rita Ann (Hoben) M.; m. Ruth Ann Cecka, Nov. 17, 1962; children— Rosemarie, Michael, Kathleen, Therese, Thomas MD, SUNY, 1963, PhD, 1968; JD, Fordham U., 1977. Bar: N.Y. 1978, D.C. 1979. Assoc. med. dir. Ayerst Labs. div. Am. Home Products Corp., N.Y.C., 1973-75, dir. clin. research, 1975-76, v.p. clin., 1977, v.p. sci., 1978-82, sr. v.p., 1982, exec. v.p., 1983-88; pres. Mullane Health Care Cons., N.Y.C. and Sarasota, Fla., 1989—; dir. drug devel. DuPont Med. Products, Wilmington, Del., 1990; sr. v.p. DuPont-Merck, 1991-94; exec. v.p. Amylin Pharms., 1994-96. Contbr. articles to profl. jours. Served to lt. col. U.S. Army, 1970-73 Recipient Upjohn Achievement award, 1970; N.Y. Heart Assn. Crawford-Maynard fellow, 1966-68 Fellow Am. Coll. Clin. Pharmacology; mem. ABA, Am. Soc. Clin. Pharmacology and Therapeutics, Am. Assn. Study of Liver Diseases, Misty Creek Country Club. Roman Catholic. Avocation: golf. Home and Office: 9047 Misty Creek Dr Sarasota FL 34241-9542

MULLANEY, JOANN BARNES, nursing educator; b. Newport, R.I., Dec. 7, 1943; d. Elliott Calvert and Betty (Dawson) Barnes; m. Charles Patrick Mullaney, June 3, 1967 (div. 1973); 1 child, Mark Andrew. Diploma in Nursing, Newport Hosp. Sch. Nursing, 1965; BSN, Salve Regina Coll., Newport, 1976; BSN/MS in Psychiat. Mental Health Nursing, Boston Coll., 1977; PhD in Edn., U. Conn., 1983. RN, R.I.; clin. specialist, ANCC. Instr. Salve Regina U., Newport, 1979-83, asst. prof., 1983-85, sr. level coord., 1983-94, assoc. prof. nursing, 1985-95, prof., 1995—. Psychiat. clin. specialist in pvt. practice The Center, Middletown, R.I., 1990—, utilization reviewer, Providence, 1990-92, ednl. cons., 1990—. Contbr. to book: Psychiatric Care Planning, 1989 (ASN Book of Yr. 1988). Mem. Atty.-Gen.'s Task Force on Domestic Violence, Providence, 1994; mem. Health Care Reform Coalition, Providence, 1993—, Nat./R.I. Action Not Gridlock Coun., 1993—; mem. R.I. House and Senate Women's Health Issues Commn., 1995. Recipient Air Force Nurse Educator award, 1988; grantee HEW, 1976, NIMH, 1977, 91-94, Lilly Co., 1994; M.A.C.N. scholar, 1995. Mem. ANA, AAUW, AAUP, NEON, ENRS, SERPA, RISNA (pres.-elect 1992-93, pres. 1993-95, pres. ex-officio 1995—), Mass. Assn. Coll. Nursing Rsch., Sigma Theta Tau (Delta Upsilon chpt.), Phi Lambda Theta. Home: 242 Gibbs Ave Newport RI 02840-2829

MULLANEY, THOMAS JOSEPH, lawyer; b. N.Y.C., Feb. 9, 1946; s. James Joseph and Dorothy Mary (Fulling) M.; m. Christine E. Hampton, Aug. 16, 1969; children: Richard, Jennette. BA, Fordham U., 1967; JD, U. Va., 1970; LLM, NYU, 1977. Bar: Va. 1970, N.Y. 1971, U.S. Dist. Ct. (so. and ea. dists.) N.Y. 1972, U.S. Ct. Appeals (2d cir.) 1972, U.S. Supreme Ct. 1975. Assoc. Brown, Wood, Ivey, Mitchell & Petty, N.Y.C., 1970-79, Law Offices of John M. Kenney, Garden City, N.Y., 1979-84; ptnr. Abrams, Thaw & Mullaney, N.Y.C., Farmingdale, 1985-91; dir., sr. counsel law dept. Merrill Lynch & Co., Inc., N.Y.C., 1991—. Capt. JAGC, U.S. Army, 1971-74. Mem. Va. State Bar Assn., N.Y. State Bar Assn. Republican. Roman Catholic. Home: 104 Huntington Rd Garden City NY 11530-3122 Office: 222 Broadway Fl 14 New York NY 10038-2510 E-mail: tmullaney@exchange.ml.com.

MULLARE, T(HOMAS) KENWOOD, JR. lawyer; b. Milton, Mass., Jan. 19, 1939; s. Thomas Kenwood and Catherine Marie (Leonard) M.; m. Joan Marie O'Donnell, May 27, 1967; children: Jennifer M. Cedrone, Tracy K., Jill M., Joyce M. AB, Holy Cross Coll., 1961; LLB, Boston Coll., 1964. Bar: Mass. 1964. Atty. New Eng. Electric System, 1964-69; v.p., gen. counsel, sec. AVX Corp., N.Y.C., 1970-73; v.p., gen. counsel, clk. Tyco Labs., Inc., Exeter, N.H., 1974-77; v.p., gen. counsel, sec. SCA Svcs., Inc., Boston, 1978-83; spl. counsel Houghton, Mifflin Co., 1984-85, v.p., dir. bus. software divsn., 1985-92; pres. North River Capital Co., Inc., Norwell, Mass., 1990—; gen. counsel, sec. Aztec Tech. Ptnrs., Inc., Braintree, 1999—. Bd. dirs. Friendship Home, Inc. Mem. regional adv. bd. Commonwealth of Mass. Dept. Mental Retardation, 1994-97; bd. dirs. Barque Hill Assn., Norwell, 1980-84, pres., 1981-83; pres. Ch. Hillers, Norwell, 1983-84; bd. dirs. South Shore Assn. for Retarded Citizens, Weymouth, Mass., 1993-98, chmn., 1995-97. Mem. Boston Bar Assn. Home: 31 Barque Hill Dr Norwell MA 02061-2815 Office: Aztec Tech Ptnrs Inc Ste 220 50 Braintree Hill Office Park 20 Braintree MA 02184-8724

MULLARKEY, MARY J. state supreme court chief justice; b. New London, Wis., Sept. 28, 1943; d. John Clifford and Isabelle A. (Steffes) M.; m. Thomas E. Korson, July 24, 1971; 1 child, Andrew Steffes Korson. BA, St. Norbert Coll., 1965; LLB, Harvard U., 1968; LLD (hon.), St. Norbert Coll., 1989. Bar: Wis. 1968, Colo. 1974. Atty.-advisor U.S. Dept. Interior, Washington, 1968-73; asst. regional atty. EEOC, Denver, 1973-75; 1st atty. gen. Colo. Dept. Law, 1975-79, solicitor gen., 1979-82; legal advisor to Gov. Lamm State of Colo., 1982-85; ptnr. Mullarkey & Seymour, 1985-87; justice Colo. Supreme Ct., 1987—, chief justice, 1998—. Recipient Alumni award St. Norbert Coll., De Pere, Wis., 1980, Alma Mater award, 1993. Fellow ABA Found., Colo. Bar Found.; mem. ABA, Colo. Bar Assn., Colo. Women's Bar Assn. (recognition award 1986), Denver Bar Assn., Thompson G. Marsh Inn of Ct. (pres. 1993-94). Office: Supreme Ct Colo Judicial Bldg 2 E 14th Ave Denver CO 80203-2115*

MULLEN, DANIEL ROBERT, finance executive; b. Swedesboro, N.J., Apr. 17, 1941; s. Harold Legrand and Gladys (DeVault) M.; m. Elizabeth A. Willers, Dec. 17, 1977; children: William H., Jonathan O. BS in Fin., Ariz. State U., 1966, postgrad., 1966-67. Appraiser Ariz. Dept. Revenue, 1966-68; financial analyst Amerco, Inc., Phoenix, 1968-70, treas., 1970-82; pres., dir. Continental Leasing Co., 1980—; v.p. Southwest Pipe and Supply Co., 1982; treas. Talley Industries, Inc., 1982-93, v.p., 1993-98; COO Friendship Publs., 1998-99. Bd. dirs. C. Myers Corp. Del. Ariz. Presdl. Dem. Conv., 1972; bd. dirs. Big Sisters of Ariz., 1975, Found. for Blind Children, 1984-90, Phoenix Little Theatre, 1985-91, Kachina Country Day Sch., 1988-94, New Way Sch., 1994-2000. With U.S. Army, 1959-62. Ariz. Soc. CPAs grantee, 1964-65 Mem. Fin. Execs. Inst. Home: 3627 E Medlock Dr Phoenix AZ 85018-1505

MULLEN, EDWARD JOHN, JR. Spanish language educator; b. Hackensack, N.J., July 12, 1942; s. Edward J. and Elsie (Powell) M.; m. Helen Cloe Braley, Apr. 2, 1971; children: Kathleen, Julie Ann. BA, W.Va. Wesleyan Coll., 1964; MA, Northwestern U., 1965, PhD, 1968. Asst. prof. modern langs. Purdue U., West Lafayette, Ind., 1967-71; assoc. prof. Spanish U. Mo., Columbia, 1971-78, prof. Spanish, 1978—. Author: La Revista Contemporáneos, 1972, Carlos Pellicer, 1977, Langston Hughes in the Hispanic World and Haiti, 1977, The Life and Poems of a Cuban Slave: Juan Francisco Manzano 1797-1854, 1981, Critical Essays on Langston Hughes, 1986, Sendas Literarias: Hispanomerica, 1988, El cuento hispánico, 1994, 96, 99, Afro-Cuban Literature: Critical Junctures, 1998; co-editor Afro-Hispanic Rev., 1987—; editor: The Harlem Group of Negro Writers (Melvin B. Tolson), 2000. Recipient Diploma de Honor Instituto de Cultura Hispánica, 1964; Woodrow Wilson fellow, 1964-65; Northwestern U. fellow, 1965-67; summer research grantee U. Mo., 1972, 76; grantee Am. Council Learned Socs., 1979 Mem. MLA, Am. Assn. Tchrs. Spanish and Portuguese, Assn. of Depts. Fgn. Langs. (pres. 1989-91). Home: 207 Edgewood Ave Columbia MO 65203-3413 Office: U Mo Dept Romance Langs 143 Arts And Sci Bldg Columbia MO 65211-0001 E-mail: mullene@missouri.edu.

MULLEN, EILEEN ANNE, human resources executive; b. Phila., Feb. 14, 1943; d. Joseph Gregory and Helen Rita (Kane) M.; m. William John Raschiatore (dec.). BS in English, St. Joseph's U., 1967; MA in English, Villanova U., 1978. Cert. tchr., Pa. Tchr. St. Anastasia Sch., Newtown Square, 1960-67, West Cath. Girls H.S., 1967-74; mgr. staff tng. and devel. ASTM, Phila., 1974-96, dir. human resources, 1996—. Instr. lit., speech and communications Widener U., Chester, Pa. and Wilmington, Del. Contbg. author articles on comms. tng. programs; contbr. articles to profl. jours. Mem. ASTD (pres. Phila./Del. Valley chpt. 1980-81, Outstanding Leadership as Pres. award 1981), Soc. for Human Resource Mgmt. Democrat. Roman Catholic. Office: ASTM 100 Barr Harbor Dr West Conshohocken PA 19428-0700 E-mail: emullen@astm.org.

MULLEN, FRANK ALBERT, former university official, clergyman; b. Lafayette, Ind., Apr. 7, 1931; s. Albert Edwin and Bernice Elizabeth (Weidlich) M.; m. Ruth Charlotte Ackerman, May 28, 1960 (dec. Oct. 1969). BA, Wabash Coll., Crawfordsville, Ind., 1953; MDiv, Yale U., 1956; DD (hon.), Yale U., New Haven, 1988. Ordained to ministry Christian Ch. (Disciples of Christ), 1956. Exec. dir. YMCA of Wilmington, Del., 1956-60, YMCA of Greater N.Y., N.Y.C., 1960-74; pastor St. Marks United Ch. of Christ, Ridgewood, N.Y., 1973-99; assoc. dir. Campaign for Yale, Yale U., N.Y.C., 1975-79; min. Cmty. Ch. of Elmhurst, N.Y., 1974-99; dir. devel. Bapt. Med. Ctr., N.Y.C., 1980-83; dir. devel. Div. Sch. Yale U., New Haven, 1984-97; dir. planned giving Guideposts, Inc., Carmel, N.Y., 1983-84. Life mem. bd. advisors Yale U. Divinity Sch., 1997—; trustee Park Avenue Christian Ch., N.Y.C., 1999—; dir. bd. ch. ext. Christian Ch., Disciples of Christ, 2000—. Recipient Liberty Bell award Queens County Bar Assn., 1969, Alumni award of merit Wabash Coll., 1970; Wright fellow Yale U., 1955, fellow Trumbull Coll., 1985—. Mem. Assn. Theol. Schs., Coun. for Advancement in Secondary Edn., Wellness Assn., Travelers' Century Club, Circumnavigators Club. Home and Office: 17833 Croydon Rd Jamaica Est NY 11432-2203 *Live for others. It is the only true way to find happiness.*

MULLEN, GRAHAM C. federal judge; b. 1940; BA, Duke U., 1962, JD, 1969. Bar: N.C. 1969. Ptnr. Mullen, Holland, Cooper, Morrow, Wilder & Sumner, 1969-90; judge U.S. Dist. Ct. (we. dist.) N.C., Charlotte, 1990—. Lt. USN, 1962-66. Mem. N.C. Bar Assn. (bd. govs. 1983-88), Mecklenburg County Bar Assn. Office: US Courthouse 401 W Trade St Rm 230 Charlotte NC 28202-1619 E-mail: gmullen@ncwd.net.

MULLEN, J. THOMAS, lawyer; b. Evanston, Ill., Aug. 27, 1940; BSE, Princeton U., 1963; JD cum laude, U. Mich., 1967. Bar: Ill. 1967. Ptnr. Mayer, Brown, Rowe & Maw, Chgo.; ptnr.-in-charge London office, 1974-78. Bd. dirs. Legal Assistance Found. Chgo., 1979-85. Mem. ABA, Chgo. Bar Assn., Chgo. Coun. Lawyers. Office: Mayer Brown & Platt 190 S La Salle St Ste 3100 Chicago IL 60603-3441 E-mail: tmullen@mayerbrownrowe.com.

MULLEN, JAMES AELRED, metal processing executive; b. Youngstown, Ohio, Mar. 24, 1941; s. James Aelred and Isabel Margaret (Ott) M.; m. Clara Mary Hudak, Mar. 6, 1965 ; children: Mary Renee, James A. III, Thomas M., Karen E., Linda E., Lesley A., Matthew B. BEE, Youngstown State U., 1971. Registered profl. engr., Ohio, Pa., W.Va. Project mgr. Pa. Engring. Corp., New Castle, 1965-70; chief. elec. engr. Alliance (Ohio) Machine Co., 1972-79; v.p. mktg. Pa. Engring. Corp., New Castle, 1979-82; v.p. engring. Swank Metacon Systems Co., Pitts., 1982-83; pres. Metacon Systems Co., Youngstown, 1983—, also bd. dirs. V.p., bd. dirs. Berthold Systems Co., Pitts. Author: Basic Oxygen Furnace Steel Making, 1982; patentee B.O.F. Suspension, 1970. Mem. Assn. Iron and Steel Engrs., Iron and Steel Soc. Republican. Roman Catholic. Avocations: woodworking, gardening. Home: 1270 Stonington Dr Youngstown OH 44505-1656 Office: Youngstown Thermal LP 205 North Ave Youngstown OH 44502-1141

MULLEN, MICHAEL T. lawyer; b. Evanston, Ill., Apr. 15, 1956; s. George Martin and Marguerite (Tully) M.; m. Patricia Reilley, Apr. 24, 1987; children: Claire, Catharine, Michael, Conor. BA, Marquette U., 1978; JD, Loyola U., 1981. Bar: Ill. 1981, U.S. Dist. Ct. (no. dist.) Ill. 1981, U.S. Ct. Appeals (7th cir.) 1981, U.S. Supreme Ct., 2000. Asst. atty. gen. Ill. Atty. Gen., Chgo., 1981-85; asst. U.S. atty. U.S. Atty., 1985-90, 90-92, dep. chief, 1990-92; ptnr. Mullen & Minella, 1992-98, Paul B. Episcope, Ltd., Chgo., 1998—. Contbr. articles to profl. jours. Trustee Village of Western Springs (Ill.), 1995—. Recipient Spl. Achievement award for sustained superior U.S. Dept. Justice, 1988, performance award 1990; named to Loyola Acad. Athletic Hall of Fame. Mem. Ill. State Bar Assn., Ill. Trial Lawyers Assn., West Suburban Bar Assn. lawyer for multiple cases with multimillion dollar jury verdicts and settlements. Office: Paul B Episcope Ltd 77 W Washington St Ste 300 Chicago IL 60602-2896 E-mail: mtm@episcopeltd.com.

MULLEN, PETER P. lawyer; b. N.Y.C., Apr. 8, 1928; m. Cecilia Kirby; 5 children. AB cum laude, Georgetown U., 1948; LLB, Columbia U., 1951. Bar: N.Y. 1951. Ptnr. Skadden, Arps, Slate, Meagher & Flom LLP, N.Y.C., 1961-98, exec. ptnr., 1981-94, of counsel, 1998—. Co-chmn. Cardinal's Com. Laity Archdiocese N.Y., 1992—; bd. dirs., sec., treas., Eye Surgery, Inc. Formerly mem., pres. Bd. Edn. Pub. Schs., Bronxville, N.Y., 1979-81; chmn. Skadden Fellowship Found., 1988—; bd. dirs., vice-chmn. Lawrence Hosp., Bronxville, 1984-89; bd. dirs. Project Orbis, Georgetown U., Washington, 1982-99, chmn., 1985-92; bd. dirs. Legal Aid Soc., 1987-93, Vols. Legal Svcs., Inc., 1988-99, United Way Bronxville, 1985-93, Practicing Attys. Law Students, 1988-99; trustee Lawyer's Commn. Civil Rights Under Law, 1984-99; chmn. Gregorian U. Found., 1989—; bd. dirs., exec. com. Vatican Obs. Found., 1993. Named Man of Yr. Cath. Big Bros., 1987; recipient John Carroll award Georgetown U., 1984, John Carroll Medal Merit, 1988, Thomas More award Lawyers Com. Cardinal's Com. of the Laity, 1996, Elizabeth Ann Seton award Nat. Cath. Edn. Assn., 1998; named Stone scholar Columbia U., 1951. Mem. Am. Bar Assn., N.Y. State Bar Assn. (com. securities regulation 1980-83), Assn. Bar City N.Y. (com. corp. law 1964-67, com. admissions 1965-68, com. securities regulation 1970-73), Soc. Friendly Sons St. Patrick (N.Y., pres. 1989-90), Knight Malta. Office: Skadden Arps Slate et al LLP 4 Times Sq New York NY 10036-6522

MULLEN, ROD, nonprofit organization executive; b. Puyallup, Wash., Aug. 2, 1943; s. Charles Rodney and Grace Violet (Fritsch) M.; m. Lois Fern Tobiska, May 3, 1963 (div. Jan. 1977); children: Cristina, Charles, Moneka; m. Naya Arbiter, Oct. 17, 1977. Student, U. Idaho, 1961-63; AB in Polit. Sci., U. Calif., Berkeley, 1966; postgrad., San Francisco Art Inst., 1968. Dir. Oakland (Calif.) facility Synanon Found., Inc., 1971-72, dir. San Francisco facility, 1972-73, dir. Tomales Bay (Calif.) facility, 1976-78, dir. Synanon edn. programs, 1973-76; treatment dir. nat. programs Vision Quest, Inc., Tucson, 1981-82; dir. resources and devel. Amity, Inc., 1982-84, exec. dir., 1984-95; founder, pres., CEO, Amity Found., Porterville, Calif., 1995—. Mem. Nat. Adv. Com. on Substance Abuse Prevention, 1990-92, 93-96; mem. sci. adv. bd. Ctr. for Therapeutic Cmty. Rsch., Nat. Devel. and Rsch. Insts., N.Y.C., 1991—; cons. Calif. Office Criminal Justice Planning, Sacramento, 1993; prin. investigator program Nat. Inst. on Drug Abuse, 1990-93. *Mr. Mullen has a 30-year career providing national leadership using the therapeutic community model for addicted women and their children; adolescents with lengthy histories of substance abuse and violent behaviors, and adult and adolescent addicts in incarcerated settings. Mullen directs Amity's recidivism reduction program at the RJ Donovan Correctional Facility in San Diego, cited by the Office of National Drug Control policy, Department of Justice, Center for Addiction and Substance Abuse at Columbia University, and numerous others for the ability to significantly reduce recidivism and violent behviors in inmates, saving millions of dollars per year and providing a national model.* Contbr. numerous articles to profl. publs., chpts. to books. Mem. Am. Correctional Assn., Therapeutic Coms. of Am. Office: Amity Found PO Box 713 Porterville CA 93258-0713 Fax: 559-783-2846. E-mail: rodm@amityfoundation.com.

MULLEN, RON, insurance company executive; b. Tex., Aug. 8, 1939; s. Durward Lacy and Blanche V. (Coulson) M.; m. Carole King, Dec, 29, 1959; children: Lacy Lynne Holcomb, Misty Kay. Student, Abilene Christian Coll., 1957-58, San Antonio Coll., 1958-59; BBA, S.W. Tex. State U., 1965. C.L.U., Chartered Fin. Cons. City council mem. City of Austin, 1977-83, mayor, 1983-85; mgr. Prin. Fin. Group, Austin, 1965-98, Ron Mullen & Assocs. Inc., Austin, 1966—, InNet Fin. Group. Chmn. TML Ins. Trust Fund Com., 1983—; mem. Gov.'s Task Force on State Employees Health Ins. Benefits, Austin, 1984 Chmn. Austin Transp. Study Com., Austin, 1983—, Greater Austin-San Antonio Corridor Coun., 1984—, Social Policy Adv. Com., Austin, 1979-80, March of Dimes campaign, Austin, 1974-75; co-chmn. Consumers United for Rail Equity, Austin, 1983—; v.p. Austin Symphony Orch., 1974-75; mem. exec. com. Capital Area Planning Coun., Austin, 1976—, exec. bd. Tex. Mcpl. League, Austin, 1983—, Gov.'s Task Force on Indigent Health Care, Austin, 1984, Tex. Adv. Commn. on Intergovtl. Rels., Austin, 1981—; chmn. Infant Parent Tng. Ctr., 1985-98; bd. dirs., chmn. South MoPac Transp. Com., 1986-87; life mem. Austin Jaycees, bd. dirs., 1974-75; vice-chmn. Mental Health Mental Retardation Bd.; vice chmn. South Tex. Audio Reader Svc.; bd. dirs. BBB, Inc., Hyde Park Bapt. Sch., 1999—; mem. nat. com. Assn. Ins. and Fin. Advisers, Austin, 1999—. Recipient Road Hand award Tex. Dept. Hwys. and Transp., 1985, award for regional statesmanship Greater Austin-San Antonio Corridor Commn.; named Boss of Yr., Treaty Oaks chpt. Am. Bus. Women's Assn., 1978, Nat. Mgr. of Yr., Bankers Life Ins. Co., 1977, 82, 84-85, Alumnus of Yr. Austin Jaycees, 1988-90. Mem. Am. Coll. Life Underwriters (pres.), Tex. Assn. Life Underwriters (pres. 1997-98), Austin Assn. Life Underwriters (pres. 1974-75), Austin Gen. Agts. and Mgrs. Assn. (pres. 1978-80), Sales and Mktg. Execs. of Austin (pres. 1972-73), Downtown Rotary (pres. 1996-97). Baptist. Home: 6902 Mesa Dr Austin TX 78731-2822 E-mail: von9991@msn.com.

MULLEN, TERRI ANN, retired special education educator; b. St. Louis, Apr. 01; d. William Earl and Sophia Kinniff; m. Thomas Patrick Mullen; children: David, Mark, Debi. BS in Edn., S.E. Mo. State U.; M in Sch. Adminstrn., Calif. State U., 1978, M in Spl. Edn., 1981; EdD in Institutional Mgmt., Pepperdine U., 1985. Cert. spl. edn., std. sec., std. elem., adminstrv. svc. K-12, cmty. coll. instr. Tchr. Irvine (Calif.) Unified Sch. Dist., 1972-84; lectr., spl. edn. Calif. State U., Fullerton, 1989-90; asst. prin. Moreno Valley (Calif.) Unified Sch. Dist., 1984-85; adminstr. of spl. svcs. Centralia Sch. Dist., Buena Park, Calif., 1984-89; elem. prin. Capistrano Unified Sch. Dist., San Juan Capistrano, 1989-93; spl. edn. tchr., dept. chair Moreno Valley (Calif.) Unified Sch. Dist., 1993—. Chair, cmty. staff ednl. planning com. Santiago Elem. Sch., Irvine Unified Sch. Dist., 1981; dir., staff devel. for spl. programs pers. Centralia Sch. Dist., Buena Park, 1984-89; workshop presenter Assn. of Calif. Sch. Adminstrs. Conf., San Francisco, 1983. Author: Resource Book of Classroom Interventions for the Collaborative Teaching Model, 1994, Tips of the Trade for the Classroom Aide, 1984; contbr. articles to profl. jours. Adv. bd. for sp. edn. Calif. State U. Fullerton, 1988-89. Recipient Cmty. Svc. award Disneyland, 1992, 93; named Outstanding Educator of Yr. Rotary Club, 1983. Mem. Coun. for Exceptional Children, Kappa Delta Pi, Phi Kappa Phi. Avocations: roller skating, fashion design, interior design, computer applications, writing. E-mail: tmullen@pacbell.net.

MULLEN, THOMAS EDGAR, real estate consultant; b. Hackensack, N.J., Feb. 10, 1936; s. Luke B. and Jean (Edgar) M.; m. Sarah Lee Huff, Aug. 17, 1984. BS in Engring., Va. Poly. Tech., 1954; grad mgmt. program, Harvard U., 1964. Cons. in field. Mgr. mktg. Eastern Airlines, N.Y.C., 1954-69; pres. Profl. Sprits Mktg., 1969-72, Shelter Devel. Corp. Am., N.Y.C., 1972-79; supr. ops. Gen. Mills, Orlando, Fla., 1980-86; cons., exec., realtor A.H.M. Graves Co. Inc., Indpls., 1986-92; pres. Pegasus Assocs. Ltd., 1992—. Inventor TV Guider Holder, patent, 1971. Fundraiser Am. Cancer Soc., Miami, 1967-70, Westchester Hosp., N.Y.C., 1967-70; pres. Brighton Found. Mem. Met. Bd. Realtors, Builders Assn. Greater Indpls. (bd. dirs.), Ind. Builders Assn. (bd. dirs.), Nat. Assn. Realtors, Inst. Residential Mktg. (pres. sales & mktg. coun., bd. dirs.). Republican. Roman Catholic. Avocations: tennis, recreational pilot. Home: 6251 Behner Way Indianapolis IN 46250-1494

MULLEN, WILLIAM COCKE, classics educator; b. Houston, Nov. 4, 1946; s. Joseph and Edith (Donnan) M. BA magna cum laude, Harvard Coll., 1968; PhD, U. Tex., 1972. Prof. Bard Coll., Annandale-on-Hudson, N.Y., 1994—. Author: Choreia: Pindar and Dance , 1982,; Enchanted Rock included in The Best Amer. Poetry, 1998; The Agenda of the Milesian School: The Post-Catastrophic Paradigm Shift in Ancient Greece, 1998. Included in Five Hundred Leaders of Influence, Amer. Biological Inst., 1998. Home and Office: Bard Coll Annandale On Hudson NY 12504

MULLEN, WILLIAM JOSEPH, III, military analyst, retired career officer; b. Plattsburg, N.Y., Dec. 26, 1937; s. William Joseph Jr. and Georgia (Cook) M.; m. Norma Sturgeon, Aug. 6, 1962; 1 child, William Joseph IV. BS, U.S. Mil. Acad., West Point, N.Y., 1959; MS in Internat. Affairs, George Washington U., 1971. Commd. 2d lt. U.S. Army, 1959, advanced through grades to brig. gen., 1987; various assignments in U.S., Vietnam, Korea, Panama, Germany, Saudi Arabia, 1959-92; mem. staff, faculty U.S. Mil. Acad., West Point, 1967-70; comdr. 1st Brigade, 1st Inf. Div., Ft. Riley, Kans., 1983-86; asst. div. comdr. 5th Inf. Div., Ft. Polk, La., 1986-87; comdg. gen. U.S. Army Combined Arms Tng. Activity, Ft. Leavenworth, Kans., 1987-89, 1st Inf. Div. (Forward), Germany, 1989-91; dep. dir. ops. J3 Forces Command, Ft. McPherson, Ga., 1991-92; sr. mgr. mil. tng. and analysis sys. BDM Fed., Inc., Monterey, Calif., 1992-98; sr. program mgr. tng. mgmt. sys. TRW (formerly BDM Fed., Inc.), 1998—. Co-author: Changing an Army, An Oral History of Gen. W.E. DePuy, 1979; contbr. articles, book revs. to Mil. Rev. Chmn. Officers of the 1st Divsn. Dinner, 1999—. Decorated D.S.C., D.S.M. Mem. Assn. U.S. Army, Soc. of 1st Div. (chpt. officer 1968, assoc. 1989-93, trustee found. 1989-93, bd. dirs.), Legion of Valor. Avocations: sports, reading. *When in doubt, I have always found direction from the guidance explicit in the 1st Infantry Division's motto, "Duty first!".*

MULLENBACH, LINDA HERMAN, lawyer; b. Sioux City, Iowa, Dec. 25, 1948; d. Verner Wilhelm and Margaretta Victoria (Grant) Herman; m. Hugh James Mullenbach, Aug. 22, 1970; children: Erika Lynn, Linnea Britt. BS in Speech, Northwestern U., 1971, MS in Speech, 1972, JD, 1979. Bar: Ill. 1979, U.S. Dist. Ct. (no. dist.) Ill. 1979, DC 1983, U.S. Dist. Ct. DC 1983, U.S. Ct. Appeals (7th, DC and fed. cirs.) 1983, U.S. Supreme Ct. 1984. Assoc. Jenner & Block, Chgo., 1979-83, Dickstein, Shapiro & Morin, Washington, 1983-85, prin., 1985-87, ptnr., 1988-93; v.p., assoc. gen. counsel Zurich Small Bus. and Zurich Comml. Legal Divsn., Balt., 1994-99; asst. gen. counsel, v.p. Corp. Law Divsn. Zurich U.S., 1999-2001; asst. gen. counsel, v.p. corp. law divsn. Zurich N.Am., 2001—02, sr. v.p., assoc. gen. counsel corp. law divsn., 2002—. Mem.: ATLA, ABA, Women's Legal Def. Fund, Women's Bar Assn., DC Bar Assn., Mortar Bd., Zeta Phi Eta. Home: 8201 Killean Way Potomac MD 20854-2728

MULLENDORE, LAWRENCE KENT, airport director; b. Independence, Mo., June 19, 1941; s. William Lawrence and Edna Cecilia (Boehm) M.; m. Bernadette Kroll, June 23, 1962; children: Randal Kent, Scott kent. BS in Aeronautical Engring., U. Wichita, 1964. Aeronautical engr. Cessna Aircraft Co., Wichita, Kans., 1962-64, regional svc. mgr., 1964-67; airport dir. Bi-State Devel. Agy., Cahokia, Ill., 1967-87; exec. dir. Naples (Fla.) Airport Authority, 1987-89; airport dir. The Ea. Iowa Airport, Cedar Rapids, 1989—. Chmn. Cedar Rapids (Iowa) Conv. & Vis. Bur., 1993-94; dir. All Iowa Agrl. Assn., Cedar Rapids, 1990-2000. Mem. Cedar Rapids C. of C., St. Louis Auto Racing Assn. Avocations: auto racing, skiing, flying radio controlled model airplanes. Office: the Ea Iowa Airport 2515 Wright Bro Blvd W Cedar Rapids IA 52404 Fax: 319-362-1670. E-mail: larrym@cedar-rapids.org.

MULLENDORE, WALTER EDWARD, economist; b. Harrah, Okla., Apr. 22, 1940; s. Newton and Ida Minnie (Lohmann) M.; m. Edra Janell Havenstrite, July 4, 1963; children— Matthew Edward, Karen Kay, Mark Andrew. BS, Okla. State U., 1961, MS, 1963; PhD in Econs, Iowa State U., 1968. Grad. asst. Okla. State U., 1961-63; instr. Iowa State U., 1965-67; mem. faculty dept. econs. U. Tex., Arlington, 1968—, prof., 1975—, dean Coll. of Bus., 1980-93. Contbr. articles to profl. jours. Served with U.S. Army, 1963-65. Mem. Mo. Valley Econ. Assn. (v.p. 1980-81, pres. 1982-83), Regional Sci. Assn., Western Regional Sci. Assn., Gt. S.W. Rotary (pres. 1989-90), Omicron Delta Epsilon. Methodist. Home: 8003 John T White Rd Fort Worth TX 76120-3611 Office: U Tex Coll Bus PO Box 19479-uta Arlington TX 76019-0001

MULLENS, WILLIAM REESE, retired insurance company executive; b. Franklin, Tenn., Sept. 12, 1921; s. William Pope and Elizabeth (Reese) M.; m. Katherine Ann Jones, Nov. 24, 1945; children: Jo Ann Mullens Sanditz, Carol Ann Mullens Slegers. BA, Vanderbilt U., 1942. With Bus. Men's Assurance Co., Kansas City, Mo., 1947-75, exec. v.p., dir., 1969-75; pres., dir. J.C. Penney Life Ins. Co., 1975-82; pres. Gt. Am. Res. Ins. Co., 1975-84, dir., 1975-89. Dir. Nat. Fidelity Life Ins. Co., 1986-89 Served to lt. comdr. USNR, 1943-46. Fellow Soc. Actuaries; mem. Phi Beta Kappa, Alpha Tau Omega. Presbyterian. Home: 2502 Broken Circle Rd Flagstaff AZ 86004-7596

MULLER, BARBARA ANN, allergist; b. Teaneck, N.J., Jan. 10, 1957; MD, Med. U. Guadalajara, 1982. Diplomate Am. Bd. Allergy and Immunology, Am. Bd. Internal Medicine. Intern U. Medicine Dentistry N.J./Hackensack Med. Ctr., 1983-84; resident in internal medicine Hackensack Med. Ctr., 1984-87, chief resident in internal medicine, 1987-88; fellow in allergy and immunology U. Iowa Hosps., Iowa City, 1988-91, assoc. allergy-immunology, 1991, asst. prof. allergy-immunology, 1995—; dir. ambulatory care programs internal medicine U. Iowa Hosps. and Clinics, 1993—; dir. U. Iowa Health Plans, 1996—; dir. care mgmt. program U. Iowa, 1997—; dir. Anticoagulation Case Mgmt. Svc., 1999—. Med. dir. Diabetes Disease Mgmt. Ctr., 2001. Mem.: ACP/ASIM, Am. Coll. Physician Execs., Am. Coll. Allergy and Immunology, Am. Acad. Allergy and Immunology. Office: U Iowa Hosps and Clinics A&I BT 1081 Iowa City IA 52242 E-mail: barbara-muller@uiowa.edu.

MULLER, CAROLYN BUE, physical therapist, volunteer; b. Crosby, N.D., Feb. 24; d. Sigurd Christian and Eleanor (Rushfeldt) Bue; m. Willard Chester Muller, Jan. 27, 1945; children: Marolyn Jean, Barbara Anne, Nancy Eleanor. BA, St. Olaf Coll., 1940; cert. in phys. therapy, Harvard U., 1944. Assoc. dir. younger girls and phys. edn. sect. YWCA, Syracuse, N.Y., 1940-43; phys. therapist Valley Forge Hosp., Phoenixville, Pa., 1944-45; med. records libr. Trust Territory of Pacific Islands, Truk, Caroline Islands, 1951-52. Founder, prin. organizer Am. Cmty. Sch., Truk, 1952, Lincoln Sch., Katmandu, Nepal, 1956, Am. Cmty. Sch., Mogadiscio, Somali Republic, 1958, Kampala, Uganda, 1966; panelist workshop Wash. Commn. for Humanities, Yakima, 1996. Author: Living in Uganda, 1967; cartographer: Maudie - An Oregon Trail Childhood, 1993. Charter registrar Clallam County Mus. and Hist. Soc., Port Angeles, Wash., 1977-87; vol. reading tutor Port Angeles Sch. Dist., 1980—; cmty. coord. UNICEF, Port Angeles, 1982-85; rep. Target Wash. Seminar, Seattle, 1984; rep. Asia-Can. Women in Mgmt. Conf., Victoria, B.C., Can., 1985; regional judge Wash. State Nat. History Day Contest, Port Angeles, 1985—; selection judge Wash. State Inquiring Mind Lecture Series, Seattle, 1989, 90, 96, organizer/coord., Inquiring Mind Lecture Series 1983—; Wash. state judge Nat. History Day Contest, Ellensburg, Wash., 1993—; bd. dirs. Wash. State Friends of the Humanities, 1991-94; trustee Wash. Commn. for the Humanities, 1995-97; pres. Am. Women's Club, Katmandu, 1957-58, Mogadiscio, 1959-60; v.p. Internat. Women's Club, Saigon, South Vietnam, 1971; mem. selection com. Evergreen State Soc. Awards, 1998, 99. Recipient Women Making a Difference award Soropimist Internat., 1984, Outstanding Vol. award Citizens' Ednl. Ctr. N.W., 1988, Evergreen award Evergreen State Soc., 1992. Mem. AAUW (br. pres. 1980-84, Edn. Found. scholarship in her name 1996). PEO (rec. sec. 1984-85, v.p. 1985-86, pres. 1987-89, chaplain 1994, Internat. Peace scholarship in her name 1990, state chmn. Internat. Peace scholarship 1989-90), Washington Athletic Club. Avocations: growing flowers, cross-country walking, oil painting, reading, travel. Home: 3624 S Mount Angeles Rd Port Angeles WA 98362-8910 E-mail: muller@tenforward.com.

MULLER, CHARLOTTE FELDMAN, economist, educator; b. N.Y.C., Feb. 19, 1921; d. Louis and Lillian (Drogin) Feldman; m. Jonas N. Muller, 1942 (dec.); m. Carl Schoenberg, 1970; children: Jeremy Lewis Muller, Sara Linda Muller. AB, Vassar Coll., 1941; A.M., Columbia U., 1942, PhD in Econs., 1946. Instr. econs. Bklyn. Coll., 1943; lectr. Barnard Coll., 1943-46; asst. prof. Occidental Coll., 1947; asst. study dir. Survey Rsch. Ctr., U. Mich., 1948; rsch. assoc. U. Calif., Berkeley, 1948-50; lectr. Yale U. Sch. Pub. Health, 1952-53; asst. prof. Columbia U. Sch. Pub. Health, 1957-67; assoc. dir. Ctr. for Social Rsch. CUNY, 1967-86, prof. econs., 1978-91, prof. emerita, 1991—, prof. sociology, 1982-91, prof. urban studies Ctr. for Social Rsch., 1967-78; v.p. CUNY Acad. for Humanities and Scis., 1985-88; prof. health econs. Mt. Sinai Sch. Medicine, 1986-91, prof. emerita, 1991—, dir. div. health econs., 1988-91, prof. dept. geriatrics, 1990-91, assoc. dir. Internat. Longevity Ctr.-USA, Ltd., 1991-97, sr. economist Internat. Longevity Ctr.-USA, Ltd., 1998—, co-dir. program Internat. Longevity Ctr.-USA, Ltd., 1999—. Cons. Health Care Financing Adminstrn., U.S. VA; disting. alumna speaker Vassar Centennial, 1971. Author: Health Care and Gender, 1990; mem. editorial bd. Am. Jour. Pub. Health, 1980-84, Women and Health, Rsch. on Aging; contbr. numerous articles on health econs. to profl. publs. Mem. N.Y.C. Mayor's Com. on Prescription Drug Abuse, 1970-73; bd. dirs. Alan Guttmacher Inst., 1972-81, CUNY Rsch. Found., 1985-91; vice chmn. Med. and Health Rsch. Assn., N.Y.C.; mem. health care tech. study sect. Nat. Ctr. Health Svcs. Rsch., 1976-79; mem. commn. on nat. policy Am. Jewish Congress, 1980-91. Ford/Rockefeller Founds. grantee, 1972-73, 75-76; Russell Sage Found. grantee, 1985-90. Mem. APHA, NOW, Am. Econ. Assn. Jewish. Office: Internat Longevity Ctr-USA Ltd 60 E 86th St New York NY 10028-1009

MULLER, DAVID WEBSTER, architectural designer; b. Norwich, Conn., Aug. 25, 1956; s. Richard Johnson and Barbara Alice (Reading) M.; m. Susan Akers, Dec. 31, 1989; 1 stepchild, Shannon. BA in Polit. Sci., George Washington U., 1978. Rsch. assoc. Rep. Nat. Com., Washington, 1978-80, dep. dir. spl. projects, 1981-83; western field dir. Nat. Rep. Congl. Com., 1983-85; v.p. Russo Watts & Rollins, Sacramento, 1985-86; campaign mgr. Chavez for U.S. Senate, Silver Spring, Md., 1986; v.p. Russo Watts & Rollins, Sacramento, 1987-89; cons., 1989; pvt. investor, 1990—. Archtl. design and restoration Muller/West, 1990—; founding mem. The M.I.N.D. Inst. Med. Investigation of Neurodevelopmental Disorders, U. Calif. Davis Med. Ctr., Sacramento. Mem. Nat. Coun. for Arts and Scis. at George Washington U. Mem. St. Francis Yacht Club. Avocations: boating, photography, fiction writing, international travel, kayaking. Home: 1309 Dolphin Ter Corona Del Mar CA 92625-1728 Office: 512 Begonia Ave Corona Del Mar CA 92625-2011 E-mail: dmuller4385@aol.com.

MULLER, EDWARD ROBERT, lawyer; b. Phila., Mar. 26, 1952; s. Rudolph E. and Elizabeth (Steiner) M.; m. Patricia Eileen Bauer, Sept. 27, 1980; children: Margaret Anne, John Frederick. AB summa cum laude, Dartmouth Coll., 1973; JD, Yale U., 1976. Assoc. Leva, Hawes, Symington, Martin & Oppenheimer, Washington, 1977-83; dir. legal affairs Life Scis. group Whittaker Corp., Arlington, Va., 1983-84; v.p. Whittaker Health Svcs., 1984-85; v.p., gen. counsel, sec. Whittaker Corp., L.A., 1985-93, chief adminstrv. officer, 1988-92, CFO, 1992-93, bd. dirs., 1993-99; v.p., gen. counsel, sec. BioWhittaker, Inc., Walkersville, Md., 1991-93; pres., CEO, bd. dirs. Edison Mission Energy, Irvine, Calif., 1993-2000. Bd. dirs. FlobalSanTaFe Corp., Houston, Interval, Inc., Santa Monica, Calif., Strategic Data Corp., Santa Monica, RigNet, Inc., Houston, The Keith Cos., Inc., Costa Mesa, Calif.; mem. Brookings Task Force on Civil Justice Reform, 1988—89; chmn. U.S.-Philippines Bus. Com., 1998—2000; adv. bd. Tennenbaum & Co., L.A., 1997—; mem. Coun. on Fgn. Rels., 1998—, Pacific Coun. on Internat. Policy, 1988—, corp. bd. advisors, 2001—; dep. chmn. Contact Energy Ltd., Wellington, New Zealand, 1990—2000. Trustee Exceptional Children's Found., L.A., 1988-94, treas., 1988-93; co-chair Internat. Energy Devel. Coun., Washington, 1993-2000; bd. govs. Jr. Achievement of Orange County and the Inland Empire, 1995-96. Home and Office: 502 20th St Santa Monica CA 90402-3028

MULLER, ERNEST H. geology educator; b. Tabriz, Iran, Mar. 4, 1923; (parents U.S. citizens); s. Hugo Arthur and Laura Barnett (McComb) M.; m. Wanda Custis, Apr. 7, 1951; children: Ruth Anne, David Stewart, Katherine Lee. BA, Wooster Coll., 1947; MS, U. Ill., 1949, PhD, 1952. Geologist U.S. Geol. Survey, Washington, 1947-54; asst. prof. geology Cornell U., Ithaca, N.Y., 1954-59; assoc. prof. Syracuse U., 1959-63, prof., 1963-89, interim chmn. dept. geology, 1970-71, 79-81, prof. emeritus, 1989—. Seasonal geologist N.Y. Geol. Survey, 1956-76; geologist Am. Geog. Soc., Chile, 1959; rsch. assoc. Natural History Mus., Rejkjavik, Iceland, 1968-69; vis. prof. Alaska Pacific U., Anchorage, 1979; Erskine vis. prof. U. Canterbury, Christchurch, New Zealand, 1974; mem. Bering Glacier (Alaska) Rsch. Group, 1988—, N.Y. Pleistocene Stratigraphy. Author: Geology of Chautauqua County, New York, 1964, Seaway Trail Rocks and Landscapes, 1987. 1st lt. USAAF, 1943-46. Fellow Geol. Soc. Am. (geomorphology panel 1962-64, 66-68, 75-77, 97-99), AAAS; mem. Am. Quaternary Assn. (counselor 1982-86), Glaciological Soc., Nat. Assn. Geology Tchrs., Sigma Xi. Home: 874 Livingston Ave Syracuse NY 13210-2936 Office: Syracuse U 204 Heroy Geology Lab Syracuse NY 13244-0001

MULLER, FRANK, mediator, arbitrator; b. Prague, Czechoslovakia, Nov. 24, 1930; m. Louise De Vel, Dec. 14, 1957; children: Robert, William, David. BE in Civil Engring., Yale U., 1952; LLB, Boston Coll., 1959. Bar: N.Y. 1973, Mass. 1959; registered profl. engr., N.Y., N.J., Mass. Field engr., field supt. Raymond Internat., Inc., N.Y.C., 1955-58; project engr. New Eng. Found., Inc., Boston, 1958-59; house counsel, chief project engr. Daniel O'Connell's Sons, Inc., Holyoke, Mass., 1959-64; v.p., dir., sec. Madigan Praeger, Inc., N.Y.C., 1964-76; dir. constrn. mgmt. svcs. and constrn. dept. Parsons Brinckerhoff Quade Douglas, Inc., 1976-79; sr. v.p. O'Brien-Kreitzberg & Assocs., 1979-89; pres. Metro Mediation Svcs. Ltd., 1989—. Industry prof. exec. 21 program Poly. Inst. N.Y., 1999—; adj. asst. prof. Sch. Cont. Edn. NYU, 1989-94; adj. instr. Polytechnic Inst. N.Y., 1975-77, adj. prof. dept. civil engring.; lectr. profl. assns.; pvt. judge The Pvt. Adjudication Ctr., Inc.; arbitrator N.Y. Small Claims Ct.; mediator Community Dispute Settlement Svc., N.Y. State; arbitrator and mediator panel Am. Arbitration Assn.; mem. mediator panels N.Y. Supreme Ct., Superior Ct. N.J., U.S. Dist. Ct. (ea. dist.) N.Y. Co-author: Construction Management: A Professional Approach, 1978; contbr. articles to profl. jours, chpts. to books. Lt. (j.g.) CEC USN, 1952-55. Recipient Constrn. Mgmt. award ASCE. Mem. Nat. Constrn. Industry Dispute Resolution Com. (past chair), Constrn. Mgmt. Assn. Am. (past pres.). Office: Metro Mediation Svcs Ltd 685 3rd Ave Ste 2100 New York NY 10017-4024

MULLER, FREDERICK ARTHUR, retired legal editor, publisher; b. Center Moriches, N.Y., Dec. 18, 1937; s. Frederick Henry and Estelle May (Reeve) M.; m. Ellen Ruth Willard, Sept. 8, 1962; children: John F., Matthew R. BA, U. Rochester, N.Y., 1960; JD, U. Chgo., 1963. Bar: Ill. 1963, N.Y. 1964, U.S. Ct. Mil. Appeals 1965, U.S. Dist. Ct. (we. dist.) N.Y. 1971. Law clk. to judge N.Y. State. Ct. Appeals, 1968-69, 72; assoc. Hodgson, Russ, Andrews, Woods & Goodyear, Buffalo, 1969-72; asst. consultation clk. N.Y. State Ct. Apls., 1972-82; dep. state reporter State of N.Y., 1982-90, state reporter, 1990—; ret.; cons. staff atty. N.Y. State Ct. on Judiciary, 1973; chmn. supervisory com. Stewart AFB Fed. Credit Union, 1964-65. Editor N.Y. State Official Style Manual, 1985, 87, 92, 96, 97. Mem. budget and allocations com. United Way Northeastern N.Y., Inc., 1975-80, bd. advisors law sch. U. Chgo., 1988—. Served with JAGC USAF, 1964-67. Mem. ABA (com. on appellate style manual 1987—), Am. Judicature Soc. (bd. dirs. 1996-97), Am. Assn. Law Librs. (task force citation formats 1994-95), Assn. Reporters of Jud. Decisions (sec. 1988-89, v.p. 1989-90, pres. 1990-91), N.Y. State Bar Assn., U. Chgo. Club (chmn. alumni schs. com., 1984-89, bd. dirs. 1986—), Phi Beta Kappa, Phi Delta Phi. Baptist. Home: 211 Milford Ln Mc Cormick SC 29835-2428

MULLER, GREGORY ALAN, retired health facilities administrator, mayor; b. Newark, Feb. 11, 1947; s. Richard Mapes and Doris J. (Morgan) M.; m. Geraldine A. Bleach, May 1, 1976; children: Laura M., Gregory P. AS in Psychology, Union Coll., 1977; BSBA, S.W. U. La., 1988; MBA, Can. Sch. Mgmt., Toronto, 1994. Lic. Realty agt., N.J.; cert. social worker, N.J. Sr. br. mgr. fin. divsn. Household Internat., Inc., 1972-84, ops. mgr. retail svcs. divsn., 1984-87, mgr. legal svcs., 1987-89; v.p., chief loan officer Lehigh Savs. Bank, Union Twp., N.J., 1989-91; program dir., bus. mgr., lectr., fin. counselor St. Barnabas Behavioral Health Hosp., Union, 1991-96, govt., cmty., pub. rels. liaison, 1996—; dir. administrative ops. behavioral health Union (N.J.) Hosp., 1991-96, cmty. and govt. rels. liaison, 1996—. Mem. Union Twp. Com., 1987-98, mcpl. drug alliance, Union ctr. spl. improvement dist., dep. mayor Union Twp., 1987, 94, mayor, 1995, 97; Fire and Police Commr., Union Twp., 1996; sec. Union County Planning Bd., 1993—; mem. Union Twp. Bd. Edn., chmn. fin., 1985-87; active Regular Rep. Club Union, bd. dirs.; mem. N.J. Coun. on Affordable Housing; bd. dirs. Kean U. Found; legis. aide to N.J. Senate pres., Donald DiFrancesco Mem. Barbershop Quartet winners N. Ctrl. Divsn. championship, 1981; named Vol. of Yr. Union County Anti-drug Alliance, 1998; recipient outstanding citizen awardCerebral Palsy League of Union County, 1998. Mem. DAV (award 1995), VFW (Citizen of Yr. 1998), Union County Coll. Alumni, Rutgers Sch. Drug & Alcohol Studies Alumni, Am. Soc. Profl. Appraisers (cert. residential real estate appraiser), Union County Assn. Realtors, Am. Psychotherapy Assn. (diplomate), Nat. Assn. Prevention Profls. and Advocates (cert. profl. ethics), Soc. Certified Consumer Credit Execs. (cert.), Am. Soc. Notary Pubs., Vietnam Vets. Am., Fireman's Mutual Benevolent Assn. (hon. life mem. 1992), Am. Legion, Masons, Shriners, Elks, Optimists. Home: 1675 Kenneth Ave Union NJ 07083-5115

MULLER, HENRY JOHN, real estate developer; b. N.Y.C., July 27, 1919; s. Henry and Anne (Wulf) M.; m. Cecelia M. Ziffer, May 19, 1943; children: Richard, Robert, Ceil Anne, Roger. BS, Bklyn. Poly. Inst., 1949. Engr. GE Co., Bloomfield, NJ, 1948-49, Prudential Ins. Co., Newark, 1949-56; dep. dir. Harvard U., 1956-64; sr. v.p. 1st Nat. City Bank, N.Y.C., 1964-71; chmn. Citicorp. Realty, 1971-72; sr. v.p. Allied Maintenance Corp., 1972-74; exec. v.p. Moorings Devel. Co., Vero Beach, Fla., 1974-77; pres. Muller & Assocs. Inc., 1977-89, Criterion Svcs. Corp., Vero Beach, 1988—, Muller Homes Inc., Vero Beach, 1998—. With AUS, 1941-46. Mem. Tau Beta Pi, Lambda Chi Alpha. Office: Criterion Svcs Corp 7412 US Hwy 1 Vero Beach FL 32967 Home: 7355 35th Ct Vero Beach FL 32967-5759

MULLER, H(ENRY) NICHOLAS, III, foundation executive, retired; b. Pitts., Nov. 18, 1938; s. Henry N. Jr. and Harriet (Kerschner) M.; m. Nancy Clagett, June 20, 1959 (div. 1985); children: Charles T., Brook W.; m. Carol A. Cook, Jan. 4, 1986. BA, Dartmouth Coll., 1960; PhD, U. Rochester, 1968. Instr. Dartmouth Coll., Hanover, N.H., 1964; lectr. Mt. Allison U., Sackville, N.B., Can., 1964-66; asst. prof. history U. Vt., Burlington, 1966-69; assoc. prof. history, 1970-73; prof. history U. Vt., Burlington, 1974-78, asst. dean Coll. Arts and Scis., 1969-70, assoc. dean Coll. Arts and Scis., 1970-73, dir. Living/Learning Ctr., 1973-78; pres. Colby-Sawayer Coll., New London, N.H., 1978-85; dir. State His. Soc. Wis., Madison, 1985-96; pres., CEO Frank Lloyd Wright Found., Spring Green, Wis. and Scottsdale, 1996—2002, ret., 2002. Chmn. State Hist. Records Adv. Bd., 1985-96, Wis. Burial Sites Bd., 1988-96, Wis. Submerged Cultural Resources, 1993-96, Standex Internat. Corp., Salem, N.H., 1984—, Nat. Trust for Hist. Preservation, 1989-98; mem. Gov. Coun. on Tourism, 1987-96. Co-author: An Anxious Democracy, 1982; co-editor: Science, Technology and Culture, 1974, In a State of Nature, 1982; sr. editor Vt. Life mag., 1975-87; editor Vt. History, 1977-85. Chmn. Bicentennial Com., Burlington, 1976, Vt. Coun. Hist. Preservation, 1975—78; fin. chmn. Vt. Bicentennial Commn., 1970—77; mem. Wis. Sesquicentennial Commn., 1995—99, N.H. Postsecondary Edn. Commn., 1983—85; trustee Vt. Hist. Soc., 1972—85, v.p., 1975—82; trustee, pres. Taliesin Preservation, Inc., 1991—2001; interim chmn. Taliesin Archs., 2000—01; trustee Frank Lloyd Wright Found., 1996—; v.p. Ind. Coll. Univ. Coun. Ariz., 1998—2000, mem. bd., 1998—2002; bd. dirs. USS Wisconsin, 1989—93, Wis. Preservation Fund Inc., 1989—; trustee Ethan Allen Homestead Trust, 2002—. Fellow Ctr. for Rsch. on Vt.; mem. Nat. Coun. on Pub. History (bd. dirs. 1988-90), Am. Assn. State and Local History (councillor 1988-91), Vt. Archeol. Soc. (pres. 1971-74), Madison Club.

MULLER, HERMAN JOSEPH, historian, educator; b. Cleve., Apr. 7, 1909; s. Joseph John and Julia (Zwilling) Muller. LitB, Xavier U., 1932; MA in History, Loyola U., 1935; S.T.L., St. Louis U., 1946; PhD in History, Loyola U., Chgo., 1951; LHD (hon.), U. Detroit Mercy, 2002. Ordained 1941. Tchr. St. Ignatius H.S., Chgo., 1935—38; lectr. Xavier U., Cin., 1943—47; asst. prof. West Baden Coll. (Loyola U.), 1941—43, John Carroll U., Cleve., 1952—56; prof. history U. Detroit, 1956—. Lectr. in History U. Coll., Dublin, 1968—69, Dublin, 1972—73, Cork, Ireland, 1977—78. Author: (History Book) The University of Detroit: 1877-1977, 75 Years of Quality Business Education, 1991, (Hist. Biography) Bishop East of the Rockies, 1994. Named one of People Who Make a Difference, U. Mercy, 2001. Mem.: Phi Alpha Theta, Alpha Sigma Nu. Roman Catholic. Avocations: fishing, golf, faculty chaplain of Univ. baseball team. Home: Lansing Reilly Hall 4001 W McNicholls Ave Detroit MI 48219 Office: Univ Detroit 4001 McNicholls Ave 48219

MULLER, JENNIFER, choreographer, dancer; b. Yonkers, N.Y., Oct. 16, 1944; d. Don Medford and Lynette (Heldman) Muller. BS, Juilliard Sch. Music, 1967. Instr. in dance H.S. Performing Arts, 1967-72, Sarah Lawrence Coll., 1968-72, The Juilliard Sch., 1969-70, Nederlands Dans Theater, 1971-76, Utah rep., 1973-74, Centre Nat. de la Dance, Paris, 1998, Acad. Isola Danzo, Venice, 1999-2001, Atelier de Paris, 1999, Barcelona State and Dance, 2001; commns.: Alvin Ailey Am. Dance Theatre, N.Y.C., 1977, 85, Festival d'Avignon, France, 1980, Lyon Opera Ballet, France, 1984, Aterballetto, 1988, 93, Ballet Stagium, 1991, Dansgroep Krisztina de Chatel, 1992, Tanz-Forum Staatsoper Koln, Sachsische Staatopera-Dresden, ARTSCAPE-Balt., 1991, 95, Aterballetto, Italy, 1993, Les Ballet Jazz de Montreal, 1994, Ballet du Nord, France, 1995, White Wave Rising, 1996, Bat Dor Dance Co., Israel, Nederlands Dans Theatre III, Ballet Contemporaneo, Argentina, Ohio Ballet, 2000; cons. Met. Mus. Art, 1971-72. Mem. Pearl Lang Dance Co., N.Y.C, 1959-63, prin. dance, Jose Limon Dance Co., N.Y.C., 1963-71, assoc. dir., choreographer, prin. dancer, Louis Falco Dance Co., N.Y.C., 1968-74; founder, dir. choreographer: Jennifer Muller/The Works, N.Y.C., 1974— ; choreographic works include: Nostalgia, 1971, Rust, 1971, Cantata, 1972, Tub, 1973, An American Beauty Rose, 1974, Biography, 1974, Speeds, 1974, Winter Pieces, 1974, Clown, 1974, Four Chairs, 1974, Wyeth, 1974, White, 1975, Strangers, 1975, Beach, 1976, Crossword, 1977, Predicaments for Five, 1977, Mondriaan, 1977, Lovers, 1978, Solo, 1979, Conversations, 1979, Chant, 1980, Terrain, 1981, Shed, 1982, Kite, 1983, Souls, 1984, The Enigma, 1986, Fields, 1986, Couches, 1986, Life/Times, 1986, Darkness and Light, 1986, Interrupted River, 1987, Occasional Encounters, 1988, City, 1988, The Flight of a Predatory Bird, 1989, Refracted Light, 1990, RIGHTeous About Passing (on the LEFT), 1990, Woman with Visitors at 3am, 1991, Regards, 1991, arm in arm in arm..., 1991, Thesaurus, 1991, Glass Houses, 1991, 2-1-1/Attic, 1992, Momentary Gathering, 1992, The Waiting Room, 1993, The Politician/Peeling the Onion, 1993, Orbs, Spheres and Other Circular Bodies, 1993, HUMAN/NATURE-A Response to the Longhouse Gardens, 1993, Pierrot, 1993, Desire-That DNA Urge, 1994, Point of View (A Case of Persimmons and Picasso), 1994, The Spotted Owl, 1995, Some Days are Like That, 1995, Promontory, 1996, Fruit, 1996, The Dinner Party, 1996, A Broken Wing, 1996, Ricochet, 1997, Degas Revisited, 1998, Dialectics Part I, 1998, Spores, Solitude & Summer Humming, 1999, Beethoven-Not Four Naught, 2000, aSOlo, 2000, Hymn for Her, 2000, Time Treading, 2000; choreographer for theatrical prodns.: Frimbo, 1980, The Death of von Richthofen..., 1982, Fame, The Musical, 1988, Up Against It, 1989, The Seven Deadly Sins, 1990, Signature, 1990, Esther, 1993, Once Around the City, 1998, 2001; dir. Le Jongleur, 2000. Recipient Best Performance award Berlin Festival, 1977, Acad. award Juilliard Sch. Music, 1967, Carbonell award, 1989; grantee Nat. Endowment for Arts, 1971-77, 80-85, 86-87, 87-88, Creative Artists Pub. Svc., 1976-77, N.Y. State Coun. on Arts, 1976-77, 78-79, 85-93, N.Y.C. Dept. Cultural Affairs, 1978-79, 94-2001, N.Y.C. Dept. Youth and Cmty. Devel., 2001-02. Mem. Am. Guild Mus. Artists, Soc. Stage Dirs. and Choreographers. Home and Office: The Muller/Works Found Inc 131 W 24th St New York NY 10011-1942 Office Fax: 212-206-6630. E-mail: jenniferm@compuserve.com., theworksnyc@compuserve.com.

MULLER, JEROME KENNETH, photographer, art director, editor; b. Amityville, N.Y., July 18, 1934; s. Alphons and Helen (Haberl) M.; m. Nora Marie Nestor, Dec. 21, 1974. BS, Marquette U., 1961; postgrad., Calif. State U., Fullerton, 1985-86; MA, Nat. U., San Diego, 1988; postgrad., Newport Psychoanalytic Inst., 1988-90. Comml. and editorial photographer, N.Y.C., 1952-55; mng. editor Country Beautiful mag., Milw., 1961-62, Reprodns. Rev. mag., N.Y.C., 1967-68; editor, art dir. Orange County (Calif.) Illustrated, Newport Beach, 1962-67, art editor, 1970-79, exec. editor, art dir., 1968-69; owner, CEO Creative Svcs. Advt. Agy., 1969-79. Founder, CEO Mus. Graphics, Costa Mesa, Calif., 1978—; tchr. photography Lindenhurst (N.Y.) High Sch., 1952-54, comic art U. Calif., Irvine, 1979, publ. design Orange Coast Coll., Costa Mesa, Calif., 1997—; guest curator 50th Anniversary Exhbn. Mickey Mouse, 1928-78, The Bowers Mus., Santa Ana, Calif., 1978; organized Moving Image Exhbn. Mus. Sci. and Industry, Chgo., Cooper-Hewitt Mus., N.Y.C., William Rockhill Nelson Gallery, Kansas City, 1981; collector original works outstanding Am. cartoonists at major mus. *Exhibitions Organized: The Cartoon Show, Laguna Beach Art Mus, 1972. Indianapolis Mus of Art, 1977, Everson Mus of Art, Syracuse, 1978, Memorial Art Gallery, Rochester, 1979; The Moving Image, San Jose Mus, 1980, Mus of Science and Industry, Chicago, William Rockhill Nelson Gallery, Kansas City, 1981, Newport Harbor Art Mus, Calif, Mus of Albuquerque, 1982, Boston Mus of Science, 1983, Pensacola Mus of Art, 1984; The American Comic Strip, U. of*

Texas, 1981, Duke U, Midwest Mus of Am Art, 1982, U of Chicago, The Parthenon, Nashville, 1983, Albrecht Art Mus, St Joseph, Mo, Wichita Art Mus, 1984, Monterey Peninsula Mus of Art, 1985. One-man shows include Souk Gallery, Newport Beach, 1970, Gallery 2, Santa Ana, Calif., 1972, Cannery Gallery, Newport Beach, 1974, Mus. Graphics Gallery, 1993, White Gallery Portland State U., 1996, U. Calif., Irvine, 1997, Nat. Telephone and Comm., Irvine, Calif., 1998, Robert Mondavi Wine and Food Center, Costa Mesa, 2000; author: Rex Brandt, 1972, Publication Design and Production, 2000; contbr. photographs and articles to mags. Mem. Cultural Arts Com., City of Costa Mesa. With USAF, 1956-57. Recipient two silver medals 20th Ann. Exhbn. Advt. and Editorial Art in West, 1965. Mem.: APA, L.A. Press Club, Laguna Beach Art Mus., Art Mus. Assn. Am., Met. Mus. Art, Mus. Modern Art (N.Y.C.), Alpha Sigma Nu. Home: 2438 Bowdoin Pl Costa Mesa CA 92626-6304 Office: PO Box 11155 Costa Mesa CA 92627-1155

MULLER, JERRY ZUCKER, history educator; b. Niagara Falls, Ont., Can., June 7, 1954; s. Henry and Bella Muller; m. Sharon Sachs, Aug. 8, 1976; children: Elisha, Sara, Joseph. BA, Brandeis U., 1977; PhD, Columbia U., 1984. From asst. prof. history to assoc. prof. history Cath. U., Washington, 1984-96, ordinary prof. history, 1996—. Author: (books) The Other God that Failed: Hans Freyer and the Deradicalization of German Conservatism, 1987, Adam Smith in His Time and Ours, 1993; editor: (book) Conservatism, 1997, The Mind and the Market: Capitalism in Modern European Thought, 2002; adv. editor: Social Science and Modern Society, 1997, Critical Rev. Fellow Bellagio Ctr., Rockefeller Found., 2001, faculty fellow Olin Found., 1987-88, 99, fellow Am. Coun. Learned Socs., 1985-86; rsch. grantee Bradley Found., 1990-91. Mem. Internat. Soc. for Intellectual History, Jewish Studies Assn., Conf. for Study of Polit. Thought, Am. Hist. Assn., Conf. on Cen. European History, 18th Century Scottish Studies Soc., German Studies Assn., Hist. Soc., Jewish. Avocations: reading, music, film. Home: 11610 Yeatman Terr Silver Spring MD 20902 Office: Cath U of Am Dept History Washington DC 20064 E-mail: mullerj@cua.edu.

MULLER, JOHN BARTLETT, university president; b. Port Jefferson, N.Y., Nov. 8, 1940; s. Frederick Henry and Estelle May (Reeve) M.; m. Barbara Ann Schmidt, May 30, 1964 (dec. 1972); m. Lynn Anne Spongberg, Oct. 10, 1987. AB in Polit. Sci., U. Rochester, 1962; postgrad. in apologetics, Westminster Sem., Phila., 1962-63; MS in Psychology, Purdue U., 1968, PhD in Psychology, 1975. Asst. prof. psychology Roberts Wesleyan Coll., Rochester, N.Y., 1964-66, acting chmn. div. behavioral sci., dir. instl. research, 1967-70; vis. asst. prof. psychology Wabash Coll., Crawfordsville, Ind., 1970-71; research assoc. Ind. U.-Purdue U., Indpls., 1971-72; prof. psychology, v.p. for acad. affairs Hillsdale (Mich.) Coll., 1972-85; pres. BMW Assocs., Osseo, Mich., 1984-85, Bellevue (Nebr.) U., 1985—. Bd. dirs. Nebr. Ind. Coll. Found., Omaha, Assn. Ind. Colls. Nebr., Lincoln; bd. advisors Wells Fargo Bank of Omaha, Applied Info. Mgmt. Inst., Am. Nat. Bank. Contbr. articles to profl. jours. and textbooks. Bd. govs. Boys Club of Omaha. Nat. Inst. Mental Health fellowship Purdue U., 1963, Nat. Tchg. fellowship Fed. Govt., 1967, Townsend fellowship U. Rochester, 1962. Mem. APA, Bellevue C. of C. (bd. dirs. 1989-95), Phi Beta Kappa, Phi Kappa Phi. Republican. Home: 13303 Lochmoor Cir Bellevue NE 68123-3770 Office: Bellevue U Office of the Pres 1000 Galvin Rd S Bellevue NE 68005-3098 E-mail: Jmuller@Bellevue.edu.

MULLER, JON, archaeologist, educator; b. Salina, Kans., Oct. 23, 1941; BA, U. Kans., 1963; PhD, Harvard U., 1967. Tchg. fellow Harvard U., Cambridge, Mass., 1965-66; prof. dept. anthropology So. Ill. U., Carbondale, 1966—, assoc. dean Coll. Liberal Arts, 1997-99. Author: Archaeology of Lower Ohio River Valley, 1986 (Delta award 1987), Mississippian Political Economy, 1997 (Soc. Am. Archaeology Book award 1999). Chmn. adv. bd. Ill. Historic Sites, Springfield, 1983-89. Office: Southern Illinois Univ Dept Anthropology 4502 Carbondale IL 62901

MULLER, KURT ALEXANDER, lawyer; b. Chgo., June 21, 1955; s. Jack and Janet (Kasten) M.; m. Sylvia Saltoon, Apr. 6, 1986; 1 child, Marissa Grace. BS, U. Wis., Parkside, 1977; JD, John Marshall Law Sch., 1986. Bar: Ill. 1986, U.S. Dist. Ct. (no. dist.) Ill. 1986, Ariz. 1987, U.S. Dist. Ct. (ea. dist.) Wis. 1989. Creative dir. Brand Advt., Chgo., 1977-80; dep. sheriff Cook County, 1978-86; broker Gerstenberg Commodities, 1980-83; assoc. Gordon & Glickson, P.C., 1986-87, Michael Harry Minton, P.C., Chgo., 1987-90; pvt. practice, 1990-92; ptnr. Law Offices of Richter-Muller, P.C., 1992-95; lawyer, CEO The Muller Firm, Ltd., 1995—. Author: In Consideration of Divorce: Giving Credit (and Debits) to Dissolution, 1991, 3d edit., 1998; contbr. The Jewish American Prince Handbook, 1986; contbr. articles to profl. jours. and newspapers; host (CBS radio show) Kurt Muller's Uncommon Law; monthly columnist for Chgo. Social: Ask Muller. Mem. ABA, ACLU, Nat. Smoker's Alliance, Chgo. Bar Assn., Masons. Avocations: interior design, films, theater, writing. E-mail: www. mullaw.com. Office: 200 N Dearborn St Apt 4602 Chicago IL 60601-1628 Fax: 312-855-9362.

MULLER, LAWRENCE GEORGE, communications consultant; b. San Francisco; s. Lawrence George Mullen Sr. and Agnes L. Meenan. AA, Skyline Coll., 1972; BA, Calif. State U., Hayward, 1974; MA with highest distinction, Calif. State U., L.A., 1976. Cert. assoc. in claims, assoc. in ins., suprvisory. mgmt. Claims adjuster Crawford & Co., San Francisco, 1980-85; litigation adjuster Maryland Casualty, Sacramento, 1985-90; corp. claims trainer Claims Unltd. Weil & Co., Oakland, Calif., 1990-93; risk mgr. MV Transp., San Francisco, 1993-95; with Infinity Ins. Co., 1997-98; comm. cons. San Francisco, 1974—. Arbitrator, mediator BBB, Oakland and San Francisco; profl. spkr Toastmasters, Calif.; comm. cons. to law enforcement and banks, Calif. Co-author: (comm. strategies) Just for the Sake of Argument, 1985; author: (comm. analysis) The Use of Ritual to Promote Officer Safety, 1990; contbr. poetry to anthologies. Grief counselor CFM, Vaccaville, 1989-98; baseball umpire Am. Softball Assn./No. Calif. Athletic Assn., Fresno and Daly City, 1988-90; dist. bd. dirs. Kiros Prison Ministry, 1990-97. Named Outstanding Toastmaster, Dist. 33, 1979-82. Mem. Pi Kappa Delta (nat. debate Gold Medal 1973, hon. Forensic Fraternity Orders of Debate, Speaking and Instruction). Avocations: photography, computers, logic problems. Office: L G Muller Jr Speech Comms Inc 1953 Manor Pl Ste 1 Fairfield CA 94533-4152 Home: Apt 104 1150 E Herndon Ave Fresno CA 93720-3118

MULLER, MARCEL W(ETTSTEIN), electrical engineering educator; b. Vienna, Austria, Nov. 1, 1922; came to U.S., 1940; s. Georg and Josephine (David) M.; m. Esther Ruth Hagler, Feb. 2, 1947; children: Susan, George, Janet. BSEE, Columbia U., 1949, AM in Physics, 1952; PhD, Stanford U., 1957. Sr. scientist Varian Assocs., Palo Alto, Calif., 1952-66; prof. elec. engring. Washington U., St. Louis, 1966-91, prof. emeritus, rsch. prof., 1991—. Vis. lectr. U. Zurich, Switzerland, 1962-63; vis. prof. U. Colo., Boulder, summer 1969; vis. scientist Max Planck Inst., Stuttgart, Fed. Republic of Germany, 1976-77; cons. Hewlett-Packard Labs., Palo Alto, 1985-89, SRI Internat., Menlo Park, Calif., 1986—. Sgt. U.S. Army, 1943-46. Recipient Humboldt prize Alexander von Humboldt Soc., 1976; Fulbright grantee, 1977, grantee NSF, 1967—. Fellow IEEE, Am. Physical Soc. Achievements include development of Maser quantum noise theory; developments in micromagnetism; contributions to magnetic information storage; invention Magneprint security system. Home: 4954 Lindell Blvd Saint Louis MO 63108-1500 Office: Washington Univ Campus Box 1127 1 Brookings Dr Saint Louis MO 63130-4899 E-mail: mwm@ee.wustl.edu.

MULLER, MERVIN EDGAR, information systems educator, consultant; b. Hollywood, Calif., June 1, 1928; s. Emanuel and Bertha (Zimmerman) M.; m. Barbara McAdam, July 13, 1963; children: Jeffrey McAdam, Stephen McAdam, Todd McAdam. AB, UCLA, 1949, MA, 1951, PhD, 1954. Instr. in math. Cornell U., 1954-56; rsch. assoc. in math. Princeton U., 1956-59; sr. statistician, dept. mgr. IBM, N.Y.C., White Plains, 1956-64; sr. scientist statis. and elec. engring. Princeton U., 1968-69; prof. computer sci. and stats. U. Wis., 1964-71; prof. computer sci. George Mason U., 1985; dept. dir. World Bank, Washington, 1971-81, sr. advisor, 1981-85; Robert M. Critchfield prof. computer info. sci. Ohio State U., 1985-98, prof. emeritus, 1994-98, dept. chair, 1985-94. Chair sci. and tech. info. bd. NRC, NAS; bd. dirs. Advanced Info. Tech. Ctr., Columbus, Ohio. Mem. editl. bd. Computation and Stats., 1990, Jour. Computational and Graphical Stats., 1990; contbr. numerous articles to profl. jours. Bd. trustees First Unitarian Ch., Bethesda, Md., 1975-79. Rsch. grantee AT&T, Columbus, Ohio, 1987. Fellow Am. Statis. Assn., World Acad. Productivity Sci.; mem. Internat. Statis. Inst. (steering com. Internat. Rsch. Ctr., 1987-89), Internat. Assn. for Statis. Computing (sci. sec. 1979-83, pres. 1977-79). Avocations: reading, jogging, walking, bridge. Home: 4571 Clairmont Rd Upper Arlington OH 43220-4501 Office: Ohio State U Dept Computer Info Sci Rm 395 2015 Neil Ave Dept Computer Columbus OH 43210-1210 E-mail: mullee@columbus.rr.com.

MULLER, PATRICIA ANN, nursing administrator, educator; b. N.Y.C., July 22, 1943; d. Joseph H. and Rosanne (Bautz) Felter; m. David G. Smith, Mar. 19, 1988; children: Frank M. Muller III, Kimberly M. Muller. BSN, Georgetown U., 1965; MA, U. Tulsa, 1978, EdD, 1983. RN. Staff devel. coord. St. Francis Hosp., Tulsa, 1978-79, asst. dir. for nursing svc., nursing edn., 1979-82, dir. dept. edn., 1982-98, St. Francis Health Sys., 1998—2002. Mem. faculty Okla. U., Northeastern U., Tulsa U.; presenter at confs. and convs. Contbg. editor JOPAN, 1992-2001; contbr. articles to profl. jours. Mem. Leadership Tulsa, 1991; bd. dirs. Am. Heart Assn., Ronald McDonald House. Mem. ANA, Nat. League for Nursing, Am. Soc. for Nursing Svc. Adminstrs., Am. Soc. for Health Manpower Edn. and Tng., Okla. Nurses Assn., Okla. Orgn. of Nurse Execs. (pres. 1992-93), Sigma Theta Tau. Address: 6203 W Utica Ct Broken Arrow OK 74011 E-mail: mullsmi@aol.com.

MULLER, PETER, lawyer, entertainment company executive, retail company executive, consultant; b. Teplitz-Sanov, Czechoslovakia, Mar. 4, 1947; came to U.S., 1949; s. Alexander and Elizabeth Rudolpha (Weingarten) M.; m. Irene Smolarski, Nov. 18, 1971 (div. 1973); children: Chloe, Aurora; m. Esther Unterman Meisler, Jan. 4, 1987 (div. 1995). BA, NYU, 1968, JD cum laude. Entertainment editor Ambience mag., N.Y.C., 1978-79, Women's Life mag., N.Y.C., 1980-81; sole practice, 1984—; entertainment writer Jewish Press; chief exec. officer Producers Releasing Corp., N.Y. and Nev., 1987-88, pres. entertainment div., 1987-88; pres., founder Muller Entertainment Group, N.Y.C. and Calif., 1988—; pres., chief oper. officer ACA Joe, Inc., San Francisco and N.Y.C.; also bd. dirs. ACA Joe Inc. Expert tech. adv. svc. for attys., Pa., 1987—; lectr. entertainment and comm. bus. to various orgns.; adj. prof. NYU, UCLA. Author: Show Business Law, 1991, The Music Business: A Legal Perspective, 1994. Bd. dirs. NYU Coll. Arts and Sci.; vol. Lawyers for the Arts, N.Y.C., 1987—. Mem. ABA (forum on entertainment and sports industries, forum on copyright, trademark and patent law), N.Y. State Bar Assn., NYU Alumni Assn. (bd. dirs. 1987—, v.p. bd. dirs., coun.), Assn. of Am. Mgmt. Assn. (pres.). Avocations: sports, swimming, history, writing, travel.

MULLER, RICHARD STEPHEN, electrical engineer, educator; b. Weehawken, N.J., May 5, 1933; s. Irving Ernest and Marie Victoria Muller; m. Joyce E. Regal, June 29, 1957; children: Paul Stephen, Thomas Richard. ME, Stevens Inst. Tech., Hoboken, N.J., 1955; MSEE, Calif. Inst. Tech., 1957, PhD in Elect. Engring. and Physics, 1962. Engr.-in-tng., 1955. Test engr. Wright Aero/Curtiss Wright, Woodridge, N.J., 1953-54; mem. tech. staff Hughes Aircraft Co., Culver City, Calif., 1955-61; instr. U. So. Calif., L.A., 1960-61; asst. prof., then assoc. prof. U. Calif., Berkeley, 1962-72, prof., 1973—. Guest prof. Swiss Fed. Inst. Tech., 1993; founder, dir. Berkeley Sensor and Actuator Ctr., 1985—. Co-author: Device Electronics for Integrated Circuits, 1977, 2d rev. edit., 1986, Microsensors, 1990; editor-in-chief IEEE/ASME Jour. Microelectromech. Sys., 1998—; contbr. more than 200 articles to profl. jours. Pres. Kensington (Calif.) Mcpl. Adv. Coun., 1992-98; trustee Stevens Inst. of Technology, 1996—. Fellow Hughes Aircraft Co., 1955-57, NSF, 1959-62, NATO postdoctoral fellow, 1968-69, Fulbright fellow, 1982-83, Alexander von Humboldt prize, 1993, Tech. U. Berlin, 1994; Berkeley citation, 1994, Stevens Renaissance award, 1995, Career Achievement award Internat. Conf. on Sensors and Actuators, 1997, Cledo Brunetti award IEEE, 1998. Fellow IEEE (life, Millennium prize 2000); mem. IEEE Press Bd., NAE, Nat. Materials (adv. bd. 1994—), Electron Devices Soc. (adv. com. 1984—), Internat. Sensor and Actuator Meeting (chmn. steering com.). Achievements include 18 U.S. and foreign patents; construction of first operating micromotor. Office: U Calif Dept EECS 401 Cory Hl Berkeley CA 94720-0001 E-mail: r.muller@ieee.org.

MULLER, ROBERT JOSEPH, gynecologist; b. New Orleans, Dec. 5, 1946; s. Robert Harry and Camille (Eckert) M.; m. Susan Philipsen, Aug. 22, 1974; children: Ryan, Matt. BS, St. Louis U., 1968; BS, MSc, Emory U., 1976; MD, La. State U., New Orleans, 1981. Cert. in emegency mgmt. Intern Charity Hosp., New Orleans, 1981-82; resident La. State U. Affiliate Hosp., 1982-85; resident staff physician La. State U. Med. Ctr., New Orleans, 1981-85; pvt. practice Camellia Women's Ctr., Slidell, La., 1985—; staff physician Tulane Med. Ctr., New Orleans, 1986—. Med. dir. Northshore Regional Med. Ctr., Slidell, 1987—, chief staff, 1998; med. dir. New Orleans Police Dept., 1981-95, S.W. La. Search and Rescue, Covington, La., 1986—, St. Tammany Parish Sheriff Dept., Covington, 1989—, commdr., 1990—, Camellia City Classic, Slidell, 1989—, Crawfishman Triathalon, Mandeville, La., 1988—, Res-Q-Med Laser Team, 1984—. Contbr. articles to profl. jours. Recipient Commendation Medal New Orleans Police Dept., 1986, 87, 89, Medal Valor St. Tammany Parish Sheriff Office, Covington, 1990, Cert. Valor S.E. La. Search and Rescue, Mandeville, 1990; named one of Outstanding Young Men of Am., 1984. Mem. Am. Coll. Ob-Gyn., La. State Med. Soc., Profl. Assn. Diving Instrs. (divemaster 1991, asst. instr. 1995), So. Offshore Racing Assn. (med. dir. 1982—), Offshore Profl. Racing Tour (med. dir. staff 1990—), Am. Power Boat Assn. (med. staff 1984-89). Roman Catholic. Avocations: scuba diving, boating, shooting. Home: 1181 Yorktown Dr Slidell LA 70461-3023 Office: Camellia Womens Ctr 105 Smart Pl Slidell LA 70458-2039

MULLER, WILLARD C(HESTER), writer; b. Havre, Mont., May 7, 1916; s. Chester Rudolph and Clara (Hansen) M.; m. Carolyn Elfrid Bue, Jan. 27, 1945; children: Marolyn Jean, Barbara Anne, Nancy Eleanor. BA, Stanford U., 1941; MPA, Maxwell Grad. Sch. Govt. Adminstrn., 1943; student, Nat. War Coll., 1961-62. Newspaper reporter, short story writer Bremerton (Wash.) Daily Searchlight, 1934-36; White House corr. Bremerton Daily Searchlight and Port Angeles Evening News, Washington, 1941; mgmt. analyst USDA, 1942, 46-47; mem. staff for food, agr. and forestry U.S. Dept. Army and U.S. High Commr. for Germany, Munich and Frankfurt, Fed. Republic Germany, 1948-50; dist. adminstr., Am. consul U.S. Trust Territory of Pacific Islands, Truk, Caroline Islands, 1951-55; dep. dir. ICA, U.S. Ops. Mission to Nepal, Kathmandu, 1956-58; dir. U.S. Ops. to Somali Republic, 1958-61, Office East and Southern African Affairs, AID, Dept. State, Washington, 1962-65, AID, Kampala, Uganda, 1965-70, assoc. dir. for land reform Saigon, Republic of Vietnam, 1970-73, ret., 1973, cons., 1974-81; free lance writer, 1973—. Author various short stories; contbr. articles to profl. jours. Chmn. steering com. 4-state program dialogue on peace Pacific NW dist. Am. Luth. Ch., Seattle, 1983-85; mem. Clallam br. Wash. State Centennial Commn., 1986-89; mem. Food Bank Bd., Port Angeles, Wash., 1986-90. Lt. USNR, 1943-45, PTO. Mem.: Am. Fgn. Svc. Assn., Am. Soc. Pub. Adminstrn., Kiwanis, Kiwanis. Avocations: horseback riding, world travel. Home and Office: 3624 S Mount Angeles Rd Port Angeles WA 98362-8910 E-mail: muller@tenforward.com.

MULLER, WILLIAM ALBERT, III, library director; b. Savannah, Ga., Jan. 1, 1943; s. William Albert Jr. and Julia Catherine (Cleary) M.; m. Claudya Barbara Burkett, Dec. 12, 1965 (div. 1986); 1 child, Martha Genevieve; m. Pamala Qualls, Apr. 9, 1988; 1 child, Tabitha Wade. BA, Ga. So. Coll., 1966; MLS, Emory U., 1969. Dir. War Woman Regional Libr., Elberton, Ga., 1969-73; rsch. libr. City of Savannah, 1973-75; dir. Mason County Pub. Libr., Point Pleasant, W.Va., 1976-78; pub. rels. cons. Eastern Shore Regional Libr., Salisbury, Md., 1978-81; dir. Brooke County Pub. Libr., Wellsburg, W.Va., 1982-84, McDowell Pub. Libr., Welch, 1984-88, Bristol (Va.) Pub. Libr., 1988—. Sec. So. W.Va. Libr. Automation Corp., Beckley, 1984-87, pres. 1987-88, S.W. Info. Network Group, Abindgdon, Va., 1990-91, treas. (swing) 1993—. Fundraiser Paramount Fund, Bristol, 1989; acct. exec. United Way Fund of Bristol, 1991; bd. dirs. Mid-Atlantic Chamber Orch., Bristol, 1988-92, treas., 1992; bd. dirs. Bristol Preservation Soc., 1988-98, Nat. Ctr. for Quality, 1992-98, Main St. Bristol, 1991-95, treas., 1994; bd. dirs. Jr. Achievement, 1992-99, pres., 1997-99; bd. dirs. Vol. Bristol, 1998—; bd. dirs., vol. chair Racefest 98, 99. Mem. ALA, Southeastern Libr. Assn., Va. Libr. Assn., Rotary Internat. (club pres. 1980-81). Democrat. Avocations: gardening, cabinetry, photography, traveling, model railroads. Home: 706 Piedmont Ave Bristol VA 24201-3446 Office: Bristol Pub Libr 701 Goode St Bristol VA 24201-4199

MULLER, WILLIAM HENRY, JR. surgeon, educator; b. Dillon, S.C., Aug. 19, 1919; s. William Henry and Octavia Elizabeth (Bethea) M.; m. Hildwin Clare Headly, Mar. 23, 1946; children: William Henry III, Marietta John Lewis. BS, The Citadel, 1940, DS (hon.), 1972; MD, Duke U., 1943; DHL (hon.), Med. U. S.C., 1977. Diplomate Am. Bd. Thoracic Surgery, Am. Bd. Surgery (rep. conf. com. grad. tng. in surgery). Intern Johns Hopkins Hosp., Balt., 1944, asst. surgery, asst. resident, 1944-46, resident gen. surgery, instr. surgery, 1948-49, resident cardiovascular surgery, 1949; practice gen. surgery Dillon, 1947-48; asst. prof. surgery UCLA, 1949-53, assoc. prof. Sch. Medicine, 1953-54; attending specialist thoracic surgery Wadsworth VA Hosp., Los Angeles; chief sect. cardiovascular surgery Los Angeles County-Harbor Gen. Hosp., Torrance, Calif.; cons. surgery St. John's, Santa Monica Hosps., 1949-54; cons. cardiovascular surgery U.S. Naval Hosp., San Diego, 1953-54; Stephen H. Watts prof. surgery, chmn. dept. U. Va. Sch. Medicine, 1954-82, v.p. health affairs, 1976-88, univ. prof. surgery and health policy, 1988-90, S. Hurt Watts prof. surgery emeritus, 1990—, v.p. for health affairs emeritus; surgeon-in-chief U. Va. Hosp., 1954-82; chmn. S.E. Surg. Congress; mem. Pres.'s Panel on Heart Disease, 1972; past chmn. surgery study sect. NIH; mem. exec. com., div. med. scis. NRC. Mem. editorial bd.: Am. Jour Surgery, Annals of Surgery, Am. Surgeon; contbr. articles to med jours. Trustee, mem. exec. com. Duke U. Served as capt. M.C. AUS, 1946-47. Named One of 10 Outstanding Young Men of Yr. U.S. Jr. C. of C., Calif. Jr. C. of C., 1952; recipient Disting. Alumni award (1st award) Duke U. Med. Ctr., 1969; Thomas Jefferson award U. Va., 1982; McCallie Sch. Alumni Achievement award, 1986; Paul Harris fellow Nat. Rotary Found., 1988. Fellow ACS (past chmn., forum com. fundamental surg. problems, regent 1971—, chmn. bd. regents 1976-78, pres.-elect 1979); mem. Internat. Soc. Surgery, Internat. Cardiovascular Soc. (past v.p.), AMA, Am. Surg. Assn. (pres. 1974-75), So. Surg. Assn. (pres. 1975), Pacific Coast Surg. Assn., Am. Assn. Thoracic Surgery, Soc. Univ. Surgeons (past pres.), Soc. Surgery Alimentary Tract, Assn. Acad. Surgeons, James IV Assn. Surgeons (v.p. U.S.), Med. Soc. Va., Albemarle County Med. Soc., Soc. Vascular Surgery (past pres.), Am. Heart Assn. (chmn. surgery research study com., mem. central research com.), Va. Surg. Soc, Halsted Soc., Johns Hopkins Soc. Scholars, Raven Soc., Sigma Xi, Alpha Omega Alpha, Phi Chi Home: 900 Flordon Dr Charlottesville VA 22901-7844

MULLER, WILLIAM MANNING, corporate lawyer; b. N.Y.C., Mar. 20, 1959; s. Eugene Lee and Patricia Anne (Manning) M. AB, Brown U., 1981; JD, Northwestern U., 1987. Bar: N.Y. 1989, Conn. 1989, Ga. 1996. Assoc. Milbank, Tweed, Hadley & McCloy, N.Y.C., 1987-90; legal counsel Rockefeller & Co., Inc., 1991-93; assoc. Reid & Priest, 1993-95; counsel Turner Broadcasting Sys., Inc., Atlanta, 1995-96, sr. counsel, 1996—. Mem. ABA, Conn. Bar Assn., State Bar Ga., Assn. Bar City of New York, TV Assn. Programmers (chmn. govt. and legal affairs com.), Univ. Club New York. Office: Turner Broadcasting Sys Inc One CNN Ctr Atlanta GA 30303

MULLETTE, JULIENNE PATRICIA, television personality and producer, astrologer, writer, health center administrator; b. Sydney, Australia, Nov. 19, 1940; came to U.S., 1953; d. Ronald Stanley Lewis and Sheila Rosalind Blunden (Phillips) M.; m. Fred Gillette Sturm, Nov. 24, 1964 (div. Dec. 1969); m. Kenneth Walter Gillman, Dec. 28, 1971 (div. Dec. 1978); children: Noah Khristoff Mullette-Gillman, D'Dhaniel Alexander Mullette-Gillman. BA, Western Coll. for Women, Oxford, Ohio, 1961; postgrad., Harvard U., 1964, U. Sao Paulo, Brazil, 1965, Inst. Philosophy, Sao Paulo, 1965, Miami U., Oxford, 1967-69. Tchr. English, High Mowing Sch., Wilton, N.H., 1962-64, Stoneleigh-Prospect Hill Sch., Greenfield, Mass., 1964; seminar dir. Western Coll. for Women, 1967-69; pres. Family Tree, Home U., Montclair, N.J., 1078-80; dir. Pleroma Holistic Health Ctr., 1980—. Dir. Astrological Rsch. Ctr., Sydney, Australia, 1983; founder Spiritual Devel. Rsch. Group, 1986—; pvt. astrology counselor, 1962—; guest on radio & TV shows, 1962—; lectr. worldwide, 1963—; prin., owner Moonlight Pond, Woodbourne, NY, 1988—; founder Pleroma Found. for Astrological Rsch. & Studies, 1990; breeder, trainer exotic animals; mem. Woodstock Pub. Access Com., 1993—. Author: The Moon-Understanding the Subconscious, 1973; contbr. articles to profl. jours.; editor (founding): KOSMOS Mag., 1968—78, Jour. Astrological Studies, 1970—; contbg. columnist mags.: ; hostess (radio talk show) The Julienne Mullette Show, 1985—, (TV series) You and the Cosmos, Woodstock, NY, 1992—, The Julienne Mullette Show Connections TV, Newark, NJ, 1985—. Founder local chpt. La Leche League, Montclair, 1974; founding pres. The Internat. Astrology Forum, 2000. Mem. AAUW (chmn. cultural affairs Montclair chpt. 1987—), NAFE, Spiritual Devel. Group (founder), Internat. Soc. Astrological Rsch. (founding pres. 1968-78), Cosmos Hyperspace Astrological Origins and Supergravity Studies (founder), Am. Fedn. Astrologers (cert.), Belgian Soc. Astrology, Am. Assn. Humanistic Psychology, Internat. Llamas Assn., Internat. Soc. Astrological Studies and Rsch. (founder 2002). Avocations competitive tennis, local theatre, singing. Home: 1019 Saw Creek Estates Bushkill PA 18324 E-mail: julienne@ptd.net.

MULLIGAN, DAVID KEITH, consulting company executive, securities arbitrator; b. Detroit, Jan. 25, 1951; s. Robert Keith and Yvonne Bette Mulligan. Student, Oakland Coll., 1973-78. Cert. data processor, quality technician, quality auditor, software quality engr.; NASD gen. securities registered rep. Pres. Atlas Prodns., N.Y.C., 1973—. Cons. info. systems, human factors, tech. and mktg. comm. Author: Human Factors in Document Design, 1982, Computer Aids to Software Engineering, 1984, Document Design and Production for the '90s, 1989, Documentation and System Maintenance, 1989, Avoiding Outsourcing and Its Demoralizing Consequences, 1990, Programmer-Analyst: Dinosaur of the '90s, 1990, Information Management: New Thinking for the '90s, 1991, Product Documentation: Key to Internat. Marketing Success, 1993, Joint Application Design Critical Success Factors, 1994, Successful Worldwide Interactive Marketing, 1995, Management Information: Lifeblood of Business, 1996, Executive Ego: Most Powerful Force in Business, 1997, Investigation Techniques in the Healthcare Industry, 1997, Oracle Data Base Adminstration: A Structured Approach, 1999, Information Management in the Entertainment Industry, 1999, Database Application Implementation in the New Millennium, 1999, Sixty Minute Methodology for Desktop Development, 2000, Broad Band Communications: A Business Blueprint, 2000, Data Design: Key To Effective Telecom Provisioning, 2001, Data Management in the Mortgage Banking Industry, 2002, Data Design: Key to Effective Mortgage Banking, 2002, Dysfunction in Corporate America, 2002; co-author: Structured Analysis and Design for the Case User, 1993. Mem. ASCAP, NARAS, Am. Soc. Quality, Am. Fedn. of Musicians, N.Y. Friars Club, Assn. Cert. Fraud Examiners, Am. Soc. for Automation in Pharmacy, The Authors Guild, Am. Mensa, NASD (bd. arbitrators). Avocations: musical composition, music performance, photography. Office: Atlas Prodns Ste 6K 372 5th Ave New York NY 10018-8109

MULLIGAN, DEANNA MARIE, management consultant; b. West Point, Nebr., July 24, 1963; d. Paul Arthur and Judith Maureen (Bottger) Predoehl; m. Stephen Edward Mulligan, Dec. 26, 1985. BS in Bus., U. Nebr., 1985; MBA, Stanford U., 1989. Cons. Woodmen Accident and Life, Hayward, Calif., 1985-87; intern Hewlett-Packard, 1988; dir., corp. planning N.Y. Life, N.Y.C., 1989-90, asst. v.p., 1990-92; prin. McKinsey & Co., Inc., 1992-97,98-2000; sr. v.p. AXA Fin. Svcs., 2000—. Dir. Project Renewal, N.Y.C., trustee Red Cross of Greater N.Y., 2000—. Vol. Freindly Visitor Program, Napa, Calif., 1987; mem. planning forum, N.Y.C. Nat. Merit scholar, 1981.

MULLIGAN, ELINOR PATTERSON, lawyer; b. Bay City, Mich., Apr. 20, 1929; d. Frank Clark and Agnes (Murphy) P.; m. John C. O'Connor, Oct. 28, 1950; children: Christine Fulena, Valerie Clark, Amy O'Connor, Christopher Criffan O'Connor; m. William G. Mulligan, Dec. 6, 1975. BA, U. Mich., 1950; JD, Seton Hall U., 1970. Bar: N.J. 1970. Assoc., Springfield and Newark, 1970-72; pvt. practice, Hackettstown, N.J., 1972; ptnr. Mulligan & Jacobson, N.Y.C., 1973-91, Mulligan & Mulligan, Hackettstown, 1976—. Atty. Hackettstown Planning Bd., 1973-86, Blairstown Bd. Adjustment, 1973-95; sec. Warren County Ethics Com., 1976-78, sec. Dist. X and XIII Fee Arbitration Com., 1979-87, mem. and chair, 1987-91, mem. dist. ethics com. XIII, 1992—; mem. spl. com. on atty. disciplinary structure N.J. Supreme Ct., 1981—; lectr. Nat. Assn. Women Judges, 1979, N.J. Inst. Continuing Legal Edn., 1988—. Contbr. articles to profl. jours. Named Vol. of Yr., Attys. Vols. in Parole Program, 1978. Fellow Am. Acad. Matrimonial Lawyers (1st woman pres. N.J. chpt. 1995-96); mem. ABA, Warren County Bar Assn. (1st woman pres. 1987-88), N.J. State Bar ASsn., N.J. Women Lawyers Assn. (v.p.

1985—), Am. Mensa Soc., Union League Club (N.Y.C.), Baltusrol Golf Club (Springfield, N.J.), Panther Valley Golf and Country Club (Allamuchy, N.J.), Kappa Alpha Theta. Republican. Home: 12 Goldfinch Way Hackettstown NJ 07840-3007 Office: 933 County Road 517 Hackettstown NJ 07840-4654 E-mail: llp-nj@mindspring.com.

MULLIGAN, JAMES FRANCIS, retired business executive, lawyer; b. Attleboro, Mass., Aug. 27, 1925; s. Henry D. and Eleanor R. (Carey) M.; m. Mary Alice Mangels, Aug. 28, 1948; 1 child, Christopher. AB, Tufts U., 1947; JD, Columbia U., 1950. Bar: N.Y. 1950, Pa. 1968, U.S. Supreme Ct. 1986. Gen. atty. Erie-Lackawanna R.R., Cleve. and N.Y.C., 1950-61; gen. counsel Monroe Internat. div. Litton Industries, Orange, N.J., 1961-67; v.p., sec., gen. counsel Lukens Steel Co., Coatesville, Pa., 1967-83; v.p. law and corp. affairs, sec. Lukens, Inc., 1983-88, ret., 1988. Pres. United Way Chester County, West Chester, Pa., 1980-81. Lt. (j.g.) USNR, 1943-46. Mem. Springhaven Country Club. Avocations: computers. Home: Riddle Village 112 Arlington Media PA 19063-6001 E-mail: jmull10565@aol.com.

MULLIGAN, JEREMIAH T. lawyer; b. Rochester, N.Y., 1944; BA, St. Bernard's Seminary and Coll., 1966; JD, Fordham U., 1970. Mem. Curtis, Mallet-Prevost, Colt & Mosle, N.Y. Office: Curtis Mallet-Prevost Colt & Mosle 101 Park Ave Fl 34 New York NY 10178-0061 E-mail: jmulligan@cm-p.com.

MULLIGAN, JOSEPH FRANCIS, physicist, science historian, educator; b. N.Y.C., Dec. 12, 1920; s. Joseph Lawrence and Mary (Collins) M.; m. Eleanor Lee Wells 1984. Student, Fordham Coll., 1938-39, 41-43; AB, Boston Coll., 1945, MA, 1946; PhD in Physics, Cath. U. Am., 1951. Instr. physics St. Peter's Coll., Jersey City, 1946-47; faculty Fordham U., 1955-68, assoc. prof. physics, 1963-68, chmn. dept., 1956-64, dean Grad. Sch. Arts and Scis., dean liberal arts faculty, 1964-67; prof. physics U. Md., Baltimore County, 1968-89, prof. emeritus, 1989—, dean for grad. studies and rsch., 1968-82. Mem. adv. com. grad. fellowship program NDEA, 1960-63 Author: Practical Physics: The Production and Conservation of Energy, 1980, Introductory College Physics, 2d edit., 1990, translated into 3-vol. Italian edit., Fisica, 1993; editor: Heinrich Rudolf Hertz (1857-1894); A Collection of Articles and Addresses, 1994; contbr. articles to profl. jours. Bd. dirs. Excel Interactive Sci. Mus., Salisbury, 1998-2000. NSF fellow U. Calif, San Diego, 1961-62 Mem. AAAS, Am. Phys. Soc., Am. Assn. Physics Tchrs., History of Sci. Soc., Sigma Xi, Sigma Pi Sigma. Home: 228 Canal Park Dr Apt G103 Salisbury MD 21804-3750 E-mail: jmull68640@aol.com.

MULLIGAN, MICHAEL DENNIS, lawyer; b. St. Louis, Mar. 9, 1947; s. Leo Virgil and Elizabeth (Leyse) M.; m. Theresa Baker, Aug. 7, 1971; children: Brennan, Colin. BA in Biology, Amherst Coll., 1968; JD, Columbia U., 1971. Bar: Mo. 1971, U.S. Dist. Ct. (ea. dist.) Mo. 1972, U.S. Ct. Appeals (8th cir.) 1982, U.S. Tax Ct. 1985. Law clk. to judge U.S. Dist. Ct. (ea. dist.) Mo., 1971-72; assoc. Lewis, Rice & Fingersh, L.C., St. Louis, 1972-80, ptnr., 1980—. Mem. editl. bd. Estate Planning Mag., 1985—. Served as cpl. USMC, 1968-70. Fellow Am. Coll. Trust and Estate Counsel; mem. ABA (mem. real property, probate and trust, and taxation sects.), Mo. Bar Assn. (mem. probate and trust, taxation sects.). Office: Lewis Rice & Fingersh LC 500 N Broadway Ste 2000 Saint Louis MO 63102-2147 E-mail: mmulligan@lewisrice.com.

MULLIGAN, MICHAEL EUGENE, physician, radiologist; b. Troy, N.Y., Feb. 26, 1954; s. Eugene Lawrence and Carolyn Anne (Roeck) M. BA summa cum laude, St. Anselm Coll., Manchester, N.H., 1976; MD, Tufts U., 1980. Diplomate Am. Bd. Radiology, Nat. Bd. Med. Examiners. Intern Tripler Army Med. Ctr., Honolulu, 1980-81, resident in diagnostic radiology, 1981-84, chief uroradiology sect., 1987, chief skeletal radiology sect., 1987-90, chief diagnostic radiology svc., 1989-90; officer in charge skeletal radiology sect. Walter Reed Army Med. Ctr., Washington, 1991-93; from asst. prof. to assoc. prof. clin. radiology Uniformed Svcs. U. Health Scis., Bethesda, Md., 1990—; asst. prof. diagnostic radiology U. Md. Med. Ctr., Balt., 1993-98, assoc. prof., 1998—; chief dept. radiology Kernan Hosp., 1996—. Author: Classic Radiologic Signs, 1996. Asst. coach Montgomery Youth Hockey Assn., 1994-98, Good Counsel H.S. Hockey Team, 1994-98; trustee Bel Pre Homeowners Assn., 1995-98. Col. U.S. Army, 1974—. Decorated Joint Svcs. Commendation medal, Meritorius Svc. medal with 2 oak leaf clusters, others. Mem. AMA, Internat. Skeletal Soc., Radiol. Soc. N.Am., Am. Roentgen Ray Soc., Am. Acad. Forensic Scis., Soc. Skeletal Radiology, Am. Coll. Radiology, Soc. Magnetic Resonance Imaging, Delta Epsilon Sigma. Avocations: chess, ice hockey. Office: U Md Med System Dept Diagnostic Radiology 22 S Greene St Baltimore MD 21201-1544 E-mail: mmulligan@umm.edu.

MULLIGAN, ROBERT, film director, producer; b. N.Y.C., Aug. 23, 1925; s. Robert Edward and Elizabeth (Gingell) M. Grad., Fordham U. Dir.: TV prodns. including Philco Playhouse, Suspense, Playhouse 90; film prodr./dir.: films Fear Strikes Out, Come September, The Spiral Road, To Kill a Mockingbird, Love with the Proper Stranger, Inside Daisy Clover, Summer of '42, Bloodbrothers, Same Time Next Year, The Other, Kiss Me Goodbye, Nickel Ride, Stalking Moon, Baby the Rain Must Fall, Pursuit of Happiness, Up the Down Staircase, Clara's Heart, The Man in the Moon. Office: Ste 675 1901 Avenue Of The Stars Los Angeles CA 90067-6098

MULLIGAN, TIMOTHY HAYDEN, public relations executive, writer; b. Wilkes-Barre, Pa., May 21, 1938; s. Edward Bowman and Celia Hayden (Rhoads) M. BA, Yale U., 1962. Sr. editor Good Housekeeping, N.Y.C., 1966-75; mng. editor Family Weekly, 1975-85; writer, 1985-88; sr. press officer Met. Mus. Art, 1988-90; dir. comm. N.Y. State Coun. on the Arts, 1990-95; dir. external affairs The Bard Grad. Ctr. for Studies in Decorative Arts, Design & Culture, 1995—. Author: Travelers Guide to the Hudson River Valley, 1985, 91, 95, 99, Virginia: A History and Guide, 1986, Travelers Guide to Western New England and the Connecticut River Valley, 1994. Office: The Bard Grad Ctr 18 W 86th St New York NY 10024-3602

MULLIKIN, THOMAS WILSON, mathematics educator; b. Flintville, Tenn., Jan. 9, 1928; s. Houston Yost and Daisy (Copeland) M.; m. Mildred Virginia Sugg, June 14, 1952; children— Sarah Virginia, Thomas Wilson, James Copeland. Student, U. South, 1946-47; AB, U. Tenn., 1950; postgrad., Iowa State U., 1952-53; A.M., Harvard, 1954, PhD, 1958. Mathematician Rand Corp., Santa Monica, Calif., 1957-64; prof. math. Purdue U., 1964-93, interim v.p., dean grad. sch., 1991-93, dean grad. sch., prof. math emeritus, 1993—. Served with USNR, 1950-52. Mem. Am. Math. Soc., AAAS, Sigma Xi. Home: 104 Club Ct Cape Carteret NC 28584-9736

MULLIN, JAMES ALBERT, executive; b. Mpls., Nov. 6, 1934; s. Gerald Thomas and Ruth Krammerer M.; m. Franchelle Collison, Apr. 20, 1968; children: John, Andrew, Charles, Anna. BA, U. Minn., 1956; MBA, U. Pa., 1960. Line & staff mgmt. Gen. Mills, Inc., Mpls., 1960-73; v.p. Ellerbe Architects & Engring., 1973-77; treas., dir. Solar Energy Resource Ctr., 1977-79; sr. v.p., CAO Opus Corp., 1979-91; dir. resource devel. Archdiocese St. Paul/Mpls., St. Paul, 1991—; exec. dir. Cath. Cmty. Found., 1992—. Dir. Opus North Corp., Chgo., 1990-2001; chmn. Archdiocesan Fin. Coun., St. Paul, 1990-91; deputy Minn. Bus. Partnership, Mpls., 1983-89. Trustee James J. Hill Ref. Libr., St. Paul, 1985-93, Mpls. Soc. Fine Arts, 1975-79, St. Thomas Acad., St. Paul, 1980-85, St. Therese Southwest, Hopkins, Minn., 1993-2001. Capt. U.S. Army, 1956-58. Decorated Commendation medal. Mem. Minikahda Club, Skylight Club, Minn. Club, Knights of Holy Sepulcher (knight comdr. 1994-2001). Roman Catholic. Home: 1700 W 26th St Minneapolis MN 55405 Office: Cath Cmty Found 328 W Kellogg Blvd Saint Paul MN 55102 E-mail: mullinj@archspm.org.

MULLIN, LEO FRANCIS, airline executive; b. Concord, Mass., Jan. 26, 1943; s. Leo F. and Alice L. (Fearns) M.; m. Leah J. Malmberg, Sept. 10, 1966; children: Jessica, Matthew. AB, Harvard U., 1964, MS, 1965, MBA, 1967. Assoc. McKinsey & Co., Washington, 1967-73, prin., 1973-76; sr. v.p. strategic planning Consol. Rail Corp., Phila., 1976-78; sr. v.p. 1st Chgo. Corp., 1981-84, exec. v.p., 1984-91; chmn. Am. Nat. Bank and Trust Co. Chgo. subs. 1st Chgo., Chgo., 1991-93; pres., COO 1st Chgo. Corp., 1993-95; vice chmn. Unicom/Commonwealth Edison, 1995—97; CEO Delta Airlines, Atlanta, 1997—, chmn. bd. dirs., 1999—. Bd. dirs. Pittway Corp., Inland Steel Industries, Inc. Vice chmn. Chgo. Urban League, 1993—; chmn. bd. trustees Field Mus. Natural History, 1994—; bd. dirs. Chgo. chpt. Juvenile Diabetes Found., 1985—, Met. Planning Coun., 1983—, Children's Meml. Hosp., Chgo., 1989—, Chgo. Coun. Fgn. Rels., 1994—; mem. Chgo. Econ. Devel. Commn., 1992-95; trustee Northwestern U., 1992—. Mem. Chgo. Club, Harvard Club of Chgo., Econ. Club of Chgo. Office: Office Of Pres 1030 Delta Blvd Dept 940 Atlanta GA 30354-1989*

MULLIN, MARY ANN, career counselor; b. Passaic, N.J., Feb. 9, 1943; d. M. Joseph and Rose M. (Rienzi) DeVita; m. John G. Mullin Jr.; children: Kathleen, John, Robert. BA in Comms., William Paterson Coll., 1991, MA in Urban Studies, 1994; postgrad., Jersey City State U., 1995—. Office mgr. Joseph DeVita, Inc., Paterson, N.J., 1978-94; grad. rsch. asst. William Paterson Coll., Wayne, 1992-94; ednl. broker/counselor Bergen County Tech. Inst., Hackensack, 1994-95; grad. admissions counselor Sch. Arch. N.J. Inst. Tech., Newark, 1995-98; sr. info. and referral specialist rsch. and eval. Girl Scouts Am., 1998—. Pres., bd. dirs. Lenni Lenape Girl Scout Coun., Bulter, N.J., 1989-96; pastoral care/eucharistic min. St. Anthony's Ch., Hawthorne, N.J., 1978—; eucharistic min. Wayne (N.J.) Gen. Hosp., 1978—. Recipient Thanks badge Girl Scouts Am., 1996, Honor pin Lenni Lenape Girl Scout Coun., 1991, Outstanding Vol. Svc. award Paterson Task Force, 1994; named Vol. of Week, The Record, 1993. Mem. Pi Lambda Theta (dir. rsch. projects Beta Chi chpt. 1994-96, Outstanding Svc. award 1995, regional chair N.E. conf. Beta Chi chpt. 1996). Democrat. Roman Catholic. Avocations: Girl Scout activities, travel. Home: 519 Goffle Hill Rd Hawthorne NJ 07506-3056 Office: Girl Scouts US Sch Arch 420 5th Ave Fl 9 New York NY 10018-2798

MULLIN, PATRICIA JONES, banker; b. Long Branch, N.J., Oct. 27, 1955; d. George Edwin and JoAn Layden Jones; m. Peter William Mullin, Apr. 5, 1986; children: Ryan Peter, Connor Patrick. BBA, St. Mary's Coll., Notre Dame, Ind., 1977; MBA, Roosevelt U., 1982. Cert. cash mgr. Officer First Chicago, 1977-83; asst. v.p. Fidelity Bank, Phila., 1983-84; v.p. State St. Bank, Boston, 1984—99, Citizens Bank, Boston, 1999-2000; v.p., team leader Sovereign Bank, 2000—. Mem. Assn. Fin. Profls., Treasury Mgmt. Assn. New Eng. (pres., bd. dirs. 1994—), Boston Club, St. Mary's Club of Boston (bd. dirs. 1994-96). Roman Catholic. Avocations: quilting, needlework, hiking, swimming. Office: Sovereign Bank 75 State St Boston MA 02109-1829

MULLIN, PATRICK ALLEN, lawyer; b. Newark, Jan. 13, 1950; s. Gerard Vincent and Frances Regina (Magnanti) M. BA, William Paterson U., 1972, MEd, 1974; JD, NYU, 1979, LLM in Taxation, 1990; postgrad., Harvard Law Sch., 1979; Gerry Spence's Trial Lawyers Coll., Duboise, Wyo., 1997. Bar: N.J. 1979, D.C. 1980, N.Y. 1990; cert. criminal trial atty. N.J. Supreme Ct. Law clk. to Hon. Dickinson R. DeBevoise, U.S. Dist. Ct. N.J., Trenton, 1979-80; assoc. Charles Morgan Assocs., Washington, 1980-81; pvt. practice, Hackensack, N.J., 1988—. Mem. Practitioners Adv. Group U.S. Sentencing Commn. Mem. ABA. Roman Catholic. Avocations: jogging, martial artist. Address: 25 Main St # 200 Hackensack NJ 07601-7015 also: 305 Madison Ave Ste 449 New York NY 10165-0006 Fax: 201-487-2840. E-mail: pmullin@bellatlantic.net.

MULLINEAUX, DONAL RAY, geologist; b. Weed, Calif., Feb. 16, 1925; s. Lester Ray and Mary Lorene (Drew) M.; m. Diana Suzanne Charais, Nov. 21, 1951; children: Peter, Lauren, Keith. Student, U. Wash., 1942, BS in Math, 1947, BS in Geology, 1949, MS in Geology, 1950, PhD in Geology, 1961. Drilling insp. U.S. Army C.E., 1948; geologist U.S. Geol. Survey, 1950-86; contracting geologist, 1987-90; scientist emeritus U.S. Geol. Survey, 1990—. Author articles on volcanic activity and hazards, Mt. St. Helens, other Cascade Range volcanoes, stratigraphy and engring. geology of Puget Sound Lowland, Wash. With USNR, 1943-54, active duty, 1943-46, 51-53. Rsch. fellow Engring. Expt. Sta. U. Wash., 1949-50. Fellow Geol. Soc. Am. (E.B. Burwell Jr. award 1983); mem. Colo. Sci. Soc. Unitarian Universalist. Home: 14155 W 54th Ave Arvada CO 80002-1513 Office: PO Box 25046 Denver CO 80225-0046 E-mail: ddmullin@attbi.com.

MULLINIX, BARBARA JEAN, special services director; b. Detroit, Nov. 1, 1949; d. John Chisholm and Elizabeth May (Nunneley) Bow; m. Barry Wayne Mullinix, Apr. 8, 1971; children: Erik, Kelley. BS in Spl. Edn., Ea. Mich. U., 1970, endorsement in emotionally impaired edn., 1984, MA, 1973, endorsement in learning disabilities, 1978, endorsement in spl. edn. adminstrn., 1987; EdD, Wayne State U., 1993. Cert. tchr., Mich. Tchr. self-contained spl. edn., mentally impaired Wayne-Westland (Mich.) Community Schs., 1970-73, tchr., cons. for emotionally impaired-learning disabilities, 1977-92, dept. head, 1986-92, program specialist pre-sch. level, 1992-94; dir. spl. svcs. Wayne-Westland (Mich.) Cmty. Schs., 1994—. Deacon Kirk of Our Savior, Westland, 1986-89. Mem. Coun. for Exceptional Children. Presbyterian. Avocations: reading, boating, genealogy. Home: 11970 Glenview Dr Plymouth MI 48170-3080 Office: Wayne Westland Schs 36745 Marquette St Westland MI 48185-3235

MULLINIX, EDWARD WINGATE, lawyer; b. Balt., Feb. 25, 1924; s. Howard Earle and Elsie (Wingate) M.; m. Virginia Lee McGinnes, July 28, 1944; children: Marcia Lee Ladd, Edward Wingate. Student, St. John's Coll., 1941-43; JD summa cum laude, U. Pa., 1949. Bar: Pa. 1950, U.S. Supreme Ct. 1955; cert. BBB Auto Line arbitrator. Assoc. Schnader Harrison Segal & Lewis LLP, Phila., 1950-55, ptnr., 1956-92, sr. coun., 1992—. Mem. adv. bds. Antitrust Bull., 1970-81, BNA Antitrust and Trade Regulation Report, 1981-94; mem. Civil Justice adv. group U.S. Dist. Ct. (ea. dist.) Pa., 1998—; mem. Civil Justice Reform Act of 1990 adv. group U.S. Dist. Ct. (ea. dist.) Pa., 1991-98; co-chmn. Joint U.S. Dist. Ct./Phila. Bar Assn. Alternative Dispute Resolution Com., 1990-2002; cons. on revision of local civil rules U.S. Dist. Ct. (ea. dist.) Pa., 1995—; mem. adv. com. U. Pa. Law Sch. Ctr. on Professionalism, 1988-92; judge pro tem Day Forward and Commerce case mgmt. programs, chmn. adv. com. Commerce program Ct. Common Pleas of Phila. County; advocate, mem. steering com. in elderly-victim-assistance program Phila. Dist. Atty.'s Office Elder Justice Project; faculty participant Pa. Bar Inst. and other CLE programs. Trustee Sta. KYW-TV Project Homeless Fund, 1985-86. Served with USMCR, 1943-44; to lt. (j.g.) USNR, 1944-46. Fellow Am. Bar Found. (life), Am. Coll. Trial Lawyers (emeritus, mem. complex litig. com. 1980-91, vice-chmn. com. 1981-83); mem. ABA (spl. com. complex and multidist. litig. 1969-73, co-chmn. com. 1971-73, coun. litig. sect. 1976-80), Pa. Bar Assn., Phila. Bar Assn., Hist. Soc. U.S. Dist. Ct. (ea. dist.) Pa. (bd. dirs. 1984—, pres. 1991-94), Juristic Soc., Order of Coif, Union League (Phila.), Socialegal Club (Phila.), Aronimink Golf Club (Newtown Sq., Pa.). Republican. Presbyterian. Home: 251 Chamounix Rd Saint Davids PA 19087-3605 Office: 1600 Market St Ste 3600 Philadelphia PA 19103-7286 Office Fax: 215-972-7262. E-mail: ewm@shsl.com.

MULLINIX, EDWARD WINGATE, JR. design and construction company executive; b. Bryn Mawr, Pa., Apr. 16, 1953; s. Edward Wingate and Virginia Lee (McGinnes) M.; m. Susan Sargent Price, July 31, 1976 (div. Aug. 1995); children: Edward Wingate III, Whitney Sargent (dec.); m. Michelle Lee Alexander, Jan. 1, 1996; stepchildren: Katie A. Crews, Patrick J. Crews. BA magna cum laude, U. Pa., 1976; MBA, U. Chgo., 1985. Various staff positions Centel Corp., Chgo., 1977—92; v.p., gen. mgr. Centel Cable TV of Iowa, 1985—87, v.p. data svcs., 1987—88; exec. v.p. adminstrn. Centel Cellular Co., 1988—89, exec. v.p. ops., 1989—90, v.p. corp. fin., 1990—92; pres. Leading Edge Bus. Svcs., St. Simons Island, Ga., 1992—93; v.p. fin. LCI, Ltd., Jacksonville Beach, Fla., 1994—95; exec. v.p. adminstrn. The Haskell Co., 1977-92, 1977-92, v.p. data svcs., 1977-92, sr. v.p. fin. and adminstrn. Fla., 1995-97, sr. v.p., 1995—; exec. v.p. ops. Paging Network, Dallas, 1997—99, pres., COO, 1999—2000. With various operating and corp. staff positions in Lincoln, Nebr., Charlottesville, Va., Chgo.; dir. daniel, Inc., 2001—. Dir. River Valley Ctr. Ind. Living, Elgin, Ill., 1990-92, Fin. Execs. Inst. N.E. chpt. Fla., 1997, Collin County United Way, 1998-2000, daniel, Inc., 2001—; fin. com. N.E. Fla. United Way, 2001--; vol. Am. Cancer Soc., Geneva, Ill., 1987-92, 90-92, Chgo. jr. achievement, 1991; with C. of C., Burlington, Iowa, 1986-87; treas., dir. Fox River Valley Ctr. Ind. Living, 1990-92; task force City of Chgo., 1992. Mem. Deerwood Country Club, Beta Gamma Sigma, Phi Eta Sigma. Republican. Avocations: bridge, golf, tennis. Home: 8166 Hollyridge Rd Jacksonville FL 32256-7104 Office: The Haskell Co 111 Riverside Ave Jacksonville FL 32202-4950

MULLINS, BARBARA J. financial executive; b. Day, Fla., Aug. 29, 1938; d. James Eli and Bessie Geraldine (Johnson) Grantham; m. Mike B. Mullins, Dec. 20, 1956; children: Ronald Lee, Richard Bryan, Mikel Duane. Acctg. Cert., Longview C.C., Lee's Summit, Mo., 1978; AS, Johnson County C.C., Overland Park, Kans., 1980; student, Avila Coll., Kansas City, Mo., 1980-84. Contr., v.p. Bride Co., Leawood, Kans., 1970-82; mgr., cons. Price Waterhouse, Atlanta, 1984-92; owner, cons. Sys. Adv. Svcs., Kansas City, Mo., 1992—99; CFO Memphis Brooks Mus. Art, 1999—. Mem. Inst. Mgmt. Accts. (chpt. pres., nat. dir., regional dir.). Avocations: reading, interior decorating, sewing.

MULLINS, CHARLES BROWN, physician, academic administrator; b. Rochester, Ind., July 29, 1934; s. Charles E. and Mary Ruth B. (Bamberger) M.; BA, N. Tex. State U., 1954; MD, U. Tex., 1958; m. Stella Churchill, Dec. 27, 1955; children— Holly, David. Diplomate Am. Bd. Internal Medicine. Intern, U. Colo. Med. Center, Denver, 1958-59; resident in internal medicine Parkland Meml. Hosp., Dallas, 1962-64; USPHS rsch. fellow U. Tex. Southwestern Med. Sch., Dallas, 1964-65; chief resident medicine Parkland Meml. Hosp., 1965-66; USPHS spl. rsch. fellow cardiology br. Nat. Heart Inst., Bethesda, Md., 1967-68; practice medicine specializing in cardiology, Dallas, 1966-81; sr. attending staff Parkland Meml. Hosp., dir. med. affairs, 1977-79; asst. prof. medicine U. Tex. Southwestern Med. Sch., Dallas, 1968-71, assoc. prof., 1971-75, dir. clin. cardiology, 1971-77, prof., 1975-79, clin. prof. medicine, 1979-81, prof., 1981— ; prof. medicine U. Tex. Health Sci. Center, Dallas, 1979-81; exec. vice-chancellor health affairs U. Tex. System, 1981—2001, spl. projects dir., 2001-; prof. medicine U. Tex. Southwestern Med. Sch., 2001-; CEO Dallas County Hosp. Dist., 1979-81. With M.C., USAF, 1959-62. Fellow ACP, Am. Coll. Cardiology (Tex. gov. 1974-77, chmn. bd. govs. 1976), Am. Heart Assn. Council on Clin. Cardiology; mem. Am. Fedn. Clin. Rsch., Assn. Acad. Health Ctrs., Assn. Univ. Cardiologists, Laennec Soc., AMA, Alpha Omega Alpha. Contbr. articles to profl. jours. Office: 5323 Harry Hines Blvd Dallas TX 75390-9166

MULLINS, EDWARD M. lawyer; b. Detroit, Mar. 20, 1965; s. Edward Huss and Barbara Ann (Murphy) Mullins; m. Rima Youakim, Aug. 24, 1991; children: Bailey Marie, Casey Ann, Riley Barbara, Connor Maurice. BA with high honors, U. Fla., Gainesville, 1986, JD with high honors, 1990. With Astigarraga Davis Mullins & Grossman, Miami, 2000—. Chmn. media and comm. law commn. Fla. Bar. Editor: Reporters Handbook, 2000—01; editor-in-chief: Fla. Law Rev.; contbr. articles to profl. jours. Mem.: ABA (standing com. silver gavel com. 1997—2000, screening com. 2001—02), Dade County Bar Assn. (vice chair appellate cts. com. 2001—02), First Amendment Found., Phi Beta Kappa, Order of Coif. Roman Catholic. Avocation: reading. Home: 6830 SW 75th Ter South Miami FL 33143 Office: Astigarraga Davis Mullins & Grossman 201 S Biscayne Blvd 20th Fl Miami FL 33131 E-mail: emullins@astidavis.com.

MULLINS, JAMES LEE, library administrator; b. Perry, Iowa, Nov. 29, 1949; s. Kenneth Wiley and Lorene (Gift) M.; m. Kathleen Stiso, May 10, 1986; 1 stepchild, Michael Stiso. BA, U. Iowa, 1972, MA, 1973; PhD, Ind. U., 1984. Instr. Ga. So. U., Statesboro, 1973-74; assoc. law librarian Ind. U., Bloomington, 1974-78, dir. library South Bend, 1978-96; dir. Falvey Meml. Libr., Villanova U., 1996-2000; assoc. dir. for adminstrn. MIT, Cambridge, 2000—. Contbr. articles to profl. publs. Mem. exec. com. South Bend Art Ctr., 1984-89; mem. Mayor's Task Force Redevel., South Bend, 1986; pres. Fischoff Nat. Chamber Music Assn., 1989-91, Gov. Conf. on Libr. Planning Com., 1989-91, Mich. Freenet bd., 1993-96; pres. Ind. Coop. Libr. Svcs. Authority, 1993-94; mem. Hugh Atkinson Award Com., 2001—; mem. planning com. Lama Nat. Inst., 2001—. Mem. ALA, LAMA (program com. 1997-2001, exec. com. 1998-2000), Ind. Libr. Assn., Assn. Coll. and Rsch. Librs. (stds. com. 1994-2000, stds. & accreditation com, 2000-02), Ind. Libr. Endowment Bd. (pres. 1988-91), Rotary. Avocations: reading, gardening, cross-country skiing, historic preservation. Home: 6 Tirrell Pl Durham NH 03824-1603 Office: MIT Libraries #14-312 77 Massachusetts Ave Cambridge MA 02139 E-mail: jmullins@mit.edu.

MULLINS, JEROME JOSEPH, real estate developer, consulting engineer; b. Reedsville, Wis., June 3, 1925; s. James Raymond and Anna (Wilhelm) M.; m. Carol M. Fessler, Sept. 12, 1949; children: Maureen, Brian, Mallory, Bradley, Jerome J. Jr. BSCE, U. Wis., 1950. Registered profl. engr., land surveyor, Wis.; lic. real estate broker and appraiser, Wis. Engr. Gen. Engring. Co., Baraboo, Wis., 1950-51; engring. mgr. George Nelson & Sons, Inc., Madison, 1951-56, Weiler & Strang Architects/Engrs., Madison, 1956-64; pres. Sample-Mullins Architects/Engrs., 1964-69; chief exec. officer J.J. Mullins & Assocs., Inc., 1969—. Pres. Bayview Found., Madison, 1968-72, Greater Madison Conv. and Visitors Bur., 1976-78; bd. dirs. Downtown Madison, Inc., 1976—, Madison Conv. and Visitors Bur., 1986-90; mem. Madison Taxicab Com., 1977-78. Officer USN, 1943-46, PTO. Recipient award Capital Community Citizens, 1974, appreciation award Madison Conv. and Visitors Bur., 1976-79, 87-89, U. Wis. Athletics, 1983, Employer of Yr. award Goodwill Industries South Cen. Wis., 1981, award Downtown Madison, Inc., 1986, award for support Badger State Games, 1989. Mem. NSPE, AIA (assoc.), Nat. Bd. Realtors, Nat. Constrn. Specifications Instr., Wis. Soc. Profl. Engrs., Profl. Engrs. in Pvt. Practice, Wis. Soc. Registered Land Surveyors. Avocations: boating, hunting, reading. Office: 401 N Carroll St Madison WI 53703-1803

MULLINS, OBERA, retired microbiologist; b. Egypt, Miss., Feb. 15, 1927; d. Willie Ree and Maggie Sue (Orr) Gunn; m. Charles Leroy Mullins, Nov. 2, 1952; children: Mary Artavia, Arthur Curtis, Charles Leroy, Charlester Teresa, William Hellman. BS, Chgo. State U., 1974; MS in Health Sci. Edn., Governors State U., 1981. Med. technician, microbiologist Chgo. Health Dept., Chgo., 1976—, now pers. asst. III, to 1999; ret., 1999. Mem. AAUW, Am. Soc. Clin. Pathologists (cert. med. lab. technician), Ill. Soc. Lab. Technicians. Roman Catholic. Home: 9325 S Marquette Ave Chicago IL 60617-4131

MULLINS, RUTH GLADYS, nurse; b. Westville, N.S., Can., Aug. 25, 1943; came to U.S., 1949, naturalized, 1955; d. William G. and Gladys H.; m. Leonard E. Mullins, Aug. 27, 1963 (dec.); children: Deborah R., Catherine M., Leonard III. BS in Nursing, Calif. State U., Long Beach, 1966; MSN, UCLA, 1973; PhD, Columbia Pacific U. Cert. pediatric nurse practitioner. Pub. health nurse Los Angeles County Health Dept., 1967-68; nure Meml. Hosp. Med. Ctr., Long Beach, 1968-72; dir. pediatric nurse practitioner program Calif. State U., 1973-97, asst. prof., 1975-80, assoc. prof., 1980-85, prof., 1985—. Health svc. credential coord. Sch. Nursing Calif. State U., Long Beach, chmn., 1979-81, coord. grad. programs, 1985-92; mem. Calif. Maternal, Child and Adolescent Health Bd., 1977-84; vice chair Long Beach/Orange County Health Consortium, 1984-85, chair 1985-86. Author: (with B. Nelms) Growth and Development: A Primary Health Care Approach; contbg. author: Quick Reference to Pediatric Nursing, 1984; asst. editor Jour. Pediatric Health Care. Tng. grantee HHS, Divsn. Nursing Calif. Dept. Health. Fellow Nat. Assn. Pediatric Nurse Assocs. and Practitioners (exec. bd., pres. 1990-91), Nat. Fedn. Nursing Splty. Orgns. (sec. 1991-93); mem. APHA, Nat. Alliance Nurse Practitioners (governing body 1990-92), Assn. Faculties Pediatric Nurse Practitioenr Programs. L.A. and Orange County Assn. Pediatric Nurse Practitioners and Assocs. (treas. 1998—), Am. Assn. Univ. Faculty, Ambulatory Pediatric Assn. Democrat. Methodist. Home: 6382 Heil Ave Huntington Beach CA 92647-4232 Office: Calif State U Dept Nursing 1250 N Bellflower Blvd Long Beach CA 90840-0001 E-mail: rgmullins@sprintmail.com., rmullins@csulb.edu.

MULLINS, W. STAN, artist, cultural ambassador; b. Cherry Point, N.C., July 1, 1964; s. Robert R. and Carolyn Hankins Mullins. BFA, U. Ga., 1987, MFA, 1989. Internat. artist Stan Mullins, Inc.; cultural amb. various orgns.; exec. dir. Athens (Ga.) Ctr. for Internat. Arts. Freelance artist, assoc. adminstr. Waters Design Group, N.Y.C., 1997; developer, mem. Mus. Modern Art, N.Y.C., 1998. One-man shows include Galleria Del Sole, Perugia, Italy, 1991, Candide Gallery, Atlanta, 1992, The Athens Coffee House, Athens, Ga., 1993, French Cultural Ctr., Kigali, Rwanda, 1994, The Main Gallery, U. Ga., Athens, Ga., 1994, The King Plow Arts Ctr., Atlanta, 1995, Alliance Francaise d'Atlanta, 1995, The Renaissance Gallery, Washington, 1995, Eklektikos Gallery, Washington, 1996, The Athens Classic Ctr., 1996, La Boulangere, N.Y.C., 1997, Hearon-Hempenstall Gallery, Jersey City, 1997, Jersey City City Hall, 1998, Galleria d'Arte G. Severini, Cortona, Italy, 1999, East/West Bistro, Athens, 1999, Classic Ctr. Main Ballroom, Athens, 1999, Belenky Gallery, N.Y.C., 2000, State Botanical Garden of Ga., Athens, 2000; exhibited in group shows at Galleria Renata, Chgo., 1990, Provincia di Perugia, Italy, 1991, Coll. Square, Athens, 1994, Mus. Contemporary Art, Washington, DC., 1995,

Kearon-Hempenstall Gallery, Jersey City, 1997, Georgetown Hilton, Washington, 1997, The Sharjah Art Mus., United Arab Emirates, 2000, Firehall Gallery, Athens, 2000, Belesky Gallery, Soho, N.Y.C., 2002; artist (children's book) Under the Back Yard Sky, 1995; sculpture presented to Gov. Kyoto, Japan. Recipient Le Depozitione, The Ch. of the Holy Spirit, Cortona, Italy, 1989; named Featured Artist, CNN, 1992-94, N.Y. Times, N.Y.C., 1999, Majii with the Mountain Gorillas of Rwanda, 2000. Home: 650 Pulaski St Athens GA 30601-2349 E-mail: stanarts@aol.com.

MULLINS, WAYMAN C. psychologist, educator, consultant; b. Little Rock, Nov. 10, 1951; s. William Wayman and Mary Anna (Beall) M.; m. Louise C. Casey, Aug. 2, 1976; children: Ruth, Rachael. BA, U. Ark., 1978, MA, 1979, PhD in Psychology, 1983. Diplomate in police psychology. Teaching and rsch. asst. U. Ark., Fayetteville, 1977-82; asst. prof. psychology Hofstra U., Hempstead, N.Y., 1982-84; asst. prof. criminal justice S.W. Tex. State U., San Marcos, 1984-87, assoc. prof., 1987-93, prof., 1993—. Cons. to various mcpl., state, and fed. law enforcement agys., 1987—. Author: Terrorist Organizations in the U.S., 1988, 1942, Issue in Doubt, 1994, Crisis Negotiations, 1996, 2d edit., 2000, A Sourcebook on Domestic and International Terrorism, 1997; editor Jour. Police and Criminal Psychology, 1984-96; contbr. articles to profl. jours. and books. Pres. N.W. Ark. Vets. Assn., Fayetteville, 1975-77, San Marcos Little League, 1989-94; mem. exec. coun. San Marcos Explorer Post, 1988-93; advisor Criminal Justice Explorer Post #120; res. police officer San Marcos Police Dept., 1987-95; res. deputy with Hays County Sheriff's Dept. Recipient grants. Mem. Soc. Police and Criminal Psychology (pres. 1984-85), Acad. Criminal Justice Scis. Avocations: baseball, ship building, tennis, fishing, camping. Office: SW Tex State U Dept Criminal Justice San Marcos TX 78666

MULLIS, KARY BANKS, biochemist; b. Lenoir, N.C., Dec. 28, 1944; s. Cecil Banks Mullis and Bernice Alberta (Barker) Fredericks; children: Christopher, Jeremy, Louise. BS in Chemistry, Ga. Inst. Tech, 1966; PhD in Biochemistry, U. Calif., Berkeley, 1973; DSc (hon.), U. S.C., 1994. Lectr. biochemistry U. Calif., Berkeley, 1972, postdoctoral fellow San Francisco, 1977—79, U. Kans. Med. Sch., Kansas City, 1973—76; scientist Cetus Corp., Emeryville, Calif., 1979—86; dir. molecular biology Xytronyx, Inc., San Diego, 1986—88; cons. Specialty Labs, Inc., Amersham, Inc., Chiron Inc. and various others, 1988—96; chmn. StarGene, Inc., San Rafael; v.p. Histotec, Inc., Cedar Rapids, Iowa; v.p. molecular biology chemistry Vyrex Inc., La Jolla, Calif. Disting. vis. prof. U. S.C. Coll. of Sci. and Math. Contbr. ; patentee in field. Named Scientist of Yr., R&D Mag., 1991, Calif. Scientist of Yr., 1992; recipient Preis Biochemische Analytik award, German Soc. Clin. Chem., 1990, Allan award, 1990, award, Gairdner Found. Internat., 1991, Nat. Biotech. award, 1991, Robert Koch award, 1992, Chiron Corp. Biotechnology Rsch. award, Am. Soc. Microbiology, 1992, Japan prize, Sci. and Tech. Found. Japan, 1993, Nobel Prize in Chemistry, Nobel Foundation, 1993. Mem.: Inst. Further Study (dir. 1983—), Am. Acad. Achievement, Am. Chem. Soc. Achievements include invention of invention of Polymerase Chain Reaction (PCR).*

MULLMAN, MICHAEL S. lawyer; b. N.Y.C., Sept. 17, 1946; s. Herbert and Harriet (Weissman) M.; m. Ellen Mullman, 1975; children: Jeremy, Cassie. BA in Polit. Sci. cum laude, Union Coll., Schenectady, N.Y., 1968; JD, Columbia U., 1971. Bar: N.Y. 1972, U.S. Ct. Appeals (2d cir.), U.S. Dist. Ct., 1975. Ptnr. Schonwald, Schaffzin & Mullman, N.Y.C., 1980-89, Tenzer Greenblatt LLP, N.Y.C., 1989-99; adminstrv. ptnr. in charge N.Y. Blank Rome Tenzer Greenblatt LLP, 2000—, mem. distbn. com., mem. ptnr. bd. Bd. editors Columbia Jour. Law and Soc. Problems, articles edition, 1970-71. Nott scholar Union Coll., 1967, Harlan Fiske Stone scholar Sch. Law Columbia U., 1971. Mem. Bar Assn. N.Y.C., Phi Beta Kappa. Avocations: tennis, skiing, reading, gardening. Office: Blank Rome Tenzer Greenblatt LLP The Chrysler Bldg 405 Lexington Ave New York NY 10174-0002

MULLONEY, PETER BLACK, retired steel, oil and gas executive; b. Boston, Oct. 24, 1932; s. Daniel Clifford and Mabel (Black) M.; m. Marie Weprich. BA, Yale U., 1954. V.p. mktg. U.S. Steel Corp., Pitts., 1978-81; v.p., asst. to chmn. USX Corp., 1981-97. Mem. adv. bd., sec. Salvation Army, Pitts.; vice chmn. World Affairs Coun. Pitts.; mem. bd. trustees La Roche Coll. Mem. Am. Iron and Steel Inst. (active com. on internat. trade, Washington, chmn. com. 1983-85), Internat. Iron and Steel Inst. (active com. on econ. studies, Brussels, chmn. com. 1983-85). Clubs: Duquesne (Pitts.), Harvard-Yale-Princeton, Pitts., Army and Navy (Washington), Pitts. Athletic Assn. Roman Catholic. Avocations: reading, walking. Home: 213 Grandview Ave Pittsburgh PA 15211-1525

MULLOY, PATRICK ALOYSIUS, lawyer; b. Wilkes-Barre, Pa., Sept. 14, 1941; s. Hugh Patrick and Ellen Mary (Meagher) M.; m. Marjorie Baumer; children: Maura Alice, Daniel Patrick, Claire Ellen. BA magna cum laude, King's Coll., 1963; MA, U. Notre Dame, 1965; JD with honors, George Washington U., 1971; LLM, Harvard U., 1978. Bar: D.C. 1972, Pa. 1972, U.S. Ct. Appeals (D.C., 2d, and 9th cirs.) 1975, U.S. Supreme Ct. 1975, U.S. Ct. Appeals (5th and 9th cirs.) 1976. Fgn. service officer U.S. Dept. State, Washington, 1965-72; trial lawyer Dept. Justice, 1973-77, sr. lawyer antitrust div., 1978-82; Congl. fellow U.S. Congress, 1983; minority gen. counsel U.S. Senate Banking Com., 1984-86, gen. counsel, 1987-89, sr. counsel, internat. affairs advisor, 1989-92, chief internat. counsel, 1993-94, chief internat. coun. (minority), 1995-98; asst. sec. market access and compliance Internat. Trade Adminstrn., U.S. Dept. Commerce, 1998-2001. Apptd. asst. sec., exec. br. commn. on security and coop. in Europe by Pres. Clinton, 1999-2001; apptd. commr. Joint House Senate U.S.-China Security Rev. Commn., Washington, 2001—; adj. prof. internat. trade law Cath. U. Law Sch., Washington, 2002--. Home: 304 W Masonic View Ave Alexandria VA 22301-2419 Office: US China Security Rev Commn Hall of States Ste 602 444 N Capitol St NW Washington DC 20001 E-mail: pamulloy@aol.com., pmulloy@uscc.gov.

MULQUIN, KIMBERLY ANN, nurse; b. Chgo., Jan. 24, 1967; d. Dennis John and Diana Lee McKay; m. Brian Keith Mulquin, Oct. 14, 1989; children: Devin Leigh, Trent Patrick. BSN, Loyola U., 1989; MBA, Keller Grad. Sch. Mgmt., 1994. RN, Ill.; cert. profl. in health care quality. Clin. nurse II Michael Reese Hosp., Chgo., 1989-91; staff nurse I Humana Healthcare Plans, 1990-95; quality coord. Rush-Presbyn.-St. Luke's Med. Ctr., 1995-97; dir. quality improvement Rest Haven Christian Svcs., South Holland, Ill., 1997—. Performance improvement cons. Health Resource Alliance, Hinsdale, Ill., 1998—. Mem. Nat. Assn. for Healthcare Quality, Ill. Assn. for Healthcare Quality. Office: Rest Haven Christian Svcs 18601 North Creek Dr Tinley Park IL 60477- E-mail: kimm@provinet.com.

MULRAIN, ANDREA E. talent scout; b. Elizabeth, N.J., Sept. 11, 1965; d. Andrew Joseph and Joan Nina M. BS, Allegheny Coll., 1987. Regl. field mktg. rep. London Records, Seattle, 1995-98; internat. A&R rep., freelance N.Y.C., 1998—. Talent scout London Records, Seattle, 1995-98; disc jockey, 2002. Breast cancer advocate NBCC Young Survival Coalition, Washington, N.Y.C., 1999—. Mem. Young Survival Coalition. Democrat. Roman Catholic. Avocations: running, travel, reading. Home: 50 Tivoli Gardens Tivoli NY 12583 Office: 8 Jefferson Ct Setauket NY 11733

MULRONEY, BRIAN (MARTIN BRIAN MULRONEY), former prime minister of Canada; b. Baie Comeau, Que., Can., Mar. 20, 1939; s. Benedict and Irene (O'Shea) M.; m. Mila Pivnicki, 1973; 4 children. BA, St. Francis Xavier U., LLD, 1979; LLL, U. Laval, Que.; LLD, Meml. U. Nfld., Nfld., 1980, U. W.I., 1993, Tel Aviv U., 1994, Ctrl. Conn. State U., 1994, Barry U., 1995. Ptnr. Ogilvy Renault, Montreal, 1965-76; exec. v.p. Iron Ore Co. Can., 1977-83, Iron Ore Co. of Can., Montreal, Que., 1976-77; pres. Iron Ore Co. Can., 1977-83; mem. Parliament Can. from Ctrl. N.S., Ottawa, Ont., 1983-84; mem. Parliament Can. from Manicouagan, 1984-88; mem. Parliament Can. from Charlevoix, 1988-93; leader of Her Majesty's Loyal Opposition, 1983-84; prime minister Can., 1984-93; royal commr. Cliche Commn. investigating violence in Que. constrn. industry, 1974; sr. ptnr. Ogilvy Renault, Montreal, 1993—. Chmn. internat. adv. bd. Barrick Gold Corp., The J.P. Morgan Chase Corp.; mem. internat. adv. coun. Power Corp. Can.; mem. adv. bd. The China Internat. Trust and Investment Corp.; mem. Bombadier/Aerospace Group N.Am., Violy Ptnrs. and Assocs., Hicks Muse Tate & Furst Ind. News and Media, PLC; trustee Freedom Found.; mem. internat. adv. coun. Inst. Internat. Studies; bd. dirs. Archer Daniels Midland Co., Barrick Gold Corp., The Trizec Properties Inc., Power Corp., Quebecor World Inc., Telesys., Inc., Cognicase; chmn. Forbes, N.Y.C. Author: Where I Stand, 1983. Trustee Montreal Heart Inst., Freedom Forum; mem. internat. adv. coun. Les Hautes Etudes Commerciales l'Université de Montréal. Recipient Companion of the Order of Can. Office: Ogilvy Renault 1981 McGill College Ave Ste 1100 Montreal QC Canada H3A 3C1 E-mail: bmulroney@ogilvyrenault.com.

MULRONEY, MICHAEL, lawyer, law educator, graduate program director; b. Chgo., Feb. 26, 1932; s. Alphonsus James and Genevieve (Moran) M.; m. Ellen Goen Mulroney, Dec. 28, 1959; children: Sean, Conor, Dermot, Kieran, Moira. BSC in Econ., State U. Iowa, 1954; JD, Harvard Law Sch., 1959. Bar: Iowa 1959, D.C. 1960, U.S. Supreme Ct., U.S. Ct. Appeals (2nd, 3rd, 4th, 5th, 6th, 7th, 8th, 9th, 10th and D.C. cirs.), U.S. Tax Ct., U.S. Dist. Ct. D.C., D.C. Ct. Appeals, D.C. Superior Ct. Atty. adv. U.S. Tax Ct., Washington, 1959-61; appellate atty. Tax Div. U.S. Dept. Justice, 1961-65; assoc. Lee, Toomey & Kent, 1965-68, ptnr., 1969-87, counsel, 1987-88; prof., dir. Grad. Tax Program Villanova (Pa.) Law Sch., 1988—; adjunct prof. Grad. Tax Program Georgetown Law Sch., Washington, 1986—. Faculty advisor fed. tax clinic Law Sch. Villanova U., 1992—; mem. joint com. on taxation acad. advisers U.S. Congress. Author: Federal Tax Examinations Manual, 1988, Foreign Taxation, 1992; mng. editor: The Tax Lawyer, 1989-96, 99—; reporter IRS/ABA Invitational Conf. on Professionalism in Tax Practice, 1993, 96; contbr. articles to profl. jours. With U.S. Army, 1954-56. Fellow Am. Coll. Tax Counsel; mem. ABA (taxation sect., chmn. tax lawyer com., mem. govt. submissions com., appt. to tax ct. com., ct. procedure com., stds. of tax practice com., tchg. taxation com.; legal edn. and admissions to the bar sect.), D.C. Bar (tax sect.), Fed. Bar Assn. (tax sect.), Iowa Bar Assn. (tax sect.), J. Edgar Murdock Am. Inn. of Ct. (founding master), Internat. Fiscal Assn. (U.S. br. coun. mem.), Washington Tax Lawyers' Study Group, Phila. Tax Conf. (mem. exec. coun.), Am. Assn. Law Schs. (tax sect., grad. legal edn. sect.). Roman Catholic. Avocation: sports car racing. Office: Villanova Law Sch Villanova PA 19085 E-mail: mulroney@law.villanova.edu.

MULROW, PATRICK JOSEPH, medical educator; s. Patrick J. and Delia (O'Keefe) M.; m. Jacquelyn Pinover, Aug. 8, 1953; children: Deborah, Nancy, Robert, Catherine. AB, Colgate U., 1947; MD, Cornell U., 1951; MSc (hon.), Yale U., 1969. Intern N.Y. Hosp., 1951-52, resident, 1952-54; instr. physiology Med. Coll. Cornell U., 1954-55; research fellow Stanford U., 1955-57; instr. medicine Yale U., 1957-60, asst. prof., 1960-66, assoc. prof., 1966-69, prof. medicine, 1969-75; chmn. dept. medicine Med. Coll. Ohio, Toledo, 1975-95, prof. medicine, 1975—. Chmn. ednl. com. Council for high blood pressure rsch. Am. Heart Assn., 1968-70, mem. exec. com., 1986-96, vice-chmn. of coun., 1990-92, chmn. 1992-94, past chmn., 1995-96; mem. study sect. NIH, 1970-74. Editorial bd. Jour. Clin. Endocrinology and Metabolism, 1966-70, 75-79, Endocrine Rsch., 1974—, Jour. Exptl. Biology and Medicine, Hypertension, 1994-98; contbr. articles to profl. jours. With USNR, 1944-46. Mem. ACP, Am. Soc. Clin. Investigation, Assn. Am. Physicians, Am. Physiol. Soc., Endocrine Soc., Am. Fedn. Clin. Rsch., Am. Clin. and Climatol. Assn., Am. Heart Assn. (nat. rsch. com., chmn. cardiovasc. regulation rsch. study com. 1986-91), Assn. Profs. Medicine, Assn. Program Dirs. in Internal Medicine, Cen. Soc. Clin. Rsch. (pres. 1988-89), Internat. Soc. Hypertension, World Hypertension League (sec.-gen. 1995—), Inter-Am. Soc. Hypertension, Sigma Xi (pres. Yale chpt. 1965-66), Alpha Omega Alpha. Home: 9526 Carnoustie Rd Perrysburg OH 43551-3501 Office: Med Coll of Ohio Dept of Medicine 3120 Glendale Ave Toledo OH 43614-5809

MULRYAN, HENRY TRIST, mineral company executive, consultant; b. Palo Alto, Calif., Jan. 6, 1927; s. Henry and Marian Abigail (Trist) M.; m. Lenore Hoag, Aug. 25, 1948; children: James W., Carol. Student, Yale U., 1945-46; AB in Econs., Stanford U., 1948; postgrad., Am. Grad. Sch. Internat. Bus., 1949, Columbia U., 1983. V.p. mktg. Sierra Talc Co., South Pasadena, Calif., 1955-65, United Sierra, Trenton, N.J., 1965-67, v.p., gen. mgr., 1967-70, pres., 1970-77; v.p. Cyprus Mines Corp., Los Angeles, 1978-80; sr. v.p. ops. Cyprus indsl. minerals div. Amoco Minerals Co., Englewood, Colo., 1980-85; pres. Cyprus Indls. Minerals Co., 1985-87; v.p. Cyprus Minerals Co., 1985-87, sr. v.p. mktg., corp. adminstr., 1987-89; pres. Mineral Econs. Internat., 1989—; chmn. Persistent Vision, LLC, 1998—; pres., CEO Carpathian Marble, Inc., 1999—. Vol. exec. Internat. Exec. Svc. Corps., Zimbabwe, 1998, Romania, 1998, Jordan, 2000, 01. Served with U.S. Army, 1944-46. Mem.: Jonathan (Los Angeles), Rotary (pres. South Pasadena club 1964-65) (bd. dirs. Princeton, N.J. club 1969-75). Office: 539 Muskingum Ave Pacific Palisades CA 90272-4252 E-mail: htmulryan@gte.net.

MULRYAN, LENORE HOAG, art curator, author; b. Lompoc, Calif., Aug. 25, 1927; d. William Thomas and Lois Lorraine (Fratis) Hoag; m. Henry Trist Mulryan; children: Patricia Trist (dec.), James William, Carrie Neal. BA, UCLA, postgrad., 1979-81; Cert., Am. Inst. Fgn. Trade, Glendale, Ariz., 1949. Art curator UCLA Fowler Mus. Cultural History, 1982—; art curator, editor, cons. Internat. Exec. Svc. Corps, 1998. Dir. fine art print calendars for Chapin Sch., Princeton, N.J., 1971-73; co-chair Fine Arts Tours, Princeton, 1973; cons. Internat. Exec. Svc. Corp., Zimbabwe, 1998, Romania, 1998. Author, curator, editor: (books/exhbns.) Mexican Figural Ceramists and Their Works, 1982, Nagual in the Garden: Fantastic Animals in Mexican Ceramics, 1996; curator Wilmot Collection of Mexican Art, 1982-91. Mem. Eisenhauer Disting. Fgn. Leader Program U. So. Calif. Mem. Delphians (pres. 1963-64), Westwood Village Rotary Club (chair Amb. Scholarship Selection com. 1996—). Avocations: music, art, yoga, travel. Office: UCLA Fowler Mus Cultural History 405 Hilgard Ave Los Angeles CA 90095-9000

MULSHINE, JAMES LAWRENCE, oncologist; b. Elizabeth, N.J., Nov. 14, 1952; children: Christine E., Michael J., Laura E., Eric B. BA, Coll. Holy Cross, 1974; MD, Loyola U., Maywood, Ill., 1977. Diplomate Am. Bd. Internal Medicine, Am. Bd. Oncology. Intern Cleve. Clinic, 1977-79, sr. med. resident, 1979-80; clin. assoc. Medicine Br. Nat. Cancer Inst., 1980-81, rsch. assoc. Navy Med. Oncology Br., 1981-82, investigator Navy Med. Oncology Br., 1982-87, sr. investigator Navy Med. Oncology Br., 1987-88, head biotherapy sect. Navy Med. Oncology Br., 1988-90; chief Biomarkers & Prevention Rsch. Br., head intervention sect. DCPC, 1991-95, head intervention sect. Cell and Cancer Biology Dept., 1997—; attending physician USN Hosp., Bethesda, Md., 1983—, Shady Grove Adventist Hosp., 1994-97. Mem. editl. bd. Internat. Jour. Cancer, Cancer Prevention Internat., Clin. Cancer Rsch., Lung Cancer, Primary Care and Cancer. Head internat. sci. bd. Roy Castle Lung Cancer Found., 1994—; bd. dirs. Alliance Lung Cancer Advocacy, Support and Edn., 1997—; liaison bd. mem. Cancer Rsch. Found. Am. Recipient Inventors Incentive award U.S. Dept. Commerce, 1984, NIH Dir.'s award, 1998; Conn. State scholar. Fellow ACP; mem. Am. Assn. Cancer Rsch., Am. Fedn. Clin. Rsch., Am. Soc. Clin. Oncology, Internat. Assn. Study Lung Cancer. Achievements include patents in Monoclonal Antibody against Non-Small Cell Lung Cancer; Intrabronchial Injection of Monoclonal Antibody Conjugates for the Detection of Lung Cancer; Technique for Early Detection of Lung Cancer, Lipoxygenase as a target for treatment and prevention of epithelial cancer; patent issued in An Epithelial Protein and DNA thereof for use in early cancer detection; PCT Application. Office: NCI Intervention Sect Cell & Cancer Biology Dept Bldg 10 Rm 12N226 NIH Clin 9000 Rockville Pike Bethesda MD 20892-1906 E-mail: mulshinj@mail.nih.gov.

MULTHAUP, MERREL KEYES, artist; b. Cedar Rapids, Iowa, Sept. 27, 1922; d. Stephen Dows and Edna Gertrude (Gard) Keyes; m. Robert Hansen Multhaup, Apr. 7, 1944; children: Eric Stephen, Robert Bruce. Student, State U. Iowa, 1942—43, Rice U., 1971. Tchg. faculty Summit (N.J.) Art Assn., 1956-60; art instr. studio classes Springfield, N.J., 1954-55, Bloomfield (N.J.) Art Group, 1955-56, Westport, Conn., 1962-63; tchg. faculty Hunterdon Art Ctr., Clinton, N.J., 1985-92. One-woman shows include Coriell Gallery, 1995; exhibited in group shows at Nat. Assn. Women Artists, N.Y.C., 1957-2000 (awards in figure painting), Hartford (Conn.) Athanaeum Mus., 1961 (1st prize), Highgate Gallery, N.Y.C., Waverly Gallery, N.Y.C., Leicester Gallery, London, Silvermine Gallery, Conn., Pendut Gallery, Tex., Benedict Gallery, Sidney Rothman Gallery, N.J., Stamford (Conn.) Mus., Bridgeport (Conn.) Mus., Montclair (N.J.) Mus., Newark Mus., Coriell Gallery, Albuquerque; (traveling exhibit) Nat. Assn. Women Artists, 1996—, Travel USA, 1999, New World Art Ctr., N.Y.C., 1998-99, Gallery Art 54, N.Y.C., 1997, Atelier 14 Gallery, N.Y.C., 2000-2002; also numerous commd. portraits. Bd. dirs., exhbn. chmn. Summit Art Assn., 1950-60, Silvermine Guild of Art, New Canaan, Conn., 1960-64; bd. dirs. Artist's Equity of N.J., 1977-84, chmn. state-wide event, 1983, 86; artist's adv. coun. Hunterdon Art Ctr., Clinton, 1988-92; pres. Four Hills Neighbors, 1998-2000. Recipient awards in juried exhbns. in Iowa, Pa., N.J., Conn., N.Y.C. Mem. Nat. Mus. for Women in Arts (charter mem.), Nat. Assn. Women Artists Inc. (awards for figure painting 1957, 80-89), Silvermine Nat. Portrait Group of Artists. Avocations: entertaining, sewing, singing, playing the piano, reading. Home: 1321 Stagecoach Rd SE Albuquerque NM 87123-4320

MULTON, KAREN DIANE, psychologist, educator; b. Chgo., Oct. 11, 1952; d. Irvin and Helen Marie (Mazurski) Richardson; m. Carl Gregory Multon, Aug. 8, 1971; 1 child, Jill Susan. BA, U. Ill., 1974; MA, St. Xavier U., Chgo., 1982; PhD, Loyola U., Chgo., 1990. Lic. psychologist, Mo. Elem. tchr. various schs., Chgo. area, 1974-83; ednl. adminstr. Interventions, Chgo., 1983-84; tchr. spl. edn. Dist. 143, Midlothian, Ill., 1984-85; grad. asst. Loyola U., Chgo., 1985-89; asst. prof. psychology U. Mo., Columbia, 1990-97, assoc. prof. psychology, 1997—. Mem. editl. bd. Jour. Counseling Psychology, 1997—, Jour. Vocat. Behavior, 1996—, Jour. Career Devel., 1993—. Contbr. articles to profl. jours. Mem. APA (Barbara A Kirk award 1991), Am. Ednl. Rsch. Assn. Office: U Mo 16 Hill Hall Columbia MO 65211-2130 E-mail: multonk@missouri.edu.

MULUKUTLA, SARMA S. engineering educator, consultant; b. Chinnaganzam, Andhra Pradesh, India, Nov. 26, 1938; s. Raghavaiah V. and Lakshmi A. Mulukutla; m. Savitri D. Vedantam, Dec. 22, 1956; 1 child Satish Muluk 1 child Santi Kumar 1 child Suresh. PhD, U. Colo., 1967; cert. of advanced tech. tng., Hitachi Ltd., Tokyo, 1961. Registered profl. engr., Mass., chartered elec. engr., Gt. Britain. Prof. Banaras Hindu U., Varanasi, India, 1971—73; prof. elec. engring. Northeastern U., Boston, 1974—. Dir. power sys. engring. Northeastern U., Boston, 1981—85; cons. engr. various orgns., including GE, Schenectady, NY, 1967—; vis. prof. U. Iowa, Iowa City, 1973—74. Author: (books) Intro. to Electrical Engineering, 2001, Power System Analysis and Design, 2001, Electric Machines, 1985, Synchronous Machines, 1979. Pres. Telugu Assn. of Greater Boston, 1998—99; Trustee New Eng. Hindu Temple, Ashland, 1996—98. Fellow: IEEE (com. mem. 1968—2002), Inst. Engring. India; mem.: HKN, Sigma Xi, Tau Beta Pi. Hindu. Avocation: travel. Office: Northeastern U 360 Huntington Ave Boston MA 02114 Office Fax: 617-373-4431. Business E-Mail: mulukutla@ece.neu.edu.

MULVA, JAMES JOSEPH, oil company executive; b. Oshkosh, Wis., June 19, 1946; m. Miriam Mulva; 2 children. BBA in Fin., U. Tex., 1968, MBA in Fin., 1969. Mgmt. trainee, treas. Phillips Petroleum Co., Bartlesville, Okla., 1973, asst. treas. London, 1974, mgr. fgn. exch. and investment Bartlesville, Okla., 1976, v.p., treas. Europe/Africa div. London, 1980, mgr. corp. and planning Bartlesville, Okla., 1984, asst. treas., 1985, treas., 1986, v.p., treas., 1988-90, chief fin. officer, 1990-1995, pres., COO, 1994-99, vice-chmn., pres. & CEO, 1999, chmn., CEO, 1999—. With USN, 1969-73. Roman Catholic. Office: Phillips Petroleum Co 18 Phillips Bldg Bartlesville OK 74003*

MULVANEY, JAMES E. lawyer; b. N.Y.C., Apr. 17, 1930; s. Thomas A. and Ann G. (Gillespie) M.; divorced; children: James Jr., Patrick J. AB, St. Peter's Coll., 1951; LLB, Cornell U., 1954; LLM, Georgetown U., 1955. Atty. V.M. McInerney, Hollis, N.Y., 1955-63; asst. dist. atty. Queens, Kew Gardens, 1963-65; ptnr. McInerney & Mulvaney, New Hyde Park, 1966-83; pvt. practice Rockaway, 1983—. Contbr. Notre Dame Law Rev., 1955, Cornell Law Forum, 1999. Democrat. Roman Catholic. Avocations: writing, theater. Home and Office: 10710 Shore Front Pkwy Rockaway Park NY 11694-2637

MULVANEY, MARY FREDERICA, systems analyst; b. N.Y., Nov. 27, 1945; d. Michael Joseph and Mary Catherine (Clapper) M. BA, Marymount Coll., 1967; MA, U. Va., 1968; MS in Computer Sci., Marymount U., 1999. Cert. data processor Inst. Certification of Computer Profls., Ill. Computer systems analyst Dept. of Def., Ft. Meade, Md., 1968-74; sr. programmer analyst Planning Rsch. Corp., McLean, Va., 1974-83; mem. tech. staff Fed. Systems Group TRW Inc., Fairfax, 1983-90; sr. mem. tech. staff GTE Govt. Systems Corp., Rockville, Md., 1990-94; engr., sci. TRW, Inc., Fairfax, Va., 1994—. Mem. IEEE, Data Processing Mgmt. Assn., Computer Measurement Group, Cath. Assn. of Scientists and Engrs. Roman Catholic. Office: TRW Sys Integration Group One Federal Systems Park Dr Fairfax VA 22033

MULVANEY, MARY JEAN, physical education educator, department chairman; b. Omaha, Jan. 6, 1927; d. Marion Fowler and Blanche Gibons (McKee) M. BS, U. Nebr., 1948; MS, Wellesley Coll., 1951; LHD (hon.), U. Nebr., 1986. Instr. Kans. State U., Manhattan, 1948-50, U. Nebr., Lincoln, 1951-57, asst. prof., 1957-62, U. Kans., Lawrence, 1962-66; assoc. prof. U. Chgo., 1966-76, prof., 1976-90, prof. emeritus, 1990—, chmn. women's divsn., 1966-76, chmn. dept. phys. edn. and athletics, 1976-90; mem. vis. com. on athletics MIT, 1978-81, Wellesley Coll., 1978-79. Recipient Honor award Nebr. Assn. Health, Phys. Edn. and Recreation, 1962, U. Nebr. Alumni Achievement award, 1998. Mem. AAHPERD, Nat. Collegiate Athletic Assn. (mem. coun. 1983-87), Collegiate Coun. Women Athletic Adminstrs., Midwest Assn. Intercollegiate Athletics for Women (chmn. 1979-81), Nat. Assn. Collegiate Dirs. of Athletics (mem. exec. com. 1976-80, Hall of Fame 1990), Ill. Assn. Intercollegiate Athletics for Women (chmn. 1978-80), Univ. Athletic Assn. (sec. 1986-90, mem. exec. com. 1986-90, mem. dels. com. 1986-90, chmn. athletic adminstr.'s com. 1986-88), Mortar Bd., Alpha Chi Omega. Home: 5821 Kenneley Ct Lincoln NE 68516-3799 E-mail: maryjeanmulvany@aol.com.

MULVANIA, WALTER LOWELL, lawyer; b. Rock Port, Mo., Sept. 20, 1905; s. Jesse L. and Eva Viola (Stewart) Mulvania; m. Eunice Mary Umbarger, Jan. 31, 1945 (dec. May 2002); 1 child Eva Jo Mulvania Van Meter. BA, William Jewell Coll., Liberty, Mo., 1927; JD, U. Mo., 1931. Pvt. practice law, Rock Port, 1931—. Fellow Am. Coll. of Trust and Estate Counsel; mem. ABA, Mo. Bar Assn. (bd. govs. 1965-71), Rotary (pres. 1951-52). Democrat. Baptist. Office: 213 S Main St Rock Port MO 64482-1531

MULVEY, GERALD JOHN, telecommunication engineer, meteorologist educator; b. Cambria Heights, N.Y., Dec. 20, 1949; s. George Patrick and Estelle Florence M.; m. Katherine Louise Strick, July 7, 1973. BS in Physics, York Coll., Jamaica, N.Y., 1971; MS in Atmospheric Sci., SUNY, Albany, 1973; PhD in Atmospheric Sci., Colo. State U., 1977. Cert. cons. meteorologist, CCM. Rsch. assoc. dept. atmospheric sci. Colo. State U., 1977-78; mgr. dept. atmospheric physics Meteorology Rsch., Inc., Altadena, Calif., 1978-80; sr. rsch. engr. Lockheed Martin Missiles and Space, Sunnyvale, 1980-97; advanced programs mgr. Lockheed Martin Western Devel. Labs., 1997-98; lectr. dept. geoscis. San Francisco State U., 1995-98; advanced programs mgr. Lockheed Martin Global Telecomm., Sunnyvale, Calif., 1998-99; prin. sys. engr. DIVA Sys. Corp., Redwood City, 1999—2002; cons., 2002—. Co-author: Environmental Impacts of Artificial Ice Nucleating Agents, 1978; contbr. articles to profl. jours. including Analytical Chemistry and Jour. Applied Meteorology. Mem. Cupertino (Calif.) Libr. Commn., 1989—93; v.p. bd. dirs. Cupertino Libr. Found., 2000—01. Mem. AAAS, Am. Meteorological Soc., Internat. Soc. Measurement and Control (v.p. Santa Clara valley 1996-97), Sigma Xi. Roman Catholic. Achievements include verifying/documenting of long range transport of active cloud nucleating agents. E-mail: gjmulvey@att.net.

MULVEY, JOHN THOMAS, JR. financial consultant; b. N.Y.C., Mar. 13, 1941; s. John T. and Jeanette (Fox) M.; m. Ruth I. Dieicks, May 5, 1962 (div. June 1982); m. Elaine R. Anderson, Oct. 6, 1984 (div. Nov. 2000). BA, Westminster Coll., Fulton, Mo., 1972. Corp. trust rsch. clk. Chem. Bank N.Y. Trust Co., 1959-60; asst. dir. personnel Fedn. Bank and Trust Co., 1960-62; personnel rep. Meadow Brook Nat. Bank, 1962-65; controller Reevesound Co., 1965-69; cost control mgr. Veco Instruments, Inc., 1972-74; supr. corp. income tax Mo. Dept. Revenue, 1974-80; asst. treas., controller Sangamon Co., 1980-82; mgr. Ford and Co. CPA, 1982-84; asst. controller Meml. Hosp., 1984-88; fin. cons. Pompano Beach, Fla.; pres. Ardus, Inc. Republican. Episcopalian. Home: Lighthouse Point Marina Slip D-14 2831 Marina Dr Lighthouse Point FL 33064 also: Ardus Inc PO Box 1178 Pompano Beach FL 33061-1178 E-mail: ardusinc@aol.com.

MULVEY, MARY CROWLEY, retired adult education director, gerontologist, senior citizens association administrator; b. Bangor, Maine, Aug. 17, 1909; d. Michael J. and Ann Loretta (Higgins) Crowley; m. Gordon F. Mulvey, Jan. 25, 1940. BA, U. Maine, 1930; MA, Brown U., 1953; EdD, Harvard U., 1961;

LHD (hon.), U. Maine, 1991. Chair R.I. Com. on Aging, 1953-65; dir. adminstrn. on aging State of R.I., 1960-63; co-founder Nat. Coun. Sr. Citizens, 1961; pres. Nat. Sr. Citizens Edn. and Rsch. Ctr., Washington, 1963—; 1st v.p. Nat. Coun. Sr. Citizens, 1976-2001; guidance counselor Providence Sch. Dept., 1963-65; dir. adult edn. City of Providence Sch. Dept., 1965-79; reg. prog. rep. Title V, Older Ams. Act, Nat. Coun. Sr. Citizens, Washington, 1980-94. Major role in enactment of Medicare and Older Americans Act, 1950-65; del., adv. com. White House Conf. on Aging, 1961, 71, 81, 95; cons. Fed. Housing for the Aging, Washington, 1963-65, mem. tech. rev. com. Older Ams. Act Title IV, 1966-70; instr. preparing for retirement, developer women's program U. R.I., 1963-80; appt. by Pres. Carter to Fed. Coun. Aging, 1979, pres. R.I. State Coun. Sr. Citizens, 1982-98; charter mem. adv. bd. Coll. Arts and Humanities, U. Maine, 1992-96. Contbr. articles to profl. jours. Charter mem. U. Maine Friends of Mus. Art, 1997—; chair sr. citizen's rally Nat. Coun. Sr. Citizens, Washington, 1998. Recipient Cert. of award as Project Dir. of Sr. AIDES Employment Program, 1968-79, Medicare award R.I. State Coun. Sr. Citizens and Nat. Coun. Sr. Citizens, 1985, Disting. Achievement award U. Maine, 1980, Disting. Achievement award Berwick Acad., 1981, Justice for All award R.I. Bar Assn., 1981, Woman of Yr. award Nat. Sr. Pageant, 1982, R.I. Women 1st R.I. Sec. of State, 1991, citation Syracuse U., 1991, R.I. Dept. Elderly Affairs, 1993, 10th, 25th and 30th Anniversaries Title V Sr. Employment award Nat. Coun. Sr. Citizens, 1978, 93, 98, Lifetime Achievement award, 1994, Co-Founder and Continuing Bd. Mem. award, 1995, Svcs. for Sr. Citizens award, 1995, 30-yr. Sr. Aides award Nat. Sr. Citizens Edn. and Rsch. Ctr., 1999; named to R.I. Heritage Hall of Fame, 1993; Citation by Gov. Lincoln Almond for contbns. to R.I., 1996; Humanitarian award U. Maine Reunion, 2000; Soroptomists fellow in rsch. in gerontology Harvard U., 1955, 57, 59. Fellow Gerontol. Soc. Am.; mem. ACA, AAUW, Am. Assn. Adult and Continuing Edn., Harvard U. Alumni Assn. (Alumni award R.I. chpt. 1986), U. Maine Alumni Assn., Brown U. Alumni Assn., Harvard 1920 Club, Charles William Elliot Soc. (charter), Charles F. Allen Soc., Stillwater Soc. U. Maine (charter, Presdl. award for achievement), Paul Hamus Soc. Harvard, Pi Lambda Theta, Delta Delta Delta. Home: 118 Evergreen Ln Windham ME 04062-4713

MULVIHILL, JAMES EDWARD, periodontist, educator; b. Cleve., Sept. 24, 1940; s. John F. and Teresa J. (Carlos) M.; m. May Jane Forino, 1963; children— Karen, Kristen, Jason BA, Coll. of Holy Cross, 1962; DMD, Harvard U., 1966. Asst. dean for student affairs, coordinator Harvard-VA continuing edn. program Harvard Sch. Dental Medicine, Boston, 1970-71; dean clin. campus L.I. Jewish-Hillside Med. Ctr., Queens Hosp. Ctr. Affiliation, Jewish Inst. for Geriatric Care, Health Scis. Ctr. SUNY-Stony Brook, 1971-80; v.p. for edn. and research L.I. Jewish-Hillside Med. Ctr., New Hyde Park, N.Y., 1975-80; v.p., provost for health affairs, exec. dir. Health Ctr., prof. periodontics U. Conn., Farmington, 1980-92; attending periodontist John Dempsey Hosp., U. Conn. Health Ctr., 1982-92; pres. John Dempsey Fin. Corp., 1988-92; sr. v.p. for health policy The Travelers Corp., Hartford, Conn., 1992-94; chmn. bd. The Travelers Health Co., 1992-93; sr. fellow in health policy Assn. of Acad. Health Ctrs., 1994; pres., CEO Managed Health, Inc., 1994, Comty. Health Plan of Queens/Nassau, New Hyde Park, N.Y., 1994-95, Forsyth Dental Ctr., Boston, 1995-96, Juvenile Diabetes Found. Internat., 1996-99; dir. instnl. advancement Am. Dental Edn. Assn., 2000—; asst. to pres. So. Maine Med. Ctr., 2000—01. Cons. in field Author: (with others) Guide to Foreign Medical Schools, 1975, Editorial Instructions for Dental Authors, 1979-80, 1979, Human Subjects Research: The Operational Handbook for IRB's, 1982, 2d edit., 1984, Japanese edit., 1987; also articles, chpt. in book Bd. dirs. William Gies Found., Nat. Fund for Med. Edn. Recipient Disting. Alumnus award Harvard Sch. Dental Medicine, 1982, Disting. alumnus award Holy Cross Coll., 1991. Fellow AAAS, Am. Coll. Dentistry, Internat. Coll. Dentistry; mem. ADA, Am. Acad. Periodontology, Harvard Dental Alumni Assn., Internat. Assn. for Dental Rsch., Alpha Sigma Nu, Sigma Psi. Avocations: golf; gardening, photography. Address: 117 Kings Hwy Kennebunkport ME 04046-5606 E-mail: mulvi@adelphia.net.

MULVIHILL, KEITHLEY D. lawyer; b. Pitts., Oct. 16, 1956; s. Bernard H. and Doris L. M.; m. Donna Colella, 1980; children: Michael, Mary Katherine. BA in History, Ind. U. Pa., 1978; JD, U. Pitts., 1981. Bar: Pa. 1981, U.S. Dist. Ct. (we. dist.) Pa. 1981, U.S. Ct. Appeals (3d cir.) 1982; CPCU. Assoc. Rose, Schmidt, Hasley & DiSalle, Pitts., 1981-88, shareholder, 1988-2001; ptnr., head litigation dept. Leech, Tishman, Fuscaldo & Lampl, 2001—. Spl. master Ct. of Common Pleas of Allegheny County, Pa.; commr. Municipality of Mt. Lebanon, Pa., 1999—, v.p. 2002. Mem. Allegheny County Dem. Com; rep. Mt. Lebanon South Hills Area Coun. of Govts.; mem. St. Bernard Roman Cath. Ch. (past mem. parish coun.). Mem. ABA, Pa. Bar Assn., Pa. Def. Inst. (treas. 1998—), Allegheny County Bar Assn., Assn. Def. Trial Attys. (Pa. state chair), Def. Rsch. Inst., CPCU Soc. (pub. rels. chmn. Allegheny chpt.). Office: Leech Tishman Fuscaldo & Lampl LLC 1800 Frick Bldg Pittsburgh PA 15219 E-mail: kmulvihill@leechtishman.com.

MULVIHILL, MAUREEN ESTHER, writer, educator, scholar; b. Detroit; d. Charles James and Esther (Byrne) M.; m. Daniel R. Harris, June 18, 1983. PhD, U. Wis., 1983; postgrad., Columbia U., Yale U., Met. Mus. Art. Instr. U. Detroit, 1968-70, Wayne State U., Detroit, 1969-70, Penn Valley C.C., Kansas City, Mo., 1970-71; project writer Office of Gov., State of Wis., Madison, 1972-82; corp. comm. dir. Gruntal & Co., N.Y.C., 1983-85; vis. asst. prof. Hunter Coll. CUNY, 1984; assoc. fellow Inst. for Rsch. in History, N.Y.C., 1984-89; vis. asst. prof. Touro Coll., 1985; mem. Princeton (N.J.) Rsch. Forum, 1991—; cons. writer-editor Securities Industry Automated Corp./NYSE, N.Y.C., 1986-94. Proposal evaluator NEH, Washington, 1989—; juror Clifford Com. Am. Soc. for 18th Century Studies, 1991; vis. faculty NYU, 1983-85, 93, Marymount Manhattan Coll., 1993-94; vis. assoc. prof. Fordham U.-Lincoln Ctr., 1994-96; vis. prof. English, St. Joseph Coll., Bklyn., 1997, Berkeley Coll., Manhattan, 2000-2001, Mercy Coll., Manhattan, 2002—; guest spkr. Bklyn. Mus., Bklyn. Pub. Libr., NYU, Princeton U., Utah State U., S.W. Tex. State U., Irish Hist. Soc., N.Y.C.; corp. liaison Irish Art Exhbn., U.S., U.K.; writer mktg. com. Saatchi & Saatchi, N.Y.C., 1998-99; cons. book devel., book proposal evaluator MLA, N.Y.C., 1998—; cons. writer Wall Street Office, Bank of N.Y., N.Y.C., 2000—. Editor: (book) Poems by Ephelia (ca. 1679), 1992, 93; contbr. to profl. publs. Recipient scholarships and awards Wayne State U., 1966, 67-68, U. Wis., 1971-81, Inst. Rsch. History, N.Y.C., 1984-89; NEH fellow, 1990-91, Princeton Rsch. Forum, N.J., 1992, 95, 97. Democrat. Roman Catholic. Avocation: rare book collecting (17th and 18th Century English, Irish and Continental women writers). Home: 1 Plaza St W Brooklyn NY 11217-3748 E-mail: mulvihill@nyc.rr.com.

MULVIHILL, MEAD JAMES, JR. lawyer; b. 1927; Mem. bd. public edn Sch. Dist. Pitts., 1972-76, Allegheny County Airport Adv. Com., 1986—, Allegheny County Airport Area Devel. Adv. Commn., 1989—. Office: Mansmann Cindrich & Titus Four Gateway Ctr 20th fl Pittsburgh PA 15222

MULVIHILL, PETER JAMES, fire protection engineer; b. Honolulu, Jan. 24, 1956; s. James H. and Jane A. (Norton) M. BSCE, Worcester (Mass.) Poly. Inst., 1978. Registered profl. engr. Fire Protection, Nev. Sr. engr. Indsl. Risk Insurers, San Francisco, 1978-84; fire protection engr. Aerojet Gen. Corp., Sacramento, 1984-87, Reno Fire Dept., 1987-93; fire protection engr., bn. chief Boise (Idaho) Fire Dept., 1993-95; cons. Rolf Jensen & Assocs., Inc., Lehi, Utah, 1995-96, fire protection engr. Las Vegas, Nev., 1996-99; mgr. western region Fire Protection Mgmt., Inc., 1999—. Part-time instr. univ. extension U. Calif., Davis, 1993-95, Truckee Meadows Community Coll., Reno, 1988-93. Mem. Gov.'s Blue Ribbon Commn. to Study Adequacy of State Regulations concerning Highly Combustible Materials, Carson City, Nev., 1988, Nev. State Bd. Fire Svcs., 2001—. Mem.: ASCE, Fire Marshals Assn. Utah, Internat. Assn. Fire Chiefs, Nat. Fire Protection Assn. (alt. com. air conditioning and profl. qualifications for fire insps.), No. Nev. Fire Marshals Assn. (pres. 1992—93), Soc. Fire Protection Engrs. Office: Ste 650 101 Convention Center Dr Las Vegas NV 89109-2001

MULVIHILL, WILLIAM J. former health science association administrator; BBA, U. Cinn.; MEd, Ohio U. V.p. Ohio River Valley chpt. Arthritis Found., 1984-87, chair, 1987-90, midwest. area vice chair, 1988-90, chair fin. devel. com., 1991-93, vice chair of couns., 1993, treas., 1994-96, sr. vice chair, 1996-98, chair, 1998—2001; mem. board Alliance for Lupus Research. Mem. com. on appointments, salary and personnel com., exec. com.; assoc. dir. athletics for external affairs U. Cinn., exec. dir. athletic team scholarships. Mem. Coun. for Advancement and Support of Edn., Nat. Assn. Collegiate Dirs. of Athletics, Nat., Assn. Athletic Devel. Dirs. Office: Alliance for Lupus Research 1270 Avenue of the Americas, Suite 609 New York NY 10020*

MULVILLE, DANIEL R. federal agency administrator; b. Washington, Dec. 7, 1939; BSME, George Washington U., 1962, M Engring., 1977; PhD in Structural Mechs., Cath. U., 1974; postgrad., Coll. Armed Forces, 1986. Mech. engr. Naval Rsch. Lab., 1962—79; program mgr. structures rsch. Office Naval Rsch., 1975; structures tech. mgr. Naval Air Sys. Command, 1979—86; dep. dir. materials and structures divsn. Office Aeronautics and Space Tech. NASA, Washington, 1986—90, dir. engring. and quality mgmt. divsn. Office Safety and Mission Assurance, 1990—94, dep. chief engr., 1994—95, chief engr., 1995—99, assoc. dep. adminstr., 1999—, acting adminstr., 2001. Office: NASA Hdqrs Mail Code A 300 E St SW Washington DC 20546

MUMAW, JAMES WEBSTER, lawyer, director; b. Youngstown, Ohio, Apr. 11, 1920; s. Daniel W. and Helen (James) M.; m. Lois M. Baird, May 28, 1948; children: Thomas, Daniel, William. AB, Coll. of Wooster, 1941; JD, U. Cin., 1948. Bar: Ohio 1949. Since practiced in, Youngstown; ptnr. Luckhart, Mumaw, Morrisroe & Zellers and predecessor firm, 1959-66; mem. firm Luckhart, Mumaw, Zellers & Robinson, 1966—2002. Dir. Ohio Bar Title Ins. Co., 1955-91, Western Res. Bank of Ohio, 1963-95. Mem. Youngstown City Bd. Edn., 1972-75; pres. Christ Mission Kindergarten Assn., Goodwill Industries, 1967-69; trustee Ohio Land Title Assn., 1975-78, v.p., 1981, pres., 1982-83, Penn Ohio Coll., 1989-96. Served with AUS, 1943-46. Mem. Ohio State Bar Found. (life), ABA, Ohio State Bar (exec. com. 1978-81), Mahoning County Bar Assn. (pres. 1963-64), Am. Judicature Soc., Phi Alpha Delta. Presbyterian (elder, trustee). Club: Kiwanian. Home: 845 Wildwood Dr Youngstown OH 44512-3244 Office: 7178 West Blvd Youngstown OH 44512

MUMFORD, CHRISTOPHER GREENE, corporate financial executive; b. Washington, Oct. 21, 1945; s. Milton C. and Dorothea L. (Greene) M. BA, Stanford U., 1968, MBA, 1975. Cons. Internat. Tech. Resources Inc., 1974; asst. v.p. Wells Fargo Bank, San Francisco, 1975-78; treas. Arcata Corp., 1978-82, v.p. fin., 1982-87, exec. v.p. fin., 1987-94. Gen. ptnr. Scarff, Sears & Assocs., San Francisco, 1986—95; mng. dir. Questor Ptnrs. Fund, L.P., San Francisco, 1995—98; v.p. bd. dirs. Triangle Pacific Corp., Dallas, 1986—88, Norton Enterprises Inc., Salt Lake City, 1988—90. Office: PO Box 1340 Mill Valley CA 94942-1340 E-mail: cgmumford@aol.com.

MUMFORD, GREG, information technology executive; B in Applied Sci., U. B in Applied Sci., M in Applied Sci., U. B.C., Can. Positions with exploratory digital switching devel. Nortel Networks, 1971, leadership positions with brand mgmt. optical products, 1991, gen. mgr., pres., pres. Optical Long Haul, chief tech. officer Canada. Office: Nortel Networks 8200 Dixie Rd Ste 100 Brampton ON L6T 5P6 Canada*

MUMFORD, MANLY WHITMAN, lawyer; b. Evanston, Ill., Feb. 25, 1925; s. Manly Stearns and Helen (Whitman) M.; m. Luigi Thorne Horne, July 1, 1961; children— Shaw, Dodge AB, Harvard U., 1947; JD, Northwestern U, Chgo., 1950. Bar: Ill. 1950, U.S. Supreme Ct. 1969. Assoc. Chapman and Cutler, Chgo., 1950-62, ptnr., 1963-90. Author: The Old Family Fire, 1997; contbr. articles to profl. jours. Served with USNR, 1942-46 Fellow Am. Coll. Bond Counsel (hon.); mem. Nat. Assn. Bond Lawyers (Bernard P. Friel medal 1987). Clubs: Cliff Dwellers, University, Chgo. Literary. Democrat. Avocation: computers. Home: 399 W Fullerton Pky Chicago IL 60614-2810 Office: 22 W Monroe St Ste 1503 Chicago IL 60603-2505 E-mail: manly@mumford.cx.

MUMFORD, RUSSELL EUGENE, biologist, educator, writer; b. Casey, Ill., May 26, 1922; s. Charles Edward Mumford, Cecile Floe Ratts; m. Vivian Alice Tate, June 7, 1947; children: James Lee, Jean Lynne, Russell Eugene. BS, Purdue U., West Lafayette, Ind., 1948; MS, Purdue U., 1952, PhD, 1961. Natural sci. tchr. Fla. Audubon Soc., Orlando, 1950—51; wildlife rsch. biologist Ind. Fish and Game Dept., 1948—50; from instr. to prof. dept. biology Purdue U., West Lafayette, Ind., 1958—88; ret., 1988. Prof. wildlife mgmt. U. Pretoria, South Africa, 1967; wildlife cons. U. Vicosa, Brazil, 1970, USAID, 1973; rsch. assoc. mammals Smithsonian Instn., Washington, 1966—75; mem. Pantanal Park site com. Brazilian Forest Svc., Mato Grosso, 1975. Co-author: (book) Mammals of Indiana, 1982, Birds of Indiana, 1984; author: Waterfowl Management in Indiana, 1954, Distribution of Indiana Mammals, 1969; contbr. Merit badge counselor Boy Scouts Am., Lafayette, Ind., 1955—60. With USN, 1942—46. Avocations: birdwatching, fishing, travel, photography, antique collecting.

MUMFORD, STEPHEN DOUGLAS, population growth control research scientist; b. Louisville, Aug. 28, 1942; s. Adrian Leroy and Mildred Margaret (Cardwell) M.; m. Judy Sheng-Ju Lee, Dec. 26, 1966; children: Christopher Lee, Sonia Lea. BS in Agr., U. Ky., 1966; MPH in Internat. Health/Population Study, U. Tex., Houston, 1971, DrPH in Health Svcs. Adminstrn., 1975. Indsl. hygienist Ky. State Dept. Health, Frankfort, 1966-67; rsch. asst. dept. ob.-gyn. Baylor Coll. Medicine, Houston, 1973-75; rsch. statis. aide population studies U. Tex., 1971-75, rsch. asst. dept. reproductive biology/endocrinology, 1971-76; dir. rsch., sr. vasectomy counselor Planned Parenthood of Houston, 1972-76; adminstr. Nat. Swine Flu Immunization Program/Houston/Harris County, Tex., 1976-77; from sect. leader design/analysis divsn. to scientist Internat. Fertility Rsch. Program, Research Triangle Park, N.C., 1977-83; pres. Ctr. for Rsch. on Population and Security, 1984—. Author: The Pope and the New Apocalypse: The Holy War Against Family Planning, 1986, American Democracy and the Vatican: Population Growth and National Security, 1984, Population Growth Control: The Next Move is America's, 1977, The Decision-Making Process that Leads to Vasectomy: A Guide for Promoters, 1977, Vasectomy Counseling, 1977, The Life and Death of NSSM 200: How the Destruction of Political Will Doomed a U.S. Population Policy, 1996; contbr. numerous articles to profl. jours., chpts. to books; contbr. editor The Churchman, 1991-98. Mem. Alan Guttmacher Inst., Assn. for Vol. Sterilization, Environ. Def. Fund, Fund for Feminist Majority, Nat. Abortion Rights Action League, Population Inst., Population Ref. Bur., Ams. United for Separation of Ch. and State, Religious Coalition for Abortion Rights. Capt. U.S. Army, 1966-70. Recipient Cert. of Appreciation for Outstanding Contbns. to Advancing the Cause of Reproductive Rights, Feminist Caucus of Am. Humanist Assn., 1986, Humanist Disting. Svc. award, 1981, Margaret Mead Leadership prize in population and ecology, 1981, Award for Outstanding Single Project in Area of Human Rels., U.S. Jaycees, 1974-75, Award for Outstanding Chmn. of a Single Project in Area of Human Rels., 1974-75. Mem. AAAS, Am. Humanist Assn., Am. Pub. Health Assn. (population sect.), Ams. for Immigration Control, Ams. for Religious Liberty, Fedn. for Am. Immigration Reform, Internat. Epidemiol. Assn., Negative Population Growth, Carrying Capacity Network, Soc. for Epidemiologic Rsch., Zero Population Growth, NOW Avocations: gardening, fruit growing, woodworking, fishing, running. Home: 322 Azalea Dr Chapel Hill NC 27517-8105 Office: Ctr Rsch Population PO Box 13067 Research Triangle Park NC 27709 E-mail: smumford@mindspring.com.

MUMFORD, WILLARD ROYAL, engineering educator, educational consultant; b. McMinnville, Oreg., Aug. 1, 1933; s. Edgar Royal and Violet (Coe) M.; m. Elaine Virginia (Lineback), Aug. 20, 1955; children: Laura, Amy, David. BS, U. Md., 1956; BSME with honors, So. Meth. U., 1964; MSME, Tex. A&M U., 1969. Commd. 2d lt. USAF, 1956, advanced through grades to lt. col., 1974; assigned to Vietnam, 1969-70; chief reliability and value engring. Ogden (Utah) Air Logistics Ctr., 1971-75, chief logistics systems mgmt. dir., 1975-76; prof. aerospace studies Angelo State U., San Angelo, Tex., 1976-79; dep. dir. Electro Magnetic Compatibility Ctr., Annapolis, Md., 1979-81; ret., 1981; prof. engring., chmn. engring. and tech. div. Anne Arundel Community Coll., Arnold, Md., 1981-93; dir. advanced tech. Chesapeake Coll., Wye Mills, 1993—. Cons. N.J. Bd. Edn., Princeton, 1987-88, NSF, Washington, 1990-92; mem. Md. Task Force on Engring. Edn., Annapolis, 1990-91. Editor Civil War Token Soc. Jour., 1980—, Md. Token and Medals Soc. Jour., 1987—. Dist. chmn. Boy Scouts Am., Balt., 1980-83; advisor Jr. Engring. Tech. Soc., Arnold, 1985—; bd. dirs., v.p. Anne Arundel County Trust for Hist. Preservation, Annapolis, 1986—; pres. Anne Arundel County Hist. Soc., 1987—; elder Presbyn. Ch. Decorated Bronze Star, Air medal; recipient George Washington Honor medal Freedoms Found., 1978. Mem. Armed Forces Communications and Electronics Assn. (pres. 1979), Am. Assn. for Engring. Edn., Md. Assn. for Higher Edn. (pres. 1988-89, editor Jour. 1987-90, Outstanding Svc. award 1990), Md. Coun. on Engring. and Techs. (founder, bd. dirs. 1989—), Soc. Old Crows, Rotary (bd. dirs. Annapolis 1984-86), Tau Beta Pi, Phi Kappa Phi, Pi Tau Sigma, Tau Alpha Pi. Avocations: archaeology, historic preservation, numismatics, public speaking. Home: 1747 Long Green Dr Annapolis MD 21401-5818 Office: Chesapeake Coll PO Box 8 Wye Mills MD 21679-0008

MUMFORD, WILLIAM PORTER, II, retired lawyer; b. Kewanee, Ill., July 13, 1920; s. Harold E. and Mary K. (Harry) M.; m. Jean N. Hagemann, Nov. 22, 1951; children— William Porter III, James F., Michael E. BS in Accounting, U. Ill., 1943, JD, 1949. Bar: Ill. bar 1949, Oreg. bar 1955; C.P.A., Ill., Oreg. Jr. accountant Price Waterhouse & Co., Chgo., 1949-51; practiced in, 1951-54, Grants Pass, Ore., 1955-57, Eugene, Oreg., 1957—; mem. firm McAdams & Kirby, 1951-55; sr. accountant B.K. Herndon & Co., 1955-57; partner Thompson, Mumford, Anderson & Fisher, 1957-86, ret., 1986. Eugene campaign mgr. Hatfield for Gov., 1960-62; Chmn. bd. trustees Oreg. State Library. Served to capt., inf. AUS, 1943-46. Mem. Am. Legion, Pi Kappa Alpha, Phi Alpha Delta. Clubs: Elk. Republican. Home: 1960 Alder St Eugene OR 97405-2938

MUMICK, INDERPAL SINGH, computer scientist, engineer; b. New Delhi, Dec. 26, 1963; came to U.S., 1986; s. Ichhpal Singh and Narinder Kaur (Batra) M.; m. Ravneet Kaur Sodhi, Dec. 21, 1989; children: Kieraj Singh, Ruhani Kaur, Saran Singh. B Tech. in Computer Sci. and Engring., Indian Inst. Tech., New Delhi, 1986; PhD in Computer Sci., Stanford U., 1991. Rsch. student assoc. IBM Rsch., San Jose, Calif., 1988-91; tech. staff AT&T Bell Labs., Murray Hill, N.J., 1991-96; prin. tech. staff AT&T Labs., 1996-97; CEO, pres., COO, chief tech. officer Savera Systems, N.J., 1997-2000; CEO KIRUSA, Berkeley Heights, 2001—. Gen. co-chair Internat. Conf. on Very Large Databases, N.Y.C., 1998. Editor: Proceedings of ACM-Sigmod Conference, 1996, Materialized Views, 1996; contbr. articles to profl. jours. Recipient Pres. India Gold medal, 1986, Gold medal in math. Ctrl. Bd. Secondary Edn., Govt. of India, 1982. Mem. IEEE, Assn. Computing Machinery. Sikh. Achievements include several patents. E-mail: mumick@acm.org.

MUMM, CHRISTOPHER ERIC, lawyer, county government official; b. Reno, Dec. 9, 1950; s. Hans Heinrich and Yolanda Victoria (Erickson) M.; m. Stephanie Wasile, Nov. 27, 1984; children: Melody Anishka, Alexander Matthew. AAS in Real Estate, Truckee Meadows Community Coll, 1976; JD, U. Nev., 1985. Bar: Nev. 1987, Calif. 1987; lic. real estate broker, Nev. Dep. appraiser Washoe County, Reno, 1976-80, dep. tax assessor, 1980—2001; ind. real estate broker Reno, 1979—; pvt. practice law, 1987—. Chief tribal ct. judge Pyramid Lake Indian Reservation, 1994-98. Pres. PTA, Sparks Mid. Sch., 1999, Alice Maxwell Elem. Sch., 1998. With U.S. Army, 1970-72. Mem. Calif. Bar Assn., Nev. Bar Assn., Soc. Real Estate Appraisers (v.p. edn. Reno chpt. 1984-86), Internat. Assn. Assessing Ofcls., Nev. Jr. C. of C. (pres. 1986), U.S. Jaycees (exec. bd. dirs. 1986, amb., sen.), Acquarian Toastmasters (pres. 1988), Sertoma. Democrat. Roman Catholic. Home: 3815 Moorpark Ct Sun Valley NV 89433-8240

MUMMA, ALBERT GIRARD, JR. architect; b. Long Beach, Calif., July 2, 1928; s. Albert Girard and Carmen (Braley) M.; m. Janeal Thomas Woolf, Dec. 24, 1973; children: Eugenia M. Villagra, Albert Girard III, Peter Brenaman. B.Arch., U. Va., 1951. Designer McLeod & Ferrara, Architects, Washington, 1951-56; assoc. Deigert & Yerkes, Architects, 1956-62; prin. Mumma & Assocs., Washington, 1962—. Archtl. designer hotel div. Marriott Corp., 1980-82 Prin. archtl. works include Nat. Arboretum Hdqrs. Bldg, 1961, Finnmark Sq., Silver Spring, Md., 1964, Inverness townhouses, Potomac, Md., 1971, Post Office and Fed. Bldg., Elkins, W.Va., 1971, U.S. Trade Fairs in Spain, Finland, Japan, El Salvador, Poland 1963-72, Fallswood housing project, Falls Church, Va., 1972, Bristow Village townhouses, Annandale, Va., 1972-73, Marriott Hotel, Dayton, Ohio, 1982, Plaza Venetia, Biscayne Bay, Miami, Fla., 1983, Houston Med. Ctr. Hotel, Newark Airport Hotel, 1984, pvt. residences, No. Neck, Rappahanock River, Lancaster County, Va., 1993-96, subdivision and townhouse projects, Washington, Md., Va., Pa., 1962—. Served with USMC, 1945-47. Recipient Design award Washington Bd. Trade, 1964; winner Newark Airport Hotel Competition, 1981. Mem. AIA (medal 1951), Rappahannock River Yacht Club.

MUMMA, MICHAEL JON, physicist, researcher; b. Lancaster, Pa., Dec. 3, 1941; s. John Henry and Violet Lyndell (Baxter) M.; m. Sage Bailey Tower, Aug. 20, 1966; children: Peter Robb, Amy Elizabeth. AB in Physics with honors, Franklin and Marshall Coll., 1963; PhD in Physics, U. Pitts., 1970. Grad. research asst. U. Pitts., 1963-70; astrophysicist NASA Goddard Space Flight Center, Greenbelt, Md., 1970-76, head br. Infrared and Radio Astronomy, 1976-84, assoc. chief Lab. Extraterrestrial Physics, 1984-85, head Planetary Systems br., 1985-90, chief scientist Lab. Extraterrestrial Physics, 1990—; adj. research assoc. in physics Pa. State U., 1978-81, prof. physics, 1981-88. Mem. numerous working groups and adv. coms. NASA, Nat. Bur. Standards, NSF, Nat. Acad. Scis., 1973—; lectr. in field. Contbr. numerous articles to profl. publs., 1970—; editor: The Study of Comets, Vols. 1, 2, 1976, Vibrational-Rotational Spectroscopy for Planetary Atmospheres, vols. 1, 2, 1982, Astrophysics from the Moon, 1990. Recipient NASA medal for Exceptional Sci. Achievement, 1988, 97, Kershner award for physics, 1962; Coll. Trustee's scholar Franklin and Marshall Coll., 1963. Fellow Am. Phys. Soc., Washington Acad. Sci.; mem. AAAS, Am. Astron. Soc., Am. Geophys. Union, Internat. Astron. Union, Sigma Pi Sigma. Achievements include discovery of natural lasers in atmospheres of Mars, Venus, and Jupiter; first detection of water vapor in comets, discovery of formaldehyde, methanol, methane, and ethane in comets; discovery of x-rays in comets; first definitive measurements of deuterium and hydrogen on Mars and Venus; first absolute wind measurements on Venus and Mars; invention of tunable diode laser heterodyne spectrometer and other advanced instruments; development of Doppler-limited infrared spectroscopy for laboratory and astrophysical applications, of absolute calibration procedures in vacuum ultraviolet, of molecular branching ratio technique for intensity calibration in vacuum ultraviolet; measurement of many absolute cross sections in vacuum ultraviolet; research on atomic and molecular physics and chemistry, on comets, on planetary atmospheres, on infrared astronomy, on high-resolution spectroscopy, and in the field of dissociative excitation of molecules. Office: Code 690 Goddard Space Flight Ctr Greenbelt MD 20771-0001

MUMMERT, WANDA JEAN, family nurse practitioner, consultant; b. McAlester, Okla., Oct. 10, 1930; d. Carl A. and Verna W. Fawcett; m. Martin G. Mummert, Aug. 27, 1948 (dec. Feb. 1994); children: Jean A., J. Anna, Mary A. AAS in Nursing, Eastern Okla. State Coll., 1974; cert. FNP, Okla. U. Coll. Nursing, 1979. RNC, ANCC; RN, Tex., Okla. Staff nurse, nead nurse, relief house supr. McAlester (Okla.) Gen. Hosp., 1974-76; substitute tchr., practical nurse Kiamichi Area Vocat. Tech., McAlester, 1975-77; staff nurse, supr. Okla. Dept. Health, Atoka, 1977-78; FNP McAlester, 1979-94; patient care coord. Hospice of McAlester Okla., Inc., 1991-94; FNP East Tex. Med. Ctr., Hughes Springs, 1994—. Mem. adv. bd. Head Start, Shawnee, Okla., 1989-90, Hospice of McAlester Okla., Inc., 1991-92. Precinct election ofcl. Pittsburg County Election Bd., McAlester, 1954-94; vol. nurse, disaster nurse ARC, McAlester, 1974-94; presenter Gov.'s Task Force on Health Care, McAlester, 1989; squadron med. officer, pilot, CAP, McAlester, 1974-75. Mem. ANA, Okla. Nurses Assn. (dist. v.p., pres. 1974—), Assn. Okla. Nurse Practitioners, Am. Acad. Nurse Practitioners, Internat. Flying Nurses Assn. (conv. co-chmn. 1980-93), Tex. Nurse Practitioners. Avocations: reading, fishing, traveling. Home: PO Box 799 Muskogee OK 74402-0799 Office: E Tex Med Ctr Rural Health Ctr 2nd and Ward Hughes Springs TX 75656

MUNAS, FILIES A. psychiatric physician; b. Colombo, Sri Lanka, Aug. 30, 1946; came to U.S., 1972; s. M.H.M. and C.P. M. MBBS, MD, Christian Med. Coll., Vellore, India, 1971. Diplomate Am. Bd. Psychiatry and Neurology. Dir. geropsychiatry Trinity Meml. Hosp., Cudahy, Wis., 1991-95; dir. clin. svcs./chief of staff De Paul Hosp., Milw., 1996-97; dir. behavioral medicine VA Med. Ctr., Marion, Ill., 1998-2000; assoc. clinical prof. of psychiatry S.I.U. Sch. Medicine, Springfield, 1999—. Pres. Extended Family Svcs. Corp., Big Bend, Wis., 1989-97; assoc. clin. prof. psychiatry So. Ill. U. Sch. Medicine, Springfield, 1999—. Home: 23107 Galatia Post Rd Pittsburg IL 62974-1832 Office: VA Med Ctr 2401 W Main St Marion IL 62959-1188 E-mail: famunasmd@hotmail.com.

MUNCEY, JAMES ARTHUR, JR. architect; b. Dallas, July 9, 1933; s. James Arthur and Thelma (Bush) M.; m. Virginia Diers, Aug. 12, 1955; children: James G., Leah V., Laura E. BArch, Tex. A & M U., 1956. Registered architect, Tex. Design assoc. Wright Rich Assoc. Architects, Dallas, 1958-70; ptnr. Manos & Muncey Architects, 1970-80; pres. James A. Muncey Inc., 1980—. Pres. 4th Generation Inc. Dallas, 1980-87; dir. Mickey Finns Inc. Dallas, 1984-87. 1st Lt. U.S. Army, 1956-58. Mem. AIA, Tex. Soc. Architects. Republican. Episcopalian. Avocation: investments. E-mail: james.muncey@fbg.net.

MUNCH, DOUGLAS FRANCIS, pharmaceutical and health industry consultant; b. Bronx, N.Y., Mar. 15, 1947; s. Robert Joseph and Isabel (Fiordelisi) M.; m. Janice Ann Davis, Apr. 3, 1976; children: Sarah Christine, Eric Christopher. BSChemE, Villanova U., 1969; MS, U. Calif., Santa Barbara, 1974; PhD, Johns Hopkins U., 1978. Project engr. Grumman Aerospace Corp., Bethpage, N.Y., 1969-73; postdoctoral fellow U. South Ala., 1978-80; program mgr. Travenol Labs., Round Lake, Ill., 1980-82; dir. Kimberly Clark Corp., Atlanta, 1982-86; pres. Biomed. Products Group Inc., Roswell, Ga., 1986-87; cons., pres. D.F. Munch & Assocs., 1986-88; pres., CEO, dir. Sphinx Pharmaceuticals, Inc., Durham, N.C., 1988-89; v.p., dir. Orthopharm Corp.-Advanced Care Products, Johnson & Johnson, Raritan, N.J., 1989-93; pres. D.F. Munch, Ltd., Basking Ridge, 1993—; pres., CEO Otowave, LLC, North Plainfield, 1996-99. Bd. dirs. Percura, Inc., Irvine, Calif.; adv. bd. mem. dept. biomed. engrng. and Whitaker Biomed. Engrng. Inst., chmn., 2001—, Johns Hopkins Sch. Medicine, 1997—; advisor Queensland N.Am. Biotech. Group, Australia, 2001—. Author: Cardiovascular Pharmacology, 1981; contbr. articles to profl. jours. Pres. Hollyberry Civic Assn., Roswell, 1980-87, Roswell Neighborhood Network, 1987, Basking Ridge (N.J.) Little League, 1992-97; elder Basking Ridge Presbyn. Ch., 1992-95; mem. BME bd. dirs. Johns Hopkins Med. Sch., Balt., 1997—; trustee Philharm. Orch. N.J., 2000—, treas., 2000—. Recipient Apollo Achievement award NASA, 1969; Profl. Achievement award Villanova U., 1987; NIH fellow, 1974-78. Fellow Royal Soc. Medicine; mem. Am. Physiol. Soc., Biomed. Engrng. Soc., Johns Hopkins Med. and Surg. Assn. Avocations: woodworking, music, camping, cycling, swimming. Home: 41 Fieldstone Dr Basking Ridge NJ 07920-1605

MUNCK, ALLAN ULF, physiologist, educator; b. Buenos Aires, Argentina, July 4, 1925; came to U.S., 1945, naturalized, 1959; s. Carl and Elisabeth (Schmidt) M.; m. Claire Brosi, Oct. 5, 1957; children— Alexander Charles, Ingrid Claire, Kirsten Tanya. BS in Chem. Engring, Mass. Inst. Tech., 1948, MS, 1949, PhD in Biophysics, 1956. Chem. engr., Ducilo, Buenos Aires, 1949-50; mem. staff Huntington Lab. Mass. Gen. Hosp., Boston, 1956-57, Worcester Found. Exptl. Biology, Shrewsbury, 1957-59; mem. med. sch. faculty Dartmouth Coll., 1959—; prof. physiology Dartmouth Med. Sch., 1967—2001, prof. physiology emeritus, 2001—. Marius Tausk prof. Leiden U., The Netherlands, 1998. Served with Argentine Army, 1949. Mem. Physiol. Soc., Endocrine Soc., Am. Soc. Biochemistry and Molecular Biology. Home: PO Box 114 Norwich VT 05055-0114 Office: Dartmouth Med Sch Dept Physiology Lebanon NH 03756 E-mail: allan.u.munck@dartmouth.edu.

MUNCK, MICHAEL GEORGE, fundraising executive; b. Newcastle, Wyo., Aug. 11, 1954; s. Elroy Delbert and Mary Pauline (Blyholder) M.; m. Kathrine Ann Anderson, Aug. 30, 1986; children: Christian Michael, Aislinn Heather. BA in English, Carroll Coll., 1976. English tchr. Harlem (Mont.) H.S., 1976-77, Hays-Lodgepole (Mont.) H.S., 1978-79; counselor Intermountain Children's Home, Helena, Mont., 1979-81, cottage coord., counselor, 1981-87, asst. dir. devel., 1987-91; exec. v.p. St. Peter's Hosp. Found., 1991—. Founder com. Festival of Trees, Helena, 1988, mem. exec. com., 1988-92; mem. alumni divsn. Carroll Coll. Mem. Assn. for Healthcare Philanthropy, Helena Advt. Fedn. (vice chair elect 1990), Helena Estate Planning Coun. (founding), Kiwanis (co-chair Helena chpt. Toys for Tots program 1993, 94), Helena C. of C. (pres.'s club 1992—). Avocations: basketball, gardening, fishing, golf. Home: 1450 Charlie Russell Dr Helena MT 59601-6122 Office: St Peters Cmty Hosp Found 2475 E Broadway St Helena MT 59601-4928

MUNCY, ESTLE PERSHING, physician; b. Tazewell, Tenn., Apr. 9, 1918; s. William Loyd and Flora Media (Monday) M.; m. Dorothy Davis, Dec. 31, 1946 (div. Apr. 1980); children: Robert H., Teresa A., Dorothy J., Estle II,James; m. Jean Marie Hayter, Mar. 19, 1985. AB, Lincoln Meml. U., 1939; MD, U. Tenn., 1943. Resident Dallas Meth. Hosp., 1948; tchg. resident Tufts Med. Sch., Boston, 1949-50; physician Jefferson City, Tenn., 1950-96. Author: The Muncys in the New World, 1988, People and Places in Jefferson County, Tennessee, 1994. Alderman Jefferson City, 1974-77; chmn. Jefferson City Planning Commn., 1976-79. Capt. M.C., U.S. Army, 1944-46. Recipient Commendation for work on Tenn. history Gov. Don Sundquist, Jefferson award Am. Inst. Pub. Svc., 1995, Covenant Health Platinum award, 2000; named to Lincoln Meml. U. Lit. and Profl. Halls of Fame, 1997. Mem. Tenn. Heart Assn. (pres. 1966-67), Hamblen County Med. Soc. (pres. 1960-61), Jefferson County Hist. Soc. (pres. 1993-94, historian 1995—). Republican. Baptist. Avocations: photography, gardening. Home: 1428 Russell Ave Jefferson City TN 37760-2216

MUND, GERALDINE, judge; b. L.A., July 7, 1943; d. Charles J. and Pearl M. BA, Brandeis U., 1965; MS, Smith Coll., 1967; JD, Loyola U., 1977. Bar: Calif. 1977. Bankruptcy judge U.S. Ctrl. Dist. Calif., 1984—, bankruptcy chief judge, 1997—2002. Past pres. Temple Israel, Hollywood, Calif.; past mem. Bd. Jewish Fedn. Coun. of Greater L.A. Mem. ABA, L.A. County Bar Assn. Office: 21041 Burbank Blvd Woodland Hills CA 91367-6606

MUND, LORRAINE G. English studies educator, writer; b. Glemsford, Suffolk, Eng. d. Mario and Joan Muselli; m. Joseph Mund, May 29, 1965; children: Jemine, Lorna, Kristin. BA in English, St. Josephs Coll., 1962; MA in English, Columbia U., 1964; PhD in English, La Salle U., 1997. Asst. prof. Five Towns Coll., Merrick, N.Y., 1976-78; instr. SUNY, Old Westbury, 1978-96. Part-time instr. SUNY, Stony Brook, 1997-99; adj. prof. Nassau Coll., Garden City, N.Y., 1974—; workshop dir. East Meadow (N.Y.) Sch., 1995, 96; dir. Old Westbury Poetry Ctr., 1994-96; guest spkr. Rotary, Hicksville, N.Y., 1997, 98, 99. Author numerous short stories; author: Poetry, Like an IV..., 2000; editor Poetry Jour. SUNY, 1994-96. Performer, singer Camcos, N.Y. chpt. Mem. Internat. Found. Freedom Women (spkr.), Women's Faculty Assn. Avocations: teaching, writing, conducting workshops. Home: 40 Alpine Ln Hicksville NY 11801

MUND, RICHARD GORDON, foundation executive; b. Balt., Feb. 11, 1942; s. Allan Winfield and Irma Louetta (Kaufman) M.; m. Joan Ann Dennis, June 24, 1967; children: Mary Jean, John Winfield, Elizabeth Anne. Student, Johns Hopkins U., 1960-63; BA, Ill. Wesleyan U., 1965; MA, U. Denver, 1967, PhD, 1970. Asst. dir. admissions Marshall U., Huntington, W.Va., 1970, dir. fin. aid, 1971, v.p. student affairs, 1971-77; coll. rels. coord. Mobil Oil Corp., N.Y.C., 1977-79; asst. sec. Mobil Found., Inc., 1979, sec., exec. dir., 1980—. Mem. contbns. coun. Conf. Bd., N.Y.C., 1980—, chmn., 1985. Trustee Huntington (W.Va.) Galleries, 1975-77, Coun. for Advancement and Support of Edn., 1987-89, Fairfax County Pub. Schs. Edn. Found., 1991—, Soc. of Yeager Scholars, Marshall U., 1995—; adv. coun. mem. ARC, BBB, Nat. Ctr. Non-Profit Bds., United Way Am. Mem. Kappa Delta Pi, Kappa Alpha Order, Phi Delta Kappa Office: Mobil Found Inc 225 Gallows Rd Fairfax VA 22037-0001

MUNDAY, ROBERT STEVENSON, priest, academic dean; b. Benton, Ill., Oct. 19, 1954; s. Robert Meade and Kathryn (McCollum) M.; m. Christina Ellen Karroll, July 31, 1976. BA, So. Ill. U., 1976; MDiv, Mid-Am. Bapt. Theol. Sem., Memphis, 1979, PhD, 1984; MLS, Vanderbilt U., 1986; postgrad., Duquesne U., U. of the South, Sewanee, Tenn. Ordained priest Episcopal Ch., 1990. Chaplain St. Jude Children's Rsch. Hosp., Memphis, 1981-84; instr. Mid-Am. Bapt. Theol Sem., 1984-86; libr. dir. Trinity Episcopal Sch. for Ministry, Ambridge, Pa., 1986—, assoc. prof. systematic theology, 1986—, assoc. dean for adminstrn., 1987-94, assoc. dean planning and policy, 1994-97, assoc. dean for libr. and info. svcs., 1997—. Dep. to the gen. conv. Episcopal Ch., 1994, 97. Chmn. bd. dirs. Life Choices, Memphis, 1984-86; bd. dirs. Cen. Pitts. Crisis Pregnancy Ctr., 1989—, pres., 1990-95; bd. dirs. Pregnancy Care Ctrs. Pitts., 1995—, pres., 1996—. Mem. Nat. Orgn. Episcopalians for Life (bd. dirs., pres. 1991-94), Fairfax Va., Theol. Edn. Commn., Episcopal Synod Am., Am. Acad. Religion, Am. Theol. Libr. Assn., Brotherhood St. Andrew (life), Fellowship of St. Alban and St. Sergius, Oblate, Order of St. Benedict. Office: Trinity Episcopal Sch for Ministry 311 11th St Ambridge PA 15003-2302 Home: 2777 Mission Rd Nashotah WI 53058-9790 *Life is about possibility and transformation—the possibility of being lifted above mere human existence to be the creatures we are ideally in the mind of God. The possiblility of that transformation is the good news of our redemption in Jesus Christ.*

MUNDAY, STEPHEN DALE, writer, artist; b. Haskell, Tex., Mar. 10, 1949; s. Edna Mae Moody; m. Joyce Laverne Stuteville, June 19, 1981. BA, West Tex. State U., 1970. Farm and ranch editor Abilene (Tex.) Reporter-News, 1971-72; field editor The Cattleman Tex. and Southwestern Cattle Raisers Assn., Fort Worth, 1972-74; info. dir. Tex. Cattle Feeders Assn., Amarillo, 1974; freelance writer Arlington, Tex., 1974-76; dir. field svcs. Simmental Shield Mag. Am. Simmental Assn., 1975; edtl. dir. The Cattleman Mag. Tex. and Southwestern Cattle Raisers Assn, Fort Worth, 1976-78; news dir. Tex. and Southwestern Cattle Raisers Assn., 1978-81, adminstrv. asst. media and govt. rels., 1981-95, exec. v.p., 1995-2001; freelance writer, artist, cons., 2001—. Mem. Tex. Farm Bur., Tarrant County, Waco; asst. sec. Tex. and Southwestern Cattle Raisers Found., Fort Worth, 1995-2001; sec.-treas. Tex. and Southwestern Cattle Raisers Assn. Ins. Svcs., Inc., Ft. Worth, 1995-2001, Tex. and Southwestern Cattle Raisers Assn. Legal Def. Fund, 1995-2001. Editor: TSCRA News Update, 1979 (1st pl. gen. excellence Livestock Pubs. Coun. 1986), TSCRA News Update, 1987 (1st pl. gen. excellence Livestock Pubs. Coun., 1 988), TSCRA News Update, 1988 (2nd pl. gen. excellence Livestock Pubs. Coun., 1989), TSCRA News Update, 1989 (1st pl. gen. excellence Livestock Pubs. Coun., 1990), TSCRA News Update, 1990 (1st pl. gen. excellence Livestock Pubs. Coun., 1991). Bd. dirs. Hist. Camp Bowie, Inc., Fort Worth, 2001. Capt. U.S. Army, 1971-99. Mem. AARP, Am. Legion, Tex. and Southwestern Cattle Raisers Assn. (treas. polit. action com. 1995-2001), Tex. Farm Bur. Avocations: reading, painting, cartooning, travel, collectibles. Home: 3415 Bristol Rd Fort Worth TX 76107 Fax: 817-878-2440. E-mail: cowscribe@msn.com.

MUNDELL, JOHN ANTHONY, environmental engineer, consultant; b. Frankfort, Ind., Apr. 11, 1957; s. Loren Sherman-Sheridan Mundell and Juanita Fern (Thompson) Rogers; m. Julia Ann Mooney, Aug. 4, 1979; children: Sarah Marie, Andrew Jacob, Daniel Isaac, James Thomas. BSCE with highest distinction, Purdue U., 1979, MSCE with highest distinction, 1980; postgrad., U. Notre Dame, 1984-88. Registered profl. engr., Ind.; licensed profl. geologist. Grad. teaching asst. Purdue U., West Lafayette, Ind., 1979-80; staff engr., then project engr. Am. Testing and Engrng. Corp. (ATEC) Assocs., Inc., Indpls., 1981-84, corp. dir. environ. svcs., 1988-89, v.p., corp. dir. tech. svcs., 1989-95; pres. Mundell & Assocs., Inc., 1995—; pvt. cons. Notre Dame, Ind., 1984-88; rsch. assoc. U. Notre Dame, 1984-88. Contbr. articles to Jour. Geotech. Engrng., Jour. Environ. Engrng., Jour. Geophys. Rsch., Soils and Founds., other profl. publs. Music group leader, guitarist, liturgist St. Elizabeth Seton Parish, Carmel, Ind., 1981-84, 88-93, Christ the King Parish, South Bend, Ind., 1985-88, St. Pius X, Indpls., 1993—, Indpls. Groundwater task force, 1994; Inpls. Wellhead Protection officer, 1995-97. Mem. ASCE, ASTM, Nat. Ground Water Assn., Am. Geophys. Union. Achievements include first to engineer the use of on-site waste fixation/stabilization approved by U.S. EPA at a Superfund site; development of multicomponent geochemical model for lead mobility analysis, of first predictive models to determine effect of waste on hydraulic properties of clay barriers at disposal sites; research in laboratory testing and field control guidelines to achieve clay liner compaction conditions to meet EPA standards of waste isolation; three-dimensional visualization techniques for assessing organic contamination at industrial sites; natural attenuation field studies for groundwater contamination. Home: 10411 White Oak Dr Carmel IN 46033-3975 Office: Mundell Assocs Inc 429 E Vermont St Ste 200 Indianapolis IN 46202-3685

MUNDHEIM, ROBERT HARRY, law educator; b. Hamburg, Germany, Feb. 24, 1933; m. Guna Smitchens; children: Susan, Peter. BA, Harvard U., 1954, LLB, 1957; MA (hon.), U. Pa., 1971. Bar: N.Y. 1958, Pa. 1979. Assoc. Shearman & Sterling, N.Y.C., 1958-61; spl. counsel to SEC Washington, 1962-63; vis. prof. Duke Law Sch., Durham, N.C., 1964; prof. law U. Pa., Phila., 1965—. Univ. prof. law and fin., 1980-93, dean, 1982-89, Bernard G. Segal prof. law, 1987-89; co-chmn. Fried, Frank, Harris, Shriver & Jacobson, N.Y.C., 1990-92; exec. v.p., gen. counsel Salomon Inc., 1992-97; sr. exec. v.p., gen. counsel Salomon Smith Barney Holdings, Inc., 1997-98; of counsel Shearman & Sterling, 1999—; gen. counsel U.S. Dept. Treasury, Washington, 1977-80, trustee and pres. Am. Acad. in Berlin, 2000—; chmn. legal adv. bd. NASDAQ; pres. Appleseed Found.; trustee New Sch. U.; bd. dirs. eCollege, Salzburg Seminar, The Kitchen; gen. counsel Chrysler Loan Guarantee Bd., 1980; mng. dir., mem. mgmt. bd. Salomon Bros. Inc., N.Y.C., 1992-97; overseer Curtis Inst. Fin., 2000—. Author: Outside Director of the Publicity Held Corporation, 1976; American Attitudes Toward Foreign Direct Investment in the United States, 1979; Conflict of Interest and the Former Government Employee: Re-thinking the Revolving Door, 1981; chmn. adv. bd. Jour. Internat. Econ. Law, 1996-97. Trustee SEC Hist. Soc. With USAF, 1961-62. Recipient Alexander Hamilton award U.S. Dept. Treasury, 1980, Harold P. Seligson award Practicing Law Inst., 1988, Francis J. Rawle award, ABA-ALI, 1992, Anti-Defamation League Human Rels. award, 1999. Mem. Am. Law Inst. (mem. coun., mem. exec. com.), Nat. Assn. Securities Dealers (gov.-at-large, vice-chmn.), San Diego Securities Regulation Inst. (chmn.), Am. Acad. in Berlin (pres. 2000—). Office: Shearman & Sterling 599 Lexington Ave Fl 16 New York NY 10022-6069

MUNDIE, CRAIG, information technology executive; BEE, M in Info. Theory and Computer Sci., Ga. Inst. Tech. Software developer Data Gen. Corp., 1972; co-founder, CEO Alliant Computer Systems Corp.; head Consumer Platforms Divsn., Microsoft, Redmond, Wash., 1992, sr. v.p. Advanced Strategies, sr. v.p., chief tech. officer of advanced strategies and policy. Mem. Nat. Security Telecom. Adv. Com., Pres. Clinton, 2000. Office: Microsoft One Microsoft Way Redmond WA 98052-6399*

MUNDIE, GENE E. nursing educator; b. Hazleton, Pa., Dec. 9, 1942; s. James J. and Priscilla I. (Smith) M. Diploma, Bellevue Hosp. Sch. Nursing, 1963; BSN, Pa. State U., 1970; MEd, Tchrs. Coll. N.Y.C., 1973; MS, SUNY, Stony Brook, 2001. Supr. ICU Columbus Hosp., N.Y.C.; supr. inservice Bellevue Hosp.; dir. continuing edn. and tng. Coney Island Hosp., Bklyn.; clin. assoc. prof. nursing Univ. Med. Ctr., Sch. Nursing, SUNY, Stony Brook. Contbr. articles to profl. jours. Mem. ANA, NLN, N.Y. State Nurses Assn., Sigma Theta Tau (pres. chpt. 1989-94), Kappa Delta Pi. Home: PO Box 336 Stony Brook NY 11790-0336 E-mail: gene.mundie@sunysb.edu.

MUNDINE, RACHEL QUINN, music educator; b. Newport, N.C., Aug. 14, 1935; d. Raymond Thomas and Ada Elizabeth (Quinn) M. Student, East Carolina U., Greenville, N.C., 1953-54. Music dir. Program Search For a Star WNCT-TV, Greenville, N.C., 1954-55, pianist various programs, 1954-55; soprano soloist Santa Monica (Calif.) Civic Opera, 1968-71; music tchr. piano, voice, organ Melody Haven Studio, Newport, N.C., 1972—; organist First United Meth. Ch., Morehead City, 1984—; guest piano soloist N.C. Symphony, 1981. Organist, pianist, vocalist various hotels and clubs throughout U.S., Can. and Thule, Greenland, 1958-71; pres., founder La Musique Club of Carteret County, N.C., 1975—; dir. Miss La Musique Pageant, Morehead City, 1993-2002; area and state chmn. music festivals N.C. Fedn. Music Clubs, Greenville and Chapel Hill, 1984-94. Composer: Our Majestic Mountains, 1986. Contbns. chmn. N.C. Symphony Carteret County chpt., Morehead City, 1980, pres., 1981; entertainment chmn. Festival of the Trees, Hospice, Morehead City, 1997-2002; mem. adv. bd. Civic Ctr., Morehead City, 1999-2001. Named Woman of Yr. in Arts Carteret County Coun. Women, Morehead City, 1990, 92. Mem. Nat. Guild Piano Tchrs., N.C. Music Tchrs. Assn., Order Eastern Star (worthy matron 1977-78, grand organist 1981-82), N.C. Music Assn. (pres., founder 1995-2002), Lions. Methodist. Avocations: hiking, sailing, skiing, swimming. Home and Office: Melody Haven Studio 580 Lake Rd Newport NC 28570-6956

MUNDINGER, DONALD CHARLES, retired college president; b. Chgo., Sept. 2, 1929; s. George Edward and Bertha (Trelkenberg) M.; m. June Myrtle Grubbe, June 17, 1951; children: Debra Sue, Donald William, Mary Ruth (dec.). Student, U. Ill., 1947-48; BA, Concordia Coll., River Forest, Ill., 1951, LLD (hon.), 1982; MA, Northwestern U., 1952; PhD, Washington U., St. Louis, 1956; DH (hon.), MacMurray Coll., Jacksonville, Ill., 1984, Ritsumeikan U., Kyoto, Japan, 1992; LLD (hon.), Ill. Coll., Jacksonville, 1993; postdoctoral study, Cambridge U. (Eng.), 1967-68. Asst. prof. polit. sci., chmn. dept. Augustana Coll., Sioux Falls, S.D., 1956-58; asst. prof. govt. Valparaiso (Ind.) U., 1958-61, assoc. prof., 1961-65, prof., 1965-73; dean Valparaiso (Ind.) U. (Coll. Arts and Scis.), 1965-67; dir. Overseas Center, Cambridge, Eng., 1967-68, v.p. acad. affairs Eng., 1968-73; pres. Ill. Coll., Jacksonville, 1973-93; chmn. Fedn. Ind. Ill. Colls. and Univs., 1975-78; chmn. non-public adv. com. Ill. Bd. Higher Edn., 1988-91. Postdoctoral fellow Center Study Higher Edn., U. Mich., 1964-65; chmn. bd. Council Ind. Colls., 1988-90. Contbr. articles to profl. jours. Mem. Ill. State Bar Assn. (com. on fed. judicial and related appointments 1983-89), Nat. Assn. Ind. Colls. and Univs. (commn. on new initiatives, 1988-90), Pi Sigma Alpha, Phi Eta Sigma. Home: 3803 Pheasant Walk Dr Valparaiso IN 46383-2205

MUNDORFF SHRESTHA, SHEILA ANN, cariologist; b. Rochester, N.Y., Dec. 14, 1945; d. Karl Mundorff and Elizabeth Mary (Braun) Ross; m. Buddhi Man Shrestha, June 18, 1988. BS in Biology, Nazareth Coll., Rochester, 1967; MS in Microbiology, U. Rochester, 1984. Lab. technician Eastman Dental Ctr. U. Rochester, 1967-69; rsch. asst. Eastman Dental Ctr., 1969-71, rsch. assoc., 1971-92, small animal expt. coord., 1984-92, sect. head animal/microbiol. rsch., 1987—, chmn. Instl. Animal Care and Use Com., 1990-97, vivarium dir., 1990-97, med. emergency program dir., 1991-92, asst. prof., 1992-97; assoc. prof. U. Rochester Eastman Dept. Dentistry, 1997—. Mem. univ. com. on animal resources U. Rochester, 1997—; mem. animal resource group ADA Health Found., Chgo., 1981-83; cons. working group Sci. Consensus Conf.-Assessment Cariogenic Potential of Foods, San Antonio, 1985; participant, reactor, co-chair animal caries models working groups Conf. on Clin. Aspects of Demineralization of Teeth, Rochester, N.Y., 1994; invited session chair symposium 2000, Univ. Leeds, 2000. Patentee in field. CPR instr. ARC, Rochester, 1978-94, cert. 1st responder, N.Y.S., 1992-95. NIH, Nat. Inst. Dental Rsch. grantee, 1986, 87, 88. Mem. Am. Assn. Dental Rsch. (sec.-treas. Rochester sect. 1977-92). Roman Catholic. Avocations: dance, sewing, swimming, flower arranging, painting on silk. Office: Eastman Dental Ctr 625 Elmwood Ave Rochester NY 14620-2913 E-mail: buddhis@msn.com.

MUNDT, BARRY MAYNARD, management consultant; b. San Francisco, June 28, 1936; s. Kenneth Francis and Janet (Doughty) M.; m. Sally Hanscom, June 13, 1960; children: Kevin Warren, Trevor Stevens, Stacey Corbin BS in Indsl. Engrng., Stanford U., 1959; MBA, U. Santa Clara, 1964. Registered indsl. engr., Calif. Statistician Aerojet-Gen., Sacramento, 1957-58; reliability engr. Lockheed Missiles, Sunnyvale, Calif., 1959-61; mgmt. engr. C-E-I-R, Inc., Los Altos, 1961-65; sr. cons. Peat, Marwick, Livingston & Co., Los Angeles, 1965-68; mgr., prin. Peat, Marwick, Mitchell & Co., Atlanta, 1968-84; ptnr.-in-charge, ops. mgmt. cons. KPMG Peat Marwick Main & Co., N.Y.C., 1984-88; internat. mgmt. cons. ptnr. KPMG Internat., N.Y.C. and Amsterdam, The Netherlands, 1988-92; mgmt. cons., ptnr. KPMG Peat Marwick U.S., Montvale, N.J., 1992-95; prin. The Strategy Facilitation Group, Rowayton, Conn., 1995—. Pres. Thomas Place Assoc., 1998—. Author-editor: Managing Public Resources, 1982; co-author Il Manager Pubblico (Italy), 1986; mem. editl. bd., contbg. author Handbook of Industrial Engineering, 3rd edit., 2001; contbr. articles to profl. jours. Mem. ann. campaign Atlanta Symphony Orch., 1974-82, Atlanta Arts Alliance, 1976-81; del. to assembly United Way of Met. Atlanta, 1974-84; bd. chmn., mem. Brandon Hall Sch., Atlanta, 1980—2002. Fellow Inst. Indsl. Engrs. (treas. 1976-81, prse. 1982-83, asst. treas. 1985-92); mem. Thomas Pl. Assn. (pres.), Norwalk Yacht Club. Episcopalian. Avocations: golf, boating. Home and Office: 21 Thomas Pl Norwalk CT 06853-1500 E-mail: bmundt@optonline.net.

MUNDY, GARDNER MARSHALL, lawyer; b. Roanoke, Va., July 19, 1934; s. Gardner Adams and Betty (Marshall) M.; m. Jean Stephens, Nov. 13, 1956 (div. 1979); children: Stephens M., Liza I.; m. Jenice Hamrick, June 21, 1980 (div. 1998); children: G. Marshall Jr., Natalie J.; m. Monika Ferguson, Aug. 28, 1999. BA, Va. Mil. Inst., 1956; LLB, U. Va., 1962. Bar: Va. 1962, U.S. Dist. Ct. (we. dist.) Va. 1962, U.S. Ct. Appeals (4th cir.) 1962. Ptnr. Woods, Rogers & Hazlegrove, Roanoke, 1962-71, Mundy & Garrison, Roanoke, 1973-76, Mundy & Strickland, Roanoke, 1976-82; pvt. practice, 1982-86; ptnr. Mundy, Rogers & Frith, 1986—. 1st lt. U.S. Army, 1957-59. Fellow Am. Coll. Trial Lawyers, Am. Bd. Trial Advocates (pres. Western Va. chpt. 1990-91), Am. Bar Found., Va. Bar Found.; mem. ABA, Va. State Bar (chmn. bd. govs. litig. sect. 1985-86, bd. govs. sr. law sect. 2000—), Roanoke Bar Assn. (bd. dirs. 1986-90, pres. 1990-91), Shenandoah Club, Roanoke Country Club, Coral Beach and Tennis Club (Bermuda). Presbyterian. Avocations: tennis, skiing, cooking, growing roses. Home: 1542 Electric Rd Roanoke VA 24018-1106 Office: Mundy Rogers & Frith 1328 3rd St SW Roanoke VA 24016-5219 Fax: 540-982-1362. E-mail: gmundy@mrf-law.com.

MUNEIO, PATRICIA ANNE, public health nurse; b. Detroit, Oct. 7, 1949; d. Charles Eli and Mary Jane (Voletti) M. BSN, Wayne State U., 1973; MS, Calif. Coll. for Health Scis., San Diego, 1994. RN, Mich., Fla. Staff nurse to head nurse Detroit Osteo. Hosp., Highland Park, Mich., 1974-75; nurse emergency rm. Grace Hosp., Detroit, 1975-77; pub. health nurse, team leader Detroit VNA, 1977-83; staff nurse, head nurse Comprehensive Health Svcs. of Detroit, 1983-85; pvt. duty nurse AbCare, Inc., Detroit, 1985; pub. health nurse, supr. Cmty. Home Care, Sterling Heights, 1985-88; home care supr. Med. Personnel Pool, Southfield, 1988-89; pub. health nurse III Macomb County Health Dept., Mt. Clemens, 1989-96; health care surveyor spl. svcs. sect. Mich. Dept. Consumer and Industry Svc., Lansing, 1996-97; owner The Pink Alligator Used Books and Consignment Store, Indian Rock Beach, Fla., 1998—2002; nurse min. St. Anthony's Hosp., St. Petersburg, 2002—. Cons., 1999—; legal nurse cons., 1999; notary pub., Fla., 2000. Bd. dirs. Indian Rocks Beach Action 2000, 1998—; charter mem. N.Am. Inst. Smithsonian. Mem. ANA, Mich. Nurses Assn. (rep. 1992, Blue Water Dist. v.p. 1990-92, pres. 1992-96), Macomb County Health Dept. Staff Coun. (pres. 1990-94). Democrat. Roman Catholic. Avocations: knitting, embroidery, painting, travel, sports. Home and Office: 309 Bahia Vista Dr Indian Rocks Beach FL 33785

MUNERA, GERARD EMMANUEL, manufacturing company executive; b. Algiers, Algeria, Dec. 2, 1935; s. Gabriel and Laure (Labrousse) M.; m. Paule A. Ramos, July 28, 1959; children: Catherine, Philippe, Emmanuelle, Jean-Marie. M Math., M Physics, M Chemistry, Ecole Poly., Paris, 1956; CE, Ecole Ponts et Chaussees, Paris, 1959. Chief county engr. Dept. Rds. and Bridges, South Algiers, 1959-62; cons. French Ministry Fgn. Affairs, Argentina, 1962-66; sr. v.p. fin. Camea Group Pechiney Ugine Kuhlmann, Buenos Aires, 1966-70, chmn. bd., chief exec. officer, 1976-77; exec. v.p. Howmet Aluminum Corp., Greenwich, Conn., 1976-77, pres., chief operating officer, 1977-79, pres., chief exec. officer, 1980-83; corporate v.p. nuclear fuels Pechiney, Brussels, 1983-85; vice chmn., chief exec. officer Union Minière, 1985-89; head corp. planning and devel. RTZ, London, 1989-90; pres., CEO Minorco USA, Englewood, Colo., 1990-94, also bd. dirs.; chmn. and CEO Latin Am. Gold, Inc., N.Y.C., 1994-96, Synergex Inc., 1996—. Bd. dirs. Nevsun Resources, Inc., Augen Capital Ltd., Dynamic Materials Corp., Inc., Twin Mining Ltd.; chmn., CEO, Synergex, Inc., Arcadia Inc. Patentee low-income housing system. Served with French Air Force, 1956-57. Decorated officer Legion of Honor (France). Roman Catholic. Office: Arcadia 60 Bonner St Stamford CT 06902-6610

MUNETZ, MARK RICHARD, psychiatrist; b. Phila., Dec. 1, 1950; s. Leon and Alice (Grossman) M.; m. Lois Sue Freedman, Apr. 11, 1976; children: Jonathan, Katherine. BA, U. Pa., 1972, MD, 1976. Diplomate Am. Bd. Psychiatry and Neurology. Asst. prof. psychiatry U. Pitts., 1979-86; assoc. prof. psychiatry U. Mass., Worcester, 1986-89, Case Western Res. U., Cleve., 1990-91, Northeastern Ohio U. Coll. Medicine, Rootstown, 1991-98, prof. psychiatry, 1998—. Fellow Am. Psychiat. Assn.; mem. Am. Assn. Cmty. Psychiatrists. Office: 100 W Cedar St # 300 Akron OH 44307-2502 E-mail: mmunetz@neoucom.edu.

MUNEVAR, GONZALO, philosophy educator, writer; b. Barranquilla, Atlantico, Colombia, Mar. 4, 1945; came to U.S., 1965; s. Gonzalo and Delia Munevar; 1 child, Ryan. BA in Philosophy, Calif. State U., Northridge, 1970, MA in Philosophy, 1971; PhD in Philosophy, U. Calif., Berkeley, 1975. Lectr. San Francisco State U., 1975-76; from asst. prof. to prof. philosophy U. Nebr., Omaha, 1976-89; prof. Evergreen State Coll., Olympia, Wash., 1989-97; chair humanities and social scis., prof. Lawrence Tech. U., Southfield, Mich.,

1999—. Vis. prof. Stanford (Calif.) U., 1983-84, Consejo Nacional, Madrid, Spain, 1987, Kobe (Japan) Shodai, 1993; vis. rsch. prof. U. Calif., Irvine, 1997-99. Author: Radical Knowledge, 1981, Evolution and the Naked Truth, 1998, The Master of Fate, 2000; editor: Beyond Reason, 1991, Spanish Studies on the Philosophy of Science, 1996, The Worst Enemy of Science?, 2000. Staff sgt. USAF, 1965-68. Fellow Stanford Humanties Ctr., 1983, Ctr. for Advanced Studies, U. Edinburgh, 1989; grantee NSF, 1979, Am. Coun. Learned Socs., 1977. Mem. AAAS, Am. Philos. Assn., Philosophy Sci. Assn. Avocations: soccer, movies, literature. Office: Lawrence Tech U 21000 W Ten Mile Rd Southfield MI 48075 E-mail: munevar@ltu.edu.

MUNGER, BENSON SCOTT, former professional society administrator; b. St. Johns, Mich., Jan. 21, 1942; s. Kenneth L. and Doris (Benson) M.; m. Bette Louise Johnson, June 15, 1963; children: Heidi Lynn, Chad Benson BA, Mich. State U., 1965, PhD, 1969. Tchr. Grand Ledge Pub. Schs., Mich., 1965-66; mem. staff Southwest Regional Lab, Los Angeles, 1969-70; dir. negotiations Mich. Edn. Assn., East Lansing, 1970-75; vis. asst.prof. Indsl. Relations Ctr., U. Minn., Mpls., 1975-76; dep. exec. dir. Am. Coll. Emergency Physicians, 1976-80; exec. dir. Am. Bd. Emergency Medicine, East Lansing, Mich., 1980-2000, chmn. com. bd. execs., 1991; exec. dir. Am. Bd. Vascular Surgery , 2002—. Commr. City of St. Johns, 1983—; bd. dirs. Old Kent Bank, St. Johns; cons. in field; chmn. com. bd. reps. and execs. Am. Bd. Med. Specialties, 1995—. Contbr. articles in field Mich. State U. fellow, 1966-69 Mem. Am. Soc. Assn. Execs., Am. Assn. Med. Soc. Execs. Office: Am Bd Vascular Surgery 221 W Walton Chicago IL 60610*

MUNGER, BRYCE LEON, physician, educator; b. Everett, Wash., May 20, 1933; s. Leon C. and Lina (Eaton) M.; m. Donna Grace Bingham, July 20, 1957; children: Ailene, D'Arcy, Gareth Torrey, Bryce Kirtley. Student, U. Wash., 1951-54; MD magna cum laude, Wash. U., 1958. Intern in pathology Johns Hopkins U., 1958-59; asst. prof. anatomy Washington U., St. Louis, 1961-65; assoc. prof. U. Chgo., 1965-66; prof. Milton S. Hershey Med. Ctr., Pa. State U., 1966-91, chmn. dept. anatomy, 1966-87; prof., head dept. anatomy U. Tasmania, Hobart, and Tasmania, Australia, 1992-96; adj. prof. anatomy Ariz. Coll. Osteo. Medicine, Midwestern U., Glendale, 1999. Bd. dirs. Pa. Spl. Olympics Inc. With M.C., USAF, 1959-61. Mem. AAAS, Am. Assn. Anatomists, Am. Soc. Cell Biology, Phi Beta Kappa, Sigma Xi, Alpha Omega Alpha.

MUNGER, EDWIN STANTON, political geography educator; b. LaGrange, Ill., Nov. 19, 1921; s. Royal Freeman and Mia (Stanton) M.; m. Ann Boyer, May 2, 1970; 1 child, Elizabeth Stanton Gibson. B.Sc., U. Chgo., 1948, M.Sc., 1949, PhD, 1951. Fulbright fellow Makerere U., 1949-50; research fellow U. Chgo.; field assoc. Am. Univs. Field Staff, 1950-60; faculty Calif. Inst. Tech., Pasadena, 1961—, prof. polit. geography, 1960—. Research fellow Stellenbosch U., 1955-56; vis. prof. U. Warsaw, 1973 *Professor Munger has traveled extensively to over 300 countries including all the nations of Africa and North and South America out of the joy of travel, professional research and to enhance his superb collection of ethnic chess sets by finding them or commissioning local artists. In pursuing knowledge of his African specialty he gas made over 80 visits to the continent, swum all its major rivers and climbed its highest mountain Kilimanjario.* Author books including Afrikaner and African Nationalsim, 1968, The Afrikaners, 1979, Touched by Africa: An Autobiography, 1983, Cultures, Chess and Art: A Collector's Odyssey Across Seven Continents, Vol. 1 Sub Saharan Africa, 1996, Vol. 2, Americas, 1997, Pacific Islands and the Asian Rim, Vol. 3, 1999, 10 short stories for kids--L.A. Times on Africa, 2001-02; editor books including Munger Africana Library Notes, 1969-82; contbr. chpts. to books and numerous articles to profl. jours. Evaluator Peace Corps, Uganda, 1966, Botswana, 1967; chmn. State Dept. Evalustion Team South Africa, 1971; trustee African-Am. Inst., 1956-62; acting pres. Pasadena Playhouse, 1966; chmn. bd. trustees Crane Rogers Found., 1979-82, fellow, 1950-54; mem. exec. com. NAACP, Pasadena, 1979—, nat. del., 1984, 85; trustee Leakey Found., 1968—, pres., 1971-84; pres. Cape of Good Hope Found., 1985—; pres. Internat. Vis. Coun., L.A., 1991-93, bd. dirs., 1979-93. Recipient Alumni Citation award for pub. svc. U. Chgo., 1993, Gandhi Martin Luther King-Ikeda award Morehouse U., 2002. Fellow South African Royal Soc., Royal Soc. Arts, African Studies Assn. (founding bd. dirs. 1963-66, Martin L. King Ikeda-Mahatma Gandhi award 2002); mem. PEN USA West (v.p.), Coun. Fgn. Rels., Cosmos Club, Athenaeum Club, Twilight Club, Chess Collectors Internat. (bd. dirs. 1998—). Office: Calif Inst Tech Divsn Humanities & Social Scis 1201 E California Blvd Pasadena CA 91125-0001 E-mail: munger@hss.caltech.edu.

MUNGER, ELMER LEWIS, civil engineer, educator; b. Manhattan, Kans., Jan. 4, 1915; s. Harold Hawley and Jane (Green) M.; m. Vivian Marie Bloomfield, Dec. 28, 1939; children: John Thomas, Harold Hawley II, Jane Marie. BS, Kans. State U., 1936, MS, 1938; PhD, Iowa State U., 1957. Registered profl. engr., Nebr., Kans., Iowa, Vt.; registered pvt. land surveyor Republic of The Philippines. Rodman St. Louis-Southwestern Ry., Ark., Mo., 1937-38; engr. U.S. Engr. Dept., Ohio, Nebr., 1938-46; missionary engr. Philippine Episcopal Ch., 1946-48; engr. Wilson & Co., Salina, Kans., 1948; tchr. Iowa State U., 1948-51, 54-58; engr. C.E., U.S. Army, Alaska, 1951-54; from tchr. to dean Norwich U., Northfield, Vt., 1958-69; prof. gen. enging. U. P.R., Mayagüez, 1969-75; prof. civil enging. Mich. Tech. U., 1975-80; ret. Mem. spl. com. on enging. Inter-Am. Devel. Bank, U. W.I., 1971. Author: (with Clarence J. Douglas) Construction Management, 1970. Fellow ASCE; mem. NSPE, Vt. Soc. Profl. Engrs., Am. Soc. Engring. Edn., Phi Kappa Phi, Sigma Tau, Tau Beta Pi, Chi Epsilon. Clubs: Masons, Shriners. Episcopalian. Home: 1527 N Washington St Hutchinson KS 67501-4077

MUNGER, HAROLD CHARLES, architect; b. Toledo, July 25, 1929; s. Harold Henry and Lela Marie (Hoffman) M.; m. Patricia Ann Billeter, Oct. 2, 1954; children: Hal Peter, Peter Charles, David James. B.Arch., U. Notre Dame, 1951; cert., Davis Bus. Coll., 1947, U. Toledo, 1949, 50, Toledo Mus. Art, 1954, Leica Sch., 1982. Registered architect, Ohio, Mich., Ind., cert. Nat. Council Arctl. Registration Bds. Draftsman atomic energy br. Giffels & Vallet, Architects and Engrs., Detroit, 1951-52; chief designer, assoc. Britsch and Munger, Architects, Toledo, 1952-55; chief architect, ptnr. Munger, Munger and Assocs., Architects, 1955-70, owner, proprieter, 1970-83; pres. Munger, Munger and Assocs., Inc., from 1983. Mem. nat. exam. evaluation com. Nat. Council Archtl. Registration Bds., Washington, 1983; presenter Ohio Assn. Sch. Officials, 1985; charter mem. Historic Dist. Design Rev. Bd., City of Perrysburg, Ohio, 1982— ; mem. mayors com. planning, City of Perrysburg, mem. downtown task force, 1985; mem. archtl. jury Nat. Sch. Bds. Assn., 1961— ; mem. pres.'s council Toledo Mus. Art, 1985— ; mem. archtl. ann. awards jury Ind. Masonry Inst., 1988. Author: Housing Physically Disabled Elderly, 1964; co-author: Lucas County Bldg. Code, 1955-56; assoc. editor: Ohio Architect, 1955-58, Architectural Graphics Standard, 8th edit., 1986— . Dist. officer, merit badge counselor, committeeman Toledo Area Boy Scouts Am., 1953— ; mem. Vocat. Tech. High Sch. Bldg. Trades Adv. Com., Toledo, 1956-79, Perrysburg 1st City Charter Commn., 1960-62; co-chmn. Chase Park Urban Renewal Adv. awards Com., Toledo, 1962-65; pres. St. Rose Bd. of Edn., Perrysburg, 1966-69; trustee Way Pub. Library, 1960-80, Historic Perrysburg, Inc., 1977-81. Recipient Pub. and Comml. award Toledo Area Concrete Assn., 1965, Indsl. award Toledo Area Concrete Assn., 1973, Boss of Yr. award Per Ro Ma chpt. Am. Bus. Women's Assn., 1977, Bus. Assoc. of Yr. award, 1985, St. George award Cath. Com. on Scouting, Diocese of Toledo, 1978, Masonry Honor award Masonry Inst. Northwestern Ohio, 1981, 85 (2 awards), 86, 87, 89 (2 awards), 92, 95, 97; Excellence in Masonry Design award Ohio Masonry Coun., 1986, 88, Man of Yr. award U. Notre Dame Alumni Club of Toledo, 1987, Best Project award Internat. Union Bricklayers, 1989, Toledo Design Forum award of excellence in architecture, 1991. Fellow AIA (nat. committeeman design, inquiry, housing, architecture for edn. 1965—, pres., past. bd. dirs., Devoted Service award 1963, Architect of Yr. award Toledo chpt. 1991); mem. Constrn. Specifications Inst. (charter mem. cert. of recognition), AIA Architects Soc. Ohio (pres., past dir. Silver Gavel award, 1969, honor award 1981, 86, 88, Gold medal award 1987 Ohio chpt., 25-Yr. Bldg. award of excellence 1991, AIA Ohio Gold Medal Firm of Yr., 1995), Toledo Club, Rotary (charter, cert. of recognition). Home: Perrysburg, Ohio. *Principles: less is more. Ideas: Judged by what we do. Goals: Self-respect and self-reliance.* Died July 17, 2001.

MUNGER, HAROLD HAWLEY, II, city engineer; b. Manila, Nov. 28, 1947; s. Elmer Lewis and Vivian Marie (Bloomfield) M.; m. Judith Ann Stacy, Aug. 27, 1977; children: Stacy J., Michelle A., Karrie R. Student, Norwich U., 1966-68; BSCE, Kans. State U., 1970. Registered profl. engr. Kans., Colo. Survey party instr. Vt. Hwy. Dept., Montpelier, 1968; design engr. Wilson & Co. Engrs., Salina, Kans., 1975-80, office mgr. Hays, 1980-85; asst. city engr. City of Hutchinson (Kans.), 1985-87, city engr., 1987—. Mem. exec. bd. Pioneer Country Devel. Inc., Hill City, Kans., 1980-85, v.p., 1984-85; mem. exec. bd. Northwestern Kans. Planning and Devel., Hill City, 1984-85; bd. dirs. Commerce Garden Apts., 1996—, v.p., 1997, pres., 1998—. Capt. U.S. Army, 1971-75. Mem. NSPE, Water Environ. Tech., Am. Water Works Assn., Am. Pub. Works Assn., Kans. Soc. Profl. Engrs. (membership chmn. 1987-88, bd. dirs. 1992—), Appaloosa Horse Club, Am. Quarter Horse Assn. Avocations: golf, skiing, horseback riding. Office: City of Hutchinson PO Box 1567 125 E Avenue B Hutchinson KS 67501-7422

MUNGER, JAMES GUY, protective services executive; b. Elyria, Ohio, Aug. 9, 1951; s. William James and Patricia Ann (Mederith) M.; m. Karen Ann Johnson, Oct. 30, 1971; 1 child, Jennifer Lisa. AAS in Fire Sci., Wallace State C.C., 1979; BS in Fire Sci., Memphis State U., 1994, PhD in Occup. Safety and Health Engring.; postgrad., U. Ala., Birmingham; MS in Fire Sci. and Safety, Western States U., 1995; D in occupational safety and health engring., Columbia So. U., 1999. Cert. Fire Fighter I, Instr. I, Fire Prevention/Investigation Officer I, Fire Prevention Officer II, III, Fire Investigation Officer II, III, Ala. Fire Fighters' Personnel Standards & Tng. Commn., Fire Protection Specialist, Fire Protection Certification Bd., Pa. Plant maintenance supr. Challenger Homes, Columbia, Tenn., 1972-74; pvt. practice Cullman (Ala.) Appliance & Refrigeration, 1972-79; fireman City of Cullman, 1980-85; dep. state fire marshal State of Ala., Montgomery, 1980-85; pvt. practice Cullman, 1985—. Bd. dirs. Soc. Nat. Fire Acad. Instrs., Ala.; adj. faculty Fed. Emergency Mgmt. Agy. Nat. Fire Acad., Emmitsburg, Md., Ala. State Fire Coll., Tuscaloosa, Ala.; expert on fire protection and investigation state and fed. cts. Fire commr. Cullman City Coun., 1992-96, City of Cullman, 1992-96. Mem. Soc. Fire Protection Engrs., Instn. Fire Engrs., Am. Fire Sprinkler Assn., Assn. Fire Protection Designers, C. of C. (pub. safety com.), Nat. Fire Protection Agy., Architects, Inst. Fire Engrs., Engrs. and Bldg. Ofcls. Sect., Fire Marshals Assn. No. Am., Internat. Assn. Elec. Insps., So. Std. Bldg. Code Congress Internat., Inc., Internat. Conf. Bldg. Ofcls., Bldg. Ofcls. and Code Adminstrs. Internat., Inc. Republican. Presbyterian. Avocations: gun collector, tropical fish collector. Office: PO Box 1773 Cullman AL 35056-1773

MUNGER, MICHAEL CURTIS, public policy educator; b. Orlando, Fla., Sept. 23, 1958; s. Herbert Elmer and Marjorie (Guernsey) M.; m. Donna Marie Gingerella, July 5, 1986; 1 child, Kevin Michael. BA, Davidson Coll., 1980; MA, Washington U., St. Louis, 1982, PhD, 1984. Rsch. analyst Ctr. Study Am. Bus., St. Louis, 1982-83; rsch. economist FTC, Washington, 1984-86; prof. econs. Dartmouth Coll., Hanover, N.H., 1985-86; prof. polit. sci. U. Tex., Austin, 1986-90, U. N.C., Chapel Hill, 1990—. Coord. policy analysis concentration Masters in Pub. Adminstrn. Program U. N.C.; cons. in field. Co-author: lSpatial Theory of Ideology, 1992; contbr. articles to profl. jours. Mem. Am. Econ. Assn., So. Econ. Assn., Pub. Choice Soc., Midwest Polit. Sci. Assn. Office: Univ North Carolina Dept Polit Sci Chapel Hill NC 27599-0001

MUNGER, PAUL DAVID, company executive, educational administrator; b. Selma, Ala., Oct. 12, 1945; s. Paul Francis and Arlene Lorraine (McFillen) M.; m. Paula Jean Dominici, May 30, 1969; children: Kimberley Beth, Christopher David. AB in Philosophy, Kenyon Coll., 1967; MA in Govt., Ind. U., 1969. Commd. 2d lt. USAF, 1969, advanced through grades to capt., resigned, 1978; asst. dir. faculty devel. Ind. U., Bloomington, 1974-77; from asst. dean to dean continuing studies Am. U., Washington, 1980-83, asst. provost acad. devel., 1983-84; dir. Commn. on Future Acad. Leadership, 1984-86; v.p. Acad. Strategies, 1986-88; pres. Strategic Edn. Svcs. Inc., Sterling, Va., 1988—. Bd. dirs. Munger Acad. Bd. advisors Madeira Sch., McLean, Va., 1993-96; treas. Bus.-Higher Edn. Fedn., Washington, 1992—; asst. scoutmaster Boy Scouts Am., 1991-93, scoutmaster, 1994-97; dir. Czech-am. LaCrosse Found., 1996—; bd. dirs. Thomas Jefferson H.S. for Sci. and Tech. Found., 1999-2001, PTSA, 1996-98, chair bus. rels. com., 1996-98. Mem. Am. Soc. Tng. & Devel. (chmn. strategic planning com. 1993-95, continuing profl. edn. electronic forum coord. 1995-97), Assn. Continuing Higher Edn., Am. Soc. Curriculum Devel. Office: Strategic Education Services Inc 624 W Church Rd Sterling VA 20164-4608 E-mail: pdmunger@strategicedservices.com.

MUNGER, PAUL R. civil engineering educator; b. Hannibal, Mo., Jan. 14, 1932; s. Paul Oettle and Anne Lucille (Williams) M.; m. Frieda Ann Mette, Nov. 26, 1954; children: Amelia Ann Munger Fortmeyer, Paul David, Mark James, Martha Jane Munger Cox. BSCE, Mo. Sch. Mines and Metallurgy, 1958, MSCE, 1961; PhD in Engring. Sci., U. Ark., 1972. Registered profl. engr., Mo., Ill., Ark., Minn. Instr. civil enging Mo. Sch. Mines and Metallurgy, Rolla, 1958-61, asst. prof., 1961-65; assoc. prof. U. Mo., 1965-73, prof., 1973-99, prof. emeritus, 2000—; dir. Inst. River Studies, U. Mo., 1976-93; exec. dir. Internat. Inst. River and Lake Systems, U. Mo., 1984-93, interim chmn. CE dept., 1998-99, prof. emeritus, 2000. Mem. NSPE, Mo. Soc. Profl. Engrs., Am. Soc. Engring. Edn., ASCE, Nat. Coun. Engring. Examiners (pres. 1983-84), Mo. Bd. Architects, Profl. Engrs. and Land Surveyors (chmn. 1978-84, 95-2002).

MUNGER, THOMAS JOGUES, lawyer; b. Detroit, Jan. 26, 1960; s. James Elliot and Patricia Ann M.; m. Virginia Gayle Morrow, July 5, 1986; children: Alexander James, Patrick Thomas. BA, Mich. State U., 1982; JD, U. N.C., 1985. Bar: Ga. 1985. Assoc. Kilpatrick & Stockton, Atlanta, 1985-89; atty. Delta Air Lines, Inc., 1989-92, sr. atty., 1992-94, gen. atty., 1995-98, asst. gen. counsel, 1998—2001; founding ptnr. Munger & Stone, LLP, 2001—. Spkr. in field. Democrat. Presbyterian. Avocations: traveling, public speaking. Home: 819 Wildwood Rd NE Atlanta GA 30324-4911 Office: 2850 First Union Plz 100 Peachtree St Atlanta GA 30309

MUNGIA, SALVADOR ALEJO, lawyer; b. Tacoma, Feb. 19, 1959; s. Salvador Alejo Sr. and Susie (Tamaki) M. BA, Pacific Luth. U., 1981; JD, Georgetown U., 1984. Bar: Wash. 1984, U.S. Dist. Ct. (we. dist.) Wash. 1985, U.S. Ct. Appeals (9th cir.) 1986, U.S. Supreme Ct. 1992. Law clk. to Justice Fred Dore Wash. State Supreme Ct., Olympia, 1984-85; law clerk to Hon. Carolyn R. Dimmick U.S. Dist. Ct. (we. dist.) Wash., Seattle, 1985-86; assoc. Gordon, Thomas, Honeywell, Malanca, Peterson & Daheim, Tacoma, 1986-91, ptnr., 1991—. Adj. prof. Pacific Luth. U., 1993-94. Vol. atty. ACLU, Tacoma, 1986—, bd. dirs., 1987-92; commr. Tacoma Human Rights Commn., 1990-96; bd. dirs. Legal Aid for Washington, 1992-96, life bd. dirs., 1997—, pres., 2002. Recipient Am. Leadership Forum fellowship, 2001—02. Mem.: ABA, Pierce County Young Lawyers Assn. (trustee 1988—90), Tacoma-Pierce County Bar Assn. (pres. 1999), Fed. Bar Assn. Western Wash., Wash. State Bar Assn., Tacoma Club, Tacoma Lawn Tennis Club. Avocations: mountain climbing, skiing, tennis, running. Home: 525 Broadway # 201 Tacoma WA 98402 Office: Gordon Thomas Honeywell Malance Peterson & Daheim PO Box 1157 Tacoma WA 98401-1157 E-mail: mungs@gth-law.com.

MUNHALL, EDGAR, retired curator, art history educator; b. Pitts., Mar. 14, 1933; s. Walter and Anna (Burns) Munhall; life ptnr. Richard Barsam. BA, Yale U., 1955, PhD, 1959; MA, NYU, 1957. Instr. art history Yale U., New Haven, 1959-64, asst. prof., 1964-65; curator The Frick Collection, N.Y.C., 1965-99; ret., 1999. Adj prof Columbia Univ, 1979, 1981—. Decorated chevalier and officer Ordre des Arts et des Lettres (France). Office: The Frick Collection 1 E 70th St New York NY 10021-4907 E-mail: munhall@frick.org.

MUNHALL, RUTH BEATRICE, business and financial consultant; b. Mendon, Mass., Feb. 8, 1929; d. Lawrence B. and Elsie B. (Gaskill) M. Grad. Salvation Army Officers Coll., Bronx, N.Y., 1951; MBA, Calif. Coast U., 1980, PhD, DBA, 1981. Civilian supr. U.S. Army and VA Hosp., Framingham, Mass., 1946-50; ordained clergywoman; officer Salvation Army centers in Mass., N.Y. and N.J., 1951-64; owner, operator acctg. and real estate firm, N.Y.C., 1964-68; supr. fiduciary and individual taxation Bank of N.Y., N.Y.C., 1968-79; cons. non profit orgns. founder R.M. Scholarship Info. Services, Ark., N.Y., Mass. and Israel, 1981-89; pres., chief exec. officer Munhall, Monahan, Chapman Fiduciary Animal Charities, Inc., 1984— ; pres. Munhall Rsch. Sci. Corp., 1985-97; cons. in field. Recipient 5 Yr. Civil Def. award Gov. N.Y. State. Author: (booklet) English, French, Hebrew, Spanish for the Traveler, 1990. Mem. DAR, Alumni Assn. Calif. Coast U. Republican.

MUNHOLLON, SAMUEL CLIFFORD, investment brokerage house executive; b. Harlan, Iowa, Jan. 12, 1948; s. Clifford Ferrell and Juanita Rosalie (Smith) M.; m. Tommie Verlene Gist, Mar. 16, 1973 (div. May 1977); m. Rosalie Jane Sholtes, May 21, 1981; stepchildren: Charles Randall Oglesby, Richard Martin Oglesby, Ronald Nelson Oglesby, Janelle Marie Oglesby Skelton, Robert Steven Oglesby. BS, Okla. State U., 1970; postgrad., So. Meth. U., 1970-71, Okla. State U., 1970-71. Cert. fgn. currency, index options, gen. securities prin., options prin.; registered rep. life-health-accident ins.; registered investment advisor; cert. estate planning specialist, retirement planning specialist, rule 144 specialist. Auditor Ernst & Ernst, Dallas, 1970-71; sr. analyst Champlin Petroleum Corp., Enid, Okla., 1971-72; chief acct., contr. Basin Petroleum Corp., Oklahoma City, 1972-75; account exec. A.G. Edwards & Sons, Inc., 1975-78; prin. ptnr. Adams, James, Foor Inc., 1978-79; v.p., br. mgr. Stix & Co. Inc., 1979-81; v.p. Smith Barney Harris Upham, 1981-82, Paine Webber Jackson Curtis, Oklahoma City, 1982-84, Stifel Nicolaus & Co. Inc., Oklahoma City, 1984-87, Morgan Stanley Dean Witter, Inc. (now Morgan Stanley), Oklahoma City, 1987-2001; 1st v.p. Morgan Stanley, 2001—. Mem. C.Am. task force U.S. Dept. Commerce, 1985—. Mem. Okla. Heritage Assn., Oklahoma City, 1988, Nat. Congl. Club, Raleigh, N.C., 1986—, Second Amendment Found., Bellevue, Wash., 1968—, Young Reps. Oklahoma City, 1966-88, Okla. Rep. Party, Oklahoma City, 1968—, Rep. Nat. Com., Washington, 1978—, Gun Owners Am., Falls Church, Va., 1979—, Okla. Coun. on Campaigning Compliance and Ethical Standards, Oklahoma City, 1988—, Rep. Sen. Inner Circle, Washington, 1988, Rep. Eagles, 1980-81, Citizens Com. for Right to Keep & Bear Arms, 1988—; bd. dirs. Okla. Shooting Sports, Inc., 1990—, Okla. Found. for Disabled, 1990-92, Northside YMCA, 1994—, Okla. Wildlife Fedn., 1994—; mem. Gov.'s Interstate Indian Affairs Coun., 1996, Lt. Gov.'s Grand Nat. Invitational Turkey Hunt Com., 1992—. Named Citizen of Yr., Presdl. Task Force, 1980, Citizen of Yr., Citizens Com. for Right To Keep and Bear Arms, 1993—; recipient award Am. Def. Inst., 1986. Mem. Sales and Mktg. Execs. Assn., NRA (life), Nat. Assn. Investment Brokers, Internat. Assn. Registered Reps. (state chair 1981-82), World Affairs Coun. Ctrl. Okla., Assn. Fin. Svc. Profls., Nat. Assn. Registered Reps., Security Industry Assn. (govt. rels. com. 1982-85), Stifel Nicolaus Club (pres. 1986, chmn. 1985, 87), Morgan Stanley Dirs. Club, Paine Webber Jackson Curtis Pace Setters Club, Nat. Wild Turkey Fed., Grand Nat. Quail Assn., N.Am. Found. Big Game, Ducks Unltd., Boone & Crockett Club, N.Am. Hunt Club, Okla. State U. Alumni Assn., Sons Confederate Vets., Safari Club Internat. (region 9 rep. 1995-96), Rotary (bd. dirs., sec. 1991, v.p. 1992, pres.-elect 1993, pres. 1994, 95, program chmn. N.W. chpt. 1989—, pres. 1994, dist. treas. 2000—, edn. rep., newsletter editor, hunt chmn.), Safari Club Internat. (chpt. bd. 1991—, dirs., chpt. v.p. 1991, pres.-elect 1992, pres. 1993-94, 94-95, membership com., ethics com., internat. bd. dirs. 1993—, ednl. rep., newsletter editor, hunt chmn.), Sierra Club, Oklahoma City Gun Club, Rotary (N.W. Oklahoma City, dist. 5750 treas., 2000-01, fin. com. chmn., 2000—), Tau Kappa Epsilon Alumni Assn. Republican. Avocations: hunting, gun collecting, sporting clays, volleyball, racquetball. Home: 10830 N Bryant Ave Oklahoma City OK 73131-5017 Office: Morgan Stanley 501 E 15th St Edmond OK 73013-5043 E-mail: smunhollon@aol.com.

MUNIAIN, JAVIER P. computer software company executive, theoretical physicist, researcher; b. Madrid, Apr. 4, 1966; came to U.S., 1989. s. Luis Perez De Muniain y Leal and Crescencia Mohedano Hernandez. BSc, U. Complutense of Madrid, 1990; M. in Physics, U. Calif., Riverside, 1992, PhD in Theoretical Physics, 1996. Rsch., tchg. asst. U. Calif., Riverside, 1992-96; pres., founder Surfernet, San Diego, 1996—, Madrid, Spain, 1996, exec. pres., CEO Spain, 1997; CEO, co-founder Adventureland.com, San Diego, 1997. Co-founder J&R Global, Ltd., Naples, Fla., 1997. Author: Gauge Fields, Knots and Gravity, 1994; contbr. articles to profl. jours. Mem. Am. Phys. Soc., Riverside Wine Tasing Soc. (co-founder 1994). Avocations: classic cars, chess, surfing, antiques, architecture. Home: Avenida General Mola 36 11 Pozuelo de Alarcon Madrid 28224 Spain

MUNIC, MARTIN DANIEL, lawyer; b. Duluth, Minn., Feb. 16, 1959; s. Robert Solomon and Pearl (Daniels) M.; m. Barbara Stimson, May 30, 1993; 1 child, Sophia Miriam. BA, Drake U., 1981; JD, U. Minn., 1984. Bar: Minn. 1984, U.S. Dist. Ct. Minn. 1986, U.S. Ct. Appeals (8th cir.) 1989. Law clk. to Hon. Harry H. MacLaughlin U.S. Dist. Ct., Mpls., 1984-86; assoc. Tanick & Heins, 1986-89, Opperman Heins & Paquin, Mpls., 1989-92; asst. county atty. Hennepin County Atty.'s Office, 1993—. Bd. dirs. Loan Assistance Repayment Program Minn., 1991-96, pres., 1991-94; arbitrator Nat. Futures Assn., Nat. Assn. Securities Dealers. Contbr. articles to profl. jours. Vol. atty. Minn. Civil Liberties Union, Mpls., 1988—92; alt. Dem.-Farmer-Labor State Conv., 1990, 2002, del., 1994; bd. dirs. Minn. NARAL, 1995—99, NARAL PAC, 1998—, pres., 2002—. Recipient William O. Douglas award U. Minn., 1984, Edward J. Devitt award, 1983. Mem. Minn. Justice Found. (bd. dirs. 1983-84, 88-92, pres. bd. dirs. 1989-91), Minn. Assn. Parliamentarians, Nat. Assn. Parliamentarians, Hennepin County Bar Assn., Order of Coif, Phi Beta Kappa. Jewish. Avocations: baseball, cross-country skiing. Office: Hennepin County Atty Office A2000 Government Ctr Minneapolis MN 55487-0001 E-mail: martin.munic@co.hennepin.mn.us.

MUNIC, RACHELLE ETHEL, health services administrator; b. Hartford, Conn., Apr. 15, 1953; d. Abe and Sara (Levenberg) M. BS in Med. Tech. summa cum laude, U. Bridgeport, 1975; physician asst. cert., Yale U., 1979; MBA in Health & Med. Svcs. Adminstrn., Widener U., 1991. Med. technologist St. Francis Hosp., Hartford, 1975-77; physician asst. Fox Chase Cancer Ctr., Phila., 1979-85; clin. dir. Fox Chase Network, 1986-92; adminstrv. dir., oncology Cooper Hosp., U. Med. Ctr., Camden, N.J., 1992-96, healthcare cons., 1996—; corp. mgr. cancer svcs. Grad. Health Sys., Phila., 1996—; cancer svc. line adminstr. Albert Einstein Med. Ctr., 1996-99; adminstrv. dir. divsn. med. oncology, hematology & genetics Jefferson U., 1999-2001; asst. v.p. Cooper Health Sys., 2001—. Mem. Cancer Prevention and Control Adv. Group to N.J. Commn. on Cancer Rsch., New Brunswick, N.J., 1993-96; mem. program com. Greater Phila. Health Assembly, 1996; presenter in field. Dana scholar U. Bridgeport, 1972; recipient Foster G. McGaw Scholarship award Assn. Univ. Programs in Health Adminstrn., 1990, Student award Hosp. Assn. Pa., 1992; Breast Cancer project grantee The Susan G. Komen Breast Cancer Found., Dallas, 1995. Mem. Am. Hosp. Assn., Am. Cancer Soc. (Camden County), Assn. Cancer Execs., Soc. Radiation Oncology Adminstrs., Assn. Cmty. Cancer Ctrs. (del.), Widener Alumni Assn. (pres. 1995), U. Bridgeport Asteria Honor Soc. Avocations: softball, golf, swimming, cross-country skiing, reading.

MUNIER, WILLIAM BOSS, medical service executive; b. Corning, N.Y., Dec. 8, 1942; s. John Hammond and Marguerite (Boss) M.; m. Sandra Lorraine Koerber, 1965 (div. 1976); m. Ann Elizabeth Wessel, 1980; children: Michael, Andrew, Laura. BA, U. Pa., 1964; MD, Columbia U., 1968; MBA, Harvard U., 1973. Diplomate Nat. Bd. Med. Examiners; lic. physician, surgeon, N.Y. Surg. intern Roosevelt Hosp., N.Y.C., 1968-69; profl. staff HEW, Washington, 1969-71, 73-75, dir. Office Quality Standards, 1975-77, dir. Office Health Practice Assessment, 1977-79; exec. v.p. Mass. Med. Soc., Boston, 1979-84; prin. Ernst & Whinney, 1984-85; pvt. practice mgmt. cons. Wellesley, Mass., 1985-86; dir. program for civilian peer rev. Commn. on Profl. and Hosp. Activities/Dept. Def., 1986-87; pres. Quality Standards in Medicine, Inc., Boston, 1986-99; chief med. officer Health Mgmt. Sys., Inc., Waltham, Mass., 1996-99; pres., CEO Wang Healthcare Info. Sys., Inc., Billerica, 1999—. Vis. prof. Harvard Sch. Pub. Health, Boston, 1980-90. Contbr. articles to profl. jours. Mem. human services com. Town of Wellesley, 1984-85. Served with USPHS, 1969-79. Mem. AMA, Mass. Med. Soc., St. Botolph Club, Capitol Hill Club. Republican. Episcopalian. Avocations: golf, skiing, music. Fax: (978) 670-1495. E-mail: bmunier@wanghealthcare.com.

MUNISTERI, JOSEPH GEORGE, construction executive; b. Rome, Sept. 24, 1930; s. Peter P. and Inez Gertrude (Ziniti) Munisteri; m. Theresa Grasso, June 7, 1952 (div. Dec. 2000); children: Joanne, Robert, Laura, Stephen, James, Richard; m. Barbra Coffman, Nov. 30, 2001. BE, Yale U., 1952. With Bechtel Corp., San Francisco, 1952-59; with The Lummus Co., N.Y.C., London and Houston, 1959-67, gen. mgr., 1964-67; sr. v.p. sales Brown & Root, Inc., Houston, 1967-75, group v.p. power div., 1975-80, group v.p. corp. devel., 1980-81, also bd. dirs.; pres. Enserch Engrs. & Constructors, Inc., 1981-85; exec. v.p. Ford, Bacon & Davis, Inc., Dallas, 1985-87; chmn., pres., CEO Comstock Group, Inc., Danbury, Conn., 1987-88; pres. Joseph G.

Munisteri Co., Houston, 1989—. Former chmn. bd. Pine-O-Pine. Former mem. Bd. dirs. Atomic Indsl. Forum; Bd. dirs. Am. Nuclear Energy Council. Mem. Atomic Indsl. Forum, Am. Inst. Chem. Engrs., Am. Nuclear Soc., Atomic Indsl. Forum, ASTM, Council Enging. Law, ASCE, Assn. Iron and Steel Engring., Assoc. Builders and Contractors (dir.), Yale Club of Houston, Yale Club of N.Y. Office: 4265 San Felipe St Ste 1100 Houston TX 77027-2998 E-mail: jmunisteri@houston.rr.com.

MUNITZ, BARRY, arts and foundation administrator; b. Bklyn., July 26, 1941; m. Anne Tomfohrde. BA, Bklyn. Coll., 1963; MA, Princeton U., 1965, PhD, 1968; cert., U. Leiden, Netherlands, 1962; hon. doctorate, Claremont U., Calif. State Univ. Sys., Whittier Coll., U. Notre Dame. Asst. prof. lit. and drama U. Calif., Berkeley, 1966-68; staff assoc. Carnegie Commn. Higher Edn., 1968-70; acad. v.p. U. Ill. System, 1971—76; v.p., dean faculties Central campus U. Houston, 1976-77, chancellor, 1977-82; pres., COO Federated Devel. Co., 1982-91; vice chmn. Maxxam Inc., L.A., 1982-91; chancellor Calif. State U. System, Long Beach, Calif., 1991-98; prof. English lit. Calif. State U., L.A., 1991—; pres., CEO, trustee J.Paul Getty Trust, 1998—. Bd. dirs. KCET-TV, SLM Holdings, KB Home; cons. in presdl. evaluation and univ. governance; trustee Princeton U. Author: The Assessment of Institutional Leadership, also articles, monographs. Mem. art mus. vis. com. Princeton and Harvard; former chair bd. dirs. ACE; former co-chair trustees planning com. Gardner Mus.; former chair Calif. Gov. Transition Team. Recipient Disting. Alumnus award Bklyn. Coll., 1979, U. Houston Alumni Pres.'s medal, 1981; Woodrow Wilson fellow. Fellow Am. Acad. Arts and Scis.; mem. Phi Beta Kappa. Office: J Paul Getty Trust 1200 Getty Center Dr Ste 400 Los Angeles CA 90049-1681 E-mail: bmunitz@getty.edu.

MUNK, PETER, mining executive; b. Budapest, Hungary, Nov. 8, 1927; arrived in Can., 1948; s. Louis L. and Katherine (Adler) M.; m. Linda Gutterson; children: Anthony, Nina; m. Melanie Jane Bosanquet, 1973; children: Natalie, Cheyne, Marc David. BASc in Elec. Engring., U. Toronto, Ont., Can., 1953, LLD, 1995, Upsala Coll., N.J., 1991, U. Toronto, Que., Can., 1995, Bishops Coll., 1995, Concordia U., Montreal, Que., 1999. Chmn., chief exec. officer So. Pacific Hotel Corp., Sydney, Australia, 1969-81; chmn. Barrick Resources, Toronto, 1981-83, Am. Barrick Resources Corp. (now Barrick Gold Corp.), Toronto, 1983—, The Horsham Corp., Toronto, 1987-96; CEO Trizec Hahn Corp., 1996—2000, chmn., 2001—. Bd. dirs. Trizec Hahn Corp. Ltd., World Gold Coun., Geneva. Trustee Toronto Hosp.; bd. dirs. U. Toronto Found. Decorated officer Order of Can. Office: Trizec Hahn Corp 181 Bay Street Ste 3900 Toronto ON Canada M5J 2T3

MUNK, ZEV MOSHE, allergist, researcher; b. Stockholm, July 14, 1950; m. Susan Deitcher; 4 children. BS, McGill U., 1972; MD, C.M., 1974. Licentiate Med. Coun. Can.; diplomate Am. Bd. Internal Medicine, Am. Bd. Allergy and Clin. Immunology. Intern Royal Victoria Hosp., Montreal, 1974-75, resident, 1975-76; resident in clin. immunology and allergy Montreal Gen. Hosp., 1976-78; practice medicine specializing in allergy/clin. immunology Houston, 1978—; founder, CEO Pharm-Olam Internat. Inc. Mem. staff Meml. City Med. Ctr., Meml. S.W., Spring Branch Meml., Cy-Fair hosps. (all Houston); clin. instr. allergy and clin. immunology Baylor Coll. Medicine, 1979—, U. Tex.-Houston, 1979—; pres. Breco Rsch. Contbr. articles to med. jours. Pres. Young Israel Synagogue of Houston, 1994-96; founder Allergy Ctr., P.A., Houston, Breco Rsch., Houston; founder, past pres. Torah and Outreach Resource Ctr. of Houston. McGill U. scholar, 1968-74. Fellow Am. Acad. Allergy, Am. Coll. Allergy and Immunogy, Royal Coll. Physician (Can.); mem. ACP, Am. Assn. Pharm. Physicians, Tex. Med. Assn., Que. Med. Assn., Am. Acad. Allergy, Tex. Allergy Soc., Harris County Med. Soc., Houston Allergy Soc. Office: 902 Frostwood Dr Ste 222 Houston TX 77024-2402 E-mail: zmunk@pharm-olam.com.

MUNKEL, WAYNE IRVIN, social worker; b. Osage, Iowa, Dec. 8, 1942; s. Irvin Walter and Roberta Genevieve (Cook) M.; m. Mary Josephine Keenan, Apr. 25, 1970; children: Christopher, Ann, Karen. BSc, Iowa State U., 1969; MSW, Washington U., St. Louis, 1972. LCSW, Mo. Social worker I Mo. Hills Home for Boys, St. Louis, 1969-72, social worker II, 1972-79; clinical social worker Cardinal Glennon Children's Hosp., 1980-96, supr. social svc., 1996—. Tchr. U. Mo., St. Louis, 1991—; with Mo. Child Fatality Review Panel, Jefferson City, 1999—. Contbr. articles to profl. jours., chpts. to books. Active City Coun. University City, Mo., 1996—. With U.S. Army, 1961-64. Recipient recognition for svc. St. Louis Circuit Atty. Office, 1987, recognition for tng. St. Charles Co. Law Enforcement Acad., 1987, Meritorious Svc. award U. Mo., St. Louis, 1998, recognition for work, Gtr. St. Louis Lead Coun., 1998. Mem. Nat. League of Cities, Mo. Mcpl. League (legis. com. 1996—), St. Louis Co. Mcpl. League, S.E. ASia Army Security Agy. Vets. Roman Catholic. Avocations: sound technician, prehistoric artifacts, hunting, wood working, travel. Home: 7543 Gannon Ave University City MO 63130 Office: Cardinal Glennon Children's Hosp 1465 S Grand Blvd Saint Louis MO 63104

MUNLU, KAMIL CEMAL, executive; b. Istanbul, Turkey, July 14, 1954; came to U.S., 1981; s. Adnan and Jale Sidika (Koniari) M. BA in Econs., Calif. State U., Long Beach, 1983; MBA in Bus. Adminstrn., Nat. U., San Diego, 1986, MS in Logistics, 1988; M in Internat. Bus. Adminstrn., U.S. Internat. U., San Diego, 1990; DPA, U. La Verne, Calif., 1995. Adj. prof. Woodbury U., Burbank, Calif., 1998—. Adj. prof. Nat. U., San Diego, 1999, U. La Verne, Calif., 2000. Mem. Turkish Army, 1984-85. Avocations: art, boating, golfing, reading, travel.

MUNN, CECIL EDWIN, lawyer; b. Enid, Okla., Aug. 8, 1923; s. Cecil Edwin and Margaret (Kittrell) M.; m. Carolyn Taylor Culver, May 8, 1948; children: Franklin Culver, Charlotte Munn Forswall. BA, U. Okla., 1945; JD cum laude, Harvard U., 1947. Bar: Okla. 1947, Tex. 1955. Practice in, Enid, 1947-54, Ft. Worth, 1954—; partner firm Cantey & Hanger, 1960-91, of counsel, 1992—. With Champlin Petroleum Co., 1954-60, v.p., atty., 1958-60, dir., 1962-75. Fellow Am. Coll. Trial Lawyers, Am. Bar Found.; mem. ABA (chmn. natural resources law sect. 1970-71), Southwestern Legal Found. (past dir.), Tex. Bar Found., Phi Delta Theta, Phi Delta Phi. Presbyterian. Office: 2100 Burnett Plz 801 Cherry St Fort Worth TX 76102-6803 Home: 1725 Hulen St fort Worth CO 76107-3828 *Some things in life are better decided wrong than left undecided. It is amazing how much one can accomplish if unconcerned with who gets the credit.*

MUNN, JANET TERESA, lawyer; b. De Funiak Springs, Fla., Nov. 7, 1952; d. Willard Ernest and Olive Pauline (Wilkinson) M.; m. Michael E. Fass, Sept. 27, 1975. BA in Anthropology, Fla. State U., 1975, MA in Social Scis., 1977; JD with high honors, Nova U., 1985. Bar: Fla. 1985, U.S. Dist. Ct. (so. dist.) Fla. 1986, U.S. Dist. Ct. (mid. dist.) Fla. 1988, U.S. Ct. Appeals (11th cir.) 1989, U.S. Supreme Ct. 1990. Jud. clerk for Judge Jose A. Gonzalez Jr. U.S. Dist. Ct. (so. dist.) Fla., Ft. Lauderdale, 1985-87; litigation assoc. Steel Hector & Davis, Miami, Fla., 1987-91, litigation ptnr., 1992—. Editor: Southern District Digest, 1987-88. Leo S. Goodwin fellow Nova U., 1983-84. Mem. ABA (co-chmn. intellectual properties litigation com. litigation sect. 1991-94, chmn. trade regulation/intellectual property com. gen. practice sect. 1990-91, vice chmn. 1989-90), Fed. Bar Assn., Fla. Bar (Pro Bono award 1988), Phi Kappa Phi. Office: 200 S Biscayne Blvd Ste 4000 Miami FL 33131-2362

MUNN, WILLIAM CHARLES, II, psychiatrist; b. Flint, Mich., Aug. 9, 1938; s. Elton Albert and Rita May (Coykendall) Munn; m. Sandra Lynn Munn; children from previous marriage: Jude Michael, Rachel Marie, Alexander Winston. Student, Flint Jr. Coll., 1958—59, U. Detroit, 1959—61; MD, Wayne State U., 1965. Diplomate Am. Bd. Psychiatry and Neurology (examiner). Intern David Grant USAF Med. Ctr., Travis AFB, Calif., 1965—66; resident in psychiatry Letterman Army Hosp., San Francisco, 1967—70; practice medicine, specializing in psychiatry Fairfield, 1972—. Flight surgeon, chief public health, chief phys. exam ctr. McGuire AFB, NJ, 1966—67; chief in-patient psychiatry David Grant Med. Ctr., 1970—71, chmn. dept. mental health, 1971—72; psychiat. cons. Fairfield-Suisan Unified Sch. Dist., 1971—, N. Bay Med. Ctr. (formerly Intercommunity Hosp.); Fairfield, 1971—, Casey Family Program, 1980—, Solano County Coroner's Office, 1981; asst. clin. prof. psychiatry U. Calif., San Francisco, 1976—; cons. Vaca Valley Hosp., Vacaville, Calif., 1988—, VA Hosp., San Francisco, 1976, David Grant USAF Hosp., 1976. Served to maj. M.C. USAF, 1964—72. Mem.: E. Bay Psychiat. Assn., No. Calif. Psychiat. Soc., Am. Psychiat. Assn. Office: 1245 Travis Blvd Ste E Fairfield CA 94533-4842 Fax: 707-422-8920.

MUNNEKE, GARY ARTHUR, law educator, consultant; b. Dec. 29, 1947; s. Leslie Earl and Margaret Frances (Fortsch) M.; children: Richard Arthur, Matthew Frederick. BA in Psychology, U. Tex., 1970, JD, 1973. Bar: Tex. 1973, Pa. 1987. Asst. dean, dir. placement U. Tex., Austin, 1978-80; asst. prof., asst. dean Del. Law Sch. Widener U., Wilmington, 1980-84, assoc. prof., 1984-87; pres. Legal Info. Sys., 1987-92; prof. Sch. Law Pace U., 1988—. Contbr. articles to profl. jours. Fellow Am. Bar Found., Coll. Law Practice Mgmt.; mem. ABA (chmn. standing com. on profl. utilization and career devel. 1981-85, chmn. law practice mgmt. sect. 1998-99, chmn. law practice mgmt. sect. pub. bd. 1992-95, articles editor Legal Econs. mag. 1984-86), State Bar Tex. Presbyterian. Office: Pace U Sch Law 78 N Broadway White Plains NY 10603-3710

MUNNEKE, RUSSELL EDWARD, music educator; b. Kansas City, Mo., Dec. 23, 1946; MusB, Baldwin-Wallace Coll., Berea, Ohio, 1969; MA, U. Iowa, 1973, D Mus. Arts, 1977. Rsch. and teaching asst. U. Iowa, Iowa City, 1969-75; vis. asst. prof. music Humboldt State U., Arcata, Calif., 1978-79; asst. prof. music Central Coll., Pella, Iowa, 1979-86; Fulbright lectr. in chamber music and theory Catholic U. Chile, Santiago, 1984; asst. prof. music Minot (N.D.) State U., 1986-92. Prin. viola Cedar Rapids (Iowa) Symphony, 1975-78; concertmaster Humboldt Symphony, Arcata, 1978-79, Minot Symphony Orch., 1986—; asst. prin. viola Des Moines Symphony, 1979-86. With U.S. Army, 1970-72. Grantee Central Coll., 1981-82, Fulbright Found., 1984, Kulas Found., Baldwin-Wallace Coll., 1965-69. Mem. Am. String Tchrs. Assn. (sec.-treas. Iowa chpt. 1984-86), Music Tchrs. Nat. Assn. (string chmn. Iowa chpt. 1980-81), Coll. Music Soc., Am. Fedn. Musicians, Pi Kappa Lambda.

MUNOZ, ALFREDO NECTARIO, emergency medicine physician, pediatrician; b. Quito, Ecuador, Feb. 28, 1944; s. Nectario and Fanny Munoz; m. Linda Marie Schlereth, May 22, 1972; children: Stephen, Mark, Kathy, Eric, Amy. MD, Ctrl. U. Ecuador, 1974. Diplomate Am. Bd. Emergency Medicine, Am. Bd. Pediatrics. Intern Allegheny Gen. Hosp., Pitts., 1970-71; resident in pediatrics Children's Hosp. Kings Daughters, Norfolk, Va., 1971-74; mem. staff Sewickley (Pa.) Valley Hosp., 1977—. Fellow Am. Acad. Pediatrics; mem. AMA. Office: Sewickley Valley Hosp Emergency Medicine Sewickley PA 15143-9117

MUÑOZ, CARLOS RAMÓN, retired bank executive; b. N.Y.C., Dec. 8, 1935; s. Alejandro and Gladys Helena (Judah) Muñoz; m. Wilhelmina Elaine North, June 8, 1957 (div. 1993); children: Carla Christine, Kyle Alexander; m. Kassie Ohtaka, Sept. 23, 2000. BA, Columbia U., 1957, MA, 1961. Insp., ofcl. asst. Citibank N.A., N.Y.C., 1959-64, from asst. mgr. to mgr. Dominican Republic, P.R., 1965-70, asst. v.p., 1971-72, v.p.. dept. head, 1972-78; sr. v.p., regional mgr. and dir. Citicorp USA, San Francisco, 1978-81, sr. v.p. mem. credit policy com., 1982-95; exec. v.p., chief credit and risk mgmt. officer Dime Savs. Bank, N.Y.C., 1995-2000; pres., dir. Dime Consulting Group, 1999-2000. Adv. coun. Credit Rsch. Ctr., 1994-2000; bd. dirs. N. Am. Mortgage Corp., 1998-2000. Mem. Columbia U. Senate, 2001—; v.p. Episcopal Mission Soc., 1995—2000; trustee Episcopal Diocese of NY, 1994—2001, Cathedral of St. John the Divine, 1998—; bd. dir. Episcopal Mission Soc., NYC, 1974—2000, Inner City Scholarship Fund, 1984—95. 1st lt. USAR, 1958—64. Recipient Productivity award State Senator Diane Watson, L.A., 1981, John Jay award for Disting. Profl. Achievement Columbia Coll., 2001; named Fairfield County Alumnus of Yr., 1989-90. Mem. Columbia Coll. Alumni Assn. (bd. dirs., treas. 1988-92, v.p., 1992-93, 1st v.p. 1994-96, pres. 1996-98), Columbia Club. Republican.

MUNOZ, JOHN JOSEPH, retired transportation company executive; b. Salinas, Calif., Jan. 18, 1932; s. John Fernando and Naomal (Smith) M.; m. Phyllis Taylor, Feb. 6, 1961 (div. 1978); children: Sam, Kathy, Toni; m. Rachel Canales, Nov. 24, 1979; children: Michelle, Monique. AA, Allan Hancock Coll., 1956; student, San Jose State U., 1981, Western Sierra Law Sch. Ops. mgr. So. Pacific Milling Co., Santa Maria, Calif., 1971-77; cons. Govt., Venezuela, 1977-78; fleet supt. Granite Rock Co., San Jose, Calif., 1978-80; plant mgr. Granite Constrn. Co., Greenfield, 1980-85; mgr. transpn. Ball, Ball & Brosmer Inc., Danville, 1985-86; ops. mgr., bd. dirs. Sorrento Ready Mix Co., Del Mar, 1986-89; trans. cons. Greenfield, 1991-96; ret., 1996. Cons. Dept. Agrl. Devel., Maricaibo, Venezuela, 1976—. Commr. Planning Commn., Greenfield, Calif., 1982-85; mem. fund raising com. Broccoli Festival, Greenfield, 1983-85; dir. Soledad Prison Vocat. Tng., 1982-85. Lt. 11th Ranger Airborne, U.S. Army, 1950-52, Korea. Mem. Am. Concrete Inst., Calif. Trucking Assn., Los Californianos, Rotary, Lions, Elks. Republican. Avocations: hunting, fishing, auto racing, photography. Home and Office: PO Box 3654 Greenfield CA 93927-3654 E-mail: 11ranger@pronet.net.

MUNOZ, LILIA ANA, lawyer; b. Bayamo, Cuba, Apr. 16, 1959; came to the U.S., 1967; d. Jose Ernesto and Lidia Rosa (Ros) M.; m. Roberto Muniz, Oct. 11, 1986; children: Lilia Cristina, Roberto Jose. BA in Polit. Sci., Seton Hall U., 1981; JD, Rutgers U., 1984. Bar: N.J. 1984, Fed. Dist. Ct. 1984. Assoc. Robert Menendez, P.A., Union City, N.J., 1984-88; ptnr. Menendez & Munoz, P.A., 1988-90; pvt. practice West N.Y., N.J., 1990—. Mem. West N.Y. Alcoholic Beverage Control Bd., 1996—; trustee Legal Svcs. Hudson County, Jersey City, N.J., 1994—; West N.Y. mpcl. prosecutor, 1997—; chief mcpl. ct. judge City of Union City, N.J., 2000—. Active Bergen County Rep. Club, Hackensack, N.J., 1995—2000, Bergen County Hispanic Rep. Orgn., 1997—2000, Bergen County Women's Rep. Club, 1997—2000. Mem. N.J. Hispanic Bar Assn. (Hudson County regional trustee 1995—2001), Hudson County Bar Assn. (membership sec. 1997-98, immediate past pres. 2001-02), Rotary Club. Roman Catholic. Avocations: tennis, swimming, travel. Office: 5202 Bergenline Ave West New York NJ 07093-5524 E-mail: lilia_16-@mns.com.

MUNOZ, MARIO ALEJANDRO, civil engineer, retired consultant; b. Havana, Cuba, Feb. 27, 1928; came to U.S., 1961, naturalized, 1968; s. Ramón and Concepción (Bermudo) M.; m. Julia Josephine Garrofe, Jan. 17, 1970. *Cuba-born wife Julia chose exile in 1960, and came to the U.S. in 1962, via Spain. Her volunteer and Philanthropic endeavors in Chicago are many: Board member of the Cardinal's Committee in the mid-1960's, Chicago Symphony Docent, Art Institute Docent, Board member of the Women's Association of the Chicago Symphony, Co-chair of the "Eternal Feminine" project at Ravinia Festival 2000, advisor of the "Crossing Boundaries" 2002 project for the Illinois Humanities Council. She and her husband are patrons of the St. James Steeplechase.* M.Arch., U. Havana, 1954; postgrad., City Colls., Chgo., 1974, U. Wis., 1974. Owner Muñoz Bermudo-Construcciones, Havana, 1954-61; designer various cos. Chgo., 1961-65; designer Chgo. Transit Authority, Mdse. Mart, 1965-69; civil engr. Dept. Water and Sewers, City of Chgo., 1969-79; supervising engr. Dept. of Sewers, 1979-85, coordinating engr., 1985-88, asst. chief engr., 1988-93. Mem. ctrl. area subway sys. utilities com. City of Chgo., 1974-93, mem. computer graphics com., 1977-78. Mem. Am. Pub. Works Assn., Western Soc. Engrs., Chgo. Architecture Found., Theodore Thomas Soc. Chgo. Symphony, Chgo. Coun. Fgn. Rels., Ground Hog Club, Execs. Club (speaker's table com.), Oak Brook Bath and Tennis Club, Barrington Polo Club. Roman Catholic. Home: 5455 N Sheridan Rd Apt 1912 Chicago IL 60640-1933 E-mail: jmmunoz@mymailstation.com.

MUNOZ, OLIVIER, artistic director; Prin. dancer Cleve. San Jose Ballet, 1987-99; artistic dir. Ballet Ark., Little Rock, 2000—. Office: Ballet Ark 1521 Merrill Dr Little Rock AR 72201*

MUNOZ, STEVEN MICHAEL, physician associate; b. Dallas, Aug. 7, 1952; s. Joseph Paul and Connie Rae (Coffman) M.; m. Paula Lou Marchant, Dec. 12, 1974 (div. 1983); 1 child, Kimberly Rene; m. Maureen Geneva Flowers, Aug. 12, 1984; children: Danielle Geneva, Sean Michael. B Med. Sci., Emory U., 1977. Physician assoc. Med. Ctr. Cen. Ga., Macon, 1977-79, William B. Martin M.D., P.C., Loganville, Ga., 1979-80, Howell Indsl. Clinic, Atlanta, 1980-81, Stanley Fineman M.D., P.C., Marietta, Ga., 1981-82; physician assoc., dir. sales and adminstrn. Family Practice Ctr./Atlanta Occupational Medicine, 1982-85; physician assoc., dir. mktg. Gwinnette Ctr. med. Clinic, Norcross, Ga., 1985-89; physician assoc. So. Orthopedic Clinic, Atlanta, 1989-90, North Fulton Health Care Assoc., Roswell, Ga., 1990-96; physician assoc. adult & pediatric care Kaiser Permanente Internal Medicine Clinic-Family Practice, Atlanta, 1996—. Asst. clin. prof. Emory U. Sch. Medicine, Atlanta, 1981—.; dir. patient edn. com. Ga. Lung Assn., 1981-82; med. adviser ARC, Atlanta, 1980-83, Ga. Statewide Hypertension Task Force, 1981-82; diabetes champion Town Park Facility; mem. med. purchasing and assoc. provider coms. Kaiser-Atlanta Region, Diabetes Disease State Mgmt. Com.; dept. medicine rep. Kaiser, Atlanta; patient care mgr. Town Park Facility, mem. patient care mgmt. com. With U.S. Army, 1972-75, Res., 1975-94. Mem. Am. Acad. Physician Assts., Am. Diabetes Assn., Assn. Family Practice Physician Assts., So. Med. Assn., Ga. Assn. Physician Assts. (bd. dirs., pub. edn. com. chair 1984), Soc. Army Physician Assts. Republican. Avocations: backpacking, camping, water sports, jogging, coaching soccer. Home: 5785 Stonehaven Dr Kennesaw GA 30152-3759 Office: Kaiser Permanente 750 Townpark Ln Kennesaw GA 30144-5824 E-mail: smunoz1952@aol.com., smunoz1952@yahoo.com.

MUÑOZ, WILLY OSCAR, language educator, researcher; b. Cochabamba, Bolivia, Apr. 6, 1949; came to U.S., 1968; s. Wilfredo and Graciela (Cadima) M. BA, Loras Coll., 1972; MA, U. Iowa, 1974, PhD, 1979. Instr. St. Ambrose Coll., Davenport, Iowa, 1976-77, Clarke Coll., Dubuque, 1978-79; sec. to the pres. Universidad Mayor de San Simón, Cochabamba, 1979-80; asst. prof. Centre Coll., Danville, Ky., 1981-84, Kent (Ohio) State U., 1984-88, assoc. prof., 1988-94, prof., 1994—. Author: (novels) Teatro boliviano contemporaneo, 1981, El personaje femenino en la narrativa de escritoras Hispanoamericanas, 1992, Polifonia de la marginalidad: La narrativa de escritoras latinoamericanas, 1999, Antologia de Cuentisias Guatemaltecas, 2001. Mem. PEN Club Internat. (Bolivia), Am. Assn. Tchrs. Spanish and Portuguese, Midwest Assn. L.Am. Studies, PEN Internat. Bolivia, Bolivian Studies Assn., Assn. de Poetas y Escritores Bolivianos, Humanities and Social Scis. Fedn. Can. Avocations: art glass collector, racquetball. Office: Dept Modern-Class Lang Studies Kent State U Kent OH 44242-0001 E-mail: wmunoz@kent.edu.

MUÑOZ-SOLÁ, HAYDEÉ SOCORRO, library administrator; b. Caguas, P.R., Dec. 27, 1943; d. Gilberto Muñoz and Carmen Haydeé (Solá) de Muñoz; m. Juan M. Masini-Soler, Jan. 8, 1966 (div. 1979); children: Juan Martín Masini-Muñoz, Haydeé Milagros Masini-Muñoz. BA in Psychology, U. P.R., Río Piedras, 1965, MLS, 1970; D in Libr. Sci., Columbia U., 1985. Asst. libr. U. P.R., Río Piedras, 1964-67; dir. libr. Interam. U., Aguadilla, P.R., 1974-75; head svcs. to pub. U. P.R., 1975-76; cataloguer Cath. U., Ponce, P.R., 1976-79, U. P.R., Río Piedras, 1982-84, head libr. and info. sci. libr., 1984-85, prof. grad. libr. sch., 1986, 99, dir. libr. sys., 1986-93, coord. external resources libr. sys., 1994-97, dir. of libr. Ponce, P.R., 1997, collection devel. officer Rio Piedras, 1998, sabbatical leave, 2000-01. Dir. P.R. Newspaper Project, Río Piedras, 1986-90; mem. Adv. Com. on Pub. Librs., San Juan, 1987-93; proposal reviewer NEH, 1990—; chmn. Puerto Rican Del. to Nat. White House Conf. on Libr. and Info. Svcs., 1991. Author: La Información y la Documentación Educativa/Informe Sobre la Situación Actual en Puerto Rico, 1991, Memorias: Sequnda Pre-Conferencia de Casa Blanca Sobre Bibliotecas y Servicios de Información en Puerto Rico, 1991, Lineamientos para Colecciones Bibliograficas Nacionales, 1997, Premio por Excelencia en Investigación Aplicada y Publicación, 1997; compiler, editor ann. Puerto Rican Bibliography, 1999—; contbr. articles to profl. jours. Mem. Ponce Sport Club, 1976-83, ARC, Ponce, 1978. Recipient plaque White House Pre-Conf. on Libr. and Info. Scis., 1990, others; French Alps Study Tour scholar Assn. Caribbean Univ. Rsch. and Instl. Librs., 1989, Germany Study Tour scholar Fgn. Rels. Office, Germany, 1991. Mem. ALA, Am. Mgmt. Assn., Grad. Sch. Libr. and Info. Sci. Alumni Assn. (pres. 1988-90), Seminar for Acquisitions L.Am. Libr. Materials, Iberoamerican Nat. Librs. Assn. (pres. 1992-93), Puerto Rican Librs. Soc. (coord. So. area 1974, Lauro award 1989, Rsch. and Pub. award 1998), Assn. Caribbean U. Rsch. and Instnl. Librs. (Parchment award 1988), Asoc. para las Comunicaciones y Tecnología Educativa, Mid. States Assn. Colls. and Schs. (collaborator), Am. Women Assn., Nat. Commn. P.R. Women, Phi Delta Kappa (chair P.R. com. 1988-90, Kappan of Yr. 1990), Eta Gamma Delta. Roman Catholic. Avocations: reading, crewel work, embroidery, knitting, movies. E-mail: hmunoz@caribe.net, hmunoz@upracd.upr.clu.edu.

MUNRO, ALICE, author; b. Wingham, Ont., Can., July 10, 1931; d. Robert Eric and Anne Clarke (Chamney) Laidlaw; m. James Armstrong Munro, 1951 (div. 1976); children: Sheila, Jenny, Andrea; m. Gerald Fremlin, 1976 BA, U. Western Ont., 1952, DLitt (hon.), 1976. Established Munro Books, 1963; writer in residence U. of British Columbia & U. of Queensland, 1980. Author: (short stories) The Dimensions of a Shadow, 1950, Dance of the Happy Shades, 1968 (Gov.-Gen.'s Lit. award 1969), A Place for Everything, 1970, Lives of Girls and Women, 1971 (Can. Booksellers award, 1972), (short stories) Something I've Been Meaning To Tell You, 1974, Who Do You Think You Are?, 1979 (pub. in U.S. as Beggar Maid: Stories of Flo and Rose, 1984, Gov.-Gen.'s Lit. award 1978), The Moons of Jupiter, 1982, The Progress of Love, 1986 (Gov. Gens. Lit. award 1987), Friend of My Youth, 1990, (short stories) Open Secrets, 1994, A Wilderness Station, 1994, Selected Stories, 1996, The Love of a Good Woman, 1998 (Fiction prize Nat. Book Critics Circle 1999), Hateship, Friendship, Courtship, Loveship, Marriage, 2001; TV scripts: A Trip to the Coast, 1973, Thanks For The Ride, 1973, How I Met My Husband, 1974, 1847: The Irish, 1978. Recipient Can.-Australia Lit. Prize 1994, Marian Engel award, 1986. Office: William Morris Agy 16th Fl 1325 Avenue of the Americas New York NY 10019*

MUNRO, DONALD JACQUES, philosopher, educator; b. New Brunswick, N.J., Mar. 5, 1931; s. Thomas B. and Lucile (Nadler) M.; m. Ann Maples Patterson, Mar. 3, 1956; 1 child, Sarah de la Roche. AB, Harvard U., 1953; PhD (Ford Found. fellow), Columbia U., 1964. Asst. prof. philosophy U. Mich., 1964-68, asso. prof., 1968-73, prof. philosophy, 1973-96, prof. philosophy and Asian langs., 1990-96; prof. emeritus philosophy and Chinese, 1996—; chmn. dept. Asian langs. and cultures U. Mich., 1993-95; vis. research philosopher Center for Chinese Studies, U. Calif., Berkeley, 1969-70; asso. Center for Chinese Studies, U. Mich., 1964—; chmn. com. on studies of Chinese civilization Am. Council Learned Socs., 1979-81. Mem. Com. on Scholarly Communication with People's Republic China, NAS, 1978-82, China Council of Asia Soc., 1977-80, Com. on Advanced Study in China, 1978-82, Nat. Com. on U.S.-China Rels., Nat. Faculty of Humanities, Arts and Scis., 1986—; Evans-Wentz lectr. Stanford U., 1970; Fritz lectr. U. Wash., 1980; Gilbert Ryle lectr. Trent U., Ont., 1983; John Dewey lectr. U. Vermont, 1989; vis. rsch.scholar Chinese Acad. Social Scis. Inst. Philosophy, Beijing, 1983, dept. philosophy Beijing U., 1990. Author: The Concept of Man in Early China, 1969, the Concept of Man in Contemporary China, 1977;, editor: Individualism and Holism, 1985, Images of Human Nature: A Sung Portrait, 1988, The Imperial Style of Inquiry in Twentieth Century China, 1996. Mem. exec. com. Coll. Literature, Sci. and The Arts U. Mich., 1986-89. Served to lt. (j.g.) USNR, 1953-57. Recipient letter of commendation Chief Naval Ops.; Disting. Svc. award U. Mich., 1968, Excellence in Edn. award, 1992; Rice Humanities award, 1993-94; Nat. Humanities faculty fellow, 1971-72; John Simon Guggenheim Found. fellow, 1978-79; grantee Social Sci. Rsch. Coun., 1965-66, Am. Coun. Learned Socs., 1982-83, China com. grantee NAS, 1990. Mem. Assn. for Asian Studies (China and Inner Asia Council 1970-72), Soc. for Asian and Comparative Philosophy. Clubs: Ann Arbor Racquet. Home: 14 Ridgeway St Ann Arbor MI 48104-1739 Office: Dept Philosophy U Mich Ann Arbor MI 48104 *I believe that much knowledge is interrelated and that academic disciplinary boundaries are transitory conveniences. The human significance of any research task I undertake should be obvious to those inside and outside my professional group (a goal I seek but do not always achieve).*

MUNRO, DONALD WILLIAM, JR. non-profit organization executive; b. Phila., Dec. 27, 1937; s. Donald William and Emily McCoy (Graham) M.; m. Joyce Eleanor Thomas, Sept. 9, 1961; children: Deborah Joy, Mark William. BS, Wheaton Coll., 1959; MS, Pa. State U., 1963, PhD, 1966. Prof. biology Houghton (N.Y.) Coll., 1966-94; exec. dir. Am. Sci. Affiliation, Ipswich, Mass., 1994—. Adj. prof. biology Gordon Coll., Wenham, Mass., 1995—; chmn. biology dept. Houghton Coll., 1972-94. Capt. U.S. Army, 1960-69. Predoctoral fellow NIH, 1964-66. Mem. Am. Philatelic Soc., Newburyport Stamp Club, Houghton Stamp Club (pres. 1988-90). Republican. Presbyterian. Avocations: stamps, piano, hiking, bioethics. Office: Am Sci Affiliation PO Box 668 55 Market St Ipswich MA 01938-2262 E-mail: don@asa3.org.

MUNRO, JANET ANDREA, artist; b. Woburn, Mass., Dec. 8, 1949; d. John Lehne, Jr. and Celina (Herbert) Baehr; m. Charles Eldon Munro II, May 16, 1968; children: Jacquelyn, David, Chad. Represented by Jay Johnson Gallery, N.Y.C., 1979-89, Frank Miele Gallery, N.Y.C., 1990-99, Sternberg Galleries, Chgo., 1990-99, Gallery 53 Artworks, Cooperstown, N.Y., 1990-99, Toad Hall Gallery, N.Y.C., 1990-99; exhbns. include Soutyby's Galleries, N.Y.C., 1986, 89, Christies Auction Galleries, N.Y.C., 1988, Bloomingdales Dept. Store,

N.Y.C., The MacArthur Found., West Palm Beach, Fla., 1987, Squibb Gallery, Princeton, N.J., 1983, Marshall Fields Dept. Store, Chgo., 1983, Jay Johnsons America's Folk Heritage Gallery, N.Y.C., 1982-84, Galerie Pro Arte Kasper , Morges, Switzerland, 1983-84, Occiental Oil Corp., San Francisco, 1980, Nassau County Mus. Fine Arts, Roslyn, N.Y., Silver Guild Ctr. Arts, New Canaan, Conn., John Judkyn Meml. Am. Mus. in Britain, Bath, Eng., Ctrl. Sch. Art and Design, London, Haworth Gallery, London, numerous others; featured in numerous pubs.; represented in permanent collections: The White House, Smithsonian Inst., The Wallace House Mus., Somerset County, N.J., Fenimore House, N.Y. State Hist. Assn., Cooperstown, N.Y.; represented in numerous pub. and pvt. collections; featured in numerous newspapers and mags., calendars and card collections. Active Cooperstown PTA, N.Y., 1985. Recipient Diploma award Internat. Naive Art Exhibit, Morges, Switzerland, 1983-84. Home: PO Box 303 Portlandville NY 13834-0303 also: 2715 48th St W Bradenton FL 34209-6127 E-mail: van@Wjlmunro.com.

MUNRO, JOHN HENRY ALEXANDER, economics educator, writer; b. Vancouver, B.C., Can., Mar. 14, 1938; s. Hector Gordon and Blanche (Almond) M.; m. Jeanette Roberta James, May 25, 1968; children: Robert Ryder, Valerie Marlene. BA with honors, U. B.C., Vancouver, 1960; MA in History, Yale U., 1961, PhD in History, 1965. Instr. in history U. B.C., 1964-65, asst. prof. history and econs., 1965-68; assoc. prof. econs. U. Toronto, 1968-73, prof., 1973—; assoc. dir. Centre for Medieval Studies, U. Toronto, 1975-78. Cons. on coinage to pub. U. Toronto Press, 1973— Author: Wool, Cloth, and Gold, 1973, Bullion Flows and Monetary Policies in England and the Low Countries, 1350-1500, 1992, Textiles, Towns and Trade: Essays in the Economic History of Late-Medieval England and the Low Countries, 1994; contbr. articles to profl. jours., essays to books; mem. editorial bd. Textile History, 1980-97, Explorations in Economic History, 1998—; Medieval area editor Oxford Ency. of Econ. History, 1996—. Can. Coun. leave fellow, Belgium, 1970-71, Social Scis. and Humanities Rsch. Coun. Can. fellow, Engl. and Holland, 1979-80, Belgium, 1986-87, Eng. and Belgium, 1992-96, 96-99, 99—, Connaught Rsch. fellow, 1993-94, 2000—. Mem. Can. Econ. Assn., Econ. History Assn. (U.S.), Econ. History Soc. (U.K.), Medieval Acad. Am. (councillor 1990-93), Instituto Internazionale di Storia Economica (comitato scientifico 1999—), Royal Flemish Acad. Belgium for Sci. and Arts (fgn.). Presbyterian. Home: 9 Woodmere Ct Toronto ON Canada M9A 3J1 Office: Dept Econs U Toronto 150 St George St Toronto ON Canada M5S 3G7 E-mail: munro5@chass.utoronto.ca., john.munro@utoronto.ca.

MUNRO, MALCOLM GORDON, obstetrician, gynecologist, educator; b. Woodstock, Ont., Can., Mar. 22, 1952; came to U.S., 1991; s. Charles Gordon and Maribelle (Logie) M.; m. Sandra June Brander-Smith, Nov. 17, 1990; children: Tyler Gordon, Megan Danielle, Justin David. MD, U. Western Ont., London, 1975. Diplomate Am. Bd. Ob-Gyn. Intern Royal Columbian Hosp., New Westminster, B.C., 1975-76; resident ob.-gyn, U. Western Ont., London, 1976-77; resident U. B.C., Vancouver, 1978-80, clin. fellow gyneolgic. oncology, 1980-81, clin. instr. ob-gyn., 1981-83, asst. clin. prof., 1983-89, assoc. clin. prof., 1988-92; assoc. prof. UCLA, 1991-95, prof., 1995—, assoc. chmn. dept. ob/gyn., 1994-95. Chmn. ob-gyn. sect. B.C. Med. Assn., Vancouver, 1984-88, Rsch. Coordinating Com. Grace Hosp., Vancouver; founding co-chmn. Gynecologic Studies Group, Washington, 1993-98; cons. Cancer Control Agy., B.C., 1981-91, Ethicon Endosuture Core Cons. Group, 1992-96; chmn. STOP-DUB Clin. Trial, 1996-2002; mem. med. adv. bd. Novacept, Inc., 1999—, Impress Med., 2000—. Author: (book) Gynecology, A Practical Approach, 1990; contbr. articles to profl. jours., chpts. to books; inventor, patentee laparoscopic loop electrodes, endoluminal ultrasound guided resectoscope, 1993; mem. editl. bd. Treating the Female Patient, 1988-94, Jour. of Gynecologic Technique, 1993—; reviewer Obstetrics and Gynecology, 1990—, Fertil Steril, 1993—, Am. Jour. Managed Care, 1996—; mem. ad hoc rev. com. Jour. Am. Assn. Gynecologic Laparoscopists, 1994—, mem. editl. adv. bd., 2000—, Am. Jour. Obstetrics Gynecology, 2000—. Med. dir. Planned Parenthood, Vancouver, 1980-85; founding dir. U. B.C. Coop. Osteoporosis Program, 1987-91, Multidisciplinary Osteoporosis Clinic, U. Hosp., Vancouver, 1987-91. Recipient Appreciation cert. Planned Parenthood of B.C., 1991; grantee Vancouver Found., 1988, P.W. Woodward Found., 1988, Ethicon Endosurgery, 1992, NIH/NIAID AIDS and Cervical Neoplasia co-investigator, 1992-94, 96, study chair AHCPR/GSG. Fellow Royal Coll. Surgeons Can., Soc. Obstetricians and Gynecologists Can.; mem. Can. Fertility and Andrology Soc., Am. Soc. Reproductive Medicine, Am. Assn. Gynecologic Laparoscopists (bd. trustees 2001-2003), Am. Coll. Obstetricians and Gynecologists (vice-chair B.C. section VIII 1987-90). Office: UCLA Med Ctr Ste 27-134 Los Angeles CA 90095-1740

MUNRO, MEREDITH VANCE, lawyer; b. Natick, Mass., Aug. 4, 1938; s. George Lawrence and Florence Estella (Murphy) M.; m. Gail Wittekind, June 10, 1960 (div. 1974); children: Susan Heidi, Elizabeth Holly, Meredith Heather. AB, Princeton U., 1960; JD, Harvard U., 1963. Bar: Mass. 1963. Assoc. atty. Gaston Snow & Ely Barlett, Boston, 1963-71, ptnr., 1971-90. Bd. dirs. Heath Cons. Inc., Stoughton, Mass., 1974—. Trustee The Tabor Acad., Marion, Mass., 1975—. Avocations: antiques, gardening, cooking. Home: 5 Patricia Rd Framingham MA 01701-3931

MUNRO, MICHAEL DONALD, air transportation executive, retired military officer; b. Kindley AFB, Bermuda, May 6, 1953; (parents Am. citizens); s. Donald M. and Marilyn Barbara (Ravenelle) M. AAS in Criminology, U. Md., 1978; BA in Sociology, SUNY, Plattsburg, 1981; MA in Aviation Mgmt., Embry-Riddle U., 1986. Cert. Project Mgmt. Profl. Commd. 2d lt. USAF, 1976, advanced through grades to capt., 1985; chief security adminstr. Plattsburg AFB, N.Y., 1979-81; ICBM launch officer Grand Forks (N.D.) AFB, 1981-83, ICBM flight comdr. N.D., 1984-86; satellite officer Colorado Springs, Colo., 1986-87; chief satellite officer U.S. Space Command, 1987; chief U.S. Space Def. Ops. Ctr., 1988-91; ret., 1991; sr. aviation project mgr. Intersyss. USA, Inc., 1998—2002; program mgr. ARINC Airport Systems, 2002—. Cons. 1980 Winter Olympics, Lake Placid, N.Y., 1979-80; sr. project mgr. Airport Info. Systems at worldwide locations. Contbr. articles to profl. jours. Mem. Pike's Peak Rodeo Com., Colorado Springs, 1987. Recipient Scholastic Achievement award Boeing Aerospace, 1988. Mem. Profl. Rodeo Cowboys Assn. (judge 1987-88, announcer, broadcaster 1988—), Crewmembers Assn. (pres. 1985-86), Grand Forks C. of C. Republican. Roman Catholic. Avocations: hunting, fishing, golf. Home: 5386 E 81st St # 811 Tulsa OK 74137

MUNRO, RALPH DAVIES, state official; b. Seattle, June 25, 1943; s. George Alexander and Elizabeth (Troll) M.; m. Karen Hansen, Feb. 17, 1973; 1 son, George Alexander. BA in History and Edn. (scholar), Western Wash. U. Indsl. engr. Boeing Co., 1966-68; sales mgr. Continental Host, Inc.; asst. dep. dir. ACTION Agy., 1971; spl. asst. to gov. State of Wash., 1970-76; gen. mgr. Tillicum Enterprises & Food Services Co.; dir. Found. for Handicapped, 1976-80; pres. Northwest Highlands Tree Farm; sec. of state State of Wash., 1980—2000; bd. dir. Votehere. Chmn. community service com. Seattle Rotary Club 4; founder 1st pres. Rotary Youth Job Employment Center, Seattle. Named Man of Yr. Assn. Retarded Citizens, Seattle, 1970 Mem. Nat. Assn. Secs. State (pres.), Nat. Assn. Retarded Children, Wash. Historic Mus. (dir.), Wash. Trust Historic Preservation (founder), Nature Conservancy. Republican. Lutheran. Office: Votehere 3101 Northrup Way Ste 250 Bellevue WA 98004-0220*

MUNRO, RODERICK ANTHONY, quality assurance professional, human performance technologist; b. Toronto, Ont., Can., Jan. 16, 1955; came to U.S., 1956; s. William George and Georgina Antionette (Schembri) M.; m. Elizabeth J. Rice, 1994. BA, Adrian Coll., 1979, secondary provisional cert., 1981; MS, Eastern Mich. U., 1984; ednl. specialist, Wayne State U., 1998; PhD, Cambridge State U., 1999. Cert. quality engr., quality auditor, hypnotherapist, cert. quality mgr. Tchr. Lincoln Park H.S., Mich., 1980-82; mgmt. trainee Fabricon Automotive, River Rouge, 1982-84; statis. process control coord. ASC, Inc., Southgate, 1984-86; quality svcs. coord. container divsn. Johnson Controls, Inc., Manchester, 1987-88; program dir. Ford Motor Co., Dearborn, 1988—2001, Stat-A-Matrix, 2001—. Cons. in field, 1986—. Served to sgt. USMCR, 1974-80. Fellow Quality Soc. Australasia, Am. Soc. for Quality (bd. dirs., past cert. com., past chmn. Greater Detroit sect., past chair human resources divsn. Testimonial award 1988, Disting. Svc. award 1989, 96), Quality Soc. of Australasia; mem. ASTD, Internat. Assn. Counselors and Therapists (cert.), Aircraft Owners and Pilots Assn., Am. Statis. Assn. (past pres. Greater Detroit chpt.), Internat. Soc. for Performance Improvement, Assn. Quality and Participation. Home: PO Box 909 Northport MI 49670-0909 Office: Stat-A-Matrix PO Box 909 9981 E Johnson Rd Northport MI 49670- Office Fax: 231-386-9256. E-mail: doctormunro@yahoo.com.

MUNRO, ROXIE JEAN, artist, educator, illustrator, writer; b. Mineral Wells, Tex., Sept. 5, 1945; d. Robert Enoch and Margaret Bissey Munro; m. Bo I. Zaunders, May 17, 1986. Student, U. Md., 1963—65, Md. Inst. Coll. of Art, 1965—66; BFA, U. Hawaii, 1969; postgrad., Ohio U., 1969—70. Lectr. photography U. Hawaii, Honolulu, 1970—71; freelance editl. illustrator Washington, 1972—80; instr. painting Paint in Italy Workshops, Lake Como, 1995—. Author, illustrator The Inside-Outside Book of New York City, 1985 (Best Illustration award N.Y. Times, 1985), Mazescapes, 2001; author: others. Fellow, Yaddo Found., 1980. Mem.: Soc. Children's Book Writers and Illustrators, N.Y. Artists Equity. Office: Roxie Munro Studio 43-01 21st St Long Island City NY 11101 E-mail: rxstudio@aol.com.

MUNROE, GEORGE BARBER, retired mining and manufacturing company executive; b. Joliet, Ill., Jan. 5, 1922; s. George Mueller and Ruth (Barber) Munroe; m. Elinor Bunin, May 30, 1968; children from previous marriage: George Taylor, Ralph W. Taylor. AB, Dartmouth Coll., 1943; LLB, Harvard U., 1949; BA (Rhodes scholar), Christ Church, Oxford (Eng.) U., 1951, MA, 1956; DHL (hon.), No. Ariz. U., 1981; LLD (hon.), Dartmouth Coll., 1993. Bar: N.Y. 1949. Assoc. Cravath, Swaine & Moore, N.Y.C., 1949; atty. Office Gen. Counsel U.S. High Commn. Germany, Frankfurt and Bonn, 1951-53; justice U.S. Ct. Restitution Appeals Allied High Commn. Germany, Nuremberg, 1953-54; assoc. Debevoise, Plimpton & McLean, N.Y.C., 1954-58; with Phelps Dodge Corp., 1958-87, v.p., 1962-66, pres., 1966-75, 80-82, chief exec. officer, 1969-87, chmn. bd., 1975-87, dir., 1966-94. Trustee emeritus Met. Mus. Art; chmn. bd. dirs. Acad. Polit. Sci. Served to lt. (j.g.) USNR, 1943—46. Mem. Mining and Metall. Soc. Am., Coun. Fgn. Rels., Century Assn., River Club, Univ. Club (N.Y.C.), Bridgehampton Club. Office: 444 Madison Ave Fl 19 New York NY 10022-6903 E-mail: e-gmunroe@worldnet.att.net.

MUNROE, TAPAN, economist, educator, consultant; b. Feb. 18, 1936; BS, U. Allahabad, India; MA, U. N.H., 1967; PhD, U. Colo., 1970. Prof. econs., chair econs. dept. U. Pacific, Stockton, Calif., 1970-80; chief economist Pacific Gas and Elec. Co., San Francisco, 1981-98; disting. prof. Pacific Rim Studies U. San Francisco, 1998-99; prin., owner Munroe Consulting, Inc., 1999—. Home: 919 Augusta Dr Moraga CA 94556-1034 Office: Munroe Consulting 1100 Moraga Way Moraga CA 94556-1146 E-mail: tapan@tapanmunroe.com.

MUNSAT, STANLEY MORRIS, philosopher, educator; b. Rutland, Vt., Apr. 12, 1939; s. Leo and Ethel (Geron) M.; children— Steven, Tobin. AB, Cornell U., 1960; MA, U. Mich., 1962, PhD, 1965. Asst. prof. U. Calgary, Alta., Can., 1963-66; asst. prof. philosophy U. Calif., Irvine, 1966-68, assoc. prof., 1968-71, prof., 1971-72; prof. philosophy U. N.C., Chapel Hill, 1972—. Author: The Concept of Memory, 1967; Editor: The Analytic Synthetic Distinction, 1971; gen. editor: (with A.I. Melden) Wadsworth Basic Problems in Philosophy Series; contbr. articles to profl. jours. Mem. Am. Philos. Assn. Home: 837 Shadylawn Rd Chapel Hill NC 27514-2007 Office: Univ NC Dept Philosophy Chapel Hill NC 27599-0001

MUNSCH, RICHARD JOHN, lawyer; b. Pitts., Dec. 14, 1946; BA in History, U. Notre Dame, 1968; JD, U. Mich., 1973. Bar: Pa. 1973, U.S. Dist. Ct. (we. dist.) Pa. 1973, U.S. Ct. Appeals (3d cir.) 1979, U.S. Ct. Appeals (8th cir.) 1980, U.S. Ct. Appeals (6th cir.) 1982, U.S. Supreme Ct. 1983. Law clk. to Hon. Harry A. Kramer Commonwealth Ct. Pa., Pitts., 1974-76; atty. U.S. Steel Corp., 1976—. Mem. Pa. Bar Assn., Allegheny County Bar Assn., Fed. Energy Bar Assn., Am. Corp. Counsel Assn. Office: 600 Grant St Ste 1500 Pittsburgh PA 15219-2800

MUNSELL, DEBRA S. physician assistant, educator; b. Pt. Arthur, Tex., June 13, 1957; d. Rosemond B. and Bettie Lawrence Schoenberg; m. Lloyd Allen Foreman III, Feb. 16, 1985 (dec. Mar. 1991); m. William Peter Munsell, July 18, 1998. BS in Biology, Stephen F. Austin State U., 1979; BS in Health, U. Tex., Galveston, 1981; MPhysician Asst. Studies in Otolaryng., U. Nebr., 2000. Cert. phys. asst. Physician asst. Angleton (Tex.) Clinic, 1981-83, Tex. Dept. Corrections, Huntsville, 1983-84; physician asst. med. br. Galveston U. Tex., 1985-90, clin. instr. med. br. Galveston, 1985—, physician asst. M.D. Anderson Cancer Ctr., 1990—, dir. physician asst. student edn. program M.D. Anderson Cancer Ctr., 1996—; clin. assoc. prof. physician asst. edn. We. U. Health Sci., Pomona, Calif., 1999—. Clin. instr. Baylor Coll. Medicine, Houston, 1999—. Author: (with others) Primary Care Oncology, 1998, Primary Care: A Collaborative Approach, 1999. Life mem. Brazoria County Fair Assn., Angleton, Tex., 1992—. Glaxo/Wellcome Leadership fellow Am. Acad. Physician Assts./Physician Asst. Found., 1997-98. Fellow: Assn. Physician Assts. in Oncology, Soc. Physician Assts. in Otolaryngology, Head and Neck Surgery (bd. dirs. 1992—94, chair continuing med. edn 1994—96, pres. 1996—, charter mem. 1991), Am. Acad. Otolaryngology, Head and Neck Surgery, Am. Acad. Physician Assts. (chair nominating com. 2000—). Home: 9807 Williams Bend Ct Missouri City TX 77459-6279 Office: U Tex MD Anderson Cancer Ctr 1515 Holcombe Blvd Houston TX 77030-4009

MUNSELL, ELSIE LOUISE, lawyer; b. N.Y.C., Feb. 15, 1939; d. Elmer Stanley and Eleanor Harriet (Dickinson) M.; m. George P. Williams, July 14, 1979. AB, Marietta Coll., 1960; JD, Marshall-Wythe Coll. William and Mary, 1972. Bar: Va. 1972, U.S. Dist. Ct. (ea. dist.) Va. 1974, U.S. Ct. Appeals (4th cir.) 1976, U.S. Supreme Ct. 1980. Tchr. Norview High Sch., Norfolk, Va., 1964-69; asst. Commonwealth atty. Commonwealth Atty.'s Office, Alexandria, 1972-73; asst. U.S. atty., 1974-79; U.S. magistrate U.S. Dist. Ct. (ea. dist.) Va., 1979-81; U.S. atty. Dept. Justice, 1981-86; sr. trial atty. Office of Gen. Counsel, Dept. Navy, Washington, 1986-89, asst. gen. counsel installations and environ. law, 1989-91; dep. asst. environ. and safety Sec. Navy, 1991-2001, ret., 2001. Mem. USEPA Clean Air Act Adv. Com., 1997—; bd. dirs. BMT Designers & Planners, 2002--. Active Va. Commn. on Status of Women, 1966-74; bd. vistors Coll. William and Mary, 1972-76; active Atty. Gen.'s Adv. Com. U.S. Attys., 1981-83; bd. dirs. Carpenter's Shelter, Inc., 1990-93; vestry St. Alban's, Annandale, Va., 1996-99; fed. preservation officer Dept. of Navy, 1999. Presdl. Meritorious Exec., 1999; recipient Spl. Achievement awrd Nat. Mil. Fish and Wildlife Assn., 2001, Disting. Civilian Svc. award, 2001. Mem. Environ. Law Inst. (assoc.), Sr. Execs. Assn. Episcopalian.

MUNSEY, VIRDELL EVERARD, JR. retired utility executive; b. Washington, Sept. 25, 1933; s. Virdell Everard and Mildred Lovenia (Wood) M.; m. Bernice Ann Wilson, Sept. 20, 1956; children: Wanda Louise, Allan Coll, Andrew Everard, Carolyn Jane. BA magna cum laude, Yale U., 1955; M.P.A., Harvard U., 1967. Reporter Washington Post, 1957-63; legis. asst. Rep. Henry S. Reuss, Washington, 1963-68; info. dir. United Democrats for Humphrey, 1968; asst. dir. public affairs Dem. Nat. Com., 1968; with Nat. Planning Assn., Washington, 1969-77, exec. v.p., 1974-76; dep. asst. sec. for public affairs Dept. Treasury, Washington, 1977-81; cons. World Bank, 1981; with Va. Electric and Power Co., 1981-86, mgr. corp. communications, 1982-83, exec. dir. pub. policy, 1983-86, v.p. pub. policy, 1986, Dominion Resources Inc., 1986-96; cons., 1996—. Mem. Va. Coal and Energy Commn., 1983-95. Chmn. Arlington County Dem. Party, 1967-69; mem. Arlington County Bd., 1972-75, chmn., 1973; vice chmn. No. Va. Transp. Commn., 1973, chmn., 1974; bd. dirs. Washington Met. Area Transit Authority, 1975; mem. transp. planning bd. Met. Washington Coun. Govts., 1973-75; treas. Competitive Power Policy Forum, 1990-96. Served with U.S. Army, 1955-57. Am. Polit. Sci. Assn. fellow, 1966-67 Mem. United Ch. Christ.

MUNSON, CHARLES LEE, university educator; b. Alexandria, VA, Feb. 24, 1966; s. Karl Franklin Munson, Barbara Louise Munson. PhD, Washington University, St. Louis, Missouri, 1991—97, MSBA, 1991—94, BSBA, 1984—88. Assistant Professor Washington State University, Pullman, WA, 1997—2002; Analyst-Revenues Contel Service Corporation, St. Louis, 1988—91. Consultant Express Scripts, St. Louis, 1996—96. Author: Operations Management, 2002; contbr. articles to profl. jours. Recipient Outstanding Article award, Wash. State U. Internat. Bus. Inst., 1998. Mem.: Decision Sciences Inst., Production and Operations Mgmt. Soc., INFORMS, Phi Eta Sigma, Beta Gamma Sigma, Psi Chi. Christian. Avocation: golf, volleyball, basketball, tennis. Office: Washington State University PO Box 644736 Pullman WA 99164-4736

MUNSON, EDWARD HARRY, JR. medical investigator; b. Birmingham, Ala., Apr. 3, 1948; s. Edward H. Sr. and Elizabeth (W.) M.; married, Dec. 6, 1968 (div. Dec. 1985); children: Laura Davis, Kathleen DeLacy Munson, Matthew Edward; m. Patricia Beth Wool, July 29, 1989. BA in Biology, Huntingdon Coll., 1971; student, U. Mo. Law Enforcemnt Tng. Nat. cert. investigator. Investigator Montgomery (Ala.) Police Dept., 1970-81; instr. Ala. Advanced Criminal Justice Acad., 1974-80; med. investigator Ala. Bd. Med. Examiners, Montgomery, 1981—. Cons. State Bd. of Health-Controlled Substance Adv. Panel, Montgomery, 1989—, Stae Methadone Authority, Fedn. of State Med. Bds., Ft. Worth, 1990—; mem. Med. Investigator Tng. Com., chair, 1994, 97. Recipient Silver Star, Am. Fedn. Police, Miami, Fla., 1975; named Firearms Expert, NRA, 1978. Mem. Internat. Narcotic Officers Assn., Nat. Assn. Drug Diversion Investigators, Nat. Criminal Justice Assn., Nat. Assn. State Controlled Substance Authorities. Jewish. Avocations: travel, cooking, shooting. Office: Ala Bd Med Examiners PO Box 946 Montgomery AL 36101-0946

MUNSON, HAROLD LEWIS, education educator; b. Windham, N.Y., Aug. 2, 1923; s. Esmond Lewis and Gladys (Disbrow) M.; m. Evelyn Claire Moore, Sept. 8, 1946; children: Michael Lewis, Jeffrey Charles. AB, Hobart Coll., 1947; MA, SUNY, Albany, 1948; Ed.D., NYU, 1961. Tchr. social studies, counselor Cairo (N.Y.) Central Sch., 1948-50; dir. guidance Williamson (N.Y.) Central Sch., 1950-54; supr. guidance N.Y. State Edn. Dept., Albany, 1954-59; prof. edn., chmn. Center for Counseling, Family and Worklife Studies, U. Rochester, N.Y., 1959-85, prof. emeritus, 1985—; prof. edn. Overseas Program, Boston U., 1985-87; pres. Munson Assocs., 1988—. Vocat. cons. Social Security Adminstrn., HEW, 1962-79 Author: (with H.W. Houghton) Organizing Orientation Activities, 1956, My Educational Plans, 1959, 70, Guidance Activities for Teachers of English, Social Studies, Science, Mathematics and Foreign Languages, 1965, (with Gilbert Gockley) Career Insights and Self Awareness Games, 1973; contbg. author: Ency. of Careers, 1967, Elementary School Guidance: Concepts, Dimensions and Practice, 1970, The Foundations of Developmental Guidance, 1971, Career Education for Deaf Students: An Inservice Leader's Guide, 1975. Served with USNR, 1944-46. Mem. Am. Counseling Assn., Nat. Career Devel. Assn., Am. Sch. Counselor Assn., Phi Delta Kappa. Home: 9 Charleston Drive Mendon NY 14506 Office: U Rochester Warner Grad Sch Edn and Human Devel Rochester NY 14627 E-mail: grampaGG1@aol.com. *Success is whatever you want it to be. By defining it in such personal terms, everyone should be able to experience some degree of success. For me, it has been being able to feel a measure of personal fulfillment through my accomplishments in helping others to define and examine their own existence.*

MUNSON, HENRY LEE, JR. anthropologist, educator; b. N.Y.C., Nov. 1, 1946; s. Henry Lee and Monique (Ruzette) M.; m. Fatima Zohra Bernikho, June 26, 1971; children: Leila, John, Michael, Nadia. BA, Columbia Coll., 1970; MA, U. Chgo., 1973, PhD, 1980. Prof. anthropology U. Maine, Orono, 1982—. Wilson fellow The Woodrow Wilson Internat. Ctr. for Scholars, Washington, 1996-97. Author: The House of S. Abdallah, 1984, Islam and Revolution in the Middle East, 1988, Religion and Power in Morocco, 1993. Fellow Am. Anthrop. Assn.; mem. Middle East Studies Assn. Office: U Maine Dept Anthropology Orono ME 04469-0001

MUNSON, HOWARD G. federal judge; b. Claremont, N.H., July 26, 1924; s. Walter N. and Helena (O'Halloran) M.; m. Ruth Jaynes, Sept. 17, 1949; children: Walter N., Richard J., Pamela A. BS in Economics, U. Pa., 1948; LL.B., Syracuse U., 1952. Bar: N.Y. With Employers' Assurance Corp., Ltd., White Plains, N.Y., 1949-50; mem. firm Hiscock, Lee, Rogers, Henley & Barclay, Syracuse, 1952-76; judge U.S. Dist. Ct. No. Dist. N.Y., 1976—. Mem., pres. Syracuse Bd. Edn.; bd. dirs. Sta. WCNY-TV; chmn. ethics com. Onondaga County Legislature. Served with U.S. Army, 1943-45, ETO. Decorated Bronze Star, Purple Heart. Mem. Am. Coll. Trial Lawyers, Nat. Assn. R.R. Trial Counsel, Am. Arbitration Assn., Justinian Soc., Alpha Tau Omega, Phi Delta Phi. Office: US Dist Ct US Courthouse P O Box 7376 Syracuse NY 13261-7376

MUNSON, JAY DONALD, statistician; b. Des Moines, Apr. 9, 1950; s. Donald Louis and W. Irma Munson; m. Margaret Ann Munson, July 2, 1994; 1 child, Matthew Haubrich. BS, Iowa State U., 1972, MS, 1980. Statis. rsch. analyst Iowa Dept. Human Svcs., Des Moines, 1996-2001; fiscal policy analyst Iowa Dept. Revenue and Fin., 2001—. Mem. ctrl. com., Story County Rep. Party, Ames, Iowa, 1998—. Mem. Am. Statis. Assn., Am. Econ. Assn., Prodn. and Ops. Mgmt. Soc., Acad. Mgmt., First Story Investment Group (pres. 2000-01). Office: Iowa Dept Revenue and Fin 1305 E Walnut St Des Moines IA 50319

MUNSON, JOHN BACKUS, computer systems consultant, retired computer engineering company executive; b. Chgo., May 1, 1933; s. Mark Frame and Catherine Louise (Cherry) M.; m. Anne Lorraine Cooper, July 6, 1957; children: David B., Sharon A. BA, Knox Coll., 1955. With Unisys Corp., McLean, Va., 1957-93, v.p. corp. software engring., 1977-81, v.p. tech. ops., 1981-84, v.p. gen. mgr. space transp. systems, 1984-89, 89-93, v.p., gen. mgr. Space Systems divsn., 1989-94, ret., 1994. Mem. sci. adv. bd. USAF, 1981-86, mem. USN panel on F14D issues, 1987-88. Mem. bd. advisors U. Houston, Clear Lake, 1988-93, chmn. 1990-92; bd. dirs. Bay Area YMCA, 1988-93, chmn. 1992, Clear Lake Am. Heart Assn., 1989-93; co-chmn. Bay Area United Way, 1988—, chmn., 1992; Disting. visitor IEEE Computing Soc., 1981-94. Capt. U.S. Army, 1955-57. Recipient Exceptional Civilian Svc. award USAF, 1986, Superior Pub. Svc. award USN, 1988, cert. of appreciation NATO, 1984; named to Mgmt. Assn. Hall of Fame, 1994. Fellow IEEE (editor Trans. of Software Engring. 1982-84, bd. dirs. tech. com. software engring. 1982—); mem. AIAA, Am. Astronautical Soc. (bd. dirs. S.W. sect. 1989-94), Aerospace Industries Assn. (space com. 1989-94), U.S. Army Assn., Nat. Security Indsl. Assn., Armed Forces Comm. Electronics Assn. (pres. Houston chpt. 1987-90), S.W. Regional Coun. Corp. CEOs. Home and Office: 1018 Westcreek Ln Westlake Village CA 91362-5462

MUNSON, JOHN CHRISTIAN, acoustician; b. Clinton, Iowa, Oct. 9, 1926; s. Arthur J. and Frances (Christian) M.; m. Elaine Hendershot, Sept. 2, 1950; children: John Christian, Holly Elizabeth. BS, Iowa State Coll., 1949; MS, U. Md., 1952, PhD, 1962; Navy Dept. scholar, MIT, 1956. Electronic scientist Naval Ordnance Lab., Washington, 1949-66; tech. dir. navy portion Practice Nine, Naval Air Systems Command, 1967; supt. acoustics divsn. Naval Rsch. Lab., 1968-85; v.p. Engring. & Sci. Assocs., 1983-94; chmn. bd. dirs., 1994; ret. Asst. extension prof. elec. engring. U. Md., 1964-66; mem. Underwater Sound Adv. Group, 1969-75, U.S. Sonar Team, 1971-85, Mobile Sonar Tech. Com., 1972-85; cons., 1985— . Editor U.S. Navy Jour. Underwater Acoustics, 1983-91; patentee in field. Mem. exec. bd. D.C. Bapt. Conv., 1973—, chmn. fin. com., 1973, v.p., 1996-97, pres., 1997-98; trustee Midwestern Bapt. Theol. Sem., 1970-80; trustee Bapt. Sr. Adult Ministries of Washington Met. Area, 1976-91, 92—, pres., 1981-88, CEO, 1991-92; mem. Gen. Bd. Am. Bapt. Chs. U.S.A., 1994-99; pres. Allied Silver Spring Interfaith Svcs. to Srs. Today, 1994-2000, bd. dirs. 1994—; bd. mgrs. Am. Bapt. Hist. Soc., 1996—, sec., 1997—; corp. mem. Am. Bapt. Homes of the West, 1999, dir., 2000—. Fellow IEEE, Signal Processing Soc. (mem. adminstrv. com. 1974-76, chmn. underwater acoustics com. 1973-76), Acoustical Soc. Am.; mem. Sigma Xi. Home: 3118 Chartwell Crescent Ln Adamstown MD 21710-9643 E-mail: johncmunson@compuserve.com. *I have a positive joy for life, and I am an incurable optimist: my basic attitude is that things will work out for the best—but only if we do our very best. Each of us has a responsibility to grow to our maximum capacity and to be of reasonable service to mankind. The proper balance among family, job, service to God, service to others, and attention to yourself is essential. Whatever you are doing, do it from the right motivation and with enthusiasm.*

MUNSON, LAWRENCE SHIPLEY, management consultant; b. N.Y.C., Jan. 10, 1920; s. Lawrence J. and Anna (Lee) M.; m. Gretchen Thannhauser, May 24, 1947; children: Catherine Anne, Shipley John. AB, Harvard U., 1942, JD, 1948. Bar: N.Y. 1948. Assoc. Willkie, Owen, Farr, Gallagher & Walton, N.Y.C., 1948-51; assoc., then partner McKinsey & Co., Inc., 1953-67; pres.

Loral Corp., Scarsdale, N.Y., 1967-69; v.p. Allegheny Power System, Inc., N.Y.C., 1969-72; v.p., mng. prin. Louis Allen Assocs., Inc., 1972-97; self-employed cons., 1998—. Author: How To Conduct Training Seminars, 1984, 2d edit., 1992. Chmn. bd. Planned Parenthood N.Y.C., 1966-70; mem. bd. Planned Parenthood Manhattan and Bronx, 1960-66, Planned Parenthood World Population, 1967-70; bd. dirs. Greater N.Y. Fund, 1966-88, chmn. mgmt. assistance com., 1970-75; pres. East Hampton Village Preservation Soc., 1982-87, trustee, 1982—, chmn., 1993-99; bd. dirs. United Way N.Y.C., 1988-89; co-founder, trustee East Hampton Healthcare Found., 1998—. Served to maj. USAAF, 1942-46; with USAF, 1951-53. Mem. Am. Soc. Tng. and Devel. (pres. N.Y. met. chpt. 1988-89, chmn. bd. dirs. 1990-93), Maidstone Club (East Hampton), Harvard Club (N.Y.C.). Home: 25 Dayton Ln East Hampton NY 11937-2415 E-mail: l.s.munson@worldnet.att.net.

MUNSON, LUCILLE MARGUERITE (MRS. ARTHUR E. MUNSON), real estate broker; b. Norwood, Ohio, Mar. 26, 1914; d. Frank and Fairy (Wicks) Wirick; m. Arthur E. Munson, Dec. 24, 1937; children: Barbara Munson Papke, Judith Munson Andrews, Edmund Arthur. RN, Lafayette (Ind.) Home Hosp., 1937; AB, San Diego State U., 1963; student, Purdue U., Kans. Wesleyan U. Staff and pvt. nurse Lafayette Home Hosp., 1937-41; indsl. nurse Lakey Foundry & Machine Co., Muskegon, Mich., 1950-51, Continental Motors Corp., Muskegon, 1951-52; nurse Girl Scout Camp, Grand Haven, Mich., 1948-49; owner, ret. Munson Realty, San Diego, 1964—2002. Mem. San Diego County Grand Jury, 1975-76, 80-81, Calif. Grand Jurors Assn. (charter). Address: 3875-18 Vista Campana S Oceanside CA 92057-8151

MUNSON, NANCY KAY, lawyer; b. Huntington, N.Y., June 22, 1936; d. Howard H. and Edna M. (Keenan) Munson. Student, Hofstra U., 1959-62; JD, Bklyn. Law Sch., 1965. Bar: N.Y. 1966, U.S. Supreme Ct. 1970, U.S. Ct. Appeals (2d cir.) 1971, U.S. Dist. Ct. (ea. and so. dists.) N.Y. 1968. Law clk. to E. Merritt Weidner, Huntington, 1959-66; sole practice, 1966—. Mem. legal adv. bd. Chgo. Title Ins. Co., Riverhead, N.Y., 1981—; bd. dirs., legal officer Thomas Munson Found. Trustee Huntington Fire Dept. Death Benefit Fund; pres., trustee, chmn. bd. Bklyn. Home Aged Men Found.; bd. dirs. Elderly Day Svcs. on the Sound, Huntington Rural Cemetery Assn., Inc. Mem. ABA, N.Y. State Bar Assn., Suffolk County Bar Assn., Bklyn. Bar Assn., NRA, DAR (trustee Ketewamoke chpt.), Soroptimists (past pres.). Republican. Christian Scientist. Office: 197 New York Ave Huntington NY 11743-2711

MUNSON, PAUL LEWIS, pharmacologist; b. Washta, Iowa, Aug. 21, 1910; s. Lewis Sylvester and Alice E. (Orser) M.; m. Aileen Geisinger, Mar. 7, 1931 (div. 1948); 1 dau., Abigail (Mrs. Mark Krumel); m. Mary Ellen Jones, Aug. 15, 1948 (div. 1971); children: Ethan Vincent, Catherine Laura; m. Yu Chen, Feb. 27, 1987; 1 stepchild, Ming An Chen. BA, Antioch Coll., 1933; MA, U. Wis., 1937; PhD, U. Chgo., 1942; MA (hon.), Harvard, 1955. Fellow, asst. biochemistry U. Chgo., 1939-42; research biochemist William S. Merrell Co., Cin., 1942-43; research biochemist, head endocrinology research Armour Labs., Chgo., 1943-48; research asst., then research asso. Yale Sch. Medicine, 1948-50; asst. prof., asso. prof. pharmacology, then prof. Harvard Sch. Dental Medicine, 1950-65; prof. pharmacology, chmn. dept. U. N.C. Sch. Medicine, 1965-77, Sarah Graham Kenan prof., 1970—. Mem. U.S. Pharmacopeia Panel on Corticotropin, 1951-55; mem. pharmacology test com. Nat. Bd. Med. Examiners, 1966-71; mem. gen. medicine B study section NIH, 1966-70, chmn., 1969-70, mem. pharmacology-toxicology rev. com., 1972-76 Author numerous articles on hormones; co-editor: Vitamins and Hormones, 1968-82; editl. bd. Endocrinology, 1957-63, Jour. Pharmacology and Exptl. Therapeutics, 1959-65, Jour. Dental Rsch., 1962-64, Biochem. Medicine, 1967-84, Am. Jour. Chinese Medicine, 1973-79, 99—, Pharmacol. Revs., 1967-70, editor-in-chief, 1977-81; editor-in-chief: Principles of Pharmacology, 1981-94. Fellow AAAS, Am. Acad. Arts and Scis.; mem. Am. Soc. Pharmacology and Exptl. Therapeutics (council 1970-73, sec.-treas. 1971-72), Am. Soc. Biol. Chemists, Endocrine Soc. (council 1963-65, Fred Conrad Koch award 1976), Am. Soc. Bone and Mineral Research (William F. Neuman award 1982), Am. Chem. Soc., Biometrics Soc., Internat. Assn. Dental Research (councillor 1957-59), AAUP, ACLU (mem. internat. confs. on calcium regulating hormones, Elsevier Sci. Pubs. award 1989), Assn. Med. Sch. Pharmacology (council 1971-73, sec. 1972-73, pres. 1974-76), Am. Thyroid Assn. (nominating com. 1973), Sigma Xi. Dem. Socialist. Unitarian. Home and Office: 1520 Taylor Ave Parkville MD 21234-5241

MUNSON, RICHARD HOWARD, horticulturist; b. Toledo, Dec. 20, 1948; s. Stanley Warren and Margaret Rose (Winter) M.; m. Joy Ellen Smith, July 8, 1972; children: Sarah Joy, David Remington. BS, Ohio State U., 1971; MS, Cornell U., 1973, PhD, 1981. Plant propagator The Holden Arboretum, Mentor, Ohio, 1973-76; asst. prof. Agrl. Tech. Inst., Wooster, 1976-78, Tex. Tech U., Lubbock, 1981-84; dir. botanic garden Smith Coll., Northampton, Mass., 1984-95; exec. dir. The Holden Arboretum, Kirtland, Ohio, 1995-2000; dir. botanic garden U. Mo., Columbia, Mo., 2001—. V.p. Childs Park Found., Northampton, Mass., 1985-95. Ret. lt. col. USAR, 1971-99. Recipient Disting. Alumnus award Ohio State U. Coll. Agr., 1998. Mem. Internat. Plant Propagators Soc., Am. Soc. for Hort. Sci., Am. Assn. Bot. Gardens and Arboreta (com. chmn. 1987-92), Internat. Assn. Plant Taxonomy, Sigma Xi, Pi Alpha Xi, Gamma Sigma Delta. Methodist. Avocations: fishing, golf, woodworking, gardening. Office: University of Missouri General Svcs Bldg Columbia MO 65211-3200

MUNSON, ROBERT DEAN, agronomist, soil scientist, consultant; b. Stockport, Iowa, Mar. 14, 1927; s. Glenn Edward and Frances Emma (Wilson) M.; m. Mary Jane Miesen, Dec. 23, 1950; children: Anthony Kirby, Susan Lee, John Simpkin. BS, U. Minn., Mpls., 1951; MS, Iowa State U., 1954, PhD, 1957; postgrad., U. Minn., St. Paul, 1965. Cert. profl. agronomist, soil scientist. Agrl. economist rsch. projects TVA, Knoxville, 1957-58; agronomist Am. Potash Inst., St. Paul, 1958-64, Midwest dir., 1964-76; North Cen. dir. Potash & Phosphate Inst., 1976-86; cons., 1987-95; project assoc. Ctr. Internat. Food and Agrl. Policy U. Minn., 1990-91; v.p. rsch., edn. and mktg. devel. Nat. Fertilizer Solutions Assn. and Fluid Fertilizer Found., Manchester, Mo., 1991-92. Adj. prof. soil, water and climate U. Minn., St. Paul, 1987-97, soil and water resources endowed fund campaign com. chair, 1988-91, endowed chair adv. coun., 1993—, food sci. and nutrition adv. coun., 1999, 2001; project scientist Potassium, Calcium and Magnesium project Internat. Fertilizer Devel. Ctr., Muscle Shoals, Ala., 1979; lectr. on soil fertility and plant nutrition Acads. of Agrl. Sci., China, 1985, 91; hon. dir. Minn. Plant Food and Chems. Assn., 1991-93; bd. dirs. Soil and Plant Analysis Coun., 1991-93; assn. cons. Internat. Fertilizer Devel. Ctr./Dhaka and Bangladesh Ministry of Agri. Project, 1993; cons. Potash & Phosphate Inst., 1999; program chair internat. potassium in agr. symposium Am. Soc. Agronomy, Soil Sci. Soc. Am., Crop Sci. Soc. Am. Editor: Potassium in Agriculture, 1985, translated into Chinese (Chinese Acad. Sci.), 1998; co-editor: Moving Off the Yield Plateau, 1971; editor-in-chief Fertilizer Issues, 1991-92; mem. editl. bd. Comms. in Soil Science and Plant Analysis, 1970-96, Soil Sci. Soc. Am. Jour., 1981-82, Jour. Potassium Rsch. (India), 1985-90; assoc. editor Jour. Agronomic Edn., 1971-72; contbr. 14 chpts. to books and articles to profl. jours., 10 tech. bulls. consulting reports, many tech. and non-referred papers. Mem. state ctrl. com. Minn. Rep. Orgn.; project ag grad bd. Minn. Conf. united Meth. Ch., 1996—2002. Recipient Merit Cert. award, Am. Forage & Grass Coun., 1983. Fellow: AAAS, Soil Sci. Soc. Am. (bd. dirs., chair extension agronomy divsn.), Crop Sci. Soc. Am., Am. Soc. Agronomy (bd. dirs., chair fertilizer tech. divsn., Agronomy Svc. award 1970, Werner L. Nelson award 1990); mem.: Farmhouse, Coun. Agrl. Sci. and Tech., Internat. Soil Sci. Soc., Wis. Fertilizer Assn. (v.p. 1962—63, organizing dir.), UN Assn. Minn. (adv. coun. 1998—2001), Wis. Fertilizer and Chem. Assn. (Recognition for Meritorious Work Related to Soil Fertility Mgmt. 1986), Minn. Plant Food and Chems. Assn. (Dedicated Svc. award 1986), Minn. Agr.-Growth Coun. (organizing dir., initial sec. and bd. dirs.), Minn. Plant Food Assn. (sec. 1962—63, pres. 1963—65, program. tech. advisor 1965—72, Valuable and Devoted Svc. hon.), Minn. Fertilizer Industry Assn. (sec. 1959—62), Minn. Forage and Grassland Coun. (organizing dir. v.p. 1976, pres. 1977, Outstanding Svc. award), Sigma Xi, Gamma Sigma Delta, Alpha Zeta, U. Minn. Coll. Agr. Alumni Soc. (Outstanding Alumnus award 1990, Outstanding Achievement award 2001). Home: 2147 Doswell Ave Saint Paul MN 55108-1731 E-mail: rdmunson@earthlink.net.

MUNSON, ROBERT SYDNEY, biomedical researcher; b. Waterbury, Conn., Jan. 18, 1947; s. Robert Sydney, Sr. and Lillian Marti M.; m. Barbara Bell, Nov. 22, 1966 (div.); children: Mary Ann, Kimberley; m. Lauren Opremcak Bakaletz, Sept. 16, 1994; stepchildren: Megan, Kelsey, Nicole. BA, U. Conn., Storrs, 1968; PhD, U. Conn., Farmington, 1976; postdoctoral fellow, Washington U., St. Louis, 1976-79. Rsch. asst. prof. pediatrics Washington U. Sch. of Medicine, St. Louis, 1980-82, asst. prof. of pediatrics, 1982-89, asst. prof. molecular microbiology, 1987-89, assoc. prof. pediatrics, 1989-94, assoc. prof. molecular microbiology, 1989-94; prof. pediatrics Ohio State U., Columbus, 1994—, prof. of molecular virology, immunology, and med. genetics, 1994—, prof. microbiology, 1999—. Mem. cons. group on vaccine devel. U.S. AID, 1989-90; co-chmn. steering com. molecular microbiology and microbial pathogenesis grad. program, Washington U. 1991-92, program coord. and chmn. steering com. molecular microbiology and microbial pathogenesis grad. program, 1992-94; mem. standing com. for the Can. Bacterial Diseases Network, 1992-93; dir. Core DNA Sequencing Facility, Children's Rsch. Inst., Columbus, 1996—, mem. prin. investigator adv. com., 1996—; mem. NIH Bacteriology/Mycology Study Sect., 1997-2000. Contbg. author book chpts.; contbr. articles to profl. jours. and publs. Recipient Grad. fellowship U. Conn., 1970-76, Conn. State Fellowship for Grad. Students, 1971-73, fellowship NIH, 1976-78, Neurosci. Tng. Grant Postdoctoral fellowship, 1978-79; grantee NIH. Fellow IDSA; mem. Am. Soc. Microbiology (counselor-at-large 1997, co-organizer Mo. br. mtg. 1991). Office: Childrens Rsch Inst 700 Childrens Dr Columbus OH 43205-2664 E-mail: munsonr@pediatrics.ohio-state.edu.

MUNSON, RONALD ALFRED, retired chemist; b. Lancaster, Pa., Aug. 12, 1933; s. Saron Erik and Millicent Edwards Munson; m. Sarah Elizabeth Robinson, June 24, 1967; children: Katherine, Elizabeth Pickens, Hilma, Erika. BS, Franklin and Marshall Coll., 1955; PhD, Northwestern U., 1958. Post-doctoral rsch. assoc. Max-Planck-Institut fuer Physikalische Chemie, Goettingen, Germany, 1958—60; rsch. chemist GE Rsch. Lab., Schenectady, NY, 1960—67; rsch. supr. US Bur. Of Mines, College Park, 1967—72; rsch. staff assistent US Bur. of Mines Hdqs., Washington, 1972—82; chief office of mineral institutes US Bur. of Mines, 1982—96; now ret. Contbr. articles to profl. jours. Pres. Arlington County Parent Tchr. Assn., Arlington, Va., 1980—81. Recipient predoctoral fellowship, NSF, 1955—58, postdoctoral fellowship, 1958—60, meritorious svc. award, Dept. of the Interior, 1991. Mem.: AIME (chmn. Washington sect. 1981—82), Am. Chem. Soc. Unitarian Universalist. Achievements include discovered and characterized transition metal disulfides having the pyrite structure using ultra-high pressure synthesis techniques. Avocations: skiing, tennis.

MUNSON, VIRGINIA ALDRICH, interior designer, decorator; b. Evanston, Ill., Oct. 10, 1932; d. Jefferson Elliott and Catherine (Stinson) Aldrich; m. John Chester Munson, Feb. 4, 1956; children: Catherine, John Jr., Laura. AA, Bennett Junior Coll., 1952. Owner, pres. Virginia Munson Interiors, Lake Forest, Ill., 1967—. Mem. Lake Forest Ctr. Infant Welfare Soc., 1957-93, pres., 1976-78; active com. candidates caucus, Lake Forest, 1984-87; mem. women's bd. Lake Forest Hosp., 1977—, Guild of Chgo. Hist. Soc., 1990—; bd. dirs. Infant Welfare Soc. Chgo., 1967-93, Ill. Regent Gunston Hall, 1988-96, Altar Guild, Ch. of the Holy Spirit, 1980—; bd. trustees St. Mary's Svcs., 1998—; chmn. landscape and grounds Lake Forest Pl., 2000—, mem. resident adv. coun., 2001—. Mem. Am. Soc. Interior Designers (Allied 1978-2002), Nat. Soc. Colonial Dames Am. (bd. dirs. 1978—, pres. State of Ill. br. 1982-84, chair landscape and ground com. Lake Forest Place 1999-2002, chair dining svcs. com. 2002—, mem. resident adv. coun. Lake Forect Place 2001—), Soc. Mayflower Descs., Contemporary Club, Onwentsia Club, Winter Club. Republican. Episcopalian. Avocations: tennis, needlepoint. E-mail: Ginmunson@aol.com.

MUNSON, WILLIAM LESLIE, insurance company executive; b. Chgo., Apr. 28, 1941; s. David Curtiss and Leona Ruth (Anderson) M.; m. Marian Lee Blanton, July 16, 1966; children: Katherine, Sandra, Deborah. Student, U. Md., 1959-62; BBA cum laude, Coll. of Ins., 1968. CPCU, 1967. Asst. mgr. N.Y. Fire Ins. Rating Orgn., N.Y.C., 1959-69; br. mgr. CNA Ins. Co., 1969-75; pres., dir. Commerce & Industry Ins. Co., 1975-83; pres. Commerce & Industry of Can., 1980-83; sr. v.p., chief underwriting officer Am. Internat. Underwriters, 1983-87; exec. v.p. Home Ins. Co., 1987-93; pres., chief exec. officer Home Indemnity Ins. Co., 1987-93, also bd. dirs.; chmn. City Internat. Ins. Co. Ltd., 1991-93; pres., COO Merc. and Gen. Reins. Co. Am., 1993-97; chmn., pres., CEO Toa-Re-Ins. Co. Am. (now named Toa Reinsurance Co. Am.), 1993—. Trustee Coll. of Ins., 1985-2001; bd. overseers Sch. of Risk Mgmt., Ins. and Actuarial Sci., St. Johns Univ., 2001—; mem. bd. visitors Drew U., 2002--; bd. dirs. Nat. Coun. Compensation Ins., 1989-92, ISO Comml. Risk Svcs., 1993; mem. comml. lines com. Ins. Svcs. Office, 1989-92; trustee Am. Inst. for Charter Property Casualty Underwriters, 1996-2002. Pres. Wyckoff (N.J.) Bd. Edn., 1979-82; chmn. bd. lay leaders Grace United Meth. Ch., Wyckoff, 1989-92, trustee, 1999—. Past mem. Soc. CPCUs (bd. dirs. N.Y. chpt.); mem., Conf. Spl. Risk Underwriters, Reinsurance Assn. Am. (bd. dirs. 1993-2002). Clubs: John St. (N.Y.C.). Republican. Home: 762 Albemarle St Wyckoff NJ 07481-1005 Office: Toa Reinsurance 177 Madison Ave Morristown NJ 07960-6016 E-mail: wmunson@toare.com.

MUNSTER, ANDREW MICHAEL, surgeon, educator; b. Budapest, Hungary, Dec. 10, 1935; came to U.S., 1965. s. Leopold S. and Marianne (Barcza) M.; m. Joy O'Sullivan, Dec. 7, 1963; children: Andea, Tara, Alexandra. MD, U. Sydney, Australia, 1959. Diplomate Am. Bd. Surgery. Rsch. fellow Harvard U. Med. Sch., Boston, 1966-67; asst. prof. surgery U. Tex., San Antonio, 1968-71; assoc. prof. surgery Med. U. S.C., Charleston, 1971-76, Johns Hopkins U., Balt., 1976-85, prof., 1985—2001; dir. Burn Ctr., Balt. City Hosp., 1976—2001; prof. emeritus Johns Hopkins U., 2001. V.p. Chesapeake Physicians, Balt., 1978-84; Hunterian prof. Royal Coll. Surgeons, 1974; chmn. Burn Sci. Pubs. Inc., 1998—; pres. ANDYPLOP Inc., LLC, 1998—. Author: Surgical Anatomy, 1971, Surgical Immunology, 1976, Burn Care for House Officers, 1980; contbr. numerous articles to med. jours. Pres. Chesapeake Ednl. Rsch. Trust, Balt., 1980-84, Charleston Symphony, 1974-75, Charleston TriCounty Arts Coun., 1975-76. Lt. col. U.S. Army, 1968-71. Recipient John Hunter prize U. Sydney, 1959. Fellow Royal Coll. Surgeons Eng., Royal Coll. Surgeons Edinburgh (Scotland), Am. Assn. Surgeons of Trauma, Colombian Coll. Surgeons (hon.); mem. Am. Burn Assn. (sec. 1990-93, 1st v.p. 1993-94, pres.-elect 1994-95, pres. 1995, found. pres. 2001), So. Surg. Assn., Soc. Univ. Surgeons, Am. Surg. Assn. E-mail: aandyplop@aol.com.

MUNTEAN, ANDREI MIHAI, legislative staff member, educator; b. Chisinau, Moldova, Sept. 4, 1976; arrived in U.S., 1996; s. Mihai Ion and Galina Andrian Muntean. Diploma in lang, Fudan U., Shanghai, China, 1994; BS magna cum laude, Drexel U., Phila., 1996; MS with honors, London Sch. Econs., 1999. Rsch. specialist Drexel U., Phila., 1997—98; govt. cons. Govt. of Moldova, Chisinau, 1999—2000; sr. strategic cons. Ecotehagro Indsl. Group, 1999—2000; asst. prof. Drexel U., Phila., 2000—; asst. to U.S. Senator, 2001—. Mentor World Affairs Coun., Phila., 2000. Mem.: European Consortium Polit. Rsch., U. London Convocation, Acad. Polit. Sci. Avocations: chess, opera, tennis, travel, books. Home: 864 N 22d St Apt 3F Philadelphia PA 19130 Office: Drexel Univ 3141 Chestnut St Philadelphia PA 19104 Office Fax: 215-895-6614. E-mail: muntean@drexel.edu.

MUNTZ, CHARLES EDWARD, school system administrator; b. Cynthiana, Ky., May 26, 1944; s. Charles Edward and Hedy Wright (Shaw) M.; m. Betty Jean Dance, June 7, 1986; children: Susan Lynn Lanter, Christopher, Laura Cox. AB, Ea. Ky. U., 1967, MA, 1968. Social sci. tchr. Harrison County Schs., Cynthiana, Ky., 1967, Georgetown (Ky.) Ind. Schs., 1968-69; spl. edn. tchr. Harrison County Schs., Cynthiana, 1969-76; dir. spl. edn. Franklin County Schs., Frankfort, Ky., 1976-94. Instr. U. Ky.; spl. edn. cons., presenter in field. Chairperson issues com. Ky. Coalition for the Handicapped, 1988. Named Outstanding Spl. Edn. Adminstr. of Yr., 1991. Mem. Coun. for Exceptional Children (past pres.), Ky. Coalition for People with Handicaps, Ky. Coun. Adminstrs. of Spl. Edn. (past pres.), Phi Delta Kappa. Avocations: reading, sports.

MUNTZ, ERIC PHILLIP, aerospace and mechanical engineering and radiology educator, consultant; b. Hamilton, Ont., Can., May 18, 1934; came to U.S., 1961, naturalized, 1985; s. Eric Percival and Marjorie Louise (Weller) M.; m. Janice Margaret Furey, Oct. 21, 1964; children: Sabrina Weller, Eric Phillip. BASc., U. Toronto, 1956, MASc., 1957, PhD, 1961. Halfback Toronto Argonauts, 1957-60; group leader Gen. Electric, Valley Forge, Pa., 1961-69; assoc. prof. aerospace engring. and radiology U. So. Calif., Los Angeles, 1969-71, prof., 1971-87, chmn. aerospace engring., 1987-97, A.B. Freeman prof. engring., 1992—, chmn. aerospace and mech. engring., 2000—. Cons. to aerospace and med. device cos., 1967—; mem. rev. of physics (plasma and fluids) panel NRC, Washington, 1983-85 Contbr. numerous articles in gas dynamics, micromech. sys., and med. diagnostics to profl. publs., 1961—; patentee med. imaging, isotope separation, nondestructive testing, net shape mfg., transient energy release micromachines, microscale vacuum sys., micropropulsion sys. Mem. Citizens Environ. Avc. Coun., Pasadena, Calif., 1972-76. Pilot RCAF, 1955-60. U.S. Air Force grantee, 1961-74, 82—; NSF grantee, 1970-76, 87—; FDA grantee, 1980-86. Fellow AIAA (aerospace Contbn. to Soc. award 1987), Am. Phys. Soc.; mem. NAE. Episcopalian. Home: 1560 E California Blvd Pasadena CA 91106-4104 Office: U So Calif Univ Pk Los Angeles CA 90089-1191 E-mail: muntz@spock.usc.edu.

MUNTZ, ERNEST GORDON, historian, educator; b. Buffalo, Nov. 15, 1923; s. J. Palmer and Laura Estelle (Wedekindt) M.; m. Marjorie Corinne Wilson, June 29, 1948; children— Carolyn Odell, Deborah Lynn, Howard Gordon. AB, Wheaton (Ill.) Coll., 1948; PhD, U. Rochester, N.Y., 1960. Asst. prof. social sci. Blue Mountain (Miss.) Coll., 1954-56; from asst. prof. to prof. history Union U., Jackson, Tenn., 1956-61; assoc. faculty U. Cin., 1961-91, prof. history, 1969-91, prof. emeritus, 1991—; dean Raymond Walters Coll., Cin., 1969-90, dean emeritus, 1991—. Cons.-evaluator North Central Assn. Colls. and Schs., 1974-91, mem. Commn. on Instns. of Higher Edn., 1983-87 Served as officer USAAF, 1943-46, ret., 1975; col. USAFR. So. Fellowships Fund fellow, 1955 Mem. Am. Hist. Assn., Am. Assn. Community and Jr. Colls. (bd. dirs. coun. 2 yr. colls. of 4 yr. instns. 1988-90), Cincinnatus Assn., Phi Alpha Theta, Pi Gamma Mu. Clubs: Cin. Literary, University. Presbyterian. Home: 7950 Indian Hill Rd Cincinnati OH 45243-3906

MUNTZ, J(OHN) RICHARD, clergyman; b. Buffalo, Dec. 14, 1927; s. J. Palmer and Laura Estelle (Wedekindt) M.; m. Marietta Hayden, June 22, 1951; children: Palmer Hayden, Laura Marie De Soer. BS, Wheaton (Ill.) Coll., 1949; BDiv, We. Conservative Bapt. Sem., Portland, Oreg., 1953; MA, Wayne State U., Detroit, 1964; ThM, No. Bapt. Sem., Chgo., 1964; MA in Libr., San Jose State U., 1976. Ordained to ministry Bapt. Ch. Pastor Grace Bapt. Ch., Rochelle, Ill., 1954-56, West Bloomfield Bapt. Ch., Orchard Lake, Mich., 1957-62; prof., libr. San Francisco Bapt. Theol. Sem., 1964-72, Denver Bible Bapt. Sem., 1972-75; libr., prof. We. Bapt. Coll., Salem, Oreg., 1975—. Accreditation team mem. Am. Assn. Bible Colls., Fayetteville, Ark., 1977-94. Author: A Suggested Theological Bibliography for AABC Colleges, Supplement I, 1994. Deacon, shepherd, tchr. Bethany Bapt. Ch., Salem, Oreg. Mem. Assn. Christian Librs., So. Bapt. Hist. Soc., Beta Phi Mu. Republican. Baptist. Home: 1095 Cayuse Cir SE Salem OR 97306-1396 Office: Western Bapt Coll 5000 Deer Park Dr SE Salem OR 97301-9330 E-mail: rmuntz@wbc.edu.

MUNYER, EDWARD A. zoologist, museum administrator; b. Chgo., May 8, 1936; s. G. and M. Munyer; m. Marianna J. Munyer, Dec. 12, 1981; children: Robert, William, Richard, Laura, Cheryl. BS, Ill. State U., 1958, MS, 1962. Biology tchr. MDR High Sch., Minonk, Ill., 1961-63; instr. Ill. State U., Normal, 1963-64; curator zoology Ill. State Mus., Springfield, 1964-67, asst. dir., 1981-98, asst. dir. emeritus, 1998—; assoc. prof. Vincennes (Ind.) U., 1967-70; dir. Vincennes U. Mus., 1968-70; assoc. curator Fla. Mus. Natural History, Gainesville, 1970-81. Mem. Mus. Accreditation Vis. Com. Roster, 1976—. Contbr. articles to profl. jours. Mem. Am. Assn. Mus. (bd. dirs. 1990-95), Assn. Midwest Mus. (pres. 1990-92, lifetime achievement award for disting. svc. 1998), Ill. Assn. Mus. (bd. dirs. 1981-86, lifetime profl. achievement award 1998), Wilson Ornithol. Soc. (life). Office: Ill State Mus Spring & Edward Sts Springfield IL 62706-0001 E-mail: eammjm@springnet1.com.

MUNZER, ALFRED, internist; b. The Hague, The Netherlands, Nov. 23, 1941; came to U.S., 1958; s. Simcha and Gisele Munzer.. BA, CUNY-Bklyn. Coll., 1963; MD, SUNY, Bklyn., 1968. Intern in internal medicine State U.-Kings County Med. Ctr., Bklyn., 1968-69, resident in internal medicine, 1969-70, U. Rochester (N.Y.)/Strong Meml. Hosp., 1970-71; fellow in pulmonary medicine Johns Hopkins U., Balt., 1971-72; chief pulmonary and infectious disease Malcolm Grow USAF Med. Ctr., Suitland, Md., 1972-74; co-dir. pulmonary medicine Washington Adventist Hosp., Takoma Park, 1974—. Contbr. chpt. to: Lippincott Manual of Nursing PRactice, 1982, Textbook of Internal Medicine, 1996. Pres. Am. Lung Assn., N.Y.C., 1993-94; trustee Action on Smoking and Health, 1996—. Maj. USAF, 1972-74. Recipient Will Ross medal Am. Lung Assn., 2000. Fellow Am. Coll. Chest Physicians (chpt. pres. 1976-77); mem. ACP, Am. Thoracic Soc. (bd. dirs. 1981-83, 92-95), Dramatists Guild (assoc.). Democrat. Jewish. Avocation: playwriting. Home: 2939 Van Ness St NW Washington DC 20008-4662 Office: Washington Adventist Hosp 7600 Carroll Ave Takoma Park MD 20912-6367

MUNZER, ANNETTE ELIZABETH, cultural affairs consultant; b. Washington, Aug. 19, 1944; d. Edward Norman and Mary Elizabeth (Snider) Munzer; children: Edward Erkin, Aaron Erkin. BA, Syracuse U., 1966; MA, U. Okla., 1970. Head libr. art libr. U. Okla., Norman, 1968-70; prof. anthropology U. Alaska, College, 1970-93, anthropologist College and Anchorage, 1973-77; rsch. libr. Phoenix Art Mus., 1978-80; curator of edn., collections, hist. sites, hispanic culture Tucson Mus. Art, spl. events and pub. program coord., 1980-85; exec. dir. Tucson Festival Soc., 1985-93; dir. cultural affairs City of Savannah, Ga., 1993; cons. El Centro Cultural de Las Americas, Tucson, 1994—2001. Cons. Cultural Olympiad , Savannah, 1993—94, Amigos de la Danza, Tucson, 1995—96, Bus. Expo, Tucson Bus. Coalition, Tucson, 1996—97, Mujer 2000, Tucson, 1996—2000; tour planner, dir. Grayline Tours/Citizen's Autostage. Author: Olaf Wieghorst, 1984; author, editor: Contact, 1972; author text (portfolio) Alaskan Eskimo Masks, 1973. Panelist Ariz. Commn. on Arts, Phoenix, 1995-96, Tucson/Pima Arts Commn., 1994-2001. Mem. Am. Assn. State and Local History, Am. Assn. Museums, Internat. Festival and Spl. Events Assn. (cert. festival exec.). Avocations: training service/assistance dogs. Home and Office: 17213 Sandwick Dr Pflugerville TX 78660

MUNZER, STEPHEN IRA, lawyer; b. N.Y.C., Mar. 15, 1939; s. Harry and Edith (Isacowitz) M.; m. Patricia Eve Munzer, Aug. 10, 1965; children: John, Margaret. AB, Brown U., 1960; JD, Cornell U., 1963. Bar: N.Y. 1964, U.S. Supreme Ct. 1974, U.S. Dist. Ct. (so. and eas. dists.) N.Y., U.S. Ct. Appeals (3d cir.). Formerly ptnr. Pincus Munzer Bizar & D'Alessandro, 1978-83; atty., real estate investor Munzer & Saunders, LLP, 1984—. Pres. Simcor Mgmt. Corp., N.Y.C., 1984—. Lt. USNR, 1965-75. Mem. Assn. of Bar of City of N.Y., N.Y. State Bar Assn., City Athletic Club, Washington Club. Jewish. Avocations: golf, skiing. Home: 99 Battery Pl New York NY 10280-1320 also: 170 Shearer Rd Washington CT 06793-1013 Office: 609 5th Ave New York NY 10017-1021

MUNZNER, ROBERT FREDERICK, biomedical engineer; b. Balt., July 3, 1936; s. Robert F. Munzner and Catherine E. (Appel) Gay; m. Jo Ann Goettee, Sept. 2, 1960 (div. 1980); children: Elizabeth Mae, Robert Victor, Ann Catherine; m. Karen E. Winstedt, Oct. 1, 1988. BS in Physics, Loyola Coll., Balt., 1963; PhD in Biomed. Engring., U. Va., 1976. Aerospace engr. Westinghouse Def. and Space, Balt., 1963-69; rsch. assoc. Johns Hopkins U., 1975-77; chief, neurol. devices br. U.S. FDA, Rockville, Md., 1977-97, expert sci. reviewer, 1998-99; regulatory affairs cons. Herndon, Va., 1999—. Exec. sec. neurol. device adv. panel. IEEE Standards Bd., 1999-2001. Co-author: Cerebellar Stimulation for Spasticity, 1984, The Physicians Perspective on Medical Law, 1997; contbr. articles to profl. jours. Postdoctoral fellow Johns Hopkins U., Balt., 1975, U. Va. fellow, Charlottesville, 1972-73, Thornton fellow, 1971. Mem. IEEE (sr.; Millennium medal 2000), Biomed. Engring. Soc. (chmn. standards com.), Engring. in Medicine and Biology Soc., Sigma Xi. Achievements include research in atrial mechanical stimulation producing vasomotor reflex. E-mail: r.munzner@ieee.org.

MURAD, FERID, physician; b. Whiting, Ind., Sept. 14, 1936; s. John and Josephine Murad; m. Carol Ann Leopold, June 21, 1958; children: Christine, Marianne, Carrie, Julie, Joseph. BA, DePauw U., 1958; MD, PhD, Case Western Res. U., 1965. Diplomate Nat. Bd. Med. Examiners. Intern and resident Mass. Gen. Hosp., Boston, 1965—67; clin. assoc. NIH, Bethesda,

Md., 1967—70; from assoc. prof. to prof. U. Va., Charlottesville, 1970—81, dir. clin. research ctr., 1971—81, dir. clin. pharmacology, 1973—81; prof. Stanford (Calif.) U., 1981—88, assoc. to acting chmn. dept. medicine, 1984—88; chief of medicine VA Med. Ctr., Palo Alto, Calif., 1981—88; v.p. pharm. divsn. Abbott Labs., 1988—92, CEO, pres. molecular geriatrics, 1993—95; prof. dept. medicine, chmn. dept. integrative biology and pharmacology U. Tex., Houston, 1997—, dir. Inst. Molecular Medicine, 1999—. Co-editor: The Pharmacological Basis of Therapeutics, 1985; contbr. articles. Recipient Lasker award, 1996, Nobel Prize for Medicine, 1998, others. Mem.: Western Assn. Physicians (Ciba award 1988, Lasker award 1996), Assn. Am. Physicians, Am. Soc. Clin. Investigation, Am. Soc. Physiology, Am. Soc. Biol. Chemists, Am. Soc. for Pharmacology and Exptl. Therapeutics, Am. Acad. Arts and Scis., Inst. of Medicine of NAS. Achievements include patents in field. Office: U Tex Med Sch Dept Integrative Biology/Pharmacology PO Box 20708 Houston TX 77225-0708 E-mail: Ferid.Murad@uth.tmc.edu.

MURADIAN, VAZGEN, composer, viola d'amore player; b. Ashtarak, Armenia, Oct. 17, 1921; came to U.S., 1950, naturalized, 1956; s. Grigor and Arusiak (Vardanian) M.; m. Arpi Kirkyasharian, Aug. 29, 1964; children: Vardges, Armen. Grad., Benedetto Marcello State Conservatory Music, Venice, 1948; studied composition with, Gabriele Bianchi; studied violin with, Luigi Ferro. Tchr. violin, solfeggio and theory of music Collegio Armeno, Venice, Italy, 1945-50. Pvt. tchr. viola d'amore. Composer numerous works including 36 symphonies, 64 concertos for all classical instruments and concertos for lesser known instruments, 12 suites for orch., 4 moto perpetuos for violin and orch., 7 sonatas for solo violin, 7 sonatas for violin and piano, 2 sonatas for piano, sonata for viola d'amore, 2 quartets, 2 trios for violin, violoncello and piano, 56 songs with orch. and 8 songs for chorus and orch. on works of Shakespeare, Goethe, Dante, Hugo, others; author articles in field; debut, N.Y. Lincoln Center, 1972; violist with various U.S. orchs. including New Orleans Philharmonic, Wagner Opera Co.; appeared as viola d'amore soloist, U.S. and abroad, compositions performed throughout Europe and Am. Recipient Tekeyan prize, 1962 Mem. ASCAP, Viola D'amore Soc. Achievements include being the only composer of music who wrote concerti for all classical instruments and many for lesser known instruments, so far 64 concerti for 35 different instruments. All major compositions written in classical sonata form. All melodies and themes are his own originals. Home: 269 W 72nd St Apt 11A New York NY 10023-2713

MURADOGLU, METIN, engineering educator; b. Andirin, Kahramanmaras, Turkey, July 15, 1971; s. Osman and Ayse Muradoglu. Doctorate, Cornell U., 2000. Registered engr. Rsch. asst. Cornell U., Ithaca, NY, 1995—2000, rsch. assoc., 2000—01; asst. prof. Koc U., Istanbul, Turkey, 2001—. Mem.: Am. Phys. Soc. Home: 204 Eastern Heights Dr Ithaca NY 14850 Office: Cornell U Upson Hall Ithaca NY 14853 Home Fax: 607-255-1222; Office Fax: 607-255-1222. Personal E-mail: metinm@mae.cornell.edu. Business E-Mail: metinm@mae.cornell.edu.

MURADOV, NAZIM ZIRADDIN, chemist, researcher; b. Akstafa, Azerbaijan, June 5, 1947; s. Ziraddin Gasan and Ramila Kashif Muradov; m. Pervin Ahmed, Oct. 6, 1981; children: Orhan N., Esther N. MSc, Inst. Oil and Chemistry, Baku, Azerbaijan, 1970; DSc, Inst. Chem. Physics, Moscow, 1990. Prin. rsch. scientist Inst. Petrochem. Processes, Baku, Azerbaijan, 1970-90, Fla. Solar Energy Ctr., Cocoa, Fla., 1990-2001. Contbr. articles to profl. jours.; patentee in field. Recipient Disting. Rschr. award U. Ctrl. Fla., 1996. Mem. Am. Chem. Soc., Internat. Assn. Hydrogen Energy. Democrat. Avocations: music, painting. Office: Fla Solar Energy Ctr 1679 Clearlake Rd Cocoa FL 32922

MURAI, NORIMOTO, plant molecular biologist, educator; b. Sapporo, Japan, Mar. 4, 1944; came to U.S., 1968; s. Nobuo and Hideko (Odagiri) M.; m. Andreana Lisca, Nov. 14, 1977; 1 child, Noki. BS, Hokkaido U., 1966, MS, 1968; PhD, U. Wis., 1973. Rsch. assoc. dept. botany U. Wis., Madison, 1974-78, project assoc. dept. bacteriology, 1979, postdoctoral fellow dept. plant pathology, 1980-82; lab. head dept. molecular biology Nat. Inst. Agrobiol. Resources, Tsukuba, Japan, 1983-84; assoc. prof. plant pathology and crop physiology La. State U., Baton Rouge, 1985-92, prof., 1992—. Adj. prof. biochemistry, full mem. grad. faculty and interdept. studies in plant physiology and genetics La. State U.; mem. study sect. on minority biomed. rsch. support program NIH, 1993; grant reviewer USDA, NSF, NIH. Reviewer manuscripts Genome, Protein Engring., Plant Cell, Plant Physiol., Planta, Plant Molecular Biology, Plant Cell Report, Australia Jour. Plant Physiol. Named Honors Rschr., Phi Delta Kappa, 1989; grantee Fulbright Found., 1968, Sci. and Tech. Agy., Tokyo, 1984, La. Edn. Quality Support Fund, 1988, 89, 91, 94, 95, 97, 98, Monsanto Co. Fund, 1992, 93, U.S. Dept. Agr., 1995, Rockefeller Found., 1995-96. Mem. AAAS, Am. Soc. Plant Physiologists, Internat. Soc. Plant Molecular Biology, Japan Molecular Biology Assn., Crop Sci. Soc. Am., Fulbright Assn., Sigma Xi, Gamma Sigma Delta, Phi Delta Kappa. Avocations: running, skiing, gardening, golf, tennis. Office: La State U Dept Plant Path Crop Baton Rouge LA 70803-0001

MURAI, RENE VICENTE, lawyer; b. Havana, Cuba, Mar. 11, 1945; came to the U.S., 1960; s. Andres and Silvia (Muñiz) M.; m. Luisa Botifoll, June 12, 1970; 1 child, Elisa. BA, Brown U., 1966; JD cum laude, Columbia U., 1969. Bar: Fla. 1970, N.Y. 1972, U.S. Supreme Ct. 1977. Atty. Reginald Heber Smith Fellow Legal Svcs. Greater Miami, Fla., 1969-71; assoc. Willkie, Farr & Gallagher, N.Y.C., 1971-73; ptnr. Paul, Landy & Beiley, Miami, 1973-79; shareholder Murai, Wald, Biondo & Moreno, 1979—. Vice-chmn. Premier Am. Bank, Miami; dir. Cuban Am. Bar Assn., 1982-96, pres., 1985; vice chmn., lectr. Internat. Conf. for Lawyers of the Ams., 1982, chmn. and lectr., 1984; mem. panel grievance com. Fla. Bar, 1983-86. Mng. editor Columbia Law Rev., 1967-69. Bd. dirs., sec. Archtl. Club of Miami, 1978-86; bd. dirs. Dade Heritage Trust, 1979-82, Facts About Cuban Exiles, Inc., 1982—, pres., 1989, Legal Svcs. of Greater Miami, Inc., 1980-90, pres. 1986-88, ARC, 1984-90, exec. com., 1988-90, Mercy Hosp. Found., 1985-91, Miami Chldn's Hosp., 2000—, United Way, 1989-95, dir. Dade Cmty. Found., 1988-93, chair grants com., 1991-93; chmn. adminstrn. of justice com. Fla. Bar Found., 1996-98, bd. dirs., 1991-2000, chmn. audit and fin. com., 1993-98, sec., 1997-98, pres. 1999-2000; mem. task force leadership Dade County Ptnrs. for Safe Neighborhoods, 1994-95, Code Enforcement Bd. City of Coral Gables, 1982-86, Bd. Adjustment, 1987-89, city mgr. selection com., 1987, charter rev. commn., 1980; trustee U. Miami, 1994-96; bd. dirs. Miami Children's Hosp., 1999—. Mem. ABA, Cuban-Am. Bar Assn., Dade County Bar Assn. (dir. 1987-88), Greater Miami C. of C., Spain-U.S. C. of C., Miami City Club (bd. dirs. 1997—, pres. 2000—). Democrat. Roman Catholic. Avocation: sports. Home: 3833 Alhambra Ct Coral Gables FL 33134-6229 Office: Murai Wald Biondo & Moreno PA 25 SE 2nd Ave Ste 900 Miami FL 33131-1600 E-mail: rmurai@mwbm.com.

MURAKAMI, CRAIG STUART, facial plastic surgeon; b. Seattle, Apr. 6, 1957; BS in Biology with honors, U. Wash., 1979, MD, 1983. Diplomate Am. Bd. Otolaryngology, Am. Bd. Facial Plastics and Reconstructive Surgery. Gen. surg. intern U. Hawaii, Honolulu, 1983-84, resident in gen. surgery, 1984-85; resident in otolaryngology-head and neck surgery Columbia Presbyn. Med. Ctr., N.Y.C., 1985-88; fellow in facial plastic and reconstructive surgery Oreg. Health Scis. U., Portland, 1988-89, clin. instr. dept. otolaryngology--head and neck surgery divsn. facial plastics and reconstructive surgery, 1988-89; clin. instr. dept. otolaryngology VA Hosp., 1988-89; asst. prof. dept. otolaryngology-head and neck surgery U. Wash., Seattle, 1989-96, assoc. prof. dept. otolaryngology-head and neck surgery, 1996-98, chief div. facial cosmetic and reconstructive surgery, 1996-98; clin. assoc. prof. dept. otolaryngology Virginia Mason Med. Ctr./U. Wash., 1998—. Attending otolaryngologist Virginia Mason Med. Ctr., Children's Orthop. Med. Ctr., VA Med. Ctr.; examiner Am. Bd. Otolaryngology, 1995, 96, 98, 99. Author: (with others) Otolaryngology-Head and Neck Surgery, 2d edit., 1992, Complications of Head and Neck Surgery, 1993, Cutaneous Surgery, 1994, Controversies in Oral and Maxillofacial Surgery, 1994, Principles of Facial Reconstruction, 1995, Office-Based Surgery in Otolaryngology, 1998, Otolaryngology-Head and Neck Surgery, 3rd edit., 1998, Current Therapy in Otolaryngology-Head and Neck Surgery, 1998; guest editor Operative Techniques in Otolaryngology-Head and Neck Surgery, vol. 4, 1993, Facial Plastic Surgery Clinics in N.Am., 1999; contbr. articles to profl. jours.; presenter in field. Fellow ACS (assoc.); mem. AMA, Am. Acad. Otolaryngology-Head and Neck Surgery, Am. Acad. Facial Plastic and Reconstructive Surgery (fellowship co-preceptor 1991—, bd. dirs. and dir.-at-large 1998—), Am. Soc. Dermatologic Surgeons (assoc.), Wash. State Med. Assn., N.W. Acad. Otolaryngology, King County Med. Soc. Avocations: tennis, hiking, music. Office: Virginia Mason MC X10-10 1100 9th Ave Seattle WA 98101-2756 E-mail: otocsm@vmmc.org.

MURAKAMI, GAEL BAXLEY, artist; b. Seattle, Nov. 26, 1946; d. William Milton and Grace Eleanor Baxley; m. Firmin Shinichi Murakami, Sept. 9, 1927. BA, U. Wash., 1970. Office: PO Box 83406 Fairbanks AK 99708-3406 Personal E-mail: murakami@mosquitonet.com. E-mail: murakami@mosquitonet.com.

MURAKAMI, MASANORI, physicist; b. Ashiya, Hyogo, Japan, May 16, 1940; came to U.S., 1965; s. Shohei and Chiyoko (Tani) M.; m. Keiko Takechi, June 6, 1968; children: Tsuyoshi, Megumi, Hiro. MS, Kyoto U., Japan, 1965; PhD, MIT, 1970. Rsch. asst. MIT, Cambridge, 1966-69; sr. mem. rsch. staff Oak Ridge (Tenn.) Nat. Lab., 1969—. Vis. scientist Plasma Physics Lab., Princeton U., 1984-85, 93-94; vis. scientist Gen. Atomics, San Diego, 1995—. Contbr. articles to sci. jours. Fellow Am. Phys. Soc. (exec. com. div. plasma physics 1987-89). Achievements include research in exptl. plasma confinement, plasma transport, plasma diagnostics. Home: 150 Cumberland View Dr Oak Ridge TN 37830 Office: Gen Atomics PO Box 85608 San Diego CA 92186-5608

MURANAKA, HIDEO, artist, educator; b. Mitaka, Tokyo, Japan, Feb. 4, 1946; s. Nobukichi and Hisae M. BFA, Tokyo Nat. U. of Fine Arts, 1970, MFA, 1972. Calif. Community Coll.- Instr. Cred. Drawing accepted for The Pacific Coast States Collection from the v.p. house, Washington, 1980, Nat. Mus. Art, Bklyn. Mus., Achenbach Found., Calif. Palace of Legion of Hon., Yergeau-Musee Internat. d'Art (Can.), Japanese Calligraphy Book, 2000. Mem. Democratic Nat. Comm., Wash., 1985—. Recipient second prize Iternat. Art Exhbn. Museo Hosio, Italy, 1984, V.J.'s Artist award Palm Springs Desert Mus., 1995; named to Hist. Preservation Am. Hall of Fame. Mem. Oakland Mus. Assn., The Fine Arts Mus. San Francisco, Lepidopterist's Soc. Avocations: collecting butterflies, music. Home: 179 Oak St Apt W San Francisco CA 94102-5948

MURANE, WILLIAM EDWARD, lawyer; b. Denver, Mar. 4, 1933; s. Edward E. and Theodora (Wilson) M.; m. Rosemarie Palmerone, Mar. 26, 1960; children: Edward Wheelock, Peter Davenport, Alexander Phelps. AB, Dartmouth Coll., 1954; LLB, Stanford U., 1957. Bar: Wyo. 1957, Colo. 1958, D.C. 1978, U.S. Supreme Ct. 1977. Assoc. then ptnr. Holland & Hart, Denver, 1961-69; dep. gen. counsel U.S. Dept. Commerce, Washington, 1969-71; gen. counsel FDIC, 1971-72; ptnr. Holland & Hart, Denver, 1972—2000. Pub. mem. Adminstrv. Conf. of the U.S., Washington, 1978-81. Bd. dirs. Ctr. for Law and Rsch., Denver, 1973-76, Acad. in the Wilderness, Denver, 1986—, Colo. Bus. Com. for Arts, 2002—; trustee Colo. Symphony Orch., 1994-2000; mem. bd. visitors Stanford U. Law Sch. Capt. USAF, 1958-61. Fellow Am. Coll. Trial Lawyers; mem. ABA (ho of dels. 1991-96), U. Club, Cactus Club. Republican. Avocations: fishing, classical music. Office: Holland & Hart 555 17th St Ste 2700 Denver CO 80202-3950

MURANO, ELSA A. federal agency administrator; b. Havana, Cuba; BS in Biol.. Sci., Fla. Internat. U.; MS in Anaerobic Microbiology, Va. Polytechnic Inst.; PhD in Food Sci. and Tech., Va. State U. Asst. prof. Iowa State U., Ames, 1990—92, prof. in charge rsch. programs linear accelertor facility, 1992—95; various positions including dir. food safety A&M U., College Station, Tex., 1995—2001, assoc. prof. animal sci., 1995—2000, prof. dept. animal sci., 2000—01; undersec. food safety USDA, Washington, 2001—. Chair food safety state initiative com. Tex. Agr. Ext. Sta., 1999—2001; nat. adv. com. meat and poultry inspection USDA, 2001; mem. Nat. Aliance for Food Safety Ops. Com., 1998—2001, chair, 2000—01. Mem.: Intenat. Assn. Food Protection, Poultry Sci. Assn., Inst. Food Technologists, Assn. Meat Sci., Am. Soc. Microbiology. Office: USDA Food Safety 1400 Independence Ave Sw Washington DC 20250 Office Fax: 202-690-4437.*

MURARKA, SHYAM PRASAD, science and engineering educator, administrator; b. Jaynagar, Bihar, India, Mar. 13, 1940; came to U.S., 1966; s. Bihari L. and Suti Murarka; m. Saroj Murarka, May 21, 1962; children: Sumeet, Amal. BS in Chemistry with honors, Bihar U., Muzaffarpur, 1958, MS in Chemistry, 1960; PhD in Chemistry, Agra (India) U., 1970; PhD in Materials Sci. and Metals, U. Minn., 1970. Lectr., rsch. assoc. Bihar U., 1960-61; trainee Atomic Energy Est., Trombay, Maharastra, 1961-62, sci. officer, 1962-66; rsch. asst. U. Minn., Mpls., 1966-70, rsch. assoc., 1970-72; mem. tech. staff, supr. Bell Labs., Murray Hill, N.J., 1972-84; prof. Rensselaer Poly. Inst., Troy, N.Y., 1984—, dir. Ctr. for Integrated Electronics and Electronics Mfg., 1994-96, dir. Ctr. for Advanced Interconnect Sci. and Tech., 1996-2000, dir. Sematech Ctr. of Excellence, 1989-96, Elaine S. & Jack S. Parker chair engring., 1997—. Cons. Bell Labs., Murray Hill, N.J., 1984-89, Applied Materials, Santa Clara, Calif., 1997-99. Author: Silicides for VLSI Applications, 1983, Metallization Theory and Practice for VLSI and ULSI, 1993; (with others) Electronic Materials Science and Technology, 1989, Chemical Mechanical Planarization of Microelectronic Materials, 1997, Copper Fundamental Mechanisms for Microelectronic Applications, 2000; co-editor: Advanced Metallizations in Microelectronics, 1990, Advanced Metallization and Processing for Semiconductor Devices and Circuits II, 1992, Interface Control of Electrical, Chemical, and Mechanical Properties, 1994, Advaned Metallization for Devices and Circuits, 1994, Microelectronics Technology and Process Integration, 1994, Low Dielectric Constant Materials Synthesis in Microelectronics, 1995; contbr. book chpt. Transition Metal Silicides, 1983. Mem. Tri-City India Assn.'s Indian Comty. Support Group, Albany, 1996. Recipient Gold medal Bihar U., 1960; Univ. Grants Commn. scholar, 1961. Fellow IEEE, Am. Vacuum Soc., Am. Soc. Metals and Electrochem. Soc. (Thomas Callinan award 1987, Electronics Divsn. award 2001); mem. Materials Rsch Soc., Bihar U. Chem. Soc. (hon. life). Achievements include 13 patents in field, over 500 rsch. papers and talks. Office: CIEEM Materials Sci & Enging Dept 110 8th St Troy NY 12180-3522

MURASE, JIRO, lawyer; b. N.Y.C., May 16, 1928; BBA, CCNY, 1955; JD, Georgetown U., 1958, LL.D. (hon.), 1982. Bar: D.C. 1958, N.Y. 1959. Sr. ptnr. Marks & Murase L.L.P., N.Y.C., 1971-97, Bingham McCutchen Murase , N.Y.C., 1997—. Legal counsel Consulate Gen. of Japan; mem. Pres.'s Adv. Com. Trade Negotiations, 1980-82; mem. Trilateral Commn., 1985—; apptd. mem. World Trade Coun., 1984-94; adv. com. internat. investment, tech. and devel. Dept. State, 1975. Editorial bd.: Law and Policy in Internat. Bus. Trustee Asia Found., 1979-83, Japanese Ednl. Inst. N.Y.; bd. dirs. Japan Soc., Japanese C. of C. in N.Y., Inc.; bd. regents Georgetown U.; bd. visitors Georgetown Law Ctr.; adv. coun. Pace U., Internat. House Japan; pres. Japanese-Am. Assn. N.Y., Inc., 1996-98—, Japan Ctr. Internat. Exch., 2001—. Recipient N.Y. Gov.'s citation for contbns. to internat. trade, 1982; named to Second Order of Sacred Treasure (Japan), 1989. Mem. ABA, Assn. of Bar of City of N.Y., N.Y. State Bar Assn., N.Y. County Lawyers Assn., Maritime Law Assn., Consular Law Soc., Fed. Bar Coun., Am. Soc. Internat. Law, World Assn. Lawyers, Japanese-Am. Soc. Legal Studies, Am. Arbitration Assn., Lic. Execs. Soc., U.S. C. of C. Clubs: Nippon (dir.); Ardsley Country; N.Y. Athletic; Mid-Ocean (Bermuda). Office: Bingham McCutchen Murase 399 Park Ave New York NY 10022-4614

MURASKI, ANTHONY AUGUSTUS, lawyer; b. Cohoes, N.Y., July 28, 1946; s. Adam Joseph and Angeline Mary (Vozzy) M.; m. Jeanne Marie Gerig; children: Adam Peter, Emily Jo, Talia Rose, Lydia Fern. BA, MA in Speech/Hearing, Sacramento State Coll., 1970; PhD in Audiology/ Hearing Sci., U. Mich., 1977; JD, Detroit Coll. Law, 1979. Bar: Mich. 1980, U.S. Dist. Ct. (ea. dist.) Mich. 1981, U.S. Ct. Appeals (6th cir.) 1982, U.S. Claims Ct. 1989, U.S. Supreme Ct. 1990, Pa. 1990. Asst. Kresge Hearing Research Inst. U. Mich., Ann Arbor, 1971-77; asst. prof. Wayne State U. Med. Sch., Detroit, 1979-82; assoc. Kitch, Suhrheinrich, Saurbier & Drutchas, 1982-83; assoc. prof. Detroit Coll. Law, 1983-85; mng. ptnr. Muraski & Sikorski, Ann Arbor, 1985—. Cons. audiology Ministry of Environment, Ont., Can., 1980-81; trustee Deaf, Speech and Hearing Ctr., Detroit, 1981—; legal adv. on air WWJ Radio, Detroit, 1984—; mem. mental health adv. bd. on deafness Dept. Mental Health, 1984, vis. com. U. Mich. Sch. Edn., 1986—. Author: Legal Aspects of Audiological Practice, 1982, Hearing Conservation in Industry: Licensure, Liability and Forensics, 1985. Mem. ABA, Mich. Bar Assn., Washtenaw County Bar Assn., Am. Speech-Lang.-Hearing Assn. (sci. merit award, 1981), Ann Arbor C. of C. Avocations: photography, writing. Home: 1603 Westminster Pl Ann Arbor MI 48104-4358

MURATA, MARGARET KIMIKO, music historian, educator; b. Chgo., July 29, 1946; d. Yoshinori and Mikiko Murata. AB, U. Chgo., 1967, AM, 1971, PhD, 1975. Prof. U. Calif., Irvine, 1973—, chair dept. music, 1995-96. Music subject test com. Grad. Record Examination, Princeton, 1995-2000. Author: Operas for the Papal Court, 1981, Source Readings Musical History: Baroque, rev. edit., 1998; contbr. articles to profl. jours. Recipient Disting. Tchg. award U. Calif. Irvine Alumni Assn., 1984, Sch. Arts, 1996; hon. fellow Woodrow Wilson Found., 1967, Dissertation fellow AAUW, 1972-73. Mem. Internat. Musicol. Soc., Am. Musicol. Soc. (bd. dirs., v.p. 1994-96), Coll. Music Soc., Soc. 17th-Century Music (pres. 2000-2003), Società Italiana di Musicologia, Japanese-Am. Citizens League. Office: U Calif Irvine Dept Music Irvine CA 92697-2775 E-mail: mkmurata@uci.edu.

MURATA, TADAO, engineering and computer science educator; b. Takayama, Gifu, Japan, June 26, 1938; arrived in U.S., 1962; s. Yonosuke and Ryu (Aomame) M.; m. Nellie Kit-Ha Shin, 1964; children: Patricia Emi, Theresa Terumi BSE.E., Tokai U., 1962; MSE.E., U. Ill., 1964, PhD in Elec. Engring., 1966. Research asst. U. Ill., Urbana, 1962-66; asst. prof. U. Ill. at Chgo., 1966-68, assoc. prof., 1970-76, prof., 1977—; assoc. prof. Tokai U., Tokyo, Japan, 1968-70. Vis. prof. U. Calif., Berkeley, 1976-77; cons. Nat. Bur. Stds., Gaithersburg, Md., 9184-85; panel mem. NAS, Washington, 1981-82, 83-85; vis. scientist Nat. Ctr. For Sci. Rsch., France, 1981; guest rschr. Gesellschaft für Mathematik und Datenverarbeitung, Germany, 1979; Hitachi-Endowed prof. Osaka (Japan) U., 1993-94. Editor IEEE Trans. on Software Enging., 1986-92; assoc. editor Jour. of Cirs., Sysems and Computers, 1990—; contbr. articles to sci. and engring. jours. Recipient C.A. Petri Disting. Tech. Achievement award Soc. Design and Process Scis., 2000; Sr. univ. scholar award U. Ill., 1990; NSF grantee, 1978— , U.S.-Spain coop. rsch. grantee, 1985-87. Fellow IEEE (golden core charter mem. IEEE Computer Soc., Donald G. Fink Prize award 1991); mem. Assn. Computing Machinery, Info. Processing Soc. Japan, European Assn. for Theoretical Computer Sci., Upsilon Pi Epsilon (hon.). Avocations: golf, travel. Office: U Ill Dept Computer Sci m/c 152 851 S Morgan St Chicago IL 60607-7042 E-mail: t.murata@ieee.org.

MURAVCHIK, JOSHUA, writer; b. N.Y.C., Sept. 17, 1947; s. Emanuel and Miriam Muravchik; m. Sally Golden, Jan. 1, 1974; children: Stephanie, Madeline, Valerie. BA, CCNY, 1970; PhD, Georgetown U., 1984. Project dir. Coalition for Dem. Majority, Washington, 1974, exec. dir., 1976-78; profl. staff mem. House Subcom. on Higher Edn., 1975; scholar-in-residence Washington Inst. for Near East Policy, 1985-86; resident scholar Am. Enterprise Inst., Washington, 1987—. Mem. editl. bd. World Affairs, Washington, 1982—, Jour. Democracy, Washington, 1990—; mem. Md. state adv. com. U.S. Commn. on Civil Rights, Washington, 1984-97. Author: The Uncertain Crusade, 1986, News Coverage of the Sandinista Revolution, 1988, Exporting Democracy, 1991, The Imperative of American Leadership, 1996, Heaven on Earth, 2002. Mem. commn. on broadcasting to People's Republic of China, U.S. Govt., Washington, 1992. Mem. Coun. on Fgn. Rels. Jewish. Avocations: softball, gardening. Home: 1932 Wallace Ave Wheaton MD 20902 Office: AEI 1150 17th St NW Washington DC 20036 E-mail: jmuravchik@aei.org.

MURAY, LESLIE ANTHONY, Episcopalian priest, educator; b. Budapest, Hungary, Dec. 30, 1948; came to U.S., 1959; naturalized, 1965; s. Remus Frederick and Marianna Margareta (Zetelaki Tohaty) M. BA, Whittier Coll., 1971; M in Religion, Sch. of Theology, Claremont, Calif., 1973; PhD, Claremont Grad. Sch., 1982. Ordained deacon Episcopalian Ch., 1974, priest, 1975; cert. c.c. tchr., Ariz. Asst. dir. Episcopal Comty. Svcs., Phoenix, 1975-79; vicar St. Luke's at the Mountain, 1975-78; priest in charge Epiphany on the Desert, Gila Bend, Ariz., 1978-79; chaplain Ariz. Ctr. for Women, Phoenix, 1980-83; interim vicar Christ Ch., Florence, Ariz., 1983-84; interim rector-vicar St. Paul' Ch., St. George's, Winslow, Holbrook, 1984-85; rector St. John's Ch., Globe, 1985-86; chaplain Episcopal Ministry at Mich. State U., East Lansing, 1986-89; rector St. John's Ch., St. John, Mich., 1990-95; part time temporary asst. prof. Ctrl. Mich. U., Mount Pleasant, 1992—. Adjunct prof. dept. religious studies Ariz. State U., Tempe, 1979-84; adj. prof. Rio Salado C.C., Paradise Valley, Ariz., 1985, Northland Pioneer Coll., Winslow, Ariz., 1985, Gila Pueblo Coll., Globe, Ariz., 1985; assoc. faculty Humanities and Religious Studies, Lansing (Mich.) C.C., 1987—; adjunct prof. U. Detroit, 1990, Religious Studies, Polit. Sci., Western Mich. U., Lansing Regional Ctr., 1990—; mem. adv. bd. Ctr. for Process Studies, 1977, 1996—. Author: (book) Introduction to the Process of Science, Society and the Self, 1988; contbr. articles to religious and profl. mags., chpts. to books. Mem. Am. Acad. Religion (mem. sect. program com. 1993—, co-chair 1995—), Am. Philos. Assn., Soc. Christian Ethics, Inst. Religion in an Age of Sci., Hungarian Philos. Assn. Democrat. Avocations: reading, sports, langs., photography, travel. Office: Lansing CC Dept Humanities Arts PO Box 40010 Lansing MI 48901-7210 Home: 34 Century Ln Milton MA 02186-4817

MURAYAMA, MAKIO, biochemist; b. San Francisco, Aug. 10, 1912; s. Hakuyo and Namiye (Miyasaka) M.; children: Gibbs Soga, Alice Myra. BA, U. Calif., Berkeley, 1938, MA, 1940; PhD (NIH fellow), U. Mich., 1953; ScD honoris causa, Open Internat. U., Sri Lanka, 1994. Rsch. biochemist Children's Hosp. of Mich., Detroit, 1943, 45-48, Bellevue Hosp., N.Y.C., 1943-45; Research biochemist Harper Hosp., Detroit, 1949-54; research fellow in chemistry Calif. Inst. Tech., Pasadena, 1954-56; research asso. in biochemistry Grad. Sch. Medicine, U. Pa., Phila., 1956-58; spl. research fellow Nat. Cancer Inst. at Cavendish Lab., Cambridge, Eng., 1958; sr. research biochemist NIH, Bethesda, Md., 1958-93. Author: (with Robert M. Nalbandian) Sickle Cell Hemoglobin, 1973; discovered DIPA (decompression-inducible platelet aggregation), 1975; discovered DIPA causes vascular occlusion in both acute mountain sickness and diver's syndrome, 1984. Fellow Am. Inst. Chemists; mem. AAAS, Am. Chem. Soc., Am. Soc. Biol. Chemists, Assn. Clin. Scientists, Undersea and Hyperbaric Med. Soc., Aerospace Med. Assn., Internat. Platform Assn., West African Soc. Pharmacology (hon.), N.Y. Acad. Sci., Sigma Xi. Achievements include patent for automatic amperometric titration apparatus, 1958; development of molecular mechanism of human red cell sickling and prevention of sickle cell crisis by oral prophylactic carbamide, 1972; discovery of decompression inducible platelet aggregation by means of simulation of decompression-inducible platelet aggregation of diving in frogs and mice that diver's disease and acute mountain sickness could be alleviated by piracetam and thymol, antiplatelet agents, 1986. Home: 5010 Benton Ave Bethesda MD 20814-2804 E-mail: mmurayama@aol.com.

MURBACH, DAVID PAUL, horticulturist; b. N.Y., July 19, 1952; s. J. Frederick and Ragna M. (Samuelsen) M. BS, U. Ariz., 1974; AAS, SUNY, Farmingdale, 1981; MS, U. Del., 1988. Cert. in Mus. Studies. Mgr. gardens div. Rockefeller Ctr. Mgmt. Corp., N.Y.C., 1985-96; mgr. gardens divsn. Tishman Speyer Properties-Rockefeller Ctr., 1997—. Computer cons. Murbach, Inc., N.Y.C., 1989—; exec. dir. Horticulture Soc. South Fla., 2000—; chmn. bd. dirs. Metro Hort. Group, N.Y.C., 1988-90; adj. asst. prof. urban landscape architecture program Sch. Architecture and Environ. Studies CUNY, 1990; chair Horticulture Com. The LongHouse Reserve, 1999, hon. trustee; adv. to bd. Old Westbury Gardens, 1997—, Ann Norton Sculpture Garden; ex-offico Monnts Botanical Garden. Author: (booklet) Directory of Computer Use in Plant Record Keeping, 1984; contbr. articles on plants and drought to profl. jours. Ex officio mem. bd. dirs. Mount Bot. Garden, West Palm Beach, Fla.; bd. dirs. Ann Norton Sculpture Garden. Recipient Cmty. Svc. award N.Y.C. Parks Coun., 1994, Presdl. citation U. Del., 2000; Loeb fellow Harvard U., 2000. Mem. Hort. Soc. N.Y., Am. Assn. Bot. Gardens Arboreta (chmn. computer svc. com. Wayne, Pa. 1988-90, profl. citation 1994), Hort. Soc. S.Fla. (exec. dir.). Avocation: opera. Office: Murbach Inc PO Box 958 East Hampton NY 11937-0705

MURCHISON, DAVID CLAUDIUS, lawyer; b. N.Y.C., Aug. 19, 1923; s. Claudius Temple and Constance (Waterman) M.; m. June Margaret Guilfoyle, Dec. 19, 1946; children: David Roderick, Brian, Courtney, Bradley, Stacy. AA, George Washington U., 1947, BA, JD with honors, George Washington U., 1949. Bar: D.C. 1949, Supreme Ct. 1955. Assoc. Dorr, Hand & Dawson, N.Y.C., 1949-50; founding ptnr. Howrey & Simon, Washington, 1956-90, counsel, 1990—. Legal asst. under sec. army, 1949-51; counsel motor vehicle, textile, aircraft, ordinance and shipbldg. divsns. Nat. Prodn. Authority, 1951-52; assoc. gen. counsel Small Def. Plants Adminstrn., 1952-53; legal adv. and asst. to chmn. FTC, 1953-55 Chmn. So. Africa Wildlife Trust. With AUS, 1943-45, ETO. Mem. ABA (chmn. com. internat. restrictive bus. practices sect. antitrust law 1954-55, sect. adminstrv. law, sect. litigation), FBA, D.C. Bar Assn., N.Y. State Bar Assn., Order of Coif, Met. Club, Chevy Chase Club, Talbot Country Club. Republican.

MURCHISON, DAVID RODERICK, lawyer; b. Washington, May 28, 1948; s. David Claudius and June Margaret (Guilfoyle) M.; m. Kathy Ann Kohn, Mar. 15, 1981; children: David Christopher, Benjamin Michael. BA cum laude, Princeton U., 1970; JD, Georgetown U., 1975. Bar: D.C. 1975, Fla. 1993. Legal asst. to vice chmn. CAB, Washington, 1975-76, enforcement atty., 1976-77; sr. atty. Air Transport Assn., 1977-80, asst. v.p., sec., 1981-85; sr. assoc. Zuckert, Scoutt and Rasenberger, 1980-81; v.p., asst. gen. counsel Piedmont Aviation, Inc., Winston-Salem, N.C., 1985-88; v.p., gen. counsel, sec. Braniff, Inc., Dallas, 1988-89, chief exec. officer Orlando, 1990-94; fed. adminstrv. law judge Office of Hearings and Appeals, Charleston, W.Va., 1994-96, chief adminstrv. law judge Mobile, Ala., 1996-99, adminstrv. law judge, 1999—. Lectr. continuing legal edn. program Wake Forest U., Winston-Salem, 1988. Contbr. articles to legal jours. Lt. USNR, 1970-72. Mem. ABA, Met. Club Washington. Republican. Roman Catholic. Office: Office Hearings and Appeals 3605 Springhill Bus Park Mobile AL 36608-1239

MURCKO, DONALD LEROY, architect; b. Warren, Ohio, Jan. 24, 1953; s. Joseph Mathew and Sophie May (Hidukawich) M.; m. Marilyn A. Infante, Oct. 3, 1998. BArch, Kent State U., 1977. Registered architect, Ohio. Archtl. draftsman Angel Constrn. Co., Garrettsville, Ohio, 1977-80; apprentice architect E.S. Jakubick & Assoc.s, Warren, 1980-82; assoc. architect Mosure & Assocs., Inc., Youngstown, 1982-90; project architect MS Consultants, Inc., 1990-91, Buchanan Ricciuti Balog, Youngstown, Ohio, 1991-96, Ricciuti Balog and Ptnrs., Youngstown, 1996—. Cons. architect VA, Cleve., 1986—. Mem. Western Pa. Conservancy, Pitts., 1985—, Mahoning Valley Hist. Soc., Youngstown, 1989—, Butler Inst. Am. Art, Youngstown, 1991—. Recipient Cert. of Merit, Ohio Edison Co., 1976. Mem. AIA, Architects Soc. Ohio, Cath. Alumni Club Youngstown (past pres.). Democrat. Roman Catholic. Avocations: architectural delineation, illustration, modelmaking, photography, travel. Office: Ricciuti Balog and Ptnrs Architects 1500 Metropolitan Tower Youngstown OH 44503

MURDEN, ROBERT A. medical administrator, physician; b. Radford, Va., May 5, 1951; s. William P. and Mabel S. Murden; children: Rob, Nick, Chelsea. BS, U. Mich., 1972; MD, U. Mo., Columbia, 1977. Diplomate Am. Bd. Internal Medicine; cert. added qualifications in geriatrics. Resident in internal medicine U. Tex., Galveston, 1977-80; fellow in geriatrics Mt. Sinai Sch. Medicine, N.Y.C., 1983-85; faculty medicine and geriatrics SUNY, Stony Brook, 1985-86, Bklyn., 1986-89, U. Kans. Med. Ctr., Kansas City, 1990-91; faculty medicine Ohio State U., Columbus, 1991-94, divsn. dir. gen. medicine, 1994—. Co-dir. Alzheimer's Disease Assistance Ctr., SUNY, Bklyn., 1988-89. Contbr. articles to profl. jours. Fellow ACP; mem. Soc. Gen. Internal Medicine, Am. Geriatrics Soc., Soc. Am. Baseball Rsch. E-mail: murden_1@medctr.ohio_state.edu. Office: Ohio State U 456 W 10th Ave Rm 4510 Columbus OH 43210-1240

MURDOCH, BERNARD CONSTANTINE, psychology educator; b. Greensboro, N.C., Dec. 5, 1917; s. Homer Odell and Hilma Caroline (Lang) M.; m. Martha Grace Hood, June 29, 1946; children: Norma, Constance, Joyce, Diana. BS, Appalachian State Tchrs. Coll., 1938; EdM, U. Cin., 1939; PhD, Duke U., 1942; postgrad., NYU, 1942-43. Licensed applied psychologist, Ga. Math. critic tchr. Appalachian State Tchrs. Coll. demonstration sch., 1938; math. and sci. tchr. Lexington (N.C.) High Sch., 1939-40; sci. tchr. Harding High Sch., Charlotte, N.C., 1945-46; also dir. Guidance and Testing Bur., Vets. Info. Center; prof. edn. and psychology Presbyn. Coll., Clinton, S.C., 1946-48, acad. dean, 1947-48; also extension prof. edn. U. S.C., 1946-48; mem. research staff Am. Council on Edn., Office of Naval Rsch., Washington, 1948-50; dean Muskingum Coll., New Concord, Ohio, 1950-54; prof., head psychology dept. Wesleyan Coll., Macon, Ga., 1954-82, prof. emeritus, 1982—, chmn. dept. behavioral scis., 1973-82, also dir. testing.; pres. Fore(In)Sight Found., 1991—. Author: Consistency of Test Responses, 1942, Love and Problems of Living, 1992, God and Positive Christianity, 1998; co-author: The Production of Doctorates in the Sciences, 1936-48; contbr. to sci., ednl. and religious publs. Served to capt. USAAF, 1942-45. Fellow AAAS; mem. APA (life), Southeastern Psychol. Assn., Ga. Psychol. Assn. (dir., pres. 1969-70), Ga. Mental Health Assn. (dir.), NEA, Ga. Mental Health Council (psychology rep. 1973-74), Ga. State Bd. Examiners Psychologists (pres. 1974-75), Am. Ednl. Rsch. Assn., Masons, Presbyterian. Home: 4966 Zebulon Rd Macon GA 31210-3059 *Opportunities vary widely, and the necessary perception to capitalize on such also is a distinct variable. Those of us who have achieved a measure of "success" in vocational or other ways must feel very humble as we recognize our good fortune. We have not only had opportunities come before us, but we were able to perceive them in such a way as to accomplish whatever recognition has been ours. Millions have not been so fortunate.*

MURDOCH, DAVID ARMOR, lawyer; b. Pitts., May 30, 1942; s. Armor M. and N. Edna (Jones) M.; m. Joan Wilkie, Mar. 9, 1974; children: Christina, Timothy, Deborah. AB magna cum laude, Harvard U., 1964, LLB, 1967. Bar: Pa. 1967, U.S. Dist. Ct. (we. dist.) Pa. 1967, U.S. Ct. Mil. Appeals 1968, U.S. Supreme Ct. 1990, U.S. Ct. Appeals (3d cir.) 1991. Assoc. Kirkpatrick & Lockhart, LLP, Pitts., 1971-78, ptnr., 1978—. Mem. adv. bd. Ctr. for Internat. Legal Edn., U. Pitt., 1997—. Co-author: Business Workouts Manual. V.p., bd. dirs. Avonworth Sch. Dist., 1977-83; mem. bd. dirs. Pitts. Expt., 1988-93, chmn., 1989-90; mem. Pa. Housing Fin. Agy., 1981-88, vice chmn., 1983-87; alt. del. Rep. Nat. Conv., 1980; elder The Presbyn. Ch. of Sewickley, 1986-92; past pres. Harvard Law Sch. Assn. W. Pa.; bd. advisors Geneva Coll., 1993-94, trustee, 1994-97; trustee Sewickley Pub. Libr., 1994-2002, vice chmn., 1997-2002; trustee World Learning, Inc., 1995—, vice chmn., 1998-2000, chmn., 2000—; dir. Allegheny County Libr. Assn., 1994-96; chair Czech Working Group, Presbyn. Ch. USA, 1995-2000; bd. visitors U. Ctr. Internat. Studies, U. Pitts., 1996—; bd. advisors The Ctr. for Bus., Religion, and Pub. Life, Pitts. Theol. Sem., 1997—; bd. dirs. World Affairs Coun. Pitts., 1998—, Am. Coun. Germany, 1998—; hon. consul Fed. Rep. of Germany in Pitts., 2002—. Capt. U.S. Army, 1968-71. Recipient Disting. Svc. award Allegheny County Libr. Assn., 2001. Fellow Am. Coll. Bankruptcy, Am. Bar Found.; mem. ABA (mem. bus. bankruptcy com., chmn. subcom. on bankruptcy coms., trust indentures and claims trading 1991-97). Office: Kirkpatrick & Lockhart LLP Henry W Oliver Bldg 535 Smithfield St Pittsburgh PA 15222-2312 E-mail: dmurdoch@kl.com.

MURDOCH, KEITH MICHAEL, physicist; b. Auckland, New Zealand, Jan. 12, 1968; s. Neil W. and Noelene A. (Charlton) M. BSc with honors, U. Canterbury, Christchurch, New Zealand, 1990, PhD in Physics, 1994. Post-doctoral fellow Lawrence Berkeley (Calif.) Nat. Lab., 1994-96; rsch. asst. U. Oxford, Eng., 1996-97; rsch. assoc., lectr. U. Wis., Madison, 1997-2000; sr. devel. engr. Coherent Inc., Santa Clara, Calif., 2001—. Contbr. articles to profl. jours. Charles Cook Warwick House Meml. scholar, U. Canterbury, 1990-91, Australian Nat. U. Vacation scholar, Canberra, Australia, 1989; Grad. Rsch. Los Alamos Nat. Lab., N.Mex., 1991. Mem. Royal Soc. New Zealand, Royal Astron. Soc. New Zealand, New Zealand Inst. Physics, Am. Phys. Soc., Optical Soc. Am., New Zealand Am. Assn. San Francisco (treas. 2001--). Avocations: astronomy, travel, hiking, reading, current affairs. Office: Coherent Inc Mail Stop P-33 5100 Patrick Henry Dr Santa Clara CA 95054 E-mail: keith.murdoch@coherentinc.com.

MURDOCH, LAWRENCE CORLIES, JR. retired banker, economist; b. Phila., June 3, 1926; s. Lawrence C. and Barbara (Boyd) M.; children: Lawrence C. III, Anne G.; m. 2d Eleanor M. Egan, June 16, 1970. BS Wharton Sch., U. Pa. in Econs., 1948; MBA, Wharton Sch., U. Pa., 1956. With Fed. Res. Bank Phila., 1954-92; ret., 1992. Bd. dirs. Cliveden Inc., 1981, Fort Mifflin, 1990. Contbr. articles to consumer and monetary publs.; producer documentary films; spokesman (radio and TV). Lt. (j.g.) USN, 1948-54. Mem. Soc. Cin. (pres. 1990-93), Little Egg Harbor Yacht Club (Beach Haven, N.J.), Beta Gamma Sigma, Zeta Psi. Home: 115 Hilltop Rd Philadelphia PA 19118-3737

MURDOCH, NORMAN HOWARD, history educator; b. DuBois, Pa., May 15, 1939; s. Walter Howard and Emma Irene (Douge) M.; m. Grace M.A. Bell, Sept. 17, 1966; children: Randall, Amy, Ryan. BA in History and Polit. Sci., Asbury Coll., 1961; MDiv, Asbury Theol. Sem., 1965, MTh, 1972; MEd, U. Cin., 1968, MA, 1975, PhD, 1985. Prof. history U. Cin., Cin., 1968—. Mem. Milford (Ohio) Bd. Edn., 1976-83. Provostal grantee, 1989, 91, 94, Ctr. on Philanthropy at Ind. U. grantee, 1991; recipient Brodie award, 1981. Mem. AAUP (pres. 1990-94, Ohio exec. com. 1992-95, nat. coun. 1992-95), Am. Hist. Assn., Orgn. Am. Historians, Internat. Communal Studies Assn., Soc. for Utopian Studies, Am. Soc. Ch. History, Ohio Acad. History, Wesleyan Theol. Soc., Social Welfare History Group, Milford Area Hist. Soc. Avocation: travel. Home: 9412 Bluewing Ter Cincinnati OH 45241-3303 Office: U Cin 206 Mill St Cincinnati OH 45215-4627

MURDOCH, RUPERT (KEITH RUPERT MURDOCH), publisher; b. Melbourne, Australia, Mar. 11, 1931; came to U.S., 1974, naturalized, 1985; s. Keith and Elisabeth Joy (Greene) M.; m. Anna Maria Torv, Apr. 28, 1967 (div.); children: Prudence, Elisabeth, Lachlan, James; m. Wendi Deng, June 25, 1999. MA, Worcester Coll., Oxford, Eng., 1953. Chmn. bd. dirs. News Corp., 1979—, chief exec., 1979—; dir. BSkyB, 1990—; CEO Fox Entertainment Group, 1995—. Dir. Phillip Morris Cos., Inc., 1989—; owner, pub. numerous newspapers, mags. and TV stas. in U.S.A., Australia, U.K., Asia. Office: The News Corp Ltd 3rd Fl 1211 Avenue Of The Americas New York NY 10036*

MURDOCH-KITT, NORMA HOOD, clinical psychologist; b. Clinton, S.C., May 16, 1947; d. Bernard Constatine and Martha Grace (Hood) Murdoch; m. Jonathan Michael Kitt, Mar. 23, 1974; children: Kelly, Michelle, Mark Jason, Sabrina Brittany, Laura Kristina. BA, Wake Forest U., 1969; MS, U. Pitts., 1971, PhD, 1975. Psychology intern Ea. Pa. Psychiat. Inst., 1972-73; asst. prof., therapist campus counseling ctr. William and Mary U., Williamsburg, Va., 1973-74; staff psychologist child psychiatry dept. Med. Coll. Va., 1974-75; pvt. practice psychotherapy, family, martial, individual Richmond, Va., 1975—. Clin. prof. psychiatry Med. Coll. Va., 1995—. Pres. Ginter Park Residents Assn., 1988—89, 1998—, North Richmond's Team of Civic Assn. Pres., 2001—03; mem. Richmond Human Rels. Adv. Commn., 1978—80, Richmond Mayor's Com. on Concerns of Women, 1987—93, chair, 1989—93; mem. Richmond Citizens' Crime Commn., 1985—88, co-chair police chief sect. com., 1994—95; mem. Richmond Dem. Com., 1978—79, 1982—85, 1988—89, 1991—97, 1999—2002; founder, 1st state chair polit. action com. ERA, 1977—78; chief lobbyist ERA Ratification Coun., 1977—79; mem. long-range planning com. Bapt. Theol. Sem., Richmond, 1993—96, 1999—; v.p. The Women's Ctr. for Christian Leadership, Inc., 1996—99, vice chair, 1997—98; mem. Presbyn. Ch. Found.; bd. dirs. Va. Psychol. Found., 1987—, North Richmond YMCA, 1999—, HOMEWARD, 2002—, Richmond Tech. Ctr., 2000—. USPHS fellow 1969-72. Mem.: APA (steering com. state leadership conf. 1986—91, chair 1991, Richmond area chair ARC/APA disaster mental health network 1993—), Internat. Soc. for Study Multiple Personality and Disassociation (chmn. edn. com. 1979—80, bd. dirs. 1980—81), Chronic Fatigue Assn., Richmond Acad. Clinical Psychologists (pres. 1995), Va. Breast Cancer Found. (rsch. chair 1992—96), Va. Acad. Clin. Psychologists (chair profl. affairs com. 1982—84), Va. Psychol. Assn. (state legis. lobbyist 1978—79, chair legis. com. 1981—83, bd. profl. affairs 1981—85, pres. 1986), Richmond First Club. Office: Murdoch-Kitt Profl Bldg 3217 Chamberlayne Ave Richmond VA 23227-4806 E-mail: shrinkrapper@juno.com.

MURDOCK, CHARLES WILLIAM, lawyer, educator; b. Chgo., Feb. 10, 1935; s. Charles C. and Lucille Marie (Tracy) M.; m. Mary Margaret Hennessy, May 25, 1963; children: Kathleen, Michael, Kevin, Sean. BSChemE, Ill. Inst. Tech., 1956; JD cum laude, Loyola U., Chgo., 1963. Bar: Ill. 1963, Ind. 1971. Asst. prof. law DePaul U., 1968-69; assoc. prof. law U. Notre Dame, 1969-75; prof., dean Law Sch. Loyola U., Chgo., 1975-83, 86—; dep. atty. gen. State of Ill., 1983-86; of counsel Chadwell & Kayser, Ltd., 1986-89. Vis. prof. U. Calif., 1974; cons. Pay Bd., summer 1972, SEC, summer 1973; co-founder Loyola U. Family Bus. Program; arbitrator Chgo. Bd. Options Exch., Nat. Assn. Securities Dealers, N.Y. Stock Exch., Am. Arbitration Assn.; co-founder, mem. exec. com. Loyola Family Bus. Ctr., 1990—; bd. dirs. Plymouth Tube Co., 1993—. Author: Business Organizations, 2 vols., 1996; editor: Illinois Business Corporation Act Annotated, 2 vols., 1975; tech. editor The Business Lawyer, 1989-90. Chmn. St. Joseph County (Ind.) Air Pollution Control Bd., 1971; bd. dirs. Nat. Center for Law and the Handicapped, 1973-75, Minority Venture Capital Inc., 1973-75. Capt. USMCR. Mem. ABA, Ill. Bar Assn. (cert. of award for continuing legal edn.), Chgo. Bar Assn. (cert. of award for continuing legal edn., bd. mgrs. 1976-78), Ill. Inst. Continuing Legal Edn. (adv. com) Roman Catholic. Home: 2126 Thornwood Ave Wilmette IL 60091-1452 Office: Loyola U Sch Law 1 E Pearson St Chicago IL 60611-2055 E-mail: cmurdoc@luc.edu.

MURDOCK, CHLOE CONGER, artist; b. Bloomington, Ill., Jan. 30; d. Tom and Lela (Conger) Keefe; m. John James Murdock (dec.). Exhibits include L.A. County Mus., San Francisco Mus. Art, Calif. State Fair, Nat. Watercolor Society, L.A., Watercolor Soc., Pitts., Pitts. Fine Arts, Butler Art Inst., Youngstown, Ohio, Pasadena Mus. Art, Santa Monica (Calif.) Art Gallery, Conejo Valley Mus., Thousand Oaks, Calif., Pa. Acad. Fine Arts, Phila., U. Calif., Camerio, 2001. Avocations: yoga, hiking.

MURDOCK, DAVID H. diversified company executive; b. Kansas City, Mo., Apr. 10, 1923; m. Maria Ferrer, Apr., 1992. LLD (hon.), Pepperdine U., 1978; LHD (hon.), U. Nebr., 1984, Hawaii Loa Coll., 1989. Sole proprietor, chmn., chief exec. officer Pacific Holding Co., L.A.; chmn. Dole Food Co. (formerly Castle & Cooke, Inc.), 1985—, also bd. dirs. Trustee Asia Soc., N.Y.C., L.A.; founder, bd. dirs. Found. for Advanced Brain Studies, L.A.; bd. visitors UCLA Grad. Sch. Mgmt.;bd. govs. Performing Arts Coun. of Music Ctr., L.A.; bd. govs. East-West Ctr., L.A.; patron Met. Opera, N.Y.C. With USAAC, 1943-45. Mem. Regency Club (founder, pres.) Bel-Air Bay Country Club, Sherwood Country Club (founder, pres.), Met. Club (N.Y.C.). Office: Dole Food Co Inc One Dole Dr Westlake Village CA 91361-4633 also: Pacific Holding Co 10900 Wilshire Blvd Ste 1600 Los Angeles CA 90024-6530*

MURDOCK, JOHN T., II, academic organization administrator, publishing company executive; b. Harrogate, Eng. came to U.S., 1987; s. John T. and Cynthia (Gell) M. Exec. dir. Nat. Valedictorian Soc., Louviers, Colo., 1996—; sr. editor Valedictorian Press, 1997—; pres. NVS Acad. Resource Corp., Redmond, Wash., 2000—. Mem. Soc. for Am. Archaeology, Royal Anthropol. Inst., Am. Horticultural Soc. Avocations: ancient history, gardening, visiting university campuses. Office: Nat Valedictorian Soc PO Drawer 250 Louviers CO 80131

MURDOCK, MARY-ELIZABETH, history educator; b. Boston, Jan. 4, 1930; d. Lester Joseph and Elizabeth Rowe (Collingwood) M. AB, Tufts U., 1952; A.M., Boston U., 1958; PhD, Brown U., 1962; S.M., Simmons Coll., 1970; cert. mgmt. inst. women in higher edn., Wellesley Coll., 1985; cert. master gardener, U. Mass., 1988. Tchr. Nat. Cathedral Sch., Washington, 1954-57; assoc. prof. Trenton State Coll, N.J., 1962-66, U. R.I., Kingston, 1966-69; archivist, dir. Sophia Smith collection Smith Coll., Northampton, Mass., 1970-84, lectr. history, 1973-86, instr. Southeast Asian ESL program, 1986-88. Guest lectr. colls. and univs., 1986—; cons. N.Y.C. YWCA, 1974-75, HEN, 1976-86, Greenfield Cmty. Coll., Mass., 1983-86, Ednl. Testing Svc., Princeton, N.J., 1985—; faculty cons. Nat. Evaluation Sys., Amherst, Mass., 1984-92; bd. reviewers Hist. Jour. Mass., 1985-88; adv. bd. Ctr. Am. Studies, Concord, Mass., 1985-88; indexer Liberty Party newspaper (1845-48). Author articles, monographs, analytical catalogs. Mem. Am. Studies Assn., New Eng. Am. Studies Assn., Orgn. Am. Historians (state membership chmn. 1980-88), Am. Assn. State and Local History, Hist. Deerfield Inc., Hist. Northampton, Nat. Trust for Hist. Preservation, Phi Alpha Theta. Avocations: choral singing, piano, painting, photography, gardening.

MURDOCK, NANCI C. women's health nurse; b. Dearborn, Mich., July 18, 1946; d. John C. (dec.) and Mildred G. (Rogan) Talpos (dec.); m. Rogan C. Murdock, July 18, 1970; children: Brant A., Meigan L. ADN, Owens Tech. Coll., Perrysburg, Ohio, 1983; BS, Mary Manse Coll., Toledo, 1968; postgrad., Ea. Mich. U., 1970—72, U. Toledo, 1992. Cert. sch. nurse. Tchr. physics, life sci. and art St. Andrews High Sch., Detroit, 1971-72; tchr. life sci., earth sci. and health Otsego Jr. High Sch., Tontogany, Ohio, 1973-77; tchr. life sci. and art Our Lady of Perpetual Help, Toledo, 1978—80; staff nurse peripheral vascular dept. St. Vincent Med. Ctr., 1983-85; staff nurse labor and delivery St Vincent Med. Ctr., Toledo, 1985-88; sch. nurse Rossford (Ohio) Bd. Edn., 1988—; outpatient surgery staff nurse Healthmark Pavilion, Toledo, 1991-95; surgery staff nurse main oper. rm. Riverside Hosp., 1995-2000. Evaluator Nat. Sci. Tchrs. Assn. Conv., Washington. Mem.: Rossford Assn. Classroom Tchrs. (past mem. exec. com.), Ohio Edn. Assn., Wood County Sch. Nurses Assn., Ohio Sch. Nurses Assn., Nat. Assn. Sch. Nurses. Home: 105 Lones Dr Perrysburg OH 43551-2331 E-mail: ncmurdock18@hotmail.com.

MURDOCK, PAMELA ERVILLA, travel and advertising company executive; b. Los Angeles, Dec. 3, 1940; d. John James and Chloe Conger (Keefe) M.; children: Cheryl, Kim. BA, U. Colo., 1962. Pres. Dolphin Travel, Denver, 1972-87; owner, pres. Mile Hi Tours, 1973—, MH Internat., 1987—, Mile Hi Advt. Agy., 1986—. Bd. dirs. Rocky Mountain chpt. Juvenile Diabetes Found. Internat., 1994-2000; exec. bd. Rocky Mountain Father's Day Coun., 1998, 99. Named Wholesaler of Yr., Las Vegas Conv. and Visitors Authority, 1984; recipient Leadership award Nat. Multiple Sclerosis Soc., 1996. Mem. NAFE, Am. Soc. Travel Agts., Nat. Fedn. Ind. Businessmen. Republican. Home: 5565 E Vassar Ave Denver CO 80222-6239 Office: Mile Hi Tours Inc 2160 S Clermont St Denver CO 80222-5007 E-mail: pamm@milehitours.com., pamelaemurdock@aol.com.

MURDOCK, PHELPS DUBOIS, JR. marketing consultant, strategic planner; b. Kansas City, Mo., May 5, 1944; s. Phelps Dubois and Betty Jane M.; m. Cathy Ann Broadfoot, 1991; children: Susan, Kathleen, Phelps DuBois III, McKenna McCosh. Sales svc. mgr. Sta. KCMO-TV, Kansas City, 1965-66; acct. exec. Fremerman-Papin Advt., 1966-71; TV prodn. mgr., 1966-70; v.p., 1970-71; mng. ptnr. New Slant Prodns., Kansas City, 1971-73; v.p., creative dir. Travis-Walz-Lane Advt., Kansas City and Mission, Kans., 1973-76; pres., CEO Phelps Murdock Mktg. and Advt., Inc., Kansas City, 1977-91; CEO Phelps Murdock Strategic/Mktg. Planning, Weston, Mo., 1992—. Exec. dir. Kansas City Indsl. Coun., 1991—99, pres., 2000—01; sec.-treas. Everlasting Seasons Corp., 1996—; ptnr. Action Internat. Heartland Region, 2001—; lectr. in field. Author: numerous articles, TV, radio commls., film, TV and radio musical compositions, radio and TV programs, film with Walter Cronkite, Union Sta. is US, 1988. Active Heart of Am. United Way, 1966-80, exec. bd., 1976, bd. dirs., 1976-80; active Help Educate Emotionally Distrubed, Inc., Kansas City, 1986-80, founder, pres., bd. dirs. HEED Found., 1979-80; active Heart of Am. coun. Boy Scouts Am., 1975-85; bd. govs. Bacchus Ednl. and Cultural Found., Kansas City, 1973-76, beneficiary selection chmn., 1974, found. chmn., 1975; active Kansas City Bicentennian Commn., 1975-76, Union Sta. Commn., 1986-88, Rebuild Am. Coalition, 1992—, Aligning for Action Conf., 1993, Blight Task Force, 1995-97, Devel. Process Rev. Task Force, 1996—, Keep KC Beautiful Task Force, 1999—, Weston Mo. Econ. Devel. Com., 1999-; founder, bd. dirs., sec. Kansas City Union Sta. Inc., 1988-96, sec., 1988-92, treas., 1992-96; founder, bd. dirs., 1st v.p. Com. for Union Sta., 1987-93; pres. Friends of Union Sta., 1994-97; mem. Bi-State Vol. Coun., Union Sta., 1994-97, Union Sta. Grand Opening Events Com., 1997-99; bd. dirs., chmn. long-range planning Hist. Kansas City Found., 1989-92, bd. dirs. Hist. Garment Dist., 1991—; mem. Kansas City Consensus, 1988—, issues select com., 1988-90, metro. area strategic planning focus group, 1989-90, bd. dirs., 1990-93, chmn. cmty. rels. com., 1990-92, 1st v.p., 1991-93, F.O.C.U.S. Kansas City Bus. and Urban Fabric Perspectives Groups, 1993-95; founder, chmn. Kansas City Bus. Retention Roundtable, 1992-96; mktg. legal com. MARC Regional Amenities Task Force, 1993-94; adv. bd. We. Mo. Mental Health Ctr., 1990-92, Mid-Am. Mfg. Tech. Ctr., 1992-95; chmn. Eco-Kansas City Steering Com., 1992-94; founding mem. steering com. COMPASS: Citizens Charting a Greater Kansas City Cmty., 1990-92, Union Station Study, 1991-92, studies for Econ. and Environ. Devel. Study, 1993-94, Westside, 1997-98, Ctrl. Indsl. Dist., 1999-2000, Kans. City Urban Core, 2000-01, Northland Plan, 2001-02, KU Sch. Arch. and Urban Design; adv. group MCC Bus. & Tech. Ctr., 1992-95; steering com. Main Link Study, 1990-91, Capital Resources Network, 1992-95, Met. Bus. and Tech. Consortium, 1996, Clean Sweep Project, 1996-97, Kansas City Bi-State Brownfields Initiative, 1996-2001, KC River Heritage Trails, 1999—, Kans. City Mo. Brownsfields Commn., 2000—, Ctrl. Indsl. Dist. Sustainable Devel. Task Force, 1999-2000; chmn. Indsl. Blight Com., 1994-95, Blight Com. Environ. Mgmt. Com., 1995-99; co-founder, sec. Kansas City River Trails, Inc., 1999—; mem. Keep KC Beautiful Task Force, 1999—, Devel. Process Rev. Task Force, 1996-2001; mem. Rebuild Am. Coalition, 1992-2001; chmn. bd. Bridging the Gap, 2000—; vol. coach local youth leagues, 1975-83; cons. Com. for County Progress Campaigns, 1966-70, Charter Campaign, Jackson County, Mo., 1970; Kansas City Magnet Schs., 1986-88, spkr. internat. conf., 1988. Recipient various awards including United Way Nat. Comm. award, 1975; Effie citation N.Y. Mktg. Assn., 1975; 1st Place Print Ad award and 1st Place Poster award 9th Dist. Addy Awards, 1975, 1st Place Regional-Nat. TV Campaign award, 1976, Omni award, 1980-82, 86, 87, Silver award KCAD, 1981, 1st Place TV Campaign award KCAF Big One Show, 1976, Best-of-Show and Gold medal award Dallas Soc. Visual Comms., 1976, Gold medal Kansas City Litho Craftsmen, 1988, CUBE award, 1995, Leadership award Union Sta. Opening, 1999; named Mic-O-Say hon. warrior, 1978. Mem. Rotary. Democrat. Home: 545 Edward St Weston MO 64098-1105 Office: PO Box 14 Weston MO 64098-0014 E-mail: cottage@earthlink.net.

MURDOCK, ROBERT MCCLELLAN, air force officer; b. Montclair, N.J., Sept. 27, 1947; s. George Rutherford and Mary (Newell) M.; m. Ann Marie Wingo, Aug. 20, 1977; 1 child, Kristen. BA, Davis and Elkins Coll., 1969; MA, Ctrl. Mich. U., 1979; postgrad., Armed Forces Staff Coll., 1983, U.S. Army War Coll., 1988. Lic. command pilot, USAF. Aide, chief of staff The Pentagon, Washington, 1980-82; ops. officer 22 Airlift Squadron, Travis AFB, Calif., 1984, comdr., 1985-87; dep. inspector gen. Hdqs. European Command, Stuttgart, Germany, 1988-90; vice comdr. 436 Airlift Wing, Dover AFB, Del., 1990-92; nat. def. fellow The Atlantic Coun., Washington, 1992-93; comdr. Air Force Inspection Agy., Kirtland AFB, N.Mex., 1993-96; dep. U.S. Mil. Rep. to NATO Brussels, Belgium, 1996-98; vice comdr. San Antonio Air Logistics Ctr., Kelly AFB, Tex., 1998-2000, comdr., 2000—01; ret., 2001; br. mgr. Guardsmark Inc., San Antonio, 2001—. Decorated D.F.C., Air medal, Legion of Merit, Disting. Svc. medal, Def. Superior Svc. medal. Mem. Air Force Assn., The Airlift and Tanker Assn., Order of Daedalians. Methodist. Avocations: skiing, golf, travel. Address: 18911 La Verita San Antonio TX 78258 E-mail: murdockr@satx.rr.com.

MURDOCK, ROBERT MEAD, curator; b. N.Y.C., Dec. 18, 1941; s. Robert Davidson and Elizabeth Brundage (Mead) M.; m. Ellen Rebecca Olson, Apr. 22, 1967 (div.); children: Alison Mead, Anne Davidson; m. Deborah C. Ryan, Apr. 28, 1995. BA, Trinity Coll., Conn., 1963; MA, Yale U., 1965; student, Mus. Mgmt. Inst., U. Calif., Berkeley, 1980. Ford Found. intern Walker Art Center, Mpls., 1965-67; curator Albright-Knox Art Gallery, Buffalo, 1967-70; curator contemporary art Dallas Mus. Fine Arts, 1970-78; dir. Grand Rapids (Mich.) Art Mus., 1978-83; chief curator Walker Art Ctr., Mpls., 1983-85; program dir. IBM Gallery of Sci. and Art, N.Y.C., 1985-87, 90-93; dir. exhbns. Am. Fedn. Arts, 1987-88. Panelist, cons. Nat. Endowment for Arts, 1974-90. Author: (with others) Tyler Graphics: The Extended Image, 1987, A Gallery of Modern Art, 1994, Paris Modern, The Swedish Ballet 1920-1925, 1995, Works by Leland Bell, 1950's-1991, 2001; contbr. articles on David Novros, William Conlon, 1985, Bill Freeland, 1989, Nassos Daphnis, 1990, Cai Guo-Qiang, 1998; exhbn. catalogues Early 20th Century Art from Midwestern Museums, 1981, Berlin/Hanover: The 1920's, 1977, Richard Tuttle: Books and Prints, 1996, Lesley Dill, 1998, Jim Torok, 1999. Nat. Endowment for Arts fellow, 1973 Home and Office: 202 1st Ave Apt 14 New York NY 10009-3726

MURDOCK, WILLIAM JOSEPH, foundation administrator, educator; b. Milw., Oct. 26, 1955; s. Joseph and Marilyn (Goetz) M.; m. Robin Anne Miller, Oct. 16, 1993. AAS, Asheville Buncombe Tech. Coll., 1979; BA in Edn. and Math., Mars Hill Coll., 1984. Cert. non-profit mgmt. Harvard U.; cert. non-profit mgmt. Duke U. Asst. mgr. Myers/Arnold Dept. Store,

Asheville, N.C., 1978-84; tchr. math. and gifted edn. Erwin Middle Sch., 1984-88; tchr. math. Cylde Erwin H.S., 1986-88; asst. v.p. JD Jackson Assocs., 1988-92; exec. dir. Eblen Found., 1992—. Instr. gifted enrichment program U. N.C., Asheville, 1986—; instr. non-profit mgmt. program Duke U., 1996—; bd. dirs. First Call for Help, Asheville, A.B. Tech. Coll. Found., Asheville, T.C. Roberson H.S. Ednl. Found., Asheville. Author: Developing Public Private Partnerships, 1996, Team Building for Non Profits, 1997; contbr. articles to profl. jours. Bd. mem., regional rep. Campaign for Human Devel., 1949-96; bd. mem. Boys and Girls Club, 1994-96; bd. dirs. Cauliflower Alley Club, L.A., 1995—, Asheville Buncombe Tech. C.C. Found., Asheville, 1996—, First Call for Help, 1994—, Children First, 1998—, Internat. Wrestling Inst., 1997—, Parents for the Advancement of Gifted Edn., 1984-88, Wresting Hall of Fame, 1998, United Way, 1995; mem. selection com. Ray Kroc Youth Scholarship Program, Asheville, 1996—. Named Outstanding Tchr. of the Gifted, N.C. Assn. of the Gifted, 1987, Congl. Outstanding Pub. Svc. award, 1994. Mem. Internat. Wrestling Inst. (mem. Hall of Fame selection com. 1997—). Roman Catholic. Office: 304 Summit St Asheville NC 28803-2725

MUREHEAD, DEBORAH ELIZABETH BETTS, gifted and talented educator, music educator; b. Shreveport, La., Sept. 10, 1952; d. George Cornelius Betts, Jr. and Jackquelyn Shaw Bicknell; m. Lester Cox Morehead, Jr., Apr. 24, 1992; children: John Morehead, Les Morehead, Sam Morehead, Douglas Pearce, Nelli Pearce. BA in Speech and English, La. Tech. U., 1974; M in Religious Edn., Southwestern Theol. Sem., 1976; MEd in English and Gifted Edn., La. State U., Shreveport, 1993. Tchr. Chapel Frafton, Baton Rouge, 1984—86; asst. prin. Natalbany (La.) Bapt. Sch., 1986—89; libr. Natalbany Middle Sch., 1989—90; tchr. gifted and talented Caddo Magnet High, Shreveport, 1990—; min. music/edn. Parkview Bapt. Ch., 2000—. SS ch. growth specialist SBC, Nebr., 1980—, La., 1980—. Author: (biography) Don't Tell Me I Can't, 1995. Named Educator of Yr., CAE & Shreveport Times, 1995; recipient Barbara Jorndan award, La. Tex. Com. Disabilities, 1996. Mem.: U.S. Timing Assn., Phi Kappa Phi. Home: 523 Applespice Dr Shreveport LA 71115

MUREN, DENNIS E. visual effects director; b. Glendale, Calif., Nov. 1, 1946; s. Elmer Ernest and Charline Louise (Clayton) M.; m. Zara Pinfold, Aug. 29, 1981; children: Gregory, Gwendolen. AA, Pasadena (Calif.) City Coll., 1966; student, Calif. State U., L.A. Freelance spl. effects expert, 1968-75; camera operator Cascade of Calif., Hollywood, 1975-76; visual effects dir. photography Indsl. Light & Magic, San Rafael, Calif., 1976-80, visual effects dir., 1980—. Guest speaker Berlin Film Festival, UCLA, Film Dept., U. Calif. Berkeley Film Series, Liverpool (Eng.) U. Film Program, Mill Valley Film Festival Program, Siggraph '86, Siggraph '87, Am. Film Inst., Portland Creative Conf. '89. Cameraman, photographer various films including Star Wars, 1977, Close Encounters of the Third Kind, 1977, Battlestar Galactica, 1978, The Empire Strikes Back, 1980 (Oscar award); visual effects supr. films include Dragonslayer, 1981 (Oscar nomination), ET: The Extraterrestrial, 1982 (Oscar award), Return of the Jedi, 1983 (Oscar award, Brit. Acad. of Film and TV award), Indiana Jones and the Temple of Doom, 1984 (Oscar award, Brit. Acad. of Film and TV award), Young Sherlock Holmes, 1985 (Oscar nomination), Captain Eo, 1986, Star Tours, 1986, Innerspace, 1987 (Oscar award), Empire of the Sun, 1987, Willow, 1988 (Oscar nomination), Ghostbusters II, 1989, The Abyss, 1989 (Oscar award), Terminator 2, 1991 (Oscar award, Brit. Film and TV award), Jurassic Park, 1993 (Oscar award, Brit. Film and TV award), Casper, 1995; effects supr. Jurassic Park-The Lost World, 1997; creative advisor Twister, 1996, Mission Impossible, 1996; visual effects supr. (TV program) Caravan of Courage (Emmy award); creative advisor Twister, 1995, Mission Impossible, 1995, Jurassic Park: The Lost World, 1997 (Academy award nomination), Star Wars: The Phantom Menace, 1999, (Acad. award nomination), A.I., 2001 (acad. award nomination), Star Wars: The Attack of the Clones, 2002, The Hulk, 2003. Recipient Academy Scientific/Technical Award for the development of a Motion Picture Figure Mover for animation photography, 1981, star on Hollywood Walk of Fame, 1999. Mem. Am. Soc. Cinematographers, Acad. Motion Picture Arts and Scis.

MURESANU, VIOLETA ANA, civil, structural engineer; b. Bucharest, Romania, May 1, 1942; came to U.S., 1981; d. Romulus and Elena (Murgescu) M.; m. Lucian Popescu, Oct. 28, 1960; 1 child, Diana Rodica. M in Civil Engring., Inst. for Construction, Bucarest, 1965. Civil engr. Inst. for Design Standard Structures, Bucharest, 1965-79; draft person Muesser, Ruthledge de Desimone, N.Y.C., 1981-83; civil engr. The L.I. RR, Jamaica, N.Y., 1983--. Achievements include the design of a bridge for railroad tracks, several pedestrian overpasses, and numerous other structures. Office: The LI RR Hillside Support Facility 93-59 183rd St Jamaica NY 11423-2323

MUREZ, JOHN, music education director, educator; b. Paterson, N.J., Feb. 14, 1943; s. John Sr. and Sophie A. Murez; m. Dorothy L. Pohlman, May 29, 1971; 1 child, Daniel C. BA in Elem. Edn., William Paterson U., 1963; MAT, Seton Hall U., 1966; MusM., Montclair State U., 1976; postgrad., Drew U. Cert. tchr., N.J. Tchr. Paterson (N.J.) Pub. Schs., 1963-68; asst. prof. William Paterson Coll., Wayne, N.J., 1968-70; tchr. Tenafly (N.J.) Pub. Schs., 1970-80; prof. Luther Coll., Teaneck, N.J., 1976-79; dir. Office of Music Edn. Newark Pub. Schs., 1988-98; dist. supr. fine and performing arts Paterson Pub. Schs., 1998—; music min. Mt. Carmel R.C. Ch., Montclair, N.J., 1998—. Organ design cons. various chs., North Jersey, 1976—; cons. music workshops Diocese of Paterson, 1984—. Mem. Newark Teen Arts Festival Com., 1988-98. Mem. N.J. Music Adminstrs., Music Educators Nat. Conf., Paterson Adminstrs. Assn. Home: 2 Berkeley Pl Montclair NJ 07042-2303 Office: Paterson Pub Schs 137 Ellison St Paterson NJ 07505-1308

MURGATROYD, ERIC NEAL, data processing executive; b. Ware, Mass., July 30, 1950; s. Howard E. and Jean Francis M.; m. Pamela Lee Swift, Aug. 14, 1976 (div. Dec. 1992); 1 child, Lisa Nicole; m. Donna K. Goodwin, Sept. 4, 1999. Student, U. Mass, 1968-70. Computer operator Hammond Organ Co., Chgo., 1972-73; systems analyst Cen. States Health, Welfare and Pension Funds, 1973-78; sr. systems analyst Gould-Fluid Components Div., Niles, 1978-80; project leader mfg. systems Motorola Corp., Schaumburg, 1980-85; mgr. billing systems Cellular Billing Systems, Inc., Park Ridge, 1985-86; info. sys. dir. Leaf, Inc., Lake Forest, 1986-97; dir. applications devel. Jockey Internat., Kenosha, Wis., 1997-98; ind. IT cons. Y2K Audit, 1998—99; mgr. IT bus. processes TeleHub Network Svcs., Gurnee, 1999-2000; data warehouse mgr. Ajilon, Inc., Itasca, Ill., 2000—01. IT bus. cons. Data Warehousing, 2000—. Author computer programs and computer architecture. Mem. Mensa. Avocations: camping, swimming, coin collecting, golf. E-mail: murgs@att.net.

MURIAN, RICHARD MILLER, book company executive; b. East St. Louis, Ill., Sept. 17, 1937; s. Richard Miller Jr. and Margaret Keyes (Gregory) M.; m. Judith Lee, Aug. 11, 1961 (dec. Apr. 1992); 1 child, Jennifer Ann. BA, U. Calif., Davis, 1969; MLS, U. Calif., Berkeley, 1972; MA, Calif. State U., Sacramento, 1975; MDiv, Trinity Evang., 1977. Cert. history instr., libr. sci. instr., Calif. History reader Calif. State U., Sacramento, 1965-66, U. Calif., Davis, 1966-68, philosophy rschr., 1968-69; bibliographer Argus Books, Sacramento, 1970-71; rsch. dir. Nat. Judical Coll., Reno, 1971-72; libr. Calif. State U., Sacramento, 1972-76; tv talk show host Richard Murian Show, L.A., 1979-80; pres. Alcuin Books, Ltd., Phoenix, 1981—. Bd. dirs. Guild of Ariz. Antiquarian Books; pres. East Valley Assn. Evangs., Mesa, Ariz., 1984-86; cons. Ariz. Hist. Soc., 1993—, cons. FBI, 2000. Contbr. articles to profl. jours. Active U. Calif. Riverside Libr., 1981-83, KAET (PBS), 1988—, Ariz. State U., 1989—. Recipient Sidney B. Mitchell fellowship U. Calif., Berkeley, 1971. Mem. Am. Assn. Mus., Am. Soc. Appraisers, Ariz. Preservation Found., Grand Canyon Nature Assn., Internat. Platform Assn., Ariz. Publ. Book Assn. (awards com.), Phi Kappa Phi. Democrat. Presbyterian. Avocations: fgn. films, jazz. Office: Alcuin Books Ltd 115 W Camelback Rd Phoenix AZ 85013-2519

MURILLO, CAROL ANN, secondary school educator; b. Portland, Oreg., Mar. 1, 1948; d. Carl Harvey and Frances Berniece Bryan; children: Michelle Frances, Adam Carlos Bryan. BA, Seattle Pacific U., 1970. Multiple subjects tchg. credential Calif., reading specialist credential Calif., secondary tchg. credential Calif. Exec. sec. Sybron Corp. - Heritage Laboratories, Inc., Seattle, 1971—72; elem. tchr. Highlands Acad., Daly City, Calif., 1973—74; dir. of childrens' ministries Resurrection City Ch., Berkeley and Oakland, 1980—82; interim prin. and tchr. Hilltop Christian Sch., Vallejo, 1982—93; cfo, ceo asst., event planner Mario Murillo Ministries, Inc., San Ramon, 1993—98; elem. sch. tchr. Vallejo City Unified Sch. Dist., 1998—2002. Mem. Falconette Academic Honors Club, Seattle, 1968—70. Editor (contributor): (book) Religious - Inspirational, 2000; editor: I'm the Christian the Devil Warned You About, 1996, Love Letters to Dangerous Christians, 1996; contbr. articles to religious magazines. Spkr. Lay Leadership conf.; worship leader religious retreats; corp. sec., trustee bd. mem. First Assembly of God, Inc., Ch. on the Hill, Vallejo, Calif., 1998—2002; mem. bd. dirs. Hilltop Christian Sch., 1997—2002. Mem.: Delta Kappa Gamma (grantee 1999). Avocation: travel. Home: 3008 Georgia St Vallejo CA 94591 Personal E-mail: carolannmurillo@msn.com.*

MURILLO, VELDA JEAN, social worker, counselor; b. Miller, S.D., Dec. 8, 1943; d. Royal Gerald and Marion Elizabeth (Porter) Matson; m. Daniel John Murillo, June 25, 1967 (div. Dec. 1987); 1 child, Damon Michael. BS, S.D. State U., 1965; MA, Calif. State U., Bakersfield, 1980. Cert. marriage, family and child counselor. Social worker adult svcs. Kern County Dept. Welfare, Bakersfield, 1965-78, social worker child protective svcs., 1978-84; asst. coord. sexual abuse program Kern County Dist. Atty., 1985-91, coord. sexual abuse program, 1991—. Mem. Calif. Sexual Assault Investigators, 1982-84, Kern Child Abuse Prevention Coun., Bakersfield, 1982-84; co-developer, presenter Children's Self Help Project, Bakersfield, 1982-87; cons. mem. Sexual Assault Adv. Com., Bakersfield, 1991-96. Democrat. Avocations: spiritual healing, travel, metaphysical pursuits, Reiki (master). Office: Kern County Dist Atty 1215 Truxtun Ave Bakersfield CA 93301-4619

MURILLO-ROHDE, ILDAURA MARIA, marriage and family therapist, consultant, educator, dean; b. Garachine, Panama; came to U.S., 1945; d. Amalio Murillo and Ana E. (Diaz) de Murillo; m. Erling Rohde, Sept. 19, 1959. BS, Columbia U., 1951, MA, 1953, MEd, 1969; PhD, NYU, 1971; hon. diploma, Escuela Nat. de Enfermeria, Guatemala, 1964; Naturopathia diploma, Centro Estudios Naturista, Barcelona, Spain, 1992. RN; lic. marriage and family therapist, N.J.; cert. mental health-psychiat. nursing, ANA; lic. sex. therapist, N.J. Instr., supr. Bellevue Psychiat. Hosp., N.Y.C., 1950-54; asst. dir., dir. psychiat. div. Wayne County Gen. Hosp., Eloise, Mich., 1954-56; chief nurse psychiat. div. Elmhurst Gen. Hosp., Queens, N.Y., 1956-58, Met. Hosp. Med. Ctr., N.Y.C., 1961-63; psychiat. cons. to govt. of Guatemala WHO, UN, Guatemala, 1963-64; assoc. prof., chmn. psychiat. dept. N.Y. Med. Coll. Grad. Sch. Nursing, N.Y.C., 1964-69; dir. mental health-psychiatry, asst. prof. NYU, 1970-72; assoc. prof. Hostos Coll., CUNY, 1972-76; assoc. dean. acad. affairs, prof. U. Wash., Seattle, 1976-81; prof., dean Coll. of Nursing SUNY, Downstate Med. Ctr., Bklyn., 1981-85; dean and prof. emeritus SUNY, 1985—. Bd. dirs. Puerto Rican Family Inst., N.Y.C., 1983—; dir. Latin Am. Oncological Nurses Fuld Fellowships, 1989-90; psychiat. cons. Sch. Nursing, U. Antioquia, Medellin, Colombia, 1972-73, WHO; psychiat./rsch. cons. for master program Sch. Nursing, U. Panama, Project Hope, 1986; dir., leader mental-psychiat. interdisciplinary group to study the Chinese family after 30 yrs. of communism People to People Amb. Program, 1985. Editor: National Directory of Hispanic Nurses, 1981, 2d edit., 1986, 3d edit., 1994; contbr. numerous articles to profl. nat. and internat. jours., chpts. to books in field. Bd. dirs. Nat. Coalition of Hispanic Mental Health and Human Svcs. Orgns., 1974-84, chmn. bd., 1980-84; mem. Wash. State adv. com. U.S. Commn. on Civil Rights, Seattle, 1971-81; nat. adv. com. White House Conf. on Families, Washington, D.C., 1979-81; pres. King County Health Planning Coun., Seattle, 1979-81; exec. com. Puget Sound Health Systems Agy., Seattle, 1979-81; mem. Mosby Consumer Health's Hispanic adv. bd., 1996. Univ. Honors scholar NYU, 1972; named Citizen of the Day, Radio Sta. KIXI and N.W. Airlines, Seattle, 1979, Disting. lectr. Sigma Theta Tau, 1988-89, Woman of Yr., N.Y. Gotham Club Bus. and Profl. Women, 1989; recipient 1st Nat. Intercultural Nursing award Coun. of Intercultural Nursing, ANA, New Orleans, 1984, Women's Honors in Pub. Svc. award Minority Fellowship Programs and Cabinet Human Rights, ANA, 1986, Disting. Alumna award Divsn. Nursing, NYU Alumni Assn., 1989, 1st Nat. Dr. Hildegard Peplau award for outstanding svcs. in mental health, psychiat. nursing, edn., rsch. and practice, Las Vegas conv. ANA, 1992, Practice award Tchrs. Coll., Columbia U. Nursing Edn. Alumni, 1994; designated Living Legend for leadership in practice, edn. and rsch. Am. Acad. Nursing, 1994; inducted into Nursing Hall of Fame, Columbia U., 1999; bd. advisors Marquis Who's Who, 1991-99. Fellow Am. Assn. Marriage and Family Therapy; mem. ANA (affirmative action task force 1974-84, commn. human rights, cabinet human rights, rep. ANA at ICN Cong. Tokyo 1977, spokesperson Nat. Health Ins., conceived and designed Coun. Intercultural Nursing), Am. Orthopsychiat. Assn. (bd. dirs. 1976-79, treas. 1986-89, Presdl. nominee 1980, 93), N.Y. Assn. Marriage and Family Therapy (pres. 1973-76), Nat. Assn. Hispanic Nurses (founder, 1st pres. 1976-80), Internat. Fedn. Bus. and Profl. Women (UN rep. to UNICEF London, 1987—, del. to World UN Summit for Children N.Y.C. 1990, UN N.Y. Com. for Internat. Yr. of Family 1994, Hall of Fame for Outstanding Achievements in Field of Sci., Rsch., Mental Health-Psychiatry, 4th edit., 1995), Am. Rsch. Inst. (dep. govt. 1987), NYU Club, Gotham Bus. and Profl. Women's Club. Democrat. Avocations: travel, reading, music, stamp collecting, skiing. Home: 300 W 108th St Apt 12A New York NY 10025-2704 Office: SUNY Bklyn Coll Nursing Box 22 450 Clarkson Ave Brooklyn NY 11203-2056 E-mail: imurillorohde@aol.com.

MURINO, CLIFFORD JOHN, atmospheric and oceanic research institute executive; b. Yonkers, N.Y., Feb. 10, 1929; s. Vincent Joseph and Marie (Fuccillo) M.; m. Janet Rosalie Spallino, Dec. 28, 1954 (div. Dec. 1983); children: John Clifford, Carolyn Ruth, Kathryn Marie; m. Fryne Irene White, Jan.28, 1984. BS, St. Louis U., 1950, MA, 1954, PhD, 1957. Mem. faculty Parks Coll. Aero. Tech., Cahokia, Ill., 1954-60; prof. meteorology St. Louis U., 1960-75, v.p., 1969-75; div. dir. Nat. Ctr. Atmospheric Research, Boulder, Colo., 1975-80; pres. Deseert Research Inst., Reno, 1980-83, pres., bd. dirs. Found., 1982-83; pres. Univ. Corp. for Atmospheric Research, Boulder, 1983--, Bd. dirs. Found., 1986--. Co-author: Weather Motions from Space, 1969; contbr. numerous articles to sci. jours. Mem. Nev. Gov.'s Adv. Com., 1980-83, Reno Mayor's Adv. Com., 1982-83; trustee Nev. Devel. Authority, 1981-83. Recipient sustained superior performance award NSF, 1969; NSF research grantee, 1965-66, NOAA research grantee, 1966. Fellow Am. Meteorol. Soc. (pres. 1985); mem. Elks Club, Sigma Xi, Pi Mu Epsilon. Home: 1590 Bradley Dr Boulder CO 80305-7377 Office: Univ Corp for Atmospheric Rsch PO Box 3000 Boulder CO 80307-3000

MURIS, TIMOTHY JOSEPH, federal agency administrator; b. Massillon, Ohio, Nov. 18, 1949; s. George William and Louise (Hood) M.; children: Matthew Allen, Paul Austin; m. Pam Harmon, June 27, 1997. BA, San. Diego State U., 1971; JD, UCLA, 1974. Bar: Calif. 1974, U.S. Supreme Ct. 1983. Asst. to dir. policy planning and evaluation FTC, Washington, 1974-76, dir. Bur. Consumer Protection, 1981-83, dir. Bur. Competition, 1983-85; exec. assoc. dir. Office Mgmt. and Budget, 1985-88, cons., 1988-89; law and econs. fellow U. Chgo. Law Sch., 1979-80; asst. prof. antitrust and consumer law U. Miami Law Sch. and Law Econs. Ctr., Fla., 1976-79, assoc. prof., 1979-81, prof., 1981-83; Found. prof. law George Mason U., Va., 1988—2001, interim dean, 1996-97; chmn. Fed. Trade Commn., Washington, 2001—. Dep. counsel Presdl. Task Force on Regulatory Relief, Washington, 1981; cons. Coun. on Wage and Price Stability, Washington, 1981; mem. Nat. Issues Forum, Brookings Inst., 1986-88; mem. adv. bd. Antitrust and Trade Regulation Report, 1990—. Editor: The Federal Trade Commission since 1970: Regulation and Bureaucratic Behavior, 1981. Mem. Reagan-Bush transition team for FTC, Washington, 1980; sr. advisor Bush-Quayle transition team, 1988-89. Am. Bar Found. affiliated scholar, 1979 Mem. ABA (antitrust law spl. com. to study role of FTC 1988-89), Calif. Bar Assn., FTC (chmn.), Order of Coif Office: Fed Trade Commn Off of the Chmn 600 Pennsylvania Ave NW Washington DC 20580 Office Fax: 202-326-2396.*

MURKETT, PHILIP TILLOTSON, human resource executive; b. Chattanooga, Apr. 3, 1931; s. Philip Tillotson and Dorothy (Ingram) M.; m. Mary Jane Brewer, Dec. 10, 1960; children: Emmette, Mary Jane Easter, Leanne. BA, Duke U., 1954; MBA, U. Pa., 1957; postgrad., Warnboro Coll., Oxford, England, 1980. Methods engr. Westinghouse Elec. Co., Staunton, Va., 1957-60; adminstrv. mgr. Vulcan Materials Co., Birmingham, Ala., 1960-68; human resources mgr. Blount, Inc., Montgomery, 1968-74; pres. Murkett Enterprises Inc., 1974—. Adj. prof. Auburn U., Montgomery, Ala.; with internat. affairs Yonok Coll., Lampang, Thailand; search cons. Murkett Assocs., Montgomery, 1974—; bd. advisors Digutech Inc. Author: Use & Value of References, 1957; editor (newsletter) H.R. Quar., 1983. Pres. Montgomery Mus. Fine Art, 1982, Cmty. Concert Assn., Montgomery, 1982, Montgomery Symphony Assn., 1987; pres. Am.-Thai Edn. Devel. Found. Inc., 1991, bd. dirs. 1990; bd. dirs. Ala. World Affairs Coun., 1997; jr. warden Episcopal Ch. of Ascension, 1972. Recipient Gov.'s Arts award Ala. Arts Coun., 1983, commendation from crown princess of Thailand, 1992. Mem. Montgomery C. of C. (task chair 1983), Montgomery Country Club, Capitol City Club, Kiwanis (bd. dirs. 1972), Delta Tau Delta (chpt. v.p. 1953). Avocations: gardening, swimming, music, tennis, geneology. Office: PO Box 527 Montgomery AL 36101-0527

MURKISON, EUGENE COX, business educator; b. Donalsonville, Ga., July 2, 1936; s. Jeff and Ollie Mae (Shores) M.; m. Marilyn Louise Adams, July 3, 1965; children: James, David, Jennifer. Grad., U.S. Army JFK Spl. Warfare Sc., 1967, U.S. Naval War Coll., 1972, U.S. Army Command/Staff Coll., 1974; BSA, U. Ga., 1959; MBA, U. Rochester, 1970; PhD, U. Mo., 1986. Surveyor USDA, Donalsonville, Ga., 1956-59; commd. 2d lt. U.S. Army, 1959, advanced through grades to lt. col., 1974, inf. bn. leader Vietnam, 1967-68; mechanized comdr. (G-3), ops. officer Brigade Exec. Officer, Korea, Europe and U.S., 1968-70; prof. leadership & psychology West Point, N.Y., 1970-73; ops. officer (J-3) Office of Chmn. Joint Chiefs of Staff, Washington, 1974-77; prof. mil. sci. and leadership Kemper Mil. Coll., 1977-81; ret. U.S. Army, 1981; instr. U. Mo., Columbia, 1981-84; asst. prof. Ga. So. U., Stateboro, 1984-89, assoc. prof., 1989-94, prof., 1995—, chair grad. curriculum & programs task force, 1996-99. Vis. prof. mgmt. and bus. U. Tirgoviste, Romania, 1994, 95, 96, 98, 99, 2000; vis. prof. human resource mgmt. Tech. U. Romania, Cluj-Napoca, 1998-99, 2000; chmn. grad. programs curriculum com. GSU, 1998-2002. Author: (with Gheorghe Ionescu) Human Behavior in Organizations, 2000; contbr. numerous articles to profl. jours. and chpts. to books. V.p. Optimist Club, 1993-94, dir., 1993, 96-97, v.p., 1994-95; trustee Pittman Pk. Meth. Ch., Statesboro, 1992-99, chmn., trustee, 1995-96, adminstrv. bd., 1986-2000. Recipient Bronze Star medal with oak leaf cluster, Devel. award Ga. So. U., 1990, Teaching award U. Mo., 1983, Albert Burke Rsch. award, 1992, Best Paper award 10th Ann. conv. of Internat. Acad. of Bus.; grantee IREX, 1994, SOROS, 1995, 96. Mem. VFW, Inst. Mgmt. Sci., So. Mgmt. Assn., Inst. for Info. and Mgmt. Sci., Internat. Acad. Bus. (program chair 1994, 95), Acad. Mgmt., Bus. History Conf., Ga. Hist. Soc., Newcomen Soc., Blue Key, Scabbard & Blade, Beta Gamma Sigma, Alpha Zeta. Republican. Avocations: bus. history, mil history, tomato prodn., hiking, boating. Office: Ga So U Coll Bus Adminstrn Statesboro GA 30460-8154 E-mail: murkison@gasou.edu.

MURKOWSKI, FRANK HUGHES, senator; b. Seattle, Mar. 28, 1933; s. Frank Michael and Helen (Hughes) M.; m. Nancy R. Gore, Aug. 28, 1954; children: Carol Victoria Murkowski Sturgulewski, Lisa Ann Murkowski Martell, Frank Michael, Eileen Marie Murkowski Van Wyhe, Mary Catherine Murkowski Judson, Brian Patrick. Student, Santa Clara U., 1952-53; BA in Econs, Seattle U., 1955. With Pacific Nat. Bank of Seattle, 1957-58, Nat. Bank of Alaska, Anchorage, 1959-67; asst. v.p., mgr. Nat. Bank of Alaska (Wrangell br.), 1963-66; v.p. charge bus. devel. Nat. Bank of Alaska, Anchorage, 1966-67; commr. dept. econ. devel. State of Alaska, Juneau, 1967-70; pres. Alaska Nat. Bank, Fairbanks, 1971-80; senator from Alaska U.S. Senate, Washington, 1981—, ranking mem. Com. on Energy and Natural Resources, mem. Com. on Fin., Vets Affairs Com., Indian Affairs Com., Japan-US Friendship Com. Rep. nominee for U.S. Congress from Alaska, 1970; chmn. Can.-U.S. Interparliamentary Group. Former v.p. B.C. and Alaska Bd. Trade; mem. U.S. Holocaust Mus. Coun. Served with U.S. Coast Guard, 1955-57. Mem. AAA, AMVETS, NRA, Am. Legion, Polish Legion Am. Vets., Ducks Unltd., Res. Officer's Assn., Alaska Geog. Soc., Alaska World Affairs Coun., Fairbanks Hist. Preservation Found., Coalition Am. Vets., Alaska Native Brotherhood, Naval Athletic Assn., Am. Bankers Assn., Alaska Bankers Assn. (pres. 1973), Young Pres.'s Orgn., Alaska C. of C. (pres. 1977), Anchorage C. of C. (bd. dirs. 1966), B.C. C. of C., Fairbanks C. of C. (bd. dirs. 1973-78), Pioneers of Alaska, Internat. Alaska Nippon Kai, Capital Hill Club, Shilla Club, Army Athletic Club, Congl. Staff Club, Diamond Athletic Club, Washington Athletic Club, Elks, Lions. Office: US Senate 322 Hart Senate Bldg Washington DC 20510-0001

MURNANE, GEORGE, III, business executive; b. N.Y.C., Jan. 27, 1958; m. George Jr. and Mary McDonnell Murnane; m. Gretchen Barlow Alexander, July 19, 1986; children: George IV, Anna-Barlow. BA, U. Pa., 1980, MBA with distinction, 1986. Asst. sec. Chem. Bank, N.Y.C., 1980-84; dir. Merrill Lynch, Inc., 1986-95; COO, Atlas Air, Inc., Golden, Colo., 1995-96; gen. ptnr. Barlow Ptnrs., LP, Atlanta, 1996—; exec. v.p., COO, Internat. Airline Support Group, Inc., 1996—2002, also bd. dirs.; COO, CFO North-South Airways, 2000—, also bd. dirs.; exec. v.p. Mesa Air Group Inc., Phoenix, 2002—, also bd. dirs. Bd. dirs. Mesa (Ariz.) Air Group. Com. mem. Arts Festival of Atlanta, 1998, Ga. Trust Hist. Preservation, 1999. Capt. USARNG, 1977-83. Mem. Beta Gamma Sigma. Republican. Roman Catholic. Office: Mesa Air Group Inc 410 N 44th St Ste 730 Phoenix AZ 85008 Fax: 770-455-7550. E-mail: george.munane@mesa-air.com.

MURNICK, DANIEL ELY, physicist, educator; b. N.Y.C., May 5, 1941; s. Jacob Michael and Lena (Tishman) M.; m. Janet Barbara George, Oct. 26, 1969; children: Jonathan, Carolyn. AB in Physics and Math., Hofstra U., 1962; PhD, MIT, 1966. Physics instr. MIT, Cambridge, 1966-67; mem. tech. staff Bell Labs, Murray Hill, N.J., 1967-88; prof. physics Rutgers U., Newark, 1988—, chmn. dept. physics, 1988-95. Cons. High Voltage Engring., Burlington, Mass., 1965-67, Diagnostics and Devices, Morristown, N.J., 1985—, Am. Standard, Piscataway, 1990-2000, Alimenterics Inc., Morris Plains, N.J., 1992-2000; mem. sci. adv. bd. Surgilase, Warwick, R.I., 1984-94; Donald H. Jacobs chair in applied physics Rutgers U., 1996-2000. Contbr. more than 120 articles to profl. jours.; inventor method and apparatus for stable isotope analysis, for localized surface glazing, and for electron beam pumped lasers and lamps. Recipient Humboldt award, Rep. of Germany, 1984, Thomas Alva Edison Patent award R&D Coun. of N.J., 1996. Fellow Am. Phys. Soc.; mem. IEEE, Am. Assn. Physics Tchrs., Am. Gastroenterological Assn., Sigma Xi. Office: Rutgers U Dept Physics 101 Warren St Newark NJ 07102-1811

MURNION, WILLIAM EDWARD, philosopher; b. N.Y.C., Jan. 27, 1933; s. William Edward and Frances Annie (Canavan) M.; m. Deborah Warren Cary, June 14, 1969; children: William Cary, Gregory Thomas. BA, St. Joseph's Coll., 1954; STL, Gregorian U., Rome, 1958, PhD, 1969. Ordained priest Roman Cath. Ch., 1957. Parish priest Roman Cath. Archdiocese of N.Y., N.Y.C., 1958-66; lectr. St. John's Sem., Little Rock, 1966-67; asst. prof. Duquesne U., Pitts., 1967-68; faculty fellow Boston Coll., Chestnut Hill, Mass., 1968-69; asst. prof. Newton (Mass.) Coll., 1969-72, Ramapo Coll., Mahwah, N.J., 1972-2000; lectr., counselor PhilosophyWorks, Bellvale, N.Y., 2000—. Dir. NEH summer seminar, 1992, 95. Author: St. Thomas's Theory of Understanding, 1969; contbr. articles to profl. jours., chpts. to books. Mem. Am. Philos. Assn., Am. Acad. Religion, N.Am. Soc. Social Philosophy, Internat. Soc. Philosophy of Law and Social Philosophy. Avocations: painting, gardening, sports. E-mail: wmurnion@warwick.net.

MURO, JONATHAN MICHAEL, director; b. Islip, N.Y., Apr. 25, 1973; s. John Patrick and Lynn Patricia Muro; m. Michelle Ann Rasor, July 25, 1998. B in Music Edn.(hon.) , U. Akron, 1996, M in Adminstrn., 2001. Instrumental music tchr. Canton (Ohio) Country Day Sch., 1997; band dir. S.E. Local Schs., Apple Creek, 1997—. Brass instr. Wooster (Ohio) Music Camp, 2000—. Nominee Tchr. award, Disney, 2002. Mem.: Ohio Music Educators Assn. (spl. events coord. 2002—), S.E. Local Tchrs. Assn. (v.p. 2002—). Avocations: fishing, motorcycling, weightlifting. Home: 1870 Sherck Blvd Wooster OH 44691 Office: SE Local Sch Dist 9050 Dover Rd Apple Creek OH 44606 Office Fax: 330-698-5000. Personal E-mail: soea_jmuro@tccsa.net. E-mail: soea_jmuro@tccsa.net.

MUROFF, LAWRENCE ROSS, nuclear medicine physician, educator; b. Phila., Dec. 26, 1942; s. John M. and Carolyn (Kramer) M.; m. Carol R. Savoy, July 12, 1969; children: Michael Bruce, Julie Anne. AB cum laude, Dartmouth Coll., 1964, B of Med. Sci., 1965; MD cum laude, Harvard U., 1967. Diplomate Am. Bd. Radiology, Am. Bd. Nuclear Medicine. Intern Boston City Hosp., Harvard, 1968; resident in radiology Columbia-Presbyn. Med. Ctr., N.Y.C., 1970-73, chief resident, 1973; instr. dept. radiology, asst. radiologist Columbia U. Med. Ctr., 1973-74; dir. dept. nuc. medicine, computed tomography and MRI Univ. Cmty. Hosp., Tampa, Fla., 1974-94, H. Lee Moffitt Cancer Hosp., Tampa, 1994—; pres. Edn. Symposia Inc.,

1975-2001, Imaging Cons. Inc., Tampa, 1994—; chmn. bd. Am. Phys. Ptnrs. Inc., Dallas, 1996-98. Clin. asst. prof. radiology U. South Fla., 1974-78, clin. assoc. prof., 1978-82, clin. prof., 1982—; clin. prof. U. Fla., 1988—. Contbr. articles to profl. jours. Lt. comdr. USPHS, 1968-70. Fellow Am. Coll. Nuclear Medicine (disting. fellow., Fla. del.), Am. Coll. Nuclear Physicians (regents 1976-78, pres.-elect 1978, pres. 1979, fellow 1980), Am. Coll. Radiology (councilor 1979-80, 91-96, 2001—, chancellor 1981-87, chmn. commn. on nuclear medicine 1981-87, fellow 1981); mem. Am. Assn. Acad. Chief Residents Radiology (chmn. 1973), AMA, Boylston Soc., Fla. Assn. Nuclear Physician (pres. 1976), Fla. Med. Assn., Hillsborough County Med. Assn., Radiol. Soc. N.Am., Soc. Nuclear Medicine (coun. 1975-90, trustee 1980-84, 86-89, pres. Southeastern chpt. 1983, vice chmn. correlative imaging coun. 1983), Fla. Radiol. Soc. (exec. com. 1976-91, treas. 1984, sec. 1985, v.p. 1986, pres. elect 1987, pres. 1988, gold medal 1995), West Coast Radiol. Soc., Soc. Mag. resonance Imaging (bd. dirs. 1988-91, chmn. ednl. program 1989, chmn. membership com. 1989-93), Clinical Magnetic Resonance Soc. (pres. elect 1995-98, pres. 1998-2000). Office: 4515 George Rd Ste 355 Tampa FL 33634-7300

MUROVIC, JUDITH ANN, neurosurgeon; b. Chgo., Mar. 23, 1949; d. Henry Francis and Mary Eva (Milosevich) Hmurovic. BA, Northwestern U., 1971, MD, 1975. Diplomate Nat. Bd. Med. Examiners. Intern in gen. surgery Northwestern U., 1976-77, resident in neurosurgery, 1978-79, U. Miami, 1979-83; fellow in neuro-oncology U. Calif., San Francisco, 1983-86; attending neurosurgeon San Francisco Gen. Hosp., 1986-87; pediat. neurosurgeon UCLA Med. Ctr., 1987-88; fellow pediat. neurosurgery Hosp. Sick Children, Toronto, Canada, 1990; fellow oncological neurosurgery Meml. Sloane Kettering, 1990-92; attending neurosurgeon Mt. Sinai Med. Ctr., Elmhurst Hosp. Ctr., 1992-96. Recipient Anne Addington rsch. award Northwestern U., 1979. Mem. Alpha Chi Omega. Roman Catholic. Home: 3679 Evergreen Dr Palo Alto CA 94303

MUROW, CHRISTINE, music educator; b. Chgo., Feb. 19, 1945; d. David R. and Dorothy B. Groth; m. Raymond J. Murow, Oct. 10, 1966. B, Susquehanna U., 1967. Budget analyst U.S. Dept. H.E.W., Washington, 1967-69, pub. info. specialist, 1969-72; tchr. piano Potomac, Md., 1972—; dir. KITS, 1985—. Author: KITS Music Theory Course, 1989-98; contbr. articles to profl. jours.; composer Sounds for One Hand, 1986, Voices of Invention, 1987; contbg. composer: Allison Contemporary Piano Collection, 1993, 96. Mem. Nat. Guild Piano Tchrs., Potomac Area Music Tchrs. (sec. 1989—). Avocations: gardening, bird watching. Office: KITS 9732 Corral Dr Potomac MD 20854-1510 E-mail: musictheory@earthlink.net.

MURPHEY, ARTHUR GAGE, JR. law educator, educator; b. Macon, Miss., June 16, 1927; s. Arthur Gage and Elizabeth (Crutcher) M.; m. Linda Chaney, May 17, 1975; children by previous marriage— Mason Alexander, Arthur Nesbit; 1 stepchild, Leslie Jo (Mrs. Thomas) Pafford. Student, Vanderbilt U., 1947-48; AB, U. N.C., 1951; JD, U. Miss., 1953; postgrad., London Sch. Econs., U. London, 1953-54; LLM, Yale U., 1962. Assoc. Satterfield, Ewing Williams and Shell, Jackson, Miss., 1953; asst. prof. U. Ga., Athens, 1956-58, Emory U., Atlanta, 1958-61, U. Akron, 1962-63, assoc. prof., 1963-67; prof. U. Ark., Little Rock, 1967-96, asst. dean Sch. Law, 1970-73, Ark. Bar Found. prof., 1996-97, Ark. Bar Found. prof. emeritus, 1997—. Vis. lectr. Case Western Res. U., Cleve., 1966; vis. prof. U. Miss., 1977 Faculty editor: Jour. Public Law, 1958-61; faculty adv.: Ga. Bar Jour., 1958-61; contbr. articles to profl. jours. Served with USAAF, 1945-47. Fulbright scholar, 1953-54; Sterling fellow, 1961-62; Ford Found. grantee, 1964 Mem. ABA, Phi Delta Phi, Beta Theta Pi, Phi Beta Kappa. Mem. Anglican Ch. Episcopalian. Home: 1918 Old Forge Dr Little Rock AR 72227-5515 Office: U Ark Sch Law 1201 McMath Ave Little Rock AR 72202-5142

MURPHEY, MARGARET JANICE, marriage and family therapist; b. Taft, Calif., July 24, 1939; d. Glen Roosevelt Wurster and Lucile Mildred (Holt) Lopez; m. Russell Warren Murphey, June 20, 1959; children: Lucinda Kalbfleisch, Rochelle Scott, Janice Sorenson. BA in Social Sci., Calif. State U., Chico, 1986, MA in Psychology, 1989; postgrad., La Salle U. Sec. Folson State Prison, Calif., 1963-66; tchr. Desert Sands Unified Schs., Indio, Calif., 1969-72; claims determiner Employment Development Dept., Redding, Calif., 1976-78; sec. Shasta County Pers., 1978-79; welfare worker Shasta County Welfare Office, 1979-85; therapy intern Counseling Ctr. Calif. State U., Chico, 1989-90; therapist Family Svc. Assn., 1987-90, Butte County Drug and Alcohol Abuse Ctr., Chico, 1989-90; mental halth counselor Cibecue (Ariz.) Indian Health Clinic, 1990-98; sch. counselor Cibucue Apache H.S. and Elem. Sch., 1998—. Mem. Kinisba Child Abuse Com., 1994—98. Vol. Pacheco Sch., Redding, 1972-76; Sunday sch. tchr., dir. vacation Bible sch. Nazarene Ch., Sacramento, Indio and Redding, 1958-85. Recipient Sch. Bell award Pacheco Sch., Indian Health Svc. Dirs. award excellence, 1997. Mem. ACA, Am. Assn. Christian Counselors, Am. Assn. Multi-Cultural Counselors, Am. Acad. Bereavement Facilitators, Ariz. Sch. Counselors Assn. Avocations: study of American Indian history, sewing, crafts, travel, canoeing. Home: PO Box 1114 Show Low AZ 85902-1114 Office: Cibecue Apache HS Apache Behavioral Health PO Box 80068 Cibecue AZ 85911-0068

MURPHEY, MURRAY GRIFFIN, history educator; b. Colorado Springs, Colo., Feb. 22, 1928; s. Bradford James and Margaret Winifred (Griffin) M.; children— Kathleen Rachel, Christopher Bradford, Jessica Lenoir. AB, Harvard U., 1949; PhD, Yale U., 1954. Asst. prof. U. Pa., Phila., 1956-61, assoc. prof., 1961-66, prof., 1966-2000, chmn. dept. Am. civilization, 1969-81, 87-94. Author: Development of Peirce's Philosophy, 1961, Our Knowledge of the Historical Past, 1973, (with E. Flower) A History of Philosophy in America, 1977, Philosophical Foundations of Historical Knowledge, 1994. Democrat. Home: 200 Rhyle Ln Bala Cynwyd PA 19004-2324

MURPHEY, ROBERT STAFFORD, pharmaceutical company executive; b. Littleton, N.C., Oct. 29, 1921; married; 2 children BS, U. Richmond, 1942; MS, U. Va., 1947, PhD in Organic Chemistry, 1949. Rsch. chemist in medicinal chemistry A.H. Robins & Co. Inc., Richmond, Va., 1948-53, dir. chemistry rsch., 1953-55, assoc. dir., 1955-57, dir. rsch., 1957-60, dir. internat. rsch., 1960-66, dir. sci. devel., 1966-82, asst. v.p., 1967-73, dir. sci. devel., v.p., 1973-82, v.p. sci. affairs and corp. devel., 1982-83, sr. v.p. sci. affairs and corp. devel., 1983-87, sr. v.p., dir. new bus. devel., 1983-90; sr. v.p., dir. bus. devel. E.C. Robins Internat., Inc., Glen Allen, 1990—. Mem. AAAS, Am. Chem. Soc., Licensing Exec. Soc. Office: E C Robins Internat Inc 4551 Cox Rd Ste 200 Glen Allen VA 23060-6740

MURPHEY, SHEILA ANN, infectious diseases physician, educator, researcher; b. Phila., July 10, 1943; d. William Joseph and Sara Esther (Mallon) M. AB, Chestnut Hill Coll., 1965; MD, Women's Med. Coll. of Pa., 1969. Diplomate Am. Bd. Internal Medicine, Am. Bd. Infectious Diseases. Intern in internal medicine Mt. Sinai Hosp. of N.Y., 1969-70, resident in internal medicine, 1970-72, instr. internal medicine, 1971-72; fellow infectious diseases U. Pa. Sch. Medicine, Phila., 1972-74, instr. dept. medicine, 1974-75, asst. prof. dept. medicine, 1975-77; chief infectious diseases sect. Phila. Gen. Hosp., 1974-77; attending physician Hosp. U. Pa., Phila. Gen. Hosp., 1974-77; dir. divsn. infectious diseases, asst. prof. medicine Jefferson Med. Coll., Phila., 1977-80, clin. assoc. prof. medicine, 1980—; dir. divsn. infectious diseases Thomas Jefferson U., 1977-88; infection control officer, attending physician Thomas Jefferson U. Hosp., 1977—. Contbr. articles to profl. jours. Fellow Coll. Physicians Phila.; mem. Am. Soc. Microbiology, Am. Coll. Physicians, Soc. Healthcare Epidemiology of Am., Infectious Diseases Soc. Am., Alpha Omega Alpha. Democrat. Roman Catholic. Office: Jefferson Med Coll 1015 Chestnut St Ste 1020 Philadelphia PA 19107-4310

MURPHREE, HAROLD T. retired minister; b. Saint Clair, Alabama, June 22, 1917; s. Soloman Cleveland and Sadie Lucas (Gibbs) Murphree; m. Sara Beatrice Smith, Dec. 1, 1940; children: Janice Elaine, Gary Doyle, Harold Wayne. Min. Bold Springs Meth. Ch., Walden County, Ga., 1962, Philadelphia & Ebenezer Chs., Rockdale City, 1963—68, Bellmont Meth. Ch., DeKalb City, 1969—70, Anvil Block Meth. Ch., Ellenwood, 1970—73, N. Covington Meth. Ch., Covington, 1974—77, Forsyth Circuit, 1977—82, Cokes Chapel Meth. Ch., Sharpsburg, Ga., 1982—83, Campbellton Meth. Ch., Fairburn, 1984—86; ret., 1986. Min. Carmel Meth. Ch., Gay, Ga., 1987—92. Author: Tried and Proven, 2000. Sgt. USAF, 1945—47, The Phillippines. Republican. Avocation: gardening. Home: 2532 Freemans Walk Path Dacula GA 30019-1390

MURPHREE, HENRY BERNARD SCOTT, psychiatry and pharmacology educator, consultant; b. Decatur, Ala., Aug. 11, 1927; s. Henry Bernard and Nancy Mae (Burrus) M.; m. Dorothy Elaine Simmons, Nov. 14, 1953 (dec.); children: Julie Elizabeth, Susan Louise, Jefferson Van; m. Dorothy Elizabeth Olson, Sept. 23, 1993. Student, MIT, 1944-45; BA, Yale U., 1950; MD, Emory U., 1959. Intern internal medicine, fellow clin. pharmacology, instr. Emory U., 1959-61; resident psychiatry Med. Sch. Rutgers U., 1972-76, mem. grad. faculty psychology, 1972-97; rsch. asst. Johns Hopkins U., Balt., 1950; asst. chief neuropharmacology Bur. Rsch., Princeton, N.J., 1961-68; from assoc prof. to prof. Univ. of Medicine and Dentistry Robert Wood Johnson Med. Sch., Piscataway, 1968-97, assoc. dean acad. affairs Univ. Medicine and Dentistry, 1977-81, chmn. psychiatry Univ. Medicine and Dentistry, 1977-91. Cons. medicinal chemistry and pharmacology FMC Chem. R&D Ctr., Princeton, N.J., 1962-68, Roche Labs., Nutley and Verona, N.J., 1968-77. Author bylaws Rutgers Med. Sch.; contbr. articles to profl. jours. Founding mem. Somerset Coun. Alcoholism, Somerville, N.J., 1974-77; founding cons. Impaired Physicians Com. Med. Soc. N.J.; mem. Sci. Adv. Com., State of N.J., 1981-97; bd. trustees Carrier Found., Belle Mead, N.J., 1981-95, vice chmn. bd., chmn. exec. com., 1989-95. Aviation cadet USNR, 1945-46; lt. MSC USN, 1951-55. Mem. Am. Soc. for Pharmacology and Exptl. Therapeutics, Am. Psychiat. Assn., Soc. Biol. Psychiatry, Am. Coll. Neuropsychopharmacology, Sigma Xi, Alpha Omega Alpha. Avocations: music, electronics. Home: 467 Ridge Rd Watchung NJ 07069-5433 E-mail: hbsmurph@msn.com. *Early on, in this sorry world, I pondered the concept of the "perfectibility of humankind". I concluded the best approach is education and devoted my career to teaching and consultation, a variant of teaching.*

MURPHREE, KENNETH DEWEY, elementary school educator; b. Memphis, July 28, 1953; s. Dewey and Garneita (Bryant) M.; m. Beverly Ann Hurt, Sept. 7, 1974. AE, N.W. Miss. Jr. Coll., Senatobia, 1973; BSE, Delta State U., 1975, ME, 1976, Ednl. Specialist degree in adminstrn. and supervision, 1992. Grad. asst. dept. elem. edn. Delta State U., 1975—76; elem. tchr. Helena West - Helena Pub. Schs., Helena, 1976—81; prin. Woodruff Elem. Sch., West Helena, 1981—93, Westside Elem. Sch., 1993—97, Barton Elem. Sch., Barton, 1997—. Mem. NAESP, ASCD, Ark. Assn. Ednl. Adminstrs., Ark. Assn. Elem. Sch. Prins., East Ark. Schoolmasters Assn., Lions (pres., past pres., 1st v.p., bd. dirs. tail twister West Helena), Phi Theta Kappa (past pres. Theta Sigma chpt.), Kappa Delta Pi, Phi Delta Kappa. Office: Barton Elem Sch Hwy 85 S Barton AR 72312

MURPHY, ANN MARGUERITE, artist; b. Arlington, Mass., Feb. 21, 1937; d. Joseph Charles and Anna Marguerite (Lynah) Donnelly; m. Paul Hughes Murphy, June 19, 1960; children: Paul Hughes Jr., Debra Donnelly, Anna Marguerite. AS, Lasell Coll., Newton, Mass., 1957. One-woman and group exhbns. include Art for Heart, Bank of Boston, Cahoon Mus., Cape Cod, Chinese Cultural Ctr., Duxbury Art Complex Mus., Fed. Res. Bank, Guild of Boston Artists, JFK Bldg., Krasdale Gallery, N.Y., Landmark Bldg., Boston, Lyme Art Assn., Conn., Priscilla Hartley Gallery, Maine, Provincetown Art Mus., Sharon Art Ctr., N.H., Symphony Hall, Ventress Libr. Gallery, Whistler House Mus. Art; represented in permanent collections at Wright Gallery, Cape Porpoise, Maine, June Weare Fine Arts, Ogunquit, Maine. Gallery artist South Shore Art Ctr. Recipient Beman Purchase award Hudson Valley Art Assn., Fawcett award for humor North River Arts Soc., 1993, 1st pl. award, 1997, Simms Marine award 1999, 2d pl. award South Shore Art Ctr., 1992, Marine Painting award Ogunquit Art Ctr., Vayana Meml. award. Mem.: North River Arts Soc. (former art com. chmn.), Copley Soc. Boston (Copley Artist), Pastel Painters Soc. Cape Cod (Wallis Corp. award 1997), North Shore Art Assn. (Walter Bollendonk Meml. award, Paul E. Goodridge Meml. award 1994, Alfred and Charlotte Movalli Meml. award 1997, Howard Curtis Marine award 2000), New Eng. Watercolor Soc. (bd. dirs.), Concord Art Assn., Cape Cod Art Assn. (awards 1990, 1993, 1996, 1998, 1999, 2001), Am. Soc. Marine Artists, Acad. Artists, Allied Artists Am. (assoc.). Office: PO Box 585 Humarock MA 02047

MURPHY, ARTHUR THOMAS, systems engineer; b. Hartford, Conn., Feb. 15, 1929; s. Arthur T. and Mary (Beakey) M.; m. Jane M. Gamble, Aug. 16, 1952; children: Thomas, Patricia, Mary, John, Sheila, Jane, Joseph. BEE, Syracuse U., 1951; MS, Carnegie-Mellon U., 1952, PhD, 1957. Registered profl. engr., Kans. Instr. Carnegie-Mellon U., Pitts., 1952-56; asst., assoc. prof., head. elec. engring. Wichita State U., Kans., 1956-61; vis. assoc. prof. mech. engring. MIT, Cambridge, Mass., 1961-62; prof., dean engring. Widener U., Chester, Pa., 1962-71, v.p., acad. dean, 1971-75; Brown prof., head mech. engring. dept. Carnegie-Mellon U., Pitts., 1975-79; prof. industry, mgr. computer and automated systems, sr. research fellow Du Pont de Nemours Co., Camp Hill, Pa., 1979-87, Du Pont fellow Wilmington, Del., 1987-96, Du Pont fellow emeritus, 1996—, cons., 1996—; acting pres. Pa. Inst. Tech., Media, 1998. Vis. rsch. fellow Sony Corp. Rsch. Ctr., Yokohama, Japan, 1991-92, Internat. Superconductivity Tech. Ctr., Tokyo, 1993; vis. prof. control engring. U. Manchester, Eng., 1968-69; cons. Boeing Co., Wichita and Morton, Pa., 1957-68; bd. dirs. Rumford Pub. Co., Chgo., 1975-90; lectr. Pa. State U., 1983-87; Dupont rep. Chem. Rsch. Coun., 1994-97; mem. sci. adv. bd. Parlec, Inc. Author: Introduction to System Dynamics, 1967; contbr. articles to profl. jours.; editor: Pergamon Press, 1966-75; patentee thick film filter connector, substrate and ceramic package, connection method for circuit bd. (ball grid array), superconducting mixer antenna array. Former mem. adv. coun. Tex. A&M U., Swarthmore Coll.; program evaluator Accreditation Bd. for Engring. and Tech., 1996—. DuPont fellow, 1987—; recipient DuPont Spl. Compensation award, 1988, Electronics Mktg. Excellence award DuPont Co., 1990. Fellow AAAS, IEEE (exec. com., treas. computer packaging), Am. Soc. Engring. Edn. (v.p. fin. 2001-, chmn. grad. studies, instrumentation, awards com., DuPont rep., Corp. Mem. Coun., We. Electric Fund award 1966); mem. ASME (exec. com. control divsn.), Sigma Xi, Tau Beta Pi, Eta Kappa Nu, Sigma Pi Sigma, Pi Mu Epsilon, Phi Kappa Phi, Phi Theta Kappa (hon.). Avocations: hiking, photography, travel, genealogy. Home: 388 Spring Mill Rd Chadds Ford PA 19317-8226 Office: Du Pont Co B-10234 1007 Market St Wilmington DE 19898-0001 E-mail: arthur.t.murphy@usa.dupont.com.

MURPHY, ARTHUR WILLIAM, lawyer, educator; b. Boston, Jan. 25, 1922; s. Arthur W. and Rose (Spillane) M.; m. Jane Marks, Dec. 21, 1948 (dec. Sept. 1951); 1 dau., Lois; m. Jean C. Marks, Sept. 30, 1954; children— Rachel, Paul. AB cum laude, Harvard, 1943; LL.B., Columbia, 1948. Bar: N.Y. State bar 1949. Asso. in law Columbia Sch. Law, N.Y.C., 1948-49; asso. dir. Legislative Drafting Research Fund, 1956, prof. law, 1963—; trial atty. U.S. Dept. Justice, 1950-52; asso. firm Hughes, Hubbard, Blair & Reed, N.Y.C., 1953-56, 57-58; partner firm Baer, Marks, Friedman & Berliner, 1959-63. Mem. safety and licensing panel AEC, 1962-73; mem. spl. commn. on weather modification NSF, 1964-66; mem. Presdl. Commn. on Catastrophic Nuclear Accidents, 1988-90 Author: Financial Protection against Atomic Hazards, 1957, (with others) Cases on Gratuitous Transfers, 1968, 3d edit., 1985, The Nuclear Power Controversy, 1976. Served with AUS, 1943-46. Decorated Purple Heart. Mem. ABA, Assn. of Bar of City of N.Y. (spl. com. on sci. and law) Office: Columbia Sch of Law 435 W 116th St New York NY 10027-7297

MURPHY, AUSTIN DE LA SALLE, economist, educator, banker; b. N.Y.C., Nov. 20, 1917; s. Daniel Joseph and Marie Cornelia (Austin) M.; m. Mary Patricia Halpin, June 12, 1948 (dec. May 1974); children: Austin Joseph, Owen Gerard; m. Lee Chilton Romero, Dec. 14, 1974; stepchildren: Thomas Romero, Robert Romero (dec.). AB, St. Francis Coll., Bklyn., 1938; AM (Hayden fellow 1938-40), Fordham U., 1940, PhD, 1949; PhD (hon.), Canisius Coll., 1986. Instr. econs. Fordham U., 1938-41; Instr. econs. Georgetown U., 1941-42; asst. statistician, statis. controls Bd. Econ. Warfare, 1942; sr. econs. research editor N.Y. State Dept. Labor, 1947-50; lectr. econs. Fordham U. Sch. Edn., 1946-55; instr. N.Y. U. Sch. Commerce, 1949-51; dean sch. bus. adminstrn. Seton Hall U., South Orange, N.J., 1950-55; Albert O'Neill prof. Am. enterprise, dean sch. bus. adminstrn. Canisius Coll., Buffalo, 1955-62; dir. edn. dept. NAM, 1962-63; exec. v.p. Savs. Banks Assn. N.Y. State, 1963-70; chmn., pres. River Bank Am. (formerly East River Savs. Bank), 1970-89, vice chmn., dir., 1989-96, chmn. adv. bd., 1996-98. Charter trustee Savs. Bank Rockland County, 1965-70; dir. Bank of Charleston (S.C.), 1989-91; chmn. bd., trustee Savs. Bank Life Ins. Fund, 1983-87; chmn. dist. I, mem. adv. coun. Conf. State Bank Suprs., 1986-93; bd. dirs. MSB Fund, Inc. Author: (with Fleming Frasca, and Mannion) Social Studies Review Book, 1946, Leading Problems of New Jersey Manufacturing Industries, (with Bullock and Doerflinger), 1953, Reasons for Relocation, 1955, Forecast of Industrial Expansion in Buffalo and the Niagara Frontier, 1956, Metropolitan Buffalo Perspective, 1958; editor Handbook of New York Labor Statistics, 1950. Mem. Livingston (N.J.) Charter Commn., 1954-55; mem. capital expenditures com., City of Buffalo, 1957-63; trustee Fordham U., 1973-79, N.Y. Med. Coll., 1978-81; bd. dirs. N.Y. council Boy Scouts Am., 1974—, Jr. Achievement of Buffalo, 1958-63, Invest-in-Am. 1st lt. U.S. Army, 1942-46. Named Knight of Malta, 1971. Mem. NAM (chmn. ednl. aids com. 1958-63), Am. Fin. Assn., Def. Transp. Assn. (life), Nat. Assn. Mut. Savs. Banks (bd. dirs., treas. 1976-81), Friendly Sons. St. Patrick (1st v.p., 1976-77), Down-Town Lower Manhattan Assn. (dir., vice chmn. 1982-93), Union League Club (pres. 1991-93), Larchmont Yacht Club, Carolina Yacht Club, KC, Alpha Kappa Psi, Pi Gamma Mu. Office: RB Asset Corp 645 5th Ave New York NY 10022-5910 Home: PO Box 396 Mamaroneck NY 10543-0396 *Through the various happy events and the difficult and sorrowful, loss of loved ones as well as the vagaries of business life, I have found that an ongoing prayerful relationship to God brings a certain detachment and peace that overcomes life's passing problems.*

MURPHY, BARBARA ANN, protective services official; b. Oct. 4, 1922; d. Thomas Henry and Charlotte Ruth (Ticer) Murphy. BS, Jersey City State Coll., 1944; MA, Columbia U., 1949. Ret. educator. Chair child placement rev. bd., Hudson County Superior Court of N.J., Chancery Divsn. Family, 1992—. Pres. bd. trustees Weehawken (N.J.) Libr., 1994—; adv. panel United Water. Recipient Gov.'s Tchr. Recognition Program award, Princeton, N.J., 1989; named to Weehawken H.S. Hall of Fame, Weehawken Bd. Edn., 1992. Mem. AAUW (pres. 1988-91), N.J. Schoolwomen's Club (v.p. 1980), Weehawken Hist. Soc. (life mem.), Weehawken Adult Club (charter), Palisade Gen. Hosp. Vols. Avocations: travel, reading, gardening, piano. Home: 107 Hauxhurst Ave Weehawken NJ 07086-6838

MURPHY, BARRY AMES, lawyer; b. Summit, N.J., Mar. 3, 1938; s. Robert Joseph and Florence C. (Ames) M.; m. Leslie Lynn Smith, June 9, 1962; children— Karen Irene, Sean Patrick, Conor Brendan, Ilana Taraleigh. BA in English, Stanford U., 1960; MBA, Harvard U., 1963; JD, U. So. Calif., 1972. Bar: Calif. bar 1973, U.S. Supreme Ct 1976, U.S. Tax Ct 1976. Fin. analyst Office of Sec. Def., 1963-65; pres. Tech. Industries Inc., Los Angeles, 1966-72; invididual practice law San Mateo, Calif., 1972-74; corp. counsel Falstaff Brewing Co., San Francisco, 1974-77; sr. partner firm Levine & Murphy, 1978-81; v.p. Microvertics, Mountain View, Calif., 1981-86; pres. Murphy Law Corp., San Anselmo, 1987—. Mem. Am., Calif. bar assns., Calif. Trial Lawyers. Address: 28 Fern Ln San Anselmo CA 94960-1807 E-mail: barry@murphy.law.com.

MURPHY, BEN CARROLL, engineering company executive; b. Aug. 21, 1931; s. Benjamin Franklin and Effie (Lett) M.; m. Vivian Inez Hancock, March 3, 1950; children: Lanny Carroll, Debra Kay Murphy Soffitri, Kathy M. Murphy David, Gregory Lynn, Jon Patrick. BS, Delta State U., 1969, MBA, 1974; grad., United Electronic Inst., 1972. With U.S. Gypsum Co., Greenville, Miss., 1951-54, 55-56, Atlantic & Pacific Tea Co., Greenville, 1954-55; cost acct. Baxter Labs., Cleveland, 1966-69; project engr. mfg. U.S. Gypsum Co., Danville, Va., 1969-72; plant personnel and safety mgr. Cook Industries, Inc., Memphis, 1972-73, divsn. safety dir., plant personnel mgr., 1973-75, corp. compensation sr. analyst, 1976, div. indsl. rels. and personnel mgr., 1975-76, corp. compensation mgr., 1976-79; divsn. asst. personnel mgr. Robertson CECO Corp., Columbus, Miss., 1979-80, structural supt., 1980-82, mgr. prodn. control sys., 1982-92, divsn. prodn. control, schedule mgr., 1992-97. Ret. night instr. bus. and econs. N.W. Jr. Coll., Southaven, Miss., 1975-79, East Miss. C.C., 1980—; cons. in compensation S.E. Memphis Mental Health Center, 1978-82. Bd. dirs. Cmty. Water Assn. Mem. Mid-South Compensation and Benefits Assn. (dir. 1977-80, mem. organizing team 1976), Univ. for Women (adv. com. for extended studies of Miss. U.), Am. Compensation Soc., Soc. Mfg. Engrs. (sr., 3d v.p. chpt.), Miss. Mfg. Assn., Am. Mgmt. Compensation Soc., Carmack Cmty. Club (pres.). Baptist. Home: PO Box 13 Kosciusko MS 39090-0013 Address: 2065 Attala Rd 3989 Vaiden MS 39176-9606 E-mail: bencm@kopower.com.

MURPHY, BENJAMIN EDWARD, actor; b. Jonesboro, Ark., Mar. 6, 1942; s. Patrick Henry and Nadine (Steele) M. Student, Loras Coll., 1960-61, Loyola U., New Orleans, 1961-62, U. Americas, 1962-63, 64-65; BA in Polit. Sci, U. Ill., 1964; student, Pasadena Playhouse, 1965-67; BA in Theatre Arts, U. So. Calif., 1968. Appeared in: TV series Name of the Game, NBC, 1968-70, Alias Smith and Jones, ABC, 1971-73, Griff, 1973-74, Gemini Man, NBC, 1976, The Chisholms, CBS, 1979-80, The Winds of War, 1983, Lottery, 1983-84, Berrenger's, NBC, 1985, The Dirty Dozen, Fox Network, 1988.

MURPHY, BETTY SOUTHARD (MRS. CORNELIUS F. MURPHY), lawyer; b. East Orange, N.J. d. Floyd Theodore and Thelma (Casto) Southard; m. Cornelius F. Murphy, May 1, 1965; children: Ann Southard, Cornelius Francis Jr. AB, Ohio State U.; student, Alliance Française and U. Sorbonne, Paris; JD, Am. U.; LLD (hon.), Eastern Mich. U., 1975, Capital U., 1976, U. Puget Sound, 1986; LHD, Tusculum coll., 1987. Bar: D.C. Corr., free lance journalist, Europe and Asia, UPI, Washington; pub. relations counsellor Capital Properties, Inc. of Columbus (Ohio); practiced in, 1959-74; mem. firm McInnis, Wilson, Munson & Woods (and predecessor firm); dep. asst. sec., adminstr. Wage and Hour Divsn. Dept. Labor, 1974-75; chmn. and mem. NLRB, 1975-79; ptnr. firm Baker & Hostetler, 1980—. Adj. prof. law Am. U., 1972-80, 99—; mem. adv. com. on rights and responsibilities of women to Sec. HHS; mem. panel conciliators Internat. Ctr. Settlement Investment Disputes, 1974-85; mem. Adminstrv. Conf. U.S., 1976-80, Pub. Svc. Adv. Bd., 1976-79; mem. human resouces com. Nat. Ctr. for Productivity and Quality of Working Life, 1976-80; mem. Presdl. Commn. on Exec. Exch., 1981-85. Trustee Mary Baldwin Coll., 1977-85, Am. U., 1980-99, George Mason U. Found., Inc., 1990-2000, George Mason U. Edn. Found., 1993-2000, 2001—; nat. bd. dirs. Med. Coll. Pa., bd. corporators, 1976-85; bd. dirs. Ctr. for Women in Medicine, 1980-86; bd. govs. St. Agnes Sch., 1981-87; mem. exec. com. Commn. on Bicentennial of U.S. Constn., chmn. internat. adv. com., 1985-92; vice chmn. James Madison Meml. Fellowship Found., 1989-96; bd. dirs. Meridian Internat. Ctr., 1992-98; trustee Friends of Congl. Law Libr., 1992—, Friends of Dept. of Labor, 1984—; mediator World Intellectual Property Orgn., 1996—. Recipient Ohio Gov.'s award, 1980, fellow award, 1981, Outstanding Pub. Service award U.S. Info. Service, 1987; named Disting. Fellow John Sherman Myers Soc., 1986, 96; fellow Nat. Acad. Human Resources, 1998. Mem.: Am. U. Alumni Assn. (bd. dirs.), Supreme Ct. Hist. Soc., Union Internat. des Advocats (gov. bd. 1997—), Rep. Nat. Lawyers Assn. (nat. v.p. 1990—95, nat. vice chmn. 1996—2000, 2001—), Am. Arbitration Assn. (bd. dirs. 1985—2000, mem. editl. bd. 1992, mem. exec. com. 1995—2000, mem. internat. arbitration com. 1997—, steering com. lawyers for Bush 2000), Bar Assn. D.C., Inter-Am. Bar Assn. (editor newsletter, co-chmn. labor law com. 1975—83, Silver medal 1967), FBA, ABA (adminstrv. law sect., chmn. labor law com. 1980—83, chmn. internat. and comparative law adminstrv. law sect. 1983—88, chmn. customs, tariff and trade com. 1988—90, employment law sect. 1990, chmn. internat. com. dispute resolution sect. 1995—), World Peace Through Law Ctr., Mortar Bd., Kappa Beta Pi. Republican. Office: Baker & Hostetler LLP Ste 1100 1050 Connecticut Ave NW Washington DC 20036-5304 E-mail: bsmurphy@bakerlaw.com.

MURPHY, BRIAN STUART, internist, consultant; b. N.Y.C., July 27; s. Walter Joseph and Veronica Mary (Nally) M. BA, NYU, 1979, MS, 1985; MD, MPH, N.Y. Med. Coll., Valhalla, 1990; MPH, Harvard U., 1996; postgrad., Columbia U. Diplomate Am. Bd. Internal Medicine. Resident in internal medicine Tufts-N.E. Med. Ctr., Boston, 1990-93; chief resident Boston U. Sch. Medicine, 1993-94; fellow in medicine Harvard Med. Sch., Boston, 1994-96, fellow in med. ethics, 1994-95; rsch. fellow Mass. Gen. Hosp., 1994-96; dir. clin. strategies program St. Vincent's Hosp., N.Y.C., 1996—; dir. med. affairs Hotel Trades Health Ctrs. N.Y., 1998—. Cons. Roche Pharms., N.J., 1996—, Merck and Co., Inc., N.J., 1996—, Roerig divsn., N.Y., 1997—; asst. prof. medicine N.Y. Med. Coll., Valhalla, 1996—. Contbg. author: Saunders Manual of Medical Practice, 1999. Mem. AMA, ACP, Am. Coll. Physician Execs., Mystery Writers of Am., Harvard Club of N.Y., Mensa, Alpha Omega Alpha. Roman Catholic. Office: St Vincents Hosp of NY 153 W 11th St New York NY 10011-8305

MURPHY, BRUCE ALLEN, government and law educator, author; b. Abington, Mass., Sept. 30, 1951; m. Carol Lynn Wright, June 14, 1975; children: Emily, Geoffrey. BA, U. Mass., 1973; PhD, U. Va., 1978. Fred Morgan Kirby prof. civil rights Lafayette Coll., Easton, Pa. Author: The Brandeis/Frankfurter Connection: The Secret Political Activities of Two Supreme Court Justices, 1982, Fortas: The Rise and Ruin of a Supreme Court Justice, 1988, (with Larry Berman) Approaching Democracy, 1996, 99, 01. Avocations: fishing, reading, sports. Office: Lafayette Coll Dept Govt and Law 200 Kirby Hall Civil Rights Easton PA 18042 E-mail: murphyb@lafayette.edu.

MURPHY, CHRISTINE, medical facility administrator; b. Jan. 2, 1956; d. Mary. I. Jackson; m. Paul Murphy, June 19, 1976; children: Christie, Jannie-Kay. Diploma, Newport (R.I.) Hosp., 1977; BS, RWU, Bristol, R.I., 1994; MS, SRU, Newport, 1997. RN, R.I. Clin. educator Newport Hosp.; firm mgr. VAMC, Providence. Bd. dirs. Newport Hosp. Alumni, West House Housing Elderly. Mem. Assn. Oper. Rm. Nurse (cert.), Nat. Assn. Ambulatory Care Mgrs. Office: PVAMC 830 Chalkstone Ave Providence RI 02908-4734

MURPHY, COLLEEN FRANCES, marketing professional, public relations executive; b. Litchfield, Ill., Mar. 17, 1960; d. Carl Maurice and Margaret Evelyn (McAnarney) M.; m. James Arnold Buck, Jan. 10, 1987. BS, So. Ill. U., 1982; MBA, U. Ill., Springfield, 1996. Pub. relations rep. Ill. Consol., Mattoon, 1982-84; mktg. mgr. Mercy Hosp., Urbana, Ill., 1984-86; account exec. Cohn & Wolfe/Burson-Marstellar, Atlanta, 1987; sr. account exec. DKB Pub. Relations, 1987-88; ind. pub. relations cons. Decatur, Ill., 1988-89; dir. clin. planning and mktg. So. Ill. U. Sch. Medicine, Springfield, Ill., 1989-94; dir. mktg. and comm. The Carle Found., Urbana, 1994-97; dir. air planning and mktg. Aydlotte & Cartwright, 1997-99; v.p. mktg. Harper Coll., Palatine, Ill., 1999—. Cons. pub. rels. Families First, Atlanta, 1987-89. Bd. dirs. YWCA, Decatur, 1989-91. Mem. Pub. Rels. Soc. Am. (bd. dirs. Cen. Ill. chpt. 1986, v.p. 1987). Home: 348 Prairie Knoll Dr Naperville IL 60565-4150 Office: Harper Coll 1200 W Algonquin Palatine IL 61801-2529

MURPHY, DANIEL IGNATIUS, lawyer; b. Phila., Mar. 14, 1927; s. John Anthony Murphy and Irene Cooper Thorn; m. Jeanne B. Genetti, July 28, 1956 (div. Aug. 1978); children: Jewel A., Daniel I. Jr.; m. Barbara Ann Uncles, Jan. 1, 1979. BS in Econs., U. Pa., 1950; LLB, Yale U., 1953. Bar: Pa. 1954, U.S. Dist Ct. (ea. dist.) Pa. 1954, U.S. Ct. Appeals (3d cir.) 1954, U.S. Tax Ct. 1956, U.S. Supreme Ct. 1959. Assoc. Evans, Bayard & Frick, Phila., 1953-55; asst. city solicitor City of Phila., Pa., 1956-59; ptnr. Cavanaugh, Murphy & Kalodner, Phila., 1958-64, Shapiro, Stalberg, Cook, Murphy & Kalodner, Phila., 1964-66, Takiff, Bolger & Murphy, Phila., 1966-72, Waters, Gallagher, Collins & Masterson, Phila., 1972-80, Stradley, Ronon, Stevens & Young, Phila., 1980-92, ret., of counsel, 1993. Tchr. Am. Soc. CLUs, Villanova, Pa., 1956-57; mem. exec. com. Phila. Estate Planning Coun., 1958-60; lectr. Pa. Bar Inst., Harrisburg, 1974-92, Pa. Coll. Orphans Ct. Judges, Harrisburg, 1978, Pitts., 1991; apptd. spl. master for trial mgmt. of complex litigation Phila. County Ct. Common Pleas, 1994—; judge pro tem Comm. Ct., Phila. County Ct. Common Pleas, 2000—; arbitrator Nat. Assn. Securities Dealers, 2001. Editor: Phila. Bar Assn. Mag. The Shingle, 1958-67; contbr. chpts. to manuals and articles to profl. jours. Chmn. Phila. Chpt. Am. Cancer Soc., 1956-63; mem. Com. of 70, Phila., 1968—, chmn., 1972-74; trustee Hahnemann U., Phila., 1983-86. With USN, 1945-46. Fellow: Pa. Bar Found. (life); mem.: ABA, Colonial Soc. Pa. (bd. dirs. 2001), Phila. Bar Assn. (vice chmn. com. censors 1971), Pa. Bar Assn., Pa. Soc. S.R., Soc. Colonial Wars, Phila. Country Club, Union League Phila. Democrat. Roman Catholic. Avocation: U.S. Civil War history. Office: 2600 One Commerce Sq Philadelphia PA 19103 E-mail: dmurphyesq@prodigy.net.

MURPHY, DAVID THOMAS, secondary school educator; b. Phila., June 18, 1950; s. Thomas Vincent Murphy and Betty Louise Nelson; m. Joanne Ezzi, Aug. 7, 1998; stepchildren: Jennifer, Jason. BS, Temple U., 1976, MEd, 1984. Shipping warehouse mgr. Emerson Quiet Kool Corp., Phila., 1973—74; part-time lectr. Temple U., 1975; tchr. Sch. Dist. Phila., 1977—82, Phila. Literacy Inst., 1981—82; English tchr., reading specialist Lenape Regional H.S., Medford, NJ, 1982—. Author: numerous poems; creator, moderator (TV) Meeting at the Writers, creator Vocations and Avocations, prodr., dir., writer The Lenape Dist: The Early Years. Grantee, NEH, 1988—89, 1995. Mem.: Nat. Coun. Tchrs. English. Avocations: Karate, music, poetry, astronomy. Office: Lenape HS 235 Hartford Rd Medford NJ 08055

MURPHY, DEBORAH JANE, lawyer; b. Clinton, Tenn., Dec. 19, 1955; d. Robert C. and Mary R. (Melton) M. BS, U. Tenn., 1977; JD, Nashville Sch. Law, 1987. Bar: Tenn. 1987, U.S. Dist. Ct. (D.C. dist.) 1988, U.S. Dist. Ct. (6th cir.) 1988. Estate tax atty. U.S. Dept. Treasury, Knoxville, Tenn., 1987—; mcpl. judge Lake City, 1997—. Bd. dirs. Tenn. Lawyers Assn. Women, Nashville, 1997-01. Mem. cmty. adv. bd. East Tenn. Children's Hosp., 1998-01. Mem. ABA, Tenn. Bar Assn., Club LeConte. Dem. Methodist. Avocations: reading, golf, travel. Home: PO Box 510 Clinton TN 37717-0510 Office: IRS 710 Locust St Fl 4 Knoxville TN 37902-2540 E-mail: Deborah902@aol.com.

MURPHY, DENNIS PATRICK, hotel business entrepreneur; b. Buffalo, Jan. 12, 1958; s. Dennis Charles and Dorothy E. Murphy; m. Carol Ann Klocke. B in Hospitality Mgmt., Fla. Internat. U., 1980. Cert. hotel exec. Mgr. hotel ops. Marriott Corp., Washington, 1979-80; dir. food and beverage Mariner Corp., Houston, 1980-83; corp. dir. Innco Hospitality, Wichita, Kans., 1984-86; ops. exec. Clubhouse Inns of Am., 1986-88; chmn. JLH Lodge Corp., Amherst, N.Y., 1988—, also bd. dirs.; founding pres. InnVest Lodging Svcs. Inc., 1990—. Bd. dirs. Hotel Baronette, Inc., Genoa Lodging, LLC, Suzuki & Son, Ltd., Penn. Investors IV, LLC; nominated Esquire mag. register, 1985; chair project devel. com. econ lodging coun. Am. Hotel/Motel Assn., 1990; dep. chair World U. Games, 1990—93; treas. World Vets. Games L/O/C, Buffalo, 1994—96, Greater Buffalo Conv. and Visitors Bur, 1992—, chmn, 1999—2001; mem. exec. com. Buffalo-Niagara Partnership, 1999—2001; trustee Gates Found., 1988—. Recipient Elsworth Statler award The Statler Found., 1978-79, Citizen of the Year award, The Buffalo News, 2002. Mem. Soc. Wine Educators (pubs. com. 1977-79), Am. Hotel and Lodging Assn., The Buffalo Club, The Buffalo Launch Club. Office: PO Box 98 Buffalo NY 14205

MURPHY, DIANA E. federal judge; b. Faribault, Minn., Jan. 4, 1934; d. Albert W. and Adleyne (Heiker) Kuske; m. Joseph Murphy, July 24, 1958; children: Michael, John E. BA magna cum laude, U. Minn., 1954, JD magna cum laude, 1974; postgrad., Johannes Gutenberg U., Mainz, Germany, 1954—55, U. Minn., 1955—58; LLD, St Johns U., 2000. Bar: Minn. 1974, U.S. Supreme Ct. 1980. Assoc. Lindquist & Vennum, 1974—76; mcpl. judge Hennepin County, 1976—78, Minn. State dist. judge, 1978—80; judge U.S. Dist. Ct. for Minn., Mpls., 1980—94, chief judge, 1992—94; judge U.S. Ct. of Appeals (8th cir.), Minneapolis, 1994—. Chair U.S. Sentencing Commn., 1999—. Bd. editors: Minn. Law Rev., Bd. editors: Georgetown U. Jour. on Cts., Bd. editors: Health Scis. and the Law, 1989—92. Dir. Nat. Assn. Pub. Interest Law Fellowships for Equal Justice, 1992—95; Bd. dirs. Mpls. United Way, 1985—2001, treas., 1990—94, vice-chmn., 1996—97, chmn. bd. dirs., 1997—98; bd. dirs. Bush Found., 1982—, chmn. bd. dirs., 1986—91, also organizer, 1st chmn. adv. coun.; bd. dirs. Amicus, 1976—80; mem. Mpls. Charter Commn., 1973—76; bd. dirs. Ops. De Novo, 1971—76, chmn. bd. dirs., 1974—75; mem., chmn. bill of rights com. Minn. Constl. Study Commn., 1971—73; regent St. Johns U., 1978—87, 1988—98, vice-chmn., chmn. bd., 1985—98. bd. overseers sch. theology, 1998—2001; mem. Minn. Bicentennial Commn., 1987—88; trustee Twin Cities Pub. TV, 1985—94, chmn. bd., 1990—92; trustee, treas. U. Minn. Found., 1990—; bd. dirs. Sci. Mus. Minn., 1988—94, vice-chmn., 1991—94; trustee U. St. Thomas, 1991—; Bd. dirs. Spring Hill Conf. Ctr., 1978—84. Recipient Amicus Founders' award, 1980, Outstanding Achievement award, U. Minn., 1983, YWCA, 1981, Disting. Citizen award, Alpha Gamma Delta, 1985, Devitt Disting. Svc. to Justice award, 2001, Disting. Alumnus award, U. Minn. Law Sch., 2002; scholar Fulbright. Fellow: Am. Bar Found.; mem.: ABA (mem. ethics and profl. responsibility judges adv. com. 1981—88, standing com. on jud. selection, tenure and compensation 1991—94, mem. standing com. on fed. jud. improvements 1994—97, Appellate Judges conf. exec. com. 1996—99, chmn. ethics and profl. responsibility judges adv. com. 1997—2000), Fed. Jud. Ctr. (bd. dirs. 1990—94, 8th cir. jud. coun. 1992—94, convener task force 1993, mem. U.S. jud. conf. com. on ct. adminstrn. and case mgmt. 1994—99, chair gender fairness implementation com. 1997—98, 8th cir. jud. coun. 1997—), Hist. Soc. for 8th Cir. (bd. dirs. 1988—91), Fed. Judges Assn. (bd. dirs. 1982—, v.p. 1984—89, pres. 1989—91), U. Minn. Alumni Assn. (bd. dirs. 1975—83, nat. pres. 1981—82), Minn. Women Lawyers (Myra Bradwell award 1996), Nat. Assn. Women Judges (Leadership Judges Jud. Adminstrn. award 1998), Nat. Assn. Governing Bds. Univs. Colls. (dir. 1998—), Am. Judicature Soc. (bd. dirs. 1982—93, v.p. 1985—88, treas. 1988—89, chmn. bd. 1989—91), Am. Law Inst., Hennepin County Bar Assn. (gov. coun. 1976—81), Minn. Bar Assn. (bd. govs. 1977—81), Order of Coif, Phi Beta Kappa. Office: 11 E US Courthouse 300 S 4th St Minneapolis MN 55415-1320

MURPHY, DICK, mayor, former superior court judge; m. Jan Murphy; children: Brian, Shannon, Kelly. BS, U. Ill.; MBA, Harvard U.; JD, Stanford U. Mem. San Diego City Coun., 1981—85; San Diego mktg. dir. Bank of Am.; corp. atty. Luce, Forward, Hamilton & Scripps; mcpl. ct. judge, 1985—89; superior ct. judge, 1989—2000; mayor City of San Diego, Calif., 2000—. Chair Mission Trails Regional Park Task Force, Met. Transit Devel. Bd. Lieut. U.S. Army. Mem.: San Diego Rotary Club. Office: 202 C St San Diego CA 92101*

MURPHY, EDDIE, comedian, actor; b. Bklyn., Apr. 3, 1961; s. Vernon and Lillian Murphy Lynch; m. Nicole Mitchell, March 18, 1993; children: Bria, Myles, Shayne. Student pub. schs., Bklyn. Began performing Richard M. Dixon's White House, L.I., N.Y.; performed at various N.Y.C. clubs, including The Comic Strip; with Saturday Night Live, N.Y.C., 1980-84; host 35th Ann. Emmy Awards, 1983. Starring roles in motion pictures include 48 Hours, 1982, Trading Places, 1983, Best Defense, 1984, Beverly Hills Cop, 1984, The Golden Child, 1986, Beverly Hills Cop II, 1987, Eddie Murphy Raw, 1987, Coming to America, 1988, Harlem Nights,1989, Another 48 Hours, 1990, Boomerang, 1992, The Distinguished Gentleman, 1992, Beverly Hills Cop III, 1994, The Vampire of Brooklyn, 1995, The Nutty Professor, 1996, Metro, 1997, Mulan (voice), 1998, Doctor Dolittle, 1998, Holy Man, 1998, Toddlers, 1999, Pluto Nash, 1999, Life, 1999, Bowfinger, 1999, Shrek (voice), 2001 (Favorite Motion Picture Star in Comedy People's Choice award 2002, Favorite Voice from Animated Movie Kid's Choice award 2002), Dr. Dollittle 2, 2001, Showtime, 2002, I Spy, 2002; one-man HBO spl., 1983; albums include Eddie Murphy, 1982, Eddie Murphy Comedian, 1983, How Could it Be, 1984, So Happy, 1989, Distinguished Gentleman, 1992, Love's Alright, 1993, Metro, 1997; writer (story) Vampire in Brooklyn, Boomerang, Another 48 Hours, Coming to America, Beverly Hills Cop II; writer Harlem Nights, Eddie Murphy Raw; exec. prodr.: The PJs (TV series), 1999, Life, Vampire in Brooklyn, What's Alan Watching Now? (TV), 1989, Harlem Nights, Eddie Murphy Raw; dir. Harlem Nights, Nutty Professor II - The Klumps, 2000; actor, prodr. The Adventures of Pluto Nash, 2002. Office: ICM c/o Jim Wiatt 8942 Wilshire Blvd Beverly Hills CA 90211-1934*

MURPHY, EDRIE LEE, hospital laboratory administrator; b. Redwood Falls, Minn., Dec. 4, 1953; d. Melvin Arthur and Betty Lou (Wenholz) Timm; m. David Joseph Murphy, July 28, 1964; children: Michael David, Scott Christopher. BS in Med. Tech. summa cum laude, Mankato State U., 1976; MBA, U. St. Thomas, 1984. Registered med. technologist. Med. technologist Children's Hosps. and Clinics, St. Paul, 1976-81, chemistry supr., 1981-85, lab. mgr., 1985-95, dir. lab. sys. Mpls., St. Paul's Campus, 1995-99; lab. mgr. Fairview Health Sys., Mpls., 2000—. Contbr. articles to profl. jours. Charles H. Cooper scholar, 1975. Mem.: Minn. Soc. Clin. Lab. Mgmt. Assn. (sec.-treas. Minn. chpt. 1994—96, bd. dirs. 1996—, pres.-elect 1998—2000, pres. 2000—02), Am. Soc. Clin. Lab. Scis., Elan Vital Ski Club (v.p. membership 1981—82), Phi Kappa Phi. Avocations: photography, sailing, skiing, tennis, travel. Office: Fairview Health Sys 2450 Riverside Ave Ste 5A Minneapolis MN 55454-1450 E-mail: emurphy2@fairview.org.

MURPHY, EDWARD FRANCIS, executive; b. Chgo., July 30, 1947; s. Edward F. and Marjorie (Mooney) M.; m. Kay A. Worcester, Apr. 17, 1970; 1 child, Dean D. BA in Mktg., No. Ill. U., 1976. Dist. mgr. Midas Internat. Corp., Chgo., 1977-85; sales mgr. Raybestos, McHenry, Ill., 1985-89, Wagner Brakes, St. Louis, 1989-99; owner Displays of Distinction, Mesa, Ariz., 1998—. V.p. Associated Roof Structures, Mesa, 1999—. Author: Vietnam Medal of Honor Heroes, 1987, Heroes of World War II, 1990, Korea's Heroes, 1990, Dak To, 1993, Semper Fi-Vietnam, 1996, Khe Sahn-The Hill Fights, 2000; hist. cons. (book) Above and Beyond, 1985. Sgt. U.S. Army, 1965-68. Recipient Dist. Svc. award Congl. Medal of Honor Soc., 1989. Mem. Medal of Honor Hist. Soc. (founder, pres. 1975—). Republican. Avocations: writing, flying. Home: 2659 E Kael St Mesa AZ 85213-2363

MURPHY, EDWARD STACK, pathologist; b. Utica, N.Y., June 8, 1923; arrived in Mexico, 1958; s. Edward Simon Murphy and Elizabeth Stack; m. Consuelo Pérez Arteaga, Aug. 6, 1953; children: Eduardo, Tomás, Roberto, Andrés, Juan Pablo. BA, U. Mich., 1945, MD, 1946. Diplomate Am. Bd. Pathology, Mexican Bd. Pathology. Intern St. Anthony Hosp., Denver, 1947; gen. practice Grand Lake, Colo., 1948; resident St. Luke's Hosp. & Denver Children's Ctr., 1949-52; Barth fellow in pathology Nat. Inst. Cardiology, Mexico City, 1952-53; chief pathologist U.S. Army Hosp., Osaka, Japan, 1953-55, Atomic Bomb Casualty Commn., Hiroshima, Japan, 1955-57, Hosp. Francés, Mexico City, 1958-61; asst. to chief pathology Nutritional Disease Hosp., 1958-59; chief pathologist Hosp. Santelena, 1962—. Founder Mexican Bd. Pathology, 1963, Mexican Soc. Nuc. Medicine, 1965, Mexican Bd. Nuc. Medicine, 1973. Author: El Linfoma, 1964; contbr. articles to profl. jours. Capt. U.S. Army Med. Corps, 1953-55, PTO. Roman Catholic. E-mail: cmurphyadata.net.mx. Home: Corregidora 110 10200 Mexico City Mexico Office: Hosp Santelena Queretaro 58 06700 Mexico City Mexico

MURPHY, EDWARD THOMAS, engineering executive; b. Boston, Nov. 20, 1947; s. Edward William and Eleanor Catherine (Brown) M.; m. Marianne Scheid, May 1, 1976; children: Edward Robert, Cynthia Kathrine. BS, Calif. Inst. Tech., 1969; MS in Nuclear Sci. and Engring., Carnegie Mellon U., 1971. Registered profl. engr., Pa., Md. Containment system engr. Westinghouse Electric Corp., Monroeville, Pa., 1969-74, fuel projects engr., 1974-80, mgr. licensing ops. Bethesda, Md., 1980-84, acting regulatory com. supr. Avila Beach, Calif., 1984-85, mgr. control system analysis and support Monroeville, 1985-88; spl. project mgr. reactor restart div. Westinghouse Savannah River Co., Aiken, S.C., 1989-92, site configuration mgmt. regulatory affairs/startup projects mgr. Engring. & Projects Divsn., 1992-94, facilities configuration mgmt. support mgr., 1994-96, acting mgr. safety svcs., 1996-97; spinoff proposal mgr., transition mgr., tech. svcs. mgr. Westinghouse Safety Mgmt. Solutions LLC, 1997—, Savannah River site tech. mgr., dep. dir. ops., 1997—. Mem. Am. Nuclear Soc. Roman Catholic. Office: Westinghouse Safety Mgmt Solutions Inc PO Box 5388 Aiken SC 29804-5388 E-mail: ed.murphy@wxsms.com.

MURPHY, ELLIS, association management executive; b. Lincoln, Nebr. s. Ellis F. and Virgie (Olson) M.; m. Judy Neel, 1975; children by previous marriage: Sharon, Michael, Edward, Randall; stepchildren: Mary, Janet, Susan BS in Agr, Purdue U., 1947; MBA, Northwestern U., 1957; postgrad., Ill. Inst. Tech., 1969-81, U. Wash., 1950-51, Mexico City Coll., 1947, U. Chgo., 1964. Assoc. editor Pacific Builder & Engr., Seattle, 1948-51; tech. editor Portland Cement Assn., 1953-55; dir. public relations Chgo. chpt. AIA, 1955-56; account exec. Carrier & Jobson, Inc., Chgo., 1956-57; pres. Ellis Murphy, Inc., 1957-73, Murphy, Tashjian & Assocs., Chgo., 1973-78; v.p. Lurie/Murphy Assocs., Inc., 1979-83; pres. Murphy & Murphy Inc., 1984—. Cons. mktg. communication to various bus. firms, 1970— ; instr. (part-time) mktg. Ill. Inst. Tech., Chgo., 1977-79; instr. (part-time) assn. mgmt. DePaul U., Chgo., 1985— ; cons. to various trade assns., 1970— Mem. Bd. Edn. Thornton Fractional Dist., Ill., 1961-67; trustee First Meth. Ch., Lansing, Ill., 1959-65; chmn. dirs. funds Purdue Club, Chgo., 1990-95. Major USMCR, 1943-46, 50-52. Mem. Public Relations Soc. Am. (citation 1963), Am. Mktg. Assn., Am. Soc. Assn. Execs., Chgo. Soc. Assn. Execs. (Disting. Service award 1986), Knights Templar, St. Bernard Commndery (past comdr.), Sigma Delta Chi. Home: 3100 N Sheridan Rd Chicago IL 60657-4954 E-mail: emememememem@aol.com.

MURPHY, ELVA GLENN, executive assistant; b. Chickasha, Okla., Aug. 21, 1934; d. Elsie Lee (Murphy) Sommer and Maynard F. Glenn; m. Calvin E. Morgan, Mar. 11, 1972 (dec. Dec. 1976); m. C. Gordon Murphy, Oct. 17, 1981. Student, UCLA, 1954-55, Columbia U., 1973. Various secretarial positions, Calif., 1956-67; fgn. svc. sec. U.S. Dept. State, Paris, 1967-69; exec. asst. to Cyrus R. Vance Simpson Thacher & Bartlett, N.Y.C., 1969-77, 80-98, U.S. Dept. State, Washington, 1977-80; asst. to pres. Coun. on Fgn. Rels., Inc., N.Y.C., 1997—. Mem. Seraphic Soc. (pres. 1990-92), Women's City Club N.Y. Avocations: sailing, skiing, cooking, reading, theater. Home: 40 W 72nd St # 118 New York NY 10023-4104 Office: Coun on Fgn Rels Inc 58 E 68th St New York NY 10021-5953

MURPHY, EUGENE FRANCIS, retired government official, consultant; b. Syracuse, N.Y., May 31, 1913; s. Eugene Francis and Mary Grace (Thompson) M.; m. Helene M. Murphy, Dec. 31, 1955 (dec. Oct. 1998); children: Anne F., Thomas E. BSME, Cornell U., 1935; MME, Syracuse U., 1937; PhD, Ill. Inst. Tech., 1948. Tchg. asst. Syracuse U., 1935-36; engr. Ingersoll-Rand Co., Painted Post, N.Y., 1936-39; instr. Ill. Inst. Tech., 1939-41; from instr. to asst. prof. U. Calif., Berkeley, 1941-48; staff engr. NAS, Washington, 1945-48; adv. fellow Mellon Inst., Pitts., 1947-48; with VA, N.Y.C., 1948-83, chief R & D divsn. Prosthetic and Sensory Aids Svc., 1948-73, dir. Rsch. Ctr. for Prosthetics, 1973-78, dir. Office of Tech. Transfer, 1978-83, sci. advisor Office of Tech. Transfer, 1983-85. Mem. coun. Alliance for Engring. in Medicine and Biology, 1970-90; mem. adv. com. U. Wis., 1978-82, Case Western Res. U., 1981, Am. Found. for Blind, 1981-83; cons. disability and rehab. rsch., 1983—. Contbg. author: Human Limbs and their Substitutes, 1954, Orthopaedic Appliances Atlas, vol. 1, 1952, vol. 2, 1960, Human Factors in Technology, 1963, Biomedical Engineering Systems, 1970, Critical Revs. in Bioengring, 1971, CRC Handbook of Materials, Vol. III, 1975, Atlas of Orthotics, 1975, 2d edit., 1985, Therapeutic Medical Devices: Application and Design, 1982, McGraw-Hill Ency. Sci. and Tech. Yearbook, 1985; contbr. to Wiley Ency. of Medical Devices and Instrumentation, 1988; editor Bull. Prosthetics Rsch., 1978-82; contbr. articles to profl. jours. Recipient Silver medal Paris, 1961; Meritorious Svc. award VA, 1971; Disting. Career award VA, 1983; Biomedical Engring. Leadership award Alliance for Engring. in Medicine and Biology, 1983; citation Outstanding Handicapped Fed. Employee, 1971; Profl. Achievement award Ill. Inst. Technology, 1983; Fulbright lectr. Soc. and Home for Cripples, Denmark, 1957-58 Fellow AAAS, ASME, Rehab. Engring. Soc. N.Am. (now RESNA), Internat. Soc. for Prosthetics and Orthotics, N.Y. Acad. Medicine; mem. NAE, ASTM, Soc. for Urology and Engring. (hon.), N.Y. Acad. Scis., Acoustical Soc. Am., Optical Soc. Am., Sigma Xi, Tau Beta Pi, Phi Kappa Phi. Home: Ithaca, NY. Died Dec. 18, 2000.

MURPHY, EVELYN FRANCES, economist; b. Panama Canal Zone, Panama Canal Zone, May 14, 1940; d. Clement Bernard and Dorothy Eloise (Jackson) M. AB, Duke U., 1961, PhD, 1965; MA, Columbia U., 1963; hon. degrees, Regis Coll., 1978, Curry Coll., Northeastern U., Simmons Coll., Wheaton Coll., Anna Maria Coll., Bridgewater State Coll., Salem State Coll., Emmanuel Coll.; hon. degree, Suffolk U. Pres. Ancon Assocs., Boston, 1971-72; ptnr. Llewelyn-Davies, Weeks, Forrester-Walker & Bor, London, 1973-74; sec. environ. affairs Commonwealth of Mass., Boston, 1975-79, sec. econ. affairs, 1983-86, lt. gov., 1987-91; mng. dir. Brown Rudnick Freed and Gesmer, 1991-93; exec. v.p. Blue Cross/Blue Shield of Mass., 1994-98; also bd. dirs. Blue Cross Blue Shield Mass.; resident scholar Branceis U. Women's Studies Rsch. Ctr., 1999—. Vis. pub. policy scholar Radcliffe Coll., 1991; vice chmn./chmn. Nat. Adv. Com. on Oceans and Atmosphere (Presdl. apptd.), 1979-80; bd. dirs. Savs. Bank Mut. Life Ins. N.Y., Citizens Energy Corp., SBLI USA Mut. Life Ins., The Commonwealth Inst., Nat. Ctr. on Women and Aging, chair; pres. Health Care and Policy Inst., 1997-98; resident scholar Brandeis U., 1998—. Recipient Dist. Svc. award New Eng. Coun., 1996, Nat. Sierra Club, 1978, Nat. Bd. Govs. Assn., 1978, Outstanding Citizen award Mass. Audobon Soc., 1978; Harvard U. fellow, 1979-80. Mem. Women Execs. in State Govt. (chair 1987), Internat. Women's Forum, 1993—. Democrat. Avocation: jogging. Office: 225 Franklin St Ste 2700 Boston MA 02110-2804 E-mail: EvMurphy1@aol.com.

MURPHY, EWELL EDWARD, JR. lawyer; b. Washington, Feb. 21, 1928; s. Ewell Edward and Lou (Phillips) M.; m. Patricia Bredell Purnell, June 26, 1954 (dec. 1964); children: Michaela, Megan Patricia, Harlan Ewell. BA, U. Tex., 1946, LLB, 1948; DPhil, Oxford U., Eng., 1951. Bar: Tex. 1948. Assoc. Baker & Botts, Houston, 1954-63, ptnr., 1964-93, head internat. dept., 1972-89. Pres. Houston World Trade Assn., 1972-74; trustee Southwestern Legal Found., 1978—; chmn. Houston Com. on Fgn. Rels., 1984-85, Inst. Transnat. Arbitration, 1985-89, Internat. and Comparative Law Ctr., 1986-87; mem. J. William Fulbright Fgn. Scholarship Bd., 1991-96, vice chmn., 1992-93, chmn., 1993-95; vis. prof. U. Tex. Law Sch., 1993-97; Disting. lectr., U. Houston Law Ctr., 1996—. Contbr. articles to profl. jours. Served to lt. USAF, 1952-54. Recipient Carl H. Fulda award U. Tex. Internat. Law Jour., 1980; Rhodes scholar, 1948-51 Mem. ABA (chmn. sect. internat. law 1970-71), Houston Bar Assn. (chmn. internat. law com. 1963-64, 70-71), Houston C. of C. (chmn. internat. bus. com. 1964, 65), Philos. Soc. Tex., Internat. Law Inst. (bd. dirs. 1994—), Fulbright Assn. (bd. dirs. 1999—, v.p. 2002-), Coun. on Fgn. Rels. Home and Office: 17 W Oak Dr Houston TX 77056-2117

MURPHY, FRANCIS, English language educator; b. Springfield, Mass., Mar. 13, 1932; s. Frank Edward and Sarah (O'Connor) M. BA, Am. Internat. Coll., 1953; MA, U. Conn., 1955; PhD, Harvard U., 1960; LittD (hon.), Am. Internat. Coll., 1986. Mem. faculty English lang. and lit. Smith Coll., 1959-99, assoc. prof., 1966-69, prof., 1970-99, prof. emeritus, 1999—. Vis. curator Springfield Mus. Fine Arts, 1975-76, Hudson River Mus., 1983-84. Editor: The Diary of Edward Taylor, 1964, Major Am. Poets, 1967, Form and Structure in Poetry, 1964, Edwin Arlington Robinson, 1970, Walt Whitman, 1969, The Uncollected Essays of Yvor Winters, 1973, The Complete Poems of Walt Whitman, 1975, Of Plymouth Plantation (William Bradford), 1981; author: Willard Leroy Metcalf, 1976, (with Dean Flower) A Catalogue of American Paintings, Water Colors and Drawings (to 1923) in the G.W.V. Smith Museum, 1976, The Landscape Within: J. Francis Murphy, 1982, The Book of Nature: American Painters and the Natural Sublime, 1983; co-editor: Norton Anthology of American Literature, 1979—, Mass. Rev., 1966-67.

MURPHY, FRANCIS SEWARD, retired journalist; b. Portland, Oreg., Sept. 9, 1914; s. Francis H. and Blanche (Livesay) M.; m. Clare Eastham Cooke, Sept. 20, 1974 (dec. Apr. 1990). BA, Reed Coll., 1936. With The Oregonian, Portland, 1936-79, TV editor, Behind the Mike columnist, 1952-79. Archeol. explorer Mayan ruins, Yucatan, Mex., 1950-87, mem. Am. Quintana Roo Expdn., 1965, 66, 68. Author: Dragon Mask Temples in Central Yucatan, 1988. With U.S. Army, 1942-46. Mem. Am. Philat. Soc. (life), Royal Asiatic Soc., City Club, Am. Club of Hong Kong, Explorer's Club, Oreg. Hist. Soc., Soc. Am. Archaeology, Hong Kong Philat Soc., World Wide Fund Nature, Hong Kong Jockey Club. Democrat. Congregationalist. Home: 4213 NE 32nd Ave Portland OR 97211-7149

MURPHY, GEORGE, special effects expert; Computer graphics artist, visual effects supr. Indsl. Light & Magic, San Rafael, Calif. Films include: Hook, 1991, Death Becomes Her, 1992, Jurassic Park, 1993, Forrest Gump, 1994 (Acad. award best visual effects, Brit. Acad. Film and TV award for best visual effects 1994), Mission Impossible, 1995, Congo, 1995, Star Trek: First Contact, 1996, Starship Troopers, 1997, Mercury Rising, 1998, Mission to Mars, 1999, Impostor, 1999, Planet of the Apes, 2001, Matrix II and III, 2002-03; commls. include 1st Union Launch (gold Clio for visual effects 1999), 1st Union Noise (silver Clio for visual effects 1999), Hefty Gingerbread Man (bronze Clio for visual effects 1999); music videos include Will Smith Willenium. Mem. Acad. Motion Picture Arts and Scis. (visual effects br.). E-mail: george@georgemurphy.com.

MURPHY, GEORGE EARL, psychiatrist, educator; b. Portland, Oreg., Oct. 17, 1922; s. George Earl and Mary Ella Murphy; m. Amanda Daniel, Mar. 24, 1976; children: Paul Douglas, Bruce Kevin. Student, U. Wash., 1940-42, U. Portland, 1946-47; BS, Oreg. State U., 1949; MD, Washington U., St. Louis,

1952. Diplomate Am. Bd. Psychiatry and Neurology. Intern Alameda County Hosp., Oakland, Calif., 1952-53, asst. resident in medicine, 1953-54; fellow in psychosomatic medicine Washington U., St. Louis, 1954-55; asst. resident in psychiatry Mass. Gen. Hosp., Boston, 1955-56, Washington U., St. Louis, 1956-57, instr. sch. of medicine, 1957-59, asst. prof. sch. of medicine, 1959-66, assoc. prof. sch. of medicine, 1966-69, prof. sch. of medicine, 1969-90, prof. emeritus psychiatry, 1990—. Dir. psychiatry clinic Washington U., 1976-90, psychiat. student health, 1978-83, coursemaster human sexuality, 1978-90. Author: Suicide in Alcoholism, 1992; contbr. articles to profl. jours. Recipient Rsch. award for Advances in Suicide Prevention Am. Suicide Found. (now Am. Found. Suicide Prevention), 1994; Louis I. Dublin award for rsch. in suicide Am. Assn. Suicidology, 1995; NIMH grantee, 1963-83, 85-88. Fellow Am. Psychiat. Assn. (life); mem. Internat. Assn. for Suicide Prevention, Am. Psychopathological assn., Sigma Xi. Avocation: archaelogy of the bronze age. Office: Washington U Sch Medicine Dept Psychiatry 4940 Childrens Pl Saint Louis MO 63110-1002

MURPHY, GERALD, retired government official, consultant; b. Washington, Aug. 25, 1938; s. Jeremiah T. and Jean (Curley) M.; m. Kathryn Beckman, Sept. 24, 1988; children by previous marriage: William Michael, Janet Marie, Kathleen Anne B.C.S. with honors, Benjamin Franklin U., Washington, 1960, M.C.S., 1963. C.P.A., D.C. Dep. div. dir. Dept. Treasury, Washington, 1970-71, div. dir., 1971-74, asst. commr., 1974-75, dep. commr., 1975-79, dep. fiscal asst. sec., 1979-86, fiscal asst. sec., 1986-98; sr. prin. Keane Pub. Enterprise Consulting, Washington, 1998-2000; ind. cons., 2000—. Lectr. in acctg. Southeastern U., Washington, 1965-70, Dept. Agr. Grad. Sch., Washington, 1970-76; mem. Govt. Acctg. Standards Adv. Council, 1984-89; mem. Fed. Acctg. Standards Adv. Bd., 1991-98. Served with U.S. Army, 1956 Recipient Disting. Alumni award Benjamin Franklin U., Washington, 1976. Mem. Am. Inst. C.P.A.s, Assn. Govt. Accts. (nat. pres. 1977-78, Robert W. King award 1983, Meritorious Exec. Rsch. award 1992), Sr. Execs. Assn., Fed. Exec. Inst. Alumni Assn. Roman Catholic.

MURPHY, GERARD NORRIS, trade association executive; b. Washington, July 10, 1950; s. Maurice J. and Marguerite (Norris) M.; m. Jacqueline F., May 26, 1973; children: Anne Marie, Michael Jonathan, Kathleen Elizabeth. BA, U. Md., 1972, MA, 1975; JD, George Mason U., 1980. Mgmt. trainee Washington Area New Automobile Dealers Assn., 1972-74, asst. CEO, 1974-82, pres., CEO, 1982—. Bd. dirs. Met. Washington BBB, chmn., 1992-97; bd. dirs. Small Bus. Legis. Coun., 2001; mem. exec. com. Washington Workforce Investment Coun., 2000—; chmn. Nat. Capital Area Transp. Fedn., Washington, 1990-2000. Co-founder, past chmn. Washington Regional Alcohol Program, Vienna, Va., 1983-86; trustee Nat. Automobile Dealers Assn. Sales Rep. Cert. Commn., 1995-99; sec. Boys & Girls Clubs Greater Washington, Silver Spring, 1987—; trustee Greater Washington Bd. Trade PACs Md. and Va., 2000—; co-founder Montgomery Students Automotive Trades Found., Montgomery Pub. Schs., 1978, sec., 1990—. Recipient Govs. citation Gov. William Donald Schaefer, 1990, Silver medal Boys and Girls Clubs Am., 1997; named Automotive Trade Exec. of Yr., Northwood U., 1997. Fellow Am. Soc. Assn. Execs. (cert., com. chmn. 1989-90, 96-97); mem. ABA, Assn. Healthcare Coalition (sec. 1995, v.p. 1996-97, pres. 1998-2000), Automotive Trade Assn. Execs. (bd. dirs. 1987-88, sec., treas. 1996, v.p. 1997, pres. 1998), D.C. Bar Assn., Greater Washington Soc. Assn. Execs. (com. chmn. 1993-94, trustee Found. 1997-2000, chmn. award 1994), Leadership Washington (8th class 1993-94), Rotary (sec. 1998-00, v.p. 2001-2002, dist. conf. chmn. 2001, pres. 2002-2003, Paul Harris fellow 1990), Delta Theta Phi, Delta Tau Delta. Democrat. Roman Catholic. Office: Washington Area New Auto Dealers Assn Ste 210 5301 Wisconsin Ave NW Washington DC 20015-2015

MURPHY, GORDON JOHN, electrical engineer, educator; b. Milw., Feb. 16, 1927; s. Gordon M. and Cecelia A. (Knerr) M.; m. Dorothy F. Brautigam, June 26, 1948; children— Lynne, Craig. BS, Milw. Sch. Engring., 1949; MS, U. Wis., 1952; PhD, U. Minn., 1956. Asst. prof. elec. engring. Milw. Sch. Engring., 1949-51; systems engr. A C Spark Plug divsn. GM, 1951-52, cons., 1959-62; instr. U. Minn., 1952-56, asst. prof. elec. engring., 1956-57; assoc. prof. elec. engring. Northwestern U., Evanston, Ill., 1957-60, prof., 1960-97, head dept. elec. engring., 1960-69, dir. Lab. for Design of Electronic Systems, 1987-97, prof. emeritus, 1997—. Cons. numerous corps., 1959—; founder, 1st chmn. Mpls. chpt. Inst. Radio Engrs. Profl. Group on Automatic Control, 1956-57, Chgo. chpt., 1959-61; pres. IPC Systems, Inc., 1975—; expert witness in numerous patent suits, 1997—. Author: Basic Automatic Control Theory, 1957, 2d edit., 1966, Control Engineering, 1959; contbr. articles, papers to profl. jours.; patentee TV, electronic timers, periodontal instruments and motion control systems. Mem. indsl. adv. com. Milw. Sch. Engring., 1971-2001. Served with USN, 1945-46. Recipient ECE Centennial medal U. Wis., 1991, Outstanding Alumnus award Milw. Sch. Engring. Alumni Assn., 1974; named One of Chgo.'s Ten Outstanding Young Men Chgo. Jaycees, 1961. Fellow IEEE (for edn. and rsch. in automatic control 1967); mem. feedback control systems com. 1960-68, discrete systems com. 1962-68, adminstrv. com. profl. group on automatic control 1966-69, chmn. membership and nominating coms. 1966-67); mem. Am. Automatic Control Coun. (edn. com. 1967-69), Engr.'s Coun. for Profl. Devel. (guidance com. 1967-69), Nat. Electronic Conf. (bd. dirs. 1983-85), Am. Electronics Assn. (exec. com. M.W. coun. 1990-93), Sigma Xi, Eta Kappa Nu, Tau Beta Pi. Home: 638 Garden Ct Glenview IL 60025-4105 Office: Northwestern U Elec Engring Dept Evanston IL 60201

MURPHY, HAROLD LOYD, federal judge; b. Haralson County, Ga., Mar. 31, 1927; s. James Loyd and Georgia Gladys (McBrayer) M.; m. Jacqueline Marie Ferri, Dec. 20, 1958; children: Mark Harold, Paul Bailey. Student, West Ga. Coll., 1944-45, U. Miss., 1945-46; LL.B., U. Ga., 1949. Bar: Ga. 1949. Pvt. practice, Buchanan, Ga., from 1949; ptnr. Howe & Murphy, Buchanan and Tallapoosa, 1958-71; judge Superior Cts., Tallapoosa Circuit, 1971-77; U.S. dist. judge No. Dist. of Ga., Rome, 1977—. Rep. Gen. Assembly of Ga., 1951-61; asst. solicitor gen. Tallapoosa Jud. Circuit, 1956; mem. Jud. Qualifications Commn., State of Ga., 1977 With USNR, 1945-46. Fellow Am. Bar Found.; mem. ABA, Ga. Bar Assn., Dist. Judges Assn. for 11th Cir. Bar Assn., Am. Judicature Soc., Tallapoosa Cir. Bar Assn., Old War Horse Lawyers Club, Am. Inns Ct. (past pres. Joseph Henry Lumpkin sect.), Fed. Judges Assn. Methodist. Home: 321 Georgia Highway 120 Tallapoosa GA 30176-3114 Office: US Dist Ct PO Box 53 Rome GA 30162-0053

MURPHY, HELEN, recording industry executive; b. Glasgow, Scotland, Oct. 2, 1962; came to U.S., 1990; d. Francis and Kathleen (Gallagher) M.; m. Michael Christopher Luksha, Apr. 1, 1989. BA in Econs. with honors, U. Guelph, Can., 1982; MBA, U. Western Ontario, Can., 1984. CFA. Asst. mgr. securities rsch. Confederation Life, Toronto, Can., 1984-86; sr. analyst entertainment & merchandising Prudential Bache Securities, Can., 1986-89; v.p. rsch. Richardson Greenshields Can., 1989-90; v.p. investor rels. Polygram Holding, Inc., N.Y.C., 1990-91; v.p., treas. Polygram Records Inc., 1991-92, sr. v.p. corp. fin., treas., 1992-95; sr. v.p. investor rels. PolyGram Internat. Ltd., 1995-97; sr. v.p. mergers and acquisitions PolyGram Holding, Inc., 1995-97, CFO, 1997-99, Westvaco Corp., 1999; CFO & chief adminstrv. officer Martha Stewart Living Omnimedia, Inc., N.Y.C., 1999—. Lectr. U. Guelph, 1982-90. Fellow Nat. Investor Rels. Inst., N.Y. Soc. Security Analysts, N.Y. Treas. Group. Office: 20 W 43rd St Fl 25 New York NY 10036-7400

MURPHY, JAMES EDWARD, public relations and marketing executive; Degree in Journalism, U. Ill. Sr. corp. comms. officer Owens-Corning Fiberglas, Beatrice, Merrill Lynch; exec. v.p. Burson-Marsteller, vice chmn., 1990, chmn., CEO, 1991-93, Murphy & Co., 1993—; global mng. dir. mktg. and comm. Accenture (formerly known as Andersen Cons.), 1993—. Mem. bd. advisors Medill Sch. Journalism, Northwestern U.; mem. adv. bd. Coll. Bus. and Commerce, U. Ill., also mem. devel. bd. Coll. Comm.; past pres., bd. dirs. Arthur Page Soc. Mem. Inst. Pub. Rels. Rsch. (trustee), Sky Club, Union League Club, Belle Haven Club, Woodway Country Club, Palmetto Golf Club, Preston Mountain Club. Office: Accenture 18th Fl 1345 Avenue Of The Americas New York NY 10105 E-mail: james.e.murphy@accenture.com.

MURPHY, JAMES BERNARD, government educator, consultant; b. N.Y.C., Aug. 23, 1958; s. Donald Hugh and Jane Brown Murphy; m. Kirsten Morgan Cronin, June 6, 1987; children: Leo, Joshua, Nora. BA, Yale U., 1980; MCP, MIT, 1983; PhD, Yale U., 1990. Assoc. prof. govt. Dartmouth Coll., Hanover, N.H., 1990—. Author: (book) The Moral Economy of Labor, 1993. Trustee Crossroads Acad., Lyme, 2000-2001. Office: Dartmouth Coll Dept Govt Hanover NH 03755

MURPHY, JAMES JEFFREY, electronics executive; b. Kenosha, Wis., Nov. 4, 1954; s. Eugene C. and Thelma M. (Jensen) M.; m. Susan M. Larson, June 10, 1978. BA in Bus. Mgmt. and Labor Econs. with honors, U. Wis., 1976. Sales rep. Inland Steel, Chgo., 1976-77, product analyst, 1977; sales rep. Joerndt & Ventura, Inc., Kenosha, 1977-78; field sales rep. Applied Power Corp., New Berlin, Wis., 1978-79; Magnavox regional mgr. Philips Consumer Electronics Co., Knoxville, Tenn., 1979-87, zone mgr., 1987-89, divsn. field sales mgr., 1989-91, natl. account dir., 1991-95, v.p. merchandising, 1995—. Mem. Lincoln Continental Owners Club (treas. 1991), Vintage Radio-Phonograph Soc. Avocations: car collecting, reading, walking. Home: 2330 Stonegate Dr Cumming GA 30041-7410 Office: Philips Consumer Electronics Co 64 Perimeter Ctr E Atlanta GA 30346-2295 E-mail: murpho54@cs.com., Jim.J.Murphy@philips.com.

MURPHY, JAMES MICHAEL, judge; b. Spokane, Wash., Jan. 21, 1943; s. Harold Eugene and Helen Elizabeth (Rauschke) M.; m. Jill Jenene Giles, Aug. 31, 1968; children: Ryan Michael, Timothy Giles. BA, Ea. Wash. U., 1965; JD, Gonzaga U., 1973; cert, Nat. Jud. Coll., Reno, 1980. Bar: Wash. 1973, U.S. Dist. Ct. (ea. dist.) Wash. 1973. Law clk. U.S. Dist. Ct. (ea. dist.) Wash., Spokane, 1972-74; asst. atty. gen. State of Wash., 1974-78; judge Spokane Dist. Ct., 1978-85; superior ct. State of Wash., Spokane, 1985—. Judge juvenile ct. State of Wash., 1988-89, 92, 95, presiding judge, 1990-91, drug ct. judge, 1996-2000; judge pro tem Ct. Appeals State of Wash.; mem. Bench Book com., Jud. Qualification Commn. State of Wash., 1984-85, Bd. for Jud. Adminstrn., 1984-85, chair Bd. Trial Ct. Edn. State of Wash., 1979-96; bd. for improvemnt of jud. adminstrn.; co-chair Wash. State Bd. for Jud. Adminstrn., 2000-01. Mem. Spokane County Programs Adminstrn. Bd., 1984, Spokane County Correction Adv. Bd., 1984, Mayor Chase Youth Awards Bd. City of Spokane, Dean's Bus. Forum Bd. Gonzaga U., Wash. State Supreme Ct. Task Force on Minority and Justice, 1987-90, exec. com., 1990—, State of Wash. Minority and Justice Commn., 1991—; mem. Trial Ct. Performance Standards Task Force, 1991-94; bd. trustees Inland Empire Bd. Athletics; counselor TAC Cultural exch. com., bd. dirs. Wash. cultural exch., del. nat. track and field conv., 1988-2000, mem. organizing com. Jr. Olympics, 1990 ; mem. Spokane Sports Unltd.; v.p. Spokane Limerick Sister City Assn.; official U.S. Track & Field Olympic Trials, 1992, 96, Olympic Games, 1996; bd. dirs. U.S.A. Track and Field; chair Cultural Exch. Com., 1997, law and legislation com., 1996—; counsel Youth Com.; co-chair Wash. State Bd. Jud. Adminstrn., 2000—; exec. com. Spokane Regional Sports Adminstrn., 2000—. Named one of Outstanding Young Men Am., 1979; recipient Disting. Alumnus award Ea. Wash. U. Sch. Pub. Affairs, 1986, 99. Mem. ABA (Wash. del. nat. conv. 1989-91), Am. Judges Assn., Wash. State Superior Ct. Judges Assn. (chmn. edn. com., benchbook com., improvement of jud. adminstrn. com., chmn. shorthand reporters com., pres. judge 1999-2001), Assn. Dist. and Mcpl. Ct. Judges (pres. 1985), Wash. State Bar Assn., Spokane County Bar Assn. (pres. young lawyers 1974-75), Native Am. Legal Svcs. (pres. 1975-78), Spokane Enological Soc., Footprinters, Spokane Track Club (pres. team 1989), Friendly Sons of St. Patrick (pres. 1983, bd. dirs.), Kiwanis (bd. dirs. Spokane club 1980-84). Avocations: skiing, golf, backpacking, boating, track and field officiating. Office: Superior Ct State of Wash County of Spokane 1116 W Broadway Ave Spokane WA 99260-2052 E-mail: jmurphy@spokanecounty.org.

MURPHY, JAMES RODNEY, playwright; b. Kenton, Ohio, Mar. 23, 1933; m. Teruko Murakami, 1958; children: Cynthia, Laurel. BS in Bus. Adminstrn., U. Tenn., Knoxville, 1962; MS in Edn., U. So. Calif., 1967, MS in Sys. Mgmt., 1983; PhD in Aerospace Studies, Union Inst., Cin., 1990; Air Command and Staff Coll. Diploma, Air U., Maxwell AFB, Ala., 1987, Air War Coll. Diploma, 1988. Enlisted USAF, 1951, advanced through grades to capt., 1968; transp. combat adv., 1968-69; transp. analyst, def. transp. policy coun. advisor Ctr. for Studies and Analyses, Hdqrs. USAF, Washington, 1989-92; hazardous cargo and packaging policy specialist Directorate of Transp., Hdqrs. U.S. Air Force, 1992-95; ret. USAF, 1995—; playwright/poet, lyricist/librettist Plays Around, Colorado Springs, Colo., 1995—. Author: (musical) Truck Stop, 1994, (opera) Luke and Sarah, (musical) Member of the Team, 1996, (biography) Peon to Pentagon, 1999, also numerous poetry, lyrics and short stories. Founder, chmn. Am. Nat. Opera, 2000. Decorated Meritorious Svc. medal, Bronze Star medal, others. Mem. Nat. Def. Transp. Assn., Coun. Logistics Mgmt., Soc. Logistics Engrs., Nat. Panel Consumer Arbitrators, Better Bus. Bur., Masons, Internat. Soc. Poets, Rockford Writers Guild, Wyo. Players, Opera Am., Dramatists Guild, Writers Guild, Songwriters Assn. Washington, Washington Area Music Assn., Nashville Songwriters Assn. Internat., Am. Soc. Composers, Authors and Pubs., Drama League, Theatre Comms. Group, Colo. Opera Festival Guild, Phi Kappa Phi, Beta Gamma Sigma, Delta Nu Alpha, Delta Sigma Pi. Address: 4745 Purcell Dr Colorado Springs CO 80922-1615 E-mail: drjrmurphy@adelphia.net.

MURPHY, JEROME EUGENE, retired communications consultant; b. Libertyville, Ill., June 16, 1935; s. William Dennis and Violet (Hitchings) M.; m. Donna Mae Du Bois; children: Mary Jeanne Cox, Jean Marie Neidig, Michael Thomas, James Patrick BS in Mgmt., Calif. We. U., 1981. Mgr. equipment, engring., supt., dir. engring., dir. spl. products GTE Comm., Northlake, Ill., 1959-86; v.p. mktg., sales, asst. to pres. Olympic Controls, Elgin, 1986, 87, 90,91; sr. dist. sales mgr. Teltone Corp., Kirkland, Wash., 1988; ctrl. office products mgr. Com Dev Inc;, Sarasota, Fla., 1989; pres. Murphy Cons., Benton, Ky., 1992-97, Glen Ellyn, Ill., 1997-2000; ret. Mem., vice-chmn., chmn. jr. staff Automatic Electric, Northlake, Ill., 1969-71. Mem. Adv. Bd. Automatic Electric Tech. Jour., Northlake, Ill., 1976-80. Served in U.S. Army, 1955-57. Republican. Roman Catholic. Avocations: golf, boating, swimming, bowling, reading. Home: 509 Lowell Ave Glen Ellyn IL 60137-4718

MURPHY, JILL LUCILLE, accountant, state official; b. Charlotte, Mich., Jan. 3, 1946; divorced; Gina, Jacqueline. BA, Mich. State U., 1975, MBA, 1977. CPA, Mich. Auditor Mich. Dept. Treasury, Lansing, 1977-78; dir. internal audit Mich. Liquor Control Commn., 1984-89, Dept. of State, Lansing, 1989—. Honors scholar Lansing Community Coll., 1973. Mem. AICPA, Mich. Assn. CPAs (chair acctg. & auditing 1994-95, strategic planning com.), Assn. Govtl. Accts. (past pres. Greater Lansing chpt.), Inst. Internal Auditors. Avocations: photography, travel. Office: Mich Dept State Internal Audit Divsn Mutual Bldg Fl 5 Lansing MI 48918-0001

MURPHY, JO ANNE, lawyer; b. Binghamton, N.Y., Oct. 23, 1957; d. William T. and Shirley Anne (Merriam) M.; m. Noureddine M. Dourafei, Jan. 2, 1986; children: Zachary Dourafei, Adam Dourafei. BA summa cum laude, SUNY, Albany, 1978; JD magna cum laude, Cornell U., 1981. Bar: N.Y. 1982, Tex. 1991, U.S. Dist. Ct. (so. dist.) N.Y. 1982. Assoc. Cleary, Gottlieb, Steen & Hamilton, N.Y.C., 1981-85, 86-90, London, 1985-86; major transactions coord. Exxon Mobil Corp., Irving, Tex., 1990—2001, Fairfax, Va., 2001—. Mem. ABA, State Bar Tex., Dallas Bar Assn., Order of Coif. E-mail: jo.a.murphy@exxonmobil.com.

MURPHY, JOANNE BECKER, writer; b. Detroit; d. Louis Norman and Gertrude Margaret (Kornmeier) Becker; m. Joseph A. Murphy, Jr., June 24, 1961; children: Michael Ellis, Joseph A. III. BA in Journalism, Mich. State U., 1958; MA in Humanities, Wayne State U., 1975. With pub. rels. dept. WBZ TV, Boston, 1958-60, The Jam Handy Orgn., Detroit, 1960-62, Detroit Symphony Orch., 1969-70; freelance writer, editor Detroit, 1978-90, Washington, 1990—. Contbg. writer: Affecting Change, 1986, Glass: State of the Art, 1989; editor: As Parents We Will, 1985 (1st Pl. award Pub. Svc. Nat. Found. for Alcoholism Comm.); writer, editor publs. for arts and human svcs. orgns.; contbr. articles to mage., newspapers. Mem. program bd. Grosse Pointe (Mich.) War Meml., 1987—90; bd. dirs. Detroit Artists Market, 1982—90, Mich. Metro coun. Girl Scouts USA, 1971—78, Family Svcs. Detroit and Wayne County, 1970—76, All Hallows Guild Grounds Oversidth Bd., Washington Nat. Cathedral, 1993—; mem. bd. canvassers Grosse Pointe Sch. Sys., 1986—90; mem. regional bd. United Way D.C., 1999—. Mem.: Washington Ind. Writers, Am. News Women's Club (Washington, bd. dirs. 1996—2001), Kappa Alpha Theta. Home and Office: 2717 O St NW Washington DC 20007-3128 E-mail: murphy.joanne@verizon.net.

MURPHY, JOHN ARTHUR, tobacco, food and brewing company executive; b. N.Y.C., Dec. 15, 1929; s. John A. and Mary J. (Touhy) M.; m. Carole Ann Paul, June 28, 1952; children: John A., Kevin P., Timothy M., Kellyann, Robert B., Kathleen. BS, Villanova U., 1951; JD, Columbia U., 1954. Bar: N.Y. 1954. Since practiced in, N.Y.C.; ptnr. firm Conboy Hewitt O'Brien & Boardman, 1954-62; asst. gen. counsel Philip Morris Co. Inc., N.Y.C., 1962-66, v.p., 1967-76, exec. v.p., 1976-78, group exec. v.p., 1978-84, pres., 1984-91, vice chmn., 1991-92, also bd. dirs.; asst. to pres. Philip Morris Internat., 1966-67, exec. v.p., 1967-71; pres., chief exec. officer Miller Brewing Co., Milw., 1971-78, chmn. bd., chief exec. officer, 1978-84. Trustee North Shore Univ. Hosp., Marquette U., 1973-91; mem. exec. com. Keep Am. Beautiful, Inc.; mem. bd. consultors Sch. Law Villanova U.; mem. bus. com. Met. Mus. Art. Decorated Knight of Malta. Mem. ABA, N.Y. State Bar Assn. Office: Philip Morris Cos Inc 100 Park Ave New York NY 10017-5516

MURPHY, JOHN B. investment company executive; b. Pitts., May 30, 1947; s. John Bernard and Knolle Cordelia (Bonham) M.; m. Lauren Osa Brown, Mar. 20, 1994; 1 child, Kira Mei Li. BA, U. New Orleans, 1970; MBA, Columbia U., 1984. CFA 1987. Dir. La. Heritage Fair, New Orleans, 1974-75, 78-80; assoc. dir. New Orleans Jazz and Heritage Festival, 1978-80; exec. dir. New Orleans Jazz and Heritage Found. Inc., 1980; assoc. editor, analyst Value Line Pubs., N.Y.C., 1984-86; equity analyst, v.p. Drexel, Burnham, Lambert, 1986-90; portfolio mgr., mng. dir. Guardian, 1990—. Head of convertible investments, mng. dir., Park Ave. Portfolio, Family Svc. Life and other Guardian subs., 1998—; mem. alumni counseling bd. Sch. Bus. Columbia U., N.Y.C., 1986—; prodn. cons. Newport Jazz Festival, Capitol Radio Jazz Festival, Memphis Heritage Festival, 1978-80. Recipient Mayoralty Merit award City of New Orleans, 1978. Mem. Assn. Investment Mgmt. and Rsch., N.Y. Soc. Security Analysts, Beta Gamma Sigma (scholar 1983). Avocations: poetry, photography, golf. Home: PO Box 243 Ardsley On Hudson NY 10503-0243 Office: Guardian 7 Hanover Sq New York NY 10004-2616 E-mail: john_murphy@glic.com.

MURPHY, JOHN CARTER, economics educator; b. Ft. Worth, July 17, 1921; s. Joe Preston and Elsie (Carter) M.; m. Dorothy Elise Haldi, May 1, 1949 (dec. Jan. 1997); children: Douglas C., Barbara E.; m. Teiko Kanazawa, June 17, 2000. Student, Tex. Christian U., 1939-41; BA, North Tex. State U., 1943, BS, 1946; AM, U. Chgo., 1949, PhD, 1955; postgrad., U. Copenhagen, 1952-53. Instr. Ill. Inst. Tech., 1947-50; instr. to assoc. prof. Washington U., St. Louis, 1950-62; vis. prof. So. Meth. U., Dallas, 1961, prof., 1962-90, prof. emeritus, 1990—, dir. grad. studies in econs., 1963-68, chmn. dept., 1968-71, faculty summer program in Oxford, 1982-91, dir., 1991, pres. faculty senate, 1988-89, co-dir. Insts. on Internat. Fin., 1982-87. Vis. prof. Bologna (Italy) Ctr., Sch. Advanced Internat. Studies, Johns Hopkins U., 1961-62; UN tech. assistance expert, Egypt, 1964; vis. prof., spl. field staff Rockefeller Found., Thammasat U., Bangkok, 1966-67; sr. staff economist Coun. Econ. Advisers, 1971-72, U.S. dels. econ. policy com. and working party III OECD, 1971-72, U.S. del. 8th meeting Joint U.S.-Japan Econ. Com., 1971; cons. Washington U. Internat. Econs. Rsch. Project, 1950-53, U.S. Treasury, 1972, Fed. Res. Bank Dallas, 1994—; referee NSF; witness and referee congl. coms.; lectr. USIA Program, Germany, 1961-62, 84, Philippines, South Viet Nam, Thailand, 1972, France, Belgium, 1984; lectr. Southwestern and Midwestern Grad. Sch. Banking; adj. scholar Am. Enterprise Inst. for Pub. Policy Rsch., 1976—. Author: The International Monetary System: Beyond the First Stage of Reform, 1979; (with R.R. Rubottom) Spain and the U.S.: Since World War II, 1984; editor: Money in the International Order, 1964; contbr. articles to profl. books and jours. Chmn. rsch. com. on internat. conflict and peace Washington U., 1959-61; lectr. mgmt. tng. programs Southwestern Bell Telephone Co., 1961-66, St. Louis Coun. on Econ. Edn., 1958-61; mem. regional selection com. H.S. Truman Fellowships, 1976-89; pres. Dallas Economists, 1981, Town and Gown of Dallas, 1980-81; mem. Dallas Com. on Fgn. Rels. Lt. USNR, 1943-46. Decorated Silver Star; Fulbright scholar to Denmark, 1952-53; Ford Found. Faculty Research fellow, 1957-58; U.S.-Spanish Joint Com. for Cultural Affairs fellow, 1981; Sr. Fulbright lectr. Italy, 1961-62 Mem. Am. Econ. Assn., So. Econ. Assn. (bd. editors Jour. 1969-71), Midwest Econ. Assn., Am. Fin. Assn., Soc. Internat. Devel., Peace Rsch. Soc., Southwestern Social Sci. Assn. (pres. econs. sect. 1971-72), AAUP (chpt. pres. 1964-65). Home: 7831 Park Ln Apt 266-D Dallas TX 75255 Office: So Meth Univ Dept Econs Dallas TX 75275-0001

MURPHY, JOHN JOSEPH, manufacturing company executive; b. Olean, N.Y., Nov. 24, 1931; s. John Joseph and Mary M.; m. Louise John; children: Kathleen A. Murphy Bell, Karen L. Murphy Rochelli, Patricia L. Murphy Smith, Michael J. AAS in Mech. Engring., Rochester Inst. Tech., 1952; MBA, So. Meth. U. Engr. Clark div. Dresser Industries, Olean, 1952-67, gen. mgr. roots blower div. Connersville, Ind., 1967-69, pres. crane, hoist and tower div. Muskegon, Mich., 1969-70, pres. machinery group Houston, 1970-75, sr. v.p. ops. Dallas, 1980, exec. v.p., 1982, pres., 1982-92, CEO, 1983—95, chmn. bd., 1983-96; mng. dir. SMG Mgmt. L.L.C., 1997-2000. Bd. dirs. W.R. Grace & Co., CARBO Ceramics, Inc.; mem. Bus. Coun.; dir. ShawCor Ltd. With U.S. Army, 1954-56. Office: 5500 Preston Rd Ste 210 Dallas TX 75205-2699

MURPHY, JOHN JOSEPH, JR. investment company executive; b. Elmhurst, N.Y., June 2, 1951; s. John Joseph and Ellen Marie (Ulrich) M.; m. Monica Marie Des Marais, 1975; children: Abigail, Dylan, Regan. AB, Coll. Holy Cross, 1973; MBA, Dartmouth Coll., 1975. V.p. Citicorp Venture Capital, Ltd., N.Y.C., 1975-83; ptnr. Adler & Shaykin, 1983-87; mng. ptnr. Murphy & Ptnrs., L.P., 1987—. Chmn. bd. Minority Equity Ccapital Corp., 1989-90; chmn. bd. dirs. June/Calendar Broadcasting, Inc., 1989-99; chmn. bd. dirs. Legend Med. Svcs., Inc., 1990-94; chmn., bd. dirs. Pacific Pub. Co., Inc., 1990—; vice chmn., bd. dirs. Nat. Mobile TV, Inc., 1992-97. Mem. Holy Cross Leadership Coun., N.Y.C.; chmn. bd. dirs. Nativity Mission Ctr.; chmn. fin. coun. Ch. of the Epiphany, 1997—2002; hon. usher St. Patrick's Cathedral; trustee Covenant of the Sacred Heart; bd. dirs. Good Shepherd Svcs., 1991—; chmn. bd. dirs. Am. Higher Edn. Devel. Corp., 1998—, Ruxton Healthcare Corp., 1998—, Mosaica Edn., Inc., 1998—; vice chmn. bd. dirs. Little Tornadoes, 1998—; trustee Coll. of the Holy Cross. Mem.: N.Y. Venture Capital Forum (bd. dirs. 1984—93, 1998—), Friendly Sons St. Patrick City of N.Y., Boston Coll. Wall St. Coun., Yale Club N.Y.C., The Leash, N.Y. Athletic Club. Democrat. Roman Catholic. Avocations: marathon running, theology. Home: 3 Stuyvesant Oval New York NY 10009-2122 Office: Murphy & Ptnrs Fund LP 45 Rockefeller Plz New York NY 10111-0100 E-mail: john@murphy-partners.com.

MURPHY, JOHN JOSEPH, English literature educator, critic, editor; b. N.Y.C., Apr. 3, 1933; s. John and Margaret B. (Shadegg) M.; m. Sarah Marie McMahon, June 30, 1962; children: Sarah, Joseph, Willa, John, Emily. BA, St. John's U., N.Y.C., 1956, MA, 1961. Instr. English lit. Coll. of St. Teresa, Winona, Minn., 1960-65; asst. prof. English lit. Merrimack Coll., North Andover, Mass., 1965-68, assoc. prof., 1969-84, chmn. dept. English, 1974—76, 1979—82; prof. English lit. Brigham Young U., Provo, Utah, 1984—, chair Am. lit. sect. dept. English, 1986—89, assoc. dir. Ctr. for Study Christian Values in Lit., 1994—. Organizer and dir. Willa Cather and Nebr. 1st Internat. U. Nebr. Cather Seminar, Hastings and Red Cloud, Nebr., 1981; bd. govs. Willa Cather Meml.; mem. editl. bd. Willa Cather Scholarly Edit., U. Nebr. Press, 1986—; vis. prof. U. Leon, Spain, 2001; presenter in field. Author: (criticism) My Antonia: The Road Home, 1989, (novels) Critical Essays on Willa Cather , 1984, Willa Cather: Family, Community, History, 1990; editor Penguin My Antonia, 1994, Death Comes for the Archbishop, 1999; co-editor Lit. and Belief, 1994—2001; editor, 2001—; contbr. profl. jours. including Am.Lit., Twentieth Century Lit., Am. Lit. Realism, Religion and Lit.; prodr.: (TV series) KTCA TV, Great ladies of the Am. Novel, 1963—, Nathaniel Hawthorne, Am. Realist, 1964—. With U.S. Army, 1958-60. Recipient R.E. Twitchell award N.Mex. Hist. Soc., 2000; NEH fellow for Coll. Tchrs, 1982. Home: 8707 Hidden Oak Dr Salt Lake City UT 84121-6128 Office: Brigham Young U English Dept 3171 JKHB Provo UT 84602 E-mail: john_murphy@byu.edu.

MURPHY, JOSEPH EDWARD, JR. broadcast executive; b. Mpls., Mar. 13, 1930; s. Joseph Edward Murphy and Ann Hynes; m. Diana Kuske, July 24, 1958; children: Michael, John. BA, Princeton U., 1952; postgrad., U. Minn., 1956-60. Chartered fin. analyst. Dir. investment rsch. Woodward-Elwood & Co., Mpls., 1961-67; v.p. Northwestern Nat. Bank, 1967-83; chmn. Midwest Communications, Inc., 1990-92; ret. Dir. Midwest Comm., Inc., 1956-89, vice chmn., 1985-89. Author: Adventure Beyond the Clouds: How We Climbed China's Highest Mountain and Survived, 1986 (Friends Am. Writers award 1986), With Interest: How to Profit From Interest Rate Fluctuations, 1987, Stock Market Probability, 1988, revised edit., 1994, South to the Pole by Ski, 1990, The Random Character of Interest Rates, 1990, To the Poles by Ski and Dogsled, 1996, Bond Tables of Probable Future Yields, 1996, The Random Character of Corporate Earnings, 1997, Why the Stock Market Rises, 1998. Vice chmn. Minn. Coun. on Quality Edn., 1971-77; trustee Macalester Coll., St. Paul, 1973-87, Mpls. Soc. Fine Arts, 1977-78, Voyageur Outward Bound, 1985-92; bd. dirs. Minn. Opera Co., 1971-80, Childrens Theater Co., 1975-80, Minn. Ctr. for Book Arts, 1987-93, Greater Mpls. coun. Girl Scouts U.S.A., 1987-93, Fund for Peace, 1988-92, Minn. Nature Conservancy, 1991-96. 2d lt. U.S. Army, 1952-55. Mem. Am. Alpine Club (life, v.p. and bd. dirs. 1975-81), Himalayan Club (life), Mpls. Club. Avocations: mountaineering (leader Am. expedition to Mt. Everest 1986, mem. internat. ski expedition to South Pole 1988-89), exploration. Home: 2116 W Lake Isle Minneapolis MN 55405-2425

MURPHY, JOSEPH JAMES, chiropractic physician; b. Newark, July 30, 1956; s. Joseph P. and Roberta (Nittolo) Murphy; m. Rebecca Lynn Swanton, June 21, 1986; children: Joseph Raymond, Alexandra Renee; m. Maria Elena Sileo, Feb. 17, 2002. BA in Biology, Rider Coll., 1978; D in Chiropractic Medicine, Palmer Coll., 1984. Diplomate Nat. Bd. Chiropractic Examiners; cert. N.J. State Bd. Med. Examiners. Rsch. chemist Mallinkrodt, Inc., Englewood, N.J., 1979-81; staff physician Mid-Island Chiropractic, Levittown, N.Y., 1984; dir., chief exec. officer Suburban Chiropractic Ctr., Chatham, N.J., 1984—. Apptd. mem. N.J. Bd. Chiropractic Examiners, 2000—. Mem. editl. bd. Am. Chiropractor Mag., 2000—; editor-in-chief newsletter The Column. Advisor Chatham High Sch. Key Club, 1986-87; trustee Early Childhood Learning Ctr., Chatham, 1999—; mem. spkrs. bur. Am. Heart Assn. D. D. Palmer scholar, 1981, 82, 83. Mem.: AAAS, APHA, Morris County Chiropractic Soc. (pres. 1987—), Bd. Chiropractic Examiners (apptd. mem. State of N.J.), Internat. Soc. Food Technologists, N.Y. Acad. Sci., N.J. Chiropractic Soc. (bd. dirs. 1987—, chmn. inter profl. rels. com. 1989—, 1st v.p. 1992—95, pres. 1995—, editor-in-chief Jersey Jour. 1986—, Meritorious Svc. award 1986, Disting. Svc. award 1987—97), Am. Chiropractic Assn., Am. Assn. Cereal Chemists, Chatham C. of C. (chmn. profl. rels. com. 1988—92, pres. 1989—92, Dist. Mem. Svc. award 1996), Kiwanis (bd. dirs. Chatham club 1986—89, Disting. Svc. award 1995), Tri Beta. Republican. Presbyterian. Avocations: skiing, photography, model building, automobiles, bicycling. Home: 301 Main St Chatham NJ 07928-2410 Office: Suburban Chiropractic Ctr 301 Main St Chatham NJ 07928-2410 E-mail: drmurphy@drmurphy.com.

MURPHY, JOSEPHINE MANCUSO, critical care nurse, adult nurse practitioner; b. Boston, Oct. 14, 1960; d. Joseph and Antionette R. (Ingegneri) Mancuso; m. Brian L. Murphy, Dec. 5, 1987. ADN, St. Petersburg (Fla.) Jr. Coll., 1983; BSN, U. South Fla., 1987, MS in Nursing, 1990. RN, Fla., Wis.; cert. adult nurse practitioner. Charge/staff nurse Edward H. White II Meml. Hosp., St. Petersburg; staff nurse ICU/critical care unit U. Cmty. Hosp., Tampa, Fla.; patient care coord. Uniphy Ltd.; nurse practitioner Family Health Plan, Elm Grove, Wis.; nurse practitioner Aurora Sinai Primary Care Clinic, Milw. Recipient Golden Key award, Nat. Honor Soc. Mem. Am. Acad. Nurse Practitioners, ACNP, Wis. Nurses Assn., Sigma Theta Tau, Phi Kappa Phi. Home: Apt 202 750 N 8th St Milwaukee WI 53233

MURPHY, JUSTIN DUANE, history educator; b. Idabel, Okla., Oct. 14, 1964; s. Hurchel Joe Murphy and Shirley L. White; m. Jessica Uvonne Rooks, Sept. 7, 1983; children: Jonathan Andrew, Jason Alexander. BA in History and Polit. Sci., Southeastern Okla. State U., 1987; MA in History, Tex. Christian U., 1989, PhD, 1999. Grad. asst. Tex. Christian U., Ft. Worth, 1987-89, tchg. asst., 1989-91; adj. instr. history Tarrant County Jr. Coll., 1989-91; instr. history Howard Payne U., Brownwood, Tex., 1991-94, from asst. prof. to assoc. prof., 1994-2001, prof., 2001—. Asst. dir. Douglas MacArthur Acad. Freedom Honors Program Howard Payne U., 1993-95, acting brand resident chair of free enterprise and pub. policy, 1995-98; dir. Douglas MacArthur Acad. of Freedom Honors program Howard Payne U., 1998—. Author: Wheelock Female Seminary, 1842-1861, Chronicles of Oklahoma, 1991; assoc. editor: The European Powers in the First World War: An Encyclopedia; contbr. numerous articles to profl. jours. Pres. scholar Southeastern Okla. State U., 1982-87, Brown scholar, 1986-87, William P. Willis scholar, 1986-87. Mem. Soc. Historians of Early Am. Republic, Okla. Hist. Soc., Soc. French Hist. Studies, Phi Alpha Theta (v.p. 1988-89), Pi Sigma Alpha, Alpha Chi, Pi Gamma Mu. Avocations: reading, coin-collecting, hunting, fishing. Office: PO Box 831 Brownwood TX 76804-0831 E-mail: jumurphy@hputx.edu.

MURPHY, KATHLEEN ANN, academic administrator, writer; b. Rock Hill, S.C., June 24, 1950; d. Elden Eugene and Patricia Ortengren Zink; married, June 8, 1974; 4 children. BA in English, Ohio Dominican Coll., 1972. Sec. Wiesman Mfg. Co., Dayton, Ohio, 1968—74; writer Daily Leader, Pontiac, Ill., 1983—85; asst. mgr. MLH Group Homes, 1993—98; tutor, instr. Heartland C.C., Normal, 1998—. Columnist: Cullom Chronicle, 1984, author (numerous poems) ; contbr. articles to profl. jours. Literacy vol. State of Ill., Pontiac, 2002. Office: Heartland Cmty Coll Pontiac IL 61764

MURPHY, KATHLEEN ANNE FOLEY, advertising agency executive; b. Fresh Meadows, N.Y., Oct. 15, 1952; d. Thomas J. and Audrey L. Finn; m. Timothy Sean Murphy, Sept. 26, 1992; 1 child, G. David. BA, Marymount Coll., 1974; postgrad., Smith Coll., 1985. V.p. acct. supr., sr. v.p. mgmt. supr., sr. v.p. group dir. Ogilvy & Mather Inc., N.Y.C., 1974-90; sr. v.p., worldwide account dir. Young & Rubicam, San Francisco, 1990-92, sr. v.p., dir. account svcs., 1992-95, exec. v.p., dir. acct. svcs., 1995-97, exec. v.p., gen. mgr., 1997—2002, COO, 2002—. Mem. Advt. Edn. Found. Roman Catholic. Home: One Brookside Ave Berkeley CA 94705 Office: Young & Rubicam 100 1st St San Francisco CA 94105-2600 E-mail: kathy_murphy@sfo.yr.com.

MURPHY, KATHLEEN JANE, psychologist, educator; b. Worcester, Mass., Nov. 9, 1962; d. Frederick George and Dorothy Jane (McGuiness) M.; m. Gary Lee Tatum, July 3, 1991. BA cum laude, Holy Cross Coll., 1984; MA, Assumption Coll., 1987; PhD, Tex. A&M U., 1991. Lic. profl. counselor, marriage and family therapist. Counselor Tex. Rehab. Commn., College Station, 1988-89, psychometrician, 1989; intern clin. psychology Worcester (Mass.) State Hosp., 1989-90; psychotherapist Sandstone Ctr., College Station, 1991-92, Luth. Social Svc., Bryan, Tex., 1992-93; instr. Blinn Coll., College Station, 1993-98; pvt. practice Danielson, 1993—. Mem. APA, Nat. Register Health Svc. Providers in Psychology, Phi Beta Kappa, Psi Chi, Phi Kappa Phi. Democrat. Roman Catholic. Avocations: swimming, walking, gardening, travel. Home: 130 Wilsonville Rd North Grosvenordale CT 06255 E-mail: kathleen.j.murphy@worldnet.att.net.

MURPHY, KATHLEEN MARY, former law firm executive; b. Bklyn., Dec. 16, 1945; d. Raymond Joseph and Catherine Elizabeth (Kearney) M. BA in Edn., Molloy Coll., 1971; MS in Edn., Bklyn. Coll., 1975. Ordained minister Ch. of the Loving Servant; cert. hypnotherapist; cert. elem. sch. tchr., N.Y. Elem. sch. tchr. various parochial schs., L.I., Bklyn., Queens, N.Y., 1969-80; from asst. prin. to prin. parochial sch. Queens, 1980-82; supr.-trainer Davis, Polk, Wardwell law firm, N.Y.C., 1982-88; mgr. Schulte Roth & Zabel, 1988-95; Reiki master (alternative healing profl.), 1996—. Trainer program for new employees, 1984; speaker edn. topics, Bklyn., Queens, 1979-81. Mem. NAFE, Reiki Alliance. Democrat. Roman Catholic. Avocations: psychic phenomenon, workings of mind, ancient histories, crossword puzzles, museums.

MURPHY, KATHRYN MARGUERITE, archivist; b. Brockton, Mass. d. Thomas Francis and Helena (Fortier) M. AB in History, George Washington U., 1935, MA, 1939; MLS, Cath. U., 1950; postgrad., Am. U., 1961. With Nat. Archives and Records Svc., Washington, 1940-89, ret., supervisory archivist Ctrl. Rsch. br., 1958-62, archivist, 1962—. Mem. fed. women's com. Nat. Archives, 1974, rep. to fed. women's com. GSA, 1975; docent, 1989—; lectr. colls., socs. in U.S., 1950—; lectr. Am. ethnic history, 1978-79; free lance author and lectr. in field. Contbr. articles on Am. ethnic history to profl. publs. Founder, pres. Nat. Archives lodge Am. Fedn. Govt. Employees, 1965—, del. conv., 1976, 78, 80, recipient award for outstanding achievement in archives, 1980. Recipient commendation Okla. Civil War Centennial Commn., 1965; named hon. citizen Oklahoma City, Mayor, 1963. Mem. ALA, Soc. Am. Archivists (joint com. hosp. libns. 1965-70), Nat. League Am. Pen Women (corr. sec. Washington 1975-78, pres. chpt. 1978-80), Bus. and Profl. Womens' Club Washington, Phi Alpha Theta (hon.). Home: 1500 Massachusetts Ave NW Washington DC 20005-1821

MURPHY, KELLY, test and operations staff; b. Orlando, Fla., Aug. 27, 1954; m. Wendy J. Brewster; children: Kellen B., McKenna B. BS in Human Resource Mgmt., Kennedy-Western U., 1997. Cert. radiol. monitor; lic. ionizing radiation equipment operator NRC. Metrologist USMC Marine Air Wing, various locations, 1973-77, ITT Arctic Svcs., Thule AB, Greenland, 1977-79; flight test avionics Boeing Aircraft Co., Seattle, 1979-83; environ. test staff Boeing Missile Sys., 1983-84; test and ops. staff Free Electron Laser Boeing Aerospace Co., 1984-95; test and ops. staff S.Q.U.I.D. tech. demonstration Boeing Def., 1995-96; test and ops. staff Digital Flight Controls Boeing Comml. Airplane Group, 1996, ground truth data collection resource 21, 1996—98, secure wide-band comm. staff, 1998—2000, equipment analyst, 2000—. Cons. vacuum tech. Great Circle Tech. Svcs., 1990—. Mem. Am. Vacuum Soc. Office: Boeing Comml Airplane Group PO Box 3707 Seattle WA 98124-2207

MURPHY, KEVIN KEITH, foundation executive; b. Bellefonte, Pa., Oct. 6, 1962; s. Raymond O. and Violet Marie (Carver) M.; m. Kimberly Jo Pedersen, Mar. 15, 1986; children: Carver Patrick, McQuillin Douglas. BA in Speech Communication, Bus. Adminstrn., Pa. State U., 1984. Asst. exec. dir. Cornwall (Pa.) Manor Found. Inc., 1984-85, exec. dir., 1985, v.p. pub. rels., devel., 1985-86, v.p. pub. rels., devel., mktg., 1986-90; spl. asst. to sec. and press sec. Pa. Dept. of Aging, 1990-91; cons., 1991-95; pres. Berks County Cmty. Found., 1994—. Cons. Hershey, Pa., 1986-91; seminar instr. Pa. State U., 1988-90. Mem. pub. rels. com. Pa. Assn. Nonprofit Homes for Aging, 1986-90; pub. rels. task force, fund devel. task force United Meth. Assn. Health Welfare Ministries, 1985-90, sec., 1988-90; mem. pers. com. St. Paul's United Meth. Ch., 1982-83, adminstrv. bd., 1980-83; chmn. Golden Cross Fund Ea. Pa. Conf. United Meth. Ch., 1986-89, Greater Harrisburg Renaissance Scholarship Com., 1987-90, Pa. State Class 1984 Gift Fund; mem. mktg. com. Pa. Easter Seal Soc., 1992-93, mem. rels. com., 1994-96, bd. dirs. Lebanon County chpt., 1987-90, strategic planning com., 1989-90, mem. Pa. Atty. Gen.'s Task Force on Elder Abuse; bd. dirs. Ctr. for Cmty. Leadership, PUSH Am., 1994-97, Berks County Com. Pa. Econ. League, Cmty. Founds. for Pa., vice chmn. 1998-2000, chmn. 2000—; bd. dirs. AIDS Net, 1995—, chmn., 1996-98; bd. trustees Pub. Edn. Found., 1995-96, Pi Kappa Phi Found., 1996-2000; mem. adv. bd. Grad. Sch. Alvernia Coll., 1999—, Kutztown U. Coll. Bus., Penn State Berks Campus, 1998-2001. Named to Ea. Pa. Bus. Jour. 20 under 40, 2002; German Marshall Fund Transatlantic Cmty. Found. fellow, 2001. Mem. Pa. State Alumni Assn. (bd. dirs. 1985-91), Mt. Nittany Soc., Mensa, Pa. State Lion Ambs., Pi Kappa Phi (chpt. advisor 1988-91, alumni corp. pres. 1991-95), Alpha Sigma Alpha. Democrat. Avocations: golf, reading, flying. Home: 128 Cross Key Rd Bernville PA 19506-8806 Office: PO Box 212 Reading PA 19603-0212 E-mail: kevinm@bccf.org.

MURPHY, KEVIN GEORGE, novelist; b. Albany, N.Y., Feb. 29, 1952; s. Matthew George and Kathleen Mary (Dvorak) M.; m. Cathy Ann Clampett, July 14, 1973 (div. 1975); m. Judith Marion Chester, Jan. 9, 1987. Student, Empire State Coll., 1972-74. Novelist Scott Meredith Literary Agy., N.Y.C., 1984—, Barbara Bauer Lit. Agy., N.J., 1990. Author: The Dawn Run, 1986, Let Freedom Ring, 1986, In Someone Else's World, 1987, The Small Adventures of a Quiet Man, 1989, Humanform 2891, 1990, The Short Stories of Kevin George Murphy, 1991, Laura and the Abyss, 1991, Emergence, 1991, Angels, 1992, Alexandre and Philomena, 1993-94, others, The Streets Below, 1997-98; (poetry) Though Villages May Sleep, 1989, Her Hands Untied the Sun, 1991, Judy in the Rain, 1992; contbr. to mags. and jours. Participant anti-nuclear marches, N.Y., Washington, 1977, anti-Klan march, Albany, 1991. Mem. Mental Health Assn. (plaque 1986), Amnesty Internat. Democrat. Mem. Soc. Of Friends. Avocations: oil and watercolor painting, music composition, softball, weight lifting, travel. Home and Office: 125 Brittany C Delray Beach FL 33446-2043

MURPHY, KEVIN JAMES, business education educator; b. Sumner, Iowa, July 27, 1957; s. Robert Milner and Zae (Kvidera) M.; m. JoAnn Villa, Aug. 18, 1979; children: Kristen, Eric, Kara. BA, UCLA, 1979; MA, U. Chgo., 1981, PhD, 1984. Asst. prof. Simon Sch. of Bus. U. Rochester, N.Y., 1983-89, assoc. prof. Simon Sch. of Bus., 1989-91; assoc. prof. Bus. Sch. Harvard U., Boston, 1991—. Vis. scholar and cons. Towers Perrin, 1994-95. Contbr. numerous articles to profl. jours. Bower fellow Harvard U., 1987-88. Mem. Am. Econ. Assn., Phi Beta Kappa. Office: Harvard U Bus Sch Soldier's Field Boston MA 02163

MURPHY, LEWIS CURTIS, lawyer, former mayor; b. N.Y.C., Nov. 2, 1933; s. Henry Waldo and Elizabeth Wilcox (Curtis) M.; m. Carol Carney, Mar. 10, 1957; children— Grey, Timothy, Elizabeth. BSBA, U. Ariz., 1955, LLB, 1961. Bar: Ariz. 1961. Pvt. practice, Tucson, 1961-66; trust officer So. Ariz. Bank & Trust Co., 1966-70; atty. City of Tucson, City of Tucson, 1970-71; mayor, 1971-87, ret., 1987. Mem. Schroeder & Murphy, Tucson, 1978-88; trustee U.S. Conf. Mayors, 1978-87, chmn. transp. com., 1984-87; pub. safety steering com. Nat. League Cities, 1973-87, transp. steering com., 1973-87; v.p. Ctrl. Ariz. Project Assn., 1978-87. Bd. dirs. Cmty. Food Bank, 1987-2000, United Way Greater Tucson, 1988-90. With USAF, 1955-58. Mem. Ariz. Bar Assn., Pima County Bar Assn., Ariz. Acad. Republican. Presbyterian.

MURPHY, MARGARET A. nursing educator, adult nurse practitioner; b. N.Y.C., Apr. 4, 1934; d. William J. and Margaret (Burchill) Allen; m. Raymond L.H. Murphy, Jr., July 12, 1958; children: Raymond L.H. III, Michael W., Ann Murphy Postell, Maureen D. Murphy Olsen, Alice M., Matthew D. BSN, St. Joseph Coll., West Hartford, Conn., 1955; MS, NYU, 1957; PhD, Boston Coll., Chestnut Hill, Mass., 1987. RN, Mass.; cert. adult nurse practitioner. Instr. Boston U. Sch. Nursing, 1971-72; pulmonary clin. nurse specialist Pulmonary Assocs., Boston, 1972-73; pulmonary nurse clinician Tufts U., Medford, 1973-76; asst. prof. Boston Coll., 1982-87, instr. prof. nursing, 1976-82, asst. prof., 1982-87, assoc. prof. nursing, 1987—2001, assoc. prof. emeritus, 2001, chmn. adult health nursing, 1988-92, dir. adult nurse practitioners program, 1987—, dir. Kennedy Audio Visual Resource Ctr., 1991-95, coord. MBA-MSN program, 1993-99. Rschr. in lung sound patterns in health and disease, women's attitudes toward menopause. Co-editor: Pharmacotherapeutics and Advanced Nursing Practice, 1998; contbr. articles to profl. jours. Fellow USPHS, 1957-58; grantee Uniformed Svcs. U. Health Scis., 1995-96, Boston Coll., 1997-98. Fellow: Am. Coll. Nurse Practitioners; mem.: ANA, Mass. Thoracic Soc. (chmn. com. on nursing practice, counselor 1989—91), Am. Thoracic Soc., Mass. Nurses Assn. (co-chmn. cabinet on legis. 1985—88), Sigma Theta Tau (chmn. awards and scholarships com. Alpha Chi chpt. 1994—96, pres. 1996—98, newsletter editl. bd. 1998—2002, Alpha Chi chpt. Mentor award 2001). E-mail: murphy@bc.edu.

MURPHY, MARK JOSEPH, enterprise sales executive; b. Rockville Centre, N.Y., Aug. 5, 1960; s. John Stephen and Barbara Ann (Seeney) M.; m. Annamaria Martin, July 19, 1986; children: Dana Martine, Kelly Gabrielle. BS in Econs. and Fin., St. John's U., 1983. Sr. tech. clk. St. John's U., Jamaica, N.Y., 1979-83; sys. engr. Property and Liability Br. IBM Corp., N.Y.C., 1983-84, sys. engr. N.Y. Ins. Br., 1984-86, mktg. rep. Manhattan Ins. Br., 1986-89, adv. mktg. staff Ea. Area, 1989, mktg. mgr. N.Y. banking, 1990-93, sys. svcs. mgr., 1993-95, mgr. client server and internet sys. mktg. N.E. area, 1995-97, client exec. fin. industry sector, 1997—2001, software sales exec., 2001—. Bd. dirs. Make-A-Wish Found., Suffolk County, N.Y., past vice-chmn., past chmn. bd. devel. com., chmn. bylaws com.; vol. Make-A-Wish Found. Mem. Am. Mgmt. Assn. Avocations: golf, family, travel. Home: 134 Parkwood Rd West Islip NY 11795-3001 Office: IBM Corp 33 Maiden Ln Fl 11 New York NY 10038-4518 E-mail: bigblue@optonline.net.

MURPHY, MARY AGNES (MEG MURPHY), adult education coordinator, artist; b. Fall River, Mass., Mar. 9, 1943; d. William Joseph and Elsie Estella (Bellows) Pelton; m. Thomas Joseph Murphy, May 21, 1966; children: Sean Patrick, Bridget Norah, Mary-Agnes. BA, U. Mass., 1964; MFA, Southeastern Mass. U., 1969. Cert. tchr., Mass. Art tchr. Springfield (Mass.) Pub. Schs., 1964-66; artist, designer Fall River, 1969—; elem. art tchr. Fall River Pub. Schs., 1970-81; instr. ESOL Bristol C.C., Fall River, 1988-92, painting instr. continuing edn., 1989—2001, program coord., team leader dept. edn., 1992-93, coord. literacy vols., coord. adult literacy program, 1992—2000; program specialist Mass. Dept. Edn., Malden, 2001—. Master trainer SABES/World Edn., Boston, 1993—, health in literacy liason, 1995-99. Artist, designer Miniature Showcase, 1991-93, International Dollhouse, 1995; exhibitor Cottage Industry Miniature Trade Assn., 1988—. Recipient Marian award Diocese of Fall River, 1994, Sceptre and Scroll award Bristol Cmty. Coll., 1996. Mem. Mass. Coalition Adult Educators, Cottage Industry Miniature Trade Assn. (sec. 1994—, exhibitor 1988—), Sacred Heart Woman's Guild (pres. 1976, 95), Fall River Art Assn. Roman Catholic. Avocations: historical preservation, swimming, crafts, nature, travel. Home: 527 Cherry St Fall River MA 02720-5054 Office: Mass Dept Edn 350 Main St Malden MA 02148

MURPHY, MARY ANN, human services administrator; b. Salt Lake City, Feb. 13, 1943; d. Wallace L. and Irene (Hummer) Matlock; m. Robert A. Glatzer, Dec. 31, 1977; children: Gabriela, Jessica, Nicholas. BA, U. Wash., 1964; MS, Ea. Wash. U., 1975. House counselor Ryther Child Ctr., Seattle, 1966-67; tchr. presch. Head Start, L.A. and Seattle, 1967-70, Children's Orthopedic Hosp., Seattle, 1970-72; faculty Ea. Wash. U., Cheney, 1973-82; exec. dir. Youth Help Assn., Spokane, Wash., 1983-88; mgr. regional ctr. for child abuse and neglect Deaconess Med. Ctr., 1988-97; dir. Casey Family Ptnrs., 1997—. Pres. Wash. State Alliance for Children, Youth and Families, Seattle, 1985-87; chairperson Gov.'s Juvenile Justice Adv. Commn., Olympia, Wash., 1987—. Mem. Nat. Coun. on Juvenile Justice, 1994-98. Recipient Alumni Achievement award Ea. Wash. U., 1994; named Outstanding Women Leader in Health Care YWCA, 1992, Outstanding Children's Advocate, Wash. State Children's Alliance, 1996. Avocations: reading, swimming, backpacking. Home: 1950 W Clarke Ave Spokane WA 99201-1306 Office: Casey Family Ptnrs 613 S Washington St Spokane WA 99204-2535 *Personal philosophy: "Take the first step in faith. You don't have to see the whole staircase, just take the first step." Dr. Martin Luther King, Jr.*

MURPHY, MARY MARGUERITE, artist; b. S.I., N.Y., Mar. 29, 1958; d. Vincent Joseph and Teresa Marie (O'Connell) M.; m. James Thomas Primosch, Apr. 5, 1986. Student, Tyler Sch. Art, 1976—78; BA cum laude, Barnard Coll., 1981; student, NY Studio Sch., 1986—87; MFA in Painting, Tyler Sch. Art, 1991; student, Skowhegan Sch. Painting/Sculp., 1990. Panel mem. Coll. New Rochelle, NY, 1985, Phila. Art Alliance, 1997; tchg. fellow Tyler Sch. Art, Phila., 1989—91, instr., 1995, Fleisher Art Meml., Phila., 1992—98; vis. artist Ohio State U., Columbus, 1993, Columbus, 97; tchg. artist Inst. for Arts in Edn., Phila., 1994, Phila., 97; sr. lectr. U. of the Arts, Phila., 1996—98, adj. asst. prof., 2000—; lectr. Washington U., St. Louis, 1998—99; panel moderator Beaver Coll., Glenside, Pa., 1995, Nat. Mus. Jewish History, 1997; vis. artist lectr. Ohio State U., 1993, 97, Tyler Sch. Art, 1994, Pa. State U., 1997, U. Alaska, 2002. One person shows include S.P.A.C.E.S., Cleve., 1994, Fleisher Art Meml., Phila., 1995, Larry Becker Contemporary Art, Phila., 1995, Schmidt/Dean Gallery, Phila., 1998, 99, U. Alaska, 2002; exhibited in group shows 80 Washington Sq. East Galleries, N.Y.C., 1985, Va. Ctr. for Creative Arts, Sweet Briar, Va., 1986, The Drawing Ctr., N.Y.C., 1989, Larry Becker Gallery, Phila., 1991, 95, Temple Univ. Gallery, Phila., 1991, State Theatre Ctr. for the Arts. Easton, Pa., 1991, Momenta Art Alternatives, Phila., 1991, Beaver Coll., Glenside, Pa., 1992, 96, 99, White Columns, N.Y.C., 1992, Moore Coll. of Art and Design, Phila., Pa., 1992, 99, 1708 E Main St. Gallery, Richmond, Va., 1992, Ohio State U., Columbus, 1993, Main Line Ctr. of the Arts, Haverford, Pa., 1993, 55 Mercer St., N.Y.C., 1994, Vox Populi, Phila., 1994, 558 Broome St., N.Y.C., 1994, Tyler Sch. Art, Phila., 1994, Larry Becker Contemporary Art, Phila., 1995, Del. Art Mus., Wilmington, 1996, Borowsky Gallery, Phila., 1996, Ohio State U., Columbus, 1997, Del. Ctr. Contemporary Art, 1997, Abington Art Ctr., 1997, Phila. Art Alliance, 1997, Fleisher Art Meml., Phila., 1998, Margaret Thatcher Projects, N.Y.C., 1998, N.J. Ctr. Visual Arts, Summit, 1998, David Beitzel Gallery, N.Y., 1998, Schmidt/Dean Gallery, 1999, U. of the Arts, Phila., 2000; permanent collections Wilmington Trust, The Brooklyn Mus., Ark. Art Ctr., Am. Express; works included in publs. Richmond Times Dispatch, Phila. City Paper, New Art Examiner, The Phila. Inquirer, The Plain Dealer, Artnews, Eyelevel; contbr. to The New Art Examiner; contbr. articles to The New Art Examiner, lectr. in field. Mem. alumni bd. Tyler Sch. Art, Elkins Park, Pa., 1994-98. Resident Va. Ctr. for Creative Arts, 1985, 86; fellow Skowhegan Sch. Painting and Sculpture, 1990, Nat. Endowment for Arts fellow in painting, 1993-94; grantee Fleisher Art Meml., Phila., 1994, Venture Fund, U. of Arts, 2002, Pa. State Coun. on Arts, 2002; fellow Pa. State Coun. on the Arts, 1998; finalist Pew Fellowship in the Arts, 1994-95. Mem. Coll. Art Assn. Roman Catholic. Home: 20 Whitemarsh Ave Erdenheim PA 19038-8230 E-mail: mary.murphy52@verizon.net.

MURPHY, MARY PATRICIA, elementary education educator; b. Buffalo, Mar. 5, 1950; d. Anthony Ralph and Lena (Tirone) Scime; m. Dennis Patrick Murphy, May 4, 1973; children: Gregory Raymond, Daniel Anthony. BS, Damien Coll., 1972; MS in Elem. Edn., SUNY, Buffalo, 1975. Cert. elem. and secondary tchr., N.Y. Tchr. grade 4 North Tonawanda (N.Y.) Sch. Dist., 1972-75; tchr. grades 1 and 2 Shenendehowa Ctrl. Sch. Dist., Clifton Park, NY, 1984-92, tchr. grade 2, 1992-97, tchr. grade 4, 1997—2002, staff devel. specialist, 2002—. Assistance tchr. mentor program Shenendehowa Sch. Dist., 1993—; presenter in field. Active PTA(life mem. award, 1998), Am. Diabetes Assn., Juvenile Diabetes Found., part. Mentor/Intern program. Shenendehowa Ctrl. Sch. Dist. grantee, 1988-90. Mem. ASCD, Am. Fedn. Tchrs., N.Y. United Tchrs., N.Y. Coun. Tchrs. English, Intergenerational Writers' Conf., Internat. Women's Writing Guild. Avocations: reading, cross-country skiing. Home: 120 East Ave Saratoga Springs NY 12866-8743 Office: Shenendehowa Ctrl Sch Dist Karigon Sch 970 Route 146 Clifton Park NY 12065-3643

MURPHY, MAX RAY, lawyer; b. July 18, 1934; s. Loren A. and Lois (Mink) M.; children: Michael Lee, Chad Woodrow. BA, DePauw U., 1956; JD, Yale U., 1959; postgrad., Mich. State U., 1960. Bar: Mich. 1960. Assoc. Glassen, Parr, Rhead & McLean, Lansing, Mich., 1960-67, Lokker, Boter & Dalman, Holland, 1967-69; ptnr. Dalman, Murphy, Bidol, & Bouwens, P.C., 1969-91, Cunningham Dalman, P.C., Holland, 1991—. Instr. Lansing Bus. U., 1963-67; asst. pros. atty. Ottawa County, Mich., 1967-69. Democratic candidate for Ingham County (Mich.) Pros. Atty., 1962, 1964. Mem. ABA, Ottawa County Bar Assn. (sec. 1970-71), Mich. Bar Assn. (mem. family law sect.). Home: 3169 E Crystal Waters 3 Holland MI 49424-8091 Office: 321 Settlers Rd Holland MI 49423-3778 E-mail: mmurphy@wmis.net.

MURPHY, MELINDA, TV host, reporter; b. Midland, Tex., Dec. 10, 1963; d. James Palmer and Natalie (Harben) M. BA in Journalism, Tex. A&M U., 1986. Account exec. CBS Radio Rep., N.Y.C., 1986-88; dir. classical music mktg. Interep Radio Store, 1988; entertainment stringer KOCO-TV, 1995-97; co-host, EP, creator SCAM pilot for USA Network, 1996; info. specialist NewsTalk TV, 1995-96; host Global Shopping Network, 1996-97; reporter News 12 N.J., 1996—. Talent booker WWOR-TV, 1991-92; prodn. coord. CBS Tony awards, 1992, 93; prodn. exec. ABC, 1992; assoc. floor prodr. CNN Dem. Nat. Conv., 1992; talent coord. PBS Internat. Emmy Awards, 1992; prodr. Multimedia Entertainment, 1993-94; coordinating prodr. Buena Vista TV, 1994; sr. prodr. Dick Clark Prodns., 1994, New World Entertainment, 1994; on-air coach Columbia TriStar, 1994; prodn. mgr. PBS, 1996; writer, field prodr. WCBS-TV, 1996-97; contbg. writer Parents mag., 1996; judge Internat. TV Festival, 1995—. Recipient Emmy award, 1997. Mem. AFTRA, NATAS, Writer's Guild Am., Alpha Delta Pi. Avocations: animal rights, cooking and entertaining, traveling, outdoor sports. Home: 68 Lydia Dr West New York NJ 07093-8368

MURPHY, MICHAEL EMMETT, retired food company executive; b. Winchester, Mass., Oct. 16, 1936; s. Michael Cornelius and Bridie (Curran) M.; m. Adele Anne Kasupski, Sept. 12, 1959; children: Leslie Maura, Glenn Stephen, Christopher McNeil. BS in Bus. Adminstrn, Boston Coll., 1958; MBA, Harvard, 1962. Financial analyst Maxwell House div. Gen. Foods Corp., White Plains, N.Y., 1962-64, cost mgr. San Leandro, Calif., 1964-65, controller Jacksonville, Fla., 1965-67, Hoboken, N.J., 1967-68, mgr. fin. planning and analysis, 1968-69; mgr. planning Hanes Corp., Winston-Salem, N.C., 1969-70, corp. controller, 1970-72; v.p. adminstrn. Hanes Corp. (Hanes Knitwear), 1972-74; v.p. fin. Ryder System Inc., Miami, Fla., 1974-75, exec. v.p., 1975-79; exec. v.p., dir. Sara Lee Corp., Chgo., 1979-93, vice chmn., 1993-97. Bd. dirs. GATX Corp., Payless Shoe Source, Inc., CNH Global N.V., Coach Inc., Bassett Furniture Industries, Inc., No. Funds. Mgmt. adviser Jr.

Achievement, 1965-66; mem. exec. com. Hudson County Tax Rsch. Coun., 1967-68; trustee Boston Coll., 1980-88; chmn. Civic Fedn. Chgo., 1984-86; bd. dirs. Jobs for Youth, Chgo., 1983-86, Lyric Opera, 1986-2002; bd. dirs. Northwestern Meml. Hosp., Chgo., 1989-2000, Big Shoulders Fund, Chgo. Ctrl. Area Com., 1995—, Chgo. Cultural Ctr. Found., 1995—; prin. Chgo. United, 1995-98. Mem. Nat. Assn. Mfrs. (bd. dirs. 1989-96, dir. Big Shoulders Fund 1995—), Fin. Execs. Inst., Hoboken C. of C., Winson-Salem C. of C., Miami C. of C., Internat. Platform Assn., UN Assn., Ouimet Scholar Alumni Group, Beta Gamma Sigma. Roman Catholic. Home: 1242 N Lake Shore Dr Chicago IL 60610-2361 Office: Sara Lee Corp 3 First National Plz Chicago IL 60602

MURPHY, MICHAEL JOSEPH, retired bishop; b. Cleve., July 1, 1915; s. William and Mary Bridget (Patton) M. BA in Philosophy, Gregorian U., Rome, 1938; S.T.L., Catholic U. Am., 1942. Ordained priest Roman Catholic Ch., 1942; prof. pro-tem St. Mary Sem., Cleve., 1943-45, prof., 1947-48, vice-rector, 1948-63, rector, 1963-76; Episcopal vicar Chancery Office, 1976-78; coadjutor bishop of Erie, Chancery office (Pa.), 1978-82; bishop of Erie, 1982-90. Mem. scripture trans. com. Nat. Conf. Cath. Bishops. Recipient first Ann. Sem. Dept. award Nat. Cath. Ednl. Assn. Home and Office: St Patrick Church 130 E 4th St Erie PA 16507-1508

MURPHY, MICHAEL R. federal judge; b. Denver, Aug. 6, 1947; s. Roland and Mary Cecilia (Maloney) M.; m. Maureen Elizabeth Donnelly, Aug. 22, 1970; children: Amy Christina, Michael Donnelly. BA in History, Creighton U., 1969; JD, U. Wyo., 1972. Bar: Wyo. 1972, U.S. Ct. Appeals (10th cir.) 1972, Utah 1973, U.S. Dist. Ct. Utah 1974, U.S. Dist. Ct. Wyo. 1976, U.S. Ct. Appeals (5th cir.) 1976, U.S. Tax Ct. 1980, U.S. Ct. Appeals (9th cir.) 1981, U.S. Ct. Appeals (fed. cir.) 1984. Law clk. to chief judge U.S. Ct. Appeals (10th cir.), Salt Lake City, 1972-73; with Jones, Waldo, Holbrook & McDonough, 1973-86; judge 3d Dist. Ct., 1986-95, pres. judge, 1990-95; judge U.S. Ct. Appeals (10th cir.), 1995—. Mem. adv. com. on rules of civil procedure Utah Supreme Ct., 1985—95, mem. bd. dist. ct. judges, 1989—90; mem. Utah State Sentencing Commn., 1993—95, Utah Adv. Com. on Child Support Guidelines, 1989—95, Utah Child Sexual Abuse Task Force, 1989—93; mem. com. on fed.-state jurisdiction Jud. Conf. of U.S., 2001—. Recipient Freedom of Info. award, Soc. Profl. Journalists, 1989, Utah Minority Bar Assn. award, 1995, alumni Achievement citation, Creighton U., 1997; named Judge of Yr., Utah State Bar, 1992. Fellow Am. Bar Found.; mem. ABA (editl. bd. Judges' Jour. 1997-99), Utah Bar Assn. (chmn. alternative dispute resolution com. 1985-88), Sutherland Inn of Ct. II (past pres.). Office: 5438 Federal Bldg 125 S State St Salt Lake City UT 84138-1102

MURPHY, MICHELE SANDRA, musician, educator; b. Houston, Jan. 10, 1950; d. William Douglas and Mary Jane Murphy; children: David Gabriel, Micah Luther Ater. Singer/songwriter self-employed, Austin, Tex., 1972—; musician Alvin Crow and Pleasant Valley, 1984—88; dir. and owner Natural Ear Music Camp and Sch., Autin, 1984—. Prodr.: (music cd) Once a Night. Avocations: bicycling, motorcycling, gardening. Office: Natural Ear Music School 3607 Manchaun Road Austin TX 78704 E-mail: natural@texas.net.

MURPHY, MICHELE SUSAN, non-profit agency executive; b. Cleve., Aug. 11, 1949; d. Edward Jerry and Violet Agnes (Lozick) M. BS in Journalism, Ohio U., 1971; M Non-Profit Orgns., Case Western Res. U., 1993. Press rep. Cuyahoga Community Coll. West, Parma, Ohio, 1971-75; pub. info. specialist Cuyahoga Community Coll., Cleve., 1975-76, news bur. mgr., 1976-77, asst. dir. info. svcs., 1977-78, cons., 1979; coord. U.S. Senate Campaign, 1981-82; communications liaison Cuyahoga County Bd. Elections, 1982-94; exec. dir. Crime Stoppers of Cuyahoga County, Inc., 1994. Founder, exec. dir. Conflict Resolution Ctr. of the West Shore, Inc.; cons. in mktg. The City Club, Cleve., 1991. Mem. Leadership Cleve., Greater Cleve. Growth Assn., 1986; editor Rep. News, Cuyahoga County Rep. Orgn., 1983-84. Recipient Appreciation award Greater Cleve. Crime Prevention Com., 1992, Ohio State Chiefs of Police Assn., 1990, Vol. Achievement award CIVAC, Cleve., 1987, Cert. of Appreciation Community Rels. Bd., City of Cleve., 1987, Sports Promotion award Nat. Jr. Coll. Athletic Assn., 1973, 74, 75. Mem. Ohio Mediation Assn., Acad. Family Mediators, Cuyahoga County Police Chiefs Assn. (hon., named Citizen of Yr. 1995). Office: CRC West Shore Inc 24700 Center Ridge Rd # 6 Westlake OH 44145-5636

MURPHY, PATRICE ANN (PAT MURPHY), writer; Former instr. Clarion Speculative Fiction Workshop, Mich. State U.; former tchr. sci. fiction U. Calif., Santa Cruz; tchr. sci. fiction writing Creative Writing Program, Stanford U., 1995, 96, 97, 98. Author: The Falling Woman, 1987 (Nebula award 1987), (novelette) Rachel in Love (Nebula award 1987, Isaac Asimov Reader's award 1987, Theodore Sturgeon Meml. award 1987), (short story collection) Points of Departure, 1990 (Philip K. Dick award 1990), (novella) Bones, 1991 (World Fantasy award 1991), (novelette) An American Childhood, Nadya-The Wolf Chronicles, There and Back Again, The City, Not Long After, By Nature's Design, The Color of Nature, 1996, The Science Explorer, 1996. Avocation: karate. Office: care Tor Books 14th Fl 175 5th Ave Fl 14 New York NY 10010-7703*

MURPHY, PATRICIA ANN, physician, otolaryngologist; b. N.Y.C., Oct. 22, 1951; d. John Francis and Teresa (Whitney) M. BS, Wagner Coll., S.I., N.Y., 1974; MD, Virgen Milagrosa, The Philippines, 1981. Biochemist N.Y.C. Dept. Health, 1976-77; internist L.I. Coll. Hosp., Bklyn., 1981-82; surgeon St. Francis Hosp. and Med. Ctr., Trenton, N.J., 1982-83; clin. asst. instr., fellow otolaryngology SUNY Health Sci. Ctr. of Bklyn., 1984-87; fellow otolaryngology SUNY Health Sci. Ctr. of Bklyn., Brookdale Hosp. Med. Ctr., 1986-87; physician Family Health Plan, Fountain Valley, Calif., 1989-90; pvt. practice Santa Cruz, 1990-98, Elkins, W.Va., 1998—. Physician Hearing, Edn. and Awareness for Rockers, San Francisco; physician rock medicine Haight Ashbury Free Clin., San Francisco. Author: (with others) Ears, Nose, Throat Emergency Treatment, 1986. Fed. Rsch. grantee N.Y.C. Dept. Health, 1976-77. Mem. Am. Women's Med. Assn. (sec. 1990—), Women in Otolaryngology, Am. Acad. Otolaryngology, Am. Acad. Otolaryngic Allergy, Am. Acad. Facial Plastic and Reconstructive Surgery. Liberal. Roman Catholic. Avocations: reading, skiing, trekking. Office: 903 Gorman Ave Elkins WV 26241-3149

MURPHY, PATRICK GREGORY, real estate company executive; b. Salina, Kans., May 21, 1947; s. Jorel Edward and Geneva Gail (Jordan) M. Student, Tulsa U., 1971-72; cert. grad. realtors inst., Okla. State U., 1977. Lic. real estate broker. V.p. Profl. Home Finder, Tulsa, 1972-77, Sunshine Properties, Tulsa, 1977-81, Robert A. McNeil Corp., Phoenix, 1981-85, Resources Property Mgmt. div. Integrated Resources, Houston, 1985-88; sr. asset mgr. G.A.C. Consultants, Atlanta and Tulsa, 1988—. Co-author: Todays Real Estate, 1979. Mem. real estate com. Tulsa Jr. Coll., 1977-81; bd. dirs. Trinity Episcopal Ch., Tulsa, 1972-81; founder Greater Atlanta Bus. Coalition, 1993, pres., 1993-96. Served with USN, 1965-70. Mem. Nat. Assn. Realtors (cert. residential specialist and broker), Inst. Real Estate Mgmt. (cert. property mgr., edn. com. Houston chpt. 1987, bd. dirs. Fla. chpt. 1989-91, pres. Fla. chpt. 1991), Nat. Apt. Assn. (cert. apt. property supr.), Tex. Apt. Assn., Houston Apt. Assn. (steering com. 1986-87), Internat. Real Estate Inst. (registered property mgr.). Democrat. Episcopalian. Avocations: travel, bridge, reading. Office: GAC Cons Ste 1 Box 302 1779 Kirby Pkwy Tulsa OK 74135 E-mail: patulsaok@aol.com., gacconsult@aol.com.

MURPHY, PATRICK J. pharmaceutical researcher; b. Chgo., June 11, 1940; s. Michael and Marcella G. Murphy; m. Rita J. Durkin, Dec. 31, 1966; children: Maureen, Meghan, Patrick, Matthew. BS, Loyola U., Chgo., 1962; MS, San Diego State Coll., 1964; PhD, UCLA, 1967. Sr. biochemist Eli Lilly & Co., Indpls., 1967-72, rsch. sci., 1973-76, head drug metabolism, 1977-79, head cardiovascular pharm., 1979-83, dir. cardiovascular pharm. and drug metabolism, 1983-86, dir. toxicology and drug metabolism, 1986-89, dir. drug metabolism and clin. analysis serv., 1989-94, rsch. advisor toxicology and drug metabolism, 1994-96; cons. drug metabolism Carmel, Ind., 1997—. Mem. AAAS, Am. Chem. Soc., Internat. Soc. Study Xenobiotics, Am. Soc. Pharmacology Exptl. Therapeutics. Office: 3589 Brumley Mews Carmel IN 46033-3021

MURPHY, PEARL MARIE, medical and surgical nurse; b. Portsmouth, Ohio, Feb. 9, 1954; d. Chester Eugene and Eunice Jean (Windsor) M. LPN, Scioto Tech. Coll., Lucasville, Ohio, 1973; ADN, Hocking Tech. Coll., Nelsonville, Ohio, 1980; BSN, Ohio U., 1989. Cert. med./surg. nurse, Am. Nursing Credentialing Ctr. Staff nurse med.-surg. unit So. Hills Hosp., Portsmouth, 1973-75, staff nurse psychiat.-alcohol unit, 1975-79, staff nurse psychiat. unit, 1980-87, Mercy Hosp., Portsmouth, 1987-88; staff nurse diabetic unit Scioto Meml. Hosp., 1988-89; staff nurse med.-surg. unit Women's Ctr., So. Ohio Med. Ctr., 1989—. Nursing asst. program coord., instr. Scioto Tech. Coll., 1991-92. Mem. Ohio Nurses Assn., Order Ea. Star. Baptist. Avocations: camping, hiking, fishing, working in church. Home: 905 Stoney Run Rd West Portsmouth OH 45663-8959 Office: So Ohio Med Ctr Portsmouth OH 45662

MURPHY, PEREGINE LEIGH, priest; b. Fowler, Calif., Sept. 29, 1954; d. Elbert Thurman Pitcock Jr. and Patricia (Dolan) Olsen. BA in Human Devel., Calif. State U., Hayward, 1979, MS in Clin. Counseling, 1980; MBA, Coll. Notre Dame, Belmont, Calif., 1982; MDiv, Gen. Theol. Sem., 1990; PhD in Psychology, CUNY, 2002. Ordained priest, Episc. Ch., 1991. Parent educator, tchr. Children's Ctr. of Stanford (Calif.) Community, Stanford U., 1980-83; human resource cons. Continental Corp., N.Y.C., 1983-85; from asst. v.p. adminstrn. to v.p. adminstrn. Continental Internat. Life, Continental Corp., 1985-86; residency pastoral care Columbia-Presbyn. Med. Ctr., 1988-89, from coord. to sr. rsch. assoc. N.Y. Neurol. Inst., 1990-96; asst. min. Cathedral Ch. of St. John the Divine, 1991-95, Ch. of the Incarnation, N.Y., 1995-96; assisting priest St. Marks Episcopal Ch., Mt. Kisco, N.Y., 1996-98; instr. psychology Hunter Coll., CUNY, 1996—2001; interim priest St. Mary's Episcopal Ch., Mohegan Lake, NY, 1998—2001; priest-in-charge Eglesia Meml. de San Andres, Yonkers, 2001—. Mem. Children's Adv. Com., 1995—96; mem. Clergy Wholeness Com., 1998—, co-chair, 1999—; mem. Commn. on Ministry Episcopal Diocese, 1996—2002; mem. Commn. on Ministry ex officio Episcopal Diocese, 2002—. Mem. APA (assoc.), Am. Acad. Neurology (affiliate), Soc. Neurosci., N.Y. Acad. Scis. Office: Eglesia Meml de San Andres 22 Post St Yonkers NY 10705 E-mail: mo.pmurphy@verizon.net.

MURPHY, PETER E. corporate financial officer; BA, Dartmouth Coll.; MBA, Wharton Sch. Bus. With The Walt Disney Co., Burbank, Calif., 1988—; sr. v.p., CFO ABC, Inc., 1997-98; exec. v.p., chief strategic officer The Walt Disney Co., 1998-99, sr. exec. v.p., chief strategic officer, 1999—. Office: The Walt Disney Co 500 S Buena Vista St Burbank CA 91521

MURPHY, PETER E. secondary education educator, writer; b. Newport, Eng., Sept. 18, 1950; arrived in U.S., 1953; s. Edward Peter and (stepmother) Marie Theresa Murphy; m. Sonya M. Murphy, June 22, 1974. BA, Richard Stockton Coll., 1976; MA, NYU, 1981. Tchr. Atlantic City (N.J.) H.S., 1976—; founder, dir. Murphy Writing Seminars, LLC, Ventnor, N.J., 1999—. Cons. Gerldine R. Dodge Found., Morristown, N.J., 1986—. Contbr.: (books) Under a Gull's Wing: Poetry of the Jersey Shore, 1996, Outsiders: Poems about Rebels, Exiles, and Renegades, 1999, A Passion for Teaching, 1999, Urban Nature: Poems About Wildlife in the City, 2000, (jour.) The Shakespeare Quar., 1984. Chairperson Baha'i Group of Ventnor, N.J., 1983-2001. Named Disting. Humanities Tchr., N.J. Coun. for Humanities, 1997, Disting. Tchr. Am., White House Commn. on Presdl. Scholars, 1991, 95; Poetry writing fellow N.J. Coun. Arts, 1985, 88, 91, 94, Robert Hayden fellow in poetry Louhelen Bahá'í Sch., 1987, Tchg. Shakespeare fellow Folger Shakespeare Libr., 1984. Mem. Acad. Am. Poets, Assn. Bahá'í Studies (sec. Mid-Atlantic regional com. 1994-2001). Bahá'í. Avocations: reading, writing, running on the boardwalk. Home and Office: 18 N Richards Ave Ventnor NJ 08406 E-mail: murphywriting@hotmail.com.

MURPHY, RAMON JEREMIAH CASTROVIEJO, physician, pediatrician; b. N.Y.C., Feb. 12, 1944; s. William J. and Angelines (Castroviejo) M.; m. Lila, Sept. 12, 1971; children: Jessica, David. BA, U. Notre Dame, 1965; MD, Northwestern U., 1969; MPH, Columbia U., 1974. Diplomate Am. Bd. Pediats. Intern in medicine Cook County Hosp., Chgo., 1969-70; resident in pediats. Children's Meml. Hosp., 1970-71, Babies Hosp.-Columbia-Presbyn. Med. Ctr., N.Y.C., 1971-73; resident in cmty. medicine Mt. Sinai Hosp., 1973-74, clin. asst. pediatrician, 1974-75, asst. attending pediatrician, 1975-83, assoc. attending pediatrician, 1983—, assoc. instr. cmty. medicine, 1974-75, asst. prof. clin. pediats., asst. prof. cmty. medicine, 1975-83, assoc. prof. clin. pediats., 1983—; pediatrician Uptown Pediats., P.C., 1976—, pres., 1990—. Co-dir. Mt. Sinai Children's Cmty. Health, 1999—; dir. Mt. Sinai Off-Site Pediatric Residency Tng. Program, 1999—; vis. clin. fellow pediats. Columbia U., Coll. Physicians and Surgeons, N.Y.C., 1971-73; pediats. cons. Oxford Health Plan, 1990-94. Contbr. articles to profl. jours. Co-med. dir. Benito Juarez People's Health Ctr., Chgo., 1970-71; dep. co-dir. Wagner Child Health Project, N.Y.C., 1973-75; sch. physician The Day Sch., 1984—, The Trinity Sch., 1992—, trustee, 1993-99. Fellow Am. Acad. Pediats; mem. N.Y. Pediat. Soc. (program chmn. 1986-89, pres. 1989-90), Soc. for Adolescent Medicine, Mt. Sinai Alumni Assn. Office: 1245 Park Ave New York NY 10128-1211

MURPHY, RANDALL KENT, training consultant; b. Laramie, Wyo., Nov. 8, 1943; s. Robert Joseph and Sally (McConnell) M.; m. Cynthia Laura Hillhouse, Dec. 29, 1978; children: Caroline, Scott, Emily. Student, U. Wyo., 1961—65; MBA, So. Meth. U., 1983. Dir. mktg. Wycoa, Inc., Denver, 1967-70; dir. Comm. Resource Inst., Dallas, 1971-72; account exec. Xerox Learning Sys., 1973-74; regional mgr. Systema Corp., 1975; pres. Performance Assocs.; pres., dir. Acclivus Corp., Dallas, 1976—; founder, chmn. Acclivus Inst., 1982—. Author: Performance Management of the Selling Process, 1979, Coaching and Counseling and Performance, 1980, Managing Development and Performance, 1982, Acclivus Performance Planning System, 1983, (with others) BASE For Sales Performance, 1983, Acclivus Coaching, 1984, Acclivus Sales Negotiation, 1985, R3 Service, 1997, BASE for Effective Presentations, 1987, BASE for Strategic Sales Presentatiions, 1988, The New BASE for Sales Excellence, 1988, Major Account Planning and Strategy, 1989, Strategic Management of the Selling Process, 1989, Building on the BASE, 1992, Negotiation Mastery, 1995, R3 Service, 1997, Co-creating R3 Value, 2002; co-inventor The Randy-Band multi-purpose apparel accessory, 1968. Active Dallas Mus. Fine Arts, Dallas Hist. Soc., Dallas Symphony Assn.; vice chmn. bd. trustees The Winston Sch., 1994-96, chmn. bd. trustees, 1997-2000; mem. adv. bd. The Women's Ctr. of Dallas, 1995-98. With AUS, 1966. Mem. ASTD, Inst. Mgmt. Scis., Soc. Applied Learning Tech., Nat. Soc. Performance and Instrn., Assn. Mgmt. Cons., Am. Assn. Higher Edn., World Future Soc., Soc. for Intercultural Edn., Tng. and Rsch., Internat. Fedn. Tng. and Devel. Orgns., Inst. Noetic Scis., Nat. Peace Inst., Amnesty Internat., Acad. Polit. Sci., The Nature Conservancy, Theosophical Soc. Am., Children's Arts and Ideas Found., So. Meth. U. Alumni Assn., U. Wyo. Alumni Assn. Roman Catholic. Home: 9323 Preston Rd Dallas TX 75225-1642

MURPHY, RICARDO, biophysicist, plant physiologist; b. London, Aug. 15, 1957; came to U.S., 1993; s. Martin Murphy and Lillian Blackwell. BSc, U. E. Anglia, Norwich, Eng., 1978, PhD, 1984. Rsch. fellow Trinity Coll., Dublin, Ireland, 1984-87; rsch. assoc. U. Edinburgh, Scotland, 1987-90; rsch. fellow U. Oxford, Eng., 1990-93; rsch. assoc. U. Colo., Denver, 1993-96, U. Del., Lewes, 1996-98, Northeastern U., Boston, 1998-2000, Rush Med. Ctr., Chgo., 2001—. Lectr., tutor, 1984-96. Peer reviewer sci. jours., 1987—; contbr. articles to profl. jours. Rsch. fellow Dept. Edn., 1984, Glasstone fellow U. Oxford, 1990, Linacre fellow Linacre Coll., 1991. Mem. Biophys. Soc., Phi Beta Delta. Office: Rush Med Ctr Dept Physiology 1653 W Congress Pkwy Chicago IL 60612

MURPHY, RICHARD PATRICK, lawyer; b. Elizabeth, N.J. AB with distinction, Cornell U., 1976; JD cum laude, AM, U. Mich., 1980. Bar: D.C. 1980, U.S. Dist. Ct. (D.C.) 1981, U.S. Ct. Appeals (D.C. cir.) 1981, U.S. Supreme Ct. 1984, Calif. 1987, U.S. Dist. Ct. (so. dist.) Calif. 1987, U.S. Dist. Ct. (cen. dist.) Calif. 1992, Ga. 1993, U.S. Dist. Ct. (no. dist.) Ga. 1993, U.S. Ct. Appeals (11th cir.) 1993. Assoc. Bergson, Borkland, Margolis & Adler, Washington, 1980-82; atty. enforcement div. SEC, 1982-84, br. chief enforcement div., 1984-87; assoc. Gray, Cary, Ames & Frye, San Diego, 1987-92; sr. trial counsel SEC, Atlanta, 1993-99, asst. dist. adminstr., 1999—. Mem. ABA, D.C. Bar Assn., Calif. Bar Assn., Ga. Bar Assn. Office: SEC 3475 Lenox Rd NE Ste 1000 Atlanta GA 30326-1239

MURPHY, RICHARD WILLIAM, retired foreign service officer, Middle East specialist, consultant; b. Boston, July 29, 1929; s. John Deneen Murphy and Jane (Diehl) Bonner; m. Anne Herrick Cook, Aug. 25, 1955; children: Katherine Anne, Elizabeth Drew, Richard McGill. Grad., Phillips Exeter Acad., 1947; AB, Harvard U., 1951, Cambridge (Eng.) U., 1953; postgrad. Arabic studies, U.S. Fgn. Service Inst., Beirut, 1959-60; LLD (hon.), New Eng. Coll., 1989, Balt. Hebrew U., 1992. Vice consul U.S. Consulate Gen., Salisbury, So. Rhodesia, 1955-58; consul Aleppo, Syria, 1960-63; polit. officer Am. Embassy, Jedda, Saudi Arabia, 1963-66, Amman, Jordan, 1966-68; pers. officer U.S. State Dept., Washington, 1968-69, dir. Office Arabian Peninsula Affairs, 1969-71, asst. sec. state for Near Ea. and South Asian affairs, 1983-89; U.S. amb. to Mauritania, 1971-74, Syria, 1974-78, The Philippines, 1978-81, Saudi Arabia, 1981-83; sr. fellow for Middle East Coun. Fgn. Rels., N.Y.C., 1989—; cons. Richard Murphy Assocs., 1993—. Chmn. Fgn. Students Svc. Coun., Washington, 1989—93, Mid. East Inst., Washington, 1993—2001, Chatham House Found., 1993—; mem. bd. advisors Naval War Coll., 1991—94; bd. dirs. Harvard Med. Internat. Trustee Am. U. of Beirut, 1995--; mem. vis. com. Harvard Mid. East Ctr., 1999—, Near East Found., 2000—. Served with U.S. Army, 1953-55. Recipient Superior Honor award, U.S. Dept. State, 1969, Pres.'s Disting. Svc. award, 1986, 88, 89. Mem. Coun. Fgn. Rels., Fgn. Svc. Assn., Century Club. Republican. Episcopalian. Avocations: tennis, scuba diving. Home: 16 Sutton Pl # 9A New York NY 10022-3057 E-mail: rmurphy@cfr.org.

MURPHY, ROBERT, search firm executive; b. Davenport, Iowa; s. James and Patricia M.; children: Lisa, Todd, Kyle. BS, U. Ill. Med. Ctr., Chgo., 1963. Registered pharmacist, Ill. With Walgreen Co., Chgo., 1963-73; corp. mgr. Coll. Rels. & Recruiting Corp.; mgr. Human Resource Planning Corp.; dir. Orgn. and Human Resource Planning & Devel.; US ptnr.-in-charge exec. search PricewaterhouseCoopers, Chgo., 1974—93; founder, chmn. Murphy Ptnrs. Internat., global exec. search firm, 1993—. With PriceWaterhouseCoopers, Chgo., 1973-92; U.S. ptnr.-in-charge Exec. Search, Chgo. Contbr. articles to profl. jours. including Wall St. Jour., Newsweek. Mem. Internat. Human Resource Assn., Soc. Human Resource Mgrs., Internat. Cons. Assn., Am. Soc. Pers. Adminstrs., Soc. Human Resource Profls., Kappa Psi. Office: 956 Shoreline Rd Barrington IL 60010-3815 E-mail: bob@mpivips.com.

MURPHY, ROBERT BLAIR, management consulting company executive; b. Phila., Jan. 19, 1931; s. William Beverly and Helen Marie (Brennan) M.; children: Stephen, Emily, Julia, David, Catherine. BS, Yale, 1953. Indsl. engr. DuPont Corp., Aiken, S.C., 1953-55; mgr. sales can divsn. Reynolds Metals Co., Richmond, Va., 1955-69; gen. mgr. corrugated divsn. Continental Can Co., N.Y.C., 1969-73; v.p. and gen. mgr. beverage divsn. Am. Can Co., Greenwich, Conn., 1973-75; assoc. Heidrick & Struggles, Inc., N.Y.C., 1976-78, v.p., 1978; v.p., mng. dir. Stamford office Spencer Stuart & Assocs., 1978-84, ptnr., 1982-84; co-founder Sullivan-Murphy Assocs., 1984—. Mem. Riverside Yacht Club (Greenwich), Yale Club (N.Y.C.), Merion Cricket Club (Haverford, Pa.), Bucks Harbor Yacht Club (Brooksville, Maine). Home: 11 Indian Mill Rd Cos Cob CT 06807-1315

MURPHY, ROBERT FRANCIS, biology educator and researcher; b. Bklyn., Aug. 25, 1953; s. Robert Francis and Marguerite Ann (McClean) M.; m. Vivian Mathilde Grosswald, Aug. 15, 1981 (div. May 1990); children: Robert Emile, Charles Francis; m. Cynthia Ann Miller, Nov. 23, 1991; 1 child, Michael James. BA, Columbia U., 1974; PhD, Calif. Inst. Tech., 1980. Rsch. assoc. Columbia U., N.Y.C., 1979-83; asst. prof. dept. biol. sci. Carnegie Mellon U., Pitts., 1983-89, assoc. prof., 1989—, dir. Carnegie Mellon Beckman scholars program, 1998-99; dir. Merck Computational Biology and Chemistry , 1999—. Cons. Becton Dickinson Immunocytometry Sys., San Jose, Calif., 1982-92; assoc. Pitts. Cancer Inst., 1986—; mem. Cell Biology study panel NSF, Washington, 1989-92, rsch. experiences for undergrads. study panel, 1997-99; Biol. Scis. study sect. NIH, 1993-97; co-chair. Cytometry Devel. workshop, 1999—. Co-editor: Applications of Fluorescence in the Biomedical Sciences, 1986, Endosomes and Lysosomes: A Dynamic Relationship, 1993; contbr. over 80 articles to profl. jours. Recipient Presdl. Young Investigator award NSF, 1984; Damon Runyon-Walter Winchell Cancer Found. fellow, 1979; grantee NIH, NSF, Am. Cancer Soc., Am. Heart Assn. Mem. AAAS, Internat. Soc. Analytical Cytology, Internat. Soc. Computational Biology, Am. Soc. Cell Biology, Sigma Xi. Achievements include co-development of flow cytometry standard data file format; development of flow cytometric methods for the study of endocytosis, computational biology curriculum; rsch. in analysis of endosome acidification and lysosome biogenesis, pattern analysis applications to fluoresence microscope images. Home: 2537 Club House Dr Wexford PA 15090-7956 Office: Carnegie Mellon U 4400 5th Ave Pittsburgh PA 15213-2617 E-mail: murphy@cmu.edu.

MURPHY, ROBERT JAMES, language educator, consultant; b. Decatur, Ind., Aug. 31, 1941; s. James William and Catherine Agnes (Schumacker) Murphy; m. Linda L. Nolan, June 28, 1975; 1 child Christina Lyn. BS in Edn., Ball State U., 1963; MS in Edn., St. Francis U., 1967; postgrad., U. Denver, 1986, Ball State U., 1972. Cert. English, speech, drama and journalism tchr. Ind. Speech and drama tchr. Rochester (Ind.) H.S., 1976—78; chair dept. English Lawrenceburg (Ind.) H.S., 1978—81, Holy Family H.S., Denver, 1981—86; prin. Randall-Moore Sch., 1986—87; dir. edn. Mansfield Bus. Sch., 1987—89; prin. St. John the Bapt. Cath. Sch., Ft. Wayne, Ind., 1989—94; pres., founder Murphy Ednl. Consulting, 1995—, D/B/A Alternative Edn. Curriculum and The Learning Kaleidoscope, Pensacola, Fla., 1995—. Cons. Am. Printing House for Blind, Louisville, 1999—; cons., writer, spkr. homeschooling groups, 1995—. Author: All in One Big Book, 1998, The Pump Man, 1998; co-author: What Does My Student See?, 2000, author reading and writing curriculum. Bd. dirs. Ft. Wayne Pub. Transp. Co., 2000—, The League for Blind and Disabled, Ft. Wayne, 2000—; chmn. bd. dirs. The United Voice Coalition, 2002—. Avocations: gardening, hiking, swimming.

MURPHY, ROSEMARY, actress; b. Munich, Germany; came to U.S., 1939; d. Robert D. and Mildred (Taylor) M. Ed. in, Paris, France and Kansas City, Mo. Broadway appearances include Look Homeward Angel, 1958, Night of the Iguana, World premier at Spoleto (Italy) Festival of Two Worlds, 1959, Period of Adjustment, 1961, King Lear, 1963, Any Wednesday, 1964-66, Delicate Balance, 1966, Weekend, 1968, Butterflies are Free, 1970, Lady Macbeth, Stratford, Conn., 1973, Ladies of the Alamo, 1977, John Gabriel Borkman, 1980, Learned Ladies, 1982, Coastal Disturbances, 1987, The Devil's Disciple, 1988, A Delicate Balance, 1996, Waiting in the Wings, 1999; motion picture appearances include To Kill a Mockingbird, 1962, Any Wednesday, 1966, Ben, 1972, Walking Tall, 1972, You'll Like My Mother, 1972, Forty Carats, 1973, Julia, 1976, September, 1987, For the Boys, 1991, And The Band Played On, 1993, The Tuskegee Airmen, 1995, Message in a Bottle, 1998, Dust, 2001; TV appearance Eleanor and Franklin, 1975 (Emmy award for best supporting actress 1976), George Washington, 1983 (Tony award nominations 1961, 64, 67, award Motion Picture Arts Club 1966), E-Z Streets, 1996, The Unicorn's Secret, 1998, Frasier, 1997, 99. Recipient Variety Poll award, 1961, 67. Address: 220 E 73rd St New York NY 10021-4319

MURPHY, SANDRA ROBISON, lawyer; b. Detroit, July 28, 1949; m. Richard Robin. BA, Northwestern U., 1971; JD, Loyola U., Chgo., 1976. Bar: U.S. Dist. Ct. (no. dist.) Ill. 1976. Assoc. Notz, Craven, Mead, Maloney & Price, Chgo., 1976-78; ptnr. McDermott, Will & Emery, 1978—. Mem. ABA (family law sect.), Ill. Bar Assn. (chair sect. family law coun. 1987-88), Chgo. Bar Assn. (chair matrimonial law com. 1985-86), Am. Acad. Matrimonial Lawyers (sec. 1990-91, v.p. 1991-92, pres. Ill. chpt. 1992-93, pres.-elect 1994-95, pres. 1995-96), Legal Club Chgo.

MURPHY, SEAN PATRICK, lawyer; b. Rochester, N.Y., Aug. 22, 1963; s. Thomas Edward and Mary Patricia (Brasted) M.; m. Susan Marie Barnes, June 10, 1989; children, Katherine Anne, Caroline Grace. BS of Fgn. Svc., Georgetown U., 1985, JD, 1989. Bar: N.Y. 1989, D.C. 1991, Fla. 1995, Maryland, 1998, U.S. Ct. Fed. Claims 1991, U.S. Ct. Appeals (fed. cir.) 1991, U.S. Supreme Ct. 1995, U.S. Ct. Appeals (9th cir.) 1994, U.S. Ct. Appeals (11th cir.) 1995, U.S. Dist. Ct. (so., mid., no. dists.) Fla. 1995, U.S. Dist. (so. dist.) N.Y. 1991, U.S. Dist. Ct. (D.C. dist.) 1997, U.S. Ct. Appeals (D.C. cir.) 1997, U.S. Ct. Appeals (4th cir.) 1999. Assoc. Dewey Ballantine, N.Y.C., 1989-91; fed. trial atty. U.S. Dept. Justice, Washington, 1991-95; sr. assoc. Annis Mitchell, Tampa, Fla., 1995-97; of counsel Muldoon, Murphy & Faucette LLP, Washington, 1997-2000, Patton Boggs, LLP, Washington, 2000—; exec. v.p., gen. counsel HealthCare Fin. Ptnrs. REIT, Inc., 2001—; gen. coun., exec. v.p. Med. Office Properties, Inc., Chevy Chase, Md., 2001—. Instr. trial preparedness courses Fla. Bar, Miami, Ft. Lauderdale and Tampa,

1995-97. Bd. dirs., dir. athletic adv. bd. Georgetown U., Washington, 1989-99; mem. bd. trustees, v.p. Serra Club of Washington, 1991-99, John Carroll Soc., Washington, 1991—; vol. trial atty. Archdiocesan Pro Bono Legal Network, 1992-99. Recipient Cardinal's medal Archdiocesan Pro Bono Legal Network, 1998. Mem. Am. Inns of Ct. (barrister William Glen Terrell 1995-97), Univ. Club Washington, Potomac Boat Club. Roman Catholic. Office: Patton Boggs LLP 2550 M St NW Washington DC 20037 also: HealthCre Fin Ptnrs REIT Inc 1133 Connecticut Ave NW Washington DC 20036 E-mail: Smurphy@pattonboggs.com., smurphy@hcfpreit.com.

MURPHY, SHARON MARGARET, educator; b. Milw., Aug. 2, 1940; d. Adolph Leonard and Margaret Ann (Hirtz) Feyen; m. James Emmett Murphy, June 28, 1969 (dec. May 1983); children: Shannon Lynn, Erin Ann; m. Bradley B. Niemcek, Aug. 7, 1999. BA, Marquette U., 1965; MA, U. Iowa, 1970, PhD, 1973. Cert. K-14 tchr., Iowa. Tchr. elem. and secondary schs., Wis., 1959-69; dir. publs. Kirkwood C.C., Cedar Rapids, Iowa, 1969-71; instr. journalism U. Iowa, Iowa City, 1971-73; asst. prof. U. Wis., Milw., 1973-79; assoc. prof. So. Ill. U., Carbondale, 1979-84; dean, prof. Marquette U., Milw., 1984-94; prof. Bradley U., Peoria, Ill., 1994—, provost, v.p. acad. affairs, 1994-97, pres. Cmty. Career and Tech. Ctr., 1997-98. Pub. rels. dir., editor Worldwide mag., Milw., 1965—68; reporter Milw. Sentinel, 1967; Fulbright sr. lectr. U. Nigeria, Nsukka, 1977—78, U. Ljubljana, Slovenia, 2002. Author: Other Voices: Black, Chicano & American Indian Press, 1971; (with Wigal) Screen Experience: An Approach to Film, 1968; (with Murphy) Let My People Know: American Indian Journalism, 1981; (with Schilpp) Great Women of the Press, 1983; editor: (with others) International Perspectives on News, 1982. Mem. Peoria Riverfront Commn., 1995—2000; co-chair Peoria Race Rels. Com., 1999—2000; bd. dirs. Dirksen Congl. Leadership Ctr., 1994—2000, Dow Jones Newspaper Fund, NY, 1986—95, Peoria Symphony, 1996—2002. Recipient Medal of Merit, Journalism Edn. Assn., 1976, Amoco Award for Teaching Excellence, 1977, Outstanding Achievement award Greater Milw. YWCA, 1989; named Knight of Golden Quill, Milw. Press Club, 1977; Nat. headliner Women in Communication, Inc., 1985. Mem. Assn. Edn. in Journalism and Mass Comm. (pres. 1986-87), Soc. Profl. Journalists, Nat. Press Club. Democrat. Roman Catholic. Office: Bradley U Global Comm Ctr Peoria IL 61625-0001 E-mail: smm@bradley.edu.

MURPHY, SHAUN EDWARD, bank executive; b. London, June 3, 1961; came to U.S., 1962; s. John Joseph and Julie (Coyle) Murphy; m. Angela Mary Murphy, July 19, 1986; 1 child Liam John Patrick. BSBA, Villanova U., 1983; MSc, London Sch. Econs., 1984. Rating analyst Fireman's Fund Ins. Co., N.Y.C., 1978-83; corp. officer Marine Midland Bank, N.A., 1985-88; v.p., mgr. Nat. Bank Washington, 1988-89; sr. v.p., divsn. mgr. Riggs Nat. Bank, Washington, 1989-96; sr. v.p., sr. credit officer Allfirst Bank Md., Balt., 1996—. Chief credit officer Riggs AP Bank, London, 1991. Senate mem. U. London Convocation, 1984—; exec. Cath. Charities Washington, 1988—. Mem. Am. Friends of London Sch. Econs., Assn. Fin. Profls., Greater Washington Ceili Club (cir.), Wolf Trap Found. (corp. com.) Republican. Roman Catholic. Avocations: golf, scuba, cross-country track, traditional Irish music, marathons. Home: 415 Council Dr NE Vienna VA 22180-4740 Office: Allfirst Bank 25 S Charles St Baltimore MD 21201-3330 E-mail: shaun.murphy@allfirst.com.

MURPHY, STEPHAN DAVID, electrical engineer; b. Cin., July 12, 1948; s. James Martin and Oswalda (Magalli) M.; m. Nancy Elizabeth Benton, Apr. 20, 1979; children: Colleen B., Brian B. BSEE, Case Western Res. U., 1971. Design engr. Gould Ocean Systems, Cleve., 1971-74; project engr. Victoreen Inst. div. Sheller-Globe, 1974-78, TRW, Inc., Euclid, Ohio, 1978-85; engring. mgr. Textron, Inc., Danville, Pa., 1985-96; prin. staff mem. Concurrent Techs. Corp., West Chester, 1997—. Instr. Pa. State U., Malvern, Pa., 1999—. Author, editor: In-Process Measurement of Control, 1990; contbr. tech. articles to profl. publs. Community chmn. Cleve. unit Am. Heart Assn., 1984; coach Am. Youth Soccer Orgn., Danville, Pa., 1992, Danville Little League, 1992. Mem. AAAS, IEEE, Soc. Mfg. Engrs. (sr.). Republican. Presbyterian. Achievements include patent in area of non-contact gaging and ultrasonic defect detection, pioneering in development of non-contact gaging. E-mails. Office: Concurrent Techs Corp 211 Carter Dr West Chester PA 19382-4501 E-mail: murphys@ctc.com., smurphpa@mindspring.com.

MURPHY, S(USAN) (JANE MURPHY), small business owner; b. Williamsport, Pa., Dec. 26, 1950; d. Jack W. and Edythe J. (Grier) M.; m. Michael J. Sanchez, Dec. 30, 1979. BBA, Pa. State U., 1978. Gen. mgr. Murphy Swift Homes, Hummelstown, Pa., 1970-75; owner, operator Murphy's Home Ctr., 1975-79, 85-91; mgr. Builder's Emporium, San Diego, 1979-80; entrepreneur Castle in the Sand, 1980-83; adminstr. Sohio Constrn., Prudhoe Bay, Alaska, 1983-85; fin. systems analyst Blue Shield, San Francisco, 1991-93; pres. San Francisco Mgmt. Svcs., Inc., 1993-99; entrepreneur Blue Skies Inn and Island Place of Olde Key West, Key West, Fla., 1999—. Cons. in field; dealer Servistar Home Ctrs. Photographs displayed at San Diego Art Inst. Vol. Hershey (Pa.) Free Ch. Donald MacIntyre scholar, 1979, Class of 1920 scholar, 1979, Congressman Kunkel scholar, 1979. Mem. Pa. Hardware Assn., Hummelstown C. of C., Better Bus. Bur. Evangelical Christian. Avocations: sailing, scuba diving, photography. Office: Blue Skies Inn 630 South St Key West FL 33045 E-mail: kwproperties@yahoo.com.

MURPHY, TERENCE MARTIN, biology educator; b. Seattle, July 1, 1942; s. Norman Walter and Dorothy Louise (Smith) M.; m Judith Baron, July 12, 1969; 1 child, Shannon Elaine. BS, Calif. Inst. Tech., 1964; PhD, U. Calif. San Diego, La Jolla, 1968. Sr. fellow dept. biochemistry U. Wash., Seattle, 1969-70; asst. prof. botany U. Calif., Davis, 1971-76, assoc. prof., 1976-82, prof. plant biology, 1982—, chmn. dept. botany, 1986-90. Author: Plant Molecular Development, 1988; co-author: Plant Biology, 1998; N.Am. exec. editor, N.Am. office, Physiologia Plantarum, 1988-98; contbr. articles to profl. jours. Mem. AAAS, Am. Soc. Plant Biologists, Am. Soc. Photobiology, Scandinavian Soc. Plant Physiology. Home: 725 N Campus Way Davis CA 95616-3518 Office: U Calif Sect Plant Biology Davis CA 95616 E-mail: tmmurphy@ucdavis.edu.

MURPHY, TERENCE ROCHE, lawyer; b. Oct. 20, 1937; s. M. Leonard and Alice Lenore (Roche) Murphy; m. Suzanne Kathryn Dupré, Oct. 14, 1967 (div. Apr. 1980); children: Braden Mathias, Fiona Elizabeth Dupré; m. Patricia Ann Sherman, May 21, 1983. AB, Harvard Coll., 1959; JD with distinction, U. Mich., 1966. Bar: D.C. 1967, U.S. Supreme Ct. 1971. Trial atty. Dept. Justice, Washington, 1966-68; assoc. Wald, Harkrader & Ross, 1968-72, ptnr., 1972-83, McDermott, Will & Emery, Washington, 1983-84, Adams, Duque & Hazeltine, Washington, 1984-86; founding ptnr. Murphy Ellis Weber and predecessors, 1986—. Bd. dirs. Am. Assn. Exporters and Importers; founding chmn. Brit.-Am. Bus. Coun., 1989-90, legal counsel, 1993-96; officer, bd. dirs. Industry Coalition of Tech. Transfer; lectr. North and South Am., Europe and Mediterranean on internat. and bus. law and on strategic trade; chmn. and lectr. ann. Globalization of Export Controls Conf., London; bd. advisors The European Inst., 1993—; advisor on munitions export policy, Ctr. for Strategic and Internat. Studies, 2000—, advisor on export regulation, U.S. Dept. Commerce, 2001—. Author, lectr. on internat. trade, antitrust and administrv. law.; co-editor: Coping With U.S. Export Controls, ann. edits., 1986, 87, 88; contbr. articles to European and Am. legal publs. Mem. com. visitors U. Mich. Law Sch., 1975—; trustee Lawyer's Com. for Civil Rights Under Law, 1975-89. Lt. USN, 1959-63. Decorated U.S. Navy Commendation, Cuban Missile Crisis, 1962, Hon. Officer, Order Brit. Empire, 1993; fellow Royal Soc. of Arts. Mem. ABA (coun. adminstrv. law sect. 1980-83, co-chmn. com. on internat. and comparative adminstrv. law 1994-97), Am. Law Inst., Internat. Bar Assn. (sec. antitrust and monopolies com. 1981-83), Am. Soc. Internat. law, Brit.-Am. Bus. Assn. (Washington, founding dir. 1987—, chmn. 1989-92, legal adv. 1992-95), Royal Inst. Internat. Affairs (London), Am. Coun. on Germany, Met. Club (Washington), Harvard Club (N.Y.C.), Miscowaubik Club (Calumet, Mich.). Home: 4425 Boxwood Rd Bethesda MD 20816-1817 Office: Murphy Ellis Weber 818 Connecticut Ave NW Washington DC 20006-2702 E-mail: tmurphy@murphyellisweber.com.

MURPHY, THOMAS BAILEY, state legislator; b. Bremen, Ga., Mar. 10, 1924; s. W.H. and Leita (Jones) M.; m. Agnes Bennett, July 22, 1946; children: Michael L., Martha L., Marjorie Lynn, Mary June. Grad., North Ga. Coll., 1943; LLB, U. Ga., 1949. Bar: Ga. 1949. Ptnr. Murphy & Murphy, Bremen, 1949—; mem. Ga. Ho. of Reps., Atlanta, 1961—, adminstrv. floor leader for gov., 1969-70, spkr. pro tem, 1971-74, spkr., 1974—. Mem. Ga. Bar Assn., Am. Legion, VFW, Ga. Peace Officers Assn. (hon. life), Ga. Fraternal Order Police (hon.), Ga. Sheriffs Assn., Moose, Gridiron. Clubs: Moose. Democrat. Baptist. Office: Ho of Reps State Capitol SW Rm 332 Atlanta GA 30334-1160

MURPHY, THOMAS J., JR. mayor; m. Mona McMahon. BS in Biology and Chemistry, John Carroll U., 1967; MS in Urban Affairs/Planning summa cum laude, Hunter Coll., 1973. Vol. Peace Corps., Paraguay, 1970-72; exec. dir. Perry Hilltop Citizen's Coun., 1973-76; chem. sales rep. Alcoa, 1967-70; exec. dir. North Side Civic Devel. Coun., 1976-78; state rep. 20th Legis. Dist., 1979-94; mayor City of Pitts., 1994—. Democrat. Office: Office of the Mayor 414 Grant St Pittsburgh PA 15219-2409

MURPHY, THOMAS JAMES, physicist, educator; b. Bklyn., Feb. 17, 1942; s. Peter Ignatius Murphy and Mary Elizabeth Buckley; m. Marie Angela Corigliano, June 30, 1968; children: Rosa Nina, Elizabeth Clara. BS, Fordham U., 1963; PhD, Rockefeller U., 1968. Rsch. staff physicist Yale U., New Haven, 1968—69; asst. prof. U. Md., College Park, 1969—75, assoc. prof., 1975—. Mem. study sect. NIH, 1991. Contbr. articles to profl. jours. Fellow, NSF, 1963; grantee petroleum rsch. fund, Am. Chem. Soc., 1970. Mem.: Phi Beta Kappa (v.p. Gamma of Md. 1989—91, pres. Gamma of Md. 1991—93). Achievements include derived Onsager theory of ionic conductivity from first principles; extended Einstein diffusion relation to the N-particle case; established maximum number of collisions among three identical hard spheres in infinite space. Avocation: sailboat racing. Home: 6714 McDonough Terr Bowie MD 20720 Office: Univ Md Dept Chemistry College Park MD 20742

MURPHY, THOMAS JOHN, publishing executive; b. Lockport, N.Y., Mar. 29, 1931; s. Matthew J. and Mary Frances (Tracy) M.; m. Maryanne Elizabeth Stadnicki, Dec. 29, 1956; children: Kevin, Janine, Peter, Thomas. BS, SUNY-Brockport, 1952; postgrad., Boston U., 1955-57, Northwestern U., 1976. Sales rep., asst. dir. advt., mgr. sales services, dir. tng., asst. dir. mktg., dir. mktg. McGraw-Hill Co., St. Louis, N.Y.C., 1954-73; v.p., gen. mgr. sch. dept. Holt, Rinehart & Winston pub. CBS, Inc., N.Y.C., 1973-78; sr. v.p. CBS Sch. Pub., 1978-80, pres., 1980-82; v.p. AICPA, 1982-88; ptnr. Profl. Pub. Svcs. Co., Westport, Conn., 1988—; pres. World Book Pubs., 1991. Contbr. articles to profl. jours. Bd. dirs. Brockport Found., 1977-83, Rec. for Blind, 1980-89, Inter-Faith Housing Assn., 1991-94; mem. social concerns com. Ch. of Assumption, Westport, 2000—. Named to Heritage Hall of Fame, SUNY. Democrat. Roman Catholic. Home and Office: 4 Ivanhoe Ln Westport CT 06880-5038

MURPHY, THOMAS MICHAEL, civil engineer; b. Hubbard, Ohio, Mar. 26, 1963; s. Michael F. Jr. and Gratia Marie (Henry) M.; m. Regina Marie Quinn, Mar. 28, 1992; 1 child, Caitlin Marie. BS, Youngstown State U., 1988. Cert. asst. team leader N.Y.C. Dept. Transp., N.Y. State Dept. Transp., N.Y. State Thruway Authority. Structural engr. Marsico & Assocs., Youngstown, Ohio, 1987; constrn. inspector Adlaka & Assocs., Boardman, 1987, Marsico & Assocs., Youngstown, 1987; structural engr. Hardesty & Hanover, N.Y.C., 1988-94, A&H Engrs., N.Y.C., 1994, Ammann & Whitney, N.Y.C., 1995-96, M.S. Cons., Youngstown, 1996; quality assurance/quality control engr. Star Aluminum Extrusions, Canfield, Ohio, 1997-99; civil engr. PSI Inc., Pitts., 1999-2000, Youngstown, Ohio, 2000—01, ACA Engring., 2001—. Mem. ASCE (affiliate mem. N.Y. met. chpt. and Youngstown State U. chpt.) Am. Soc. Cert. Engring. Technicians (mem., sec.-tres. Youngstown State U. Steel Valley chpt. 1985-86), KC (3d and 4th degree). Democrat. Roman Catholic. Avocations: photography, new technology in bridge design and construction. Home: 210 Christian Ave Hubbard OH 44425-2010 Office: ACA Bldg 10B 590 Western Reserve Rd Poland OH 44514

MURPHY, THOMAS MILES, pediatrician, educator; b. Sioux City, Iowa, Dec. 5, 1945; s. Charles Thomas and Madeline Elizabeth (McGovern) M.; m. Priscilla Rollin Coit, Oct. 4, 1969; 1 child, Nicholas Charles. AB in Math., Harvard Coll., 1969; MD, U. Rochester, 1973. Diplomate Am. Bd. Med. Examiners, Am. Bd. Internal Medicine, Am. Bd. Pediatrics, subbd. pulmonology; lic. physician, N.C. Intern Georgetown U. Med. Divsn., D.C. Gen. Hosp., Washington, 1973-74; resident in internal medicine Georgetown U. Med. Ctr., 1974-76, fellow pediat. pulmonary medicine, 1976-78; asst. prof. pediat. Georgetown U. Sch. Medicine, 1979-80, asst. prof. clin. pediat., 1980-85, U. Chgo., 1985-87, asst. prof. pediat. and medicine, 1990-93; asst. prof. pediat. U. Chgo. Pritzker Sch. Medicine, 1987-90, chief sect. pulmonary medicine dept. pediat., 1992-93; assoc. prof., chief divsn. pediat. pulmonary diseases Duke U., Durham, N.C., 1993—. Assoc. dir. Pediatric Pulmonary and Cystic Fibrosis Ctr., Georgetown U., 1978-80; asst. prof. child health and devel. George Washington U. Sch. Medicine and Health Scis., Washington, 1980-85; assoc. chmn. dept. pulmonary medicine, co-dir. Cystic Fibrosis Ctr. for Care, Teaching and Rsch., Children's Hosp. Nat. Med. Ctr., Washington, 1980-85; dir. pediatric pulmonary fellowship tng. program U. Chgo., 1990-93, dir. Cystic Fibrosis Ctr., 1991-93, assoc. chief sect. allergy, immunology and pulmonology, dept. pediatrics, 1991-92; editor ATS Pediat. Assembly Website, 2000—. Contbr. articles to profl. jours., chpts. to books; cons. referee editor New Eng. Jour. Medicine, 1989, Am. Rev. Respiratory Disease, 1989—, Am. Jour. Physiology: Lung Cellular and Molecular Physiology, 1990—, Pediatric Rsch., 1991—, Jour. Applied Physiology, 1991—, Pediat. Pulmonology, 1993—, mem. editl. bd., 1996—; contbg. editor The Hudson Monitor. Mem. ctr. com. Cystic Fibrosis Found., 1992-97, 2000-2002; chmn. childhood lung disease com. D.C. Lung Assn., 1980-83, lung disease com., 1984; mem. adv. coun. D.C. Sudden Infant Death Syndrome, 1981-83, chmn. med. adv. com., 1982-83. Recipient Cmty. Svc. award So. Md. Lung Assn., 1980, Media award Am. Acad. Pediatrics, 1980, Svc. award homicide br. Met. Police Dept. D.C., 1983, Svc. award Met. D.C. chpt. Cystic Fibrosis Foun., Washington, 1985, Nat. Cystic Fibrosis Found., 1997; Rsch. grantee Am. Lung Assn., N.Y.C., 1992, NIH, Bethesda, Md., 1993, 98. Mem.: AAAS, European Respiratory Soc., Am. Thoracic Soc. (program com. assembly on respiratory structure and function 1993—96, chair long range planning com. 2000—02, chair subcom. on physician scientists, pediat. assembly 1997—, liaison officer pediat. assembly 2000—), N.Y. Acad. Scis., Am. Physiol. Soc., Soc. Pediatric Rsch. Avocations: refereeing soccer, jazz. Office: Duke U Med Ctr PO Box 2994 Durham NC 27710-2994

MURPHY, THOMAS PATRICK, lawyer; b. Syracuse, N.Y., Feb. 12, 1952; s. George Edward and Sara Eileen (Murphy) M.; m. Susan Hollis Francher, Oct. 19, 1976 (div. Oct. 1992); m. Lise M. Adkins, Aug. 6, 1994; children: Casey Marie, Matthew Thomas. BS, Clarkson U., 1974; JD, Vermont Law Sch., 1978. Bar: N.Y. 1978, D.C. 1981, Md. 1988, Va. 1989. Asst. U.S. atty. U.S. Atty.'s Office, Washington, 1982-85; assoc. Highsaw & Mahoney, 1985-87, McGuire, Woods, Battle & Boothe, Washington, 1987-90; ptnr. Reed Smith Shaw & McClay, McLean, Va., 1990-99, Hunton & Williams, McLean, 1999—. Contbr. articles to profl. jours. Chmn. bd. profl. responsibility D.C. Ct. Appeals. With USN, 1978-82, USNR, 1978-90. Recipient Spl. Achievement Award U.S. Dept. Justice, 1984; named one of Best Lawyers in Am. for employment law. Mem. ABA, Fed. Bar Assn., N.Y. State Bar Assn., D.C. Bar Assn. (chmn. pro se litigants com.), Md. Bar Assn., Asst. U.S. Attys., Bd. Profl. Responsibility D.C. Ct. Appeals (hearing com.). Office: Hunton & Williams 1751 Pinnacle Dr Ste 1700 Mc Lean VA 22102-3836

MURPHY, TIMOTHY JAMES, lawyer; b. Topeka, Sept. 30, 1946; s. Miles J. and Norine D. Murphy; m. Patricia MacKinnon, Apr. 7, 1990. BA, U. Ga., 1968; JD, Washington & Lee U., 1970; LLM, Harvard U., 1976. Bar: Va. 1970, Fla. 1972. Atty. Shutts & Bowen, Miami, Fla., 1976—. Mem. Fla. Ho. of Reps., 1982-84; bd. dirs. Cath. Charities, Inc., 1982-97, Cath. Charities Legal Svcs., Inc., Miami, 2000-02; mem. adv. bd. Miami-Dade County Pub. Libr., 1988-2002. Col. JAG Corps USAFR, 1970-95. Mem.: Biscayne Bay Yacht Club, Army and Navy Club (Washington). Democrat. Roman Catholic. Office: Shutts & Bowen 201 S Biscayne Blvd Ste 1500 Miami FL 33131-4308

MURPHY, VIVYAN PATRICIA, engineer; b. Birmingham, Ala., Oct. 25, 1948; d. William W. and Ellamai V. (Grizzard) M.; m. Ollie D. Kennedy, June 26, 1965 (div. Mar. 1976). B.S. in Engring., Auburn U., 1965, M.B.A., 1968. Environ. engr. J.B. Converse, Mobile, Ala., 1970-73; dist. rep. Nalco Chem., Mobile, 1973-77; foreman-in-tng. pulp and paper mill Container Corp. Am., Fernandina Beach, Fla., 1977-79, foreman pulp mill, 1979-82, asst. supt. power dept., 1982-84; group leader utilities Internat. Paper Co., Mansfield, La., 1984— . Editor: Auburn Engr., 1964-65. Drug abuse vol. United Way, 1966-82; leader candystripers Hosp. Aux., Opelika, Ala., and Fernandina Beach, 1978-81; membership chair Young Democrats, Fernandina Beach, 1980-82. Mem. Am. Inst. Aerospace and Aero. Engrs. (pres. 1963-64; Outstanding Engr. 1965), Nat. Assn. Female Execs., NOW, Soc. Am. Mgrs., Am. Bus. Women's Assn. (v.p. 1981-82; award 1981), AAUW, Pi Beta Phi, Tau Beta Phi. Democrat. Baptist. Avocations: painting; aerobics; tennis. Home: 3120 17th St Eureka CA 95501-1504 Office: PO Box PO Box 999 Mansfield LA 71052-0999

MURPHY, WILLIAM ALEXANDER, JR. diagnostic radiologist, educator; b. Pitts., Apr. 26, 1945; s. William Alexander and LaRue (Eshbaugh); m. Judy Marie Lang, June 18, 1977; children: Abigail Norris, William Lawrence, Joseph Ryan. BS, U. Pitts., 1967; MD, Pa. State U., 1971. Diplomate Am. Bd. Radiology. Intern Barnes Hosp., St. Louis, 1971-72, staff radiologist, 1975-93; radiology resident Washington U., 1972-75, prof. radiology, 1983-93; sec. chief Mallinckrodt Inst. Radiology, St. Louis, 1975-93; cons. Office Med. Examiner City and County St. Louis, 1993—. Radiologist, prof. radiology, John S. Dunn Sr. prof., disting. chair MD Anderson Cancer Ctr. U. Tex., 1993—, v.p. hosp. and clinics, 1996-97, COO, 1997. Fellow Am. Acad. Forensic Scis., Am. Coll. Radiology; mem. Radiol. Soc. N.Am. (1st. v.p. 1997-98), Am. Roentgen Ray Soc., Am. Soc. Bone and Mineral Rsch., Internat. Skeletal Soc., Assn. Univ. Radiologists. Methodist. Home: 4808 Bellview St Bellaire TX 77401-5306 Office: U Texas Anderson Cancer Ctr Div Dx Imaging 057 1515 Holcombe Blvd Houston TX 77030-4009 E-mail: wmurphy@di.mdacc.tmc.edu.

MURPHY, WILLIAM M. pathologist, educator, consultant; b. Des Moines, Oct. 5, 1942; s. William and Mary D. Murphy; m. Barbara K. Murphy; children: Jamar, Shawn. BA, Drake U., 1963; MD, Harvard Med. Sch., 1967. Intern Med. Coll. Va. (now Va. Commonwealth U.), Richmond, Va., 1967-68; resident Case Western Res. U., Cleve., 1968-71; from asst. to assoc. prof. U. Tenn. Med. Ctr., Memphis, 1974-80, prof., 1980-92; prof., dir. anatomic pathology Tulane U. Med. Ctr., New Orleans, 1993; prof. anatomic pathology U. Fla. Med. Ctr., Gainesville, 1994—. Author, editor: Urologic Pathology, 1989, 2d edit., 1997, AFIP Fascicle on Tumors of Kidney and Bladder, 1994; author: Bladder Carcinoma, 1986, Urinary Cytopathology, 2000. Lt. comdr. USN, 1964-77. Recipient Papanicolaou award 1998. Fellow Coll. Am. Pathologists (alternate del. 1979); mem. AMA (Physician Recognition award 1974—), Am. Soc. Clin. Pathology (anatomic pathology coun. 1990-96), Am. Soc. Cytopathology (pres. 1992-93, Cert. of Merit 1993). Avocations: golf, history. Office: CAD 2400 Sand Lake Rd Orlando FL 32809

MURPHY, WILLIAM MICHAEL, literature educator, biographer; b. N.Y.C., Aug. 6, 1916; s. Timothy Francis and Florence Catherine (McDonald) M.; m. E. Harriet Doane, Sept. 2, 1939; children: David Timothy Michael, Susan Doane, Christopher Ten Broeck. BA magna cum laude, Harvard U., 1938, MA, 1941, PhD, 1947. Instr. English Harvard U., 1938-40, 42-43, sec. univ. com. ednl. relations, 1940-42; asst. prof. English Union Coll., Schenectady, 1946-48, assoc. prof., 1948-60, prof., 1960-78, Thomas Lamont prof. ancient and modern lit., 1978-83, rsch. prof., 1983-94, prof. emeritus, 1995—. Mem. adv. bd. Cornell Yeats Series, Ithaca, N.Y., 1978—; resident fellow Rockefeller Found. Study and Conf. Ctr., Bellagio, Italy, 1991. Author: David Worcester (1907-1947): A Memorial, 1953, The Yeats Family and the Pollexfens of Sligo, 1971, Prodigal Father: The Life of John Butler Yeats (1839-1922), 1978, 2nd edit., Family Secrets: William Butler Yeats and His Relatives, 1995. Mem. N.Y. State com. U.S. Commn. on Civil Rights, 1962-74. Served to lt. USNR, 1943-46. Recipient Meritorious Service award United Negro Coll. Fund, 1967; fellow Am. Council Learned Soc., 1968; grantee Am. Philos. Soc., 1968, 75 Mem. MLA, AAUP, Am. Com. on Irish Studies, Can. Assn. Irish Studies, N.S. Bird Soc., Phi Beta Kappa (pres. Alpha chpt. 1954-56) Clubs: Harvard of Eastern N.Y. (pres. 1960-62); Fortnightly (Schenectady) (pres. 1966-67). Home: Reubens Hill Shag Harbor NS Canada Office: Union Coll English Dept Humanities Bldg Schenectady NY 12308

MURPHY, WILLIAM PATRICK, lawyer, editor, writer; b. Scranton, Pa., Feb. 17, 1952; s. William James and Mildred Mary (Ferguson) M. AB, U. Scranton, 1973; JD, U. Pa., 1976. Jud. law clk. U.S. Dist. Ct. (ea. dist.) Pa., U.S. Ct. Appeals (3rd cir.); Pa. Supreme Ct., Phila., Erie, 1976-79; from asst. to assoc. prof. law St. John's U., Queens, N.Y., 1979-81, 83; atty. Beasley, Casey, Colleran, Erbstein, Thistle, Kline & Murphy, Phila., 1982, 84-89; pvt. practice, 1989-94; legal editor Pa. Law Weekly, 1994-95, editor-in-chief, 1995-96; legal editor Pa. Dist. & County Reports, 1994-96; pvt. practice, 1996—. Instr. Temple U., Phila., 1987-88; mem. faculty continuing legal edn. Pa. Bar Inst., Harrisburg, 1989—. Author: White Dogs, 1996, columnist, 1999—. U. Pa. scholar, 1977. Mem. Pa. Bar Assn. Roman Catholic. Avocations: running, wolves. Office: Two Penn Ctr Plz Ste 200 Philadelphia PA 19102

MURPHY COLUCCI, MARION, writer, poet; b. Queens, N.Y., Mar. 6, 1940; s. Frank and Ida (Giotta) Colucci; children: Carrie, Maureen, Raygen, Erin. Writer. Free-lance profl. painter, N.Y., 1950's-80's; freelance costume mask designer, N.Y., 1969-78 Writer numerous poems; lyric recs. Petunia Revival, D.O.A. Dog, 1998, Fun Baby, Up Shoes, 1999. Mem. Internat. Soc. Poets, Songwriters Guild Am., Internat. Poetry Hall Fame. Avocations: solitude, music, innovating, walking and loving God's creations.

MURPHY-DANIELS, KAREN ILENE, environmental, safety and health professional; b. Oak Ridge, Tenn., May 20, 1955; d. Charles Everett and Charlotte Wilson Murphy; m. Richard C. Daniels, Dec. 5, 1997. BS in Transp. and Mktg., U. Tenn, 1977; MS in Occupl. Safety & Health, U. Tenn., 1982. Assoc. safety profl. BSCP, REM & CEA Nat. Registry Environ. Profls., CHMM Inst. Hazardous Material Mgmt., ISO 14001 environ. mgmt. systems provisional auditor, cert. AHERA asbestos bldg. inspector, fall protection component person. Project mgr. comml. market Analysas Corp./DPRA, Oak Ridge, 1988—96; owner, mgmt. cons. SAFE Systems, Seattle, 1996—97; corp. gen. analyst Boeing, 1997—. Vol. cons. Wash. Dept. Ecology, Lacey, 1997. Mem.: Am. Soc. Quality, Am. Indsl. Hygiene Assn., Am. Soc. Safety Engrs. (treas., sec. East Tenn. chpt. 1988—90). Democrat. Methodist. Avocations: kayaking, snowshoeing, horse training, dog training. Home: 1976 McDonald Ave Dupont WA 98327 Office: Boeing P.O. Box 3707 MC 46-89 Seattle WA Home Fax: 253-912-8320; Office Fax: 206-544-2854. Business E-Mail: karen.i.murphy-daniels@boeing.com.

MURPHY-LIND, KAREN MARIE, health educator, dermatology nurse; b. Boston, Oct. 7, 1953; d. William Joseph and Mary Catherine (Mulcahy) Murphy; m. Gary W. Lind, Feb. 28, 1976; 1 child, Nicholas. RN, AS, Laboure Coll., Dorchester, Mass., 1993. Health edn./cmty. outreach coord. Mass. Gen. Hosp., Charlestown Health Care Ctr., 1993-96, dermatology nurse, 1993—, Dept. Pub. Health breast cancer initiative outreach worker, 1992-96, advisor cmty. adv. bd., 1992—, substance abuse initiative dir. cmty. health, 1996—. Mem. Health Charlestown Coalition, 1993—; bd. dirs. Am. Cancer Soc. Cen. Boston Breast, 1995-96, co-chair cancer control core team, 1995-96. Recipient Lifesaver pub. edn. award Am. Cancer Soc., Metro North, Mass., 1994, Make A Difference award, 1995. Mem. Am. Cancer Soc. (Ctrl. Boston bd. dirs. 1995-96, co-chair Boston breast cancer control team 1995-96), Mass. Nurses Assn., Dermatology Nurses Assn., Soc. Pub. Health Edn. Home: 387 Central Ave Milton MA 02186-2803 Office: MGH Bunker Hill Health Ctr 73 High St Charlestown MA 02129-3037

MURR, JAMES COLEMAN, retired federal government official; b. Lake Charles, La., Oct. 29, 1944; m. Connie Paige Chadwell, Sept. 21, 1968; children: Christopher David, Richard Reno. BA, Tex. Tech U., 1966; MPA, Am. U., 1974. With Sears, Roebuck & Co., Tex., 1971-72, Dept. Labor, Washington, 1972-74, U.S. Customs Svc., Treasury, Washington, 1975-76; legis. analyst Office Mgmt. and Budget, 1977-81, br. chief, 1982-89, assoc. dir. adminstrn., 1990-93, asst. dir. legis. reference, 1994-98. Capt. USAF, 1967-70. Roman Catholic. E-mail: jcmurr@ktc.com.

MURRAY, ALBERT LEE, writer, educator; b. Nokomis, Ala., May 12, 1916; s. John Lee and Sudie (Graham) Young; m. Mozelle Menefee, May 31, 1941; 1 child, Michele. BS in Edn., Tuskegee Inst., 1939; MA in English, NYU, 1948; postgrad., U. Mich., 1940, Northwestern U., 1941, U. Paris, 1950; LittD (hon.), Colgate U., 1975, Tuskegee U., 1999, SUNY, Stony Brook, 2000. Tchr. undergrad. composition and lit. Tuskegee Inst., 1940-43, 46-51, also dir. Coll. Little Theatre, cons. on jazz; lectr. Grad. Sch. Journalism, Columbia U., N.Y.C., 1968; O'Connor prof. lit. Colgate U., 1970, O'Connor lectr., 1973, prof. humanities, 1982; vis. prof. lit. U. Mass., Boston, 1971; Paul Anthony Brick lectr. U. Mo., 1972; writer-in-residence Emory U., 1978; adj. assoc. prof. creative writing Barnard Coll., N.Y.C., 1981-83; lectr., participant symposia in field. DuPont vis. scholar Washington and Lee U., 1993. Author: The Omni Americans, 1970, South to a Very Old Place, 1972, The Hero and the Blues, 1973, Train Whistle Guitar, 1974 (Lillian Smith award for fiction), Stomping the Blues, 1976 (ASCAP Deems Taylor award for music criticism), Good Morning Blues: The Autobiography of Count Basie as told to Albert Murray, 1985, The Spyglass Tree, 1991, The Seven League Boots, 1996, The Blue Devils of Nada, 1996, From the Briarpatch File, 2001, (poems) Conjugations and Reiterations, 2001; also numerous articles. Served to maj. USAAF, World War II; ret. USAAF. Woodrow Wilson fellow Drew U., 1983; recipient Lincoln Ctr. Dirs. Emeriti award, 1991, Nat. Book Critic's Cir. Lifetime Achievement award, 1996, Doctor of Humane Letters Spring Hill Coll., 1996, Doctor Letters Hamilton Coll., 1997, Harper Lee award Ala. Writer's Forum, 1998, Clarence Cason award for non-fiction U. Ala., 2001. Mem. Am. Acad. Arts and Letters, Am. Acad. Arts ans Scis.

MURRAY, ALICE PEARL, data processing company executive; b. Clearfield, Pa., Aug. 4, 1932; d. James Clifford and Leah Mae (Williams) M.; BS, Pa. State U., 1954. With IBM, 1954—, systems svc. rep., Pitts., 1954-56, computer test ctr. rep., Endicott, N.Y., 1956-58, edn. devel. coord., Endicott, 1958-59, adv. instr., L.A., 1959-63, staff instr., L.a., 1963-68, exec. edn. coord., 1968-74, sr. instr. Info. Systems Mgmt. Inst., L.A., 1974-84, sr. edn. rep. IBM Americas Far East Corp., 1984-87; sr. staff mem. customer exec. edn., 1989; cons., 1990-95; ind. cons., 1995—; coord. exhibit Calif. State Mus. Sci. and Industry; guest speaker before civic and profl. groups; guest instr. various univs. and colls.; profl. lectr. Recipient Distinguished Educator award IBM, 1974, also Outstanding Professionalism award, 1975; hon. citizen Tex., Alaska. Mem. Los Angeles County Art Mus., Pa. State Alumni Assn., Wilshire Country Club, Assistance League of So. Calif., L.A. Libr. Found., Delta Delta Delta. Republican. Home and Office: 514 S Gramercy Pl Los Angeles CA 90020-4969

MURRAY, ALLEN EDWARD, deceased oil company executive; b. N.Y.C., Mar. 5, 1929; s. Allen and Carla (Jones) M.; m. Patricia Ryan, July 28, 1951; children: Allen, Marilyn, Ellen, Eileen, Allison. BS in Bus. Adminstrn, NYU, 1956. Trainee Pub. Nat. Bank & Trust Co., N.Y.C., 1948-49; acct. Gulf Oil Corp., 1949-52; various fin. positions Socony-Vacuum Overseas Supply Co. (Mobil), 1952-56; with Mobil Oil Corp. (subs. Mobil Corp.), 1956-94, v.p. planning N.Am. div., 1968-69, v.p. planning, supply and transp. N.Am. div., 1969-74, exec. v.p. N.Am. div., 1974, pres. U.S. mktg. and refining div., exec. v.p., 1975-82, pres. worldwide mktg. and refining, 1979-82, corp. pres., 1983-84, COO, 1984-86, CEO, COO, chmn. exec. com., 1986—2002, chmn. bd., 1986—2002, also dir., 1976—2002; pres., chief operating officer Mobil Corp., N.Y.C., 1984-86, chmn., pres., chief exec. officer, 1986—2002, dir., 1977—2002, Met. Life Ins. Co., 3M Co., Morgan Stanley Dean Witter & Co., St. Francis Hosp. Found. Trustee NYU. Served with USNR, 1946-48. Mem. Am. Petroleum Inst. (hon. dir.), Coun. Fgn. Rels., Bus. Coun. Clubs: Huntington Country. Died Aug. 11, 2002.

MURRAY, ANDY, professional hockey coach; Coach Phila. Flyers, 1988-90, Minn. North Stars, 1990-92, Winnipeg Jets, 1993-95; head coach Can. Nat. Team, 1996-98, L.A. Kings, 1999—. Office: Staples Ctr 111 S Figueroa St Los Angeles CA 90012-2465*

MURRAY, ANNE, singer; b. Springhill, N.S., Can., June 20, 1945; d. Carson and Marion (Burke) M.; m. William M. Langstroth, June 20, 1975; children: William Stewart, Dawn Joanne. B.Phys. Edn., U. N.B., 1966, D.Litt. (hon.), 1978, St. Mary's U., 1982. Rec. artist for Arc Records, Canada, 1968, Capital/EMI Records, 1969—. Appeared on series of TV spls. CBC, 1970—81, 1988—93; star CBS spls., 1981—85; toured N. Am., Japan, Englan, Germany, Holland, Ireland, Sweden, Australia and New Zealand, 1977—82. Singer: (31 albums including) A Little Good News, 1984, (albums) As I Am, 1988, Greatest Hits, vol. I, 1981, vol. II, 1989, Harmony, 1987, You Will, 1990, Yes I Do, 1991, Croonin', 1993, The Best So Far, 1994, Now and Forever, Anne Murray, 1996, An Intimate Evening with Anne Murray-Live, 1997, What A Wonderful World, 1999, What A Wonderful Christmas, 2001. Hon. chmn. Can. Save the Children Fund, 1978-80. Recipient Juno awards as Can.'s top female vocalist, 1970-81; Can.'s Top Country Female Vocalist, 1970-86; Grammy award as top female vocalist-country, 1974; Grammy award as top female vocalist-pop, 1978; Grammy award as top female vocalist-country, 1980, 83; Country Music Assn. awards, 1983-84; named Female Rec. Artist of Decade, Can. Rec. Industry Assn., 1980, Top Female Vocalist 1970-86; star inserted in Hollywood Walkway of Stars, 1980; Country Music Hall of Fame Nashville; decorated companion Order of Can.; inducted Juno Hall of Fame, 1993. Mem. AFTRA, Assn. Canadian TV and Radio Artists, Am. Fedn. Musicians. Office: Bruce Allen Talent 406-68 Water St Vancouver BC Canada V6B 1A4 also: EMI Music Distbn 21700 Oxnard St Ste 700 Woodland Hills CA 91367-3617

MURRAY, ARTHUR JOSEPH, engineering executive, speaker; b. Portsmouth, Va., Jan. 12, 1954; s. Arthur Patrick and Regina Agneta (Lescavage) M.; m. Deborah Marie Moyer, Sept. 6, 1975; children: Arthur III, Andrew. BSEE, Lehigh U., 1975; MEA, George Washington U., 1982, DSc, 1989. Electronics engr. USN Ordnance Sta., Indian Head, Md., 1975-81; rsch. engr. Inst. for Artificial Intelligence, Washington, 1985-87; sr. tech. staff The Titan Corp., Vienna, 1982-89; professorial lectr. Sch. Engring. and Applied Sci., The George Washington U., Washington, 1985—2001; mgr. advanced technology McDonnell Douglas Electronic Sys. Co., McLean, Va., 1989-91; sr. tech. cons. Gemini Industries, Inc., Vienna, 1991-93; CEO Telart Techs., Boyce, 1993—; mng. dir. Inst. for Knowledge Mgmt. The George Washington U., 2001—. Conf. com. Artificial Intelligence Sys. in Govt. Conf., Washington, 1986, 90, Am. Soc. Info. Sci., Atlanta, 1988; referee Interfaces, 1993—; founder, bd. dirs. BCN Group, Inc. Mem. editl. bd. Knowledge and Innovation, 2000—. Named First Titan fellow Titan Sys., Inc., 1985. Mem. Am. Assn. for Artificial Intelligence, Am. Soc. for Performance Improvement (bd. dirs. 1978-79), Russian Am. Chamber of Commerce, Lambda Chi Alpha. Mem. Constitution Party. Roman Catholic. Roman Catholic. Achievements include development of a knowledge management system for global virtual enterprises. Home: 652 Solitude Ln Boyce VA 22620-3136 Office: 652 Solitude Ln Boyce VA 22620-3136

MURRAY, BARBARA OLIVIA, writer, retired psychologist; b. Summit, N.J., July 8, 1947; d. Archibald and Anna Cutler (Mattison) M. Student, Inst. d'Etudes Francaises Pour Estrangers, France, 1965, U. de Grenoble, 1968; BA in Psychology, Lake Erie Coll., 1969; MA in Clin. Psychology, Cleve. State U., 1971; postgrad., Gestalt Inst. Cleve., 1971-73; PhD in Clin. Psychology, Calif. Sch. Profl. Psychology, Fresno, 1976. Lic. psychologist, Calif. Mental health worker Cleve. Clinic Hosp., 1970-71, assoc. psychologist, 1971-73; psychiat. intake worker Cleve. Free Clinic, 1971, group leader, 1972; cons. St. John's Coll., Cleve., 1972-73; psychology intern Fresno County Dept. Health, 1973-75, student profl. worker, 1974; mem. faculty U.Calif. Fresno Sch. Profl. Psychology, 1974; psychology intern Calif. State U. , Fresno, 1975; lectr. Calif. State U., 1976—77; treatment program dir. E. Ross Clark Home for Children, Inc., Modesto, Calif., 1976-77; clin. psychologist Santa Cruz County (Calif.) Cmty. Mental Health Svcs., 1977-79, dir. psychol. svcs., 1979-83; pvt. practice psychotherapy Soquel, Calif., 1979—96; oral commr. Calif. State Psychology Licensing Exam, 1988—96. Designated expert Calif. Med. Bd., 1991—96; mem. med. staff Dominican Hosp., 1983—93, vice chmn dept. psychiatry/psychology, 1985—87, chair dept. psychiatry/psychology, 1987—88; mem. Citizens' Involvement Assocs., 1984—87; adj. faculty Pacific Grad. Sch. Psychology, 1984—89; mem. faculty San Francisco State U., 1987; cons. NOW, 1973—76, Cmty. Hosp., Fresno, 1974; expert witness Santa Cruz, Monterey, Santa Clara and San Francisco counties, 1979—96; participant Law and Ethics Workshop, 1984, CP-MMPI workshop, 1986, Child Sexual Assault Workshop, 1986, The Role of the Profl. in Complex Custody Disputes, 1993. Contbr. articles to jours. in psychology. Mem. Women's Studies Adv. Bd., Fresno, 1975-76. Recipient Disting. Psychologist award Calif. State Psychol. Assn., 1982, recognition for contbns. to the field of psychology and Mid-Coast Psychol. Assn., 1996; Hill scholar, 1968, Smith scholar, 1969, Fritz Perls scholar, 1970. Mem. APA, Calif. Psychol. Assn. (bd. dirs. Observer 1981-83), Mid-Coast Psychol. Assn. (pres. 1981, forensic chmn. 1983-96), Psychol. Inst., Forensic Mental Health Assn., No. Calif. Psychologists for Social Responsibility, Laurel Soc., Psi Chi (v.p. 1968-69), Kappa Alpha Sigma, Cotuit Mosquito Yacht Club, Mt. Women Investment Club. Home and Office: 4595 Fairway Dr Soquel CA 95073-3010

MURRAY, BARRY WAYNE, economics educator; b. Dublin, June 1, 1946; s. Archie Guy and Helen Avis (Smith) M.; m. Laurie Lee Yoder, Sept. 11, 1976; children: Elisabeth Hope, Jonathan Guy, Caitlin Anna. BS in Econs., Auburn U., 1968; MEd in Econs. Edn., West Ga. Coll., 1978, EdS in Econs. Edn., 1980. Tchr. social studies Cobb County Bd. Edn., Marietta, Ga., 1968-85; dir. gifted program Osborne H.S., 1985—, tchr. econs., 1989—. Coach, advisor stock market game Ga. Coun. Econ. Edn., Atlanta, 1987—, advisor 8th State Stock Market Game Championship, 1996; coord. gov.'s honors selection Gov.'s Honors Program, Atlanta, 1985—. Author: (periodical) Level of Economic Understanding of Teachers, 1980 (Student Rsch. award 1980, 7 Star Tchr. awards). Active Citizenship Coun. Cobb County, Marietta, 1985-86, Ga. Coun. Econ. Edn., Atlanta, 1987—. Mem. Ga. Acad. Team Assn., Ga. Assn. Educators. Office: 1065 Polo Club Dr NW Marietta GA 30064-1283

MURRAY, BERTRAM GEORGE, JR. biology educator; b. Elizabeth, N.J., Sept. 24, 1933; s. Bertram George and Laura Estelle Murray; m. Patti Aylward, June 9, 1973. BA, Rutgers U., 1961; MS, U. Mich., 1963, PhD, 1967. Lectr. Cornell U., Ithaca, N.Y., 1967-68; asst. prof. Mich. State U., E. Lansing, 1968-71; asst. prof. biology Rutgers U., New Brunswick, N.J., 1971-74, assoc. prof. biology, 1974-81, prof. biology, 1981-2000. Author: Population Dynamics, 1979; assoc. editor: Am. Midland Naturalist, 1979-84. Airman USN, 1951-52; sgt. USAF, 1954-57. Fellow Am. Ornithologists Union; mem. Brit. Ornithologists' Union, Wilson Ornithol. Soc., Cooper Ornithol. Soc. Avocations: nature photography, scuba diving, bird watching. Home: 249 Berger St Somerset NJ 08873-2861 E-mail: bmurray@rci.rutgers.edu.

MURRAY, BRIAN VICTOR, investment banker; b. Teaneck, N.J., Oct. 17, 1947; s. Harry Lawrence and Marie Antoinette (Brizzi) M.; m. Dec. 14, 1974; children: B. Patrick, Megan, Sean, Matthew. BS in Econs., Villanova U., 1970; MBA with hons., U. Chgo., 1975. Ptnr. H.C. Wainwright & Co., N.Y.C., Boston, 1974-78; sr. mng. dir. Bear, Stearns & Co., N.Y.C., 1978-96; pres. B.V. Murray & Co., Englewood Cliffs, N.J., 1996—. Chmn. First Hungary Fund, Isle of Jersey, 1996—, Carlson Bolivia Fund, 1997—; bd. dirs. 4 Front Tech., Del., U.S., 1996—, Renal Tech. DVT. N.Y.C., 1998—; founder, bd. dirs. Ascent/Meredith Asset Mgmt., N.Y.C., 1998—. Trustee, mem. exec. com. Elizabeth Morrow Sch., Englewood, N.J., 1991—. Lt. U.S. Navy, 1970. Named Internat. Dealer of Yr., Instnl. Investment Mag., 1989. Mem. Union League (N.Y.), Inst. of Chartered Fin. Analysts (chartered). Avocation: judging horses (recognized judge Am. Horse Show Assn.). Office: BV Murray & Co Inc 560 Sylvan Ave Englewood Cliffs NJ 07632 E-mail: Bvm@bvmurray.com.

MURRAY, BRYAN CLARENCE, professional sports team executive; b. Shawville, Que., Can., Dec. 5, 1942; came to U.S., 1980; s. Clarence Herbert and Rhoda (Schwartz) M.; m. Geraldine Frances Sutton, July 8, 1967; 1 dau., Heide Alicia. Grad., McGill U., 1964. Former athletic dir., hockey coach McGill U.; athletic dir. MacDonald Coll., Ste. Anne de Bellevue, Que., 1968-72; coach, tchr. Rockland Nat.-Pontiac High Sch., Rockland, Ont., 1974-76; coach Pembroke-Kings, Pembroke, 1976-79, Regina Pats, Sask., 1979-80, Hershey (Pa.) Bears, 1980-81; former coach Washington Capitals, Landover, Md., from 1981; coach, gen. mgr. Detroit Red Wings, 1990-94; gen. manager Florida Panthers, Fort Lauderdale, Fla., 1994—2001; head coach Mighty Ducks Anaheim, 2001—. Recipient Jack Adams award as NHL Coach of Yr., 1983-84. Office: Anaheim Mighty Ducks Disney Sports Enterprises Inc. 2695 E. Katella Avenue Anaheim CA 92803*

MURRAY, CHRISTOPHER CHARLES, III, architect; b. Bklyn., July 6, 1950; s. Christopher Charles and Gertrude Rose (Marr) M.; m. Ann Herring, Nov. 16, 1974. BArch, U. Notre Dame, 1973. Registered architect, N.Y., Md., D.C., Va., Ga. Project architect Hibner Architects, Garden City, N.Y., 1973-76; project mgr. BBM Architects, N.Y.C., 1976-79; project dir. Gensler & Assocs., 1979-84; office dir., v.p., mem. nat. mgmt. com. Gensler, Washington, 1984-96, internat. practice leader profl. svc. firms, 1996—. Prin. works include interior design Sidley & Austin Worldwide, Freshfields, Latham & Watkins, Piper & Marbury, Covington & Burling. Asst. scoutmaster Boy Scouts Am., also NCAC unit commr.; active Greater Washington Bd. Trade, 1986. Mem. AIA, Md. Soc. Architects, Notre Dame Club, Club at Franklin Sq (bd. dirs.). Roman Catholic. Home: 12517 Knightsbridge Ct Rockville MD 20850-3732 Office: Gensler 2020 K St NW Washington DC 20006-1806 E-mail: christopher_murray@gensler.com.

MURRAY, DANIEL CHARLES, trial lawyer; b. Evanston, Ill., Jan. 21, 1949; s. John Joseph and Marjorie Ellen (Pequignot) M.; m. Martha Jane Gerity, Dec. 18, 1971; children: Michaela, Tyler, Brian. BA in Econs., Marquette U., 1971; JD, Loyola U., Chgo., 1976. Bar: Ill. 1976, U.S. Ct. Appeals (7th cir.) 1979, U.S. Dist. Ct. (no. dist.) Ill. 1980, U.S. Dist Ct. (ea. dist.) Mich. 1992, U.S. Dist. Ct. (ea. dist.) Wis. 1994. Jud. law clk. U.S. Ct. Appeals for 7th Cir., Chgo., 1976-78; asst. U.S. atty. Office U.S. Atty. U.S. Dept. Justice (no. dist.) Ill., 1978—91; shareholder, chmn. pro bono program Johnson & Bell, Ltd., 1991—. Trial instr. U.S. Atty. Gen.'s Advocacy Inst., Washington, 1989; mem. Environ. Crimes Task Force, 1991. Active Chgo. Vol. Legal Svcs. Found., 1977—, Chgo. Legal Advocacy to Incarcerated Mothers, 1995—; participant Chgo. North-of-Howard Task Force. Recipient Disting. Svc. award Chgo. Vol. Legal Svcs. Found., 1983, 87, award for significant contbns. in drug law enforcement U.S. Drug Enforcement Adminstrn., 1988, Insp. Gen.'s nat. award GSA, 1989, Spl. Achievement award U.S. Dept. Justice, 1990. Mem. Fed. Bar Assn. (bd. dirs. Chgo. chpt.), 7th Fed. Cir. Bar Assn. Office: Johnson & Bell Ltd Ste 4100 55 E Monroe St Chicago IL 60603-5896 E-mail: murrayd@jbltd.com.

MURRAY, DANIEL RICHARD, lawyer; b. Mar. 23, 1946; s. Alfred W. and Gloria D. Murray. AB, U. Notre Dame, 1967; JD, Harvard U., 1970. Bar: Ill. 1970, U.S. Dist. Ct. (no. dist.) Ill. 1970, U.S. Ct. Appeals (7th cir.) 1971, U.S. Supreme Ct. 1974. Ptnr. Jenner & Block, Chgo., 1970—. Trustee Chgo. Mo. and Western Rlwy. Co., 1988-97; adj. prof. U. Notre Dame, 1997—. Co-author: Secured Transactions, 1978, Illinois Practice: Uniform Commercial Code with Illinois Code Comments, 1997, Uniform Laws Annotated—Uniform Commercial Code Forms , 2001. Bd. regents Big Shoulders Fund, Archdiocese of Chgo., Bernadin Ctr., Cath. Theol. Union. Mem.: Assn. Transp. Practitioners, Transp. Lawyers Assn., Am. Coll. Comml. Fin. Lawyers, Am. Bankruptcy Coll., Am. Law Inst., Am. Bankruptcy Inst., Cath. Lawyers Guild (bd. dirs.), Lawyers' Club Chgo. Roman Catholic. Home: 1307 N Sutton Pl Chicago IL 60610-2007 Office: Jenner & Block One IBM Plz Chicago IL 60611-3605 E-mail: dmurray@jenner.com.

MURRAY, DAVE, marketing professional, editor; V.p. fin. comm. Wells Fargo Bank; city editor major daily newspaper San Francisco Bay area; exec. v.p., prin. Neale-May & Ptnrs. Inc., 1987—. Cons. with AboveNet, Amdahl Corp., A.T. Kearney, Borland, Brobeck, Phleger & Harrison, Business-land, Cheyenne Software, Concentric Network Corp, Ernst & Young, others. Office: Neale May & Ptnrs Inc 409 Sherman Ave Palo Alto CA 94306 Office Fax: 650-328-5016.*

MURRAY, DAVID GEORGE, architect; b. Tulsa, Nov. 9, 1919; s. Lee Cloyd and Marion (Bennett) M.; m. Margaret Elizabeth Oldham, Sept. 23, 1944; children: Michael Allen, Lucy Margaret (Mrs. Norman Scheer), Patrick David. BArch, Okla. State U., 1942. Registered architect, Okla. Ptnr. Atkinson & Murray, Tulsa, 1949-52; prin. David G. Murray & Assocs., 1952-56; pres. Murray, Jones, Murray, Inc., 1957-85, chmn., 1986-89. Chmn., bd. govs. Licensed Architects, Oklahoma City, 1964-74. Prin. works include Cities Service Technology Ctr., Broken Arrow, Okla., Terminal Bldg. Tulsa Internat. Airport, St. Patrick's Ch., Oklahoma City, Coll. of Osteopathic Medicine and Surgery, Tulsa, First Nat. Tower, Tulsa, Hillcrest Med. Ctr., Tulsa, Thomas Gilcrease Mus., Tulsa, Tulsa Civic Ctr. Bldgs. Chmn., dir. Goodwill Industries of Tulsa, 1966-87; chmn., exec. com. Downtown Tulsa Unltd., 1975-87; v.p., exec. com., dir. Met. Tulsa C. of C., 1979-85. Served to 1st lt. USAF, 1942-45. Named to Hall of Fame Coll. Engring. Okla. State U., 1969. Fellow AIA (pres. Tulsa chpt. 1964, mem. com. office practice 1983-87); mem. Southern Hills Country Club (dir. 1977-80). Republican. Methodist. Avocations: travel, golf.

MURRAY, DELBERT MILTON, manufacturing engineer; b. Fordland, Mo., Aug. 22, 1941; s. Chester Augustus and Iris Morene (Hamilton) M.; m. Orilla Maxine Stoaks, Sept. 15, 1962; children: Cynthia Ann, Norman Lee, Orilla Mae, Delbert Lynn. BS, S.W. Mo. State U., 1963. Prodn. planner McDonnell Douglas Corp., St. Louis, 1963-65; tool planning engr. The Boeing Corp., Wichita, Kans., 1965-70; indsl. engr. NCR Corp., 1972-77; sr. mfg. engr. Emerson Electric Co., Ava, Mo., 1977-96; mfg. engr. Copeland Corp., 1997—. Chmn. Mt. Zion Ch. of God., Mo., 1977-97; fire chief Ava Rural Fire Dept., 1998—. Mem. NRA, N.Am. Hunting Club, Gideons. Republican. Avocations: hunting, fishing, photography, woodworking. Home: RR 1 Box 305 Ava MO 65608-9720 Office: Copeland Corp 1400 NW 3D St Ava MO 65608 E-mail: dmmurray@fidnet.com.

MURRAY, DIANE ELIZABETH, librarian; b. Detroit, Oct. 15, 1942; d. Gordon Lisle and Dorothy Anne (Steketee) LaBoueff; m. Donald Edgar Murray, Apr. 22, 1968. AB, Hope Coll., 1964; MLS, Western Mich. U., 1968; MM, Aquinas Coll., 1982; postgrad., Mich. State U., East Lansing, 1964-66. Catalog libr., asst. head acquisitions sect. Mich. State U. Librs., East Lansing, 1968-77; libr. tech. and automated svcs. Hope Coll., Holland, Mich., 1977-88; dir. librs. DePauw U., Greencastle, Ind., 1988-91; acquisitions libr. Grand Valley State U., Allendale, Mich., 1991—. Sec., vice chair, chairperson bd. trustees Mich. Libr. Consortium, Lansing, 1981-85. Vice pres. Humane Soc. of Putnam County, Greencastle, 1990-91; bd. dirs., Loutit Dist. Libr., 1999—. Mem. ALA. Methodist. Avocations: dog breeding and showing, handbell ringing. Office: Grand Valley State U Zumberge Libr Allendale MI 49401 E-mail: murrayd@gvsu.edu.

MURRAY, DOROTHY SPEICHER, educator; b. Garrett, Pa., Oct. 27, 1913; d. Harry Blaine and Ada Chloe (Brumbaugh) Speicher; m. Ralph F. Murray, June 4, 1937. AB, Juniata Coll., 1934; MS, Queen's Coll., 1963. Cert. secondary tchr., Pa.; cert. tchr./ supr. secondary edn., N.Y. Tchr., librarian Boswell (Pa.) High Sch., 1934-37; sec. to pres. Cornell Iron Works, Inc., L.I., N.Y., 1939-52; instr. reading clinic NYU, 1953; instr. Poppenhusen Inst., College Point, N.Y., 1954-59; tchr. Union Free Sch. Dist. 15, Jericho, 1958-62; supr. English dept. Jericho High Sch., 1962-65, coordinator reading, 1965-72; vol. tchr. Adams County Prison, Gettysburg, Pa., 1982-89. Author: Reading in the Content Area, 1968, The English Language, 1983, Crashing the Language Barrier, 1987, A Library For Adams Co., 1988, One Man's Shadow: The H.B. Speicher Story, 1997, An Open Invitation to Explore the Wily Ways of Words, 1997, Chronicles of a Word Watcher at Work, 1999, Word Work Ahead; contbr. articles to profl. jours. Bd. dirs. Office for the Aging, 1976-79, sec. Adams County Prison Task Force, 1986-91; sec. Friends of Library, Gettysburg, 1987-90. Linguistics grantee Inst. for Tchrs. English Columbia U., 1964-65, Adult Basic Edn. grantee Pa. Dept. Edn., 1989-90; recipient citation South Cen. Reading Coun. Internat. Reading Assn., 1989. Mem. Adams County Hist. Soc., N.Y. State Ret. Tchrs. Assn. Republican. Presbyterian. Avocations: writing, teaching, public speaking.

MURRAY, EDWARD ROCK, insurance broker; b. Bklyn., Jan. 31, 1947; s. Garrett Francis and Anne M. (Rock) M.; m. Barbara Marie Robotti; children: Pamela Jean, Stephanie Elise. BA in Bus. Adminstrn., St. Bonaventure U., 1968. Claims examiner N.Y.C., 1970-72; agt. and mgr. John Hancock Life Ins., Albany, N.Y., 1972-76; regional dir. Colonial Life Insur, 1976-80; ptnr. Murray & Zuckerman, Inc., Schenectady, N.Y., 1980—. Bd. dirs. Am. Med. Ins., Hicksville, N.Y., 1988—, Northeast Mgmt. Forum, 1990—; treas. The Mktg. Alliance. 1st lt. U.S. Army, 1968-70, Vietnam. Mem. Mohawk Club (past chmn.), Nat. Assn. of Ind. Life Brokerage Agys. (bd. dirs., chmn. bd.), Edison Club (bd. dirs., treas.). Roman Catholic. Avocation: golf. Office: Murray & Zuckerman Inc 128 Erie Blvd Ste 2 Schenectady NY 12305-2283

MURRAY, ERNEST DON, artist, educator; b. Asheville, N.C., Apr. 21, 1930; s. Ernest Burgin and Daisy Ann (Bishop) M.; m. Katherine H. Shakeshaft, 1997. Student, Asheville-Biltmore Jr. Coll., 1950; AA, BA, U. Tenn., 1952; student, Art Students League, 1953; MFA, U. Fla., 1957, MEd, 1958. Instr. art Chipola Jr. Coll., Marianna, Fla., 1958, head div. humanities, 1964-68; instr. humanities U. Fla., Gainesville, 1969-72, prof. humanities, asso. chmn. dept. humanities, 1974-78, prof. fine art and humanities dept. fine art, 1978-96, prof. emeritus, 1997—; co-owner Round Earth Studio, 1996—. Cons. Holt, Rinehart & Winston, Inc., N.Y.C., 1963-76, Harcourt Brace, Jovanovich, Inc., N.Y.C., 1964-76 One-man shows in Knoxville, Tenn., 1952, N.Y.C., 1953, Gainesville, 1968, 71, 72, 75, 90, 93, Pub. Sculpture Commns., 1989, 90, 91, 93, 95, Fla. Mus. Natural History, Fla. State Fire Coll., Mathieson Hist. Ctr.; exhibited in group shows Asheville, 1949, Knoxville, 1951, 65, N.Y.C., 1953, 61, 67, Gainesville, Miami, Tallahassee, 1979—; represented in pvt. collections. With C.E. U.S. Army, 1954-56, USNR, 1949-54. Mem. So. Highlands Craftsman's Guild, Fla. Artists Assn., Phi Theta Kappa, Phi Kappa Phi, Phi Beta Kappa, Omicron Delta Kappa. Unitarian Universalist. E-mail: roundear@mindspring.com.

MURRAY, FLORENCE KERINS, retired state supreme court justice; b. Newport, R.I., Oct. 21, 1916; d. John X. and Florence (MacDonald) Kerins; m. Paul F. Murray, Oct. 21, 1943 (dec. June 2, 1995); 1 child, Paul F. AB, Syracuse U., 1938; LLB, Boston U., 1942; EdD, R.I. Coll. Edn., 1956; grad., Nat. Coll. State Trial Judges, 1966; LLD (hon.), Bryant Coll., 1956, U. R.I., 1963, Mt. St. Joseph Coll., 1972, Providence Coll., 1974, Roger Williams Coll., 1976, Salve Regina Coll., 1977, Johnson and Wales Coll., 1977, Suffolk U., 1981, So. New Eng. Law Sch., 1995; D (hon.), New England Inst. Tech., 1998. Bar: Mass. 1942, R.I. 1947, U.S. Dist. Ct. 1948, U.S. Tax Ct. 1948, U.S. Supreme Ct. 1948. Sole practice, Newport, 1947-52; mem. firm Murray & Murray, 1952-56; assoc. judge R.I. Superior Ct., 1956-78; presiding justice Superior Ct. R.I., 1978-79; assoc. justice (ret.-active) R.I. Supreme Ct., 1979—. Staff, faculty adv. Nat. Jud. Coll., Reno, Nev., 1971-72, dir., 1975-77, chmn., 1979-87, chair emeritus, 1990—; mem. com. Legal Edn. and Practice and Economy of New Eng., 1975—; former instr. Prudence Island Sch.; legal adv. R.I. Girl Scouts; sec. Commn. Jud. Tenure and Discipline, 1975-79; apptd. by Pres. Clinton to bd. dirs. State Justice Inst., 1994-99; participant, leader various legal seminars; presdl. appointment R.I. State Justice Inst. Mem. R.I. Senate, 1948-56; chmn. spl. legis. com.; mem. Newport Sch. Com., 1948-57, chmn., 1951-57; mem. Gov.'s Jud. Coun., 1950-60, White House Conf. Youth and Children, 1950, Ann. Essay Commn., 1952, Nat. Def. Adv. Com. on Women in Service, 1952-58, Gov.'s Adv. Com. Mental Health, 1954, R.I. Alcoholic Adv. Com., 1955-58, R.I. Com. Youth and Children, Gov.'s Adv. Com. on Revision Election Laws, Gov.'s Adv. Com. Social Welfare, Army Adv. Com. for 1st Army Area; mem. civil and polit. rights com. Pres.'s Commn. on Status of Women, 1960-63; mem. R.I. Com. Humanities, 1972—, chmn., 1972-77; mem. Family Ct. Study Com., R.I. com. Nat. Endowment Humanities; bd. dirs. Newport YMCA; sec. Bd. Physicians Service; bd. visitors Law Sch., Boston U.; bd. dirs. NCCJ; mem. edn. policy and devel. com. Roger Williams Jr. Coll.; trustee Syracuse U.; pres. Newport Girls Club, 1974-75, R.I. Supreme Ct. Hist. Soc., 1988—; chair Supreme Ct. Mandatory Continuing Legal Edn. Com., 1993—; apptd. bd. dirs. Touro Synague; apptd. R.I. Found. Served to lt. col. WAC, World War II. Decorated Legion of Merit; named named Judge of Yr., Nat. Assn. Women Judges, 1984, Outstanding Woman, Bus. and Profl. Women, 1972, Citizen of Yr., R.I. Trial Lawyers Assn., Newport courthouse renamed in her honor, 1990; recipient Arents Alumni award, Syracuse U., 1956, Carroll award, R.I. Inst. Instn., 1956, Brotherhood award, NCCJ, 1983, Herbert Harley award, Am. Judicature Soc., 1988, Silver Citizenship award, DAR, R.I., 1980s, Gold Citizenship award, DAR, 1990s, Merit award, R.I. Bar Assn., 1994, John Manson/Carl Robinson award, Nat. Probation Officers Assn., 1996, Longfellow Humanitarian award, ARC, 1997. Mem. ABA (chmn. credentials com. nat. conf. state trial judges 1971-73, chair judges adv. com. on standing com. on ethics and profl. responsibility 1991—, joint com. on jud. discipline of standing com. on profl. discipline 1991-94), R.I. Found. (bd. dirs. 1998—), AAUW (chmn. state edn. com. 1954-56), Am. Arbitration Assn., Nat. Trial Judges Conf. (state chmn. membership com., sec. exec. com.), New Eng. Trial Judges Conf. (com. chmn. 1967), Boston U. Alumni Coun., Am. Legion (judge adv. post 7, mem. nat. exec. com.), Bus. and Profl. Women's Club (past state v.p., past pres. Newport chpt., past pres. Nat. legis. com.), Auota Club (past gov. internat., past pres. Newport chpt.), Alpha Omega, Kappa Beta Pi.

MURRAY, FRED F. lawyer; b. Corpus Christi, Tex., Aug. 1, 1950; s. Marvin Frank and Suzanne Louise Murray. BA, Rice U., 1972; JD, U. Tex., 1974. Bar: Tex. 1975, U.S. Dist. Ct. (so. dist.) Tex. 1976, U.S. Ct. Claims 1976, U.S. Tax

Ct. 1976, U.S. Ct. Appeals (5th, D.C. and fed. cirs.) 1976, U.S. Supreme Ct. 1978, U.S. Ct. Internat. Trade 1985, N.Y. 1987, D.C. 1987, U.S. Dist. Ct. (ea. dist.) Tex. 1987; CPA, Tex. Ptnr. Chamberlain, Hrdlicka, White, Williams & Martin, P.C., Houston, 1985-92; spl. counsel (legislation) U.S. Dept. Treasury, IRS, Washington, 1992-96; v.p. tax policy Nat. Fgn. Trade Coun., 1996—2002; gen. counsel, dir. tax affairs Tax Execs. Inst., Inc., 2002—. Mem. Tax Law Adv. Commn., Tex. Bd. Legal Specialization, 1984-99, vice chmn., 1987-92; mem. Commn. Tax Law Examiners, 1984-99, vice chmn., 1987-92; adj. prof. U. Houston Law Ctr., 1984-92, U. Tex. Sch. Law, 1987; faculty lectr. Rice U. Jones Grad. Sch. Adminstrn., 1987-92; spkr. various assns. and univs.; mem. bd. advisors Houston Jour. Internat. Law, 1986-92, chmn., 1987-91; mem. Taxpayer Adv. Coun., N.Y. Commr. of Taxation and Fin., 2002—; mem. BNA Tax Mgmt. Adv. Bd., 2002—. Author various publs. Del. Bishop's Diocesan Pastoral Coun., 1979-80; chmn. parish coun. Sacred Heart Cathedral, Cath. Diocese Galveston-Houston, 1979-81, 89, mem. Red Mass steering com., 1986-92; mem. exec. com., bd. dirs., 1987-91, chmn. deferred giving com. Houston Symphony Soc., 1987-88, chmn. govt. and pub. affairs com., 1988-91; co-trustee Houston Symphony Soc. Endowment Fund, 1987-91; mem. fund coun. Rice U., 1987-96, exec. com. 1988-92, chmn. Major Gifts Com., 1988-92; gen. counsel, bd. dirs., com. on fin. and adminstrn. S.E. Tex. chpt. Nat. Multiple Sclerosis Soc.; mem. Red Mass com. Archdiocese Washington, 1993—; bd. dirs. John Carroll Soc., Archdiocese of Washington, 1996—, chmn. pilgrimage com. Knighted equestrian order Holy Sepulchre Jerusalem, 1998—. Fellow Am. Coll. Tax Counsel; mem. ABA (chmn. formation tax policy com. 1998--), FBA (mem. steering com. tax sect. 1995—, chmn. tax sect. 1998-99), AICPA, Am. Arbitration Assn. (panels comml. and internat. arbitrators 1980—), Internat. Bar Assn., Houston Bar Assn., State Bar of Tex. (various coms.), N.Y. State Bar Assn., D.C. Bar Assn., Tex. Soc. CPA, Internat. Tax Forum of Houston (sec. 1981-84, pres. 1984-92), Internat. Fiscal Assn., Am. Soc. Internat. Law, Am. Fgn. Law Assn., Am. Law Inst. (tax adv. group 1990—), Am. Tax Policy Inst. (bd. dirs.).

MURRAY, GEORGE WILLIAM, university president; b. Wilmington, Del., Apr. 22, 1945; s. John Wier and Eleanor (Stephens) M.; m. Esther Annette Brice, June 14, 1969; children: Heather, Laura, Frank, Julie. BA, Columbia Bible Coll., 1967; MA, Columbia Bibl. Sem., 1981; postgrad., U. Perugia, Italy, 1971-73, Bibl. Theol. Sem., Hatfield, Pa., 1975, 76; D of Missiology, Trinity Evangel. Div. Sch., Deerfield, Ill., 1995. Asst. to pres. Columbia (S.C.) Bible Coll., 1968, 69; missionary Bible Christian Union, Inc., Italy, 1971-83, dir. So. Europe Italy, Spain, Portugal and Greece, 1980-83, gen. dir. Europe, 1983-94; exec. dir. The Evangelical Alliance Misson, 1994-99; pres. Columbia Internat. U., S.C., 2000—. Trustee Columbia Bible Coll. and Sem., 1985-99. Office: Columbia Internat U 7435 Monticello Rd PO Box 3122 Columbia SC 29230-3122 E-mail: gmurray@ciu.edu.

MURRAY, JAMES DICKSON, mathematical biology educator; b. Moffat, Scotland, Jan. 2, 1931; s. Peter and Sarah Jane (Black) M.; m. Sheila Todd Campbell, Oct. 1959; children: Mark Woodeaton, Sarah Corinne. BSc in Math. with 1st class honors, U. St. Andrews, Scotland, 1953, PhD in Applied Math., 1956; MA, U. Oxford, Eng., 1961, DSc in Math., 1968; DSc (hon.), U. St. Andrews, 1994, U. Strathclyde, 1999. Lectr. applied math. King's Coll. Durham U., Newcastle, Eng., 1955-56; Gordon McKay lectr. and rsch. fellow Harvard U., Cambridge, Mass., 1956-59, rsch. assoc. engring., applied physics, 1963-64; prof. engring. mechanics U. Mich., Ann Arbor, 1965-67; prof. math. NYU, N.Y.C., 1967-70; lectr. Univ. Coll., London, 1959-61; fellow in math. Hertford Coll. U. Oxford, 1961-63, reader, 1972-86, prof. math. biology, 1986-92, fellow Corpus Christi Coll., 1970-92, dir. Ctr. Math. Biology, 1983-92, emeritus prof., 1992—2001, hon. fellow, 2001—. Vis. prof. applied math. MIT, 1979, U. Utah, Salt Lake City, 1979, 85, Calif. Tech. U., 1983; vis. rsch. prof. Nat. Tsing Hua U., Taiwan, 1975, U. Florence, Italy, 1976, Winegard Guelph U., 1980; guest prof. U. Heidelberg, Fed. Republic Germany, 1980; disting. vis. prof., Scott Hawkins lectr. So. Meth. U., Dallas, 1984; adj. prof. zoology U. Wash., 1988-2000, prof. applied math., 1988-2000, emeritus, 2000—, Robert F. Philip prof., 1988-94, Boeing prof., 1997-2000; ULAM scholar Los Alamos Nat. Lab., 1985; Lansdowne lectr. U. Victoria, 1990, Ostram lectr. Wash. State U. Author: Asymptotic Analysis, 1974, Nonlinear Differential Equation Models in Biology, 1977, Russian translation, 1983, Mathematical Biology, 1989, 3d edit., 2 vols., 2002; co-author: (with L. Wolpert and S. Brenner) Theories of Biological Pattern Formation, 1981, (with W. Jäger) Modelling Patterns in Space and Time, 1983, (with H.G. Othmer and P.K. Maini) Experimental and Theoretical Advances in Biological Pattern Formation, 1993; contbr. over 200 articles to profl. jours. Recipient Naylor prize for applied math. London Math. Soc., 1989; vis. fellow St. Catherine's Coll., U. Oxford, 1967, Guggenheim fellow, 1967-68; La Chaire Européene, U. Paris, 1994, 95, 96. Fellow Royal Soc., Royal Soc. Edinburgh, European Soc. for Math. and Theoretical Biology (pres. 1991-94); mem. Acad. Scis. France (fgn. mem.). Office: U Wash Dept Applied Math PO Box 352420 Seattle WA 98195-2420 E-mail: murrayjd@amath.washington.edu.

MURRAY, JAMES ALAN, urban and environmental consultant, investor; b. Evansville, Ind., Oct. 2, 1942; s. William Dewey and Dorothy Marie (Gleason) M.; children: Heidi Lynn, Paul Alan, Kendra Leigh. BS, U. N.Mex., 1964; MBA, Harvard U., 1969; MA (NDEA fellow), U. Oreg., 1971, PhD, 1972. Dir. fin. City of Boulder (Colo.), 1972-73, dir. adminstrv. svcs., 1973-74; v.p. Briscoe, Maphis, Murray & Lamont, Inc., Boulder, 1974-78, pres., 1978-84, also dir.; dir. fin. City and County of Denver, 1984-86, CEO, 1986-87, asst. to mayor, 1987-89; pres., dir. Murray Lamont & Assocs., Inc., 1990-98, Colo. Scientific Investments, Inc., 1993-96; chmn. Lanzhou Murray Clothing Co., China, 1994-95, Lanzhou Murray Electronics Co., Ltd., China, 1995—. Adj. assoc. prof. Grad. Sch. Public Affairs, U. Colo., Boulder, 1972-80, Denver, 1985-91; dir. regional/urban design assistance team program of AIA, 1994—. Mem. open space adv. com. City of Boulder, 1972-74; bd. dirs. Met. Denver Sewage Authority, 1984-85, Colo. Baseball Commn., 1989-93. Mem. ASPA, Am. Econ. Assn., Western Econ. Assn., Water Pollution Control Fedn., Denver Athletic Club, Kappa Mu Epsilon, Pi Alpha Alpha. Home: 99 S Downing St Apt 602 Denver CO 80209-2407 E-mail: Jim99s@earthlink.net.

MURRAY, JAMES DOYLE, accountant, educator; b. Rochester, N.Y., July 24, 1938; s. William Herbert and Mildred Frances (Becker) M.; m. Mary Louise Goodyear, June 22, 1962; children: William Doyle, Robert Goodyear. BS, U. Rochester, 1961. CPA, N.Y. With Ernst & Whinney, Rochester, N.Y., 1963—, ptnr., 1977-86; pvt. practice, 1986—; former mem. faculty NYSCPA. Contbr. articles to profl. jours. Treas. William Warfield Scholarship Fund, Inc.; bd. dirs. March of Dimes, Rochester chpt.; trustee B. Thomas Golisano Found.; active fund raising Boy Scouts Am., Rochester Philharm., Rochester Mus. and Sci. Ctr., U. Rochester; former bd. dirs., treas. Downstairs Cabaret; mem. Eagle bd. of rev. Boy Scouts Am.; elder Presbyn. Ch.; pres. Egypt Vol. Fire Dept. Lt. (j.g.) USN, 1961-63. Named Acct. Adv. of Yr. for region II, SBA, 1996. Mem. AICPA, N.Y. State Soc. CPAs (pres. Rochester chpt. 1982-83), Inst. Mgmt. Accts. (bd. dirs. 1978-80). Republican. Home: 42 Black Watch Trail Fairport NY 14450-3702 Office: 349 W Commercial St Ste 3000 East Rochester NY 14445-2407

MURRAY, JAMES J. textiles executive; b. 1961; CPA. Tax acct. pvt. industry; mng. dir. KPMG Corp. Trans. Svc. Practice; exec. v.p., CFO, sec. Johnston Industries, Inc., 1997—. Office: Johnston Industries Inc 105 13th St Columbus GA 31901 Fax: 706-641-3159.

MURRAY, JAMES JOSEPH, III, association executive; b. Boston, Dec. 31, 1933; s. James Joseph Jr. and Anne Louise (Gurvin) M.; children: James Arthur, Paul, Douglas Joseph, Laura Anne. AB, Harvard U., 1955. Regional editor Prentice Hall, Inc., 1957-60, editor, 1960-64, v.p., exec. editor, 1964-69; pres. Winthrop Pubs., Inc. subs. Prentice Hall, Cambridge, Mass., 1969-82, also bd. dirs.; spl. mng. cons. Am. Coun. Edn., Washington, 1983-84, dir. external affairs, 1984—, v.p., 1997—. Chmn. N.J. Heart Fund; spl. cons. NEH, 1975—. Mem. editorial bd. Capitol Pub., 1992—; author, editor: American Colleges and Universities, 2000. Mem. Dem. Nat. Com. from N.J., 1968; del. Dem. Nat. Conv., 1968; mem. gov. bd. Marine Mil. Acad., 1995—. 1st lt. USMCR, 1955-57. Mem. Am. Polit. Sci. Assn., Assn. Physical Plant Adminstrs. (bd. dirs.), Am. Assn. of Higher Edn., Harvard Club, Harvard Varsity Club, Pi Eta. Office: One DuPont Circle Ste 800 Washington DC 20036

MURRAY, JEAN RUPP, communications executive, writer, speaker; b. Portland, Oreg., Aug. 29, 1943; d. Edward Howard and Dorothy Eugenia (Ross) Brown. BA in English, Portland State U., 1965. Cert. tchr., Oreg. Tchr., dept. head Beaverton (Oreg.) Sch. Dist., 1967-88; pres., founder Write Communications, Portland, 1988—. Adj. faculty Portland C.C., Concordia U., Portland State U.; nat. trainer, cons.State of Oreg., City of Portland, Nike, Inc., Oreg. Health Scis. U., Oreg. Mil. Acad., Oreg. Fin. Instns. Assn., Freightliner, Automated Data Processing, Calif. State U. Systems, others, 1988—; spkr. Tektronix, Fred Meyer, Pacific Power, Am. Inst. of Banking, Utah Power, Pacific Telecom, Inc., other; writing dir. U.S. Army C.E., USDA Forest Svcs., PacifiCare, LawTalk MCLE, Wash. State Bar Assn., others, 1989-90; owner Wiggles & Wags Self and Full-Svc. Dog Wash. Author; Flawless Grammar at Your Fingertips: An Instant Guide to Perfect Grammar for Everybody in Business, 1994; TV appearances include Stas. KATU-TV and KGW-TV. Vol. Dove Lewis Emergency Vet. Clinic, Portland, 1989—, Doerbecher Children's Hosp., Oreg. Humane Soc. Mem. Oreg. Speakers Assn. (pres. bd. dirs. 1997—), Nat. Speakers Assn., Ctr. for Marine Conservation. Republican. Avocations: target-shooting, travel, speaking, exercise, animals. Office: Write Comm PMB 201 14845 SW Murray Schools Dr #110 Beaverton OR 97007 E-mail: jean@paws4thoughts.com.

MURRAY, JEANNE MORRIS, information scientist, educator, consultant, researcher; b. Fresno, Calif., July 6, 1925; d. Edward W. and Augusta R. (French) Morris; m. Thomas Harold Murray, June 19, 1964; children: Jeanne, Margaret, Barbara, Thomas, William. BS in Math., Morris Harvey Coll., 1957; MS in Info. and Computer Sci., Ga. Inst. Tech., 1966; PhD in Pub. Adminstrn. and Tech. Mgmt., Am. U., 1981, postgrad., 1993. Rsch. scientist Ga. Inst. Tech., Atlanta, 1959-68; adj. prof. Am. U., Washington, 1968-73; info. scientist U.S. Dept. Def., 1968-69; staff scientist Delex Sys., Inc., Arlington, Va., 1969-70; mgmt. analyst GSA, Washington, 1971-74; assoc. prof. No. Va. C.C., 1975-76, U. Va., 1976—; pres. Sequoia Assocs., Arlington, 1981—. Guest lectr. computer and society U. Md., 1986—; guest lectrl govtl. rels. Marymount U., Arlington, 1990; cons. TechDyn Sys., ABA Corp., Orkand Corp., 1978—80; panelist Inst. Agr., Akadamgorodok, Siberia, 1991. Inst. Nuc. Physics, 1991, M. Ulughbek Inst., Samarkand, Uzbekistan, 1991; chmn. confs. on Future of Fin. Structure and Pvt. Industry for Uzbekistan, 1994; rsch., developer cons. large info. warfare project, 1995—; developer indirect personality profiles for spl. internat. persons, 1995—; pres. R&D Alt. Med. Approaches, 1996; sponsor, mem. team devel. and testing vaccine for specific infectious diseases, 95; active U.S. Global Strategy Coun., 1993—. Author: Development and Testing of a System of Encoding Visual Informatino Based on Optimization of Neural Processig in Man—With Application to Pattern Recognition in the Computer, 1966, Development of a General Computerized Forecasting Model, 1971, Cybernetics and the Management of the Research and Development Function in Society, 1971, Cybernetics as a Tool in the Control of Drug Abuse, 1972, The Doctrine of Management Planning, 1973, Political Humankind and the Future of Governance, 1974, Policy Design, 1980, Computer Futures, 1982, A Search for Positive Response Leval Indicators (PRLI's) under Stress, 1987, Strategic Planning: Pathfinder to the Future, 1988, Strategic Planning: A Systems Perspective, 1988, Electronic Control Systems for Railroads, 1988, Technology Forecasting Methodologies for Use on Personal Computers, 1989, Japan's Burgeoning Rates of Economic Expansin in the U.S. and Other Western Countries, 1990, Technology Transfer and National Security, 1992, Privatization Mechanism for the Former Soviet Union and Central European Countries, 1992, Curriculum Development for Privatization Training of Entrepreneurs in Siberia, 1993, Development of Training Courses for Automated Acquisition Management Systems, 1994, Presentations of Methods of Achieving More Effective, Less Costly Federal Government, 1994; panel participant in field; co-developer TV program Cybernetics and You, Fairfax County, Va., 1995. OPSEC and Info. Warfare, 1996—; participant in panels on econ. espionage and its impact upon sci. and engring. competitiveness in the U.S., 1997. Mem. Carter Transition Team, 1976-77, Arlington CD Com., 1983—, Washington Met. Area Emergency Assistance Com., Arlington County Com. on Sci. and Tech. Mem. IEEE (sr. mem., vice chmn. Washington sect., chmn. panel on internat. mitg. high tech. in presence of def. tech. controls 1983, nat. com. on a tech. transfer policy for U.S. 1986, mem. land transp. com. Vehicular Tech. Soc. 1992-94), AAAS, ASPA, N.Y. Acad. Scis., Assn. for Computing Machinery, Washington Evolutionary Sys. Soc., Inst. Noetic Scis., Soc. Gen. Rsch., World Future Soc., Better World Soc., Acad. Polit. Sci., Personality Assessment Sys. Found., Soc. for Advancement Socio-Econs. Episcopalian. Achievements include rsch. on application of neural nets to specific areas of psychology, several areas of information security related to computers, research and application of subjective probability assessment testing. Home and Office: 2915 27th St N Arlington VA 22207-4922

MURRAY, JOHN DANIEL, lawyer; b. Cleve., Feb. 13, 1944; s. Clarence Daniel and Mary Anne (Bormann) M.; m. Pamela Mary Seese, Aug. 20, 1966 (div. Sept. 1978); children: Laura Jane, Joshua Daniel, Katherine Anne; m. Marilyn Nohren, June 15, 1979. BA, Marquette U., 1965, JD, 1968. Bar: Wis. 1968, Ill. 1968, U.S. Dist. Ct. (ea. and we. dist.) Wis. 1968, U.S. Supreme Ct. 1971, U.S. Ct. Appeals (7th cir.) 1979. Assoc. Law Offices of Elmo Koos, Peoria, Ill., 1968-70; ptnr. Coffey, Lerner & Murray, Milw., 1970-72, Coffey, Murray & Coffey, Milw., 1972-76, Murray & Burke, S.C., Milw., 1983-85; pvt. practice, 1976-83; shareholder Habush, Habush & Rottier, S.C., Appleton, Wis., 1985—. Adj. prof. law Marquette U., Milw., 1993—; lectr. Law Sch. U. Wis., Madison, 1976-80. Contbg. author: Wisconsin Trial Practice, 1999. Mem. ABA, ATLA, Nat. Bd. Trial Advocacy (cert.), Am. Bd. Trial Advocates, Am. Soc. Law and Medicine, Wis. State Bar (chmn. criminal law sect. 1977-78, tort law com. 1990-94, bd. dirs. litigation sect. 1995-2001, chmn. 1997-98), Wis. Acad. Trial Lawyers (bd. dirs. 1990-99), Woolsack Soc. Roman Catholic. Avocations: golf, travel. Office: Habush Habush Davis Rottier PO Box 1915 Appleton WI 54912-1915 Home: Apt 3 1170 Christopher Dr Neenah WI 54956-6337

MURRAY, JOHN EINAR, lawyer, retired army officer, federal official; b. Clifton, N.J., Nov. 22, 1918; s. Joseph Michael and Maru Elizabeth (Liljeros) M.; m. Elaine Claire Riehlmann (dec. 1970); 1 dau., Valerie Anne; m. Phyllis Irene Harris (div. 1989). Student, St. Johns U., 1938-41; LLB, N.Y. Law Sch., 1949, LLD, 1975; MA, George Washington U., 1961. lectr. U.S. Marine Corps Nat. Def. U.; mem. sci. panel of White House Agent Orange Working Group, Def. Intelligence Agy. Task Force on POWS and MIAS; participant Georgetown U. Panel on Crisis Mgmt. Drafted pvt. U.S. Army, 1941, advanced through grades to maj. gen., 1972; comdr. truck group Europe Mil. Ports, Vietnam and maj. logistic units, 1968; dir. Army Transp., 1969-70; chief logistics Pacific Command, 1970-72, Mil. Assistance Command, Vietnam, 1972-73; def. attache Vietnam, 1973-74; ret., 1974; v.p. Assn. Am. Railroads, Washington, 1974-84; spl. counsel Am. Internat. Underwriters, 1985; prin. dep. asst. sec. of def. for spl. ops. and low intensity conflict, 1988-89; with Am. Internat. Group Cos., Washington, 1989; spl. counsel Snavely, King & Assocs., Inc. (econ. cons.), 1990—. Adv. bd. U.S. Army Transp. Mus.; lectr. Nat. Def. U.; mem. sci. panel of White House Agent Orange Working Group, Def. Intelligence Agy. Task Force on POWs and MIAs; participant Georgetown U. Panel on Crisis Mgmt. Author: (with A.M. Chester) Orders and Directive, 1952, (with V.F. Caputo) Quick on the Vigor, 1966, The Myths of Business and the Business of Myths, 1975, The Third Curse of Moses, 1975, The Military Mind and the New Mindlessness, 1976, Lawyers, Computers and Power, 1977, Pothole Plague and Knothole Outlook, 1978, Railroads, Terrorism and the Pinkerton Legacy, 1978, Raising Corn and Beans and Hell, 1979, Remembering Who You Are, 1979, Running A Muck— The Folly of Coal Slurry, 1979, The Railroads and the Energy Crisis, 1980, U.S. Security Assistance— The Vietnam Experience, 1980, Hopeless Cause or Cause of Hope, 1980, War, Transport and Show Biz, 1981, Forget Everything You Ever Knew About the Japanese Railroads, 1981, Sweet Adversity: The U.S. Army-How It Motivates, 1982, Random Danger: The Railroad Response, 1983, Vietnam Logistics: An American Debacle, 1984, Dead Headheads and Warheads, 1987 ; Operation Desert Shield: The Smart Way to War, 1991; He Was There, 1992, The Logistics of Limited Wars, 1992, The United Nations: Sizing Up Consultant Prospects, 1992, How to Win a Lost War, 1997; contbr.: book revs. to Nat. Def. Transp. Mag., Time-Life books., Vietnam mag. Decorated D.S.M., Legion of Merit with 4 oak leaf clusters, Bronze Star medal, Joint Services Commendation medal with oak leaf cluster, Army Commendation medal with 2 oak leaf clusters, Sec. of Def. medal for Outstanding Pub. Svc., Italian Cross of War, Knight Order of Crown of Italy, Korean Chung Mu with gold star, Vietnamese Kim Khanh medal 1st class, Vietnamese Army Distinguished Service Order 1st class, Vietnamese Navy Distinguished Service Order 1st class, Vietnamese Air Force Distinguished Service Order 1st class, Vietnamese Gallantry Cross with palm, 1998, US Army Transportation Corps Hall of Fame. Mem. Spl. Forces Assn., Nat. Def. Transp. Assn., Army War Coll. Grad. Assn., Army and Navy Club, WWII Meml. Soc. (charter). Home: 3823 Bosworth Ct Fairfax VA 22031-3807 Office: Murray and Murray Fed Prac Govt Relations 444 N Capitol St NW Ste 840 Washington DC 20001-1512

MURRAY, JOHN F. priest; b. Flushing, N.Y., Jan. 25, 1923; s. John P. and Margaret M. (Redden) Murray. B.Sacred Theology, Cath. U. Am., Washington, 1957; MDiv, Immaculate Conception Sem., Mahwah, N.J., 1979. Vocation soc. dir. S.M.A. Fathers, Tenafly, NJ, 1967—77; chaplain Holy Name Hosp., Teaneck, 1962—90; state father prior of jr. K.C. K.C., Tenafly, 1968—; priest Soc. of African Missions, 1990—. Contbr. With USAAF, 1941—46. Recipient Testamonial, K.C., 1975, 1992. Roman Catholic. Avocation: golf. Home and Office: 23 Bliss Ave Tenafly NJ 07670

MURRAY, JOHN PATRICK, psychologist, educator, researcher; b. Cleve., Sept. 14, 1943; s. John Augustine and Helen Marie (Lynch) M.; m. Ann Coke Dennison, Apr. 17, 1971; children: Jonathan Coke, Ian Patrick. PhD, Cath. U. Am., 1970. Rsch. dir. Office U.S. Surgeon Gen. NIMH, Bethesda, Md., 1969-72; asst. to assoc. prof. psychology Macquarie U., Sydney, Australia, 1973-79; vis. assoc. prof. U. Mich., Ann Arbor, 1979-80; dir. youth and family policy Boys Town Ctr., Boys Town, Nebr., 1980-85; prof., dir. Sch. Family Studies and Human Svcs. Kans. State U., Manhattan, 1985-98, interim assoc. vice provost rsch., 1998—. Scholar-in-residence Mind Sci. Found., San Antonio, 1996-97; mem. children's TV com. CBS, 1996-99. Author: Television and Youth: 25 Years of Research and Controversy, 1980, The Future of Children's TV, 1984, (with H.T. Rubin) Status Offenders: A Sourcebook, 1983, (with E.A. Rubenstein, G.A. Comstock) Television and Social Behavior, 3 vols., 1972, (with A. Huston and others) Big World, Small Screen: The Role of Television in American Society, 1992, (with C. Fisher and others) Applied Developmental Science, 1996; contbr. numerous articles to profl. jours. Mem. Nebr. Foster Care Rev. Bd., 1982-84; mem. Advocacy Office for Children and Youth, 1980-85; mem. Nat. Coun. Children and TV, 1982-87; trustee The Villages Children's Homes, 1986—, Menninger Found., 1996—; mem. children's TV adv. bd. CBS-TV, 1996—. Fellow Am. Psychol. Assn. (pres. div. child youth and family svcs. 1990); mem. Internat. Comm. Assn., Soc. Rsch. in Child Devel., Royal Commonwealth Soc. (London), Manhattan Country Club. Home: 1731 Humboldt St Manhattan KS 66502-4140 Office: Kans State U Office Vice Provost Rsch 101 Fairchild Hall Manhattan KS 66506-1100 E-mail: jpm@ksu.edu.

MURRAY, JOHN WILLIAM, JR. writer, legal investigator; b. Apr. 8, 1934; s. John William and Frances (Bryan) M.; m. Norma Sousa, Oct. 30, 1959 (div. Apr. 1989); children: John William III, James Patrick, Jeffrey Dean, Jerome Bryan, Jay Joseph. BS, U. Hartford, 1968; MBA, U. Conn., 1971. Cert. fraud examiner, legal investigator, criminal def. investigator. Legal investigator, Dallas, 1974—. Author: Accident Investigation in the Private Sector, 1994 (Best New Investigative Book of Yr., 1994), Accident Investigation in the Private Sector, vol. 2, 1997, Forensic Photography in the Private Sector, 1995, Sex Crimes, 1995, Photographing Vehicles for Litigation, 1995, Guide to Depositions and Trials for Police Officer and Accident Reconstructionists, 1999, Guide to the Internet for Accident Investigators, 2001. 1st lt. USMC, 1957-60. Named One of Top 5 Investigators in Am. PI Mag., 1998, One of Top 25 Investigators of the Century, Nat. Assn. Investigative Specialists. Mem. Nat. Assn. Legal Investigators (cert., chmn. nat. cert. 1987-89, nat. chmn. editor-pub. awards com. 1992-96, regional dir. 1999-00, Editor-Pub. award Legal Investigator mag. 1989, 91, Nat. Dirs. award 1997), Evidence Photographers Internat. Coun., Nat. Assn. Investigative Specialists (cert. expert in investigative photography, expert in accident investigation, Outstanding Spkr. of Yr. award 1995, Lifetime Achievement award 1996), Nat. Acad. for Continuing Edn. (co-founder), North Tex. Pvt. Investigators Assn. (pres. 2000). Avocations: photography, stamp collecting. Office: 3942 Rochelle Dr Dallas TX 75220-1814 E-mail: jwmpi@aol.com.

MURRAY, JOSEPH EDWARD, retired plastic surgeon; b. Milford, Mass., Apr. 1, 1919; s. William Andrew and Mary (DePasquale) Murray; m. Virginia Link, June 2, 1945; children: Virginia, Margaret, Joseph Link, Katharine, Thomas, Richard. AB, Holy Cross Coll., 1940, DSc, 1965; MD, Harvard, 1943; DSc, Rockford (Ill.) Coll., 1966, Roger Williams Coll., 1986; PhD (hon.) , Anna Marie Coll., 1993, SUNY, Albany, 1993, U. Suffolk, 1993, Magill U., Montreal, 1996. Diplomate Am. Bd. Surgery, Am. Bd. Plastic Surgery . Chief plastic surgeon Peter Bent Brigham Hosp., Boston, 1951—86; chief plastic surgeon Children's Hosp. Med. Center, 1972—85; prof. surgery Harvard Med. Sch., 1970—86; ret., 1986. Chmn. Am. Bd. Plastic Surgery , 1969. Maj. M.C. U.S. Army, 1944—47. Recipient Gold medal, Internat. Soc. Surgeons, 1963, Nobel prize for medicine or physiology, 1990, Sabin award, 1994, Lifetime Achievement award, Mass. Med. Soc., 1988. Fellow: AMA, AAAS (hon.), Royal Coll. Surgeons Edinburgh, Royal Coll. Surgeons Ireland, Royal Coll. Surgeons of Eng., Royal Australasian Coll. Surgeons; mem.: NAS, ACS (regent 1970—79, v.p. 1983), Am. Acad. Arts and Scis. (Hon. award 1962), Am. Assn. Plastic Surgeons (pres. 1964—65, Hon. award 1969), Soc. U. Surgeons, Boston Surg. Soc. (pres. 1975), New Eng. Surg. Assn. (pres. 1986—87), Am. Surg. Assn. (v.p. 1979), Harvard Med. Sch. Alumni Coun. (pres. 1984), Tavern Club, Badminton and Tennis Club, Wellesley Country Club, Alpha Omega Alpha. Home: 108 Abbott Rd Wellesley MA 02481-6104

MURRAY, JOSEPH WILLIAM, banker; b. Alamosa, Colo., July 20, 1944; s. Joseph A. and Virginia (Wood) M.; m. Helen Hoberg, Jan. 20, 1970; children: Brian, Beth, Meghan. BS in Bus. with hon., U. Colo., 1966; MBA with hon., Northwestern U., 1967. Various positions with Continental Ill. Nat. Bank, Chgo., 1967-82; sr. v.p. AllFirst Bank, Balt., 1982—. Bd. dirs. Politzer & Haney, Clarity Incentive Systems; faculty mem. U. N.C. Exec. Programs on Cash Mgmt., Chapel Hill, 1982—; lectr. cash mgmt.; mem. corp. svcs. commn. Bank Adminstrn. Inst., 1992-94. Assoc. editor: Essentials of Cash Management, 4th edit., 1992, 5th edit., 1995. Pres. Wakefield Improvement Assn., Timonium, Md., 1987, 96, bd. dirs., 1996—; pres. Glen Ellyn (Ill.) Libr., 1978-82, trustee; pres. Glen Ellyn Tennis Assn., 1981, bd. dirs.; bd. trustees, sec. Ctr. Stage, 1987—; bd. dirs., Baltimore Chamber Jazz Soc., 2001. Mem. Treasury Mgmt. Assn. (editl. adv. bd., payments adv. grp., 1999), L'Hirondelle Club (Ruxton, Md.), Beta Gamma Sigma. Avocations: tennis, jazz piano, reading, racewalking. Office: AllFirst Bank PO Box 1596 Baltimore MD 21203-1596

MURRAY, JOSEPH JAMES, JR. zoologist; b. Lexington, Va., Mar. 13, 1930; s. Joseph James and Jane Dickson (Vardell) M.; m. Elizabeth Hickson, Aug. 24, 1957; children: Joseph James III, Alison Joan, William Lister BS, Davidson Coll., 1951; BA, Oxford U., Eng., 1954, MA, 1957, D.Phil., 1962. Instr. biology Washington & Lee U., Lexington, Va., 1956-58; asst. prof. biology U. Va., Charlottesville, 1962-67, assoc. prof., 1967-73, prof., 1973-77, Samuel Miller prof. biology, 1977-98, prof. emeritus, 1998, chmn. dept. biology, 1984-87. Co-dir. Mountain Lake Biol. Sta., Pembroke, Va., 1963-91. Author: Genetic Diversity and Natural Selection, 1972; contbr. articles to profl. jours. Served with U.S. Army, 1955-56 Rhodes scholar, 1951-54 Fellow AAAS, Va. Acad. Sci.; mem. Am. Soc. Naturalists, Genetics Soc. Am., Soc. Study Evolution, Am. Soc. Ichthyologists and Herpetologists, Va. Acad. Sci. (pres. 1986-87), Va. Soc. Ornithology (pres. 1976-79) Avocations: walking; mountaineering; shooting. E-mail: jjm5a@virginia.edu.

MURRAY, KATE SHAKESHAFT, artist; b. Washington, Aug. 18, 1958; d. Alston Jerrett and Emmy Hammond Shakeshaft; m. E. Donald Murray, Nov. 8, 1997. BA in English, Grinnell Coll., 1980; BFA in Ceramics, Sculpture and Drawing, U. Iowa, 1984; MFA in Ceramics, U. Fla., 1994. Potter, cook U. Iowa, Iowa City, 1983-88; potter Belmont, Vt., 1988-91; grad. asst. U. Fla., Gainesville, 1991-94; temp. instr. Francis Marion U., Florence, S.C., 1994-95, asst. prof., 1995-97; artist, potter Round Earth Studio, Gainesville, 1997—; area dir. Fla. Craftsmen, Inc., 2000—01. Contbg. artist to Ceramic Design Book, 1998, Clay Times mag., 1998, 99, The Art of Contemporary American Pottery, 2001, The Glaze Book, 2002. Grinter fellow, 1991-94; recipient Purchase award Shimpo Corp., 1994, Lagrange Nat. XX Biennial Exhbn.,

1998, Amaco prize Miami Valley Crossroads in Clay Competition, 1998, Functional Pottery award USA Craft Today, 1999; named Emerging Artist NCECA Conf., 2002. Mem. Nat. Coun. for Edn. in Ceramic Arts. Avocations: cooking, gardening, reading, critic. Home: 1854 NW 41st Ave Gainesville FL 32605-1924 E-mail: roundear@mindspring.com.

MURRAY, KATHLEEN, municipal official; b. Phillipsburg, N.J., Nov. 1, 1960; d. Joseph A. and Joann P. (Sepple) M. BS, Rosemont Coll., 1983. Legis. asst. Office of Anna C. Verna, Phila., 1983-86, aide to fin. com., 1989-94, chief of staff, 1994—; head of circulation Haverford (Pa.) Coll., 1987-88; asst. dir. Outreach Coord. Ctr., Phila., 1988-89. Staff mem. select com. of fiscal stability, Phila., 1992-94; mem. pub. affairs com. Local Emergency Planning Commn., Phila., 1995-98; staff Mayor's Commn. of Phila. Naval Base, 1997; mem. Mayor's Commn. on Homelessness, Phila., 1993-96. Mem. Police Commrs. Gay and Lesbian Liaison Com., 1998—2001; bd. dirs. Southwest Task Force, Inc., Phila., 1983—86, Voyage House Inc., Phila., 1991—96, PrideFest Am., 1998—2001, Pride of Phila. Election Com., 1999—2001, Phila. Housing Devel. Corp., 2001—, Phila. Reinvestment Commn., 2001—, Eighteenth St. Devel. Corp., 2001—. Democrat. Episcopalian. Avocations: tennis, golf, reading, U.S. history. Office: Office of Pres 494 City Hall Philadelphia PA 19107-3201

MURRAY, KEVIN DENNIS, surgeon; b. Paterson, N.J., June 22, 1953; s. Robert Emmet and Florence Sophie (Nordman) M. BS in Chemistry, Mt. St. Mary's Coll., 1974; MD, U. Md., 1978. Cert. Am. Bd. of Surgery, 1995, Am. Bd. of Thoracic Surgery, 1997. Intern U. Chgo.-Pritzker Med. Sch., 1978-79; resident in surgery U. Chgo.-Pritzker Med. Sch. Hosps. and Clinics, 1979-82; Cardiothor resident Yale-New Haven (Conn.) Hosp.-Yale U. Sch. Medicine, 1984-86; fellow in bioengring. U. Utah, 1982-84; asst. prof. Ohio State U., 1986-93; staff Arthur James Cancer Inst., Columbus, Ohio, 1990-93; staff cardiothoracic surgery Barnes-Jewish Hosp., St. Louis, 1996-97; faculty cardiothoracic surgery Washington U., 1996-97; assoc. prof., chief cardiothoracic surgery U. Nev. Sch. of Medicine, Las Vegas, 1997—. Med. dir. dept. circulation tech. Sch. Allied Health, Ohio State U., 1988-93; cons. Inst. Bioengring., Salt Lake City, 1995—; dir. The Heart and Lung Inst., U. Nev. Sch. Medicine, 1999—. Fellow Am. Coll. Surgery, Am. Coll. Cardiology, Am. Coll. Chest Physicians, Internat. Soc. Heart and Lung Transplantation, Soc. Thoracic Surgeons; mem. Am. Soc. Artificial Internal Organs, Assn. Thoracic Surgeons, Alpha Omega Alpha. Home: 7870 Dana Point Las Vegas NV 89117-3215 Office: U Nev Sch of Medicine 2040 W Charleston Blvd Ste 601 Las Vegas NV 89102-2245 E-mail: kmurray@med.unr.edu.

MURRAY, LAWRENCE, management consultant; b. N.Y.C., May 10, 1939; s. Gilbert and Edna (Blatt) M.; children: Robert, Stacy, David, Daniel, Abigail. BA, Cornell U., 1961; MBA, U. Okla., 1966; PhD, Pacific Western Univ., 1993. Cert. Pa. Food Mgmt. Account exec. Merrill Lynch, Paramus, N.J., 1965-69; chmn., pres. Murray, Lind & Co., Inc., Jersey City, 1969-72; dir. investor rels. IU Internat. Corp., Phila., 1972-73, dir. spl. projects, 1974-75; dir. fin. comm., mem. exec. staff, chmn. bd. ARA Svcs., Inc., 1975-78; chmn., chief exec. officer Century Mgmt. and affiliated cos., West Chester, 1976-82; chmn. bd., CEO Creative Mgmt. Corp., Bala Cynwyd and West Chester, 1982-87, Fin. Mgmt. Profl. Corp., West Chester, 1983-89; chmn. bd. dirs. Venture Frontiers Co., Denver, 1984-89; chmn. bd., CEO Fin. Intelligence Corp., West Chester, 1989-95; CEO, Healthy Living Ctrs. , Pa., 1995—; CEO, chmn. bd. dirs. Tax Dr. Corp., 2002—. Lectr. bus. orgn. and mgmt. Bergen C.C., 1971-72; chmn. bd. dirs. Med. Intelligence Corp., West Chester, 1993-95, Tax Doctor Corp., 2002—; chmn. bd., CEO Healthy Living Ctrs., 1993--; bd. dirs. Miramax, Health Scis. Corp., Brown Paper Bag Harry's Corp. Author: The Organized Stockbroker, 1970; A New Era in Mergers and Acquisitions, 1974; Communications: Management's Newest Marketing Skill, 1976, Powerful Tax-Saving Strategies for Honest People, 1992, Teach Your Children How to Eat Properly and Add 20 Years to Their Lives, 1999; contbr. articles to profl. jours. Pres., Congregation Beth Israel, Media, Pa., 1977-78, Parents Without Partners, Valley Forge, Pa., 1982-83; v.p. Cornell U. Class of 1961, 1981-86; mem. White House Conf. on Bus. Ethics in Am., 1986; active Beth Chaim Reform Synagogue. Served to 1st lt. arty., U.S. Army, 1963-64. Decorated U.S. Army Commendation medal. Mem. Nat. Investor Rels. Inst. (pres. Phila. chpt. 1976-78), Internat. Coun. Shopping Ctrs., Am. Health Info. Mgmt. Assn., C. of C. of Greater West Chester. Home: 924 Hollyview Ln West Chester PA 19380-1376

MURRAY, LOWELL, Canadian senator; b. New Waterford, N.S., Can., Sept. 26, 1936; s. Daniel and Evelyn (Young) M.; m. Colleen Elaine MacDonald; children: William, Colin. BA, St. Francis Xavier U., Antigonish, N.S., Can.; MA in Pub. Adminstrn., Queen's U., Kingston, Ont., Can. Chief of staff Minister of Justice and Minister of Pub. Works Can., Ottawa, Ont., Senator M. Wallace McCutcheon, Ottawa; leader of opposition Can.; dep. minister Premier N.B. (Can.); mem. Senate of Can., Ottawa, Ont., 1979—, co-chmn. joint Senate-House of Commons com. ofcl. langs., 1980-84, chmn. standing Senate com. on banking, trade and commerce, 1984-86, chmn. standing senate com. on nat. fin., 1995, 99—, chmn. standing senate com. on social affairs, sci. and tech., 1997-99. Bd. dirs. SONY Can. Inc.; trustee Inst. Rsch. Pub. Policy, 1984-86, mem. Trilateral Commn., 1985-86. Sworn of the privy coun., appointed leader of Govt. in the Senate, 1986—93; Min. of State Fed.-Provincial Rels., 1986—91; min. responsible for Atlantic Can. Opportunities Agy., 1987—88, acting min. comms., 1988—89; nat. campaign chmn. gen. election Progressive Conservative Party Can., 1977—79, 1981—83. Roman Catholic. Office: The Senate Ottawa ON Canada K1A 0A4

MURRAY, LYNNE CHRISTINE, writer; b. Decatur, Ill., Aug. 19, 1948; d. Channing Wayne Murray, Dorothy Leone Korneisel; m. Charles William Powell (dec. June 25, 1991). BA in Psychology, San Francisco State U., 1975. Author: (book) Termination Interview, 1988, Death Flower (pub. in German as Mit anderen Mitteln), 1995, Larger Than Death, 1997, Large Target, 2000, At Large, 2001, A Ton of Trouble, 2002. Recipient Disting. Achievement award, Nat. Assn. to Advance Fat Acceptance), 1999. Mem.: Mystery Writers of Am. (bd. dirs. Norcal chpt. 1997—99), Sisters in Crime. Buddhist. Personal E-mail: murraymade@aol.com.

MURRAY, MARY, early childhood, elementary; b. Beverly, Mass. d. Edward James and Anne (Dowd) M. AS in Nursing, Endicott Coll.; AB, Boston Coll., 1985; MSEd in Early Childhood & Elem. Edn., Wheelock Coll., 1993. Cert. tchr., Mass. Tchr. Glen Urquhart Sch., Beverly Farms, Mass., 1982-87, kindergarten asst., 1982-83; kindergarten tchr., 1983-85; first grade tchr., 1985-87; dir. extended day program Glen Urquhart Sch., Beverly Farms, Mass., 1982-85, coord. summer camp program, 1984-86; lower sch. assoc. Shady Hill Sch., Cambridge, 1987-88; rsch. asst. Wheelock Coll., Boston, 1987-91; tchr. kindergarten, curriculum coord. Prospect Hill Parents' and Childrens' Ctr., Waltham, 1988-91; ednl. cons. Beverly Farms, 1992—; mentor, tchr., faculty summer compass program Lesley Coll. Grad. Sch. of Edn., Cambridge, 1994-96; tchr. 6th grade sci. tech. and engring. Briscoe Mid. Sch., Beverly, 1999—2002. Buyer Cottage & Castle LLC, Pride's Crossing, Mass., 1997-98; founder, dir. Summer Enrichment at Lanesville, Mass., 1987-89; adv. bd. Power Industries, Wellesley Hills, Mass., 1989-92; cons. Activities Club, Inc., Waltham, 1986-91; mem. Early Childhood Adv. Coun., Medford, Mass., 1990-93; lifeguard supr. West Beach Corp., 1980-86; mem. cert. team Nat. Assn. Educators Young Children, 1989-91, Ind. Sch. Assn. Mass., 1983-88; presenter workshops. Author curriculum materials, activity kits for children. Tchr. religious edn. program St. Margaret Parish, Beverly Farms, 1970—, dir., coord., 1989—; synod group leader Archdiocese of Boston, 1987; water safety instr. ARC, parish pastor visitation com., 1995, 2001; active Mass. Spl. Olympics; youth activities coord. Farms/Prides Cmty. Orgn., Feed the Hungry Project, Beverly, Mass., Good Friday Walk Orgnl. Com.; Friends of Beverly Farms Libr. Wheelock Coll. grad. grantee, 1993. Mem. ASCD, Nat. Sci. Tchrs. Assn., Assn. Childhood Edn. Internat., Boston Coll. Alumni Assn. (mem. B.C.-Young Alumni Club 1987-95, program coord./spl. event 1988-90). Democrat. Roman Catholic. Avocations: reading, gardening, travel, seasonal sports, children's literature. Home: 650 Hale St Beverly Farms Beverly MA 01915-2117

MURRAY, MICHAEL DENNIS, pharmacist; b. Blairsville, Pa., Apr. 13, 1952; s. Howard Jacob and Elizabeth Murray; m. Jennifer Jayne Chumbler, Aug. 4, 1979; children: Ryan Michael, Kristin Elizabeth. BSc in Pharmacy, Duquesne U., 1975, D of Pharmacy, 1977; M of Pub. Health, Ind. U., 1992. Registered pharmacist, Ind., Pa. Asst. prof. Purdue U. Sch. of Pharmacy, West Lafayette, Ind., 1982-88, assoc. prof., 1988-99, prof., 1999—2001, Bucke prof. pharmacy, 2002—. Adj. asst. prof. Purdue U. Sch. of Pharmacy, West Lafayette, 1977—82; adj. assoc. prof. Ind. U. Sch. Medicine, 1992—2001, adj. prof., 2001—; dir. rsch. Ind. Drug Evaluation and Analysis Ctr., Indpls., 1995—98; faculty Health Svcs. R&D, Indpls., 1995—98; dir. healthcare data and epidemiology Regenstrief Inst., Indpls., 1996—; faculty scholar Purdue U., 1999. Commr. Saints Football Club, Lawrence, Ind., 1996-97; v.p. Ind. Soccer League, Carmel, Ind., 1996-97. Mem.: U.S. Pharmacopia (safe medicine use and therapeutic decision expert panels 2000—), Am. Soc. Clin. Pharmacology and therapeutics (pharmacoepidemiology chair 1998—2001, chair com. on coordination of sci. sects. 2001—, bd. dirs., exec. com.), Internat. Soc. Pharmacoepiemiology (sci. programs 1989—2001, membership chair 1990—93, bd. dirs. 1991—94). Democrat. Roman Catholic. Avocations: stained glass crafts, arts, hiking, bicycling. Home: 6309 Cromwell Rd Indianapolis IN 46250-2715 Office: Regenstrief Inst RHC 6th Fl 1050 Wishard Blvd Indianapolis IN 46202-2872 E-mail: mmurray@regenstrief.org.

MURRAY, MICHAEL KENT, lawyer; b. Missoula, Mont., Feb. 14, 1948; s. Paul R. and Virginia F. Murray; children: Britton M., Spencer J. BA, U. Calif., Santa Barbara, 1970; JD, U. Santa Clara, 1974. Bar: Wash. 1974, U.S. Ct. Claims 1975, U.S. Tax Ct. 1976, U.S. Dist. Ct. Wash. 1977, U.S. Ct. Appeals (fed. cir.) 1982. Trial atty. honor law grad. program U.S. Dept. Justice, Washington, 1974-76; atty. Foster Pepper & Riviera, Seattle, 1976-79, ptnr. Seattle and Bellevue, 1980-86, ptnr.-in-charge Bellevue, 1983-86; atty., pres. Michael K. Murray, P.S., Seattle, 1986—. Pres. N.W. Properties Devel. Corp., Seattle, 1986-92; of counsel Lasher Holzapfel Sperry & Ebberson, Seattle, 1992-2001; v.p. BELFOR USA Group, Inc., Seattle, 2001—. Articles editor Santa Clara Lawyer, U. Santa Clara Sch. Law, 1973-74. Trustee Pacific Northwest Ballet, Seattle, 1979-81; dir. Bellevue Downtown Assn., 1984-87. Mem. Wash. State Bar Assn., King County Bar Assn., Seattle Yacht Club, Seattle Tennis Club. Avocations: sailing, fly fishing, biking, computing. Home: 1570 9th Ave N Edmonds WA 98020-2627 Office: 3826 Woodland Park Ave N Seattle WA 98103-7926 E-mail: mmurray@US.belfor.com.

MURRAY, MICHAEL PETER, economist, educator; b. N.Y.C., Sept. 15, 1946; s. Thomas John and Marie Fitzgerald; m. Rosanne Ducey, June 21, 1969; children: Sarah, Anna, Adam, Ben, Seth, Peter. BA, U. Santa Clara, 1968; MS, Iowa State U., 1971, PhD, 1974. Acting asst. prof. U. Calif., San Diego, 1972-73; asst. prof. U. Va., Charlottesville, 1973-77; vis. asst. prof. U. Calif., Berkeley, 1977-78; assoc. prof. Duke U., Durham, N.C., 1978-80; prof. Claremont (Calif.) Grad. Sch., 1980-86; sr. economist The RAND Corp., Santa Monica, Calif., 1980-86; Charles Franklin Phillips prof. econs. Bates Coll., Lewiston, Maine, 1986—. Vis. prof. econs. Harvard U., 1999—; cons. HUD, Washington, 1973, The World Bank, Washington, 1981—. Author: Subsidizing Industrial Location, 1988, Building Organizational Decision Support Systems, 1992; contbr. articles to profl. jours. NDEA fellow U. Calif., San Diego, 1971; vis. scholar HUD, Washington, 1979, World Bank, 1985-86. Mem. Am. Econ. Assn., Order of Silver Spade. Democrat. Roman Catholic. Avocations: soccer, bridge, theater. Office: Bates Coll Dept Econs Lewiston ME 04240 Home: 111 Buker Rd Litchfield ME 04350-3323

MURRAY, MICHELLE LINDA, perinatal nursing specialist; BSN, UCLA, 1975; MSN, U. N.Mex., 1981, PhD, 1992. Nurse instr. Peace Corps, Manama, Bahrain, 1975-76; staff nurse nurse corps USAF, 1976-78; staff nurse labor and delivery Parkview Episcopal Hosp., Pueblo, Colo., 1978-79; lectr., clin. instr. U. Albuquerque, 1980-81, coord. maternity nursing, 1982; nurse educator St. Joseph Hosp., Albuquerque, 1982-84, nurse quality assurance, risk mgmt., 1984; nursing edn. specialist Southwest Community Health Svcs., 1984-86; pres., founder Learning Resources Internat., 1986—. Clin. specialist and part-time staff nurse Lovelace Med. Ctr., Albuquerque, 1979-80, 88-2000; educator, staff nurse Presbyn. Hosp., Albuquerque, 1986-87, 2000—; edn. cons. nutritional divsn. Mead Johnson, 1986-88; cons. Utah Med. Products, Inc., Midvale, 1988—, DataChem, Inc., 1992—, Hollister, 1994—; mem. sci. adv. bd. LMS, Quebec, 1999—. Author: Antepartal and Intrapartal Fetal Monitoring, 2d edit., 1997, Essentials of Fetal Monitoring, 2000, 2d edit., 2001. 1st lt. USAF Nurse Corps, 1976-78. Mem. N.Mex. Nursing Assn. (treas., bd. dirs., conv. del. 1986), Assn. Women's Health, Obstetric, and Neonatal Nurses (state edn. coord., N.Mex. Nurse of Yr. 1990, sec.-treas. 1995-98, sect. chair 1998—), Albuquerque Perinatal Nurses Coun. (founding mem.), Sigma Theta Tau. Office: Learning Resources Internat Inc PO Box 92050 Albuquerque NM 87199-2050

MURRAY, NEIL VINCENT, computer science educator; b. Schenectady, N.Y., July 14, 1948; s. Robert Emslie and Eileen Marie (Milano) M. BS in Engring. Physics, Cornell U., 1970; MS in Computer and Info. Sci., Syracuse U., 1974, PhD in Computer and Info. Sci., 1979. Rsch. asst. Syracuse (N.Y.) U., 1977-78; instr. computer sci. dept. LeMoyne Coll., Syracuse, 1978-79, asst. prof., 1979-82; asst. prof. computer sci. SUNY, Albany, 1982-87, assoc. prof., 1987-97, prof., 1997—, dept. chair, 1999—. Treas. CADE, Inc., Assn. Automated Reasoning; presenter in field. Contbr. articles to profl. jours. Mem. IEEE Computer Soc., Am. Assn. Artificial Intelligence, Assn. Automated Reasoning, Assn. Computing Machinery. Home: 1125 Glenmeadow Ct Niskayuna NY 12309-2511 Office: SUNY Dept Computer Sci L1 67A Albany NY 12222-0001 E-mail: nvm@cs.albany.edu .

MURRAY, PATTY, senator; b. Bothell, Wash., Oct. 10, 1950; d. David L. and Beverly A. (McLaughlin) Johns; m. Robert R. Murray, June 2, 1972; children: Randy P., Sara A. BA, Wash. State U., 1972. Sec. various cos., Seattle, 1972-76; citizen lobbyist various ednl. groups, 1983-88; legis. lobbyist Orgn. for Parent Edn., 1977-84; instr. Shoreline Community Coll., 1984-88; mem. Wash. State Senate, 1989-92; senator from Wash. U.S. Senate, 1993—. Mem. Appropriations Com. ranking minority mem. subcom. mil. constrn.; vice chmn. Dem. Senatorial Campaign Com.; mem. Com. on Labor and Human Resources, Budget Com., Health, Edn., Labor and Pensions Com., Com. on Vets. Affairs. Mem. bd. Shoreline Sch., Seattle, 1985-89; mem. steering com. Demonstration for Edn., Seattle, 1987; founder, chmn. Orgn. for Parent Edn., Wash., 1981-85; 1st Congl. rep. Wash. Women United, 1983-85. Recipient Recognition of Svc. to Children award Shoreline PTA Coun., 1986, Golden Acorn Svc. award, 1989; Outstanding Svc. award Wash. Women United, 1986, Outstanding Svc. to Pub. Edn. award Citizens Ednl. Ctr. NW, Seattle, 1987. Democrat. Office: US Senate 173 Russell Senate Office Bldg Washington DC 20510-0001*

MURRAY, PETER, metallurgist, manufacturing company executive; b. Rotherham, Yorks, Eng., Mar. 13, 1920; came to U.S., 1967, naturalized, 1974; s. Michael and Ann (Hamstead) M.; m. Frances Josephine Glaisher, Sept. 8, 1947; children: Jane, Paul, Alexander. BSc in Chemistry with honors, Sheffield (Eng.) U., 1941, postgrad., 1946-49; PhD in Metallurgy, Brit. Iron and Steel Research Bursar, Sheffield, 1948. Research chemist Steetley Co., Ltd., Worksop, Notts, Eng., 1941-45; with Atomic Energy Research Establishment, Harwell, Eng., 1949-67, head div. metallurgy, 1960-64, asst. dir., 1964-67; tech. dir., mgr. fuels and materials, advanced reactors div. Westinghouse Electric Corp., Madison, Pa., 1967-74; dir. research Westinghouse Electric Europe (S.A.), Brussels, 1974-75; chief scientist advanced power systems divs. Westinghouse Electric Corp., Madison, Pa., 1975-81, dir. nuclear programs Washington, 1981-92; sr. cons. Nuc. Programs, 1992—2001. Mem. divisional rev. coms. Argonne Nat. Lab., 1968-73; Mellor Meml. lectr. Inst. Ceramics, 1963 Contbr. numerous articles to profl. jours.; editorial adv. bd.: Jour. Less Common Metals, 1968—. Recipient Holland Meml. Research prize Sheffield U., 1949 Fellow Royal Inst. Chemistry (Newton Chambers Research prize 1954), Inst. Ceramics, Am. Nuclear Soc.; mem. Brit. Ceramics Soc. (pres. 1965), Am. Ceramic Soc., Nat. Acad. Engring. Roman Catholic. Home: 20308 Canby Ct Montgomery Village MD 20886-4014

MURRAY, PETER WILLIAM, airline executive, educator, college administrator; b. Boston, Mar. 24, 1942; s. William Andrew Murray and Carlotta Catherine (Cenedella) Catusi; m. Carolyn Pfaff, Feb. 23, 1967; children: Eric, Trevor. AB, U. Notre Dame, South Bend, Ind., 1964; MBA, U. Pa., 1966. Analyst Delta Airlines, Atlanta, 1966-67; mgr. So. Airways, 1969-72; sr. analyst Eastern Airlines, N.Y.C., 1968-69, mgr. Miami, Fla., 1972-89; dir. Discovery Airways, Honolulu, 1989-90; dean sch. bus. Chaminade U. Honolulu, 1990-94, dir. MS in Japanese bus. studies, 1990-93; assoc. prof. mgmt., dir. grad. adminstrn. Winthrop U., Rock Hill, S.C., 1995-96; dir. divsn. of lifelong learning Johnson C. Smith U., Charlotte, N.C., 1996-98; mgr. Bur. of Census, 1998-99; pres. Peter W. Murray & Assocs., 1999—; realtor Mathers Realty.com, 2000—; asst. mgr. SBIC/Charlotte Libr., 2002—; asst. mgr. Small Bus. Info. Ctr., Main Pub. Libr., Charlotte. Adj. prof. U. Miami, Fla. Internat. U., Barry U., U. Hawaii, Pfeiffer U., Montreat Coll., Belmont-Abbey Col., Embry-Riddle Aero. U., Limestone Coll., 1975—, Keller Grad. Sch. Mgmt., Strayer U. Mem. Wharton Grad. Alumni Club, Notre Dame Alumni Club, Am. Mktg. Assn., Nat. Assn. Realtors, Charlotte Regional Realty Assn., N.C. Assn. Realtors. Republican. Home: 6701 Alexander Rd Charlotte NC 28270-1808 E-mail: petemurray@hotmail.com.

MURRAY, PHILIP EDMUND, JR. lawyer; b. Floral Park, N.Y., Mar. 4, 1950; s. Philip Edmund and Anne Marie (Mackin) M.; m. Karen Anne McLeavey, Aug. 14, 1976; children: Erin Anne, Philip E. III. BS cum laude, Boston Coll., 1972, JD, 1975. Bar: Mass. 1975, U.S. Dist. Ct. Mass. 1976, U.S. Supreme Ct. 1992. Law clk. to presiding justices Mass. Superior Ct., Boston, 1975-76; sr. ptnr. Martin Magnuson McCarthy & Kenney, 1976—. Hearing officer Bd. of Bar Overseers of the Supreme Judicial Ct., Boston, 1990-96. Editor: Boston Coll. Law Rev., 1973-75; contbr. articles to profl. jours. Mem. Mass. Bar Assn., Mass. Bar Found.; mem. Am. Soc. Law and Medicine, Am. Coll. Legal Medicine. Office: Martin Magnuson McCarthy & Kenney 101 Merrimac St Ste 700 Boston MA 02114-4716

MURRAY, PHYLLIS CYNTHIA, educator; b. Farmville, Va., Nov. 3, 1938; d. Claude and Frazure Young; m. Robert William Murray, Dec. 14, 1963; 1 child, Sidney Adolphus. BA, CUNY-Hunter Coll., 1960; MS, U. Pa., 1961; diploma, Cornell U., 1980; cert., Vassar Coll., 1991. Tchr. D.C. Bd. Edn., Washington, 1961-63, N.Y. Bd. Edn., 1963—. TV prodr. TCI, Mamaroneck, N.Y., 1990—; radio host Sta. WVOX Radio, New Rochelle, N.Y., 1994—; founder One Love Tennis, White Plains, 1994—. Author: Huggy Bean Visits Ethiopia, 1985, The Colorful World of Huggy Bear, 1985; co-author: UFT Martin Luther King Instructional Package, 1990, Encounters in Living History: Activity Based Lessons on the Enslaved Africans of the North, 1996; author: Oral History of James Austin; contbr. Mem. Town and Village Civic Club, Scarsdale, N.Y., 1994—; mem. African adv. bd. Philipsburg Manor, 1999; alumna Women's Cmapaign Sch., Yale U., 1999; dir. First Vacation Bible Sch., Trinity Luth. ch., Scarsdale. Mem. NAACP (life), U.S. Tennis Assn., , United Fedn. of Tchr. (del. unity 1993, mem. unity com. 1994—), Ea. Tennis Assn. (at-large), Alpha Kappa Alpha (Silver Star 1991). Home: 1181 Post Rd Scarsdale NY 10583-2023 Office: Bd of Edn PS75X 984 Faile St Bronx NY 10459-3703 E-mail: pmur75@aol.com.

MURRAY, PIUS CHARLES WILLIAM, priest, librarian, educator; b. Worcester, Mass., July 24, 1957; s. Charles William and Ann Frances (Donoghue) Murray. BA, Coll. Holy Cross, 1979; MLS, U. R.I., 1982; MA, Holy Apostles Coll. and Sem., 1990, MDiv, 1991; postgrad., Hebrew U. Jerusalem, 1992-93; Lic. in Sacred Scripture, Pontifical Bibl. Inst., Rome, 1995, postgrad., Fordham U., 2001—. Ordained priest Roman Cath Ch, 1992. Libr. supr. Holy Cross Coll. Libr., Worcester, Mass., 1980-86; libr. dir. Greenfield (Mass.) Pub. Libr., 1982-83; town libr. West Springfield (Mass.) Pub. Libr., 1985-86; instr. sacred scripture, assoc. libr. Holy Apostle Coll. and Sem., Cromwell, Conn., 1995-96; prof. Old Testament, dir. libr. svcs. Pope John XXIII Nat. Sem., Weston, Mass., 1996-99; prof. New Testament Pontifical Inst. Regina Mundi, Rome, 1999—2000. Adj prof Old Testament, dir library Servs Pope John XXIII Nat Sem, Weston, Mass., 1995—96; chaplain cruises Princess Lines, 1996—, Royal Caribbean Cruises; leader pilgrimages to Holy Land, 1997—. Author: (by laws) Cath Theological Library Consortium; book reviewer: America, book reviewer: Choice, book reviewer: Cath Biblical Quart, book reviewer: Medievalia et Humanistica, book reviewer: The National Catholic Register, book reviewer: Religion and the Arts, abstractor: Old Testament Abstracts, 1996—99; contbr. articles to profl jours. Participant Ctr French-Am Studies Library Sci, Paris, 1986; mem Theology Faculty Pastoral Provision, 1997—99; trustee Worcester Pub Library, 1983—86. Mem.: Authors Guild, Stigmatine Fathers and Bros, Equestrian Order Holy Sepulchre Jerusalem, Ancient Order Hiberians, Phi Beta Kappa, Beta Phi Mu, Phi Sigma Iota, Alpha Sigma Nu. Avocations: autograph collecting, bowling, movies, tennis, theater . E-mail: fatherpius57@hotmail.com.

MURRAY, RAYMOND CARL, geologist, educator; b. Fitchburg, Mass., July 2, 1929; s. Henry C. and Hattie (Mindt) Murray; m. Maureen J. Fleming, Aug. 20, 1988; children: Robert, Martha. AB, Tufts U., 1951; PhD, U. Wis., 1955. Head prodn. geol. research Shell Devel. Co., 1955-66; prof. geology U. N.Mex., 1966-67; prof. geology, head dept. Rutgers U., New Brunswick, NJ, 1967-77; forensic geologist, 1972—; v.p. research U. Mont., Missoula, 1977-96. Contbr. articles to books, profl. jours. Home: 106 Ironwood Pl Missoula MT 59803-2425 E-mail: rcm@selway.umt.edu.

MURRAY, RAYMOND HAROLD, physician; b. Cambridge, Mass., Aug. 17, 1925; s. Raymond Harold and Grace May (Dorr) M.; children— Maureen, Robert, Michael, Margaret, David, Elizabeth, Catherine, Anne. BS, U. Notre Dame, 1946; MD, Harvard U., 1948. Diplomate Am. Bd. Internal Medicine, also Sub-bd. Cardiovascular Disease. Practice medicine, Grand Rapids, Mich., 1955-62; asst. prof. to prof. medicine Ind. U. Sch. Medicine, 1962-77; prof. dept. medicine Coll. Human Medicine Mich. State U., Lansing, 1977-95, chmn. dept. medicine Coll. Human Medicine, 1977-89, emeritus, 1995—. Chmn. aeromed.-bioscis. panel Sci. Adv. Bd., USAF, 1977-81; mem. adv. coun. Office Alternative Medicine/NIH, 1997-99. Contbr. numerous articles to profl. publs. Served with USNR, 1942-45; Served with USPHS, 1950-53. Fellow ACP (gov. Mich. chpt. 1994-98); mem. Am. Heart Assn. (fellow coun. clin. cardiology), Am. Fedn. Clin. Rsch. E-mail: Raymondmur@aol.com.

MURRAY, RAYMOND LEE, retired clothing designer, writer; b. Decatur, Tenn., July 27, 1920; s. Floyd Lester and Ida Mae (McClure) M.; m. Melba Lee Murray, Dec. 21, 1947; 1 child, Alice Marie. Cert. indsl. engring., U. Tenn., 1946; cert. clothing designer, Am. Gentlemen Sch. Design, N.Y.C., 1947. Foreman, designer Hardwick Clothes, Cleveland, Tenn., 1938-55; designer Sears Roebuck Plant, Rutherford, 1956-59; designer, plant mgr. McGregor Sportswear, Corinth, Miss., 1960-67; plant mgr. Cable Industries, Tuskegee, Ala., 1968-69; gen. mgr. T&W Mfg. Co., Bremen, Ga., 1969; mem. R&D staff Hardwick Clothes, Cleveland, Tenn., 1970-86; pres. Murray-Wright Protection Clothing, 1985-95. Cons. textiles and bullet-proof fabric Murray Textile Anaylsts, Cleveland, Tenn., 1985-95. Author: Grandpa Saw it Happen WWII Normandy Beach, To Elbe, 1993, How We Uprooted Our Roots and What We Found, 1996, Bradley Divided: During Civil War, 1992; contbr. articles to profl. jours. Bd. dirs. ARC, Cleveland chpt., 1980-83, Cleveland YMCA, 1950-54. With U.S. Army, ETO. Decorated 5 Bronze Stars. Mem. VFW, Internat. Assn. Clothing Designers (pres. 1977; pres. So. chpt. 1972), Am. Soc. Quality Control (chair Tenn. chpt. 1952), Am. Legion, Elks, Vets. Battle of the Bulge, Kiwanis. Presbyterian. Avocations: fishing, hunting. Home: 102 Ridley Howard Ct Decatur GA 30030-2374 E-mail: raymurray102@mac.com.

MURRAY, RICHARD BENNETT, physics educator; b. Marietta, Ga., Dec. 5, 1928; s. William Moore and Ruth (Mozley) M.; m. Clella Bay, Apr. 1, 1956; children: Ada, Annette. BA, Emory U., 1947; MS, Ohio State U., 1950; PhD, U. Tenn., 1955. Rsch. asst. Gaseous Diffusion Plant, Oak Ridge, Tenn., 1947-48; rsch. physicist Oak Ridge Nat. Lab., 1955-66; vis. assoc. prof. physics U. Del, Newark, 1962-63, assoc. prof., 1966-69, prof., 1969-98, prof. emeritus, 1999—, acting chmn. dept. physics, 1975-76, univ. coord. for grad. studies, 1979-85, assoc. provost grad. studies, 1986-88, acting provost, v.p. acad. affairs, 1988-91, provost, 1993-94. Lectr. physics U. Tenn., Knoxville, 1963-66; vis. rsch. physicist U.S. Naval Rsch. Lab., 1991-92; vis. scientist Clarendon Lab., Oxford U., 1992; cons. to industry, 1957-93; councillor Oak Ridge Associated Univs., 1979-88, bd. dirs., 1983-94, vice chmn. coun., 1983-85, chmn. coun., 1985-88; sec.-treas. NE Assn. Grad. Schs., 1982-84; dir. U. Del. Press, 1979-82. Contbr. numerous articles on exptl. nuclear and solid state physics to profl. publs., 1948-85. Trustee Sanford Sch., Hockessin, Del., 1981-85; chmn. bd. dirs. Oak Ridge Associated Univs. Found., 1989-94; bd. dirs. Del. Inst. for Med. Edn. and Rsch., 1989-91. Predoctoral fellow Oak Ridge Inst. Nuclear Studies, 1953-55; grantee AEC, NSF, Dept. Energy, 1967-84. Fellow AAAS, Am. Phys. Soc.; mem. Southeastern Univs. Rsch.

Assn. (bd. dirs. 1989-97), Phi Beta Kappa, Sigma Xi, Sigma Pi Sigma, Phi Kappa Phi, Cosmos Club. Home: 4 Bridlebrook Ln Newark DE 19711-2058 Office: U Del Dept Physics & Astronomy Newark DE 19716

MURRAY, RICHARD KEITH, marketing executive; b. Pittsfield, Mass., June 7, 1960; s. William Keith and Sarah Murray. BS in Bus. Mgmt., Bradley U., 1982, MA in Edn., 1983. Dir. student activities Bradley U., Peoria, Ill., 1983-84; leg. asst. Commonwealth of Mass., Boston, 1984-85; spl. projects mgr. Films Inc., Chgo., 1985-86; nat. sales mgr. Coll. Satellite Network, Dallas, 1986-88; pres. Greylock Entertainment, Pittsfield, 1988-94; dir. mktg. Country Music Assn., Nashville, 1994—. Bd. dirs. Pittsfield Cmty. TV, 1992-94; active Nashville Cares, 1996, Carter-Mondale Presdl. campaign, 1980, Leadership Music, 1997-98. Mem. NARAS, Nashville Songwriters Assn., Promotion Mktg. Assn. (bd. dirs. 2000—), Nashville Advt. Fedn. Democrat. Roman Catholic. Office: Country Music Assn 1 Music Cir S Nashville TN 37203-4312 E-mail: rmurray@cmaworld.com.

MURRAY, RICHARD MAXIMILIAN, insurance executive; b. Vienna, Austria, Nov. 21, 1922; came to U.S., 1955, naturalized, 1961; s. and Elizabeth Helen Peiker. Grad. in world commerce studies, U. Vienna; postgrad., Columbia U. Asst. sec. Sterling Offices Ltd. (reins. intermediaries), London, Toronto, N.Y.C., 1951-59; v.p. Guy Carpenter, Inc. (reins. intermediaries), N.Y.C., 1959-68, Travelers Ins. Cos., 1968-87, ret., 1987. Mng. dir. La Metropole Ins. Co., Brussels, ret., 1987; chmn. bd. Nippon Mgmt. Corp., N.Y.C., ret., 1991; chmn. bd. Travelers Marine Corp., ret., 1987; pres. Travelers Reins Co. Bermuda Ltd., ret., 1987; pres. Travelers of Asia Ltd., Hong Kong, ret., 1987; vice-chmn. bd. La Prov Corp., N.Y.C.; bd. electors Ins. Hall of Fame; bd. dirs. United Am. Inst. Co., United Am. Holdings Co., Inc.; mem. adv. bd. Firemark Global Ins. Fund, L.P.; dir. emeritus Davis Internat. Total Return Fund.; guest prof. Donau U., Krems, Austria. Contbr. articles to profl. publs. Decorated for promotion of pvt. ins. (Peru); Knight Order of St. John, Knights of Malta (ambassador at large). Mem. Internat. Ins. Coun. (chmn. 1979-81, award 1990). Home: 60 Remsen St Brooklyn NY 11201-3453 Office: 1 Penn Plz Ste 3600 New York NY 10119-2108

MURRAY, ROBERT FOX, lawyer; b. Burlington, Vt., Feb. 28, 1952; s. Robert and Mary (Fox) M.; m. Ann Marie Bevilacqua, Aug. 20, 1988. BA, Colgate U., 1974; JD, Boston U., 1978. Bar: Mass. 1978, U.S. Dist. Ct. Mass. 1979. Assoc. Law Offices of George Howard, Dedham, Mass., 1978-80, from assoc. to ptnr. Fairbanks & Silvia Koczera, Fountain, Murray, New Bedford, Mass., 1980-84; pvt. practice, New Bedford, 1984—. Bd. dirs., clk. Downtown New Bedford, Inc. Mem. New Bedford C. of C., Waterfront Hist. Area League, Assn. Trial Lawyers Am., Mass. Acad. Trial Attys., Mass. Bar Assn., New Bedford Bar Assn., Bristol County Bar Assn. Democrat. Office: One Johnny Cake Hill New Bedford MA 02740

MURRAY, ROBERT WALLACE, chemistry educator; b. Brockton, Mass., June 20, 1928; s. Wallace James and Rose Elizabeth (Harper) M.; m. Claire K. Murphy, June 10, 1951; children: Kathleen A., Lynn E., Robert Wallace, Elizabeth A., Daniel J., William M., Padraic O'D. AB, Brown U., 1951; MA, Wesleyan U., Middletown, Conn., 1956; PhD, Yale U., 1960. Mem. tech. staff Bell Labs., Murray Hill, N.J., 1959-68; prof. chemistry U. Mo., St. Louis, 1968-81, chmn. dept., 1975-80, Curators' prof., 1981-2000, Curators' prof. emeritus, 2001—. Vis. prof. Engler-Bunte Inst. U. Karlsruhe, Fed. Republic Germany, 1982, dept. chemistry Univ. Coll., Cork, Ireland, 1989; cons. to govt. and industry. Co-editor: Singlet Oxygen, 1979; contbr. articles to profl. jours. Mem. Warren (N.J.) Twp. Com., 1962-63, mayor, 1963; mem. Planning Com. and Bd. Health, 1962-64, Bd. Edn., 1966-68. Served with USN, 1951-54; Lt. comdr. USNR. Grantee EPA, NSF, NIH, Office of Naval Research. Fellow AAAS, Am. Inst. Chemists, N.Y. Acad. Scis.; mem. Am. Soc. Photobiology, Am. Chem. Soc., The Oxygen Soc., Sigma Xi. Home: 1810 Walnutway Dr Saint Louis MO 63146-3659 Office: Univ Mo Dept Chemistry Saint Louis MO 63121

MURRAY, ROBERT GRAY, sculptor; b. Vancouver, B.C., Can., Mar. 2, 1936; U.S. Citizen; s. John Gray and Vera (Meakin) M.; m. Cintra Wetherill Lofting, Jan. 23, 1971; children: Rebecca and Megan (twins), Claire, Hillary. Student, U. Sask., Can., 1956-58. One man shows Betty Parsons Gallery, N.Y.C., 1965, 66, 68, David Mirvish Gallery, Toronto, 1967, 68, 72, 73, 74, 75, Jewish Mus., N.Y.C., 1967, Hammarskjold Plaza, N.Y.C., 1971, Paula Cooper Gallery, N.Y.C., 1974, Janie Lee Gallery, Houston, 1977, Hamilton Gallery, N.Y.C., 1977, 79, 80, Klonaridis Inc., Toronto, 1979, 81, 82, Rice U., 1978, Dayton Mus., 1979, Columbus Mus., 1979, Lamont Gallery, Phillips Acad., Exeter, N.H., 1983, Art Gallery Greater Victoria, 1983, Gallery One, Toronto, 1985, Culturale Canadese Roma, 1985, Gallery 291, Atlanta, 1986, Richard Greene Gallery, N.Y.C.,1986, L.A., 1987, Del. Art Mus., Wilmington, 1990, Muhlenberg Coll., Allentown, Pa., 1992, Mira Godard Gallery, Toronto, Reading (Pa.) Pub. Mus., 1994, 96, Andre Zarre Gallery, N.Y.C., 1994, spl. showing Hillary Ground for Sculpture, Trenton N.J., 1997, Moore Gallery, Toronto, 1999, 2001, Ericson Gallery, Phila., 1999, McLaren Gallery, Barrie, 2001, retrospective, Grounds for Sculpture, Trenton, 1997, Nat. Gallery of Can., Ottawa, 1999; exhibited in group shows at Whitney Mus. 1996— Am., Art, N.Y.C., 1964-66, Tibor de Nagy Gallery, N.Y.C., 1965, Musée cantonal des Beaux Arts, Lausanne, Switzerland, 1966, World House Gallery, N.Y.C., 1966, Betty Parsons Gallery, 1966, Sch. Visual Arts, N.Y.C., 1967, Los Angeles County Mus., 1967, Nat. Gallery Can., Toronto, 1967, Inst. Contemporary Art, Boston, 1967, U. Toronto, 1967, Guggenheim Mus., N.Y.C., 1967, Inst. Torcuato Di Tella, Buenos Aires, 1967, Musée d'Art Moderne, Paris, 1968, Whitney Mus., 1967, Walker Art Gallery, 1969, X Sao Paulo Biennial, Brazil, 1969, Boston City Hall, 1971, Artist and Fabricator, Amherst, Mass., 1975, Met. Mus., N.Y.C., 1983, Del. Art Mus., 1990, GrandRapids (Mich.) Mus., 1994; represented in permanent collections, Montreal Mus. Fine Arts, Nat. Gallery Can., Joseph Hirshhorn Collection, Art Gallery Ont., Larry Aldrich Mus., Ridgefield, Conn., New Brunswick Mus., Whitney Mus. Am. Art, Met. Mus., N.Y.C., Columbus Mus., Dayton Art Inst., Storm King Art Centre, Del. Art. Mus., Wilmington, Muhlenberg Coll., Allentown, Pa., others; major commns. include, Everson Mus., Syracuse, N.Y., Fredonia (N.Y.) State Coll., Canadian Dept. External Affairs, Ottawa, Ont., U. Mass., U. Toronto, Ont., State Mus., Juneau, Alaska, Honeywell Corp., Mpls., CNIB, Toronto, also others. Mem. Order of Can. Fax: 610-869-4403.

MURRAY, ROBERT WAYNE, artist, writer; b. Circleville, Ohio, Dec. 20, 1964; s. Kennith Wayne Murray and Brenda Lee Murray-Mason. Pvt. practice, Florence, Ariz., 1992—; cons. Ala., 1992—. Pub. rels. Pvt. and MGM Club, Muscle Shoals, Ala., 1982—88. Campaign supporter Dem. Party, Muscle Shoals, Ala., 1984—88. Mem.: NRA, Coalition of Arizonans to Abolish Death Penalty, Nat. Geog. Soc. Independent. Sikhism. Avocations: meditation, personal consulting, personal consulting, reading periodicals, thinking. Home: ADC #94261 SMU2 PO Box 3400 Florence AZ 85232-3400 Office: Arizona State Prison Death Row Adc #94261 Smu2 3g28 Florence AZ 85232-3400

MURRAY, RODERICK CHARLES, manufacturing executive; b. Johannesburg, S. Africa, Jan. 29, 1945; came to U.S., 1987; s. Charles Victor Murray and Yvonne Margaret Sherriffs; m. Yvonne Edna Bennett, Feb. 26, 1966; children: Sandra Leigh, Stuart Charles. BS, Witwatersrand U., Johannesburg, 1967; MBA, Calif. Coast U., 1990. Qualtiy assurance S. African Breweries, Johannesburg, 1971-75; tech. mgr. Hens Paper, Eerbeek, Holland, 1975-80; dir. mktg. and sales Metal Box, Barlow Rand, Johannesburg, 1980-87; v.p. mktg. ARPAC L.P., Chgo., 1987-89; pres. BMI Machinery, Milw., 1990-96; v.p. Klockner Packaging, 1990—96; CEO, pres. PPi Techs., Sarasota, Fla., 1996—. Author: Label Paper Technology, 1976, Brand Introductions, 1989; contbr. articles to profl. jours. Fellow British Bottlers; mem. Inst. Packaging Profls. (chmn. 1976), Internat. Beverage Tech. (vice chmn. 1978). Republican. Anglican. Avocations: golf, tennis, boating, travelling. Office: PPi Techs 1100 Ben Franklin Dr # 804 Sarasota FL 34236 E-mail: rcmpp@aol.com.

MURRAY, ROYCE WILTON, chemistry educator; b. Birmingham, Ala., Jan. 9, 1937; s. Royce Leeroy and Justina Louisa (Herd) M.; m. Judith Studinka, 1957 (div.); children: Katherine, Stewart, Debra, Melissa, Marion; m. Mirtha X. Umana, Dec. 11, 1982. BS in Chemistry, Birmingham So. Coll., 1957; PhD in Analytical Chemistry, Northwestern U., 1960. Instr. U. N.C., Chapel Hill, 1960-61, asst. prof., 1961-66, assoc. prof., 1966-69, prof., 1969—, vice chmn., 1970-75, acting chair dept. chemistry, 1970-71, dir. undergrad. studies, 1978-80, dept. chmn., 1980-85, chmn. curriculum applied scis., 1995-98, div. chmn., 1987-93, Kenan prof., 1980—. Contbr. articles to jours. in field. Recipient award, Japanese Soc. for Promotion Sci., 1978, Electrochem. Group medal, Royal Soc. Chemistry, 1989, N.C. award in Sci., 2001, Pitts. Analytical Chemistry award, 2002; fellow Alfred P. Sloan, 1969, 1972, Guggenheim, 1980, 1982. Fellow AAAS, Am. Inst. Chemists, Am. Acad. Arts and Scis., Electrochem. Soc.; mem. NAS, Soc. for Electroanalytical Chemistry (bd. dirs., co-founder 1982-84, Charles N. Reilley award 1988, pres. 1991-93), Am. Chem. Soc. (Electrochemistry award 1990, Analytical Chemistry award 1991, editor in chief Analytical Chemistry 1991—), Electrochem. Soc. (hon. life, Carl Wagner Meml. award 1987, Palladium medal 1997). Presbyterian. Office: U NC Dept Chemistry Chapel Hill NC 27599-0001

MURRAY, RUSSELL, II, aeronautical engineer, defense analyst, consultant; b. Woodmere, N.Y., Dec. 5, 1925; s. Herman Stump and Susanne Elizabeth (Warren) M.; m. Sally Tingue Gardiner, May 22, 1954; children: Ann Tingue, Prudence Warren, Alexandria Gardiner. BS in Aero. Engring, MIT, 1949, MS, 1950. Guided missile flight test engr. Grumman Aircraft Engring. Corp., Bethpage, N.Y., 1950-53, asst. chief operations analysis, 1953-62; prin. dep. asst. sec. of def. for systems analysis The Pentagon, Washington, 1962-69; dir. long range planning Pfizer Internat., N.Y.C., 1969-73; dir. review Center for Naval Analyses, Arlington, Va., 1973-77; asst. sec. of def. for program analysis and evaluation Dept. of Def., The Pentagon, Washington, 1977-81; prin. Systems Research & Applications Corp., Arlington, Va., 1981-85; spl. counsellor Com. on Armed Services U.S. Ho. of Reps., 1985-89, nat. security cons., 1989—. Served with USAAF, 1944-45. Recipient Sec. of Def. Medal for meritorious civilian service, 1968; Disting. Public Service medal Dept. Def., 1981 Home: 210 Wilkes St Alexandria VA 22314-3839

MURRAY, STEPHEN JAMES, lawyer; b. Phila., Jan. 27, 1943; s. Paul Martin and Hannah (Smith) M.; m. Linda Sanders, June 20, 1970; children: Gordon Joshua, Cara Sanders. AB cum laude, Brown U., 1963; LLB, Harvard U., 1966; LLM, George Washington U., 1967. Bar: N.Y. 1968, U.S. Ct. Appeals (2nd cir.) 1971, U.S. Ct. Appeals (fed. cir.) 1998, U.S. Dist. Ct. (so. and ea. dists.) N.Y. 1972, U.S. Ct. Claims 1974, U.S. Supreme Ct. 1975, Conn. 1988, U.S. Dist. Ct. Conn. 1988, U.S. Ct. Internat. Trade 1998. Spl. asst. SEC, Washington, 1966-67, Maritime Adminstrn., Washington, 1967-68; assoc. Hill, Betts & Nash, N.Y.C., 1970-76; transp. atty. Union Carbide Corp., 1976-78, sr. transp. atty., 1978-85, chief transp. counsel Danbury, Conn., 1985—2001, group counsel, 1986—2001, real estate counsel, 1992—2001, comml. counsel, 1993—2001, customs and internat. trade counsel, 1997—2001; of counsel Mahoney & Keane, New York City, 2001—, 2001—. Spkr. in field. Contbr. articles to profl. jours. Lt. JAGC, USN, 1968-70. Mem. ABA, Conn. State Bar Assn., U.S. Naval Inst., Navy League of U.S., Maritime Law Assn., U.S. Transp. Lawyers Assn., N.Y. State Bar Assn., Am. Corp. Counsel Assn. (co-chair real estate com. Westchester-So. Conn. chpt.), Conn. Maritime Assn., Harvard Club, Brown Club (co-pres.), Brown Faculty Club, Brown Alumni Schs. Commn. (chmn. Fairfield County), Brown Alumni Assn. (bd. govs.). Home: 14 Pilgrim Ln Weston CT 06883-2412 Office: Mahoney & Keane 14 Pilgrim Ln Weston CT 06883 E-mail: lsmurray@erols.com., sjmurray@snet.net.

MURRAY, SUSAN JULIANO, director of school and community affairs; b. Scarborough Twp., Ontario, Can., Feb. 5, 1964; came to U.S., 1964; d. Frank and Frances (Palermo) Juliano; m. John T. Murray II, Apr. 27, 1991. BA, Montclair State Coll., 1986. Exec. dir. Rep. Exec. Com., Somerville, N.J., 1983-91; dir. cultural affairs Somerset County Vocat. Tech. Schs., Bridgewater, 1991—. Fund raising cons. SELF, Bound Brook, N.J., 1986—; mem. adv. bd. Commn. on Women, Somerville, N.J., 1988—. Sec. Somerset County Rep. Orgn.,, 1986-92, treas. Bound Brook Rep. Club, 1986-88; alternate del. 34th Nat. Rep. Conv., New Orleans, 1987; mem. Bound Brook Bd. of Health, County Wellness Com., Somerville, N.J., 1993—; vol. fund raiser Make a Wish Found., The Valerie Fund. Recipient Women's Equality award, N.J. Commn. on the Status of Women, Trenton, 1988. Mem. Nat. Soc. Fund Raising Execs., Nat. Alliance of Bus., Somerset County C. of C. Republican. Roman Catholic. Avocations: sailing, ice skating, water skiing, reading, painting, sketching, tennis, golf. Home: 1025 Vosseller Ave Martinsville NJ 08836-2391

MURRAY, TERRY (TERENCE RODNEY MURRAY), former professional hockey team coach; b. Shawville, Que., Can., July 20, 1950; m. Linda Murray; children: Megan, Lindsey. Hockey player Calif. Golden Seals, 1972-75, Phila. Flyers, 1975-77, 78-81, Detroit Red Wings, 1977, Washington Capitals, 1981-82, asst. coach, 1982-88, head coach, 1990-94, Balt. Skipjacks, 1988-90, Philadelphia Flyers, 1994-97, Florida Panthers, Sunrise, Fla., 1998—2000. Named to 3 Am. Hockey League all-star teams; named most valuable defenseman Am. Hockey League, 1978, 79.*

MURRAY, THERESE, state legislator; one child. Student, El Camino Coll., Northeastern U., U. Mass., Midwest Acad., IL. Mitigation mgr. Mass. Hwy. Dept., 1984-91; mem. Mass. Senate, Boston, 1993—2000; chair. Joint Cmtee. on Insurance, 2001—. Chmn. joint com. onf human svcs. & elderly affairs Mass. State Senate, 1993—, transp. com., 1993—, pub. safety com., 1993—; past market assoc. Coldwell Banker, Plymouth Port, Mass.; former cmty. rels. & coord. Am. Cablesys. Dir. Mcpl. Women's Project Inc., Boston; mem. Dem. State Com. Named among Ten Women Who Make Things Happen in Mass., Redbook Mag. Mem. Vis. Nurses Assn. (bd. dirs.), Women's Transp. Seminar, Plymouth County Dem. League, LWV. Address: Rm 511C State House Boston MA 02133

MURRAY, THOMAS HENRY, bioethics educator, writer; b. Phila., July 30, 1946; s. Thomas Henry and Colombia Rita (Lucci) M.; m. Sharon Marie Engelkraut, Jan. 1968 (div. Sept. 1975); children: Kathleen Elizabeth, Dominique Maria, Peter Albert; m. Cynthia Sarah Aberle, Apr. 1, 1978; 1 child, Emily Sarah Aberle. BA in Psychology, Temple U., 1968; PhD in Social Psychology, Princeton, 1976. Instr. New Coll., Sarasota, Fla., 1971-75; asst. prof. Interdisciplinary Studies Miami U., Oxford, Ohio, 1975-80, assoc. prof., 1980; assoc. social behavioral studies The Hastings Ctr., Hastings-on Hudson, N.Y., 1980-84; assoc. prof. Inst. Med. Humanities U. Tex Med. Br., Galveston, Tex., 1984-86, prof., 1986-87; prof., dir. Ctr. Biomed. Ethics Case We. Reserve U., Cleve., 1987-99, Susan E. Watson prof. bioethics, 0198—1999; pres. The Hastings Ctr., Garrison, N.Y., 1999—. Mem. Nat. Bioethics Adv. Commn., 1996-2001; mem. ethical, legal and social issues working group Human Genome Project NIH/Dept. Energy, 1989-95. Author: The Worth of a Child, 1996; founder, editor Med. Humanities Rev.; mem. editl. bd. Human Gene Therapy, Cloning, Politics and the Life Scis., Hastings Center Report; editor: Encyclopedia of Ethical, Legal, and Policy Issues in Biotechnology. Fellow NEH, 1977-78, 1979-80, Aspen Inst., 1989. Fellow Hastings Ctr.; mem. APHA, Assn. Practical and Profl. Ethics, Am. Soc. Law Medicine and Ethics (bd. dirs. 1993-97), Assn. Integrative Studies (bd. dirs. 1980-87, pres. 1983), Soc. Health and Human Values (chair program dirs. sect. 1989-90, faculty assn. 1989-90, SHHV program com. 1990, pres.-elect 1992-93, pres. 1993-94), Am. Soc. Human Genetics (chair social issues com. 1998-99), Am. Coll. Ob-Gyn. (com. on ethics 1996-2001), Am. Soc. Bioethics and Humanities (pres.-elect 1998-99, pres. 1999-2000), Human Genome Orgn. (ethics com.), World Anti-Doping Agy. (ethics and edn. com.). Office: The Hastings Ctr 21 Malcolm Gordon Rd Garrison NY 10524-5555

MURRAY, THOMAS J. advertising executive; b. Bridgeport, Conn., Mar. 12, 1924; s. Thomas and Mary (Diskin) M.; m. Mary Elizabeth Cull, Feb. 22, 1945; children: Joshua Francis, Mary Elizabeth, Katherine Diskin. AB, Dartmouth Coll., 1947. Instr., Dartmouth Coll., 1947-48; with Warwick & Legler, N.Y.C., 1948-68, sr. v.p., mgmt. account supr., 1964-68; sr. v.p. group supr. Gaynor & Ducas, Inc., 1968-74, exec. v.p., 1974—, chief fin. officer and gen. mgr., 1978-87; pres. TJM & Assn., 1987—. Pres., trustee Hillcrest Gen. Hosp., N.Y.C.; Westchester Inst. for tng. in Psychoanalysis and Psychotheraphy, Mt. Kisco, N.Y. Served as 1st lt. USAAF, 1942-45. Decorated D.F.C., Air medal with 4 oak leaf clusters. Mem. Nat. Wholesale Druggists Assn., Propriety Assn., Nat. Assn. Chain Drug Stores, Am. Mktg. Assn. Home and Office: 65 Norfield Rd Weston CT 06883-2213

MURRAY, THOMAS JAMES, financial planner, publisher; b. Jamestown, R.I., Mar. 26, 1924; s. Daniel Peter and Margaret (McPartland) M.; m. Jean Shaw, July 2, 1948 (dec. June 1985); children: Thomas, Carolyn, Elizabeth, John, Peter; m. Evelyn Ayers, Apr. 19, 1986. Student, Brown U., 1942-44; BA in Social Sci., George Washington U., 1964. Commissioned ensign USN, 1944, advanced through ranks to lt. comdr., 1964, ret., 1964; sales rep. J.D. Marsh & Assoc., Washington, 1964—78; pres. TJM Securities Inc., Chevy Chase, Md., 1985—92, Thomas Murray Assocs. Inc., Chevy Chase, 1985—, TMA Ins., Chevy Chase, 1978—; pub. Social List Washington Inc., Kensington, 1985—. Mem. Am. Legion (comdr. Thad Dulin post 1975-76), Rotary (pres. Wheaton Kensington chpt. 1966-67), Knights of Malta, St. Andrew's Soc. (Washington)(pres. 1997-99). Roman Catholic. Home: 10500 Rockville Pike Apt 1702 N Bethesda MD 20852-3356 Office: Social List Washington 9620 E Bexhill Dr Kensington MD 20895-3103 also: Thomas Murray Assocs 6935 Wisconsin Ave Chevy Chase MD 20815-6113 E-mail: TJM@webfirst.com.

MURRAY, THOMAS JOHN (JOCK MURRAY), medical humanities educator, medical researcher, neurologist; b. Halifax, N.S., Can., May 30, 1938; m. Janet Kathleen Pottie; children: Shannon, Bruce, Suellen, Brian. Grad. pre-med, St. Francis Xavier U., 1958, LLD (hon.), 1989; MD, Dalhousie U., 1963; DSc (hon.), Acadia U., 1991. Family physician, Nashwaaksis, N.S., 1963-65; chief of medicine Camp Hill Hosp., Halifax, 1974-79; chief of neurology Dalhousie U., 1979-85, dir. multiple sclerosis rsch. unit, 1980—, dean of medicine, 1985-92; prof. med. humanities, 1992—. Emeritus chmn. ACP Bd. Regents; mem. working group on Diability in U.S. Pres., 1994-96. Co-author: (textbook) Essential Neurology; author over 200 pub. works, including 5 books and contbns. to 12 textbooks. Bd. dirs. St. Francis Xavier U., Pictou Acad. Found., Robert Pope Found., Nat. Coun. on Bioethics and Health Rsch. Decorated officer Order Can. Fellow Royal Coll. Physicians (Can. and London), ACP (gov. 1985-90, chmn. bd. govs. 1990-91, bd. regents, chmn. 1995-97, master); mem. Can. Neurol. Soc. (pres. 1982-84), Am. Acad. Neurology (v.p. 1981-83), Can. Med. Assn., N.S. Med. Soc., Assn. Can. Med. Colls. (pres. 1991-92), Can. Med. Forum (chmn. 1992-95), Consortium of Multiple Sclerosis Ctrs. (pres. 1997-99), Can. Soc. for History of Medicine (pres. 1997-99). Avocations: medical history, piano, windsurfing, beer-making. Home: 16 Bobolink St Halifax NS Canada B3M 1W3 Office: Dalhousie Med Sch Clin Rsch Ctr Halifax NS Canada B3H 4H7 E-mail: jock.murray@dal.ca.

MURRAY, THOMAS VEATCH, lawyer; b. Phoenix, July 17, 1947; s. Robert Morrison Jr. and Jane Veatch (Murray) Barber and Richard A. Barber; m. Cynthia Ann Burnett, June 2, 1971; children: Anne Caroline, Thomas Veatch Jr. BA, U. Kans., 1969; JD, U. Mich., 1972. Bar: Kans. 1972, U.S. Dist. Ct. Kans. 1972, U.S. Ct. Appeals (10th cir.) 1983, U.S. Supreme Ct. 1976. Assoc. Barber, Emerson, Six, Springer & Zinn, Lawrence, Kans., 1972-76; mem. Barber, Emerson, Springer, Zinn & Murray, L.C., 1976—. Dir. The First Nat. Bank of Lawrence, 1980-91, Hall Ctr. for the Humanities, Lawrence, 1988—; adj. prof. U. Kans. Sch. Law, 1990-91. Contbr. articles to profl. jours. Mem. adv. bd. Lawrence Consumer Affairs Assn., 1974—77, Sta. KANU, Lawrence, 1976—80; mem. Bd. Edn. Unified Sch. Dist. 497, 1991—95; mem. Kans. Bd. Law Examiners, 1995—, Lawrence Emergency Svcs. Coun., 1998—; dir. Lawrence C. of C., 1993—95; trustee First Presbyn. Ch., 1978. Mem. ABA, Fedn. Ins. and Corp. Counsel (regional v.p. 1994-97, dir. 1997-99), Kans. Assn. Def. Counsel (dir. 1993-97), Kans. Bar Assn. (pres. corporation, banking and bus. law sect. 1983), Kans. Bar Found. (trustee 1999—), Douglas Co. Bar Assn., Coaches' Corner (Lawrence), Lawrence Lions Alumni Assn., Kansas City Club, Lawrence Rotary Club, Lawrence Country Club, The Fortnightly Club (Lawrence). Republican. Presbyterian. Avocations: classical and operatic music. Office: Barber Emerson Springer Zinn & Murray LC 1211 Massachusetts St Lawrence KS 66044-3351

MURRAY, TIMOTHY P. mayor; m. Tammy L. Sullivan. BA in Am. Studies, Fordham U.; JD, Western New England Sch. Law. Pvt. law practice State of Mass., Worchester, Mass., councillor-at-large Worcester, mayor, 2002—. Office: 455 Main St Worcester MA 01608-1821 E-mail: mayor@ci.worcester.ma.us.*

MURRAY, WALLACE SHORDON, publisher, educator; b. Dorchester, Mass., May 9, 1921; s. Wallace Jennings and Ina (Shordon) M.; m. Eleanor Muriel Grandy, Oct. 30, 1948; children: Patricia Ann, William Howard. BS, MIT, 1942; M.Ed., Boston U., 1949; Litt.D. (hon.), Western New Eng. Coll., 1965. Tchr. Bolles Sch., Jacksonville, Fla., 1945-46, head math. dept., asst. prin., 1946-49; headmaster Berwick Acad., South Berwick, Maine, 1949-50; sales rep. D.C. Heath & Co., Boston, 1950-52, editor, 1952-53, head elementary editorial dept., 1953-55, editor in chief, 1955-66, v.p., 1962-66, dir., 1956-66, sec. of corp., 1957-66; dir. Erica Corp., 1956-66; exec. v.p. Heath de Rochemont Corp., 1960-66, dir., 1960-66; editor-in-chief, mgr. materials devel. dept. Raytheon Edn. Co., 1966-68; v.p., editorial dir. domestic and internat. ops. Grolier Inc., 1968-80, dir., 1969-82, cons., 1980-82; dir. Grolier Edn. Corp., 1968-80, Scarecrow Press Inc., 1969-80. Chmn. elementary and high sch. research com. Am. Ednl. Pubs. Inst., 1966-68, chmn. elem. and high sch. sect., 1968-69 Lay leader Boston dist. Meth. Ch., 1952-56; mem. adv. bd. Boston U. Student Christian Assn., 1954-62, treas., 1957-59, chmn., 1959-61; mem. president's adv. council St. Joseph's Coll., North Windham, Maine, 1973-88; mem. corp. New Eng. Deaconess Assn., 1965-95, exec. com., 1965-68; mem. corp. New Eng. Deaconess Hosp., 1967-93; dir. Japan America Soc. of Maine, 1981-91, pres., 1984-86; merit badge counselor Pine Tree Coun., Boy Scouts Am., 1984-95; dir. Children's Mus. of Maine, 1987-89; dir. Leisure Ctr. for the Handicapped, Inc., Portland, Maine, 1987-93, treas. 1988-93; mem. adv. council So. Maine Retired Sr. Vol. Program, 1987-90, chmn. fin. com., 1987-89; mem. Foster Care Case Review Panel Maine Dept. Human Services, 1987-91; dir. Foreside Common Condominium Assn., Falmouth, Maine, 1986-89, 1991-92, pres., 1987-89; vol. staff mem. Vol. Lawyers Project of Maine, 1987-90; vol. math. instr. Adult Basic Learning Exchange, Portland, 1987-91. Served to capt. AUS, 1942-46, to maj. USAR. Mem. Newcomen Soc., Masons, Shriners, Phi Delta Kappa. Republican. Episcopalian. Home: PO Box 17 Sebago Lake ME 04075-0017

MURRAY, WARREN JAMES, philosophy educator; b. St. Paul, Dec. 3, 1936; s. James Bernard and Louise (Robertson) M.; m. Mary Ann McAulay, July 18, 1959; children: Mark, Anne, Kathleen. Student, St. Thomas Coll., 1954-55; BA in Chemistry, Wis. State Coll., River Falls, 1962; B.Ph. in Philosophy, Universite Laval, Que., Can., 1964, Ph.L., 1965, scolarite PhD, 1966. Analytical chemist 3M Co., St. Paul, 1957-61, research chemist, 1961-63; prof. philos. sci. U. Laval, Sainte-Foy, 1966—, vice dean, 1979—. Invited prof. Faculte de philosophie Comparee, Paris, 1969, 72, Universite libre des sciences de l'homme, Paris, 1975—, Ecole des Hautes Etudes, Paris, 1976, Universidad Nacional de Tucuman, Argentina, 1991. Fgn. exchange teaching grantee Province Que., 1969 Mem. Soc. Aristotelian Studies (pres.), Can. Soc. History and Philosophy Sci., Soc. Ancient Greek Philosophy. Office: Faculte De Philosophie Universite Laval Sainte Foy QC Canada G1K 7P4 E-mail: warren.murray@fp.ulaval.ca.

MURRAY, WILLIAM BRUCE, opera singer; b. Schenectady, N.Y., Mar. 13, 1935; s. John Allison and Jessie Chrystal (Gray) M.; m. Nancy Lee Adams, Mar. 1, 1958; children: John Horton, Christopher Andrew, Judith Leora. BA in Music Edn., Adelphi U., 1956; Cert. di Studio, U. Perugia, Italy, 1957; grad., Goethe Inst., 1960. Opera singer Landestheater Detmold, Germany, 1960-61, Staatstheater Braunschweig, Germany, 1961-64, Nat. Theater Mannheim, Germany, 1964-66, Staatsoper München, Germany, 1966-78, Deutsche Opera Berlin, Germany, 1969—, Houston Grand Opera, 1994—. Opera singer numerous other theaters including N.Y. State Opera, Catania, Italy, Marseille, France, L.A. Opera, Teatro Reggio Torino (Italia), 1992; prof. voice Shepherd Sch. Music Rice U., Houston. Recordings include Salome, Die Bassariden, Hochzeit des Camacho, Schöne Müllerin, Die Totestadt. With U.S. Army, 1958-60. Named Kammersänger Senate Berlin Germany, 1980; Fulbright fellow, 1956. Mem. Lions Club. Avocations: hiking, cooking, swimming. Home: 113 Homeyer Rd Sparrow Bush NY 12780-8302 also: 2400 N Braeswood Blvd Apt 306 Houston TX 77030-4358 E-mail: wbmurray@ruf.rice.edu.

MURRAY, WILLIAM JAMES, anesthesiology educator, clinical pharmacologist; b. Janesville, Wis., July 20, 1933; s. James Arthur and Mary Helen (De Porter) M.; m. Therese Rose Dooley, June 25, 1955; children: Michael, James, Anne. BS, U. Wis., 1955, PhD, 1959; MD, U. N.C., 1962. Diplomate Am. Bd. Anesthesiology. Rsch. asst. U. Wis., Madison, 1955-59; instr. pharmacology U. N.C., Chapel Hill, 1959-62, resident and fellow in surgery (anesthesiology), 1962-64, instr., 1964-65, asst. prof., 1965-68; asst. to dir. for drug availability FDA, Washington, 1968-69; assoc. prof. pharmacology, clin. pharmacology and anesthesiology U. Mich., Ann Arbor, 1969-72; assoc. prof. anesthesiology Duke U., Durham, N.C., 1972-81, prof., from 1981. Assoc. dir. Upjohn Ctr. for Clin. Pharmacology, Ann Arbor, 1969-72. Mem. AMA, Am. Soc. Anesthesiologists, Internat. Anesthesia Rsch. Soc., Soc. for Ambulatory Anesthesia, Am. Pharm. Assn., N.Y. Acad. Scis., N.C. Soc. Anesthesiologists, Am. Soc. Hosp. Pharmacists, U.S. Pharmacopeial Conv., Am. Coll. Clin. Pharmacology, Am. Soc. for Clin. and Therapeutic Pharmacology, Am. Soc. Pharmacology and Exptl. Therapeutics, N.C. Soc. Hosp. Pharmacists, So. Med. Assn., Annals Pharmacotherapy, Am. Med. Writers Assn. Republican. Roman Catholic. Home: Durham, NC. Deceased.

MURRAY, WILLIAM MICHAEL (MIKE MURRAY), lawyer; b. Ottumwa, Iowa, Dec. 28, 1947; s. William Bernard and Thelma Jean (Hart) M.; m. Ann Elizabeth Wawzonek, Oct. 11, 1973; children: Kathleen Elizabeth, Daniel Webster. BA, U. Iowa, 1970; JD, 1973. Bar: Iowa 1973, U.S. Dist. Ct. (so. dist.) Iowa 1976, U.S. Dist. Ct. (no. dist.) Iowa 1978, U.S. Ct. Appeals (8th cir.) 1978. Staff counsel Iowa Civil Rights Commn., Des Moines, 1973-76; assoc. Bertroche & Hagen, 1976-78; ptnr. Murray, Jankins & Noble, 1978—. Spkr., co-author: Workers' Compensation Claims in Iowa, 1999. Bd. dirs. Iowa Civil Liberties Union, Des Moines, 1978-83, pres., 1982-83; bd. dirs. Polk County Legal Aide Soc., Des Moines, 1984-88. Mem. ABA, Asn. Trial Lawyers Am., Assn. Trial Lawyers Iowa, Iow Assn. Workers' Compensation Lawyers, Iowa State Bar Assn., Polk County Bar Assn., Des Moines Jaycees Club (bd. dirs. legal counsel 1980-81). Democrat. Home: 600 SW 42nd St Des Moines IA 50312-4605 Office: Murray Jankins & Noble 2903 Ingersoll Ave Des Moines IA 50312-4014 E-mail: murray@iowa-law.com.

MURRAY, WILLIAM MICHAEL, lawyer; b. Buffalo, Dec. 21, 1953; s. William Joseph and Mary Ann (Lichtenthal) M.; m. Suzanne M. Raynor; children: Colleen Elizabeth, William Michael Jr., Caitlin Anne, Matthew Francis Johnson. BA, U. Notre Dame, 1975; JD, U. Detroit, 1978. Bar: N.Y. 1978, U.S. Dist. Ct. (we. dist.) N.Y. 1980. Asst. county atty. Erie County, Buffalo, 1978-79; ptnr. Stamm & Murray, Williamsville, N.Y., 1979-96, Renaldo Myers & Palumbo, Williamsville, 1996-98; dep. atty. Town of Amherst, 1993-96; gen. counsel Town of Amherst Indsl. Devel. Agy., 1996—. Mem. Amherst (N.Y.) Rep. Com., 2000—; chmn. Amherst Zoning Bd. Appeals, 1986-93. Mem. N.Y. State Bar Assn., Erie County Bar Assn., Williamsville Bus. Assn. (bd. dirs., v.p. 1985-96), Rotary (pres. Williamsville 1989). Roman Catholic. Office: 130 John Muir Dr Amherst NY 14228-1148 E-mail: wmurray@amherstida.com.

MURRAY-JOHNSON, LISA M. communications educator, consultant; b. Bryn Mawr, Pa. married. PhD, Mich. State U., 2001. Contbr. articles to profl. jours. Office: The Ohio State University 3016 Derby Hall, 154 N. Oval Mall Columbus OH 43210

MURRAY-PARKER, KAREN S. journalist, newspaper editor; b. Tampa, Fla., Dec. 5, 1953; d. Jack Vernon and Jacqueline Louise (Holder) Murray; m. William L. Parker, Apr. 21, 1978 (div. Apr. 1982); m. Katharine Crystal Willow. BA in Journalism, BS in Pre-disciplinary Sci., U. South Fla., 1975. Lic. capt, USCG; lic. airplane pilot, FAA. Journalist, photographer Oracle, Tampa, Fla., 1972-75; art specialist Dept. Recreation City of Tampa, 1976-80; journalist Tampa Tribune, 1980-82; editor, assoc. pub. Roofer Mag., Ft. Myers, Fla., 1982-85; owner, designer Oceanographics Design, Boca Grande, 1986-87; journalist Ft. Myers (Fla.) News-Press, 1987-88, Boca Beacon Newspaper, Boca Grande, 1988-96; editor, gen. mgr. Gasparilla Gazette Newspaper, 1996—, exec. editor, gen. mgr., 1996—, Gasparilla Mag. and Island Angler Mag., Boca Grande, 1996—. Actress, set. designer Royal Palm Player Inc., Boca Grande, 1987—; exhibiting artist Boca Grande Art Alliance, 1986—; editor (mags.) History of Boca Grande, 1996, First Drift, 1997. Sec., treas. Barrier Island Pks. Soc., Boca Grande, 1990—. Recipient 21 awards for editl. content Fla. Mag. Assn., Orlando, 1982-85; named one of 85 Most Interesting People in Fla., Gulfshore Life Mag., Naples, 1985. Mem. Fla. Press Assn. (18 writing awards 1988—). Democrat. Roman Catholic. Avocations: painting, sailing, writing, scuba diving, flying. Home: PO Box 1258 Boca Grande FL 33921-1258 Office: Gasparilla Gazette PO Box 929 Boca Grande FL 33921-0929

MURRELL, DEBORAH ANNE, music educator, speaker, writer; b. Louisville, July 7, 1942; d. James Howard and Mayme Ruth (Manning) M. AB, Ea. Ky. U., 1964; MA, Western Ky. U., 1975; MACE, So. Bapt. Theol. Sem., Louisville, 1983; postgrad. in music, Ind. U. Band and choral dir. Hardin County Pub. Schs., Elizabethtown, Ky., 1964-66; dir. instrumental and vocal music Bullitt County Schs., Shepherdsville, 1966-74; band dir. Clark County Schs., Winchester, 1974-76; band and choral dir., head coach h.s. girls basketball Carroll County Schs., Carrollton, 1978-81; cons., speaker Nat. Single Adults, Louisville, 1981—; minister of single and sr. adults Temple Terr. First Bapt. Ch., Tampa, Fla., 1983-88; minister of adults First Bapt. Ch., Winston-Salem, N.C., 1988-91; minister of adults and evangelism Taylors (S.C.) First Bapt. Ch., 1991-93; music specialist Bullitt County Pub. Schs., Shepherdsville, Ky., 1993—; interim min. of music Bullitt Lick Bapt. Ch., 1999-2000; music specialist Pleasant Grove Elem. Sch., Mt. Washington , 2000—. Bd. dirs. Good News Clubs, Inc., Louisville, 1966-73; task force mem. single adults Bapt. Sunday Sch. Bd., Nashville, Tenn., 1991-93; Master's Men Orch., Inc., Louisville, 1993-99—; internat. spkr. to single adults, Eng. and Brazil, 1987-93, 2000. Author: (with others) Single Adult Resource and Recipient, 1986, Single Adult Ministry, 1987; interviewee (video) Bapt. Sunday Sch. Bd., 1983-93; contbg. writer Christian Single Mag., 1980-93; prodr., dir.: PGE Sings the Music of America, 2002. Band hostess Ky. Derby Festival Commn., Louisville, 1980-83; internat. and nat. spkr. single adult ministries, 1981—; founder, organizer Bullitt County Music Festival, 1968—. Named Ky. Col. Commonwealth of Ky., Frankfort, 1978. Mem. NEA, Music Educators Nat. Conf., Ky. Edn. Assn., Ky. Music Educators Assn. (dist. officer 1964-81, 97-2001), Bullitt County Edn. Assn., Bullitt County Music Tchrs. Assn. (v.p. 1994-98, pres. 1998-99, sec. 2000-2001), Religious Educators Assn., N.C. Religious Edn. Assn. (publicity, promotion com. 1990-91), Pilot Mt. Bapt. Assn. (mem. exec. com. 1989-91), Ea. Ky. U. Alumni Assn., Nat. Alumni Band (chmn. 1975-78), Fern Creek High Sch. Alumni Assn., Phi Delta Kappa. Home: 2805 Alice Ave Louisville KY 40220-1703 Office: Pleasant Grove Elem Sch 6415 Hwy 44 E Mount Washington KY 40047 Business E-Mail: dmurrell@bullitt.k12.ky.us.

MURRELL, SUSAN DEBRECHT, librarian; b. St. Louis, Aug. 10, 1951; d. Edward August and Edith (Keeney) DeB.; m. Harry Thornton Murrell, Oct. 18, 1974; children: Brian, Katherine. BA in History, U. Ky., 1973; MLS, U. Mo., 1976. Children's libr. Louisville Free Pub. Libr., 1974-76, talking book libr. head, 1976-83; lower/mid. sch. libr. Ky. Country Day Sch., Louisville, 1983-84; children's libr. Emmet O'Neal Libr., Mountain Brook, Ala., 1984-86, asst. dir., 1986-89, dir., 1989—. Active Jefferson County Pub. Libr.; mem. allocations com. United Way; bd. dirs. Mountain Brook Libr. Found., 1993—, Ala. Ctr. for Book. Mem. ALA, Ala. Libr. Assn. (mem. publicity com. 1992-93, pub. libr. chair 1995-96), Rotary Internat. Roman Catholic. Office: Emmet O'Neal Libr 50 Oak St Birmingham AL 35213-4295

MURRELL, WILLIAM IVAN, accountant; b. Bessemer, Ala., Dec. 28, 1923; s. Virgil Stewart Murrell and Mae (Rutledge) Ferguson; m. Virginia Byrd Reynolds, May 27, 1944; children: Melinda Ann, Barbara Kay, Shirley Sue. Student, Walton Sch. Commerce, 1941-46, Tex. Christian U., 1947-48, So. Meth. U., 1949-50. CPA. Bookkeeper Continental Oil Co., Ft. Worth, 1942-43; staff acct. Patterson & Leatherwood, 1946-48; sr. acct. Coopers & Lybrand, Dallas, 1949-51; sr. ptnr. Parish, Murrell & Co., 1951-85; cons., 1986—. Bd. dirs. Rancho Oil Co., Dallas, Nat. Industries Corp., Dallas, Warehouse Properties Corp., Dallas. Author: World War II Love Letters, 1993, This Is It, Men, 1991, Murder for Profit or Loss, 1992. With U.S. Army, 1943-46. Mem. AICPA (life), Accts. Computer Users (Devoted Svc. award 1971), Tex. Soc. CPA (life, pres. 1968-69), Horatio Alger Soc. (Rags to Riches award 1990). Baptist. Avocations: travel, writing, music, oil painting, gardening. Home: 4321 W Lawther Dr Dallas TX 75214-2921

MURRELLE, RONALD KEMP, architectural firm executive; b. Greensboro, N.C., Aug. 14, 1940; s. George Kemp and Marian (Lewis) M.; Betsy Blackburn Stevens, Oct. 1960 (div. Aug. 1982); children: Brett Stevens, Mary Anna. Student, N.C. State Sch. Design, 1958-60. Dept. mgr. Kirkman and Koury, Inc., Greensboro, 1961-70; v.p. Wm. B. Owen Constrn. Co. Inc., Banner Elk, N.C., 1970-76, M and B Constrn. Inc., Vansant, Va., 1976-77; multifamily dept. mgr. Harmon Assoc., Greensboro, 1978-80; pres. Diversified Residential Svcs., Inc., Banner Elk, 1980-82; project designer Harmn Assoc., Greensboro, 1984-85; with Hotel Designs, 1986-88, Nu-Stone Surfacing, Orlando, Fla., 1989, Fellowship Facilities Designs, Orlando, Myrtle Beach, 1990; founder Fulfilled Mansions, Greensboro, 1997—; pres. Diversified Residential Svcs., 1998. Author: His Father's Temple, 1994, God Experience, 1996, Recovery Words with Definitions, 1996. Avocations: chess, golf. Address: PO Box 66055 Greensboro NC 27403-6055 E-mail: ronm-drs@triad.rr.com.

MURRIAN, ROBERT PHILLIP, retired judge, lawyer, educator; b. Knoxville, Tenn., Apr. 1, 1945; s. Albert Kinzel and Mary Gilbert (Eppes) M.; m. Jerrilyn Sue Boone, Oct. 29, 1983; children: Kimberley Ann, Jennifer Rebecca, Albert Boone, Samuel Robert. BS, U.S. Naval Acad., 1967; JD, U. Tenn., 1974. Bar: Tenn. 1974, U.S. Dist. Ct. (ea. dist.) Tenn. 1975, U.S. Ct. Appeals (6th cir.) 1982. Law clk. to judge U.S. Dist. Ct. (ea. dist.) Tenn., 1974-76; assoc. Butler, Vines, Babb & Threadgill, Knoxville, 1976-78; magistrate, judge U.S. Dist. (ea. dist.) Tenn., 1978—2002; ptnr. Kramer, Rayson, Leake, Rodgers & Morgan, LLP, 2002—. Adj. prof. U. Tenn. Coll. Law, 1990-93, 95-96, 2002. Lt. USN, 1967-71. Green scholar, 1973-74, Nat. Moot Ct. scholar, 1974. Fellow Tenn. Bar Found.; mem. ABA, Tenn. Bar Assn., Knoxville Bar Assn. (bd. govs. 1994), Order of Coif, Am. Inn of Ct. (master of the bench, pres. 1997-98), Phi Kappa Phi. Presbyterian. Office: Kramer Rayson Leake Rodgers & Morgan LLP PO Box 629 Knoxville TN 37901-0629 Address: First Tennessee Plz 800 S Gay St Ste 2500 Knoxville TN 37929 Fax: 865-522-5723. E-mail: rpmurrian@kramer-rayson.com.

MURRISH, CHARLES HOWARD, oil and gas exploration company executive, geologist; b. Rochester, Minn., Dec. 27, 1940; s. Richard John and Emily Louise (Marsh) M.; m. Brigitte Marie Furlotte, Oct. 23, 1965; children: Stephanie, Stephen, Brian. Student, Mexico City Coll., 1962; BS, Mich. State U., 1963, MS, 1966. Exploration geologist and geophysicist Chevron, New Orleans, 1966-71; mgr. exploration Odeco, 1971-77; v.p. McMoRan Offshore Exploration Co., Metairie, La., 1977-79, sr. v.p., 1979-81; pres. McMoRan-Freeport Oil Co., 1981-83, McMoRan Exploration Co., Metairie, 1983-86; exec. v.p. McMoRan Oil & Gas Co., 1986, sr. exec. v.p., 1986-90, Freeport-McMoRan Oil & Gas Co., 1990-92; ptnr. CLK Co., 1992-94; pres., COO McMoRan Oil & Gas Co., New Orleans, 1994-98, McMoRan Oil & Gas LLC, New Orleans, 1998-2001; exec. v.p. McMoRan Exploration Co., 1998—, vice-chmn., 2001—. Chmn. bd. Hysell Ballet Arts, Inc., New Orleans, 1982-83; chmn. petroleum majors campaign United Way, 1996, 98; bd. dirs. Lenpac, Metairie, 1983; chmn. citizenship com. McMoRan Exploration Co., 2000—. Mem. New Orleans Geol. Soc., Geol. Soc. Am., Am. Assn. Petroleum Geologists, Petroleum Club of New Orleans (bd. dirs. 1988, 89, 90), Houston Geol. Soc., La. Assn. Ind. Producers, Mid-Continent Oil and Gas Assn. Office: McMoRan Oil & Gas LLC 1615 Poydras St New Orleans LA 70112-1254 also: PO Box 60004 New Orleans LA 70160-0004

MURROW, WAYNE LEE, communications educator, dean; b. Alva, Okla., Jan. 23, 1935; s. Everett Emmet Murrow and Stella Jean McGlothlin; m. Marti L. Rogers, Aug. 19, 1956 (dec. Sept. 1966); children: Sherri, Randal, Cynthia, Jeffrey; m. Nila Arlene West, Jan. 19, 1968. BA, Bethany Nazarene Coll., 1956; M of Tchg., Ctrl. State U., 1968; PhD, U. Okla., 1972. Min. Ch. of the Nazarene, Tex., Okla.; prof. So. Nazarene U., Bethany, 1968-80, dean, prof., 1980—. Evaluation team mem. Okla. State Dept. Edn., Oklahoma City, 1980-94. Mem. Nat. Comm. Assn, Ctrl. States Comm. Assn. (adv. coun. 1977-90), Okla. Theatre Speech Comm. Assn. (pres. 1976-77, Outstanding Tchr. award 1980), Christian Adult Higher Edn. Assn. (coun. mem. 1994-2000, pres. 1997-98), North Ctrl. Assn. (evaluation team mem. 1968-80, cons.-evaluator for colls. and univs. 1994—). Avocation: family history. Home: 8105 Bridgeport Ln Bethany OK 73008 Office: So Nazarene Univ 6729 NW 39th Exp Bethany OK 73008 E-mail: wmurrow@snu.edu.

MURRY, CHARLES EMERSON, lawyer, official; b. Hope, N.D., June 23, 1924; s. Raymond Henry and Estelle Margarete (Skeim) M.; m. Donna Deane Kleve, June 20, 1948; children: Barbara, Karla, Susan, Bruce, Charles. BS, U. N.D., 1948, JD, 1950. Bar: N.D. 1950. Mem. firm Nelson and Heringer, Rugby, N.D., 1950-51; dir. N.D. Legis. Council, 1951-75; adj. gen. with rank of maj. gen. State of N.D., Bismarck, 1975-84; mgr. Garrison Diversion Conservancy Dist., 1985-93. Cons. Council State Govts.; mem. res. forces policy bd. Sec. of Def. Vice-pres. Mo. Slope Luth. Home of Bismarck, 1965-66. Served with AUS, 1942-45. Decorated D.S.M., Legion of Merit, Meritorious Service medal, Bronze Star, Army Commendation medal; Fourragere Belgium; Orange Lanyard Netherlands; recipient Sioux award U. N.D., 1970; Gov.'s award of excellence, 1971; Nat. Leadership award Bismarck C. of C., 1971 Mem. Adjs. Gen. Assn. (exec. com., sec. 1983-84), Nat. Legis. Conf. (past chmn.), N.G. Assn., Am. Bar Assn., N.D. Bar Assn., Commrs. Uniform State Laws. Lodges: Elks, Masons. Lutheran. Office: 5505 Ponderosa Ave Bismarck ND 58503-9159 E-mail: murryce@webtv.net.

MURRY, HAROLD DAVID, JR. lawyer; b. Holdenville, Okla., June 30, 1943; s. Harold David Sr. and Willie Elizabeth (Dees) M.; m. Ann Moore Earnhardt, Nov. 1, 1975; children: Elizabeth Ann, Sarah Bryant. BA, Okla. U., 1965, JD, 1968. Bar: Okla. 1968, D.C. 1974. Asst. to v.p. U. Okla., Norman, 1968-71, legal counsel Research Inst., 1969-71; atty. U.S. Dept. Justice, Washington, 1971-74; spl. asst. U.S. Atty., 1972; assoc. Clifford & Warnke, 1974-78, ptnr., 1978-91, Howrey & Simon, Washington, 1991-98, Baker Botts LLP, Washington, 1998—. Mem. ABA, Okla. Bar Assn., D.C. Bar Assn., Fed. Bar Assn., Met. Club (Washington), Chevy Chase Club (Md.), Phi Alpha Delta. Democrat. Home: 8931 Bel Air Pl Potomac MD 20854-1606 Office: Baker Botts LLP Ste 1300 1299 Pennsylvania Ave NW Washington DC 20004-2408

MURTAGH, FREDERICK REED, neuroradiologist, educator; b. Phila., Nov. 20, 1944; s. Frederick and Mary (Shaner) M.; (div.); children: Ryan David, Kevin Reed; m. Dorothy Rossi. BA, William and Mary Coll., 1966; MD, Temple U., 1971. Prof., dir. neuroradiology U. S. Fla., Tampa, 1978—. Author: Imaging Anatomy of Head and Spine, 1991. Author: Imaging Anatomy of Head & Spine, 1991. Lt. USNR, 1972-74. Mem. Am. Coll. Radiology (cert. added qualification in neuroradiology 1995), Assn. Univ. Radiologists, Am. Soc. Neuroradiology (sr. mem.), Radiol. Soc. N.Am., Southeastern Neuroradiology Soc. Office: U South Fla 3301 Alumni Dr Tampa FL 33612-9413

MURTAGH, JOHN EDWARD, alcohol production consultant; b. Wallington, Surrey, Eng., Sept. 12, 1936; arrived in U.S., 1982; s. Thomas Henry and Elsie (Kershaw Paterson) M.; m. Eithne Anne Fawsitt, July 18, 1959; children: Catherine, Rhoda, Sean, Aidan, Doreen. BSc, U. Wales, 1959, MSc, 1970, PhD, 1972. Rsch. coord. House of Seagram, Long Pond, Jamaica, 1959-63, whisky distillery mgr. Beaupre, Que., Can., 1963-65, rum distillery mgr. Richibucto, N.B., Can., 1965-68, rsch. mgr. Montreal, Que., 1968-70; alcohol prodn. cons. Murtagh & Assocs., Buttevant, Ireland, 1972-77, 79-82, Winchester, Va., 1982—; vodka distillery mgr. Iran Beverages, Tehran, 1977-79. Ethanol tech. cons., adv. bd. Info. Resources, Inc., Washington, 1988—; lectr. Alltech Ann. Alcohol Sch., Lexington, Ky., 1982-97; chmn. Ann. World Ethanol Conf., London, 1998–; cons. in field. Author: Glossary of Fuel-Ethanol Terms, 1990; co-author, editor: The Alcohol Textbook, 1995; editor: Worldwide Directory of Distilleries, 1996; contbr. articles to profl. jours. Adv. bd. Byrd Sch. Bus., Shenandoah U., Winchester, Va., 1989-95. Recipient Millers Mut. prize, U. Wales, 1959. Fellow Am. Inst. Chemists, Inst. Chemistry of Ireland, Inst. Food Sci. and Tech. of Ireland; mem. Royal Soc. Chemistry (chartered), Am. Arbitration Assn. (arbitrator nat. comml. panel 1990-2000). Achievements include development of processes for the prodn. of high-quality neutral alcohol from a wide range of feedstocks. Home and Office: 160 Bay Ct Winchester VA 22602-4700 E-mail: murtagh@murtagh.com.

MURTAGH, MICHAEL PAUL, psychologist; b. Washington, Sept. 23, 1959; s. Hugh Hunter and Margaret (Payne) M.; m. Anne Marie Murtagh, Nov. 30, 1985. BS magna cum laude, James Madison U., 1981; MS, Villanova U., 1983; PhD, U. Mont., Missoula, 1991. Lic. psychologist, N.Y. Staff psychologist Eagleville (Pa.) Hosp., 1984-87; dir. psychol. svcs. Mont. State Prison, Deer Lodge, 1991-94; staff psychologist, coord. forensic svcs. Madison County Dept. Mental Health, Wampsville, N.Y., 1994-2000; asst. prof. Bridgewater State Coll., 2000—. Part-time faculty Salish-Kootenai Coll., Pablo, Mont., 1988; vis. prof. U. Mont., Missoula, 1992; adj. faculty Onondaga C.C., Syracuse, N.Y., 1998-2000; coord. graduate program in psychology Bridgewater (Mass.) State Coll., 2000—; consultant sex offender treatment program Madison County Dept. Mental Health, 2000—; lectr., presenter in field. Contbr. articles to profl. jours. Vol. crisis counselor Listening Ear Svc., Harrisonburg, Va., 1980-81. Recipient Disting. Svc. award Southea. Pa. Mental Health Assn., 1985. Mem. Am. Psychol. Assn. Avocation: baseball. Home: 57 Seymour St Berkley MA 02779

MURTAGH, WILLIAM JOHN, preservationist, educator; b. Phila., May 2, 1923; s. Frederick and Maude Elizabeth (Rhoad) M.; m. Mary Louise Morton (div.). BArch, U. Penn., 1950, MA in Archtl. History, 1953, PhD in Archtl. History, 1963. Exec. dir. Annie S. Kemmerer Mus., Bethlehem, Pa., 1956-58; exec. sec. Hist. Bethlehem, Inc., 1956-58; asst. to pres. Nat. Trust for Hist. Preservation, Washington, 1958-59; dir. edn. Nat. Trust Hist. Preservation, 1959-67, v.p. preservation svcs., 1981-84; keeper nat. register historic places U.S. Dept. Interior-Nat. Park Svc., 1967-79; dir. hist. preservation program Columbia U., N.Y.C., 1979-81; prof. dept. Am. studies, founder hist. preservation program U. Hawaii Manoa, Honolulu, 1986-93, dir. Pacific preservation consortium, 1990—. Bd. dirs. Preservation Inst., Nantucket, Mass. Author: Moravian Architecture and Town Planning, 1967, 2d edit., 1998, Keeping Time, 1988, 2d edit., 1997. Pres. Victorian Soc. Am., Phila., 1974-80. Recipient Louise DuPont Crowninshield award, 1980, Disting. Svc. award Sec. of Interior, 1976; Benjamin Franklin fellow Royal Soc. Arts, London, 1974, Fulbright fellow, U. Bonn, Germany, 1954, U. Freiburg, Germany, 1955, U.S. Com. Internat. Coun. on Monuments and Sites, Paris, 1988. Mem. Cosmos Club (Washington). Episcopalian. Avocations: photography, music, gardening, travel, house restoration. Home and Office: 6 W Cedar St Alexandria VA 22301-2618 E-mail: kepperwjm@aol.com.

MURTAUGH, CHRISTOPHER DAVID, lawyer; b. Darby, Pa., Oct. 25, 1945; s. John Michael and Rita (Sullivan) M.; m. Nancy R. Hanauer, Nov. 30, 1968; children: Jason C., Colin M., Alison M. AB, U. Ill., 1967, JD, 1970. Bar: Ill. 1970, Fla. 1973, U.S. Dist. Ct. (no. dist.) Ill. 1975. Ptnr. Winston & Strawn, Chgo., 1974—, capital ptnr., 1987—, real estate dept. chmn., 1994—. Mem. Glen Ellyn (Ill.) Capital Improvements Com., 1985-89, Glen Ellyn Plan Com., 1989-96, Met. Planning Coun., 1995—; bd. visitors U. Ill. Coll. of Law, 1998-2001. Lt. USNR, 1971-74. Mem. ABA, Am. Coll. Real Estate Lawyers, Fla. Bar Assn., Ill. State Bar Assn., Chgo. Bar Assn., Urban Land Inst., Internat. Coun. Shopping Ctrs., Order of Coif. Office: Winston & Strawn 35 W Wacker Dr Ste 4200 Chicago IL 60601-1695 E-mail: cmurtaug@winston.com.

MURTHA, JOHN PATRICK, congressman; b. New Martinsville, W.Va., June 17, 1932; s. John Patrick and Mary Edna (Ray) M.; m. Joyce Bell; three children. BA in Econs., U. Pitts., 1961; postgrad., Indiana U. of Pa., 1962-65; H.H.D. (hon.), Mt. Aloysius Jr. Coll. Mem. Pa. Ho. of Reps., 1969-73, 93rd-106th Congresses from 12th Pa. dist., Washington, 1974—; mem. appropriations com. Served to lt. USMC, 1952-55, as maj. 1966-67, Vietnam; ret. col. Res. Decorated Bronze Star, Purple Heart (2); Cross of Gallantry Vietnam; Pa. Disting. Svc. award, 1978, Pa. Meritorious Svc. medal, numerous service awards for work during Johnstown flood, 1977, Iron Mike award Marine Corps League, 1988, Disting. Am. award Nation's Capital chpt. Air Force Assn., 1989, Outstanding Veteran award Vets. Caucus of Am. Acad. Physician Assts., 1989, Man of Steel award Cold Finished Steel Bar Inst., 1989; named Man of Yr. Johnstown Jaycees, 1978 Office: US Ho of Reps 2423 Rayburn Ho Office Bldg Washington DC 20515-0001 also: PO Box 780 Johnstown PA 15907-0780*

MURTHA, PAMELA BERRY, secondary education educator; b. Oct. 24, 1941; d. Joseph Charles and Elenor (Kucharski) B.; 1 child, Katie Julia. BA, Western Mich. U., 1965; MA, U. Mich., 1975; Edn. Specialist, Wayne State U., 1985, postgrad. Lic. profl. tchr. Tchr. East Prairie Jr. H.S., Vicksburg, Mich., 1965-66, Allen Park (Mich.) H.S., 1966—, English dept. chair, 1969-81, tchr. English, 1993—. Rsch. asst. U. Mich., Ann Arbor, 1973-75, Wayne State U., Detroit, 1981-82, dir. politics in edn., 1981-82; spl. projects dir. Allen Park Pub. Schs., 1981-92; cons. Humanistic Mgmt. Sys., Columbus, Ohio, 1981-82; mem. Internat. Yr. of the Child, Wayne State U., Detroit, 1981-82; mem. std. setting com. Mich. Dept. Edn., Lansing, 1998, content adv. com., 1998—, mem. task force State Bd. Edn., 2002; tech. liaison Allen Park Pub. Schs.; trainer Trainers County Mentoring Program. Pres. Young Dems., 1978-82; precinct dir. Dem. Party, del., 1985—. Nominee Phoebe Apperson award, Nat. PTA, 1985, Disney Tribute to Tchrs.; recipient Disting. Tchr. of Writing, Northwood U., 2001. Mem. Nat. Coun. Tchrs. English, Mich. Coun. Tchrs. English, Mich. Reading Assn., Phi Delta Kappa. Avocations: golf, reading, travel, theater, writing.

MURTHY, ANDIAPPAN K.S. technology manager; b. Sivakasi, India, Nov. 24, 1943; came to U.S., 1967; parents: K. Andiappan and Janaki Nadar; m. Mohana Rajendran, Apr. 17, 1970; children: Rajan, Vale. BTech with honors, Indian Inst. Tech., Khargpur, 1966; MS, Columbia U., 1968, ScD in Engring., 1974. Registered profl. engr., N.J. Engr. Digvijay Cement Co., India, 1966-67; process engr., project mgr., then mgr. R & D Allied Chem. Corp., Morristown, N.J., 1968-86; sr. technologist Allied Signal Corp., 1986-88; process engring mgr. Jacobs Engring. Group, Baton Rouge, 1989-93; dir. tech. BOC Group, Murray Hill, N.J., 1993—. Adj. prof. Columbia U., N.Y.C., 1979-89, N.J. Inst. Tech., Newark, 1979-84; course dir. Ctr. for Profl. Advancement, East Brunswick, N.J., 1981—. Patentee in field; contbr. articles to tech. publs. Mem. Am. Inst. Chem. Engrs. Avocations: photography, travel. Home: 8 Pilgrim Ct Morristown NJ 07960-5737

MURTHY, KURUKUNDI KRISHNA, neurosurgeon; b. Hopset, India, June 6, 1937; came to U.S., 1963; MD, Bangalore (India) Med. Coll., 1961. Diplomate Am. Bd. Neurol. Surgery. Intern Victoria Hosp., Bangalore, 1962-63, Unity Hosp., Bklyn., 1963-64; resident L.I. Coll. Hosp., 1964-65; resident in neurol. surgery VA Hosp., Bronx, N.Y., 1965-66, 67-69, Neurol. Inst., Columbia Presbyn. Med. Ctr., N.Y.C., 1966-67; fellow U. Toronto (Can.)/Toronto Western Hosp., 1969-71; neurosurgeon Neurol. and Neurosurg. Assocs., Poughkeepsie, N.Y. Instr. neurosurgery Coll. of Medicine and Dentistry of N.J., N.J. Med. Sch., 1971-72; attending physician St. Francis Hosp., Poughkeepsie, Vassar Bros. Hosp., Poughkeepsie; dir. dept. neurosurgery St. Francis Hosp., Poughkeepsie, 1980-82, sec.-treas. med./dental staff, 1983, v.p. med./dental staff, 1985, pres. med./dental staff 1987-89; presenter in field. Contbr. articles to profl. jours. Fellow Royal Coll. Surgeons Can., Internat. Coll. Surgeons; mem. ACS, Am. Assn. Neurol. Surgeons, Congress Neurol. Surgeons, Am. Assn. Fgn. Med. Grads., N.Y. State Soc. Surgeons, N.Y. State Neurosurg. Soc., Dutchess County Med. Soc., Mid-Hudson Surg. Soc., N.Y. Acad. Scis. Office: Neurol and Neurosurg Assocs PC 74 W Cedar St Poughkeepsie NY 12601-1310

MURTHY, VADIRAJA VENKATESA, biochemist, researcher, educator; b. Bombay, Mar. 27, 1940; came to U.S., 1961; s. Ramanathpur Venkatesa and Saroja (Bai) M.; m. Jayashree Deshpande, Sept. 21, 1969; children: Deepti, Seema. BSc with honors, U. Bombay, 1959, MSc, 1961; PhD in Biochemistry, U. Md., 1968. Clin. chemist Nat. Registry of Clin. Chemists; lic. dir. clin. chemistry, N.Y.C. and N.Y. state. Sr. rsch. biochemist, asst. group leader USV Pharms., Yonkers, N.Y., 1970-71; rsch. assoc. Toxicology Ctr., U. Iowa, Iowa City, 1971-72; vis. scientist NIH-Environ., Research Triangle Park, N.C., 1972-74; sr. rsch. assoc. Emory U. Sch. Medicine, Atlanta, 1974-75; adj. asst. prof. Atlanta (Ga.) Univ., 1975-76; prof., co-dir. Talladega (Ala.) Coll., 1976-83; clin. assoc. prof. Albert Einstein Coll. Medicine, Bronx, N.Y., 1993—, co-dir., 1983-95; dir. spl. chem. lab., coord. mgr. labs. Jacobi Med. Ctr., N.Y., 1995—, assoc. prof. pathology, 1996—. Chmn. sci. rev. San Diego (Calif.) Conf. on Nucleic Acids, 1992; chmn. sci. symposium on molecular diagnostics Am. Assn. Clin. Chemistry Nat. Meetings, N.Y., 1993. Contbr. chpt. to book and articles to profl. jours. Hon. sec. Vishwa Kalyana Trust, Washington, 1989—. Named Fogarty Internat. Vis. Scientist Nat. Inst. Environ. Health Scis., NIH, 1972-74; rsch. grantee NIH, 1976-83, Resource Ctr. grantee NSF, 1981-83. Mem. Am. Assn. for Clin. Chemistry (chmn.-elect molecular pathology divsn. 1992-93, chair 1993-94), Am. Assn. Cancer Rsch., Am. Chem. Soc., Assn. Clin. Lab. Physicians and Scientists. Hindu. Achievements include U.S. patent for spectrophotometric attachment for analyzing two-phase systems. Avocations: painting, writing popular science articles. Home: 100 Lindbergh Blvd Teaneck NJ 07666-5347 Office: Jacobi Med Ctr Dept Pathology Rm 603 Bronx NY 10461

MURTHY, VANUKURI RADHA KRISHNA, civil engineer; b. Hyderabad, India, June 20, 1928; came to U.S., 1963; s. Rama Vannkuri and Sita (Dittakavi) Rao; m. Lakshmi Gruha Gadiraju, Mar. 12, 1952; children: Siva, Prabha, Jyothy, Lata. BE in Civil, Osmania U., 1949; MS in Engring., U. Fla., 1964; PhD, U. Pa., 1967. Registered profl. engr., Tex. Engr. Govt. of Andhra Pradesh, Hyderabad, 1949-62; grad. rsch. asst. U. Fla., Gainesville, 1963-64, U. Del., Newark, 1964-66, U. Pa., Phila., 1966-67, instr., 1967-68; hydrologist Tex. Water Rights Commn., Austin, 1968-71, head hydraulics design sect., 1972-77; head basin modeling Tex. Water Commn., 1978-90, chief engr., 1990-91; cons. water resources, 1991—. Engr. advisor to commr. Pecos River Compact Commn., Austin, 1987-91, chmn. engring. adv. com., 1987-91; prin. expert witness in interstate law suit for Tex. against N.Mex., 1977-90. Author: Allocation of Pecos River Basin Water, 1991; contbr. articles to profl. jours. Travel grant NSF, 1975. Mem. ASCE (life, editor Jour. Pipeline Div. 1969-74), Sigma Xi. Achievements include development of water availability models for all major river basins in Texas. Home: 5910 Mountain Villa Dr Austin TX 78731-3753 Office: 600 W 28th St Austin TX 78705-3700

MURTON, WILLIAM NORMAN, II, telecommunications executive; b. Lakewood, Ohio, Sept. 12, 1944; s. William Norman Sr. and Marica Lydia (Elkins) M.; m. Margaret Ann Cavan, Sept. 9, 1967; children: Margaret Sibley, Amy Elkins, Joshua William, Nathan Douglas, Alexander David. Student, Syracuse U., 1962-64; BSBA, Ohio State U., 1977. Programmer SCOA Industries, Columbus, Ohio, 1969; mgr. systems programming Ohio State U. Hosp. Computer Ctr., 1969-73; sr. systems planner and program mgmt. Horizons Data Systems, 1973-77; mgr. Arthur Andersen & Co., 1977-83; mgr. info. systems Chillicothe (Ohio) Telephone Co., 1983-90, profitability analysis mgr., 1990—. V.p. fin. Boy Scouts Am., Chillicothe, 1988-90, v.p. adminstrn., 1990-92, pres.-elect, 1992-93, pres., 1993, svc. area chair, 1993-95, advanced chair, 1995—, area v.p., 1995—, Webelos den leader, 1988-90, chmn. troop advancement com., 1987-89, chmn. troop com., 1989-92; chmn. publicity com. Ross County Ctrl. Ohio Diabetes Assn., 1987-88; chmn. Boy Scout com. Chillicothe Rotary Club, 1988-94. Recipient Dist. Merit award Boy Scouts Am., Chillicothe, 1987, Statuette award, 1988, Silver Braver award, 1993. Mem. Assn. for Computing Machinery (pres., founder Ohio State U. chpt. 1966), Assn. for Sys. Mgmt. (long-range planning com. 1985-88, Ctrl. Ohio chpt. pres. 1988-89, membership adv. com. 1988-89, chmn. 1989-90, Div. 14 sec.-treas. 1989-90, chmn. 1990-91, constl. bylaws com. 1990-92, chmn. 1992-94, internat. dir. 1992-94, internat. external affairs v.p. 1994-95, internat. treas. 1995—, chpt. svc. award 1986, merit award 1987, chpt. pres. award 1988, achievement award 1988, disting. svc. award 1990), Ohio Telephone Assn. (cert. sys. profl. 1984—, data processing com. 1986-90, fin. com. 1990-94). Republican. Avocations: camping, chess. Office: Chillicothe Telephone Co 68 E Main St Chillicothe OH 45601-2503

MURTY, HEMA S. aerospace engineer, researcher; b. Calcutta, India, Apr. 5, 1960; arrived in Can., 1962; d. Nirmalamba (Maddali) M. B of Engring., Carleton U., Ottawa, Ont., Can., 1982; MASc, U. Toronto, 1983, PhD in Aerospace Engring., 1992. Rsch. asst. U. Toronto, 1982-90; engring. contractor NRC of Can., Ottawa, 1990-94; rsch. assoc. Rensselaer Poly. Inst., Troy, N.Y., 1994-96; sr. aerodynamicist Sikorsky Aircraft, Stratford, Conn., 1996—. Bd. dirs. South Shore Music and Arts Ctr. Humanities. Contbr. articles to profl. jours. Mem. AIAA, ASME, Am. Helicopter Soc. (pres. Stratford chpt.), Can. Aeronautics and Space Inst. Avocations: singing East Indian classical music, East Indian classical dancing, classical piano, tennis. Office: 6900 Main St M/S S317a5 PO Box 9729 Stratford CT 06615-9129

MUSA, JOHN DAVIS, computer and infosystems executive, software reliability engineering researcher and expert, independent consultant, educator; b. Amityville, N.Y., June 11, 1933; s. Khan Hussein and Ione Geraldine (Ryan) M.; m. Marilyn Laurene Allred, June 24, 1959. BA, Dartmouth Coll., 1954, MSEE, 1955. With AT&T Bell Labs., Murray Hill, N.J., 1958-96, mem. tech. staff, 1958-63, supr. guidance program devel., 1963-68, supr. command and control program devel., 1968-69, supr. mgmt. control and new software tech., 1969-72, supr. human factors test, 1972-74, supr. computer graphics, 1974-80, supr. computer measurements, 1980-85, supr. software quality, 1985-90, tech. mgr. software reliability engring., 1991-96. Mem. N.J. Coun. R&D; lectr., spkr. in field. Author: Software Reliability: Measurement, Prediction, Application, 1987, Software Reliability Engineering: More Reliable Software, Faster Development and Testing, 1998; editor: (book series) Software Quality Institute; contbr. numerous articles to prof. jours. and books. Lt. USN, 1955-58. Fellow IEEE (Third Millenium medal for outstanding achievements and contbns.); mem. IEEE Computer Soc. (2d v.p. 1986, v.p. publs. 1984-85, v.p. tech. activities 1986, chair tech com. software engring. 1982-84, founding mem. editl. bd. IEEE Software Mag., Disting. lectr. 1980-83, Meritorious Svc. award 1984, 85, 87, Golden Core award, founding officer com. on software reliability engring., mem. editl. bds. Spectrum mag., 1984-86, Proc. of the IEEE 1983-90, Technique et Science Informatiques jour., sr. editor Software Engring. Inst. book series, sr. founding editor Software Quality Inst. book series, chair steering com. Internat. Conf. on Software Engring.), IEEE Reliability Soc., Assn. for Computing Machinery. Achievements include internat. leader in software engring. and in creation new tech. software reliability engring.; created two software reliability models; developed concepts and practice of operational profile, software-reliability engineered testing, concept of execution time; reduced operation software (ROS), and operational development; created concept of fault exposure ratio; developed approach for choosing software development strategies to meet different reliability objectives; international leader in reducing software reliability engineering to practice. Office: 39 Hamilton Rd Morristown NJ 07960-5341 E-mail: j.musa@ieee.org.

MUSA, SAMUEL ALBERT, university executive; m. Judith Friedman; children: Gregory, Jeffrey. BA, BSEE, Rutgers U., 1961; MS in Applied Physics, Harvard U., 1962, PhD in Applied Physics, 1965. Rsch. scientist Gen. Precision Inc., Little Falls, N.J., 1965-66; asst. prof. elec. engring. U. Pa., Phila., 1966-71; project leader Inst. for Def. Analyses, Arlington, Va., 1971-78; dep. dir. Office of Under Sec. Def., Washington, 1978-83; dir. rsch. and advanced tech. E-Systems, Inc., Dallas, 1983-86, v.p. rsch. and advanced tech., 1986-95; exec. dir. Ctr. Display Tech. and Mfg. U. Mich., 1995-99; assoc. v.p. for strategic initiative Northwestern U., Evanston, Ill., 1999—. Mem. sci. adv. bd. USAF, 1987-91; mem. adv. bd. Def. Intelligence Agy., Army Sci. Bd. Contbr. articles to profl. jours. Recipient Exceptional Civilian Svc. award, Sec. of Air Force, cert. of appreciation, Sec. Def. Fellow IEEE; mem. AIA (tech. and ops. coun. 1986-95, vice chmn. 1993, chmn. 1994), Sigma Xi, Tau Beta Pi, Pi Mu Epsilon. Office: 1801 Maple Ave Evanston IL 60208-0001

MUSACCHIA, X(AVIER) J(OSEPH), physiology and biophysics educator; b. Bklyn., Feb. 11, 1923; s. Castrense and Orsolina (Mazzola) M.; m. Betty Cook, Nov. 23, 1950; children: Joseph, Mary, Thomas, Laura Ann. BS, St. Francis Coll., Bklyn., 1944; MS, Fordham U., 1947, PhD, 1949. Instr. biology Marymount (N.Y.) Coll., 1948-49; from instr. to prof. biology St. Louis U., 1949-65; prof. physiology U. Mo., Columbia, 1965-78; prof. physiology and biophysics U. Louisville, 1978-91, prof. emeritus, 1991—, dean Grad. Sch., 1978-89, assoc. provost for rsch., 1985-89. Bd. dirs. Coun. Grad. Schs., 1986-89. Author: Depressed Metabolism, 1969, Regulation of Depressed Metabolism and Thermogenesis, 1976, Survival in Cold, 1981; also articles. Bd. govs. J. Graham Brown Cancer Ctr., Louisville, 1978-83; bd. dirs. Oak Ridge Associated Univs. Served with AUS, 1943-45. Research grantee NIH; Research grantee NASA. Fellow AAAS; mem. Am. Physiol. Soc., Am. Soc. Zoologists, Am. Soc. for Space and Gravitational Biology (v.p. 1988-89, pres. 1989-90), Soc. Exptl. Biology and Medicine, Corp. Marine Biol. Lab., Sigma Xi. (past chpt. pres.) Address: PO Box 5054 Bella Vista AR 72714-0054

MUSACCHIO, LAURA R. planning and design educator; b. N.Y., Oct. 28, 1966; d. Bruce W. and Rose Marie E. Musacchio. Student, Le Moyne Coll., Syracuse, N.Y., 1984—86; B of Landscape Arch., 1989; M of Landscape Arch., SUNY, 1993; PhD in Urban and Regional Sci., Texas A&M U., College Station, 1999. Designer design and planning firms, Orange County, Calif., 1989—91; grad. asst. SUNY Coll. Environ. Sci. and Forestry, Syracuse, 1991—93; asst. prof. Utah State U., Logan, 1993—95; grad. asst. Tex. A&M U., College Station, 1995—96, asst. lectr., 1996—99; asst. prof. Ariz. State U., Tempe, 2000—. Cons., intern Lower Colo. River Authority, Austin, 1996—98; coord. 16th ann. symposium program U.S. Regional Chapter, International Association of Landscape Ecology, Tempe, 1999—2001; rschr. Cen. Ariz. Phoenix Long-Term Ecol. Rsch. Project, 2000—. Contbr. articles to profl. jours. Mem. S.W. Riparian Mgmt. and Restoration Task Force, Phoenix, 2000—. Named prin. investigator, Nat. Endowment of Arts, 2000, co-prin. investigator, S.W. Ctr. for Environ. Rsch. and Policy/EPA, 2000; recipient, 2001. Mem.: Am. Soc. Landscape Archs. (mem.-at-large Utah chpt. 1994—95, Merit award 1989), Am. Planning Assn., Soil and Water Conservation Soc., Soc. for Conservation Biology, Ecol. Soc. Am., Internat. Assn. Landscape Ecology (councillor-at-large U.S. Regional chpt. 2002—, NASA/Mich. State U. Profl. Enhancement award 1999), Sigma Lambda Alpha, Beta Beta Beta. Office: Ariz State U PO Box 872005 Tempe AZ 85287-2005 Business E-Mail: Laura.Musacchio@asu.edu.

MUSACCHIO, MARILYN JEAN, nurse midwife, educator; b. Louisville, Dec. 7, 1938; d. Robert William and Loretta C. (Liebert) Poulter; m. David Edward Musacchio, May 13, 1961; children: Richard Peter, Michelle Marie. BSN cum laude, Spalding Coll., 1968; MSN, U. Ky., 1972, cert. in nurse-midwifery, 1976; PhD, Case Western Res U., 1993. RN; cert. nurse-midwife; advanced registered nurse practitioner; registered nurse-midwife. Staff nurse gynecol. unit St. Joseph Infirmary, Louisville, 1959-60, staff nurse male gen. surgery unit, 1960; instr. St. Joseph Infirmary Sch. Nursing, 1960-71; from asst. prof. to assoc. prof., dir. dept. nursing edn. Ky. State U., Frankfort, 1972-75; asst. prof. U. Ky. Coll. Nursing, Lexington, 1976-79, assoc. prof., coord., 1979-92, acting coordinator nurse-midwifery, 1982-84, coordinator for nurse-midwifery, 1987-92; assoc. prof., dir. nurse-midwifery U. Ala., Birmingham, 1992-96, assoc. prof., 1997-98; dean, prof. Tenn. Technol. U., Cookeville, 1998—. Cons. in field. Mem. editorial bd. Jour. Obstet., Gynecol. and Neonatal Nursing, 1976-82; author pamphlet; contbr. articles to profl. jours. Mem.Louisville Safety Coun., 1973-80. Brig. Gen. Army Nurse Corps, USAR, 1992-95. Recipient Disting. Citizen award City of Louisville, 1977, Jefferson Cup award Jefferson County, Ky., 1991; named Outstanding Alumna, Mercy Acad., 1993; named to Hall of Disting. Alumni, U. Ky., 1995; recipient scholarships and fellowships, other awards. Fellow Am. Acad. Nursing; mem. AWHONN, NAFE, ANA, Nurse Assn. Am. Coll. Ob-Gyn. (charter; nat. sec. 1970-72, chmn. dist. V 1969), Am. Coll. Nurse-Midwives, Res. Officers Assn., Assn. Mil. Surgeons U.S., Sr. Army Res. Comdr. Assn., Assn. U.S. Army, Army Nurse Corps. Assn., Army War Coll. Alumni Assn. (life). Roman Catholic. Avocations: reading, candy making, cake decorating, cooking, sewing. Home: PO Box 5001 Cookeville TN 38505-0001 Fax: 931-372-6244. E-mail: mmusacchio@tntech.edu.

MUSANTE, PATRICIA W. library director; b. Pitts., June 15, 1944; d. Edward Anthony and Katherine (Webber) Wagner; m. Guido J. Musante, Ap4. BA, Carlow Coll., Pitts., 1967; MA, Carnegie Mellon U., 1970; MLS, U. Pitts., 1991. Tchr. Canevin H.S., Pitts., 1967-69; flight attendant Capitol Internat. Airways, Nashville, 1971-79; adj. prof. Carlow Coll., 1990-91; pub./editor Ft. Covington (N.Y.) Sun, 1982-89; asst. dir. Potsdam (N.Y.) Pub. Libr., 1991-99, dir., 1999—. Bd. dirs. North Country Dist. PTA, Potsdam, 1996—; founding trustee Ft. Covington Reading Ctr., 1984-89. Recipient Jos. Schubert Moving Toward Excellence award N.Y. State Libr., Albany, 1997, North Country Reference and Rsch. Resources award for excellence in libr. svcs., 2001. Mem. AAUW (chair book discussion group 1993—), Beta Phi Mu. Home: 871 River Rd Norwood NY 13668-3155

MUSANTE, TONY (ANTHONY PETER MUSANTE JR.), actor; b. Bridgeport, Conn. s. Anthony Peter and Natalie Anne (Salerno) M.; m. Jane Ashley Sparkes, June 2, 1962. BA (Baker scholar), Oberlin Coll., 1958; postgrad., Northwestern U., 1957; student, HB Studios, N.Y.C., 1961-65. Appearances include: (off Broadway prodns.) Borak, 1960, Zoo Story, Night of the Dunce, The Collection, Match-Play, Kiss Mama, L'Histoire du Soldat, A Gun Play, Falling Man, Cassatt, Grand Magic, The Big Knife, The Taming of the Shrew, Two Brothers, The Archbishop's Ceiling, Souvenir, A Streetcar Named Desire, Double Play, Dancing in the End Zone, Snow Orchid, Wait until Dark, Widows, Anthony Rose, Mount Allegro, Frankie and Johnny in the Clair de Lune, Breaking Legs, The Flip Side, Love Letters, The Sisters, Italian Funerals and Other Festive Occasions (Broadway prodns.) PS Your Cat is Dead, 1975 (N.Y. Drama Desk nomination), Memory of Two Mondays, 27 Wagons Full of Cotton, The Lady from Dubuque; films: Once a Thief, 1964, The Incident (Best Actor award Mar del Plata Internat. Film Festival), 1967, The Detective, The Mercenary, One Night at Dinner, Bird with the Crystal Plumage, Grissom Gang, Anonymous Venetian, The Last Run, Pisciotta Case, Goodbye and Amen, Break-Up, Collector's Item, The Repenter, Devil's Hill, Appointment in Trieste, Nocturne, The Pope of Greenwich Village, The Deep End of the Ocean, The Yards; TV appearances include Ride with Terror, 1963, star series Toma, 1973-74 (Photoplay Gold medal award 1974), scriptwriter several episodes; star HBO series Oz, A&E series 100 Centre Street; also starred in TV miniseries and movies: Exiled, The Seventh Scroll, Deep Family Secrets, A Kiss In the Dark, High Ice, Breaking Up is Hard to Do, The Baron, Legend of the Black Hand, The Story of Esther, My Husband is Missing, Nowhere to Hide, The Quality of Mercy (Emmy nominee 1975), Court Martial of Lt. William Calley, Night Heat, Rearview Mirror, Nutcracker: Money, Madness and Murder, Acapulco HEAT, Nothing Sacred, American Playhouse: Weekend, Last Waltz on a Tightrope; daytime TV (guest star): Loving, ABC, 1993, As The World Turns, CBS, 2000. Mem. SAG, AFTRA, ATAS, Actors Equity Assn., Writers Guild Am. West, Acad. Motion Picture Arts and Scis.

MUSCARELLA, CHRISTOPHER JAMES, finance educator; b. New Brunswick, N.J., Aug. 30, 1952; s. Mark Benjamin and Virginia (Pickert) M.; m. Bobbie Jean Weidner, June 1, 1985; children: Sarah Anne, Aaron Matthew BSEE, U. Notre Dame, 1974, MBA, 1976; PhD, Purdue U., 1983. Asst. prof. So. Meth. U., Dallas, 1984-90; sr. fin. economist U.S. Securities & Exch. Commn., Washington, 1990-91; prof., L.W. Roy and Mary Lois Clark tchg. fellow Pa. State U., University Park, 1991—. Vis. asst. prof. U. Notre Dame (Ind.), 1979, U. Oreg., Eugene, 1980-82, U. Utah, Sale Lake City, 1982-84; Dale S. Coenen vis. prof. free enterprise, Darden Grad. Sch. Bus. Adminstrn., U. Va., 2000. Assoc. editor Jour. Fin. Rsch., 1993—. Mem. Am. Fin. Assn., Fin. Mgmt. Assn. (northeast regional dir. 1994-96), European Fin. Assn. Avocations: genealogy. Office: Coll Bus Adminstrn 609 BAB University Park PA 16802 E-mail: cmuscarella@psu.edu.

MUSCATINE, CHARLES, English educator, author; b. Bklyn., Nov. 28, 1920; m. Doris Corn, July 21, 1945; children: Jeffrey, Alison. BA, Yale U., 1941, MA, 1942, PhD, 1948; L.H.D. (hon.), New Sch. for Social Research, 1982; Litt.D., SUNY, 1989, Rosary Coll., 1991. Mem. faculty dept. English U. Calif., Berkeley, 1948—, prof., 1960-91, prof. emeritus, 1991—, dir. Collegiate Seminar Program, 1974-80. Vis. prof. Wesleyan U., 1951-53; Ward Phillips lectr. U. Notre Dame, 1969; mem. com. of selection J.S. Guggenheim Found., 1969-89, chmn. 1985-89. Author: Chaucer and the French Tradition, 1957, The Book of Geoffrey Chaucer, 1963, Poetry and Crisis in the Age of Chaucer, 1972, The Old French Fabliaux, 1986, Medieval Literature, Style, and Culture, 1999; co-author, editor: Education at Berkeley, 1966, (with M. Griffith) The Borzoi College Reader, 1966, 7th edit., 1992, First Person Singular, 1973; co-editor Integrity in the Coll. Curriculum, 1985. Bd. dirs. No. Calif. chpt. ACLU, 1959-62, 63-66, Assn. Am. Colls., 1979-82, Ctr. for the Common Good, 1994-99 ; bd. dirs. Fedn. State Humanities Couns., 1989-94, chair, 1991-93; mem. Commn. on Humanities, Rockefeller Found., 1978-79, Calif. Coun. Humanities, 1986-94. With USNR, 1942-45. Recipient Navy Commendation ribbon, 1945, Berkeley citation, 1991; Fulbright fellow, 1958, 62, ACLS Rsch. fellow, 1958, Guggenheim fellow, 1962, NEH Sr. fellow, 1968. Fellow Am. Acad. Arts and Scis., Medieval Acad. of Am.; mem. MLA, New Chaucer Soc. (pres. 1980-81), Aircraft Owners and Pilots Assn., Phi Beta Kappa. Home: 2812 Buena Vista Way Berkeley CA 94708-2016 E-mail: chasm@uclink4.berkeley.edu.

MUSCATO, ANDREW, lawyer; b. Newark, Aug. 28, 1953; s. Salvatore and Bertha (Kubilus) M.; m. Ann Marie Hughes, Aug. 19, 1978; children: Amy, Andrew Joseph, Amanda. AB magna cum laude, Brown U., 1975; JD, Seton Hall U., 1978. Bar: N.J. 1978, U.S. Dist. Ct. N.J. 1978, U.S. Ct. Appeals (3d cir.) 1981, N.Y. 1984, U.S. Dist. Ct. (so. and ea. dists.) N.Y. 1984, U.S. Dist. Ct. (no. dist.) N.Y. 1998. Law clk. to presiding judge, appellate div. N.J. Superior Ct., Somerville, 1978-79; staff atty. Adminstrv. Office of Cts., Trenton, N.J., 1979-80; assoc. Simon & Allen, Newark, 1980-86; ptnr. Kirsten & Simon, 1987-89, Whitman & Ransom, Newark, 1989-93, Whitman Breed Abbott & Morgan, LLP, Newark, 1993-99; counsel Skadden, Arps, Slate, Meagher & Flom LLP, 1999—; commr. N.J. Pub. Employee Rels. Commn., 1999—. Atty. Irvington (N.J.) Rent Leveling Bd., 1980—; mem. N.J. Banking Adv. Bd., 2002—. Author: Executing on a Debtor's Interest in a Tenancy by the Entirety, 1986. Mem. ABA, Essex County Bar Assn., Trial Attys. N.J., N.J. Inst. Mcpl. Attys., Def. Rsch. Inst. Republican. Roman Catholic. Home: 66 Addison Dr Basking Ridge NJ 07920-2202 Office: Skadden Arps Slate Meagher & Flom LLP One Newark Ctr Newark NJ 07102-5297

MUSCHEL, LOUIS HENRY, immunologist, educator; b. N.Y.C., July 4, 1916; s. Maurice and Betty (Tobey) M.; m. Anne Orzel, Oct. 22, 1946; 1 child, Ruth Josephine. BS, NYU, 1936; MS, Yale U., 1951, PhD, 1953. Joined U.S. Army, 1941, advanced through grades to lt. col., 1961; chief dept. serology (Walter Reed Army Inst. Research), Washington, 1958-62; faculty U. Minn., Mpls., 1962-70, prof. microbiology, 1964-70; prof. bacteriology U. Calif., Berkeley, 1965, 67; with research dept. Am. Cancer Soc., 1970-88. Adj. prof. microbiology Columbia U., 1977-83; adj. prof. pathology NYU, 1983—. Mem. Am. Assn. Immunologists, Brit. Soc. Immunology, N.Y. Acad. Scis., Am. Soc. Microbiology, Soc. Exptl. Biology and Medicine, Am. Assn. for Cancer Research, Phi Beta Kappa, Sigma Xi, Phi Lambda Upsilon. Achievements include research, publs. on bactericidal action of serum and its role in host defs., natural bactericidal and viral neutralizing antibodies, applications of complement fixation technique. Home: 3333 Henry Hudson Pkwy W Apt 8A Bronx NY 10463-3255

MUSCHENHEIM, FREDERICK, retired pathologist; b. N.Y.C., July 9, 1932; s. Carl and Haroldine (Humphreys) M.; m. Linda Alexander, Mar. 29, 1958; children: Alexandra Lydia, Carl William, David Henry. AB, Harvard U., 1953; MDCM, McGill U., Montreal, Can., 1963. Intern Santa Clara County Hosp., San Jose, Calif., 1963-64; resident in pathology U. Colo. Med. Ctr., Denver, 1964-68, chief resident in clin. pathology, 1968-69; pathologist Freeman, Hanske, Munkittrick & Foley PA, Mpls., 1969-77; clin. pathologist Union-Truesdale Hosp., Fall River, Mass., 1977-78; chief pathologist St. Clare's Hosp., Denville, N.J., 1978-83, Oneida Healthcare Ctr., 1984-99, ret., 1999; cons. pathologist St. Jude Hosp., Vieux Fort, St. Lucia, West Indies, 1999—. Clin. asst. prof. SUNY Health Sci. Ctr., Syracuse, 1984-90, clin. assoc. prof., 1990-97, clin. prof., 1998-99, clin. prof. emeritus, 1999-2001; chief med. staff Oneida City Hosps., 1991; pres. Sunderman Fund, Bermuda Biol. Sta. for Rsch., v.p. Madison County (N.Y.) bd. health, 1995-96, pres., 1997-2000. Choir 1st Presbyn. Ch. of Cazenovia, N.Y., 1984-2000, trustee, 1985-89; choir Wayzata (Minn.) Cmty. Ch., 2001—. Mem.: Syracuse ARC Blood Svcs. (chmn. med. adv. coun. 1995—99), Minn. Soc. Pathologists (sec. 2002—), N.Y. State Soc. Pathologists (councilor 2nd dist. 1991—2000, chmn. legis. com. 1991—2000, del. to MSSNY 1998—99), N.Y. State Assn. Pub. Health Labs. (v.p. 1992—93, pres. 1993—94, edn. chmn. 1994—95), Med. Soc. Madison County (v.p. 1990—91, pres. 1991—93), Med. Soc. State of N.Y. (mem. legis. com. 1991—2000), Coll. Am. Pathologists (mem. govt. affairs com. 1994—97, nominating com. 1995, steering com. ho. dels. 1999—), Assn. Clin. Scientists (v.p. 1989, pres. 1990, rec. sec. 1995—, Diploma of Honor 1991). Home: 1159 Hollybrook Dr Wayzata MN 55391-1364

MUSCHLER, AUDREY LORRAINE, insurance broker; b. New Britain, Conn., May 24, 1928; d. Leonard Marl and Carolyn Dorothy (Low) Jackson; m. Arthur F. Muschler, Aug. 28, 1954; children: George F., James A., John L. Grad., Edgewood Coll., 1948. Agt. Fidelity Mut. Life Ins. Co., Chgo., 1953-63; ins. broker Oak Brook, Ill., 1975—. Co-author: Oak Brook, a concise history of the Village, 1990. Co-founder, 1st pres. Oak Brook Hist. Soc., 1975—, Fullersburg Hist. Found., Oak Brook, 1986—; co-founder, v.p., treas. Salt Creek Greenway Assn., Oak Brook, 1988-97; co-founder, co-dir, Mayslake Landmark Conservancy, Oak Brook, 1993-2000; active Grace Episcopal Churchwomen, 1970—, pres., 1987-89. Mem. Nat. Assn. Life Underwriters, DuPage Life Underwriters, PEO Sisterhood (pres. 1985-87). Republican. Avocation: historic preservation. Home: 55 Yorkshire Woods Oak Brook IL 60523-1472 E-mail: artimusm@aol.com.

MUSE, JAMES MICHAEL, bank executive, finance educator; b. Salem, Mass., June 22, 1960; s. James Joseph and Gertrude Marie (Coté) M.; m. Patricia Ann Tyrrell, May 30, 1986; children: Kristine Amy Kmiec, Michael Thomas Kmiec. BS in Bus. Adminstrn., Salem State Coll., 1983; CFP, Fairfield U., 1990, postgrad. Nat. Sch. Banking, 1995; postgrad. Sch. Bank Mktg., U. Colo., 1999; MBA, Fairfield U., 2002. Cert. Fin. Mktg. Profl., Inst. of Cert. Bankers; cert. employee plan specialist. Retail sales mgr. Salem (Mass.) 5 cents Saving Bank, 1982-84; retirement plans mgr. Andover (Mass.) Savings Bank, 1984-86; asst. treas. Bank 5 For Savings, Arlington, Mass., 1986-91; asst. v.p., trust officer Cambridge (Mass.) Savings Bank, 1991-97; v.p., dir. retail fin. svcs. Beverly (Mass.) Nat. Bank, 1997—. Chmn., treas. Mass. Retirement Plans Consortium, Boston, 1987; mem. faculty Endicott Coll., Beverly, Mass., New Eng. Coll. Fin., Boston, The Financial Planning Assn. Chair bd. dirs. ARC, Beverly, Mass.; bd. dirs. Beverly Teen YMCA, North Shore United Way; bd. dirs., vice chair North Shore Music Theatre Corp. Circle; former moderator, trustee First Federated Ch., Beverly, Mass., 1992—2002; treas. Babe Ruth Baseball, 1992—94; pres. basketball booster club Beverly H.S., 1994, 1995, 1996; treas. Friends of Emma Found.; bd. dir. ABA Mktg. Network NE chpt.; mem. United Ch. of Christ. Mem.: Bank Mktg. Assn., Mass. Bankers Assn (bd. dir.s). Avocations: kayaking, skiing, golf, the ocean, community involvement. Home: 7 Cross St Beverly MA 01915-3808 Office: Beverly Nat Bank 240 Cabot St Beverly MA 01915

MUSE, WILLIAM VAN, academic administrator; b. Marks, Miss., Apr. 7, 1939; s. Mose Lee and Mary Elizabeth (Hisaw) M.; m. Anna Marlene Munden, Aug. 22, 1964; children: Amy Marlene, Ellen Elizabeth, William Van. BS (T.H. Harris scholar), Northwestern La. State U., 1960; MBA (Nat. Def. Grad. fellow), U. Ark., 1961, PhD (Nat. Def. Grad. fellow), 1966. Instr. U. Ark., 1962-63; field supr. Tau Kappa Epsilon Fraternity, 1963-64; asst. prof. Ga. Tech., 1964-65; assoc. prof., chmn., dir. rsch. Ohio U., 1965-70; dean Coll. Bus. Appalachian State U., Boone, N.C., 1970-73; dean Coll. Bus. Adminstrn. U. Nebr., Omaha, 1973-79, Tex. A&M U., College Station, 1979-82, vice chancellor, 1983-84; pres. U. Akron, Ohio, 1984-92, Auburn U., Ala., 1992-2001; chancellor East Carolina U., 2001—. Author: Business and Economic Problems in Appalachia, 1969, Management Practices in Fraternities, 1965; Contbr. articles to profl. jours. Found. for Econ. Edn. fellow, 1967. Mem. Blue Key, Omicron Delta Kappa, Phi Kappa Phi, Delta Sigma Pi, Beta Gamma Sigma, Pi Omega Pi, Tau Kappa Epsilon, Phi Beta Kappa. Clubs: Rotarian. Office: Chancellors Office East Carolina Univ 103 Spilman Bldg Greenville NC 27858-4353 E-mail: musew@mail.ecu.edu.

MUSEKAMP, LINDA NOE, television producer, volunteer; b. Campbellsville, Ky., July 31, 1951; d. Charles Simpson and Audrey Ethel (Akin) Noe; m. George Justin Musekamp, Sept. 8, 1979 (dec.); children: George Brookshire, Charles Oliver Justin. Cert. exec. sec., Patricia Stevens Coll., Tampa, Fla., 1970. Cert. property mgr. Exec. sec. Sta. WLWT-TV, Cin., 1975-77, talent coord., 1977-80; prodr. Musekamp Prodns., 1980-83, cons., 1983-85; chmn., vol. Am. Cancer Soc., 1992—, bd. dirs., 1993—; pres., vol. PTO, 1992—; publicity chmn. Kindervelt, 1993—; real estate agt., 1994-96. Prodr.: (TV show) Real Cincinnati, 1996—. Republican. Baptist. Avocations: tennis, piano.

MUSEN, MARK ALAN, computer science educator, physician; b. Providence, Feb. 22, 1956; s. Frederick Norton and Dolores (Shechtman) M.; m. Elyse Ann Barnett, June 5, 1983; children: Jay Derek, Kate Hannah. BSc in Biology, Brown U., 1977, MD, 1980; PhD in Med. Info. Scis., Stanford (Calif.) U., 1988. Intern in medicine Stanford U. Hosp., 1980-81, resident in medicine, 1981-83, Henry J. Kaiser Family Found. fellow in gen. internal medicine, 1983-87; vis. scientist dept. med. informatics Erasmus U., Rotterdam, Netherlands, 1987-88; asst. prof. medicine and computer sci. Stanford U., 1988-95, assoc. prof., 1995—2002, prof., 2002—; head sect. on med. informatics Stanford U. Sch. Medicine, 1993—. Mem. biomed. libr. rev. com. Nat. Libr. of Medicine, 1992-96. Author: Automated Generation of Model-Based Knowledge Acquisition Tools, 1989, (with J. van Bemmel) Handbook of Medical Informatics, 1987; mem. editl. bd.: Knowledge Acquisition,

1989-94, IEEE Expert, 1990-94, Artificial Intelligence in Medicine, 1990—, Internat. Jour. of Expert Sys., 1990—, Methods of Information in Medicine, 1991—, Medical Decision Making, 1992-94, Internat. Jour. Human-Computer Studies, 1995—. Recipient NSF Young Investigator award, 1992. Fellow ACP, Am. Coll. Med. Informatics; mem. Am. Med. Informatics Assn., Am. Assn. for Artificial Intelligence, Assn. for Computing Machinery, Am. Fedn. for Clin. Rsch., Soc. for Med. Decision Making, Soc. for Clin. Trials, Am. Soc. for Clin. Investigation. Office: Stanford U Sch of Medicine Sect on Med Informatics Stanford CA 94305-5479 Home: PO Box 19797 Stanford CA 94309-9797

MUSER, TONY, former manager professional athletics; b. L.A., Aug. 1, 1947; m. Nancy Muser; children: Tony Jr., Michael, Kristi. Student, San Diego Mesa Jr. Coll. Maj. league baseball player Boston, 1969, White Sox, 1971-75, Balt., 1975-77, Milw. Brewers, 1978; profl. baseball player Seibu Lions, Japanese Pacific League, 1979; mgr. Stockton A, Calif. League, 1980, El Paso AA then Vancouver AAA, 1983; 3rd base coach Milw. Big League Staff, 1985-88, hitting instr., 1987-89; amateur, maj. league crosschecker Milw. West Coast, 1991; mgr. Denver AAA, Am. Assn., 1991-92, Milw. Brewers; bullpen coach Chgo. Cubs, 1993, 3rd base coach then hitting coach, 1994-97; mgr. Kansas City Royals, 1997—2002. Named Calif. League Champions, 1980, Mgr. of Yr., Am. Assn., 1991. Office: Kansas City Royals Baseball Club PO Box 419969 Kansas City MO 64141-6969*

MUSGRAVE, ANNA MIRIAM, charitable organization administrator; b. Santiago de Cuba, Cuba, Aug. 6, 1939; came to U.S., 1958; d. Moises and Ernestina (Hernandez) Suarez; m. Fred A. Musgrave, July 22, 1961; children: Vincent Kirk, Vonda Kali Musgrave Mathews. BS in Home Econs., U. Havana, Cuba, 1957; ordination as officer, The Salvation Army Sch. for Officers Tng., Atlanta, 1960; AA in Mental Health, Essex Community Coll., Balt., 1977. Ordained to ministry Salvation Army, 1959. Dir. office of children with spl. needs The Salvation Army, Balt., 1973-78, cons. juvenile delinquency Atlanta, 1978-80, dir. supplies and purchasing Buenos Aires, 1980-84, dir. prison ministries divisional hdqrs. Charlotte, N.C., 1984-85, coord. women's activities, 1985-91, Jacksonville, Fla., 1991—. Cons. Rehab. Ctr., The Salvation Army, Charlotte, 1984-91; cons. for children with emotional problems, Johns Hopkins Hosp., 1975-78. Rep. Women's Aux., Charlotte, 1985-91, Jacksonville, 1991—. Mem. Am. Assn. Counselors, Am. Assn. Family Therapy, United Fedn. Doll Clubs, Queen Charlotte Doll Club (corr. sec. 1991—), Altrusa Club, Meninak Internat. Club. Democrat. Avocations: doll collecting, reading, travel, music. Office: The Salvation Army 328 N Ocean St Jacksonville FL 32202-3220

MUSGRAVE, FRANK WEBSTER, economics educator; b. Newark, Mar. 28, 1932; s. William Edward and Margaret (Hacker) M.; m. Eva Mae Gifford, Oct. 15, 1960; children: Scott Kenneth, Marcia Carol. AB, Muhlenberg Coll., Allentown, Pa., 1954; MBA, Rutgers U., Newark, 1961; PhD, Rutgers U., New Brunswick, 1968. Tchr. Lakewood (N.J.) High Sch., 1958-68; asst. prof. Ithaca (N.Y.) Coll., 1968-72, assoc. prof. econs., 1972-79, prof. econs., 1979—. Editor: Health Care and Health Economics, 1979. Assoc. dir. So. Tier Ctr. Econ. Edn., Binghamton, N.Y., 1977—; bd. dirs. N.Y. State Coun. Econ. Edn., 1974—, Tompkins Community Hosp., Ithaca, 1977-88. With U.S. Army, 1955-57. Students in Free Ent. Inc. fellow, 1989—, others. Mem. AAUP, N.Y. State Econ. Assn. (pres. 1989-90), Am. Econ. Assn. Lutheran. Avocation: travel. Home: 6 Main St Candor NY 13743-1615 Office: Ithaca Coll Dept Econs Ithaca NY 14850

MUSGRAVE, LEE, artist, museum administrator; b. Perth, Australia, June 13, 1944; came to U.S., 1946; s. Cecil Beryl and Dulse Joan (Aldersea) M.; m. Heidi Orbitz, Dec. 19, 1964; children: Timothy Devon, Christopher Kim. AA, L.A. Valley Coll., 1965; BA, Calif. State U., Northridge, 1967; MA, Calif. State U., L.A., 1970. Cert. secondary art tchr., Calif. Prof. art. L.A. Mission Coll., Sylmar, Calif., 1974-95; dir. L.A. Mission Coll. Campus Gallery, San Fernando, 1974-82, Mcpl. Gallery, Agoura Hills, 1983-86, Merging One Gallery, Santa Monica, 1986-88; curator County of Los Angeles Century Gallery, Sylmar, 1983-86, dir., 1991-95; curator contemporary exhibitions Maryhill Mus. Art, Goldendale, Wash., 1996—. One man shows include Heritage Gallery, L.A., 1985, Orlando Gallery, L.A., 1986, Chemetka Gallery, Salem, Oreg., 1986, Ersgard Gallery, Santa Monica, Calif., 1992. Founding pres. Santa Monica/Venice Art Dealers Assn., 1987-88, Cultural Affairs Commn., Agoura Hills, 1983-86; dir. N.E. Valley Arts Coun., Sylmar, 1991-95. Fellow NEA Wash. Arts Commn., 1996; recipient cert. of appreciation Calif. Art Edn. Assn., 1992, Calif. Legis. Assembly, 1987, cert. of recognition Calif. State Senate, 1987. Mem. Nat. Art Educators Assn., Wash. Art Educators Assn., Columbia Gorge Regional Arts Assn. Avocations: writing, hiking. Home: PO Box 256 Lyle WA 98635-0006 Office: Maryhill Mus Art 35 Maryhill Hwy Goldendale WA 98620-4604

MUSGRAVE, MICHAEL G. musicologist, musician; b. London, Aug. 26, 1942; came to U.S., 1997; s. Albert Henry and Phillis Mary Musgrave; m. Celia Helen Terrington, July 31, 1965 (div. Mar. 1983); children: Stephen Michael, Jonathan Mark; m. Janie Elizabeth Bailey. Grad. diploma, Royal Schs. of Music, 1963; cert. music tchr., U. London, 1964, MusB with 1st class honors, 1973, PhD, 1980. Dir. music Eltham Hill Sch., London, 1964-74; lectr. in music U. London, 1974-80, prin. lectr., 1980-89, reader in music, 1989-94, prof. music, 1994-98, prof. emeritus, 1998—. Vis. rsch. fellow Royal Coll. Music, 1998—; acad. adv. coun. Manhattan Sch. Music, N.Y.C., 1999. Author: (book) The Music of Brahms, 1985, The Music of Brahms, 2d edit., 1994, The Musical Life of the Crystal Palace, 1994, Brahms: A German Requiem, 1996, A Brahms Reader, 2000; editor (contbr.): Brahms 2: Biographical, Documentary and Analytical Studies, 1987, The Cambridge Companion to Brahms, 1999; rev. editor (jour.) Music Analysis jour., 1982—93, mem. adv. bd., 1993—; contbr. Fellow Royal Coll. Organists, Royal Soc. Arts; mem. Royal Coll. Music (assoc.), Trägerverein, Johannes Brahms Gesamtausgabe. Avocations: musical performance, literature, theatre, travel.

MUSGRAVE, R. KENTON, federal judge; b. 1927; Student, Ga. Inst. Tech., 1945-46, U. Fla., 1946-47; BA, U. Wash., 1948; JD with distinction, Emory U., 1953. Asst. gen. counsel Lockheed Internat., 1953-62; v.p., gen. counsel Mattel, Inc., 1963-71; mem. firm Musgrave, Welbourn and Fertman, 1972-75; asst. gen. counsel Pacific Enterprises, 1975-81; v.p., gen. counsel Vivitar Corp, 1981-85; v.p., dir. Santa Barbara Applied Rsch., 1982-87; judge U.S. Ct. Internat. Trade, N.Y.C., 1987—. Trustee The Dian Fossey Gorilla Fund, Dolphins of Sharks Bay (Australia); hon. trustee Pet Protection Soc.; mem. United Way, Save the Redwoods League; active Palos Verdes Community Assn. Mem. Internat. Bar Assn., Pan Am. Bar Assn., State Bar Calif. (chmn. corp. law sect. 1965-66, del. 1966-67), L.A. County Bar Assn., Fng. Trade Assn. So. Calif. (bd. dirs.). Office: US Ct Internat Trade 1 Federal Plz New York NY 10278-0001

MUSGRAVE, STORY, astronaut, surgeon, pilot, physiologist, educator; b. Boston, Aug. 19, 1935; children: Lorelei Lisa, Bradley Scott, Holly Kay, Christopher Todd, Jeffrey Paul, Lane Linwood. BS in Math. and Stats., Syracuse U., 1958; MBA, UCLA, 1959; BA in Chemistry, Marietta Coll., 1960; MD, Columbia U., 1964; MS in Biophysics, U. Ky., 1966; MA in Lit., U. Houston, 1987, MA in Humanities, 1989. Surg. intern U. Ky. Med. Ctr., Lexington, 1964-65; scientist-astronaut NASA, Houston, 1967-97, backup sci.-pilot 1st Skylab mission, 1973, flew on first Challenger flight, STS-6, 1983, flew on Spacelab 2, 1985, flew on space shuttle mission STS-33, 1989, flew on STS-44, 1991, flew as payload comdr. STS61 Hubble Telescope Repair Mission, 1993, flew on STS-80 last flight, 1996; Walt Disney fellow, 1997—; creative designer Applied Minds Inc., 2000—; performing artist, 1997—; poet and writer, 1997—. Contbr. articles to profl. jours. With USMC, 1953-56. Recipient Reese AFB Comdr.'s trophy, 1969, NASA exceptional svc. medal, 1974, 83, 90, NASA disting. svc. medal, 1992, 94, 97, NASA spaceflight medal, 1983, 85, 89, 91, 93, 96, Space award Aviation Week and Space Tech., 1997; USAF postdoctoral fellow, 1965-66, Nat. Heart Inst. postdoctoral fellow, 1966-67. Mem. AAAS, AAS, AIAA, Flying Physicians Assn. (Airman of Yr. award 1974, 83), Civil Aviation Med. Assn., N.Y. Acad. Sci., Nat. Geog. Soc., Soaring Soc. Am., U.S. Parachute Assn., Marine Corps Assn., Alpha Kappa Psi, Phi Delta Theta, Omicron Delta Kappa, Beta Gamma Sigma. E-mail: storymusgrave@hotmail.com. *From subatomic particles, to the stardust from which I was created, from the forming galaxies, to the universes beyond our own, I live to participate physically and spiritually in every aspect of this cosmic creation and evolution.*

MUSGRAVE, THEA, composer, conductor; b. Edinburgh, Scotland, May 27, 1928; m. Peter Mark, 1971. Ed., Edinburgh U., Paris Conservatory; Mus.D. (hon.). Composer: (opera) The Abbot of Drimock, 1955, The Decision, 1964-65, The Voice of Ariadne, 1972-73, Mary, Queen of Scots, 1975-77, (first performed Scottish Opera) A Christmas Carol, 1978-79 (first performed Va. Opera Assn., 1979), An Occurrence at Owl Creek Bridge, 1981, Harriet, The Woman Called Moses, 1981-84 (first performed Va. Opera 1985), Simon Bolivar, (ballet) Beauty and the Beast, 1969, (symphony and orchestral music) Obliques, 1958, Nocturnes and Arias, 1966, Concerto for Orch., 1967, Clarinet Concerto, 1968, Night Music, 1969, Scottish Dance Suite, 1969, Memento Vitae, 1969-70, Orfeo II, 1975, Soliloquy II and III, 1980, From One to Another, 1980, Peripeteia, 1981, The Seasons, 1988, (marimba concerto) Journey through a Japanese Landscape, (bass-clarinet concerto) Autumn Sonata, (oboe concerto) Helios, Phoenix Rising, 1997, (chamber and instrumental music) String Quartet, 1958, Trio for flute, oboe and piano, 1960, Monologue, 1960, Serenade, 1961, Chamber concerto No. 1, 1962, Chamber Concerto No. 2, 1966, Chamber Concerto No. 3, 1966, Music for horn and piano, 1967, Impromptu No. 1, 1967, Soliloquy I, 1969, Elegy, 1970, Impromptu No. 2, 1970, Space Play, 1974, Orfeo I, 1975, Fanfare, 1982, Pierrot, 1985, Narcissus, 1987, Niobe, 1987, (vocal and choral music) Two Songs, 1951, Four Madrigals, 1953, Six Songs: Two Early English Poems, 1953, A Suite O'Bairnsangs, 1953, Cantata for a Summer's Day, 1954, Song of the Burn, 1954, Five Love Songs, 1955, Four Portraits, 1956, A Song for Christmas, 1958, Triptych, 1959, Sir Patrick Spens, 1961, Make Ye Merry for Him That Is to Come, 1962, Two Christmas Carols in Traditional Style, 1963, John Cook, 1963, Five Ages of Man, 1963-64, Memento Creatoris, 1967, Primavera, 1971, Rorate Coeli, 1973, Monologues of Mary, Queen of Scots, 1977-86, O Caro M'e Il Sonno, 1978, The Last Twilight, 1980, Black Tambourine, 1985, For the Time Being, 1986, Echoes Through Time, 1988, Wild Winter for Viols & Voices, 1993, On the Underground Sets 1, 2 & 3, 1994, 95, (Robert Burns' poems for soprano & orch.) Songs for a Winter's Evening, 1995, Phoenix Rising for orchestra, 1996-97, Voices from the Ancient World for 3 flutes and percussion, 1998, Celebration Day for chorus and orchestra, 1998-99, Lamenting With Ariadne for 8 instruments, 1999. Office: VA Opera Assn PO Box 2580 Norfolk VA 23501-2580

MUSGROVE, DAVID RONALD, governor; b. Sardis, Miss., July 29, 1956; s. Henry and Nina (Rogers) M.; m. Melanie Ballard, Aug. 12, 1977; children: Jordan, Carmen, Rae. AA, Northwest Miss. C.C., 1976; BS, U. Miss., 1978, JD, 1981. Bar: Miss. Ptnr. Smith, Musgrove & McCord, Batesville, Miss., 1981-2000; lt. gov. State of Miss., 1996-2000, gov., 2000—. State sen. Miss. State, 1988-96; chair Nat. Conf. Lt. Govs., 1998-99. Pres. Batesville Jaycees, 1982-83; chair Panola County Heart Fund, 1985-86; deacon First Bapt. Ch., Batesville, 1983-2000. Democrat. Fellow Miss. Bar Found; mem. Am. Inns Ct., Panola County Bar Assn., Tri-County Bar Assn., Miss. Young Lawyers Assn. Office: PO Box 139 Jackson MS 39205-0139*

MUSGROVE, KAY AWALT, school system administrator; b. Mineral Wells, Tex., Mar. 20, 1942; d. Pat O. T. and Mary Lee Morse; m. Robert Musgrove; children: Stacy (dec.), Bradley. BS, Tex. Wesleyan Coll., 1966; MS in Edn., Baylor U., 1972; PhD, Vanderbilt U., 1988. Cert. tchr., prin., supr. Elem. tchr. San Antonio Pub. Schs., 1966, LaVega Pub. Schs., Waco, Tex., 1966-68; with reading clinic Baylor U., 1969-70; thcr. reading Franklin Spl. Schs., Tenn., 1970-71, first grade tchr., 1971-80, asst. prin., 1980-84, prin., 1984-90, Moore Elem. Sch., Franklin, 1990-97, assoc. supt., 1997—. Mem. adv. coun. for tchr. cert. and edn. Tenn. State Sch. Bd., 1977-86; adminstr. career level III State of Tenn., 1987—; chmn. for revision elem. cert. State of Tenn. Co-author Religious Christian Day Sch. Curriculum, 1978; author: Study Book for 6-8 Year Olds, 1980. Tenn. spl. scholar, 1983-84; named Tenn. Elem. Prin. of Yr., 1994, Nat. Disting. Prin. Tenn., 1996, So. Assn. Disting. Educator, 2002. Mem. ASCD (bd. dirs. 1992-95, exec. coun. 1995-98, internat. pres.-elect 2000-01, pres. 2001-2002), Internat. Reading Assn., Mid. Tenn. Coun. Internat. Reading Assn., Tenn. Assn. Supervision and Curriculum Devel. (pres. 1986-87, 92-93, exec. sec. 1993—), Tenn. Bd. Examiners for State for Approval of Tchr. Edn., Delta Kappa Gamma (pres. Rho chpt.). Baptist. Office: Franklin Schs 507 New Highway 96 W Franklin TN 37064-2470

MUSHATT, DAVID MICHAEL, medical educator; b. Boston, Dec. 1, 1959; s. Cecil and Margaret (Allsop) Mushatt; m. Mary Anne Blaszczak; children: John Edwin, Jacob Michael. BA, Yale U., 1982; MD, Harvard U., 1986; MPH in Tropical Medicine, Tulane U., 1991. Intern in medicine Brigham & Womens Hosp., Boston, 1986-87, resident in medicine, 1987-89; fellow in infectious diseases Tulane U. Sch. of Medicine, New Orleans, 1989-91, assoc. prof., 1991—. Albert Schweitzer fellowship, 1985. Mem. ACP, Infectious Diseases Soc. Am., Am. Soc. for Microbiology. Avocations: squash, tennis. Office: Tulane U Sch Medicine 1430 Tulane Ave New Orleans LA 70112-2699

MUSICH, ROBERT LORIN, motivational speaker; b. Glendale, Calif., Feb. 15, 1969; s. Richard and Zola (Nickel) M. MBA, M, La Salle U. Sr. asst. mgr. Am. Gen. Fin., Upland, Calif., 1988-89; mgmt./corp. trainer Mortgage Link, Pasadena, 1989-94; mgr. AT&T, L.A., 1994-96; owner Musich & Assocs., West Covina, Calif., 1989—. Singer (tenor) So. Calif. Mormon Choir, 1994—; cand. Calif. State Assembly, 59th Dist., 1995; vol. Am. Cancer Soc., 1994-96; coach Youth League Football, 1987-92; elder's quorum pres. LDS Ch., sec., 1992-93, 2d and 1st counselor, 1995-96, mem. stake single adult com., 1993-95, mem. regional single adult com. bi-regional chmn., 1993-95. Republican. Avocations: singing, dancing, theatre, volleyball, football. Office: Musich and Associates 3447 E Hillhaven Dr West Covina CA 91791-1718

MUSICK, GERALD JOE, retired entomology educator; b. Ponca City, Okla., May 24, 1940; s. Arlie A. and Leona (Beier) M.; m. Florene Ione Thompson, May 11, 1962; children: Linda Kaye, Mary Louise. BS, Okla. State U., 1962; MS, Iowa State U., 1964; PhD, U. Mo., 1969. Grad. asst. Iowa State U., 1962-64; instr. U. Mo., 1964-69; asst. prof. Ohio State U., Wooster, 1969-71, assoc. prof., 1971-76; dept. head U. Ga., Tifton, 1976-79; prof., dept. head U. Ark., Fayetteville, 1979-86, interium dir. agrl. exptl. sta., 1986-87, dean, assoc. v.p. agrl. rsch., 1987-93, univ. prof. entomology, 1993—2002, chmn.-elect faculty coun. Dale Bumpers Coll. Agrl., Food and Life Scis., 1997, chmn., 1998, prof. emeritus, 2002—, ret., 2002—; chmn. faculty coun. Dale Bumpers Coll. of Agrl. Food and Life Scis., 1998. Author and co-author numerous publs. Vice-chairperson com. Coop. States Rsch. Svc., 1993, So. Expt. Sta.; chairperson steering com. Midwest Food Safety Consortium, 1991-93; mem. U. Ark. Faculty Senate, 1994—, chair campus faculty, 1998-99, chair faculty sentate 1999-2000, faculty exec. com., 1999—; coord. Pest Mgmt. Programs, 1998—. Mem. Entomol. Soc. Am. (pres. S.E. br. 1983-84), Ark. Acad. Sci., Ctrl. States Entomol. Soc. (v.p. 1995-96, pres. 1996-97), Sigma Xi, Gamma Sigma Delta. Lutheran. Avocation: golf. Office: University of Arkansas AG-321 Dept Entomology Fayetteville AR 72701

MUSICK, PAT, artist, sculptor, art educator; b. L.A., Sept. 14, 1926; d. Mark Melvin and Emma Lucille (Ferguson) Tapscott; m. John Elmore Musick, Aug. 18, 1946 (dec. Nov. 1977); children: Cathleen M. Goebel, Melinda M. King, Laura M. Wright; m. Gerald Paul Carr, Sept. 14, 1979. MA, Cornell U., 1972, PhD, 1974. Rsch. asst. Cornell U., Ithaca, N.Y., 1971-73; prof. SUNY, Oswego, 1974-76, U. Houston, 1976-85; postdoct. fellow Med. Sch. U. Tex., Galveston, 1978. Adj. prof. Syracuse (N.Y.) U., 1974-76, U. Ark., Fayetteville, 1986—; mem. nat. adv. coun. Rocky Mountain Coll., Billings, Mont., 1996-97; mem. com. site integrated art planning, art selection com. Walton Arts Ctr., Fayetteville, Ark., 1988-90; pres. CAMUS, Inc., Huntsville, Ark., 1995—. One-woman exhibns. include Tulsa Ctr. Contemporary Arts, 1989, Huntsville (Ala.) Mus. Art, 1992, Springfield (Mo.) Mus. Art, 1992, Ark. Arts Ctr., Little Rock, 1992, Walton Arts Ctr., Fayetteville, Ark., 1992, 95, Amarillo (Tex.) Mus. Art, 1995, Goddard Gallery State Fair C.C., Sedalia, Mo., 1996, Charles B. Goddard Ctr., Ardmore, Okla., 1997, U. Ark., Little Rock, 1997, Albrecht Kemper Mus., 1998, tour of 7 Tex. museums, 1998—; group exhibns. include Senator David Pryor's Offices, Washington, 1991-93, Ark. Art Ctr., Little Rock, 1994, Walton Arts Ctr., 1994; permanent collections Jewish Theol. U., Ark. Aerospace Edn. ctr., Ark. Arts Ctr., Dartmouth Coll., Huntsville (Ala.) Mus. Art, Internat. Ctr. Transp. Studies, Promus Hotels, U. Houston, Springfield (Mo.) Art Mus., U. Ozarks, Walton Arts Ctr. Fine Arts scholar U. So. Calif., 1944; Touring grantee Ark. Arts Coun., NEA, 1987-88, Assistance grantee Ark. Arts Coun., 1997; Connemara Found. fellow, 1998; recipient Gold Medal Pizzo Calabro (Italy) Internat. Invitational, 1983, Gold Medal Southeastern Mus. Conf., 1993, Richard A. Florsheim Art Fund award, 1997; winner 9th Ann. Outdoor Sculpture Competition, Miami U., Ohio, 1998. Avocations: cooking, swimming, reading, writing poetry. Home: 2 Pack McClain Rd Huntsville AR 72740 Office: CAMUS Inc PO Box 919 Huntsville AR 72740-0919

MUSICK, ROBERT LAWRENCE, JR. lawyer; b. Richlands, Va., Oct. 3, 1947; s. Robert Lawrence and Virginia (Brooks) M.; m. Beth Pambianchi, 1996; children: Elizabeth, Robert. BA in History with honors, U. Richmond, 1969; JD, MA in Legal History, U. Va., 1972; LLM, Coll. William and Mary, 1986. Bar: Va. 1972, U.S. Ct. Appeals (4th cir.) 1974. Law clk. Supreme Ct. Va., Richmond, 1972-73; assoc. Williams, Mullen & Christian, 1973-78; ptnr. Williams, Mullen, Christian & Dobbins, 1978-99, Williams Mullen Clark & Dobb, Richmond, 1999—. Bd. govs. estates and property sect. Va. State Bar, 1977-80, chmn., 1980. Author: RIA Non Qualified Deferred Compensation, 1997, (with others) CCH Federal Tax Service, 1989; contbr. articles to profl. jours. Trustee U. Richmond, 1991-94, Va. Intermont Coll., 2002—; mem. Estate Planning Coun. Richmond, 1981—, U. Richmond Estate Planning Coun., 1984—; bd. dirs. Va. Bapt. Homes, Inc., 1994—. Lt. col. USAR. Fellow Am. Coll. Employment Benefit Counsel; mem. ABA, Va. Bar Assn., Richmond Bar Assn., So. Pension Conf., Va. Assn. Professions (pres. 1980-81), Commonwealth Club, Willow Oaks Country Club (dir. 1999—, pres. 2002). Baptist. Avocations: tennis, golf, scuba. Office: Williams Mullen Clark & Dobbins 2 James Center PO Box 1320 Richmond VA 23218-1320

MUSIHIN, KONSTANTIN K. electrical engineer; b. Harbin, China, June 17, 1927; came to U.S., 1967, naturalized, 1973; s. Konstantin N. and Alexandra A. (Lapitsky) M.; m. Natalia Krilova, Oct. 18, 1964; 1 child, Nicholas. Student, YMCA Inst., 1942, North Manchurian U., 1945, Harbin Poly. Inst., 1948. Registered profl. engr., Calif., N.Y., Pa., Wash. Asst. prof. Harbin Poly. Inst., 1950-53; elec. engr. Moinho Santista, Sao Paulo, Brazil, 1955-60; constrn. project mgr. Caterpillar-Brazil, Santo Amaro, 1960-61; mech. engr. Matarazzo Industries, Sao Paulo, 1961-62; chief of works Vidrobras, St. Gobain, Brazil, 1962-64; project engr. Brown Boveri, Sao Paulo, 1965-67; sr. engr. Kaiser Engrs., Oakland, Calif., 1967-73, Bechtel Power Corp., San Francisco, 1973-75; supr. power and control San Francisco Bay Area Rapid Transit, Oakland, 1976-78; chief elec. engr. L.K. Comstock Engring. Co., San Francisco, 1978-79; prin. engr. Morrison Knudsen Co., 1979-84, Brown & Caldwell, Cons. Engrs., Pleasant Hill, Calif., 1984-85; cons. engr. Pacific Gas and Electric Co., San Francisco, 1986-89; sr. engr. Bechtel Corp., 1989. Mem. IEEE (life, sr.), NSPE, Calif. Soc. Profl. Engrs. Christian Orthodox Ch. Home: 5666 Ocean View Dr Oakland CA 94618-1533

MUSIL, ROBERT KIRKLAND, professional society administrator; b. N.Y.C., Oct. 27, 1943; s. Ralph A. and Margaret Hooker (Kirkland) M.; m. Caryn Lynne McTighe, June 15, 1968; children: Rebecca McTighe, Emily Kirkland. BA, Yale U., 1964; MA, Northwestern U., 1966, PhD, 1970; MPH, Johns Hopkins U., 2001. Instr. Def. Info. Sch., Ft. Benjamin Harrison, Ind., 1969-71; co-dir. CCCO/An Agy. for Mil. and Draft Counseling, Phila., 1971-74; dir. mil. affairs project Ctr. for Nat. Security Studies, Washington, 1974-75; asst. prof. English and Am. studies Temple U., Phila., 1976-78; prodr., host Consider the Alternatives Radio, 1978-92; exec. dir. SANE Edn. Fund, Phila. and Washington, 1984-88, Profls. Coalition for Nuclear Arms Control, Washington, 1988-92; dir. policy and programs Physicians for Social Responsibility, 1992-95, exec. dir., CEO, 1995—. Adj. prof. Sch. Internat. Svc., Am. U., 1997—. Prodr.: (documentary series) Shadows of the Nuclear Age: American Culture and the Bomb, 1980 (NEH grantee). Bd. dirs. Scoville Fellowships, Washington, 1989-92, 95—, SANE, 1978-84. Capt. U.S. Army, 1969-71. Recipient Maj. Armstrong award for radio Armstrong Found., Columbia U., N.Y.C., 1988, 89. Mem. United Ch. of Christ. Home: 8600 Irvington Ave Bethesda MD 20817-3604 Office: Physicians for Social Resp Ste 1012 1875 Connecticut Ave NW Washington DC 20009 E-mail: bmusil@psr.org.

MUSKIN, VICTOR PHILIP, lawyer; b. N.Y.C., Mar. 1, 1942; s. Jacob Cecil and Fanya (Solomonoff) M.; m. Odette Cheryl Spreier, June 10, 1979; children: Adam James, Liana Jeanne. BA, Oberlin Coll., 1963; JD, NYU, 1966. Bar: N.Y. 1969, U.S. Dist. Ct. (so. and ea. dists.) N.Y. 1972, U.S. Ct. Appeals (2d cir.) 1974, U.S. Supreme Ct. 1974, U.S. Ct. Appeals (9th and 10th cirs.) 1978, U.S. Ct. Appeals (3d cir.) 1987. Asst. corp. counsel divsn. gen. litigation City of N.Y., 1969-73; assoc. Wolf, Popper, Ross, Wolf & Jones, N.Y.C., 1973-74, Reavis and McGrath, N.Y.C., 1974-78; pvt. practice, 1979; ptnr. Gruen & Muskin, 1980-81, Gruen, Muskin & Thau, N.Y.C., 1981-89, Munves, Tanenhaus & Storch, N.Y.C., 1989-90, Solin & Breimdel, N.Y.C., 1991-92; pvt. practice, 1992—. Served with Peace Corps, 1966-68. Mem. N.Y.C. Bar Assn. (com. computer law 1982-84, com. internat. law 1996-99). Home: 529 E 84th St New York NY 10028-7330 Office: 445 Park Ave Fl 14 New York NY 10022-2606 E-mail: vp.muskin@verizon.net.

MUSKOPF, BETH A. curriculum consultant; b. Hicksville, Ohio, July 25, 1943; d. Claron Lavon Laub and Florence Elizabeth Laub; m. David Earl Muskopf, June 26, 1965; children: Richard, Stephen. BS in Edn., Miami U., Oxford, Ohio, 1965, MEd, 1973, PhD, 1998. Tchr. Mason (Ohio) Local Schs., 1967-68, Mason Local/City Schs., 1982-95; asst. prof. Cin. Bible Coll., 1996-98; supr. curriculum Clermont County Edn. Svc. Ctr., Batavia, Ohio, 1999—. Recipient Excellence in Tchg. award Warren County (Ohio) Area Progress Coun., 1990; Morrison scholar Dept. Edn. Leadership, Miami U., Oxford, 1997. Mem. ASCD, Internat. Reading Assn., Nat. Coun. Tchrs. English, Ohio Coun. Internat. Reading Assn., Phi Delta Kappa (rsch. chair 1999-2001, treas. 2001—). Avocations: reading, hiking, traveling. Home: 8060 Crest Acres Dr Mason OH 45040-9656 Office: Clermont County Ednl Svc Ctr 2400 Clermont Center Dr Batavia OH 45103-1957

MUSLIN, LEE, artist; b. Palmerton, Pa., Aug. 25, 1951; d. Charles H. and Jean (Marek) Lowry; m. Stephen Joseph Muslin, Feb. 25, 1977 (div. May 1979); 1 child, Jessica Marie. AAS, Parsons Sch. of Design, N.Y.C., 1996. Art dir. Simmons-Boardman Pub., N.Y.C., 1978-84, Broadband Info. Svcs., N.Y.C., 1984-85, Dealers' Digest, N.Y.C., 1985-86; real estate salesperson Hillary & Stephens Realty, 1986-88; travel coord. New Sch. for Social Rsch., 1988-97; owner, dir. Nexus Gallery, 1997—2002; founder Ctr. for Digital Art, 1999—. Mem. Nat. Mus. Women in the Arts, Washington, 1997, Guggenheim Mus., N.Y.C., 1997, Whitney Mus., N.Y.C., 1998-2000, Artists Talk on Art, N.Y.C., 1999. Recipient awards from Photographer's Forum, 1994, Manhattan Arts Internat., 1997. Mem. Nat. Assn. Women Arts., Profl. Women Photographers. Avocation: ballroom dancing. E-mail: mail@leemuslin.com.

MUSMANN, KLAUS, librarian; b. Magdeburg, Germany, June 27, 1935; came to U.S., 1957; s. Ernst Hans and Eva (Grunow) M.; m. Gladys H. Arakawa, June 15, 1963 (div. 1973); children: Carlton, Michelle; m. Lois Geneva Steele, Dec. 27, 1986. BA, Wayne State U., 1962; MALS, U. Mich., 1963; MA, Mich. State U., 1967; PhD, U. So. Calif., 1981. Libr. Detroit Pub. Libr., 1962-65; asst. serials libr. Mich. State U., East Lansing, 1965-67; head of acquisitions Los Angeles County Law Libr., L.A., 1968-84; coll. devel. libr. U. Redlands, Calif., 1984—2001, acting dir., 1994-96, dir., 1996—2001; dir. libr. svcs. Notre Dame de Namur U., Belmont, 2001—. Author: Helen and Vernon Farquhar Collection: A Bibliography, 1987, Diffusion of Innovations, 1989, Technological Innovations in Libraries, 1850-1950, 1993; contbr. articles to profl. jours. Grantee Coun. on Libr. Resources, 1990. Mem. ALA, Assn. Coll. and Rsch. Librs., Soc. for History of Tech. Avocations: photography, travel. Home: 975 Pizzaro Ln Foster City CA 94404 Office: Notre Dame de Namur U 1500 Ralston Ave Belmont CA 94002 E-mail: kmusmann@ndnu.edu.

MUSOLF, LLOYD DARYL, political science educator, institute administrator; b. Yale, S.D., Oct. 14, 1919; s. William Ferdinand and Emma Marie (Pautz) M.; m. Berdyne Peet, June 30, 1944; children— Stephanie, Michael, Laura. BA, Huron Coll., 1941; MA, U. S.D., 1946; PhD, Johns Hopkins U., 1950. Mem. faculty Vassar Coll., Poughkeepsie, N.Y., 1949-59, assoc. prof. polit. sci., 1955-59; chief of party adv. group Mich. State U., Republic South Vietnam, 1959-61, prof. polit. sci., 1961-63, U. Calif.-Davis, 1963-87, dir. Inst. Govtl. Affairs, 1963-84, prof. emeritus, 1988—. Vis. prof. Johns Hopkins U., Balt., 1953, U. Del., 1954, U. Mich., 1955-56; U.S. Nat. rapporteur for Internat. Congress Adminstrv. Scis., Berlin, 1983; cons. and lectr. in field Author: Federal Examiners and the Conflict of Law and Administration, 1953, Public Ownership and Accountability: The Canadian Experience, 1959, Promoting the General Welfare, Government and the Economy, 1965, (with others) American National Government-Policies and Politics, 1971, Mixed Enterprise-A Developmental Perspective, 1972, (with Springer) Malaysia's Parliamentary System-Representative Politics and Policymaking in a Divided Society, 1979, Uncle Sam's Private Profitseeking Corporations-Comsat, Fannie Mae, Amtrak and Conrail, 1983; editor: (with Krislov) The Politics of Regulation, 1964, Communications Satellites in Political Orbit, 1968, (with Kornberg) Legislatures in Developmental Perspective, 1970, (with Joel Smith) Legislatures in Development-Dynamics of Change in New and Old States, 1979; contbr. monographs, chpts. to books, articles to profl. jours. Served to lt. USNR, 1942-45 Johnston scholar Johns Hopkins U., 1946-48; Faculty fellow Vassar Coll., 1954-55; sr. assoc. East-West Ctr., Honolulu, 1968-69; vis. scholar Brookings Instn., Washington, 1980. Mem. Am. Soc. Pub. Adminstrn. (exec. council 1967-70), Nat. Assn. Schs. Pub. Affairs and Adminstrn. (exec. council 1972-75), Western Govtl. Research Assn. (exec. bd. 1966-68), Am. Polit. Sci. Assn., Nat. Assn. State Univs. and Land Grant Colls. (rsch. com. fdiv. urban affairs 1980-81). Home: 844 Lake Blvd Davis CA 95616-2611 Office: U Calif Dept Polit Sci Davis CA 95616

MUSON, HOWARD HENRY, writer, consultant; b. Mt. Vernon, N.Y., Mar. 19, 1935; s. Joseph Ernest and Beatrice (Hakmaier) M.; m. Dorothy Regina Tyor, May 21, 1967; children: Eve, Stephanie, Nickolas, Alice. AB magna cum laude, Harvard U., Cambridge, Mass., 1956; cert., Johns Hopkins Sch. Advanced Internat. Studies, Bologna, Italy, 1956-57; postgrad., U. Calif., Berkeley, 1957-58. Dir. program research CARE Inc., N.Y.C., 1960-62; bur. chief Hartford Courant, Conn., 1962; newsman, columnist AP, Boston, 1963-66; contbg. editor Time mag., N.Y.C., 1966-70; articles editor N.Y. Times mag., 1970-77; exec. editor Psychology Today mag., 1977-82; editor Across The Board, 1983-89; editor, pub. Family Bus. mag., Phila., 1992-2000; rsch. assoc. Lansberg Gersick & Assocs., New Haven, 1998—. Vis. lectr. in residential colls. Yale U., New Haven, 1982-83; instr. in sci. & environ. reporting program NYU, 1992. Author: Media Violence, 1972, Triumph of the American Spirit: Johnstown, Pennsylvania, 1989; contbr. articles to profl. jours., popular mags. Dir. Project Concern/No. Westchester Walk for Mankind, Mt. Kisco, N.Y., 1986-90. Mem. Nat. Assn. Sci. Writers E-mail: hmuson@earthlink.net.

MUSSANO, THEODORE ANTHONY, court services supervisor; b. Paterson, N.J., Dec. 15, 1943; s. Theodore Anthony Sr. and Theresa Marie M.; m. Susan Fay Janusewski, May 24, 1980; 1 child, Theodore Edward. BA cum laude, Seton Hall U., 1965; MA, St. John's U., 1967. Probation officer Passaic County Probation Dept., Paterson, N.J., 1971-77, sr. probation officer, 1977-83; ct. svcs. supr. Superior Ct. N.J., 1873—. Weaver fellow, 1967, Teaching fellow, 1967-68, 65-67. Mem.: Probation Assn. NJ (pres. 1977), Soc. Ancient Numismatists, Am. Numis. Assn., KC. Roman Catholic. Avocations: ancient and medieval studies, reading. Home: 17 Fenner Pl Wayne NJ 07470-2809 Office: Passaic County Probation Divsn 19-31 Henry St Passaic NJ 07055 E-mail: mussano@aol.com.

MUSSEHL, ALLAN ARTHUR, program director; b. Edgerton, Wis., Aug. 12, 1942; s. Arthur John and Ruth Anna (Miller) M. BA, Milton Coll., 1965; MA, U. Wis., Madison, 1971, U. Wis., Milwaukee, 1973. Chairperson speech dept. Cumberland (Wis.) High Sch., 1965-71; asst. prof. mass communications Milton (Wis.) Coll., 1971-74; asst. prof. communications media Bemidji (Minn.) State U., 1974-79; assoc. prof. mass communications Middle Tenn. State U., Murfreesboro, 1979-85; dir. Learning Resources, assoc. prof. humanities Southeastern U., Washington, 1985-87; dean of instrn. Learning Resources Nicolet Coll., Rhinelander, Wis., 1987—. Vocat. tech. adult edn. rep. Coun. Wis. Librs., 1990-99. Author: Man, Media and Society, 1976; also articles. Disting. Mellon fellow, Vanderbilt U., 1981; named Sch. of Libr. and Info. Sci. Notable Alumnus, U. Wis., Milw., 1993. Mem. ALA, ACLU, Coun. Wis. Librs. (elected). Democrat. Lutheran. Avocations: history and collection of classic animated films. Home: W2148 Eagle Dr Neshkoro WI 54960-8412 Office: Nicolet Coll Learning Resource Ctr Rhinelander WI 54501 E-mail: amussehl@nicolet.tec.wi.us.

MUSSEHL, ROBERT CLARENCE, lawyer; b. Washington, May 1, 1936; s. Chester Carl and Clara Cecelia (Greenwalt) Mussehl; children: Debra Lee (dec.), David Lee; m. Misook Chung, Mar. 22, 1987; 1 child, Omar. BA, Am. U., 1964, JD, 1966. Bar: Wash. 1967, U.S. Dist. Ct. (we. dist.) Wash. 1967, U.S. Ct. Appeals (9th cir.) 1968, U.S Supreme Ct. 1971. Sr. ptnr. Thom, Mussehl, Navoni, Hoff, Pierson & Ryder, Seattle, 1967-78, Neubauer & Mussehl, Seattle, 1978-80, Mussehl & Rosenberg, Seattle, 1980—2001. Speaker law convs. and other profl. orgns.; moot ct. judge Nat. Appelate Advocacy Competition, San Francisco, 1987; panel mem. ABA Symposium on Compulsory Jurisdiction of World Ct., San Francisco, 1987. chair dispute resolution com., 2001-02; chmn. bd., chief exec. officer The Seattle Smashers profl. volleyball club, 1976-80. Contbr. numerous articles to legal publs. Mem. Wash. Vol. Lawyers for Arts, 1976-80; statewide chair Lawyers for Durning for Gov., 1976; mem. task force on the single adult and ch. Ch. Coun. Greater Seattle, 1976-78; bd. dirs. Wash. State Pub. Interest Law Ctr., 1976-81; founder, past chair Lawyers Helping Hungry Children campaign, Wash. State Lawyers Campaign for Hunger Relief, 1991—. Recipient Jefferson award for cmty. and pub. svc. State of Wash., Am. Inst. for Pub. Svc., 1997. Fellow Am. Bar Found. (life), Am. Acad. Matrimonial Lawyers; mem. ABA (ho. of dels. 1979-91, spl. adv. com. on internat. activities 1989-91, chair marriage and family counseling and conciliation com. family law sect. 1981-83, mem. world order under law standing com. 1983-89, chair, 1986-89, chair ad hoc com. on the assembly 1986-89, mem. assembly resolutions com. 1979-91, mem. blue ribbon com. for world ct. 1987-88, mem. standing com. on dispute resolution, 1992-93; exec. coun. sect. dispute resolution 1993-95, asst. budget officer, 1995-97, budget officer 1997-99, vice-chair 1999—, chair 2001-02), Wash. State Bar Assn. (exec. com. family law sect. 1973-75, chmn. internat. law com. 1974-76, sec.-treas., exec. com. world peace through law sect. 1980—, chair 1981-82, mem. edit. bd. Family Law Deskbook 1987-89), Wash. State Trial Lawyers Assn., Seattle-King County Bar Assn. (family law sect. 1971-90, other coms. 1970—, chmn. young lawyers sect. 1971-72, sec. 1972-73, trustee), Am. Arbitration Assn. (panel arbitrators), World Assn. Lawyers of World Peace Through Law Ctr. (founding mem.), Heritage Club YMCA Greater Seattle (charter 1977—), UN Assn. U.S.A. (bd. dirs. Seattle chpt. 1989-91). Avocations: biking, tennis, weight training, painting, religious studies. Home: One Pacific Tower 2000 1st Ave Apt 902 Seattle WA 98121-2167 Office: Ste 3000 1000 2nd Ave Seattle WA 98104-1093 E-mail: bobmussehl@earthlink.net.

MUSSELMAN, ERIC, professional basketball coach; b. Ashland, Ohio, Nov. 19, 1964; m. Wendy Musselman; children: Michael, Matthew. BS, U. San Diego, 1987. Asst. dir. scouting L.A. Clippers, 1987—90; asst. coach Minn. Timberwolves, 1990—91; gen. mgr. Fla. Beach Dogs, Continental Basketball Assn., 1990—98, head coach, 1991—98, Fla. Sharks. U.S. Basketball League, 1995—96; asst. coach Orlando Magic, 1998—2000, Atlanta Hawks, 2000—02; head coach Golden State Warriors, 2002—. Office: Golden State Warriors 7000 Coliseum Way Oakland CA 94621*

MUSSELMAN, LARRY L. chemical engineer; b. Erie, Pa., Aug. 16, 1947; s. Lloyd H. and Lyda Musselman; m. Susan E., Nov. 25, 1966; children: Cheri A., Jason L., Lucy A., Gavin A., Lauren A. BSChemE magna cum laude, Akron U., 1971, MS in Engring., 1972. Rsch. engr. Timken Co., 1971-77; sr. rsch. engr. Alcoa Co., Alcoa Center, Pa., 1977-79, sr. scientist, 1979-81, staff engr., 1981-83, tech. svc. mgr., 1983-86, tech. mgr., 1986-89; dir. tech. and ops. Polymer Additives Group, Apollo, Pa., 1989-93, v.p. tech. and ops. polymer additives group, 1993—. Mem. tech. adv. com. Ohio Legislature. Author: Handbooks of Science and Technology of Alumna Chemicals, Plastics Additives; contbr. over 50 articles on polymers and fire retardants to profl. jours.; numerous patents in field. Akron U. scholar. Mem. ASME (sect. dir.), ASTM (fire testing coms.), Am. Soc. Lubrication Engrs., Soc. Plastics Engrs., Fire Retardant Chems. Assn., Soc. Plastics Industry Coms., Sigma Xi, Sigma Tau, Alpha Chi Sigma. Office: Polymer Additives Group 321 Markle Rd Apollo PA 15613-8703

MUSSELMAN, ROBERT METCALFE, lawyer; b. N.Y.C., June 12, 1914; s. Joseph Franklin and Susan M. (Metcalfe) Musselman; m. Lucie Carolyn Clarke, Sept. 6, 1958; 1 child Susan Carole. BS, U. Va., 1934, MA in Polit. Sci., 1940, LLB, 1945. Bar: Va. 1945, U.S. Dist. Ct. (ea. dist.) Va. 1948, U.S. Tax Ct. 1948, U.S. Dist. Ct. (we. dist.) Va. 1951, U.S. Ct. Appeals (4th cir.) 1953, U.S. Supreme Ct. 1964, U.S. Claims Ct. 1986, U.S. Ct. Appeals (11th cir.) 1987, U.S. Ct. Appeals (fed. cir.) 1988, U.S. dist. Ct. (ctrl. dist.) Ill. 1994, U.S. Ct. Appeals (7th cir.) 1994. Instr., lectr. U. Va., Charlottesville, 1936-59, chief acct., 1943-46; law clk. to judge U.S. Ct. Appeals (4th cir.), 1945-46; ptnr. Michael and Musselman, Charlottesville, 1946-53, Musselman and Drysdale, Charlottesville, 1953-56; pvt. practice, 1956—. Lectr. in field. Editor-in-chief: Alexander's Federal Tax Handbook, 1955—61, bd. editors: Jour. Taxation, 1954—73. Pres. Charlottesvill-Albermarle Young Dem. Club, 1940—43; mem. Albemarle County Dem. Com., 1978—. Mem.: AICPA, ABA, Va. Soc. CPAs (bd. dirs.), Charlottesville-Albermarle Bar Assn., Va. Bar Assn., Am. Assn. Atty.-CPAs (charter, bd. dirs.), 4th Cir. Jud. Conf., Phi Sigma Kappa. Episcopalian. Home: 1438 Lilac Ct Charlottesville VA 22901-6403 Office: 413 7th St NE PO Box 254 Charlottesville VA 22902-0254 E-mail: rmmesquire@aol.com.

MUSSENDEN, GERALD, psychologist; b. N.Y.C., June 1, 1941; s. Geraldo and Adele (Gimenez) M.; m. Iris Manuela Prado, Aug. 11, 1967; children: Gerald, Ricardo-Antonio, Gina. BA, Tarkio Coll., 1968; MS, Brigham Young U., 1971, PhD, 1974. Diplomate Am. Bd. Profl. Disability Cons., Am. Bd. Forensic Examiners, Am. Bd. Forensic Clin. Psychology. Dir. child program Albert Einstein Coll. Medicine, N.Y.C., 1974-76; psychologist Mental Health Ctr., Bartow, Fla., 1976-77, Norside Community Mentala Health Ctr., Tampa, 1977-80; pvt. practice Brandon (Fla.) Counseling Ctr., 1980—. Criminal ct. psychologist Fla. Cts., Hillsborough, Fla., 1978—; with children's svcs. State Rehab., Hillsborough, 1977—; rehab. psychologist Vocat. Rehab., Hillsborough; psychologist Div. Blind Svcs., Hillsborough. Fellow Ford Found., 1972-73. Mem. APA, Fla. Psychol. Assn., Bay Area Psychol. Assn., Soc. Personality Assessment. Home: 317 Cactus Rd Seffner FL 33584-6105 Office: Brandon Counseling Ctr 134 N Moon Ave Brandon FL 33510-4420

MUSSER, SANDRA G. retired lawyer; b. Hollywood, Calif., July 23, 1944; d. Donald Godfrey Gumpertz and Gloria G. (Rosenblatt) King; m. Michael R.V. Whitman, Feb. 19, 1980. BA, UCLA, 1965; JD, Hastings Coll. of Law, 1970. Bar: Calif. 1971, U.S. Dist. Ct. (no. dist.) Calif. 1971, U.S. Ct. Appeals (9th cir.) 1971. Clk. 9th Cir. Ct. of Appeals, 1971-72; lawyer pvt. practice of family law, 1972-86; ptnr. Musser & Ryan, San Francisco, 1986-97; pvt. practice, 1997-98; ret., 1998. Judge pro tem San Francisco County Superior Ct., 1988-98; dealer antique Chinese rugs and textiles, 1996—. Contbr. articles to profl. jours. Mem. adv. coun. Textile Mus., Washington, 1996—. Fellow Acad. Matrimonial Lawyers; mem. ABA (chair litig. sect. domestic rels. and family law com. 1993-94), State Bar Calif. (state bar family law sect. 1977—, chair 1982-83, advisor 1983-84), Bar Assn. San Francisco. Office: 361 Oak St San Francisco CA 94102-5615

MUSSER, SAUNDRA JEANNE (BERRY MUSSER), music educator, composer; b. Bluffton, Ohio, July 23, 1937; d. Dallas Herbert and Frances Miriam (Gilbert) Berry; children: Trisha, David, Steven. BSc in Edn., Bluffton Coll., 1959; MSc in Edn., U. Dayton, 1979. Cert. music tchr. Vocal music tchr. Glenwood Jr. High, Findlay, Ohio, 1959-64, 76-97; pvt. practice, 1959—2002; cooperative tchr. various Colls., Ohio, 1959-89; vocal music tchr. Whittier Elem., Adams Elem., Findlay, 1974-75; supr. student tchrs. Bowling Green State U., Findlay City Schs., Ohio, 1989-96. 31 published vocal compositions including: Music and Kids! (sung in World's Largest Concert via PBS TV, 1986, 96, sung at OMEA state convention 1985, 86, 87, performed at Constitution Hall, Washington), Kids of the U.S.A.! (opening song for World's Largest Concert, 1987, sung via PBS TV, sung at OMEA state convention, 1987), Kids!, Barbershop Blues, Til We Meet Again, R-A-G-T-I-M-E!, Joy! Joy! The Christ Child is Born, Gospel Jubilee!, Everybody Singing One Song!, others. Recipient Bruce Hill award Findlay City Schs., Composer awards ASCAP, 1987-2002; Martha Jennings scholar Findlay City Schs., 1982-83. Mem. Nat. Edn. Assn. (Ohio chpt., Findlay chpt.), Am. Soc. Composers, Ohio Music Educators Assn., Music Educators Nat. Conference, Findlay City Schs. curriculu com., in-service com., staff devel. com., Glenwood Jr. High adv. com., performance ensembles, North Central Evaluation Team, Alpha Gamma, Pi Delta.

MUSSETT, RICHARD EARL, city official; b. Erie, Pa., June 24, 1948; s. Clarence Harold and Elva (Brueckner) M.; m. Alaine Kathleen Rau, Aug. 14, 1971; children: Matthew, Mark. BPA, U. N.D., 1974; M of Urban Planning, U. Mich., 1975. Chief planner City of Largo, Fla., 1976-77; chief long-range planning Pinellas County Planning Dept., Clearwater, 1977-80; planning dir. City of St. Petersburg, 1980-85, dep. city mgr., adminstr., 1987—; adminstr. cmty. devel. City of Bloomington, Minn., 1985-87. Chmn. Pinellas County Planners Adv. Com., 1982. Alternate del. N.D. Dem. Conv., 1972; mem. Tampa Bay Study Commn., 1984-85; mem. environ. quality com. Fla. League of Cities, 1984-85, devel. strategies legis. policy com., 1986; bd. dirs. Mahaffey Theater, 1994—, Tampa Bay Partnership, 1997—. Rackham grantee, 1975. Mem. Am. Inst. Cert. Planners (charter), Am. Planning Assn. (chmn. Suncoast sect. 1984, mem. legis. policy com. Fla. chpt. 1984-85, editor Suncoast sect. newsletter 1985). Lutheran. Avocations: reading, sports, politics. Office: City of St Petersburg 175 5th St N Saint Petersburg FL 33701-3708 E-mail: remusset@stpete.org.

MUSSMAN, CAROL LYNNE, lawyer; b. Salt Lake City, Oct. 6, 1957; d. S. Mark and Barbara (Rampton) Johnson; m. William E. Mussman III; children: Katherine Anne, Laura Lynne, Elizabeth Ashley. AB, Bryn Mawr Coll., 1979; JD, Duke U., 1982. Bar: Tex. 1982, Calif. 1987. Assoc. Strasburger & Price, Dallas, 1982-86, Pettit & Martin, San Francisco, 1986-89, Carr, McClellan, Ingersoll, Thompson & Horn, Burlinghame, Calif., 1991—. Asst. city atty. Hillsborough, Calif., 1991—. Mem. State Bar Tex., State Bar Calif., Phi Delta Phi. Republican. Mem. Lds Ch. Home: 604 Bing Way Modesto CA 95356-9585 Office: 216 Park Rd Burlingame CA 94010-4206

MUSSMAN, WILLIAM EDWARD, III, lawyer; b. San Francisco, Jan. 31, 1951; s. William Edward and Janet John (Skittone) M.; m. Carol Lynne Johnson, Jan. 9, 1988; children: Katherine Ann, Laura Lynne, Elizabeth Ashley. BS cum laude, Stanford U., 1973; JD, U. Calif.-San Francisco, 1976. Bar: Calif. 1976, U.S. Dist. Ct. (cen. dist.) Calif. 1982, U.S. Dist. Ct. (ea. dist.) Calif. 1998, U.S. Supreme Ct. 1985, U.S. Ct. Appeals (9th cir.) 1987. Assoc. Lasky, Haas, Cohler & Munter, San Francisco, 1980-82, Pillsbury, Madison & Sutro, San Francisco, 1982-84, Carr & Mussman, San Francisco, 1984-91, ptnr., 1991-95, Carr, Mussman & Harvey, LLP, San Francisco, 1996-99, Mussman & Mussman, LLP, Modesto, 2000—. Contbr. articles to profl. jours. Vol., rep., Ch. Jesus Christ Latter Day Sts., Tokyo, 1977-78. Mem. Calif. State Bar Assn. (litigation sect., law practice mgmt. sect.), Stanislaus County Bar Assn., Stanford Alumni Assn. (life), Tau Beta Phi. Office: Mussman & Mussman LLP 1101 Sylvan Ave Ste C106 Modesto CA 95350-1687 E-mail: wmussman3@mussmanlaw.com.

MUST, DENNIS PATRICK, writer, editor; b. New Castle, Pa., May 4, 1934; s. Joseph Francis and Margaret Elenor (Daugherty) M.; m. Beverly Ann Davis, July 15, 1955 (div. Jan. 1970); children: Kim, Kathy, Shawn; m. Aviva Sara Cohen, July 18, 1975; children: Shoshanna, Ariel. BA, Washington and Jefferson U., 1956; postgard., Princeton Theol. Sem., 1956-58, U. Iowa, 1958-59. Instr. NYU, Bronx, 1969; chair English dept. Barnard Sch. for Boys, N.Y.C., 1960-68, Elisabeth Irwin H.S., N.Y.C., 1968-71; exec. v.p., owner Corporate Space, Inc., Boston, 1980-93; founder, editor Flying Horse LIt. Jour., Marblehead, Mass., 1993—. Author: (plays, produced off-off-Broadway) Nightmoths, Blue Horse, Mexican Bird Act, Deaths Balloon, (short stories) Banjo Grease, 2000; contbr. short stories to lit. jours. Recipietn 1st place Fiction award The Oval Mag., 1996, Taproot Lit. Jour., 1998, Alsop Review, 1999. Mem. Nat. Writers Union, Authors Guild. Avocation: jazz piano. Home: 1 Valiant Way Salem MA 01970- E-mail: must@attbi.com.

MUSTACCHI, PIERO, preventive medicine physician, educator; b. Cairo, May 29, 1920; came to U.S., 1947; naturalized, 1962; s. Gino and Gilda (Rieti) M.; m. Dora Lisa Ancona, Sept. 26, 1948; children: Roberto, Michael. BS in Humanities, U. Florence, Italy, 1938; postgrad. in anatomy, Eleve Interne, U. Lausanne, Switzerland, 1938-39; MB, ChB, Fouad I U., Cairo, Egypt, 1944, grad. in Arabic lang. and lit., 1946; D Medicine and Surgery, U. Pisa, 1986; D Honoris Causa, U. Aix-Marseilles, France, 1988; hon. degree, U. Alexandria, Egypt, 1985. Qualified med. examiner, Calif. Indsl. Accident Commn., 1994. House officer English Hosp., Ch. Missionary Soc., Cairo, 1945-47; clin. affiliate U. Calif., San Francisco, 1947-48; intern Franklin Hosp., 1948-49; resident in pathology U. Calif., 1949-51; resident in medicine Meml. Ctr. Cancer and Allied Diseases, N.Y.C., 1951-53; rsch. epidemiologist Dept. HEW, Nat. Cancer Inst., Bethesda, Md., 1955-57; cons. allergy clinic U. Calif., San Francisco, 1957-70, clin. prof. medicine and preventive medicine, 1970-90, clin. prof. medicine and epidemiology, 1990-96, head occupl. epidemiology, 1975-90, head divsn. internat. health edn. dept. epidemiology and internat. health, 1985-90; médecin agréé, official physician Consulate Gen. of France, San Fransisco, 1995—; sr. cons. internat. health care U. Calif., San Francisco. Med. cons., vis. prof. numerous ednl. & profl. instns., U. Marseilles, 1981—82, U. Pisa, Italy, 1983, U. Gabon, 1984, U. Siena, Italy, 1985; cons U. Calif., 1975—, sr. cons. internat. med. care, 2000—. Contbr. chpts. to books, articles to profl. jours. Editorial bd. Medecine d'Afrique Noire, Ospedali d'Italia. Served with USN, USPHS, 1953-55 Decorated Order of Merit (Commander) (Italy), Ordre de la Legion d'Honneur (France), Medal of St. John of Jerusalem, Sovereign Order of Malta, Order of the Republic (Egypt); Scroll, Leonardo da Vinci Soc., San Francisco, 1965; award Internat. Inst. Oakland, 1964; Hon. Vice Consul. Italy, 1971-90. Fellow ACP, Am. Soc. Environ. and Occupational Health; mem. AAAS, Am. Assn. Cancer Rsch., Calif. Soc. Allergy and Immunology, Calif. Med. Assn., San Francisco Med. Soc., West Coast Allergy Soc. (founding), Mex. Congress on Hypertension (corr.), Internat. Assn. Med. Rsch. and Continuing Edn. (U.S. rep.), Acad. Italiana della Cucina. Democrat. Avocations: mathematics, music, languages. Home: 3344 Laguna St San Francisco CA 94123-2208 Office: U Calif Parnassus Ave San Francisco CA 94143-0560 also: 3838 California St San Francisco CA 94118-1522

MUSTAFA, ALI SYED, structural engineer, consultant; b. Hyderabad, India, Oct. 21, 1935; came to U.S., 1962; s. Syed Inayat and Habib-Un-Nissa (Begum) Husain; m. Abida Meher Sultana, July 26, 1964; children: Rohina, Rubina, Sameena, Raabia, Arjumund. BCE, U. Peshawar, Pakistan, 1957; MS in Structural Engring., Okla. State U., 1963. Registered profl. structural engr., Ill. Asst. engr. Burlington R.R., Chgo., 1963-66; structural engr. Sargent & Lundy Engrs., 1966-74; project mgr. Bur. Engring. Dept. Pub. Works, 1974-91; project mgr. Divsn. Planning & Design Dept. of Aviation, 1991-94; chief structural engr. Divsn. of Engring., Dept. of Aviation, 1995—. Bd. dirs. Delta Engring. Inc., Chgo. Bd. dirs. Muslim Community Ctr., Chgo., 1974-84. Fellow ASCE. Home: 6900 N Minnetonka Ave Chicago IL 60646-1518 Office: Dept Aviation O'Hare Internat Airport PO Box 66142 Chicago IL 60666-0142

MUSTAFA, SHAKIR, English and Arabic educator; b. Baghdad, Iraq, June 15, 1952; came to U.S., 1990; s. Mahmoud Mustafa and Zakiya Mahdi; m. Nawal Nasrallah, Apr. 15, 1979. BA in English Lit., Baghdad U., 1974, MA in English Lit., 1977; PhD, Ind. U., 1999. Vice chmn. English dept. Mosul (Iraq) U., 1988-90; vis. asst. prof. Ind. U., 1999-2000; vis. prof. Boston U., 2000—. Author: To the Promised Land through Gas Chambers: Zionism and the Jewish Novel in America, 1980, Literary Translation, 2 vols., 1984, 85, Seventeenth-Century English Poetry, 1988; contbr. articles to profl. jours.; co-editor: A Century of Irish Drama, 2000; translator Arabic lit. Mem. Modern Fgn. Langs., Union of Writers in Iraq. Moslem. Office: Boston U 718 Commonwealth Ave Boston MA 02215 E-mail: mustafa@bu.edu.

MUSTAPHA, TAMTON, gastroenterologist; b. Calicut, Kerala, India, Oct. 17, 1941; s. Mahamood and Asmabi (Tamton) Thoosikannan; m. Rahma Marikar, June 15, 1969; children: Monisha, Mumtaz, Nigel. Student, Malabar Christian Coll., India, 1958; MD, Calicut Med. Coll., 1963. Diplomate Am. Bd. Internal Medicine, Am. Bd. Gastroenterology. Resident in internal medicine VA Hosp., Bklyn., 1967-68, Grasslands Hosp., Valhalla, N.Y., 1968-70; resident in gastroenterology Montefiore Hosp., Bronx, 1970-72; practice medicine, specializing in gastroenterology Hudson, 1972—; attending physician Columbia Meml. Hosp., 1972—; chief dept. medicine Columbia Greene Med. Ctr., 1989-91; instr. Albany Med. Ctr., 1972—. Mem. med. adv. com. N.Y. State Health Dept.; bd. dirs., chmn. auditing assurance Hudson Valley PSRO; pres. No. Columbia Assocs., Columbia Greene Med. Assocs., Cairo Med. Realty, Prime Med. Assocs., Hudson, 1997—; bd. Greene Health Care Assocs.; bd. dirs. Regional Heart Assn. Mem. town planning bd. kinderhook, 1987-96; chmn. bd. trustees Columbia Greene C.C., 1995-97. Fellow Am. Coll. Gastroenterologists; mem. AMA, ACP, Columbia County Med. Soc., N.Y. State Med. Soc. (med. adv. com.), Am. Gastroent. Assn., Am. Soc. Internat. Medicine, Acad. Scis., Am. Heart Assn. (bd. dirs.), Am. Coll. Physician Execs., Columbia and Dutchess Lung Assn., Assn. for Mentally Retarded, Am. Assn. Physicians and Dentists of India (pres. Capital Dist. 1986), Rotary (dir. 1976-78, pres.-elect 1986-87, pres. 1987—, Paul Harris fellow, gov. dist. 7210 1999—), Mason (master), Shriners, Cypres Temple. Republican. Home: 2575 Rte 21 Valatie NY 12184 Office: Prime Med Assocs 949 Columbia St Hudson NY 12534-2624 E-mail: mustapha@mhmline.net.

MUSTARD, MARY CAROLYN, financial executive; b. North Bend, Nebr., Sept. 21, 1948; d. Joseph Louis and Rosalie Margaret (Emanuel) Smaus; m. Ronald L. Mustard, Apr. 19, 1969 (div. 1988); children: Joel Jonathan, Dana Marie. Student, Creighton U., 1966-67, C.E. Sch. Commerce, 1967-68, Coll. of St. Mary, 1983-84, Met. C.C., Omaha, 1988-90, Bellevue U., 1991-92. With Platte County Dept. Pub. Welfare, Columbus, Nebr., 1968-69; sec. to plant mgr. B.L. Montague Steel Co., Sumter, S.C., 1969-70; property disposal technician Property Disposal Office, Shaw AFB, 1970-71; libr. technician Hdqs. Strategic Air Command Libr., Offutt AFB, Nebr., 1971-76; sec.-steno Hdqs. Strategic Air Command Comm./Frequency Mgmt., 1976-79; security specialist/program analyst Hdqs. Strategic Air Command Security Police, 1979-88; budget analyst Hdqs. Strategic Air Command Fin. Mgmt., 1988-92; funds control analyst Hdqs. Air Mobility Command, Scott AFB, Ill., 1992-93, chief hdqs. and comm. account, 1993-94, chief hdqs. relocation, transition assistance/comm. programs, 1994-95; chief base realignment and closure program Air Mobility Command, 1995-96; sys. adminstr. Def. Fin. and Acctg. Svc., Kansas City, Mo., 1996-2000, fin. sys. mgmt., 2000—02, fin. mgmt. bus. mgmt. office, 2002—. Mem. Am. Soc. Mil. Comptrollers (SAC Budget Analyst of Yr. 1990). Democrat. Roman Catholic. Avocations: walking, reading, biking. Office: DFAS-KC/ADB 1500 E Bannister Rd Kansas City MO 64197-0001 E-mail: mmustard1@msn.com.

MUSTELIER, ALINA OLGA, travel consultant, music educator; b. Havana, Cuba, Sept. 28, 1949; d. Carlos Enrique and Olga Castellanos Mustelier; children: Antonio Freire, Ana Freire. MusB, U. Miami, 1971; MS, Fla. Internat. U., , 1982. Cert. ednl. leadership. Customer care rep. So. Bell, Miami, Fla., 1973—74; music tchr. Shenandoah Elem., 1974—75; music tchr. Coral Way Elem., 1975—78, Fairlawn Elem., Miami, 1979—88; tchr. Whispering Pines Elem., 1988—93; music tchr. Claude Pepper Elem. Sch., 1998—2001. Singer: Miami Opera Guild Chorus, 1970, Church By the Sea Choir, 1979. Recipient Sword of Honor, Sigma Alpha Iota, 1968-1971. Office: Claude Pepper Elem Sch 14550 SW 96 St Miami FL 33186 Office Fax: (305) 382-7150. Personal E-mail: musteliera@aol.com.*

MUSTIN, BOB, retired civil engineer, writer; b. Shreveport, La., July 19, 1944; s. Amos Burdette and Miriam Pauline Mustin; m. Rebecca Rose Gifford, June 10, 1947. BS in Civil Engring., La. Tech. U., 1966. Registered profl. engr., Ga. Transp. engr., team leader Ga. Dept. Transp., Atlanta, 1973—85, asst. state bridge engr., 1985—91, asst. engring. svcs. adminstr., 1991—93, engring. svcs. adminstr., 1993—99; ret. Editor: (lit. jour.) The Rural Sophisticate, 1993; author: (novels) A Reason to Tremble, 1996, poetry. Midshipman USN, 1962—64. Recipient Third prize, Byron Herbert Reece Internat. Awards, 1997. Home: 14 Zachary Ridge Rd Asheville NC 28804 Personal E-mail: bobmust@earthlink.net.

MUSTION, ALAN LEE, pharmacist; b. Oklahoma City, Feb. 6, 1947; s. Granville E. and Iris E. (Graham) M.; children: Jeffrey Alan, Jennifer Chere; m. Mary Jane Bozek, Dec. 4, 1982. BS in Pharmacy, Southwestern Okla. State U., 1970. Staff pharmacist VA Med. Ctr., Oklahoma City, 1970-74, dir. pharmacy, Saginaw, Mich., 1974-76, asst. dir. pharmacy, Richmond, Va., 1976-77, dir. pharmacy, Iowa City, Iowa, 1977-90; dir. pharmacy svcs. VA Hosp., Houston, 1990-2002; mgr. pharmacy Integris Baptists Med. Ctr., 2002-; clin. instr. clin./hosp. div. U. Iowa, 1977-90; adj. asst. prof. pharmacy practice U. Houston, 1990-2002. Contbr. articles to profl. jours. Served to lt. col. USAR. Recipient VA Spl. Achievement awards, 1973, 77, 86, 87, 88, 89, 92, 93, 94, 95, 96, 97, Special Contbn. award, 1998, 99, 2000, VA Suggestion awards, 1979, 81, 83, VA Cost Reduction award, 1983, VA Contbr. award, 1987; rsch. grantee Travenol Labs., 1980-87, VA HSR&D grantee, 1984, 88.

Mem. Am. Soc. Hosp. Pharmacists, Tex. Soc. Hosp. Pharmacists, Gulf Coast Soc. Hosp. Pharmacists, Assn. Mil. Surgeons of U.S., Am. Assn. Colls. Pharmacy, Res. Officers Assn., Kappa Psi. Methodist. Home: 1919 E Second St Apt 378 Edmond OK 73034 Office: 3300 NW Expressway Oklahoma City OK 73112 E-mail: alan.mustion@integris-health.com.

MUSTO, DAVID FRANKLIN, physician, educator, historian, consultant; b. Tacoma, Jan. 8, 1936; s. Charles Hiram and Hilda Marie (Hanson) Mustoe; m. Emma Jean Baudendistel, June 2, 1961; children: Jeanne Marie, David Kyle, John Baird, Christopher Edward. BA, U. Wash., 1956, MD, 1963; MA, Yale U., 1961. Lic. physician, Conn., Pa. Clerk Nat. Hosp. for Nervous Disease, London, 1961; intern Pa. Hosp., Phila., 1963-64; resident Yale U. Med. Ctr., New Haven, 1964-67; spl. asst. to dir. NIMH, Bethesda, Md., 1967-69; vis. asst. prof. Johns Hopkins U., 1968-69; asst. prof. Yale U., 1969-73, assoc. prof., 1973-78, sr. rsch. scientist, 1978-81, prof., 1981—, exec. fellow Davenport Coll., 1983-88; mem. adv. editorial com. Yale Edits. Private Papers James Boswell, 1975—; cons. Exec. Office of Pres., 1973-75; mem. White House Strategy Coun., 1978-81; mem. panel on alcohol policy NAS, Washington, 1978-82; cons. White House Conf. on Families, 1979-80. Vis. fellow Clare Coll., Cambridge U., 1994; mem. alcohol adv. com. Nat. Assn. Broadcasters, 1994—; DuMez lectr. U. Md.; Walter Reed meml. lectr. Richmond Acad. Medicine; Galdston lectr. N.Y. Acad. Medicine; Sirridge lectr. U. Mo. Med. Sch.; Clendening lectr. U. Kans. Med. Sch. Author: The American Disease: Origins of Narcotic Control, 1973, expanded edit., 1987, 3rd edit., 1999; co-author: (with P. Korsmeyer) The Quest for Drug Control: Politics and Federal Policy in a Period of Increasing Drug Use, 1963-1981, 2002; editor: One Hundred Years of Heroin, 2002, Drugs in America: A Documentary History, 2002. Historian Pres.'s Commn. on Mental Health, 1977-78; adv. U.S. Del. to UN Commn. Narcotic Drugs, Geneva, 1978-79; mem. nat. coun. Smithsonian Instn., Washington, 1981-90, hon. mem., 1991—; hist. cons. Presdl. Commn. Human Immuno-deficiency Virus Epidemic, 1988; mem. nat. adv. com. on anti-drug program Robert Wood Johnson Found., 1989-2002; mem. nat. adv. com. on internat. narcotic policy UN Assn. of U.S.A., 1991; mem. adv. com. causes drug abuse Office Tech. Assessment, Congress U.S., 1992-94; commr. Conn. Alcohol and Drug Abuse Commn., 1992-93; bd. dirs. Coll. on Problems of Drug Dependence, 1990-94; trustee Assocs. of Cushing-Whitney Med. Libr., 1994—. With USPHS, 1967-69. Fellow: Coll. Problems of Drug Dependence, Am. Psychiat. Assn.; mem.: Soc. of Cin. in the State of Conn. (pres. 1998—2001), English-Speaking Union (pres. New Haven br. 1995—98), Am. Assn. History of Medicine (William Osler medal 1961), Am. Hist. Assn., Am. Inst. History of Pharmacy (Kraemers award 1974), New Haven County Med. Assn. (chmn. bicentennial com. 1983), Century Assn., Athenaeum Club (London), Cosmos Club. Office: Yale U PO Box 207900 New Haven CT 06520-7900

MUSTO, JOSEPH JOHN, lawyer; b. Pittston, Pa., Nov. 22, 1943; s. James and Rose Musto; m. Fortunata Giudice, July 5, 1969; children: Laura, Joseph Robert. BA, King's Coll., Wilkes-Barre, Pa., 1965; JD, Dickinson Sch. Law, Carlisle, Pa., 1968. Bar: Pa. 1968, U.S. Ct. Appeals (3d cir.) 1968, U.S. Dist. Ct. (mid. dist.) Pa. 1971. Asst. dist. atty. City of Phila., 1968-69; assoc. Bedford, Waller, Griffith, Darling & Mitchell, Wilkes-Barre, 1969-73; ptnr. Griffith, Darling, Mitchell, Aponick & Musto, 1973-75; prin. Griffith, Aponick & Musto, 1975-90; ptnr. Rosenn, Jenkins & Greenewald, 1990-93; judge Ct. Common Pleas of Luzerne County, 1993-94; mem. Hourigan, Kluger, Spohrer & Quinn, Wilkes-Barre, Pa., 1994-97; prin. Musto & Saunders, PC, Plymouth, 1997—. Solicitor Yatesville (Pa.) Borough, 1973-80, Duryea (Pa.) Borough, 1975-80, Pittston Area Sch. Dist., 1973-93. Mem. Luzerne County Gov. Study Com., Wilkes-Barre, 1973-74; mem., chmn. No. Luzerne Health Adv. Coun., Wilkes-Barre, 1976-80; pres., mem. Health Sys. Agy. of N.E. Pa., Avoca, 1980-86; pres. Pa. Health Planning Assn., Harrisburg, 1985-86; mem. civil justice reform act adv. com. Fed. Dist. Ct. Pa. Ct., 1991-95. Mem. Fed. Bar Assn. (past pres. Ctrl. Pa. chpt.), Pa. Bar Assn., Wilkes-Barre Law and Libr. Assn. Democrat. Roman Catholic. Home: 7 Prospect Pl Pittston PA 18640-2627 Office: Musto & Saunders 117 W Main St Plymouth PA 18651-2926

MUSTOE, THOMAS ANTHONY, physician, plastic surgeon; b. Columbia, Mo., June 29, 1951; s. Robert Moore and Carolyn (Swett) M.; m. Kathryn Claire Stallcup, Aug. 13, 1977; children: Anthony, Lisa. BA cum laude in biology, Harvard Coll., 1973, MD cum laude, 1978. Diplomate Am. Bd. Otolaryngology, Am. Bd. Plastic Surgery. Rsch. assoc. dept. microbiology Harvard Med. Sch., Cambridge, Mass., 1976-77; intern in medicine Mass. Gen. Hosp., Boston, 1978-79; resident in surgery Peter Bent Brigham Hosp., 1979-80; resident in otolaryngology Mass. Eye and Ear Infirmary, 1980-82, chief resident, 1982-83; resident in plastic surgery Brigham and Women;s Hosp., Children's Hosp., 1983-84, chief resident, 1984-85; asst. prof. in surgery Wash. U. Sch. Medicine, St. Louis, 1985-89, assoc. prof., 1989-91; prof., chief divsn. plastic surgery Northwestern U. Med. Sch., Chgo., 1991—; plastic surgeon Northwestern Meml. Hosp., 1991—, Evanston Hosp., 1991—, Children's Meml. Hosp., 1992—, Shriner's Hosp. Chgo., 1994—. Co-chmn. Gorden Rsch. Conf., 1995; spl. cons. FDA, 1994—98; mem. sci. adv. panel Biologies, 1997, NCI, 1998; lectr. seminars, 2001. Editl. bd. Archives of Surgery, 1992—, Plastic and Reconstructive Surgery, 1993-2001, Wound Repair and Regeneration, 1992—, Jour. Surg. Rsch., 1997—; contbr. articles to profl. jours., more than 200 publs., book chpts.; book reviewer. Harvard Nat. scholar, 1969-73; Rhodes scholar candidate, Harvard Coll., 1973. Fellow: ACS (adv. coun. plastic surgery 1999—2002, surg. forum com. 1999—2002, surg. biology club III); mem.: AMA, Coun. Plastic Surger Org., Double Boarded Soc. (pres. 1995—98), Chgo. Surg. Soc., Chgo. Plastic Surg. Soc. (sec. 1996—97), Wound Healing Soc. (program com. 1990, audit com. 1992, program com. 1992, bd. dir. 1993—96, program com. 1994, fin. com. 1994—96, program com. 1997, pres. 1997—99), Assn. Acad. Chmn. Plastic Surgery (matching program and ctrl. application svc. com. 1994), Soc. U. Surgeons, Soc. Head and Neck Surgeons (membership com. 1993—95), Plastic Surgery Rsch. Coun. (rep. coun. acad. surgeons 1991—94, com. indsl. rels. 1992, program com. 1992—94, 1995, Judge Snyder & Crikelair awards 1991), Midwest Assn. Plastic Surgeons, Lipoplasty Soc. N.Am. (lipoplasty ednl. rsch. found. 1998—2000), Am. Assn. Plastic Surgery (rsch. and edn. com. 1994—96, chmn. 1996, mem. com. 1998—, co-chmn.ASPRS-ASAPS task force on emerging trends 1999—2000, chmn. instl. coun. com. 1999—), Am. Soc. Plastic and Reconstructive Surgery (rsch. fund proposal com. 1987—92, plastic surgery device com. 1989—93, resource book for plastic surgery residents com. 1991—93, socioecon. 1992—94, sci. program com. 1993—95, chmn. device and tecyhnique assessment com. 1994—96, co-chmn. gen. reconstruction subcom. 1995, ultrasonic lipectomy task force 1995—96, task force for outcomes and guidelines 1995—98, devices and tech. com. 1995—98, chmn. instrnl. com. 1999—2002, chmn. edn. com. 1999—, chmn. resource book com.), Aesculapian Club, Sigma Xi. Avocations: reading, golf, gardening, sports. Home: 144 Greenwood St Evanston IL 60201-4712

MUSZYNSKA, AGNIESZKA (AGNES MUSZYNSKA), mechanical engineering researcher, consultant; b. Warsaw, Poland, Oct. 10, 1935; came to U.S., 1980; d. Zdzislaw E. and Wida-Wanda (Jellinek) Galinowski; m. Jerzy Muszynski, Dec. 2, 1954 (div. July 1974); 1 child, Roman. MSME, Warsaw Tech. U., Poland, 1960; PhD in Tech. Scis., Polish Acad. Scis., Warsaw, 1966, habilitation, 1977; prof. tech. scis., Poland, 1998. Designer Machine Tool Design Co., Warsaw, 1960-61; asst. prof. Inst. Fundamental Tech. Rsch., Polish Acad. Scis., 1961-78, assoc. prof., 1978-82; sr. rsch. scientist Bently Nev. Corp., Minden, Nev., 1981-82; rsch. mgr. Bently Rotor Dynamics Rsch. Corp., 1982-99; cons. A.M. Cons., 1999—. Vis. prof. Inst. Nat. Scis., Lyon, France, Swiss Fed. Inst. Tech., Zurich, 2000—01, U. Franche Comte, Besancon, France, 2001; vis. rsch. scientist U. Dayton, Ohio, 1980—81; fac. mem. U. Nev., Reno, 1984—89. Editor 5 books; sci. editor: Dynamics of Machines (in Polish), 1974, Dynamics of Machines: Vibration Control in Machines (in Polish and English), 1978, (with D. E. Bently, R.C. Hendricks) Instability of Rotating Machinery, 1985, (with J.C. Simonis) Rotating Machinery Dynamics, 1987, Don Bently Through the Eyes of Others, 1995, Procs. of 7th Internat. Symposium on Transport Phenomena and Dynamics of Rotating Machinery, 1998; regional editor Internat. Jour. Rotating Machines, 1994—; contbr. articles to profl. jours. Recipient Gold Cross of Merit Polish Acad. Scis., 1975, Innovation award NASA, 1990, Outstanding Rsch. award Pacific Ctr. Thermal Fluids Engring., 1996; titled Prof. of Tech. Scis., Pres. of Poland, 1998. Fellow ASME (assoc. editor Transactions of the ASME 1988-94); mem. NAFE, Am. Acad. Scis. Achievements include contributions to the new discipline of mechanical engineering; vibrational diagnostics of rotating machines. Avocations: music, cross-country skiing, photography, stamp collecting. E-mail: agnes@gbis.com.

MUSZYNSKI, CHERYL ANN, neurosurgeon; b. Detroit; d. Harry Jerome Jr. and Patricia Marie Muszynski. BA, Kalamazoo Coll., 1984; MD, Washington U., St. Louis, 1988. Diplomate Am. Bd. Neurol. Surgery. Intern and resident in gen. surgery Hosp. St. Raphael, New Haven, 1988-90; resident, chief resident neurosurgery Baylor Affiliated Hosp. Sys., Houston, 1990-95; fellow divsn. pediatric neurosurgery NYU Med. Ctr., N.Y.C., 1995-96; attending physician dept. neurosurgery Beth Israel Med. Ctr., 1996-2000, Med. Coll. of Wis., Milw., 2000—. Co-contbr. articles to profl. jours. Neurotrauma Soc. Travel fellow, Houston, 1993. Fellow ACS; mem. AMA, Am. Assn. Neurol. Surgeons, Congress Neurol. Surgeons, Internat. Soc. Pediatric Neurosurgery. Office: Childrens Hosp of Wis Neurosurgery 9000 W Wisconsin Ave PO Box 1997 MS#405 Milwaukee WI 53201 E-mail: cmuszynski@neuroscience.mcw.edu.

MUSZYNSKI, JANE, interior designer, colorist, space planner; b. Memphis, Dec. 4, 1950; m. Jerry Muszynski. BA in Interior Design and Home Econs., Calif. State U., 1973. Profl. status Nat. Coun. Interior Design Qualification, 1986; cert. Calif. Coun. Interior Design, 1993. Graphic designer Stewart Woodard Arch., Irvine, Calif., 1973-74; interior designer Interior Space Design, Newport Beach, 1974-76; office mgr. purchasing Lockheed Marine Lab., Diablo Canyon, 1976-77; realtor assoc. Century 21 Real Estate, Los Osos, 1977-79, Sierra Madre, 1979-80; v.p. mktg., designer S.K. Young Assocs., Tustin, 1979-88; sales acct. exec. Entouch Bus. Interiors, Rancho Cucamonga, 1988-89; sr. interior designer Walt Disney Imagineering - Disneyland, Anaheim, 1989-98; interior designer Universal Studios, Hollywood, 1998-2000; mktg. exec., owner Staffease & Advance Concepts, Walnut, 1991—2001; interior designer cons. Snow Creek Resources, 2001—; interior designer Interiors, Big Bear Lake, Calif. Realtor, sales assoc. Anthony Real Estate, Santa Maria, Calif., 1977, Santa Maria, Calif., 1977—; instr. Mt. San Antonio Coll., Walnut, 1985, Walnut, 87, Walnut, 2002—03, Calif. Poly. U., Pomona, 1988—89, adv. bd. interior design, 1988—90; chmn. nominating com. Bus. Devel. Assn. Orange County, Irvine, 1988—89; dir. pub. rels. NEWH-So. Countries, 2001—02. Mem. host program Bear Mountain Ski Resort, Big Bear, Calif., 1993, 94; cookie chmn. Girl Scouts Am., Walnut, 1993. Mem. Am. Soc. Interior Designers, Network Exec. Women in Hospitality. Avocations: golf, snow skiing, camping, hiking. Office: Advance Concepts Employer Svcs 325 S Lemon #E 253 Walnut CA 91789-3038 E-mail: jane_muszynski@hotmail.com.

MUTALIPASSI, LOUIS RICHARD, psychologist, educator; b. Kansas City, Kans., Jan. 23, 1937; s. Louie R. Mutalipassi and Cleda E. (Miller) Wolverton; m. Edalee Kenworthy, July 14, 1962 (div. 1970); 1 child, Annemarie; m. Laura Ruth Posner, July 17, 1976; children: Michael, Anthony. BA in Psychology, U. Calif., Santa Barbara, 1962; MA in Psychology, UCLA, 1965, PhD in Psychology, 1969. Lic. psychologist, Calif. Staff psychologist VA Med. Ctr., L.A., 1969-76, chief psychology svc. Albany, N.Y., 1976-80; clin. assoc. prof. psychology UCLA, U. So. Calif., L.A., 1980—; chief psychology svc. VA Med. Ctr., Long Beach, Calif., 1980-97, ret., 1997; clin. psychologist in pvt. practice Cypress, 1982—. Oral commr. State Bd. Med. Examiners, Calif., 1996—. Contbr. articles to profl. jours.; presenter in field. With USAF, 1954-58. Mem. APA. Avocations: golf, photography. E-mail: lrmteetime@aol.com.

MUTCH, JAMES DONALD, health therapist; b. Portland, Oreg., Mar. 6, 1943; s. Keith William and Dorothy (Wones) M.; m. Judith Ann Thompson, June 12, 1965; children: William James, Alicia Kathleen. BS in Pharmacy, Oreg. State U., 1966. Registered pharmacist Calif., Oreg., cert. hypnotherapist Nat. Guild Hypnotists, massage therapist Ctr. for Body Harmonics, zero balancer Zero Balancing Assn., process acupressure practitioner Process Acupressure Unltd. Mgr. regulatory affairs Syntex Labs., Palo Alto, Calif., 1970-72, assoc. dir. regulatory affairs, 1972-76, dir. regulatory affairs, 1976-80; dir. regulatory affairs and clin. devel. Cooper Vision, Inc., Mt. View, 1980-86; dir. regulatory affairs and pre-clin. devel. Salutar, Inc., Sunnyvale, 1987-89, v.p. product devel., 1990-91; pres. Altos Biopharm. Inc., Los Altos, 1991-92; v.p. regulatory affairs and product devel. Pharmacyclics, Inc., Mountain View, Calif., 1992-96; Reiki master tchr., cons. herbal pharmacist Palo Alto, 1996—; craniosacral therapist, 1998—; hypnotherapist, massage therapist, 1998—; zero balancer, 1999—; process acupressure practitioner, 2001—. Bd. advisors Process Acupressure Assn. Contbr. articles to profl. jour. Pres. bd. dirs. Woodland Vista Swim & Racquet Club, Los Altos, Calif., 1982-83, 2002--. With USPHS, 1966-68. Mem. Am. Pharm. Assn., Internat. Assn. Health Care Profls., Associated Body Work and Massage Profls., Nat. Guild Hypnotists, Zero Balancing Assn. Democrat. Achievements include co-development of Naprosyn, Lidex, Polycon, CSI, Clerz, Clerz-2, Omniscan. Office: Integrated Healing Arts Ste B 4161 El Camino Way Palo Alto CA 94306 E-mail: JDMutch@aol.com.

MUTH, ERIC PETER, ophthalmic optician; b. Munich, Germany, July 25, 1940; came to U.S., 1948, naturalized 1955; s. Erich Walter and Anna Lisa (Pentenrieder) M.; m. Rachel Hubbard, Apr. 4, 1971; children: Eric Van, Karl George, Ellen Anna. BS, Charter Oak Coll., 1978; MBA, PhD, Columbia Pacific U., 1983; degree (hon.), Anoka-Hennipen Tech. Coll., 1995. Lic. optician, Conn. Optician Park Lane Eye Care, Inc., Milford, Conn., 1968—. Sr. rsch. fellow Internat. Soc. for Philosophical Inquiry, 1991—96, pers. cons., 1996; cons. Nat. Acad. Opthamology Found. Mus., San Francisco, 1982—88, Nat. Mus. Hist. Smithsonian Inst., 1983—94, Gesell Inst. Human Devel., 1984—89; mem. adv. com. South. Cen. Cmty. Coll., Seattle, 1984—89; mem. adv. bd. internat. Scientific Inst., PR, 1989; adv. bd. Middlesex C.C. (vice chmn.), 1989; vol. VA, West Haven, Conn. Mem. editl. rev. bd. (U.S.A.) Dispensing Opticians, Butterworths Heinmann, 1998, co-author 2nd edit., 1998; contbr. the Social History of Eyeglasses in Japan, 1991, die Brille, Leipzig, 1989, Thinking on the Edge Agamennon, 1993; pub. over 250 papers in 6 langs.; contbg. editor Optical Mgmt., 1979-80, OpticScan Canada, 1981-82, Indian Optician, 1982, Prism Mag., Can., 1988, 92; tech. editor Optical Index, 1980-82; reviewer optical books. Presdl. appointment U.S. Selective Svc. Sys., 1991-92; Scoutmaster Boy Scouts Am., 1960-62; bd. dirs. ARC Conn. chpt., 1988; advisor Tri Hi-Y YMCA, 1964; founder, chmn. Korea-Vietnam Meml. com., Milford, 1985-86; organizer WWII Monument Com. 1991; trustee Conn. Visual Health Ctr., 1982-84; commr. Nat. Commn. on Opticianry Edn., 1989-93; life mem. Soc. 3d. U.S. Inf. Div., 1987; hon. Capt. 25th Bn. Royal Fusiliers, 1999. Served with AUS, 1957-59, Conn. Army N.G., 1960-69. Decorated Roman Cath. Knight Malta, Equestrian Knight of The Order of the Holy Sepulchre; recipient Eng. Nelson/Wingate prize, 1983, Service Above Self award, Rotary, 1986, Optician of the Yr., Guild of Prescription Opticians Am., 1993, Senate Citation, State of Conn., 1993, German-Am. Friendship award, Germany, 1995, State of Conn. Justice of the Peace, 1995, cert. of appreciation, Nat. Libr. Medicine, Bethesda, Md., 1995, Med. Scis. Divsn. Nat. Mus. History, 1995, NRA Legion of Honor, 1996, Mayoral Proclamation, Milford, Conn., 1998, Bronze medal of merit, Austrian Albert Schweitzer Soc., 1998, Chemical Corps Regimental Assn. Order of the Dragon, 1999, Oeuvre Humanitaire Croix d'Honneur, 1999, medal of merit, El Salvador Red Cross, 1999, Award of Merit, Army and Navy Union of USA, 2000. Fellow: Conn. Opticians Assn. (amb., pres. 1974, chmn. membership and ethics coms., Optician of Yr. 1975), Opticians Assn. Am. (honored fellow, historian citation 1993, advancing opticinary award 1994, disting. svc. award 2000, diploma in refractometry 1995), Nat. Acad. Opticianry (regional membership chmn., faculty speakers bur., citation 1988), Internat. Acad. Opticianry; mem.: Nat. Contact Lens Examiners (cert.), Guild Prescription Opticians Am. (councilor 2001—), Royal Lifesaving Soc. Can. (hon. assoc. 1998), Soc. Am. Mil. Engrs., Calif. Soc. Dispensing Opticians (hon.), Ari. Soc. Dispensing Opticians (hon.), Am. Bd. of Opticianry (master of ophthalmic optics 1972), Internat. Platform Assn., Contact Lens Soc. Am., Contact Lens Soc. Conn., Internat. Found. in Ophthalmics Optics, Conn. Guild Dispensing Opticians (pres. 1980, Optician of Yr. 1981), Charter Oak Coll. Alumni Assn. (bd. dirs. 1987, alumni citation 1995), Milford C. of C. (chmn. law and safety com. 1975, Cmty. Svc. award 1986), Am. Legion (parade marshal 1998, life mem. Post 196, citation 1986). Avocations: skydiving, para-sailing, ballooning, motorcycling, Tae Kwan Do (presdl. sports award, 1973). Home: 25 Parkland Pl Milford CT 06460-7723 Office: Park Lane Eye Care Inc 50 Broad St Milford CT 06460-3358 E-mail: muth@nyc.com.

MUTH, JOHN FRASER, economics educator; b. Chgo., Sept. 27, 1930; s. Merlin Arthur and Margaret Fraser (Ferris) M. BSI.E., Washington U., St. Louis, 1952; MS, Carnegie-Mellon U., 1954, PhD, 1962. Research fellow Carnegie-Mellon U., 1956-59, asst. prof. econs., 1959-62, assoc. prof., 1962-64; prof. Mich. State U., 1964-69, Ind. U., 1969-94; ret., 1994. Author: (with others) Planning Production, Inventories, and Work Force, 1960, (with G. K. Groff) Operations Management: Analysis for Decision, 1972; editor: (with G. L. Thompson) Industrial Scheduling, 1963, (with G. K. Groff) Operations Management: Selected Readings, 1969; contbr. articles to profl. jours. Fellow Econometric Soc. Home: 21028 4th Ave Summerland Key FL 33042-4033 E-mail: muthjohn@aol.com.

MUTH, RICHARD FERRIS, economics educator; b. Chgo., May 14, 1927; s. Merlin Arthur and Margaret Ferris Muth; m. Helene Louise Martin, Dec. 23, 1955; children: Lisa Helene, Laurianne Martin Love. Student, USCG Acad., 1945-47; AB, Washington U., St. Louis, 1949, MA, 1950; PhD, U. Chgo., 1958; M of Theol. Studies, Emory U., 1995. Lectr. polit. economy Johns Hopkins U., Balt., 1955-56; economist Resources for Future, Washington, 1956-58; assoc. prof. urban econs. U. Chgo., 1959-64; economist Inst. Def. Analyses, Arlington, Va., 1964-66, cons., 1966-69; prof. econs. Washington U., St. Louis, 1966-70, Stanford U., (Calif.), 1970-83; Callaway prof. econs. Emory U., Atlanta, 1983—2001, chmn. dept., 1983-90, prof. emeritus, 2001—. Vis. assoc. prof. econs. Vanderbilt U., 1958—59; vis. sr. fellow Urban Inst., Washington, 1976—77; vis. prof. Sch. Bus. U. Calif., Berkeley, 1991. Author (with others): Regions, Resources and Economic Growth, 1960, Cities and Housing, 1969, Public Housing, 1974, Urban Economic Problems, 1975; co-author (with Allen C. Goodman): The Economics of Housing Markets, 1989. Mem. Presdl. Task on Urban Renewal, 1969, Presdl. Task Forces on Urban Affairs and Housing, 1980—81, Presdl. Commn. on Housing, 1981—82. With USCG, 1951—52. Mem.: Am. Real Estate and Urban Econs. Assn. Libertarian. Methodist. Office: Emory U Dept Econs Atlanta GA 30322-2240

MUTH, WILLIAM HENRY HARRISON, JR. medical/surgical nurse, nurse practitioner; b. Allentown, Pa., May 28, 1953; s. William Henry Harrison Sr. and Katie (Martin) M. BA in Psychology, BA in German, Wheaton (Ill.) Coll., 1979; MDiv, Luth. Theol. Sem., 1987; BSN, Cath. U. Am., 1990, MSN, 1998. RN; cert. med.-surg. nurse; cert. adult nurse practitioner; cert. RNC, ACLS, BCLS, EMT. Vicar, chaplain Evangelical Luth. Ch. of Am., Allentown, Pa., 1985-87; neuro med-surg. nurse VA, Washington, 1990-91; commd. USAF, 1991-95; with Washington Hosp. Ctr., 1996—; med.-surg. staff nurse 7th Med. Group, Dyess AFB, Tex., 1991-93, staff nurse-staff devel., 1993, obstetric staff nurse, 1993-94, med-surg. staff nurse, 1994-95; lt. comdr. (0-4) USPHS, 1997—. Adult nurse practitioner Fed. Bur. Prisons, Fed. Correctional Instn., Sandstone, Minn.; neurol. med.-surg. nurse VAMC, Washington, 2000—. AIDS edn. vol. Dyess AFB and Local Schs., Abilene, Tex., 1993—; clin. pastoral educator Lehigh Valley Hosp., Allentown, 1986. Health profl. scholarship program VA, 1989-90. Mem. ANA, Am. Acad. Nurse Practitioners, Am. Assn. Nurse Practitioners, Am. Legion, Officers Christian Fellowship, Reserve Officers Assn., Sigma Theta Tau Internat. (Kappa chpt.). Republican. Lutheran. Avocations: travel, reading, racquet ball, tennis, running. Home: PO Box 29139 Washington DC 20017-0139 E-mail: whhmjr@aol.com.

MUTO, SUSAN ANNETTE, religion educator, academic administrator; b. Pitts., Dec. 11, 1942; d. Frank and Helen (Scardamalia) M. BA in Journalism and English, Duquesne U., 1964; MA, U. Pitts., 1967, PhD in English Lit., 1970. Asst. dir. Inst. of Formative Spirituality Duquesne U., Pitts., 1965-80, dir., 1980-88, faculty coord. grad. programs in foundational formation, 1979-88, prof., 1981—. Guest lectr. formative reading various colls. and cmty. orgns., 1970—. Author: Catholic Spirituality from A to Z: An Inspirational Dictionary, 2000, Deep Into the Thicket: Soul Searching Meditations Inspirted by the Spiritual Canticle of Saint John of the Cross, Praying the Lord's Prayer with Mary. Mem. Soc. for Sci. Study of Religion, Epiphany Assn. (exec. dir. 1988—), Phi Kappa Phi. Home: 820 Crane Ave Pittsburgh PA 15216-3050 E-mail: samuto@epiphanyassociation.org.

MUTTERS, DAVID RAY, real estate broker; b. Ashland, Ky., Apr. 2, 1949; s. Frank R. and Ruth Evelyn (Duncan) M. AB, U. Ashland, 1974. Lic. real estate broker, Fla. Mil. police sgt. U.S. Army, 1968-70; painter Ashland (Ky.) Oil Inc., 1970-73; asst. purchaser Ky. Road Oiling Inc., Ashland, 1973-77; v.p. Anderson Radio Inc., Bluefield, W.Va., 1977-80; pres., owner Advanced Comm. Inc., 1980-82; broker, salesman Douglas Realty Inc., Cape Coral, Fla., 1982-91; pres., broker Coldwell Bankers David R. Mutters Realty Group, Inc., 1991—. Mem. Cape Coral Bd. Realtors, Nat. Assn. Realtors, Cape Coral C. of C., Naples C. of C., Rush Lodge, Araba Temple, Cape Coral Shrine. Republican. Methodist. Avocations: boating, tennis. Home: Unit 106 2601 Marina Isle Way Jupiter FL 33477-9426 Office: Arvida Realty Svcs 902 S US Hwy 1 Jupiter FL 33477 Fax: 561 744-1694. E-mail: david@jupiterproperties.com.

MUTTI, ALBERT FREDERICK, minister; b. Hopkins, Mo., Feb. 13, 1938; s. Albert Frederick and Phyllis Margaret (Turner) M.; m. Etta Mae McClurg, June 7, 1959; children: Timothy Allen, John Frederick, Martin Kent. AB, Cen. Meth. Coll., 1960; MDiv., Garrett-Evang. Theol. Sem., 1963; DMin., St. Paul Sch. Theology, 1975; DD, Baker U., 1993, Ctrl. Meth. Coll., 2000. Civ pastor Union Star Charge, Mo., 1963-65; sr. pastor Crossroads Parish, Savannah, 1965-74; assoc. coun. dir. Mo. West Conf. UMC, Kansas City, 1974-80, coun. dir., 1980-82; sr. pastor First United Meth. Ch., Blue Springs, Mo., 1982-87; dist. supt. Cen. Dist. UMC, 1987-89; dist. supr. Kansas City N. Dist., 1989-92; bishop Kans. Area United Meth. Ch., Topeka, 1992—. Chair Savannah Cmty. Betterment, 1971; bd. mem. St. Mary's Hosp., Blue Springs, 1986; dir. ARC, Savannah, 1968; bd. Discipleship, Nashville, bd. Global Ministries, N.Y.; pres. Mo. Coun. Chs., Jefferson City, Gen. Commn. on Christian Unity, Dean Mo. Area Ministers Sch., Curator, Ctrl. Meth. Coll.; trustee St. Paul Sch. Theology; organizer Rural, Religion and labor Coun. Kans. Named Disting. Alumni Ctrl. Meth. Coll.; recipient Grad. award St. Paul Sch. Theology. Home: 6841 SW Dunstan Ct Topeka KS 66610-1406 Office: 4201 SW 15th St Topeka KS 66604-2412 E-mail: ksbishumc@mindspring.com.

MUTTI, JOHN HARMON, economics educator; b. Urbana, Ill., Nov. 5, 1947; s. Ralph Joseph and Kathryn (Harmon) M.; m. Janet Ruth Clark, Apr. 11, 1971; children: James, Michael, Glenn. BA, Earlham Coll., Richmond, Ind., 1968; PhD, U. Wis., 1974. Vol. Peace Corps, Fundación, Colombia, 1968-70; economist U. Wyo., Laramie, 1974-87, asst. prof., 1974-78; assoc. prof. U. Iowa, 1978-82, prof., 1982-87; Sidney Meyer prof. econs. Grinnell (Iowa) Coll., 1987—. Economist Office Internat. Taxation, U.S. Treasury Dept., Washington, 1977, 83; sr. staff internat. economist Pres.'s Coun. Econ. Advisers, Washington, 1985-86; cons. U.S. Dept. State, Washington, 1974, U.S Treasury Dept., 1984, Volume Shoe Corp., Topeka, 1984-85, Govt. of Colombia, Bogota, 1987-88. Author: Changing Patterns of U.S. Indusrial Activity, 1983, U.S. Adjustment Policies in Trade Impacted Industries, 1985; contbr. articles to econ. jours. Bd. dirs. Greater Grinnell Devel. Corp. Recipient Outstanding Tchr. award U. Wyo. Coll. Commerce and Industry, 1986. Mem. Am. Econ. Assn. Home: 1433 Broad St Grinnell IA 50112-1422

MUTUNAYAGAM, N. BRITO, architecture and planning educator, associate dean; b. Quilon, Kerala, India; came to U.S., 1976; BSc in Engring., Kerala U., Trivandrum, India, 1963; D.T.C.P., Sch. Planning, New Delhi, 1967; M Engring., Asian Inst. Tech., Bangkok, 1974; D.E.D.P., Va. Tech., Blacksburg, 1981. Jr. engr. Kerala Govt., 1963-64, town planner, 1964-77; instr. Va. Tech., Blacksburg, 1977-81; assoc. prof. Coll. Architecture, U. Nebr., Lincoln, 1981-90, prof., 1990—, assoc. dean, 1994—. Cons. several archtl. firms, Nebr., Iowa, Tex., Mass., Mo., Ariz., Wash., Calif., 1984—; mem. Speakers Bur., U. Nebr., Lincoln, 1996—. Co-author: Cartography and Site Analysis, 1985, Designing With Solid Models Study Guide, 1995, Dimensions Reference Guide, 1995, Command Reference Manual, 1995. Fellow Ctr. for Great Plains Studies, 1985—; grad. fellow U. Nebr., 1988—. Mem. Am. Planning Assn., Nat. Geog. Soc. Avocations: computer graphics, music, television, video recording, model ships. Office: U Nebr 210 Architecture Hall Lincoln NE 68588-0106

MUTZ, GREGORY THOMAS, insurance company executive; b. Indpls., Dec. 19, 1945; BA, DePauw U., 1967; JD, U. Mich., 1973. Chmn. bd. dir. AMLI Realty Co. subs. UICI, Chgo., 1980—; chmn. bd. trustees AMLI

Residential Properties Trust; pres., CEO UICI, Dallas, 1999—. Bd. dirs. Nat. Multifamiy Housing Coun., Chgo., 1995—, Alleghany/Chgo. Trust, 1996—. Lt. U.S. Army, 1968-69, Vietnam. Office: UICI 4001 McEwen Dr Ste 200 Dallas TX 75244

MUTZ, OSCAR ULYSSES, manufacturing and distribution executive; b. Edinburg, Ind., Feb. 12, 1928; s. Harold Winterberg and Laura Belle (Sawin) M.; m. Jean Greiling, Aug. 22, 1948; children: Marcia, H. William. BS, Ind. U., 1949. Vice pres. Peerless Corp., Indpls., 1954-63; v.p., gen. mgr. Space Conditioning, Inc., Harrisonburg, Va., 1964-66; v.p., treas. Cosco, Inc., Columbus, Ind., 1966-67; exec. v.p., 1967-69; pres., 1969-71; chmn. bd. Court Manor Corp., Columbus, 1971-73; pres. Jenn Air Corp., Indpls., 1973-75; pres., CEO Mutz Corp., 1975-81; pres., dir. Haag Drug Co., 1977-78; pres. Forum Group, Inc. (merger Mutz Corp. and Excepticon, Inc.), Indpls., 1981-91; chmn., CEO, bd. dirs. Capital Industries, Inc., 1991-96; chmn. Lakeland Auto Mall, 1996—. Pres. Ct. Manor Corp., co-chmn. bd. dirs. Sargent & Greenleaf, Safemasters; pres. Security Group, Inc., 1991—, also bd. dirs. Nat. trustee Fellowship Christian Athletes, 1985-91, chmn. nat. conf. ctr., 1994-96; mem. pres. coun. and dean's adv. coun. Ind. U. Mem. Ind. Mfrs. Assn. (chmn. 1980), Acad. Alumnae Fellows Ind. U. Sch. Bus., Naples Yacht Club, Port Royal Club, Royal Poinciana Country Club. Republican. Baptist. Office: Mutz Corp 625 Admiralty Parade Naples FL 34102-7802

MUTZ, STEVEN HERBERT, lawyer; b. Rockville Centre, N.Y., July 9, 1958; s. Herbert Edward and Theresa A. M.; m. Bernadette Jane Shaw, Aug. 8, 1987. BA in Econs., St. John's U., 1979, JD summa cum laude, 1982. Bar: N.Y. 1983, U.S. Dist. Ct. (ea. and so. dists.) N.Y. 1983. Law intern to presiding justice N.Y. Supreme Ct., Mineola, 1982; assoc. Sandback & Birnbaum, 1982-84, Salvatore R. Gerbasi, Mineola, 1984, Schiavetti, Geisler, Corgan, Socia, DeVito et al, N.Y.C., 1984—; mng. atty. Schiavetti, Geisler, Corgan, Soscia, DeVito, Gabriele & Nicholson, White Plains, N.Y., 1989—, ptnr., 1991-99; mng. and trial atty. Wolf & Fuhrman, N.Y.C., 1999-2000; sr. assoc. Gordon & Silber, 2000—. Counsel to Senator Dean G. Skelos, Rockville Centre, 1986. Mem. ABA, N.Y. State Bar Assn., Omicron Delta Epsilon. Avocations: swimming, tennis, travel. Office: Wolf & Fuhrman Ste 210 855 Ave of the Americas New York NY 10001

MUUSS, ROLF EDUARD, retired psychologist, educator; b. Tating, Germany, Sept. 26, 1924; came to U.S., 1953, naturalized, 1992. s. Rudolf A. and Else M.; m. Gertrude Louise Kremser, Dec. 22, 1953 (dec. April 1999); children: Michael John (dec.), Gretchen Elise. Diploma, Tchr. Coll., Flensburg, Germany, 1951; student, U. Hamburg, Germany, 1951, Ctrl. Mo. State Coll., 1951-52, Columbia Tchrs. Coll., 1952; MEd, Western Md. Coll., 1954; PhD, U. Ill., 1957. Tchr. pub. sch., Germany, 1945-46, 51, 52-53; substitute prin. Germany, 1952-53; tchr. trainee U.S. Office Edn., 1951-52; houseparent Child Study Ctr., Balt., 1953; grad. asst. U. Ill., 1954-57; rsch. assoc. prof. Iowa Child Welfare Rsch. Sta., State U. Iowa, 1957-59; rsch. cons., 1960, 61; mem. faculty Goucher Coll., 1959-95, prof. edn., 1964-95, chmn. dept., 1972-75, dir. spl. edn., 1977-92, Elizabeth C. Todd disting. prof., 1980-85, chmn. dept. sociology and anthropology, 1983-85, prof. emeritus, 1995—. Rsch. assoc. edn. Johns Hopkins, 1962-63; part-time or summer tchr. U. B.C., 1962, Johns Hopkins U., 1962, 65, U. Del., 1965, Towson U., 1967, U. Ill., 1967; tchg. assoc. Sheppard and Enoch Pratt Hosp., 1969-80; guest lectr. Tchrs. Coll., Kiel, Fed. Republic Germany, 1977-78; hearing officer spl. edn. cases State of Md., 1980-96. Author: First-Aid for Classroom Discipline Problems, 1962, Theories of Adolescence, 1962, 5th edit., 1988, 6th edit., 1996, Grundlagen der Jugendpsychologie, 1982; also numerous articles; editor: Adolescent Behavior and Society: A Book of Readings, 1971, 4th edit., 1990, 5th edit., 1998. Served with German Air Force, 1942-45. Recipient award for disting. scholarship Goucher Coll., 1979; grantee Andrew W. Mellon Found., 1976-77 Fellow Am. Psychol. Soc., Am. Psychol. Assn., Md. Psychol. Assn. (treas. 1971-73); mem. Balt. Psychol. Assn. (chmn. membership com. 1966, v.p. 1970-71), Soc. Rsch. Child Devel., Soc. Rsch. on Adolescence, Kappa Delta Pi (v.p. Alpha chpt. 1956-57), Phi Delta Kappa. Home: 1540 Pickett Rd Lutherville Timonium MD 21093-5822 E-mail: rmuuss@goucher.edu.

MUZYKA, JENNIFER LOUISE, chemist, educator; b. Fredericksburg, Va., Nov. 9, 1963; d. Kie Muzyka and Jo Anne (Martin) Cepeda; m. Mark Stephan Meier, June 4, 1994; 1 child, Maxwell Stephan Meier. BS in Chemistry, U. Dallas, 1985; PhD in Organic Chemistry, U. Tex., 1990. Asst. prof. Roanoke Coll., Salem, Va., 1990-94, Centre Coll., Danville, Ky., 1994-98, assoc. prof., 1998—. Petroleum Rsch. Fund summer faculty fellow U. Ky., 1992. Contbr. articles to profl. jours. Grantee NSF, 2000, Ky. NSF EPSCOR, 1995, Petroleum Rsch. Fund, 1992; Engrs. Club Dallas scholar, 1981-82. Mem. AAUP, Am. Chem. Soc. (chair-elect Lexington sect. 1995-96, chair 1996-97, sec. Va. Blue Ridge sect. 1993-94), Ky. Acad. Sci. (Marcia Athey Rsch. grantee 1995, phys. scis. rep. to bd. 2001—), Coun. Undergrad. Rsch., Iota Sigma Pi (sec. Argentum chpt. 1993-94). Avocations: scuba diving, beading, hiking. Office: Centre Coll Chemistry Dept 600 W Walnut St Danville KY 40422-1309 E-mail: muzyka@centre.edu.

MUZYKA, RAY, application developer; MD, U. Alta., Can. Joint CEO BioWare Corp., Edmonton, Canada, 1995—. Software developer (electronic game) Baldur's Gate. Office: BioWare Corp 302 10508 82d Ave Edmonton AB T6E 6HZ Canada*

MUZYKA-MCGUIRE, AMY, marketing professional, nutrition consultant; b. Chgo., Sept. 24, 1953; d. Basil Bohdan and Amelia (Rand) Muzyka; m. Patrick J. McGuire, June 3, 1977; children: Jonathan, Elizabeth. BS, Iowa State U., 1975, postgrad., 1978—; registered dietitian, St. Louis U., 1980. Cert. dietitian. Home economist Nat. Livestock and Meat Bd., Chgo., 1975-77; dietary cons. various hosps. and nursing homes, Iowa, 1978-79; supr. foodsvc. Am. Egg Bd., Park Ridge, Ill., 1980-83; assoc. dir., mgr. foodsvc. Cole & Weber Advt., Seattle, 1984-85; prin., owner Food and Nutrition Comms., Federal Way, Wash., 1986—. Co-author: Turkey Foodservice Manual, 1987; editor: (newsletter) Home Economists in Business, 1975-77, Dietitians in Business and Industry, 1982-85; Food Net on Internet, 1995—; contbr. articles to profl. jours. Active Federal Way Women's Network, 1986-87. Named Outstanding Dietitian of Yr. North Suburban Dietetic Assn., 1983. Mem. Am. Dietetic Assn., Internat. Foodsvc. Editorial Coun., Consulting Nutritionists, Vegetarian Nutrition, Home Economists in Bus. Avocations: gardening, travel, music, food and beverage tastings. Home: 5340 SW 315th St Federal Way WA 98023-2034

MWENDA, KENNETH KAOMA, legal consultant, advisor, educator; LLB, U. Zambia, 1990; Gr.Dip, LCCI, U.K, 1991; DMS, IoC, U.K, 1992; BCL, U. Oxford, U.K., 1994; MBA, U. Hull, U.K, 1995; DBA, Pacific Western U., L.A., 1996, PhD in Publs., 1999; PhD, U. Warwick, U.K., 2000. Cert. Bar, Zambia, 1991; cert. cumpolsory edn., devels. in comml. securities, intellectual property law. Worked in trust funds and co-financing dept. Vice-Presidency of World Bank, Washington, 1998-99, worked in poverty reduction, mgmt. and pub. sector reform unit, 1999; worked as counsel in legal dept. World Bank, 1999-2000, projects officer, 2000—. Vis. prof. U. Miskolc Sch. Law, Hungary, 1996; lectr. U. Zambia Law Sch., 1991—95, vis. prof., 2001; lectr. Warwick U. Law Sch., 1995—98; spkr. and presenter in field. Author: Legal Aspects of Corporate Capital and Finance, 1999, Contemporary Issues In Corporate Finance and Investment Law, 2000, Banking Supervision and Systemic Bank Restructuring, 2000, Zambia's Stock Exchange and Privatization Programme, 2001, The Dynamics of Market Integration: African Stock Exchange's in the New Millennium, 2000, Banking and Microfinance Regulation and Supervision: Lessons from Zambia, 2002. Tutor U. Zambia Law Sch., 1991-95. Staff Devel. fellow in law U. Zambia, 1991, U. Yale Law Faculty fellow, 1998; Rhodes scholar U. Zambia, 1992, U. Oxford, 1992-94, U. Hull, 1994-95. Fellow Royal Soc. Arts. of England, Inst. Commerce of England; mem. Internat. Bar Assn., Law Assn. of Zambia, Brit. Assn. Lawyers for Def. of Unborn. Office: The World Bank 1818 H St NW Washington DC 20433-0001 E-mail: kmwenda@yahoo.com., kmwenda@worldbank.org.

MYCIELSKI, JAN, mathematician, educator; b. Wisniowa, Poland, Feb. 7, 1932; s. Jan and Helena (Bal) M.; m. Emilia Przezdziecka, Apr. 25, 1959. MS, U. Wroclaw, Poland, 1955, PhD, 1957. With Inst. Math., Polish Acad. Scis., Wroclaw, 1956-68; prof. math. U. Colo., Boulder, 1969—. Vis. prof. Case Western Res. U., Cleve., 1967, U. Colo., 1967, Inst. des Hautes Etudes Scientifiques, Bures-sur-Yvette, 1978-79, dept. math. U. Hawaii, 1987; attache de recherche Centre National de la Recherche Scientifique, Paris, 1957-58; asst. prof. U. Calif., Berkeley, 1961-62, 70; long-term vis. staff mem. Los Alamos Nat. Lab., 1989-90. Author over 150 rsch. papers. Recipient Stefan Banach prize, 1965, Alfred Jurzykowski award, 1977, Waclaw Sierpinski medal, 1990. Mem. Am. Math. Soc., Polish Math. Soc., Assn. for Symbolic Logic. Office: U Colo Dept Math Boulder CO 80309-0001

MYCOSKIE, CHRISTOPHER RYAN, reporter; b. Arlington, Tex., Dec. 15, 1978; s. Philip John and Cynthia (Sansing) M.; stepson of Gary Glenn Wood and Diane King Rudy. Student, U. Mo., 1997-2000. Sports corr. WBAP-AM, Dallas, 1997-2000; sports dir. KCOU-FM, Columbia, Mo., 1998-2000; tv news reporter KOMU-TV, 1998-2000, WOI-TV, West Des Moines, Iowa, 2000—; sports reporter KESN-FM, Arlington, Tex., 2001—. Recipient Excellence in Sports Writing award Journalism Edn. assn., 1994, 95. Mem. Soc. Profl. Journalists, U. Mo. Alumni Assn. Presbyterian. Home: 3008 James Ave Fort Worth TX 76110 E-mail: sportslounge@yahoo.com.

MYDLAND, GORDON JAMES, judge; b. nr. Hetland, S.D., May 12, 1922; s. Jacob and Anna (Hetl) M.; m. Lorrie Grange, May 29, 1958; 1 child, Gabriel. BS, S.D. State U., 1947; JD, U. S.D., 1956. Bar: S.D. 1956. Pvt. practice law, Brookings, S.D., 1956-69, Lake Preston, 1973; S.D. circuit judge, 1973-87; presiding judge (3d Jud. Circuit), 1975, 79-80; S.D. state's atty. Brookings County, 1959-62; mem. S.D. State Senate, 1963-68; atty. gen. S.D., 1968-72; ret., 1987. Part-time instr. constl. and bus. law S.D. State U., 1956-65 Mem. S.D. Code Compilation Commn., 1964-68. Served with USNR, 1943-46. Mem. Am. Legion. Lutheran.

MYDLO, JACK HENRY, surgeon, researcher; b. Phila., June 12, 1956; s. Morris and Helen (Finkelstein) M.; m. Jolie Lynn Kanter, June 15, 1986; 1 child, Ariel. BA, SUNY, Buffalo, 1977; MD, SUNY, Bklyn., 1981. Diplomate Am. Bd. Urology. Intern in surgery Montefiore/Einstein, Bronx, 1981-82, resident in surgery, 1982-83, resident in urology, 1983-86; fellow in urology Meml. Sloan-Kettering, N.Y.C., 1986-89; asst. prof. urology SUNY Health Sci. Ctr., Bklyn., 1989-98, assoc. prof. urology, 1998—; head uro-oncology Kings County Hosp., 1989—; chief urology divsn. Woodhull Med. Ctr., 1994—; prof., chmn. dept. urology Temple U. Sch. Medicine, Philadelphia, 2000—. Mem. operating room com. Kings County Hosp., Bklyn., 1990-93; mem. urology selection com. SUNY Health Sci. Ctr., Bklyn., 1990—, med. sch. interview com., 1994—, med. student mentor program, 1994—. Contbr. articles to profl. jours. Recipient 2nd prize for rsch. Valentine Competition, N.Y.C., 1985; Urology fellow F.C. Valentine Assn., 1986-88. Fellow ACS (1st prize for rsch. 1985), Internat. Coll. Surgeons; mem. Am. Assn. Cancer Rsch., Am. Urological Assn. (scholar 1986-88), Am. Assn. Clin. Urologists, Soc. Univ. Urologists. Avocations: photography, cycling, audiophile, drums. Office: Temple U Hosp Dept Urology 3401 N Broad St Philadelphia PA 19140

MYER, DONALD BEEKMAN, architect; b. Cleve., Aug. 25, 1937; s. Beekman Walter and Jennie Helen (Gimpel) M.; m. Ellen Jane Schwartz, June 10, 1970; 1 child, Jamie Beekman. BArch, U. Ill., 1961, MArch, 1962. Registered architect Va., D.C. Supervisory architect Nat. Park Svc., Phila., Washington, Cape, Mass., 1962-65; asst. sec. Commn. Fine Arts, Washington, 1965-97; adminstrn., budget and grants cons. Keyes, Lethbridge & Condon, Architects, 1968-70; clk. of works Washington Nat. Cathedral, 1998-2001; curator bldg. and grounds Tudor Place, Georgetown, 2001—02; strategic counsel cons., 2002—. Cons. Preservation Galveston (Tex.) History Found., 1968-69, Joint Com. on Landmarks, Washington, 1969; faculth cons. Sch. of Arch., Cath. U. of Am., 1990—. Author: Bridges and the City of Washington, 1974, Building Potomac Aqueduct, 1975; editor: Centennial History of Washington AIA, 1987. Mem. faculty Smithsonian Resident Assocs., Washington, 1973-81; pres. Washington Archtl. Found., 1998-2000; trustee Com. of 100 on the Fed. City, 1997-2000. Grantee Europa-Nostra Seminar Smithsonian Fgn. Currency Program, Poland, 1974; named one of 77 People to Watch award, Washingtonian Mag., 1987. Fellow AIA (chair hist. resources 1976, v.p. found. 1980, chpt. pres. 1987, fellows selection jury 1998-2000); mem. Woodley Park Men's Club (pres. 1979-82), Lambda Alpha (hon.). Republican. Avocations: bridge history, travel, photography, furniture and clock restoration. E-mail: emyer@erols.com.

MYER, DONNA GAIL, writer, health researcher; b. Otsego, Mich., Aug. 19, 1931; d. Herbert H. and Ruth V. (Bottomley) Haifley; m. Robert Eugene Myer, Aug. 20, 1950; children: Phillip, Daryl, Fritz. Diploma, White Pigeon (Mich.) High Sch., 1949; student, Kellog C.C., Battle Creek, Mich., 1959-97, We. Mich. U., 1967-94. Mushroom broker Mushroom Cave, Inc., Battle Creek, Mich., 1969-77; sales www.featherart4you.com and pvt. parties. Author: Answers to Your Mushroom Questions Plus Recipes, 1977. Mem.: Battle Creek Soc. of Artists, Holistic Health Resources Assn. (editor newsletter 1995—2001, contbr.), Inst. for Learning in Retirement (curriculum com., bd. dirs.), Sturgis (Mich.) Hist. Soc., Am. Soc. Dowsers, Inc. Avocation: collecting books. Home: 319 Cornell Dr Battle Creek MI 49017-4611 Office: Holistic Health Resource Assn 181 North Ave Battle Creek MI 49017-3418 E-mail: morel7@aol.com.

MYER, JOHN DANIEL, II, small business owner; b. Columbus, Ohio, Apr. 25, 1950; s. John Daniel and Virginia Lee (Julian) M.; m. Mary Lynn Ivy Vickerman, Oct. 9, 1976; children: J. Daniel, Carolyn Ivy. BA, Ohio State U., 1973. Underwriter Continental Ins. Co., Columbus and Detroit, 1973-78; regional underwriting mgr. Universal Underwriters Inc., Columbus, 1978-80; prin., owner Julian-Myer Ins. Agy., 1980-85; v.p., owner-operator Lynn Enterprises Inc., Asheville, N.C., 1985-99; owner, operator Mighty Mac, Inc., Hilton Head Island, S.C., 2000—. Founder, chmn. Buncombe County Young Reps., Asheville, 1988-90; cons., bd. dirs. Jr. Achievement, Asheville, 1989-2000, chmn. 1993-94; chmn. bd. Buncombe County Am. Heart Assn., Western N.C., 1990-94; bd. dirs. Leadership Asheville IX, 1990-91; v.p. leadership Asheville Found., 1992-94; pres. Buncombe County Rep. Men's club, 1994-95; bd. dirs. WNC Better Bus. Bur., 1996-2000. Named Agt. of Month, Ind. Ins. Agts., 1983, Golden Ladle award Little Caesars, 1990. Mem. Ohio Jaycees (govt. affairs program mgr. 1983-85, Outstanding Program Mgr. award 1984, Seiji Horiuchi award 1984), Asheville C. of C., Young Bus. Club (show dir. 1982-84), Highlands Sportscar Club, Henderson Ville C. of C. (small bus. leader 1997). Avocations: skiing, photography, sports car racing. Home: 8 Whitetail Deer Ln Hilton Head Island SC 29926-1832 Office: Mighty Mac Inc PO Box 5160 15 Palmetto Office Park Hilton Head Island SC 29938 E-mail: itzapie@aol.com.

MYER, WARREN HITESH, mortgage broker, internet advertising executive; b. New Delhi, India, Sept. 8, 1961; s. Hana N.S. and Veena Myer; m. Suki Myer, Aug. 15, 1991. MS, U. Del., 1986; MBA, U. Chgo., 1990. Instr. U. Del., Newark, 1984-86; mem. tech. staff Lachman Assoc., Naperville, Ill., 1986-88; sys. mgr. Pyramid Tech., San Jose, Calif., 1988-91; pres. Loan World Inc., 1991—, Bestrate.com, Inc., San Jose, 1995—. Inventor in field. Avocation: windsurfing. Home: 1421 Old Piedmont Rd San Jose CA 95132-2417 Office: Myers Internet Inc 2160 Lundy Ave Ste 128 San Jose CA 95131

MYERBERG, MARCIA, investment banker; b. Boston, Mar. 25, 1945; d. George and Evelyn (Lewis) Katz; m. Jonathan Gene Myerberg, June 4, 1967 (div. Mar. 1994); 1 child, Gillian Michelle. BS, U. Wis., 1966. Corp. trust adminstr. Chase Manhattan Bank, N.Y.C., 1966-67; asst. cashier Glore Forgan, Wm. R. Staats, Phoenix, 1967-68; bond portfolio analyst Trust Co. of Ga., Atlanta, 1969-72; asst. v.p. 1st Union Nat. Bank, Charlotte, N.C., 1973-78; dir. cash mgmt. Carolina Power & Light Co., Raleigh, 1978-79; sr. v.p., treas. Fed Home Loan Mortgage Corp., Washington, 1979-85; dir. Salomon Bros. Inc., N.Y.C., 1985-89; sr. mng. dir. Bear, Stearns & Co. Inc., 1989-93; mng. dir. Bear, Stearns Home Loans, London, 1989-93; chief exec. Myerberg & Co., L.P., N.Y.C., 1994—. Home: 37 W 12th St Apt 6K New York NY 10011-3205 Office: 780 3rd Ave New York NY 10017-2024

MYERHOLTZ, RALPH W., JR. retired chemical company executive, chemist, researcher; b. Bucyrus, Ohio, July 29, 1926; s. Ralph W.E. and Vera (Kirkland) M.; m. Lois Ellen Corgan, June 24, 1951; children: Carl Alan, Lynne Elaine Myerholtz Patterson. BS, Purdue U., 1950; PhD in Organic Chemistry, Northwestern U., 1954. Project chemist Standard Oil Co. (Ind.), Whiting, Ind., 1954-58; group leader Amoco Chem. Corp., 1958-66, rsch. assoc., 1966-69, dir. polymer physics divsn. Naperville, Ill., 1969-86. Contbr. articles to profl. jours.; holder 7 patents. Trustee Greenfield (Ind.) Pub. Libr., 1995—; radio officer CD, Naperville, 1971-81; scoutmaster Boy Scouts Am., Hammond, Ind., 1955-59. Sgt. U.S. Army, 1944-46, PTO. Mem. Am. Chem. Soc., Sigma Xi, Pi Kappa Phi, Phi Lambda Upsilon. Avocations: photography, electronics, woodcarving, nature/environment. Home: 1125 Cricket Reel Greenfield IN 46140-2805

MYEROWITZ, P(AUL) DAVID, cardiac surgeon; b. Balt., Jan. 18, 1947; s. Joseph robert and Merry (Brown) M.; m. Susan Karen Macks, June 28, 1967 (div.); children: Morris Brown, Elissa Suzanne, Ian Matthew. BS, U. Md., 1966; MD, 1970; MS, U. Minn., 1977. Intern in surgery U. Minn., Mpls., 1970-71, resident in surgery, 1971-72, 74-77; resident in cardiothoracic surgery U. Chgo., 1977-79; practice medicine specializing in cardiovascular surgery Madison, Wis., 1979—; asst. prof. thoracic and cardiovascular surgery U. Wis., 1979-85; assoc. prof., 1985; chief sect. cardiac transplantation, 1984-85; Karl P. Klassen prof., 1985-97; chief thoracic and cardiovascular surgery Ohio State U. and Hosps., Columbus, 1985-97. Author: Heart Transplantation; contbr. articles to profl. jours. Served with USPHS, 1972-74. Mem. ACS, Am. Coll. Cardiology, Soc. Thoracic Surgeons, Am. Assn. Thoracic Surgeons. Jewish. E-mail: hrttx1@aol.com.

MYERS, A. MAURICE, transportation executive; b. Long Beach, Calif., May 20, 1940; s. Walter Ray and H. Priscilla (Larsen) M.; m. Elizabeth Jean Ashburn, July 16, 1960; children: Michele, Tracy, Leanne. BA, Calif. State U., Fullerton, 1964; MBA, Calif. State U., Long Beach, 1972. Fin. mgr. Ford Motor Co., Newport Beach, Calif., 1964-72; fin. cons. Merrill Lynch, 1972-75; mktg. dir. Continental Airlines, L.A., 1975-82; v.p. ops. On TV, 1982-83; pres., CEO Aloha Airgroup, Honolulu, 1983-93; pres. Am. West Airlines, Phoenix, 1993-95; chmn., pres., CEO, bd. dirs. Yellow Corp., Overland Park, Kans., 1996-99; chmn., pres., CEO Waste Mgmt., Houston, 1999—. Bd. dirs. Hawaiian Elec. Industries, Honolulu, Tetoro Petroleum Inc., San Antonio, Pleasant Holidays, West Lake Village, Calif., Tegoro Petroleum. Bd. dirs. Greater Houston Partnership, Keep Am. Beautiful. Mem. Waialae Country Club (Honolulu). Avocations: reading, golf, travel. Office: Waste Management 1001 Fannin St Ste 4000 Houston TX 77002-6711

MYERS, ADELE ANNA, artist, educator, nun; b. Bklyn., Oct. 4, 1925; d. Everett Ecil and Anna Maria (Menig) M. Student, U. Notre Dame; BS in Edn., Fordham U., 1956; MA in Fine Arts, Villa Schifanoia, Florence, Italy, 1962; postgrad., NYU, Pratt Graphics Ctr., Columbia U. Cert. permanent tchr. art, grades K-12, N.Y.; joined Sparkill Dominican Sisters, Roman Cath. Ch., 1944. Tchr. art Monsignor Scanlon H.S., Bronx, N.Y., 1956-60, Albertus Magnus H.S., Bardonia, 1961-62; founder, dir. Thorpe Intermedia Gallery, Sparkill, 1976-91; prof., chairperson art dept. St. Thomas Aquinas Coll., 1962-78, adj. prof., 1978-99. Design cons. sr. housing devels. Thorpe Village and Dowling Gardens, Sparkill, N.Y., 1981—; mem. adv. bd. Bogliasco Found., N.Y.C. and Italy, 1997—; freelance curator contemporary art exhbns., 1986—. Commd. works include cross in fresco and cement St. Peter's Ch., Yonkers, N.Y., 1990, outdoor sidewalk mosaic Thorpe Village, 1997, stained glass windows for meditation rm. Dowling Gardens, 1996, outdoor mosaic, meditation garden Dominican Sisters, Sparkill, 2001, stained glass windows Our Lady of Rosary Chapel, Dominican Convent, 2001; exhibited sculpture in fresco and cement, most recently at ArtBldrs. Gallery, Jersey City, 1994-95, Rockland Ctr. for Arts, 1995, 96, 99, St. John's Chapel Gallery, Newark, 1996, Piermont Flywheel Gallery, N.Y., 2002, Azarian-McCullough Gallery, Sparkill, N.Y., 2001, Visions Gallery, Albany, N.Y., 2001; one-woman shows include Hopper Ho. Art Ctr., Nyack, 1992, Piermont Flywheel Gallery, 1996, 98, 2000, 01, 02, ArtBldrs. Gallery, 1996, Old Ch. Cultural Ctr. Gallery, Demarest, N.J., 1997; represented in pub. and pvt. collections; works and exhibits reviewed in various publs., including N.Y. Times, Star Ledger, Suburban People, Arts Happenings; featured on cable TV program, N.J., 1988. Apptd. art in pub. places com. Rockland County, 1987-92; founding bd. dirs. Arts Fund Rockland, 1989-91. Postgrad. studies scholar Villa Schifanoia, 1960; Sister Adele Myers Scholarship established in her name St. Thomas Aquinas Coll., 1986; recipient award for Outstanding Contbn. in Field of Art, Rockland County Women's Network, Rockland C.C., Suffern, N.Y., 1980, 1st Ann. Arts award Rockland County Execs., 1987. Mem. Nat. Mus. Women in Arts, Internat. Sculpture Ctr., Christians in Visual Arts. Democrat. Avocations: reading, travel, visiting places of historical interest. Home: Dominican Convent 175 Route 340 Sparkill NY 10976-1041

MYERS, ALFRED FRANTZ, retired state education official, educator; b. Crooked Creek State Park, Pa., Feb. 19, 1936; s. Jacob Alfred Jr. and Ida Gertrude (Schaeffer) M. BA, Lehigh U., 1958, MA, 1966; postgrad., George Peabody Coll., 1971-72. Instr. Grand River Acad., Austinburg, Ohio, 1966, Culver (Ind.) Mil. Acad., 1966-68, Kiskiminetas Springs Sch., Saltsburg, Pa., 1968-71; asst. prof. social studies Ind. State U., Terre Haute, 1972-73; divsn. trainer Ency. Britannica, Rochester, N.Y., 1973-75; mgr. Rupp's, Kittanning, Pa., 1976-77; criminal justice sys. planner Pa. Commn. on Crime and Delinquency, Harrisburg, 1977-80; rsch. assoc. Pa. Dept. Edn., 1980-89, basic edn. assoc., 1989-98; assoc. EdVise, 1998-2001; ret. Vol. tchr. Global Vols., Xi'an, China, 1999. Social work Dominican Rep., 1958. Served to 1st lt. USAF, 1958-63, capt. USAFR, 1963-71. Mem.: ACLU, AAUP, Pa. Fedn. Tchrs., Pa. Coun. for Social Studies, Pa. Assn. Adult Continuing Edn., Pa. Ednl. Rsch. Assn., Nat. Coun. Social Studies, Mid. States Coun. for Social Studies (pres. 1987—88), Gay Lesbian and Straight Edn. Network, Conf. Latin Americanist Geographers, Am. Hist. Assn., Am. Fedn. Tchrs., Am. Evaluation Assn., Am. Ednl. Rsch. Assn., Am. Acad. Polit. and Social Sci., Acad. Polit. Sci., People for Am. Way., Pa. Hist. Assn., Orgn. Am. Historians, Nat. Braille Assn., Phi Beta Kappa, Phi Delta Kappa. Home: 849 Melissa Ct Enola PA 17025-1551

MYERS, ALLEN RICHARD, rheumatologist; b. Balt., Jan. 14, 1935; s. Ellis Benjamin and Rosina (Blumberg) M.; m. Ellen Patz, Nov. 26, 1960; children: David Joseph, Robert Todd, Scott Patz. BA, U. Pa., 1956; MD, U. Md., 1960. Diplomate Am. Bd. Internal Medicine, Am. Bd. Rheumatology. Intern Univ. Hosp., Balt., 1960-61, resident in medicine Ann Arbor, Mich., 1961-64; fellow in rheumatology Mass. Gen. Hosp. and Harvard Med. Sch., Boston, 1966-69; dir. clin. tng. rheumatology U. Pa. Sch. Medicine, Phila., 1969-72, chief rheumatology sect., 1972-78; dep. chair medicine Temple U. Sch. Medicine, 1978-84, acting chmn. medicine, 1984-86, dean, 1991-95, prof. medicine, 1978—, assoc. v.p. Health Scis. Ctr., 1988-95. Vis. prof. Cardiothoracic Inst., U. London, 1988; mem. med. adv. bd. Scleroderma Rsch. Found., Santa Barbara, Calif., 1986. Mem. editl. bd. Arthritis & Rheumatism, 1985—90, Brit. Jour. Rheumatology, 1989—94; editor: Systematic Scleroderma, 1985, Medicine, 1986, 1993, 1996, 2000. Pres. Phila. Health Care Congress, 1994—; mem. adv. com. Pa. Lupus Found., 1976—. With USPHS, 1964-66. Recipient Margaret Whitaker prize U. Md. Sch. Medicine, 1960, Lindback Found. award Temple, 1981; named Physician of Yr. Temple U. Hosp., 1986. Fellow: Am. Coll. Rheumatology (master 2000, master), ACP, Phila. Coll. Physicians (pres. 2000); mem.: Brit. Soc. Rheumatology, N.Y. Acad. Scis., Am. Fedn. Clin. Rsch., Phila. Rheumatism Soc. Avocations: walking, classical music, reading. Office: Temple U Sch Medicine 3400 N Broad St Philadelphia PA 19140-5104

MYERS, ARTHUR B. journalist, author; b. Buffalo, Oct. 24, 1917; s. Edward A. and Isabelle (Baker) M.; m. Irma H. Ashley, 1972. BA, Hobart Coll., 1939. Journalist Rochester (N.Y.) Times Union, 1948-52, Washington Post, 1956-57, Berkshire (Mass.) Eagle, 1957-64; contbg. editor Coronet mag., 1965-68; columnist Bergen Record, Hackensack, N.J., 1969-71; exec. editor Berkshire Sampler, Pittsfield, Mass., 1971-77; tchr. writing Mass. U. extension program and Berkshire Community Coll., 1958-62, Fairleigh Dickinson U., Teaneck, N.J., 1970, Cambridge (Mass.) Coll., 1989. Author: (with J. O'Connell) Safety Last: An Indictment of Auto Industry, 1966, Journalism Careers for the 70's, 1971, Analysis: The Short Story, 1975, Analysis: The Personal Profile Magazine Article, 1976, Kids Do Amazing Things, 1980, The Ghost Hunters, 1980, Sea Creatures Do Amazing Things, 1981; (with Irma Myers) Why You Feel Down and What You Can Do About It, 1982, The Ghostly Register, 1986, Ghosts of the Rich and Famous, 1988, The Ghostly Gazetteer, 1990, Ghost Hunter's Guide, 1993, The Cheyenne, 1992, The Pawnee, 1993, The First Movies, 1993, The First Baseball Game, 1993, The First Football Game, 1993, Drugs and Peer Pressure, 1995, Communicating with Animals, 1997; also short stories, articles. Mem. PEN, Nat. Writers Union, Mensa, Boston Authors Club. Home: 60 Grove St Apt 6202 Wellesley MA 02482-7716 E-mail: artmyers17@aol.com.

MYERS, C. ROBERT, association executive, marketing professional; b. New Brunswick, N.J., Dec. 16, 1949; s. Carleton I. and Alice H. Myers; m. Hilanne J. Myers, Apr. 27, 1974; children: Eric J., C. Ryan, Craig R. BS in Gen. Design, Drexel U., 1973. Dist. exec. Boy Scouts Am., Oakhurst, N.J., 1973-76, sr. dist. exec. Rochester, N.Y., 1976-78, asst. scout exec. Boston, 1991-97, dir. fin. and mktg. svcs., v.p. devel. Balt., 1997—; account exec. Giltspur Exhibits, Rochester, 1978-83; sr. account exec. Creative Prodns., Pittsburgh, Pa., 1983-84, DCA Exhibits, Horsham, 1984-87, GWF Assocs., Holmdel, N.J., 1987-90, Denby Assocs., Princeton, 1990-91. Chmn. ch. coun. Trinitarian United Ch. of Christ, Norton, Mass., 1996-97; asst. scoutmaster Boy Scouts of Am., Texas, Md., 1997—; deacon Hunt Valley Ch., 2000—. Mem. Ind. Order of Odd Fellows, Order of the Arrow (Vigil Honor award 1994). Avocations: jogging, hiking, photography. Home: 123 E Padonia Rd Lutherville Timonium MD 21093-2521 Office: Balt Area Coun Boy Scouts Am 701 Wyman Park Dr Baltimore MD 21211-2805 E-mail: bmyers@baltimoreBSA.org., crmscout@aol.com.

MYERS, CAROL MCCLARY, retired sales administrator, editor; b. Dawson, N.Mex. d. Joseph Franklin and Alberta Lenore (McGarvey) McClary; m. Dwight Andrew Myers, Sept. 16, 1950 (dec. Sept. 1995); children: Robert Andrew, Debra Ann, James Allen. MusB, U. Redlands, 1950. Cert. tchr., Calif. Tchr. music Barstow (Calif.) Pub. Schs., 1950-52; sec., acct. U.S. Army, Columbus, Ga., 1952-54; part-time sec. Robert Lafollette, Atty., Albuquerque, 1954-57; sec., acct. Midland Specialty Co., 1957-60; pvt. tchr. piano Oakland, N.J., 1960-70; organist, choir dir., ch. sec. Ramapo Valley Bapt., 1965-70; order fulfillment/invoicing U. N.Mex. Press, Albuquerque, 1974-76, sales mgr., 1976-88, ret., 1988. Editor (mag.) Book Talk, 1971-2001; (7 books) In Celebration of the Book: Literary New Mexico, 1982, Literary New Mexico: Essays From Book Talk, 1998. Recipient Edgar Lee Hewett award Hist. Soc. N.Mex., 1985, Paso Por Aquí award Rio Grande Hist. Collections, 1990. Mem. N.Mex. Libr. Assn. (hon. life, treas. 1989-91, bd. dirs. 1992-94), Rocky Mountain Book Pubs. Assn. (Jack D. Rittenhouse award 1994), Mountains and Plains Booksellers Assn. Republican. Avocations: piano playing, New Mexico Book League (vol. editor). Home: 8632 Horacio Pl NE Albuquerque NM 87111-3218

MYERS, CHARLES LAWRENCE, anesthesiologist; b. Houston, June 17, 1954; s. Charles Robert and Betty June (Simpson) M.; m. Deborah Louise Remont, Dec. 20, 1976; children: James, Brian, William. BS, La. State U., Baton Rouge, 1975; MD, La. State U., Shreveport, 1979. Diplomate Am. Bd. Anesthesiology. Intern La. State U. Med. Ctr., Shreveport, 1979-80; resident Parkland Meml. Hosp., Dallas, 1980-82; anesthesiologist Anesthesiology Assocs., Shreveport, 1982-85, Alexandria (La.) Anesthesia Svc., 1985-93, Profl. Anesthesiology Cons., Alexandria, 1993—. Col. La. Air NG. Home: 4914 Windermere Blvd Alexandria LA 71303-2458

MYERS, CLARK EVERETT, retired business administration educator; b. Rossville, Kans., Oct. 19, 1915; s. Thad James and Rose I (Page) M.; m. Cora Henley Hepworth, May 7, 1942; children— Clark Everett, Richard G. Hepworth. BS, U. Kans., 1939, MBA, 1946; D.C.S., Harvard, 1956. Tchr. Auburn (Kans.) Sch., 1932-34, prin., 1934-36; instr. U. Kans., 1939-41; asst. prof. U. Tex., 1947-49, asso. prof., 1949-53, chmn. dept. mgmt., 1950-53; lectr. Harvard Grad. Sch. Bus. Adminstrn., 1953-54; dean Coll. of Commerce, prof. bus. adminstrn. Ohio U., 1954-57; dir. mgmt. devel. inst. Lausanne, Switzerland, 1957-60; lectr. Harvard Grad. Sch. Bus., 1960-61; dean Sch. Bus. Adminstrn., prof. mgmt. U. Miami, Coral Gables, Fla., 1961-68; dean Grad. Sch. Bus. Adminstrn., Emory U., Atlanta, 1968-75, prof. bus. adminstrn., 1975-85, prof. emeritus, 1985—. Editor: (with William R. Spriegel) The Writings of the Gilbreths, 1953. Served as lt. USNR, 1942-45. Fellow Acad. Mgmt.; mem. Am. Assn. Collegiate Schs. Bus. (exec. com. 1965-68, 1969-70, pres. 1970-71), Phi Kappa Phi, Sigma Iota Epsilon, Delta Sigma Pi, Beta Gamma Sigma, Phi Gamma Delta, Beta Alpha Psi. Home: 1082 Vistavia Cir Decatur GA 30033-3413

MYERS, CLAY, retired investment management company executive; b. Portland, Oreg., May 27, 1927; s. Henry Clay and Helen (Mackey) M.; m. Elizabeth Lex Arndt, Oct. 1, 1955; children: Richard Clay (dec.), Carolyn Elizabeth, David Hobson. BS, U. Oreg., 1949; postgrad., Northwestern Coll. Law, 1950-52; LHD (hon.), Ch. Div. Sch. of the Pacific, 1992. With 1st. Nat. Bank, Portland, 1949-53; with Conn. Gen. Life Ins. Co., Hartford and Portland, 1953-62, state mgr., 1960-62; v.p. Ins. Co. Oreg., Portland, 1962-65; asst. sec. state State of Oreg., Salem, 1965-67, sec. state, 1967-77, state treas., 1977-84; v.p. J.P. Morgan Investment Mgmt. Co., N.Y.C., 1984-89, Capital Cons. Inc., Portland, Oreg., 1989-92. Chmn. Oreg. House Adv. Com. Legis. Reapportionment, 1961; chmn. Oreg. Gov.'s Commn. on Youth, 1969-74 Author: (with others) Population Reapportionment Initiative Constitutional Amendment, 1952. Bd. dirs., treas. Ch. Divinity Sch. of Pacific, 1977-83; trustee Pacific U., 1989-92; vestryman Trinity Parish, Wall St., 1986-93; pres. Nat. Interfrat. Conf., 1986-87; mem. social responsibility in investing com. Nat. Episcopal Ch., 1983-87; trustee Ch. Pension Fund; bd. dirs. Ch. Life Ins. Co., 1991-97; sr. warden St. Andrew's, Nogales, Az., 2002—. Mem. Nat. Assn. State Treas. (past pres.), Multnomah Athletic Club (Portland), DeMolay Club (Legion of Honor), Lambda Chi Alpha (nat. pres. 1974-78), Sigma Nu Phi. Episcopalian. Home: PO Box 237 Tumacacori AZ 85640-0237

MYERS, DALE DEHAVEN, government, industry, aeronautics and space agency administrator; b. Kansas City, Mo., Jan. 8, 1922; s. Wilson and Ruth (Hall) M.; m. Marjorie Williams, Sept. 18, 1943; children— Janet Louise Myers Westling, Barbara Toby Myers Curtis. Student, Kansas City Jr. Coll., 1939-40; BS in Aero. Engring, U. Wash., Seattle, 1943; PhD (hon.), Whitworth Coll., 1970. Chief engr. missile devel. div. N. Am. Aviation, 1946-57, v.p., weapons systems mgr., 1957-63; asst. div. dir. advanced systems Rockwell Internat. Corp., El Segundo, Calif., 1963-64; v.p., program mgr. Rockwell Internat. Corp. (Apollo CSM programs), 1964-69, Rockwell Internat. Corp. (space shuttle program), 1969-70; asso. adminstr. manned space flight NASA, 1970-74; pres. N.Am. Aircraft ops. Rockwell Internat. Corp., corporate v.p.; Rockwell Internat., 1974-77; under-sec. Dept. Energy, Washington, 1977-79; pres., chief oper. officer Jacobs Engring. Group Inc., Pasadena, Calif., 1979-84; pres. Dale D. Myers & Assoc. Cons. Aerospace & Energy, 1984-86; dep. adminstr. NASA, Washington, 1986—. Mem. adv. com. NASA, Washington, 1984-86; responsible for Apollo Command and Svc. Module constrn. and launch, 1960's, for overall Apollo program Apollo 13 through 17, for complete Skylab program, for concepts and initiation of the Shuttle program. Contbr. articles to profl. jours. Dist. mgr. United Way, Greater L.A., 1983; U.S. rep. 22d conf. Internat. Atomic Energy Agy., Geneva, 1979; bd. dirs. Internat. Aero. Hall of Fame, San Diego, 1989. Recipient Meritorious Service award Compton (Calif.) Schs., 1977, Achievement award Los Angeles City Schs., 1976, Public Service award, 1969, Disting. Service medal Dept. Energy, 1979, Von Karman award Mus. of Sci. and Industry, L.A., 1987. Fellow AIAA (nat. dir.), Am. Astronautics Soc.; mem. Nat. Acad. Engring., Newcomen Soc. in N.Am., Calif. C. of C. (dir.), Calif. Roundtable, Sigma Alpha Epsilon. Presbyterian (elder). Clubs: Century Flying, Calif., (Los Angeles). Achievements include rsch. in and development of aerospace vehicles and mgmt. of large high tech. projects. Office: NASA 400 Maryland Ave SW Washington DC 20202-0001

MYERS, DANE JACOB, lawyer, podiatrist; b. Murray, Utah, June 20, 1948; s. Lorin LaVar Myers and Irma Lee (Bell) Willette; m. Mary Jo Jackson, June 22, 1970; children: Troy, Chad, Melissa, Apryll, Tristan, Remington. DPM, Pa. Coll. Podiatric Medicine, 1977; BA, U. Utah, 1983; JD, U. Ark., 1986. Bar: Ark 1986. Pres. Tooele (Utah) Foot Clinic, 1977-83; owner N.W. Ark. Foot Clinic, Rogers, Ark., 1983—; pvt. practice law Fayetteville, 1986-97. Served to maj med serv corps USAR, 1977—94. Mem.: APHA, ABA, Ark Podiatric Med Asn, Am Podiatric Med Asn, Am Soc Law and Med, Ark Bar Asn, Am Diabetes Asn, Am Col Foot and Ankle Surgeons (assoc.), Delta Theta Phi. Republican. Mem. Lds Ch. Avocations: golf, computers, history. Home: 2005 Oakhill Dr Springdale AR 72762 Office: NW Ark Foot Clinic 700 N 13th St Rogers AR 72756-3436 E-mail: danejmyers@hotmail.com.

MYERS, DANIEL WILLIAM, II, lawyer; b. Camden, N.J., Mar. 21, 1931; s. Charles Rudolph II and Myrtle Henrietta (Kress) M.; m. Eileen Ethel Kohn, Nov. 22, 1959; children: Susan Leigh, Meredith Ann Myers Winner, Kathryn Kress. BS in Commerce, U. Va., 1952, LLB, 1957. Bar: Va. 1957, N.J. 1958, U.S. Dist. Ct. N.J. 1958, U.S. Supreme Ct. 1980. Assoc. Lewis & Hutchinson, Camden, 1958-60; ptnr. Myers, Matteo, Rabii, Norcross & Landgraf, predecessors, Cherry Hill, N.J., 1960-89, Montgomery, McCracken, Walker & Rhoads, 1989-94, of counsel, 1994-98, Steven J. Jozwiak, Cherry Hill, N.J., 1998—. 1st lt. U.S. Army, 1952-54. Mem. N.J. Bar Assn., Va. Bar Assn., Camden County Bar Assn., Am. Arbitration Assn., Exch. Club (pres. Cherry Hill chpt. 1969). Republican. Lutheran. Home: 1 E Atlantic Ave Harvey Cedars NJ 08008 Office: 2201 Route 38 Ste 200 Cherry Hill NJ 08002-4370 Fax: 856-667-5322. E-mail: jozco@aol.com.

MYERS, DARLENE MARIE, dance studio owner, choreographer; b. Schenectady, N.Y., July 25, 1950; d. Raymond Charles and Marie (Walsh) M. Grad. high sch., Schenectady, N.Y. Dancer Pa. Ballet Co., Phila., 1968-70; tchr., choreographer Schenectady Civic Ballet, 1970-76, Electronic Body Arts, Albany, N.Y., 1978-79; dir. dance Schenectady Arts Council, 1978-79; ballet mistress, choreographer Saratoga Ballet Co., Saratoga Springs, N.Y., 1980-81; artistic dir. Guilderland (N.Y.) Ballet Workshop, 1980-84; head dance program SUNY, Albany, 1981-85; founder, dir. Myers Studio and Art Gallery, Schenectady, 1985—. Adj. prof. arts Union Coll., Schenectady, 1980-84, adj. prof. dance; cons. Proctors Theater, Schenectady, 1985—; dir. Myers Dance Co., Schenectady, 1985—, annual summer dance camp hiring guest tchrs. from. N.Y.C. Ballet; artistic dir. N.E. Ballet Co.; choreographer, producer annual full-length Nutcracker, Schenectady. Contbr. (jour. collection) Ariadne's Thread, 1982; choreographer ann. full-length Nutcrackers and a spring concert of new repetoire. Grantee CETA, 1978, 80, Adirondack Jr. Ballet, 1982, 83. Mem. Albany League of Arts. Avocations: hiking, walking, herbal gardening. Office: 1020 Barrett St Schenectady NY 12305-1102

MYERS, DARYL RONALD, engineer; b. Denver, July 12, 1948; s. James Elmer Myers and Betty Mae (Gannon) Welborn; m. Donna Lee Olsen, Oct. 3, 1990 (dec. Oct. 1995); m. Barbara Jane Bowker, Sept. 5, 1997. BS in Applied Math., U. Colo., 1970, postgrad., 1974-75. Staff physicist Smithsonian Radiation Biology Lab., Rockville, Md., 1974-78; metrology engr. Solar Energy Rsch. Inst. (now Nat. Renewable Energy Lab.), Golden, Colo., 1978-93; sr. staff scientist, team leader Photovoltaic Radiometric Measurements & Evaluation, 1993—. Project leader Joint U.S.-Saudi Arabian Solar Radiation Resource Assessment, 1997-2000, Joint Saudi Arabian/NASA Remote Sensing Validation Project, 1998—. Editor Optical Radiation News; contbr. articles to Solar Energy, Solar Cells and other profl. publs. Russian and German interpreter, Cultural Diversity Com., Arvada, Colo., 1992. With U.S. Army, 1970-74. Mem. ASTM, Precision Measurement Assn. (John Quincy Adams award 1979-80), Am. Solar Energy Soc., Coun. Optical Radiation Measurement, Math. Assn. Am. Democrat. Achievements include contribution of significant algorithms for interpolation and corrections to measured precipitable water, aerosol optical depth, and radiometric data used in developing national solar radiation data base and international projects to establish global climate change trends via ground and satellite based instrumentation; development of revised terrestrial of spectral solar radiation reference standards. Office: Nat Renewable Energy Lab 1617 Cole Blvd Golden CO 80401-3305

MYERS, DAVID RICHARD, youth organization financial executive; b. Plainfield, N.J., Oct. 5, 1948; s. George Kelsall and Margaret (Story) M.; 1 child: Christina Marie. BSBA, U. Kans., 1971; MBA in Fin., U. Mo., 1981. Check processor No. Trust Bank, Chgo., 1971; officer trainee Commerce Bank Kansas City, Mo., 1973-74; sales mgr. Sun Life of Can. Ins. Co., Kansas City, 1974-75; dist. exec. Boy Scouts Am., Des Moines, 1975-78, Kansas City, 1978-81, dir. fin. svcs. N.Y.C., 1981-84, dir. fin. and mktg. Phila., 1984-89; scout exec. Green Mountain Coun. Waterbury, Vt., 1989-98; dir. fin. mktg. Conn. Yankee Coun., Milford, Conn., 1998—. Guest lectr. Iowa State U., Ames, 1976-78, Pace U., N.Y.C., 1982-84; tech. 17 nat./regional meetings Boy Scouts Am., 1977-92, leader 3 overseas trips. Producer 12 in-house booklets, contbr. monthly in-house publs. Boy Scouts Am. Area chmn. United Way Phila., 1986-87; mem. cabinet United Way, Milford, 1999-2002; mem. Congl. redistricting com., 1980; bd. dirs. Jaycees, Iowa, Mo., 1972-81; lay reader, mem. vestry, Eucharistic minister Episcopalian Ch. 1st lt. USMC, 1971-72. James E. West fellow, 1994, Paul Harris fellow, 1997; recipient Medal of Peace, Govt. of Egypt, 1984, St. George award Episcopal Ch., 1997; named Man of Yr., Beta Theta chpt. Phi Kappa Tau, 1969, Keyman, Kansas City Jaycees, 1974. Mem. Nat. Soc. Fund Raising Execs., Phila. Ad Club, U. Kans. Alumni Assn. N.Y. (treas. 1982-84), U. Mo. Kansas City Alumni Assn., Rotary (past pres., bd. dirs.), SAR. Republican. Episcopalian. Avocations: camping, travel, art. Home: 79 Blue Hills Rd Monroe CT 06468-2053 Office: Conn Yankee Coun BSA 60 Wellington Rd PO Box 32 Milford CT 06460-0032 E-mail: dmyers04@snet.net.

MYERS, DEBRA TAYLOR, elementary school educator, writer; b. Balt., Feb. 5, 1953; d. James Zachary and Gene Elizabeth (Blubaugh) Taylor; m. Kenneth Lee Myers Jr., June 18, 1977; children: Kenneth Andrew, Katherine Elizabeth. BS in Elem. Edn., Towson State U., 1975, MEd, 1983. Cert. tchr., Md. 5th grade tchr. N.W. Mid. Sch., Taneytown, Md., 1975-80; home and hosp. sch. tchr. Balt. County Schs., 1992-93; tchr. educator in elem. edn. dept. Towson (Md.) State U., 1993-94; 2d grade tchr. Balt. County Pub. Schs., 1994—, mentor/trainer. gifted and talented resource tchr. Workshop leader, guest lectr. Harford (Md.) County Schs., Balt. County Schs., United Meth. Commn. on the Young Child, Balt.; primary talent devel. cadre mem., workshop dir., spkr. Contbr. articles to children's mags. and jours. Mem. Renew, A Randallstown Cmty. Group Assn., Balt., 1993—; bd. dirs. Child Devel. Ctr., Milford Mill United Meth. Ch., 1992—; coord. Jr. Fieldstone Garden Club. Recipient Outstanding Vol. award Balt. County PTA, 1992, 93, 94; named N.W. Area Educator of Yr., 1999. Mem. Kappa Delta Pi. Avocations: travel, reading, writing for children, volunteering, spending time with family. Home: 3607 Blackstone Rd Randallstown MD 21133-4213 Office: Randallstown Elem Sch 9103 Liberty Rd Randallstown MD 21133-3521

MYERS, DONALD LEE, university chief financial officer; b. Feb. 28, 1945; BS in Bus. Adminstrn., Shepherd Coll., 1968; MBA in Fin., Am. U., Washington. Asst. v.p. for fin., asst. treas. Am. U., Washington, 1975-80, treas., 1980-82, v.p. fin. and treas., 1982—. Bd. cons. Riggs Nat. Bank; treas., bd. mem. Washington Rsch. Libr. Consortium. Mem. DC C. of C., Econ. Club of Washington, Greater Washington Bd. of Trade, Nat. Ea. and So. Assns. of Coll. and Univ. Bus. Officers, Soc. of Coll. and Univ. Planners, Consortium of Univ. Treas. Office: Am U 4400 Massachusetts Ave NW Washington DC 20016-8033

MYERS, DOROTHY ROATZ, artist; b. Detroit, Mar. 24, 1921; d. Harry Agustus and Lola May (Kelly) Roats; children: Bruce, Leslie Ann, Douglas. Student, Antioch Coll., 1941, Corcoran Gallery Art Sch., 1943, Art Students League, 1965—. Asst. to design dir. Harper & Row Pub., N.Y.C., 1981-87. Lectr. and writer on art-related affairs. Contbr. revs. to profl. publs.; exhibited works in numerous shows including N.Y. ArtExpo, 1992, Art Miami, 1992, Cornell Med. Libr. Ann., 1992, Hellenic Art Inst. Exhbn., 1991, Vt. Inst. Natural Sci., 1983, Montserrat Gallery Internat. Exhbn. (hon. mention 1993); represneted in permanent collection Ward-Nasse Gallery, N.Y.C. Recipient 1st place award for drawing Brookdale Coll., 1994, 2d place award for sculpture, 1993, Bronze medal for animal art, 1986, 20th Century award for Achievement Internat. Biog. Ctr.; appointed corr. academician Acad. Internazionale Dept. Arts, Italy. Mem.: Academia del Verbano, Italy (academical ofcl. knight), N.Y. Artists Equity, Garrison Art Ctr., Hellenic Art Inst., League Sci. et Edn. Sociale, Arts, Scis., Lettres: Soc. Academique de Edn. et Encouragement, Art Students League (life), Salmagundi Club. Studio: 1701 Ocean Ave #20A Asbury Park NJ 07712-0518

MYERS, DOUGLAS GEORGE, zoological society administrator; b. L.A., Aug. 30, 1949; s. George Walter and Daydeen (Schroeder) Myers; m. Barbara Firestone Myers, Nov. 30, 1980; children: Amy, Andrew. BA, Christopher Newport Coll., 1981. Tour and show supr. Anneheuser-Busch (Bird Sanctuary), Van Nuys, Calif., 1970-74, mgr. zool. ops., 1974-75, asst. mgr. ops., 1975-77, mgr. ops., 1977-78; gen. services mgr. Anneheuser-Busch (Old Country), Williamsburg, Va., 1978-80, park ops. dir., 1980-81; gen. mgr. wild animal park Zool. Soc. San Diego, 1981-83, dep. dir. ops., 1983-85, exec. dir., 1985—; chief exec. ofcr. San Diego Wild Animal Park, Escondido, Calif. Cons. in field. Mem. adv. com. of pres.' assn. Am. Mgmt. Assn. Fellow Am. Assn. Zool. Parks and Aquariums (profl., bd. dirs.), Internat. Union Dirs. Zool. Gardens; mem. Internat. Assn. Amusement Parks and Attractions, Am. Mgmt. Assn. (adv. com. pres. assn.), Calif. Assn. Zoos and Aquariums, Rotary. Office: San Diego Zoo PO Box 120551 San Diego CA 92112-0551

MYERS, EDDIE EARL, clinical psychologist; b. Ardmore, Okla., Nov. 24, 1937; s. Finis Weldon and Fern Durrell (Johnson) M.; m. Ineta June Moore, July 2, 1955 (div. Mar. 1988); children: Richard Weldon, Ronald Leland, Marilyn June, Rebecca Jean; m. Ann Clymer Taylor, July 15, 1988 (div. May 1996); Clark Clymer Taylor, Katy Ann Taylor; m. Katherine Call Emch, Dec. 28, 1996. BSEd, Tex. Christian U., 1958; MEd, U. N. Tex., 1967, EdD, 1969. Lic. psychologist, Ohio; Nat. Drug Edn. Leadership Tng. Adlephi U., 1970. Machinist Chance Vaught Aircraft, Grand Prairie, Tex., 1957-58; 5th grade tchr., jr. high coach Ft. Worth Christian Schs., 1958-59; 6th grade tchr., jr. high coach Corpus Christi (Tex.) Ind. Sch. Dist., 1959-60; youth, music, ednl. min. Norton St. Ch. Christ, Corpus Christi, 1960-61, Procter St. Ch. Christ, Port Arthur, Tex., 1963-65; min. Cameron (Tex.) Ch. Christ, 1961-63; high sch. English tchr. Christian Schs., Inc., Dallas, 1965-66; psychology instr. Tex. Women's U., Denton, 1968-69; sr. rsch. assoc., dir. psychology dept. Ednl. Rsch. Coun. Am., Cleve., 1969-78; clin. psychologist pvt. practice, 1978—. Faculty dept. guidance anc counseling U. Oreg. Workshop, Frankfurt, German, 1972; Ea. U.S. drug abuse task force Am. Soc. Health Assn., N.Y.C., 1971-73; chmn. drug abuse and alcoholism task force Fedn. Cmty. Planning, Cleve., 1970-71; adv. bd. Freedom House Rehab. Ctr., Cleve., 1993—; adj. assoc. prof. ednl. specialists Cleve. State U., 1970-74; mem. med. staff St. John Westshore Hosp., West Lake, Ohio, Fairview Hosp., Cleve. Author: Social Isolation and Personality, 1973, Handy Asks the Psychologist, 1974, (tchr. manual) Human Persons and Use of Psychoactive Agents, 1974; co-author: (tchr. manual) New Model Me: Operator's Guide to Coping with Aggression, 1974; contbr. articles to profl. jours. R & D grantee NIMH, Washington, 1974-78, Nat. Def. Edn. Rsch. Tng. grantee U.S. Dept. Edn., Washington, 1965-69. Mem. APA, Cleve. Psychol. Assn. (bd. trustees 1981-85), Cleve. Acad. Consulting Psychologists (pres. 1984-86), Ohio Psychol. Assn. (bd. trustees 1978—), Phi Delta Kappa. Avocations: computers, golf, jet boating. Office: 3865 Rocky River Dr Ste 2 Cleveland OH 44111-4114

MYERS, ELISSA MATULIS, publisher, association executive; b. Munich, Aug. 4, 1950; (parents Am. citizens); d. Raymond George and Anne Constance (Moley) Matulis; m. John Wake Myers, Sept. 13, 1967 (div. 1972); 1 child, Jennifer Anne Myers Bick. BA in English Lit., George Mason U., 1972, MA in English Lit., 1982. Dir. rsch. and info. Am. Soc. Assn. Execs., Washington, 1972-80, dir. mem. svcs., 1980-88, v.p., pub. Assn. Mgmt. mag., 1988-97; pres., CEO Nat. Informercial Mktg. Assn., 1997—, Electronic Retailing Assn., Washington, 1998—. Pub. Principles of Association Management, 1976, 3d edit., 1996; columnist Footnotes, 1988-97. Bd. dirs. Ethics Resource Ctr., Washington, 1982-86; mem. Universal Postal Union Adv. Group 2000-; mem. Fed. Adv. Commn. on e-commerce; appointee DofC 1fac-4 Ecommerce, 2001-. Mem. Am. Soc. Assn. Execs. (cert.), Assn. Conv. Mktg. Execs., Greater Washington Soc. Assn. Execs. (bd. dirs. 2000—), Nat. Assn. Hispanic Mktg. Profls. (adv. bd.), Soc. Nat. Assn. Publs., Com. of 100 U.S. C. of C., Soc. Scholarly Pubs. Roman Catholic. Avocations: running, scuba diving. Home: 5315 Moultrie Rd Springfield VA 22151-1915 Office: Electronic Retailing Assn 2101 Wilson Blvd Arlington VA 22201-3062 E-mail: emyers@retailing.org.

MYERS, ELIZABETH ROUSE, management consultant; b. Grand Island, Nebr., July 14, 1923; d. William Wayne Rouse and Lulu Zella Trout; m. Richard Roland Myers, June 25, 1943; children: Diane Marie Berndt, Richard Wayne. Student, Kearny State Tchrs. Coll., Nebr., 1942-43. Draftsman Borg-Warner Corp., Kalamazooo, 1944; acct. CFI Steel Corp., Pueblo, Colo., 1950-52; sec., treas. Standard Paint, Yakima, Wash., 1954-86; pres. Pied Piper Childrens Books, 1985-96; federal oil leases, 1980—. Docent Yakima Valley Mus. & Gilbert House, Wash. 1984—. Editor: H.S. Paper. Tchr., supt. First Presbyn. Ch., Yakima, Wash., 1958-70; mem. bd. Parent Tchrs.; bd. dirs., teen chmn. YWCA; pres. Gilbert House. Mem. Yakima Valley Mus. (awarded Doll 1985, Show 1986, vol. of yr. 1994). Republican. Presbyterian. Avocations: gardening, doll and toy collecting, world traveling, walking, flying. Home and Office: 106 N 25th Ave Yakima WA 98902-2807

MYERS, ELMER, psychiatric social worker; b. Blackwell, Ark., Nov. 12, 1926; s. Chester Elmer Myers and Irene (Davenport) Lewis; widowed; children: Elmer Jr., Keith, Kevin. BA, U. Kans., 1951, MA, 1962; student, U. Calif., Santa Barbara, 1977-78. Lic. clin. social worker; C.C. counselor credentials. Psychiat. social worker Hastings (Nebr.) State Hosp., 1960-62, State of Calif. Bur. Social Tng. Com., Sacramento, 1962-75; supr. psychiat. social worker State of Calif., 1975-80, Alta Calif. Regional Ctr., Sacramento, 1980-85. Exec. dir. Tri-County Family Svcs., Yuba City, Calif., 1966-69; cons. to four convalescent Hosps., Marysville and Willows, Calif., 1969-71; lectr. Yuba Coll., Marysville, 1971-76; assoc. prof. Calif. State U., Chico, 1972-73; cons. in field, Marysville, 1985—; group therapist Depot Homeless Shelter, 1996—, facilitator HIV support group, 1993-2002, counselor, 1995—; cons., therapist New Millennium Group Home, 2000. Bd. dirs. Habitat for Humanity, 1993; juror Yuba County Grand Jury, Marysville, 1965, 1987—88; sec. Y's Men's Club, Yuba City, 1964—65; chmn. Tri-County Home Health Agy., 1974—76; vice-chmn. Gateway Projects, Inc., 1974—75; bd. dirs. Yuba County Truancy Bd., Marysville, 1964—67; asst. dir. Marysville Adult Activity Ctr., 1990—; active Yuba-Sutter United Way, 1971—73, 1991—92; active, sec. Tri-County Ethnic Forum, 1991—93; steering com. Yuba County Sr. Ctr. Assn., 1992, 1995—; chmn. Yuba County Cmty. Svcs. Commn., 1997—99, Yuba-Sutter Gleaners, 1997—, bd. dirs., 1998, 2001; chmn. Yuba-Sutter Commn. on Aging, 1996, bd. dirs., 1998, 2001; chmn. H.E.L.P. Working Group, HIV Prevention, 2000; bd. dirs. Christian Assistance Network, 1993, Golden Empire Health Sys. Agy., Sacramento, 1972—76, Youth Svcs. Bur., Yuba City, 1967, Bi-County Mental Retardation Planning Bd., Yuba City, 1972, Yuba County Juvenile Justice Commn., Marysville, 1982—90, Am. Cancer Soc., Marysville, 1985—92, Yuba County Rep. Ctrl. Com., 1983—90, Salvation Army, 1990—, facilitator care proj., 1992. Recipient Cert. Spl. Recognition, Calif. Rehab. Planning Project, 1969, Cert. Spl. Recognition, State of Calif., 1967, Cert. Spl. Recognition, Alta Calif. Regional Ctrs., 1985; named Vol. of Week, Appeal Dem. newspaper, 1999. Mem. Nat. Assn. Social Workers (cert.), Kern County Mental Health Assn. (chmn. 1978-79). Lodges: Rotary (bd. dirs. Marysville club 1975-76). Avocations: fgn. lang. study, gardening, reading, computers. Home and Office: 3920 State Hwy 20 Marysville CA 95901-9003 E-mail: elm@syix.com.

MYERS, EUGENE NICHOLAS, otolaryngologist, otolaryngology educator; b. Phila., Nov. 27, 1933; s. David and Rosalind (Nicholas) Myers; m. Barbara Labov, June 10, 1956; children: Marjorie Rose, Jeffrey N. BS in Econs., U. Pa., 1954; MD, Temple U., 1960. Diplomate Am. Bd. Otolaryngology. Intern Mt. Sinai Hosp., N.Y.C., 1960—61; resident Mass. Eye and Ear Infirmary, Boston, 1963—65; asst. prof. clin. otolaryngology U. Pa., 1968—72; prof. clin. oncology dept. oral pathology U. Pitts. Sch. Dental Medicine, 1975—82, prof. dept. diagnostic services, 1982—2000, prof. dept. oral and maxillofacial surgery, 2000—; prof., chmn./chief dept. otolaryngology U. Pitts. Med. Ctr., 1972—. Cons. VA Med. Ctr., Pitts., 1972—, Children's Hosp., Pitts., 1972—. Editor: Cancer of the Head and Neck, 1981, 1989, 1996, Tracheotomy, 1985, 1998; mem. editl. bd. Laryngoscope, 1973—95, exec. editl. bd., 1995—, mem. editl. bd. Head and Neck Surgery, 1978—92, 1998—, AMA Archives of Otolaryngology, 1981—, Annals of Otology Rhinology and Laryngology, 1984—, Oncology, 1986—, European Archives of Oto-Rhino-Laryngology, 1990—97, editor-in-chief (book) Advances in Orolaryngology, 1985—2001; co-editor: Butterworth's Intern Med. Revs., 1981—; internat. editor Otolaryngology-Head and Neck Surgery, 1996—. Mem. adv. bd. Pa. Lion Hearing Rsch. Found., Pitts., 1983—99. Capt. M.C. U.S. Army, 1965—67. Recipient Cert. of Merit Com. Rsch., Am. Acad. Otolaryngology-Salicylate Otoxicity, 1965, Award of Merit, Am. Acad. Otolaryngology-Head and Neck Surgery Inc., 1978, Robert E. Shoemaker Rsch. award, Pa. Acad. Ophthalmology and Otolaryngology, 1979, Disting. Svc. award, Am. Acad. Oto-HNS, 2001. Fellow: Am. Acad. Otolaryngology (chmn. com. on head and neck surgery 1981—83, bd. dirs. 1985—88, 1990—, pres. 1994—95, internat. coord. 1996—), Am. Laryngol. Assn. (sec. 1982—88, pres. 1989—90, mem. coun. 1990—93, James Newcomb award 1993, DeRoaldes award 2001, award 2001), ACS (bd. govs. 1981—87, mem. adv. coun. 1985—87); mem.: Pitts. Athletic Assn., Triological Soc. (mem. coun. 1989—92, v.p. Ea. sect. 1994—95), Am. Soc. Head and Neck Surgery (mem. coun. 1977—93, pres.

1988—90), Nat. Cancer Inst. (chmn. upper aerodigestive tract working group 1986—89), Assn. Acad. Depts. Otolaryngology (mem. coun. 1978—80), Am. Bd. Otolaryngology (bd. dirs. 1981—99, pres.-elect 1994—96, pres. 1996—98), Pitts. Golf Club. Republican. Jewish. Office: U Pitts Sch Med Eye and Ear Inst Ste 500 200 Lothrop St Pittsburgh PA 15213-2546 E-mail: myersen@msx.upmc.edu.

MYERS, FRANKLIN, oil industry executive; b. Pensacola, Fla., Nov. 2, 1952; s. T. F., Sr. and D. Bernice (Brewer) Myers; children: Amanda C., Adam F., Anne Marie M. BS, Miss. State U., 1974; JD, U. Miss., 1977. Bar: Miss. 1977, Tex. 1978. Ptnr. Fulbright and Jaworski, Houston, 1978-88; sr. v.p., gen. counsel Baker Hughes Inc., 1988-95; sr. v.p. Cooper Cameron Corp., 1995—. Adj. prof. U. Tex. Sch. Law, 1990—; bd. dirs. Reunion Industries, Inc., Metals USA, Inc., InPut Output Inc. Fellow: Houston Bar Assn., Miss. Bar Assn., Tex. Bar Assn., Houston Bar Found. Office: Cooper Cameron Corp 1333 W Loop South Ste 1700 Houston TX 77027

MYERS, FRANKLIN LEWIS, II, ophthalmologist; b. Wichita, Kans., Mar. 20, 1933; s. Kermit Whitney and Bertha Alice (Perkins) M.; m. Gloria Joyce Johnston, Sept. 2, 1955 (div. 1993); children: Jeffrey, Jennifer; m. Helen Elizabeth Lyngaas, July 23, 1994. BA, U. Iowa, 1954, MD, 1957. Diplomate Am. Bd. Ophthalmology. Intern Highland-Alameda County Hosp., Oakland, Calif., 1957-58; resident in ophthalmology U. Wis., Madison, 1964-67, fellow, 1967-68, from instr. to prof. dept. ophthalmology, 1968-97, prof. emeritus, 1997—. Ophthalmologist, dir. Davis Duehr Eye Assn., Madison, 1968-95. Lt. comdr. USNR, 1959-61. Mem. Retina Soc., Vitreous Soc., Phi Beta Kappa, Omicron Delta Kappa, Alpha Omega Alpha. Avocations: gardening, photography, sailing, lapidary. Home: 4946 Lake Mendota Dr Madison WI 53705-1376 Office: U Wis Dept Ophthalmology 2870 University Ave Ste 206 Madison WI 53705-3611 E-mail: flmyers@facstaff.wisc.edu.

MYERS, GARY, public relations executive; BS, U. Mo., 1971. Pres., CEO Morgan & Myers, Jefferson, Wis., 1997—. Recipient Founder award Agrl. Rels. Coun., 1984. Mem. Pub. Rels. Soc. Am., Coun. Pub. Rels. Firms, Nat. Agrl. Mktg. Assn. Office: Morgan & Myers 146 E Milwaukee St Jefferson WI 53549-1696*

MYERS, GERALD E. humanities educator; b. Central City, Nebr., June 19, 1923; s. Harold W. and Mary (Ferguson) M.; m. Martha Coleman, Aug. 7, 1948; 1 son, Curt. BA, Haverford Coll., 1947; MA, Brown U., 1949, PhD, 1954. Instr. Smith Coll., 1950-52; asst. prof. Williams Coll., 1952-61; assoc. prof. Kenyon Coll., 1961-65; prof. C.W. Post Coll., L.I. U., 1965-67, Queens Coll. and Grad. Center, City U. N.Y., 1967—; also dep. exec. officer Ph.D. program Queens Coll. and Grad. Center, City U. N.Y. (Grad. Center); dir. intro. philosophy into N.Y.C. High Schs. project.; emeritus CUNY. Dir. humanities-and-dance projects, philosopher-in-residence Am. Dance Festival, Durham, N.C., 1979; project dir. African-Am. Perspectives in Am. Modern Dance, Am. Dance Festival/NEH. Author: Self, Religion and Metaphysics, 1961, Self: An Introduction to Philosophical Psychology, 1969, The Spirit of American Philosophy, 1970, William James: His Life and Thought, 1986; editor: The Black Tradition in American Modern Dance, 1988, African American Genius in Modern Dance, 1992; co-editor: Emotion Philos. Studies, 1983, Echoes from the Holocaust, 1988; cons. Free to Dancd PBS documentary, 2001; contbr. articles to profl. jours. NEH fellow, 1981-82. Mem. Am. Philos. Assn. (past sec.-treas. Western div.), Metaphys. Soc. Am., Soc. Phenomenology and Existential Philosophy, Phi Beta Kappa. Home: 36 Gardner Ave New London CT 06320-4313 Office: 33 W 42nd St New York NY 10036-8003

MYERS, GREGORY EDWIN, aerospace engineer; b. Harrisburg, Pa., Jan. 1, 1960; s. Bernard Eugene and Joyce (Calhoun) M.; m. Susan Ann Hayslett, Dec. 30, 1983 (div. 1999); children: Kimberly, Benjamin. BS in Aerospace Engring., U. Mich., 1981; MS in Aerospace Engring., Air Force Inst. Tech., 1982. Aerospace engr. Sperry Comml. Flight Systems group Honeywell, Inc., Phoenix, 1987-90, sr. project engr. satellite systems ops. Glendale, Ariz., 1990-92, sr. project engr. air transport systems Phoenix, 1992-93, prin. engr., 1993-97; prin. software engr. Orbital Scis. Corp., Chandler, Ariz., 1997—, sr. prin. software engr., 1999—. Presenter in field. Contbr. articles to profl. jours. Active Aviation Week Rsch. Adv. Panel, 1990-91. Recipient Certs. of Recognition and Appreciation Lompoc Valley Festival Assn., Inc., 1983, Arnold Air Soc. (comdr. 1979), Cert. of Appreciation Instrument Soc. Am., 1991. Mem. AIAA (sr.). Lutheran. Avocations: softball, tennis, reading, computer programming. Office: Orbital Scis Corp 3380 S Price Rd Chandler AZ 85248-3534 *Personal philosophy: My 3 principles to live by: ask questions, be honest and try.*

MYERS, HARDY, state attorney general, lawyer; b. Electric Mills, Miss., Oct. 25, 1939; m. Mary Ann Thalhofer, 1962; children: Hardy III, Christopher, Jonathan. AB with distinction, U. Miss., 1961; LLB, U. Oreg., 1964. Bar: Oreg., U.S. Ct. of Appeals (9th cir.), U.S. Dist. Ct. Law clerk U.S. Dist. Judge William G. East, 1964—65; pvt. practice Stoel Rives LLP, 1965—96; atty. gen. State of Oreg., 1997—. Mem. Oreg Ho. of Reps., 1975—85, spkr. of the ho., 1979—83. Pres. Portland City Planning Commn., 1973—74; chair Oreg. Jail Project, 1984—86, Citizen's Task Force on Mass Transit Policy, 1985—86, Oreg. Criminal Justice Coun., 1987—91, Portland Future Focus, 1990—91, Metro Charter com., 1991—92, task force on state employee benefits, 1994; co-chair gov. task force on state employee compensation, 1995. Office: Oreg Atty Gen Justice Dept 1162 Court St NE Salem OR 97310-1320

MYERS, HAROLD MATHEWS, academic administrator; b. Doylestown, Pa., Apr. 13, 1915; s. Carl and Alice W. Myers; m. Margaret F. Smith, July 19, 1946 (dec. Sept. 1963); children: Donald Smith, Dean Chappell, Deborah Kay; m. L. Marjorie Bellau, Nov. 28, 1964. BS in Commerce, Drexel Inst. Tech., 1938, DSc in Commerce (hon.), 1983; postgrad., Temple U., 1940-41, U. Omaha, summer 1957. Instr. coop. edn., dir. grad. placement Drexel U., Phila., 1938-46, asst. dean men, dir. student bldgs., adj. instr. labor econs., 1946-52, dean of men, 1952-55, treas., 1955-57, v.p., treas., 1957-80, sr. v.p., 1980-82, sr. v.p. emeritus, 1982-87, interim pres., 1987-88, pres. emeritus, 1988—, life trustee, 1986—. Regional dir. First Pa. Banking and Trust Co., 1959-76; dir. Sadtler Rsch. Labs., Inc., 1963-69, Almo Indsl. Elecs., Inc., 1966-68; dir., treas. Uni-Coll Corp., 1974-81; bd. dirs. Beulah Cemetary Assn., asst. treas., 1984-89, treas., 1989-90, v.p. and treas., 1980—; bd. dirs., mem. exec. com. Univ. City Sci. Ctr., 1974-90, dir. emeritus, 1991—, chmn. fin. com., 1976-88, vice chmn., 1988-90. Contbr. articles to profl. jours. Bd. dirs. Internat. House of Phila. Inc., 1954-81, exec. com., 1972-81; active Phila. coun. Boy Scouts Am., 1953—, hon. chmn., 1985-97, pres., 1982, 83; mem. citizens fire prevention com. Phila. Fire Dept., 1970-86; bd. dirs. United Fund Greater Phila., 1983-87, Luth. Ch. of Am. Common Investing Fund, 1976-82, NCCJ, Inc., Phila. and S. Jersey region NCCJ, 1959-65; dir. Phila. Coun. of Chs., 1954-61, pres. jr. coun., 1950-51; bd. dirs., pres. Ea. Assn. Coll. and Univ. Bus. Officers, 1971-72; treas. Lambda Chi Alpha Found., 1970-84, dir. emeritus, 1984—; pres. Broadmoor Pines Home Owners Assn., 1993-94; dir. PalmAire Cmty., Inc., 1993-95, chmn. security com., 1995—. Served to comdr. USNR, ret. Recipient Silver Beaver award Boy Scouts Am., 1963, Mary M. Hart award Phila. coun. Boy Scouts Am., 1986, Drexel Alumni Varsity Club award, 1966, Drexel U. Evening Coll. Alumni Assn. award, 1973, Drexel U. Anthony J. Drexel Paul award, 1988, Dept. of Army Cert. of Appreciation for Patriotic Civilian Svc., 1979, Disting. Bus. Officer award Nat. Assn. Coll. and Bus. Officers, 1989, Disting. Svc. in Trusteeship award Assn. Governing Bd. Univs. and Colls., 1989; named Educator of Yr., Phila. coun. Boy Scouts Am., 1989; named to Legion of Honor, Chapel of Four Chaplins; Drexel U. student dormitory named Myers Hall in his honor, 1984; 1 of 100 alumni honored Centennial of Drexel U., 1992. Mem. AARP, Am. Legion, Mil. Order World Wars (perpetual, comdr. Phila. chpt. 1958-59), Ret. Officers Assn. (life), Swedish Colonial Soc. Phila. (sec. 1968), Welsh Soc. Phila. (life), Internat. Frat. Lambda Chi Alpha (pres. 1966-70), Vet. Corps 1st Regiment Infantry, N.G.P. (hon.), Penn Club, Union League Phila. (pres. 1980-81), Sarasota Yacht Club, Masons, Rotary (Paul Harris fellow), Gulf Coast Curvate Club.

MYERS, HARRY J., JR. retired publisher; b. Denver, Aug. 7, 1931; s. Harry J. and Edith M. (Reed) M.; m. Mary Kay Racine, June 21, 1958; children: Harry J., Hans R. (dec.), Peter C. BA, Colo. U., 1957; postgrad., U. Mo., 1959-60. Pub., or pub. dir. Meredith Corp., 1962-82, Geo, Archtl. Digest, Bon Appetit, Home, Sci. Am., Cowles Mag, 1982-95. Served with USMC, 1953-56. Mem. Kappa Tau Alpha, Phi Gamma Delta. Home: 46 W Ranch Trl Morrison CO 80465-9504 E-mail: hmyersb@aol.com.

MYERS, HELEN PRISCILLA, music educator; b. Palo Alto, Calif., June 5, 1946; d. Henry Alonzo Myers and Elsie (Phillips) Myers-Stainton; children: Ian Alister Woolford, Adam Robert Woolford, Sean Patrick Woolford. MusB, Ithaca Coll., 1967; M in Mus. Edn., Syracuse U., 1971; MA, Ohio State U., 1975; PhD, U. Edinburgh, Scotland, 1984; MPhil, Columbia U., 1993. Cert. instrumental mus. K-12, N.Y. Clarinettist Am. Wind Symphony Orch., Pitts., 1966-67; rsch. fellow Columbia U., N.Y.C., 1973-75, lectr., 1975-76; lectr. Goldsmiths' Coll. U. London, 1981-89; assoc. prof. Trinity Coll., Hartford, Conn., 1989—, St. Anthony Hall prof., 1994—. Ford Found. lectr. ethnomusicology Nat. Ctr. Performing Arts, Bombay, India, 1988; vis. assoc. prof. music Columbia U., N.Y.C., 1993; ethnomusicologist cons. Oxford U. Press, London, 1981-83, The New Grove Dictionary of Music, 7th edit., London, 1993—; resident ethnomusicologist Grove's Dictionaries of Music and Musicians, 1976-89; guest lectr. Guildhall Sch. of Music, London, 1982-89. Author: Felicity, Trinidad: Musical Portrait of a Hindu Village, 1984, (with Bruno Nettl) Folk Music in the United States: An Introduction, 1976; author introductions to facsimile reprints of Alice Cunningham Fletcher's Omaha Indian Music, 1994, Indian Games and Dances, 1994, Native Songs, 1994, others; editor, contbr.: Ethnomusicology: An Introduction, 1992, Ethnomusicology: Historical and Regional Studies, 1993; gen. editor, contbr. South Asia Vol. VI, The Garland Ency. of World Music. Grantee Am. Inst. Indian Studies, 1986-87, 88-89, Brit. Acad., 1988-89, Ford Found., 1988, Am. Philosophical Soc., 1989-90, Wenner-Gren Found. for Anthropological Rsch., 1989-90. Mem. Am. Anthrop. Assn., Am. Musciological Soc., Soc. Ethnomusicology (coun. mem. 1992—), Assn. Asian Studies, Internat. Coun. Traditional Music, Indian Musicological Soc., Sangeet Natak Akademi, Earthwatch, English Folk Dance and Song Soc. (editorial bd. Polk Music Jour.), Phi Kappa Lambda. Home: 207 Old Main St Rocky Hill CT 06067-1505 also: Grove Dictionaries Macmillan Press 4 Little Essex St London WC2R 3LF England

MYERS, HOWARD, aerospace scientist, systems analyst; b. N.Y.C., Jan. 27, 1928; s. Howard G. and Sally (Kline) M.; m. Lois Marie Lowe, July 19, 1948 (dec. Apr. 1969); children: Susanna, William, Sally Joy. PhB, U. Chgo., 1948, BS, 1950, MS, 1958. Scientist Hughes Rsch. Labs., Culver City, Calif., 1953-57; tech. specialist Douglas Aircraft Co., Santa Monica, 1957-61; program mgr. Aerospace Corp., El Segundo, 1961-66; mem. tech. staff TRW Inc., Redondo Beach, 1966-69; sr. tech. specialist McDonnell Douglas, St. Louis, 1969-80; sr. systems engr. GE, 1980-92; pres. CPRL, Boardman, Ohio, from 1968. Leader, scientist supporters NASA's Project Galileo, 1972-78. Contbr. articles to profl. jours.; patentee elastometer. Prin. collaborator Nobel prize for chemistry, 1983. Mem. AAAS, Am. Chem. Soc., Am. Geophys. Union, Math. Assn. Am., N.Y. Acad. Sci., Sigma Xi. Democrat. Died Sept. 13, 2000.

MYERS, IONA RAYMER, real estate property manager; b. Guymon, Okla., Sept. 18, 1931; m. Harold Rudolph Myers, Mar. 28, 1953; children: Richard Galen, Sandra Dawn, Paula Colleen. BS magna cum laude, So. Nazarene U., 1952; MEd, U. Okla., 1959; postgrad., McNeese State U., 1970. Tchr. home econs. Can. County Pub. Schs., Mustang, Okla., 1952-53; tchr. elem. Oklahoma City Pub. Schs., 1955-61, Transylvania County Pub. Schs., Brevard, N.C., 1961-67; elem. tchr., student tchr. supr. Allen Parish Pub. Schs., Oakdale, La., 1967-71; mgr. DeRidder Tracts and Comml. Property, Metairie, 1968-94; tchr. elem. and jr. high history Lafourche Parish Pub. Schs., Raceland and Lockport, La., 1974-76; tchr. elem. sci. Jefferson Parish Pub. Schs., Metairie, 1976-80; treas. Harold R. Myers Engring. (divsn. Harold R. Myers, Inc.), 1993—; mgr. Harion Properties, L.L.C., 1980—. Vol. founding bd. dirs. Jefferson Performing Arts Soc., Metairie, 1977-83; vol. founding mem. community adv. coun. East Jefferson Gen. Hosp., Metairie, 1980-87. Vol. scout leader S.E. La. Girl Scouts U.S. coun., Metairie, 1977-89, fund raising com., 1992-93; vol. tchr. music Harold Keller Elem. Sch., Metairie, 1981-83; life mem. Rep. Nat. Com., Washington, 1980-91, mem. fin. com., 1988; jubilee chmn., fundraiser Jefferson Performing Arts Soc., Metairie, 1987; candidate La. Ho. of Reps. Dist. 88, Baton Rouge, 1991; com. YWCA New Orleans Role Model Luncheon, 1994-95; financier Bus. and Profl. Women USA Found., 1990-95, Golden Circle donor, 1996-2001; sec. East Jefferson Rep. Parish Coun., 1998-99; parlimentarian Nat. Women's Polit. Caucus Greater New Orleans Region, 1998-99. New Orleans Mus. of Art fellow, 1984-94, So. Nazarene U. fellow, 1985-94; recipient Rice in the Ear award S.E. La. Girl Scouts U.S., 1982, Great Lady/Great Gentleman award Ladies Aux. East Jefferson Gen. Hosp., 1987, Commendation award Jefferson Performing Arts Soc., 1988, Women as Winners award YWCA New Orleans, 1993. Mem. AAUW (pres. 1988-90, vol. coord. Metairie chpt. 1990-91, del. 5 nat. and 5 regional convs. 1987-94, 98, 99, corr. sec. La. chpt. 1989-91, scholar and grantee 1989, Magnolia editor 1991-96, Magnolia co-editor 1996-97, chair nominating com. 1992-93, 98-99, sec. 1998-2000, state parliamentarian 2000-01, state pres. elect 2001-02, state pres. 2002—, grant honoree La. 1994, program v.p. Metairie br. 1997-99, Parliamentarian br. 1999-2000, chmn. fin. 2000-2001, br. pres. 2002—), Jefferson Hist. Soc. (life), La. Landmarks Soc. (life), Nat. Assn. Parliamentarians (pres. Metairie unit 1996-97, 98-99, del. nat. conv., 1997-99, v.p. program chair, 1999-2000, parliamentarian 2000-2001, pres. 2002—), La. Assn. Parliamentarians (2d v.p., edn. chair 1997-2001, state 1st v.p. 2001—), La. Fedn. Bus. Profl. Women's Clubs, Inc., La. Fedn. Bus. Profl. Women's Clubs, Inc. (auditor, legis. chmn. 1990-91, rec. sec. 1991-92, membership v.p. 1992-93, state newsletter Pelican editor 1995-2000 (pres. Jefferson Parish chpt. 1980-82, 1st v.p. 1993-94, state pres. 1995-96, pres.-elect 1994-95, state historian, 2001—, program v.p. 1993-94, mem. v.p. 1992-93, rec. sec. 1991-92, auditor and legis. chmn. 1990-91, Vision editor 1993-96, Jefferson Parish Voice editor 1993—, sec. 1998-99, parliamentarian 1999-2001, pres. 2001-02, Outstanding Dist. Dir. award 1985, Nike award 1991, Highest Mem. honor 1992-93, Best Membership Recruiter 1993-94), Metairie Woman's Club (corr. sec. 1994-96); New Orleans Mus. Art (fellow 1984-94), E. Jefferson Parish Republican Coun., 1998-99, Nat. Women's Political Caucus (New Orleans region pres. 1999-2000, v.p. polit. activity, 2000-2001, del. nat. conv., 1997, 99), Jefferson bd. (Patty Strong award 1997, Woman of Yr. 2001). Methodist. Avocations: plate collector, gardening, lobbyist. Home: 4701 Chastant St Metairie LA 70006-2059

MYERS, IRA LEE, physician; b. Monrovia, Ala., Feb. 9, 1924; s. Ira W. and Azelea Juanita (Cobbs) M.; m. Dorothy Will Foust, Sept. 4, 1943; children: Martha Crystal, Ira Grady, Stephen Allen, Joanna Lynn. BS, Howard Coll., Birmingham, Ala., 1945; MD, U. Ala., 1949; postgrad., Harvard U. Sch. Public Health, 1953. Diplomate: Am. Bd. Preventive Medicine. Commd. officer USPHS, 1949-55; intern USPHS Marine Hosp., Seattle, 1949-50; epidemic intelligence officer Charleston, W.Va., 1950-52, Erie County Health Dept., Buffalo, 1952, Center Communicable Disease, Atlanta, 1952-55; resigned, 1955; adminstrv. health officer Ala. Dept. Health, Montgomery, 1955-63, state health officer, 1963-86. Sec. Ala. Bd. Med. Examiners, 1962-73; chmn. Ala. Bd. Registration Sanitarians, 1964-81, Ala. Air Pollution Control Commn., 1969-82; v.p. Ala. Pollution Control Fin. Authority, 1971-81; assoc. clin. prof. preventive medicine and pub. health U. Ala. Med. Sch.; mem. Ala. vol. med. adv. com. SSS, 1968-86; chmn. Ala. Health Care Hall of Fame, 1998—. Pres. Ala. div. Am. Cancer Soc., 1991-93; chmn. bd. dirs. Dalraida Health Ctr., 1992-98; chmn. awards com. Ala. Sr. Citizens Hall of Fame, 1997—. Recipient Ala. Sr. Citizens Hall of Fame Golden Eagle award, 1986, St. George medal Nat. Divisional award Am. Cancer Soc., 1989, 1st Ann. Vol. award Montgomery Bapt. Assn., 1993. Mem. AMA, Med. Assn. Ala. (William Henry Saunders award 1968, 1st annual Ira L. Myers Service award, 1986), Montgomery County Med. Soc., Ala. Pub. Health Assn. (D.G. Gill award 1967, established Ira L. Myers Scholarship Endowment), Am. Assn. Pub. Health Physicians, Assn. State and Territorial Health Officers (Arthur N. McCormick award 1976), Ala. Hosp. Assn. (hon.), State. Ala. Acad. Honor, Tuberculosis Assn. (Heacock Gold medal 1986), Montgomery Coun. of Aging (Srs. of Achievement award 1998, Gov.'s Lifetime Achievement award 1998). Lodges: Montgomery Kiwanis. Republican. Baptist. Achievements include initiating state narcotic control program, 1967, state hosp. service for indigent, 1958. Home and Office: 925 Green Forest Dr Montgomery AL 36109-1515

MYERS, JACK FREDRICK, artist, educator, author; b. Lima, Ohio, Feb. 17, 1927; s. Harold Frank and Lesta Arvilla (Ross) M.; m. Frances Dydek, Apr. 30, 1949; children: Steven Ross, David Gene, Kevin Douglas. Student, Cleve. Inst. Art, 1947-49; MFA, Kent State U., 1980. Staff artist Bill Ripley & Assocs., Cleve., 1951-57; art dir. Premier Indsl. Corp., 1957-70; instr. Cooper Sch. Art, 1970-80; assoc. prof. art U. Dayton, Ohio, 1982-87; ret., 1992. Author: The Language of Visual Art, 1989, Windy Side of Care, 2002. With USNR, 1945-46, PTO. Recipient First prize in art Newsweek/Paillard S.A., 1969. Home and Office: 22269 Country Meadows Ln Strongsville OH 44149-2000

MYERS, JAMES CLARK, advertising and public relations executive; b. Chgo., Aug. 26, 1941; s. Herbert George Myers and Lenore (Goldberg) Levi; m. Judy Anne Schnitzer, Feb. 9, 1964; children: Jeffrey Stephan, Jeremy H. BA, Washington U., St. Louis, 1964. Acct. exec. Nahas, Blumberg, Zelikow, Houston, 1967-69; mgr. spl. events Houston Post, 1969-73; pres., creative dir. Motivators, Inc., Houston, 1973—. Vice-chmn. Internat. Sci. and Engring. Fair Coun., Washington, 1972-73; bd. dirs. Sci. Engring. Fair of Houston, 1969-73; spl. corrs. Navy Times Newspaper; pres. S.W. Houston 2000, Inc., 1999—. Contbr. articles to newspapers. Chmn. Boy Scouts Am., Houston Chpt. Served to capt. USNR, 1964-96. Recipient Wood Badge award, Boy Scouts Am., 1979, Shofar award, 1981; named Pindren SW Citizen of Yr., 2002. Mem. Pub. Relations Soc. Am. (Silver Anvil award 1983, 87, Excalibur 2001). Jewish. Avocations: model railroading, square dancing, photography. Home: 8006 Duffield Ln Houston TX 77071-2017 Office: Motivators Inc 7171 Harwin Dr Ste 206 Houston TX 77036-2119 E-mail: motivators.inc@juno.com.

MYERS, JAMES R. lawyer; b. Valdosta, Ga., Aug. 29, 1952; s. J. Walter Jr. and Mary (Gallion) M.; m. Monica Faeth Myers, Sept. 19, 1992. BA cum laude, Harvard U., 1972, JD, 1975. Bar: Mass. 1975, U.S. Dist. Ct. (D.C. dist.) 1976, D.C. 1977, U.S. Ct. Appeals (D.C. cir.) 1977, U.S. Supreme Ct. 1983, U.S. Ct. Appeals (fed. cir.) 1991, Va. 1992, U.S. Ct. Appeals (4th cir.) 1992. Assoc. Wald, Harkrader & Ross, Washington, 1976-77; assoc. solicitor U.S. Dept. Energy, 1977-79; assoc. Andrews & Kurth, 1980-85; ptnr. Steele, Simmons & Fornaciari, 1985-86, Robbins & Laramie, Washington, 1986-89, Venable, Baetjer, Howard & Civiletti, Washington, 1990-97, Kilpatrick Stockton LLP, 1997—. Author Jour. Space Law, 1984, Space Mfg., 1983. Office: Kilpatrick Stockton LLP Ste 300 11130 Sunrise Valley Dr Reston VA 20191-4329 Fax: 703-648-8501. E-mail: jmyers@kilpatrickstockton.com.

MYERS, JEFFERY MARK, music educator,musician; b. Grenada, MS, Sept. 14, 1957; s. Robert Carl Myers, Norma Grey Myers; m. Angela Renee Yopp; children: Audra. Master of Music, University of Miami, Coral Gables, Florida, 1979—81; Bachelor of Music, University of Mississippi, University, MS, 1975—79. Keyboard performer Tupelo Symphony Orchestra, Tupelo, MS, 1994—2002; Music education instructor Itawamba Community College, Fulton, 1989—2002. Teacher/piano instruction Mississippi Keyboard Camp, Raymond, MS, 1997—2002. Ordained Deacon Ellistown Baptist Church, Ellistown, MS, 1996—98; Music Director Westside Baptist Church, Cincinnati, OH, 1981—83; Music and Youth director Central Baptist Church, Grenada, MS, 1982—91; Music director Ellistown Baptist Church, Ellistown, 1996—98; Music Director Belden Baptist Church, Belden, 1999—2001; Keyboard and rehearsal pianist Entertainment for Education, Amory, 1997—2000. Mem.: Music Teacher's National Association. Independent Baptist. Avocation: musician, swimming, . Office: Itawamba Community College 602 West Hill Street Fulton MS 38843 Business E-Mail: jmmyers@icc.cc.ms.us.

MYERS, JERRY ALAN, computer engineer; b. Dayton, Ohio, May 11, 1958; s. Gleason Harold and Loretta P. (Phillips) M. BS in Computer Engring., Wright State U., 1983, MS in Computer Engring., 1993. Electronics engr. USAF, Wright Patterson AFB, Ohio, 1983-84; firmware engr. Digital Tech., Inc., Dayton, 1984-85; computer engr. Comml. Flight Systems Div. Honeywell, Phoenix, 1985-88; computer engr. USAF, Wright Patterson AFB, 1989—. Office: USAF WL AAA #2 Wright Patterson AFB OH 45433

MYERS, JESSE JEROME, lawyer; b. Anthony, Kans., Sept. 30, 1940; s. Claud Lewis and Lucille S. (Robertson) M.; m. Claire H. Conni, Nov., 1966; children: Timothy Todd, Jessica Joy. BS, McPherson Coll., 1963; JD, Washburn U., 1970. Bar: Kans. 1970, Mo.1996, U.S. Dist. Ct. Kans. 1970. Law clk. U.S. Dist. Ct. Judge Frank Theis, Wichita, Kans., 1970—72; individual practice law, 1972—74, 1995—; lawyer Cessna Aircraft Co., 1974—75; v.p., dir., gen. counsel Martin K. Eby Constrn. Co., 1975—95. Served with USN, 1963-67. Mem. Am. Bar Assn., Kans. Bar Assn.

MYERS, JOHN HERMAN, investment company executive; b. Queens, N.Y., July 2, 1945; s. John Howard and Edna May (Strodthoff) Myers; m. JoAnn Barbara Eikamp, Sept. 29, 1973; children: Jennifer Ann, David John, Christina Marie, Kimberly Grace. BS in Math., Wagner Coll., 1967. With GE, 1970—, fin. program trainee GE Internat., 1970-74, fin. mgr. Compagnia Generale di Elettricita Milan, 1974-77, fin. mgr. Fairfield, Conn., 1977-81, dep. treas., 1981-84, group fin. mgr. N.Y.C., 1984-86, exec. v.p. GE Investments Stamford, Conn., 1986-96; chmn., pres. GE Asset Mgmt., 1997—. Bd. dirs. Peable Beach Co., GE Capital Svcs., Inc., Hilton Hotels Corp., Laffer Investments, XO Comm. Inc.; mem. pension mgrs. adv. com. NYSE, 1997; mem. Warburg Pincus Adv. Bd. Trustee Wagner Coll., 1993—. Lt. (j.g.) USN, 1967—70, Vietnam. Mem.: Aspetuck Valley Country Club. Republican. Lutheran. Avocations: tennis, basketball, golf.

MYERS, JOHN MOORE, fraternal organization administrator; b. Urbana, Ohio, Jan. 24, 1946; s. Louis Walter and Dorothy Caroline (Vordermark) M.; m. Nancy Lee Huff, Dec. 30, 1971; children: David Lawrence, Edward Louis. BS in Edn., Bowling Green State U., 1968; postgrad., U. Kansas, 1968-71, Columbia Sch. Broadcasting, 1971-72. Pub. svc. dir. KAKE Radio, Wichita, Kans., 1972-79; pub. svc. dir. Morning Dr. KFH Radio, 1979-81, community rels. dir., 1985-87; dir. devel. Kans. Masonic Home, 1981-84; ops. mgr. Morning Dr KAKZ Radio, 1984-85; sec.-treas. Scottish Rite Bodies of Wichita, 1987—; bd. dirs. Episcopal Social Svcs., 1990-96. Bd. dirs. Sta. KPTS-TV; sec./treas. Kans. Scottish Rite Found., 1987—; bd. dirs. Kans. Masonic Found., 1988—; owner Planetalk Airshow Announcers. Author: (play) MacArthur - Duty, Honor, Country, 1993—. Speakers Bur. United Way, Sedgwick County; co-host Children's Miracle Network Telethon, Wichita, 1985-87; bd. dirs. Sedgwick Co. Hist. Mus. Named Broadcaster of Yr., Kans. Assn. Broadcasters, 1979, Wichitan Mag., 1980-91; col. Commemorative Air Force. Fellow Titanic Hist. Mus.; mem. Sir John Falstaff Lit. Soc., Rotary (sec. 1989, chmn. membership 1990-91), Kans. Aviation Mus., Exptl. Aircraft Assn. Episcopalian. Avocations: aviation, historical reading, biking, hiking, air show announcing. Home: 3 High Point Airpark Rd Valley Center KS 67147-8566 Office: Scottish Rite Bodies 332 E 1st St Wichita KS 67202-2495 E-mail: jmyers@powwwer.net.

MYERS, JOHN THOMAS, retired congressman; b. Covington, Ind., Feb. 8, 1927; m. Carol Carruthers; children: Carol Ann, Lori Jan. BS, Ind. State U., 1951. Cashier, trust officer Fountain Trust Co.; owner, operator farm; mem. 90th-104th Congresses from 7th Dist. Ind., 1967-96; former chmn. subcom. on energy & water, appropriations com.; ret., 1997. Served with AUS, World War II, ETO. Mem. Am. Legion, VFW, Wabash Valley Assn., Res. Officers Assn., C. of C., Sigma Pi. Clubs: Mason, Elk, Lion. Republican. Episcopalian.

MYERS, JOHN WESCOTT, aviation executive; b. L.A., June 13, 1911; s. Louis Wescott and Blanche (Brown) M.; m. Lucia Raymond, Mar. 21, 1941 (dec. Mar. 1999); children: Louis W. (dec.), Lucia E. AB, Stanford U., 1933; JD, Harvard U., 1936. Bar: Calif. 1936. Ptnr. law firm O'Melveny & Myers, L.A., 1936-42; from test pilot to sr. v.p., dir. Northrop Corp., 1942-54, 1954-79; chmn. bd. Pacific Airmotive Corp., 1954-79, Airflite, Long Beach, Calif., 1970-89, Flying M Assocs., Long Beach, 1989—. Owner Flying M Ranches, Merced, Calif., 1959—. Dir. Smithsonian Nat. Air and Space Dulles Ctr. Project. Fellow Soc. Exptl. Test Pilots; mem. Calif. Bar Assn., Los Angeles Bar Assn., Inst. Aerospace Scis., Order of Daedalians (hon.). Clubs: Bohemian, California, Los Angeles Country, Los Angeles Yacht, Sunset, Aviation Country, Conquistadores del Cielo. Republican. Home: 718 N Rodeo Dr Beverly Hills CA 90210-3210 Office: 3200 Airflite Way Long Beach CA 90807-5312

MYERS, JOHNNIE DUMAS, law educator; b. Macon, Ga., Dec. 18, 1948; d. Ella Pearl Bryant and Johnny Dumas; children: Badru, Akii. BA, Clark Atlanta U., 1970, PhD, 1995; MS, Ga. State U., 1976; cert., Hers Women

Higher Edn. Adminstrn., 1997. Parole supr. Ga. Pardons and Paroles, Atlanta, 1973—76; instr. Kennesaw (Ga.) State U., 1977—83; asst. prof. criminal justice Albany (Ga.) State U., 1983—88; chairperson criminal justice dept. Morris Brown Coll., Atlanta, 1988—; Advisor to Beta Chi chpt. Alpha Phi Sigma Morris Brown Coll., Atlanta, 1993—, faculty athletics rep. to NCAA, 1992—, former pres. faculty coun., 1997—98; presenter United Negro Coll. Fund PEJER Project, Augusta, Ga.; panelist substance abuse edn. in instns. higher learning Lonnie Mitchell Conf. Substance Abuse, Balt., 2002. Mem. personnel com. Rainbow Pk. Bapt. Ch., Decatur, Ga., 1999—2001, mem. nomination com., 2000—02; exec. bd. Nat. Historically Black Colls. and Univs. Substance Abuse Consortium, Atlanta, 1999—2002; governance coun. CORK Inst., Morehouse Sch. Medicine, 1989—2002; participant selection com. Ga. Police Corps, Forsyth, 2002. Recipient Outstand Svc. and Dedication to Orgn., National HBCU Substance Abuse Consortium, 2001; fellow Particia Robert Harris, U. S. Dept. Edn. through Clark Atlanta U., 1990-1993. Mem.: Nat. Assn. Blacks in Criminal Justice, Acad. Criminal Justice Scis., Am. Correctional Assn., Nat. Conf. Black Polit. Scientist (2002 conv. local arrangements com. 2001—02), Delta Sigma Theta (life; chairperson career day com. 1995—97). Baptist. Avocations: reading, bowling, travel. Home: 4925 Thames Ct Lithonia GA 30038 Office: Morris Brown Coll 643 Martin Luther King Jr Dr Atlanta GA 30314 Office Fax: 404-739-1175. Personal E-mail: jdmyers6@juno.com. Business E-Mail: johnnie.myers@morrisbrown.edu.

MYERS, KENNETH ELLIS, hospital administrator; b. Battle Creek, Mich., Jan. 1, 1932; s. Orlow J. and Kathryn (Brown) M.; m. Nancy Lee Lindgren, June 9, 1956; children— Cynthia Lynn, Anne Lisa, Thomas Scot, Susan Elaine. BBA, U. Mich., 1956, MBA, 1957. Research analyst Bur. Bus. Research, U. Mich., 1956-57; in financial mgmt. Burroughs Corp., Detroit, 1957-66; controller William Beaumont Hosp., Royal Oak, Mich., 1966-68, asso. dir., 1968-69, hosp. dir., 1969-80, exec. v.p., 1976-80, pres., 1981-97; retired. Pres. Trinity Loss Prevention Systems, 1980-81. Elder Bloomfield Hills Christian Ch., 1979-82, Grace Chapel, 1988-92, 1995-99, 2001-02; bd. visitors Oakland Sch. Bus. Adminstrn., 1978-92; adv. bd. Salvation Army, 1985-99; bd. dirs. William Tyndale Coll., 1992—, West Bloomfield Bldg. Authority, 1978—, William Beaumont Hosp., 1971—; trustee St. Mary's Hosp., 1992-97. Mem. Mich. Hosp. Assn. (past chmn.), Vol. Hosps. Am. Enterprises (bd. dirs. 1984-87), Full Gospel Businessmen's Fellowship, Bloomfield Hills Country Club, Belleair Country Club, Old Club, Phi Delta Theta, Beta Gamma Sigma. Home: 6085 Simsbury Ct West Bloomfield MI 48322-3567

MYERS, KENNETH JEFFREY, physician; b. Washington, July 29, 1957; s. Herschel Kenneth and Carolyn Sue Myers; m. Erin Bethany Wills, Oct. 28, 1989; children: Bethany, Grace. BS in Chemistry, U. Evansville, 1977; MD, Ind. U., Indpls., 1981; MS, Wright State U., 1987. Bd. cert. emergency medicine Am. Bd. Emergency Medicine, bd. cert. aerospace medicine, occupl. medicine and med. toxicology Am. Bd. Preventive Medicine. Gen. surgery resident Mayo Clinic, Rochester, Minn., 1981-84; aerospace medicine resident Wright State U., Dayton, Ohio, 1985-88; mgr. med. ops. Bionetics Corp., Kennedy Space Ctr., Fla., 1988-95; physician, emergency medicine cons. EG&G Fla., 1995-98; physician, toxicology cons. Comp Health Svcs., 1998—. Med. cons. Emergency Egress and Rescue Working Group, Kennedy Space Ctr., 1987—; emergency med. svcs. coord., Kennedy Space Ctr., 1994—, triage physician, 1995—; cons., reviewer Annals of Emergency Medicine, Dallas, 1996—; toxicology cons. Fla. Poison Ctr., Jacksonville, 1997—; adj. prof. space flight physiology Fla. Inst. Tech., Melbourne, 1996—. Hoosier boys state del. Am. Legion, Terre Haute, Ind., 1973; student union bd. Ind. U. Sch. Medicine, Inpdls., 1979. Maj. USAF, 1990-91, Desert Storm. Recipient Pres.'s citation Soc. NASA Flight Surgeons, 1999. Mem. Aerospace Med. Assn. (pres. space medicine br. 1998-99), Pan Am. Med. Assn. (pres. sect. for space and underwater medicine 1990—). Avocations: astronomy, running, model aeronautics, cross country skiing, scuba. Office: Comprehensive Health Svcs. Mail Code Chs 005 Kennedy Space Center FL 32899-0001

MYERS, KENNETH L(EROY), secondary education educator; b. Auburn, Nebr., Oct. 5, 1954; s. Kenneth E. and Erma F. (Hardwick) M.; m. Willo Kay Dykstra, July 1, 1995; children: Kendra, Kayla. BS in Edn., Peru State Coll., 1985, mid. sch. endorsement, 1990, MS in Edn., 1992. Cert. tchr., Nebr., Mo., Iowa. Tchr. math., coach Nodaway-Holt High Sch., Graham, Mo., 1985-87, Nebraska City (Nebr.) Lourdes High Sch., 1987-89; tchr. math., social studies, coach Newcastle (Nebr.) High Sch., 1989-97; tchr. math., coach Schaller/Crestland H.S., Early, Iowa, 1997—. Chair Newcastle Math. Curriculum Team, 1991-97; master tchr. N.E. Nebr. Masters Tchrs. Project, 1991-97; past mem. N.E. Nebr. Math. Cadre; mem. Nebr. State Coll. Evaluation Visitation Team, 1984. Mem. Iowa Coaches Assn., Newcastle Faculty Orgn. (pres. 1992-95). Achievements include development of reverse FOIL method of factoring using grid structure. Office: Schaller Crestland HS Early IA 50535

MYERS, LAWRENCE STANLEY, JR. radiation biologist; b. Memphis, Apr. 29, 1919; s. Lawrence Stanley and Jane Myers; m. Janet Vanderwalker, June 13, 1942; children: David Lee, Frederick Lawrence, Lee Scott. BS, U. Chgo., 1941, PhD, 1949. Jr. chemist Metall. Lab. of Manhattan Engring. Dist., U. Chgo., 1942-44; asst. chemist Clinton Labs. of Manhattan Engring. Dist., Oak Ridge, Tenn., 1944-46; chemist Inst. for Nuclear Studies, U. Chgo., 1947-48; assoc. chemist Argonne (Ill.) Nat. Lab., 1948-52; asst. prof. radiology UCLA, 1953-70, assoc. rsch. phys. chemist Atomic Energy project, 1952-59, lectr. in radiol. scis., 1970-76, adj. prof. radiol. scis., 1976-82; rsch. radiobiologist, chief radiobiology div. UCLA Lab. Nuclear Medicine and Radiation Biology, 1959-76; prof. radiology and nuclear medicine Uniformed Svcs. Univ. of Health Scis., 1982-88; sci. advisor Armed Forces Radiobiology Rsch. Inst., 1982-87; cons. Oak Ridge Assoc. Univs., 1987-94. Vis. scientist AFRRI, 1987-93; adj. biophysicist Radiation Biology Br. Nat. Cancer Inst. NIH, 1993—; co-organizer UCLA Internat. Conf. on Radiation Biology, 1957, 59; participant in three major Fed. Govt. planning exercises related to energy rsch. and devel. in U.S., 1973-74; mem. adv. com. Ctr. for Fast Kinetic Rsch. U. Tex., Austin, 1975-81, chmn., 1977-81; mem. adv. bd. Radiation Chemistry Data Ctr., U. Notre Dame, 1976-84, sec. 1979-81, chmn. 1981-83; chmn. Long Range Planning Com., Radiation Rsch. Soc., 1976-78; dir. Issues and Requirements Workshop for Analysis of the 1976 "Inventory of Fed. Energy Related Environ. and Safety Rsch.", 1977. Contbr. more than 100 sci. articles and abstracts to profl. jours. Com. mem. Boy Scouts of Am., Pacific Palisades and Malibu, Calif., 1956-67. Fellow AAAS; mem. Radiation Rsch. Soc., N.Y. Acad. Sci., Soc. for Free Radical Rsch., Sigma Xi. Home: 11810 Coldstream Dr Potomac MD 20854-3612 Office: NIH Nat Cancer Inst Radiation Biology Br Bethesda MD 20892-1002 E-mail: lmyers@mail.nih.gov.

MYERS, LAWRENCE W. neurologist; b. Rome, Apr. 8, 1938; m. Shirley Ann Liebi, June 17, 1961; children: Brian, Bruce, Lorraine. BA, Hobart Coll., 1960; MD, SUNY, Syracuse, 1964. Diplomate Am. Bd. Psychiatry and Neurology. Intern in medicine U. Tex. Med. Br., Galveston, 1964-65; resident in neurology UCLA, 1967-71, rsch. fellow in neurology, 1971-73, asst. prof. of neurology, 1973-77, assoc. prof. neurology, 1977-83, prof. neurology, 1983—. Asst. dir. UCLA Multiple Sclerosis Clin., L.A., 1973-75, co-dir., 1975—; med. adv. bd. Nat. Multiple Sclerosis Soc., L.A., 1978—, N.Y.C., 1991-94, 96—. Contbg. author chpts. in books; author rsch. papers. Capt. USAF, 1965-67. Fellow Am. Acad. Neurology; mem. Am. Neurol. Assn., Clin. Immunology Soc., Soc. for Clin. Trials.

MYERS, LIBBY ANN, retired nurse; b. Hutchinson, Kans., July 22, 1936; d. Edwin Eugene and Verna Maxine (Craig) Schroeder; m. William Wayne Osborne, Apr. 1950 (div. 1960); m. William Andrew Myers III, June 21, 1962; children: Linda Kay, Lloyd Lee, Diana Gaye, Joe Lyle, Delbert Matthew. MSN, Okla. Bapt. U., 1958. RN, Okla. Nurse Bapt. Meml. Hosp., Oklahoma City, 1967-70, Doctors Gen. Hosp., Oklahoma City, 1970-73, Mercy Hosp., Oklahoma City, 1973-79; nurse, team leader PICU Hutchinson (Kans.) Hosp., 1979-87; pvt. practice pvt. duty nurse Oklahoma City, 1987-93; ret., 1993. Owner, operator Day Care Facility, Oklahoma City, 1977-79. Precinct poll inspector Precinct 238 Oklahoma City Election Bd., 1988-96, precinct com. chair Precinct 238 Oklahoma City Rep., 1992-96; exec. com. Oklahoma County Rep. Hdqrs., Oklahoma City, 1994-96; pres., former block capt. Epworth Neighborhood Assn., Oklahoma City, 1991-96; counselor Homicide Survivors Support Group, Oklahoma City, 1991-96, lobbyist for victims bills, 1992-96; Sunday sch. tchr., Bible sch. tchr. Crestwood Bapt. Ch., Oklahoma City; rescue worker during Oklahoma City bombing aftermath, also mem. survivor notifcation team, 1st Christian Ch., and victim advocate, Save Haven, Oklahoma City, during trials; candidate for Okla. Ho. of Reps., Dist. 88, 1998. Mem. Tri-City Rep. Women, Bapt. Women. Avocations: reading, poetry writing, watching ball games, cooking, crafts.

MYERS, LONN WILLIAM, lawyer; b. Rockford, Ill., Nov. 14, 1946; s. William H. and Leona V. (Janvrin) M.; m. Janet L. Forbes, May 14, 1968; children: Andrew, Hillary, Corwin. BA, Mich. State U., 1968; MBA, Ind. U., 1973; JD, Harvard U., 1976. Bar: Ill. 1976, U.S. Ct. of Fed. Claims 1977, U.S. Tax Ct. 1977, U.S. Ct. Appeals (7th cir.) 1977. Ptnr. McDermott, Will & Emery, Chgo., 1976—. Served to maj. USAR, 1968-80. Mem. ABA (capital recovery and leasing com. tax sect., tax exempt fin. com. tax sect.). Episcopalian. Home: 1711 Highland Ter Glenview IL 60025-2284 Office: McDermott Will & Emery 227 W Monroe St Chicago IL 60606-5096

MYERS, MADELEINE BECAN, secondary school educator; b. Waco, Tex., Feb. 17, 1944; d. Jaromir J. and Willie Mae (Hejl) Becan; m. James Dale Myers, Dec. 27, 1966; children: Steven, Melanie, Justin. BA in English, U. Dallas, 1966, MA in English, 1971. Cert. tchr., Tex. Elem. tchr. St. Andrew Sch., Ft. Worth, 1966-67; adminstrv. asst. U. Dallas, 1978-84; tchr. English MacArthur H.S., Irving, Tex., 1985-97, The North Hills Sch., Irving, 1997-98; tchr. Lewisville (Tex.) H.S., 1998—. Mem. SAT II lit. com. Ednl. Testing Svc., Princeton, N.J., 1997-2000; mem. textbook com. State Bd. Edn., Tex., 1986; adj. prof. U. Tex., Arlington, summer 1998. Contbg. author: Talking to Learn, 1997. Pres. Irving LWV, 1992-94, natural resources chair, 1983-92; mem. Coppell Cmty. Theater. Mem. Nat. Coun. Tchrs. English, Tex. Coun. Tchrs. English, Tex. Classroom Tchrs. Assn., Tex. Ednl. Theatre Assn., Tex. Assn. Gifted and Talented, Coppell Friends of the Libr., Kappa Delta Pi (v.p. 1985-86). Roman Catholic. Avocations: travel, needlework, writing. Office: Lewisville High Sch North 2103 Savage Ln Lewisville TX 75057-2149

MYERS, MARILYN GLADYS, pediatric hematologist and oncologist; b. Lyons, Nebr., July 17, 1930; d. Leonard Clarence and Marian N. (Manning) M.; m. Paul Frederick Motzkus, July 24, 1957 (dec. Aug. 1982). BA cum laude, U. Omaha, 1954; MD, U. Nebr., 1959. Diplomate Am. Bd. Pediatrics. Intern Orange County Gen. Hosp., Orange, Calif., 1959-60, resident, 1960-62; fellow in hematology/oncology Orange County Gen. Hosp./Children's Hosp. L.A., 1962-64; assoc. in rsch., chief dept. hematology/oncology Children's Hosp., Orange, 1964-80, dir. outpatient dept., 1964-73, assoc. dir. leukapheresis unit, 1971-80; clin. practice hematology, oncology, rheumatology, 1964-80; instr. Coll. Medicine U. Calif., Irvine, 1968-71, asst. clin. prof. pediatrics, 1971—; pvt. practice hematology, oncology, rheumatology Santa Ana, Calif., 1980—. Clin. rschr. exptl. drugs. Contbr. articles to med. jours. Mem. med. adv. com. Orange County Blood Bank Hemophiliac Found. Grantee Am. Leukemia Soc., 1963, Am. Heart Assn., 1964. Fellow Am. Acad. Pediatrics; mem. AMA, Calif. Med. Assn., L.A. County Med. Assn., Orange County Med. Assn., Orange County Pediatric Soc., Southwestern Pediatric Soc., L.A. Pediatric Soc., Internat. Coll. Pediatrics, Orange County Oncologic Soc., Am. Heart Assn. (Cardiopulmonary Coun.). Republican. Methodist. Avocation: reading. Office: 2220 E Fruit St Ste 217 Santa Ana CA 92701-4459

MYERS, MARSHALL DEAN, English educator; b. Platteville, Wis., Dec. 4, 1943; s. Clarice Myers Jr. and Carol Jane Agnes (Cushman) Clement; m. Lynn Gillaspie; children: Mitzi Carol Kreisle, Marti Alice Brown. AA, Lindsey Wilson Coll., Columbia, Ky., 1963; BA, Ky. Wesleyan U., 1965; MA, Ea. Ky. U., 1966; PhD, U. Louisville, 1994. Instr. Elizabethtown (Ky.) C.C., 1966-68; asst. prof. English Ky. Wesleyan Coll., Owensboro, 1968-70, 74-88, Tex. Tech. U., Lubbock, 1993-95; assoc. prof. English Ea. Ky. U., Richmond, 1995—. Instr. Tell City (Ind.) Schs., 1977-79, Ky. Tech., Owensboro, 1979-88. Author: (book of poetry) On the Inside, (collection of short stories) Barefoot; editor Ellipsis newsletter, 1990-91, Ky. Assn. Continuing Edn. newsletter, 1985; author 200 poems, essays and articles in jours. and mag. Sec. Literacy Coun., Owensboro, 1987-88; mem. coun. Faith Luth. Ch., Owensboro, 1980-85. Winner Ohio Valley Writing Club, Evansville, Ind., 1983; recipient Cert. of Recognition, Owensboro-Daviess County Literacy Coun., 1986. Mem. Nat. Coun. Tchrs. English, Madison County Civil War Roundtable (pres. 1998—), Coll. Conf. on Composition and Comm. Home: 207 Keystone Dr Apt 5 Richmond KY 40475-8571 Office: Eastern Ky Univ Dept English Case Annex 467 Richmond KY 40475

MYERS, MARY A. public relations consultant; b. Waukesha, Wis., July 28, 1936; d. Willard R. and Ruth Hardaker Evans; m. Ralph Payton Myers, June 14, 1958 (dec. Sept. 1969); children: Marsha Ruth, Evan Scott. BS, Northwestern U., Evanston, Ill., 1957; MBA, De Paul U., Chgo., 1984. Mng. editor Pioneer Press, Wilmette, Ill., 1969-73; dep. bus. editor Chgo. Sun-Times, 1973-84; v.p. Hill & Knowlton, Chgo., 1984-86; dep. bus. editor The Washington Post, 1986-88; sr. v.p. Hill & Knowlton, 1988-92; dir. Burson-Marsteller, Chgo., 1992-96, mng. dir., chair Midwest corp. practice, 1996-2001. Mem.: Nat. Investor Rels. Inst., Soc. Profl. Journalists, Univ. Club, Exec. Club Chgo., Chgo. Headline Club. Presbyterian. E-mail: maryamyers@earthlink.net.

MYERS, MARY KATHLEEN, publishing executive; b. Cedar Rapids, Iowa, Aug. 19, 1945; d. Joseph Bernard and Marjorie Helen (Huntsman) Weaver; m. David F. Myers, Dec. 30, 1967; children: Mindy, James. BA in English and Psychology, U. Iowa, 1967. Tchr. Lincoln H.S., Des Moines, 1967-80; editor Perfection Learning Corp., 1980-87, v.p., editor-in-chief, 1987-93; pres., founding ptnr. orgn. to promote Edward de Bono Advanced Practical Thinking Tng., 1992—. Pres. Innova Tng. & Cons., Inc., 2000—. Editor: Six Thinking Hats, 1991, Lateral Thinking, 1993, Direct Attention Thinking Tools, 1997, Total Creativity, 1997. Adv. bd. Sch. Bus., Econs. and Acctg., Simpson Coll., 1998—. Mem. ASTD, Am. Creativity Assn. (bd. dirs. 1997—, pres. 1999), Instrnl. Systems Assn. (v.p. mem. svcs. 2002—). Home: 813 56th St West Des Moines IA 50266-6314 Office: APTT 2882 106th St # 200 Des Moines IA 50322-3771 E-mail: kymers@aptt.com.

MYERS, MICHELE TOLELA, college president; b. Rabat, Morocco, Sept. 25, 1941; came to U.S., 1964; d. Albert and Lilie (Abecassis) Tolela; m. Pierre Vajda, Sept. 12, 1962 (div. Jan. 1965); m. Gail E. Myers, Dec. 20, 1968; children: Erika, David. Diploma, Inst. Polit. Studies, U. Paris, 1962; MA, U. Denver, 1966, PhD, 1967; MA, Trinity U., 1977; LHD, Wittenberg U., 1994, Denison U., 1998, U. Denver, 1999. Asst. prof. speech Manchester Coll., North Manchester, Ind., 1967-68; asst. prof. speech and sociology Monticello Coll., Godfrey, Ill., 1968-71; asst. prof. communication Trinity U., San Antonio, 1975-80, assoc. prof., 1980-86, asst. v.p. for acad. affairs, 1982-85, assoc. v.p., 1985-86; assoc. prof. sociology, dean Undergrad. Coll. Bryn Mawr (Pa.) Coll., 1986-89; pres. Denison U., Granville, Ohio, 1989-98, Sarah Lawrence Coll., Bronxville, N.Y., 1998—. Comm. analyst Psychology and Commn., San Antonio, 1974-83; chmn. bd. dirs. Am. Coun. on Edn., 1997-98, Sherman Fairchild Found., 1992--; mem. Fed. Res. Bank of Cleve., 1995-98; pres.'s commn. Nat. Collegiate Athletic Assn., 1993-97, JSTOR, 1999—. Author: (with Gail Myers) The Dynamics of Human Communication, 1973, 6th and internat. edits., 1992, transl. into French, 1984, Communicating When We Speak, 1975, 2d edit., 1978, Communication for the Urban Professional, 1977, Managing by Communication: An Organizational Approach, 1982, transl. into Spanish, 1983, internat. edit., 1982. Trustee Phila. Child Guidance Clinic, 1988-89; trustee assoc. The Bryn Mawr Sch., Balt., 1987-89; v.p., bd. dirs. San Antonio Cmty. Guidance Ctr., 1979-83. Am. Coun. Edn. fellow in acad. adminstrn., 1981-82, Bank One Columbus, 1990-94. Mem. Am. Coun. Edn. (commn. on women in higher edn. 1990-92, bd. dirs. 1993-99, chmn. 1997-98). Home: 935 Kimball Ave Bronxville NY 10708-5507 Office: Sarah Lawrence Coll One Mead Way Bronxville NY 10708 E-mail: mmyers@slc.edu.

MYERS, MILES ALVIN, educator, educational association administrator; b. Newton, Kans., Feb. 4, 1931; s. Alvin F. and Katheryn P. (Miles) M.; m. Celeste Myers; children: Royce, Brant, Roslyn. BA in Rhetoric, U. Calif., Berkeley, 1953, MAT in English, 1979, MA in English, PhD in Lang. and Literacy, U. Calif., Berkeley, 1982. Cert. secondary tchr. English. Tchr. English Washington Union High Sch., Fremont, Calif., 1957-59, Oakland (Calif.) High Sch., 1959-67, 69-74, Concord High Sch., Mt. Diablo, Calif., 1967-69; chmn. bd. dirs. Alpha Plus Corp. Preschs., Piedmont, 1968—; dir. All City High, 1973-74; tchr. English Castlemont High Sch., Oakland, 1974-75; mem. faculty U. Calif., Berkeley, 1975-85; adminstrv. dir. Bay Area writing project Sch. Edn. U. Calif.., 1976-85; adminstrv. dir. nat. writing project Sch. Edn. U. Calif., 1979-85; pres., CEO Calif. Fedn. Tchrs., 1985-90; exec. dir. Nat. Coun. Tchrs. of English, Urbana, Ill., 1990-97, Edschool.com of Edvantage/Riverdeep, 1999—2001; dir. Inst. Rsch. on Learning and Tchg., Berkeley, Calif., 2001—. Co-dir. Nat. Standards Project for English Language Arts, 1992-96; adj. prof. English U. Ill., Champaign-Urbana, 1991-94; exec. dir. Calif. Subject Matter Projects, U. Calif., 1997-98, Edn. Sch. com., 1999—; vis. lectr. at numerous colleges and Univs.; rschr. in field. Author: The Meaning of Literature, 1973; co-author: Writing: Unit Lessons in Composition, Book III, 1965, The English Book-Composition Skills, 1980; author: A Procedure for Holistic Scoring, 1980, Changing our Minds, 1996; co-author: Exemplars of Standards for English Language Arts, 3 vols., 1997; editor Calif. Tchr., 1966-81; contbr. articles to profl. jours.; pub. monographs. Sgt. U.S. Army, 1953-56. Recipient cert. of Merit, Ctrl. Calif. Coun. Tchrs. of English, 1969, Commendation award Oakland Fedn. Tchrs., 1970, First Place award Internat. Labor Assn., 1971, Disting. Svc. award Calif. Coun. Classified Employees, 1991, Svc. award Nat. Writing Project, 1996. Fellow Nat. Conf. Rsch. in English; mem. Nat. Coun. Tchrs. of English, Nat. Conf. on Rsch. in English, Am. Fedn. of Tchrs. (legis. dir. Calif. Fedn. of Tchrs. 1971-72, Union Tchr. Press awards 1969-75, 86-89, 91, Ben Rust award Calif. Fedn. of Tchrs. 1994), Am. Edn. Rsch. Assn., Calif. Assn. Tchrs. of English (Disting. Svc. award 86), Internat. Reading Assn., U. Calif./Berkeley Alumni Assn., Phi Delta Kappa. Home: 5823 Scarborough Dr Oakland CA 94611-2721 Office: Dir Inst Rsch on Learning & Tchg Berkeley CA 94704 Fax: 510-531-1734. E-mail: milesmye@pabell.net.

MYERS, MILLER FRANKLIN, finance company executive, retail executive; b. Aberdeen, S.D., Sept. 26, 1929; s. Burton Franklin and Virginia (Miller) M.; m. Janet Arlene Rylander, June 16, 1951; children: Leslie Ann, Burton F., Claudia Ann, Georgianna. Student, Grinnell Coll., 1947-49; BA, U. Minn., 1951-53, LLD, 1953. From v.p. to pres. Internat. Dairy Queen, Mpls., 1961-65, Dairy Queen of Can., Hamilton, Ont., 1953-70; chmn., chief exec. officer Internat. Dairy Queen, Mpls., 1970-74; pres. Econo-Therm Energy Systems, 1975-84; chmn. Franklin Investments, Inc., 1984-93. Pres., chmn. Dairy Queen Nat. Devel. Corp., St. Louis, 1960-64, Bayview Capital Corp., 1980-95; bd. dirs. Northwestern Nat. Bank, Mpls., 1965-69, Northwestern Teleprodns., Mpls., 1969-77, Keller Grad. Sch. Mgmt., 1974—. Del. Rep. Conv., St. Paul, 1968; student organizer Stassen for Pres., 1948. Mem. Young Pres. Orgn., 1966-82, World Bus. Counsel, Minn. Execs. Orgn., Mpls. Club, Minikahda Club, Wilderness Country Club, Lafayette Club, Hole in the Wall Golf Club. Republican.

MYERS, MINOR, JR. academic administrator, political science educator; b. Akron, Ohio, Aug. 13, 1942; s. Minor and Ruth (Libby) M.; m. Ellen Achin, Mar. 21, 1970; children: Minor III, Joffre V.A. BA, Carleton Coll., Northfield, Minn., 1964; MA, Princeton U., 1967, PhD, 1972. From instr. to assoc. prof. Conn. Coll., New London, 1968-81, prof. govt., 1981-84; provost, dean of faculty, prof. polit. sci. Hobart and William Smith Colls., Geneva, 1984-89; pres., prof. polit. sci. Ill. Wesleyan U., Bloomington, 1989—. Adv. Numismatic Collection Yale U., 1975-84; chmn. adv. coun. Lyman Allyn Mus., 1976-81, 82-84, pres., 1982-84. Author: Liberty Without Anarchy: A History of the Society of the Cincinnati, 1983, The Insignia of the Society of the Cincinnati, 1998; (with others) Arnold O. Beckman, One Hundred Years of Excellence, 2000, (with others) New London County Furniture, 1974, (with others) The Princeton Graduate School: A History, 1978, 2nd edit., 1997, (with others) American Interiors: A Documentary History from the Colonial Era to 1915, 1980. Asst. sec. gen. Soc. of the Cin., 1983-86, sec.-gen., 1986-89; trustee Inst. for Internat. Edn. Students, 1992-98, Found. for Ind. Higher Edn., 1999—, Nat. Merit Scholarship Corp., 1999-2002; pres. Associated Colls. Ill., 1999-2001. Mem. Grolier Club (N.Y.C.), Princeton Club (N.Y.C.), University Club (Chgo.), Caxton Club (Chgo.), Phi Beta Kappa, Sigma Xi. Office: Ill Wesleyan U PO Box 2900 Bloomington IL 61702-2900

MYERS, NORMAN LEWIS, fund development consultant; b. Xenia, Ohio, Oct. 21, 1932; s. Norman Theodore and Effie Marie (DeLawder) M.; m. Sue Anne Hanlon, Nov. 7, 1953; children: John Norman, Jeffrey Alan, Joseph Brian. Stuent, U.S. Armed Forces Inst., 1956. Chief dep. clk. Ohio Supreme Ct., Columbus, 1957-66; divsn. dir. United Way, 1966-69; sr. assoc. dir. Children's Hosp. Found., 1970-94. Cons. Arnold Palmer Children's Hosp., Orlando, Fla., 1995, Orland Amateur Athletic Assn., Orlando, 1996. Author: The Buck Starts Here, 1999. Bd. dirs. various ch. and civic assns.; trustee Children's Miracle Network, 1983-85. Served with USN and USNR, 1952-76, comdg. Naval Res. unit, Zanesville, Ohio. Recipient Best Total Devel. award Nat. Assn. for Hosp. Devel., 1977; Norman L. Myers Staff award for support of devel. of volunteerism named in his honor, 1994. Fellow Assn. Healthcare Philanthropy (Harold J. Seymour honors award 1991); mem. Univ. Club (Winter Park, Fla.) (2d vice chair 1998—), Sigma Phi Epsilon (hon.) Methodist. Avocations: golf, genealogy. Home: 1500 Gay Rd Apt 20B Winter Park FL 32789-2962

MYERS, PHILLIP FENTON, financial services and technology company executive; b. Cleve., June 24, 1935; s. Max I. and Rebecca (Rosenblum) M.; m. Hope Gail Strum, Aug. 13, 1961 B in Indsl. Engring., Ohio State U., 1958, MBA, 1960; D in Bus. Adminstrn., Harvard U., 1966. Staff indsl. engr. Procter & Gamble Co., Cin., 1958; sr. cons. Cresap, McCormack & Paget, N.Y.C., 1960-61; staff assoc. Mitre Corp., Bedford, Mass., 1961; cons. Sys. Devel. Corp., Santa Monica, Calif., 1963-64; dir. long range planning Electronic Specialty Co., Los Angeles, 1966-68; chmn. Atek Industries, 1968-72; pres. Myers Fin. Corp., 1973-82; chmn. Amvid Comm. Svcs., Inc., 1975-79, Omni Resources Devel. Corp., 1979-83; chmn., pres. Am. Internat. Mining Co., Inc., 1979-83; pres. Advent Internat. Mgmt. Co., Inc., 1982—; chmn. Global Bond Mktg. Svcs., Inc., 1987-90; pres., CEO Whitehall Container Mfg. Corp., 1988-91; pres. Whitehall Motors Co., 1989-97, Allied Metamatter Tech. Corp., 1994—; chmn. U.S. Water Resources, Inc., 1994-96; pres. Am. Tech. Venture Fund Mgmt., Inc., Advent Internat. Realty Corp., 1996—, First Internet. Capital Corp., 1996—. Pres. Turbogen, Inc., 1995—, Blue Star Material Techs. Inc., 1997-2000, founding dir. Warner Ctr. Bank, 1980-83; bd. dirs. Cyber Security Systems, Inc.; lectr. bus. adminstrn. U. So. Calif., L.A., 1967-74; prof. Grad. Sch. Bus. Adminstrn. Pepperdine U., 1974-81. Trustee, treas. Chamber Symphony Soc. Calif., 1971-78; mem. campaign issues com. Reagan for Pres., 1976, 80; pub. safety commr. City of Hidden Hills, Calif., 1976-83, chmn., 1982-83; co-chmn. budget adv. com. Las Virgenes Sch. Dist., 1983-86; mem. Mayor's Blue Ribbon Fin. Com., 1981-82; mem. dean's select adv. com. Coll. Engring., Ohio State U., 1984-94; mem. state exec. com. Calif. Libertarian Party, chmn. region 61, 1989-90, chmn. strategic planning com.; dep. chmn. Los Angeles County Libertarian Party, 1991-92; chairperson campaign issues com. Marrou for Pres., 1991-92; chmn. bd. trustees WWII Hist. Soc., 1992—, new Sousa Band, Inc., 1998—; pres. Harvard Bus. Club Columbus, 1996-98, dir.; dir. Harvard Bus. Sch. Club of Columbus, 1998—, Ohio State Alumni Club, Franklin County, 1996—, pres. , 1998-99. Capt. USAF, 1958-60. Ford Found. fellow, 1961-64 Mem. Soc. Automotive Engrs., Harvard Bus. Sch. Assn., Ohio State Alumni Assn., Harvard Club (bd. dirs. 1970-74, treas. 1971-73). E-mail: pmyers@istcap.com. *Personal philosophy: All out all the time. I stand for the creation of a new system of global governance which stresses individual liberty, freedom and responsibility, and which leads to a world that works for everyone with no one left out. In business, I stand for exceptional vision, creativity, innovation, and contribution.*

MYERS, PHILLIP SAMUEL, mechanical engineering educator; b. Webber, Kans., May 8, 1916; s. Earl Rufus and Sarah Katharine (Breon) M.; m. Jean Frances Alford, May 26, 1943; children: Katharine Myers Muirhead, Elizabeth Myers Baird, Phyllis Myers Rathbone, John, Mark. BS in Math. and Commerce, McPherson Coll., 1940; BSME, Kans. State Coll., 1942; PhDME, U. Wis., 1947. Registered profl. engr., Wis. Instr. mech. engring. Ind. Tech. Coll., Ft. Wayne, summer 1942; instr. U. Wis., Madison, 1942-47, asst. prof., 1947-50, assoc. prof., 1950-55, prof., 1955-86, emeritus prof., 1986—, chmn. dept. mech. engring., 1979-83. Cons. Diesel Engine Mfrs. Assn., U.S. Army, various oil and ins. cos. Contbr. articles to profl. jours. Chmn. Pine Lake com. W. Wis. Conf. Meth. Ch., 1955-60; Mem. Village Bd., Shorewood Hills, 1962-67. Recipient B.S. Reynolds Teaching award, 1964, McPherson Coll. Alumni citation of merit, 1971; Dugald Clerk award, 1971 Fellow ASME (Diesel Gas Power award 1971, Soichiro Honda award 1993), Soc. Automotive Engrs. (Colwell award 1966, 79, Horning award 1968, nat. pres. 1969, hon. mem.), AAAS; mem. NAE, Am. Soc. for Engring. Edn., Blue Key, Sigma Xi, Phi Kappa Phi, Sigma Tau, Pi Tau Sigma (Gold medal 1949), Tau Beta Pi (Ragnar Onstad Svc. to Soc. award 1978). Mem. Brethren Ch. Achievements include patents in field.

MYERS, PHILLIP WARD, otolaryngologist; b. Evanston, Ill., Nov. 11, 1939; s. R. Maurice and Vivian (Ward) M.; m. Lynetta Sargent, Dec. 22, 1963; children: Andrea, Ward, Alycia, Amanda, Andrew. BS, Western Ill. U., 1961; MD, U. Ill., 1965. Diplomate: Am. Bd. Otolaryngology. Intern St. Paul-Ramsey Hosp., 1965-66; resident in otolaryngology U. Louisville, 1966-68; resident Northwestern U., 1968-70, fellow, 1970-71; practice medicine specializing in otolaryngology Springfield, Ill., 1973—; clin. prof. otolaryngology So. Ill. U., 1973—. Served to maj. M.C. AUS, 1971-73. Fellow Am. Soc. for Head and Neck Surgery, Am. Acad. Facial Plastic and Reconstructive Surgery; ACS, Am. Acad. Otolaryngology-Head and Neck Surgery. Achievements include research in perilymphatic fistulas. Home: 3423 N Oak Hill Rd Rochester IL 62563-9273 Office: 331 W Carpenter St Springfield IL 62702-4901

MYERS, R. DAVID, library director, dean; b. Hutchinson, Kans., Mar. 27, 1949; s. William Raymond and Elizabeth (Haas) M.; m. Barbara Jean Burridge, Sept. 15, 1973; 1 child, John David. BA, U. No. Colo., 1972, MA, 1974; ABD, U. Mich., 1976; MA, U. Denver, 1979. Manuscript curator Western History Collection, Denver, 1976-79; rsch. assoc. Colo. Legis. Coun., 1979-81; reference specialist Libr. of Congress, Washington, 1981-84, reference supr., 1984-88; libr. dir. State Hist. Soc. of Wis., Madison, 1988-94; assoc. dean univ. libr. N.Mex. State U., Las Cruces, 1994-2001; dir. Fogelson libr., prof. history Coll. Santa Fe, 2001—. Editor Am. history Macmillan Pub., N.Y.C., 1991-94; cons. history of medicine dept. U. Wis., Madison, 1993-94. Author bibliographies for Libr. of Congress, 1987, 88. Mem. ALA, Am. Hist. Assn., Orgn. Am. Historians, Wis. Libr. Assn. Avocations: research, writing, baseball, mysteries. Office: Fogelson Libr Coll Santa Fe 1600 St Michaels Dr Santa Fe NM 87505

MYERS, R(ALPH) CHANDLER, lawyer; b. L.A., Jan. 9, 1933; s. Ralph Cather and Winifred (Chandler) M.; m. Rebecca Blythe Borkgren, Jan. 11, 1963. BA, Stanford U., 1954, JD, 1958; LLD (hon.), Whittier Coll., 1988. Bar: Calif. 1959, U.S. Dist. Ct. (cen. dist.) Calif. 1959, U.S. Supreme Ct. 1971. Law clk., then assoc. Parker, Stanbury, Reese & McGee, L.A., 1958-63; assoc. Nicholas, Kolliner & Van Tassel, 1963-65; ptnr. Myers & D'Angelo and predecessors, L.A. and Pasadena, Calif., 1965—. Nat. panelist Am. Arbitration Assn., L.A., 1964— ; bd. visitors Stanfor d U. Law Sch., Calif., 1970-73; mem. judge pro tem panel L.A. Mcpl. Ct., 1971-81; mem. Los Angeles County Dist. Atty.'s Adv. Coun., 1976-83 Nat. vice chmn. Keystone Gifts, Stanford Centennial Campaign, 1987—92; trustee Whittier Coll., Calif., 1973—2001, chmn. bd. trustees, 1981—87, trustee emeritus, 2001—; trustee Flintridge Prep. Sch., LaCanada-Flintridge, 1981—88, chmn. bd. trustees, 1985—88; co-founder Whittier Law Sch., 1975, trustee, 1975—2001, chmn. bd. trustees, 1981—87, trustee emeritus, 2001—; bd. dirs. Opera Guild So. Calif., L.A., 1971—83, pres., 1980—82; bd. dirs. Guild Opera Co. L.A., 1974—83, pres., 1975—77; bd. dirs. Western Justice Ctr. Found., 1993—, treas., 1996—99, 2d v.p., 1999—2001, 1st v.p., 2001—; bd. dirs. L.A. Child Guidance Clinic, 1972—83, pres., 1977—79; bd. dirs. Opera Assocs. of the Music Ctr., L.A., 1976—78. Recipient Stanford Assocs. award, 1984, Centennial Medallion award, 1991, Gold Spike award Stanford U., 1989, Disting. Svc. award Whittier Law Sch., 1993, Outstanding Achievement award Stanford Assocs., 1998. Mem. Wilshire Bar Assn. (bd. govs. 1972-81, pres. 1979-80), L.A. County Bar Assn. (trustee 1979-81), Stanford Law Soc. So. Calif. (bd. dirs. 1967-72, pres. 1970-71), Stanford Assocs. (bd. govs. 1992-97, treas. 1995-97), Jonathan Club, University Club (Pasadena), Stanford Club of L.A. (bd. dirs. 1963-70, pres. 1968-69). Home: La Canada 5623 Burning Tree Dr La Canada Flintridge CA 91011-2861 Office: Myers & D'Angelo 301 N Lake Ave Ste 800 Pasadena CA 91101-4108

MYERS, R(ALPH) THOMAS, chemist, educator; b. Maidsville, W.Va., Mar. 28, 1921; s. Harrison Lonzo and Martha Jane (Nuce) M.; m. Dorothy Kraus (div.); m. Evelyn Lightfoot (div.); children: Paul, Alice, Mary; m. Dorothy Amelia VanWert, Mar. 22, 1986. AB in Chemistry, W.Va. U., 1941, PhD in Chemistry, 1949. Rsch. assoc. Manhattan Project Columbia U., N.Y.C., 1944-45; assoc. prof. Waynesburg Coll., Wagnesburgh, Pa., 1948-51; asst. prof. chemistry Colo. Sch. Mines, Golden, 1951-56; prof. chemistry Kent (Ohio) State U., 1956-87, prof. emeritus, 1987—. Co-author: Chemistry: Visualizing Matter, 2d edit. Bd. edn., Kent, 1990-93, pres., 1993. Mem. AAAS, Am. Chem. Soc., Ohio Acad. Sci., Sigma Xi. Democrat. Unitarian-Universalist. Avocations: skiing, golf. Home: 1641 S Lincoln St Kent OH 44240-4448 Office: Kent State U Dept Chemistry Kent OH 44242-0001 E-mail: rtmyers@aol.com.

MYERS, REX CHARLES, history educator, retired college dean; b. Cleve., July 1, 1945; s. Charles F. and Merial W. (Jones) M.; m. Susan L. Richards, Jan. 10, 1987; children: Gary W., Laura M. BA, Western State Coll., 1967; MA, U. Mont., 1970, PhD, 1972; postgrad., U. Wash., 1983, Harvard U., 1990. Instr. Palo Verde Coll., Blythe, Calif., 1972-75; reference librarian Mont. Hist. Soc., Helena, 1975-78; prof., divsn. chmn., dean Western Mont. Coll., Dillon, 1979-86; dean S.D. State U., Brookings, 1986-91; acad. dean Lyndon State Coll., Lyndonville, Vt., 1991-95; lectr. Western State Coll., Gunnison, Colo., 1995-98, Mesa State Coll., 1998-99, Lawrence U., 1999—. Author: Montana Symbols, 1976, Montana Trolleys, 1970, Lizzie, 1989; co-author: Marble Colorado, 1970, Montana: Our Land and People, 1978, Montana and the West, 1984; contbr. articles to profl. jours. Bd. dirs. Ctr. for Western Studies, Sioux Falls, SD, 1990—, Gunnison Arts Ctr., Gunnison County Libr., Fox Valley Arts Alliance, Meml. Park Arboretum and Gardens. Summer stipend NEH, 1973; fellow James J. Hill Library, 1985. Mem.: AAUW, Mont. Oral History Assn. (chmn. 1980—83), Am. Conf. Acad. Deans, Western History Assn. (chmn. membership com. 1980—83), N.E. Kingdom C. of C. (bd. dirs.), Masons (master 1984), Kiwanis (pres. Dillon 1983, lt. gov. 1984, 1997), Phi Alpha Theta, Phi Kappa Phi. Unitarian Universalist. Home: PO Box 783 Appleton WI 54912-0783

MYERS, RICHARD KELLEY, family physician; b. Decatur, Ga., Dec. 26, 1968; s. Charles Hugh Myers and Judy Thomas. AA, Gainesville Coll., 1989; BS, U. Ga., 1993; MD in Microbiology and Psychology, Med. Coll. Ga., 1997. House officer Self Meml. Hosp., Greenwood, S.C., 1997-98; emergency rm. physician Abbeyville (S.C.) Hosp., 1998—; family physician Montgomery Ctr. for Family Medicine, Greenwood, 1998—. Physician Nat. Health Care Nursing Home, Greenwood, 1997—. Pres. student body, Med. Coll. Ga., 1996-97. Scholar Ty Cobb Ednl. Found., 1993-97, Dan Printup Meml. Trust, 1993-97, Sch. Med., 1993-94, Gainesville Coll. Found. Mem. AMA, Am. Acad. Family Physicians, Gideons Internat., Phi Beta Kappa, Phi Kappa Phi. Address: 112 Robusta Ct Harlingen TX 78552-6634

MYERS, ROBERT A, music educator; s. Kennety O and Irene E Myers; m. Marilyn Sue Jones, Sept. 2, 1967; children: Jason Earl, Amy Megan. Associater Arts, South Plains Coll., Leveland, Texas, 1965—67; Bachelor Music Edn., Ea. N.Mex U., Portales, New Mexicl, 1982—90; Masters Secondary Educaton, U. N.Mex, Albequerque, New Mexico, 1980—80. Cert. Music K-12, N.Mex Bd. Edn. Band dir. Santa Fe mcpl. schools, Santa Fe, 1972—82; music edn. specialist Washburn Musicland, Mesa, Ariz., 1982—90; band dir. Cloudcroft mcpl. schools, Cloudcroft, N.Mex., 1990—. Band v.p. N.Mex Educators Association, N.Mex., 1999—2001. Specialist fourth class U.S. Army, 1969—71, Fort Leonard Wood, Missouri. Recipient Music Educator Yr., N.Mex Edn. Assn., 1999. Mem.: Music Educators Nat. Conf., Tex. Bandmasters Assn., N.Mex Music Educators Assn. Methodist. Achievements include first to Incorporated small school all-. Avocations: music technology, outdoor activities, outdoor activities. Home: PO Box 1307 Cloudcroft NM 88317-1307 Office: Cloudcroft High School PO Box 198 Cloudcroft NM 88317 Personal E-mail: bibmarilynmyers@aol.com.

MYERS, ROBERT DAVID, judge; b. Springfield, Mass., Nov. 20, 1937; s. William and Pearl (Weiss) M.; m. Judith G. Dickenman, July 1, 1962; children— Mandy Susan, Jay Brandt, Seth William. AB, U. Mass., 1959; JD, Boston U., 1962. Bar: Ariz. 1963. Practice in, Phoenix, 1963-89; presiding judge civil dept. Superior Ct. of Arizona in Maricopa County, 1991-92; presiding judge probate and mental health dept. Superior Ct. of Ariz., Maricopa County, Ariz., 1992-95, presiding judge, 1995-2000; pro tem judge Ariz. Ct. Appeals; judge Ariz. Superior Ct., 1989—. Adj. prof. Ariz. State U. Sch. Law, 1997—; chmn. com. on exams and admissions Ariz. Supreme Ct., 1974-75, chmn. com. on character and fitness, 1975-76, mem. multi-state bar exam. com., 1976-85; bd. dirs. Nat. Conf. Met. Judges, 1997—, pres., 1998-99. Pres. Valley of Sun chpt. City of Hope, 1965-66, Cmty. Orgn. for Drug Abuse Control, 1972-73, Valley Big Bros., 1975; chmn. Mayors Ad Hoc Com. on Drug Abuse, 1974-75; bd. dirs. Maricopa County Legal Aid Soc., 1978. Recipient award for outstanding svc. and dedication to improving the legal profession and professionalism of the bar and bench Maricopa County Bar Assn., 1999, Superior Svc. award Ariz. chpt. ASPA, 2000, Justice Tom C. Clark award Nat. Conf. Metro. Cts., 2000. Mem. ATLA (nat. chmn. gov.), Ariz. Bar Assn. (gov., com. chmn., sect. pres.), Maricopa County Bar Assn. (dir., pres. 1979-80,Judge of yr., 1999, Henry S. Steven award 2000), Ariz. Trial Lawyers Assn. (pres., dir., co-editor newsletter), Phoenix Trial Lawyers Assn. (pres., dir.), Western Trial Lawyers Assn. (pres. 1977), Am. Judicature Soc. (spl. merit citation outstanding svc. improvement of adminstrn. justice 1986), Am. Bd. Trial Advocates (Phoenix chpt. Judicial Officer of Yr. award 2001), Sandra Day O'Connor Inn of Ct. (pres. 1991-92). Office: Justice Ctr 201 W Jefferson St Phoenix AZ 85003-2205

MYERS, ROBERT EUGENE, writer, educator; b. L.A., Jan. 15, 1924; s. Harold Eugene and Margaret (Anawalt) M.; m. Joyce E. Daily, 1946 (div. 1949); 1 child, Kathleen; m. Patricia A. Tazer, Aug. 17, 1956; children: Edward E., Margaret A., Hal R., Karen I. AB, U. Calif., Berkeley, 1955; MA (Crown-Zellerbach fellow), Reed Coll., 1960; EdD, U. Ga., 1968. Employed in phonograph record bus., 1946-54; tchr. elem. sch. Calif., Oreg., Minn., 1954-61; rsch. asst. U. Minn., 1961-62; asst. prof. Augsburg Coll., 1962-63, U. Oreg., 1963-66; elem. tchr. Eugene, Oreg., 1966-67; assoc. prof. U. Victoria, 1968-70; assoc. rsch. prof. Oreg. System of Higher Edn., 1970-73; film maker, producer ednl. filmstrips, books, recs., 1973-77; learning resources specialist Oreg. Dept. Edn., Salem, 1977-81; with Linn-Benton Edn. Svc. Dist., Albany, Oreg., 1982-87; ret., 1987. Author: (with E. Paul Torrance) Creative Learning and Teaching (Pi Lambda Theta award 1971), 1970, La Ensenanza Creativa, 1970, Can You Imagine?, 1965, Invitations to Thinking and Doing, 1964, Invitations to Speaking and Writing Creatively, 1965, Plots, Puzzles, and Ploys, 1966, For Those Who Wonder, 1966, Timberwood Tales, Vol. II, 1977, Wondering, 1984, Imagining, 1985, What Next?, 1994, Facing the Issues, 1995, Cognitive Connections, 1996, Mind Sparklers, 1997, Multiple Ways of Thinking with Social Studies, 1997, Character Matters, 1999, A Matter of Respect, 2000, It's Your Attitude That Counts, 2000, Mind Stretchers, 2001, Stories That Build Character, 2001, Think and Write, 2002, Now What, 2002, Spurs to Creative Thinking, 2002, Word Play, 2002; films: Feather (CINE Golden Eagle award), 1972, The Magic Net, 1972, Elephants, 1973. Mem. exec. bd. Nat. Assn. Gifted Children, 1974-77. With U.S. Mcht. Marine, 1944-45. Recipient CINE Golden Eagle award Coun. Internat. Non-theatrical Events, 1973. Mem. Internat. Reading Assn. Democrat. Home: 1357 Meadow Ct Healdsburg CA 95448-3347 E-mail: rorpmyers@mymailstation.com.

MYERS, ROBERT JAY, retired aerospace company executive; b. Bklyn., Oct. 15, 1934; s. John J. and Clara S. (Martinsen) M.; m. Carolyn Erland, Aug. 10, 1963; children: Susan, Kenneth. BCE, NYU, 1955, postgrad., 1957-65; P.MD, Harvard U., 1972. With Grumman Corp., Bethpage, N.Y., 1964-94, v.p. resources, 1980-83, sr. v.p. bus. and resource mgmt., 1983-85, sr. v.p. corp. svcs., 1985-86; pres. Grumman Data Systems Corp., 1986-90; pres., chief operating officer, bd. dirs. Grumman Corp., 1991-94, ret., 1994. Mem. sci. adv. coun. Ala. Space and Rocket Ctr., 1986-91. Mem. adv. panel on econ. devel. N.Y. State Project 2000, 1985-86; mem. L.I. Project 2000; mem. adv. bd. L.I. Youth Guidance, 1986-91; bd. dirs. Poly. U., 1991-98, North Shore Health System, 1994—, L.I. Mus. of Sci. and Tech., 1994-96; chmn. Huntington Hosp., 1996—. 1st lt. U.S. Army, 1955-57. Fellow Poly. U., 1987, Disting. Alumni award, 1989. Mem. Am. Def. Preparedness Assn. (dir. 1992-94), Navy League, Industry Exec. Bd., Nat. Space Club (bd. govs. 1986-89), Huntington Country Club (N.Y.), Audubon Country Club (Naples, Fla.). Presbyterian. Home: 200 Cheshire Way Naples FL 34110

MYERS, ROBERT LUTHER, architect, artist; b. Macon, Ga., May 29, 1926; s. John Henry and Ada (Leake) M. BArch, Cornell U., 1950; MArch, Harvard U., 1951. Cert. Nat. Coun. Archl. Registration Bds. Project designer The Architects Collaborative, Cambridge, Mass., 1951-53; instr. archtl. design Cornell U., Ithaca, N.Y., 1954-56; project designer Lashmit, James, Brown & Pollack, Winston-Salem, N.C., 1956-60, Charles Luckman Assocs., N.Y.C., 1962-67, Eggers Group Architects, N.Y.C., 1970-72; asst. head design dept. Russell, Gibson, Von Dohlen, Architects, Farmington, Conn., 1977-88; artist New Preston, 1988—. Co-founder S.E. Ctr. Contemporary Art, Winston-Salem; mem. nat. adv. bd. Ackland Art Mus. U. N.C., Chapel Hill, 1983—. With. inf. U.S. Army, 1944-45, M.C., 1945-46. Prix de Rome in architecture Am. Acad. Rome, 1954; Eidlitz travel fellow Cornell U., 1950. Mem. Washington-Conn. Art Assn., Chancellor's Club U. N.C., Gerrard Soc. U. N.C. Avocations: art collecting, gardening. Home: 144 Curtiss Rd New Preston Marble Dale CT 06777-1007

MYERS, ROBERT MANSON, English educator, author; b. Charlottesville, Va., May 29, 1921; s. Horwood Prettyman and Matilda Manson (Wynn) M. BA summa cum laude, Vanderbilt U., 1941; MA, Columbia, 1942, Harvard, 1943; PhD, Columbia, 1948. Instr. English Yale, 1945-47; asst. prof. Coll. William and Mary, 1947-48, Tulane U., 1948-54; tchr. English Brearley Sch., N.Y.C., 1954-56; chmn. dept. English Osbourn High Sch., Manassas, Va., 1956-59; mem. faculty U. Md., College Park, 1959—, prof. English, 1968-86, prof. emeritus, 1986—. Author: Handel's Messiah, 1948, From Beowulf to Virginia Woolf, 1952, rev., 1984, Handel, Dryden, and Milton, 1956, Restoration Comedy, 1961, The Children of Pride, 1972, abridged edit., 1984 (Nat. Book award 1973), A Georgian at Princeton, 1976, Quintet: Five Plays, 1991. Fulbright Postdoctoral Research fellow U. London, 1953-54; Fulbright lectr. Rotterdam, Netherlands, 1958-59 Mem. Modern Lang. Assn. Am., Am. Soc. 18th Century Studies, Jane Austen Soc. N.Am., Phi Beta Kappa. Home: 3804 Deckford Pl Charlotte NC 28211-3408

MYERS, ROBERT NORMAN, JR. financial executive; b. Altoona, Pa., July 19, 1949; s. Robert Norman and Elizabeth Ellen (Miller) M.; m. Janet Mae Weaver, Dec. 4, 1971; children: Michael, Patrick. BS in Acctg., Pa. State U., 1971; MBA, Xavier U., 1981. Bus. analyst Dun & Bradstreet, Columbus, Ohio, 1972-74; cost pricing analyst Rockwell Internat., 1974-79; fin. analyst Battelle Meml. Inst., 1979-81, bus. mgr., 1981-83, mgr. adminstrn. Duxbury, Mass., 1983-85, mgr. fin. and program mgmt. systems Columbus, 1985-87, mgr. fin., 1987-89, dir. of bus. ops., 1989-92, v.p. bus. ops., 1993-2001; CFO Edison Welding Inst., 2001—. Cons. fin. analysis, Columbus, 1986—. Capt. U.S. Army, 1971-80. Lutheran. Avocations: sports, woodwork, auto mechanics. Office: Edison Welding Inst 1250 Arthur E Adams Dr Columbus OH 43221 E-mail: myersr@battelle.org.

MYERS, ROBERT T. anesthesiologist; b. Peoria, Ill., Feb. 15, 1928; MD, U. Ill., 1954. Diplomate Am. Bd. Anesthesiology. Intern Cook County Hosp., Chgo., 1954-55; resident in anesthesiology Hines VA Hosp., 1958-60; pvt. practice Peoria; clin. asst. prof. Peoria Sch. Medicine; active staff Meth. Med. Ctr., Peoria; courtesy staff St. Francis Med. Ctr., 1960—; proctor Cmty. Hosp., 1960—. Mem. AMA, Am. Soc. of Anesthesiologists, Peoria Med. Soc.

MYERS, RODMAN NATHANIEL, lawyer; b. Detroit, Oct. 27, 1920; s. Isaac Rodman and Fredericka (Hirschman) Myers; m. Jeanette Polisei, Mar. 19, 1957 (dec. 1996); children: Jennifer Myers Grabenstein, Rodman Jay. BA, Wayne State U., 1941; LLB, U. Mich., 1943. Bar: Mich. 1943, U.S. Supreme Ct. 1962. Agt. IRS, Detroit, 1943; from assoc. to ptnr. Butzel, Keidan, Simon, Myers & Graham, 1943-90; of counsel Honigman Miller Schwartz and Cohn, 1991—. Mem. blue ribbon task force Mich. Dept. Edn., 1988—90; founding mem., trustee Mich. chpt. Leukemia and Lymphoma Soc., founding pres., 1984—86, nat. trustee, 1984—; founding mem., trustee Detroit Sci. Ctr.; commr. Detroit Mcpl. Parking Authority, 1963—71; pres., trustee Bloomfield Twp. Pub. Libr.; trustee Temple Beth El, Bloomfield Hills, Mich.; bd. dirs. United Cmty. Svcs. of Met. Detroit, 1978—85, v.p., 1981—85, chmn. social svcs. divsn., 1982—85; bd. dirs. Children's Ctr. of Wayne County, Mich., 1963—88, pres., 1969—72. Mem. ABA, State Bar Mich. (chmn. atty. discipline panel, past vice chmn. unauthorized practice of law com., past mem. character and fitness com.). Home: 3833 Lakeland Ln Bloomfield Hills MI 48302-1328 Office: 2290 1st National Bldg Detroit MI 48226

MYERS, ROLLAND GRAHAM, investment counselor; b. St. Louis, Aug. 30, 1945; s. Rolland Everett and Lurilien (Graham) M. Diploma, St. Louis Country Day Sch., 1963; AB cum laude in History and Lit., Harvard U., 1966; postgrad. Faculties of Social Scis. and Law, U. Edinburgh, Scotland, 1966-67; postgrad. Fondation Nationale des Sciences Politiques and Faculte de Lettres et des Sciences Humaines, U. Paris, 1967-68. Trainee global credit dept. The Chase Manhattan Bank, N.A., N.Y.C., 1968-69, mem. 32nd spl. devel. program, 1969, strategic planner internat. dept., 1969-70, securities analyst, mktg. rep., fiduciary investment dept., 1970; assoc. Smith, Barney & Co., Inc., 1971, account exec. N.Y. sales dept., 1971-72, instl. account exec. N.Y. internat. sales dept., 1972-74, 2nd v.p., stockholder, 1975-76; v.p., stockholder Smith Barney, Harris Upham & Co., Inc. (subs. SBHU Holdings, Inc.), 1976-78; prin. W.H. Graham & Sons, family investment office, 1977-82, investment counsel, 1982—. Ltd. ptnr. Croke Patterson Campbell, Ltd., Denver, 1975—; joint founder, gen. ptnr. Mansion Disbursements, Denver, 1979—; pres., chmn. exec. com., bd. dirs. Fifty-Five Residents Corp., N.Y.C., 1980-84; bd. dirs. Fifty-Six Danbury Rd. Assn., Inc., New Milford, Conn. Trustee, mem. corp. Bishop Rhinelander Found. (Episcopal Chaplaincy at Harvard and Radcliffe Colls.), Cambridge, 1973-75; v.p., treas., bd. dirs. The Whitehill Graham Found., St. Louis, 1976—; bd. dirs., fin. com., bylaws com., mem. corp. Eliot Pratt Edn. Ctr., Inc. (The Pratt Ctr.: Your Connection with the Natural World), New Milford, 1987-94; bd. dirs., mem. corp. Kent (Conn.) Land Trust, Inc., 1989—, treas., 1989-93; project financier Restoration of 1851 Samuel Curtiss Hosford House, Nat. Register Historic Dist., Falls Village, Conn., 1984-86; commr. Housatonic River Commn., Warren, Conn., 1985-93, vice chmn., 1986-87, chmn., 1988-92; commr. Conservation, Inland Wetlands and Watercourses Commn., Kent, 1988-93, vice chmn., 1988-92; mem. schs. and scholarships com., Office of Admissions and Fin. Aid, Harvard and Radcliffe Colls., 1991—. Mem. Cum Laude Soc., Mary Inst. and St. Louis Country Day Sch. Alumni Assn., Harvard Alumni Assn., Capitol Hill Club (Washington), Harvard Club (N.Y.C.), Hasty Pudding-Inst. of 1770 (Cambridge), Wyo. Bus. Alliance, Wyo. Heritage Found., St. Andrew's Soc., New Eng. Soc. in City N.Y. Republican. Episcopalian. Office: W H Graham & Sons Investment Counsel 1818 Evans Ave Ste 207 Cheyenne WY 82001-4664

MYERS, RONALD KOSTY, manufacturing executive, inventor; b. Mercer, Pa., Aug. 31, 1946; s. Cecil Charles and Mildred Elma (Hrisak) M.; m. Carol Lee Hunter, July 31, 1964; children: Tammy Lynn, Ronald K., Thomas Christopher. Cert. scuba diver. Mailbox painter, Hermitage, Pa., 1960-61; drive in usher Hickory Drive In, 1961-63; clk. Oscars Drive Thru, Masury, Ohio, 1963-64; gas station shift leader Kayo Oil Co., Warrenton, Va., 1967-68; clk. Erie R.R., Ferrona, Pa., 1968-70; diesel mechanic Sharon Steel Corp., Farrell, 1969-70, craneman, 1970-93; roofer contractor R&R Roofing, Sharon, 1978-79; asst. wrestling coach Sharon High Sch., 1979-85; chief exec. officer Flick It Mfg., Sharon, 1991—. Clk. B&O R.R., Youngstown, Ohio, 1973; coord. tour guide Army Security Agy., Va., 1967-68; participant Long Shot nuclear test, 1965. Author: How to Flick It, 1991, Refraction From a Patagonia Fragmentary, 1997; inventor Flick It trick rope. Chmn. armwrestling activities Hartford Apple Festival, 1988—. With U.S. Army, 1964-69. Mem. DAV, Nat. Assn. Atomic Vets., Army Security Agy. Chitose Alumni Assn., F.H. Buhl Club, VFW Post No 1835. Democrat. Roman Catholic. Avocations: writing, fishing, designing and inventing, armwrestling officiating, swimming. Home and Office: 440 N State Line Rd Sharon PA 16146-1471

MYERS, SHARON DIANE, auditor; b. Lawrence, Kans., Sept. 18, 1955; d. Richard Paul and Helen Carol (Overbey) M. AA, Mt. San Antonio Coll., Walnut, Calif., 1981; BSBA, Calif. State U., Pomona, 1983, MBA, 1986. Cert. fraud examiner; cert. govt. fin. mgr. Revenue agt. IRS, Glendale, Calif., 1984-85; auditor Def. Contract Audit Agy., L.A., 1985-92; auditor Office Inspector Gen. FDIC, Newport Beach, Calif., 1992—. Instr. Azusa (Calif.) Pacific U., 1987, 88, West Coast U., San Diego, 1992. Musician, Sunday sch. supt. Covina (Calif.) Bapt. Temple, 1975-95, Liberty Bapt. Ch., Irvine, Calif., 1995—. Mem. Assn. Govt. Accts. Republican. Avocations: piano, traveling. Home: 2702 44th Ave NW Olympia WA 98502-3692

MYERS, SHIRLEY DIANA, art book editor; b. N.Y.C., Jan. 6, 1916; d. Samuel Archibald and Regina (Edelstein) Levene; m. Bernard Samuel Myers, Aug. 11, 1938 (dec. Feb. 1993); children: Peter Lewis, Lucie Ellen. BA, NYU, 1936, MA, 1938. Editorial asst. Am. Dancer mag., N.Y.C., 1936-38; asst. to dir. Nat. Art Soc., 1938-42; freelance, art book editor N.Y.C. and Austin, Tex., 1947—. Editor: Modern Art in the Making, 1950, 59, Mexican Painting in Our Time, 1956, The German Expressionists, 1957, 63, Understanding the Arts, 1958, 63, Bruegel, 1976, Manet, 1977, (with B.S. Myers) Dictionary of 20th Century Art, 1974; asst. editor Ency. of Painting, 1955, 70, 79; asst. editor, contbr. McGraw-Hill Dictionary of Art, 5 vols., 1960-69; contbg. editor: Art and Civilization, 1956, 67; coord., picture editor Ency. World Art: Supplement, Vol. XVI, 1982, 83. Vol. archives New Sch. for Social Rsch. Libr., 1993-95. Mem. NOW, Older Women's League (rec. sec. Greater N.Y. chpt. 1993-95, co-chair 1995-97, mem. steering com. 1997—), Quest (coord. archaeology 1995-97, coord. cultural anthropology 1997-98, assoc. editor newsletter 1997-2000, mem. coun. 1997-2001, co-chair curriculum com. 1998-2001).

MYERS, STEPHEN HAWLEY, lawyer; b. Washington, Mar. 28, 1953; s. Robert Holt and Antoinette (Hawley) M.; children: Stephen, Hampton, Brielle; m. Laura Lee Fuller, Dec. 1, 1989. BA in Polit. Sci. with honors, Union Coll., 1976; JD, Loyola U., 1979. Bar: D.C. 1979, La. 1979, U.S. Dist. Ct. D.C. 1980, U.S. Tax Ct. 1980, U.S. Ct. Claims 1980, U.S. Ct. Appeals (fed. and D.C. cirs.) 1980, U.S. Ct. Appeals (5th cir.) 1985, U.S. Dist. Ct. (we., mid. and ea. dists.) La. 1985, U.S. Supreme Ct. 1989. Atty. advisor to hon. judge Edward S. Smith U.S. Ct. Appeals (Fed. cir.), Washington, 1979-80; assoc. Duncan Allen & Mitchell, 1980-82; atty. advisor to Judge Jules G. Körner U.S. Tax Ct., 1982-84; assoc. Davidson Meaux Sonnier & McElligott, Lafayette, La., 1984-85; ptnr. Roy Forrest, Lopresto, DeCourt & Myers and predecessor firms, 1985-97; pvt. practice Stephen Hawley Myers, LLC, La., 1997—. Lectr. for continuing legal edn. seminars on corp., bus. and sales tax litigation; chmn. Nat. Bus. Adv. Coun., Washington, 2002--. Vice chmn., bd. dirs. La. Coun. for Fiscal Reform, New Orleans, 1986-96; bd. dirs., treas. Acadiana Youth, Inc., Lafayette, 1986-94; mem. La. State Police Commn., 2002--. Mem. ABA, Am. Platform Assn., Lafayette Bar Assn., La. Counsel Def. Attys., La. Trial Lawyer's Assn., Phi Delta Phi. Avocations: writing, photography, skeet shooting, sports clay shooting, hunting. Office: 600 Jefferson St Ste 401 Lafayette LA 70501-8919 also: 15 W Lenox St Chevy Chase MD 20815-4208 Home: 105 Mill Valley Run Lafayette LA 70508-7027

MYERS, THOMAS ARTHUR, accountant; b. Long Branch, N.J., Jan. 12, 1945; s. Arthur Louis and Gladys (Kampf) M.; m. Rose Terrez, June 19, 1976; children: Kristen, Rhonda, Rhoda. BS in Math., N.Mex. Sch. Mines, 1966; BS in Acctg., U. No. Colo., 1977. Prodr. surfing films, Honolulu, 1970-76; tax cons. Touche Ross & Co., Denver, 1977-82; founding ptnr. T.A. Myers & Co., 1980—. Lectr., cons. Fed. Home Loan Bank, profl. orgns.; chmn. Northwest Ctr. Pres. Colo. Coun. for Self Esteem; co-founder Imagine Programs for Non-Violence. Author: Tax Planning for Canadian Investment in the United States, Imagine Program for Non-Violence, Taxation of Foreign Inestments in the United States, American Bankers Association Construction Policy and Lending Manual, Loan Workouts for Problem Real Estate, The Problem Loan Action Plan, The Longevity Revolution; contbr. articles to profl. jours. Pres. Nat. Assn. Self Asteem. Mem. IACPA, Colo. Soc. CPAs, Inernat. Tax Group, Denver Athletic Club. Republican. Methodist. Achievements include winner masters mountain bike racing series, Winter Park and Thunder Valley, Colo. Home: 7 S Mcintyre Way Golden CO 80401-5062

MYERS, VIRGINIA ANNE, art educator; b. Greencastle, Ind., May 8, 1927; d. Everett Clark and Bessie Hurst (McKann) M. BA in Fine Arts, George Washington U., Corcoran Sch. Art, 1949; MFA in Drawing and Painting, Calif. Coll. of Arts & Crafts, Oakland, 1951; postgrad. in print making. U. Ill., 1953-55, U. Iowa, 1955-61; studied with Stanley William Hayter, Paris, 1961-62. Rsch. asst. Sch. Art and Art History U. Iowa, Iowa City, 1958-61; instr. arts and crafts, phys. edn. Tucson Indian Tng. Sch., 1949-50; teaching asst. dept. art and architecture U. Ill., Champaign-Urbana, 1954-55; instr. printmaking U. Iowa, Iowa City, 1962-69, asst. prof. printmaking, 1969-74, assoc. prof., 1974-82, prof., 1982—. Artist: A Time of Malfeasance (21 engravings and drypoints), 1976, The Views from Tenacre: The Seasons (66 paintings and drawings), 1979, Landscape in Iowa (36 paintings and drawings), 1986; inventor Iowa Foil Printer, 1992; contbr. articles to profl. jours.

Recipient Fulbright fellowship, Paris, 1961-62; grantee U. Iowa, 1973, 78, 84, 89, 93, Iowa Arts Coun., 1974-77, 80, 85, Stanley Found., 1984-88, Thorson Found., 1984, 86. Mem. Foil Stamping and Embossing Assn. (charter), Nat. Mus. of Women in Arts (charter). Avocations: gardening, reading, swimming. Home: Tenacre Print 4244 210th St NE Solon IA 52333-9657 Office: Univ Iowa Sch Arts & Art History Iowa City IA 52242

MYERS, VIRGINIA LOU, education educator; b. Indpls., July 18, 1940; d. John Rentschler and Bonnie Mae (Powell) Jones; m. James W. Rose Jr., Aug. 2, 1966 (div. Nov. 1986); m. Byron P. Myers, Sept. 11, 1987. BS in Edn., U. Indpls., 1966; MS in Edn., Butler U., 1971; PhD in Edn. Psychology, U. South Fla., 1991. Cert. elem. tchr., reading specialist and prin., Ind. Tchr. Indpls. Pub. Schs., 1966-72; pvt. tutor Self, Indpls., 1972-74; tchr.'s tchr. Urban/Rural Sch. Devel. Project, Indpls, 1974-77; reading techr. Met. sch. dist. Pike Twp., Indpls., 1977-80; curriculum specialist Met. sch. Dist. Washington Twp., 1980-82; tchr. chpt. I Noblesville (Ind.) Pub. Schs., 1982-83; instr. social scis. Manatee C.C., Venice, Fla., 1983-87; asst. prof. edn. Mo. So. State Coll., Joplin, 1990-91, East Carolina U., Greenville, N.C., 1992-96; ednl. cons. Cath. Diocese of Venice, Fla., 1996-99; program mgr. child devel. and edn. Manatee Cmty. Coll., 1999—2001; sr. rsch. assoc. Fla. Inst. Edn., 2001—. Cons. Bertie County Schs., Windsor, NC, 1994—96; program mgr. early childhood and edn. Manatee C.C., 1999—2001, mem. early childhood adv. bd., 1996—2001; lead coach early literacy and learning model project Fla. Inst. Edn., 1990—2001; cons. Early Learning Accelerates Total Edn. Treas. Smart Start Initiative, Greenville, 1993—96; chair Birth Through Kindergarten Higher Edn. Consortium, 1994—96; mem. Fla. C.C. Early Childhood Network, 1999—, Manatee County Early Childhood Trainers Adv. Coun., 2000—, Lakewood Ranch H.S. Child Devel. Lab. Sch. Adv. Bd., 2000—, Sch. Readiness Coalition of Sarasota County, Inc., 2001—, exec. dir., 2002. Mem. ASCD, Nat. Assn. for Edn. Young Children, Orton Dyslexia Soc., Assn. Childhood Edn., Internat., Venice Area C. of C. (edn. com. 2001-02), Phi Theta Kappa (advisor 2000-01). Presbyterian. Avocations: needle work, reading. Home: 334 Woodvale Dr Venice FL 34293-4161 E-mail: drvmyers@comcast.net.

MYERS, WARREN POWERS LAIRD, physician, educator; b. Phila., May 2, 1921; s. John Dashiell and Mary Hall (Laird) M.; m. Katharine Van Vechten, July 1, 1944; children: Warren Powers Laird, Jr., Anne Van Vechten Myers Evans, Duncan McNeir, Sara Myers Gormley. Grad., Episcopal Acad., 1939; BS, Yale U., 1943; MD, Columbia U., 1945; MS in Medicine, U. Minn., 1952; postgrad. (Eleanor Roosevelt Found. fellow), U. Cambridge, Eng., 1962-63. Diplomate: Am. Bd. Internal Medicine. Rotating intern Phila. Gen. Hosp., 1945-46; intern medicine Maimonides Hosp., N.Y.C., 1948-49; resident fellow in medicine Mayo Clinic, Rochester, Minn., 1949-52; clin. asst. Meml. Hosp., N.Y.C., 1952-54, asst. attending physician, 1954-58, assoc. attending physician, 1959, attending physician, 1959-90; instr. Cornell U. Med. Coll., 1955-56, asst. prof., 1956-59, asso. prof., 1959-68, prof. medicine, 1968-86, prof. emeritus, 1986—, assoc. dean, 1977-86; chmn. dept. medicine Meml. Sloan-Kettering Cancer Ctr., N.Y.C., 1967-77; v.p. for ednl. affairs Meml. Hosp., 1977-81, Eugene W. Kettering prof., 1979-86; attending physician N.Y. Hosp., N.Y.C., 1968-86; mem. Sloan-Kettering Inst. Cancer Rsch., 1969-90; mem. emeritus Meml. Sloan-Kettering Cancer Ctr., 1990—; cons. Rockefeller U. Hosp., 1977-86. Mem. clin. cancer tng. com. Nat. Cancer Inst., 1970-73, chmn., 1971-73, chmn. clin. cancer edn. com., 1975-78; adj. prof. medicine Dartmouth Med. Sch., 1987-96, prof. medicine emeritus, 1996—; cons. staff Mary Hitchcock Meml. Hosp., Hanover, N.H., 1987-96. Contbr. articles on cancer, bone metabolism, internal medicine, and med. edn. to med. jours. Bd. dirs. Rye (N.Y.) United Fund, 1969-72, chmn. budget com., 1968-69; bd. dirs. Damon Runyon-Walter Winchell Cancer Fund, 1976-86, pres., 1985-86; trustee Hitchcock Clinic, Lebanon, N.H., 1983-96, Dartmouth-Hitchcock Med. Ctr., Lebanon, 1983-95, chmn. exec. com., 1992-95, tchr.'s coll. Columbia U., 1980-86; trustee Friends of Norris Cotton Cancer Ctr., Dartmouth-Hitchcock Med. Ctr., Lebanon, 1997-2000, v.p., 1999-2000—; elder Presbyn. Ch., 1969-86, Norwich Congregational Ch., deacon, 1998—. With M.C., USNR, 1946-47. Recipient Alumni award for research Mayo Clinic, 1952, Margaret Hay Edwards Achievement medal Am. Assn. Cancer Edn., 1993. Fellow ACP, N.Y. Acad. Medicine (v.p. 1983-85); mem. Am. Clin. and Climatological Assn., Am. Assn. Cancer Research, Endocrine Soc., Harvey Soc., Am. Fedn. Clin. Research, Practioners' Soc. of N.Y., AMA, Am. Assn. Cancer Edn. (pres. 1984-85), Am. Soc. Clin. Oncology, Founders and Patriots Pa., Yale Club, Charaka Club, Century Assn. (N.Y.C.), Alpha Omega Alpha. Presbyterian (elder 1969—). Clubs: Yale, Charaka, Century Assn. (N.Y.C.). Address: 436 Joshua Rd White River Junction VT 05001-9028 E-mail: wplm@dartmouth.edu.

MYERS, WILLIAM GERRY, III, federal agency administrator; BA, Coll. William and Mary, 1977; JD, U. Denver, 1981. Bar: Idaho, Wyo., Colo., D.C., U.S. Ct. Appeals (9th cir.), U.S. Ct. Appeals (10th cir.), U.S. Supreme Ct. Legis. counsel U.S. Senator Alan K. Simpson, 1985; asst. to U.S. Atty. Gen., 1989—92; dep. gen. counsel for programs U.S. Dept. Energy, 1992—93; asst. to atty. gen. Dept. Justice, 1989—92; exec. dir. Pub. Land Coun.; dir. fed. lands Nat. Cattlemen's Beef Assn.; atty. Holland & Hart, Boise, Idaho; solicitor U.S. Dept. Interior, Washington, 2001—. Chmn. Idaho Fed. Lands Working Group. Mem.: ABA (past vice chmn. pub. lands com. environment, energy and resources sect), Boise Area C. of C. (chmn. state affairs and natural resources com.). Office: US Dept Interior Solicitor 1849 C St Nw Washington DC 20240*

MYERS, WILLIAM RICHARD, minister, educator; b. Oil City, Pa., June 19, 1942; s. William Alfred Myers and Margaret Elizabeth Kuntz; m. Barbara Kimes, June 20, 1964; children: Michal Elaine, Melissa Anne, Jason William. MDiv, Pitts. Theol. Sem., 1967; MEd, R.I. Coll., 1972; EdD, Loyola U., Chgo., 1981. Ordained min., Lake Erie Presbytery, 1967. Dir. coll. union Barrington (R.I.) Coll., 1969-72; youth min. Flossmoor (Ill.) Cmty. Ch., 1971-81; prof. religious edn. Chgo. Theol. Sem., 1981-99, acad. dean, 1992-99; dir. leadership edn. The Assn. of Theol. Schs. in the U.S. and Can., Pitts., 1999—. Assoc. pastor Hiland Presbyn. Ch., Pitts., 1967-69. Author: Theological Themes of Youth Ministry, 1987, Black and White Styles of Youth Ministry, 1990, Research in Ministry, 1993, Becoming and Belonging, 1993. Office: The Assn Theol Schs 10 Summit Park Dr Pittsburgh PA 15275 E-mail: myers@ats.edu.

MYERS, JR. GEORGE JOSEPH STEPHEN, historical archaeologist, researcher; b. The Bronx, NY, Mar. 26, 1952; s. George Joseph Stephen Myers, Adelaide Martha Urquhart. BA Anthropology, Stony Brook University, Stony Brook, New York, 1976—80. Researcher Parsons ES, New York, NY, 1999—2002; Field Historical Archaeology Panamerican Consultants, Inc., Tuscaloosa, AL, 2001—01; Field Archaeology Grossman and Associates, Inc., New York, NY, 1989—94; Field Archaeology Greenhouse Consultants, Inc, 1984—89, Various , New York, 1981—84; Field Archaelogy National Park Service, Various, CO, 1978—81. Mem.: Council for Northeast Historical Archaeology. Avocation: Watching New Hampshire. Home: 1918 Holland Ave. Bronx NY 10462-3226 Personal E-mail: georgejmyersjr@hotmail.com.

MYERS/BOYCE, MICHAEL ALLEN, computer technician, consultant; b. Flint, Mich., Mar. 20, 1965; s. Patricia Marrie Kelly, Alferd E. Boyce; life ptnr. Tracy Ellen McCann; children: Nathan McCann, Kaiti McCann; children: Michael. B. of Open Systems Tech.(hon.) , Baker Coll., Flint, Mich., 2001. Cert. Novell engr. 2000. Electronic technician Clio Area Schs., Clio, Mich., 1988—96, computer technician, 1996—. Mem.: Baker Network Club. Home: 1167 W Wilson Rd Clio MI 48420 Office: Clio Area Schools 430 N Mill St Clio MI 48420 Personal E-mail: mmyers@admin.clio.k12.mi.us. Business E-Mail: mmyers@admin.clio.k12.mi.us.

MYERSON, ALAN, film and television director; b. Cleve., Aug. 8, 1936; s. Seymour A. and Vivien I. (Caplin) M.; m. Irene Ryan, June 2, 1962; 1 son, Lincoln; m. Leigh French, May 15, 1977; children: Sierra Jasmine French-Myerson, Darcy Anna French-Myerson. Student, Pepperdine Coll., 1956-57, UCLA, 1957. Mem. drama faculty U. Calif., Berkeley, 1966, San Francisco State U., 1967 Dir. Broadway and Off Broadway Prodns., 1958-64, including This Music Crept By Me Upon the Waters, The Committee; dir.: Second City, N.Y.C. and Chgo., 1961, 62; founder, producer, dir. The Committee, San Francisco, L.A. and N.Y., 1963-74; dir.: (films) Steelyard Blues, 1972, Private Lessons, 1981, Police Academy 5, 1988, It's Showtime, 1976; numerous TV shows, 1975—, including Ally McBeal, Larry Sanders Show, Friends, Frazier, Picket Fences, Miami Vice, Dynasty, Laverne and Shirley; TV films The Love Boat, 1976, Hi, Honey, I'm Dead, 1991, Bad Attitudes, 1991, Holiday Affair, 1996. Active in civil rights, anti-war, anti-nuclear power movements, 1957— . Recipient Emmy nomination 1997, Cable ACE award nominations, 1995, 96, 97, TV Comedy award nomination Dirs. Guild, 1997. Mem. ASCAP, Acad. Motion Picture Arts and Scis., Acad. TV Arts and Scis., Dirs. Guild Am.

MYERSON, ALBERT LEON, physical chemist; b. N.Y.C., Nov. 14, 1919; s. Myer and Dora (Weiner) M.; m. Arline Harriet Rosenfield, May 10, 1953; children: Aimee Lenore, Lorraine Patrice, Paul Andrew. BS, Pa. State U., 1941; postgrad., Columbia U., 1942-45; PhD, U. Wis., 1948. Rsch. asst. Manhattan Project Columbia U., N.Y.C., 1941-45; sr. rsch. chemist Franklin Inst. Labs., Phila., 1948-56; mgr. phys. chemistry Gen. Electric Co., 1956-60; prin. phys. chemist Aero. Lab. Cornell U., Buffalo, 1960-68; rsch. assoc. Exxon Rsch. and Engring. Co., Linden, N.J., 1969-79; head phys. chemistry sect. Mote Marine Lab., Sarasota, Fla., 1979-85. Cons. in field. *Dr.Myerson determined, for the Manhattan Project, the correct of two contradictory values for the viscosity of gaseous uranium hexafluoride, as previously measured in England and the United States. He studied the explosion properties of carbon disulfide-oxygen mixtures for aircraft applications. Introduced a new method (known as ARAS) for studying the reaction rates of many atomic species at very high (i.e. re-entry) temperatures (needed by NASA). Studied the mechanism by which atomic oxygen and certain molecules re-combine on surfaces. Discovered two non-catalytic methods (and developed one of them) for removing highly undesirable nitric oxide from automotive exhaust using only very small quatities of an effective agent.* Co-editor: Physical Chemistry in Aerodynamics and Space Flight, 1961; contbr. articles in field to profl. jours.; patentee in field. Mem. Am. Phys. Soc., Am. Chem. Soc., Combustion Inst., Pa. State U. Alumni Assn., Sigma Xi, Phi Lambda Upsilon. Avocations: violin, fine antique china and porcelain. Home and Office: 4147 Rosas Ave Sarasota FL 34233-1614 *It has always seemed to me that one's satisfaction with life can be expessed as an integral of the intensity of his or her pursuit of contributions to the world as a function of time, throughout one's life.*

MYERSON, JACOB MYER, former foreign service officer; b. Rock Hill, S.C., June 11, 1926; s. Solomon and Lena (Clein) M.; m. Nicole Neuray, June 10, 1965 (dec. Oct. 1968); 1 child, Sylvie Anne; m. Helen Hayashi, Mar. 9, 1974 (dec. Jan. 1995). Student, Pa. State Coll., 1944; BA with distinction, George Washington U., 1949, MA, 1950; grad., Fgn. Service Inst., 1953. Joined U.S. Fgn. Service, 1950; 3d sec. (Office U.S. High Commr. Germany), Berlin, 1950-52; 2d sec. (U.S. Mission to NATO and European Regional Orgn.), Paris, France, 1953-55; also mem. U.S. permanent del. to coordinating com. InterGovtl. Consultative Group on EastWest Trade; internat. economist, internat. relations officer State Dept., 1956-60; adviser U.S. del. GATT session, Geneva, Switzerland, 1958; ministerial session OEEC, Paris, 1958; 1st sec., chief polit. section U.S. Mission to European Communities, Brussels, Belgium, 1960-65; spl. asst. to under sec. state, 1965-66; officer-in-charge NATO Polit. Affairs, Dept. State, 1966-68; adviser U.S. delegation ministerial sessions North Atlantic Council, 1966-67; dep. polit. adviser, counselor U.S. Mission to NATO, Brussels, Belgium, 1968-70; counselor econ. affairs U.S. Mission to European Communities, 1970-74, minister counselor, from 1974; U.S. rep. to UN Econ. and Social Council with rank of ambassador, 1975-77; alt. U.S. del. 30th and 31st sessions UN Gen. Assembly, 1975, 76; alt. U.S. rep. 4th session UN Conf. on Trade and Devel., 1976; minister-counselor for econ. and comml. affairs Am. Embassy, Paris, 1977-80; ret., 1980; dep. sec. gen. OECD, Paris, 1980-88. Served with inf. AUS, 1944-46, ETO. Decorated Bronze Star; Order of the Sacred Treasure Gold and Silver medal (Japan). Recipient Meritorious Service award State Dept., 1960 Mem. Fgn. Service Assn. (Rivkin award 1969), Phi Beta Kappa, Artus, Pi Gamma Mu, Phi Eta Sigma. Address: 2 rue Lucien Gaulard 75018 Paris France

MYERSON, ROBERT J. radiation oncologist, educator; b. Boston, May 12, 1947; s. Richard Louis and Rosemarie M.; m. Carla Wheatley, Aug. 8, 1970; 1 child, Jacob Wheatley. BA, Princeton U., 1969; PhD, U. Calif., Berkeley, 1974; MD, U. Miami, 1980. Diplomate Am. Bd. Radiology. Asst. prof. dept. physics Pa. State U., State Coll., 1974-76; fellow Inst. Advanced Studies, Princeton, N.J., 1976-78; resident U. Pa. Hosp., Phila., 1981-84; assoc. prof. radiology Washington U. Sch. Medicine, St. Louis, 1984-97, prof. radiology, 1997—. Contbr. articles to profl. jours. Recipient Career Devel. award Am. Cancer Soc., 1985. Fellow Am. Coll. Radiology; mem. Am. Coll. Radiation, Am. Soc. Therapeutic Radiologists, Am. Phys. Soc. Democrat. Jewish. Avocation: bicycling. Office: Washington U Radiation Oncology Ctr Box 8224 4921 Parkview Pl Saint Louis MO 63110-1001 E-mail: myerson@radonc.wustl.edu.

MYERSON, ROGER BRUCE, economist, game theorist, educator; b. Boston, Mar. 29, 1951; s. Richard L. and Rosemarie (Farkas) M.; m. Regina M. Weber, Aug. 29, 1982; children: Daniel, Rebecca. AB summa cum laude, SM, Harvard U., 1973, PhD, 1976. Asst. prof. decision scis. Northwestern U., Evanston, Ill., 1976-78, assoc. prof., 1979-82, prof., 1982-2001, Harold Stuart prof. decision scis., 1986-2001, prof. econs., 1987-2001; W.C. Norby prof. econs. U. Chgo., 2001—. Guest researcher U. Bielefeld, Federal Republic of Germany, 1978-79; vis. prof. econs. U. Chgo., 1985-86, 2000-01. Author: Game Theory: Analysis of Conflict, 1991; mem. editorial bd. Internat. Jour. Game Theory, 1982-92, Games and Econ. Behavior, 1988-97; assoc. editor Jour. Econ. Theory, 1983-93; also articles. Guggenheim fellow, 1983-84; Sloan rsch. fellow, 1984-86. Fellow Econometric Soc., Am. Acad. Arts and Scis. (Midwest v.p. 1999-2002). Office: U Chgo Dept Econs 1126 E 59th St Chicago IL 60637

MYHERA, MICHAEL G. computer scientist, computer company executive; b. Fort Francis, Ont, Can., Jan. 30, 1958; s. Henrietta Dee Myhera-Blaha and Vernon Barnes Blaha(Stepfather), William Michael Myhera. BBA, Northwood U., Midland, Mich., 1979; postgrad., Cen. Mich. U., 1983—86, BS in Computer Sci., 1986. Cert. Veritas vol. mgr. expert, Veritas file sys. expert, Veritas cluster server expert. Sr. programmer, analyst Brit. Telecom., Rockville, Md., 1986—90; sr. integration arch. cons. EDS/McDonnell Douglas/DoD, Heidelberg, Germany, 1990—92; experienced sr. cons. Andersen Consulting, McLean, Va., 1992—95; sr. enterprise arch. cons. Hewlett-Packard, Profl. Services Orgn., Palo Alto, Calif., 1995—97; sr. data warehouse integration arch. cons. IRS, New Carrollton, Md., 1997; DCE/CORBA arch. cons. SBC/Pacific Bell, San Ramon, Calif., 1998—2000; sr. arch., Sun Solaris sys. adminstr. AT&T/Excite@Home, Redwood City, 1999—2000; sr. arch., Sun Solaris sys. adminstr., global wireless Internet platforms Vodafone/Airtouch, Walnut Creek, 2001—01. Integration arch. (software) ENGNET+, 1992 (commendation, Dep. Chief of Staff Engrs., U.S. Army, Europe, 1992); contbr. software (Letter of Appreciation, CEO Brit. Telecom., 1989); "live wire" infrastructure arch., enterprise arch. ($250M Contract award, 1996); contbr. integration. Mem.: IEEE, Automated Computing Machinery, Lambda Chi Alpha (pres. cen. Mich. U. chpt. 1984). Roman Catholic. Achievements include invention of Sun Solaris Jumpstart Enhancement. Avocations: snow and water skiing, international travel, writing, foreign languages, Linux. Home: Apt 216 3180 Oak Rd Walnut Creek CA 94596

MYHRE, BYRON ARNOLD, pathologist, educator; b. Fargo, N.D., Oct. 22, 1928; s. Ben Arnold and Amy Lillian (Gilbertson) M.; m. Eileen Marguerite Scherling, June 16, 1953; children: Patricia Ann, Bruce Allen. BS, U. Ill., 1950, MS, Northwestern U., 1952, MD, 1953; PhD, U. Wis., 1962. Intern Evanston (Ill.) Hosp., 1953-54; resident Children's Meml. Hosp., Chgo., 1956-57, U. Wis. Hosp., Madison, 1957-60; assoc. med. dir. Milw. Blood Ctr., 1962-66; sci. dir. L.A. Red Cross Blood Ctr., 1966-72; dir. Blood Bank Harbor-UCLA Med. Ctr., Torrance, Calif., 1972-85, chief clin. pathology, 1985-2000; prof. pathology UCLA, 1972-2000, prof. emeritus, 2000—. Author: Quality Control on Blood Banking, 1974, (with others) Textbook of Clinical Pathology, 1972, Paternity Testing, 1975; editor seminar procs.; contbr. articles to med. jours., chpts. to books. Served with USAF, 1954-56. Mem.: Harbor-UCLA Faculty Soc. (past pres.), Wis. Blood Bank Assn. (past pres.), L.A. Acad. Medicine (past pres.), Calif. Blood Bank Sys. (past pres.), Calif. Med. Assn., Assn. Clin. Scientists, Coll. Am. Pathologists (chmn. blood bank survey com.), Am. Assn. Blood Banks (pres. 1978—79), Am. Soc. Clin. Pathology (dep. commr. commn. on continuing edn.), AMA, Palos Verdes Breakfast Club (past pres.). Home: 4004 Via Larga Vis Palos Verdes Estates CA 90274-1122 Office: Harbor UCLA Med Center 1000 W Carson St Torrance CA 90502-2004

MYHRE, JANET, mathematician, educator; b. Tacoma, Sept. 24, 1932; d. Leif Christian Klippen, Thelma Gladys Klippen; m. Philip Cushman Myhre, June 12, 1954 (div. Dec. 1984); 1 child Karin Elizabeth ; m. Leon Hollerman, May 29, 1988; 1 child Jeremy Hollerman. BA summa cum laude, Pacific Luth. U., 1954; MA, U. Wash. Seattle, 1956; PhD of Math. Stats., U. Stockholm, 1968. Prof. math. Claremont McKenna Coll., Claremont, Calif., 1962—. Vis. prof. U. Stockholm, Stockholm, 1971—72, Swiss Fed. Inst. Tech., Zurich, 1971—72, Wash. State U., Pullman, 1978; prof. math. Claremont Grad. U., 1968; founder, pres. Math. Analysis Rsch. Corp., Claremont, 1973—; dir. Reed Inst. for Decision Sci. Claremont McKenna Coll., Claremont, 1975—; cons. Strategic Sys. Programs USN, Washington, 1968—; cons. EPA, Washington, 1976—77. Contbr. . Bd. trustees mem. The Webb Schs., Claremont, 1984—88; officer Padua Hills Homeowners Assn., 1988—94. Recipient Austin Bonis award, Am. Soc. Quality Control, 1984; grantee Rsch. grants, Office Naval Rsch., 1973—85. Mem.: Inst. Math. Stats., Am. Statis. Assn. (assoc. editor Technometrics 1969—75, coun. rep. 2001), Padua Hills Mus. Com., Phi Beta Kappa. Achievements include development of models/statistical theory used since 1972 by USN Ballistic Missile Program for reliability assessments; software/theory used by Fleet Ballistic Missile Program since 1990 for safety and risk assessment. Avocations: gardening, cooking, hiking, weaving. Office: Claremont McKenna Coll Adams Hall 9th St Claremont CA 91711

MYHREN, TRYGVE EDWARD, communications company executive; b. Palmerton, Pa., Jan. 3, 1937; s. Arne Johannes and Anita (Blatz) M.; m. Carol Jane Enman, Aug. 8, 1964; children: Erik, Kirsten, Tor; m. 2d Victoria Hamilton, Nov. 14, 1981; 1 stepchild, Paige. BA in Philosophy and Polit. Sci., Dartmouth Coll., 1958, MBA, 1959. Sales mgr., unit mgr. Procter and Gamble, Cin., 1963-65; sr. cons. Glendinning Cos., Westport, Conn., 1965-69; pres. Auberge Vintners, 1970-73; exec. v.p. Mktg. Continental, Westport, 1969-73; v.p., gen. mgr. CRM, Inc., Del Mar, Calif., 1973-75; from v.p. mktg. to pres. Am. TV and Comm. Corp., Englewood, Colo., 1975-80, chmn. bd., CEO, 1981-88; pres. Myhren Media Inc., Denver, 1989—. V.p., then exec. v.p. Time Inc., N.Y.C., 1981-88; mem. exec. com., treas., vice chmn., then chmn. bd. dirs. Nat. Cable TV Assn., Washington, 1982-91; mem. adv. com. on HDTV, FCC, 1987-89, pres. Providence Jour. Co., pres., 1990-96; bd. dirs. Advanced Mktg. Svcs., Inc., La Jolla, Calif., ; Founders Funds, Inc., J. D. Edwards, Inc., Verio, Inc., Formus Inc., Nat. Cable TV Ctr., Denver, Cable Labs, Inc., Boulder, Colo., Peapod, Inc., Skokie, Ill.; pres. Myhren Media, 1989—, Greenwood Cable Mgmt., 1989-91; pres., CEO King Broadcast Co., 1991-96. Mem. Colo. Forum, 1984—, chmn. higher edn. com., 1986, chmn. Scandinavian channel, 1998—; bd. dirs., co-founder Colo. Bus. Com. for the Arts, 1985-91; mem. exec. coun. Found. for Commemoration U.S. Constn., 1987-90; mem. Nat. GED Task Force, 1987-90, Colo. Baseball Commn., 1989-91, Colo. Film Commn., 1989-91; trustee Nat. Jewish Hosp., 1989— (Humanitarian award 1996), R.I. Hosp., 1991-95, Lifespan Health Sys., 1994-97, U. Denver, 1996—, U.S. Ski and Snowboard Team Found., 1998—; chmn. Local Organizing Commn. 1995 NCAA Hockey Championship; trustee, exec. com., chmn. fin. com. U. Denver, 1997—. Lt. (j.g.) USNR, 1959-63. Recipient Disting. Leader award Nat. Cable TV Assn., 1988, ann. humanitarian award Nat. Jewish Hosp., 1996. Mem. Cable TV Adminstrn. and Mktg. Soc. (pres. 1978-79, Grand Tam award 1985, One of A Kind award 1994), Cable Adv. Bur. (co-founder 1978), Cable TV Pioneers. Episcopalian. Address: Myhren Media Inc 280 Detroit St # 200 Denver CO 80206-4807

MYKLES, DONALD LEE, biology educator, zoologist, crustacean biologist; b. Stockton, Calif., Oct. 23, 1950; s. Norman and Dorothy (Alldredge) M.; m. Vicki Fogel, Sept. 10, 1978. AB, U. Calif., Santa Barbara, 1973; PhD, U. Calif., Berkeley, 1979. Postdoctoral fellow Oak Ridge (Tenn.) Nat. Lab., 1979-85; asst. prof. biology Colo. State U., Ft. Collins, 1985-88, assoc. prof., 1988-93, prof., 1993—. Panel mem. physiol. processes NSF, 1988-90. Contbr. articles to profl. jours. Recipient Presdl. Young Investigator award, 1989, Fulbright award, 1991; grantee NIH, 1979-82, 92-93, NSF, 1987—; Disting. Rsch. fellow U. Calif., Davis, 1999. Home: PO Box 247 Bodega Bay CA 94923-0247 E-mail: don@lamar.colostate.edu.

MYLER, HARLEY ROSS, electrical engineer, educator; b. Pitts., Nov. 28, 1953; s. Harley Ross and Anna (Krivka) M.; m. Nancy Coleman, Aug. 13, 1975; children: Krifka Alexandra, Logan Ross. BSEE, Va. Mil. Inst., Lexington, 1975; MSEE, N.Mex. State U., 1981, PhD in Elec. Engring., 1985. Registered profl. engr., Fla. Digital sys. project engr. Gen. Instrument Corp., El Paso, Tex., 1979-80; grad. research asst. N.Mex. State U., 1980-81; digital sys. engr. Space Comm. Co., Las Cruces, N.Mex., 1981-82; instr., grad. research asst. N.Mex. State U., 1982-85; staff engr. Image and Signal Processing dept. Martin Marietta Orlando Aerocpace, Orlando, Fla., 1985-86; prof. elec. and computer engring. dept. U. Ctrl. Fla., 1986—2001; prof. & chair elec. engring. Lamar U., Beaumont, Tex., 2001—. Cons. in field; bd. dirs. Ocular Imaging Corp., Winter Park, Fla.; pres. I-Math Assocs., Inc., Orlando, 1998-99. Author: Pocket Handbook of Image Processing Algorithms in C, 1993, Computer Imaging Recipes in C, 1993, Fundamentals of Machine Vision, 1998, Fundamentals on Engineering Programming with C Fortran, 1998; contbr. articles to profl. jours.; patentee in field. Capt. U.S. Army, 1975-79. NASA grantee, 1987—; Ctr. Research in Electro-Optics and Lasers grantee, 1986-87, others. Mem. IEEE (sr.). Republican. Avocations: swimming, boating, flying. Home: 2495 Evalon St Beaumont TX 77702 Office: Dept Elec Engring Lamar U Beaumont TX 77710-0049 E-mail: h.myler@myler.org.

MYLES, KEVIN MICHAEL, metallurgical engineer; b. Chgo., July 18, 1934; s. Michael J. and Ursula (May) M.; m. Joan Christine Ganczewski, Dec. 16, 1967; children: Kathleen, Gary, Jennifer. BS in Metallurgical Engring., U. Ill., 1956, PhD in Phys. Metall. Engring., 1963. Asst. mgr. nuclear fuel reprossing program Argonne (Ill.) Nat. Lab., 1977-79, dep. dir. fossil energy program, 1982-87, dir. fuel cell program, 1987-88, dir. electrochem. tech. program, 1988—, assoc. dir. chem. tech. div., 1992—. Adj. prof. materials sci. U. Ill., Chgo., 1967-69; prof. materials sci. Midwest Coll. Engring., Lombard, Ill., 1969-81. Contbr. articles to Jour. Phys. Chemistry, Chem. Engring. Sci., Jour. Electrochem. Soc., Jour. Fusion Energy, Jour. Power Sources. Mem. Sch. Bd. Dist. #58, Downers Grove, Ill., 1964-70. Capt. USAR, 1956-68. Mem. Am. Soc. for Metals, AIME, Alpha Sigma Mu. Achievements include 10 patents in field. Office: Argonne Nat Lab 9700 Cass Ave Argonne IL 60439-4803

MYLNECHUK, LARRY HERBERT, financial executive; b. Littlefork, Minn., Mar. 9, 1948; s. William and Marjorie (Raco) M.; m. Sandy L. Henderson, Mar. 14, 1970; children: Kendra Elizabeth, Scott William. BA, Lewis & Clark Coll., Portland, 1970; JD, Lewis & Clark Coll., 1974. Legal specialist Oreg. Dept. Edn., Salem, 1976-82; sr. v.p., dir. Morley Capital Mgmt. Inc., Portland, 1982-89; founder, pres. Integra Assocs., Inc., Lake Oswego, Oreg., 1989—; exec. dir. The Stable Value Assn., Inc., 1990-96; co-founder, prin. Residential Capital Mgmt., LLC, 2000. Cons. Hueler Analytics, Inc., Mpls., 1989—; conf. chmn. GIC Nat. Forum Conf., Washington, 1993-95; guest lectr. Portland State U., 1978, U. Oreg., 1980; cert. arbitrator NASD SEries 7, 63, 2000—. Contbr. articles to profl. jours. Founder Woodstock Neighborhood Assn., 1975; mem. Multnomah County (Oreg.) Charter Rev. Commn., 1978; mem. Tualatin (Oreg.) City Coun., 1980—84, Portland Com. on Fgn. Rels., 1976—98, bd. dirs., 1993—96; mem. Gov.'s Commn. on Adminstrv. Hearings, State of Oreg., 1988—89, Tchrs. Standards and Practices Commn., State of Oreg. , 2000—02; mem. vestry, lay eucharistic min., del. State Episcopal Conv., 1996; mem. Diocesan Coun., 1996—98; mem. vestry Christ Ch. Parish, 1995—2000, Christ Episcopal Ch., 1998—2000; founding mem. St. Margaret's Ch., 2000—; trustee St. Francis of Assisi Endowment Fund, 1993; bd. dirs. Patriot Found., 2002—. Fellow NEH, 1979, ednl. policy fellow George Washington U., 1980. Mem. NASD, SAR (pres. Lewis and Clark chpt.,pres. Oreg. State Soc. 1997, nat. trustee, 1997-98, v.p. Gen.-Pacific dist. 1999-2001), Western Pension Conf., Assn. Soc. Execs., World Affairs Coun. Oreg., Citizen Amb. Program to Western Europe, Gen. Soc. The War of 1812, Soc. Colonial Wars, Sons and Daus. of Pilgrims, Oregon Soc. Sons of the Revolution (co-founder, treas. 1996), Internat. Bus. Forum (mem. adv. bd. 1996), Sons of the Bench and Bar (charter), N. Am.

Soc. Securities Adminstrs. (profl. stds. com. 1998), Oreg. Assn. Adminstrv. Law Judges, Soc. Magna Charta Barons, Crown of Charlegmagne Soc., Soc. Charlemagne's Descendants. Democrat. Episcopalian. Avocations: hiking, diving. Office: Residential Capital Mgt LLC PO Box 1594 Lake Oswego OR 97035-0013

MYLONAKIS, STAMATIOS GREGORY, patent agent, polymer science consultant; b. Athens, Aug. 18, 1937; s. Gregory S. and Vassiliki (Charalambopoulos) Mylonakis; m. Pamela H. Morton, May 5, 1965 (dec. Mar. 1978); 1 child Gregory (dec.). BS, Nat. U. of Athens, 1961; MS, Ill. Inst. of Tech., 1964; PhD, Mich. State U., 1970. Rsch. assoc. Ill. Inst. of Tech., Chgo., 1964-65; rsch. scientist Brookhaven Nat. Lab., Upton, N.Y., 1965-68; instr. U. Calif., Berkeley, 1971-73; group leader Rohm and Haas Co., Springhouse, Pa., 1973-76; supr. DeSoto, Inc., Des Plaines, Ill., 1976-79; staff scientist Borg-Warner Corp., 1979-82, mgr., 1982-87; dept. head Enichem Am., Monmouth Junction, N.J., 1988-94; tech. advisor, registered patent agt. law firm Oblon, Spivak, Arlington, Va., 1994-2000; cons., patent law practitioner, 2000—; sci. fellow Nuc. Rsch. Ctr. Democritos, Athens, 1960—62. Tech. adv. bd. Ctr. Applied Polymer Rsch. Case Western Res. U., Cleve.; adv. bd. NSF Ctr. Polymer Interfaces Lehigh U. Assoc. editor: Jour. Applied Polymer Sci.; contbr. articles to profl. jours. Lt. Greek Army. Fellow Sci., Nuc. Rsch. Ctr. Democritos, Athens, Greece, 1960—62, NSF, Mich. State U., 1968—70, U. Calif., 1971—73. Mem.: AAAS, Am. Chem. Soc., N.Y. Acad. Scis., Sigma Xi. Greek Orthodox. Achievements include patents in field of in polymer sci. tech. Avocations: photography, painting, travel. Home and Office: 7009 Cashell Manor Ct Derwood MD 20855-1201 E-mail: mylonakis@msn.com.

MYMIT, CHUCK W. music educator, musician; b. N.Y.C., Dec. 15, 1948; s. Jack Mymit, Gloria Epstein; m. Maria Laura Asuaje, Aug. 16, 1993. BMus in Composition, Berklee Coll. of Music, Boston, 1971; MA in Composition, NYU, 1982. Asst. prof. Five Towns Coll., Seaford, NY, 1973—87, prof. jazz studies Dix Hill, 1973—87, 2000—; tchr. music N.Y.C. Bd. Edn., 1987—97; coord. music Peninsula Counceling Ctr., L.I., 1997—2000; house pianist Nordstroms Dept. Store, 1997—2000. Jazz comml. pianist AF of M, Local 802, N.Y.C., 1973—; freelance arranger/composer, N.Y.C., 1973—; editor FTC Press Five Towns Coll., 2000—; guest condr. NMEA All State Jazz Ensemble, NY, 2002. Author: (book) A Beginner's Approach to Jazz Improvisation, 1973, Contemporary Harmony I and Workbook, 1977, Contemporary Harmony II and Workbook, 1979, Arranging for Small Band, 1980, Club Date Pianist, 1981, Voicing Techniques for the Arranger, 1997, Contemporary Concepts in Jazz Harmony, 2001; composer (pianist, arranger): (CD's) Tú Eras Mi Corazon, 1995, The Romantic Pianist, 1995, Reflection, 1998, Ambience, 2001, music score. Named Most Valuable Player, Nordstroms Dept. Store, N.Y., 1997. Mem.: ASCAP, Internat. Assn. Jazz Educators. Avocation: sports. Office: Five Towns College 305 N Service Rd Dix Hills NY 11746

MYNATT, CECIL FERRELL, psychiatrist; b. Knoxville, Tenn., May 10, 1920; s. Cecil Ferrell and Ethel (May) Mynatt; m. Minnie Lee Rouser, Dec. 8, 1945 (div. Nov. 1988); children: Matthew, Cecilia, Melissa, Martha, Richard; m. Yong Cha Lee, Oct. 10, 1990; children: Katherine, John. BS, U. Tenn., 1950, MD, 1951. Pvt. practice in gen. medicine, Morristown, Tenn., 1952-61; resident Menninger Sch. Psychiatry, 1961-65; suprt. Ea. State Hosp., Knoxville, 1965-67; pvt. practice Wright Ferry Hosp., 1967-68; pvt. practice, co-owner Pvt. Hosp., 1968-73, Las Vegas, 1973-84; dir. Taliferro Mental Health Ctr., Lawton, Okla., 1984-89; supt. Western State Hosp., Woodward, 1989-91; med. dir. Rolling Hills Psychiat. Hosp., Ada, 1991-96; med. dir. behavioral medicine Mercy Meml. Hosp., Ardmore, 1996—. CEO Sun Enterprises, Inc., Ada, 1987—; cons. Pononotoc County Mental Health Assn., Ada, 1992-96, Valley View Meml. Hosp., Ada, 1992-96. Editor, pub. Voice of Experience, 1993—; contbr. articles to profl. jours. Maj. OSS, 1941-45. Decorated Silver star, Bronze star, (2) Purple Hearts. Mem. VFW, AMA, Okla. Med. Assn., Pononotoc County Med. Assn. Republican. Baptist. Avocations: motocycling, bowling, walking with wife. Home: 126 Kings Rd Ada OK 74820

MYNTTI, JON NICHOLAS, software engineer; b. Virginia, Minn., Mar. 11, 1940; s. William and Irene Myntti; m. Gail Bartolas, July 10, 1965; children: William, Mike, Donald. AS, Virginia Jr. Coll., 1960; BSEE, N.D. State U., 1963, MSEE, 1966. Assoc. engr. Control Data Corp., Mpls., 1963-65; engr. Univac, St. Paul, 1966-68; sr. engr. Electro Magnetic Rsch., Bloomington, 1968-69; prodn. devel. mgr. Copycomposer, Rockville, Md., 1969-71, Standard Register Co., Dayton, Ohio, 1971-77; cons. analyst Nat. Cash Register Co., Wichita, Kans., 1977-78; dir. prodn., engring. and acquisition Reporter Times Inc., Martinsville, Ind., 1978—; pres. control brain COTC, Newark, 1994—, divsn. chair engring. tech., 1997-99. Chmn. electronics Ind. Vocat. Coll., Indpls., 1985-88; chmn. electronics Wright State U., Dayton, 1988-94, editor computer paper, 1988-92; chmn. bd. Newsmate Products, Martinsville, 1979-90. Author: Automatic Control of A Manual Shift Transmission, 1966; contbr. articles to profl. jours. Mem. IEEE, Minutemen Assn. Inc., Mooresville, Ind. (pres. 1975—). also: 1964 Birchwood Ln Tower MN 55790-8146 Address: 1964 Birchwood Ln Tower MN 55790-8146

MYRA, HAROLD LAWRENCE, publisher; b. Camden, N.J., July 19, 1939; s. John Samuel and Esther (Christensen) M.; m. Jeanette Austin, May 7, 1966; children: Michelle, Todd, Gregory, Rick, Joshua, Lindsey. BS, East Stroudsburg State Coll., 1961; Litt.D., John Wesley Coll., 1976; D.Lit., Biola U., 1984; DLitt, Gordon Coll., 1992. Tchr. Pocono Mountain Jointure, Cresco, Pa., 1961; editorial asst. Youth for Christ Internat., Wheaton, Ill., 1961-62, asso. editor, 1962-64, mng. editor, 1964-65, dir. of lit., 1965-66; v.p. lit. div., pub. Campus Life, Wheaton, 1966-75; pres., chief exec. officer Christianity Today, Inc., Carol Stream, Ill., 1975—. Author: No Man in Eden, 1969, Michelle, You Scallawag, I Love You, 1972, The New You, 1972, The Carpenter, 1972, Elsbeth, 1975, Is There a Place I Can Scream?, 1976, Santa, Are You For Real?, 1979, Love Notes to Jeanette, 1979, The Choice, 1980, Halloween, 1982, Your Super-Terrific Birthday, 1985, Living By God's Surprises, 1988, Children in the Night, 1991, The Shining Face, 1993, Morning Child, 1994, Surprised by Children, 2001. Presbyterian. Home: 1737 Marion Ct Wheaton IL 60187-3319 Office: Christianity Today 465 Gundersen Dr Carol Stream IL 60188-2498

MYRDAL, ROSEMARIE CARYLE, state official, former state legislator; b. Minot, N.D., May 20, 1929; d. Harry Dirk and Olga Jean (Dragge) Lohse; m. B. John Myrdal, June 21, 1952; children: Jan, Mark, Harold, Paul, Amy. BS, N.D. State U., 1951. Registered profl. first grade tchr., N.D. Tchr., N.D., 1951-71; bus. mgr. Edinburg Sch. Dist., 1974-81; mem. N.D. Ho. of Reps., Bismarck, 1984-92, mem. appropriations com., 1991-92; lt. gov. State of N.D., 1993—2001. Sch. evaluator Walsh County Sch. Bds. Assn., Grafton, N.D., 1983-84; evaluator, work presenter N.D. Sch. Bds. Assn., Bismarck, 1983-84; mem. sch. bd. Edinburg Sch. Dist., 1981-90; adv. com. Red River Trade Corridor, Inc., 1989—. Co-editor: Heritage '76, 1976, Heritage '89, 1989. Precinct committeewoman Gardar Twp. Rep. Com., 1980-86; leader Hummingbirds 4-H Club, Edinburg, 1980-83; bd. dirs. Camp Sioux Diabetic Children, Grand Forks, N.D., 1980-90, N.D. affiliate Am. Diabetes Assn., Families First-Child Welfare Reform Initiative, Region IV, 1989-92; dir. N.D. Diabetes Assn., 1989-91; chmn. N.D. Ednl. TelecommunicationsCoun., 1989-90; vice chmn. N.D. Legis. Interim Jobs Devel. Commn., 1989-90. Mem. AAUW (pres. 1982-84 Pembina County area), Pembina County Hist. Soc. (historian 1976-84), Northeastern N.D. Heritage Assn. (pres. 1986-92), Red River Valley Heritage Soc. (bd. dirs. 1985-92). Clubs: Agassiz Garden (Park River) (pres. 1968-69). Lutheran. Avocations: gardening, architectural history, ethnic foods, historic/cultural preservation. Home: 12987 80th St NE Edinburg ND 58227-9635*

MYREN, DAVID JAMES, aeronautical engineer; b. Eau Claire, Wis., July 30, 1960; s. Gerald Vernon and Donna Mae (Stuber) M.; m. Beth Marjorie Olsen, May 25, 1985; children: Sarah Beth, Brent David. BS, U. Minn., 1984. Mgr. inventory control Sears Bus. Sys. Ctr., Mpls., 1983-85; test engr. FluiDyne Engring. Corp., 1985-89, project leader, aerotest mktg., 1989-97, aerotest mktg. mgr., 1997-2001, dir. Aerotest Lab., 2001—. Mem. AIAA (mem. coun. 1987-89, sect. treas. 1989, sect. sec. 1990, vice chmn. 1991, chmn. 1992, hons. and awards chmn. 1993—, dep. dir. region 5 1999—), U. Minn. Alumni Assn., Air Force Assn. Exptl. Aircraft Assn. Methodist. Avocations: music, reading, softball, wood working, swimming. Office: Aero Systems Engring Inc FluiDyne Aerotest Lab 358 Fillmore Ave E Saint Paul MN 55107-1204 E-mail: dmyren@aerosysengr.com.

MYREN, RICHARD ALBERT, criminal justice consultant; b. Madison, Wis., Aug. 9, 1924; s. Andrew Olaus and Olyanna (Olson) M.; m. Patricia Ross Hubin, June 12, 1948; children: Nina Ross Schroepfer, Tania Ellis, Kristina Albee Myren Sheldon, Andrew James. BS, U. Wis., 1948; LLB, Harvard U., 1952; LLD (hon.), U. New Haven, 1976. Bar: N.C. 1954. Research chemist U.S. Dept. Agr., No. Regional Research Lab., Peoria, Ill., 1948-49; asst. to assoc. research prof. pub. law and govt. Inst. Govt., Chapel Hill, N.C., 1952-56; asst. to assoc. prof. Ind. U., 1956-66; dean, prof. Sch. Criminal Justice, State U. N.Y., Albany, 1966-76, Sch. Justice, Am. U., Washington, 1976-86, prof. emeritus, 1986—; cons., 1987—. Vis. prof. Inst. Criminology, Cambridge (Eng.) U., 1973-74, East China Inst. for Politics and Law, Shanghai, People's Republic of China, 1988; cons. law enforcement programs for children and youth Children's Bur., HEW, Washington, 1960-62; cons. Pres.'s. Com. on Juvenile Delinquency and Youth Crime, 1962-64, Pres.'s Commn. on Law Enforcement and Adminstrn. Criminal Justice, 1966, U.S. Law Enforcement Assistance Adminstrn., 1968-82, N.Y. State Temp. Commn. on Constl. Conv., 1967, N.Y. State Dept. Edn., 1967, 69, Calif. Coordinating Council for Higher Edn., 1969-70, Nat. Adv. Commn. on Criminal Justice Standards and Goals, 1971-72, Tenn. Higher Edn. Commn., 1976, Ky. Dept. Justice, 1977-78, NSF, 1978— , U.S. Civil Rights Commn., 1978, others. Author: Coroners in North Carolina: A Discussion of Their Problems, 1953, Indiana Sheriffs' Manual of Law and Practice, rev. edit, 1959, Indiana Conservation Officers' Manual of Law and Practice, 1961; (with Lynn D. Swanson) Police Work With Children, 1962; (with Carroll L. Christenson) The Walsh-Healey Public Contracts Act: A Critical Review of Prevailing Minimum Wage Determinations, 1966, Education in Criminal Justice, 1970, Law and Justice: An Introduction, 1988, Investigation for Determination of Fact: A Primer on Proof, 1989; contbr. to: Bases for Justice Systems: Law and the Social Sciences (Gordon E. Misner), 1980, Five Year Outlook: Problems, Opportunities and Constraints in Science and Technology, 1980; assoc. editor: Jour. Criminal Justice; contbr. articles to profl. jours. Bd. dirs. Sex Info. and Edn. Council U.S., 1972-75. Served with inf. AUS, 1943-46, ETO; with USNR, 1954-58. Fulbright research scholar to Argentina Cordoba, 1964-65 Mem. N.C. Bar Assn., Sociedad Argentina de Sociología Home: 8017 Saint Andrews Way Mount Dora FL 32757-9127 E-mail: rpmyren@aol.com.

MYRICK, BISMARCK, diplomat; b. Portsmouth, Va., Dec. 23, 1940; children: Bismarck, Jr., Wesley Todd, Allison Elizabeth. BA, U. Tampa, 1972; MA, Syracuse U., 1973, postgrad., 1979-80; LHD (hon.) , Spelman Coll., 2002. Enlisted U.S. Army, 1959; desk officer for Somalia, U.S. Dept. State, Washington, 1980-82; advanced through grades to maj., 1975; ret., 1979; polit. officer Am. Embassy, Monrovia, Liberia, 1982-84; action officer office strategic nuclear policy bur. politico-milit. affairs U.S. Dept. State, 1985-87, dep. dir. policy plans and coordination bur. inter-Am. affairs, 1987-89, Una Chapman Cox fellow US-African Policy, 1988-90; consul gen. Am. Consulate Gen., Durban, South Africa, 1990-93, Capetown, South Africa, 1993-95; amb. to Lesotho, Am. Embassy, Maseru, 1995-98; diplomat-in-residence Atlanta U. Ctr. at Spelman Coll., 1998-99; U.S. amb. to Liberia Dept. of State, Monrovia, Liberia, 1999—. Author: Three Aspects of Crisis in Colonial Kenya, 1975. Decorated Silver Star, Purple Heart, 4 Bronze Stars; named to U.S. Army Hall of Fame, 1996; named Ambassador Bismarck Myrick Days, City of Portsmouth, Va., 2000, Bismarck Myrick St and Bismarck Myrick Crescent St. named in his honor, 2002. Address: Dept State Monrovia Washington DC 20521

MYRICK, HELEN ESTELLE, civic worker; b. Vancouver, B.C., Can., Feb. 4, 1952; came to U.S., 1964; d. Guy Vernon and Vera Loretto (Tacey) M. BA in Cmty. Svcs., Seattle U., 1973; MPA, Pacific Luth. U., 1984. Counselor Renton (Wash.) Area Youth Svcs., 1973-79; probation officer Kitsap County, Bremerton, Wash., 1979-82; social worker III, Wash. State Dept. Social and Health Svcs., Tacoma, 1982-85; mgr. human resources Tacoma-Pierce County Health Dept., 1985-93; legis. aide Wash. State Ho. of Reps., Olympia, 1993-94; polit. cons. Save Our Sealife Initiative Campaign, Tacoma, 1994-95; cons., project mgr. Greater Pierce County Cmty. Network, 1995—; owner The People's Bus. Employment counselor King County Work Tng. Program, Seattle, summer 1995; owner The People's Bus., contract with Greater Pierce County Cmty. Network, 1995—. Mem. adv. bd. Pierce County Cmty. Action Agy., 1987-95, Tacoma Hate Crimes Task Force, 1991-93; adult advisor Students Against Violence Everywhere, Federal Way, Wash., 1994-95; candidate Wash. State Ho. of Reps., 1990, 94; bd. dirs. Wash. State Women's Polit. Caucus, Seattle, 1993-95, endorsement chmn., 1995-97; rep. legis. action com. 30th Dist. Dems., Federal Way, 1992-94; bd. dirs. Port of Tacoma Citizen's Work Group, 1995—; bd. dirs. Federal Way Youth and Family Svcs., 1990—, also past pres.; mem. tech. adv. bd. Family Policy Coun., 1995—; commr. City of Tacoma Human Rights Commn., 1996. Recipient Disting. Svc. award N.W. Dispatch newspaper, 1991; leadership fellow Tacoma-Pierce County C. of C., 1988-89. Mem. NOW, Coalition To Stop Gun Violence, Toastmasters (Most Enthusiastic Speaker award Tacoma 1990), City Club Tacoma (bd. dirs. 1991—). Home and Office: 15411 9th Ave E Tacoma WA 98445-1291

MYRICK, SUE, congresswoman, former mayor; b. Tiffin, Ohio, Aug. 1, 1941; d. William Henry and Margaret Ellen (Roby) Wilkins; m. Jim Forest (div.); children: Greg, Dan; m. Wilbur Edward Myrick Jr., Sept. 11, 1977. Student, Heidelberg Coll., 1959-60, LLD (hon.), 1995. Exec. sec. to mayor and city mgr. City of Alliance, Ohio, 1962-63; dir. br. office Stark County Ct. of Juvenile and Domestic Rels., Alliance, 1963-65; pres. Myrick Agy., Charlotte, N.C., 1971-95; mayor City of Charlotte, 1987-91; mem. 104th Congress from 9th N.C. Dist., Washington, 1995—. Candidate for U.S. Senate from N.C., 1992. Active Heart Fund, Multiple Sclerosis, March of Dimes, Arts and Scis. Fund Dr.; past mem. adv. bd. Uptown Shelter, Uptown Homeless Task Force, bd. dirs. N.C. Inst. Politics; v.p. Sister Cities Internat.; mem. Pres. Bush's Affordable Housing Commn.; founder, coord. Charlotte vol. tornado relief effort; former bd. dirs. Learning How; former mem. adv. bd. U.S. Conf. Mayors; mem.-at-large Charlotte City Coun., 1983-85, Strengthening Am. Commn.; lay leader, Sunday sch. tchr. 1st United Meth. Ch.; treas. Mecklenburg Ministries; former trustee U.S. Conf. of Mayors. Recipient Woman of Yr. award Harrisonburg, Va., 1968; named one of Outstanding Young Women of Am., 1968. Mem. Women's Polit. Caucus, Beta Sigma Phi. Republican. Home and Office: Myrick Enterprises 9169 Bonnie Briar Cir Charlotte NC 28277-1576 also: US House Reps 230 Cannon Hob Washington DC 20515-0001

MYSAK, LAWRENCE ALEXANDER, oceanographer, climatologist, mathematician, educator; b. Saskatoon, Sask., Can., Jan. 22, 1940; s. Stephen and Nettie (Trojan) M.; m. Diane Mary Eeles, Aug. 15, 1974; children: Paul Alexander, Claire Anastasia. BSc, U. Alta., Can., 1961; MSc, U. Adelaide, Australia, 1963; AM, Harvard U., 1964, PhD, 1967. Rsch. fellow Harvard U., 1966-67; mem. faculty U. B.C., Vancouver, 1967-86, prof. math. and oceanography, 1976-86; Atmospheric Environ. Svc./Natural Scis. Engring. Rsch. Coun.; sr. indsl. rsch. prof. climatology McGill U., Montreal, Que., Can., 1986-96, dir. Climate Rsch Group Can., 1986-90, Can. Steamship Lines prof. meteorology Can., 1989—, founding dir. Ctr. for Climate and Global Change Rsch. Can., 1990-96. Vis. rsch. assoc. Oreg. State U., summer 1968; sr. visitor Cambridge (Eng.) U., 1971-72; vis. scientist Inst. Ocean Sci., Sidney, B.C., fall 1976, Nat. Ctr. Atmospheric Rsch., Boulder, Colo., 1977; vis. prof. U.S. Naval Postgrad. Sch., Monterey, Calif., summer 1981, Swiss Fed. inst., Tech., Zurich, 1982-83, 2000-2001; George's Lemaître vis. prof. Cath. U. Louvain, Belgium, 1995; invitation fellowship for rsch. in Japan, Japan Soc. for Promotion of Scis., 1997; vis. prof., supr. 62 grad. and postdoctoral students, 1967—; vis. prof. Italian Nat. Inst. Geophysics and Volcanology, Bologna, 2001; exch. lectr. Royal Soc. Can. Nat. Acad. Scis. of Ukraine, 2002. Co-author: Waves in the Ocean, 1978; also articles in profl. jours.; assoc. editor Jour. Phys. Oceanography, 1977-92, Atmospheric-Ocean, 1988-91, Climatol. Bull., 1992-93; contbg. editor Am. Geophys. Union books on coastal and esturaine studies, 1987-2000; mem. editl. bd. Geophys. and Astrophys. Fluid Dynamics, 1983-96; series editor: Kluwer Acad. Pubs. Atmospheric and Oceanog. Scis. Libr., 2001-. Recipient Patterson Disting. Svc. medal Environ. Can. Atmospheric Environment Svc., 1997; appt. Order of Can., 1996. Fellow Acad. of Sci. of Royal Soc. Can. (v.p. Acad. of Sci. 1991-93, pres. 1993-96), Am. Meteorol. Soc., Am. Geophys. Union; mem. Can. Applied Math. Soc., Can. Meteorol. and Oceanog. Soc. (co-recipient Pres.'s prize 1980, J.P. Tully medal Oceanography 1997, inaugural fellow 1999), Royal Soc. Can. (life), European Geophys. Soc., Academia Europaea (fgn.). Office: McGill U 805 Sherbrooke St W Montreal QC Canada H3A 2K6 E-mail: mysak@zephyr.meteo.mcgill.ca.

MYSEROS, JOHN SOCRATES, pediatric neurosurgeon; b. Washington, Jan. 12, 1964; s. Socrates John and Euridiki S. Myseros; m. Wendy MacKay, May 14, 1990; children: Alexandra, Sophia. BA, Johns Hopkins U., 1986, MD, 1990. Diplomate Am. Bd. Pediat. Neurol. Surgery, Am. Bd. Neurol. Surgery. Surg. intern Med. Coll. Va., Richmond, 1990-91, resident in neurosurgery, 1991-96; fellow in pediatric neurosurgery Hosp. for Sick Children, Toronto, 1996-97; asst. prof. neurosurgery, staff pediatric neurosurgery Allegheny U. Hosp., Pitts., 1997-98; staff pediatric neurosurgeon Inova Fairfax (Va.) Hosp. for Children, 1998-99, asst. prof. neurosurgery and pediat.; staff. pediatric neurosurgeon Children's Hosp. Med. Ctr., Cin., 1999—. Fellow ACS, Am. Acad. Pediats.; mem. Am. Assn. Neurol. Surgeons, Congress Neurol. Surgeons, Joint Sect. Pediatric Neurol. Surgery, Am. Soc. Pediat. Neurosurgeons. Greek Orthodox. Office: Children's Hosp Med Ctr 3333 Burnet Ave Cincinnati OH 45229-3026

MYSLINSKI, NORBERT RAYMOND, medical educator; b. Buffalo, Apr. 14, 1947; s. Bernard and Amelia Joan (Lesniak) M.; m. Patricia Ann Byrne, June 19, 1970 (dec. 1980); m. René Carter, Nov. 21, 1993; children: Matthew Ryan, Kelly Lynn. BS in Biology, Canisius Coll., Buffalo, 1965-69; PhD in Pharmacology, U. Ill., Chgo., 1973. Rsch. assoc. Tufts U., Boston, 1973-75; asst. prof. U. Md., Balt., 1975-80, assoc. prof. physiology, 1980—, co-dir. Facial Pain Clinic, 1980-84, instr. nursing, 1982-84; rsch. fellow U. Bristol, Eng., 1984-85; adj. assoc. prof. U. Md. Sch. Nursing, 1997—. Instr. C.C. Balt., 1980—82; dir. grad. program dept. physiology U. Md., 1981—97, dir. h.s. biomed. rsch. program, 2000—, mem. faculty Marine-Estuarine Environ. Scis. grad. program, 1988—97; founder, dir. Patricia Byrne Nursing Scholarship Fund Trocaire Coll., Buffalo, 1985; dir. NIH Minority Rsch. Apprentice Program Balt. Coll. Dental Surgery, 1988—99; mem. grant rev. com. Nat. Inst. Nursing Rsch., 1993—94; grant reviewer Dept. Health and Human Svcs., 1993—94; cons. in field; appeared on more than 20 live TV and radio programs; founder, dir. Internat. Brain Bee, 1999—. Editor newsletters Med. Soc. Md. Rsch., 1977-82, Brain Storm, 1999—; author book chpts., revs. and numerous abstracts on pharmacology and neurosci.; inventor in field; reviewer 7 jours. Rep. task force on aging U. Md., 1979—84; instr. Am. Heart Assn., Balt., 1978, ARC, Balt., 1977—83; dir. Md. Brain Awareness Week, 1996—; eucharistic min., pastoral visitor Cath. Ch., 1983—93. Capt. U.S. Army, 1969—77. Grantee NIH, various drug cos. and founds.; USPHS fellow, 1969-73; recipient Alumni of Yr. award St. Mary's H.S., Lancaster, N.Y., 1996, Disting. Alumni award for outstanding career Canisius Coll., Buffalo, 1997, Time to Care Cmty. Svc. award U. Md., 1998, Founders Day Pub. Svc. award U. Md., 2000. Mem.: Am. Soc. Pharmacology and Exptl. Therapeutics, Soc. for Neurosci. (pres. Balt. chpt. 1990—92, editor newsletter 1990—97, neurosci. literacy com. 1997—2001), Am. Physiol. Soc., Internat. Assn. Dental Rsch. (adv. 1980—81), Md. Soc. Med. Rsch. (exec. com. 1978—86, bd. dir. 1978—86), Internat. Brain Rsch. Orgn., European Brain and Behavior Soc. (hon.). Republican. Home: 9395 Carrie Way Ellicott City MD 21042-1701 Office: U Md OCBS Dept 666 W Baltimore St Baltimore MD 21201-1510 Fax: (410) 706-0193. E-mail: nrm001@dental.umaryland.edu.

MYTELKA, ARNOLD KRIEGER, lawyer; b. Jersey City, July 24, 1937; s. Herman Donald and Jeannette (Krieger) M.; m. Rosalind Marcia Kaplan, Dec. 17, 1961; children: Andrew Charles, Daniel Sommer. AB, Princeton U., 1958; LLB cum laude, Harvard U., 1961; postgrad., London Sch. Econs., 1961-62. Bar: N.J. 1961, U.S. Dist. Ct. N.J. 1963, U.S. Supreme Ct. 1970, U.S. Ct. Appeals (3d cir.) 1978, U.S. Dist. Ct. (so. and ea. dist.) N.Y. 1983. Law sec. Chief Justice N.J. Supreme Ct., Newark, 1962-63; assoc. Clapp & Eisenberg, 1963-68, ptnr., 1968-94; prin. Kraemer, Burns, Mytelka, Lovell & Kulka, Springfield, N.J., 1994—. Lectr. Rutgers Law Sch., Newark, 1973; mem. Am. Law Inst., Phila., 1989—; mem. cons. group The Law Governing Lawyers, 1990-99; founding trustee Newark Legal Svcs. Project, 1965-68; trustee Edn. Law Ctr., 1974-75; chmn. dist. V ethics com. Supreme Ct. N.J., 1983-84, mem. 1981-84; trustee Legal Svcs. Found. Essex County, 1982—, pres., 1990-92; lectr. in land use law. Mem. editorial bd. N.J. Law Jour., 1991—; contbr. legal articles to profl. jours. Chmn. bd. trustees Ramapo Coll. N.J., 1979-80, mem. 1975-80; mediator chancery divsn. N.J. Superior Ct., 1990—, trustee, 1998-2000, spl. fiscal agt., 1997, spl. master, 1999, 2000. Frank Knox Meml. fellow Harvard U., London Sch. Econs. and Polit. Sci., 1961-62. Mem. ABA (mem. litigation sect.), N.J. State Bar Assn. (chmn. appellate practices study com. 1977-79, chmn. land use sect. 1984-85). Home: 56 Hall Rd Chatham NJ 07928-1723 Office: Kraemer Burns Mytelka Lovell & Kulka 675 Morris Ave Springfield NJ 07081-1523 E-mail: amytelka@kraemerburns.com.

MYTNIK, HALINA ZOFIA, retired librarian; b. Cracow, Poland, Apr. 20, 1935; d. Stanislaw and Aniela Cecylia (Fijak) M. MA, Jagiellonian Univ., 1957. Chartered libr. Sci. worker dept. linguistics Cracow Polish Acad. Scis., 1955-59; libr. Ctrl. Libr., U. Mining and Metallurgy, Cracow, 1959-70, libr. Inst. Mining and Dressing Machines, 1970-92, libr. Dept. Mining Machines Libr., 1993-96. Sec. Solidarity Trade Union, 1980-81. Recipient gold cross of merit State Coun. Poland, 1981. Mem. Assn. of Jagellonian Univ. Grads., Polish Libr. Assn. (Cracow chpt.). Roman Catholic. Home: Lwowska 18/6 30-548 Cracow Poland

NA, TSUNG SHUN (TERRY NA), Chinese studies educator, writer; b. Beijing, Nov. 3, 1932; came to U.S., 1964; s. Chi-L and Hui (Hu) N.; m. Yen Yen Chao, 1964. BA, Taiwan Normal U., 1956; MA, U. B.C., 1970; PhD, U. Minn., 1978. Assoc. prof. Taipei Normal Coll., Taiwan, Republic of China, 1956-64; vis. lectr. Ind. U., Bloomington, 1964-66; asst. prof. U. Minn., Mpls., 1970-80; vis. prof. Sun Yat-sen U., Taiwan, 1981-84; prof., dir. Am. Inst. Chinese Studies, Charles Town, W.Va., 1985—. Author: (English books) A Linguistic Study of P'i-pa Chi, 1969, Studies on Dream of the Red Chamber: A Selected and Classified Bibliography, 1979, Supplement, 1981, Taiwan Studies on Dream of the Red Chamber: A Selected and Classified Bibliography, 1983, Chinese Studies in English: A Selected Bibliography, 1991, (Chinese) Mandarin Pronunciation, 1966, Teaching Chinese in the U.S.A., 1983, Studies on Chinese Classical Novels, 1985, A Collection of Short Stories, 1987; contbr. numerous articles, short stories, and research essays to jours. and newspapers in U.S., Taiwan, ROC, and China. Mem. MLA, Assn. Asian Studies. Office: Am Inst Chinese Studies PO Box 453 Charles Town WV 25414-0453

NA'ALLAH, ABDUL-RASHEED, writer, educator; b. Ilorin, Kwara, Nigeria, Dec. 21, 1962; s. Ahmad Alabi and Bilkisu Olohuntoyin Na'Allah; m. Rahmat Olohuntoyin Kamaldeen, July 27, 1995; children: Saarah Asabi, Haleemah Aduke, Rabiah Abio. BA in English and Edn. with honors, U. Ilorin, 1988, MA in Lit.-in-English, 1992; PhD, U. Alta., Edmonton, Can., 1999. GRD II tchr.'s cert. Tchr. Ilorin Schs. Bd., 1981—84; lectr. U. Ilorin, 1989—94; co-founder The Africa Soc. U. Alberta, Alberta, Canada, 1997—98; asst. prof. Western Ill. U., Macomb, 1998—2002, assoc. prof., 2002—. Founder, faculty adviser Creative Writers Soc. Western Ill. U., Macomb, 1998—. Co-author: Introduction to African Oral Literature, 1991; editor: (book) Ogoni's Agonies, 1998; author: Almajiri: A New African Poetry, 2001; editor: The People's Poet: Emerging Perspectives on Niyi Osundare, 2002. Co-founder Ilorin Vanguard, 1990—94. Mem.: Can. Comparative Lit. Assn., Flora Nwapa Soc., Internat. Comparative Lit. Assn., African Studies Assn., African Lit. Assn. Moslem. Avocations: poetry performance, story telling, reading. Office: Western Ill U 1 University Cir Macomb IL 61455 Office Fax: 309-298-2181. Business E-Mail: a-naallah@wiu.edu.

NAAOUSH, SABAH FARAJ, economist, consultant; b. Baghdad, Iraq, Nov. 28, 1945; s. Faraj Satar and Zahra (Amin) N.; m. Michele Henriette Nicollet, Sept. 15, 1984. BA in Law, Baghdad U., 1968; M in Law, Montpellier U., France, 1972; D in Fin., Poitiers U., France, 1977. Lawyer Lawyer Union, Baghdad, 1968-70; lectr. Hassan II U., Casablanca, Morocco, 1978-82, sr. lectr. Morocco, 1982-87; mem. editl. staff Liberal, 1988-95; journalist Marches tropicaux jour., Paris, 1990—, Fgn. Ministry, Paris, 1990—. Cons. CEEP Co., Cardiff, Gt. Britain, 1986-88. Author: Public Finance, 1983, Arab Economic Organization, 1986, Direct Taxes in Morocco, 2 vols., 1986, Taxes in Arab Countries, 1987, External Debt in Arab Countries, 1989, Economy and Finance in Arab Countries, 1994, External Finance Crisis in Arab Countries,

1998. Avocations: chess, arts, photography, music, sports. Home: 103 Duchere-Chateau 69009 Lyon France Office: 103 rue Jean Fournier 69009 Lyon France E-mail: snaaoush@free.fr.

NAAR, HARRY I. fine arts educator, artist; b. New Brunswick, N.J., July 28, 1946; s. Isidore B. and Dorothy Naar; m. Barbara Jean Naar, June 25, 1972; children: Devin, Aaron. BFA, Phila. Coll. Art, 1968; MFA, Ind. U., 1970; pvt. study, Jean Helion, Paris, 1970-71. Tchg. assoc. Ind. U., Bloomington, 1968-70; instr. Middlesex County Coll., Edison, N.J., 1972-77, Beaver Coll., Glenside, Pa., 1975-78, Moore Coll. Art, Phila., 1978, Rutgers U., Newark, 1979-80; instr. fine arts Rider U., Lawrenceville, N.J., 1980-93, assoc. prof., 1993, prof., 1993—; gallery dir. Rider U. Art Gallery, NJ. Tchr. Gill-St. Bernard's Upper Sch., Gladstone, N.J., 1972-74, Princeton (N.J.) Art Assn., 1974-76, Art Ctr. No. N.J., Tenafly, 1975-76, Princeton Adult Sch., 1976, Somerset Art Assn., Bernardsville, N.J., 1977-78; vis. artist, instr. Phila. Coll. Art, 1978, 84; juror numerous shows, latest being Ellarslie Open XVII, XX, Trenton (N.J.) City Mus., 1999; guest lectr. Westminster Coll., New Wilmington, Pa., 1976; mem. symposium panel Montgomery Coll., Rockville, Md., 1983; lectr. Kean Coll., Newark, 1988, Western Carolina U., Cullowhee, N.C., 1989, Somerset Art Assn., Far Hills, N.J., Rider U., 1998, Trenton (N.J.) City Mus., 1999, also others; vis. artist-juror Princeton Regional H.S., 1991. Numerous one-man shows, 1968—, including N.J. State Mus., Trenton, 1977, Princeton Gallery Fine Art, 1979, Rider Coll., 1980, 93, Western Carolina U., 1989, NIH Clin. Ctr. Galleries, Bethesda, Md., 1992, Rowan Coll., Glasboro, N.J., 1994, Gallery South Orange, N.J., 1995, Les Malaut Art Gallery, Union, N.J., 1999; 2-man show Rider U., 1997; exhibited in numerous group exhbns., 1967—, including Indpls. Mus. Art, 1970, Corcoran Gallery Art, 1970, N.J. State Mus., Trenton, 1974, 75, 79, Rider Coll., 1974, 99, Hunterdon Art Ctr., Clinton, N.J., 1977, 86, 87, 90, Barbara Glaberson Gallery, New Brunswick, N.J., 1981, More Gallery, Phila., 1982, Carimor Galleries, N.Y.C., 1984, David Adamson Gallery, Washington, 1984, Bergen (N.J.) Mus. Art and Sci., 1987, Boca Raton Mus. Art, 1987, Princeton Gallery Fine Arts, 1988, Western Carolina U., 1989, USSR Artists Union Gallery, Moscow, 1990, Trenton City Mus., 1991, 92, Scanticon, Princeton, 1992, 93, 95, Hardcastle Gallery, Wilmington, Del., 1997, Coll. of N.J., Trenton, 2000, Sussec County Coll., Newton, N.J., 2000, Trenton City Mus., 2001, N.J. State Mus., Trenton, 2001, Gallery of South Orange,N.J., 2001, Blair Acad. Blairsbotn, N.J., 2001; represented in permanent collections Ind. U., Morris Mus. Art and Scis., Morristown, N.J. State Mus., Jane Voorhees Zimmerli Art Mus., Rutgers U., New Brunswick, also corp. collections; work reviewed in numerous articles and interviews and represented in catalogs. Recipient Best in Show/drawing, Trenton City Mus., 2002, Dorothy Malloy Meml. award for painting Trenton City Mus., 1992; fellow Ind. U., 1968-69; rsch. grantee Rider Coll., summers 1982, 88, grantee TAWA-Soviet Exch. Program summer 1990, Rider U., 1999, 2001. Mem. Printmaking Coun. N.J. (bd. dirs. 1984-86), Assoc. Artists N.J., Trenton Artists Workshop Assn. Home: 4 Tracey Ct Lawrenceville NJ 08648-1543 Office: Rider U Fine Arts Dept Lawrenceville NJ 08648

NABEL, ELIZABETH G. medical researcher, cardiologist; BA summa cum laude, St. Olaf Coll., 1974; postgrad., Union Theol. Sem., 1974-75, Columbia U., 1975-77; MD, Cornell U., 1981. Diplomate Am. Bd. Internal Medicine and cardiovascular diseases. Intern & resident in internal medicine Brigham and Women's Hosp.-Harvard Med. Sch., Boston, 1981—84, clin. and rsch. fellow cardiovasc. divsn., 1984-87; asst. prof. internal medicine U. Mich., Ann Arbor, 1987-91, assoc. prof. internal medicine, 1991-94, prof. internal medicine, 1994—, dir. Cardiovasc. Rsch. Ctr., 1992—, prof. physiology, 1995—, chief divsn. cardiology, 1997-99; Scientific dir. clinical rsch. NIH/NHLBI, Bethesda, Md., 1999—. Mem. sci. adv. bd. Vical Inc., San Diego, 1992—; mem. arteriosclerosis, hypertension, and lipid metabolism adv. com. NHLBI, NIH, 1991-93, parent program project grant rev. com., 1995—, mem. task force on human gene therapy, 1992, mem. cardiology adv. com., 1993-94, mem. spl. emphasis panel arterial thrombosis, 1996; chair Scientific Pub. Com., Am. heart assn., 1996-98, (bd. of dir, 1996-98), Atherosluosis Thrombosis and Vascular Biology Coun., 2002-03, Gordon Conf. on Vascular Cell Biology, 1996; pres. N.Am. Vascular Biology Orgn., 1996-97; Scientific adv.bd. Keystone Symposia, 1999-2006, (bd. of dir. 2001-06), com. on Space Med. Instit. of Med., 1991-2001, Coun. & Sec. Treas., Am. soc. of Clinical Investigation, 2001-03; Lectr. Mayo Clinic, 1996, Yale Univ., 1997, Univ. of Texas, 1997, Womens Hosp., 1997, 2001, Univ. of Hawaii, 1980, Temple Univ., 1999, John Hopkins, 1999, 2000, 2002, Am. Heart Assoc. 1999, Univ. of Mich., 2001, Vanderbilt Univ., 2001, Univ, of Va., 2002, among many others. Assoc. editor Jour. Molecular Medicine; mem. editl. bd. Circulation, 1993—, Jour. Vascular Rsch., 1993-95, Circulation Rsch., 1994—, Hypertension, 1994—, Trends in Cardiovasc. Medicine, 1995—, Am. Soc. Clin. Investigation, 1995—, Jour. of Clinical Investigation, 1997-2002 (Editl. bd., 2002—); guest editor Current Protocols in Human Genetics, 1995—; bd. of reviewing editors, Sci., 1998—; Editl. bd. New England Jour. of Med., 2001—; editor Trends in Cardiovascular Med., 2001—; Cons. Editor circulation rsch. Ather. Thrombosis and Vascular Biology, 2000— Fellow Am. Coll. Cardiology, Am. Heart Assn. (basic sci. coun., clin. cardiology coun., circulation coun., atherosclerosis coun., bd. dirs. 1996-97, sci. adv. and coord. com. 1996-97, chair sci. pub. com. 1996-97, sci. pub. com. 1994-96, sci. sessions program com. 1994-95; rsch. fellowship com. Mich. chpt. 1993-95, rsch. grant-in-aid com. 1994-96, vice chair rsch. grant-in-aid com. 1995-96, rsch. exec. com. 1995-96, rsch. com. 1995-96, chair peer rev. rsch. com. 1996-97); mem. AAAS, ACP, Am. Soc. for Biochemistry and Molecular Biology (Amgen Sci. award 1996), Am. Fedn. Clin. Rsch., Am. Soc. Investigative Pathology, Am. Soc. Clin. Investigation, N.Y. Acad. Scis., Am. Soc. Gene Therapy (bd. dirs. 1996), Assn. Am. Physicians, N.Am. Vascular Biology Orgn. (councillor 1994-95, sec., treas. 1994-95, pres. 1996-97), Inst. of Medicine, Ctrl. Soc. Clin. Rsch., Phi Beta Kappa, Alpha Omega Alpha. Office: NIH/NHLBI Bldg 10 Rm 8C103 10 Ctr Dr Bethesda MD 20892

NABERS, CLAUDE LOWREY, retired periodontist, writer; b. Vernon, Tex., Mar. 29, 1924; s. John Bradford and Mae (Moore) N.; m. Blanche Lillian Eaton, Sept. 28, 1951; children: Marquis Eaton, Bradford Claude. DDS, U. Tex., 1946; MS in Dentistry, Northwestern U., Chgo., 1949. Diplomate Am. Bd. Periodontology (bd. dirs. 1965-71, chmn. 1971). Civilian cons. Brook Army Hosp., 1958-84, Lackland Air Force Hosp., 1958-75, Sch. Aerospace Medicine, 1975-80. Pres. Nabers Eaton Properties, San Antonio, 1983—; nat. cons. Surgeon Gen. USAF, 1969-71; mem. ADA Coun. on Dental Rsch., Chgo., 1983-87; lectr. in field worldwide. Author: (in Japanese) Periodontal Therapy, 1980; co-author: Periodontal Therapy, 1990; originator procedures in field. Mem. devel. bd. U. Tex. Health Sci. Ctr., San Antonio, 1989-94; trustee Cancer Therapy and Rsch. Ctr. Found. Bd., San Antonio, 1998—; elder 1st Presbyn. Ch., San Antonio, 1960; v.p. Alamo Kiwanis, San Antonio, 1990-91; bd. dirs. The 100 Club, San Antonio, 1993-96, McFarland Tennis Found., San Antonio, 1994-97, San Antonio Salvation Army, 1998—; bd. govs. Cancer Therapy and Rsch. Ctr., San Antonio, 1999—. Capt. U.S. Army, 1946-48. Recipient 1st Holler's Disting. Lectureship award, San Antonio, 1984; recipient Outstanding Civilian Svc. medal Dept. of the Army, 1978, 1st Meml. G.R. Landquist Lectureship Northwestern U., 1979. Fellow Am. Coll. Dentists, Am. Acad. Periodontology (pres. 1972-73, exec. coun. 1962-74, Gold medal 1978, Master Clinician award 1990), Acad. Internat. Dentistry; mem. S.W. Soc. Periodontists (pres. 1961), San Antonio Country Club, Town Club, Argyle, European Acad. Dentistry (hon.), South African Soc. Periodontology (hon.), Omicron Kappa Upsilon (hon.). Republican. Avocations: tennis, golf, hunting, bridge, travel.

NABHOLZ, JOSEPH VINCENT, biologist, ecologist; b. Memphis, Nov. 3, 1945; s. Martin Peter and Helen Kathleen (Garbacz) N.; m. Sue Ann Winterburn, Aug. 12, 1972; children: Karen Stacey, Pamela Michelle. BS, Christian Bros. U., Memphis, 1968; MS, U. Ga., 1973, PHD, 1978. Sr. biologist EPA, Washington, 1979—. Reviewer NSF and profl. jours., 1973—, Standards Methods Com., Am. Water Works Assn., Denver 18th through 21st edits.; evaluator Office Exptl. Learning U. Md., College Park, Md., 1984-86. Author: ECOSAR computer program to predict aquatic toxicity of chemicals, 2001; co-author: Methods of Ecological Toxicology, 1981, Testing for Effects of Chemicals on Ecosystems, 1981; author: Estimating Toxicity of Industrial Chemicals to Aquatic Organisms Using Structure Activity Relationships, 1988, 94; contbr. articles to profl. jours. Bd. dirs. Comty. Assn. Rollingwood Village (4th sect.), Woodbridge, Va., 1981-90, v.p. 1981-82, pres. 1983-90, maintainence chmn. 1990—. Decorated Army Commendation medal with oak leaf cluster, U.S. Army, Vietnam, 1969, '70. Mem. AAAS, Am. Inst. Biol. Scis., Assn. Southeastern Biologists, Internat. Assn. Ecology, Ecol. Soc. Am. (life), Soc. Environ. Toxicology and Chemistry, Phi Kappa Phi (life). Roman Catholic. Achievements include pragmatic application of theory of chemical structure activity relationships for routine risk assessment of industrial chemicals for environmental toxicity. Home: 13627 Bentley Cir Woodbridge VA 22192-4340 Office: EPA 7403 1200 Pennsylvania Ave NW Washington DC 20460-0001 Fax: 202-564-9063. E-mail: nabholz.joe@epa.gov.

NABHOLZ, MARY VAUGHAN, rehabilitation nurse; b. Memphis, July 4, 1938; d. George E. Jr. and Anna Marie (Hannifin) Vaughan; m. William James Nabholz, Jr.; children: Kathleen Marie, William James III, Michael Vaughan. Diploma, St. Joseph Hosp., Memphis, 1959; BA, Webster U., 1978. Cert. CDMS, CCM. Staff nurse St. Joseph Hosp., St. Charles, Mo., 1965-77; supr. Always Care Nursing Svc., St. Louis, 1977-78; home care nurse Jewish Hosp., 1979-81; regional med. mgr. Md. Casualty Co., 1981-88; case mgr. Am. Health Network, 1988-91; regional mgr., 1990; cons., owner Nabholz & Assocs., Bridgeton, Mo., 1991—. Bd. dirs. Ctr. Head Injury Svcs. Bd. dirs. Ctr. Head Injury Svcs. Mem. Nat. Head Injury Assn., Nat. Spinal Cord Assn., Assn. Rehab. Nurses, Nat. Rehab. Assn., CMSA.

NABI, STANLEY ANDREW, investment executive; b. Baghdad, Iraq, Sept. 17, 1930; came to U.S., 1947; s. Moshi S. and Victoria T. (Mukamal) N.; m. Bette E. Miller, Mar. 31, 1968; children: Deborah Susan, Lisa Meryl. BA, Columbia U., 1952; postgrad., NYU, 1954-58. Gen. ptnr. Schweickart & Co., N.Y.C., 1954-72; gen. ptnr., chief investment officer Lazard Freres & Co., 1973-84; exec. v.p. Bessemer Trust Co., N.A., 1985-95; pres., CEO, Bessemer Investors Svcs., 1985-95; vice chmn., chmn. investment policy com. Wood, Struthers & Winthrop, N.Y.C., 1995-2000; chief investment officer DLJ Asset Mgmt. Corp., 1996-2000; mng. dir., sr. advisor Credit Suisse Asset Mgmt., 2000—. Lectr. New Sch. Social Research, N.Y.C., 1963-68; investment cons. U.S. Steel and Carnegie Pension Fund, N.Y.C., 1979— ; dir. Bargain Town U.S.A., N.Y.C., 1962-69; mem. pres.'s coun. New Sch. U., N.Y.C., 1989—; adj. prof. fin. Grad. Sch. Bus., Fordham U., N.Y.C., 1992-97. Editor: weekly jour. The Analyst, 1957-72; assoc. editor: jour. The Fin. Analysts Jour., 1971-83. Trustee NABI Found., 1964—. Served with U.S. Army, 1952-54. Mem. N.Y. Soc. Security Analysts (pres. 1971-72), Inst. Chartered Fin. Analysts, Assn. for Investment Mgmt. and Rsch. Office: 466 Lexington Ave New York NY 10017 Home: Ph 1 1 Kensington Gate Great Neck NY 11021-1202 E-mail: Stanley.a.nabi@csam.com.

NABIRAHNI, DAVID M.A. chemical scientist, educator, administrator; b. Tehran, Iran, July 10, 1956; came to U.S., 1979; BS, Nat. U. Iran, 1979; MS with honors, Ea. N.Mex. U., 1980; PhD, U. New Orleans, 1985. Chmn. and English tchr. Armaghan Tarbiat Sch., Tehran, 1975-79; teaching and rsch. asst. Ea. N.Mex. U., Portales, 1979-80; from teaching and rsch. asst. to sr. rsch. chemist U. New Orleans, La., 1981-86; asst. prof. analytical chemistry Pace U., Pleasantville, N.Y., 1986-89, assoc. prof., 1990-92, prof., 1992—, dir. ctr. applied analytical chemistry, 1988—, adj. prof. environ. law, 1992—. Vis. prof. II U. Rome, 1987—, Inst. Analytical Chemistry, U. Florence, Italy, 1990; adj. rsch. chemist Am. Health Found., Valhalla, N.Y., 1987; adj. prof. chemistry Manhattanville Coll., Purchase, N.Y., 1990-93; vis. scientist IBM T.J. Watson Rsch. Ctr., Yorktown Heights, N.Y., 1991-92, Ciba Giegy Corp., 1993; adj. prof. dermatology N.Y. Med. Coll., Valhalla, 1995—; dir. grad. program environ. Sci. Pace U., Pleasantville, N.Y., 1996—. Contbr. 100 articles /presentation to profl. jours. Environ. advisor to Congresswoman Nita M. Lowey, 1990-92; co-founder Persion Watch Cat: Iranian-Am. Anti-Discrimination Coun.; mem. Fulbright Com. Rev. Bd., Scandinavian Countries. Fulbright Sr. rsch. scholar Tech. U. Denmark, 1993, vis. faculty fellow Oxford U., U.K., 1994. Mem. AAUP, Am. Chem. Soc. (Disting. Scientist of Yr. award 1996, Kenan award for tchg. excellence 1998), Am. Chem. Soc. N.Y. (chair), Am. Assn. Clin. Chemistry, Persian Am. Chemists Assn. (founder 1990-92, chmn., sec. bd. dirs. 1988—, ran for chmn. N.Y. sect. 2000, chmn. Westchester div. 1991), Soc. Electroanalytical Chemistry, N.Y. Acad. Sci., Soc. Neurosci., Sigma Xi. Moslem. Avocations: soccer, swimming, hiking, pro-environ. quality, computers. Office: Pace U Dept Chemistry Pleasantville NY 10570 E-mail: nrahni@pace.edu.

NABORS, BRIAN KEITH, music educator, religious organization administrator; b. Columbus, Ohio, May 4, 1967; s. Lou J. and Barbara J. Nabors. MusB in Edn., Ohio State U., 1994. Cert. tchr. edn. Dir. h.s. choral activities Mansfield (Ohio) Sr. H.S., 1995—; dir. contemporary worship; youth mus. dir. Mansfield Playhouse, 1995—; organist 1st Christian Ch., 1995—97; mus. dir. Ashland (Ohio) U. Summer Theatre Festival, 2002—. Grant bd. mem. Richland County Found., Mansfield, 2000—02; lectr. in field. Mem. Mansfield City Schs. Task Force, 1999—2001. Grantee theater grantee for mus., Richland County Found., 1997. Mem.: I A Jazz Educators, Am. Choral Dir.'s Assn., Ohio Music Educators Assn., Phi Mu Alpha. Avocations: bowling, walking, comic book collecting. Home: Apt 207 40 South Linden Rd Mansfield OH 44906 Office: Mansfield Sr H S 145 W Park Blvd Mansfield OH 44906 Personal E-mail: bnaborschoirs@cs.com..

NABORS, ROBERT L. military officer; b. Boston; married; children: Robert, Richard, Jonathan. BS in Systems Engring., U. Ariz.; MS in Systems Mgmt., U. So. Calif.; grad. Sr. Officials in Nat. Security, Harvard U.; grad., Armed Forces Staff Coll. Commd. 2d lt. U.S. Army, advanced through grades to maj. gen., with 67th Signal Battalion Kans., overseas tours in Vietnam and Worms, Germany, also active duty tours N.J., Aberdeen Proving Grounds, Md., aide-de-Camp for Comdg. Gen., VII Corps, 1979-81; with Office of Dir. of Plans, Programs and Policy U.S. Army Readiness Command, 1983; then comdr. 509th signal Battalion U.S. Army, Italy; spl. asst. to U.S. Army's Dir. of Info. Sys. for Command Control. Comm. and Computers; chief Integration div. Architecture Directorate U.S. Army, dep. comdr. White House Comm. Agy., comdr. 2d Signal Brigade, 1990, comdr. 5th Signal Command, 1995-98, comdr. Comm.-Electronics Command and comdr. Ft. Monmouth N.J., 1998-2001. Decorated DSM, Def. Superior Svc. medal, Legion of Merit with 4 oak leaf clusters, Bronze Star, Meritorious Svc. medal with 4 oak leaf clusters, others; recipient Roy Wilkins award of Reknown, NAACP, 2000, Fed. Asian-Pacific Am. Coun. award, 2000, others. Mem. Mensa.

NABRIT, SAMUEL MILTON, retired embryologist; b. Macon, Ga., Feb. 21, 1905; BS, Morehouse Coll., 1925; MS, Brown U., 1928, PhD in Biology, 1932; 13 hon. degrees, various U.S. univs. Instr. zoology Morehouse Coll., 1925—27, prof., 1928—31, Atlanta U., 1932—55; pres. Tex. So. U., 1955—66; commr. U.S. AEC, 1966—67; exec. dir. So. Fellows Fund, 1967—81. Exch. prof. Atlanta U., 1930, dean Grad. Sch.; gen. edn. bd. fellow Columbia U., 1943; rsch. fellow U. Brussels, 1950; coord. Carnegie Expn. Grant-in-Aid Rsch. Program; mem. sci. bd. NSF, 1956—60; mem. corp. Marine Biol. Lab., Woods Hole; mem. Marine Biol. Labs., AEC, 1966—67; exec. dir. Nat. Fellows Fund, 1967—81; interim dir. Atlanta U. Ctr., 1989—91. Named to Hall of Fame Black Scientists, NSF, Sayles Hall of Fame Brown U. Fellow: AAAS; mem.: Inst. Medicine-NAS, Societ+248 d'honneur Francaise, Am. Soc. Zoology, Nat. Inst. Sci. (pres. 1945), Nat. Assn. Rsch. Sci. Tchg., Soc. Devel. Biology, Sigma Xi, Pi Delta Phi, Phi Beta Kappa.

NACCHIO, JOSEPH P. former communications executive; m. Anne Nacchio; children: David, Michael. BSEE, MBA, NYU; MS in Mgmt., MIT. Former head consumer and bus. market divsns. AT&T; chmn., CEO Qwest Comm. Internat. Inc., Denver, 1997—. Bd. dirs. Qwest Comm. Corp. Avocation: running.*

NACE, BARRY JOHN, lawyer; b. York, Pa., Nov. 28, 1944; s. John Harrison and Mildred Louise (Orwig) N.; m. Andrea Marcia Giardini. Apr. 28, 1973; children: Christopher Thomas, Jonathan Barry, Matthew Andrew. BS, Dickinson Sch. of Law, 1965, JD, 1969, DL, 1994. Bar: Md. 1970, D.C. 1971, Pa. 1972, W.Va. 1997, U.S. Ct. Appeals (3d, 4th and D.C. cirs.); U.S. Supreme Ct. Ptnr. Davis & Nace, Washington, 1972-78, Paulson & Nace, Bethesda, Md., 1978-85, 98—; sr. ptnr. Paulson, Nace & Norwind, Washington, 1986-97. Fellow Roscoe Pound Found. (trustee); mem. Nat. Bd. Trial Advocacy in Civil Litigation (bd. govs. 2001—), D.C. Bar Assn., Montgomery County Bar Assn., Assn. Trial Lawyers Am. (gov. 1976-87, pres. 1993-94), Met. D.C. Trial Attys. (pres. 1977-78, 87-88, Atty. of Yr. 1976), Trial Lawyers for Pub. Justice, Internat. Acad. Trial Lawyers, Lambert Soc., Am. Inns of Ct., Am. Law Inst. Am. Bd. of Profl. Liability Attorneys. Avocations: golf, tennis, reading, racquetball. Home: 6208 Garnett Dr Bethesda MD 20815-6618 Office: Paulson & Nace 1814 N St NW Washington DC 20036-2404 E-mail: BJN@Lawtort.com.

NACE, MORTON OLIVER, JR. human resources professional, performance consultant; b. Tampa, Fla., June 30, 1937; s. Morton Oliver and Penelope Adele (Holland) N.; m. Eleanor Hart Moslow, June 27, 1964; children: Morton Oliver III, Jennifer Ann. BS, Boston U., 1964; MS, Syracuse U., 1974. Cert. literacy tutor Laubach Literacy Internat., Syracuse, N.Y. Exec. dir. Episcopal Diocese Chgo., 1964-70; dir. comm. Laubach Literacy Internat., Syracuse, N.Y., 1970-80; tng. and devel. specialist Rochester (N.Y.) Inst. Tech., 1980-96; adminstrv. asst., cons. City of Rochester, 1997—. Cons. tng. and orgn. devel., Rochester, 1982-98; facilitator retreats/tng. for new parish model The Apostle, 1990—; asst. prof. Rochester Inst. Tech., Henrietta, N.Y., 1994; sales and consulting staff Human Resource Svcs., Rochester, 1995-97. Facilitator planning retreat City Coun. of Rochester, 1993; regional planning cons. Mayor-elect City Coun., Rochester, 1997, performance cons. and trainer, 1998—. With USAF, 1957-61. Mem. ASTD (Genesee Valley chpt., conf. presenter 1981-96), Profl. and Orgn. Devel. in Higher Edn. (nat. presenter on faculty/staff devel. 1993-96). Episcopalian. Avocations: photography, piano, physical exercise, history, travel. Home and Office: 2271 Westfall Rd Rochester NY 14618-3126

NACHAZEL, JOHN, pathologist; b. Milw., Aug. 29, 1938; s. Delbert Peter and Jane Mary N.; m. Susan Chuchhill, Oct. 28, 1972; children: Heather, Brooke. BA, Marquette U., 1960; MD, Marquette U. Med. Coll. Wis., 1964. Cert. Am. Bd. Pathology. Partner Clin. Lab. Med. Group, L.A., 1972—; lab. med. dir. Calif. Hosp. Med. Ctr., 1988—. Capt. U.S. Army, 1965-67. Fellow Coll. Am. Pathologist, Am. Soc. Clin. Pathologist, Calif. Soc. Pathologist, Am. Soc. Cytology; mem. AMA, Calif. Med. Assn. Home: 1401 Lachman Ln Pacific Palisades CA 90272-2233 Office: Calif Hosp Med Ctr 1401 S Grand Ave Los Angeles CA 90015-3010

NACHMAN, GERALD WEIL, columnist, critic, author; b. Oakland, Calif., Jan. 13, 1938; s. Leonard Calvert and Isabel (Weil) N.; m. Mary Campbell McGeachy, Sept. 3, 1966 (div. 1979). Student, Merritt Coll., 1955-57; BA in Journalism, San Jose State U., 1960. TV and humor columnist San Jose (Calif.) Mercury, 1960-63; feature writer N.Y. Post, N.Y.C., 1963-66; drama critic Oakland (Calif.) Tribune, 1966-71; syndicated humor columnist N.Y. Daily News, 1973-79; critic and columnist San Francisco Chronicle, 1979-93. Juror Pulitzer Prize Com. to choose best play, 1991. Author: The Portable Nachman, 1960, Playing House, 1978, Out on a Whim, 1983, The Fragile Bachelor, 1989; contbr. to (book) Snooze, 1986, Raised on Radio, 1998; contbr. articles to newspapers, mags.; author, co-lyricist (revues) Quirks, 1979, Aftershocks, 1992, New Wrinkles, 1999. Recipient Page One award N.Y. Newspaper Guild, 1965, Deems Taylor award ASCAP, 1989. E-mail: nachnach@aol.com.

NACHMAN, JOSEPH FRANK, metallurgical consultant; b. Toledo, Jan. 22, 1918; s. Frank and Jane (Wujciak) N.; m. Rosemary Anderson, May 4, 1943; children: Richard Joseph, Ronald James. BS in Chemistry, U. Toledo, 1940; MS in Metallurgy, Ohio State U., 1947. Registered profl. engr., Calif., Colo., Md. Chief metallurgy branch U.S. Naval Ordnance Lab., Silver Spring, Md., 1948-56; mgr. alloy devel. U. Denver Research Inst., 1956-63; group leader Atomics Internat., Canoga Park, CA, 1963-66; chief applied scis. Solar Turbines, San Diego, 1966-77, research staff specialist, 1977-81; pres. Metall. Cons. Services, Inc., 1981—. Editor: Rare Earth Research, 1961, Proceeding of 7th Conference on Rare-Earth Research vols. I & II., 1968; patentee in field; contbr. articles to profl. jours. Served to lt. commdr. USNR, 1943-46. Recipient Meritorious Civilian Service award, USN Ordnance Lab., 1953; spl. commendation for improvement of ordnance equipment, 1945. Mem. Am. Soc. Metals (life), AAAS, Nat. Assn. Corrosion Engrs., Sigma Xi, Alpha Sigma Phi (v.p. 1939-40). Republican. Methodist. Avocations: travel, photography, geneal. research. Home: Metall Cons Services Inc The Woodlands 123 Robindale Cir Conroe TX 77384-4654

NACHMAN, MERTON ROLAND, JR. lawyer; b. Montgomery, Ala., Dec. 21, 1923; s. Merton Roland and Maxine (Mayer) N.; m. Martha Street, June 8, 1968; children: Nancy Nachman Yardley, Linda Nachman Connelly, Betsy Wild, Amy N. DeRoche, Karen Vann. AB cum laude, Harvard U., 1943, JD, 1948. Bar: Ala. 1949, U.S. Supreme Ct. 1953, U.S. Ct. Appeals (5th and 11th cirs.), U.S. Ct. Claims, U.S. Tax Ct. Asst. atty. gen. State of Ala., 1949-54; ptnr. Knabe & Nachman, Montgomery, 1954-59; adminstrv. asst. to Senator John Sparkman, Ala., 1956; ptnr. Steiner, Crum & Baker, Montgomery, 1959-86, counsel mem., 2000—; from ptnr. to coun. mem. Balch & Bingham, 1986-2000. Chmn. human rights com. Ala. Prison System, 1976-78. With USN, 1943-46. Recipient Merit award Ala. State Bar, 1974;, cert. of appreciation Supreme Ct. of Ala., 1974. Fellow Am. Coll. Trial Lawyers; mem. ABA (com. on fed. judiciary 1982-88, bd. govs. 1978-81), Ala. State Bar (pres. 1973-74), Am. Judicature Soc. (dir. 1976-80, Herbert Lincoln Harley award 1974), Am. Law Inst., Ala. Law Inst., Unity club (Montgomery), Am. Acad. Appellate Lawyers. Episcopalian. Office: PO Box 668 8 Commerce St Ste 8 Montgomery AL 36101-0668 E-mail: bburkett@steinercrum.com.

NACHMAN, RALPH LOUIS, physician, educator; b. Bayonne, N.J., June 29, 1931; s. Samuel Nachman and Ethel Nelson; m. Nancy Rubin; children: Susan, Steve. BA, Vanderbilt U., 1953, MD, 1956. Lic. physician N.Y., diplomate Am. Bd. Internal Medicine, subsplty. hematology, med. oncology. Intern in medicine Vanderbilt U. Hosp., 1956—57; asst. resident in medicine Montefiore Hosp., 1960—62; asst. resident in pathology N.Y. Hosp.-Cornell U. Med. Ctr., N.Y.C., 1957—58, rsch. fellow in medicine, 1962—63; dir. labs. for clin. pathology N.Y. Hosp., 1963—69, assoc. attending physician, 1968—72, attending physician, 1972—; from instr. to asst. prof. to assoc. prof. medicine Cornell Med. Ctr., 1963—72, chief divns. hematology, 1968—93, prof. medicine, 1972—; vice chmn. dept. medicine Cornell U. Med. Coll., 1974—78, acting chmn. dept. medicine, 1974—75, dir. Specialized Ctr. Rsch. in Thrombosis, 1976—97, acting co-chmn. dept. medicine, 1980—81, bd. overseers, 1987—89, chmn. dept. medicine, 1990; physician-in-chief N.Y.-Presbyn. Hosp./Cornell Campus, 1990. Guest investigator Rockefeller U., 1969—70; Wiessberg lectr. Case Western Res. U., 1978; Aggeler lectr. U. Calif. , San Francisco, 1981; Patek lectr. Boston U., 1981; Rosenthal lectr. Mt. Sinai, 1982; Beaumont lectr. Wash. U., 1983; Wiener lectr. N.Y. Blood Ctr., 1983; chmn. Gordon Conf. on Hemostasis, 1984; Alpha Omega Alpha lectr. N.Y. Med. Coll., 1985; Sharp lectr. Wayne State U., 1986; Roon lectr. Scripps Rsch. Inst., 1987; Johnson lectr. Internat. Soc. on Thrombosis, 1987; Merck lectr. Cleve. Clinic, 1987; vis. prof. Harvard U., 1991; E. Stanley Emery Jr. Meml. lectr., physician-in-chief pro tempore, 91; chief resident's vis. prof. Baylor Coll. Medicine, 1991; Samuel S. Riven vis. prof. Vanderbilt U., 1992; Hymie Nossel Meml. lectr. Columbia U., 1992; Pfizer vis. prof. Royal Soc. Medicine, 1992; disting. lectr. Am. Heart Assn., 1994; Seckler lectr. Mt. Sinai Med. Ctr., 1994; Runme Shaw Meml. lectr. Acad. Medicine, Singapore, 1994; chmn. hematology study panel Health Rsch. Coun., N.Y.C., 1973—75; mem. NIH-Program Project Com. Heart and Lung Inst., 1975—79; bd. govs. Am. Bd. Internal Medicine, 1985—88; cons. Manhattan VA Hosp.; vis. physician Rockefeller U. Hosp. Author: Genetics of Coronary Heart Disease, 1992, Systemic Lupus Erythematosus, 1993, (jours.) Blood, 1994, Ann. Internal Medicine, 1993; assoc. editor: Beeson McDermott Textbook of Medicine, XIV edit., 1975, assoc. editor: Beeson McDermott Textbook of Medicine, XV edit., 1979, assoc. editor: Blood, 1976—82, assoc. editor: Am. Jour. Medicine, 1978, adv. editor: Jour. Exptl. Medicine, 1976, editl. bd.: Arteriosclerosis, 1983; contbr. articles to med. jours. With USN, 1958—60. Fellow: ACP; mem.: AAAS, N.Y. Acad. Medicine, Inst. Medicine NAS, Am. Soc. Biol. Chemists, Soc. Exptl. Biology and Medicine, Internat. Soc. Thrombosis and Hemostasis (coun. 1986—92), Am. Physiol. Assn., Harvey Soc. (coun. 1980), Am. Soc. Hematology (exec. coun. 1978—79), N.Y. Soc. for Study of Blood (pres. 1975), N.Y. Acad. Sci., Am. Clin. and Climatol. Assn., Am. Fedn. Clin. Rsch., Am. Soc. Clin. Investigation, Assn. Am. Physicians, Cornell Med. Alumni (hon.), Peripatetic Club, Nat. Blood Club (pres. 1981—82), Phi Beta Kappa, Alpha Omega Alpha. Office: NY Presbyn Hosp Weill Medical Coll Cornell U 525 E 68th St # M-52- Box 130 New York NY 10021-4870

NACHMAN, RONALD JAMES, research chemist; b. Takoma Park, Md., Feb. 1, 1954; s. Joseph Frank and Rosemary (Anderson) N.; m. Lita Rose Wilson, Dec. 18, 1976 (div. 1987); m. Isidora Austria Panis, May 6, 1989. BS in Chemistry, U. Calif., San Diego, 1976; PhD in Organic Chemistry, Stanford U., 1981. Rsch. asst. Scripps Inst. Oceanography, La Jolla, Calif., 1974-76; chemist Western Regional Rsch. Ctr., USDA, Berkeley, 1981-89, Vet. Toxicology and Entomology Rsch. Lab., College Station, Tex., 1989—. Vis. scientist dept. molecular biology Salk Inst., La Jolla, 1985, Scripps Rsch. Inst., La Jolla, 1988-89. Mem. editl. adv. bd. The Jour. Peptides; mem. organizing com. Ann. Invertebrate Neuropeptide Conf.; contbr. sci. articles to profl. jours. Recipient USDA Cert. of Merit, 1988, 91, 94-98, Arthur S. Flemming award for sci. achievement, 1994. Fellow Internat. Neoropeptide Soc. (bd. dirs. 2000—); mem. AAAS, Internat. Neuropeptide Soc., Am. Chem. Soc., N.Y. Acad. Scis., Sigma Xi. Avocations: travel, photography, jogging, racketball. Home: 14891 Pollux Dr Willis TX 77318-5079 Office: USDA Southern Plains Agrl Rsch Ctr 2881 F And B Rd College Station TX 77845-4988

NACHT, SERGIO, biochemist; b. Buenos Aires, Apr. 13, 1934; came to U.S., 1965; s. Oscar and Carmen (Scheiner) N.; m. Beatriz Kahan, Dec. 21, 1958; children: Marcelo H., Gabriel A., Mariana S., Sandra M. BA in Chemistry, U. Buenos Aires, 1958, MS in Biochemistry, 1960, PhD in Biochemistry, 1964. Asst. prof. biochemistry U. Buenos Aires, 1960-64; asst. prof. medicine U. Utah, Salt Lake City, 1965-70; rsch. scientist Alza Corp., Palo Alto, Calif., 1970-73; sr. investigator Richardson-Vicks Inc., Mt. Vernon, N.Y., 1973-76, asst. dir., dir. rsch., 1976-83, dir. biomed. rsch. Shelton, Conn., 1983-87; sr. v.p. rsch. and devel. Advanced Polymer Sys., Redwood City, Calif., 1987-93, sr. v.p. sci. and tech., 1993-98, sr. v.p. dermatology and skin care, 1998-2000, Enhanced Derm Techs., Redwood City, 2000—02; ptnr. Riley-Nacht, LLC, 2002—. Lectr. dermatology dept. SUNY Downstate Med. Ctr., Blkyn., 1977-87. Contbr. articles to profl. jours.; patentee in field. Mem. Soc. Cosmetic Chemists (award 1981), Dermatology Found., Am. Acad. Dermatology. Democrat. Jewish. Home and Office: 409 Wembley Ct Redwood City CA 94061-4308

NACHT, STEVE JERRY, geologist; b. Cleve., July 8, 1948; s. Max and Elfrida (Kamm) N.; m. Patricia Katherine Osicka, Aug. 3, 1976; 1 child, David Martin. BS in Geology, Kent State U., 1971, MS in Geology, 1973; MS in Urban Studies, Cleve. State U., 1979. Registered geologist, S.C., Va., Wyo.; environ. assessor, Calif.; cert. geologist, Ind.; lic. drinking water treatment class III, Ohio; cert. environ. mgr., Nev. Geologist Cleve. Utilities Dept., 1974-78; geologist, hydrologist Dalton, Dalton & Newport, Cleve., 1979-82; prin. scientist Lockheed-Emsco, Las Vegas, Nev., 1983-86; sr. geologist, project mgr. Earth Tech. Inc., Long Beach, Calif., 1986-87, The MARK Group, Las Vegas, 1987-90; dir. waste tech., sr. geologist Reynolds Elec. & Engrng. Co., 1990-92, chief environ. remediation sect., 1992-95; asst. project mgr. Bechtel Nev. Corp., 1996-97, project mgr., 1997-99, project engr., tech. mgr., 1999-2001, dep. project mgr., 2001—. Contbr. articles to profl. jours. Mem. AAAS, ASTM (groundwater com., past chmn. sect., well maintenance, rehab. and decommissioning sect.), Am. Inst. Profl. Geologists (cert.), Assn. Ground Water Scientists and Engrs., Assn. Engrng. Geologists, Project Mgmt. Profl. (cert.), Project Mgmt. Inst. Home: 4184 Del Rosa Ct Las Vegas NV 89121-5011 Office: Bechtel Nev PO Box 98521 Las Vegas NV 89193-8521 E-mail: snacht@worldnet.att.net.

NACHTIGAL, PATRICIA, lawyer; b. 1946; BA, Montclair State U.; JD, Rutgers U.; LLM, NYU. Tax atty. Ingersoll-Rand Co., Ltd., Hamilton, Bermuda , 1979—83, dir. taxes and legal, 1983—88, sec., mng. atty., 1988—91, v.p., gen. counsel, 1991—2000, sr. v.p., gen. counsel, 2000—, bd. dirs., 2002—. Office: Ingersoll-Rand Co 200 Chestnut Ridge Rd Woodcliff Lake NJ 07677

NACHWALTER, MICHAEL, lawyer; b. N.Y.C., Aug. 31, 1940; s. Samuel J. Nachwalter; m. Irene, Aug. 15, 1965; children: Helynn, Robert. BS, Bucknell U., 1962; MS, L.I. U., 1967; JD cum laude, U. Miami, 1967; LLM, Yale U., 1968. Bar: Fla. 1967, D.C. 1979, U.S. Dist. Ct. (so. dist.) Fla. 1967, U.S. Dist. Ct. (mid. dist.) Fla. 1982, U.S. Ct. Appeals (5th and 11th cirs.) 1967, U.S. Supreme Ct. 1975. Law clk. to judge U.S. Dist. Ct. (so. dist.) Fla.; shareholder Kelly, Black, Black & Kenny; now shareholder Kenny Nachwalter Seymour Critchlow & Spector, P.A., Miami. Lectr. Law Sch. U. Miami. Editor-in-chief U. Miami Law Rev., 1966-67. Fellow Am. Coll. Trial Lawyers; mem. ABA, FBA, Am. Bd. Trial Advs., Fla. Bar Assn. (bd. govs. 1982-90), Internat. Soc. Barristers (dir.), Dade County Bar Assn., Jud. Qualifications Commn. (vice chmn. 1995-2000), Iron Arrow, Soc. Wig and Robe, Omicron Delta Kappa, Phi Kappa Phi, Phi Delta Phi. Office: Kenny Nachwalter Seymour Arnold Critchlow & Spector PA 201 S Biscayne Blvd Ste 1100 Miami FL 33131-4327

NACK, CLAIRE DURANI, artist, author; b. N.Y.C. d. Myron Irving and Rachel Rita Adele (Feldman) N. Student, NYU, 1975, Sculpture Ctr., N.Y.C., 1975, Arts Student League. Pres., owner, founder Claire Durani Nack Corp. subs. Princess Enterprs./Durani Co., N.Y.C., 1993; pres. Books of Poetry by Claire Durani Nack, Mystery Stories by Claire Durani Nack, Books of Science Fiction by Claire Durani Nack, Works of Art by Claire Durani Nack, C.D.N. Co. Prof. N.Y. State Mus., Albany, 1992, Hudson Valley C.C., 1986-92, Schenectady (N.Y.) Mus.; lectr. Troy Arts League, 1989. Artist sketchbooks; author/artist: Something Happened in the Kitchen, 1981, European Journey, Book II, 1981, Cat Book, 1994, Diary, 2, 1980, Diary, Vol. 4, 1994, Vol. 5, 1994, The Journals of Claire Durani Nack, 1994, Art Book 1, 1982, Art Book 2, 1982, My World, 1999, Blue Book, Upwards Bent (books 1-5), 1993-94, Spiders Web Unspun, 1994, An Unfamiliar Place, 1993, The Adventures of Cora, 1994 (books 1-5), Cahiers de Dessins de Paris, 1994, Big City Lights, 1991, Something Happened in the Bathroom, 1981, Something Happened in the Living Room, 1981, Children's Coloring Book, 1995, Animal Book, 1995, The Adventures of Cora, Plot, Counterplot, Plot, 1997, All About Life, Sorrow and Joy, Essays and Soliliquis, Stoolie the Ghoulie, The Small Book of Art, The Gold Book, 1997, The Book of Art, 1997, Conversations with Myself, 1997, Facts, Fools and Ghools, 1997, All About Life, 1997, Sorrow and Joy, 1997, The Silver Book, 1997, A Light's Work, 1997, Being C, 1997, Alive, 1998, The Cheerful Book, 1998, Essays and Soliloquis, 1998, Questions and Answers, 1998, The Prosecuting Lawyer, 1998, Life's a Theatre, 1999, The Cheetah, 1999, Toulouse Lautrec and Claire Durani Nack, 1999, The Scrapbook of Claire Durani Nack, 1998, The Album of Claire Durani Nack, 1999, Life's a Theatre, 1999, The Portfolio of Claire Durani Nack in Paris, 1999, Conversations with Myself, Garden of the Orient, 2001, Dating, Waiting & Mating, The Orange Book, Excavations and Illuminations. Recipient poetry award Nat. Libr. of Poetry, Calif., 1991; scholar Art Students League, 1985. Mem. Nat. Mus. of Women in the Arts (charter mem.), Art Students League (life), N.Y. State Mus. Avocations: travel, collecting model airplanes, collecting hats, art and rare books, jewelry, Am. and European real estate. Office: 416 East St Rensselaer NY 12144-2303

NACKEL, JOHN GEORGE, technology executive; b. Medford, Mass., Nov. 4, 1951; s. Michael and Josephine (Maria) N.; m. Gail Helen Becker, Oct. 30, 1976; children: Melissa Anne, Allison Elizabeth. BS, Tufts U., 1973; MS in Pub. Health and Indsl. Engring., U. Mo., 1975, PhD, 1977. Sr. mgr. Ernst & Young, Chgo., 1977—83; nat. dir. health care cons. Cleve., 1983—87; regional dir. health industry svcs., 1987—91; mng. dir. health care Ernst & Young, 1991—93; mng. dir. Health Consulting, LA, 1993—99, New Ventures, 1999—2000; CEO Sogeti USA, LLC, 2000—01; chmn., CEO Sértan Corp., Santa Fe Springs, Calif., 2002—. Editorial bd. Jour. Med. Systems, 1983—. Author: Cost Management for Hospitals, 1987 (Am. Hosp. Assn. book award 1988); contbr. articles to profl. jours. Grantee Dept. Health Edn. Welfare, Washington, 1973-76. Fellow Am. Coll. Healthcare Execs., Healthcare Info. and Mgmt. Systems Soc. (articles award); mem. Inst. Indsl. Engrs. (sr.), U. Mo. health Svcs. Mgmt. Alumni Assn. (pres.), Canterbury Golf Club (Cleve.), L.A. Country Club, Annandale Golf Club. Republican. Avocations: golf, tennis, squash, paddle, photography. Home: 666 Linda Vista Ave Pasadena CA 91105-1145 E-mail: jnackel@sertan.net.

NACKNOUCK, JAMES D. management executive; b. Newark, May 7, 1950; BS, Montclair State Coll., 1972; MBA, Fairleigh Dickinson U., 1984. Asst. art dir. Markal Corp., Montclair, N.J., 1972-75; art educator Phillipsburg (N.J.) Pub. Sch., 1975; prodn. mgr. Landmark Assocs. Ltd., Orange, N.J., 1975-77; graphic designer Exxon Rsch. and Engring. Co., Florham Park, 1977-81, supr. graphic design, 1981-88; unit head accounts payable Exxon Central Svcs., 1988-92; process leader Exxon Rsch. and Engring. Co., 1992-93, acctg. group head, 1993-95, acctg. leader, 1995-97, fin. govt. and tax reporting process leader, 1997-98; earnings reporting process leader Exxon Co., Internat., Fla., 1998-2000; controls and planning analyst Exxon Mobil, 2000—. Pres. The Users Group, N.J., 1986-88. Home: 3750 Ottawa Ln Hollywood FL 33026-4619 Office: ExxonMobil Global Svcs 396 Alhambra Cir Coral Gables FL 33134-5007

NACLERIO, ROBERT MICHAEL, otolaryngologist, educator; b. N.Y.C., Mar. 30, 1950; s. Albert Paul and Lee Ann (Rabinowitz) N.; m. Sharon Ann Silhan, Mar. 30, 1983; children: Jessica, Daniel. BA, Cornell U., 1972; MD with honors, Baylor U., 1976. Diplomate Am. Bd. Otolaryngology. Intern in surgery Johns Hopkins Hosp., Balt., 1976-77, resident in surgery, 1977-78; resident in otolaryngology Baylor Coll. Medicine, Houston, 1978-80, chief resident in otolaryngology, 1982-83; fellow in clin. immunology divsn. Johns Hopkins U. Sch. Medicine, Balt., 1980-82, asst. prof. medicine and otolaryngology, 1983-87, asst. prof. pediat., 1986-87, dir. divsn. pediat. otolaryngology, 1986-94, assoc. prof. otolaryngology, medicine and pediat., 1987-92, prof. otolaryngology, medicine and pediat., 1992-94; chief of otolaryngology, head and neck surgery U. Chgo., Chgo., 1994—. Cons. Richardson-Vicks Inc., 1986-89, 90, NIH, 1987, Proctor & Gamble, 1987, 94, Sandoz Rsch. Inst., 1988, Schering Rsch., 1988, Wallace Labs., 1989, Joint Rhinologic Conf., 1989, Internat. Congress Rhinology, 1991, Norwich-Eaton Pharm. Inc., 1991-92, Ciba-Geigy Corp., 1991-92, Mktg. Corp. Am., 1993—, Astra, others; mem. med. bd. Children's Ctr., 1991-94, other local comms.; reviewer Am. Jour. Rhinology, others; lectr. in field. Editor: Rhinoconjunctivitis: New Perspectives in Topical Treatment, 1988; asst. editor: Am. Jour. Rhinology, 1986—, Rhinology, 1988—; mem. editl. bd. Otolaryngology-Head and Neck Surgery, 1990-97, Laryngoscope, 1990—, Jour. Allergy and Clin. Immunology, 1992-97; contbr. numerous chpts. to books, papers and abstracts to profl. jours. and procs. Fellow ACS, Am. Acad. Otolaryngology-Head and Neck Surgery (mem. com. 1985-90, 90-92, subcom. 1987-92), Am. Laryngol., Rhinol. and Otol. Soc., Inc.; mem. Am. Acad. Allergy and Immunology (mem. com. 1983-88, 88-89, 88-95, chmn. com. 1990-91, 91—, Jerome Glazer Meml. lectureship), Am. Fedn. Clin. Rsch., Am. Soc. Pediat. Otolaryngology (mem. rsch. com. 1990-94, chmn. subcom. 1990), Soc. Univ. Otolaryngologists-Head and Neck Surgeons, Pan-Am. Assn. Otorhinolaryngology, Internat. Symposium on Infection and Allergy of the Nose (v.p.). Office: U Chgo Section of O-HNS 5841 S Maryland Ave # 1035 Chicago IL 60637-1463 E-mail: rnacleri@surgery.bsd.uchicago.edu.

NACOL, MAE, lawyer; b. Beaumont, Tex., June 15, 1944; d. William Samuel and Ethel (Bowman) N.; children: Shawn Alexander Nacol, Catherine Regina Nacol. BA, Rice U., 1965; postgrad., South Tex. Coll. Law, 1966. Bar: Tex. 1969, U.S. Dist. Ct. (so. dist.) Tex. 1969. Pvt. practice law, Houston, 1969—; escrow officer Commonwealth Land Title Co.; mem. bd. devel. Prosperity Bank. Author, editor ednl. materials on multiple sclerosis, 1981-85. Nat. dir. A.R.M.S. of Am. Ltd., Houston, 1984-85. Recipient Mayor's Recognition award City of Houston, 1972. Mem. Houston Bar Assn. (chmn. candidate com. 1970, membership com. 1971, chmn. lawyers referral com. 1972), Assn. Trial Lawyers Am., Tex. Trial Lawyers Assn., Am. Judicature Soc. (sustaining), Houston Fin. Coun. Women, Houston Trial Lawyers Assn. Presbyterian. Office: 600 Jefferson St Ste 750 Houston TX 77002 also: 8401 Westheimer Ste 104 Houston TX 77063

NADAS, JOHN ADALBERT, psychiatrist, educator; b. Innsbruck, Austria, Mar. 14, 1949; came to U.S., 1950; s. Julius Zoltan and Ibolya Erzsebet (Szöllösy) N.; m. Gabriella Ilona Ormay, Apr. 11, 1981; children: János, Miklós, István. BA, Case Western Res. U., Cleve., 1970; MD, Duke U., Durham, N.C., 1974. Diplomate Am. Bd. Psychiatry and Neurology. Resident in psychiatry U. Chgo., 1974-77; pvt. practice Munster, Ind., 1977-84, Canton, 1984—; instr. psychiatry Northeastern Ohio U. Coll. Medicine, Rootstown, 1985-86; coord. psychiat. edn. Mercy Med. Ctr., Canton, Ohio, 1985-87, clin. dir. psychiat. svcs., 1990-91; asst. prof. Northeast Ohio U. Coll. Medicine, Rootstown, 1986—. Cons. Crisis Ctr., Canton, 1985-92. Author: Philosophical Basis of Depth Psychotherapy, 1983, Journey Toward Energy, 1995, Transformation, 1999. Trustee Sisters of Charity Found., Canton, 1996—. NCAA nat. collegiate epee champion, 1970; mem. All-Am. Fencing Team, 1969, 70. Mem. AMA, Am. Psychiat. Assn., Hungarian Assn. (pres. 2000-). Roman Catholic. Avocations: basketball, computer programming. Office: 1330 Mercy Dr NW Ste 320 Canton OH 44708-2624

NADASKAY, RAYMOND, architect; b. Newark, Aug. 26, 1938; s. Charles and Marie (Roncskevitz) Nadaskay; m. Nancy Searle, 1962; 1 child Cathy. BArch, Washington U., St. Louis, 1962. Registered architect, N.J., Conn., Vt., Mass., Ill., Ohio, S.C., Vt., Del.; registered planner; cert. NCARB. Designer Rotwein and Blake, Architects, Union, N.J., 1962-63, I.M. Pei, N.Y.C., 1963-64; designer, assoc. McDowell Goldstein, Morristown, N.J., 1964-72; pres. Nadaskay Kopelson Architects, P.A., 1972—. Chair Mendham (N.J.) Twp. Hist. Preservation Commn.; mem. Mendham Twp. Roadscape Commn., Mendham Twp. Facilities Com., Mendham Twp. Open Space Com., Morristown Streetscape Com. Recipient numerous spl. commendations, awards of merit for variety of works. Mem.: NJ Soc. Archs. (conv. chmn. 1985—86, past pres. Newark Suburban chpt. 1984), Porsche Club (No. NJ). Avocations: woodworking, sailing, auto rally events, swimming. Office: Nadaskay Kopelson Architects 95 Washington St Morristown NJ 07960-6816 E-mail: nadaskayr@nkarchitects.com.

NADEAU, BERTIN FELIX, diversified company executive; b. May 26, 1940; s. J.-D. and Irene (Daigle) N.; m. Juliette Angell, July 24, 1971; children: Eric, Shahn, Stephanie. BA, Coll. St-Louis, 1961; grad., Ecole des Hautes Etudes Commerciales de Montreal, 1964; postgrad., Harvard U.; DBA, Ind. U., 1969; LLD (hon.), Queen's U.; D in Fin. (hon.), Moncton U.; DBA (hon.), Sainte-Anne U.; D in Civil Law (hon.), Bishop's U. Chmn., CEO Unigesco Inc., 1982-94, Provigo Inc., 1989-93; chmn., CEO, Gescolynx Inc., Montreal, 1994—. Bd. dirs. Sun Life Fin. Svcs. of Can. Inc., Sun Life Assurance Com. Can., Lafarge N.Am. Inc. Bd. dirs. Montreal Gen. Hosp. Found. Office: GescoLynx Inc 606 Cathcart Ste 1035 Montreal QC Canada H3B 1K9

NADEAU, JERRY, race car driver; b. Danbury, Conn., Sept. 9, 1970; m. Jada Nadeau. Racecar driver Richard Jackson, 1997, Hendrick Motorsports. Named winner, NAPA 500, 2000, Rookie of the Yr., Skip Barber Ea. Series, 1991; recipient 4th pl., European Formula Ford Festival, 1993, Silver medal, Nations Cub VII, Eng., 1996. Avocations: skiing, golf. Office: c/o Hendrick Motorsports 4400 Papa Joe Hendrick Blvd Charlotte NC 28262*

NADEAU, JOHN, marketing and corporate communications consultant; b. N.Y.C., Apr. 22, 1934; m. Beryl Green, July 11, 1962; children: Louise, Philip. BA, Emerson Coll., 1956; MA, Harvard U., 1957. Announcer WGBH-TV-FM, Boston, 1954-57; tchr. English Lynnfield (Mass.) H.S., 1957-60; announcer WBCN-FM, Boston, 1960; English tchr. Whitman H.S., South Huntington, N.Y., 1961-64; pub. rels. dir. Dutchess Coll., Poughkeepsie, 1964-69; editor Berkshire Life, Pittsfield, Mass., 1969-76; mgr. advt., pub. rels. Gen. Am. Life, St. Louis, 1976-86, dir. corp. comm., 1986-92, dir. comm. svcs., 1993-98, GenAm. Mgmt. Co., St. Louis, 1999. Editor Gen. Am. Solutions mag., 1994-99; contbr. articles to profl. jours. Reader Wash. Talking Book and Braille Libr., Seattle, 2002—; co-chmn. pub. rels. com. Boston Symphony Orch. Coun. Tanglewood Friends; bd. dirs. Mo. Concert Ballet, St. Louis, 1978—85. Recipient Telly award for corp. video, 1990, 97, 98, Golden Reel award for script writing 1998 Internat. TV Assn., Spl. Appreciation award Mathews-Dickey Boys Club, St. Louis, 2001; Fulbright fellow, Padiham, Eng., 1960-61. Mem.: Life Ins. Communicators Assn. (mem. exec. com. 1985—87, faculty mem. and dir. comm. workshop and ann. meeting, Excellence awards, Best of Show awards 1996, 1997, Spl. Recognition for Outstanding Contbns. award 1987), Harvard Club of Western Wash. Unitarian Universalist. Avocations: reading, travel, French language and literature, cycling. E-mail: nadeaujandb@juno.com.

NADEAU, JOSEPH EUGENE, health care management consultant, information systems consultant; b. Portland, Maine, Sept. 23, 1937; s. Edwin Tustin and Beatrice Margaret (Spiller) N.; m. Mary Lou Prendible, Dec. 2, 1961; children: Laura, Keith, Michael. BS in Math., Boston Coll., 1960. Cert. computer profl. Dir. sys. devel. Mass. Hosp. Assn., Burlington, 1967-72; S.E. regional mgr. Automatic Data Processing, Miami, Fla., 1972-73; S.E. regional mktg. mgr. Space Age Computer Sys., Louisville, 1973-74; prin. COMPUTERx Cons., Miami, 1974—. Asst. scoutmaster South Fla. coun. Boy Scouts Am., 1972-81. 1st lt. U.S. Army, 1960-64, Germany. Mem. Am. Hosp. Assn., Soc. Computer Medicine, Data Processing Mgmt. Assn., Hosp. Mgmt. Sys. Soc., Assn. Sys. Mgmt. (pres. 1971-72), Hosp. Fin. Mgmt. Assn. (chmn. data processing com. 1967-84), Am. Arbitration Assn. (arbitrator 1980—). Home: 10260 SW 144th St Miami FL 33176-7034 Office: COMPUTERx Consulting 9719 S Dixie Hwy Ste 1 Miami FL 33156-2834

NADEAU, JOSEPH P. Supreme Court Judge; AB, Dartmouth Coll.; LLB, Boston U., 1962. Pvt. practice trial atty., 1962—81; justice Durham Dist. Ct., 1968-81; judge N.H. Superior Ct., 1981-92, chief justice, 1992; assoc. justice N.H. Supreme Ct., 2000—. Mem. Jud. Br. Adminstrv. Coun., Supreme Ct. Jud.Ednl. Svcs. Com., Supreme Ct. Accreditation Commn.; pres. Am. Acad. Jud. Edn., 1990-92; participant ct. study program former Soviet Union, facutly jud. edn. program, Latvia, study programs in Russia, Georgia, Armenia; involved in jud. edn. seminars and legis. activities in Albania, Bulgaria, Kazakhstan, Poland. Mem. Gov.'s Commn. on Domestic Violence. Office: Supreme Ct Bldg One Noble Dr Concord NH 03301-6160*

NADEAU, MICHAEL JOSEPH, staff assistant; b. Glens Falls, N.Y., Dec. 19, 1949; s. John Long and Mary Catherine (Cimo) N. Student of Eli Siegel's Aesthetic Realism, N.Y.C., 1977-81; AA in English with honors, Borough of Manhattan C.C., N.Y.C., 1992. Orderly Glens Falls (N.Y.) Hosp., 1969-72; record storage clk. Continental Ins. Co., Glens Falls, 1972-75; purchasing agt. Maersk Inc., Madison, N.J., 1975-93; coll. svc. asst. Passaic County C.C., Paterson, 1993-99, staff asst. Wanaque Acad. Ctr., 1999—. Author: The Adventures of Prudence Longface, 1993. Actor, singer Elbee Audio Players, N.Y.C., 1979-81. With USN, 1969-70. Mem. Am. Legion. Democrat. Roman Catholic. Avocations: bowling, swimming, boating, woodworking, singing. Home: 15 Overlook Ave Mine Hill NJ 07803-3100

NADEAU, REGINALD ANTOINE, medical educator; b. St. Leonard, N.B., Can., Dec. 18, 1932; married, 1957; 2 children. BA, Loyola Coll., Montreal, 1952; MD, U. Montreal, 1957. From asst. prof. to assoc. prof. Faculty Medicine, U. Montreal, 1964-70, prof. physiology, 1972-75, prof. medicine, 1975-99; cardiologist Hopital Sacre Coeur, Montreal, 1972—2002. Career investigator Med. Rsch. Coun. Can., 1965. Fellow Royal Coll. Physicians (Can.); mem. Can. Physiol. Soc., Can. Cardiovasc. Soc., Am. Coll. Cardiology. Achievements include research in basic and clinical cardiology. Office: Sacre Coeur Hosp Montreal 5400 Gouin Blvd W Montreal QC Canada H4J 1C5 E-mail: r-nadeau@crhsc.umontreal.ca.

NADEAU, ROBERT BERTRAND, JR. lawyer; b. Miami Beach, Fla., July 15, 1950; s. Robert B. and Ernestine Inez (Nicholson) N. BBA magna cum laude, U. Notre Dame, 1972; JD with honors, U. Fla., 1975. Bar: Fla. 1975, U.S. Dist. Ct. (mid. dist.) Fla. 1976, U.S. Dist. Ct. (so. dist.) Fla. 1982, U.S. Ct. Appeals (11th cir.) 1982. Asst. to pres. The Fla. Bar, Tampa, Fla., 1975-76; ptnr. Akerman, Senterfitt & Eidson, P.A., Orlando, 1976—. Arbitrator Am. Arbitration Assn., Orlando, 1987—. Mem. ABA, The Fla. Bar (chmn. student edn. and admission to bar com., vice chmn. 9th cir. grievance com.), Notre Dame Club Greater Orlando (pres. 1979-80). Avocations: golf, running. Office: Akerman Senterfitt & Eidson PA 255 S Orange Ave Orlando FL 32801-3445

NADEAU, STEVEN C. lawyer; b. Schenectady, N.Y., July 6, 1954; AB magna cum laude, Boston Coll., 1974, JD cum laude, 1977. Bar: Mich. 1977. Mediator Wayne County Cir. Ct., 1983-88; mem. Honigman Miller Schwartz and Cohn, Detroit. Coord. dir. Sediment Mgmt. Work Group, 1998—. Mem. ABA (sect. natural resources), State Bar Mich. (sect. environ. law), Detroit Bar Assn. Office: Honigman Miller Schwartz and Cohn 660 Woodward Ave Ste 2290 Detroit MI 48226-3506 E-mail: snadeau@honigman.com.

NADEINE, VLADIMIR, journalist, editor; b. Donetzk, Ukraine, USSR, Apr. 19, 1938; s. Dimitri and Sofia Nadeine; m. Olga Krassouska; 1 child, Olga. MA, Lviv State U., Ukraine, 1960, journalist degere, 1961, Moscow State U., 1961, MA, 1963. Mng. editor Crocodile mag., Moscow, 1963-71; satire columnist Izvestia, 1971-89, bur. chief Washington, 1989-97; dir. programming Ethnic Am. Broadcasting Co., Ft. Lee, N.J., 1997—. Author: (short stories) How To Sell Rams, 1965, Non-Dimenional Pants, 1967, Three Carats for You Only, 1976, You Will Be Surprised, 1978. Recipient award for best Moscow journalist Union Journalists, 1968, for best Russian satire writer, 1974, for best journalist of USSR, 1988. Avocations: gardening, fishing. Home: 188 Hiawatha Blvd Oakland NJ 07436-3643 Office: EABC One Bridge Plz Fort Lee NJ 07024

NADEL, ELLIOTT, investment firm executive; b. N.Y.C., Nov. 23, 1945; s. Archie and Faye (Braverman) N.; children: Lindsey, Amanda. BBA, Baruch Coll., 1969, MBA, 1971. Portfolio mgr. SwissRe Advisors, N.Y.C., 1973-74; v.p., stockbroker E. F. Hutton, 1975-84, Shearson Lehman Bros., N.Y.C., 1984-85, Oppenheimer & Co., N.Y.C., 1985, Rooney Pace Inc., N.Y.C., 1986-87, Philips Appel & Walden, N.Y.C., 1987-88; sr. v.p. investments Moore, Schley & Cameron, 1988-90, Prudential-Securities, N.Y.C., 1990-94; sr. v.p. Gilford Securities, 1994—; with EN Investments; sr. v.p. Chgo. Investment Group. With U.S. Army, 1969-74. Jewish. Avocations: jogging, reading, cars, golf, travel.

NADEL, KAY CHANEY, small business owner; b. Charleston, Ill., Apr. 2, 1945; d. Jack and Eleanor (Gardner) C.; m. Brown Harris, II (div. 1972); 1 child, Brown; m. Ed Nadel, 1984. AA, Stephens Coll., 1965; BS, U. Mo., Columbia, 1967; MS, U. Mo., Kansas City, 1976. Tchr. curriculum writer, adminstr., St. Louis and Kansas City, 1968-74; dir. alumnae programs Stephens Coll., Columbia, Mo., 1974-78; v.p. univ. rels. U. Charleston, W.Va., 1978-79; v.p. McCluney/Brewer Advt., Kansas City, 1979-80; sr. v.p. Hickerson/Powell Advt., 1980-82; pres., owner Harris & Assocs., 1982-85, C-N Communications, Inc., N.Y.C., 1985-94; owner, pres. Chaney LLC Fine Golf Jewelry, White Plains, N.Y., 1994—. Lectr. in field. Contbg. writer: The Best of CASE Currents: A Marketing Approach to Student Recruitment, 1979, 3d edit. 1985; Sourcebook, Guide to Alumnae Admissions program, 1976. Board dirs. Family Svc. Westchester, United Way, Columbia, 1976-78, YWCA of Kansas City, 1981; charter mem. Columbia Ambs., 1976; vol. Girl Scouts U.S., 1980-83; adv. bd. dirs. Rsch. Med. Ctr., Kansas City, 1982; hon. trustee Truman Med. Ctr., Kansas City, 1982; mem. pers. and fundraising com. Cen. Exch., Kansas City, 1981—; mem. coun. N.Y. Hosp.-Cornell Med. Ctr., 1989—. Recipient Best of Class award for advt. Mo. Gov.'s Conf., 1978, Pres.'s award Am. Soc. Interior Design, 1982. Mem. Pub. Rels. Soc. Am., Coun. for Advancement and Support Edn. (Nat. Merit award 1978), Westchester Assn. Retarded Citizens (bd. dirs.), Westchester Putnam Girl Scout Coun., Inc. (bd. dirs. 1994—). Roman Catholic. Home: 10801 E Happy Valley Rd Scottsdale AZ 85255-8171 also: 10801 E Happy Valley Rd # 63 Scottsdale AZ 85255-8171

NADEL, LAURIE, journalist, psychotherapist; b. Bklyn., May 26, 1948; d. Alfred and Midred (Eisman) Nadel; m. Theophile van Dijk, Nov. 1, 1980 (div. June 1993); 1 child Charlene. BA Creative Writing, Sarah Lawrence Coll.; MA Psychology, Internat. Inst. Advanced Studies, St. Louis, 1989; PhD Psychology, Greenwich U., 1991; D Clin. Hypnotherapy, Am. Inst. Hypnotherapy, Irvine, Calif., 1993. Diplomate Nat. Bd. Cert. Clin. Hypnotherapists. Author, journalist various orgns., 1969—; psychotherapist pvt. practice N.Y.C., 1991—; journalist New York Times, 2001—. Advisor UN Fedn. for Mental Health, 1993—95; cons. various orgns., 1995—; adj. prof. NYU Sch. Journalism, N.Y.C., 2001—. Author: (novels) Sixth Sense, 1990, 2002, Dancing With the Wind, 2001; contbr. articles to profl. jours. Fellow: Nat. Bd. Cert. Clin. Hypnotherapists; mem.: Am. Soc. Journalists and Authors. Buddhist. Avocations: windsurfing, meditation, raising a child. Office: 56 7th Ave 7G New York NY 10011 Address: 57 Dalton St Long Beach NY 11561-2518 Fax: 516-889-0144. Business E-mail: drlaurie@laurienadel.com.

NADEL, NORMAN ALLEN, civil engineer; b. N.Y.C., Apr. 10, 1927; s. Louis and Bertha (Julius) N.; m. Cynthia Esther Jereski, July 6, 1952; children: Nancy Sarah Frank, Lawrence Bruce. B.C.E., CCNY, 1949; postgrad., Columbia U., 1949-50. Registered profl. engr., N.Y., Conn. Engr. Arthur A. Johnson Corp., N.Y.C., 1950-53; engr. Slattery Contracting Corp., 1953-56; mgr., estimator Hartsdale Constrn. Corp., Hartsdale, N.Y., 1956-59; engr.

MacLean Grove & Co., Inc., Greenwich, Conn., 1959-63, project mgr., 1963-66, v.p., 1966-70, pres., 1970-94; chmn. Nadel Assocs., Inc., Brewster, N.Y., 1988—. Cons. tunnel and underground constrn.; dir. United Am. Energy Corp., mem. com. on tunneling Transp. Rsch. Bd., Washington, 1974-75; mem. U.S. Nat. Com. on Tunneling Tech., Washington, 1976-82, chmn., 1980-81; chmn. adv. com. Superconducting Super Collider Underground Tech., 1992-94. Trustee Tunnel Workers Welfare Fund, N.Y.C., 1976-88; mem. adv bd. CCNY Engring. Sch., 1992—. With USNR, 1945-46 Named Heavy Constrn. Man of Yr., United Jewish Appeal, 1984; Benjamin Wright award Conn. Soc. Civil Engrs., 1984, Townsend Harris medal City Coll. of N.Y. Alumni Assn., 1987. Fellow ASCE (Constrn. Mgmt. award 1986); mem. NAE, Conn. Acad. Sci. and Engring., The Moles (pres. 1982-83, Outstanding Achievement in Constrn. award 1985), Am. Arbitration Assn., Tau Beta Pi, Chi Epsilon. Home: Reynwood Manor Greenwich CT 06831

NADELBERG, ERIC PAUL, brokerage house executive; b. Providence, Dec. 14, 1947; s. Arnold and Sandra (Schwartz) N.; m. Evelynne Luberoff, Dec. 12, 1968; children: Amanda, Ariel. BA, Bklyn. Coll., 1973; MA, Sch. of Journalism, N.Y.U., 1994. Registered commodities rep. News analyst The Wall Street Jour., N.Y.C., 1973-76; reporter Reuters Ltd., 1976-77; sr. analyst E.F. Hutton & Co., Inc., 1977-79, v.p., 1983-85, Gill & Duffus Svcs., Inc., N.Y.C., 1979-81, Rudolf Wolff Futures, Inc., N.Y.C., 1981-83; pres. Tropical Trader, Inc., Hoboken, N.J., 1985-90; 1st v.p. Merrill Lynch Inc., N.Y.C., 1990-96; sr. v.p. Latin Am. divsn. ABN-AMRO Chgo. Corp., 1996-98; mng. dir. ADM Investor Svcs. Inc., 1998—. Dir. Futures Rsch. co., 1991—; cons. UNCTAD, 1993—, World Bank, 1993—. Contbr. Barrons Fin. Mag., 1976-79; contbg. editor Commodity Rsch. Bur., 1986-93; columnist Cotton Mag., Memphis, 1977-88. With U.S. Army, 1968-71. Democrat. Avocations: fishing, walking, writing. Office: ADM Invesor Svcs Inc 140 Broadway New York NY 10005-1101

NADELLA, SATYA, information technology executive; MS in Computer Sci., U. Wis.; MBA, U. Chgo. Software devel. engr. Sun Microsystems Inc.; from group product mgr. to leader bCentral mktg. & bus. devel. Microsoft, Redmond, Wash., leader bCentral mktg. & bus. devel. Office: One Microsoft Way Redmond WA 98052-6399*

NADELSON, EILEEN NORA, lawyer; b. N.Y.C., Sept. 10, 1938; d. Morton and Sally (Malkin) N. BA in Econ./Polit. Sci., Ariz. State U., 1960; postgrad., CUNY, 1964-69, New Sch., N.Y.C., 1979-81; JD, Touro Coll., 1984. Bar: N.Y. 1985, U.S. Dist. Ct. (so. and ea. dists.) N.Y. 1987, U.S. Supreme Ct. 1990. Tchr. Massapequa (N.Y.) Sch. Dist., 1962-67, N.Y.C. Bd. Edn., 1967-68, 71-73; adminstrv. asst. Cox & Co. Inc., N.Y.C., 1968-71; mng. editor, reporter Our Town Newspaper, 1972-75; bus. mgr. Eng-Hill Drug Plan, Inc., Plainview, N.Y., 1973-78; legal asst. Traub & Lesser, N.Y.C., 1978-79, 81-85, assoc., 1987-89; community dist. rep. N.Y. State Senator Goodman, 1979-81; asst. dir. law and taxation NYU, 1986-87; pvt. practice, 1988—2001; judge N.Y. Civil Ct., 2002—. Arbitrator Am. Arbitration Assn., N.Y.C., 1986-2000, Better Bus. Bur., N.Y.C., 1987-90; adj. instr. law and taxation divsn. NYU, N.Y.C., 1987—; reporter CBS Network Election Svc., Massapequa, 1964; tutor, supr. Vol. Svcs. for Children, N.Y.C., 1971-73; moderator civic program WNYC Radio, N.Y.C., 1973; tutor Jewish Child Care, N.Y.C., 1979-80, Fortune Soc., N.Y.C., 1981; legal counsel Rep. Vols., 1987-89, Fed. Rep. Club, 1987-96; lectr. Nat. C. of C. Women, 1994-2001. N.Y.C. Dept. Bus. Svcs., 1994-97; mem. N.Y. Ednl. Priorities Panel, 1997-98. Contbr. articles to profl. jours. Vol. advisor Consumer Affairs Bur., Mineola, N.Y., 1975; researchist, editor Common Cause, N.Y.C., 1976; researchist transp. Community Bd. #8, N.Y.C., 1978-79; alt. del. Jud. Conv., N.Y.C., 1979, 80, 86; researcher, writer LWV, N.Y.C., 1980-82, 87, chair alt. to incarceration, 1992; campaign mgr. N.Y. State Assembly Candidate, N.Y.C., 1988; mem. Regional Plan Assn.; candidate N.Y.C. Coun., 1993; chair Com. for Campaign Reform, 1993; mem. exec. bd. League of Women Voters, N.Y.C., 1993-2000, pres., 1999—; del., chair com. on taxation White House conf. on Small Bus., 1994-95. Mem. ABA, N.Y. State Bar Assn., N.Y. Women's Bar Assn., Assn. of Bar of N.Y., Touro Coll. Law Alumni Assn. Jewish. Avocations: tennis, poetry, philos. and polit. analysis. E-mail: enadelson@nyc.rr.com.

NADER, LAURA, anthropology educator; b. Winsted, Conn., Sept. 30, 1930; m. Norman Milleron, Sept. 1, 1962; 3 children BA, Wells Coll., 1952; PhD, Radcliffe Coll., 1962. Mem. faculty U. Calif.-Berkeley, 1960—, now prof. anthropology; vis. prof. Yale Law Sch., New Haven, fall 1971; Henry R. Luce prof. Wellesley Coll., Mass., 1983-84; Henry R. Luce prof. Sch. Law Howard U., 1987-89, Stanford U., 1987-89. Field work in Mex., Lebanon, Morocco; mem. adv. com. NSF, 1971-75; mem. cultural anthropology com. NIMH, 1968—, chmn. to 1971, chmn. social scis. research tng. rev. com., 1976-78; mem. NAS-NRC assembly behavioral and social scis., 1969-71, 73-75, 75—; mem. com. Nuclear and Alternative Energy Forms, NAS , 1976-77. Editor: Law in Culture and Society, 1969; The Disputing Process, 1978, No Access to Law-Alternatives to the American Judicial System, 1980, Harmony Ideology, 1990; contbr. articles to profl. jours.; author ednl. films; mem. editorial com. Law and Society Rev., 1967— Mem. Calif. Council for the Humanities, 1975-79; mem. Carnegie Council on Children, 1972-77; active Coun. Librs. at Libr. of Congress, Washington, 1988—. Radcliffe Coll. grantee, 1954-59; Thaw fellow Harvard U., 1955-56, 58-59; Peabody Mus. grantee, 1954-59; Am. Philos. Assn. grantee, 1955; Mexican Govt. grantee, 1957-58; Milton Fund grantee, 1959-60, Wellness Found. grantee, 1993-96; fellow Ctr. Advanced Study in Behavioral Scis., Stanford, Calif., 1963-64; NSF grantee, 1966-68; Wenner Gren Found. grantee, 1964, 66, 73; Carnegie Corp. grantee, 1975; Woodrow Wilson fellow, 1979-80; Wells Coll. Alumnae award, 1980; Radcliffe Coll. Alumnae award, 1984 Mem. AAAS, Am. Acad. Arts and Scis., Am. Anthrop. Assn. (planning and devel. com. 1968-71, 75-76), Social Sci. Research Council, Law and Soc. Assn. (trustee 1967-72), Ctr. for Study of Responsive Law (trustee 1968—), Soc. Women Geographers. Office: U Calif Dept Anthropology 313 Kroeber Hl Berkeley CA 94720-0001

NADER, ROBERT ALEXANDER, judge, lawyer; b. Warren, Ohio, Mar. 31, 1928; s. Nassef J. and Emily (Nader) N.; m. Nancy M. Veauthier. BA, Western Res. U., 1950, LL.B., 1953. Bar: Ohio 1953. Ptnr. Paul G. Nader, Warren, 1953-83. Pres. Warren City Police and Fire Pension Bds., 1960-66; trustee Office Econ. Opportunity, 1970-72; mem. Warren City Coun., 1960-66, pres. pro tem, 1964-66; mem. Ohio Ho. of Reps., 1971-83, chmn. reference com., 1977-81, chmn. judiciary com., 1981-83; presiding judge Trumbull County Ct. Common Pleas, 1983-91; judge Ohio 11th Dist. Ct. Appeals, 1991—; trustee Family Svc. Assn., 1959-65. With AUS, 1946-48. Recipient Outstanding Young Man of Yr. award, 1964, award Am. Arbitration Assn., 1965, Community Action award Warren Area Bd. Realtors, 1967, Outstanding Svc. award Kent State U., Trumbull campus. 1978, Outstanding Svc. award Children's Rehab. Ctr., 1980; named to Warren H.S. Disting. Alumni Hall of Fame, 1993. Mem. Ohio State Bar Assn., Trumbull County Bar Assn. (past pres.), Ct. Appeals Judges Assn. (chmn. legis. com. 1995-98), Trumbull County Law Libr. Assn. (trustee 1958-72), Trumbull New Theatre (past pres.), KC, Elks, Lambda Chi Alpha. Roman Catholic. Home: 798 Wildwood Dr NE Warren OH 44483-4458 Office: 11th Dist Ct # Appeals 111 High St NE Warren OH 44481 *My parents provided me with a strong moral background and the inspiration to improve. I will never feel that I have achieved success and thus may continue to improve.*

NADER, SUZANNE NORA BEURER, elementary education educator; b. Detroit, July 6, 1947; d. Victor James and Patricia Kathleen (Perry) Beurer; m. Joseph Samuel Nader, Sept. 12, 1969; 1 child, Joseph Samuel Jr. BA, Eastern Mich. U., 1982, MA, 1990. Cert. elem. tchr., prin., Mich. English tchr. jr. high alternative program Wayne-Westland (Mich.) Sch. Dist., adult basic edn. tchr.; tchr. 5th grade Our Lady of Grace Sch., Dearborn Heights, Mich.; tchr. adult basic edn. Willow Run (Mich.) Sch. Dist., 1986-87; substitute tchr. Plymouth-Canton (Mich.) Sch. Dist., 1983; tchr. grades 2-3 Wayne-Westland (Mich.) Schs., 1993-94, tchr. grade 5, 1994-98, tchr. grade 3, 1998-2000, tchr. grades 2-3, 2000-01, tchr. grade 3, 2001—. Instr. Sch. Craft Coll.; English tutor for Japanese engrs.; tutor Best of Friends Learning Inst., Plymouth. Grant AAUW. Mem. ASCD, Women in Leadership Network. E-mail: JoeSueNader1@prodigy.net.

NADER-HEIKENFELD, RITA MARIA, culinary educator, food writer; b. Cin., July 15, 1946; d. Charles Michael and Mary (Calim) Nader; m. Frank J. Heikenfeld, Jr., Mar. 7, 1970; children: Jason Charles, Shane Andrew. Grad., Marian H.S., Cin., Internat. Assn Cooking Profl. Cert. tchr., trainer. Food editor Clermont Sun Newspapers, Batavia, Ohio, 1987-97; co-owner, operator Country Gourmet Catering, 1988—; food and hist. contbg. editor Gannett Papers, Cin., 1989-93; food columnist Eastside Weekend Mag., 1993-97, Sunbury (Ohio) News, 1995-97, Women Alive! mag., 1994—; cooking tchr. Lazarus Creative Kitchen, Cin., 1990-95; resident culinary expert McAlpin's Simply Cooking Sch., 1995-98; syndicated columnist Cmty. Press Newspapers, 1997—. Lectr., motivational speaker, 1987—, cons., test kitchen team, Mercantile Stores, Cin., 1995-98; culinary expert, educator Lazarus Stores, 1999—. Co-author: The Official Snack Guide for Beleaguered Sports Parents, 2001; syndicated author Shaker Christmas Series Cin. Enquirer, 1993; contbr. (booklet) Herbal Friends, 1993; contbr. (booklet) Herbs to Grow, 1994; radio and TV personality. Mem. adv. bd. YWCA Clermont County, Ohio, 1978-80; pres. Mother's Day Out, Inc., Batavia, Ohio, 1978-80; pres., adv. bd. mem. Cancer Family Care, Inc., Clermont City, Ohio, 1981-90; pres. St. Louis sch. PTA, 1983-84; vol. tchr. Kids in the Kitchen, Cin., 1995—; mem. adv. bd. Ohio State Extension Agy., Clermont County. Named Cin.'s Best Kept Secret in Food-Tchg. Area, Cin. Ballet, 1997; recipient Profl. Journalists award, 1999. Mem. Soc. Profl. Journalists, Internat. Assn. Culinary Profls. (cert. culinary profl., level III instr.), Assn. Food Journalists, Chef's Collaborative (Cin. chpt.). Democrat. Roman Catholic. Avocations: gardening, foraging wild edibles, ethnic food history, culinary and medicinal herbs.

NADICH, JUDAH, rabbi; b. Balt., May 13, 1912; s. Isaac and Lena (Nathanson) N.; m. Martha Hadassah Ribalow, Jan. 26, 1947; children: Leah N. (Mrs. Aryeh Meir), Shira A. (Mrs. James L. Levin), Nahma M. Nadich (Mrs. David Belcourt). BA, CCNY, 1932; MA, Columbia U., 1936; rabbi, M.H.L., Jewish Theol. Sem. Am., 1936, D.H.L., 1953, D.D. (hon), 1966. Rabbi Temple Beth David, Buffalo, 1936-40; co-rabbi Anshe Emet Synagogue, Chgo., 1940-42; lecture tour U.S., South Africa and Rhodesia, 1946-47; rabbi Kehillath Israel Congregation, Brookline, Mass., 1947-57, Park Ave. Synagogue, N.Y.C., 1957-87, rabbi emeritus, 1987—. Conducted first Bat Mitzvah in People's Republic of China, 1990. Author: Eisenhower and the Jews, 1953, Jewish Legends of the Second Commonwealth, 1983, Legends of the Rabbis, 2 vols., 1994, Rabbi Akiba and His Contemporaries, 1998; editor, translator: (Menachem Ribalow) The Flowering of Modern Hebrew Literature, 1959; editor: (Louis Ginzberg) Al Halakha v'Aggada, 1960. Pres. Rabbinical Assembly, 1972-74; pres. Jewish Book Coun. Am., 1968-72; hon. bd. dirs. Jewish Theol. Sem. Am.; past bd. dirs., mem. exec. com. Nat. Jewish Welfare Bd., Fedn. Jewish Philanthropies N.Y.; former mem. hospice com. Beth Israel Med. Ctr.; past mem. N.Y.C. Holocaust Meml.; hon. v.p. bd. dirs. Jewish Braille Inst.; bd. dirs. Friends of Jewish Hist. Mus., Warsaw; past pres. Assn. Jewish Chaplains Armed Forces; adv. to Gen. Eisenhower on Jewish affairs, ETO, 1945; com. 50th anniversary World War II U.S. Dept. Defense. Lt. col., chaplain AUS, 1942-46, ETO. Assimilated rank of Maj. Gen. South Vietnam, 1971. Decorated Order Brit. Empire, 1943, ETO with battle star medal, 1944, Croix de Guerre (France), 1945, Occupation of Germany medal, 1945, Victory medal, 1945, Ittur Lohamai Hamedinah (Israel), 1975; fellow Herbert Lehman Inst. Talmudic Ethics, 1958; Jewish Theol. Sem. Am. honoree, 1997. Mem. Mil. Chaplains Assn., Phi Beta Kappa. Lodges: Masons. Home: 1040 Park Ave New York NY 10028-1032 Office: Park Ave Synagogue 50 E 87th St New York NY 10128-1099 *Live so that your life will make a difference for the better in the lives of other people.*

NADIEN, MARGOT BALLON, psychology educator, researcher; b. Montreal, May 25, 1930; came to U.S., 1945; d. David Herbert and Lillian Glauberson Ballon; m. David William Nadien, June 11, 1950. BA, Hunter Coll., 1967; PhD, CUNY, 1974. Adj. prof. Fordham U., N.Y.C., 1971-73, asst. prof. psychology, 1974-88, assoc. prof. psychology, 1989—, dir. gerontology cert. program, 1989-94. Author: Child's Psychosocial Development, 1980, Adult Years and Aging, 1989; sr. editor Females and Autonomy: Life-Span Perspective, 2000; contbr. chpts. to books. Mem. Internat. Coun. Psychologists (area chmn. for N.Y. state, orgnl. rep. to UN, 2000-), N.Y. State Psychol. Assn. (pres. acad. divsn. 1995-96, pres. social & cross cultural issues 1992-93, Kurt Lewin award 1995, Svc. award 1995-96), N.Y. Acad. Scis. (mem. adv. com. for psychology 1993—, vice-chair adv. com. 1996-98, chair adv. com. 1998-2000), Phi Beta Kappa, Psi Chi. Office: Fordham U 113 W 60th St New York NY 10023-7484

NADIG, GERALD GEORGE, manufacturing executive; b. Astoria, N.Y., May 9, 1945; s. Charles Edwin and Louise (Hahn) N.; m. Nancy Hanford Stewart, June 20, 1970; children: Sara Hanford, Jennifer Stewart. AB cum laude, Harvard Coll., 1967, MBA, 1974. Fin. mgr. Rockwell Internat., Hopedale, Mass., 1974-76, materials mgr. Oshkosh, Wis., 1976-78, Marysville, Ohio, 1978-79, ops. mgr., 1979-80, plant mgr., 1980-82, regional mgr. Atlanta, 1984-85; mng. dir. Rockwell Maudslay Ltd., Great Alne, Eng., 1982-84; dir. mfg. Toyoda Machinery USA, Arlington Heights, Ill., 1985-87, v.p., gen. mgr., 1987-88; v.p., gen. mgr. Littell div. Allied Products Corp., Chgo., 1988-89; exec. v.p. pre finish metals Material Scis. Corp., 1989-90; pres. Pre Finish Metals Materials Scis. Corp., 1990-91; pres., chief oper. officer Material Scis. Corp., Chgo., 1991-96, pres., CEO, 1997—, chmn. bd. dirs., 1998—; bd. dirs. Tokheim Corp., 2000—. Bd. dirs. Chgo. chpt. Nat. Assn. Corp. Dirs.; trustee Village of Lake Barrington, 1989-91. With U.S. Army, 1966-70. Mem. Soc. Mfg. Engrs. (sr.), Biltmore Country Club (bd. dirs.). Avocations: golf, tennis, game theory. Home: 24354 N Grandview Dr Barrington IL 60010-6218 Office: Material Scis Corp 2200 Pratt Blvd Elk Grove Village IL 60007-5917

NADIG, SANDHYA MAHESH, computer engineer; b. Gorakhpur, India, Nov. 27, 1965; came to U.S., 1991; d. Ramachandra Honnenahalli and Susheela (Narasimhamurthy) Ramachandra; m. Mahesh Kumar Nadig, June 12, 1989; 1 child, Megha Priya. BS in Electronics, Dayananda Sagar Coll. Engring., Bangalore, india, 1988; postgrad., Pace U., 1991-94. Pvt. tutor, Bangalore, 1988-91; software engr. MCI Internat., Rye Brook, N.Y., 1992—. Lectr. electronics Vasavi Edn. Trust, Bangalore, 1988-91. Recipient cert. Red Cross Soc. India, UN Info. Orgn. Home: 15 Marlborough Rd Norwalk CT 06851-2611 Office: MCI Internat 1 International Dr Rye Brook NY 10573-1059

NADIM, FARHAD, writer, researcher; b. Tehran, Iran, Aug. 10, 1956; s. Abolhassan Nadim and Zinatosadat Keliddarzadeh; m. Afarin Rahmanifar; 1 child Avishen. M Architectural Engring., Tehran U., 1980; postgrad. Diploma, Internat. Inst. of Hydraulic and Environ. Engring., Delft, The Netherlands, 1986; M Environ. Engring., U. Conn., 1996, U. New Haven, 1991. City planner Ministry of Housing and City Planning, Tehran, Iran, 1981—82; instr. Ministry of energy Abbaspour Edn. and Rsch. Ctr., Iran, 1982—89; rsch. asst. Uniroyal Chem. Co., Middlebury, Conn., 1991—92; technical writer U. Conn. Environ. Rsch. Inst., Storrs, 1996—. Mem.: Ground Water Assn. N.Am. Office: U Conn ERI 270 Middle Tpke Rte 44 Storrs Mansfield CT 06269 Office Fax: 860-486-5488. Personal E-mail: fnadim@eri.uconn.edu.

NADIRI, M. ISHAQ, economics educator, researcher, lecturer, consultant; b. Kabul, Afghanistan, Oct. 16, 1936; s. M. Alam and Gul-Nasa N.; m. Tahira Homayun, Sept. 9, 1978; children: Youssof, Khalid. BS with highest distinction, U. Nebr., 1958; MA, U. Calif.-Berkeley, 1960, PhD, 1965; postgrad., Yale U., 1962-63. Asst. prof. Northwestern U., Evanston, Ill., 1964-66, U. Chgo. Bus. Sch., 1966-67; research fellow Nat. Bur. Econ. Research, N.Y.C., 1968-70, research assoc., 1969—; full prof. econs. NYU, 1970—, Jay Gould prof. econs., 1975—, chmn. dept. econs., 1972-78; Disting. vis. prof. Am. U. Cairo, 1993. Cons. in field; participant seminars NSF Ctr. Strategic Studies, UN Assn.; adviser to Afghanistan Interim Govt. and Pres. Hamid Karzai; CEO, Global Partnership for Afghanistan; mem. Pvt. Sector Devel. Task Force for Afghanistan; mem. Aid Coordination Com. of Afghanistan; mem. Afghanistan-Am. Found. Author: books, including A Disequilibrium Model of Demand for Factors of Production, 1974; research, numerous publs. in field; editor books including The Importance of Technology and the Permanence of Structure in Industrial Growth, 1978, Commodity Markets and Latin American Development: A Modeling Approach, 1980; editorial bd.: Annals of Econs. and Social Measurement. Mem. Com. to Upgrade Central Park, N.Y.C.; mem. Com. to Help Afghan Refugees in the U.S. C. Miller fellow, 1958-59; U. Calif. fellow, 1959-60; Earnhart fellow, 1962-63, 63-64; grantee NSF, Ford Found., IBM Corp., AT&T Mem. Am. Econs. Assn., Econometrica Soc., Univs.-Nat. Bur. Econ. Research, Internat. Assn. Research in Income and Wealth; mem. AAAS, Am. Statis. Assn., Council Fgn. Relations, Phi Beta Kappa, Pi Sigma Alpha, Beta Gamma Sigma Office: NYU Dept Econs 269 Mercer St Fl 7 New York NY 10003-6633 E-mail: min1@nyu.edu.

NADKARNI, ASHOK B. electrical engineer; b. Sept. 12, 1946; married; 2 children. BE, Gujarat U., 1968; MS, Tex. A&I U., 1985. Chartered engr., India; registered profl. engr., Tex. Sr. elec. engr. Navasari Mills, Navasari, India, 1969-77; deputy chief engr. Gaekwar Mills, Bilimora, India, 1977-80; elec. engr. Goldston Engring., Corpus Christi, Tex., 1981-87, BMW Engring., Corpus Christi, 1987-89; elec. engr. support Indtech Engring., 1989—. Mem. IEEE (chair Corpus Christi sect. 1997-98), NSPE, Tex. Soc. Profl. Engrs., Inst. of Engrs. (India). Avocations: reading, walking, gardening. Home: 5529 Fox Run Cir Corpus Christi TX 78413-4827

NADLER, GERALD, management consultant, educator; b. Cin., Mar. 12, 1924; s. Samuel and Minnie (Krumbein) N.; m. Elaine Muriel Dubin, June 22, 1947; children: Burton Alan, Janice Susan, Robert Daniel. Student, U. Cin., 1942-43; BSME, Purdue U., 1945, MS in Indsl. Engring, 1946, PhD, 1949. Instr. Purdue U., 1948-49; asst. prof. indsl. engring. Washington U., St. Louis, 1949-52, assoc. prof., 1952-55, prof., head dept. indsl. engring., 1955-64; prof. U. Wis., Madison, 1964-83, chmn. dept. indsl. engring., 1964-67, 71-75; prof., chmn. dept. indsl. and sys. engring. U. So. Calif., L.A., 1983-93, IBM chair engring. mgmt., 1986-93, IBM chair emeritus, prof. emeritus, 1993—; v.p. Artcraft Mfg. Co., St. Louis, 1956-57; dir. Intertherm Inc., 1969-85. Pres. Ctr. for Breakthrough Thinking Inc., L.A., 1989—; vis. prof. U. Birmingham, Eng., 1959, Waseda U., Tokyo, 1963, Ind. U., 1964, U. Louvain, Belgium, 1975, Technion-Israel Inst. Tech., Haifa, 1976; speaker in field. Author: The Planning and Design Approach, 1981; (with S. Hibino) Breakthrough Thinking, 1990, 2d edit., 1994, Creative Solution Finding, 1995; (with G. Hoffherr, J. Moran) Breakthrough Thinking in Total Quality Management, 1994; contbr. articles to profl. jours.; reviewer books, papers, proposals. Mem. Ladue Bd. Edn., St. Louis County, 1960-63, L.A. County Quality and Productivity Commn., 1997—; chmn. planning com. Wis. Regional Med. Program, 1966-69; bd. dirs. USC Credit Union, 1994—. Served with USN, 1943-45. Gilbreth medal Soc. Advancement Mgmt., 1961, Editl. award Hosp. Mgmt. Mag., 1966, Disting. Engring. Alumnus award Purdue U., 1975, Outstanding Indsl. Engr. award, 1997; Book of Yr. award Inst. Indsl. Engrs., 1983, Frank and Lillian Gilbreth award, 1992; Phi Kappa Phi Faculty Recognition award U. So. Calif., 1990, Engring. Disting. Svc. award U. Wis. Madison, 2000. Fellow AAAS, Inst. Indsl. Engrs. (pres. 1989-90), Inst. for Advancement Engrs., Am. Soc. Engring. Edn.; mem. NAE, Inst. Operations Rsch. and Mgmt. Scis., Japan Work Design Soc. (hon. adv. 1968—), World Future Soc., Acad. Mgmt. Soc., Engring. Mgmt. Soc., Sigma Xi, Alpha Pi Mu (nat. officer), Pi Tau Sigma, Omega Rho, Tau Beta Pi. Office: Univ Park GER 240 Dept Of I&se Los Angeles CA 90089-0193 E-mail: nadler@usc.edu.

NADLER, HENRY LOUIS, pediatrician, geneticist, medical educator; b. N.Y.C., Apr. 15, 1936; s. Herbert and Mary (Kartiganer) N.; m. Benita Weinhard, June 16, 1957; children: Karen, Gary, Debra, Amy. AB, Colgate U., 1957; MD, Northwestern U., 1961; MS, U. Wis., 1965. Diplomate: Am. Bd. Pediatrics, Am. Bd. Med. Genetics. Intern NYU Med. Ctr., 1961-62, sr. resident pediatrics, 1962-63, chief resident, 1963-64; teaching asst. NYU Sch. Medicine, 1962-63, clin. instr., 1963-64, U. Wis. Sch. Medicine, 1964-65; practice medicine specializing in pediatrics Chgo., 1965—; fellow Children's Meml. Hosp. dept. pediatrics Northwestern U., 1964-65; assoc. in pediatrics Northwestern U. Med. Sch., 1965-66, asst. prof., 1967-68, assoc. prof., 1968-70, prof., 1970-81, chmn. dept. pediatrics, 1970-81; prof. Northwestern U. Med. Sch. (Grad. Sch.), 1971-80; mem. staff Children's Meml. Hosp., 1965-81, head div. genetics, 1969-81, chief of staff, 1970-81; dean, prof. pediatrics, ob-gyn Wayne State U. Med. Sch., Detroit, 1981-88; prof. U. Chgo., 1988-89, U. Ill., 1989—; pres. Michael Reese Hosp. and Med. Ctr., Chgo., 1988-91; market med. dir. Aetna Health Plans, Phoenix, 1993-94, mktg. v.p., CEO, 1994-95; v.p. managed care/physician integration, med. dir. Am. Healthcare Sys., San Diego, 1995. Mem. vis. staff, div. medicine Northwestern Meml. Hosp., 1972-81; staff Children's Hosp. of Mich., 1981-88. Mem. editorial bd. Comprehensive Therapy, 1973-84, Am. Jour. Human Genetics, 1979-83, Pediatrics in Rev., 1980-83, Am. Jour. Diseases of Children, 1983-91; contbr. articles to profl. jours. Recipient E. Mead Johnson award for pediatric rsch., 1973, Meyer O. Cantor award for Disting. Svc. Internat. Coll. Surgeons, 1987; Irene Heinz Given and John La Porte Given rsch. prof. pediatrics, 1970-81. Fellow Am. Acad. Pediatrics; mem. Am. Soc. for Clin. Investigation, Am. Soc. Human Genetics, Am. Pediatric Soc., Soc. for Pediatric Rsch., Midwest Soc. for Pediatric Rsch., Pan Am. Med. Assn., Alpha Omega Alpha. Home and Office: 25150 N Windy Walk Dr Unit 23 Scottsdale AZ 85255-8105 E-mail: hlnadler@aol.com.

NADLER, JERROLD LEWIS, congressman, lawyer; b. Brooklyn, N.Y., June 13, 1947; m. Joyce L. Miller, 1976; 1 child, Michael. JD, Fordham U., 1978; AB, Columbia Coll., 1969. Mem. Community Planning Bd. No. 7, Manhattan, 1967-71; Dem. leader 67th Assembly Dist. Part C, 1969-71; exec. dir. Community Free Dem., 1972; law clerk Morgan, Finnegan, Pine, Foley & Lee, 1976; Dem. dist. leader 69th Assembly dist. Part A, 1973-77; assemblyman N.Y. State 69th dist., 1977-82, 67th dist., 1983-92; mem. 102d Congress from 17th N.Y. dist., Washington, 1992, 103d-106th Congress from 8th N.Y. Dist., Washington, 1993—; subcoms. comml./adminstrv. law, cts. intellectual property 103d-105th Congress from 8th N.Y. Dist., 1995-96, ranking Dem. subcom. on comml./adminstrv. law, 1997-2000, mem. subcom. on constn., 1997—, mem. subcoms. on surftace transp., water resources, environ., 1993-94, mem. subcoms. on railroads/aviation, 1995—, mem. subcoms. on surface transp. and railroads, 1997-2000; mem. Judiciary com., transp. infrastructure com., Regional Whip 106th Congress from 8th N.Y. Dist., 1999—. Mem. coms. on judiciary and pub. works and transp. U.S. Ho. Reps., 1995—, subcom. on constl. law and immigration, 1993-94, jud. com., ranking mem. comml. and adminstr. law subcom., transp. and infrastructure com., chmn. Assembly Com. on Corps, Authorities and Commn., 1991-92, Assembly Consumer Affairs and Protection Com., 1987-90, Assembly Com. on Ethics and Guidance, 1985-86, Assembly Subcom. on Mass Transit and Rail Freight, 1979-86, mem. Assembly Com. on Judiciary, Gov. Ops., Legis. Tax Study Commn.; mem. Assembly Com. Ways and Means, Housing, Real Property Tax, Health, Election Law, Ins., ranking mem. subcom. on constn., subcom. on comml. and admintrv. law, subcom. on hwys. and transit, subcom. on railroads. Founder, chmn. West Side Peace Com., 1969-71; former mem. exec. coun. N.Y. State New Dem. Coalition; pres. Zionist Orgn. Am. dist. 7A; active Common Cause, Met. Coun. on Housing, West Side Tenants Union, Community Free Dems.; mem. nat. governing coun. Am. Jewish Congress; former bd. dirs. N.Y. State Nat. Abortion Rights Action League, Women's InterArts Ctr. Recipient hon. recognition award N.Y. State Nurses Assn., 1982, Disting. Svc. award Coalition on Domestic Violence, 1989; named Assembly Mem. of Yr. N.Y. chpt. NOW, 1980; Pulitzer scholar Columbia U. Mem. NOW, NAACP, N.Y. Bar Assn., N.Y. Civil Liberties Union (honor roll), Citizens Union, League Conservation Voters, New Dem. Coalition, Ams. for Dem. Action (bd. dirs., nat. v.p.). Office: US Ho of Reps 2334 Hob Washington DC 20515-0001 E-mail: jerrold.nadler@mail.house.gov.*

NADLER, MYRON JAY, lawyer, director; b. Youngstown, Ohio, July 22, 1923; s. Murray A. and Jean (Davis) N.; m. Alice Blue, Nov. 4, 1951; children: Jed M., Wendy D., John M.S. Student, N.Mex. State Coll., 1943-44; BS in Econs. Wharton Sch., U. Pa., 1947; JD with distinction, U. Mich., 1949. Bar: Ohio 1950. Pres., shareholder Nadler, Nadler & Burdman Co., L.P.A., Youngstown, 1950-95, pres., 1950-95; ret., 1996. Asst. editor Mich. Law Rev., 1949; instr. Youngstown U. Law Sch., 1952-59. Author: (with Saul Nadler) Nadler on Bankruptcy, 1965, April's Bankruptcy Forms and Practice, 1964; contbr. articles to profl. jours. Chmn. exec. budget com. United Appeal, Youngstown, 1964-66, v.p., 1967-70; co-chmn. Mayor's Commn. Human Rights, 1957; mem. Mahoning County Planning Commn., 1965-71, Nat. Budget and Consultation Com., 1967-70; trustee Cmty. Corp., Youngstown, v.p., 1977-82, chmn. pers. com., 1974-92; bd. dirs. Ctr. for Learning, Villa Maria, Pa., 1969-95, pres., 1981-89, chmn. bd., 1989-94. With AUS, 1943-45. Decorated Purple Heart with oak leaf cluster. Mem. Fellows of Ohio Bar Assn. Found., ABA, Ohio Bar Assn., Mahoning County Bar Assn., Scribes Assn. Legal Writers, Comml. Law League Am., Squaw Creek Country Club (pres. 1966-68), Hamlet Country Club. Clubs: Squaw Creek Country (pres. 1966-68); Hamlet Country. Home: 601 Pine Lake Dr Delray Beach FL 33445-9042 Office: 20 Federal Plz W Ste 600 Youngstown OH 44503-1423

NADLER, SIGMOND HAROLD, physician, surgeon; b. Bklyn., May 16, 1932; s. Morris and Rose (Levine) N.; m. Beverly Melcher, June 20, 1954; children: Geoffrey, Shail, Tamara, Kimberly. BA, State U. Iowa, 1955, MD, 1957. Intern Menorah Med. Ctr., Kansas City, Mo., 1957-58, resident in surgery, 1958-61, Roswell Park Meml. Inst., 1961-63, mem. staff, 1962-68, clin. coord. Ea. region clin. drug evaluation program, 1966-68, project dir. nat. adj. studies, 1966-68, assoc. chief cancer rsch. surgery, 1966-68; assoc. prof. surgery Jefferson Med. Coll., Phila., 1968-70; also dir. clin. cancer tng., asst. clin. prof. surgery SUNY, Buffalo, 1970-94, prof. emeritus, 1994—. Mem. Am. Soc. Clin. Oncology (ret.). Achievement include research in human tumor immunotherapy. Home: 9513 Preston Trl W Ponte Vedra Beach FL 32082-3311

NADOLSKI, STEPHANIE LUCILLE, artist, designer; b. Sacramento, Feb. 21, 1945; d. Robert Emmett and Barbara Lucille (Kramer) Jones; m. Michael Edward Nadolski, Jan. 9, 1970; 1 child, Jason Edward Nadolski. Student, Glassell Sch. Art, Houston, 1972-76, San Jose State Coll., 1963-68. Computer programmer Lawrence Radiation Lab., Livermore, Calif., 1964-70; electron microscopy technician Ocean Springs (Miss.) Rsch. Lab., 1970-72; artist, gallery dir., owner Archway Gallery, Houston, 1973-86; artist, owner Nadolski Fine Art & Design, Annapolis, Md., 1986—. One-woman shows include Mus. Am. Art and Architecture Houston Bapt. U., 1997, Gallery 18, Chesterton, Ind., 1997, Pranschke and Holderle, St. Louis, 1997, Clair E. Smith Gallery, Barrington, Ill., 1999, Chesapeake Ctr. Creative Arts, Brooklyn, M.D., 2002, Future Care, Chesapeake, Md., 2002; exhibited in group shows at Deer Path Gallery, Lake Forest, Ill., 1990-99, Art Independent, Lake Geneva, Wis., 1995—, Niemi Gallery, Lake Villa, Ill., 1997-2002, Gallery West, Alexandria, Va., 2002, Md. Fedn. Art, Annapolis, 2002, Benfield Gallery, Severna Park, Md., The Art League, Alexandria, 2002, Creative Ptnrs., Bethesda, Md., 2002; represented in permanent collections Kane County Courthouse, Mus. Art of Am. West, Houston, U. Miss., Oxford, Baylor Coll. Medicine, Houston, Stora N.Am. Corp., Schaumburg, Ill., Wausau Ins. Co., Wis., Westerville Pub. Libr., Ohio, Barrington Pub. Libr., Marshfield (Wis.) Clinic, Prairie Cardiovasc. Assocs., Springfield, Ill., Towne Bank, Portsmouth, Va.; display designer, curator art exhbn. and collections. Bd. advisors N.W. Cultural Coun., Rolling Meadows, Ill., 1992-95, Barrington (Ill.) Arts Coun., 1993—; bd. dirs., mem. Chgo. Artists Coalition. Recipient 1st annual Flo Bash award Barrington, Ill. Area Arts Coun., 1989, award of excellence, 1995, best of show award Watertown, Wis. Arts Coun., 1996, best of category award Oconomowoc, Wis. Fest. of Arts, 1997, Excellence award Lake Geneva Arts Assn., 1998, Best of Mixed Media, Boston Mills Artfest, Ohio, 2000. Mem.: Md. Printmakers, The Art League, Md. Fedn. Art, Soc. Layerists in Multi Media, Mich. Guild Artists and Artisans, Chgo. Artists Coalition, Nat. Coll. Soc. Avocations: scuba diving, tennis, golf, hiking, travel. Home: 4785 Idlewilde Rd Shady Side MD 20764 E-mail: stephn@artlover.com.

NADY, JOHN, electronics company executive; b. Agfalva, Hungary, Feb. 13, 1945; came to U.S., 1951; s. John and Hermine Nady. BSEE, Calif. Inst. Tech., 1965; MSEE, U. Calif., Berkeley, 1968. Elec. engr. Lawrence Radiation Lab., Livermore, 1966-71, Westinghouse Corp., Oakland, Calif., 1971-72; owner, chief exec. officer Nady Systems, Inc., 1976—, Calif. Concerts, Inc., Oakland, 1985-93. Patentee in field. Recipient Emmy award Pioneering Devel. Wireless Microphones, 1996. Mem. Nat. Assn. Broadcasters, Audio Engring. Soc., Nat. Assn. Music Merchants. Avocations: electric guitar, skiing, tennis, golfing. Office: Nady Systems Inc 6701 Shellmound St Emeryville CA 94608-1023

NADZICK, JUDITH ANN, accountant; b. Paterson, N.J., Mar. 6, 1948; d. John and Ethel (McDonald) N. BBA in Acctg., U. Miami, 1971. CPA, N.J. Staff acct., mgr. Ernst & Whinney, C.P.A.s, N.Y.C., 1971-78; asst. treas. Gulf & We. Industries, Inc., 1979-83; asst. v.p., 1980-82; v.p., 1982-83; v.p., corp. contr. United Mchts. and Mfrs. Inc., N.Y.C., 1983-85; sr. v.p., 1985-86; exec. v.p., CFO, 1986-97; pres., 1997—; also bd. dir. Mem. U. Miami Alumni Assn., Delta Delta Delta. Roman Catholic. Home: 280 Lincoln Ave Elmwood Park NJ 07407-2824 E-mail: judenadz@aol.com.

NAEGELE, CARL JOSEPH, university academic administrator, educator; b. Newark, Jan. 1, 1939; s. Carl Joseph Sr. and Mabel (Flood) N.; m. Elizabeth C. McVey, June 19, 1971; children: Jennifer, Erin. BS, Kean Coll., 1965; MS, Syracuse U., 1969; PhD, Cornell U., 1974. Tchr. physics Summit (N.J.) High Sch., 1965-68; instr. physics Kean Coll., Union, N.J., 1968-70; physics instr. Cornell U., Ithaca, N.Y., 1973-75; prof. Mich. State U., East Lansing, 1975-79; program dir. NSF, Washington, 1979-81, 91-92; dean coll. arts and scis. U. San Francisco, 1981-91; dir. Sci. Inst., 1984—; prof. physics and computer sci. U. San Francisco, 1981—. Computer cons. San Rafael, Calif., 1981—. Author: Physics for the Life and Health Sciences, 1974, Laboratory Experiment in General Physics, 1976, Electronic Mail and Communications Networks, 1984, Computer Systems and Applications, 1998, Experiments in Physical Science, 1998; contbr. articles to profl. jours. Served with U.S. Army, 1959-61, Korea. Recipient Outstanding Tchg. award Mich. State U., 1978, Leadership award U. San Francisco, 1985; grantee NSF, 1968, 78, 94-99, Coun. for Basic Edn., 1984-89. Mem. Am. Phys. Soc., Am. Assn. Physics Tchrs., Am. Assn. Univ. Adminstrs., Assn. for Computing Machinery. Avocations: flying, boating, skiing, tennis, running. Office: U San Francisco Coll Arts & Scis Ignatian Heights San Francisco CA 94117-1080

NAEGELE, ELIZABETH MARIE, musician, educator; b. Minot, N.D., July 17, 1951; d. George Eugene and Margaret Lenora (Wiens) Faul; m. Michael Dean Naegele, June 17, 1972; children: Heidi Marie, Nicholas Michael. Diploma, Moody Bible Inst., 1972; MusB, Mich. State U., 1975, MusM, 1976; MusD, Northwestern U., Evanston, Ill., 1989. Prof. music Moody Bible Inst., Chgo., 1976—. Organ recitalist, Ill., Mich. Dir. music Eastminster Presbyn. Ch., East Lansing, Mich., 1975-76, Carter Westminster Presbyn., Skokie, Ill., 1976-82, 1st Presbyn. Ch., Waukegan, Ill., 1990—; organist Winnetka (Ill.) Bible Ch., 1982-89. Mem. Assn. Am. Guild Organists (bd. dirs. Chgo. chpt. 1977-79, 88-91, 96—), Chgo. Club Woman Organists (bd. dirs. 1986-94), Phi Kappa Phi. Avocation: word games. Home: 2516 Edina Blvd Zion IL 60099-2702 Office: Moody Bible Inst 820 N La Salle Dr Chicago IL 60610-3263 E-mail: SocratesNaegele@att.net., enaegle@moody.edu.

NAEGELE, PHILIPP OTTO, violinist, violist, music educator; b. Stuttgart, Fed. Republic Germany, Jan. 22, 1928; came to U.S., 1940; s. Reinhold and Alice (Nordlinger) N.; m. Susanne Russin (div. 1980); 1 child, Matthias Dominic; m. Barbara Wright, Mar. 1992. BA, Queens Coll., 1949; MFA, Princeton U., 1950, PhD, 1955. Violinist, violist Marlboro (Vt.) Music Festival, 1950—; violinist Cleve. Orch., 1956-64; from asst. prof. to assoc. prof. to prof. violin dept. music Smith Coll., Northampton, Mass., 1964-78, William R. Kenan Jr. prof. music, 1978-2000, William R. Kenan Jr. prof. music emeritus, 2000—; violist Cantilena Piano Quartet, 1980-96; mem. Boccherini Ensemble, 1980-84. Mem. resident string quartet Kent (Ohio) State U., 1960-64; mem. violin faculty Cleve. Inst. Music, 1961-64, Vegh String Quartet, 1977-79; rec. artist Columbia Mus. Heritage Soc., Pro Arte, Nonesuch Records, Bis Records, Marlboro Rec. Soc., Arabesque Records, Da Camera, Spectrum Records, Bayer Records, Sony Classical, Philomusica, Qualitone Records. Contbr. to New Groves Dictionary of Music, also articles to profl. jours. With U.S. Army, 1955-56. Fellow Am. Council Learned Socs., 1949-50, Proctor fellow, 1952-53, Fulbright fellow, 1953-54. Mem. Phi Beta Kappa. Home: 57 Prospect St Northampton MA 01060-2130

NAEGLE, MADELINE ANNE, mental health nurse, educator; b. Penn Yan, N.Y., Feb. 2, 1942; d. Lester Lawrence and Nona Caroline (Muir) N.; m. James Michael McGowan, Aug. 6, 1966 (div. 1984); children: Amanda Allen, Benjamin Logan. BS, Nazareth Coll. Rochester, 1964; MA, NYU, 1967, PhD, 1980. Staff nurse Syracuse (N.Y.) Meml. Hosp., summer 1964; staff nurse, asst. head nurse Payne Whitney Clinic, N.Y.C., 1964-65; instr. nursing Herbert H. Lehman Coll., Bronx, N.Y., 1972-75, part-time instr. nursing, 1975-78; asst. clin. prof. Sch. Nursing U. Pa., Phila., 1979-83; pvt. practice N.Y.C., 1980—; assoc. prof. Leinhard Sch. Nursing Pace U., Pleasantville, N.Y., 1983-85; assoc. prof. div. nursing NYU, N.Y.C., 1985—. Cons. The Day Sch., 1980-84; mem. N.Y. State Gov.'s Health Care Adv. Bd., 1991-94. Author: Nursing Process with Clients Using Drugs, 1993, Patterns of Substance Abuse, 1996; author, editor: (model curriculum) Substance Abuse Education in Nursing, 1991; editor Addictions Nursing, 1988-98, Addictions and Substance Abuse: Stratgies for Advanced Nursing Practice, 2000; contbr. articles to profl. jours. Recipient Presdl. Citation award N.Y. County RN Assn., 1986, Amanda Silver Disting. Svc. award N.Y. County RN Assn., 1994; named Outstanding Alumna, Nazareth Coll. of Rochester, 2000; inducted into Acad. Women Achievers, YWCA, 1991; USPHS fellow, 1978-79, Pres.'s award Nat. Nurses Soc. on Addiction; grantee Nat. Inst. Alcohol Abuse and Alcoholism, Nat. Inst. Drug Abuse, 1989-90, Ctr. for Substance Abuse Prevention, 1990-95, U.S. Human Resources Adminstrn., 1999; Fulbright scholar U. Malta, 1995. Fellow: Am. Acad. Nursing; mem.: ANA (com. chair 1987—89, com. on addiction 1999, nominating com. 1996—2000, pres.-elect 1987—89, pres. 1989—91, Hildegard Peplav award 2002), Assn. Med. Educators and Rschrs. in Substance Abuse, N.Y. State Nurses Assn. (chair com. on impaired nursing practice 1986—88), Sigma Theta Tau. Democrat. Avocations: hiking, running, dancing, theatre, music. Office: NYU Div Nursing 246 Greene St New York NY 10003-6677 Business E-Mail: MAN1@nyu.edu.

NAEHER, LUKE PETER, science educator; b. NY, 1966; married. PhD, Yale U. Asst. prof. U. of Ga., Athens, Ga., 2001—. Office: Dept of Environmental Health Science EHS Building Athens GA 30602

NAEVE, MILO MERLE, museum curator and trustee; b. nr. Arnold, Kans., Oct. 9, 1931; s. Bernhardt and Fern (Yasmer) N.; m. Nancy Jammer, July 18, 1954. BFA, U. Colo., 1953; MA, U. Del., 1955. Curatorial asst. Henry Francis duPont Winterthur Mus., 1957, asst. curator, 1958, sec. of mus., 1959-63, registrar, 1963-65; editor Winterthur Portfolio, 1965-66; asst. dir. dept. collections Colonial Williamsburg, Va., 1967-69, curator, dir. dept. collections, 1970; dir. Colorado Springs (Colo.) Fine Arts Ctr., 1971-74; curator Am. arts Art Inst. Chgo., 1975-91; ret. Am. Arts, Art Inst. Chgo., 1991. Curator emeritus Field McCormick. Author: The Classical Presence in American Art, 1978, Identifying American Furniture: A Pictorial Guide to Styles and Terms, Colonial to Contemporary, 1981, 3rd edit., 1998, John Lewis Krimmel: An Artist in Federal America, 1987, 150 Years of Philadelphia Painters and Painting: Selections from the Sewell C. Biggs Museum of American Art, 1999; mem. editl. bd. Am. Art Jour.; contbr. articles to profl. jours. Trustee Skowhegan Sch. Painting and Sculpture, Libr. Co. of Phila., Nat. Coun. of the Fine Arts Mus. of San Francisco, Calif. Recipient Robert C. Smith award for most disting. article pub. in field in U.S., Decorative Arts Soc., 1996. Fellow Royal Soc. Arts; mem. Coll. Art Assn. Am., Nat. Trust Hist. Preservation, Am. Assn. Museums, Museums Assn. (Eng.), Ill. Acad. Fine Arts (Lifetime Achievement award 1991), Grolier Club.

NAEYE, RICHARD L. pathologist, educator; b. Rochester, N.Y., Nov. 27, 1929; s. Peter John and Gertrude Ellen (Lookup) N.; m. Patricia Ann Dahl, June 4, 1955; children: Nancy Ellen, Susan Amy, Robert Peter. AB, Colgate U., 1951; MD, Columbia U., 1955. Diplomate: Am. Bd. Pathology. Intern N.Y. Hosp., N.Y.C., 1955-56; resident Columbia-Presbyn. Med. Ctr., 1956-58, Mary Fletcher Hosp., Burlington, Vt., 1958-60; practice medicine, specializing in pathology, 1960-67, Hershey, Pa., 1967—; asst. attending pathologist Mary Fletcher Hosp., 1960-63; assoc. prof. U. Vt., 1963-67, prof. pathology, 1967; prof. dept. pathology M.S. Hershey Med. Ctr., Pa. State U. Coll. Medicine, 1967—, chmn. dept. pathology, 1967-97. Mem. NIH study sect. USPHS, 1968-72. Mem. editl. bd. Human Pathology, 1982-96, Pediatric Pathology, 1983-96, Pediatric and Perinatal Epidemiology, 1987-94, Modern Pathology, 1993-96; contbr. articles to med. jours. Markle scholar in acad. medicine, 1960-65. Mem. Am. Soc. Exptl. Pathology, U.S. Can. Acad. Pathology, Am. Soc. Pathologists, Am. Soc. Clin. Pathologists, Coll. Am. Pathologists, Pediatric Pathology Soc., Pa. Soc. Clin. Pathologists, Investigative Pathology. Home: 50 Laurel Ridge Rd Hershey PA 17033-2513 Office: Pa State U Coll Medicine Dept Pathology 500 University Dr Hershey PA 17033

NAFRIA AZNAR, VITALINO, bank executive; BS in Bus. Adminstrn., MBA, Universidad Comercial de Deusto. CEO Grupo Financiero BBV-Probursa; regional dir. BBV, Pais Vasco, Spain, dir. middle mkt. risks; CEO Grupo Financiero BBVA Bancomer SA, Mexico City. Office: Grupo Financiero BBVA Bancomer SA Montes Urales 424 Col Lomas de Chapultep 11000 Mexico City Mexico*

NAFTALIS, GARY PHILIP, lawyer, educator; b. Newark, Nov. 23, 1941; s. Gilbert and Bertha Beatrice Naftalis; m. Donna Arditi, June 30, 1974; children: Benjamin, Joshua, Daniel, Sarah. AB, Rutgers U., 1963; AM, Brown U., 1965; LLB, Columbia U., 1967. Bar: N.Y. 1967, U.S. Dist. Ct. (so. dist.) N.Y. 1969, U.S. Ct. Appeals (2d cir.) 1968, U.S. Ct. Appeals (3d cir.) 1973, U.S. Ct. Appeals (D.C. cir.) 1993, U.S. Supreme Ct. 1974. Law clk. to judge U.S. Dist. Ct. So. Dist. N.Y., 1967-68; asst. U.S. atty. So. Dist. N.Y., 1968-74, asst. chief criminal divsn., 1972-74; spl. asst. U.S. atty. for V.I., 1972-73; spl. counsel U.S. Senate Subcom. on Long Term Care, 1975, N.Y. State Temp. Commn. on Living Costs and the Economy, 1975; ptnr. Orans, Elsen, Polstein & Naftalis, N.Y.C., 1974-81, Kramer, Levin, Naftalis & Frankel, N.Y.C., 1981—. Lectr. Law Sch. Columbia U., 1976-88; vis. lectr. Law Sch. Harvard U., 1979; mem. deptl. disciplinary com. Appellate div. 1st Dept., 1980-86. Author: (with Marvin E. Frankel) The Grand Jury: An Institution on Trial, 1977, Considerations in Representing Attorneys in Civil and Criminal Enforcement Proceedings, 1981, Sentencing: Helping Judges Do Their Jobs, 1986, SEC Actions Seeking to Bar Securities Professionals, 1995, SEC Cease and Desist Powers Limited, 1997, The Foreign Corrupt Practices Act, 1997, Prosecuting Lawyers Who Defend Clients in SEC Actions, 1998, Obtaining Reports from a Credit Bureau for Litigation May be a Crime, 1999; editor: White Collar Crimes, 1980. Trustee Boys Brotherhood Rep., 1978—, Blueberry Treatment Ctr., 1981-91, Joseph Haggerty Children's Fund, 1991—; bd. dirs. The Legal Aid Soc., 2000—. Fellow: Am. Coll. Trial Lawyers; mem.: ABA (white collar crime com. criminal justice sect. 1985—), N.Y. Coun. Def. Lawyers (bd. dirs. 2000—), Internat. Bar Assn. (bus. crimes com. 1988—), N.Y. Bar Assn. (com. state legis. 1974—76, exec. com. comml. and fed. litigation sect.), Fed. Bar. Coun. (com. cts. 2d cir. 1974—77), Assn. of Bar of City of N.Y. (com. criminal cts. 1980—83, com. judiciary 1984—87, com. on criminal law 1987—90, 1997—2001, coun. criminal justice 1985—88). Home: 1125 Park Ave Apt 7B New York NY 10128-1243 Office: Kramer Levin Naftalis & Frankel 919 3rd Ave New York NY 10022-3902

NAFTOLIN, FREDERICK, physician, reproductive biologist educator; b. Bronx, N.Y., Apr. 7, 1936; s. Nathan and Jean (Pesacov) N.; children: Michael Eugene, Joshua Joseph; m. Marcie Myerson, Nov. 1, 1987. AA, UCLA, 1957; BA with honors, U. Calif., Berkeley, 1958; MD with honors, U. Calif., San Francisco, 1961; DPhil, U. Oxford, 1970. Intern King County Hosp., Seattle, 1961-62; resident in ob-gyn UCLA, 1962-66; asst. chief gynecology, endocrine fellow USPHS, Seattle, 1966-68; NIH fellow Oxford (Eng.) U., 1968-70; asst. prof. ob-gyn U. Calif., San Diego Sch. Medicine, 1970-73; asso. prof. ob-gyn Harvard Med. Sch., 1973-75; prof., chmn. ob-gyn dept. McGill Faculty Medicine, Montreal, 1975-78; prof., chmn. dept. ob-gyn Yale Med. Sch., New Haven, 1978-2000, prof. dept. biology, 1983—; dir. Yale U. Ctr. for Research in Reproductive Biology, 1986—, head reproductive neuroscience unit, 2000—. Vis. prof. U. Geneva, 1982-83, Weizmann Inst., 1991-92, Complutense U., Spain, 1999; prof extraordinaire Complutense U., 1999. Author 15 books including: Subcellular Mechanisms in Reproductive Neuroendocrinology, 1976, Abnormal Fetal Growth, 1978, Clinical Neuroendocrinology, 1979, Dilatation of the Uterine Cervix, 1980; 2-vol. series Basic Reproductive Medicine, Vol. I, Basis of Normal Reproduction, Vol. II, 1981, Male Reproduction, Vol. III, Metabolism of Steroids by Neuroendocrine Tissues, Follicle Stimulation and Ovulation Induction, 1986; editor Jour. Exptl. Zoology, 2002--; mem. editl. bd. Jour. Soc. Gynecologic Investigation, Menopause, Endocrine Revs.; contbr. more than 500 articles to med. jours. Recipient Arnaldo Bruno prize Lincei Acad., Italy, 2002; Fogarty Internat. fellow, 1982, John Simon Guggenheim fellow, 1983; Berlex Internat. scholar, 1991; fellow ad enundem Royal Coll. Ob-Gyn. Fellow Royal Coll. Ob-Gyn.; mem. Am. Gynecol. and Obstet. Soc., Soc. Gynecol. Investigation (pres. 1991-92), Endocrine Soc., Internat. Soc. Neuroendocrinology, New Haven Ob-Gyn. Soc., Can. Fertility Soc., Soc. for Neurosci., N.Am. Menopause Soc. (pres. 1998-99). Office: Yale Med Sch Dept Ob-Gyn FMB 331 333 Cedar St Dept Ob New Haven CT 06520-8063

NAFZIGER, ESTEL WAYNE, economics educator; b. Bloomington, Ill., Aug. 14, 1938; s. Orrin and Beatrice Mae (Slabaugh) N.; m. Elfrieda Nettie Toews, Aug. 20, 1966; children: Brian Wayne, Kevin Jon. BA, Goshen Coll., 1960; MA, U. Mich., 1962; PhD, U. Ill., 1967. Rsch. assoc. Econ. Devel. Inst., Enugu, Nigeria, 1964-65; asst. prof. Kans. State U., Manhattan, 1966-73, assoc. prof., 1973-78, prof., 1978-99, univ. disting. prof., 1999—; Fulbright prof. Andhra U., Waltair, India, 1970-71; fellow East West Ctr., Honolulu, 1972-73. Vis. scholar Cambridge U., 1976; vis. prof. Internat. U. Japan, Yamato-machi, 1983; external rsch. fellow World Acad. Devel. and Coop., College Park, Md., 1984-85; Indo-Am. Found. scholar Andura U., Waltair, India, 1993; World Inst. for Devel. Econ. Rsch., UN Univ., Helsinki, Finland, 1996-98. Author: African Capitalism, 1977, Class, Caste and Entrepreneurship, 1978, (with others) Development Theory, 1979, Economics of Political Instability, 1983, Economics of Developing Countries, 1984, 2d edit., 1990, 3d edit., 1997, Entrepreneurship Equity and Economic Development, 1986, Inequality in Africa, 1988 (named one of Outstanding Acad. Books, Choice 1989-90), The Debt Crisis in Africa, 1993, Poverty and Wealth, 1994, Learning From the Japanese, 1995, Fathers, Sons, and Daughters: Industrial Entrepreneurs under India's Liberalization, 1998; co-editor: War, Hunger, and Displacement, 2 vols., 2000, Prevention of Humanitarian Emergencies, 2002. Sec. bd. overseers Hesston Coll., Kans., 1980-85; chmn. Lou Douglas Lecture Series, 1984-91, 92-93; pres. faculty senate Kans. State U., 1990-92. Recipient Honor Lectr. award Mid Am. State U.'s Assn., 1984-85; grantee Social Sci. Found., 1969 Mem. Am. Econ. Assn., AAUP (pres. chpt. 1981-82), African Studies Assn., Assn. Comparative Econ. Studies, Omicron Delta Epsilon (hon.), Phi Kappa Phi (hon.) Democrat. Avocations: reading; running. Home: 1919 Bluestem Ter # 785 Manhattan KS 66502-4508 Office: Kans State U Dept Econs Waters Hall Manhattan KS 66506-4001

NAFZIGER, JAMES ALBERT RICHMOND, lawyer, educator; b. Mpls., Sept. 24, 1940; s. Ralph Otto and Charlotte Monona (Hamilton) N. BA, U. Wis., 1962, MA, 1969; JD, Harvard U., 1967. Bar: Wis. 1967. Law clk. to chief judge U.S. Dist. Ct. (ea. dist.) Wis., 1967-69; fellow Am. Soc. Internat. Law, Washington, 1969-70, adminstrv. dir., 1970-74; exec. sec. Assn. Student Internat. Law Socs., 1969-70; lectr. Sch. Law Cath. U. Am., Washington, 1970-74; assoc. prof. law Coll. Law Willamette U., Salem, Oreg., 1977-80, prof., 1980-95, Thomas B. Stoel prof., 1995—, assoc. dean, 1985-86, dir. internat. programs, 1984—. Scholar-in-residence Rockefeller Found. Ctr., Bellagio, Italy, 1985; vis. assoc. prof. Sch. Law, U. Oreg. 1974-77; vis. prof. Nat. Autonomous U. Mex., 1978; hon. prof. East China U. of Politics and Law, 1999—; lectr. tutor Inst. Pub. Internat. Law and Internat. Rels., Thessaloniki, Greece, 1982; cons. Adminstrv. Conf. U.S., 1988-90, Internat. Com. Migration, 1997—; mem. bd. advisors Denver Jour. Internat. Law and Policy, Am. Jour. Comparative Law (bd. dirs. 1985—). Editor Procs. of Am. Soc. Internat. Law 1977; Am. author: Conflict of Laws: A Northwest Perspective, 1985, International Sports Law, 1988; contbr. articles to profl. jours. Bd. dirs. N.W. Regional China Coun., 1987-89. 1st lt. U.S. Army, 1962-64. Recipient Burlington No. Faculty Achievement award, 1988, Willamette U. Pres.'s award for excellence in scholarship, 2000. Mem. ABA (legal specialist ctrl. and east European law initiative 1992—), Am. Soc. Internat. Law (exec. coun. 1983-86, 92-95, exec. com. 1994-95, chmn. ann. meeting 1988, chmn. nominating com. 1989), Am. Soc. Comparative Law (bd. dirs. 1985—, treas. 1997—), Internat. Acad. Comparative Law, Internat. Law Assn. (rapporteur cultural heritage law com. 1990—, Am. br. exec. com. 1986—, pres. 2000—, v.p. 1994-2000, co-dir. studies 1991-95, chmn. human rights com. 1983-88), UNA-USA (pres. Oreg. divsn. 1987-90, bd. dirs. 1990—, exec. com. coun. chpt. and divsn. prof., v.p. 1990-94), Washington Fgn. Law Soc. (v.p. 1973-74), Internat. Studies Assn. (exec. bd. 1974-77, internat. law sect.), ACLU (pres. chpt. 1980-81, mem. state bd. 1982-88, sec. 1983-87), Assn. Am. Law Schs. (chmn. law and arts sect. 1981-83, 89-91, chmn. immigration law sect. 1990-91, chmn. internat. law sect. 1984-85, com. on sects. and ann. meeting 1995-98, chmn. internat. law workshop, 1995), Am. Law Inst., Oreg. Internat. Coun. (pres. 1990-92), Internat. Sports Law Assn. (v.p. 1992—), Nat. Sports Law Inst. (bd. advisors 2002-), Phi Beta Kappa, Phi Kappa Phi. Home: 3775 Saxon Dr S Salem OR 97302-6041 Office: Willamette U Coll Law Salem OR 97301

NAGAICH, AKHILESH KUMAR, biomedical researcher, researcher; b. Kalpi, India, June 24, 1966; came to US, 1993; s. Shrigopal and Kishori Devi (Budhaulia) Nagaich; m. Kamalpreet Arora, Mar. 26, 2000; 1 child Amitoj. BS, Bundelkhand U., Jhansi, Uttar Pradesh, India, 1983, MS, 1985; PhD, Allahabad U., Uttar Pradesh, 1989. Sr. rsch. fellow Allahabad U., 1987-89; rsch. assoc. Indian Inst. Sci., Bangalore, 1990-93; sr. rsch. assoc. U. Nev., Reno, 1993-96; exchange scientist Nat. Cancer Inst./NIH, Bethesda, Md., 1996-2000. CTRA fellow Nat. Cancer Inst./NIH, Bethesda, Md., 2000—01; cons. Bioneer Biotech Co., Reno and Korea, 1996—97; sr. rsch. fellow Coun. Scientific and Indsl. Rsch., India, 1988. Recipient Young Scientist award Indian Nat. Sci. Acad., 1992. Mem. ACS, AAAS, Am. Assn. Biochemist and Molecular Biologists. Achievements include discovery of bending in P53-DNA complexes; development of methods for the efficient synthesis of oligonucleotides; laser crosslinking technology to study protein-DNA interactions. Avocations: golf, tennis, creative writing. Home: 1001 Spring St # 928 Silver Spring MD 20910 Office: NIH Bethesda MD 20892

NAGAO, NORRIS SADATO, political science educator, consultant; b. Sacramento, June 9, 1954; s. Sadao and Misao (Iwahashi) N. AA, Sacramento City Coll., 1973; AB, U. Calif., Berkeley, 1975; MA, cert. East Asian Inst., Columbia U., 1979, EdM, 1980, MA, 1983. Legis. aide Calif. State Assembly, Sacramento, 1976-77; exec. dir. N.Y.-Tokyo-Beijing Nanshiki Baseball Friendship Series, N.Y.C., 1981-84; exec. sec. N.Am.-Japan Promotions, Inc., 1986-89; pres. Mediagenesis Inc., L.A., 1988-91; prof. polit. sci. and ethnic studies/history Southwestern Coll., Chula Vista, Calif., 1991—. Adj. instr. history Chaffey Coll., Rancho Cucamonga, Calif., 1998; originator cert. in diversity mgmt. program Southwestern Coll.; mem. Ctr. for Lesbian and Gay Studies, Grad. Ctr. CUNY. Columnist Update So. Calif.'s Gay and Lesbian Newspaper, 1997. Treas. San Diego County Log Cabin Club, 1993, v.p., 1993-94; polit. action chair Calif. Republican League of San Diego County, 1994; selection chair The Harvey Milk/Tom Homann Scholarship Fund-The Imperial Ct. de San Diego, 1993-96; pub. comms. chair The Lesbian and Gay Men's Cmty. Ctr., 1994-96; mem. Mayor Susan Golding's Gay and Lesbian adv. bd. City of San Diego, 1994-97; bd. libr. commrs. City of San Diego, 1994—, scholarship com. Greater San Diego Bus. Assn. Charitable Found. , 1997-99, The City of San Diego Diversity Commitment, 1998; active Friends of San Diego Pub. Libr., Human Rights Campaign; chair Internet Policy Adv. Com.-City of San Diego, 1998; mem. Perfect Libr. Mem. Alumni Fedn. of Columbia U., Tchrs. Coll. Columbia U., Assn. Asian Am. Studies, Calif. Alumni Assn., Calif. Libr. Assn., Internat. House N.Y., Japan Soc., San Diego and Tijuana, Japanese Am. Citizens League, Japanese Am. Hist. Soc. San Diego, Sacramento City Coll. Alumni Assn., Uptown Dist. Owners' Assn., U.S. Postal Svc. Commemorative Stamp Club, Kappa Delta Pi. Office: PO Box 3643 San Diego CA 92163-1643 E-mail: nnagao@swc.cc.ca.us., ps91nagao@aol.com.

NAGARAJAN, RADHAKRISHNAN, medical researcher; b. Chennai, Tamil Nadu, India, July 1, 1969; s. Nagarajan Venkatraman and Lalitha Balasubramaniam. PhD in Applied Sci., U. Ark., Little Rock , 2001. Rsch. asst. U. Ark., LittleRock, 1998—2001; postdoctoral fellow U. Ark. Med. Scis., Little Rock, 2001—02. Reviewer Israel Sci. Found., other confs. in field. Contbr. to jour. including Internat. Jour. Bifurcation and Chaos (Best Researcher Award at University of Arkansas at LittleRock, 2000). Mem.: IEEE. Iyer. Office: U Ark Med Sci COA 629 S Elm St Rm no: 3105 Little Rock AR 72205 Office Fax: (501) 526-5830. Business E-Mail: nagarajanradhakrish@uams.edu.

NAGATA, AKIRA, publishing executive; b. Tokyo, Aug. 8, 1929; s. Koichi and Mikiko (Minami) N.; m. Tomoko Iida, Apr. 21, 1958; children: Junko, Hidehiko, Kazuhiko. BS in Econs., Jiyu-Gakuen Coll., Tokyo, 1953. Gen. mgr. for N.Am. Nihon Keizai Shimbun, Inc., Tokyo, 1973-77, spl. asst. to pres., 1977-80; dir. Nikkei-McGraw-Hill, Inc., 1980-88; sr. exec. dir. Nikkei Bus. Publs., Inc., 1988-90, pres., CEO, 1990-94, chmn., 1994-98, spl. advisor, 1998—; pres., CEO Nikkei Nat. Geog. Inc., 1994-96. Pres./CEO Nikkei Nat. Geographic Inc., 1994-96; dep. chmn. Internat. Fedn. Periodical Press, London, 1995-97, vice chmn., 1997-99; chmn. Postal Coop. Assn. of Shin-Tokyo, 1992-98, Postal Coop. Assn. of Harumi, Tokyo, 1983-90; chmn. bd. Jiyu Gakuen, 2001—. Co-author: Japanese Agriculturl Industry Off for a New Start, 1961, Revaluation of the Japanese Yen, 1971, Business Culture in the U.S., 1978, The Nine Years in New Delhi, London and New York, 1980. Mem.

Japan Mag. Pubs. Assn. (exec. dir. 1993-99), Rotary (Tokyo Club). Avocations: golf, tennis, opera. E-mial. Office: Nikkei Bus Publs Inc 2-7-6 Hirakawa cho Tokyo 102-8622 Japan E-mail: nagata@nikkeibp.co.jp.

NAGEL, EDWARD MCCAUL, lawyer, former utilities executive; b. Geneva, Sept. 6, 1926; s. Edward Samuel and Helen Veronica (McCaul) N.; m. Mary Elizabeth Klein, Sept. 11, 1950; children— Christopher, Linda, Michael, Jeffrey, Ellen. AB, Harvard, 1949; LL.B., U. Pa., 1952; postgrad., Cornell U. Bus. Sch., 1962. Bar: Pa. 1953. Assoc. Simpson, Thacher & Bartlett, N.Y.C., 1953-54; atty. Pa. Power & Light Co., Allentown, 1952, 54-62, asst. counsel, 1962-68, asst. gen. counsel, 1968-71, gen. counsel, 1971-85, sec., 1971-89, v.p., 1973-91; prin. Edward M. Nagel Atty. at Law, 1991—. Exec. dir., dir. Exec. Svc. Corps of Lehigh Valley. Chmn. Mayor's Citizens Adv. Com., Allentown, 1968-72; assoc. counsel, bd. dirs. Minsi Trails council Boy Scouts Am. Served with USNR, 1945-46. Mem. Pa. Bar Assn., Lehigh County Bar Assn. Home: 417 N 28th St Allentown PA 18104-4838

NAGEL, M. CONSTANCE, poet; Office mgr. Remington Rand Dist. Office, Peoria; adminstrv. sec. St. Mary's Hosp., Decatur, Ill.; exec. sec. Great Ctrl. Ins. Co., Peoria; office assoc. State of Ill. Author: (poems) The Second Mile; contbr. poems. Docent hist homes Peoria Hist Soc; team capt Peoria Heart Fund Dr; vol Broadway Theater League, Peoria, Ill., Burnham Hosp Aux, Champaign, Lakeview Mus., Peoria; church organist, dir choirs. Episcopalian.

NAGEL, PETER BORDEN, research scientist; b. Libertyville, Ill., Mar. 16, 1971; s. Mark and Marilyn Nagel. PhD, U. Tex., 1999. Rsch. assoc. Ctr. for Space Rsch., Austin, Tex., 1999—. Fellow Fulbright fellow, Inst. Internat. Edn., 1996. Lutheran. Avocation: cycling. Office: Ctr for Space Rsch Ste 200 3925 W Braker Ln Austin TX 78759 Office Fax: 512-471-3570. Business E-Mail: nagel@csr.utexas.edu.

NAGEL, SIDNEY ROBERT, physics educator; b. N.Y.C., Sept. 28, 1948; s. Ernest and Edith (Haggstrom) N. BA, Columbia U., 1969; MA, Princeton U., 1972, PhD, 1974. Rsch. assoc. Brown U., Providence, 1974-76; asst. prof. physics U. Chgo., 1976-81, assoc. prof., 1981-84, prof., 1984—, assoc. dean divsn. phy. scis., 1997-2000, Louis Block prof., 1998-2000, assoc. dean divsn. phy. scis., 1997-2000, Stein-Freiler disting. svc. prof., 2001—. Contbr. articles to profl. jours. Recipient Klopsteg Meml. Lecture award Am. Assn. Physics Tchrs., 1998; Alfred Sloan Found. fellow, 1978-82. Fellow AAAS, Am. Phys. Soc. (Oliver E. Buckley prize 1999), Am. Acad. Arts and Scis. Home: 4919 S Blackstone Ave Chicago IL 60615-3003 Office: U Chgo 5640 S Ellis Ave Chicago IL 60637-1433

NAGEL, STEVEN R. astronaut, retired military officer; b. Canton, Ill., Oct. 27, 1946; s. Ivan R. and Nagel; m. Linda M. Godwin; 2 children. BS in Aero. and Astro. Engring., U. Ill., 1969; MS in Mech. Engring., Calif. State U., Fresno, 1978. Commd. 2d lt. USAF, 1969; advanced through grades to col.; ret. USAF, 1995; ret. NASA, 1995; pilot F-100 jets 68th Tactical Air Force Squadron, England AFB, La., 1970—71; instr. Laotian Air Force, Utorn RTAFB, Thailand, 1971—72; student test pilot sch. Edwards AFB, Calif., 1975—76; instr. pilot USAF, England AFB, 1976—79; astronaut NASA, 1979—95; dep. dir. ops/ devel., safety, reliability, and quality assurance office Johnson Space Ctr., Houston, 1995; rsch. pilot Aircraft Ops. Divsn., 1996. Decorated Disting. Flying Cross and Air medal with 7 Oak Leaf Clusters USAF; recipient 4 NASA Space Flight medals, Flight Achievement award, AAS, 1992, Outstanding Alumni award, U. Ill., 1992, Disting. Alumni award, Calif. State U. (Fresno), 1994, Lincoln Laureate, State of Ill., 1994. Mem.: Order of Daladiens (life), Phi Eta Sigma (hon.), Sigma Tau (hon.), Sigma Gamma Tau (hon.), Tau Beta Pi (hon.), Alpha Delta Phi (life). Achievements include 4 space missions, 773 hours spent in space contributing to knowledge of that environment. Avocations: flying, music. Office: Astronaut Office NASA Johnson Space Ctr Houston TX 77058

NAGEL, THOMAS, philosopher, educator; b. Belgrade, Yugoslavia, July 4, 1937; came to U.S., 1939, naturalized, 1944; s. Walter and Carolyn (Baer) N.; m. Doris Blum, June 18, 1958 (div. 1973); m. Anne Hollander, June 26, 1979. BA, Cornell U., 1958; B.Phil., Oxford (Eng.) U., 1960; PhD, Harvard, 1963. Asst. prof. philosophy U. Calif., Berkeley, 1963-66; asst. prof. Princeton U., 1966-69, assoc., 1969-72, prof., 1972-80, NYU, 1980—, prof. philosophy and law, 1986—, Fiorello LaGuardia prof. law, 2001—, Univ. prof., 2002—. Vis. prof. Rockefeller U., 1973, U. Mex., 1977, U. Witwatersrand, 1982, UCLA, 1986. Author: The Possibility of Altruism, 1970, Mortal Questions, 1979, The View from Nowhere, 1986, What Does It All Mean?, 1987, Equality and Partiality, 1991, Other Minds, 1995, The Last Word, 1997; author: (with Liam Murphy) The Myth of Ownership, 2002; author: Concealment and Exposure, 2002; assoc. editor: Philosophy and Public Affairs, 1970—82. Guggenheim fellow, 1966, NSF fellow, 1967-69, NEH fellow, 1978, 84-85, vis. fellow All Souls Coll., Oxford, Eng., 1990. Mem. Am. Philos. Assn., Am. Acad. Arts and Scis., Brit. Acad.

NAGEL, WILLIAM LEE, management consultant; b. Youngstown, Ohio, May 17, 1949; s. William Edward and Helen Patricia (Shingledecker) N.; m. Margaret Carol Spotts, June 11, 1978; children: William French, Margaret Alicia. BS, Ohio State U., 1972, MBA, 1979. Program specialist Mahoning County Welfare Dept., Youngstown, 1972-74, Ohio Bur. Vocat. Rehab., Toledo, 1974-76; exec. dir. Epilepsy Assn. of S.E. Ohio, Athens, 1976-77; programmer, analyst Deere & Co., Moline, Ill., 1979-83; mng. assoc. Conley, Canitano & Assocs., Inc., Beachwood, Ohio, 1983-91, Systems Solutions (now Impaxt Tech.), Cleve., 1991—. Info. systems advisor Coop. Extension Svc., Ohio State U., Cuyahoga County, Ohio, 1990—. Area coord. White House Conf. on Handicapped Individuals, Toledo, 1976. Mem. ACM, Internat. DB2 Users Group, N.E. Ohio Visual Basic SIG. Avocations: tennis, golf, classical guitar, public speaking. Home: 20186 Westover Ave Cleveland OH 44116-4065 Office: Impaxt Technologies 19885 Detroit Rd Ste 176 Cleveland OH 44116-1815

NAGENDRAN, SUKUMAR, physician; b. Colombo, Sri Lanka, Jan. 27, 1966; came to U.S. 1987; s. Parayerawar and Wijeyaeswari (Tyagaraja) Nagendran; m. Christine Anne Nagendran, July 11, 1992; children: Sanjay, Amrit, Arjun. MBBS, N. Colombo Med. Coll., Ragama, Sri Lanka, 1987; BA in Biochemistry, Psychology magna cum laude, Rutgers U., 1990; MD, U. Medicine and Dentistry N.J.- Robert Wood Johnson Med. Sch., Piscataway/Camden, N.J., 1994. Cert. Am. Bd. Internal Medicine, Ariz., Minn. Physician Mayo Clinic, Rochester, Minn., 1994-97, Ariz. Physicians Ctr., Phoenix, 1997-98; cons. in internal medicine, 1998-2000; cons. Thunderbird Internal Medicine, 2000-01; dir. RMRS metabolic team Pfizer Pharms. Group, 2001—. Recipient Robert Wood Johnson Alumni award N.J., 1994, Cooper Hosp. Staff award, N.J., 1994. Mem. ACP, AMA. Hindu. Avocations: tennis, cricket, reading. Home: 1434 W Port Au Prince Phoenix AZ 85023-3580

NAGER, CHARLES WILLIAM, obstetrician, gynecologist; b. Wheeling, W.Va., 1956; s. William R. and Jean S. Nager; m. Karen Ditzler Nager, May 19, 1984; children: Andrew, Julie. BS, Stanford (Calif.) U., 1978; MD, UCSD, 1982. Cert. ob/gyn, 1988-98. Intern UCSD Med. Ctr., San Diego, 1982-83; resident ob/gyn, 1982-86; fellow urogynecology and reconstructive pelvic surgery St. George's Hosp., London, 1997—; MD UCSD Med. Ctr., San Diego, 1997, prof. Fellow Am. Coll. Ob-gyn.; mem. Am. Urogynecologic Soc. Office: UCSD Med Ctr 8433 200 W Arbor Dr San Diego CA 92103-9000

NAGER, ELIZABETH EILEEN, clinical social worker; b. Duluth, Minn., May 5, 1956; d. Sam and Fay (Passon) N.; m. Charles S. Greenberg, June 12, 1983. BA in Social Work, U. Wis., 1978, MS in Social Work, 1979. Lic. ind. clin. social worker, Minn. Clin. social worker Mpls. Clinic of Neurology, 1982—2002, Sanctuary: A Ctr for Psychotherapy, Spiritual Direction, and Edn., Inc., Golden Valley, Minn., 2002—. Cons. Lakeview Clinic, Waconia, Minn., 1982—, Minn. chpt. Nat. Multiple Sclerosis Soc., Mpls., 1982—. Contbr. author: Symptom Management in Multiple Sclerosis, 1987. Recipient Ednl. award Multiple Sclerosis Soc., 1990. Mem. NASW. Office: Sanctuary 8100 Wayzata Blvd Golden Valley MN 55426

NAGERA, HUMBERTO, psychiatrist, psychoanalyst, educator, author; b. Havana, Cuba, May 23, 1927; m. Gloria Maria Hernandez, Sept. 8, 1952; children: Lisette Maria, Humberto Felipe, Daniel. B.Sc., U. Havana, 1945; MD, Havana Med. Sch., 1952. Intern, resident in psychiatry Havana U. Hosp., 1950-55; sr. staff, chmn. research Anna Freud's Clinic, London, 1958-68; prof. psychiatry U. Mich., Ann Arbor, 1968-87, chief youth services, 1973-79, prof. emeritus, 1987; prof. psychiatry U. South Fla., 1987—, dir. adolescent inpatient unit and children's inpatient unit, 1987-97, dir. Carter Jenkin Ctr., 2002—. Author: Early Childhood Disturbances, Problems of Developmental Psychoanalytic Psychology, 1966, Vincent Van Gogh, 1966, Basic Psychoanalytic Concepts on the Libido Theory, 1969, Basic Psychoanalytic Concepts on the Theory of Instincts, 1970, Basic Psychoanalytic Concepts of Metapsychology Conflicts, Anxiety, and Other Subjects, 1970, Female Sexuality and the Oedipus Complex, 1975, Obsessional Neurosis: Developmental Psychopathology, 1977, 2nd edit., 1993, The Developmental Approach in Child Psychopathology, 1981; Contbr. articles to profl. jours. Mem. Am. Psychiat. Assn., Internat. Psychoanalytic Assn., Mich. Psychoanalytic Inst. (pres. 1975-77), Am. Assn. Child Psychoanalysis, Cuba Med. Assn. in Exile, South Fla. Tampa Bay Psychoanalytic Soc. (pres. 1992-93). Home: 5202 Dwire Ct Tampa FL 33647-1016 Office: U South Fla Dept Psychiatry 3515 E Fletcher Ave Tampa FL 33613-4706 E-mail: hnagera@hcs.usf.edu.

NAGEY, DAVID AUGUSTUS, physician, researcher; b. Oct. 14, 1950; s. Tibor Franz and Patricia Ann (Griffin) N.; m. Elaine Traicoff, Aug. 7, 1971; children: Stefan Anastas, Nicholas Tibor. Student, Cornell U., 1966-67; BS with distinction, Purdue U., 1969; PhD in Bioengring., Duke U., 1974, MD, 1975. Diplomate Am. Bd. Obstetrics and Gynecology, Am. Bd. Maternal-Fetal Medicine; registered profl. engr., Md. Resident in ob/gyn. Duke U. Sch. Medicine, Durham, N.C., 1975-79, fellow in maternal-fetal medicine, 1979-81; from asst. prof. to prof. U. Md. Sch. Medicine, Balt., 1981-95, prof., 1995-96, asst. dir. divsn. maternal-fetal medicine, 1981-85, dir. divsn. maternal-fetal medicine, 1985-96; assoc. prof., dir. perinatal outreach Johns Hopkins Hosp. and Sch. Medicine, from 1996. Adj. assoc. prof. dept. elec. engring., U. Md., Balt., 1986-92; assoc. prof. dept. population and family health sci., Johns Hopkins U., Balt., 1986—; rsch. assoc. Nat. Inst. Child Health & Human Devel., 1991-92; assoc. examiner Am. Bd. Obstetrics and Gynecology, 1991-92, examiner, 1993-99, Am. Bd. Maternal-Fetal Medicine, 1996-99, mem. perinatal adv. com.; adv. com. chair Md. Inst. for Emergency Med. Svcs. Sys. (MIEMSS), 2000—. Assoc. editor: Computers in Medicine and Biology, 1984—; mem. editl. bd. Jour. Maternal-Fetal Investigation, 1991-98, Ob/Gyn., 1995-98, Birth, 1997—; contbr. articles to profl. jours. ACOG/Syntex grantee, 1987. Fellow Am. Coll. Obstetricians and Gynecologists (com. sci. program 1989-95, chair 1993-94, mem. com. on practice Bulletins, 1995-99, chmn. 1998-99, document rev.-panel obstetrics vice chair 1999-2001, chair 2001—, Md. sect. vice-chair 1995-98, chair 1998-01, Edith Potter lectr. 2002); mem. AAAS, IEEE (healthcare engring. policy com. 1987-91), Nat. Perinatal Assn. (bd. dirs. 1986-90), Bayard Carter Assn. Ob/Gyn. (pres. 2000-01), Md. Ob/Gyn. Soc. (pres. 1990-91, exec. com. 1987—). Avocation: sailing. Home: Sherwood Forest, Md. Died Apr. 21, 2002.

NAGI, CATHERINE RASEH, retired educational administrator, financial planner; b. Bklyn., Oct. 13, 1940; d. Massed and Catherine (Irato) N. BS, Bklyn. Coll., 1962, MS, 1964, postgrad., 1965-67, 76, Hofstra U., 1967-76, St. Johns U., Queens, N.Y., 1976-78. Cert. dist. sch. adminstr., supr., prin., asst. prin., tchr. health/phys. edn., N.Y.; CFP. Tchr. health/phys. edn. Jr. High Sch. 211-Dist. 18, Bklyn., 1962, Bay Ridge High Sch., Bklyn., 1962-63; tchr., acting chair Jr. High Sch. 78-Dist. 22, 1963-70; acting asst. prin. Intermediate Sch. 302-Dist. 19, 1970-71; narcotics edn. tchr. trainer Dist. 19 Bd. of Edn., 1971-73, supr. health/drug edn./svcs., 1973-75; supr. reimbursable programs Dist. 22 Bd. of Edn., 1975-79, supr. comprehensive planning, 1979-84, dep. supt., 1984-90; acting prin. Pub. Sch. 217-Dist. 22, 1980; sch. supt. Dist. 28 Bd. of Edn., Queens, N.Y., 1990-97; ret., 1997. Tchr. Adult Edn./Community Ctrs., N.Y.C., 1959-65; presenter N.Y.C. and N.Y. State Ednl. Confs., Univs.; grant writer N.Y.C. Bd. Edn., 1973—. Co-author, cons. (math. workbook) Get Ahead in Math, 1985; creator, editor (ednl. mag.) Gateways to Learning, 1977-90; creator, developer ednl. data system, 1976; developer first N.Y.C./N.Y. State early identification learning disabilities program, 1975. Named Educator of Yr. Assn. Tchrs. N.Y., 1980; recipient City Coun. Proclamation N.Y.C. Coun., 1991, 97, Legis. resolution N.Y. State Assembly/Senate, 1991, 97, Congl. Record recognition U.S. Congress, 1991, 97, Recognition award Forestdale Foster and Adoptive Parents Assn., Queens, 1992, Queensboro Pres. Proclamation, Supts.' Network Recognition, Fordham U., N.Y.C., Recognition, 112 Pct. Cmty. Coun. Mem. ASCD, Am. Assn. Sch. Adminstrs., N.Y.C. Assn. Supts., N.Y.C. Adminstrv. Women in Edn., Bklyn./N.Y. State Reading Coun./Assn., Thomas Jefferson Dem. Club, Kings County Dem. Com. Avocations: languages, sports, singing, gourmet cooking, collecting stamps, coins and pens. Office: 122 Crispell Rd Krumville NY 12461-5408

NAGI, RAKESH, engineering educator; s. Madan Lal and Brij Mohini Nagi; m. Nidhi Nagi; 1 child Sohum 1 child Karm Vir. B in Engring., U. Roorkee, India, 1987; MS, PhD, U. Md., 1991. Vis. rschr. INRIA-Lorraine, Inst. Nat. Rsch. Info. and Automation, Nancy and Metz, France, 1988—91; rsch. assoc. Inst. Systems Rsch., U. Md., College Park, 1991—93; asst. prof. SUNY, Buffalo, 1993—98, assoc. prof., 1998—. Cons. The Ctr. for Indsl. Effectiveness, Amherst, NY, 1993—; participant 5th Ann. Symposium on Frontiers of Engring. Nat. Acad. Engring., 1999. Contbr. articles to profl. jours. Recipient CAREER award, NSF, 1996—2001. Mem.: Inst. Indsl. Engrs. (chair comm., mfg. divsn. 1998—99, Outstanding Young Indsl. Engr. in Academia award 1999), Soc. Mfg. Engrs. (assoc.; faculty advisor, Milton C. Shaw Outstanding Young Mfg. Engr. award 1999), ASEE. Office: SUNY at Buffalo Dept Indsl Engring 342 Bell Hall Buffalo NY 14260 Office Fax: 716-645-3302. Business E-Mail: nagi@buffalo.edu.

NAGIN, C. RAY, mayor; m. Seletha Nagin; children: Jeremy, Jarin, Tianna. BSc in Acctg. , Tuskegee U., 1978; MBA, Tulane U., 1994. V.p., gen. mgr. Cox Comm. S.E. La. cable sys.; mayor City of New Orleans , 2001—. Mem. bd. dirs. United Way, Convenant Ho.; chmn. United Negro Coll. Fund Walkathon fundraising campaign; pres. 100 Black Men Metro New Orleans. Recipient La. State Bd. Edn. Disting. Bus. Ptnr. award, 1994, Young Leadership Coun. Diversity and Role Model award, 1995, Gambit weekly New Orleanian of Yr. award, 1998. Office: 1300 Perdido St Rm 2E04 New Orleans LA 70112*

NAGLE, DAVID EDWARD, lawyer, columnist; b. Natick, Mass., May 31, 1954; s. Edward G. and Eleanor (Fitz) N.; m. Sue Ellen Southard, Oct. 1, 1988. BS in Govt. and Philosophy, Coll. William and Mary, 1976; JD, U. Richmond, 1981; LLM in Labor Law, Georgetown U., 1983. Bar: Va. 1981. Police officer City of Richmond (Va.), 1976-79; atty. Williams, Mullen & Christian, Richmond, Va., 1981-86; sole practice, 1986-89; ptnr. Hazel & Thomas, 1989-93; columnist Richmond News-Leader, 1986-90; ptnr. LeClair Ryan, Richmond, 1993—. Lectr. U. Richmond Sch. Law and Sch. Bus., Med. Coll. Va. Sch. Hosp. Adminstrn.; appelate practice before U.S. Supreme Ct. and Ct. of Appeals. Contbr. articles to law revs. Mem. Va. Polygraph Bd., 1985-89, Richmond Corrections Bd., 1988-92; dir. Fan Dist. Assn., 1995-97, Monument Ave. Preservation Soc., 1994-97, Richmond Area Assn. Retarded Citizens, 1993-99. Mem. ABA, Va. Bar Assn., Bar Assn. City of Richmond, Am. Arbitration Assn. (arbitrator 1982-94). Office: LeClair Ryan 707 E Main St Richmond VA 23219-2814

NAGLE, JEFFREY KARL, chemist, educator; b. Marietta, Ohio, Mar. 12, 1953; s. Kenneth Lee and Hope (Wells) Nagle; m. Constance Ruth Eaton, June 12, 1976; children: Eric Kenneth, Jannah Allyn. BA, Earlham Coll., 1975; PhD, U. N.C., 1979. Vis. asst. prof. Bucknell U., Lewisburg, Pa., 1979-80; asst. prof. chemistry Bowdoin Coll., Brunswick, Maine, 1980-86; vis. assoc. prof. chemistry U. Calif., Davis, 1986-87; assoc. prof. Bowdoin Coll., Brunswick, 1986-92, prof., 1992—. Fulbright vis. prof. U. Regensburg, Germany, 1993-94; vis. prof. Free U., Amsterdam, The Netherlands, 2000-01. Contbr. articles to profl. jours. Mem. Am. Chem. Soc. Office: Bowdoin Coll Dept Chemistry 6600 College Sta Brunswick ME 04011-8466 E-mail: jnagle@bowdoin.edu.

NAGLE, JOHN FREDERICK, physicist; b. Easton, Pa., Sept. 29, 1939; s. Edgar Eugene and Julia Elizabeth (Meeder) N. BA, Yale U., 1960, MS, 1962, PhD, 1965. Asst. prof. physics Carnegie-Mellon U., 1967-72, asso. prof. physics and biol. scis., 1972-78, prof., 1978—. NATO Fellow, 1965-66; Alfred P. Sloan fellow, 1969-71; Guggenheim fellow, 1979-80. Fellow Am. Phys. Soc. (chair divsn. biol. physics 1992-93); mem. AAUP, Biophys. Soc., Phi Beta Kappa, Sigma Xi. Office: Physics Dept Carnegie-Mellon U Pittsburgh PA 15213

NAGLER, ARNOLD LEON, pathologist, scientist, educator; b. N.Y.C., 1935; s. Max and Esther (Finkel) N.; m. Rosalie Groden, Feb. 18, 1961; children: Stephen Marc, Melissa Sue. BS, CCNY, 1953; MD, NYU, 1958, PhD, 1960. Lic. dir. labs., N.Y. Postgrad. tng. NYU-Bellevue Med. Ctr., 1958-61; research assoc. Mt. Sinai Hosp., N.Y.C., 1960-61; mem. faculty Albert Einstein Coll. Medicine, Bronx, N.Y., 1961—, assoc. prof. pathology, surgery, 1975—; sr. assoc. dean, prof. and chmn. pathology N.Y. Coll. Osteo. Medicine, Old Westbury, 1978—. Trustee Robert Chambers Microsurgery Research Labs., 1978— ; founder, trustee Esther Nagler Dystrophy Research Fund, N.Y. Coll. Osteo. Medicine Mem. editorial bd.: Circulatory Shock; contbr. articles to profl. jours. Chmn. Jericho council Boy Scouts Am., 1971-73; mem. Pres.'s Task Force, 1981— , Nat. Republican Congressional Com., U.S. Senatorial Club; trustee Liberal Jewish Day Sch., N.Y.C.; corp. mem. Nassau-Suffolk Health Systems Agy., mem. Primary Care Task Force. Served with U.S. Army, 1953-55. NIH grantee, 1961— Fellow Am. Soc. Clin. Pathologists; mem. N.Y. Acad. Sci., N.Y. Acad. Medicine, AAAS, Am. Trauma Soc. (founder), Sigma Xi Jewish. Home: 72 Hazelwood Dr Jericho NY 11753-1704 Office: Albert Einstein Coll Medicine 1300 Morris Park Ave Bronx NY 10461-1926 *I was guided by my parents when they were alive and directed by their teachings and precepts after their death to strive to do the best that I possibly may, in any and every endeavor that I undertake. They provided the armoury: Do no harm to anyone— achieve by dedicating yourself to excellence/performance. Do not rally in relegating someone to a lesser state; this is only relative success and is neither satisfying nor worthwhile to the soul, nor is it real.*

NAGLER, HARRIS M. urologic surgeon; b. Bklyn., Dec. 23, 1949; s. Simon H. and Thelma N.; m. Freema Gluck, May 25, 1978; children: Arielle Rachel, Gabrielle Marin. BS, Union Coll., 1971; MD, Temple U., 1975. Diplomate Nat. Bd. Med. Examiners, Am. Bd. Urology. Intern in gen. surgery Columbia-Presbyn. Med. Ctr., N.Y.C., 1975-76, resident in urology, 1976-80, fellow in reproductive medicine, 1980-81; instr. urology Columbia U. Coll. Physicians and Surgeons, N.Y.C., 1981-82, asst. prof. urology, 1982-87, assoc. prof. urology, 1987-89; dir. dept. urology Beth Israel Med. Ctr., N.Y.C., 1989-94, chmn. dept. urology, 1995—, lab. dir., 1996—, chief grad. med. edn. and acad. affairs, 1991—; prof. urology Mt. Sinai Sch. Medicine, 1989-94, Albert Einstein Coll. Medicine, Bronx, N.Y., 1995—. Co-dir. N.Y. Male Reproductive Ctr., 1981-84, dir., 1984-89; chief Vanderbilt Urology Clinic, 1982-87; asst. attending urologist Presbyn. Hosp., N.Y.C., 1982-87, assoc. attending urologist, 1987-89; chmn. dept. urology Beth Israel Med. Ctr., N.Y.C., 1989—, com. of surgery, 1989—, med. bd. com., 1989—, adminstrv. adv. com., 1989—, faculty practice plan adv. coun., 1989-92, chmn. faculty practice plan adv. coun., 1992—. Editl bd. Molecular Andrology, 1989, Assisted Reproductive Reviews, 1991, Gyneologic and Obstetric Investigation, 1992-2000, Fertility and Sterility, 1993-2001. Bd. dirs. Coalition to Save City & Suburban Housing, N.Y.C., 1993-94. Ferdinand C. Valentine fellow, 1981. Fellow ACS, N.Y. Acad. Medicine (pres. sect. urology); mem. AMA, Am. Assn. Med. Colls. (task force inegrating edn. and patient care 1999—), Am. Urol. Assn. (1st prize in clin. rsch. 1982), Am. Soc. Andrology, Soc. Productive Surgeons (sec. 1993, treas. 1993-94, v.p. 1995, pres. 1996), Soc. for Study of Male Reprodn. (pres. 1993), N.Y. County Med. Soc., Harvey Soc., Am. Fertility Soc. (Pacific Coast chpt., urology com. 1984, urology-andrology com. 1985, movies com. 1987—, co-chmn. male reproduction/urology com. 1986-88, award selection com. 1987-88, program com. 1988-90, co-chmn. male reproduction/urology com. 1988-90, program chair N.Y. sect. annual meeting 1991, exec. com. N.Y. chpt., 2000—, urology prize 1985), ACMI (urology prize 1982), Alpha Omega Alpha. Office: Beth Israel Med Ctr 1st Ave at 16th St New York NY 10003

NAGLER, LEON GREGORY, management consultant, business executive; b. Buenos Aires, Argentina, Jan. 29, 1932; (parents Am. Citizens); s. Morris and Jennie (Golden) N.; m. F. Elise Charness, Dec. 20, 1953; children: Jeri Lynn, Sandra Michelle. BS cum laude, Boston U., 1953, MBA, 1954; JD, Cleve. State U., 1961. Bar: Ohio 1961. Tchr. psychology Cameron State Agrl. Jr. Coll., Lawton, Okla., 1956-57; supr. employment and tng. Jones & Laughlin Steel Corp., Cleve., 1957-65; exec. dir. indsl. rels. Charles Corp., 1965-67; dir. personnel ITT Svc. Industries Corp., 1967-72; v.p. personnel Builder Svcs. Corp., Clearwater, Fla., 1972-73; v.p. adminstrn. Damon Corp., Needham Heights, Mass., 1973-77; pres. Nagler & Co., Inc., Wellesley Hills, 1977-95, Nagler, Robins & Poe Inc., 1995—. Mem. Mayfield Heights (Ohio) Planning and Zoning Commn., 1965-67; sec. Mayfield Heights Zoning Bd. Appeals, 1963-65; chmn. Combined Health Fund, Mayfield Heights, 1963; pres. N.E. Ohio region, mem. nat. gov. coun. Am. Jewish Congress, 1972-73; bd. dirs. New Eng. region Anti-Defamation League, 1977-80, Jewish Community Ctr. Greater Boston, 1988—, bd. dirs. Jewish Vocat. Svc., Boston, 1977—, sec., 1980-83, v.p., 1983-88; bd. dirs. Am. Friends Wingate Inst., 1987—, v.p. fin., 1987—; trustee Temple Beth Avodah, Newton, 1978—, v.p., 1979-83, pres., 1983-85; trustee Combined Jewish Philanthropies, Boston, 1985-1992; bd. overseers Combined Jewish Philanthropies, 1992—. Served with AUS, 1955-57. Mem. Ohio, Cleve. bar assns., Soc. for Human Resource Mgmt., Internat. Assn. Corp. and Exec. Recruiters, Boston U. Alumni Assn. (pres. N.E. Ohio 1969-73, nat. council 1973—), Masons, Wyclidd Golf & Country Club (bd. govs. 1999—). Democrat. Office: Nagler Robins & Poe Inc 65 William St Wellesley MA 02481-3802

NAGLER, STEWART GORDON, insurance company executive; b. Bklyn., Jan. 30, 1943; s. Henry and Mary Nagler; m. Bonnie Lawrence, Aug. 9, 1964 (dec.); children: David, Ellen; m. Ronnie Hendler, Jan. 9, 2000. BS summa cum laude, Poly. U., 1963. With Met. Life Ins. Co., N.Y.C., 1963—, exec. v.p., 1983-85, sr. exec. v.p., 1985-93, sr. exec. v.p., CFO, 1993-98, vice chmn. bd., CFO, 1998—. Fellow Soc. Actuaries, Acad. Actuaries. Office: Met Life Ins Co 1 Madison Ave New York NY 10010-3603

NAGLIERI, EILEEN SHERIDAN, special education educator; b. Queens, N.Y., Oct. 3, 1962; d. Raymond J. and Julia C. (Giusani) Sheridan; m. Raymond M. Naglieri, May 2, 1987. BA, St. Joseph's Coll., 1984; MS in Edn., St. John's U., 1987; postgrad., U. Cen. Fla., 1988—. Cert. elem. tchr., reading, mentally handicapped. Tchr. 1st grade Incarnation Sch., Queens Village, N.Y., 1984-87; tchr. exceptional students Denn John Mid. Sch., Kissimmee, Fla., 1987-91; resource compliance specialist Denn John Mid. Sch. and Ventura Elem. Sch., 1991-93; resource compliance specialist, program specialist emotionally handicapped Lakeview Elem. Sch., 1993—2001; program specialist for mentally handicapped and autistic Sch. Dist. Osceola County, Fla., 2001—. Instr. adult basic edn. Vocat., Adult and Community Edn. Osceola County, Kissimmee, 1988-91. Vol. spl. religious edn. program Our Lady Lourdes, Queens, 1976-85, Queens Children's Psychiat. Ctr., 1979-80; vol. counselor autism and devel. delays, Queens, 1984-86. Blanche A. Knauth scholar, 1980. Mem. NEA, Coun. Exceptional Children, Delta Epsilon Sigma. Roman Catholic. Avocations: sailing, reading, music.

NAGORSKI, ANDREW ZYGMUNT, journalist; b. Edinburgh, U.K., May 3, 1947; came to U.S., 1948; s. Zygmunt and Marie (Bogdaszewska) N.; m. Christina Cecilia Kowalska, Jan. 23, 1969; children: Eva, Sonia, Adam, Alexander. BA, Amherst Coll., 1969. Social studies tchr. Wayland (Mass.) H.S., 1969-73; editor Newsweek, N.Y.C., 1973-78, Hong Kong bur. chief, Moscow bur. chief, 1981-82, 95-96, Rome bur. chief, 1982-85, Bonn bur. chief, 1985-88, Warsaw bur. chief, 1990-94, Berlin bur. chief, 1996-99; sr. assoc. Carnegie Endowment for Internat. Peace, Washington, 1988-89; sr. editor Newsweek Internat., 2000—. Author: Reluctant Farewell, 1985, The Birth of Freedom, 1993; contbr. articles to profl. publs. Recipient Best Bus. Reporting from Aboard Overseas Press Club, 1978, Citation Best reporting from abroad, 1980. Mem. Coun. on Fgn. Rels. E-mail: anagorenewsweek.com. Office: Newsweek Internat 251 W 57th St New York NY 10019

NAGORSKI, LEONARD EDWARD, radiologist; b. Omaha, June 12, 1952; s. Edward Leonard and Dorothy Ann (Buman) N.; m. Hilda M. Diaz, Mar. 3, 1979; children: Edward, Patrick, Lani, Stephen. BS in Biology, Creighton U., 1974, MD, 1978. Diplomate Am. Bd. Radiology, Am. Bd. Nuclear Medicine, Am. Bd. Pediatrics, also cert. in nuclear radiology; lic. physician, Nebr.

Commd. 2nd lt. U.S. Army, 1978, advanced through grades to col., 1996; intern, then resident in pediat. Brooke Army Med. Ctr., Ft. Sam Houston, Tex., 1978-81, resident in radiology, 1990-93; resident in nuc. medicine Walter Reed Army Med. Ctr., Washington, 1986-88; chief pediat. U.S. Army MEDDAC, Ft. Leavenworth, Kans., 1982-85, Ft. Sill, Okla., 1985-86, chief nuc. medicine Ft. Hood, Tex., 1988-89, chief diagnositc radiology, 1993-96, chief radiology Ft. Knox, Ky., 1996—. Mem. Am. Coll. Radiology, Tex. Radiology Soc., Soc. Amateur Radio Astronomy. Roman Catholic. Office: Ireland Army Hosp Dept Radiology Fort Knox KY 40121

NAGORSKI, ZYGMUNT, political scientist, writer; b. Warsaw, Poland, Sept. 27, 1912; came to U.S., 1948, naturalized, 1953; s. Zygmunt Julian and Maria Nagorski; m. Marie Bogdaszewski, Nov. 22, 1938; children: Maria, Andrew, Teresa. MA, U. Cracow (Poland), 1935; postgrad., U. Geneva, 1937-38, Internat. Inst. Trade and, Berne, Switzerland, 1937-38. Reporter Chattanooga Times, 1948; editor-in-chief Fgn. News Svc., Inc., N.Y.C., 1949-56; chief Internat. Br. Office Rsch. USIA, Washington, 1956-59; fgn. svc. officer Cairo, 1959-61, Seoul, 1961-64, Paris, 1964-66; spl. asst. to pres. Fgn. Policy Assn., Inc., N.Y.C., 1966-68; mem. profl. staff Hudson Inst., Inc., 1968-69; dir. members meetings program Coun. Fgn. Rels., N.Y.C., 1969-78; v.p. Lehrman Inst., 1978-80; spl. advisor Aspen Inst. Adj. asst. prof. polit. sci. dept. Queens Coll., 1974-75; v.p. Human Resource Svcs., Inc., 1980-81; guest lectr. Wilton Park, Sussex, Eng., Fgn. Svc. Inst., Ctr. Study Human Values, Tanglewood, N.C., Experiment in Internat. Living (Vt.), also nummerous univs.; v.p., dir. exec. seminars programs Aspen Inst. Humanistic Studies, 1981-85; pres. Ctr. Internat. Leadership, N.Y.C., 1986—. Author: Armed Unemployment, 1945, The Psychology of East-West Trade, 1975; co-author U.S.-Japan Economic Relations, 1979; contbr. articles to newspapers and mags. Pres. Am. Friends Wilton Park, 1967-70, 94-96, Mid-Atlantic Club N.Y., 1972-90; bd. dirs. Scarsdale Adult Sch., 1968-72, Internat. U. Found. Served with Polish Army, 1939-45, under French and Brit. command. Decorated Brit. War medal, officer's cross Order of Merit (W. Germany); comdr. Order of Leopold II (Belgium); recipient Meritorious Svc. award USIA, 1965, Outstanding Fgn. Born Am. award Internat. Ctr. N.Y., 1988. Mem. Coun. Fgn. Rels., Am. Polit. Sci. Assn., Internat. Studies Assn., Polish Inst. Arts and Scis., Am. Fgn. Svc. Assn., Fgn. Svc. club, Nat. Press Club (Washington). Democrat. Roman Catholic. Home: 5208 MacArthur Ter NW Washington DC 20016-2617 Fax: (202) 686-3769.

NAGOURNEY, HERBERT, publishing company executive; b. N.Y.C., Jan. 30, 1926; s. Isidor and Tillie (Burstein) N.; children: Adam, Beth, Eric, Sam. BS, Columbia U., 1946, MS, 1947. Pres. Profl. and Tech. Programs, N.Y.C., 1951-65; v.p. Macmillan Co., 1965-69; pres. Quadrangle/New York Times Book Co., 1969-76, New York Times Book Co., N.Y.C., 1971-76, Quartet Books, Inc., N.Y.C. and London, 1976-81, Knowledge Tree Group Inc., 1979-89; v.p., dir. Sci. DataLink, 1981-88, Comtex Sci., 1981-90; pres. Profl. and Tech. Pub. Inc., 1989—, Sci. Datalink, 1990—. Served with AUS, 1944. Home: 320 Joshuatown Rd Lyme CT 06371-3000 Office: 45 Christopher St New York NY 10014-3533 E-mail: hnagourney@aol.com.

NAGPAL, MADAN LAL, biochemist, educator, researcher; b. Kurram, Pakistan, Dec. 15, 1939; m. Raman Verma, Oct. 14, 1943; 1 child, Manish. PhD, Panjab Agrl. U., 1968. Asst. prof. Panjab Agrl. U., Ludhiana, India, 1968-75; rsch. assoc. prof. U. S.C., Columbia, 1987—. Scientist, chemist Dorn Vets. Hosp., Columbia, 1990-95. Rsch. grant U. S.C., 1989-91. Fellow Linnean Soc. of London. Avocations: golf, fishing, travel, photography, hiking. Home: 709 Skylane Dr Hopkins SC 29061 Office: U SC Sch Medicine Garner's Ferry Rd Columbia SC 29209 E-mail: madan@med.sc.edu.

NAGPURWALA, QUAMBER HUSAIN, scientist; b. Ujjain, India, Apr. 14, 1945; s. Yusuf Ali and Khairunnisa N.; m. Zaitoon Naz, Nov. 17, 1975; children: Zeenat, Nuzhat. B of Engring., U. Indore, India, 1968; M in Tech., IIT, Madras, India, 1972. From scientist to asst. dir. Nat. Aerospace Labs., Bangalore, India, 1972-94, dep. dir. India, 1994—. Group head axial compressor group Nat. Aerospace Labs., Bangalore, 1992—, project leader sponsored projects, 1975—; chmn. Internat. Symposium on Aerothermodynamics of Internal Flows, 1996, Internat. Symposium on Fluid Machinery and Fluid Engring., 1996. Contbr. rsch. papers and tech. reports to profl. jours. Deutscher Akademicher Austauschdienst fellow German Acad. Exch. Svc., 1977-79, 1998. Mem. Instn. Mech. Engrs., Aero. Soc. India, Instrument Soc. India (life). Avocations: reading, music, photography. Home: E1 Staff Qtrs Nal Airport 560017 Bangalore India Office: Nat Aerospace Labs Airport Rd 560017 Bangalore India

NAGRIN, DANIEL, dancer, educator, choreographer, lecturer, writer; b. N.Y.C., May 22, 1917; s. Harry Samuel and Clara (Wexler) N.; m. Helen Tamiris, 1946 (dec. 1966); m. Phyllis A. Steele, Jan. 24, 1992. BS in Edn., CCNY, 1940; DFA, SUNY, Brockport, 1991; DHL, Ariz. State U., 1992; studied dance with Martha Graham, Anna Sokolow, Helen Tamiris, Mme. Anderson-Ivantzova, Nenette Charisse and Edward Caton, studied acting with Miriam Goldina, Sanford Meisner and Stella Adler, , 1936-56. Tchr. Silvermine Guild Art, New Canaan, Conn., 1957-66, SUNY, Brockport, 1967-71, U. Md., College Park, 1970, Davis Ctr. Performing Arts, CCNY, 1973-75, Nat. Theatre Inst., Eugene O'Neill Found., Waterford, Conn., 1974, Hartmann Theatre Conservatory, Stamford, 1975-77; long-term resident tchr., Nat. Endowment for Arts sponsorship U. Hawaii, 1978-80, tchr., 1981, Bill Evans Dance Workshop, Seattle, 1981; prof. dance dept. Ariz. State U., Tempe, 1982-92; tchr. grad. liberal studies program Wesleyan U., Middletown, Conn., 1984, Dance Workshop for Movement Rsch., N.Y.C., 1984, Improvisation Workshop, Seattle, 1985, Improvisation, Choreography and Acting Technique for Dancers, Seattle, 1985, Dance Workshop, Glenwood Springs, Colo., 1990; prof. emeritus dance Ariz. State U., 1992. Tchr. summer sessions Conn. Coll., New London, 1959, 74; Am. Dance Festival at Conn. Coll., 1960, 77, Duke U., Durham, N.C., 1978, 80, 82, 87, 88, 92, Balasaraswati/Joy Ann Dewey Beinecke Chair Dising. Tchg., 1992; summer dance program Conn. Coll., 1979, E. La Tour Dance Workshop, Sedgewick, 1982, 83; dance workshop U. Minn. at Mpls., 1984, Stanford U., 1990; co-dir. Tamiris-Nagrin Summer Dance Workshop, Sedgewick, 1960-61, (with Tamiris) summer dance session C. W. Post Coll., Greenville, N.Y., 1962-63; dir. summer dance workshop Johnson (Vt.) State Coll., 1972, 73, 75, 76. Dancer (featured dance soloist on Broadway) Annie Get Your Gun, Lend an Ear, Touch and Go, Plain and Fancy (Billboard Donaldson award, 1954), (appearance in film) Just for You, (adapted and performed one-man theater piece) The Fall, from novel by Albert Camus, 1977—79, choreographer (solo works) Spanish Dance, 1948, Man of Action, 1948, Strange Hero, 1948, Indeterminate Figure, 1957, With My Eye and With My Hand, 1968, Jazz: Three Ways, 1958, 1966, Path-Silence, 1965, Not Me, But Him, 1965, The Peloponesian War, 1967—68, Untitled, 1974, Ruminations, 1976, Getting Well, 1978, Poems Off the Wall, 1981, Apartment 18C, 1993, Crosscurrents, 1997, Lost and Never Found, 1998, Someone for Theater X, Tokyo, Japan, What Did You Say?, 2001, others, (for groups) Faces from Walt Whitman, 1950, An American Journey, 1962, asst. choreographer (original Broadway prodns.) Up in Central Park, Stovepipe Hat, Show Boat, Annie Get Your Gun, By the Beautiful Sea, others; dir.: (off-Broadway) Volpone, 1957, The Firebugs, 1960, The Umbrella, 1961, Emperor Jones (Boston, 1963, others; (film choreography) His Majesty O'Keefe; actor: (video) The Art of Memory, 1985; (plays) Three Stories High, others; extensive touring U.S., Europe, The Pacific and Japan, 1957—84, conceived and directed (videos) Steps, 1972, The Edge is Also a Circle, 1973, Nagrin Videotape Library of Dances, 1985; author: How to Dance Forever: Surviving Against the Odds, 1988, Dance and the Specific Image: Improvisation, 1993, The Six Questions: Acting Technique for Dance Performance, 1997, Choreography and the Specific Image: Nineteen Essays and a Workbook, 2001. With spl. svcs. Army Airforce, 1942-43. Grantee Rebekah Harkness Found., 1962, Logan Found., 1965, N.Y. State Coun. on Arts and Nat. Found. for Arts and Humanities, 1967-68, N.Y. State Coun. on Arts, 1971-72, 73-74, 75-76, 76-77, 78-79, 80-81, Anne S. Richardson Fund, 1971, 73, 74, 75, 76, 78, Nat. Endowment for Arts, 1975, 79, 81, 83, Ariz. State U., 1983, 84, 85, 86, 88; CAPS fellow N.Y. State Coun. on Arts, 1977-78; fellow NEA, 1977-78, 80, 82, 83, 90, 91, Minn. McKnight Nat. fellow, 1996-97; commd. ballet Rebekah Harkness Ballet Found., 1986. Mem. Actors' Equity, Phi Kappa Phi (hon.). Avocation: reading. Home and Office: 208 E 14th St Tempe AZ 85281-6707 Fax: (480) 829-3933. E-mail: nagrin@imap2.asu.edu.

NAGTALON-MILLER, HELEN ROSETE, humanities educator; b. Honolulu, June 27, 1928; d. Dionicio Reyes and Fausta Dumbrigue (Rosete) N.; m. Robert Lee Ruley Miller, June 15, 1952. BEd, U. Hawaii, 1951; Diplôme, The Sorbonne, Paris, 1962; MA, U. Hawaii, 1967; PhD, Ohio State U., 1972. Cert. secondary education educator. Tchr. humanities Hawaii State Dept. Edn., Honolulu, 1951-63; supr. student tchrs. French lab. sch. Coll. of Edn. U. Hawaii, 1963-66, instr. French, coord. French courses Coll. Arts and Scis., 1966-69; teaching asst. Coll. Edn. Ohio State U., Columbus, 1970-72; instr. French lab. sch. Coll. Edn. U. Hawaii, Honolulu, 1974-76; adminstr. bilingual-bicultural edn. project Hawaii State Dept. Edn., 1976-77; coord. disadvantaged minority recruitment program Sch. Social Work, U. Hawaii, 1977-84; coord. tutor tng. program U. Hawaii, 1984-86; program dir. Multicultural Multifunctional Resource Ctr., 1986-87; vis. prof. Sch. Pub. Health, ret. U. Hawaii, 1987-92. Bd. dirs. Hawaii Assn. Lang. Tchrs., Honolulu, 1963-66, Hawaii Com. for the Humanities, 1977-83; mem. statewide adv. coun. State Mental Health Adv. Com., Honolulu, 1977-82; task force mem. Underrepresentation of Filipinos in Higher Edn., Honolulu, 1984-86. Author: (with others) Notable Women in Hawaii, 1984; contbr. articles to profl. jours. Chairperson edn. and counseling subcom. First Gov.'s Commn. on Status of Women, Honolulu, 1964; vice chairperson Honolulu County Com. on the Status of Women, 1975-76, Hawaii State Dr. Martin Luther King Jr. Commn., Honolulu, 1982-85; pres. Filipino-Am. Hist. Soc. of Hawaii, 1980—; mem. Hawaii State Adv. Com. to U.S. Commn. on Civil Rights, 1981—, chairperson, 1982-85; bd. dirs. Japanese Am. Citizens League Honolulu chpt., 1990—, mem. Hawaiian Sovereignty com., 1994-98, Protect Our Constitution, Hawaii; mem. Pro-Choice Polit. Action Com., 1989-92. Women of Distinction, Honolulu County Com. on Status of Women, 1982; recipient Nat. Edn. Assn. award for Leadership in Asian and Pacific Island Affairs, NEA, 1985, Alan F. Saunders award ACLU in Hawaii, 1986, Disting. Alumni award U. Hawaii Alumni Affairs Office, 1994. Mem. Filipino Am. Nat. Hist. Soc., Filipino Coalition for Solidarity, Gabriela Network (Hawaii chpt.), Filipino Cmty. Ctr., Philippine Centennial Coordinating Com./Hawaii, NOW, Alliance Française of Hawaii, Rainbow Peace Fund. Democrat. Avocations: social-political advocacy, reading, classical music, theater, literary presentations. Home and Office: 47-543 Halemanu St Kaneohe HI 96744-4604 E-mail: rlrmiller@earthlink.net.

NAGY, CHRISTA FIEDLER, biochemist; b. Marienbad, Czech Republic, July 8, 1943; d. Herbert A. Fiedler and Anna C. (Gluth) Rathmann; m. Bela Imre Nagy, Aug. 22, 1969; 1 child, Byron. BS in Biology, Fairleigh Dickinson U., 1967, MS in Biochemistry, 1974; PhD in Biochemistry, Rutgers U., 1981. Sr. scientist Hoffmann-La Roche Inc., Nutley, N.J., 1981-88, assoc. rsch. investigator, 1988-95; contract med. writer, 1996-97; asst. dir. preclin. rsch. Eisai Inc., Teaneck, N.J., 1997-98, asst. dir. clin. pharmacology, 1998—2002, assoc. dir. clin. pharmacology NJ, 2002—. Mem. AAAS, N.Y. Acad. Scis., Am. Soc. Biol. Chemists, Am. Med. Writers Assn., Drug Info. Assn., Am. Soc. Clin. Pharmacology and Therapeutics, DIA. Roman Catholic. Avocations: traveling, skiing, tennis, hiking. Office: Eisai Inc Glenpointe Ctr E 300 Franklin Burr Blvd Teaneck NJ 07666-6741

NAGY, IMRE V. civil engineer, educator; b. Fuzesgyarmat, Hungary, Nov. 2, 1927; s. Istvan V. Nagy and Eszter Dajka; m. Imrene Szucs Jolan; children: Imre, Laszlo, Edina, Zoltan. MS in Civil Engring., Tech. U., Budapest, 1952, PhD in Civil Engring., 1956; DSC, Hungarian Acad. Scis., Budapest, 1963. Head Dept. foe Edn. Tech. U., Budapest, 1952-53; prin. investigator U. Moscow, 1953-56; cons. engr. Design Office, Budapest, 1957-58; vice dir. Rsch. Inst., 1958-64; dep. head Tech. U., 1964—. Author: (book) Hydrology, 1965, Probability and Statistics in Hydrology, 1984, Internat. Trade in Hazardous Wastes, 1996. Sec. gen. Comm. of Hydr. Science, Budapest, 1958-63; sec. Hung Hydrological Soc., 1960-62; chmn. Nat. Comm. for Environment Protection, 1964-92. Recipient Order of Labour award Hungarian Govt., 1984. Mem. Hungarian Acad. (mem. water resources com. 1957—), Hungarian Soc. Environ. Protection (chmn. 1964—). Home: Etele U 19 H-1119 Budapest Hungary Office: Technical U Budafoki U 4 Kmf 8 H1111 Budapest Hungary E-mail: vnagy@rektori.bme.hu.

NAGY, LOUIS LEONARD, engineering executive, researcher; b. Detroit, Jan. 15, 1942; s. Alex and Helen Nagy; m. Dianna M. Skarjune, Aug. 5, 1961; children: Tammy, Kimberly, Kristine, Amanda. BSEE, U. Mich., Dearborn, 1965; MSEE, U. Mich., Ann Arbor, 1969, PhDEE, 1974. Registered profl. engr. Rsch. engr. U. Mich., Ann Arbor, 1962-69; staff rsch. engr. GM R & D Ctr., Warren, Mich., 1969-98; sr. staff rsch. engr. Delphi Rsch. Labs., 1999—. Contbr. articles to profl. jours.; patentee in field. Bd. dirs. Convergence Ednl. Found., Birmingham, Mich., 1990-97, Convergence Transp. Electronics Assn., Birmingham, 1990-97. Recipient 1998 R&D 100 award R&D Mag. Fellow IEEE; mem. Convergence Fellowship (bd. dirs. 1988-96), Vehicular Tech. Soc. (Spl. Recognition award 1979, Avant Garde award 1986, Paper of Yr. 1975), Soc. Automotive Engrs., Tau Beta Pi, Eta Kappa Nu. Avocations: electronics, antennas, radar, automotive radar, microwaves. Office: Delphi Rsch Labs MC 483-478-105 51786 Shelby Pkwy Shelby Township MI 48315

NAGYS, ELIZABETH ANN, environmental issues educator; b. St. Louis; d. Dallas and Miriam (Miller) Nichols; m. Sigi Nagys, Feb. 7, 1970; children: Eric M., Jennifer R., Alex E. BS., So. Ill. U. Extension, Edwardsville, 1970. Cert. tchr., Mo., Ill. Announcer Sta. KMTY, Clovis, N.Mex., 1970-71; substitue tchr. Ritneour Sch. Dist., Overland, Mo., 1977-78; instr. biology, environ. issues Southwestern Mich. Coll., Dowagiac, Mich., 1988-92; exec. v.p. Profl. Sound Designers, Goshen, Ind., 1994-96; customer svc. coord. Meijer, Inc., 1995-96; constrn. sales adminstr. Trans Eastern Homes, Weston, Fla., 1997-98; constrn. adminstr. Trafalger Assocs., 1998-99. Reviewer textbooks Harcourt, Brace & Co., 1993; notary pub. State of Fla., 1999—. Active Nat. Arbor Day Found.; mem. Hazardous Waste Com. for Elkhart County, Ind., 1991—94; asst. dir. South Fla. Folk Festival, 1998—; bd. dirs. United Meth. Ch., Marvin Park, 1979—84; coord. United Meth. Women, 1980—87; bd. dirs., corr. sec. Broward Folk Club, 1998—2002; charter mem. Holocaust Meml. Mus.; assoc. mem. Art Inst. Chgo. Mem. AAUW (v.p. Goshen 1994-96), Nat. Audubon Soc., Nat. Women's History Mus. (charter mem.), Sierra Club, Welcome Wagon Club. Avocations: reading, gardening.

NAH, FIONA FUI-HOON, information technology educator, researcher; BSc, Nat. U. Singapore, 1988, BSc with honors, 1989, MSc, 1992; PhD, U. B.C., 1997. Asst. prof. Purdue U., West Lafayette, Ind., 1996-98, U. Nebr., Lincoln, 1998—. Contbr. articles to profl. jours. E-mail: fnah2@unl.edu.

NAHAS, GABRIEL GEORGES, pharmacologist, educator, writer; b. Alexandria, Egypt, Mar. 4, 1920; came to U.S., 1947, naturalized, 1962; s. Bishara and Gabrielle (Wolff) N.; m. Marilyn Cashman, Feb. 13, 1954; children: Michele, Anthony, Christiane. BA, U. Toulouse, France, 1937, MD, 1944; MS, U. Rochester, 1949; PhD, U. Minn., 1953; DSc (hon.), U. Uppsala, 1988. Rockefeller Found. fellow U. Rochester, 1947-48; Mayo Found. fellow Mayo Clinic, 1949-50; rsch. fellow U. Minn., 1950-53, mem. faculty, 1955-57; mem. staff Walter Reed Army Inst. Rsch., 1957-59; faculty George Washington U. Med. Sch., 1957-59; mem. faculty Columbia U. Coll. Physicians and Surgeons, N.Y.C., 1959-92, prof. anesthesiology, 1962-92; prof. emeritus, 1992; rsch. prof. anesthesiology NYU Med. Sch., N.Y.C., 1992—. Disting. vis. scientist Addiction Rsch. Ctr., NIDA, 1987; adj. rsch. prof. anesthesiology U. Paris, 1968-71; fellow Coun. Circulation and Basic Sci., Am. Heart Assn., 1961—; mem. com. on trauma NRC, 1964-66; mem. adv. bd. Cousteau Soc.; cons. commn. on narcotics, drug control program UN. Author 700 sci. publs. and 40 books and monographs in English and French. Decorated Presdl. Medal of Freedom with gold palm Govt. of U.S.; comdr. Legion of Honor, Croix de Guerre with 3 palms (France), Order Brit. Empire, Order Orange Nassau Netherlands, Silver medal City of Paris; recipient Medal of Honor, Statue of Liberty Centennial, 1986; Fulbright scholar, 1966. Fellow AAAS, N.Y. Acad. Sci.; mem. Am. Physiol. Soc., Harvey Soc., Am. Soc. Pharmacology and Exptl. Therapeutics, Soc. Physiol. Langue Française, French Acad. Medicine (laureate 1995, 96), Brit. Pharm. Soc., Sigma Xi. Achievements include research on med. instrumentation, pharmacology Tham, acid-base regulation, pharmacology of cannabis and cocaine, drug dependence, consciousness, college problem on drug dependence. Home: 40 E 74th St New York NY 10021-2732 Office: NYU Med Ctr Dept Anesthesiology 550 1st Ave New York NY 10016-6402 *Courage is to stand by one's own conviction unheeding the trends of fashion or pressure groups. It is to suffer alone and be scorned for a lifetime. But, in the end, one will hear "he was right!".*

NAHAVANDI, AMIR NEZAMEDDIN, retired engineering firm executive; b. Tehran, Iran, Apr. 6, 1924; came to U.S., 1956, naturalized, 1970; s. Ahmad and Fatima (Razaghi) N. Electromech. Engring. degree, Tehran U., 1947; MS in Mech. Engring, Carnegie Inst. Tech., 1957, PhD, 1960. Registered profl. engr., Pa. Engr. Tehran U., 1948-50; head design group Nat. Iranian Oil Co., Tehran, 1950-56; adv. engr. Westinghouse Electric Corp., Pitts., 1957-66; prof., chmn. dept. mech. engring. U. Vt., 1967-68; research prof. N.J. Inst. Tech., 1969-77; prof. engring. and applied Sci. Columbia U., N.Y.C., 1977-81; chief scientist Electronic Assocs., Inc., West Long Branch, N.J., 1981-82; pres. Mazen, Inc., Long Branch, 1982-92. Decorated Sci. medal 1st degree Iran). Fellow ASME; mem. N.Y. Acad. Scis., Phi Kappa Phi, Sigma Xi, Tau Beta Pi. Achievements include research and devel. in dynamics of steam generators and boiling systems, dynamic and accident analysis of conventional and nuclear power plants, vibration of reactor structures, thermal pollution of lakes and rivers, solid-fluid interaction, development of analytical models for stock market forecasting. Home: 532 Meridian Way Carlsbad CA 92009-5400

NAHIGIAN, ROBERT JOHN, real estate development broker; b. Boston, Feb. 24, 1956; s. John Moses and Theresa (Zeytoundjian) N.; m. Donna P. Dewar, Oct. 23, 1993; children: Jessica Lee, Kimberly Patricia. BA cum laude, Lehigh U., 1978; MS in Urban Planning, Columbia U., 1980. Cert. real estate mediator Mass. Property mgr. Auburndale (Mass.) Realty Co., 1972-77; jr. planner Bethlehem (Pa.) Redevel. Authority, 1978; planner, tech. analyst Perkins & Will Archtl. Firm, N.Y.C., 1978-80; city planner, econ. developer City of Bowie, Md., 1980-81; v.p. The Norwood Group, Inc., Burlington, Mass., 1981-88; v.p., dir. The Robbins Group, Cambridge, 1988-89; pres. Auburndale Realty Co., Newton, 1989—. Dir., lectr. real estate studies Northeastern U., Boston, 1982-93; instr. real estate Boston U., 1994—; lectr., spkr. at convs. in field; Boston U. lectr. U. of Hong Kong Polytech.; 1st SIOR spkr. at Mexico's Nat. Bd. Realtors Conv., 1997; 1st U.S. Real Estate Practitioners & SIOR to be nat. conv. spkr. at Latin America's First Real Estate Conf., Bogota, Columbia, 1998; invited lectr. Czech Republic, Poland; mem. Greater Boston Real estate Bd. Commerical Broker Assn. Investment Affairs rep., bd. dirs. 2002—. Co-author: Master Office Leasing, 1993, rev. edit., 2000; contbr. articles to profl. jours. Mem. Wang Ctr. for the Performing Arts, Boston, 1985. Recipient Cert. of Appreciation, The Exch. Club, 1991, Alumni award Lehigh U., 1993, N.E. Constrn. Show, So. Calif. Constrn. Show, Mex. Nat. Bd. Realtors, 1997, Plaque for Grateful Appreciation for serving as pres. New England chpt. SIOR from 1998-99, Disting. Achievement in cml. leasing Greater Boston Real Estate Bd., 1999, Greater Boston Real Estate Bd. medal of appreciation New Eng. chpt. Soc. Indsl. and Office Realtors, 1998-99, Broker Achievement Bronze award, Broker Achievement Gold award, Comml. Broker Assn., 2000, 2001Comml. Leasing Achievement Gold award, 2001, Indsl. Deal of Yr. award, 2001; named Nat. Real Estate Instr. of Yr., Soc. Indsl. and Office Realtors, 1994, First Mass. Comml. Broker as Cert. Instr., Banker and Tradesman Top 125 Bus. Leaders in Mass. for 1999, 1st Comml Broker as Cert. Mass. Real Estate Mediator, 2001. Mem.: Comml. Brokers Assn. (govt. affairs rep. to Mass. Assn. Realtors 2002, rep. to Commonwealth of Mass. 2002), Nat. Assn. Indsl. and Office Parks (New Eng. chpt. membership com. 1993—96, membership com. chmn. 1996, exec. com. 1996, cert. appreciation Mass. chpt.), Am. Soc. Real Estate (counselors of real estate 1996, nat. conv. spkr. 1997, com. mem. nat. edn. com., nat. presdl. task force 1998—2000, vice chmn. pub. rels. com. 1998—2000, nat. bd. dir. 2001, nat. spl. task force 2001, nat. chmn. pub. rels. & comm. 2001—), Soc. Indsl. and Office Realtors (nat. vice chmn. office courses 1993—94, edn. exec. com. 1993—94, nat. regional v.p. 1994—96, nat. exec. com. 1994—96, nat. bd. dir. 1994—96, nat. chmn. edn. com. 1994—98, ex officio edn. fund 1995—97, nat. chmn. instrs. com. 1994—97, nat. chmn. edn. exec. com. 1995—97, nat. nominating com. 1995—98, Presdl. edn. task force 1995—99, bd. dir. New Eng. chpt. 1995—, pres. New Eng. chpt. 1998—99, spl. adv. and immediate past pres. 2000—, nat. budget and fin. com. 2000—, v.p. nat. com. programs 2001, nat. convention co-chair 2001, nat. bd. dirs. 2001—, nat. vice chmn. designation courses edn. com. 2002—, nat. nominating com. 2002—, sr. instr., instrs. com. and office mktg. forum, task force indsl. office leasing handbook, property evaluation forum, expert roundtable com., cert. appreciation, cert. profl. edn. com., cert. appreciation as outgoing nat. ednl. chair), Mass. Assn. Realtors (mem. various coms. 2001—, govt. affairs com. for CBA), Nat. Assn. Realtors (cert. of appreciation 1992, Mass. mediation officer award 2001), Counselors of Real Estate (bd. dirs. 2002), Algonquin Club, Lehigh Club (class '78 pres. 1993—98). Republican. Mem. Armenian Apostolic Ch. Home: 365 Highland St Weston MA 02493-2624 Office: Auburndale Realty Co PO Box 66125 335 Auburn St Newton MA 02466-1902

NAHIGIAN, RUSSELL ARA, mathematician; b. Brookline, Mass., Apr. 20, 1934; s. Moses Hovenes and Rose (Ashjian) N.; m. Carol Jane Paboojian, July 16, 1960; children: Thomas, Susan, Laura. BA in Math. disting. mil. grad., Colby Coll., Waterville, Maine, 1956; postgrad., MIT, 1957; MS in Engring. Mgmt., Northeastern U., Boston, 1971. Technician Minn-Honeywell, Brighton, Mass., 1960-61; analyst Edgerton, Germeshausen & Grier, Boston, 1961-65; sci. programmer Minn-Honeywell, 1965-67; sr. sci. programmer Service tech. Corp., Cambridge, Mass., 1967-70; mathematician U.S. Dept. Transp., 1970-85; currier Anacomp Inc., Medford, Mass., 1986-96; data entry staff Prostaff, Adecco, Waltham, 1996-99, Boston Co., Woburn, 1996-99; pricer MVP Sports, Wilmington, 1999—. Tchr. computer programming U.S. Dept. Transp., Cambridge, 1970-85. Contbr. articles to profl. jours. Deacon First Armenian Ch., Belmont, Mass., 1994-96; eagle scout, 1952. 1st lt. USAF, 1956-60. Named Father of the Yr., First Armenian Ch., 1995. Republican. Home: 3 Monadnock Rd Arlington MA 02476-8026 Office: 326 Ballardvale St Wilmington MA 01887-1012

NAHIGYAN, DEBI ROGERS, marketing professional; b. Meriden, Conn., Sept. 9, 1960; d. Edward Clarence and Geri Floyd Rogers; m. Peter Dana Nahigyan, May 28, 1983; children: Pierce, Derek, Holly. BSBA, Cen. Conn. State U.; MBA, Pepperdine U., 1988. Dir. mkgt. Allergan Inc., Irvine, 1981-92; dir. mktg. Summit Tech., Waltham, Mass., 1993-94; dir. managed care mktg. CIBA Vision Ophthalmics - Novartis, Duluth, Ga., 1994-97; dir. mktg. Autonomous Techs., Orlando, 1997-99, PacifiCare, Cypress, Calif., 1999-2000; dir. mktg., cons., dir. rsch. Gallup Orgn., Irvine, 2000—02; group accounts Allergan, Inc., 2002—. Contbr. articles to profl. jours. Mem. Am. Mktg. Assn., Med. Mktg. Assn., Soc. Regulatory Affairs Profls., Mktg. Rsch. Assn. Avocations: writing, kickboxing. Office: 575 Anton Blvd Costa Mesa CA 92714 E-mail: nahigyan-debi@pacific-com.com.

NAHMAN, NORRIS STANLEY, electrical engineer; b. San Francisco, Nov. 9, 1925; s. Hyman Cohen and Rae (Levin) N.; m. Shirley D. Maxwell, July 20, 1968; children: Norris Stanley, Vicki L., Vance W., Scott T. BS in Electronics Engring, Calif. Poly. State U., 1951; MSE.E., Stanford U., 1952; PhD in Elec. Engring, U. Kans., 1961. Registered profl. engr., Colo. Electronic scientist Nat. Security Agy., Washington, 1952-55; prof. elec. engring., dir. electronics rsch. lab. U. Kans., Lawrence, 1955-66; sci. cons., chief pulse and time domain sect. Nat. Bur. Standards, Boulder, Colo., 1966-73, chief time domain metrology, sr. scientist, 1975-83, group leader field characterization group, 1984-85; v.p. Picosecond Pulse Labs, Inc., Boulder, 1986-90, scientific advisor, co-chair tech. adv. bd., 1990—; cons. elec. engr., 1990—; prof., chmn. dept. elec. engring. U. Toledo, 1973-75;; prof. elec. engring. U. Colo., Boulder, 1966—; affiliate staff Los Alamos (N.Mex.) Nat. Lab., 1990—. Disting. lectr., prin. prof. Ctr. Nat. d' Etude des Telecomm. Summer Sch., Lannion France, 1978; disting. lectr. Harbin Inst. Tech., Peoples Republic China, summer 1982; mem. faculty NATO Advanced Study Inst., Castelvecchio, Italy, 1983, Internat. Radio Sci. Union/NRC; chmn. Internat. Intercomm. Group Waveform Measurements, 1981-90, chmn. Commn. A, 1985-86. Contbr. rsch. articles profl. jours.; patentee in field. Asst. scoutmaster Longs Peak coun. Boy Scouts Am., 1970-73, 75-89. With U.S. Mcht. Marine, 1943-46, U.S. Army, 1952-55. Ford Found. faculty fellow MIT, 1962; Nat. Bur. Standards sr. staff fellow, 1978-79; recipient Disting. Alumnus award Calif. Poly. State U., 1972, Order of Arrow Boy Scouts Am., 1976. Fellow IEEE (life), Internat. Sci. Radio Union; mem. Instrumentation and Measurement Soc. of IEEE (admstrv. com. 1982-84, editorial bd. Trans., 1982-86, Andrew H. chi Best Tech. Paper award 1984, Tech. Leadership and Achievement award 1987), Am. Assn. Engring. Edn., U.S. Mcht. Marine Veterans

World War II, Am. Legion, Calif. Poly. State U. Alumni Assn. (life), Stanford U. (life), U. Kans. (life), Am. Radio Relay League Club (life), Sigma Pi Sigma, Tau Beta Pi, Eta Kappa Nu, Sigma Tau, Sigma Xi. E-mail: nsnahman@ieee.org.

NAHMIAS, STEVEN, finance educator, writer; b. New York, Ny, June 19, 1945; s. Morris and Elizabeth Nahmias; m. Vivian Saukwan Loh, Aug. 21, 1988; children: Mitchell Aaron; m. Susan Lynn Esses, Aug. 13, 1972 (div. July 1, 1979). BA, Queens Coll., New York, NY, 1963—66; BS, Columbia U., New York, NY, 1966—68; MS, Northwestern U., Evanston, IL, 1968—71, PhD, 1972. Sci. programmer, analyst IBM Corp., Armonk, NY, 1967—68, 1970—70; grad. rsch., tchg. asst. Northwestern U., Evanston, Ill., 1968—72; asistant prof. U. Pitts., Pittsburgh, Pa., 1972—76, assoc. prof., 1976—79, Santa Clara U., Santa Clara, Calif., 1979—81, prof., 1981—; dir. Competitive Mfg. Inst., 1991—98. Vis. assoc. prof. Stanford U., 1978—79, vis. prof., 1982—82, Ga. Inst. Tech., Ga., 1986—86, U. Tel Aviv, 1987—87; chmn. Dept. of Decision and Info. Sciences, Sch. of Bus., Santa Clara U., Santa Clara, Calif., 1987—91; vis. scholar U. Haifa, 1994—94, Stanford U., 1994—94. Mem.: Arrangements Com., Fifth Internat. Symposium Multivariate Stats., U. Pitts., Omega Rho (hon.), Sigma Xi (hon.), Alpha Pi Mu (hon.). Achievements include development of inventory control system for spare parts stocking policies for Chanslor and Lyon Corporation (a subsidary of the Lex Corporation which is involved in the automotive aftermarket) (1980); developed and analyzed mathematical models for internal mail delivery systems for Xerox Corporation (1979-1980); assisted in analysis and development of integrated multi-level supply and distribution system for Shaklee Corporation (1982-1984); developed model and software for planning the optimal size of the salesforce for Hyundai Electronics America (1984-1985); preliminary model for the inclusion of a battery or pumped storage facility into an electrical system for Lotus Consulting Group on a contract with Electric Power Research Institute (1985); model for planning work force sizing based on queuing theory for Smith-Kline Beecham Pharmaceuticals (1992); worked with Avulet, a start-up based in Santa Clara, to develop queuing models to determine capacity requirements for web-based training systems (1999). Avocations: jazz trumpeter, jazz trumpeter, jazz trumpeter, biking. Home: 332 Arden Road Menlo Park CA 94025 Office: Santa Clara University Santa Clara CA 95053 Office Fax: 408-554-5157. E-mail: snahmias@mailer.scu.edu.

NAHRWOLD, DAVID LANGE, surgeon, educator; b. St. Louis, Dec. 21, 1935; s. Elmer William and Magdalen Louise (Lange) N.; m. Carolyn Louise Hoffman, June 14, 1958; children: Stephen Michael, Susan Alane, Thomas James, Anne Elizabeth. AB, Ind. U., 1957, MD, 1960. Diplomate Am. Bd. Surgery, Am. Bd. Thoracic Surgery. Intern, then resident in surgery Ind. U. Med. Ctr., Indpls., 1960-65; postdoctoral scholar in gastrointestinal physiology VA Ctr., UCLA, 1965; asst. prof. surgery Ind. U. Med. Sch., 1968-70; assoc. prof. Coll. Medicine Pa. State U., 1970-73; vice-chmn. dept. surgery Pa. State U., 1971-82, assoc. provost, dean health affairs, 1981-82, prof., chief divsn. gen. surgery, 1974-82; Loyal and Edith Davis prof., chmn. dept. surgery Northwestern U. Med. Sch., Chgo., 1982-97; surgeon-in-chief Northwestern Meml. Hosp., 1982-97; pres., CEO Northwestern Med. Faculty Found., Inc., 1996-99; prof. surgery, exec. assoc. dean clin. affairs Northwestern U. Med. Sch., 1997-99, prof. emeritus, 1999—. Mem. Nat. Digestive Disease Adv. Bd., 1985—89; bd. dirs. Am. Bd. Surgery, vice chmn., 1994—95, chmn., 1995—96; bd. dirs. Northwestern Healthcare Network; mem. exec. bd. Am. Bd. Med. Spltys., 1997—, pres., 2002—; mem. exec. com. Accreditation Coun. for Grad. Med. Edn., 1999—2000. Editor emeritus Jour. Laparoendoscopic Surgery, 1997—; mem. editl. bd. Surgery, 1981-94, Archives of Surgery, 1983-93, Digestive Surgery, 1986-99, Am. Jour. Surgery, 1994-2000, Jour. Gastrointestinal Surgery, 1996-2000, Current Opinion in Gen. Surgery, Jour. Lithotripsy and Stone Disease, 1988-92; contbr. articles to profl. jours. With M.C., U.S. Army, 1966-68. Fellow: ACS (bd. govs. 1992—98, vice chmn. 1994—96, chmn. bd. govs. exec. com. 1996—98, interim dir. 1999—2000, bd. regents, Disting. Svc. award 2001), Philippine Coll. Surgeons (hon.); mem.: AMA, Chgo. Surg. Soc. (pres. 1993—94), Chgo. Med. Soc., We. Surg. Assn., Soc. Univ. Surgeons, Soc. Surgery Alimentary Tract (pres. 1989—90, trustee), Soc. Clin. Surgery (sec. 1984—88), Internat. Biliary Assn., Ill. Surg. Soc., Ill. State Med. Soc., Internat. Fedn. Surg. Colls. (hon.; treas. 1999—2002), Gastroenterology Rsch. Group, Collegium Internat. Chirurgiae Digestive (pres. U.S. chpt. 1988—90), Ctrl. Surg. Assn. (sec. 1994—97, pres.-elect 1997—98, pres. 1998—99, pres. Found. 2002—), Assn. Surg. Edn., Assn. Acad. Surgery, Am. Surg. Assn. (2d v.p. 1993—94), Am. Phys. Soc., Alpha Omega Alpha, Sigma Xi. Office: Dept Surgery Galter 10-105 251 E Huron St Chicago IL 60611-2908 E-mail: dnahrwol@nmh.org.

NAIDICH, THOMAS PAUL, neuroradiologist, educator; b. Bklyn., Apr. 8, 1944; s. James and Rose (Bitko) N.; m. Rochele Miriam Pudlowksi, Feb. 2, 1975 (div. Nov. 1981); children: 1 child, Sandra Rebecca; m. Michele W. Levin, Dec. 29, 1990. BA, Cornell U., 1965; MD, NYU, 1969. Diplomate Am. Bd. Radiology; cert. Added Qualification Neuroradiology. Intern Bronx (N.Y.) Mcpl. Hosp. Ctr., 1969-70; resident in radiology Montefiore Hosp., Bronx, 1970-73; fellow in neuroradiology NYU Sch. Medicine, 1973-75; prof. radiology, neurosurgery and anatomy and functional morphology . Mt. Sinai Med. Ctr. NYU, 1998—, dir. neuroradiology, 1998—, vice chmn. radiology for acad. affairs, 2001—, Irving and Dorothy Regenstreif Rsch. prof. of neurosci., 2002—; asst. prof. Albert Einstein Coll. Medicine, Bronx, 1975-77; from asst. prof. to assoc. prof. Mallinckrodt Inst. Radiology, St. Louis, 1978-80; from assoc. prof. to prof. Northwestern U. Sch. Medicine, Chgo., 1980-88; clin. prof. neuroradiology U. Miami (Fla.) Sch. Medicine, 1988-98; dir. neuroradiology Bapt. Hosp. Miami, 1988-98. Author: (with R. M. Quencer) Clinical Neurosonography, 1987; (with Valavanis, Schubiger) Clinical Imaging of the Cerebello-Pontine Angle, 1987; (with Daniels, Haughton) Cranial and Spinal Magnetic Ressonance Imaging, 1987; editor-in-chief Neuroradiology, 1980-91, chmn. editl. bd., 1991-93; assoc. editor Surg. and Radiol. Anatomy, 1991-97; founding editor Internat. Jour. Neuroradiology, 1994-00; contbr. articles to profl. jours. Recipient John Caffey award Soc. Pediatric Radiology, 1983. Mem. Am. Soc. Neuroradiology (treas. 1991-93, Cornelius Dyke award 1975), Am. Soc. Pediatric Neuroradiology (pres. 1994-95), European Soc. Neuroradiology (hon.) Avocation: antique furniture. Office: Mt Sinai Med Ctr Dept Radiology Box 1234 1 Gustave Levy Pl New York NY 10029 E-mail: thomas.naidich@mountsinai.org.

NAIDORF, LOUIS MURRAY, architect; b. Los Angeles, Aug. 15, 1928; s. Jack and Meriam (Abbott) N.; m. Dorise D. Roberts, June 1948 (div.); children: Victoria Beth Naidorf-Slifer; m. Patricia Ann Shea, June 1, 1968 (div.); m. Patricia Ruth Allen, Dec. 6, 1992 (dec.). BA, U. Calif., Berkeley, 1949, MA, 1950; Doctorate (hon.), Woodbury U., 2000. Registered architect, Calif. Designer Welton Becket Assocs., L.A., 1950-51, Pereira and Luckman, L.A., 1951-52; project designer Welton Becket Assocs., 1952-55, sr. project designer, 1955-59, v.p. asst., dir. design, 1959-70, sr. v.p., dir. rsch., 1970-73; sr. v.p., design prin. Ellerbe Becket Assocs., 1973-95; dean Sch. Architecture and Design Woodbury U., 1990-2000. Mem. peer rev. panel Nat. Endowment Arts, 1995—; vis. lectr. Calif. Poly. Sch. Architecture, San Luis Obispo, 1975-82; instr. UCLA Sch. Architecture, 1985, UCLA Landscape Archtl. Program, 1980-85, Otis-Parsons, L.A., 1986-92. Prin. works include Capitol Records Bldg., Century City, Los Angeles, Hyatt Regency, Dallas, Restoration Calif. State Capitol Bldg. Bd. dirs. Inst. for Garden Studies, L.A., 1986—, ARC, 2000; trustee Woodbury U., 2000. Recipient Honor award Nat. Trust for Hist. Preservation, 1985. Fellow AIA (bd. dirs. Los Angeles chpt. 1977-79, Silver Medal 1950, Nat. Honor award 1985, Educator of Yr. 1997). *Leadership often requires decisions based on limited information. Course corrections can be made but only after action is taken because you can't steer a car that isn't moving.*

NAIFEH, JAMES O. (JIMMY NAIFEH), state legislator, speaker of the house; b. Covington, TN, June 16, 1939; m., three children. , U. Tennessee, Knoxville, TN. Pres. Covington Wholesale Comp., Inc., Covington, TN; partner Naifeh Realty Comp.; congressman TN General Assembly, Dist.-81, Nashville, 1978—; majority floor leader TN General Assembly, 1979-83, majority leader, 1983-85, speaker of the house, 1986—. Formerly chrm., Rural West TN Dem. Caucus, House Ethics Comm., House Rules Comm.; former v-chrm., Select Oversight Comm. on Corrections; mem., House/Senate Joint Managment Comm. Former pres., mem., Bd. Dirs. Covington-Tipton County Chamber of Comm., mem., South Tipton Chamber of Comm., Bd. Dirs. TN Wholesale Grocers' Assn.; former pres., Covington Rotary Club, Tipton County U. TN Alumni Assn.; bd. mem., First State Bank - Covington, TN; bd. govrns. dirs., ALSAC - St. Jude Childrens' Research Hosp. Recipient of NCSL Leadership Awd, 1990; TN State Employees Assn, 1990; Legislator of the Year Awd, by TN Assn. of Human Resource Agencies, TN Dist. Attr. Generals' Conf., TN School Bds. Assn., and TN Court Clerks' Assn. Am. Legion Post # 67. Episcopal Home: PO Box 97 Covington TN 38019-0097 Office: 19 Legislative Plz Nashville TN 37243*

NAIK, PRASAD ANAND, marketing educator; b. Bombay, July 15, 1962; arrived in U.S., 1991; BSChemE, U. Bombay, 1984; MBA, Indian Inst. Mgmt., 1987; PhD, U. Fla., 1996. Sales exec. Dorr Oliver, Bombay, 1984-85; brand exec. SmithKline Beecham, Delhi, India, 1987-91; asst. prof. mktg. U. Calif., Davis, 1996—2002, assoc. prof. mktg., 2002—. Contbr. articles to profl. jours. Recipient Frank Bass award Inst. Ops. Rsch., 1999. Mem. Am. Mktg. Assn., Assn. Consumer Rsch., Inst. for Ops. Rsch. and Mgmt. Scis. Office: U Calif One Shields Ave Davis CA 95616

NAIMARK, ARNOLD, medical educator, physiologist, educator; b. Winnipeg, Man., Can., Aug. 24, 1933; s. Harvey and Lisa N.; m. Barbara Jean Alder, Feb. 28, 1960; children: David, Mila. MD, BSc in Medicine, U. Man., Winnipeg, 1957, MSc, 1960; postgrad., U. London, 1962-63, U. Calif., 1960-62; LLD (hon.), Mt. Allison U., 1986, U. Toronto, 1997. Registrar in medicine Hammersmith Hosp., London, 1962-63; asst. prof. physiology U. Man., 1963-64, assoc. prof., 1965-66, prof., 1967-71, acting head dept. physiology, 1966-67, head dept., 1967-71, dean Faculty Medicine, 1971-81, pres. and vice chancellor, 1981-96, prof. medicine and physiology, 1971—, dir. Ctr. for Advancement Medicine, 1996—. Dir. Health Scis. Ctr., 1971-99; cons. to govt. agys. and founds.; chmn. Can. Health Svcs. Rsch. Found., Can. Biotech. Adv. Com.; dir. Can. Imperial Bank of Commerce, Urban Idea Ctr., Inspiraplex Ltd.; mem. adv. coun. Order of Can., 1988-89; v.p., Can., Inter-Am. Orgn. for Higher Edn., 1993-95. Contbr. articles to profl. jours. Mem. nat. hon. bd. dirs. Juvenile Diabetes Fedn. Internat. Can. Lt. Royal Can. Arty., 1950-53. Decorated officer Order of Can.; recipient Queen Elizabeth Silver Jubilee medal; Symons medal Commonwealth Univs.; medal in physiology U. Man., 1955; Stefansson Meml. prize, 1957; Prowse prize in clin. rsch., 1959; Isbister scholar, 1950-53, 54-56 Fellow Royal Coll. Physicians, AAAS, Royal Soc. Can. (G. Malcolm Brown award 1987, com. univ. rsch. 1989-91); mem. Can. Med. Assn., Can. Physiol. Soc., Am. Physiol. Soc., Can. Soc. Clin. Investigation, Med. Rsch. Soc. Gt. BRit., Assn. Chairmen Depts. Physiology, Can. Tb and Respiratory Disease Assn., Assn. Commmonwealth Univs. (coun. 1985-91), Assn. Univs. and Colls. Can. (pres. 1986-88), Am. Heart Assn., Assn. Commonwealth Univs. (chmn. 1988), Can. Soc. for Acad. Medicine. Office: U Man Ctr for Adv Medicine 730 William Ave Ste 230 Winnipeg MB Canada R3E 3J7

NAIMARK, GEORGE MODELL, marketing and management consultant; b. N.Y.C., Feb. 5, 1925; s. Myron S. and Mary (Modell) N.; m. Helen Anne Wythes, June 24, 1946; children: Ann, Richard, Jane. BS, Bucknell U., 1947, MS, 1948; PhD, U. Del., 1951. Rsch. biochemist Brush Devel. Co., Cleve., 1951; dir. quality control Strong, Cobb & Co., Inc., 1951-54; dir. sci. svcs. White Labs., Inc., Kenilworth, N.J., 1954-60; v.p. Burdick Assocs., Inc., N.Y.C., 1960-66; pres. Rajah Press, Summit, N.J., 1963—, Naimark and Barba, Inc., Florham Park, 1966—, Naimark & Assocs., Inc., Florham Park, 1994—; dir. Alteon, Inc., 2000—. Bd. dirs. Alteon Inc., Ramsey, N.J. Author: A Patent Manual for Scientists and Engineers, 1961, Communications on Communication, 1971, 3d edit., 1987, A Man Called Skeeter, 1996; patentee in field; contbr. articles in profl. jours. With USNR, 1944-46. Fellow AAAS, Am. Inst. Chemists; mem. Am. Chem. Soc., N.Y. Acad. Scis., Am. Mktg. Assn. Home: 87 Canoe Brook Pky Summit NJ 07901-1404 Office: Naimark & Barba Inc 248 Columbia Tpke Ste 1 Florham Park NJ 07932-1210

NAIMI, SHAPUR, cardiologist, educator; b. Tehran, Iran, Mar. 28, 1928; came to U.S., 1959; s. Mohsen and Mahbuba (Naim) n.; m. Amy Cabot Simonds, May 11, 1963; children: Timothy Simonds, Susan Lyman, Cameron Lowell. MB, ChB, Birmingham (Eng.) U., 1953. Diplomate Royal Coll. Physicians (London), Royal Coll. Physicians (Edinburgh), Am. Bd. Internal Medicine (subsplty. bd.cardiovascular disease). House physician Royal Postgrad. Med. Sch. London, 1955; sr. house officer Inst. Diseases of the Chest, London, 1956; fellow in grad. tng. New Eng. Med. Ctr. and MIT, 1961-64; cardiologist Tufts New Eng. Med. Ctr., Boston, 1966—; dir. intensive cardiac care unit, 1973—; assoc. prof., 1970-93; prof., 1993—. Contbr. articles to profl. jours. Recipient disting. Inst. award, 1972, Tchg. citation, 1976, Excellence in Tchg. award, 1982 (all Tufts Med. Sch.). Fellow royal Coll. Physicians (Edinburgh), ACP, Am. Coll. Cardiology; mem. Am. Soc. Exptl. Biology and Medicine, AHA, Mass. Med. Soc., Country Brookline, Cohaset Yacht. Home: 265 Woodland Rd Chestnut Hill MA 02467-2204 also: 55 Lothrop Ln Cohasset MA 02025-1425 Office: 750 Washington St Boston MA 02111-1526

NAIMOLI, VINCENT JOSEPH, diversified operating and holding company executive; b. Paterson, N.J., Sept. 16, 1937; s. Ralph A. and Margaret R. (Calabrese) N.; children— Christine, Tory Ann, Alyson, Lindsey. BSM.E., U. Notre Dame, 1959; MSM.E., N.J. Inst. Tech., 1962; MBA, Fairleigh Dickinson U., 1964; grad. Advanced Mgmt. Program, Harvard Bus. Sch., 1974. With Continental Group, 1965-77, v.p., gen. mgr. ops., 1975-77; pres., chief oper. officer Allegheny Beverage Corp., Balt., 1977-78; sr. v.p., group exec. Jim Walter Corp., Tampa, Fla., 1978-81; group v.p. packaging Anchor Hocking Corp., Lancaster, Ohio, 1981-83; chmn. bd., pres., chief exec. officer Anchor Glass Container Corp., 1983-89; chmn., pres., CEO Anchor Industries Internat., Tampa, Fla., 1990—; chmn., chief exec. officer Electrolux Corp., Atlanta, 1990-91; chmn., CEO Doehler Jarvis Corp., Toledo, 1991-95; CEO Ladish, Inc., Milw., 1992-95; chmn., pres., CEO Harvard Industries, 1993-97; mng. gen. ptnr., CEO Tampa Bay Devil Rays, 1992—. Bd. dirs. JLM Industries. Roman Catholic. Office: Anchor Industries Internat 1 Tropicana Dr Saint Petersburg FL 33705-1703

NAIR, BALA RADHAKRISHNAN, engineer; b. Belgaum, Mysore, India, Feb. 14, 1936; came to U.S., 1967; s. Cherukatt Balakrishnan and Malamal Parvathy Nair; m. Indira Rajagopal Menon, Dec. 9, 1963; children: Nandita, Sarita. BS in Mech. Engring., U. Madras, 1959; MS in Indsl. Engring., Kansas State U., 1969. Jr. engr. Larsen & Toubro, Ltd., Bombay, 1959-60; trainee AEC, 1960-61, scientific officer, 1961-64; asst. engr. Voltas Ltd., 1964-67; sr. engr. Crane Co., Chgo., 1969-72; design engr. Rockwell Internat., Pitts., 1972-74; sr. prin. engr. Westinghouse Electric Corp., 1978—85, engring. mgr., 1986—. Patentee in field; contbr. articles to profl. jours. Recipient grand prize Excellence in Design, Design News Mag., Chgo., 1988, R & D Mag. award, 1993. Mem. ASME, Am. Nuclear Soc., Laser Inst. Am., Titanium Devel. Assn. Republican. Hindu. Avocations: reading, travel. Home: 610 Charles Dr Irwin PA 15642-1987 Office: Westinghouse Govt Svcs Co Cheswick PA 15024

NAIR, KRISHNAKUMAR R. software engineer, researcher; b. Trivandrum, Kerala, India; s. Raghavan N.S. and Vijayamma R. Nair; m. Shyama R. Nair; 1 child Srijith K. BS, U. Kerala, 1980; MTech, Cochin U. Sci & Tech., 1988; MS, U. Ill., Chgo., 1994. Mem. rsch. and devel. group Ctrl. Elecrochem. Rsch. Inst., Karaikudi, 1983-90; computer cons. U. Ill., Chgo., 1990-95; engring. intern Motorola, Inc., Boynton, Fla., 1995; mem. tech. staff Lucent Technolologies, Naperville, Ill., 1996; software engr. Motorola, Inc., Boynton Beach, 1996-98, sr. software engr., 1998-99, lead/staff software engr., 1999—2002, sr. staff software engr., 2002—. Referee, reviewer tech. articles Motorola, Jours., Confs. Contbr. Mem.: AAAS, IEEE (sr.), Inst. Engrs. India, Assn. Computing Machinery. Avocations: reading, sports, numismatics. Home: 4327 Juniper Ter Boynton Beach FL 33436-3024 Office: Motorola Inc 3301 Quantum Blvd # Q10C Boynton Beach FL 33426-8622 E-mail: kknair@hotmail.com.

NAIR, RAMACHANDRAN P.K. agroforestry educator, researcher; b. Trivandrum, Kerala, India, Mar. 12, 1942; came to U.S., 1987. s. Krishna Kittu Pillai and Parukutty Amma; m. Vimala Devi Pillai, Aug. 29, 1973; children: Bindu, Deepa, Rekha. BS in Agr., Kerala Agrl. U., 1961, MS in Agr., 1968; PhD, Pantnagar U., India, 1971; Dr. Sci. Agr., U. Goettingen, W. Germany, 1978; D (hon.) , Kyoto U., 2002. Research asst. Kerala Agrl. U., 1961-66, lectr. in agronomy, 1966; post-doctoral fellow Rothamsted Experimental Sta., Harpenden, Eng., 1971-72; agronomist ICAR (CPCRI), Kasaragod, Kerala, 1972-76; Humboldt fellow U. Goettingen, 1976-78; prin. sci. Internat. Centre for Rsch. in Agroforestry, Nairobi, Kenya, 1978-87; prof. agroforestry U. Fla., Gainesville, 1987-2001, Disting. prof., 2001—. Cons., rschr. numerous orgns. Author: Intensive Multiple Cropping with Coconuts in India, 1979, Agroforestry Species: A Crop Sheets Manual, 1980, Soil Productivity Aspects of Agroforestry, 1984, An Introduction to Agroforestry, 1993; co-editor: Agroforestry: A Decade of Developments, 1987; editor: Agroforestry Systems in the Tropics, 1989, Agroforestry Systems, 1982—, chief editor, 1994. Recipient Internat. Soil Sci. award, 2001, Internat. Agronomy award, 2000. Fellow Am. Soc. Agronomy (chair divsn. A-6 internat. agronomy 1995-96), Nat. Acad. Agrl. Scis. India, Soil Sci. Soc. Am.; mem. Internat. Soil Sci. Soc., Internat. Soc. Tropical Foresters, Soc. Am. Foresters. Office: U Fla 118 Newins Ziegler Hall Gainesville FL 32611-0410 E-mail: pknair@ufl.edu.

NAIR, RAMACHANDRAN S. urologist; b. Vazhoor, Kerala, India, Feb. 23, 1937; came to U.S., 1966; s. K.K. Sankunny and R. Ponnamma Nair; m. Rema A. Nair, Aug. 18, 1971; children: Giju R., Deeptha. B.Sc., Madras U., Cochin, Kerala, 1957; M.B.BS, Madras U., Pondicherry, India, 1963; MBA, Madonna U., Livonia, Mich., 1998. Diplomate Am. Bd. Urology. Urologist Millard Filmore Hosp., Buffalo, 1971-74; chief of urology VA Hosp., Topeka, 1974-75; pvt. practice urology Mercy Meml. Hosp., Monroe, Mich., 1976—; pres. Monroe Urology Assocs., 1978—. Bd. dirs. Mercy Meml. Hosp., Monroe, 1991—98; chmn. Mercy Meml. Hosp. Found., 2001—. Fellow: ACS, Am. Coll. Internat. Physicians, Internat. Coll. Surgeons; mem.: Mich. State Med. Soc. (del. 1989—, chair utilization com. 1985—), Monroe County Med. Soc. (sec. 1981—, pres. 1989—91, 2001—), Mich. Urol. Soc., Am. Urol. Assn., Rotary. Republican. Hindu. Avocations: photography, travel. Home: 245 Maywood Ave Monroe MI 48162 Office: Monroe Urology Associates PO Box 2165 Monroe MI 48161 E-mail: rnair@tdi.net.

NAIR, SARASWATHI, physician, pathologist; b. Cochin, Kerala, India, Sept. 1, 1951; came to U.S., 1977. d.Govindan Padmanabhan and Malathi N.; m. Kesav Gopal Nair, Sept. 14, 1977; children Sidharth, Sangeetha. MD, Patrice Lumumba Friendship U., Moscow, 1975. Pathologist Norwalk (Conn.) Hosp., 1985—, pathologist, dir. hematology, 1993—, pathologist, dir. immunology, 1995; pathologist dir., cons. Lab. Silver HIll Hosp., New Canaan, Conn., 1988—. Sci. vol. elementary. schl., 1992,-94, 97-98. Fellow Coll. Am. Pathology; mem. Am.Soc. Clin. Pathologists, State, County Medical Socs., AMA Office: Norwalk Hosp Maples St Norwalk CT 06856 E-mail: saraswathi.nair@norwalkhealth.org.

NAIR, VELAYUDHAN, pharmacologist, medical educator; arrived in U.S., 1956, naturalized, 1963; m. Jo Ann Burke, Nov. 30, 1957; children: David, Larry, Sharon. PhD in Medicine, U. London, 1956, DSc, 1976. Research assoc. U. Ill. Coll. Medicine, 1956-58; asst. prof. U. Chgo. Sch. Medicine, 1958-63; dir. lab. neuropharmacology and biochemistry Michael Reese Hosp. and Med. Center, Chgo., 1963-68, dir. therapeutic research, 1968-71. Vis. assoc. prof. pharmacology FUHS/Chgo. Med. Sch., 1963—68, vis. prof., 1968—71, prof. pharmacology, 1971—, vice chmn. dept. pharmacology and therapeutics, 1971—76, dean Sch. Grad. and Postdoctiral Studies, 1976—, v.p. for rsch., 1999—, disting. prof., 2001; vis. prof. Harvard U., 1994, Johns Hopkins Sch. Medicine, 1995. Contbr. articles to profl. jours. Recipient Morris Parker award, U. Health Scis./Chgo. Med. Sch., 1972. Fellow: AAAS, Am. Coll. Clin. Pharmacology, N.Y. Acad. Scis.; mem.: AAUP, Internat. Soc. Devel. Neurosci., Am. Coll. Toxicology, Internat. Soc. Chronobiology, Soc. Neurosci., Soc. Exptl. Biology & Medicine, Pan Am. Med. Assn. (coun. on toxicology), Royal Inst. Chemistry (London), Brit. Chem. Soc., Am. Chem. Soc., Soc. Toxicology, Radiation Rsch. Soc., Am. Soc. Clin. Pharmacology & Therapeutics, Am. Soc. Pharmacology & Exptl. Therapeutics, Internat. Soc. Biochem. Pharmacology, Internat. Brain Rsch. Orgn., Cosmos Club (Washington), Alpha Omega Alpha, Sigma Xi. Office: FUHS Chgo Med Sch 3333 Green Bay Rd North Chicago IL 60064-3037 *Success like happiness is relative and can only be gauged by one's own standards and ideals. There is probably no universal formula for either of them, but I have been guided by the following tenets: Dedication and committment to one's responsibilities and in the conduct of everyday life, honesty and sincerity in personal relations. One must have tolerance for those in less fortunate situations. As one grows older, one recognizes that no one makes it alone. As for me, I have received help from many; some of whom I can never repay except by passing on the gift which I was privileged to share. Above all, a faith that looks beyond the immediate helps to bear the inevitable ups and downs in life.*

NAIR, VELUPILLAI KRISHNAN, cardiologist; b. Kerala, India, Dec. 30, 1941; came to U.S., 1973; s. Veupillai and Bharathy Nair; m. Sathy C. Nair, Apr. 22, 1971; children: Parvathy, Pradeep. BSc, Kerala U., Trivandum, India, 1961, MB BS, 1965, MD, 1971. Diplomate Am. Bd. Internal Medicine, Am. Bd. Cardiology. Intern, resident, fellow in cardiology Bergen Pines County Hosp., Paramus, N.J.; asst. prof. N.Y. Med. Coll. Lincoln Hosp., Bronx, 1979-80; cardiologist, dir. cardiology svc. Somerset (Pa.) Hosp., 1980—, chief of med. dental staff, 1990-93. V.p. bd. dirs. Somerset Hosp., 1997, Somerset Health Svcs., 2000—; clin. asst. prof. MCP Hahnemann Med. Coll., 1996—. Former pres. Somerset County divsn. Am. Heart Assn.; bd. dirs. Somerset Hosp. Fellow ACP, Am. Coll. Cardiology; mem. AMA, Pa. Med. Soc., Somerset County Med. Soc. (former pres.), Soc. Hypertension, Soc. Echocardiography, Cardiac Club (advisor). Avocations: reading, tennis, travel. Office: 223 S Pleasant Ave Somerset PA 15501-2188 E-mail: vknair@pol.net.

NAIRN, CHARLES EDWARD, librarian, pastor, religious educator; b. Columbus, Ohio, Aug. 26, 1926; s. William Elden and Hariette (Basbagill) N.; m. Margaret Lucille Prentiss, Aug. 2, 1952; children: Elizabeth, Barbara Kay, Stephen, Michael, Ronald. BA in Philosophy and Religion, Kent (Ohio) State U., 1950, MLS, 1951; BDiv in Philosophy and Religion, Oberlin (Ohio) Coll., 1958; MDiv in Philosophy and Religion, Vanderbilt U., 1972. With various chs., 1960-84; libr., tchr. philosophy and religion Lake Superior State U., 1968-88, ret., 1988. Leader Boy Scouts Am. With USN, 1944-46. Mem. Am. Acad. Religion, Am. Philosophy Assn., Soc. Bibl. Lit., Soc. Christian Philosophy, Metaphys. Soc. Am., Sault Ste. Marie Internat. Libr. Assn. (co-bd. dirs. 1968-88), Mich. Libr. Assn. (rep. Sault Ste. Marie and Lansing, Mich. chpt.). *Life is a gift from God. In life we discover and come to know that, as Jesus taught and lived, this Being in whom we live, and move and have our being is "Our Father." Thus we and all forms of life are one in the family of God.*

NAISMITH, JAMES POMEROY, civil engineer; b. Dallas, Aug. 4, 1936; s. James S. and Frances (Pomeroy) N.; m. Beverly Mozeney, Feb. 2, 1957; children: Anne Elizabeth, James Mozeney, Robert Alan, Margaret Lynn. B of Civil Engring., Cornell U., 1958, MS, 1959. Registered profl. engr. Tex., N.Y., Mo.; registered pub. land. surveyor Tex. Instr. Cornell U., Ithaca, N.Y., 1959-60; asst. engr. Calif. Water Pollution Control Bd., San Luis Obispo, 1960-61; engr. to chief exec. officer Naismith Engrs. Inc., Corpus Christi, Tex., 1961-89; mgr., dist. engr. San Patricio Mcpl. Water Dist., Ingleside, 1989—. Trustee Calallen Ind. Sch. Dist., Corpus Christi, 1985-91; chmn. Zoning Bd. of Adjustment, Corpus Christi, 1970. Fellow ASCE (dir. 1982-85); mem. ASCE Tex. Sect. (pres. 1973). Office: San Patrico Mcpl Water Dist PO Box 940 Ingleside TX 78362

NAISMITH, ROBERT WILLIAM, investment banker; b. N.Y.C., Sept. 26, 1944; s. Robert Thomas and Elizabeth Margaret (Hoyer) N.; m. Claudia Rae Bialkowski, Nov. 19, 1966; children: Robert Thomas II, Nadia Rae, Arianne Ameila. BS, East Stroudsburg U., 1966; PhD, Pa. State U., 1971. Assoc. prof. Pa. State U., 1971-82; co-founder, exec. v.p. Pharmakon Rsch., Internat., Inc., Waverly, Pa., 1981-87; v.p. Scherer Healthcare, Inc., Atlanta, 1986-95; chmn. The MicroCap Fund, N.Y.C., 1996; mng. dir. Healthcare BlueStone Capital Ptnrs., 1996-98; chmn., CEO, mng. dir. Genome Securities Inc, 1998-99; chmn., CEO eMedSecurities, Inc., 2000—. Founder, pres., CEO, Biofor, Inc., Waverly, 1986-95; chmn. William Naismith & Assocs., Scranton, 1995—; bd. dirs. Penn Security Bank Trust, St. Charles Pharms.; adj. prof. Case Western Res. U., 1988—, Pa. State U., 1984—, U. Scranton, 1996—. Trustee William Harvey Med. Rsch. Found., London, 1996—; Cmty. Med. Ctr., Scranton, 1980-92; dir. United Neighborhood Svcs., Scranton, 1982-84. Avocations: jogging, downhill skiing. Office: 800 James Ave Ste 201 Scranton PA 18510-1551 also: 27 E 40th St New York NY 10016 E-mail: rwn@emedsecurities.com.

NAITO, MICHIRO, financial analyst; b. Tokyo, Aug. 13, 1957; s. Takeshi and Teruko Naito; m. Anna Moeling. PhD, U. Tex., 1992. Rsch. asst. U. Tex., Austin, 1988—92; analyst BZW Securities Japan, Tokyo, 1994—97; sr. analyst Merrill Lynch Japan, 1998—99; sr. investment analyst Tchr. Retirement Sys. Tex., Austin, 2000—.

NAITO, TAKESHI, investment company executive; b. Yakata, Japan, May 17, 1929; s. Shoji and Tsune (Haseba) N.; m. Yasuko Minami, Nov. 22, 1956; children: Naomi (Mrs. J.W. Morris Jr.), Mary Ann Goto, Walter Ray Akira. BA, Osaka (Japan) U. Commerce, 1953; postgrad., UCLA, 1958. Dir. Seibu Securities, L.A., 1962; dir., mng. dir. Yamaichi Securities, Tokyo, 1980-87; chmn., CEO Yamaichi Investment Trust Mgmt. Co., Ltd., 1988-92, statutory auditor, 1992-95; ptnr. Naito & Morris Consulting, Kawasaki and Oakland, Calif.; sr. mng. dir. Yamaichi Internat. (Am.), N.Y.C., 1983—88. Mem.: Aoyama (Japan) Golf Club, Tsuru Country Club, Fgn. Corr. Club (Tokyo), Scarsdale Golf (N.Y.). Home and Office: 1-1 Ogura, D-2104 Saiwai-Ku Kawasaki 212-0054 Japan Office: 65 Schooner Hill Oakland CA 64618 Fax: 510-549-0498.

NAJAR, LEO MICHAEL, conductor, arranger, educator; b. Grand Rapids, Mich., Jan. 29, 1953; s. Ammiel George and Claire Elizabeth (Grant) Najar; children: John Andrew, Erik. MusB in Viola Performance, U. Mich., 1976, MusM in Viola Performance, 1977. Asst. condr. Flint (Mich.) Symphony Orch., 1975-80; dir. Flint Community Music Sch., 1976-80; music dir. Saginaw (Mich.) Symphony Orch., 1980—; conductor The Gazebo Orch., 1993—; gen. dir. Ohio Chamber Orch., Cleve., 1998-2000; artistic dir. New Am. Orch., 2000—; prin. guest condr. Nat. Symphony Orch. El Salvador, 2001—. Lectr. music Wayne State U., Detroit, 1983-86; guest asst. prof. music U. Mich., Ann Arbor, 1986-87; artistic adviser Dearborn (Mich.) Symphony Orch., 1987-89, Traverse Symphony Orch., 1988-90; spl. artistic adviser Flint Inst. Music, 1991-92; asoc. prof. Ctrl. Mich. U., 1995-97; artistic dir. Midland Symphony Orch., 1996-97. Prodr., host radio program Preludio: The String Thing, 1978-80; co-prodr. After Glow, 1994-96; prodr.: Preludio, 1996-99. Mem. adv. panel Mich. Coun. for Arts, 1989-91; rev. panel Mich. Coun. for Arts & Cultural Affairs, 1996-2000. Mem. Am. Symphony Orch. League (various coms. 1980—, Helen M. Thompson award 1982), Mich. Orch. Assn. (pres. 1985-88), Condrs. Guild Am. (bd. dirs. 1991-93), Assn. Can. Orchs., Rowfant Club Cleve. Home: 2697 Raven Trail NE Marietta GA 30066 Office: Saginaw Bay Symphony Orch PO Box 415 Saginaw MI 48606-0415 Home: 2697 Raven Trail NE Marietta GA 30066 E-mail: leonajar@aol.com., leonajar@concenter.net.

NAJARIAN, BETTY JO, music educator; b. Samson, Ala., Nov. 6, 1929; d. Edward Bryan and Ida (Cox) Murdock; m. Zovak Najarian, July 25, 1953; children: Pamela Najarian Whitehead, Brian Keith Najarian. BA in Music Edn., Troy (Ala.) State U., 1951; student, Fla. State U., Tallahassee, 1952, Auburn U., 1956. Ind. music tchr., ch. musician, Destin, Fla., 1955-99; pres. Okaloosa County Music. Tchrs., Ft. Walton Beach, 1987-89, Fla. State Music Tchrs. Assn. Dist. I, Ft. Walton Beach, 1993-95, Choctaw Bay Music Club, Ft. Walton Beach, 1983-85, Niceville, 1993-95, Fla. Fedn. Music Capital Dist., Destin, 1985-87, 95-97, Fla. Fedn. Music Clubs, Destin, 1997-99. Composer: The Auxiliary Song, 1987. Pres. Am. Legion Aux #296, Destin, Fla., 1958-2002; mem. Sarasota Music Archives, 1997-2002; mem. Fla. League of the Arts, Inc. Named Tchr. of Yr., Destin Elem. Sch., Okaloosa County Sch. Bd., Destin. Fla., 1956-57. Mem. Am. Coll. Musicians, Music Tchrs. Nat. Assn., Nat. Fedn. Music Clubs (chmn. 1999—), Am. Folk Music (chmn. 1999—2002), Fla. State Music. Tchrs. Assn., Okaloosa County Music Tchrs. Assn., Choctaw Bay Music Club (chaplain 2002-), Fla. League Arts, Fla. Fedn. of Music Clubs. (state pres., 1997-99, chmn. coun. dist. and club presidents 1999—). Democrat. Presbyterian. Avocations: collecting old music and hymn books, collecting music boxes, collecting glass bluebirds, collecting baskets, word games, crossword puzzles. Home: 130 Calhoun Ave Destin FL 32541-1504

NAJARIAN, JACK GEORGE, investment banker; b. Beirut, Lebanon, Jan. 11, 1956; came to U.S., 1970, naturalized, 1976; s. George O. Najarian and Marie Keuftejian; m. Victoria A. Dickson, Oct. 6, 1984; 1 child, Emily Jane Marie. BBA in Pub. Acctg., Bernard Baruch Coll., 1976; JD, Hofstra U., 1979. Internat. tax cons. Arthur Andersen & Co., N.Y.C., 1979-81; internat. banking cons. Deloitte & Touche, 1981-82; v.p. internat. treasury and capital markets Societe Generale, 1982-94; acting treas. treasury and capital markets Nat. Australia Bank, 1994-96; chmn. Griffin Securities, Inc., 1997-99; pres. Weatherly Securities Corp., 1999—. Chmn. acctg., fin. and taxation dept. World Trade Inst.; mem. Securities Ins. Protection Corp.; bd. dirs. Uni-Marts, Inc., Weatherly Internat. Plc. Mem. Securities Industry Assn. (bd. dirs. 1997—), Nat. Assn. Securities Dealers.

NAJARIAN, JOHN SARKIS, surgeon, educator; b. Oakland, Calif., Dec. 22, 1927; s. Garabed L. and Siranoush T. (Demirjian) N.; m. Arlys Viola Mignette Anderson, Apr. 27, 1952; children: Jon, David, Paul, Peter. AB with honors, U. Calif., Berkeley, 1948; MD, U. Calif., San Francisco, 1952; LHD (hon.), Univ. Athens, 1980; DSc (hon.), Gustavus Adolphus Coll., 1981; LHD (hon.), Calif. Luth. Coll., 1983. Diplomate Am. Bd. Surgery. Surg. intern U. Calif., San Francisco, 1952-53, surg. resident, 1955-60, asst. prof. surgery, dir. surg. research labs., chief transplant service dept. surgery, 1963-66, prof., vice chmn., 1966-67; spl. research fellow in immunopathology U. Pitts. Med. Sch., 1960-61; NIH sr. fellow and assoc. in tissue transplantation immunology Scripps Clinic and Research Found., La Jolla, Calif., 1961-63; Markle scholar Acad. Medicine, 1964-69; prof., chmn. dept. surgery U. Minn. Hosp., Mpls., 1967-93; med. dir. Transplant Ctr., clin. chief surgery Univ. Hosp., 1967-94; chief hosp. staff U. Minn. Hosp., Mpls., 1970-71, Regents' prof., 1985-95, Jay Phillips Disting. Chair in Surgery, 1986-95, prof. emeritus, prof. surgery, 1995—. Spl. cons. USPHS, NIH Clin. Rsch. Tng. Com., Inst. Gen. Med. Scis., 1965-69; cons. U.S. Bur. Budget, 1966-68; mem. sci. adv. bd. Nat. Kidney Found., 1968; mem. surg. study sect. A div. rsch. grants NIH, 1970; chmn. renal transplant adv. group VA Hosps., 1971; mem. bd. sci. cons. Sloan-Kettering Inst. Cancer Rsch., 1971-78; mem. screening com. Dernham Postdoctoral Fellowships in Oncology, Calif. div. Am. Cancer Soc. Editor: (with Richard L. Simmons) Transplantation, 1972; co-editor: Manual of Vascular Access, Organ Donation, and Transplantation, 1984; mem. editorial bd. Jour. Surg. Rsch., 1968—, Minn. Medicine, 1968—, Jour. Surg. Oncology, 1968—, Am. Jour. Surgery, 1967—, assoc. editor, 1982—; mem. editorial bd. Year Book of Surgery, 1970-85, Transplantation, 1970—, Transplantation Procs, 1970—, Bd. Clin. Editors, 1981-84, Annals of Surgery, 1972—, World Jour. Surgery, 1976—, Hippocrates, 1986—, Jour. Transplant Coordination, 1990—; assoc. editor: Surgery, 1971; editor-in-chief: Clin. Transplantation, 1986—. Bd. dirs., v.p. Variety Club Heart Hosp., U. Minn.; trustee, v.p. Minn. Med. Found. Served with USAF, 1953-55. Hon. fellow Royal Coll. Surgeons of Eng., 1987; hon. prof. U. Madrid, 1990; named Alumnus of Yr., U. Calif. Med. Sch., San Francisco, 1977; recipient award Calif. Trudeau Soc., 1962, Ann. Brotherhood award NCCJ, 1978, Disting. Achievement award Modern Medicine, 1978, Internat. Gt. Am. award B'nai B'rith Found., 1982, Uncommon Citizen award, 1985, Sir James Carreras award Variety Clubs Internat., 1987, Silver medal IXth Centenary, U. Bologna, 1988, Humanitarian of Yr. award, U. Minn., 1992, Najarian Festschrift award Am. Jour. Surgery, 1993, Jubilee medal Swedish Soc. Medicine, 1994. Fellow ACS; mem. Internat. Pediat. Transplantation Assn. (pres. 1998—), Soc. Univ. Surgeons, Soc. Exptl. Biology and Medicine, AAAS, Am. Soc. Exptl. Pathology, Am. Surg. Assn. (pres. 1988-89), Am. Assn. Immunologists, AMA, Transplantation Soc. (v.p. western hemisphere 1984-86, pres. 1994-96), Am. Soc. Nephrology, Internat. Soc. Nephrology, Am. Assn. Lab. Animal Sci., Assn. Acad. Surgery (pres. 1969), Internat Soc. Surgery, Soc. Surg. Chairmen, Soc. Clin. Surgery, Central Surg. Assn., Minn., Hennepin County med. socs., Mpls., St. Paul, Minn., Howard C. Naffziger, Portland, Halsted surg. socs., Am. Heart Assn., Am. Soc. Transplant Surgeons (pres. 1977-78), Council on Kidney in Cardiovascular Disease, Hagfish Soc., Italian Research Soc., Minn. Acad. Medicine, Minn. Med. Assn., Minn. Med. Found., Surg. Biology Club, Sigma Xi, Alpha Omega Alpha, others. Office: U Minn Surgery Dept Mayo Meml Bldg Box 195 516 Delaware St SE Minneapolis MN 55455-0374

NAJITA, TETSUO, history educator; b. Honokaa, Hawaii, Mar. 30, 1936; s. Niichi and Kikuno (Manpuku) N.; m. Elinor Moon, Aug. 2, 1958; children: Mie Kim, Kiyoshi Young. BA, Grinnell Coll., 1958; MA, Harvard U., 1960, PhD, 1965; LLD, Grinnell Coll., 1989. Asst. prof. Carleton Coll., Northfield, Minn., 1964-66, Wash. Univ., St. Louis, 1966-68; assoc. prof. U. Wis., Madison, 1968-69; Robert S. Ingersoll disting. prof. History/Japanese studies U. Chgo., 1969—, dir. Ctr. for East Asian Studies, 1974-80, assoc. dean, 1983-87, master collegiate div. social scis., 1983-87. John A. Burns disting. visiting chair U. Hawaii, Manoa, 1994; chair dept. history U. Chgo., 1994-97; Ena H. Thompson lectr. Pomona Coll., 1996; Catherine Gould Chism vis. prof. U. Puget Sound, Tacoma; Maruyame Masao lectr. U. Calif., Berkeley, 2000. Author: Hara Kei in the Politics of Compromise, 1969 (J.K. Fairbank prize Am. Hist. Assn.), Intellectual Foundations of Modern Japanese Politics, 1974, Visions of Virtue in Tokugawa Japan, 1987, Tokugawa Political Writings, 1998. Recipient Yamagata Banto prize Prefecture of Osaka, 1989; grantee NEH 1973-74, 1980-81; Fulbright fellow 1961-63, 68, Guggenheim fellow 1980-81. Fellow Am. Acad. Arts and Scis.; mem. Am. Hist. Assn., Assn. for Asian Studies (v.p., pres. 1991-93), Phi Beta Kappa. Office: U Chgo Dept History 1126 E 59th St Chicago IL 60637-1580

NAJJAR, MOHAMED KHALIL, architect, consultant; b. Amman, Jordan, Sept. 27, 1959; s. Khalil Sulieman and Khadijah Khader Najjar; m. Lamya Kamil Al-Ajou, Jan. 28, 1983; children: Dima, Lubna, Khalil, Islam. BS, Kent State U., 1986, BArch, 1989; Total Quality Mgmt. degree, Quality Mgmt. Cons., Akron, Ohio, 1993. Pres. MN Design Build Group, Akron, 1989—99; chief op. officer UAE, Inc., 1994—; pres. MCC Am., Kent, 2001—. Bus. com. mem. Congressman Tim Davis, Akron, 2001, bus. adv. bd., 2001—. Recipient Best Design award, Islamic Ctr. Cleve., 1988. Mem.: Contract Mgmt. Assn. Avocations: golf, reading. Home: 1684 Olympus Dr Kent OH 44240-4632 Office: MCC America Inc 117 S Water St Kent OH 44240 Office Fax: 330-673-3809. Business E-Mail: mknajjar@mknajjar.com.

NAKAGAWA, ALLEN DONALD, radiologic technologist; b. N.Y.C., Mar. 14, 1955; s. Walter Tsunehiko and Alyce Tsuneko (Kinoshita) N. BS in Environ. Studies, St. John's U., Jamaica, N.Y., 1977; MS in Marine Biology, C.W. Post Coll., 1980. Cert. radiologic technologist, in fluoroscopy, Calif.; cert. Am. Registry Radiol. Technologists. Research asst. environ. studies St. John's U., 1976-78; lab. asst. Bur. Water Surveillance, Nassau Co. of Health Dept., Wantaugh, N.Y., 1978; clin. endocrinology asst. U. Calif. VA Hosp., San Francisco, 1981-83; student technologist St. Mary's Hosp., 1985-86; radiologic technologist Mt. Zion Hosp., 1986-88; sr. radiologic technologist U. Calif., 1989—, urosurg. radiologic technologists, 1988-89. Attendee U. Calif. San Francisco Trauma and Emergency Radiology Conf., 1995, U. Calif. San Francisco Musculoskeletal MRI Conf., 1996, PACS for Hour Hosp., 1998, Breast Imaging for Technologists and Health Care Providers, U. Calif. Stanford Health Care, 1999, Clinical MRI 2000, U. Calif., San Francisco, 2000, Resident Rev. Diagnostic Imaging, U. Calif., San Francisco, 2001, Digital X-ray & PACs: An Ednl. Forum, 2002. Mem. ACLU, Calif. Soc. Radiologic Technologists, Calif. Acad. Scis., Japananese -Am. Nat. Mus., Sigma Xi. Democrat. Methodist. Avocations: photography, music, computer illustration, studying advanced technology. E-mail: datarover@onebox.com. *If you know, believe and have faith in yourself first, only then can you endeavor to assist someone else. Otherwise, you have wasted your efforts and may have even caused a loss of life.*

NAKAGAWA, KOJI, endocrinologist, educator; b. Sapporo, Hokkaido, Japan, June 5, 1932; s. Satosu and Michi (Yokoyama) N.; m. Keiko Hirato, Oct. 20, 1962; children: Shin, Tamao Yamaguchi. MD, Hokkaido U., 1957, PhD, 1962. Lic. endocrinologist, Japan. Staff scientist Worcester Found. for Experimental Biology, Shrewsbury, Mass., 1964-65; rsch. staff Syntex Rsch. Ctr., Palo Alto, Calif., 1965; rsch. fellow U. Utah Med. Ctr., Salt Lake City, 1965-66; rsch. assoc. 2d dept. medicine Hokkaido U. Sch. Medicine, Sapporo, 1967-83, asst. prof., 1983-89; prof. Health Adminstrn. Ctr., Hokkaido U. Edn., 1989-96, dir. Health Adminstrn. Ctr., 1990-96; prof. dept. nutrition Tenshi Coll., 2000—. Contbr. articles to profl. jours. Fellow Japan Endocrine Soc.; mem. Endocrine Soc., Japanese Soc. Internal Medicine, Japan Diabetes Soc. Home: 2-8 4-chome Yamanote 1-jo Nishi-ku Sapporo 063-0001 Japan Office: Tenshi Coll North 13 East 3 Higashi-Ku Sapporo 065-0013 Japan

NAKAJIMA, HIROSHI, education educator; b. Hiroshima, Japan, June 12, 1923; s. Iwao and Tamae (Takenaka) N.; m. Sei Sakao, May 2, 1966; children: Akihiko, Takehiko. Student, Nishogakusha Coll., 1942-44; BA, Waseda U., 1950; MA, 1954, EdD (hon.), 1989. Asst. prof. Japan women's Coll. Econs., 1954-59; lectr. Waseda U., 1954-63; asst. prof., 1963-68; prof. comparative and internat. edn., 1968-94; prof. emeritus, 1994—. Vis. prof. U. Helsinki, 1962-63; advisor Japanese Inst. Social Studies on Sweden, 1989—; vice-chmn. youth com. Higashikurumeshi, 1978-83; mem. bd. edn. Higashikurumeshi, 1983-91. Served with Japanese Army, 1943-46. Recipient Acad. Hon. Medal U. Helsinki, 1963; decorated Nat. 3rd Order, 2000. Mem.: Finnish Acad. Sci. and Letters (fgn.). Home: 1-4-37 Minamisawa Higashikurume-shi Tokyo 203-0023 Japan

NAKAMOTO, CAROLYN MATSUE, principal; b. Hilo, Hawaii, Oct. 28, 1947; d. Matsuichi and Kiyoko Sugimoto; m. Glenn Sunao Nakamoto, June 15, 1985. BEd in Secondary Edn., U. Hawaii, 1969, MEd in Ednl. Adminstrn., 1994. Cert. prof. sch. adminstr., Hawaii; cert. profl. tchr. secondary tchr. phys. sci. and gen. sci., Hawaii. Tchr. sci. Kalani H.S., Honolulu, 1971-77, Kaiser H.S., Honolulu, 1977-87; vice-prin. McKinley H.S., 1987-90; acting prin. Royal Elem., 1989; prin. Hahaione Elem., 1990—. Mem. ASCD, Nat. Assn. Secondary Sch. Prins., Phi Delta Kappa.

NAKAMURA, HIDEO, law educator; b. Tokyo, Mar. 2, 1926; s. Muneo and Fumiko (Mitani) N.; m. Mitsuko Terai, Feb. 25, 1958; children: Eri, Akiyoshi. LLB, Waseda U., Tokyo, 1947, LLD, 1980; Dr. honoris causa, Athens U., 1995. Assoc. prof. Faculty of Law Waseda U., tokyo, 1955-60, prof., 1960, dean Grad. Sch. Law, 1980-82, dir. Inst. Comparative Law, 1984-88, pres. Law Assn., 1990-94; dir. Inst. Comparative Civil Law, 1975—; ret. hon prof. Waseda U., 1996. Author: (in German) The Japanese Criminal Procedure Code, 1970, Japan and German Civil Procedure, 1995, (in Japanese) Collected Works on Civil Procedure, Vols., 1-5, 1975-86; Civil Procedure, 1987; co-author: (in German) The Japanese Civil Procedure Code, 1978; editor: Family Law Litigation, 1984. Recepient Honor of Freedom award City of Athens, 1998. Mem. Japanese Assn. of Law of Civil Procedure (exec. com. 1960-80, hon.), Japanese Assn. of Law of Pub. Notary (coun. 1978—), Japan Fedn. of Bar Assn. (commr. disciplinary com. 1984-87), Acad. Assn. of Law of Internat. Procedure. Avocation: photography. Home: 2-6-6 Kamitakata Nakano-ku Tokyo 164-0002 Japan Office: Inst Comparative Civil Law 43 Waseda-Minamicho Shinjuku-ku Tokyo 162-0043 Japan

NAKAMURA, HIROSHI, urology educator; b. Tokyo, Mar. 22, 1933; s. Yataroh and Hideko (Tanaka) N.; m. Miyoko Kodachi, Aug. 13, 1966. MD, Keio U., Tokyo, 1960; PhD, Grad. Sch. Medicine, Keio U., 1966. Med. diplomate. Asst. resident Mt. Sinai Hosp., N.Y.C., 1962—63; rsch. fellow Cornell U. Med. Coll., 1966—68; asst. Sch. Medicine Keio U., Tokyo, 1968—70; chmn. urology dept. Tokyo Elec. Power Hosp., 1970—73; vis. asst. prof. surgery Cornell U. Med. Coll., N.Y.C., 1973; chmn. urology Kitasato Inst. Hosp., Tokyo, 1973—77; chmn. dept., prof. urology Nat. Def. Med. Coll., Tokorozawa, Japan, 1977—98, dir. dept. acad. affairs, 1994—96, prof. emeritus, 1999—; emeritus dir. Tokorozawa Ishikawa Clinic, 1998—. Author: Bedside Urology, 1991, Modern Clinical Point-Urology, 1993; editor: Up-to-date Urology, 1983, Caveats & Pitfalls in Clinical Urology, 1999, Medical Ethics Q&A, 2002. Recipient Tamura award Keio U. Sch. Medicine, 1967, All-around Med. award, Igaku-Shoin, Ltd., Tokyo, 1967. Buddhist. Avocations: jazz, audiophile, travel, fishing, baseball. Home: 11-1-1204 Higashicho Tokorozawa Saitama 359-1116 Japan Office: Tokorozawa Ishikawa Clin Iseki Bldg 4F 9-22 Hiyoshicho Tokorozawa Saitama 359-1123 Japan

NAKAMURA, JAMES I. economics educator; b. Toppenish, Wash., Mar. 16, 1919; s. Ichihei and Suya (Hirayama) N.; m. Tetsuko Fujii; children— Richard Ken, Leonard Isamu AA, Santa Maria Jr. Coll., 1939; BS, Columbia U., 1952, PhD, 1964. Asst. prof. Columbia U., N.Y.C., 1964-68, assoc. prof., 1968-80, prof. econs., 1980-89, prof. emeritus, 1989—; vis. research scholar Kobe U., Japan, 1971-72; co-founder, co-dir., sec.-treas. Japan Econ. Seminar (supported by Columbia U., Harvard U., George Washington U.), 1965-90. Author: Agricultural Production and Economic Development of Japan, 1966, Nihon no Keizai Hatten to Nogyo, 1968; mem. editorial bd. Japan Econ. Studies, 1972-90; contbr. numerous articles to profl. jours. Editor newspaper War Relocation Ctr., Gila River, Ariz., 1943-44; legal researcher Shanks Village Com. to Fight Closure, Orangeburg, N.Y., 1952. Served to lt. U.S. Army, 1945-48, PTO. Ford Found. fellow 1952-55, 62-63; Fulbright-Hays fellow, 1967. Mem. Econ. History Assn., Am. Econ. Assn., Assn. for Asian Studies, Japan Econ. Research Ctr., Phi Beta Kappa. Buddhist. Home: 35 Claremont Ave New York NY 10027-6802 E-mail: jinl@columbia.edu.

NAKAMURA, KAZUO, artist; b. Vancouver, Can., Oct. 13, 1926; s. Toichi and Yoshiyo (Uyemoto) N.; m. Lillian Yuriko Kobayakawa, Sept. 15, 1967; children— Elaine Yukae, Bryan Kazuto. Student, Central Tech. Sch., Toronto, 1948-51. Exhibited in one man shows at, Picture Loan Soc., 1952, Hart House, U. Toronto, 1953, Gallery of Contemporary Art, Toronto, 1956, 58, Jerrold Morris Gallery, Toronto, 1962, 65, 67-70, R. McLaughlin Gallery, Oshawa and Can. Tour, 1974-75, Christopher Cutts Gallery, Toronto, 1991, 96; exhibited in group shows at, Fifth Internat. Hallmark Art Award Exhbn., N.Y.C., 1960, Canadian Prints, Drawings and Watercolor, Am. Fedn. Arts Tour, 1960, Seconde Biennale, Musee d'Art Moderne, Paris, France, 1961, Canadian Painting, Polish Tour, 1962, Canadian Painting, Central Africa, 1962, Nineteen Canadian Painters, Louisville, 1962, Commonwealth Painting, London, Eng., 1962, Recent Acquisitions, Mus. Modern Art, N.Y.C., 1963, Canadian Painting, London, 1963, Member's Loan Gallery Acquisitions, Albright-Knox Gallery, Buffalo, 1963, World Show, Washington Sq. Gallery, N.Y.C., 1964, Cardiff Commonwealth Exhbn. of Drawings, Wales, 1965, Centennial Exhbn. of Canadian Prints and Drawings, Australian Tour, 1967, Painters Eleven in Retrospect, Can. tour, 1979-81, Ont. Heritage Found. Firestone Collection, European tour, 1983-84, Nat. Gallery Can., Ottawa, 1989, Nat. Gallery Can., Ottawa, Can. tour, 1993, Mead Mus., Amherst Coll., 1994, Art Forum, Berlin, 1998, others; represented in permanent collections at Nat. Gallery Can., Mus. Modern Art, N.Y.C., Art Gallery of Ont., Toronto, Musée d'Art contemporain, Montreal, R. McLaughlin Gallery, Oshawa, Hirshhorn Mus., Washington, British Mus., London, Art Gallery of Hamilton, Winnipeg Art Gallery, MacKenzie Art Gallery, Regina Edmonton Art Gallery, Vancouver Art Gallery, Beaverbrook Art Gallery, Fredericton, N.B., Windsor (Ont.) Art Gallery, Lugano Collection, Hart House, U. Toronto, Victoria Coll., U. Toronto, U. Western Ont., U. Guelph, Concordia U., Univ. Club Montreal, commd. 2 sculptures, Toronto Internat. Airport. (Recipient prize 4th Internat. Exhbn. Drawings and Engravings, Lugano, Switzerland 1956, Purchase award 5th Internat. Hallmark Art Award Exhbn., N.Y.C. 1960).

NAKAMURA, RICHARD, mental health services professional; BA Psychology, Earlham Coll.; MA Psychology , NYU; PhD Psychology, SUNY, Stony Brook. Postdoctoral fellow intramural lab. neuropsychology Nat. Inst. Mental Health, 1976, chief behavioral and integrative neurosci., 1990, dir. sci. policy and program planning, 1990, acting dir., 2001—02. Recipient Disting. Svc. award, Dept. Health and Human Svcs. Sec., 2000, Outstanding Achievement award, NIH Asian/Pacific Am. Orgn.'s, 2001. Mem.: NIH Office Equal Employment Opportunity (dir.), NIH Office Behavioral and Social Scis. (rsch. dir.), Nat. Inst. Aging (dep. dir. , chmn.), NIH Ctr. Sci. Review (chmn.), NIH Evaluation Policy and Oversight Com., NIH Info. Tech. Bd. Dirs. Office: 6001 Executive Blvd Rm 8184 Bethesda MD 20892*

NAKAMURA, ROBERT MOTOHARU, pathologist; b. Montebello, Calif., June 10, 1927; s. Mosaburo and Haru (Suematsu) N.; m. Shigeyo Jane Hayashi, July 29, 1957; children: Mary, Nancy. AB, Whittier Coll., 1949; MD, Temple U., 1954. Cert. of spl. qualification in pathologic anatomy, clin pathology, immunopathology, Am. Bd. Pathology. Prof. pathology U. Calif., Irvine, 1971-74, adj. prof. pathology, 1974-75; chmn. dept. pathology Scripps Clinic and Rsch. Found., La Jolla, Calif., 1974-92; sr. cons., 1992—; pres. Scripps Clinic Med. Group, La Jolla, 1981-91; prof. dept. immunology and exptl. and molecular medicine Scripps Rsch. Inst., 1997—; chmn. pathology Scripps Clinic, 1998-99, chmn. emeritus pathology, 1999—. Adj. prof. pathology U. Calif., San Diego, 1975-93. Author, editor profl. publs.; co-editor Jr. Clin. Lab. Analysis, 1989—. Fellow: Coll. Am. Pathologists, Am. Soc. Clin. Pathologists, Assn. Clin. Scientists, Am. Coll. Nutrition; mem. Internat. Acad. Pathology. Avocation: reading. Home: 8841 Nottingham Pl La Jolla CA 92037-2131

NAKANISHI, KOJI, chemistry educator, research institute administrator; b. Hong Kong, May 11, 1925; came to U.S., 1969; s. Yuzo and Yoshiko (Sakata) N.; m. Yasuko Abe, Oct. 25, 1947; children: Keiko, Jun. BSc, Nagoya U., Japan, 1947; PhD, Nagoya U., 1954; DSc (hon.), Williams Coll., 1987, Georgetown U., 1992. Asst. prof. Nagoya U., 1955-58; prof. Tokyo Kyoiku U., 1958-63, Tohoku U., Sendai, Japan, 1963-69; prof. chemistry Columbia U., N.Y.C., 1969-80, Centennial prof. chemistry, 1980—; dir. research Internat. Ctr. Insect Physiology and Ecology, Nairobi, Kenya, 1969-77; dir. Suntory Inst. for Bioorganic Research, Osaka, Japan, 1979-91. Hon. prof. Shanghai Inst. Materia Medica, 1995. Author: Infrared Spectroscopy-Practical, 1962, rev. edit., 1977, Circular Dichroic Spectroscopy-Exciton Coupling in Organic Stereochemistry, 1983, A Wandering Natural Products Chemist, 1991; co-editor, contbr. chpt. Comprehensive Natural Products Chemistry, vol. 1-9, 1999; contbr. chpts. to books. Recipient Asahi cultural prize, 1968, Sci. Workers Union medal, Bulgaria, 1978, E.E. Smissman medal U. Kan., 1979, H.C. Urey award Columbia U., 1980, Alcon ophthalmology award, 1986, Paul Karrer gold medal U. Zurich, 1986, E. Havinga medal Havinga Found., Leiden, 1989, Imperial prize Japan Acad., 1990, Japan Acad. prize, 1990, R.T. Major medal U. Conn., 1991, L.E. Harris award U. Nebr., 1991, award in chem. scis. NAS, 1994, J. Heyrovsky hon. gold medal Czech Acad. Scis., 1995, Robert A. Welch award in chemistry, 1996, Person of Cultural Merit award Japanese Govt., 1999; Nakanishi prize established in his honor, 1996. Fellow N.Y. Acad. Scis., Nat. Acad. Sci. Italy (fgn.); mem. Chem. Soc. Japan (hon., award in pure chemistry 1954, award 1979, Nakanishi prize established 1996), Am. Chem. Soc. (E. Guenther award 1978, Remsen award Md. sect. 1981, A.C. Cope award 1990, Nichols medal N.Y. sect. 1992, Mosher award Santa Clara Valley sect. 1995, internat. award in agrochems. 1995), Brit. Chem. Soc. (Centenary medal 1979), Swedish Acad. Pharm. Scis. (Scheele award 1992), Am. Acad. Arts and Scis., Am. Soc. Pharmacognosy (rsch. achievement award 1985), Internat. Chirality Symposium (Chirality gold medal 1995), Pharm. Sc. Japan (hon.), Am. Mus. Soc. of Natural History (1st environ. award 2000). Home: 560 Riverside Dr New York NY 10027-3202 Office: Columbia U Dept Chemistry Mail Code 3114 3000 Broadway New York NY 10027-6941

NAKANISHI, YUKO JULIE, engineering educator, consultant; b. Westland, Mich. d. Ukyo Stanley and Tatsuko Ann Nakanishi; life ptnr. Larry Lifschultz. BA in English Lit., Harvard U., 1987; MBA, Columbia U., 1993; MSCE, CCNY, 1997. Chair N.Y. Area Data Coun., N.Y.C., 1997-99; sr. tchg. assoc., cons. Rensselaer Poly. Inst., Troy, N.Y., 1999-2000; program mgr. Urban ITS Ctr. Poly. U., Bklyn., 2000—. Chair Freight and Intermodal Transp. Data Com., N.Y., 1997-2000; asst. dir. Univ. Transp. Rsch. Ctr., N.Y.C., 1996-99; mem. info. svc. com. Transp. Rsch. Bd., 1998—. Contbr. articles to profl. jours. Fellow Eisenhower fellow, 1997—2000, Eno fellow, 2001. Mem. IEEE, ASCE, Inst. Transp. Engrs., Office: Poly U 6 Metrotech Ctr Brooklyn NY 11201 E-mail: ynakanis@poly.edu., ynakan@aol.com.

NAKANO, DANIEL KEN, mathematician, educator; b. Seattle, July 30, 1964; s. Akira and Ruth Kanae (Ikeda) N. AB in Math. with highest honors, U. Calif., Berkeley, 1986; PhD in Math., Yale U., 1990. Asst. prof. Auburn U., Auburn, Ala., 1990-91, Northwestern U., Evanston, Ill., 1991—. Contbr. articles to Jour. of Algebra, Memoirs of the Am. Math. Soc. Recipient Percy Lionel Davis award U. Calif., Berkeley, 1986. Mem. Am. Math. Soc., Phi Beta Kappa. Office: Dept Math Northwestern U Evanston IL 60201

NAKARAI, CHARLES FREDERICK TOYOZO, music educator, adjudicator; b. Indpls., Apr. 25, 1936; s. Toyozo Wada and Frances Aileen N. *Grandfather Tashiro Furukawa invented a method of teaching the deaf and dumb in Japan and was principal of the first school for the deaf and blind in Japan. Father Toyozo Wada Nakarai, reared as a Shintoist and Buddhist priest, as well as a Samurai, became a Christian minister and professor of Semitic languages and Old Testament in seminaries. Mother Frances Aileen Nakarai was a librarian and became Assistant Librarian for the State of Indiana, heading three divisions of that library. Brother Frederick Leroy Nakarai served as a lawyer in the USAF and as a legal editor.* BA cum laude, Butler U., 1958, Mus.M., 1967; postgrad., U. N.C., 1967-70. Organist, dir. choirs Northwood Christian Ch., Indpls., 1954-57; minister music Allisonville Christian Ch., 1957-58; asst. prof. music Milligan Coll., Tenn., 1970-72; pvt. instr. organ, piano Durham, 1972—. Mem. faculty piano camp U. N.C.-

Greensboro, 1996, 97, 2000, 01; adjudicator N.C. Fedn. Music Clubs, Raleigh Music Tchrs. Assn., Charlotte Piano Tchrs. Forum, Chapel Hill Music Tchrs. Assn. *Sang in a choir at the age of three. Studied piano with Vilora P. Kelley, whose teacher studied with Josef Lhévinne, and Felix Witzinger of Switzerland. Studied organ with Ellen English and Ernest White, both of whom studied with Lynnwood Farnam. Studied voice with Margaret Friermood and Farrell Scott. Awarded "Director of the Month" and "Instructor of the Quarter" in the USAF. Interested in preparing students to enjoy music as adults, with knowledge of reading and interpretation. Students have been awarded numerous honors and prizes in music. Featured in a pictorial essay in the Durham, NC, Herald Sun, May 1, 1998.* Composer: Three Movements for Chorus, 1971, Bluesy, 1979. Served with USAF, 1958-64. Mem. Am. Musicol. Soc., Coll. Music Soc., Am. Guild Organists, Music Tchrs. Nat. Assn., Music Library Assn., N.C. Music Tchrs. Assn., Organ Hist. Soc., Durham Music Tchrs. Assn. (chair student activities), Triangle Guitar Soc. Address: 2312 Anthony Drive Durham NC 27705

NAKATA, GARY KENJI, lawyer; b. Okinawa, Japan, Nov. 13, 1964; came to the U.S., 1971; s. Hiroshi Nakata and Miwako Kin; m. Jo Ann Akiko Tengan, Aug. 22, 1998. BBA in Fin., U. Hawaii, 1988; JD with distinction, U. of the Pacific, 1995. Bar: Hawaii 1996, Calif. 1996, U.S. Dist. Ct. Hawaii, 1996; cert. mgmt. acct.; cert. fin. mgr.; cert. grad. Am. Banker's Assn. Nat. Sch. Regulatory Compliance. Credit analyst Bank of Hawaii, Honolulu, 1988-90, sr. credit analyst, 1990-92; law clk. Hawaii Atty. Gen. Tax Divsn., 1994; sr. assoc. Kobayashi, Sugita & Goda, 1995—. Mem. new product devel. adv. bd. Warren Gorham & Lamont, N.Y.C., 1997-98. Editor-in-chief: The Transnational Lawyer, 1994, 95. Pres., enlisted adv. coun. Hawaii Air Nat. Guard, Honolulu, 1986-92; mem. ex officio alumni coun., mem. membership com., mem. membership benefits subcom. U. Hawaii Alumni Assn., Honolulu, 1990-91; mem. fin. com. and bylaws subcom. Soc. Coll. Bus. Alumni and Friends, U. Hawaii Coll. Bus. Adminstrn. Alumni Affairs, Honolulu, 1990-91, founding mem., treas., 1990-91, mem. steering com. to form alumni orgn., 1997—, pres., 1998—; at-large rep., treas., legis. liaison Neighborhood Bd., Kaneohe, Hawaii, 1991-92. Mem. ABA (bus. law sect., comml. fin. svcs. com., consumer fin. svcs. com.), Hawaii State Bar Assn. (mem. real property and fin. svcs. sect. 1997—), Calif. State Bar Assn., Inst. Cert. Mgmt. Accts. (bd. dirs. 1998-2000, dir. mem. acquistion 1998-2000), Hawaii Fin. Regulatory Compliance Assn. (bd. dirs. 1997—, chairperson fair credit reporting act regulatory update com. 1998—), Hawaii Bus. Jaycees (charter mem. 1991—, charter pres. 1991-92, chmn. bd. 1992-93, R. Allen Watkins Outstanding Chpt. Pres. award 1992, Hampton Whetsell award 1992, Clarence Howard award 1992), Hawaii Jaycees (legal counsel 2000-2001). Office: Kobayashi Sugita & Goda 999 Bishop St Ste 2600 Honolulu HI 96813-4430

NAKAYAMA, MINEHARU, language professional/educator Japanese; b. Nagano, Japan, Dec. 11, 1958; s. Minematsu and Hiroko (Kuribayashi) N.; m. Jennifer E. Workman. BA in English Lang. & Lit., Waseda U., Tokyo, 1983; MA in Linguistics, U. Conn., 1986, PhD in Linguistics, 1988. Japanese Oral Proficiency Interview Tester, 1991-94. Lectr. U. Conn., Storrs, 1984-86; vis. instr. Conn. Coll., New London, 1985-88; asst. prof. Ohio State U., Columbus, 1988-94, assoc. prof., 1994—, dir. Inst. for Japanese Studies, 2002—. Cultural Adv. WBNS-TV Nagano Winter Olympics coverage team, 1998. Author: Acquisition of Japanese Empty Categories, 1996; co-author: Let's Play Games in Japanese, 1991; editor: Issues in East Asian Language Acquisition, 2001, Sentence Processing in East Asian Languages, 2002; co-editor: Proceedings of the Japanese Syntax Workshop, 1988, Japanese/Korean Linguistics, vol. 9, 2001. Recipient Awards for Study Papers of the Waseda Centennial Celebration, Waseda U., 1982, award for internat. understanding Rotary Found., 1983, Outstanding Internat. Faculty award Office Internat. Edn., 1998; conf. grantee N.E. Asia Coun., 1989, rsch. assistance grantee N.E. Asia Coun., 1990, Study-in-Japan grantee Japan Found., 1994, workshop and conf. grantee Japan Found. Lang. Ctr., Tchg. Material grantee Gogaku Kyoiku Shinko Zaidan, 1995, conf. grantee Japan Found., Korea Rsch. Found., 1999. Mem. Assn. for Asian Studies, Assn. Tchrs. of Japanese, Linguistic Soc. Am., Ctrl. Assn. Tchrs. of Japanese, Assn. of Lang. Sci., Ohio Assn. Tchrs. of Japanese, Japan Second Lang. Assn. Office: Dept East Asian Langs & Lits Ohio State U 1841 Millikin Rd Columbus OH 43210-1229 E-mail: nakayama.1@osu.edu.

NAKAYAMA, PAULA AIKO, state supreme court justice; b. Honolulu, Oct. 19, 1953; m. Charles W. Totto; children: Elizabeth Murakami, Alexander Totto. BS, U. Calif., Davis, 1975; JD, U. Calif., 1979. Bar: Hawaii 1979. Dep. pros. atty. City and County of Honolulu, 1979-82; ptnr. Shim, Tam & Kirimitsu, Honolulu, 1982-92; judge 1st Cir. Ct. State of Hawaii, Oahu, 1992-93; justice State of Hawaii Supreme Ct., Honolulu, 1993—. Mem. Am. Judicature Soc., Hawaii Bar Assn., Sons and Daughters of 442. Office: Hawaii Supreme Ct Ali'iolani Hale 417 S King St Honolulu HI 96813-2902*

NAKAYAMA, WATARU, engineering educator, consultant; b. Kamakura, Kanagawa, Japan, Jan. 7, 1936; s. Shiroh and Haru N.; m. Michiko Aoyagi, Jan. 8, 1967. BS, Defense Acad., Yokosuka, Japan, 1958; MS, Tokyo Inst. Tech., 1963, DEng, 1966. Lectr. U. Sherbrooke, Que., 1969-70; rschr. Hitachi, Ltd., Tokyo, 1970-71, chief rschr. Tsuchiura, Japan, 1971-78, sr. rschr. Japan, 1978-88, sr. chief rschr. Japan, 1988-91, hon. engr. Japan, 1991-92; Hitachi chair prof. Tokyo Inst. Tech., 1989-92, prof., 1992-96; vis. prof. U. Md., 1996-98; pres. ThermTech Internat., 1998—. Lectr. in field. Author: (with others) Heat Transfer in Electronic and Microelectronic Equipment, 1990, High Performance Computing in Japan, 1992, Computers and Computing in Heat Transfer Science and Engineering, 1993; contbr. articles to profl. jours. Recipient New Tech. Innovation award Ichimura Found., 1978, best paper award Gas Turbine Soc. of Japan, 1984. Fellow ASME (K-16 com. 1981—, chmn. Japanese chpt. 1990-92, Best Paper award 1981, Heat Transfer Meml. award 1992, Electronic Packaging award 1996, Achievement award Intersoc. Conf. Thermal Phenomena Electronic Sys., 2000, achievement award Pacific Rim Internat. Electronic Packaging Conf. 2001); mem. IEEE (sr.; achievement award Internat. Intersoc. Elec. Packaging Tech./Bus. conf. 2001), Japanese Soc. Mech. Engrs. (vice chmn. thermal engring. divsn. 1989-90, chmn. 1990-91, Best Paper award 1965, 80, Tech. award 1978), Heat Transfer Soc. Japan (pres. 1994). Achievements include patents for industrial application of heat transfer enhancement techniques to heat exchangers, rotating machinery, cooling systems of computers. E-mail: WatNAKAYAMA@aol.com.

NAKAZAWA, PAUL WESLEY, architect, consultant; b. Chgo., Feb. 8, 1951; s. Yoshio and Yuri Lily (Takahashi) N.; m. Maria Laura Rocha, Jan. 24, 1951; children: Natalia, Marie-Nicole, Isabella. BA, U. Chgo., 1973, MBA, 1974; MArch, Harvard U., 1979. Registered architect Ill., N.J., N.Y., Conn., Mass., N.C. Archtl. designer Yosh Nakazawa & Assocs., Inc., Evanston, Ill., 1968-75, Edward Larabee Barnes, N.Y.C., 1979; mgr. fin. and adminstrn. B.A. Capital Corp., 1979-81; exec. v.p. Nakazawa Corp., Charlotte, N.C., 1982-87; adj. to chmn. acquisitions, corp. strategic planning and fin., corp. sec. Office of Chmn. Tribble Harris Li Inc., 1987-90; mng. prin. Clark Tribble Harris & Li Architects, P.A., N.Y.C., 1989-90, Moshe Safdie & Assocs., Inc., Boston, 1990-93, Nakazawa Cons., Boston, 1993—. Bd. dirs. Machado and Silvetti Assocs., Inc., Boston, Office for Met. Architecture, Rotterdam, The Netherlands, AMO, Inc., Cambridge, Mass.; lectr. (studio) in architecture U. N.C., Charlotte, 1982; chmn. designer selection bd. Commonwealth of Mass., 1994-95; lectr. archtecture Grad. Sch. Design, Harvard U., 1996—; chmn. designer selection panel Mass. Tech. Collaborative, 1998-2000, Mass. Conv. Ctr. Authority, Boston, 1998-2000; bd. overseers Boston Archl. Ctr., 2000—. Mem. AIA, Boston Soc. Architects (exec. com. and dir. 1994-96), Am. Phys. Soc., N.Y. Acad. Scis., Am. Assn. for Artificial Intelligence. Avocations: numismatics, world travel, photography, classical and ancient music, art collecting.

NAKER, MARY LESLIE, legal firm executive; b. Elgin, Ill., July 6, 1954; d. Robert George and Marilyn Jane (Swain). BS in Edn., No. Ill. U., 1976, MS in Edn., 1978, postgrad., 1980, Coll. Fin. Planning, 1990. Cert. tchr., Ill., fin. paraplanner. Retail sales clk. Fin'n Feather Farm, Dundee, Ill., 1972-75; pvt. practice tchr. South Elgin, 1974-78; tchg. asst. Sch. Dist #13, Bloomingdale, 1976-78, substitute tchr.; office mgr. Tempo 21, Carol Stream, 1978-82, LaGrange, 1982-85; sales coord. K&R Delivery, Hinsdale, 1986-89; fin. planner coord. Elite Adv. Svcs., Inc., Schaumburg, 1989-90; adminstrv. coord. Export Transports, Inc., Elk Grove Village, 1990-98; adminstrn. mgr. SBS Worldwide Chgo. Inc., Bensenville, 1998-99; office adminstr. DiMonte & Lizak, Attys. at Law, Park Ridge, 2000—. Leader Girl Scouts U.S.A., 1972-77, camp counselor, 1972-79. Music Scholar PTA, U. Wis., 1967, PTA, U. Iowa, 1968-69. Mem. Nat. Geographic Soc., Smithsonian Assn. Lutheran. Avocations: ceramics, bowling, knitting, camping, sewing. Home: 2020 Clearwater Way Elgin IL 60123-2588 Office: DiMonte & Lizak 216 Higgins Rd Park Ridge IL 60068-5706

NAKHLA, ATIF MOUNIR, scientist, biochemist; b. Cairo, Oct. 23, 1946; came to the U.S., 1981; s. Mounir and Afifa (Nagib) N.; 1 child, Ashraf. BS (hon.) in Biochemistry, Cairo U., 1967, MS, 1971, PhD, 1975. Instr., lectr. Cairo U., 1967-80, assoc. prof., 1980-85; rsch. scientist Coll. Physicians and Surgeons Columbia U., N.Y.C., 1985—. Postdoctoral fellow Aarhus (Denmark) U., 1976-79; fellow in residence Rockefeller U., N.Y.C., 1981-85. Contbr. more than 50 articles to profl. jours. Fellow Danish Internat. Devel. Agy., 1976, World Health Orgn., 1981. Mem. AAAS, Am. Soc. Biochemistry and Molecular Biology, Endorcine Soc. U.S.A., Am. Recorder Soc., Egyptian Biochem. Soc., N.Y. Acad. Scis., Sigma Xi. Avocations: music, drawing, horseback riding, swimming, tennis. Home: PO Box 6292 Jersey City NJ 07306-0292 E-mail: AMNAKHLA@yahoo.com.

NAKHLEH, EMILE A. political science educator; b. Galilee, Palestine, May 25, 1938; came to U.S., 1960; s. Abdullah J. and Labibeh (Shiban) N.; m. Mary Bird, Dec. 25, 1965 (div. Aug. 1993); children: Charles, Richard; m. Ilonka Lessnau, Dec. 30, 1993. BA in Polit. Sci., St. John's U., 1963; MA in Polit. Sci., Georgetown U., 1966; PhD in Internat. Rels., Am. U., 1968. From asst. prof. to prof. Mt. St. Mary's Coll., Emmitsburg, Md., 1967-93, chmn. dept., 1975-89, dir. internat. studies, 1981-93, chmn. dept. govt. and internat. studies, 1989-93, John L. Morrison prof. in internat. studies, 1990-93; exec. dir. Inst. for Internat. and Contemporary Affairs, 1990-93; scholar-in-residence, sr. analyst U.S. Govt., Washington, 1993—. Adj. scholar Am. Enterprise Inst., Washington, 1981-90, Ctr. for Strategic and Internat. Studies, Washington, 1986-90. Author: Gulf Cooperation Council: Policies, Problems and Prospects, 1986, Persian Gulf and American Policy, 1982, A Palestinian Agenda for West Bank and Gaza, 1980, Bahrain: Political Development in a Modernizing Society, 1976. Founding mem. Cumberland Valley Fgn. Policy Study Group, Waynesboro, Pa., 1981-93, Soc. for Gulf Arab Studies, 1989-93; commr. Town of Emmitsburg Coun., 1977; chmn. City Bd. Commrs., Emmitsburg, 1978-79. Fulbright Sr. Rsch. fellow, Bahrain, 1972-73, Jerusalem, Israel, 1987, Sr. Rsch. fellow NEH, Washington, 1979-80; resident scholar Woodrow Wilson, Washington, 1979, U.S. Govt., Washington, 1990-91, 93-94. Mem. Md. Assn. for Higher Edn. (Outstanding Educator award 1989), Coun. for Advancement and Support of Edn., Soc. for Gulf Arab Studies (founding mem., pres. 1992-93), Am. Polit. Sci. Assn., Coun. Fgn. Rels. Roman Catholic. Avocations: reading, traveling, gardening. Home: 11415 Bedfordshire Ave Potomac MD 20854-2009 Office: US Govt CIA Washington DC 20505 E-mail: enakhleh@erols.com.

NAKONECZNY, MICHAEL MARTIN, artist; b. Detroit, Oct. 30, 1952; s. Michael and Edithe (Pheil) N.; 1 child, Alysha. Student, Kent State U., 1972-74; BA, Cleve. State U., 1979; MFA, Univ. Cin., 1981. Artist in residence Pub. Sch. 1, Long Island City, N.Y., 1986; instr. Cuyahoga C.C., Cleve., 1987, Cleve. Inst. of Art, 1988; vis. artist Herron Sch. of Art Ind. U., Indpls., 1990, Kansas City (Mo.) Art Inst., 1991; artist in residence Bemis Found., Omaha, 1992; vis. artist Tamarind Inst., Albuquerque, 1995, Ill. State U., 1997; asst. prof. U. Alaska, Fairbanks, 2002—. Vis. artist Mont. State U., 1998. Artist: solo exhibns. include: Graham Modern Gallery, N.Y.C., 1988, Cleve. Ctr. for Contemporary Art, 1993, Zolla Lieberman Gallery, Chgo. 1991, 92, 93, 96, 97, 98, 99, 2000, 2001, Horwitch LewAllen Gallery, Santa Fe, 1995, Purdue U., West Lafayette, Ind., 1995, Clark Gallery, Boston, 1999, Anchorage Mus. of History and Art; exhibited in group shows at Corcoran Gallery of Art, Washington, 1985, The Alternative Mus., N.Y., 1986, LA County Mus. of Art, 1987 (travelling exhbn.), Graham Modern Gallery, N.Y.C., 1989, Machida City Mus. of Graphic Arts, Tokyo, 1993, Galleria De Arte, Sao Paulo, Brazil, 1994, Weatherspoon Art Gallery, U. N.C., 1995 (travelling exhbn.), Chgo. Ctr. Book & Paper Arts, Columbia Coll., 1996, Banco Ctrl., Cuenca, Ecuador, 1996, Calif. Mus. Art, Santa Rosa, 1997. Fellow, U. Cin., 1979—81, Ohio Arts Coun., 1990, Arts Midwest NEA Regional fellow, 1994—95, Ill. Arts Coun., 1995, Visual Arts 7 in Conjunction with Traveling Exhbn., 1987. Address: 660 Rebecca St Apt 16 Fairbanks AK 99709-3563

NALBANDIAN, E. CAROLYN, social worker; b. Boston, July 3, 1933; d. William Michael and Emily (O'Kane) Tatten; 1 child, David Allen; m. John Nalbandian, Dec. 12, 1969. BA in Philosophy, Trinity Coll., 1975, MA in Philosophy, 1978; MSW, U. Conn., 1980. Diplomate Am. Bd. Clin. Social Work. Actress Claire-Tree Maj. Theatre Co., Plainville, N.Y., 1950-54; social worker Mass. Adoption Resource Exch., Boston, 1960-65; mem. grant writing adminstrn. Harvard U. Sch. Dental Medicine, 1965-70; rsch. intern dept. community medicine Health Ctr. U. Conn., Farmington, 1976-78, clin. intern social work dept. psychiatry, 1978-79, social worker mental health Hartford, 1980-83, lectr. social work dept. sociology Storrs, Waterbury and West Hartford, 1981-99, instr. dept. behavioral sci. and community health Sch. Dental Medicine, 1987-99, social work interviewer Sch. Dental Medicine, 1987-88; clin. intern social work Elmcrest Psychiat. Inst., Portland, Conn., 1979-80; pvt. practice Farmington, 1981—; psychiat. social worker, inpatient unit Johns Dempsey HOsp., 1997-99. Mem. Regional Mental Health Bd. Planning Com., 1982-84, Regional Mental Health Bd. North Cen. Conn., 1983-86; bd. dirs. Health Systems Agy. North Cen. Conn., 1980-83. Mem. NASW (chair ethics com. Conn. chpt. 1986-88), Am. Group Psychotherapy Assn., Hastings Ctr. Inst. Soc. (ethics and life scis.), Soc. for Study Profl. Ethics, Am. Philos. Soc., Conn. Assn. for Human Svcs., Trinity Club Hartford. Avocations: theater, music. Home and Office: 350 W 4th St Apt 303 South Boston MA 02127-2674 E-mail: jecnalbandian@earthlink.net.

NALCIOGLU, ORHAN, physics educator, radiological sciences educator; b. Istanbul, Turkey, Feb. 2, 1944; came to U.S., 1966, naturalized, 1974; s. Mustafa and Meliha Nalcioglu. BS, Robert Coll., Istanbul, 1966; MS, Case Western Res. U., 1968; PhD, U. Oreg., 1970. Postdoctoral fellow dept. physics U. Calif., Davis, 1970-71; rsch. assoc. dept. physics U. Rochester, N.Y., 1971-74, U. Wis., Madison, 1974-76; sr. physicist EMI Med. Inc., Northbrook, Ill., 1976-77; prof. depts. radiol. scis., elec. engring., medicine and physics U. Calif., Irvine, 1977—, head divsn. physics and engring., 1985—, dir. biomed. magnetic resonance rsch., 1987—, dir. Rsch. Imaging Ctr., 1992—. Cons. UN, 1980-86; gen. chmn. IEEE Nuclear Sci. Symposium and Med. Imaging Conf., 1996, 99. Editor several books; guest editor IEEE Nuclear Sci. Symposium and Med. Imaging Conf., 1997; contbr. articles to profl. jours. Mobil scholar, 1961-66; recipient Athalie Clarke award for rsch. excellence, 2001. Fellow IEEE (pres. Nuclear and Plasma Scis. Soc. 1993-94, Millennium medal 2000, NPSS Richard Shea award 2000), Am. Assn. Physicists in Medicine, Internat. Soc. Magnetic Resonance in Medicine; mem. Nuclear and Plasma Scis. Soc., Internat. Soc. Maj. Rsch. in Medicine. Office: U Calif Health Scis Rsch Imaging Ctr Irvine CA 92697-0001

NALDRETT, ANTHONY JAMES, geology educator; b. London, June 23, 1933; emigrated to Can., 1957; s. Anthony George and Violet Ethel (Latham) N.; m. Sylvia Robb Clark, Apr. 23, 1960 (div.); children: Anne, Jennifer, Penelope; m. Galina Stanislavovna Rylkova, July 6, 1991. BA, U. Cambridge, 1956, MA, 1962; MS, Queens U., Can., 1961, PhD, 1964; DS (hon.), Laurentian U., Sudbury, Can., 2000, U. Pretoria, South Africa, 2001. Geologist Falconbridge Nickel Mines, Ltd., Sudbury, 1957-59; fellow Carnegie Inst. Washington, Geophys. Lab., 1964-67; asst. prof. U. Toronto, Ont., 1967-68, assoc. prof., 1968-72, prof. mineral deposits geology, 1972-84, univ. prof., 1984-98, univ. prof. emeritus, 1998—. Mine geologist Falconbridge Nickel, 1957-59, exploration geologist, summers 1959-63, sr. prin. rsch. officer CSIRO, Australia, 1972-73; vis. prof. U. Pretoria, South Africa, 1979-80; chercheur associé CNRS, Orleans, France, 1986-87; stagiére BRGM, Orleans, France, 1993-94. Contbr. articles to profl. jours.; editor: Jour. Petrology, 1974-82. Served with Royal Air Force, 1951-53. Recipient Barlow medal Can. Inst. Mining/Metallurgy, 1974, Duncan Derry medal Geol. Assn. Can., 1980, Logan medal Geol. Assn. Can., 1994, Bownocker gold medal Ohio State U., 1986. Fellow: Internat. Mineral. Assn. (1st v.p. 1994—98, pres. 1998—), Societé de Mineralogie et Crystallogrphie (v.p. 1987), Russian Mineral. Soc. (hon. fellow 1999), Mineral. Assn. Can. (pres. 1982, 1983), Soc. Econ. Geologists (v.p. 1982, pres. 1991—92, medal 1982, Disting. lectr. 1996), Geol. Assn. Can., Geol. Soc. Am. (v.p. 2000, pres. 2001—02), Mineral Soc. Am., Royal Soc. Can., European Union Geoscientists (hon.; fgn.). Avocations: sailing, skiing, carpentry. Home: 70 Cambridge Ave Ste 2225 Toronto ON Canada M4K 2L5 Office: Dept Geology University of Toronto Toronto ON Canada M5S 1A1

NALE, JULIA ANN, nursing educator; b. Chgo., Oct. 27, 1948; d. Anthony John and Mary Elizabeth (Magrady) Doheny; m. Robert Douglas Nale, Feb. 27, 1971; children: Daniel, Kerry. Diploma, St. Francis Sch. Nursing, Evanston, Ill., 1969; BS, U. S.C. Coastal Carolina Coll., Conway, 1989. Staff nurse St. Francis Hosp., 1969-71; charge nurse McDonough Dist. Hosp., Macomb, ill., 1971-72; supr. surg. ICU Victory Meml. Hosp., Waukegan, 1973-78; charge nurse St. Mary's Hosp., Galesburg, 1978-79; assoc. dir. nursing Community Meml. Hosp., Monmouth, Ill., 1979-85; staff nurse Loris (S.C.) Community Hosp., 1987-91; instr. health occupations Horry County Sch. Dist., Conway, S.C., 1985-89, instr. LPNs, 1989—; staff nurse Conway Hosp., 1992—. Mem. S.C. Textbook Selection Com., 1988-90. Lectr., tchr. Tommy Trauma Program for Pub. Sch. Children, Monmouth, 1982-84; charter mem. Com. to Combat Alcohol/Drug Abuse, Monmouth, 1985. Named Tchr. of the Yr. Finklea (S.C.) Career Ctr., 1989, Aynor-Conway Career Ctr., 1991, other awards. Mem. AACN, NEA, S.C. Ednl. Assn., Horry County Vocat. Assn., S.C. Vocat. Assn. (pres. health occupations div. 1990-91), Am. Vocat. Assn. Roman Catholic. Avocations: swimming, cross-stitch, reading. Office: Aynor-Conway Career Ctr Four Mile Rd Conway SC 29526

NALEN, CRAIG ANTHONY, government official; b. Montclair, N.J., Apr. 17, 1930; s. Paul Anthony and Mildred A. (Tucker) N.; m. Katherine Andrews, Dec. 30, 1953; children: Katherine M., David A., Peter H. BA, Princeton U., 1952; MBA, Stanford U., 1957. Mktg. exec. Procter & Gamble, Cin., 1957-62, Foremost-McKesson, San Francisco, 1962-64; divisional gen. mgr., corp. v.p. Gen. Mills Inc., Mpls., 1964-72; pres., also bd. dirs. Am. Photograph Corp., Great Neck, N.Y., 1972-75; pres., chmn. bd. dirs. STP Corp., Ft. Lauderdale, Fla., 1975-80; pres., chief exec. officer Overseas Pvt. Investment Corp. (govt. agy.), Washington, 1981-89, also bd. dirs.; chmn. AES Transpower, 1989-92. Bd. dirs. Glendale Internat. Corp., Ont., Can., Sonex Corp. Bd. dirs., founder Children's World, Denver. Lt. USNR, 1952-55. Mem. Chevy Chase (Md.) Club, Gulf Stream Golf Club (Fla.), Gulf Stream Bath & Tennis Club (Delray Beach, Fla.), Valley Golf Club (Sun Valley, Idaho). Republican. Home: 532 Banyan Rd Gulf Stream FL 33483-7404 also: 3101 New Mexico Ave NW Apt 844 Washington DC 20016-5917 also: PO Box 2439 Ketchum ID 83340-2439

NALIN, DAVID ROBERT, retired pharmaceutical executive; b. N.Y.C., Apr. 22, 1941; s. Edward Murray Nalin and Hilda (Cumsky) Mehlman. BA, Cornell U., 1961; MD, Albany Med. Coll., 1965. Intern, resident Montefiore Hosp., Bronx, N.Y., 1965-67; rsch. assoc. internat. rsch. NIH, Bethesda, Md., 1967-70; sr. resident medicine Harvard U., Boston, 1970-71; rsch. assoc. pathobiology, instr. medicine Johns Hopkins U. Med. Coll., Balt., 1971-73, asst. prof. medicine and pathobiology, 1973-76; ass. prof. medicine Med. Coll. U. Md., 1976-79, chief physiology sect. ctr. vaccine devel., 1978-79, assoc. prof. internat. medicine, dir. Pakistan Med. Ctr., 1979-82, clin. assoc. prof. epidemiology and preventive medicine, 1981-82; dir. clin. rsch. Merck Rsch. Lab., West Point, Pa., 1983-98; dir. vaccine sci. affairs Merck Vaccine Divsn., 1998—2002; ret., 2002. Cons. WHO, Geneva, 1969—90, USAID, Washington, 1970—82; sr. asst. surgeon USPHS, 1965—70. Contbr. Co-founder Bangladesh Info. Ctr., Washington, 1970—72. Recipient medals and plaques, Govts. of Bangladesh and Pakistan, Internat. Ctr. for Diarrheal Diseases Rsch., Bangladesh, 1972, 1981, 1992, Pollin prize for Pediatric Rsch., Columbia U., 2002. Mem.: ACP, Royal Soc. Tropical Medicine & Hygiene, Am. Soc. Microbiology, Am. Soc. Tropical Medicine & Hygiene. Avocation: Avocation: art collector.

NALITZ, WILLIAM ROBERT, judge; b. Pitts., Oct. 16, 1944; s. Stanley Robert and Clare P. Nalitz; m. Linda Ann White, June 29, 1968; children: Jennifer (dec.), Thaddeus, Carolyn. BA, Georgetown U., 1966; JD, Duquesne U., 1973. Claims adjuster Travelers Ins., Pitts., 1968-70; field agt. Pa. Bd. Probation/Parole, 1970-73; assoc. Sayers, King & Keener, Waynesburg, Pa., 1973-75; ptnr. King and Nalitz, 1975-97; judge Greene County Ct. Common Pleas, 1998—. 1st lt. U.S. Army, 1966-68, Vietnam. Home: Cabin Rd Waynesburg PA 15370 Office: Greene County Courthouse High St Waynesburg PA 15370

NALL, LAWANDA CAROL, healthcare company executive, consultant; b. Monroeville, Ala., July 19, 1964; d. Charles Edward and Willie Earline (Brantley) Nall. AA, Pensacola Jr. Coll., 1983, AS, 1984; BS, MS, Columbia Pacific U., 1986; DSc, London Inst. Applied Rsch., 1991. Cert. nursing adminstr. advanced; cert. ACLS, BTLS; cert. long term care nurse. Nursing supr. Columbia Regional Med. Ctr., Andalusia, Ala., 1984-85, dir. edn., 1984-85; nursing dir. Perry Community Hosp., Marion, 1985; nursing instr. S.W. Va. Community Coll., Logan, 1986; clin. dir. nursing Med. Ctr. Baton Rouge, 1987-88; asst. adminstr. for nursing Terrell (Tex.) Community Hosp., 1988, clin. rsch. assoc. Drug Rsch. and Analysis, 1988-90; nursing adminstr. Copper Basin Med. Ctr., Copperhill, Tenn., 1990-92; dir. patient care svcs. Man Appalachian Regional Hosp., Man, W.Va., 1993-95; corp. dir. nursing and quality improvement MHS Health Svc., Riyadh, Saudi Arabia, 1995-97; pres., CEO Com Enterprises, Pensacola, Fla., 1998—. Author: Manual of Inservice Education, 1985, Manual of Effective Communication and Management Techniques for Nursing Adminstrators, 1986, others. Mem. AACN, NAFE, ANA (cert. nursing adminstr. advanced 1988), Emergency Nurses Assn., Am. Heart Assn., Am. Coll. of Health Care Execs. Avocations: oil painting, interior decorating, music, flying.

NALLS, GAYIL LYNN, artist; b. Washington, July 17, 1953; d. Hampton Roberts and Doris Winifred (Fields) N.; m. Winfred Overholser III, Feb. 17, 1979 (dec. Oct. 1983); m. John William Steele, Aug. 15, 1992; 1 child, Morgan Nalls. Student, Va. Commonwealth U., 1971-72, Parsons Sch. Design, 1972-74, Am. U., Washington, 1974, Corcoran Sch. Art, 1975-76. Tchr. Parsons Sch. Design, N.Y.C., 1986—. Ptnr. Election Satellite Network, Tribeca Film Ctr., N.Y.C., 1991—; co-founder Digital Network TV, N.Y.C., 1993—; spkr., panelist Aspen Inst. Soc. of Fellows, Feb. 1998; pres. 18th Internat. Sculpture Conf., Houston. One-person shows include Susan Caldwell Gallery, N.Y.C., 1983, U. Richmond, Va., 1988, Baumgartner Galleries, Washington, 1990, Phillipe Staib Gallery, N.Y.C., 1992, Downtown Cmty. TV Ctr., N.Y.C., 1992, Steffany Martz Gallery, N.Y.C., 1998; exhibited in group shows at Indpls. Mus. Art, 1984, Corcoran Gallery Art, Washington, 1988, U.S. Mission, Berlin, West Germany, 1988, Bruce Mus., Greenwich, Conn., 1988, Southeastern Ctr. Contemporary Art, Winston-Salem, 1989, Monastery of Santa Clara, Seville, Spain, 1992, Pretoria Art Mus., South Africa, 1994, Hand Workshop, Richmond, 1995, NGO Forum on Women '95 Film Festival, Huairou, China, 1995, (Internet exhibition) Inst. Studies in the Arts Ariz. State U., 1995, Internat. Ctr. N.Y., 1996, Steffany Martz Gallery, 1997, 98, 99; represented in permanent collections at Met. Mus.Art, Nat. Mus. Am. Art, Corocoran Gallery, World Sensorium, N.Y.C.; author: World Sensorium, 1998, The Laments, 1990, (screenplay) X-tips, 1994; author, producer: Permutatude, 1988-94, Gal Gaia/Mother Right, 1990; producer, dir. The Laments, 1994; dir., prodr. (documentary) A Common Destiny: Thomas Banyacya, The Hopi Prophecy, Jewell Praying Wolfe James, Walking in Both Worlds, 1989, Tom Dostou Speaking for Traditional Chief William Commanda: Message from the Elders of the Seven Fires Prophecy, 1995; choreographer (video) Wheels Over Indian Trails, 1993. Conceiver, designer, constructor Commn. Fine Arts and Landmark, Winfred Overholser III Meml. Sculpture Garden, Georgetown U. Hosp., Washington, 1983-85; conceier The Lab Sch. Portfolio for Lab. Sch. Washington, 1986; bd. dirs., curator 10thAnniversary Exhbn. Washington Project for the Arts, 1985-88. Recipient award EarthPeace Internat. Film Festival, Burlington, Vt., 1991, award of merit 20th Biennial Exhbn., U. Del., Newark, 1982, Purchase award Richard B. Russell Bldg. and U.S. Ct. House, Atlanta, 1982, Bay Bank Valley Trust Co. award 66th Nat. Exhbn. George Walter Vincent Smith Art Mus., Springfield, Mass., 1985; D.C. Commn. Arts. and Humanities fellow, Washington, 1987. Address: Steffany Martz Gallery 529 W 20th St Fl 6 New York NY 10011-2800

NALWA, HARI SINGH, materials scientist, polymer chemist; b. Soop, Meerut, Uttar Prad, India, Jan. 15, 1954; arrived in U.S., 1998; s. Kadam and Sukh (Devi) Singh; m. Beena Singh Rani, Apr. 25, 1989; children: Surya Singh, Ravina Singh, Eric Singh. BSc in Bioscis., Meerut (India) U., 1974; MSc in Organic Chemistry, U. Roorkee, India, 1977; PhD in Polymer Sci.,

Indian Inst. Tech., Delhi, 1983. Guest scientist Hahn Meitner Inst., Berlin, 1983-84; rsch. assoc. U. So. Calif., L.A., 1984-87, SUNY, Buffalo, 1987-88; lectr. Tokyo U. Agr. and Tech., 1988-90; scientist Hitachi (Japan) Ltd., 1990-99; R&D mgr. Ciba Splty. Chems. Corp., L.A., 1999-2000; mng. dir. Stanford Sci. Corp., 2000—; pres., CEO Am. Sci. Pub., 2000—. Hon. vis. prof. Indian Inst. Tech., New Delhi, 1996—98. Editor: (book) Ferroelectric Polymers, 1995, Handbook of Organic Conductive Molecules and Polymers, Vols. 1-5, 1997; co-editor: Nonlinear Optics of Organic Molecules and Polymers, 1997; editor (with Seizo Miyata): Organic Electroluminescent Materials and Devices, 1997, Handbook of Nanostructural Materials and Nanotechnology, Vols. 1-5, 1999, Handbook of Low and High Dielectric Constant Materials and Their Applications, Vols. 1-2, 1999, Advanced Functional Molecules and Polymers, Vols. 1-4, 2001; editor: Handbook of Advanced Electronic and Photonic Materials and Devices, Vols. 1-10, 2000, Handbook of Surfaces and Interfaces of Materials, Vols. 1-5, 2001, Handbook fo Thin Films Materials, Vols. 1-5, 2001, Silicon-Based Materials and Devices, Vols. 1-2, 2001, Photodetectors and Optical Fibers, 2001, Supramolecular Electroactive and Photosensitive Materials, 2001, Polymer Optical Fibers, 2002, Nanostructured Materials and Nanotechnology, 2001; founder, editor-in-chief: Jour. Porphyrins and Phthalocyanines, 1997—2000, editor-in-chief: Jour. Nanosci. and Nanotechnology, 2001—, mem. editl. bd.: Applied Organometallic Chemistry, 1993, mem. editl. bd.: Photonic Sci. News, 1994, mem. editl. bd.: Jour. Macromolecular Sci.-Physics, 1995, mem. editl. bd.: Internat. Jour. Photoenergy, 1998—2001, referee: Jour. Am. Chem. Soc., referee: Jour. Phys. Chemistry, referee: Jour. Polymer Sci., referee: Applied Organometalic Chemistry, referee: Applied Phys. Letter, referee: Jour. Electronic Materials, referee: Jour. Macromolecular Sci.-Physics, referee: Jour. Materials Sci.: Material in Electronics, referee: Jour. Applied Physics, referee: Optic Comms.; contbr. chapters to books, articles to profl. jours.; editor: (book) Handbook of Polyelectrolytes and Their Applications, vols. 1-3, 2002, Magnetic Nanostructures, 2002, Quantum Dots and Nanowires, 2002, Nanoclusters and Nanocrystals, 2002. Fellow Rsch., indian Space Rsch. Orgn., 1978—81, Cou. Sci. and Indsl. Rsch., 1982—83, NEC, 1988—89, Japanese Gov. Sci. and Tech. Agy., 1989—90; scholar Govt. India Merit, 1970—72. Mem.: AAAS, Am. Chem. Soc. Achievements include patents in field. Avocations: jogging, swimming, volleyball, hockey, kabbaddi. E-mail: nalwa@mindspring.com.

NAM, CHARLES BENJAMIN, sociologist, demographer, educator; b. Lynbrook, N.Y., Mar. 25, 1926; s. Samuel and Yetta (Huff) N.; m. Marjorie Lee Tallant, Jan. 1, 1956; children: David Wallace, Rebecca Jane. BA, NYU, 1950; MA, U. N.C., 1957, PhD, 1959. Statistician U.S. Bur. Census, Washington, 1950-53, chief edn. and social stratification br., 1957-64; statistician USAF, Montgomery, Ala., 1953-54; rsch. asst. U. N.C., Chapel Hill, 1954-57; prof. sociology Fla. State U., Tallahassee, 1964—96, chmn. dept. sociology, 1968—71, disting. rsch. prof., 1994—96, disting. rsch. prof. emeritus, 1996—; rsch. assoc. Ctr. for Study of Population, 1967—, dir., 1967—82; mem. population adv. com. U.S. Bur. Census, 1978-81. Cons. population divsn. Orgn. for Econ. Coop. and Devel., 1968-70, UNESCO, 1978-83, Indonesian Ministry of Population and Environment, Jakrarta, 1988-90; Social Sci. Rsch. Coun., 1981-88. Author: (with John K. Folger) Education of the American Population, 1967, Population and Society, 1968, (with Susan Gustavus) Population: The Dynamics of Demographic Change, 1976, Nationality Groups and Social Stratification, 1981, (with Susan Philliber) Population: A Basic Orientation, 1983, (with Mary Powers) The Socioeconomic Approach to Status Measurement, 1983, Our Population: The Face of America, 1988, Understanding Population Change, 1994, (with Richard Rogers and Robert Hummer) Living and Dying in the USA, 2000; (with Janusz Balicki and Ewa Fratczak) Mechanisms of Population Changes and Population Policy (in Polish), 2002; editor: Demography, 1972-75; co-editor: (with David Sly, William Serow) International Handbook of Internal Migration, 1990, Handbook of International Migration, 1990; assoc. editor jour. Population Research and Policy Review, 1993-94. Fellow AAAS (rep. sect. K 1999-); mem. Am. Sociol. Assn. (chmn. sect. on population 1976-78), Population Assn. Am. (pres. 1979), Internat. Union for Sci. Study Population, Am. Statis. Assn. (chmn. social statistics sect. 1974), So. Sociol. Soc. (pres. 1981-82), So. Demographic Assn. (vice chmn. 1974-75; fellow 2001), Soc. Study Social Biology (bd. dirs. 1996—, exec. com. 1998-99). Home: 820 Live Oak Plantation Rd Tallahassee FL 32312-2413 E-mail: charlesnam@earthlink.net.

NAM, SEHYUN, polymer engineer; b. Seoul, Korea, Feb. 11, 1949; arrived in U.S., 1975; s. Kidong Nam, Okjoon Park; m. Kuisook Nam, Aug. 13, 1975; children: Brian T., Edwin T. BS in Applied Chemistry, Seoul Nat. U., 1971; MS in Chem. Engring., Oreg. State U., 1975; MSE in Materials and Metall. Engring., U. Mich., 1978; PhD in Polymer Engring., U. Tenn., 1982. Tchg./rsch. asst. U. Oreg., Corvallis, 1973—75, U. Mich., Ann Arbor, 1975—78, U. Tenn., Knoxville, 1979—82; sr. engr. 3M Co., St. Paul, 1982—86, rsch. specialist, 1987—2001, sr. rsch. specialist, 2002—. Adj. prof. 3M Co., St. Paul, 1992—95; strategic tech. advisor Rheosense Inc., Woodbury, Minn., 2001—. Contbr. Pres. Minn. chpt. Korean-Am. Scientist and Engrs. Assn., Vienna, 1986—88; exec. councilor Korean Soc. of Minn., Mpls., 2001—. Mem.: Soc. of Internat. Polymer Processing, Soc. of Rheology, Soc. Plastics Engrs. (sr.). Presbyterian. Achievements include patents for in field. Avocations: reading, golf. Home: 4890 Wild Canyon Dr Woodbury MN 55129 Office: 3M Company 3 Center Saint Paul MN 55144-0001

NAMBISAN, SATISH, management educator; b. Kerala, India, May 31, 1965; came to U.S., 1993. m. Priya Nambiar. BTech, Calicut U., India, 1987; PhD, Syracuse U., 1997. Asst. prof. Nat. U. Singapore, 1997-99, Rensselaer Poly. Inst., Troy, N.Y., 1999—. Rsch. assoc. Ctr. for Telemedia Strategy, Singapore, 1997—. Contbr. articles to profl. jours. Ernst & Young fellow Internat. Conf. on Info. Sys., 1996. Mem. Acad. Mgmt. Office: Rensselaer Poly Inst Lally Sch Mgmt 110th and 8th St Troy NY 12180 Fax: (518) 276-6881. E-mail: nambis@rpi.edu.

NAMBOODIRI, KRISHNAN, sociology educator; b. Valavoor, Ind., Nov. 13, 1929; s. Narayanan and Parvathy (Kutty) N.; m. Kadambari Kumari, Sept. 7, 1954; children: Unni (dec.), Sally. B.Sc., U. Kerala, 1950, M.Sc., 1953; MA, U. Mich., 1962, PhD, 1963. Lectr. U. Kerala, India, 1953-55, 58-59; tech. asst. Indian Statis. Inst., Calcutta, 1955-58; reader demography U. Kerala, 1963-66; asst. prof. sociology U. N.C., Chapel Hill, 1966-67, asso. prof., 1967-73, prof., 1973-84, chmn. dept., 1975-80; Robert Lazarus prof. population studies Ohio State U., Columbus, 1984—, chmn. dept. sociology, 1989-93. Author: (with L.F. Carter and H.M. Blalock) Applied Multivariate Analysis and Experimental Designs, 1975; editor: Demography, 1975-78, Survey Sampling and Measurement, 1978, Auth. Matrix Algebra: An Introduction, 1984, (with C.M. Suchindran) Life Table Techniques and Their Applications, 1987, (with R.G. Corwin) Research in Sociology of Education and Socialization: Selected Methodological Issues, 1989, Demographic Analysis: A Stochastic Approach, 1991, (with R.G. Corwin) The Logic and Method of Macrosociology, 1993, Methods for Macrosociological Research, 1994, A Primer of Population Dynamics, 1996; contbr. articles to profl. jours. Fellow Am. Statis. Assn.; mem. Population Assn. Am. (dir. 1975-76), Internat. Union Sci. Study Population, Am. Sociol. Assn., Indian Sociol. Assn., Am. Statis. Assn., Sociol. Research Assn. Home: 3107 N Star Rd Columbus OH 43221-2366 E-mail: namboodiri.2@osu.edu.

NAMBU, YOICHIRO, physics educator; b. Toyko, Jan. 18, 1921; arrived in U.S., 1952; m. Chieko Hida Nambu, Nov. 3, 1945; 1 child Jun-ichi. Research asst. U. Tokyo, 1945—49; prof. physics Osaka City U., Japan, 1950—56; mem. Inst. Advanced Study, 1952—54; research assoc. U. Chgo., 1954—56, mem. faculty, 1956—, prof. physics, 1958, Disting. prof., 1971—; emeritus, 1991—. Contbr. articles to profl. jours. Recipient J.J. Sakurai prize, Am. Phys. Soc., 1994, Wolf prize in Physics, 1994. Mem.: NAS, Am. Phys. Soc., Am. Acad. Arts and Scis. Office: Univ of Chicago Enrico Fermi Inst 5740 S Ellis Ave Chicago IL 60637-1434

NAMDARI, BAHRAM, surgeon; b. Oct. 26, 1939; s. Rostam and Sarvar Namdari; m. Kathleen Wilmore, Jan. 5, 1976; children: Mondona, Mietra, Ariana. MD, 1966. Diplomate Am. Bd. Surgery. Resident in gen. surgery St. John's Mercy Med. Ctr., St. Louis, 1969-73; practice medicine specializing in gen. and vascular surgery Milw., 1976—. Mem. staff St. Mary's Hosp., Milw., St. Luke's Hosp., Milw., St. Michael Hosp., Milw.; founder, pres. Famous Mealwaukee Foods Enterprises. Contbr. articles; patentee med. instruments and other devices. Cardiovascular Surgery fellow with Michael DeBakey, Baylor Coll. Medicine, Houston, 1974-75. Fellow ACS, Internat. Surgeons; mem. AMA, Med. Soc. Milwaukee County, Milw. Acad. Surgery, Wis. Med. Soc., Wis. Surg. Soc., Royal Soc. Medicine Eng. (affiliate), Am. Soc. Bariatric Surgery, World Med. Assn., Internat. Acad. Bariatric Medicine (founding mem.), Am. Acad. Cosmetic Surgery, Michael DeBakey Internat. Cardiovascular Soc. Office: Great Lakes Med and Surg Ctr 6000 S 27th St Milwaukee WI 53221-4805

NAMI, THOMAS ANTHONY, music educator; b. Syracuse, N.Y., July 23, 1965; s. Ottavio Peter and Dorothy Helen Nami. AAS, Onondaga C.C., 1985; MusB, SUNY, Potsdam, 1988; MS in Edn., Coll. St. Rose, 1995. Cert. elem. music tchr. N.Y. Elementary Music Teacher Catholic Schools, Syracuse, NY, 1988—89, Mohawk Central Schools, Mohawk, 1989—92; Elementary/High School Vocal Music Teacher Mount Markham Central Schools, West Winfield, 1992—95; High School Vocal Music Teacher Fulton Consolidated Schools, Fulton, 1995—. Recipient Rookie award, Fulton Tchr.'s Assn., 1997. Home: 116 Oswego St #5 Baldwinsville NY 13027 Office: G Ray Bodley H S 6 William Gillard Dr Fulton NY 13069 Office Fax: 315-593-5427. Personal E-mail: eighth@dreamscape.com. Business E-Mail: tnami@fulton.cnyric.org.

NAMIKAS, STEVEN, geography educator; b. Bellingham, Wash., Jan. 13, 1966; s. Gediminas and Jessie Namikas; m. Lise Namikas, July 8, 1990. BA, U. Windsor, Ont., Can., 1988; MS, Rutgers U., 1992; PhD, U. So. Calif., L.A., 1999. Vis. instr. dept. geography Tex. A&M U., College Station, 1998-99; asst. prof. dept. geography and anthropology La. State U., Baton Rouge, 1999—. Contbr. articles to profl. jours. Grantee NSF, 1997-98, Acad. Reward Coll. Scientists Found., 1997, 98. Mem. Internat. Assn. Sedimatologists, Assn. Am. Geographers, Am. Geophys. Union, Coastal Edn. Rsch. Found. Office: La State U Dept Geography-Anthropology Baton Rouge LA 70803

NAMYSLOWSKI, JAN, physician, interventional radiologist; b. Warsaw, Poland, May 29, 1957; s. Leszek and Izabella Namyslowski. MD, Warsaw Med. Acad., 1981. Diplomate Am. Bd. Radiology. Rsch. asst. in pathology SUNY Downstate Med. Ctr., Bklyn., 1982-84; resident in surgery Interfaith Med. Ctr., 1984-87; resident in radiology Boston U. Med. Ctr., 1988-92; fellow in interventional radiology Tufts U., New Eng. Med. Ctr., Boston, 1992-93, mem. staff, 1993-96, Ind. U., Univ. Hosp., Indpls., 1996—. Contbr. articles to sci. and profl. jours. Mem. Soc. of Cardiovascular and Interventional Radiology, Cardiovascular and interventional Radiol. Soc. of Europe. Avocations: skiing, photography, climbing, hiking. Office: Ind U Univ Hosp 550 University Blvd Rm 279 Indianapolis IN 46202-5149

NANAGAS, MARIA TERESITA CRUZ, pediatrician, educator; b. Manila, Jan. 21, 1946; came to U.S., 1970; d. Ambrosio and Maria (Pasamonte) Cruz; m. Victor N. Nanagas, Jr.; children: Victor III, Valerie, Vivian. BS, U. of the Philippines, 1965, MD, 1970. Diplomate Am. Bd. Pediat. Intern, resident St. Elizabeth's Hosp., Boston, 1971-74; fellow in ambulatory pediat. North Shore Children's Hosp., Salem, Mass., 1974-75; active staff medicine Children's Med. Ctr., Dayton, Ohio, 1976—, head divsn. gen. pediat., 1988-90, 95-97, co-interim head ambulatory pediat., 1989-90, med. dir. ambulatory pediat., 1990—. Clin. asst. prof. pediat. Wright State U., Dayton, 1977-83, clin. assoc. prof. pediat., 1983—, selective dir., 1989—, assoc. prof. pediat., 2000—; clin. asst. prof. family practice Wright State U., Dayton, 1999—; dir., preceptor Wright State U. residents continuing clinic Children's Med. Ctr., 1989—, attending physician family practice programs, 1978—. Active Miami Valley Lead Poisoning Prevention Coalition, 19926. Fellow Am. Acad. Pediat.; mem. Western Ohio Pediat. Soc., Ambulatory Pediat. Assn. Office: Children's Med Ctr Health Clinic 1 Childrens Plz Dayton OH 45404-1898

NANAGAS, VICTOR N., JR. pediatric surgeon; b. Manila, Nov. 2, 1940; came to U.S., 1969; s. Victor T. and Amparo B. (Navarrete) N.; m. Maria Teresita Cruz, Dec. 26, 1970; children: Victor III, Valerie, Vivian. MD, U. Philippines, Manila, 1964; MS in Surgery, Tufts U., 1972. Diplomate Am. Bd. Surgery. Clin. prof. surgery Wright State U. Coll. Medicine, Dayton, Ohio, 1988-2000, 2000—; chmn. dept. sci. Children's Med. Ctr., Dayton, 1991-94. Author: Prognosis and Outcomes in Surgical Diseases, 1999; contbr. chpt. to book. Mem. Am. Pediat. Surg. Assn., Am. Coll. Surgeons, Am. Acad. Pediats. (mem. exec. bd. Ohio chpt. 1991-92), Ohio State Med. Assn., We. Ohio Pediat. Soc. (pres. 1991-92). Roman Catholic. Avocations: tennis, chess. Office: Pediat Surgeons Dayton Inc One Children's Plz Dayton OH 45404

NANAO, KENJILO, artist, educator; b. Aomori, Japan, July 26, 1929; came to U.S., 1960; s. Yosaburo Hirano and Tama Nanao; m. Gail Carol Chadell, Aug. 24, 1965; 1 child, Max Harunobu. Student, Nihon U., Tokyo, 1950-53, Calif. Sch. Fine Arts, San Francisco, 1960-63; MFA, San Francisco Art Inst., 1970. Lectr. art San Jose (Calif.) State U., 1970; prof. art Calif. State U., Hayward, 1970-91, prof. emeritus, 1991—. Vis. prof. U. N.H., 1973, Stanford U., 1992. One-man shows include Tsubaki Kindai Gallery, Tokyo, 1965, Smith Andersen Gallery, Palo Alto, Calif., 1971, 74, 78, 90, 98, Santa Barbara Mus., 1972, Achenbach Found. Legion Honor, 1973, Dubins Gallery, L.A., 1985, 86, 89, 92, others; exhibited in group shows at Gump's Gallery, San Francisco, 1971-76, Anchorage Fine Arts and Hist. Mus., 1976, Bklyn. Mus., 1976, 78, Crocker Art Mus., Sacramento, Calif., 1980, Palo Alto Cultural Ctr., 1992, Galerie Sho, Tokyo, 1994, J.J. Brookings Gallery, San Francisco, 1997, others; represented in permanent collections Biblioteque National, Paris, Mus. Modern Art, N.Y.C., Libr. of Congress, Washington, Nat. Gallery of Art, Washington, others. Recipient 4 Purchase prizes Honolulu Acad. Arts, 1973-78, Purchase prize City of Phila., 1973, Bklyn. Mus. Art, 1972; Ford Found. grantee, 1968; Nat. Endowment for the Arts fellow, 1980. Home: 640 Santa Rosa Ave Berkeley CA 94707-1547

NANAY, BENCE, writer; b. Budapest, Hungary, Oct. 3, 1974; s. Istvan Nanay, Marianne Blazso. MA, Eotvos Lorand U., Budapest, 1999; MPhil, Cambridge U., Eng., 2001; PhD, U. Calif., Berkeley, 1999. Faculty Dept. Philosophy, U. Calif., Berkeley. Author: (bbok) Mind and Evolution, 2000 (Various); editor: (jour.) Metropolis, 1997 (Various). Recipient Pro Scientia Gold Medal, Hungarian Acad. Sci., 1999; fellow Hewlett fellow, Hewlett Found., 1999—2002, Benefactors' fellow, St John's Coll. Cambridge, 2000—01, Republic of Hungary fellow, Republic of Hungary, 1998—99. Fellow: Collegium Budapest (Fellow 2001—02); mem.: Cambridge Overseas Trust (hon.; Fellow 2000).

NÁNAY, JULIA, oil and gas consulting company executive; b. Budapest, Hungary, Mar. 15, 1951; came to U.S., 1957; d. Endre and Marta (Medvegy) N.; 1 child, Ilona Clara. BA, UCLA, 1973; MA in Law and Diplomacy, Tufts U., 1976. Asst. v.p. N.E. Petroleum Co., Boston, 1976-83; v.p. Charter Oil Co., Washington, 1983-85; dir. Petroleum Fin. Co., 1985—. Author: Transylvania: The Hungarian Minority in Rumania, 1974; contbr. articles to profl. jours., chpts. to numerous books; appearances on TV, radio, conf. on oil and gas. Mem. Phi Beta Kappa. Lutheran. Home: 2808 Olive Ave NW Washington DC 20007-3327 E-mail: jnanay@pfcenergy.com.

NANCE, ALLAN TAYLOR, retired lawyer; b. Dallas, Jan. 31, 1933; s. A.Q. and Lois Rebecca (Taylor) N. BA, So. Meth. U., 1954, LLB, 1957; LLM, NYU, 1978. Bar: Tex. 1957, N.Y. 1961. With Simpson Thacher & Bartlett, N.Y.C., 1960-65; asst. counsel J.P. Stevens & Co., Inc., 1965-70, sec., 1970-78, asst. gen. counsel, 1970-89; counsel J.P. Stevens & Co. Inc. and WestPoint-Pepperell Inc., 1989-93; asst. gen. counsel WestPoint Stevens Inc., N.Y.C., 1993-98, ret., 1998. With USNR, 1957-59. Woodrow Wilson fellow Columbia U., 1959-60. Mem. Phi Beta Kappa. Home: 201 E 66th St New York NY 10021-6451

NANCE, BETTY LOVE, librarian; b. Nashville, Oct. 29, 1923; d. Granville Scott and Clara (Mills) N. BA in English magna cum laude, Trinity U., 1967; AB in LS, U. Mich., 1958. Head dept. acquisitions Stephen F. Austin U. Libr., Nacogdoches, Tex., 1958-59; libr. 1st Nat. Bank, Ft. Worth, 1959-61; head catalog dept. Trinity U., San Antonio, 1961-63; head tech. processes U. Tex. Law Libr., Austin, 1963-66; head catalog dept. Tex. A&M U. Libr., College Station, 1966-69; chief bibliographic svcs. Washington U. Libr., St. Louis, 1970; head dept. acquisitions Va. Commonwealth U. Libr., Richmond, 1971-73; head tech. processes Howard Payne U. Libr., Brownwood, Tex., 1974-79; libr. dir. Edinburg (Tex.) Pub. Libr., 1980-91. Pres. Edinburg Com. for Salvation Army. Mem. ALA, Pub. Libr. Assn., Tex. Libr. Assn., Hidalgo County Libr. Assn. (v.p. 1989-81, pres. 1981-82), Pan Am. Round Table Edinburg (corr. sec. 1986-88, assoc. dir. 1989-90), Edinburg Bus. and Profl. Womens Club (founding bd. dirs., pres. 1986-87, bd. dirs. 1987-88), Zonta (bd. dirs. San Antonio 1996-97), Alpha Lambda Delta, Alpha Chi. Home: 5359 Fredericksburg Rd # 806 San Antonio TX 78229-3549 E-mail: bettynance@webtv.net.

NANCE, DAVID W. minister; b. Lubbock, Tex., Aug. 19, 1956; s. James Wilson and Carole Delia Nance; m. LaDonna Ann Coulston, Nov. 18, 1983; children: Zachary Wilson, Rachel Marie. AA, Memphis Sch. of Preaching, 1981; BA, Ala. Christian Sch. Religion, Montgomery, 1983; MA, Harding U., 1991; D Ministry, So. Christian U., Montgomery, 1996. Min. Clyattville (Ga.) Ch. of Christ, 1981-83, Elem Grove Ch. of Christ, Burlison, Tenn., 1983-89, Cape Coral (Fla.) Ch. of Christ, 1989-92, Hinesville (Ga.) Ch. of Christ, 1992-97, Parkway Ch. of Christ, Naples, Fla., 1997—. Sgt. USAF, 1974-78. Recipient Scholarly Achievement award Am. Bible Soc., 1996. Avocations: scuba diving, reading, fishing, cooking. Business E-Mail: prkwycoc@gate.net.

NANCE, JOHN JOSEPH, lawyer, writer, air safety analyst, broadcaster, consultant; b. Dallas, July 5, 1946; s. Joseph Turner and Margrette (Grubbs) N.; m. Benita Ann Priest, July 26, 1968; children: Dawn Michelle, Bridgitte Cathleen, Christopher Sean. BA, So. Meth. U., 1968, JD, 1969; grad., USAF Undergrad. Pilot Tng., Williams AFB, Ariz., 1971. Bar: Tex. 1970, U.S. Ct. Appeals (fed. cir.) 1994. News reporter, broadcaster, newsman various papers and stas, Honolulu and Dallas, 1957-66; news anchorman Sta. WFAA-AM, Dallas, 1966-70; newsman including on camera Sta. WFAA-TV; pvt. practice, 1970—; news dir. Newscom Network, 1970; airline pilot Braniff Internat. Airways, 1975-82, Alaska Airlines, Inc., Seattle, 1985—; chmn., pres. Exec. Transport, Inc., Tacoma, 1979-85; chmn., CEO EMEX Corp., Kent, Wash., 1987—; mng. ptnr. Phoenix Ptnrs., Ltd., Tacoma, 1995—; project devel. assoc. Columbia Tristar TV, 1997—; with Nance & Carmichael, PLLC, Austin, Tex., 1997—. Spkr. Human Mgmt., 1984—, Teamwork and Comms. in the Med. Profession; airline safety, advocate Ind. Cons., earthquake preparedness spokesman Ind. Cons.; dir. steering com. Found. for Issues Resolution in Sci. Tech., Seattle, 1987-89; speaker Northwestern Transp. Ctr. Deregulation and Safety Conf., 1987; cons. NOVA Why Planes Crash, PBS, 1987, ABC World News Tonight Crash of US AIR 427, 1994; aviation analyst ABC-TV and radio, 1995—; aviation editor: ABC Good Morning Am., 1995—; broadcast analyst, 1986—; spkr. in field. Author: Scorpion Strike, 1982, Splash of Colors, 1984, Blind Trust, 1986, On Shaky Ground, 1988, Final Approach, 1990, What Goes Up, 1991, Operating Handbook USAF Air Carrier Safety and Inspection, 1991, Phoenix Rising, 1994, Medusa's Child, 1997, The Last Hostage, 1998, Blackout, 2000, Headwind, 2001; contbr. ; : Turbulence, 2002 actor: appeared in Sheep on the Runway, 1975; (TV series) Pandora's Clock, 1996; tech. advisor (TV series) Pandora's Clock, 1996; actor: (TV series) Medusa's Child, 1997; prodr.: USF Video Prodns.: ANG Introduction to CRM, 1992, USAF SOC CRM Program, 1992, The Teamwork Connection, 1996; author: USF Video Prodns.: ANG Introduction to CRM, 1992, USAF SOC CRM Program, 1992, The Teamwork Connection, 1996; dir.: USF Video Prodns.: ANG Introduction to CRM, 1992, USAF SOC CRM Program, 1992, The Teamwork Connection, 1996. Pres. Fox Glen Homeowners Assn., Tacoma, 1974-77; cons. Congl. Office Tech. Assessment, Tacoma, 1987; witness air safety hearings U.S. Congress, Washington, 1986-88; bd. dirs. St. Charles Borromeo Sch., Tacoma, 1975-78, Nat. Patient Safety Found. of AMA, 1997—; mem. Mayor's Vets. Task Force, Tacoma, 1991; bd. advisors Jour. Air Law and Commerce So. Meth. Sch. Law, 1995—, exec. bd. Sch. of Law, 1998—; bd. advisors Pacific Northwest Writer's Conf., 1994—; adv. bd. supply and logistics mgmt. program Portland State U., 1997-98. Capt. USAFR, 1975-94; lt. col. Persian Gulf. Decorated Merit Svc. medal; named Airline Safety Man of Year Wash. State Div. of Aeronautics, 1987. Fellow Chartered Inst. Transport (Canberra, Australia); mem. ABA, SAG, Tex. Bar Assn., Author's Guild Am., Res. Officers Assn. (life), Aircraft Owners' and Pilots' Assn., Phi Alpha Delta, Delta Chi. Home and Office: John Nance Prodns 4512 87th Ave W Tacoma WA 98466-1920 Office: Phoenix Ptnrs Ltd PO Box 24465 Federal Way WA 98093-1465

NANCE, RICHARD J. health facility administrator, social worker; b. Newport, Ark., Apr. 17, 1956; s. Richard Jackson and Beth Shirlene Nance; life ptnr. Susan Melissa Peyser. AB, Point Loma Coll. (now Point Loma Nazarene U.), 1978; MSHHA, U. Ala., Birmingham, 1981; MSW, Brigham Young U., 1995. Lic. clin. social worker Utah, designated mental health examiner Utah. Dir. divsn. human svcs. Utah County Govt., Provo, 1998—. Exec. bd. dirs. Utah Behavioral Healthcare Network, Salt Lake City; bd. dirs. Brigham Young U. Sch. Social Work Faculty Adv. Bd., Provo, 2000—, Utah Behavioral Healthcare Network, Salt Lake City. Author: (booklet) Passage of Time: A Brief History of Social Work and Social Welfare in Utah Since Statehood, 1996. Bd. dirs. Substance Abuse Technical Advisory Group, Utah Health Policy Commission, Salt Lake City, 1998—2000. Mem.: NASW, Assn. Family Practice Adminstrs. (founding mem., treas. 1983—84), Med. Group Mgmt. Assn., Assn. Mental Health Adminstrs., Nat. Assn. Cmty. Behavioral Health Dirs. Avocations: running, horseback riding, mountain biking, hiking, skiing. Home: 2885 N Marrcrest Cir Provo UT 84604 Office: Utah County Divsn Human Svcs 100 E Center St Provo UT 84606 Office Fax: 801-370-8498. Business E-Mail: ucadm.richardn@state.ut.us.

NANCE, ROBERT LEWIS, oil company executive; b. Dallas, July 10, 1936; s. Melvin Renfro Nance and Ruth Natlie (Seibert) Nowlin; m. Penni Jane Warfel; children: Robert Scott, Amy Louise, Catherine Leslie. BS, So. Meth. U., 1959; LLD (hon.), Rocky Mountain Coll., 1989. V.p. geology Oliver & West Cons., Dallas, 1960-66; ptnr. Nance & Larue Cons., 1966-69; pres., CEO Nance Petroleum Corp., Billings, Mont., 1969—. Bd. dirs. First Interstate Bank, Mont., MDU Resources, St. Mary Land and Exploration Co., Rocky Mountain Coll., Billings, chmn., 1986-91; mem. Nat. Petroleum Coun., 1992-94; chmn. Petroleum Technology Transfer Coun., 1996-99. Coun. pres. Am. Luth. Ch., Billings, 1980; trustee, chmn. Deaconess Med. Ctr., Billings; chmn. Deaconess Billings Clinic Healty Sys. Recipient Hall of Fame award Rocky Mountain Coll. Alumni, 1987, Disting. Svc. Trusteeship, Assn. Governing Bds. Univs. Colls., 1988. Mem. Am. Assn. Petroleum Geologists, Ind. Petroleum Assn. Am. (exec. com., nat. bd. govs.), Ind. Petroleum Assn. Mountain States (v.p. Mont. 1977-79, Wildcatter of Yr. 1999), Mont. Petroleum Assn., Hilands Golf Club, Billings Petroleum Club. Avocations: fly fishing, scuba diving, skiing. Office: Nance Petroleum Corp PO Box 7168 550 N 31st St Billings MT 59103

NANCE, SANDRA JUNE TADDIE, blood service administrator; b. Balt., Nov. 21, 1953; d. John Anthony and Elizabeth Arlene (Warfel) Taddie; m. Robert Daniel Nance; 1 child Danielle Elizabeth stepchildren: Christa Darleen, Amy Rebecca Boeke. BS, Ind. U. of Pa., 1975; MS in Pathology, U. Md., 1982. Lic. clin. immunohematology tech., Calif., 1981, med. tech., Am. Soc. Clin. Pathologists, 1975, spl. in blood banking, Am. Soc. Clin. Pathologists, 1979. Instr. U. Md., Balt., 1979-80, grad. student researcher pediatric research dept., 1979-80; lead tech. Johns Hopkins Blood Bank, 1979-81; research tech. ARC Blood Svc., L.A., 1981-85, faculty, rsch. assoc., 1985-90; asst. dir., faculty ARC Blood Svc./Penn Jersey Region, Phila., 1990—2001; dir. ARC Bid Sen, 1994—, Nat. Ref Lab. for Blood Group Serology, 1995—; faculty mem. U. Pa., 1995—. Mem. Invitational Conf. of Investigative Immunohematologists, mem. steering com., 1996—. Editor: Methods in Immunohematology, 1988, Immune Destruction of Red Blood Cells, 1989, Transfusion Medicine in the 1990s, 1990, Basic Science and Clinical Aspects of Immunohematology, 1991, Blood Safety: Current Challenges, 1992. Ch. tchr. St. Peter's by the Sea Presbyn. Ch., Rancho Palos Verdes, 1987-90. Recipient AABB John Elliott Meml. award, 1996; scholar, Alpha Mu Tau, Md. Soc. Med. Tech., 1978, Hyland Therapeutics, Travenol Labs., Inc., 1978. Mem.: Pa. Assn. Blood Banks (sci. program com. 1990—94, bd. dirs. 1994—2002), Calif. Blood Bank Soc. (adminstrv. program com. 1982—83, sci. program com. 1982—84, abstract rev. com. 1986—87, sci. program com. 1986—88, publs. com. 1986—89), L.A. Serum Cell. Soc., Am. Assn. Blood Banks (ann. sem. com. 1986—90, sci. program abstract reviewer 1986—, chmn. 1988—90, chmn. sci. program com. 1990—98, bd. dirs. 1998—, Found. Rsch. grantee 1989, NBF scholar 1994), Am. Soc. Clin. Pathologists (nominating com. 2000—01, teleconf. com. 1990—, transfusion medicine coun. 2001—). Democrat. Presbyterian. Avocations: skiing, water skiing, photography, dog obedience/agility.

NANCE, WELDON BAILEY, petroleum engineer; b. Alice, Tex. s. Weldon Bailey and Viola (Freeman) N.; m. Frances Kay Bourriague, June 20, 1969 (div. Oct. 1987); 1 child, David Wayne; m. Donna Marie Villarrubia, Aug. 3, 1989; 1 child, Olivia Eleanor. BS, U. Southwestern La., 1968; MS, Australian Nat. U., Canberra, 1976. Product devel. supr. Milchem Inc., Houston, 1975-79; drilling engr. Tenneco Oil Co., Lafayette, La., 1979-84, engring. cons., 1984-86, chem. svcs. mgr., 1986-87; drilling engring. supr. Brit. Gas, Houston, 1989-92; gen. mgr. Brit. Gas Gabon, Port Gentil, 1992-94, Amerada Hess Gabon, Libreville, 1994—, also bd. dirs. Contbr. articles to sci. publs. With USMCR, 1961-67. Mem. Soc. Petroleum Engrs. Roman Catholic. Achievements include 2 patents in field. Avocations: fishing, tennis, jogging. Home: PO Box 2040 Houston TX 77252-2040 Office: Amerada Hess PO Box 2040 Houston TX 77252

NANCREDE, SARAH ELIZABETH (SALLY NANCREDE), reporter; b. Bloomington, Ind., Mar. 7, 1944; d. George Riley and Elizabeth Clare (May) Boardman; m. Richard Allen Falk, Jan. 27, 1969 (div. May 1979); m. David Henry Nancrede, Apr. 1, 1992. AB in English Lit., Ind. U., 1966, MS in English, 1973. Lic. tchr., Ind. Tchr. Bloomfield (Ind.) Sch. System, 1966-67; writer Ind. U. News Bur., Bloomington, 1967-69, South Ctrl. Bell Telephone Co., Louisville, 1969; copy editor, reporter The News Sentinel, Ft. Wayne, Ind., 1970-72; home furnishings editor The Indpls. Star, 1973-90, arts & entertainment writer, 1990-95, weekend editor, 1994-95; cityside neighborhood reporter The Indpls. Star & News, 1995-99; neighborhood reporter The Indpls. Star, 1999—2001. Chmn. food com. St. Joan of Arc French Market, Indpls., 1996—. Named to Furniture Writers Hall of Fame, 1979. Mem. Delta Delta Delta. Avocation: travel. Home: 4164 N Washington Blvd Indianapolis IN 46205-2617 Office: 4164 N Washington Blvd Indianapolis IN 46205-2617 E-mail: hoosierhabitat@yahoo.com.

NANDA, VED PRAKASH, law educator, university official; b. Gujranwala, India, Nov. 20, 1934; came to U.S., 1960; s. Jagan Nath and Attar (Kaur) N.; m. Katharine Kunz, Dec. 18, 1982; 1 child, Anjali. MA, Punjab U., 1952; LLB, U. Delhi, 1955, LLM, 1958, Northwestern U., 1962; postgrad., Yale U., 1962-65; LLD, Soka U., Tokyo, 1997, Bundelkhand U., Jhansi, India, 2000. Asst. prof. law U. Denver, 1965-68, assoc. prof., 1968-70, prof. law, dir. Internat. Legal Studies Program, 1970—, Thompson G. Marsh prof. law, 1987—, Evans Univ. prof., 1992—, asst. provost, 1993-94, vice provost, 1994—; sst. prof. law . Denver, 965-68, ssoc. prof., 968-70, rof. law, dir. Internat. Legal Studies Program, 970—, hompson G. Marsh prof. law, 987—, vans Univ. prof., 992—, sst. provost, 993-94, ice provost, 994—. ls. prof. Coll. Law, U. Iowa, Iowa City, 1974-75, Fla. State U., 1973, U. San Diego, 1979, U. Colo., 1992; disting. vis. prof. internat. law Chgo. Kent Coll. Law, 1981, Calif. We. Sch. Law, San Diego, 1983-84; disting. vis. scholar Sch. Law, U. Hawaii, Honolulu, 1986-87; cons. Solar Energy Rsch. Inst., 1978-81, Dept. Energy, 1980-81. Uthor: (with David Pansius) Litigation of International Disputes in U.S. Courts, 1987; editor: (with M. Cherif Bassiouni) A Treatise on International Criminal Law, 2 vols., 1973, Water Needs for the Future, 1977; (with George Shepherd) Human Rights and Third World Development, 1985; (with others) Global Human Rights, 1981, The Law of Transnational Business Transactions, 1981, World Climate Change, 1983, Breach and Adaption of International Contracts, 1992, World Debt and Human Conditions, 1993, Europe Community Law After 1992, 1993, International Environmental Law and Policy, 1995; (with William M. Evan) Nuclear Proliferation and the Legality of Nuclear Weapons, 1995, (with others) European Union Law After Maastricht, 1996, (with S.P. Sinha) Hindu Law and Legal Theory, 1996, (with D. Krieger) Nuclear Weapons and the World Court, 1998; editor, contbr.: Refugee Law and Policy, 1989; editl. bd. Jour. Am. Comparative Law, Indian Jour. Internat. Law, Transnational Pubs. O-chmn. Colo. Pub. Broadcasting Fedn., 1977-78; mem. Gov.'s Commn. on Pub. Telecommunications, 1980-82. Em. World Jurist Assn. (v.p. 1991—, pres. 1997—), World Assn. Law Profs. (pres. 1987-93), UN Assn. (v.p. Colo. divsn. 1973-76, pres. 1986-88, 93-96, nat. coun. UNA-USA 1990—, mem. governing bd. UNA-USA 1995—), World Fedn. UN Assns. (vice-chmn. 1995—), Am. Assn. Comparative Study Law (bd. dirs. 1980—), Am. Soc. Internat. Law (v.p. 1987-88, exec. coun. 1969-72, 81-84, bd. rev. and devel. 1988-91, hon. v.p. 1995—), Assn. Am. Law Schs., U.S. Inst. Human Rights, Internat. Law Assn. (mem. exec. com. 1986—), Colo. Coun. Internat. Orgns. (pres. 1988-90), Assn. U.S. Mems. Internat. Inst. Space Law (bd. dirs., mem. exec. com. 1980-88), Internat. Acad. Comparative Law (assoc.), Order St. Ives (pres.), Rotary, Cactus Club. Office: U Denver Coll Law 1900 Olive St Denver CO 80220-1857 E-mail: vnanda@mail.law.du.edu.

NANDAGOPAL, MALLUR R. engineer; b. Kolar, Karnataka, India, May 14, 1938; came to U.S., 1976; s. M. Ramanuja Iyengar and Garudammal; m. Sreedharani K. Ramamurthy; children: Radha, Meena, Sudha. BS, Cen. Coll., Bangalore, India, 1958; B of Tech., Indian Inst. Tech., Bombay, 1962; ME, Indian Inst. Sci., Bangalore, 1963, PhD, 1974. Registered profl. engr., Wash.; cert. water distbn. mgr. 4, Wash. Mem. faculty Indian Inst. Sci., 1963-77; engr. City of Spokane, Wash., 1977—. Coord. summer sch. Indian Inst. Sci., 1974-75. Contbr. articles to profl. jours. Mem. restoration adv. bd. Fairchild AFB. Mem. IEEE (sr., Engr. of Yr. award 1995), Inst. Sci. (sec. Staff Club 1972-74), Fed. Emergency Mgmt. Agy. (mitigation com.). Hindu. Avocations: tennis, astrology, reading, movies. Home: 410 E Shiloh Hills Dr Spokane WA 99208-5819 E-mail: mallur@hotmail.com. *Motto: "It is better that managers lose face than the public lose money."*.

NANGIA, SHASHI BHUSHAN, executive; b. New Delhi, Mar. 24, 1948; s. Mitra Bhushan and Sushila Devi (Mohan) N.; m. Vandana Bhan, Jan. 26, 1952; children: Shalini, Sheetal, Kulbhushan. Dir. Ashish Pub. House, New Delhi, 1974—, APH Exports, New Delhi, 1995—. Home: 8/81 Punjabi Bagh New Delhi 110 026 India Office: APH Exports Ansari Rd New Delhi 110 002 India

NANGLE, JOHN FRANCIS, federal judge; b. St. Louis, June 8, 1922; s. Sylvester Austin and Thelma (Bank) N.; m. Jane Adams, June 7, 1986; 1 child, John Francis Jr. AA, Harris Tchrs. Coll., 1941; BS, U. Mo., 1943; JD, Washington U., St. Louis, 1948. Bar: Mo. 1948. Pvt. practice law, Clayton, 1948-73; judge U.S. Dist. Ct., 1973—, chief judge, 1983-90, sr. judge, 1990—91, Ga., 1991—. Mem. 8th Cir. Jud. Coun.; mem. exec. com. Jud. Conf. U.S.; chmn. Jud. Panel on Multidist. Litigation, mem. working group on mass torts, mem. jud. resources working group. Mem. Mo. Rep. Com., 1958-73; mem. St. Louis County Rep. Cen. Com., 1958-73, chmn., 1960-61; pres. Mo. Assn. Reps., 1961, Reps. Vets. League, 1960; mem. Rep. Nat. Com., 1972-73; bd. dirs. Masonic Home Mo. With AUS, 1943-46. First Sgt. USAR. Named Mo. Republican of Year John Marshall Club, 1970, Mo. Republican of Year Mo. Assn. Reps., 1971; recipient Most Disting. Alumnus award Harris-Stowe Coll., Most Disting. Alumnus award Washington U. Sch. Law, 1986. Mem. ABA, Legion of Honor DeMolay, Mo. Bar Assn., St. Louis Bar Assn., St. Louis County Bar Assn.

NANK, LOIS RAE, financial executive; b. Racine, Wis., Jan. 06; d. Walter William August and Lanora Elizabeth (Freymuth) N. BS in Econs., U. Wis., 1962; postgrad. in profl. mgmt., Fla. Inst. Tech., 1977. Contract specialist U.S. Naval Ordnance Sta., Forest Park, Ill., 1963-66, U.S. Army Munitions Command, Joliet, 1966-72, plans/program specialist, 1972-73, U.S. Army Armament Command, Rock Island, Ill., 1973-77; chief budget office U.S. Army Auto Log Mgmt. System Act, St. Louis, 1977-81; sr. budget analyst U.S. Army Materiel Command, Alexandria, Va., 1981-87; sr. fin. mgr. Def. Mapping Agy., Reston, 1987-93; cons. Springfield, Va, 1993-96, Leesburg, Fla., 1996—. Coun. mem. chairperson bldg. com. Bread of Life Luth. Ch., Springfield, Va., 1986-90, Christ Luth. Ch., Fairfax, Va., 1990-96; bd. dirs. Cedar Wood Homeowners' Assn., Bettendorf, Iowa, 1975-77, Oak Homeowners' Assn., Chesterfield, Mo., 1980-81. Mem. Order of Ea. Star. Avocations: travel, people, fashion, interior design, architecture.

NANKO, RAYMOND S. physician; b. Inglewood, Calif., Feb. 13, 1962; s. John and Veronica Marie (Thunder) N. DC, Cleve. Chiropractic Coll., 1985; MD, Ross U., 1994. Diplomate Am. Bd. Disability Analysts, Am. Bd. Family Practice, Am. Bd. Chiropractic Orthopedics, Am. Bd. Pain Mgmt. With ActiveCare Med. Spine & Pain Ctr., Muncie, Ind. Fellow Am. Back Soc.; mem. AMA, Ind. State Med. Assn., Ind. State Chiropractic Assn., Am. Chiropractic Assn., Am. Acad. Orthop. Medicine, Nat. Headache Found., Ind. State Med. Assn., Ind. State Chiropractic Assn., Coun. Orthop., Acad. Chiropractic Orthopedics, Arthritis Found., Internat. Spinal Injection Soc., Am. Assn. Orthopedic Medicine. Office: Active Care Med Spine & Pain Ctr 919 W Jackson St Muncie IN 47305-1554

NANNE, LOUIS VINCENT, professional hockey team executive; b. Sault Ste. Marie, Ont., Can., June 2, 1941; s. Michael and Evelyn N.; m. Francine Yvette Potvin, Aug. 27, 1962; children: Michelle, Michael, Marc, Marty. BS in Mktg., U. Minn., 1963. Mem. Minn. North Stars hockey club, 1967-78, v.p., gen. mgr., 1978-88, pres., 1988-91; sr. v.p. Piper Capital Mgmt., Mpls., 1991-95; exec. v.p. Voyageur Asset Mgmt., 1995—. Bd. govs. Nat. Hockey League, 1981-91; mem. internat. com. USA Hockey. Bd. dirs. Mpls. C.C. Found., 1986-90, Children's Home Soc., 1998—. Recipient Lester Patrick award NHL, 1989; named among Top 50 Players in 50 Yrs.; inducted into U. Minn. Hall of Fame, U.S. Hockey Heritage Hall of Fame award, Sault St. Marie Hall of Fame, U.S. Hockey Hall of Fame. Mem. Interlachen Country Club (bd. dirs. 1992-95), Spring Hill Golf Club (bd. dirs. 1996—). Roman Catholic. Office: Voyageur Asset Mgmt 90 S 7th St Minneapolis MN 55402-3903

NANNEY, DAVID LEDBETTER, genetics educator; b. Abingdon, Va., Oct. 10, 1925; s. Thomas Grady and Pearl (Ledbetter) N.; m. Jean Kelly, June 15, 1951; children: Douglas Paul, Ruth Elizabeth Beshears. AB, Okla. Bapt. U., 1946; PhD, Ind. U., 1951; Laurea honoris causa, U. Pisa, Italy, 1994. Asst. prof. zoology U. Mich., Ann Arbor, 1951-56, asso. prof., 1956-58; prof. zoology U. Ill., Urbana-Champaign, 1959-76, prof. genetics and devel., 1976-86, prof. ecology, ethology and evolution, 1987-91, prof. emeritus, 1991—. Sr. postdoctoral fellow Calif. Inst. Tech., 1958-59; predoctoral fellow NIH, Ind. U., 1949-51 Author: (with Herbert Stern) The Biology of Cells, 1965, Experimental Ciliatology, 1980. Recipient Disting. Alumnus award Okla. Bapt. U., 1972; named Disting. Lectr. Sch. Life Scis., U. Ill., 1981; Preisträger, Alexander von Humboldt Stiftung, Fed. Republic Germany, 1984. Fellow AAAS, Am. Acad. Arts and Scis.; mem. Genetics Soc. Am., Am. Genetic Assn. (pres. 1982), Soc. Protozoologists. Home: 703 W Indiana Ave Urbana IL 61801-4835 Office: U Ill Dept Animal Biology 505 S Gregory St Urbana IL 61801 E-mail: d-nanney@uiuc.edu.

NANTO, ROXANNA LYNN, marketing professional, management consultant; b. Hanford, Calif., Dec. 17, 1952; d. Lawson Gene Brooks and Bernice (Page) Jackson; m. Harvey Ken Nanto, Mar. 23, 1970; 1 child, Shea Kiyoshi. AA, Chemeketa Community Coll., 1976; BSBA, Idaho State U., 1978. PBX operator Telephone Answer Bus. Svc., Moses Lake, Wash., 1965-75; edn. coord. MimiCassia Community Edn., Rupert, Idaho, 1976-77; office mgr. Lockwood Corp., 1977-78; cost acct. Keyes Fibre Co., Wenatchee, Wash., 1978-80; acctg. office mgr. Armstrong & Armstrong, 1980-81; office mgr. Cascade Cable Constrn. Inc., East Wenatchee, 1981-83; interviewer, counselor Wash. Employment Security, Wenatchee, 1983-84; pres. chief exec. officer Regional Health Care Plus, East Wenatchee, 1986-88; dist. career coord. Eastmont Sch. Dist., 1984-90; prin. Career Cons., 1988-90; exec. dir. Wenatchee Valley Coll. Found., 1990-91; ednl. cons. Sunbelt Consortium, East Wenatchee, 1991-93; cons. CC Cons. Assocs., 1993—; ptnr. Cmty. Devel. Mktg. and Mgmt. Resource Group, Wenatchee, Wash., 1994—, also bd. dirs.; ptnr. Bus. Consulting and Rsch., Malaga, Wash., 1997-99. Speaker North Cen. Washington Profl. Women, Wenatche, 1987, Wen Career Women's Network, Wenatchee, 1990, Wenatchee Valley Rotary, 1990, Meeting the Challenge of Workforce 2000, Seattle, 1993; cons., speaker Wash. State Sch. Dirs., Seattle, 1987; speaker Wenatchee C. of C., 1989; sec. Constrn. Coun. of North Cen. Washington, Wenatchee, 1981-83; bd. dirs. Gen. Vocat. Adv. Bd., Wenatchee, 1986-88, Washington Family Ind. Program, Olympia, 1989-91; mem. econ. devel. coun. Grant County, 1992—; ptnr. low income housing devel. Bus. Cons. & Rsch., Wenatchee, 1996-99. Mem. at large career Women's Network, 1984—, mem. Econ. Devel. Coun. of No. Cen. Washington; mem. Steering Com. to Retain Judge Small. Recipient Nat. Paragon award, 1991, Wash. State Gov.'s award for achievement in farmworker housing, 2001; grantee Nat. Career Devel. Guidelines Wash. State, 1989; named Wenatchee Valley Coll. Vocat. Contbr. of Yr., 1991. Fellow Dem. Women's Club; mem. Nat. Assn. Career Counselors, Nat. Assn. Pvt. Career Counselors, Nat. Coun. Resource Devel., NCW Estate Planning Coun. Avocations: self improvement books, staff and organizational development, cmty. improvements advocate, housing development for elderly and special needs individuals. Home and Office: 2961 Riviera Blvd Malaga WA 98828-9733

NANTS, BRUCE ARLINGTON, lawyer; b. Orlando, Fla., Oct. 26, 1953; s. Jack Arlington and Louise (Hulme) N. BA, U. Fla., 1974, JD, 1977. Bar: Fla. 1977. Asst. state's atty. State Atty.'s Office, Orlando, 1977-78; pvt. practice, 1979—. Columnist The Law and You, 1979-80. Auctioneer pub. TV sta., 1979; campaign coord. cen. Fla. steering com. Bob Dole for Pres., 1988; bd. dirs. Cystic Fibrosis Found. Mem. Acad. Fla. Trial Lawyers, Am. Arbitration Assn., Fellowship Christian Athletes (past bd. dirs. Cen. Fla.), Tiger Bay Club Cen. Fla., Orlando Touchdown Club, Fla. Blue Key, Omicron Delta Kappa, Phi Beta Kappa, Phi Delta Theta. Democrat. Baptist. Avocations: tennis, golf, swimming, scuba diving. Home: 1112 Country Ln Orlando FL 32804-6934 Office: PO Box 547871 Orlando FL 32854-7871

NANULA, RICHARD, health products executive; BA in economics, U. Calif., Santa Barbara; MBA, Harvard Bus. Sch. Chmn. and CEO Broadband Sports; pres. and COO Starwood Hotels; various positions Walt Disney Co.; exec. v.p. - fin., strategy and comm. Amgen, 2001—. Office: Amgen Amgen Ctr Thousand Oaks CA 91320*

NAN YU, XIAO, dancer; b. Dalian, China; Trained at, Shen Yang Sch. of Dance, Beijing Dance Acad., China, Nat. Ballet Sch., Can., 1995—96. Apprentice ballerina Nat. Ballet Can., Toronto, Canada, 1996—2000, first soloist, 2000—. Office: Walter Carsen Ctr for Nat Ballet Canada 470 Queens Quay West Toronto ON M5V 3K4 Canada*

NANZ, ROBERT HAMILTON, petroleum consultant; b. Shelbyville, Ky., Sept. 14, 1923; s. Robert Hamilton and Willie Virginia (O'Brien) N.; m. Norma Lee Peters, Dec. 21, 1944; children— Robert H., Loren P. BA in Geology, Miami U., Oxford, Ohio, 1944; PhD, U. Chgo., 1952. With Shell Oil Co., 1947-83, exploration mgr., 1964-66, exploration mgr. Pacific Coast area Los Angeles, 1966-67, dir. exploration research Houston, 1959-64, v.p. exploration and prodn. research center, 1967-70, v.p. exploration N.Y.C., Houston, 1970-75, v.p. Western exploration and prodn. ops. Houston, 1975-81, v.p. tech., 1982-83. Fellow Geol. Soc. Am.; mem. Am. Petroleum Inst. (past chmn. gen. com. exploration affairs, chmn. public lands task force), Am. Assn. Petroleum Geologists (select com. on OCS). Clubs: Lakeside Country (Houston). Presbyterian. Home: 10102 Briar Dr Houston TX 77042-1209

NAOR, DANIEL, food products executive; b. Paris, July 1, 1960; s. Shlomo and Sarah (Puderbeutel) N.; 1 child, Nathalie. BS in Elec. Engring., MS in Elec. Engring. and Computer Sci., MIT, 1981; MBA, INSEAD, 1990. Cert. engr. Project mgr. ELOP, Rehovot, Israel, 1985-87, mktg. mgr. Israel, 1988-89; assoc. McKinsey & Co., Paris, 1990-95, prin., 1995-98, Dallas, 1998—2002; v.p. strategy, planning and bus. devel. Frito Lay N.Am., Plano, 2002—. Contbr. articles to profl. jours. Mem. bd. dirs. Dallas Theater Ctr. Bd., 1999-2002, Variety, 1997—. Capt. Israeli Air Force, 1981-85. Mem. IEEE, Tau Beta Pi, Sigma Xi (assoc.). Jewish. Avocations: ballroom dancing, cinema, theater, philately. Office: Frito Lay 7701 Legacy Dr Plano TX 75024 Business E-Mail: DanielNaor@FritoLay.com.

NAPADENSKY, HYLA SARANE, engineering consultant; b. Chgo., Nov. 12, 1929; d. Morris and Minnie (Litz) Siegel; m. Arnaldo I. Napadensky; children: Lita, Yafa. BS in Math., MS in Math., U. Chgo. Design analysis engineer Internat. Harvester Co., Chgo., 1952-57; dir. rsch. Ill. Inst. Tech. Rsch. Inst., 1957-88; v.p. Napadensky Energetics Inc., Evanston, Ill., 1988-94; engring. cons., Lutsen, Minn., 1994-98. Contbr. numerous articles to profl. jours. Bd. overseers Armour Coll. Engring. Ill. Inst. Tech., 1988-93. Mem. NAE, Sigma Xi. Home and Office: 3284 W Highway 61 Lutsen MN 55612-9537

NAPALA, PHIL, aerospace engineer; BS in Mgmt. Engring., U. Pacific, Stockton, Calif., 1974; grad., Navy Logistics Tng. program, Mechanicsburg, Pa., 1977. Cert. reliability engr. Dep. for reliability and maintainability Naval Air Systems Command, U.S. Army; prodn. and operational analysis engr. Office of Sec. Def.; aerospace engr. AST Safety, Reliability, Maintainability and Quality Assurance NASA, 1990—. Mem.: Am. Soc. Quality. Office: NASA Hdqrs Mail Code Q 300 E St SW Washington DC 20546*

NAPIER, BRUCE ALAN, physicist; b. Pitts., July 14, 1953; s. Robert McMunn Napier, Doris Ann Napier; m. Judith Ann Bamberger; children: Alexandra, Jonathan. BS, Kans. State U., 1975, MS, 1977; PhD, Oreg. State U., 2002. Cert. health physicist American Board of Health Physics, 1986. Staff scientist Pacific Northwest Nat. Lab., Richland, Wash., 1977—. Chair U.S./Ukraine Bi-Nat. adv. com. Chernobyl studies U.S. Nat. Cancer Inst., Kiev, Ukraine, 1998—2001; chair U.S./Belarus Bi-Nat. adv. com. Chernobyl studies US National Cancer Institute, Minsk, Belarus, 1998—; chair Chernobyl thyroid adv. group U.S. Nat. Cancer Inst., Bethesda, Md., 2001—; chief scientist Hanford Environ. Dose Reconstruction Project, Richland, 1987—94; Principle Investigator US/Russia Joint Coordinating Committee for Radiation Effects Research, Chelyabinsk, Russia, 1995—2002. Author: (computer code) GENII - The Hanford Environmental Dosimetry Software System, 1986; contbr. articles to profl. jours. Named Health Physicist of Year, Columbia Chpt. Health Physics Soc., 1987. Mem.: Health Physics Soc. (sec. 1999—2000), Northview Swim Club (treas. 2000—02). Avocations: water sports, skiing, hiking. Office: Pacific Northwest Nat Lab PO Box 999 Richland WA Business E-Mail: Bruce.Napier@PNL.GOV.

NAPIER, CAMERON MAYSON FREEMAN, historic preservationist; b. Shanghai, China, Dec. 5, 1931; d. Hamner Garland and Cameron Middleton (Brame) Freeman; m. John Hawkins Napier III, Sept. 11, 1964. Student, L'Ecole des Artes Municipale, Paris, 1950-51; BA, U. Ala., 1955. Photographer's asst. Scott, Demott & Perry, Montgomery, Ala., 1951; art dir. WCOV-TV, 1955; self-employed graphic designer Dallas, 1956-64; self-employed designer Alexandria, Va., 1965-71; restoration chmn. White House Assn. Ala., Montgomery, 1973-76, 1st vice regent, 1976-80, regent, 1980—. Co-founder Friends of Stratford Hall for No. Va., Alexandria, late 1960s; docent chmn. Lee's Boyhood Home, Alexandria, late 1960s; bd. dirs. Landmarks Found., Montgomery, 1971-75; advisor Conde Charlotte House, Mobile, Ala., 1994-95. Author, designer booklet: The First White House of the Confederacy, 1978 (nat. printers award 1979). Bd. dirs. English Speaking Union, Montgomery, 1980-83. Named Hon. First Lady, by the Gov.'s wife, Montgomery, Ala., 1985; recipient Awards of Excellence, Advt. Artists Assn., Dallas, 1960, 1961, 1962, disting. svc. award, Ala. Hist. Commn., Montgomery, 1977, Cert. of Commendation, Gov. Ala., 1986, So. Patriot award, 1997, Lifetime Achievement award, Ala. Preservation Alliance, 2001, Jefferson Davis award, 1984, Winnie Davis award, United Daus. of Confederacy, 1985. Mem.: Antiquarian Soc. (pres. 1981—82), Sojourners Lit. Club (pres.), Militi Templi Scotia (dame 1993), Daus. of Barons Runnymede, Am. Soc. Most Venerable Order of the Hosp. of St. John of Jerusalem (assoc. officer sister 1995), Nat. Soc. Colonial Dames in Am. (hist. properties com. 1994—95, state bd. mgrs. 1998—2000, ctr. vice chmn. 1998—2000), Sovereign Mil. Order Temple of Jerusalem (aumoniere 1995, dame comdr. 1996), Soc. Desc. of Colonial Clergy, Kappa Delta. Episcopalian. Avocations: crossword puzzles, afternoon tea. Office: First White House Confed 644 Washington St Montgomery AL 36130-3057

NAPIER, JOHN HAWKINS, III, historian; b. Berkeley, Calif., Feb. 6, 1925; s. John Hawkins and Lena Mae (Tate) N.; m. Cameron Mayson Freeman, Sept. 11, 1964. BA, U. Miss., 1949; MA, Auburn U., 1967; postgrad., Georgetown U., 1971; D (hon.), Napier U., Edinburgh, 2000. Journalist, tchr. Picayune (Miss.) H.S., 1946; commd. 2d lt. U.S. Air Force, 1949, advanced through grades to lt. col., 1966; ret., 1977. Staff dir. Congressional Com. on S.E. Asia, 1970; faculty Air War Coll., 1971-74; Air U. Command historian, 1974-77; asst. to exec. dir. Ala. Commn. on Higher Edn., Montgomery, 1977-78; adj. history faculty Auburn U., Montgomery, 1980-85; columnist Montgomery Advertiser, 1980-87; lectr. in field. Author: Lower Pearl River's Piney Woods: Its Land and People, 1985; The Air Force Officers Guide, 30th edit., 1995, Dr. Patrick Napier: His Ancestors and Some Descendants, 1991; contbr. articles to profl. jours. With USMC, 1943-46, col. Ala. State Defense Force, 1991-97, brig. gen., dep. comdr., 1997-99. Decorated Legion of Merit; Order of St. John of Jerusalem, Milit. and Hospitaller Order of St. Lazarus of Jerusalem, Sovereign Mil. Order of Temple of Jerusalem; recipient award of merit Ala. Hist. Commn., 1976, Ala. Disting. Svc. medal, 1999, merit award English-Speaking Union U.S., 1983; Taylor medal and grad. fellow U. Miss., 1949; Storrs scholar Pomona Coll., 1942-43. Fellow Soc. Antiquaries Scotland; mem. English-Speaking Union (pres. 1978-87, nat. dir. 1980-86, 87-90, 91-94), Royal Order Scotland, Ala. Hist. Assn. (pres. 1979-80), Soc. Pioneers Montgomery (pres. 1979-80), Soc. Colonial Wars, SCV (vice comdr. Ala. 1979-80), Soc. War of 1812 (pres. Ala. 1980-82), St. Andrews Soc., S.R. SAR (pres. 1974-75), Clan Napier in N.Am. (lt. to chief 1985—), Order 1st Families Va., Gov. Ala. Soc. Order Founders Patriots Am., Jamestowne Soc., Soc. Cincinnati, Ala. Assn. (pres. 1998-2001), Montgomery Country Club, Aztec 1847, Mil. Order Carabao, Royal Scots (Edinburgh), Scabbard and Blade, Sigma Chi, Phi Kappa Phi, Omicron Delta Kappa, Phi Alpha Theta, Pi Sigma Alpha. Home: Kilmahew 158 Mt Zion Rd Ramer AL 36069-6505

NAPIER, MICHELLE H. nursing educator; b. Mansfield, Ohio, June 13, 1963; d. Herbert and Kathryn (Shortridge) Hatfield; m. Doyle Napier, May 21, 1983. Diploma, St. Marys Sch. Nursing, Huntington, W.Va., 1983; BSN, Ohio U., Ironton, 1988; MSN, Bellarmine Coll., 1990. Critical care nurse St. Mary's Hosp., Humana Hosp. Louisa, Ky.; instr. nursing Ashland (Ky.) Community Coll. Mem. ANA, Ky. Nurses Assn., Ohio U. Honor Soc. for Nursing, Sigma Theta Tau Internat. Home: PO Box 249 Fort Gay WV 25514-0249

NAPIER, PETER CHARLES, manufacturing company consultant; b. Bryn Mawr, Pa., July 5, 1936; s. Charles Campbell and Violet Burnie Napier; m. Elena Nikolaeva, Oct. 5, 1996; children: Arianne, Tanya, Anna, Lydia. BA, BS, Swarthmore Coll., 1958; MS, Technische Hochschule, Munich, Germany, 1959. Dir. ops. The Gillette Co., London, 1968-81, Schering-Plough Inc., London, 1981-87; pres. Advent Mfg. Internat., 1987-90; v.p. internat. ops. Tambrands Inc., White Plains, N.Y., 1990-96; dir. internat. ops. Am. Saw, East Longmeadow, Mass., 1997—. Part-time lectr. Ashridge Coll., Berkhamstead, Eng., 1985-87. Mem. Hurlingham Club. Avocations: skiing, motorcycling, traveling. Home: 42 Pinckney St Boston MA 02114-4800

NAPIER, RONALD LEWIS, lawyer; b. Alexandria, Va., Oct. 12, 1954; s. William Wilson and Lee Elizabeth (Moore) N.; m. Katherine Winston Pritchard, May 27, 1979; children: Andrew Lewis, William Hamilton, Mary Katherine. BS in Math., Mary Washington Coll., Fredericksburg, Va., 1977; JD, U. Va., 1981. Bar: Va. 1981, U.S. Dist. Ct. (we. dist.) Va. 1981. Ptnr. Napier & Napier, P.C., Front Royal, Va., 1981-98; pres. Napier, Pond, Athey & Athey, P.C., 1998—. Mem. Warren County Bar Assn. (pres. 1994-96), Rotary (bd. dirs. Front Royal Club 1987-94, pres. 1993-94, asst. gov. Internat. Dist. 7570 1996-98, Paul Harris Fellowship award Rotary Found. 1993). Baptist. Home: 545 Locust Dale Rd Front Royal VA 22630-4531 Office: Napier Pond Athey & Athey PC 35 N Royal Ave Front Royal VA 22630-2662 E-mail: ron@npaalaw.com.

NAPIER, THOMAS M. electrical engineer; b. Forfar, Scotland, Jan. 20, 1941; came to U.S., 1981; BS in Physics, Aberdeen (Scotland) U., 1962, MS in Electronics, 1963. Rsch. asst., sr. exptl. officer Leeds (Eng.) U., 1963-70; payload engr. ESTEC, Netherlands, 1970-72; electronics engineer CERN, Geneva, 1972-79; devel. mgr. Nuc. Enterprises Ltd., Edinburgh, Scotland, 1979-81; sr. engr. LeCroy Rsch. Sys., Spring Valley, N.Y., 1981-85; engr. mgr. Aydin Monitor Sys., Ft. Washington, Pa., 1985-88; prin. engr. Aydin Computer and Monitor Sys., Horsham, 1988-96; electronics cons., 1996—. Contbr. articles to profl. jours. Achievements include patent. Mem. Mensa, Phila. Assn. Critical Thinking (mem. coun. 1994—). Home and Office: 1 Lower State Rd North Wales PA 19454

NAPIER, WILLIAM JAMES, JR. marine oil and gas construction consultant; b. Dallas, July 19, 1952; s. William James and Frankie (Hanchey) N.; m. Christine Ann Douget, June 18, 1977; children: Jay, Stephanie, George, Catherine. BS in Marine Biology, U. So. Miss., 1974; BS in Civil Engring., La. Tech. U., 1976. Project engr., field engr. inland svcs. divsn. McDermott Internat. Inc., Harvey, La., 1976-80, project coord. New Orleans and Houston, 1982-86, sr. project coord./project coord. worldwide bus. devel. New Orleans, 1986-89; project engr. McDermott Nigeria, Ltd., Warri, 1980-82; mgr. marine sales/dir. marine sales, nat. accounts mgr. Bailey Controls Co., New Orleans,

1989-92; pres. COO Balehi Marine, Inc., Lacombe, La., 1992-94; pres., owner Fairwinds Internat. Inc., Mandeville, 1994—. Elder Lakeview Christian Ctr., New Orleans, 1985-92. Mem. Soc. Naval Architects and Marine Engrs., Franco's Athletic Club. Republican. Baptist. Avocations: weight lifting, racquetball, bicycling. Home: 913 Beau Chene Dr Mandeville LA 70471-1505 Office: Fairwinds Internat Inc 4045 De Soto St Mandeville LA 70448

NAPLES, CAESAR JOSEPH, law and public policy educator, lawyer, consultant; b. Buffalo, Sept. 4, 1938; s. Caesar M. and Fannie A. (Occhipinti) N.; children: Jennifer, Caesar; m. Sandra L. Harrison, July 16, 1983. AB, Yale U., 1960; JD, SUNY, 1963. Bar: N.Y. 1963, Fla. 1977, Calif. 1988, U.S. Supreme Ct. 1965. Assoc. Moot & Sprague, Buffalo, 1965-69; asst. dir., employee rels. N.Y. Gov. Office, Albany, 1969-71; asst. v. chancellor SUNY, 1971-75; vice chancellor and gen. counsel Fla. State U. System, 1975-82; v. chancellor Calif. State U. System, 1983-92; vice chancellor emeritus Calif. State U., 1992—; prof. law and fin. Calif. State U. System, Long Beach, 1983—; bd. dirs., gen. counsel, corp. sec. Open U., Denver and Wilmington, Del., 1999—. Cons. Govt. of Australia, U. Nev. Sys., Assn. Can. Colls. and Univs., Que., also other univs. and colls. Contbr. articles to profl. jours.; co-author: Romanov Succession, 1989 with J.Victor Baldridge. Bd. dirs., gen. counsel Walden U., 1997—; mem. Metlife Resources Adv. Bd., 1986—, chmn., 1992—; mem. Meml. Heart Inst. Long Beach Meml. Hosp., 1993—, bd. dirs., chmn. 1998—, found. bd., 1996—; bd. dirs. Calif. Acad. Math. and Scis., 1995—. Capt. U.S. Army, 1963-65. Mem. Acad Pers. Adminstrn. (founder), Nat. Ctr. for Study Collective Bargaining Higher Edn. (bd. dirs.). Avocations: opera, tennis. Office: 816 N Juanita Ave Ste B Redondo Beach CA 90277-2200 Fax: 310-798-0065. E-mail: cjnaples@csulb.edu.

NAPLES, MARY CECILIA, mental health services professional, health facility administrator; b. Ocana, Colombia, Oct. 31, 1954; d. Efrain and Olga (Rodriguez) Pineres; m. Anthony Louis Naples Jr., May 30, 1981; children: Marina Nicole, Alysia Marie. BA, Coll. of Comm. and Fine Arts, 1992, MEd in Counselor Edn., 1994; PhD in Family Therapy, Nova Southeastern U., 2002. Lic. mental health counselor; nat. cert. counselor; bd. cert. clin. hypnotherapist; bd. cert sex therapist. Owner, CEO Every Woman's Place, Boca Raton, Fla., 1997-99, Family Life Counseling Ctr., Boca Raton, 1999—. Profl. mem. Am. Counseling Assn. Roman Catholic. Avocations: movies, connecting with family and friends. Office: Family Life Counseling Ctr 400 S Dixie Hwy Ste 100 Boca Raton FL 33432 E-mail: napleslmhc@aol.com.

NAPLES, NANCY A. sociology and women's studies educator; b. S.I., N.Y., Dec. 20, 1951; d. Donald V. and Margaret J. Naples. BA, Springfield (Mass.) Coll., 1972; MA in Dance Edn., NYU, 1974; MSW, Hunter Coll., 1979; PhD in Sociology, CUNY, 1988. With YWCA of N.Y.C., 1972-80; lectr. sociology SUNY, Purchase, N.Y., 1986-87; social work rschr. Sloan Kettering Cancer Inst., N.Y.C., 1987-88; asst. prof. sociology SUNY, Old Westbury, N.Y., 1988-89, U. Calif., Irvine, 1989-92, assoc. prof. sociology and women's studies, 1998—, U. Conn., 2001—. Author: Grassroots Warriors: Activist Mothering, Community Work and the War on Poverty, 1998; editor: Cmty. Activism and Feminist Polit. Organizing Across Race, Class, and Gender, 1998; editor: (with Manesha Desai) Women's Activism and Globalization, 2002. Mem. Am. Sociol. Assn., Soc. for Study of Social Problems, Nat. Women's Studies Assn., Social Sci. History Assn., Rural Sociol. Assn. Home: 82 Kenyon St Hartford CT 06105

NAPLES, RONALD JAMES, manufacturing company executive; b. Passaic, N.J., Sept. 10, 1945; s. James V. and Lee A. N.; m. Suzanne Lorraine Shoudy, June 17, 1967; children: Regen Jeffrey, Marcus Jamison, Tiffany Marie. BS, U.S. Mil. Acad., 1967; MA, Fletcher Sch. Law, 1972; MBA with distinction, Harvard U., 1974. Assoc. in corp. fin. Loeb Rhoades Co., 1973; fellow, spl. asst. to counselor to Pres. The White House, 1974; spl. asst. to adminstr. Fed. Energy Adminstrn., 1975; exec. dir. Presdl. Task Force on Energy, Washington, 1975-76; v.p. internat. Hunt Mfg. Co., Phila., 1976, exec. v.p., 1980-81, vice chmn., pres., CEO, 1981-86, chmn., CEO, 1987-95; also dir.; pres. Hunt Internat. Co., 1977-82; pres., CEO Quaker Chem. Corp., 1995-97, chmn., pres., CEO, 1997—. Dir. Glatfelter Paper Co.; chmn. U. of Arts; bd. dirs. Fed. Res. Bank Phila.; CEO DF Decade Bus. Equipment Fin. World mag., 1989. Bd. dirs. Rock Sch. Pa. Ballet, ARC, Fgn. Policy Rsch. Inst., Phila., Phila. Mus. Art Franklin Inst., Friends Ctrl. Sch. With U.S. Army, 1967-71. Decorated Bronze star with oak leaf cluster, Army Commendatin medal with oak leaf cluster, Air medal, Cross of Gallantry (Vietnam); recipient Mil. Order World Wards award U.S. Mil. Acad., 1967, Phila. Inc. Cmty. Leadership award, 1990, Human Rels. Civic Achievement award Am. Jewish Com., 1989, Semper Fidelis award Marine Corps Scholarship Fedn., 1991; named Outstanding Young Man Am., U.S. Jaycees, 1977, Stephen Girard award Phila. Fin. Assn., 1992, Touching a Life award Boys and Girls Clubs Am., 1994; Walter Heller fellow, Harvard U., 1974; White Ho. fellow, 1974-75. Mem. White House Fellows Assn., World Pres.' Orgn., Chief Execs. Orgn., Assn. Grad. U.S. Mil. Acad., Harvard Bus. Sch. Alumni Assn., Racquet Club, Pyramid Club, Harvard Bus. Sch. Club (Phila.), Phila. Country Club. Office: Quaker Chem Corp Elm & Lee Sts Conshohocken PA 19428

NAPLETON, ROBERT JOSEPH, lawyer; b. Evergreen Park, Ill., Jan. 13, 1963; s. Francis Edward and Elizabeth (Raynor) N.; m. Clare Therese McEnery, June 6, 1992; children: Martin Joseph, Nora Elizabeth, Patricia Clare, Francis James, Luke John. BBA, Loyola U., Chgo., 1985, JD, 1988. Bar: Ill. 1988, U.S. Dist. Ct. (no. dist.) Ill. 1988, U.S. Dist. Ct. (ctrl. dist.) Ill. 1995, U.S. Dist. Ct. (we. dist.) Wis. 1998, U.S. Supreme Ct. 1999. Law clk. to Chief Judge James E. Murphy Circuit Ct. of Cook County, Chgo., 1985-87; mem. staff State's Atty. Office of Cook County, Markham, Ill., 1987-88; assoc. Motherway & Glenn, Chgo., 1988-98; ptnr. Motherway, Glenn & Napleton, 1999—. Spkr., presenter in field. Treas. campaign Citizens to Elect James Brosnahan State Rep. for 36th Dist., Ill., 1996—. Fellow Roscoe Pound Found.; mem. ATLA (aviation law com.), Ill. Trial Lawyers Assn. (bd. advocates 1993-97, bd. mgrs. 1997—, med. negligence and product liability coms. 1994—, civil practice com. 1995—), Ill. State Bar Assn. (bd. govs. 1994-2000, tort law sect. coun. 1992-95), Southwest Bar Assn., Chgo. Bar Assn. (trial techniques com. 1991-92), Catholic Lawyers Guild, Brother Rice H.S. St. Thomas More Soc. Democrat. Roman Catholic. Avocations: golf, skiing, ice hockey, reading. Home: 400 Sunset Ave La Grange IL 60525-6115 Office: Motherway Glenn & Napleton 100 W Monroe St Ste 200 Chicago IL 60603-1923

NAPOLEON, DONALD PAUL, b. Niagara Falls, N.Y., Apr. 10, 1954; s. Vincent Dominic and Lucy Ann (Manuse) N.; m. Justine Ann Wieszczyk, May 7, 1977; children: Rachel Marie, Rebecca Ann, Paul Vincent John. Assoc., Nat. Radio Inst., Washington, 1979. Night mgr. Tops Friendly Markets, Niagara Falls, 1972-76, asst. mgr., 1976-80, grocery mgr., 1980-93; owner, prin. Cataract Refrigeration Co., 1993—95; grocery staff support coord. TOPS Friendly Markets, 1995-96, sr. merchandising analyst, 1996-2001; v.p. ops. VSCO, Inc., 2001—. Mem. Niagara Coun. of Arts, 1989; mem. Parent Network, Buffalo, 1989; pres. bd. dirs. United Cerebral Palsy Assn. of Niagara, Inc., 1989—. Mem. Refrigeration Svc. Engrs. Soc. Republican. Roman Catholic.

NAPOLI, DONNA JO, linguistics educator, writer; b. Miami, Fla., Feb. 28, 1948; d. Vincent Robert and Helen Gloria Napoli; m. Barry Ray Furrow, Dec. 29, 1968; children: Elena, Michael Enzo, Nicholas Umberto, Eva, Robert Emilio. BA in Math., Harvard U., 1970, MA in Italian Lit., 1971, PhD in Gen. and Romance Linguistics, 1973. Instr. Italian Berlitz, Seattle, 1970, Concord (Mass.) Pub. Schs., 1970; tchg. fellow dept. linguistics, math. and romance langs. Harvard U., 1970-73; lectr. dept. philosophy, dept. romance langs. and lit. Smith Coll., Northampton, Mass., 1973-74; lectr. dept. math. and dept. romance langs. and lit. U. N.C., Chapel Hill, 1974-75; asst. prof. linguistics Georgetown U., 1975-80, U. Mich., Ann Arbor, 1980-82, assoc. prof., 1982-84, prof., 1984-87; prof., dir. linguistics Swarthmore (Pa.) Coll., 1987—. Linguistics cons. Ednl. Testing Svc., Princeton, N.J., 1971-72; S.W. Brooks vis. lectr. dept. English U. Queensland, St. Lucia, Australia, summer 1992; instr. First Australian Linguistic Inst., U. Sydney, Australia, 1992, U. Geneva, 1993; vis. prof. English dept. San Francisco State U., summer 1994; vis. lectr. linguistics U. Witwatersrand, Johannesburg, South Africa, summer 1995; prof. Coll. English Tchr. Tng. Inst., summer 1997. Author: The Two si's of Italian: An Analysis of Reflexive, Inchoative, and Indefinite Subject Sentences in Modern Standard Italian, 1976, (with E. Rando) Syntactic Argumentation, 1979, Predication Theory: A Case Study for Indexing Theory, 1989, Syntax: Theory and Problems, 1993, (with S. Davis) Phonological Factors in Historical Change: The Passage of the Latin Second Conjugation into Romance, Linguistics: Theory and Problems, 1996, over 40 fiction books for children; editor: Elements of Tone, Stress, and Intonation, 1978; co-editor: (with J. Kegl) Bridges Between Psychology and Linguistics: A Swarthmore festschrift for Lila Gleitman, 1991; contbr. articles to profl. jours. Recipient Briggs award Radcliffe Coll., 1970; Fulbright-Hays Jr. lectr. in linguistics, Italy, 1974-75, Fulbright-Hays sr. lectr. in linguistics, Italy, 1975-76; NEH fellow, 1979-80, 90-91, Eugene Lang Faculty fellow, 1994-95; grantee Radcliffe Inst., 1970, 72, Nederlandse Organisatie voor Zuiverwetenschappelijk Onderzoek, Amsterdam, 1976, NSF, 1981-83, Rackham Faculty grantee, 1983-84, Sloan Found. grantee, 1988, Curricular Devel. grantee Swarthmore, 1989; scholar Radcliffe Coll., 1966-70. Office: Linguistics Dept Swarthmore Coll Swarthmore PA 19081 E-mail: dnapoli1@swarthmore.edu.

NAPOLI, MARY, education educator; b. Dover, N.J., Jan. 4, 1969; d. Patrick and Josephine N. BS in Elem. Edn., East Stroudsburg (Pa.) U., 1991; MS in Reading, Marywood U., 1997. Tchr. K-1st grade Pocono Mountain Sch. Dist., Swiftwater, Pa., 1987-98; asst. prof. Elizabeth Town Coll., 2001—. Bd. dirs. East Stroudsburg U. Alumni, 1997—; judge Monroe County Math Fair, 1993-97; lector Our Lady of Victory Ch., Tannersville, Pa., 1992-97; founding pres. Nat. Coun. of Tchrs. of English Pa. State U.; co-creator Partners in Literacy. Recipient Nat. Writing Project fellow, 1994. Mem. Am. Ednl. Rsch. Assn., Children's Lit. Assn., Internat. Reading Assn., Nat. Coun. of Tchrs. of English, Am. Ed. Rsch., Kappa Delta Pi., Omicron Delta Kappa, Phi Delta Kappa, Pi Delta Theta, Alpha Epsilon Lamba. Roman Catholic. Avocations: basketball, reading.

NAPOLIELLO, DANIEL ANDREW, nursing administrator; b. Omaha, Sept. 27, 1944; Ceasare Dan and Therese Mary (Sierszynski) N.; m. Sally Ann Rodak, Jan. 7, 1967; children: John, Ann Marie, Michael. Diploma in nursing, St. Joseph Hosp., Omaha, 1965; BS in Nursing, U. S.C., 1975; MEd, Chapman Coll., 1977. Commd. 2nd lt. U.S. Army, 1964; advanced through grades to capt. Nurse Corps U.S. Army, 1994, chief nurse 8th combat support hosp. Calif., 1975-77, resigned, 1977; commd. officer USPHS, 1977-94; retired, 1994; advanced through grades to comdr. USPHS, 1988, dir. nursing Indian Hosp. S.D., 1977-78, Winnebago, Nebr., 1984-87, assoc. hosp. dir. nursing edn. Balt., 1978-81, evening supr. nursing, coord. quality assurance, 1981-84; retired, 1994; area hosp. nursing cons. Phoenix Area Indian Health Svc., 1987-94; nurse cons. Peoria, 1994—; quality mgmt. specialist Intergroup of Ariz., 1996—2001; internal auditor med. care Triwest Healthcare Alliance, 2001—. Mem. USPHS Nursing Continuing Edn. Rev. Com., Rockville, Md., 1979—81, Indian Health Svc. Nursing Profl. Splty. Group, Rockville, 1984—90, Ind. Health Svc. Coun. of Nursing Svcs., 1987—94, chmn., 1988—92; managed care orgn. adv. com. chmn. Greater Ariz Ctrl. Credentialing Program, 1996—98; mem. Ariz. Diabetes Control Coun., 1997—; mem. rules task force Ariz. Dept. Health Svcs. Hosp., 1999—2001. Contbr. articles to profl. jours. Asst. scoutmaster Sioux coun. Boy Scouts Am., 1977—78, scoutmaster Balt. coun., 1978—81, asst. dist. commr. Prairie Gold area coun., 1982—87, asst. dist. commr. Theodore Roosevelt coun., 1987—93, chmn. dist. health and safety com., 1978—81, mem. health careers subcom. nat. exploring com., 1989—94, mem. coun. health and safety com., 1989—, dist. commr. Grand Canyon coun., 1993—97, co-chmn. exploring svc. team, 1998—99, asst. coun. commr., 1999—, mem. coun. risk mgmt. com., 2001—; instr. CPR ARC, 1982—87; mem. Hebr. Hist. Soc., Union Pacific R.R. Hist. Soc. Recipient citation USPHS, 1987, 94, commendation medal, 1989, Chief Nurse Office award, 1991, Outstanding Svc. medal, 1992, Nursing Excellence award for Nursing Practice, 1991, Wood Badge Boy Scouts Am., 1981, Exploring Leadership award, 1996, St. George Emblem, 1982, 3 Bead Wood Badge, 1989, Disting. Commr. award, 1991, Disting. Svc. Team award, 1998, Silver Beaver award, 1992, Surgeon Gen.'s Exemplary Svc. medal USPHS, 1993, Dirs. award for Excellence and EEO Excellence award, Indian Health Svc., Phoenix, 1994. Powder Horn award Boy Scouts Am., 2002. Mem. ANA, Nebr. Nurses Assn., Balt. Chpt. Commd. Officers Assn. of USPHS (nurse officers rep. 1980, v.p. 1981), Aberdeen Area Coun. on Nursing (pres. 1986-87), Nat. Model Railroaders Assn., Nat. Scout Collectors Soc., Camerail Club, Commd. Officers Assn. (sec.-treas. Phoenix chpt. 188-89, v.p. Phoenix chpt. 1990-91, pres. 1991-92, nat. del. 1987, 88, 92), Am. Legion. Democrat. Roman Catholic. Avocations: camping, photography, model railroading, philately, computers. Home: 8880 W Christopher Michael Ln Peoria AZ 85345-5687 Office: Triwest Healthcare Alliance Inc 15451 N 28th Ave Phoenix AZ 85053

NAPOLITAN, JOSEPH, political consultant; b. Springfield, Mass., Mar. 6, 1929; s. Pasquale and Lucy (Anzalotti) N.; m. Mary T. Nelen, Oct. 13, 1952; children: Christine, Joseph Jr., Luke, Martha. BA, Am. Internat. Coll., Springfield, Mass., 1952, DHL (hon.), 1971; LLD (hon.), Our Lady of the Elms Coll., Chicopee, Mass., 1994. Reporter Springfield Union, 1946-56; pres. Joseph Napolitan Assocs., Inc., Springfield, 1956—. Advisor to nine fgn. heads of state. Author: The Election Game, 1952, 100 Things I've Learned in 30 Years as a Political Consultant, 1986. Campaign staff Pres. John F. Kennedy, Pres. Lyndon B. Johnson, V.P. Hubert H. Humphrey. Named one of 100 Most Influential Pub. Rels. People of the Century, PR Week, 1999; Pew Found. honoree, 2000. Mem. Internat. Found. for Election Sys. (treas. 1994—, bd. dirs.), Internat. Assn. Polit. Cons. (pres., dir.), Am. Assn. Polit. Cons. (Hall of Fame 1991). Democrat. Office: Joseph Napolitan Assocs Inc 121 Chestnut St Springfield MA 01103-1500 E-mail: cigar777@aol.com.

NAPOLITANO, GRACE F. congresswoman; b. Brownsville, Tex., Dec. 4, 1936; d. Miguel and Maria Alicia Ledezma Flores; m. Frank Napolitano, 1982; 1 child, Yolando M., Fred Musquiz Jr., Edward M., Michael M., Cynthia M. Student, Cerritos Coll., L.A. Trade Tech, Tec Southwest Coll. Mem. Calif. Assembly, 1993-98, U.S. Congress from 34th Calif. dist., Washington, 1999—; mem. resources com., sml. bus. com. U.S. Ho. Reps. Councilwoman City of Norwalk, Calif., 1986-92, mayor, 1989-90; active Cmty. Family Guidance. Mem. Cerritos Coll. Found., Lions Club. Democrat. Roman Catholic. Office: US Ho Reps 1609 Longworth Ho Office Bldg Washington DC 20515-0001 also: PO Box 408 Sacramento CA 95812-0408*

NAPOLITANO, JANET ANN, state attorney general; b. N.Y.C., Nov. 29, 1957; d. Leonard Michael and Jane Marie (Winer) Napolitano. BS summa cum laude, U. Santa Clara, Calif., 1979; JD, U. Va., 1983. Bar: Ariz. 1984, U.S. Dist. Ct. Ariz. 1984, U.S. Ct. Appeals (9th cir.) 1984, U.S. Ct. Appeals (10th cir.) 1988, U.S. Ct. Appeals (5th cir.), U.S. Ct. Appeals, U.S. Ct. Appeals (7th cir.), U.S. Ct. Appeals (8th cir.). Law clk. to Hon. Mary Schroeder U.S Ct. Appeals 9th Cir., 1983—84; assoc. Lewis & Roca, Phoenix, 1984—89, ptnr., 1989—93; U.S. atty. Dist. Ariz., 1993—97; atty. Lewis and Roca, 1997—98; atty. gen. State of Ariz., 1999—. Mem. Atty. Gen.'s Adv. Com., 1983—, chair, 1995—96; chair victims rights subcom. Ariz. Criminal Justice Commn.; chair Ariz. High Intensity Drug Traficking Area; mem. Ariz. Peace Officer Stds. and Tng. Bd., Ariz. Pros. Attys.' Adv. Coun.; past com. to study civil litigation abuse, cost and delay Ariz. Supreme Ct.; past pres. Ariz. Cmty. Legal Svcs. Corp.; past judge pro tem Ariz. Ct. Appeals. Contbr. articles to profl. jours. Chmn. Nucleus, 1989—91; active Phoenix Design Stds. Rev. Com., 1989—91, Ariz. Women's Forum, Charter 100; hon. chmn. Camp Fire Boys and Girls, 1999; 1st vice-chmn. Ariz. Dem. Com., 1990—92; active Dem. Nat. Com., 1990—92; chmn. Ariz. del. Dem. Nat. Conv., 1992, chmn., 2000; active Ariz. Bd. Tech. Registration, 1989—92; bd. dirs. Ariz. Fire Fighters and Emergency Paramedics Meml., Phoenix Children's Hosp., Actors' Lab Ariz., Inc., Ariz. Peace Officers Meml.; bd. regents Santa Clara U., 1992—. Named Ariz. Dem. of Yr., 1989; recipient Leader of Distinction award, Anti-Defamation League, Human Betterment award, Roots and Wings, Golden Apple award, West Valley NOW, Nat. Network To End Domestic Violence award, Woman of Distinction award, Crohns and Colitis Disease Found., Women Making History award, Nat. Mus. Women's History, Tribute to Women award, YWCA; fellow Dillard fellow; scholar, Truman Scholarship Found, 1977. Fellow: Ariz. Bar Found.; mem.: ABA, Raven Soc., Sandra Day O'Connor Inn of Ct. (barrister), Ariz. Women Lawyers Assn., Ariz. State Bar (chmn. civil practice and procedure com. 1991—92), Am. Judicature Soc., Maricopa County Bar Assn. (past long range planning com.), Ariz. Bar Assn. (past com. on minorities in law, past chmn. civil practice and procedure com.), Nat. Assn. Attys. Gen. (exec. com., tobacco bankruptcy working group, health care fraud group, co-chmn. civil rights com., stop underage smoking com., exec. working group on prosecutorial rels.), Am. Law Inst., Alpha Sigma Nu, Phi Beta Kappa. Avocations: hiking, walking, travel, reading, film. Office: 1275 W Washington St Phoenix AZ 85007-2926

NAPOLITANO, LENA MARIE, surgeon, educator; b. Waterbury, Conn., Oct. 31, 1957; d. Carmine and Mary (Dell'Anno) N. BA, Boston U., 1979; MD, George Washington U., 1984. Diplomate Nat. Bd. Med. Examiners, Am. Bd. Surgery. Rsch. asst. dept. surgery Yale U. Med. Ctr., New Haven, 1979-80; resident in gen. surgery George Washington U. Med. Ctr., Washington, 1984-87, sr. resident in gen. surgery, asst. in surgery, 1988-89, chief resident in gen. surgery, clin. instr. in surgery, 1989-90; clin. and rsch. fellow dept. anesthesia and surgery Mass. Gen. Hosp./Harvard Med. Sch., Boston, 1987-88; instr., fellow in surg. critical care and trauma U. N.C. Hosps., Chapel Hill, 1990-91; trauma rsch. fellow dept. surgery U. N.C., 1991-92, attending in surgery, trauma and critical care, 1991-92; asst. prof. surgery and anesthesia U. Mass. Med. Ctr., Boston, 1992-95, dir. surg. critical care, co-dir. surg. ICU, trauma svcs., 1992-95; asst. prof. surgery U. Md. Med. Ctr. and Balt. VA Med. Ctr., 1995-97, assoc. prof., 1997—2000, prof. surgery, 2000—, dir. surg. critical care, nutrition support svcs., 1995—; divsn. chief surg. critical care U. Md. Med. Systems. Program dir., surg. critical care fellow U. Md. Med. Sys.; mem. disaster med. assistance team Internat. Inst. for Disaster and Emergency Medicine, U. Mass. Med. Ctr., 1993—; rschr., lectr. in field. Contbr. chpts. to books and articles to profl. publs.; reviewer Critical Care Medicine, Jour. Intensive Care Medicine, Chest. Conn. State scholar, 1975-79, Davis & Geck scholar, 1991; recipient Outstanding Resident award Holy Cross Hosp., 1988, Surg. Resident award Alpha Omega Alpha, 1989; grantee U. Mass. Med. Ctr., 1993, Burroughs Wellcome, Sterling Winthrop Inc., Soc. Critical Care Medicine, Cetus Corp., Alpha-Beta Tech., Inc., Healthcare Innovation. Fellow ACS (Harry Zehner Jr. Meml. Travelling Fellowship award Wash. chpt. 1989), Am. Coll. Chest Physicians; mem. AMA, Assn. for Acad. Surgery (mem. exec. coun. 1993—, mem. nominations com. 1994—), Surg. Infection Soc. (mem. edn. and fellowship com. 1995—), Assn. Women Surgeons (specialty rep. for trauma and critical care), Nathan Womack Surg. Soc., Soc. Critical Care Medicine, Worcester Med. Soc., Am. Med. Women's Assn., Ea. Assn. for Surgery of Trauma, Am. Soc. Parenteral and Enteral Nutrition, Am. Burn Assn., Shock Soc., Assn. VA Surgeons, Phi Beta Kappa. Office: Balt VA Med Ctr/ U Md Med Ctr 10 N Greene St Baltimore MD 21201-1524 E-mail: lnapolitano@smail.umaryland.edu.

NAPOLITANO, SUSAN, psychologist; b. Sept. 27, 1963; BS, LeMoyne Coll., 1985; MA, Fairleigh Dickinson U., 1988; PhD, Calif. Sch. Profl. Psychology, 1991. Asst. dir. Sullivan Ctr. for Children, Fresno, Calif., 1991—. Asst. prof. Calif. Sch. Profl. Psychology, Fresno, 1996—; chief of staff Cedar Vista Hosp., Fresno, 1999. Editor: San Joaquin Psychologist, Fresno, 1992-2000, Juvenile Diabetes Found. Newsletter, 1999-2001. Bd. dirs. Juvenile Diabetes Found., Fresno, 1999—. Mem. Fresno Area Psychol. Assn.. Office: Sullivan Ctr for Children 3443 W Shaw Ave Fresno CA 93711-3204 E-mail: snapoli@attbi.com.

NAPP, GUDRUN F. artist; b. Kiel, Germany, Aug. 14, 1929; came to the U.S., 1986; d. Walter Alexander and Erika Elisabeth (Burchard) Rode; m. Edmund Carl Napp, Dec. 29, 1951 (dec. Dec. 2002); children: Helenita F., Johann Christian, Anneke J., Florian D. Student, Art Sch., Kiel, 1949, Escuela Artes Plastias, Caracas, Venezuela, 1950, Toronto (Can.) Coll. Art, 1950-51. Assoc. dir. One Ear Soc., 1999-2001. Exhibited in group shows at Miami Beach Conv. Ctr., 1997, Art Expo L.A., 1997, 98, Art Expo N.Y., 1998, Art Expo Fla., 2000; one-woman shows include Art Am., 1997. Recipient cert. of excellence Art Horizon, N.Y.C., 1988, hon. mention Royal Poinciana Fiesta, Miami, 1993, The Fla. Mus. of Hispanic and L.Am. Art, Miami, 1994, Miami Watercolor Soc. exhibit, 1999, One Ear Soc. exhibit. Mem. Nat. Collage Soc., Internat. Soc. Exptl. Artists (signature mem.), Miami Watercolor Soc. (pres. 1995-96, trustee 1997, publicity chair 1998-99, 3rd place 1990), Art Expo Fla. Lutheran. Avocations: painting. Home: 1586 Passion Vine Cir Weston FL 33326 Studio: Studio Gallery Napp Inc 1388 Weston Rd Weston FL 33326 E-mail: art1100@aol.com.

NAPPI, JAMES FRANCIS, hand surgeon, educator; b. Ashtabula, Ohio, June 3, 1951; s. Samuel and Caroline Rose Nappi; children: Justin, Veronica, Celia, Samuel. BS cum laude, John Carroll U., 1973; MD, Ohio State U., 1976. Diplomate Am. Bd. Plastic Surgery C.A.Q. Hand Surgery. Instr. surgery Ohio State U., Columbus, 1980-82, asst. prof. surgery, 1983-86, clin. asst. prof. surgery, 1987—; mem. provisional staff Curtis Hand Ctr., Balt., 1982-83; founder Hand and Microsurgery Assocs., Columbus, 1987—; instr. Agee Endoscopic Carpal Tunnel Release Sys., 1993—. Sect. head plastic surgery Grant/Riverside Hosps., Columbus, 1994-98, sect. head hand surgery Grant/Riverside Meth. Hosps., 1999—. Contbr. chpts. to books, articles to profl. jours. Active Animal Rsch. vs. Animal Rights, Ohio State U., 1990—. Recipient Edwin Ellison award Dept. Surgery Ohio State U., 1982. Mem.: Am. Soc. Peripheral Nerve, Assn. Acad. Surgery, Plastic Surgery Rsch. Coun., Am. Soc. Reconstructive Microsurgery (edn. com. 1994—96), Am. Soc. Surgery of the Hand (self assessment exam com. 1991—, vice chair 2000), Sigma Xi. Avocations: golf, sailing, woodworking, children. Office: Hand & Microsurgery Assocs 3400 Olentangy River Rd Columbus OH 43202-1576

NAPUK, KERRY F. management executive; b. Great Falls, Mont., Oct. 5, 1939; s. David and Bernice (Manheim) N.; m. Angela Mary Bryant, July 31, 1970; children: Sarah, David. BS, U. Calif., 1961, MA, 1963. Intern AFL-CIO, Washington, 1963-64, rsch. dir. packinghouse workers Chgo., 1964-68; project mgr. SAC, San Francisco, 1968-72; non exec. dir. group of cos., Edinburgh, Scotland, 1973—. Dir. Open Futures Ltd., Scottis Dir. Centre. Author: The Strategy Led Business, 1993. Fellow Inst. Dirs. (London). Office: NAP Assocs Ltd 10 W Savile Rd Edinburgh EH16 5NG Scotland

NAQUIN, PATRICIA ELIZABETH, employee assistance consultant; b. Houston, Jan. 28, 1943; d. Louie Dee and Etha Beatrice (English) Price; m. Hollis James Naquin, Mar. 23, 1961; children: Price Naquin, Holli Campbell. BS, U. Houston, 1969, MS, 1982; PhD, Tex. Woman's U., 1988. Lic. profl. counselor; lic. chem. dependency counselor; nat. cert. counselor; cert. chem. dependency specialist; cert. employee assistance profl. Purchasing agt. Internat. Affairs U. Houston, 1966-68; elem. sch. tchr. Pasadena (Tex.) Ind. Sch. Dist., 1969-82; spl. edn. counselor Alvin (Tex.) Ind. Sch. Dist., 1982-85, drug-free schs. coord., 1988-92; marriage and family therapist Lifespan Counseling, Pasadena, 1985-92; employee assistance cons. DuPont, LaPorte, Tex., 1992—. Adv. com. mem. Sam Houston U., Huntsville, Tex., 1983; trainer and instr. Bay Area Coun. on Drugs and Alcohol, Houston, 1988—92; supr. State Bd. Profl. Counselors, Houston, 1988—; cons. Alvin Ind. Sch. Dist., 1989—92, DuPont Valuing People Core Team, 1993—; adj. prof. U. Houston, Clear Lake, 2001—. Co-author: Life is for Everyone Manual, 1990. Com. co-chair Alvin S.A.P. Task Force, 1988-92; com. mem. Tri-Dist. Task Force, Alvin, 1990-91; com. chmn. Alvin Bus./Edn. Partnership, 1992; bd. dirs. Brazoria (Tex.) County Coun. Drugs and Alcohol, 1991. Mem. Am. Assn. Marriage and Family Therapists, Tex. Assn. Counselors of Alcohol and Drug Abuse, Am. Counseling Assn., Employee Assistance Program Assn., Nat. Disting. Svc. Registry/Libr. of Congress, Phi Delta Kappa. Republican. Methodist. Avocations: quilting, playing piano, genealogy, computer games.

NAQUIN, SHARON SMITH, personnel director, educator; b. Baton Rouge, Dec. 9, 1961; d. James Edwards and Marjorie (Chustz) Smith; m. Al Joseph Naqin, May 26, 1984; 1 child Laura Blair. BS in Fin., La State U., Baton Rouge, 1982; BS in Mgmt., 1984, MA, 1995, PhD in Human Resource Devel., 1999. V.p. Pelican Homestead, Metaire, La., 1982—99; regional mgr. RTC, Dallas, 1991—93; asst. prof., rschr. La. State U., Baton Rouge, 1998—; pres. Assessment and Rsch. Assocs., 1998—. Author: (Book) How to Succeed in Your First Job, 2001, Helping Your New Employee Succeed, 2001, So You're New Again: How to Succeed When You Change Jobs, 2001; contbr. articles to profl. jours. Mem.: others, Soc. Human Resouce Mgmt., So. Mgmt. Assn., Southwest Acad. Mgmt., Cert. Knowledge and Info. Mgmt. Profl. Soc., Assn. Leadership Educators, La. Cert. Pub. Mgmt. Soc., Nat. Cert. Pub. Mgmt. Soc., Acad. Human Resource Dirs. Republican. Roman Catholic. Achievements include development of La. managerial and supervisor survey; new research constructive motivation to improve work through learning. Avocations: canoeing, hiking, travel.

NAQVI, IQBAL MEHDI, electrical engineering educator, consultant; b. New Delhi, India, Jan. 6, 1939; came to U.S., 1958; s. Mehdi Hasan and Nazar Amna (Zaidi) N.; m. Alice L. Smith, Dec. 19, 1964 (div. May 1975); children: Javed Iqbal, Jasmin Noor; m. Carol Ann Hildreth, Dec. 17, 1988. B.S., U. Panjab, Pakistan, 1958; B.E., Youngstown U., 1960; M.S., U. Pa., 1961; Ph.D., Cornell U., 1970. Sr. prin. engr. Honeywell Inc., Waltham, Mass., 1961-66; asst. prof. U. Hawaii, Honolulu, 1970-73; mem. research staff Fairchild Semiconductor, Palo Alto, Calif., 1973-75; mem. sr. tech. staff Rockwell Internat., Anaheim, Calif., 1975-78; head device engring. Hughes Aircraft Co., Newport Beach, Calif., 1978-82; vis. lectr. Calif. State U.-Fullerton, 1977, Calif. State Poly. U., 1978, U. Calif.-Irvine, 1981—; sr. cons. engr., head VLSI devel. MAI Basic Four, Tustin, Calif., 1982-85; cons. Western Digital Corp., Irvine, 1985-89; lectr. tech. presentation Device Research Conf., 1968, 70; moderator panel discussion Engring. Workstations, 1984, Silicon compilers, 1985. Contbr. articles to tech. jours. Research scholar U. Pa., 1961; research fellow Cornell U., 1966-69; research grantee U. Hawaii, 1971-73. Fellow Inst. for the Advancement of Engring.; mem. IEEE (sr. mem., chmn. Orange County sect. 1988—, program chmn. Orange County 1984-85, edn. chmn. 1984-85, chmn. circuits and systems/electron devices chpt. 1985-86), Computer Soc., Circuits and Systems Soc., Electron Devices Soc. Clubs: Sierra (San Francisco). Current work: Directing microelectronic chip development activity for computer applications; responsible for computer-aided design; lecturer, organizer of profl. courses and workshops; device physics. Subspecialties: Electronics; Computer-aided design. Home: 5742 Cardale St Lakewood CA 90713-1508

NAQVI, TASNEEM ZEHRA, cardiologist, researcher, consultant; b. Karachi, Sind, Pakistan, Jan. 19, 1960; came to U.S., 1991; d. Shaiq Hussain and Laila (Rajabali) Zaidi; m. Syed Shujat A. Naqvi, June 30, 1985; children: Ali A., Kazim A. BS, St. Joseph's Coll., Karachi, 1976; MBBS, Dow Med. Coll., Karachi, 1984. Diplomate Am. Bd. Internal Medicine, Am. Bd. Cardoivasc Disease, Nat. Bd. Echocardiography. House officer internal medicine & gen. surgery Civil Hosp., Karachi, 1984—85; resident med. officer internal medicine Aga Khan U. Hosp., 1985—86; registrar, instr. Civil Hosp., 1986—87; sr. house officer Lister Hosp., Stevenage, England, 1988—89; registrar Queen Elizabeth U. Hosp., Birmingham, England, 1989—91; asst. clin. instr. in medicine Stony Brook U. Hosp., NY, 1991—93; fellow in clin. cardiology Cedars Sinai Med. Ctr., L.A., Calif., 1993—96, staff cardiologist, 1996—, assoc. dir. cardiac non-invasive lab, 1996—. Asst. prof. medicine UCLA Sch. Medicine, 1997—; mem. instl. review bd. Cedars-Sinai Med. Ctr.; spkr. in field. Reviewer: Jour. Am. Coll. Cardiology , : Am. Jour. Cardiology, : Jour. Am. Soc. Echocardiography, : Am. Jour. Med. Scis., : Archives of Internal Medicine. Co-recipient Young Investigator award Am. Heart Assn., 1995; recipient Laverna Titus Young Investigators award Am. Heart Assn., 1995; fellow Am. Coll. Cardiology/Merck, 1996-97, L.A.Echo Soc., 1997. Fellow Am. Coll. Cardiology (cardiovasc. imaging com., edn. com. 2002-, Merck Rsch. Fellowship award 1996-97, Jr. Faculty award), L.A. Soc. Echocardiography (bd. dirs. 1997-, adv. bd. mem.); mem. Royal Coll. Physicians U.K., Am. Heart Assn., Am. Soc. Echocardiography (vascular task force), Pakistan Med. and Dental Coun. Office: Cedars Sinai Med Ctr 8700 Beverly Blvd Rm 5341 Los Angeles CA 90048 E-mail: tasneem.naqvi@cshs.org.

NARAD, JOAN STERN, psychiatrist; b. N.Y.C., June 21, 1943; d. Victor and Grete (Metzger) S.; m. Richard M. Narad; children: Christine, Laurie, Michael. BA, NYU, 1964; MD, Woman's Med. Coll., Pa., 1968. Diplomate Am. Bd. Psychiatry, Am. Bd Child Psychiatry. Intern pediatrics Stanford (Calif.) U. Hosp., 1968-69; resident adult psychiat. Med. Coll., Phila., 1969-71, chief resident in child psychiatry, 1971-73; grad. in psychoanalysis and child psychoanalysis Phila. Psychoanalytic Inst., 1978; practice medicine specializing in child and adolescent psychiatry Westport, Conn., 1973-98; chief Adolescent and Young Adult Svc., Silver Hill Found., New Canaan, 1980-84, 89-93, sr. adolescent cons., 1993-94; unit chief Riverview Hosp. for Children and Youth, Middletown, 1994—, assoc. med. dir., 1998—. Cons. Cath. Home Girls, Phila., 1971-78, Germantown Friends Sch., 1973-79; asst. prof. Child Psychiat. Med. Coll. Pa., 1975-79; asst. clin. prof. Yale Child Study Ctr., 1979-92, assoc. clin. prof., 1992—. Fellow NIMH, 1968. Fellow Am. Acad. Child and Adolescent Psychiat., Am. Acad. Pediats.; mem. Am. Psychiat. Assn., AMA, Alumnae Assn. Med. Coll. Pa., Western New Eng. Psychoanalytic Soc., Conn. Coun. Child Psychiatry. Home: 7 N Cove Rd Old Saybrook CT 06475-2538 Office: Riverview Hosp Middletown CT 06457

NARAD, RICHARD M. safety engineer; b. Niagara Falls, N.Y., July 7, 1935; s. Marian F. and Mary (Blum) N.; m. Faye Erhard, June 16, 1962 (dec. 1977); children: Christine, Laurie; m. Joan Gabrielle Stern, June 2, 1978; 1 child, Michael. BS, U. New Haven, 1976. Safety engr. Aetna Life & Casualty, Buffalo, Boston, 1962-71; corp. safety mgr. Scovill Mfg. Co., Waterbury, Conn., 1971-77; dir. safety Brinks, Inc., Darien, 1977-79; dir. indsl. safety, hygiene and security Gulf & Western, N.Y.C., 1981-86; dir. corp. safety Wickes Cos., Inc., N.Y.C., Santa Monica, 1986-88; owner R.M. Narad & Assocs., Old Saybrook, Conn., 1988—. Cons. in field; aj. instr. U. New Haven, 1975-81. With USAF, 1954-58. Mem. Nat. Safety Mgmt. Soc., Nat. Fire Protection Assn., Am. Soc. Safety Engrs. Avocations: boating, swimming. Address: 7 N Cove Rd Old Saybrook CT 06475-2538

NARAHASHI, TOSHIO, pharmacology educator; b. Fukuoka, Japan, Jan. 30, 1927; arrived in U.S., 1961; s. Asahachi and Itoko (Yamasaki) Ishii; m. Kyoko Narahashi, Apr. 21, 1956; children: Keiko, Taro. BS, U. Tokyo, 1948, PhD, 1960. Instr. U. Tokyo, 1951-65; research assoc. U. Chgo., 1961, asst. prof., 1962, Duke U., Durham, N.C., 1962-63, 65-67, assoc. prof., 1967-69, prof., 1969-77, head pharmacology div., 1970-73, vice chmn. dept. physiology and pharmacology, 1973-75; prof., chmn. dept. pharmacology Northwestern U. Med. Sch., Chgo., 1977-94; Alfred Newton Richards prof. Med. Sch. Northwestern U., 1983—, John Evans prof. Evanston, 1986—. Mem. pharmacology study sect. NIH, 1976-80; mem. rsch. rev. com. Chgo. Heart Assn., 1977-82, vice chmn. rsch. coun., 1986-87, chmn., 1988-90; mem. Nat. Environ. Health Scis. Coun., 1982-86; rev. com. Nat. Inst. Environ. Health Scis., 1991-95. Editor: Cellular Pharmacology of Insecticides and Pheromones, 1979, Cellular and Molecular Neurotoxicology, 1984, Insecticide Action: From Molecule to Organism, 1989, Ion Channels, 1988—; specific field editor Jour. Pharmacology and Exptl. Therapeutics, 1972-97; assoc. editor Neurotoxicology, 1994—; contbr. articles to profl. jours. Recipient Javits Neurosci. Investigator award, NIH, 1986. Fellow AAAS; mem. Am. Soc. for Pharmacology and Exptl. Therapeutics (Otto Krayer award 2000), Am. Physiol. Soc., Soc. for Neurosci., Biophys. Soc. (Cole award 1981), Soc. Toxicology (DuBois award 1988, Merit award 1991, 1st Ann. Disting. Investigator Lifetime Achievement award 2001), Agrochem. Divsn. Am. Chem. Soc. (Burdick L. Jackson Internat. award 1989). Home: 175 E Delaware Pl Apt 7911 Chicago IL 60611-7745 Office: Northwestern U Med Sch Dept Mol Pharmaco Biol Chem 303 E Chicago Ave Chicago IL 60611-3008 E-mail: tna597@northwestern.edu.

NARAIN, PREM, agricultural scientist, educator, researcher; b. Lucknow, India, Jan. 3, 1934; s. Govind Narain Verma and Lalli Devi; m. Krishna Srivastava, June 14, 1955; 1 child, Dhirendra Verma. BSc (hons.), Lucknow U., 1953, MSc, 1954; PhD, Edinburgh (Scotland) U., 1969, DSc, 1984. Stats. investigator Ministry of Transport, New Delhi, 1955-58; asst. rsch. officer Indian Vet. Rsch. Inst., Izatnagar, 1958-61; asst. prof. Indian Agrl. Rsch. Stats., New Delhi, 1961-70, from prof. to sr. prof., 1970-78; joint dir. Indian Agrl. Stats. Rsch. Inst., 1978-81, dir., 1981-92; prin. scientist Indian Agrl. Rsch. Inst., 1992-93, dean, joint dir., 1993-94, prof. emeritus, 1994—. Author: Statistical Genetics, 1990; editor, chair Indian Soc. Agrl. Stats. Jour., 1983, Impact Of P.V. Sukhatme On Agricultural Statistics And Nutrition, 1984. Recipient Rafi Ahmad Kidwai prize Indian Coun. Agrl. Rsch., 1977, Sankhyiki Bhushan award Indian Soc. Agrl. Stats., 1991, O.P. Bhasin Found. award, 1992, Dr. M.S. Randhawa Meml. medal, Nat. Acad. Agrl. Sci., 1999. Fellow Indian Nat. Sci. Acad. (G.P. Chatterji Meml. prize 1987), Indian Acad. Sci.; mem. Nat. Acad. Agrl. Sci. (founding), Internat. Statis. Inst. (mem. coun. 1989-93), Internat. Biometric Soc. (mem. coun. 1988-91). Home: B-3/27 A Lawrence Rd Keshav Puram New Delhi 110035 India E-mail: pnaraim@bol.net.in.

NARANGAJAVANA, KANTHAKA, analytical chemist; b. Bangkok, 1945; came to U.S., 1975; s. Chand Narangajavana and Prasertsri Tangknasing; m. Khaunchai Narangajavana, Nov. 12, 1973; 1 child, Kittiboon. Assoc., Analytical Chem. Tng., Bangkok, 1966; BSc, Mahidol U., Bangkok, 1973; MSc, St. Joseph's U., 1982. Chemist dept. sci. Ministry of Industry, Bangkok, 1968-75; analytical chemist water dept. City of Phila., 1977—. Mem. Am. Chem. Soc. Buddhist. Office: City of Phila Water Dept Organic Lab 1500 E Hunting Park Ave Philadelphia PA 19124

NARANJA, ROGELIO DARUSIN, SR. psychiatrist; b. Manila, Philippines, Feb. 1, 1939; came to U.S., 1964; s. Maximo and Consolacion (Darusin) N.; m. Antonietta Tobias, June 12, 1965 (dec. Jan. 1971); children: Rogelio Jr., Anthony; m. Imelda Tanada, Sept. 15, 1973. AA, U. Santo Tomas, Manila, 1958, MD, 1963. Diplomate in gen. psychiatry, child and adolescent psychiatry, forensic and geriatric psychiatry Am. Bd. Psychiatry and Neurology. Intern Meth. Hosp., Peoria, Ill., 1964-65; resident in gen. psychiatry Medfield State Hosp., Mass., 1965-68; spl. fellow in legal psychiatry Boston U. Medicine Inst., 1967-68; fellow in child psychiatry Kans. City Gen. Hosp. Med. Ctr. U. Mo. Sch. Medicine, 1968-70; med. dir. N.D. State Hosp. Children's Ctr., Jamestown, 1970-77; chief psychiat. svcs., chief med. svcs. USAF, Phoenix, also Minot, N.D., 1977-84; med. dir. forensic unit N.D. State Hosp., Jamestown, 1984-89; med. dir. mental health unit Mercy Hosp., Williston, N.D., 1989-95, N.W. Human Svc. Ctr., Williston, 1989—; pvt. practice. Cons. N.D. State Penitentiary, Bismarck, 1986-89, USAF, Minot AFB, N.D., 1984—, Good Samaritan Nursing Home, Crosby, N.D., 1990—. Col. USAF, 1977-99, ret. Mem. Am. Psychiat. Assn. Roman Catholic. Avocations: gardening, sightseeing, travel, reading, listening to music. Home: 2304 14th Ave W Williston ND 58801-3106 Office: Mercy Med Ctr and NW Human Svc Ctr 1301 15th Ave W Williston ND 58801-3821

NARASIMHAM, PRABHALA LAKSHMI, civil engineering and management consultant; b. Draksharama, India, Jan. 8, 1941; s. Prabhala Subbarao and Prabhala Sitadevi Challa; m. Prabhala Laxmi Addanki, June 26, 1967; children: Anupama Prabhala Kapse, Madhav Prabhala. B of Engring. with honors, Andhra U., Visakhapatnam, India, 1961; M of Engring., Indian Inst. Sci., Bangalore, 1962; Diploma of Imperial Coll., U. London, 1970. Cert. specialist course in foundation engring., U. Roorkee, India, 1966; cert. in Urdu, Urdu Acad., Delhi, India, 1994; cert. proficiency in carnatic music Sangeeta Janakulam, 2000; registered individual cons. Asian Devel. Bank. Extra asst. dir. Ctrl. Water & Power Commn., Govt. India, New Delhi, 1963-64, asst. dir., 1964-75, dep. dir., 1975-76; sr. engr. Howe (India) Pvt. Ltd., 1977-87, sr. cons., 1987-94, dep. chief, project mgmt., 1994-2000; civil engring. and mgmt. cons., 2000—. Asst. in tech. capacity various adv. coms., Govt. of India, New Delhi, 1963-76; advisor in formulation of design stds. for dams, Indian Stds. Instn., New Delhi, 1963-76; organizer rsch. activities for R & D in the irrigation sector all centrally-funded rsch. orgns./labs. in India, including the premier hydraulic rsch. inst. The Ctrl. Water & Power Rsch. Sta., Pune, 1975-76. Contbr. articles to profl. jours. and conf. procs. V.p. Residents' Welfare Assn., Sector-26, Noida, India, 1984-85, 86-87. Hindu. Avocations: Hindu philosophy, religion and theosophy, languages, journalism and literary pursuits, reading. Home: A-149/Sector 26 Noida 201301 India

NARASIMHAN, PARTHASARATHY, physician; b. Cuddapah, India, June 15, 1935; Grad., Govt. Coll. Kumbakpnam, India, 1952; MD, Madras Med. Coll., India, 1956. Diplomate Am. Bd. Oncology, 1979, Am. Bd. Hematology, 1980, Am. Bd. Internal Medicine, Am. Bd. Medicine. Intern Knickerbocker Hosp., N.Y.C., 1959, resident, 1960, Luth. Med. Ctr., Bklyn., 1961-62; fellow hematology Meth. Hosp., 1969-71; pvt. practice Managed Care-HMO; dir. hematology, oncology, assoc. dir. medicine Northshore U. Hosp., Forest Hills, N.Y. Clin. asst. prof. Cornell U. Med. Sch. Fellow ACCP, ACP, RCPCan. Office: GLIMG 96-10 Metropolitan Ave Forest Hills NY 11375 Fax: 718-286-3922. E-mail: narasu@aol.com.

NARATH, ALBERT, retired laboratory administrator; b. Berlin, Mar. 5, 1933; came to U.S., 1947; s. Albert Narath and Johanna Agnes Anna (Brueggemann) Bruckmann; m. Worth Haines Scattergood (div. 1976); children: Tanya, Lise, Yvette; m. Barbara Dean Camp (div. 1993); 1 child, Albert; m. Shanna S. Lindeman. BS in Chemistry, U. Cin., 1955; PhD in Phys. Chemistry, U. Calif., Berkeley, 1959. Mem. tech. staff, mgr. phys. sci. Sandia Nat. Labs., Albuquerque, 1959-68, dir. solid state sci., 1968-71, mng. dir. phys. sci., 1971-73, v.p. rsch., 1973-82, exec. v.p. rsch. and adv. weapons sys., 1982-84, pres., 1989-95; pres. energy and environ. sect. Lockheed Martin Corp., 1995-98; ret., 1998. Contbr. sci. articles to profl. jours. Fellow AAAS, Am. Phys. Soc. (George E. Pake prize 1991); mem. NAE. E-mail: anarath@compuserve.com.

NARAYAN, BEVERLY ELAINE, lawyer; b. Berkeley, Calif., June 19, 1961; d. Jagjiwan and Alexandra Mataras Narayan; m. James Dean Schmidt, Jan. 7, 1989 (div. May 2002); children: Sasha Karan Schmidt, Kaiya Maria Schmidt. Student, San Francisco State U., 1979—80; BA, U. Calif., Berkeley, 1983; JD, U. Calif., San Francisco, 1987. Bar: Calif. 1987, U.S. Dist. Ct. (no. dist.) Calif. 1987, U.S. Dist. Ct. (ctrl. dist.) 1988. Atty. Daniels Barratta & Fine, L.A., 1988-89, Kornblum Ferry & Frye, L.A., 1990-91, Clapp Moroney Bellagamba Davis & Vucinich, Menlo Park, Calif., 1991-93, pvt. practice, Burlingame, 1993—; mng. dir. KarmaTek, 1999—2000. Arbitrator Nat. Assn. Securities Dealers, San Francisco, 1987—, Pacific Exch., San Francisco, 1994—; mediator Peninsula Conflict Resolution Ctr., San Mateo, Calif., 1995—; appellate mediator First Dist. Ct. Appeals, 2000—; neutral San Mateo County Multi-Option ADR Project. Candidate Sch. Bd. San Mateo (Calif.) Unified Sch. Dist., 1993; mem. San Mateo County Task Force Violence Against Women. Recipient U. Calif. Hastings Coll. Law Achievement award, 1986; named Barrister of Yr., San Mateo County, 1996. Mem. ABA, San Mateo County Bar Assn. (co-chair women lawyers 1995, bd. dirs. 1994-96), South Asian Bar Assn., Nat. Women's Polit. Caucus (bd. dirs., diversity chair 1993-96), San Mateo County Barristers Club (bd. dirs. 1993-99, child watch chair 1995-99). Avocations: baking, cooking, reading, travel, motorcycles, family. Office: 1508 Howard Ave Burlingame CA 94010-5216

NARAYAN, RAJ K. neurosurgeon, educator; b. Secunderabad, India, Nov. 9, 1952; came to U.s., 1976; s. Brij K. and Rathna Narayan; m. Tina Mathias, Sept. 19, 1979; children: Tara, Neil, Gita. , f. Diplomate Am. Bd. Neurol. Surgery. Resident in neurosurgery Med. Coll. Va., Richmond, 1977-82; spl. expert NIH, Bethesda, Md., 1982-85; asst. prof. neurosurgery Baylor Coll. Medicine, Houston, 1985-89, assoc. prof. neurosurgery, 1989-94, prof. neurosurgery, 1994-95; prof. and chmn. neurosurgery Temple U., Phila., 1995—. Nat. faculty mem. ATLS; cons. NIH, Ctr. for Disease Control, FDA; mem. editl. bd. Neurosurgery. Editor: Neurotrauma, 1996; contbr. over 80 articles to profl. jours., over 40 chpts. to books. Fellow ACS; mem. Am. Assn. Neurol. Surgeons (chmn. sect. on neurotrauma 1992-94), Soc. Neurol. Surgeons, Soc. Univ. Neurosurgeons, Congress of Neurol. Surgeons. Office: Temple U Hosp Dept Neurosurgery 3401 N Broad St Philadelphia PA 19140-5103

NARAYAN, VADUVUR SRINIVASAN, preventive medicine physician; b. Tanjore, India, Aug. 8, 1944; came to U.S., 1977; BS, U. Bombay, 1963, MB, BS, 1969; diploma in pub. health, U. Liverpool, Eng., 1974; MS, U. Cin., 1979. Diplomate Am. Bd. Preventive Medicine, Am. Bd. Occupl. Medicine. Intern Sir J.J. Group, Bombay, 1968-69; provincial officer medicine Zambia, 1970-76; resident in preventive medicine U. Cin. Med. Ctr., 1977-79; staff physician GE, Cin., 1979-81; asst. corp. dir. medicine Atlantic Richfield Co., Louisville and Phila., 1981-84; med. dir. Monsanto Co., Pensacola, Fla., 1993-95; pvt. practice, 1996—. Cons. in preventive medicine. Address: 6830 Madrid Ave Jacksonville FL 32217-2680

NARAYANAN, RAMASWAMY, biomedical engineer; b. Mohanur, India, Mar. 15, 1952; s. Anandhachari and Jayalakshmi R.; m. Jeanine Bouchard, Apr. 29, 1982, 1 child, Anndal. BS in Chemistry and Physics, Bombay U., 1972, MS in Clin. Biochemistry, 1974; PhD in Biochemistry, U. Coll., Dublin, 1980. Teaching asst., jr. lectr. U. Bombay, 1972-75; med. coord. Themis Pharm. Co., Bombay, 1975-76; teaching asst. dept. biochemistry Univ. Coll. of Dublin, 1977-80; vis. fellow Lab. Viral Carcinogenesis/Cellular Molecular Bio Nat. Cancer Inst. NIH, Bethesda, Md., 1981-83; vis. scientist AIDS Rsch. Lab. Ctrs. for Disease Control, Atlanta, 1983-85; assoc. rsch. scientist dept. pharmacology Sch. Medicine Yale U., New Haven, 1985-87; asst. lab. mem. Meml. Sloan-Kettering Inst., N.Y.C., 1987-88, adj. asst. mem., 1988-94; rsch. investigator dept. molecular genetics Hoffmann-La Roche, Inc., Nutley, N.J., 1988-94; rsch. leader divsn. oncology Hoffman-LaRoche Inc., 1994-98; prof. dept. biol. scis. Fla. Atlantic U., Boca Raton, Fla., 1998—, assoc. dir. Ctr. for Molecular Biology and Biotech., 1998—2001; founder, pres., CEO, Forseti Bioscis., Inc., Boca Raton , Fla., 2001—. Vis. prof. Rutgers U., New Brunswick, N.J., 1993-98. Mem. editorial bd. Antisense Rsch. Devel., 1994—, In Vivo, 1995—, Anticancer Rsch., 1996—; contbr. numerous chpts. to books, articles to profl. jours. Bd. Advisors Am. Biographic Inst., 1996—; panel mem. NCI study sect., 1995—, Dept. Def. Breast Cancer Rsch., 1995—. Fellow Med. Rsch. Coun. Ireland, 1980; grantee Am. Cancer Soc., 1986. Mem. AAAS, Am. Assn. Advancement Cancer Rsch., Am. Soc. Microbiology, Am. Soc. Hematology, N.Y. Acad. Scis., Internat. Soc. Hematology, Internat. Soc. Comparative Oncology. Office: 777 Glades Rd Boca Raton FL 33431-6424 E-mail: rnarayanan@fau.edu.

NARAYANAN, VADAKE K. management educator, consultant; b. Cohin, Kerala, India, June 20, 1949; came to U.S., 1974; s. Thadavillil Madhava Menon and Akilandam Subrahmanyan; m. Rajagopal Sunanda Narayanan, July 15, 1984; 1 child Shriram. BTech, Indian Inst. of Tech., Madras, 1971; postgrad. diploma in bus. adminstrn., Indian Inst. of Mgmt., Ahmedabad, India, 1973; PhD, U. Pitts., 1979. Prof. U. Kans., 1978—2000; assoc. prof. Rutgers U., Newark, 1988—90; Stubbs prof. strategy and entrepreneurship Drexel U., Phila., 2000—. Author: Managing Technology, 2000. Dir. Kans. Internat., Lawrence. Mem. Strategic Mgmt. Soc., Acad. of Mgmt. (sec., treas. TIM divsn.). Office: 9 Bailey Dr Princeton NJ 08540-7956

NARAYANASWAMY, ONBATHIVELI SUBRAHMANYAN, computer engineer, consultant; b. Chennai, TamilNadu, India, May 13, 1936; s. Onbathiveli Ramaswamy and Akilandam Subrahmanyan; m. Padmini Sreenivasan. PhD, Case Western Res. U., 1965. Jr. sci. officer Atomic Energy Establishment, Mumbai, India, 1959—60; lectr. Indian Inst. Tech., Chennai, 1960—61; sr. rsch. scientist Ford Motor Co., Dearborn, Mich., 1966—72, prin. rsch. engr. assoc., 1972—81, staff scientist, 1981—86; pres. Computer Simulations, Dearborn Heights, 1986—. Contbr. chapters to books. Recipient Ross Coffin Purdy award, 1973. Fellow: Am. Ceramic Soc.; mem.: Soc. for Exptl. Mechanics. Hindu. Avocation: travel. Personal E-mail: osnswamy@comcast.net. Business E-Mail: osnswamy@comcast.net.

NARDELLI, CHRISTY ANN, research scientist; b. Youngstown, Ohio, Mar. 14, 1955; d. Charles Howard and Ruth Evelyn (Laughlin) Haggis; m. James Anthony Nardelli, Aug. 26, 1978; children: Beth, James Jr. BS, Youngstown State U., 1977. Rsch. scientist Electrochem. divsn. Dart Industries, Youngstown, Ohio, 1977-81; asst. chemist Ross Products Divsn. Abbott Labs., Columbus, 1985-89, assoc. chemist, 1989-92, chemist, 1989-92, sr. chemist, 1992-96, rsch. scientist, 1995-96; sr, rsch. scientist Abbott Labs., North Chicago, Ill., 1996—2001, rsch. investigator, 2001—02, sr. internat. regulatory assoc. Abbott Park, 2002—. Mem. Visiting Wizards, Columbus, Ohio, 1991-95; panel mem. Women in Science, Columbus, 1992-95. Contbr. articles to profl. jours. Mem. Am. Chem. Soc. Achievements include patents for 5 patents on processes to remove phytate antinutrient from protein sources; 2 patents on processes to reduce phosphorous content in milk; patent on processes to remove metals from proteins, improvements in electroplating of tin. Office: Abbott Labs 200 Abbott Park Rd Abbott Park IL 60064

NARDELLI, ROBERT L. consumer home products executive; BS in Bus., Western Ill. U.; MBA, U. Louisville. With GE, 1971-88; exec. v.p., gen. mgr. worldwide parts and components Case Corp., Racine, Wis., 1988-91; pres., CEO Can. Appliance Mfg. Co. subs. GE, Toronto, Ont., Can., 1991-92, GE Transp. Sys., Erie, Pa., 1992-95, GE Power Sys., 1995-2000, The Home Depot, 2000—. Office: The Home Depot 2455 Paces Ferry Rd Atlanta GA 30339*

NARDELLI-OLKOWSKA, KRYSTYNA MARIA, ophthalmologist, educator; b. Myslowice, Poland, June 23, 1939; d. Walerian and Stefania (Jasinska) Nardelli; m. Zbigniew L. Olkowski, Apr. 15, 1963. MD, Silesian U. Med. Sch., 1964. Diplomate: Am. Bd. Ophthalmology; 1983. Intern, resident ophthalmology Emory U. Med. Sch., Atlanta, 1977-80, fellow in glaucoma, 1980-81, asst. prof. dept. ophthalmology, 1972—; pvt. practice ophthalmology, 1982—. Postdoctoral fellow Fight for Sight, 1974-75. Fellow Am. Soc. Research in Ophthalmology; mem. AMA, Royal Micros. Soc. (Eng.). Home: Villa Sadyba 1018 McConnell Dr Decatur GA 30033-3402 Office: 724 Holcomb Bridge Rd Bldg 4 Norcross GA 30071-1325

NARDI, MICHAEL ARTHUR, research scientist, medical educator; b. Williamsport, Pa., Jan. 22, 1949; s. Angelo Arthur and Flora Mae (Pagana) N. BS, U. Pitts., 1971, MS, 1972. Asst. rsch. prof. dept. pediat. NYU Med. Ctr., N.Y.C., 1992—. Contbr. articles to sci. jours. Mem. Am. Soc. Hematology, Am. Soc. Clin. Pathology, Internat. Soc. Thrombosis andHaemostasis. E-mail: Michael.Nardi@med.nyu.edu.

NARDI, STEPHEN J. lawyer; b. Kalispell, Mont., Feb. 11, 1951; s. Micheal Stephen and Grace Elaine N.; m. Darlene R. Nardi, May 26, 1979. BA in History, U. Mont., 1974, BA in Polit. Sci., JD, 1977. Bar: Mont. 1977, U.S. Dist. Ct. Mont. 1977, U.S. Ct. Appeals (9th cir.) 1977. Ptnr. Sherlock & Nardi, Kalispell, 1977—. Instr. Flathead Valley C.C., Kalispell, 1979-84. Mem.: NACDL, Mont. Trial Lawyers Assn., Mont. Assn. Criminal Def. Attys., Mont. State Bar Assn. Avocations: boating, golf, skiing, scuba diving. Office: Sherlock & Nardi 30 5th St E Ste 101 Kalispell MT 59901-4999 E-mail: stevenardi@centurytel.net.

NARDI RIDDLE, CLARINE, association executive; b. Clinton, Ind., Apr. 23, 1949; d. Frank Jr. and Alice (Mattioda) Nardi; m. Mark Alan Riddle, Aug. 15, 1971; children: Carl Nardi, Julia Nardi. AB in Math with honors, Ind. U., 1971, JD, 1974; LHD (hon.), St. Joseph Coll., 1991. Bar: Ind. 1974, U.S. Dist. Ct. (so. dist.) Ind. 1974, Conn. 1979, Fed. Dist. Ct. Conn. 1980, U.S. Supreme Ct. 1980, U.S. Ct. Appeals (2d cir.) 1986, U.S. Ct. Appeals (D.C. cir.) 1994. Staff atty. Ind. Legis. Svc. Agy., Indpls., 1974-78, legal counsel, 1978-79; dep. corp. counsel City of New Haven, 1980-83; counsel to atty. gen. State of Conn., Hartford, 1983-86, dep. atty. gen., 1986-89, acting atty. gen., 1989, atty. gen., 1989-91, judge Superior Ct., 1991-93; sr. v.p., gen. counsel Nat. Multi-Housing Coun., Nat. Apartment Assn., 1995—. Asst. counsel state majority Conn. Gen. Assembly, Hartford, 1979, legal rsch. asst. to prof. Yale U., New Haven, 1979; legal counsel com. on law revision Indpls. State Bar Assn., 1979; mem. Chief Justice's Task Force on Gender Bias, Hartford, 1988-90; mem. ethics and values com. Ind. Sector, Washington, 1988-90; co-organizer Ind. Continuing Legal Edn. Forum Inst. Legal Drafting Legislature and Pvt. Practice; Internat. Women's Yr. panelist Credit Laws and Their Enforcement; mem. Atty. Gen.'s Blue Ribbon Commn., Chief Justice's Com. Study Publs. Policy Conn. Law. Jour., Law Revision Commn. Adminstrv. Law Study, Chief Justice's Task Force Gender, Justice and Cts., Gov.'s Task Force Fed. Revenue Enhancements; mem. exec. com. Jud. Dept.; mem. panel arbitrators Am. Arbitration Assn., 1994; gen. counsel Nat. Multi Housing Coun.; lectr. in field. Author: (with F.R. Rembusch) Drafting Manual for the Indiana General Assembly, 1976; sr. editor Ind. U. Law Sch. Interdisciplinary Law Jour.; contbr. articles to profl. jours. Bd. visitors Ind. U., Bloomington, 1974-92; mem. Gov.'s Missing Children Com., Hartford, Conn. Child Support Guidelines Com., Gov.'s Task Force on Justice for Abused Children, Hartford, 1988-90; mem. Mayor's City of New Haven Task Force Reorganization Corp. Counsel's Office, Gov.'s Child Support Commn., Mayor of New Haven's Blue Ribbon Commn.; former bd. dirs. New Haven Neighborhood Music Sch.; bd. dirs., mem. youth adv. com. Gov.'s Partnership Prevent Substance Abuse Workforce-Drugs Don't Work. Recipient Women in Leadership Recognition award Hartford Region YWCA, 1986, Award of Merit, Women & Law Sect. Conn. Bar Assn., 1989, Fellowship award South End Ladies Dem. Club, 1989, Woman of Yr. award Greater Hartford Fedn. of Bus. & Profl. Women's Clubs, 1990, Conn. Original award Somers-Mabelle B. Avery Sch., 1990, Cert. of Recognition, Consortium Law-Related Edn., 1990, Citizen award Conn. Task Force Children's Constl. Rights, 1991, Ann. award Hartford Assn. Women Attys., 1993; named Conn. History Maker, U.S. Dept. Labor, Women's Bur. & Permanent Commn. Status Women, 1989, Impact Player, The Conn. Law Tribune, 1992; inductee Ind. U. Sch. Law Alumni Acad. Fellow, 1999. Mem. ABA, Conn. Bar Assn. (chair com. on gender bias, Citation of Merit women and law sect. 1989), Nat. Assn. Attys. Gen. (chair charitable trusts and solicitation 1988-90), New Haven Neighborhood Music Sch. (bd. dirs.), Am. Arbitration Assn. (arbitration panel 1994), Ind. Bar Assn., Conn. Bar Assn. (chair com. gender bias legal profession), Indpls. Bar Assn., Ind. Civil

Liberties Union (bd. dirs., mem. exec. com., chair long range planning com., mem. women's rights project, membership v.p., Disting. Svc. award), Conn. Consortium Law and Citizenship Edn., Inc. (bd. dirs.), Conn. Judges Assn. (mem. legislation com.), Ind. U. Law Sch. Alumni Assn. (bd. dirs.), Enomene Hon. Soc., Pleiades Hon. Soc., Mortar Bd. (nat. fellow), Alpha Lambda Delta. Democrat. Presbyterian. Office: Nat Multi Housing Coun 1850 M St NW Ste 450 Washington DC 20036-5803

NARDONE, RICHARD, lawyer, consultant; b. Poughkeepsie, N.Y., Dec. 29, 1945; s. Michael and Rosemary (Murden) N.; m. Tracy J. Nardone; children: Richard David, Jorinda Suzanne. BA, Syracuse U., 1970; JD, Albany Law Sch., 1973. Bar: N.Y. 1974, U.S. Dist. Ct. (no. dist.) N.Y 1974, U.S. Dist. Ct. (so. dist.) N.Y. 1977. Ptnr. Nardone & Nardone, Highland, N.Y., 1977-79; sole practice, 1979—. Fellow mem. ABA, N.Y. State Bar Assn., N.Y. State Trial Lawyers Assn., Ulster County Bar Assn., Dutchess County Bar Assn. Avocations: fishing, hunting, boating, auto racing. Office: N Roberts Rd Highland NY 12528-2003

NARDONE, WILLIAM ANDREW, lawyer; b. Groton, Conn., June 16, 1954; s. Henry Joseph and Mary Frances (Herley) N.; m. Diane Ruth Hall, July 1, 1988; children: Madison Catherine, William Chase. BA, U. R.I., 1976; JD, Suffolk U., 1980. Bar: R.I. 1981, U.S. Dist. Ct. R.I. 1981, U.S. Supreme Ct. 1991. Assoc. Law Office of M.L. Lewiss, Westerly, R. I., 1980-83; ptnr. Orsinger & Nardone Law Offices, 1983—. Solicitor Westerly Sch. Dept., 1984-90, 94-96, 98—. Mem. com. Westerly YMCA, 1980, bd. dirs., 1991—, exec. com., 1994—; bd. dirs., pres. Westerly Adult Day Care Ctr., 1985-93; trustee Westerly Hosp., 1993—, sec., asst. treas., 1999-2001, treas. and v.p., 2002—; trustee SNEPHO, 1994—. Mem. Nat. Coun. Sch. Attys., R.I. Bar Assn. (rep. Ho. of Dels. 1984-90), Nat. Assn. Legal Problems in Edn. Republican. Roman Catholic. Home: 38 Wicklow Rd Westerly RI 02891-3644 Office: Orsinger & Nardone 53 High St Westerly RI 02891-6001

NARELL, IRENA, freelance writer, history educator; b. Sanok, Poland, Sept. 17, 1923; came to U.S., 1939; d. Abraham and Antonina Penzik; m. Murray Narell, June 29, 1945 (dec. Jan. 1991); children: Jeff, Andrew. BS, Columbia U., 1969. Asst. to Polish UN Delegation, N.Y.C., 1945-51; owner Art Originals Gallery, 1961-63, 1964-69; co-mgr. The Steel Bandits—a mus. group. Project dir. San Francisco Jews-Old Traditions on a New Frontier, bicentennial exhibit Judah L. Magnes Mus., Cmty. and Diversity, Bay Area Jewish Families, 1989, Inst. for Hist. Study. Mem. editl. bd.: Western States Jewish History; author: Ashes to the Taste, 1961, The Invisible Passage, 1969, Joshua Fighter for Bar Kochba, 1978 (Nat. Jewish Book award 1979), Our City: The Jews of San Francisco, 1981, History's Choice, 1996; contbr. numerous short stories, revs. and articles to profl. jours. and mags.; translator: Holy Week (Jerzy Andrzejewski) Samson (Kazimierz Brandys), Summer in Nohant (Jaroslaw Iwaszkiewicz), Poetry by Julian Tuwim. Mem. Jewish Arts Cmty. of the Bay, San Francisco, 1975-96. Mem. Inst. Hist. Study. Jewish. Avocations: swimming, collecting art and antiques. Home: 5949 Estates Dr Oakland CA 94611-3113 E-mail: irenapn@aol.com.

NARENDRA, KUMPATI SUBRAHMANYA, electrical engineer, educator; b. Madras, India, Apr. 14, 1933; came to U.S., 1954, naturalized, 1974; s. Subrahmanya and Sarada (Alladi) Kumpati; m. Barbara Lamb, Nov. 3, 1961. BEE with honors, U. Madras, 1954; MS, Harvard U., 1955, PhD, 1959; MA (hon.), Yale U., 1968; DSc (hon.), Anna U., Madras, 1995. Lectr., postdoctoral asst. Harvard U., Cambridge, Mass., 1959-61, asst. prof., 1961-65; assoc. prof. Yale U., New Haven, 1965-68, prof. elec. engring., 1968—, chmn. dept. elec. engring., 1984-87, dir. Neuroengring. and Neurosci. Ctr., 1995-96. Cons. to comml. firms, 1961—; dir. Ctr. for Systems Sci., 1981—; disting. lectr. Tex. A&M Coll., 1997; disting. vis. scientist Jet Propulsion Lab., 1994—; hon. vis. prof. Anna U., Madras, India, 1993; mem. adv. bd. Inst. Advanced Engring., Republic of Korea; disting. lectr. U.N.Mex., 1999, U. Va., 2001; plenary spkr. Am. Control Conf., 2000; keynote spkr. Conf. on Intelligent Control, U. Va., 2001, Internat. Conf. of Soc. of Indsl. and Control Engring., Osaka, Japan, 2002. Author: Frequency Domain Criteria for Absolute Stability, 1973, Stable Adaptive Systems, 1989, Learning Automata-An Introduction, 1989; editor: Applications of Adaptive Control, 1980, Adaptive and Learning Systems: Theory and Applications, 1987, Advances in Adaptive Control, 1991; editor issue on learning automata Jour. Cybernetics and Info. Sci., vol. I, 1977. Recipient John R. Ragazzini Edn. award Am. Automatic Control Coun., 1990, Leadership award Neural Network Soc., 1994, Hendrik W. Bode prize/Lectr. award Control Sys. Soc., 1995. Fellow AAAS, IEEE (life, Franklin V. Taylor award 1973, George S. Axelby award 1988, Outstanding Paper of neural network coun. 1991), Inst. Elec. Engrs. (U.K.); mem. Conn. Acad. Sci. and Engring., Sigma Xi. Home: 35 Old Mill Rd Woodbridge CT 06525-1523 Office: Yale U Ctr Systems Sci PO Box 2157 New Haven CT 06520-2157 E-mail: kumpati.narendra@yale.edu.

NARIN, STEPHEN B. lawyer; b. Phila., Nov. 23, 1929; s. Bernard E. and Anne (Lipsius) N.; m. Sandra C. Goldberg, Sept. 29, 1963; children: Howard Glen, Brenda Teri. BS, Temple U., 1951, LL.B., 1953; LL.M. in Taxation, NYU, 1960. Bar: Pa. 1954, U.S. Supreme Ct. 1958; CPA, Pa. Dep. atty. gen. Commonwealth of Pa., Harrisburg, 1955-57; instr. acctg. Temple U., Phila., 1954-55; lectr. in law grad. legal studies div. Temple U. Sch. Law, 1976-85; lectr. Practicing Law Inst., 1967-69; ptnr. Narin & Chait, Phila., 1970-89, Predecessor Ptnrships., Phila., 1955-70; v.p., gen. counsel Travelco Assocs., 1989-90; of counsel Krekstein, Wolfson & Krekstein, 1989-92; v.p., gen. counsel Eagle Nat. Bank, 1990-91; counsel Schachtel, Gerstley, Levine & Koplin, Phila., 1993-98; pvt. practice, Ardmore, 1998—. Mem. Phila. County Bd. Law Examiners, 1961-65. Mem. nat. governing council Am. Jewish Congress, 1963-84, nat. exec. com., 1978-84, pres. Greater Phila. council, 1965-67; mem. Nat. Commn. on Law and Social Action, 1964-84. Mem. Phila. Bar Assn., Phi Alpha Delta. Office: 631 Kenilworth Rd Ardmore PA 19003-2914

NARITA, HIRO, cinematographer; b. Seoul, Republic of Korea, June 26, 1941; arrived in Japan, 1945,arrived in U.S., 1957; s. Masao and Masako (Kojima) Morikawa; m. Barbara Parker, Sept. 8, 1971. BFA in Design, San Francisco Art Inst., 1964. Lectr. Mill Valley Film Festival, 1984, Hawaii Internat. Film Festival, 1984. (dir. photography): (films) Farewell to Manzanar, 1976 (Emmy nomination, 1976); Never Cry Wolf, 1983 (Best Cinematography award Nat. Soc. Film Critics, 1983); Solomon Northrup's Odyssey, 1984; Go Tell It on the Mountain, 1985; Amerika, 1987; Honey, I Shrunk the Kids, 1989; The Rocketeer, 1991; Star Trek VI, 1992; Hocus Pocus, 1993; White Fang II, 1994; James & The Giant Peach, 1995; The Arrival, 1995; Stones & Paper, 1997; Conceiving Ada, 1998; Shadrach, 1998; I'll Be Home for Christmas, 1998; Dirty Pictures, 1999 (Emmy nomination, 2000); Half Past Autumn, 2001 (Emmy nomination, 2001); Technolust, 2002. With U.S. Army, 1964—66. Mem.: Acad. TV Arts and Scis., Acad. Motion Picture Arts and Scis., Am. Soc. Cinematographers, Internat. Photographers Guild. E-mail: bphnarita@earthlink.net.

NARKIEWICZ-LAINE, CHRISTIAN K. GF. museum director, painter, poet; Student , U. de Strasbourg, France, 1970—72, Athens, Greece, 1972—73; grad., Lake Forest (Ill.) Coll., 1975. Arch. critic Chgo. Sun-Times, 1978—81; editor Inland Arch., 1979—81; pub. Met. Press Ltd., 1983; dir., pres. Chgo. Athenaeum, 1988—. Arch. cons.; tchr. arch. history and aesthetics Ill. Inst. Tech. Author: Helmut John, 1984, Landmark Springfield, 1985; author: (anthology of poetry) Distant Fires, 1997; author: Inspiration: Nature and the Poet (The Collected Poems of the Chicago architect, Louis H. Sullivan), 1999, Baltic Hours, 1999, Greenland, 2002. Office: c/o Chicago Athenaeum 307 N Michigan Ave Chicago IL 60601

NARMONT, JOHN STEPHEN, lawyer; b. Auburn, Ill., June 24, 1942; s. Stephen and Luriel (Welle) N.; m. Sondra J. Nicholls, Feb. 12, 1978. BBA magna cum laude, U. Notre Dame, 1964; JD, U. Ill., Champaign, 1967. Bar: Ill. 1967, U.S. Dist. Ct. (so. dist.) Ill. 1967, U.S. Ct. Appeals (7th cir.) 1967, U.S. Supreme Ct. 1973, U.S. Tax Ct. 1978. Pvt. practice, Springfield, Ill. Founder, pres., owner Richland Ranch, Inc., Auburn; originator, pres. The Solid Gold Futurity, Ltd. Mem. Sangamon Valley Estate Planning Coun. Mem. ABA, Sangamon County Bar Assn., Ill. State Bar Assn., Assn. Trial Lawyer Am., Am. Agrl. Law Assn., Ill. Inst. for Continuing Legal Edn., Internat. Livestock Exposition (pres., founder). Office: 209 N Bruns Ln Springfield IL 62702-4612

NARRETT, CARLA MARIE, university administrator; b. Iron Mountain, Mich., June 26, 1956; d. Peter Michael and Lucille Ann (Beitel) Belpedio; m. Walter Richard Ott, May. 27, 2000. BS, No. Mich. U., 1978; MS, Syracuse U., 1981, PhD, 1982. Lic. psychologist, N.Y.; permanent cert. sch. psychologist, N.Y.; nat. cert. sch. psychologist. Sch. psychologist East Syracuse (N.Y.)-Minoa Cen. Sch. Dist., 1981-82; from asst. prof. to assoc. prof. to prof. psychology Alfred (N.Y.) U., 1982-96, chairperson divsn. sch. psychology, 1985-96, assoc. dean Coll. Engring. and Profl. Studies, 1995-96; dean Grad. Sch. and Rsch. Montclair State U., Upper Montclair, N.J., 1996—. Program dir. Crisis Intervention Svcs., Alfred, 1985-90; dir. The Child and Family Svcs. Ctr., Alfred, 1986-89; sr. rsch. fellow Oreg. Social Learning Ctr., Eugene, 1989-90. Contbr. articles to profl. jours. Grantee U.S. Dept. Edn., 1991-96, A&L Powell Found., 1994-96, N.Y. State Office of Mental Retardation and Developmental Disabilities, 1985-90. Mem. Nat. Assn. Sch. Psychologists (co-chair accreditation credentialling and tng. 1994-97, exec. bd. program approval bd. 1995-99), Sch. Psychology Educators Coun. (pres. 1988-89, 91-92), Nat. Coun. for Accreditation of Tchr. Edn., Mid. State Assn. (mem. accreditation team 1999—), Multidisciplinary Acad. Clin. Edn. Avocations: tennis, opera. Office: Montclair State U College Hall-203 Valley and Normal Aves Upper Montclair NJ 07043 Home: 165 Clarken Dr West Orange NJ 07052-3429 E-mail: narrettc@mail.montclair.edu.

NARULA, RAM GOPAL, engineer; b. Fazilka, India, Oct. 8, 1938; came to U.S., 1970; s. Sohan Lal and Vidya Bai (Gilhotra) N.; m. Pushpa Bubber, Dec. 11, 1962; children: Sushma, Komal, Uma, Avlok. BSME, Panjab U., 1961; MS in Nuclear Engring., U. Mich., 1975; MBA, EAstern Mich. U., 1977. Registered profl. engr. Ill., Mich., Pa. Lectr. Punjab Polytech, Nilokheri, India, 1961-62; sr. engr. Bharat Heavy Electricals, Hardwar, India, 1962-70, Sargent & Lundy, Chgo., 1970-72; engring. mgr. Bechtel Power Corp., Gaithersburg, Md., 1972—, prin. v.p., 1998—. Contbr. over 40 tech. papers to profl. publs. Vol. local ch., Ann Arbor, Mich., 1986-91, local hosp., Gaithersburg, 1996; Bechtel fellow, 1996. Mem. ASME (v.p. bd. on standardization, chmn. B133 code com. 1996, chmn. turbine water damage prevention com. 1997—, coun. on codes and stds., bd. pressure tech., Prime Mover award for Best Tech. Paper 1994, mem. nat. coal coun. adv. body to U.S. Sec. Energy 1999—), Am. Power Conf. (indsl. com. 1991—), Power-GEN (indsl. com. 1987—, prin. v.p. 1998). Hindu. Avocations: gardening, bridge. Home: 10 Letterman Ct Gaithersburg MD 20878-1031 Office: Bechtel Power Corp 5275 Westview Dr Frederick MD 21703-8306

NARULA, SUBHASH CHANDER, management science and statistics educator; b. Bannu, India, Jan. 20, 1944; came to U.S., 1968, naturalized; s. Har Dial and Sumitra Devi Narula. B Engring. in Mech. Engring., U. Delhi, India, 1964; MS in Indsl. and Mgmt. Engring., U. Iowa, 1969, PhD in Indsl. and Mgmt. Engring., 1971. Supr. Hindustan Machine Tools Ltd., Pinjore, India, 1965-68; asst. prof. dept. indsl. engring. SUNY, Buffalo, 1971-77; assoc. prof. Rensselaer Poly. Inst. Sch. Mgmt., Troy, N.Y., 1977-83; prof. mgmt. sci. and stats. Va. Commonwealth U., Richmond, 1983—. Chair optimization dept. math. Linkoping (Sweden) Inst. Tech., 1991-93; mem. organizing com. Internat. Symposium on Locational Decision VI, Chios, Greece, 1993; mem. organizing com. founding meeting Mid. East Forum, Chios, 1995; mem. adminstrv. com. Inst. Mid. East Studies Al-Mamun, 1994—; presenter numerous profl. meetings, univs. and confs., including Aarhus (Denmark) U., Asian Inst. Tech., Bangkok, Charles U., Prague, Czechoslovakia, Swiss Fed. Inst. Tech., Zurich, Helsinki U. Econs., U. Lisbon, Bulgarian and Polish acacs. scis., Nat. U. Singapore, Tech. U., Sofia, Bulgaria, U. Brasilia, Brazil, Univs. Bergen, Norway, Bielefeld, Germany, Birmingham, Eng., Bremen, Germany, Hong Kong, Ioannina, Greece, Liverpool, Eng., Nanjing, China, Seville, Spain, Sao Paulo, Brazil, Stockholm, Zurich; participant numerous regional, nat. and internat. confs., latest being 15th Internat. Conf. of Internat. Fedn. Ops. Rsch., Beijing, 1999. Author: (with G. Stangenhaus) Analise de Regessao L, 1988; assoc. editor Jour. Quality Tech., 1989-91, Studies in Locational Analysis, 1992—, Zimbabwe Jour. Sci. and Tech., 1999—; editor Internat. Jour. Math. and Statis. Scis., 1991—; assoc. editor, mem. adv. bd. Mid. East Forum-Jour. Inst. Mid. East Studies, 1995—; contbr. over 125 articles to stats., ops. rsch. and mgmt. sci. jours. and procs., chpts. to books. Scholar, Va. Commonwealth U., 2000. Fellow Am. Statis. Assn. (com. on internat. rels. in stats. 1989-94, vice chmn. 1994; sec.-treas. Buffalo-Niagara chpt. 1974-75, v.p. 1975-76, pres. 1976-77), Am. Soc. for Quality, Royal Statis. Soc.; mem. Constantine Porphyrogenetus Internat. Assn. (chmn. sci. com. 1995—, award 1994), Decision Scis. Inst., Inst. for Ops. Rsch. and Mgmt. Scis., Internat. Soc. on Multiple Criteria Decision Making, Internat. Statis. Inst. (life), Internat. Working Group on Environ., Locational Decision Scis. and Regional Planning (founding), Math. Programming Soc., Sigma Xi, Tau Beta Pi, Beta Gamma Sigma, Omega Rho (regional dir. 1988-98, treas. 1998—). Office: Va Commonwealth U Sch Bus 1015 Floyd Ave # 844000 Richmond VA 23284-4000

NARVAEZ, HEATHER RENEE, cultural organization administrator, consultant; b. Allentown, Pa., June 28, 1972; d. Celeste Billheimer Kramer and Robert Samuel Skeleton, Jr.; m. Alfonso Augustine Narvaez. BA in Eng. and Comm., DeSales U., 1995; MA in Philanthrophy & Develop., St. Mary's U. Mo., Winona, 2000. Develop. assoc. Nat. Soc. DAR, Washington, 1997—2001; dir. develop. The Cultural Landscape Found., 2001—. Cons. St. John's Episcopal Ch. Broad Creek, Fort Washington, 2001—; fundraising cons., 2001—. Dir. religious edn. St. John's Episcopal Ch. Broad Creek, Ft. Washington, 2001, Sunday sch. tchr., 2001. Mem.: Assn. Fundraising Profls., Women of Faith. Episcopalian. Avocations: reading, writing, basket weaving, travel. Office: The Cultural Landscape Found 1909 Que St NW Third Flr Washington DC 20009

NARVER, JOHN COLIN, business administration educator emeritus; b. Portland, Oreg., Aug. 5, 1935; s. Ursel Colin and Merle (Wells) N.; children: Gregory, Allison Ann, Colin. BS, Oreg. State U., 1957; MBA, U. Calif.-Berkeley, 1960; PhD, 1965. With Boise Cascade Corp., Portland, 1960-61; asst. prof. U. B.C., Can., 1964-66; asst. prof. dept. mktg. and internat. bus. U. Wash., Seattle, 1966-68, assoc. prof., 1968-71, prof., 1971-99, chmn. dept., 1974-78. Vis. prof. Norwegian Sch. Econs., 1973, Bogazici U., Istanbul, Turkey, 1974, U. Helsinki, 1995; cons. in field. Author: Conglomerate Mergers and Market Competition, 1967, (with R. Savitt) The Marketing Economy: An Analytical Approach, 1971, (with S. Slater) The Effect of a Market Orientation on Business Profitability, 1990. Served to lt. U.S. Army, 1957-59. Mem. Phi Delta Theta. Democrat. Episcopalian. Home: 2015 Federal Ave E Seattle WA 98102-4141

NARVESON, JOYCE ANN, public services administrator; b. Madison, Wis., Mar. 22, 1942; d. Oscar N. and Ada S. Narveson. BS, U. Wis., 1964; MBA, No. Ill. U., 1976. Mgmt. info. specialist dept. health and social svcs. State of Wis., Madison, 1982—85, fin. officer dept. industry labor and human rels., 1985—86; adminstr. adminstrv. svcs. Pub. Svc. Commn. Wis., 1986—93, adminstr. water and consumer affairs, 1993—2000; fiscal mgr. for child support Dept. Workforce Devel., 2000—. Sec., vice chair, then chair Wis. Adminstrv. Officers Coun., 1989-91. Bd. dirs., fin. chair Black Hawk coun. Girl Scouts U.S., 1985-87; mem. pers. com. Lake Edge Luth. Ch., 1999—. Mem. Phi Beta Kappa, Phi Kappa Gamma, Beta Gamma Sigma. Avocations: antiques, cross-country skiing, golf, U. Wis. sports, Green Bay Packers football. Office: Dept Workforce Devel PO Box 7935 201 E Washington Ave Madison WI 53707-7935 Home: Apt 114 5815 American Pkwy Madison WI 53718-8349 E-mail: narvejo@dwd.state.wi.us.

NARWOLD, LEWIS LAMMERS, paper products manufacturer; b. Cleve., Sept. 4, 1921; s. Lewis Lammers and Dorothy Marie (Andrus) N.; m. Marilyn Ebner, Oct. 26, 1944; 1 dau., Christine. BBA, Western Res. U., 1942; MBA, Harvard, 1947. Salesman Hoerner Boxes, Inc., 1950-54, gen. sales mgr., 1954-57, v.p., gen. mgr., 1957-62; v.p. So. div. Hoerner Waldorf Corp., St. Paul, 1962-70; sr. v.p., container div. Hoerner Waldorf Corp., 1970-72; CEO, founder, pres. SouthWest Packaging Inc., Tulsa, 1972—. Dir. UNCA Bankshares, Utica Nat. Bank & Trust, Thermo Chem. Corp., Sooner Box Corp., Hoerner Boxes, Inc., So. Mo. Container Corp.; organizer 1st Bank & Trust Co. of Okla. Chmn. United Fund of Sand Springs, Okla.; pres., trustee Tulsa Charity Horse Show.; Trustee Children's Med. Center of Tulsa, Tulsa Psychiat. Clinic, U. of the Ozarks. Capt. USMC, 1943-45. Decorated Purple Hearts; recipient Presdl. Citation. Mem. Sand Springs C. of C. (dir.), Tulsa C. of C. (dir.), N.A.M., Tulsa Mfg. Club, Mason Club, Summit Club (dir.), So. Hills Country Club, Union League Club (Chgo.), Coves Golf Club. Home: 7116 S College Ave Tulsa OK 74136-5601 Office: 6106 W 68th St Tulsa OK 74131-2429

NAS, TEVFIK FIKRET, economics educator; b. Mardin, Turkey, Nov. 17, 1947; came to U.S., 1972; s. Ahmet and Hamdiye N.; m. Paula L. Duey, July 7, 1990; children: Megan, Jonathan. BS, Mid. East Tech. U., Ankara, Turkey, 1970; MBA in Mktg., Fla. State U., 1973, PhD in Econs., 1977. Instr. Fla. State U., Tallahassee, 1976-78; asst. prof. Winthrop Coll., Rock Hill, S.C., 1978-79, Mid. East Tech. U., Ankara, 1979-81; vis. asst. prof. Calif. State U., San Bernardino, 1981-82; vis. prof. Semester at Sea U. Pitts., 1989; asst. prof. U. Mich., Flint, 1982-85, chmn. econs. dept., 1987—90, 1999—2002, assoc. prof., 1986—93, prof., 1993—. Author: Cost-Benefit Analysis, 1996; editor: Liberalization and Turkish Economy, 1988, Economics and Politics of Turkish Liberalization, 1992; contbr. articles to profl. publs. Fellow Salzburg Seminar; mem. Am. Econ. Assn. Avocations: photography, travel.

NASAR, SYED ABU, electrical engineering educator; b. Gorakhpur, Uttar Pradesh, India, Dec. 25, 1932; came to U.S., 1956; s. Syed M. and Syeda (Begum) Y.; m. Sara Samad, Sept. 3, 1961; children— Naheed, Sajida BSc, Agra U., 1951; BSEE, Dacca U., 1955; MSEE, Tex. A&M U., 1957; PhD, U. Calif., Berkeley, 1963. Chartered elec. engr., U.K. Assoc. prof. U. Ky., Lexington, 1968-70, prof. elec. engring., 1970—, Univ. Rsch. prof., 1989-97, chmn., 1980-87, dir. grad. studies, 1980-87. Visitor Brit. Council, London, 1964 Author or co-author 35 books on elec. engring., 1970-98; editor Elec. Machines and Power Systems Jour., 1976—; contbr. articles to profl. jours. Recipient Aurel Vlaicu award Romanian Nat. Acad., 1978; NSF rsch. grantee, 1966-87, 92—, Fellow IEEE (life; Nikola Tesla award 2000), Instn. Elec. Engrs. London. Office: U Ky 453 Anderson Hl Lexington KY 40506-0001 E-mail: snasar@engr.uky.edu.

NASGAARD, ROALD, museum curator; b. Denmark, Oct. 14, 1941; s. Jens Larsen and Petra (Guldbaek) N. BA, U. B.C., 1965, MA, 1967; PhD, Inst. Fine Arts, N.Y. U., 1973. Lectr., asst. prof. U. Guelph, 1971-75; curator contemporary art Art Gallery of Ont., Toronto, 1975-78, chief curator, 1978-89, deputy dir., chief curator, 1989-93, sr. curator rsch., 1993; chair dept. art Fla. State U., Tallahassee, 1995—; co-dir. programming Inst. of Modern and Contemporary Art, Calgary, Alta., Can. Vis. lectr. U. Guelph, York U., U. Toronto; adj. prof. U. Toronto. Author, curator: Ron Martin: World Paintings, 1976, author, curator: Structures for Behavior, 1977, author, curator: Garry Neill Kennedy: Recent Work, 1978, author, curator: Ten Canadian Artists in the 1970's, 1980, author, curator: Yves Gaucher: A Fifteen Year Perspective, 1978, author, curator: The Mystic North: Symbolist Landscape Painting in Northern Europe and North America, 1890-1940, 1984, author, curator: Gerhard Richter: Paintings, 1988, Individualities: 14 Contemporary Artists from France, 1991, author, curator: Free Worlds: Metaphors and Realities in Contemporary Hungarian Art, 1991, author, curator: Concealing/Revealing: Voices from the Canadian Foothills, 1997, author, curator: Pleasures of Sight and States of Being: Radical Abstract Painting, 2001, co-organizer: The European Iceberg: Creativity in Germany and Italy Today, 1985. Mem. Toronto Pub. Art Commn., Gershon Iskowitz Found. Can. Council fellow, 1967-68, 70-71 Mem. Coll. Art Assn., Univ. Art Assn. Can., Internat. Art Critics Assn.

NASH, ALANNA KAY, critic, writer; b. Louisville, Aug. 16, 1950; d. Allan and Emily Kay (Derrick) N. BA, Stephens Coll., 1972; MS, Columbia U., 1974. Music critic Louisville Courier Jour., 1977; writer, producer Sta. WHAS, Louisville, 1980; pres. Alandale Prodns., 1981—. Freelance writer specializing in the arts Stereo Rev., Esquire, N.Y. Times, Entertainment Weekly, TV Guide, Wired, Amazon.com, Ms., Glamour, Working Woman, Good Housekeeping, Saturday Evening Post, Video, Disney Adventures, Penthouse, Playgirl, The Perfect Vision, 1964—; country music editor Musicmaker.com, 2000-01. Author: Dolly, 1978, rev. edit. Dolly Parton: The Early Years, 1994, Behind Closed Doors: Talking with the Legends of Country Music, 1988, Golden Girl: The Story of Jessica Savitch, 1988, 96 (became feature film Up Close and Personal 1996), Elvis Aaron Presley: Revelations from the Memphis Mafia, 1995; (ghostwriter) Elvis: From Memphis to Hollywood, 1992; co-producer: (TV documentary) The Deaners: Cause without a Rebel; introduction: Branson, Mo.: Las Vegas of the Ozarks, 1998; primary on-camera source Lifetime Cable documentary Intimate Portrait: Jessica Savitch, 1995; writer, producer: network and syndicated specials; contbr. to books. Recipient Nat. Prodn. awards Alpha Epsilon Rho, 1971. Mem. Soc. Profl. Journalists (bd. dirs. Louisville chpt. 1987—, v.p. 1992-93, pres. 1993-94, Nat. Mem. of Yr. award 1994, Howard Dubin award 1994), Authors Guild, Am. Soc. Journalists and Authors, Country Music Assn. Republican. Methodist. Home and Office: 649 Breckenridge Ln Louisville KY 40207-4556 E-mail: talkshak@iglou.com.

NASH, ALICIA, computer programmer, physicist; b. San Salvador, Jan. 1, 1933; came to U.S., 1944; d. Carlos Roberto and Alicia (Lopez-Harrison) Larde; m. John Forbes Nash, Jr., Feb. 16, 1957; children: John Charles Martin. BS in Physics, MIT, 1955, postgrad., 1959. Physicist Nuclear Devel. Corp. of Am., White Plains, N.Y., 1956-57, Tech. Ops., Burlington, Mass., 1957-58; rsch. assoc. MIT Computation Ctr., Cambridge, 1958-59; physicist, aerospace engr. R.C.A. Astro Divsn., Hightstown, N.J., 1960-66; programmer, analyst Mgmt. Data Processing, N.Y.C., 1972-74, Con Edison, N.Y.C., 1974-80, Blue Cross Blue Shield of N.Y., N.Y.C., 1980-82; systems/analyst programmer specialist N.J. Transit, Newark, 1983—. Mem. AAUW, MIT Club of Princeton (past pres., bd. dirs.), Soc. of Women Engring. Home: 932 Alexander Rd Princeton Junction NJ 08550-1002 Office: NJ Transit One Penn Plaza East Newark NJ 07105

NASH, CHARLES D. investment banker; b. Atlanta, Feb. 8, 1943; s. Floyd Johnson and Ida Lee (Camp) N.; m. Augusta Horsey; 1 child, Paren J. BBA in Fin., Ga. State U., 1968. V.p. Courts & Co., Atlanta, 1961-70, The Dornbush Co., Atlanta, 1970-76; pres., chief exec. officer So. Turf Nurseries, Inc., Tifton, Ga., 1976-83, Neville & Gladstone, Inc., Atlanta, 1984-86; sr. v.p. Wheat First Securities, 1987-91, Interstate/Johnson Lane, Atlanta, 1991-97; investment banker Nash Equity Capital, 1997—. Mem. Ansley Golf club. Republican. Episcopalian. Avocations: tennis, boating, travel, golf.

NASH, CHARLES PRESLEY, chemistry educator; b. Sacramento, Mar. 15, 1932; s. Clarence and Mildred Vida (Johnson) N.; m. Lois Olive Brown, May 29, 1955 (dec. May 1999); children: Nancy Caroline, Sandra Lee, James Roy. BS, U. Calif., Berkeley, 1952; PhD, UCLA, 1958. Instr. chemistry UCLA, 1956-57; from instr. to assoc. prof. U. Calif., Davis, 1957-70, prof., 1970-93, prof. emeritus, 1993—, chmn. acad. senate, 1987-90, chmn. faculty assn., 1993-97; v.p. external rels. Coun. U. Calif. Faculty Assns., 1997—. Vis. sr. lectr. Imperial Coll., London, 1968-69; disting. vis. prof. USAF Acad., Colorado Springs, 1979-80. Contbr. articles to profl. jours. Bd. pres. Explorit Sci. Ctr., 1995-97. Recipient Disting. Teaching award U. Calif. Davis, 1978; named Disting. Alumnus of Yr. Sacramento City Coll., 2000. Mem. Am. Chem. Soc., Sigma Xi, Phi Lambda Upsilon. Office: U Calif at Davis Dept Chemistry Davis CA 95616

NASH, DONALD GENE, commodity investigator; b. Paris, July 20, 1945; s. Lelan and Mildred (Washburn) N.; m. Jo Ann Bellew, Aug. 29, 1964; children— Stacey Alan, Ryan Christopher, Shaun Christian BS, So. Ill. U., 1967, MS, 1969; postgrad., DePaul U., 1970-71. Farm mgr., test farms So. Ill. U., Carbondale, 1968-69; economist Commodity Futures Trading Commn., Chgo., 1969-77; v.p.-ops. Mid. Am. Commodity Exch., 1977-86; sr. investigator divsn. enforcement Commodity Futures Trading Commn., 1986—. Bd. trustees Friends of Danada, Wheaton, Ill., 2001—. With N.G. U.S. Army, 1968—74. Recipient Outstanding Mktg. award Wall St. Jour., 1966, award of merit Am. Farm Econ. Assn., 1967, cert. of merit Commodity Exch. Authority, merit award Naperville Art League, 1994, Honorable Mention award Danada Nature Show, 1995. Methodist. Avocations: photography; woodworking; sketching. Home: 923 Bainbridge Dr Naperville IL 60563-2002 Office: Commodity Futures Trading Commn 300 S Riverside Plz Ste 1600N Chicago IL 60606-6615 E-mail: dnash@cftc.gov.

NASH, EDGAR MASON, writer; b. Hilo, Hawaii, June 16, 1920; s. Edgar Mason and Mildred Evalina Nash; m. Rae Ethel Campbell Nash, Aug. 11, 1971; 1 child Lesley Rae. BS, Yale U., 1948. Cert. REB dept. real estate State of Calif. . Mfrs. rep. self employed, Pitts., 1949—58, L.A., 1958—66, real estate broker Visalia, 1966—96, inventor Modesto, 1999—2002, author, 2000—02. Designer machinery self employed, Pitts., 1951—58, con., Visalia, Calif., 1990—94. Author: Patent Your Idea Yourself..Without An Attorney, 2000, The Court-Martial of Ensign Mason, 2001. Lt. (jg) USCG, 1941—46. Achievements include design of and building of machinery and equipment for steel industry, including 250-ton hydraulic shear; patents in field; patents pending in field. Avocations: reading, exercising. Home and Office: 2800 Braden Ave #35 Modesto CA 95356 E-mail: ramblersoup@bigvalley.net.

NASH, EDGAR MASON, writer; s. Edgar Mason and Mildred Evalina Nash; m. Rae Ethel Campbell, Aug. 11, 1971; children: Leslie Rae. BS, Yale U., New Haven, CT, 1948. Cert. Department of Real Estate State of Calif. Mfr. / rep. self, Los Angeles, Calif., 1958—66, Pittsburgh, Pa., 1949—58, real estate broker Visalia, Calif., 1966—96, author Modesto, 2000—, inventor, 1999—. Consulting self, Visalia, Calif., 1990—94, machinery designer, Pittsburgh, Pa., 1951—58. Author: (book) Patent Your Idea Yourself.Without An Attorney, The Court-Martial of Ensign Mason. Lt. USCG, 1941—46, Various. Achievements include patents for Two patents granted, four patents pending. Avocations: reading, excercise at gym. Home: 2800 Braden Avenue # 35 Modesto CA 95356 Personal E-mail: ramblersoup@bigvalley.net.

NASH, EDWARD L. advertising agency executive; b. N.Y.C., Nov. 8, 1936; s. Irving and Mina (Koppel) N.; m. Diana R. Kithcart, June 2, 1968; 1 child, Amelia. BA, CCNY, 1953. Dir. advt. Crowell, Collier, Macmillan, Inc., N.Y.C., 1961-62; v.p. mktg. LaSalle Extension U., Chgo., 1962-64; pres. Capitol Record Club, Inc., Los Angeles, 1964-69; founder, pres. Nash Pub., 1969-74; exec. v.p. Rapp & Collins, N.Y.C., 1975-82; pres., chief exec. officer BBDO Direct, 1982-86; owner, pres. Nash Direct Inc., 1986-91; chmn. Nash, Wakeman & de Forrest, Inc., 1991-92; exec. v.p. Bozell, Jacobs, Kenyon & Eckhardt, N.Y.C., 1992-95; CEO, mng. ptnr. Team Nash, Inc., 1996—. Lectr. in field; chmn. Direct Mktg. Day, N.Y.C., 1985, Internat. Direct Mktg. Conf., 1996; instr. NYU, 1998—, Va. Commonwealth U., 1998—. Author: Direct Marketing: Strategy/Planning/Execution, 1982, 2d edit., 1986, 3d edit., 1995, 4th edit., 2000; editor: The Direct Marketing Handbook, 1984, 2d edit., 1991, Database Marketing, 1993. Mem. Direct Mktg. Assn. (chmn. mktg. coun. 1980-82, Silver Apple award 1999). Office: Team Nash Inc 104 E 40th St New York NY 10016-1801

NASH, ELIZABETH HAMILTON, music and theater educator, vocalist, writer; b. New Rochelle, N.Y., July 13, 1934; d. Allan Benjamin and Renee Nash. BFA, Columbia U., 1957, MA, 1971; PhD, Ind. U., 1975. Assoc. instr. Sch. Music Ind. U., 1971-74; assoc. prof. dept. theater arts U. Minn., Mpls., 1975—. Vis. prof. U. Tex., Austin, 1991, 92, Theaterhochschule Hans Otto, Leipzig, 1989, 92; voice prodn. coach/presentation stylist to Christian Sci. Monitor and Herold World Radio, 1975—; lectr., presenter, and panelist in field. Leading coloratura soprano Pfalztheater, Kaiserslautern, 1961—62, Theater am Domhof, Osnabrück, 1962—63, Landestheater, Detmold, 1963—64, Hessisches Staatstheater, Kassel, 1964—67, guest artist Mozart's Magic Flute, Amiens, Nancy, Strasbourg, Bruges, Ghent, Luxembourg, Lugano, Salzburg, 1968—70; leading singer/actress: Children's Theater Co., 1979—80; soloist Vt. Philharm. Orch., Montpelier, 1963, 1965, 1982; TV and radio interviews, essay readings and commls.: ; author (biographies): Always First Class, The Career of Geraldine Farrar, 1981, The Luminous Ones, A History of the Great Actresses, 1991, Pieces of Rainbow, 1994, The Memoirs of Sylvia Olden Lee, Premier African-American Classical Vocal Coach, 2001; contbr. articles and essays to profl. publs. Nat. Honor Soc. grantee, 1952; Fulbright grantee Staatliche Hochschule für Musik und Darstellende Kunst, Stuttgart, Germany, 1959-61, Bush Found. sabbatical grantee Guildhall Sch. Music and Drama, London, 1982-83; Bush Found. summer fellow Inst. in Arts Adminstrn., Harvard U., 1978. Mem. Nat. Assn. Tchrs. of Singing, Voice and Speech Trainers Assn., Women Historians of the Midwest, German Equity, Berkshire Conf. of Women Historians. Christian Scientist. Home: 4504 Oak Dr Edina MN 55424-1531 Office: U Minn Dept Theater Arts & Dance Minneapolis MN 55455 E-mail: nashx001@tc.umn.edu.

NASH, HENRY WARREN, marketing educator; b. Tampa, Fla., Sept. 19, 1927; s. Leslie Dikeman and Mildred (Johnson) N.; m. Frances Lora Venters, Aug. 20, 1950; children: Warren Leslie, Richard Dale. BS in Bus. Adminstrn, U. Fla., 1950, MBA, 1951; postgrad., Ind. U., 1951-53; PhD, U. Ala., 1965. Student asst. U. Fla., 1948-50, grad. asst., 1950-51, Ind. U., 1951-53; salesman Field Enterprises, Inc., Chgo., 1953; assoc. prof. bus. and econs. Miss. Coll., 1953-57; assoc. prof. marketing Miss. State U., 1957-66, prof., head dept., 1966-96; emeritus prof. mktg.; emeritus head dept. mktg., quantitative analysis, bus. law; dir. Coll. Bus. and Industry Acad. Advising Ctr., 1995-2000; ptnr. Southland Cons. Assos., 1968-84; bd. dirs. Govt. Employees Credit Union, 1969-92, v.p., 1969-73, pres., 1973-78. Author: (with others) Principles of Marketing, 1961. Served with USNR, 1945-46. Loveman's Merchandising fellow U. Ala., 1961-62 Mem. Am. Mktg. Assn., Am. Acad. Advt., Acad. Internat. Bus., So. Econ. Assn., So. Mktg. Assn. (sec. 1974-75, pres. 1976-77), Sales and Mktg. Execs. (internat. chmn. educators com. 1967-70), Miss. Retail Mchts. Assn. (bd. dirs.), Pi Sigma Epsilon (Nat. educator, v.p. 1967-69, nat. pres. 1967-71), Kiwanis (treas. Starkville club 1969-70, v.p. 1973-74, pres. 1974-75, lt. gov. 1977-78, gov. 1982-83), Blue Key, Beta Gamma Sigma, Omicron Delta Kappa, Mu Kappa Tau (nat. v.p. 1977-79, 86-88, pres. 1979-81, 88-90), Alpha Kappa Psi, Phi Kappa Phi (v.p. Miss. State U. 1990-91, pres. 1991-92). Baptist (tchr., deacon). Home: 2800 W Main St Cottage 302B Tupelo MS 38801-3027

NASH, HOWARD ALLEN, geneticist, researcher; b. N.Y.C., Nov. 5, 1937; s. Harvey and Harriet (Ratner) N.; m. Dominie Maria Shortino, Aug. 31, 1963; children: Janet Elisabeth, Emily Julia. BS, Tufts U., 1957; MD, U. Chgo., 1961, PhD, 1963. Intern U. Chgo. Clinics, 1963-64; rsch. assoc. NIMH, Bethesda, Md., 1964-68, med. officer (res), 1968-84, chief, sec. molecular genetics, 1984—. Chmn. Gordon Conf. on Nucleic Acids, 1988; vice-chair FASEB Conf. on Genetic Recombination, 1993, chair, 1995. Assoc. editor Cell Jour., 1985-91; editl. bd. Current Biology Jour., 1993—, Genes to Cells, 1996—, Jour. Neurogenetics, 1998—. Lt. comdr. USPHS, 1964-68. Recipient Superior Svc. award USPHS, 1985, Disting. Svc. award HHS, 1990, Alumni award for Disting. Svc., U. Chgo., 1994. Fellow Am. Acad. Arts and Sci.; mem. NAS. Office: Lab Molecular Biology NIMH 36 Convent Dr Bethesda MD 20892-0001 E-mail: nash@codon.nih.gov.

NASH, JAMES LEE, poet, security official; b. Lynchburg, Va., Oct. 1, 1957; s. James Belvy and Marjorie Lea Glden (Campbell) N. Grad., Brookville H.S., Lynchburg, 1977. VIP transp.-info. aide de camp Greater Ft. Lauderdale Broward County Conv. Ctr.; with Brookville H.S., Lynchburg, 1977. Author: (poetry) Casus Belli, 1993, Enduring Significance, 1996; contbg. author: T.P.O.A., 1994, Treasure the Moment, 1996, A Shadow in the Light, 1999, Love and Other Observations, 1999, Melodies and Madness, 1999, Explanations, 2000, Other Planets are Places Too, 2000, The Erotic Adventures of a White Trash Southern Boy, 2002. Mem. at large Dem. Exec. Com., Broward County, Fla., 1997-2000; mem. Croissant Park Civic Assn., Ft. Lauderdale, Fla., 1997-2000. Mem. Titanic Hist. Soc., Soc. Am. Magicians. Avocations: playing piano, juggling. Home: 1114 F St NE # 108 Washington DC 20002 Office: Trover 221 Pennsylvania Ave SE Washington DC 20003 E-mail: jlnashpoet@aol.com.

NASH, JANET RAE, geriatrics nurse; b. Taylorville, Ill., Aug. 12, 1953; d. Rayford C. and Dorothy L (Chlebus) Hurtte; m. James V. Nash, Sept. 17, 1976; children: Cherise, Brian, Brandon, Amanda. Diploma, Decatur Meml. Hosp. Sch. Nsg., 1975. RN, Ill. Staff nurse, charge nurse Decatur (Ill.) Meml. Hosp., 1976-81; clin. coord./head nurse long term care Decatur Meml. Hosp., 1985-91; dir. nursing Americana Healthcare Ctr., Decatur, 1981, Lincoln Manor Nursing Home, Decatur, 1991-92, Cedarwood Healthcare Ctr., Decatur, 1993-94; nurse restorative nursing Ea. Star Home, Macon, Ill., 1992-93; dir. nursing Pershing Estates Psychiat. Facility, Decatur, 1994; supr. Friendship Manor, Mt. Zion, Ill., 1994-95; resident care coord. Fairhaven's Christian Home, Decatur, 1995—.

NASH, JOHN ARTHUR, bank executive; b. Indpls., Mar. 12, 1938; s. Basil and Harriet Nash; m. Susan Moss; children: John, Bill, Stacia. BS, Ind. U., 1960, MBA, 1961. Account officer Nat. City Bank, Cleve., 1961-66; v.p. Irwin Union Bank, Columbus, Ind., 1966-71, exec. v.p., 1971-75, pres., 1975-79, Irwin Fin. Corp., Columbus, 1975—, also bd. dirs. Ind., 1972—. Bd. dirs. Irwin Union Bank, Irwin Mortgage Corp., Irwin Ventures, Irwin Home Equity Corp., Irwin Cap. Holdings. Chmn. bd. trustees Columbus Regional Hosp., Columbus Econ. Devel. Bd.; past chmn. Heritage Fund Bartholomew County, Columbus; mem. adv. bd. Ind. U.-Purdue U., Indpls. 2d lt. U.S. Army, 1961-63. Recipient Sagamore of Wabash award Gov. of Ind., 1991. Mem. Am. Bankers Assn. (mem. bank leadership coun.), Ind. Bankers Assn. (bd. dirs., past chmn., chmn. govt. rels. com.), Ind. U. Alumni Assn. (pres. 1991-92). Office: Irwin Fin Corp 500 Washington St Columbus IN 47201-6230 E-mail: john.nash@irwinfinancial.com.

NASH, JOHN DAVIDSON, JR. economist; b. Houston, Apr. 12, 1953; s. John Davidson and Virginia (Bryant) N.; m. Sarah Hendrickson, June 26, 1982. BS, Tex. A&M U., 1975; MA, U. Chgo., 1978, PhD, 1982. Asst. prof. econs. Tex. A&M U., College Station, 1980-83; economist Bur. Econs., FTC, Washington, 1982-83, dep. asst. dir. consumer protection, 1983-84, asst. dir. trade regulation rules, 1984-86; agrl. sector economist Latin Am. and Caribbean Agrl. Projects div. The World Bank, Washington, 1986—, economist trade policy div., 1987—. Author: (with others) Strategic Minerals for Defense Needs, 1979, Colombia: External Sector and Agriculture Policies for Adjustment and Growth, 1985; contbr. articles to profl. jours. Mem. Am. Econs. Assn., We. Econs. Assn., So. Econs. Assn., Phi Kappa Phi, Omicron Delta Epsilon, Phi Eta Sigma, Libertarian. Avocations: scuba diving, tennis, running. Home: 3307 Brandy Ct Falls Church VA 22042-3705 Office: The World Bank 18th And H Sts NW Washington DC 20433-0001

NASH, JOHN FORBES, JR. research mathematician; b. Bluefield, W.Va., 1928; MS, Carnegie-Mellon U., 1948, BS in Math., 1945, PhD (hon.), Princeton U., 1950, U. Athens. Rsch. asst., instr. Princeton (N.J.) U., 1950—51; Moore instr. MIT, 1951—53, asst. prof., 1953—57, assoc. prof., 1957—59; sr. rsch. mathematician Princeton U. Cons. RAND Corp., 1950, 52, 54; vis. mem. Inst. Advanced Study Princeton U., 1956—57, 1961—62, 1963—64; rsch. assoc. math. MIT, 1966—67. Co-recipient Nobel Prize in Econ. Scis., 1994, Bus. Week award, Erasmus U., Rotterdam, 1998, Leroy P. Steele prize in math., 1999; recipient von Neumann Theory prize, Ops. Rsch. Soc. Am., Pres.'s award, Nat. Alliance for the Mentally Ill, 1999; fellow Sloan fellow, NSF fellow; scholar Westinghouse scholar. Fellow: Am. Acad. Arts and Scis., Econometric Soc.; mem.: NAS. Office: Princeton U Fine Hall Math Dept Princeton NJ 08544-0001

NASH, JUNE CAPRICE, anthropology educator; b. Salem, Mass., May 30, 1927; d. Joseph and M. Josephine Bousley; children: Eric, Laura; m. Herbert Menzel, July 1, 1972; m. Frank Reynolds, 1997. BA, CUNY, 1948; MA, U. Chgo., 1953, PhD, 1960. Asst. prof. Chgo. Tchrs. Coll., Chgo., 1960-63, Yale U. New Haven, Conn., 1963-68; assoc. prof. NYU, 1968-72; prof. CUNY, 1972—; disting. vis. prof. Am. U., Cairo, 1978, U. Colo., Boulder, 1988—; vis. prof. SUNY, Albany, 1988-89; disting. prof. CUNY, N.Y.C., 1990; Neilson prof. Smith Coll., 1996. Author: In the Eyes of the Ancestor, 1970, We Eat the Mines and the Mines Eat Us: Dependency and Exploitation in Bolivian Mining Communities, 1979, From Tank Town to High Tech: The Clash of Community and Industrial Cycles, 1989; editor: Crafts in the World Market: The Impact of Global Exchange on Middle American Artisans, 1993, La explosíon de comunidades en chiapas, México, 1995; co-editor: (with Helen I. Safa) Sex and Class in Latin America, 1976, Women and Change in Latin America, 1986, (with Juan Corradi and Hobard Spalding) Ideology and Change in Latin America, 1976, (with Jorge Dandler and Nicholas Hopkins) Popular Participation in Change: Cooperatives, Collectives and Self-Management, 1976. Mem. Soc. for the Anthropology of Work (pres. 1988—), Assn. Polit. and Legal Activities (pres. 1983), Am. Anthropology Assn. (Disting. Svc. award 1995), Am. Ethnographic Soc., Assn. for Feminist Anthropology (pres. 1990-93). Avocations: skiing, hiking. Home: 2166 Broadway 18D New York NY 10024 Office: CUNY 137th Convent New York NY 10031

NASH, KAREN MARSTELLER MYERS, sculptor, designer, systems analyst; b. Washington, Aug. 30, 1943; d. Frederick Arell and Ruth Mary (Quinn) M.; m. Christian W. Myers, Oct. 4, 1963 (div. 1973); children: Christian W. III, Meredith Kennedy. Student, U. Va., Fredericksburg, 1961-63. Boatbuilder Solna Corp., Newport, 1974-75; boatbuilder, purchase mgr. Coddington Yachts, Jamestown, R.I., 1975-77, Williams & Manchester Shipyard, Newport, 1983-87; boatbuilder, dir. purchasing Shannon Boat Co., Bristol, R.I., 1987-89, Aries Powercraft Ltd., Fall River, Mass., 1989-90; systems designer, mgr. Ronaco Internat. Inc., New Bedford, 1990-96, Guatemala and Nicaragua, 1990-96; programmer, analyst, designer Wildcat Cons. & Design, Newport, R.I., 1996—; sr. programmer/analyst Sys. Resource Mgmt., Middletown, 1997—. Designer, cons. The Grand Design, Newport, 1975—; costume designer The R.I. Shakespeare Theatre, Newport, 1978-90, Am. Renaissance Theatre, N.Y.C., 1982-84; design and systems cons. Blue Pelican Jazz Club, Newport, 1983-91; artist/mem. Newport Art Mus. Bd. dirs. The R.I. Shakespeare Theatre, Newport, 1981-84, Cultural Affairs Commn., Newport, 1982-84, The Hill Assn., Newport, 1983-85. Recipient Rhody award Providence Jour., 1984; U.S. Dept. Interior grantee, 1978. Episcopalian. Avocations: computers, sailing, fishing, camping, parrots. Home: The Gothic Cottage 104 John St Newport RI 02840-3108 Office: Wildcat Consulting & Design 104 John St Newport RI 02840-3108

NASH, LEONARD DAVID, writer, consultant; b. Miami Beach, Fla., Dec. 2, 1965; s. Raymond and Rose Levy Nash; m. Dalia Stein (div. Nov. 1, 1994). AA, U. Fla., 1986; BA in Eng., Fla. Internat. U., 1987, MFA in Creative Writing, 1996. Cert. Engl. tchr. Fla., 1988, lic. real estate realtor 1988. Eng. tchr. Dade County Pub. Schs., Miami, 1988—93; adj. lectr. Fla. Internat. U., 1994—99. Writing and editing cons., Hollywood, 1993—. Author: (short stories) Dad's Fish, 1996, (poem) Eighteen Wheels Across America, 1998, (short stories) No Deposit, No Return, What More Do You Want?, 1998. Participant Ednl. Civic Inst., Hollywood, 2002, Citizen's Police Acad., Hollywood, 2002. Avocations: tennis, hiking, bicycling, travel, reading.

NASH, LEONARD KOLLENDER, chemistry educator; b. N.Y.C., Oct. 27, 1918; s. Adolph and Carol (Kollender) N.; m. Ava Byer, Mar. 3, 1945; children— Vivian C., David B. BS, Harvard, 1939, MA, 1941, PhD, 1944. Rsch. asst. Harvard U., Cambridge, Mass., 1943-44, instr., 1946-48, asst. prof., 1948-53, assoc. prof., 1953-59, prof. chemistry, 1959-86, chmn. dept., 1971-74; rsch. assoc. Columbia, 1944-45; instr. U. Ill., 1945-46; ret. Staff Manhattan Project, 1944-45 Author: Elements of Chemical Thermodynamics, 1962, The Nature of the Natural Sciences, 1963, Stoichiometry, 1966, Elements of Statistical Thermodynamics, 1968, ChemThermo, 1972. Recipient Mfg. Chemists' award, 1966; James Flack Norris award, 1975 Home: 11 Field Rd Lexington MA 02421-8014

NASH, MARY HARRIET, artist, educator; b. Washington, May 8, 1951; d. Richard Harvey and Janet Rose (Nivinski) Nash; m. Richard Day, 1980. BA, George Washington U., 1973; MFA, Wsh. State U., 1976. Guest lectr. Mus. Art, Wash. State U., Pullman., 1976, 2d St. Gallery, Charlottesville, Va., 1980, U. Ala., Tuscaloosa, 1981, SEWSA Conf., Charlottesville, 1983; artist-in-residence Va. Mus. Fine Arts, Richmond, 1984—; guest juror Twinbrook Art Show, Fairfax, Va., 1978; tchg. asst. Wash. State U., 1975-76 vis. artist, lectr. Johnson (Vt.) State Coll., 1995; guest lectr. Julian Scott Meml. Gallery, 1995, Stetson U., DeLand, Fla., 1997, Emerson Gallery, McLean (Va.) Project for the Arts, 1997. Author: (artist's book) Skulls Are Forever, 1986; contbr. articles to profl. jours.; painting commd. by Nat. Hockey League, 2001. Recipient cert. for outstanding achievement Women in Design Internat., 1983, 3 gubernatorial citations Gov. of Va., Richmond, 1995-96; named Jinx Hazel Arts Citizen of Yr., Arts Coun. Fairfax County, 2001. Mem. Southeastern Ctr. for Contemporary Art (hon. mention 1979), MacDowell Colony Fellows, Phi Kappa Phi.

NASH, MELVIN SAMUEL, lawyer; b. Atlanta, Aug. 26, 1949; s. Ralph Samuel and Mary Pauline (Quarles) N.; m. Cynthia Joanna Hamrick, Aug. 21, 1980 (div.); m. Kristine Marie Clark, Nov. 22, 1997. A.B., Ga. State U., 1974; J.D., U. Fla., 1976. Bar: Ga. 1978, U.S. Ct. Claims 1983, U.S. Ct. Internat. Trade 1983, U.S. Tax Ct. 1982, U.S. Ct. Appeals (5th cir.) 1978, U.S. Ct. Appeals (11th cir.) 1981, U.S. Supreme Ct. 1985. Asst. solicitor State Ct., Cobb County, Marietta, Ga., 1977-78; assoc. Milam & Smith, Austell, Ga., 1978; ptnr. Milam, Smith & Nash, Austell, 1978-79; sole practice, Marietta, 1979—; spl. master Cobb Superior Ct., 1982—; dir. Nash Trucking Co., Inc., Marietta, Security Fiedelity Mortgage, Marietta, Nash Properties, Marietta. Magistrate Prohac Vice State Ct. Cobb County, Marietta, 1980-82; candidate state rep. State of Ga. Dist. 21, Marietta, 1982. Served with USAF, 1967-71. Mem. ABA, Acad. Fla. Trial Lawyers, Assn. Trial Lawyers Am., Nat. Assn. Criminal Def. Lawyers, Ga. Assn. Criminal Def. Lawyers, Cobb County Bar Assn. (com. 1983-84), Cobb Criminal Def. Bar Assn. (sec., Seminar award 1984), State Bar Ga. (fee arbitrator 1982—). Democrat. Presbyterian. Clubs: Atlanta Ski, Atlanta Track (Marathon finisher). E-mail: melvinsnash@msn.com.

NASH, MIKE, information technology executive; married. B in Computer Sci., Cornell U.; MBA (Palmer scholar), Wharton Sch. Bus. Project leader, software developer Gen. Data Corp.; various pos. in Windows mktg. Microsoft, Redmond, Wash., 1991, gen. mgr., bus. Windows product mgmt., corp. v.p., content devel. and delivery group, corp. v.p., security bus. unit. Office: One Microsoft Way Redmond WA 98052-6399*

NASH, NICHOLAS DAVID, retailing executive; b. Mpls., June 11, 1939; s. Edgar Vanderhoef and Nancy (Van Slyke) N. AB, Harvard U., 1962; MEd, Bowling Green State U., 1970; PhD, U. Minn., 1975. Head lower sch. Maumee Valley (Ohio) Country Day Sch., 1965-71; assoc. dir. Univ. Council for Ednl. Adminstrn.; adj. asst. prof. Ohio State U., 1975-78; v.p. programming Minn. Public Radio, St. Paul, 1978-82, Am. Pub. Radio, St. Paul, 1982-85; pres. The Nash Co., 1985—. Bd. dirs. Artspace Projects, Inc. Author works in field. Bd. dirs. Nash Found., 1975—. Mem. University Club St. Paul. Episcopalian. Home: 1340 N Birch Lake Blvd Saint Paul MN 55110-6716 Office: 2179 4th St Ste 2H Saint Paul MN 55110-3041

NASH, PAUL LENOIR, lawyer; b. Poughkeepsie, N.Y., Jan. 29, 1931; s. George Matthew and Winifred (LeNoir) N.; m. Nancy Allyn Thouron, Dec. 30, 1961; children: Andrew Gray, Laurie LeNoir, Daphne Thouron. BA, Yale U., 1953; LLB, Harvard U., 1958. Bar: N.Y. 1959. Assoc. Dewey Ballantine, N.Y.C., 1958-66, ptnr., 1966—. Pres. bd. trustees Peck Sch., Morristown, N.J., 1978-82. Served to capt. USMC, 1953-55; Japan. Mem. Assn. of Bar of City of N.Y. Republican. Home: 4 Westminster Pl Morristown NJ 07960-5810 Office: Dewey Ballantine LLP 1301 Avenue Of The Americas New York NY 10019-6022 E-mail: pnash@deweyballantine.com., pnash65131@aol.com.

NASH, RICHARD EUGENE, aerospace engineer; b. San Diego, Feb. 18, 1954; s. Clifford Arthur Jr. and Dorothy Fay (Johnson) N.; m. Lynn Elora Martin, Aug. 5, 1978. BSCE, U. Ky., 1981; MSCE, U. So. Calif., 1988; MSEM, West Coast U., 1995; EMBA, U. LaVerne, 2001. Registered profl. civil engr., Calif.; cert. profl. mgr. Mem. tech. staff Boeing, Downey, Calif., 1982—, lead engr. space shuttle propulsion systems, 1986-88; engr. Nat. Aero-Space Plane, Long Beach, 1988-89, space shuttle orbiter project engr., 1989-95; project mgr. problem action ctr., product mgr., problem reporting and corrective action, orbiter shuttle program Boeing, Huntington Beach, 1995—2001, sys. engring. staff on future shuttle between space launch initiative and future shuttle, project mgr. future shuttle program Huntington, 2001—. Pvt. practice civil engring., Calif., 1985-87. Scoutmaster Boy Scouts Am., Covington, Ky., 1972-74, Williamstown, Ky., 1976-82, asst. scoutmaster, Ft. Hood, Tex., 1975-76. Sgt. U.S. Army, 1976. Decorated Nat. Def. Svc. medal, Armed Forces Expeditionary medal; recipient Quality Spotlight award, 1971, Space Flight Awareness award, 1992, 95, Manned Space Flight Awareness award 1996, NASA Group Achievement award, 1997, Sustained Superior Performance award, 1985, Divsn. Quality award, 1997; named to Hon. Order of Ky. Cols., 1985. Mem. Nat. Mgmt. Assn. (series facilities), Nat. Eagle Scout Asst. (advisor 1983), Masons (32 degree, sr. warden), Chi Epsilon. Republican. Avocations: backpacking, scouting. Office: Boeing Human Space Flight and Exploration 5301 Bolsa Ave MC H017-D414 Huntington Beach CA 92647-2099 *Personal philosophy: If you want to be a doctor; talk to a doctor, she has already done it. If you want to be an engineer; talk to an engineer, he has already done it. If you want to be a success; talk to yourself, for only you know how to define success.*

NASH, RUTH S. foundation administrator; b. Westfield, Mass., May 7, 1916; d. George Whitney and Marguerite (Mueller) Searle; m. Clayton Richmond Nash, Sept. 7, 1940 (dec. 1990); children: Roberta Marie, Marguerite Louise, Gail Winifred; m. Charles Williams, Mar. 13, 2002. Student, Simmons Coll., 1935-37; Diploma, Sch. Handicraft and Occupl. Therapy, 1937-39; B in Liberal Studies, Fla. So. Coll., 1996. Leader Girl Scouts, Winthrop, Mass., 1934-40, field dir., exec. dir. Greater Lynn (Mass.), 1940-43; leader, bd. mem. Reading, Mass., 1940-60; field dir., exec. dir. Naumkeag Area Girl Scouts, Salem, 1949-56, field dir., tng. dir. Greater Lawrence (Mass.), 1958-63; leader Mystick Side Medford, Mass., 1960-63; field dir., pub. rels., tng. dir., camping svcs. dir. Merrimack River Coun., Andover, 1963-78. Author: High Seas to High Stakes, 2000, Tales & Tails From Stagecoach Lodge, 2002; editor: Monthly Civic Newspaper Beacon, 1984-99; contbr. articles to profl. jours. Vol. Meals on Wheels, 1991-96, Cmty. Svc., 1978-98; sec., mem. choir, handbell ringer Harbour Heights (Fla.) United Meth. Ch., 1991—; mem., founder H.H. Kitchen Band, 1990—; trail guide Charotte Harbor Environ. Ctr., Punta Gorda, Fla., 1997—; leader disadvantaged girls Girl Scouts USA, 1998—, study ptnr. for disadvantaged children, 1998—. Mem. AAUW (sec. 1998-), Learning in Retirement (sec. bd.), Alzheimers Assn. (support leader, bd. dirs. 1992-97). Republican. Methodist. Avocations: writing, watercolors, canoeing, golf, camping. Home: 3524 Peace River Dr Harbour Heights FL 33983-3523 also: RR 1 Box 70A Alton NH 03809-9719

NASH, SEYMOUR CY, surgeon, urologist; b. N.Y.C., Nov. 18, 1931; s. Annette (Gersten) Cook; m. Sally Anne Kugler, Aug. 6, 1958; children: Allison, Elizabeth, Gregory. BS, U. Fla., 1952; MD, Washington U., St. Louis, 1956. Diplomate Am. Bd. Urology. Surg. intern Yale Med. Ctr., New Haven, 1956-57, surg. resident, 1957-59; clin. assoc. Nat. Cancer Inst., Bethesda, Md., 1959-61; urology resident Georgetown U. Hosp., Washington, 1961-64; pvt. practice in urology Miami Beach, Fla., 1964—; assoc. clin. prof. U. Miami Med. Sch., 1964-94; chmn. dept. urology Mt. Sinai Hosp., Miami Beach. Co-author: Prostate Cancer Making Survival Decisions, 1994. Capt. USPHS, 1959-61. Fellow Am. Coll. Surgeons; mem. AMA, Am. Assn. Clin. Urologists, Fla. Med. Assn., Dade County Med. Assn. Republican. Jewish. Avocation: tennis. Office: 4302 Alton Rd Ste 670 Miami Beach FL 33140-2877

NASH, TED RUSSELL, musician; b. L.A., Dec. 28, 1959; s. Richard Taylor and Barbara Margaret Nash; children: Emily, Lisa. Alto sax Mel Lewis Jazz Orch., N.Y.C., 1981—91; tenor sax Carnegie Hall Jazz Band, 1993—95; alto sax Lincoln Ctr. Jazz Orch., 1997—; leader Ted Nash and Odeon, 1999—. Composer-in-residence Jazz Composers Collective, N.Y.C., 1992—; artistic dir. Jazz in Nevada County, Grass Valley, Calif., 2001—. Leader (CD recording) Sidewalk Meeting, 2001 (Top 10, 2001), Rhyme & Reason, 1999 (Top 10, 1999), Out Of This World, 1993. Grantee composing grantee, Mary Flagler Charitable Trust, 1998, recording grantee, 1999, composing grantee, Davos Musik Festival, 1994. Mem.: SEGAC, Local #802 Musicians Union. Avocations: photography, videography.

NASH, WARREN LESLIE, banker; b. Jackson, Miss., Aug. 26, 1955; s. Henry Warren and Frances Lora (Venters) N.; m. Valerie Ann Roberts, Nov. 22, 1980; children: John Wilson, Warren Graham, William Dixon. Student, U.S. Naval Acad., 1973-75; BS in Banking and Fin., Miss. State U., Starkville, 1978; MBA, U. Ala., Birmingham, 1982; profl. cert., Stonier Grad. Sch. Banking, Newark, Del., 1987. Asst. br. mgr. 1st Nat. Bank of Birmingham, Ala., 1978-80, br. officer, 1980-81, asst. v.p., 1981-84; v.p. AmSouth Bank, N.A., Birmingham, 1984-86, v.p., regional retail banking mgr. Montgomery, Ala., 1986-89; sr. v.p. AmSouth Bank, 1989-91; sr. v.p. consumer banking AmSouth Bank, N.A., Birmingham, 1991-93; v.p. productivity AmSouth Bank, 1993-94, sr. v.p. tech., 1994-95, sr. v.p. retail delivery, 1995-98; pres. Retail BancAssocs., LLC, 1998—. Instr. fin. Samford U., Birmingham, 1982-84; v.p., Ala. Automated Clearing house, 1983-84. Counselor Jr. Achievement, Birmingham, 1980-82; loaned exec. United Way, Birmingham, 1980; com. chmn. Birmingham Festival Arts, 1985-86. Named one of Outstanding Young Men of Am., 1984, 85, 86. Mem. Am. Mktg. Assn. (bd. dirs. 1983-84), Am. Inst. Banking, Birmingham C. of C. (dept. coord. 1985), Newcomen Soc., Young Montgomerians Bus. Club, Summit Club, Kiwanis (local pres. 1985-86), Alpha Kappa Psi, Beta Gamma Sigma. Republican. Methodist. Home: 3772 Rockhill Rd Birmingham AL 35223-1560 Office: Retail BancAssocs 2100 Southbridge Pkwy Birmingham AL 35209-1310

NASH, WILLIAM ARTHUR, civil engineer, educator; b. Chgo., Sept. 15, 1922; s. William A. and Rose (Keck) N.; m. Verna Lucile Baer, Aug. 8, 1953; children: Rebecca Ann, Phillip Arthur. BSCE, Ill. Inst. Tech., 1944, MS, 1946; PhD, U. Mich., 1949. Rsch. engr. David W. Taylor Model Basin, Navy Dept., Washington, 1949-54; mem. faculty U. Fla., Gainesville, 1954-67, head dept. engrng. mechanics, 1964-67; prof. civil engring. U. Mass., Amherst, 1967—. Cons. to govt. and industry; hon. prof. Shanghai Inst. Tech., 1985; pres. Cons. Engrng., Amherst, 1992—. Author: Theory and Outline of Strength of Materials, 3rd edit., 1994, 4th edit., 1998, Statics and Mechanics of Materials, 1991, Hydrostatically Loaded Structures, 1995; contbr. over 100 rsch. articles to profl. jours.; editor Internat. Jour. Nonlinear Mechanics. Recipient Humboldt U.S. Sr. Scientist award to Fed. Republic Germany, 1986. Fellow ASME; mem. Internat. Assn. Shell and Spatial Structures, Am. Soc. Engrng. Edn. (Curtis W. McGraw Rsch. award 1961), AIAA, Earthquake Engrng. Rsch. Inst. Congregationalist. Office: 235 Marston Hall U Mass Amherst MA 01003

NASH, WILLIAM LEWIS, III, retired music education educator; b. Kingston, Pa., July 5, 1946; s. Ray S. and Margaret (Zimmerman) N.; m. Janet Nossal, Dec. 29, 1979; children: Adrienne, William James. B of Music Edn., Westminster Choir Coll., 1968; MA in Music Performance, Trenton State Coll., 1970; PhD, Columbia State U., 1997. Cert. elementary and secondary edn. educator. Music tchr. Milford Mid. Sch. Quakertown (Pa.) Cmty. Sch. Dist., 1968-98; coord. of music Quakertown Cmty. sch. dist., 1974-98. Organist, choirmaster St. John's Luth. Ch., Boyertown, Pa., 1968-87; organist, music dir., dir. concert series Emmanuel Luth. Ch., Pottstown, Pa., 1987—; organist Am. Legion Baseball World Series, Boyertown, Pa., 1990—; organist St. David's Soc., 1998—, v.p., 2000, pres., 2001. Mem. Bucks County Music Educators Assn. (pres. 1978-80), Antique Classic Boat Soc. (N.E. chpt. founder, bd. dirs., pres. 1991-94, pres. 2002), Pa. Music Educators Assn. (Citation of Excellence, 1997, bd dirs. 1992-2002) Republican. Avocations: restoration of antique cars, boats, antique furniture; painting, fishing gardening, cooking, composing music. Home: 285 E Moyer Rd Pottstown PA 19464-1534 Office: Emmanuel Lutheran Ch Hanover and Walnut Sts Pottstown PA 19464 E-mail: nashr455@aol.com.

NASHIF, TAYSIR N. researcher; b. Tayyiba, near Jerusalem, Mar. 22, 1940; came to U.S., 1969; s. Najm A. and Aisha A. Nashif; m. Mayyada I. Nashif, Apr. 15, 1968; children: Fawz, Fayruz, Hanin. BA in Polit. Sci./Arabic Lang. & Lit., Hebrew U., Jerusalem, 1964, MA in Internat. Rels., 1968; MA in Islamic Studies, U. Toronto, 1969; PhD in Polit. Sci., SUNY, Binghamton, 1974. Prof. U. Oran, Algeria, 1974—76, UN, N.Y.C., 1976—77, polit. affairs officer, 1980—81, reviser, editor, 1982—96; prof. Essex County Coll., Newark, 1985—93; chief Arabic verbatim reporting sect. UN, N.Y.C., 1996—2002. Author: The Palestine Arab and Jewish Political Leaderships, 1979, Nuclear Warfare in the Middle East, 1984, Nuclear Weapons in Israel, 1996, The Arabs and the World in the Next Century, 1999, Authority, Intellectual Freedom and Society, Palestinian Thinkers in the Twentieth Century; contbr. articles on strategic and polit. issues to profl. jours. Grantee SUNY, 1971-73. Mem.: Third World Studies Assn., Am. Translators Assn., Mid. East Studies Assn., Am. Polit. Sci. Assn. Avocations: sea cruising, fishing, mountain climbing. Home: 350 George Dye Rd Hamilton NJ 08691 E-mail: tnnashif@aol.com.

NASHMAN, ALVIN ELI, computer company executive; b. N.Y.C., Dec. 16, 1926; s. Joseph and Fay (Portnoy) N.; m. Honey Weinstein, May 29, 1960; children: Jessica Rachel, Pamela Wynne, Stephanie Paige. BEE, CUNY, 1948; MEE, NYU, 1951; ScD (hon.), Pacific U., 1968, George Washington U., 1986. With Ketay Mfg. Corp., N.Y.C., 1951-52; dir. missile systems lab, dir. rsch. and devel. programs ITT Fed. Labs., Nutley, N.J., 1952-62; dir. ops., systems engrng. and tech. advisor Defense Comms. Agency ITT Intelcom, Inc., Falls Church, Va., 1962-65; pres. Computer Scis. Corp., 1965-67, bd. dir., 1968-95, v.p., 1969-92. Patentee in field; contbr. articles to profl. jours. Trustee Inova Hosp. System Found. With USN, 1944-46. Fellow IEEE; mem. Armed Forces Communications and Electronics Assn. (dir., internat. v.p. 1976-79, chpt. pres. 1979-80, exec. com. 1980-84, chmn. bd. 1984-86), AIAA, Nat. Space Club, Nat. Security Indsl. Assn., Tau Beta Pi, Eta Kappa Nu. Republican. Jewish. Home: 3609 Ridgeway Ter Falls Church VA 22044-1308

NASILOWSKI, PAUL, geriatrician; b. Krasnik, Poland, Feb. 3, 1968; s. Zbigniew and Joanna N. MD, Med. Acad. Lublin, 1992. Resident Flushing (N.Y.) Hosp. Med. Ctr., 1995-96, Newark Beth Israel Med. Ctr., 1996-99; fellow in geriatrics U. Ill. Chgo., 1999—; pvt. practice Chgo., 2000—; with Adv. Health Ctr., Orland Park, 2001—. Mem. ACP, AMA, Polish Med. Assn. Home: Ste 3108 3660 N Lake Shore Dr Chicago IL 60613 Office: 29 Orland Sq Dr Orland Park IL 60462

NASLUND, ALAN JOSEPH, communications educator; b. Chinook, Mont., Apr. 12, 1941; s. Harvey Clifford and Thelma Ruth Naslund; m. Sarah Agnes Riley, Feb. 13, 1994; m. Sena Jetter Naslund (div.); children: Flora Kathryn; m. Charlotte Ferree (div.); children: Andra. BA English Lang. and Literatures, U. Mont., Missoula, MT, 1970, MA English Lang. and Literatures, 1973; PhD English Lang. and Lit., U. Louisville, Louisville, KY, 1982. Grad. tchg. asst. English Dept., U. Louisville, Louisville, 1976—78, asst. to dir., grad. rhetoric program, 1980—81; instr. English Dept., Bellarmine Coll., 1981—82; devel. writing coord. English Dept., Hanover Coll., Hanover, Ind., 1982—85; asst. prof. English Dept., Pikesville Coll., Pikesville, Ky., 1985—86; english instr. Bellarmine Coll., Louisville, 1987—89; writing and lit. instr. English Dept., Stephens Coll., Columbia, Mo., 1989—92; english instr. Moberly Area CC, Moberly, 1983—83, English Dept., Columbia Coll., Columbia, 1993—93; instr., speech and writing in english for non-native speakers Comm. Dept., Sanyo Gakuen U., Okayama City, Japan, 1994—95; world lit. and writing instr. English Dept., So. Ill. U., Carbondale, Carbondale, Ill., 1996—96; basic english and coll. reading instr. Three Rivers CC Consortium PREP Program, Cape Girardeau, Mo., 1997—97; composition, lit., bus. comm. and tech. writing instr. U. Md. Coll. Overseas Program, Seoul, Korea (South), 1998—98; bus. comm. instr. for internat. studies SE Mo. State U., Cape Girardeau, Mo., 1998—99; composition and bus. communication instr. English Dept., U. Louisville, Louisville, 2000—00; composition and grad. bus. comm. instr. English Dept., Sullivan U., 2000—01; full-time grad. faculty Sullivan U. Grad. Sch., 2002—. Sec. Composition Com., Ind. Coll. English Assn., Ind., 1983—84; chmn. of sect.: authors reading poetry and fiction Twentieth-Century Lit. Conf., U. Louisville, Louisville, 1988—88; chmn. of sect. xid: remedial composition Second Miami U. Conf. on Sentence Combining and the Tchg. of Writing, Miami U., Oxford, Ohio, 1983—83; poetry judge Kentuckiana Metroversity Writing Contest, Ind. U. SE, 1983—83. Author: (book) Silk Weather; contbr. numerous short stories, poetry and book reviews to mags. Recipient Winning Entry (campus wide playwriting contest), Bellarmine Coll. Players, 1988, Winning Entry (campus-wide playwriting contest), Mont. Masquers, U. Mont., 1961; fellow Ficiton Writing Fellowship, Vt. Studio Ctr., 1993, Tenn. Williams Fellowship, Sewanee Writers Conf., U. South, 1991; grantee Al Smith Fellowship in Fiction (support grant), Ky. Arts Coun., 1990, Hanover Coll. Faculty Grant in Aid, Ninth Ann. Seminar on Rhetoric and Current Theories of Tchg. Composition, 1984; scholar Charles Merrill Smith Scholarship in Playwriting, Ill. Wesleyan U. Writers' Conf., 1986. Home: PO Box 5014 Louisville KY 40255 Office: Sullivan University 3101 Bardstown Rd Louisville KY 40205 Office Fax: 502-456-0040. E-mail: anaslund@sullivan.edu.

NASO, VALERIE JOAN, automobile dealership executive, travel company operator, artist, photographer, writer; b. Stockton, Calif., Aug. 19, 1941; d. Alan Robert and Natalie Grace (Gardner) McKittrick Naso; m. Peter Joralemon, May 31, 1971 (div.). Student pub. schs., Piedmont, Calif. Cert. graphoanalyst. Pres., Naso Motor Co. (formerly Broadway Cadillacs, Oakland, Calif.) Bishop, Calif., 1964—; freelance artist, 1965—; owner, operator Wooden Horse Antiques, Bishop, 1970-82; editor, writer, photographer Sierra Life Mag., Bishop, 1980-83; freelance writer, photographer, 1972—; owner, operator Boredom Tours, Bishop, 1981—; owner, sole photographer, Renaissance Photography, N.Y.C. and Bishop, Calif., 1982—, Keyboard Colors, 1986; cons. graphoanalyst, 1976—. Fiction, non-fiction work pub. in Horse and Horseman, Am. Horseman, Horse & Rider Mag., Cameo Mag., Desert Mag., Sierra Life Mag. Mem. Nat. Assn. Female Execs., Authors Guild, Inc., Authors League Am., Am. Film Inst., Archives of Am. Art, Lalique Soc. Am., Musical Box Soc. Internat., Alliance Francaise (N.Y. chpt.), Bishop C. of C., Victorian Soc. Am., Nat. Trust for Hist. Preservation, Am. Craft Coun., Nat. Rifle Assn. Clubs: Cadillac LaSalle (nat. and so. calif. chpts.); Wagner Soc. (N.Y.C.). Office: 783 N Main St Bishop CA 93514-2427 also: PO Box 1625 Bishop CA 93515-1625

NASON, CHARLES TUCKEY, diversified financial services company executive; b. Apr. 22, 1946; s. Raymond W. and Helen (Tuckey) Nason; m. Elizabeth Lucille Rabun, May 1, 1999; children: Rebecca Ann, Jill Nicole. BA, Washington and Jefferson Coll., 1968; MBA, U. Pitts., 1969. Cert. fin. planner, charterd fin. cons. Dist. sales mgr. Met. Life Ins. Co., Pitts., 1971-77; mng. dir. Acacia Group Cos., 1977-88; founder, pres. Coordinated Capital Ltd., 1982-85; chmn., pres., CEO Acacia Life Ins. Co., Washington, 1988—. Chmn. devel. coun. exec. com. Washington and Jefferson Coll., 1982—85, trustee, 1988—2000, chmn. Nat. Ann. Giving Fund, 1992—96; trustee Washington Fed. City Coun., 1988—; bd. dirs. Greater Washington Bd. Trade, 1990—, chmn.-elect, 1993, chmn., 1994; bd. dirs. Blue Cross Blue Shield Washington, 1991—93, Greater Washington Boys and Girls clubs, 1991—, Am. Coun. Life Ins., 1993—2000, Medlantic Healthcare Group, 1997—98. Lt. USAF, 1970—71. Mem.: Ins. Mktg. Stds. Assn. (bd. dirs. 1999—, chmn.-elect 2001, chmn. 2002), Inst. Cert. Fin. Planners (bd. dirs.), Nat. Assn. Securities Dealers, Estate Planning Coun. (bd. dirs.), Am. Soc. CLUSs (pres. 1981—82), Gen. Agts. and Mgrs. Assn. (pres. 1984—85), Talbout Country Club, Congl. Country Club, Burning Tree Club. Republican. Roman Catholic. Home: 8015 Quarry Ridge Way Bethesda MD 20817 Office: Acacia Group 7315 Wisconsin Ave Fl 10W Bethesda MD 20814-3202

NASON, DOLORES IRENE, computer company executive, social services administrator, eucharistic minister; b. Seattle; d. William Joseph Lockinger and Ruby Irene (Church) Gilstrap; m. George Malcolm Nason Jr.; children: George Malcolm III, Scott James, Lance William, Natalie Joan. Student, Long Beach (Calif.) City Coll.; cert. in Religious Edn. for elem tchrs., cert. teaching, cert. secondary teaching, Immaculate Heart Coll.; attended, Salesian Sem. Buyer J. C. Penney Co., Barstow, Calif.; prin. St. Cyprian Confraternity of Christian Doctrine Elem. Sch., Long Beach; prin. summer sch. St. Cyprian Confraternity of Christian Doctrine Elem. Sch.; pres. St. Cyprian Confraternity Orgn.; dist. co-chmn. L.A. Diocese; v.p. Nason & Assocs., Inc., Long Beach, 1978—; pres. L.A. County Commn. on Obscenity & Pornography, 1984—; eucharistic minister St. Cyprian Ch., Long Beach, 1985—; bd. dirs. L.A. County Children's Svcs., 1988—; assoc. dir. social svcs. Disabled Resources Ctr., Inc., Long Beach, 1992—. Vol. Meml. Children's Hosp., Long Beach, 1977—; mem. scholarship com. Long Beach City Coll., 1984-90, Calif. State U., Long Beach, 1984-90. Pres. St. Cyprian's Parish Coun., 1962—; mem. Long Beach Civic Light Opera, 1973-96, Assistance League of Long Beach, 1976—. Mem. U. of Pacific Club, KC (Family of Month award 1988). Roman Catholic. Avocations: physical fitness, theater, choir, travel.

NASON, LEONARD YOSHIMOTO, lawyer, writer, publisher; b. N.Y.C., Feb. 17, 1954; s. Leonard Hastings and Mary Yukiko (Yoshimoto) N.; m. Linda Thayer, Sept. 26, 1981; children: Victoria, Kelsey, Jennifer. BA, Tufts U., 1975; JD, Northeastern U., Boston, 1979. Bar: Mass. 1979, U.S. Dist. Ct. 1979, U.S. Ct. Appeals (1st cir.) 1985. Assoc. Ricklefs & Uehlein, Natick, Mass., 1979-84; ptnr. Uehlein, Nason & Wall, 1985-95, Nason, Wall & Wall, P.C., Lexington, Mass., 1995—. Pres. Legal Info. Svcs., Inc., Lexington, 1986—; interviewer admissions Tuft U. Author: (handbook) Mass. Workers' Compensation, 1986, (statute book) Mass. Workers' Compensation, 1987; co-author: Massachusetts Practice Series, Vol. 29, 1989, 95; contbg. author: A Judicial Guide to Labor and Employment Law, 1990. Bd. dirs. Newton Community Service Ctr., 1981; coach soccer, basketball and softball, Little League. Mem. ABA, Mass. Bar Assn., Boston Bar Assn., Assn. Trial Lawyers Am. Avocations: tennis, sailing, softball, music. Office: Nason Wall & Wall PC 113 The Great Rd Bedford MA 01730 E-mail: Lyn@Legalinfosysinc.com., LNASON1750@aol.com.

NASON, ROCHELLE, conservation organization administrator; b. Oakland, Calif., May 21, 1959; d. Milton and Ann Frances (Reed) Nason. BA, U. Calif., Berkeley, 1984; JD, U. Calif., San Francisco, 1987. Bar: Calif. 1987. Law clk. to Chief Justice Malcolm Lucas Supreme Ct. of Calif., San Francisco, 1987-88; litigation assoc. Morrison & Foerster, 1988-92; staff lawyer League to Save Lake Tahoe, South Lake Tahoe, 1992-93, exec. dir., 1993—. Adj. instr. Sierra Nev. Coll., Incline Village, 1992—94, Lake Tahoe C.C., 1992—96. Editor: The Traynor Reader, 1987; sr. rev. editor: Hastings Law Jour., 1986—87; editor: (jour.) Keep Tahoe Blue, 1992—; columnist: newspaper Tahoe Daily Tribune; contbr. articles to profl. jours. Mem. leadership coun. Tahoe-Truckee Regional Econ. Coalition, Stateline, Nev., 1992—94; v.p., bd. dirs. Jewish Cmty. South Lake Tahoe/Temple Bat Yam, 1992—99; bd. dirs. Tahoe Ctr. Sustainable Future, Glenbrook, Nev., 1995—98, Earthshare Calif., 2002—. Mem.: Thurston Soc., Order of Coif. Jewish. Avocations: backpacking, skiing. Office: League to Save Lake Tahoe 955 Emerald Bay Rd South Lake Tahoe CA 96150-6410

NASR, NABIL ZAKI, national center executive; b. Cairo, Apr. 6, 1954; came to U.S., 1981; s. Zaki and Monera (Sherbini) N.; m. Gwendolyn Susan Breon, June 15, 1986; children: Laura, Amy. BS, Helwan U., Cairo, 1978; MS, Rutgers U., 1983, PhD, 1990; M Engrng., Pa. State U., 1985. Instr. Helwan U., Cairo, 1978-81; design engr. Uni-Peak Cons., 1978-81; teaching asst. Rutgers U., New Brunswick, N.J., 1985-89; asst. prof. indsl. engrng. Rochester (N.Y.) Inst. Tech., 1989-95, Earl W. Brinkman prof., 1996—, dir. Nat. Ctr. for Remfg. and Resource Recovery, 1997—. Ind. cons. Piscataway, N.J., 1985-89; cons. Advanced Mfg. Systems, Pittsford, N.Y., 1989—. AMIDEAST fellow, Washington, 1981. Sr. mem. Inst. Indsl. Engrng., Soc. Mfg. Engrs. (chpt. chair 1985-87, Outstanding Student Svc. award 1987), Computer and Automated Systems Assn. Avocations: reading, tennis, swimming, soccer. Office: Rochester Inst Tech Nat Ctr Remfg 133 Lomb Memorial Dr Rochester NY 14623-5608 E-mail: nzneie@rit.edu.

NASRALLAH, HENRY ATA, psychiatry researcher, educator; b. Apr. 30, 1947; came to U.S., 1972; s. Ata George and Rose G. (Yameen) N.; m. Amelia C. Tebsherani, June 9, 1972; children: Ramzy George, Rima Alice. BS in Biology, Am. U. of Beirut, 1967; MD, Am. U. Coll Medicine, Beirut-Lebanon, 1971. Intern Am. U. Med. Ctr., Beirut, Lebanon, 1972; resident in psychiatry U. Rochester, N.Y., 1972-75; rsch. assoc. NIMH, Washington, 1975-77; asst. prof. psychiatry U. Calif., San Diego, 1977-79; from assoc. prof. to prof. psychiatry U. Iowa, Iowa City, 1979-85; prof. psychiatry Ohio State U., Columbus, 1985-98, U. Miss. Med. Ctr., Jackson, 1998—. Staff psychiatrist VA Med. Ctr., La Jolla, Calif., 1977-79; chief psychiatry svc. VA Med. Ctr., Iowa City, 1979-85. Editor: (5 vol. book series) Handbook of Schizophrenia, 1986-90; co-editor: NMR Spectroscopy in Psychiatric Brain Disorders, 1995; editor-in-chief Schizophrenia Rsch., 1987—, Jour. Psychiatry Disorders, 1996—; author and co-author over 200 published articles, 1976—. Pres. Psychiat. Rsch. Found. of Columbus, 1985—; mem. Alliance for the Mentally Ill, Columbus, 1987—. Recipient VA grants, 1979-84, NIMH, 1983—. Fellow Am. Psychiat. Assn. (coun. on rsch.), Am. Coll. Neuropsychopharmacology (chmn. pubs. com. 1992-95), Am. Coll. Psychiatrists (Deans Award com. 1996—), Am. Acad. Clin. Psychiatrists (pres. 1989-90), Soc. Biol. Psychiatry (awards com. 1988-90). Avocations: photography, tennis, poetry. Office: U Miss Med Ctr Dept Psyc & Human Behavior 2500 N State St Jackson MS 39216-4500

NASRUDDIN, JOHN, computer company executive; b. Woodhaven, Ny, Jan. 14, 1967; s. Abdul and Jamilla Nasruddin. BS, St. John's U., Queens, NY, 1985—89. Bus. owner Quantum Virtue LLC, Scottsdale, Ariz., 1990—. Home: 6633 E Greenway Pkwy Apt 205 Scottsdale AZ 8524-2027 Home Fax: 400-659-4479. Personal E-mail: keepfit2@cox.net.

NASS, CONNIE KAY, state auditor; m. Alan Nass; 3 children. V.p. Nass & Son, Inc., 1974—; auditor State of Ind., 1999—. Bd. Senator Richard Lugar's Excellence in Pub. Svc. Program. Bd. mem. Huntingburg Utility Bd., 1975—; city coun. mem., Huntingburg, 1979-88, mayor, 1988-96; mgr. municipally owned utility cos., Huntingburg, 1988-96; candidate for lt. gov. State of Ind., 1995-96; mem. GOP Platform Com., 1992; del. Rep. Nat. Conv., 1996; bd. dirs. Welborn Found. Evansville, S.W. Ind. Regional Health Care Ctr., Inc.; adv. bd. AAA, Evansville, 1990—; mem. fin. com. and emergency svcs. com. ARC Greater Indpls., 1999—; nat. gen. synod del. Ind.-Ky. Conf. United Ch. of Christ, 1981, com. on planning and evaluation, 1990—, bd. dirs., 1996—; Sunday sch. tchr., music dir. Salem United Ch. of Christ. Recipient Protect Our Woods Environtl. award, 1995; named Outstanding Rep. Woman Ind. Reps Mayor's Assn., 1995. Mem. Nat. Automated Clearing House Assn. (internet coun., electronic benefits coun., strategic expansion bd.), Nat. Assn. State Auditors, Comptrs. and Treas., Network Women in Bus., Women Execs. in State Govt., Ind. State Auditor Adv. Coun., Ind. Farm Bur., Ind. Assn. of Cities and Towns (bd. dirs.), Dubois County GOP Women's Club (pres. 1996-98), Marion County GOP Women's Club, Huntingburg C. of C. Office: State House Rm 240 200 W Washington St Indianapolis IN 46204-2728

NASS, LEONARD IRA, chemist, consultant; b. N.Y.C., Apr. 23, 1927; s. Irving and Sylvia Nass; m. Irene Shirley Wurman, June 3, 1950; children: Meryl, Hillary Atzori, Laura. BS in Chemistry, Syracuse U., 1949; postgrad., Poly. Inst., N.Y.C., 1950—54. Quality control chemist Consolidated Film Industries, Ft. Lee, NJ, 1949—51, Cineque Color Film Labs, N.Y.C., 1951—53; synthetic rsch. chemist Advance Solvents and Chems. Corp., 1953—65; mgr. specialty chems. Nat. Starch & Chem. Corp., Plainfield, NJ, 1965—68; pvt. cons. Warren, 1968—; founder, pres. Tech. Info. Exch., Gouldsboro, 1983—. Contbr. articles to profl. jours.; editor, author: Encyclopedia of PVC, 3 vols., 1975; ; editor: (rev. edit.) Encyclopedia of PVC, 4 vols., 1986; author: Modern Vinyl Compounding and Stabilization, 1964. Pharmacist mate 3d class USN, 1945—47. Fellow: Soc. Plastics Engrs. (pres. Palisades sect. 1965—66, founder, councilor polymer modifiers and additives divsn. 1984—87, councilor Palisades sect. 1980—83, Outstanding Achievements award Polymer Modifiers and Additives Divsn. 1987, Contbns. to Vinyl award Vinyl Plastics Divsn. 1997); mem.: ASTM, Plastics Inst. Am., Am. Chem. Soc. Achievements include patents for polyurethane foam and benzotriazole u.v. absorbing monomers and polymers. Avocations: jazz, photography. Home: PO Box 242 Gouldsboro PA 18424 Office: Tech Info Exch 33 Louis Ln Gouldsboro PA 18424 Fax: 570-842-2586. E-mail: l.nass@att.net.

NASSAR, CARL RUDOLPH, engineering executive; b. Lebanon, May 15, 1968; arrived in Can., 1971; came to US, 1997; s. Rudolph Carl and Mona N.; m. Gretchen Brooks, July 13, 1996. B, McGill U., Montreal, Quebec, Can., 1989, M, 1990, PhD, 1997. Design engr. CAE Electronics, Montreal, 1991; tchg. asst. McGill U., 1993-96, prof., 1996-97, Colo. State U., Ft. Collins, 1997—. Mem. bd. advs. Idris Comms., Boulder, Colo., 1999—. Author: Telecommunications Demystified, 2000, The Spirit of Joy: A Transformational Journey to Awaken the Soul, 2001; contbr. articles to profl. jours. Founder, bd. dirs. The Miracle Ctr., Ft. Collins, 1998—; founder Miracle Books, 2000—. Rsch. grantee Colo. State Govt., 1999-01, NSF, 2000-2002; recipient Nat. Sci. and Engrng. Rsch. Coun. award Canadian Govt., 1990, 92-96, Exemplary Project award Colo. Advanced Software Inst. Mem. IEEE. Office: Colo State U Fort Collins CO 80523-0001 E-mail: carln@engr.colostate.edu.

NASSAR, EUGENE PAUL, humanities educator; b. Utica, N.Y., June 20, 1935; s. Michael Joseph and Mintaha (Kassouf) N.; m. Karen L. Nocian, Dec. 30, 1969; children: Anne, Laura, Paul. BA, Kenyon Coll., 1957; MA in English Lang. and Lit., Worcester Coll., Oxford U., 1960; PhD, Cornell U., 1962. Instr. in English Hamilton Coll., 1962-64; asst. prof. Utica Coll. Syracuse (N.Y.) U., 1964-66, assoc. prof., 1966-71, prof., 1971—. Dir. Ethnic Heritage Studies Ctr. Author: Wallace Stevens: An Anatomy of Figuration, 1965, 2d printing, 1968, The Rape of Cinderella: Essays in Literary Continuity, 1970, Selections from a Prose Poem: East Utica, 1971, Wind of the Land: Two Prose Poems, 1979, The Cantos of Ezra Pound: The Lyric Mode, 1975, Essays: Critical and Metacritical, 1983, Illustrations to Dante's Inferno, 1994, A Walk Around the Block, 1999; contbr. articles to profl. jours. Rhodes scholar 1958-60; Woodrow Wilson fellow 1960-62, NEH fellow 1974. Home: 918 Arthur St Utica NY 13501-5302 E-mail: pnassar@dreamscape.com.

NASSAR, RAJA, statistics educator, researcher, consultant; b. Lebanon, 1936; came to U.S., 1958; naturalized, 1971; m. Ita G. Schaeffer, 1965; 1 child, Mark BS, Am. U., Beirut, Lebanon, 1958; MS, U. Idaho, 1960; PhD, U. Calif., Davis, 1963. Rsch. fellow U. Idaho, Moscow, 1958-60; rsch. asst. U. Calif., Davis, 1960-63, rsch. assoc., 1963-64; mem. vis. faculty U. Minn., St. Paul, 1964-66; asst. prof. Kans. State U., Manhattan, 1966-68, assoc. prof., 1968-74, prof. stats., 1974—. Vis. prof. Govt. Research Inst., Hamburg, Fed. Republic Germany, 1969-70, Nat. Research Inst., Toulouse, France, 1974-75, U. Kiel, Fed. Republic Germany, 1982-83, U. Giessen, Germany, 1992-93. Contbr. numerous artilces to sci. jours. Alexander von Humboldt fellow, 1969, 82, French Govt. fellow, 1974. Mem. Am. Statis. Assn., Biometric Soc., Sigma Xi, Pi Mu Epsilon. Greek Orthodox. Avocations: tennis, travel, piano, reading. Office: La Tech U Math and Stats 305 Wisteria St Ruston LA 71270-4235

NASSAR, VICTOR HANNA, pathology educator; b. Nazareth, Palestine, Sept. 10, 1937; s. Hanna Nasser and Mateel (Mastouri) N.; m. Jane Brannon, June 15, 1968; children: Paul B., Timothy V. BSc, Am. U. of Beirut, 1961, MD, 1964. Diplomate Am. Bd. Pathology. Resident Emory Un. Hosp., Atlanta, 1964-67; fellow in surg. pathology Columbia U., N.Y.C., 1967-68; fellow in pathology Johns Hopkins U., Balt., 1968-70; asst. prof. of pathology Am. U. of Beirut, Lebanon, 1970-75, chmn. pathology dept. Sch. of Medicine Lebanon, 1973-75; assoc. prof. Emory U., Atlanta, 1975-82, prof., 1982—. Mem. steering com. Mediterraiean lympoma WHO, Geneva, 1976—; collaborative scientist Yerkes Primate Ctr., Atlanta, 1977—. Contbr. articles to profl. publs., chpts. to books. Co-founder Lebanese Cancer Soc., Beirut, 1973; bd. dirs. Antiochian Ch. of N.Am., Atlanta, 1983. Yerkes Primate Ctr. grantee. Mem. Arab Am. Med. Assn. (pres. Atlanta chpt. 1990-93), Am. U. Alumni Assn. (founder Atlanta chpt. 1986), Order of St. Ignatius. Achievements include first to describe the pathology of new disease Mediterranean Abdominal Lymphoma, or Small Intestinal Immuno-proliferative Disease. Office: VA Med Ctr 1670 Clairmont Rd Decatur GA 30033-4098

NASSAU, MICHAEL JAY, lawyer; b. N.Y.C., June 3, 1935; s. Benjamin and Belle (Nassau) N.; m. Roberta Bluma Herzlich, June 26, 1971; children: Stephanie Ellen, William Michael. BA summa cum laude, Yale U., 1956, LLB cum laude, 1960. Bar: N.Y. 1960, U.S. Ct. Appeals (2d cir.) 1963, U.S. Tax Ct. 1963, U.S. Supreme Ct. 1965, U.S. Dist. Ct. (so. dist.) N.Y. 1978. Asst. instr. in constl. law Yale U., 1959-60; law clk. to judge U.S. Ct. Appeals 2d Cir., 1960-61; assoc. tax dept. Paul, Weiss, Rifkind, Wharton & Garrison, N.Y.C., 1961-73; ptnr. Kramer Levin Naftalis & Frankel LLP, and predecessor, 1974—. Mem. adv. bd. Matthew Bender Fed. Pension Law Service, 1975-76; mem. adv. com. NYU Ann. Inst. Employee Plans and Exec. Compensation, 1976-79; mem. steering com. Am. Pension Conf., 1981-83; lectr. in field; panelist various seminars on employee benefits; panelist Pension Video Seminar, 1983; mem. N.E. region pension liaison group IRS. Mem. editl. bd. Bank and Corp. Governance Law Reporter, 1989—; contbr. chpts. to books and articles to profl. jours. Charter fellow Am. Coll. Employee Benefits Counsel; mem. ABA (sect. taxation, employee benefits com. 1993—), N.Y. State Bar Assn. (co-chmn. employee benefits sect. taxation 1976-78, mem. exec. com. sect. taxation 1976-79), Assn. of Bar of City of N.Y. (chmn. subcom. pension legis. of com. taxation 1975-76, employee benefits com. 1987-92), WEB (N.Y. chpt. bd. dirs. 1990—, pres. 1993-94), Phi Beta Kappa. Office: Kramer Levin Naftalis & Frankel LLP 919 3rd Ave New York NY 10022-3902

NASSTROM, ROY RICHARD, retired education educator, consultant; b. Oakland, Calif., Oct. 28, 1930; s. Roy Richard and Edith Dolores (Spilman) N.; m. Sally Louise Shaw, Aug. 29, 1964; children: Karen, Eric. AA, U. Calif., Berkeley, 1955, BA, 1956, MA, 1964, PhD, 1971. Asst. to supt. Ravenswood Sch. Dist., East Palo Alto, Calif., 1964-65; acting instr. edn. U. Calif., Berkeley, 1965-68; asst. prof. ednl. adminstrn. U. Ky., Lexington, 1969-70; asst. prof. edn. Purdue U., West Lafayette, Ind., 1971-76; mediator, fact finder Ind. Edn. Employment Rels. Bd., 1974-76; asst. grad. dean Winona (Minn.) State U., 1976-77, chmn. ednl. adminstrn. dept., 1976-88, prof., 1976-01, prof. emeritus, 2001—, chmn. ednl. leadership dept., 1998-01. Cons., spkr. various orgns. and schs., 1969—; mem. bd. abstractors Ednl. Adminstrn. Abstracts, 1976-83; dir. post-masters studies, Winona State U., 1992-99. Bd. editors AASA Prof., 1979-82; manuscript reviewer Edn. Rschr., 1983-87; contbr. articles and revs. to profl. jours., chpts. to books. With U.S. Army, 1952-54. Recipient numerous grants, 1969-98. Mem. Midwest Coun. Ednl. Adminstrn., Am. Ednl. Rsch. Assn. (paper reviewer 1983-2000), Am. Assn. Sch. Adminstrs., Am. Assn. Colls. for Tchr. Edn. (instnl. rep., paper reviewer), Nat. Coun.

Profs. Ednl. Adminstrn., Nat. Assn. Scholars, Nat. Rural Edn. Assn., Minn. Licensing Collaboration in Ednl. Adminstrn., Phi Delta Kappa, Pi Sigma Alpha . Avocation: photography. Home: 1702 Edgewood Rd Winona MN 55987-2149

NAST, DIANNE MARTHA, lawyer; b. Mount Holly, N.J., Jan. 30, 1948; d. Henry Daniel and Anastasia (Lovenduski) N.; m. Joseph Francis Roda, Aug. 23, 1980; children: Michael, Daniel, Joseph, Joshua, Anastasia. BA, Pa. State U.; JD, Rutgers U., 1976. Bar: Pa. 1976, U.S. Dist. Ct. Pa. 1976, N.J. 1976, U.S. Dist. Ct. N.J. 1976, U.S. Ct. Appeals (3d, 5th, 6th, 7th, 8th and 11th cirs.) 1976, U.S. Supreme Ct. 1982, U.S. Dist. Ct. Ariz. 1985. Dir., v.p. Kohn, Nast & Graf, P.C., Phila., 1976-95, Roda & Nast, P.C., Lancaster, Pa., 1995—. Mem. lawyers adv. com. U.S. Ct. Appeals (3d cir.), 1982-84, chmn., 1983-84, mem. com. on revision jud. conf. conduct rules, 1982-84; mem. U.S. Ct. Appeals for the 3d Cir. Jud. Conf. Permanent Planning Com., 1983-90; bd. dirs. 3d Cir. Hist. Soc., 1993—; bd. dirs. Phila. Pub. Def., 1980-89; dir. U.S. Fed. Judicial Ctr. Found., 1991—, chair, 1996—; chmn. lawyers adv. com. U.S. Dist. Ct. (ea. dist.) Pa., 1982-90. Pres. Hist. Soc., 1988-91. Fellow ABA (coun. litigation sect. 1986-89, co-chmn. anti-trust com. litigation sect. 1984-86, div. dir. 1990-91, practical litigation editl. bd. 1989—, ho. of dels. 1992-94, mem. task force state justice initiatives, mem. task force state of justice system, 1993, mem. task force long range planning com. 1994), Am. Law Inst. (chair internat. professionalism com. 1991-94, civil justice task force 1993-95), Am. Arbitration Assn. (bd. dirs., mem. alt. dispute resolution and mass torts task force), Am. Judicature Soc., Pa. Bar Assn. (bd. of dels. 1983-95), N.J. Bar Assn., Pa. Trial Lawyers Assn., Phila. Bar Assn. (bd. govs. 1985-87, chmn., bicentennial com. 1986-87, chmn. bench bar conf. 1988-89), Lancaster Bar Assn. (co-chair civil litigation and rules com. trial law sect.), Rutgers Law Sch. Alumni Assn. Home: 1059 Sylvan Rd Lancaster PA 17601-1923 Office: Roda & Nast PC 801 Estelle Dr Lancaster PA 17601-2130 E-mail: dnast@rodanast.com.

NASTA, PHYLLIS F. school counselor, writer; b. N.Y.C., Aug. 31, 1950; d. Phillip R. and Yolanda Danieli Nasta; 1 child, Jeremy. BA, Fordham U., 1971; M in Counseling, Ariz. State U., 1976; cert. in massage therapy, Desert Inst. Healing Arts, 1986. Prevention specialist Maricopa Youth Svc. Ctr., Phoenix, 1972-74; psychiat. social worker Kino Hosp., Tucson, 1982-84; children's therapist La Frontera Mental Health Ctr., 1983-84, Las Familias Ctr. for Treatment of Sex Abuse, 1985-86; children's play therapist Tucson Psychiat. Inst., 1985-86; children's therapist Family Counseling Agy., Tucson, 1987-89; sch. counselor Amphi Sch. Dist., 1989—. Author: (book) Aaron Goes to the Shelter, 1989, Bill of Rights for Children Whose Parents Are Divorced, 1997, Touching Is Important, 1984. Vol. asst. Tucson Symphony Orch. Recipient Essay Contest award N.Y. Soc. Med. Massage Therapists, 1997. Avocations: music, volunteer work. Office: Wilson Sch 2330 W Glover Rd Tucson AZ 85742 E-mail: pfnasta@prodigy.net.

NASTAC, LAURENTIU, materials and metallurgy engineer; b. Bucharest, Romania; came to US, 1991; m. Mihaela Nicoleta Nastac; children: Gabriel Cristian, Michael Lucian. Diploma in engrnig., U. Poly., Bucharest, 1985; MS in Metall. and Materials Engring., U. Ala., 1993, PhD in Metall. and Materials Engring., 1995. Project mgmt. cert. Concurrent Techs. Corp. Plant metall. engr. Fine Mechanisms Unit, Spl. Foundry, Sinaia, Romania, 1985-87; jr. rschr. Inst. for Hot Processes, Bucharest, 1987-89, sr. rschr., 1989-90; asst. prof. dept. metall. and materials engring. U. Poly., 1990-91; grad. rsch. asst. dept. metall. and materials engring. U. Ala. Solidification Lab., Tuscaloosa, 1991-94; cons., co-investigator Automated Techs. Corp., Peoria, Ill., 1991-94, project engr., 1994-96; sr. tech. staff Concurrent Techs. Corp., Johnstown, Pa., 1996-99, prin. process modeling engr., 1999—. Cons. Caterpillar, Inc., Peoria, Carpenter Technology Corp., Reading, Pa., 2000; co-investigator NASA, Huntsville, Ala. Contbr. articles to profl. jours. Recipient Bunshah Best Paper award Am. Vacuum Soc. Vacuum Metallurgy Divsn., Santa Fe, 1999; Spain-Hickman scholar Rotary Internat., Tuscaloosa, 1993; Sullivan, Long and Hagerty Endowed fellow U. Ala., Tuscaloosa, 1993. Mem. Am. Foundrymen's Soc., The Materials Soc., Am. Soc. Metals, Sigma Xi. Achievements include patent in field. Avocations: skiing, chess, traveling, tennis. Home: 1204 Ridgewood Rd Upper St Clair Pittsburgh PA 15241-2840 Office: Concurrent Techs Corp Regional Enterprise Tower 425 6th Ave 28th Fl Pittsburgh PA 15219 Fax: (412) 577-2660. E-mail: nastac@hotmail.com., nastac@ctc.com.

NASTALI, BERNADETTE THERESA, music educator; b. Chgo., Sept. 29, 1933; d. Henry and Adeline (Balut) N. B Music Edn., Mundelein Coll., 1955; MEd, DePaul U., 1963. Tchr., chair music dept. St. Edward Sch., Chgo., 1955—. Pres Citywide Orch. Bd., Chgo., 1980-93. Pres. St. Hyacinth Sch. Bd., Chgo., 1983—. Recipient Heart of the Sch. award Archdiocese of Chgo., 1991. Mem. Nat. Cath. Bandmaster Assn., Nat. Sch. Orch. Assn., Music Educators Nat. Conf., Ill. Music Educators Assn. Roman Catholic. Avocations: stamp collecting, reading, needlework. Home: 2914 N Harding Ave Chicago IL 60618-7216 Office: St Edward Sch 4343 W Sunnyside Ave Chicago IL 60630-4198

NASTASI, ALDO A. judge; b. N.Y.C., Sept. 18, 1932; s. Anthony and Santina N.; m. Marie A. Nastasi, Dec. 26, 1954; children: Aldo, Robert, Marc, Anthony, David. B in Social Sci., Fordham U., 1954, LLD, 1959. Bar: N.Y. 1960, U.S. Supreme Ct. 1974. City ct. judge, Yonkers, N.Y., 1975-79; judge Westchester County Ct., 1980-83, N.Y. State Supreme Ct., 1984-97, 98—. Councilman City of Yonkers, 1972-75, selected coun. majority leader. 1st lt. USMC, 1954-56. Mem. N.Y. State Lawyers Trial Assn., Westchester County Bar Assn., Columbia Lawyers Assn. (bd. dirs. 1992-98). Republican. Roman Catholic. Avocations: reading historical novels, accounts and biographies, golf. Office: 9th Jud Dist Ct NY Westchester County Ct House 111 MLK Jr Blvd White Plains NY 10601

NASZÁLYI, BARON PHILIPPE JACQUES, economics educator, publication director; b. Savigny, Orge, France, Apr. 7, 1955; s. François and Monique (Moine) N. BA in History, Sorbonne U., Paris, 1976, MA in History, 1977, BA in Lit., 1978, PhD in History, 1982. Cert. tchr. capes and agregation. Tchr. St. Charles Coll., Athis-Mons, France, 1981—93; dep. dir. Jeanne d'Arc Sch., Bretigny, France, 1983—84; lectr. Justice Ministry, Paris, 1988—92; prof. C. of C. EGC, Evry, France, 1994—95; prof. econs. U. Evry, Telecomms. Nat. Inst., 1995—2000; dir. mgmt. master dept. CFA U. Evry; dir. Direction et Gestion La Revue des Scis. de Gestion, Epinay sur Orge, France, 1990—. V.p. Credit Mutuel Bank, Epinay Sur Orge, 1981-86, chmn. bd., 1986-89, 92-93, fed. adminstr., 1986-89; mgmt. Nat. Inst. Telecoms. Evry. Author: Computers for Everyone, 1985, Guide du Pèlerin de Compostelle, 1989, L'Euro, APE, PUF, 1997, L'Hopital et la Santé publique, APE, 1998, Investment in China, AFPA, 1999, editor-in-chief Politique et Technologies, Paris, 1986-89. Councillor City Coun., Epinay Sur Orge, 1983-95. Recipient 2nd prize on French revolution Regional Coun. of Ile de France, 1989; Bronze Medal of Essonne, 1989, Mot d'or du Français des Affaires, 1996. Mem. Syndicate of Econ. Press (exec. com. 1992—), Fedn. of Press (exec. com. 1992—), Assn. Press et Enseignement (asst. gen. sec. 1996), Malta Order, Computer Mgmt. Assn. (founding pres. 1980-93), Alumni Club (pres. 1978-89, 92-93). Roman Catholic. Avocation: resting in the country. Home: 31 Rue de L'Esplanade F 91360 Epinay Sur Orge France Office: Direction et Gestion BP 49 F 91360 Epinay Sur Orge France E-mail: revue-sciences-gestion@wanadoo.fr.

NATALE, JOE, financial consultant; Sr. v.p., country leader Can., global leader automotive and transp. industries KPMG Consulting Inc., Toronto. Office: KPMG Ste 3300 Commerce Ct W 199 Bay St Toronto Canada M5L 1B2*

NATALE, LAUREL ARMITAGE, nursing case manager; b. N.Y.C., Apr. 25, 1945; d. Laurence C. and Grace O. (McIntyre) Armitage; m. Carmen J. Natale, Feb. 13, 1964; children: Julia Ann Gerson, Christine Cartwright, Kathryn Natale. Diploma, Charity Hosp. Sch. Nursing, New Orleans, 1978; BSN, U. Tex., Galveston, 1984; MSN, U. Tex., Houston, 1990. RN, Tex.; cert. case mgr. Staff nurse SICU trauma Hermann Hosp., Houston, asst. head nurse renal transpant intensive care unit; patient care supr. hospice Vis. Nurse Assn.; instr. clin. nursing U. Tex. Health Sci. Ctr.-Houston Sch. Nursing; staff nurse emergency dept. Meml. Hosp. System; case mgr. Worklink, 1994-95, supr. case mgmt., 1996-97; divsn. case mgr. Nat. Convenience Stores, Houston, 1995-96; utilization review CorVel Corp., 1997-98; legal nurse cons., paralegal Gallagher & Howard, Atys. at Law, Tampa, 1999—2002; patient case mgr. LifePath Hospice and Palliative Care, Lakeland, Fla. E-mial. E-mail: laurelnatale@hotmail.com.

NATALICIO, DIANA SIEDHOFF, academic administrator; b. St. Louis, Aug. 25, 1939; d. William and Eleanor J. (Biermann) Siedhoff. BS in Spanish summa cum laude, St. Louis U., 1961; MA in Portuguese lang., U. Tex., 1964, PhD in Linguistics, 1969. Chmn. dept. modern langs. U. Tex., El Paso, 1973-77, assoc. dean liberal arts, 1977-79; acting dean liberal arts, 1979-80; dean Coll. Liberal Arts U. Tex., El Paso, 1980-84, v.p. acad. affairs, 1984-88, pres., 1988—. Bd. dirs. El Paso br. Fed. Res. Bd. Dallas, chmn., 1989; mem. Presdl. Adv. Commn. on Ednl. Excellence for Hispanic Ams., 1991; bd. dirs. Sandia Corp., Trinity Industries; bd. dirs. Nat. Action Coun. for Minorities in Engring., 1993—; mem. Nat. Sci. Bd. 1994-2000; mem. NASA Adv. Coun., 1994-96; bd. mem. Fund for Improvement of Post-Secondary Edn., 1993-97; bd. dirs. Fogarty Internat. Ctr. of NIH, 1993-96; bd. chair Am. Assn. Higher Edn., 1995-96; bd. dirs. U.S.-Mexico Commn. for Ednl. and Cultural Exch., 1994—. Co-author: Sounds of Children, 1977; contbr. articles to profl. jours. Bd. dirs. United Way El Paso, 1990-93, chmn. needs survey com., 1990-91, chmn. edn. divsn., 1989; chmn. Quality Edn. for Minorities Network in Math. Sci. and Engring., 1991-92; chairperson Leadership El Paso, Class 12, 1989-90, mem. adv. coun., 1987-90, participant, 1980-81; mem. Historically Black Colls. and Univs./Minority Instns. Consortium on Environ. Tech. chairperson, 1991-93. Recipient Harold W. McGraw. Jr. prize in edn., 1997, Torch of Liberty award Anti-Defamation League B'nai B'rith, 1991, Conquistador award City of El Paso, 1990, Humanitarian award El Paso chpt. NCCJ, 1990; mem. El Paso Women's Hall of Fame, 1990. Mem. Philos. Soc. Tex. Avocations: hiking, bicycling, skiing, skating. Home: 711 Cincinnati Ave El Paso TX 79902-2616 Office: U Tex at El Paso Office Of President El Paso TX 79968-0001

NATALIE, RONALD BRUCE, lawyer; b. Lynn, Mass., Nov. 29, 1935; s. John Richard and Cecelia Lucy (Fish) N.; m. Betty Ann McEnteggart, Aug. 22, 1958; children: Ronald Bruce Jr., Karen Lorraine Walker, Donna Leslie Lee, John Francis. AB, Tufts Coll., 1957; JD with highest honors, George Washington U., 1962. Bar: D.C. 1962, U.S. Ct. Appeals (D.C. cir.) 1964, U.S. Ct. Appeals (2d cir.) 1970, U.S. Ct. Appeals (5th cir.), 1991, U.S. Ct. Appeals (3d cir.) 1992, U.S. Supreme Ct. 2000. Atty. Office of Gen. Counsel, U.S. Commn. on Civil Rights, Washington, 1962-64; assoc. Verner, Liipfert, Bernhard, McPherson and Hand, 1964-68, ptnr., 1968-81; shareholder Verner Liipfert, Bernhard, McPherson & Hand, 1981—, gen. counsel, dir., 2001—. Chief counsel Pres.'s Commn. to Investigate the Accident at Three Mil Island, Washington, 1979; vice chmn. Close Up Found., Alexandria, Va., 1971-98, chmn., 1998—. Lt. USN, 1957-62. Mem. ABA, D.C. Bar Assn., Ba Assn. of D.C., Assn. for Transp., Law, Logistics and Policy, Phi Alpha Delta. Democrat. Home: 3307 39th St NW Washington DC 20016-3711 Office: Verner Liipfert Bernarhd McPherson & Hand 901 15th St NW Ste 600 Washington DC 20005-2306 E-mail: bnatalie@msn.com., rbnatalie@verner.com.

NATALONI, ANDREW HECTOR, obstetrician, gynecologist; b. Bologna, Italy, Feb. 24, 1955; s. Marino and Faustina (Minarelli) N.; m. Zeinab Fath-el-Bab. MD, U. Bologna, 1981. Intern Flushing Hosp. and Med. Ctr., N.Y.C., 1981-82, resident in ob-gyn., 1982-85, chief resident in ob-gyn., 1984-85; full attending staff Ctrl. Suffolk Hosp., Riverhead, N.Y., 1985—, chmn. dept. ob-gyn., 1991—, also bd. dirs. Bd. dirs. Peconic Health Corp., Riverhead. Mem. AAAS, N.Y. State Med. Soc., N.Y. State Soc. Ob-Gyn., N.Y. Acad. Scis., Suffolk County Med. Soc. Office: Central Suffolk Hosp 1333 Roanoke Ave Riverhead NY 11901-2029

NATANI, KIRMACH, psychologist; b. Milw., June 5, 1935; s. Whit Baer Naabane and Natasha Rucoss Nabona. MSc in Clin. Psychology, Okla. U., 1974; PhD in Biopsychology, Okla. U. Health Sci. Ctr., 1977; postgrad., USAF Sch. Aerospace Medicine, San Antonio, 1977—79. Cert. psychologist, health svc. provider. Physics tech./profl. Lawrence Berkeley Lab., Berkeley, Calif., 1958—63; vol. Peace Corps, Thailand, 1963—65; clin. rschr. Oklahoma City VA Hosp., 1965—77; human factors engr. McDonnell-Douglas, St. Louis, 1980—92; postodoctoral resident/cons. St. Mary's Hosp., East St. Louis, Ill., 1992—97; pvt. practice clin. neuropsychologist, cons. Bi-State Neurometric Svcs., various cities, 1998—. Clin. mgr. Mo. Dept. Corrections, Farmington, Mo., 1999—2001; sr. care mgr. Magellan Behavior Health, St. Louis, 2001—02; ad hoc peer reviewer profl. psychology, rsch., practice, 2001; mem. adv. com. NRC, 1978—83. Contbr. With USAF, 1955—63. Recipient, Roche Labs. awards, 1973; grantee Rsch. grantee, Divsn. Polar Programs, NSF, 1966—75. Fellow: Am. Coll. Forensic Examiners, Am. Coll. Forensic Examiners; mem.: APA, Soc. for Neuronal Regulation. Avocations: computer graphics, digital photographic restoration. Office: PO Box 97 Hazelwood MO 63042-0097

NATARAJAN, ARUNA, physician, educator, researcher; b. Madras, Tamilnadu, India, Nov. 5, 1960; came to U.S., 1994; d. R. and Bama N.; m. Rajiv N. Sheth, July 12, 1998. BS, MB, Armed Forces Med. Coll., Poona, Maharashtra, India, 1984. Diplomate Am. Bd. Pediatrics. Chief resident, instr. Dartmouth Med. Sch., Hanover, N.H., 1995-96; fellow pediat. intensive care U. Tex. Southwestern Med. Ctr., Dallas, 1996-99; asst. prof. pediat. Georgetown U. Med. Ctr., Washington, 1999—. Contbr. author: Clinics in Primary Care, 1995, Jour. Molecular and Cellular Cardiology, 2001. Mem. Soc. Critical Care Medicine. Avocations: reading, writing, listening to Indian classical music. Office: Georgetown U Med Ctr CCC Bldg Rm 5414 3800 Reservoir Rd Washington DC 20007 E-mail: AN5@gunet.georgetown.edu.

NATARUS, BURTON F. lawyer, municipal legislator; b. Wausau, Wis. BS in Polit. Sci., U. Wis., 1956, JD, 1960; postgrad., John F. Kennedy Sch. Govt., 1993. Chair qualified arbitrator: Cir. Ct. Cook County, Ill. Pvt. practice law, Chgo.; elected alderman 42d Ward, 1971; chmn. Chgo. City Coun. Com. Traffic Control and Safety, 1997—; mem. Chgo. Plan Com. State St. Com., 1997—. Mem. Mayor's Zoning Reform Commn.; mem. Ctrl. Area Planning Task Force. Mem. 2000 Yr. Chgo. Trade Del. to China. Capt. USAR, ret. Mem. City Club, Greater North Mich. Ave Assn., Streeterville C. of C., River North Assn., North Dearborn Assn., North State, Astor, Lake Shore Dr. Assn., Streeterville Orgn. Active Residents, Washington Sq. Assn., State Street Coun., Ctrl. Mich. Ave. Assn. Address: 30 N La Salle St Ste 2900 Chicago IL 60602-2584 Office: City Hall Rm 306 121 N Lasalle St Chicago IL 60602-1202

NATCHER, STEPHEN DARLINGTON, lawyer, business executive; b. San Francisco, Nov. 19, 1940; s. Stanlus Zoch and Robena Lenore Collie (Goldring) N.; m. Carolyn Anne Bowman, Aug. 23, 1969; children: Tanya Michelle, Stephanie Elizabeth. AB in Polit. Sci., Stanford U., 1962; JD, U. Calif., San Francisco, 1965. Bar: Calif. 1966. Assoc. firm Pillsbury, Madison & Sutro, San Francisco, 1966-68; counsel Douglas Aircraft div. McDonnell Douglas Corp., Long Beach, 1968-70; v.p., sec. Security Pacific Nat. Bank, 1971-79; asst. gen. counsel Security Pacific Corp., 1979-80; v.p., sec., gen. counsel Lear Siegler, Inc., Santa Monica, Calif., 1980-87; v.p., gen. counsel Computer Sci. Corp., El Segundo, 1987-88; exec. v.p., gen. counsel, sec. CalFed Inc., 1989-90; sr. v.p. adminstrn., gen. counsel, sec. Wyle Electronics, Irvine, Calif., 1991-98; gen. counsel VEBA Electronics LLC, Santa Clara, 1998—. With USCG, 1965-71. Mem.: St. Francis Yacht Club (San Francisco). Republican. E-mail: snatcher@starstream.net.

NATELLO, GREGORY WILLIAM, cardiologist, educator; b. Phila., Mar. 30, 1954; s. Americo Vespucci and Catherine (Logan) N.; m. Judy Marie Cutcliffe; children: Logan Angelina, Connolly Claire. BA in Biology, Gettysburg Coll., 1976; DO, Phila. Coll. Osteo. Medicine, 1980. Diplomate Nat. Bd. Examiners, in internal medicine, geriatric medicine, cardiovascular disease, interventional cardiology Am. Bd. Internal Medicine. Intern Detroit Osteo. Hosp., 1980-81; gen. practice medicine Pennsauken, N.J., 1981-82; resident in internal medicine Cleve. Clinic Found., 1982-85; fellow in geriatrics Case Western Res. U., Cleve., 1985-86; assoc. in cardiovascular disease U. Ala., Birmingham, 1986-89; fellow in interventional cardiology Thomas Jefferson U., Phila., 1989-91; instr. phys. diagnosis Case Western Res. U., 1984-85; acting co-dir. labs. cardiac catheterization U. Mo. Health Sci. Ctr., Columbia, 1992—93; asst. prof. medicine U. Mo., 1991—93, U. Tenn., Chattanooga, 1993-96; assoc. West Fla. Med. Ctr. Clinc, P.A., 1996-99, CardioVascular Assocs., P.C., Birmingham, Ala., 1999—2001, CompHealth, 2001—. Cardiology cons. Dept. athletics U. Mo.-Columbia, 1991-93, U. Tenn., Chattanooga, 1993-96, co-leader heart failure continuous quality improvement team, 1995-96; mem. sleep disorders com. and quality assurance com. W. Fla. Med. Ctr. Clinic, 1997-99; bd. dirs. Prin. Healthcare Fla., 1997-99. Contbr. articles to profl. jours. Recipient award of Merit for Outstanding Achievement, Detroit Osteo. Hosp., 1981, Disting. Sr. Resident award Cleve. Clinic Found., 1985. Fellow Am. Coll. Cardiology; mem. AMA, Am. Heart Assn. (bd. dirs. Escambia unit 1997-99), Phila. Coll. Osteo. Medicine Alumni Assn. (life), Fla. Osteo. Med. Assn. (pres. dist. I 1997-99), Ala. State Med. Assn., Phi Kappa Psi. Republican. Episcopalian.

NATELSON, STEPHEN ELLIS, neurosurgeon; b. N.Y.C., Dec. 23, 1937; s. Samuel R. and Ethel D. (Nathan) N.; m. Laurie Lou Acred, 1990; children from previous marriage, Lea Jane, Jamie Ann, Jessica Ilana, Benjamin Henry, Marissa Claire. BA magna cum laude, Carleton Coll., 1958; MD, U. Rochester, 1963. Diplomate Am. Bd. Neurol. Surgery. Intern USAF Hosp., Wright-Patterson AFB, 1963-64; resident in neurosurgery Ohio State U., 1967-71; chief resident in neurology U. N.Mex., 1971-72; pvt. practice specializing inneurosurgery Knoxville, Tenn., 1972—. Clin. assoc. prof. U. Tenn. Contbr. articles to profl. jours. Served with USAF, 1962-67. Decorated Air Force Commendation medal; Fulbright scholar in Math., Westfalische-Wilhelms U., Germany, 1958-59. Fellow ACS; mem. AMA, Am. Assn. Neurol. Surgeons, Congress Neurol. Surgeons, Knoxville Acad. Medicine, Tenn. Neurosurg. Soc. (past pres.), Am. Physicians Fellowship, Undersea Med. Soc., Phi Beta Kappa, Sigma Xi, Alpha Omega Alpha. Republican. Jewish. Office: 103 Newland Profl Bldg Knoxville TN 37916

NATES, JEROME HARVEY, publisher, lawyer; b. N.Y.C., Sept. 19, 1945; s. Louis and Lillian (Berger) N.; m. Marilyn Arlene Weiss, June 6, 1971; children: Lori Jennifer, Scott Eric. BA, Hunter Coll., 1968; JD, Bklyn. Law Sch., 1972. Bar: N.Y. 1973. Assoc. atty. Natiss & Rogers, Long Island, N.Y., 1972-73; editorial dir. Matthew Bender & Co., N.Y.C., 1973-84; editor-in-chief Kluwer Law Book Pub., 1984-88; legal pub. cons., 1988-98; edtl. dir. Aspen Law & Bus., N.Y.C., 1998—. Co-author: Damages in Tort Actions, 1982; editor: Personal Injury Deskbook-1983, Personal Injury Deskbook-1984. Avocations: tennis, golf. Home: 19 Hummingbird Ct Marlboro NJ 07746-2510

NATH, JOGINDER, genetics and biology educator, researcher; b. Joginder Nagar, Panjab, India, May 12, 1932; came to U.S. 1957; s. Moti Ram and Vira Wali (Khorana) N.; m. Charlotte Lynn Reese, Apr. 5, 1969; children— Pravene, Brian BS with honors, Panjab U, Amritsar, India, 1953, MS with honors, 1955; PhD, U. Wis., 1960. Research assoc. Am. Inst. Biol. Research, Madison, Wis., 1960-63; asst. prof. So. Ill. U., Carbondale, Ill., 1964-66; from asst. to assoc. prof. W.Va. U., Morgantown, 1966-72, prof., chmn. dept. genetics and devel. biology, 1972—. Contbr. articles on cytogenetics, mutagenesis, biochem. genetics and cryobiology to profl. jours. Chmn. bd. Morgantown Day Sch., 1977-79 Recipient Alexander Hollaender award, Environ. Mutagen Soc., 1997, Edn. and Student Mems. Com. award, 2000, Mehra Meml. award, Panjab U., 2000; grantee, NSF, 1967—68, DOE, 1992—95, Nat. Inst. Occupl. Safety and Health, 1985—95, Nat. Inst. of Health, 2002—. Mem. Soc. Cryobiology, Environ. Mutagen Soc., Sigma Xi. Office: WVa U Coll Agr Dept Genetics & Devel Biology Morgantown WV 26506 E-mail: jnath@wvu.edu.

NATH, RAGHU, management consultant, educator; b. Rawalpindi, Pakistan, Nov. 3, 1932; arrived in U.S., 1959; s. Ram Chand and Som Rani; m. Lily Nath; children: Ritika, Nitika. BSc in Physics, Delhi (India) U., 1953; degree, Indian Inst. Sci., Bangalore, 1956; PhD, MIT, 1964. Cons. Bus. and Engring. Consultants, Bombay, 1956—59; exec. dir. World Tech. Ctr., Pitts., 1985—95; prof. bus. adminstrn. U. Pitts., 1964—, prof. emeritus, 2001—; pres. Inst. for Devel. of Orgnl. and Human Potential, 1966—. Organizer confs. in field. Author: Comparative Management, 1988, Organization Theory, 1993. Chair program com. Partnerships for Devel., Pitts., 1982—90; pres. UN Assn., 1991—94. Recipient Golden Key and Prefecture Book, Gov. of Hygo Prefecture, Kobe, Japan, 1985. Mem.: The Acad. of Mgmt. (chair internat. divsn. 1977—78, Outstanding Svc. award 1978), Acad. Brasileira de Ciencias Sociais e Politicas (hon.), Educators for World Peace, Triveni Internat. Club (bd. dirs., pres. 1987—93, Svc. award 1995). Avocations: tennis, hiking, swimming, yoga, gardening. Office: Katz Grad Sch of Bus U Pitts Pittsburgh PA 15260 Fax: 412-276-9210.

NATHAN, CHERIE-ANN OLYMPIA, surgeon, educator; b. Bombay, Dec. 17, 1963; d. Jeffrey Victor and Gema Maria Menezes; m. Raghu Parthasarathy Nathan, Dec. 29, 1991; children: Sean, Neil. MD, Bombay U., 1986. Diplomate Am. Bd. Otolaryngologist; lic. La. State Bd. Med. Examiners; bd. cert. otolaryngology/head and neck surgery. Intern U. Bombay, 1986-87, resident in otolaryngology, 1987-88; postdoctoral rsch. fellow Johns Hopkins U., 1988-89; intern in gen. surgery Butterworth Hosp. Mich. State U., 1989-90; resident in otolaryngology U. Calif., San Diego, 1990-94, clin. instr. head and neck, 1994-95; chief of ENT VA Med. Ctr. La. State U. Health Sci. Ctr., Shreveport, 1995-97, asst. prof., dir. head and neck cancer surgery, 1997-99, assoc. prof. otolaryngology, 1999—. Contbr. chpts. to books, numerous articles to profl. jours. Rhodes scholar finalist, 1987; recipient Travel awards, 1991, 93; NIH grantee, 1999. Fellow Am. Coll. Surgeons; mem. AMA, AAAS, ACS, Am. Rhinol. Soc., Am. Assn. Cancer Rsch., Soc. U. Otolaryngologists Head and Neck Surgeons, S.W. Oncology Group, So. Med. Soc., am. Acad. Otolaryngology Head and Neck Surgery. Avocations: piano, dancing, hiking, table tennis. Office: La State U Health Sci Ctr Dept Otolaryngol Head Neck 1501 Kings Hwy Shreveport LA 71103-4228 E-mail: cnatha@lsuhsc.edu.

NATHAN, FREDERIC SOLIS, lawyer; b. N.Y.C., June 24, 1922; s. Edgar Joshua and Mabel (Unterberg) N.; m. Frances E., Oct. 28, 1956; children: JEan E., Frederic S. Jr., William E. BA, Williams Coll., Williamstown, Mass., 1943; LLD, Yale U., 1948. Bar: N.Y. 1948, U.S. Dist. Ct. (so. and ea. dists) N.Y. 1948, U.S. Ct. Appeals (2d cir.) 1953, U.S. Supreme Ct. 1968. Instr. Williams Coll., Williamstown, 1948; assoc. Rathbone Perry Kelley & Drye, N.Y.C., 1948-53; asst. U.S. atty. U.S. Attys.' Office (so. dist.), 1953-56; assoc. Greenbaum, Wolff & Ernst, 1956-58, ptnr., 1959-65, 70-82; 1st asst. corp. counsel N.Y.C. Law Dept., 1966-69; ptnr. Kelley, Drye & Warren, 1982—. Mem. N.Y. Rep. County Com., N.Y.C., 1948-66; trustee Mt. Sinai Hosp., N.Y.C., 1970—; chmn. bd. FOJP Svc. Corp., N.Y.C., 1977-85, bd. dirs., 1979—; bd. dirs., v.p. Am. Jewish Soc. for Svc., N.Y.C., 1950—. With U.S. Army, 1943-45, ETO. Fellow Am. Coll. Trial Lawyers; mem. ABA, Assn. of Bar of City of N.Y. (exec. com. 1979-81), Fed. Bar Council (pres. 1975-76), N.Y. State Bar Assn. Clubs: Century Assn., Yale of N.Y.C.; Sunningdale Country. Republican. Jewish. Home: 180 East End Ave New York NY 10128-7763 Office: Kelley Drye & Warren 101 Park Ave New York NY 10178-0062 E-mail: fnathan@kelleydrye.com.

NATHAN, IRWIN, business systems company executive; b. N.Y.C., June 24, 1932; s. Albert Y. and Sarah Nathan; m. Sandra Alpert, June 18, 1955 (dec. June 1989); children: Alan Bradley, Mitchell Jordan; m. Phyllis Davis, Feb. 16, 1992. BSME, Stevens Inst. Tech., Hoboken, N.J., 1953; MSEE, N.Y.U., 1955, MS in Indsl. Engring., 1960; PhD, Poly. U., Bklyn., 1984. Registered profl. engr., N.Y. R & D engr. Dynamics Corp. of Am., Garden City, N.Y., 1953-56; sr. systems engr. Am. Bosch ARMA, Inc., 1956-63; prin. engr. Gen. Precision, Inc., Totowa, N.J., 1963-66; from section mgr. to mgr. svc. maintenance strategy Xerox Corp., Stamford, Conn., 1967-94; ret., 1994. Guest lectr. George Washington U., 1969, UCLA, 1971, The Wharton Sch., 1985; cons. OR/RAM Assoc. Westport, 1994—. Mem. IEEE, Ops. Rsch. Soc. Am. Avocations: boating, fishing, woodworking. Home: 121B N Country Rd Mount Sinai NY 11766-1503

NATHAN, JAMES A. political science educator; b. Chgo., May 1, 1942; s. Samuel and Dorothy (Goldsmith) N.; m. Lisa Harry; children: Michael, Alexander. AB with honors, Ind. U., 1960; MA, Johns Hopkins U., 1966, PhD, 1972. With U.S. Fgn. Svc., 1966-70; asst. prof. U. Del., Newark, 1972-75, assoc. prof., 1976-78, prof. polit. sci., 1978-90, Auburn U., Montgomery, Ala., 1991—. Vis. prof. Am. U., Washington, 1979, U. Adelaide, 1982, Army War Coll., 1982-85, Johns Hopkins U., 1986; rsch. assoc. Columbia U., 1980-83; Fulbright prof. U. New South Wales, 1987, Curtin U., Perth, Australia, 1987; Disting. Fulbright prof. fgn. affairs Coll. Beijing, 1999-2000. Author: (with others) The Future of United States Naval Power, 1979 (Furness prize 1979),

The United States Foreign Policy and World Order, 1976, 2d edit., 1981, 3d edit., 1985, 4th edit., 1989, Foreign Policy Making and the American Political System, 1983, 2d edit., 1987, 3rd edit., 1994; editor: The Cuban Missile Crisis Revisited, 1992, Anatomy of the Cuban Missle Crisis, 2001; contbr. numerous articles to profl. jours. Exec. dir. Ala. World Affairs Coun., 1991—. Faculty scholar Naval War Coll., 1976, Johns Hopkins U., 1979, Khaled bin Sultan Eminent scholar, 1991—, NDEA fellow, Melville Locker fellow, Sch. Advanced Internat. Studies, 1964-66, 68-72, Arms Control and Disarmament Agy. fellow, 1969-71, Spencer fellow, 1973-75, Naval War Coll. fellow, 1973-76, Fulbright-Hays fellow, 1976, NATO fellow, 1982-85, Dept. Def. fellow, 1983-86; grantee U. Del., 1972-82, 87, 94, 99-2000. Home: PO Box 244023 Montgomery AL 36124-4023 E-mail: jnathan@mindspring.com.

NATHAN, LAURA E. sociology educator; b. L.A., Oct. 28, 1951; d. Monroe and Sheila (Solomon) Engelberg; m. Mark D. Nathan, April 9, 1978; children: Justin, Michael. BA in Sociology, U. Calif., Santa Barbara, 1973; MA in Sociology, U. Calif., L.A., 1975, PhD in Sociology, 1981. Teaching assoc. in sociology Univ. Calif., L.A., 1975-76; acting asst. prof. sociology Calif. State Univ., Fullerton, Calif., 1977-81; coord., instr. Univ. Calif., L.A., 1979-80; assoc. prof. sociology and psychology Antelope Valley Coll., Lancaster, Calif., 1981-82; asst. prof. sociology Mills Coll., Oakland, 1982-87, assoc. prof. sociology, 1987-93, prof. of sociology Calif., 1993—, Robert J. and Ann B. Wert prof. of sociology, 1993-96, head dept. sociology and anthropology, 2000—. Lectr. in sociology and womens studies Calif. State Univ., Long Beach, 1978; program evaluator U.S. Dept. Health, Edn. and Welfare, L.A., 1974-75, program dir. 1975-76; mem. conf. planning com. Womens Leadership Conf., Mills Coll., also com. chair, 1992-93; bd. dirs. Am. Cancer Soc., Alameda County, Calif., 1985-96; bd. dirs. Am. Cancer Soc. East Bay Metro Unit, 1996—, pres., 1999-2001. Author: (with others) Secondary Analysis of Survey Data, 1985; contbr. chpts. to books. Regents Rsch. grantee, 1979, Mellon Found. grantee, 1983, Faculty Devel. Rsch. grantee Mills. Coll., 1985, 86, 87, 90, 91, 94, 95, 99) W.K. Kellogg Nat. fellow, 1988, Thornton Bradshaw Humanities fellow Claremont Grad. Sch., 1990, Graduate Leadership Am., 1997; recipient Disting. Leadership award Am. Cancer Soc., 1995, Unit and Region Lifetime Achievement award, 2000, ten Broek Soc. award for Excellence in Teaching, 1996. Mem. Pacific Sociol. Assn. (mem. nominating com. 1985-88, mem. program com. 1995-96, exec. coun., 1997-99), Am. Sociol. Assn. (membership com. 1988-92, com. soc. and persons with disabilities 1997-2000, chair), Soc. for the Study of Social Problems (chmn. poverty, class inequality div. 1987-88). Jewish. Avocations: traveling, mysteries, vol. work, beading, pilates. Office: Mills Coll 5000 Macarthur Blvd Oakland CA 94613-1301 E-mail: laura@mills.edu.

NATHAN, PAUL S. editor, writer; b. Oakland, Calif., Apr. 2, 1913; s. Alfred Jacobs and Frances (Strause) N.; m. Dorothy Goldeen, July 14, 1935 (dec. Dec. 1966); children: Andrew J., Carl F., Janet D. Souza; m. Ruth Wilk Notkins, May 26, 1972. BA, U. Calif., Berkeley, 1934. Reporter Oakland Post-Enquirer, 1929-36; asst. play editor Paramount Pictures, N.Y.C., 1937-48; hosp. pub. relations Will, Folsom & Smith, 1948-61; sci. editor Nat. Cystic Fibrosis Research Found., N.Y.C., Atlanta, 1963-73; columnist Rights and Permissions (subsequently Rights) Pubs. Weekly, N.Y.C., 1946-98. U.S. liaison Jerusalem Internat. Book Fair, 1976-77 Author: (play) Ricochet, 1980 (Edgar Allan Poe award of Mystery Writers Am. for best play of 1980), Texas Collects: Fine Arts, Furniture, Windmills & Whimseys, 1988; co-editor: (anthology) View: Parade of the Avant-Garde, 1991; author: (novels) Protocol for Murder, 1994, No Good Deed, 1995, Count Your Enemies, 1997; columnist Pub. News, London, 1998—; contbr. fiction and articles to Story, N.Y. Times mag., Saturday Evening Post, Saturday Rev., others. Mem. P.E.N., Dramatists Guild, Authors Guild, Authors League, Mystery Writers Am., Phi Beta Kappa. Office: 141 E 33rd St New York NY 10016-4606 E-mail: paulnathanny@aol.com.

NATHAN, PETER E. psychologist, educator; b. St. Louis, Apr. 18, 1935; s. Emil and Kathryn (Kline) N.; m. Florence I. Baker, Nov. 26, 1959; children: David Edward, Anne Miller, Laura Carol, Mark Andrew. AB, Harvard U., 1957; PhD, Washington U., 1962. Research fellow psychology Harvard U., 1962-64, research asso., 1964-68, asst. prof. psychology, 1968-69; research psychologist Boston City Hosp., 1964-68, dir. alcohol study unit, 1967-70; prof. Rutgers U., New Brunswick, N.J., 1969-89, dir. clin. psychology tng., 1969-87, dir. Alcohol Behavior Research Lab., 1970-87, chmn. dept. clin. psychology, 1976-87, dir. Ctr. Alcohol Studies, 1983-89, Henry and Anna Starr prof. psychology, 1983-89; sr. program officer, health program MacArthur Found., 1987-89; v.p. acad. affairs, found. disting. prof. psychology U. Iowa, 1990—, dean faculties, 1990-93, provost, 1993-95, acting pres., 1995. Mem. advisory council VA, 1972-76; chmn. alcoholism com. Nat. Inst. on Alcohol Abuse and Alcoholism, 1973-76, co-chmn. spl. rev. com., 1985, mem. nat. adv. coun., 1990-94; mem. psychol. scis. fellowship rev. com. NIMH, 1977-79; chmn. N.J. State Community Mental Health Bd., 1981-84; mem. working group substance use disorders, DSM-IV. Author: Cues, Decisions, and Diagnoses, 1967, Psychopathology and Society, 1975, 2d edit., 1980, Experimental and Behavioral Approaches to Alcoholism, 1978, Alcoholism: New Directions in Behavioral Treatment and Research, 1978, Clinical Case Studies in the Behavioral Treatment of Alcoholism, 1982, Professionals in Distress, 1987, Neuropsychological Deficits in Alcoholism, 1987, Introduction to Psychology, 1987, 2d edit., 1990, Abnormal Psychology, 1992, 2d edit., 1996, A Guide to Treatments that Work, 1998, 2d edit., 2002; exec. editor: Jour. Studies Alcohol, 1983—90; assoc. editor Am. Psychologist, 1977—85, Contemporary Psychology, 1991—97, Prevention and Treatment, 1998—2001, Psychol. Bull., 2002—, mem. editl. bd. Jour. Clin. Psychology, 1969—95, Jour. Cons. Clin. Psychology, 1973—95, Profl. Psychology, 1976—89. Fellow Am. Psychol. Assn. (chmn. sect. 3 div. 12 1976-77, rep. to council 1976-79, 82-85, pres. div. 12 1984-85; Disting. Contbns. to Knowledge award 1999). Democrat. Jewish. Home: 248 Black Springs Cir Iowa City IA 52246-3800 Office: Univ Iowa E119 Seashore Hall Iowa City IA 52242-1316 E-mail: pnathan@blue.weeg.uiowa.edu.

NATHAN, RICHARD P(ERLE), political scientist, educator; b. Schenectady, N.Y., Nov. 24, 1935; s. Sidney Robert and Betty (Green) N.; m. Mary McNamara, June 5, 1957; children: Robert Joseph, Carol Hewit. AB, Brown U., 1957; M in Pub. Adminstrn., Harvard U., 1959, PhD, 1966. Legis. asst. U.S. Senator Kenneth B. Keating, Washington, 1959-62; dir. domestic policy rsch. Nelson A. Rockefeller, 1963-64; rsch. assoc. The Brookings Instn., Washington, 1966-69, sr. fellow, project dir. monitoring studies gen. revenue sharing, community devel. block grant and pub. svc. employment programs, 1972-79; associated staff The Brookings Inst., 1980-85; asst. dir. U.S. Office of Mgmt. and Budget, 1969-71; dep. undersec. U.S Dept. Health, Edn. and Welfare, 1971-72; prof. pub. and internat. affairs Woodrow Wilson Sch. Pub. and Internat. Affairs Princeton (N.J.) U., 1979-89, also dir. Princeton Urban and Regional Rsch. Ctr., 1979-89; Disting. prof. polit. sci. and pub. policy SUNY, Albany, 1989-97; provost Rockefeller Coll. Pub. Affairs and Policy, 1989-98. Bd. dirs. Rockefeller Inst. Govt., Fleet Nat. Bank; assoc. dir. Nat. Adv. Commn. on Civil Disorders, 1967-68; vis. prof. govt. and fgn. affairs U. Va., 1972-77; chmn. Nixon Adminstrn. Transition Task Forces on Poverty and Intergovtl. Fiscal Rels., 1968, Domestic Coun. Com. on Welfare Reform Planning, 1969-70; mem. Commn. on Orgn. Govt. of D.C., 1970-72; bd. overseers New Sch. for Social Rsch., 1982-88; mem. working seminar on family and welfare Marquette U., 1986-87; selection com. Rockefeller Pub. Svc. Awards Program, 1976-78; income maintenance task force Nat. Urban Coalition, 1975-78; treas. Manpower Demonstration Rsch. Corp., 1974-81, chmn., 1981-98; mem. coun. scholars U.S. Libr. of Congress, 1989—; mem. N.Y. State Temp. Commn. Constl. Revision, 1993-94; mem. U.S. Adv. Commn. on Intergovtl. Rels., 1998-2000; vis. fellow GAO, 1998; cons. U.S. Gen. Acctg. Office, 1998-2000. Author: Jobs and Civil Rights, The Role of the Federal Government in Promoting Equal Opportunity in Employment and Training, 1969, The Plot That Failed: Nixon and the Administrative Presidency, 1975, Monitoring Revenue Sharing, 1975, Revenue Sharing, The Second Round., 1977, Monitoring the Public Service Employment Program, 1978, America's Government: A Fact Book of Census Data on the Organization, Finances, and Employment of Federal, State, and Local Governments, 1979, Public Service Employment: A Field Evaluation, 1981, The Administrative Presidency, 1983, Reagan and the States, 1987, Social Science in Government Uses and Abuses, 1988, A New Agenda for Cities, 1992, Turning Promises into Performance: The Management Challenge of Implementing Workfare, 1993; co-author: (with Thomas L. Gais) Implementing the Personal Responsibility Act: A First Look, 1999, Social Science in Government, 2000; (with Gerald Benjamin) Regionalism and Realism, A Study of Governments in the New york Metropolitan Area, 2001; contbr. chpts. to books; editor: (with Harvey S. Perloff) Revenue Sharing and the City, 1968; (with John D. DiJulio, Jr.) The View From the States, Making Health Reform Work, Brookings Instn., 1994; mem. editl. bd. Urban Affairs Quar., 1978-85. Eisenhower fellow European Econ. Commn., 1977. Mem. ASPA (Intergovtl. Mgmt. award 1985), Nat. Acad. Social Inst., Nat. Acad. Pub. Adminstrn. (James E. Webb award 1986), Am. Pub. Human Svcs. Assn., Am. Polit. Sci. Assn. (Charles E. Merriam award 1987), Assn. for Pub. Policy Analysis and Mgmt., Ft. Orange Club, Phi Beta Kappa, Theta Delta Chi. Republican. Jewish. Avocations: reading, travel, movies. Home: 9 Ridgefield Dr Voorheesville NY 12186-9798 Office: SUNY Rockefeller Inst Dir Office 411 State St Albany NY 12203-1003 E-mail: nathanr@rockinst.org.

NATHAN, RICHARD ARNOLD, technology company executive; b. N.Y.C., Sept. 25, 1944; s. Joseph and Mildred (Heller) N.; m. Shelly Ann Michaels, Sept. 5, 1966 (div. Mar. 1992); children: Wendy Beth, Daniel Scott; m. Onalee Louise Bodi, Apr. 27, 1994. BS in Chemistry, MIT, 1965; PhD in Chemistry, Poly. U., Bklyn., 1969. Researcher Polaroid Corp., Cambridge, Mass., 1969; chemist Battelle Meml. Inst., Columbus, Ohio, 1970-74, project mgr., 1974-76, mgr. environ. chem. sect., 1976-79, dir. programs, 1979-80, mgr. nuclear tech. dept., 1980-85, dir. tech. mgmt., 1985-86, div. gen. mgr., 1986-87, corp. v.p., div. pres., 1987-89, group v.p., gen. mgr., 1989-92; sr. v.p., dir. Mason & Hanger Corp., Lexington, Ky., 1993—. Bd. dirs. VersaTech Engring., Inc., Mason & Hanger Nat., Inc., Ensycon Internat., Inc. Editor: Fuels from Sugar Crops, 1976; contbr. articles to profl. publs.; patentee in field. Bd. dirs. Ctrl. Ohio coun. Boy Scouts Am., 1981-90, Ctrl. Sci. and Industry, Columbus, 1988—; chmn. Ohio Sci. Tech. and Industry Hall of Fame, 1989-93. Recipient award Indsl. Rsch. Mag., 1976. Mem. Am. Soc. Macro-Engring. (bd. dirs. 1986-92), Am. Nuclear Soc., Am. Mgmt. Assn., Ohio Acad. Sci., Sigma Xi, Phi Lambda Upsilon. Avocations: golf, reading. Office: Ensycon Internat 99 Canal Center Plz Ste 230 Alexandria VA 22314-1588

NATHANIEL, ALVITA KAY, nurse practitioner; b. Beckley, W.Va., Dec. 31, 1950; d. Zane Franklin and Nina Gretchen (Redden) Griffith; m. Timothy Charles Nathaniel, Sept. 23, 1972; children: Joshua Andrew, Maggie Corinne. BSN, Alderson-Braddus Coll., 1972; MSN, W.Va. U., 1984. Cert. FNP, ANA, Am. Acad. Nurse Practitioners. Instr. W.Va. Inst. of Technology, Montgomery, 1972-76; insvc. edn. staff nurse Charleston (W.Va.) Area Med. Ctr., 1981-84, 72, 76; FNP W. Va. Health Right, Charleston, 1984-87, Mercer Health Right, Bluefield, W.Va., 1990—, Ind. Practice, Princeton, 1995—, Bluefield (W.Va.) Regional Med. Ctr., 1994—; lectr. W.Va. U., Charleston, 1987—. Founding dir., bd. dirs. Mercer Health Right. Co-author: Ethics & Issues in Contemporary Nursing, 1998; contbr. articles to profl. jours. Mem. med. adv. bd. Office of Maternal and Child Health, W.Va. Bur. of Pub. Health, Charleston, 1995—, W.Va. Med. Office, Charleston, 1993—, Rural Health Initiative, Charleston, 1992-96; mem. drug utilization rev. com. W.Va. Dept. of HHS, Charleston, 1993-95. Recipient Hats Off award Nat. Coun. Jewish Women, W.Va., 1993, award of appreciation Gov. Gaston Caperton, W.Va., 1996; named W.Va. Polit. Active Nurse of Yr., W.Va. Nurses Assn., 1991. Mem. ANA, W.Va. Nurses Assn. 9bd. dirs. 1986-92, chair legis. com. 1986-93), Am. Acad. Nurse Practitioners, Sigma Theta Tau. Democrat. Baptist. Home: 209 E Grandview Dr Princeton WV 24740-3844

NATHANIEL, archbishop; b. Aurora, Ill., June 12, 1940; s. Joseph and Vera (Boytor) P. BA, St. Propcopius Coll., 1962; MDiv, Pontifical Gregorian U., Rome, 1966. Ordained priest Romanian Greek Cath. Ch., 1966; consecrated bishop Romanian Orthodox Episcopate of Am., 1980; elevated to archbishop, 1999. Asst. pastor St. Michael Byz Ch., Aurora, 1967; parish priest Holy Cross Romanian Orthodox Ch., Hermitage, Pa., 1975-80; aux. bishop Romanian Orthodox Episcopate of Am., Orthodox Ch. in Am., Jackson, Mich., 1980-84, ruling bishop Detroit, 1984—; mem. Holy Snyod Orthodox Ch. in Am., Syosset, N.Y., 1980—; Episcopal moderator Pastoral Life Ministries, O.C.A., 1991—. Bd. dirs. Moldovita Romanian Orthodox Ch., Hayward, Calif, 1982; tchr. summer youth programs Romanian Diocese; confessor to sisterhood Holy Transfiguration Monastery; rep. Conf. on Monasticism, Cairo, 1978; participant Monastic Consultation, Cairo, 1979, Seventh Assembly, Vancouver, Can., 1983; active mem. diocesan liturgical commn.; spkr., lectr. in field. Author: Holy Icons, 1969; editor newspaper Solia; contbr. numerous articles to profl. jours. Chmn. Romanian-Am. Heritage Ctr., Grass Lake, Mich.; organizer, chmn. Help for Romania Nat. Relief Fund and Help the Children of Romania Relief Fund; chmn. Congress of Romanian Ams., 1991—; mem. adv. bd. Orthodox Christian Laity, 1999—; pres. Ctr. for Orthodox Christian Studies, St. Andrew, Detroit, 2000. Home and Office: Romanian Orthodox Episcopate Am 2535 Grey Tower Rd Jackson MI 49201-9120 also: PO Box 185 Grass Lake MI 49240-0185 E-mail: hg.bnpopp@aol.com.

NATHANSON, HARVEY CHARLES, electrical engineer; b. Pitts., Oct. 22, 1936; s. David Benjamin and Ella (Sachs) N.; m. Esther Janet Mishelevich, Oct. 13, 1963; children: Marc Elliot, Elinor Sharon. BSEE, Carnegie Inst. Tech., 1958, MSEE, 1959, PhD, 1962. Sr. engr. Junction Device Physics, Westinghouse, Research/Devel. Center, Pitts., 1962-67, fellow engr., 1968-72, mgr. silicon junction physics, 1972-77, mgr. microelectronics dept., 1978-90, chief scientist electronic div., 1990-95; chief scientist Northrop Grumman Sci. Tech. Ctr., 1996—2001; cons. Northrop Grumman, 2002—. Instr. Carnegie Inst. Tech., Pitts., 1959-60; chmn. Westinghouse Sat. Sci. Honors Inst. for High Sch. Students, 1970-76; mem. adv. group on electron devices U.S. Dept. Def., 1976-86; adviser to Nat. Materials Bd., 1986-87. Contbr. articles to profl. jours.; mem. editorial bd. Solid State Electronics, 1985—; patentee in field. Bd. dirs. Temple Sinai, 1981-83, 95-97; pres. Brotherhood, 1993-95. Recipient IR100 award, 1965, hon. mention Outstanding Young Engr. award Eta Kappa Nu, 1967, Best Display Paper award Soc. Info. Display, 1972, Carnegie-Mellon Alumni award, 1982, Westinghouse Top Corp. Patent award, 1990; named to Westinghouse Order of Merit, Westinghouse Electric Corp., 1987. Fellow IEEE (editl. bd. Spectrum mag. 1989-91, 3e Millennium medal 2000, Pitts. Inventor of Yr. 2002); mem. IEEE Electron Device Soc. (pres. 1978-80), Fedn. Materials Socs. (bd. dirs. 1987-90), Sigma Xi, Eta Kappa Nu. Democrat. Jewish. Home: 5635 Marlborough Rd Pittsburgh PA 15217-1404 Office: Northrop Grumman Sci-Tech Ctr Advanced Tech Lab PO Box 1521-MS 3B10 Baltimore MD 21203 E-mail: harvey_c_nathanson@mail.northgrum.com.

NATHANSON, LARRY, medical educator, physician; b. Boston, Dec. 23, 1928; s. Robert Bernard and Leah (Rabin) N.; m. Anna Bloch, May 27, 1962; children: Andrew, Aran, Nicholas. AB, Harvard Coll., 1950; MD, U. Chgo., 1955. Diplomate Am. Bd. Internal Medicine, Am. Bd. Med. Oncology. Instr. medicine Harvard Med. Sch., Boston, 1966-68; from asst. to prof. Tufts U. Sch. Medicine, 1968-79; prof. medicine SUNY Stony Brook Sch. of Medicine, 1980-96, prof. emeritus, 1996—. Pres., CEO Oncology Cons., Cambridge, Mass., 1996—; cons. John Wayne Cancer Inst., Santa Monica, Calif., 1996—; councilor Cambridge Hist. Soc. Editl. bd. Cancer, 1977—, Jour. Clin. Oncology, 1995-98, Seminars in Oncology, 1979-83, Med. & Pediat. Oncology, 1977-96, Jour. Cancer Edn., 1986-92; editor 6 books; contbr. over 280 articles to profl. jours. Trustee Cold Spring Harbor Lab., 1990-94, Soc. Preservation L.I. Antiquities, Setauket, N.Y., 1982-92, Cambridge Sch. of Weston, 1997—. Capt. U.S. Army Med. Corps., 1956-58. Nat. Cancer Inst. fellow, 1964-66; recipient Disting Svc. award Vet. Affairs Rev. Bd. in Cancer Rsch., 1974-78, Winthrop U. Hosp., 1993. Fellow ACP; mem. Harvard Club (Boston, N.Y.), Seawanhaka Corinthian Yacht Club (race com. 1990-96), Harvard Faculty Club. Avocations: sailing, squash, tennis, history. Office: Oncology Cons 3 Gray Gdns E Cambridge MA 02138-1401 Fax: (617) 441-0043. E-mail: larrymd@ix.netcom.com.

NATHANSON, LINDA SUE, publisher, author, technical writer; b. Washington, Aug. 11, 1946; d. Nat and Edith (Weinstein) N.; m. James F. Barrett. BS, U. Md., 1969; MA, UCLA, 1970, PhD, 1975. Tng. dir. Rockland Research Inst., Orangeburg, N.Y., 1975-77; asst. prof. psychology SUNY, 1978-79; pres. Cabri Prodns., Inc., Ft. Lee, N.J., 1979-81; rsch. supr. Darcy, McManus & Masius, St. Louis, 1981-83; mgr. software tng., documentation On-Line Software Internat., Ft. Lee, 1983-85; pvt. practice, 1985-87; founder, exec. dir. The Edin. Group, Inc., Gillette, N.J., 1987-98; founder, pres. Edin Books, Inc., 1994—. Author: (with others) Psychological Testing: An Introduction to Tests and Measurements, 1988; (with S.J. Thayer) Interview with an Angel, 1997; (with S.J. Thayer) The Heart of Interview with an Angel, 1998; publ. A Funny Thing Happened at the Interview (G.F. Farrell), 1996, Angel Talk (R. Crystal), 1996; (audiobook with W. Barnes) I Built the Titanic: Past-Life Memories of a Master Shipbuilder, 1999, Thomas Andrews, Voyage into History, 2000; (audio book with W. Barnes and F. Baranowski) A Past-Life Interview with Titanic's Designer, 1999. Recipient Rsch. Svc. award 1978; Albert Einstein Coll. Medicine Research fellow, 1978-79. Jewish. Home and Office: 102 Sunrise Dr Gillette NJ 07933-1944 E-mail: edinbooks@rcn.com.

NATHANSON, MELVYN BERNARD, university provost, mathematician; b. Phila., Oct. 10, 1944; s. Israel and Sophia (Manstein) N.; m. Marjorie Jane Frankel, Jan. 29, 1978; children: Alexander Philip, Rebecca Anne. BA, U. Pa., 1965; postgrad., Harvard U., 1965-66; MA, U. Rochester, 1968, PhD, 1972. Prof. So. Ill. U., Carbondale, 1971-81; dean Rutgers U., Newark, 1981-86; provost, v.p. acad. affairs Lehman Coll. CUNY, Bronx, 1986-91, prof. math. Grad. Sch., 1986—; pres. Short Hills Math. Vis. prof. Moscow State U., USSR, 1972-73, Inst. for Advanced Study, Princeton U., N.J., 1974-75, 76, 90-91, 99-2000, Harvard U., Cambridge, Mass., 1977-78, Rockefeller U., 1982-85, Rutgers U., 1991-93, Tel Aviv U., 2001. Author, editor fifteen books; contbr. articles to profl. jours. Fellow N.Y. Acad. Sci.; mem. AAAS, Am. Math. Soc., Math. Assn. Am., Assn. Mems. Inst. for Advanced Study (pres.). Office: CUNY Lehman Coll Dept Math Bronx NY 10468 E-mail: melnathanson@hotmail.com.

NATHANSON, NEAL, virologist, epidemiologist, educator; b. Boston, Sept. 1, 1927; s. Robert B. and Leah (Rabinowitch) N.; m. Constance Allen, June 8, 1954; children— Katherine L., John A., Daniel R.; m. Phoebe Starfield, Oct. 7, 1984. BA, Harvard U., 1949, MD, 1953. Chief polio surveillance unit USPHS, 1955-57; rsch. assoc., asst. prof. anatomy Johns Hopkins, Balt., 1957-63, assoc. prof. epidemiology, 1963-68, prof., 1968-79; chmn. dept. microbiology U. Pa., Phila., 1979-93, vice dean rsch., 1993-95, dir. Office of AIDS Rsch., 1998-2000, vice provost, rsch., 2000—. Editor-in-chief: Am. Jour. Epidemiology, 1964-79, Microbial Pathogenesis, 1985-88. Achievements include research in pathogenesis, immunology, and epidemiology of viral infections. Home: 1600 Hagys Ford Rd Apt 9W Narberth PA 19072-1049 E-mail: nathanson@mail.med.upenn.edu.

NATHANSON, P. RACHEL, land use planner; b. Madison, Wis., Mar. 9, 1955; d. Yaron Simon and Ruthanne Elizabeth (Mescar) N.; m. Kevin Edward Conley, Sept. 5, 1993; 1 child, Sasha Natana. AA, Coll. of Marin, 1977; BA, Evergreen State Coll., 1979. Cons. Clallam County Planning Dept., Port Angeles, Wash., 1980; land use planner Jefferson County Planning Dept., Port Townsend, 1980-86, sr. planner, 1986-89; land use legal asst. Hillis Clark Martin Peterson, Seattle, 1989-91; planning mgr. Lowe Enterprises, 1991-93; land use cons. Nathanson Assocs., 1993—. Mem. Am. Inst. Cert. Planners (cert.), Am. Planning Assn. (treas. Wash. state chpt. 1996—). Avocations: swimming, hiking. Office: Nathanson Assocs 2581 NE 85th St Seattle WA 98115 E-mail: rachel@nwlink.com.

NATHANSON, THEODORE HERZL, aeronautical engineer, architect; b. Montreal, Que., Can., Apr. 20, 1923; came to U.S., 1949, naturalized, 1983; s. Henry and Minnie (Goldberg) N. Student, McGill U., 1940-42; SB in Aero. Engring., MIT, 1944; MArch, Harvard U., 1955. Rsch. engr. Noorduyn Aviation Ltd., Montreal, 1944-45; stress engr. Canadair Ltd., 1945-46; structural engr. A.V. Roe (Can.) Ltd., Malton, Ont., 1946-47; with Mies van der Rohe, Chgo., summer 1949, Buckminster Fuller, Forest Hills, N.Y., summer 1951; cons. engr., arch. Montreal, Boston, L.A., 1955—. Mem. tech. staff Rockwell Internat., 1979-92, structural analysis and advanced design Space Transp. Systems divsn., Downey, Calif., 1979-86, mission ops. and advanced concepts Space Sta. Systems divsn., 1986-87, space sta. elec. power system Rocketdyne div., Canoga Park, Calif., 1987-92; cons. Aerospace Engr., L.A., 1992—; lectr. arch. McGill U., 1967-68. Projects and models included in group shows: Mus. Fine Arts, Springfield, Mass., 1961, N.Y. World's Fair, 1965, Winterfest, Boston, 1966, Boston Artists' Project '70. Fellow Brit. Interplanetary Soc.; mem. Order Engrs. Que., Order Archs. Que., Soc. Am. Registered Archs., Nat. Soc. Profl. Engrs., AIAA, AIA (assoc.), Royal Archtl. Inst. Can., Nat. Mgmt. Assn., Copley Soc. Boston, MIT Club So. Calif. (bd. govs.), Can. Soc. (L.A.). Jewish. Home: 225 S Olive St Apt 1502 Los Angeles CA 90012-4906 E-mail: thanso@hotmail.com.

NATHWANI, BHARAT N. pathologist, consultant; b. Bombay, Jan. 20, 1945; came to U.S., 1972; s. Narottam Pragji and Bharti N. (Lakhani) N. MBBS, Grant Med. Coll., Bombay, 1969, MD in Pathology, 1972. Intern Grant Med. Coll., Bombay U., 1968-69; asst. prof. pathology Grant Med. Coll., 1972; fellow in hematology Cook County Hosp., Chgo., 1972-73; resident in pathology Rush U., 1973-74; fellow in hematopathology City of Hope Med. Ctr., Duarte, Calif., 1975-76, pathologist, 1977-84; prof. pathology, chief hematopathology U. So. Calif., L.A., 1984—. Contbr. numerous articles to profl. jours. Recipient Grant awards Nat. Libr. Medicine, Bethesda, Md., Nat. Cancer Inst., 1991. Mem. Internat. Acad. Pathology, Am. Soc. Clin. Pathology, Am. Soc. Hematology, Am. Soc. Oncology. Office: Hmr 209 2011 Zonal Ave Los Angeles CA 90033

NATION, DAVID ARTHUR, retired computer scientist, sculptor; b. Waterloo, Iowa, Aug. 23, 1947; s. Harold Stanley and Martha Elizabeth (Loonan) N.; m. Jean Lea Bielefeldt, Aug. 9, 1969 (div. May 1979); 1 child, Justin David; m. Rebecca L. Johnson, Oct. 27, 1979. BS in Computer Sci., Iowa State U., 1970; MS, Johns Hopkins U., 1979. Computer scientist U.S. Govt., Washington, 1975—2001; ret., 2001. Author mapping software, pattern classication software, Web software, information visualization software; sculptor;solo shows: Dave Nation's Art Gallery, 1995—; Bay Country Art Guild Member Show, 2000, Treas., Emmanuel United Meth. Ch., Dorsey, md., 1987—. Sgt. USAF, 1970-73. Mem. SAG, Assn. for Computing Machinery. Democrat. Methodist. Achievements include 2 U.S. patents on Selective Polygon Map Display Method. Avocations: sculpture, bird watching, genealogy, Volksspport, photography. E-mail: dave@davenation.com., dnation@acm.org.

NATION, EARL F. retired urologist, educator; b. Zephyr, Tex., Jan. 16, 1910; s. Joseph Madison and Alma Emily (Johnson) N.; m. Evelyn Stapp Poynter, Aug. 11, 1936; children: William Earl, Robert Joseph. BA, San Diego State U., 1931; MD, Western Res. U., 1935. Lic. urologist, Calif.; diplomate Am. Bd. Urology. Internship, resident in urology Los Angeles County Gen. Hosp., 1935-39; pvt. practice Pasadena, Calif., 1941-90; ret., 1990. Instr., assoc. prof. urology U. So. Calif., L.A., 1941-55; sr. attending staff Huntington Meml. Hosp., Pasadena, 1941—, St. Luke Hosp., Pasadena, 1941—, also past pres.; pres. Pasadena Dispensary, 1946; lectr. Coll. Med. Evangelists (now Loma Linda U.), 1941-48. Mem. editorial bd. Jour. of Urology, 1958-66, Calif. Medicine, 1965-69, Forum on Medicine; contbr. articles to profl. jours., contbg. author to numerous books. Sec.-treas. Pasadena Breakfast Forum, 1970-73, pres. 1974-75. Crile rsch. scholar Western Res. U., 1931. Mem. ACS, AMA, Am. Urol. Assn. (past pres., Ramon Guiteras award 2002), Am. Osler Soc. (past pres.), L.A. County Med. Assn., Calif. Med. Assn., Pasadena Hist. Soc., So. Calif. Hist. Soc., Am. Soc. Clin. Urologists, Pasadena U. Club, Zamorano Club (v.p. L.A. chpt. 1991), Twilight Club, Alpha Omega Alpha. Republican. Avocations: book collecting, reading, writing, gardening, fishing. Home: # E 311 E Sierra Madre Blvd Apt E Sierra Madre CA 91024-2669 E-mail: enoitan@gte.net.

NATION, JAMES EDWARD, retired speech pathologist; b. Springfield, Ill., Aug. 22, 1933; s. John Herbert and Margaret Josephine (Weiss) N. BS, Ill. State U., 1959; MS, U. Wis., 1960, PhD, 1964. Asst. prof. U. Ga., 1964-66; asst. prof., assoc. prof., prof. Case Western Res. U., Cleve., 1966-86, prof., chmn. dept. communication scis., 1979-85; dir. speech pathology Cleve. Hearing and Speech Center, 1970-74; sr. clin. instr. dept. pediatrics Case Western Res. Sch. Medicine, 1979-86; speech-lang. pathologist Tucson Unified Sch. Dist. #1, 1985-95; ret., 1995. Chief speech-lang. pathologist craniofacial defects team Rainbow Babies and Childrens Hosp., Univ. Hosps., Case Western Res. U., 1978-85; exec. bd. Nat. Council Grad. Programs in Speech-Lang. Pathology and Audiology; cons. in field. Author: Diagnosis of Speech and Language Disorders, 1977, Child Language Disorders, 1982, 2d rev. edit., 1984; editorial cons.: Cleft Palate Jour.; contbr. chpts. to books; editor: Ohio Speech and Hearing Jour., 1969-73; contbr. articles to profl. jours. Served with U.S. Army, 1953-55. Recipient Wittke award for disting. undergrad. teaching, 1977, Outstanding Service award Ill. State U. Alumni

Assn., 1982 Fellow Am. Speech-Lang. and Hearing Assn. (cert. speech-lang. pathologist); mem. Am. Cleft Palate Assn., Ohio Speech and Hearing Assn., Aphasiology Assn. Ohio, Nat. Council Grad. Programs in Speech-Lang. Pathology and Audiology. (Disting. Service award 1982) Home: Apt 19 2600 E Skyline Dr Unit 19 Tucson AZ 85718-3065 E-mail: jamesenation@yahoo.com.

NATION, PHILIP DAVID, financial planner; b. London, May 31, 1962; came to U.S., 1965; s. John A. and Sally G. (Leeds) N.; m. Cynthia Anne Bateman, Apr. 19, 1986. BA in Econs., Cornell U., 1984; M in Estate Planning, Coll. Fin. Planning, 1993. CFP. Sr. fin. advisor Am. Express Fin. Advisors, Raleigh, N.C., 1987—. Mem. Fin. Planning Assn., Cornell Alumni Club. Avocations: fitness, theatre. Office: Am Express Fin Advisors Inc 3720 Benson Dr Raleigh NC 27609-7321 Home: 1401 Ballyclare Ct Raleigh NC 27614-7168

NATIONS, HOWARD LYNN, lawyer; b. Dalton, Ga., Jan. 9, 1938; s. Howard Lynn and Eva Earline (Armstrong) Lamb; m. Ella Lois Johnson, June 4, 1960 (div. Nov. 1976); children: Cynthia Lynn Nations Garcia, Angela Jean Gordon. BA, Florida State U., 1963; JD, Fla. State U., 1966. Bar: Tex. 1966; cert. trial atty. Tex. Bd. Legal Specialization. Assoc. Butler, Rice Cook & Knapp, Houston, 1966-71; pres. Nations & Cross, 1971—; v.p., dir., co-founder Ins. Corp. Am., 1972—; pres. Caplinger & Nations Galleries, 1973—, Nations Investment Corp., Houston, 1975—, NCM Trade Corp., Houston, 1975; v.p. Delher Am. Inc., 1975—; pres. Howard L. Nations, PC, 1971—, Trial Focus, Inc., 1995—. Founder Nations Found.; adj. prof. So. Tex. Coll. Law, Houston, 1967—; speaker in field. Author: Structuring Settlements, 1987; co-author: Texas Workers' Compensation, 1988, (with others) The Anatomy of a Personal Injury Lawsuit, 3rd rev. edit. 1991; editor: Maximizing Damages in Wrongful Death and Personal Injury Litigation, 1985; contbr. articles to profl. jours. Chmn., trustee Nat. Coll. Advocacy, Washington, 1985-92. With M.I. Corps, U.S. Army, 1957-60. Recipient Gene Cavin Excellence award State Bar Tex., 2000. Fellow Tex. Bar Found., Houston Bar Found. (life); mem. ATLA (exec. com. 1991-95), Nat. Bd. Trial Advocacy (diplomate civil trial advocacy), So. Trial Lawyers Assn. (pres. 1994-95), Tex. Trial Lawyers Assn. (pres. 1992-93). Office: The Sterling Mansion 4515 Yoakum Blvd Houston TX 77006-5821

NATKIN, ROBERT, painter; b. Chgo., Nov. 7, 1930; s. Phillip and Betty Natkin; m. Judith Dolnick; children: Joshua, Leda. BA, Art Inst. Chgo., 1952. Exhibited paintings in numerous one-man shows, including Andrè Emmerich Gallery, N.Y.C., Holburne of Menstrie Mus., Bath, Eng., Art Inst. Chgo., Moore Coll. Art, The Reele Galleries, N.Y.C., Phila., Ivory/Kimpton Gallery, San Francisco, Gimpel Fils Gallery, London, Gimpel & Weitzenhoffer Gallery, N.Y.C., A.B.C.D. Gallery, Paris, Tortue Gallery, Santa Monica, Calif., Butler Inst. Am. Art, Ohio, Galerie Brusberg, Hannover, Fed. Republic Germany, Hirshhorn Mus. and Sculpture Garden, Washington, Okla. Art Ctr., Oklahoma City, 1982 , Gloria Luria Gallery, Miami, 1984, Klonarides Gallery, Toronto, 1985; group shows include Mus. Art, Pa. State U., 1973, Poindexter Gallery, N.Y.C., 1976; represented in permanent collections, including Art Inst. Chgo., Mus. Modern Art, N.Y.C., Solomon R. Guggenheim Mus., N.Y.C., Whitney Mus. Am. Art, Hirshhorn Mus. and Sculpture Garden, Smithsonian Instn., Washington, Mus. Fine Arts, Houston, Mus. Art, R.I. Sch. Design, San Francisco Mus. Art, Mus. Art, Carnegie Inst., Duke U. Mus. Art, Centre Georges Pompidou (Beaubourg), Paris, Milw. Art Ctr., Fogg Mus. Harvard U., Met. Mus. Art, N.Y.C., Akron (Ohio) Inst., Albright-Knox Art Gallery, N.Y.C., Butler Inst. Am. Art, L.A. County Mus. Art, Mint Mus. Art, N.C., Wadsworth Atheneum, Conn.

NATOLI, JOE, newspaper publishing executive; Pres. The Miami Herald, Fla., 1994—2001; pres., pub. San Jose Mercury News, 2001. Mem., bd. dir. United Way-Silicon Valley. Office: The San Jose Mercury News 750 Ridder Park Dr San Jose CA 95190*

NATOLI, JOSEPH, English language educator; b. Brooklyn, N.Y., Aug. 24, 1943; m. Elaine Tuminelli, June 6, 1970; children: Amelia, Brenda. BA, Bklyn. Coll., 1965, MA, 1968; PhD, SUNY, Albany, 1973. Asst. prof. English New Eng. Coll., Henniker, N.H., 1971-73, 1973-75; acting dir. libr., adj. lectr. English Bluefield (W.Va.) State Coll., 1975-77; head reference and bibliography libr. Wake Forest U., Winston Salem, N.C., 1977-81; bibliographer, adj. lectr. humanities U. Calif., Irvine, 1981-83, Mich. State U., East Lansing, 1983—, dir. study abroad program Europe, 1996—. Series editor SUNY Press Postmodern Culture, Albany, 1990—. Author: Mots D'Ordre, 1992, Hauntings, 1994, Primer to Postmodernity, 1997, Speeding to the Millenium, 1998, Postmodern Journeys, 2000; editor: Twentieth Century Blake Criticism, 1982, Psychological Perspectives on Literature, 1984, Psychocriticism, 1984, Tracing Literary Theory, 1987, Literary Theory's Future(s), 1989, A Postmodern Reader, 1993, Postmodernism: The Key Figures, 2002. Mem. MLA. Home: 620 Baldwin Ct East Lansing MI 48823-3230 Office: Ctr Integrative Studies 304 Linton Hall Mich State U East Lansing MI 48824 E-mail: natoli@pilot.msu.edu.

NATORI, JOSIE CRUZ, apparel executive; b. Manila, May 9, 1947; came to U.S., 1964; d. Felipe F. and Angelita A. (Almeda) Cruz; m. Kenneth R. Natori, May 20, 1972; 1 child, Kenneth E.F. BA in Econs., Manhattanville Coll., 1968. V.p. Merrill-Lynch Co., N.Y.C., 1971-77; owner, CEO The Natori Co., 1977—. Bd. dirs. The Alltel Corp. Bd. dirs. Philippine Am. Found., Jr. Achievement, Inc., 1992, Ednl. Found. for Fashion Industries; trustee Manhattanville Coll., Asian Cultural Coun.; commr. White House Conf. on Small BUs., 1993. Recipient Human Relations award Am. Jewish Com., N.Y.C., 1986, Harriet Alger award Working Woman, N.Y., 1987, Castle award Manhattanville Coll., Purchase, 1988, Galleon award Pres. Philippines, N.Y.C. Asian-Am. award, Friendship award Philippine-Am. Found., Hall of Fame award Mega Mags., Salute to Am. Fashion Designers award Dept. of Commerce, Ellis Island medal of Honor, 1994; named Bus. Woman of Yr. N.Y.C. Partnership and C. of C., 1997. Mem. CFDA, Young Pres.'s Orgn., Fashion Group, Com. of 200. Avocations: pianist, tennis player. Home: 45 E 62nd St New York NY 10021-8025 Office: Natori Co 40 E 34th St Fl 18 New York NY 10016-4563

NATOWITZ, JOSEPH B. chemistry educator, research administrator; b. Saranac Lake, N.Y., Dec. 24, 1936; BS in Chemistry, U. Fla., 1958; Cert. in Meteorology, UCLA, 1959; PhD in Nuc. Chemistry, U. Pitts., 1965. Staff meteorologist, 1st lt. USAF, 1958-61; grad. teaching asst. U. Pitts., 1961-62, grad. rsch. asst., 1962-65; postdoctoral rsch. assoc. SUNY, Stony Brook, 1965-67; rsch. collaborator Brookhaven Nat. Lab., 1965-67; asst. prof. Tex. A&M U., College Station, 1967-72, assoc. prof., 1972-76, prof., 1976—, head dept. chemistry, 1981-85, dir. Cyclotron Inst., 1991—. Part-time instr. SUNY-Stony Brook, 1966-67; rsch. collaborator Lawrence Radiation Lab., Berkeley, Calif., 1966, Los Alamos (N.Mex.) Nat. Lab., 1973-74; Alexander Von Humboldt sr. scientist Max Planck Inst. für Kernphysik, Heidelberg, Germany, 1978; vis. prof. Inst. for Nuc. Studies, U. Tokyo, 1979, U. Claude Bernard, Inst. de Physique Nucleaire, 1983, U. de Caen, 1985, Ctr. des Etudes Nucleaires de Saclay, 1986, U. Cath. de Louvain, 1987; former mem. accelerator review com. TASCC, Chalk River, Can.; former mem. adv. com. LBL Superhilac, ORNL Cyclotron, Nat. Superconducting Cyclotron Lab.; mem. program adv. com. Ganil Lab; mem. nuc. sci. vis. com. Lawrence Berkeley Nat. Lab. Contbr. over 150 articles to profl. jours., also to approx. 40 books and procs. Chmn. Cub Scout Pack 802, 1973-75; v.p. College Hills PTO, 1974-75; mem. A&M Consol. Sch. Bd., 1975-78, pres., 1977-78; pres. A&M Consol. Band Boosters, 1980-81. NSF summer fellow, 1962; NASA predoctoral fellow, 1964-65; recipient Disting. Achievment award-rsch. Tex. A&M U., 1988, Am. Chem Soc. award for Nuc. Chemistry, 1995. Fellow Am. Phys. Soc.; mem. Am. Chem. Soc. (vice chmn. div. nuc. chemistry and tech. 1993, chmn. 1994, award in nuc. chemistry 1995, S.W. Regional award 2000), Sigma Xi, Phi Lambda Upsilon. Office: Tex A&M U Cyclotron Inst College Station TX 77843-0001

NATSIOS, ANDREW, federal agency administrator; b. Mass. m. Elizabeth Natsios; children: Emily, Alexander, Phillip. BA, Georgetown U., 1971; MPA, Harvard U., 1979. State rep. Mass. Ho. Reps.; exec. dir. Northeast Pub. Power Assn.; chief fin. and adminstrv. officer Commonwealth of Mass.; v.p. World Vision U.S., 1993—98; chmn. Mass. Turnpike Authoruty; adminstr. Agy. Internat. Devel., Washington. Author book. Lt. col. USAR. Fellow, U.S. Inst. PEace, 1998—99. Office: AID 1300 Pennsylvania Ave NW Washington DC 20523*

NATSIOS, NICHOLAS ANDREW, retired foreign service officer; b. Lowell, Mass., July 31, 1920; s. Andrew and Fanny (Papageorgiou) N.; m. Mitzi Peterson, Sept. 2, 1951; children: Christine Daphne, Deborah Diane, Valerie Sophia, Alexandra Roxanne. Student, Lowell Technol. Inst., 1939-40; BA cum laude, Ohio State U., 1948; MAL.D., Fletcher Sch. Law and Diplomacy, 1983. Civilian spl. adviser polit. problems U.S. Mil. Mission, Salonika, Greece, 1948-50, polit. adviser mil. secretariat Athens, Greece, 1951-56; polit. officer, 1st sec. embassy, spl. asst. to ambassador Am. embassy, Saigon, Viet Nam, 1956-60, attache Paris, 1960-62, spl. asst. to ambassador Seoul, Korea, 1962-65; 1st sec. American embassy, Buenos Aires, Argentina, 1965-69; spl. asst. to ambassador Am. embassy, The Hague, The Netherlands, 1969-72, regional affairs officer. Tehran, Iran, 1972-74; mgmt. cons., 1977—. Served to capt. AUS, 1942-47; comdg. officer Italian Frontier Control Detachment, U.S. Occupation Forces, 1945-47, Milan, Italy. Decorated Medal of Merit; decorated Bronze Star U.S.; knight comdr. of Italy; Knight comdr. Order of St. George; Cross of Mil. Valor, Cross of Mil. Merit (Italy); D.S.C. 1st class Knights of Malta; Order of Eagle Yugoslavia; Disting. Svc. medal Greece; Order of Svc. Merit Korea); recipient Ellis Island medal of honor, 2002. Mem. Phi Beta Kappa, Phi Eta Sigma. Address: 77 Lincoln Pky Lowell MA 01851-3405

NATSUYAMA, HARRIET HATSUNE, mathematician, educator; b. Honolulu, Sept. 2, 1937; d. Kenjiro and Yakue Natsuyama; children: Julia, Conan. BA, U. Hawaii, 1959, MS, 1960; PhD, Kyoto U., 1965. Math. Rand Corp., Santa Monica, Calif., 1961-68, cons., 1968-77; adj. assoc. prof. U. So. Calif., L.A., 1974-79; sr. scientist Hughes Aircraft Co., El Segundo, 1979-87; chief engr. Infotec Devel. Inc., Camarillo, 1987-89; prof. systems engring. Calif. State U., Fullerton, 1990-96; v.p. Advanced Indsl. Materials, 1996-97; co-founder Planet Aura, Inc., 2002—. Fgn. spl. vis. prof. Oita U., 1995, Kyoto Sch. of Computer Sci., 1997—; vis. prof. Sci. U. Tokyo, 1998. Author: Invariant Imbedding and Time-Dependent Transport Processes, 1963, System Identification: Methods and Applications, 1974, Integral Equations via Imbedding Methods, 1974, Multiple Scattering Processes: Inverse and Direct, 1975, Numerical Derivatives and Nonlinear Analysis, 1986, Terrestrial Radiative Transfer: Modeling, Computation, Data Analysis, 1998. Mem. Grad. Women in Sci. (pres. 1990-91), Phi Beta Kappa, Phi Kappa Phi.

NATTEL, STANLEY, cardiologist, research scientist; b. Haifa, Israel, Jan. 28, 1951; arrived in Can., 1952; s. William and Julie (Zwirek) N.; m. Celia Anne Reich, Sept. 25, 1973; children: Jonathan, Ilana, Daniel, Sarah. BSc magna cum laude, McGill U., 1972, MD, 1974. Diplomate Am. Bd. Internal Medicine, Am. Bd. Cardiology. Intern in medicine Royal Victoria Hosp., 1974-75, resident in internal medicine, 1975-76; resident in clin. pharmacology Montreal (Que., Can.) Gen. Hosp., 1976-78, cardiologist, clin. pharmacologist, 1981-87, dir. coronary care unit, 1983-87; fellow in cardiology Ind. U., 1978-80; fellow in physiology U. Pa., 1980-81; asst. prof. pharmacology, medicine McGill U., Montreal, 1981-87, assoc. prof., 1987—; cardiologist Montreal Heart Inst., 1987—, dir. rsch. ctr., 1990—; prof. Dept. Medicine, U. Montreal, 1995—. External reviewer Med. Rsch. Coun., 1981—, Ont. Health Ministry, 1983-84, NSF, 1992, others; chmn. libr. com. dept. pharmacology McGill U., 1982-86, mem. grad. com., 1984-89, chmn. grad. tng. com., 1986-89, departmental rep. grad. faculty coun., 1989-91, coord. grad. teaching pharmacology, 1989-91; mem. oper. grants com. Can. Heart Found., 1983-86; chmn. clin. trials com. Montreal Gen. Hosp., 1983-87, chmn. pharmacy and therapeutics com., 1984-87, sec. clin. chemistry rev. com., 1984, course dir. drug therapy, 1984-87, acting dir. divsn. clin. pharmacology, 1984-85, mem. various coms., 1985-87; mem. fellowship awards com. FRSQ, 1988-90, mem. ctr. grants pharmacology/pharmacy com., 1989-90; chmn. pharmacology com. Montreal Heart Inst., 1988-90, mem. search com. pharmacist-in-chief, 1989-90, mem. ethics com., 1991—, chmn. internal rsch. com., 1991—, mem. consultative com. exec. dir., 1991—, chmn. consultative com. rsch. ctr., 1991—; consulting coun. pharmacology Province of Quebec, 1989-90; mem. safety monitoring com. CAMIAT Study, 1990-95; assoc. prof. medicine U. Montreal, 1991-95, prof. 1995—, chmn. search com. dir. rsch. Sacré-Coeur Hosp., 1991, mem. rsch. com. Cormes faculty medicine, 1991—, mem. rsch. com. dept. medicine, 1991—; chmn. search com., dir. rsch. Maisonneuve Rosemont Hosp., 1996; mem. site visit team program project grant NIH, 1991, cons. program project grant, 1993, spl. reviewer cardiovascular study sect., 1993, 95; mem. oper. grants com. Med. Rsch. Coun. Can., 1988-93; mem. sr. personnel awards com. Can. Heart Found., 1994-96; lectr. in field. Assoc. editor Can. Jour. Physiology and Pharmacology, 1990-95; mem. editl. bd. Jour. Cardiovasc. Electrophysiology, 1991—, Drugs, 1993—, Cardiovasc. Drugs and Therapy, 1993—, Circulation Rsch., 1995—, JACC, 1995—, Cardiovascular Rsch., 1999—; manuscript reviewer Am. Jour. Cardiology, Can. Med. Assn. Jour., European Jour. Pharmacology, New Eng. Jour. Medicine, others; contbr. chpts. to books and articles to profl. jours. Chmn. edn. com. Hebrew Acad. Sch., Montreal, 1991-92. Grantee Que. Heart Found., 1981—, Nordic Pharms., 1985-87, Knoll Pharms., 1991-93, others; fellow Med. Rsch. Coun. Can., 1979-81; McGill U. scholar, 1967-74, Sir Edward Beatty scholar McGill U., 1967-70, Rsch. scholar Med. Rsch. Coun., 1982-87, Sr. Rsch. scholar Fonds de la Recherche en Santé du Quebec, 1990-93. Fellow Am. Coll. Cardiology, Royal Coll. Physicians Can. (cert. medicine, cardiology); mem. Am. Heart Assn. (coun. basic sci.), Am. Soc. Pharmacology and Exptl. Therapeutics, Can. Cardiovasc. Soc. (councilor 1992-95), Can. Soc. Clin. Pharmacology (Kenneth M. Piafsky Young Investigator award 1985), Pharm. Soc. Can. Biophys. Soc. Avocations: studying Jewish religious works, sports. Home: 5609 Alpine Ave Côte Saint Luc QC Canada H4V 2X6 Office: Montreal Heart Inst 5000 Belanger St E Montreal QC Canada H1T 1C8 E-mail: nattel@icm.umontreal.ca.

NATTRESS, DEBRA LYNN, computer systems analyst; b. Easton, Pa., Mar. 13, 1954; d. Ronald Ramon and Dorothy Francis Nattress. BS in Bus. Adminstrn., Penn State U., 1979. Database admintr. Dept. Defense, Mechanicsburg, Pa., 1979—. Chmn. Children's Christmas Party, Mechanicsburg, 1997. Mem. Fed. Employees Leadership Assn. (v.p. 1997), Pa. Guild Craftspersons. Roman Catholic. Avocations: photography, gardening, travelling, crafts. Home: 315 Mount Airy Rd Lewisberry PA 17339-9189 Office: Naval Supply Info Sys Activity PO Box 2010 5450 Carlisle Pike Mechanicsburg PA 17055-0787 E-mail: debranattress@yahoo.com.

NATVIG, CONNIE BEA, clinical psychologist; b. Oct. 15, 1964; BA in Psychology, Notre Dame U., 1986; MS in Clin. Psychology, Purdue U., 1989, PhD in Clin. Psychology, 1992. Lic. clin. psychologist. Staff psychotherapist Purdue U., West Lafayette, 1988-91; clin. psychologist Southlake Ctr. for Mental Health, Hobart, Ind., 1992-96, Hoover & Assocs., Orland Park, Ill., 1995—. Adj. faculty St. Xavier U., Oak Lawn, Ill., 1996-98. Mem. APA, Ill. Psychol. Assn., Nat. Register of Health Svc. Providers in Psychology. Office: Hoover & Assocs 15010 S Ravinia Ave Ste 14 Orland Park IL 60462-5353 E-mail: cnatvig@juno.com.

NATZKE, KIRK ROLAND, poet, author; b. Cedar Falls, Iowa, Sept. 13, 1943; s. Roland Felton Lange Natzke and Mae Clark Arnold; m. Vicki Gritton, June 30, 1973 (div. Oct. 1979). Student, U. No. Iowa, Cedar Falls, 1967-68, 2001—, Elmhurst (Ill.) Coll., 1968-69, Hawkeye C.C., Waterloo, Iowa, 1969—70, Hawkeye C.C., 2001. Laborer John Deere Co., Waterloo, 1972-95; ret. Editor Post-Modern Art, 2000; author poetry: Human Spirituality, 1965-00; actor stage musical: "Hero," A Funny Thing, 1968; author: Differences of Modern & Post-Modern Thinking, 2001. Charter dir. Cedar Falls Cmty. Playhouse, 1978-80, also budget dir. With U.S. Army, 1964-66. Christian Existentialist. Avocations: folk music, jazz, coffee. Home: 418 Cutler St Waterloo IA 50703-2452

NATZKE, PAULETTE ANN, manufacturing executive; b. Wausau, Wis., Oct. 23, 1943; d. Milton L. and Geraldine J. (Henrichs) Marth; m. Kenneth A. Natzke, June 29, 1963; children: Jerome E., Julie J. Cert. ceramic tchr. Sec. Marth Wood Shavings Supply, Marathon, Wis., 1973—85, pres., 1985—; v.p. Marth Transp. Inc., 1984—; adminstr. Marth Found., 1982—; owner Privacy Point on Lake Nokomis, Tomahawk, Wis., 1992—97; treas. Marth Mfg., Inc., 2000. Dir. Marathon Area Credit Union, 1985-87. Republican. Lutheran. Avocations: decorating chicken eggs, framing. Home: 6752 State Highway 107 Marathon WI 54448-9444 Office: Marth Wood Shavings Supply Inc Marathon WI 54448-9802

NAU, DON H. fraternal organization administrator; b. Seattle, Aug. 5, 1931; s. Fern B. and Evelyn Nau; m. Betty Jean Arnold (div.); 1 child Denise Gervais-Shari (dec.) ; m. Marlene Ann Boyle, Dec. 27, 1975; children: Denise Gervais, Kathryn Carey, Janet Huttals, Patty Boyle. BBA, U. Puget Sound. Sales rep. Tidewater Oil, Seattle, 1959—66; advt. sales promotion mgr. Phillips Petroleum, 1966—70, sales mgr., 1970—76; dist. sales mgr. Tosco, 1976—84, R. W. Wade, 1984—89; mgr. Afifi Shrine Ctr., Tacoma, 1989—. With USN, 1950—54. Avocation: golf. Home: PO Box 1529 Milton WA 98354 Office: Afifi Shrine Ctr 815 S Vassault St Tacoma WA 98465-2097 Office Fax: 253-565-3580. E-mail: ashrine@aol.com.

NAUDZIUS, ALDONA KANAUKA, pianist, music educator; b. Kaunas, Lithuania, Sept. 18, 1933; came to U.S., 1949; d. Vincas and Ona (Razmaite) Kanauka; m. Victor K. Naudzius, Dec. 1961; children: Ingrid Aldona, Renata Victoria. BA, Bennington Coll., 1955; MA, Columbia U., 1957; EdD, U. Ill., 1983; studied piano with, C. Freidberg, J. DeGray, C. Frank, V. Bacevicius, T. Richner, A. Forte, R. McDowell, S. Dorfman, S. Stravinsky, V. Leyetchkiss. Cert. music tchr. Ill., Ind., N.Y., M ass., social studies tchg. cert. Ill., N.Y. Tchr. music Pub. Schs., N.Y., 1958-59, N.Y.C., 1959-62, East Chicago, Ind., 1963-67; tchr. piano Morton East H.S., Cicero, Ill., 1985-86; tchr. music De Lourdes Coll., Des Plaines, 1986, Chgo. Pub. Elem. Schs., 1989-94, Near North Metro H.S., Chgo., 1994-96, William Taft H.S., Chgo., 1996-98; pvt. piano tchr., 1998—. Participant internat. piano seminars, Graz, Austria, 1992, Lyon, France. Musician: Nelita True's Master Class, Dmitry Paperno's Master Class, 2000; piano soloist: various cmty. functions. Mem. Am.-Lithuanian Cmty., Lithuanian Scouts Assn. (collegiate divsn.), Am.-Lithuanian Music Soc., Wagner Music Soc. Roman Catholic. Home: 5733 N Sheridan Rd Chicago IL 60660-8767 E-mail: aldona_n@yahoo.com.

NAUGHTEN, ROBERT NORMAN, pediatrician; b. Stockton, Calif., Oct. 13, 1928; s. Norman Stafford and Junetta (Doherty) N.; m. Ann Louise Charkins, June 26, 1954; children: Robert James, Annette Marie Naughten-Dessel, Patricia Louise Schoof. AA, San Jose City Coll., San Jose, Calif., 1948; BA, U. Calif., Berkeley, 1950; MA, Stanford U., 1955; MD, Hahnemann U., 1959. Lic. physician and surgeon, Calif. Intern Highland-Alameda County Hosp., Oakland, Calif., 1959-60; rsch. fellow Nat. Cancer Inst., Stanford, 1960-61; resident pediat. Stanford Med. Ctr., 1961-63; pvt. practice specializing in pediat. Los Gatos, Calif., 1963—. Instr. Santa Clara Valley Med. Ctr., San Jose, 1963—, Dept. of Pediat., Stanford, 1963-73; cons. drug abuse San Jose Police Dept., 1963-68; cons. child abuse Dist. Atty., San Jose, 1984—; cons. dept. social svcs. State of Calif., 1989—. Contbr. articles to profl. jours. Bd. dirs., v.p. Outreach and Escort, Inc., San Jose, 1985-88. Named Alumnus of Yr. San Jose City Coll., 1967, Chef of the West Sunset Mag., 1989; fellow Coll. of Physicians, Phila., 1986. Mem. AMA, Calif. Assn., Santa Clara Med. Assn. (v.p. 1986-88), Am. Acad. Pediatrics, Am. Acad. Allergy and Clin. Immunology, Calif. Alumni Assn. (Berkeley), Stanford Alumni Assn., Commonwealth Club (San Francisco), Soc. of the Sigma Xi. Democrat. Roman Catholic. Avocations: gourmet cooking, stamp collecting, sailing, art. Home: 13601 Riverdale Dr Saratoga CA 95070-5229 Office: 777 Knowles Dr Ste 3 Los Gatos CA 95032-1417

NAUGHTON, ANN ELSIE, educator; b. N.Y.C., Apr. 27, 1942; d. George and Wilma (Lubitz) Bruning; m. Gerald Richard Naughton, Dec. 26, 1965 (dec. Apr. 1983); 1 child, Jonathan. BA, CUNY, 1963; MA, Columbia U., 1965; postgrad., Greenburgh Inst. Tchrs.; ESL Cert., Long Island (N.Y.) U., 1990. Social worker div. child and family welfare Westchester County, Yonkers, N.Y., 1963-64; tchr. Hastings On Hudson (N.Y.) Pub. Schs., 1965—. Tchr. Lincoln Ctr. Inst., N.Y.C., 1986—. Mem. Hastings Tchrs. Union (mem.-at-large exec. com. 1982—, state facilitator and trainer N.Y. parent tchrs. confs. 1988—, exec. com. 1982-88, corr. sec. 1989—), N.Y. Zool. and Ecol. Habitat (trainer 1991—), Impact II Grant Winner 1993-94, Scarsdale (N.Y.) Woman's Club (pres.), Investment Club, Montauk Art Assn. Avocations: gardening, horseback riding, swimming, painting, art history. Home: 31 Walbrooke Rd Scarsdale NY 10583-2743 E-mail: anaug67171@aol.com.

NAUGHTON, JAMES LEE, internist; b. 1946; AB, Dartmouth Coll., 1968; MD, Harvard U., 1972. Intern U. Calif. Moffitt Hosp., San Francisco, 1972-73; resident in medicine U. Calif. Affiliated Hosps., 1973-75, San Francisco Gen. Hosp., 1975-76; fellow in nephrology U. Calif., San Francisco, 1976-77, assoc. clin. prof. medicine, 1982—; pvt. practice internal medicine, ptnr. Alliance Med. Group, Pinole, Calif., 1982—. Mem. Am. Bd. Internal Medicine (bd. dirs. 1995-2002, exec. com. 1997-2002, trustee found. 2000—). Office: Alliance Med Group 2160 Appian Way Ste 200 Pinole CA 94564-2524

NAUGHTON, JAMES MARTIN, journalist; b. Pitts., Aug. 13, 1938; s. Francis Patrick and Martha Ann (Clear) N.; m. Diana Marie Thomas, Sept. 5, 1964; children: Jenifer Mary Naughton Genovesi, Lara Marie, Michael Thomas, Kerry Marie. BA cum laude, U. Notre Dame, 1960. Reporter, photographer Painesville (Ohio) Telegraph, summer, 1955-60; reporter Cleve. Plain Dealer, 1962-69; Washington corr. N.Y. Times, 1969-77; nat. editor Phila. Inquirer, 1977-79, met. editor, 1979-83, assoc. mng. editor, 1980-86, dep. mng. editor, 1986-90, mng. editor, 1990-91, exec. editor, 1991-96; pres. The Poynter Inst. for Media Studies, St. Petersburg, Fla., 1996—. Marsh prof. U. Mich., 1977 Served with USMC, 1960-62. Recipient Disting. Service award Sigma Delta Chi, 1973 Roman Catholic. Home: 2500 Coffee Pot Blvd NE Saint Petersburg FL 33704-3466 Office: 801 3rd St S Saint Petersburg FL 33701-4920 E-mail: swami@poynter.org.

NAUGHTON, JOHN ALEXANDER, lawyer; b. Chgo., Jan. 26, 1947; s. Hugh and Margaret (Durkin) N.; m. Raydeen E. Banfi, Dec. 27, 1969; children: Teryn Alisa, Tysen Anne, Ryan Eric, Justen Aran. BS in Commerce, De Paul U., 1970; JD, John Marshall Law Sch., Chgo., 1977. Bar: Ill. 1977, U.S. Dist. Ct. (no. dist.) Ill. 1978. Assoc. Kusper & Raucci, Chartered, Chgo., 1978-81; city atty. Berwyn, 1981-82; pvt. practice Ill., 1981—. Twp. atty. Berwyn Health Dept., 1982-85. Bd. dirs. Altenheim, Forest Park, Ill., 1977-88; alderman Berwyn City Council, 1977-80, mayor, 1980-81. Mem. Ill. Bar Assn., W. Suburban Bar Assn.

NAUGHTON, JOHN PATRICK, cardiologist, educator; b. West Nanticoke, Pa., May 20, 1933; s. John Patrick and Anne Frances (McCormick) N.; children: Bruce, Marcia, Lisa, George, Michael, Thomas. AA, Cameron State Coll., Lawton, Okla., 1952; BS, St. Louis U., 1954; MD, Okla. U., 1958; MD (hon.), Kosin U., 1995. Intern George Washington U. Hosp., Washington, 1958-59; resident U. Okla. Med. Center, 1959-64; asst. prof. medicine U. Okla., 1966-68; assoc. prof. medicine U. Ill., 1968-70; prof. medicine George Washington U., 1970-75, dean acad. affairs, 1973-75, dir. div. rehab. medicine and Regional Rehab. Research and Tng. Center, 1970-75; dean sch. Medicine, SUNY, Buffalo, 1975-96, prof. medicine, physiology, social, preventive and rehab. medicine, 1975—; acting v.p. for health scis. SUNY, 1983-84, v.p. clin. affairs, 1984-96. Dir. Nat. Exercise and Heart Disease Project, 1972-83; chmn. policy adv. bd. Beta-blocker Heart Attack Trial Nat. Heart, Lung and Blood Inst., 1977-82; pres. Western N.Y. chpt. Am. Heart Assn., 1983-85, v.p. N.Y. State affiliate, 1985, pres. N.Y. State affiliate, 1988-90; chmn. clin. applications and preventions adv. com. Nat. Heart, Lung and Blood Inst., 1984; mem. Fed. COGME working group on consortia, 1996-97, N.Y. Gov.'s Commn. on Grad. Med. Edn., 1985, N.Y. State Coun. on Grad. Med. Edn., 1988-90, chmn. 1996—; pres. Assoc. Med. Schs. N.Y., 1982-84, mem. adminstrv. com. Coun. of Deans, 1983-89; mem. N.Y. State Dept. of Health Adv. Com. on Physician Recredentialing; mem. exec. coun. Nat. Inst. on Disability and Rehab. Rsch. 1991-92; v.p. James H. Cummings Found.; bd. dir. Academic Health Profls. Ins. Assn. Author: Exercise Testing and Exercise Training in Coronary Heart Disease, 1973, Exercise Testing: Physiological, Biomechanical, and Clinical Principles, 1988 Career devel. awardee Nat. Heart Inst., 1966-71; recipient Brotherhood-Sisterhood award in medicine NCCJ, N.E. Minority Educators award, 1990, Acad. Alumnus of Yr. award Okla. U., 1990, award for svc. to minorities in med. edn., 1991, Frank Sindelar award N.Y. State Am. Heart Assn., 1995, James Platt White Soc. award, 1995, Outstanding Contbns. in the field of Health Care award Sheehan Meml. Hosp., 1995, Chancellor Charles P. Norton medal, SUNY, Buffalo, 1997, AMS Disting. Svc. award, 2001. Fellow ACP, Am. Coll. Cardiology, Am. Coll. Sports Medicine (pres. 1970-71,

Citation award 2000), Am. Coll. Chest Physicians; Am. Coll. Preventive Medicine, Am. Heart Assn. (epidemiology coun. 2000—, coun. on nutrition, phys. activity and metabolism). Office: SUNY Buffalo 128 Farber Hall 3435 Main St Buffalo NY 14214-3099 E-mail: jpn@buffalo.edu.

NAUGHTON, KRISTEN DOLIBOIS, accountant; b. Columbus, Ohio, Apr. 17, 1972; d. John Michael and Alison Millar (Hodgson) Dolibois; m. Brian Curran Naughton, Aug. 23, 1997. Student, Miami U. Dolibois European Ctr, Luxembourg City, Luxembourg, 1992; BSBA, U. Colo., 1994. CPA, Ill. Gen. ledger clk. Lincoln Trust Co., Englewood, Colo., 1995, accts. payable clk., 1995-96; staff accountant Friedman, Eisenstein, Raemer & Schwartz, LLP, Chgo., 1996—. Mem. AICPA, Internat. Women's Insolvency and Restructuring Confederation, Assn. Certified Fraud Examiners, Ill. CPA Soc., Turnaround Mgmt. Assn. Office: Friedman Eisenstein Raemer & Schwartz LLP 401 N Michigan Ave Ste 2600 Chicago IL 60611-4246

NAUGLE, JEAN MARIE, legal nurse consultant; b. Huron, S.D., Aug. 11, 1955; d. Duane Burton and Dorothy Ann (Davies) Carson; m. Duane Douglas Naugle, June 15, 1985. AA in Nursing, L.A. City Coll., 1979; diploma, Calif. Hosp., L.A., 1979; cert. in legal nurse cons., U. Calif., San Diego. RN, Calif.; cert. gastrointestinal clinician; cert. CPR. Clin. nurse orthopedics and neurology Sharp Meml. Hosp., San Diego, 1979-81, clin. nurse cardiovascular and post cardiac care units, 1981-83, clin. nurse endoscopy unit, 1983-87; supr. nursing, nurse specialist endoscopy Western Health Med. Clinic, 1987-88; clin. nurse endoscopy U. Calif. San Diego Med. Ctr., 1988-93; clin. nurse specialist endoscopy Children's Hosp. San Diego, 1993-95; legal nurse cons., g.i. cons., 1995—; ptnr. JK & Assocs., San Diego, 1997—. Speaker in field. Editor: (newsletter) MediLegal Links, 1996-2000. Mem. Soc. Gastroenterology Nurses and Assocs. (legis. spl. interest group chmn. 1997-99), So. Calif. Soc. Gastroenterology Nurses and Assocs. (edn. chmn. 1991-96, publicity chmn. 1992-94, editor newsletter 1996, pres. 1997), Am. Assn. Legal Nurse Cons. (edn. com. San Diego chpt. 1996—, editor Medi-Link newsletter, 1996-99, membership com. 1996, hospitality com. 1996), Consumer Attys. Calif., Consumer Attys. of San Diego, Am. Radio Relay League, PEO (pres. chpt. PT 2000—). E-mail: jeannaugle@yahoo.com.

NAUGLE, ROBERT PAUL, dentist; b. Cleve., May 3, 1951; s. Paul Franklin Albert and Olga (Bigadza) N.; m. Nancy Elaine Baker, June 14, 1975; 1 child, Jennifer Elaine. BS, Heidelberg Coll., Tiffin, Ohio, 1973; DDS, Case Western Res. U., 1977. Pvt. practice, Uniontown, Ohio, 1980—. Capt. USAF, 1977-80. Mem. ADA, Am. Soc. Dentistry for Children, Ohio Dental Assn., Acad. Gen. Dentistry, Acad. Sports Dentistry, Stark County Dental Soc., Akron Dental Soc., Air Force Assn., Rotary (past program chmn. Uniontown, Student of Month chmn., past pres., past v.p., past treas., Paul Harris fellow, past sgt.-at-arms, cmty. svc. chmn., cmty. svc. chmn.). Republican. Mem. United Church of Christ. Office: 13027 Cleveland Ave NW Uniontown OH 44685-8430

NAUHEIM, STEPHEN ALAN, lawyer; b. Washington, Nov. 17, 1942; s. Ferdinand Alan and Beatrice Lillian (Strasburger) N.; children: Terry Beth, David Alan. BS in Acctg., U. N.C., 1964; JD, Georgetown U., 1967; LLM, George Washington U., 1970. Bar: D.C. 1968, U.S. Ct. Claims 1968, U.S. Tax Ct. 1971. Atty. adviser office chief counsel IRS, Washington, 1967-71, asst. br. chief, 1970-71; assoc. Surrey & Morse, 1971-75, ptnr., 1975-81; prin. Anderson, Hibey, Nauheim & Blair, 1981-91, Schall, Boudreau & Gore, Washington, 1991-93; pres., gen. counsel CMW Group, Ltd., 1994-96; dir. Pricewaterhouse Coopers LLP, 1996—. Mem. adv. bd. World Trade Inst., N.Y.C., 1978—, Tax Mgmt. Adv. Bd., Washington, 1980—. Mem. editl. bd. Internat. Tax Jour., N.Y.C., 1982—; contbr. to profl. publs. Mem. ABA (former com. chmn. taxation sect.), Internat. Fiscal Assn., D.C. Bar Assn. (mem. steering com. tax sect. 1987-92, chmn. tax sect. 1990-92), Am. Coll. of Tax Counsel. Avocations: traveling, sailing. Office: Pricewaterhouse Coopers 1301 K St NW Ste 800W Washington DC 20005-3317

NAULIN, JOHN ARTHUR, entertainment company executive; b. Euclid, Ohio, Mar. 21, 1956; s. Arthur Arnold and Verne Lou Naulin; m. Shayna Lin Klickstein, Jan. 3, 1976; children: Daniel Patrick, Juliet Christine. AA in Theatre arts, Phoenix (Ariz.) Coll., 1976; student, Sherwood Oaks Coll., Hollywood, Calif., 1978. Mgr. Shop of 1000 Faces Universal Studios, Inc., University City, Calif., 1976-78; supr. R&D Don Post Studios, Inc., North Hollywood, 1978-83; owner M.T.S.D. Design, Newbury Park, 1983—; supr. 3-D design Landmark Entertainment, North Hollywood, 1989-92; co-owner M.B.C. Entertainment, Oxnard, Calif., 1993-95; supr. practical design and devel. Santa Monica (Calif.) Pictures, 1996-99; co-founder DzynZ, 1999—. Design cons. Walt disney Imagineering, Burbank, Calif., 1990, Sci-Fi Cafe, Inc., Thousand Oaks, Calif., 1995-96; design submissions to NASA Mars Program, Washington, 1990. West Coast editor: Questar, 1983-85; scriptwriter Ghosts, 1986, Magic and Mischief, 1987, The Wolf Pack, 1987, Soapbox, 1989, Scared Witless, 1995; co-scriptwriter Corporate States, 1990, The Oath, 1994, Mates, 1997. Float design and coun. mem. YMCA, Thousand Oaks, 1996. Recipient Tech. Achievement award for film spl. effects Canne's Film Festival, 1985; named Hon. Congl. Mem. U.S. Congress, 1972. Republican. Avocations: Disney and film collectibles, writing. Home: 133 Hope Rd Newbury Park CA 91320-4717 E-mail: Mtsddesign@aol.com.

NAULT, ROBERT D. legislator; married. Student, U. Alta., Winnipeg, Can. Trainman CP Rail, 1980-86; chmn. Local 431 United Transp. Union, 1986; head Kenora Dist. Liberal Assn., 1984-86; parliamentary sec. Min. Human Resources Devel., 1996—; elected House of Commons, 1988—; min. Indian affairs & no. devel. Canadian Govt. Mem. several parliamentary coms. including chair standing com. natural resources, chair govt. task force CN Commercialization. Office: House of Commons West Confederation Bldg Rm 707 Ottawa ON Canada K1A OA6

NAULT, WILLIAM HENRY, publishing executive; b. Ishpeming, Mich., June 9, 1926; s. Henry J. and Eva (Perrault) N.; m. Helen E. Matthews, Nov. 28, 1946; children: William Henry, Rebecca Nault Marks, Ronald, George, Peter, Julia Nault Doyle, Robert, David. AB, No. Mich. U., 1948, LittD (hon.), 1988; MA, U. Mich., 1949; EdD, Columbia U., 1953, LHD (hon.), 1980, LLD (hon.), 1986, LittD (hon.), 1988. Dir. adult edn., Battle Creek, Mich., 1948-49; guidance counselor, 1949-50; prin. W.K. Kellogg High Sch., Battle Creek, 1950-53; research assoc. Columbia U., 1953-54; asst. supt. Ridgewood, N.J., 1954-55; adj. prof. Patterson State Coll., 1954-55; dir. research World Book, Inc. (formerly Field Enterprises Edn. Corp.), Chgo., 1955-63, v.p., 1963-66, sr. v.p., editorial dir., 1966-68, exec. v.p. and editorial dir., 1968-83; pres., pub., chief operating officer World Book, Inc., 1983-84, gen. chmn. editorial adv. bds., 1968-99, pub., 1983-95, pub. emeritus, 1995—. Past vice chmn. Govt. Adv. Com. on Internat. Library and Book Programs, U.S. Dept. State; past mem. nat. adv. bd. Ctr. on Ednl. Media and Materials for Handicapped; past mem. exec. bd. Commn. Instns. Higher Edn., North Central Assn. Colls. and Secondary Schs.; mem. dean's adv. council Coll. Bus. and Pub. Adminstrn., U. Mo., Columbia; mem. nat. council Inst. Internat. Edn. Author material on courses of study. Mem. alumni com. Columbia Tchrs. Coll. Capital Campaign; mem. White House Conf. on Youth, White House Conf. on Librs., White House Conf. on Edn.; pres. Oak Park (Ill.) Bd. Edn., 1960-63; v.p. LaGrange (Ill.) Libr. Bd.; bd. regents Lincoln Acad., Ill.; past trustee Adler Planetarium, De Paul U., Chgo. Geol. Soc.; bd. dirs. H.V. Phalin Found. Grad. Study, World Book, Inc., A.J. Nystrom Co., Field Edn. Co., Libr. Movens, Inc.; mem. adv. bd. Rosary Coll.; mem. liberal arts and scis. adv. council De Paul U. Served with F.A., AUS, 1944-45. Recipient Columbia U. Tchrs. Coll. medal for disting. svc. in edn.; named Disting. Alumnus No. Mich. U., U. Mich., Columbia U. Fellow AAAS; mem. ALA, Chgo. Planetarium Soc. (trustee), Chgo. Geog. Soc. (dir.), Am. Acad. Polit. and Social Sci., Am. Edn. Rsch. Assn., Am. Assn. Sch. Adminstrs., ASCD, Chgo. Pubs. Assn. (past pres.), Ill. Assn. Sch. Adminstrs., Ill. Acad. Sci., NSTA, Nat. Council Tchrs. English, Assn. Am. Geographers, Assn. Childhood Edn. Internat., NAESP, Nat. Assn. Secondary Sch. Prins., Council for Advancement Sci. Writing, Internat. Platform Assn., Nat. Council Social Studies, Nat. Soc. Study Edn. Clubs: Mid-Am, Mchts. and Mfrs. Roman Catholic. Office: World Book Inc 525 W Monroe St Chicago IL 60661-3629 E-mail: naultwh@aol.com.

NAULTY, SUSAN LOUISE, archivist; b. Abington, Pa., May 28, 1944; d. Charles J. and Ruth E. (Schick) N. BA, Whittier Coll., 1967; MA, Loyola U., L.A., 1972. Tchr. history and English, Whittier (Calif.) H.S., 1968-70; from libr. asst. to asst. curator Huntington Libr., San Marino, Calif., 1972-91; archivist Richard Nixon Libr. and Birthplace, Yorba Linda, 1991—. Office: Richard Nixon Libr and Birthplace 18001 Yorba Linda Blvd Yorba Linda CA 92886-3903

NAUM, CHRISTOPHER JOHN, fire protection management and training consultant, educator; b. Syracuse, N.Y., Feb. 8, 1957; s. John and Florence (Karafile) N.; m. Ann M. McCabe, July 21, 1984 (div.); children: Lauren K., Ashley C.; m. Lori A. Drosi, Sept. 13, 1997; 1 child, Emily N. BA, Syracuse U., 1981; student, SUNY-Onondaga C.C., 1980-86, Nat. Fire Acad., Emmitsburg, Md., 1982-92, 99-01, U. Md., 1982-84. Cet. fire instr., hazardous materials technician, fire prevention and bldg. code enforcement officer and instr., fire protection engr.; cert. fire officer; safety specialist. From fire explorer to fire lt. Moyers Corners Fire Dept., Town of Clay, NY, 1975-81; fire capt. Moyers Corners Fire Dept., Onondaga County Fire System, 1981—93, tng. instr., 1991-99, FD tng. officer, 1999—; project architect Maniktala Assocs., P.C., Syracuse, 1981-91; pres., exec. cons. Americana Fire Cons., Inc., 1988-91; fire protection engr. James A. FitzPatrick Nuclear Power Plant, Lycoming, 1992-93, fire protection specialist, 1993-98, fire and safety specialist, 1998-99, fire and safety specialist II, 2000—, dep. fire chief, 1995—; acting fire protection supr. N.Y. Power Authority, James A. Fitzpatrick Nuc. Power Plant, 1999-2000. Coord. dept. fire protection tech. Onondaga C.C., SUNY, Syracuse, 1984-89; co-dir. Onondaga County Fire Rescue Inst., 1987-89, Town of Clay Fire Tng. Tower, 2000—; pres. L.A. Emergency Mgmt. and Tng. Cons., Syracuse, 1992—; adj. faculty instr. U.S. Fire Adminstrn., Nat. Fire Acad., Md., 2000—. Contbg. editor Firehouse Mag., 1988—, On-Call Mag., 1995-96, Nat. Fire Protection Assn. Handbook, 18th edit., 1997; contbr. articles to profl. jours. Mem. FEMA US&R Task Force Working Group, 1989-92. Recipient Kodak/KINSA internat. medallion for excellence in photography, 1977, FEMA cert. of appreciation, 1991; others. Mem. AIA, Internat. Soc. Fire Svc. Instrs. (George D. Post award 1987, Nat. Fire Instr. of Yr. award 1987), World Safety Orgn., Internat. Assn. Fire Chiefs (nat. com. on urban rescue and structural collapse 1988-98, Cert. of Appreciation 1993), Internat. Fire Photographers Assn., Nat. Fire Protection Assn. (nat. com. 1988—, chair tech. rescue com., trench rescue working group), Nat. Assn. for Search and Rescue, Soc. Fire Protection Engrs., N.Y. State Assn. Fire Chiefs, Alliance for Fire and Emergency Mgmt. (steering com. for Nat. Search and Rescue Assn. 1996-97, Internat. Fire Instr. Exch. fellow 1996), Soc. Fire Protection Engrs. Greek Orthodox. Avocations: downhill skiing, drawing and painting, photography. Home and Office: LA Emergency Mgmt & Tng Cons 4286 Ironwood Cir Liverpool NY 13090-2402 E-mail: cnaum@twcny.rr.com.

NAUMAN, ANN KEITH, education educator, department chairman; b. Greensboro, N.C., Aug. 2, 1931; d. Erle Almon and Santa Maria Keith; m. William Logan Nauman, Sept. 15, 1951; children: Richard Logan, Gerald Keith. BA, La. State U., 1961, MA, 1965, BS, 1966, MS, 1969, PhD, 1974; postgrad., Southeastern La. U., 1976-78, Cath. U., Santiago, Chile. Sch. libr. Parish Sch. Sys., Baton Rouge, 1966-76; asst. prof. ednl. founds. Southeastern La. U., Hammond, 1976-80, assoc. prof., 1986-89, prof., 1989—; prof., head dept. St. Joseph Sem. Coll., St. Benedict, La., 1980—. Author: Biographic Handbook of Educators, 1981, Guide to Latin American Archives, 1982, Time Management for Librarians, 1991, Inés de Suarez, Conquistadora, 2000. Fellow La. State U., 1972, OAS, Santiago de Chile, 1973; Mellon grantee Tulane U. Office: Southeastern La U PO Box 659 Hammond LA 70402-0001

NAUMANN, HANS J. manufacturing company executive; b. Germany, May 5, 1935; arrived in U.S., 1960; s. Herbert and Elfriede (Heydenreich) N.; m. Edith Huempel; children: Irene, Michelle, Jacqueline, John. MME, U. Hamburg, Fed. Rep. Germany, 1960; MBA, Rochester (N.Y.) U., 1965. Registered profl. engr., NY. Mgr. engrng. Farrell Corp., Rochester, 1961-66; exec. v.p. Hegenscheidt Corp., Troy, Mich., 1966-70; pres., CEO, stockholder Hegenscheidt GmbH, Erkelenz, Germany, 1970—82; chmn., CEO Internat. Knife Corp., Erlanger, Ky., 1982—84; chmn. bd., CEO, stockholder Simmons Machine Tool Corp., Albany, NY, 1984—; chmn., CEO, stockholder Niles-Simmons Industrieanlagen, GmbH, Chemnitz, Germany, 1992—; chmn., CEO Niles-Simmons-Hegenscheidt Gmbh, Germany, 2001. Author: Tool and Manufacturing Engineering Handbook, 1976; patentee roller finishing and deep rolling. Bd. dirs. U. Albany Fund, Inc., 1986—. Mem. ASME, SAE, Am. Inst. Mgmt. (pres.'s coun.), Am. Mgmt. Assn., Am. Pub. Transit Assn., Verein Deutscher Ingenieure, Soc. Mech. Engrs., Capital Region Tech. Devel. Coun., Capital Region World Trade Coun., Assn. for Mfg. Tech., Albany Colonie Regional C. of C., Rwy. Supply Assn., N.Y. R.R. Club Inc., Lions (past pres.). Avocations: sailing, tennis, golf, skiing. Home: 26 Folmsbee Dr Albany NY 12204-1206 Office: Simmons Machine Tool Corp 1700 Broadway Albany NY 12204-2701 also: Niles-Simmons Industrieanlagen Zwickauer Str 355 09117 Chemnitz Germany E-mail: hnaumann@smtgroup.com., hj.naumann@niles-simmons.de.

NAUMANN, JOSEPH FRED, bishop; b. St. Louis, June 4, 1949; BA, Cardinal Glennon Coll., St. Louis, 1971; degree in theology, Kenrick Sem., St. Louis, 1975. Transitional deacon St. Christopher's Parish, Florissant, Mo., 1974-75; assoc. pastor St. Dominic Savio Parish, Affton, 1975-79, Our Lady of Sorrows Parish, St. Louis, 1979-84; part-time assoc. pastor Most Blessed Sacrament Parish, 1984-89; pastor Ascension Parish, Normandy, 1989-94; apptd. Vicar Gen. with responsibilities for fins. of the ArchdioceseArchdiocese of St. Louis, 1994—; Aux. Bishop of St. Louis/Titular Bishop of Caput Cilla, 1997—. Office: 4445 Lindell Blvd Saint Louis MO 63108-2403

NAUMANN, ROBERT BRUNO ALEXANDER, chemistry and physics educator; b. Dresden, Germany, June 7, 1929; came to U.S., 1932, naturalized, 1951; s. Eberhard Bruno and Elsa Henriette (Haege) N.; m. Marina Grot Turkevich, Sept. 16, 1961; children: Kristin Ragnhild Naumann Juros, Andrew John Bruno. BS, U. Calif., Berkeley, 1949; MA, Princeton U., 1951, PhD, 1953. Faculty Princeton U., 1953—, prof. chemistry and physics, 1973-92, prof. emeritus, 1992—. Mem. vis. staff Los Alamos Nat. Lab., 1970-86; rsch. collaborator Brookhaven Nat. Lab., 1984-87; sci. assoc. CERN, Geneva, 1985-96; vis. prof. physics dept. Tech. U. Munich, 1988; vis. scholar physics Dartmouth Coll., 1992-96, adj. prof. physics and astronomy, 1996—. Author articles electromagnetic isotope separation, nuclear structure via radioactive and charged particle nuclear spectroscopy, implantation radioactive isotopes into solids, formation and properties of muonic atoms. Recipient Alexander von Humboldt Stiftung Sr. U.S. Scientist award, 1978, 83; Allied Chem. and Dye Corp. fellow, 1951-52, Procter and Gamble faculty fellow, 1959-60; Deutsche Forschungsgemeinschaft grantee, 1988. Fellow Am. Phys. Soc., AAAS; mem. Am. Chem. Soc. (chmn. Princeton U. sect. 1975, Chmn. Div. Nuclear Chemistry and Technology 1984), Sierra Club, Phi Beta Kappa, Sigma Xi (chmn. Princeton, N.J. sect. 1986-87). Episcopalian. Home: 387 Hawk Pine Rd Norwich VT 05055-9631

NAUMANN, WILLIAM CARL, consumer products company executive; b. Peoria, Ill., Mar. 25, 1938; s. William Louis and Emma (Bottin) N.; m. Polly Roby, May 20, 1962 (div. 1980); children: Jeff, Heather, Derek; m. Patricia Gallagher, Sept. 9, 1993. BSCE, Purdue U., 1960; MBA, U. Chgo., 1975. With Inland Steel Products Co., Chgo., 1960-74, N.Y. dist. mgr., 1968-70, div. gen. mgr., 1971-74; group v.p., bd. dirs. Inryco, Melrose Park, Ill., 1974-81; asst. chief engr. Inland Steel Co., Chgo., 1981-82, asst. gen. mgr. corp. planning, 1982-83, asst. gen. mgr. sales, 1983-85, gen. mgr. sales and mktg., 1985-87; exec. v.p. internat. ops. Hussmann Corp., Bridgeton, Mo., 1987, exec. v.p. sales and mktg., 1987; pres. Hussmann Food Svc. Co., 1987-89; corp. v.p., chief quality officer Whitman Corp., Chgo., 1990-91; CEO Ranger Industries, 1992; sr. v.p., COO Pexco Holdings, Inc., Tulsa, 1993-96; chmn. bd. dirs., CEO Sports Holdings Corp., Montreal, Can., 1996-97; pres., CEO Hatteras Yachts, Inc., New Bern, N.C., 1997—. Mem. U. Chgo. Exec. Program Club (past pres.), U. Chgo. Alumni Assn. (past pres., bd. govs. 1986-95), Eastern Carolina Yacht Club, Tarheel Bus. Forum, New Brer Aves C. of C. (chmn.), Ocean Reef Club, New Bern Golf and Country Club, Beta Gamma Sigma. Avocations: boating, travel, cooking. Home: 406 Wexford Pl Trent Woods NC 28562-7105 Office: Hatteras Yachts Inc 110 N Glenburnie Rd New Bern NC 28560-2703 E-mail: bnaumann@hatterasyachts.com.

NAUMOVA, ELENA NIKOLAEVNA, medical educator; b. Novosibirsk, Russia, Sept. 15, 1960; d. Nikolai Fedorovich Nazarenko; m. Yuri Nikolaevich Naumov; children: Ekaterina, Mikhail Naumov. PhD, Novosibirsk State Tech. U., Russia, 1988. Investigator Inst. Clin. Immunology, Novosibirsk, 1982—91; sr. investigator Inst. Patology of Blood Circulation, 1991—92; rsch. asst. Med. Coll. Wis., Milw., 1993—97; asst. prof. Tufts U. Sch. Medicine, Boston, 1997—. Grant proposal rev. com. NIH, Washington, 2002—; mem. info. sys. faculty adv. com. Tufts U., Boston, 2000—. Contbr. articles. Mem. Communicable Disease Surveillance Adv. Com., Boston, 2000. Recipient First prize for Innovation, Sect.: Statis. Processing and Software in Med. Applications, Soc. Innovation and Rsch., 1987. Mem.: Internat. Environmetrics Soc., Am. Statis. Assn. Avocations: hiking, ice skating, travel. Office: Tufts Univ Sch Medicine 136 Harrison Ave Boston MA 02111 Business E-Mail: elena.naumova@tufts.edu.

NAURATH, DAVID ALLISON, engineering psychologist, researcher; b. Houston, Mar. 11, 1927; s. Walter Arthur and Joy Frances (Bradbury) N.; m. Barbara Ellen Coverdell; children: Kathleen Ann, David Allen, Cynthia Ellyn, Randall Austin. BA, Simpson Coll., Indianola, Iowa, 1948; MA, Southern Meth. U., 1949; postgrad., U. Denver, 1955-57. Job analyst U.S. Air Force, San Antonio and Denver, 1951-55, rsch. psychologist Lowry AFB, Colo., 1955-60, Navy, Life Scis. & Systems div., Point Mugu, Calif., 1960-76; engrng. psychologist Navy Systems Engrng., 1976-83; ret. Presenter at profl. socs. and orgns. in field. Contbr. articles to Jour. Engrng. Psychology, jour. Soc. for Info. Display, jour. Soc. Photo-optical Instrument Engrs. With USAAF, 1944-46. Mem. AAAS (life), IEEE (sr.), Am. Psychol. Assn., N.Y. Acad. Sci. (emeritus), Human Factors Soc. (panel mem. Certification of Human Factors Engrs. 1976), Soc. Engrng. Psychologists, Soc. for Info. Display (life). Methodist. Home: 5633 Pembroke St Ventura CA 93003-2200

NAUWELAERS, PAUL LOUIS, engineer; b. Brussels, Oct. 18, 1962; s. Guy Herman Nauwelaers and Denise Léontine Walckiers; m. Marilia Madeira Craveiro, July 14, 1984; children: Isabel Denise, Ines Carolina. MS in Electromech., Inst. Technique Superieur Cardinal Mercier, Brussels, 1983. Inspector Vinçotte, Brussels, 1983-84; sales engr. Klockner-Humboldt-Deutz, 1985-87; prodn. engr. Snecma Sabena, Zaventem, Belgium, 1987—. Mem. Am. Soc. Materials, Soc. Automotive Engrs. Home: Groenlaan 12 3080 Tervuren Belgium E-mail: paul.nauwelaers@wanadoo.be.

NAVA, ELOY LUIS, financial planner, financial consultant; b. N.Y.C., May 19, 1942; s. Eloy and Dolores Nava; m. Diane Margret Binder, Dec. 21, 1968; children: Alyson Beth, David Eloy. BMgmt Engrng., Rensselaer Poly. Inst., 1964, BMech. Engrng., 1965, MSMgmt., 1970. Cert. fund specialist, CFP. Indsl. engr. Johnson & Johnson Inc., Troy, N.Y., 1965-66; nuclear project engr. and chief nuclear test engr. to ops. analysis project mgr. Electric Boat Div., Gen. Dynamics Corp., Groton, Conn., 1966-78; ptnr., chief fin. officer Collado Ozamiz Co., N.Y.C., 1978-88; pres., chmn. bd. JB Apparel Corp., 1984-93; v.p., sr. fin. cons. Cruice Investment Advisors, Ltd., 1994-97; sr. assoc. Fleming, Relyea & Cox, Inc., Stamford, Conn., 1996-2000; pres. Nava Investment & Fin. Svcs., LLC, 2000—. Bd. dirs. Jose Blanco Inc., Santo Domingo, Dominican Republic; mgmt., fin. cons. various orgns. in Dominican Republic. Chmn. water, sewer com. City of Waterford, Conn., 1975-77; mem. Rep. Nat. Com.; swimming ofcl. YMCA, USS. Mem. NRA, Am. Philatelic Soc., Internat. Assn. Fin. Planners, Inst. CFPs (Fairfield County chpt. trustee), Western Conn. Estate and Tax Planning Coun., Midwest Decoy Collectors Assn. Roman Catholic. Avocations: fishing, golf, skiing, stamp and antique decoy collecting. Home: 15 Pasture Ln Darien CT 06820-5618

NAVA, JEAN ANTHES, writer, farmer; b. Inglewood, Calif., July 11, 1940; d. Jacob C. Anthes and Gatha Mary Parks; m. Phillip Nava, Jan. 31, 1960; children: Ruth Stack, Jonathan. BA in English, U. Calif., Santa Barbara, 1961. Tchr. El Camino Elem. Sch., Lompoc, Calif., 1961—62; staff Gospel Pub. Ho., Springfield, Mo., 1962—64; Elementary School Teacher Chgo. Christian Acad., 1970—73; Spanish tchr. Mountain Grove (Mo.) Christian Acad.; English Teacher; TESOL tchr. English Lang. Inst. China, Chengdu, 1992; home schooling Tri-County Homeschoolers Assn., Mo. Author: (book) Learning - Life in the Castle, 1997, Laboring - Life in the Outpost, 1998, Leading - Life at the Battlefront, 1999; editor: (novels) A Tree in Winter, 2001. Ind. missionary. Mem.: St. Louis Pubs. Assn., Calif. Scholarship Fedn. (life). Avocations: canoeing, travel, reading. Home and Office: 1869 Top Rd Mountain Grove MO 65711-2571 Personal E-mail: navajean@fidnet.com. Business E-Mail: navajean@fidnet.com.

NAVA, PATRICIA ANN, electrical engineering educator, researcher; b. Las Cruces, N.Mex., Oct. 17, 1958; d. Jose Encarnacion Nava and Margarita Renteria; children: Marcela Osorno, Ileana Osorno. BSEE, N.Mex. State U., 1980, MSEE, 1982, PhD, 1995. Registered profl. engr., Tex. Design engr. office products divsn. IBM, Boulder, Colo., 1979-80; electronics engr. Office Advanced Tech. White Sands (N.Mex.) Missile Rsch., 1982-84; mem. computer engrng. faculty No. Ariz. U., Flagstaff, 1984-88; asst. prof. elec. and computer engrng. Calif. State U., L.A., 1988-91; coll. asst. prof. N.Mex. State U., Las Cruces, 1995-96; asst. prof. elec. and computer engrng. U. Tex., El Paso, 1996—, Forrest and Henrietta Lewis prof. elec. engring., 1998-2000. Rschr. in fuzzy neural networks. Contbr. articles to sci. jours. Recipient Ariz. Educator of Yr. award collegiate divsn. LULAC, 1987; Crimson scholar N.Mex. State U., 1980; fellow N.Mex. Commn. on Higher Edn., 1992-95; grantee NSF, 1996, U. Tex., 1996-97, NASA-Jet Propulsion Lab., 1999-2002. Mem. IEEE (faculty counselor student sect. U. Tex. 1996—, treas. El Paso-Las Cruces sect. 1998—, svc. award 2000), Phi Kappa Phi (life), Tau Beta Pi (faculty co-advisor to student chpt. 1998—). Democrat. Avocations: classical music, martial arts. Office: U Tex at El Paso 500 W University St El Paso TX 79968-0523 Fax: 915-747-7871. E-mail: pnava@ece.utep.edu.

NAVAR, LUIS GABRIEL, physiology educator, researcher; b. El Paso, Tex., Mar. 24, 1941; s. Luis and Concepcion (Najera) N.; m. Randa Ann Bumgarner, Oct. 15, 1965; children: Tonia, Tess, Gabriel, Daniel. BS, Tex. A&M U., 1962; PhD, U. Miss., 1966, postdoctoral study, 1966-69. Instr. dept. physiology/biophysics U. Miss., Jackson, 1966-67, asst. prof., 1967-71, assoc. prof., 1971-74, U. Ala., Birmingham, 1974-76, prof., 1976-88, assoc. prof. Nephrology Rsch. and Tng. Ctr., 1979-83, prof., 1983-88; prof., chmn. dept. physiology Tulane U. Med. Sch., New Orleans, 1988—. Vis. scientist Duke U. Med. Ctr., Durham, N.C., 1972-73; adv. bd. NIH Ctr. Sci. Rev., 1998-99; bd. dirs. Fedn. Am. Socs. Exptl. Biology, 1997—. Assoc. editor News in Physiol. Scis., 1994—, Am. Jour. Physiology, 1983-89, mem. editl. bd., 1982-83, 97—; mem. editl. bd. Kidney Internat., 1976-87, Jour. Am. Soc. Nephrology, 1996-2001, Am. Jour. Kidney Disease, 1997-2001; mem. editl. bd. Hypertension, 1980-83, assoc. editor, 1993-2000; editl. bd. Kidney, 1992—, Clin. Sci., 1994-99, Am. Jour. Hypertension, 1999—; contbr. sci. papers, book chpts., slides and tapes to profl. publs. Chmn. cardiorenal rsch. study com. Am. Heart Assn., 1994—95, mem. nat. rsch. com., 1994—99; mem. cardiovascular and renal study sects. NIH, 1998—, chmn., 2000—; bd. dirs. Consortium for Southeastern Hypertension Control, 1998—2000. Recipient Rsch. Career Devel. award, Nat. Heart, Lung and Blood Inst., 1974—79, Merit award, 1988—97. Fellow: AAAS; mem.: Assn. Chmn. Depts. Physiology (councillor 1993—95, pres.-elect 1995—96, pres. 1996—97), Internat. Soc. Hypertention, Am. Soc. Hypertension (coun. 1992—94, chmn. basic. sci. com. 1997, treas. 1997—2001, Richard Bright award 2001), Internat. Soc. Nephrology, Am. Soc. Nephrology, Am. Heart Assn. (profl. and pub. edn. com. 1999—, kidney, high blood pressure couns., Lewis K. Dahl Lectr. 1997, Sci. Coun. Disting. Achievement award 1999, Corcoran Lectr. award 2001), Am. Physiol. Soc. (coun. 1991—94, pres.-elect 1997—98, pres. 1998—99, Gottschalk Disting. Lectr. Renal Physiology 1997). Democrat. Roman Catholic. Home: 10020 Hyde Pl New Orleans LA 70123-1522 Office: Tulane U Med Sch Dept Physiology 1430 Tulane Ave New Orleans LA 70112-2699 E-mail: navar@tulane.edu.

NAVARRO, BRUCE CHARLES, lawyer; b. West Lafayette, Ind., Oct. 30, 1954; s. Joseph Anthony and Dorothy Gloria (Gnazzo) N.; children: Philip Joseph, Joanna Christina. BA, Duke U., 1976; JD, Ind. U., 1980. Bar: D.C. 1980. Asst. counsel U.S. Senate Labor Subcom., Washington, 1981-84; acting dep. undersec. for legis. affairs Dept. Labor, 1984-85; atty. advisor EEOC, 1985-86; dir. Office of Congl. Rels. Office of Pers. Mgmt., 1986-89; prin. dep. asst. atty. gen. for legis. U.S. Dept. of Justice, 1989-91; spl. asst. to gen. counsel U.S. Dept. HHS, 1991; expert cons. U.S. Dept. Def., 1992; counsel to the vice chmn. U.S. Consumer Product Safety Commn., Bethesda, Md., 1992-95; prin. Navarro Regulatory and Legis. Affairs, Washington, 1995—. Mem. Arlington County Republican Com. (Va.), 1983; bd. dirs. Prince

William Cmty. Safe Kids Coalition, 1997-99. Mem. D.C. Bar Assn. Roman Catholic. Avocation: music, golf. Office: 2121 K St NW Ste 800 Washington DC 20036 Home: 12580 Cricket Lane Woodbridge VA 22192

NAVARRO, J. RENEE, anesthesiologist; b. June 5, 1960; PharmD, U. Pacific, 1982; MD, U. Calif., San Francisco, 1986. Internal medicine intern Cedars Sinai Med. Ctr., L.A., 1986-87; resident in anesthesiology U. Calif., San Francisco, 1987-90; attending anesthesiologist San Francisco Gen. Hosp., 1990—; assoc. prof. anesthesia and perioperative care U. Calif., San Francisco, 1997—; chief med. staff San Francisco Gen., 2001—. Contbr. articles to profl. jours. Mem. Alpha Omega Kappa, Alpha Kappa Alpha. Office: San Francisco Gen Hosp 1001 Potrero Ave Rm 3c38 San Francisco CA 94110-3594

NAVARRO, JANYTE JANINE, real estate executive; b. LaJara, Colo., Apr. 14, 1935; d. John Charles Blissard and Mary Margaret (Mathias) Tedesco; m. Daniel David Myers (div. 1968); children: Kelli, Keith, Kim; m. Rafael Fowler Navarro (div. Sept. 1994); children: Eric, Marshall, Laura Lynne, Mitchell. Student, Colo. U., 1954-55, U. N.Mex. Owner Poodle Breeding Bus., Albuquerque, 1964-67, Jan-Knits, Albuquerque, 1973-74, Sharing Is Caring, Albuquerque, 1980—; mng. ptnr. Land-Ho Enterprises, 1988—. Regional dir. EXCEL Telecoms., 1996; bd. dirs. Fieseta de Shaklee, Albuquerque. Producer: (video) The Sponsoring Process, 1981; articles, newsletters in field. Bd. dirs. Sandia Ch. Religions Sci. Mem. Rio Grande Sales Leaders Assn. (pres. 1984, 86). Avocations: walking, metaphysical research, teaching self-image classes, environ. issues. Home and Office: 1505 Gretta St NE Albuquerque NM 87112-4319 E-mail: blacjacjan@aol.com.

NAVARRO, JOSEPH ANTHONY, statistician, consultant; b. New Britain, Conn., July 6, 1927; s. Charles C. and Josephine V. (Bianco) N.; m. Dorothy G. Gnazzo; children: Kenneth M., Bruce C., Joseph S. BS, Cen. Conn. State U., 1950; MS, Purdue U., 1952, PhD, 1955. Rsch. staff, cons. GE, 1955-59; rsch. staff, mgmt. IBM, 1962-64; sr. staff mem., asst. dir. Inst. Def. Analyses, Alexandria, Va., 1964-72; pres., chief oper. officer System Planning Corp., Arlington, 1972-86; dep. undersec. test and evaluation Dept. Defense, Washington, 1986-87; now pvt. practice cons., 1987—; pres. Wackenhut Applied Technologies Ctr., Fairfax, Va., 1989-90. Contbr. articles to profl. jours. Mem. Bd. Trade, Washington, 1983-85. Mem. Internat. Test and Evaluation Assn. Clubs: COSMOS (Washington). Republican. Roman Catholic. E-mial. Office: JAN Assocs 7825 Fulbright Ct Bethesda MD 20817-3119 E-mail: jadgnav@aol.com.

NAVARRO, SAMUEL ENRIQUE, investment research executive; b. Matagalpa, Nicaragua, Dec. 27, 1955; came to U.S., 1973, naturalized, 1986; s. Ernesto Navarro and Perla Amador; m. Alexandra Suarez de Sola; children: Samuel R., Alejandro Enrique, Sylvia. BS, U. Tex., 1976; MS, Stanford U., 1978; MBA, U. Pa. Wharton Sch., 1983. Registered profl. engr., Calif. Assoc engr. URS/John A. Blume Assoc., San Francisco, 1978-80; sr. engr. Chemplant Designs, N.Y.C., 1980-81; jr. analyst Equity Research Assocs., 1982, sr. analyst, 1983-84; mng. dir., ptnr. Ladenburg, Thalmann & Co., 1984—. Sr. v.p. Ladenburg, Thalmann Asset Mgmt., N.Y.C., 1984-86, chmn., chief investment officer, 1987-89; mng. dir. Health Care Group Health Care and Med. Tech. Rsch., Needham & Co., Inc., 1992—; mng. dir. med. tech. rsch. Furman Selz, Inc., 1993—. Sustaining mem. Nat. Rep. Com., Washington, 1983—; treas. Am.-Nicaraguan Found. Mem. Investment Assn. N.Y. Clubs: Wharton Sch. (N.Y.C.); Stanford U. Roman Catholic. Office: Furman Selz Incorp 230 Park Ave Fl 13 New York NY 10169-0005

NAVAS, WILLIAM ANTONIO, JR. federal agency administrator, retired military officer; b. Mayaguez, P.R., Dec. 15, 1942; s. William Antonio Sr. and Ethel Ines (Marin) N.; m. Wilda Margarita Cordova Navas, Aug. 7, 1965; children: William Antonio III, Gretchen Maria. BSCE, U. P.R., 1965; MS in Engring. Mgmt., U. Bridgeport, 1979. Registered profl. engr., P.R. Commd. 2d. lt. U.S. Army, 1966, advanced through grades to maj. gen., 1990; served in U.S. Army Corps of Engrs., 1966-70; project engr. Empresas Navas, Inc., Mayaguez, P.R., 1970-72; ptnr., prin. W.A. Navas Jr. & Assocs., 1972-80; dir. Navas & Moreda, Inc., 1973-81; with Interamerican Def. Coll., Washington, 1981-82; dir. ops. P.R. Army Nat. Guard, San Juan, 1982-84, 84-87; comdr. Engr. Task Force, Panama, 1984; dep. dir. Army Nat. Guard Bur., Washington, 1987-97; vice chief Nat. Guard Bur., 1990; mil. exec. res. forces policy bd. Office of Sec. of Def., 1992-94, dep. asst. sec. of def., 1994-95; dir. Army Nat. Guard, 1995-97, ret., 1997; asst. secy. navy manpower reserve affairs U.S. Dept. Defense, Washington, 2001—. Chmn. Dept. of Army Hispanic Employment Commn., Washington, 1988. Decorated Knight Eq. Order of Holy Sepulchre. Mem. Nat. Guard Assn. of the U.S. (del. 1980-86), Nat. Guard Assn. of P.R., Soc. of Am. Mil. Engrs. Roman Catholic. Avocations: militaria collection, reading, running, travel, tennis. Office: US Dept Defense Manpower Reserve Affairs 1000 Navy Pentagon Washington DC 20350-1000 Office Fax: 703-614-4103. E-mail: bnavas@aol.com.*

NAVASKY, VICTOR SAUL, magazine editor, publisher; b. N.Y.C., July 5, 1932; s. Macy and Esther Blanche (Goldberg) N.; m. Anne Landey Strongin, Mar. 27, 1966; children: Bruno, Miri, Jenny. AB, Swarthmore Coll., 1954; LL.B., Yale U., 1959. Spl. asst. to Gov. G. Mennen Williams, Mich., 1959-60; editor, pub. Monocle Mag., 1961-65; editor N.Y. Times mag., 1970-72, The Nation mag., N.Y.C., 1978-94; editl. dir. and pub. The Nation, 1995—; Delacorte prof. of mag. journalism Columbia U., 1999—. Vis. scholarRussell Sage Found., 1975—76; Ferris prof. journalism Princeton U., 1976—77. Author: Kennedy Justice, 1971 (Nat. Book Award nominee), Naming Names, 1980 (Am. Book award 1981), rev. edit., 1991; editor: (with C. Cerf) The Experts Speak, 1984; playwright: (with Richard R. Lingeman) Starr's Last Tape, 1999. Mem. bd. mgrs. Swarthmore Coll., 1991-94. Served with U.S. Army, 1954-56. Guggenheim fellow, 1974-75; fellow Inst. of Politics, Harvard U., 1994; Sr. fellow Freedom Forum, 1994. Mem. Author's Guild (coun.), Com. To Protect Journalists (exec. com.), Phi Beta Kappa. Democrat. Jewish. Office: The Nation 33 Irving Pl Fl 8 New York NY 10003-2332 E-mail: vic@thenation.com.

NAVIA, LUIS E. philosopher, writer; b. Cali, Colombia, Jan. 28, 1940; s. Jose V. and Juanita Navia; m. Alicia S. Cadena, May 15/*; children: Monica Stella Navia-Farrell, Olga Lucia Navia-Pioreck, Melissa Celeste, Soraya Emilia. MA, NYU, 1967, PhD, 1972; BA, CUNY, 1963. Prof. of philosophy NY Inst. of Tech., Old Westbury, 1968—, dean of arts, sciences, and communication, 1993—98. Evaluator, cons. Commn. on Higher Edn., Phila., 1974—. Editor: (book) Journeys Through Philosophy, 1977; author: A Bridge to the Stars, 1977, Das Abenteuer Universum: Der Weg zur kosmischen Gesellschaft, 1978; editor: Ethics and the Search for Values, 1980, The Fundamental Questions, 1985; author: Socrates: An Annotated Bibliography, 1988, Pythagoras, 1990, The Presocratics: An Annotated Bibliography, 1993, The Socratic Presence: A Study of the Sources, 1993, The Philosophy of Cynicism: An Annotated Bibliography, 1995, Classical Cynicism: A Critical Study, 1996, Diogenes of Sinope: The Man in the Tub, 1998, The Adventure of Philosophy, 1999, Antisthenes of Athens: Setting the World Aright, 2001, Socratic Testimonies, 2002. Named Honoree for Accomplishments and Contributions, Nassau County Hispanic Am. Cmty., 1996; named to Outstanding Educators of Am., 1975; recipient Founders' Day ward, NYU, 1972; fellow, N.E.H, 1977. Mem.: Sigma Delta Pi, Phi Beta Kappa. Office: NY Institute of Technology Northern Blvd Old Westbury NY 11568 E-mail: lnavia@nyit.edu.

NAVICKAS, JOHN, fluid dynamics engineer, researcher, consultant; b. Raseiniai, Lithuania, Nov. 26, 1933; came to U.S., 1949; s. John and Ona (Remeikis) N.; m. Marija D. Masionis Navickas, Sept. 1, 1985; children: Rima, Rymante, Tadas, Dalia. BS, UCLA, 1957; MS, 1961. Tech. fellow The Boeing Co., Huntington Beach, Calif., 1957—. Cons. Lloyd's Registry of Shipping, Eng., 1982, Am. Bur. Shipping, 1992, Nippon Kokan, Japan, 1979-82, Lithuania Acad. Sci., 1978, 82. Editor: Conference Proceedings Computational Experiments, 1989; author more than 40 articles on multiphase fluid dynamics, computational methods and space systems. Com. mem. Lithuanian Childrens Hope, L.A., 1992—. Capt. U.S. Army, 1957-65. Mem. ASME, AIAA. E-mail: jm.navickas@verizon.net.

NAVLANI, ANITA A. small business owner; b. Indore, India, Jan. 27, 1968; arrived in U.S., 1991; d. Ghanshyamdas and Rajkumari Keswani; m. Ashok Navlani; children: Rohit, Pooja. BA, Devi Ahiiga Vishov Vidyalay, 1987. Mktg. staff Ashok Pharma, Indose, India, 1991—94; treas. Unique Auto Corp., Levittown, NY, 2000—02; owner Uniondale (N.Y.) Car Care, 2002—. Home and Office: Unique Auto Corp 606 Wantagh Ave 18 Sanford St Huntington Station NY 11746

NAVON, IONEL MICHAEL, mathematics educator; b. Bucharest, Romania, Apr. 28, 1940; s. David and Sarah (Schwartzman) N.; m. Lily Marcu, May 11, 1967; children: Daria, Livia. BSc in Math., Hebrew U. Jerusalem, 1967, MSc in Atmospheric Scis., 1971; PhD in Applied Math., U. Witwatersrand, Johannesburg, South Africa, 1979. Sr. rsch. meteorologist Israel Meteorol. Office, Tel Aviv, 1973-74; head applied math. sect. Tamam/Israel Aircraft Industry, 1974-76; sr. rsch. officer Counc. Sci. and Indsl. Rsch., Pretoria, South Africa, 1976-78, chief rsch. officer South Africa, 1979-80, sr. chief rsch. officer South Africa, 1981-83; sr. vis. scientist NASA/Goddard Space Flight Ctr., Greenbelt, Md., 1983-84; cons. NASA/Goddarad Space Flight Ctr., 1984-85; sr. specialist researcher Coun. Sci. and Indsl. Rsch., Pretoria, 1984-85; assoc. rsch. scientist Supercomputer Rsch. Inst., Tallahassee, 1985-87; assoc. prof. math. Fla. State U., 1987-1990, prof., 1991—, program dir. optimization and optimal control, 1993—, hon. prof. dept. meteorology Supercomputer Rsch. Inst., 1987—, faculty assoc. Supercomputer Computation Rsch. Inst., 1988—, faculty assoc. Geophys. Fluid Dynamics Inst., 1989—, dir. applied math dept. math, 1998—. Dir. applied math. Fla. State U., 1998—; cons. Ctr. Analysis Prediction of Storms, Norman, Okla., 1989, French Navy, 1995; leader Argonne Nat. Lab.; co-organizer Internat. Conf. Element Methods in Geophysics, Tallahassee, 1991; summer lecture series scientist NASA, 1991—; mem. panel nat. experts to rev. and conduct site visiting Okla. Sci. and Tech. Ctr.; keynote spkr. Internat. Conf. on Finite Element Methods, South Africa, 1992, Internat. Conf. on Optimization Techniques and Applications, Singapore, 1992, Assimilation of Meteorological and Oceanographic Observations, France, 1993; dir. applied math. dept. math. Fla. State U., 1998. Editor spl. issues Computer and Math. with Applications; editor Monthly Weather Rev., 1991-94; assoc. editor Monthly Weather Rev., 2001, Jour. for Numerical Linear Algebra with Applications, 1991, Computational Fluid Dynamics Jour., 1992; chief editor spl. issue Dynamics of Atmospheres and Oceans, 1998; contbr. over 95 refereed articles to sci. jours. Lt. Israel Civil Def., 1960-63. Grantee NSF, 1988, 91, 94—, 98—, NASA, 1991, 94, 97-99; rsch. grantee Air Force Office Sci., 1989, 91, 94. Fellow Am. Meteorol. Soc.; Nat. Rsch. Coun. NASA/GSFC Delta Assimilation Office, 2000 (sr.); mem. Am. Math. Soc., Am. Geophys. Union, Soc. Indsl. and Applied Math., Israel Assn. Profl. Engrs., Am. Computing Machinery Assn. Avocations: ping-pong, photography, books. Home: 3138 Ferns Glen Dr Tallahassee FL 32309-2304 Office: Fla State U Love Building Rm 415 Tallahassee FL 32306 Fax: 850/644-0098. E-mail: navon@math.fsu.edu., navon@csit.fsu.edu.

NAVON, ROBERT, real estate investor, former book publisher; b. N.Y.C., May 18, 1954; s. Jack and Estelle N. AB, CUNY, Bronx, 1975; MLS, SUNY, Geneseo, 1978; MA, PhD, U. Kans., 1987; postgrad., U. N.Mex., 1991-93. Coll. libr. N.Y. Inst. Tech., N.Y.C., 1978-79; tchr. history and English N.Y.C. Schs., 1983-86; pub. Selene Books, N.Y.C., 1984-86, Lawrence, Kans., 1986-88, El Paso, Tex., 1988-93, Marianna, Fla., 1996-99; tchr. ESL, Evergreen Inst., Korea, 1993-94; real estate investor, Panama City, Fla., 1995—. Author: Patterns of the Universe, 1977, Autumn Songs, 1983, The Harmony of the Spheres, 1991, Cosmic Patterns, 1993, Tales of the Future, 1999. Mem. Internat. Soc. for Comparative Study of Civilizations, Phi Beta Kappa. Avocations: chess, international travel, collecting movies. Home: PO Box 634 Panama City FL 32402

NAVONE, EDWARD WILLIAM, artist, educator; b. Richmond, Calif., Oct. 5, 1937; s. Julio Mario and Helen Marie (Gianelli) N. BA in art, San Jose (Calif.) State Coll., 1959, MA in art, 1961; postgrad., U. Calif., Berkeley, 1961-62. Vis. instr. Ea. Wash. State Coll., Cheney, 1962-63; from instr. to prof. Washburn U., Topeka, 1964—. Asst. dir. Mulvane Art Mus., Topeka, 1964-79; taught and conducted course on Italian Renaissance Art History including 20-day trip to Italy, 1972, 73, 90-94, 2000; cons. Salina Arts and Humanities Commn., 1989; mem. various coms. including acad. policy com., 1981-84, athletic com., 1978-79, spl. instructional program com., 1974-81, libr. com., 1966-81. One-person shows include Topeka/ Shawnee County Pub. Libr. Gallery, 1993, Art Gallery Univ. No. Iowa, 1998, Benedictine Coll., Atchinson, Kans., 1965, Sheldon Art Gallery, Lincoln, Nebr., 1969, U. Calif. Davis Gallery, 1971, U. Mo., Kansas City, 1976, Mabee-Gerrer Mus., Shawnee Okla., 1987, Swarthmore Coll., 1988, Mulvane Art Ctr. Gallery, 1989, U. No. Iowa, 1998, Mulvane Art Mus., 1999; group exhbns. Ancestral Legacy, Drury Coll., Springfield, Mo., 1992, Mulvane Art Mus., 1997, Shafer Gallery Barton County Comty. Coll., 1998; murals commd. for White Concert Hall/Washburn U., 1997, Lawrence Art Ctr., 2002, E. Cen. Univ., Ada, Okla., 2002, Birger Sandzen Gallery, 2002. Recipient numerous grants including Sweet Summer Sabbatical Italy, France, 1994, Sweet Sabbatical Italy, Austria, 1999, Italy, Belgium, France, 2002, Univ. Rsch. Com. joint project to design, execute and install a ceramic mural in corridor of Garvey Fine Arts Ctr., 1990, Summer Sweet Sabbatical N.Y., 1970. Mem. Coll. Art Assn., Kansas City Artists Coalition, Phi Kappa Phi, Phi Beta Delta. Roman Catholic. Avocations: travel, classical music, photography. Home: 1325 SW Jewell Ave Topeka KS 66604-2731 Office: Washburn U 1700 SW College Ave Topeka KS 66621-0001

NAVRAN, LESLIE, retired clinical psychologist; b. Bklyn., June 30, 1921; s. Frank and Mollie Navran; m. Calypso Hawley, Oct. 9, 1943 (div. 1965); children: Katherine Lesley Navran Sakurada, Brent Hawley; m. Marca Leu, Apr. 30, 1966; children: Michelle Gigi Navran Dalton, Nicholas Peter. AB, Stanford U., 1947, MA, 1949, PhD, 1952. Lic. psychologist, Calif.; diploma in clin. psychology Am. Bd. Profl. Psychology. Staff psychologist VA Neuropsychiat. Hosp., American Lake, Wash., 1952-55, clin. psychologist Sepulveda, Calif., 1955-61, West Los Angeles, 1976-85; sr. staff psychologist Kaiser Permanente Gen. Practice Clinic, L.A., 1961-67; vis. assoc. prof. U. So. Calif., 1967-68; assoc. prof. psychology Royal Roads Mil. Coll., Victoria, B.C., Can., 1968-73, U.S. Internat. U., San Diego, 1973-76; pvt. practice, Westlake Village, Calif., 1985-90, Rancho Mirage, 1990-95, Temecula, 1995-2000; ret., 2000. Editl. cons. Western Psychol. Svcs., L.A., 1967-68; clin. prof. UCLA, 1977-85, Fuller Theol. Sem., Pasadena, Calif., 1982-85; clin. dir. Assn. for Advanced Tng. in Behavioral Sci., L.A., 1977-82. Author: Marital Evaluation Checklist, 1975. Lt. (j.g.) USCG, 1944-45; comdr. USCG, ret. Recipient citation President's Com. To Employ Handicapped, 1961; rsch. grantee Can. Def. Rsch. Bd., 1968-69. Fellow: APA, Acad. Clin. Psychology, Soc. Personality Assessment; mem.: Calif. Psychol. Assn., Phi Beta Kappa. Home: 735 Kappock St Apt 9D Bronx NY 10463

NAVRATIL, GERALD ANTON, physicist, educator; b. Troy, N.Y., Sept. 5, 1951; s. Lloyd George and Frances Mary (Scalise) N.; m. Joan Frances Etzweiler, Sept. 4, 1976; children: Frances, Alexis, Paula. BS, Calif. Inst. Tech., 1973; MS, U. Wis., 1974, PhD, 1976. Project assoc. dept. physics U. Wis.-Madison, 1976-77; asst. prof. engring. sci. Columbia U., N.Y.C., 1977-78, asst. prof. applied physics, 1978-83, assoc. prof., 1983-88, prof., 1988—, chmn. 1988-94, vice dean Sch. Engring. and Applied Sci., 1994-95; vis. fellow Princeton U., 1985-86; cons. MIT, 1984-86, Fusion Systems, Inc., 1988, Inst. Def. Analysis, 1992—; chmn. program adv. com. TFTR, 1994-97, NSTX, 1996—. Assoc. editor Physics of Plasmas, 1994—. Patentee in field. Cottrell Rsch. grantee, 1978; U.S. Dept. Energy High Beta Tokomak Research contract, 1982—; NSF grantee, 1978-88; Alfred P. Sloan rsch. fellow, 1984. Fellow Am. Phys. Soc., Univ. Fusion Assn. (sec./treas. 1988-89, v.p. 1990, pres. 1991), Sigma Xi. Office: Columbia U Dept Applied Physics 500 W 120th St Rm 215 Mudd New York NY 10027-6623

NAWAZ, SHAH, physician; b. Mar. 26, 1961; m. Shama Shah Nawaz; children: Aliana Shah, Alishia Shah. BA, BS, U. Punjab, Lahore, Pakistan; MD/MBBS, Allama Iqbal Med. Coll., Lahore, Pakistan. Chief med. officer Punjab Civil Secretariat Med. Ctr., Pakistan, 1990-91; sr. staff fellow FDA, Washington, 1997-99; chief med. resident dept. internal medicine D.C. Gen. Hosp.; fellow nuc. cardiology, fellow cardiac imaging St. Luke's Roosevelt Hosp., N.Y.C.; fellow in hypertension Mt. Sinai Hosp. Mem.: Allama Iqbal Patient Welfare Soc. Office: Mt Sinai Med Ctr Cardiovasc Inst Dept Cardiology New York NY

NAWROCKI, H(ENRY) FRANZ, propulsion technology scientist; b. Pueblo, Colo., Dec. 10, 1931; s. Henry Vincent and Verna Ella (Weyand) N.; m. Marlene Charlotte Kryak, Sept. 1, 1973. BS Aero. Engring., U. Colo., 1953; MS Aerospace Engring., U. So. Calif., 1968. Group supr. for RJ43 qualification Marquardt, Van Nuys, Calif., 1953-64; flight test analyst engr. for L-1011 cert. Lockheed, Palmdale, 1964-72; flight test program coord. for B-1 qualification Rockwell Internat., El Segundo, 1972-77; propulsion group supr. for CL600 cert. Canadair Ltd., Montreal, Que., Can., 1977-80; design mgr. for LF2000 devel. Lear Fan Ltd., Reno, 1980-82; staff scientist Gulfstream Aerospace Corp., Savannah, Ga., 1982-97; aerospace engr. aircraft cert. office FAA, Atlanta, 1997-98; cons. Propulsion Tech., Inc., Savannah, 1998—. Fellow AIAA (assoc.). Avocations: mineralogy, model railroading, lapidary, metal working. Home: 18 Landon Ln Savannah GA 31410-3830 E-mail: ptfranz@aol.com.

NAWY, EDWARD GEORGE, civil engineer, educator; b. Baghdad, Iraq, Dec. 21, 1926; came to U.S., 1957, naturalized, 1966; s. George M. and Ava (Marshall) N.; m. Rachel E. Shebbath, Mar. 23, 1949; children: Ava Margaret, Robert M. DIC, Imperial Coll. Sci. and Tech., London, 1951; CE, MIT, 1959; D of Engring., U. Pisa, Italy, 1967. Registered profl. engr. N.J., N.Y., Pa., Calif., Fla. Head structures Israel Water Planning Authority, Tel-Aviv, 1952-57; faculty Rutgers U., New Brunswick, N.J., 1959—, grad. faculty, 1961—, prof. civil engring., 1966-72, Disting. prof. (prof. II), 1972—, chmn. dept. civil and environ. engring., dir. grad. programs, 1980-86. Chmn. Coll. Engring. Del. Assembly, 1969-72; mem. Univ. Senate, 1973-80, exec. com., faculty rep., bd. govs., trustee; guest prof. Nat. U. Tucaman, Argentina, summer 1963, Imperial Coll. Sci. and Tech., summer 1964; vis. prof. Stevens Inst. Tech., Hoboken, N.J., 1968-72; hon. prof. Nanjing Inst. Tech., China, 1987; mem. N.J. Chancellor Higher Edn. for Higher Edn. Master Plan; mem. Rutgers U. rep. Transp. Rsch. Bd., 1974-2001, Bridge Com., chmn. com. on concrete materials; cons. to industry; U.S. mem. commn. on cracking Comitè EuroInternat. du Beton; mem. Civil Engring. Tech. Adv. Coun. N.J., 1966-72; concrete sys. cons. FAA, Washington; cons. energy divsn. U.S. Gen. Acctg. Office, Washington; gen. chmn. Internat. Symposium on Slabs and Plates, 1971; hon. presidium internat. conf. Reunion Internat. des Lab. d'Essais et de Rsch. sur Les Materiaux et les Constructions, Budapest, 1977; mem. Accreditation Bd. Engring. and Tech. Author: Reinforced Concrete, 4th edit., 2000, Simplified Reinforced Concrete, 1986, Prestressed Concrete, 3d edit., 2000, High Performance Concrete, 1996, 2d edit., 2001; author, editor-in-chief: Concrete Construction Engineering Handbook, 1998; contbr. over 170 articles to profl. jours. V.p. Berkeley Twp. Taxpayers Assn., Ocean City, N.J., 1966-70. Recipient Merit citation and award N.J. Concrete Assn., 1966; C. Gulbenkian Found. fellow, 1972. Fellow ASCE (joint com. on slabs), Instn. Civil Engrs. (London), Am. Concrete Inst. (pres. N.J. chpt. 1966, 77-78, chmn. nat. com. on cracking 1966-73, bd. com. chpts. 1969-72, ACI rep. internat. commn. fractures, H.L. Kenneday award 1972, award of recognition N.J. chpt. 1972, chpt. activities award 1978, chmn. nat. com. on deflection 1989-96, Concrete Rsch. Coun. Philleo award 2001); mem. NSPE, AAUP (chmn. budget and priorities com. Rutgers U. chpt. 1972), Am. Soc. Engring. Edn., Prestressed Concrete Inst. (Bridge Competition award 1971, tech. activities com.), N.Y. Acad. Scis., Tall Bldgs. Coun., N.J. Contractors Assn. (cons. ednl. com., tall bldgs. coun.), Rotary, Sigma Xi, Tau Beta Pi, Chi Epsilon (hon.). *Success is normally the result of honesty and continuous setting and updating of high goals which have to be perseverely pursued.*

NAYAR, BALDEV RAJ, political science educator; b. Gujrat Dist., India, Oct. 26, 1931; emigrated to Can., 1964; s. Jamna Das and Durga Devi (Marwah) N.; m. Nancy Ann Skinner, Aug. 27, 1961; children— Sheila Jane, Kamala Elizabeth, Sunita Maria. BA, Punjab U., 1953; MA, 1956, U. Chgo., 1959, PhD, 1963. Asst. prof. Calif. State Coll., Hayward, 1963-64; mem. faculty dept. polit. sci. McGill U., 1964-94, assoc. prof., 1966-71, prof., 1971-94, prof. emeritus, 1996—, assoc. chmn., 1990-93. Research assoc. Internat. Devel. Research Centre, 1978 Author: Minority Politics in the Punjab, 1966, National Communication and Language Policy, 1969, The Modernization Imperative and Indian Planning, 1972, American Geopolitics and India, 1976, India's Quest for Technological Independence, 1983, India's Mixed Economy, 1989, The Political Economy of India's Public Sector, 1990, Superpower Dominance and Military Aid, 1991, The State and International Aviation in India, 1994, The State and Market in India's Shipping, 1996, Globalization and Nationalism, 2001, India and the Major Powers After Pokhran II, 2001. Bd. dirs. Shastri Indo-Canadian Inst., 1970-72, sr. fellow, 1978, 86. Recipient Watumull prize Am. Hist. Assn., 1966; Charles E. Merriam fellow, 1957; Carnegie Study New Nations fellow, 1962; Can. Council sr. fellow, 1967, 74; SSHRC leave fellow, 1982 Mem. Can. Asian Studies Assn. Office: McGill Univ Dept Polit Sci Montreal QC Canada H3A 2T7 E-mail: bnayar@po-box.mcgill.ca.

NAYAR, SAMEER, investment banker; b. New Delhi, India, Dec. 16, 1970; s. Ashok and Nirmal Nayar; m. Archana Rohatgi. MS in Real Estate, MIT, 1995—96. Sr. v.p. Moody's Investors Svc., N.Y.C., NY, 1996—2001; dir. Credit Suisse First Boston, 2001—. Personal E-mail: snayar@nyc.rr.com.

NAYDAN, WILLIAM J. music educator; b. Trenton, Nj, June 11, 1956; s. Wiliam and Anna Naydan; m. Catena Messina, June 11, 1983; children: William M., Mary K. BA, Lafayette Coll., Easton, PA, 1974—78; MA, Temple Univ., Philadelphia, PA, 1979—81. Choir dir. Ctrl. Bucks H.S. West, Doylestown, Pa., 1982—91, Hatboro-Horsham H.S., Horsham, 1991—, Lafayette Coll., Easton, 1992—2000; adjuct prof., music ed. Chestnut Hill Coll., Philadelphia, 2000—. Pres. Dist. II PMEA, Pa., 1988—90. Recipient Tchr. of the Yr., Hatboro-Horsham H.S., 1990, Disting. Tchr., PMEA/Music Educators Nat. Conf., 2000. Mem.: Nat. Assn. of Teachers of Singing, Am. Choral Directors Assn., PA Music Educators Assn. Avocations: golfing, playing guitar, traveling. Home: 625 North Wales Road North Wales PA 19454-1724 Office: Hatboro-Horsham High School 899 Horsham Road Horsham PA 19044 Office Fax: 215-441-7940. E-mail: wnaydan@hatboro-horsham.org.

NAYERAHMADI, HABIB, psychologist; b. Tehran, Iran, Apr. 4, 1949; came to U.S., 1975; s. Younes Nayerahmadi and Nasimeh (Sheikhzadeh) Tavassoli; m. Mitra Farzaneh, Aug. 6, 1979; children: Kooshan, Poorya. BA in Psychology, Pars Coll., Tehran, 1973; MA in Clin. Psychology, Ball State U., 1978; PhD, U. Pa., 1989. Psychologist, counselor Imperial Iranian Air Force, Tehran, 1973-75; rsch. asst. U. Pa., Phila., 1980-82; assoc. Uni-Marts, Inc., 1981-88; rsch. cons. CON-RAIL, 1986-87; sr. clin. psychologist North Princeton Devel. Ctr., 1988, 98; clin. psychologist New Lisbon Devel. Ctr., 1998-2000, Ann Klein Forensic Ctr., Trenton, N.J., 2000—. Author: Development of a Homesickness Scale for Iranian Population, 1989; contbr. articles to profl. jours., U.S. and Iran. Mem. APA, Am. Ednl. Rsch. Assn., Iranian Cultural Soc. Am. (trustee 1997-00, pres. 1998-99). Home: 3521 Hale Rd Huntingdon Valley PA 19006-3230 Office: Ann Klein Forensic Ctr PO Box 7717 Stuyvesant Ave Trenton NJ 08628 E-mail: nayerahmad@aol.com., hnayerahm@dhs.state.nj.us.

NAYFEH, ALI HASAN, mechanical engineering educator; b. Shuweikah, Jordan, Dec. 21, 1933; arrived in U.S., 1958; s. Hasan Ahmad and Khadrah (Said) N.; m. Inam A. Zibdeh, Aug. 4, 1965; children: Mahir, Tariq, Samir, Nader. BS with Great Distinction, Stanford U., 1962, MS, 1963, PhD, 1964; Doctorate (hon.), Marine Tech. U., St. Petersburg, Russia, 1996, Tech. U. Munich, Germany, 1999. Prin. research scientist KMS Industries, Van Nuys, Calif., 1964-68, Accurex, Mountain View, 1968-71; prof. Va. Poly. Inst. and State U., Blacksburg, 1971-76, Univ. Disting. prof., 1976—. Dean Sch. Engring.; Disting. prof., v.p. Yarmouk U., Irbid, Jordan, 1980-84. Author: Perturbation Methods, 1973, Russian edit., 1976, (with others) Nonlinear Oscillations, 1979, Introduction to Perturbation Techniques, 1981, Russian edit., 1984, Problems in Perturbation, 1984, Method of Normal Forms, 1993, Applied Nonlinear Dynamics, 1995, Perturbation Methods with Mathematica, 1999, Pertubation Methods with Maple, 1999, Nonlinear Interactions, 2000, Linear and Nonlinear Structural Mechanics, 2000; also more than 350 articles. Recipient Pendray Aerospace Literature award Am. Inst. of Aeronautics and Astronautics, 1995 Fellow Soc. Design and Process Sci., Am. Phys. Soc., Am. Acad. Mechanics, AIAA, ASME (J.P. Den Hartog award 1997); mem. Phi Beta Kappa, Sigma Xi, Tau Beta Pi. Moslem. Office: VA Poly Inst and State U Dept Engring Scis-Mechanics MC 0219 Blacksburg VA 24061 Home: 300 Murphy St Blacksburg VA 24060 E-mail: anayfeh@vt.edu.

NAYLON, BETSY ZIMMERMANN, artist; b. Buffalo, Jan. 27, 1934; d. Gerard M. and Marion G. (McDonald) Zimmermann; m. Bernard M. Naylon, Aug. 11, 1956; children: Lisa, Bernard, Claire. BA, Rosary Hill Coll., 1955; postgrad., Daemen Coll., 1976; studied with, William Paden, N.Y.C., 1986. Instr. Daemen Coll., Buffalo, 1969-70, SUNY, Buffalo, 1974-79, Niagara U., 1981-83, Trinity Ch., 1990-91. Tchr. tutorial studio classes, 1999-2001; art exhbn. judge Niagara Arts Guild Spring Exhibit, 1997, Internat. Children's Art Exhibit, Niagara Falls, Ont., Can., 1991, Lewiston Art Festival, 1982, 86, Castellani Art Gallery, Niagara U., 1982, 85, 89, Niagara Falls Soc. Artists, 1992-94; Am. judge for internat. art exhibit Niagara on the Lake, Ont., 1977; judge ann. group show Grand Island Art Group Exhibit, 1982, 88. One-woman shows include O'Keefe Ctr., Toronto, 1981, Rainbow Ctr., Niagara Falls, 1983, EW Brydges Libr., Niagara Falls, 1983, 84, Occidental Hooker Bldg., Niagara Falls, 1984, The Buffalo Forge Co., 1984, Chautauqua Inst. Art Gallery, 1986, Capen Hall, SUNY, Buffalo, 1986, Carnegie Cultural Ctr., Tonawanda, N.Y., 1987, CP Chelsea Gallery, 1988, Kenan Gallery, Lockport, N.Y., 1989-90, Stella Niagara, 1994-97, Wilhelmenia Gallery, Seneca Falls, N.Y., 1997, 98; exhibited in group shows at Albright-Knox Gallery, Buffalo, 1980-2001, Burchfield Art Ctr., Buffalo, 1980-2001, O'Keefe Ctr., 1982, AAO Galleries, Buffalo, 1984, A-K WNY exhbn. 1984, NAWA Nat. Exhbn., N.Y.C., 1997, NLAPW Nat. Exhbn., Washington, 1996, NFWS Internat. Exhbn., Lockport, N.Y., 1996, ALMC Internat. Fine Arts Exhbn., Fla., 1997, U. Wis. Nat. Art Exhbn., 1987, Nat. NAWA Exhbn., Soho, N.Y.C., 1998, Western N.Y. Artists Group, Art Dialogue Gallery, 1998, 99, 2000, Nat. Assn. Women Artists, Sarasota, Fla., 2000, 02, D'Youville Coll. Art Gallery, 2001, Art Loft Gallery, BSA, 2001, Gallery 12, BSA, 2001; executed mural Niagara Falls Meml. Med. Ctr., 1995, Peller & Mure Co., Buffalo, 1985, JNW Ent., Lewiston, N.Y., 1997, Woman Free, Seneca Falls, N.Y., 1998; artwork and articles about artwork entered into the Women's History Collection, U. Buffalo Archives, 1998, 99, 2000. Recipient Grumbacher Gold Medal award, 1996. Mem. Nat. Assn. Women Artists (traveling printmaking exhibit U.S. 1987-89, 2002, India 1989-90), Nat. League Am. Penwomen (1st Place award 1991, Merit award 1989), Nat. Mus. Women in Arts, Nat. Women's Caucus for Art, Niagara Coun. Arts (bd. dirs. 1983-84), Niagara Frontier Watercolor Soc. (painting award 1989, 1st prize 1994), Buffalo Soc. Artists. Home: 25 Melbourne Pl Buffalo NY 14222-1455 Studio: Our Lady of Loretto 172 15th St Buffalo NY 14213-2606

NAYLON, MICHAEL EDWARD, retired army officer; b. Rochester, N.Y., Jan. 15, 1943; s. Edward M. and Patricia (Brennan) N.; m. Beverly Marzano, Mar. 27, 1965; children: Michelle A. Faber, Colleen M. Burgos. BA, John Carroll U., 1965; MBA, Marymount U., 1986; grad., U.S. Army War Coll., 1989. Indsl. rels. specialist Gen. Railway Signal Co., Rochester, N.Y., Farrell Co., Rochester; manpower adminstr. City of Rochester; employment mgr. U. Rochester; personnel dir. Interstate Brands Corp., Rochester; office mgr., dir. adminstrn., regional tng. coord. Nat. Machine Tool Builders Assn., McLean, Va.; chief U.S Army Res. Hdqs. Dept. of Army, Washington; staff officer Joint Chiefs of Staff, col., sr. res. advisor Dept. Def.; with U.S. Southern Command, Panama City, Panama. Dir. ops. Nat. Assn. Ret. Fed. Employees; nat. exec. dir. AMVETS; exec. dir. Presdl. Spl. Oversight Bd., Dept. Def. investigations of Gulf War chem. and biol. incidents; chief of staff Nat. Com. Employer Support of Guard and Res., Arlington, Va. Mem. VFW, AMVETS, U.S. Army War Coll. Alumni Assn., John Carroll U. Alumni Assn., Res. Officers Assn. USA, Ret. Officers Assn., Am. Legion, Vietnam Vets. Home: 1434 Aldenham Ln Reston VA 20190-3901

NAYLOR, AUBREY WILLARD, botany educator; b. Union City, Tenn., Feb. 5, 1915; s. Harry Joseph and Clara Mae (Isbell) N.; m. Frances Valentine Lloyd, Dec. 26, 1940 (dec. May 1998); children: Virginia Dawson Naylor Kirby, Edith-Margaret Naylor DeWitt. BS, U. Chgo., 1937, MS, 1938, PhD, 1940. Mem. staff, bur. plant industry U.S. Dept. Agr., Chgo., 1938-40; instr. botany U. Chgo., 1940-44, Northwestern U., Evanston, Ill., 1944-45; asst. prof. U. Wash., Seattle, 1946-47, Yale U., 1947-52; assoc. prof. Duke U., 1952-59, prof., 1959-72, James B. Duke prof., 1972-85, James B. Duke prof. emeritus, 1985—. Program dir. for metabolic biology NSF, Washington, 1961-62, cons., 1960-63; chmn. com. examiners for Grad. (Sch.) Record Examination on Biology, Edn. Testing Svc., Princeton, N.J., 1966-72; cons. Oak Ridge Nat. Lab., 1957-58, Rsch. Triangle Inst., N.C., 1968—, TVA, 1969-75, Schaper and Brümmer Pharm. Co., Salzgitter, Fed. Republic of Germany, 1986-92, Akzo Salt Co., 1991-96; mem. summer faculties U. N.C., Chapel Hill, 1960-61, Greensboro, 1964-65; mem. summer faculties Bennett Coll., Greensboro, N.C.; vis. prof. U. Bristol, Eng., 1958-59, U. Tex., Austin, 1977 Contbr. chpts. to books, articles and book revs. to profl. jours. NRC fellow Boyce Thompson Inst. for Plant Rsch., Yonkers, N.Y., 1945-46, Guggenheim fellow, 1958-59; NSF sr. fellow, 1958-59; grantee, 1956-86, Am. Cancer Soc. grantee, 1953-57, Herman Frasch Found. grantee, 1957-72. Fellow AAAS (life mem.); mem. Am. Soc. Plant Physiologists (life, chmn. bd. trustees 1962-74, pres. 1961, exec. com. 1959-60, 62-74, 81-82, Disting. Svc. award So. sect. 1981, Charles Reid Barnes life membership 1981, archivist 1987—), Am. Inst. Biol. Scis., Am. Soc. Cell Biologists, Bot. Soc. Am. (life, cert. of merit 1988), Scandinavian Soc. Plant Physiologists, Japanese Soc. Plant Physiologists, Australian Soc. Plant Physiologists, Cosmos Club (Washington), Sigma Xi (life, pres. chpt. 1968-69). Home: Box 2818 2701 Pickett Rd Durham NC 27705-5688 E-mail: anaylor1@nc.rr.com. *Almost everything interests me. For this reason, I am seldom bored. Channeling my curiosity has been best achieved through a burning desire to learn how living things grow from a single cell, differentiate into a distinct multicellular organism and reproduce. The joy of discovery feeds upon itself and motivates me to work, work, and work some more.*

NAYLOR, JAMES CHARLES, psychologist, educator; b. Chgo., Feb. 8, 1932; s. Joseph Sewell and Berniece (Berg) N.; m. Georgia Lou Mason, Feb. 14, 1953; children— Mary Denise, Diana Darice, Shari Dalice. BS, Purdue U., 1957, MS, 1958, PhD, 1960. Asst. prof. Ohio State U., 1960-63, asso. prof., 1963-67, prof. vice chmn. dept. psychology, 1967-68; prof. Purdue U., Lafayette, Ind., 1968-86, head dept. psychol. scis., 1968-79; prof., chmn. dept. psychology Ohio State U., Columbus, 1986-98, prof. emeritus, 1999—. Fulbright rsch. scholar, Umea, Sweden, 1976; Disting. scholar, vis. scientist Flinders U., South Australia, 1982-83, UNESCO ednl. cons. to Hangzhou U., Peoples Republic of China, 1984; chmn. Coun. Grad. Depts. Psychology, 1993-94; lead reviewer Psychology Program Rev., State U. Sys. Fla., 1996. Author: Industrial Psychology, 1968, A Theory of Behavior in Organizations, 1980; founder, editor: Organizational Behavior and Human Decision Processes; mem. editorial bd.: Prof. Psychology; Contbr. articles to profl. jours. Served with USN, 1950-54. Fellow AAAS, Am. Psychol. Soc., Am. Psychol. Assn.; mem. Psychonomic Soc., Psychmetric Soc., Internat. Assn. Applied Psychology, Soc. Organizational Behavior (founder), Midwestern Psychol. Assn. (coun. 1994-97), Phi Beta Kappa, Sigma Xi. Home: 176 Tucker Dr Columbus OH 43085-3064 Office: Ohio State U Dept Psychology Columbus OH 43210 E-mail: naylor.2@osu.edu.

NAYLOR, JOHN THOMAS, telephone company executive; b. Orillia, Ont., Can., Jan. 30, 1913; s. Fred Addison and Ethel (Thompson) N.; m. Ruth Louisa Tissot, Dec. 21, 1934; children: Joan Crosby, Carol Manka. BSEE, Oreg. State U., 1934. Registered profl. engr., Calif., Oreg., Wash. Chief accountant McKesson & Robbins, Inc., Portland, Oreg., 1934-38; engr. Pub. Service Comm. Oreg., 1938-41; v.p. Gen. Telephone Co. Calif., 1941-50; v.p., gen. mgr. Philippine Long Distance Telephone Co., Manila, 1950-56; also dir.; v.p. United Utilities, Inc., 1956-59; pres., dir. United Telephone Co.; v.p. Internat. Tel. & Tel. Corp., N.Y.C., 1959-61; pres., dir. Telectronic Systems, Inc., Manila, Philippines, 1962-73; cons., 1973—. Author articles on engring., finance, mgmt., pub. service. Active Boy Scouts Am., YMCA; pres. Am. Sch., Manila; mem. coun. regents Oreg. State U., 1981—. Mem. IEEE, NSPE, Philippine Assn. Mech. and Elec. Engrs., Phi Kappa Phi, Tau Beta Pi, Eta Kappa Nu. Clubs: Army and Navy. Address: 1451 NE Meier Dr Grants Pass OR 97526-3805

NAYLOR, LARRY LEE, anthropologist, educator; b. Corning, N.Y., Mar. 14, 1940; s. Harry Earnest Naylor, Francis Jennette McGee; m. Alma Diane Bennett. BS Edn., SUNY, 1962, MS Edn., 1968; DPhil Anthropology, So. Ill. U., 1974. Cert. tchr. N.Y., 1962, N.Mex., 1966. Tchr. elem. sch. Newark Pub. Schs., Newark, 1962—63; tchr. high sch. history Grants Mcpl. Sch. Dist., Grants, N.Mex., 1966—67; asst. prof. anthropology U. Alaska, Fairbanks, 1974—78; asst. prof., dir. anthropology North Tex. State U., Denton, 1978—83; assoc. prof., dir. anthropology U. North Tex., 1983—86, assoc. prof. anthropology dept. georgraphy & anthropology, 1986—90, assoc. prof., chair anthropology, 1990—93, assoc. prof. , chair Inst. Anthropology and Cultural Sensitivity Tng. & Rsch. Ctr., 1993—97, prof. anthropology, 1997—. Dir. Cultural Sensitivity Tng. & Rsch. Ctr., U. North Tex., Denton, 1994—97; cons. Native affairs Institute of Social, Econ. and Govt. Rsch., U. Alaska, Fairbanks, 1974—78; advisor Native alcohol abuse Alaska Concern Citizens on Alchhol Abuse, 1975—77; cons. criminal justice program U. Alaska, 1975—76; Consultant Alcan Pipeline Company, Anchorage, 1976—77; Consultant - Pipeline Impact on Native Canadians Canadian Government, Canada, 1976—77; Consultant - Alaskan Pipeline Impact Gulf State Engineering, Houston, 1976—78; Consultant Alaska Native Foundation on Culture Change, Anchorage, 1976, on Gas Pipeline Impact - Tanana Development Corporation, Fairbanks, AK, 1978; Consultant and Member of Emergency Management Projects Advisor Board Texas A & M University, TX. Translator: Eskimos, Reindeer and Land, 1981; author: Science and the Future (Anthropology), 1993, Cultural Anthropology, 1993, Science and the Future (Anthropology), 1994, Anthropology: Study Guide, 1994, Science and the Future (Anthropology), 1995, Culture Change: An Introduction, 1996, Science and the Future (Anthropology), 1996, Interative Study Guide for Anthropology, 1996, Culture Diversity in the United States, 1997, Science and the Future (Anthropology), 1997, American Culture: Myth and Reality of a Culture of Diversity, 1998, Issues and Problems of Culture Diversity in the United States, 1999, Anthropology Study Guide (CD-ROM), 2001; co-author: Applied Social Science for Environmental Planners, 1983; contbr. articles to profl. jours. Mayor City of Krugerville, Tex., 1999—2000. Grantee, Arctic Gas Corp., 1976, Nat. Park Svc., 1976, Gulf Interstate Engring. Corp., 1976—77, Berger Commn., Can. Govt., 1976—77, Inst. of Arctic Biology, 1976, Nat. Park Svc., 1977—78, Bur. Indian Affairs, 1977—78, U. North Tex., 1982, U. North Tedx. Internat. Affairs, 1982, U. North Tex. Internat. Program Office, 1983, U.S. Corp Engrs., 1987, City Mgr.'s Office, Dallas, 1985, U. North Tex., 1989, Harcourt Brace Publ., 1992, 1993, Higher Edn. Assistance Fund, U. North Tex., 1993. Fellow: Soc. Applied Anthropology, Am. Anthrop. Assn.; mem.: AAAS, N.Y. Acad. Scis., Tex. Coop. Edn. Assn., Current Anthropology (assoc.), Ctrl. State Anthropology Assn. (assoc.), Alaska Anthropology Assn., Coun. Edn. and Anthropology. Home: 106 Brumley Dr Krugerville TX 76227 Office: U North Tex Anthropology 410 Ave C Chilton Hall Rm 330B Denton TX 76203 Office Fax: 940-369-7833. Personal E-mail: naylor@scs.cmm.unt.edu. Business E-Mail: naylor@scs.cmm.unt.edu.

NAYLOR, NATALIE, history educator; b. Peekskill, N.Y., Aug. 20, 1937; d. Colin T. and Anna W. Naylor. AB, Bryn Mawr Coll., 1959; MA, Columbia U., 1962, EdD, 1971. Rsch. asst. Nat. Bur. Econ. Rsch., N.Y.C., 1959-62; social studies tchr. Tuckahoe H.S., Eastchester, N.Y., 1962-65; from instr. to prof. Hofstra U., Hempstead, 1968-2000, prof. emerita, 2000—. Dir. L.I. Studies Inst. Hofstra U., 1985-2000. Editor Nassau County Hist. Soc. Jour., 1996—. Mem. Am. Ednl. Studies Assn. (exec. coun. 1980-83), History Edn. Soc. (dir. 1984-87), Nat. Coun. Religion and Pub. Edn. (editl. bd. jour. 1982-88). Presbyterian. Home: 496 Clarendon Rd Uniondale NY 11553-2106 E-mail: nucnzn@hofstra.edu.

NAYLOR, PAUL DONALD, lawyer; b. St. Bernard, Ohio, May 28, 1925; s. David Frederick and Erna Helen (Miller) N.; m. Geraldine L. Lacy, Jan. 20, 1945; children: Linda S., Paul Scott, Todd L. JD, U. Cin., 1948. Bar: Ohio 1948. Ptnr. Pulse & Naylor, Cin., 1949-65; pvt. practice, 1965—. Mem. Nat. Rep. Com. Lt. (j.g.) USN, 1943-46. Recipient Svc. to Mankind award Sertoma Internat. Mem. Cin. Bar Assn. (real property com. 1966-86), Ohio Bar Assn., Cin. Lawyers Club (pres. 1955), Order of the Coif. Office: 30 E Central Pky Ste 210 Cincinnati OH 45202-1118

NAYLOR, PHYLLIS REYNOLDS, author; b. Anderson, Ind., Jan. 4, 1933; d. Eugene Spencer and Lura Mae (Schield) Reynolds; m. Thomas A. Tedesco, Jr., Sept. 9, 1951 (div. 1960); m. Rex V. Naylor, May 26, 1960; children: Jeffrey, Michael. Diploma, Joliet Jr. Coll., 1953; BA, Am. U., 1963. Author more than 115 books including Crazy Love: An Autobiographical Account of Marriage and Madness, 1977, Revelations, 1979, A String of Chances, 1982 (ALA notable book), The Agony of Alice, 1985 (ALA notable book), The Keeper, 1986 (ALA notable book), Unexpected Pleasures, 1986, Send No Blessings, 1990 (YASD best book for young adults), Shiloh, 1991 (ALA notable book, John Newbery medal 1992). Recipient Golden Kite award Soc. Children's Book Writers Am., 1985, Child Study award Bank St. Coll., 1983, Edgar Allan Poe award Mystery Writers Am., 1985, Internat. book award Soc. Sch. Librs., 1988, Christopher award, 1989, Newbery award ALA, 1992, Nat. Endowment of Arts Creative Writing fellow, 1987. Mem. Children's Book Guild of Washington (pres. 1974-75, 83-84), Soc. Children's Book Writers, Authors Guild, PEN, Council for a Livable World, Physicians for Social Responsibility, Amnesty Internat. Unitarian Universalist. Avocations: theater, swimming. Home and Office: 9910 Holmhurst Rd Bethesda MD 20817-1618

NAYLOR, SUSAN EMBRY, music educator; b. Huntington Park, Calif., Feb. 21, 1951; d. Hollie J. and Sara Mozelle (Maddox) Embry. BM in Piano Performance, Converse Coll., 1973; MM, Ga. State U., 1975. Cert. music tchr. Ga. Prof. piano & music theory Reinhardt Coll., Waleska, Ga., 1975—, coord. music program, 1995-2000. Pvt. piano tchr., Waleska, Marietta, Kennesaw, Ga., 1973—. Performer solo piano and ensemble recitals colls., chs. and profl. orgns., 1973—; pianist Spartanburg (S.C.) Symphony Orch., 1970-73, featured soloist, 1972; guest pianist Nat. Pub. Radio, 1988. Ch. pianist Bapt., Meth. Chs., Marietta, Dallas, Kennesaw, 1973—. Recipient Cobb County Young Artist award Cobb County Arts Coun. Parks & Recreation & Jr. League, 1983, 86. Mem. Ga. Music Tchrs. Assn. (adjudicator 1976—, coll. faculty chair 1996-98, cert. credentials chair 1997—, pres. elect 1998-2000, pres. 2000—), Ga. Fedn. Music Clubs (adjudicator 1976—), Cherokee Music Tchrs. Assn. (pres. 1988-91, 1st v.p. program 1997-99), Cherokee County Arts Coun. (exec. bd., v.p. 1993-95), Music Tchrs. Nat. Assn. (nat. coll. faculty cert., nat. cert. evaluation team 1993-96, hon. dels. 2000—). Baptist. Avocations: collecting antiques, reading. Home: 109 Myrtle Ct Waleska GA 30183-4202 Office: Reinhardt Coll 7300 Reinhardt College Cir Waleska GA 30183-2981 E-mail: sen@reinhardt.edu.

NAYLOR, THOMAS HERBERT, economist, educator, consultant; b. Jackson, Miss., May 30, 1936; s. Thomas Hector and Martha (Watkins) N.; m. Magdalena Raczkowska, Dec. 14, 1985; children: Susanne, Alexander. BS in Math., Millsaps Coll., 1958; BS in Indsl. Engring., Columbia U., 1959; MBA in Quantitative Bus. Analysis, Ind. U., 1961; PhD in Econs., Tulane U., 1964. Instr. Sch. Bus. Adminstrn. Tulane U., 1961-63; asst. prof. econs. Duke U., 1964-66, assoc. prof. econs., 1966-68, prof. econs., 1968-93, prof. emeritus econs., 1994—. Vis. prof. U. Wis., 1969-70, Middlebury Coll., 1993-94, U. Vt., 1994-96; pres. Social Systems, Inc., 1971-80; mng. dir. Naylor Group, 1980; cons., lectr. worldwide. Co-author: (with Eugene Byrne) Linear Programming, 1963, (with Joseph L. Balintfy, Donald S. Burdick and King Chu) Computer Simulation Techniques, 1966, translated into Japanese, Portuguese and Spanish, (with John Vernon) Microeconomics and Decision Models of the Firm, 1969, translated into Spanish, (with James Clotfelter) Strategies for Change in the South, 1975, (with John M. Vernon and Kenneth Wertz) Managerial Economics: Corporate Economics and Strategy, 1983, (with William H. Willimon) The Abandoned Generation: Rethinking Higher Education, 1995, Downsizing the U.S.A., 1997, (with Rolf Österberg and William H. Willimon) The Search for Meaning in the Workplace, 1996, others; author or co-author of 29 books including: Computer Simulation Experiments with Models of Economic Systems, 1971, translated into Spanish, Polish, and Russian, Corporate Planning Models, 1979, Strategic Planning Management, 1980, The Corporate Strategy Matrix, 1986, translated into Hungarian, The Gorbachev Strategy, 1988, The Cold War Legacy, 1991, (with William H. Willimon and Magdalena R. Naylor), The Search for Meaning, 1994; editor: The Impact of the Computer on Society, 1967, The Design of Computer Simulation Experiments, 1969, The Politics of Corporate Planning and Modeling, 1978, Simulation Models in Corporate Planning, 1979, Simulation in Business Planning and Decision Making, 1981, others; co-editor: (with H. Brandt Ayers) You Can't Eat Magnolias, 1972, (with Michele H. Mann) Portfolio Planning and Corporate Strategy, 1983, (with Celia Thomas) Optimization Models for Strategic Planning, 1984, (with John DeGraff), Affluenza, 2001, (with David Wann), The Vermont Manifesto, 2002, others; contbr. numerous articles to profl. publs.; mem. editl. bd. jours. Exec. dir., founder. L.Q.C. Lamar Soc., Washington, 1969-73. Named to Lambda Chi Alpha Alumni Hall of Fame, 1996. Mem.: Lambda Chi, Beta Gamma Sigma, Omicron Delta Kappa. Home: 202 Stockbridge Rd Charlotte VT 05445-9358

NAYLOR-JACKSON, JERRY, public relations consultant, retired, entertainer, broadcaster; b. Chalk Mountain, Tex., Mar. 6, 1939; s. William Guy and Mary Bernice (Lummus) Jackson; m. Pamela Ann Robinson, Jan. 30, 1966; children: Geoffrey K. Naylor, Kelli A. Naylor-Dobrzynski, Gregory K. Naylor. Grad., Elkins Electronics Inst., Dallas, 1957. Life first class radio/TV engring. lic. FCC. Broadcaster various local TV and AM radio stas., San Angelo, Texas, 1955-57; lead singer Buddy Holly and the Crickets, 1960-65; solo entertainer, performer, recording artist and producer, 1965-87; sr. v.p. corp. devel. Newslink Internat. Satellite Broadcast Comms. Co., Inc., Washington, 1986-88; pres. Internat. Syndications, Inc. subs. Newslink, Inc., 1986-88; pres., CEO, owner The Jerry Naylor Co., McMinnville, Oreg., 1984—; v.p. capital programs, sr. cons. Calif. Luth. Univ., Thousand Oaks, 1990-92. Sr. cons., dir. ann. fund Calif. Luth. U., 1989-90; polit./media cons. various Rep. candidates and orgns., 1968-93; spl. cons. to Violeta Barrios de Chamarro, Pres. of Republic of Nicaragua, 1990-92; disc jockey Sta. KHEY-AM, Sta. KINT-AM, El Paso, Tex., 1959; on-air personality Sta. KRLA-AM, Sta. KDAY-AM, L.A., 1960; on-air disc jockey, air personality, celebrity host KLAC-AM, L.A., 1974-83; on-camera and voice-over spokesman for Safeway Stores, Inc., Avis Rent-a-Car, Mut. of Omaha, Wrigley Co., 1968-83; U.S. presdl. appointee, chmn. Job Tng. Partnership Act work group/youth at risk subcom. Nat. Commn. for Employment Policy, 1985-91; nat. dir. spl. events Reagan for Pres., 1979-81; apptd. mem. commn. for employment policy Pres. Ronald Reagan, 1985-91. Recording artist maj. labels including Capitol/Tower Records, Mercury/Smash Records, CBS/Columbia Records, Mole Club Prodns., Motown Records, Warner Bros. Records, EMI Records, 1965-84; solo recording artist, prodr. Phonograph Records and TV Documentaries; host weekly nat. and internat. radio program Continental Country (Number 1 syndicated country music radio show in Am., Billboard Mag., Country Music Assn., 1974), (weekly variety show syndicated tv Desilu Prodns.) Music City, USA, 1966-67. Nat. dir. spl. events Reagan for Pres., 1975-76, 79-80; sr. cons. to White House, 1981-88, 89-92. With U.S. Army, 1957-58, Germany. Named to Top 40 Male Vocalists of Yr., Billboard Mag., 1970, named #1 Rock Group (Crickets), Billboard Mag./New Musical Express Mag., 1958, 62. Mem. NARAS, Country Music Assn., Acad. Country Music (Telly award for TV documentary 1991, 92), Pi Kappa Phi (alumni). Avocation: writing prose and poetry. Home and Office: Jerry Naylor Co 1279 SW Russ Ln Mcminnville OR 97128-5699 *Know no boundaries. Experience the world and become enriched from its varied inhabitants.*

NAYMARK, SHERMAN, consulting nuclear engineer; b. Duluth, Minn., May 12, 1920; s. David N. and Lena (Naymark); children by previous marriage: Ronald L., Janet Naymark Stone. BS in Engring., U.S. Naval Acad., 1941; MS in Engring. and Constrn., MIT, 1946. Sr. scientist Argonne Nat. Lab., (Ill.), 1948-52; dir. reactor div. project, engring. mgr. Schenectady office AEC, 1952-56; with Gen. Electric Co., 1956-70; engring. mgr. nuclear turnkey plants San Jose, 1967-69; pres. Quadrex Corp., Campbell, Calif., 1970-86, chmn., 1986. Lectr. U. Va., MIT, U.S. Naval Res. Officer tng. Schs.; adviser to U.S. del. 3d Internat. Conf. on Peaceful Uses of Atomic Energy, Geneva, 1964; sr. examiner Profl. Engrs. State of Calif., 1960-70 ; mem. fusion power coordinating com. Dept. Energy Contbr. numerous articles on nuclear research, devel., engring. to profl. jours. Served to capt. USN, 1941-54. Fellow Am. Nuclear Soc. (gen. chmn. ann. meeting, nat. treas. 1978-80), nat. treas. (mem. governing bd. Nuclear Tech. 1979-81); mem. AAAS, Am. Pub. Power Assn. (assoc.), U.S. Naval Inst. (hon. life) Democrat. Jewish. Home: 218 Forrester Rd Los Gatos CA 95032-6509 E-mail: snaymark@aol.com.

NAYYAR, MOHINDER LAL, mechanical engineer; b. Jullundur, Punjab, India, Dec. 16, 1943; came to U.S., 1971; s. Dina Nath and Lila (Wati) N.; m. Surendra Prabha Suri, May 23, 1970; children: Mukta Mohi, Manav Mohi, Mahak Mohi. BS in Physics, Chemistry and Math., Agra (Ind.) U., 1963, MA in History, 1969; BE, U. Roorkee, India, 1966. Registered profl. engr., Va.; lic. boiler installer, Mich. Lectr. mech. engring., cons. engr. Tech. Coll., Agra, 1966-71; jr. engr. Charles Besseler Co., Florham Park, N.J., 1971-72; dir. engring. Internat. Inventors, Inc., Alexandria, Va., 1973-74; prin. engr. Bechtel Corp., Gaithersburg, Md., 1974—. Author: (collections of poems) Ghatayen, 1983, Ehsas, 1995, (engring. manual) BPC ISI Manual, 1986, 89; editor-in-chief, author: (engring. handbooks) Piping Handbook, 1992, 1999, Piping Databook, 2002; editor mags. Recipient Outstanding Participation award Nat. Engrs. Week, 1990-91. Fellow ASME (sect. XI task force 1980-81, power piping code com. 1991—, B16 subcom. C 1993—, subcom. B16 N valves 1996—, main com. B16, standardization of valves, flanges, fittings and gaskets, chmn. materials group B31.1, chair B31 materials tech. com., chair B16 redesign task group, vice chair B16 Main com. 2001); mem. Engring. Assn. (sr. pres. 1966-71), UN Club (founding mem.), Internat. Hindi Assn. (founding mem.), Metrication Task Force for Am. Nat. Stds. Inst./ B16.10. Avocations: reading, writing, music, social work. Home: 19405 Prospect Point Ct Brookeville MD 20833-2246 Office: Bechtel Power Corp 5275 Westview Dr Frederick MD 21703-8306

NAZAIRE, MICHEL HARRY, physician; b. Jérémie, Haiti, Sept. 29, 1939; s. Joseph and Hermance N.; m. Nicole Lamarque, Dec. 28, 1968; children: Hannick and Carline (twins). *Daughters Carline and Hannick, born in 1970, are living in New York: Carline is currently employed as administrative assistant by Rheinbraun Thyssen Inc. Carline is also married and has a son named Gabriel.Hanick attended City College during four years,studying education.* BS, DOE, Port-Au-Prince, Haiti, 1959; MD Faculty of Medicine and Pharmacology, State U. Haiti, 1966. Intern State U. Hosp., Port-Au-Prince, Haiti, 1965-66; resident physician Sanitarium, Haiti, 1966-68; practice medicine specializing in pneumology, 1966-68; practice medicine specializing in pneumo-physiology Port-Au-Prince, 1966—; physician fellow Klinik Havelhohe and Heckeshorn, Berlin, 1969-70, 89-91; attending physician Sanitarium, Port-Au-Prince, 1976-91. Dep. mem. Internat. Parliament for Safety and Peace, envoy-at-large Internat. State Parliament, mem. global environ. technol. newtwork Who. Contbr. articles to Jour. Indsl. Hygiene, Pneumology and Respiratory Protection. Fellow Internat. Soc. for Respiratory Protection, Am. Coll. Chest Physicians (assoc.), mem. Am. Pub. Health Assn., Am. Conf. Govtl. Indsl. Hygienists, Internat. Union Against Tuberculosis, Internat. Platform Assn., Physicians for Social Responsibility. Address: 2455 "F" St SE Apt 57 Auburn WA 98002 also: 1115-25 Dorchester Rd #3C Brooklyn NY 11218

NAZARIAN, JOHN, academic administrator, mathematics educator; b. Pawtucket, R.I., Sept. 6, 1932; s. Zakie and Amenia (Nahas) N. EdB, R.I. Coll., 1954; AM, Brown U., 1956; MA, U. Ill., 1961; PhD, NYU, 1967. Instr. math. R.I. Coll., Providence, 1954-58, asst. prof., 1958-67, assoc. prof., 1967-71, prof., 1971—, assoc. dean Arts and Scis., 1970-72, spl. asst. to pres., 1971-77, v.p. adminstrn. and fin., 1977-90, pres., 1990—. Chmn., vice-chmn. Arabic Ednl. Found., Pawtucket, 1966-72; chmn. Sargeant Rehab. Ctr, Providence, 1983-86, Diocesan Pastoral Coun., West Newton, Mass., 1974-78; chmn. Diocesan Fin. Coun., 1996-. Recipient Cross of Jerusalem, Patriarch of Melkite Ch., 1976. Avocations: music, golf, reading. Office: RI Coll Roberts Hall 404 600 Mount Pleasant Ave Providence RI 02908-1924 E-mail: jnazarian@ric.edu.*

NAZARIAN, LAWRENCE FRED, pediatrician; b. N.Y.C., May 17, 1940; s. Samuel George and Winifred Lucia (Zotian) N.; m. Sharon Louise Carlson, June 22, 1963; children: Douglas, Stephen, Sarah. BA, Yale U., 1960; MD, U. Rochester, 1964. Pediatrician Panorama Pediatric Group, Rochester, N.Y., 1969—; clin. prof. pediatrics U. Rochester (N.Y.) Sch. Medicine and Dentistry, 1969—. Bd. dirs. James P. Wilmot Found., Rochester. Contbr. articles to profl. jours.; assoc. editor Pediatrics in Rev. Jour., 1990—. Mem. troop com. Boy Scouts Am., Penfield, N.Y., 1978-88; mem. coun. com. Luth. Ch. of Reformation, Rochester, 1969—. Maj. USAR, 1967-69. Fellow Am. Acad. Pediatrics; mem. Med. Soc. State of N.Y., Ctrl. N.Y. Pediatric Club, Monroe County Med. Soc., Rochester Acad. Medicine, Rochester Pediatric Soc. Avocations: hiking, camping, canoeing, gardening, cross-country skiing. Office: Panorama Pediatric Group 220 Linden Oaks Rochester NY 14625-2839

NAZAROFF, WILLIAM W. engineering educator; b. Lynwood, Calif., Sept. 3, 1955; s. William George and Barbara J. Nazaroff; m. Ingrid Elsa Hamann; children: Rani Hamann-Nazaroff, Alexis Hamann-Nazaroff, Daniela Hamann-Nazaroff. AB in Physics, U. Calif., Berkeley, 1978, MEng in Elec. Engring. and Computer Sci., 1980; PhD in Environ. Engring. Sci., Calif. Inst. Tech., 1989. Staff scientist Lawrence Berkeley Lab., Berkeley, Calif., 1980—84; prof. U. Calif., 1989—. Author: Environmental Engineering Science, 2001; editor: Radon and Its Decay Products in Indoor Air, 1988. Mem.: Internat. Acad. Indoor Air Scis. (chair membership com. 1996—99), Am. Assn. Aerosol Rsch. (bd. dirs. 1999—2002). Office: U Calif CEE Dept 631 Davis Hall Berkeley CA 94720-1710 Business E-Mail: nazaroff@ce.berkeley.edu.

NAZEM, FEREYDOUN F. venture capitalist, financier; b. Tehran, Iran, Dec. 29, 1940; came to U.S., 1960; naturalized, 1976; s. Hassan and Afsar N.; m. Susie Gharib, Jan. 20, 1973; children: Alexander, Taraneh. BS, Ohio State U., 1964; MSc, U. Cin., 1967; MBA, Columbia U., 1971. Sr. rsch. chemist Matheson Coleman & Bell, Norwood, Ohio, 1967-68; asst. v.p., investment analyst Irving Trust Co., N.Y.C., 1969-74; v.p., venture capital officer Charter N.Y., 1974-75; mng. dir. Collier Enterprises, 1976-81; mng. ptnr. Nazem & Co., 1981—, Explorer Fund, N.Y.C., 1997—, Transatlantic Venture Fund, 1998—. Bd. dirs. Genetix Corp., Boston, IQ Net Solutions, Boston, Oxford Health, Norwalk, Conn., Aliaswire, Boston, Munshee Corp., N.Y.C. Author: The Chemical Industry and Energy Shortage; author monthly Market Letter. Mem. N.Y. Soc. Security Analysts, Venture Investor Assn. N.Y. Office: Nazem & Co 645 Madison Ave New York NY 10022-1010 E-mail: fnazem@nazem.com. *Don't take activity for progress or comfort for civility. Set aside a peaceful hour a day to get in touch with the divinity within you.*

NAZETTE, RICHARD FOLLETT, lawyer; b. Eldora, Iowa, July 27, 1919; s. Hilmer H. and Genevieve A. (Follett) N.; m. Joan Chehak, June 20, 1942; children— Ronald D., Randall A. BA, U. Iowa, 1942, JD with distinction, 1946. Bar: Iowa bar 1946. Practiced in, Cedar Rapids, 1946—; partner firm Nazette, Marner, Wendt, Knoll & Usher, 1968—; asst. atty. Linn County, Iowa, 1951-56; county atty., 1957-63. Dir. United States Bank, Cedar Rapids, 1968-91, State Surety Co., Des Moines, 1966-78 Bd. dirs. Linn County Health Center, 1968-73, chmn., 1968-69; mem. Iowa Bd. Parole, 1981-84. Served with AUS, 1942-44. Fellow Am. Bar Found., Iowa Bar Assn. (bd. govs. 1972-76), Iowa State Bar Found.; mem. Linn County Bar Assn. (pres. 1963), Iowa County Attys. Assn. (pres. 1959), Iowa Acad. Trial Lawyers (pres. 1964), Sigma Phi Epsilon. Clubs: Masons, Shriners, Jesters, Elks, Optimists (internat. v.p. 1955). Republican. Presbyterian. Home: 2224 Country Club Pkwy SE Cedar Rapids IA 52403-1639 Office: 100 1st St SW Cedar Rapids IA 52404-5701 E-mail: r.nazette@nazmar.com.

NAZZARO, DAVID ALFRED, sales executive; b. Malden, Mass., Sept. 15, 1940; s. Alfred Anthony and Louise (Cunningham) N.; m. Jane Valentine, June 26, 1971; one child, David Thomas. BME, U.S. Mcht. Marine Acad., 1962; MS, Columbia U., 1965; MBA, Pepperdine U., 1975. Regional mgr. Turbo Power and Marine Systems divsn. United Techs., Hardford, Conn., 1965-74; mgr. bus. devel S & Q Corp., San Francisco, 1974-78; v.p. and gen. mgr. Con-Val, Oakland, Calif., 1978-85; pres. and chief exec. officer Dasa Controls, Belmont, 1985-87; mgr. bus. devel Johnson Yokogawa Corp., San Francisco, 1987-94; prin. Nazzaro and Assocs. Fin. Cons., 1994—. Bd. dirs. Community Action Agy., 1998—, Peninsula Exch. Contbr. papers to profl. publs. Bd. dirs. Clearview Homeowners Assn., San Mateo, 1976; pres. St. Bartholomew's Parish Council, San Mateo, 1986. Lt. USNR, 1963-69. Sr. Mem. Instrument Soc. Am. (pres. No. Calif. Sec. 1987-88); mem. ASME, Am. Water Works Assn., Elks, Jaycees, St. Bartholomew's Mens Club (pres. 1977). Avocations: skiing, tennis, racquetball, handball, bridge. Home: 30 Tollridge Ct San Mateo CA 94402-3730 E-mail: danazzaro@aol.com.

NDEGWA, PIUS MWANGI, agricultural engineer, researcher; b. Nyeri, Kenya, Nov. 23, 1961; came to U.S., 1988; s. Ndegwa Nyanja and Sabina Wangui Ndegwa; m. Grace Naesiae, July 1, 1995; 1 child, Ndegwa Mwangi. BS in Agrl. Engring., U. Nairobi, Kenya, 1986; MS in Agrl. Engring., U. Ga., 1990, PhD Biology & Agrl. Engring., 1999. Engr. in tng., Minn. Asst. engr. Dept. Agrl., Nairobi, 1986-88, project engr., 1990-93; rsch. asst. U. Ga., Athens, 1988-90, 95-99; lectr. U. Nairobi, 1993-95; rsch. assoc. U. Minn., Waseca, 1999—. Contbr. articles to profl. jours. Mem. Am. Soc. Agrl. Engrs., Kenyan Soc. Agrl. Engrs. (assoc.), Gamma Sigma Delta. Avocations: travel, reading. Office: Oklahoma State Univ 120th Ag Hall Stillwater OK 74078 E-mail: ndegw001@tc.umn.edu.

NDENGA, LUCY VIOLA, librarian; b. Manning, Ark., Aug. 1, 1933; d. Samuel Peter and Naomi Tommie Lee Watson; 1 child, Peter Andrew Watson Ndenga. BS cum laude, Philander Smith Coll., 1957; MLS, U. Wash., 1962; postgrad., U. Minn., 1973-76. Mem. faculty reference libr. Lewis & Clark Coll., Portland, Oreg., 1962-63; reference libr. U. Wash., Seattle, 1963-67; head reference libr., instr. U. Minn., St. Paul, 1967-73; head libr., faculty, audio visual dir. Bishop Whipple Schs., Faribault, Minn., 1976-78; head libr., computer tape libr. Jud. Data Ctr. Mich. Supreme Ct., Detroit, 1978-80; asst. editor Gale Rsch. Publ. Co., 1982-83; dir. McGregor Pub. Libr., Highland Park, Mich., 1983—. Bd. dirs. YWCA No. Br., Detroit, Detroit Unity Temple, sec. 1990-93; active Democrats. Mem. ALA (pub. rels. com.), Nat. Assn. Univ. Women (v.p. 1990-93), Mich. Libr. Assn. (continuing edn. and profl. stds. com.), Detroit Assn. Libr. Coop. (exec. staff), Mich. Libr. Consortium (trustee). Office: McGregor Pub Libr 12244 Woodward Ave Highland Park MI 48203-3320

NDIBO, IRENE N. investment advisor; BA in Polit. Sci., Bryn Mawr Coll., 1996. Analyst Goldman Sachs & Co., N.Y.C., 1996—98, assoc., 1999—. Active Abysinnian Bapt. Ch., N.Y.C., 1999—. Mem.: Bryn Mawr Coll. Alumnae Assn. Home: 7 Whalen Ct West Orange NJ 07052

NDIKUM, PHILIP FORSANG, barrister; Grad. in Econs., History and Geography, Cameroon Coll. Arts Sci. and Tech., 1979; diploma in Airline Safety, Internat. First Aid, Hotel Mgmt., Ecole Nat. D'Aviation Civile/Air France, 1980; diploma in Internat. Human Rights and Jurisprudence, Internat. Human Rights Program, Strasbourg, France, 1996; LLB with honors, U. Luton, Eng., 1997; LLM, U. Minn., 1999; program in Fin. Acctg., Met. State U., 2001; JD, William Mitchell Coll. of Law, 2002; diploma in Profl. Legal Skills, City U., London, 2002; postgrad., Inns of Court Sch. Law, London. Flight attendant Cameroon Airlines, 1979—95; entrepreneur, founder, pres. Gen. Modern Enterprises, Internat. Ltd., 1980—95; lawyer Macha Sinegre-David/Agnes Pannier, Paris, 1994—2000; grad. asst. U. Minn. Human Rights Ctr., 1998—99; law clk. to Judge Nancy Dreher U.S. Bankruptcy Ct., Mpls., 1998—99. Prodr., editor Cameroon Copyright Corp. Mem.: ABA, Nat. Health Assn., Minn. Bar Assn., Hennepin County Bar Assn., Minn. Black Lawyers Assn., Minn. State Bar Assn., Am. Immigration Lawyers Assn., Assn. Trial Lawyers Am., Lincoln's Inn, Rotary Club Internat., Toast Masters Internat., Lions Club Internat., Phi Delta Phi. Home: 286 W Arlington Ave # 303 Saint Paul MN 55117

NEADERLAND, LOUISE ODES, artist, educator, professional society executive; b. Bklyn., Aug. 23, 1932; m. Ralph Neaderland, July 13, 1967; children: Zoe, Ben. BA, Bard Coll., 1954; MFA in Printmaking, State U. Iowa, 1957. Artist, tchr. various instns., 1957—. Founder, dir. Internat. Soc. Copier Artists, Ltd., 1982—. Artist (book) Lifesense/License (NEA award), 1985, Where is Home?, 1989; creater, prodr. visual books: Artist at Work, 1982, A Book of Short Stories, 1986, The Case for Gun Control, 1994, Desert Storm/Desert Sand, 1991, Dialogues, 1990, The Disposable History of the World, 1986, Distress Signals, 1985,m Empress Bullet 1982, Farewells, 1990, Hazardous Waste, 1996, The Heart of Lightness, 1983, High Falls, 1982, numerous others; painter, printmaker Fellowship Huntington Hartford, 1960, 62; books represented in collections at the Met. Mus., N.Y.C., Bklyn. Mus. Art, Tate Galleries, London, King Stephan Mus., Budapest, Minn. Ctr. for Book Arts, Columbia Coll., South Bend Ind. Mus. Yale/Norfolk scholar, Yale U. Art Sch., Norfolk, Conn., 1953; recipient scholarship Bard Coll., 1950-54. Avocations: photography, wood carving, carpentry. Address: ISCA 759 President St Apt 2H Brooklyn NY 11215-1362 E-mail: isca4art2b@aol.com.

NEAL, ALAINE (DIANN NEAL), nursing administrator; b. Seaside, Oreg., Jan. 25, 1942; d. Alan Welch Jr. and Beatrice June (Wisdom) Smith; m. Kelly Sayre Neal Jr., July 31, 1965; children: Kelly III, Karter B. BS, U. Portland, 1964; MS, U. Ariz., 1970. RNC in in-patient obstetrics, nursing adminstrn. advanced. Head nurse Family Childbirth Ctr. St. Joseph's Hosp. and Med. Ctr., Phoenix, 1982-87, nurse mgr. maternal-newborn svcs., 1987-90, dir. nursing women's and children's svcs., 1990-95; dir. pediatrics and nursery, pediatric intensive care Desert Samaritan Med. Ctr., Mesa, Ariz., 1995-2000; dir. women's nad infants svcs. St. Joseph's Hosp., Carondelet Health Network, Tucson, 2000—. Author: (with others) High-Risk Intrapartum Nursing, 1992. Capt. Nurse Corps, U.S. Army, 1964-67. Mem. Sigma Theta Tau. Episcopalian. Avocations: equestrian, genealogy, cooking. Office: 225 W Spring Valley Dr Tucson AZ 85737-6745 E-mail: dneal@carondelet.org.

NEAL, ANITA, artist; b. Glendale, Calif., June 13, 1929; d. Frank Bartholdy and Dora Mae (Jones) Mendelssohn; m. James Truman Dowdle, Jan. 17, 1948 (dec. Nov. 1969); children: Doug Dowdle, Wendy Grobe; m. Albert Dale Neal, July 2, 1971. AA, Golden West Coll., 1981; ind. study art, culture and calligraphy, China, 2000; ind. study, Alphonsa Mucha, Chez Republic, 2002. Lic. real estate agt., Calif.; cert. Coastline C.C. Dist. Tchg. Host Friends of Artists for Cultural Exch., 1988; judge Ms. Sr. Am. Pageant, 1989—91; founder The ANCA Group. Exhibited in group shows New Calif. Mus. of Sci. and Industry, L.A., 1968, New Art in N.Y., N.Y.C., 1985, Laguna Art Mus., Laguna Beach, Calif., 1986, Loyola Marymount U., Orange, Calif., 1986, Bowers Mus., Santa Ana, Calif., 1987, Expo Site Plaza of Nations, Vancouver, 1988, Irvine (Calif.) Fine Arts Ctr., 1989, Chautauqua Invitational Exhibit U. Calif., Irvine, 1989, Berkley (Calif.) U., 1994, U. Calif., Irvine, 1999; artist in charge of Orange County, Calif., children's mural Imagination Celebration, NEA, Washington, 1987-96; performance artist Richard Bennett Gallery, L.A., 1989; prodr.: (shows) Coconut Grove-Calif. Girl, L.A., 1970; prodr., publicist Airport, City of Santa Monica, 1968; featured artist: How to Market Fine Art by Sally Prince Davis. Sponsor 32 artists Anita Neal Contemporary Art, Laguna Beach, 1986-87; mem. artist coun. bd. Laguna Art Mus., Laguna Beach, 1986; mem. allied arts bd. City of Huntington Beach, Calif., 1988; sponsor So. Calif. Artists, Anita Neal Gallery, Fawnskin, Calif., 1994—. Co-winner Mademoiselle mag. writing contest, 1970; recipient LULU award Women in Advt., 1968, New Art in New York (NANY) award, 1985. Mem. Am. Portrait Soc., Artist's Equity Assn. (L.A. chpt.), Orange County Visual Artists, L.A. Inst. Contemporary Art, Nat. Mus. Women in Arts (charter), L.A. Contemporary Art Assocs., Coun. of Arts State of Calif. Artist Registry, Alpha Gamma Sigma (Sigma Pi chpt.). Republican. Avocations: airplane pilot, European museum studies, helping emerging artists, writing poetry. Home: 17272 Blue Fox Cir Huntington Beach CA 92647-5602 Studio: Anita Neal Gallery 1063 Fawnskin Dr Fawnskin CA 92333 E-mail: fineart4u2@aol.com.

NEAL, BENNIE F. secondary school administrator; b. Manchester, Ga., June 13, 1956; s. Issac and Arrie Bell (Dunn) N.; m. Dianna Lynn Thompson; children: Tiffany Annette, Bennie Jr., Brittany Denette, Joseph Edward. BS, Ft. Valley State Coll., 1979; MEd in Adminstrn., Cleve. State U., 1997. Cert. tchr. reading, K-12 history. Reading tchr., boys track coach Glenville H.S., 1989-91; tchr., boys jr. varsity basketball coach Willson Middle Sch./E. Cleve. Pub. Schs., Cleve., 1991-95; asst. prin. Shaw H.S. Adj. prof. Bryant & Stratton Coll. Contbg. writer: Stakeholders, 1992—. Chaplain East 92d St. Club, Cleve., 1985—; chmn. deacon bd., fin. sec. Fidelity Bapt. Ch., Cleve., 1992; mem. Summer Writing Inst., Cleve., 1990, Project Elan, Cleve., 1992-93, Lillian Hinds Reading Orgn., Cleve., 1989-94; cubmaster Boy Scouts Am., 1990—; del., leader Lake Erie Girl Scouts, 1996—. Recipient Plain Dealer Crystal Apple award, 1992-95, Cleve. Cavaliers Tchr. of Mo., 1995, Tchr. of the Yr., Ashland Oil Co., 1996. Mem. Emerald Necklace Tchr. Network (pres. 1995), Cleve. Tchrs. Union (union bldg. chair 1992-93), Phi Delta Kappa, Alpha Phi Alpha (v.p. 1977-78, 93—). Baptist. Avocations: chess/checkers, coaching, reading, teaching. Home: 1347 E 92nd St Cleveland OH 44106-1035

NEAL, BONNIE JEAN, real estate agent; b. Kansas City, Mo. d. David Ira and Juanita Mae (Duncan) Johnson; m. Howard Stranton Neal, July 24, 1948 (div. Oct. 1972); children: Randall Stranton, William Scott, Douglas Kelly. Student, U. Omaha, 1980-86, Londay Sch. Real Estate, Omaha, 1987. Lic. real estate broker. Data processing supr. Enron Corp., Omaha, 1980-85, adminstrv. support analyst, 1985-86; real estate sales agt. Allen, Young Assocs., 1987, Home Real Estate (merger Allen Young Assocs. and Wurdeman & Maenner), Omaha, 1988; with Coldwell Banker Action Real Estate, 1988-91, Coldwell Banker BJ Brown, La Vista, Nebr., 1991-92. Active PTA, Council Bluffs, Iowa, 1957-59; vol. March of Dimes, Council Bluffs, 1963; mem. Realtors Polit. Action Com.; mem. pub. rels. com. Bd. Realtors, 1994-2000, mem. forms com., 1995-96. Fellow Omaha Bd. Realtors, Women's Bowling Assn., Order Ea. Star (25-Yr. award 1980); mem. Women's Coun. Realtors. Democrat. Baptist. Avocations: music, piano, water sports, bicycling, motor sports. Home and Office: CBS Home Real Estate 14250 W Maple Rd Omaha NE 68164-2436

NEAL, DARWINA LEE, government official; b. Mansfield, Pa., Mar. 31, 1942; d. Darwin Leonard and Ina Belle (Cooke) N. BS, Pa. State U., 1965; postgrad., Cath. U, 1968-70. Registered landscape architect. Landscape architect nat. capital region Nat. Pk. Svc., 1965-69, office of White House liaison, 1969-71, office of profl. services, 1971-74, div. design svcs., 1974-89, chief design svcs., 1989-95, chief landscape arch. office of stewardship and partnership, 1996-98, chief cultural resource preservation svcs. nat. capital reg., 1998—. Judge numerous award juries. Contbr. articles to profl. jours.; co-author sects. of profl. bull., mag.; author introduction to book Women, Design and the Cambridge School; columnist: Land monthly, 1975-79. Treas. U.S. Internat. coun. on Monuments and Sites, 1998—. Recipient Merit award Landscape Contractors Met. Washington; recipient hon. mention Les Floralies Internat. Montreal, 1980 Alumni Achievement award Pa. State U. Arts and Architecture Alumni Soc., 1981 Fellow Am. Soc. Landscape Architects (v.p. 1979-81, pres. elect 1982-83, pres. 1983-84, trustee 1976-77, nat. treas. 1977-79, legis. coord. 1975-79, sec. Coun. Fellows 1988-90, del. to Internat. Fedn. Landscape Architects 1989-92, 2000—, ex-officio rep. to U.S./internat. coun. on monuments and sites 1985-98, liaison to historically black coll. and univ. program Dept. Interior, chair internat. task force 1999-2000, Pres.' medal 1987); mem. Landscape Archtl. Accreditation Bd. (roster vis. evaluators), Nat. Recreation and Parks Assn., Nat. Soc. Park Resources (bd. dirs. 1978-80), Nat. Trust Hist. Preservation, Pa. State U. Alumni Assn. (Washington met. chpt. trustee 1972-74), Am. Arbitration Assn. (nat. panel arbitrators), Com. 100 for the Fed. City, Preservation Action, Nat. Assn. Olmsted Parks, Beekman Pl. Condominium Assn. (bd. dirs. 1985-91, archtl. control com. 1977-2000, landscape com. 2000-02), Alliance for Historic Preservation, Garden Conservancy, Scenic Am., Preservation Action, Preservation Roundtable, Hist. Soc. Washington. Office: Nat Park Svc/Nat Capital Region Off Lands Resources & Plan 1100 Ohio Dr SW Washington DC 20242-0001

NEAL, DENNIS MELTON, middle school administrator; b. Lakeland, Fla., Feb. 7, 1966; s. M. H. and Alice Marie (Twiddy) N.; m. Christine Anne Rufo, Oct. 21, 1989; children: Lauren Elizabeth, Waverly Rose, Emma Katherine. AA, Polk C.C., Winter Haven, Fla., 1987; BS, Fla. So. Coll., 1991; MEd, Stetson U., 1995. Cert. elem. tchr., ednl. leader, prin., Fla. Guest svcs. Cypress gardens, Winter Haven, 1985-86; entertainer Boardwalk and Baseball, Baseball City, Fla., 1986-88; guest svcs. Hilton Walt Disney World, Orlando, 1988-91; tchr. Deltona (Fla.) Middle Sch., 1991-95, asst. prin., 1995-99, Heritage Middle Sch., Deltona, Fla., 1999-2000; prin. intern Pine Ridge H.S., 2000—. Chair correlate com., team leader Deltona Middle Sch., sch. adv. coun. Tchr. Lith. Ch. of Providence, Orange City, Fla., 1992-93; active Parent, Tchr., Student Assn. Named One of Top 100 Beginning Tchrs. in Nation, Sallie Mae Student Loan Assn., 1992. Avocations: soccer, racquetball, drawing, painting. Home: 2939 Owen Ct Deltona FL 32738-1846

NEAL, EDWARD GARRISON, lawyer; b. Abingdon, Va., Mar. 20, 1940; s. James Wiley Neal and Edna Mae (Felty) Millsap; children: Jay Garrison, Heather Leigh; m. Diane T. Neal, Feb. 16, 2002. BA, Fla. State U., 1962; JD, U. Balt., 1966; LLM, George Washington U., Washington, 1969. Bar: Md. 1966, U.S. Dist. Ct. Md. 1968, U.S. Supreme Ct. 1972. Asst. trust officer Md. Nat. Bank, Balt., 1964-66; gen. counsel Hatch Act Study Commn., Washington, 1967; exec. asst. U.S. Sen. Daniel Brewster, 1966-68; asst. states atty. Office of States Atty., Balt., 1968-71; chief criminal div. States Atty. Prince George's County, Upper Marlboro, 1971-76; assoc. county atty. Prince George's County Office of Law, 1976-79; pvt. practice College Park, Md., 1979—. Law lectr. Prince Georges County and Md. State Police Acads., 1971—76, U.S. Secret Svc., Fed. Law Enforcement Tng. Ctr., 2000—; legal advisor Office Tech. Assistance U.S. Treasury Dept., Moldova, 1999. Vice chmn. Women's Sexual Assault Commn., Upper Marlboro, Md., 1974—75; pres. PTA Concordia Luth. Sch., Hyattsville, 1976—77; Dem. precinct chmn. University Park, 1972—80; trustee Rossborough Festival, Kapell Internat. Piano Competition, College Park, 1986—89, 1989—. Recipient cert. of Appreciation, Prince George's County Coun., Upper Marlboro, Md., 1975. Mem.: Nat. Dist. Attys. Assn. (scholarship award 1968, 1970, 1975, 1976), Md. State's Attys. Assn. (legislative liaison Md. Gen. Assembly 1972—76), Md. State Bar Assn. (various coms.), George Washington U. Alumni Assn. (bd. dirs. 1980—), Kiwanis, Phi Alpha Delta (dist. v.p. 1962—, pres. 1963). Episcopalian. Avocations: music, reading, tennis, basketball, bridge. Home: Ste 1613 6100 Westchester Park Dr College Park MD 20740-2847 Office: 7309 Baltimore Ave Ste 117 College Park MD 20740-3200

NEAL, E(VERETT) G(ILBERT), sculptor, clown, small business owner; b. Nov. 8, 1946; BSBA, U. Tulsa, 1976. Gen. coord. Praxis Project, Tulsa, 1977-78; owner, mgr. NEAL HT, Inc., 1982—; pres. Nonprofit Exhibits, Inc., 1996—. Pres. Tulsa Artists' Coalition, 1995-96. Work recorded in archives of Mus. of Am. Folk Art, N.Y.C. Office: 5916 E Tecumseh St Tulsa OK 74115-4322 E-mail: everettneal@hotmail.com.

NEAL, FLORENCE ARTHUR, artist; b. Columbus, Ga., Nov. 12, 1954; d. Edward Warner and Mary Ann Neal; m. W. Scott Pfaffman, July 14, 1979 (div. Mar. 1995); m. Michael J. Kowalski, Oct. 28, 2000. BFA, Auburn U., 1976. Established Everglade Press, Bklyn., 1985—; co-founder, dir. Kentler Internat. Drawing Space, Bklyn., 1990—; artist-in-residence Mid-Atlantic States Arts Consortium, Balt., 1987. Exhibited in group shows at White Columns, N.Y.C., 1981, Orgn. Internat. Artists, Hanalei, Hawaii, 1985, Socrates Sculpture, L.I., N.Y., 1985, Willis Gallery, Detroit, 1988, Art Omaha, 1990, Hermit Internat. Art Symposium, Czech Republic, 1993, Kunstinitiatief L5, Roermond, The Netherlands, 1995. Pollock-Krasner Found. grantee, 1989; recipient Honoria N.Y. State Coun. Arts-Prospect Park, 1988. Mem. Red Hook Civic Assn. Office: Kentler Internat Drawing Space 353 Van Brunt St Brooklyn NY 11231-1245 E-mail: florence@kentlergallery.org.

NEAL, GAIL FALLON, physical therapist, educator; b. New Haven, May 6, 1938; d. Edward Francis and Ruth Alexina (Hutchinson) Fallon; m. Marcus Pinson Neal Jr.; children: Sandra Neal Dawson, Marcus Pinson III, Ruth-Catherine Neal Perkins. Student, Mary Washington Coll., 1955-57; BS in Phys. Therapy, Med. Coll. Va., 1959. Lic. phys. therapist. Staff phys. therpist Univ. Hosps., U. Wis., Madison, 1959-61; chief phys. therapy Stoughton (Wis.) Cmty. Hosp., 1961-63; vol. phys. therapy Cerebral Palsy Ctr., Richmond, Va., 1963-64; pvt. practice in phys. therapy, 1965-68; interim dir. Stuart Cir. Hosp., 1968-69; phys. therpist on call St. Mary's Hosp., 1968-74; pres., owner Capital Phys. Therapy Assocs., 1989—. Part-time phys. therapist St. Mary's Hosp., Richmond, 1975-88; lectr. Med. Coll. Va., Richmond, 1992, 93, John Tyler C.C., Richmond, 1992, 93, 94; mem. adv. bd. phys. therapy Va. State Bd. Medicine, 1990-96, vice chmn., 1992-93, chmn. 1995-96. Mem. adv. bd. Va. Opera, 1979—; bd. visitors Mary Washington Coll., Fredericksburg, Va., 1980-82, rector bd. visitors, 1982-84; pres. Richmond Symphony Orch. League, 1986-88. Named Clubwoman of Yr., Richmond Newsleader, 1972. Mem. Am. Phys. Therapy Assn., Richmond Acad. Medicine Aux. (pres. 1967-68), Med. Soc. Va. Alliance (pres. 1980-81), Med. Coll. Va. Hosps. Aux. (pres. 1973-75), Va. Cultural Laureate Soc. Avocations: reading, music, skiing, Indian folklore. Office: Capital Phys Therapy Assocs 1919 Huguenot Rd Ste 201 Richmond VA 23235-4321 Home: 7301 Riverside Dr Richmond VA 23225-1066

NEAL, HOMER ALFRED, physics educator, researcher, university administrator; b. Franklin, Ky., June 13, 1942; s. Homer and Margaret Elizabeth (Holl) Neal; m. Donna Jean Daniels, June 16, 1962; children: Sharon Denise, Homer Alfred. BS in Physics with honors, Ind. U., 1961; MS in Physics (John Hay Whitney fellow), U. Mich., 1963, PhD in Physics, 1966. Asst. prof. physics Ind. U., 1967—70, assoc. prof., 1970—72, prof., 1972—81, dean research and grad. devel., 1976—81; prof. physics SUNY, Stony Brook, 1981—87, provost, 1981—86; prof. physics, chmn. U. Mich., Ann Arbor, 1987—93, v.p. rsch., 1993—97, interim pres., 1996—97, prof. of physics, 1987—2000, Samuel A. Goudsmit disting. prof. physics, 2000—, dir. of atlas project, 1997—. Bd. dirs. Ford Motor Co., Covanta Corp.; mem. Nat. Sci. Bd., 1980—86; mem. adv. coun. Oak Ridge Nat. Lab., 1993—99; mem. external adv. coun. Nat. Computational Sci. Alliance, 1997—; mem. applications strategy coun. Univ. Corp. for Advanced Internet Devel., 2000—; chmn. Argonne Zero Gradient Synchrotron Users Group, 1970—72; trustee Argonne Univs. Assn., 1971—74, 1977—80; physics adv. panel NSF, 1976—79, chmn. physics adv. panel, 1987—89; high energy physics adv. panel U.S. Dept. Energy, 1977—81. Contbr. articles to profl. jours. Mem. bd. regents Smithsonian Instn., 1989—; trustee Ctr. for Strategic and Internat. Studies, 1990—2000; Oak Ridge (Tenn.) Nat. Lab., 1993—; mem. bd. overseers Superconducting Super Collider, 1989—93; trustee Environ. Rsch. Inst. of Mich., 1994—96; N.Y. Sea Grant Inst., 1982—86. Recipient Stony Brook medal, 1986, Ind. U. Disting. Alumni award, 1994; fellow NSF, 1966—67, Sloan, 1968, Guggenheim, 1980—81. Fellow: AAAS, Am. Acad. Arts and Scis., Am. Phys. Soc.; mem.: Univs. Rsch. Assn., Sigma Xi. Office: Dept of Physics Rm 2477 Randall Lab 500 East University Ann Arbor MI 48109-1120

NEAL, IRENE COLLINS, artist, educator; b. Greensburg, Pa., May 14, 1936; d. Oliver Shupe and Betsey Cowap (Mann) Collins; m. Paul Whitaker Neal, Nov. 24, 1960; children: Paul Collins Gordon, Betsey Whitaker. BA, Wilson Coll., 1958; student, Sch. Visual Arts, Rio de Janeiro, 1976-77, Memphis State U., 1979-80, U. Bridgeport, 1982-83; participant, Triangle Art Workshop, Pine Planes, N.Y., 1985. Guest spkr. Coll. Santa Fe, Albuquerque, N.Mex., 1994. One-woman shows include Allied Chem. Corp., Morristown, N.J., 1975, Planetarium Rio de Janeiro, 1977, Pat Ackerman Gallery, Memphis, 1980, Westmoreland Mus. Art, Greensburg, 1986, Wilson Coll., 1993, Cooper Classics Collections, N.Y.C., 2001, 02; group exhbns. include Jersey City Mus., 1975, N.J. State Mus., 1975, Somerset (N.J.) Tri-State Mus., 1975, Nat. Arts Club, N.Y.C., 1975, Garden State Watercolor Soc., 1975, Salao de Marinhas, Rio de Janeiro, 1977, Stamford Mus., 1984, 85, 89, Branchville Soho Gallery, Ridgefield, Conn., 1984, Silvermine Guild, New Canaan, Conn., 1984, Stamford Libr., 1985, Shippee Gallery, N.Y.C., 1986, 110 Greene St., N.Y.C., 1986, Wilton (Conn.) Libr., 1986, Aldrich Mus. Contemporary Art, Ridgefield, 1987, Visual Arts Festival, Edmonton, Alta., Can., 1989, Mus. Art, Ft. Lauderdale, Fla., 1991-92, Salander-O'Reilly Galleries, Inc., N.Y., 1994, Vanderleelie Gallery, Edmonton, 1996, Galerie Piltzer, Paris, 1996, Fine Art 2000 Gallery, Stamford, 1996, 97, York Coll., Queens, N.Y., 1997, Ctr. for Performing Arts, Stamford, 1997, Mus. Contemporary Art, Palm Beach, Fla., 1997, Griffis Art Ctr., New London, 1997, Vero Beach (Fla.) Mus., 1998, Flint (Mich.) Inst. Art, 1999, Mus. Contemporary Art, Denver, 1999, Gelabert Studios Gallery, N.Y.C., 2000, Hotel de Ville, Brussels, 2000, 69th Regiment Armory, N.Y.C., New New Painters, The Real Avant Garde, 2000, Nat. Gallery, Prague, The Czech Repub., 2001, 2002 Galerie Anne-Lettrie, Paris, 2001; represented in permanent collections Planetarium Rio de Janeiro, Internat. Paper, N.Y.C., Westmoreland Mus. Art, Greensburg, Pepperdine U., Malibu, Calif., Newport Harbor Art Mus., Newport Beach, Calif., Hoover Instn. Stanford U., St. Matthew's Episcopal Ch., Wilton, Columbia U., Ctr. Arts, Vero Beach, Fla., Mus. Art, Ft. Lauderdale, Alamo Renta A Car, Ft. Lauderdale, Denver Ctr. Performing Arts, Louis P. Cabot, Boston, Flint (Mich.) Inst. Art, The Nat. Gallery, Prague, The Czech Repub.; pub., contbr. art to book New New Painting, 1996, catalog, 2000, Cooper Classics Collection, 2001, 2002. Republican. Episcopalian. Avocations: ocean diving, tennis, golf, gardening. Home: 700 River Rd Cos Cob CT 06807-1907

NEAL, JAMES PRESTON, state senator, project engineer; b. Cin., July 1, 1935; s. James Preston and Desha Frank (Thompson) N.; m. Nancy Joan Tyner, June 11, 1961; children: Leslie Neal Driscoll, Karen Desha, James P. BSME, U. Ill., 1960. Registered profl. engr., Del. Project engr. DuPont Co., 1960-92; dir. Tetra Tech Inc., Christiana, Del., 1992-95; pres. Tech. Mgmt., 1994—2001. Mem. Del. Ho. of Reps., 1978-80; mem. Del. Senate, 1980-94; bd. trustees U. Del., 2002—. Patentee in field. Councilman City of Newark, 1973-78. With U.S. Army, 1954-56. Recipient Disting. Svc. award Forum to Advance Minorities in Engring., 1989, Disting. Svc. citation Del. Libr. Assn., 1994, Appreciation award Del. Autistic Program, 1999. Mem. Am. Legis. Exch. Coun. (sr. fellow, nat. officer 1991-94, Outstanding Leader 1989,

Outstanding Legis. mem. 1994), Conf. World Regions (sr. fellow), IEEE (sr.), Del. Engring. Soc. (Engr. of Yr. 1989), Instrument Soc. Am. Republican. Presbyterian. Avocations: photography, reading. Home and Office: 50 Bridlebrook Ln Newark DE 19711-2061

NEAL, JOSEPH LEE, vocational school educator; b. Memphis, Feb. 17, 1948; s. James Henry and Minnie Rue (Waldrop) N.; children: Janice Celeste Neal, Mary Joanne; m. Lou Alice Smith, Apr. 10, 1999. AAS, N.W. C.C., Senatobia, Miss., 1979, AS in Bus., 1980; BS, U. S. Miss., 1984, MS, 1986. Cert. tchr. Miss. Police officer City of W. Memphis, Ark., 1970-72; customer svc. rep. Biomed. Labs., Little Rock, 1972-75; sales, svc. rep Moore Ford Co., N. Little Rock, 1975-77; electronics technician N.W. Miss. C.C., Senatobia, 1979-82, electronics inst., 1982-83; electronics engr. U. So. Miss., Hattiesburg, 1983-85; electronics instr. Tex. State Tech. Inst., Sweetwater, 1985-87, De Soto County Vo-Tech. Ctr., Southaven, Miss., 1988-97, South Panola H.S., Batesville, 1997—. Cons. engr. various radio ops., Hattiesburg, 1982-85; mem. curriculum com. De Soto County Schs., 1990-95; steering com. N.W. Miss. Tech. Prep., Senatobia, 1992-95, participant in Learn to Work Workshop Miss. St. U. and Pealey Electronics, 1997, tchr. trainer for Tech. Discovery, 1998, 99. Bd. dirs. Optimist Club, Sweetwater, Tex., 1987. Named Outstanding Tchr., Horn Lake So. C. of C., 1992. Mem. Am. Vocat. Assn., Miss. Trade and Tech. Assn. (v.p. 1994-95, pres. 1995-96), Miss. Assn. Vocat. Educators (pres. dist. 1 1991-92, 95-96, bd. dirs. 1991-92, 95-96, sec. dist. 1 1993-94, v.p. 1994-95), Vocat.-Indsl. Clubs of Am. (100% Advisor 1990, 91, 92, VICA state advisor of yr. 1993), N.Am. Hunting Club (life). Baptist. Avocations: hunting, fishing, pub. speaking. Home: PO Box 172 1578 Freeman Rd Como MS 38619 Office: South Panola HS Batesville MS 38606

NEAL, LEORA LOUISE HASKETT, social services administrator; b. N.Y.C., Feb. 23, 1943; d. Melvin Elias and Miriam Emily (Johnson) Haskett; m. Robert A. Neal, Apr. 23, 1966; children: Marla Patrice, Johnathan Robert. BA in Psychology and Sociology, City Coll. N.Y., 1965; MS in Social Work, Columbia U., 1970, cert. adoption specialist, 1977; IBM cert. community exec. tng. program, N.Y., 1982. Cert. social worker N.Y. Caseworker N.Y.C. Dept. Social Service, 1965-67, Windham Child Care, N.Y.C., 1967-73; exec. dir., founder Assn. Black Social Workers Child Adoption Counseling and Referral Service, 1975-96; adoption tng. specialist Ctr. for Devel. Human Svcs., SUNY-N.Y. State Office Children and Family Svcs., Yonkers, 1996—. Cons. in field; founder Haskett-Neal Publs., Bronx, N.Y., 1993. Co-author: Transracial Adoptive Parenting: A Black/White Community Issue, 1993; contbr. articles to profl. jours. Pres. bd. dirs. Fountain Ave. Cmty. Devel. Corp. Child Welfare League Am. fellow, 1976; recipient cert. No Time to Lose cert. N.Y. State Dept. Social Svcs., 1989. Mem. NAFE, Nat. Assn. Black Social Workers, Columbia U. Alumni Assn., CCNY Alumni Assn., Missionary Com. Revival Team (outreach chair 1982-88). Democrat. Avocations: writing, history and religious studies, travel, cultural activities. Office: NY State Office of Children and Family Svcs SUNY 525 Nepperhan Ave Yonkers NY 10703-2857

NEAL, MARCUS PINSON, JR. radiologist, medical educator; b. Columbia, Mo., Apr. 22, 1927; s. M. Pinson and Mathilda (Evers) N.; m. Gail S. Fallon, May 27, 1961; children: Sandra G. Neal Dawson, M. Pinson III, Ruth-Catherine Neal Perkins. AB, U. Mo., 1949, BS, 1951; MD, U. Tenn., 1953. Intern Med. Coll. Va., Richmond, 1953-54; resident U. Wis. Hosp., Madison, 1954-57; instr. dept. radiology Sch. Medicine U. Wis., 1957-59; mem. staff U. Wis. Hosps., 1957-63; asst. prof. radiology, dir. dept. radiology Cen. Wis. Colony, 1959-63; radiologist Wis. Diagnostic Ctr., 1962-63; mem. staff Med. Coll. Va. Hosps., Va. Commonwealth U., 1963-99; assoc. prof. radiology Med. Coll. Va., Va. Commonwealth U., 1963-66, prof. radiology, 1966-97, prof. emeritus, 1997—, dir. postgrad. edn. dept. radiology, 1964-73, chmn. divsn. diagnostic radiology, 1965-68, asst. dean Sch. Medicine, dir. grad. med. edn., dir. regional med. program, 1968-71, dir. continuing edn. Sch. Medicine, 1969-72, interim dean Sch. Medicine, 1971, asst. v.p. for health scis., 1971-73, provost Health Scis. campus, 1973-78, assoc. dean for continuing med. edn. and quality assurance Sch. Medicine, 1978-79, dir. housestaff edn. Dept. Radiology, 1979-93, dir. section genitourinary radiology, Dept. Radiology, 1981-92. Bd. dirs. Common Wealth Bank, Richmond; cons., radiologist Va. Hosp., Madison, 1962-63, USAF Hosp., Truax Field, Madison, 1962-63, McGuire VA Hosp., Richmond, 1963-99; bd. forestry Commonwealth of Va., 1990-94, chmn. bd. forestry, 1993-94. Editor: Emergency Interventional Radiology: Practical Aspects, 1988; contbr. articles to profl. jours. Pres. Oxford Civic Assn., Richmond, 1965-67, Three Ridges Condominium Assn., Wintergreen, Va., 1979-84. Served as pharmacist mate USNR, 1945-47. Fellow Oak Ridge Inst. Nuc. Studies, Am. Coll. Radiology (councilor Va. chpt. 1977-83, 85-91, 93-97); mem. AMA, Radiol. Soc. N.Am., Am. Roentgen Ray Soc., Med. Soc. Va., So. Med. Assn. (pres. 1982-83, Disting. Svc. award 1994), Richmond Acad. Medicine, Capital Club (bd. dirs.), Commonwealth Club, Bull and Bear Club, Willow Oaks Country Club, Sigma Xi. Avocations: hunting, fishing, gardening, skiing. Home: 7301 Riverside Dr Richmond VA 23225-1066 Office: Med Coll Va PO Box 980615 Richmond VA 23298-0615

NEAL, MARGARET SHERRILL, writer, editor, graphics designer, web designer; b. Memphis, Apr. 13, 1950; d. Wilburn Franklin and Merle Aileen (Willis) N. BA, Memphis State U., 1972, postgrad., 1973; MS, Columbia Pacific U., 1984. Cert. internet webmaster. Air traffic contr. FAA, Memphis, 1974-76, New Bern, N.C., 1976-81, Vero Beach, Fla., 1981-83; detection sys. specialist U.S. Customs Svc., Miami, 1983-87, intelligence rsch. specialist, 1987-89; ret., 1989. Editor newsletter Highlands Neighborhood Watch. Sec. Pompano Beach Highlands Civic Improvement Assn., 1998; mem. Highlands Neighborhood Watch. Mem. NOW, Smithsonian Instn., Mensa, Nat. Trust Hist. Preservation, Greenpeace, Clan Macneil Soc., Environ. Def., Nature Conservancy, Lighthouse Point Writers' Workshops, Save the Manatee Club. Democrat. Presbyterian. Avocations: genealogy, growing orchids. E-mail: sayitwithstyle@care2.com.

NEAL, PHIL HUDSON, JR. manufacturing company executive; b. Birmingham, Ala., Nov. 17, 1926; s. Phil Hudson and Amy (Gross) N.; m. Sarah Swift Britton, Sept. 19, 1959; children: Amy Neal Ager, Phil Hudson, III, Samuel Abney Britton. AB, Duke U., 1950; MBA, Harvard U., 1952. Investment analyst First Nat. Bank, Birmingham, 1952-55; procedures analyst Gen. Electric Co., Hendersonville, N.C., 1955-58; with Ala. By-Products Corp., Birmingham, 1958-79, asst. treas., 1964-68, treas., 1968-79; dir., v.p. Utility Tool Co., Birmingham, 1979-86; dir., pres. Nutec Metal Finishing Inc., 1986-92, chmn., 1992—. Trustee Advent Episcopal Sch., 1967—, pres., 1968-89, trustee charitable endowment trust, 1981—; treas. Cathedral Ch. of Advent, 1981-82, mem. chpt., 1983-85, 86-89; bd. dirs. Greater Birmingham Ministries, 1975-77, Advent Episcopal Assn. for Edn., 1968-89, Jefferson County chpt. Ala. Soc. Crippled Children and Adults, Inc., 1977-79; trustee Ala. Found. for Hearing and Speech, 1967-74, v.p., 1968-69, pres., 1969-71. Served with USNR, 1945-46. Mem. Newcomen Soc. N.Am., Birmingham Country Club, The Club, The Summit Club, Phi Beta Kappa, Sigma Nu, Phi Eta Sigma. Episcopalian (vestryman, sr. warden). Home: 3336 Hermitage Rd Birmingham AL 35223-2004 also: 81 Old Duck Hole Rd East Orleans MA 02643 Office: 3669 Indsl Pkwy PO Box 170746 Birmingham AL 35217-0746

NEAL, PHILIP MARK, diversified manufacturing executive; b. San Diego, Aug. 28, 1940; s. Philip Mark and Florence Elizabeth (Anderson) N.; children: Brian, Kevin. BA, Pomona Coll., 1962; MBA, Stanford U., 1964. Mgr. financial planning and analysis CBS, Hollywood, 1964-66; cons. McKinsey & Co., L.A., 1966-73; v.p., contr. Avery Internat. Corp., 1974-78, sr. v.p. fin. Pasadena, Calif., 1979-88, group v.p. materials group, 1988-90, exec. pres., 1990, pres., COO, 1990-98, pres., CEO, 1998-2000, chmn., CEO, 2000—. Bd. dirs. L.A. Bus. Advisors, Edwards Lifescis. Corp. Trustee Pomona Coll.; bd. govs. Town Hall of Calif.; bd. dirs. Calif. Inst. Tech., Pacific Basin Inst., L.A. C. of C., L.A. World Affairs Coun., Music Ctr. Los Angeles County. Mem.: Calif. Bus. Roundtable (bd. dirs.). Republican. Episcopalian. Office: Avery Dennison Corp 150 N Orange Grove Blvd Pasadena CA 91103-3534

NEAL, RICHARD EDMUND, congressman, former mayor; b. Worcester, Mass., Feb. 14, 1949; s. Edmund J. and Mary H. (Garvey) N.; m. Maureen Conway, Dec. 20, 1975; children— Rory, Brendan, Maura, Sean BS, Am. Internat. Coll., Springfield, Mass., 1972; M.P.A., U. Hartford, Conn., 1976; postgrad., U. Mass., Amherst, 1982. Adminstrv. aide to Mayor City of Springfield, Mass., 1973-78, mem. city council, 1978-83, mayor, 1984-88; mem. U.S. Congress from 2nd. Mass. dist., 1989—; mem. ways and means com. Lectr. history and politics Springfield Tech. Community Coll., Mass., 1973-83; lectr. bus. and govt. Western New Eng. Coll., Springfield, 1979-82; project dir. Springfield Tech. Community Coll., 1979-82 Trustee ARC, YMCA, Springfield Named to Outstanding Young Men in Am., U.S. Jr. C. of C., Springfield Mem. Am. Internat. Coll. Alumni Assn. (pres. 1980, Alumni Achievement award 1985). Springfield Library and Mus. Assn. (trustee) Clubs: Valley Press. John Boyle O'Reilly (Springfield). Democrat. Roman Catholic. Office: US House of Reps 2133 Rayburn House Ofc Bldg Washington DC 20515-0001*

NEAL, ROBERT LEE, JR. government official; m. Beverly N.; 1 child, Aja. BS in bus. mgmt., U. Md., Coll. Pk., 1976; MBA in fin., Am. U., Washington, D.C., 1992; postgrad., Am. U. Mgr. analyst, chemist Def. Mapping Agy.; various positions Mgmt. and Budget office; assoc. dep. adminstr. Govt. Contracting/Minority Enterprise; assoc. Adminstr. Gen. Svcs. Adminstr.; dir. Under Sec. of Def. Office, 1996—. Recipient Outstanding and Disting. Pub. Svc. medals, Outstanding Achievement award Sec. of Def., Spl. Performance awards, EEO award, Hammer award, Spl. Performance Divsnl. awards Office of Mgmt. and Budget.

NEAL, TERESA SCHREIBEIS, secondary education educator; b. Wheatland, Wyo., Mar. 19, 1956; d. Gene L. and Bonnie Marie (Reed) Schreibeis; m. Michael R. Neal, Apr. 7, 1990; 1 child, Rianna Michele. BA in Am. Studies and English Edn., U. Wyo., 1978; MA in History, U. So. Calif., 1989, PhD, 1994, Cert. Studies of Women/Men in Soc., 1995. Cert. secondary edn. tchr., Wyo., Colo. Tchr. lang. arts and social studies, asst. coach Carbon County Sch. Dist. 1, Rawlins, Wyo., 1978-86; asst. lectr. freshmen writing program U. So. Calif., L.A., 1986-90; prof. history Palomar (Calif.) C.C., San Diego, 1991; software support specialist Dynamic Data Systems, Westminster, Colo., 1992-93; tchr. humanities gifted and talented classes Arvada (Colo.) West H.S., 1993-98; tchr., program developer New Montessori Mid. Sch., 1998-00, Mountain Shadows Mid. Sch., Boulder, Colo., 1998-2000. Participant critical thinking and humanities secondary edn. project NEH, Wyo., 1985-86; adj. prof. English Composition, Front Range Cmty. Coll., Westminster, Colo., 2000—. Mem., chmn. Reading Is Fundamental Program, Rawlins, 1983-85, Women of the West Mus., 2001—; tchr., sponsor Denver-Metro YMCA Youth and Govt., 1994-97, Close Up, Washington, 1984-86, 97; tchr., advisor Nat. History Day Contest, 1995—; tchr., sponsor World Affairs Challenge, Denver U., 1998. Mem. AAUW, Western Assn. Women Historians, G. Autrey Mus. Western Art, Phi Beta Kappa. Avocations: travel, fine arts, baseball, reading. E-mail: tneal@javakats.com.

NEAL-BARNETT, ANGELA MARIE, psychology educator; b. Youngstown, Ohio, Feb. 13, 1960; d. Andrew Lee and Doris Lucille Neal; m. Edgar J. Barnett Jr., July 17, 1995; 1 child, Reece. BA, Mt. Union Coll., 1982; MA, DePaul U., 1985, PhD, 1988. Lic. psychologist, Ohio. Clin. therapist ECHO Community Health Orgn., Chgo., 1985-87; post-doctoral fellow U. Pitts. (Pa.), Western Psychiat. Inst., 1988-89; asst. prof. Kent (Ohio) State U., 1989—, 1989-95, assoc. prof., 1995—. Pres., founder Rise Sally Rise Prodn.; founder, CEO Rise, Sally, Rise, Inc.; bd. dirs. King-Kennedy Ctr., Ravenna, Ohio, 1989—95; rsch. fellow Inst. African Am. Affairs, Kent, 1991—; co-chair Allied Health Edn. Com., 1994—; mem. NIMH Child Psychopathology and Treatment Rev. Panel, 1996—99; spkr. in field. Author: Forging Limits: African American Children Clinical Developmental Perspectives; contbr. articles to profl. jours. Mem. alumni coun. Mt. Union Coll.; mem. governing bd. Ida B. Wells Cmty. Acad., 1998-2000. Urban Rsch. grantee Ohio Bd. Regents, 1990, biomed. support grantee NIH, 1991, small grantee NIMH, 1994-96. Mem. APA (Kenneth & Marie Clark award), Ohio Pscyhol. Assn., Assn. Advancement Behavior Therapy, Assn. Black Psychologists, African Am. Lit. Guild Kent. Methodist. Avocations: tennis, reading. Office: Kent State U Dept Psychology 118 Kent Hl Kent OH 44242-0001 also: Rise Sally Rise Inc 361 Starr Line Dr Tallmadge OH 44278 E-mail: aneal@kent.edu.

NEALE, E(RNEST) R(ICHARD) WARD, retired university official, consultant; b. Montreal, Que., Can., July 3, 1923; s. Ernest John and Mabel Elizabeth (McNamee) N.; m. Roxie Eveline Anderson, June 3, 1950; children— Richard Ward, Owen Curtis B.Sc., McGill U., Montreal, 1949; MS, Yale U., 1950, PhD, 1952; LL.D. (hon.), Calgary U., Alta., Can., 1977; DSc (hon.), Meml. U., Nfld., Can., 1989. Asst. prof. geology U. Rochester, N.Y., 1952-54; sect. chief Geol. Survey Can., Ottawa, Ont., 1954-63, div. chief, 1965-68, Calgary, 1976-81; commonwealth geol. liaison officer London, 1963-65; prof., head geology Meml. U., St. John's, Nfld., Can., 1968-76, v.p. acad., 1982-87; cons., Calgary, Alta., Can., 1987—. Chmn. nat. adv. bd. on sci. publs. NRC-Natural Scis. and Engring. Rsch. Coun., Ottawa, 1982-88. Author: Geology and Geophysics in Canadian Universities, 1980. Editor: Some Guides to Mineral Exploration, 1967, Geology in the Atlantic Region, 1968, The Geosciences in Canada, 1968; Editor: Can. Jour. of Earth Science, 1974-79, Science and the Public, 1988. Bd. dirs. Unitarian Ch. Calgary, 1993—, pres., 1995-96. Petty officer Royal Can. Navy, 1943-45. Decorated officer Order of Can., 1990; recipient Queen's Jubilee medal Govt. of Can., 1977, Can. 125 medal, 1992 Fellow Royal Soc. Can. (coun. 1972-75, chmn. com. pub. awareness of sci. 1987-91, Bancroft medal 1975), Geol. Assn. Can. (pres. 1973-74, Ambrose medal 1986, 1st E.R. Ward Neale medal 1995), Can. Geosci. Coun. (pres. 1975-76, R.T. Bell medal Can. Mining Jour. 1977), Geol. Soc. Am.; mem. Assn. Earth Sci. Editors, Nat. Def. (chmn. biol. and chem. def. rev. com. 1990-93), Univ. Club Calgary, Chancellor's Club, Crows Nest Club, Calgary Sci. Network (pres. 1989), Sigma Xi (nat. lectr. New Haven 1976, chmn. Avalon chpt. 1986). Avocations: golf, cross-country skiing, hiking, canoeing. Home and Office: 5108 Carney Rd NW Calgary AB Canada T2L 1G2

NEALE, GAIL LOVEJOY, non-profit organization management consultant; b. Detroit, Feb. 8, 1935; d. Elijah Parish and Jane Appleton (Howell) Lovejoy; m. Richard Potter (div.); m. Anthony Astrachan (div.); children: Owen Lovejoy Astrachan, Joshua Howell Astrachan; m. Robert Edward Neale, June 23, 1984. Student, Vassar Coll., 1952-54. Rsch. aide, dir. devel., corp. sec., v.p. Hudson Inst., Inc., Croton on Hudson, N.Y., 1962-76; v.p. Aspen Inst., N.Y.C., 1976-78; dir. external affairs Middlebury (Vt.) Coll., 1978-80; pres. Hudson Inst., Croton on Hudson, 1980-82; corp. sec. Commonwealth Fund, N.Y.C., 1983-86; project adminstr. Mt. Holyoke Coll., South Hadley, Mass., 1986-88; dir. devel. Hampshire Coll., Amherst, 1988-91; exec. v.p., COO Salzburg Seminar, Middlebury, Vt., 1991-96; pres., founder The Lovejoy Consulting Group, Inc., Burlington, 1997—. Trustee JL Found., L.A.; bd. dirs. Capital Income Builder, L.A., Capital World Growth and Income Fund, L.A., Fundamental Investors, L.A., Growth Fund Am., Vera Inst. for Justice, N.Y.C.; trustee Endowments, Inc., L.A.; dir., chair campaign Shelburne Farms, 1997-2000; dir. Circus Smirkus. Bd. dirs. Conern for Dying, N.Y.C., 1986-90; dir. Frances Clark Ctr. for Keyboard Pedagogy, 1997-2000; mem. Preservation Land Trust Vt., Mozart Festival Vt., Flynn Theatre. Mem. Origami U.S.A. Democrat. Episcopalian. Avocations: reading, cooking, knitting, origami, magic. Office: The Lovejoy Consulting Group Inc 154 Prospect Pkwy Burlington VT 05401-4148 Fax: 802-658-6189. E-mail: neale@together.net.

NEALE, GARY LEE, utilities executive; b. Lead, S.D., Mar. 3, 1940; s. Vearl J. and Gladys M. (Trenkle) N.; m. Sandra C. Lovell, June 16, 1962; children: David G., Julie C. BA in Econs., U. Wash., 1962, MBA, 1965. Loan examiner Wells Fargo, 1966-69; sr. fin. analyst Kaiser Industries, 1969-70; chmn., pres., chief exec. officer Planmetrics, Chgo., 1970-89; pres., chief oper. officer No. Ind. Pub. Svc. Co., Hammond, 1989-93; chmn., pres., CEO Ni Source Inc. (formerly No. Ind. Pub. Svc. Co.), 1993—. Bd. dirs. Modine Mfg., Racine, Wis., Am. Gas Assn., Arlington, Va., Ind. Gas Assn./Ind. Electric Assn., Indpls., Nipsco Industries Inc., Hammond. Bd. dirs. N.W. Ind. Symphony, 1990; mem. Ind. Energy Policy Forum, 1991. Lt. (j.g.) USN, 1962-64. Mem. Econ. Club Chgo., Chgo. Univ. Club, NYU Club. Office: NiSource Inc 801 E 86th Ave Merrillville IN 46410-6272*

NEALE-MAY, DONOVAN, marketing professional; Degree in journalism, Rhodes U., South Africa. Leader pub. rels. ops. Ogilvy & Mather, Calif.; pvt. practice as pres., founder, 1987—. Mem. adv. bd. pub. rels. degree program San Jose State U., Calif.; cons. with various clients; several acct. mgmt., sr. exec. positions comm. agys., England. Mem. bd. Travelzoo.com; mem. bd. Rhodes U. Charitable Trust. Scholar Cape Times . Office: Donovan Neale-May 409 Sherman Ave Palo Alto CA 94306 Office Fax: 650-328-5016.*

NEALON, WILLIAM JOSEPH, JR. federal judge; b. Scranton, Pa., July 31, 1923; s. William Joseph and Ann Cannon (McNally) N.; m. Jean Sullivan, Nov. 15, 1947; children: Ann, Robert, William, John, Jean, Patricia, Kathleen, Terrence, Thomas, Timothy. Student, U. Miami, Fla., 1942-43; BS in Econs, Villanova U., 1947; LL.B., Cath. U. Am., 1950; LL.D. (hon.), U. Scranton, 1975. Bar: Pa. 1951. With firm Kennedy, O'Brien & O'Brien (and predecessor), Scranton, 1951-60; mem. Lackawanna County Ct. Common Pleas, 1960-62; U.S. dist. judge Middle Dist. Pa., 1962—, chief judge, 1976-88, sr. judge, 1989—. Mem. com. on adminstrn. of criminal law Jud. Conf. U.S., 1979— ; lectr. bus. law and labor law U. Scranton, 1951-59; mem. jud. council 3d Cir. Ct. Appeals, 1984—; dist. judge rep. from 3d Cir. Jud. Conf. of U.S., 1987—. Mem. Scranton Registration Commn., 1953-55; hearing examiner Pa. Liquor Control Bd., 1955-59; campaign dir. Lackawanna County chpt. Nat. Found., 1961-63; mem. Scranton-Lackawanna Health and Welfare Authority, 1963—; assoc. bd. Marywood Coll., Scranton; pres. bd. dirs. Cath. Youth Center; pres. Father's Club Scranton Prep. Sch., 1966; chmn. bd. dirs. Mercy Hosp., 1991-95; chmn. bd. trustees U. Scranton; vice chmn. bd. trustees Lackawanna Jr. Coll., Scranton; bd. dirs. St. Joseph's Children's and Maternity Hosp., 1963-66, Lackawanna County unit Am. Cancer Soc., Lackawanna County Heart Assn., Lackawanna County chpt. Pa. Assn. Retarded Children, Scranton chpt. ARC, Lackawanna United Fund, Mercy Hosp., Scranton, 1975— ; trustee St. Michael's Sch. Boys, Hoban Heights; adv. com. Hosp. Service Assn. Northeastern Pa. Served to 1st lt. USMCR, 1942-45. Recipient Americanism award Amos Lodge B'nai B'rith, 1975; Cyrano award U. Scranton Grad. Sch., 1977; Disting. Service award Pa. Trial Lawyers Assn., 1979; named one of 50 Disting. Pennsylvanians Greater Phila. C. of C., 1980, Outstanding Fed. Trial Judge Assn. Trial Lawyers Am., 1983 Mem. Pa. Bar Assn., Lackawanna County Bar Assn. (Chief Justice Michael J. Eagen award 1987), Friendly Sons St. Patrick (pres. Lackawanna County 1963-64), Pi Sigma Alpha. Clubs: Scranton Country (Clarks Summit, Pa.) (bd. dirs.). Lodges: K.C. Office: US Courthouse PO Box 1146 Scranton PA 18501-1146

NEAL-PARKER, SHIRLEY ANITA, obstetrician and gynecologist; b. Washington, Aug. 28, 1949; d. Leon Walker and Pearl Anita (Shelton) Neal; m. Andre Cowan Dasent, June 21, 1971 (div. Feb. 1978); 1 child, Erika Michelle Dasent; m. James Carl Parker, Feb. 11, 1979; 1 child, Amirah Nabeehah. BS in Biology, Am. U., 1971; MD, Hahnemann U., 1979. Lic. Md., Calif., Wash. Intern Howard U. Hosp., 1979-80, resident, 1980-84; physician Nat. Health Svc. Corp., Charleston, W. Va., 1984-86; clin. instr. W. Va. U., 1985-86; pvt. practice ob./gyn. Sacramento, 1986-95; pvt. practice Chehalis, Wash., 1995—; chair dept. perinatology Providence Centralia Hosp., 1999-2000. Bd. dirs. Ruth Rosenberg Dance Ensemble, Sacramento, 1992-95, Human Response Network, Chehalis, 1995-97. Mem.: Wash. State Obstet. Soc., Lewis County Med. Soc., Wash. State Med. Assn., Nat. Assn. Gynecol. Laparoscopists, Am. Med. Women's Assn. (comty. svc. award Mother Hale br. 1994), Nat. Med. Assn., Am. Reproductive Health Profls., Am. Assn. Gynecologic Laparoscopists, Soroptimist Internat. Avocations: traveling, reading, crocheting, collecting ethnic dolls, magnets. Home: 1725 S Madcel Blvd B3 Chehalis WA 98532 Office: 1725 South Market Blvd B3 Chehalis WA 98532-0997 E-mail: parker@localaccess.com.

NEAL-VITTIGLIO, CYNTHIA KAREN, clinical psychologist; b. Detroit, Dec. 30, 1952; d. Gaston O. and Evelyn Jewel (Dunn) N.; m. Thomas Anthony Vittiglio, July 10, 1988; 1 child, Anthony. BA, Wayne State U., 1975, MA, 1977, PhD, 1983. Licensed psychologist. Clin. researcher Sinai Hosp., Detroit, 1977-78; clin. asst. Dept. Neuropsychology Lafayette Clinic, 1974-75; faculty mem. Inst. for Sex Rsch., Bloomington, Ind., 1975, 80; sch. psychologist Lakeshore Pub. Schs., St. Clair Shores, Mich., 1979-80; staff psychologist Evergreen Counseling Ctr., 1979—. Consulting psychologist St. John Hosp., Detroit, 1983—. Mem. Jr. Coun., Founders Soc., Detroit, 1985—, Cranbrook Women's Soc., Bloomfield Hills, Mich., 1987—, Am. Ballet Soc., N.Y.C., 1980—. Recipient Grad. Fellowship Wayne State U., 1988. Mem. APA, DAR (Louise St. Clair chpt.). Republican. Avocations: exercise, boating, downhill skiing. Office: Associated Psychologists 21929 E 9 Mile Rd Saint Clair Shores MI 48080-2906 also: Evergreen Counseling Svcs Ste 210B 53950 Van Dyke Ave Shelby Township MI 48316-1815

NEAME, RONALD, director, producer; b. Hendon, Middlesex, Eng., Apr. 23, 1911; s. Stuart Elwin and Ivy Lillian (Close) N.; m. Beryl Yolanda Heanly, Oct. 15, 1933; 1 son, Christopher Elwyn; m. Donna Friedberg, Sept. 12, 1993. Student pvt. schs., London and Sussex, Eng. Asst. cameraman Brit. Internat. Pictures, Estree, Eng., 1928-35, chief cameraman, 1935-45. Dir.: photography, prodn. supr. various films, including In Which We Serve, 1942, This Happy Breed, 1943, Blithe Spirit, 1944; co-writer, producer: films Brief Encounter, 1945, Great Expectations, 1946; producer: film Oliver Twist, 1947; dir.: films Take My Life, 1948, Golden Salamander, 1949, The Promoter, 1952, Man with a Million, 1953, The Man Who Never Was, 1954, Windom's Way, 1957, The Horse's Mouth, 1958, Tunes of Glory, 1960, I Could Go On Singing, 1962, The Chalk Garden, 1963, Mr. Moses, 1964, Gambit, 1966, The Prime of Miss Jean Brodie, 1968, Scrooge, 1970, The Poseidon Adventure, 1972, The Odessa File, 1974, Meteor, 1978, Hopscotch, 1979, First Monday in October, 1980-81, Foreign Body, 1985, The Magic Baloon, 1989; co-founder film co. Cineguild Co., Denham, Eng., 1943-44. Decorated Comdr. of the Order of the Brit. Empire, 1996. Mem. Dirs. Guild Am., Am. Film Inst., Acad. Motion Picture Arts and Scis. (gov. 1977-79), Brit. Acad. Film and TV Arts (London and Los Angeles), Savile Club (London). *When I am asked which film I consider to be my best, I reply, "I haven't made it yet. Perhaps next time".*

NEARINE, ROBERT JAMES, educational psychologist; b. Fitchburg, Mass., May 15, 1930; s. Raymond Johns and Beatrice Aileen (Strickland) N.; children: Luke, Martha, Amy. BS, Fitchburg State Coll., 1951; EdM, Tufts Coll., 1952; cert. advanced grad. specialization, Boston U., 1961; MA, U. Conn., 1965, profl. diploma, 1996; EdD, Boston U., 1972. Tchr. pub. schs., Holbrook, Mass., 1952-54, Groton, 1954-55, Winchester, 1955-59, supr. Inverness, Mont., 1959-60, guidance counselor Manchester, Conn., 1961-66, supr. of evaluation, 1966-73, adminstr. for funding and evaluation, 1973-76, spl. asst. for funding Hartford, 1976-78; spl. asst. for evaluation rsch. and testing Bd. Edn., 1978-93; ednl. cons. Glastonbury, Conn., 1993—. Mem. requirements adv. com., 1991-92. Contbr. articles to profl. jours. Col., USAR. NDEA fellow Boston U., 1960-61, GE fellow Syracuse U., 1971, Ednl. Policy Inst. fellow George Washington U., 1979-80. Mem. APA, Nat. Assn. Test Dirs., Am. Ednl. Rsch. Assn., Nat. Coun. on Measurement in Edn., Res. Officers Assn. (nat. councilman 1994—), Sr. Army Res. Comdrs. Assn., Amvets, Civitan (pres. 1998-99, Conn. state com. employee support of Guard and Res.), Army and Navy Club, Victory Svcs. Club U.K., Assn. of U.S. Army, NG Assn. U.S., Gov.'s Foot Guard, Phi Delta Kappa. Avocations: military history, travel. E-mail: rjnear@ntplx.net.

NEARY, BRUCE WAYNE, bank executive; b. New Brunswick, N.J., Oct. 14, 1950; s. John Runyon and Jennievieve (Harget) N.; m. Patricia Kay Drinkard, July 11, 1970 (div. Jan. 1981); 1 child, Angela Kay; m. Laura Ann Kneeland, Sept. 20, 1986; 1 child, William Covert. BBA, So. Meth. U., 1973, MBA, 1974. Zone mgr. Ford Motor Co., Dallas, 1974-77; employee rels. specialist Exxon Co. USA, Houston, 1977-83; owner B.W. Constrn., 1983-84; pers. coord. Gulf States Asphalt Co., 1984-90; pers. supr. Comiskey Kaufman Inc., 1990-95; asst. v.p., comm. specialist Chase Bank Tex., 1995—. Dance instr. North Harris C.C., Houston, 1982-88; resident dir. Northwoods Repertory Co., Houston, 1982—. Extra in films and TV program; contbr. poetry to lit. publs. Mem. steering com. United Way of Tex., Houston, 1996, 97; membership chmn. Playhouse 1960 Theatre, Houston, 1997; minister Universal Life Ch., 1969. Mem. Delta Sigma Pi. Republican. Presbyterian. Avocations: country and western dancing, hunting, edged weapons, acting, softball. Home: 4215 Glenchase Ln Houston TX 77014-1808 Office: Chase Bank Tex 1111 Fannin 10th PO Box 2558 Houston TX 77252-2558

NEARY, PATRICIA ELINOR, ballet director; b. Miami; d. James Elliott and Elinor (Mitsitz) N. Corps de ballet Nat. Ballet of Can., Toronto, Ont., 1957-60; prin. dancer N.Y.C. Ballet, 1960-68; ballerina Geneva Ballet, Switzerland, 1968-70, ballet dir. Switzerland, 1973-78; guest artist Stuttgart Ballet, Germany, 1968-70; asst. ballet dir., ballerina West Berlin Ballet, 1970-73; ballet dir. Zurich Ballet, Switzerland, 1978-86, La Scala di Milano ballet co., Italy, 1986-88; tchr. Balanchine ballets, Balanchine Trust, 1987—. E-mail: laneary@aol.com.

NEARY, VINCENT SINCLAIR, engineering educator; b. Vineland, N.J., May 20, 1964; s. James Vincent Neary and Carol Lucille Sinclair; m. Jessica Graydon Taylor, June 23, 1990; 1 child, Liam James. BS in Agrl. Engring., Rutgers U., 1987; MS, Univ. Iowa, 1992, PhD, 1995. Cert. profl. engr., Tenn. Engr.-in-tng. Sadat Assocs., Inc., Princeton, N.J., 1987-88, Post, Buckley, Schuh & Jernigan, Inc., Princeton, 1988-89; sr. assoc. Philip Williams & Assocs., Ltd., San Francisco, 1996-97; asst. prof. dept. civil and environ. engring. Tenn. Technol., Cookeville, Tenn., 1997—. Advisor Napa-Sonoma Marsh Restoration Com., San Francisco, 1996-97; sec. Environ. Hydraulics Tech. Com., Am. Soc. Civil Engrs., Washington, 1999—. Contbr. articles to profl. jours. Founder, coord. Ralston Creek Watershed Ptnrship, Iowa City, 1995. Recipient Ralph E. Power Jr. Faculty Enhancement award in Engring., Oak Ridge Assoc. Univs., 1999, Iowa Engring. Dean's scholarship U. Iowa, 1990. Mem. Am. Soc. Civil Engrs., Internat. Assn. of Hydraulic Rsch. Democrat. Avocations: soccer, cooking, reading, gardening. Office: Tenn Tech Univ PO Box 5015 Cookeville TN 38505-0001

NEAS, JOHN THEODORE, investment company executive; b. Tulsa, May 1, 1940; s. George and Lillian J. (Kaspar) N.; m. Sally Jane McPherson, June 10, 1966; children: Stephen, Gregory, Matthew. BS, Okla. State U., 1967, MS, 1968. With acctg. dept. Rockwell Internat., 1965; with contr.'s dept. Amoco Prodn. Co., 1966—67; mem. audit and tax staf Deloitte, Haskins & Sells, 1968—75; pres. Nat. Petroleum Sales, Inc., Tulsa, 1975—, John Neas Tank Lines, Inc., 1986—. McPherson Fuels & Asphalts, Inc., 1981—88, sec., 1989—; prin. Neas Investments Ltd. Partnership, 1997—, Sebring Investments Ltd. Partnership, 1997—. Mem. Bailey Ranch estates LLC, 1994—; stockholder N-H Dealership Investments, Inc., 1996—; mem. coun. Oak Bldg. Mgmt., LLC, 1997—; mem. Brad Noe Autoplex, LLC, 1997—; mem. Vet. Properties, LLC, 1994—; asst. instr. U. Tulsa, 1974; former mem. bd. dirs. Waterways Bd. Okla. Dept. Transp., 1989-96.

NEAS, LINDSEY RUTLEDGE, legislative assistant; b. St. Louis, Apr. 20, 1959; s. Robert Earl and Lois Eleanora (Warner) N. BA in Polit. Sci., Grinnell Coll., 1986; MPA, U. Mo., St. Louis, 1994. Mil. legis. asst. Congressman James M. Talent, Ho. of Reps., Washington, 1995-2000, legis. dir. Congress W. Todd Akin, 2001—. 1st lt. U.S. Army, 1987-92; capt. USAR, 1996-2002. Presbyterian. Office: Ho of Reps 501 Cannon HOB Washington DC 20515-0001

NEASE, JUDITH ALLGOOD, marriage and family therapist; b. Arlington, Mass., Nov. 15, 1930; d. Dwight Maurice Allgood and Sophie (Wolf) Allgood Morris; m. Theron Stanford Nease, Sept. 1, 1962; children: Susan Elizabeth, Alison Allgood. Student, Rockford Coll., 1949-50; BA, NYU, 1953, MA, 1954; MS, Columbia U. Sch. Social Work, 1956. Psychiat. social worker Bellevue Psychiat. Hosp., N.Y.C., 1956-59, St. Luke's Hosp., N.Y.C., 1959-62; asst. psychiat. social work supr. N.J. Neuropsychiat. Inst., Princeton, 1962-64; group co-leader Ctr. for Advancement of Personal and Social Growth, Atlanta, 1973-76; asst. dir., social work supr., group co-leader Druid Hills Counseling Ctr., Columbia Theol. Sem., 1973-82; marriage and family therapist Cath. Social Svcs., Atlanta, 1978-87; chief Cmty. Mental Health Svc., Ft. McPherson, Atlanta, 1987-92; master's level clinician Ctr. for Psychiatry, Smyrna, Ga., 1990-92; pvt. practice Grayson, 1992—. Democrat. Episcopalian. Home and Office: 1557 Bennett Rd Grayson GA 30017-1046 Office Fax: 770-978-8281.

NEASE, STEPHEN WESLEY, college president; b. Everett, Mass., Jan. 15, 1925; s. Floyd William and Madeline Anzelette (Nostrand) N.; m. Dorothy Christine Hardy, June 17, 1946; children: Linda Carol Nease Scott, Floyd William II, Stephen Wesley Jr., David Wayne, Melissa Jo Nease Wallace. AB, Brown U., 1946; Th.B., Eastern Nazarene Coll., 1947, D.D., 1966; Ed.M., Boston U., 1956; postgrad., Harvard Div. Sch., 1946-48. Ordained to ministry Ch. of the Nazarene, 1951; pastor East Side Ch. of the Nazarene, Newark, 1948-50; dean men, instr. religion Ea. Nazarene Coll., Wollaston, Mass., 1950-53, dir. devel., 1953-66, pres. emeritus; founding pres. Mt. Vernon (Ohio) Nazarene Coll., 1966-72, pres. emeritus; pres. Bethany (Okla.) Nazarene Coll., 1973-76, Nazarene Theol. Sem., Kansas City, Mo., 1976-80, Eastern Nazarene Coll., Wollaston, Mass., 1981-89; edn. commr. Ch. of the Nazarene, 1989-94; exec. dir. Capital and Endowment Devel., Mt. Vernon, Ohio, 1994—. Served with USNR, 1943-46. Office: 51 Haverhill Rd Windham NH 03087-1515

NEATE, ROBERT EDWARD, lawyer; b. Sandusky, Ohio, June 15, 1957; s. Paul Raymond and Ann Rau Neate; m. Tracey Joanne Harken, July 8, 2000. AB, Harvard U., 1979; JD, U. Notre Dame, 1982. Bar: Wash. 1982, Idaho 1986. Assoc. Paine Hamblen, Coffin, Brooke & Miller LLP, Spokane, 1982-1997, ptnr., 1998-2000; asst. gen. counsel Puget Sound Energy, Inc., Bellevue, Wash., 2000—. Office: Puget Sound Energy OBC-14E PO Box 97034 Bellevue WA 98009

NEAVES, WILLIAM BARLOW, cell biologist, educator; b. Spur, Tex., Dec. 25, 1943; s. William Fred and Revvie Lee (Hefner) N.; m. Priscilla Wood, Jan. 28, 1965; children: William Barlow, Clarissa D'laine. AB magna cum laude, Harvard U., 1966; postgrad., Med. Sch., 1966-67, PhD, 1969. Lectr. vet. anatomy U. Nairobi, 1970-71, vis. prof., 1978; lectr. anatomy Harvard U., 1972; asst. prof. cell biology U. Tex. Health Sci. Ctr., Dallas, 1972-74, assoc. prof., 1974-77, prof., 1977—, Doris and Brian Wildenthal Prof. of Biomed. Sci., 1993—, dean Grad. Sch. Biomed. Scis., 1980-88, interim dean Southwestern Med. Sch., 1986-88, dean Southwestern Med. Sch., 1989-98, exec. v.p. acad. affairs, 1998—. Rsch. assoc. herpetology Los Angeles County Mus., 1970-73; vis. lectr. U. Chgo., 1976-77. Assoc. editor Anat. Record, 1975-87; mem. editl. bd. Biology of Reprodn., 1983-86, Jour. Andrology, 1987-89; contbr. chpts. to books, articles to profl. jours. Bd. dirs. Dallas Zool. Soc., 1989-94, Dallas Mus. Natural History, 1993-95, Damon Runyan-Walter Winchell Cancer Fund, 1986-92, v.p., 1990-92, Sarnoff Endowment, 1998—. Rockefeller Found. fellow, 1970-71; Milton Fund grantee, 1970-71; Population Council grantee, 1973-75; NIH grantee, 1973-89; Ford. Found. grantee, 1976-78. Fellow AAAS; mem. Am. Assn. Anatomists, Am. Soc. Andrology (Young Andrologist award 1983), Dallas Assembly, N.Y. Acad. Scis., Soc. Study of Reprodn., Liaison Com. on Med. Edn. (joint com. of AMA and Assn. Am. Med. Colls.), Sigma Xi, Alpha Omega Alpha. Methodist. Office: 5323 Harry Hines Blvd Dallas TX 75390-7208

NEAVOLL, GEORGE FRANKLIN, writer; b. Lebanon, Oreg., Aug. 20, 1938; s. Jesse Hunter and Mazie Maude (Meyer) N.; m. Laney Lila Hunter Hough, June 21, 1969 (dec. Nov. 2000). BS, U. Oreg., 1965. Reporter, photographer Lebanon (Oreg.) Express, 1969-70; state editor Idaho State Jour., Pocatello, 1970-72; editorial writer The Jour.-Gazette, Ft. Wayne, Ind., 1972-75, Detroit Free Press, 1975-78; editorial page editor The Wichita (Kans.) Eagle, 1978-91, Portland (Maine) Press Herald, Maine Sunday Telegram, 1991-99. Vol. Peace Corps, India, 1967-69; bd. councilors Save-the-Redwoods League, 1980—. Recipient Edward J. Meeman award Scripps-Howard Found., 1973, Honor Roll award, Izaak Walton League Am., 1974, Jamaica Daily Gleaner award Inter Am. Press Assn., 1985, Global Media award, The Population Inst.,1996, Henri A. Benoit award for leadership in pvt. sector Greater Portland (Maine) C. of C., 1999; named Hon. Pk. Ranger, Nat. Pk. Svc., 1988. Mem. Nat. Press Club. Home: 3279 Hillrise Dr Las Cruces NM 88011-4707 E-mail: gneavoll@zianet.com.

NEAVOR, JEFFREY PAUL, music educator; b. Rock Island, Ill., Sept. 4, 1975; s. Linda M. and William F. Cain(Stepfather); m. Ann Jeanette Braun, June 6, 1998; children: Erin. MusB in Edn., Millikin U., 1997. Cert. tchr. music grades K-12 Ill. Instrumental music tchr. grades 4-12 Hartsburg-Emden CUSD 21, Hartsburg, Ill., 1997—2001; dir. of bands Morton H.S., 2001—. Composer: (musical compositions) A Score For The Renaissance, 2000 (lic. for scores of two ind. films., 2000). Grantee Woods grantee, The Woods Found., 2000. Mem.: ASCAP (musician and composer 2000—), MENC. Avocations: music, soccer. Office: Morton HS 350 N Illinois Ave Morton IL 61550 Office Fax: 309-263-2168. Personal E-mail: saxophone4@hotmail.com.

NEBEL, SARA DROUGHT, artist, poet; b. Norwalk, Conn., Oct. 25, 1961; d. James William and Lorna Beryl (Carlson) Drought; m. Emil B. Nebel, May 5, 1984; children: James Blakely, Corrado Carlson, Franceska Nereise. Student, Bennington Coll., 1979-80; Fine Arts Cert., Silvermine Guild Sch. Arts, New Canaan, Conn., 1982. Commercial artist, illustrator, 1980—; owner Earthspirit Gallery, Westport, 1996—. One-woman exhibns. include The Inn at Longshore, Westport, Conn., 1982, Carmen's Country Homes, Westport, Conn., 1982; group shows include Westport Downtown Art Show, 1981, 91, 94, 96, 97, Kent (Conn.) Art Assn. Gallery, Town Hall, Westport, 1986, Earthspirit Art Gallery, Westport, 1996, 98; illustrator Christmas card., 1980, (book cover, design) So Long Chicago, 1982, Queen of Spades, 1982, (cover, interior) Mexamerica Mag., 1980, Writer in Exile, Centennial issue; commd. portraits, mural, landscapes; designer billboard; creator, designer backdrops Sesame St. Children's TV Workshop, 1996. Recipient award The Madison Art Soc., 2000. Mem. Shoreline Arts Alliance, Kent Art Assn. Home: 101 Fort Path Rd Madison CT 06443 Studio: Earthspirit Art Studio 101 Fort Path Rd Madison CT 06443

NEBEL, WILLIAM ARTHUR, obstetrician, gynecologist; b. Charlotte, N.C., Dec. 23, 1936; s. Arthur Ernest and Marie (Hunter) N.; m. Ann Elizabeth Bonner, June 20, 1959; children: Ann Marie Nebel, William Arthur Jr. AB in History, U. N.C., 1958, MD, 1962. Diplomate Am. Bd. Ob-Gyn. Intern Duke Univ. Med. Ctr., Durham, N.C., 1962-63, asst. clin. prof. ob-gyn, 1973—; resident in ob-gyn U. N.C., Chapel Hill, 1963-67, clin. instr. Sch. Med., 1969-70, clin. prof., 1989—; pvt. practice medicine specializing in ob-gyn, 1970—; chmn. ob-gyn dept. Durham County Gen. Hosp., 1978-80, pres. med. staff, 1988-89, cons. staff, 1992—. Mem. Steering Com. Chapel Hill Health Maintenance Orgn. Planning Project, 1973; mem. Orange County Health Bd., 1977, 80; mem. Birth, Neonatal Task Force, State of N.C. Dept. Human Resources, 1985; mem. organizing com. Coordinated Med. Svcs. N.C., 1985; bd. dirs. Triangle Bd. N.C. Med. Mut., 1998—; bd. dirs. Ctrl. Carolina Physicians Health, Village Bank, chmn. bd. 1987-89; pres. Women's Health Network, 1997-99. Contbr. numerous articles to profl. jours.; author numerous presentations to profl. assns. Chmn. troop com. Boy Scouts Am., Troop 39, 1975-78; basketball coach Chapel Hill Recreation Dept., 1975-79; mem. Orange County Com. of N.C. 2000; bd. dirs. U. N.C. Ednl. Found.; vestryman Ch. of the Holy Family, 1973-76; pres. orange County unit Am. Cancer Soc., 1975-76, N.C. divsn. bd. dirs. 1977-78; bd. dirs. N.C. Blue CrossBlue Shield Personal Care Plan, 1985, Ctrl. Carolina Physicians Health, 1985-88, Found. for Better Health of Durham, 1988-89. Recognized by Am. Acad. Family Physicians, 1976-80; named Chapel Hill-Carrboro Father of Yr., 1977; United Cerebral Palsy Med. student fellow, 1960-61, Am. Cancer Soc. fellow, 1965-66. Mem. Internat. Corr. Soc. of Obstetricians and Gynocologists, Am. Fertility Soc., Am. Cancer Soc., S. Cen. Ob-Gyn. Soc. (pres. 1984-85), N.C. Med. Soc. (sect. chmn. 1983-84), N.C. Ob-Gyn. Soc. (pres. 1982-83), Piedmont Ob-Gyn. Soc., Durham-Orange County Med. Soc., Robert A. Ross Ob-Gyn. Soc. (pres. 1976), Village Med. Soc. (pres. 1970-80), Womens Health Alliance (pres. 1999—), Def. Orientation Conf. Assn., Chaine des Rotisseurs, Rotary (past pres., Paul Harris fellow), Alpha Omega Alpha, Phi Alpha Theta, Phi Chi, Pi Kappa Alpha. Democrat. Episcopalian. Avocations: swimming, history, travel. Office: Chapel Hill Ob-Gyn PO Box 3317 Chapel Hill NC 27515-3317

NEBELKOPF, ETHAN, psychologist; b. N.Y.C., June 13, 1946; s. Jacob and Fannie (Carver) N.; m. Karen Horrocks, July 27, 1976; children: Demian David, Sarah Dawn. BA, CCNY, 1966; MA, U. Mich., 1969; PhD, Summit U., 1989. Social worker Project Headstart, N.Y.C., 1965; coord. Project Outreach, Ann Arbor, 1968-69; program dir. White Bird Clinic, Eugene, Oreg., 1971-75; counseling supr. Teledyne Econ. Devel. Corp., San Diego, 1976-79; dir. planning and edn. Walden House, San Francisco, 1979-89, dir. tng., 1990-93; program evaluator United Indian Nations, Oakland, Calif., 1994-96; clin. dir., Family and Child Guidance Clinic Indian Health Ctr., 1997—; clin. dir. Family and Child Guidance Clinic Native Am. Health Ctr., 1997—. Adj. prof. dept. social work San Francisco State U., 1982-87; cons. Berkeley (Calif.) Holistic Health Ctr., 1979-84, Medicine Wheel Healing Co-op, San Diego, 1976-79; alternate del. Nat. Free Clinic Coun., Eugene, 1972-74; clin. dir. Urban Indian Health Bd., Oakland, Calif., 1997. Author: White Bird Flies to Phoenix, 1973, The New Herbalism, 1980, The Herbal Connection, 1981, Hope Not Dope, 1990. Mem. Mayor's Task Force on Drugs, San Francisco, 1988; mem. treatment com. Gov.'s Policy Coun. on Drugs, Sacramento, 1989; task force Human Svcs. Tng., Salem, Oreg., 1972; organizer West Eugene Bozo Assn., 1973; founder Green Psychology, 1993. Named Outstanding Young Man of Am., U.S. Jaycees, 1980; recipient Silver Key, House Plan Assn., 1966. Fellow Am. Orthopsychiat. Assn.; mem. Calif. Assn. Family Therapists, World Fedn. of Therapeutic Communities, Nat. Writer's Club, N.Y. Acad. Scis., Internat. Assn. for Human Rels. Lab. Tng., Calif. Assn. of Drug Programs and Profls. (pres. 1988-90), Phi Beta Kappa. Avocations: herbs, rocks, cactus, yoga, baseball cards. Office: 6641 Simson St Oakland CA 94605-2220

NEBENZAHL, KENNETH, rare book and map dealer, author; b. Far Rockaway, N.Y., Sept. 16, 1927; s. Meyer and Ethel (Levin) N.; m. Jocelyn Hart Spitz, Feb. 7, 1953; children: Kenneth (dec.), Patricia Suzanne Nebenzahl Frish, Margaret Spitz Nebenzahl Quintong, Suzanne Spitz Nebenzahl Nichol. Student, Columbia U., 1947-48; L.H.D. (hon.), Coll. William and Mary, 1983. Solicitor new bus. United Factors Corp., N.Y.C., 1947-50; sales rep. Fromm & Sichel, Inc., 1950-52; v.p. Cricketeer, Inc., Chgo., 1953-58; pres. Kenneth Nebenzahl, Inc., 1957—. Bd. dirs. Imago Mundi, Ltd., London, 1976— ; cons. Rand McNally and Co., 1966-97. Author: Atlas of the American Revolution, 1974, Bibliography of Printed Battle Plans of the American Revolution, 1975, Maps of the Holy Land, 1986 (German edit. 1995), Atlas of Columbus and the Great Discoveries, 1990, also edits. in Spanish, German, Italian, Portugese and French langs.; contbr. articles to profl. jours. and monographs. Trustee Glencoe Pub. Libr., 1963-69, pres., 1966-69; bd. dirs. North Suburban Libr. System, 1966-69, Beverly Farm Found., Godfrey, Ill., 1961-67, Nature Conservancy of Ill., 1980-88; trustee Adler Planetarium, 1969—, chmn., 1977-81; mem. exec. com. Northwestern U. Libr. Coun., 1973-75; sponsor Kenneth Nebenzahl Jr. lectures history cartography Newberry Libr., Chgo., 1965—; mem. assoc. coun. John Crear Libr., Chgo., 1972-99, trustee, 1976-84; trustee U. Chgo., 1982—, mem. vis. com. to libr., 1978-96, chmn., 1987-95; co-chair Phillips Soc.-Libr. of Congress, Washington, 1995-98; bd. dirs. Evanston Hosp. Corp., 1978-85, Am. Himalayan Found., 1994—; mem. U.S. nat. adv. coun. World Wildlife Fund, 1993—. With USMCR, 1945-46. Recipient IMCoS-Tooley award (London), 1984. Fellow Royal Geog. Soc., Royal Soc. for Asian Affairs; mem. Manuscript Soc. (dir. 1965-71), Am. Library Trustees Assn. (nat. chmn. com. intellectual freedom 1967-68), Bibliog. Soc. Am., Newberry Library Assocs. (bd. govs. 1965-78, chmn. 1976-78), Newberry Library (trustee 1978—, vice chmn. 1994—), Antiquarian Booksellers Assn. Am. (bd. govs. 1965-67, v.p. 1975-77), Am. Antiquarian Soc. (gov. 1981-85), Soc. History Discoveries (dir. 1974-76), Chgo. Map Soc. (dir. 1976-86), Ill. Ctr. for the Book (pres. 1986-88), N.Am. Elk Breeders Assn., Caxton Club (Chgo.) (bd. govs. 1961-68, 74-80, pres. 1964-66), Wayfarers Club (Chgo.) (pres. 1970-80), Lake Shore Country Club, Century Club (N.Y.C.), Grolier Club (N.Y.C.) (bd. govs. 1998-99). Clubs: Caxton (Chgo.) (bd. govs. 1961-68, 74-80, pres. 1964-66), Wayfarers (Chgo.) (pres. 1979-80); Lake Shore Country (Glencoe); Century (N.Y.C.), Grolier (N.Y.C., gov. 1998-99), Mid-Day (Chgo.). Office: PO Box 370 Glencoe IL 60022-0370

NEBENZAHL, PAUL, fundraising executive, museum executive; b. Chgo., Nov. 1, 1954; s. Irving Arthur and Norma (Waggett) N.; m. Christina Marie Senese, Sept. 17, 1982; children: Ian, Aria. B of Philosophy, Grand Valley State U., 1979. Dir. Channing-Murray Found., Urbana, Ill., 1981-82; dir. devel. The Peace Mus., Chgo., 1982-83, The Acad. - Art, Music, Dance, Theatre, Chgo., 1983-84; co-dir. Chgo. Filmmakers Inc., 1984-85; asst. dir. Gateway Found. Inc., 1985-87; dir. corp./found. rels Field Mus. Nat. History, 1987-89; asst. exec. dir. Boys and Girls Clubs of Chgo., 1989-90; assoc. dir. WTTW/Chgo., 1990-91, dir. devel., 1991-92, v.p. devel., 1992-97, Lincoln Park Zoo, Chgo., 1997-2001; dir. devel. Temple Sholom of Chgo., 2001—. Bd. com. Donors Forum Chgo., 1991-92. Composer, performer with Joseph Jarman, Leroi Jenkins, Carei Thomas, Big Walter Horton, Homesick James, Fred Simon, Ella Jenkins, Corky Siegal, Art Hoyle, Jim Galliretto, City Lights Orch., Satisfaction Blues Band; composer soundtrack Chicago Matters, Dread (nomination Emmy), A Man and His School, 1994; composer, recorder (soundtrack) Journey of Rememberance, 1996. Bd. dirs. Circle Pines Ctr., Delton, Mich., 1987-90, chair 60th Anniversary Celebration com., 1996—; bd. dirs. Joseph Holmes Dance Theatre, Chgo., 1990-91, CHALK Chgo. Art Link for Kids, 1999-2001; mem. fundraising com. Greater Chgo. Food Depository, 1990; mem. com. bd. Issues Com. Donors Forum, Chgo., 1993—, Arts and Bus. Coun., 1993—; mem. Chgo./Osaka Sister City Com., City of Chgo., Dept. Cultural Affairs, 2001-02. Mem. Assn. Fundraising Profls. (mem. Chgo. chpt. ethics com./membership com. 1990-92, long range planning com., co-chair support com. 1993—, faculty 1st course in fundraising 1993, faculty midwestern conf. 1996, ind. track chair Midwest Region Conf. 2000), 410 Club, Econ. Club (Chgo.) (reception com. 1999-, host reception com. 2001, 5th night reception com. 2002). Avocation: musician. Home: 550 Barton Ave Evanston IL 60202-2109 Office: 3480 N Lake Shore Dr Chicago IL 60657 E-mail: paul@sholomchicago.org.

NEBERGALL, DONALD CHARLES, rural consultant; b. Davenport, Iowa, Aug. 12, 1928; s. Ellis W. and Hilda (Bruhn) N.; m. Shirley Elaine Williams, Apr. 12, 1952; children: Robert W., Nancy L. Nebergall Bosma. BS, Iowa State U., 1951. With Poweshiek County Nat. Bank, 1957-72, sr. v.p., to 1972; founding pres., CEO Brenton Bank and Trust Co., Cedar Rapids, Iowa, 1972-82, chmn. bd., 1982-86; v.p. Chapman Co., 1986-88. Bd. dirs. Telephone & Data Systems, Inc.; bd. dirs. Guaranty Bank and Trust, Barlow Investment Co.; former vice chmn. bd. Iowa Transfer Svc. V.p., bd. dirs. Iowa 4-H Found., 1972-76; divsn. campaign chmn. United Way; former bd. dirs., past pres. Methwick Retirement cmty.; founding trustee Cedar Rapids Cmty. Sch. Dist. Found.; past pres. Cedar Rapids Greater Downtown Assn. With AUS, 1946-48. Recipient Ptnr. in 4-H award Iowa 4-H, 1983, charter 4-H Found. Ct. of Honor, 1989. Mem. Rotary, Alpha Zeta, Gamma Sigma Delta, Delta Upsilon. Republican. Methodist. Office: 2919 Applewood Pl NE Cedar Rapids IA 52402-3323 E-mail: dneber@jmbest.net.

NEBGEN, STEPHEN WADE, stage producer; b. Austin, Tex., Dec. 13, 1955; s. Andrew Paul and Jane (Wade) N.; m. Jill Annette Alpert, June 28, 1991; children: Austin Wade, Lindsay Emily. BA summa cum laude, Fordham U., 1996; JD, U. Tex., 1998. Bar: N.Y. 1999, N.J. 2000, U.S. Dist. Ct. (so. and ea. dists.) N.Y. 1999, U.S. Dist. Ct. N.J. 2000, Ariz. 2001, U.S. Dist. Ct. Ariz. 2001. Artistic dir. Quicksilver Co., Phoenix, 1977-84; founder, artistic dir. Astoria Arts Ctr., N.Y.C., 1984-88; prodr., gen. mgr. Fortune & Men's Eyes, 1987-88; gen. mgr. The Lamb's Theatre Co., 1988-89; co. mgr. Lettic & Lovage, 1989-90; pub. rels., mktg. cons. Strategic Mktg., Atlas Pub., 1990-91; producer, gen. mgr. Bert Sees the Light, 1991-92; atty. Togut Segal & Segal LLP, 1999-2000; pvt. practice, 2000-01; atty. Quarles & Brady Stretch Lang LLP, Scottsdale, Ariz., 2001—. William Randolph Hearst vis. lectr. U. Tex., 2001; panelist South by Southwest film. Contbr. articles to profl. publs. Mem. Vol. Lawyers for the Arts. Mem. ABA (sect. entertainment law), Assn. Bar City N.Y. (com. on entertainment law 2000—), N.Y. State Bar Assn. (coms. on theater film and rec. industry). Office: Quarles & Brady Stretch Lang LLP One Rena Scance Sq Two N Central Ave Phoenix AZ 85004 Home: 13311 N 94th Pl Scottsdale AZ 85260-4362

NEBLETT, CAROL, soprano; b. Modesto, Calif., Feb. 1, 1946; m. Philip R. Akre; 3 children. Studies with, William Vennard, Roger Wagner, Esther Andreas, Ernest St. John Metz, Lotte Lehmann, Pierre Bernac, Rosa Ponselle, George London, Jascha Heifetz, Norman Treigle, Sol Hurak, Dorothy Kirsten, Maestros Julius Rudel, Claudio Abbado, Daniel Barenboin, Erich Leinsdorf, James Levine, others. Soloist with Roger Wagner Chorale; performed in U.S. and abroad with various symphonies; debut with Carnegie Hall, 1966, N.Y.C. Opera, 1969, Met. Opera, 1979; sung with maj. opera cos. including Met. Opera, N.Y.C., Lyric Opera Chgo., Balt. Opera, Pitts. Opera, Houston Grand Opera, San Francisco Opera, Boston Opera Co., Milw. Florentine Opera, Washington Opera Soc., Covent Garden, Cologne Opera, Vienna (Austria) Staatsoper, Paris Opera, Teatro Regio, Turin, Italy, Teatro San Carlo, Naples, Italy, Teatro Massimo, Palermo, Italy, Gran Teatro del Liceo, Barcelona, Spain, Kirov Opera Theatre, Leningrad, USSR, Dubrovnik (Yugoslavia) Summer Festival, Salzberg Festival, others; rec. artist RCA, DGG, EMI; appearances with symphony orchs., also solo recitals, (film) La Clemenza di Tito; filmed and recorded live performance with Placido Domingo, La Fancuilla del West; numerous TV appearances. Office: 622 Glorietta Blvd Coronado CA 92118-2304

NECARSULMER, HENRY, investment banker; b. N.Y.C., Mar. 6, 1914; s. Edward and Manuela Fortlouis (Maas) N.; m. Elizabeth Louise Borden, Mar. 21, 1946; children: Susan N. Goldsmith, John B., Peter B. AB, Dartmouth Coll., 1934. With Kuhn, Loeb & Co., N.Y.C., 1935-77, gen. partner, 1956-77, mng. partner, 1969-77; vice chmn. Kuhn, Loeb & Co., Inc., 1977; mng. dir. Lehman Bros. Kuhn Loeb Inc., 1977-81, adv. dir., 1981-84, Shearson Lehman Bros. Inc., 1984-85, mng. dir., 1986-88, adv. dir., 1988-90, cons., 1990-93, Lehman Bros., Inc., 1993-96. Past dir. various corps. Mem. Am. Stock Exchange, 1973-78; mem. governing council Securities Industry Assn., 1972-75; mem. State of N.Y. Judiciary Relations Com., Appellate Div., 1st Jud. Dept., 1973-77; Trustee Jewish Child Care Assn. N.Y. Served to capt. AUS, 1942-46. Office: 590 5th Ave New York NY 10036-4702

NECCO, ALEXANDER DAVID, lawyer, educator; b. Gary, Ind., Jan. 31, 1936; s. Alesandro Necco and Mary Millonovich; m. Caroline Chappel, Apr. 20, 1958 (dec. Mar. 1978); 1 child, Laurie Ann Necco Stansbury; m. Edna Joanne Painter, July 1, 1989. BA in Philosophy, U. Nev., 1958; JD, Oklahoma City U., 1965. Bar: Okla. 1965, U.S. Dist. Ct. (we. dist.) Okla. 1965, U.S. Ct. Appeals (10th cir.) 1987), U.S. Ct. Claims 1989, U.S. Ct. Vets. Appeals 1994. Assoc. Robert Jordan, Oklahoma City, 1965-66, Stuckey & Witcher, Oklahoma City, 1968-69; atty. Okla. Hwy. Dept., 1966, Oklahoma City Urban Renewal, 1966-67; ptnr. Stuckey & Necco, Oklahoma City, 1969-71, Necco & Dyer, Oklahoma City, 1978-82, Dyer, Necco & Byrd, Oklahoma City, 1982-88; pvt. practice, 1965—; ptnr. Necco & Byrd, 1988—. Adj. prof. Oklahoma City U. Sch. Bus., 1965—, Webster U., 1995—. Cubmaster Boy Scouts Am., Oklahoma City. With USMC, 1953-82, lt. col. Res. ret. Named Pro-bono Atty. of Month Okla. County. Mem.: ABA, Okla. Trial Lawyers Assn., Assn. Trial Lawyers Assn., Marine Corps Res. Officers Assn. (pres. Oklahoma City chpt. 1984—85), Sigma Nu, Phi Delta Phi. Republican. Roman Catholic. Avocations: golf, swimming, tennis. Office: Necco & Byrd PC 5700 N Portland Ave Ste 121 Oklahoma City OK 73112-1662 E-mail: dnecco@neccoandbyrd.com.

NECCO, E(DNA) JOANNE, school psychologist; b. Klamath Falls, Oreg., June 23, 1941; d. Joseph Rogers and Lillian Laura (Owings) Painter; m. Jon F. Puryear, Aug. 25, 1963 (div. Oct. 1987); children: Laura L., Douglas F.; m. A. David Necco, July 1, 1989. BS, Cen. State U., 1978, MEd, 1985; PhD in Applied Behavioral Studies, Okla. State U., 1993. Med.-surg. asst. Oklahoma City Clinic, 1961-68; spl. edn. tchr. Oklahoma City Pub. Schs., 1978-79, Edmond (Okla.) Pub. Schs., 1979-83; co-founder, owner Learning Devel. Clinic, Edmond, 1983-93; asst. prof. profl. tchr. edn. U. Ctrl. Okla., 1993-97; assoc. prof. U. Ctr. Okla., 1998—2001, prof. profl. tchr. edn., 2002—. Adj. instr. Ctrl. State U., Edmond, 1989-93, Oklahoma City U., 1991-93; mem. rsch. group Okla. State U., Stillwater, 1991-93; faculty senator U. Ctrl. Okla., 1998-2000; Coll. Edn. rep. AAUP, 2000-01; presenter in field. Contbr. articles to profl. jours. Com. mem. Boy Scouts Am., SCUBA Post 604, Oklahoma City, 1981-86; mem. Edmon TAsk Force for Youth, 1983-87, Edmond C. of C., 1984-87; presenter internat. conf. Okla. Ctr. for Neurosci., 1996; evaluator for Even Start Literacy Program, 1994-96, reviewer Okla. Even Start applicants, 1997, presenter internat. conf., Singapore, 1996, Alta., Can., 1996, 98. Mem. AAUP, ASCD, PEO, APA, Nat. Assn. for Sch. Psychologists, Am. Bus Women's Assn., Coun. for Exceptional Children, Learning Disabilities Assn., Am. Assn. for Gifted Underachieving Students, Am. Tchr. Educators, Okla. Learning Disabilities Assn., Okla. Ctr. Neurosci., Okla. Assn. for Counseling and Devel., Okla. Psychol. Soc., U. Ctrl. Okla. Assn. Supervision & Curriculum Develop., Golden Key Nat. Honor Soc., Internat. Soc. for Scientific Study of Subjectivity, Am. Coun. on Rural Spl. Edn., Ctrl State U. (Okla., life), Phi Delta Kappa. Republican. Avocations: scuba diving, underwater photography, water skiing, travel, golf. Home: 3624 Equestrian Ct Edmond OK 73034-5871 Office: U Ctrl Okla Coll Edn 100 N University Dr Edmond OK 73034-5207 E-mail: jnecco@ucok.edu.

NECESSARY, JEFFREY TODD, physician assistant; b. Malvern, Ark., Oct. 26, 1960; s. James Edward and Marilyn (Lewis) N.; m. Pamela Dell Andritsos, June 9, 1984; 1 child, Jeffrey Tyler. BA, U. Ark., 1983; BS, U. Tex., Galveston, 1995. Cert. physician asst. Physician asst. U. Tex. Med. Br., Galveston, 1995—. Lectr. European Fedns. of Orthopedics and Traumatology, Brussels, 1999; clin. trials coord. divsn. spine surgery, U. Tex., 1996—. Contbr. articles to sci. and profl. jours. Fellow Am. Acad. Physician Assts., Tex. Acad.

Physician Assts. Avocations: golf, running, basketball, U. Ark. coll. sports fan. Home: 9 Campeche Dr Galveston TX 77554-9359 Office: U Tex Med Br Divsn Spine Surgery 301 University Blvd Galveston TX 77555-0792 E-mail: Jnecessa@utmb.edu.

NECHEMIAS, STEPHEN MURRAY, lawyer; b. St. Louis, July 27, 1944; s. Herbert Bernard and Toby Helen (Wax) N.; m. Marcia Rosenstein, June 19, 1966 (div. Dec. 1981); children: Daniel Jay, Scott Michael; m. Linda Adams, Aug. 20, 1983. BS, Ohio State U., 1966; JD, U. Cin., 1969. Bar: Ohio 1969. Ptnr. Taft, Stettinius & Hollister, Cin., 1969—. Adj. prof. law No. Ky. U., Chase Coll. Law. Tax comment author: Couse's Ohio Form Book, 6th edit., 1984. Mem. Ohio State Bar Assn. (chmn. taxation com.), Cin. Bar Assn. (chmn. taxation sect. 1985), Legal Aid Soc. Cin. (pres., trustee). Democrat. Jewish. Home: 3122 Walworth Ave Cincinnati OH 45226-1047 Office: 1800 Star Bank Ctr 425 Walnut St Cincinnati OH 45202-3923

NECHIN, HERBERT BENJAMIN, lawyer; b. Chgo., Oct. 25, 1935; s. Abraham and Zelda (Benjamin) N.; m. Susan Zimmerman (div.); 1 child, Jill Rebecca; m. Roberta Fishman, Oct. 24, 1976; 1 child, Stefan. BA with distinction, honors in History, Northwestern U., 1956; JD, Harvard U., 1959. Bar: Ill. 1960. From assoc. to ptnr. Brown Fox & Blumberg, Chgo., 1960-75; ptnr. Taussig Wexler & Shaw, 1975-79, Fink Coff Stern, Chgo., 1979-81, Holleb & Coff, Chgo., 1981-2000; prin. Levin & Schreder, 2000—. Contbr. articles to profl. jours. Pres. Emanuel Congregation, Chgo., 1994-97. Staff sgt. USAR, 1960-66. Mem. ABA, Ill. Bar Assn., Chgo. Bar Assn. (chmn. trust law com. 1990-91), Am. Coll. Trust and Estate Counsel, Standard Club, Cliff Dwellers Club, Phi Beta Kappa. Office: Levin & Schreder 120 N Lasalle St Ste 3800 Chicago IL 60602-2417 E-mail: Herb@LevinSchreder.com.

NECKERS, DOUGLAS CARLYLE, chemistry educator; b. Corry, Pa., Aug. 15, 1938; m. Suzanne Ames Evans, June 18, 1960; children: Pamela, Andrew. AB, Hope Coll., 1960; PhD, U. Kans., 1963. Fellow Harvard Corp., 1963-64; asst. prof. Hope Coll., Holland, Mich., 1964-67, assoc. prof., 1967-71; assoc. prof. chemistry U. N.Mex., Albuquerque, 1971-73; prof. and chmn. dept. chemistry Bowling Green (Ohio) State U., 1973—, Disting. rsch. prof., 1986—; McMaster Disting. rsch. prof., 1993; exec. dir. Ctr. for Photochem. Scis. Bowling Green (Ohio) State U., 1986—. Vis. lectr. Ohio State U., Columbus, 1965, U. Ill., Urbana, 1970; vis. prof. U. Groningen, The Netherlands, 1968-69, U. Nijmegen, The Netherlands, 1975. Co-author: Organic Chemistry, 1977, Programmed Introduction to Organic Chemistry, 1977, Organic Chemistry: Structure, Mechanism and Synthesis, 1973; author: Mechanistic Organic Photochemistry, 1967. Recipient Paul R. Block Jr. award Toledo sect. Am. Chem. Soc., 1987, Paul and Ruth Olscamp Rsch. award, 1987, Leo Friend award for Chem. Tech., 1978, Honors Disting. Alumnus award U. Kans., 1982, Morley medal Cleve. sect. Am. Chem. Soc., 1994; named McMaster Prof. Photochem. Scis., 1993, hon. alumnus Bowling Green State U., 1995. Fellow AAAS. Office: Bowling Green State U/Ctr Photochem Scis/Dept Chem 141 Overman Hl Dept Chem Bowling Green OH 43403-0001

NEDELKOFF, RICHARD R. federal agency administrator; b. Ohio; BS in Criminal Justice, Bowling Green State U., 1980; MS in Adminstrn. of Justice with high honors, U. Louisville; JD, Capital U., 1986. Dir. Bur. Justice Assistance U.S. Dept. Justice, Washington, 2001—. Instr. criminal justice and juvenile justice Capital U. Office: US Dept Justice Bur Justice Assistance 810 7th St NW Washington DC 20531*

NEDERLANDER, JAMES MORTON, theater executive; b. Detroit, Mar. 31, 1922; s. David T. and Sarah L. (Applebaum) N.; m. Charlene Saunders, Feb. 12, 1969; children: James Laurence, Sharon, Kristina. Student, Detroit Inst. Tech. Chmn. Nederlander Orgn., Inc. (formerly Nederlander Producing Co. Am., Inc., N.Y.C., 1966—. Owner and operator of numerous theaters including Palace Theatre, Lunt-Fontanne Theatre, Nederlander Theatre, Brooks Atkinson Theatre, Gershwin Theatre, Neil Simon Theatre, Marquis Theatre, Minskoff Theatre, Richard Rodgers Theatre, N.Y.C., Greek Theatre, Pantages Theatre, Henry Fonda Theatre, L.A., Shubert Theatre, Chgo., Fisher Theatre, Masonic Temple, Detroit, Aldwych Theatre, Adelphi Theatre, Dominion Theatre, London; producer numerous shows for Broadway including She Loves Me, Will Rogers Follies, Me and My Girl, Orpheus Descending, Les Liaisons Dangereuses, Nicholas Nickleby, Annie, La Cage aux Folles, Nine, Applause, Not Now Darling, See Saw, Oliver, Abelard and Heloise, Sherlock Holmes, Treemonisha, Habeus Corpus, Otherwise Engaged, Whose Life is it Anyway?, Betrayal, Woman of the Year, Lena Horne: The Lady and Her Music, The Dresser, Noises Off, Merlin, Night and Day, My Fat Friend, Shirley MacLaine on Broadway, Sweet Charity, Benefactors, Breaking the Code; numerous road show prodns.; revivals: Peter Pan, She Loves Me, Hello Dolly, Porgy and Bess, The Music Man, I Do! I Do!, Oklahoma, On a Clear Day You Can See Forever, Fiddler on the Roof. Office: Nederlander Orgn Inc 1450 Broadway Fl 6 New York NY 10018-2201

NEDERLANDER, MARJORIE SMITH, retired interior designer and decorator; b. Springfield, Mo., Nov. 10, 1922; d. Laurence Jabe and Harriet George S.; m. William Howard Breech, Mar. 16, 1945 (div. Sept. 1971); children: William Kimball Breech, Kathryn Breech Raft; m. Harry Jay Nederlander, July 2, 1976. Student, Sullins Coll., 1938-40, U. Mo., 1940-41, Am. Acad. of Dramatic Art, 1941-42. Prin. Marjorie Breech Interiors, Bloomfield Hills, Mich., 1970-95; ret. Mem. Village Club. Episcopal.

NEDERVELD, RUTH ELIZABETH, retired real estate executive; b. Hudsonville, Mich., Oct. 29, 1933; d. Ralph and Hattie (Ploeg) Schut; m. Terrill Lee Nederveld, June 6, 1952; children: Courtland Lee, Valerie Lynn Nederveld Heisey, Darwin Frederic. Degree in Real Estate, U. Mich., 1979; student, Pa. State U., Centre Hall, 1973, Aquinas Coll., Grand Rapids, Mich., 1974; degree, Grad. Realtors Inst., 1979. Cert. residential specialist; registered securities agt. With sales dept. Field Enterprises, Lancaster, Pa., 1962-72; sales assoc. E. James Hogan, 1972-74, C-21 Packard, Grand Rapids, Mich., 1974-80; assoc. broker comml. divsn. Markland Devel., Inc., 1980-86, Am. Acquest Realty, Inc., Grand Rapids, 1986-89; broker, owner R.E. Nederveld Realtors, Ada, Mich., 1989-94; ret., 1994. Pres. Civic Nucomers of Grand Rapids, 1978; trustee, elder Forest Hills Presbyn. Ch., Cascade, Mich., 1983-86. Named Poet Laureate, 2002. Mem. Nat. Assn. Realtors (mem. comml. dept. 1973—), Mich. Assn. Realtors, Grand Rapids Real Estate Bd., Woman's Council Realtors (corr. sec. 1986-87), Nat. Assn. Female Execs., Assn. Sales and Mktg. Execs. (exec. dir. internat. chpt. 1977-84, pres. Grand Rapids chpt. 1986-87). Republican. Avocations: poetry, hammered dulcimer and banjo, sailing, art, author.

NEDOM, H. ARTHUR, petroleum consultant; b. Lincoln, Nebr., Aug. 19, 1925; s. Henry Arthur and Pearle Bertrick (Swan) N.; m. Patricia Margaret Rankin, July 4, 1974; children: Richard A., Robert L., Nicole C. BS, U. Tulsa, 1949, MS, 1950; postgrad. in bus. adminstrn., Northwestern U., Evanston, Ill., 1968. Chief engr. Amerada Petroleum Corp., Tulsa, 1961-65, v.p., 1965-70, Natomas Co., San Francisco, 1971-74; also dir.; pres. Norwegian Oil Co., Houston, 1974-75; pres., mng. dir. Weeks Petroleum Ltd., Westport, Conn., 1975-82; cons., 1982—; chmn. bd. arbitration Prudhoe Bay Unit, 1983-85. Chmn. Offshore Tech. Conf., 1971; bd. dirs. Engrs. Joint Council, 1978 Contbr. articles to profl. jours. Served with inf. U.S. Army, 1943-45, ETO. Decorated Bronze Star; named Disting. Alumnus U. Tulsa, 1972 Mem. Soc. Petroleum Engrs. (dir. 1965-68, pres. 1967, Disting. Lectr. 1973, Disting Svc. award 1978, DeGolyer Disting. Svc. medal 1981, Disting. mem. 1983, Disting. lectr. emeritus 1989, Legion of Honor 1998, v.p. SPE Found. 1988-89), AIME (dir. 1966-69, 76-79, pres. 1977, hon. mem. 1982, Disting. Svc. award 1993), Am. Assn. Engring. Soc. (dir. 1980-82, chmn. 1981, Spl. award 1979, Engring. Svc. award 1980). Episcopalian. Home: 21 Deerwood Ln Westport CT 06880-2648

NEDUV, EUGENE, mathematician, researcher; b. Odessa, Ukraine, Feb. 28, 1972; s. Eduard and Inna Neduv. PhD, Columbia U., 2002. Instr. Columbia U., N.Y.C., NY, 1996—. Fellow Courant, NYU, 1992—94; grantee Travel, Columbia U., 1998. Mem.: Am. Math. Soc.

NEDZA, SANDRA LOUISE, manufacturing executive; b. Chgo., Aug. 20, 1951; d. Thomas and Ina Louise (Wilson) Ingle; m. James Owen Earnest, May 5, 1973 (div. Nov. 1984); m. Ronald Edward Nedza, Nov. 22, 1986; 1 child, Thomas Edward. Student acctg., Met. Sch. Bus., Chgo., 1970. Accounting clk. Gane Bros. & Lane, Inc., Chgo., 1967-72; advanced from expeditor to buyer Hammond Organ Co., 1972-84; purchasing/prodn. control supr. IRP-Profl. Sound Products, Addison, 1984-2000; purchasing agt. ANI Safety and Supply, Inc., Lincolnwood, 2000; adminstrv. asst. to v.p. mktg. svcs. and mktg. The Willy Wonka Candy Factory, Itasca, 2001—. Mem. Jobs Daughters, 1967—. Mem. Lions (pres. 2000—), Alpha Iota (scholarship key 1970). Clubs: Juke Box Sno-Riders (sec. 1986-87) (Fox Lake, Ill.), Lakeview Sno-Riders. Lodges: Lioness (pres. 1988-89) (Chgo.). Lutheran. Home: 1418 S Robert Dr Mount Prospect IL 60056-4542 E-mail: buzzylion@juno.com.

NEE, D. Y. BOB, think tank executive, engineering consultant; b. Shanghai, Dec. 13, 1935; came to U.S., 1953; m. Flora Hsu, Sept. 19, 1959; children: Winifred, Vivian, William BS, Purdue U., 1957; PhD, 1963; MS, U. Mo., Rolla, 1959. Sr. engr. Westinghouse Electric, Pitts., 1967-83; project mgr. U.S. Govt., San Francisco Bay, 1984-91; founder, pres. Inst. for Sys. Monitor, Tiburon, Calif., 1992—; pres. World Humanity Inst., Honolulu, 1995—. Pres. Acad. for Critical Edn.; sci. and tech. cons. ASTM, 1994. Author: Radicalizing the World Through Social Engineering, 1993, Destiny of Humanity, 1998, The New Globalism, 2002. Mem. adv. bd. Reagan for Pres., Washington, 1980. Mem. ASME. Office: Inst for Sys Monitor PO Box 26723 San Francisco CA 94126-6723 E-mail: whi187114@aol.com.

NEE, KAY BONNER, advertising executive; b. Plummer, Minn., Oct. 26; d. David Thomas and Helena Mary (Franken) Bonner; m. William Joseph Nee, Apr. 19, 1947; children: Christopher, Nicole, Lisa, Rachel. BA in English and Speech, Coll. St. Catherine, St.Paul, 1941; postgrad., U. Minn., 1947—50. Program dir. Sta. KATE, Albert Lea, Minn., 1941-43; with Spl. Svc. Forces, ETO, ETO, 1943-45; mgr. radio sta. Armed Forces Network, Pilsen, Czechoslovaki, 1945; actress Sta. WTCN, Mpls., 1945-50; freelance radio and T.V. actress, 1950-52; radio/TV dir. Manson-Gold-Miller, Mpls., 1952-54; dir. Sta. WCCO-TV, 1954-56; pres. North State Advt. Co., 1956-70; radio writer and prodr. Target Stores, Inc., 1970-72; writer, prodr. Sta. KTCA-TV, St. Paul, 1970-72; exec. dir. Minn. Assn. Vol. Social Svc. Agencies, 1972-81; pres. North State Advt. Co., Mpls., 1981—. V.p. Pederson, Herzog & Nee, Inc.; cons. in field. Author: Powhatan, 1971; co-author: Eugene J. McCarthy, U.S. Senator, 1964; contbr. stories to profl. publs. Mem. Gov. Minn. Commn. on Status of Women, 1965-77; mem.-at-large Minn. Dem. Farm Labor Exec. Com., 1963-65; chmn. Anoka County Com.; mem. Ctrl. Com. 3d dist., 1962-65; del. Dem. Nat. Conv., 1964; mem. Guthrie Theatre Found.; T.V. dir. McCarthy for Pres. campaign, 1968, press sec., 1982; bd. dirs. North Suburban Ctr. for Arts, pres., 1984-88; chair hist. prevention com. Banfill Locke Ctr. Arts, 1988—; mem. Congl. Health Care adv. com. Decorated Bronze Star; recipient Best Actress award Fridley Theatre, 1960, 65, Citation U.S. Holocaust Meml. Coun., 1981, N.W. Met. Bus. and Profl. Club award, 1983; Kay Bonner scholarship est. in her name Sch. Dist. 14, 1996. Mem. AFTRA, N.W. Advt. Coun., LLWV, Bus. and Profl. Women, Sister City Assn., Smithsonian Assocs., Minn. Press Club, Delta Phi Lambda. Home: 219 Logan Pkwy NE Minneapolis MN 55432-3056 Office: PO Box 32007 Minneapolis MN 55432-0007 E-mail: kbnee@mninter.net.

NEE, LINDA ELIZABETH, social science analyst; b. Boston, Dec. 29, 1938; d. Thomas Markham and Ellen Thomas (Jamieson) Nee. BA, Russell Sage Coll., 1961; MS in Social Work, Va. Commonwealth U., 1968. Social worker, social svc. dept., N.Y. Neurol. Inst., Columbia Presbyn. Med. Ctr., N.Y.C., 1961-66; med. social worker Tb San., Med. Coll. Va., Richmond, summer 1967; clin. social worker social work dept. Clin. Center, NIH, Bethesda, Md., 1968-74, clin. rsch. social worker sect. exptl. therapeutics, lab. clin. sci., NIMH, Bethesda, 1974-84, clin. genetics rsch. assoc. Nat. Inst. Neurol. Disorders and Stroke, 1984, social sci. analyst, 1984—; mem. ethics com. Md. State Bd. Social Work Examiners, 1979—. Adv., organizer, bd. dirs. Met. D.C. chpt. Alzheimer's and Related Diseases Assn., 1979-88, pres., 1982-86; mem. sci. bd. Familial Alzheimer's Disease Rsch. Found., Tulsa, 1987—; bd. dirs. Friends of Clin. Ctr., Bethesda, 1989—, pres., 1992; trustes The Sage Colls., Troy, N.Y., 1993—. Mem. NASW (chmn. ethics and grievances 1977-79; pres. Met. Washington 1975-77). Editor: Jour. Social Work Met. Washington, 1975-77; columnist: The Bulletin newsletter Nat. Assn. Social Workers, 1975-77; contbr. articles to profl. jours. Office: Clin Ctr Ninds Bethesda MD 20892-0001

NEE, SISTER MARY COLEMAN, college president emeritus; b. Taylor, Pa., Nov. 14, 1917; d. Coleman James and Nora Ann (Hopkins) N. AB, Marywood Coll., 1939, MA, 1943; MS, Notre Dame U., 1959. Joined Order of Sisters, Servants of Immaculate Heart of Mary, 1941; assoc. prof. math. Marywood Coll., Scranton, Pa., 1959-68, pres., 1970-88, pres. emerita, 1988—. Apostolic coord. Sisters, Servants Immaculate Heart of Mary, Scranton, Pa., 1968-70. Home and Office: Cathedral Convent 333 Wyoming Ave Scranton PA 18503-1223

NEECE, OLIVIA HELENE ERNST, investment company executive, consultant; b. L.A., Jan. 3, 1948; d. Robert and Beatrice Pearl Ernst; m. Huntley Lee Bluestein, 1967 (div. 1974); children: Melissa Dawn, Brendon Wade; m. Anthony Ray Neece, Mar. 20, 1976. Cert. interior design, UCLA, 1972-75; BSBA, U. So. Calif., 1990; MBA, UCLA, 1993; postgrad., Claremont U., 1998—. Cert. interior designer Calif. Coun. for Interior Design; lic. gen. contractor, real estate broker, Calif. Staff designer Frances Lux Designs, L.A., 1974; project designer Yates Silverman Inc., 1974-77; owner Olivia Neece Planning & Design, Tarzana, Calif., 1977-86; v.p. project devel. Design Services/Aircoa, Englewood, Colo., 1986-87; v.p. project adminstrn. Hirsch-Bedner Assoc., Santa Monica, Calif., 1987-88; treas.-sec. EON Corp., L.A., 1980—; owner Olivia Neece Planning & Design, Tarzana, 1988-93; dir. ops. The Ernst Group, L.A., 1980—85. Instr. ext. program UCLA, 1981—83; part-time prof. Calif. State U., Northridge, 1994—99; acad. rschr. Jet Propulsion Lab., 2000—02; spkr. in field. Co-author: A Step by Step Approach to Hotel Development, 1988; contbr. chapters to books, articles to profl. jours. Bd. dirs., chmn. advt. L.A. Music Ctr. Opera League; co-chair L.A. Master Chorale Gala; founder Performing Arts Ctr. L.A., Hollywood Bowl Soc.; inner cir. mem. Ctr. Theatre Group; charter mem. L.A. County Mus. Art; vol. restoration of San Diego R.R. Mus., 1985—92; patron L.A. Philharmonic; gold patron L.A. Opera Soc.; bd. dirs. Master Choral Assocs. Recipient Holiday Inn Devel. award, Foster City, Calif., 1986, Warwick, R.I., 1988, 1st and 2d place awards Lodging Hospitality Designers Circle, 1987, Gold Key award Russell St. Inn, 1986. Mem. Am. Soc. Interior Designers (1st pl. portfolio competition 1974), Acad. Mgmt., Fin. Mgmt. Assn., Internat. Inst. Designers & Arch. (profl., v.p., bd. dirs.), We. Acad. Mgmt., Assn. Info. Sys., Inst. Ops. Rsch. and Mgmt. Scis. Office: Neece Assoc 18200 Rosita St Tarzana CA 91356-4622 E-mail: olivia.neece@hotmail.com.

NEEDHAM, CAROL ANN, lawyer, educator; b. Chgo., Nov. 1, 1957; d. Robert Michael and Loretta Ann (Grabowy) Needham; m. Thomas Joseph Timmermann, July 23, 1994; 1 child, Genevieve. BA in English, Northwestern U., 1979, JD, 1985; MA in English, U. Va., 1982. Bar: Calif. 1987, D.C. 1989, Ill. 1985. Jud. law clk. U.S. Dist. Ct., Honolulu, 1985-86; assoc. Gibson, Dunn & Crutcher, L.A., 1986-90, Chadbourne & Parke, L.A., 1990-91; prof. law St. Louis U. Sch. Law, 1992—. Mem. corp. ethics com. St. Mary's Health Sys. Bd. Co-author: Lawyers and the Legal Profession; contbr. articles to profl. jours. Chair scholarship com. Verbum Dei H.S., L.A., 1987-95. Mem. ABA, Ctrl. States Law Assn. (treas. 1995-96, v.p. 1996-98, pres. 1998-99), Mo. Bar (vice chmn. com. on lawyers' advt. 1995-98, com. on multidisciplinary practice 2000, professionalism com. 2000—, com. on multijurisdictional practice 2001—), Am. Assn. Law Schs. (profl. responsibility exec. com. 1995-98). Office: St Louis U Sch Law 3700 Lindell Blvd Saint Louis MO 63108-3412 E-mail: needhamc@slu.edu.

NEEDHAM, GEORGE AUSTIN, investment banker; b. Beverly, Mass., Jan. 27, 1943; s. Everett Austin and Edith Strode (Walton) N.; m. Ellen Ann Levin, July 9, 1978; children— Michael Austin, Sarah Elisabeth, Paul Everett. BS in Bus. Adminstrn., Bucknell U., 1965; MBA, Stanford U., 1971. Portfolio mgr. Bankers Trust Co., N.Y.C., 1967-69; mng. dir. First Boston Corp., 1971-84; chmn., CEO Needham & Co. Inc., 1985—. Trustee Stanford Bus. Sch. Trust, Palo Alto, Calif., 1983-89. Served to 1st lt. U.S. Army, 1965-67. Mem. Fin. Analysts Fedn., Bond Club N.Y., The Links, Univ. Club, Sleepy Hollow Country Club, Coral Beach Club. Republican. Home: 79 E 79th St New York NY 10021-0202 Office: Needham & Co Inc 445 Park Ave New York NY 10022-2606

NEEDHAM, GEORGE MICHAEL, association executive; b. Buffalo, July 3, 1955; s. Paul James and Dolores Ann (Duffy) N.; m. Joyce Elaine Leahy, Nov. 28, 1992; 1 stepchild, Katherine Callison. BA in English, SUNY, Buffalo, 1976, MLS, 1977. Various profl. positions Charleston (S.C.) County Libr., 1977-84; dir. Fairfield County Dist. Libr., Lancaster, Ohio, 1984-89; mem. svcs. dir. Ohio Libr. Assn., Columbus, 1990-92; exec. dir. Pub. Libr. Assn., Chgo., 1993-96; state librarian State of Mich., Lansing, 1996-99; v.p. mem. svcs. OCLC Online Computer Libr. Ctr., Dublin, 1999—. Mem. adv. bd. Libr. Video Project, 1996—. Co-author: A Director's Checklist for Connecting Public Libraries to the Internet, 1995; author (book revs.) Booklist, 1994—, (video revs.), Libr. Jours., 1979—. Bd. dirs. Fairfield County chpt. ARC, Lancaster, 1984-88, Mt. Prospect Theatre Soc., Mt. Prospect, Ill., 1993-96, Lib. Media Project, 1997—. Mem. ALA, Pub. Libr. Assn., Ohio Libr. Assn. Avocations: acting, traditional folk music, writing, 2-time Jeopardy champion. Office: OCLC Online Computer Libr Ctr 6565 Frantz Rd Dublin OH 43017-3395 E-mail: needhamg@oclc.org.

NEEDHAM, GLEN RAY, entomology and acarology educator, researcher; b. Lamar, Colo., Dec. 25, 1951; s. Robert Lee and Evor Elaine (Kern) N.; m. Karla Marie Lohr, May 28, 1983; children: Kathleen Marie, John Harrison, Elizabeth Anne. BS, S.W. Okla. State U., 1973; MS, Okla. State U., 1975, PhD, 1978. Grad. rsch. asst. Okla. State U., Stillwater, 1974-78; asst. prof. Ohio State U., Columbus, 1978-84, assoc. prof., 1984—, co-organizer and coord. acarology summer program. Co-editor: Africanized Honey Bees and Bee Mites, 1988, Acarology IX: Proceedings and Symposia. Donor ARC, Columbus. Recipient Dist. Alumnus award Okla. State U., 1992. Mem. Acarology Soc. Am. (pres. 1994), Entomol. Soc. Am., Soc. Vector Ecology, Ohio Acad. Sci., Gamma Sigma Delta, Sigma Xi. Methodist. Achievements include research in tick and dust mite biology and control. Office: Ohio State U 484 W 12th Ave Columbus OH 43210-1214 E-mail: needham.1@osu.edu.

NEEDHAM, JAMES JOSEPH, retired financial services executive; b. Woodhaven, N.Y., Aug. 18, 1926; s. James Joseph and Amelia (Pasta) N.; m. Dolores A. Habick, July 1, 1950 (dec. Feb. 1993); children: James, Robert, Ravenna, Michael, Catherine; m. Patricia Henry Campo, May 24, 1995. Student, Cornell U., 1946; BBA, St. John's U., 1951, LLD (hon.), 1972. CPA, N.Y. Acct. Price Waterhouse & Co., N.Y.C, 1947-54; ptnr. R. T. Hyer & Co., Port Washington, N.Y., 1954-57; ptnr., mem. exec. com. A. M. Pullen & Co., N.Y.C., 1957-69; commr. SEC, Washington, 1969-72; chmn., chief exec. officer N.Y. Stock Exch., 1972-76; v.p. Internat. Fedn. Stock Exchs., 1973-75; pres. Internat. Fedn. Stock Exchanges, 1976-90; councilman Town of Southampton, N.Y., 1986—. Disting. prof., grad. div. Coll. Bus. Adminstrn., St. John's U., Jamaica, N.Y.; U.S. amb. to Japan Expo '85, 1982—; bd. dirs. Mut. of Am. Mut. Funds. Treas. Central Sch. Dist. 4, 1951-52, mem. budget and finance com., 1951, 63, chmn. high sch. planning com., 1947; active local Boy Scouts Am., 1962-65; mem. bishop's com. of laity Catholic Charities, Rockville Center, N.Y., 1960-68; mem. lay adv. bd. Cath. Youth Orgn., 1964-67; bd. advs. Coll. Bus. Adminstrn., St. John's U.; mem. hon. com. Am. Cancer Soc.; N.Y. State co-chmn. fin. Reagan for Pres. Campaign, 1980; Past dir., auditor Plainview (N.Y.) Republican Club.; Bd. govs. Fed. Hall Meml. Assos.; trustee N.Y. Foundling Hosp. Served with USNR, 1944-46. Recipient Disting. Citizen award N.Y. U. Law Sch., Disting. Service award in investment edn. Nat. Assn. Investment Clubs; named Bus. Person of Year Bus. Adminstrn. Soc. St. John's U., 1975; fellow Aspen Inst. for Humanistic Studies. Mem. N.Y. Soc. CPA's (past dir., treas., past pres. Nassau-Suffolk chpt., recognition award), Am. Inst. CPA's (past mem. council), L.I. Assn., N.Y. Chamber Commerce and Industry, Internat. C. of C. (U.S. council), Downtown-Lower Manhattan Assn. (dir., mem. exec. com.), N.Y. Credit and Fin. Mgmt. Assn. (Laurel award), Cath. Accountants Guild (past pres.), Accountants Club Am. Clubs: Serra (Nassau) (past pres.); Cornell of Nassau County, Wheatley Hills Golf (past treas.), Siwanoy Country; Burning Tree. Home: 97 Coopers Farm Rd Unit 1 Southampton NY 11968-4066

NEEDHAM, JUDY LEN, artist, art educator; b. Big Spring, Tex., Dec. 1, 1941; d. Carl Granvil and Mary Louise (Grilliette) Hill; m. Andrew James Needham III, Jan. 1, 1960; children: Andy, Jack, Johnny, Joshua. Grad. high sch., Tuscola, Tex., 1960. Workshop dir., coord. Fine Arts League Coleman (Tex.) County, 1990-96, art exhbn. dir. 1992-96, pres., 1992, 93. Exhibited in group shows Citizens Nat. Bank, Brownwood, Tex., 1992, 1st Coleman (Tex.) Nat. Bank, 1992-95, Coleman County State Bank, 1992-96, Security State Bank, Abilene, Tex., 1995, John Selmon Gallery, Stamford, Tex., 1995, Gage Hotel Emporium, Marathon, Tex., 1994-95, West Tex. Art Gallery, San Angelo, 1994-95, Kendall Art Gallery, San Angelo, 1995, Breckenridge (Tex.) Fine Arts Gallery, 199.4. Troop leader Heart of Tex. coun. Girl Scouts Am., Brownwood, 1965-70; den mother, asst. camp dir. Chisholm Tr. coun. Boy Scouts Am., Abilene, 1972-79; pres. Band Boosters Coleman H.S., 1990, 91, 92. Recipient Dist. Award of Merit Boy Scouts Am. Chisholm Trail Coun., 1979, Best of Show Cross Plains (Tex.) Paint and Palett, 1993, Best of Show Coleman County Fine Arts League, 1994, Best of Show Comanche County Art Assn., 1995. Avocations: crochet, photography, reading. Home: 427 Sunrise Dr Coleman TX 76834-2107

NEEDHAM, MAUREEN, dance educator, writer; b. Washington, June 11, 1938; d. Maurice d'Arlan and Thyria (Hughart) Needham; children: Terri, Jon, Sarah; m. Terry Charles Aldrich, 1999. BA, Harvard U., 1960; MA, U. Ill., 1972; PhD, NYU, 1989. Dancer New Orleans Opera Assn., 1952-56; choreographer, tchr. Harand Theatre Arts, Lake Elkhart, Wis., 1957-59; choreographer Hasty Pudding Theatricals, Cambridge, Mass., 1959; tchr. Jewish Found. Sch., Staten Island, 1961-62, Dwight Sch. for Girls, Englewood, N.J., 1962-63, Tenafly (N.J.) Pub. Schs., 1963-65; dance therapist Adler Zone Ctr., Champaign, Ill., 1971-75; asst. prof. U. Ill., 1975-77; assoc. prof. Vanderbilt U., Nashville, 1984—2001; writer Sarasota (Fla.) Style Mag., 2001—. Cons. day care ctrs. for handicapped, Ill., 1974; advisor U.S. Rsch. Internat. Music, 1987—. Editor, contbr.: Therapy in Motion, 1978, I See America Dancing, 2001; contbr. articles to profl. jours., chpts. to books and encys.; editor Channels newsletter, Am. World Dance Alliance, 1994-95; dance reviewer Champaign-Urbana Courier, 1976-78; critic, writer Nashville Scene, 1996-2001. Sen. Vanderbilt Faculty Senate, 1985-89, 96-97; bd. dirs. Nashville City Ballet, 1986-88; active Mayor's Task Force on Arts, Nashville, 1988-90, 94; bd. dirs. Coun. Cmty. Svcs., Nashville, 1995—, Ctr. Health Coalition, Nashville, 1995-2001; mem. grants allocations com. Metro Arts Coun., 1990, 94; chair faculty adv. coun., Blair Sch. Music, 1991-2001. Edmund James scholar U. Ill., 1972; Tenn. Endowment for Humanities grantee, 1987; NEH summer rsch. fellow, 1993. Mem. Soc. Dance History Scholars (bd. dirs. 1991-95), World Dance Alliance (North/South Am. rep. 1990—, co-editor calendar 1990-93), Woman's Faculty Orgn. (chair 1991-92, bd. dirs. 1996-2001).

NEEDHAM, NANCY JEAN, management consultant; b. Chgo., July 21, 1941; d. Robert Leonard and Grace Irene (Bennett) N.; children: Thomas, Charles, Catharine, Jessica. BA, Wellesley Coll., 1964; MBA, Harvard U., 1972, DBA, 1977. Pubs. specialist MIT, Cambridge, Mass., 1964-65; editor SRA, Chgo., 1966; sr. editor Ency. Britannica, 1967; cons. ABT Assocs., Cambridge, 1968; program mgr. Am. Sci. & Engring., Boston, 1969; faculty Harvard Bus. Sch., Cambridge, 1973-75; cons. CRI, 1977-78; prof. mgmt. Poly. U. N.Y., N.Y.C., 1986-96; assoc. dir. Ctr. for Advanced Tech. in Telecommunications, 1986-96; pres. ICGS Inc., 1978—. Pres. Global Initiatives, Inc., 1997—. Contbr. articles to profl. jours. Mem. Am. Soc. Macro Engring. (bd. dirs. 1984-92), C.G. Jung Found. (bd. dirs. 1988-94), Phi Beta Kappa. Presbyterian. Home: 548 Passuello Rd Delhi NY 13753-9643

NEEDHAM, RICHARD LEE, magazine editor; b. Cleve., Jan. 16, 1939; s. Lester Hayes and Helen (Bender) N.; m. Irene Juechter, Aug. 7, 1965; children: Margaret, Richard, Trevor. BA, Denison U., 1961; MA, U. Mo., 1967. Copy editor Sat. Rev., N.Y.C., 1967-68; editor-in-chief Preview Internat., 1968-69; financial and N.Y. editor Instns. mag.; also editor Service World Internat., N.Y.C., 1969-70; copy dir. American Home mag., 1970-71; exec. editor Ski Mag., 1971-74, editor, 1974-92, editor-in-chief, 1992-94, sr. contbg. editor, 1994—; contbg. editor Yachting Mag., 1996; editor Ency. of Skiing, 1978, Ski Fever, 1995; edit. dir. Times Mirror Mags. Conservation Coun., 1994-96; editor-in-chief Inside Tracks, 1996—2002; automotive writer Gannett Suburban Newspapers, 1995—; editor Arthritis Advisor, 2002—, Skiing Heritage, 2002—. Broadcaster: Ski Spot, CBS Radio, N.Y.C., 1978-83, On the Slopes, Audio Features Syndicate, 1984-87; author: Ski--50 Years in North

America, 1992, Ski Fever!, 1995. Served to lt. USNR, 1961-65. Recipient Lowell Thomas award, 1985 Mem. N.Am. Ski Journalists Assn., Ea. Ski Writers Assn., Internat. Assn. Ski Journalists, Internat. Motor Press Assn. Home and Office: 481 Sandy Point Ave Portsmouth RI 02871-3515 E-mail: rneed76476@aol.com.

NEEDLE, JEFFREY LOWELL, lawyer; b. Gt. Neck, N.Y., Feb. 21, 1947; BSBA, Boston U., 1969; JD, Am. U., 1972. Bar: Wash. 1975, U.S. Dist. Ct. (ea. and we. dist.) Wash. 1978, U.S. Ct. Appeals (9th cir.) 1984, U.S. Supreme Ct. 1991. VISTA atty. Pierce County Legal Svcs., Tacoma, 1972-73; pvt. practice, Seattle, 1977—. Adj. instr. law and justice dept. Cen. Wash. U., Seattle, 1989-92; commentator on Constn., Sta. KIRO, 1990-98. Civil rights columnist Trial News, 1986-92. Bd. dirs. Country Doctor Health Clinic, Seattle, 1981-85; mem. legal com. ACLU-Wash., Seattle, 1984—. Mem. Wash. State Bar Assn., ATLA (chmn. civil rights sect. 1992-93, bd. govs. 1993-96, chair employment rights sect. 1999-2000, amicus com. 2001—), Wash. State Trial Lawyers Assn. (chmn. civil rights sect. 1986-92), Trial Lawyers for Pub. Justice, Nat. Employment Lawyers Assn., Wash. Employees Lawyers Assn. (chair amicus com. 1997—). Avocations: music, reading, camping, sailing. Office: 119 1st Ave S Ste 200 Seattle WA 98104-3416

NEEDLEMAN, ALAN, mechanical engineering educator; b. Phila., Sept. 2, 1944; s. Herman and Hannah (Goodman) N.; m. Wanda Sapolsky, Apr. 12, 1970; children: Deborah, Daniel BS, U. Pa., 1966; MS, Harvard U., 1967, PhD, 1970. Instr. applied math. MIT, Cambridge, 1970-72, asst. prof., 1972-75; asst. prof. engring. Brown U., Providence, 1975-78, assoc. prof., 1978-81, prof., 1981—, dean engring., 1988-91; Florence Pirce Grant Univ. prof. Vis. asst. prof. Tech. U. Denmark, Lyngby, 1973; vis. fellow Clare Hall, U. Cambridge, Eng., 1978; vis. prof. MIT, Cambridge, 1991. Contbr. articles to profl. jours. Guggenheim fellow, 1977 Fellow ASME, Am. Acad. Mechanics, Danish Ctr. for Applied Math. and Mechanics (fgn.), Groupe Francais de Macanique des Matèriaux (hon.); mem. NAE. E-mail: alan. Home: 24 Elton St Providence RI 02906-4106 Office: Brown U Div Engring Providence RI 02912-0001 E-mail: Alan_Needleman@brown.edu.

NEEDLEMAN, JACOB, philosophy educator, writer; b. Phila., Oct. 6, 1934; s. Bemjamin and Ida (Seltzer) Needleman; m. Carla Satzman, Aug. 30, 1959 (div. 1989); children: Raphael, Eve; m. Gail Anderson, Dec. 1989. BA, Harvard U., 1956; grad., U. Freiburg, 1957-58; PhD, Yale U., 1961. Clin. psychology trainee West Haven (Conn.) Veterans Hosp. Adminstrn., 1960-61; rsch. assoc. Rockefeller Inst., N.Y., 1961-62; from asst. prof. to assoc. prof. philosophy San Francisco State U., 1962-66, prof philosophy, 1967—, chair dept. philosophy, 1968-69. Vis. scholar Union Theol. Seminary, 1967-68; dir. Ctr. Study New Religions, 1977-83; lectr. psychiatry, cons. med. ethics U. Calif., 1981-84. Author: Being-in-the-World, 1963, The New Religions, 1970, Religion for a New Generation, 1973, A Sense of the Cosmos, 1975, On the Way to Self-Knowledge: Sacred Tradition and Psychotherapy, 1976, Lost Christianity, 1980, Consciousness and Tradition, 1982, The Heart of Philosophy, 1982, Sorcerers, 1986, Sin and Scientism, 1986, Lost Christianity: A Journey of Rediscovery to the Centre of Christian Experience, 1990, Money and the Meaning of Life, 1991, Modern Esoteric Spirituality, 1992, The Way of the Physician, 1993, The Indestructible Question, 1994, A Little Book on Love, 1996, Time and the Soul, 1998; The American Soul, 2002; (trans.) The Primary World of Senses, 1963, Essays on Ego Psychology, 1964; editor Care of Patients with Fatal Illness, 1969, The Sword of Gnosis, 1973, Sacred Tradition and Present Need, 1974, Understanding the New Religions, 1978, Speaking of My Life: The Art of Living in the Cultural Revolution, 1979, Real Philosophy: An Anthology of the Universal Search for Meaning, 1991, The American Soul, 2002; contbr. Death and Bereavement, 1969, To Live Within, 1971, My Life with a Brahmin Family, 1972, The New Man, 1972, The Universal Meaning of the Kabbalah, 1973, The Phenomenon of Death. Grantee Religion in Higher Edn., Marsden Found., 1967—68, Ella Lymna Cabot Trust, 1969, Far West Inst., 1975. Office: San Francisco State U Dept Philosophy 1600 Holloway Ave San Francisco CA 94132-1722

NEEDLES, BELVERD EARL, JR. accountant, educator; b. Lubbock, Tex., Sept. 16, 1942; s. Belverd Earl and Billie (Anderson) N.; m. Marian Powers, May 23, 1976; children: Jennifer Helen, Jeffrey Scott, Annabelle Marian, Abigail Marian. BBA, Tex. Tech. U., 1964, MBA, 1965; PhD, U. Ill., 1969. CPA, Ill.; cert mgmt. acct. Asst. prof., assoc. prof. acctg. Tex. Tech. U., Lubbock, 1968-72; dean Coll. Bua. and Adminstn., Chgo. State U., 1972-76; prof. acctg. U. Ill., Urbana, 1976-78; dir. Sch. Accountancy DePaul U., Chgo., 1978-86, prof. acctg., 1976-88, Arthur Andersen & Co. alumni disting. prof. acctg., 1988—. Author: Accounting and Organizational Control, 1973, Modern Business, 2d edit., 1977, Principles of Accounting, 1980, 8th edit., 2002, Financial Accounting, 1982, 7th edit., 2001, The CPA Examination: A Complete Review, 7th edit., 1986, Comparative International Auditing Standards, 1985, Financial and Managerial Accounting, 5th edit., 2002; editor Accounting Instructor's Report, 1981—, The Accounting Profession and the Middle Market, 1986, Creating and Enhancing The Value of Post-Baccalareate Accounting Education, 1988, A Profession in Transition: The Ethical and Responsibilities of Accountants, 1989, Comparative International Accounting Educational Standards, 1990, Accounting Education for the 21st Century: The Global Challenges, 1994, Financial Acctg.: A Global Approach, 1999. Treas., bd. dirs. CPAs for Pub. Interest, 1978-86. Gen. Electric fellow, 1965-66, Deloitte Haskins and Sells fellow, 1966-68; named Disting. Alumnus Tex. Tech. U., 1986; recipient Award of Merit DePaul U., 1986, Faculty Award of Merit Fedn. of Schs. of Accountancy, 1990, Excellence in Tchg. Award DePaul U., 1998; named among 100 most influential accts. Acctg. Today, 2001. Fellow Am. Acctg. Assn. (sec. internat. sect. 1984-86, vice chmn. 1986-87, chmn. 1987-88, named outstanding internat. acctg. educator 1996); mem. AICPA (named Outstanding Educator 1992), Fedn. Schs. Accountancy (bd. dirs. 1980-87, pres. 1986), Acad. Internat. Bus., Ill. CPA Soc. (bd. dirs. 1994-96, vice chair 2001—, Outstanding Acctg. Educator 1990), European Acctg. Assn. (exec. com. 1986-89), Intenrat. Assn. for Edn. & Rsch. in Acctg. (v.p. 1989-92, sec.-treas. 1992-97, pres. 1997—), Phi Delta Kappa, Phi Kappa Phi, Beta Alpha Psi (named Acct. of Yr. for Edn. 1992), Beta Gamma Sigma.

NEEL, HARRY BRYAN, III, surgeon, scientist, educator; b. Rochester, Minn., Oct. 28, 1939; s. Harry Bryan and May Birgitta (Bjornsson) N.; m. Ingrid Helene Vaga, Aug. 29, 1964; children: Carlton Bryan, Harry Bryan IV, Roger Clifton. BS, Cornell U., 1962; MD, SUNY-Bklyn., 1966; PhD, U. Minn., 1976. Diplomate Am. Bd. Otolaryngology. Intern Kings County Hosp., Bklyn., 1966-67; resident in gen. surgery U. Minn. Hosps., Mpls., 1967-68; resident in otolaryngology Mayo Grad. Sch. Medicine Mayo Clinic, Rochester, Minn., 1970-74, cons. in otorhinolaryngology, 1974—, cons. in cell biology, 1981—, assoc. prof. otolaryngology and microbiology Med. Sch., 1979-84, prof., 1984—, also chmn. dept. otolaryngology. Mem. adv. com. Pitts. Eye and Ear Found. Author: Cryosurgery for Cancer, 1976; contbr. chpts. to books, articles to profl. jours. V.p. bd. dirs. Minn. Orch. in Rochester, Inc., 1982, pres., chmn., 1983—84; mem. devel. com. Minn. Orchestral Assn., 1983, Mayo Found., 1983—86; bd. dirs. Mayo Health Plan, 1986—92, chmn., 1990—92; mem. bd. Mayo Mgmt. Svcs., Inc., 1992—94; mem. bd. regents U. Minn., 1991—, chair faculty staff, student affairs com., 1993—95, 1999, vice chmn. bd., 1995—97, chmn. fin. and ops. com., 1999—2001, mem. audit com., 1995—2000, chair litigation com., 2001—; bd. dirs. Greater Rochester Area Univ. Ctr., 1993—; trustee U. Minn. Found., 1996—, mem. fin. com., 1999—2001; chmn. U. Minn. Investment Adv. Com., 1999—2002; mem. State Commn. on U. Minn. Excellence, 2002, commn. on U. Minn. Excellence, 2002—. With USPHS, 1968—70. Recipient travel award Soc. Acad. Chmn. Otolaryngology, 1974, Ira J. Tresley rsch. award Am. Acad. Facial and Reconstructive Surgery, 1982, Master Tchr. award in surgery Alumni Assn. Coll. Medicine, SUNY, Health Sci. Ctr., Bklyn., 1991, The Best Doctors in Am. Assn. Collegiate Women Athletic Admisntrs., 1992, The Best Doctors in Am. award Woodward/White, 1992-93, 94-99. Mem. AMA, ACS (bd. govs. 1985-90, devel. bd. 1988—, treas. 1990-98, sec.-treas. Minn. chpt. 1983-85, pres. 1988-89), Am. Acad. Otolaryngology-Head and Neck Surgery (prize for basic rsch. in otolaryngology 1972, bd. dirs. 1988-91, established Neel Disting. Rsch. Lectureship Endowment Fund 1994, audit com. 1998-2000, chair investment adv. com. 1995—, chmn. audit com. 1999-2000), Minn. Med. Assn., Zumbro Valley Med. Soc., Am. Broncho-Esophagological Assn. (pres.-elect 1988, pres. 1989-90), Am. Laryngological, Rhinological and Oto. Sco. (Mosher award 1980, pres.-elect 1995-96, centennial pres. 1996-97, investment com. 1994—), Am. Laryngological Assn. (Casselberry award 1985, sec. 1988-93, v.p. 1994, pres. 1994—, Newcomb award 1996, Baker lectr. 1998), Assn. for Rsch. in Otolaryngology, Assn. Acad. Depts. in Otolaryngology (sec.-treas. 1984-86, pres.-elect 1986, pres. 1988-9), Alumni Assn. Cornell U. (Outstanding Alumni award 1985), Collegium ORL Amicitiae Sacrum (bd. dirs. 2000—), Am. Bd. Otolaryngology (bd. dirs. 1986—, treas. 1998—), Am Laryngol. Voice Rsch. and Edn. Found. (charter bd. dirs. 1996—). Clubs: Rochester Golf and Country. Republican. Presbyterian. Home: 828 8th St SW Rochester MN 55902-6310 Office: Mayo Clinic 200 1st St SW Rochester MN 55905-0002

NEEL, JOHN DODD, memorial park executive; b. McKeesport, Pa., Aug. 7, 1923; s. Harry Campbell and Anna (Dodd) N.; m. Jean Wyatt, Feb. 11, 1948; children: Harry C., John Dodd II, W. Wyatt (dec.), Jeffrey J. BA, Pa. State U., 1946. From salesman to pres. Jefferson Meml. Park, Pitts., 1946-88, chmn. bd. dirs., 1988—. Alternate mem. Zoning Hearing Bd., Pleasant Hills, Pa., 1970—. Mem. adv. bd. Pa. State U., McKeesport; former mem. Pa. State Real Estate Commn. 1st lt. USAAF, 1943-45. Decorated Air medal with 4 clusters, D.F.C.; recipient George Washington cert. Freedom Found., 1974. Mem. Pa. Cemetery Fun. Assn. (pres. 1963-65), Internat. Cemetery and Funeral Assn. (pres. 1973-74), West Jefferson Hills C. of C. (pres. 1984), VFW, Am. Legion 57th Bomb Wing Assn., South Hills Country Club, Indian Lake Golf Club, Aero Club, OX-5CLUB, Kiwanis (pres. 1959), Masons, Shriners, Tau Kappa Epsilon. Presbyterian. Office: 401 Curry Hollow Rd Pittsburgh PA 15236-4636

NEEL, JUDY MURPHY, association executive; b. Rhome, Tex. d. James W. and Linna B. (Vess) Neel; m. Ellis F. Murphy, Jr., Dec. 30, 1975; children from previous marriage: Mary B. Schmidt, Janet E. Wescott, Susan E. Salinas. BS, Northwestern U., 1976; MBA, Roosevelt U., 1983. V.p. Murphy, Tashjian & Assocs., Chgo., 1960-73; exec. dir. Automotive Affiliated Rep. Assn., 1973-78; mgr. Automotive Svc. Ind. Assn., 1978-80; exec. dir. Am. Soc. Safety Engrs., Des Plaines, Ill., 1980-98, Am. Assn. Diabetes Educators, 1999—. Recipient Assn. Leadership award Bus. Women's Network/Assn. Trends Mag., 1998. Mem. Chgo. Soc. Assn. Execs. (bd. dirs. 1979—, pres. 1985—, Shapiro award 1991), Am. Soc. Assn. Execs. (sec.-treas. 1994, found. dir. 1986-90, bd. dirs. 1990-95, Key award 1986). Republican.

NEEL, RICHARD EUGENE, economics and business educator; b. Bluefield, Va., Jan. 7, 1932; s. Charles Richard and Zell LaVerne (Bowling) Neel; m. Binnie Jo LeFever, June 10, 1961; children: Jeffrey Richard, Cynthia Jo. BS, U. Tenn., 1954, MS, 1955; PhD, Ohio State U., 1960. Instr. econs. Ohio State U., 1958-60; asst. prof. econs. Coll. William and Mary, 1960-61; asst. prof. U. South Fla., 1961-63, assoc. prof., 1963-66, chmn. econs. and fin. programs, 1964-66, acting chmn. grad. program Coll. Bus Adminstrn., 1965-66; dir. instl. planning Fla. Tech. U., 1966-68, chmn. dept. econs., prof. econs., 1968-69; assoc. dean Sch. Bus. Adminstrn. Ga. State U., 1969-77, dean grad. studies Sch. Bus. Adminstrn., 1973-77, prof. econs. Sch. Bus. Adminstrn., 1969-78; dean Coll. Bus. Adminstrn. U. N.C., Charlotte, 1978-93, prof. econs., 1978-97, dean emeritus Belk Coll. Bus. Adminstrn., 1997—, prof. econs. emeritus, 1997—. Author (contbg auth): (book) The Case Study of Off-Campus Postsecondary Education on Military Bases, 1980; contbr. articles, monographs to profl publs; editor: (book) Readings in Price Theory, 1973. Mem fin and admin comt United Way Cent Carolinas Inc; bd dirs Charlotte Foreign Trade Zone. Mem.: Beta Gamma Sigma, Phi Kappa Phi. Presbyterian. Office: U NC at Charlotte Dept Economics Charlotte NC 28223 E-mail: reneel@email.uncc.edu.

NEEL, SAMUEL ELLISON, lawyer; b. Kansas City, Mo., Feb. 22, 1914; s. Ellison Adger and Serena (Smith) N.; m. Mary Wilson, Oct. 11, 1941; children: James Adger, Amy Bowen, Wilson (dec. 1947), Wendy Busselle, Mary Ellison, Sophia Talbot. BA, Westminster Coll., Mo., 1935, LLD, 1995; LLB, Yale U., 1938. Bar: Mo. 1938, D.C. 1946, Va. 1953. Spl. asst. to atty. gen. anti-trust div. U.S. Dept. Justice, Washington, 1938-40, rep. State-War Dept. Mission on Japanese Combines, 1946; legal staff adv. commn. Coun. Nat. Def., OPM, WPB, 1940-42; pvt. practice Washington and McLean, Va., 1946-93. Bd. dirs. emeritus Rouse Co.; v.p., dir. Image Hunter Publ. Co., 1997-99. Mem. Fed. City Coun., Washington, 1954-58; pres. McLean Citizens Assn., 1953-54, Pub. Utilities Commn., Fairfax County, Va., 1956-57, The Squam Lakes Assn., N.H., 1987-89; chmn. Fairfax County Water Authority, 1957-63, Fairfax County Housing Authority, 1970-72; mem. adv. com. mortgage fin. FHA, 1956-66; pres. Neel Found.; trustee Westminster Coll. Comdr. USNR, 1942-46; staff comdr. air forces Pacific Fleet. Mem. Mortgage Bankers Assn. Am. (exec. v.p. 1965-66, gen. counsel 1946-74), Soc. Cin., Beta Theta Pi, Omicron Delta Kappa. Democrat. Episcopalian (past trustee). Clubs: Lawyers (Washington), Metropolitan (Washington); N.Y. Yacht. Home: 1157 Chain Bridge Rd Mc Lean VA 22101 Office: PO Box 385 Mc Lean VA 22101

NEEL, SPURGEON HART, JR. physician, retired army officer; b. Memphis, Sept. 24, 1919; s. Spurgeon Hart and Pyrle (Womble) N.; m. Alice Glidewell Torti, Nov. 18, 1939; children: Spurgeon Hart III, Alice Leah Neel Zartarian. Student pre-med., Memphis State U., 1939; MD, U. Tenn., 1942; MPH, Harvard U., 1958; MSBA, George Washington U., 1965. Diplomate: Am. Bd. Preventive Medicine. Intern Meth. Hosp., Memphis, 1943; resident x-ray Santa Ana (Calif.) AFB, 1944; resident aviation medicine USAF Sch. Aerospace Medicine, 1960; commd. 2d lt. U.S. Army, 1942, advanced through grades to maj. gen., 1970; various assignments U.S., 1943-44, 47-48, ETO, 1944-47; chief surgeon service Ft. McPherson, Ga., 1949; med. service, 1949; div. surgeon (82d Airborne Div.), Ft. Bragg, N.C., 1949-51; comdr. (30th Med. Group), Korea, 1953-54; dep. dir. div. physiology and pharmacology (WRAIR, WRAMC), 1956; chief aviation br. (OTSG), 1957; chief aviation medicine Ft. Rucker, Ala., 1960; comdg. officer U.S. Army Hosp., post surgeon, 1961-64; stationed in Vietnam, 1965-66, 68-69; dep. surgeon gen. U.S. Army, Washington, 1969-73; comdr. (U.S. Army Health Services Command), 1973-77. Clin. assoc. prof. family practice U. Tex. Health Sci. Ctr., San Antonio, now prof. emeritus occupl. and aerospace medicine U. Tex. Sch. Pub. Health; med. cons. U.S. Automobile Assn., other industries, San Antonio. Contbr. articles med. jours. Decorated D.S.M. with oak leaf cluster, Legion of Merit with 4 clusters, Bronze Star with oak leaf cluster, Air medal with 3 oak leaf clusters, Joint Service Commendation medal, USAF Commendation medal, Purple Heart, others.; recipient Seaman award Assn. Mil. Surgeons U.S., 1950, Gary Wratten award, 1967; McClelland award Army Aviation Assn. Am., 1962; named to U.S. Army Aviation Hall Fame, 1976; recipient Lyster award Aerospace Med. Assn., 1977, Nat. Soc. DAR medal of honor, 1999. Fellow A.C.P., Am. Coll. Preventive Medicine (past v.p.), Royal Soc. Health, Aerospace Med. Assn. (past pres.), Internat. Acad. Aviation and Space Medicine, Am. Acad. Med. Adminstrs., Am. Coll. Health Care Execs.; mem. AMA (past-sec. sect. mil. medicine), Assn. Mil. Surgeons U.S., Assn. U.S. Army, Army Aviation Assn. Am., Dustoff (Hall of Fame 2001), Phi Chi (assoc.). Home: 4106 Tarlac Dr San Antonio TX 78239-3072

NEELD, MICHAEL EARL, health facility administrator; b. Portland, Oreg., May 13, 1955; s. Carl Eugene and Frances Karlene (Riggers) N.; m. Ann Pelissier. BA in Journalism and Polit. Scis., U. Oreg., 1977. Advt. rep. Post Publs., Camas, Wash., 1977; chpt. cons. Kappa Sigma Internat. Fraternity, Charlottesville, Va., 1977-79; fundraising dir. Am. Cancer Soc., Richmond, 1979-80; news editor, polit. rep. Sta. KYXI, Portland, 1980-84; comms. dir. Moshofsky for Congress, 1984; pub. info. officer Wash. State Ho. of Reps., Olympia, 1984-85; comms. dir. Paulus for Gov., Portland, 1985-86; sr. info. officer Wash. State Ho. of Reps., Olympia, 1986-91, rep. staff coord., 1991-96, pub. rels. coord., 1996-99; pub. affairs dir. Washington Health Care Assn., 1999—2001. Exec. dir. Wash. Health Care Assn., 2001—; founder, ptnr. Pacific N.W. Advocates Pub. Affairs Cons., Olympia, 1989-96; instr. polit. strategy, tactics, fundraising and media Wash. State Rep. Party, Tukwila, 1991-92; campaign dir. House Rep. Orgnl. Com., Olympia, 1991-92. Mem. Downtown Olympic Rotary. Recipient Best Coverage of Breaking News award Oreg. AP/Broadcast, 1982. Mem. U. Oreg. Alumni Assn., Trumpeters, City Club of Portland, Fremont Grove Soc. (founder), Indian Summer Golf and Country Club (v.p. 1998-2000), Wash. State Golf Assn. (club rep. 1999—), Pacific N.W. Golf Assn. (club rep. 1999—), Kappa Sigma (alumni, housing corp. bd. dirs. 1980-84). Presbyterian. Avocations: politics, reading, golf. Home: 7224 Deerfield Park Dr NE Olympia WA 98516-2132 Office: Wash Health Care Assn 2120 State Ave NE # 102 Olympia WA 98506-6514 Personal E-mail: m.neeld@worldnet.att.net. Business E-Mail: mikeneeld@whca.org.

NEELEY, BEVERLY EVON, sociologist, consultant; b. Oakland, Calif., June 14, 1947; d. Chester Arthur Neeley Jr. and Thalia Evon Littlefield; m. Niles Bruce, Sept. 13, 1970 (div. Aug. 1977); children: Autumn Yvonne, Bruce Curd. BA, U. Calif., Berkeley, 1970, MPH, 1972; PhD, U. Calif., San Diego, 1983. Eligibility supr. W. Oakland Health Ctr., 1970-72; health edn. supr. San Diego County Drug Edn., 1972-74; proposal writer, cons. Cmty. Crisis Ctr., San Diego, 1974-77; sociologist, dir., sec., treas. Image Mind, Inc., Oakland, 1993—. Instr. Calif. State U., San Diego, 1976; health planner Health Sys. Agy., San Diego, 1978; mem. adv. bd. Help Other People Evole Inst., Oakland, 2000—. Author: The Ethiopian Grail, 1994. Founder S.E. Drug Coalition, San Diego, 1974, Nu-Way Yougth Svc. Ctr., San Diego, 1976. Mem. NAACP, Sojourner Truth Tenants Assn. Avocations: reading, walking, cooking. Home and Office: 5915 Martin Luther King Jr Way B10 Oakland CA 94609 E-mail: drbneeley3@hotmail.com.

NEELEY, DELMAR GEORGE, mediator, pastoral counselor; b. Charleston, Ill., June 4, 1937; s. Glenn Truman and Gladys Bernice (Dittman) N.; m. Yvonne Tamara Penrod, Mar. 2, 1957 (div. Feb. 1969); children: Timothy Del, Kimberly Yvonne, Terry; m. Terry Anne Barbour, Aug. 28, 1971; children: Robert James, Stephen Edward. BA in Philosophy, Olivet Nazarene U., 1965, MA in Lit., 1969; EdD, U. Sarasota, 1996. Cert.: Fla. Bar Assn. (mediator); diplomate Am. Psychotherapy Assn., in marriage and family counseling Am. Soc. Christian Therapists, lic. mental health counselor-intern Fla. , cert. clin. pastoral counselor advanced cert.; mediator and arbitrator. Mgr. mgmt. devel. Rauland Divsn. Zenith Corp., Chgo., 1967-70; sr. personnel cons. Mid. West Svc. Co., 1971-73; dir. human resources Nichols-Homeshield Inc., West Chicago, Ill., 1974-76, Gould Inc./Ind. Battery Divsn., Langhorne, Pa., 1976-81; pres., owner Barbour-Neeley Inc., Sarasota, Fla., 1982-91. Stephen Ministries leader. Recipient Meritorious Svc. award Chgo. Boys Club, 1970, Svc. award Chgo. Jaycees, 1967-71. Mem.: Nat. Conservative Christian Ch. (ordained min. counseling), Am. Soc. Christian Therapists, Nat. Assn. of Masters in Psychology, Fla. Assn. Christian Counselors (cert.), Fla. Acad. Profl. Mediators, Am. Assn. Profl. Chaplains, Ctr. for Study of Presidency, Am. Assn. Christian Counselors, Am. Psychotherapy Assn., Nat. Christian Counselors Assn. (lic. clin. pastoral counselor). Congregationalist. Home: 3778 Bonaventure Ct Sarasota FL 34243-4862

NEELEY, JAMES KAME, credit agency executive; b. Visalia, Calif., Dec. 4, 1955; s. James M. and Dorothy Neeley; m. Lynn Travioli, Aug. 13, 1977; children: Janessa, Jimmy. BS in Bus. Adminstrn., Calif. State U., Fresno, 1978. Lic. personal property appraiser. Loan officer Visalia Prodn. Credit Assn., Tipton, Calif., 1978-82; asst. br. mgr. Visalia (Calif.) Prodn. Credit Assn., 1982-83; v.p., br. mgr. Valley Prodn. Credit Assn., Visalia, 1983-91, FarmCreditWest, Visalia, 1991—. Advisor Redwood Future Farmers of Am., Visalia, 1988-90; advisor computer software devel. Western Farm Credit Bank, Sacramento, 1990-91; mem., advisor Kit Fox Adv. Com., Visalia, 1995-96. Mem. Ctrl. Dem. Com., Visalia, 1975-77; soccer coach Am. Youth Soccer Orgn., Tulare, Calif., 1990-96, 99; coach Tulare Little League, 1996-97; parent vol. St. Alyosios Sch., Tulare, 1993-96; mem. coun. on fin., head audit com. Calif./Nev. United Meth., 1990-96; layleader Tulare United Meth. Ch., 1994-96, mem. adminstrv. bd., 1996-97. Scholar So. Calif. Edn., 1974. Mem. Tulare Host Lions Club (pres. 1982-83, ag leader alumni com. 1999—), Phi Kappa Phi. Avocations: collecting old and rare books, soccer, basketball, skiing. Office: FarmCreditWest PO Box 4379 Visalia CA 93278-4379 E-mail: james.neeley@farmcreditwest.com.

NEELY, CHARLES B., JR. lawyer; b. Raleigh, N.C., Dec. 11, 1943; AB with honors, U. N.C., 1965; JD, Duke U., 1970. Bar: N.C. 1970. Lawyer Maupin, Taylor & Ellis P.A., Raleigh. Mem. 4th Cir. Jud. Conf. Mem. N.C. Ho. of Reps., 1995-99. Capt. USNR, JAGC, 1965-89. Fellow Am. Bar Found.; mem. ABA (taxation sect.), N.C. Bar Assn. (chmn. law office mgmt. sect. 1986-88, bd. govs. 1995-98), Inst. for Profls. in Taxation. Address: Maupin Taylor & Ellis PA PO Drawer 19764 Ste 500 3200 Beechleaf Ct Raleigh NC 27619 E-mail: cneely@maupintaylor.com.

NEELY, JOHN GAIL, otolaryngologist; b. Oklahoma City, Dec. 10, 1939; MD, U. Okla., 1965. Intern U. Oreg. Med. Ctr., Portland, 1965-66; resident in surgery Baylor Hosp., Houston, 1968-69, resident in otolaryngology, 1969-72; fellow Otologic Med. Group, L.A., 1972-73; staff Barnes Hosp., St. Louis, 1992—, Jewish Hosp., St. Louis, 1992—; prof., dir. rsch. Washington U., 1992—. Mem. ACS, Am. Neurotology Soc., Am. Otol. Soc., Am. Acad. Otolaryngology, Head and Neck Surgery, Soc. Univ. Otolaryngologists, Triologic Soc. Office: Washington U Sch Medicine Dept Oto Head-Neck Surgrey 660 S Euclid Ave Rm 8115 Saint Louis MO 63110-1010 E-mail: neelyg@msnotes.wustl.edu.

NEELY, MARION VICTORIA, community volunteer; b. Prescott, Mich., Apr. 5, 1937; d. Robert John and Marie Caroline (Koch) Fabera; divorced; children: Rebekah, Nathan, Sally. Student, Lake Superior State Coll., Sault Ste. Marie, Mich., 1954-56, Lincoln U., 1981-85. Lab. tech., acctg. clk., prodn. worker Chesebrough Ponds, Inc., Jefferson City, 1967-86; supr. for telephone book delivery Directory Distributing Assocs., Inc., St. Louis, 1986-95. Innovative recycler, Holts Summit, 1997—. Editor: (newsletter) Another Look Unltd., Holts Summit, 1992—; contbg. author: (anthology) The Simple Life, 1998; designer: Memory Quilts, 1993—, Broken Levees Sampler Quilt (1993 Flood Memoir) 1994, Miniature Books, 1999, others; contbr. articles to mags. Quilt donation to Habitat for Humanity, Jefferson City, Mo., 1998, Fulton, Mo., 1995; active cmty. recycling projects. Mem. Co-op Am., Phi Alpha Theta. Avocations: writing, travel, community volunteerism.

NEELY, ROBERT ALLEN, retired ophthalmologist; b. Temple, Tex., Mar. 1, 1921; s. Jubal A. and Almeida (Fordtran) N.; m. Eleanor V. Stein, June 29, 1944 (dec.); m. Joy S. Brown, Aug. 24, 1990; children: Byron D., Warren F. BA, U. Tex., 1942, MD, 1944; postgrad., Washington U., St. Louis, 1951-52. Intern, then resident Hermann Hosp., Houston, 1944-45, 55-57; gen. practice medicine, 1846-51; specializing in ophthalmology, Bellville, Tex., 1955-92; ret., 1992. Trustee, staff mem. Bellville Hosp., Inc.; pres. Mid-Tex. Nursing Homes, Inc.; ret., 1992. Mem. Bellville Ind. Sch. Dist. Sch. Bd., 1948-53; past pres. Bellville Area United Fund; mem. adv. bd. Sam Houston Area coun. Boy Scouts Am., also past mem. Nat. coun.; mem. chancellor's coun. U. Tex. Sys.; pres. Bellville Econ. Devel. Corp., 2000-01. With USNR, 1943-46, 53-55. Recipient Silver Beaver award Boy Scouts Am. Fellow Am. Acad. Ophthalmology; mem. AMA, Austin-Grimes-Waller Counties Med. Soc. (past pres.), 9th Dist. Med. Soc. (psst pres.), Tex. Med. Assn., Tex. Ophthal. Assn., Tex. Soc. Ophthalmology and Otolaryngology, Belleville C. of C., Littlefield Soc. (U. Tex., Austin), VFW, Bellville Golf Club (past pres.), Doctors Club, LIons (past pres.). Republican. Lutheran. Home: 105 E Hacienda St Bellville TX 77418-3103

NEELY, SALLY SCHULTZ, lawyer; b. L.A., Mar. 2, 1948; BA, Stanford U., 1970, JD, 1971. Bar: Ariz. 1972, Calif. 1977. Law clk. to judge U.S. Ct. appeals (9th cir.), Phoenix, 1971-72; assoc. Lewis and Roca, 1972-75; asst. prof. Law Sch. Harvard U., Cambridge, Mass., 1975-77; assoc. Shutan & Trost, P.C., L.A., 1977-79; ptnr., sr. counsel Sidley & Austin, 1980—99; sr. counsel Sidley Austin Brown & WoodLLP, 1999—. Mem. faculty Am. Law Inst.-ABA Chpt. 11 Bus. Reorgns., 1989-95, 97—, Banking and Comml. Lending Law, 1997-99, Nat. Conf. Bankruptcy Judges, 1988, 90, 95, 96, 97, 99, 2002, Fed. Jud. Ctr., 1989, 90, 94-95, Southeast Bankruptcy Law Inst., 2002, Workshop Bankruptcy and Bus. Reorgn. NYU, 1992—; rep. 9th cir. jud. conf., 1989-91; mem. Nat. Bankruptcy Conf., 1993—, co-chair com. on legislation, 2001--. Chair Stanford U. Law Sch. Reunion Giving, 1996; bd. vis. Stanford U. Law Sch., 1990-92; atty. mem. editl. bd. Am. Bankruptcy Law Jour. Mem. ABA, Am. Coll. Bankruptcy, Calif. Bar Assn. Office: Sidley Austin Brown & Wood LLP 555 W 5th St Ste 4000 Los Angeles CA 90013-3000 E-mail: sneely@sidley.com.

NEELY, VICKI ADELE, accountant, legal assistant, poet; b. Dallas, Nov. 29, 1962; d. Robert Theodore and Linda Carolyn (Vogtsberger) Kissel; 1 child, Travis Wade. Student, Richland Coll., 1981-82, Austin C.C., 1983, San Antonio Coll., 1983, Am. Coll. Real Estate, 1983. Asst. mgr., leasing cons. Nash Phillips/Copus, Inc., 1983-85; loan processor Univ. Nat. Bank, 1985-87; co-owner Reels on Wheels, 1987; loan sec. Tex. Am. Bank/Richardson, N.A., 1987-88; legal sec., paralegal Clements, Allen & Warren, 1988-89; legal sec. Jackson & Walker, A Profl. Corp., 1989-90, Robins, Kaplan, Miller & Ciresi, 1990-91; freelance litigation sec. Smith & Underwood, 1991-92, legal asst.,

1992-94, Collins, Norman & Basinger, P.C., Dallas, 1994, Law Offices of Arlen D. (Spider) Bynum, 1995; pvt. practice cons. Richardson, Tex., 1996—. Author: (poems) Animal Love, Believe, 1993; co-author: Texas Rent-A-Bank, 1993. Methodist. Avocations: sailing, reading, dancing, painting. Home and Office: 1911 Eastfield Dr Richardson TX 75081-5435 E-mail: vneely@attbi.com.

NEELY, WILLIAM CHARLES, science educator, consultant; b. Cave City, Ark., Nov. 22, 1931; s. Kenneth Andrew and Sara Virginia Neely; m. Betty Jean Tibi, Dec. 7, 1956; 1 child Virginia Stringfellow 1 child William (dec.). D, La. State U., 1962. Rsch. chemist Chemstrand Rsch. Ctr. Inc., Research Triangle Park, NC, 1962—66; prof. Auburn (Ala.) U., 1962—. Cons. Auburn Chem. Co. Inc., 1986—, Sci. Applications Internat., San Diego, 1995—. Contbr. articles to profl. jours.; inventor in field. Chmn. Bd. Zoning Adjustment, Auburn, 1986—96. Served with U.S. Army, 1955—66, Germany. Mem.: Sigma Xi (life). Home: 415 Hare Ave Auburn AL 36830 Office: Auburn U Dept Chemistry 257 Chemistry Bldg Auburn AL 36849 E-mail: neelywc@auburn.edu.

NEEMAN, YUVAL, information technology executive; b. Israel; married; 3 children. BSEE, MS, Technion, Israel Inst. Tech. With Products Computers, Israel; various sr. devel. pos. Microsoft, Redmond, Wash., 1989, gen. mgr. MIcrosoft Visual Langs., corp. v.p., developer divsn. Avocations: beach house, kayaking, reading, travel. Office: One Microsoft Way Redmond WA 98052*

NEENAN, PETER ANTHONY, state agency administrator; b. Sioux City, Iowa, Dec. 12, 1946; s. Edward W. and Margaret B. Neenan; m. Linda J. Fisher, Feb. 5, 1947. BA, Creighton U., 1969; MA, U. Iowa, 1972; PhD, U. Wis., 1982. Asst. prof. Simmons Coll., Boston, 1978—82, U. of NC, Chapel Hill, 1982—86, sr. rsch. assoc., 1987—97; rsch. scientist Rsch. Triangle Inst., Research Triangle Park, 2000—01; dir., labor market info. Employment Security Commn. of NC, Raleigh, 2002—. Contbr. articles to profl. jours. Precinct chair Dem. Party of NC, 1985—86. Mem.: ALA, Nat. Assn. State Workforce Agys., Nat. Assn. Welfare Rsch. and Stats., Am. Assn. Pub. Opinion Rsch., Am. Evaluation Assn. (co-chair human services tig 2001—02). Democrat. Roman Catholic. Avocations: travel, history, philately. Office: Employment Security Commission of North 700 Wade Ave Raleigh NC 27611

NEER, CHARLES SUMNER, II, orthopedic surgeon, educator; b. Vinita, Okla., Nov. 10, 1917; s. Charles Sumner and Pearl Victoria (Brooke) N.; m. Eileen Meyer, June 12, 1990; children: Charlotte Marguerite, Sydney Victoria, Charles Henry. BA, Dartmouth Coll., 1939; MD, U. Pa., 1942. Diplomate Am. Bd. Orthopaedic Surgery (bd. dirs. 1970-75). Intern U. Pa. Hosp., Phila., 1942-43; asso. in surgery N.Y. Orthopedic-Columbia-Presbyn. Med. Center, N.Y.C., 1943-44; instr. in surgery Coll. Physicians and Surgeons, Columbia U., 1946-47, instr. orthopaedic surgery, 1947-57, asst. prof. clin. orthopaedic surgery, 1957-64, asso. prof., 1964-68, prof. clin. orthopaedic surgery, 1968-90, prof. clin. orthopaedic surgery emeritus, spl. lectr. orthopaedic surgery, 1990—. Attending orthopaedic surgeon Columbia-Presbyn. Med. Ctr., N.Y.C.; chief adult reconstructive svc. N.Y. Orthopaedic Hosp.; chief shoulder and elbow clinic Presbyn. Hosp.; cons. orthopaedic surgeon emeritus N.Y. Orthopaedic-Columbia-Presbyn. Med. Ctr., 1991—; chmn. 4th Internat. Congress Shoulder Surgeons; chmn. Internat. Bd. Shoulder Surgery, 1992—. Founder, chmn. bd. trustees Jour. Shoulder and Elbow Surgery, 1990—; contbr. articles to books, tech. films, sound slides. Served with U.S. Army, 1944-46. Recipient Disting. Svc. award Am. Bd. Orthopaedic Surgeons 1975. Fellow ACS (sr. mem. nat. com. on trauma), Am. Acad. Orthop. Surgeons (com. on upper extremity, shoulder com.); mem. AMA, ACS (mem. com. trauma), Am. Bd. Orthop. Surgeons (bd. dirs. 1970-75, Disting. Svc. award 1975), Am. Shoulder and Elbow Surgeons (inaugural pres.), Am. Assn. Surgery Trauma, Am. Orthop. Assn., Mid-Am. Orthop. Assn. (hon.), N.Y. Acad. Medicine, Allen O. Whipple Surg. Soc., N.Y. State Med. Soc., N.Y. County Med. Soc., Pan Am. Med. Assn., Am. Trauma Soc., Soc. Latino Am. Orthop. y Traumatology, Internat. Soc. Orthop. Surgery and Traumatology, Va. Orthop. Soc. (hon.), Carolina Orthop. Alumni Assn. (hon.), Conn. Orthop. Club (hon.), Houston Orthop. Assn. (hon.), Soc. Française de Chirurgie Orthop. et Traumatology (hon.), Soc. Italiana Orthop. Etravmatologia e Traumatologia; patron, Shoulder and Elbow Soc. Australia, South African Shoulder Soc., Giraffe Club, Internat. Bd. Shoulder Surgery (chmn. 1992—), Alpha Omega Alpha, Phi Chi. Home and Office: 231 S Miller St Vinita OK 74301-3625 E-mail: elmcreekacres@hotmail.com. *Forever grateful I could be a doctor and especially to work in the exciting area of shoulder surgery.*

NEESE, KRISTAL ANN, comptroller; b. Milton, Fla., June 29, 1968; d. Arthur Bill and Helen Margaret Bailey; m. Edward Terrell Neese Jr., June 25, 2000; m. John Leamon Ramos, Oct. 11, 1985 (div. Dec. 1991); children: John Leamon Jr., Shawn Michael. BS cum laude in Acct., U. South Ala., 1996. CPA. Tax acct. Sirmon, Frankel & Pawlowski, CPA, Mobile, Ala., 1995—96; cost acct. So. Aluminum Casting Co., Bayminette, 1996—97; staff mgr. Gulf States Airgas, Mobile, 1997; comptroller, acct. mgr., fin. adv. Lake Forest Property Owner's Assn. Inc., Daphne, 1997—; also bd. dirs. Mem.: Ala. State Bd. Acct., Daphne H.S. Quarterback Club. Methodist. Avocations: reading, football, crocheting, raising children. Home: 30529 Pine Ct Daphne AL 36527 Office: Lake Forest POA Inc One Golf Place Terr Daphne AL 36527

NEEWOOR, ANUND PRIYAY, ambassador; b. Mauritius, June 26, 1940; married; 3 children. BA in English with honors, Delhi U.; attended, Makerere U., Uganda, UN Inst. Tng. and Rsch. Tchr., prin. secondary sch.; in charge UN affairs, West Asia Fgn. Ministry, Mauritius, 1970-73; served Mauritius High Commn., London; 1st sec. Mauritian Embassy, New Delhi, min. counselor Washington, 1982; high commr. for Mauritius India, Sri Lanka, Bangladesh, 1983-93; amb. to Russia, Myanmar, Nepal, Thailand, 1983-93; amb. to U.S Govt. of the Rep. of Mauritius, Washington, 1993—; sec. fgn. affairs Govt. of Mauritius, 1996-98; amb., permanent rep. to UN, 1999—. Fellow Carnegie Endowment for Internat. Peace. Office: Permanent Mission of Mauritius to UN 211 E 43rd St Fl 15 New York NY 10017-4707 Home: Apt 108 7420 Lakeview Dr Bethesda MD 20817-6450

NEFF, BONITA DOSTAL, communication developmental facilitator; b. Grinnell, Iowa, Aug. 16, 1942; d. Lester Ernest and Mary Margaret (Hudnut) Dostal; m. Gregory Pall Neff, Apr. 27, 1974; 1 child, Kristiana. BA, U. N. Iowa, 1964, MA, 1966; PhD, U. Mich., 1973; AA cum laude, Lansing (Mich.) C.C., 1980. Edn. leadership fellow George Washington U., Washington, 1976-77; specialist Mich. State U., East Lansing, 1977-80, co-investigator family and child inst. energy rsch. team, 1980-82; asst. prof. comm. Purdue U., Hammond, Ind., 1982-87; pres. Pub. Comm. Assocs., Munster, 1986—; assoc. prof. comm. Valparaiso (Ind.) U., 1991—. Co-founding mem. Internat. Interdisciplinary and Intercultural Annual Conf. in Pub. Rels.; presenter over 125 rsch. papers to regional, nat., and internat. profl. confs.; cons. in field. Mem. adv. bd., reviewer Jour. Applied Comm. Rsch., Jour. Promotional Mgmt.; reviewer Mgmt. Comm. Quar.: An Internat. Jour.; editor procs. on accreditation for nat. conf.; contbr. chpts. to books, profl. articles and poetry to jours.; editl. bd. Jour. of Pub. Rels. Rsch. Mem. Nat. Steering Commn. for Revision of Pub. Rels. Curriculum, 1996—, mem. Nat. Task Force Pub. Rels. Conf. 1998; mem. Lake County (Ind.) Community Devel. Com., 1984—; bd. dirs. Big Bros. and Big Sisters N.W. Ind., 1984, 87; pres., chmn. bd. dirs. N.W. Ind. Youth Chorus, 1985—; bd. dirs., mem. mktg. com. N.W. Ind. Symphony, bd. dirs. PBS56-Ind., sec. exec. com., 2000—. Faculty rsch. grantee U. Mich., 1971, Consumer Product Safety Coun. grantee, 1976-77, Ind. Arts Commn./Nat. Endowment for Arts grantee, 1990-92, Valparaiso U. Diversity grantee, 1996; recipient top rsch. honors regional confs. Mem.: Nat. Commn. on Undergrad. and Grad. Pub. Rels. Curriculum (nat. task force for conf. 1998), Pub. Rels. Soc. Am. (advisor 2001, established student chpt.), Internat. Acad. Bus. Disciplines (co-chair pub. rels. divsn.), World Comm. Assn., Assn. Educators in Journalism Mass Comm. (chair internat. com. 1994—96, scholarly liaison com. 1995—), Ctrl. States Comm. Assn. (founder and chmn. 1988—89, pub. rels. officer 1989—92), Nat. Comm. Assn. (founder and twice chair of pub. rels. divsn. 1988, chmn. nat. Pub. Rels. Rsch. awards com. PRIDE 1988, nat. legis. coun. rep. 1993—, nat. com. on convs. allied orgns., task force on nat. policy), Internat. Pub. Rels. Assn., Internat. Comm. Assn. (chmn. task force on accreditation 1988, newsletter editor 1997, chair planning pub. rels. divsn. internat. conf. South Korea, chair dissertation thesis award com. pub. rels. divsn.), Assn. Women in Comm. (assoc.; pres. Calumet chpt. 1985—90, advisor Valparaiso Student AWC, Inc. 1994—, Outstanding Communicator 1990, Nat. Outstanding chpt. advisor 1999). Democrat. Roman Catholic. Avocations: ballet, tap, piano, reading, professional clown. Home: 8320 Greenwood Ave Munster IN 46321-1813 Office: Pub Comm Assocs 8320 Greenwood Ave Munster IN 46321-1813 E-mail: bonita.neff@valpo.edu.

NEFF, DIANE IRENE, university administrator; b. Cedar Rapids, Iowa, Apr. 26, 1954; d. Robert Mariner and Adeline Emma (Zach) N. BA in Psychology and Home Econs., U. Iowa, 1976; MA in Sociology, U. Mo., 1978; MEd in Ednl. Leadership, U. West Fla., 1990. Contract compliance officer, dir. EEO, City of Cedar Rapids, 1979-81; commd. ensign USN, 1981, advanced through grades to lt. comdr.; asst. legal officer Naval Comm. Area Master Sta., Guam, 1982-83; comm. security plans and requirements officer Comdr.-in-Chief US Naval Forces in Europe, London, 1983-85; dir. standards and evaluation dept. Recruit Tng. Command, Orlando, Fla., 1985-89; rsch. and analysis officer Naval Res. Officers Tng. Corps Office Chief Naval Edn. and Tng., Pensacola, 1989-91; tech. tng. officer Recruit Tng. Command, Great Lakes, Ill., 1991-92, mil. tng. officer, 1992-93, dir. apprentice tng., 1993-95; coord. ednl. and tng. programs U. Ctrl. Fla., Orlando, 1995—. Founding mem. Unity of Gulf Breeze, Fla., 1990; performer various benefits for chs., mus., others, Orlando, 1988, 91, 95, 96, 97. Fellow Adminstrn. on Aging, 1977. Mem. ASTD. Unitarian Universalist. Avocation: piano. E-mail: dneff@mail.ucf.edu.

NEFF, DONALD LEROY, computer software executive; b. Portland, Oreg., Dec. 5, 1950; s. Lester LeRoy and Avon Maxine Neff; m. Josefina S. Carpio, Apr. 23, 1988; 1 child, Justin Leroy. Student, Ambassador Coll., 1972. Cert. data processor. Computer programmer Ambassador Coll., Pasadena, Calif., 1969-78; cons. San Jose, 1979-92; CEO Tellan Software, Inc., 1992—. One man art shows include Carnegie Mus., 1981, Ambassador Coll., 1979. Recipient numerous awards in art shows. Office: Tellan Software Inc 3286 Knightswood Way San Jose CA 95148-3151

NEFF, DONALD LLOYD, news correspondent, writer; b. York, Pa., Oct. 15, 1930; s. Harry William and Gertrude Marie N.; m. Abigail Trafford; 1 son, Gregory Harry. Student, Trinity Coll., San Antonio, 1949, York Coll., 1950-52, N.Y. U., 1953. Reporter York Dispatch, 1954-56, L.A. Mirror-News, 1956-57, UPI, L.A., 1957-61; with L.A. Times, 1961-64, bur. chief, 1964; with Time mag., 1965-81, corr. Vietnam, 1965-66, writer, 1966-68, bur. chief Houston, 1968-70, L.A., 1970-73, Jerusalem, 1975-78, N.Y.C., 1978-79, sr. editor, 1973-75; news svcs. editor Washington Star, 1979-80. Author: Warriors at Suez: Eisenhower Takes America into the Middle East, 1981, Warriors for Jerusalem, The Six Days That Changed the Middle East, 1984; Warriors Against Israel, 1988, Fallen Pillars; U.S. Policy Toward Palestine and Israel since 1945, 1995, Fifty Years of Israel, 1998. Served with AUS, 1948-50. Recipient Theta Sigma Phi Matrix award, 1962, Calif.-Nev. AP Writing Contest best met. spot news story award, 1962, Overseas Press Club award for best fgn. article in a mag., 1979; finalist Am. Book Award History category, 1982. Mem. Fgn. Press Assn. (Israel pres. 1977, v.p. 1978)

NEFF, FRED LEONARD, lawyer; b. St. Paul, Nov. 1, 1948; s. Elliott Ira and Mollie (Poboisk) N.; m. Christa Ruth Powell, Sept. 10, 1989; 1 child, Lena. BS with high distinction, U. Minn., 1970; JD, William Mitchell Coll. Law, 1976. Bar: Minn. 1976, N.D. 1994, U.S. Dist. Ct. Minn. 1977, U.S. Ct. Appeals (8th cir.) 1985, U.S. Supreme Ct. 1985, Wis. 1986, U.S. Dist. Ct. (ea. and we. dists.) Wis. 1992. Tchr. Hopkins (Minn.) Pub. Schs., 1970-72; instr. U. Minn., Mpls., 1974-76; pvt. practice, 1976-79; asst. county atty. Sibley County, Gaylord, Minn., 1979-80; mng. atty. Hyatt Legal Svcs., St. Paul, 1981-83, regional ptnr., 1983-85, profl. devel. ptnr., 1985-86; pres. Neff Law Firm, PA, Mpls., 1986—; CEO Profl. Devel. Inst. Inc., Edina, Minn., 1994—, also bd. dirs. Instr. Inver Hills Coll., 1973-77; counsel Am. Tool Supply Co., St. Paul, 1976-78; cons. Nat. Detective Agy., Inc., St. Paul, 1980-83; CEO A Basic Legal Svc., Bloomington, 1990—; CEO, bd. dirs. Profl. Devel. Inst., Inc., Edina, Minn., 1994—; lectr., guest instr. U. Wis., River Falls, 1976-77; spl. instr. Hamline U., St. Paul, 1977; vis. lectr. Coll. St. Scholastica, Duluth, Minn., 1977; program. faculty, cons. Employment Law Seminar for Colo., Fla., La., Oreg., Employment and Labor Law Seminar for Ala., Alaska, Calif., Conn., Ind., N.C., Ohio, Va., N.C. Safety and Health at the Workplace, S.C. Labor Law, Ohio Safety at the Workplace; bd. dirs. Acceptance Ins. Holdings, Inc., Omaha; active Internat. Confederation Jurists, 1993; mem. faculty sem. Ariz. Safety at Workplace, Hawaii Employment & Labor, Miss. Employment & Labor Law, Del. Employment & Labor, Alaska Employment and Labor Law, Ga. Employment & Labor Law, N.J. Employment & Labor, Wash. Employment Law, Mass. Employment & Labor Law, 1995—, Ark. Employment and Labor Law, Mo. Employment and Labor Law, Iowa Employment and Labor Law, Utah Employment and Labor Law; pres. Martial Arts Bookstore Internat., Inc., 1998; pres. Endless Fist Soc., Inc., 1998. Author: Fred Neff's Self-Defense Library, 1976, Everybody's Self-Defense Book, 1978, Karate Is for Me, 1980, Running Is for Me, 1980, Lessons from the Samurai, 1986, Lessons from the Art of Kempo, 1986, Lessons from the Western Warriors, 1986, Lessons from the Fighting Commandos, 1990, Lessons from the Ancient Japanese Masters of Self-Defense, 1990, Lessons from the Eastern Warrors, 1990, Mysterious Persons of the Past, 1991, Great Mysteries of Crime, 1991; host TV series Great Puzzles In History; co-host TV series Great Unsolved Crimes, Minn.; asst. editor: Hennepin County Lawyer, 1992—. Advisor to bd. Sibley County Commrs., 1979-80; speaker civic groups, 1976-82; mem. Hennepin County Juvenile Justice Panel, 1980-82, Hennepin County (Minn.) Pub. Def. Conflict Panel, 1980-82, 86—, Hennepin County Bar Assn. Advice Panel Law Day, 1987, mem. dist. ethics com., 1990—; mem. Panel Union Privilege Legal Svcs. div. AFL-CIO, 1986—, Montgomery Wards Legal Svcs. Panel, 1986—, Edina Hist. Soc., Decathlon Athletic Club; charter mem. Commn. for the Battle of Normandy Mus.; founding sponsor Civil Justice Found., 1986—; mem. com. for publ. Hennepin County Lawyer, 1992; pres. Endless Fist Soc., Inc., 1998. Recipient Outstanding Tchr. award Inver Hills Coll. Student Body, 1973, St. Paul Citizen of Month award Citizens Group, 1975, Kempo Club award U. Minn., 1975, U. Minn. Student Appreciation award Kempo Club, 1978, Sibley County Atty. Commendation award, 1980, Good Neighbor award WCCO Radio, 1985, Lamp of Knowledge award Twin Cities Lawyers Guild, 1986, N.W. Cmty. TV Commendation award, 1989-91, Presdl. Merit medal Pres. George Bush, 1990, N.W. Cmty. TV award, 1991, HLS Leadership award, 1984, Mng. Attys. Guidance award, 1985, Creative Thinker award Regional Staff, 1986, HLS Justice award, 1986, Honors cert. for Authors, Childrens Reading Round Table of Chgo., 1988, Wisdom Soc. Wisdom award, 1998. Fellow Roscoe Pound Found., Nat. Dist. Attys. Assn.; mem. ABA, ATLA, Minn. Bar Assn. (com. on ethics 1994—, com. on alternative dispute resolution 1994—), Minn. Trial Lawyers Assn., Hennepin County Bar Assn. (dist. ethics com. 1990—), Wis. Bar Assn., Ramsey County Bar Assn., Am. Judicature Soc., Internat. Platform Assn., Am. Arbitration Assn. (panel of arbitrators 1992), Minn. Martial Arts Assn. (pres. 1974-78, Outstanding Instr. award 1973), Nippon Kobudo Rengokai (bd. dirs. North Ctrl. States 1972-76, regional dir. 1972-76), Endless Fist Soc. (pres. 1998), Internat. Confedn. Jurists, Edina C. of C., Southview Country Club, Masons, Kiwanis, Scottish Rite, Sigma Alpha Mu. Avocations: reading, Far Eastern and Oriental studies, civic activities, physical conditioning, gardening. Home: 4515 Andover Rd Minneapolis MN 55435-4031 Office: 5930 Brooklyn Blvd Ste 206 Brooklyn Center MN 55429-2518 also: 1711 County Road B W Ste 340N Roseville MN 55113-4077 also: Minn Ctr 7760 France Ave S Ste 720 Bloomington MN 55435-5921

NEFF, GREGORY PALL, mechanical engineering educator, consultant; b. Detroit, Nov. 23, 1942; s. Jacob John and Bonnie Alice (Pall) N.; m. Bonita Jean Dostal, Apr. 27, 1974; 1 child, Kristiana Dostal Neff. BS in Physics, U. Mich., 1964, MA in Math., 1966, MS in Physics, 1967; MSME, Mich. State U., 1982. Registered profl. engr., Ind.; cert. mfg. engr.; cert. mfg. technologist; cert. sr. indsl. technologist. Rsch. asst. cyclotron lab U. Mich., Ann Arbor, 1968-72, teaching fellow physics dept., 1973; instr. sci. dept. Lansing (Mich.) C.C., 1976-82; guest lectr. Purdue U. Calumet, Hammond, Ind., 1982-83, asst. prof., 1984-91, assoc. prof. mech. engrng. tech., 1991—. Cons. Inland Steel Co., Indsl. Engrng., East Chicago, Ind., 1984-86, Polyurethane divsn. Pinder Industries, East Chicago, 1990-92, Elevated divsn. Pitts. Tank & Tower, Henderson, Ky., 1990-91; program evaluator for tech. accreditation commn. Accreditation Bd. for Engrng. and Tech., 1996—. Author textbook chpts.; contbr. articles to profl. jours. County commr. Ingham County Bd. of Commr., Mason, Mich., 1977-80, Tri-County Regional Planning Commn., Lansing, 1978-80, chair, non-motorized adv. coun. Mich. Dept. Transp., Lansing, 1982-83. Mem. ASHRAE, ASME (sec. MET dept. heads com. 1999, vice chair 2000, chair 2001, webmaster 1999--, bd. on engrng. edn.), Soc. Mfg. Engrs. (chpt. 112 bd. dirs. 1986—, webmaster 1999--, Appreciation award 1990, 92, Outstanding Faculty Advisor award 1991,), Am. Soc. for Engrng. Edn. (Merl K. Miller award 1994), Nat. Assn. Indsl. Tech., Order of Engr., Sigma Alpha Epsilon, Tau Alpha Pi. Democrat. Roman Catholic. Office: Purdue U Calumet 2200 169th St Hammond IN 46323-2068 E-mail: gneff@purdue.edu.

NEFF, JACK KENNETH, apparel manufacturing company executive; b. N.Y.C., Feb. 23, 1938; s. William K. and Rose T. N.; m. Barbara Joan Neff, Nov. 4, 1961; 1 son, Craig William. AAS., Queens Coll., 1968; postgrad., Stanford Advanced Mgmt. Coll., 1973. Gen. mdse. mgr. youthwear Levi Strauss & Co., 1973-78, v.p. mktg., 1978-80; pres. Salant & Salant Co., N.Y.C., 1980-81; exec. v.p. Salant Corp., 1981-84; pres., chief exec. officer Thomson Co., 1984-87; exec. v.p., chief operating officer Stanley Blacker Co., 1987-90; with Inside Mgmt. Assocs., 1991-93; v.p. and gen. mgr. Reebok Worldwide Apparel Div., 1993-94; sr. v.p., 1994-96; ptnr. The Muller Sports Group, N.Y.C., 1996—. Served in USN, 1956-59.

NEFF, MARY ELLEN ANDRE, elementary school educator; b. Indiana, Pa., July 6, 1943; d. Frank Vincent and Marie Isabel (Elrick) Andre; children: Gary V. Jr., Traci Dawn. BS, Indiana U. Pa., 1965, MEd, 1971. Elem. sch. tchr. Blairsville (Pa.)-Saltsburg Sch. Dist., Derry (Pa.) Area Sch. Dist. Sec., bd. dirs. Westmoreland County Hist. Soc. Mem. NEA, PTA, Pa. State Edn. Assn., Blairsville-Saltsburg Edn. Assn. (past sec.), Nat. Soc. DAR (past vice regent Wm. Kenly chpt., regent), Delta Kappa Gamma (pres. 1986-90, treas. 1992—). Home: 17 Carriage Rd Greensburg PA 15601-9014

NEFF, P. SHERRILL, venture capitalist; b. Balt., Dec. 18, 1951; s. Paul Heston and Mary (Poulnot) N.; m. Sarah B. Barrett, June 20, 1976 (div. 1985); 1 child, Jacob Colin; m. Alicia Phyll Felton, May 26, 1988; children: Michael Felton, Jonathan Felton. BA, Wesleyan U., 1974; JD magna cum laude, U. Mich., 1980. Bar: Pa. 1980. Atty. Morgan Lewis & Bockius, Phila., 1980—84; investment banker Alex Brown & Sons, Inc., Balt., 1984—93, mng. dir., 1992—93; sr. v.p. corp. devel. U.S. Healthcare, Blue Bell, Pa., 1993—94; pres., CFO Neose Techs., Inc., Horsham, 1994—2000, pres., COO, 2000—02; mng. ptnr. Quaker Bio Ventures, Phila., 2002—. Bd. dirs. Resource America, Inc., Phila., Bancorp.com., Inc., Phila., Biotechnology Inst., BioRexis Pharms., Inc.; bd. dirs., v.p. Greater Phila. Venture Group. Trustee Zero Moving Dance Co., Phila., 1984-93; bd. dirs. Univ. City Sci. Ctr., 1998—. Mem. Pa. Biotech. Assn. (bd. dirs. 1996-2002, pres.-elect 1997-98, pres. 1998-99). Democrat. Jewish. Home: 619 Revere Rd Merion Station PA 19066-1007 Office: Quaker Bio Ventures 1811 Chestnut St Philadelphia PA 19103

NEFF, RAY QUINN, electric power educator, consultant; b. Houston, Apr. 29, 1928; s. Noah Grant and Alma Ray (Smith) N.; m. Elizabeth McDougald, Sept. 4, 1982. Degree in Steam Engrng., Houston Vocat. Tech., 1957; BSME, Kennedy Western U., 1986. Various positions Houston Lighting & Power Co., 1945-60, plant supr., 1960-70, plant supt. asst., 1970-80, tech. supr., 1980-85, tng. supr., 1985-87; owner, operator Neff Enterprises, Bedias, Tex., 1987—; tng. supr. Tex. A&M U., 1991—. Cons. Houston Industries, 1987-89. Author: Power Plant Operation, 1975, Power Operator Training, 1985, Power Foreman Training, 1986. Judge Internat. Sci. and Engrng. Fair, Houston, 1982, Sci. Engrng. Fair Houston, 1987. Mem. ASME, Assn. Chief Operating Engrs., Masons. Republican. Methodist. Avocations: farming, ranching, classic cars. Home: Hwy 90 Rte 2t PO Box 193A Bedias TX 77831-0193 Office: Tex A&M U Power Plant College Station TX 77843-0001

NEFF, ROBERT CLARK, SR. lawyer; b. St Marys, Ohio, Feb. 11, 1921; s. Homer Armstrong and Irene (McCulloch) N.; m. Betty Baker, July 3, 1954 (dec.); children: Cynthia Lee Neff Schifer, Robert Clark Jr., Abigail Lynn (dec.); m. Helen Picking, July 24, 1975. BA, Coll. Wooster, 1943; postgrad., U. Mich., 1946-47; LLB, Ohio No. U., 1950. Bar: Ohio 1950, U.S. Dist. Ct. (no. dist.) Ohio, 1978. Pvt. practice, Bucyrus, Ohio, 1950—; ptnr. Neff Law Firm Ltd.; law dir. City of Bucyrus, 1962-95. Chmn. blood program Crawford County (Ohio) unit ARC, 1955-89; life mem. adv. bd. Salvation Army, 1962—; clk. of session 1st Presbyn. Ch., Bucyrus, 1958-96; bd. dirs. Bucyrus Area Cmty. Found., Crawford County Bd. Mental Retardation and Devel. Disabilities, 1977-82. With USNR, WWII; comdr. Res. ret. Recipient "Others" plaque for 30 yrs. adv. bd. svc. Salvation Army, Ohio No. U. Coll. Law Alumni award for cmty. svc., 1996; inducted Ohio Vets. Hall Fame, Columbus, 1996. Mem. Ohio Bar Assn., Crawford County Bar Assn., Naval Res. Assn., Ret. Officers Assn., Am. Legion, Bucyrus Area C. of C. (past bd. dirs., Outstanding Citizen award, 1973, Bucyrus Citizen of Yr. 1981), Kiwanis (life mem., past pres.), Masons. Republican. Home: 1085 Mary Ann Ln Bucyrus OH 44820-3145 Office: 840 S Sandusky Ave PO Box 406 Bucyrus OH 44820-0406 Fax: 419-562-1660. E-mail: nefflaw@cybrtown.com.

NEFF, ROBERT WILBUR, academic administrator, educator, minister; b. Lancaster, Pa., June 16, 1936; s. Wilbur Hildebr and Hazel Margaret (Martin) N.; m. Dorothy Rosewarne, Aug. 16, 1959; children: Charles Scott, Heather Lynn. BS, Pa. State U., 1958; BD, Yale Div. Sch., 1961, MA, 1963, PhD, 1969; DD, Juniata Coll., 1978, Manchester Coll., 1979; DHL, Bridgewater Coll., 1979. Asst. prof. Bridgewater Coll., 1964-65; mem. faculty dept. Bibl. studies Bethany Theol. Sem., 1965-77, prof., 1973-77; gen. sec. Ch. of the Brethren, Elgin, Ill., 1978-86; pres. Juniata Coll., 1986-98, pres. emeritus, 1998—. Vis. prof. Pa. State U., 1998—; mem. faculty North Park Sem., No. Bapt. Sem., Theol. Coll. No. Nigeria; bd. dirs. Mellon Bank (Ctrl.) Nat. Assn., exec. com., 1989, chair exec com., 1993, chair CRA com., 1994-2001; mem. pres.'s com. NCAA, 1996-99; resource assoc. Village at Morrison's Cove, 1999—; bd. dirs. Susquehanna Valley Satellite, 2002--; adj. faculty Bethany Theol. Sem., 1999—; lectr. Young Ctr. at Elizabethtown Coll., 2002; mem. USDA Del. to Baltic States, 2000. Mem. governing bd. Nat. Coun. Chs. of Christ, 1976-86, mem. exec. com., 1979-86; mem. Mid-East panel, 1980, 2d v.p., 1985-86; mem. ctrl. com. World Coun. Chs., 1983-92; rep. Assembly of World Coun. Chs., 1983, mem. exec. com. on interch. rels., 1980-84, mem. del. to China, 1981, chmn. presdl. panel, 1982-84; bd. dirs. Bethany Theol. Sem., 1978-86; campaign chmn. United Way, Huntington County, 1989; chair higher edn. com. Ch. of Brethren, 1993-98. Danforth fellow, 1958-69 Mem. Soc. Bibl. Lit., Soc. Old Testament Study, Chgo. Soc. Bibl. Rsch., Soc. Values in Higher Edn., Coun. Ind. Colls. (nat. bd. dirs. 1991-94, treas. 1995-98), Pa. Coun. Ind. Colls. and Univs. (exec. com. 1988-90, 92-96, chair ann. conf. nominating com. 1993-94), Mid Atlantic Athletic Conf. (sec., mem. exec. com. 1994-97). Democrat. Home: RR 1 Box 437 Alexandria PA 16611-9652 Office: Village at Morrisons Cove 429 Market St Martinsburg PA 16866

NEFF, THOMAS JOSEPH, executive search firm executive; b. Easton, Pa., Oct. 2, 1937; s. John Wallace and Elizabeth Ann (Dougherty) N.; m. Susan Culver Paull, Nov. 26, 1971 (dec.); children: David Andrew, Mark Gregory, Scott Dougherty; m. Sarah Brown Hallingby, Jan. 20, 1989; stepchildren: Brooke, Bailey BS in Indsl. Engrng., Lafayette Coll., 1959; MBA, Lehigh U., 1961. Assoc. McKinsey & Co., Inc., N.Y.C. and Australia, 1963-66; dir. mktg. planning Trans-World Airlines, N.Y.C., 1966-69; pres. Hosp. Data Scis., Inc., 1969-74; prin. Booz, Allen & Hamilton, Inc., 1974-76; regional ptnr. Spencer Stuart, Inc., N.Am., 1976-79; bd. dirs. Spencer Stuart & Assocs., 1976-79, pres., 1979-96, also bd. dirs., chmn. U.S., 1996—. Bd. dirs. Lord Abbett Mut. Funds, Ace Ltd., Exult, Inc.; chmn. Brunswick Sch., 1991-95. Trustee, exec. com. Lafayette Coll., 1992—. 1st lt. U.S. Army, 1961-63. Mem. Links Club, Sky Club, Blind Brook Club, Quogue (N.Y.) Beach Club, Quogue Field Club, Round Hill Club, Coral Beach Club, Quantuck Beach Club, Nat. Golf Links, Lost Tree Club. Republican. Roman Catholic. Home: 925 Park Ave New York NY 10028 Office: Spencer Stuart & Assocs 277 Park Ave Fl 29 New York NY 10172-2998

NEFF BALCH, BETTY MARIE, retired nursing educator; b. Durkee, Oreg., Oct. 9, 1925; d. Charles F. and Blanche O. (Hickerson) Schuck; m. William F. Neff, Oct. 6, 1946 (div.); children: Charles, Susan, Doris Ann, Bill Jr.; m. George E. Balch, Jr., Sept. 1998. Diploma, St. Elizabeth Hosp., 1946; BS, St. Joseph's Coll., 1981; MEd, Northern Mont. Coll., 1986; M in Career Guidance and Planning, No. Mont. Coll., 1989; EdD, Mont. State U., 1995. RN Mont., cert. tchr. Mont. Staff nurse USAF Hosp., Great Falls, Mont., 1960-75, De Paul Hosp., Cheyenne, Wyo., 1963; 22 USAF Hosp., Wiesbaden, Germany, staff nurse Great Falls, Mont.; ind. contractor tchg. nurse aides, 1976-98;

headmaster cert. nurse aides Distance Learning Instrn. by Computer, Helena, Mont., 1993—98; ret., 1998. Presenter Motivational Workshop, Mont. Health Care Assn., 1989; speaker and piloting nurse's aides program in field. Contbr. articles to profl. jours. Named Tchr. of Yr., Mont. Health Occupation, 1986, grantee 5 Carl Perkins grants. Mem. Mt. Voc. Assn. (am. voc. assn. nat. bylaws com., speaker N. Mex. convention, 1988), Sons of Norway, Friendship Force, Beta Sigma Phi. Home: 806-68 Ave SW Tacoma WA 98499

NEFF-SINCLAIR, JAN A. software engineer; b. Chgo., Sept. 12, 1957; d. Jerome Price and Joan Ruth (McKeown) Neff. Student, Ill. Inst. Technology, Chgo., 1975-78, De Anza Coll., Cupertino, Calif., 1980-81, San Diego Community Coll., 1985-89, Mira Costa Community Coll., 1991-92, Calif. State U., 1992. Computer programmer Cortron Div. Ill. Tool Works, Inc., Elmhurst, 1977-78; systems programmer Olivetti Advanced Technology Ctr., Cupertino; software engr. Lomac Corp., San Jose, Calif., Shasta Gen. Systems, Sunnyvale, Omex, Santa Clara, Calif.; sr. software project engr. Metacomp, Inc., San Diego, 1983-86; prin. programmer analyst Fusitsu Systems Am., Inc., 1986-89; mem. tech. staff Bluebird Systems, Carlsbad, 1989-91; systems engr. II Nat. Systems & Rsch. Co., Oceanside, 1991—93; IT specialist Marine Corps Tactical Sys. Support Activity, 1995—. Mem. NAFE, Mensa, Theatre Goers of San Diego, Athletic Singles Assn. Avocations: travel, athletics, computers. Home: # 108A-200 300 Carlsbad Village Dr Carlsbad CA 92008-2900

NEFSKE, DONALD JOSEPH, engineer; b. Detroit, Dec. 18, 1938; s. Frank J. and Esther M. N.; m. Susan Sung, Dec. 10, 1983. BS magna cum laude, U. Detroit, 1962; MS, U. Mich., 1964, PhD, 1969. Engr. Ford Motor Co., Dearborn, Mich., 1960-61; rsch. engr. GM, Warren, 1969-70, sr. rsch. engr., 1970-85, sr. staff engr., 1985-93; prin. engr., 1993—. Mem. ASME, AIAA, Acoustical Soc. Am., Soc. Automotive Engrs., Sigma Xi. Roman Catholic. Office: Gen Motors R&D Ctr Engring Mechs Dept 30500 Mound Rd Warren MI 48092-2031

NEFT BYERS, SUZI TERRY, television producer, marketing, public relations executive, advertising executive; b. Pitts., Sept. 17, 1957; d. Harris Rosenberg and Fannie Rachel Neft; m. Paul Alan Byers, June 14, 1986 (div. 2002); 1 child Charles Alexander II Byers. BA in Journalism and Comm., Point Park Coll., 1979. Announcer, writer WNUF-FM, Millvale, Pa., 1979-80; news reporter WESA-AM, Charleroi, 1980-81; ops. coord. WQED-TV, WQEX-TV, WQED-FM, Pitts., 1981-87; location prodn. mgr. You TV Cable Network, 1988; tv prodr. The Mercy Hosp., 1992-93; dir. internship devel., sr. tv prodr. Reliance Tng. Networks, 1996-2000; freelance TV prodr., writer, pub. rels./mktg. profl., 1977—. Assoc. prodr. KDKA/Children's Hospital Free Care Fund Benefit Show, 1994, 95, Lucille's Car Care Clinic, 1994; prodr. HealthVision, 1998-99. Pub. rels., mktg. Jewish Assn. Aging; mem. publicity com., intergenerational choir Temple Sinai, trustee. Recipient Emmy Mid-Atlantic Region Best Live Show, Acad. TV Arts and Scis., 1991, 1st pl. best tv comml. Women in Comm., 1994, 1st pl. spl. events promo under $20,000 Women in Comm., 1995, 1st pl. spl. events budgets under $20,000 Women in Comm., 1996. Mem.: Press Club Western Pa. (bd. dirs. 1994—95), Am. Women in Radio and TV (pres. chpt. 1995—97). Home and Office: 633 Montclair St Pittsburgh PA 15217-2808

NEGLEN, NILS PETER, surgeon; b. Helsingborg, Sweden, July 30, 1948; came to U.S., 1996; s. Malte and Ewy Ingeborg (Karlsson) N.; m. Linda Pamela Ohnell, July 19, 1975; children: Niclas Peter, Nils Pontus. MD, U. Lund, Sweden, 1974, PhD in Surgery, 1980, Docent, 1988. Rotating intern Danderyd, Sweden, 1974-76; resident Helsingborg/Lund, Sweden, 1976-81; clin. rsch. fellow Duke U., N.C., 1981-82; cons. surgeon Helsingborg, 1982-83; asst. prof. Kuwait U., 1983-88, assoc. prof., 1988-90; prof. United Arab Emirates U., Al Ain, 1991-96; sr. resident Temple U., Phila., 1996-97; attending vascular surgeon River Oaks Hosp., Jackson, Miss., 1997—. Vis. prof. U. Miss. Med. Ctr., Jackson, 1990-91. Contbr. chpts. to books and articles to profl. jours. Mem. Soc. Vascular Surgery, Am. Venous Forum, Am. Assn. Vascular Surgery, Internat. Soc. Surgery, European Soc. Vascular Surgery, Internat. Soc. Endovascular Specialists. Avocations: tennis, motorcycle riding. Office: 1020 River Oaks Dr Ste 480 Jackson MS 39232-9536 E-mail: neglenmd@earthlink.net.

NEGOITA, CONSTANTIN VIRGIL, computer scientist, educator; b. Bucharest, Romania, Feb. 3, 1936; arrived in U.S., 1982; s. Athanasie Negoita and Ileana Popescu; m. Seta Shishmanian, Mar. 10, 1986. PhD, Poly. U., Bucharest, 1969. Rschr. City U. Inst. Informatics, Bucharest, 1972-82; prof. Hunter Coll. CUNY, N.Y.C., 1983—. Chmn. 8th Internat. Congress Cybernetics and Sys., NY, 1990. Author: (book) Fuzzy Systems, 1981, Expert Systems and Fuzzy Systems, 1985 (award IEEE, 1985), Cybernetic Conspiracy, 1988, Fuzzy Sets, 2000, Postmodern Logic, 2002; editor: Kybernetes, 1972—, Jour. of Fuzzy Sets and Systems, 1978—96. Office: Hunter Coll 695 Park Ave New York NY 10021-5024 Fax: 212-772-5219. E-mail: cnegoita@hunter.cuny.edu.

NEGRO, SANDRA ELIZABETH, librarian; b. Elysburg, Pa., Oct. 12, 1947; d. Roy Clark and Evelyn Mae (Schlegel) Vought; m. Frank J. Negro Jr., Jan. 27, 1973; children: Michael, Jennifer. BS in Edn., Kutztown (Pa.) State U., 1969; postgrad., Cath. U. of Am., 1979. Cert. pub. libr., Md. Aquisitions/cataloging libr. Frederick (Md.) Cancer Rsch. Ctr., 1973-77; libr. II/cataloger Montgomery County Dept. Pub. Librs., Rockville, Mo., 1983-92, Sunday svc. supr., 1992-94, health info. libr., 1994—, health info. ctr. mgr., 1997—. Mem. Healty Montgomery Coalition, Rockville; adv. com. Nat. Network/Librs. of Medicine, 1997-98, pub. libr. pilot, 1998-99; ad hoc group Nat. Libr. of Medicine, 1999—. Author: County Resource Provides Health Information-Montgomery Medicine. Mem. Md. Assn. of Health Sci. Librs. (nominating com. 1994—), Med. Libr. Assn. Democrat. Avocations: reading, needlework. Home: 18717 Flower Hill Way Gaithersburg MD 20879-1535 Office: Wheaton Regional Libr 11701 Georgia Ave Wheaton MD 20902-1997 E-mail: negros@mont.lib.md.us.

NEGRON, JAIME, performing arts center sales director; b. San Juan, P.R., Dec. 23, 1939; came to U.S., 1952; s. Rito and Tomasa (Otero) N.; m. Barbara Charlotte Stovall, Nov. 5, 1959; children: Jeannette Michelle, Victoria Frances. BA in Econs., Howard U., 1987. Lic. realtor. Chief receiving & shipping Am. Univ., Washington, 1960-62; book dept. mgr. Am. U., 1968-71; bookstore mgr. Follett Corp., Chgo., 1962-68, Cath. U., Washington, 1971-74; dir. Howard U. stores Howard Univ., 1974-87; dir. aux. enterprises Howard U., 1987-91; real estate agt. Weichert Referral Assocs., Vienna, 1993—; asst. dir. aux. enterprises DeKalb Coll., Atlanta, 1992-96; dir. retail operations J.F. Kennedy Ctr. for Performing Arts, Washington, 1996—. Cons. U. Del., Newark, 1988, Wesley Sem., Washington, 1984, R.R. Moton Meml. Inst., N.Y.C., 1974-79. Active Vienna Jaycees, 1970-80. With USN, 1958-60. Mem. Middle Atlantic Coll. Stores (pres. 1984), Nat. Assn. Coll. Stores, Nat. Bd. Realtors, Va. Bd. Realtors. Episcopalian. Avocation: dancing. Office: JFK Ctr Performing Arts 2700 F St NW Washington DC 20566-0002

NEGROPONTE, JOHN DIMITRI, ambassador; b. London, July 21, 1939; s. Dimitri John and Catherine (Coumantaros) N.; m. Diana Mary Villiers, Dec. 14, 1976; children: Marina, Alexandra, John, George, Sophia. BA, Yale U., 1960. Commd. fgn. svc. officer U.S. Dept. of State, 1960; vice consul Hong Kong, 1961-63; 2nd sec. Saigon, 1964-68; mem. U.S. Del. to Paris Peace Talks on Viet-Nam, 1968-69; mem. staff NSC, 1970-73; polit. counselor Quito, Ecuador, 1973-75; consul gen. Thessaloniki, Greece, 1975-77; dep. asst. sec. of state for oceans and fisheries affairs Washington, 1977-79; dep. asst. sec. for East Asian and Pacific affairs U.S. Dept. State, 1980-81; U.S. amb. to Honduras, 1981-85; asst. sec. for oceans and internat. environ. and sci. affairs, 1985-87; dep. asst. Pres. for Nat. Security Affairs, 1987-89; U.S. amb. to Mexico, 1989-93; U.S. amb. to The Philippines, 1993-96; spl. coord. for post-1999 U.S. presence in Panama, 1996-97; exec. v.p. global markets McGraw-Hill Cos., N.Y.C., 1997—2001; repr. to the UN U.S. Dept. State, Washington, 2001—. Co-pres. U.S./Mexico Commn. for Ednl. and Cultural Exch., 1997—; chmn. The French-Am. Found., 1998—; mem. exec. com. U.S. Coun. for Internat. Bus., 1998—. Mem. Am. Fgn. Svc. Assn., Coun. on Fgn. Rels., Am. Acad. Diplomacy, Fgn. Policy Assn. Greek Orthodox. Office: US Mission to the UN 799 United Nations Plaza New York NY 10017-3505 E-mail: jdneg@erols.com.*

NEGUS, LUCY NEWTON BOSWELL, foundation executive; b. Charlottesville, Va., Apr. 27, 1937; d. William Ward and Lucy Tyler (Newton) Boswell; m. Sidney Stevens Negus, Jr., Dec. 23, 1957 (div. Nov. 1971); children: Sidney Stevens III, Lucy Tyler Negus Snidow, Tayloe Newton. Student, Randolph-Macon Woman's Coll., 1955-57; BS in Mass. Comm., Va. Commonwealth U., 1985. Cert. fundraising exec. Adminstrv. asst. St. Paul's Episcopal Ch., Richmond, Va., 1972-77; coord. comm. Westminster-Canterbury Corp., 1977-78; corp. sec. Westminster-Canterbury Found., 1980—; dir. cmty. rels. and devel. Westminster-Canterbury Mgmt. Corp., 1978-95, dir. devel., 1995-99, dir. major gifts and planned giving, 1999—. Writer/editor Coming of Age insert Va. Churchman, 1978-79, The Lamp, 1978-95; contbr. articles, poetry to profl. jours.; writer/rschr. books by other authors including Christpower, 1974. Mem. Leadership Metro Richmond Class, 1996, Citizens Coalition for Greater Richmond, 1996—; exec. bd. Collegiate Schs. Alumni Assn., Richmond, 1980-83, 91-94; bd. assocs. St. Paul's Coll., Lawrenceville, Va., 1985-88. Mem. Am. Assn. Homes and Svcs. for the Aging (retirement housing profl.), Va. Assn. Fundraising Execs. (founding mem., pres. 1983-84, Devel. Recognition award 1993), Va. Planned Giving Study Group (bd. dirs. 1992-95), Estate Planning Coun. of Richmond, Va. Writers Club, The Woman's Club, The Laurels Honor Soc., Phi Kappa Phi, Kappa Tau Alpha. Republican. Episcopalian. Avocations: writing, history, genealogy, travel, local economic development. Home: 5404 Queensbury Rd Richmond VA 23226-2120 Office: Westminster-Canterbury Mgmt 1600 Westbrook Ave Apt 1 Richmond VA 23227-3324

NEHAMAS, ALEXANDER, philosophy educator; b. Athens, Greece, Mar. 22, 1946; came to U.S., 1964; s. Albert and Christine (Yannuli) N.; m. Susan Glimcher, June 22, 1983; 1 child, Nicholas Albert Glimcher. BA, Swarthmore Coll., 1967; PhD, Princeton U., 1971; D in Philosophy (hon.), Athens, 1993. Asst. then assoc. prof. philosophy U. Pitts., 1971-81, prof., 1981-86; prof. philosophy U. Pa., 1986-90; vis. prof. Princeton (N.J.) U., 1978-79, 89, Edmund Carpenter prof. humanities, 1990—, prof. philosophy and comparative lit., 1990—, chair humanities coun., 1994—2002, chmn. program in Hellenic studies, 1994—2002. Dir. Princeton Soc. Fellow in Liberal Arts, 1999-2002; Mills vis. prof. U. Calif., Berkeley, 1983; Sather vis. prof., 1993; vis. prof. U. Calif., Santa Cruz, 1988; bd. dirs. Princeton U. Press; trustee Nat. Humanities Ctr., 1996-99, Athens (Greece) Coll., 1996–. Author: Nietzche: Life as Literature, 1985, The Art of Living: Socratic Reflectionsfrom Plato to Foucault, 1998, Virtues of Authenticity: Essays on Plato and Socrates, 1999; translator Plato's Symposium, 1989, Plato's Phaedrus, 1995; co-editor: Aristotle's Rhetoric: Philosophical Essays, 1994; contbr. articles to profl. jours.; mem. editl. bd. Am. Philos. Quar., 1981-86, History of Philosophy Quar., 1983-88, Ancient Philosophy, 1984—, Jour. Modern Greek Studies, 1986—, Arion, 1989—, Philosophy and Lit., 1989—, Philosophy and Phenomenological Rsch., 1990—. Recipient Lindback Found. Tchg. award, U. Pa., 1989, Behrman award in humanities, Princeton U., 1999, Ann. prize in Hellenic Studies Acad., Athens, 2000, Internat. Nietsche prize, 2001, Mellon Disting. Achievement award, 2001; grantee Guggenheim fellow, 1983, NEH, 1978. Mem. MLA, Am. Philos. Assn. (chmn. program 1982-83, exec. com. 1990-92, v.p. ea. divsn. 2002, pres.-elect ea. divsn.), Modern Greek Studies Assn. (exec. com. 1983-89), Am. Soc. Aesthetics, N.Am. Nietzche Soc. (exec. com. 1988-91), Phi Beta Kappa (vis. prof. 1989, vis. scholar 1995). Office: Princeton U Dept Philosophy Princeton NJ 08544-0001

NEHER, MARY TIMMONS, nursing consultant, former nursing administrator; b. New Madison, Ohio, Dec. 20, 1930; d. Benjamin Willard and Treva Marie (Longanecker) Timmons; m. Robert Trostle Neher, June 12, 1954; children: Kenneth Edward, Jon Oscar, Daniel Allen. Student, Manchester Coll., 1948-50; diploma, Miami Valley Hosp. Sch. Nursing, 1954; BS, U. La Verne, Calif., 1981. Gen. staff nurse Bloomington (Ind.) Hosp., 1954-55; nursery and delivery rm. nurse Bethany Hosp., Chgo., 1955-57; staff nurse Woods Meml. Convalescent Hosp., LaVerne, Calif., 1973-75; charge nurse Brethren Hillcrest Homes, La Verne, 1975-81, dir. staff devel., 1981-91, asst. dir. nursing, 1981-91, acting DON, 1991-92, dir. of resident svcs., quality assurance coord., 1991-97; ednl. cons., 1998-2000. Vol. nurse ARC, Pomona chpt., 1967-68. Mem. Am. Nursing Found. Home: 2373 Bonita Ave La Verne CA 91750-4932

NEHER, ROBERT TROSTLE, biology educator; b. Mt. Morris, Ill., Nov. 1, 1930; s. Oscar Warner and Etha Mae (Trostle) N.; m. Mary Rebecca Timmons, June 12, 1954; children: Kenneth, Jon, Daniel. BA in Sci., Manchester Coll., Ind., 1953; MAT in Biology, Ind. U., 1955, PhD in Botany, 1963; MRE in Counseling, Bethany Sem., Chgo., 1957. Assoc. Christian edn. Ch. of Brethren, Elgin, Ill., 1956; asst. prof., then assoc. prof. biology U. LaVerne, Calif., 1958-62, prof. biology, 1966—, chmn. nat. sci. divsn., 1978—, provost, v.p. acad. affairs, 2000-01; dir. U. LaVerne Field Sta. Magpie Ranch, Drummond, Mont., 1994—. Dep. dir. Nat. Energy Rsch. and Info. Inst., 1982-88, chair pre-health sci. com., program dir., academic coun., 1985—; aquaculture cons. Bolsa Aquaculture Consortium, 1973-76, AM China Corp., 1981; cons. devel. of in-svc. tchg. tng. in environ. edn. L.A. Pub. Schs.; dir. coll. level curriculum program Montclair High Sch., Van Nuys, Calif. Co-editor: Energy from Biomass, 1979; contbr. articles to profl. jours. City councilman LaVerne City Coun., 1976-84, mayor pro tem, 1980-84; commr. L.A. County Watershed Commn., 1976-91; bd. dirs. Pomona Valley Youth Svcs.; juvenile divsn. chmn. 1978-79; chmn. San Gabriel Valley Get-About Transp. Bd., 1980-84; mem. L.A. County Solid Waste Curbside Recycling Task Force, 1980-82; chmn. La Verne City Commn. on Environ. Quality, 1972-75; mem. La Verne City Planning Commn., 1966-72; moderator La Verne Ch. of Brethren, 1966-75, chmn. bd. 1977-80, mem. ch. bd. dirs., 1966-84; trustee, officer San Gabriel Valley Mosquito and Vector Control Dist., 1991—. Named Outstanding Tchr. of Yr. LaVerne Coll., 1969-70, NSF grantee, 1960-61; NSF faculty fellow Ind. U., Bloomington, 1961-62. Mem. AAAS (life mem), Am. Soc. Plant Taxonomists, Calif. Bot. Soc., San Bernardino County Mus. Assn., Audubon Soc., Sierra Club, Nat. Geog. Soc., Sigma Xi. Office: U La Verne Natural Science Divsn 1950 3rd St La Verne CA 91750-4401 E-mail: neherr@ulv.edu.

NEHLS, ROBERT LOUIS, JR. school system administrator; b. Berkeley, Calif., Dec. 27, 1944; s. Robert Louis and Inda May (Kean) N.; m. Diana Jean Smith, June 17, 1967; 1 child, Patrick Robert. AA, Coll. Marin, 1965; BS, San Jose State U., 1967, MA, 1976; EdD, U. San Francisco, 1991. Cert. tchr., sch. adminstr., Calif. Tchr. Diablo Valley Coll., Pleasant Hill, Calif., 1979-86; acct. Kelly and Tama, CPAs, Walnut Creek, 1978-79; tchr. Pleasanton (Calif.) Unified Sch. Dist., 1970-78, 79-81, dir. fiscal svcs., 1981-83; dep. supt. San Leandro (Calif.) Unified Sch. Dist., 1983-87, 90-2001; asst. supt. Acalanes Union H.S. Dist., Lafayette, Calif., 1987-89; supt. Orinda (Calif.) Union Sch. Dist., 1989-90; tchr. St. Marys Coll. Sch. Edn., Moraga, Calif., 1997; chief bus. official Tahoe Truckee Sch. Dist., 2001—. Exec. adv. com. Calif. Found. Improvement of Employee/Employer Relationships, Sacramento, 1992-97. Contbr. articles to profl. jours. Mem. Assn. Calif. Sch. Adminstrs. (comptroller 1992-95, pres. 1996-97), Calif. Assn. Sch. Bus. Ofcls. (bd. dirs. no. sect. 1984-89), No. Calif. Sch. Bus. Ofcls. (past pres.), Acad. of Sci., Phi Kappa Phi. Avocations: fishing, skiing, performing Irish and Scottish music. Home: 12688 Falcon Point Pl Truckee CA 96161 Office: Tahoe Truckee Unified Sch Dist 11839 Donner Pass Rd Truckee CA 96161 E-mail: rnehls@ttusd.k12.ca.us.

NEHORAI, ARYE, electrical engineering educator, researcher; b. Haifa, Israel, Sept. 10, 1951; s. Aharon and Victoria Nehorai; m. Shlomit Nehorai, June 28, 1979; children: Elad, Sharon. BSc in EE, Technion Inst., Haifa, Israel, 1976, MSc in EE, 1979; PhD, Stanford U., 1983. Rsch. asst. Stanford U., Palo Alto, Calif., 1979-83, rsch. assoc., 1983-84; rsch. engr. Sys. Control Tech., Inc., 1984-85; asst. prof. Yale U., New Haven, 1985-89, assoc. prof., 1989-95; prof. U. Ill., Chgo., 1995—. Assoc. editor IEEE, 1987-2001; mem. editl. bd. Signal Processing, Europe, 1999—; editor-in-chief IEEE Trans. Signal Processing, 2000—. Grantee USN, USAF, 1987—, NSF, 1986—, ONR, 1991—. Fellow IEEE, Royal Statis. Soc. Avocations: sports, travel. Office: U Ill ECE Dept 851 S Morgan St Chicago IL 60607-7042 E-mail: nehorai@ece.uic.edu.

NEHRA, GERALD PETER, lawyer; b. Detroit, Mar. 25, 1940; s. Joseph P. and Jeanette M. (Bauer) N.; m. children: Teresa, Patricia; m. Peggy Jensen, Sept. 12, 1987. B.I.E., Gen. Motors Inst., Flint, Mich., 1962; JD, Detroit Coll. Law, 1970. Bar: Mich. 1970, N.Y. 1972, Colo. 1992, U.S. Dist. Ct. (ea. dist.) Mich. 1970, U.S. Dist. Ct. (so. dist.) N.Y. 1972, U.S. Dist. Ct. (no. dist.) N.Y. 1976, U.S. Ct. Appeals (6th cir.) 1978. Successively engr., supr., gen. supr. Gen. Motors Corp., 1958-67; mktg. rep. to regional counsel IBM Corp., 1967-79; v.p. gen. counsel Church & Dwight Co., Inc., 1979-82; dep. chief atty. Amway Corp., 1982-83; dep. gen. counsel, 1983-92; dir. legal div., 1989-91; sec., dir. corp. law, 1991-92; v.p. gen. cousnel Fuller Brush, Boulder, Colo., 1991-92; pvt. practice, 1992—. Adj. instr. Dale Carnegie Courses, 1983-91. Recipient Outstanding Contbn. award Am. Cancer Soc., 1976. Mem. ABA, Mich. Bar Assn., Colo. Bar Assn., N.Y. State Bar Assn. Home and Office: 1710 Beach St Muskegon MI 49441-1008 E-mail: gnehra@mlmatty.com.

NEHRBASS, RICHARD GEORGE, literature educator, writer; b. Sacramento, May 3, 1943; s. George Lamar and Lois Nehrbass; m. Marilynn Louise Nehrbass, Aug. 31, 1968 (div. Nov. 2000); children: David, Dan, Ken. BS, Sacramento State U., 1965; MBA, U. So. Calif., L.A., 1970, DBA, 1976. Acct. GM, L.A., 1967—69; prof. Calif. State Dominguez Hills, Carson, Calif., 1974—. Mgmt. cons. U. So. Calif. Sch. Dentistry, 1974—85. Author: A Perfect Death for Hollywood, 1991, Dark of Night, 1992; author: (under pseudonym of Zachary Alan Fox) Cradle and All, 1998, All Fall Down, 1997, When the Wind Blows, 1998. Mem.: Nat. Assn. Scholars. Avocations: reading, walking.

NEHRBASS, SETH MARTIN, patent lawyer; b. Lafayette, La., Nov. 10, 1960; s. Neil Martin and Janet (Himbert) N.; m. Mary Elizabeth Dennis, Aug. 12, 2000; children: Gabriel, Fabian. Student, U. Catholique de l'Ouest, Angers, France, 1980, U. Paul Valéry, Montpellier, France, 1981; BS in Physics summa cum laude, U. Southwe. La., 1982; JD cum laude, Loyola U., 1990. Bar: U.S. Patent & Trademark Office 1984, La. 1990, U.S. Dist. Ct. (ea., mid., and we. dists.) La. 1990, U.S. Ct. Appeals (5th and fed. cirs.) 1990; cert. notary public, La. Patent examiner U.S. Patent & Trademark Office, 1982-84; patent agt. with law firm New Orleans, 1986-87; assoc. Pravel, Hewitt, Kimball & Krieger, 1987-97, shareholder, 1997-98, Garvey, Smith, Nehrbass & Doody, L.L.C., Metairie, La., 1998—. Adj. law faculty Tulane Law Sch., 1997—; judge practice round moot ct. teams Loyola Law Sch., 1992—; preparer questions patent bar exam PTO Q & A Bd., 1992-93; presenter in field. Contbr. articles to profl. jours. Den leader 2d grade Cub Scouts, Boy Scouts Am., Lusher Sch., Audubon Dist., 1991-92, 3d grade, 1994-95, asst. den leader 3d grade, 1992-93, 4th grade, 1993-94; soccer coach Carrollton Booster Club, New Orleans, 1993-95, Lakeview Soccer Club, New Orleans, 1995-96; adv. mem. La. Ctr. for Law and Civic Edn., 1996-98. Recipient Hornbook award West Pub. Co., 1986-87, 87-88, Corpus Juris Secundum award, 1986-87, Am. Jurisprudence awards (2), 1986; scholar La. State U. Alumni Fedn., 1978, Coun. Devel. French La./French Govt., 1980-81, Loyola Law Sch., 1986. Mem. ABA (sect. law, sci., tech. 1988-91, law student divsn. liaison patent trademark and copyright law 1988-90, intellectual property law sect. 1988—, chmn. law student com. 1996-98, chmn. spl. com. drug crisis 1990-93, co-chmn. ann. meeting arrangements com. 1993-94, internat. treaties and laws com. 1994—, co-chmn. young lawyers com. 1998-99), Am. Intellectual Property Law Assn. (ADR com., internat. and fgn. law com., patent law com. 1994-2000), La. Bar Assn. (internat. law sect. 1992—, intellectual property law sect. 1996—, vice chmn. 1997-98, chair-elect 1998-99, chair 1999-2000), New Orleans Bar Assn. (interim chmn. ad hoc com. drug crisis 1991-92, chmn. intellectual property law com. 1991-95, chmn. law related edn. com. 1995-97), Loyola Law Sch. Moot Ct. Alumni Assn., Sigma Pi Sigma, Pi Delta Phi, Alpha Sigma Nu. Democrat. Roman Catholic. Avocations: gardening, dancing, traveling, hunting, fishing. Home: 453 Audubon Blvd New Orleans LA 70125-3503 E-mail: Nehrbass@aol.com.

NEHRING, LISA MARIE, secondary school educator; b. Charleston, S.C., June 30, 1966; d. Roy Andrew and Lilian (Nunnen) Olson; m. C. Mark Nehring, June 15, 1991. BA in Math., Lake Forest Coll., 1988; MEd in Adminstrn. summa cum laude, Nat.-Louis U., 1994. Cert. tchr., Ill.; cert. supr. adminstrn., Ill. H.S. math. tchr. Wykeham Rise, Washington, 1988-89, Wamogo Regional H.S., Litchfield, 1989-90; math. tchr. Waukegan (Ill.) H.S., 1990-94, Adlai E. Stevenson H.S., Lincolnshire, Ill., 1994—. Mem. Nat. Coun. Tchrs. Math., Ill. Coun. Tchrs. Math. Avocations: skiing, tennis, travel, dance. Office: Adlai E Stevenson HS Two Stevenson Dr Lincolnshire IL 60069 E-mail: lnehring@district125.k12.il.us.

NEHRING, WENDY MARIE, pediatrics nurse; b. Waukegan, Ill., Aug. 17, 1957; d. Virgil M. and R. Allene (Nelson) Nehring. BSN, Ill. Wesleyan U., Bloomington, 1979; MS, U. Wis., Madison, 1983; PhD, U. Ill., Chgo., 1989. Primary nurse level III pediatrics Evanston (Ill.) Hosp., 1979-81; staff/charge nurse pediatrics Kishwaukee Community Hosp., DeKalb, Ill., 1981; staff/charge nurse geriatrics Madison (Wis.) Convalescent Ctr., 1982; instr. parent-child nursing Ill. Wesleyan U., Bloomington, 1983-85; clin. nurse specialist/rsch. asst. U. Ill. Chgo. and Peoria, Coll. Nursing, 1985-87; rsch. asst./nurse cons. U. Ill. at Chgo., Early Intervention Project, 1987-89; sr. rsch. specialist, project dir. U. Ill. Chgo. U. Affiliated Prog. in Devel. Disabilities, 1989-90; sr. rsch. specialist child and family studies U. Ill. at Chgo., Coll. Nursing, Ctr. for Narcolepsy Rsch., 1990-92; pediatric clin. instr. U. Ill., Chgo., 1992, asst. prof. maternal-child nursing, 1992-98, coord. undergrad. pediatric nursing program, 1994-95, coord. undergrad. maternal-child nursing programs, 1995-98; assoc. prof. So. Ill. U., Edwardsville, 1998-2001, dir. undergrad. programs, 2000—02, prof., 2001—, acting assoc. dean for ednl. svcs., 2002—. Lectr. in field; conductor workshops in field; cons. in field. Cons. editor: Mental Retardation, 1996—, assoc. editor: Simulation and Gaming, 2001, mem. editl. bd., column editor: Jour. Child and Family Nursing, 1998—2001; contbr. articles to profl. jours. HEW traineeship, 1981-82, 82-83; Downs Syndrome Rsch. fund grantee, 1988, 93-96, NIH, NINR grantee, 1999—. Mem.: Am. Acad. Nursing, Midwest Nursing Rsch. Soc. (co-chmn. pediat. sect. 1995—96, chmn. 1996—97), Soc. Pediat. Nurses, Am. Assn. on Mental Retardation (prevention com. 1989—92, chair com. on health promotion and prevention 2001—, pres. nursing divsn. 1992—94, awards and fellowship com. 1997—2001, bd. dirs. 1998—2000, pubs. com. 1998—2000), Nat. Assn. on Down Syndrome (bd. dirs. 1990—98, 2d v.p. 1991—94), Nat. Down Syndrome Congress (profl. adv. com. 1988—). Office: SIUE Sch Nursing Rm 2330 Alumni Hl Edwardsville IL 62026-1066 Fax: 618-650-3854. E-mail: wnehrin@siue.edu.

NEHRIR, M. HASHEM, electrical engineer, educator; b. Shiraz, Fars, Iran, Aug. 16, 1946; s. Mohammad Hossein Nehrir; m. Maryam Nehrir, Oct. 15, 1970; children: Ali Reza, Sara, Amin Reza. BSEE, Oreg. State U., 1969, MSEE, 1971, PhD, 1978. Instr. Shiraz U., 1971—75, asst./assoc. prof., 1978—86; vis. scholar Univ. of Idaho, 1986—87; asst./assoc. prof. Mont. State U., Bozeman, 1987—96, prof., 1996—. Vis. scholar, prof. U. Idaho, Moscow, 1986—87. Rschr.: textbook Hybrid Simulation of Engineering Systems, 1986 (Mont. State U. Alumini Assn. and Bozeman Area C.of C. award Excellence, 2001); author: Basic Electric Circuits, 1981; contbr. articles to profl. jours. Fellow Rsch., Kumamoto U., 1998; grantee, NSF, 1992, 1997, 2000, U.S. Dept. Energy, 1994, Mont. State U., 1997, 2000. Mem.: IEEE (vice chair 1997, chair Mont. sect. 1998). Avocations: travel, hiking. Office: Mont State U Elec and Computer Engring Dept Bozeman MT 59717 Office Fax: 406-994-5958. Business E-Mail: hnehrir@ece.montana.edu.

NEHRLING, ARNO HERBERT, JR. retired chemical company executive; b. Richmond, Ind., Mar. 5, 1928; s. Arno Herbert and Irene Thelma (Dahlberg) N.; m. Mary Helen Mudd, Jan. 11, 1958; children: Amy Irene Nehrling Belz, Dorothy Louise Nehrling Murphy. BA, Cornell U., 1950; MBA, Harvard U., 1955. Various supervisory and mgmt. positions E.I. DuPont de Nemours & Co., Wilmington, Del., 1955-64, dir. fin. Dusseldorf, Fed. Republic Germany and Mexico City, 1965-71, asst. mgr. credit div., asst. mgr. treasury div., asst. mgr. fgn. and banking div. Wilmington, Del., 1972-76, asst. treas., dir. employee compensation and benefits, 1977—. Former pres. Geriatric Svcs. of Del., Inc.; chmn. Del. Health Info. Network. Mem. Health Resources Bd., Tuition Savings. Bd. Del., Health Care Com. Del. Mem. Fin. Execs. Inst. (past chmn. employee benefits com., past chmn. com. on other post employment benefits), Pension Investment Com. Del. Home: 25 Shipcarpenter Sq Lewes DE 19958-1246

NEHRT, LEE CHARLES, management educator; b. Baldwin, Ill., Sept. 12, 1926; s. Martin William and Amanda Fredarika (Tillock) N.; m. Ardith Ann Saltzman, Mar. 26, 1952; children: Chadwick Charles, Philip Lee, Dana Ann. BS, USCG Acad., 1949; cert. d'etudes politiques, U. Paris, 1955; MBA,

Columbia U., 1956, PhD, 1962. Fgn. ops. supr. Atomics Internat., Canoga Park, Calif., 1956-60; prof. internat. bus. Ind. U., 1962-65, 67-69, 71-74; Ford Found. adv. to minister planning, economy and industry Tunisia, 1965-67; chief adv. group U. Dacca, E. Pakistan, 1969-71; R.P. Clinton prof. internat. mgmt. Wichita (Kans.) State U., 1974-78; pres. World Trade Inst., N.Y.C., 1978-81; Owens-Ill. prof. internat. mgmt. Ohio State U., Columbus, 1981-86. Cons. UN, World Bank, advisor Ministry Planning Govt. Indonesia, 1987-89; dir., curator The Blacksmith Mus., 1991-92. Author: Education in International Business, 1963, Foreign Marketing of Nuclear Power Plants, 1965, Financing Capital Equipment Exports, 1966, International Finance for Multinational Business, 1967, 2d rev. edit. 1972, International Business Research: Past, Present and Future, 1969, The Political Climate for Private Investment in North Africa, 1970, Managerial Policy and Strategy for Developing Countries, 1973, Managerial Policy, Strategy and Planning for South-East Asia, 1974, Managerial Policy and Strategy for the Philippines, 1976, 3d rev. edit. 1989, Business and International Education, 1977, The Internationalization of the Business School Curriculum, 1979, Case Studies in the Internationalization of the Business School Curriculum, 1981, The Politico-Economic Analysis of Countries, 1981; contbr. articles to profl. jours. Chmn. bd. dirs. Monroe County ARC, 1996-98. Lt. (j.g.) USCG, 1949-53. Mem. Acad. Internat. Bus. (pres. 1972-74, dean fellows 1978-81), Soc. Internat. Devel. (gov. 1968-71)

NEIBEL, OLIVER JOSEPH, JR. retired medical services executive; b. Kansas City, Mo., Apr. 17, 1927; s. Oliver Joseph and Eula Lee (Durham) N.; m. Patricia Helen O'Keefe, June 24, 1950 (div. 1971); children: Oliver Joseph III, Deborah Sue; m. Diane Bachus Nelson, Apr. 11, 1981. BS, U. Ariz., 1949; JD, U. Va., 1952. Bar: Wash. 1953, Ill. 1961, Nebf. 1973. Instr. U. Wash., Seattle, 1952-53; private practice, 1953-57; asst. atty. gen. State Of Wash., 1957-61; legis. atty. AMA, Chgo., 1961-63; exec. dir., gen. counsel Coll. Am. Pathologists, 1963-72; v.p., gen. mgr. Physicians Lab., Omaha, 1973-97; ret., 1997. Justice of peace, Mountlake Terrace, Wash., 1955-57. With USNR, 1945. Mem.: Med. Group Mgmt. Assn., Nat. Health Lawyers Assn., Ill. Bar Assn., Nebr. Bar Assn., Wash. Bar Assn., Omaha Press Club, Rotary, Wash. Athletic Club (Seattle), Tavern Club, Shriners, Masons, Delta Sigma Rho, Alpha Kappa Psi, Delta Theta Phi, Phi Kappa Psi. Home: 7918 Potter Plz Omaha NE 68122-1449 E-mail: ojn-dbn-bear@att.net.

NEIBERG, ALAN DAVID, physician; b. Pitts., July 22, 1942; s. Morris Joseph and Ethel (Zerelstein) N.; m. Vicki Barbara Evans, Mar. 1, 1964 (div.); children: Maurine, Forrest; m. Judy A. Neiberg. BS, U. Pitts., 1962; MA, U. Cin., 1963, PhD, 1967; MD, Mich. State U., 1973. Intern Yale-New Haven Hosp., 1973-76; resident in internal medicine Mich. State U. Affiliated Hosps., Lansing, 1973-76; rsch. scientist USAF, 1966-67; asst. prof. U. Mich., E. Lansing, 1967-69; clin. asst. prof. Mich. State U., 1976-82, clin. assoc. prof., 1982-95, clin. prof., 1995—; pvt. practice Lansing, Mich., 1976—. Office: Lansing Internal Medicine 1200 E Michigan Ave Ste 500 Lansing MI 48912-1899 E-mail: neiberg@pilot.msu.edu.

NEIBERGER, RICHARD EUGENE, pediatrician, nephrologist, educator; b. Onaga, Kans., Nov. 16, 1947; s. Earl Edward and Margaret Bell (Grim) N.; m. Mary June Chamberlin, Oct. 31, 1971; children: Ami, Eric, Chris, Robert. BS in Physics, U. Ctrl. Fla., 1971; PhD, U. Louisville, 1979, MD, 1982. Diplomate Am. Bd. Pediat., Nat. Bd. Med. Examiners. Intern, then resident in pediat. Albert Einstein Coll. Med., Bronx, N.Y., 1982-85, fellow in pediat. nephrology, 1985-88; asst. prof. U. Fla. Coll. Med., Gainesville, 1988-93, assoc. prof., 1993—; med. dir. pediatrics Renal Stone Disease Clinic, 1996—. Assoc. med. dir. Children's Kidney Ctr., Gainesville, 1989—; co-investigator on 8 rsch. studies, dir. Pediatric Rsch. Stone Disease Clin. U. Fla., rsch. peer rev. com. Am. Heart Assn., 1997-99; physician advisor Fla. Med. Quality Assurance, Tampa, 1994—. Contbr. articles to profl. jours. Sunday Sch. tchr. Trinity United Meth. Ch., Gainesville, 1992—; bd. dirs. Children's Home Soc., Gainesville, 1994—, Ronald McDonald House, 1996—; asst. scoutmaster Boy Scouts Am. Trinity Ch., Gainesville, 1994—. Grantee CoInvest, Bethesda, Md., 1995—. Mem. AMA, Fla. Med. Assn., So. Med. Assn., Am. Soc. Nephrology, Internat. Pediat. Nephrology Assn., Am. Soc. Pediat. Nephrology, Fla. Soc. Pediat. Nephrology (pres. 1998). Republican. Methodist. Avocations: camping, skiing, traveling. E-mail: neibere@peds.ufl.edu.

NEIDERT, DAVID LYNN, administrator; b. Akron, Ohio, Nov. 4, 1954; s. William K. and Violet P. (Barker) N.; married; children: Sarah, David, Mariah. BA, Anderson U., 1977, MA, 1987. Dir. human resources Anderson (Ind.) U., 1978-85, dir. aux. svcs., 1985-2000; dir. Ctr. Christian Leadership, 2000—. Author: (book) Four Seasons of Leadership, 1999; co-author: A New Paradigm of Leadership, 1997; contbr. articles to profl. jours. Chair Jr. Achievement, Anderson, 1995-96. Mem.: Inst. Cert. Profl. Mgrs. (bd. govs., chair bd. dirs. 2000—01), Anderson Area Leadership Acad. (Disting. Svc. award 1987, 1995, Servant Leadership award 2002), Internat. Mgmt. Coun. (nat. pres. 1994—95, program chair 1996—, Nat. Disting. Svc. award 1999). Republican. Avocations: writing, public speaking, facilitation, consulting. Office: Anderson U 1100 E 5th St Anderson IN 46012-3495 E-mail: dneidert@anderson.edu.

NEIDERT, KALO EDWARD, accountant, educator; b. Safe, Mo., Sept. 1, 1918; s. Edward Robert and Margaret Emma (Kinsey) N.; m. Stella Mae Vest, June 22, 1952; children— Edward, Karl, David, Wayne, Margaret. BS in Bus. Adminstrn. with honors, Washington U., St. Louis, 1949, MS in Bus. Adminstrn, 1950; postgrad., U. Minn., 1950-54. CPA, Nev. Mem. faculty U. Minn., 1950-54; mem. faculty U. Miss., 1954-57, U. Tex., Austin, 1957-61, Gustavus Adolphus Coll., St. Peter, Minn., 1961-62; prof. acctg. and info. systems U. Nev., 1962-90, prof. emeritus, 1990—; auditor Washoe County Employee Fed. Credit Union, 1969-82, dir., treas., 1982-86. Author: Statement on Auditing Procedure in Decision Tree Form, 1974. Asst. scoutmaster local Boy Scouts Am., asst. dist. commr. New Area coun.; bd. dirs. Tahoe Timber Trails, 1980-82, treas., 1981-82, v.p. fin., 1982-84; Bd. dirs. St. Johns Child Care Center, 1982-84; cen. com. mem. Washoe County Rep. Party, Reno, 1986-88, 90—. Mem. AICPA, Assn. System Mgmt. (treas. Reno chpt. 1984—), Am. Acctg. Assn., Am. Econ. Assn., Am. Fin. Assn., Fin. Mgmt. Assn., Nev. Soc. CPAs, Western Fin. Assn., Oddfellows, Beta Alpha Psi, Beta Gamma Sigma. Presbyterian. Office: U Nev Coll Bus Adminstrn Reno NV 89557-0001 *I am the descendent of a second generation American. In addition I was raised on a farm in rural America. Early in life, I learned that achievements come only with hard work and taking advantage of each opportunity that comes along, not waiting to see if there was a better opportunity around the corner. All through life this has been my philosophy; take advantage of each opportunity and work hard to make it succeed.*

NEIDHARDT, FREDERICK CARL, microbiologist, educator; b. Phila., May 12, 1931; s. Adam Fred and Carrie (Fry) N.; m. Elizabeth Robinson, June 9, 1956 (div. Sept. 1977); children: Richard Frederick, Jane Elizabeth; m. Germaine Chipault, Dec. 3, 1977; 1 son, Marc Frederick. BA, Kenyon Coll., 1952, DSc (hon.), 1976; PhD, Harvard U., 1956; DSc (hon.), Purdue U., 1988, Umea U., 1994. Research fellow Pasteur Inst., Paris, 1956-57; H.C. Ernst research fellow Harvard Med. Sch., 1957-58, instr., then assoc., 1958-61; mem. faculty Purdue U., 1961-70, assoc. prof, then prof., assoc. head dept. biol. scis., 1965-70; mem. faculty U. Mich., Ann Arbor, 1970—, chmn. dept. microbiology and immunology, 1970-82, F.G. Novy disting. univ. prof., 1989-99, F.G. Novy disting. univ. prof. emeritus, 2000—, assoc. dean faculty affairs, 1990-93, assoc. v.p. for rsch., 1993-96, acting v.p. for rsch., 1996-97, interim v.p. for rsch., 1997, v.p. for rsch., 1998. Cons. Dept. Agr., 1964-65; mem. grant study panel NIH, 1965-69, 88-92; mem. commn. scholars Ill. Bd. Higher Edn., 1973-79; mem. test com. for microbiology Nat. Bd. Med. Examiners, 1975-79, chmn., 1979-83; mem. sci. adv. com. Neogen Corp., 1982-92; mem. basic energy scis. adv. com. U.S. Dept. Energy, 1994-98; Wellcome vis. prof. in microbiology U. Ky., 1986. Author books and papers in field; mem. editorial bd. profl. jours. Recipient award bacteriology and immunology Eli Lilly and Co., 1966; Alexander von Humboldt Found. award for U.S. sr. scientist, 1979; NSF sr. fellow U. Copenhagen, 1968-69 Mem. Am. Soc. Microbiology (pres. 1981-82), Am. Acad. Arts and Scis., Am. Soc. Biochemistry and Molecular Biology, Am. Inst. Biol. Scis., Genetics Soc. Am., Bavarian Acad. Sci., Soc. Gen. Physiology, Waksman Found. for Microbiology (bd. dirs. 1996—, pres. 2001—), Phi Beta Kappa, Sigma Xi. Office: U Mich Med Sch Dept Microbiology and Immunology Ann Arbor MI 48109-0620 E-mail: fcneid@umich.edu.

NEIDHART, CAROL LYNN, pharmaceutical company official; b. Mt. Vernon, OH, Sept. 18, 1953; d. Clair Edwin and Merry Evelyn (Burke) Neidhart. BA, Miami U., Oxford, Ohio, 1975. Sr. med. rep. CIBA-Geigy Co., Summit, N.J., 1976—; clin. conf. moderator, 1980—. Speaker Pharm. Mfrs. Assn. Mem. NAFE. Republican. Methodist. Avocations: snow skiing, swimming. Home: 9165 Symmes Landing Dr Loveland OH 45140-8200

NEIDICH, GEORGE ARTHUR, lawyer; b. N.Y.C., Feb. 22, 1950; s. Hyman and Rosalyn N.; m. Alene Wendrow, Jan. 10, 1982; 1 child, Hannah Lauren. BA, SUNY, Binghamton, 1971; JD magna cum laude, SUNY, Buffalo, 1974; MLT, Georgetown U., 1981. Bar: N.Y. 1975, D.C. 1979, Va. 1996, Conn. 1990. Assoc. Runfola & Birzon, Buffalo, 1973-75, Duke, Holzman, Yaeger & Radlin, Buffalo, 1975-77; gen. counsel subcom. on capital, investments and bus. opportunity, com. on small bus. U.S. Ho. of Reps., Washington, 1977-79, subcom. on gen. oversight, 1979-80; sr. legal advisor Task Force Product Liability and Accident Compensation Office of Gen. Counsel, Dept. Commerce, 1980-81; assoc. Steptoe & Johnson, 1981-86, of counsel, 1986-89; gen. counsel, sr. v.p. Preferred Health Care, Ltd., Wilton, Conn., 1989-93; COO Value Behavioral Health, Inc., Falls Church, Va., 1993-95; counsellor at law, 1995—; gen. counsel CareAdvantage, Inc., Iselin, NJ, 1999—. Adj. prof. Georgetown U. Law Ctr., 1985-87. Author: Report on Product Liability, 1980; contbr. articles to profl. jours. Office: 9301 Morison Ln Great Falls VA 22066-4153 E-mail: gneidich@aol.com.

NEIDIGK, DIANNE, management consultant; b. Monette, Ark., June 28, 1945; d. William Thomas and Thelma Elizabeth (Wells) Wilkerson; m. Lester Dale Neidigk, Feb. 28, 1964; children: Tami Elizabeth, Scott Alan, Lance Dale, Byron Ross. Student, Sam Houston State U., 1963-65, U. Houston, 1969-70. Sub. tchr. Tomball Ind. Sch. Dist., Tex., 1970-74; owner Total Image & Assocs., Houston, 1980— ; dir. Colorific, Houston, 1983-85; v.p. L.D. Neidigk Inc., Magnolia, 1978—; dir. pub. relations, corp accounts Travel Depot, Tomball, 1987-88; bd. dirs. The Discovery Fields, 1987; pres. Excel Tng. Dynamics, 1987-94; CEO Am. Inst. Learning and Productivity, 1994—. Author: Scarves: How to Tie One On, 1987, 1987; (newspaper) Total Image, 1984; Total Image, 1986. Mem. ASTD, NAFE, Exec. Women's Network, Assn. Image Cons., Tomball Bus. and Profl. Women, Tomball C. of C., Fedn. Profl. Women, Internat. Platform Assn. (bd. dirs.), PALS of Tex. (bd. dirs. 1996), Houston Women's Bus. Coun. (bd. dirs. 1996), Beta Sigma Phi. Republican. Club: Study (Tomball). Avocations: private pilot; tennis; sewing; reading. Home: 1543 Virgie Magnolia TX 77355 Office: 363 N Sam Houston Pkwy E Houston TX 77060-2404

NEIDLE, CAROL, language educator, researcher; b. N.Y.C., May 31, 1956; d. Amos and Estelle Laura Neidle. BA, Yale U., 1978; MA, Middlebury French Sch., Vt., 1973—76; PhD, MIT, 1982. Faculty mem. Middlebury Coll., Vt., 1983, 1985—88; dir. PhD program in applied linguistics Boston U., 1988—94, prof. linguistics, 1982—. Dir. Am. Sign Lang. Linguistic Rsch. Project, Boston, 1994—. Author: The Role of Case in Russian Syntax, 1988; co-author: The Syntax of American Sign Language, 2000; prin. designer SignStream (software). Grantee, NSF, 1994—. Office: Boston Univ 718 Commonwealth Ave Boston MA 02215

NEIFELD, JAMES PAUL, surgical oncologist; b. Paterson, N.J., June 5, 1948; s. Herbert S. and Elinor (Charney) N.; m. Ramona S. Simmons, Apr. 27, 1985; children: Emily Claire, Jillian Rose. Student, Lafayette Coll., 1965-68; MD, Med. Coll. Va., 1972. Intern Med. Coll. Va., Richmond, 1972-73, resident in surgery, 1973-74, 76-78, asst. prof. surgery, 1978-82, assoc. prof., 1982-86, prof., 1986—. Lt. comdr. USPHS, 1974-76. Office: PO Box 980011 Richmond VA 23298-0011

NEIGHBORS, IRA ARTHELL, social work educator; b. L.A., Oct. 10, 1946; s. Richard Neighbors and Eliza Beaviory Peyton. BA in Psychology, Calif. State U., Dominguez Hills, 1973; MSW in Social Welfare Adminstrn., UCLA, 1983; D of Social Work, Howard U., 1994. Diplomate Am. Bd. Clin. Social Work; lic. clin. social worker, Calif.; adult edn. credential, Calif. Dept. Edn. Psychiat./clin. social worker Dept. Devel. Svcs. State of Calif., Pomona and Porterville, 1984-90; adult correctional tchr. County of Riverside (Calif.) Dept. Edn., 1987-90; grad. tchg. asst. Howard U., Washington, 1991-93; social worker-adoption and quality assurance Dist. Govt., 1992-94; asst. prof. dept. social work Calif. State U., San Bernardino, 1995-99; assoc. prof. So. U., New Orleans, 1991—. Tchr. ESL Porterville Adult Schs., 1984-86, Moreno Valley (Calif.) Schs., 1997-98; cons. Option Ho., San Bernardino, 1998; social work counselor Vasquez Mgmt. Consulting, Redlands, Calif., 1999; mem. faculty forensic social work Tulane Sch. Social Work Ctr. for Lifelong Learning, New Orleans, 2000. Contbr. articles to profl. jours., chpts. to books. Bd. dirs. Inland Behavioral Svcs., San Bernardino, 1995-98, L.A. Inst. Black Parenting, 1997-2000. Mem. NASW, Nat. Orgn. Forensic Social Work (bd. dirs., pres. 2000-01), Inst. for Black Parenting (bd. dirs., adv. bd.), Inland Area Assn. Black Social Workers (pres. 1995-2001), Calif. Assn. Black Social Work (pres. 1998-2000), Coun. on Social Work Edn. Avocations: reading, jazz, swimming, walking, gymnastics. Home: 1122 W 56th St Sn Bernrdno CA 92407-5346 E-mail: ineighbo@csusb.edu.

NEIGHBORS, PATSY JEAN, school counselor; b. Overton, Tex., May 22, 1936; d. Jackson A. and Alta Lois McQuaid; m. Richard Lon Neighbors, May 30, 1957; children: Sharon Elaine, Richard Lon Jr., Kelly Dianne. BS, East Tex. State U., 1957, MS, 1965. Lic. counselor, Tex.; cert. libr., Tex. Tchr., coach Hawkings (Tex.) Ind. Sch. Dist., 1958-60, Quitman (Tex.) Ind. Sch. Dist., 1962-91, counselor, 1991—, also ednl. bds. and adv. coms. Mem. Tex. Profl. Counselors Assn., Tex. High Sch. Counselors Assn., Tex. Classroom Tchrs. Assn., Tex. Coaches Assn., Piney Woods Counselors Assn. (membership chair 1989—), Delta Kappa Gamma (chair project com. 1988—). Avocations: watching sports, classic cars, sewing, fishing.

NEIHARDT, HILDA, foundation administrator, writer, educator; b. Bancroft, Nebr., Dec. 6, 1916; d. John Gneisenau and Mona (Martinsen) N.; m. Albert Joseph Petri, Apr. 18, 1942 (div. Oct. 1963); children; Gail Petri Toedebusch, Robin, Coralie Joyce Hughes. AB, U. Nebr., 1937; postgrad., Letitia Barnum Sch. Theatre, Chgo., 1943-44; JD, U. Mo., 1963. Bar: Mo. 1963. Adminstrv. asst. Consulate of Switzerland, St. Louis, 1937-42; pvt. practice Columbia, 1963-85, Lake Ozark, 1985-88; pres. John G. Neihardt Found., Bancroft, 1987—2000, chmn. bd. dirs. Lectr. in field. Author: Black Elk and Flaming Rainbow, 1995, Black Elk Lives, 2000; editor: The Giving Earth, 1991, The End of The Dream, 1991, The Ancient Memory, 1991. Trustee John G. Neihardt Trust, Columbia and Tekamah, Nebr., 1973-99; chmn. bd. dirs. Black Elk Lives, 2000; with USN, 1944-45. Mem. AAUW, Westerners, Internat. P.E.O. Avocations: boating, camping, horses. Home: PO Box 358 504 Pennsylvania Ave Bancroft NE 68004 also: 4235 E McDowell #88 Phoenix AZ 85008 Office: John G Neihardt Found PO Box 344 Bancroft NE 68004-0344

NEIKIRK, WILLIAM ROBERT, journalist; b. Irvine, Ky., Jan. 6, 1938; s. Lewis Byron and Nancy Elizabeth (Green) N.; m. Ruth Ann Clary, Sept. 10, 1960; children: Paul Gregory, John Stuart, Christa Lynn. BA in Journalism, U. Ky., 1960. Reporter Lexington (Ky.) Herald, 1959-60; state capital corr. AP, Frankfort, Ky., 1961-66, Baton Rouge, 1966-69; econ. corr. AP (Washington Bur.), 1970-74; nat. econ. writer Chgo. Tribune, Washington, 1974-83, White House corr., 1977, 94-98—, econ. columnist, 1980—, news editor Washington bur., 1983, fin. editor, 1988-91, sr. writer, 1991—, chief Washington corr., 1998—. Author: The Work Revolution, 1983, Volcker: The Money Man, 1987. Recipient Beck award Chgo. Tribune, 1975, Bus. Writing award U. Mo., 1978, 80, Bus. Writing award Amos Tuck Grad. Sch. Bus., Dartmouth Coll., 1980, John Hancock Bus. Writing award Wharton Sch. Fin., U. Pa., 1979, finalist, 1990, 91, John Hancock Bus. Writing award U. Houston, 1980, Loeb Bus. Writing award UCLA Grad. Sch. Mgmt., 1979, Chgo. Headliner Club award, 1979, 84, Raymond Clapper Meml. award, 1981, Barnet Nover award, 1994, Merriman Smith award, 1995, White House Correspondents Assn.; named to Ky. Journalism Hall of Fame, 1998, One of Top 100 Bus. News Luminaries of the Century, TJFR mag., 2000; co-recipient Pulitzer Prize, 2001. Mem. Gridiron Club. Mem. United Ch. of Christ Home: 5121 38th St N Arlington VA 22207-1827

NEIL, FRED APPLESTEIN, public relations executive; b. Balt., Nov. 26, 1933; s. Frank and Mollie (Schapiro) Applestein; m. Sheila Tilles, Aug. 30, 1959 (div. May 1980); children: Jay Alan, Brian Mark Applestein, Gail Renee Murphy; m. Dawn Francis Fisher, July 6, 1986. BA, U. Md., 1959. News and sports editor Sta. WITH, Balt., 1959-60; dir. news and sports Sta. WCBM, Metromedia, 1960-69; press officer Mayor William Donald Schaefer, 1970-71; gen. mgr. Balt. Banners World Team Tennis League, 1971-72; pres. Fred Neil Assocs., Pub. Rels., Balt., 1972—. Staff specialist pub. info. Md. Rehab. Ctr., Balt., 1980-91; owner Cruising for Mems., Ellicott City, 1987—, P.I.O. Office of Comm. and Cmty. Rels., Divsn. Rehab. Svcs., Balt., 1980—; co-owner Carrolltowne Card & Gift Shop. Author: It's a Very Simple Game!, The Life and Times of Charles Eckman II, 1995, A Funny Thing Happened on the Way to the Health Fair, 2002; editor, contbr. Lafayette Sq. Newsletter, 1974-82, Fed. Hill Newsletter, 1974-82, Greater Penn Ave. Newsletter, 1974-82, MPCA News Letter, 1982—, Md. Rehab. Assn. News Letter, 1985—, Front and Center newsletter, 1980-92, Rehab Digest, 1992—; contbr. articles to mags., newspapers, and newsletters. Bd. dirs. Liberty Showcase Theater, 1985-87, Howard County Summer Theatre, 1992-99, pres. 1995-99. With U.S. Army, 1956-58. Recipient award for spot reporting Chesapeake AP, 1967, award for in-depth sports reporting, 1967, 69, Media Appreciation award U.S. Intercollegiate Lacrosse Assn., 1970, Humanitarian award Md. Rehab. Assn., 1982, Appreciation award 1986, Profl. Svc. award Md. Rehab. Counseling Assn., 1985, Ams. with Disabilities Act award The Task Force on the Rights and Empowerment of Ams. with Disabilities, 1991, Outstanding Contbns. award, 1994, Md. Gov.'s Com. on Employment of People with Disabilities Print Media award, 1996, Golden Radio Buffs' Golden Mike award, 1996. Mem. Md. Rehab. Assn. (pres. 1985, 87), Md. Press Club (pres. 1988-89, 97-98, bd. dirs. 1990-91), Balt. Sports Reporters Assn. (pres. 1964), Balt. Press Reporters Assn. (pres. 1965), Mid-Atlantic Rehab. Adminstrs. Assn. (pres. 1990). Home: 4029 Pebble Branch Rd Ellicott City MD 21042-5348

NEIL, ROBERT F. broadcast executive; Pres., CEO Cox Radio Inc., Atlanta, 1986—. Office: Cox Radio Inc 6205 Peachtree Dunwoody Rd Atlanta GA 30328

NEILD, ROBERT RALPH, economist, educator; b. Peterborough, U.K., Sept. 10, 1924; s. Ralph and Josephine Neild; m. Elizabeth W. Griffiths (div.); 5 children. Ed. Charterhouse and Trinity Coll., Cambridge. Sec. UN Econ. Commn. for Europe, Geneva, 1947-51; mem. staff econ. sect. Cabinet Office (later Treasury), 1951-56; lectr. econs., fellow Trinity Coll., Cambridge U., 1956-58, prof. econs., 1971-84; mem. staff Nat. Inst. Econ. and Social Research, 1958-64; econ. adviser to Treasury, 1964-67; mem. Fulton Com. on Civil Service, 1966-68; dir. Stockholm Internat. Peace Research Inst., 1967-71, mem. governing bd., 1972-82; lectr. in field. Author: Pricing and Employment in the Trade Cycle, 1964; The Measurement and Reform of Budgetary Policy (with T.S. Ward), 1978; How to Make Up Your Mind About the Bomb, 1981, An Essay on Strategy, 1990; co-editor: The Foundations of Defensive Defense, 1990, The English, The French and the Oyster, 1995. Mem. governing body Queen Elizabeth Coll., Oxford, 1978-86. Served with RAF, 1943-45.

NEILL, DENIS MICHAEL, international consultant; b. Grand Rapids, Mich., Apr. 27, 1943; s. Thomas Patrick and Agnes Josephine (Weber) N.; m. Mary Kathleen Golden, June 11, 1966; children: Mark, Erin. AB cum laude, St. Louis U., 1964, JD cum laude, 1967. Bar: Mo. 1967, D.C. 1969. Gen. atty. Office of Asst. Regional Counsel IRS, Newark, 1967-68; assoc. Arent, Fox, Kintner, Plotkin & Kahn, Washington, 1969-71, Morgan, Lewis & Bockius, Washington, 1971-72; atty. advisor office gen. counsel AID, 1972-73, asst. gen. counsel legis. and policy coordination, 1973-75, asst. adminstr. legis. affairs, 1975-77; sr. v.p., gen. counsel Aeromaritime Internat. Corp., 1977-80; counsel Surrey & Morse, 1980-81; sr. ptnr. Neill & Shaw, 1981-92; sr. law ptnr. Dalley, Neill, Assevero, Carroll & Nealer, 1992-93; pres. Neill & Co., Inc., 1981—; counsel Fin. Markets Internat., Inc., 1998—. Bd. dirs. Barker Found., 1981-86, Fed. City Nat. Bank, Washington, 1987. Lt. USCG, 1968-71. Recipient Superior Unit Citation AID, 1976, Disting. Honor award, 1977. Mem. ABA, FBA, D.C. Bar Assn., Mo. Bar Assn., Nat. Security Indsl. Assn. (bd. dirs. 1982-90), Capitol Hill Club, Columbia Country Club (Chevy Chase, Md.), Jefferson Islands Club. Democrat. Home: 5945 Searl Ter Bethesda MD 20816-2022 Office: Neill & Co 5945 Searl Ter Bethesda MD 20816-2022 E-mail: denisneill@aol.com.

NEILL, RICHARD ROBERT, retired publishing company executive; b. N.Y.C., June 20, 1925; s. Robert Irving and Mildred Mary (Hall) N.; m. Patricia Mae Robinson, Dec. 27, 1952; 1 son, Robert Kenneth. AB summa cum laude, Princeton U., 1948; MA, N.Y. U., 1953. With Prentice-Hall, Inc., N.Y.C. and Englewood Cliffs, N.J., 1948-85, advt. mgr., 1953-58, v.p. advt., 1958-62; pres. Executive Reports Corporation, 1962-85, ret., 1985. Regional chmn. Princeton Alumni Giving, Yonkers, N.Y., 1960-63, Tarrytown-Irvington, N.Y., 1977-80 Pres. Tarrytown (N.Y.) Jr. High Sch. PTA, 1971-72; bd. dirs. Martling Owners, Tarrytown, 1980-84, 89-93. Lt. (j.g.) USNR, 1943-46, PTO. Mem. USN Meml. Found., Princeton Terrace Club (bd. govs. 1986-92), Phi Beta Kappa. Republican. Mem. Reform Ch. Home: Apt 6E 222 Martling Ave Tarrytown NY 10591-4756 *A thought acquired from one of my first bosses: "Everything happens for the best - or can be made to do so." This has been a lifelong help.*

NEILL, VE, make-up artist; b. Riverside, Calif., May 13, 1951; d. Charles and Eileen Anne (Bernasco) Flores. Grad., Louisville H.S., Woodland Hills, Calif. Credits include (TV movies) Cry for Help, 1978, The London Affair, 1978, Sultan and the Rock Star, 1979, Muppets Go to the Movies, 1981, First Lady of the World, 1982, Money on the Side, 1982, Jane Doe, 1986; (TV Spls.) Sold Out-Lily Tomlin, 1981, Lily for President, 1982, Comedy Store 15th Yr. Reunion, 1988; (TV pilots) One Night Band, 1981, T.J. Hooker, 1981, Madeline (Madeline Kahn), 1982, Girls Life, 1982, A-Team, 1982, Rock & Roll Mom, 1987, Kowalski Loves, 1987, Stephen King's The Shining, 1996 (Emmy award Best Make Up), From the Earth to the Moon, 1997 (Emmy award nomination); (TV show) Pee Wee's Playhouse (Emmy award 1988, Emmy award nominee 1989); (feature films) Star Trek: The Motion Picture (Saturn award 1981), The Incredible Shrinking Woman, 9 to 5, Monty Python at the Hollywood Bowl, Sword and the Sorcerer, The Last Star Fighter, All of Me, The Lost Boys, 1986 (Saturn award 1987), Beetlejuice, 1987 (Acad. award 1987, Saturn award 1988, Brit. Acad. award nominee 1988), Cocoon II, 1988, Big Top Pee Wee, 1988, Dick Tracy, 1989, Flatliners, 1989, Edward Scissorhands, 1990 (Acad. award nominee 1989, Brit. Acad. award nominee 1990), Curly Sue, 1990, Hook, 1991, Batman Returns, 1991 (Saturn award 1992, Acad. award nominee 1992, Brit. Acad. award nominee 1992), Hoffa, 1992 (Acad. award nominee 1992), Rising Sun, 1992, Mrs. Doubtfire, 1993 (Acad. award 1993), Ed Wood, 1993 (Acad. award 1994), Cobb, 1994, Junior, 1994, Batman Forever, 1995, Matilda, 1995, Evening Star, 1996, Mars Attack, 1996, Gattaca, 1996, Batman and Robin, 1996, Amistad, 1997, Stigmata, 1998, Man on the Moon, 1998, Galaxy Quest, 1999, How the Grinch Stole Christmas, 1999, Blow, 2000, A.I., 2000, Death to Smochy, 2001, (commercial) Sony Mini Disc, 1997, (mag.) Vanity Fair Hollywood Issue, 1998. Mem.: Brit. Acad. Film and TV, Acad. Motion Picture Arts and Scis. Avocations: collecting antiques, beading with antique Am. trade beads, hiking, traveling the U.S. Office: IATSE Local 706 828 N Hollywood Way Burbank CA 91505

NEILL, WILLIAM HAROLD, JR. biological science educator and researcher; b. Wynne, Ark., Oct. 21, 1943; s. William H., Sr. and Shirley A. (Ellis) N.; m. Charlotte A. Jackson, Dec. 20, 1964; 1 child, Amanda K. BS in Zoology, U. Ark., 1965, MS in Zoology, 1967; PhD in Zoology/Statis., U. Wis., 1971. Rsch. fishery biologist Southwest Fisheries Ctr. Nat. Marine Fisheries Svc., Honolulu, 1971-74; assoc. prof. Tex. A&M U./Tex. Agrl. Expt. Sta., College Station, 1975-83; prof. Tex. A&M U./TAES, 1983—; interim head Dept. Wildlife and Fisheries Sci., 1992-93; faculty assoc. Bush Inst. Sci., Tech. and Pub. Policy, Tex. A&M U., 1999—. Mem. organizing com. Advanced Rsch. Inst. on Mechanisms Fish Migration, NATO, 1980-82; mem. tech. com. So. Regional Aquaculture Ctr., USDA, 1987-89; mem. sci.-tech. adv. com. Corpus Christi Bay Nat. Estuary Program, 1994-97. Editor Tex. Jour. Sci., 1983-85; mem. editl. adv. bd. Critical Revs. in Aquatic Sci., 1986-90; assoc. editor Transactions of the Am. Fisheries Soc., 1995-97; contbr. numerous articles to sci. jours. and books. Grantee numerous orgns., 1975—. Fellow Tex. Acad. Sci.; mem. AAAS, Am. Fisheries Soc. (life, Award of Excellence com. 1987, 89, chair Publ. Awards com. 1993, editl. bd. 1995), Am. Inst. Fishery Rsch. Biologists, Internat. Soc. Ecol. Modelling, Internat.

Soc. Ecosystem Health, Phi Beta Kappa, Sigma Xi, Phi Sigma. Office: Texas A&M U Dept Wildlife & Fisheries Scis 2258 TAMUS College Station TX 77843-0001 E-mail: w-neill@tamu.edu.

NEILSON, BENJAMIN REATH, lawyer; b. Phila., July 11, 1938; s. Harry Rosengarten and Alberta (Reath) N.; m. Judith Rawle, June 20, 1959 (div. May 1983); children: Benjamin R. Jr., Theodora C., Johanna K., Alberta R., Marshall R.; m. Meta B. Grace, Dec. 26, 1983. AB magna cum laude, Harvard U., 1960, LLB, 1963. Bar: Pa. 1964. Law clk. to chief justice Pa. Supreme Ct., Phila., 1963-64; assoc. Ballard, Spahr, Andrews & Ingersoll, 1964-71, ptnr., 1971—. Sec.-treas. The Chanticleer Found., Wayne, Pa.; pres. bd. trustees St. Paul's Sch., Concord, N.H. Mem. ABA, Pa. Bar Assn., Phila. Bar Assn., Am. Coll. Estate & Trust Counsel,Phi Beta Kappa. Episcopalian.

NEILSON, ELIZABETH ANASTASIA, deceased health sciences educator, association executive, author, editor; b. Medford, Mass., Oct. 13, 1913; d. William H. and Anastasia (Mahony) N. Diploma, Tufts U., 1933; BS in Edn, Boston U., 1934, MEd, 1945, EdD, 1957. Tchr. pub. schs., Medford, 1934-43; instr. health and phys. edn. Boston Coll., 1954-55; mem. faculty State Coll., Lowell, Mass., 1944-72, prof. edn., chmn. dept. health and phys. edn., 1966-72; dir. continuing edn. Am. Sch. Health Assn., Kent, Ohio, 1972—2001; adj. prof. Kent State U., 1971-77; adj. prof. health edn. Boston-Bouvé Coll. Human Devel. Professions, Northeastern U., 1974—2001; lectr. extension div. Harvard U., 1975—2001. Vis. prof. Boston U., 1960-62, Ind. U., summers 1966-72, Utah State U., summer 1968; del. Internat. Conf. Health and Edn., Madrid, 1965, Pa., 1962, Dusseldorf, Germany, 1959; health edn. cons. to govt. agys., industry, ednl. instns.; del. White House Conf. Children and Youth, 1970; mem. membership com. Am. Nat. Council for Health, 1967-73; chmn. resources council Mass. Sch. Health Council, 1964-69; mem. Nat. Adv. Council on Smoking and Health Edn., 1966-74, Gov.'s Council for Health and Fitness, 1964-69, Gov.'s Council for Nutrition Edn., 1971-74; mem. program evaluation team N.H. State Bd. Edn. Author: Health Living Program, 1977, also school health textbooks; contbg. author: coll. text Personal and Community Health; editor in chief coll. text Journal-Health Values: Achieving High Level Wellness, 1976—; contbr. articles to profl. jours. V.p. bd. dirs. March Against Dental Disease Found.; bd. dirs. Middlesex TB and Health Assn., Mass. Cancer Soc., Lowell MEntal Health Assn., Lowell Heart Assn., Lowell Diabetes Assn., New Hampshire Lung Assn.; mem. Jackson Sch. Bd.; trustee Jackson Libr.; pres., bd. dirs. Flintlock Village Assn.Inc., Wells, Maine, 1988—; founder Elizabeth A. Neilson-George H. Neilson Advanced Grad. Endowed Scholarship Fund for the Promotion of Health Edn., dept. physiology and health scis., Ball State U., 1992. Recipient William A. Howe award Am. Sch. Health Assn., 1969, Disting. Svc. award 1965, Disting. Svc. award ea. dist. AAHPER, 1967, Profl. Svc. award Mass. chpt. 1965, Svc. award Nat. ARC, 1960, Disting. Alumni award Northeastern U., Boston, 1983, Profl. Svc. award Am. Alliance for Health Edn., 1987; inducted into Mass. Hall of Fame, Medford High, 1990; hon. fellow Ball State U., Muncie, Ind., 1993, named to Fellows Soc. and Pres.'s Cir., 1996. Fellow Am. Sch. Health Assn. (life, pres. 1964-66, chmn. study coms. 1969-72, mem. governing assn. 1960-65, Howe award), Royal Soc. Health; mem. Am. Assn. Higher Edn., Am. Soc. Assn. Execs., Nat. Bus. and Profl. Women's Club, Assn. Supervision and Curriculum Devel., UN Assn. U.S.A., Internat. Union for Health, Smithsonian Assocs., Nat. Parks and Conservation Assn., New Eng. Health Assn., Am. Coll. Health Assn. (research council 1954-57), Am. (editorial bd. 1958-60, chmn. coll. health com. Eastern dist. 1948-51, chmn. resolutions com. sch. health div. 1951-53), Mass. assns. health, phys. edn. and recreation, Am. Pub. Health Assn., Soc. Pub. Health Educators, Fellows Soc. Ball State U., Pres. Cir. Ball State U., Phi Lambda Theta. *Since childhood my life has been guided by the concept that it is best to prevent illness by healthful living. On this premise I have devoted my life toward achieving a high level of wellness for myself and my family. As a professor of health education and an exemplar of the concepts associated with the daily application of scientific health information, I have worked toward helping others achieve the level of health their inherited potential would permit.* Died Oct. 4, 2001.

NEILSON, ERIC GRANT, physician, educator, health facility administrator; b. Bklyn., Sept. 14, 1949; s. Jack Drew and Lynette Elsie (Lundquist) N.; m. Linda Rae Apolzon, May 27, 1972; children: Tinsley, Sigrid. BS magna cum laude, Denison U., 1971; MD magna cum laude, U. Ala., 1975; MD (hon.), U. Pa., 1987. Asst. prof. U. Pa., Phila., 1980-87, assoc. prof., 1987-91, prof., 1991-98, C. Mahlon Kline prof., 1993-98, chief renal-electrolyte & hypertension divsn. dept. medicine, 1988-98; Hugh Jackson Morgan prof., chmn. dept. medicine Vanderbilt U. Med. Ctr., Nashville, 1998—. Attending physician Hosp. of U. Pa., 1980-98; physician-in-chief Vanderbilt U. Hosp., 1998—; cons. in field. Med. editorial bds. on sci. jours.; assoc. editor Kidney Internat., 1997—; contbr. numerous articles to profl. jours. Chmn. med. adv. bd. Lupus Found. of Phila., 1985-95; chmn. pathology A study sect. NIH, Bethesda, Md., 1990-92; chmn. grant rev. com. Nat. Kidney Found. of Delaware Valley; mem. adv. coun. NIDDK, NIH; mem. bd. sci. advisors Polycystic Kidney Found., 1997-2000; mem. postdoctoral fellowship com. Howard Hughes Med. Inst., 1997-2000. Recipient Clin. Scientist award Am. Heart Assn., 1980, Young Investigator award Am. Soc. Nephrology/Am. Heart Assn., 1985, Established Investigator award Am. Heart Assn., 1985-90, President's medal Am. Soc. Nephrology, 1994, AN Richard Disting. Achievement award, 1998. Fellow: ACP; mem.: Assn. Prof. Medicine (chmn. rsch. com. 2000—), Assn. Subsplty. Profs. (pres. 1994—96), Am. Fedn. Clin. Rsch., Am. Assn. Immunologists, Am. Clin. Climatol. Assn., Am. Soc. Nephrology, Assn. Am. Physicians, Am. Soc. Clin. investigation. Mem. Soc. Of Friends. Office: Vanderbilt U Med Ctr Dept Medicine D3100 Med Ctr N Nashville TN 37232-0001

NEILSON, WINTHROP CUNNINGHAM, III, communications executive, financial communications consultant; b. N.Y.C., Jan. 7, 1934; s. Winthrop Cunningham, Jr. and Frances Fullerton (Jones) N.; m. Ilse Rossenbeck, Jan. 4, 1957; children: Luise R., Victoria F.; m. Demaris King Hetrick, July 5, 1985; 1 child, Whitney C. C.; stepchildren: Norman P. Hetrick Jr., D. Page Hetrick BA, Harvard U., 1956; grad. in security analysis, N.Y. Inst. Finance, 1963. Asst. producer, asst. dir. Rangley Lakes Theater, 1955; gen. assignment reporter Albany (N.Y.) Times-Union, 1959-60; pub. info. writer, speaker Consol. Edison, 1960-61; asst. dir. pub. relations Union Service Corp., 1962; with Georgeson & Co., N.Y.C., 1962-81, prin., 1969-81; sr. v.p. D.F. King & Co. Inc., 1982-86; founder, mng. dir. Krone Communications, Harrisburg, Pa., 1986-89; pres. Krone Group Inc., 1987-89; mng. dir. Neilson/Hetrick Group, Montclair, N.J., 1990—, Harrisburg, Pa., 1993—, chmn. Chambersburg, 1997—; mng. dir. Corp. Investor Communications, Carlstadt, N.J., 1991-93; guest lectr. NYU, 1991. Author: series Aunt Jane, 1971, 73, The Reluctant Marriage, 1978, Investorism, 1981, Annual Reports, The Agony and the Ecstasy, 1985, Individual Investors, a Counterbalance to Institutional Investors, 1986; writer, assoc. editor: Trends, 1965-81; contbr. articles to profl. jours. Mem. Mountain Lakes (N.J.) Econ. Devel. Council, 1974-79, chmn., 1977-79; pres. Robert A. Taft Republican Club, Queens, N.Y., 1964-65, chmn., 1966-67; treas. 23d Assembly Dist. Rep. Party, 1966-67; county committeeman, 1964-67; del. N.Y. State Nominating Conv., 1966; campaign mgr. for 2 assemblymen and state senator. Served with AUS, 1956-59. Recipient Investor Edn. Disting. Service award Nat. Assn. Investors Clubs, 1986. Mem. Nat. Investor Rels. Inst. (charter dir. 1980-84, v.p. manpower 1980-81, v.p. long-range planning 1981-84), Pub. Rels. Soc. Am. (charter, exec. com. investor rels. 1982-90, chmn. 1987, Pres. award 1987, charter inductee into Hall of Fame for Investor Rels.), Corp. Rels. Soc. Ctrl. Pa. (v.p. 1986-89, pres. 1994-95), Ctrl. Pa. Entrepreneurial Assn. (bd. dirs. 1988-89, adv. bd. tech. coun. Ctrl. Pa. 1994-96), Chambersburg Country Club, DU Club, Hasty Pudding Club, Ausable Club. Lutheran. Home and Office: 3333 Carnoustie Dr Chambersburg PA 17201-8116 Home (Summer): Ausable Club Saint Huberts NY 12943 E-mail: neil@supernet.com.

NEIMAN, GARY S. university administrator; b. Chgo., Oct. 2, 1947; s. David J. and Miriam (Factor) N.; m. Margalit C. Buchsbaum, June 11, 1972; children: Emily R., Lisa R. BS, U. Ill., MA, 1971, PhD, 1973. Cert. of clin. competence Am. Speech-Lang.-Hearing Assn. Rsch. and clin. assoc. Ctr. for Craniofacial Anomalies U. Ill./Abraham Lincoln Sch. of Medicine, Chgo., 1972; speech, pathologist, facial deformity team Carle Found. Hosp., Urbana, 1972-73; asst. prof. speech Kans. State U., Manhattan, 1973-77, dir. Speech and Hearing Clinic, 1974-77; assoc. prof. Sch. of Speech Pathology and Audiology Kent (Ohio) State U., 1977-92, dir. Sch. of Speech Pathology and Audiology, 1979-90; assoc. dean for grad. affairs and health-related programs Kent State U., 1990-99, prof., speech pathology and audiology, 1992-99. Co-dir. and speech pathologist Akron Craniofacial Ctr., Children's Hosp. Med. Ctr. of Akron, 1977-99; mem. med. adv. bd. Kent Vis. Nurse Assn., 1979-85; dean Coll. Health and Human Svcs. Ohio U., 1999—, prof. Sch. Hearing and Speech Scis., 1999—. Author: (book) A Parent's Guide: Cleft Lip and Palate and Other Craniofacial Problems, 1985; contbr. articles to profl. jours.; presenter in field. Vice-pres. bd. dirs. Portage County Unit, Am. Cancer Soc., Kent, 1980-85; pres. Temple Beth Shalom, Hudson, Ohio, 1992-94. Mem. Am. Cleft Palate-Craniofacial Assn., Am. Speech Lang. Hearing Assn., Internat. Assn. of Logopedics and Phoniatrics, Internat. Soc. for the Study of Behaviour Devel., Phi Beta Delta. Office: Coll Health and Human Svcs Ohio U W 381 Grover Ctr Athens OH 45701-1711 E-mail: neiman@ohio.edu.

NEIMAN, JOHN HAMMOND, lawyer; b. Des Moines, Jan. 8, 1917; s. Donald Edwin and Bessie A. (White) N.; m. Madeline Clare Flint, July 2, 1941; children— Richard F., Donald F., Nancy J. BA, Drake U., 1939, JD, 1941. Bar: Iowa 1941. Ptnr. Neiman, Neiman, Stone & Spellman, Des Moines, 1946-92, Neiman, Stone, McCormick, Attys., Des Moines, 1992—; exec. v.p., sec. Nat. Assn. Credit Mgmt., 1956-83. Mem. ethics com. Iowa Senate, 1969-73, probate rules com. Iowa Supreme Ct., 1977-81; mem., chmn. Client Security and Atty. Disciplinary Commn., Iowa, 1974-85. Pres. bd. councilors Drake U. Law Sch., 1968; pres. Northwest Community Hosp., Des Moines, 1974-77 Recipient Centennial award Drake U., 1981 Fellow Am. Bar Found., Comml. Law Found., Iowa State Bar Found. (50 Yr. award 1995); mem. ABA (bd. govs. 1984-85, ho. of dels. 1978-87, profl. discipline com. 1979-84, forum com. 1985-89, responsibility for clients protection 1989-90), Iowa Bar Assn. (bd. govs. 1963-67, pres. 1967-68, award of merit 1975), Polk County Bar Assn. (pres. 1960-61), Comml. Law League Am., Iowa State Bar Found. (sec. 1975-78, pres. 1988-92, 50 Yr. Svc. award 1995), Wakonda Club (pres. 1973), Met. Club (pres. 1981-82, 84-86). Republican. Methodist. Home: 3514 Wakonda Ct Des Moines IA 50321-2648 Office: Neiman Stone & McCormick 7405 University Ave Ste 10 Des Moines IA 50325-1343 *There are talkers and doers, it's more important to be a doer. Their accomplishments live long after they are gone.*

NEIMAN, KENNETH PAUL, judge; b. N.Y.C., July 4, 1945; s. Julius and Gertrude (Fox) N.; m. Jan Dumond, May 24, 1987; children: Jennifer Gottlieb, Anna L. Neiman, J. Matthew Gowdy, Kerri Escudero. BA, Tufts U., 1967; JD, Harvard Law Sch., 1971. Bar: N.Y. 1972, Mass. 1974, U.S. Dist. Ct. Mass. 1974, U.S. Ct. Appeals (1st cir.) 1981, U.S. Supreme Ct. 1978. Staff atty. Mental Health Info. Svcs., N.Y.C., 1971, Ctr. Social Welfare, Policy & Law, N.Y.C., 1971-73; rsch. fellow Legal Svcs. Corp. Rsch. Inst., Washington, 1978; mng. atty. Western Mass. Legal Svcs., Holyoke, 1973-81; ptnr. Fierst & Neiman, Northampton, Mass., 1981-94; U.S. magistrate judge Dist. Mass., Springfield, 1995—. Mem. ABA, Mass. Bar Assn., Mass. Bar Found., Hampshire County Bar Assn. Office: US Dist Ct 1550 Main St Springfield MA 01103-1422

NEIMAN, LEROY, artist; b. St. Paul, June 8, 1927; s. Charles and Lydia (Serline) Runquist; m. Janet Byrne, June 22, 1957. Student, Sch. Art Inst., Chgo., 1946-50, U. Ill., 1951, DePaul U., 1951; LittD (hon.), Franklin Pierce Coll., 1976; D (hon.), St. John's U., 1980, Iona Coll., 1985, Hofstra U., 1997, St. Francis Coll., 1998, St. Bonaventure U., 1999. Instr. Sch. Art Inst. Chgo., 1950-60, Saugatuck (Mich.) Summer Sch. Painting, 1957-58, 63, Sch. Arts and Crafts, Winston-Salem, N.C., 1963; instr. painting Atlanta Youth Council, 1968-69; printmaker-graphics, 1971—; artist Olympics, ABC-TV, Munich, 1972, ofcl. artist Montreal, 1976, U.S. Olympics, 1980, 84; computer artist CBS-TV (Superbowl), New Orleans, 1978; ofcl. artist Goodwill Games CNN-TV, Moscow, 1986; 1st ofcl. artist Ky. Derby, Louisville, 1997; ofcl. artist Mardi Gras, New Orleans, 2002. Mem. adv. com. LeRoy Neiman Ctr. for Print Studies Sch. of the Arts Columbia U., 1995; mem. adv. com. for N.Y.C. Commn. for Cultural Affairs, 1995, UCLA LeRoy Neiman Ctr. for Study of Am. Soc. and Culture, 1998; established LeRoy Neiman Art Ctr. for Youth, San Francisco, 2000, Watsonville, Calif., 2002. Exhibited one-man shows: Oehlschlaeger Gallery, Chgo., 1959, 61, O'Hana Gallery, London, Gallerie O. Bosc, Paris, 1962, Hammer Gallery, N.Y.C., 1963, 65, 67, 70, 72, 76, 78, 79, 81-83, 85-87, 89, 92, 94, 97, 2000, Huntington-Hartford Gallery Modern Art, N.Y.C., 1967, Heath Gallery, Atlanta, 1969, Abbey Theatre, Dublin, Ireland, 1970, Museo de Bellas Artes, Caracas, Indpls. Inst. Arts, 1972, Hermitage Mus., Leningrad, Tobu Gallery, Tokyo, 1974, Springfield (Mass.) Mus. Fine Arts, 1974, 84, Knoedler Gallery, London, 1976, Casa gratica, Helsinki, 1977, Renée Victor, Stockholm, 1977, Okla. Art Ctr., Oklahoma City, 1981, Harrod's, London, 1982; retrospective show, Minn. Mus. Art, St. Paul, 1975, Meredith Long Galleries, Houston, 1978, Hanae Mori Gallery, Tokyo, 1988, New State Tretyakov Mus., 1988, Butler Inst., Youngstown, Ohio, 1990, Galerie Marcel Bernheim, Paris, 1993, Ky. Derby Mus., Louisville, 1995, 1997, Marlborough Gallery, N.Y.C., 2000, The Fairfield, Sturgeon Bay, Wis., 2001, Nat. Art Mus. of Sport, Ind. U.-Purdue U., 2001; two-man show, Neiman-Warhol, Los Angeles Inst. Contemporary Art, 1981; exhibited in group shows, Art Inst. Chgo., 1954-60, Carnegie Internat., 1956, Corcoran Gallery Am., Washington, Walker Art Center, Mpls., 1957, Ringling Mus., Sarasota, Fla., 1959, Salon d'Art Mus., Paris, 1961, Nat. Gallery Portraiture, Smithsonian Instn., Washington, Minn. Mus. Art, 1969, Rotunda Della Basana, Milan, Italy, 1971, Royal Coll. Art, London, 1971, Minn. Mus. Art Nat. Tour, 1976-77, Whitney Mus., 1985 ; Master Prints of 19th and 20th Centuries, Hammer Galls., N.Y., 1987, Salon d'Automne, Paris, 1992, 93; represented in permanent collections, Mpls. Inst. Arts, Ill. State Mus., Springfield, Joslyn Mus., Omaha, Wodham Coll., Oxford, Eng., Nat. Art Mus. Sport, N.Y.C., Museo De Ballas Artes Caracas, Hermitage Mus., Indpls. Inst. Arts, U. Ill., Balt. Mus. Fine Art, The Armand Hammer Collection, Los Angeles, Edwin & Ruth Kennedy Mus. of Am. Art at Ohio U., Midwest Mus. Am. Art, Elkhart, Ind., Nat. Art Mus. of Sport, Indpls.; executed murals at, Merc. Nat. Bank, Hammond, Ind., Continental Hotel, Chgo., Swedish Lloyd Ship S.S. Patricia, Stockholm, ceramic tile mural, Sportsmans Park, Chgo.; author: LeRoy Neiman—Art and Life Style, 1974, Horses, 1979, LeRoy Neiman. Posters, 1980, LeRoy Neiman. Catalogue Raisonné, 1980, Carnaval, 1981, LeRoy Neiman: Winners, 1983, Japanese translation, 1985, LeRoy Neiman, Monte Carlo Chase, 1988, The Prints of LeRoy Neiman, 1980-90, Big Time Golf, 1992, LeRoy Neiman, An American in Paris, 1994, LeRoy Neiman on Safari, 1997, The Prints of LeRoy Neiman 1991-2000; illustrator: 12 paintings deluxe edit. Moby Dick, 1975, 35 charcoal drawings deluxe edit. Casey at the Bat, 2000, trade edit., 2002. Served with AUS, 1942-46. Recipient 1st prize Twin City Show, 1953, 2d prize Minn. State Show, 1954, Clark Meml. prize Chgo. Show, 1957, Hamilton-Graham prize Ball State Coll., 1958, Municipal prize Chgo. Show, 1958, Purchase prize Miss. Valley Show, 1959, Gold medal Salon d'Art Modern Paris, 1961; award of merit as nation's outstanding sports artist AAU, 1976; Olympic Artist of Century award, 1979, Gold Medal award St. John's U., 1985. Address: 1 W 67th St New York NY 10023-6200

NEIMAN, NORMAN, aerospace business and marketing executive; b. Phila., May 23, 1935; s. Harry and Clara (Schuller) N.; m. Sandra Elaine Berk (dec. 1989); children: Nadene Lori Eisaman, Andrea Neiman-Pearce, David Michael; m. Bonnie Gail McCoy, Sept. 5, 1990. BSME, U. Miami, 1957; postgrad., Alexander Hamilton Inst., N.Y.C., 1959; postgrad. real estate law, Brevard C.C., Cocoa, Fla., 1973. Lic. real estate broker, Fla.; lic. fed. firearms dealer. Engr. Sperry Gyroscope Corp., Gt. Neck, N.Y., 1957-59; lead mech. engr. Convair Aerospace Co., Cape Canaveral, Fla., 1959-62; engring. scientist Douglas Aircraft Corp., 1962-65; chief support engr. Grumman Aerospace Corp., Kennedy Space Center, Fla., 1965-73, mgr. Cocoa Beach (Fla.) ops., 1973-74, mgr. Orlando (Fla.) ops., 1974-79; pres. Neiman and Co., Inc., Orlando, 1980—90. Pres. Sunshine State Realty, Inc., Cocoa Beach, 1972—76; v.p. Vitality Workshop, Inc., Orlando, 1978—80, Reconnaissance Techs., Arlington, Va., 1985—89; U.S. Govt. sales agt. Calico Light Weapon Systems, 1989—91; dir. program devel. NYMA Inc., Cocoa Beach, 1990—97, Fed. Data Corp., Orlando, 1998—2000; COO Neiman & Assocs., Inc., 2000—. Patentee waveguide disconnect. Mem. NRA, AIAA, Tech. Mktg. Soc., Range, Missile and Space Pioneers (life), Am. Meteorol. Soc., Am. Numismatic Assn., Air Force Assn., Mensa, Intertel. Republican. Jewish. Avocations: shooting, model railroading, coin collecting, foreign travel. Office: Neiman and Assocs PO Box 140094 Orlando FL 32814-0094 E-mail: nsquareinwp@att.net.

NEIMARK, SHERIDAN, lawyer; b. Youngstown, Ohio, Apr. 7, 1935; s. David and Anne (Kamisar) N.; m. Dana Ellen Perlzweig, Jan. 5, 1963; children: David, Rebecca, Matthew. BS in Chem. Engring, Carnegie-Mellon U., 1957; JD, George Washington U., 1961. Bar: Va. 1962, D.C. 1962, U.S. Ct. of Customs and Patent Appeals 1963, U.S. Ct. Appeals (Fed. cir.) 1982, U.S. Supreme Ct. 1973. Patent examiner U.S. Patent Office, Washington, 1957-62; practiced in, 1962—; patent atty. firms K. Flocks and A. Browdy, 1962-68; mem. firm Browdy and Neimark, 1969—, sr. ptnr., 1989—. Contbr. articles, papers to profl. jours. Charter mem. Gov.'s Planning and Adv. Coun. on Devel. Disabilities, State of Md., 1971-86, vice chmn., 1975-77; mem. Legal and Human Rights Task Force, Montgomery County (Md.) Com. for Employment of Handicapped, 1972-73; bd. dirs., co-founder Cmty. Svcs. for Autistic Adults and Children; past bd. dirs. Tifereth Israel Congregation. Recipient Gov.'s citation State of Md., 1986. Mem. Am. Bar Assn. (mem. adv. bd. developmental disabilities model legis. project 1977-81, mem. adv. bd. mental and phys. disabilities law reporter 1979—), D.C. Bar, Va. State Bar, Am. Intellectual Property Law Assn. (mem. com. patent law 1965-69, chem. practice 1970—), Md. Patent Law Assn., Internat. Assn. Jewish Lawyers and Jurists, Patent Office Soc., Autism Soc. Am. (nat. dir. 1973-77, dir. Montgomery County chpt. 1970-72, nat. Plaque awards 1972, 77), Md. State Soc. for Autistic Children (founder, dir. 1971-73), Am. Jewish Com., Am. Jewish Congress, B'nai Brith. Home: 12908 Ruxton Rd Silver Spring MD 20904-5278 Office: 624 9th St NW Washington DC 20001-5303

NEIMS, ALLEN HOWARD, university dean, medical scientist; b. Chgo., Oct. 24, 1938; s. Irving Morris and Ruth (Geller) N.; m. Myrna Gay Robins, June 18, 1961; children: Daniel Mark, Susan Roberta, Nancy Elizabeth. BA, BS, U. Chgo., 1957; MD, Johns Hopkins U., 1961, PhD, 1966. Intern, resident in pediatrics Johns Hopkins Hosp., 1961-62, 66-68; research asso. Lab. Neurochemistry, NIH, 1968-70; asst. prof. physiol. chemistry and pediatrics Johns Hopkins Med. Sch., 70-72; assoc. prof. McGill U., 1972-77, prof. pharmacology and pediatrics, 1977-78; dir. Roche developmental pharmacology unit, 1972-78; prof., chmn. dept. pharmacology and therapeutics, prof. pediatrics U. Fla., Gainesville, 1978-89, dean Coll. Medicine, 1989-96, prof. pharmcology, pediat., 1996—. Fulton Bequest prof. U. Melbourne, Australia, 1974; mem. human embryology and devel. study sect. NIH, 1979-83; sci. cons. Can. Found. for Study of Sudden Infant Death, 1974-77, Nat. Soft Drink Assn., 1976-78, Internat. Life Scis. Inst., 1978-89; bd. sci. counsellors Nat. Inst. Child Health and Human Devel., 1984-89. Contbr. chpts. to books, articles to med. jours. Served to comdr. USPHS, 1968-70. NIH, Can. Med. Research Council grantee. Mem. Can. Assn. Research in Toxicology (pres. 1976-78), Am. Soc. Pharmacology and Exptl. Therapeutics (past mem. exec. coms. clin. pharmacology and drug metabolism), Am. Pediatric Soc., Am. Acad. Pediatrs. Office: U Fla Coll Medicine PO Box 100267 Gainesville FL 32610-0267 E-mail: ahneims@ufl.edu.

NEIS, ARNOLD HAYWARD, pharmaceutical company executive; b. N.Y.C., Feb. 13, 1938; s. Harry H. and Mary Ruth (Bishop) N.; m. Lucy de Puig, Dec. 8, 1989; children by previous marriage: Nancy R., Robert C. BS cum laude, Columbia U., 1959; MBA, NYU, 1967. With Scott Chem. Co., 1959-64; v.p. mktg., then v.p. Odell, Inc., N.Y.C., 1964-71, pres. Thayer Knomark div., 1969-71; pres., chief exec. officer E.T. Browne Drug Co., Inc., Englewood Cliffs, N.J., 1971—, chmn., 2000—. Dir. Esquire A.B. Stockholm, Knomark Can. Ltd., E.T. Browne Internat. Fellow Royal Soc. Chemists, Royal Geog. Soc., Am. Inst. Chemists, N.Y. Acad. Scis.; mem. AAAS, Am. Chem. Soc., Am. Pharm. Assn., New Eng. Soc. (v.p., bd. dirs.), Explorers Club (v.p., bd. dirs., Sweeney medal 1997), Chemists Club, Lotos Club, Soldiers, Sailors and Airmans Club (bd. dirs.), St. Georges Soc., Ch. Club, Pilgrims of the U.S. Episcopalian. Home: 898 Park Ave New York NY 10021-0234 Office: PO Box 1613 440 Sylvan Ave Englewood NJ 07632-2700

NEIS, ARTHUR VERAL, healthcare and development company executive; b. Lawrence, Kans., May 30, 1940; s. Veral Herbert and Louise (Schlegel) N.; m. Fleeta Weigel, Apr. 12, 1969 (dec. 1999); children: Frederich Arthur, Benjamin Jason, Sarah Louise. BS in Bus., U. Kans., 1962, MS in Acctg., 1963. CPA, Kans., Iowa. Mgmt. cons. Arthur Andersen & Co., Kansas City, Mo. and Mpls., 1963-74; chief corp. acctg. Carlson Co., Mpls., 1974-76; contr. The Fullerton Cos., 1976-78; asst. treas. Fru-Con Corp., St. Louis, 1978-80, asst. contr., 1981, contr., 1982-86; corp. contr. LCS Holdings, Inc. (Weitz Corp. and Subsidaries), Des Moines, 1986-87, v.p., treas., CFO, 1987—; treas., CFO Weitz Co., 1987-93, Life Care Services LLC, Des Moines, 1987—; v.p., treas., CFO, mem. exec. com. LCS Holdings and Subs., Inc., 1995—, also trustee retirement plan, bd. dirs. Mem. adv. group Nat. Assn. Ins. Com., 1990-93. Treas. Villa de Maria Montessori Sch., St. Louis, 1984—86, exec. com. bd., 1984—86; trustee Fin. Execs. Rsch. Found., 1994—2000, chair audit com., 1997—98, vice chair rsch., 1998—2000, chmn., 2000—01; bd. dirs. Inst. Humane Studies, George MAson U., Fairfax, Va., exec. com., 1975—83, chmn., 1978—83; bd. dirs. Lake Country Sch., Mpls., 1973—78, Alliance for Arts and Understanding, co-chair, 1993—96, chair, 1996—. Note, corporate directorships are not dated and only current ones are listed, per style. Mem. AICPA, Kans. Soc. CPAs, Iowa Soc. CPAs, Fin. Execs. Inst. (bd. dirs. Iowa chpt. 1986, 88-94, sec. 1988-90, v.p. 1990-91, pres. 1991-92). Avocations: bibliophile, Kans. history, orientalia. Home: 1575 NW 106th St Clive IA 50325-6604 Office: Life Care Svcs LLC Capital Sq 400 Locust St Des Moines IA 50309-2334

NEISER, BRENT ALLEN, public affairs and personal finance consultant, speaker, foundation executive; b. Cin., Sept. 16, 1954; s. Rodger and Hazel Neiser; m. Marion, Apr. 1, 1978; children: Christy Jean, Steven José, April Reneé. BA in Pub. Affairs, George Washington U., 1976; MA in Urban Studies, Occidental Coll., 1978; MBA, U. Louisville, 1979; postgrad. in internat. affairs, U. Denver, 1987-90. Cert. fin. planner, 1985; cert. assn. exec., 1994; chartered mut. fund counselor, 1996; accredited asset mgmt. specialist, 1998. Project mgr., analyst Legis. Research Com., Frankfort, Ky., 1978-84; pres. Moneyminder, Denver and Frankfort, 1983-91; dir. edn., govt. affairs Inst. Cert. Fin. Planners, Denver, 1985-91, exec. dir., 1991-94; pub. affairs, govt. rels. bus. strategies cons. The Brent Neiser Co., Englewood, 1994—; dir. collaborative programs Nat. Endowment for Fin. Edn., 1995—. Mng. dir. Fin. Products Stds. Bd., Denver, 1985-91; co-creator Personal Econ. Summit '93, Washington. Author: EPCOT/World Showcase External Directions, Walt Disney Imagineering, 1977, Personal Management, 1996, 2000; co-inventor: Trivia Express (game) Denver, 1986; developer over 100 publs. for disaster victims, low income families and children. Vol., v.p. Big Bros./Big Sisters, Frankfort, 1982; del. Colo. Model Constn. Conv., 1987; mem. citizens budget rev. com. Greenwood Village; mem. long range planning com. Adoption Exch., Denver, 1992-93, bd. dirs., 1993-99; polit. action dir. Frankfort NAACP, 1983, legis. chmn. state conf., 1984; troop com. mem., asst. scoutmaster Boy Scouts Am., Englewood, 1993-99; bd. dirs. Young Ams. Bank Edn. Found., 1993-99, chair edn. coun.; vol. host com. Denver Summit of the Eight, 1997; nat. spokesperson Protect our Children Campaign, 1996; active Annie E. Casey Found.: Nat. Foster Care Awareness Project, 1999-2002; citizen's panelist News Hour with Jim Lehrer (PBS), 1998—; founding ptnr. Social Venture Ptnrs., Denver, 2000-02, Colo. Coun. of Advisors on Consumer Credit, 2000—; mem. CFP bd. Consumer Adv. Coun. on Fin. Planning, 2001— ; bd. advisors Coll. Visual and Performing Arts, Winthrop U., 2002-; scholarship com. Invesco Funds Group, 2002-. Lt. (j.g.) USNR, 1985-92. Recipient Leadership Denver award, 1993, Assn. Advance Am. award Excellence, 1996, 1998,; Pub. Affairs fellow Coro Found., 1976-77; named Eagle Scout. Mem. Investors Edn. Assn. Colo. (bd. dirs. 1995-2001), Nat. Assns. in Colo., Denver C. of C. (pub. affairs coun.), Adoptive Families of Am., Assn. for Fin. Counseling and Planning Edn., Am. Soc. Assn. Execs., Inst. Mgmt. Cons., N.Am. Securities Adminstrs. Assn. (investment adviser and fin. planner adv. com.), Nat. Soc. Compliance Profls. (bd. dirs. 1987-89), Am. Film Inst. (writers workshop), Am. Polit. Items Collectors, Fin. Planning Assn., Snowboard Outreach Soc. Avocations: snowboarding, drums (jazz) and latin percussion music, golf, swimming, modern design. Office: 5860 Big Canyon Dr Englewood CO 80111-3516 E-mail: ban@nefe.org.

NEISLER, OTHERINE JOHNSON, education educator, consultant; b. St. Louis, Apr. 27, 1954; d. Robert Louis and Ruth (Wilson) Johnson; m. Anton Ross Neisler, Sr. (div. 1988); children: Maiya Rose Neisler Benda, Anton Ross Jr. BA, Brandeis U., 1972; MA, Fairfield U., 1991; PhD, Syracuse U., 1994. Tchr. social studies Warren H.S., Newton, Mass., 1974-76; mktg. mgr./analyst IBM, White Plains, N.Y., 1976-88; asst. prof. instrnl. tech. Boston Coll.,

Chestnut Hill, Mass., 1994-2000; assoc. dir. tchr. preparation program Yale U., New Haven, 2000—. Curriculum cons. numerous schs., 1994—. Contbr. articles to profl. jours. Pres. bd. dirs. Erie County (Pa.) Domestic Abuse Agy., 1978-80; bd. dirs. The Multicultural Resource Ctr., Phila., 1996—, Primary Source, Inc., Boston, 1996-98. Mem. ASCD, Am. Edn. Rsch. Assn. (equity com. 1992—), Nat. Coun. Social Studies (citizenship com. 1992—), Links, Inc. Avocations: hiking, tennis. Office: Yale Univ PO Box 208362 New Haven CT 06520-8362 E-mail: otherine.neisler@yale.edu.

NEISSER, HORST, library director; b. Nuernberg, Germany, July 30, 1943; s. Heinrich and Eleonore (Mergner) Neisser; m. Barbara Friedrich. Student, U. Frankfurt, Germany, 1965-68; DPhil, U. Tuebingen, Germany, 1973. Subject specialist EKZ, Reutlingen, Germany, 1973-76; dir. City Libr. Saarbrücken, Germany, 1976-86, City Libr. Cologne, Germany, 1986—. Lectr Fochhochschule für Sozialwesen, Esslingen, Germany, 1973—76, Fachhochschule für Bibliotheken, Cologne, Germany, 1987—; mem various library communications, Berlin, 1982—; mem various adv comts, 1974—. Author: (book) Die Jugendzeitschrift, 1975, Diskotheken in Deutschland, 1979, Traumzeiten, 1984, Der Gott der Ameise, 1993, Centratur, 1996, Centratur II, 1997. Mem.: Deutschen Gesellschaft fuer Informations wissenschaft und Informationspraxis (pres 1999), Verband Deutscher Schriftsteller. Avocations: painting, music. Home: Luebecker Str 17 50858 Cologne Germany Office: City Libr Cologne Josef-Haubrich-Hof 1 50676 Cologne Germany E-mail: horst@neisser-online.de.

NEITER, GERALD IRVING, lawyer; b. L.A., Nov. 11, 1933; s. Harry and Ida Florence (Alperin) N.; m. Margaret P. Rowe, Mar. 5, 1961; children: David, Karen, Michael. BSL, JD, U. So. Calif., 1957. Bar: Calif. 1958. Judge pro tem Mcpl. Cts., L.A. and Beverly Hills, 1970-94; judge pro tem and mediator Calif. Superior Ct., L.A. County, 1974-94, family law mediator, 1976—; prin. Gerald I. Neiter, P.C., L.A., 1981—. Lectr. State Bar of Calif., 1968, 76, 79, 81; former referee State Bar Ct.; arbitrator Am. Arbitration Assn. Mem. Am., Los Angeles County (arbitrator), Beverly Hills, Century City bar assns., State Bar Calif. Office: 1925 Century Park E Ste 200 Los Angeles CA 90067-2701 E-mail: Neitlaw@aol.com.

NEITHERCUT, MARK EDWARD, foundation executive; b. Flint, Mich., June 26, 1951; s. Edward John and Elizabeth Koegel Neithercut; m. Helen Patrick Lownie, Oct. 6, 1990. BA with high honors in history, U. Mich., 1974; MA, Mich. State U., 1977; PhD, U. B.C., Vancouver, Can., 1984. From instr. to asst. prof. U. Ala., Tuscaloosa, 1982-85; dir. Mich. Met. Info. Ctr. Wayne State U., Detroit, 1985-93, assoc. prof. rsch., 1993; program officer Kresge Found., Troy, Mich., 1993-95; v.p. program Cmty. Found. for Southeastern Mich., Detroit, 1995—. Adj. prof. urban planning Wayne State U., Detroit, 1990-95; mem. adv. bd. Mich. Nonprofit Rsch. Program, Aspen Inst., Washington, 1999—; membership com. Coun. on Founds., Washington, 1999—; bd. dirs. Cmty. Devel. Funders Collaborative, Detroit; mem. exec. com., fund raising chmn. Arts Centered Edn. Program, Detroit, 1996-99. Author: (monographs) Status of Detroit Youth, 1993, Patterns of Mortgage Lending in the City of Detroit, 1990. Bd. dirs. Mich. Housing Trust Fund, Lansing, 1994-98, Detroit Inst. Arts, 1993-94, Detroit Artists Market, 1993-95; membership com. Detroit Inst. Arts, 1995--; pres. Founders Jr. Coun., Detroit Inst. Arts, 1993-94; chmn. Detroit Area Grantmakers, 2001--; mem. cmty. found. leadership team Coun. of Found., 2001--. Named NSFRE Vol. of Yr., Detroit Inst. Arts, 1994; recipient Cmty. Spirit award Mich. Gay and Lesbian Ann. Pride Banquet, 1999; James B. Angell scholar U. Mich., 1974; Internat. Schoolboy fellow English Spkg. Union, 1969-70, doctoral fellow U. B.C., 1978-80; grantee Kresge Found., 1998-2004. Mem. Phi Beta Kappa. Avocations: steelhead fly fishing, tennis. Office: Cmty Found for Southeastern Mich Ste 2010 333 W Fort St Detroit MI 48226

NEITZEL, GEORGE PAUL, engineer, educator; b. Atlanta, Nov. 28, 1947; s. George Paul Sr. and Bettymae Irene (Chapman) N.; m. Evelyn Kathleen Heaps; children: Erik Paul, Jason Ward, Michael Brent, Timothy Jacob. BS, Rollins Coll., 1969; MS, Johns Hopkins U., 1974, PhD, 1979. Mathematician, engr. U.S. Army Ballistic Research Lab., Aberdeen Proving Ground, Md., 1969-79; asst. to full prof. engring. Ariz. State U., Tempe, 1979-90; prof. mech. engring. Ga. Inst. Tech., Atlanta, 1990—. Cons. Monsanto Corp., St. Peters, Mo., 1984-86, Rockwell Internat., Thousand Oaks, Calif., 1987; vis. prof. U. Karlsruhe, Fed. Republic Germany, 1985-86, Imperial Coll., London, 1986, U. d'Aix-Marseille II, 1995. Contbr. articles to sci. jours. Recpipient Presdl. Young Investigator award NSF, 1984; Alexander Von Humboldt fellow, 1985. Fellow Am. Phys. Soc.; assoc. fellow AIAA; mem. ASME, Sigma Xi. Democrat. Unitarian Universalist. Avocations: phys. fitness, backpacking, music. Home: 8165 Grogans Ferry Rd Atlanta GA 30350-3107 Office: Ga Inst Tech George Woodruff Sch Mech Eng Atlanta GA 30332-0001

NEITZEL, LISA ANN, newscaster, reporter; b. Watertown, Wis., Jan. 5, 1970; d. Deane Allen and Ruth Emma (Johnson) N. BA in Broadcast Journalism, BA in Polit. Sci., U. Wis., 1993. News reporter, anchor WBKB-TV (CBS), Alpena, Mich., 1994-95; reporter, weathercaster WDIO-TV (ABC), Duluth, Minn., 1995—. Mem. Soc. Profl. Journalists, Women in Comms, Inc. Avocations: skiing, mountain biking, reading, swimming.

NEITZKE, ERIC KARL, lawyer; b. Mobile, Ala., Dec. 10, 1955; s. Howard and Otti S. Neitzke; m. Kathryn Sloan; children: Kyle, Blake, Blaire. BA, U. Fla., 1979, JD, 1982. Bar: Fla. 1982, U.S. Dist. Ct. (mid. dist.) Fla. 1987. Asst. state atty. 7th Jud. Cir., State Atty., Daytona Beach, Fla., 1982; atty. Dunn, Smith & Withers, 1982-88, Monaco, Smith, Hood and Perkins, Daytona Beach, 1988—. Adj. faculty family law and criminal law Daytona C.C.; chmn. adv. com. Juvenile Detention Ctr. Contbr. articles to profl. jours. Mem. Fla. Acad. Trial Lawyers, Assn. Trial Lawyers Am., Volusia Bar Assn., Fla. Assn. Criminal Def. Lawyers, Phi Beta Kappa. Avocations: water sports, shooting, travel. Home: 19 Lost Creek Ln Ormond Beach FL 32174-4840 Office: Eric K Neitzke PA 444 Seabreeze Blvd Ste 900 Daytona Beach FL 32118-3953

NEJELSKI, PAUL ARTHUR, retired judge, freelance writer; b. Chgo., Feb. 24, 1938; s. Leo Lawrence and Rena Grace (Martin) N.; m. Marilyn Ray Mills, Oct. 2, 1965; children: Nicole Rena, Stephen Downing. BA magna cum laude, Yale U., 1959, LLB, 1962; MPA, Am. U., 1969; cert. of theol. studies, Georgetown U., 1989. Bar: N.J. 1963. Law clk. appellate div. N.J. Superior Ct., 1962-63; asst. U.S. atty. U.S. Dist. Ct. N.J., 1964-65; atty., later chief immigration unit Dept. Justice, Washington, 1965-69; chief cts. desk Nat. Inst. Justice, 1969-70; asst. dir. Criminal Justice Ctr., Harvard U., 1970-71; dir. planning phase Inst. Jud. Adminstrn.-ABA Juvenile Justice Standards Project, N.Y.C., 1971-73; dir. Inst. Jud. Adminstrn., NYU, 1973-76; dep. ct. adminstrn. Conn. Jud. Dept., Hartford, 1976-77; dep. asst. atty. gen. Office for Improvements in Adminstrn. Justice, Dept. Justice, Washington, 1977-79; dir. Action Commn. to Reduce Ct. Costs and Delay, ABA, 1979-81; cir. exec. 3rd Cir., Phila., 1981-84; ct. adminstr. U.S. Tax Ct., 1984-89; immigration judge Dept. Justice, Arlington, Va., 1989-98. Mem. faculty law NYU, 1972-74, U. Conn., 1976-77, U. Md., 1981-82; cons. Author: (with C.O. Philip) Where Do Judges Come From?, 1976; editor: Social Research in Conflict With Law and Ethics, 1976; contbr. articles to profl. and popular jours. With U.S. Army, 1963-64. Home: 4628 Western Ave Bethesda MD 20816-2749

NEL, PHILIP W. English educator, writer; b. Saugus, Mass., Mar. 29, 1969; s. Pierre E. and Gloria D. (Hardman) N.; m. Karin E. Westman, May 24, 1997. BA in English and Psychology, U. Rochester, 1992; MA in English, Vanderbilt U., 1993, PhD in English, 1997. Grad. tchg. fellow Vanderbilt U., Nashville, 1993-97, adj. prof. English and Am. studies, 1997-98; adj. prof. English, comms. and women's studies Coll. of Charleston, S.C., 1998-99, vis. prof. English, 1999—. Book reviewer Post and Courier, Charleston, 1998—; reader Syracuse UP and Addison Wesley, 1999. Contbr. articles to Modern Fiction Studies, Children's Lit., others. Mem. MLA, Don DeLillo Soc. (sec. and webmaster), Children's Lit. Assn., Phi Beta Kappa. Democrat. Episcopalian. Avocations: research, running, playing the guitar. Office: Coll of Charleston Dept English 66 George St Charleston SC 29424-1407

NELIPOVICH, SANDRA GRASSI, artist; b. Oak Park, Ill., Nov. 22, 1939; d. Alessandro and Lena Mary (Ascareggi) Grassi; m. John Nelipovich Jr., Aug. 19, 1973. BFA in Art Edn., U. Ill., 1961; postgrad., Northwestern U., 1963, Gonzaga U., Florence, Italy, 1966, Art Inst. Chgo., 1968; diploma, Accademia Universale Alessandro Magno, Prato, Italy, 1983. Tchr. art Edgewood Jr. High Sch., Highland Park, Ill., 1961-62, Emerson Sch. Jr. High Sch., Oak Park, 1962-77; batik artist Calif., 1977—; illustrator Jolly Robin Publ. Co., Anaheim, 1988—2001, Assistance League of Anaheim, 2000—. Supr. student tchrs., Oak Park, 1970-75; adult edn. tchr. ESL, ceramics, Medinah, Ill., 1974; mem. curriculum action group on human dignity, EEO workshop demonstration, Oak Park, 1975-76; guest lectr. Muckenthaler Ctr., Fullerton, Calif., 1980, 92, Niguel Art Group, Dana Point, Calif., 1989, Carlsbad A.A., 1990, ARt League, Oceanside Art Group, 1992; 2d v.p. Anaheim Hills Women's Club, 1990-91, rec. sec. 1991-92; fabric designer for fashion designer Barbara Jax, 1987; illustrator Assistance League Anaheim (Calif.), 2000—. One-Woman shows include Lawry's Calif. Ctr., L.A., 1981-83, Whittier (Calif.) Mus., 1985-86, Anaheim Cultural Ctr., 1986-88, Ill. Inst. Tech., Chgo., 1989, Muckenthaler Cultural Ctr., Fullerton, 1990; also gallery exhibits in Oak Brook, 1982, La Habra, Calif., 1983, Millard Sheets Gallery, Pomona, Calif., 1996; represented in permanent collections McDonald's Corp., Oak Brook, Glenkirk Sch., Deerfield, Ill., Emerson Sch., Oak Park, Calif.; poster designer Saratoga Fine Arts. Active Assistance League, Anaheim, Calif., 1992—, 2d v.p. ways and means com., 1995—96, 1997—98, historian, 2002—. Recipient numerous awards, purchase prizes, 1979—; featured in Calif. Art Rev., Artists of So. Calif., Vol. II, Nat. Artists' Network, 1992, Batik for Artists and Quilters, 2001. Mem. AAUW (hospitality chmn. 1984-85), Soc. Children's Book Writers and Illustrators, Assistance League Anaheim, Orange Art Assn. (jury chmn. 1980). Roman Catholic. Avocations: cooking, gardening, travel. Home and Office: 5922 E Calle Cedro Anaheim CA 92807-3207

NELKIN, DOROTHY, sociology and science policy educator; b. Boston, July 30, 1933; d. Henry and Helen (Fine) Wolfers; m. Mark Nelkin, Aug. 31, 1952; children: Lisa, Laurie. BA, Cornell U., 1954. Research assoc. Cornell U., Ithaca, N.Y., 1963-69, sr. research assoc., 1970-72, assoc. prof., 1972-76, prof. sci. tech. sociology program, 1976-90, prof. sociology, 1977-90; univ. prof., prof. sociology, affiliate prof. law NYU, 1990—, Clare Boothe Luce vis. prof., 1988-90. Cons. OECD, Paris, 1975-76, Inst. Environ., Berlin, 1978-79; maitre de conference U. Paris, 1975-76; maitre de recherche Ecole Polytechnique, Paris, 1980-81. Author: The Atom Besieged, 1981, The Creation Controversy, 1982, Science as Intellectual Property, 1983, Workers at Risk, 1984, Selling Science: How the Press Covers Science and Technology, 1987, 2d edit., 1995, Dangerous Diagnostics: The Social Power of Biological Information, 1989, 2d edit., 1994, A Disease of Society: Cultural Impact ofAIDS, 1991, The Animal Rights Crusade, 1991, Controversy: Politics of Technical Decision, 3d edit., 1992, The DNA Mystique: The Gene as Cultural Icon, 1995, Body Bazaar: The Market for Body Tissue in the Biotechnology Age, 2001. Adviser Office Tech. Assessment, 1977-79, 82-83; expert witness ACLU, Ark., 1982; mem. Nat. Adv. Coun. to NIH Human Genome Project, 1991-95; mem. exec. com. NIH Ethical, Legal and Social Issues Working Group, Commn. on Embryo Rsch., 1998-99; mem. Working Group for Nat. Commn. on Future of DNA Evidence, 1998-2000. Vis. scholar Resources for the Futures, 1980-81; vis. scholar Russell Sage Found., N.Y.C., 1983; Guggenheim fellow, 1983-84. Fellow AAAS (bd. dirs.), Hastings Inst. Soc. Ethics and Life Scis.; mem. NAS Inst. of Medicine, Soc. for Social Studies Sci. (pres. 1978-79). Home: 684 Broadway Apt 12W New York NY 10012-1836 Office: NYU Dept Sociology 269 Mercer St New York NY 10003-6633 E-mail: dorothy.nelkin@nyu.edu.

NELL, JAMES LEO, association administrator; b. N.Y.C., Oct. 4, 1948; s. Sidney Watts and June Sybil (Suesskind) n.; m. Patricia Jean Falkowski, May 11, 1974 (div. Feb. 1992); children: Daniel Alexander, Christopher Eric; m. Julie Ann Vaniman, Jun 4, 1996. BA, Rutgers U., 1970; MHA, U. Mich., 1972. Staff specialist N.J. Hosp. Assn., Princeton, N.J., 1972-75, asst. dir., 1975-78; dir. Monmouth-Ocean Hosp. Shared Services Assn., Wall Twp., N.J., 1978-79; pres. S. Cen. Mich. Hosp. Council, Lansing, 1979-83, Seattle Area Hosp. Council, 1983-93; exec. dir. Apartment Assn. Seattle-King County, 1996—. Mem. steering com. Community Obstets. Referral Program, Seattle, 1985—, State Issues Forum, Washington, 1986-89; mem. adminstrv. com. Found. Health Care Quality, Seattle, 1988—. Pres. Rep. Club, Matawan, N.J., 1978-79. Lt. USAFR, 1972-80. Mem. Allied Hosp. Assn. (mem. com.), Am. Hosp. Assn., Am. Soc. Assn. Execs., Am. Coll., Healthcare Execs., Rotary. Avocations: model railroads, fishing, golf.

NELL, PATRICIA ANN, retired allergist; b. Marshfield, Wis., Aug. 10, 1935; d. Harry William (dec.) and Sarah Alice (Ingraham) N.; m. Lewis Edwards Gibson, Dec. 27, 1986. BA, State U. of Iowa, 1957, MD, 1960. Rotating intern Phila. Gen. Hosp., 1960-61; resident in pediatrics Cin. Children's Hosp., 1961-62, St. Christopher's Hosp., Phila., 1964-65; resident in allergy and immunolgy U. Wis., Madison, 1969-71; practice medicine specializing in allergy immunology West Side Clinic, Green Bay, Wis., 1971-73; tng. program faculty, chief allergy St. Christopher Hosp., Temple U., Phila., 1973-78; chief pediatric allergy dept., asst. prof. pediatrics U. Ill., Chgo., 1978-86; clin. office dir., allergist Anchor HMO, Oak Park, Ill., 1986-92; pvt. prac., 1992-98; chief aerospace medicine USAF Hdqrs. AFRC/SGP, Robins AFB, Ga., 1998—. Asst. prof. Rush-Presbyn. St. Luke Med. Ctr., Chgo., 1986-98. Contbr. articles to profl. jours. Served to maj. USAF, 1962-68, res. 1981-98, served to col. USAFR. Fellow Am. Acad. Pediatrics, Am. Acad. Asthma and Allergy-Immunology; mem. Am. Med. Assoc., Aerospace Med. Assn., Phila. Allergy Soc. (sec. 1975-78). Clubs: St. Christopher (Phila.) (treas. 1974-78), Chgo. Lit. Methodist. Avocations: cross country skiing, training labrador retrievers for hunt and field trials. E-mail: nellgibson@mac.com.

NELLER, EARL HENRY, archaeologist; b. Alton, Ill., June 28, 1943; s. Earl Henry Neller and Doris Mae (Deckelman) Landfather. B.S., U. N.Mex., 1971; M.A., U. Hawaii, 1979. Archaeologist Nat. Park Service, Chaco Canyon, N.Mex., 1975-76, Bur. Land Mgmt., Santa Fe, 1976-78; forest archaeologist U.S. Forest Service, Russellville, Ark., 1978-79; state archaeologist State of Hawaii, Honolulu, 1980-86, archaeologist Office Hawaiian Affairs, Honolulu, 1987—. Adviser Hui Lama High Sch. Hiking Club, Kamehameha High Sch., 1984—. Served with U.S. Army, 1966-70. Mem. Soc. Am. Archaeology, Am. Soc. Conservation Archaeology, N.Mex. Archeol. Council, Nat. Speleological Soc. Home: RR 2 Box 58 Auxvasse MO 65231-9802 Office: Office Hawaiian Affairs 711 Kapiolani Blvd Ste 500 Honolulu HI 96813-5255

NELLIGAN, ANNETTE FRANCES, clinical coordinator; b. Bangor, Maine, Sept. 20, 1954; d. Paul James and Laura Jenny (Sumner) N.; m. Peter Jamie Smith, June 22, 1985 (dec. June, 1997); children: Angelica Grace Nelligan-Smith, Acatia Faith Nelligan-Smith. AA, U. Maine, Bangor, 1974; BS, U. Maine, 1977, MEd, 1978, EdD, 1995. Lic. clin. profl. counselor; lic. marriage and family counselor; lic. social worker; cert. secondary sch. tchr., Maine. Tchr. Bangor H.S., 1978, Etna (Maine)-Dixmont Sch., 1979-80; residential advisor Penobscot Job Corps, Bangor, 1980-84; group life worker St. Andre's Home, 1984; caseworker, supr. Maine Dept. Human Svcs., 1984-96; clin. coord. Old Town Regional Program, 1996—. Mem. Homeless Edn. Adv. Bd., Bangor, 1992-95; instr. counselor edn. U. Maine, 1996—. Mem. ACA, Assn. for Specialists in Group Work. Roman Catholic. Avocations: doll collecting, camping, downhill skiing, sailing. Home: 385 Hancock St Bangor ME 04401-5505 Office: Main St Old Town ME 04468

NELLIGAN, KATE (PATRICIA COLLEEN NELLIGAN), actress; b. London, Can., Mar. 16, 1951; d. Patrick Joseph and Alice (Dier) N. Attended, York U., Toronto, Ctrl. Sch. Speech and Drama, London. Appeared in plays in Bristol, London, and New York: Barefoot in the Park, 1972, Misalliance, A Streetcar Named Desire, The Playboy of the Western World, London Assurance, Lulu, Private Lives, Knuckle, 1974, Heartbreak House, 1975, Plenty, 1975, As You Like It, A Moon for the Misbegotten, 1984, Virginia, 1985, Serious Money, 1988, Spoils of War, 1988, Bad Habits; films include: The Count of Monte Cristo, 1979, The Romantic Englishwoman, 1979, Dracula, 1979, Mr. Patman, 1980, Eye of the Needle, 1980, Agent, 1980, Without a Trace, 1983, Eleni, 1985, White Room, 1990, Bethune: The Making of a Hero, 1990, Frankie and Johnnie, 1991 (BAFTA Film award, 1992), The Prince of Tides, 1991, Shadows and Fog, 1992, Fatal Instinct, 1993, Wolf, 1994, Into the Deep, 1994, How to Make an American Quilt, 1995, Margaret's Museum, 1995, Up Close and Personal, 1996, U.S. Marshals, 1998, (voice) Stolen Moments, 1998 Boy Meets Girl, 1998, The Cider House Rules, 1999; TV appearances include: The Arcata Promise, 1974, The Onedin Line, The Lady of the Camellias, Licking Hitler, Measure for Measure, Therese Raquin, 1980, Forgive Our Foolish Ways, 1980, Kojak: The Price of Justice, 1987, Control, 1987, Love and Hate: A Marriage Made in Hell, 1990, Terror Strikes the Class Reunion, 1992, The Diamond Fleece, 1992, Liar Liar, 1993, Shattered Trust: The Shari Karney Story, 1993, Spoils of War, 1994, Million Dollar Babies, 1994, A Mother's Prayer, 1995, Captive Heart: The James Mink Story, 1996, Calm at Sunset, Calm at Dawn, 1996, Love Is Strange, 1998, Swing Vote, 1999, Blessed Stranger: After Flight 111, 2000, Walter and Henry, 2001, A Wrinkle in Time, 2002; TV guest appearance Road to Avonlea, 1990. Recipient Best Actress award Evening Standard, 1978. Avocations: reading, cooking. Office: Innovative Artists Ste 2850 1999 Avenue Of The Stars Los Angeles CA 90067-4612*

NELLIGAN, WILLIAM DAVID, professional association executive; b. Halstead, Kans., Aug. 10, 1926; s. William D. and Katherine (Roberts) N.; m. Dorothy Meyer, Aug. 17, 1952; children: Richard, Arthur, Mark. Student, U. Wichita, 1944-46; BS, U. Kans., 1949. Display advt. salesman Kansas City Star and Times, Mo., 1949-51; mgr. SW Kans. Extension Ctr. U. Kans., Garden City, 1951-55, exec. dir. dept. postgrad. med. edn. Sch. Medicine Kansas City, Kans., 1955-64; asst. to pres. Med. Coll. Ga., Augusta, 1964-65; exec. v.p. Am. Coll. Cardiology, Bethesda, Md., 1965-92; v.p. Marion Merrell DOW, Inc., Kansas City, Mo., 1992-94; exec. dir. Am. Soc. Nuc. Cardiology, Bethesda, 1994-2001, Cert. Bd. Nuclear Cardiology, Damascus, Md., 1996—. Mem. Nat. Commn. Diabetes, 1975-76, adv. council Nat. Diabetes and Digestive and Kidney Diseases, 1987-88; bd. dirs. Arthur E. Hertzler Research Found., Halstead, Kans., 1961—. Recipient Man with a Heart award N.Y. Cardiol. Soc., 1970, Presdl. citation Am. Coll. Cardiology, 1975, Disting. Service award Am. Coll. Cardiology, 1986, CLC Hall of Leaders award, 1986. Fellow Am. Coll. Cardiology; mem. AMA (citation of layman for disting. svc. 1993), Profl. Conv. Mgmt. Assn. (pres. 1974-75, Disting. Svc. award 1990), Am. Med. Writers Assn. (dir., exec. com., treas. 1970-78, Harold Swanberg Disting. Svc. award), Am. Soc. Assn. Execs. (cert., dir. 1975-78, sec.-treas. 1987-88, Key award 1984), Am. Assn. Med. Soc. Execs. (pres. 1986-87), Brit. Cardiac Soc. (hon.), Alliance for Continuing Med. Edn. (Pres.'s award 1994), Masons. Office: 9929 C Main St Damascus MD 20872-2068 E-mail: cbnc@starpower.net.

NELLIS, JOSEPH LEON, lawyer, writer; b. Chgo., Dec. 10, 1916; s. Leo Max and Tania (Goberman) N.; m. Muriel Gollon, Dec. 12, 1963; children—Barbara, David; stepchildren— Amy Weiss, Adam Pressman. Student U. Wis., 1934-36, U. Mich., 1936-37; B.S., Northwestern U., 1938, J.D., 1940. Bar: Ill. 1941, U.S. Dist. Ct. (no. dist.) Ill. 1941, D.C. 1947, U.S. Supreme Ct. 1946, U.S. Ct. Appeals (D.C. cir.) 1947, U.S. Dist. Ct. Md. 1963, U.S. Ct. Clms. 1965, U.S. Ct. Appeals (7th cir.) 1970, U.S. Ct. Apls. (4th cir.) 1965. Assoc. counsel U.S. Senate Crime Com., 1950-52; spl. counsel N.Y. State Crime Commn., 1952; chief counsel House Reps. Small Bus. Subcom., 1957-58; mem. Lyon and Nellis, Washington, 1966-75; counsel Batzell, Nunn and Bode, Washington, 1975-82, Spriggs, Bode & Hollingsworth, 1982— ; spl. counsel Ho. Reps. Crime Com., 1969-70; spl. counsel Senate Antitrust Com., 1958-59; chief counsel Ho. of Reps. Select Com. Narcotics Abuse, 1976-79; gen. counsel Ho. Reps. Judiciary Com., 1979-81; lectr. George Washington U., Am. U. Dep. dir., state coordinator Citizens for Humphrey-Muskie, 1968. Contbr. articles to popular mags. Served to capt. JAG, USAFR, 1950-55. Mem. ABA, D.C. Bar Assn., Decalogue Soc. Lawyers, Nat. Abortions Rights League (bd. trustees 1973-74). Club: Outrigger (Honolulu). Author: (with others) Private Lives of Public Enemies, 1974; contbr. articles to profl. jours. Office: Suite 1100 1015 15th St NW Ste 1100 Washington DC 20005-2619

NELLIS, M. DUANE, dean, geography educator; b. Spokane, Wash., July 26, 1954; s. Marvin B. and Sophie Ann Nellis; m. C. Ruth Nellis, June 21, 1975; children: Jonathan Duane, Jason Scott. BS, Mont. State U., 1976; MS, Oreg. State U., 1977, PhD, 1980. Asst. prof. dept. geography Kans. State U., Manhattan, 1980-86, assoc. prof. dept. geography, 1986-90, prof. dept. geography, 1990-97, dept. head dept. geography, 1987-94, dir. Inst. for Social and Behavioral Rsch., 1990-94, assoc. dean Coll. Arts and Scis., 1994-97; dean Eberly Coll. Arts and Scis. W.Va. U., Morgantown, 1997—. Bd. dirs. W.Va. U. Rsch. Corp., Morgantown, 1997—, Snowshoe Inst., Charleston, W.Va. Co-author: Perspective on Applied Physical Geography, 1997; co-editor: Contemporary Rural Systems in Transition, 1993; co-editor Geocarto Internat. Jour., 1999—; contbr. chpts. to books and articles to profl. jours. Pres. Kans. Acad. Sci., Emporia, 1990. Recipient Outstanding Contbns. award Assn. Am. Geographers Remote Sensing Specialty Bd., 1995; grantee NASA, NSF, U.S. Agy. for Internat. Devel., 1985—. Mem. Coun. Colls. Arts and Scis. (rsch. univs. com. mem. 1999—), Assn. Am. Geographers (nat. councilor 1996-99, pres. 2002--, John Fraser Hart award for rsch. excellence contemporary agr. and rural land use spity. group 1991, Honors award 2001), Nat. Coun. for Geog. Edn. (pres. 1994), Am. Soc. Photogrammetry and Remote Sensing, Gamma Theta Upsilon (pres. 1999-2000), Phi Kappa Phi. Avocations: travel, running, reading. Office: WVa Univ PO Box 6286 Morgantown WV 26506

NELMS, LEWIS CALDWELL, minister; b. Millen, Ga., July 2, 1957; s. Mack and Nan Nelms; m. Leah Mae Nelms, June 26, 1979; children: Stephen, Adam, Caleb, Hannah. BS, Hyles-Anderson Coll., 1979. Assoc. pastor Chestertown (Md.) Bapt. Ch., 1979-83, Des Moines Bapt. Ch., 1983-84; sr. pastor Calvary Chapel, S.I., 1984-90; dir. devel. and expansion Final Frontiers Found., Louisville, 1990-98; founder, pres. Gospelink Inc., Wrens, 1998—. Prin. Chestertown Christian Acad., 1979-83; instr. Des Moines Bible Inst., 1990-91; cons. Sunday sch. orgn. Decatur (Ala.) Bapt. Ch., 1992-94. Contbr. articles to ch. jours. Office: Gospelink Inc PO Box 889 Wrens GA 30833

NELSEN, HART MICHAEL, sociologist, educator; b. Pipestone, Minn., Aug. 3, 1938; s. Noah I. and Nova (Ziegler) N.; m. Anne Kusener, June 13, 1964; 1 dau., Jennifer. BA, U. No. Iowa, 1959, MA, 1963; M.Div., Princeton Theol. Sem., 1963; PhD (NSF faculty fellow), Vanderbilt U., 1972. Asst. prof. sociology Western Ky. U., Bowling Green, 1965-70, assoc. prof., 1970-73, Catholic U. Am., 1973-74, prof., 1974-81, chmn. dept. sociology, 1974-77, mem. Boys Town Ctr. for Study Youth Devel., 1974-81; prof. sociology La. State U., Baton Rouge, 1981-84, chmn. dept. sociology, head dept. rural sociology, 1981-84, coordinator rural sociology research, 1981-84; dean Coll. Liberal Arts Pa. State U., 1984-90, prof. sociology, 1984—. Author: (with Anne K. Nelsen) Black Church in the Sixties, 1975; co-author: The Religion of Children, 1977, Religion and American Youth, 1976; editor: (with others) The Black Church in America, 1971; adv. editor: Sociol. Quar, 1976-82; assoc. editor: Sociol. Analysis, 1977-80, Rev. Religious Research, 1977-80, 84—, editor, 1980-84; mem. editorial bd.: Social Forces, 1983-86. Co-rec. sec. Capitol Hill Restoration Soc., 1979-80, v.p., 1980-81; mem. exec. bd. Lafitte Hills Assn., 1983-84; pres. Midtown Sq. Condo. Assn., 1996-99, treas., 1999—. Presbyterian Chs. grantee, 1966-69; NIMH co-grantee, 1969-72; Russell Sage Found. co-grantee, 1972-73; La. Gov.'s Commn. on Alcoholism and Drug Abuse grantee, 1982 Mem. Assn. Sociology Religion (exec. council 1974-76, 78-82, v.p. 1978-79, pres. 1980-81), Religious Research Assn. (dir. 1977-80, pres.-elect 1985-86, pres. 1987-88), Soc. Sci. Study Religion (council 1981-83, exec. sec. 1984-87), Am. Sociol. Assn., So. Sociol. Soc. (chmn. membership com. 1983-85), AAAS (rep. 1984-2000). Presbyterian. Office: Pa State U Oswald 306 Dept Sociology University Park PA 16802

NELSEN, MARTIN CLAUDE, management services professional; b. Kankakee, Ill., Nov. 12, 1942; s. Claude Brink and Mildred Pauline (Paraday) N.; m. Darlene Marie Buckardt, Mar. 31, 1962; children: Dawn Therese (dec.), Deena Marie Nelsen Hyatt, Martin Arthur. AS, Waubonsee C.C., Sugar Grove, Ill., 1973; B in Mgmt., Elmhurst Coll., 1983; cert. gen. mgr., Planty Sr. Seminar. Cert. laundry/linen mgr. Nat. Assn. Instnl. Linen Mgmt., advanced devel. program for mgrs. Prodn. control mgr. Lyon Metal Products, Aurora, Ill., 1969-72, plant mgr., 1972-80, dir. mfg., 1980-85; gen. mgr. Marriott Mgmt. Svcs., Opa Locka, Fla., 1985—. Contbr. articles to profl. jours. and in-house news periodicals. Active Mens Rep. Club Boca Raton, Fla., 1986-94. Named Laundry Mgr. of Yr., Nat. Assn. Instl. Linen Mgmt. South Fla. Chpt., 1987, 92, 95. Mem. Am. Soc. ASHES, South Fla. Healthcare Exec. Forum, South Fla. Chpt. Nat. Assn. Instnl. Linen Mgmt. (pres. 3 terms, sec.-treas. 5 terms), Elks, Moose. Lutheran. Avocations: golf, boating, corvette restoration, travel. Office: Marriott/Combined Svcs 2358 NW 151st St Opa Locka FL 33054-2712

NELSEN, ROGER BAIN, mathematician; b. Chgo., Dec. 20, 1942; s. Howard Ernest and Ann Maxwell (Bain) N. BA, DePauw U., 1964; PhD, Duke U., 1969. Prof. maths. Lewis and Clark Coll., Portland, Oreg., 1969—. Vis. prof. Mt. Holyoke Coll., South Hadley, Mass., 1986, 88, 90-91, U. Mass.-Amherst, 1983-84, 93; assoc. editor Coll. Math. Jour., Washington, 1989—; referee Math. Mag., Am. Math. Monthly. Contbr. articles to profl. jours. Mem. AAUP, Am. Math. Soc., Math. Assn. Am., Phi Beta Kappa, Sigma Xi. Avocations: sailing, bicycling, hiking, photography, numismatics. Home: 28 Atwood Rd South Hadley MA 01075-1602 Office: Lewis and Clark Coll PO Box 110 Portland OR 97207-0110

NELSEN, WILLIAM CAMERON, foundation executive, former college president; b. Omaha, Oct. 18, 1941; s. William Peter and Ellen Lucella (Cameron) N.; m. Margaret Leone Rossow, May 30, 1981; children by previous marriage: William Norris, Shawna Lynn; 1 adopted dau., Sarah Ruth. BA, Midland Luth. Coll., Fremont, Nebr., 1963; MA, Columbia U., 1966; PhD, U. Pa., 1971; Fulbright scholar, U. Erlangen, W. Ger., 1964; D (hon.), Midland Luth. Coll., 1995. Program exec. Danforth Found., St. Louis, 1970-73; asst. dean, then v.p., dean coll. St. Olaf Coll., Northfield, Minn., 1973-80; dir. Project on Faculty Devel. Assn. of Am. Colls., 1979; pres. Augustana Coll., Sioux Falls, S.D., 1980-86, Citizens' Scholarship Found. of Am., St. Peter, Minn., 1986—. Bd. dirs. 1st Nat. Bank and Bancommunity Svc. Corp., St. Peter, Minn. Author: Effective Approaches to Faculty Development, 1980, Renewal of the Teacher Scholar, 1981, also articles. Bd. dirs. S.D. Symphony, 1980-85, Sioux Falls YMCA, 1980-86, Luth. Ednl. Conf. N.Am., 1982-86, Sioux Falls United Way, 1983-86; nat. bd. advisors Coun. Aid to Edn.; mem. nat. coun. Connect Am., Points of Light Found; chmn. bd. U.S. Dream Acad.; mem. exec. bd. Nat. Assembly; charter bd. dirs. Nat. Scholarship Providers Assn.. Recipient McKee award for outstanding nat. leadership in edn. Nat. Assn. Ptnrs. in Edn., 1999; Danforth Grad. fellow, 1963, Woodrow Wilson fellow, 1963. Mem. Am. Assn. Higher Edn., Assn. Am. Colls. (bd. dirs. 1984-86), Shoreland Country Club (pres. 1996-99), Consortium for Advancement of Pvt. Higher Edn., Coun. of Ind. Colls., Nat. Dollars for Scholars, Rotary Club. Republican. Lutheran. Home: 804 Spruce Pl Saint Peter MN 56082-1598 Office: Citizens' Scholarship Found Am PO Box 297 Saint Peter MN 56082-0297 E-mail: wcnelsen@csfa.org.

NELSON, ALAN RAY, internist, medical association administrator; b. Logan, Utah, June 11, 1933; s. Ray J. and Leah B. (Olson) Nelson; m. Gwen L. Sparrow, Jan. 2, 1959; children: John R., Shannon, Alan L. Student, Utah State U., 1951—54; MD, Northwestern U., 1958. Diplomate Am. Bd. Internal Medicine, Am. Bd. Endocrinology and Metabolism. Intern Highland Alameda County Hosp., Oakland, Calif., 1958—59; resident in internal medicine U. Utah, Salt Lake City, 1959—62, assoc. clin. prof., 1964—89, clin. prof., 1989—92; practice medicine specializing in internal medicine and endocrinology Salt Lake City, 1964—91; assoc. Meml. Med. Ctr., 1964—91; exec. v.p. Am. Soc. Internal Medicine, Washington, 1992—98; assoc. exec. v.p. Am. Coll. Physicians Am. Soc. Internal Medicine, 1998—2000, spl. advisor to exec. v.p., 2000—. Mem. Nat. Profl. Std. Rev. Coun., 1973—77; pres. Utah Profl. Rev. Orgn., 1971—75; mem. AMA Coun. on Legis., 1977—80, trustee, 1980—, chmn., 1986—88, pres.-elect, 1988—89, pres., 1989—90; commr. Joint Commn. on Accreditation of Hosps., 1982—86, sec.-treas., 1985—86. Chair Health Care Quality Alliance, 1992—96. With M.C. USAF, 1962—64. Recipient Spl. Recognition award, Am. Soc. Internal Medicine, 1973, Disting. Internist award, 1989, Coble award, Am. Assn. Clin. Endocrinology, 1999. Master: ACP; mem.: World Med. Assn. (pres.-elect 1990—91, pres. 1992), Med. Payment Adv. Commn., Inst. Medicine of NAS (governing coun. 1984—87), Utah Med. Assn. (pres. from 1976, award 1973, 1979). Home: 11905 Parkside Dr Fairfax VA 22033-2648 Office: ACP - ASIM 2011 Pennsylvania Ave NW Washington DC 20006-1813 E-mail: anelson@mail.acponline.org.

NELSON, ALFRED JOHN, retired pharmaceutical company executive; b. Dalmuir, Scotland, Jan. 24, 1922; came to U.S., 1972; s. John and Mary Catherine (Duncan) N.; m. Frances C. Hillier, Dec. 5, 1952; children: J. Stuart, Andrew D. MBChB, U. Glasgow, Scotland, 1945, MD with commendation, 1957; DPH, Royal Inst. Pub. Health and Hygiene, London, 1948. Resident Ayr County Hosp., 1945, Belvidere Fever Hosp., Glasgow, Scotland, 1948; cons. N.Y. State Dept. Health, Albany, 1950-51; dir. venereal disease control B.C. Dept. Health and Welfare, Vancouver, Can., 1952-54, cons. epidemiology Can., 1954-55; asst. dean medicine U. B.C., Can., 1955-57, clin. assoc. prof. pub. health Can., 1954-70; dir. health services B.C. Hydro and Power Authority, Vancouver, Can., 1957-70; v.p. Hoechst-Roussel Pharm., Inc., Somerville, N.J., 1972-81, sr. v.p., med. dir., 1981-87, ret., 1987. Hon. cons. staff Vancouver Gen. Hosp. Served with RCAF, 1953-56. Recipient John J. Sippy Meml. award APHA, 1959, Spl. award, Order St. John of Jerusalem, 1960; named officer brother Order St. John of Jerusalem, 1966. Fellow ACP, Royal Coll. Physicians and Surgeons Can., Am. Coll. Preventive Medicine, N.Y. Acad. Medicine. Presbyterian. Home: 29436 Port Royal Way Laguna Niguel CA 92677-7947

NELSON, ALLEN F. proxy solicitation company executive; b. Portland, Oreg., Oct. 17, 1943; s. Roy August and MIldred Mary (Jensen) N.; m. Johanna Molenaar, Dec. 8, 1973. BS, U. Iowa, 1965, MA, 1968. V.p. Shareholder Comm. Corp., N.Y.C., 1970-72; v.p. Trafalgar Capital Corp., 1973; pres. Nelson, Lasky & Co., Inc., 1974-76; account exec. Corp. Comm., Inc., Seattle, 1976-77; pres. Allen Nelson & Co., Inc., 1977—. Mem. Fin. Analysts Fedn., Nat. Investor Rels. Inst., Nat. Security Traders Assn., Practicing Law Inst. (presdl. rank rev. bd. 2001), Pub. Rels. Soc. Am., Am. Soc. Corp. Secs., Can. Corp. Secs., Ranier Club, Montana Club, Vancouver Club. Home: 4400 Beach Dr SW Seattle WA 98116-3937 Office: Allen Nelson & Co Inc PO Box 16157 Seattle WA 98116-0157 E-mail: anelson@worldproxy.com.

NELSON, ARTHUR HUNT, real estate management development company executive; b. Kansas City, Mo., May 21, 1923; s. Carl Ferdinand and Hearty (Brown) N.; m. Eleanor Thomas, Dec. 27, 1954; children: Carl F., Frances, Pamela. AB, U. Kans., 1943; JD, Harvard U., 1949. Bar: Mass. 1949. Staff radiation lab. MIT, 1943-44; sr. engr., cons. Raytheon Mfg. Co., Boston, 1948-52; pvt. practice, 1949; v.p., treas., dir. Gen. Electronic Labs., Inc., Cambridge, 1951-64, chmn. bd., 1959-63; treas., dir. Sci. Electronics, Inc., 1955-64, Assocs. for Internat. Rsch., Inc., Cambridge, 1954—, pres., 1968—; treas., dir. Victor Realty Devel., Inc., 1959-76, pres., 1972-76, gen. ptnr., 1976—, Prospect Hill Exec. Office Park, Waltham, Mass., 1977—; chmn. Nelson Cos., 1990—, Cambridge Devel. Lab., Cambridge, 1994—2001. Bd. dirs. Internat. Data Group, Inc., Sterling Bank. *Since 1954, Arthur Nelson has founded or cofounded nine business firms and ten nonprofit organizations. Most of his nonprofit organizations involve the application of technology to help solve social problems. He has found over the years that business entrepreneurialism and social entrepreneurialism are very similar. He believes that business entrepreneurs can make substantial contributions to society by using their entrepreneurial skills to found and support nonprofit organizations.* Pres., trustee Tech. Edn. Rsch. Ctrs., Inc., 1965—; trustee Winsor Sch., Boston, 1978-88, treas., 1978-82; bd. dirs. Charles River Mus. Industry, Waltham, 1986—, pres. 1994—, pres., dir. 128 Bus. Coun. Inc., 1987—, Hist. Waltham Inc., 1996—, Am. Computer Fedn. Inc., 1996—, Charles River Pub. Internet Ctr. Inc., 1996—. Ensign USNR, 1944-46. Recipient Ernst & Young New Eng. Master Entrepreneur of Yr. award, 1999. Mem. ABA, Mass. Bar Assn., Boston Bar Assn., Boston Computer Soc. (bd. dirs. 1985-97, chmn. 1994-97), Greater Boston C. of C., Harvard Club Boston, Beta Theta Pi, Phi Beta Kappa, Sigma Xi. Home: 75 Robin Rd Weston MA 02493-2436 Office: care The Nelson Cos Prospect Place 230 3rd Ave Waltham MA 02451-7528

NELSON, AUDREY MAY, physician; b. Austin, Minn., Apr. 1, 1940; d. Glen Stanley and Clara May (Torgerson) N. BA, U. Minn., 1962, BS, 1963, MD, 1965. Diplomate in internal medicine and rheumatology Am. Bd. Internal Medicine. Assoc. cons. Mayo Clinic, Rochester, Minn., 1972, cons. in internal medicine and rheumatology, 1972—; instr. medicine Mayo Med. Sch., 1973-76, from asst. prof. to assoc. prof. medicine, 1976-2000, prof., 2000—, chair pediat. rheumatology, 1993-2001. Bd. govs. Mayo Clinic, 1982-89; trustee Mayo Found., 1982-93, v.p., 1989-92. Trustee Christ United Meth. Ch., Rochester, 1995—2002, vice chair, 1999—2001, chair, 2001—02. Recipient Woman of Achievement award YWCA, Alumni Recognition award U. Minn. Alumni Med. Soc., 2002; named Woman Physician of Yr., Alpha Epsilon Iota. Fellow ACP, Am. Coll. Rheumatology (bd. dirs. 1995-99), Am. Acad. Pediatrics; mem. AMA, Minn. Med. Assn. (trustee, Disting. Svc. award 1999), Am. Med. Group Assn. (chair bd. dirs. 1997-98), Phi Beta Kappa, Alpha Omega Alpha. Avocation: sailing. Office: Mayo Clinic 200 1st St SW Rochester MN 55905-0002

NELSON, BARBARA ANNE, judge; b. Mineola, N.Y., Jan. 16, 1951; d. Richard William and Dorothee Helen (Thorne) N. BA, Inter Am. U. P.R., 1972; JD, New Eng. Sch. Law, 1975. Legal editor Prentice Hall Pub. Co., Englewood Cliffs, N.J., 1976-77; assoc. Antonio C. Martinez Law Firm, N.Y.C., 1977-79, Pollack & Kramer, N.Y.C., 1979-83; pvt. practice, 1983-95; immigration judge U.S., 1995—. Author, spkr., tng. film. Mem. ACLU, Legal Aid Soc. N.Y., Amnesty Internat., Asia Soc., Internat. Assn. Refugee Judges. Avocations: travel, yoga, foreign languages. Home: 324 W 14th St Apt 5A New York NY 10014-5003 Office: 26 Federal Plz New York NY 10278-0004 E-mail: nelsonferrets@yahoo.com.

NELSON, BARBARA LOUISE, secondary education educator; b. Indpls., Apr. 18, 1935; d. Dennis Arthur Chandler and Bertha Louise (Drane) Hill; children: Edwin Robert Swanson, III, Patricia Marie Swanson, Barbara Michelle Swanson Clure. BA, Ind. U., 1956; tchrs. cert., Millikin U., 1964; MA, U. Denver, 1969. Cert. English tchr. Tchr. AL Jr. High Sch., Jefferson Co.; tchr., dept. chair O'Connell Jr. High; tchr. Alameda High Sch., Jefferson County R-1, Lakewood, Colo. Exch. tchr. ITF, Melbourne, Australia, 1976, Lakewood-Sutherlandshire Sister City Tchr. Visitation Exch., 1989; mem. writing com. Jefferson County Commn. Chalice, min., lector, Stephen min., prayer min., mem. stewardship commn., evangelism commn. Christ Episc. Ch. Mem. NEA, Colo. Internat. Tchr. Exch. League, Colo. Edn. Assn., Jefferson County Edn. Assn., Delta Kappa Gamma (advisor, past pres., v.p., rec. sec. and treas., corr. sec. Pi chpt.), Phi Delta Kappa (scholarship chmn., svc. key 1998, Sanders scholarship com.), Delta Delta Delta. Home: 3100 S Race St Englewood CO 80110-3032 E-mail: blnelson@jeffco.k12.co.us.

NELSON, BARRY, actor; b. San Francisco; s. Trygve and Betsy (Chritophison) Neilsen. BA, U. Calif., Berkeley. Broadway appearances include Light Up the Sky, 1949, The Rat Race, 1950, The Moon is Blue, 1951-53, No Time For Sergents, London, Eng., 1956, Mary-Mary, 1960-61, Cactus Flower, 1965-67, Everything in the Garden, 1967, The Only Game in Town, 1970, Seascape, 1975, The Norman Conquest, 1975, The Act, 1978 (nominated for Tony award); nat. co. 42d Street, 1983-86, Broadway co., 1986-87; motion pictures appearances in Mary-Mary, 1963, Airport, 1970, Pete and Tillie, 1972, The Shining, 1979; TV series The Hunter, 1953, My Favorite Husband, 1954-55. Office: Fifi Oscard Agency, Inc. Rm 1601 110 W 40th St New York NY 10018-8512

NELSON, BEN, JR. retired air force officer; b. Ft. Lewis, Wash., Jan. 31, 1942; s. Ben and Marie (Warn) N.; m. Suzanne Wiseman, Dec. 22, 1963; 1 child, William Bryant. BBA, U. Tex., 1964; MPA, Golden Gate U., 1976. Commd. 2d lt. USAF, 1964, advanced through grades to brig. gen., 1988; instr. pilot 3525th Fighter Tng. Squadron, Williams AFB, Ariz., 1965-70; flight comdr. 390th Tactical Fighter Squadron, DaNang, Vietnam, 1970-71, Sheppard AFB, Tex., 1971-74; chief pers. tng. br. Office Dep. Chief of Staff for Pers., Hdqrs. Tactical Air Command, Langley AFB, Va., 1974-77; ops. officer, comdr. 428th Tactical Fighter Squadron, Nellis AFB, Nev., 1977-81; student Naval War Coll., Newport, R.I., 1981-82; chief fighter plans br. Office Dep. Chief of Staff Plans, Hdqrs. USAF, Washington, 1982-84; vice comdr. 32d Tactical Fighter Group, Soesterberg Air Base, The Netherlands, 1984-85; vice comdr., then comdr. 50th Tactical Fighter Wing, Hahn Air Base, Fed. Republic Germany, 1985-88; asst. dep. chief of staff for plans Hdqrs. Tactical Air Command, Langley AFB, 1988-89; comdr. 56th Fighter Wing, MacDill AFB, Fla., 1989-92; dep. comdr. 5th Allied Tactical Air Forces (NATO), Vicenza, Italy, 1992-94; CEO regional office ARC, Tampa Bay, Fla., 1994—. Bd. dirs. CMS, Inc., Tampa, Fla.; COO, Skylynx Comm., Inc., San Jose, Calif., 1998—99; ptnr. Harrod Properties, Inc., 1999—; 0044. Recipient Phoenix award Dept. Def., 1987, O'Malley award Dept. Air Force. Mem. Air Force Assn., Tampa C. of C. (bd. dirs. 1989-92), Order of Daedalians. Episcopalian. Avocation: golf.

NELSON, BENJAMIN, senator, former governor, lawyer; b. McCook, Nebr., May 17, 1941; s. Benjamin Earl and Birdella Ruby (Henderson) N.; m. Diane C. Gleason, Feb. 22, 1980; children from a previous marriage: Sarah Jane, Patrick James; stepchildren: Kevin Michael Gleason, Christine Marie Gleason. BA, U. Nebr., 1963; MA, 1966, JD, 1970; LLD (hon.), Creighton U., 1992, Peru State Coll., 1993. Bar: Nebr. 1970. Instr. dept. philosophy U. Nebr., 1963-65; supr. Dept. Ins. State of Nebr., Lincoln, 1965-72; dir. ins., 1975-76; asst. gen. counsel, gen. counsel, sec., v.p. The Ctrl. Nat. Ins. Group Omaha, 1972-75; exec. v.p., 1976-77; pres., 1978-81; CEO, 1980-81; of counsel Kennedy, Holland, DeLacy & Svoboda, Omaha, 1985-90; gov. State of Nebr., Lincoln, 1991-98; of counsel Lumson, Dugan and Murray, Omaha, 1999—; U.S. Senator from Nebr., 2001—. Co-chmn. Carter/Mondale re-election campaign, Nebr., 1980; chair Nat. Edn. Goals Panel, 1992-94; co-founder Gov.'s Ethanol Coalition, chair, 1991, 94; pres. Coun. of State Govs., 1994. Recipient Disting. Eagle award Nat. Eagle Scout Assn., 1994; named Amb. Plenipotentiary, 1993. Mem. ABA, Nat. Assn. Ind. Insurers, Nat. Assn. Ins. Commrs. (exec. v.p. 1982-85), Nebr. Bar Assn., Consumer Credit Ins. Assn., Midwestern Govs. Assn. (chair 1994), Western Govs. Assn. (vice chair 1994, chair 1995), Happy Hollow Club, Omaha Club, Hillcrest Country Club. Democrat. Methodist. Avocations: reading, hunting, fishing. Office: US Senate 720 Hart Senate Office Bldg Washington DC 20510

NELSON, BILL, senator, former state treasurer; b. Miami, Fla., Sept. 29, 1942; s. C.W. and Nannie (Merle) N.; m. Grace H. Cavert, Feb. 19, 1972; children: C. William, Nan Ellen. BA, Yale U., 1965; JD, U. Va., 1968. Bar: Fla. 1968. Practice law, Melbourne, Fla., 1970-79; mem. Fla. Ho. of Reps., 1972-78, U.S. Congress, 1979-91; flew on 24th Flight of Space Shuttle, 1986; treas. State of Fla., Tallahassee, 1995—2000, U.S. senator, 2000—; vice chmn. Dem. Senatorial Campaign com. , 2000—. Served to capt. USAR, 1965-75, with U.S. Army, 1968-70. Office: US Senate 716 Hart Sen Office Bldg Washington DC 20510 Address: 225 E Robinson St Ste 410 Orlando FL 32801*

NELSON, BRUCE, consumer products company executive; Sr. mgmt. positions Boise Cascade, 1968-90; pres., CEO BT Office Products USA, 1991-94, Viking, 1995—98; pres. Office Depot Internat., 1998—2000, CEO, 2000—, chmn., 2001. Office: Office Depot 2200 Old Germantown Rd Delray Beach FL 33445-8299

NELSON, BRYCE EAMES, journalist, educator; b. Reno, Dec. 16, 1937; s. H.V. and Jennie Nelson; m. Martha Streiff, Sept. 23, 1961; children: Kristin, Matthew. BA, Harvard Coll., 1959; MPhil (Rhodes Scholar), U. Oxford, Eng., 1962. Instr. U. Pitts., 1962-63; fgn. affairs asst. Senator Frank Church, Washington, 1963-65; reporter Washington Post, 1965-66, Sci. Mag., Washington, 1966-69; midwest bur. chief, corr. L.A. Times, Chgo., Washington, 1969-82; writer human behavior N.Y. Times, 1982-84; prof. journalism U. So. Calif., L.A., 1984—. Dir. U. So. Calif. Sch. Journalism, 1984-88. Mem. editl. bd. Am. Oxonian, Claremont, Calif., 1996—; contbr. articles to publs. Recipient award Calif. Assoc. Press Contest for Investigative Reporting, 1980, Disting. Contbr. award APA, 1983, Deutsch award for Disting. Journalism Am. Orthopsychiat. Assn., 1970. Mem. Assn. Am. Rhodes Scholars, Soc. Profl. Journalists, Assn. Edn. in Journalism and Mass Comm., Am. Hist. Assn., We. History Assn. Episcopalian. Avocations: history and literature of Western America, hiking, biking, music. Office: Univ So Calif Sch Journalism Annenberg Sch Los Angeles CA 90089-0281 Fax: (213) 740-8036. E-mail: benelson@usc.edu.

NELSON, C. JERRY, agronomy educator; b. Mona, Iowa, Mar. 25, 1940; s. Harlan Leroy and Joy Isabelle (Watkinson) N.; m. Barbara Ann Finholdt, Sept. 17, 1960; children: Daniel C., Deborah A. BS, U. Minn., 1961, MS, 1963; PhD, U. Wis., 1966. Rsch. assoc. Cornell U., Ithaca, N.Y., 1966-67; asst. prof. U. Mo., Columbia, 1967-71, assoc. prof., 1971-75, prof., 1975-89, Curators' prof., 1989—. Chair continuing com. Internat. Crop Sci. Congress, 1992—. Editor: Forages, Vol. I, 1995, Vol. II, 1995; contbr. chpts. to books, more than 170 articles to profl. jours. Mem. Am. Forage and Grassland Coun. (Medallion award 2002); mem. Coun. Agrl. Sci. and Tech. Recipient Disting. Faculty award U. Mo. Alumni Assn., 1987; named hon. scientist Rural Devel. Adminstrn., Suweon, Korea, 1994. Mem. Internat. Crop Sci. Soc. (pres. 2000—), Am. Soc. Agronomy (pres. 1996), Crop Sci. Soc. Am. (pres. 1988), Am. Soc. Plant Biology. Lutheran. Avocations: jogging, golf, fishing. Home: 1606 Limerick Ln Columbia MO 65203-5465 Office: U Mo Dept Agronomy 210 Waters Hall Columbia MO 65211-6140 E-mail: nelsoncj@missouri.edu.

NELSON, CANDICE JEAN, political science educator; b. New Bedford, Mass. d. Richard Theodore and Jean (Roscow) N.; children: David, Peter, Michael. BA, Wheaton Coll., 1971; MA, UCLA, 1974; PhD, U. Calif., Berkeley, 1982. Asst. prof. dept. govt. Georgetown U., Washington, 1980-86; congl. fellow Office of Senator Alan Cranston, 1986-87, spl. asst., 1987-88; vis. fellow The Brookings Instn., 1988-90; asst. prof. dept. govt. Am. U., 1990-96, assoc. prof., 1996—. Mem. adv. com. money & politics project League of Women Voters Ednl. Fund, Washington, 1995-97. Co-author: The Money Chase, 1990, The Myth of the Independent Voter, 1992; co-editor: Campaigns and Elections American Style, 1995, Crowded Airwaves, 2000, Campaign Warriors, 2000, Shades of Gray, 2002. Mem. nat. governing bd. Common Cause, Washington, 1994-97. Mem. Nat. Capital Area Polit. Sci. Assn. (exec. coun. 1992-93, 2d v.p. 1993-94, 1st v.p. 1994-95, pres. 1995-96), Am. Polit. Sci. Assn. Democrat. Episcopalian. Avocations: tennis, skiing. Office: Am U Dept Govt 4400 Massachusetts Ave NW Washington DC 20016-8003 E-mail: cnelson@american.edu.

NELSON, CAREY BOONE, sculptor; b. Lexington, Mo. d. William M. and Carey (Butler) Boone; m. Kenneth Warwick Nelson; children: Caren, Kenneth Warwick II, Kimberley, Keith, Kyle, Craig. Student, U. Mo.; BA, Wellesley Coll.; MS in Edn., Wagner Coll. Cert. tchr., N.Y.C., N.Y. State. Tchr. N.Y.C. Pub. Schs.; instr. sculpture Snug Harbor Cultural Ctr., N.Y.C., 1982-84. Per diem col., artist USAF, 1974—; artist USCG, 1974—. One-woman shows include Pietrantonio Galleries, N.Y.C., St. Bartholomew's, Salmagundo Club, Poly. Prep. Country Day Sch., Bklyn., Shug Harbor Cultural Ctr., N.Y.C., Epiphany Libr., exhibited in group shows at Internat. Art Exch., Monte Carol, Paris, Cannes, Athens, Victoria Mus. Libr., Melbourne, Australia, numerous others, Represented in permanent collections Victoria Libr. Mus., Australia, Sheldon Swope Mus., Terre Haute, Ind., Esperanza, Antarctica, Durban Mus., South Africa, numerous others, commd., , , , . Bd. dirs. Cerebral Palsy Assn., S.I., N.Y., Vis. Nurse Assn., S.I. Named Woman of Achievement, Wagner Coll., 1978; recipient Hon. Life Artist, Catharine Lorillard Wolfe Art Club, 1990, awards, Salmagundi, 1995, 1996, 1997, 1997, 1998, 1999, 2000, Anna Hyatt Huntington award, Catharine Lorillard Wolfe Art Club, Horsehead Trophy, 1980, Coun. of Am. Artists award, Hudson Valley, 1996, Medal of Achievement, USCG, 1991, Nat. Arts Club award, 1998, Salmagundi Peter Helch award, 1998, 1st Pl. Sculpture award, 1999, M. Soroka Meml. award, 1999, Cert. of Appreciation, USCG, 1999, Achievement award, 1999, George Gray award, 1999. Fellow Am. Artists Profl. League (cert. of appreciation 1999); mem. Nat. Arts Club (life, award 1998), Royal Soc. Arts (London, life), Composers, Authors and Artists Am. (nat. bd. dirs. 1981-90, 1st pl. award 1982, 84, 86), Soc. Illustrators, Burr Artists (bd. dirs.), Catharine Lorillard Wolfe Art Club (pres. 1978-81, bd. dirs., sculpture chmn., Creative Hands award 1987, Artist of Yr. 1985, tour U.S. Mus., Colls., 1996—), Nat. League Am. Pen Women (pres. N.Y.C. br. 1981-84, Manhattan-N.Y.C. br. 1990-94, 96-98, Woman of Achievement award 1988), Wellesley Coll. Club (pres. S.I.), Kappa Kappa Gamma (Woman of Achievement award 1978). Episcopalian. Avocations: jewelry design, snorkeling, travel. Home: 282 Douglas Rd Staten Island NY 10304-1526

NELSON, CARL ROGER, retired lawyer; b. Gowrie, Ia., Dec. 26, 1915; s. Carl Helge and Inez Olivia (West) N.; m. Elizabeth Boswell Campbell, Apr. 27, 1946; children: Thomas C., Nancy L. AB, Grinnell Coll., 1937; MA, Columbia, 1938, LLB, 1941. Bar: N.Y. 1941, D.C. 1947, U.S. Supreme Ct. 1947. Law clk. to Chief Justice Stone, 1941-42; Washington asso. firm Root, Ballantine, Harlan, Bushby & Palmer, 1946-51; mem. firm Purcell & Nelson, Washington, 1951-80, Reavis & McGrath, 1980-83, Nelson Thurston Jones & Blouch, 1984-86. Mem. Adminstrv. Conf. U.S., 1967-73 Served to capt. AUS, 1942-46. Fellow Am. Bar Found.; mem. ABA (mem. ho. dels. 1964-66, mem. coun. 1960-66, chmn. sect. adminstrv. law 1963-64), Mediation Panel U.S. Ct. Appeals (D.C. cir.), Chevy Chase (Md.) Club, Lawyers Club (Washington), Met. Club (Washington), Phi Beta Kappa. Mem. United Ch. of Christ.

NELSON, CHARLES A. physicist, educator; b. Chadron, Nebr., Oct. 11, 1943; s. Arnold W. and Martha J. (Brackman) N.; m. Nancy Kneller, May 21, 1988; 4 children. BS in Engring. Physics, U. Colo., 1965; PhD in Theoretical Physics, U. Md., 1968. Rsch. assoc. City Coll. CUNY, N.Y.C., 1968-70; cons. Ctr. for Particle Theory, U. Tex., Austin, 1970-72; rsch. assoc. La. State U., Baton Rouge, 1970-72, Nat. Bur. Stds., Gaithersburg, Md., 1972-73; prof. physics SUNY at Binghamton, 1973—. Vis. scientist Fermilab, Batavia, Ill., 1980-81, Kyoto U., Japan, 1981. Author 90 sci. papers. Grantee NSF, 1978-81, U.S. Dept. Energy, 1982—. Univ. Excellence Rsch. award, 2000. Mem. Am. Phys. Soc. Office: SUNY Binghamton Dept Physics Binghamton NY 13902-6016 E-mail: cnelson@binghamton.edu.

NELSON, CHARLES ARTHUR, publisher, author; b. Berwyn, Ill., Dec. 21, 1922; s. Arthur A.R. and Florence Dorothy (Lagergren) N.; m. Anne Ballou Higgins, July 1946; children: Christopher, Janet, Colin, Edward. BA, St. John's Coll., Annapolis, Md., 1947. Dir. liberal arts program, humanities lectr. U. Chgo., 1947-52; exec. dir. Am. Found. For Polit. Edn., Chgo., 1947-56; sr. cons. Cresap, McCormick & Paget, N.Y.C., 1956-58; pres. Nelson Assocs., 1958-68; prin. Peat Marwick Mitchell & co., 1968-83; pub. Croton-Cortlandt Gazette, Croton-on-Hudson, 1986—. Author: Developing Responsible Public Leaders, 1963; co-author: The University, The Citizen, & World Affairs, 1956, Financial Management for the Arts, 1975, Ratio Analysis in Higher Education, 1980, Ethics, Leadership and the Bottom Line, 1991, Scott Buchanan: A Centennial Appreciation of His Life and Work, 1995, Stringfellow Barr: A Centennial Appreciation of His Life and Work, 1997, Radical Visions, 2001; contbr. articles to jours. Chmn. bd. Exec. Council on Fgn. Diplomats, N.Y.C.; trustee St. John's Coll., Annapolis, Md., Santa Fe, 1952-91, chmn. bd., 1978-83. Mem.: Asian and Western Studies Initiative (pres. 1997—99). Democrat. Home and Office: Bay Woods Apt 609 Bembe Beach Rd Annapolis MD 21403

NELSON, CHARLOTTE BOWERS, public administrator; b. Bristol, Va., June 28, 1931; d. Thaddeus Ray and Ruth Nelson (Moore) Bowers; m. Gustav Carl Nelson, June 1, 1957; children: Ruth Elizabeth, David Carl, Thomas Gustav. BA summa cum laude, Duke U., 1954; MA, Columbia U., 1961; MPA, Drake U., 1983. Instr. Beaver Coll., 1957-58, Drake U., Des Moines, 1975-82; office mgr. LWV of Iowa, 1975-82; exec. asst. Iowa Dept. Human Svcs., 1983-85; exec. dir. Iowa Commn. on Status of Women Dept. Human Rights, 1985—. Bd. dirs., pres. LWV, Beloit, Wis., 1960-74; bd. dirs. LWV, Des Moines, 1974-82, Westminster House, Des Moines, 1988-97, pres. 1996-97. Recipient Gov.'s Golden Dome award as Leader of the Yr., 2002; named Visionary Woman, Young Women's Resource Ctr., 1994. Mem. Am. Soc. Pub. Adminstrn. (mem. exec. coun. 1984-92, 98-99, past pres., Mem. of Yr. 1993), Phi Beta Kappa, Pi Alpha Alpha. Home: 1141 Cummins Cir Des Moines IA 50311-2113 Office: Human Rights Dept Lucas State Office Bldg Des Moines IA 50319-0001 E-mail: charlotte.nelson@dhr.state.ia.us, nelson514@aol.com.

NELSON, CLARA SINGLETON, human resources consultant; b. Union Ridge, Tenn., Apr. 10, 1935; d. Ernest Caldwell and Willie Emma (Hord) Singleton; m. Joe Edward Nelson, July 26, 1953; children: Drexel Edward, Dorissia Lynett. Student, Tenn. State U., 1961-62, Middle Tenn. State U., 1984; AS, Motlow Coll., 1978; BS in Edn. with highest honors, U. Tenn., Knoxville, 1991. Cert. personnel specialist. Sec., adminstrv. asst. Bedford County Sch., Shelbyville, Tenn., 1957-64; sec., personnel asst. Aro, Inc., Arnold Air Force Sta., 1964-71; mem. pub. rels. staff, job interviewer Employment Security, Shelbyville, 1971-81; mgr. employment EEO Calspan Corp., Arnold Air Force Sta., 1981-94; with Micro Craft Tech., 1994-95; employment and recruiting mgr. Sverdrup Tech., 1995-97; pvt. practice human resource cons., 1998—. Cons. dir. Career Devel. Workshops, Shelbyville. Mem. adv. bd. Tenn. Area Vocat. Sch., Shelbyville, 1979—; chmn. adv. commn. Equal Employment Opportunity, 1983—, chmn. employer com. Tullahoma Job Svc., Tenn., 1985—; mem. Patrons Coun. Argie Cooper Libr., Shelbyville; trustee Motlow Coll. Found.; former mem. Shelbyville Regional Planning Commn. Recipient cert. of appreciation ARC, 1985. Mem. Am.

Mgmt. Assn., Highland Rim Human Resources Mgmt. Assn. (treas. 1983-84, 87, sec. 1988, 94, chair program com. 1989, 1994—, pres. 1998-2000), Nat. Assn. Female Execs. (network dir. 1985, charter), Nat. Mgmt. Assn., Nat. Assn. Bus. and Profl. Women's Clubs, Inc. (charter; chair membership 1991-93), Am. Assn. Affirmative Action, Tenn. State U. Cluster (chmn. com. 1984—), Better Homes and Gardens Shelbyville Club. Methodist. Avocations: reading, gardening, writing. Home and Office: 105 Sun Cir Shelbyville TN 37160-2519

NELSON, CRAIG ALAN, management consultant; b. San Rafael, Calif., July 11, 1961; s. Kenneth Alfred and Anne Catherine (Laurie) N. BS in Fin., San Diego State U., 1984. Loan assoc. Union Bank, San Diego, 1984-85, comml. loan officer, 1985-86, corp. banking officer, 1986-87, asst. v.p., 1987-89, v.p. corp. banking, 1989-93; v.p. Alexander & Alexander, 1993-95; sr. assoc. Goreham-Moore & Assocs., 1995-98; v.p. Sedgwick Tech. Group Sedgwick of Calif., Inc., 1998; v.p., dir. tech. Marsh Inc., La Jolla, Calif., 1998—; regional v.p. Comerica Tech. Banking Group, San Diego. V.p. Sedgwick Tech. Group, 1997. Corp. recruiter United Way, San Diego, 1988; community group chair San Diego chpt. Am. Cancer Soc., 1989; mem. com. Juvenile Diabetes Assn.; bd. dirs. San Diego State Found., 1989—; pres. Am. Lung Assn., San Diego and Imperial counties, San Diego State U. Athletic Found. Mem. San Diego State U. Young Alumni Assn. (pres. 1988-89, bd. dirs. emeritus 1989). Home: 1233 San Dieguito Dr Encinitas CA 92024-5116 Office: Comerica Tech Group 11512 El Camino Real Ste 350 San Diego CA 92130

NELSON, CYNTHIA KAYE, information security analyst; b. Kearney, Nebr., May 8, 1949; d. LeRoy J. and W. Eileen (Schmidt) Wacker; m. James C. Nelson (div. 1987); children: Alexis Ann, Whitney Eileen. BA, U. No. Iowa, 1971; postgrad., No. Ill. U., 1973. Cert. tchr., Ill., Mo. Tchr. Dixon (Ill.) Pub. Schs., 1972-74, Maplewood (Mo.)-Richmond Heights Sch. Dist., 1974-75; counselor Mo. Bus. Men's Clearing House, St. Louis, 1975-76; dir. edn. Deltex Co., Naperville, Ill., 1982-84; trainer Electronic Data Systems Co., LaGrange, 1985-86; learning technologist Bellcore Tng. and Edn. Ctr., Lisle, 1988-90; sr. tech. tng. engr. Fujitsu Network Comm., Raleigh, N.C., 1990-98; sr. network engr. Signal Corp., 1998-2000; network design engr. Nortel Networks, 2000—01; info. tech. security infrastructure engr. Northrop Grumman, 2002—. Mem. ASTD, AAUW, Internat. Soc. of Performance and Improvement, Alpha Chi Omega, Beta Sigma Phi. Republican. Lutheran. Home: 7404 Rainwater Rd Raleigh NC 27615-3743 Office: 4200 Wake Forest Rd Raleigh NC 27668-9700 E-mail: cknelson@aol.com., cknelsoll@email.usps.gov.

NELSON, DARRELL WAYNE, university administrator, scientist; b. Aledo, Ill., Nov. 28, 1939; s. Wayne Edward and Olive Elvina (Peterson) N.; m. Nancyann Hyer, Aug. 27, 1961; children: Christina Lynne, Craig Douglas. BS in Agriculture, U. Ill., 1961, MS in Agronomy, 1963; PhD in Agronomy, Iowa State U., 1967. Cert. profl. soil scientist. Div. chief U.S. Army Chem. Corps., Denver, 1967-68; asst. prof. Purdue U., West Lafayette, Ind., 1968-73, assoc. prof., 1973-77, prof. agronomy, 1977-84; dept. head U. Nebr., Lincoln, 1984-88, dean for agr. rsch. and dir. Nebr. Agrl. Experiment Sta., 1988—. Cons. U.S. EPA, Washington, 1977-79, Ind. Bd. of Health, Indpls., 1977-83, Eli Lilly Co., Indpls., 1976. Editor: Chemical Mobility and Reactivity in Soils, 1983. Served to capt. U.S. Army, 1967-68. Fellow AAAS, Am. Soc. Agronomy (bd. dirs., pres.-elect, pres. 2001, CIBA-Geigy award 1975, Agronomic Achievement award 1983, Environ. Quality Rsch. award 1985), Soil Sci. Soc. Am. (bd. dirs., pres. elect 1992, pres. 1993, past. pres. 1994); mem. Internat. Soil Sci. Soc., Lions Lodge (treas. 1980-83, Lafayette, Ind. chpt.). Presbyterian. Avocations: fishing, skiing, jogging. Office: Univ of Nebr Agrl Rsch Divsn Lincoln NE 68583-0704 E-mail: dnelson1@unl.edu.

NELSON, DAVID ALDRICH, judge; b. Watertown, N.Y., Aug. 14, 1932; s. Carlton Low and Irene Demetria (Aldrich) Nelson; m. Mary Dickson, Aug. 25, 1956; 3 children. AB, Hamilton Coll., 1954; postgrad., Cambridge U., Eng., 1954—55; LLB, Harvard U., 1958. Bar: Ohio 1958, N.Y. 1982. Atty.-advisor Office of the Gen. Counsel, Dept. of the Air Force, 1959—62; assoc. Squire, Sanders & Dempsey, Cleve., 1958—67, ptnr., 1967—69, 1972—85; judge U.S. Ct. Appeals (6th cir.), Cin., 1985—99, sr. judge, 1999—. Gen. counsel U.S. Post Office Dept., Washington, 1969—71; sr. asst. postmaster gen., gen. counsel U.S. Postal Svc., Washington, 1971; nat. coun. Ohio State U. Coll. Law, 1988—98. Trustee Hamilton Coll., 1984—88. Served to maj. USAFR, 1959—69. Recipient Benjamin Franklin award, U.S. Post Office Dept., 1969; scholar Fulbright, 1954—55. Fellow: Am. Coll. Trial Lawyers; mem.: Cin. Bar Assn., Ohio Bar Assn., Fed. Bar Assn., Emerson Lit. Soc., Ct. of Nisi Prius (sgt. emeritus), Phi Beta Kappa. Office: US Ct Appeals 6th Cir Potter Stewart US Ct House 5th and Walnut St Cincinnati OH 45202-3988

NELSON, DAVID EVAN, performing arts educator, director; b. Bellefonte, Pa., Oct. 6, 1966; m. Mary Frances Deldin, June 13, 1998; children: Michaela. BA, So. Conn. State U., 1988; MusM, U. of Conn., 1992. Music tchr. Ezra Acad., Woodbridge, Conn., 1993—94; tchr. Mooreland Hill Sch., Kensington, 1994—98; computer dept. buyer The Bookstore at the U. of Mont., Missoula, Mont., 1998—2000; tchr. Casady Sch., Okla. City, Okla., 2000—01; dir. of performing arts Avon Old Farms Sch., Avon, Conn., 2001—. Cantor The Cathedral of St. Joseph, Hartford, Conn., 1997—98, St. Francis Ch., Missoula, Mont., 1998—2000; pvt. music tchr., New Britain, Conn., 1992—98, Missoula, Mont., 1998—2000; bass singer Conn. Choral Artists, New Britain, Conn., 1989—95; chorister Conn. Opera, Hartford, Conn., 1994—95. Sect. leader South Congl. 1st Bapt. Ch., New Britain, Conn., 1989—96, dir. children's choir, 1989—96. Recipient The Richard Coakley Acting award, So. Conn. State U. Theater Dept., 1986, Choir award for Excellence, So. Conn. State U. Music Dept., 1987, 1988. Mem.: Conn. Music Union, Actor's Equity, Music Educator's Nat. Conf., Conn. Music Educator's Assn. Conservative. Roman Catholic. Office Fax: 860-404-4135. E-mail: nelsond@avonoldfarms.com.

NELSON, DAVID HERMAN, biologist, educator, researcher; b. Houston, Mar. 28, 1943; s. John Edward and Dorothy Ann (Lindemann) Eaves; m. Cynthia Hood Scardamalia, Sept. 4, 1999; children: Amy Elizabeth, David Scott. BA, Baylor U., 1966, MA, 1968; PhD, Mich. State U., 1974. Predoctoral fellow Savannah River Ecology Lab., Aiken, S.C., 1970-73, rsch. assoc., 1975-77; asst. prof. biology Adrian (Mich.) Coll., 1973-75, U. South Ala., Mobile, 1977-80, assoc. prof. biology, 1981—. Contbr. articles to profl. jours. Recipient Roosevelt Meml. award Am. Mus. Natural History, 1970; predoctoral fellow AEC, 1970-73; rsch. grantee NSF, 1974, Ala. Dept. Conservation, 1990-99, U.S. Fisheries and Wildlife Svc., 1995-97. Mem. Ecol. Soc. Am., Am. Inst. Biol. Scis., Am. Soc. Ichthyologists and Herpetologists, Southwestern Assn. Naturalists, Ala. Acad. Scis., Soc. Study Amphibians and Reptiles, Herpetologists League, Sigma Xi. Baptist. Home: 306 Belrose Ave Daphne AL 36526-4612

NELSON, DAVID K. lawyer; b. Baton Rouge, Sept. 9, 1959; s. Robert E. Jr. and Helen C. Nelson; m. Desiree Vila, May 16, 1981; children: David K. Jr., Danny, McKenzie. BS, La. State U., 1982, JD, 1985. Bar: La. 1985. Ptnr. Kean, Miller, Hawthorne, D'Armond, McCowan & Jarman, Baton Rouge, 1989—. Bd. dirs., atty. La. Coun. on Child Abuse, Baton Rouge, 1993-94; instr. Nat. Inst. Trial Advocacy for Gulf Coast Regional Program, Loyola, New Orleans, 1993-99, La. State U. Trial Advocacy Program, Baton Rouge, 1993-97; tech. presenter for Internat. Tech. Corp., Ann. Indsl. Hygiene Conf., 1993. Pres. Round Oak Homeowners Assn., Baton Rouge, 1989-90; legal coord. Baton Rouge H.S. and Baker High Mock Trial, 1989-90; mock trial coord. Cath. H.S., 1999—; lectr. La. Assn. Educators, Baton Rouge, 1990—; pres. St. Jude the Apostle Sch. Bd., 2000—. Mem. ABA, La. Bar Assn., La. Assn. Def. Counsel, Baton Rouge Bar Assn. Office: Kean Miller Hawthorne D Armond McCowan & Jarman LLP One American Pl 22nd Fl Baton Rouge LA 70825

NELSON, DAVID LEON, foundation administrator, lawyer, accountant; b. Lubbock, Tex., Nov. 25, 1944; s. Edmund Leon and Emma Leata Nelson; m. Martie Sue Lowry, Aug. 28, 1967; children: Amy LaVerne, Rachel Ann. BBA, Tex. Tech. U., 1967; JD, So. Meth. U., Dallas, 1970. CPA; bar: Tex. 1970. Capt., judge adv. USMC, Okinawa, 1971—73; mem. tax staff Ernst & Young, Houston, 1974—81, tax ptnr., 1981—91; v.p., grant dir. Houston Endowment Inc., 1991—. Chair legis. com. Conf. SW Founds., Dallas, 1993—97; mem. planning com., spkr. ann. non-profit orgns. inst. U. Tex. Sch. Law, Austin, 1983—; participant joint civilian orientation conf. Dept. Def., Washington, 1999. Contbr. articles to profl. jours. Bd. dirs. Cystic Fibrosis, Houston, 1981—82. Capt. USMC, 1971—73. Mem.: ABA, Am. Inst. CPAs, Naval Order U.S., Def. Orientation Conf. Assn., Houston Club. Avocations: travel, reading military novels, 50's and 60's music. Office: Houston Endowment Inc 600 Travis St Ste 6400 Houston TX 77002

NELSON, DAVID LEONARD, process management systems company executive; b. Omaha, May 8, 1930; s. Leonard A. and Cecelia (Steinert) N.; m. Jacqueline J. Zerbe, Dec. 26, 1952; 1 child, Nancy Jo. BS, Iowa State U., 1952. Mktg. adminstr. Ingersoll Rand, Chgo., 1954-56; with Accuray Corp., Columbus, Ohio, 1956-87, exec. v.p., gen. mgr., 1967, pres., 1967-87, chief exec. officer, 1970-87; pres. process automation bus. unit Combustion Engring., Inc., 1987-90; pres. bus. area process automation Asea Brown Boveri, Stamford, Conn., 1990-91, v.p. customer satisfaction Ams. region, 1991-93, v.p. customer support Ams. region, 1994-95; chmn. bd. dirs. Herman Miller Inc., Zeeland, Mich., 1995-2000, counsel, 2000—. Patentee in field. Served to capt. USMCR, 1952-54. Mem. IEEE, Instrument Soc. Am., Newcomen Soc. N.Am., Tau Beta Pi, Phi Kappa Phi, Phi Eta Sigma, Delta Upsilon. Home: 1113 Roundhouse Ln Alexandria VA 22314-5935

NELSON, DAVID LOREN, geneticist, educator; b. Washington, June 25, 1956; s. Erling Walter and Marlys Joan (Jorgenson) N.; m. Claudia Jane Hackbarth, July 31, 1982; children: Jorgen William, Erik Alexander. BA, U. Va., 1978; PhD, MIT, 1984. Staff fellow NIH, Bethesda, Md., 1985-86; sr. assoc. Baylor Coll. Medicine, Houston, 1986-89, instr., 1989-90, asst. prof., 1990-94, assoc. prof., 1994-99, prof., 1999—. Dir. Human Genome Ctr., 1995-96. Editor: Genome Data Base, 1992-2000; assoc. editor Genomics, 1994— Achievements include development of Alu PCR; discovery of fragile X syndrome gene (FMR-1), new form of genetic mutation (simple repeat expansion); identification of gene defects in Lowe Syndrome and Incontinentia Pigmenti. Office: Baylor Coll Dept Medicine Molecular & Human Genetics 1 Baylor Plz Houston TX 77030-3411 E-mail: nelson@bcm.tmc.edu.

NELSON, DAVID ROBERT, physics educator; b. Stuttgart, Federal Republic of Germany, May 9, 1951; came to U.S., 1953; s. Robert Charles and Faye Scott (Abernethy) N.; m. Patricia Schneider, Dec. 30, 1975; children: Meredith, Leigh, Christopher David, Peter Charles. AB, Cornell U., 1972, MS, 1974, PhD, 1975; MA (hon.), Harvard U., 1980. Jr. fellow Harvard Soc. Fellows, Cambridge, Mass., 1975-78; assoc. prof. physics Harvard U., 1978-80, prof., 1980-91, Mallinckrodt prof. physics, 1992-97, prof. applied physics, 1997—. Cons. IBM, Yorktown Heights, N.Y., 1976-82, Mitre Corp., Bedford, Mass., 1985—, AT&T Bell Labs., Murray Hill, N.J., 1988—, Exxon Rsch. & Engring., 1994-95. Author: Defects and Geometry in Condensed Matter Physics, 2002; co-author: Phase Transitions and Critical Phenomena, Vol. 7, 1983; co-author, editor: Statistical Mechanics of Membranes and Interfaces, 1989. A.P. Sloan Found. fellow, 1979-83, MacArthur Found. Prize fellow, 1984-89, Guggenheim fellow, 1993-94; recipient award for initiatives in rsch. NAS, 1986, Ledlie prize, 1995. Fellow Am. Phys. Soc., Harvard Soc. Fellows (sr.); mem. APS, AAAS, NAS, Am. Acad. Arts and Scis. Office: Harvard U Dept Physics Cambridge MA 02138

NELSON, DEBRA L. consultant for non-profit organizations; b. Williston, N.D., Sept. 14, 1953; d. Duane Robert Leroy and Ida M. (Lester) Evanson; m. Kenneth E. Nelson, Nov. 8, 1975; children: Brian Paul, Brent Allen. BS in Secondary Edn., Minot State U., 1975. Classroom instr. Donnybrook (N.D.) H.S., 1976-82, Dickinson (N.D.) H.S., 1982-83; mgr. B. Dalton Bookseller, Dickinson, 1983-88; traffic safety coord. City of Dickinson, 1988-93; prevention and traffic safety coord. Cmty. Action and Devel., Dickinson, 1993-98; state and fed. hwy. safety cons. State N.D. Dept. Transp./Nat. Hwy. Traffic Safety Adminstrn., Bismarck, N.D. and Denver, 1998—; owner, mgr. DLN Consulting, Inc., Dickinson, N.D. Editor: (manuals) N.D. Cmty. Traffic Safety Program Manual, 1996, N.D. Safe Cmtys. Coords. Handbook, 1998, 2000. Adult coord. Teen Action Group, 1990-2000; bd. dirs. children's svcs. coord. com., Dickinson, 1993-99, Sunrise Youth Bur., Dickinson, 1998-99; mem. City of Dickinson Traffic Commn., 1994-97, N.D. Safety Belt Coalition, 1989-93, N.D. Children's Caucus, 1996-99. Recipient N.D. Gov.'s Hwy. Safety award, Bismarck, 1998, Gold Belt award N.D. Safety Belt Coalition, 1993. Mem. AAUW, Roughrider Country Kiwanis (fellow, bd. dirs. 1992-97, pres. 2001, chmn. orientation com. 1989—, Builders award 1996). Avocations: volunteering with Boy Scouts Am., reading, gardening, concerts, plays, sporting events. Home and Office: 130 7th Ave W Dickinson ND 58601-5013

NELSON, DENNIS LEE, finance educator; b. Randall, Minn., Nov. 4, 1929; s. George Otto and Emma Ida (Schwanke) N.; m. Joyce Marie Prozinski, Aug. 25, 1956; children: Constance, Kristin, Norma Joan. BS, St. Cloud State U., 1954; MA, U. Minn., 1964, PhD in Econs., 1970. Prof. econs. U. Minn., Duluth, 1964—, dir. ctr. for econ. edn., 1967-71, grad. faculty, 1970—, head dept. econs., 1971-77, assoc. chancellor, 1977-88, vice chancellor fin. ops., 1987-88. Mem. faculty Westhill Coll., U. Birmingham, Eng., 1996-97; instnl. rep. for adminstrs. on Nat. Collegiate Athletic Assn., 1978-87; adminstr., vis. faculty Oxford U., Eng., 1997, Yonsei U., Seoul, 1988, Moscow U., 1978, 84. Author econ. textbooks. Recipient Disting. Alumnus award U. Minn. Mem. Duluth Blueline Club, Duluth Quarterback Club, UMD Rasmussen Fund, UMD Hoop Club, Pres. Club U. Minn. Lutheran. Avocations: gardening, writing, reading, woodworking, bridge. Home: On the Lake 21190 Forest Rd Little Falls MN 56345-4065 Office: U Minn 10 University Dr Duluth MN 55812-2403

NELSON, DON HARRIS, gas and oil industry executive; b. Phila., Mar. 18, 1932; s. Morris Daniel and Catherine (Kaplan) N.; m. Ruth Kaiser Nelson, Aug. 31, 1959 (div. 1981); children: Michael Stewart, Pamela Blair, Randolph Miles, Timothy Blake; m. Karen Fulton, Feb. 12, 1982 (div. 1998); m. Sara Louise Rothman, July 10, 1998. BA, Yale U., 1953; MBA, U. Pa., 1957. Project engr. GE, Phila., 1957-60; mgr. exploration Kaiser Francis Oil Co., Tulsa, 1960-77; CEO Sanguine, Ltd., Greenwich, Conn., 1977—. Mem. Yale Devel. Bd., 1988—; chmn. Mus. African Art, N.Y.C., 1991-94. Pres. Family and Childrens Svc. Agy., Tulsa, 1975. Capt. USMC, Korea. Mem. Am. Assn. Petroleum Geologists, Stanwich Club, Yale Club (N.Y.C.), Tulsa Tennis Club. Avocations: post-impressionistic and African art, tennis, skiing, scuba diving, golf. Home: 1121 Lake Ave Greenwich CT 06831-2748 Office: Sanguine Ltd 95 E Putnam Ave Greenwich CT 06830-5611

NELSON, DONALD ARVID (NELLIE NELSON), professional basketball coach; b. Muskegon, Mich., May 15, 1940; Student, U. Iowa. Player NBA teams, Chgo. Zephyrs, 1962-63, Los Angeles Lakers, 1963-65, Boston Celtics, 1965-76; from asst. to head coach Milw. Bucks NBA, 1976-87, also dir. player personnel; exec. v.p., part owner Golden State Warriors, NBA, Oakland, Calif., 1987-95; mem. Nat. Basketball championship teams, 1966, 68, 69, 74, 76; head coach Golden State Warriors, 1988-95, New York Knicks, 1995-96; coach Dream Team II, 1994; coach, gen. mgr. Dallas Mavericks, Dallas, 1996—. Named Coach of Yr. NBA, 1983, 85, 92. Office: Dallas Mavericks 2909 Taylor St Dallas TX 75207-4411*

NELSON, DORA GILMORE, educator; b. N.C., June 30, 1954; d. Brooks Webster and Dawn (Leach) Gilmore; m. John M. Zeigler Jr., Mar. 18, 1978 (div. Apr. 1990); children: Paul Brooks, John M. V; m. William M. Nelson Jr., July 24, 1993. BS in Zoology, N.C. State U., 1976; cert. sci., U. N.C., Asheville, 1981; MEd in Supervision and Tech., Western Carolina U., 2000. Math. tchr. Asheville (N.C.) City Schs., 1981-82; sci. tchr. St. Genevieve/Gibbons Halla, Asheville, 1982-87; asst. to admissions and devel. Carolina Day Sch., 1987-90, sci. and math. tchr., 1990-92, tech. coord., tchr. math. and sci., 1992—. Recipient Woodrow Wilson Fellowship Found. scholarship, 2001. Mem. NSTA, Nat. Coun. Tchrs. Math., N.C. Tech. Educators Assn., So. Appalachian Mineral Soc., Pi Gamma Nu, Delta Kappa Pi, Pi Lambda Theta. Avocation: natural history. Home: 17 Colonial Pl Asheville NC 28804 Office: Carolina Day Sch 1435 Hendersonville Rd Asheville NC 28803 E-mail: redeft@hotmail.com.

NELSON, DOREEN KAE, educator, mental health counselor, reserve military officer; b. Duluth, Minn., Oct. 18, 1957; d. Norman G. Nelson and Carola Gerene (Sunneli) Cooper. B Applied Scis., U. Minn., 1983; MS in Human Resources Mgmt. Devel., Chapman U., 1988; MAEd in Mental Health Counseling, Western Ky. U., 1995. Commd. 2nd lt. U.S. Army, 1983, advanced through grades to lt. col., 2001, pers. officer 62nd Med. Group Wash., 1987—88, med. pers. officer Acad. Health Scis. Ft. Sam Houston, Tex., 1989, chief adminstrv. svcs. div. Med. Dept. Ctr. and Sch., 1989—92; med. advisor Readiness Group Knox, Ft. Knox, Ky., 1992—94; counselor intern Ireland Army Hosp., 1995; mental health counselor IV Meridian Behavioral HealthCare, Inc., Gainesville, Fla., 1995—97; substitute tchr. Ind. Sch. Dist. #381, Silver Bay, Minn., 1997—2001, Title I tchr., 2001—. Lutheran. Avocation: family genealogy. Home: 31 Marks Dr Apt 13 Silver Bay MN 55614-1114

NELSON, DOROTHY WRIGHT (MRS. JAMES F. NELSON), federal judge; b. San Pedro, Calif., Sept. 30, 1928; d. Harry Earl and Lorna Amy Wright; m. James Frank Nelson, Dec. 27, 1950; children: Franklin Wright, Lorna Jean. BA, UCLA, 1950, JD, 1953; LLM, U. So. Calif., 1956; LLD (hon.) , U. San Diego, 1997, U. So. Calif., 1983; LLD (hon.) , Georgetown U., 1988; LLD (hon.) , Whittier U., 1989, U. Santa Clara, 1990, Whittier U., 1989. Bar: Calif. 1954. Rsch. assoc. fellow U. So. Calif., 1953—56, instr., 1957, asst. prof., 1958—61, assoc. prof., 1961—67, prof., 1967—, assoc. dean., 1965—67, dean., 1967—80; judge U.S. Ct. Appeals 9th Cir., 1979—95, sr. judge, 1995—. Com. to consider stds. for admission to practice in fed. cts. Jud. Conf. U.S. , 1976—79; cons. project STAR Law Enforcement Assistance Adminstrn.; select com. on internal procedures Calif. Supreme Ct., 1987—; co-chair Sino-Am. Seminar on Mediation and Arbitration, Beijing, 1992. Contbr. articles to profl. jours.; author: Judicial Adminstration and The Administration of Justice, 1973; author: (with Christopher Goelz and Meredith Watts) Federal Ninth Circuit Civil Appellate Practice, 1995. Co-chair Confronting Myths in Edn. for Pres. Nixon's White House Conf. on Children, Pres. Carter's Commn. for Pension Policy, 1974—80; pres. Reagon's Madison Trust; active Nat. Spiritual Assembly of Bahais of U.S., 1967—; bd. dirs. Dialogue on Transition to a Global Soc., Weinacht, Switzerland, 1992; bd. vis. U.S. Air Force Acad., 1978; bd. dirs. Coun. on Legal Edn. for Profl. Responsibility, 1971—80, Constnl. Right Found., Am. Nat. Inst. for Social Advancement; adv. bd. Nat. Ctr. for State Cts., 1971—76; adv. com. to promote equality for woman and men in cts. Nat. Jud. Edn. Program; bd. dirs. Pacific Oaks Coll., Childrens Sch. & Rsch. Ctr., 1996—98; adv. bd. World Law Inst., 1997—, Tahirih Justice Inst., Washington, 1998—; chmn. bd. Western Justice Ctr., 1986—; chair 9th Cir. Standing Com. on Alternative Dispute Resolution, 1998—. Named Law Alumnus of Yr., UCLA, 1967, Woman of Yr., Times, 1968, Disting. Jurist, Ind. U. Law, 1994; recipient Profl. Achievement award, 1969, AWARE Internat. award, 1970, Humanitarian award, U. Judaism, 1973, Ernestine Stalhut Outstanding Woman Lawyer award, 1972, Pub. Svc. award, Coro Found., 1978, Pax Orbis ex Jure medal, World Peace thru Law Ctr., 1975, Hollzer Human Rights award, Jewish Fedn. Coun., 1988, Medal of Honor, UCLA, 1993, Emil Gumpert Jud. ADR Recognition award, L.A. County Bar Assn., 1996, Julia Morgan award, YWCA, 1997, Samuel E. Gates Litigation award, Am. Coll. Trial Lawyers, 1999, Bernard E. Witkin award, State Bar Assn. Calif., 2000; fellow Lustman fellow, Yale U., 1977, Davenport Coll. Fellow: Davenport Coll., Am. Bar Found.; mem.: ABA (sect. on jud. adminstrn., chmn. com. on edn. in jud. adminstrn. 1973—89, D'Alemberte/Raven award 2000), Assn. Am. Law Schs. (chmn. com. edn. in jud. adminstrn.), Am. Judicature Soc. (bd. dirs., Justice award 1985), Bar Calif. (bd. dirs. continuing edn. bar commn. 1967—74), Order of Coif (nat. v.p. 1974—76), Phi Beta Kappa. Office: US Ct Appeals Cir 125 S Grand Ave Ste 303 Pasadena CA 91105-1621

NELSON, DOUGLAS CLARENCE, lawyer, consultant; b. Norfolk, Nebr., May 30, 1946; s. Clarence Nels Peter and DeLoris Ella (Kleveland) N. BS, U. Nebr., 1968, JD, 1971, MS, 1973, PhD in Resource Econs., 1981. Bar: Nebr. 1971, Ariz. 1976, U.S. Dist. Ct. Nebr., U.S. Dist. Ct. Ariz. Lectr. U. Nebr., Lincoln, 1971-73; property mgr. Northwestern Mut. Life Ins. Co., Milw., 1973-78; assoc. Rawlins, Ellis, Burris & Kiewit, Phoenix, 1978-81; pres. Douglas C. Nelson PC, 1981—. Mem. Maricopa County Flood Control Adv. bd., Phoenix, 1988-92; mem. adv. bd. Ariz. Water Resources Rsch. Ctr., 1987—; active Valley Leadership Assn., PHoenix; chmn. Ariz. Water Quality Appeals Bd., Phoenix, 1998. Recipient cert. of appreciation Am. Right of Way Assn., 1978, Hohakam Resource Conservation and Defel. Area, 1988, Prescott C. of C., 1990, Ariz. Planning Assn., 1991. Mem. FBA (pres. Ariz. chpt. 1983-84), Am. Water Resources Assn. (chmn. water law sect. 1983-87), Ariz. Agrl. Law Assn. (founder, chmn. 1982-86), Ariz. Rural Water Assn. (exec. v.p. 1984—). Home: 7525 N 21st Pl Phoenix AZ 85020-4751 Office: PMB 307 7000 N 16th St Ste 120 Phoenix AZ 85020-5547 E-mail: dcn@netwrx.net.

NELSON, DOUGLAS MICHAEL, school system administrator, educator; b. Seattle, Feb. 20, 1948; s. Donald Edgar and Helen Thomasina (Manarino) N.; m. Virginia Jude Smith, Aug. 4, 1973; children: Kourtney, Karly, Jenna. BA, Whitman Coll., 1970; MEd, U. Puget Sound, 1974; EdD, Seattle U., 1986. Tchr. history Auburn (Wash.) Sr. H.S., 1970-75; asst. prin. Pioneer Jr. H.S., Walla Walla, Wash., 1975-78; prin. Highland Middle Sch., Kennewick, 1978-80, Meridian Jr. H.S., Kent, 1980-85; asst. supt. Franklin Pierce Sch. Dist., Tacoma, 1985-89; supt. Pullman (Wash.) Sch. Dist., 1989-2000, mem. livability task force, 1998-2000. Adj. prof. Wash. State U., Pullman, 1990-2000. Pres. Wash. Sch. Admin. Polit. Action Com., State of Wash., 1996; cmty. svc. mem., bd. dirs. Pullman Cmty. Found., 1989-2000; bd. dirs. Pullman Edn. Found., 1995-2000; supt. Bend-La Pub. Schs., 2000—. Recipient Excellence in Edn. award State of Wash., 1994, Outstanding Adminstr. award Wash. State PTA Region 9, Kent, Wash., 1985, Excellence in Edn. Leadership award Univ. Coun. for Ednl. Adminstrn., 1997. Mem. Pullman (Wash.) C. of C. (pres. 1994; Mem. of Yr. 1999), Parkland-Spanaway (Wash.) C. of C. (exec. bd., pres. elect 1986-89, community growth award 1988), Northeast Washington Assn. Sch. Adminstrs. (pres. 1999), Wash. Assn. Sch. Adminstrs. (regional officer 1988-89), Future of Wash. Schs. (exec. comm. 1995-97), Wash. ASCD (outstanding educator award 1984), Rotary Club, Phi Delta Kappa (scholarship award 1985). Roman Catholic. Avocations: golf, snow skiing, reading, travel. Home: 20328 Donkey Sled Rd Bend OR 97702-2644 Office: Bend-La Pine Pub Schs 520 NW Wall St Bend OR 97701-2608 E-mail: dvnelson@bendnet.com., dnelson@bend.k12.or.us.

NELSON, DREW VERNON, mechanical engineering educator; b. Elizabeth, N.J., Oct. 11, 1947; s. Andrew K. and Myra G. (Kempson) N. BSME, Stanford U., 1968, MSME, 1970, PhDME, 1978. Research asst. Stanford U., Calif., 1971-74, asst. prof., 1978-83, assoc. prof., 1983-96, prof., 1996—; engr. Gen. Electric Co., Sunnyvale, Calif., 1975-76, sr. engr., 1977-78. Cons. in field. Co-editor: Fatigue Design Handbook, 1989; contbr. articles to profl. jours. Recipient Spergel Meml. award for Most Outstanding Paper, 32d Internat. Wire and Cable Symposium, 1984, Hetenyi award for Best Rsch. Paper Pub in 1994 in the jour. Exptl. Mechanics. Mem. ASTM, Soc. Automotive Engrs., Soc. for Exptl. Mechanics, Sigma Xi, Tau Beta Pi. Home: 840 Cabot Ct San Carlos CA 94070-3464 Office: Stanford U Dept Mech Engring Stanford CA 94305-4021 E-mail: dnelson@stanford.edu.

NELSON, DUANE JUAN, minister; b. Urbana, Ill., Nov. 19, 1939; s. Elmer Andrew and Mabel Mae (Jones) N.; m. Marlys Mavis Klaustermeier-Hawkinson, Aug. 30, 1974; children: Matthew, Joshua, Joel. BA, Wartburg Coll., Waverly, Iowa, 1961; MDiv, Wartburg Theol. Sem., Dubuque, 1965. Ordained to ministry Luth. Ch., 1966. Pastor St. Paul's Luth. Ch., Massillon, Ohio, 1966-67, Hope Luth. Ch., Indpls., 1967-69, Grace Luth. Ch., Westchester, Ill., 1977-78; sr. chaplain Minn. Rec./Diag. Ctr., Lino Lakes, 1970-75; criminal justice chaplain Luth. Social Svc., Washington, 1975-77; staff chaplain Unity Med. Ctr., Fridley, Minn., 1978-81; sr. chaplain Anoka (Minn.) Metro-Reg. Treatment Ctr., 1981—. Sec. bd. Ch. in Soc., St. Paul Synod, 1986-90; mem. specialized pastoral com., bd. for ministry St. Paul Area Synod, 1991—; mem. chaplaincy adv. bd. HHS, 1990—; program chmn. Assn. of Mental health Chaplains, Midwest states, 1973-75. Writer, producer Multi-Media presentation, Celebrate Life, 1986, Your Part in God's World, 1988, Aging: Keenagers in Prime Time, 1996, others. Pres. Coalition for Criminal Justice Reform, Washington, 1976; co-founder Pastoral Care sect. Minn. Chem. Dependency Assn., St. Paul, 1983; lectr. health care workshops; v.p. Guardian Angel Corp., St. Paul; mem. State of Minn. AIDS Steering Com., 1985-86; co-prs. MVHS Boosters, 1994-95; actor Cmty. Theater. Mem. Assn. for Clin. Pastoral Edn., Minn. State Chaplains Assn. (chmn. 1990-96, treas. 1990—, vol. prison chaplain 1989-90), Anoka County Corrections Outpatient Treatment Program, Castle Singers (pres. 1960). Office: Anoka Metro-Reg Trtmt Ctr 3301 7th Ave Anoka MN 55303-4516 E-mail: duane.nelson@state.mn.us.

NELSON, EDITH ELLEN, dietitian; b. Vicksburg, Mich., Sept. 26, 1940; d. Edward Kenneth and Anna (McManus) Rolffs; m. Douglas Keith Nelson; children: Daniel Lee, Jennifer Lynn. BS, Mich. State U., 1962; MEd in Applied Nutrition, U. Cin., 1979. Lic. dietitian, Fla. Clin. dietitian Macon (Ga.) Gen. Hosp., Blodgett Meml. Hosp., Grand Rapids, Mich.; grad. teaching asst. U. Cin., 1978-79; dir. nutrition svcs. Dialysis Clinic, Inc., Cin., 1979-88; cons. dietitian Panama City Devel. Ctr., Ft. Walton Beach Devel. Ctr., Fla., 1988-94; renal dietitian Dialysis Svcs. Fla., Ft. Walton Beach, 1989-92; cons. dietitian N.W. Fla. Community Hosp., Chipley, Fla., 1993-94, Beverly Enterprises, Panama City Beach, 1994-96, pvt. practice, Panama City, Fla., 1996—. Mich. Edn. Assn. scholar, 1958; Nat. Kidney Found. grantee, 1986. Mem. Am. Dietetic Assn., Fla. Dietetic Assn., Panhandle Dist. Dietetic Assn., Nat. Kidney Found. (coun. on renal nutrition, Fla. coun. on renal nutrition), Omicron Nu. Home and Office: 150 Grand Lagoon Shores Dr Panama City FL 32408-5132

NELSON, EDWARD HUMPHREY, architect; b. Winchester, Mass., Sept. 2, 1918; s. Richard MacDonald and Evelyn Miller (Humphrey) N.; m. Lois Whitaker Renouf, Sept. 24, 1948 (dec.); children: Susan, David, Sarah; m. Miriam P. Ketcham, Jan. 2, 1988. Grad., Lenox Sch., 1936; B.Arch., Yale, 1950. Pvt. archtl. practice, Tucson, 1953-61; sr. v.p. CNWC Architects, 1961-88, pres., 1989-94; ret., 1994. Mem. adv. com. U. Ariz. Coll. Architecture, 1984-93. Works include: design for Tucson Community Ctr. Pres. Tucson Cmty. Coun., 1969-71, Tucson Art Ctr., 1960, Tucson Housing Found., 1969—; bd. dirs. Tucson Trade Bur., 1976-91, pres., 1984, Tucson Symphony, 1977-84, Tucson United Way, 1980, NBA Tucson Housing, 2002—; trustee Green Fields Sch., 1960-74, Tucson Art Mus.; vestry St. Philips Episc. Ch., 1967-69, sr. warden, 1987-90, parish warden, 1993-94; convenor Episcopal Interparish Coun., 1990-92; mem. Episcopal Diocese of Ariz., S.W. Regional Parish; 1st Phila. City Troop, 1940—, horse cavalry, 1940-42. Served to capt. AUS, 1940-41, WWII, ETO. Decorated Bronze Star with oak leaf cluster, Purple Heart; recipient Disting. Citizen award U. Ariz., 1981, St. Philips medal St. Philips Episc. Ch., 2000. Fellow AIA (pres. So. Ariz. chpt. 1962, emeritus 1994; chmn. Ariz. fellows 1986-94); mem. Ariz. Soc. Architects (pres. 1963), Yale Club (pres. Tucson chpt. 1962, 83, dir. 1979—), U. Ariz. Pres.'s Club. Home: 2020 E 4th St Tucson AZ 85719-5114 E-mail: miriamned@dakotacom.net.

NELSON, EDWARD BLAKE, medical products executive; b. Altoona, Pa., Dec. 12, 1943; s. Edward Julius and Elizabeth Jane (Blake) N.; m. Kirsten Ravn, Dec. 12, 1964; children: Edward R., Inga Kirsten. BS in Biochemistry, Pa. State U., 1965; PhD in Biochemistry, Mich. State U., 1970; MD, U. Tex. Med. Sch., 1974. Diplomate Am. Bd. Internal Medicine. Asst. prof. pharm. SUNY, Buffalo, 1976-79; attending faculty Baylor Coll. of Medicine, Houston, 1979-89; sr. dir. Merck Rsch. Lab., West Point, Pa., 1989-94; v.p. med. R&D McNeil Consumer Products, Fort Washington, 1994—. Edit. bd. Clin. Pharmacology and Therapeutics, 1992; patentee in field. Pres. Sping Br. Sch. Bd., Houston, 1985-89. Fellow ACP; mem. Am. Soc. for Clin. Pharmacology and Therapeutics, Alpha Omega Alpha. Office: McNeil Consumer Products Co Camp Hill Rd Fort Washington PA 19034 E-mail: enelson@mccus.jnj.com.

NELSON, EDWARD GAGE, merchant banking investment company executive; b. Nashville, May 17, 1931; s. Charles and Polly (Prentiss) N.; m. Carole Olivia Frances Minton, Sept. 17, 1960; children— Carole Gervais, Emily Minton, Ellen Prentiss BA in Polit. Sci., U. of South, Sewanee, 1952. Exec. v.p. Clark, Landstreet & Kirkpatrick, Inc., Nashville, 1955-64, Commerce Union Bank, Nashville, 1968-72, pres., 1972-82, cons., 1985—, chmn., chief exec. officer, 1982-84; chmn., pres. Nelson Capital Corp., 1985—. Hon. consul gen. Japan; bd. dirw. Werthan Packaging, Consumers Ins., Franklin Industries, Trans Arabian Investment Bank, ClinTrials, Inc., Berlitz Internat., Inc. Ctrl. Parking Sys., Advocat Inc., Micro Craft, Inc., Nashville Scene; mem. 1st adv. coun. Japan/Tenn. Soc. Trustee Vanderbilt U., Nashville, 1979—, chmn. med. ctr. bd., 1984—; vice chmn. Pub. Edn. Nashville Citizens; mem. De Tocqueville Soc. of United Way. Spl. agt. U.S. Army, 1955, Japan. Mem. Belle Meade Country Club, Cumberland Club, River Club (N.Y.C.). Republican. Episcopalian. Home: 1305 Chickering Rd Nashville TN 37215-4521 Office: Nelson Capital Corp 3401 W End Ave Ste 300 Nashville TN 37203-1085

NELSON, EDWARD SHEFFIELD, lawyer, former utility company executive; b. Keevil, Ark., Feb. 23, 1941; s. Robert Ford and Thelma Jo (Mayberry) N.; m. Mary Lynn McCastlain, Oct. 12, 1962; children: Cynthia, Lynn (dec.), Laura. BS, U. Cen. Ark., 1963; LLB, Ark. Law Sch., 1968; JD, U. Ark., 1969. Mgmt. trainee Ark. La. Gas Co., Little Rock, 1963-64, sales engr., 1964-67, sales coordinator, 1967-69, gen. sales mgr., 1969-71, v.p., gen. sales mgr., 1971-73, pres., dir., 1973-79, pres., chmn., chief exec. officer, 1979-85; ptnr., chmn. bd., chief exec. officer House, Wallace, Nelson & Jewel, Little Rock, 1985-86; pvt. practice law, 1986—; of counsel Jack, Lyon & Jones, P.A., 1991—. Bd. dirs. Fed. Res. Mem. N.G., 1957-63, Fellowship Bible Ch.; bd. dirs. U. Ark., Little Rock, vice chmn. bd. visitors, 1981; bd. dirs. Philander Smith Coll., 1981; chmn. Ark. Indsl. Devel. Commn., 1987, 88; past chmn. Little Rock br. Fed. Res. Bd. St. Louis; chmn. Econ. Expansion Study Commn., 1987—; bd. dirs. Ark. Ednl. TV Found., Ark. Game and Fish Commn. Found.; founder, 1st pres. Jr. Achievement Ark., 1987-88; Rep. nominee for Gov. of Ark., 1990, 94; co-state chmn. Ark. Reps., 1991-92, nat. committeeman Ark. GOP, 1993-2000; mem. Ark. Higher Edn. Coord. Bd., 1997-99; apptd. commr. Ark. Game and Fish Commn., 2000—. Named Ark.'s Outstanding Young Man Ark. J. C. of C., 1973; One of Am.'s Ten Outstanding Young Men U.S. Jr. C. of C., 1974; Citizen of Yr. Ark. chpt. March of Dimes, 1983; Humanitarian of Yr. NCCJ, 1983; Best Chief Exec. Officer in Natural Gas Industry Wall Street Transcript, 1983; recipient 1st Disting. Alumnus award U. Cen. Ark., 1987. Mem. Am., Ark., Pulaski County bar assns., Ark. C. of C. (dir.), Little Rock C. of C. (dir., pres. 1981), Sales and Mktg. Execs. Assn. (pres. 1975, Top Mgmt. award 1977), U. Ark. Law Sch. Alumni Assn. (pres. 1980), Sigma Tau Gamma (Ben T. Laney Leadership award for leadership and achievment 2000). Fellowship Bible Ch. Office: 6th and Broadway 3400 TCBY Bldg Little Rock AR 72201

NELSON, EDWIN STAFFORD, actor; b. New Orleans, Dec. 21, 1928; s. William Jackson and Aimee (Robelot) N.; m. Patricia Amelia Miller, June 9, 1951; children— Gregory, Christopher, Cynthia, Elizabeth, Mary, Anne. BA in Media Arts, Tulane U., 2000; degree, Sch. Radio Technique, N.Y.C., 1953. Asst. dir. WDSU-TV, New Orleans, 1953-56. Adj. prof. Tulane U., 2001. Free-lance actor, 1956-62, actor, under contract to, Universal Studios, Cal., 1962-64, 72, contract with, 20th Century Fox, Calif., 1964-69; starred on TV series Peyton Place, 1965-70, Silent Force; series, 1971-72, ABC's Ed Nelson show, 1976, daytime series Capital, 1982-87. Mem. L.A. County Sheriff's Res., 1968-73, Mountain Rescue Unit, 1968-71; Pres. Univ. Calif. Polytech. Inst. Pomona Assocs., 1973-75. Served with USN, 1946-49. Named TV Father of Year, 1968; presented George award, 1968 Mem. AFTRA, SAG, Equity, Acad. Motion Picture Arts and Scis. Office: care Marvin Josephson 16 W 22nd St Fl 3 New York NY 10010-5803 E-mail: edpaedpactor@aol.com. *Consider your critics more accurate than your complimentors. Success is building on attempts that failed.*

NELSON, ELINOR S. human resources consultant, labor arbitrator; b. Mar. 12, 1953; BA magna cum laude, Marshall U., 1974; MA, U. Cin., 1976, PhD, 1980. Rschr. U. Minn., St. Paul, 1978-80; adminstr. St. Cloud (Minn.) Schs., 1980-81; prof. St. Louis U., 1981-86; human resources cons., arbitrator, mediator, fact finder The Employment Relationship, Dublin, 1981—. Office: 5146 S Forestdale Cir Dublin CA 94568

NELSON, ELIZABETH HAWKINS, public association administrator; b. Rockville Centre, N.Y., N.Y., Jan. 27, 1931; arrived in Eng., 1951; d. Harry Dadmun and Gretchen (Hawkins) N.; m. Ivan Piercy, Dec. 7, 1960 (div. 1972); children: Catherine, Christopher, Nicholas; m. Claude Jacob Esterson, July 26, 1975 (div. 1998). BA, Middlebury Coll., 1951; PhD, U. London, 1953; D (hon.), City U., London, 1994. Rsch. psychologist Mars Ltd., London, 1954-55; dir., mng. dir. rsch. unit Benton & Bowles, 1955-64; dir. Mass Observation Ltd., 1964-65; founder dir., chmn. Taylor Nelson/Sofres plc, 1965-92; chief exec. The Princess Royal Trust for Carers, 1992-95; chair coun. U. Surrey Roehampton, 1995—2001; chmn. South West London Cmty. NHS Trust, 1997—2002. Chair exec. com. wellbeing Royal Coll. Ob-Gyns., 2002—; non-exec. dir. Royal Bank Scotland, Edinburgh, 1988—97; chmn. bd. UK Ecolabelling, 1992—98; pres. World Assn. Pub. Opinion Rsch., 1990—92; coun. mem. City & Guilds, 1998—; mem. adv. com. on degree awarding powers Quality Assurance Agy., 1998—. Vice chair coun. Open U., Milton Keynes, England, 1991—2001; dir. U.S. Open U., 1998—2001; Mem. Doctors and Dentists Pay Rev. Bd., London, England, 1992—97. Decorated Order Brit. Empire, 1997; City & Guilds hon. fellow, 1993. Fellow: Market Rsch. Soc., Royal Soc. Arts; mem.: Freedom City of London, Internat. Women's Forum (bd. mem. 2001—), Forum U.K. Avocations: choral singing, opera, bridge. Home: 57 Home Park Rd London SW19 7HS England Office: WellBeing Royal Coll Ob-Gyn 27 Sussex Pl London NW1 4SP England E-mail: liznlson53@aol.com.

NELSON, ELMER KINGSHOLM, JR. educator, writer, mediator, consultant; b. Laramie, Wyo., Sept. 14, 1922; s. Elmer Kingsholm and Alice (Downey) N.; m. Jane Beckwith Oliver, Aug. 4, 1945; 1 son, Elmer Kingsholm III (Kirk). BA, U. Wyo., 1943, JD, 1948, MA, 1949; Dr. Pub. Adminstrn., U. So. Calif., 1959. Instr. psychology U. Wyo., 1947-49; psychologist, staff psychologist dept. probation Contra Costa County, Calif., 1949-51; sr. psychologist Cal. State Dept. Corrections, San Quentin and Chino Prisons, 1951-52; asst. prof. criminology U. B.C., Can., 1952-54, assoc. prof., 1954-56, head criminology div., 1953-56; warden Haney Correctional Instn., B.C., 1956-58; assoc. dir. Youth Studies Ctr. U. So. Calif., 1958-59, dir. Youth Studies Ctr., 1959-64, assoc. prof. pub. adminstrn., 1958-61, prof., 1961—, dean Sch. Pub. Adminstrn., 1971-76, prof., co-dir. Sacramento Pub. Affairs Ctr.; head Bay Area Research Center, Berkeley, 1979—; prof. emeritus U. So. Calif. Dep. adminstr. Youth and Adult Corrections Agy., State of Calif., Sacramento, 1964-65; interim exec. dir. Office Criminal Justice Planning, spring 1975; dir. Nat. Study Probation and Parole, 1976-77; chmn. task force on corrections, asso. dir. Pres.'s Commn. on Law Enforcement and Adminstrn. of Justice, Washington, 1966-67; dir. nat. study of correctional adminstrn. U. So. Calif. for Joint Commn. on Correctional Manpower and Tng., 1967-69 Co-author: Corrections in America, 1975; contbr. articles, monographs, research reports to profl. jours. Advisor on mgmt. Boys Republic, Chino, Calif., 1967—; bd. dirs., v.p. Am. Justice Inst., Sacramento; bd. dirs. Human Interaction Rsch. Inst., L.A. Recipient Disting. Alumnus award U. Wyo., 1975, Exemplary Alumni award U. Wyo. Coll. Arts and Scis., 1994; Ford Found. Travel Study grantee, 1970-71; E. Kim Nelson endowed doctoral fellowship established at U. So. Calif., 1987. Sr. fellow Nat. Acad. Pub. Adminstrn.; mem. Wyo. Bar Assn., Alpha Tau Omega, Phi Beta Kappa, Phi Kappa Phi, Psi Chi. Home: 355 St Augustine Ct Benicia CA 94510-2866

NELSON, FLORENCE ELY, civic leader; b. N.Y.C., June 3, 1931; d. Albert H. and Constance (Jennings) Ely; m. Jerry Nelson, Nvo. 21, 1964; children: Nicolos Jennings, Thomas Burr, James Pollock. Stage, screen technician various theaters, 1949-64. Design cons. Oaxaca Rest/Le Relais, Scottsdale, Ariz., 1986, Corp. Bldg. of Pinnacle Paradise Inc., 1986, pvt. residences, Scottsdale, 1986. Bd. dirs. Ariz. Mus. Sci. and Tech., Phoenix, 1984—, Ballet Ariz., Phoenix, 1985—, Scottsdale Prevention Inst., 1987—; coordinator Boy Scouts Am., Ariz., 1977—; mem. Ariz. Opera, 1985; learning leader Paradise Valley Sch. Dist., Ariz., 1987—. Named Women of Achievement Jr. League of Ariz., 1987. Mem. Charter 100 (program chair 1985-86, membership com. 1986-87, v.p. 1987-88), Scottsdale Chairwomen (co-founder), Phoenix Com. Fgn. Relations (founder), Ariz. Assn. Gifted and Talented (hon. bd. dirs. 1986, pres. 1987—), Nat. Space Soc. (bd. dirs. 1984—). Clubs: Troon Golf and Country (Scottsdale), Skyline Golf and Country (Tucson), Pinnacle Peak Golf and Country (Scottsdale). Democrat. Episcopalian. Avocations: scuba diving, bicycling, cross country skiing, joint rehab., cooking. Home: 8711 E Pinnacle Peak Rd Scottsdale AZ 85255-3517

NELSON, FLORENCE G. retired secondary school educator; b. N.Y.C., July 6, 1915; m. Benjamin Nelson (dec.); children: Carolyn, Judith, Jeffrey. BA in Sci. and Econs., St. John's U., 1936; MA in Edn., NYU, 1939; profl. cert. in secondary edn., 1963. Tchr. various secondary schs. Julia Rich H.S., Thomas Jefferson H.S., Erasmus N.J., NY, 1938—65; guidance counselor N.Y.C. Bd. Edn., 1965—76; ret., 1976. Active Grey Panthers, Miami Beach, Fla.; vol. counselor muscular dystrophy victims; mem. adv. bd. Fla. Internat. U. Mem.: N.Y.C. Ret. Tchrs. Orgn. (mem. exec. bd.), Sigma Tau Delta, Delta Mu Delta. Democrat. Avocations: reading, community service. Home: 10275 Collins Ave Miami FL 33154

NELSON, FREDA NELL HEIN, librarian; b. Trenton, Mo., Dec. 16, 1929; d. Fred Albert and Mable Carman (Doan) Hein; m. Robert John Nelson, Nov. 1, 1957 (div. Apr. 1984); children: Thor, Hope. Nursing diploma, Trinity Luth. Hosp., Kansas City, Mo., 1950; B. Philosophy, Northwestern U., 1961; MS in Info. and Libr. Sci., U. Ill., 1986. RN. Operating rm. nurse Trinity Luth. Hosp., Kansas City, Mo., 1950-53, Johns Hopkins Hosp., Balt., 1952, Wesley Meml. Hosp., Chgo., 1952-58, Tacoma Gen. Hosp., 1958-59, Chgo. Wesley Hosp., 1959-61; libr. asst. Maple Woods Campus Met. Community Colls., Kansas City, 1987-89, libr., libr. mgr. Blue Springs Campus, 1989-96; ret., 1996. Co-founder Coll. for Kids, Knox Coll., Galesburg, Ill., 1982. Nurses scholar Edgar Bergen Found., 1947; recipient Award of Merit, Chgo. Bd. Health, 1952. Avocations: swimming, walking, cross-word puzzles. Home: 7000 N Elm St Pleasant Valley MO 64068-9571

NELSON, FREDERICK CARL, mechanical engineering educator; b. Braintree, Mass., Aug. 8, 1932; s. Carl Edwin and Marjorie May (Miller) N.; m. Delia Ann Dwaresky; children: Jeffrey, Karen, Richard (dec.), Christine. BSME, Tufts U., 1954; MS, Harvard U., 1955, PhD, 1961. Registered profl. engr., Mass. Instr. Tufts U., Medford, Mass., 1955-57, asst. prof. mech. engring., 1957-64; assoc. prof. mech. engring., 1964-71; prof. mech. engring. Tufts U., Medford, 1971—, dean engring., 1980-94. Translator: (book) Mechanical Vibrations for Engineers, 1983. Recipient Career Achievement award Tufts U. Dept. Mech. Engring., 1996. Fellow ASME (centennial medal award 1980), AAAS, ASA, Nat. Inst. Applied Scis. of Lyon (medal 1988), Korea Advanced Inst. Sci. and Tech. (medal 1988), Tufts U. Alumni Assn. (medal 1991), The Vibration Inst. (bd. dirs. 1999—). Office: Tufts U Sch Engring Medford MA 02155-5555 E-mail: frederick.nelson@tufts.edu.

NELSON, FREDERICK HERBERT, lawyer; b. Ft. Bragg, N.C., Sept. 19, 1960; s. Grant H. II Nelson and Sandra J. (Dexter) Bergen. BA magna cum laude, Toccoa Falls (Ga.) Coll., 1989; JD, Stetson U., 1993. Bar: Fla. 1993, U.S. Dist. Ct. (ea. dist.) Wis. 1993, U.S. Ct. Appeals (11th cir.) 1993, U.S. Dist. Ct. (mid. dist.) Fla. 1994, U.S. Ct. Appeals (D.C., 6th, 7th, 9th, 10th cirs.) 1994, U.S. Dist. Ct. (no. and so. dists.) Fla. 1995, U.S. Ct. Appeals (2d, 3d, 4th, 5th, 8th cirs.) 1995. Rsch. asst. Stetson U. Coll. Law, St. Petersburg, Fla., 1992-93; exec. counsel Liberty Counsel, Orlando, 1993—; pres., gen. counsel Am. Liberties Inst., 1994—. Contbg. editor: The International Sale of Goods, 1994; contbr. articles to profl. jours. Bd. dirs. Cmty. Issues Forum, Orlando, 1994—. Ctrl. Fla. CLS, Orlando, 1994—. Mem. ABA (mem. bd. dirs.), ATLA (Fla. bar appellate practice & advocacy sect., Fla. bar fed. appellate practice com.), Phi Delta Phi. Avocations: scuba diving, snow skiing, sky diving. Office: Liberty Counsel 1900 Summit Tower Blvd Ste 540 Orlando FL 32810-5912

NELSON, GARY MICHAEL, lawyer; b. Mpls., July 12, 1951; s. Emery Marshal and Henrietta Margaret (Flategraff) Nelson; m. Deb Snyder; 1 child Courtney Snyder ; children: Rachel Mary, Amy Margaret. BA, Gustavus Adolphus Coll., St. Peter, Minn., 1973; JD, Harvard U., 1976. Bar: Minn. 1976, U.S. Dist. Ct. Minn. 1976. Ptnr., CEO Oppenheimer Wolff & Donnelly, Mpls., 1976-97; exec. v.p., gen. counsel, corp. sec. Ceridian Corp., 1997—. Chair corp. practice inst. Minn. Inst. Legal Edn., Mpls., 1978-93. Sec., v.p. Mpls. Girls' Club, 1978-83. Recipient Significant Contbns. award Am. Girls' Clubs Am., 1982. Mem. ABA. Lutheran. Avocations: fishing, hunting, hiking, reading. Home: 2685 Maplewood Rd Wayzata MN 55391 Office: Ceridian Corp 3311 E Old Shakopee Rd Minneapolis MN 55425-1640

NELSON, GAYLORD ANTON, former senator, association executive; b. Clear-Lake, Wis., June 4, 1916; s. Anton and Mary (Bradt) N.; m. Carrie Lee Dotson, Nov. 14, 1947; children— Gaylord, Cynthia, Jeffrey. Grad., San Jose State Coll., Calif., 1939, U. Wis. Law Sch., 1942. Bar: Admitted Wis. bar 1942. Practiced in, Madison, 1946-58; mem. Wis. Senate, 1949-58, Democratic leader, 1948-52; gov. Wis., 1958-62; U.S. senator from Wis., 1963-81. Mem. finance com., chmn. subcom. on Social Security; chmn. employment, poverty and migratory labor subcom. of human resources com.; chmn. select com. on small bus., chmn. monopoly subcom. Author: Environmental Education Act, 1970, Nat. Environmental Education Act, 1972; co-author: The National Teacher Corps, 1965. Counselor Wilderness Soc., Washington, 1981—; founder Earth Day. 1st lt. AUS, World War II. Recipient Conservationist of the Year Award, Nat. Wildlife Fedn., 1989, Only One Earth Award, Environmental Leadership Award, UN Environment Prog., 1992, 95, Presdl. Freedom medal, 1995. Mem. State Bar Assn. Wis. Home: 3611 Calvend Ln Kensington MD 20895-3154 Office: Wilderness Soc 1615 M St NW Washington DC 20036

NELSON, GEORGE DALMAN, JR. banker; b. Shreveport, La., May 28, 1950; s. George Dalman and Nell Carolyn (Querbes) N.; m. Clare deNelle Morgan, May 8, 1982; children: George D. III, Catherine, Morgan, Spencer. BA, Tulane U., 1972; MBA, Harvard U., 1974; JD, Georgetown U., 1977, LLM, 1980. CPCU. V.p., mng. dir. Querbes & Nelson, Shreveport, 1979-95; chmn. Bank One, 1995-2000, chmn. adv. bd., 2000—. Dir. La. Cos. Inc., Baton Rouge, 1980-95, Premier Bancorp Inc., Baton Rouge, 1990-95. Pres., dir. Shreveport Symphony, 1985-87; chmn. campaign United Way of N.W. La., Shreveport, 1988; chmn. Downtown Devel. Authority, Shreveport, 1988. Named Rising Young Bus. Leader Shreveport C. of C., 1987. Mem. Shreveport Club (dir. 1997-99), Shreveport Country Club, Boston Club, Cambridge Club, Rotary Club of Shreveport (pres.). Episcopalian. Avocations: golf, baseball, football, children. Home: 3315 Fairfield Ave Shreveport LA 71104-4103 Office: PO Box 5 Shreveport LA 71161-0005

NELSON, GLEN DAVID, medical products executive, physician; b. Mpls., Mar. 28, 1937; s. Ralph and Edna S. Nelson; m. Marilyn Carlson, June 30, 1961; children: Diana, Curtis, Wendy. AB, Harvard U., 1959; MD, U. Minn., 1963. Diplomate Am. Bd. Surgery, also sub-bd. bariatric and peripheral vascular surgery. Intern Hennepin County Gen. Hosp., Mpls., 1963-64, resident in gen. surgery, 1964-69; staff surgeon Park Nicollet Med. Ctr. (formerly St. Louis Park Med. Ctr.), 1969-86, pres., chmn. bd. trustees, 1975-86; chmn., CEO Am. Med Ctrs., 1984-86; exec. v.p. Medtronic, Inc., 1986-88, vice chmn., 1988—2002, also bd. dirs.; prin., owner GDN Holdings, LLC, Minnetonka, 2002—. Bd. dirs. Carlson Cos., Inc., Mpls., St. Paul Cos., Medtronic, Inc., Mpls., Advanced BioSurfaces, Inc., Itamar Med. Ltd. Bd. visitors Johns Hopkins U.; mem. deans coun. Harvard. Fellow ACS (del.); mem. AMA, Am. Acad. Med. Dirs., Am. Coll. Physician Execs., Hennepin County Med. Assn., Greater Mpls. C. of C. (chmn. 1987), Jackson Hole Group. Office: GDN Holdings LLC 301 Carlson Parkway Ste 315 Minnetonka MN 55305

NELSON, GLENDA KAY, special education educator; b. Crosby, Miss., Oct. 11, 1942; d. John and Nellie (McDonald) Jackson; m. Ralph Gordon Nelson, Nov. 26, 1964; children: Karl Christian, Andrew Jon. BS, U. Houston, 1964; MEd, Incarnate Word Coll., San Antonio, 1985. Cert. sch. counselor; lic. profl. counselor. Tchr. history Houston Ind. Sch. Dist., 1964-70; tchr. spl. edn. San Antonio Ind. Sch. Dist., 1985—. Vol. counselor Bexar County Women's Ctr.; coach Spl. Olympics, 1987-92; mem. San Antonio Conservation Soc., 1983—. Mem. AAUW, UDC, Delta Kappa Gamma. Avocations: tennis, swimming, reading, ballet, symphony. Home: 13403 Southwalk St San Antonio TX 78232-4867

NELSON, GLENIS HILLARD, software engineer, consultant; b. Knoxville, Tenn., Nov. 27, 1951; s. Fred Hillard and Martha Ann (Robertson) N.; m. Rachel Ann Kosier, Aug. 25, 1975 (div. Nov. 1981). Student, Dranglons Jr. Coll., Knoxville, 1975-77, State Tech. Inst., 1977-79. Computer specialist City of Knoxville, 1974-84; programmer, analyst Holston Valley Hosp., Kingsport, Tenn., 1983-84, C & S Bank, Ft. Myers, Fla., 1985-89; cons., 1989-90; sys. analyst Tropical Shipping, West Palm, Fla., 1990-91; software engr. Geac Software, Atlanta, 1991-97; MIS analyst III Lowes Co., North Wilkesboro, N.C., 1997-98; ind. cons., 1999—. Tchr. Knoxville Bus. Coll., 1977-79, Geac Software, Atlanta, 1991-97; cons. Maxim Group, Knoxville. Scout leader Boy Scouts Am., Knoxville, 1974-80. With USN, 1970-76, 81. Mem. Am. Legion, Data Prcessing Mgmt. Assn. State Tech. (charter). Home: 2300 Mount Olive Rd Knoxville TN 37920-4851

NELSON, GORDON LEIGH, chemist, educator; b. Palo Alto , Calif., May 27, 1943; s. Nels Folke and Alice Virginia (Fredrickson) N. BS in Chemistry, U. Nev., 1965; MS, Yale U., 1967, PhD, 1970; DSc (hon.), William Carey Coll., 1988. Staff research chemist corp. research and devel. Gen. Electric Co., Schenectady, N.Y., 1970-74, mgr. combustibility tech. plastics div. Pittsfield, Mass., 1974-79, mgr. environ. protection plastics div., 1979-82; v.p. materials sci. and tech. Springborn Labs. Inc., Enfield, Conn., 1982-83; prof., chmn. dept. polymer sci. U. So. Miss., Hattiesburg, 1983-89; dean Coll. Sci. and Liberal Arts, prof. chemistry Fla. Inst. Tech., Melbourne, 1989—, mem. coun. sci., soc. pres., sec., 1989-90, chair-elect, 1991, chair, 1992. Cons. in field. Author: Carbon-13 Nuclear Magnetic Resonance for Organic Chemists, 1972, Carbon-13 Nuclear Magnetic Resonance for Organic Chemists, 2d edit., 1980; co-author: Polymeric Materials-Chemistry for the Future, 1989, Carbon Monoxide and Human Lethality, 1993; editor: Fire and Polymers-Materials and Tests for Hazard Prevention, 1990, 1995; co-editor: Fire and Polymers-Materials and Solutions for Hazard Prevention , 2001, editor books on coating sci. tech.; contbr. articles to profl. jours. Mem.: ASTM (E5 cert. of appreciation 1985, D1 1997), Soc. Advancement of Scandinavian Study, Coun. Colls Arts and Scis., Soc. Plastics Industry (structural plastics divsn., Man of Yr. 1979), Internat. Electrotech. Commn. (U.S. tech. adv. group on info. processing equipment), So. Soc. for Coatings Tech., Ctr. Sci. Tech. and the Media (bd. dir. 1991—94), Info. Tech. Industry Coun. (chmn. plastics task group), Am. Chem. Soc. (bd. dirs. 1977—85, 1987—89, pres. 1988, bd. dirs. 1992—94), Am. Inst. Chemists (Henry Hill award 1986, 1st Nelson award Orlando sect. 1996, Charles Holmes Herty medal Ga. sect. 1998, Mems. and Fellows lectr. award 1989), Nev. Hist. Soc., Yale Chemists Assn. (pres. 1981—), Sigma Xi. Republican. Presbyterian. Avocations: travel, western U.S. history. Office: Fla Inst Tech Coll Sci & Liberal Arts 150 W University Blvd Melbourne FL 32901-6975

NELSON, GRANT STEEL, lawyer, educator; b. Mitchell, S.D., Apr. 18, 1939; s. Howard Steel and Clara Marie (Winandy) N.; m. Judith Ann Haugen, Sept. 22, 1962; children: Mary Elizabeth, Rebekah Anne, John Adam. BA magna cum laude, U. Minn., 1960; JD cum laude, 1963. Bar: Minn. 1963, Mo. 1971. Assoc. Faegre & Benson, Mpls., 1963-67; mem. law faculty U. Mo., Columbia, 1967-91, assoc. prof., 1970-72, prof., 1972-91, Enoch H. Crowder prof. law, 1974-91; prof. UCLA, 1991—. Mem. bd. legal advisors Gt. Plains Legal Found., 1978-85; vis. asst. prof. U. Mich., Ann Arbor, 1969-70, Brigham Young U., Provo, Utah, summer 1976; vis. prof. U. Minn., Mpls., 1981-82, UCLA, 1989-90; disting. vis. prof. Pepperdine U., 1987-88; vis. endowed Campbell prof. U. Mo., Columbia, 1996-98; commr. Nat. Conf. Commrs. Uniform State Laws, 1983-91; mem. West Pub. Law Sch. Adv. Bd. Author: (with Van Hecke and Leavell) Cases and Materials on Equitable Remedies and Restitution, 1973, (with Whitman) Cases and Materials on Real Estate Finance and Development, 1976, Cases and Materials on Real Estate Transfer, Finance and Development, 1981, (with Osborne and Whitman) Real Estate Finance Law, 1979, (with Leavell and Love) Cases and Materials on Equitable Remedies and Restitution, 1980, (with Whitman) Land Transactions and Finance, 1983, rev. edit., 2001, (with Whitman) Real Estate Finance Law, 1985, rev. edit., 1994, (with Leavell and Love) Cases and Materials on Equitable Remedies, Restitution and Damages, 1986, rev. edit., 1994, rev. edit., 2000, (with Whitman) Cases and Materials on Real Estate Transfer, Finance and Development, 1987, (with Browder, Cunningham, Stoebuck and Whitman) Basic Property Law, 1989, (with Stoebuck and Whitman) Contemporary Property, 1996, (with Whitman) Cases and Materials on Real Estate Transfer, Finance and Development, 1992, rev. edit., 1998; co-reporter ALI Restatement of Property-Mortgages; contbr. articles to profl. jours. 1st lt. AUS, 1964-65. Recipient award for meritorious service and achievement U. Mo. Law Sch. Found., 1974; recipient Disting. Faculty Service award U. Mo.-Columbia Alumni Assn., 1978, Disting. Faculty award, 1986, Disting. Non-Alumnus award, 1991, Rutter award for excellence in tchg. UCLA Law Sch., 2000. Mem. Am. Law Inst., Assn. Am. Law Schs. (sect. chmn. 1976-77), Am. Coll. Real Estate Lawyers, Mo. Bar Assn. (vice chmn. property law com. 1974-75, chmn. 1975-77), Order of Coif, Phi Beta Kappa, Phi Delta Phi. Office: UCLA Sch Law Hilgard Ave PO Box 951476 Los Angeles CA 90095-1476

NELSON, H. H. RED, insurance company executive; b. Herman, Nebr., June 2, 1912; m. Ruth Hansen; children: John, Steve. BA, U. Nebr., 1934, JD, 1937. Bar: Iowa, Nebr. 1938; CLU, 1948. Asst. mgr. life accident group depts. Travelers Inc. Co., Omaha, 1939-44; chmn. bd. Redlands Ins. Co., 1945—, Ins. Agts. Inc., Council Bluffs, Iowa, 1945—, Am. Agrisurance Co., Council Bluffs, 1969—, Am. Growers Ins., Council Bluffs, 1995—, Acceptance Ins., Tex., Council Bluffs, 1988—; chmn. Silverstone Group, 1997-2001, chmn. emeritus, 2001—. Chmn. Redland Group Cos. Pres. United Fund, Western Iowa council Boy Scouts Am.; bd. dirs. Nat. Scout Council; pres. Christian Home Orphanage, Council Bluffs Indsl. Found. Named to, Iowa Ins. Hall of Fame, 1997. Office: Silverstone Group 300 W Broadway Ste 200 Council Bluffs IA 51503-9099 E-mail: hhnelson@ssgi.com.

NELSON, HARLAND STANLEY, retired English educator; b. Hawley, Minn., Aug. 11, 1925; s. Hartvig and Selma Mabel N.; m. Corinne Lois Rye, Dec. 3, 1954; children: Hilary Mark, Sarah Marie, Catherine Louise. BA, Concordia Coll., 1949; MA, Wash. State U., 1951; PhD, U. Minn., 1959. Instr. English U. Mo., Columbia, 1951-53; tech. writer Honeywell Co., Mpls., 1953; pub. rels. newswriter Evang. Luth. Ch., 1953-55; instr. English U. Conn., Storrs, 1959-62; asst. prof. English Luther Coll., Decorah, Iowa, 1962, assoc. prof. English, 1963-67, prof. English, 1967-92; ret., 1992. Fulbright prof. Am. lit. U. Bergen, Norway, 1967-68, U. Innsbruck, Austria, 1972-73; symposium evaluator Iowa Humanities Bd., Grinnell, 1987; curriculum cons. Luth. Ednl. Conf., 1980-81; hon. vis. rsch. fellow Victorian studies ctr. U. Leicester, Eng., 1985. Author: Charles Dickens, 1981; contbr. articles to profl. jours. Dir. Consortium Agr. and World Hunger Luther Coll., Coe Coll., Cornell Coll., Grinnell Coll., 1981-86; congl. liaison County affiliate Habitat for Humanity, 1992—; mem. Norwegian-Am. Hist. Assn., 1985—; ch. coun., endowment com. Decorah Luth. Ch., 1986-2001, pres., 2001; bd. dirs. Decorah Betterment Assn., 1980-86. With USAF, 1944-45. Recipient Faculty Growth award Am. Luth. Ch., 1978. Mem. AAUP, MLA, Soc. Values Higher Edn., Phi Beta Kappa, Phi Kappa Phi. Democrat. Avocations: reading, golfing, theatre, travel, volunteering. Home: 507 Ohio St # 5 Decorah IA 52101-1120 Office: Luther Coll 700 College Dr Decorah IA 52101-1039 E-mail: nelsonhs@luther.edu.

NELSON, HAROLD BERNHARD, museum director; b. Providence, May 14, 1947; s. Harold B. and Eleanor (Lavina) N. BA, Bowdoin Coll., 1969; MA, U. Del., 1972. Rsch. fellow NMAA Smithsonian Inst., Washington, 1976-77; curator Am. art Mus. Art & Archeol., U. Mo., Columbia, 1977-79; registrar Solomon R. Guggenheim Mus., N.Y.C., 1979-83; exhibition program dir. Am. Fedn. Arts, 1983-89; dir. Long Beach (Calif.) Mus. of Art, 1989—. Juror Annual Art Exhibition Mus. Art, Sci. & Industry, Bridgeport, Conn., 1988, Annual Art Exhibition, Clark County Dist. Libr., Las Vegas, Nev., 1984; speaker Am. Assn. Mus. Annual Conf., Detroit, 1985, annual meeting Western Mus. Conf., Portland, Oreg., 1987, Grantmakers in Art Symposium, N.Y.C., 1986, annual meeting Western Mus. Conf., Salt Lake City, 1985; mem. adv. com. APA, Assn. Sci. and Tech. Ctrs.; panelist Aid to Spl. Exhibitions, NEA, Washington, 1986; participant Am. Legal Assn., ABA Conf., San Francisco, 1986; observer, respondent Mus. Symposium, NEA, Dallas, 1985. Author: Sounding the Depths: 150 Years of American Seascape, 1989, New Visions: Selina Trieff, 1997, Bountiful Harvest: American Decorative Arts from the Gail-Oxford Collection, 1997, For a New Nation: American Decorative Arts from the Gail-Oxford Collection, 1998, In Ye Grandest Manner and After Ye Newest Fashion, 2000, Conjunction: The Melba and Al Langman Collection, 2000, Tulips, Pomegranates and Kings: Delftware from the Collection of Benjamin F. Edwards III, 2000, Imps on a Bridge: Wedgwood Fairyland and Other Lustres, 2001. Office: Long Beach Mus Art 2300 E Ocean Blvd Long Beach CA 90803-2442

NELSON, HARRY LOUNSBURY, JR. property development and management executive; b. Mt. Kisco, N.Y., Jan. 23, 1928; s. Harry L. and Elizabeth McQueen Nelson; m. Joyce Wilson, Aug. 23, 1953; children: Anne, Nancy, Susan, Hunt. BA, Pomona Coll., 1951; LLB, U. Calif., Berkeley, 1956; cert., Harvard Bus. Sch., 1983. Atty. Adams Duque & Hazeltine, L.A., 1956-62, Nelson, Tilson & Trevithick, L.A., 1967-68, MacDonald, Halsted & Laybourne, L.A., 1968-74; CEO Almar Ltd., Rolling Hills Estates, Calif., 1974—. Author monograph: Dutch Republic and Evolution of Maritime Art, 2000. Trustee Ventura County Maritime Mus., Oxnard, Calif., 1990—; pres., bd. dirs. Marina Recreation Assn., Sacramento, 1980-84; bd. dirs. Am. Land and Devel. Assn., Washington, 1981-83; commr. Calif. Dept. Boating and Waterways, Sacramento, 2001. Cpl. U.S. Army, 1951-52. Mem. Calif. Club. Avocations: collecting maritime art, woodworking. Office: Almar Ltd 28441 Highridge Rd # 110 Rolling Hills Estates CA 90274 E-mail: almarltd@almar.com.

NELSON, HEDWIG POTOK, marketing executive; b. Detroit, Oct. 6, 1954; m. Richard Alan Nelson. BA with honors, U. Mich., 1976; MBA, Am. U., 1980. Fin. asst. antitrust div. U.S. Dept. Justice, Washington, 1979-80; fin. analyst corp. treasury Martin Marietta Corp., Bethesda, Md., 1980-81, fin. adminstr. aggregates div., 1981-83, sr. fin. adminstr. bus. devel. data systems div., 1983, mgr. fin. planning and analysis, 1983-85; mgr. mergers and acquistions M/A-COM Devel. Corp., Rockville, 1985-88; sr. analyst group fin. Marriott Corp., Bethesda, 1988-89, mgr. bus. planning, hotel div., 1989-90; mgr. planning and analysis, geon vinyl div. BF Goodrich, Cleve., 1990-91, bus. contr. molding, geon vinyl dv., 1991-93; bus. mgr. extrusions The GEON Co., 1993-96; dir. planning and analysis Elsag Bailey, Inc., Wickliffe, Ohio, 1996-98; product mgr. Saint-Gobain, Aurora, 1998-2001, mktg. mgr., 2001—. Mem. NAFE (treas. Montgomery County chpt. 1987-88). Home: 325 Middlebush Cir Akron OH 44321-2778 Office: Saint-Gobain 1199 S Chillicothe Rd Aurora OH 44202-8001 E-mail: hedwig.p.nelson@sgppl.com.

NELSON, HERBERT LEROY, psychiatrist; b. Eddyville, Iowa, June 15, 1922; s. Albert and Bessie Mae (Durham) Nelson; m. Carol Lorayne Hofert, Dec. 23, 1943; children: Richard Kent, Vicki Lurae, Thadeus Leroy, Cylda Vermae. BA, U. Iowa, 1943, MD, 1946. Diplomate Am Bd Psychiatry and Neurology. Intern Univ Hosps. of U. Iowa, Iowa City, 1946-47; resident Brooke Army Med. Ctr, Fort Sam Houston, Tex, 1947-49, U.S. VA Hosp., Knoxville, Iowa, 1949-51, Oreg. State Hosp., Salem, 1951-52, clin. dir., 1952-63; asst. prof. psychiatry U. Iowa, Iowa City, 1963-66, assoc. prof., 1966-73, prof., 1973-84, prof. emeritus, 1984—; dir. Iowa Mental Health Authority, Iowa City, 1968-82; med. dir. Mideast Iowa Community Mental Health Ctr., 1969-84. Adj prof Tulane Univ, New Orleans, 1974—77. Co-author: 4 monographs; contbr. articles to profl jours. Served as capt MC U.S. Army, 1947—49. Fellow: Am Psychiat Asn; mem.: AMA, Am Col Mental Health Adminrs, Am Asn Psychiat Adminrs, Johnson County Med Soc, Iowa Psychiat Soc (pres 1970—71, chmn subcom psychiat care 1973—77). Republican. Methodist. Avocations: gardening, fishing, woodworking, painting, travel. Home and Office: Melrose Meadows #1009 350 Dublin Dr Iowa City IA 52246 Personal E-mail: hlnelson@mehsi.com.

NELSON, HOWARD JOSEPH, geographer, educator; b. Gowrie, Iowa, Jan. 12, 1919; s. Joseph A. and Hannah (Swanson) N.; m. Betty Marie Garlick, June 18, 1944; children: Linda Ann, James Allan. BA with high honors, Iowa State Tchrs. Coll., 1942; MA, U. Chgo., 1947, PhD, 1949. Mem. faculty UCLA, 1949—, prof. geography, 1963-86, prof. emeritus, 1986—, chmn. dept., 1966-71. Author: (with W.A.V. Clark) Los Angeles, The Metropolitan Experience, 1976, The Los Angeles Metropolis, 1983. Served with AUS, 1943-46. Mem. Assn. Am. Geographers (regional councillor 1968-71), Sigma Xi. Home: 6136 Kentland Ave Woodland Hills CA 91367-1719 Office: Univ Calif Dept Geography Los Angeles CA 90024

NELSON, IRIS DOROTHY, retired guidance and rehabilitation counselor; b. N.Y.C., July 5, 1937; d. Simon and Bertha (Rapkine) N. BA, Barnard Coll., 1959; MA, Columbia U., 1964, Ed.M., 1980; postgrad., Inst. Rehab. Medicine, 1983-84, NYU, 1983-84. Cert. tchr., guidance and rehab. counselor, N.Y. Rsch. asst. to chmn. zoology dept. Columbia U., N.Y.C., 1959-64; tchr., activity therapist Psychiat. Treatment Ctr., 1964-67; tchr., guidance counselor gen., spl. edn. programs N.Y.C. Pub. Schs., 1967-77; assoc. chmn. com. on handicapped Cmty. Sch. Dist. Divsn. Spl. Edn. and Pupil Personnel Svcs., 1977-78; sch. and rehab. counselor youth employment and tng. program N.Y.C. Bd. Edn. Office Career Edn., 1978-82; Bronx Ctr. for Career and Occupl. Svcs. Office f Career Edn., 1982-83; sch. and rehab. counselor divsn. spl. edn. N.Y.C. Bd. Edn., 1984-90; sch. and rehab. counselor citiwide programs spl. edn. dist. # 75 P.S. 186, Bronx, N.Y., 1990-95; ret., 1995. Vocat. rehab. counselor Internat. Ctr. for the Disabled, N.Y.C., 1988-89. Annual cmty. sponsor West Side Cmty. Conf.; mem. alumnae adv. vocat. com. Barnard Coll., 1974-76. Mem. ACLU, Am. Counseling Assn., Am. Sch. Counselor Assn. (divsn. mem.), Am. Rehab. Counselors Assn. (divsn. mem.), Nat. Career Devel. Assn. (divsn. mem.), Assn. Religious and Values Issues in Counseling (divsn. mem.), Assn. Adult Devel. and Aging (divsn. mem.) Nat. Rehab. Assn., Nat. Rehab. Counseling Assn. (divsn. mem.), N.Y.C. Metro Chpt. Bd., Jewish Labor Com. (educators chpt.), United Fedn. Tchrs. Guidance Counselors (del. to del. assembly retiree chpt.), Women's Am. Orgn. Rehab. through Tng. (educators chpt.), N.Y. Counseling Assn. (v.p. profl. rels. 2000-01), N.Y. State Mental Health Counselors Assn. (divsn. mem.), Assn. Profl. Sch. Counselors N.Y. (divsn. mem.), N.Y. State Sch. Counselors Assn., N.Y. State Rehab. Counselors Assn. (divsn. mem.), N.Y. State Career Devel. Assn. (divsn. mem., v.p.), N.Y.C. Assn. Counseling and Devel. (bd. dirs.), Joint Coun. for Mental Health Svcs., Chi Sigma Iota (life), Kappa Delta Pi (bd. dirs. Kappa chpt.). Home: 235 W 102d St #7B New York NY 10025-8400

NELSON, IVORY VANCE, academic administrator; b. Curtis, La., June 11, 1934; s. Elijah H. and Mattie (White) N.; m. Patricia Robbins, Dec. 27, 1985; children: Cherlyn, Karyn, Eric Beatty, Kim Beatty. BS with distinction, Grambling (La.) State U., 1959; PhD with distinction, U. Kans., 1963. Assoc. prof. chemistry So. U., Baton Rouge, 1963-67, head div. sci., 1966-68; prof. chemistry Prairie View (Tex.) A&M U., 1968-83, asst. acad. dean, 1968-72, v.p. rsch., 1972-82, acting pres., 1982-83; exec. asst. Tex. A&M U. System, College Station, 1983-86; chancellor Alamo C.C. Dist., San Antonio, 1986-92; pres. Cen. Wash. U., Ellensburg, 1992-99, Lincoln U., Pa., 1999—. DuPont teaching fellow U. Kans., 1959; rsch. chemist Am. Oil Co., 1962; sr. rsch. chemist Union Carbide Co., 1969; vis. prof. U. Autonomous Guadalajara, Mex., 1966, Loyola U., 1967; Fulbright lectr., 1966; cons. evaluation coms. Oak Ridge (Tenn.) Assoc. Univs., NSF, Nat. Coun. for Accreditation Tchr. Edn., So. Assn. Colls. and Schs.; mem. regional policy coms. on minorities Western Interstate Com. on Higher Edn., 1986-88; mem. exec. com. Nat. Assn. State Univs. and Land Grant Colls., 1980-82. Contbr. articles to profl. jours. Bd. dirs. Target 90, Goals San Antonio, 1987-89, coun. of pres.NAIDA,(1993-96) Commn. on Student Learning, Wash., 1992—, United Way San Antonio, 1987-89, Alamo Area coun. Boy Scouts Am., 1987-89, San Antonio Symphony Soc., 1987-91, Key Bank of Wash.; mem. bd. dirs. assn. Western U., (1995—) mem. com. for jud. reform State of Tex., 1991; mem. edn. adv. bd. Tex. Rsch. Park, 1987-89; bd. givs. Am. Inst. for character Edn., Inc., 1988-91; mem. adv. com. Tex. Ho. of Reps., 1978; chmn. United Way Campaign Tex. A&M U. System, 1984, others. Staff sgt. USAF, 1951-55, Korea. T.H. Harris scholar Grambling State U., 1959; fellow Nat. Urban League, 1969. Mem. AAAS, Am. Chem. Soc., Tex. Acad. Sci., NAACP, Phi Beta Kappa, Sigma Xi, Phi Lambda Upsilon, Beta Kappa Chi, Alpha Mu Gamma, Kappa Delta Pi, Sigma Pi Sigma, Omega Psi Phi, Sigma Pi Phi, Phi Kappa Phi. Avocations: fishing, photography, sports. Office: Lincoln U Office of Pres PO Box 179 Lincoln University PA 19352-0999 E-mail: inelson@lu.lincoln.edu.

NELSON, J. GORDON, geography educator; Adj. prof. planning and geography, disting. prof. emeritus U. Waterloo, Ont., Can., 1998—. Recipient Massey medal Royal Can. Geog. Soc., 1993. Office: U Waterloo Dept Geography Waterloo ON Canada N2L 3G1

NELSON, JACK LEE, education educator; b. Cheyenne, Wyo., Nov. 2, 1932; s. Myron Alfred and Mary Elizabeth (Baker) N.; m. Gwen Margret Names, Mar. 13, 1953; children: Barbara Louise Nelson Vollmer, Steven Lee. BA, U. Denver, 1954; MA, Calif. State U.-Los Angeles, 1958; Ed.D., U. So. Calif., 1961. Tchr. pub. schs., Riverside, Calif., 1956-58; instr. Calif. State U., Los Angeles, 1958-59, asst. prof., 1959-63; instr. Citrus Community Coll., Glendora, Calif., 1959-63; assoc. prof. SUNY, Buffalo, 1963-68, chmn. dept., 1966-68; prof. edn. Rutgers U., New Brunswick, N.J., 1968—, Disting. prof., 1975; dean, prof. Sch. Edn. San Jose (Calif.) State U., 1986-87. Chmn. dept. sci. and humanities edn. Rutgers U., 1972-75; vis. prof. Cambridge U., Eng., 1974, 75, 79, 80, 83, 84, 85; vis. scholar U. Calif., Berkeley, 1975-76, Stanford U., 1982-83, Western Australia Inst. Tech., 1985, U. Colo., 1989, U. Wash., 1993, U. Sydney, Australia, 1994-95, Edith Cowan U., Australia, 1997; cond. editor Random House Inc., McGraw-Hill Inc., Primis Pubs.; mem. adv. coun. New World Dictionary; mem. San Diego County Supt. Com. on Tchr. Quality, 2000—. Author: (with J. Michaelis) Secondary Social Studies, 1980, (with V. Green) International Human Rights, 1980, (with Frank Besag) Foundations of Education, 1984, (with S. Palonsky and K. Carlson) Critical Issues in Education, 1990, 4th edit., 2000; contbr. numerous articles to profl. jours.; editor: Social Sci. Rsch., 1964-68, Theory and Rsch. in Social Edn., 1982-85. Mem. exec. bd. ACLU, Middlesex County, N.J., 1968-83; mem. Erie County Dem. Com., 1967-68, N.J. Gov.'s Task Force on Rehab. Edn. for Prisoners, 1970-74; mem. Highland Park Bd. Edn., N.J., 1972-75, pres., 1974-75; mem. Highland Park Hist. Commn., 1980-86; mem. nat. panel Project Censored, 1976—; mem. N.J. Rural Adv. Commn., 1992—. Robert Taft Found. grantee Inst. in Govt., 1970, 86; Inst. for World Order grantee Rutgers U., 1973— ; Rutgers U. grantee; SUNY-Buffalo grantee, 1967-68; ACLU of N.J. grantee, 1972-73; U.S. Office Edn. grantee, 1967-68; N.J. Dept. Higher Edn. grantee, 1985-86 Mem. Am. Acad. Polit. and Social Sci., AAUP (editorial bd. 1977-80, rep. nat. council 1982-85, com. on acad. freedom and tenure 1983-86, com. on legis. affairs 1992-95, 96—, exec. bd., state confs. 1996—), Am. Ednl. Research Assn., Internat. Studies Assn., Nat. Council for Social Studies, Social Sci. Edn. Consortium (bd. dirs. 1983-85), Phi Delta Kappa Home: 1360 Las Flores Dr Carlsbad CA 92008-1031 Office: Rutgers U Grad Sch Edn Rutgers U Grad Sch Edn New Brunswick NJ 08903 E-mail: Cinderjackie@netscape.com.

NELSON, JACQUELINE DUNHAM, elementary education educator; b. Catawba, S.C., Jan. 20, 1937; d. John Ervin and Jessie Gazree (Walker) D.; m. Raymond Talmadge Nelson, Nov. 20, 1967 (div. June 1970); 1 child: Ouinette Michelle Willingham. BS, Morgan State U., 1960; MA, George Washington U., 1977, EdD, 1991. Kindergarten tchr. Dept. Def., Kaneohe, Hawaii, 1962-64; tchr. reading, health educator Cleveland County Pub. Schs., Shelby, N.C., 1964-66; tchr. health and phys. edn. Prince Edward County Schs., Cumberland, Va., 1966-67; tchr. health and phys. edn., curriculum writer D.C. Pub. Schs., Washington, 1967—. Advisor Montgomery Elem. Sch., Washington, 1993-94. Author: Teacher/Student Behavior, 1991. Named Coach of Yr., Va. Intercollegiate Assn., 1966. Avocations: photography, skiing, fishing, antique collecting. Office: Maury Elem Sch 13th & Constitution Ave NE Washington DC 20002

NELSON, JAMES ALONZO, radiologist, educator; b. Cherokee, Iowa, Oct. 20, 1938; s. Joe George and Ruth Geraldine (Jones) N.; m. Katherine Metcalf, July 16, 1966; children: John Metcalf, Julie Heaps. AB, Harvard U., 1961, MD, 1965. Asst. prof. radiology U. Calif., San Francisco, 1972-74; assoc. prof. U. Utah, Salt Lake City, 1974-79, prof., 1979-86, U. Wash., Seattle, 1986-2000, prof. emeritus, 2000—. Dir. radiol. rsch. U. Calif./Ft. Miley VA Hosp., 1973—74, U. Utah, 1974—85, U. Wash., 1986—98; mem. bd. sci. advisors NeoVision, 1995—96, Oreg. Life Scis., 1995—; co-founder Circulation, Inc., 1996; mem. adv. panel on non-radioactive diagnostic agts. USP, 1984—96; mem. NIH RSN study sect., 1998—. Contbr. chpts. to books, articles to Am. Jour. Roentgenology, Radiology, Investigative Radiology, others. Capt. USAF, 1967-69. John Harvard scholar, 1957-61, James Picker Found. scholar, 1973-77; recipient Mallinkrodt prize Soc. Body Computerized Tomography, 1990, Roscoe Miller award Soc. Gastrointestinal Radiology, 1991. Fellow Am. Coll. Radiology (diplomate); mem. Radiol. Soc. N.Am., Assn. Univ. Radiology. Achievements include patents (with others) for Non-Surgical Peritoneal Lavage, Recursive Band-Pass Filter for Digital Angiography, for Unsharp Masking for Chest Films, Oral Hepatobiliary MRI Contrast Agent, non-surgical myocardial revascularization. Office: U Wash Dept Radiology Diagnostic Imaging Sci Ctr PO Box 357115 Seattle WA 98195-7115 E-mail: jimnel@mindspring.com.

NELSON, JAMES AUGUSTUS, II, real estate executive, architect, banker; b. Damrascotta, Maine, July 26, 1947; s. Robert Maynard and Margret Rebbeca (Harmision) Nelson; 1 child Jennifer Alexandria. BArch, Columbia U., 1973, MBA, 1974. Resident v.p. Citibank, N.Y.C., 1974-77; group v.p. Bank of Am., San Francisco, 1977-82; assoc. John Portman and Assocs., Atlanta, 1983-85; pres. J.A. Nelson and Assocs., L.A., 1986-88; dir. real estate planning and devel. Universal Studios, 1988-94; founder Mother Co., Hollywood, Calif., 1995. Master planner, Internat. Gateway of the Ams., San Yisedro, Calif. Author: Banker's Guide to Construction, 1978, Doing Business in Saudi Arabia, 1979. Chmn. Eco. Dev. Com., L.A. Conservancy-Broadway Iniative, Laurel Canyon Coalition, L.A.; bd. dirs. Laurel Canyon Assn., Hollywood Heritage, Hillside Fedn., L.A., Lookout Mountain Assocs., L.A.; developer Universal CityWalk Project. Recipient Innovative Design award for Universal CityWalk, Internat. Coun. Shopping Ctrs., 1994, best new home of yr. award Metro. Home, 1989, commendation and pres.'s award Hillside Fedn., 1989, 1992. Avocations: gardening, architecture. Office: Mother Co 8306 Grand View Dr Los Angeles CA 90046-1918 E-mail: motherco@aol.com.

NELSON, JAMES C, state supreme court justice; b. Idaho, Feb. 20, 1944; m. Chari Werner; 2 children. BS, U. Idaho, 1966; JD cum laude, George Washington U., 1974. Fin. analyst SEC, Washington; pvt. practice Cut Bank; county atty. Glacier County; assoc. judge Mont. Supreme Ct., 1993—. Former mem. State Bd. Oil and Gas Conservation, also chmn.; former mem. State Gaming Adv. Counsel, Gov. Adv. Coun. on Corrections and Criminal Justice Policy; liaison to Commn. of Cts. of Ltd. Jurisdiction, mem. adv. com. Ct. Assessment Program. Served U.S. Army. Office: Supreme Ct. PO Box 203001 Helena MT 59620*

NELSON, JAMES CARMER, JR. writer, advertising executive; b. Denver, Nov. 10, 1921; s. James Carmer and Helen (McClelland) N.; m. Mary-Armour Ransom, Sept. 9, 1950; children— James Carmer III, Marie-Louise Nelson Graves, Jeffrey Armour, Sophia McClelland (dec.), Rebecca McClelland Nelson Sylla. AB, Yale, 1943. Mktg. editor Bus. Week mag., N.Y.C., 1946-48, illustration editor, 1948-52; freelance author Sonoma, Calif., 1952-57; copy chief Hoefer, Dieterich & Brown, Inc., San Francisco, 1957-59, v.p., creative dir., 1959-66, exec. v.p., 1966-76, pres., 1976-79, vice chmn., 1979-80; ptnr. John H. Hoefer & Assocs., 1972—82; vice chmn. Chiat/Day/Hoefer, 1980; pvt. advt. cons., 1980—87. Bd. dirs. McKinney, Inc., Phila.; instr. Golden Gate Coll., San Francisco, 1958-59, Nat. Advt. Rev. Bd., 1971-75. Author: The Trouble With Gumballs, 1957, Great Cheap Wines: A Poorperson's Guide, 1977, Great Wines Under $5, 1983; contbr. articles and fiction to popular mags. Mem. Harold Brunn Soc. for Med. Research, Mt. Zion Hosp., San Francisco; bd. assos. Linus Pauling Inst. Sci. and Medicine, Palo Alto, Calif.; mem. Colony Found., New Haven; trustee Coro Found., 1965-75, Marin Art Complex; bd. mgrs. Marin County YMCA. Served with USNR, 1942-46. Mem. ASCAP. Clubs: Villa Taverna (San Francisco). Home: 649 Idylberry Rd San Rafael CA 94903-1231

NELSON, JAMES E. lawyer; b. Jan. 3, 1943; BS, U. Notre Dame, 1965; MS, U. Denver, 1968, JD, 1973. With Ball Corp., London, Singapore, 1973-82; ptnr. Schafer, Rooke & Nelson, Denver, 1983-87; from internat. counsel to v.p., gen. counsel The Gates Corp., 1987—. E-mail: jmsdgrnlsn@aol.com.

NELSON, JAMES HAROLD, health sciences administrator; b. Gosnell, Ark., Apr. 26, 1936; s. J.D. and Louise (Gann) N.; m. Betty Sue Leonard, Sept. 21, 1974; children: Amelia Rebecca, Rachel Louise. BS, Ark. State U., 1961, MS, 1969; PhD, Okla. State U., 1972. Br. chief U.S. Army Environ. Hygiene Agy., Edgewood, Md., 1972-76; from rsch. area mgr. to div. chief U.S. Army Biomed. R & D Lab., Fort Detrick, 1976-92; project mgr. applied med. systems U.S. Army Med. Materiel Devel. Activity, 1992-96, dir., 1996-2000; chief liaison office U.S. Army Med. Rsch. & Materiel Command, U.S. Army Med. Dept. Ctr. and Sch., Fort Sam Houston, Tex., 2000—. Mem. Fed. Work Group Pest Mgmt., Washington, 1977-81; chmn. equipment com. Armed Forces Pest Mgmt. Bd., Washington, 1979-83; cons. dir. engrs. Ft. Detrick, Frederick, 1976-2000; guest lectr. Acad. Health Scis., U.S. Army, Ft. Sam Houston, Tex., 1986-88. Contbr. articles to profl. jours.; assoc. editor: Jour. Am. Mosquito Control Assn., 1982-88; chmn. editorial bd.: Equipment & Insecticides-Mosquito Control, 1989. With USN, 1954-58. Recipient numerous commendations U.S. Army, Ft. Detrick, 1981-93, R&D Achievement award Asst. Sec. of the Army, 1988, Order of Mil. Med. Merit, 1992. Mem. AAAS, AMVETS, Am. Pub. Health Assn., Assn. Mil. Surgeons U.S., Am. Legion, Internat. Platform Assn., N.Y. Acad. Scis., Sigma Xi (pres. 1987-88). Presbyterian. Achievements include patent for far-forward surgical table. Home: 1315 Brook Bluff San Antonio TX 78248 Office: US Army Med Res & Materiel Command US Army Med Dept Ctr & Sch 2250 Stanley Rd Ste 334 Fort Sam Houston TX 78234-6100 E-mail: dhnelson@prodigy.net., james.nelson@amedd.army.mil.

NELSON, JAMES LINDEMANN, philosophy educator, bioethicist; b. Williamsport, Pa., Apr. 2, 1954; s. David C. and Jeanne Gormley Nelson; m. Hilde Lindemann, Jan. 18, 1986; children: Eric, Laura, Melissa, Elise Robinson, Ellen Robinson, Paul Robinson. PhD, SUNY, Buffalo, 1980; BA, Canisius Coll., 1974. Assoc. for ethical studies The Hastings Ctr., Garrison, N.Y., 1990-95; prof. philosophy U. Tenn., Knoxville, 1995-2000, Mich. State U., East Lansing, 2000—. Vis. prof. philosophy Duke U., 2001-02. Co-author: Alzheimer's: Answers to Hard Questions, 1996, The Patient in the Family, 1995; author: Hippocrates' Maze, 2002; contbr. articles to profl. jours. Summer seminar grantee NEH, 2000. Mem. Am. Philos. Assn., Am. Soc. Bioethics and Humanities, Brit. Soc. Ethical Theory (assoc.). Home: 1117 Wildwood Dr East Lansing MI 48823 Office: Philosophy Dept Mich State U 503 S Kedzie Hall East Lansing MI 48824 E-mail: jlnelson@msu.edu.

NELSON, JANICE EILEEN, paralegal; b. Worcester, Mass., Oct. 1, 1943; d. Joseph and Sally (Kosakowski) Rubler; m. Henry T. Knittel, Jr., Oct. 16, 1965 (div. 1979); children: Christie, Robin, Marcelle, Gary; m. David Nelson, Apr. 11, 1980 (div.). Grad., North High Sch., Worcester, 1961; student, Lyme Acad. Fine Art, 1985-86. Respiratory therapist St. Vincent Hosp., Worcester, 1963-65, Nassau Community Hosp., Mineola, N.Y., 1966-67, Good Samaritan Hosp., West Islip, 1968-69; campaign mgr. Former Selectman Thomas Collimore, Fairfield, Conn., 1975, Former State Senator Myron Ballen, Fairfield, 1976; respiratory therapist VA Med. Ctr., West Haven, Conn., 1980-82; med. asst. Reproductive Med. Assocs., New London, 1983-86; paralegal O'Brien & Shafner, Groton, 1986-99, Young Moore & Henderson, Columbus, Ohio, 1999-2000, Agee, Cymer et al, Columbus, 2000-2001, Squire, Sanders & Dempsey, Columbus, 2001—. Author poetry in Am. Poetry Anthology, 1986-87; artist of pastels, acrylic; photographer of landscapes, portraits; exhibited artwork at Mysic (Conn.) Art Assn. Members Show, 1987-89, Mayflower Hotel Washington, 1991; photography exhibited Duke U. Ctr. Documentary Studies, 1999, published in mags.; back stage properties Am. Musical Theatre, 1986; mem. scene study workshop Eugene O'Neill Theatre, 1993; published photographer. Mem. Rep. Town Mtg., Dems., Groton, 1987-89, Dem. Town Com., 1987-89, Ctr. for Study of the Presidency, Rep. Presdl. Task Force, 1989—, Acad. Polit. Sci., 1988-89; founding sponsor Challenger Ctr., 1990; mem. Environ. Def. Fund; founding mem. Am. Air Mus. in Britain; hospitality hostess Rep. Women's Club; elected mem. rep. Town Com., 1976, dist. leader; usher Eugene O'Neill Playwright's Conf., 1988—; mem. studio class Yale U., 1997—. John F. Kennedy Libr. hon. fellow, 1989; recipient Merit award for Photography IPA, Washington; named Juror's Asst. Curator, White House/Curator U.S. Senate. Mem. Am. Acad. Polit. and Social Sci., Internat. Sculpture Ctr., Sotheby's (charter), Nat. Trust, Folio Soc., Internat. Platform Assn., Friends of Hartford Ballet, UNA-USA, Newcomen Soc., Nat. Space Soc., Copley Soc. of Boston, World Affairs Coun., Friends of the Garde Arts Ctr., Charter Oak Cultural Ctr., Am. Film Inst., Libr. of Congress Assocs., Nat. Archives (charter). Avocations: art, literature, attending ballet and theatre. Home: 135 Georgetown Dr Apt B Columbus OH 43214-1624 Office: Agee Clymer et al 89 E Nationwide Blvd Columbus OH 43215

NELSON, JANIE RISH, hospital executive; b. Gloster, Miss., Mar. 1, 1941; d. William Hubert and Essie Dell (Davis) Rish; m. John Preston Nelson, Jr., Aug. 19, 1984. Student S.W. Miss. Jr. Coll., 1959-61, Stephens Coll., 1981— . Accredited record technician. Admissions clk. Field Hosp., Centreville, Miss., 1963-68, asst. dir. med. records, 1968-73; dir. med. records West Feliciana Parish Hosp., St. Francisville, La., 1976— . Med. records cons. Beverly Enterprises & Centreville Health Care, 1983-84. Mem. nat. adv. bd. Am. Security Council, 1984-85; mem. U.S. Congl. Adv. Bd. for La., 1985; fund raiser Republican Com., 1984. Mem. Am. Med. Records Assn., La. Med. Records Assn., Nat. Assn. Female Execs., Tumor Registration Assn. La., Miss. Sheriffs Assn. (hon.). Republican. Presbyterian. Club: Civic. Avocations: Reading; public speaking; gardening. Home: PO Box 374 Centreville MS 39631-0374

NELSON, JEANNE M. coordinator multicultural healthcare; b. Escanaba, Mich. BS in Biology, Fine Arts, Mt. Mary Coll., 1976; BSN, U. Md., Balt., 1985; MSN, Villanova U., 1990. RN, Minn. Staff nurse burn ctr. St. Christopher's Hosp. for Children, Phila., 1985-86; staff nurse emergency dept. Osteo. Med. Ctr. Phila., 1986-88, nursing edn. coord., 1988-89; emergency dept. pool nurse Chestnut Hill Hosp., Phila., 1989-90; ednl. nurse specialist Children's Hosp. of Phila., 1989-90; emergency trauma relief nurse emergency trauma ctr. Abington (Pa.) Meml. Hosp., 1991-95; faculty Meth. Hosp. Sch. Nursing, Phila., 1990-92; critical care edn. coord./CNS Cooper Hosp., Camden, N.J., 1992-95; nursing edn. specialist Mayo Med. Ctr., Rochester, Minn., 1995-97; coord. Multicultural Healthcare Alliance Mayo Clinic-Rochester/Pub. Health Svcs./Olmsted Med. Group, 1997—. Lectr. nat. nursing confs. Contbr. articles to profl. jours., chpts. to textbooks. Mem. edn. task force Nat. Emergency Nurse's Assn., 1994. Avocations: photography, Christian ministry. Home: 1121 20th St NW Rochester MN 55901-1585 Office: Multicultural Healthcare Alliance OCPHS 2100 Campus Dr SE Rochester MN 55904-4717

NELSON, JERYL L. finance educator, consultant; b. West Point, Nebr., May 10, 1964; s. James L. and Judy A. Nelson; m. Rochelle Escue; children: Emily, Angela. BS, Wayne State Coll., Wayne, 1986; MBA, U. S.D., Vermillion, 1989; PhD, U. Nebr., 2000. SBDC dir. Wayne State Coll., 1986—89, assoc. prof., 1989—. Author: (Academic Paper) Resource Dependency and Corporate Directors: A test of the Business Week Best and Worst Boards, 2001 (N.Am. Mgmt. Soc. Disting. Paper award, 2001). Dir. Wayne Childcare Bd., Nebr., 1996—2001. Mem.: Soc. for Case Rsch. (pres. 1999—2000). Republican. Lutheran. Avocation: camping. Office: Wayne State Coll 1111 Main Wayne NE 68787 Business E-Mail: jenelso1@wsc.edu.

NELSON, JILL ELAINE, nurse attorney, health care consultant, health facility administrator, instructor, researcher; b. Ashland, Ohio, Jan. 1, 1952; d. John Robert and Phyllis Rae (Williams Hardesty) N. Assoc. summa cum laude, Cuyahoga C.C., 1975; BA cum laude, Baldwin-Wallace Coll., MBA, 1993; JD, Case Western Res. U., 1999. Bar: Ohio 2000; RN, Ohio; cert. healthcare mediator, compliance profl., profl. coder. RN Emergency/Trauma rm. St. Luke's Hosp., Cleve., 1982-87; rsch. asst. div. of neurosci. Case Western Reserve U.; RN, rsch. asst. dept. Artificial Organ Rsch. Cleve. Clinic, 1975-82; coord., adminstr. rsch. Met. Health Med. Ctr. Case Western Res. U., Cleve., 1983-93, consulting asst. dir. Office of Rsch. Adminstrn., 1993-94, project dir. dept. family medicine, 1994-95, adminstrv. dir. cancer ctr. clin. trials unit, 1994-97; cons. West Hudson, Inc., Dallas, 1997; patent coord. affiliates at STERIS Corp., 1997-98; paralegal specialist Ctr. Devices Radiol. Health, FDA, 1998; intern Food & Drug Law Inst., Washington, 1998; nurse legal cons./paralegal Kremb's & Alkire LLP, 1998-99; legal intern Supreme Ct. Ohio, 1998-99; dir. corp. compliance and privacy, chmn. mgmt. engring. Comprehensive Health Care of Ohio, Inc. (EMH) Regional Healthcare Sys. , 2001—. Instr. legal nurse cons. program, divsn. bus. and tech. Cuyahoga C.C. legal nurse cons. program, 2000—; instr. Baldwin-Wallace Coll., 2002-. Assoc. editor Health-Matrix: Jour. Law Medicine. Mem. ABA, AAAS, NAFE, Am. Health Lawyers Assn., Am. Coll. Healthcare Execs., Assocs. Clin. Pharmacology, Am. Trial Lawyers Assn., Am. Assn. Profl. Coders, Am. Health Info. Mgmt. Assn., Nat. Coun. Univ. Rsch. Adminstrs., Mental Health Assn., ENA (cert. clin. rsch. coord., past pres.-elect), Inst. for Personal Health Skills, Ohio State Bar Assn., Cuyahoga County Bar Assn., Lorain County Bar Assn., Healthcare Compliance Assn., Internat. Assn. Privacy Officers, Alpha Sigma Lambda. Home: 19291 Trillium Trl Strongsville OH 44149-3146 E-mail: jillenelso@aol.com.

NELSON, JIMMIE DIRK, kinesiology administrator, educator, researcher; b. Wichita, Kans., July 23, 1962; s. Ronald Paul and Bonnie Lou (Horton) N.; m. Renda Joy Colglazier, May 27, 1989; children: Philip Alexander, Emalee Joy. BS, Mont. State U., 1984; MS in Edn., U. Kans., 1986, PhD, 1990. Tchg. asst. U. Kans., 1987-89; asst. prof. Mo. So. State Coll., Joplin, 1989-94, assoc. prof., 1994-99, head dept. kinesiology, 1992-99; chair divsn. kinesiology, assoc. prof. LeTourneau U., Longview, Tex., 1999—2001, asst. v.p. acad. affairs, prof., 2000—. Dietary and fitness and health cons. Mo. Day Care Workers, 1989—99; textbook reviewer Brown & Benchmark Pubs., Allyn & Bacon Pub., Prentice Hall Pub., Brooks/Cole Pub. Co., Benjamin/Cummings Pub. Co., McGraw-Hill Cos.; acad. editor Coursewise Pub., 1997—; reviewer minority health rsch. and edn. grant program Tex. Higher Edn. Coord. Bd., 2001. Tchr. jr. and sr. high edn. coord. 4th and Forrest Ch. of Christ, Joplin, 1989-99; tchr. Pine Tree Ch. of Christ, Longview, 1999—; vol. Spl. Olympics, 1989-2000, youth sports coach, 1998-2000. Named to, Wendy's of Mont./Mont. State U. Athletic Hall of Fame, 1994, All 20th Century Football Team, Mont. State U., 2001. Mem. Nat. Acad. Advising Assn., Nat. Collegiate Honors Coun., Soc. of Centennial Alumni Mont. State U. Mem. Ch. of Christ. Avocations: aviation, zoology, military history, jazz music, old house renovation. Home: 905 Sunshine Sq Longview TX 75601-3237 Office: LeTourneau U 2100 S Mobberly Ave Longview TX 75602-3564

NELSON, JOAN MARIE, social worker; b. Boston, Dec. 23, 1947; d. I. Joseph and Aurea E. (Franz) Guccione; m. Peter A. Nelson, May 15, 1971; children: Erik, Adam, Jennifer. BA in Psychology, Duquesne U., 1969; MSW, Cath. U., 1973; MA in Child Clin. Psychology, George Mason U., 1978. Lic. clin. social worker, Va.; diplomate Nat. Bd. Examiners in Clin. Social Work. Social worker No. Va. Tng. Ctr., Fairfax, 1977-79, Woodmont Ctr., Arlington, Va., 1979-87, Fairfax County Schs., 1988—; pvt. practice social work Oakton, Va., 1980—. Mem. Acad. Cert. Social Workers. Home: 3108 Trenholm Dr Oakton VA 22124-1328 Office: 10470 Armstrong St Fairfax VA 22030

NELSON, JOHN CHARLES, retired educator; b. Rome, Oct. 9, 1925; came to the U.S., 1926; s. Claud Dalton and Maud Sparks Nelson; m. Bruna Marchi, July 24, 1948; 1 child, Marcella Simonetta Nelson de la Fontaine. BA, Columbia Coll., 1944; MA, Columbia U., 1950, PhD, 1954. Instr. U. Rochester, N.Y., 1953-56; lectr. Columbia U., N.Y.C., 1956-57, assoc. prof., 1962-66, prof., 1966-88; instr. Harvard U., Cambridge, Mass., 1957-58, asst. prof., 1958-62. Dir. music dept. War Prisoners Aid of YMCA, N.Y.C., 1945-46; lectr. to trainees for Somalia, Peace Corps, N.Y.C., 1966; co-founder Columbia U. Tennis Ctr., N.Y.C. Author: Renaissance Theory of Love, 1958; editor: Francesco Patrizi L'Amorosa Filosofia, 1963; co-editor: (with H. Hayden) A Renaissance Treasury, 1953; assoc. editor: Philosophy and Humanism: Renaissance Essays in Honor of Paul Oskar Kristeller, 1976. Fulbright scholar Fulbright Commn., U. Rome, 1950-51; Guggenheim fellow Guggenheim Found., Italy, 1960-61. Mem. Phi Beta Kappa. Avocation: tennis tournaments. Home: 1100 Gulf Shore Blvd N Apt 305 Naples FL 34102-5364

NELSON, JOHN GUSTAF, lawyer; b. Denver, Jan. 29, 1965; s. Carl R. and Dorothy M. (Harris) N. BA, U. Colo., 1987, JD, 1990. Bar: Colo. 1990, U.S. Dist. Ct. Colo. 1991, U.S. Ct. Appeals (10th cir.) 1992, U.S. Fed. Claims Ct. 1993, U.S. Ct. Appeals (9th cir.) 1993, Tribal Ct. Omaha Tribe Nebr. 1996, U.S. Dist. Ct. Hawaii, 1997, U.S. Ct. Appeals (8th cir.) 2000, U.S. Supreme Ct. 2002. Staff atty. Mountain States Legal Found., Denver, 1990-94; atty. Law Offices of John D. Musick Jr. and Assocs., 1994-98; pvt. practice, 1998-2001; atty. Brega & Winters, P.C., 2001—. Contbr. articles to profl. jours. Bd. dirs. Colo. Rep. Bus. Coalition; mem. Jefferson County Corrections Bd. Mem. Colo. Bar Assn., Denver Bar Assn., The Federalist Soc., Rocky Mountain Mineral Law Found., Denver Athletic Club, Univ. Club Denver, Masons (Highlands lodge) Lutheran. Avocations: reading, backpacking, scuba diving. Home: 10574 Pierson Cir Broomfield CO 80021-3524 Office: Ste 2222 1700 Lincoln St Denver CO 80203 Fax: 303-861-9109. E-mail: jnelson@brega-winters.com.

NELSON, JOHN HOWARD (JACK HOWARD NELSON), journalist; b. Talladega, Ala., Oct. 11, 1929; s. Howard Alonzo and Barbara Lena (O'Donnell) N.; m. Virginia Dare Dickinson, Aug. 4, 1951 (div. Nov. 1974); children: Karen Dare, John Michael, Steven Howard; m. Barbara Joan Matusow, Dec. 7, 1974. Student econs., Ga. State Coll., 1953-57; Nieman fellow, Harvard U., 1961-62. Reporter, Biloxi (Miss.) Daily Herald, 1947-51; Reporter Atlanta Constitution, 1952-65; So. bur. chief Los Angeles Times, Atlanta, 1965-70; with Washington bur. Los Angeles Times, 1970—, Washington bur. chief, 1975-96, chief Washington corr., 1996—2002. Author: (with Gene Roberts, Jr.) The Censors and the Schools, 1963, (with Jack Bass) The Orangeburg Massacre, 1970, (with R.J. Ostrow) The FBI and the Berrigans, 1972, Captive Voices, Shocken Books, 1974, Terror in the Night, 1993. Mem. vis. com. U. Miami Sch. Communications. With AUS, 1951-52. Recipient Pulitzer prize for local reporting under deadline pressure, 1960; Drew Pearson award for gen. excellence in investigative reporting, 1974 Mem. The Gridiron Club. Home: 4 Wynkoop Ct Bethesda MD 20817-5936

NELSON, JOHN KEITH, electrical engineer, educator; b. Oldham, Lancashire, Eng., July 3, 1943; s. John Collins and Joyce Palfrey (Simmons) N.; m. Christine Anne Baker, Feb. 10, 1968; children: David John, Peter Mark. BS in Engring., U. London, 1965, PhD, 1969. Rsch. fellow U. London, 1966-69, lectr., 1969-78, reader, 1978-79; rsch. mgr. GE, Schenectady, NY, 1979-82; prof. elec. power engring. Rensselaer Poly. Inst., Troy, 1982—, Philip Sporn prof., 2001—. Head dept., 1997-2001; examiner U. Sri Lanka, 1970-85; cons. in field. Contbr. articles to profl. jours.; patentee in field. Recipient Snell premium, IEE, London, 1972, J.R. Beard award, 1976, Rsch. award, Brit. Coun., 1974, 76, Travel award, Royal Soc., London, 1976, Power Engring. Educator award Edison Elec. Inst., 1994, Fellowship award Am. Soc. Nondestructive Testing, 1997. Fellow Inst. Elec. Engrs. (U.K.), IEEE (tech. v.p. Dielectrics and Elec. Insulation Soc. 1991-92, adminstrv. v.p. 1993-94, pres. 1995-96, Meml. lectr. 1993, tech. activities bd. 1995-96, membership devel. com. 1997—, Forster Disting. Svc. award 1998, IEEE Millenium medal 2000); mem. Engring. Inst. (coun.). Episcopalian. Avocations: squash, sailing, scuba diving, flying. Office: Rensselaer Poly Inst Dept Elec Power Engring Troy NY 12180-3590 E-mail: k.nelson@ieee.org.

NELSON, JOHN MARSHALL, medical information services company executive; b. Madison, Wis., Oct. 28, 1941; s. Russell Arthur and Dorothea (Smith) N.; m. Linda Taylor, Oct. 13, 1962 (div. June 1968); children: Ann, David; m. Katherine Dianne Hoagland, Sept. 24, 1972; children: James, George AB, Harvard Coll., 1963; MD, Case Western Reserve U., 1967; MBA, U. Chgo., 1983. Diplomate Am. Bd. Internal Medicine. Staff assoc. NIH, Bethesda, Md., 1968-71; rsch. assoc., asst. prof. medicine Promis Lab. Med. Sch. Univ. Vt., 1973-76; med. dir. Madison Gen. Hosp., 1976-84; assoc. clin. prof. Med. Sch. U. Wis., 1976-84; v.p. corp. med. affairs Gen. Health Mgmt. Co., Madison, 1984-86; dir. med. and ednl. affairs Washington Hosp. Ctr., 1986-87; pres. Nelson Info. Systems, Bethesda, Md., 1987—. Cons. Med. Sch. U. Utah, Salt Lake City, 1985-86; med. reviewer FDA, 1990-91. Contbr. articles to profl. jour. Coach youth soccer, 1984-85; merit badge counselor Boy Scouts Am., 1987; mem. Harvard Schs. Com., Md., 1988-91; vestry St. John's Episcopal Ch., Bethesda, 1988-91. Harvard Hon. Nat. Scholar, 1959-62; recipient Steuer Meml. award Case Western Reserve U., Cleve., 1967; grantee Nat. Libr. Medicine, NIH, 1992-97. Fellow ACP, Am. Coll. Physician Execs.; mem. AMA, Univ. Club Chgo., Harvard Club (Washington), Alpha Omega Alpha. Republican. Episcopalian. Avocations: swimming, reading, cycling. Home: 6616 Millwood Rd Bethesda MD 20817-6058 Office: 4740 Chevy Chase Dr Chevy Chase MD 20815-6461

NELSON, JOHN MARTIN, corporate executive; b. N.Y.C., Aug. 9, 1931; s. Martin H. and Margaret (Larkin) N.; m. Linda Crocker Moore, Aug. 30, 1992; children: Murrey E., Christopher L. AB, Wesleyan U., 1953; MBA, Harvard U., 1959. With Norton Co., Worcester, Mass., 1959-90; pres., chief exec. officer Norton Christensen Inc. subs. Norton Co., Salt Lake City, 1978-86; pres., chief operating officer Norton Co., Worcester, 1986-88, chmn., chief exec. officer, 1988-90; chmn., CEO Wyman-Gordon Co., 1991-94, chmn. Mass., 1995-97, The TJX Cos., Inc., Framingham, 1995-99, Brown & Sharpe Mfg. Co., Kingstown, RI, 2000—01, Commonwealth Nat. Bank, 2001—. Bd. dirs. Brown & Sharpe Mfg. Co., Kingston, RI, 2000-20001, Eaton Vance Corp., Boston, Commerce Holdings, Inc., Webster, Mass; chmn. Commonwealth Nat. Bank, Worcester, Mass., 2001-. Trustee Wesleyan U., 1978-81, Worcester Poly. Inst., 1986—, chmn. 1995-2000; bd. dirs. Worcester Mcpl. Rsch. Bur., 1989—, pres., 1998-99; bd. dirs. Greater Worcester Cmty. Found., 1990-98, pres., 1990-94; bd. dirs. Alliance for Edn., 1991—, United Way Ctrl. Mass., 1993-98, chmn., 1993; trustee Worcester Found. for Biomed. Rsch., 1993-2000, Worcester Art Mus., 1988-99, chmn., 1996-99; trustee Worcester Area C. of C., 1992-97, chmn., 1994; trustee Meml. Hosp. Med. Ctr., 1991-98. Home: 7 Massachusetts Ave Worcester MA 01609-1622 Office: Office J Nelson 446 Main St Worcester MA 01608-2359

NELSON, JOHN ROBERT, theology educator, clergyman; b. Winona Lake, Ind., Aug. 21, 1920; s. William John and Agnes Dorothy (Soderborg) N.; m. Dorothy Patricia Mercer, Aug. 18, 1945; children: Eric Mercer, William John. AB, DePauw U., 1941, LHD, 1960; BD, Yale U., 1944; DTheol, U. Zürich, Switzerland, 1951; LLD, Wilberforce U., 1954; DD, Ohio Wesleyan U., 1964; LHD, Loyola U., 1969; DH, Hellenic Coll., 1985. Ordained to ministry Meth. Ch., 1944; dir. Wesley Found., Chapel Hill, N.C., 1946-48, assoc. dir. Urbana, Ill., 1950-51; study sect. United Student Christian Council, N.Y.C., 1951-53; sec. commn. on faith and order World Council Chs., Geneva, Switzerland, 1953-57, chmn. working com. Switzerland, 1967-75; dean, prof. theology Vanderbilt Div. Sch., 1957-60; vis. prof. ecumenics Princeton Theol. Sem., 1960-61; vis. prof. United Theol. Coll., Bangalore, India, and Leonard Theol. Coll., Jabalpur, India, 1961-62; Fairchild prof. Christian theology Grad. Sch. Theology, Oberlin Coll., Ohio, 1962-65; prof. systematic theology Boston U. Sch. Theology, 1965-84, dean, 1972-74. Peyton lectr. So. Meth. U., 1961; Merrick lectr. Ohio Wesleyan U., 1964; Lowell lectr., 1966; Burke lectr. U. Calif.-San Diego, 1985; Willson lectr. Centenary Coll., 1985; Nobel lectr. Gustavus Adolphus U., 1985; vis. prof. Pontifical Gregorian U., Rome, 1968-69; Mendenhall lectr. DePauw, 1974; Russell lectr. Tufts U., 1976, Wattson lectr., Cath. U., 1989; cons. Pres.'s Commn. for Study Ethical Problems in Biomed. Research, 1980-82; dir. Inst. Religion, Tex. Med. Ctr., Houston, 1985-92; adj. prof. medicine Baylor Coll. Medicine, 1985-98, adj. prof. religious studies Rice U., 1987-91; program dir. Genetics, Religion and Ethics, Baylor Coll. Medicine, 1990-94. Author: The Realm of Redemption, 1951, One Lord, One Church, 1958, Overcoming Christian Divisions, rev. edit, 1962, Criterion for the Church, 1963, Fifty Years of Faith and Order, (with J. Skoglund), 1963, Crisis in Unity and Witness, 1968, Church Union in Focus, 1968, Science and Our Troubled Conscience, 1980, Human Life: a Biblical Perspective for Bioethics, 1984, On the New Frontiers of Genetics and Religion, 1994; editor: The Christian Student and the World Struggle, 1952, Christian Unity in North America, 1958, No Man Is Alien, 1971, Life as Liberty, Life as Trust, 1992; editor-at-large, The Christian Century, 1958-91; assoc. editor: Jour. Ecumenical Studies; mem. editorial bd. Human Gene Therapy. Del. all 8 assemblies World Coun. Chs., 5th World Conf. on Faith and Order, 1993, United Meth. Gen. Conf., 1968, 72; mem. commn. on faith and order Nat. Coun. Chs.; mem. U.S. Commn. for UNESCO, 1974-80. Lt. USNR, 1944-46. Fellow Am. Acad. Arts and Scis.; mem. Am. Theol. Soc. (past pres.), N.Am. Acad. Ecumenists (past pres.), Soc. Europeenne de Culture (v.p.), Houston Philosophy Soc., Country Club of Brookline (Mass.), Phi Beta Kappa, Beta Theta Pi. Home: 1111 Hermann Dr Apt 19 A Houston TX 77004-6930 *The sequence of my persuasions and commitments has been from Christian unity to human unity to basic concern for the value of human life itself; and these are cumulative convictions from which I cannot deviate.*

NELSON, JOHN WOOLARD, neurology educator, physician; b. Hagerstown, Ind., Mar. 9, 1928; s. John Hans and Marvel May (Woolard) N.; m. Nancy Louise Elam, July 21, 1966; 1 son, John Hancock. AB, Earlham Coll., 1950; MD, Ind. U., 1953. Diplomate in neurology and clin neurophysiology Am. Bd Psychiatry and Neurology . Instr. neurology U. Tenn. Coll. Medicine, 1959-61; asst. prof. neurology W. Va. U. Sch. Medicine, 1961-63; assoc. prof. neurology U. Tenn., 1963-66; assoc. prof. to prof. Med. Coll. Wis., Milw., 1966-72; clin. prof. neurology U. Minn., Duluth, 1972-73; prof., head dept. neurology U. Okla. Coll. of Medicine, Oklahoma City, 1973-88, prof. emeritus neurology, 1989—. Served with M.C. U.S. Army, 1955-56. Mem. Okla. County Med. Soc., Okla. Med. Soc., AMA, Am. Acad. Neurology, Am. Electroencephalographic Soc., Am. Med. Electroencephalographic Soc. Home: 14901 N Pennsylvania Ave Apt 2B Oklahoma City OK 73134-6080

NELSON, JON PAUL, economics educator; b. Hinsdale, Ill., Aug. 9, 1941; s. Everett W. and Helen W. (Halvorson) N.; m. Naomi Higa, Jan. 21, 1967; children: Bradley R., Steven E. BS, U. Wis., 1964, MS, 1967, PhD, 1970. Rsch. asst. State of Wis., Madison, 1964-67; rsch. fellow U. Wis., 1967-69; prof. econs. Pa. State U., University Park, 1969—. Cons. Pa. Dept. Justice, Harrisburg, 1980—. Author: Economic Analysis of Transportation Noise Abatement, 1978; contbr. articles to profl. pubs. Ford. Found. fellow, 1967-68, Am. Iron and Steel Inst. fellow, 1968-69. Mem. Am. Econ. Assn., Indsl. Orgn. Soc., Assn. Resource and Environ. Economists, Am. Canoe Assn., Pa. State Outing. Home: 642 Glenn Rd State College PA 16803-3474 Office: Pa State U 518 Kern Bldg University Park PA 16802-3305 E-mail: jpn@psu.edu.

NELSON, K. BONITA, literary agent; b. Austin, Minn., July 5, 1945; d. Wallace Arthur and Opal Rebecca (Lastine) N. BA, Hunter Coll., 1969; B in laws, LaSalle U., 1982. Literary agent trainee Am. Play Co., Inc., N.Y., 1970-75; legal sec., reviewer Eastman & DaSilva, Esqs., 1975-79; founder, pres. BK Nelson Literary Agy., 1983—, BK Nelson Lect. Bureau, N.Y., 1988—, BK Nelson Wordprocessing, Pleasantville, N.Y., 1994—; pres., publ. Internat. Media Comm., Inc., 1998. Bd. dirs. Dynaray, N.Y.; founder BK Nelson, Inc., 1995, Nelson Am. Movies Ptnrs., 1997; founder Literacy Inst. for Edn. (Life) Inc., 1996. Collaborator: Looking for Canterbury, 1994; author: My Literary Agent, 1998; exec. prodr. (movie) Paradise FOUND. Pres. True Story Network Found. and Wellness Ctr., Breckenridge, Colo. Mem. Authors Guild (assoc.), NAFE (assoc.), Nat. Assn. Campus Activities (assoc.), AAUW, (assoc.), Dramatists Guild (assoc.), Am. Booksellers Assn. (assoc.), Minority and Woman Owned Businesses. Avocations: aerobics, yoga, needlepoint, stamp collecting. Home and Office: 1565 Paseo Vida Palm Springs CA 92264 E-mail: bknelson4@cs.com.

NELSON, KAY ELLEN, speech and language pathologist; b. Milw., Apr. 14, 1947; d. John A. and Magaret B. (Janke) Strobel; m. Dale Kuglitisch, Mar. 2, 1974 (div. Dec. 1981); 1 child Ashley Lara ; m. Ronald P. Anderson, Sept. 7, 2002. BA with distinction, U. Wis., Madison, 1969; MA, U. Wis., Milw., 1972. Speech and lang. pathologist Sch. Dist. 146, Dolton, Ill., 1970-71, Waukesha County Handicapped Children's Edn. Bd., Waukesha, Wis., 1972-77, 79-80, Kettle Moraine Area Schs., Wales, 1980-94; dir. speech/lang. pathology MJ Care, Inc., Fond du Lac, 1994-96; speech-lang. pathologist, team leader NovaCare, Inc., New Berlin, 1996-97, clin. specialist, 1996-98, Prism Rehab Systems, Glendale, 1998-99, Mariner Health Care, Greenfield, 1999—; clin. supr., instr. U. Wis.-Whitewater, 2000—. Pvt. practice, Dousman, Wis., summers 1991-93. Fellow Herb Kohl Found., 1993. Mem.: Internat. Soc. for Augmentative and Alternative Comm., U.S. Soc. for Augmentative and Alternative Comm., Wis. Soc. for Augmentative and Alternative Comm. (sec. 1990—92, membership chmn. 1990—93, v.p. profl. affairs 1993), Wis. Speech, Lang. and Hearing Assn. (sch. rep. dist. VII 1991—94, chmn. sch. svcs. com. 1992—94, v.p. sch. svcs. 1994—95, rep.-at-large 1995—96, v.p. healthcare 1998—99), Am. Speech, Lang. and Hearing Assn. (ACE award 1990, 1991, 1992, 1994, 1995, 1996, 1997, cert. of clin. competence, ACE award 2001). Unitarian Universalist. Avocations: sewing, computers, nature activities, travel. Office: SouthPointe Health Care Ctr 4500 W Loomis Rd Greenfield WI 53220

NELSON, KAY HOYLE, communication educator; b. Jackson, Mich., Oct. 24, 1939; d. Thomas Joseph and Helen May (Exposito) Hoyle; m. Malcolm Maxwell Nelson, Apr. 9, 1972 (dec. 1984). PhD in English Lang. and Lit., U. Chgo., 1978. Asst. prof. English St. Cloud (Minn.) State U., 1987-91; assoc. prof. comm. and humanities Aurora (Ill.) U., 1991—. Bd. dirs. Hyde Park-Kenwood Cmty. Conf., 1996-99. Mem. Univ. Chgo. Club Met. Chgo. (bd. dirs., treas. 1998-2000). Home: 5529 S University Ave Chicago IL 60637-1534 Office: Aurora Univ 347 S Gladstone Ave Aurora IL 60506-4892

NELSON, KAYE LYNN, healthcare consultant; b. Bismarck, N.D., Oct. 5, 1935; d. Charles and Carolyn Phyllis (Thorne) Staiger; m. Roy Franklin, Dec. 29, 1959; children: Dana Lynn, Erik Roy. BS with honors, Mont. State Coll., Bozeman, 1958; MS with honors, Eastern Mont. Coll. Edn., Billings, 1962. Instr. Mont. State U., Bozeman, 1958-60; insvc. educator Deaconess Med. Ctr., Billings, 1975-83, risk mgr., 1983-88, dir. nursing, 1988-93. Mem. Sigma Theta Tau.

NELSON, KEITHE EUGENE, state court administrator, lawyer; b. Grand Forks, N.D. m. Shirley Jeanne Jordahl, June 10, 1955; children: Kirsti Lynn Nelson Hoerauf, Scott David, Kenen Edward, Karen Lee Nelson Strandquist. PhB, U. N.D., 1958, JD, 1959. Bar: N.D. 1959, U.S. Ct. Mil. Appeals 1967., U.S. Supreme Ct. 1967. With Armour & Co., Grand Forks, 1958-59; commd. 2d lt. USAF, 1958, advanced through grades to maj. gen., 1985, judge advocate N.D. and, Fed. Republic Germany and Eng., 1959-73, chief career mgmt., 1973-77; comdt. USAF JAG Sch., Montgomery, Ala., 1977-81; staff judge adv. Tactical Air Command USAF, Hampton, VA., 1981-82, SAC, Omaha, 1984-85; dir. USAF Judiciary, Washington, 1982-84; dep. JAG USAF, 1985, JAG, 1988-91, JAG, 1988, ret. JAG, 1991; dir. jud. planning Supreme Ct. N.D.; state ct. adminstr., 1992—. Chmn. editorial bd. USAF Law Rev., 1977-81. Decorated D.S.M., Legion of Merit with two oak leaf clusters. Mem. ABA. Lutheran. Avocations: skeet shooting, hunting, tennis, theater. Home: 800 Munich Dr Bismarck ND 58504-7050

NELSON, KIMBERLY TERESE, federal agency administrator; B, Shippensburg U.; M, U. Pa. Spl. asst. to sec., spl. asst. to deputy sec. adminstrn., spl. asst. deputy sec. field ops. Pa. Dept. Environ. Resources, 1987—95; dir. program integration and effectiveness then chief info. officer Pa. Dept. Environ. Protection, 1999—2001; asst. adminstr. environ. info. EPA, Washington, 2001—. Office: EPA 1200 Pennsylvania Ave NW MC 2810A Washington DC 20460*

NELSON, L. BRUCE, lawyer; b. Mpls., Aug. 6, 1946; s. Leo W. and Sylvia E. Nelson; m. Nancy E. Cook, Aug. 23, 1969; 1 child, Andrew C. AB, Hamilton Coll., 1968; JD, U. Colo., 1971. Bar: Colo., D.C., U.S. Ct. Appeals (10th cir.). Assoc./ptnr. Sherman & Howard, Denver, 1972-83; dir., shareholder Isaacson, et al, 1983-91; counsel Inverness Properties, 1991-94; dir., shareholder Ducker, Montgomery, et al, 1994—. Clk. Judge Jean Breitenstein, 10th Cir. Ct. Appeals, Denver, 1971. Mem. ABA, Colo. Bar Assn., Colo. Corp. Counsel. Office: Ducker Montgomery 1560 Broadway Ste 1500 Denver CO 80202-5151

NELSON, LARRY A. statistics educator, consultant; b. Omaha, Oct. 28, 1932; s. Rudolph Lawrence and Elizabeth Coleman (Lewis) N. BS in Agronomy, Iowa State U., 1954; MS in Soil Sci., Tex. A&M U., 1958; PhD in Soil Sci.-Stats., N.C. State U., 1961. Soil scientist Iowa Agrl. Exptl. Sta., Ames, 1954-55; soils instr. Tex. A&I Coll., Kingsville, 1955; rsch. soil scientist Tex. A&M Rsch. Found., College Station, 1956; soils lab. instr. Tex. A&M U., 1956-58; rsch. asst. N.C. State U., Raleigh, 1959-61; asst. specialist in land classification Land Study Bur., U. Hawaii, Honolulu, 1961-64; asst. prof. exptl. stats. N.C. State U., Raleigh, 1964-66, assoc. prof. exptl. stats., 1966-71, prof. stats., 1971-89, prof. emeritus stats., 1989—, coord. Concade Project (Bolivia), 1999—, interim coord. internat. programs Coll. Agr. and Life Scis., 2002—. Lectr., tchr., cons. in field; spl. advisor head dep. stats. Kasetsart U., Bangkok, Thailand, 1973; evaluator quantitative skills IADS, Bangladesh, 1984; mem. rev. team Ctr. for Agrl. Econs. and Ctr. for Data Processing, Winrock Internat., Indonesia, 1985; statis. cons. PROCAFE, El Salvador, 1993-96, ICRAF, Nairobi, Kenya, 1991—; cons. Potash and Phosphate Inst. Can., China and India, 1990, 94, 96; ptnr. Statis. Rsch. Assocs., Honolulu, 1962-63. Assoc. editor Geoderma, 1976-84, Agronomy Jour., 1981-87; contbr. numerous articles to profl. publs. NATO fellow Data Analysis Lab., Lynbgy, Denmark, 1978. Fellow AAAS, Am. Statis. Assn. (mem. biometrics sect. com. 1989-90, mem. com. on internat. rels. in stats. 1996-98), Am. Soc. Agronomy, Soil Sci. Soc. Am.; mem. Statis. Assn. Thailand (life), Internat. Biometric Soc. (bus. mgr. and treas. 1969-79, awards com. 1987-94, chmn. 1990-93, com. on edn. 1997-99), Sigma Xi, Gamma Sigma Delta (internat. pres. 1984-86, award of merit 1973-74, rep. to AAAS 1978-86), Phi Kappa Phi, Sigma Iota Rho. Baptist. Avocations: music, genealogy, diving, bicycling, travel. Home: 2816 Wycliff Rd Raleigh NC 27607-3035 Office: NC State U Office Internat Programs PO Box 7608 Raleigh NC 27695-7608 E-mail: lan@unity.ncsu.edu., lnelson460@worldnet.att.net.

NELSON, LARRY DEAN, telecommunications and computer systems company executive, consultant; b. Newton, Kans., Aug. 5, 1937; s. Carl Aaron and Leta V. (Van Eaton) N.; m. Linda Hawkins, June 2, 1972. BA, Phillips U., 1959; MS, Kans. State U., 1962; PhD, Ohio State U., 1965. From rsch. asst. to rsch. assoc. Rsch. Found., Ohio State U., Columbus, 1962—65; mathematician II Batelle Meml. Inst., 1962—65; from mem. tech. staff to supr. math. dept., data sys. devel. Bellcomm, Inc., Washington, 1965—72; supr. mgmt. info. sys. dept. Bell Telephone Labs., Murray Hill, NJ, 1972—77; supr. rate and tariff planning divsn. AT&T, N.Y.C., 1977—79; dep. adminstr. rsch. and spl. programs adminstrn. U.S. Dept. Transp., Washington, 1979—81; pres. MCS, Inc., 1981—; supr. govt. comm. ctr. AT&T Bell Labs., 1985—89; mgr. govt. mktg. AT&T Network Sys., 1989—90, supr. secure info. sys. engring., 1990—94, disting. mem. tech. staff, secure sys. engring., 1995—96; tech. cons. AT&T Labs, Info. Security Ctr., AT&T, 1996—98. Cons. Contel Info. Sys., Denver, 1982-85, Martin Marietta Corp., Denver, 1982-85; mem. info. assurance task force, info infrastructure group, intrusion detection task force, cybercrime subgroup Nat. Security Telecomms. Advisory Com. Contbr. articles to profl. jours. Organizer, sponsor Odd Jobs Club, Washington, 1967-72; pres. Mountain County Condominiums Assn., Dillon, Colo., 1975-83, 85—; treas. Chris' Landing Condominium Assn., 1986-90; mem. Am. del. 5th Meeting of U.S.-USSR Working Group on Transp., Moscow, 1979; head Am. del. 5th Meeting of U.S.-USSR Working Group on Transport of Future, Moscow, 1979; head meeting Am. Del. to ISO/IEC TCI/SC27 Working Group 1 of Info. Tech., Security Methodology Stds., editor Intrusion Detection Project, Germany 1997, Kista, Sweden, 1998, Rio De Janeiro, 1998, Spain, 1999, Brazil, 1999, U.S., 1999, Eng. and Tokyo, 2000, Oslo, Norway, 2001, Berlin Germany, 2002; internat. rep. Am. Stds. Inst.-Tech. Com. on Info. Tech. Security Methodology. Mem. ABA (assoc., info. security com.), Am. Nat. Stds. Inst. (info. tech. security tech. stds. com., internat. rep. tech. com. on info. tech. security mgmt.), IEEE (sec. D.C. sect. 1982, cert. appreciation 1968), Sys., Man and Cybernetics Soc. (sec. 1981, v.p. 1982-83), Math. Programming Soc, Am. Math Soc., N.Y. Acad. Scis., Assn. Computing Machinery, Sigma Xi, Phi Kappa Phi, Pi Mu Epsilon. Democrat. Mem. Disciples of Christ. Current work: information systems, networks and network management, digital signature, public key infrastructure, and electronic commerce technology. Subspecialties: secure information technology systems and networks; systems engineering. Office: MCS Inc 440 New Jersey Ave SE Washington DC 20003-4008 E-mail: ldcnelson@att.net.

NELSON, LAWRENCE EVAN, business consultant; b. Chgo., Dec. 3, 1932; s. Evan Thomas and Elizabeth Marie (Stettka) N.; m. Jean H. Clayton, July 11, 1953; children: Lori Jean, Lawrence Evan. BS with honors, So. Ill. U., 1959; MBA, U. Chgo., 1969. CPA, Ill. Sr. acct. Price Waterhouse & Co., CPA's, Chgo., 1959-65; sec.-treas. Bradner Cen. Co., 1965-73; pres. Protectoseal Co., Bensenville, Ill., 1973-84, Plan Ahead Inc., Palos Park, Ill, 1984—. Author: (book) Personal Financial Planning, 1985. Treas. City of Palos Heights, Ill., 1964-68, alderman, 1970-71; trustee Palos Heights FPD, 1977—. Served with USNR, 1952-56. Mem. Am. Inst. CPA's, Ill. Soc. CPA's. Office: Plan Ahead Inc PO Box 164 Palos Park IL 60464-0164

NELSON, LEANN LINDBECK, small business owner; b. McCook, Nebr., Jan. 27, 1937; d. Clifford Roy Lindbeck and Elizabeth J. (Downs) Rollstin; m. Lawrence L. Nelson, June 21, 1958; children: Glen Lindbeck, Todd Alan. BS in Dietetics, U. Tex., 1960. Dietitian Parkview Bapt. Hosp., Yuma, Ariz., 1960-61; instr. foods and nutrition Jefferson County Schs., Lakewood, Colo., 1969-71; dir. education and consumer programs, cons. nutrition Dairy Coun., Inc., Denver, 1971-74; coord. low-income foods and nutrition programs Emily Griffith Opportunity Sch., 1974-76; dir., asst. dir. edn./info. and product publicity Am. Sheep Prodrs. Coun., 1976-83; pres. Natural Accents, 1983-90; pres., owner LeAnn Nelson Presents, 1988—; sales mgr. Weekenders, U.S.A., Inc., 2001—. Cons. fixed income counseling program City of Denver, Denver County, 1975-76, comm. cons., 1989—; co-chairperson Home Econs. Nat. Task Force on Profl. Unity and Identity, 1992-93; prof. home econs., mem. adv. com. Coll. Applied Human Scis., Colo. State U., 1994-96. Author: Accessories... What a Finish!, 1988. Chmn. home econs. adv. com. U. No. Colo., 1980-82; v.p. Clock Tower Mchts. Assn., Denver, 1983-85; chmn., buyer Denver Symphony Guild Gift Shop, 1984-87; mem. adv. bd. State Bd. Cmty. Colls. Occupational Edn., Home Econ. Tech. Adv. Com., 1986-95, Coll. Applied Human Scis. Colo. State U., Ft. Collins, 1986-87; mem. consumer & family studies adv. com. Emily griffith Opportunity Sch., 1993—, chair profl. sewing adv. com., 1996—. Named Colo. Home Economist of Yr. Colo. Home Econs. Assn., 1979, Colo. Bus. Home Economist of Yr. Colo. Home Econs. Assn., 1980; recipient Leadership award Colo. Home Econs. Assn. Mem. Nat. Assn. Women Bus. Owners, Home Economists in Bus. (nat. chmn.-elect 1981-82, nat. chmn. 1982-83, Nat. Bus. Home Economist of Yr. 1986), Colo. Assn. of Profl. Saleswomen, Profl. Aux. Assistance League of Denver (corr. sec. 1994-96), Denver Fashion Group (regional dir. 1984-86), Am. Women in Radio & TV (treas. Denver chpt. 1978-79). Clubs: Penrose, Executive, PEO. Home and Office: 1250 Humboldt St Apt 1001 Denver CO 80218-2416

NELSON, LINDA BEATRICE D'ANDREA, volunteer worker; b. Waterbury, Conn., Apr. 27, 1926; d. Consalvo August and Margaret Donata (Santoro) D'Andrea; m. Robert Andrew Nelson, June 20, 1949; children: Eric Robert, Forrest Andrew. Grad. high sch., Terryville, Conn. Mem. staff Am. Bd. Anesthesiology, Hartford, Conn., 1958-82. Author: (poetry) Satan's Beat, 1975, Rhyme Remembrances, 1990. Charter mem. Burlington (Conn.) Land Trust, 1989; founder Burlington Concerned Citizens, 1987. Mem. Farmington (Conn.) Watershed Assn. Avocations: environmental activist, writing, communications. Home: 472 Jerome Ave Burlington CT 06013-2314

NELSON, LINDA BENEFIELD, writer, secretary; b. Mobile, Ala., Jan. 23, 1949; d. William Jackson Benefield and Lucille Josephine Maples; divorced; 1 child, Chris Whatley. AAS with honors, Phillips Jr. Coll., 1991. Med. sec. Springhill Meml. Hosp., 1975-89, U. South Ala., 1990-93; ret. Am. General Life/Accident Co Insurance Agent, 1993—98; med. sec. Mobile Infirmary Hosp., 1998—2001. Recipient Pres.'s award for best lit. work, 1996. Mem. Smithsonian Instn. (assoc.), Libr. of Congress (assoc.), Nat. Registry Authors, Nat. Trust Historic Preservation. Home: PO Box 2593 Semmes AL 36575-2593

NELSON, LINDA CAROL, corporate chief executive; b. Knoxville, Tenn., Feb. 18, 1954; d. Solon Morris and Dorothy Thelma (Randles) Woods. BA in Polit. Sci. and Psychology magna cum laude, U. Tenn., 1975; BS in Acctg. summa cum laude, Ga. State U., 1978. Cert. of mgmt. acct.; enrolled agt. Pvt. investigator Hanover Security Systems, Knoxville, 1968-74; office mgr. Dale Carnegie Inst., 1969-75, instr. Dale Carnegie course and profl. devel. series Atlanta, 1980-88; legal asst. office of regional atty. H.E.W., 1975; tech. support staff Dist. Conf. U.S. Treasury Dept., 1976, instr., tng. analyst continuing profl. edn., 1976-88, recruiter, 1979-86, team coord. large case exam, 1980-85, resident lead instr. S.E. Region, 1984, fed. racketeering investigator, 1985-86, coord. Joint Com. Taxation in Congress, 1986-87; internal revenue agt., tax technician of exam. div. IRS, 1976-79; consolidations tax dept. staff mgr. Bellsouth, 1984-85; ind. mgmt. cons. Ga., 1980-86; pres., CEO Exec. Svcs. Inc., Atlanta, 1988—. Active Speakers' Bur., Atlanta, 1993—. Hospitality com. mem. Atlanta Women's Network, 1990-92; vol. worker Eagles Boy's Ranch, Atlanta, 1986—; River of Life Family Ch.; vol. counselor Atlanta Home for Abused Children, 1980-83; Sunday sch. tchr., choir, nursery, various chs., 1975—; fundraiser Atlanta Symphony Orch., 1985-86; cons. adopt-a-student program, 1985-86; vol. missions program 1st Bapt. Ch., Atlanta, 1986; key person United Way Atlanta Combined Fed. Campaign, 1978-84; calling com. Norcross (Ga.) United Meth. Ch., 1983-84; coord. blood drive ARC, Atlanta, 1984; vol. counselor Helen Ross McNabb Ctr., Knoxville, 1970-72; campaign com. mem. Senator Paul Coverdell. Recipient citation U.S. Sec. Labor Brennan, Superior Instr. award Dale Carnegie, 1988; named one of Outstanding Young Women of Am., 1984. Mem. ASTD (vol. placement com. 1988-92), NAFE, Inst. Mgmt. Accts. (program speaker Atlanta chpt., bd. dirs. 1989), High Mus. Art Young Career Mems. Guild, Young Women of the Arts, Nat. Assn. Enrolled Agts., Nat. Soc. Tax Profls., Profl. Info. Network (mem. spkr.'s bur.), Gwinnett County Leads Network (founder), Women's Life Underwriters' Assn. (program spkr.), Altanta C. of C., Ga. State U. Alumni Assn., U. Tenn. Alumni Assn., Golden Key Nat. Honor Soc., Mortar Bd., U.S. Tennis Assn., Atlanta Lawn Tennis Assn., So. Bicycle League, Sierra Club, Phi Beta Kappa, Beta Alpha Psi, Pi Sigma Alpha, Pi Kappa Phi, Alpha Lambda Delta, Delta Gamma (social chair), Chi Phi Little Sisters (pres.). Avocations: serving others, cooking, public speaking, outdoor activities, tennis. Home: 6001 Meadowbrook Dr Norcross GA 30093-3729 Office: Exec Svcs Inc PO Box 450822 Atlanta GA 31145-0822

NELSON, LINDA SHEARER, child development and family relations educator; b. New Kensington, Pa., Dec. 8, 1944; d. Walter M. and Jean M. Shearer; m. Alan Edward Nelson, Dec. 29, 1973; children: Amelia (Amy), Emily. BS in Home Econs. Edn., Pa. State U., 1966; MS in Child Devel. and Family Rels., Cornell U., 1968; PhD in Higher Edn. and Child Devel., U. Pitts., 1982. Head tchr.-lab. nursery sch. Dept. of Psychology, Vassar Coll., Poughkeepsie, N.Y., 1968-69; instr. child devel. dept. home econs. edn. Indiana (Pa.) U., 1969-72, asst. prof., 1972-77, assoc. prof., 1977-84, prof. child devel. and family rels., 1984-93, prof. child devel. and family rels., human devel. and family environ. studies dept., 1993—, chmn. dept., 1991—93, 1998—. Ind. cons., trainer Head Start Programs, Pa., 1970—, Child Care Programs and Agys., Pa., 1970—; child devel. assoc. rep. Coun. for Early Childhood Profl. Recognition, Washington, 1989—91; field rep. Keyston U. Rsch. Corp., Erie, 1990—91; spkr. in field. Co-author (with A. Nelson): Child Care Administration and Instructor's Manual, 2000; mem. adv. bd.: Early Childhood Education Annual Editions, 1985—, mem. adv. bd. interface: Home Economics and Technology Newsletter, 1993—96; contbr. articles to profl. jours. Bd. dirs. Indiana County Child Care Program, 1970-92; guest spkr. Delta Kappa Gamma, Indiana, 1990, Bus. and Profl. Women, Indiana, 1991, IUP's The Marriage Project, 1996, AAUW, Ind., 1996. Grantee in field, 1985—. Mem. Nat. Assn. for Edn. Young Children, Pitts. Assn. for Edn. Young Children (conf. co-chair 1983-85, in-svc. tng. spkr. 1995), Assn. Pa. State Coll. and Univ. Faculties, Kappa Omicron Nu, Phi Upsilon Omicron. Democrat. Presbyterian. Avocations: photography, reading, Chautauqua Instn. programs. Office: Indiana U of Pa Human Devel and Environ Studies Dept 207 Ackerman Hl Indiana PA 15705-0001 E-mail: lnelson@iup.edu.

NELSON, LISA LOUISE, art therapist, artist; b. Jamestown, N.Y., Jan. 18, 1956; d. Carl Lenart and Jane (Kerr) N. BFA, Sch. Art Inst. Chgo., 1988; MS, Ill. State U., 1985. Lic. clin. profl. counselor, Ill.; registered art therapist, Ill. Artist, Chgo., 1980—; specialized foster care therapist Cath. Social Svcs., Peoria, Ill., 1994-98, Children's Home Assoc., Peoria, 1998-00; pvt. practice, 2000—. Spkr., presenter in field including St. Latvian/Norway Weavers Conv., Riga, Latvia, 1990, Ill. Art Therapy Assn. Conf., Chgo., 1994, 2000, Ill. Coun. on Tng., 1995, 98, Am. Art Therapy Conv., San Diego, 1995. Exhbns. include Muse Gallery, San Antonio, 1985, Norris Gallery, St. Charles, Ill., 1986, 88, Lakeside Group at Navy Pier, Chgo., 1990, Ruth Volid Gallery, Chog., 1991, SAIC, Chgo., 1991, Textile Arts Ctr., Chgo., 1992, Adler Cultural Ctr., Libertyville, Ill., 1991, Elgin C.C., 1993, Suburban Fine Arts Ctr., Highland Park, Ill., 1993, Ill. State U., Normal, 1994, Circa Gallery, Chgo., 1996, Ill. Art Therapy Assn., Oak Park, Ill., 1996, Eureka Coll., 1997, Peoria Art Guild, 1997, Creative Devel. Ctr., Chgo., 1997, First United Meth. Ch., Peoria, 1997, Quad City Arts, Rock Island, Ill.,1 998, Truman State U., Mo., 1998, Quincy (Ill.) U., 1998, Peoria Art Guild, 1998, ARC Gallery, Chgo., 1999, Ill. Ctrl. Coll., East Peoria, 1999, Lakeview Mus., Peoria, 2000, State of Ill. Bldg., Chgo., 2000, Phoenix Gallery, Peoria, 2000, Quincy Art Ctr., 2000, Bradley U., Peoria, 2000, among others; contbr. articles to profl. jours. Mem. edn. com. Contemporary Art Ctr., Peoria, Ill., 2000; mem. program com. Cancer Ctr. for Health Living, Peoria, 2000; mem. Peoria Art Guild. Recipient Elizabeth Stein Art scholarship Ill. State U., 1995, Karen Deske Art Therapy scholarship, 1995, Mary Packwood Art scholarship, 1994. Mem. Ill. Art Therapy Assn. (membership co. 1996-97, pres.-elect 2001, pres. 2002-03), Am. Art Therapy Assn., Am. Counseling Assn., Coalition Ill. Counselor Orgns. Avocations: singing, gardening. Home: 1015 N Flora Ave Peoria IL 61606-1405 Office: Art Therapy Studio 305 SW Water St Peoria IL 61602 E-mail: babawalla@aol.com.

NELSON, LOUIS, design and planning consultant; b. N.Y.C., Oct. 8, 1936; s. Louis and Ingrid (Gjerstal) N.; m. Sandra Balestracci, Nov. 1, 1970 (div. May 1979); m. Judy Collins, Apr. 16, 1996. B.Indsl. Design, Pratt Inst., 1958, M.Indsl. Design, 1963. Mgr. exhibit design Corning Glass Works, N.Y., 1963-68; exec. v.p. R.P. Gersin Assocs., N.Y.C., 1968-80; pres. Louis Nelson Assocs., N.Y.C., 1980—; design cons. AT&T, Corning, IBM, Met. Transit Authority, Calif. Mus. Sci. & Industry, Port Authority Soc. for Savs., L.A. Conservancy, others; mem. panel Nat. Endowment of Arts; mem. design adv. com. Pratt Indsl. Inst.; chair Kostellow Fund, Pratt Inst.; vis. lectr., critic Pratt Inst., Phila. Coll. Art, N.Y. Sch. Interior Design; jury mem. Clio, Print, Indsl. Design Ann. Rev.; mem. mgmt. com. Worldesign/Internat. Congress Socs. Indsl. Design, 1985. Artist Korean War Vets. Meml. Mural, Washington; contbr. articles to profl. jours. Regent Cathedral St. John Devine. Served to capt. U.S. Army, 1958-62. Recipient awards Art Dirs. Club Los Angeles, Clio, Internat. Assn. Bus. Communicators, Indls. Design Ann. Rev., Print Ann. Rev., Printing Industries Am., Printing Industries Met. N.Y., USIA Traveling Show, Western Electronic Soc. Congress Creativity awards Art Direction Mag., 1983, 84, 85. Mem. Indsl. Designers Soc. Am. (chmn. awards N.Y. chpt. 1984, IDEA Silver), Am. Inst. Graphic Artists (award), Am. Nat. Standards Inst. (graphic symbols com.), Nat. Fire Protection Assn. (graphic symbols com.). Democrat. Clubs: North Shore Yacht (Manor Haven, N.Y.); The Players. Avocations: gardening; sailing; watercolors. Office: 80 University Pl New York NY 10003-4564

NELSON, LUTHER SULLIVAN, radiologist; b. Lasker, N.C., 1926; s. charles Wesley and Maggie Virginia (Collier) N.; m. Thelma Olivia Joyner, June 23, 1951; children: James Elliott, Stuart Edward, Glenda Ann Nelson Rogers. BA, BS, East Carolina U., 1950; MD, U. N.C., 1958. Diploamte Am. Bd. Radiology. Intern U. Mich., Ann Arbor, 1958-59; resident U. N.C., Chapel Hill, 1965-68; pvt. practice; radiologist St. Anthony's Hosp., Amarillo, Tex., 1968—. Mem. AMA, Am. Coll. Radiologists. Republican. Methodist.

NELSON, MARCELLA MAY, volunteer; b. Schaunavon, Sask., Can., Oct. 11, 1928; d. Ilmer Alexander and Zylpha May (Geier) Madson; m. William Robert Nelson, June 12, 1951 (dec. Nov. 2000). Stenographer Idaho Employment Security, Bonners Ferry, 1947-50, interviewer, 1950-51, mgr., 1951-63; supr., asst. mgr. Employment Security Agy., Sandpoint, Idaho, 1963-83, program supr. Coeur d'Alene, 1983-84; ret., 1984. Events asst. Sandpoint C. of C., 1984—, membership coord., 1984—; tutor illiteracy program NIC Coll., Coeur d'Alene, 1985-91; v.p. solicitations Festival at Sandpoint, 1988—. Campaign mgr. state rep. candidate for Vi Sims, Sandpoint and Bonners Ferry, 1984; pres. Pend Oreille Arts Coun., 1993-95, bd. dirs.; bd. dirs. Clean Air Coalition; bd. dirs. fundraising com. Panida Theatre; mem. Cmty. Assistance League, 1994—; mem. Sandpoint Centennial Commn., 2001; chairperson Sandpoint C. of C., 2001-02. Named Vol. of the Month, Sandpoint C. of C., 1987, 2000, Citizen of Yr., 1990, Retiree of Yr. Idaho chpt. 1985, Internat. Assn. Personel in Employment Security, Woman of Wisdom Women Honoring Women, 2000; recipient Woman of Distinction award, sr. category, Women's Forum Inc. of N. Idaho, 1999. Mem. Employment Security Agy. Rets., Internat. Personnel in Employment Security (sec., treas. 1970), Idaho State Employees Assn. (v.p. 1977, pres. elect 1978, pres. 1979, Employee of the Yr. 1968). Republican. Avocations: dressmaking, skiing, swimming, aerobics, reading. Home: PO Box 54 Sandpoint ID 83864-0054 Office: Sandpoint C of C PO Box 928 Sandpoint ID 83864-0887

NELSON, MARCELLA SIMONETTA, artist; b. Rochester, N.Y., Mar. 13, 1955; d. John Charles and Bruna (Marchi) N.; m. Jean de la Fontaine, Feb. 28, 1997. BA in Liberal Arts, Sarah Lawrence Coll., 1977; MA in Painting, NYU, 1979. Tchr. art St. Ann's Sch., Brooklyn Heights, N.Y., 1979-82; apprentice, part-time asst. John Kacere, N.Y.C., 1979-82. One-woman show 80 Washington square East Gallery, NYU, 1979; 2-person show Joy Berman Gallery, Phila., 1991; exhibited in group shows at NYU, 1979-80, Kamikaze, nightclub, N.Y.C., 1984, RVS Gallery, Southampton, N.Y., 1988, SUNY, L.I., 1988, Keith Green Gallery, N.Y.C., 1988, Joy Berman Gallery, Phila., 1989, Gallery Madison 90, N.Y.C., 1990, 92, Max Fish, N.Y.C., 1991, Hampton Square Gallery, Westhampton, N.Y., 1993, Gallery Factor 44, Antwerpen, Belgium, 1998, 2000, 2001, Installation, Karn Vyncke Dance Company, Brussels, 1999. Recipient hon. mention NYU Ann. Small Works Competition, 1980. Home: care Jean de la Fontaine 125 Rue Defacqz, bt. 2 1060 Brussels Belgium E-mail: marcella@miniature-pet-portrait.com.

NELSON, MARGUERITE HANSEN, special education educator; b. S.I., N.Y., June 23, 1947; d. Arthur Clayton and Marguerite Mary (Hansen) Nelson. AB magna cum laude, Boston Coll., 1969; MS in Edn., SUNY, Plattsburgh, 1973; cert. in gerontology, Yeshiva U., 1982; PhD, Fordham U., N.Y.C., 1995. Cert. elem. and spl. edn. tchr. N.Y. Pre-primary tchr. Pub. Sch. 22R S.I., N.Y.C. Bd. Edn., 1969-70; primary tchr. Oak Street Sch., Plattsburgh, 1971-73, Laurel Plains Sch., Clarkstown Cen. Schs., New City, 1973-78, Resource Rm. Lakewood Sch., Congers, 1978—2002; assoc. prof. St. Thomas Aquinas Coll., Sparkill, 2002—. Adj. faculty St. Thomas Aquinas Coll., Sparkill, 1985—89, Sparkill, 1995—2002, Fordham U., N.Y.C., 1990; presenter in field. Author: (book) Teacher Stories, 1993, Research on Teacher Thinking, 1993, Metaphor as a Mode of Instruction, 1995; contbr. articles to profl. jours. Recipient Impact II Tchr. Recognition award, 1984; grantee, Chpt. II, 1983—84, Clarkstown Ctrl. Schs., 1986—91, Office Spl. Edn., 1992, 1995, N.Y. Assn. Comprehensive Edn., 1997. Mem.: APA, AAUW, Assn. Retarded Citizens, Assn. Children with Learning Disabilities, Am. Ednl. Rsch. Assn., N.Y. State Congress Parents and Tchrs. (hon.). Avocations: reading, poetry, ballet, gardening, flower arranging. Home: PO Box 395 Valley Cottage NY 10989-0395 Office: Saint Thomas Aquinas Coll Rt 340 Sparkill NY 10976

NELSON, MARIAN EMMA, education educator; b. Brockton, Mass., Apr. 4, 1932; d. Carl V. and Lillian M. (Smith) N. AS, Boston U., 1952; BS in Edn., Bridgewater State Coll., 1956, MS in Edn., 1962. Cert. gen. tchr., elem., elem. libr. Tchr. 1st grade Brockton Pub. Schs., 1956-62; assoc. prof. edn. Bridgewater (Mass.) State Coll., 1962-96, ret., 1996. Founder, bd. dirs., pres. of bd. Children's Art Presch., Brockton. Author primary pod phonics program; contbr. articles to profl. jours. Tchr. ch. sch. 1st Evang. Luth. Ch.; mem. Coun. on Aging, Town of Bridgewater, 1998—. Luth. Brotherhood grantee. Mem. NEA, Mass. Tchrs. Assn., Nat. Assn. Lab. Schs., Delta Kappa Gamma (pres. Alpha Kappa chpt.), Phi Delta Kappa. Home: 60 Trailwood Dr Bridgewater MA 02324-2079

NELSON, MARILYN (MARILYN NELSON WANIEK), education educator, poet; b. Cleve., Apr. 26, 1946; d. Melvin Moton and Johnnie Edwina (Mitchell) Nelson; m. Erdmann Waniek, 1970 (div. 1979); m. Roger B. Wilkenfeld, 1979 (div. 1998); children: Jacob, Dora. BA, U. Calif., Davis, 1968; MA, U. Pa., 1970; PhD, U. Minn., 1979. With Lane C.C., Eugene, Oreg., 1970-72; vis. prof. Reed Coll., Portland, 1971-72, Nr. Nissum Seminarium, Denmark, 1972-73, St. Olaf Coll., Northfield, Minn., 1973-78, Universitat Hamburg, Fed. Republic of Germany, spring 1977, U. Conn., Storrs, 1978—2002, Trinity Coll., Hartford, Conn., 1982-83; adj. prof. NYU, 1986—87, 1994—95; instr. MFA program Vt. Coll., 1988-89; Fulbright tchg. fellow France, 1995; vis. prof. U.S. Mil. Acad., West Point, NY, 2000, U. Del., 2002—. Resident faculty Frost Place, Franconia, N.H., 1986. Author: For the Body, 1978, The Cat Walked Through the Casserole, 1984, Mama's Promises, 1985, The Homeplace, 1990, Partial Truth, 1992, Magnificat, 1994, The Fields of Praise: New and Selected Poems, 1997, Carver: A LIfe in Poems, 2001, Triolets for Triolet, 2001, She-Devil Circus, 2001; translator: Literary Sex Roles, 1975, Hundreds of Hens and Other Poems, 1983, "Hecuba" in Euripides I of Penn Greek Drama Series. Recipient Annisfield-Wolf award, 1992, The Poets prize, 1998, The Boston Globe-Horn Book award, 2001; Kent fellow, 1976, NEA fellow, 1981, 90; Danish Ministry of Culture grantee, 1984; Guggenheim fellow, 2001; nominee Pulitzer prize, 1985, 91, Nat. Book award finalist, 1991. Mem. AAUP, Associated Writing Programs, Soc. for the Study of Multi-Ethnic Lit. of the U.S., Soc. for Values in Higher Edn., Third World Villanell Soc., Phi Kappa Phi. Avocation: quilting, travel, contemplation.. Office: U Del Dept English Newark DE

NELSON, MARILYN C. hotel executive, food service executive, travel services executive, marketing professional; b. Mpls. m. Glen Nelson; children: Diana, Curtis C., Wendy. Student, U. Sorbonne, Paris, Inst. Hautes Etudes Econ., Geneva; degree in internat. econs. with honors, Smith Coll., 1961; DBA (hon.), Johnson & Wales U.; DHL (hon.), Coll. St. Catherine, Gustavus Adolphus Coll. Securities analyst Paine Webber, Mpls.; co-owner Citizens State Bank, Waterville, Minn., 1971—; COO Carlson Cos., Inc., Mpls., 1997—, pres., CEO, chmn., 1998—, also bd. dirs. Co-chair Carlson Holdings, Inc., 1991—; dep. chair Thomas Cook Holdings; co-chair Carlson Wagonlit Travel, 1994—; disting. vis. prof. Johnson & Wales U.; bd. dirs. Exxonmobil Corp., Qwest, Inc. Pres. United Way Mpls., campaign chair, 1984; bd. dirs. United Way Am.; chair Super Bown Task Force, Mpls.; bd. dirs. U.S. Nat. Tourism Orgn., 1996—, Ctr. for Internat. Leadership, 1990—; mem. Internat. Adv. Coun., 1996—; mem. disting. adv. coun. Coll. of St. Catherine, 1989—; mem. Bretton Woods Com., 1986—; hon. bd. dris. Svenska Inst., Stockholm, 1993—; mem. adv. bd. Hubert H. Humphrey Inst. Pub. Affairs, 1992-96; co-founder Minn. Women's Econ. Roundtable, 1974—; chair Minn. Super Bowl Task Force, 1992; chair, founder Midsummer Internat. Festival of Music; co-chair New Sweden '88; past bd. dirs. Guthrie Theatre, Greater Mpls. coun. Girl Scouts U.S., Jr. Achievement, Jr. League Mpls., KTCA Pub. TV, Minn. Congl. Award, Minn. Opera Co., Women's Assn. Minn. Symphony Orch.; trustee Smith Coll., Northampton, Mass., 1980-85, Macalester Coll., St. Paul, 1974-80. Named Woman of Yr., Minn. Exec. Women in Tourism, Sales Exec. of Yr., Sales and Mktg. Exec. of Mpls., Person of Yr. Travel Agt. mag., 1997, Woman of Yr. Roundtable for Women in Foodsvc., 1995, Outstanding Individual in Tourism, Minn. Office of Tourism, 1992, Woman of Yr., Minn. Exec. Women in Tourism, 1991-92, The Top 25 Execs. Yr. Bus. Week, 1999, Exec. Yr. Corp. Report Minn., 1999; recipient Minn. Congl. award for initiative and svc. to cmty., cert. of commendation State of Minn., Cmty. Svc. award YWCA, Independence award Vinland Nat. Ctr., Cmty. Svc. award Park-Nicollet Med. Ctr., Outstanding Mktg. Exec. of Yr. award, Minn. Distributive Edn. Club Am., Career Achievement award Sales and Mktg. Execs. Mpls., Outstanding Achievement award United Way Mpls., Extraordinary Leadership award Greater Mpls. C. of C., Disting. Svc. award United Way of Am., 1984-90, Nat. Caring award Caring Inst., 1995, Outstanding Bus. Leader award Northwood U., 1995, The 50 Most Powerful Women award in Am. Bus. Fortune, 1998, United Way Minn. Disting. Svc. award United Way's highest vol. honor, 1998, Good Neighbor award WCCO Radio, 1999, Caring Heart award charitable contbns. by Larry King Cardiac Found., 1999, Am.'s 100 Most Important Women award Ladies' Home Jr., 1999, The 50 Most Powerful Women in Bus. Fortune 1999, The Most Powerful Women in Travel #1 Travel Agent, 1999, Svc. Above Self award The Rotary Club Downtown, Minn., 1999, The Top 500 Women-Owned Bus.'s award Working Women, 2000, The 25 Most Influential Executives award Leisure Travel News, 2000, Northwest Airlines Disting. World Traveler award Hospitality Sales and Mktg. Assn. Internat., 2000. Mem. Hennepin County Med. Soc. Auxiliary, Jr. League Mpls., Minn. Meetings, Smith Coll. Alumni Assn., Smith Club Mpls., Woodhill Country Club, Mpls. Club, N.W. Tennis Club, Nat. Ctr. for Social Entrepreneurs, Com. of 200, Minn. Orchestral Assn., Orphei Dranger, Alpha Kappa Psi. Office: Carlson Cos Inc Carlson Parkway Minneapolis MN 55459-8215*

NELSON, MARITA LEE, anatomist, educator; b. Torrance, Calif., Aug. 8, 1934; d. Lee George and Marie Blanche (Waples) N. BS, UCLA, 1957, MS, 1959; PhD in Anatomy, U. Calif., Berkeley, 1968. Instr. Ill. State U., 1960-64; assoc. U. Calif., Berkeley, 1965-68, instr., 1968-69, acting asst. prof., 1969, asst. prof., 1972-74, Georgetown U. Schs. Medicine and Dentistry, 1969-72; assoc. prof. anatomy and reproductive biology John A. Burns Sch. Medicine, U. Hawaii, 1974-82, prof., 1982-97, prof. clin. anatomy and pathology, 1997-99, prof. emerita, 1999—. Recipient Tchg. award Kaiser Found., 1977, Golden Pineapple award John A. Burns Sch. Medicine, 1979, Basic Sci. Tchr. of Yr. award, 1986, 88, 92, 94, Excellence in Tchg. Regent's medal, 1984, Disting. Tchg. award U. Calif., Berkeley, 1983, Regent's medal U. Hawaii, 1984. Mem. AAUP, Am. Assn. Anatomists, Am. Assn. Clin. Anatomists, Assn. Women in Sci., Hawaiian Assn. Women in Sci., Sigma Xi, Pi Lambda Theta. Achievements include research on environmental endocrinology, effects of high altitude on maturation and pituitary function, extracranial arteriosclerosis and stroke risk. Office: 1960 E West Rd Honolulu HI 96822-2319 E-mail: mnelson@hawaii.edu.

NELSON, MARK BRUCE, interior designer; b. Los Angeles, Dec. 8, 1921; s. Mark Bruce and Rubie (Henrionnet) N. BA in Art, U. Calif., Los Angeles, 1943, postgrad., 1949-50, Art Center Sch., 1946-49. Tchr. Pasadena (Calif.) City Coll., 1950-54; propr. Mark Nelson Interiors, Los Angeles, 1954—; designer DuPont Corp. exhibit N.Y. World's Fair, 1964; co-chmn. Los Angeles show com. Am. Inst. Interior Designers, 1960-67, Living with Famous Paintings, 1964-65. Mem. Los Angeles adv. council Am. Arbitration Assn., 1971-72; chmn. Los Angeles N.C.I.D.Q., 1973-80, Design House West, 1978 Mem. Los Angeles Beautiful Com., 1966. Served as officer USNR, 1942-46, 52-53, ETO, Korea. Fellow Am. Soc. Interior Designers (life mem., exam. chmn. 1972— , chmn. nat. by-laws com. 1973, pres. Los Angeles 1969-71, Calif. regional v.p. 1970-73, pres. Los Angeles found. 1980, Presdl. citation 1973); mem. Phi Kappa Sigma. Home and Office: 554 Lillian Way Los Angeles CA 90004-1106 *During my thirty years as a interior designer, I have* *enjoyed many successes, while watching the profession grow and improve. Designing the homes of rich and famous Americans has not altered my concept that it is the middle class American consumer who needs and can afford the services of professional designers.*

NELSON, MARTHA JANE, magazine editor; b. Pierre, S.D., Aug. 13, 1952; d. Bernard Anton and Pauline Isabel (Noren) N. BA, Barnard Coll., 1976. Mng. editor Signs: Jour. of Women in Culture, N.Y.C., 1976-80; staff editor Ms. Mag., 1980-85; editor-in-chief Women's Sports and Fitness Mag., Palo Alto, Calif., 1985-87; exec. editor Savvy, N.Y.C., 1988-89, editor-in-chief, 1989-91; asst. mng. editor People, 1993; founding editor In Style Mag., N.Y.C., 1993—2002, exec. prodr. TV program Celebrity Weddings, 1997—2002, exec. prodr. TV programs Celebrity Moms, Celebrity Homes, 2001; mng. editor People Mag., 2002—. Editor: Women in the American City, 1980; cons. editor Who Weekly, Sydney, 1992; contbr. articles to profl. jours. Bd. dirs. Painting Space 122, N.Y.C., 1982—85, 1995—96, Urban Athletic Assn. , 1986; accessories coun. adv. bd. NYU Grad. Sch.; mem. ACRIA, Comm. Rsch. Inst. on AIDS. Mem.: N.Y. Women in Comm., Women in Film, Am. Soc. Mag. Editors, Athletic and Swim Club.

NELSON, MARVIN DALE, JR. radiologist, educator; b. Hastings, Nebr., June 16, 1954; s. Marvin Dale Sr. and Patricia J. (Pingenot) N.; m. Mary C. Baron, Sep. 30, 1990; children: Kevin James, Andrew John. BS, MD, Loma Linda U., 1978; MBA, U. So. Calif., 1999. Diplomate Am. Bd. Radiology, Am. Bd. Diagnostic Radiology, Am. Bd. Pediat. Radiology, Am. Bd. Neuroradiology. Intern, resident in radiology Loma Linda U. Med. Ctr., 1978-82; fellow in neuroradiology Nat. Hosp. for Nervous Disease, London, 1985-86, Rothschild Founds., Paris, 1986; fellow in pediat. neuroradiology Children's Mem. Hosp., Chgo., 1986-87; asst. prof. radiology Children's Hosp.-USC Sch. Med., 1987-93, assoc. prof., 1993-2001; chmn. dept. radiology Children' Hosp., L.A., 1998—, prof., 2001—, John L. Gwinn prof. pediat. radiology, 2002—. Maj. USAF, 1982-85. Recipient Cornelius Dyke award for original rsch. Am. Soc. Radiology, 1990, Gabriel Wilson award for best paper Western Neuroradiol. Soc., 1997. Fellow Am. Coll. Radiology; mem. Am. Soc. Neurol. Radiology, western Neuroradiog. Soc. (pres. 2001). Office: Children's Hosp 4650 W Sunset Blvd Los Angeles CA 90027-6062 E-mail: mdnelson@chla.usc.edu.

NELSON, MARVIN RAY, retired life insurance company executive; b. Thornton, Iowa, Aug. 29, 1926; s. Clarence Anton and Rose Bessie (Nicolet) N.; m. Juanita Mae Brown, May 26, 1951; children: Nancy, Kenneth. BS, Drake U, 1951. Actuary Security Mut. Life Ins. Co., Lincoln, Nebr., 1951-58; assoc. actuary Life Ins. Co. N.Am., Phila., 1958-59; group actuary Bankers Life of Nebr., Lincoln, 1959-66; actuary Mut. Service Life Ins. Co., St. Paul, 1966-68; sr. v.p. Horace Mann Educators Corp., Springfield, Ill., 1968-77, Security Life of Denver, 1977-83, exec. v.p., 1988-91; pres., chief oper. officer, dir., mem. investment com. Midwestern United Life Ins. Co., Ft. Wayne, Ind., 1983-89; ret., 1991. Bd. dirs., treas. Ft. Wayne Urban League, 1983-87; bd. dirs. Taxpayers Research Assn., Ft. Wayne, 1984-88. Served with U.S. Army, 1946-47. Fellow Soc. Actuaries; mem. Am. Acad. Actuaries, Pi Kappa Phi. Home: 7636 E Windford St Parker CO 80134-5927

NELSON, MARY CARROLL, artist, writer; b. Bryan, Tex., Apr. 24, 1929; d. James Vincent and Mary Elizabeth (Langton) Carroll; m. Edwin Blakeley Nelson, June 27, 1950; children: Patricia Ann, Edwin Blakely. BA in Fine Arts, Barnard Coll., 1950; MA, U. N.Mex., 1963. Juror Am. Artist Golden Anniversary Competition, 1987, Don Ruffin Meml. Art Exhbn., Ariz., 1989, N.Mex. State Fair Profl. Exhbn., 1999. Guest instr. continuing edn. U. N.Mex., 1991; conf. organizer Affirming Wholeness, The Art and Healing Experience, San Antonio, 1992, Artists of the Spirit Symposium, 1994. Group shows include N.Mex. Mus., 1987, N.Mex. Lightworks, 1990, Level to Level, Layering, Ohio, 1987, Artist as Shaman, Ohio, 1990, The Healing Experience, Mass., 1991, Art is for Healing, The Universal Link, San Antonio, 1992, Fuller Lodge Art Ctr. Los Alamos, N.Mex., 1993, Layering, Albuquerque, 1993, Crossings, Bradford, Mass., 1994, The Layered Perspective, Fayetteville, Ark., 1994, Tree of Life, San Miguel de Allende, Mex., 1996, Honoree, Magnifico, Albuquerque, 1997, Guardian Spirits, Marlborough, Eng., 1997, Memories in Multi-Media, Columbus, Ohio, 1998, Agora Gallery, N.Y.C., 1998, Celtic Connections, Mass., 1998, Bridging Time and Space, Calif., 1999, Musings on the Millennium, Ohio, 2000, Layerists in Multi-Media/Affirming Wholeness, Albuquerque, 2000, The Birth of Wisdom, N. Mand Gordes, France, 2000, Tides of Change, Tex., 2001, EarthSpirit, Ohio, 2001, Shadow & Light, Albuquerque, 2001, Landscape and Memory, Sedona, Ariz., 2002, dsg Gallery, Albuquerque, 2002others; represented in pvt. collections in U.S., Germany, Eng. and Australia; author: American Indian Biography Series, 1971-76, (with Robert E. Wood) Watercolor Workshop, 1974; (with Ramon Kelley) Ramon Kelley Paints Portraits and Figures, 1977, The Legendary Artists of Taos, 1980, (catalog) American Art in Peking, 1981, Masters of Western Art, 1982, Connecting, The Art of Beth Ames Swartz, 1984, Artists of the Spirit, 1994, Doris Steider, A Vision of Silence, 1997, Beyond Fear, A Toltec's Guide to Freedom and Joy, 1997, Layering, An Art of Time and Space, 1985, (catalog) Layering/Connecting, 1987; contbg. editor Am. Artist, 1976-91, Southwestern Art, 1987-91; editor (video) Layering, 1990; arts correspondent Albuquerque Jour., 1991-93; contbr. One Source Sacred Journeys, 1997, Bridging Time and Space, Essays on Layered Art, 1998; co-author: Bridging Time and Space, Essays on Layered Art, 1998. Mem. Albuquerque Arts Bd., 1984-88. Mem. Soc. Layerists in Multi-Media (founder 1982). Home: 1408 Georgia St NE Albuquerque NM 87110-6861 E-mail: mcn50@swcp.com.

NELSON, MARY KATHRYN, bilingual counselor, artist, singer, comedienne; b. Chgo., May 28, 1954; d. James C. Nelson and Leila R. Cooke. BS in Social Work, So. Ill. U., 1978; MS in Rehab. Counseling, U. Ariz., 1982. Cert. rehab. counselor, substance abuse counselor, profl. counselor, Ariz.; nat. cert. counselor. Bilingual counselor Ill. Migrant Council, 1975-76; social worker Child Protective Svcs., 1980-85; bilingual clinician pvt. nonprofit agys., 1985-96; bilingual counselor contractor, counselor Suprme Ct. Ariz., Phoenix, 1995—; owner, mgr. Valleywide Inhome Bilingual Counseling, Scottsdale, Ariz., 1985—; actress, comedienne, singer, 1995—. Exhibited in group shows at Franciscan Renewal Ctr., Scottsdale, 2001, exhibitions include Artareas.com, 2001—; performer: Talent Show at Crossroads, 1999—2001; singer: Franciscan Renewal Ctr., 2000—01;exhibitions include Fountain Hills Ariz. Art Exhibit, 1995, Channel 22 Phoenix Cable Amateur Hr., Spanish Songs, 1996, Iberoamericana Internat. Art Exhibit, Miami, Fla., 1997, Phoenix K Lite Radio TV Commn., 1997, Peoria Sportscomplex Art Fair, Ariz., 1998, Franciscan Renewal Ctr. Art Fair, Scottsdale, Ariz., 1999, 2001, ArtAreas.com. Vol. Big Bros.-Big Sisters, Tucson, 1999; family advocate Cesar Chavez Farmworkers Union Labor Movement; art donator Ariz. Foster Care Assn., Paradise Valley, Ariz., 2001, donor original oil painting with World Trade Ctr. motif, 2001; vol. campaign worker Jon Kyle for Senator, Phoenix, 1996—99; fundraiser John Shadegy for Congreeeman, 2002; choir mem. Franciscan Renewal Ctr., Paradise Valley, 1999—2002. Recipient humanitarian award Inst. Arts Plastiques, 1997. Mem. Drama Beat Acting Club. Republican. Avocation: singing live Spanish and English, comedy, acting. Web site: www.artareas.com. Home and Office: PO Box 3435 Scottsdale AZ 85271-3435 E-mail: binkyink@webtv.net.

NELSON, MARY ELLEN DICKSON, retired actuary; b. Mpls., Mar. 24, 1933; d. William Alexander and Laura Winona (Baxter) Dickson; m. David Aldrich Nelson, Aug. 25, 1956; children: Frederick Dickson, Claudia Baxter, Caleb Edward. BA, Vassar Coll., 1954; postgrad., Cambridge (Eng.) U., 1954-55. Rsch. assoc. N.Am. Life & Casualty Co., Mpls., 1955-56; actuarial asst. John Hancock Mut. Life Ins. Co., Boston, 1956-58; actuary David R. Kass & Assocs., Cleve., 1973-74; pres. Nelson & Co., 1975, Conrad, Nelson & Co., Cleve., 1975-81, Nelson & Co., Cleve./Cin., 1981-99. Bd. dirs. Blount Internat. Inc. and its subs. Blount, Inc., Montgomery, Ala., 1986—99, Broadwing, Inc., Union Ctrl. Life Ins. Co., Cin. Scholar Fulbright, 1954—55. Fellow: Soc. Actuaries, Phi Beta Kappa; mem.: Am. Acad. Actuaries, Midwest Benefits Conf. (chair 1991), Cin. Actuaries Club. Republican.

NELSON, MERLIN DEAN WILLIAM, accountant; b. Norfolk, Nebr., Nov. 22, 1943; s. Oscar Reuben and Esther L. (Schmidt) N.; ed. public schs.; m. Sandra Lee Davalos, Feb. 27, 1965 (div. Feb. 1985); children— Renee Marie, Ramon Reuben; m. Susan E. Snowden Richay, Apr. 19, 1985. Sales clk. Katz Drug Co., Topeka, 1964-65; with Frito Lay Inc., Topeka, 1965-66, Pacific Gamble Robinson, Topeka, 1966-68; cost accountant Ohse Meat Products, Inc., Topeka, 1968— , office mgr., acctg. supr., 1980— . Served with U.S. Army, 1961-64. Roman Catholic. Home: 427 NE Emmett St Topeka KS 66616-1206 Office: PO Box PO Box 1658 Topeka KS 66601-1658

NELSON, MERLIN EDWARD, international business consultant, company director; b. Fargo, N.D., Jan. 30, 1922; s. Theodore G. and Eva C. (Hultgren) N.; m. Nancy Ellen Craig, June 1952 (div. June 1962); children: Craig Edward, Brian Anthony; m. Janet April Pope, Aug. 30, 1963; children: Claudia Jane, Rolf Merlin. BS in Polit. Sci., U. Oreg., 1943; postgrad., Fordham U., 1943-44; JD, Yale U., 1948. Bar: Oreg. 1948, N.Y. 1954, U.S. Dist. Ct. D.C. 1954. Atty. Office Gen. Counsel, ECA, Washington and Paris, 1949-52; assoc. Davis, Polk, Wardwell, Sunderland & Kiendl, 1952-59; exec. asst. to v.p. AMF, Inc., N.Y.C., 1960-62; chmn., mng. dir. AMF Internat., Ltd., London, 1962-63; v.p., group exec. AMF, Inc., 1963-70, exec. v.p., vice chmn., dir., 1970-84, now cons., 1984—; ret., 1984. Bd. dirs. Indsl. Bank Japan Trust Co., Mitsui Found., IBJ Found.; chmn., pres. Tuckernuck Land Trust. Mem. Coun. Fgn. Rels.; mem. nat. adv. coun. Trust for Pub. Land. Decorated Purple Heart. Mem. Phi Beta Kappa. Home and Office: 16 W 77th St Apt 12E New York NY 10024-5126 E-mail: nelsonmj@earthlink.net.

NELSON, MICHAEL UNDERHILL, association executive; b. Balt., May 5, 1932; s. Cyril Arthur and Elise (Macy) N.; m. Barbara Gail Hutchins, June 25, 1960; children: Kevin Underhill, Bronwyn Hastings, Gayle Hutchins, Corey Williams. AB, Rutgers U., 1957, EdM, 1968. Salesman J & N Distbg. Co., New Brunswick, N.J., 1957-59; extension assoc. Univ. Coll., Rutgers U., 1959-61; asst. dir. summer session Rutgers U., 1961-68; asst. dean sch. continuing edn., dir. summer sch. Washington U., St. Louis, 1969-81, dir. div. of profl. and community programs sch. continuing edn., 1975-78; exec. sec. N.Am. Assn. Summer Sessions, 1979—; account exec. Trio Printing Co., 1982-84; sr. procedures analyst McDonnell Douglas Corp, St. Louis, 1984-96. Bd. dirs. Adult Edn. Council of Greater St. Louis, 1975-78. Served with USMC, 1951-54. Mem. North Ctrl. Conf. Summer Schs. (pres. 1974-75), Am. Assn. Univ. Adminstrs., Assn. Univ. Summer Sessions, Am. Summer Sessions Senate, N.Am. Assn. Summer Sessions (pres. 1978), Alpha Sigma Lambda, Phi Delta Kappa. Episcopalian. Home and Office: 43 Belanger Dr Dover NH 03820-4602 E-mail: NAASS@aol.com.

NELSON, MURRY ROBERT, education educator; b. Chgo., May 12, 1947; s. H. Cyril and Beatrice (Lissner) N.; m. Elizabeth Jane Rose, June 15, 1973; children: Rebecca Meredith, Daniel Zachary. AB in Sociology, Grinnell (Iowa) Coll., 1969; MA in Teaching, Northwestern U., 1972; MA in Anthropology, PhD in Edn., Stanford U., 1975. Tchr. Chgo. Pub. Schs., 1970-72; supr. tchr. interns Stanford (Calif.) U., 1972-75; asst. prof. edn. The Penn State U., University Park, 1975-82, assoc. prof. edn., 1982-87, coord. elem. program, 1984-90, prof. edn., 1987—, coord. grad. edn. curriculum and instrn., 1992-98, head dept. curriculum and instrn., 2000—; Fulbright lectr. in edn. U. Iceland, 1983. Disting. vis. prof. U. Wyo., 1989; Fulbright Sr. Lectureship in Am. Studies, Ministry of Edn., Norway, 1990-91; workshop presenter in field; cons. in field. Author: Law in the Curriculum, 1978, Children and Social Studies, 1992, 98, The Originals - The New York Celtics Invent Modern Basketball, 1999; editor: Critical Issues in Curriculum, 1988, Curriculum History, 1989, The Future of the Social Studies, 1994, The 1916 Report of the Committee on Social Studies of the Commission on the Reorganization of Secondary Education of the National Education Association, 1994; contbr. numerous articles to profl. jours.; mem. editorial bd. Theory and Rsch. in Social Edn., 1978-84, 87-90, Social Studies Jour., 1980-83, Social Edn., Internat. Social Studies Forum, 2000—. Named Outstanding Young Man of Am., 1975, 79; named Vis. Phi Delta Kappa scholar, 1979; recipient Harry J. Carmen Gold medal for Outstanding Achievement in Social Studies, 1985, Outstanding Rsch. award Rural Edn. Assn., 1982, Fulbright Sr. Lectureship, U. Iceland, 1983, Norwegian Ministry of Edn., 1990-91. Mem. Am. Edn. Rsch. Assn. (program chair Rsch. in Social Studies Edn. 1988, com. on spl. interest groups 1992-94, chair 1993-94), Coun. for Anthropology and Edn., Nat. Coun. for Social Studies (chmn. rural social studies com. 1979-80, bd. dirs. 1997-2000. chair acad. freedom com. 1981-82, coll. and univ. faculty assembly bd. dirs. 1981-83, chairperson 1983), Pa. Coun. for Social Studies (pres. 1987-88, bd. dirs. 1983-89), Social Sci. Edn. Consortium, Phi Delta Kappa. Avocations: basketball, skiing, baseball cards, travel. E-mail: mrn2@psu.edu.

NELSON, NANCY ELEANOR, pediatrician, educator; b. El Paso, Apr. 4, 1933; d. Harry Hamilton and Helen Maude (Murphy) N. BA magna cum laude, U. Colo., 1955, MD, 1959. Intern, Case Western Res. U. Hosp., 1959-60, resident, 1960-63; pvt. practice medicine specializing in pediats., Denver, 1963-70; clin. prof. U. Colo. Sch. Medicine, Denver, 1988—, assoc. dean student affairs U. Colo. Sch. Medicine, 1988—. Mem. Am. Acad. Pediats., AMA (sect. med. schs. governing coun. 1994-96), Denver Med. Soc. (pres. 1983-84), Colo. Med. Soc. (bd. dirs. 1985-88, mem. jud. coun. 1992—, mem. liason com. med. edn. 1995—). Office: 4200 E 9th Ave Denver CO 80220-3706

NELSON, NEVIN MARY, interior designer; b. Cleve., Nov. 5, 1941; d. Arthur George Reinker and Barbara Phyllis (Gunn) Parks; m. Wayne Nelson (div. 1969); children: Doug, Brian. BA in Interior Design, U. Colo., 1964. Prin. Nevin Nelson Design, Boulder, Colo., 1966-70, Vail, 1970—, Denver, 2002—. Program chmn. Questers Antique Study Group, Boulder, 1969. Coord. Bob Kirscht for Gov. campaign, Eagle County, Colo., 1986; state del. Rep. Nat. Conv., 1986-88; county coord. George Bush for U.S. Pres. campaign, 1988, 92; chmn. Eagle County Reps., 1989-93; v.p. bd. dirs. Park Lane Condo Assn., Denver, 1995-96; pres. Save Our Imperiled Land, Vail, 1998. Mem. Am. Soc. Interior Designers, City Club of Denver, Chaine des Rotisseurs; Fndr. Denver Dollies Red Hat Soc., 2001. Episcopalian. Avocations: party planning, cooking, reading, travel, skiing. Home: 1440 S Dahlia St Denver CO 80222

NELSON, NORMAN DANIEL, government official; b. Dec. 30, 1968; BSBA, U. Fla., 1991; MBA, U. Miami, 1997; MA, Georgetown U., 2000. Intern corp. fin. divsn. mergers and acquisitions Commerzbank AG, Frankfurt, 1992; intern corp. fin. divsn. internat. leasing and new stock issues Deutsche Bank AG, 1992; commd. 2d lt. disting. mil. grad. USAR, 1991; advanced through grades to capt. USAR, C.E. and Civil Affairs, 2000; econ. plans and program officer U.S. Dept. of State, 1997—; pres., CEO Nelson Systems Internat. Corp., 1998—. Mem. Boy Scouts Am. (Eagle Scout). Decorated Army Commendation medal (2); Fed. Chancellor scholar Alexander-von-Humboldt Found., 1991-92. Mem. Sigma Chi.

NELSON, PAUL JAMES, educator; b. Porter County, Ind., Dec. 1, 1932; s. Forrest Ross and Bessie Marie (Kline) N.; m. Judith Ann Benda, Feb. 14, 1956; children: Douglas Ross, Paula Ann, Daniel Forrest. Grad. high sch., Chesterton, Ind. Lic. comml. pilot; cert. tchr., Ind. With U.S. Steel Co., Gary, Ind., 1951-54, 59-83; pilot, instr. Phillips Airlines, Michigan City, 1983-85; tchr. Gary Cmty. Sch. Corp., 1985-95; profl. grant writer for edn. Employed Bethlehem Steel, Chesterton, Ind., 1997—. Author: (text book) Machinist Study Guides, 1980. Trustee Town of Pines, 1970; pres. Pines Planning Commn., Inc., 1973, v.p., 1991—; Pines Bd. Zoning Appeals, 1978; mem. Ind. Dunes Nat. Lakeshore Task Forces, 1980, Gary Regional Airport Task Force, 1988; cert. airlift vol. Am. Cancer Soc., 1981; Dem. precinct com. person Pine Twsp., Ind.; treas. Porter County Dem. Ctrl. Com., 1997—. With USAF, 1954-56. Democrat. Avocations: restoration old aircraft, building scale locomotives. Home: 1545 Ash St Michigan City IN 46360-6652 Office: Burns Harber Divsn PO Box 248 Chesterton IN 46304-0248

NELSON, PAULA MORRISON BRONSON, educator; b. Memphis, Mar. 26, 1944; d. Fred Ford and Julia (Morrison) Bronson: m. Jack Marvin Nelson, July 13, 1968; children: Eric Allen, Kelly Susan. BS, U. N.Mex., 1967; MA, U. Colo., Denver, 1985. Physical edn. tchr. Grant Union Sch. Dist., Sacramento, 1967-68, Denver Pub. Schs., 1968-74, with program for pupil assistance, 1974-80; tchr. ESL Douglas County Pub. Schs., Parker, Colo., 1982-83; chpt. 1 reading specialist Denver Pub. Schs., 1983-96, computer/reading specialist, 1996-98, reading specialist, gifted and talented tchr., 1998-99, lead tchr. in charge instrn., 1999-2001, edn. cons., 2001—. Demonstration tchr. Colo. Edn. Assn., 1970-72; mem. curriculum com. Denver Pub. Schs., 1970-72; mem. Douglas County Accountability Com., Castle Rock, Colo., 1986-92; mem. educators rev. panel Edn. for Freedom; computer trainer Denver Pub. Schs. Tech. Team, 1992—. Co-author: Gymnastics Teacher's Guide Elementary Physical Education, 1973, Applauding Our Constitution, 1989; editorial reviewer G is for Geography, Children's Literature and the Five Themes. 1993; producer slide shows Brotherhood, 1986, We the People...Our Dream Lives On, 1987, Celebration of Cultures, 1988. Named Pub. Edn. Coalition grantee, Denver, 1987, 88, 89, 90, grantee Rocky Mountain Global Edn. Project, 1987, Wake Forest Law Sch., Winston-Salem, N.C., 1988, 89, 90, 92, Read to Achieve grantee Colo. State Dept. Edn., 2000; recipient chpt. II grant, 1991, Tech. grant, 1993, Title VI Reading grant, 1999, 2000, Three R's of Freedom award State Dept. Edn., 1987, Nat. Recognition award Commn. on Bicentennial of Constitution., 1987, Distinguished Tchr. award City of Denver, 1994. Mem.: Denver Fedn. Tchrs., Am. Fedn. Tchrs., Tech. in Edn. Republican. Methodist. Avocations: snow and water skiing, tennis. Home: 10488 E Meadow Run Parker CO 80134-6220

NELSON, PHILIP EDWIN, food scientist, educator; b. Shelbyville, Ind., Nov. 12, 1934; s. Brainard R. and Alta E. (Pitts) N.; m. Sue Bayless, Dec. 27, 1955; children: Jennifer, Andrew, Bradley. BS, Purdue U., 1956, PhD, 1976. Plant mgr. Blue River Packing Co., Morristown, Ind., 1956-60; instr. Purdue U., West Lafayette, 1961-76, head dept. food sci., 1984—. Cons. PEN Cons., West Lafayette, 1974; chair Food Processors Inst., Washington, 1990-93. Editor: Fruit Vegetable Juice Technology, 1980, Principles of Aseptic Processing and Packaging, 1992. Recipient Pers. Achievement award USDA, 1997. Fellow Inst. Food Techs. (Indsl. Achievement award 1976, Nicholas Appert award 1995, 49'er Svc. award 1995, Tanner Lectr. 1999, pres. 2002—); mem. AAAS, Sigma Xi, Phi Tau Sigma (pres. 1976-77). Achievements include 11 U.S. and foreign patents. Office: Purdue U Dept Food Sci 1160 Food Sci Bldg West Lafayette IN 47907-1160 E-mail: pen@purdue.edu.

NELSON, PHILIP FRANCIS, musicology educator, consultant, choral conductor; b. Waseca, Minn., Feb. 17, 1928; s. Elmer Philip and Frances (Bretzke) N.; m. Georgia Ann Yelland, June 5, 1950; children: Curtis Ann, Philip Francis Jr. *Philip Nelson's father, E.P. Nelson, a native Minnesotan, was a successful motion picture theatre owner in the Midwest for 50 years. Philip's wife, a Phi Beta Kappa Grinnell College 1951 graduate, has devoted her professional life to student affairs in several universities. She is noted for her distinguished tenure as Dean of Freshmen at Yale. Philip's daughter, Curtis Ann, is a graduate of Yale University and Smith College. She is a senior staff member of the John F. Kennedy School of Government at Harvard. Philip's son, Phil Jr. is a graduate of Pomona College and UCLA and is a practicing architect with Cesar Pelli Associates in New Haven.* AB, Grinnell Coll., 1950; AM, U. N.C., 1956, PhD, 1958; Diplome (Fulbright scholar), U. Paris, 1957; student, Conservatoire Nat. de Paris, 1956-57; MA (hon.), Yale U., 1971; LHD (hon.)., Grinnell Coll., 1981. Asst. prof. Ariz. State U., 1958-62, assoc. prof., 1962-63; prof., chmn. dept. music SUNY, Binghamton, 1963-70; prof., dean Sch. Music, Yale U., 1970-81; prof., provost, dean U. Calif., Santa Cruz, 1981-83; chmn. trustee com. Curtis Inst., 1982-83; sr. v.p. AED, N.Y.C., 1984-87; v.p. Aspen Inst. for Humanistic Studies, 1987-89; interim chancellor Sch. Arts, U. N.C., 1989-90; assoc. fellow Nat. Humanities Ctr., 1990-91; interim vice chancellor U. N.C., Chapel Hill, 1991; cons. edn., arts, 1992-93; chmn. grad. sch. adv. coun. U. N.C., Chapel Hill, 1993-96, cons. arts and humanities, 1996—; interim dir. N.C. Sch. Sci. and Math., 1999-2000. Music critic Phoenix Gazette, 1959-62; music cons. Taliesin West, 1959-63; chmn. Nat. Screening Com. for Fulbright Awards in Musicology, 1965-68; cons. Nat. Endowment for Arts, 1984-90; vis. lectr. Duke U., 1992—. Contbg. editor: College and Adult Reading List, 1962, Nicolas Bernier, Principles of Composition, 1964, Recherches sur la musique Française classique, 1979, 80; contbr. to Groves Dictionary of Music, 6th edit.; editor publs. in the arts for The Aspen Inst. for the Humanities, 1987-89. Bd. dirs. various symphonies, chamber music socs., arts groups; trustee Curtis Inst. Music, Phila., 1980-83; mem. exec. com. Conn. State Golf Assn., 1975-81; founder Seven Springs Soc., 1975; bd. dirs. Conn. Hospice, 1983-87, Nat. Soc. to Prevent Blindness, 1987-93;, bd. dirs., v.p., 1987-93; mem. Chapel Hill Arts Ctr., 1992—; mem. Triangle J. Coun. Govt., 1992-95. Served from ensign to lt. comdr. USCGR, 1952-72. Found. grantee. Mem. Am., Internat. musicol. socs., Coll. Music Soc. (nat. council, editor jour. 1966-69), Société Française de Musicologie, Soc. Ethnomusicology, U.S. Srs. Golf Assn. Clubs: Mory's (New Haven); Yale (N.Y.C.); Elizabethan Grads., Carolina Club, New Haven Country, Yale Golf, Finley Golf, Chapel Hill Country. Home: 621 Greenwood Rd Chapel Hill NC 27514-5921 *Keep casting bread on the waters-it may come back as French toast.*

NELSON, PRINCE ROGERS See PRINCE

NELSON, RALPH ALFRED, physician; b. Mpls., June 19, 1927; s. Alfred W. and Lydia (Johnson) N.; m. Rosemary Pokela, Aug. 7, 1954; children— Edward Ancher, Audrey Anne, Elizabeth Marie, Andrew William, Evan Robert. BA, U. Minn., 1949, MD, 1953, PhD, 1961. Diplomate Am. Bd. Internal Medicine. Intern Cook County (Ill.) Hosp., 1953-54; resident U. Minn. Hosps., Mpls., 1954-55, U. Minn., Mpls., 1955-56; fellow in physiology Mayo Grad. Sch., Rochester, Minn., 1957-60, resident in internal medicine, 1976-78; practice medicine specializing in internal medicine and clin. nutrition Sioux Falls, S.D., 1978-79, Urbana, Ill., 1979—. Bd. dirs. Scott Research Lab., Fairview Park Hosp., Cleve., 1962-67; assoc. in physiology Western Res. U., Cleve., 1962-67; asst. prof. physiology Mayo Grad. Sch., 1967-73, Mayo Med. Sch., 1973, assoc. prof. nutrition, 1974; cons. in nutrition Mayo Clinic, 1967-76; assoc. prof. medicine U. S.D. Sch. Medicine, Sioux Falls, 1978-79; prof. nutrition U. Ill. Coll. Medicine, Urbana-Champaign, 1979— , chmn. dept. medicine prof. nutritional sci., physiology, biophysics dept. food sci. Sch. Agr., 1979—, also prof. medicine, exec. head dept. internal medicine , 1989—, exec. head four sites of Coll. Medicine, 1989-2000; dir. research Carle Found. Hosp., Urbana, 1979— ; cons. nutritional support service Danville (Ill.) VA Hosp., 1980—. Co-author: The Mayo Clinic Renal Diet Cookbook, 1974; contbr. articles on nutrition, physiology, and hibernation to sci. jours.; editor: Geriatrics, 1980— , The Physician and Sportsmedicine, 1980-88, Am. Jour. Clin. Nutrition, 1980-83. Cons. in nutrition Nat. Cancer Inst., 1976; cons. in nutrition HEW, 1976, 79, 89, Nat. Heart and Lung Inst., 1976. Served with USAF, 1945-47. Fulbright scholar, Morocco, 1988. Fellow ACP; mem. Am. Physiol. Soc., Am. Inst. Nutrition, Am. Soc. Clin. Nutrition, Central Soc. Clin. Research, Am. Gastroent. Assn. Lutheran. Home: 2 Illini Cir Urbana IL 61801-5813 Office: Carle Foundation Hospital 611 W Park St Urbana IL 61801-2529 E-mail: r-nelson@staff.UIUC.edu.

NELSON, RALPH ERWIN, investment company executive, coin dealer; b. Chgo., July 30, 1946; s. Vernon Leslie and Astrid Lorene (Seagren) N.; BS, McPherson Coll., 1971; MBA, U. Sarasota, 1980, MFM, 1981; MHS, U. Sarasota, 1983; PhD, Columbia Pacific U., 1984; m. Elarie Marie Fletcher, Oct. 14, 1967; 1 child, Anne Marie. Chief planning dept. Roberts & Zoller Inc., Bradenton, Fla., 1971-76; v.p., supr. planning div. Dan Zoller Engring. Inc., Bradenton, 1976-78; pres. Ralph Nelson & Assocs., Inc., Landscape Architects, Planners, Architects and Engrs., Bradenton, 1978-88, Nelson Investments, Inc., 1981—. Baptist. Address: PO Box 14777 Bradenton FL 34280-4777

NELSON, RALPH STANLEY, lawyer; b. Mpls., Mar. 15, 1943; s. Stanley L. and Louise M. Nelson; m. Judy E. Nelson, July 8, 1867; children: Sara C., Amy E., David A. BS in Bus. Adminstrn., U. Minn., 1966; JD with honors, Drake U., 1972. Bar: Minn. 1973, Wash. 1982, Tex. 1985. Assoc. Wiese and Cox, Ltd., Mpls., 1973-76; atty. Burlington No. R.R., St. Paul, 1976-81; sr. corp. counsel Burlington No. Inc., Seattle, 1981-85; v.p. law and adminstrn. Burlington Motor Carriers Inc., Ft. Worth, 1985-88, exec. v.p. and gen. counsel, 1988-93, sr. v.p., gen. counsel Daleville (Indpls.), Ind., 1993-96, Trism Inc., Kennesaw, Ga., 1996-2001, exec. v.p., gen. counsel, 2001—, pres., CEO, 2001—. Mem. law rev. Drake U. Capt. USMC, 1966-70. Mem. Order of the Coif. E-mail: ralphneslo@yahoo.com.

NELSON, RANDY SCOTT, lawyer; b. Milw., Dec. 4, 1952; s. Seymour and Mildred (Rosen) N.; m. Judy Ann, Jan. 4, 1975; children: Stefanie, Jeffrey. BBA, U. Wis., Milw., 1974; JD cum laude, Marquette U., 1977. Bar: Wis., U.S. Dist. Ct. (ea. dist., we. dist.) Wis. 1977, U.S. Tax Ct. 1984. Tax acct. Arthur Andersen & Co., Milw., 1977—80; atty. Weiss Berzowski Brady LLP, 1980—. Adj. prof. Marquette U. Law Sch., 1985—; continuing edn. instr. State Bar Wis., Wis. Inst. CPAs, 1982—. Co-author: Workbook for Wisconsin

Estate Planners, 1990. Mem. ABA, State Bar Wis. (chairperson real property, probate and trust law sect. 1998-99), Milw. Bar Assn., Am. Coll. Trust and Estate Counsel, AICPA, WICPA (Outstanding Instr. 1987-94). Office: Weiss Berzowski Brady 700 N Water St Ste 1500 Milwaukee WI 53202-4273 E-mail: rsn@wbb-law.com.

NELSON, REX, communications executive; b. Arkadelphia, Ark., Sept. 2, 1959; s. Robert and Carolyn N.; m. Melissa Garcia, Oct. 14, 1989; children: Austin, Evan. BA in Comm., Ouachita U., 1981. Chief Washington bur. Ark. Dem., Washington, 1986-89; comm. dir. U.S. Rep. Tommy Robinson, Little Rock, 1989-91; editor Ark. Bus. Jour., 1991-92; polit. editor Ark. Dem.-Gazette, 1992-96; comm. dir. Govs. Office, 1996—. Pres. Soc. Profl. Journalists, Little Rock, 1994-95. Author: The Hillary Factor, 1993. Republican. Baptist. Avocations: duck hunting, fishing, reading, traveling. Office: Gov's Office State Capitol Little Rock AR 72201-1088 E-mail: rex.nelson@gov.state.ar.us.

NELSON, RICHARD ALAN, financial executive; b. N.Y.C., Apr. 15, 1954; m. Hedwig Potok. BBA summa cum laude, U. Mich., 1976; MBA in Fin. Mgmt. and Internat. Bus., George Washington U., 1979. Mktg. rep. Wometco Enterprises, Inc., Miami, Fla., 1976-78; v.p. Gen. Investment Funds, Chevy Chase, Md., 1982-90; asst. to chmn. fin. GenCorp. (formerly The Gen. Tire and Rubber Co.), 1980-86; dir. investor rels. GenCorp., Fairlawn, Ohio, 1990-95; v.p. investor rels. Dix & Eaton, Inc., Cleve., 1995-99, sr. v.p. investor relations, 1999-00, mng. dir. investor rels., 2000—. Mem. Nat. Investor Rels. Inst. Home: 325 Middlebush Cir Akron OH 44321-2778 Office: Dix & Eaton 1301 E 9th St Ste 1300 Cleveland OH 44114-1820 E-mail: rnelson@dix-eaton.com.

NELSON, RICHARD ALVER, contractor; b. Greeley, Colo., Sept. 13, 1942; s. Alver Samuel and Ila Georgina (Armitage) N.; m. Christine Marie Rishell, Dec. 30, 1967; children: Nathan Paul, Steven Douglas, Robin Lee, Amy Lyn. BA in Psychology cum laude, Chico (Calif.) State Coll., 1966; MA in Vocat. Edn., Calif. State U., Long Beach, 1979. lic. tchr. gen. secondary, cmty. coll., Calif.; lic. gen. contractor, Denver, Calif., Tenn.; lic. real estate affiliate broker, Tenn.; lic. real estate agt., Calif. Tchr. Watts L.A. City Schs., 1967-71, dept. chmn. indsl. arts, 1969-71; pres. Bros. Constrn. Assocs., Denver, 1972-74; gen. contractor Morning Star Constrn. Co., Denver-Nashville-Anaheim, Calif., 1974—; ptnr. Body-Care, Nashville, 1992—, NPH Builders, Nashville, 1992—; pub. Morning Star Press, 1994—. Tchr. women's constrn. mgmt. Cerritos (Calif.) Jr. Coll., 1977-78; tchr. psychology Draughons Coll., Nashville, 1985-86. Author: Family, 1994, The Protestant Work Ethic: Its Origin, 1995, Where Are You?, 1998, Work Usually Is, 1998; contbr. column to newspaper, articles to profl. jours. Pres. Inter-Varsity Christian Fellowship, Chico, 1965-66; student del. Presdl. Prayer Breakfast, 1966; patron Acad. Am. Poets; ch. youth sponsor, L.A., Nashville, 1967—; ch. elder, Denver. Named Poet Laureate, Poetry Acad., Beverly Hills, Calif., 1993; recipient Editors Choice award Nat. Libr. Poetry, Balt., 1993. Mem. Oxford Club (life, chmn.'s cir.), Internat. Soc. Poets (5 Poet of Merit awards), Home Builders Assn., Tenn. Writers Assn. Republican. Avocations: family gatherings, church service, writing, economics, nutrition. Home and Office: Morning Star Constrn Co 13405 Old Hickory Blvd Antioch TN 37013-4803

NELSON, RICHARD ARTHUR, lawyer; b. Fosston, Minn., Apr. 8, 1947; BS in Math., U. Minn., 1969, JD, 1974. Bar: Minn. 1974, U.S. Ct. Appeals (D.C. cir.) 1975, U.S. Dist. Ct. Minn. 1975. Law clk. U.S. Ct. Appeals (D.C. cir.), Washington, 1974-75; ptnr. Faegre and Benson, Mpls., 1975—. Seminar lectr. in employee benefits and labor laws, 1983—. Note and articles editor Minn. Law Rev., 1973-74. Active Dem.-Farmer-Labor State Cen. Com., Minn., 1976—, del. dist. and local coms. and convs., 1970—, state exec. com., 1990—; student rep. bd. regents U. Minn., Mpls., 1973-74; mem. adv. coun. IRS Mid-States Key Dist. EP/EO, 1996-2000, IRS Ctrl. Mountains Region TE/GE, 2001—; chair Mpls. Pension Coun., 1999-2000. Served with U.S. Army, 1970-72. Mem. ABA, Minn. Bar Assn. (chair employee benefits sect. 1997-98), Order of Coif, Tau Beta Pi. Lutheran. Office: Faegre and Benson 90 S 7th St Ste 2200 Minneapolis MN 55402-3901 E-mail: rnelson@faegre.com.

NELSON, RICHARD DAVID, lawyer; b. Chgo., Jan. 29, 1940; s. Irving E. and Dorothy (Apolsky) N.; m. Davida Distenfield, Dec. 17, 1960; children: Cheryl, Laurel. BS in Acctg., U. Ill., 1961, LLB, 1964. Bar: Ill. 1964. Ptnr. Defrees & Fiske Law Offices, Chgo., 1964-81; ptnr., counsel, chief adminstrv. officer Heidrick & Struggles, Inc., 1981—2001; pres. Galrk Sheridan, Inc., Highland Park, 2001—. Bd. dirs., exec. com. Heidrick & Struggles, Inc., Chgo., 1981-99. Pres. Jewish Cmty. Ctrs. of Chgo., 1987-89; chmn. Sign Graphics Task Force, Highland Park, Ill., 1986-88, Bus. and Econ. Devel. Commn., Highland Park; chmn. Econ. Devel. Commn. Highland Park, 1993-96, Ft. Sheridan Joint Plan Commn., 1997-2000, Bus. and Econ. Devel. Commn., Highland Park, 2000—. Mem. ABA, Ill. State Bar Assn., Chgo. Bar Assn., Standard Club, Northmoor Country Club. Office: Galrk Sheridan Inc 1896 Sheridan Rd Ste 200 Highland Park IL 60035-4635

NELSON, RICHARD LLOYD, systems engineer, consultant; b. Mansfield, Ohio, Nov. 18, 1934; s. Harold Francis Nelson, Billie Clara (Nussel) Nelson; m. Susan Frances Benzing, June 6, 1953 (div. Apr. 1972); children: Miriam Louise, James Harold; m. Sandra Lin Dunkle, Feb. 23, 1986. MSEE, U. Cin., 1957; MS in Econs. and Sys. Engring., Ohio State U., 1964. Cert. artificial intelligence U. N.C., 1958. Sr. engr. rsch. Battelle Meml. Inst., Columbus, Ohio, 1960—67; dir. rsch. Gilbarco divsn. Exxon Corp., Greensboro, NC, 1967—69, mgr. New Venture Devel. N.Y.C., 1970—77, v.p. New Tech., 1977—81; pres. Quest Rsch., Inc., Trout Run, Pa., 1981—. Co-author: Reliability Engineering, 1962; contbr. Bd. dirs. Holotron Corp., Columbus, Ohio, 1964—67, Zito Co., Inc., Derry, NH, 1972—74; bd. dirs., chmn. bd. Qwip Sys. divsn. Exxon, N.Y.C., 1977—81; elec. cons. City Coun., Worthington, Ohio, 1965—66; supr. township planning Bd. Suprs., Cascade Township, Pa., 1992—94. Lt. USN, 1957—60. Fellow: AAAS. Achievements include patents in fields of optics, electronics and mechanics; discovery of method for creating holograms using non-coherent source; invention of first practical convenience-facsimile sys. Avocations: music, cooking, mathematics. Home: 3110 Kellyburg Rd Trout Run PA 17771 Office: Quest Rsch Inc 3110 Kellyburg Rd Trout Run PA 17771

NELSON, RICHARD WILLIAM, economist; b. Washington, May 17, 1945; s. James Cecil and Helen Catherine (Sands) N.; m. Sallie Beth Bregman, June 22, 1969; children: Jonathan Eric, Kenneth Charles. BA summa cum laude, Yale U., 1967, MPhil, 1969, PhD, 1971. Economist Exec. Office Pres., Washington, 1971-72; mgr. banking studies Fed. Res. Bank N.Y., N.Y.C., 1972-81; v.p., economist Chem. Bank, 1981-85; prof. econs. and fin. SUNY, Binghamton, 1985-87; v.p., chief economist Fed. Home Loan Bank of San Francisco, 1987—. Contbr. articles on banking to profl. jours. 1st lt. U.S. Army Res., 1972-78. Woodrow Wilson fellow, 1967-71, NSF fellow, 1967-71. Mem. Am. Econ. Assn., Nat. Assn. Bus. Economists, Phi Beta Kappa. Republican. Unitarian Universalist. Avocations: music, reading, running, tennis, gardening. Home: 74 Charles Hill Rd Orinda CA 94563-1524 Office: Wells Fargo Bank 343 Sansome St Ste 300 San Francisco CA 94104-1395

NELSON, ROBERT E. geology educator; b. June 25, 1949; 1 child, Christopher Daniel. BA, San Francisco, 1972; MS, U. Wash., 1979, PhD, 1982; MA (hon.), Colby Coll., 1996. Technician U.S. Geol. Survey, Menlo Park, Calif., 1972-75, geologist Seattle, 1975-82; MacArthur asst. prof. Colby Coll., Waterville, Maine, 1982-88, assoc. prof., 1988-96, prof., 1996—, dept. chmn., 1990-99. Adj. prof. U. Colo., 1994-2001. Mem. editl. bd. Northeastern Naturalist, 1995—2001. Office: Colby Coll Dept Geology 5804 Mayflower Hl Waterville ME 04901-8858 E-mail: renelson@colby.edu.

NELSON, ROBERT ARTHUR, civil engineer; b. Davis, S.D., Sept. 9, 1939; s. Kermit George and Georgia Alice Nelson; m. Mary Jean Ellsworth, Aug. 5, 1960; children: David, Michael, Karen, Chris. BSCE, S.D. Sch. Mines, 1961; cert. bus. mgmt., U. Calif. Riverside, 1971; MPA, U. So. Calif. LA, 1974. Project engr. S.D. Highway Dept., Vermillion, 1961-62; from jr. engr. to assoc. engr. Riverside (Calif.) County Flood Control Dist., 1965-67; sr. engr. Pub. Utilities City of Riverside, 1967-9—; planning engr. Riverside County Flood Control Dist., 1969-77, asst. chief flood control engr., 1977-88; gen. mgr., chief engr. Riverside County Waste Mgmt. Dept., 1988—. Bd. trustees First United Meth. Ch. of Riverside, chmn. 2000-01. 1st lt. U.S. Army, 1962-65. Mem. ASCE (Young Engr. of Yr. 1974), Solid Waste Assn. N.Am., So. Calif. Waste Mgmt. Forum (pres. 1998-99), Riverside County/San Bernardino City Engrs. (pres. 1992), Kiwanis (pres. Uptown Riverside chpt. 1998-81, Golden Rule award 1979). Office: Riverside County Waste Mgmt Dept 1995 Market St Riverside CA 92501

NELSON, ROBERT CHARLES, retired publishing executive; b. Phila., Dec. 10, 1924; s. Charles Emil and Florence E. (Kelly) N.; m. Jeanne H. Wallace, Mar. 10, 1945; children— John R., Barbara J., Nancy A. Student, The Citadel, 1942-43; ME, Stevens Inst. Tech., 1949. Asst. mech. supt. N.Y. News, N.Y.C., 1949-52; with Detroit News, 1952—, prodn. mgr., 1952-69, ops. mgr., 1969-75, v.p., 1973-79, gen. mgr., 1975-81, pres., 1981-87, pres., pub., 1982-87, spl. asst. to chmn., 1987—90; exec. v.p. newspaper div. Evening News Assn., 1978-87; ret., 1990. Bd. dirs., sec. Greater Detroit Safety Council, 1973— ; bd. dirs. Engring. Sci. Fair, Detroit, 1975— ; bd. dirs., mem. exec. com. Better Bus. Bur., Detroit, 1976— Vol. All Children's Hosp., 1997—; trustee New Detroit, 1980—. With USNR, 1943-46, PTO. Mem. Engring. Soc. Detroit, Greater Detroit C. of C. (bd. dirs. 1980—, vice chmn. 1985—), Acad. Sr. Profls. at Eckerd Coll., Detroit Club, Orchard Lake Country Club, Adcraft Club of Detroit, Econ. Club, St. Petersburg Yacht Club, St. Anthony's Hosp. Aux., Brookwood, SCORE; vol. All Children's Hosp.

NELSON, ROBERT EDDINGER, management and development consultant; b. Mentone, Ind., Mar. 2, 1928; s. Arthur Irven and Tural Cecile (Eddinger) N.; m. Carol J., Nov. 24, 1951; children: Janet K., Eric P. BA, Northwestern U., 1949; LHD, Iowa Wesleyan Coll., 1969, North Ctrl. Coll., 1987. Asst. dir. alumni rels. Northwestern U., Evanston, Ill., 1950-51; v.p., dir. pub. rels. Iowa Wesleyan Coll., Mt. Pleasant, 1955-58; vice chancellor for devel. U. Kansas City, 1959-61; v.p. instl. devel. Ill. Inst. Tech., Chgo., 1961-68; pres. Robert Johnston Corp., Oak Brook, Ill., 1968-69, Robert E. Nelson Assocs., Inc., Oak Brook, 1969—. Bd. dirs. Chautauqua Workshop in Fund Raising and Instl. Relations, Continental Bank of Oak Brook Terr., The Sun Cos.; nat. conf. chmn. and program dir. Am. Coll. Pub. Relations Assn., 1961; trustee, Iowa Wesleyan Coll., 1962-68; faculty mem. Ind. U. Workshops on Coll. and Univ. Devel., 1963-65, Lorretto Heights Summer Inst. for Fund Raising and Pub. Relations, 1964-68; mem. Pub. Review Panel for Grants Programs, Lilly Endowment, Inc., 1975. Contbr. chpt. to Handbook of College and University Administration, 1970. With U.S. Army, 1951-54. Mem. Coun. on Fin. Aid to Edn. (bd. dirs. 1957-63), Pub. Rels. Soc. Am., Nat. Soc. Fund Raisers, Nat. Small Bus. Assn., Chgo. Soc. Fund Raising Execs., Blue Key, Execs. Club, Econ. Club, Union League, DuPage Club, Masons, Delta Tau Delta. Methodist. Home and Office: 5 Oakbrook Club Dr N101 Oak Brook IL 60523-1348

NELSON, ROBERT LOUIS, lawyer; b. Dover, N.H., Aug. 10, 1931; s. Albert Louis and Alice (Rogers) N.; m. Rita Jean Hutchins, June 11, 1955; children: Karen, Robin Andrea. BA, Bates Coll., Lewiston, Maine, 1956; LLB, Georgetown U., 1959. Bar: D.C. 1960. With U.S. Commn. Civil Rights, 1958-63, AID, 1963-66; program sec. U.S. Mission to Brazil, 1965-66; exec. dir. Lawyers Com. Civil Rights Under Law, 1966-70; dep. campaign mgr. Muskie for Pres., 1970-72; v.p. Perpetual Corp., Houston, 1972-74; sr. v.p., gen. counsel Washington Star, 1974-76; pres. broadcast div. Washington Star Communications, Inc., 1976-77; asst. sec. of army U.S. Dept. Def., 1977-79; spl. advisor to chief N.G. Bur., Dept. Def., 1980-85; pres., dir. Mid-Md. Communications Corp., 1981-85; ptnr. Verner, Liipfert, Bernhard, McPherson and Hand, 1979-87; gen. counsel Paralyzed Vets. Am., 1988-99, sr. counsel, 2000—. Vice chmn. D.C. Redevel. Land Agy., 1976-77; bd. dirs. Community Found. Greater Washington, 1977-78 ; bd. dirs. Friends of Nat. Zoo, 1975—89, pres., 1982-84; bd. dirs. Downtown Progress, 1976-77, Fed. City Coun., 1976-77, 83-87, Pennsylvania Ave. Devel. Corp., 1976-77; trustee Wolfe's Neck Farm Found., 2001--. Served with AUS, 1953-54. Mem. ABA, D.C. Bar Assn., Army Navy Club (Washington). Democrat. Episcopalian. Home: Robins Nest PO Box 52 Orrs Island ME 04066-0052 Office: 801 18th St NW Washington DC 20006-3517

NELSON, ROBERT R. hotel, restaurant and tourism educator; b. Buffalo, June 4, 1961; s. Richard Peter and Carol Jean (McVeigh) N.; m. Genevieve Murphy, Oct. 19, 1985; children: Madeline Murphy, Erica Rose. BS in Hotel Adminstrn., Cornell U., 1983; MBA, Drexel U., 1989; PhD, U. Del., 2000. Restaurant mgr. Bennigan's Restaurants, Phila., 1985-87; instr. Drexel U., 1987-89; food svc. dir. Canteen Corp., 1989-90; asst. prof. U. Del., Newark, 1990—. Adj. prof. Drexel U., Phila., 1989-90; advisor Vision for the Rivers Project, Wilmington, Del., 1995—. Author: (with others) New Dimensions in Marketing/Quality of Life Research, 1995; contbr. articles to profl. jours.; host TV series Culinary Survival Skills and Food Facts, 1998. Bd. dirs., chair nominating com. Del. Coun. for Internat. Visitors, Wilmington, 1993-98; tourism com. leader Gov.'s Internat. Trade Coun., Wilmington, 1992—; mem. Wilmington Cmty. Devel. Partnership, 1994—. Mem. Acad. Mktg. Sci., Soc. Quality-of-Life Studies, Coun. of Hotel, Restaurant and Instnl. Educators, Internat. Coun. Del., Cornell Soc. Hotelmen. Avocations: promoting peace, understanding and trade through international tourism, cooking. Office: U Del Rextrew House-HRIM Program Newark DE 19716

NELSON, ROGER HUGH, management educator, business executive; b. Spring City, Utah, Mar. 7, 1931; s. Hugh Devere and Maudella Sarah (Larsen) N.; m. DeEtte Munk, Aug. 26, 1955 (dec. Sept. 1998); children— Steven R., Deanne, Mark L. BS, U. Utah, 53, MS, 1953; Ed.D., Columbia U., 1958. Mem. faculty U. Utah Coll. Bus., 1953-97, prof. mgmt., 1970-97, prof. emeritus, 1997—, dir. programs in emerging bus., 1989-97, chmn. mgmt. dept., 1976-82, asst. dean, 1969-74; dir. MBA integrative field studies, 1993-96; pres. David Eccles Sch. of Bus. Faculty, 1995-96; mem. faculty Utah Mgmt. Inst., 1968-75; v.p. Computer Logic Corp., 1970-73; pres. Am. Leisure & Sports Investment Corp., 1973-75, Oil Resources, Inc., 1980-88, Puma Energy Corp., 1981-88, The Ultimate Choice Catalog Co., 1986—. Fin. and mgmt. cons., 1965— ; founder Utah Small Bus. Devel. Center, U. Utah, 1979; trustee Utah Tech. Fin. Corp., 1998—; chmn. Am. Recreation and Sports, Inc., 1996—. Author: Personal Money Management, 1973, The Utah Entrepreneur's Guide, 1995, also articles, reports, manuals. Active local Am. Heart Assn., Am. Cancer Soc. campaigns; mem. exec. bd. Utah Opera Co., 1981-85, gen. bd., 1985-89. Danforth Teaching fellow, 1957 Mem. Acad. Mgmt., Adminstrv. Mgmt. Soc., NEA, AAUP, Phi Kappa Phi, Beta Gamma Sigma, Phi Delta Kappa, Delta Phi Epsilon. Inventor comml. color separation camera and related dye-transfer processes. Home: 2662 Skyline Dr Salt Lake City UT 84108-2855 Office: U Utah David Eccles Sch Bus Salt Lake City UT 84112

NELSON, ROGER THEODORE, surgeon; b. Oct. 7, 1920; MD, Loma Linda U., 1945. Diplomate Bd. Thoracic Surgery, Am. Bd. Surgery. Intern White Meml. Hosp., L.A., 1944-45, resident surgery, 1945-46, 48-51, fellow thoracic surgery, 1956-58; surgeon Wildwood (Ga.) Lifestyle Ctr., 1983—. Home: HC 65 Box 580 Dunlap TN 37327-9341 Office: Dunlap Med Clinic 8 Cates Rd Dunlap TN 37327

NELSON, RON, composer, conductor, educator; b. Joliet, Ill., Dec. 14, 1929; s. Walter E. and Lois (Fulton) N.; m. Helen Mitchell, 1954 (dec. 1967); children: Marc W., Kristen R. Mus.B., Eastman Sch. Music, 1952, Mus.M., 1953, Mus.D., 1956; postgrad., L'École Normale, Normale, Paris, 1954-55; MA, Brown U., 1959. Prof. Brown U., Providence, chmn. dept. music, 1963-73, Acuff chair of excellence in creative arts, 1991, prof. emeritus, 1993—. Film composer, HEW, Eastman Kodak, ARC, Columbia Pictures, commns. from, Cin. Symphony, Lima Symphony, Rochester Philharmonic, R.I. Philharm., Am. Bapt. Soc., U. Minn., Dartmouth Coll., Brown U., New Music Ensemble, LaSalle Coll., Western Mich. U., Classic Chorale, U.S. Air Force Band, Nat. Symphony Orch.; composer (for orch.) Savannah River Holiday, 1954, Sarabande: For Katherine in April, 1954, (opera) The Birthday of the Infanta, 1956; (cantata) The Christmas Story, 1958: (for orch.) Toccata for Orchestra, 1963; (oratorio) What is Man?, 1964; (orch./wind ensemble) Rocky Point Holiday, 1968-69; This is the Orchestra; (orch. and tape trilogy) Trilogy: JFK-MLK-RFK, 1969; (choral) Prayer of Emperor of China, 1973; (choral) Thy Truth is Great, 1973; (choral) Psalm 95, 1974; (orch.) Five Pieces for Orchestra after Paintings by Andrew Wyeth, 1975; (choral) Prayer of St. Francis of Assisi, 1976; (orch.) Meditation and Dance for Orch., 1976; (choral) Six Pieces for Chamber Ensemble, 1977, Four Choral Pieces After the Seasons, 1978, Three Autumnal Sketches, 1979, Here We Come As in The Beginning, 1979, Mass in Honor of St. LaSalle, 1981, Three Nocturnal Pieces, 1982, Three Seasonal Reflections, 1982; composer: Fanfare for a Celebration, 1982; (choral) On Christmas Night, 1982; Medieval Suite, 1983; (choral) Dreams, 1982; (band) Fanfare for a Celebration, 1983; (cello-piano) And the Moon Rose Golden, 1983; (band) Medieval Suite, 1983; composer: Aspen Jubilee, 1984; (organ-brass) Pebble Beach Sojourn, 1984; (chorus-band) Te Deum Laudamus, 1985; (choral) Lost and Found, 1985, Light Years, 1985, Three Settings of the Moon, 1985, (strings-trumpet) Elegy, 1986, (brass) Brevard Fanfare, 1986, (chorus/band) Prime: The Hour of Sunrise, 1987, (choral) White, 1987, (choral) Another Spring, 1987, (choral) Miniatures from a Bestiary Parts I and II, 1988, (saxophone-band) Danza Capriccio, 1988, (choral) Three Pieces after Tennyson (1988), (choral) Three Mountain Ballads, 1989, (brass-winds-percussion) Fanfare for the Hour of Sunrise, 1989, (band) Morning Alleluias for the Winter Solstice, 1989, (band) Resonances, 1990; (chorus) And This Shall Be for Music, 1990, Invoking the Powers, 1991, Songs of Praise and Reconciliation, 1991, The Meadow, 1991, (band) Lauds: Praise High Day, 1992, To the Airborne, 1991, Passacaglia (Homage on B-A-C-H), 1992, Chaconne (In Memoriam), 1994, Sonoran Desert Holiday, 1994, (band), Epiphanies (Fanfares and Chorales bands), 1995, Courtly Airs and Dances, 1995, (orch.) Resonances II, 1996, (orch., band) Resonances III, 1996,(orch.) Panels (Epiphanies II), 1996, The Music of Ron Nelson, 1996, (euphonium and winds) Night Song, 1998, (band) Fanfare for the New Millennium, 1999, Proclaim This Day for Music, 2002. Recipient ASCAP awards, 1962-97, Found. award for World tour, 1965-66, Nat. Band Assn. award, 1992, John Philip Sousa medal of merit, 1994; Fulbright fellow, 1954; Ford Found. commn., 1962, NEA grantee, 1973, 76, 79; awarded Acuff Chair of Excellence on the Creative Arts, 1991; winner Am. Bandmasters Assn. Ostwald Contest, 1993, Am. Band Assn. contest, 1992, Sudler Internat. Wind Band Competition, 1993. Office: Brown U Dept Music Providence RI 02912-0001

NELSON, RONALD HARVEY, animal science educator, researcher; b. Union Grove, Wis., Aug. 10, 1918; s. Harvey August and Myra Frances (Sheen) N.; m. Elizabeth Jane Lappley, Apr. 13, 1940; children: David Peter, Marjorie Jean, Linda Louise, Ronda Elizabeth. BS, U. Wis., 1939; MS, Okla. A&M U., 1941; PhD, Iowa State U., 1943. Mem. faculty Mich. State U., 1946-85, prof., head, animal sci. dept., 1950-84, prof. emeritus, 1985—; chief of party Mich. State U. tech. assistance project Balcarce, Pcia, Buenos Aires, 1966-68. Recipient Grad. Distinction award Okla State U., 1987, Nat. Saddle and Sirloin Portrait award, 1990. Fellow Am. Soc. Animal Sci. (Internat. Animal Agr. award 1978, Animal Industry award 1984); mem. Am. Angus Assn. (chmn. research advisory com. 1956-60), Mich. Angus Assn. (pres. 1977-78), Animal Sci. Assn., Sigma Xi, Phi Kappa Phi, Alpha Zeta. Home: 1545 N Harrison Rd East Lansing MI 48823-1801

NELSON, ROY HUGH, JR. lawyer, mediator, arbitrator; b. St. Paul, May 13, 1955; s. Roy H. and Helen S. Nelson; m. MaryJean G. Froehlich, Aug. 13, 1994; children: Benjamin, Calla. BS, U. Wis., Milw., 1979, MS, 1985; JD, U. Wis., 1988. Bar: Wis. 1988, U.S. Dist. Ct. (ea. and we. dists.) Wis. 1988, U.S. Dist. Ct. (ea. dist.) Mich. 1991, U.S. Ct. Appeals (7th cir.) 1988, U.S. Ct. Appeals (fed. cir.) 1996, U.S. Supreme Ct. 1999. Police officer City of Brookfield, Wis., 1978-88; assoc. Borgelt, Powell, Peterson & Frauen, Milw., 1988-92; shareholder, dir. Petrie & Stocking SC, 1992—; mediator, arbitrator, dir. Conflict Resolution Svcs., 1997—. Exec. dir. Conflict Mgmt. Edn. Project, 1999; chair adv. bd. Mediation Ministries, Sun Prairie, Wis., 1998—. Mem. Wis. Bar Assn., Milw. Bar Assn., Christian Legal Soc., Acad. Family Mediators, Bus. Network Internat., Wis. Intellectual Property Law Assn., Wis. Assn. Mediators. Lutheran. Office: Petrie & Stocking SC 111 E Wisconsin Ave Ste 1500 Milwaukee WI 53202-4808 E-mail: rnelson@petriestocking.com.

NELSON, RUSSELL MARION, surgeon, educator; b. Salt Lake City, Sept. 9, 1924; s. Marion C. and Edna (Anderson) N.; m. Dantzel White, Aug. 31, 1945; children: Marsha Nelson McKellar, Wendy Nelson Maxfield, Gloria Nelson Irion, Brenda Nelson Miles, Sylvia Nelson Webster, Emily Nelson Wittwer (dec.), Laurie Nelson Marsh, Rosalie Nelson Ringwood, Marjorie Nelson Helsten, Russell Marion Jr. BA, U. Utah, 1945, MD, 1947; PhD in Surgery, U. Minn., 1954; ScD (hon.), Brigham Young U., 1970; DMS (hon.), Utah State U., 1989; LHD (hon.), Snow Coll., 1994. Diplomate: Am. Bd. Surgery, Am. Bd. Thoracic Surgery (dir. 1972-78). Intern U. Minn. Hosps., Mpls., 1947, asst. resident surgery, 1948-51; first asst. resident surgery Mass. Gen. Hosp., Boston, 1953-54; sr. resident surgery U. Minn. Hosps., Mpls., 1954-55; practice medicine (specializing in cardiovascular and thoracic surgery), Salt Lake City, 1959-84; staff surgeon Latter-day Saints Hosp., 1959-84, dir. surg. research lab., 1959-72, chief cardiovascular-thoracic surg. div., 1967-72, also bd. govs., 1970-90, vice chmn., 1979-89; staff surgeon Primary Children's Hosp., Salt Lake City, 1960; attending in surgery VA Hosp., 1955-84, Univ. Hosp., Salt Lake City, 1955-84; asst. prof. surgery Med. Sch. U. Utah, 1955-59, asst. clin. prof. surgery, 1959-66, asso. clin. prof. surgery, clin. prof., 1966-69, research prof. surgery, 1970-84, clin. prof. emeritus, 1984—; staff services Utah Biomed. Test Lab., 1970-84. Dir. tng. program cardiovascular and thoracic surgery at Univ. Utah affiliated hosps., 1967-84; mem. policyholders adv. com. New Eng. Mut. Life Ins. Co., Boston, 1976-80 Contbr. articles to profl. jours. Mem. White House Conf. on Youth and Children, 1960; bd. dirs. Internat. Cardiol. Found.; bd. govs. LDS Hosp., 1970-90, Deseret Gymnasium, 1971-75, Promised Valley Playhouse, 1970-79; mem. adv. com. U.S. Sec. of State on Religious Freedom Abroad, 1996-99. 1st lt. to capt. M.C., AUS, 1951-53. Markle scholar in med. scis., 1957-59; Fellowship of Medici Publici U. Utah Coll., 1967; Gold Medal of Merit, Argentina, 1974; named Hon. Prof. Shandong Med. U., Jinan, People's Republic of China, 1985; Old People's U., Jinan, 1986; Xi-an (People's Republic of China) Med. Coll., 1986, Legacy of Life award, 1993. Fellow A.C.S. (chmn. adv. council on thoracic surgery 1973-75), Am. Coll. Cardiology, Am. Coll. Chest Physicians; mem. Am. Assn. Thoracic Surgery, Am. Soc. Artificial Internal Organs, AMA, Dirs. Thoracic Residencies (pres. 1971-72), Utah Med. Assn. (pres. 1970-71), Salt Lake County Med. Soc., Am. Heart Assn. (exec. com. cardiovascular surgery 1972, dir. 1976-78, chmn. council cardiovascular surgery 1976-78), Utah Heart Assn. (pres. 1964-65), Soc. Thoracic Surgeons, Soc. Vascular Surgery (sec. 1968-72, pres. 1974), Utah Thoracic Soc., Salt Lake Surg. Soc., Samson Thoracic Surg. Soc., Western Soc. for Clin. Research, Soc. U. Surgeons, Am., Western, Pan-Pacific surg. assns., Inter. Am. Soc. Cardiology (bd. mgrs.), Phi Beta Kappa, Sigma Xi, Alpha Omega Alpha, Phi Kappa Phi, Sigma Chi. Mem. Ch. of Jesus Christ of Latter-day Saints (pres. Bonneville Stake 1964-71, gen. pres. Sunday sch. 1971-79, regional rep. 1979-84, Quorum of the Twelve Apostles 1984—). Home: 1347 Normandie Cir Salt Lake City UT 84105-1919 Office: 47 E South Temple Salt Lake City UT 84150-1200

NELSON, SARAH MILLEDGE, archaeology educator; b. Miami, Fla., Nov. 29, 1931; d. Stanley and Sarah Woodman (Franklin) M.; m. Harold Stanley Nelson, July 25, 1953; children: Erik Harold, Mark Milledge, Stanley Franklin. BA, Wellesley Coll., 1953; MA, U. Mich., 1969, PhD, 1973. Instr. archaeology U. Md. extension, Seoul, Republic Korea, 1970-71; asst. prof. U. Denver, 1974-79, assoc. prof., 1979-85, prof. archaeology, 1985—, chair dept. anthropology, 1985-95, dir. women's studies program, 1985-87, John Evans prof., dir. Asian studies, 1996, vice provost for rsch., 1998—2002, interim vice provost grad. studies and rsch., 2001—02. Vis. asst. prof. U. Colo., Boulder, 1974; resident Rockefeller Ctr. in Bellagio, Italy, 1996. Co-editor: Powers of Observation, 1990, Equity Issues for Women in Archaeology, 1994; author: Archaeology of Korea, 1993, Gender in Archaeology: Analyzing Power and Prestige, 1997, (novel) Spirit Bird Journey, 1999; co-author: Denver: An Archaeological History, 2001; editor: The Archaeology of Northeast China, 1995, Ancestors for the Pigs: Pigs in Prehistory, 1998; co-editor: In Pursuit of Gender: Worldwide Archaeological Perspectives, 2001, Ancient Queens: Archaeological Perspectives, 2002. Active Earthwatch, 1989. Recipient Outstanding Scholar award U. Denver, 1989; grantee S.W. Inst. Rsch. on Women, 1981, Acad. Korean Studies, Seoul, 1983, Internat. Cultural Soc. Korea, 1986, Colo. Hist. Fund, 1995-97, Rockefeller Found. Residency, Bellagio, Italy, Wenner-Gren Found., 2000-02, Nat. Geographic Soc., 2000—. Fellow Am. Anthrop. Assn.; mem. Soc. Am. Archaeology, Assn. Asian Studies, Royal Asiatic Soc., Sigma Xi (sec.-treas. 1978-79), Phi Beta Kappa. Democrat. Avocations: skiing, gardening. Home: 5878 S Dry Creek Ct Littleton CO 80121-1709 Office: U Denver Dept Anthropology Denver CO 80208-0001 E-mail: snelson@du.edu.

NELSON, STEPHEN D. music educator; b. Clearwater, Fla., Apr. 5, 1957; s. Brasher Parker and Catherine Land (Kit) Nelson. BA, U. Cen. Fla., 1982. Dir. music 1st Presbyn. Ch. Apopka; performer, co-founder Ars Antiqua - an Early Music Ensemble, Orlando, 1986—; dir. music 1st Presbyn. Ch. Apopka, 1983—; creative music cons. Nelson Music Svcs., Apopka, 1976—. Musician orch. arrangement of ednl. mus. materials, composer 2 For The Road; contbr. Arrangements for Harcourt Texts; musician: (ednl. video) Ars Antiqua - Music from a Distant Tyme, 1996. Mem.: Bears of Cen. Fla. (pres. 2001—02). Office: Park Maitland Sch 1450 S Orlando Ave Maitland FL 32751 Personal E-mail: nelsonmusic@cfl.rr.com.

NELSON, STEVEN DWAYNE, lawyer; b. Austin, Minn. m. Vicky L. Staab, July 6, 1990. BA in English, SUNY, Buffalo, 1972; JD, U. Mont., 1978. Bar: Mont. 1978, U.S. Dist. Ct. Mont. 1978. Sole practice, Bozeman, Mont., 1978—; city prosecutor City of Bozeman, 1979-82; city atty. City of Ennis (Mont.), 1980-82; prof. U. Great Falls, Mont., 1990—, mediator, 1998—. Mem. ABA, Mont. State Bar Assn., Phi Delta Phi. Avocations: fishing, skiing, hiking. Home and Office: 4590 Maiden Rock Rd Bozeman MT 59715-7769 E-mail: Nelsonsvl@cs.com.

NELSON, STEVEN LESLIE, surgeon; BA in Chemistry, Pacific Union Coll., Angwin, Calif., 1975; MD, Loma Linda U., 1978. Diplomate Am. Bd. Surgery. Intern Loma Linda U. Med. Ctr., 1979, resident in gen. surgery, 1980-83; surgeon U.M. Bryner M.D., Inc., Yreka, Calif., 1984—. Mem. staff Fairchild Med. Ctr., Yreka. Mem. Siskiyou County Pub. Health Adv. Bd., Yreka, 1990—. Fellow ACS; mem. AMA, Calif. Med. Assn., Alpha Omega Alpha, Rotary. Office: U M Bryner MD Inc 814 N Main St Yreka CA 96097-2538

NELSON, STUART OWEN, agricultural engineer, researcher, educator; b. Pilger, Nebr., Jan. 23, 1927; s. Irvin Andrew and Agnes Emilie (Nissen) N.; m. Carolyn Joye Fricke, Dec. 27, 1953 (dec. Nov. 1975); children: Richard Lynn, Jana Sue; m. Martha Ellen White Fuller, Apr. 8, 1979. BS in Agrl. Engring., U. Nebr., 1950; MS in Agrl. Engring., 1952; MA in Physics, U. Nebr., 1954; PhD in Engring., Iowa State U., 1972; DSc (hon.), U. Nebr., 1989. Grad. asst. U. Nebr., Lincoln, 1952-54, rsch. assoc., 1954-60, assoc. prof., 1960-72, prof., 1972-76. Project leader Farm Electrification Rsch., Agrl. Rsch. Svc., USDA, Lincoln, 1954-59, rsch. investigations leader, 1959-72, rsch. leader 1972-76, rsch. agrl. engr. Russell Rsch. Ctr., Athens, Ga., 1976—; adj. prof. U. Ga., 1976—; sci. adv. coun. Am. Seed Rsch. Found.; mem. CAST Task Force on Irradiation for Food Preservation and Pest Control; adv. com. grain moisture measurement Nat. Coun. Weights and Measures; mem. sci. bd. 4th Internat. Conf. on Phys. Properties Agrl. Materials, Prague, 1985. Assoc. editor Jour. Microwave Power 1975-76, 95-2000; contbr. more than 400 articles to sci. and tech. jours. With USN, 1946-48. Recipient HM Crops and Soils award Am. Soc. Agronomy, 1966, Founders Gold medal Fed. Engr. of Yr. NSPE, 1985, Superior Svc. award USDA, 1986, Profl. Achievement Citation Engring. award Iowa State U., 1987, Ga. Engring. Found. medal of honor, 1999; named to U. Nebr. Biol. Systems Engring. Hall of Fame, 1999. Fellow IEEE, Am. Soc. Agrl. Engrs. (Tech. Paper award 1965, 94, Engr. of Yr. award Ga. sect. 1988, chmn. Ga. sect. 1988-89, Cyrus Hall McCormick-Jerome Increase Case Gold Medal award 2000), Internat. Microwave Power Inst. (Decade award 1981); mem. AAAS, The Electromagnetics Acad., Internat. Soc. Agromaterials Sci. and Engring., Ga. Soc. Profl. Engrs. (Engr. of Yr. in Govt. award 1991, Engr. of Yr. 1998), Nat. Acad. Engring., Nat. Soc. Profl. Engrs., Orgn. Profl. Employees of Dept. of Agrl. (pres. Athens area chpt. 1984-86, nat. coun. rep. 1988-95, Profl. of Yr. award 1987), Athens Optimist (pres. 1980-81, 2000-2001, lt. gov. Ga. dist. 1983-84, Optimist of Yr. award 1982, disting. and outstanding lt. gov. Ga. dist. 1985), Assn. for Microwave Power in Europe for Rsch. and Edn., Sigma Xi, Sigma Tau, Gamma Sigma Delta, Tau Beta Pi. Methodist. Home: 270 Idylwood Dr Athens GA 30605-4635 Office: USDA Agrl Rsch Svc Russell Rsch Ctr PO Box 5677 Athens GA 30604-5677

NELSON, STUART JAMES, internist, medical informatician; b. Santa Monica, Calif., Apr. 25, 1947; s. Clair Edmund and Ruth (Gibson) N.; m. Linda K. F. Mui, June 18, 1978; children: Victoria, Mark, Elizabeth. AB in Math., U. Calif., Berkeley, 1970; MD, SUNY, Bklyn., 1975. Diplomate Nat. Bd. Med. Examiners, Am. Bd. Internal Medicine. Intern Phila. Gen. Hosp., 1975-76; resident Met. Hosp., N.Y.C., 1976-78; instr. medicine SUNY, Stony Brook, 1978-82, asst. prof. clin. medicine, 1982-86, clin. assoc. prof. medicine, preventive medicine, 1986-91, assoc. head divsn. gen. internal medicine, 1985-90; assoc. prof. medicine Med. Coll. Ga., Augusta, 1991-96; head med. subject headings Nat. Libr. Medicine, Bethesda, Md., 1996—. Reviewer for profl. jours. Contbr. articles to profl. jours. Fellow: Am. Coll. Physicians, Am. Coll. Med. Informatics; mem.: Med. Libr. Assn. Presbyterian. Office: Nat Libr Medicine Rm B 2 E17 Bldg 38A Bethesda MD 20894-0001 E-mail: nelson@nlm@nih.gov.

NELSON, THOMAS ADAMS, electrical engineer, transportation consultant; b. Berkeley, Calif., Aug. 26, 1921; s. Thomas Fleming and Mabel Margaretta (Adams) N.; m. Mary Anne Mares, July 12, 1958. AA, Los Angeles City Coll., 1942; BS, U. So. Calif., 1949, MS, 1953; postgrad. cert. bus. mgmt., UCLA, 1970. Registered profl. engr., Calif. Design engr. Los Angeles Dept. Water and Power, 1950-53, quality assurance engr. U.S., Europe and Japan, 1953-65, asst. chief quality assurance engr., 1965-68, chief quality assurance engr., 1968-72, engr. in charge oper. engring., 1972-77, mgr. communications, transmission lines, sta. maintenance and distbn. trouble, 1977-80; rail transp. cons. Ariz. and Nev., 1973-79; rep. to Calif. Power Pool, 1975-77; cons. engr., transp. cons. Los Angeles, 1980—. Reviewer rail transit plans So. Calif. Rapid Transit Dist., Los Angeles County Transp. Commn., L.A. County Metro. Transp. Auth., Orange County Transit Dist., Caltrans, San Diego Met. Transit Devel. Bd., 1978—. Editor, major author Railroad Chronology Compendium, 1976, 50 Years of Railroading in Southern California, 2001; editor Jour. Pacific R.R. Soc., 1980-84, 87-94, cons. editor, 1994—; contbr. articles to profl. jours. Mem. Citizens Adv. Commn. for Met. Rail, Hollywood, Calif., 1982-84, Met. Rail CORE Forum, 1987. Served to capt. USAAF, 1942-45, ETO. Mem. IEEE (sr.), Vehicular Tech. Soc., Pacific R.R. Soc. (bd. dirs. 1977-80, 82-85, v.p. 1986, pres. 1987-89, publs. mgr. 1981-94), Eta Kappa Nu, Tau Beta Pi, Phi Kappa Phi.

NELSON, THOMAS G. federal judge; b. Idaho Falls, Idaho, 1936; Student, U. Idaho, 1955—59, LLB, 1962. Ptnr. Parry, Robertson, and Daly, Twin Falls, Idaho, 1965—79, Nelson, Rosholt, Robertson, Tolman and Tucker, Twin Falls, 1979; judge U.S. Ct. of Appeals (9th cir.), Boise, 1990—. With Idaho Air N.G., 1962—65, with USAR, 1965—68. Mem.: ABA, Idaho Law Found., Am. Bd. Trial Advocates (pres. Idaho chpt.), Idaho Assn. Def. Counsel, Idaho State Bar (pres., bd. commrs.), Am. Coll. Trial Lawyers, Am. Bar Found., Phi Alpha Delta. Office: US Ct Appeals 9th Circuit 304 N Eighth St PO Box 1339 Boise ID 83701-1339*

NELSON, THOMAS GEORGE, consulting actuary; b. Mason City, Iowa, Mar. 27, 1949; s. George Burton and Bonny Sue (Sharp) N.; m. Beverlee Joan Trindl, Sept. 28, 1974; children: Kristen Elizabeth, Joseph Charles. BA in Math., U. Iowa, 1971; MA in Math., U. Mich., 1972. Actuary CNA, Chgo., 1972-80; consulting actuary William M. Mercer, Inc., 1980-82, A.S. Hansen, Inc., Chgo., 1982-83; sr. consulting actuary, prin., nat. dir. health, bd. dirs. Milliman & Robertson, Inc., 1983—. Mem. task force on acctg. for non-pension retiree benefits Fin. Acctg. Standards Bd., Norwalk, Conn., 1986-90. Contbr. articles to profl. jours. Fellow, 1972, teaching fellow, 1972, U. Mich. Fellow Soc. Actuaries; mem. Am. Acad. Actuaries (bd. dirs. 1989-92, chmn. com. on health and welfare plans 1984-89, com. on rels. with accts. 1987-89, budget and fin. com. 1987-89, chmn. audit subcom. 1991-92, task force on taxation employee benefits 1986), Conf. of Consulting Actuaries (bd. dirs. 1989-95, v.p. 1991-92, exec. com. 1991-95, treas. 1992-95, chmn. com. on recognition of continuing profls. 1989-92, com. on health issues 1985-91), Chgo. Actuarial Soc. Roman Catholic. Avocations: tennis, golf, music. Home: 820 N Waiola Ave La Grange Park IL 60526-1452 Office: Milliman & Robertson Inc 55 W Monroe St Ste 4000 Chicago IL 60603-5001

NELSON, TOZA, elementary school educator; b. Beaumont, Tex., Feb. 25, 1948; d. Silas Bailey and Mary Eula (Prudhomme) Estes; m. Don W. Nelson, Oct. 26, 1974; 1 child, Bryan Alan Jones. BS, West Tex. State U., 1972; MEd, Tex. Tech U., 1975. Cert. elem. tchr., reading specialist, supr., Tex. Elem. tchr. Lubbock (Tex.) Ind. Sch. Dist., 1972-78, elem. demonstration tchr., 1978-83, coord. elem. reading and lang. arts., 1983-93, elem. prin., 1993—. Mem. Tex. Assn. for Improvement Reading, Tex. Elem. Prins. and Suprs. Assn., Lubbock Elem. Prins. and Suprs. Assn. Office: Lubbock Ind Sch Dist Maedgen Elem 4401 Nashville Ave Lubbock TX 79413-3313

NELSON, VICKI G. volunteer; b. Racine, Wis., Dec. 5, 1945; d. Myron Max and Betty (Donner) Goldberg; m. John L. Nelson, June 22, 1969; children: Sarah, Rachel. AB, Brandeis U., 1968; postgrad., U. Chgo., 1968. Loan agreement analyst Harris Bank, Chgo., 1969-74; credit analyst Harris Bank Internat., N.Y.C., 1974-75; expansion coor. Brandeis U. Nat. Women's Com., Waltham, Mass., 1985-87; temple adminstr. Temple B'nai Or, Morristown, N.J., 1993; gen. mgr. Historic Speedwell, 1996-98. Mem. New Providence (N.J.) Bd. Edn., 1983; pres. Temple B'nai Or, 1993-95; vice chair Morris Ednl. Found., Morristown, 1994—; v.p. N.J. region Union Am. Hebrew Congregations, 1998—.

NELSON, VITA JOY, editor, publisher; b. N.Y.C., Dec. 9, 1937; d. Leon Abraham and Bertha (Sher) Reiner; m. Lester Nelson, Aug. 27, 1961; children: Lee Reiner, Clifford Samuel, Cara Ritchie. BA, Boston U., 1959. Promotion copywriter Street & Smith, N.Y.C., 1958-59; asst. to mng. editor Mademoiselle Mag., 1959-60; mcpl. bond trader Granger & Co., 1960-63; founder, editor, pub. Westchester Mag., Mamaroneck, N.Y., 1968-80, L.I. Mag., 1973-78; founder, editor, pub., pres. Moneypaper, Mamaroneck, 1981—. Pub. The Guide to Dividend Reinvestment Plans, Direct Investing; founder MP63 Fund; pres. Moneypaper Advisor Inc., 1999—. Author: (with Donald Korn) Create and Manage Your Own Mutual Fund, 1994. Bd. dirs. United Way of Westchester/Putnam County, 1998—2002; bd. govs., v.p. Am. Jewish Com. , Westchester, 1979—89. Recipient citation Coun. Arts, 1972, Media award Pub. Rels. Soc. Am., 1974. Mem. Women in Comms. (Outstanding Communicator award 1983). Democrat. Home: Pleasant Ridge Rd Harrison NY 10528-1004 Office: The Moneypaper Inc 555 Theodore Frend Ave Rye NY 10580 E-mail: vitajoy@aol.com.

NELSON, VIVIENNE E. artist, office manager; b. Mandeville, Jamaica; d. William A. Irwin and Doris Lampart; m. Louis T. Nelson; 1 child John. Grad., Mt. St. Joseph Acad., Mandeville, Jamaica, 1968. Office mgr. Marcel Dekker Inc., N.Y.C., 1972—. Contbg. author: poetry Falling Star, contbg. author: poetry Best Poems, 2001; author: Lift Him Up In Poetry, 2001, Experience the Glory on the Rise, 2002. Recipient Editors Choice award, Internat. Soc. Poetry, 2001, 2002. Avocations: writing, working with youth. Home: 199 William St Hempstead NY 11550

NELSON, W. MICHAEL, III, psychologist, educator; b. Cin., June 29, 1949; s. William M. and Marjorie A. N.; m. Sarah B. Nelson, Aug. 5, 1972; children: William M. IV, Meredith A. BS, Xavier U., 1971; MA, Va. Commonwealth U., 1974, PhD, 1976. Diplomate Am. Bd. Profl. Psychology. Psychology intern U. Tenn. Ctr. Health Scis., Memphis, 1974-75; clin. psychology trainee Petersburg (Va.) Fed. Reformatory, 1975-76; clin. psychologist U. Tex. Health Sci. Ctr., Dallas, 1976-78, Millcreek Psychiat. Ctr. for Children, Cin., 1978-80, dir. psychology, 1980-83; asst. prof. Xavier U., 1978-82, assoc. prof., 1982-86, dir. psychol. svcs., 1984-89, prof., 1986—, chairperson dept. psychology, 1987—2001. Lectr. in field; Midwest regional exam coord. Am. Bd. Profl. Psychology, 1994—, mem. founding com. of bd. certification of clin. child psychology specialty, 2000—, pres. elect. Author: Keeping Your Cool: The Anger Management Video, 1998; co-author: Cognitive-Behavioral Procedures with Children and Adolescents, 1993, (with A.J. Finch) Keeping Your Cool: The Anger Management Workbook, Parts 1 and 2, 1996, Managing Anxiety in Youth: The Coping Cat Video; contbr. articles to profl. jours. Acad. Clin. Psychology fellow, 1994. Fellow: APA; mem.: Cin. Acad. Profl. Psychology, Cin. Psychol. Assn. (pres. 1987—88), Ohio Psychol. Assn. (chair continuing edn. 1984—87, program com. 1985—87), Southeastern Psychol. Assn. Roman Catholic. Avocations: golf, basketball, hunting. Office: Xavier U Dept Psychology Cincinnati OH 45207 E-mail: nelsonwm@xu.edu.

NELSON, WALDEMAR STANLEY, civil engineer, consultant; b. New Orleans, July 8, 1916; s. Bernard Stanley and Mary Lockett (Hutson) N.; widowed; children: Mary Sue Nelson Roniger, Martha Nelson Frost, Charles W., Virginia Nelson Dodge, Kenneth H. BS in Mech. and Elec. Engring., Tulane U., 1936. Registered civil, elec. and mech. engr., 44 states. Jr. engr. A. M. Lockett & Co., 1936-37; civil engr. Jeff. Lake Sulphur Co., Brazoria, Tex., 1937-38; chief survey party N.O. Pub. Belt. R.R., New Orleans, 1938; resident engr. James M. Todd, Buras, La., 1938-39; pvt. practice New Orleans, 1939-40; asst. chief engr. W. Horace Williams Co., Camp Claiborne, La., 1940-41; sr. engr. U.S. Engr. Dept., 1941-44; prin. Waldemar S. Nelson and Co. Inc., New Orleans, 1945—, chmn. bd. dirs. Past chmn. La. State Bd. Registration Profl. Engrs. and Land Surveyors; founding mem., pres. bd. advisors sch. engring. Tulane U. Chmn. Tulane Alumni Fund, Mems' Coun., 1984; mem. bd. visitors Tulane U.; active The Chamber/New Orleans, Boy Scouts Am.; past chmn. Com. of 50; past pres. bd. commrs. New Orleans City Pk. Improvement Assn.; mem. exec. bd. Christmas New Orleans, 1988; past sr. warden of vestry St. Andrew's Episcopal Ch., mem. property com.; past chmn. bd. dirs. St. Andrew's Episcopal Sch.; past pres. bd. trustees St. Martin's Protestant Episcopal Sch.; trustee Tulane Engring. Found.; bd. dirs. River Region, MetroVision. Recipient Outstanding Engring. Alumnus award Tulane U., 1976, Honor award Constrn. Industry Assn. New Orleans, Inc., 1982, Role Model of Yr. award Young Leadership Coun., 1987, Vol. of Yr. award Tulane U. Alumni Affairs, 1992, George Washington Honor medal Freedom's Found. at Valley Forge New Orleans chpt., 1998, Weiss award Nat. Conf. for Cmty. and Justice, 1998. Fellow: NSPE (past. v.p., past chmn. bd. ethical rev.), ASME (life; past. chmn. New Orleans sect.), ASCE (life); mem.: French-Am. C. of C. (pres. La. chpt. 1992—93, chmn. 1994, pres. 1996—97, 1998, named to Bus. Hall of Fame 1997, UNO's First Citizen of the Learning Soc. award 1998), Soc. Tulane Engrs. (past pres.), La. Engring. Found. (trustee 1990, treas. 1991, sec. 1994—95, pres. 1995—96, 1997—99), Soc. Naval Archs. and Marine Engrs., La. Engring. Soc. (hon.; past pres., Charles M. Kerr Pub. Rels. award, Leo M. Odom Profl. Svcs. award, A.B. Paterson medal, Andrew M. Lockett medal), Am. Pub. Works Assn. (life), Soc. Am. Mil. Engrs., Nat. Coun. Engring. Examiners (past treas., Disting. Svc. award), Am. Acad. Environ. Engrs. (diplomate), IEEE, La. Southeast Council, Engrs. Club New Orleans (past pres.), Tulane Alumni Assn. (past. pres.), Boy Scouts of Am. (Disting. Citizen award 2001), Eta Kappa Nu, Pi Tau Sigma, Tau Beta Pi. Avocations: fishing, boating, gardening, shop work, photography. Office: Waldemar S Nelson & Co Inc 1200 Saint Charles Ave New Orleans LA 70130-4334 E-mail: Waldemar.Nelson@wsnelson.com.

NELSON, WALLACE JAY, patent attorney; b. Patrick County, Va., Aug. 1, 1926; s. Willie Everitt and Mollie Jane (Tudor) N.; m. Helen Nixon Blount Nelson, Oct. 27, 1951; children: Jane Elizabeth Shuart, Wallace J. Nelson Jr. BS, Va. Tech., Blacksburg, 1951; JD, The Am. U., Washington, 1960. Patent atty., U.S. Patent Office, Va. State Bar. Chem. lab. tech., analytical chemist Dept. U.S. Army, Radford, Va., 1951-55; patent examiner U.S. Patent Office, Washington, 1955-61; patent atty. Nat. Aeronautics and Space Adminstrn., Hampton, Va., 1961-86, pvt. practice, Hampton, 1986—2002. Inventor Slosh Alleviator, 1969. Mem. AF&AM #306 Masonic Lodge (past master), Scottish Rite of Freemasonry USA, Va. State bar. Methodist. Avocations: spectator sports, reading, golf, fishing. Home: 34 Salt Pond Rd Hampton VA 23664-1736 E-mail: walheln@aol.com.

NELSON, WALTER WILLIAM, computer programmer, consultant; b. Seattle, May 7, 1954; s. Arne A. and Helen R. (Truitt) N.; m. Paula E. Truax, Dec. 21, 1985; m. Joy E. Dalquist, Oct. 27, 2001. BA in Zoology, U. Wash., 1976, BS in Psychology, 1977; PhC in Psychology, U. Minn., 1982. Systems analyst Dept. of Social and Health Svcs., State of Wash., Seattle, 1986-89; computer info. cons. Dept. of Health, State of Wash., 1989-90; pres. Data Dimensions, Inc. (name now Nelson Consulting, Inc.), 1990—. Pres. Tech. Alliance, Renton, Wash., 1990-91, Nelson Family Homes, Inc., 1996—, Women's Fin. Resources, Inc., 1998—. Contbr. articles to profl. jours. Mem. Tech Alliance, Berkeley Macintosh Users Group, Seattle Downtown Macintosh Bus. Users Group, 4th Dimension Spl. Interest Group (founder, pres. 1990—), Am. Singles Golf Assn. (founder Seattle chpt. 1999). Avocations: tennis, golf, thoroughbred horse racing. Office: 7637 Dogwood Ln SE Snoqualmie WA 98065-9733

NELSON, WALTER GERALD, retired insurance company executive; b. Peoria, Ill., Jan. 2, 1930; s. Walter Dennis and Hazel Marie (Tucker) Nelson; m. Mary Ann Olberding, Jan. 28, 1952 (dec. Nov. 1989); children: Ann Larkin, Michael, Susan Boor, Patrick, Thomas, Timothy, Molly Edwards; m. Mary Jo Sunderland, Apr. 6, 1991. Student, St. Benedict's Coll., Atchison, Kans., 1947-49, Bradley U., Peoria, Ill., 1949; JD, Creighton U., Omaha, 1952. Bar: Nebr 1952, Ill 1955. Practice in, Peoria, 1955-56; with State Farm Life Ins. Co., Bloomington, Ill., 1956—, counsel, 1968—, v.p., 1970-96; adj. prof. Ill. State U., Bloomington, 1996—. Past dir Ill Life Ins Coun; past chmn legal sect Am Coun Life Ins; spkr in field. Contbr. articles to profl jours. Community bd dirs St Joseph Med Ctr, Bloomington, Ill., 1994. Mem.: ABA, Nat. Orgn. Life and Health Ins. Guaranty Assn. (past pres.), Assn. Life Ins. Counsel (past pres.), Nebr. Bar Assn., Ill. Bar Assn., Bloomington Country Club, KofC. Republican. Roman Catholic. E-mail: WGN1930@aol.com.

NELSON, WALTER HENRY, communications consultant, author; b. Munich, Mar. 23, 1928; parents Am. citizens; s. Casimir Thaddeus and Eugenie (Simon) Zawadzki; m. Rose Marie Carson, Mar. 4, 1950; children: Roger Stuart, Gregory Eugene, Victoria Eugenie; 2d marriage to Rita L. Christoffersen, June 30, 1962; 1 child, Samantha Christine. Student, NYU, 1944, Norwich U., 1944-46, Columbia U., 1949-50. News editor, info. analyst Radio Free Europe, N.Y.C., Munich, 1950-53; dir. mag. info. Am. Heritage Found., N.Y.C., 1953-55; mag. pub. dir., editor quar. Am. Petroleum Inst., 1955-57; dir. pub. rels. Reach, McClinton & Co., Inc., N.Y.C., 1957-59; v.p., gen. mgr. Candygram, Inc., Chgo., 1959-60; asst. to pres. Stevens Candy Kitchens, Inc., 1960-61; assoc. in pub. rels. Fred Rosen Assocs., Inc., 1961-62; ptnr. Prittie and Nelson Internat. Pub. Rels., London, 1975-81; chmn. Nelson Assocs. Ltd., 1981-93; freelance author and comms. cons., 1993—. Pub. rels. dir. William H. Rentschler for U.S. Senator, 1959-60. Author: Small Wonder: The Amazing Story of the Volkswagen Beetle, 1965, rev., 1998, German edit., 1966, Br. edit., 1967, rev., 1971, Dutch edit., 1968, Spanish edit., 1974, revised edit., 1998, The Great Discount Delusion, 1965, The Berliners: Their City and Their Saga, 1969, Br. edit., 1969, The Soldier Kings: The House of Hohenzollern, 1970, Br. and Italian edits., 1971, German edit., 1972, 98, Ernest Hemingway, 1971, Germany Rearmed, 1972, The Londoners: Life in A Civilized City, 1974, Br. edit., 1975, Japanese edit., 1976, 77, (with Terence Prittie) Economic War Against the Jews, 1977, Br. Edit., 1978, the Siege of Buckingham Palace, 1980, The Minstrel Code, 1979, Spanish edit., 1982, Gautama Buddha: His life and his Teaching, U.K. edit., 1998, Buddha: Life & Teaching, U.S. edit., 2000; contbr. articles to popular mags., newspapers. Served in U.S. Army, 1946-49. Address: 23 Clifford Ave London SW14 7BT England E-mail: walter@words.softnet.co.uk.

NELSON, WILLIAM EUGENE, lawyer; b. Roland, Iowa, Sept. 23, 1927; s. Sam J. and Katherine A. (Coffey) N.; m. Sherlee M. Stanford, July 11, 1959; children: Anne, Kristin, William. BA, U. Iowa, 1950; JD, Drake U., 1957. Bar: Iowa 1957, D.C. 1965, Md. 1976. Trial atty. civil divsn. U.S. Dept. Justice, 1957-65, asst. chief tort sect., 1966-70, chief r.r. reorgn. unit, 1970-71; gen. counsel Cost of Living Coun. Phase I, 1971, chief econ. stblzn. sect., 1971-74; ptnr. Nelson and Nelson, LLP, Washington, Bethesda, Md., 1975—. Gen. counsel the Communicators, Inc., Myersville, Md. Assoc. editor Drake Law Rev., 1955-57. With USN, 1945-46. Recipient Atty. Gen.'s Disting. Svc. award, 1972. Mem. Order of Coif, Omicron Delta Kappa. Home: 511 Colston Dr Falling Waters WV 25419 Office: Nelson & Nelson LLP 3 Bethesda Metro Ctr Ste 700 Bethesda MD 20814-6300 E-mail: sswen@aol.com.

NELSON, WILLIAM GEORGE, IV, software company executive; b. Phila., May 26, 1934; s. William George III and Eleanor (Boyle) N. BA in Chemistry, Swarthmore Coll., 1956; MBA in Finance, U. Pa., 1958; PhD in Econs., Rice U., 1965. Various positions Du Pont Co., 1957-62, Monsanto Co., St. Louis, 1965-76; vis. asst. prof. Washington U., 1966-75; sr. v.p. Chase Econs./Interactive Data, Waltham, Mass., 1976-83; pres. Pansophic Systems, Lisle, Ill., 1983-90; pres., CEO OnLine Software, Ft. Lee, N.J., 1990-91, bd. dirs.; pres., CEO Pilot Software, Boston, 1992-94; CEO Harris Data Corp., 1990—; pres., CEO Clarendon Capital Corp., Boston, 1995-96; chmn. GEAC Computer Corp. Ltd., North York, Ont., Can., 1996—, CEO Can., 1996-99. Bd. dirs. GEAC, Toronto, Manugistics, Rockville, Md., Harris Data, Waukesha, Wis., HealthGate Data, Boston. Bd. dirs. Swarthmore Coll. NFS fellow in econs., 1963-65. Office: HarrisData 611 N Barker Rd Brookfield WI 53045-5977

NELSON, WILLIAM O. retired pharmaceutical company executive; b. Gold Canyon, Ariz., Mar. 30, 1941; s. William Orestas and Glenice Irene (Pearson) N.; m. Sue Farmer, Jan. 27, 1962 (div. Jan. 1971); 1 child, Terri Lynn; m. Deborah Marie Goodwin, Oct. 5, 1985. AA, Pima Coll., Tucson, 1976; BS, U. Phoenix, 1980. Sales rep. Sandoz Pharms., Riverside, Calif., 1966-71, Tucson, 1971-79, regional sales mgr. Phoenix, 1979-87, western area mgr., med. scis. liaison, 1987-94; assoc. dir. oncology bus. ops. Novartis Pharm. Corp., East Hanover, N.J., 1994-97, ret., 1997. With USN, 1959-63. Republican. Avocations: golf, trap shooting, audiophile. Home: 10955 E Vista Del Cielo Gold Canyon AZ 85218-4842

NELSON, WILLIAM RANKIN, surgeon, educator; b. Charlottesville, Va., Dec. 12, 1921; s. Hugh Thomas and Edith (Rankin) N.; m. Nancy Laidley, Mar. 17, 1956 (div. 1979); children: Robin Page Nelson Russel, Susan Kimberly Nelson Wright, Anne Rankin Nelson Cron; m. Pamela Morgan Phelps, July 5, 1984. BA, U. Va., 1943, MD, 1945. Diplomate Am. Bd. Surgery. Intern Vanderbilt U. Hosp., Nashille, 1945-46; resident in surgery U. Va. Hosp., Charlottesville, 1949-51; fellow surg. oncology Meml. Sloan Kettering Cancer Ctr., N.Y.C., 1951-55; instr. U. Colo. Sch. Medicine, Denver, 1955-57, asst. clin. prof., 1962-87, clin. prof. surgery, 1987—. Asst. prof. Med. Coll. Va., Richmond, 1957-62; mem. exec. com. U. Colo. Cancer Ctr.; mem. nat. bd., nat. exec. com. Am. Cancer Soc. Contbr. articles to profl. jours. and chpts. to textbooks. Capt. USAAF, 1946-48. Recipient Nat. Div. award Am. Cancer Soc., 1979. Fellow Am. Coll. Surgeons (bd. govs. 1984-89); mem. AMA, Internat. Soc. Surgery, Brit. Assn. Surg. Oncology, Royal Soc. Medicine (U.K.), Soc. Surg. Oncology (pres. 1975-76), Soc. Head and Neck Surgeons (pres. 1986-87), Am. Cancer Soc. (pres. Colo. div. 1975-77, exec. com., nat. bd. dirs., del. dir. from Colo. div. 1985-94), Am. Soc. Clin. Oncology, Western Surg. Assn. Colo. Med. Soc., Denver Med. Soc., Denver Acad. Surgery, Rocky Mt. Oncology Soc., Univ. Club, Rotary. Republican. Episcopalian. Avocations: skiing, backpacking, travel, bicycling, fly fishing. E-mail: wrn3@msn.com .

NELSON, WINIFRED HARRISON, singer, actress, computer programmer; b. Oak Park, Ill., Dec. 29, 1924; d. Fred and Florence Harrison; m. Robert Hartley Nelson, May 5, 1945 (dec. Feb. 24, 1994); children: Richard, Wendy, Steven (dec.), Jonathan, Elizabeth. BA, Knox Coll., 1945; MusM, Northwestern U., 1970. Tchr. voice, 1972-78, Chgo., 1976-80; computer programmer U. Ill., Champaign, 1978-82, Tex. A&M U., College Station, 1982-90. Mem. Chgo. Symphony Chorus, 1972-80. Mem. Briarcrest Country Club. Presbyterian. Avocations: community theater, music, golf. Home: 2505 Oak Cir Bryan TX 77802-2009

NELSON-COLLINS, ELLA M. foundation administrator, consultant; b. Carthage, Tex., Aug. 25, 1950; d. Anthony and Nellie (Delaney) Collins; divorced; children: Makeba Collins, Brittany Collins. BSc, Tex. Coll., 1971; postgrad., U. Houston, 1978-80, Tex. Women U., 1989. Tchr. biology, earth and life sci. Lamar Fleming Jr. High Sch. Houston Ind. Sch. Dist., 1975-86, coord. sci. dept., 1975-86; drug edn. specialist Tarrant Coun. Alcoholism and Drug Abuse, Ft. Worth, 1987-89; drug coord. Ft. Worth Housing Authority, 1987-91; regional coord. Texans' War Drugs, Ft. Worth, 1991-93; pres./CEO Neighborhoods Organized Substance Abuse Prevention, Inc., 1993—. Coach girl's basketball Lamar Fleming Jr. High Sch., Houston Ind. Sch. Dist., 1975-86. Pres. Matilda Tolbert Perkins Delaney Found.; mem. North Tex. inter-alumni coun. United Negro Coll. Fund; mem. citizen's crime commn. Tarrant County Gangs Task Force. Recipient Valuable Svc. to Assn. award Houston Tex. Coll. Alumni Assn., 1986, Human Svcs. award Phi Beta Sigma, 1989, Region VI Housing and Urban Devel. award, 1990, Gov.'s award Gov. Bill Clements, 1990, Leadership award United Negro Coll. Fund, 1992, U.S. HUD award, 1992. Mem. NAFE, Tex. Coll. Alumni (pres.), Ft. Worth Lions Club, Zeta Phi Beta (pres.). Home: 1524 Hollowbrook Ct Fort Worth TX 76103-1735

NELSON-HUMPHRIES, TESSA, writer, educator; b. Wakefield, Yorkshire, Eng. came to U.S., 1955; m. Kenneth Nelson Brown, June 1, 1957 (dec. July 1962); m. C. H. Unthank, 1963 (dec. 1979). PhD, U. Liverpool, 1974. Prof. Cumberland Coll., Williamsburg, Ky., 1964-90, N.Mex. State U., Las Cruces, 1990-92; writer, lectr., poet. Author poetry; contbr. anthologies. Life mem. Las Cruces Humane Soc., 1990—. Fulbright scholar, 1955; recipient Clemence Dane Cup for dramatic monologue, 2000; scholarship named in honor Cumberland Coll., 1997. Mem. Soc. Women Writers and Journalists (London, article prize 1998, 99, other prizes, Garrod Prize, 2001), Soc. Children's Book Writers and Illustrators, S.W. Writers Assn., Albuquerque, N.M., Vegetarian Soc. U.K. (life). Episcopalian. Avocations: dogs, vegetarian cooking, travel, reading. Home: 4 Hills 3228 Jupiter Rd Las Cruces NM 88012-7742

NELSON-SMALL, KATHY ANN, foundation administrator; b. Williamsport, Pa., Sept. 21, 1954; d. Dan LeRoy and Shirley Joann (Klein) Hoover; m. Robert Joseph Small, Feb. 14, 1996. BS in German Edn., Ind. U. of Pa., 1976; postgrad., Pa. State U., 1978-83. Tchr. German Hollidaysburg (Pa.) Area Sch. Dist., 1977-85; adminstr. Carlisle (Pa.) Project, 1985; dir. fin. devel. and pub. rels. Am. Lung Assn., York, Pa., 1986; chief profl. officer Adams County United Way, Gettysburg, 1987—. Press sec. Nancy Kulp's campaign for 9th Congl. Dist., Pa., 1984; mem. Main Street Gettysburg, 1987—, mem. pub. rels. com., 1996-98, 125th Battle of Gettysburg Anniversary Commn., 1988; treas. Adams County Coun. Cmty. Svcs., 1987-89, sec. 1995-99, Pa. State Club of Adams County, 1989—; mem. adv. bd. Adams County Job Ctr., 1989-91, Minority Youth Ednl. Inst., 1988-91, Intercultural Resource Ctr., Gettysburg Coll., 1989-91; mem. Adams Area Postal Customer Coun., 1987-89; dir. Adams Cmty. TV, 1988-89; mem. profl. adv. coun., chmn. small cities task force United Way Pa., 1990—, mem. network com., 1992-94, now mem. pub. sector impact com. and pers. com.; mem. planning com. United Way Leaders' Conf., 1995, also participant; mem. collaborative bd. Family Svc. Sys. Reform Initiative; bd. dirs. Adams County Interfaith Housing Corp., Adams County Coop. Ext., bd. dirs., 1996—, v.p., 2001—, sec., 1999-2000, strategic planning com. chair, 1999—; bd. dirs. Adams County Partnership for Cmty. Health, 1996—. Fulbright/Goethe Haus scholar, Stuttgart, Germany, 1982; named citizen of yr. Gettysburg-Adams County Area C. of C., 2000. Mem. Ctrl. Pa. Assn. Women Execs. (charter), Kiwanis (pres. Hist. Gettysburg chpt. 1989-95, chmn. dist. conv. Pa. chpt. 1992, dist. maj. emphasis program chairperson 1992-93), Gettysburg Rotary (club svc. chair 1998-2000, sec. 2000—), Pa. State Alumni Assn. (life), Gettysburg-Adams County Area C. of C. (pub. rels. com. 1989-98, strategic planning com. 1998—), Alpha Omicron Pi (endowment com. 1993—). Democrat. Lutheran. Avocations: traveling, skiing, antiquing, sewing, gardening. Home: 2566 Old Route 30 Orrtanna PA 17353-9417 Office: Adams County United Way PO Box 3545 Gettysburg PA 17325-0545

NELSON-THORPE, CARLON JUSTINE, engineering and operations executive; b. Siloam Springs, Ark., May 26, 1960; d. Robert F. and Jean (Caroom) Toenges. BS in Indsl. Engring., U. Ark., 1982; MBA, Houston Bapt. U., 1988. Registered profl. engr., Tex. Supr. codes and regulatory compliance Tex. Ea., Houston, 1982-85, supr. ops. spl. projects, 1985-87, mgr. project devel., 1987-90; dir. spl. projects, tech. asst. to pres. Enron, 1990-91, dir. throughput engring., 1991-92, project dir., 1992-95; v.p. engring. So. Union Gas Co., Austin, 1995-96; v.p. ops. Mo. Gas Energy, Kansas City, Mo., 1996-99; gen. mgr. Shell Tech. Ventures, Houston, 1999—2002. Mem. NSPE, Tex. Soc. Profl. Engrs. Home: 5334 Indian Shores Ln Houston TX 77041-4298 Office: 200 N Dairy Ashford St Houston TX 77079-1101 E-mail: carlon@sbcglobal.net.

NELSON-WALKER, ROBERTA, management software company executive; b. N.Y.C., Sept. 1, 1936; d. Richard E. and Esther (McBride) Martin; m. Robert L. Nelson, July 20, 1957 (div.); children: Carol, Craig, Robert H.; m. Dan Walker, Nov. 1978 (div.). BA, DePaul U., 1976, MS in Mgmt. with distinction, 1977. Dir. devel. Ray Graham Assocs., Elmhurst, Ill., 1970-76; dir. human resources Nat. Easter Seal Soc., Chgo., 1979-81; v.p. Butler Walker Inc., Oak Brook, Ill., 1981-85; pres. CNR, Inc., 1985-91; spl. agt. Prudential Ins., 1991-95; mng. dir. Visimark L.L.C., 1995—. Author: Creating Acceptance for Handicapped People, 1975, Creating, Planning, and Financial Housing for Handicapped People, 1979. Founder, organizer Found. for Handicapped, 1970-76,; pres. DuPage County Pub. Health Coun., 1974; bd. dirs. DuPage County Mental Health Assocs., 1970, Forest Found. DuPage County, 1976-86, Shakespeare Globe, London and Chgo., 1982—; mem. DuPage County Bd. Health, 1975, Ill. Gov.'s Com. for Handicapped, 1976, women's coun. Chgo. Heart Assn., 1979—. Recipient Meritorious Svc. award, Chgo. Heart Assn., 1968, 70, Fond du Coer award AHA, 1968, Cursade of Mercy Achievement awards, 1974-76, State of Ill. procalmation by Gov. James Thompson, Ill. Epilepsy Assn., 1978.

NELTNER, MICHAEL MARTIN, lawyer; b. Cin., July 31, 1959; s. Harold John and Joyce Ann Neltner; m. Barbara Ann Phair, July 9, 1988; children: Brandon August, Alexandra Nicole. BA, Mercy Coll., 1981; MA, Athenaeum of Ohio, 1987; JD, U. Cin., 1994. Bar: Ohio 1994, U.S. Dist. Ct. (so. dist.) Ohio 1995. Tchr. Elder H.S., Cin., 1985-91; ins. agt. Ky. Ctrl., 1987-91; mediator City of Cin., 1992-94; tchg. asst. Ohio Gov.'s Inst., Cin., 1992; legal extern to Chief Justice Thomas Moyer Ohio Supreme Ct., 1993; assoc. Eagen, Wykoff & Healy, LPA, Cin., 1994-99, Thompson Hine & Flory, Cin., 1999-2000, Freund, Freeze & Arnold, Cin., 2000—. Editor-in-chief Mercy Coll. Lit. Mag., 1980-81, U. Cin. Law Rev., 1993-94. Campaign coord. Rep. Orgn. Detroit, 1980. Recipient Merit scholarship Cin. Enquirer, 1977-81, Sage scholarship Mercy Coll., 1980, Am. Jurisprudence award Lawyers Coop. Publishing, 1994. Mem ABA, Ohio Bar Assn., Cin. Bar Assn. (mem. acad. medicine com. 1995—, chair Ct. Appeals com. 1998-2000). Home: 3344 Milverton Ct Cincinnati OH 45248-2865 Office: Freund Freeze & Arnold LPA 105 E 4th St Cincinnati OH 45202-4006 E-mail: mneltner@ffalaw.com.

NEMARA, VANESSA ANNE, federal official; b. Middle Village, N.Y., Aug. 24, 1953; d. Frank Joseph and Ann Margaret (O'Mara) Nemara; 1 child, Sophia Marie. BS in Police Sci., John Jay Coll., 1975, MA in Criminal Justice, 1980. Salesperson Lane Bryant Dept. Store, N.Y.C., 1973-74; from procurement clk. to supervisory contract specialist Gen. Svcs. Adminstrn., 1974-85, procurement analyst, 1986-88; supr. contract specialist U.S. Dept. Agr., Orient Point, NY, 1985-86, USCG, Governor's Island, 1988—97, Norfolk, Va., 1996—. Roman Catholic. Avocation: baseball. Home: 1446 Shortleaf Ln Chesapeake VA 23320-0656 Office: 300 E Main St Ste 600 Norfolk MA 23510-9102

NEMAT-NASSER, SIA, engineering educator, researcher; b. Tehran, Apr. 14, 1936; married. BS, Calif. State U., Sacramento, 1960; MSCE, U. of Calif., Berkeley, 1961, PhD in Structural Mechanics, 1964. Asst. prof. civil engring. Calif. State U. , Sacramento, 1961—62; tchg. fellow U. of Calif., Berkeley, 1963—64; postdoctoral fellow Northwestern U., Evanston, Ill., 1964—65; asst. prof. applied mechanics U. of Calif. , San Diego, 1966—69; assoc. prof. applied mechanics U. of Calif., 1969—70; prof. civil engring. and applied math. Northwestern U., Evanston, Ill., 1970—85; prof. applied mechanics and engring. scis. U. of Calif., San Diego, 1985—99; prof. mech. and aerospace engring. dept. U. of Calif. , 1999—. Dir. of the ctr. of excellence for advanced materials U. of Calif. San Diego, San Diego, 1986—2002, program dir. of the materials sci. grad. program, 1989—94, dir. of the inst. for mechanics and materials, 1998—2000; cons. Jet Propulsion Lab., Pasadena, CALIF., 1967—67, Systems Exploration, San Diego, 1967—67, Gulf-General Atomic, San Diego, 1969—69, BDM Corp., McLean, VA., 1983—83, S-Cubed, La Jolla, CALIF., 1985—89, ANatech Research Corp, La Jolla, CALIF., 1989—95, Trw, Redondo Beach, CALIF., 1990—91, Engring. Sci. Software Inc, Smithfield, RI, 1992—92, Trans-Science Corp., La Jolla, CALIF., 1987—98, Sandia Nat. Laboratories, Albuquerque, 1993—98, Alpha Star Corp., West Los Angeles, CALIF., 1995—97, Gen. Atomics, San Diego, 1995—97, BP Exploration, Houston, 1998—99, Logicon, Albuquerque, 1998—2000; vis. prof. Tech. U. Denmark, Lyngby, 1972—73. Author: (book) On Elastic Stability Under Noconservative Loads, 1972, Micromechanics: Overall Properties of Heterogeneous Materials, 1993, Micromechanics: Overall Properties of Heterogeneous Materials, 2d edit., 1999; editor: Mechanics Today, Vol. 1, 1974, Mechanics Today, Vol. 2, 1975, Mechanics Today, Vol. 3, 1976, Mechanics Today, Vol. 4, 1978, Mechanics Today, Vol. 5, 1980, Mechanics Today, Vol. 6, 1981, (seven book series) Mechanics of Elastic and Inelastic Solids, 1980, (book) Three Dimensional Constitutive Relations and Ductile Fracture, 1981, Hydraulic Fracturing and Geothermal Energy, 1983, Theoretical Foundation for Large-Scale Computations of Nonlinear Material BehaviorDordrecht, 1984, Large Deformations of Solids: Physical Basis and Mathematical Modeling, 1986. Named John Dove Isaacs Chair in Natural Philosophy, U. of Calif. San Diego, 1995—2000; recipient Alburz Ednl. Found. prize, Iran, 1975, Gold medal, Tech. U. of Crete, Greece, 1997; fellow Arthur Gould Tasheira fellow, U. of Calif., 1962—63, Forth Found. fellow, 1963—64, rsch. fellow, Tech. U. of Denmark, 1972—73, Fgn. fellow, Danish Ctr. for Applied Math. and Mechanics, 1987. Fellow: ASME (chair-materials divsn. 1997—98, Lifetime Membership Certification and Life Fellow Designation 2001), Soc. of Engring. Sci. (v.p. 1978—79, dir. 1976—82, pres. 1979—80, William Prager medal in Solid Mechanics 2002), Am. Acad. of Mechanics (pres. 1996—97, sec. 1988); mem.: NAE, ASCE, Internat. Soc. for Optical Engring., Minerals, Metals and Materials Soc., Soc. of Engring. Sci. Office: U Calif San Diego 9500 Gilman Dr La Jolla CA 92093-0416 Office Fax: 858-534-2727. Business E-Mail: sia@shiba.ucsd.edu.

NEMATOLLAHY, VIOLET, physician, pediatrician; b. Tehran, Iran, Nov. 24, 1953; came to U.S., 1979; d. Ahmad and Mahrokh (Milani) Nematollahy; 1 child, Pooneh. MD, Tehran U., 1978. Resident in pediatrics Georgetown U., Washington, 1978-83; pediatrician Nova Pediatrics, Springfield, Va. Fellow Am. Acad. Pediatrics. Office: Nova Pediatrics 6120 Brandon Ave Springfield VA 22150-2504

NEMBHARD, DAVID A. engineering educator, researcher; b. Cleve., Oct. 20, 1964; s. Horace O. Nembhard, Carren S. Nembhard; m. Harriet Black Black; children: Olivia, Naomi. BS in Sys. and Control Engring., Case Western Res. U., 1987, MS in Sys. Engring., 1990; PhD in Indsl. and Ops. Engring., U. Mich., 1994. Asst. prof. ops. mgmt. Auburn U., Auburn, Ala., 1994—98; asst. prof. indsl. engring. U. Wis., Madison, 1998—. Contbr. articles. Fellow Rackham Merit, U. Mich., 1991—94; grantee, NSF and Decision Risk and Mgmt. Sci. Program, 2000—, Space and Naval Warfare Sys. Command and Dept. Def., 2000; scholar, Great Lakes Ctr. Truck and Transit Rsch., 1994, Nat. Achievement, Case Western Res. U., 1983—87. Mem.: IEEE, Am. Soc. Quality, Inst. Indsl. Engrs., Inst. Ops. Rsch. and Mgmt. Sci., Soc. Mfg. Engrs. (trea. chpt. 75 2001). Avocation: piano, racquetball, cycling. Office: Univ Wis Madison 1513 University Ave Rm 360 Madison WI 53706

NEMBHARD, HARRIET BLACK, engineering educator; b. Ft. Worth, Dec. 7, 1967; d. Charles Eldred Black, Helen Eastman Black; m. David Arthur Nembhard; children: Olivia, Naomi. BA, Claremont McKenna Coll., 1987; BSE, Ariz. State U., 1990; MSE, PhD, U. Mich., 1994. Asst. prof. Auburn (Ala.) U., 1994—98, U. Wis., Madison, 1998—. Contbr. articles to profl. jours. Recipient Rsch. award, NSF, 2001—; fellow Rackham Merit fellow, U. Mich. Grad. Sch., 1991—94, New Faculty fellow, Alfred P. Sloan Found., 1997. Mem.: Institute of Industrial Engineers, INstitute for Operations Research and the Management Sciences, American Society for Quality, American Society for Engineering Education. Office: U Wis Madison 1513 University Ave Madison WI 53706 Business E-Mail: hbnem@engr.wisc.edu.

NEMBHARD, JESSICA GITT GORDON, economist; b. N.Y.C., July 3, 1956; d. Edmund W. and Susan E. (Gitt) Gordon; children: Stephen M. Nembhard, Susan R. Nembhard. BA, Yale U., 1978; MAT, Howard U., 1982; MA, U. Mass., 1989, PhD, 1992. Tchr. San Pedro Roman Cath. Sch., Belize, 1978-79; asst. to the chair African Am. studies program Yale U., New Haven, 1979-80; rsch. asst. Sch. Edn. Howard U., Washington, 1980-81; dir. St. Philip's Tutorial Program, 1981-82; spl. asst. to pres. Children's Def. Fund, 1982-84; cons. editor disweek Newspaper, Belize City, Belize, 1984-85; rsch. asst. dept. econs. U. Mass., Amherst, 1987-88; econ. devel. analyst, acting dep. dir. Black Cmty. Crusade for Children, Children's Def. Fund, Washington, 1993-96; sr. economist Inst. for Urban Rsch., Morgan State U., Balt., 1997—. Cons. New Econ. Equation, Radcliffe Pub. Policy Inst., Cambridge, Mass., 1996; cons. econ. edn. working group Edn. Dept. AFL-CIO, Washington, 1997; sr. fellow Annenberg Inst. for Sch. Reform, Brown U., Providence, 1998—. Author: The Nation We Are Making: A Junior History of Belize, 1990, Capital Control, Financial Regulation, and Industrial Policy in South Korea and Brazil, 1996; co-editor: Creating a New World Economy, 1993; contbr. articles to profl. jours. Asst. treas., corr. sec. Shepherd Elem. PTA, Washington, 1996—. Minority grad. fellow NSF, Washington, 1988-91; Minority dissertation fellow Am. Econ. Assn., Fed. Res. Sys., 1991-92. Mem. Nat. Econ. Assn. (bd. mem. 1996—), Am. Econ. Assn., Athena Telamatics (bd. mem. 1995—), Kappa Delta Pi. Office: Inst for Urban Rsch Morgan State Univ Baltimore MD 21251-0001

NEMEC, DAVID JOSEPH, writer, baseball historian; b. Cleve., Dec. 10, 1941; MA, Ohio State U. Writer, San Francisco, 1976—. Baseball history cons., 1986—; tchr., tennis pro, 1978—. Author: (novels) Stonesifer, 1999, Early Dreams, 2000, Remember Me to My Father, 2001, (baseball histories) The Great American Baseball Team Book, 1992, The Rules of Baseball and How They Came to Be, 1994, The Beer and Whisky League, 1995, The Great Encyclopedia of 19th Century Major League Baseball, 1997 (Sporting News SABR Baseball Rsch. award 1998), The Great Book of Baseball Knowledge, 1999, The Ultimate Baseball Book, 2000. Mem. Soc. for Am. Baseball Rsch.

NEMEC, JOSEF, retired organic chemist, researcher; b. Ostresany, Czechoslovakia, Sept. 7, 1929; came to U.S., 1969; s. Josef Nemec and Marie (Joskova) Nemcova; m. Anna Pastush, Aug. 29, 1975; 1 child, Marketa. MS, Inst. Chem. Tech., Prague, Czechoslovakia, 1954; PhD, Czechoslovak Acad. Scis., Prague, 1958. Organic chemist Inst. Chem. Tech., Prague, 1954-61; sr. rsch. chemist Czechoslovak Acad. Scis., 1961-69; rsch. fellow in organic chemistry Wayne State U., Detroit, 1969-70; sr. rsch. scientist Squibb Inst. Med. Rsch., New Brunswick, N.J., 1970-75; staff mem. St. Jude Children's Rsch. Hosp., Memphis, 1975-84; sr. scientist Nat. Cancer Inst.-Program Resources, Inc. Cancer R&D Ctr., Frederick, Md., 1984-95; ret., 1995. Adj. prof. med. chemistry U. Tenn., Memphis, 1979-91; external examiner U. Zimbabwe, Harare, 1994—; cons. in field. Contbr. articles to scholarly and profl. jours. Grantee Nat. Cancer Inst., 1975-85. Mem. AAAS, Am. Chem. Soc., Royal Soc. Chemistry, Czechoslovak Soc. Arts and Scis. Achievements include patents in fields of anticancer agents, organic chemicals, semimicroequipment in organic chemistry; research in natural products, synthetic anticancer agents, monosaccharides, experimental semimicrotechniques in organic chemistry.

NEMEC, MICHAEL LEE, lawyer; b. Tulsa, Aug. 1, 1949; s. Milton L. and Betty D. (Lawrence) N.; m. Vivian Strobel, Dec. 26, 1970; children: Adam, Jennifer, David. BA in Polit. Sci., U. Tulsa, 1971, JD, 1976. Bar: Okla. 1976. Pvt. practice law, Tulsa, 1976-78; dir. deferred giving Okla. State U. Found., Stillwater, 1978-80; asst. v.p., trust officer Bank Okla. N.A., Tulsa, 1980; v.p., trust officer Bank Commerce & Trust Co., 1980-85; pvt. practice law, 1985-89; assoc. Hall, Estill, Hardwick, Gable, Golden & Nelson P.C., 1989-93, shareholder, 1993—. Mem. fin. com. Monte Cassino Sch., Inc., Tulsa, 1987; vol. Boy Scouts Am., Tulsa, 1984-86, 97-2001; participant U.S. Naval Acad. Fgn. Affairs Conf., 1971; founders chorus, Soc. for the Preservation and Encouragement of Barber Shop Singing in Am., Tulsa Boys' Home; mem. Planned Giving Coun.; mem. Major Gifts Coun., AHA, 1998-99. Named Family of Yr., LDS Ch., Tulsa, 1985. Mem. ABA, Okla. Bar Assn., Tulsa County Bar Assn. (sec. tax sect. 1988), Tulsa Title and Probate Lawyers (bd. dirs. 2001—), Tulsa Estate Planning Forum (bd. dirs. 2000—), Tulsa Tax Forum (pres. 1994, 95), Soc. for Preservation and Encouragement of Barber Shop Quartet Singing in Am., Univ. of Tulsa Coll. of Law Alumni Assn. (bd. dirs. 2002—), Mensa. Roman Catholic. Office: Hall Estill Hardwick Gable Golden & Nelson PC 320 S Boston Ave Ste 400 Tulsa OK 74103-3704

NEMEC, VERNITA ELLEN (VERNITA N'COGNITA), artist, curator; b. Painesville, Ohio, Nov. 30; d. Vernon William McClish and Ellen Ludway; m. David Joseph Nemec, Apr. 18, 1964 (div. July 1970). BFA cum laude, Ohio U., 1964; MA, NYU, 1966; postgrad., Naropa Inst., 1978. Asst. to dir. Susan Caldwell Gallery, N.Y.C., 1982; exec. dir. Artists Talk on Art, 1989-98; dir. Viridian Artists, 1998—. Vis. artist Rutgers U., 1997, Mich. State U., 1999; art cons. Middlesex County Arts Coun., Edison, N.J., 1988-90; pres. bd. dirs. Artists Talk on Art, N.Y.C., 1988-97; v.p. Heresies, Art and Politics, N.Y.C., 1992-96; guest curator Henry St. Art Ctr., N.Y.C., 1992—; curator Art from Detritus, N.Y.C., 1994—; art writer Cover Mag., N.Y.C., 1998, Zing mag., 2000; interviewer/producer How to Survive in the Art World, WBAI radio, N.Y.C., 1994. Author: (performance art) Bohemian Barbie, 1998; actor: (performance art) Bohemian Barbie, 1998; author: (performance art) How To Be The Perfect Woman, 1999; actor: (performance art) How To Be The Perfect Woman, 1999; author: (performance art) It All Goes So Quickly, 2001; actor: (performance art) It All Goes So Quickly, 2001;one-woman shows include NIH, Bethesda, 1995, Westchester C.C., N.Y., 1999, Gallery 128, N.Y.C., 2000, S.E. Mo. State U., 2001, 11 E. Ashland, Phoenix, 2001. Active Lower Manhattan Loft Tenants, N.Y.C., 1975—. Curatorial grantee Muriel McBrien Kauffman Found., Kansas City, Mo., 1995, Artist Performance Collaborative grantee The Field, N.Y.C., 1997; grantee Jerome Found., 1986. Avocations: travel, writing Haiku and poetry. Home: 361 Canal St New York NY 10013-2216 E-mail: ncognita@earthfire.org.

NEMECEK, ALBERT DUNCAN, JR. retail company executive, investment banker, management consultant; b. Helena, Mont., Mar. 10, 1936; s. Albert Duncan and Geneva (Reindle) N.; m. Marilyn Ann Shaughnessy, Sept. 7, 1963 (div.); children: Maureen Ann, Steven Mathew; m. Judith Eileen Swift, Sept. 18, 1981 (div.); 1 child, Jennifer Eileen. BS, U. Md., 1960, postgrad. in econs., 1961. Agt. IRS, Washington, 1961-65; tax dir. Macke Co., 1965-69; tax dir., then sec. Garfinckle, Brooks Bros., Miller & Rhoads, Inc., 1969-76, treas., 1976—, v.p., 1979—; mng. ptnr. Nemecek & Falleroni, 1987, Nemecek & Jacknis, investment bankers, mgmt. cons., Falls Church, Va., 1989; founder Nemecek & Co., Inc., 1990. Founder Entrepreneurial Growth Fund, Falls Church, 1990. Founder The Leadership Group, 1996. Home: PO Box 21 Occoquan VA 22125-0021 E-mail: fixit00001@aol.com. *A man's success is measured by the respect he has gained from his peers, his understanding and compassion, respect for the feelings of others, appreciation of the world's beauty, and his attempts to leave the world better than he found it.*

NEMECEK, GEORGINA MARIE, molecular pharmacologist; b. Mineola, N.Y., Aug. 27, 1946; d. George and Frances Valerie (Masaryk) N. AB, Mt. Holyoke Coll., 1968; PhD, U. Pa., 1972. Rsch. assoc. dept. biochemistry U. Mass. Med. Sch., Worcester, 1972-73, postdoctoral fellow of Am. Heart Assn., dept. biochemistry, 1974, asst. prof., 1974-80, assoc. prof., 1981-83; sr. scientist platelet dept. Sandoz Pharm. Corp., East Hanover, N.J., 1983-85, mem. sr. sci. staff, platelet dept., 1986, fellow, sect. head molecular biology, 1987-91, fellow diabetes, 1991-93, study dir. regulatory toxicology, 1993-96; internat. project mgr. preclin. safety Novartis Pharm. Corp., 1997, assoc. dir. project mgmt., 1997-2000, dir. project mgmt., 2000—. Vis. scientist dept. molecular biology, Princeton (N.J.) U., 1987, Sea Pharm. Inc., 1985, NATO, U. Libre, Brussels, 1979, biotechnology dept. Sandoz AG, Basel, Switzerland, 1988. Contbr. articles to profl. jours. Named Nat. Heart, Lung, and Blood Inst. Young Investigator, NIH, 1977-81. Mem. Am. Soc. Pharmacol. Exptl. Therapeutics, N.Y. Acad. Scis. (chmn. biochem. sect. 1992-94), Tissue Culture Assn., Soc. Toxicology, Soc. Toxicol. Pathologists, Sigma Xi. Avocations: boating, gardening, riding, needlework. Office: Novartis Pharm Corp 1 Health Plz East Hanover NJ 07936-1005

NEMECHEK, JOE, race car driver; b. Lakeland, Fla., Sept. 26, 1963; m. Andrea Nemechek; 1 child, John Hunter. Student, Fla. Inst. Tech. Founder, racecar driver NEMCO Motorsports, Mooresville, NC, 1990—. Entered NASCAR driving ranks in 1990 with the family-operated NEMCO Motorsports team, competed fulltime in NASCAR Busch Series Grand Nat. Divsn. through 1993; formed own team in 1994, securing a Burger King sponsorship for the season; moved to SABCO in 1996-2000; driver with Andy Petree's No. 33, 2000, sponsored by Oakwood Homes. Career includes: NASCAR finishes between 26th and 34th in every full season of his career; won first place NASCAR Winston Cup Series, N.H., 1999; recipient All-Pro Late Model Rookie of Year, 1989, Rookie of Year award NASCAR Busch Series Grand Nat., 1993, 3rd place in a field of candidates for NASCAR Winston Cup Rookie of the Year award 1994. Avocations: racing, snow skiing, fishing, boating. Office: Nemco Motorsports 128 S Iredell Indsl Park Rd Mooresville NC 28115*

NEMEC-KESSEL, CHARLENE, artist, educator; b. Milw., Apr. 2, 1970; m. Peter Kessel. BFA, Sch. of Art Inst. Chgo., 1993; MFA, Sch. of Art Inst. of Chgo., 1997. Assoc. lectr. fiber art Concordia U., Mequon, Wis., 1997—98, U. Wis., Milw., 1997—98. One-woman shows include Lyons Wier Gallery, Chgo., 1999, Evanston (Ill.) Art Ctr., 1999, art work featured in. Recipient Award of Excellence, Coalition of Creative Orgns., 1993, Expressions of Culture, 1997; fellow James Nelson Raymond fellow, 1997.

NEMENMAN, MARK YEFIM, mathematics and computers educator, consultant; b. Minsk, Belarus, Nov. 6, 1936; s. Yefim L. and Pesya N. (Shukhman) N.; m. Nataliya A. Verzhbitskaya M+Nemenman, Jan. 25, 1974; children: Ilya, Matvey. MS, Belarussian State U., Minsk, Belarus, 1958; PhD, Acad. Sci., Tallinn, Estonia, 1975. Head. dept. Computer Rsch. Inst., Minsk, Belarus, 1962-94; prof. Sakharov Coll., Belarus, 1992-94; prof. math. Ohlone Coll., Fremont, Calif., 1997—. Author: 5 books; editor: AKI Computer Programming Language, 1964, M32, an operating system, 1968. Home: 6159 Thornton Ave # B Newark CA 94560 E-mail: mark@menem.com.

NEMEROFF, CHARLES BARNET, neurobiology and psychiatry educator; b. Bronx, N.Y., Sept. 7, 1949; s. Philip Peace and Sarah (Greenberg) N.; m. Melissa Ann Pilkington, May 24, 1980 (div.); children: Matthew P. (dec. 1997), Amanda P., Sarah-Frances P.; m. Gayle Applegate, June 11, 2001. BS, CCNY, 1970; MS, Northeastern U., 1973; PhD, U. N.C., 1976, MD, 1981. Diplomate Am. Bd. Psychiatry and Neurology; lic. physician, N.C., Ga. Rsch. asst. ichthyology Am. Mus. Natural History, N.Y.C., 1968-71; neurochemistry lab. McLean Hosp., Belmont, Mass., 1971-72; rsch. assoc. surgery Beth Israel Hosp., Boston, 1972-73; tchg. asst. biology Northeastern U., 1972-73; postdoctoral fellow Biol. Scis. Rsch. Ctr., U. N.C., Chapell Hill, 1976-77, rsch. fellow, 1977-83, clin. instr. psychiatry, 1983; resident psychiatry N.C. Meml. Hosp., Chapel Hill, 1981-83; asst. prof. dept. psychiatry and pharmacology Duke U., Durham, N.C., 1983-85, assoc. prof. psychiatry, 1985-89, assoc. prof. pharmacology, 1986-89, prof. depts. psychiatry and pharmacology, 1989-91, chief divsn. biol. psychiatry, 1988-91; prof., chmn. dept. psychiatry and behavioral scis. Emory U. Sch. Medicine, 1991—, Reunette W. Harris prof. psychiatry and behavioral scis., 1994—. Vis. prof. physiology Cath. U., Santiago, Chile, 1978; sci. coun. Nat. Alliance for Rsch. Schizophrenia and Depression, 1997—; mem. coun. NIMH, 1999—; mem. biomed. rsch. counl NASA, 2000—; bd. dirs. George West Mental Health Found., 1999—, Cypress Bioscis. Inc. Editor: (with A.J. Prange Jr.) Neurotensin, a Brain and Gastrointestinal Peptide, 1982, (with A.J. Dunn) Peptides, Hormones and Behavior, 1984, (with P.T. Loosen) Handbook of Clinical Psychoneuroendocrinology, Neuropeptides in Psychiatric and Neurological Disorders, 1987, Neuropeptides in Psychiatric Disorders, 1991, Neuroendocrinoogy, 1992, (with P. Kitabgi) The Neurobiology of Neurotensin, 1992, (with A.F. Schatzberg) Textbook of Psychopharmacology, 1995, 2nd edit., 1998, (with A. F. Schatzberg) Recognition and Treatment of Psychiatric Disorders, 1999; editor-in-chief: Depression, 1993-2000, Psychopharmacology Bull., 2001—, Neuropsychopharmacology, 2002--; co-editor-in-chief: Critical Revs. in Neurobiology, 1992-2001; contbr. chpts. to books and articles and abstracts to profl. jours. Recipient Michiko Kuno award U. N.C., 1978, 79, Merck award for acad. excellence, 1981, Merck award for young investigators Am. Geriatrics Soc., 1985, 2nd prize Anna Monica Found. for Rsch. in Endogenous Depression, 1987, merit award NIMH, 1987, rsch. prize World Fedn. Socs. Biol. Psychiatry, 1991, Edward J. Sachar award Columbia U., 1993, Edward A. Strecker prize Instnl. Pa. Hosp., 1993, Outstanding Alumni award in health scis. Northeastern U., 1995, Disting. Alumni award U. N.C. Sch. Medicine, 1999, George Ham Alumni award dept. psychiatry U. N.C., 2000; grantee Nat. Inst. Aging, 1982-83, NIMH, 1983—, NIDA, 1996-98; predoctoral fellow Schizophrenia Rsch. Found., Soc. Scottish Rite, Lexington, Mass., 1975-76, postdoctoral fellow Nat. Inst. Neurol., Communicative Disorders and Stroke, 1977, Nanaline Duke fellow Duke U. Med. Ctr., 1985-87. Fellow Am. Coll. Neuropsychopharmacology (Mead Johnson Travel award 1982, Efron award 1987, coun. mem. 1993—, pres. 1997), Am. Coll. Psychiatrists (chmn. contbns. com. 1991-93, 95—, edn. com. 1993-96, 96—, bd. regents 1994-97, first v.p. 1999, pres.-elect 2000, pres. 2001, Mood Disorders Rsch. award 1998, Bowis award 1999); mem. AAAS, AMA, Soc. Neurosci. (program com. 1993-95), Internat. Soc. Psychoneuroendocrinology (pres. 1993-96, Curt P. Richter award 1985), Internat. Soc. Neuroendocrinology, Internat. Soc. Neurochemistry, Am. Soc. Neurochemistry (Jordi-Folch-Pi award 1987), Endocrine Soc., Soc. Neuroendocrinology, Soc. Biol. Psychiatry (A.E. Bennett award 1979, Gold medal award 1996), Am. Fedn. Clin. Rsch., Am. Pain Soc., Am. Psychiat. Assn. (coun. rsch. 1993-98, chmn. 1994-95, bd. dirs. rsch. inst. 1999—, chair coun. rsch. subcom. on psychiat. treatments 1999—, Kempf award 1989, Samuel Hibbs award 1991, Rsch. prize 1996, 99—, Disting. Psychiatrist Lecture Ann. Meeting 1999), Am. Coll. Physicians (William C. Menninger award 2000), Anxiety Disorders Assn. Am. (chmn. adv. bd. 2001—), Argentine Assn. Psychoneuroendocrinology (sci. coun.), Nat. Depressive and Manic Depressive Disorders Assn. (vice chair 1996-98, bd. dirs. 1999—, chair 1999-2000, Gerald L. Klerman Lifetime Achievement award 1997), N.Y. Acad. Scis., Am. Found. for Suicide Prevention (scientific adv. bd. 1997—, bd. dirs. 1998—), Sigma Xi. Democrat. Jewish. Office: Emory U Sch Medicine Dept Psychiatry 1639 Pierce Dr Atlanta GA 30322-0001

NEMEROFF, MICHAEL ALAN, lawyer; b. Feb. 16, 1946; s. Bernard Gregor and Frances (Gotleib) N.; m. Sharon Lynn Leininger, Sept. 22, 1974; children: Theodore, Patrick, James. BA, U. Chgo., 1968; JD, Columbia U., 1971. Asst. counsel Subcom. on Juvenile Delinquency of Senate Jud. Com., Washington, 1971-73; assoc. Sidley & Austin, 1973-78; ptnr. Sidley Austin Brown & Wood, 1978—. Treas. Friends of Jim Sasser, 1978-96, Andy Ireland Campaign Com., 1984-92. Office: Sidley Austin Brown & Wood LLP 1501 K St NW Washington DC 20005

NEMEROV, JEFFREY ARNOLD, lawyer; b. Bklyn., Sept. 2, 1942; s. David and Florence Nemerov; m. Susan Ellen Fiorentino, Sept. 8, 1968; 1 child, Jennifer Courtney Nemerov Cahill. BS, Bucknell U., 1964; LLB, JD, Bklyn. Law Sch., 1967. Bar: U.S. Dist. Ct. (so. and ea. dists.) N.Y. 1967, U.S. Supreme Ct. Mng. ptnr. Segan Nemerov and Singer P.C., N.Y.C., 1968—. Mem. Assn. Trial Lawyers Am., N.Y. County Lawyers Assn. Avocations: tennis (ranked), golf, biking. Office: Segan Nemerov & Singer 112 Madison Ave New York NY 10016-7416

NEMETH, DIAN JEAN, secondary school educator; b. Lakewood, Ohio, Mar. 5, 1949; d. Alex Ray and Doris Jean (Sakach) N.; 1 child, Kymberlee Marie. BS, Kent State U., 1971, MEd, 1994. Cert. home econs. tchr., vocat. consumer-homemaking tchr., Ohio. Tchr. vocat. family and consumer scis. Cleve. Bd. Edn., 1972—. Piloted modern design fine arts course Cleve. Bd. Edn., 1989-90; writer course of study for hospitality and facility care svcs. Active Tchrs.-Leader Inst., 1994-97, Urban Task Force. Mem. Greater Cleve. Assn. Family and Consumer Sci. (auditor 1994-95, treas. 1995-98), Ohio Hotel and Motel Assn., Sigma Sigma Sigma (chpt. adv. bd. 1992, chpt. housing coord. 1992), Omicron Tau Theta. Democrat. Roman Catholic. Home: 9505 N Church Dr Apt 122 Cleveland OH 44130-4773

NEMETH, PATRICIA MARIE, lawyer; b. Flint, Mich., Sept. 18, 1959; d. Gyula Nemeth and Marie (Glaska) Adkins. BA, U. Mich., 1981; JD, Wayne State U., 1984, LLM, 1990. Bar: Ill. 1987, Mich. 1984, U.S. Ct. Appeals (6th cir.), U.S. Dist. Ct. (ea. dist.) Mich., U.S. Dist. Ct. (we. dist.) Mich. Teaching asst. Wayne State U., Detroit, 1982; intern. U.S. Dist. Ct. (ea. dist.) Mich., 1983; assoc. Bloom & Bloom, Birmingham, Mich., 1984-85, Stringari, Fritz, Kreger, Ahearn, Bennett & Hunsinger, Detroit, 1985-92; prin. Law Offices of Patricia Nemeth, P.C., 1992-97, Nemeth Burwell, P.C., Detroit, 1998—. Lectr. in field; adj. prof. Walsh Coll., 1992—94. Guest appearance (TV) Straight Talk, 1994, 95, 2002; contbr. articles to profl. jours. Mem. adv. bd. Vista Maria, 2001-02, bd. dirs., 2002—. Named one of Top 10 Best Places to Work in Southeastern Mich., Crain's/IRI, 2001. Mem. ABA (labor sect.), Mich. Bar Assn. (labor sect.), Ill. Bar Assn., Nat. Order Barristers, Nat. Assn. Women Bus. Owners (sec., exec. bd., bd. dirs., named One of Top Ten Women Bus. Owners of Distinction 2002), Women Lawyers Assn. Mich., Detroit Bar Assn., Health Care Assn. of Mich., Small Bus. Assn. Mich. Roman Catholic. Avocations: sailing, golf, rollerblade. Office: 243 W Congress St Ste 1060 Detroit MI 48226-3214 E-mail: nemethburwell@michbar.org.

NEMETH, VALERIE ANN, lawyer; b. Sutton Surrey, Eng., Mar. 23, 1954; d. Gerald Arnold and Louise Marian (Ross) N.; m. Larry Nagelberg, Dec. 28, 1978 (div. Nov. 1979); m. Hyman Joseph Zacks, Oct. 28, 1984 (div. 1997). BA, UCLA, 1976; JD, Whittier Coll., 1979. Assoc. Grayson, Gross, Friedman, L.A., 1979-80; gen. counsel Red Wind Prodns., 1979-80; sole practice L.A., San Diego, 1980—; gen. counsel, ptnr. MarValUs Entertainment Co., L.A., 1984—; arbitrator Los Angeles County Superior Ct., 1985—, San Diego Superior Ct., 1985—. Legal cons. Centre Devel., San Diego, 1985-87; adj. prof. mgmt. and bus. U. Redlands, 1994—. Mem. legal com. Fairbanks Ranch Assn., Rancho Santa Fe, Calif., 1987-92; adminstrv. dir. community svcs. dist. Fairbanks Ranch, 1988-92. Mem. Am. Film Inst., State Bar Calif. (mem. intellectual property sect.), Variety Clubs Internat., Hadassah (life), Zool. Soc. San Diego. Republican. Jewish. Avocations: film, art, outdoors, travel. Office: 619 S Vulcan Ave Ste 215 Encinitas CA 92024-3654 Fax: 760-942-6043. E-mail: vanemeth@cs.com.

NEMETS, BORIS LVOVICH, programmer; b. Moscow, Mar. 21, 1953; came to the U.S., 1991; s. Lev Markovich and Sophia Aronovna (Shifrina) N.; m. Elena Sergeevna Kantorovitch, Dec. 18, 1976 (div.); 1 child, Anna; m. Marina Urievna Chekis, Nov. 10, 1987 (div. Apr. 1991); 1 child. MS in Mech. Engring., Moscow Automech. Inst., 1975; postgrad., Rsch. Inst. Pipelines, Moscow, 1978, 81. Rschr. Ctrl. Engine Toxity Rsch. Lab., Moscow, 1975, 78, Rsch. Inst. Pipelines, Moscow, 1979, 81; project leader Hydromechanic Equipment Design, 1981, 91, sys. adminstr., 1986, 91; computer ops. staff PC Help Svc., Clark, N.J., 1993; cons. Tribase Sys., Florham Park, 1994; sr. programmer Realistic Techs. Inc., 1994-97, Automated Wagering Internat., Inc., Hackensack, N.J., 1997—. Patentee in field. Mem. IEEE. Home: 14 Royal Ave Livingston NJ 07039-3122 Office: Automated Wagering Internat Inc # 200 1255 Broad St Clifton NJ 07013-3398

NEMETZ, PETER NEWMAN, economics researcher, policy analysis educator; b. Vancouver, B.C., Can., Feb. 19, 1944; s. Nathan Theodore and Bel Nemetz; m. Roma E.S. Kellock, July 16, 1994; 1 stepchild, Fiona Susan. BA in Econs. and Polit. Sci., U. B.C., 1966; AM in Econs., Harvard U., 1969, PhD in Econs., 1973. Tchg. fellow, tutor Harvard U., Cambridge, Mass., 1971-73; lectr. Sch. Planning U. B.C., Vancouver, 1973-75, asst. prof. to assoc. prof. policy analysis, 1975-96, prof., 1996—, chmn., 1984-90. Non-resident faculty Green Coll., 1993-94, 95-97, St. John's Coll., 1997—; vis. scientist Dept. of Health Scis. Rsch. Mayo Clinic, 1988—; cons. consumer and corp. affairs, Can., 1977-80, B.C. Hydro, 2000-02; program chmn. The Vancouver Inst., 1990—; mem. bd. advisors evidence-based practice ctr. rsch. project U. Calif., San Francisco, 2000-01; mem. rsch. mgmt. com. Ctr. Health Svcs. and Policy Rsch., U. B.C., 1990—, mgmt. com. Ctr. Southeast Asia Rsch., 1992-99, assoc. mem. dept. health care and epidemiology, 1995—; bd. dirs. U. B.C. Press, 1993—; faculty assoc. U. B.C. dept. resource mgmt. and environ. studies, 1979—, Ctr. Japanese Studies, 1992—, dept. healthcare and epidemiology; mem. Inst. for Resources and Environment, U. B.C., 1997—; selection com. U.B.C. Rhodes Scholarship, 1991-99; mem. U.B.C. Senate, 1998—; assoc. Ctr. Pacific Basin Monetary and Econ. Studies, Econ. Rsch. Dept., Fed. Reserve Bank of San Francisco, 1991—. Editor Jour. Bus. Adminstrn., 1978—; mem. editl. bd. Jour. Internat. Bus. Edn., 2001—; contbr. articles to sci. jours. Life mem. BC-Yukon divsn. Can Nat. Inst. for Blind. Postdoctoral fellow Westwater Rsch. Ctr., Vancouver, 1973-75; grantee Natural Scis. and Engring. Rsch. Coun. of Can., 1976-92, Consumer and Corp. Affairs Can., 1978-80, Econ. Coun. of Can., 1979-80, Max Bell Found., 1982-84. Mem. Am. Econ. Assn., Internat. Epidemiol. Assn., Harvard Club of B.C. (pres. 1986-94), Vancouver Club. Jewish. Avocations: swimming, photography. Office: U BC Faculty Commerce Vancouver BC Canada V6T 1Z2 E-mail: peter.nemetz@commerce.ubc.ca.

NEMFAKOS, CHARLES PANAGIOTIS, defense industry executive; b. Athens, Greece, Oct. 21, 1942; s. Panagiotis Soterios and Mirka (Kyriakakis) N.; children: Mirka Leigh, Charles Jr.; m. Pamela Durrant; 1 child: Alexandra. BA, Pan Am. U., 1964; MA, Georgetown U., 1982. Cert. in nat. security. Health advisor USPHS, Washington, 1965-66; fed. mgmt. intern Dept. Navy, 1966-67; budget analyst Naval Ordnance Systems Command, 1967-71; supervisory budget analyst Naval Ship Systems Command, 1971-73; sr. budget analyst Office of Sec. of Def., 1973-75; divsn. dir. Office Budget and Reports, Dept. Navy, 1975-76, assoc. dir., 1976-93, dep. asst. sec., 1994-95, dep. under sec., 1995—2001, sr. civilian official for fin. mgmt., comptr., 1998—2001; dir. internal programs devel. Lockheed Martin Corp., Manassas, Va., 2001—. Bd. dirs. First Command Ednl. Found., Am. Automar and Atlantic Marine; lectr. Naval Postgrad. Sch., Monterey, Calif., 1984—, Georgetown U., Washington, 1987—, Ind. U. Grad. Sch., 1996—, Def. Acquisition U., 2001—; mem. base structure com. Dept. Navy, Washington, 1990-91, mem. sr. advisors group, 1991-92, vice-chmn. base structure com., 1992-95; gen. adminstrn. bd. USDA Grad. Sch., 2000—. Contbr. articles to profl. jours. Coach McLean (Va.) Youth Soccer, 1978-93, chmn., 1982-85; bd. dirs. McLean Youth, Inc., 1980-84; registrar Va. Youth Soccer Assn., 1984-86. Recipient Dept. Navy Superior Civilian Svc. award Asst. Sec. of Navy, 1980, Dept. Navy Disting. Civilian Svc. award Sec. of Navy, 1985, 87, 93, 2000, 01, Dept. Def. Disting. Civilian Svc. award Sec. of Def., 1990, 2000, 2001, Dept. Navy Disting. Pub. Svc. award Sec. of Navy, 1995, Roger W. Jones award exec. leadership Am. U., 2000; named to Rank of Disting. Exec. Pres. of U.S., 1986, 95, to Rank of Meritorious Exec., Pres. of U.S., 1981, 91; sr. fellow Ctr. for Naval Analyses, Adj. Nat. Def. U. Mem. Am. Assn. Budget and Program Analysis (dir.-at-large 1980-83), Am. Soc. of Mil. Comptrs. (v.p. 1988-90), Fed. Execs. Inst. Alumni Assn., Tau Kappa Epsilon (chpt. pres. 1964-65). Greek Orthodox. Avocations: golf, tennis, coaching soccer. Office: Lockheed Martin Naval Electronics & Surveillance Sys 9500 Godwin Dr Manassas VA 20110

NEMHAUSER, GEORGE L. industrial, systems engineer, operations research educator; b. N.Y.C., July 27, 1937; s. Martin and Rose (Schwartz) N.; m. Ellen Krupsaw, Sept. 14, 1959; children: Wendy, Dennis. B.Chem.Engring., CCNY, 1958; MS, Northwestern U., 1959, PhD, 1961. Prof. ops. research Johns Hopkins U., Balt., 1961-69; prof. Cornell U., Ithaca, N.Y., 1969-84, Leon C. Welch prof. engring., 1984-85, dir. Sch. Ops. Research and Indsl. Engring., 1977-83; Chandler prof. indsl. and systems engring. Ga. Inst. Tech., 1985—, inst. prof., 1992—. Vis. prof. U. Leeds, U.K., 1963-64; vis. prof., dir. research Center for Ops. Research and Econometrics, U. Louvain, Belgium, 1975-77; cons. NSF (others.) Author: Introduction to Dynamic Programming, 1966, Integer Programming, 1972, Integer and Combinatorial Optimization, 1988; editor-in-chief: Ops. Research, 1975-78, Ops. Research Letters, 1981—; contbr. articles to profl. jours. NSF faculty fellow, 1969-70 Mem. NAE, Ops. Research Soc. Am. (pres. 1981-82, Lanchester prize 1977, 89, Kimball medal 1988), Inst. Mgmt. Sci., Soc. Indsl. and Applied Math., Am. Inst. Indsl. Engrs., Math. Programming Soc. (chmn. 1989-1992). Home: 1208 Villa Dr NE Atlanta GA 30306-2567

NEMICKAS, RIMGAUDAS, cardiologist, educator; b. Kaunas, Lithuania, Mar. 10, 1938; came to U.S., 1949; s. Romualdas and Elena (Saulyte) N.; m. Joan A. McLee, Feb. 16, 1965; children: Rimas Jonas, Kristina Nemickas Tomlinson, Tomas Edward, Nikolas. Student, Ind. U., 1954-57; MD magna cum laude, Loyola U., 1961; MD (hon.), Kaunas Med. Acad., 1993. Diplomate in internal medicine and cardiovascular diseases Am. Bd. Internal Medicine; lic. physician, Ill., Ind. Intern U. Chgo. Clinics, 1961-62; med. resident U. Ill. Rsch. and Edn. Hosps., 1966—67; fellow in cardiology Cook County Hosp., Chgo., 1962-63, U. Chgo. Hosp., 1967-69; assoc. chief cardiology Loyola U., Maywood, Ill., 1972-77, clin. prof. medicine, 1979—. Dir. cardiology Ill. Masonic Med. Ctr., Chgo., 1980—2001, emeritus, 2001—. Mem. Task Force for Health Care Reform, Ministry of Health, Vilnius, Lithuania, 1994-97. Capt. USAF, 1963-66. Fellow ACP, Am. Coll. Cardiology, Am. Coll. Chest Physicians; mem. Am. Heart Assn., Chgo. Soc. Internal Medicine, Chgo. Cardiology Group. Republican. Roman Catholic. Avocations: walking, travel, fishing, collecting art. Office: Ill Masonic Med Ctr 836 W Wellington Chicago IL 60657-5188 E-mail: rnemickas@msn.com., rimgaudas.nemickas-md@advocatehealth.com.

NEMIR, DONALD PHILIP, lawyer; b. Oakland, Calif., Oct. 31, 1931; s. Philip F. and Mary (Shavor) N. AB, U. Calif., Berkeley, 1957, JD, 1960. Bar: Calif. 1961, U.S. Dist. Ct. (no. dist.) Calif. 1961, U.S. Ct. Appeals (9th cir.) 1961, U.S. Dist. Ct. (ctrl. dist.) Calif. 1975, U.S. Supreme Ct. 1980. Pvt. practice, San Francisco, 1961—. Pres. Law Offices of Donald Nemir, A Profl. Corp. Mem. Calif. State Bar Assn. Home: PO Box 1089 Mill Valley CA 94942-1089

NEMIRO, BEVERLY MIRIUM ANDERSON, author, educator; b. St. Paul, May 29, 1925; d. Martin and Anna Mae Anderson; m. Jerome Morton Nemiro, Feb. 10, 1951-75; children: Guy Samuel, Lee Anna, Dee Martin. Student, Reed Coll., 1943-44; BA, U. Colo., 1947; postgrad., U. Denver. Tchr. Seattle Pub. Schs., 1945-46; fashion coord., dir. Denver Dry Goods Co., 1948-51; fashion dir. Denver Market Week Assn., 1952-53; free-lance writer Denver, 1958—. Moderator TV program Your Presch. Child, Denver, 1955-56; instr. writing and comm. U. Colo. Denver Ctr., 1970—, U. Calif., San Diego, 1976-78, Met. State Coll., 1985; dir. pub. rels. Fairmont Hotel, Denver, 1979-80; freelance fashion and TV model. Author, co-author: The Complete Book of High Altitude Baking, 1961, Colorado a la Carte, 1963, Colorado a la Carte, Series II, 1966, (with Donna Hamilton) The High Altitude Cookbook, 1969, The Busy People's Cookbook, 1971 (Better Homes and Gardens Book Club selection 1971), Where to Eat in Colorado, 1967, Lunch Box Cookbook, 1965, Complete Book of High Altitude Baking, 1961, (under name Beverly Anderson) Single After 50, 1978, The New High Altitude Cookbook, 1980. Co-founder, pres. Jr. Symphony Guild, Denver, 1959-60; active Friends of Denver Libr., Opera Colo.; mem. Friends of Painting and Sculpture, Denver Art Mus. Recipient Top Hand award Colo. Authors' League, 1969, 72, 79-82, 100 Best Books of Yr. award N.Y. Times, 1969, 71; named one of Colo.'s Women of Yr., Denver Post, 1964. Mem. Am. Soc. Journalists and Authors, Colo. Authors League (dir. 1969-79), Authors Guild, Authors League Am., Friends Denver Libr., Opera Colo. Guild, Denver Women's Press Club, Rotary, Kappa Alpha Theta. Address: Park Towers 1299 Gilpin St Apt 15W Denver CO 80218-2556

NEMIROFF, MAXINE CELIA, art educator, gallery owner, consultant; b. Chgo., Feb. 11, 1935; d. Oscar Bernard and Martha (Mann) Kessler; m. Paul Rubenstein, June 26, 1955 (div. 1974); children: Daniel, Peter, Anthony; m. Allan Nemiroff, Dec. 24, 1979. BA, U. So. Calif., 1955; MA, UCLA, 1974. Sr. instr. UCLA, 1974-92; dir., curator art gallery Doolittle Theater, Los Angeles, 1985-86; owner Nemiroff Deutsch Fine Art, Santa Monica, Calif. Leader of worldwide art tours; cons. L'Ermitage Hotel Group, Beverly Hills, Calif., 1982—, Broadway Dept. Stores, So. Calif., 1979—, Security Pacific Bank, Calif., 1978—, Am. Airlines, Calif. Pizza Kitchen Restaurants; art chmn. UCLA Thieves Market, Century City, 1960—, L.A. Music Ctr. Mercado, 1982—; lectr. in field. Apptd. bd. dirs. Dublin (Calif.) Fine Arts Found., 1989; mem. Calif. Govs. Adv. Coun. for Women, 1992; mem. art selection com. Calif. State Office Bldgs., 1997—. Named Woman of Yr. UCLA Panhellenic Council, 1982, Instr. of Yr. UCLA Dept. Arts, 1984; elected to Fashion Circle of the Costume Coun., L.A. County Mus. Art, 1997—. Mem. L.A. County Mus. Art Coun., UCLA Art Coun., UCLA Art Coun. Docents, Alpha Epsilon Phi (alumnus of yr. 1983). Avocations: tennis, horseback riding, skiing, piano and guitar. E-mail: mumseyart@aol.com.

NEMIROW, LAWRENCE H. lawyer; b. Bklyn., Dec. 4, 1948; s. Hyman W. Nemirow and Irma Carver; m. Sharz Dee Nemirow; children: Jennifer, Adam, Jaime. JD, Western State U., Fullerton, Calif., 1995; BBA, U. Detroit, 1978, MBA, 1980. V.p., ins. mgr. Ford Motor Co., Dearborn, Mich., 1973-80; dir. ins. and benefits John Morrell & Co., Northfield, Ill., 1980-84; dir. risk mgmt. Honda North Am., Torrance, Calif., 1985-88; prin., risk mgmt. Windes & McClaughry, Long Beach, 1988-89; risk mgmt. cons. The Nemirow Group, Los Alamitos, 1989-95; pvt. practice, 1995—. Amb. Cypress Chamber, Calif., 1988-98. Mem. ATLA, ABA, Orange County Bar Assn. Office: 5242 Katella Ave Ste 104 Los Alamitos CA 90720-2862 E-mail: nemirow@aol.com.

NEMITZ, PATRICIA ANNE, artist, homemaker; b. Detroit, Mar. 26, 1930; d. Harold Edgar and Nora Bertha (Harke) Conley; m. Earl Arnold Nemitz, June 21, 1952; children: Barbara, Diane, David, Mark. AA, Macomb C.C., Warren, Mich., 1984; BFA cum laude, Wayne State U., 1991. Part time artist, St. Clair Shores, Mich., 1984—. Commnd. pastel portraits, 1992, 97; sold water color at Grosse Pointe Woods Presbyn. Ch., 1997. Recipient hon. mention Mich. State Fair, 1997. Mem. Lakeside Palette Club (2d prize 1990, 3d prize 2002). Avocations: reading, gardening, swimming, cycling. Home: 23432 Playview St Saint Clair Shores MI 48082-2090

NEMO, ANTHONY JAMES, lawyer; b. St. Paul, May 18, 1963; s. Joseph Marino Jr. and Dianne Marie (Wegner) N.; m. Mary Rose Mazzitello, July 17, 1987; children: Anne Marie, Katherine Mary, Anthony James Jr. BA in English Lit., U. St. Thomas, 1986; JD, William Mitchell Coll. Law, 1991. Bar: Minn. 1991, U.S. Dist. Ct. Minn., U.S. Dist. Ct. Ariz., U.S. Dist. Ct. (ea. dist.) Wis., U.S. Ct. Appeals (4th cir.), U.S. Supreme Ct. Account exec. div. info. svcs. TRW, Mpls., 1986-90; ptnr. Meshbesher & Spence, Ltd., St. Paul, 1990—. Assoc. editor William Mitchell Law Rev., 1988-90; author law rev. note. Recipient R. Ross Quaintance award, Douglas K. Amdahl-Mary O'Malley Lyons Trial Advocacy award. Mem. ABA, Minn. Trial Lawyers Assn., Assn. Trial Lawyers Am., Minn. State Bar Assn., Hennepin County Bar Assn., John P. Sheehy Legal History Soc. Roman Catholic. Home: 2125 Heath Ave N Oakdale MN 55128-5207 Office: Meshbesher & Spence Ltd 1616 Park Ave Minneapolis MN 55404

NEMSER, EARL HAROLD, lawyer; b. N.Y.C., Jan. 17, 1947; s. Harold Summers and Eleanor Patricia (Beckerman) N.; m. Randy Lynn Lehrer, June 17, 1974 (div.); children: Eliza Sarah, Maggie Lehrer. BA, NYU, 1967; JD magna cum laude, Boston U., 1970. Bar: N.Y. 1970, U.S. Supreme Ct. 1975, U.S. Claims Ct. 1979, U.S. Tax Ct. 1985. Law clk. hon. Collins J. Seitz chief judge U.S. Ct. Appeals 3rd Cir., 1970-71; ptnr. Cadwalader, Wickersham & Taft, N.Y.C., 1971-95, Swidler Berlin Shereff Friedman, LLP, N.Y.C., 1996—2002, of counsel, 2002—; pres. Park and 76th Street Co., Inc., 1998—. Vice chmn. Interactive Brokers Group, LLC, Greenwich, Conn., 1995—; dir. Timber Hill, LLC, Greenwich, Caribbean Cellular Telephone Ltd., Tortola, BVI. Spl. town atty. Town of Southampton, NY; mem. bd. advisors Lenox Hill Hosp. Mem. ABA, Nat. Assn. Criminal Def. Lawyers, Assn. Bar City N.Y.; dir. The Quogue Assn. Office: Swidler Berlin Shereff Friedman LLP 405 Lexington Ave New York NY 10174-0002 E-mail: ehnemser@swidlaw.com.

NEMSER, ROBERT SOLOMON, visual communications consultant, art director, creative director, designer, writer, educator; b. Bklyn., May 30, 1938; s. Leo Lewis Nemser and Mae (Silver) Wolf; m. Fredda Carol Siegel, Oct. 15, 1960; children: Lori, Adam, Alec, Ian. AAS, N.Y. Coll. Arts and Scis., 1960; MFA, Syracuse U., 1990. Designer Inst. Life Ins., N.Y.C., 1960, Dell Pub. Co., N.Y.C., 1962-65; art. dir. Universal Pub. Co., 1965-67; v.p. Corp. Ann. Reports, 1967-73; pres., owner Robert S. Nemser Assocs., N.J. and N.Y., 1974—. Mem. adj. faculty Rutgers U. Mason Gross Sch. Arts, 1987-91; asst. prof. art Trenton (N.J.) State Coll., 1993-94, Baruch/SUNY, 1996-98, Gibbs Coll., 2000—; spkr. on Psychodelic Art in the '60s and the San Francisco Music Scene, The Art of Seeing: Creating with Your Camera, The Psychology and Design of Coffee-Table Books, Photoluminescence: Painting with the Camera. Designer, photo editor (books) Martin Luther King Jr., 1976 (Gold medal 1977), The Eternal Sea (Gold medal 1977), Your Future in Space, 1986, King Remembered, 1986, He Had a Dream: Martin Luther King Jr. and the Civil Rights Movement, 1995 (Silver medal 1995); designer Ctrl. N.J. Jewish Home for Aged logo, 1975, East Brunswick (N.J.) Libr. logo, 1976; work exhibited at Art Dirs. Club N.J., 1970—, Rutgers U., 1990; prodr.: (concerts) From the Heart, 1996, 97, 99, 2000—. Bd. dirs. East Brunswick Jewish Ctr., 1975-77, publicity chmn., 1976; TV photo show host East Brunswick Channel 8 Cable TV, 1986. Served to sgt. U.S. Army, 1960-62. Recipient numerous design awards from various profl. orgns.; invited to White House to present Portrait of a President to Pres. Gerald Ford, 1976. Mem. Art Dirs. Club N.J. (life, pres. 1976-77, chmn. edn. coun. 1987-92, numerous awards), Advt. Club N.Y. (Andy award 1973). Avocations: collecting military medals and paraphernalia, elephants and police badges, racquetball, paddleball, noted authority on Rock and Roll and Doo Wopp music of 1950's and 1960's. Office: PO Box 2229 Fort Lee NJ 07024-0497 E-mail: resmen@aol.com.

NENNEMAN, RICHARD ARTHUR, retired publishing executive; b. Chgo., Oct. 13, 1929; s. William T. and Fannie (Peterson) N.; m. Katherine Ann LaBrunerie, June 29, 1954; children: Ann Walker, Mary Lisa, Katherine Conley. AB magna cum laude, Harvard U., 1951, MA in Internat. Affairs, 1953. With No. Trust Co., Chgo., 1957-58; v.p., treas., dir. First Fed. Savs. & Loan Assn., St. Joseph, Mo., 1958-60; with Valley Nat. Bank. Phoenix, 1960-65; asst. v.p., 1963-65; bus. and financial editor Christian Sci. Monitor, Boston, 1965-74; v.p., dir. investment research Girard Bank, Phila., 1974-77, sr. v.p., chmn. trust investment policy com., 1977-82; mng. editor Christian Sci. Monitor, Boston, 1983-86; editor, exec. prodr., TV broadcasting Christian Sci. Pub. Soc., 1987; editor-in-chief Christian Science Monitor, 1988-93; ret., 1993. Mem. investment com. Gen. Accident Ins. Group., until 1982; dir. DLB Fund Group, 1994—. Contbr. to Understanding Our Century, 1984; editor: (with Earl Foell) How Peace Came to the World, 1986, The New Birth of Christianity, 1992, Persistent Pilgrim: The Life of Mary Baker Eddy, 1997. Trustee Barnes Found., until 1982; selectman Town of Weston, Mass., 1973-74; vice chmn. Boston Com. on Fgn. Rels. Served with AUS, 1954-57. Mem. Coun. on Fgn. Rels., Am. Coun. Ger., Harvard Grad. Coun. Home: 314 Hemlock Cir Lincoln MA 01773-4923

NENNER, VICTORIA CORICH, nurse, educator; b. Marshall, Tex., Mar. 17, 1945; d. Bernard Paul and Mary DeLayne (Bowen) Corich; m. Paul Edwin Nenner, Aug. 12, 1970. BSN, Tex. Women's U., 1966; cert., U. Paris, summer 1966; MSN, U. San Diego, 1984. Mem. nursing staff St. Thomas Hosp., London, 1966-67, Parkland Meml. Hosp., Dallas, 1967-68; coord. nursing continuing edn. Scripps Meml. Hosp., La Jolla, Calif., 1974-85; owner, pres. Marvik Ednl. Svcs., Inc., 1985—. Mem. part-time faculty U. Calif., San Diego; mem. vis. faculty U. B.C.; mem. Inservice Coun. San Diego and Imperial Counties, 1974-80, pres., 1976-77; mem. San Diego C.C. Health Edn. Adv. Bd., 1976-84. Contbg. author in healthcare software; prodr. oncology nursing ednl. videotapes; contbr. articles to profl. jours. Bd. dirs. San Diego Performing Arts League, 1990-92; chair Star Awards Luncheon, 1995; mem. Puente de Oro com. Girl Scouts, 1998—; bd. dirs. Vietnam Vets. San Diego, 1998—. Capt. Nurse Corps, USAF, 1968-77. Named Tex. Student Nurse of Yr., 1966; Regents scholar, Krost-Freeman scholar, Mary Gibbs Jones Nursing scholar. Mem. ANA, Am. Soc. Health Edn. and Tng., Nat. League Nursing (Leadership award 1995), Calif. League for Nursing (pres. 1993-94), Sigma Theta Tau. Office: 1677 1/2 Los Altos Rd San Diego CA 92109-1322 E-mail: vcnenner@cs.com.

NENTWICH, MICHAEL ANDREAS ERHART, educator, consultant; b. Prague, Czech Republic, Sept. 6, 1941; came to U.S., 1994; s. Walter Joseph and Charlotte Rosina (Hawle) N. Student, schs. in Linz, Schörfling, Austria, Wellingborough, Eng., Karlsruhe, Germany, Nuremberg (Germany) U., Heidelberg (Germany) U., 1960-64, 65-69, PhD, 1973. German tchr. St. Olave's and St. Saviour's Grammar Sch., London, 1964-65; English lectr. Mannheim (Germany) U., 1969-75; vis. lectr. in German, Chinese U. Hong Kong, 1975-80; rsch. scholar in English Tech. U. Berlin, 1980-81; educator, cons. Goethe-Inst., Bremen, Germany, 1982, Madrid, 1983-85, Düsseldorf, Germany, 1985-88, São Paulo, 1988-92, Munich, 1992-94, N.Y.C., 1994-2000, exec. dir. Atlanta, 2000—. Author: Der schottische Shaw, 1973, Werbemappe—Advocacy Binder for Teachers of German in the USA, 1999; editor Modern Germany Update; contbr. articles to profl. jours. Recipient Sophie Bernsthen scholarship U. Heidelberg, 1968. Avocations: music, painting, travel, theatre. Office: Goethe-Inst Atlanta Colony Sq Plaza Level 1197 Peachtree St NE Atlanta GA 30361-3502 E-mail: goetheatlanta1@mindspring.com.

NEOGI, ARUP, physics educator, researcher; b. Calcutta, Bengal, India, Feb. 13, 1967; s. Samir Kumar and Rekha (Ghosh) N.; m. Purnima Basu. BSc, R.D. U., Jabalpur, India, 1986, MSc, 1988; PhD, Viram U., Ujjain, India, 1992. Rsch. assoc. D.A. U., Indore, India, 1992-94; vis. scientist Ymagata U., Yonezawa, Japan, 1994—. Contbr. articles to profl. jours. Recipient M.P. Young Scientist award, M.P. Coun. of Sci. & Tech., Ujjan, India, 1990; Japanese Govt. scholarship, Menbusho, 1993, fellowshp Japan Soc. for Promotion of Scis., 1994-95. Mem. OSA, JSAP. Avocations: reading, music, sight seeing. Home: 2902/A Saket Nagar Ranjhi Jabalpur 482005 India

NEPOMUCENO, CECIL SANTOS, physician; b. The Philippines, Feb. 1, 1936; came to U.S. 1967; s. Dominador and Augustina (Santos) N.; m. Edna Manacsa, Dec. 4, 1963; children: Joy, Regina, Celeste. MD, U. Santo Tomas, Manila, The Philippines, 1962. Diplomate Am. Bd. Physical Medicine and Rehab. Intern St. Francis Hosp., Wichita, Kans., 1963; resident Baylor U. Med. Ctr., Dallas, 1967-70; staff physician HealthSouth Lakeshore Rehab. Hosp., Birmingham, Ala., 1994-99; prof. medicine U. Ala. Former cons. Social Security Adminstrn.; oral bd. examiner Am. Acad. Physical Medicine and Rehab. Lt. col. USAMR, 1982-94, ret. Mem. Ala. Soc. Phys. Medicine and Rehab.(past pres.). Roman Catholic. Home: 1070 Country Club Cir Birmingham AL 35244-1478 E-mail: nepomuceno@charter.net.

NEPPE, VERNON MICHAEL, neuropsychiatrist, psychopharmacologist, forensic specialist, author, educator, playwright; b. Johannesburg, Rep. South Africa, Apr. 16, 1951; came to U.S., 1986; s. Solly Louis and Molly (Hesselsohn) N.; m. Elisabeth Selima Schachter, May 29, 1977; children: Jonathan, Shari. BA, U. South Africa, 1976; MB, BCh, U. Witwatersrand, Johannesburg, 1973, diploma in psychol. medicine, 1976, M in Medicine, 1979, PhD in Medicine, 1981; MD, U.S., 1982. Diplomate Am. Bd. Psychiatry and Neurology, specialties in psychiatry, geriatric psychiatry, forensic psychiatry, Am. Bd. Psychol. Specialties in Psychopharmacology; registered psychiatry specialist U.S., Republic of South Africa, Can. Specialist in tng. dept. psychiatry U. Witwatersrand, Johannesburg, 1974-80; sr. cons. U. Witwatersrand Med. Sch., 1980-82, 83-85; neuropsychiatry fellow Cornell U., N.Y.C., 1982-83; div. dir. U. Wash. Med. Sch., Seattle, 1986-92; dir. Pacific Neuropsychiat. Inst., 1992—. Mem. clin. faculty dept. psychiatry and behavioral scis. U. Wash. Med. Sch., 1992-2002; adj. prof. psychiatry St. Louis U. Sch. of Medicine, dept. psychiatry and human behavior, 1994—; attending physician N.W. Hosp., 1992—; neuropsychiatry cons. South African Brain Rsch. Inst., Johannesburg, 1985—; chief rsch. cons. Epilepsy Inst., N.Y.C., 1989; mem. faculty lectr. Epilepsy: Refining Med. treatment, 1993-94. Author: The Psychology of Déjà Vu: Have I Been Here Before, 1983, Innovative Psychopharmacotherapy, 1990, Cry the Beloved Mind: A Voyage of Hope, 1999, Psychology of Déjà Vu: All Over Again, 2001, (text) BROCAS SCAN, 1992; (plays) Tomorrow the Earthquake, 2001, Quakes, 2002; (with others) 33 book chpts.; editor 14 jours. issues; contbr. articles to profl. jours. Recipient Rupert Sheldrake prize for rsch. design (2d prize) award New Scientist, 1983, Marius Valkhoff medal South African Soc. for Psychical Rsch., 1982, George Elkin Bequest for Med. Rsch., U. Witwatersrand, 1980; named Overseas Travelling fellow, 1982-83. Fellow Psychiatry Coll. South Africa (faculty), Royal Coll. Physicians of Can., North Pacific Soc. for Neurology, Neurosurgery and Psychiatry, Coll. Internat. Neuropharmacologicum, Am. Coll. Forensic Examiners; mem. AMA, Parapsychologic Assn., Am. Psychiat. Assn. (U.S. transcultural collaborator diagnostic and statis. manual 1985-86, cons. organic brain disorders 1988—), Am. Epilepsy Soc., Soc. Biol. Psychiatry, Can. Psychiat. Assn., Soc. Sci. Exploration, Am. soc. Clin. Psychopharmacology, Am. Neuropsychiat. Assn. Jewish. Avocations: chess, table tennis, tennis, computers, scrabble. Office: Pacific Neuropsychiat Inst 10330 Meridian Ave N Ste 380 Seattle WA 98133-9463

NEPPL, WALTER JOSEPH, retired retail store executive; b. Halbur, Iowa, June 15, 1922; s. Frank and Anna (Halbur) N.; m. Marian Maher, Oct. 15, 1945; children: Eugenie Neppl Kauffman, Marilee Neppl Cumming, Deborah Neppl Johnson, John, Thomas (dec.), Christina Neppl Totino, Nancy Neppl Tripucka. Grad. h.s., Carrol, Iowa. With J.C. Penney Co., Inc., 1940—, mgr. store, 1954-55, dist. mgr. Pitts., 1955-61, store coordination mgr. N.Y.C., 1961-64, asst. to dir. dist. mgmt. dept., 1964-65, gen. mdse. mgr. hard lines, 1965-67, v.p., 1967-68, gen. sales and mdse. mgr., 1968-71, dir. merchandising, 1971-72, exec. v.p., 1972-76, pres., chief operating officer, 1976-81, vice-chmn. bd., 1981-82, ret., 1982, dir., 1968-85. Bd. dirs. emeritus J.C. Penney Co. Inc. Trustee emeirtus Geraldine R. Dodge Found. Served to capt. USAAF, 1943-45. Decorated D.F.C. Roman Catholic. Home: The Enclave 5345 Annabel Ln Plano TX 75093-3428

NEPPLE, JAMES ANTHONY, lawyer; b. Carroll, Iowa, Jan. 5, 1945; s. Herbert J. and Cecilia T. (Irlmeier) N.; m. Jeannine Ann Jennings, Sept. 9, 1967; children: Jeffrey B., Scott G., Carin J., Andrew J. BA, Creighton U., 1967; JD, U. Iowa, 1970; postgrad. in bus., Tex. Christian U., 1971; LLM in Taxation, NYU, 1982. Bar: Iowa 1970, Ill. 1973, U.S. Dist. Ct. (so. dist.) Iowa 1972, U.S. Dist. Ct. (cen. dist.) Ill. 1972, U.S. Dist. Ct.(no. dist.) Iowa 1975, U.S. Ct. Appeals (7th and 8th cirs.) 1975, U.S. Supreme Ct. 1975, U.S. Ct. Claims 1976, U.S. Tax Ct. 1976. Tax acct. Arthur Young & Co., Chgo., 1970; v.p., treas., bd. dirs. Stanley, Rehling, Lande & VanDerKamp, Muscatine, Iowa, 1972-92; pres. Nepple, VanDerKamp & Flynn, P.C., Rock Island, Ill., 1992-98; prin. Nepple Law Offices, P.L.C., 1999—. Scoutmaster Boy Scouts Am., Muscatine, 1982-85; trustee State Hist. Soc. Iowa, 1986-92, vice-chmn., 1991-92; bd. dirs. Iowa Hist. Found., 1988-95, pres., 1991-93. Capt. U.S. Army, 1971-72. Recipient Gov.'s Vol. award State of Iowa, 1988, 90, Jr. Achievement of the Quad Cities Bronze award, 1996, Silver award, 2000. Fellow Am. Coll. Trust and EstateCounsel, Am. Bar Found., Iowa Bar Found.; mem. ABA (tax sect. 1972—, chair agrl. tax com. 2001—); mem. Ia (tax com. 1979-91, chmn. 1988-91), Fed. Bar Assn., Ill. Bar Assn. (mem. fed. tax sect. coun. 1993-99, chair 1997-98), Muscatine Bar Assn. (pres. 1982-83), Scott County Bar Assn., Rock Island County Bar Assn., Iowa Assn. Bus. and Industry (tax. com. 1978—, chmn. 1986-88, leadership Iowa award 1985), Quad City Estate Planning Coun. (pres. 1987), Muscatine C. of C. (pres. 1985), Geneva Golf and Country Club (pres. 1990-91), Kiwanis (pres. Muscatine chpt. 1978), Elks. Republican. Roman Catholic. Home: 2704 Mulberry Ave Muscatine IA 52761-2746 Fax: 563-264-6844. E-mail: jim@nepplelaw.com.

NEPTUNE, JOHN ADDISON, chemistry educator, consultant; b. Barnesville, Ohio, Nov. 27, 1919; s. George Addison and Lola Mae (Skinner) N.; m. Ruth Elizabeth Dorsey, Aug. 24, 1947; 1 child, Benjamin BS summa cum laude, Muskingum Coll., 1942; MS, U. Wis., 1949, PhD, 1952. Instr. chemistry Muskingum Coll., New Concord, Ohio, 1943-44, 45-48; foreman Tenn. Eastman Corp., Manhattan Project, 1944-45; asst. prof. chemistry Bowling Green State U., Ohio, 1949-50; instr. pharm. chemistry U. Wis.-Madison, 1952-55; asst. prof. chemistry San Jose State U., Calif., 1955-58, assoc. prof., 1958-61, prof., 1961-90, chmn. dept., 1973-86. Mem. Am. Chem. Soc., AAUP Methodist. Home: 50 Cherokee Ln San Jose CA 95127-2513 Office: San Jose State U Dept Chemistry San Jose CA 95192-0001

NEQUIST, JOHN LEONARD, retired food company executive; b. Sparta, Mich., July 31, 1929; s. John Ormond and Leola Irene (Fessenden) N.; m. Patricia Ann Kelley, Jan. 7, 1950; children: Eric Martin, Kelley Jo; m. Donna Jean Williams, 1990. BBA, U. Mich., 1956. With Kellogg Co., Battle Creek, Mich., 1957-88, chief accountant, then asst. controller, 1967-75, controller, 1975-79, v.p., controller U.S. Foods Products div., 1979-84, dir. spl. assignments McCanly Sq. div., hotel and retail area, 1984-88. Chmn. planning and budget com. Battle Creek United Fund, 1969-70, Battle Creek Family/Childrens Service, 1973, Battle Creek United Arts Council, 1975; dir. spl. assignments Gov.'s Exec. Corps, 1984-85; bd. dirs. ARC, Battle Creek; chmn. bd. Downtown Bus. Assn., Battle Creek., 1987-88; mem. South Haven (Mich.) City Council. Served with USAF, 1948-52. Mem. Beta Alpha Psi. Home: 36 Lake Shore Dr South Haven MI 49090-1131 also: 2103 Tara Circle #102 Naples FL 34112

NEREBERG, ELIOT JOEL, lawyer; b. N.Y.C., May 15, 1949; s. Harry and Muriel (Gravitz) N.; m. Amy V. Jaffe, June 1, 1973; children: Rebecca, Kate. BS, CCNY, 1970; JD, NYU, 1973. Bar: Conn. 1973, U.S. Dist. Ct. Conn. 1973, U.S. Ct. Appeals (2d cir.) 1975. Clin. supr. sch. law. U. Conn., West Hartford, 1973-75; pvt. practice, 1975—. Spl. masters Hartford County Family Ct., 1985—. Mem. ABA (bd. dirs. publ. bd. family law sect.), Conn. Bar Assn. (chair family law sect.), Hartford County Bar Assn. (co-chmn. family law sect. 1990-92). Democrat. Jewish. Home: 62 Walbridge Rd West Hartford CT 06119-1343 Office: 10 N Main St West Hartford CT 06107-1968 E-mail: enerenberg@rcn.com.

NEREM, ROBERT MICHAEL, engineering educator, consultant; b. Chgo., July 20, 1937; s. Robert and Borghild Guneva (Bakken) Nerem; m. Jill Ann Thomson, Dec. 21, 1958 (div. 1977); children: Robert Steven, Nancy Ann Nerem Chambers; m. Marilyn Reed, Oct. 7, 1978; stepchildren: Christina Lynn Maser, Carol Marie Maser. BS, U. Okla., 1959; MS, Ohio State U., 1961, PhD, 1964; D (honoris causa), U. Paris, 1990. Asst. prof. Ohio State U., Columbus, 1964-68, assoc. prof., 1968-72, prof., 1972-79, assoc. dean Grad. Sch., 1975-79; prof. mech. engring., chmn. dept. U. Houston, 1979-86; Parker H. Petit prof. Ga. Inst. Tech., Atlanta, 1987—, Inst. prof., 1991—, dir. Inst. for Bioengring. and Biosci., 1995—; dir. Ga. Tech/Emory Ctr. for the Engring. of Living Tissues NSF Engring. Rsch. Ctr., 1998—. Mem. Ga. Gov.'s Adv. Coun. on Sci. and Tech. Devel., Atlanta, 1992—95; Alza disting. lectr. Biomed. Engring. Soc., 1991; ASME Thurston lectr., 94; mem. sci. bd. FDA, 2000—. Contbr. articles. Fellow: AAAS, ASME, Am. Inst. Med. and Biol. engring. (founding pres. 1992—94); mem.: Polish Acad. Scis., U.S. Nat. Com. on Biomechanics (chmn. 1988—91), Internat. Fedn. for Med. and Biol. Engring. (pres. 1988—91), Internat. Union for Phys. and Engring. Scis. in Medicine (pres. 1991—94), Inst. Medicine, Biomed. Engring. Soc., Am. Acad. Arts and Scis., NAE. Home: 2950 Waverly Ct SE Atlanta GA 30339-4200 E-mail: robert.nerem@ibb.gatech.edu.

NERENZ, TIMOTHY THEODORE, accounting executive; b. Mpls., June 22, 1954; s. Kenneth Lester and Janet (Wray) N.; m. Joanne s. Schleicher, Sept. 8, 1984. Student, Carthage Coll., 1972-75, U. Wis., Madison, 1975-84. Warehouse supr. Gettys Mfg., Racine, Wis., 1975-78, prodn. mgr., 1978-81; materials mgr. Rayovac Corp., Madison, 1981-84, dir. bus. sys. Portage, 1984-90; dir. info. sys. Lake Shore, Inc., Kingsford, Mich., 1990-92, dir. info. sys. and contract acctg., 1992-95, gen. mgr. mining products, 1995—. Mfg. sys. cons. I.S.S., Inc., Racine, 1978-81; bd. dirs. SST Contractors, LaCrosse, Wis., 1986-89; ptnr. H.O.T.D. Assocs., Kingsford, 1993-94. Vol. Middleton (Wis.) Fire Dept., 1986-90; bd. dirs. Ducks Unltd., Kingsford, 1990-94; scout leader Cub Scouts, Middleton, 1984-87. Mem. Am. Prodn. and Inventory Control Soc., Data Processing Mgmt. Assn., Wis. Firefighers Assn., Oak Crest Country Club. Avocations: golf, hunting, skiing, hiking, photography. Office: Lake Shore Inc 900 W Breitung Ave Iron Mountain MI 49802-5316

NERHOOD, ROBERT CLARKE, obstetrician-gynecologist; b. Altoona, Pa., Aug. 27, 1944; s. Albert and Jeanne (VanOrmer) N.; m. Carolyn Haught, Aug. 27, 1965; children: Robert, Timothy; m. Deborah Brooks, Nov. 30, 1984. Student, W.Va. U., 1962-65, MD, 1969. Diplomate Am. Bd. Ob-Gyn. Intern Polyclinic Hosp., Harrisburg, Pa., 1969-70; resident in ob-gyn. W.Va. Hosp., Morgantown, 1970-73, Kessler Air Force Med. Ctr., 1973-75; clin. assoc. prof. Sch. Medicine Marshall U., Huntington, 1977-87; dir. resident edn. Allegheny Gen. Hosp./Med. Coll. Pa.; assoc. prof. ob-gyn. Med. Coll. Pa., 1989-92; chief ob-gyn. Berkshire Health Sys.; assoc. prof. Med. Sch. U. Mass.; with Mass. Bd. Perinatal Medicine; vice chmn. bd. Cabell Huntington Hosp., 1997—; prof. chmn. ob-gyn. divsn. Sch. Medicine Marshall U., Huntington, W.Va., 1992—. Mem. W.Va. Bd. Perinatal Medicine, 1977-87. Ob-gyn. editor Postgraduate Medicine, 1997—. Maj. USAF, 1973-75. Mem. Am. Coll. Ob-Gyn. (vice chair W.Va. sect. 1992-95, chair W.Va. sect. 1995-98, 2001-, mem. adv. coun. dist. IV 1992-98, 2001-). Office: Marshall U Sch Medicine Ob-Gyn 1600 Medical Center Dr Huntington WV 25701-3655 Fax: (304) 691-1453.

NERLINGER, JOHN WILLIAM, retired trade association administrator; b. Detroit, June 22, 1920; s. John W. and Bessie Prudence (Beith) N.; m. Pearl Pauline Procup, Nov. 4, 1943; children: John Charles, Ruth Marie Nerlinger Blazevich. Grad., Detroit Bus. Inst., 1939; BA, Detroit Inst. Tech., 1950; LLD (hon.), Northwood U., Midland, Mich., 1990. Bus. mgr. Retail Gasoline Dealers Assn. Mich., Detroit, 1939-51, exec. sec., 1951-63, Nat. Congress Petroleum Retailers, Detroit, 1951-63; asst. exec. v.p. Automotive Service Industry Assn., Chgo., 1963-73, exec. v.p., 1973-80, pres., 1981-91; ret., 1991. Vice chmn. Automotive Hall of Fame; advisor Nat. Hwy. Users Fedn. Served with AUS, 1942-45, PTO. Recipient Petroleum Man of Yr. award Gasoline News, 1961, Automotive Replacement Edn. award Northwood U., Midland, Mich., 1975, Disting. Svc. citation Automotive Hall of Fame, 1978, Industry Leadership award Automotive Svc. Industry Assn., 1978. Mem. Am. Soc. Assn. Execs. (mem. edn. com.), Chgo. Soc. Assn. Execs., Automotive Old Timers, Automotive Info. Council (dir.), Automotive Boosters Clubs Internat., Chgo. Assn. Commerce and Industry (mem. govt. relations com.), Nat. Assn. Wholesalers-Distbrs. (exec. com., dir. distbn. research and edn. found), Automotive Acad. Clubs: Mid-America, Inverness Golf. Lodges: Masons (32 deg.), Shriners. Lutheran. Home: 601 E Fairview St Arlington Heights IL 60005-2770

NERLOVE, MARC LEON, economics educator; b. Chgo., Oct. 12, 1933; s. Samuel Henry and Evelyn (Andelman) N.; children: Susan, Miriam. BA, U. Chgo., 1952; MA, Johns Hopkins U., 1955, PhD, 1956. Analytical statistician USDA, Washington, 1956-57; assoc. prof. U. Minn., Mpls., 1959-60; prof. Stanford (Calif.) U., 1960-65, Yale U., 1965-69; prof. econs. U. Chgo., 1969-74; F.W. Taussig rsch. prof. Harvard Coll., Cambridge, Mass., 1967-68; vis. Cook prof. Northwestern U., Evanston, Ill., 1973-74, Cook prof., 1974-82; prof. econs. U. Pa., Phila., 1982-86, Univ. prof., 1986-93; prof. agr. and resource econs. U. Md., College Park, 1993—. Author: Dynamics of Supply, 1958, Distributed Lags and Demand Analysis, 1958, Estimation and Identification of Cobb-Douglas Production Functions, 1965, Analysis of Economic Time Series: A Synthesis, 1979, Household and Economy: Welfare Economics of Endogenous Fertility, 1987, Essays on Panel Data Econometrics, 2002; contbr. numerous articles to profl. jours. 1st lt. AUS, 1957-59. Recipient award Am. Farm Econ. Assn., 1956, 58, 61, 79, P.S. Mahalanobis medal Indian Econ. Soc., 1975. Fellow Am. Statis. Assn., Econometric Soc. (v.p. 1980, pres. 1981), Am. Acad. Arts and Scis., Am. Agrl. Econ. Assn.; mem. NAS, Am. Econ. Assn. (mem. exec. com. 1977-79, John Bates Clark medal 1969), Royal Econ. Soc., Phi Beta Kappa, others. Achievements include research on economics of agriculture with particular reference to developing countries, population and economic growth; analysis of categorical data, particularly business and household surveys. Office: U Md Dept Agr and Resource Econs College Park MD 20742-0001 E-mail: mnerlove@arec.umd.edu.

NERN, CHRISTOPHER CARL, lawyer; b. N.Y.C., Sept. 30, 1944; s. William Francis and Jule Anne (Allison) N.; m. Kathleen Jean Brogan, Aug. 24, 1974 (div. Nov. 1985). BA, Mich. State U., 1967; JD, Wayne State U., 1972. Bar: Mich. 1973, U.S. Dist. Ct. (ea. and we. dists.) Mich. 1973, U.S. Ct. Appeals (6th cir.) 1974, U.S. Supreme Ct. 1979. Asst. atty. gen. State of Mich., Lansing, 1972-73; staff atty. corp. affairs div. Detroit Edison Co., 1973-74, sr.atty. rates and regulatory div., 1975-78, gen. atty. regulatory affairs div., 1978-82, assoc. gen. counsel, mgr., 1982-89, asst. v.p., asst. gen. counsel, 1989-93, v.p., gen. counsel, 1993-2000, DTE Energy, 1993-2000; adj. prof. St. Mary's Coll., 2001—. Adj. prof. Lawrence Tech. U., 2002—. Mem. allocation com. United Found., Detroit, 1983, 86-87; bd. dirs. Oakland Parks Found., Oakland County, Mich., 1985, Mich. Opera Theatre, 1996—; trustee Music Hall Ctr. for the Performing Arts, 1987-93. Served with USAF, 1967-69. Mem. ABA (bd. trustees), Detroit Met. Bar Assn. (trustee found.), Am. Corp. Counsel Assn. (pres. Mich chpt. 1986-88), Econs. Club (Detroit), Detroit Golf Club, Detroit Athletic Club. Roman Catholic. Home: 1052 Stratford Ln Bloomfield Hills MI 48304-2930 E-mail: nernchris@aol.com.

NEROD, STEVE (SCHEZEPAN ALEXANDER NEROD), entrepreneur, designer; b. Anchorage, June 15, 1952; s. Steve (Schezepan) and Eleanor (Maytak) Nierodzik. Student, U. Wash., 1970-72, U. Alaska, 1978-82, U. Calif., Berkeley, 1983-85. Owner Eldorado Placers, Eldorado Creek, Alaska, 1970-83, Nerod & Assocs. Apparel, San Francisco, Seattle, N.Y., 1971-82, Nerod Orthopedics, San Francisco and Seattle, 1982—, DoNots ATV, 1991—, RadGear Bicycles, 1992—, VAS-Comp, Hong Kong, 1993—, OrthoSys, Everett, Wash., 1994—, N.A.S.T.I., Everett, 1994—. Cons. OrthoTech, San Leandro, Calif., Orthopedic Systems, Hayward, Calif., Med. Device Engring., Hayward, Israel Med. Products Devel., Tel Aviv, 1991—. Patentee in field. Mem. Am. Acad. Cosmetic Surgery, Am. Soc. Plastic and Reconstructive Surgery, Am. Orthopedic and Prosthetic Assn., Am. Assn. Orthopedic Medicine, Am. Acad. Orthopaedic Surgeons, Alaska Miners Assn. Avocations: writing, art, archaeology, travel. Office: 275 Coulson Rd Chehalis WA 98532-8704

NERODE, ANIL, mathematician, educator; b. L.A., June 4, 1932; s. Nirad Ranjan and Agnes (Spencer) N.; m. Sondra Raines, Feb. 12, 1955 (div. 1968); children: Christopher Curtis, Gregory Daniel; m. Sally Riedel Sievers, May 16, 1970; 1 child, Nathanael Caldwell. BA, U. Chgo., 1949, BS, 1952, MS, 1953, PhD, 1956. Group leader automata and weapons systems Lab. Applied Sci., U. Chgo., 1954-57; mem. Inst. for Advanced Study, Princeton, 1957-58, 62-63; vis. asst. prof. math. U. Calif. at Berkeley, 1958-59; mem. faculty Cornell U., 1959—, prof. math., 1965—, Goldwin Smith prof. math., 1990—, chmn. dept. math., 1982-87, dir. Math. Sci. Inst., 1986-97; acting dir. Center for Applied Math., 1965-66; vis. prof. Monash U., Melbourne, Australia, 1970, 74, 78, 79, U. Chgo., 1976, M.I.T., 1980, U. Calif., San Diego, 1981; disting. vis. scientist EPA, 1985-87; dir. Ctr. for Found. of Intelligent Sys. Cornell U., 1997—2001. Prin. investigator numerous grants; mem. sci. adv. bd. EPA, 1988-93, chair tech. adv. panel Global Change, 1990-92; mem. sci. adv. bd. Ctr. for Intelligent Control, Harvard-MIT-Brown U., 1988-94; cons. to govt. and industry; co-founder Hynomics Corp., 1995. Author: (with John Crossley) Combinatorial Functors, 1974, (with Richard Shore) Logic for Applications, 2d edit., 1996, (with G.A. Metakides) Principles of Logic and Logic Programming, 1996, (with B. Khoussainov) Automata Theory and its Applications, 2001; editor Advances in Mathematics, 1967-70, Jour. Symbolic Logic, 1967-82, Annals of Pure and Applied Logic, 1983-96, Future Generation Computing Systems, 1983-97, Jour. Pure & Applied Algebra, 1988—, Annals of Math. and Artificial Intelligence, 1989—, Logical Methods in Computer Sci., 1991-94, Computer Modelling and Simulation, 1991—, Constraints, 1995-2001, Grammers, 1997-2001, (with J. Remmel, S. Goncharov, Y. Ershov) Handbook of Recursive Algebra, 1998. Mem. AIII, IEEE, Assn. Computing Machinery, Am. Math. Soc. (assoc. editor procs. 1962-65, v.p. 1992-95), Soc. Indsl. and Applied Math., Math. Assn. Am., Assn. Symbolic Logic, European Assn. for Theoretical Computer Sci. Home: 406 Cayuga Heights Rd Ithaca NY 14850-1402 Office: Cornell U 545 Mallott Hall Dept Math Ithaca NY 14853-4201 E-mail: anil@math.cornell.edu.

NES, DAVID GULICK, retired diplomat; b. York, Pa., Feb. 17, 1917; s. Charles Motier and Ethel (Billmeyer) N.; m. Elizabeth Taylor Houghton, Dec. 7, 1946; children: Victoria, Nancy, Margaret, Audrey, Wendy. AB in History with hons., Princeton U., 1939; postgrad., Harvard U., 1939-40. With Balt. Sun, 1940-41; div. asst. Dept. State, Washington, 1941-42, fgn. svc. officer, 1946-68, assigned to Washington, 1952-54, 56-59; vice consul Am. Consulate, Glasgow, Scotland, 1946-49; 2d sec. Am. Embassy, Paris, 1949-52; dep. chief mission, counselor Tripoli, 1954-56, Rabat, 1959-62; dep. chief mission min. Saigon, Vietnam, 1963-64, Cairo, 1965-67; ret., 1968. Columnist, lectr. in field, 1968—. Capt. AUS, 1942-46, CBI. Decorated Bronze Star. Mem. Chevy Chase Golf Club, Green Spring Valley Hunt Club, West River Sailing Club, N.Y. Yacht Club. Home: 15 Crestline Ct Owings Mills MD 21117-4336

NESBARY, DALE K. social sciences educator; b. Twin Lake, Mich., June 2, 1955; s. Admiral Dural and Sadie Mae Nesbary; m. Connie Rose Obits; children: Nicole, Matthew. BA, Mich. State U., 1977; MPA, We. Mich. U., 1981; PhD, Northeastern U., 1994. Fiscal analyst Mich. Senate Fiscal Agy., Lansing, 1978—83; prin. staff assoc. Nat. Conf. State Legis., Denver, 1983—86; asst. dir. budget and program evaluation City of Boston, 1986—90; rsch. dir. Boston Police Dept., 1990—92, tech. svcs. dir., 1992—94; prof. polit. sci. Oakland U., Rochester, Mich., 1994—, dir. master pub. adminstrn. program, 2001—; Technical Services Director Boston Police Department, Boston, 1992—94. Dir. contract mgmt. City of Boston, 1988—90; prin. Nesbary Cons. Group, Southfield, 1994—. Author: Survey Research and the World Wide Web, 2002, Quick Guide to the Internet for Criminology and Criminal Justice, 1998; contbr. articles. Bd. trustees Blue Lake Fine Arts Camp, Twin Lake, 1980—2002; mem. Southfiedl Pub. Sch. Fine Arts Acad., 1998—2002; polit. cons. City of Southfield, 1982—2002. Mem.: NAACP, Social Sci. Computer Rev., Oakland U. Tech. Security Task Force, Oakland U. Instl. Tech. Task Force. Avocations: photography, jazz. Office: Oakland Univ 421 Varner Hall Rochester MI 48309-4488 Business E-Mail: nesbary@oakland.edu.

NESBEITT, SARAH LYNN (LEWIS), librarian, editor; b. New Britain, Conn., Oct. 21, 1969; d. Stephen Harry and Judith Ann (Orman) Lewis. BA in French, Drew U., 1991; MA in Linguistics, Ohio State U., 1992; M Info. and Libr. Studies, U. Mich., 1994. Reference and sys. libr. Bridgewater (Mass.) State Coll., 1995—2002; asst. prof. libr. svcs. Ea. Ill. U., Charleston, 2002—. N.Am. regional editor jour. Reference Revs., 2001—; coord. editor Hist. Novels Rev., 2000—; hist. fiction editor NoveList Readers Adv. Svc., 2001—, Electronic Resources Rev., 2000. Co-author: The Information Professionals Guide to Career Development Online, 2002. Mem. ALA, Assn. Coll. and Rsch. Librs. Office: Eastern Illinois Univ Booth Library Charleston IL 61920 Fax: 217-581-7534. E-mail: cfsln@eiu.edu.

NESBIT, GARY MERLIN, neuroradiologist, educator; Student, Winona State U., 1978-79; BA in Chemistry, St. Olaf Coll., 1982; MD, U. Minn., 1986. Diplomate Am. Bd. Radiology added qualification in neuroradiology, Nat. Bd. Med. Examiners. Radiology resident Mayo Grad. Sch. Medicine, Rochester, Minn., 1986-90, neuroradiology fellow, 1990-91; asst. clin. prof. U. Calif. Sch. Medicine, San Diego, 1992-94; dir. neuroradiology and spl. studies U.S. Naval Med. Ctr., 1993-94; interventional neuroradiology fellow Oreg. Health Scis. U., Dotter Interventional Inst., Portland, Oreg., 1994-96, instr., 1994-95, asst. prof., 1995-99, assoc. prof., 1999—; interim chief neuroradiology and MRI Oreg. Health Scis. U., 1995-96, chief neuroradiology and MRI, 1996—. Assoc. cons. neuroradiology Mayo Clinic, Rochester, 1991; presenter in field. Manuscript reviewer Am. Jour. Neuroradiology, 1994—; guest editor Neuroimaging Clinics of North America, 1999. Mem. Am. Soc. Neuroradiology (sr. mem. 1992—, mem./chmn. sci. exhibits com. 1998—), Radiol. Soc. N.Am., Western Neuroradiol. Soc. (chmn. membership com. 1997-98), Soc. Cardiovascular and Interventional Radiology, Am. Soc. Interventional and Therapeutic Neuroradiology, Alpha Omega Alpha. Office: Oreg Health Scis Univ CR 135 3181 SW Sam Jackson Park Rd Portland OR 97201-3011 Fax: 503-494-7129. E-mail: nesbitg@ohsu.edu.

NESBIT, PHYLLIS SCHNEIDER, judge; b. Newkirk, Okla., Sept. 21, 1919; d. Vernon Lee and Irma Mae (Biddle) Schneider; m. Peter Nicholas Nesbit, Sept. 14, 1939. BS in Chemistry, U. Ala., 1948, BS in Law, 1958, JD, 1969. Bar: Ala. 1958. Ptnr. Wilters, Brantley and Nesbit, Robertsdale, Ala., 1958-74; pvt. practice, 1974-76; dist. judge Baldwin County Juvenile Ct., 1977-88; supernumerary dist. judge and juvenile ct. judge Baldwin County, 1989—. Bd. dirs. Baldwin Youth Svcs.; bd. dirs., v.p. women's activities So. Ala. chpt. Nat. Safety Coun., 1978-83; chmn. quality assurance com. The Homestead Retirement Village, 1992-95. Mem. Nat. Assn. Women Lawyers, Nat. Assn. Women Judges, N.Am. Judges Assn., Ala. Dist. Judges Assn., Ala. Coun. Juvenile Judges, Am. Judicature Soc., Baldwin County Bar Assn., Baldwin Sr. Travelers (sec. 1994-98), Spanish Fort, Fairhope Bus. and Profl. Women's, Phi Alpha Delta. Democrat. Methodist.

NESBIT, ROBERT GROVER, management consultant; b. Scranton, Pa., Feb. 8, 1932; s. George Archibald and Mildred Maude (Bohl) N.; m. Nancy Elizabeth Wilson, June 17, 1961; children: Robert, Jonathan. BS, U. Scranton, 1957; MS, NYU, 1958. Asst. to dean NYU, N.Y.C., 1960-64; mdse. mgr. Associated Merchandising Corp., 1964-67; dir. corp. mktg. Genesco, Inc., Nashville, 1968-77; v.p., div. gen. mgr. Levi Straus & Co., San Francisco, 1977-79; sr. partner Korn/Ferry Internat., N.Y.C., 1979—. Trustee Rollins Coll., 1992-95, U. Scranton, 1995—. With U.S. Army, 1953-55. Mem. Orchid Island Golf and Tennis Club, Sigma Nu. Clubs: N.Y. Athletic. Presbyterian. Home: 939 Orchid Pt Way Vero Beach FL 32963

NESBIT, ROBERT RAYMOND, JR. surgeon; b. New Haven, Apr. 1, 1939; BA, Harvard U., 1961; MD, U. Rochester, 1965. Diplomate Am. Bd. Surgery. Intern Strong Meml. Hosp., Rochester, 1965-66, resident in surgery, 1966-67, 69-74; chief vascular surgery Med. Coll. Ga. Hosps., Augusta, 1994-2000; prof. surgery Med. Coll. Ga., 1994-2000, prof. surgery emeritus, 2000—, dir. med. student edn. dept. surgery, 2002—. Fellow ACS; mem. Am. Assn. for Vascular Surgery, So. Surg. Assn., Assn. VA Surgeons, So. Assn. Vascular Surgery, Augusta-Richmond County Hist. Soc. (pres. 2003—), Phi Beta Kappa, Alpha Omega Alpha. Office: Med Coll Ga Dept Surgery Augusta GA 30912 E-mail: rnesbit@mail.mcg.edu.

NESBIT, WILLIAM TERRY, small business owner, consultant; b. Pitts., Jan. 30, 1945; s. William Frank and Glenna (Cleeton) N.; divorced. Owner, CEO Narrow Gauge Car Shop, Evergreen Outdoor Ctr., Shiremanstown, Pa., 1972—; mem. faculty Millersville (Pa.) U., 1976-81, Temple U., Phila., 1979, Nat. Aquatic and Small Craft Sch., Bemis Point, N.Y., 1980, Harrisburg (Pa.) Area C. C., 1981-82, 91, Dickinson Coll., Carlisle, Pa., 1982-83. Judge 32d Capital Area Sci., Engring. Fair, Dickinson Coll., Carlisle, Pa., 1989; mem. tech. briefs reader adv. panel NASA, 2000—. Co-developer ARC basic and whitewater canoeing programs for instrn., 1977-79; inventor, developer The Z Drag for Boat Rescues, 1980; developer, mfr. first HOn3 ready-to-run plastic rolling stock having NMRA warrant. Vol. ARC, 1961—; contbr. A.C. Kalmbach Meml. Libr., Chattanooga; benefactor Carlyton Sch. Dist. Libr., Carnegie, Pa. Recipient award for Humanity ARC, 1967, award for 30 Yrs. Vol. Svc., 1991; named Class I Radiological Protection Officer, U.S. Dept. of Defense and Nuclear Regulatory Commn., 1993. Mem. Math. Assn. Am., Nat. Assn. Canoe Liveries and Outfitters (founding), Nat. Model Railroad Assn. (life, mid-eastern region bd. dirs. 1997-2001, supt. Susquehanna divsn.

1996-2000, edn. chair 2002-), Conewago Canoe Club (canoe tng. officer 1999—). Episcopalian. Avocation: ferroequinology. Office: Evergreen Outdoor Ctr PO Box 3081 Shiremanstown PA 17011-3081 E-mail: wnesbit@ddc.dla.mil.

NESBITT, CHARLES RUDOLPH, lawyer, energy consultant; b. Miami, Okla., Aug. 30, 1921; s. Charles Rudolph and Irma Louise (Wilhelmi) N.; m. Margot Dorothy Lord, June 6, 1948; children: Nancy Margot Nesbitt Nagle, Douglas Charles, Carolyn Jane Nesbitt Gresham-Feagle. BA, U. Okla., 1942; JD, Yale U., 1947. Bar: Okla. 1947, U.S. Supreme Ct. 1957. Pvt. practice, Oklahoma City, 1948-62, 67-69, 75-91, 95—; atty. gen. Okla., 1963-67; mem. Okla. Corp. Commn., 1968-75, chmn., 1969-75; sec. of energy State of Okla., Oklahoma City, 1991-95; pvt. practice, 1995—. Okla. rep., v.p. Interstate Oil and Gas Compact. Trustee endowment fund St. Gregory's Coll.; pres. Hist. Preservation, Inc.; pres. bd. trustees Okla. Mus. Art; v.p., bd. dirs. Western History Collections Assocs., U. Okla. Librs.; mem. panel arbitrators Am. Arbitration Assn., NASD, NYSE. With AUS, 1942-46. Mem. ABA, Okla. Bar Assn., Oklahoma City C. of C., Phi Beta Kappa, Phi Delta Phi. Episcopalian. Home: 1703 N Hudson Ave Oklahoma City OK 73103-3428 Office: 125 NW 6th St Oklahoma City OK 73102-6014

NESBITT, DEETTE DUPREE, small business owner, investor; b. Houston, May 5, 1941; d. Raymond Benjamin DuPree and Alice Lula (Cade) Foster; children: Alice L., Charles S. Massey Nesbitt; m. Ernest V. Nesbitt, Aug. 20, 1971. Student, Sam Houston State U., 1960-61, U. Houston, 1961-62, 81-83. Lic. real estate, Tex. Co-owner K & N Perforators, Inc., Houston. Contbr. articles to various publs. Former bd. trustees Pace Soc. Am., Inc., 1992-95, Ladies Oriental Shrine N.Am., Inc.; bd. dirs. Evergreen Friends, Inc., 1991-92; dir., sec. competitive swim team Dad's Club YMCA, Houston, 1981-83; vol. adminstrv. asst. numerous orgns., Houston; patron Houston Jr. League. Recipient Varina Howell Davis medal Mil. Order Stars and Bars, 1992, Silver Good Citizenship medal SAR, 1992, Honor award Tex. SCV, 1992; featured on Eyes of Texas, NBC, 1992; Ky. Col. Mem. Nat. Soc. DAR, Huguenot Soc., S.C. Soc. Descendants of the Colonial Clergy, Nat. Soc. Magna Charta Dames (Houston Colony historian 1992-95), Plantagenet Soc., Col. Order of the Crown, The Sovereign Colonial Soc. Am. Royal Descent, Nat. Jamestown Soc. (coun. 1993-95, auditor gen. 1995-97, lt. gov. gen. 1997-98, gov. gen. 1998-2000), First Tex. Co. Jamestowne Soc. (lt. gov., gov. 1985-93, hon. gov. life), Soc. First Families of Ga. 1733-1797 (libr. gen. Tex. State Soc. 1987—), Soc. First Families of S.C. 1670-1700 (life rec. sec.), Order of First Families of Va. 1607-1624, (life, coun. 2001—), Nat. Gavel Soc. (founder 2001, organizing dep. gov. 2001—, Dames of Colonial Cavaliers 1640-60), Order of First Families of Miss. 1699-1817 (life), Daus. Rep. Tex. (Appreciation award 1996), Colonial Dames Am. (pres. chpt. VIII 1995-97), United Daus. Confederacy (Jefferson Davis chpt., Confederate Ball com. 1985-95, co-chmn. ball 1988, adv. to chmn. 1989, 90, Jefferson Davis Hist. award, Winnie Davis medal, Spl. Recognition award, hon. chmn. Houston's Confederate Ball 1995), Sons and Daus. of Pilgrims (nat. com. 1993-97), Freedoms Found. Valley Forge (George Washington Honor medal 1994), Nat. Soc. Sons and Daus. Antebellum Planters 1607-1861, Sons and Daus. of Colonial Antellum Bench and Bar 1565-1861, Harris County Hist. Commn., Petroleum Club Houston, Galveston Yacht Club. Republican. Episcopalian. Avocation: taking continuing adult educational classes. Home: 15411 Old Stone Trail Houston TX 77079-4206

NESBITT, JOHN ARTHUR, recreation service educator, recreation therapy educator; b. Detroit, Mar. 29, 1933; s. John Jackson and Anna Maye (Hartley) N.; m. Dolores Antonia Gutierrez, Apr. 8, 1961; children: John Arthur, Victoria Bowen. Student, Howe Mil. Sch., 1945-51, Olivet Coll., 1952-53; BA, Mich. State U., 1955; MA, Columbia U., 1961, EdD, 1968. Registered hosp. recreation dir.; cert. therapeutic recreation specialist. Program dir. Jaycees Internat., Miami, Fla., 1957-60; therapeutic recreation specialist Rusk Inst. Rehab. Medicine, NYU-Bellevue Med. Ctr., 1960-61; dir. World Commn. on Vocat. Rehab., Rehab. Internat., N.Y.C., 1963—65; dep. dir. gen. World Leisure and Recreation Assn., 1964—68; asst. sec. gen. Rehab. Internat., 1966-68; asst. prof., coordinator rehab. svcs., leisure studies San Jose State U., 1968-69, assoc. prof., dir. Inst. interdisciplinary studies, 1969-72; assoc. prof., chmn. recreation edn. program U. Iowa, Iowa City, 1972-76, prof. therapeutic recreation svc. dept. leisure studies, 1976-91, prof. emeritus therapeutic recreation svc. dept. leisure studies, health and physical edn. studies, 1991—; prof., chmn. dept. leisure studies, 1986-87. Pres., CEO Spl. Recreation disABLED Internat., Inc., 1978—; dir. Com. for U.S. People to People Program, 1964—; chmn. com. recreation and leisure U.S. Pres.'s Com. on Employment of Handicapped, 1972-81; dir. Internat. Ctr. on Spl. Recreation, 1978—; vice chmn. People to People Com. Disability, 1996—. Author, editor books in field; editor Alert Mag., 1956, Jaycees Internat. World, 1957-60, Internat. Rehab. of Disabled Rev., 1965-68, Therapeutic Recreation Jour., 1968-70, Jour. Iowa Pks. and Recreation, 1974-76, Play, Recreation and Leisure for People Who Are Disabled, 1977, Fed. Funding for Spl. Recreation, 1978, New Concepts and New Processes in Spl. Recreation, 1978, New Horizons in Profl. Tng. in Recreation Service for Handicapped Children and Youth, 1983, Nisbet/Nesbitt Family Surname Assn. Newsletter, 1983-86, Spl. Recreation for disABLED Digest, 1983—, Spl. Recreation Compendium, 1986, USA Ban Fireworks and Fireworks Safety Campaign Bull., 1988—, UNAGRAM, 1997-99; sr. editor Recreation and Leisure Service for Disadvantaged, 1969; editor, compiler Spl. Recreation Compendium of 1,500 Resources for Disabled People, 3d edit., 1989, Special Recreation for disABLED Press, University Heights, Iowa, 1989. Bd. dirs., treas. United Cerebral Palsy Assn., San Mateo and Santa Clara County, 1970-72; bd. dirs. Harold Russell Found., 1971-73, Goodwill Industries Santa Clara County, 1969-72, rehab. counselor, master therapeutic recreation specialist; bd. dirs. Hawkeye Area Poverty Cmty. Action Program, Iowa, Iowa Pk. and Recreation Assn., Am. Leisure and Recreation Assn., Washington, others; bd. dirs., state v.p. Iowa Aging Coalition, Iowa; bd. dirs., founding pres. Santa Clara County Assn. on Recreation Handicapped, Iowa; bd. dirs., tech. adv. Disability Internat. Found., 1997—. With USAFR, 1955-57; maj. Ret. Recreation Svc. Ill and Handicapped fellow; recipient numerous awards and citations for work with handicapped, including Torch of Gold award Nat. Boy Scouts Am., Appreciation award Philippines Found. Mem. Nat. Therapeutic Recreation Soc. (pres. 1970-71, Disting. Svc. award), Nat. Rehab. Assn., Am. Assn. Leisure and Recreation (bd. dirs. 1977-80), Nat. Consortium on Phys. Edn. and Recreation for Handicapped (pres. 1976-77), Nat. Forum Comml. Recreation and Handicapped (chmn. 1979), AAHPER, Iowa Parks and Recreation Assn. (bd.dirs. 1973-75, 89-90), Nat. Rehab. Counseling Assn., Council Exceptional Children, Pi Sigma Epsilon. Presbyterian. Avocations: arts, gardening, travel, genealogy, community service. Office: Spl Recreation Disabled Internat 701 Oaknoll Dr Iowa City IA 52246 E-mail: john-nesbitt@uiowa.edu.

NESBITT, LLOYD IVAN, podiatrist; b. Toronto, Ont., Can., Sept. 24, 1951; s. Allan Jay and Rose (Shuster) N.; m. Marlene Cindy Wegler, May 13, 1984; children: Hilary Liza, Andrea Eve, Jeffrey Ryan. D in Podiatric Medicine, Calif. Coll. Podiatric Medicine, San Francisco, 1975. Diplomate Internat. Soc. Podiatric Laser Surgery. Residency program Vancouver (B.C.) Gen. Hosp., Can., 1975-76; pvt. practice podiatric medicine Toronto. Lectr. numerous colls., fitness ctrs. and sports medicine confs., Ont., 1979—; bd. dirs. Cumba Ins. Co., Toronto. Contbr. numerous articles to sports medicine books and jours; editor Canadian Podiatrist Jour., 1979-88. Bd. dirs. Cumba Charitable Found. Fellow: Am. Acad. Podiatric Sports Medicine, Can. Podiatric Sports Medicine Acad. (pres. 1979—89, editor newsletter 1977—89); mem.: Ont. Podiatric Med. Assn. (past pres.), Am. Podiatric Med. Assn., Am. Soc. Laser Medicine & Surgery (diplomate), Sierra Club. Avocations: skiing, in-line skating, hockey, sailing, cycling, gardening. Home: 122 Argonne Crescent Willowdale ON Canada M2K 2K1 Office: Madison Ctr Office Tower 4950 Yonge St Ste 2414 Toronto ON Canada M2N 6K1 E-mail: foothealth@lloydnesbitt.com.

NESBITT, MARK, management consultant; b. Ottawa, Ont., Can., Dec. 31, 1952; s. William Alonzo and Barbara (Ellis) N.; 1 child, Karen Elizabeth. BSc, Carleton U., Ottawa, 1973, BA, 1974; MBA, Harvard U., 1978. Cert. Mgmt. Cons. Cons. Peat Marwick & Ptnrs., Ottawa, 1978; assoc./ mgr. Veritas Cons. Inc., Toronto, Ont., Can., 1978-86, pres. Can., 1986-93; pres., CEO Vertex Cons. Inc., 1993—. IS com. mem. YMCA Metro Toronto, 1992-93; bd. dirs. Inst. Cert. Mgmt. Cons. Can. Mem. Am. Mktg. Assn., Inst. Cert. Mgmt. Cons. Ont., Inst. Cert. Mgmt. Cons. Can. (pres. 1997-98, chmn. 1998), Assn. for Creative Change, Internat. Mgmt. Devel.: Internat. Consulting (1st v.p., sec.-treas. 1995-98, pres. 1998—). Anglican. Avocations: bicycling, photography, programming. Office: Vertex Cons Inc 14 Dundonald St Toronto ON Canada M4Y 1K2

NESBITT, ROBERT EDWARD LEE, JR. physician, educator, scientific researcher, writer, poet; b. Albany, Ga., Aug. 21, 1924; s. Robert E.L. and Anne Louise (Hill) N.; m. Ellen Therese Morrissey. BA, Vanderbilt U., 1944, MD, 1947. Diplomate: Am. Bd. Ob-Gyn (asso. examiner). Asst. prof. Johns Hopkins U., 1954-56, chief obstetric pathology lab., acting chief obstetrics, 1955-56; prof., chmn. dept. ob-gyn Albany (N.Y.) Med. Coll., Union U., 1956-61, SUNY Health Sci. Ctr., Syracuse, 1961-81, dir. gen. gynecology service, 1982-84, prof. and chmn. emeritus dept. ob-gyn; obstetrician-gynecologist-in-chief Albany Hosp., 1956-61; obstetrician, gynecologist-in-chief Syracuse Meml. Hosp., 1961-65; obstetrician-gynecologist-in-chief Crouse-Irving Hosp., 1963-70, attending staff, 1970-84; prof. surgery U. South Fla., Tampa, 1988-92, prof. ob.-gyn., 1988-92. Chief ob-gyn State U. Hosp., 1964-81, chmn. med. staff and med. bd., 1964-66; attending staff St. Joseph's Hosp.; cons., chief gynecology sect. surg. service Syracuse VA Hosp., 1984-88; chief gynecology sect., asst. chief surgery, dir. uro-gynecology VA Med. Ctr., Bay Pines, Fla., 1988-92, acting chief of staff, 1990, interim chief surgery, 1991-92, chmn. O.R. com. surg. svc., 1988-92, chmn. patient care evaluation com., 1989-90, chmn. clin. exec. bd., 1990, chmn. drug usage evaluation com., 1990-91, chmn. profl. standards bd., 1990; cons. Syracuse Psychiat. Inst.; mem. cancer tng. grants and edn. com. Nat. Cancer Insts.; mem. adv. com. Bur. Maternal and Child Health, N.Y. State Dept. Health, 1957-61; nat. adviser to Children, publ. of Children's Bur., HEW, 1959-63; cons. Children's Bur., 1959-62; mem. prenatal care guide subcom. Am. Pub. Health Assn., 1962-64; cons. to regional adviser in maternal and child health Pan Am. San. Bur., WHO, 1963-65; numerous guest professorships including univs. in Mex., Chile, Uruguay, Colombia, St. Vincent (W.I.), Venezuela, People's Republic of China, Western Europe, Panama, Australia, Canada; numerous guest professorships including univs. and others. Author: Perinatal Loss in Modern Obstetrics, 1957, Last Twig on the Bush?, 1999, In the Fullness of Time, 1999, Hearts of Flesh, 2001, (poetry collections) Chorales for Arid Souls, 1999, The Fullness Search, 2000, Visions Shared, 2000, Daily Relevance, 2000, Marked Off from Pagans, 2000, Puppet or Saint, 2001, Glimpses, 2002, (poetry collection) Latent Harvest, 2002, over 300 published poems, also poems in numerous anthologies (14 Editor's Choice awards), sect. on ob-gyn in Rypin's Med. Licensure Exams; co-author: Infant, Perinatal, Maternal and Childhood Mortality in U.S, 1968; editor: sect. on obstetrics and gynecology Stedman's Medical Dictionary, 1958—64, sect. on fetus Funk and Wagnalls Universal Std. Ency., 1959; 1st guest editor: sect. on fetus Clinics in Perinatology, 1974; 1st editor sect. on fetus Clinical Diagnosis Quiz for Obstetrics and Gynecology, 1976, Clini-Pearls in Obstetrics and Gynecology, 1977; contbr.: sect. on fetus Attorneys' Textbook of Medicine. Capt. M.C., U.S. Army, 1952-54. Named One of Ten Outstanding Young Men in Am., U.S. Jr. C. of C., 1957; Robert E.L. Nesbitt Jr. scholarship, Sr. Resident in Ob-Gyn, and Robert E.L. Nesbitt Jr. student scholarship established in his honor, SUNY Health Sci. Ctr. at Syracuse, 1987; recipient Wisdom award, named to Hall of Fame, Wisdom Soc., 2001, recipient Winston Churchill medal of wisdom, 2002. Fellow: A.C.S. (com. forum fundamental surg. problems 1962—67), N.Y. Acad. Scis., Am. Coll. Obstetricians and Gynecologists (chmn. com. mental retardation and perinatal health 1966), Am. Assn. Maternal and Child Health, Venezuelan Obstetrics-Gynecol. Soc. (hon.); mem.: AMA (mem. residency accreditation com., site visit team mem.), Internat. Soc. Poets (Disting. mem.), Pub. Health Council N.Y. State, Am. Soc. Cytology, Onondaga County Med. Soc., Med. Soc. N.Y. State (regional obstetrics chmn., subcom. Maternal and Child Welfare), Pan Am. Med. Assn. (med. ambassador goodwill, life mem. sect. on cancer), Soc. for Gynecol. Investigation (coun.), Internat. Soc. Poets, others, Alpha Omega Alpha, Southwest, Fla. obstet. and gynecol. socs. (hon.). Achievements include research and 230 publications on cytologic, cytochemical and histochemical study of early cervical cancer, perinatal and placental pathology, cytologic and hormonal studies in normal and high-risk obstetrics patients, experimental production of abruptio placentae, reproductive endocrinology, animal experimentation, induced endocrine insults upon pregnant and nonpregnant ewes and hormonal influence on placentation, invitro placenta perfusion, fetal growth and development, female urology, surgical techniques for restoration of female pelvic floor integrity; human spirituality; inspirational poetry. Home: 3743 Roscommon North Martinez GA 30907

NESBITT, VANCE GORDON, computer software company executive; b. May 5, 1959; Student, U. Tex., 1977-82. Operator Seismic Data Ctr. Tex. Instruments, Austin, 1983-84; facilities and tech. svcs. assoc. Microelectronics & Computer Tech. Corp., 1984-85; v.p. product devel. Kent * Marsh Ltd., Houston, 1985-90; chmn., CEO Kent & Marsh Ltd., 1990—. Author: (software) MacSafe, 1990, FolderBolt, 1992, Cryptomatic, 1993, WinShield, 1995. Vol. caregiver Omega House Hospice, Names Project Friend of the Quilt, Human Rights Campaign, Tex. Human Rights Found. Named Outstanding Vol. of Yr., Omega House Hospice, 2001. Mem. IEEE Computer Soc., Computer Security Inst., Nat. Computer Security Assn., Assn. Computing Machinery, Electronic Frontier Found., Computer Profls. for Social Responsibility, Info. Systems Security Assn., Microsoft Developer Network, Houston Area Apple Users Group, Houston Area League of PC Users, Apple Programmers and Developers Assn., Assn. Corp. Computing Tech. Profls., Data Processing Mgmt. Assn., Optimist Club, Alpha Phi Omega. Office: Kent & Marsh Ltd 2109 Driscoll St Ste 304 Houston TX 77019-6824

NESBITT, VERONICA A. management executive; b. Henderson, Tenn., June 10, 1959; d. Hiawatha Daniel and Laura Mae (Green) Thompson; divorced; children: Shemenya A. Davis, Maleka L. Cert. stenographer, Miller-Hawkins B. Coll., 1979; Cert. data transcriber, IRS, Memphis, Tenn., 1981; Cert. computer operator, U.S. Army, Newport News, Va., 1985, Cert. computer programmer, 1987; postgrad., Columbia Coll., 1990. Cert. computer opr. Stenographer Memphis & Shelby County Health Dept., Memphis, 1979-80; cash clk./data transcriber IRS, 1980-82; data transcriber U.S. Army, Fort Sheridan, Ill., 1982-83, work order clk., 1984-85, quality control clk., 1985-89; mgmt. asst. HQ USAREC, Ill., 1989-92; data transcriber Selective Svc., North Chicago, 1983-84; telemarketer Allstate Ins. Co., Northbrook, 1986-88, unit supr. Glenview, 1988-92; employee coun., 1994; total quality facilitator Allstate Ins. Co., Glenview, Ill., 1992; mgmt. asst. Hdqs. US Army Recruiting Command, Ft. Knox, Ky., 1992-94, 233d Base Support Bn., Darmstadt, Germany, 1994-97; staffing specialist Snelling Staffing Network, Columbia, Md., 1997-99; exec. adminstrv. asst. GSE Sys., Inc., 1999; mgmt. analyst Navy Internat. Programs/INS, Inc., 1999-2001; internat. jr. analyst/adminstr. Jil Info. Sys., Inc., 2001—. Mgmt. analyst, INS, Inc., Washington, 1999-2001—; chmn. task force Allstate, Glenvie, 1990; interviewer Mathematica Policy Rsch., Inc., Columbia, Md., 1998-99, supr., 1999—. Mem. Am. Heart Disease Found., 1991-92, Easter Seal Soc., 1991-92, March of Dimes, 1991—, Nat. Heart Rsch., 1991-95; mem. Nat. Cancer Rsch., 1991-95, fed. women's program mgr., 1995-97; treas. Second Glance Thrift Store, 1996-97; welfare com., continuing edn. grants Darmstadt Women's Club, 1995-96, chmn. Second Glance Thrift Store; counselor Equal Employment Opportunity, 1995-97; mem. Equal Opportunity Adv. Action Team, 1995-97; asst. supt. ch. schs. Asbury Town Neck United Meth. Ch., Severna Park, Md. Mem. NAFE, Am. Cancer Soc., Am. Heart Disease Prevention Found., Jack Anderson Internat. Platform Assn., Order Ea. Star (assoc. matron 1997). Baptist. Avocations: reading, knitting, drama, bicycling, sewing. Office: Office Under Sec Def (ATSC) Rm 2D173 3070 Defense Pentagon Washington DC 20301-3070

NESBITT, VIRGINIA, special education educator, poet; b. Blackwell, Okla., Nov. 22, 1944; d. Earl Raymond and Myrtle Iva Combs; m. Raymond Lee Delaney, Dec. 24, 1964 (div. Sept. 1977); m. Emmanuel William Benjamin Nesbitt, June 20, 1992 (div. Feb. 1997). BS in Spl. Edn., Ctrl. Okla. State U., 1975. Cert. tchr. Tex., Pa. Tchr. 5-County Coop, McAlester, Okla., 1985—86, Cotton-Comanche Coop, Faxon, 1986—88; tchr., cons. Vision Guest Sch., Franklin, Pa., 1990—92; tchr. Houston Ind. Sch. Dist., 1996—98, Mrs. Wagner's Pvt. Sch., Houston, 2000—01. Contbr. . Bd. dirs. Ch. Daycare, Oklahoma City, 1973—75, dir., 1975—78. With U.S. Army, 1963—65. Mem.: Internat. Soc. Poets. Avocations: dancing, reading, cooking, sewing, baking.

NESHEIM, DENNIS WARREN, art educator, artist, writer, instructional materials producer; b. Decorah, Iowa, Nov. 24, 1948; s. Kenneth H. and Adelle N.; m. Lavonne Selene Jones, Mar. 29, 1968. AA, Rochester State Jr. Coll., Minn., 1970; BS in Art/Art Edn., Winona (Minn.) State U., 1972; MA in Spl. Edn., U. Colo., Denver, 2000. cert. art tchr. K-12, Minn., Wis., Ark., Colo. Dept. Def. Dependent Schs. Tchr. art Cassville (Wis.) Pub. Schs., 1972-74, Franklin Mid. Sch., Shawano, Wis., 1974-76; substitute tchr., tchr. 4th grade Dept. Def. Dependent Schs., Neu Ulm, Germany, 1977-78, tchr. art Ulm. Am. Sch., 1978-80, tchr. art and video arts, 1980-87; tchr., artist art ctrs., Fla., 1987-89; owner, producer Nesheim Arts & Video, Lakeland Fla., Lakewood, Colo., 1989—2001; tchr. art, tchr. aide Synergy Sch., Denver; tchr. spl. edn. Euclid Mid. Sch., Littleton, 2000—. Presenter workshops and seminars, 1980-86; video tng., cons., Lakeland, 1988-93. Author, illustrator: (workbook) Making Waves, An Imagination Starter, 1994; creator, producer: (instrnl. video/handbook kits) Look and Draw series, 1990—; editor lit. quar. Onionhead, 1989-93, others; cons. writer, editor Frugal Times, 1992; part-time writer, editor Free Shopping News, 1985-87, S&N Advertising, 1985-87; prodr. (videos) Fantastic Realism, The Video, 1989, Epic Silence, 1989, Verbal Science, 1989, October 26, 1970, 1990, See in the Dark, 1990, Look and Draw, 1990, Head in the Clouds, 1990, Look and Draw Faces and Figures, 1991, Look and Draw Space In Perspective, 1992; prodr. (with David Lee Jr.) Produce Better Video, 1989; one-man shows include Donau Casino, Neu Ulm, Germany, 1977, Maas Brothers Gallery, Lakeland, 1990; exhibited in group shows Wurzburg (Germany) Milcom, 1979, Oberstube Gallery, Ulm, Germany, 1985, 86, Ridge Art, Winter Haven, Fla. (Merit award), 1988, Arts on the Park, Lakeland, (Honorable Mention award) 1988, 89, 90, 91, Arts Ctr., St. Petersburg, Fla. 1989, Art League Manatee, Bradenton, Fla., 1989, Ridge Art Assn., Winter Haven, Fla., 1990, Mt. Dora (Fla.) Ctr. for the Arts, 1990, Imperial Artists Gallery, Lakeland, 1990, 1991; contbr. articles to profl. jours. including Jour. Adolexcent and Adult Literacy, Prin. Leadership. Mem. Arts on Park, Lakeland Ctr. for Creative Arts, 1987-95, bd. dirs., 1991-93; mem. Green Mountain Park Vols. Recipient various commendations and appreciation awards from schs. and cmty. orgns. Mem. Nat. Art Edn. Assn., Fine Art Forum, Compuserve. Avocations: hiking, reading, creative cooking. Office: Euclid Mid Sch 777 W Euclid Ave Littleton CO 80120

NESHEIM, MALDEN C. academic administrator, nutrition educator; Provost emeritus Cornell U., Ithaca, N.Y., prof. emeritus nutrition, 1997—. Office: Cornell U 311 Savage Hall Ithaca NY 14853-7601 E-mail: mcn2@cornell.edu.

NESHEIM, ROBERT OLAF, retired food products executive; b. Monroe Center, Ill., Sept. 13, 1921; s. Olaf M. and Sena M. (Willms) Nesheim; m. Emogene P. Sullivan, July 13, 1946 (div.); children: Barbara Mowry, Susan Yost(dec.) , Sandra Rankin; m. Doris Howes Calloway, July 4, 1981 (dec.). BS, U. Ill., 1943, MS, 1950, PhD, 1951; postgrad. in advanced mgmt. program, Harvard U., 1971. Farm mgr. Halderman Farm Mgmt. Svc., Wabash, Ind., 1946-48; instr. U. Ill., 1951; mgr. feed rsch. The Quaker Oats Co., Barrington, Ill., 1952-64; prof., head of dept. animal sci. U. Ill., 1964-67; dir. nutrition rsch. The Quaker Oats Co., Barrington, Ill., 1967-69, v.p. R & D, 1969-78, v.p. sci. & tech. Chgo., 1978-83; sr. v.p. sci. & tech. Avadyne, Inc., Monterey, Calif., 1983-85; pres. Advanced Healthcare, 1985-91; ret., 1991. Mem. food and nutrition bd. NAS, 1972—78, chmn. com. in mil. nutrition rsch. FNB, 1982—97; bd. mem. Bioscis. Info. Svcs., 1978—84, chmn., 1982—84. Capt. U.S. Army, 1943-46, South Pacific. Fellow Am. Inst. Nutrition (treas. 1983-86), AAAS; mem. Inst. Food Technologists, Fed. Socs. Exptl. Biologists (treas. 1973-79), APHA, Corral de Tierra Club (Salinas, Calif.). Avocations: gardening, golf.

NESIN, BARBARA, artist, art educator; b. N.Y.C., Jan. 5, 1951; d. Lazare and Simone (Esteve) N. BFA, Pratt Inst., 1974; MBA, L.I. U., Bklyn., 1984; MFA, Ind. State U., 1996. Instr. art N.H. Coll., Brunswick, Maine, 1988-90; art specialist K-3 MSAD 75, Topsham, 1988-90; art specialist K-8 Augusta (Maine) Sch. System, 1990-91; youth program coord. Stanwood (Wash.)-Camano Family Ctr., 1992-93; instr. art Whidbey Island Naval Air Sta., Oak Harbor, 1993, Skagit Valley Coll., Oak Harbor, 1991-93; grad. teaching asst. Ind. State U., Terre Haute, 1993-96; assoc. prof. visual arts faculty, program dir. Front Range C.C., Fort Collins, Colo., 1996—. Pub. rels. coord. Tedford-Oasis Programs, Brunswick, Maine, 1988-90; panel presenter Founds. Art Theory and Edn. Conf., St. Louis, 1995; mem. gallery com. Ctr. for Arts at the Chocolate Ch., Bath, Maine, 1989-91; intern cross-cultural visual literacy program Bronx (N.Y.) Mus. of Arts, 1995; panel presenter Ctr. Caribbean Studies, Havana, 1995, Haitian Studies Assn., Montrouis, 1996, Detroit, 1997, Port-au-Prince, 1998, Atlanta, 1999, W. Palm Beach, Fla., 2000; curator Bas Bleu Gallery, Ft. Collins, 1999-2002. Exhibited in shows at Ind. State U., 1994-96, Arts Illiana, 1995, Miss. State U., 1995, Ind. U. Gallery, Bloomington, 1994-95, Indpls. Mus. of Art Rental Gallery, 1995, Art Place, Chgo., 1996, St. John's U., Jamaica, N.Y., 1996, SFA Gallery, Nacogdoches, Tex., 1996, Jardin Culturel, Cambria Heights, N.Y., 1996, St.-Mary-of-the-Woods Coll. Art Gallery, 1996, Ashwell Gallery, Beverly, Mass., 1996, Galeria Coqui, Seattle, 1997, Urban Inst. Contemporary Art, Grand Rapids, Mich., 1997, U. Colo., Boulder, 1997, Ceres Gallery, N.Y.C., 1998, Puffin Found., Teaneck, N.J., 1999, Gallery of Social/Polit. Art, Boston, 1999, C.C. of R.I., Lincoln, 1999, Holter Mus. Art, Helena, Mont., 2000, Green Gallery, Colo. State U., 2001, others; represented in permanent collection at U. Ill., Ind. State U. Chair No. Colo. Multicultural Corp. Ft. Collins. Recipient Cmty. Svc. (VISTA) award State of Maine, 1988, Peoples Choice award Ind. U. Fine Art Gallery, 1994; grad. rsch. grantee, 1995-96. Mem. Nat. Assn. Women Artists, Coll. Art Assn., Haitian Studies Assn., Founds. in Art Theory and Edn. (v.p. biennial conf. 1997-99, Col. Art Assn. rep. 1999—). Office: Front Range Cmty Coll Arts & Humanities 4616 S Shields St Dept Arts& Fort Collins CO 80526-3812

NESLER, MITCHELL SCOTT, psychology researcher; b. Bklyn., Mar. 9, 1966; m. Megan Nesler, Oct. 11, 1992. PhD, U. Albany, 1993. Assoc. dean for outcomes assessment and rsch. Excelsior Coll., Albany, NY, 1994—. Adj. faculty Siena Coll., Saratoga Springs, N.Y., 1991-93, Empire State Coll., Saratoga Springs, 1991-93. Contbr. articles to profl. jours. Assn. for Instnl. Rsch/. Nat. Ctr. for Edn. Stats. grantee, 1998. Mem. APA, Am. Psychol. Soc. Office: 7 Columbia Cir Albany NY 12203-5156

NESMELOVA, IRINA VLADISLAVOVNA, research scientist, physicist; b. Kazan, Russia, Sept. 8, 1968; d. Vladislav Nikolaevich and Tamara Alexandrovna (Frolova) Serebrennikov; m. Yuriy Eugenévich Nesmelov, Aug. 10, 1990; 1 child, Andrei. BS, Kazan State U., 1990, PhD, 1998. Jr. rsch. scientist Kazan Med. Inst., 1990-92, Kazan Biol. Inst. and State U., 1995-98; postdoctoral assoc. U. Minn., Mpls., 1999—. Kazan Inst. Biology grant, 1997-98.

NESMITH, KIMBLIN EUGENE, law educator; b. Jacksonville, Fla., Sept. 19, 1963; s. James and Elizabeth (Crawley) N.; m. Lisa Jeanette Brown, Jan. 1, 1994 (div. Jan. 3, 1997); 1 child, Lana Imani Jene'. BS in Experimental Psychology, Morehouse Coll., Atlanta, 1985; JD in Corp. Bus. Transactions, U. Miami Law Sch., 1991; postgrad., Yale U., 1987-89, Northwestern U., 1994. Adj. prof. U. North Fla. Coll. Bus., Jacksonville, 1992-94; assoc. prof. Edward Waters Coll., 1993—; asst. prof., chmn. Divsn. Criminal Justice, 1993—; adjunct prof. Webster U., 1996; exec. dir. Ctr. for Commerce and Trade at Edwards Waters Coll., 1996—, Inst. for Global Entrepreneurship at Edwards Waters Coll., Jacksonville, 1996—; v.p. Henry Roberts Gourmet Food Co., 1998—. Faculty rep., mem. Bd. Trustees Edward Waters Coll., Jacksonville, 1996—; vice chmn. Cmty. Alliance Devel. Corp., Jacksonville, 1996—. Mem. Jacksonville Chpt. NAACP. Recipient Outstanding Achievement, William R. Raines Sr. H.S., Jacksonville, 1998, Recognition of Disting. Accomplishment Boys & Girls, Inc., Jacksonville Housing Authority and The Tenant Adv., Jakcsonville, 1998, Outstanding Accomplishment, S.P. Livingston Elem., Jacksonville, 1998; named Outstanding Guest Spke., Fla. C.C. of Jacksonville, Downtown Campus, 1998. Mem. Daniel Webster Perkins Bar Assn., First Coast Micro Loan Program, First Coast African-Am. C. of C., Morehouse Coll. Alumni Assn. Avocations: writing and reading books and articles on wealth, lecturing on entrepreneurship, exercising. E-mail address. Home: 6161 Pettiford Dr W Jacksonville FL 32209-1843 Office: Edward Waters Coll 1658 Kings Rd Jacksonville FL 32209-6167 Fax: 904-366-2723. E-mail: kenesmith@lib.ewc.edu.

NESOFF, IRWIN, social work educator, management consultant; b. Mexico City, Jan. 28, 1948; s. Hyman and Sally Leah Nesoff; m. Paula Moszenberg, Feb. 1, 1970; 1 child, Jeremy. BA in Sociology, CUNY, 1970; MSW, Hunter Coll. Sch. Social Work, 1978; D of Social Welfare, CUNY, 1998. Cert. social worker, social work mgr. Exec. dir. Sunnyside (N.Y.) Cmty. Svcs., 1983-90; dir. Bur. Cmty. Svcs., N.Y.C. Dept. for Aging, 1990-92; assoc. exec. dir. Ednl. Alliance, N.Y.C., 1992-94; assoc. prof. social work Kean U., Union, NJ, 1995—. Mgmt. cons. Nesoff Assocs., Mgmt. Support for Non-profits, Congers, N.Y., 1994—. Author: Reaching Out to Older New Yorkers: A Handbook for Service Providers, 1998; contbr. articles to profl. jours. Pres. Nat. Ctr. for Creative Aging, Bklyn., 1996-2002, Park Slope Geriatric Day Ctr., Bklyn., 1999-2002; mem. commn. on racial, ethnic and cultural minorities, Council on Social Work Edn. Mem. NASW (chair nominating com. 1994-96, N.Y.C. chpt. exec. bd. polit. action for candidate election 1995-98), Nat. Network for Social Work Mgrs., Coun. on Social Work Edn., CUNY Grad. Ctr. Alumni Assn. Jewish. Avocations: Tai Chi, cycling, scuba diving, travel. Office: Kean Univ 1000 Morris Ave Union NJ 07083 E-mail: INAssoc@aol.com.

NESOFF, ROBERT, newspaper publisher; b. Bronx, N.Y., July 6, 1938; s. Hyman and Sally Leah (Reznikoff) N.; m. Sandra Roberta Levine, June 27, 1965; children: Wendy Naimaister, Barbara Thorson, Karen Nesoff. Editor Country Wide Publs., N.Y.C., 1964-65; reporter The Record, Hackensack, N.J., 1965-66, Newark News, 1966-72; pub. Metro Publs. Group/Metro Feature Syndicate, Oradell, N.J., 1972—, Palisadian Newspaper, East Bergen, 1984—. Pub. rels. cons. U.S. Homes Corp., 1973, Best Western Internat. Hotels, 1979, tourism ministries Republics of Guatemala, 1979-80, Panama, 1979-81, Kenya, 1985; former N.Y. State pub. rels. dir. Common Cause, N.Y.C. Mcpl. Svcs. Adminstrn., 1974-75; pub. rels. dir. N.J. State Assn. Chiefs of Police, Bergen County Police Chiefs Assn.; com. dir. Bergen County Sheriff's Dept., 2000-01; instr. police-press rels. Bergen County Police Acad., 1970-75; nat. rep., spokesman Fed. Criminal Investigators Assn., 1974-85; mem. Stein Commn., N.Y. State Commn., dir. info. and investigations.; dir. investigations into funeral home abuses; expert witness FTC, 1975; appeared on numerous radio and TV shows including 20/20, Sta. KABC, L.A., Sta. WABC Radio, N.Y., Eleanor Guggenheim Consumer show on Channel 5, Richard Bey, Jackie Mason shows on Sta. WWOR-TV; capt., exec. officer Bergen County SPCA Law Enforcement Divsn., 1997—. Author: Never a Doubt, 1996; contbg. editor Lifestyles mag., 1997—; columnist Metro Feature Svc., 1972—; radio and TV appearances. Pres. sch. bd. New Milford, N.J., 1983-90, Ctrl. Bergen Crime Stoppers Orgn.; councilman City of New Milford, 1990-99, pres. coun., 1996-98, 99; pres. New Milford Jewish Ctr., 1991-92, past bd. dirs.; past trustee New Milford Swim Club, past sec., v.p., 1980-83; former coach Princess League Softball, 1983; scoutmaster Boy Scouts Am., New Milford; mem. N.J. Dem. State Com., 1997—, Dem. County Com., 1998—, Bergen County Task Force on Youth Violence, Bias Crimes sub-com., 1994, Bergen County Bicentennial Com., 1976, Family Life Curriculum Com.; commr. New Bridge Landing Pk. Commn., 1996-98; v.p. Bergen County SPCA. Sgt. U.S. Army 11th Spl. Forces Group (Green Berets), 1962-64. Recipient Heroism award N.Y.C. Police Dept., cert. of recognition Newark Police Dept., Voice of Democracy award VFW, cert. of appreciation NCCJ, Citizenship award Am. Legion, cert. of appreciation Kiwanis, Pax Et Justicia plaque Royal St. Vincent Police Force, Grenadine Islands, 30 awards from various press assns.; named hon. mem. Fed. Criminal Investigators Assn., Leonia (N.J.) Police Dept. SWAT Team. Mem. N.Am. Travel Journalists Assn. (pres. 1989-96, Best Profile Feature, 1996, other awards), Working Press Assn. N.J. (pres. 1987-90, Best Edtl. Writer 1985-86, 90-91, 93, 95, Best Column 1990, Best Critical Rev. 1991-95, Gold Medal award), North Jersey Press Assn. (pres. 1972-73, 76-77, 81-83), N. Am. Ski Journalists Assn., Ea. Ski Writers Assn. (bd. dirs. 1998-2001—), Jewish War Vets. (comdr. Wallch-Gold-Moses Post #773 1996-97). Democrat. Jewish. Avocations: skiing, scuba diving. Office: Metro Publs Group/Metro Feature Syndicate PO Box 104 Oradell NJ 07649-0104

NESPOLI, PAOLO ANGELO, astronaut; b. Milan, Apr. 6, 1957; s. Luigi and Maria Nespoli. BS in Aerospace Engring., Poly. U. N.Y., 1988, MS in Aeronautics and Astronautics, 1989; laurea in ingegneria meccanica, U. degli Studi di Firenze, Italy, 1990. Registered profl. engr.; lic. pvt. pilot, advanced scuba diver, NitrOx diver, master parachutist, cert. parachutist instr., jump master, demolition expert. Non-commd. officer, parachute instr. Scuola Militare de Paracudutismo, Pisa, Italy, 1977—80; spl. forces operator 9[00b0] Btg d'Assalto "Col Moschin", Livorno, Italy; mem. multinat. peacekeeping force Italian Army, Beirut, 1982—84, ret., 1987; design engr. Proel Tecnologie, Florence, Italy, 1989—91; mem. astronaut tng. divsn., European Astronaut Ctr. European Space Agy., Cologne, Germany, 1991—98; mem. EUROMIR project European Space Tech. Ctr., Noordwijk, Netherlands, 1995—96; mem. spaceflight tng. divsn. NASA, Johnson Space Ctr., Houston, 1996—98; astronaut Italian Space Agy., 1998; astronaut, mission specialist candidate NASA, Johnson Space Ctr., Houston, 1998—. Avocations: scuba diving, aircraft piloting, assembling computer hardware and electronic equipment, computer software. Office: Astronaut Office NASA Johnson Space Ctr Houston TX 77058*

NESS, ANDREW DAVID, lawyer; b. San Francisco, Oct. 29, 1952; s. Orville Arne and Muriel Ruth (Trendt) N.; m. Rita M. Kobylenski, May 25, 1980; children: Katherine, Austin, Emily. BS, Stanford U., 1974; JD, Harvard U., 1977. Bar: Calif. 1977, D.C. 1979, Va. 1986, U.S. Dist. Ct. (no. dist.) Calif. 1977, U.S. Dist. Ct. D.C. 1983, U.S. Dist. Ct. (ea. dist.) Va. 1988, U.S. Ct. Appeals (4th cir.) 1989. Law clk. U.S. Dist. Ct., San Francisco, 1977-78; assoc. Lewis, Mitchell & Moore, Vienna, 1979-82, ptnr., 1982-87, Morgan, Lewis & Bockius LLP, Washington, 1987-2000, Thelen Reid & Priest LLP, Washington, 2000—, mng. ptnr. D.C. office, 2001—. Instr. U. Md., College Park, 1987-90; mem. faculty constrn. exec. program Stanford (Calif.) U., 1984-87. Contbr. chpt. to books, articles to profl. jours. Mem. ABA (forum on constrn. industry, pub. contract law sect.). Avocations: hiking, bicycling. Office: Thelen Reid & Priest LLP 701 Pennsylvania Ave NW Washington DC 20004-2608 E-mail: adness@thelenreid.com.

NESS, ARTHUR JOSEPH, musicologist; b. Chgo., Jan. 27, 1936; s. Martin J. and Rosetta Ness; m. Charlotte A. Kolczynski, Dec. 29, 1982. MusB in Music Theory, U. So. Calif., L.A., 1958; AM in Music, Harvard U., 1961; PhD in Musicology, NYU, 1984. Asst. prof. U. So. Calif., L.A., 1963-76; prof., dept. chmn. Daemen Coll., Buffalo, 1976-84; faculty SUNY, 1984-86, State U. Coll. N.Y., Fredonia, 1984-86. Editor: Lute Works of Francesco Canova da Milano, 1970, Lute Works of Marco dall'Aquila, 1999; contbr. New Grove Dictionary, 1970, New Harvard Dictonary of Music, 1980; contbr. articles to profl. jours. With USNR, 1954-62. Fulbright fellow, Munich, 1965-68. Mem. Am. Musicol. Soc. (chpt. sec.-treas. 1964-66), Lute Soc. Am., Lute Soc. U.K., Internat. Assn. Music Librs., Internat. Musicol. Soc. Home and Office: 2039 Commonwealth Ave Apt 10 Boston MA 02135-5163 E-mail: 71162.751@compuserve.com.

NESS, BRYAN DOUGLAS, biologist, educator; b. Seattle, June 6, 1961; s. Iver L. and Nancy J. (Anderson) N.; m. Judy Lynn Egnew, June 7, 1981; children: Tara Lynn, Reuben David. BS in Biology, Walla Walla Coll., 1983, MS in Biology, 1985; PhD in Botany, Wash. State U., 1992. Assoc. prof. biology Pacific Union Coll., Angwin, Calif., 1989—. Contbg. author: The Jepson Manual, 1993, Flora of North America, 2001; editor: Encyclopedia of Plant Life; contbr. articles to profl. jours. Recipient N.W. Sci. Assn. award, 1986; Sigma Xi grantee, 1986, NSF grantee, 1987-89; Hannah Aase fellow, 1986-88. Mem. AAAS, Am. Soc. Plant Taxonomists, Bot. Soc. Am., audubon Soc., Adventist Sci. Educators Soc., Nature Conservancy, Am. Philatelic Soc. Avocations: backpacking, stamp collecting, music, computers, writing poetry. Home: 46 Mobile Mnr Angwin CA 94508-9710 Office: Pacific Union College 1 Angwin Ave Angwin CA 94508-9797 E-mail: bness@puc.edu.

NESS, GARY GENE, accountant; b. Fargo, N.D., Feb. 7, 1948; s. Gene Stanley and Myrtle (Lattimore) N.; m. Janet Lynn, Jan. 30, 1971; children: Jennifer Lynn, Kam Elizabeth. BA in Acctg., Moorhead State U., 1973. CPA. Supr. corp. taxes Nat. Rental Systems, Inc., Mpls., 1973-76; sr. tax specialist Maine LaFrentz and Co., 1976-77; tax mgr. Mason Folkert and Co., Detroit Lakes, 1999—; ptnr. in charge of Fargo office, chmn. mgmt. com. Eide Bailly LLP, Fargo, 1979—; pres. Acctg. Ctrs. Am., Inc., 1991—. Author: (pamphlet) Tax Guide for North Dakota Legislature, 1985. Treas. N.D. State U. Bison Hockey Club, Inc., Fargo, 1988-95; treas. Ea. N.D. Synod Evang. Luth. Ch. Am., Fargo, 1988-96; chmn. found. dir. Moorhead State U. Devel. Coun. and Moorhead State U. Found., 1993—. With U.S. Army, 1969-71. Mem.: AICPA, Fargo Country Club, Minn. Soc. CPAs, N.D. Soc. CPAs, Gateway Lions. Avocations: running, sailing, racquetball. Office: Eide Bailly LLP 406 Main Ave Fargo ND 58108 Home: 4906 Meadow Creek Dr Fargo ND 58104-7116

NESS, JAMES JOSEPH, protective services official, consultant; b. Stevens Point, Wis., July 6, 1941; s. Lawrence Joseph and Eleanor Thresa (Hojnacki) Niespodziani; m. Sandra Jean Peters Feverston, Apr. 11, 1964 (div. Sept. 1985); 1 child, Peter James; m. Ellyn Katherine Buikema, Nov. 29, 1986; 1 child, Jamie (dec.). BA in Liberal Arts, Northeastern Ill. U., 1975; MS in Law Enforcement, So. Ill. U., 1979, PhD in Ednl. Admin., 1989. Patrol officer Wis. Dells Police, 1964-66, Drake U. Police, Des Moines, 1966-69; police lt. Triton Police Dept., River Grove, Ill., 1969-77; rschr. So. Ill. U., Carbondale, 1977-79, dir. police mgmt. study, 1979-81, prof. law enforcement, 1983-89; chief of police Villa Grove (Ill.) Police, 1981-83; dir. AJ programs Barton County C.C., Great Bend, Kans., 1989-95; dean of academics Haitian Nat. Police Tng. Ctr., Port-au-Prince, Haiti, 1995; internat. police task force UN, Bosnia, Yugoslavia, 1996-97; dean acad. Commonwealth Internat. U., Mesa, Ariz., 1997-99; chief Specialized Tng. Unit, OSCE, Kosovo, Yugoslavia, 1999-2000; cons., trainer Ness, Ness & Assocs., Mesa, 2000—. Author: Introduction to Law Enforcement, 1994; contr. articles to profl. jours. Staff sgt., USAF, 1959-64. Mem. Internat. Assn. Chiefs of Police, Central Kans. Ct. Appointed Spl. Advocates (pres. 1990-94), Ctrl. Kans. Cmty. Corrections (pres. 1993-95). Avocations: civil war reenactor, trail riding. Home and Office: 9241 E Grandview St Mesa AZ 85207

NESS, NORMAN FREDERICK, astrophysicist, educator, administrator; b. Springfield, Mass., Apr. 15, 1933; s. Herman Hugo and Eva (Carlson) N.; children: Elizabeth Ann, Stephen Andrew. BS, Mass. Inst. Tech., 1955, PhD, 1959. Space physicist, asst. prof. geophysics UCLA, 1959-61; NAS-NRC postdoctoral rsch. assoc. NASA, 1960-61; rsch. physicist in space scis. Goddard Space Flight Center, Greenbelt, Md., 1961-86, head extraterrestrial physics br., 1968-69, chief Lab. for Extraterrestrial Physics, 1969-86; prof. Bartol Rsch. Inst., U. Del., Newark, 1987—, pres. Bartol Rsch. Inst., 1987-2000; dir. NASA Space Grant Coll. Consortium, Del., 1991—. Lectr. math. U. Md., 1962-64, assoc. research prof., 1965-67 Contbr. articles prof. jours. Recipient Exceptional Sci. Achievement award NASA, 1966, 81, 86, Arthur S. Flemming award, 1968, Space Sci. award AIAA, 1971, Disting. Svc. medal NASA, 1986, Nat. Space Club Sci. award, 1993, Emil Wiechert medal German Geophys. Soc., 1993, Space Sci. award COSPAR, 1996. Fellow Am. Geophys. Union (John Adam Fleming award 1965); mem. NAS, Academia Nazionale dei Lincei, Royal Ocean Racing Club. Achievements include research, experimental studies of interplanetary and planetary magnetic fields by satellites and space probes. Home: 9 Wilkinson Dr Landenberg PA 19350-9359 Office: U Del Bartol Rsch Inst 215 Sharp Lab Newark DE 19716-4793 E-mail: nfness@bartol.udel.edu.

NESSAN, CRAIG LEE, minister, educator; b. Lansing, Mich., June 9, 1952; s. Lee A. and Lucy E. (Welford) N.; m. Cathy Sue Gee, Dec. 16, 1972; children: Benjamin, Nathaniel, Sarah, Andrew, Jessica, Mary Catherine. BA, Mich. State U., 1974; M. Div., Wartburg Theol. Sem., 1978; S.T.M., 1978; ThD., U. Munich, 1986. Ordained to ministry Am. Luth. Ch., 1978. Pastor Trinity Luth. Ch., Phila., 1978-82, St. Mark Luth. Ch., Cape Girardeau, Mo., 1987-94; univ. asst. U. Regensburg, Fed. Republic of Germany, 1982-86; prof. contextual theology Wartburg Theol. Sem. (E.L.C.A.), Dubuque, Iowa, 1994—, acad. dean, 1999—. Author: Orthopraxis or Heresy, 1989, Wer bist du Christus?, 1998, Beyond Maintenance to Mission, 1999, Who is Christ for Us?, 2002; contbr. articles to profl. jours. Mem. Bread for the World, Fellowship of Reconciliation, Luth., Peace Fellowship, Phi Beta Kappa. Office: 333 Wartburg Pl Dubuque IA 52003-7769 E-mail: cnessan@wartburgseminary.edu.

NESSEL, EDWARD HARRY, swimming coach; b. Roselle, N.J., 1945; s. Irving Meyer Nessel and Ruth Elliott; m. Eileen Robin Berstein, 1973; children: Lee Allyson, Jason Eric (dec.), Matthew Scott (dec.). BS in Chemistry, Rutgers U., 1967, degree in pharmacy chemistry, 1968, postgrad., 1971, Jersey City State, 1970; MS in Bacteriology, MPH, Wagner Coll., 1978. Registered pharmacist, Calif., N.J., Fla.; cert. U.S. Swimming Coach. Researcher, product developer Mennen Cos., Morrisplains, N.J., 1967; pharmacist supr. Pathmark Pharmacies, 1968-79; pharmacist, mgr. Roxy Drug Co., Inc., Irvington, 1979-90. Diet and nutrition cons. Fanwood Scotch Plaines YMCA, 1985-91, masters swim coach, 1984-91, swimming and racing cons., head age group coach, asst. sr. coach, 1989-91; head swim coach Jewish Cmty. Ctr. Metrowest, West Orange, 1991-2001; head masters swim coach Rutgers U., New Brunswick, N.J., 2000—; head swim coach Maccabi, 1990-91, 92, 93, 94, head coach swimming USA Nat. Team World Maccabi Games, Israel, 1997; coach N.J. Masters Swimming, 1985—; physiology and sports medicine cons. Nat. Health and Fitness; health and fitness chmn. N.J. Masters Swimming; nat. masters swimming coaches com. Nat. Com. for Sports Medicine; nat. libr. U.S. Masters Swimming; chair N.J. Masters Swimming Com.; pres. Jersey Masters Swimming Inc.; sports chair age group and masters swimming Garden State Games; summer coord. long-course 50 meter swim season Rayway YMCA, 1987-2001. Contbr. articles on swimming, self def. and physiology to profl. jours.; two patents adjustable hand-swim paddle. Athletic and swimming cons. N.J. Spl. Olympics, 1986; cons. Essex County Narcotic Strike Force; Garden State Games ofcl.; chair govs. coun. phys. fitness for swimming events Garden State Games, 1989-96. Recipient Presdl. Series award 1986; winner N.J. State Pentathlon champion Masters Swimming, 1986, 87, YMCA Masters Nat. Swim champion, 1988, 91, 95, 98, 2000, 01, Masters All-Am. Relay, 1998-99, Nat. Svc. award U.S. Masters Swimming, 1999; apptd. head swim coach U.S. Jr. Nat. Swim Team, World Maccabi Games, Israel, 1997; named Coach of Yr., U.S. Masters Swimming, Inc., 1998, mentor coach, 2000. Mem. NRA (disting. expert rating in pistol shooting), Am. Assn. Microbiologists, N.J. Pharm. Assn., N.J. Guild Pharmacists, Internat. Practical Shooters Confedn. (N.J. State Champion 1982, 83), Am. Swimming Coaches Assn. (master level, cert. level 5 coach), Am. Masters Aquatic Coaches Assn. (pres. 1999—), U.S. Swimming Coaches Assn. (cert. level 5, masters swimming coaches and sports medicine coms.), Master Swim Coaches Assn. Am., Rutgers Coll. Alumni Assn., Am. Med. Athletic Assn. (life, contbg. editor quar. 1993—), Masters Aquatic Coaches Assn. Am. (pres.), N.J. Masters Swimming Inc. (chmn. 1999—), Willow Grove Swim Club (bd. dirs. 1986-90), South River Pistol Club. Avocations: playing clarinet, saxophone and flute, museum quality ship builder. Home: 10 Irene Ct Edison NJ 08820-1024 E-mail: Ednessel@aol.com.

NESSETH, JEFFREY DAVID, music educator; b. Sparta, Wis., Jan. 21, 1971; s. David James and Cardyn Louise Nesseth. Bachelors of Music, No. Ill. U., Dekalb, IL, 1995. Bd classroom aide Clinton Rosette Mid. Sch., Dekalb, Ill., 1995—96; choral / theater educator Ctrl. H.S., Burlington, 1996—. Imea dist. #9 rep. Ill. Music Educators Assn., Ill., 2000—; rep. Student Assistance Team, Burlington, Ill., 2000—; play / musical dir. Crimson Masque, Burlington, Ill., 1996—. Recipient Kane County Educator of the Yr. Nominee, Regional Superintendent's Office, 2000. Mem.: Music Educators Nat. Conf., Am. Choral Directors Assn. Avocations: singing, outdoor activity. Office: Central High School 44W625 Plato Road Burlington IL 60109 Office Fax: 847-464-6039.

NESSIM, BARBARA, artist; b. Bronx, N.Y., Mar. 30, 1939; d. Garrett and Claire N.; m. Jules Demchick. BFA, Pratt Inst., 1960. Pres., owner Nessim & Assocs., N.Y.C., 1960-92; instr. Sch. Visual Arts, 1967-92, Fashion Inst. Tech., N.Y.C., 1974-92; chmn. illustration dept. Parsons Sch. Design, 1992—. Vis. asst. prof. Pratt Inst., Bklyn., 1977-84; dir. R & D (212) Studios, Inc., Long Island City, N.Y., 1982; cons. Time Life Video Info. Svcs. N.Y.C., 1982-84; art juror ann. student show Soc. Illustrators, N.Y.C., 1985; art juror graphic arts contest ABA Software, Inc., 1988, 4th Ann. N.Y. Digital Salon, N.Y. Siggraph 1996, 5th Ann. Digital Salon, 1997, , 6th Ann. Digital Salon, S.P.D. 33d Ann. Design Competition, 1998. Exhibited in one man shows including Grace Gallery, N.Y. Tech. Coll., 1989, Vertown Gallery, San Diego, 1991, Sangre de Cristo Arts Ctr., Peublo, Colo., 1991, Rempire Fine Art and Galley, Soho, N.Y., 1991, Ariz. State U., 1993, Colo. State U., 1992, Bogata, Colombia, 1995, Adams Landing Art Ctr., Ohio, 1994, Ariz. State U., 1993; exhibited in group shows including Smithsonian Inst., Washington, 1990, Rempire Gallery, Soho, 1990, Berkshire Art Mus., Bklyn., 1990, Kunstmuseum Dusseldorf, Germany, 1990, Rogue Gallery, Medford, Oreg., 1991, U. Western Ont.-McIntosh Gallery, London, 1991, Art Exch. Show, N.Y.C., 1997, Norman Rockwell Mus., 1998, and many pvt. and pub. collections. Bd. dirs. H.S. of Art and Design, N.Y.C., 1982; trustee Norman Rockwell Mus., 1999—; mem. bd. advisors N.Y. Found. of the Arts, 1999—. Artist-in-residence, Md. Inst. Coll. Art, Balt., 1989, Atlanta Coll. Art, 1990, Ctr. Creative Imaging, 1991, 92. Mem. Soc. Publ. Designers, Artist's Fellowship, Soc. Illustrators, Graphic Artist's Guild, YLEM, Art Dirs. Club. Studio: Nessim & Assoc 63 Greene St Ste 503 New York NY 10012-4372 E-mail: bnessim@interport.net., nessimb@newschool.edu.

NESSMITH, H(ERBERT) ALVA, dentist; b. Miami, Fla., Nov. 27, 1935; s. William Boyd and Florence Editha (Lowe) N.; m. Paula Ann Fox, Oct. 1, 1960 (div. 1984); children: Amy Susan, Lynn Margaret, Mark Alva. Student, U. Miami, Fla., 1953-56; DDS, Northwestern U., 1960. Gen. practice dentistry, Tequesta, Fla., 1963—; dental cons. Palm Beach-Martin County Med. Ctr., Jupiter, 1970—; rsch. assoc. Colgate Palmolive Co., 1997—. Calibrated caries examiner, cons. Colgate Dental Rsch., 1997—. Mem. advminstrv. bd. United Meth. Ch. Tequesta, Jupiter, 1970—, chmn., 1988-90; pres. Meth. Men, 1982; chmn. Coun. on Ministries, 1992-94, mem. staff parish rels. com. 1999—; pres. Jupiter Elem. PTO, 1972; clarinetist Symphonic Band of Palm Beaches, Fla. Concert Band; pianist and clarinetist United Meth. Ch.; active Village of Tequesta Hist. Commn., 1992-96, Jupiter (Fla.) Cmty. Resource Ctr., 1994—; mem. adminstrv. bd., v.p. Christian Dental Soc., 1994—, v.p., 1995—, Andean Rural Health Care, 1999—. Mem. ADA, North Palm Beach County Dental Soc., Fla. Dental Assn., Jupiter-Tequesta-Juno Beach C. of C. Lodges: Kiwanis (pres. Jupiter/Tequesta chpt. 1980-81). Democrat. Avocations: mission dentistry, Latin American studies, gardening, music, travel. Home: 196 River Dr Tequesta FL 33469-1934 Office: Inlet Profl Bldg 175 Tequesta Dr Jupiter FL 33469-2733

NESTER, WILLIAM RAYMOND, JR. retired academic administrator and educator; b. Cin., Feb. 19, 1928; s. William Raymond and Evelyn (Blettner) N.; m. Mary Jane Grossman; children: William Raymond, Mark Patrick, Brian Philip, Stephen Christopher. BS, U. Cin., 1950, EdM, 1953, EdD, 1965. Dir. student union U. Cin., 1952-53, asst. dean of men, 1953-60, dean of men, 1960-67, assoc. prof. edn., 1965-70, dean of students, 1967-69, vice provost student and univ. affairs, 1969-76, prof. edn., 1970-78, assoc. sr. v.p., assoc. provost, 1976-78; v.p. student svcs. Ohio State U., Columbus, 1978-83, prof. edn., 1978-83; pres. Kearney State Coll., Nebr., 1983-91, prof. edn., 1983-93; chancellor U. Nebr., Kearney, 1991-93, prof. emeritus, chancellor emeritus, 1993—; v.p. university relations devel. No. Ky. U., 1996-99. Pres. emeritus Mus. Nebr. Art, 1991—; cons. on higher edn., 1993—. Pres. Metro-Six Athletic Conf., 1975-76, Ctrl. States Intercollegiate Conf., 1986-89. Mem. Am. Assn. State Colls. and Univs. (bd. dirs.), Ctrl. States Intercollegiate Conf. (pres.), Nat. Assn. Student Pers. Adminstrs. (past regional v.p., mem. exec. com.), Am. Assn. Higher Edn., Ohio Assn. Student Pers. Adminstrs. (past pres.), Nat. Intrafrat. Conf. (pres. 1991-92), Frat. Scholarship Officers Assn. (past pres.), Mortar Bd., Pi Kappa Alpha Found. (nat. pres. 1978-80, past pres. ednl. found.), Omicron Delta Kappa, Phi Delta Kappa, Phi Alpha Theta, Phi Eta Sigma, Sigma Sigma. Episcopalian. Home: 7674 Coldstream Dr Cincinnati OH 45255-3932 E-mail: wrnchanem@cs.com.

NESTOR CASTELLANO, BRENDA DIANA, real estate company executive; b. Palm Beach, Fla., Nov. 10, 1955; d. John Joseph and Marion O'Connor Nestor; m. Robert Castellano. Student, U. Miami, Fla., 1978. Lic. real estate broker, Fla. Salesman Oscar E Dooley, Inc., Miami, Fla., 1978-80; prin. Brenda Nestor Assocs, Inc., Miami Beach, 1980—. Exec. v.p., bd. dirs. D.W.G. Corp., 1988-94, N.V.F. Corp., Salem Corp., 1988-97, Southeastern Pub. Svc., Graniteville Corp., 1988-94, Essex Ins., Chesapeake Ins.; exec. v.p., dir. Security Mgmt. Bd. dirs. Vizcayan Mus.; dir. Miami's Jackson Meml. Found. Named Ms. Charity, City of Miami, 1985, Lady Comdr., State of Fla. Mem. Miami Beach Bd. Realtors (bd. dirs. 1984—), Real Estate Securities and Exch. Com., Knights of Malta, Doubles Club (N.Y.C.), La Gorce Country Club, Fisher Island Club, Bath Club, Surf Club. Roman Catholic. Avocations: golf, tennis, boating, skiing. Home and Office: 39 Palm Ave Miami FL 33141-3263

NESTVOLD, ELWOOD OLAF, oil and gas industry consultant; b. Minot, N.D., Mar. 19, 1932; came to Netherlands 1979; s. Ole Enevold and Ragnhilda (Quanbeck) N.; m. Simone Chriqui, Dec. 6, 1955 (dec. Jan. 1990); children: Rebecca Lynn, Paul Stephen; m. Jeannette Garvin, Mar. 23, 1991; stepchildren: Michele Marie, Jennifer Ann, Michael Dennis. BA, Augsburg Coll., Mpls., 1952; postgrad., U. Wash., 1952-53; MS, U. Minn., 1959, PhD, 1962. Physics instr. U. Minn., Mpls., 1956-61; physicist and section leader Shell EP Rsch. Lab., Houston, 1962-68, mgr. geophysics rsch., 1968-71; mgr. geophysics Shell Western Div., Denver, Houston, 1971-74, Pecten Internat., Houston, 1974-77; chief geophysicst Woodside Petroleum, Perth, Australia, 1977-78; mgr. EP processing ctr. Shell EP Rsch. Lab., Rijswijk, Netherlands, 1979-81; chief geophysicst Shell Internat. Petroleum, The Hague, 1981-86, dir. geophysics and topography, 1986-92; chief geophysicist Geco-Prakla div. Schlumberger Ltd., Paris, 1992-94, v.p. mktg. Geco-Prakla div., 1993-94; sr. geophysics cons. Schlumberger Oilfield Svcs., Houston, 1994-95; exploration and prodn. sector exec. IBM Corp., 1995-97; prin. Nestvold Cons. Internat. Inc., 1997—. Cons. Lighting and Transients Rsch. Inst., Mpls., 1957-61; lectr. Australian Petroleum Exploration Assn, 1991, Internat. Assn. Geophysical Contractors, 1992, European Assn. Exploration Geophysicists, 1994 and others. Presenter keynote addresses; contbr. articles to profl. and trade jours. 1st lt. USAF, 1952-56. Recipient award of appreciation Internat. Assn. Geophys. Contractors, 1992. Mem. Am. Assn. Petroleum Geologists (Disting. lectr. 1993-94), European Assn. Petroleum Geoscientists, European Assn. Exploration Geophysicists, Soc. Exploration Geophysicists (OTC tech. program com. rep. 1995-2000, Spl. Commendation award 1998, Certificate of Appreciation 2000), N.Y. Acad. Scis., Soc. Petroleum Engrs. (Disting. lectr. 1994-95), Sigma Xi. Avocations: hiking, museums. Home and Office: 9059 Briar Forest Dr Houston TX 77024-7220 E-mail: nestvold@hal-pc.org.

NESWALD, BARBARA ANNE, advertising executive, writer, printmaker, artist; b. Jan. 14, 1935; d. Edward and Veronica (Presby) Lutz; m. Ronald Neswald, Nov. 15, 1952 (div. Jan. 1957); children: Kurt Thomas, Linda Neswald Hunt, Elizabeth Williams Gann. Student, Hunter Coll. Media dir. R.M. Klosterman Inc., L.A., 1960-64, copy writer, 1964-73; copy chief Broadway Dept. Stores, 1973-76; creative dir. Lucky Stores, Inc., Buena Park, Calif., 1976-79; v.p. advt. and comm. Top Value Enterprises Co., Dayton, Ohio, 1979-82; sales promotion dir. Strawbridge & Clothier Clover divsn., Phila., 1982-96. Mem. adv. bd. L.A. Trade Tech. Coll., 1976-77. Author: (poetry) Iconography, 1997, Dream Truth, 1997, Hermit of Time, 1998; etchings and paintings shown at numerous venues, Phila. and N.J., 1997—. Bd. dirs. Logan Square Neighborhood Assn., 1984-97, Pa. chpt. UNICEF, 1985-89, Am. Poetry Ctr., 1985-92, Women in Transition, Inc., 1986-92, Friends of the Children, 1993-94; bus. and profl. funding com. Acad. Vocal Arts; alumna Cmty. Leadership Seminars, Phila. Recipient various advt. awards, Benton Spruance award for disting. printmaking, 2000; N.Y. Regents scholar, 1952-53. Mem.: Am. Soc. Bot. Illustrators, Phila. Soc. Bot. Illustrators (bd. dirs. Phila. chpt. 1989—91), Internat. Mass Retailing Assn. (chair steering retail com. advt., mktg. and sales promotion 1988—93, named Retail Advertiser of Yr. 1990), Women in Comm., Am. Mktg. Assn.

NETERER, CHRISTOPHER DEAN, mural painter, manufacturing company official; b. Goshen, Ind., Feb. 19, 1974; s. Dean Lamar and Johnnie Louisa (Stevens) N. BA in English, Goshen Coll., 1996. Mural painter, Goshen, 1993—; plant supr. Bower Mfg. Inc. (divsn. of Goshen Rubber Inc.), 1996—. Author: Unknown Soldiers, 1996. Democrat. Mem. Brethren Ch. Avocations: reading, writing, drawing, collecting comic books, listening to music. Home: 1304 Prairie Ave Goshen IN 46526-2261 Office: Bower Mfg Inc 2515 Industrial Park Dr S Goshen IN 46526-5371

NETHERCUT, WILLIAM ROBERT, classicist, educator, baritone; b. Rockford, Ill., Jan. 11, 1936; s. Robert C. and Constance E. (Stanley) N.; m. Jane Lillian Swann, July 27, 1977; children: William Andrew, Amanda Jane, Robert Christopher, Jason Scott. AB magna cum laude, Harvard U., 1958; student, New Eng. Conservatory of Music, 1959-60; MA (Henry Drisler fellow, Pres.'s fellow), Columbia U., 1961, PhD, 1963. Instr., Greek and Latin Columbia U., 1961-66, asst. prof., 1966-67, Lawrence H. Chamberlain fellow,

1967; assoc. prof. classics U. Ga., Athens, 1967-72, prof., 1972-75; prof. classics U. Tex., Austin, 1975—, prof. epyptology, 1997—, undergrad. adv., 1977-82, 98-00; vis. fellow classics U. New Eng., Armidale, Australia, 1985; vis. prof. Brigham Young U., 1986; NEH vis. lectr. Inst. on Vergil Miami U., 1986; supr. for secondar cert. in Latin U. Tex. Coll. of Edn., 1996—. Announcer radio sta. WROK, Rockford, 1957-58; cons. on Greece and Rome Pathescope Ednl. Films, N.Y.C., 1965-66; appearance ednl. program TV sta. WGTV, Athens, 1970-72; lectr. 1st Internat. Conf. on Ovid, Constanta, Rumania, 1972, Internat. Soc. Homeric Studies, Athens, Greece, 1973, 74, 3d Internat. Congress S.E. European Studies, Bucharest, 1974, Conf. on Ancient Novel, Bangor, Wales, 1976 Soloist, New Eng. Opera Theatre, Boston, 1958-59; debut as Figaro in: Barber of Seville, 1958; soloist recital, Carnegie Hall, N.Y.C., 1966, Atlanta Opera Co., 1968, Austin Lyric Opera Theatre, 1987-88; translator: De Praestigiis Daemonum (Johan Weyer), 1964, Almanach Perpetuum Celestium Motuum (Rabbi Abraham Zacuto), 1973; editor: Tex. Classics in Action, 1976-82; asso. editor The World and Its Peoples, Italy, 1964, Latina et Graeca, 1974, Helios, Jour. Classical Assn. Southwestern U.S, 1977-81; author: A Course in the Derivation of English Words from Greek and Latin, 1981; contbr. articles on classical lit., antiquity to profl. jours. Coach community youth soccer and baseball, 1985—; chmn. com. for chaplaincy Breckenridge Hosp., Austin, Tex., 1985; trustee Austin Acad. Liberal Arts, 1991—; deacon 1st Bapt. Ch., Austin, chair bd. deacons, 2000—. Am. Coun. Learned Socs. grantee, 1972; recipient U. Tex. Alumni award for teaching excellence, 1982, U. Tex. Pres. award for teaching excellence, 1990, 98; named to U. Tex. Hall of Fame, 1992. Mem. Rocky Mountain Modern Lang. Assn. (sec. classics 1986, pres. classics 1987), Am. Philol. Assn. (campus adv. service 1975-78), Archaeol. Inst. Am. (pres. Athens chpt. 1972-74), Vergilian Soc. Am. (life mem., trustee 1974-79, 1st v.p. 1981-82, pres. 1983-84, dir. Egypt, Greece, Italy 1983), Classical Assn. Southwestern U.S. (pres. elect 1991-92), Classical Assn. Middle West and South (nat. com. for promotion of Latin 1978-81, pres. elect 1991-92), Tex. Classical Assn. (pres. 1979-81, hon. life mem. 1983—), Am. Classical League, Met. Club, Harvard Club, Univ. Club, Explorers of N.Y.C. Club, Masons, KT. Home: 1003 The High Rd Austin TX 78746-2224 *Dedication to work tunes the soul. In creative vision there is eager pride, exaltation. One is humbled in the face of rejection, then taught to behave nobly, choosing, in pain, not to quit the contest, but to serve the vision more effectively.*

NETHERCUTT, GEORGE RECTOR, JR. congressman, lawyer; b. Spokane, Wash., Oct. 7, 1944; s. George Rector and Nancy N.; m. Mary Beth Socha Nethercutt, Apr. 2., 1977; children: Meredith, Elliott. BA in English, Wash. State U., 1967; JD, Gonzaga U., 1971. Bar: D.C. 1972. Law clk. to Hon. Raymond Plummer U.S. Dist. Ct. Alaska, Anchorage, 1971; staff counsel to U.S. Senator Ted Stevens Washington, 1972; chief of staff to U.S. Senator Ted Stevens, 1972-76; pvt. practice Spokane, Wash., 1977-94; mem. 104th-107th Congresses from 5th Wash. dist., Washington, 1994—. Mem. house appropriations and sci. coms. Chmn. Spokane County Rep. Party, 1990-94, co-founder Vanessa Behan Crisis Nursery, pres. Spokane Juvenile Diabetes Found., 1993-94. Mem. Masons (lodge #34), Lions Club (Spokane Ctrl.), Sigma Nu. Republican. Presbyterian. Avocations: running, handball, squash. Office: US House Reps 223 Cannon HOB Washington DC 20515-0001

NETHERY, JOHN JAY, government official; b. Mpls., June 4, 1941; s. Ronald Jay and Mary Vesta (McVeety) N.; m. Sonya Elisabeth Magin, July 27, 1968; children: William Jay, Mary Elisabeth (dec.), Sarah Ann. BA, U. Denver, 1963, MPA, 1968. Mgmt. intern USAF Logistics Command, San Antonio, 1969-71, budget analyst Dayton, Ohio, 1971-72; chief, fiscal analysis USAF Hdqrs., Washington, 1973-80, chief, investment div., 1980-81, chief budget mgmt., 1981-85; dep. asst. sec. programs and budget Dept. of USAF, 1986-88, asst. to undersecretary, 1988-89, dep. asst. sec. fin. ops., 1989—. Mem. Air Force bd. for the correction of mil. records, Washington, 1980—. Recipient Gov.'s Scholastic award Gov. of Colo., 1968, Presdl. Rank award, 1988. Mem. Sr. Execs. Assn., Air Force Assn. Presbyterian. Avocations: history, military minatures. Home: 12349 Coleraine Ct Reston VA 20191-1627 Office: Dept USAF SAF/FM The Pentagon Washington DC 20330-1130 E-mail: Jnethery@aol.com.

NETI, SUDHAKAR, mechanical engineering educator; b. Bapatla, India, Sept. 27, 1947; came to U.S., 1968; naturalized, 1977. s. Chiranjeeva Rao and Meenakshi Neti; m. Kathy Gibson, Jan. 11, 1974. BME, Osmania U., 1968; MS, U. Ky., 1970, PhD, 1977. Research asst. U. Ky., 1968-77; asst. prof. mech. engring. Lehigh U., Bethlehem, Pa., 1978-83, assoc. prof., 1983-92, prof., 1992—. Vis. fellow Wolfson Coll., Oxford U., Eng.; vis. rsch. assoc. U.K. Atomic Energy Rsch. Establishment, Harwell, Eng.; fallout shelter analyst Fed. Emergency Mgmt. Adminstrn.; chair Mech. Engring. Thermal-Fluids Divsn., 1996—, dir. Lehigh U. Indsl. Assessment Ctr., 2000—, mem. Lehigh Valley Planning Commn., 1996, 97; bd. dirs. ANS, PANE; cons. to industry. Contbr. articles to profl. jours. Summer faculty fellow NASA-Am. Soc. Engring. Edn., 1978; grantee electric Power Research Inst., NSF, NRC. Mem. ASME, AAAS, Sigma Xi (chpt. treas. 1997-2002), Phi Beta Delta. Office: Lehigh U Mech Engring Dept 19 Memorial Dr W Bethlehem PA 18015-3006 E-mail: sn01@lehigh.edu.

NETTELBECK, DIRK MANFRED, biomedical scientist; b. Wuppertal, Germany, May 28, 1969; s. Manfred and Lieselotte Nettelbeck. MSc, Philipps U. of Marburg, Germany, 1996, PhD, 2000. Postdoctoral fellow Gene Therapy Ctr., U. Ala., Birmingham, 2000—. German Rsch. Assn. fellow, 2001-02. Mem. AAAS, Am. Soc. Gene Therapy, Am. Assn. Cancer Rsch., European Soc. Gene Therapy, Internat. Union of Biochemistry and Molecular Biology. Achievements include research in targeting gene therapy vectors for specific cancer treatment; development of new and optimized adenoviral gene transfer vectors and oncolytic adenoviruses; patentee in targeting gene therapy vectors for specific cancer treatment. Avocations: travel, hiking, reading. Office: Gene Therapy Ctr U Ala BHR II # 564 901 19th St S Birmingham AL 25294 Fax: 205 975-7949. E-mail: dirk.nettelbeck@ccc.uab.edu.

NETTELBECK, FRED ARTHUR, poet; b. Chgo., Nov. 9, 1950; s. Manfred Emil Nettelbeck and Thelma Anderson; m. Billy Joe Nettelbeck, July 17, 1999; children: James, Danny, Amandla. Student, El Camino Coll., 1969-71. Poet, 1966—. Editor This is Important mag., Beatty, Oreg., 1980—. Author numerous books including The Quick and The Dead, 1970, Spectator, 1977, Large Talk, 1983, Americruiser, 1983, The Kiss Off, 1984, Hands on a Mirror, 1987, Albert Ayler Disappeared, 1989, Ecosystems Collapsing, 1992, Hurting Music, 1998. Democrat. Avocations: angling, marksmanship, entheogenic plants. Home and Office: PO Box 69 Beatty OR 97621 E-mail: aftermathbooks@cs.com.

NETTELHORST, ROBIN PAUL, academic administrator, writer; b. Ohio, Mar. 14, 1957; s. Paul Merrit and Naomi Jean (Saylor) N.; m. Ruth Williamson, June 25, 1983; children: Vanessa Rachel, Nichole Antoinette, Sarah Brittany. BA, L.A. Bapt. Coll., 1979; MA, UCLA, 1983. Lectr. Christian Heritage Coll., El Cagon, Calif., 1984; lectr. old testament and bibl. langs. L.A. Bapt. Coll., 1984-87; novelist, 1987—; v.p. Quartz Hill (Calif.) Sch. Theology, 1992—. Webmaster Quartz Hill Sch. Theology, 1996—. Editor Quartz Hill Jour. Theology, 1994-99; author short stories; contbr. articles to mags.; host (internet and FM Radio broadcast) Beyond the Box, 1999—; author: What Dreamers Be These Rocks: Tableland, Book I, 2000, Dreams of Nothingness: Tableland, Book II, 2000, Awakens the Dreamer: Tableland, Book III, 2000, The Wrong Side of Morning, 2000, With a Rod of Iron, 2000, Antediluvian, 2000, Somewhere Obscurely, 2000, Does God Have a Long Nose? vol. I, 2001, Does God Have a Long Nose? vol. 2, 2001. Ordained deacon Quartz Hill Cmty. Ch., 1989—. Mem. Am. Acad. Religion, Soc. Bibl. Lit. Baptist. Avocations: camping, reading, philately, numismatics. Office: Quartz Hill Sch Theology 43543 51st St W Quartz Hill CA 93536-5608 E-mail: robin@theology.edu. *To hold the hand of God, to listen to his heart, to feel his pain, to taste his joys, to long for his happiness—that is to love God.*

NETTELS, ELSA, English language educator; b. Madison, Wis., May 25, 1931; d. Curtis Putnam and Elsie (Patterson) N. BA, Cornell U., 1953; MA, U. Wis., 1955, PhD, 1960. From instr. to asst. prof. English Mt. Holyoke Coll., South Hadley, Mass., 1959-67; from asst. prof. to prof. English Coll. William and Mary, Williamsburg, Va., 1967-97, prof. emeritus, 1997—. Author: James and Conrad, 1977 (South Atlantic Modern Lang. Assn. award 1975), Language, Race and Social Class in Howells' America, 1988, Language and Gender in American Fiction: Howells, James, Wharton, and Cather, 1997; contbr. articles to profl. jours. NEH fellow, 1984-85. Mem. Modern Lang. Assn., South Atlantic Modern Lang. Assn. (edit. bd. 1977-83), Henry James Soc. (edit. bd. 1983—), Am. Studies Assn. Office: Coll William and Mary Dept English Williamsburg VA 23187 E-mail: exnett@wm.edu.

NETTELS, GEORGE EDWARD, JR. mining executive; b. Pittsburg, Kans., Oct. 20, 1927; s. George Edward and Mathilde A. (Wulke) N.; m. Mary Joanne Myers, July 19, 1952; children: Christopher Bryan, Margaret Anne, Katherine Anne, Rebecca Jane. BSCE, U. Kans., Lawrence, 1950. With Black & Veatch Engrs., Kansas City, Mo., 1950-51, Spencer Chem. Co., Kansas City, 1951-55, Freeto Constrn. Co., Pittsburg, 1955-57; pres. Midwest Minerals, Inc., 1957—; chmn. bd. McNally Pittsburg Mfg. Corp., 1970-76, pres., CEO, 1976-87, ret., 1987. Past chmn. bd. Nat. Limestone Inst.; bd. dirs. Pitts. Indsl. Devel. Com. Mem. bd. advisors U. Kans. Endowment Assn.; mem. Kans. U. Chancellor's Club, Kans., Inc.; past pres. Bd. Edn. 250, Pittsburg; past chmn. bd. trustees Mt. Carmel Hosp.; past mem. Kans. Commn. Civil Rights; chmn. Kans. Republican Com., 1966-68; Kans. del. Rep. Nat. Conv., 1968, Kans. Bus. and Industry Com. for Re-election of Pres., 1972. With AUS, 1946-47. Recipient Disting. Svc. citation U. Kans., 1980, Disting. Engring. citation U. Kans., 1985; named Kansan of Yr. Natives Sons and Daus. Kans., 1986. Mem. ASCE, NAM (past. dir.), Kans. C. of C. and Industry (dir., chmn. 1983-84), Kans. Right to Work (dir.), Pittsburg C. of C. (past dir.), Kans. U. Alumni Assn. (pres. 1977), Kans. Leadership Com., Crestwood Country Club, Wolf Creek Golf Club (Olathe), Tau Beta Pi, Omicron Delta Kappa, Beta Theta Pi. Office: Midwest Minerals Inc 509 W Quincy St Pittsburg KS 66762-5689 E-mail: george@midwestminerals.com.

NETTERVILLE, GEORGE BRONSON, retired minister; b. McComb, Miss., Dec. 31, 1929; s. George Irving and Eula Hazel (Bronson) N.; m. Mary Elbridge Bogie, Mar. 15, 1957 (dec.). BA with honors, Southeastern La. U., 1951; BD, Lexington Theol. Sem., 1957, ThM, 1958; PhD, Sussex Coll., Eng., 1971. Ordained to ministry Christian Ch. (Disciples of Christ) 1952. Min. various chs., Miss., Ky., 1953-59; min. 1st Christian Ch., Clarksdale, Miss., 1959-64, Univ. Christian Ch., Starkville, 1964-68; assoc. regional min. Christian ch. in Tenn., Nashville, 1968-80, regional min., pres., 1980-90; ret., 1990; sr. min. emeritus East Ridge Christian Ch., Chattanoooga, 1992; min. 1st United Ch., Nashville, 1993—94, 2001—; regional min. Christian Ch. in Ala. and N.W. Fla., Birmingham, Ala., 1995-96; min. 1st Christian Ch., Hartselle, 1989-99, min. emeritus, 1999—; min. Ctrl. Christian Ch., Springfield, Tenn., 1999-2001. Bd. dirs. Christmount Christian Assembly, Black Mountain, N.C., 1975-90; mem. gen. bd. Christian Ch., Indpls., 1980-90, 95; pres. Tenn. Assn. Chs., Nashville, 1982-84; bd. dirs. Ch. Fin. Council, Indpls., 1986-90; treas. So. Christian Services, Macon, Ga., 1986-88, 98-99, v.p., 1999—. Instr. Am. Assn. Ret. Persons 55 Alive-Mature Driving, 1992—. With U.S. Army, 1951-53, Korea. Mem. Conf. Regional Mins., Am. Acad. Religion, Soc. Bibl. Lit., Am. Schs. Oriental Rsch., Coun. Mins. Christian Ch., Masons.

NETTL, BRUNO, anthropology and musicology educator; b. Prague, Czechoslovakia, Mar. 14, 1930; s. Paul and Gertrud (Hutter) N.; m. Wanda Maria White, Sept. 15, 1952; children: Rebecca, Gloria. AB, Ind. U., 1950, PhD, 1953; MA in L.S, U. Mich., 1960; LHD (hon.) , U. Chgo., 1993; LHD (hon.) , U. Ill., 1996, Carleton Coll., 2000, Kenyon Coll., 2002. Mem. faculty Wayne State U., Detroit, 1953-64, asst. prof., 1954-64, music librarian, 1958-64; mem. faculty U. Ill., Urbana, 1964—, prof. music and anthropology, 1967—, chmn. div. musicology, 1967-72, 75-77, 82-85. Vis. lectr., Fulbright grantee U. Kiel, Fed. Republic of Germany, 1956-58; cons. Ency. Britannica, 1969—, also on ethnomusicology to various univs.; vis. prof. Williams Coll., 1971, Wash. U., 1978, U. Louisville, 1983, U. Wash., 1985, 88, 89, 93, 95, 98, 2000, Fla. State U., 1988, Harvard U., 1989, U. Alta., 1991, Colo. Coll., 1992, Northwestern U., 1993, U. Minn., 1994, U. Chgo., 1996, Carleton Coll., 1996, U. So. Calif., 2002. Author: Theory and Method in Ethnomusicology, 1964, Music in Primitive Culture, 1956, Folk and Traditional Music of the Western Continents, 1965, 2d edit., 1973, Eight Urban Musical Cultures, 1978, The Study of Ethnomusicology, 1983, The Western Impact on World Music, 1985, The Radif of Persian Music, 1987, rev. edit., 1992, Blackfoot Musical Thought, 1989, Comparative Musicology and Anthropology of Music, 1991, Heartland Excursions, 1995, In the course of Performance, 1998, Encounters in Ethnomusicology, a Memoir, 2002; co-author Excursions in World Music, 1992, 3rd edit., 2000; editor Ethnomusicology, 1961-65, 98-2002, Yearbook of the International Folk Music Council, 1975-77; sr. adv. editor Garland Ency. of World Music; contbr. articles to profl. jours. Recipient Koizumi prize in ethnomusicology, Tokyo, 1994. Fellow Am. Acad. of Arts and Scis.; mem. Soc. Ethnomusicology (pres. 1969-71), Am., Internat. musicol. socs., Internat. Coun. for Traditional Music, Coll. Music Soc. Home: 1423 Cambridge Dr Champaign IL 61821-4958 Office: U Ill Sch Music Urbana IL 61801

NETTLES, BERT SHEFFIELD, lawyer; b. Monroeville, Ala., May 6, 1936; s. George Lee and Blanche (Sheffield) N.; m. Elizabeth Duquet, Sept. 16, 1967; children: Jane, Mary Katherine, Susan, Anne. BS, U. Ala., Tuscaloosa, 1958, JD, 1960. Bar: Ala. 1960. Asst. atty. gen. State of Ala., Montgomery, 1961-62; ptnr. Johnston, Johnston & Nettles, Mobile, Ala., 1962-69, Nettles & Cox, Mobile, 1969-81, Nettles, Barker, Janecky & Copeland, Mobile, 1981-89, Spain, Gillon, Grooms, Blan & Nettles, Birmingham, Ala., 1989-94, London & Yancey, Birmingham, 1995—. Contbr. articles to profl. jours. Mem. Ala. Ho. of Reps., 1969-74; bd. dirs. U. South Ala. Med. Sci. Found., Mobile, 1982-89, U. So. Ala. Health Svcs. Found., 1985-89; chancellor Episcopal Diocese of Cen. Gulf Coast, Mobile, 1983-88; asst. chancellor Episcopal Diocese of Ala., 2000—. 2d lt. inf. U.S. Army, 1960-61. Recipient Exceptional Performance citation Def. Rsch. Inst. and ATLA, 1987. Mem. ABA (chmn. standing com. on legis. 1978), Ala. Bar Assn. (chmn. young lawyers divsn. 1966-67, chair task force on appellate restructuring 1988-91), Am. Right of Way Assn. (sr.), Ala. Def. Lawyers Assn. (pres. 1986-87), Ala. Supreme Ct. (com. on appellate rules 2001—, pattern jury instructions/civil, 1990—). Republican. Avocations: reading, children. Home: 1416 Windsor Cir Birmingham AL 35213-3434 Office: London & Yancey 2001 Park Pl Birmingham AL 35203-2735

NETTLES, GAYLON JAMES, lawyer, social work consultant; b. Detroit, Jan. 16, 1947; s. Lemuel James and Florence Junell Nettles; m. Bungon Sookka, May 18, 1970; children: Linda, Catherine. BS, Campbell Coll., 1974; MS in Counseling, Am. Tech. U., Killeen, Tex., 1978; MSW, Our Lady of Lake Coll., San Antonio, 1981; JD, Ind. U., Indpls., 1997. Bar: Ind. 1998; lic. clin. social worker, Ind. Enlisted man U.S. Army, 1967, advanced through grades to capt.; assignments included Thailand, Korea, Germany; ret., 1989; social work cons. Ind. Dept. Edn., Indpls., 1989—, state attendance officer; pvt. practice, 1997—. Judge pro tem, 1999-2002. Capt. USAR, 1981-89. Mem. NASW, ATLA, Ind. State Bar Assn. (com. on civil rights of children 1998, chmn. lawyers assistance com.), Indpls. Bar Assn. Avocations: music, collecting art. Office: 197 N Shertridge Indianapolis IN 46219 E-mail: gnettles@justice.com.

NETTLES, JOHN BARNWELL, obstetrics and gynecology educator; b. Dover, N.C., May 19, 1922; s. Stephen A. and Estelle (Hendrix) N.; m. Eunice Anita Saugstad, Apr. 28, 1956; children: Eric, Robert, John Barnwell; m. 2d, Sandra Williams, Sept. 14, 1991; stepchildren: Steven Williams, Clayton Williams. BS, U. S.C., 1941; MD, Med. Coll. S.C., 1944. Diplomate: Am. Bd. Obstetrics and Gynecology. Intern Garfield Meml. Hosp., Washington, 1944-45; research fellow in pathology Med. Coll. Ga., Augusta, 1946-47; resident in ob-gyn. U. Ill. Rsch. and Ednl. Hosps., Chgo., 1947-51; instr. to asst. prof. ob-gyn. U. Ill. Coll. Medicine, 1951-57; asst. prof., assoc. prof., prof. ob-gyn. U. Ark. Med. Ctr., Little Rock, 1957-69; dir. grad. edn. Hillcrest Med. Ctr., Tulsa, 1969-73; prof. ob-gyn Coll. Medicine, U. Okla., Oklahoma City, 1969-78; chmn. dept. ob-gyn. U. Okla.-Tulsa Med. Coll., 1975-80, prof., 1980—, mem. coun. on residency edn. in ob-gyn., 1974-79. Dir. Tulsa Obstet. and Gynecol. Edn. Found., 1969-80; Coordinator med. edn. Nat. Def., Ark., 1961-69; mem. S.W. regional med. adv. com. Planned Parenthood Fedn. Am., 1974-78; mem. adv. com. Health Policy Agenda Am. People, 1982-85, rev. com. Accrediation Coun. for Continuing Med. Edn., 1987-92. Contbr. articles on uterine malignancy, kidney biopsy in pregnancy, perinatal morbidity and mortality, human sexuality sch. age pregnancy to profl. jours. Served as lt. (j.g.) M.C. USNR, 1945-46; as lt. 1953-54. Fellow Am. Coll. Obstetricians and Gynecologists (dist. sec.-treas. 1964-70, dist. chmn. exec. bd. 1970-73, v.p. 1977-78, Disting. Svc. award 1998), A.C.S. (bd. govs. 1969-71, program com. 1970-71, Surg. forum 1977-84, adv. com. gyn/ob 1985-92), Royal Soc. Health, Royal Soc. Medicine; mem. Ark. Obstet. and Gynecol. Soc. (exec. sec. 1959-69), Ctrl. Assn. Obstetrics and Gynecology (exec. com. 1966-69, pres. 1978-79), Internat. Soc. Advancement Humanistic Studies in Gynecology, Assn. Mil. Surgeons U.S., AMA (sect. coun. on obstetrics and gynecology 1975-96, chmn. 1982-96, del. from Am. Coll. Obstetricians and Gynecologists 1987—, Young at Heart award Young Physicians sect. 1994), Nurses Assn. Am. Coll. Obstetricians and Gynecologists (exec. bd. 1970-73, assoc. 1980-95), So. Med. Assn. (chmn. obstetrics 1973-74), Okla. Med. Soc., Tulsa County Med. Soc., Chgo. Med. Soc., Am. Assn. for Maternal and Infant Health, Assn. Am. Med. Colls., Am. Public Health Assn., Am. Assn. Sex Edn. Counselors and Therapists (S.W. regional bd. 1976-79), Soc. for Gynecol. Investigation, AAAS, Am. Soc. for Study Fertility and Sterility, Internat. Soc. Gen. Semantics, So. Gynecol. and Obstet. Soc. (pres. 1981-82), Am. Cancer Soc. (pres. Okla. div. 1979-83, St. George's medal 1991), Com. on In-Tng. Exam. in Obstetrics and Gynecology, Am. Coll. Nurse Midwives (governing bd. examiners 1979-83), Sigma Xi (pres. Tulsa chpt. 1992-93), Phi Rho Sigma. Lutheran. Office: U Okla Health Sci Ctr 1145 S Utica Ave Ste 600 Tulsa OK 74104-4070 *To live life fully, with faith and trust in God and his people, working with others to make our world a little better, and willing to fill the gaps wherever they are.*

NETZEL, PAUL ARTHUR, fund raising management executive, consultant; b. Tacoma, Sept. 11, 1941; s. Marden Arthur and Audrey Rose (Jones) N.; BS in Group Work Edn., George Williams Coll., 1963; m. Diane Viscount, Mar. 21, 1963; children: Paul M., Shari Ann. Program dir. S. Pasadena-San Marino (Calif.) YMCA, 1963-66; exec. dir. camp and youth programs Wenatchee (Wash.) YMCA, 1966-67; exec. dir. Culver-Palms Family YMCA, Culver City, Calif., 1967-73; v.p. met. fin. devel. YMCA Met. Los Angeles, 1973-78, exec. v.p. devel., 1979-85; pres. bd. dirs. YMCA Employees Credit Union, 1977-80; chmn. N.Am. Fellowship of YMCA Devel. Officers, 1980-83; adj. faculty U. So. Calif. Coll. Continuing Edn., 1983-86, Loyola Marymount U., L.A., 1986-90, Calif. State U., L.A., 1991-92, UCLA Extension, 1991—; chmn., CEO Netzel Assocs., Inc., 1985—; pvt. practice cons., fund raiser. Chmn. Culver-Palms YMCA, Culver City, 1991-93, chmn. 1989-91, bd. mgrs. 1985—; pres. bd. Culver City Guidance Clinic, 1971-74; mem. Culver City Bd. Edn., 1975-79, pres., 1977-78; mem. Culver City Edn. Found., 1982-91; bd. dirs. Los Angeles Psychiat. Svc., 1971-74, Goodwill Industries of So. Calif., 1993-97; mem. Culver City Council, 1980-88, vice-mayor, 1980-82, 84-85, mayor, 1982-83, 86-87; mem. Culver City Redevel. Agy., 1980-88, chmn., 1983-84, 87-88, vice chmn, 1985-86; bd. dirs. Los Angeles County Sanitation Dists., 1982-83, 85-87, Western Region United Way, 1986-93, vice chmn, 1991-92; chmn. bd. dirs. Calif. Youth Model Legislature, 1987-92; mem. World Affairs Coun., 1989-99; mem. adv. bd. Automobile Club of So. Calif., 1996-2002. Recipient Man of Yr. award Culver City C. of C., 1972. Mem. Nat. Soc. Fund Raising Execs. (nat. bd. dirs. 1989-91, vice chmn. 1994, v.p. bd. dirs. Greater L.A. chpt. 1986-88, pres. bd. dirs. 1989-90, Profl. of Yr. 1983), Calif. Club, Rotary (L.A. # 5, pres. 1992-93, treas. L.A. found. 1995-96), Rotary Internat. (gov. dist. 5280 1997-98), Mountain Gate Country. Address: Netzel Assocs Inc 9696 Culver Blvd Ste 204 Culver City CA 90232-2753

NETZER, DICK, economics educator; b. N.Y.C., May 14, 1928; s. Solomon and Sue (Dick) N.; m. Carol Risika, Dec. 30, 1945; children: Jenny, Katherine. BA, U. Wis., 1946; MA, M.P.A., Harvard U., 1948, PhD, 1952. Successively economist, sr. economist, asst. v.p. Fed. Res. Bank Chgo., 1948-60; econ. cons. Regional Plan Assn., N.Y.C., 1960-80; assoc. prof. N.Y. U., 1961-64, prof. econs., 1964—, dean Grad. Sch. Pub. Adminstrn., 1969-82, dir. Urban Research Center, 1981-86. Cons. in field, 1960— Author: Economics of the Property Tax, 1966, The Economics of Public Finance, 1974, The Subsidized Muse, 1978, Urban Politics New York Style, 1990; editor: N.Y. Affairs, 1973-88. Mem. Mayor N.Y.C. Fiscal Adv. com., 1969-73; treas. Colony-South Bklyn. Houses, 1968-73; mem. Mcpl. Securities Rulemaking Bd., 1978-81, vice chmn., 1980-81; bd. dirs. Mcpl. Assistance Corp., N.Y.C., 1975-97, Citizens Union Found., 1981—; bd. dirs., treas. Adolph and Esther Gottlieb Found., 1975—, v.p., 1979-88, pres. 1989—. Fellow Assn. Cultural Econs. Internat. (pres. 1993-94), Am. Inst. Cert. Planners; mem. Am. Econs. Assn., Regional Sci. Assn., Nat. Tax Assn.. Home: 41 Huckleberry Ln East Hampton NY 11937-2830 Office: 4 Washington Sq N New York NY 10003-6671 E-mail: dick.netzer@nyu.edu.

NETZHAMMER, EMILE CONRAD, III, academic administrator, department chairman; b. New Orleans, Mar. 24, 1959; s. Emile Conrad Jr. and Anna Belle (Basanez) N.; life ptnr. Lee Mitchell Faver. BA in Comm. magna cum laude, Loyola U., New Orleans, 1981; MS in Mass Comm., U. Utah, 1984, PhD in Comm., 1987. News asst. Sta. WWL-TV, CBS, New Orleans, 1978-79; engr., videographer So. Mobile Video, 1978-82; prodr., dir. media ctr. Jefferson Parish Sch. Bd., Marrero, 1982; grad. teaching asst. U. Utah, Salt Lake City, 1981-84, grad. teaching fellow, 1984-87; asst. prof. comm. SUNY, Buffalo, 1987-93, assoc. prof., dept. chmn., 1993-98, assoc. chmn. dept., 1991-93, prof., dean arts and humanities, 1999—. Conv. presenter in field. Contbr. articles to profl. jours. Bd. dirs. Arts Coun. Buffalo and Erie Counties. Univ. fellow Loyola U., 1979-80, Marriner S. Eccles rsch. fellow U. Utah, 1984, 85, 86; faculty devel. grantee Ctr. for Devel. Human Svcs., 1989, 90, 93, profl. devel. and quality of working life grantee, 1990. Mem. Assn. for Edn. in Journalism and Mass Comm., Nat. Comm. Assn. (mass comm. divsn. gay and lesbian caucus), Kappa Tau Alpha, Alpha Sigma Nu. Home: 12 Radcliffe Rd Buffalo NY 14214-1221 Office: Buffalo State Coll Arts and Humanities RH222 1300 Elmwood Ave Dept Comm Buffalo NY 14222-1004 E-mail: netzhaec@bscmail.buffalostate.edu.

NETZLOFF, MICHAEL LAWRENCE, pediatric educator, endocrinologist, geneticist; b. Madison, Wis., Sept. 11, 1942; s. Harold Harvey Netzloff and Garnet Lucille (Wilson) MacFarlane; m. Cheryl Lynne Crandall, July 20, 1963; children: Michelle Lynne, Rochelle Anne, Cherie Lucille. BS with high honors, Eckert Coll., 1964; MS, U. Fla., 1968, MD, 1969. Diplomate Am. Bd. Pediatrics, Am. Bd. Pediatric Endocrinology, Am. Bd. Med. Genetics. Rsch. fellow, rsch. trainee dept. of anat. scis. U. Fla. Coll. Medicine, Gainesville, 1965-69, intern and resident in pediat., 1969-71, clin. and rsch. fellow divsn. genetics, endocrinology and metabolism, dept. pediat., 1971-73, instr. in pediat., 1973-74, asst. prof. of pediat., 1974-79; assoc. prof. of pediat. and human devel. Mich. State U. Coll. of Human Medicine, East Lansing, 1979-85, dir. of pediatric endocrinology, pediat. and human devel., 1981-89, dir. divsn. of human genetics, genetic toxicology, endocrinology and oncology, pediat. and human devel., 1982-89, prof. dept. pediat. and human devel., 1985—, chmn. dept., 1987-91; vis. prof. dept. pediat. U. Mich., 1992-93, dir. divsn. clin. genetics, 1993—, acting dir. pediat. endocrinology, diabetes & metabolism, 1999—. Cons. Juvenile Diabetes Found., Lansing, 1981-95; mem. diabetes adv. coun. Mich. State Dept. Pub. Health and Chronic Disease Control, Lansing, 1980-90. Recipient Carithers award for Child Health and Human Dev., U. Fla. Coll. Medicine, 1969, Edward Bogen fellowship U. Fla. Coll. Med., 1972, Basil O'Connor rsch. grant Nat. Found. March of Dimes, 1973, pediatric residency teaching award, Grad. Med. Edn., Inc., Mich. State U.. Affiliated Residency program, 1982, 86. Fellow Am. Acad. Pediatrics; mem. Assn. Clin. Scis. Inst. (sci. com. 1979-96), Am. Diabetes Assn. (coun. on diabetes in youth 1979-96), Am. Pediatric Soc., Lawson-Wilkins Pediatric Endocrine Soc., Mich State Med. Soc., Midwest Soc. for Pediat. Rsch., Ingham County Med. Soc., Soc. for Pediatric Rsch., Teratology Soc., Sigma Xi. Democrat. Lutheran. Home: 4432 Greenwood Dr Okemos MI 48864-3044 Office: Mich State U Dept Pediatrics B240 Life Scis East Lansing MI 48824-1317 E-mail: netzlof1@msu.edu.

NETZLY, DWIGHT H. lawyer; b. Navarre, Ohio, May 7, 1919; s. Harry E. Netzly and Lillian N. Ramsey; m. Martha L. Emerick, Jan. 29, 1949; children: Duane, Dwight K., Doyle, Derek. BSBA, Kent State U., 1948; LLB, William McKinley Law Sch., 1952. Bar: Ohio 1952. Acct. H.C. Schwitzgebul, Canton, Ohio, 1948-52; pvt. practice law and acctg. Massillon, 1952—. Sgt. U.S. Army, 1941-45. Mem. Am. Assn. Atty. CPAs, Ohio State Bar Assn., Ohio Soc. CPAs, Am. Legion (state treas. 1993-94). Republican. Home: 6179 Pigeon Run Rd SW Navarre OH 44662-8738 Office: 1237 Lincoln Way E Massillon OH 44646-6954 E-mail: dhnetz@aol.com.

NEU, CARL HERBERT, JR. management consultant; b. Miami Beach, Fla., Sept. 4, 1937; s. Carl Herbert and Catherine Mary (Miller) N.; BS, MIT, 1959; MBA, Harvard U., 1961; m. Carmen Mercedes Smith, Feb. 8, 1964; children— Carl Bartley, David Conrad. Cert. profl. mgmt. cons. Indsl. liaison officer MIT, Cambridge, 1967-69; coord. forward planning Gates Rubber Co., Denver, 1969-71; pres., co-founder Dyna-Com Resources, Lakewood, Colo., 1971-77; pres., founder Neu & Co., Lakewood, 1977— ; mng. dir. Pro-Med Mgmt. Systems, Lakewood, 1981— ; lectr. Grad. Sch. Pub. Affairs, U. Colo. Denver, 1982-84. Mem. exec. coun. Episcopal Diocese Colo., 1974; mem. Lakewood City Coun., 1975-80, pres., 1976; chmn. Lakewood City Charter Commn., 1982, Lakewood Civic Found., Inc., 1986-91; pres. Lakewood on Parade, 1978, bd. dirs., 1978-80; pres. Classic Chorale, Denver, 1979, bd. dirs., 1978-83; pres. Lakewood Pub. Bldg. Authority, 1983—; bd. dirs. Metro State Coll. of Denver Found., 1990—, treas., 1994-97; bd. dirs. Kaiser Permanente Health Adv. Com., 1990—, chair, 1997. With U.S. Army, 1961-67. Decorated Bronze Star medal, Army Commendation medal; recipient Arthur Page award AT&T, 1979; Kettering Found. grantee, 1979-80. Mem. Internat. City Mgrs. Assn., Lakewood-So. Jefferson County C. of C. (bd. dirs. 1983-89, chmn. 1988, chmn. 1987-88), Jefferson County C. of C. (chmn. 1988). Republican. Episcopalian. Contbr. articles to profl. jours. Home: 8169 W Baker Ave Denver CO 80227-3129

NEU, CHARLENE ANN, labor union administrator; b. Ayer, Mass., Nov. 11, 1958; d. Robert and Joan W. Neu. BA, Trinity Coll., 1991; postgrad., Am. U. Legis. asst. Rep. Chester Atkins U.S. Ho. of Reps., Washington; legis. rep. Internat. Fedn. Profl. and Tech. Employees; legis. field instr. Nat. Assn. Letter Carriers; congl. liaison Dept. Commerce; dir. legis. field ops. Nat. Treas. Employees Union. Mem.: Pub. Rels. Soc. Am., Nat. Press Club. Democrat. Roman Catholic. Office: 901 E St NW Washington DC 20004-2037 E-mail: neuchar@aol.com.

NEU, CHARLES ERIC, historian, educator; b. Carroll, Iowa, Apr. 10, 1936; s. Arthur Nicholas and Martha Margaret (Frandsen) N.; m. Deborah Dunning, Sept. 2, 1961 (div. 1978); children: Hilary Adams, Douglas Bancroft.; m. Sabina deWerth Tuck, Mar. 27, 1999. BA, Northwestern U., 1958; PhD, Harvard U., 1964. Instr. history Rice U., 1963-64, asst. prof., 1964-67, asso. prof., 1968-70; asso. prof. history Brown U., Providence, 1970-76, prof., 1976—, chmn. dept. history, 1995—98, 1999—2002. Dir. summer seminar NEH, 1979, 1986—87, 1989, 92. Author: An Uncertain Friendship: Theodore Roosevelt and Japan, 1906-1909, 1967, The Troubled Encounter: The United States and Japan, 1975; co-editor: The Wilson Era: Essays in Honor of Arthur S. Link, 1991; editor: After Vietnam: Legacies of a Lost War, 2000. Recipient, Woodrow Wilson Found. fellowship, 1958—59, Am. Coun. Learned Socs. fellowship, 1975—76, Charles Warren Ctr. fellowship, 1971—72, Howard Found. fellowship, 1976—77, Guggenheim fellowship, 1981—82, NEH scholarship, 1968—69, guest scholarship, Woodrow Wilson Ctr., 1988. Mem. Am. Hist. Assn., Orgn. Am. Historians, Soc. Historians of Am. Fgn. Policy, Phi Beta Kappa. Clubs: Agawam Hunt (Providence). Democrat. Home: 346 Rochambeau Ave Providence RI 02906-3516 Office: Brown U Dept History Providence RI 02912-0001 E-mail: Charles_Neu@brown.edu.

NEU, PETER S. music educator; b. Bethlehem, Pa., Sept. 27, 1962; s. Charles Edwin Neu, Elisabeth (Uhler) Neu; m. Michaeline Anne Botti, Nov. 27, 1993; 1 child Nicholas Peter. BA in Music, B in Music Edn., Phila. U. Arts, 1985; postgrad., West Chester U., 1986—89, Temple U. Tchr. music, dir. bands North Penn Sch. Dist., Lansdale, Pa., 1985—. Musician, Phila., 1985—; profl. musician trumpet Valley Forge Music Fair, Devon, Pa., 1986—96; asst. dir., music arranger Upper Moreland H.S., Willow Grove, Pa., 1990—. Composer: Five 2-act musicals, 1998—. Mem. jazz com. Cavalcade of Bands Assn., 1999—. Recipient Citation of Excellence, Pa. Music Educators Assn., 2001. Mem.: NARAS, Music Educators Nat. Conf., Internat. Assn. Jazz Educators. Avocations: skiing, travel. Home: 107 Usher Ln North Wales PA 19454 Office: North Penn Sch Dist 1201 E Walnut St North Wales PA 19454

NEUBAUER, CHARLES FREDERICK, investigative reporter; b. Berkeley, Ill., Feb. 13, 1950; s. Fred Charles and Dolores Jeanne (Pries) N.; m. Sandra Carol Bergo, Oct. 4, 1975; 1 child, Michael Frederick. BSJ., Northwestern U., 1972, MSJ., 1973. Investigator Better Govt. Assn., Chgo., 1971-73; investigative reporter Chgo. Today, 1973-74, Chgo. Tribune, 1974-83, Chgo. Sun Times, 1983—2001; investigative reporter Washington bur. L.A. Times, 2001—. Recipient Pulitzer prize local reporting, 1976; Edward Scott Beck award for domestic reporting Chgo. Tribune, 1980 Office: 401 N Wabash Ave Chicago IL 60611-5642

NEUBAUER, DEAN VERAL, statistician; b. Battle Creek, Iowa, Oct. 8, 1955; s. Virgil Albert and Fanchon Kay Neubauer; m. Kimberly Jean Rennie, May 15, 1982; children: Jason Dean, Bryan Andrew, Laura Jean. BS in Stats., Iowa State U., 1981; MS in Applied and Math. Stats., Rochester Inst. Tech., 1988. Math. statistician U.S. Bur. of Census, Washington, 1979-80; statis. engr. II Corning (N.Y.) Glass Works, 1981-83, sr. statis. engr. I, 1983-86, sr. statis. engr. II, 1986-89; project engr. Corning Incorp., 1989-91, sr. project engr., 1991-95, engring. assoc., 1995—. Adj. prof. stats. Rochester (N.Y.) Inst. Tech., 1992—. Co-author: Process Quality Control, 3d edit. Fellow Royal Statis. Soc. (chartered statistician), Am. Soc. Quality (cert. quality engr., program chmn. 1983-84, sect. chmn. 1985-86, examining chmn. 1994-2001, mem. T.A.G. to ISO/TC-69 com. on statis methods 1993-2001, treas. chem. and proc. indsl. divsn. 2001—); mem. ASTM (mem. E-11 com. quality and stats. com. 1993—, mem.-at-large, chmn. E11.10 on sampling and data analysis 1999-, sec. e-11 com 2001—), Am. Statis. Assn. Achievements include research in applications of statistical mixture designs to exploring and discovering new glass and ceramic compositions, exact critical factors for simplified analysis of means; patents (2) for liquid crystal display glass composition. Office: Corning Incorp HP ME 02 A11B Corning NY 14831-0001 E-mail: neubauerdv@corning.com., dneubaue@stny.rr.com.

NEUBAUER, DEANE, academic administrator; PhD, Yale U. Interim chancellor U. Hawaii, interim v.p. acad. affairs; adj. prof. U. Hawaii, U. Sydney; dean coll. social sci. U. Hawaii, 1980—88. Served Western Assn Sch. & Coll., 1983—, mem. sr. commn., 1995—2001. Recipient Robert W. Clopton award, 1997. Office: U Hawaii-Manoa 2444 Dole St Honolulu HI 96822*

NEUBAUER, HUGO DUANE, JR. computer network engineer; b. Mankato, Minn., Oct. 31, 1959; s. Hugo Duane and Joan Marie (Habinger) N.; m. Susan A. May, July 7, 1990. Student, U. Miami, 1978-80; AA, U. Fla., 1981; AS, Santa Fe C.C., 1984; student, U. Fla., 1984—. Microsoft cert. profl. Aquaculture specialist, technician Aqualife Rsch. Inc., 1979-80; automotive dept. K-Mart, 1981-82; electronic technician Synergetics, Inc., 1983-84; water resources equipment technician Environ. Sci. and Engring., Inc., Gainesville, Fla., 1984-89, tech. ops. equipment mgr., 1990-91, geosciences divsn. equipment mgr., 1992-93, ctr. 3 equipment mgr., 1994-95; office mgr. Keck Instruments, Inc., Newberry, Fla., 1996-98; founder, owner, web master and designer Innovative Computer and Instrument Svcs., Alachua, 1996—; co-founder, co-owner Dances with Hooves Farm, 1997—; info. tech. systems adminstr. CPAmerica Internat. (formerly Acctg. Firms Associated Inc.), 1999—. Cons. in field. Mem. IEEE, IEEE Computer Soc., NRA, Internat. Webmasters Assn. Guild. Avocations: computer programming and Internet, horses, gun collecting and shooting, videography and photography (including underwater), scuba diving (cert. Profl. Assn. Diving Instrs.). Home and Office: 14108 NW 195th St Alachua FL 32615-8023 Fax: 253-276-5435. E-mail: hdneubauer@ieee.org., hdneubauer@cpamerica.org.

NEUBAUER, JOSEPH, food services company executive; b. Oct. 19, 1941; s. Max and Herta (Kahn) N.; children: Lawrence, Melissa. BS in Chem. Engring, Tufts U., 1963; MBA in Fin, U. Chgo., 1965. Asst. treas. Chase Manhattan Bank, 1965-68, asst. v.p., 1968-70, v.p., 1970-71; asst. treas. Pepsico Inc., Purchase, N.Y., 1971-72, treas., 1972-73, v.p., 1973-76; v.p. fin. and control Wilson Sporting Goods Co., River Grove, Ill., 1976-77, sr. v.p., gen. mgr. team sports div., 1977-79; exec. v.p. fin. and devel., chief fin. officer, dir. ARA Svcs., Inc., Phila., 1979-81; pres., chief operating officer, dir. ARA Services, Inc., 1981-83, pres., chief exec. officer, 1983-84; chmn., CEO ARA Svcs., Inc. (in 1994, name changed to Aramark Corp.), 1984—. Bd. dirs. 1st Fidelity Bancorp, Bell Atlantic, Federated Dept. Stores; trustee Penn Mut. Life Ins. Co. Chmn., CEO Phila. Orch. Assn., Mann Music Ctr., Inroads/Phila., Inc.; trustee Hahnemann U., Tufts U., Mus. Am. Jewish History, Greater Phila. First Corp., Com. for Econ. Devel., U. Chgo.; bd. govs. Joseph H. Lauder Inst. Mgmt. and Internat. Studies, U. Pa. Mem. Phila. C. of C., Union League Club, Locust Club, Phila. Club, Bus. Coun., Bus. Roundtable. Office: ARAMARK Corp 1101 Market St Philadelphia PA 19107*

NEUBAUER, PETER BELA, psychoanalyst; b. Krems, Austria, July 5, 1913; came to U.S., 1941, naturalized, 1946; s. Samuel and Rose (Blau) N.; m. Susan Rachlin, Nov. 25, 1953 (dec.); children— Joshua Rachlin, Alexander Lewis. MD, U. Berne, 1938. Intern Lawrence Meml. Hosp., New London, Conn., 1941, Beth-El Hosp., Bklyn., 1942; resident in psychiatry Bellevue Hosp., N.Y.C., 1943-45; dir. Child Devel. Ctr., Jewish Bd. Family and Children's Services, 1951-83; clin. prof. psychiatry Psychoanalytic Inst., N.Y. U., 1979—. Lectr. child psychoanalysis Psychoanalytic Inst. for Tng. and Research Columbia U., 1973 Author: Children in Collectives: Child Rearing Aims and Practices in Kibbutzim, 1965, Early Child Day Car, 1974, Process of Child Development, 1976, (with Alexander Neubauer) Nature's Thumbprint, 1990; contbg. author: Fathers and Their Families, 1989; mem. editorial bd. Psychoanalytic Study of the Child, 1978. Recipient Hulse award N.Y. Council Child Psychiatry, 1975, Heinz Hartmann award N.Y. Psychoanalytic Soc., 1981, Mary S. Sigourney award, 1994. Mem. Am. Psychoanalytic Assn., Am. Acad. Child Psychiatry, Assn. Child Psychoanalysis, Internat. Assn. Child and Adolescent Psychiatry, Assn. for Child Psychoanalysis (pres. 1974-76). Office: 33 E 70th St New York NY 10021-4941

NEUBAUER, RICHARD A. library science educator, consultant; b. Meadville, Pa., Oct. 9, 1933; s. Carl Gustave and Velma Winston (Watson) N.; m. Janice Ernest; children: David, Lynda, Karl, Jennifer; m. Carol Barton. BS, Clarion U., 1955; MLS, SUNY, Geneseo, 1966; attended, Kent St. U., 1966-68, Simmons Coll., 1970-72. Cert. profl. libr., sch. libr., tchr. Tchr. geography Franklin (Pa.) Sch. Dept., 1957-58, N. Bedford County Schs., Woodbury, Mass., 1958-60; tchr. history Hornell (N.Y.) Jr. High Sch., 1960-62, sch. libr., 1962-65; prof. libr. sci. Edinboro (Pa.) U., 1965-68, assoc. libr. Hamilton Libr., 1965-68; dir. sch. librs. Duxbury (Mass.) Sch. Dept., 1968-69; dir., cons. Pub. Libr., Lincoln, Mass., 1969-70; prof. libr. sci. Bridgewater (Mass.) State Coll., 1969-78, chair dept. libr. sci., 1978-80, prof. libr. sci., 1980-91, coord. libr. media program, 1991-95; prof. emeritus libr. sci., 1996—. Adj. prof. libr. sci. U. R.I., Kingston, 1975-88; cons. Tabor Acad., Marion, Mass., 1970-71, Abington (Mass.) Pub. Libr. Trustees, 1973-76, Duxbury Free Libr., 1968-72. Author: Planning the Elementary School Library, 1968; author, editor Exploring the U.S.-Northeast, 1994. Chmn. Mass. Dept. Edn. Cert., Quincy, 1989-90; resource cons. Project Contemporary Competitiveness, Bridgewater, Mass., 1973-83. 1st lt. USMC, 1955-57. Inst. grantee HEA of 1965 Edinboro U., 1968. Mem. NEA, Am. Libr. Assn., Intellectual Freedom Found., Mass. Assn. of Edn. Media, Mass. Sch. Libr. Media Assn., Mass. Tchrs. Assn. Democrat. Avocations: gardening, woodworking, reading. Home: 22 Pleasant St Carver MA 02330-1013

NEUBERG, HANS W. internist, educator; b. Hanover, Germany, Mar. 26, 1921; came to U.S., 1937, naturalized, 1943. s. George and Gertrude (Dux) N.; m. Birgit Aron, Apr. 8, 1949; children: Peter G., Gerald W. BS, Wagner Coll., 1941; MD, Columbia U., 1950. Diplomate Am. Bd. Internal Medicine. Intern Presbyn. Hosp., N.Y.C., 1950-53, asst. resident, NRC fellow in medicine, 1953-54, asst. attending physician, 1966-80, assoc. attending physician, 1980-91, attending physician, 1992—; pvt. practice, 1954-83. Instr. medicine Columbia U. Coll. Phys. and Surg., N.Y.C., 1954-63, assoc. in medicine, 1963-67, asst. prof. clin. medicine, 1967-80, assoc. clin. prof. medicine, 1980-91, clin. prof. medicine, 1992—, instnl. rev. bd. With AUS, 1943-46. Fellow ACP; mem. Alpha Omega Alpha. Mem. Am. Diabetes Assn. Home: 85 Erledon Rd Tenafly NJ 07670-2503 Office: 620 W 168th St New York NY 10032-3702 E-mail: NeubergH@aol.com.

NEUBERG, JOEL GARY, librarian; b. Chgo., June 11, 1945; s. LeRoy and Sari (Platt) N.; m. Pamela Susan Haas, June 12, 1970; 1 child, Jacob Michael. BA in English, U. Calif., Berkeley, 1967; MA in English and Creative Writing, San Francisco State U., 1972; AA in Forest Tech., Santa Rosa (Calif.) Jr. Coll., 1979; MLS, San Jose State U., 1997. Corres. Press Dem., Santa Rosa, 1972-74; park ranger Sonomoa County and Calif. State Parks, Bodega Bay, 1977-81; exec. dir. Holocaust Libr. & Rsch. Ctr., San Francisco, 1983-91; libr. El Molino High Sch., Forestville, 1991—2002, Sonoma Acad., Santa Rosa, 2002—. Instr. Santa Rosa Jr. Coll., 1973—. Author: Out of the Promised Land Into the Wilderness, 1972; (with Jacob Boas) Kristallnacht: The Night of Broken Glass, 1988; editor: Kobrin Memorial Book, 1992. Vol. U.S. Peace Corps., Niger, West Africa, 1967-69; field supr., asst. dir. Student Conservation Assn., Charlestown, N.H., 1972-88; bd. dirs. Gold Ridge Resource Conservation Dist., Sebastopol, Calif., 1978-81; bd. dirs. Holocaust Ctr. No. Calif., San Francisco, 1991—, treas. 1994. Recipient Beyond War award, 1987, Cert. of Appreciation, ALA, 1991; Weyerhaeuser Lumber Co. scholar, 1963-67; Calif. Coun. Humanities grantee, 1986. Mem. Alliance For Study of Holocaust (bd. dirs. 1983—, treas. 1984, pres. 1999-), Assn. of Holocaust Orgns. (bd. dirs. 1988-94). Mem. Reform Party. Jewish. Avocations: back-packing, cross-country skiing, swimming, photography, foreign languages. Office: Sonoma Acad 50 Mark West Springs Rd Santa Rosa CA 95403 E-mail: jneuberg@santarosa.edu.

NEUBERGER, EGON, economics educator; b. Zagreb, Croatia, Yugoslavia, Feb. 27, 1925; came to U.S., 1940; s. Paul and Ann (Freund) N.; m. Florence Perlmutter, Dec. 22, 1949; children: Leah Ruth, Marc Joseph. BA, Cornell U., 1947; MA, Harvard U., 1949, PhD, 1958. Econ. analyst State Dept., Washington, 1949-54; asst. prof. econ. Amherst (Mass.) Coll., 1957-60; economist RAND Corp., Santa Monica, Calif., 1960-67; prof. econ. SUNY, Stony Brook, 1967-81, leading prof. econs., 1982-97, emeritus, 1998—, dean social and behavioral scis., 1982-88, vice provost for undergraduate studies, 1989-90. Econ. officer Am. Embassy, Moscow, 1952-53; vis. prof. U. Mich., Ann Arbor, 1965-66, U. Konstanz, Germany, 1995, U. Tuebingen, Germany, 1996. Served with U.S. Army, 1943-46, ETO. Mem. Assn. Comparative Econ. Studies (mem. exec. com. 1974-76, pres. 1990-91), Am. Econ. Assn., Assn. Study of Grants Economy (adv. bd.), Omicron Delta Epsilon (pres. 1979-81, exec. bd., Disting. Ser. award 1981). Democrat. Jewish. Home: 5 Somerset Ct East Setauket NY 11733-1831 Office: SUNY Dept Econs Stony Brook NY 11794-0001

NEUBERGER, JEROME M. lawyer; b. N.Y.C., Apr. 7, 1928; s. Hyman D. and Anne (Musinger) N.; m. Gail L. Mandel, July 14, 1957 (wid. Jan. 1993); children: Ned, Andrew, Hallie. BA, Bklyn. Coll., 1949, JD, 1951, LLM, 1955. Bar: N.Y., Pa. Pvt. practice, N.Y.C., 1953—; counsel to pres. Boro Pres. of Staten Island, 1974-77; asst. dist. atty. S.I./N.Y.C., 1964-74. Past pres. North Shore Kiwanis, S.I., 1963, B'Nai Brith, S.I., 1984; trustee Temple Emanuel of S.I.; vice commodore Am. Legion, N.Y., 1980; v.p. N.Y. State Young Dems., 1958, 59. Cpl. U.S. Army, 1951-53. Democrat. Jewish. Avocation: tennis. Home: 14 Merrick Ave Staten Island NY 10301-4620

NEUEFEIND, WILHELM, economics educator, university administrator; b. Viersen, Germany, Mar. 6, 1939; came to U.S., 1977; m. Ingrid Leuchtenberg, Mar. 30, 1966; children: Nicole, Bettina. MBA, U. Cologne, Germany, 1962, MA in Math., 1969; PhD in Econs., U. Bonn, 1972. Lectr. econs. U. Bonn, 1973—77; prof. econ. Washington U., St. Louis, 1977; chmn. dept. econs. Wash. U., 1983—99. Contbr. articles to profl. jours. Mem. Econometric Soc., Am. Econ. Assn., Assn. for Advancement Econ. Theory. Office: Washington U Dept Econs 1 Brookings Dr # 1208 Saint Louis MO 63130-4899

NEUENSCHWANDER, DANIEL PAUL, music educator; b. Monroe, Wis., Dec. 18, 1958; s. Virgil Will and Clareoa Mae Neuenschwander; m. Mary Diane Krantz, July 20, 2002. MMA, U. Akron, Akron, OH, 1997; BS, U. Wisconsin-Maozson, Maozson, WI, 1993. Grad. tchg. asst. U. Akron, Akron, Ohio, 1993—97; h.s. band dir. Canfield Local Schools, Canfield, 1997—. Charter mem. Sch. of Music Alumni Com., Akron, Ohio, 2000—. Mem.: Ohio Music Educators Assn., Kappa Kappa Psi (hon.).

NEUENSCHWANDER, PIERRE FERNAND, medical educator; BS in Chemistry, 1985; PhD in Biochemistry & Molecular Biology, SUNY, Stony Brook, 1990. Lab. tchg. asst. SUNY, Stony Brook, 1985-86, lecture tchg. asst. in biochemistry, 1986, 87; assoc. rsch. scientist Cardiovascular Biology Rsch. Program Okla. Med. Rsch. Found., Oklahoma City, 1990-93, sr. rsch. scientist, 1993-94, found. rsch. scientist, 1994-95, asst. mem., 1995-2001; assoc. prof. biochemistry U. Tex. Health Ctr., Tyler, 2001—. Co-editor Trigger newsletter; rev. Jour. Biol. Chemistry; contbr. articles to profl. jours. Recipient Am. Heart Assn. Travel stipend, 1994, Internat. Soc. Haematology Travel award, 1992, Am. Soc. Hematology Travel award, 1989, 90. Mem. Am. Heart Assn. (coun. on thrombosis), Am. Chem Soc. (divsn. biol. chemistry), Internat. Soc. Thrombosis and Haemostasis, Sigma Xi, Alpha Chi Sigma. Office: Univ Tex Health Ctr Biomed Rsch Lab C7 11937 US Hwy 271 Tyler TX 75708 E-mail: Pierre.Neuenschwander@uthct.edu.

NEUER, PHILIP DAVID, lawyer, real estate consultant; b. Bklyn., May 31, 1946; s. Murray and Adele (Jacobs) N.; m. Rena Donna Levine, July 30, 1972 (div. 1987); children: Jeremy Evan, Linzy Michelle, Sari Faith. BBA, CCNY, 1968; postgrad., Boston U., 1968-69; JD, Seton Hall U., 1976. Bar: N.J. 1976, U.S. Dist. Ct. N.J. 1977, U.S. Supreme Ct. 1980. Asst. town atty. Town of West Orange (N.J.), 1976-77; assoc. Margolis and Bergstein, Verona, N.J., 1979-80; ptnr. Slavitt and Slavitt, West Orange, 1980-81; assoc. Mandelbaum and Targan, 1981-83; ptnr. Margolis Neuer, Verona, 1984-91; of counsel Slavitt Simon & Neuer, Parsippany, 1991-2000; exec. v.p., gen. counsel Safer Textiles Group, Safer Devel. and Mgmt. Co., Newark, 1993—; of counsel Lum, Danzis, Drasco, Positan & Kleinberg, LLC, Roseland, 2000—02. Mem. editl. bd. Internat. Jour. for Corp. Real Estate, 1998—. With USN, 1969-73. Named to, Internat. Corp. Real Estate Hall of Fame, 2002. Mem. ABA, N.J. State Bar Assn., Essex County Bar Assn., Internat. Assn. Corp. Real Estate Execs. (pres., bd. dirs., gen. counsel N.J. chpt., designated internat. assoc., Mem. of Yr. 1993, N.J. Corp. Real Exec. of Yr. 1993, internat. bd. dirs.), Inst. Corporate Real Estate (bd. dirs., pres. 1998-2002), Internat. Real Estate Inst. (registered internat. mem.), Urban Land Inst., Mensa. Office: 1875 McCarter Hwy Newark NJ 07104-4211 E-mail: pdneuer@aol.com.

NEUFELD, ELIZABETH FONDAL, biochemist, educator; b. Paris, Sept. 27, 1928; married, 1951. PhD, U. Calif., Berkeley, 1956; DHc (hon.) , U. Rene Descartes, Paris, 1978; DSc (hon.) , Russell Sage Coll., Troy, N.Y., 1981; DSc (hon.) , Hahnemann U. Sch. Medicine, 1984; DSc (hon.) , Queens Coll., 1996. Asst. research biochemist U. Calif., Berkeley, 1957—63; with Nat. Inst. Arthritis, Metabolism and Digestive Diseases, Bethesda, Md., 1963—84, research biochemist, 1963—73, chief sect. human biochem. genetics, 1973—79, chief genetics and biochem. br., 1979—84; prof., chmn. dept. biol. chemistry UCLA Sch. Medicine, 1984—. Named Passano Found. sr. laureate, 1982, Calif. Scientist of Yr., 1990; recipient Dickson prize, U. Pitts., 1974, Hillenbrand award, 1975, Gairdner Found. award, 1981, Albert Lasker Clin. Med. Rsch. award, 1982, William Allan award, 1982, Elliott Cresson medal, 1984, Wolf Found. prize, 1988, Christopher Columbus Discovery award for biomed. rsch., 1992, Nat. Medal of Sci., 1994. Fellow: Fellow AAAS; mem.: NAS, Am. Soc. Gene Therapy, Am. Soc. Clin. Investigation, Am. Soc. Cell Biology, Am. Soc. Biochemistry and Molecular Biology (pres. 1992—93), Am. Chem. Soc., Am. Soc. Human Genetics, Am. Philos. Soc., Am. Acad. Arts and Scis, Inst. Medicine of NAS. Office: UCLA Sch Medicine Dept Biol Chemistry Los Angeles CA 90095-1737 E-mail: eneufeld@mednet.ucla.edu.

NEUFELD, HOWARD B. foundation administrator; b. N.Y.C., Mar. 1, 1956; s. Helmuth and Nina N.; m. Joan Nina, Aug. 7, 1994; children: Elise Joy, Jennifer Michell. BA in Psychology, Queens Coll.; M, Yeshiva U., 1981. Pres. Young Israel of Coop., N.Y., 1987—; treas. BY Jewish Cmty. Coun., 1989—; pres. Coop. Jewish Cmty. Coun., 1990—; exec. dir. Chelsea Assisted Living, N.Y.C., 1998—; pres. Bronx (N.Y.) Jewish Home Care Agy., 1999—. Exec. v.p. Young Israel Ohab Zedek. Recipient cert. Nat. Coun. Sr. Citizens, 1992, proclamation City of N.Y., 1993, congressional record Ho. Reps., 1991. Mem. Gerontol. Soc. Am., Am. Assn. Counseling and Devel., Rotary. Jewish. Home: 12 Fanshaw Ave Yonkers NY 10705-3713 E-mail: wibey@aol.com.

NEUFELD, MICHAEL JOHN, curator, historian; b. Edmonton, Alta., Can., July 7, 1951; s. Henry John and Isabel Grace (Mitchell) N.; m. Sheila Faith Weiss, May 29, 1983 (div. Dec. 1992); m. Karen Lee Levenback, June 14, 1994. BA with 1st class honors, U. Calgary, Alta., 1974; MA, U. B.C., Vancouver, Can., 1976, Johns Hopkins U., 1980, PhD in History, 1984. Hist. rschr. Dept. Supply and Svcs., Ottawa, Ont., Can., summer 1973, 74; teaching asst. Johns Hopkins U., Balt., 1979-80; instr. Clarkson U., Potsdam, N.Y., 1983-84, from part-time instr. to part-time asst. prof., 1983-85; vis. asst. prof. SUNY, Oswego, 1985-86, Colgate U., Hamilton, N.Y., 1986-88; Verville fellow Nat. Air and Space Mus., Washington, 1988-89, Smithsonian postdoctoral fellow, 1989-90, curator aeronautics, 1990-99, curator space history, 1999—. Curator Air Power in WWII series, 1991-94; sr. lectr. Johns Hopkins U., 2001. Author: The Skilled Metalworkers of Nuremberg, 1989, The Rocket and the Reich, 1995; editor: Planet Dora, 1997; co-editor: The Bombing of Auschwitz, 2000; contbr. articles and book revs. to profl. jours. Recipient History Manuscript award AIAA, 1995, Dexter Prize SHOT, 1997, NSF Scholar's award History of Sci. and Tech. Program, 1989-90. Mem. German Studies Assn., Conf. Group on Ctrl. European History, Soc. Mil. History, Soc. for History Tech., History of Sci. Soc. Avocation: amateur astronomy. Office: Nat Air & Space Mus Divsn Space History Smithsonian Instn Washington DC 20560-0311 E-mail: mike.neufeld@nasm.si.edu.

NEUGEBAUER, MARCIA, physicist, administrator; b. N.Y.C., Sept. 27, 1932; d. Howard Graeme MacDonald and Frances (Townsend) Marshall; m. Gerry Neugebauer, Aug. 25, 1956; children: Carol, Lee. BS, Cornell U., 1954; MS, U. Ill., 1956; D of Physics (hon.), U. New Hampshire, 1998. Grad. asst. U. Ill., Urbana, 1954-56; vis. fellow Clare Hall Coll., Cambridge, Eng., 1975; sr. research scientist Jet Propulsion Lab. Calif. Inst. Tech., Pasadena, 1956-96, disting. vis. scientist Jet Propulsion Lab., 1996—; vis. prof. planetary sci. Calif. Inst. Tech., 1986-87. Mem. com. NASA, Washington, 1960-96, NAS, Washington, 1981-94; Regents lectr. UCLA, 1990-91; adj. sr. rsch. sci. Lunar & Planetary Lab., U. Ariz., 2002-. Contbr. numerous articles on physics to profl. jours. Named Calif. Woman Scientist of Yr. Calif., Mus. Sci. and Industry, 1967, to Women in Tech. Internat. Hall of Fame, 1997; recipient Exceptional Sci. Achievement medal NASA, 1970, Outstanding Leadership medal NASA, 1993, Disting. Svc. medal NASA, 1997, COSPAR award for space sci., 1998. Fellow Am. Geophys. Union (sec., pres. solar planetary relationships sect. 1979-84, editor-in-chief Rev. Geophysics 1988-92, pres.-elect 1992-94, pres. 1994-96) mem. governing bd. Amer. Inst. Physics, 1919-97. Democrat. Home: 7519 S Eliot Ln Tucson AZ 85747-9627 Office: U Ariz Lunar & Planetary Lab 1629 E Univ Blvd Tucson AZ 85721

NEUGEBAUER, VOLKER EDGAR, biomedical scientist, neuroscientist, physician; b. Werneck, Bavaria, Germany, June 11, 1964; came to U.S., 1995; s. Erich Karl and Rosemarie (Gehring) N.; 1 child, Benjamin David. MD, U. Würzburg, Germany, 1991, PhD equivalent, 1992. Med. lic., Germany. Intern U. Würzburg, 1991-92, postdoctoral fellow, 1992-95; rsch. scientist U. Tex. Med. Br., Galveston, 1995-97, asst. prof. dept. anatomy and neuroscis., 1998—2002, clin. asst. prof. dept. anesthesiology, 1996-99, mem. Marine Biomed. Inst., 1999—, assoc. prof., 2002—. Instr. Acad. Phys. Therapy, Schweinfurt, Germany, 1993-95; invited lectr. nationally and internationally. Author 10 book chpts. and revs.; contbr. over 30 rsch. articles to biomed. jours. including Jour. Neurosci., European Jour. Neurosci. Jour., Neurophysiology, Jour. Pharmacology and Exptl. Therapeutics. Recipient 1st award Lower Franconia Meml. Endowment for Sci., Würzburg, 1993, Rsch. Career Devel. award German Rsch. Coun., Bonn, 1995, Pain Rsch. award German Soc. for Study of Pain, Heidelberg, 1995. Mem. Internat. Assn. for Study of Pain, German Neurosci. Assn., Soc. for Neurosci., Sigma Xi. Roman Catholic. Achievements include development of animal (rat) model for acute arthritis; discovery of antinociceptive and analgesic potencies of drugs acting on spinal neurotransmitter and neuropeptide receptors; discovery of antiepileptogenic potency of metabotropic glutamate receptor agonists (presynaptic) as novel anticonvulsants; definition of the role of neuropeptides and glutamate receptors in cocaine sensitization; discovery of metabotropic glutamate receptors as novel targets for pain relief; identification of the amygdala as a key player in the emotional component of pain. Avocations: books, classical music, piano, travel, outdoors. Office: Marine Biomed Inst Dept Anatomy and Neuroscis U Tex Med Rsch Bldg 2.138 Galveston TX 77555-1069 E-mail: voneugeb@utmb.edu.

NEUGEBOREN, JAY, author; b. Bklyn., May 30, 1938; s. David and Anne (Nassofer) N.; m. Betsey Bendorf, June 7, 1964 (div. Oct. 1982); children: Miriam, Aaron, Eli. BA, Columbia U., 1959; MA, Ind. U., 1963. Preceptor Columbia U., N.Y.C., 1964-66; vis. prof. Stanford (Calif.) U., 1966-67; prof. SUNY, Old Westbury, 1969-71; prof., writer-in-residence U. Mass., Amherst, 1971-2001. Author: Big Man, 1966, Corky's Brother, 1969, Sam's Legacy,

1977, An Orphan's Tale, 1976, The Stolen Jew, 1981, Before My Life Began, 1985, Poli, 1989, Imagining Robert, 1997, Don't Worry About the Kids, 1997/Transforming Madness, Madness, 1999; editor: Story of Story Magazine, 1980. Pres. Cong. Bnai Israel, Northampton, Mass., 1978-80; exec. com. Fifth Ave. Peace Parade, N.Y.C., 1963-66; bd. dirs. Pathways to Housing, N.Y.C., Art in Edn., others. Recipient Ken award Nat. Alliance for Mentally Ill, 1999, Best Novel of Yr. award, 1981, 85; Guggenheim fellow, 1978, NEA fellow. Democrat. Jewish. Avocations: swimming, tennis, guitar, piano. Office: care Richard Parks Agy 138 E 16th St New York NY 10025-1945

NEUGROSCHEL, ARNOST, electrical engineering educator; b. Prešov, Czechoslovakia, June 18, 1942; came to U.S., 1973; s. Ludovit and Irene (Gottfried) Neugröschl; m. Susan M. Pertz, June 20, 1982. Diploma in engring., Slovak Tech. U., Bratislava, Czechoslovakia, 1965; PhD, Technion-Israel Inst. Tech., Haifa, 1973. Engr. Tesla, Inc., Pieštany, Czechoslovakia, 1966-67; instr. Technion-Israel Inst. Tech., 1969-73; postdoctoral rsch. assot. dept. elec. engring. U. Ill., Urbana, 1973-75; asst. prof. U. Fla., Gainesville, 1975-79, assoc. prof., 1979-83, prof., 1983—. On leave Interuniv. Microelectronic Ctr., Leuven, Belgium, 1986; mem. summer faculty IBM T.J. Watson Rsch. Ctr., Yorktown Heights, N.Y., 1982. Contbr. over 100 articles to profl. jours.; patentee in field. Fellow IEEE. Avocations: tennis, travel. Office: U Fla Dept Elec/Computer Engring Benton 325 Gainesville FL 32611

NEUHARTH, DANIEL J., II, psychotherapist; b. Sioux Falls, S.D., Nov. 10, 1953; s. Allen Harold and Loretta Faye (Helgeland) N. BA, Duke U., 1975; MS in Journalism, Northwestern U., 1978; MA, John F. Kennedy U., 1988; PhD in Clin. Psychology, Calif. Sch. Profl. Psychology, 1992. Lic. marriage, family and child counselor. Reporter USA Today, Washington, 1982-83; lectr. San Diego State U., 1983-84; talk show host KSDO-AM, San Diego, 1983-84; pres. Dialogues, San Francisco, 1987—; psychotherapist pvt. practice, 1992—. Vis. prof. U. Fla., Gainesville, 1980-81, U. Hawaii, Honolulu, 1981-82; adj. faculty U. San Francisco, 1989-92. Host, prodr. radio talk show Saturday Night People, 1984; Author: If You Had Controlling Parents, 1998, (with others) Confessions of an S.O.B., 1989. Office: PO Box 1015 Cloverdale CA 95425-1015

NEUHAUS, CHRISTIAN E.O.S. writer; b. Red Wing, Minn., Dec. 18, 1974; s. Ronald Leroy Neuhaus and Lucinda Carol Sonvidge. BS English , U. Wis., 1997. Proposal writer Epic Sys. Corp., Madison, Wis., 1998—. Playwright (plays) Phoust, 1997 (2nd place award the one minute playwright rosebud, 1997), Bearbating Will Not Be Seen Tonight, 1998. Active Luther Meml. Ch., 1997—. Lutheran. Avocations: creative writing, old time radio re creations, Karate. E-mail: cneuhaus@badger.alumni.wisc.edu.

NEUHAUS, PHILIP ROSS, investment banker; b. Houston, Dec. 25, 1919; s. Hugo Victor and Kate Padgitt (Rice) N.; m. Elizabeth Lacey Thompson, Oct. 31, 1942 (div. 1967); children: Philip Ross (dec.), Lacey Neuhaus Dorn, Elizabeth Neuhaus Armstrong, Joan Neuhaus Schaan; m. Barbara R. Haden, Aug. 14, 1968; 5 stepchildren. Grad., St. Mark's Sch., Southborough, Mass., 1938; BA, Yale, 1942. With Nat. City Bank of Cleve., 1946-47, McDonald & Co., Cleve., 1947; with Neuhaus & Co., 1947; chmn. Underwood, Neuhaus & Co., Inc., Houston, 1948-89; hon. chmn. Lovett Underwood Neuhaus & Webb, 1989-92; sr. v.p. Kemper Securities Inc., 1992-95, Everen Securities, Inc., Houston, 1995-99, Wachovia Securities Inc. (formerly First Union Securities, Inc.), Houston, 1999—. Chmn. bd. Voss-Woodway, Inc., 1994—. Mem. adv. bd. Tex. Children's Hosp., 1973-; assoc. Rice U.; advisory bd. Salvation Army, Houston, 1969-91. Served to capt., cav. AUS, 1942-45. Mem. Securities Industry Assn. Am. (bd. govs., chmn. Tex. dist. 1973, exec. com. 1975), Houston Soc. Financial Analysts (pres. 1959), Stock and Bond Club Houston (past pres.), Nat. Fedn. Financial Analysts (v.p. 1963, dir.) Clubs: Bayou, Houston Country, Houston, Eagle Lake Rod and Gun. Home: 407 Thamer Ln Houston TX 77024-6939 Office: Wachovia Securities Inc 909 Fannin Ste 2100 Houston TX 77010-1001

NEUHAUSER, DUNCAN VONBRIESEN, medical educator; b. Phila., June 20, 1939; s. Edward Blaine Duncan and Gernda (vonBriesen) Neuhauser; m. Elinor Toaz, Mar. 6, 1965; children: Steven, Ann. BA, Harvard U., 1961; MHA, U. Mich., 1963; MBA, U. Chgo., 1966, PhD, 1971. Research assoc. U. Chgo., 1965—70; asst. prof. Sch. Pub. Health, Harvard U., Boston, 1970—74, assoc. prof., 1974—79; cons. in medicine Mass. Gen. Hosp., Boston, 1975—80; assoc. dir. Health Systems Mgmt. Ctr. Case Western Res. U., Cleve., 1979—85, prof. epidemiology, biostats., orgnl. behavior, 1979—, prof. medicine, 1981—, prof. family medicine, 1990—, Charles Elton Blanchard prof. health mgmt., 1995—, co-dir. Health Systems Mgmt. Ctr., 1985—. Mem. biomedical staff Metrohealth Med. Ctr., 1981—; adj. mem. med. staff Cleve. Clinic Found., 1984—99; vis. prof. Vanderbilt U. Sch. Nursing, 1998—, Karolinska Med. Sch., Stockholm, 2002—. Author: numerous books, sci. papers; editor (jours.): Health Matrix, 1982—90, Med. Care, 1983—87. Vice chmn. bd. dirs. Vis. Nurse Assn. Greater Cleve., 1983—84, chmn., 1984—85; bd. dirs. New Eng. Grenfell Assn., Boston, 1972—, Braintree (Mass.) Hosp., 1975—86; trustee Internat. Grenfell Assn., St. Anthony, Canada, 1975—83, Blue Hill (Maine) Hosp., 1983—94, Hough Norwood Health Ctr., 1983—94, chmn., 1993—94; mem. vis. com. Columbia U. Sch. Nursing, 2000—. Recipient E.F. Meyers Trustee award, Cleve. Hosp. Assn., 1987, Hope award, Nat. Multiple Sclerosis Soc., 1992, Neuhauser lectr., Soc. Pediatric Radiology, 1982, Freedlander lectr., Ohio Permanente Med. Group, 1986, Univ. medal, Tohoku Med. U., Sendi, Japan, 2001; fellow Kellogg, 1963—65; scholar Keck Found., 1982—. Mem.: Soc. for Clin. Decision Making, Inst. Medicine NAS, Cleve. Skating Club, Kollegewidgwok Yacht Club (Blue Hill) (commodore 1991—93), St. Botolph Club (Boston), Beta Gamma Sigma. Home: 2655 N Park Blvd Cleveland Heights OH 44106-3622 Office: Case Western Reserve U Med Sch 10900 Euclid Ave Cleveland OH 44106-4945 Fax: 216-368-3970. E-mail: dvn@po.cwru.edu.

NEUHÄUSER, MARY HELEN, artist, writer, playwright; b. San Antonio, Feb. 17, 1943; d. Gotthelf Friedrich and Edna Earl (Walling) N.; m. Federico Andrea Canuto, Jan. 6, 1972 (div. June 1981. Student, Cath. U. Am., 1957-58; student of drama, Cath. U., 1957-58; student, Carnegie-Mellon U., 1962-64, Studio Nera Simi, Florence, Italy, 1964-65. Official portraits in FBI Bldg., Rayburn House Reps. Office Bldg., Trinity Coll., Sidwell Friends Sch., Washington; one-person shows include Potters House Gallery, Washington, AAUW, Bethesda, Md., Martha Washington Library, Alexandria, Va., Thirty-Year Retrospective, Friendship Gallery, Chevy Chase, 1989; exhibited at Nat. Mus. Fine Arts, Smithsonian Instn., Nat. Cathedral, Lincoln Meml., Corcoran Gallery of Art, Monroe House, Arena Stage, Nat. Dem. Club, Veerhoff Galleries, Washington, Curl Gallery, Washington, Capricorn Galleries, Bethesda, Md., Lorenz Gallery, Bethesda, Gallery Orlov, Alexandria, Seloff Gallery of Fine Art, Brownsville, Tex., Art and Design Gallery, Chantilly, Va., 1994-95; work reproduced in newspapers The Washington Post (1st place 1961, 64), The Washington Daily News, The Evening Star, Capitol Hill Roll Call; represented in numerous pvt. collections; contbr. op-ed articles to Washington Post, Bethesda Almanac, Am. Enterprise Inst. Mag.; author: (plays) The Great Sin, 1993, Awkwright and Murgatroyd, 1994, (screenplay) Crusade Against Hitler, 2000. Active St. Joseph's Home for Boys, Washington, 1965-66, Lincolnia (Va.) Day Care Ctr., 1966-67, Meriwether Home for Children, Washington, 1969-70, congl. campaign of Stewart Bainum; active supporter, writer Dem. Presdl. campaign, 1988, 92; vol. with Vietnam casualties, Nat. Naval Med. Ctr., Bethesda ARC, 1970-71; active supporter and writer on homeless, 1984—; health care advocate writer, U.S. Senate, 1986—; donator art works to Fed. City Shelter, Washington, Bapt. Home for Women and Children, Bethesda, Md.; vol. 3 shelters for homeless, Washington and Md., 1984—; health care advocate, writer U.S. Senate; writer campaign for Nat. Health Ins. Act, 1989—. Recipient Best-in-Show award, first profl. competition, 1961, 11 awards for abstracts, numerous others; ofcl. portraits in FBI Bldg., Rayburn Ho. of Rep. Office Bldg., Trinity Coll., Sidwell Friends Sch. Democrat. Avocation: fgn. langs. Home: 2107 Belvedere Blvd Apt 6 Silver Spring MD 20902-5677

NEUKIRCHEN, KAJO, industry executive; Dr.rer.pol, Bonn U., 1973. With Kabelwerke Reinshagen GmbH, Wuppertal, 1973-77, Felten & Guilleaume Carlswerke AG, Cologne, 1977-81, SKF Kugellagerfabriken GmbH, Schweinfurt, 1981-87, KHD Aktiengesellschaft, Cologne, 1987-91; CEO Hoesch AG, Dortmund, 1991-92, mg technologies ag, Frankfurt, Germany, 1993—. Office: mg technologies ag 60325 Frankfurt Germany E-mail: info@mg-technologies.com.

NEULS-BATES, CAROL, business executive, musicologist; b. Bklyn., Dec. 1, 1939; d. Frederick Carl and Edith (Tindall) Neuls; m. William Boulton Jr. Bates, Sept. 1, 1962; 1 child Julia Barstow Bates. BA cum laude, Wellesley Coll., 1961; PhD, Yale U., 1970; postgrad., NYU Sch. Bus. Adminstrn., 1979. Mng. editor RILM: Abstracts of Music Lit., Grad Ctr. CUNY, 1972—75; project dir., co-prin. investigator Women in Am. Music, 1976—79; adj. asst. prof. music Hunter Coll., CUNY, 1973—75; asst. to curator Lincoln Ctr. Libr. Performing Arts, 1975—76; asst. editor Coll. Music Symposium, 1975—78; asst. prof. music Bklyn. Coll., CUNY, 1978—82; account supr. John O'Donnell Co., N.Y.C., 1982—85, v.p., 1986—. Author: (books) Women in Music: An Anthology of Source Readings from the Middle Ages to the Present, 1982, 1995, Women in American Music: A Bibliography of Music and Literature, 1979; contbr. articles. Fellow, Yale U., 1962—67; grantee, Radcliffe Inst., 1968—70, Nat. Endowment for the Humanities, 1976—79, Ford Found., 1977—79, Nat. Fedn. Music Clubs, 1978. Mem.: NOW, Women in Devel., Nat. Soc. Fund Raising Execs., Nat. Women's Studies Assn., Inst. Rsch. in History, Sonneck Soc., Am. Musicol. Soc., Coll. Music Soc. (coun. 1975—78).

NEUMAIER, GERHARD JOHN, environment consulting company executive; b. Covington, Ky., July 27, 1937; s. John Edward and Elli Anna (Raudies) N.; m. Ellen Elaine Klepper, Oct. 24, 1959; children: Kevin Scott, Kirsten Lynn. BME, Gen. Motors Inst., 1960; MA in Biophysics, U. Buffalo, 1963. Research ecologist, project mgr. Cornell Aero. Lab., Buffalo, 1963-70; pres., chief exec., chmn. bd. Ecology and Environment Inc., 1970—. Recipient Theodore Roosevelt Citizen of Yr. award City of Buffalo, 1990, Paul McClennan Environ. Citizen of Yr. award Erie County, 2000. Mem. APHA, Air Pollution Control Assn., Internat. Assn. Gt. Lakes Research, Inst. Environ. Scis., Ecol. Soc. Am., Am. Inst. Biol. Scis., Urban Land Inst., Arctic Inst. N.Am., Nat. Parks and Conservation Assn., Defenders of Wildlife, Nat. Wildlife Fedn., Wilderness Soc., Am. Hort. Soc., Smithsonian Assocs., Nat. Audubon Soc. Home: 284 Mill Rd East Aurora NY 14052-2805 Office: Ecology & Environment Inc 368 Pleasant View Dr Lancaster NY 14086-1316

NEUMAIER, MARK ADAM, lawyer; b. Johnson AFB, Japan, Apr. 2, 1958; (parents Am. citizens); s. Richard Eugene and Alice Jane (Allen) N. BA in Psychology, U. Fla., 1979, JD with honors, 1984. Bar: Fla. 1984, U.S. Dist. Ct. (mid. dist.) Fla. 1984, U.S. Ct. Appeals (11th cir.) 1988. Assoc. E.F. Gerace, P.A., Tampa, Fla., 1984-85, Muga & Real, P.A., Tampa, 1985-88; pvt. practice, 1988—. Home: PO Box 16661 Tampa FL 33687-6661 Office: 5118 N 56th St Ste 100 Tampa FL 33610-5481 Fax: 813-620-0353.

NEUMAN, CHARLES P. electrical and computer engineering educator; b. Pitts., July 26, 1940; s. Daniel and Frances G. Neuman; m. Susan G. Neuman, Sept. 4, 1967 BS in Elec. Engring. with honors, Carnegie Inst. Tech., 1962; S.M., Harvard U., 1963, PhD in Applied Math., 1968. Tchg. fellow Harvard U., Cambridge, Mass., 1962-64, rsch. asst., 1964-67; mem. tech. staff Bell Telephone Labs., Whippany, N.J., 1967-69; asst. prof. elec. engring. Carnegie-Mellon U., Pitts., 1969-71, assoc. prof., 1971-78, prof. elec. engring., 1978-83, prof. elec. and computer engring., 1983—, undergrad. advisor, 1994—. Mem. editorial bd. Internat. Jour. Modelling and Simulation, Control and Computers; contbr. numerous articles to profl. jours. Mem. IEEE (sr., assoc. editor Trans. on Systems, Man and Cybernetics), Inst. Mgmt. Scis., AAAS, Instrument Soc. Am. (sr.), Soc. Harvard Engrs. and Scientists, Soc. Indsl. and Applied Math., Sigma Xi, Phi Kappa Phi, Tau Beta Pi, Eta Kappa Nu Office: Carnegie-Mellon U Dept Elec & Computer Engring Pittsburgh PA 15213 E-mail: cpn@gauss.ece.cmu.edu.

NEUMAN, LINDA KINNEY, state supreme court justice; b. Chgo., June 18, 1948; d. Harold S. and Mary E. Kinney; m. Henry G. Neuman; children: Emily, Lindsey. BA, U. Colo., 1970, JD, 1973; LLM, U. Va., 1998. Ptnr. Betty, Neuman, McMahon, Hellstrom & Bittner, 1973-79; v.p., trust officer Bettendorf Bank & Trust Co., 1979-80; dist. ct. judge, 1982-86; supreme ct. justice State of Iowa, 1986—. Mem. adj. faculty U. Iowa Grad. Sch. of Social Work, 1981; part-time jud. magistrate Scott County, 1980-82; mem. Supreme Ct. continuing legal edn. commn.; chair Iowa Supreme Ct. commn. planning 21st Century; mem. bd. counselors Drake Law Sch., time on appeal adv. com. Nat. Ctr. State Cts. Trustee St. Ambrose U. Recipient Regents scholarship, U. Colo. award for disting. svc. Fellow ABA (chair appellate judges conf., mem. appellate standards com., JAD exec. coun.); mem. Am. Judicature Soc., Iowa Bar Assn., Iowa Judges Assn., Scott County Bar Assn., Nat. Assn. Woman Judges (bd. dirs.), Dillon Am. Inn of Ct., U.S. Assn. Constl. Law. E-mail: linda.k.neuman@jb.state.ia.us.*

NEUMAN, MAXINE DARCY, cellist, educator; b. Phila., July 1, 1948; d. Marvin Memorial and Helga (Hennigson) N.; m. Reinhard Humburg, Oct. 16, 1987; children: Julia Vera Neuman, Mark Daniel Humburg. MusB, Manhattan Sch. Music, 1968, MusM, 1969. Cellist N.J. Symphony Orch., Newark, 1969-71; cellist with variety of groups including Mostly Mozart Festival, Am. Ballet Theatre, "Y" Chamber Symphony, Martha Graham, Dance Theatre of Harlem, Am. Composers Orch., N.Y.C., 1971-80; cellist Walden Trio (Vanguard Records), Leonia, N.J., 1972—, Contemporary Trio (Crest Records), N.Y.C., 1975-80; cellist U.S. and European tours Crescent Quartet (Leonarda Records) U.S. & European tours, 1979—; cellist St. Luke's Chamber Ensemble, 1981—; prof. music Bennington (Vt.) Coll., 1981-95, Williams Coll., Mass., 1994-95, 98—; mem. faculty Sch. for Strings, N.Y.C., 1996—; cellist Claremont Duo, Artek Records, Germany, 1998—, Bermont Trio Thorofon Records, Germany, 2002. Mem. faculty Chamber Music Conf. N.E. Bennington, 1982—, bd. dirs.; chmn. dept. music Bennington Coll., 1985-86, 90-91; touring solo cellist yearly to Europe, Mex., S.Am., Japan, 1980—, Montreux Jazz Festival, 1993, 94, N.Y. Film Festival, 1995; founder Bennington Cello Quartet; panelist Chamber Music Am. Nat. conv., 2000, Jazz at Lincoln Ctr., 2001. Rec. artist: Swiss,French, Australian, German, Italian, Ecuadorian, Colombian radio and TV, 1980—, rec. artist: also Columbia, Orion, CRI, Opus One, Albany Records. Sony/Virgin, Koch Internat., CBS World, Nonesuch, AMC, Biddulph Records, B.E. Records, Angel, Mus. Heritage, CBS Records, Deutsche Grammophon, PBS Gt. Performers , 1995—97; performer: Sat. Night Live, 1998, Metallica Concert, Madison Sq. Garden, 1999, Live from Lincoln Center, 2000. Bd. dirs. Bronx (N.Y.) Opera Co., 1972-85. Recipient Double Award of Merit Nat. Fedn. Music Clubs, 1976, award Internat. Congress on Women in Music, UN, 1990, prize Am. Soc. for Jewish Music, 1998; Ford Found. grantee, 1971-72. Mem. Am. Fedn. Musicians, Chamber Music Conf. of the East (bd. dirs.), Kulturforum (artistic advisor). Avocations: photography, traveling, cooking, hiking. Home: 200 Claremont Ave Apt 52 New York NY 10027-4070 Office: Box 42 Park St North Bennington VT 05257 E-mail: cellomax@aol.com.

NEUMAN, MICHAEL ROBERT, biomedical engineer; b. Milw., Nov. 25, 1938; s. Robert B. and Jane G. N.; m. Judith H. Borton, Aug. 2, 1973; 1 child, Elizabeth Ann. BSEE, Case Inst. Tech., 1961, PhD, 1966; MD, Case Western Res. U., 1974. Asst. prof., then assoc. prof. Case Western Res. U., Cleve., 1966-74, assoc. prof. reproductive biology, 1974—; adj. prof. biomed. engring. Duke U. Guest prof. U. Zurich (Switzerland) Women's Hosp., 1980; Lilly vis. prof. Duke-N.C. ERC, Durham, 1990; adj. prof. biomed. engring. Duke U., 1995—; adv. bd. Wash. Regional Primate Ctr., Seattle, 1989—; mem. device adv. panel FDA, Rockville, Md., 1992—; presenter at profl. confs. Editor in chief IEEE Trans. Biomed. Engring., 1989-95; contbg. author: Biomedical Instrumentation, 1978, 2d edit., 1992; contbr. articles to sci. publs. U.S. Steel Found. fellow, 1966; recipient Career Devel. award NIH, 1970-74; grantee NIH, NSF. Fellow Am. Inst. Med. and Biol. Engrs.; mem. IEEE (sr., v.p. engring. in medicine and biology soc. 1987-88), Internat. Soc. Biotelemetry (pres. 1984-88), Biomed. Engring. Soc. Achievements include development of biotelemetry for fetal monitoring, infant monitoring devices, biomedical sensors for infant monitoring and for feedback control of paralyzed hand, implantable electrochemical pH sensors; 2 patents in field. Office: Case Western Res U MetroHealth Med Ctr 2500 MetroHealth Dr Cleveland OH 44109-1900

NEUMAN, NANCY ADAMS MOSSHAMMER, civic leader; b. Greenwich, Conn., July 24, 1936; d. Alden Smith and Margaret (Mevis) Mosshammer; m. Mark Donald Neuman, Dec. 23, 1958; children: Deborah Adams, Jennifer Fuller, Jeffrey Abbott. BA, Pomona Coll., 1957; LLD, 1983; MA, U. Calif., Berkeley, 1961; LHD, Westminster Coll., 1987. Disting. lectr. Am. govt. Pomona Coll., 1990; disting. vis. prof. Washington and Jefferson Coll., 1991, 94, Bucknell U., 1992. Editor A Voice of Our Own: Leading American Women Celebrate the Right to Vote, 1996, True to Ourselves: A Celebration of Women Making a Difference, 1998. Pres. Lewisburg (Pa.) LWV, 1967-70; bd. dirs. LWV Pa., 1970-77, pres., 1975-77; bd. dirs. LWV U.S., 1977-90, 2nd v.p., 1978-80, 1st v.p., 1982-84, pres., 1986-90; mem. Pa. Gov.'s Commn. on Mortgage and Interest Rates, 1973, Pa. Commonwealth Child Devel. com., 1974-75, Nat. Commn. on Pub. Svc., 1987-90; bd. dirs. Housing Assistance Coun., Inc., Washington, 1974—, pres., 1978-80; bd. dirs. Nat. Coun. Agrl. Life and Labor, 1974-79, Nat. Rural Housing Coalition, 1975-95, Pa. Housing Fin. Agy., 1975-80, Jud. Inquiry and Rev. Bd. Pa., 1989-93; disciplinary bd. Supreme Ct. Pa., 1980-85; mem. Pa. Gov.'s Task Force on Voter Registration, 1975-76, Nat. Task Force for Implementation Equal Rights Amendment, 1975-77; mem. adv. com. Pa. Gov.'s Interdepartmental Coun. on Seasonal Farmworkers, 1975-77; mem. Appellate Ct. Nominating Commn. Pa., 1976-79; mem. Fed. Jud. Nominating Commn. Pa., 1977-85, chmn., 1978-81, 82-83; mem. Pa. Gov.'s Study Commn. on Pub. Employee rels., 1976-78; del. Internat. Women's Yr. Conf., 1977; bd. dirs. ERAmerica, Inc., 1st v.p., 1977-79, Nat. Low Income Housing Coalition, 1979-82; Rural Am., 1979-81, Fed. Home Loan Bank Pitts., 1979-82; mem. Nat. adv. Com. Women, 1978-79; mem. nat. adv. com. Pa. Neighborhood Preservation Support Sys., 1976-77; bd. dirs. Pa. Women's Campaign fund, 1984-86, 92—, pres., 1992-96, 2001-02, Rural coalition, Washington, 1984-90, Com. on the Constitutional Sys., 1988-90, Am. Judicature Soc., 1989-93; exec. com. Leadership Conf. Civil Rights, 1986-90; bd. dirs. Pennsylvanians for Modern Cts., 1986—; trustee Citizen's Rsch. Found., 1989-99; mem. mid. dist. Pa. adv. com. judicial and U.S. atty. nominations, 1993-94; bd. dirs. Pathmakers, 1993-97, pres. 1993-95; bd. dirs. Capital Concerts, 1997—. Virginia Travis lectureship Bucknell U., 1982; Woodrow Wilson vis. fellow, 1993-2000; recipient Disting. Alumna Award MacDuffie Sch. Girls, 1979, Liberty Bell award Pa. Bar Assn., 1983, Barrows Alumni Award Pomona Coll., 1987, Thomas P. O'Neill Jr. award for Exemplary Pub. Svc., 1989; named Disting. Daughter of Pa., 1987. Mem. ABA (com. election law and voter participation 1986-90, accreditation com. 1990-96, coun. sect. of legal edn. 1997—, sec. 2000—), Cosmos Club. Home: 190 Verna Rd Lewisburg PA 17837-8747

NEUMAN, PAULA ANNE YOUNG, cultural organization administrator; b. Tiffin, Ohio, Sept. 15, 1960; d. Paul Everett and Mary Virginia (Brosious) Young; children: Nichole Adele, Jessica Theresa, Samantha Rebekah, Mary Elizabeth; m. Russell M. Neuman, Aug. 19, 2000. BS in Psychology, Heidelberg Coll., 1982; MA in Polit. Sci., Bowling Green (Ohio) State U., 1987; MA in Adult Edn., Ball State U., 1996; EdD, Nova Southeastern U., Ft. Lauderdale, Fla., 2000; cert. in fundraising mgmt., Ind. U., 1997. Cert. fundraising exec. Child therapist Sandusky (Ohio) Youth Referral Svc., 1982-83; parole officer State of Ohio, Columbus, 1983-86; dep. dir. Seneca, Sandusky and Wyandot Commn. Mental Health Bd., Tiffin, 1987-88; program dir. WSOS Cmty. Action Commn., Fremont, Ohio, 1988-90; exec. dir. Tiffin Area C. of C./Seneca Indsl. & Econ. Devel. Corp., Tiffin, 1988-90; pres. Chapman Cmty. Devel. Cons., 1990-2000; dir. devel. St. Francis Health Care Ctr., Green Springs, Ohio, 1993-94, St. Francis Coll., Fort Wayne, Ind., 1994-95; dir. of fund devel. Girl Scout Coun., Inc., 1995-97; exec. dir., CEO McMillen Ctr. for Health Edn., 1997-2000; pres., owner edn. and devel. cons., 2000—. Adj. prof. econs. Tiffin U., 1987—94; adj. prof. non-profit mgmt. Ivy Tech. State Coll., 1999—; mem. ednl. adv. bd. Vanguard/Sentinel Vocat Sch., Fremont, 1989—90; chmn. Tiffin Fair Housing Bd., 1985—90; bd. dirs. Ohio Indsl. Tng. Program, Sandusky, 1988—90, Pvt. Industry Coun., Fremont, Seneca County Revolving Loan Fund, Tiffin; chair adv. bd. WSOS; cons. in field. Candidate Seneca County Commr., 1992; mem. Grad. Ft. Wayne Leadership Works, 1994; bd. dirs. Purdue U. Ext., 2000-02. Mem. Nat. Soc. Fundraising Execs. (bd. dirs. Ind. chpt. 1999-2002), Bus. and Profl. Women's Assn. (Young Career Woman of Yr. 1987, 89), Rotary (Ft. Wayne). Avocations: philanthropic studies. Home: 6217 Spy Glass Run Fort Wayne IN 46804 E-mail: neumans2000@yahoo.com.

NEUMAN, ROBERT HAROLD, communication executive; b. Phila. s. Otto and Bessie Neuman; m. Joan Elizabeth Huhn, June 3, 1978 (dec. Feb. 1996). Cert. sys. application, U. So. Calif., Arlington, Va., 1981; BA, U. Md., 1972; MLA, Johns Hopkins U., 1983, cert. advanced study, 1987. Photographer Photo Corp. Am., Rockville, Md., 1973; retail mgr. various firms, 1974-77; acct. rep. Kastle Security Inc., Arlington, Va., 1977-80; sr. data technician Mantech Internat. Corp., Rockville, 1981-82; computer programmer Harry Diamond Lab., Adelphi, Md., 1982-86; program analyst Lab. Command, 1986-88; analyst internat. programs Army Rsch. Lab., 1988-93; owner, mgr. Neu-Enterprise Prodns., Potomac, Md., 1993—. Prodr., program dir. Laurel (Md.) Cable Network, 1990-98, bd. dirs. Vol. Hospice Caring, Inc., Gaithersburg, Md., 2000—; bd. dirs. Vistas Condominium, Laurel, Md., 1993-95. With U.S. Army, 1960-63. Mem. Alliance for Cmty. Media, Internat. TV Assn. Avocations: videography, travel. E-mail: robh4life@aol.com.

NEUMAN, ROBERT HENRY, lawyer; b. N.Y.C., Oct. 14, 1936; s. Sydney A. and Ethel (Pekelner) N.; m. Emily Mann, Dec. 30, 1960 (div. 1975); children: David Marshall, Anthony Howard, Amanda Sarah; m. Joyce Thompson, May 5, 1975; 1 child, Nicole Sydney. AB magna cum laude, Harvard U., 1958, JD, 1961. Bar: N.Y. 1962, D.C. 1962. Ford Found. fellow, West Africa, 1961-62; assoc. Meyers & Batzell, Washington, 1962-64; asst. legal adviser U.S. Dept. of State, 1964-70; ptnr. Arent, Fox, Kintner, Plotkin & Kahn, 1970-93, Baker & Hostetler, Washington, 1993-98. Adj. prof. The George Washington U., Elliott Sch. Internat. Affairs, 2001-02. U.S. rep. to UN Conf. on Marine Pollution, 1969. Recipient Superior Honor award Dept. State, 1965. Mem. ABA, FBA, Am. Soc. Internat. Law, Internat. Bar Assn., Phi Beta Kappa. Avocation: sailing. Home: 7915 Sandalfoot Dr Potomac MD 20854-5476

NEUMAN, ROBERT STERLING, art educator, artist; b. Kellogg, Idaho, Sept. 9, 1926; s. Oscar C. and Katherine (Samuelson) N.; m. Helen Patricia Feddersen, Apr. 6, 1947 (div. 1971); children— Ingrid Alexandra, Elizabeth Catherine; m. Sunne Savage, June 3, 1979; 1 dau., Christina Mary. Student, U. Idaho, 1944-46; BAA., M.F.A., Calif. Coll. Arts and Crafts, 1947-51; student, San Francisco Sch. Fine Arts, 1950-51, Mills Coll., 1951. Assoc. prof. art Brown U., 1962-63; lectr. drawing Carpenter Center for Visual Arts, Harvard, 1963-72; prof. art, chmn. dept. Keene (N.H.) State Coll., 1972-90. Exhbns. include, Mus. Modern Art, Whitney Mus. Am. Art, Carnegie Internat., San Francisco Mus. Art, Boston Mus. Fine Arts, Worcester (Mass.) Art Mus., also, Japan and Europe. Served with AUS and USAAF, 1945-46. Recipient Howard Found. award for painting, 1967; Fulbright grantee, 1953-54; Guggenheim fellow, 1956-57; Bender grantee San Francisco Art Assn., 1952. Home: 135 Cambridge St Winchester MA 01890-2411

NEUMAN, SHLOMO P. hydrology educator; b. Zilina, Czechoslovakia, Oct. 26, 1938; came to U.S., 1963, naturalized, 1970; s. Alexander Neumann and Klara (Pikler) Lesny; m. Yael B. Neuman, Jan. 30, 1965; children: Gil, Michal, Ariel. BSc in Geology, Hebrew U., Jerusalem, 1963; MS in Engring. Sci., U. Calif., Berkeley, 1966, PhD in Engring. Sci., 1968. Cert. profl. hydrogeologist. Acting asst. prof., asst. rsch. engr. dept. civil engring. U. Calif., Berkeley, 1968-70, vis. assoc. prof. dept. civil engring., 1974-75; sr. scientist, assoc. rsch. prof. Inst. Soil and Water Agrl. Rsch. Orgn., Bet-Dagan, Israel, 1970-74; prof. hydrology dept. hydrology and water resources U. Ariz., Tucson, 1975-88, Regents' prof. dept. hydrology and water resources, 1988—. Cons. to U.S., Can. and Swedish govts. on hydrologic issues concerning nuc. waste disposal; vis. scientist dept. isotope Weizmann Inst. Sci., Rehovot, Israel, 1976; maître de rsch. Ctr. d'Informatique Geologique, Ecole Mines Paris, Fontainebleau, France, 1978, dir. rsch., 1981; vis. prof. dept. fluid mechanics and heat transfer Tel-Aviv U., 1981; hon. appointment concurrent prof. Nanjing U., China, 1989—; disting. lectr. in field; hon. prof. Nanjing Hydraulic Rsch. Inst., China, 1998—. Mem. editl. bd. Jour. Hydrology, 1977-84, Water Sci. and Tech. Libr. (The Netherlands), 1983-86, Stochastic Hydrology and Hydraulics, 1992—; mem. editl. bd. Water Resources Rsch. Jour., 1987-93, Hydrogeology Jour., 1999—; guest editor spl. issue in memory of Eugene S. Simpson Hydrogeology Jour., 1997-98; contbr. over 250 articles to profl. publs., chpts.

to books. Hebrew U. scholar, 1962-63, Edwin Letts Oliver scholar, 1965-66; Jane Lewis fellow, 1966-68; recipient Cert. of Appreciation award USDA, 1975, C.V. Theis award Am. Inst. Hydrology, 1990. Fellow Geol. Soc. Am. (O.E. Meinzer award 1976, Birdsal Disting. Lectr. 1987), Am. Geophys. Union (4th Walter B. Langbein lectr. hydrology 1996, Robert E. Horton award 1969, original mem. ISI highly cited rschrs. database 2000); mem. Soc. Petroleum Engrs. of AIME, NAE, Assn. Groundwater Scientists and Engrs. of Nat. Well Water Assn. (Sci. award 1989), Ariz. Hydrol. Soc., Internat. Assn. Hydrogeologists. Jewish. Office: U Ariz Dept Hydrology & Water Resou Tucson AZ 85721-0001 E-mail: neuman@hwr.arizona.edu.

NEUMAN, SUSAN B. federal agency administrator; Grad., Am. U.; master's, Calif. State U., Hayward; doctorate, U. Pacific. Reading specialist; tchr. elem. sch.; instr. Boston Coll., U. Mass., Yale U.; prof. Temple U., Phila.; dir. Ctr. Improvement Early Reading Achievement U. Mich., Ann Arbor, prof.; asst. sec. elem. and secondary edn. Dept. Edn., Washington, 2001—. Office: Dept Edn Office Elem and Secondary Edn 400 Maryland Ave SW FOB 6 Washington DC 20202-6100*

NEUMAN, SUSAN CATHERINE, public relations and marketing consultant; b. Detroit, Jan. 29, 1942; d. Paul Edmund and Elsie (Goetz) N. AB, U. Miami, Fla., 1964; MBA, Barry U., Miami Shores, Fla., 1985. Journalist, writer The Miami Herald, 1962-65; editor Miamian Mag., 1965-69; pres. Susan Neuman Inc., Miami, 1969—; ptnr. Neuman Enterprises Unltd., 1994—. Mem. Fla. Gov.'s Pyb. Rels. Adv. Coun., 1978-86. Mem. Pub. Rels. Soc. Am. (accredited, past officer, bd. dirs.), Miami C. of C., Counselors Acad., Miami City Club (founder, bd. govs.), Miami Internat. Press Club (charter, founder, pres. 1985-86), Com. of One Hundred (bd. dirs., sec.). Democrat. Roman Catholic. E-mail: s. Home: 13540 NE Miami Ct Miami FL 33161-2739 Office: Susan Neuman Inc Venetia 25th Fl 555 NE 15th St Ste 25K Miami FL 33132-1404 E-mail: neuman@hotmail.com.

NEUMAN, TOM S. emergency medical physician, educator; b. N.Y.C., July 23, 1946; s. Otto and Susan Ann (Baltaxe) N.; m. Doris Rubin, Aug. 24, 1969; children: Allison Rachel, Russell Solomon. AB, Cornell U., 1967; MD, NYU, 1971. Diplomate Nat. Bd. Med. Examiners, Am. Bd. Internal Medicine, Am. Bd. Pulmonary Diseases, Am. Bd. Preventive Medicine in Occupl. Medicine and Underseas and Hyperbaric Medicine), Am. Bd. Emergency Medicine. Intern Bellevue Hosp., N.Y.C., 1971-72, resident, 1972-73; commd. med. officer USN, 1973; advanced through grades to capt. USNR, 1990; instr. Naval Undersea Med. Inst., New London, Conn., 1973-74; staff med. officer Submarine Devel. Group One, San Diego, 1974-76, 78-80; emergency room physician Chula Vista (Calif.) Community Hosp., 1975-80; attending physician VA Med. Ctr., La Jolla, Calif., 1976-78; fellow in pulmonary medicine and physiology U. Calif. Sch. Medicine at San Diego, 1976-78, clin. instr., 1978-80, asst. clin. prof., 1980-84, flight physician Life Flight Aeromed. Program, 1980-86, asst. dir. dept. emergency medicine, 1980-94, assoc. dir. dept. emergency medicine, 1994—, attending physician pulmonary divsn., 1980-99, assoc. clin. prof. medicine and surgery, 1984-87, base hosp. physician, 1984—, dir. Hyperbaric Med. Ctr., 1984—; med. officer UDT/SEAL Res. Unit 119, San Diego, 1980-84, Mobile Diving and Salvage Unit One, USNR, San Diego, 1984-86, PRIMUS Unit 1942-A, U. Calif. at San Diego, 1988-90; sr. med. officer Seal Teams 1/3/5, USNR, Coronado, Calif., 1986-87; asst. officer in charge Med. Unit 1942-A U. Calif. Sch. Medicine, San Diego, 1990-95, prof. clin. medicine, 1996—. Mem. med. adv. bd. western regional underwater lab. program U. So. Calif. Marine Sci. Ctr., Catalina, 1982—85; assoc. adj. prof. medicine and surgery U. Calif. Sch. Medicine at San Diego, 1987—90, adj. prof. medicine and surgery, 1990—96, prof. clin. medicine and adj. prof. surgery, 1996—; mem. San Diego Coroner's com. for investigation of diving fatalities, 1974—; mem. diving cons. Vocat. Diver Tng. Facility, Calif. Inst. Med., Chino, 1967; mem. task force City Mgr. on Carbon Monoxide Poisoning, San Diego, 1991; mem. com. for minimal course content for recreational scuba instr. cert. Am. Nat. Stds. Inst., 1992—94, chmn. emergency med. physician quality improvement com., 1992—94; mem. undersea and hyperbaric medicine exam subcom. Am. Bd. Preventative Medicine, 1999—; mem. com. on creating vision for space medicine beyond earth orbit, mem. com. on extreme environments NAS; cons. NASA. Author book chpts.; contbr. articles to profl. jours. Fellow ACP, Am. Coll. Preventive Medicine; mem. Am. Thoracic Soc., Am. Lung Assn., Undersea and Hyperbaric Med. Soc. (program com. 1981-82, nominations com. 1982-83, chmn. 1988-89, mem. edn. com. 1982-87, chmn. awards com. 1983-84, v.p. exec. com. 1983-84, co-chmn. credentials com. 1984-85, editor-in-chief Undersea and Hyperbaric Medicine 1995—), Profl. Assn. Diving Instrs. (emeritus), NAS-IOM (com. on extreme environ.). Avocations: scuba diving, fishing, photography. Office: U Calif Med Ctr Dept Emergency Medicine 200 W Arbor Dr Dept 8676 San Diego CA 92103-8676 E-mail: tneuman@ucsd.edu.

NEUMAN, WILLIAM LAWRENCE, JR. sociology educator; b. Phila., Oct. 1, 1950; s. William Lawrence and Elizabeth Ruth (Mearkle) N.; m. Diane Kathryn Mertens, June 16, 1984; m. Deanna Sue Livingstone, Aug. 18, 1970 (div. 1976). BA with honors, Ind. U., Bloomington, 1972; MS, U. Wis., Madison, 1975, PhD, 1982. Lectr. U. Wis., Madison, 1976-82; vis. asst. Oberlin Coll., 1983; prof. sociology U. Wis., Whitewater, 1983—, asst. dean, 1985-91; adminstrv. assoc. Office Acad. Affairs U. Wis. System, 1992; vis. prof. Tohoku U., Sendai, Japan, 1995-96. Dir. Pacific Asia Ednl. Resource Ctr., 1999—. Grantee Fulbright Coun. for Exch. Internat. Scholars, 1995. Mem.: Assn. Asian Studies, Midwest Sociol. Assn. (bd. dirs. 1995—97), Wis. Sociol. Assn., Am. Sociol. Assn. (pres. 1993—94), Internat. House of Japan, Phi Kappa Phi (U. Wis. Whitewater pres. 2001—). Democrat. Unitarian Universalist. Home: 2935 Forest Down Madison WI 53711-5294

NEUMAN FELDBAUM, SANDRA FAYE, communal worker, nurse; b. St. Paul, Apr. 18, 1946; d. Joseph and Dorothy (Rifkin) Lipschultz; m. Richard Neuman, Apr. 7, 1941 (div. Aug. 1988); children: Jennifer, Marc; m. Stephen Feldblum, Aug. 19, 2001. AS, St. Mary's Coll., Mpls., 1967; student, U. Minn., 1967—. RN, Minn. Operating rm. nurse U. Minn. Hosps., Mpls., 1967-68; staff nurse Twin Cities Airport Med. Clinic, 1968; mem. fin. staff Durenberger for Senate, 1987-88; asst. dir. maj. gifts United Jewish Appeal, Fedn. of Jewish Philanthropies of Greater N.Y., N.Y.C., 1988-89; dir. east coast region The Jerusalem Found., 1989-91; Ea. regional dir. Israel Tennis Ctrs., 1991—. Nat. officer, chair women's young leadership cabinet United Jewish Appeal, N.Y.C., 1985-86; owner Back Door Art Studio. Mem. exec. coun. Am. Israel Pub. Affairs Com., Washington, 1985-86; mem. nat. com. Joint Action Com. for Polit. Affairs, Chgo.; trustee Temple Shalom, Naples, Fla. Recipient Outstanding Young Leadership award Coun. Jewish Fedns., 1981. Mem. Nat. Soc. Fund Raising Execs., Nat. Coun. Jewish Women, Women in Fin. Devel. Home: 24030 Copperleaf Blvd Bonita Springs FL 34135-8169 E-mail: sandyneuman@email.msn.com.

NEUMANN, ALFRED JOHN, music director; b. Bklyn., Dec. 15, 1928; s. Erich Paul and Elsa (Kleiber) N. BS, Davidson Coll., 1951; MMus, U. Mich., 1954. Asst. to music dir. Brevard (N.C.) Music Ctr., 1948-52; dir. of bands Furman U., Greenville, S.C., 1951-52; asst. instr. in music U. Mich., Ann Arbor, 1952-54; music dir. Nat. Conv. of United Ch. of Christ, Washington, 1976, Christ Congregational Ch., Silver Spring, Md., 1958-94; accompanist Washington Performing Arts Soc. Concerts in Schs., Washington, 1972-97, Todd Duncan Voice Studio, Washington, 1992-98. Mem. adv. bd. to select the Bicentennial hymn, U.S. Army, Washington, 1976; student condr. U. Mich. Choirs, Ann Arbor, 1952-54; accompanist U. Mich. Opera Dept., Ann Arbor, 1952-54, The Mozart Trio, Washington, 1958-68. Composer: (church anthems) Truly, We Shall Be in Paradise, 1970, I Sing to Thee, 1983, (sacred opera) An Opera for Christmas, 1961, An Opera for Easter (both premeired on NBC-TV, Washington); contbr. articles to profl. jours. Organizer, dir. concerts to benefit AMA Colls., Washington, 1974, 75; music dir. Nat. Conv. of the United Ch. of Christ, Washington, 1976. Recipient Cert. commendation Can. Internat. Exhbn., Montreal, Can., 1967, Performance award WGMS Good Music Sta., Washington, 1980, 1981. Democrat. United Ch. of Christ. Home: Ste 1515 1400 E West Hwy Apt 1515 Silver Spring MD 20910-3264

NEUMANN, BRUCE RUSSELL, emergency physician; b. St. Louis, Dec. 3, 1949; s. Roland F. Neumann Jr. and Ruth Mary (Herleman) Sullivan. BA cum laude, Colo. Coll., 1972; MD, U. Minn., 1976. Diplomate Am. Bd. Emergency Medicine, Am. Bd. Family Practice. Resident in family practice Bethesda Luth. Med. Ctr., St. Paul, 1976-79, med. dir. emergency dept., 1979-83; emergency physician Meth. Hosp., Mpls., 1983—, Vail (Colo.) Valley Med. Ctr., 1985-87, Seven Mile Clinic, Winter Park, Colo., 1989-94; with Snowmass (Colo.) Clinic, 1996—. Mem. Wilderness Med. Soc. Avocation: songwriting. Office: Snowmass Clinic PO Box 5338 Snowmass Village CO 81615-5338

NEUMANN, CHARLES HENRY, mathematics educator; b. Washington, Jan. 30, 1943; s. Bernhardt Walter and Emma (Habitz) N.; m. Cheryl Elaine Girard, June 18, 1965; children: Matthew Roy, Kristen Elizabeth. AS, Alpena (Mich.) C.C., 1962; BS in Math., Mich. State U., 1964, MAT. in Math., 1965. Sci. tchr. Alpena Pub. Schs., 1965-66; instr. math. Alpena C.C., 1966-84, math. sci. dept. chair, 1969-84; prof. math. Oakland C.C., Bloomfield Hills, Mich., 1984—. Scoutmaster troop 92 Boy Scouts Am., Alpena, 1981-84; bd. dirs. Mich. Vision Svc. Assn., Columbus, 1985-89, Ohio Vision Svc. Assn., 1988-89, Blue Cross Blue Shield Mich., 1986-94; mem. exec. com. Oakland County (Mich.) Dem. Com., 1995-96; bd. dirs. Luth. Social Svcs. of Mich., 1996—, v.p., 1999—. Mem. NEA (del. 1974-80, adv. com. on membership 1993-96), Math. Assn. Am., Am. Math. Assn. of Two-Yr. Colls., Mich. Edn. Assn. (bd. dirs. 1974-80), Mich. Edn. Spl. Svcs. (trustee 1975-93, pres. 1976-93), Mich. Math. Assn. of Two-Yr. Colls., Mich. Assn. Higher Edn. (v.p. two-yr. colls. 1970-96, 2002—), Oakland C.C. Faculty Assn. (v.p. 1994-95, 98-01, pres. 1995-98), Phi Kappa Phi. Lutheran. Avocations: collecting antique books, racquetball, cross country skiing. Home: 5871 Warbler Clarkston MI 48346-2973 Office: Oakland CC 2900 Featherstone Rd Auburn Hills MI 48326-2817

NEUMANN, FORREST KARL, retired hospital administrator; b. St. Louis, Oct. 7, 1930; s. Metz Earl and Ruth (McGhee) N.; m. Erika Stefanie Turkl, Feb. 11, 1955; children: Tracey Neumann Liberson, Karen Neumann Kruger, Scott, Lisa BS, Roosevelt U., 1953; MS in Hosp. Adminstrn., Northwestern U., 1955. Adminstrv. resident Louis A. Weiss Hosp., Chgo., 1954-55; mem. staff Sparrow Hosp., Lansing, Mich., 1958-90; CEO, pres., dir. Edward W. Sparrow Hosp., 1962-90; pres., chief exec. officer, dir. Mason Gen. Hosp., 1973-85; chmn. bd. Caymich Ins. Co. Ltd., Cayman Islands, 1979-91, emeritus dir. Cayman Islands, 1991—; chmn. bd. Caymich Ins. Co. (Barbados) Ltd., 1986-91; pres., CEO, Mich. Hosp. Assn. Ins. Co., 1990-96; dir. Mich. Hosp. Assocs. Ins. Co., 1976-98; pres., CEO, Sparrow, Inc., 1984-90. Chmn. bd. Mich. Hosp. Assn. Ins. Co., 1979-90; dir. First of Am. Bank Corp., 1980-95, Auto Owners Ins. Co., 1980-90. Chmn. hosp. div. United Community Chest, 1965-68, chmn. budget steering com., 1970-71, bd. dirs., mem. exec. com., 1969-75; mem. adv. com. Capitol Area Comprehensive Health Planning Assn., 1969, bd. dirs., 1971-75, treas., 1974-75; mem., vice chmn. Mich. Arbitration Adv. Com., 1975-80; bd. dirs. Grad. Med. Edn., Inc., 1971-80, pres., 1972-73, treas. 1973 Fellow Am. Coll. Hosp. Adminstrs. (life); mem. Southwestern Mich. Hosp. Council (trustee 1968-73, pres. 1970-71), Am. Hosp. Assn. (del. 1979-87), Mich. Hosp. Assn. (1st v.p. 1972-73, bd. dirs., exec. com., treas. 1974-75, chmn. 1976-77, Meritorious Key award 1979), Rotary.

NEUMANN, HARRY, philosophy educator; b. Dormoschel, Germany, Oct. 10, 1930; came to U.S., 1937, naturalized, 1948; s. Siegfried and Frieda (Lion) N.; m. Christina Sopher, Sept. 25, 1959. BA, St. John's Coll., 1952; MA, U. Chgo., 1954; PhD, Johns Hopkins U., 1962; postgrad., U. Heidelberg, Germany, 1956-58. Mem. faculty Mich. State U., 1962-63, Lake Forest Coll., 1963-65; prof. philosophy, and govt. Claremont Grad. U. Scripps Coll., Claremont (Calif.) Grad. Univ., 1966—. Research assoc. Rockefeller Inst., N.Y.C., 1963 Author: Liberalism, 1991; contbr. articles profl. jours. With AUS, 1954-56. Classical Philosophy fellow Ctr. Hellenic Studies, Dumbarton Oaks, Washington, 1965-66, rsch. fellow Salvatori Ctr. for Study of Individual Freedom in the Modern World, 1970; rsch. fellow Earhart Found., 1973-74, 78, 82, 86, 90, 94, 98. Mem. AAUP, Univ. Ctrs. Rational Alternatives, Univ. Profs. for Acad. Order, John Brown Cook Assn. for Freedom (advisor). Office: Scripps Coll Claremont CA 91711 E-mail: harry_neumann@scrippsscol.edu.

NEUMANN, HERMAN ERNEST, elementary and special education educator; b. Winona, Minn., Nov. 11, 1931; s. Herman Ferdinand and Dena Matilda (Peterson) N.; m. Juanita Evelyn, Sept. 11, 1954; children: Mary Evelyn, Herman Ernest Jr., Martin Andrew, Amy Louise. BS, Winona State U., 1961; MA, Calif. State U., Bakersfield, 1976; postgrad., San Jose U., 1977, Calif. State U., San Barbara, 1978. Cert. early childhood, spl. edn., elem. edn., ESL instr. Classroom tchr. grades K-6, resource specialist Bakersfield (Calif.) City Schs., 1980-82; classroom tchr. Kern County, Bakersfield, 1982-84; resource specialist Bakersfield (Calif.) City Schs., 1984-92; lectr. in edn. Calif. State U., Bakersfield, 1994—. Lectr. Calif. State U., Bakersfield, 1996—. Contbr. articles to profl. jours. 1st class airman USAF, 1952-56. NSF fellow, 1966, Internat. Biog. Assn. fellow, Cambridge, Eng., 1993; named to Hall of Fame Teaching Excellence Kern County, 1990, Tchr. of Yr., 1990. Mem. NEA (grantee 1969), Bakersfield Elem. Tchrs. Assn., ASCD, Calif. Tchrs. Assn. Home: 3209 Apollo St Bakersfield CA 93306-2129 Office: Bakersfield City Schs 1300 Baker St Bakersfield CA 93305-4326

NEUMANN, HERSCHEL, physics educator; b. San Bernardino, Calif., Feb. 3, 1930; s. Arthur and Dorothy (Greenhood) N.; m. Julia Black, June 15, 1951; 1 child, Keith. BA, U. Calif., Berkeley, 1951; MS, U. Oreg., 1959; PhD, U. Nebr., 1965. Theoretical physicist Gen. Electric Co., Richland, Wash., 1951—57; instr. physics U. Nebr., Lincoln, 1964—65; asst. prof. physics U. Denver, 1965—71, assoc. prof. physics, 1971—85, prof. physics, 1985—, chmn. physics and astronomy, 1985—97, assoc. chmn. physics and astronomy, 2001—. Contbr. over 20 articles to profl. jours. Dir. numerous pub. outreach programs in physics. Mem. Am. Assn. Physics Tchrs. Home: 2425 S St Paul St Denver CO 80210-5516 Office: U Denver Dept Physics Astronomy Denver CO 80208-2238 E-mail: hneumann@du.edu.

NEUMANN, JEFFREY JAY, photographer, minister; b. Cleve., Aug. 6, 1948; s. Fred and LaVerne (Vavra) N.; m. Charlene Rose Sparrow, Apr. 21, 1968 (dec.); children: Stephan, Corene, Lara; m. Carolyn Hannah, Nov. 4, 1972; 1 son, Jeffrey. Ordained to ministry, 1962. Lithographer, camera operator Advertype, Inc., Cleve., 1972; lab. technician Vista Color Lab., 1972-73; prodn. mgr. Mort Tucker Photography, 1973-78; owner, photographer Photography by Jeffrey Neumann, Wadsworth, OH, 1978—. Lectr. in field. Author: Thirty Years as Jehovah's Slave, 1999, To Have and Remember the Perfect Wedding, 2000, Forty Years as Jehovah's Willing Slave, 2002., 120 Years Preaching the Good News of the Kingdom, 2002. Mem. Sm. Bus. Mgmt. Adv. Com., 1980-83. Mem. Internat. Platform Assn., Profl. Photographers Am. (awards), Wedding and Portrait Photographers Internat. (awards), Profl. Photographers Ohio (awards). Jehovah'S Witness. Home and Office: 9960 Mount Eaton Rd Wadsworth OH 44281-9028 E-mail: jneumann@neo.rr.com.

NEUMANN, LINDA KAY, marketing executive; b. Wyandotte, Mich., Feb. 5, 1959; d. Michael and Raelene Fern (Bongart) Goldman; m. David Dewain Neumann, Mar. 31, 1980; children: Rachel Anne, Kyle Wayne. Student, Mesa C.C., San Diego, 1976-86; grad. with honors, Bank Mktg. Sch., 1991. Mail clk., securities clk. Hawaiian Trust Co. Ltd., Honolulu, 1977-78, supr., 1979-81; securities vault clk., bank card clk. Union Bank Calif., San Diego, 1981-82, sales adminstrv. asst., 1983-86, mktg. adminstrv. asst., mktg. officer, 1986-88, from mktg. asst. v.p. to mktg. v.p., 1992-94, mktg. v.p., mgr., 1994-96, bus. and sales planning mgr., v.p., 1996—. Chmn. San Diego Ednl. Coun. Am. Banking Assn. Am. Inst. Banking, 1996-97; owner Brilliant Mktg. Ideas, 1999—. Pres. Rolling Hills Elem. PTA, 1995—96; parliamentarian Deer Canyon Elem. PTA; nat. del. San Diego Imperial Coun. Girl Scouts; bd. dir. San Diego Safety Coun., Pacific Safety Coun. Mem. Am. Soc. Autism, Direct Mktg. Assn., Advt. Club San Diego, San Diego Direct Mktg. Assn., Bank Mktg. Assn., Advt. Splty. Inst. Promotional Products Assns., Nat. Soc. Fundraising Execs., San Diego Employers Assn., Am. Soc. Autism. Office: Brilliant Marketing Ideas Ste 109 8340 Clairemont Mesa Blvd San Diego CA 92111-1320 E-mail: ideas@adexec.com.

NEUMANN, PETER GABRIEL, computer scientist; b. N.Y.C., Sept. 21, 1932; s. J.B. and Elsa (Schmid) N.; m. Elizabeth Susan Neumann; 1 child, Helen K. AB, Harvard U., 1954, SM, 1955; Dr rerum naturarum, Technische Hochschule, Darmstadt, Fed. Republic Germany, 1960; PhD, Harvard U., 1961. Mem. tech. staff Bell Labs, Murray Hill, N.J., 1960-70; Mackay lectr. Stanford U., 1964, U. Calif., Berkeley, 1970-71; prin. scientist SRI Internat., Menlo Park, Calif., 1971—. Adj. prof. U. Md., 1999. Author: Computer-Related Risks, 1995. Fulbright grantee, 1958-60; Nat. Computer Sys. Security award, 2002. Fellow AAAS, IEEE, Assn. for Computing Machinery (editor jour. 1976-93, chmn. com. on computers and pub. policy 1985—). Avocations: music, tai chi, holistic health. Office: SRI Internat EL-243 333 Ravenswood Ave Menlo Park CA 94025-3493 E-mail: pneumann@acm.org.

NEUMANN, RONALD DANIEL, nuclear medicine physician, educator; b. Watertown, Wis., Oct. 10, 1947; BS summa cum laude, Carroll Coll., 1970; MD with highest honors, Yale U., 1974. Diplomate Nat. Bd. Med. Examiners, Am. Bd. Nuclear Medicine; lic. physician, Md., D.C. Resident in pathology Yale-New Haven Hosp., 1974-77, resident in nuclear medicine, 1977-79, chief resident in nuclear medicine, 1978-79, attending physician, 1979-85; asst. prof. diagnostic radiology Sch. Medicine Yale U., 1979-83, assoc. prof. diagnostic radiology and pathology, 1983-86; dep. chief dept. nuclear medicine NIH, Bethesda, Md., 1985-88, chief. dept. nuclear medicine, 1988—, dir. nuclear medicine residency tng. program, 1986-92; clin. prof. diagnostic radiology and nuclear medicine Sch. Medicine George Washington U., Washington, 1986—. Chmn. med. isotopes and radiation safety com. West Haven VA Med. Ctr., 1979-85; mem. clin. rsch. panel Nat. Inst. Diabetes and Digestive and Kidney Diseases, 1987-88; mem. radiation safety com. NIH and Nat. Ctr. for Health Stats., 1987-89. Patentee Antigen-specific composition and in-vivo methods for detecting and localizing an antigenic site and for radiotherapy; contbr. over 200 articles and abstracts to med. and sci. jours., 30 chpts. to books and conf. proceedings. Nat. Merit scholar; NASA summer fellow. Fellow Am. Coll. Chest Physicians; mem. AAAS, Am. Soc. for Investigative Pathology, Soc. Nuclear Medicine (co-chmn. C.M.E. program 1995-96, pres.-elect 1997, pres. Mid.-Atlantic chpt. 1998), Internat. Acad. Pathology (U.S. and Can. divsns.), European Assn. Nuclear Medicine, Sigma Xi., Delta Sigma Nu. Office: NIH-CC Dept Nuclear Medicine 10 Center Dr Ms 1180 Bethesda MD 20892-0001

NEUMANN, RONALD ELDREDGE, diplomat; b. Washington, Sept. 30, 1944; s. Robert G. N. and Marlen Eldredge; m. Margaret Elaine Grimm, Jan 23, 1966; children: Helen, Brian. BA, U. Calif., Riverside, 1966, MA, 1967; student, Nat. War Coll., 1991. Joined Fgn. Svc., 1970; vice-consul Am. Embassy, Dakar, Senegal, 1971-73; from vice-consul to consul Am. Consulate, Tabriz, Iran, 1973-76; desk officer office of so. European affairs Dept. State, Washington, 1976-77, aide to asst. sec. Near East and South Asian Affairs, 1977-78, desk officer Jordanian Affairs, 1978-81, dep. dir. Arabian Peninsula Affairs, 1983-86, dir. No. Gulf affairs, 1991-94; dep. chief mission Am. Embassy, Sana'a, North Yemen, 1981-83; with Arabic Lang. Tng., Washington, 1986-87; dep. chief mission Am. Embassy, Abu Dhabi, United Arab Emirates, 1987-90; amb. to Algeria, 1994-97; dep. asst. sec. of state for Mid. East Dept. State, 1997-2000, amb. to Bahrain, 2001—; spl. negotiator with Spain, 2000—01. 1st. lt. US Army, 1969-70, Vietnam. Decorated Bronze star, Combat Infantry Badge, Superior Honor medal. Mem. Am. Fgn. Svc. Assn., U. Calif. Riverside Alumni Assn., Officer Candidate Sch. Alumni Assn., Assn. of 5th Divsn. Nat. War Coll. Alumni, Phi Beta Kappa. Avocations: reading, backpacking, bicycling, hiking. Office: US Embassy Manama PCS-451 FPO AE 09834-5100

NEUMANN, ROY COVERT, architect; b. Columbus, Nebr., Mar. 1, 1921; s. LeRoy Franklin and Clara Louise (Covert) N.; m. Hedy Charlotte Schultz, Aug. 28, 1948; children: Tali, Scott. Student, Midland Coll., 1939-40, U. Calif.-Berkeley Armed Forces Inst., overseas, 1942-43; AB, U. Nebr., 1948, BArch, 1949; MA, Harvard U., 1952; postgrad., U. Wis., Iowa State U. Registered profl. architect, Iowa, Nebr., Kans., Minn., S.D., N.Y., N.J., Mass., Ohio, Pa., Tenn., Ky., Va., W.Va., Ga., Mich., Mo., Ill., Wis., Tex., Colo. Ptnr., architect R. Neumann Assocs., Lincoln, Nebr., 1952-55; officer mgr. Sargent, Webster, Crenshaw & Folley, Schenectady, N.Y., 1955-59; dir. architecture, ptnr. A.M. Kinney Assocs., Cin., 1959-65; officer mgr. Hunter, Campbell & Rea, Johnstown, Pa., 1965-66; dir. architecture, ptnr. Stanley Cons., Muscatine, Iowa, 1966-76; pres., chmn. bd. Neumann Monson P.C., Iowa City, 1976—. Ptnr. Clinton St. Ptnrs., Iowa City, 1983—, Iris City Devel. Co. Mt. Pleasant, Iowa, 1986, Linn Mar Elem./Mid. Sch., Marion, Iowa. Prin. works include Harbour Facilities, Antigua, W.I., S.C. Johnson Office Bldg., Racine, Wis., Iowa City Transit Facility Bldg., addition to Davenport Ctrl. High Sch., V.A. Adminstrv. Office Bldg., Iowa City, Johnson County Office Bldg., Iowa City Mercer Park Aquatic Ctr., Iowa City, Coll. Bus. U. Iowa, Iowa City, renovation Lawrence County Courthouse, Deadwood, S.D., H.S. and Elem. Schs., Mt. Pleasant, Iowa. Mem. bd. edn. Muscatine Community Sch. Dist., 1974-76. Served with USN, 1942-46, PTO. Recipient Hönor award Portland Cement Assn., 1949, Lorraine D. Wright award for outstanding constrn. Camanche (Iowa) H.S., 1998-99. Mem. AIA (Honor award 1975), Constrn. Specifications Inst. (pres. 1974-76, Honor award 1983, 84, 85, 86), Soc. Archtl. Historians, Archtl. Assn. London, U. Nebr. Alumni Assn., Harvard U. Alumni Assn., Iowa City C. of C., Phi Kappa Psi, Univ. Athletic Club (Iowa City), Masons, Ea. Star, Elks Republican. Presbyterian. Avocations: golf, fishing, medieval history, big band music. Home: 2014 Burnside Dr Muscatine IA 52761-3510 Office: Neumann Monson Architects 111 E College St Iowa City IA 52240-4012

NEUMANN, THOMAS WILLIAM, archaeologist; b. Cin., Aug. 30, 1951; s. William Henry and Virginia Marie Neumann; m. Mary Louise Spink, Sept. 3, 1988. BA in Anthropology, U. Ky., 1973; PhD in Anthropology, U. Minn., 1979. Instr. U. Minn., Mpls., 1977-79; asst. prof. Syracuse U., 1979-86, dir. archaeology field program, 1979-86; sr. ptnr. Neumann & Sanford Cultural Resource Assessments, Syracuse, 1985-87; sr. scientist R. Christopher Goodwin & Assocs., Inc., Frederick, Md., 1987-92. Rsch. assoc. Terrestrial Environ. Specialists, Phoenix, N.Y., 1980-83, SUNY Rsch. Found., Potsdam, 1985-87; external reviewer NSF, Washington, 1982-85; dir. Ctr. for Archaeol. Rsch. and Edn., Houston, Minn., 1982-84; vis. assoc. prof. Emory U., 1991-93, 96, 97-2000, 2002-03, U. Ga., 1997; ind. cons., 1991—; mgr. Diachronics divsn. Pocket Park-Wentworth Analytical Facility, 1993—. Author, co-author more than 80 monographs including 2 winners of the Anne Arundell County Hist. Preservation award; asst. editor Amanuensis, 1972-73; contbr. more than 40 articles to profl. jours. Nat. Trust Historic Preservation honor award. Recipient Oswald award U. Ky., 1973; co-recipient Vt. Gov.'s medal for Stonewalls and Cellarholes; grantee Am. Philos. Soc., 1981, Appleby-Mosher Found., 1983, Landmarks Assn. Ctrl. N.Y., 1984. Mem. AAAS, N.Y. Acad. Sci., Soc. for Am. Archaeology, Ea. States Archaeol. Fedn., Mid. Atlantic Archaeol. Conf., Ga. Coun. Profl. Archaeologists, Register of Profl. Archaeologists, Phi Beta Kappa. Roman Catholic. Achievements include development of use of vegetation successional stages for cultural resource assessments; identification of cause of passenger pigeon extinctions, microlithic compound tool industry in the eastern prehistoric U.S., contingency planning budget system for Archdiocese of Atlanta. Home and Office: Ind Archeol Cons 3859 Wentworth Ln SW Lilburn GA 30047-2260

NEUMANN, WALTER DAVID, mathematician; b. Cardiff, Wales, Jan. 1, 1946; arrived in Australia, 1993; s. Bernhard and Hanna (Von Caemmerer) N.; m. Anne Waldron, Aug. 26, 1972; 1 child, Hannah. BA, Adelaide U., 1966, MA, 1968; PhD, Bonn U., 1969. Lectr. Bonn U., Germany, 1969-75; asst. prof. to prof. U. Md., College Park, 1975-87; prof. Ohio State U., Columbus, 1987-93, U. Melbourne, Australia, 1993—, personal chair Australia, 1997—. Rsch. fellow Princeton (N.J.) Univ., 1992-93. Grantee NSF, 1977—, Australian Rsch. Coun., 1993—. Mem. Am. Math. Soc., Australian Math. Soc. Avocations: music, cycling. Office: U Melbourne 3042 Parkville Victoria Australia

NEUMARK, DAVID, economics educator; b. Chgo., July 7, 1959; s. George A. and Miriam Neumark; m. Donna Edwards, June 9, 1983; children: Noam, Eitan. BA, U. Pa., 1982; PhD, Harvard U., 1987. Economist Fed. Res. Bd., Washington, 1987-89; asst. prof. U. Pa., Phila., 1989-94; prof. econs. Mich. State U., East Lansing, 1994—. Rsch. assoc. Nat. Bur. Econ. Rsch., Cambridge, Mass., 1989—; vis. fellow Pub. Policy Inst. of Calif., 2000—01. Contbr. articles to profl. jours., including Jour. Polit. Economy, Quar. Jour. Econs., Jour. Labor Econs., Jour. Human Resources. Tchr. religious sch. Kehillat Israel, Lansing, Mich., 1999-00; cmty. soccer coach OAKS, Okemos, Mich. Grad. fellow NSF, 1982-87. Democrat. Jewish. Avocations: squash, weightlifting, softball. Office: Mich State U Dept Econs East Lansing MI 48824

NEUMARK, GERTRUDE FANNY, materials science educator; b. Nuremberg, Germany, Apr. 29, 1927; came to U.S., 1939; d. Siegmund and Bertha (Forchheimer) N.; m. Henry Rothschild, Mar. 18, 1950. BA, Barnard Coll., 1948; MA, Radcliffe Coll., 1949; PhD, Columbia U., 1951. Advanced rsch. physicist Sylvania Rsch. Labs., Bayside, N.Y., 1952-60; sr. mem. tech. staff Philips Labs., Briarcliff Manor, 1960-85; prof. materials sci. Columbia U., N.Y.C., 1985-99, Howe prof. materials sci. and engring., 1999—. Cons. Am. Inst. Physics, N.Y.C., 1968-69; NSF vis. prof., 1982; panelist NRC; panelist, reviewer NSF. Contbr. Encyclopedia of Advanced Materials, numerous articles to sci. jours., chpt. to books; inventor in field. Rice fellow, 1948, Dana fellow, 1948, AAUW Anderson fellow, 1951. Fellow Am. Phys. Soc. (Goeppert-Meyer award com. 1987-89); mem. Materials Rsch. Soc., Soc. Women Engrs. (sr.), Am. Chem. Soc.

NEUMARK, MICHAEL HARRY, lawyer; b. Cin., Oct. 28, 1945; s. Jacob H. and Bertha (Zubor) N.; m. Sue Daly, June 5, 1971; children: Julie Rebecca, John Adam. BS in Bus., Ind. U., 1967; JD, U. Cin., 1970. Bar: Ohio 1970, D.C. 1972. Atty. chief counsel's office IRS, Washington, 1970-74, acting br. chief, 1974-75, sr. atty. regional counsel's office, 1975-77; assoc. Paxton & Seasongood Legal Profl. Assn., 1977-80; ptnr. Thompson, Hine & Flory, 1980—, mem. mgmt. com., 1993—. Chmn. So. Ohio Tax Inst., 1987; mem. IRS and Bar Liaison Com., 1991-93; spkr. at profl. confs. Contbr. articles to profl. jours. Bd. dirs. 1987 World Figure Skating Championship, Cin., 1986-89; precinct exec. Hamilton County Rep. Orgn., 1980-86; vol. referee Hamilton County Juvenile Ct., 1980-86; trustee Cin. Contemporary Arts Ctr., St. Rita Sch. for Deaf, 1991-97, Legal Aid Soc. Cin., 1997—, v.p., 2002—; bd. visitors U. Cin. Coll. Law. Recipient Commendation Resolution Sycamore Twp., 1987. Mem. ABA (ho. of dels. 1998-2002), Ohio State Bar Assn., Cin. Bar Assn. (pres. 1996-97, recognition award 1985, treas., bd. trustees 1988-91, trustee 1992—, chair tax sect., 1990-91), Leadership Cin., Ohio Met. Bar Assn. (pres. 1996-97), Kenwood Country Club, Indian Hill Club, Ohio Met. Bar (pres. 1996-97), Cin. Acad. of Leadership for Lawyers (founder, chair). Republican. Avocations: golf, travel. Office: Thompson Hine & Flory 312 Walnut St Ste 1400 Cincinnati OH 45202-4089

NEUMEIER, JOHN, choreographer, ballet company director; b. Milw., Feb. 24, 1942; s. Albert and Lucille N. BA, Marquette U., 1961, DFA (hon.), 1987; student, Stone-Camryn Ballet Sch., Chgo., 1957-62, Royal Ballet Sch., London, 1962-63; student of Vera Volkova, Copenhagen, 1962-63. Dancer Sybil Shearer Co., Chgo., 1960-62, Stuttgart (Fed. Republic Germany) Ballet, 1963-69; artistic dir. Frankfurt (Fed. Republic Germany) Opera Ballet, 1969-73, Hamburg (Fed. Republic Germany) State Opera Ballet, 1973—; prof. City of Hamburg, 1987; dir. Hamburg Ballet, 1996, ballettintendant, 1997—. Found. ballet sch. Hamburg State Opera, 1978; found. ballet ctr. John Neumeier, ballet sch., Hamburg State Opera co. tng. under one roof., 1989. Guest choreographer for various cos. including Am. Ballet Theatre, Royal Ballet London, Royal Danish Ballet, Nat. Ballet Can., Royal Winnipeg Ballet, Stuttgart Ballet, Munich Opera, Vienna Opera, Ballet du XX siecle, Brussels, Opera de Paris, Opera of Stockholm, Mariinsky Theatre, St. Petersburg; guest opera dir. Otello, Munich Opera, Hamburg State Opera; ballet dir. (films) Rondo, 1971 (Prix Italia 1972), Third Symphony of Gustav Mahler (Golden Camera award 1978), Legend of Joseph, Wendungen (String Quintet in C major by Schubert), 1979, Scenes of Childhood, The Lady of the Camellias, 1986, Othello, 1987; choreographer Romeo and Juliet, The Nutcracker, 1971, Daphnis and Chloé, 1972, Third Symphony of Gustav Mahler, 1975, Illusions-Like Swan Lake, 1976, A Midsummer Night's Dream, 1977, Sleeping Beauty, The Lady of the Camelias, 1978, Matthaeus-Passion, 1981, Giselle, 1983, Sixth Symphony of G. Mahler, 1984, Peer Gynt, 1989, Fifth Symphony of G. Mahler, 1989, Requiem, 1991, A Cinderella Story, 1992, Odyssee, 1995, Vivaldi Or What You Will, 1996, Sylvia, 1997, Images from Bartók, 1998, Messias, 1999 (Danza Danza award 2001), Nijinsky, 2000, Giselle, 2000, Sounds of Empty Pages, 2001. Decorated knight's cross Danebrog Order (Denmark); recipient Dance mag. award, 1983, Fed. German Cross of Merit, 1987, German Dance prize, 1988; title of Prof. conferred by City of Hamburg, 1987, Deutscher Tanzpreis, Fed. Republic of Germany, 1988; recipient Prix Diaghilev award, France, 1988, Order Des Arts et des Lettres award French Minister Culture, 1991, Carina Ari award, Stockholm, 1994, Nijinsky medal Polish Minister Culture, 1996, Danebrog Order in Gold, Denmark, 2000. Mem. Acad. der Kuenste Hamburg, Acad. der Kuenste Berlin, Golden Mask. Roman Catholic. Office: Ballettzentrum Hamburg Caspar-Voght-Strasse 54 D-20535 Hamburg Germany E-mail: intendanz@hamburgballett.de.

NEUMEIER, LEANDER ANTHONY, mining engineer, researcher; b. St. Louis, Feb. 15, 1933; s. Martin Joseph Neumeier and Lona Martha Anhalt; m. Joanne McDaniel, Nov. 30, 1963; 1 child Kimberly Renee. BS Metallurgical Engring., U. Mo., 1959, MS Metallurgical Engring., 1960. Registered profl. engr., Md., 1974. Project leader Bur. Mines, U.S. Dept. Interior, Rolla, Mo., 1960—74, rsch. supr., 1974—88, acting rsch. dir., 1979, ret., 1988. Rep. for FEMA U.S. Dept. Interior, Rolla, Mo., 1978—85. Contbr. articles to profl. jours. With USAF, 1952—56. Mem.: TMS-AIME, K of C. Achievements include 4 patents in metallurgical research. Avocations: literature, history, current affairs, music, sports. Home: 301 Lariat Ln Rolla MO 65401-4711 Personal E-mail: lenmr@tidnet.com.

NEUMEIER, MATTHEW MICHAEL, lawyer, educator; b. Racine, Wis., Sept. 13, 1954; s. Frank Edward and Ruth Irene (Effenberger) N.; m. Annmarie Prine, Jan. 31, 1987; children: Ruthann Marie, Emilie Irene, Matthew Charles. B in Gen. Studies with distinction, U. Mich., 1981; JD magna cum laude, Harvard U., 1984. Bar: N.Y. 1987, Mich. 1988, Ill. 1991, U.S. Dist. Ct. (ea. dist.) Mich. 1988, U.S. Dist. Ct. (ea., no. dists. and trial bar) Ill. 1991, U.S. Ct. Appeals (7th cir.) 1992, U.S. Ct. Appeals (fed. cir.) 1998, U.S. Supreme Ct. 1991. Sec.-treas. Ind. Roofing & Siding Co., Escanaba, Mich., 1973-78; mng. ptnr. Ind. Roofing Co., Menominee, 1977-78; law clk. to presiding justice U.S. Ct. Appeals (9th cir.), San Diego, 1984-85; law clk. to chief justice Warren E. Burger U.S. Supreme Ct., Washington, 1985-86; spl. asst. to chmn. U.S. Constn. Bicentennial Commn., 1986; assoc. Cravath, Swaine & Moore, N.Y.C., 1986-88; spl. counsel Burnham & Ritchie, Ann Arbor, Mich., 1988; assoc. Schlussel, Lifton, Simon, Rands, Galvin & Jackier, P.C., 1988-90, Skadden, Arps, Slate, Meagher & Flom, Chgo., 1990-96; ptnr. Jenner & Block, 1996—. Adj. prof. computer law and high tech. litig. John Marshall Law Sch., Chgo., 1999—. Editor Harvard Law Rev., 1982-84. Pres., bd. dirs. Univ. Cellar Inc., Ann Arbor, 1979-81; bd. dirs. Econ. Devel. Corp., Menominee, 1978-79, Midwestern divsn. Am. Suicide Found., sec., 1992-97, Commonwealth Plaza Condominium Assn., dir., 1999—, pres., 2000—; mem. vestry Ch. of Our Savior, 1997-2000; bd. dirs. Chgo. Children's Mus., 1999—; chmn. Harvard Law Sch. 15 Yr. Reunion Gift Fund, 1999. Mem. ABA, State Bar Mich., Assn. of Bar of City of N.Y., Chgo. Bar Assn., Def. Rsch. Inst., The 410 Club, Econ. Club Chgo. Republican. Avocations: classic automobiles, piano, choir. Office: Jenner & Block Ste 4200 One IBM Plz Chicago IL 60611 E-mail: mneumeier@jenner.com.

NEUMEIER, RICHARD L. lawyer; b. Boston, Nov. 22, 1946; s. Victor L. and Crystal Gladys (Mueller) N.; m. Mary Edna Malcolm, Mar. 15, 1975; children: Hannah Catherine, Edmund Malcolm, Thomas Richard. AB, AM, U. Chgo., 1968; JD, Columbia U., 1971. Bar: N.Y. 1972, U.S. Dist. Ct. (so. dist.) N.Y. 1972, Mass. 1973, U.S. Dist. Ct. Mass. 1973, U.S. Ct. Appeals (1st cir.) 1974, R.I. 1979, U.S. Supreme Ct. 1985. Assoc. Hart & Hume, N.Y.C., 1971-73; from assoc. to ptnr. Parker, Coulter, Daley & White, Boston, 1973-95; ptnr. McDonough, Hacking, Neumeier, & Lavoie LLP, 1995—. Mem. editl. bd. Def. Counsel Jour., 1989-92, editor, chmn. bd. editors, 1992—; mem. editl. bd. Boston Bar Jour., 1988-94; contbr. articles to profl. jours. Bd. dirs. Common Cause/Mass., Boston, 1980-91, 94-96, chmn., 1990-91; active Town Meeting, Lexington, Mass., 1989—. Fellow Am. Bar Found.; mem. ABA, Fed. Bar Assn. (pres. Mass. chpt. 1989-90), Am. Law Inst., Mass. Bar Assn., Boston Bar Assn. (chmn. ethics com. 1991-94, chmn. torts com. 1994-96), Internat. Assn. Def. Counsel (exec. com. 1992-97). Democrat. Home: 2 Pitcairn Pl Lexington MA 02421-7134 Office: McDonough Hacking Neumeier & Lavoie LLP 11 Beacon St Ste 1000 Boston MA 02108-3013 E-mail: rneumeier@mhnattys.com.

NEUMEYER, JOHN LEOPOLD, research company administrator, chemistry educator; b. Munich, Germany, July 19, 1930; came to U.S., 1945, naturalized, 1950; s. Albert and Martha (Stern) N.; m. Evelyn Friedman, June 24, 1956; children: Ann Martha, David Alexander, Elizabeth Jean. BS, Columbia U., 1952; PhD, U. Wis., 1961. Rsch. chemist Ethicon Inc., New Brunswick, N.J., 1952-57, FMC Corp., Princeton, 1961-63; sr. staff chemist Arthur D. Little, Inc., Cambridge, Mass., 1963-69; prof. medicinal chemistry, chemistry Northeastern U., Boston, 1969-91, dir. grad. sch., 1978-85, disting. emeritus prof., 1992—; chmn. bd., chief sci. officer, co-founder Rsch. Biochem. Internat., Natick, 1981-97; pres., co-founder Brain Rsch. Labs., Inc., 1999—2002. Mem. com. of revision U.S. Pharmacopeia, 1970-85; lectr. in psychiatry dept. psychiatry Harvard Med. Sch., 1996—; Boudewijn Tieboel vis. prof., Groningen-Utrecht Inst. for Drug Exploration, Holland, 1997, dir. medicinal chemistry program Alcohol and Drug Abuse Rsch. Ctr. McLean Hosp., Belmont, Mass., 1996—; cons. in field. Contbr. articles to profl. jours., chpts. to books in field; patentee in field. Mem. Bd. Health, Wayland, Mass., 1968-75, Pesticide Bd., Mass., 1972-75; mem. panel to sec. HEW Commn. on Pesticides and their Relationship to Environ. Health, 1969; mem. Mass. Tech. Collaborative, 1996—. Served to cpl. U.S. Army, 1953-55. Recipient Lunsford Richardson award, 1961, Marie Curie award in Nuclear Medicine, 1992; sr. Hayes Fulbright fellow, 1975-76, Henry A. Hill award for Outstanding Svc. to the Northeastern Sect., Am. Chem. Soc., 1998. Fellow: AAAS (mem. at large 1983—87, chmn. pharm. sci. sec. 1992—93), Am. Assn. Pharm. Scis.; mem.: Am. Chem. Soc. (bd. editors Jour. Medicinal Chemistry 1974—88, chmn. divsn. med. chem. 1982, councilor 1985—, trustee 1989—93, N.E. sect. chmn.-elect 2002), Am. Soc. Exptl. Pharm. and Exptl. Therapeutics, Am. Soc. Neurosci., Acad. Pharm. Scis. (Rsch. Achievement award in medicinal chemistry 1982, Northeastern U. faculty lectr. award 1978, univ. disting. prof. 1982—). Office: Harvard Med Sch/McLean Hosp ADARC 115 Mill St Belmont MA 02478-1041 E-mail: neumeyer@mclean.harvard.edu.

NEUMEYER, SUSAN LEE, lawyer; b. Wolf Point, Mont., Dec. 27, 1945; BA magna cum laude, St. Olaf Coll., Northfield, Minn., 1967; JD with honors, U. Ariz., 1975. Tchr. H.S., West Branch, Iowa, 1968-71; assoc. Curtin, Emerick & Mahoney, Mpls., 1975-91; ptnr. Hanbery, Neumeyer & Carney, 1991—. Author: Minnesota Wills and Estate Planning, 1993. Bd. dirs. Greater Mpls. Girl Scout Coun., Brooklyn Center, Minn., 1979-84. Mem. Minn. State Bar Assn. (chair bus. and profl. corps. com. 1997-2000), Hennepin County Bar Assn. (sects. corp., banking and bus., employee benefit, probate and trust, co-chair gen. practice, solo and small firm com. 1991-93). Office: Hanbery Neumeyer & Carney PA 3725 Multifoods Tower Minneapolis MN 55402

NEUNZIG, CAROLYN MILLER, elementary, middle and high school educator; b. L.I., May 5, 1930; kd. Stanley and Grace (Walsh) Miller; m. Herbert Neunzig, May 28, 1955; children: Kurt Miller, Keith Weidler. BA, Beaver Coll., Glen Side, Pa., 1953; MSSc, Syracuse U., 1989; postgrad., Adelphi U.; Cert., N.C. State U., Raleigh. Cert. in elem. edn., reading, history and English, N.C., permanent cert. in secondary English, N.Y. Reading tchr. grades K-6 St. Timothy's Sch., Raleigh, N.C., 1971-83, 5th grade tchr., 1983-88, 5th grade lead tchr., 1986-88; tchr. English and geography 7th grade St. Timothy's Mid. Sch., 1991—; tchr Am. govt. 12th grade St. Timothy's Mid. Sch./Hale H.S., 1991-93. Instr. continuing edn. program history Meredith Coll., Raleigh, 1990-91, spl. high sch. registration commr., 1991-93, instr. presdl. classroom, 1998, 99; mem. Ctr. for Study of Presidency, 1998-01. Asst. election ofcl. Wake County, N.C., 2000. Mem. AAUW, Am. Acad. Polit. and Social Sci., Acad. Polit. Sci., Ctr. for Study of the Presidency. E-mail: c.neunzig@gte.net.

NEUROCK, MITCHEL, lawyer; b. Kindley AFB, Bermuda, Mar. 31, 1966; s. Isadore and Frances Neurock; m. Kara Elizabeth Koller, May 26, 1990; children: Aryn Grace, Bennett Edwards. Student, Hebrew U., 1987-88; BA, Rice U., 1989; JD, Washington & Lee U., 1992. Bar: Tex., 1992, U.S. Ct. Appeals Armed Forces, 1993, Colo., 1994, U.S. Supreme Ct., 1997, D.C. 1999. Claims officer USAF, Whiteman AFB, Mo., 1992-94, dep. staff judge adv. Izmir Air Sta., Turkey, 1994-96; appellate govt. counsel Air Force Legal Svcs. Agy., Washington, 1996-98; counsel adminstrv. affairs Overseas Pvt. Investment Corp., 1998-99; assoc. Howrey, Simon, Arnold & White, LLP, 1999—2001; asst. U.S. atty. Laredo, Tex., 2001—. Appellate govt. counsel USAFR, 1998—. Capt. USAF, 1992-98. Mem. ABA, Fed. Bar Assn. (chair young lawyers divsn. 2001—, sec. Pentagon chpt. 1998-99). Republican. Jewish. Office: US Atty's Office PO Box 1179 Laredo TX 78042-1179 E-mail: mitchel.neurock@usdoj.gov.

NEUSCHATZ, JEFFREY SCOTT, psychology educator; b. Boston, Apr. 1970; s. Joseph Simon and Rita N. PhD, Binghamton (N.Y.) U., 1999. Asst. prof. St. Mary's Coll. of Md., 1999-2000; asst. prof. psychology U. Ala., Huntsville, 2000—. Contbr. articles to profl. jours. UAH rsch. grant U. Ala., 2001—. Mem. Am. Psychol. Assn., Psychonomic Soc., Am. Psychol. Soc. Office: U Ala at Huntsville Sparkman Dr Huntsville AL 35899

NEUSNER, JACOB, humanities and religious studies educator; b. Hartford, Conn., July 28, 1932; m. Suzanne Richter, Mar. 15, 1964; children: Samuel Aaron, Eli Ephraim, Noam Mordecai Menahem, Margalit Leah Berakhah. AB in History magna cum laude, Harvard U., 1953; postgrad. (Henry fellow), Lincoln Coll., Oxford, Eng., 1953-54; postgrad. (Fulbright scholar), Hebrew U., 1957-58; M.H.L., Jewish Theol. Sem. Am., 1960; PhD in Religion (Univ. scholar), Columbia U., 1960; A.M. ad eudem, Brown U., 1969; L.H.D., U. Chgo., 1978; D.Phil. (hon.), U. Cologne, 1979; Hon. Doctorate, U. Bologna, Tulane U., St. Louis U., U. Rochester. Instr. religion Columbia U., 1960-61; asst. prof. Hebrew U. Wis.-Milw., 1961-62; research asso. Brandeis U., 1962-64; asst. prof. religion Dartmouth Coll., 1964-66, assoc. prof., 1966-68; prof. religious studies Brown U., 1968-75, prof. religious studies, Ungerleider Disting. scholar Judaic studies, 1975-82, Univ. prof., Ungerleider Disting. scholar, 1982-90; Disting. Rsch. prof. religious studies U. S. Fla., Tampa, 1990-2000; rsch. prof. religion and theology Bard Coll., Annandale-on-Hudson, N.Y., 2000—. Vis. prof. Jewish Theol. Sem. Am., summer 1977, Iliff Sch. Theology, Denver, summer 1978, U. Frankfurt, 1991, Cambridge (Eng.) U., 1992, Abo Akademi U., 1993, U. Canterbury, Eng., 1994, U. Goettingen, Germany, 1995; Hill vis. prof. U. Minn., 1978; pres. Max Richter Found., 1969—; mem. Nat. Coun. for Humanities; governing bd. Nat. Endowment Humanities, 1978-84, Nat. Coun. for the Arts, 1984-90; lectr. in field. Author 650 books including: A Life of Yohanan ben Zakkai, 1962 (Abraham Berliner prize in Jewish History), A History of the Jews in Babylonia, 1965-70, Development of a Legend: Studies on the Traditions Concerning Yohanan ben Zakkai, 1970, Aphrahat and Judaism: The Christian-Jewish Argument in Fourth Century Iran, 1971, The Rabbinic Traditions about the Pharisees before 70, 1971, Eliezer ben Hyrcanus: The Tradition and the Man, 1973, The Idea of Purity in Ancient Judaism, 1973, A History of the Mishnaic Law of Purities, 1974-80, Judaism: The Evidence of the Mishnah, 1981, others; author numerous textbooks including American Judaism, Adventure in Modernity, 1972, From Politics to Piety: The Emergence of Pharisaic Judaism, 1973, 78, Invitation to the Talmud: A Teaching Book, 1974, Between Time and Eternity: The Essentials of Judaism, 1976, Form-Analysis and Exegesis: A Fresh Approach to the Interpretation of Mishnah, 1980; editor numerous books including Studies in Judaism in Late Antiquity, 1973—, Studies in Judaism in Modern Times, 1975—, Library of Judaic Learning, 1975—, Brown Judaic Studies, 1976-90, Chicago Studies in the History of Judaism, 1980-90; founder, editor-in-chief Brown Studies on Jews and Their Societies, 1985-90. Kent fellow Nat. Council for Religion in Higher Edn., 1957-60; Lown fellow, 1962-64; Guggenheim Found. fellow, 1973-74, 79-80; Am. Council Learned Socs. fellow, 1966-67, 70-71; research grantee Am. Philos. Soc., 1965, 67; recipient Univ. Medal for Excellence Columbia U., 1974, Von Humboldt prize Von Humboldt Found., 1981, Disting. Humanitarian award Ohio State U., 1983. Fellow Royal Asiatic Soc.; mem. Am. Acad. Religion (v.p., program chmn. 1967-68, pres. 1968-69, chmn. sect. on history of Judaism 1979-81, dir. 1981—), Soc. Bibl. Lit., Phi Beta Kappa. Home: 39 Kalina Dr Rhinebeck NY 12572-1022 Office: Bard Coll Dept Religion Annandale On Hudson NY 12504 E-mail: neusner@webjogger.net.

NEUSPIEL, DANIEL ROBERT, pediatrician, epidemiologist; b. Haifa, Israel, May 15, 1952; came to U.S., 1953; s. William and Miriam (Schwerstein) N.; m. Cathy Canepa, Apr. 12, 1987; children: Juliana, Samuel. BA, Rutgers U., 1975; MD, N.J. Med. Sch., 1979; MPH, U. Pitts., 1984. Diplomate Nat. Bd. Med. Examiners, Am. Bd. Pediatrics, Am. Bd. Preventive Medicine; cert. Am. Soc. Addiction Medicine. Resident in pediatrics Children's Hosp., Pitts., 1979-82; fellow in epidemiology U. Pitts., 1982-84; asst. prof. Albert Einstein Coll. of Medicine, Bronx, 1984-90, assoc. prof., 1990—; med. dir. U. Avenue Family Practice, 1995-97; chief pediat. ambulatory svcs., physician-in-charge Beth Israel Pediat. Assocs., 1997-99; assoc. chmn. pediats. Beth Israel Med. Ctr., 1998—; med. dir. Phillips Ambulatory Care Ctr., Beth Israel Med. Ctr., 1999—2002. Founding dir. early family outreach program North Cen. Bronx Hosp. Contbg. sect. editor AAP Grand Rounds, 1998—; contbr. articles to Jour. AMA, Am. Jour. Pub. Health, Neurotoxicol. Teratol, Devel. Behavior Pediatrics. Fellow Am. Acad. Pediatrics (chmn. sect. on epidemiology 2000—), N.Y. Acad. Medicine. Office: Phillips Ambulatory Care Ctr 10 Union Sq E Ste 2J21 New York NY 10003-3314 E-mail: dneuspiel@aol.com.

NEUSTADT, RICHARD ELLIOTT, political scientist, educator; b. Phila., June 26, 1919; s. Richard Mitchells and Elizabeth (Neufeld) N.; m. Bertha Frances Cummings, Dec. 21, 1945 (Dec. 1984); children: Richard Mitchells (Dec. 1995), Elizabeth Ann; m. Shirley Williams, Dec. 19, 1987. AB, U. Calif., Berkeley, 1939; MA, Harvard U., 1941, PhD, 1951. Economist OPA, 1942; mem. staff Bur. Budget, 1946-50, White House, 1950-53; prof. pub. adminstrn. Cornell U., 1953-54; prof. govt. Columbia U., 1954-64, Harvard U., 1965-78, Lucius N. Littauer prof. pub. adminstrn., 1978-87, Douglas Dillon prof., 1987-89, assoc. dean John F. Kennedy Sch. Govt., 1965-75, dir. Inst. Politics, 1966-71, prof. emeritus, 1989—. Spl. cons. subcom. on nat. policy machinery U.S. Senate, 1959-61; mem. adv. bd. Commn. Money and Credit, 1960-61; spl. cons. to Pres. elect Kennedy, 1960-61; to subcom. on nat. security staffing and ops. U.S. Senate, 1962-68; cons. to Pres. Kennedy, 1961-63, Pres. Johnson, 1964-66, Dept. State, 1962-69, Bur. Budget, 1961-70, AEC, 1962-68, Rand Corp., 1964-79, Pres.'s Reorgn. Project, Office Mgmt. and Budget, 1977-79; chmn. adv. com. candidate selection Commn. Presdl. Debates, 1988, 92, 96; vis. lectr. Nuffield Coll., Oxford, Eng., 1961-62, assoc. mem., 1965-67, 90-92; vis. prof., Princeton U., 1957, U. Calif., Berkeley, 1986, Cornell U., 1992, U. Essex, UK, 1994-96. Author: Presidential Power, 1960, rev., 1990, Alliance Politics, 1970; (with Harvey V. Fineberg) The Swine Flu Affair, 1978, reissued as The Epidemic That Never Was, 1983; (with Ernest R. May) Thinking in Time, 1986, Report to JFK, 1999, Preparing to be President, 2000; contbr. articles to mags., revs. Mem. staff Dem. Platform Com., 1952, 56, chmn., 1972; trustee Radcliffe Coll., 1976-80; mem. exec. bd. Coll. Letters & Scis., U. Calif., Berkeley, 1994-97. With USNR, 1942-46. Fellow Ctr. Advanced Study in the Behavioral Scis., 1978-79; recipient Grawemeyer award U. Louisville, 1988, Paul Peck prize Smithsonian Instn., 2002. Fellow Am. Acad. Arts Scis; mem. Am. Polit. Sci. Assn. (Woodrow Wilson award 1961, Hubert H. Humphrey award 1993), Nat. Acad. Pub. Adminstrn., Council Fgn. Rels., Inst. Strategic Studies, Am. Philos. Soc., Cosmos Club. Office: Harvard U Kennedy Sch Govt 79 Jfk St Cambridge MA 02138-5801

NEUSTADTER, RUDOLF PETER, retired engineer; b. Nottingham, Pa., Mar. 10, 1939; s. Gerhard and Susanna (Krueger) N.; m. Janet Louise Espenshade, Apr. 9, 1965; 1 child, Amy Elizabeth Fowler. BA in Physics, Millersville U., 1969; cert. in nuc. power, cert. protype reactor, USN, 1958. Registered profl. engr., Pa., N.H., Calif. Reactor operator, electronic specialty R.I. Nuc. Sci. Ctr., Narragansett, R.I., 1964-66; sr. test engr. Raymark, Manheim, Pa., 1969-74; instrumentation and control engr. Raytheon Engrs. & Constructors, Inc., Phila., 1974-80, supervising instrumentation and control engr., 1980-2000, ret., 2000. With USN, 1958-64. Recipient Presdl. Unit citation Pres. Eisenhower, 1960. Mem. Internat. Soc. Measurement & Control (sr., tech. session developer 1985, 89—, chmn. stds. and practices of various nuc. stds. 1989—, Achievement award 1993). Republican. Avocations: hiking, travel, model railroading, antique cars. E-mail: rjneust@aol.com.

NEUTRA, DION, architect; b. Los Angeles, Oct. 8, 1926; s. Richard Joseph and Dione (Niedermann) N.; children: Gregory, Wendy, Haig, Nicholas. Student, Swiss Inst. Tech., 1947-48; B.Arch. cum laude, U. So. Calif., 1950. With Richard J. Neutra (architect), Los Angeles, 1942-55; assoc. Neutra & Alexander, 1955-60; asso. Robert E. Alexander, 1960-62; prin. Richard & Dion Neutra, Architects and Assos., 1962—; pres. Richard J. Neutra, Inc., 1970—. Exec. cons. Inst. for Survival Through Design, L.A.; lectr. Calif. State U., L.A., Sacramento City Coll., Mira Costa State U., Cabrillo State U., Soka U., Tokyo, San Diego City Coll., Germany, Switzerland, Eng., Austria; vis. prof. Calif. State U.-Pomona, 1970, 85-86, U. Minn., 2000, Fullerton U., 2001, Nat. Bldg. Mus., 2002; vis. lectr. U. So. Calif., Va. Commonwealth U., 1998. Prin. works include various residential, ednl., religious and instnl. facilities including Am. Embassy Karachi, Pakistan, Gettysburg Meml., Simpson Coll. Libr., Adelphi Univ. Libr., Libr. and Resource Ctr. for City of Huntington Beach, Calif., Treetops Townhouses, 1980; exhbns. "View from Inside", 1984, 86, 92, 98, 99, travelling show, 2000, Visions & Exiles", Vienna, 1995, Am. Century Art and Culture, Whitney Mus., N.Y.C., 1999. Mem. Silver Lake-Echo Park Dist. Plan Adv. Com., Master Plan City of Los Angeles, 1970-71; mem. Citizens to Save Silver Lake, 1973-76; dir. Child Care and Devel. Services, 1970-71, Preservation and Maintenance of Existing Neutra Projects. Served with USNR, 1944-46. Street named Neutra Pl. in firm's honor, Silverlake, 1992; Neutra Centennial, 1992. Mem. AIA, Nat. Council Archtl. Registration Bds., Alpha Rho Chi. Studio: Richard & Dion Neutra 2440 Neutra Pl Los Angeles CA 90039-4400 E-mail: dionn@aol.com.

NEUWIRTH, ALAN JAMES, lawyer; b. N.Y.C., July 4, 1943; s. Bernard and Audrey (Hattenbach) N.; m. Patricia E. Neuwirth, Sept. 4, 1966; children: John A., Daniel P. BA, Lehigh U., 1965; JD, NYU, 1969. Bar: N.Y. 1970, U.S. Dist. Ct. (so. and ea. dists.) N.Y. 1972, U.S. Ct. Appeals (2d cir.) 1972, U.S. Ct. Internat. Trade 1983, U.S. Ct. Appeals (Fed. cir.) 1984, U.S. Supreme Ct. 1988. Assoc. Miller & Summit, N.Y.C., 1970-72, Ratheim, Hoffman, Kassel & Silverman, N.Y.C., 1973-75; ptnr. Kassel, Neuwirth & Geiger, 1976-86, Webster & Sheffield, N.Y.C., 1987-90; sr. ptnr. Morgan, Lewis & Bockius LLP, 1990—. Bd. dirs. various cos. With U.S. Army, 1969-74, USAR. Mem. ABA, Assn. of Bar of City of N.Y., N.Y. County Lawyers Assn., Internat. Trade Commn., Trial Lawyers Assn. Office: Morgan Lewis & Bockius LLP 101 Park Ave New York NY 10178-0060

NEUWIRTH, ALLAN CHARLES, designer, director, screenwriter; b. N.Y.C., Jan. 21; s. David Osias and Bella Jenta (Gajzt) N. BFA, Pratt Inst., 1977. Designer, dir. Studios of Diamond & Diaferia, N.Y.C., 1979-84; producer Klassy Prodns., 1984-92, Neuwirth Design, N.Y.C., 1992—; freelance comedy writer, 1984—; ptnr. Two Idioms, 1995—. Poster designer, The Phoenix Theater, N.Y.C., 1983-84. TV logo and title designer World Series, 1979, ABC News Nightline, 1980, ABC News This Week, 1982, ABC News Closeup, 1983; art dir. (TV) Mother's Day, 1983-88, Mother's Minutes, 1984-89; animator (home video) Your Newborn Baby, 1985; effects animator: (films) Sgt. Kabukiman, NYPD, 1990, King's Ransom, 1991; author: (book) Makin' Toons, 2003; illustrator: (book) Where in America is Carmen Sandiego, 1992; co-author: (screen story) Haunted Hacienda, 1995; (TV) The Wubbulous World of Dr. Seuss, 1996-97, Steven Spielberg Presents: Toonsylvania, 1998, Courage the Cowardly Dog, 2001, G-Man and the Gadgetinis, 2001; (cartoon) Koki, 1996—; co-developer TV series Big Bag, 1996, assoc. animation prodr., story editor, 1997—; supervising prodr., story editor TV series Fix and Foxi, 1999-2001; co-developer TV series Lab Rats, 1998; co-writer, dir., prodr. (short animated film) Hoppin' Jon, 2001; author (comic books) The Flinstones & The Jetsons, 1998-99, co-author (comic book) Wonder Woman vs. The Red Menace, 2000; co-creator (comic strip): Chelsea Boys, 1998—; storyboard artist (cartoon) Courage the Cowardly Dog, 1999; developer (TV) One Tree Hill, 1999; co-developer (TV) JuniorNet TV Show, 2000. Avocations: collecting vintage animation and cartoon art. E-mail: allanneuwirth@aol.com.

NEUWIRTH, GLORIA S. lawyer; b. N.Y.C., Aug. 16, 1934; d. Nathan and Jennie (Leff) Salob; m. Robert S. Neuwirth, June 9, 1957; children: Susan Madeleine Guerra, Jessica Anne, Laura Helaine, Michael Jonathan. BA, Hunter Coll., 1955; JD, Yale U., 1958. Bar: N.Y. 1959, Fla. 1979, U.S. Supreme Ct. 1976, U.S. Dist. Ct. (so. and ea. dists.) N.Y. 1976. Assoc. dir. Joint Rsch. Project on Ct. Calendar Congestion Columbia U., N.Y.C., 1958-61; assoc. Kridel & Friou, 1974-76; ptnr. Kridel, Slater and Neuwirth, 1976-82, 87-94; assoc. Kaye, Scholer, Fierman, Hays and Handler, 1982-84, Graubard Moskovitz McGoldrick Dannett & Horowitz, N.Y.C., 1984-86; ptnr. Davidson, Dawson & Clark, 1995—. Vol. arbitrator Better Bus. Bur. Author: (with R.B. Hunting) Who Sues in New York City: A Study of Automobile Accident Claims, 1962; contbr. articles to profl. jours. Trustee Blueberry Inc., 1962-70, Riverdale Country Sch., 1981-86; trustee, v.p., sec. Nat. Kidney Found., Inc., N.Y./N.J., 1980—, trustee nat. office, 1980-90; dir. Estate Planning Coun. N.Y.C., Riverdale Mental Health Assn., Bronx Opera Co., The

Ruth Turner Fund, Fin. Women's Assn. Recipient C. LaRue Munson prize Yale Law Sch., 1958. Fellow Am. Coll. Trust & Estate Counsel; mem. ABA, N.Y. State Bar Assn. (vice chmn. com. on law of the elderly), Assn. Bar City N.Y. (bd. dirs.), Estate Planning Coun. N.Y., Nat. Health Lawyers Assn., Appalachian Mtn. Club. Office: Davidson Dawson & Clark LLP 330 Madison Ave Fl 35 New York NY 10017-5094 Fax: 212-286-8513. E-mail: gsneuwirth@davidsondawson.com.

NEUWIRTH, MATTHEW ANTHONY, marketing executive; b. Sept. 14, 1965; BBA in Mktg., St. Mary's U., San Antonio, 1987. Ter. mgr. Procter & Gamble, Mpls., 1987-93; bus. mgr. ctrl. region Bausch & Lomb, Cin., 1993-98; dir. mtkg. Fielding Pharm. Co., St. Louis, 1998-99; pres. MB Packaging, 2000, ctrl. dist. mgr., 2001—. E-mail: mneuwirth@fieldingcompany.com.

NEUWIRTH, ROBERT SAMUEL, obstetrician, gynecologist; b. N.Y.C., July 11, 1933; s. Abraham Alexander and Phyllis Neuwirth; children from previous marriage: Susan, Jessica, Laura, Michael, Alexander. BS, Yale U., 1955, MD, 1958. Intern Presbyn. Hosp., N.Y.C., 1958-59, resident, 1959-64; asst. prof. ob-gyn. Columbia U., 1964-68, assoc. prof., 1968-71, prof., 1972-2001, Babcock prof., 1977-2001, Babcock prof. emeritus, 2001—. Dir. ob-gyn. Bronx Lebanon Hosp., N.Y.C., 1967-72, Woman's Hosp., N.Y.C., St. Luke's Hosp. Ctr., 1974—, St. Luke's Roosevelt Hosp., 1981-91; prof. Albert Einstein Coll. Medicine, 1971-72; cons. WHO, NIH, AID, FDA; interim dir. St. Luke's Roosevelt Hosp., 1998-2000. Author: Hysteroscopy, 1975; contbr. articles to profl. jours. Mem.: ACOG, Assn. Vol. Sterilization (chmn. biomed. com. 1971—), Am. Assn. Profs. Ob-Gyn., N.Y. Obstet. Soc., Soc. Gynecologic Investigation, Am. Gynecol. and Obstetric Soc. Office: St Lukes Roosevelt Hosp 1000 10th Ave Dept Ob New York NY 10019-1147

NEVANS, LAUREL S. rehabilitation counselor; b. N.Y.C., Aug. 1, 1964; d. Roy N. and Virginia (Place) Nevans; m. Russell Baird Palmer III, Oct. 12, 1991 (div. Jan. 2001). BA in English, Secondary Edn. cum laude, U. Richmond, 1986, postgrad., 1989-92; MA in Edn. and Human Devel., George Washington U., 1991, cert. in job devel. and placement, 1992. Group leader S.E. Consortium for Spl. Svcs., Larchmont, NY, 1980—85; vocat. instr. Assn. for Retarded Citizens Montgomery County, Rockville, Md., 1986—89; edn. specialist George Washington U. Out of Sch. Work Experience Program, Washington, 1989—90; rsch. asst. George Washington U. Dept. Tchr. Prep. & Spl. Edn., 1989—91; employability skills tchr., rsch. intern Nat. Rehab. Hosp. Rehab. Engring. Dept., 1991; vocat./ind. living skills specialist The Independence Ctr., Rockville, Md., 1991—93; leadership team mgr. Career Choice project The Endependence Ctr. of No. Va., Arlington, 1993—94; program dir. United Cerebral Palsy of D.C. and No. Va., Washington, 1994—97; sr. assistive tech. specialist Tech., Automation & Mgmt., Inc., Greenbelt, Md., 1997—98; owner WebLaurels Designs, Silver Spring, 1998—, ArtistCrafts, 2001—, Clayers with Disabilities Listserv (electronic discussion list), 2002—, Artist Crafts, Silver Spring, 2001—. Teaching asst. Rehab. Counseling Program, George Washington U., 1991; moderator FPList Electronic Discussion List, 2000—. Bd. mem., newsletter editor Cameron Hill Owners Assn., 2002—. Recipient traineeship GWU Counseling Dept., 1990, 91. Mem. Nat. Rehab. Assn., Nat. Rehab. Counselors Assn., D.C. Met. Area Assn. Person's in Supported Employment (editor newsletter 1995-97), Nat. Career Devel. Assn., Nat. Employment Counseling Assn., Nat. Assn. Ind. Living, Am. Assn. Counseling and Devel., Am. Rehab. Counseling Assn., Nat. Polymer Clay Guild. Democrat. Avocations: writing, photography, music, travel, jewelry making. Home: 8501 Cameron St Silver Spring MD 20910-3466 E-mail: laurel@artistcrafts.com.

NEVANS, ROY NORMAN, food products executive, producer; b. N.Y.C., July 1, 1931; s. Al Nevans and Lillian (Schiff) Margolis; m. Virginia Place, Dec. 31, 1961; children: Lisa Ann, Laurel Sue, Judith Lynn. BS, U. Pa., 1953; MBA, Columbia U., 1957. Mgmt. trainee Henningsen Foods, Inc., N.Y.C., 1958-60, mgr. export sales div., 1960-65, mgr. nat. sales div., 1965-70, v.p. mktg. White Plains, N.Y., 1970-90; mng. dir. Henningsen Van Den Burg, Waalyk, Holland, 1979-90, Henningsen Nederland B.V., Waalyk, 1984-90, Henningsen Foods, Ltd., London, 1977-90; pres. Royco Internat. Inc., Stamford, Conn., 1991—. Pres Royal Productions, Ltd, New York, NY, 1966, New York, 73, Int TV Productions, Ltd, London, 1978—; exec producer NCM Entertainment, Inc, New York, NY, 1982—; bd dirs Global Educ Mgt, Wall St Inst, World Trade Club. Prodr.: (Broadway plays) Gandhi, 1969, Solitaire Double Solitaire, 1972; (TV series) Juke Box, 1978—79; exec. prodr.: (TV miniseries) Roots of Rock and Roll, 1981. Lt comdr USN, 1953—56. Mem.: NATAS, US Naval Order, US Naval War Col, Univ Pa Club, Jaguar Touring Club, River Club. Avocations: classic cars collector, boating, theatre. Home: 74 Greenwich Hills Dr Greenwich CT 06831 also: 1945 Gulf of Mexico Dr #108 Longboat Key FL 34228 also: 302 W 12th St New York NY 10014 Office: Royco Internat Inc 1177 High Ridge Rd Stamford CT 06905-1203 Fax: 941-387-7304; Office Fax: 203-321-1295. E-mail: roycointl@att.net.

NEVAREZ, MIGUEL A. university president; Pres. U. Tex.-Pan Am., Edinburg, 1981—. Office: U Tex-Pan Am 1201 W University Dr Edinburg TX 78539-2909 E-mail: info@www.panam.edu.

NEVELOFF, JAY A. lawyer; b. Bklyn., Oct. 11, 1950; m. Arlene Sillman, Aug. 26, 1972; children: David, Kevin. BA, Bklyn. Coll., 1971; JD, NYU, 1974. Bar: N.Y. 1975, D.C. 1992, U.S. Dist. Ct. (so. and ea. dists.) N.Y. 1975, U.S. Ct. Appeals (2d cir.) 1975, U.S. Supreme Ct. 1982. Assoc. Marshall, Bratter, Greene, Allison & Tucker, N.Y.C., 1974-82, Rosenman, Colin, Freund, Lewis & Cohen, N.Y.C., 1982-83, ptnr., 1983-88, Kramer, Levin, Naftalis, Nessen, Kamin & Frankel, N.Y.C., 1988—. Editor N.Y. Real Property Service. Mem. planning bd. Briarcliff Manor, 1995—. Mem. ABA (vice chmn. com. partnerships, joint ventures and other investment vehicles 1988-95), Am. Law Inst., Am. Coll. Real Estate Attys., N.Y. State Bar Assn. (financing com.), Practising Law Inst. (lectr. 1988—, mem. adv. bd. 1991—), N.Y. County Lawyers Assn. (lectr. 1984—), Assn. of Bar of City of N.Y. (real property law com., lectr. 1984-88), Cmty. Assns. Inst. (lectr. 1986), Law Jours. Seminars (lectr. 1987—), Strategic Resources Inst. (lectr. 1994—), Internat. Health Network Soc. (vice chmn. 1995-2000), Inst. Internat. Rsch. (lectr. 1994—). Home: 134 Alder Dr Briarcliff Manor NY 10510-2218 Office: Kramer Levin Naftalis & Frankel LLP 919 3rd Ave New York NY 10022-3902 E-mail: jneveloff@kramerlevin.com.

NEVERSON, NORMAN C. political organization administrator; Chair D.C. Dem. Party. Office: Democratic Party Chmn 499 S Capitol St SE Fairchild Ste 110B Washington DC 20003*

NEVES, KERRY LANE, lawyer; b. San Angelo, Tex., Dec. 19, 1950; s. Herman Walter and Geraldine (Ball) N.; m. Sharon Lynn Briggs, July 28, 1973; 1 child, Erin Lesli. BBA, U. Tex., 1975, JD, 1978. Bar: Tex. 1978, U.S. Dist. Ct. (so. and ea. dists.) Tex. 1979, U.S. Ct. Appeals (5th cir.) 1979, U.S. Dist. Ct. (we. dist.) 1980; cert. personal injury trial law, Tex. Bd. Legal Specialization, 1994. Ptnr. Mills, Shirley, Eckel & Bassett, Galveston, Tex., 1978—93, Neves & Crowther, Galveston, 1993—2002; pvt. practice Law Offices of Kerry L. Neves, 2002—. Vice-chmn. Bldg. Stnds. Commn., Dickinson, Tex., 1991-98; mem. City Coun. Dickinson, Tex., 1998—. Sgt. USMC, 1969-72. Fellow Tex. Bar Found. (life); mem. ABA, State Bar Tex. (grievance com. 1989-92, disciplinary rules profl. conduct com. 1990-92, dir. dist. 5 1997-2000), Galveston County Bar Assn. (pres. 1989-90), U. Tex. Law Alumni Assn. (pres. 1991-92). Avocations: gardening, wine, reading. Home: RR 2 Box 95 Dickinson TX 77539-9204 Office: 1802 Broadway St Ste 206 Galveston TX 77550-4953

NEVES-ELBAUM, STELLA BOUDRIAS, design company representative; b. Boston, Mar. 3, 1949; d. Albert Joseph and Stella Ann (Shimkus) Boudrias; m. Alfred F. Neves, June 14, 1969 (div. 1978); children: Alexandria Lee, Jennifer Lynn; m. Marvin B. Elbaum, July 23, 1994. BA, U. Hartford, 1970. Pres. Home Nursing Svc., Hartford, 1973-80, Koenig's Art Supply, Old Saybrook, Conn., 1980-83, The Freelance Exch., Inc., Glastonbury, 1983—. Chmn. bd. dirs. ARC, Hartford, 1984-85. Mem. Conn. Women's Coun. (bd. dirs.), Les Chefs Femmes, Inc. (bd. dirs.). Avocations: skiing, gourmet cooking, gardening, golf. Office: Freelance Exchange Inc PO Box 1165 Glastonbury CT 06033-6165

NEVEU, JEAN, printing company executive; Chmn. Quebecor Inc., Montreal, Que., Can. Office: Quebecor Inc 300 Viger Ave E 6th Fl Montreal QC Canada H2X 3W4

NEVIASER, ROBERT JON, orthopaedic surgeon, educator; b. Washington, Nov. 21, 1936; s. Julius Salem and Jane Frances (Gibbons) N.; m. Anne Maclean Shedden, Dec. 3, 1966; children: Jeanne Nicole, Robert Jon Jr., Ian Maclean, Andrew Shedden. Grad., Phillips Acad., Andover, Mass., 1954; AB, Princeton U., 1958; MD, Jefferson Med. Coll., 1962. Diplomate Am. Bd. Orthop. Surgery with cert. of added qualification in surgery of hand. Intern N.Y. Hosp., Cornell Med. Ctr., N.Y.C., 1962-63, asst. resident, 1963-64; asst. resident in orthopaedic surgery N.Y. Orthop. Hosp., Columbia-Presbyn. Med. Ctr., 1964-66, jr. Annie C. Kane fellow, resident, 1966-67; fellow in surgery of the hand Orthop. Hosp., L.A., 1969-70; asst. prof. divsn. orthop. and hand surgery, chmn. dept. U. Conn., Hartford, 1970-71; assoc. prof. orthop. surgery George Washington U., Washington, 1971-76, prof., 1976—, dir. orthop. edn., assoc. chmn. dept. orthop. surgery, 1984-87, chmn. dept. orthop. surgery, 1987—; chmn. governing bd. Med. Faculty Assocs. George Washington U. Med. Ctr., 1995-98, bd. trustees, 2000—. Editor-in-chief Jour. of Shoulder and Elbow Surgery, 1997—; contbr. articles in field to profl. jours. Lt. comdr. USNR, 1967-69. Fellow Am. Soc. Surgery of the Hand, Am. Acad. Orthop. Surgeons, Ea. Orthop. Assn., Am. Shoulder and Elbow Surgeons, Am. Orthop. Assn.; mem. Alpha Kappa Kappa. Clubs: Princeton (N.Y), Manor Country Club, Cosmos. Republican. Office: 2150 Pennsylvania Ave NW Washington DC 20037-3201

NEVIL, LINDA, nursing administrator; b. Lowville, N.Y., Mar. 18, 1950; d. L.D. Jr. and Alice (MaKuch) Barnum; m. Terry Nevil, May 1, 1971; children: Michael, Amy. AAS, Agr. Tech. Canton Coll., 1970; BS, St. Joseph's Coll., North Windham, Maine, 1989. RN, N.Y.; cert. in ACLS, BLS. Nursing mgr. emergency dept., operating room, cen. supply Myers Community Hosp., Sodus, N.Y.; nursing mgr. gen. medicine unit, clin. practice mgr. Genesee Valley Group Health, Rochester; dir. ops., dir. patient svcs. Wilson Med. Ctr., Group Health Med. Ctrs.; dir. patient svcs. Lifetime Health. Home: 6093 Independence Way Ontario NY 14519-9156

NEVILL, WILLIAM ALBERT, chemistry educator; b. Indpls., Jan. 1, 1929; s. Irwin Lowell and Mary Marie (Barker) N.; m. Nancy Neiman Roll, May 19, 1979; children: Paul David, John Michael, Steven Joseph, Anne Marie, Deborah Ruth. BS magna cum laude, Butler U., 1951; PhD, Calif. Inst. Tech., 1954. Research chemist Proctor-Gamble, Cin., 1954; prof. chemistry, chmn. dept. Grinnell Coll., 1956-67; prof. chemistry Ind. U.-Purdue U., Indpls., 1967-83, chmn. dept., 1967-72, dean Sch. Sci., 1972-79, dir. grad. studies, 1979-83; pres. B&N Cons. Co., 1972-93; vice chancellor acad. affairs La. State U., Shreveport, 1983-85, prof., 1983-94; pres. Catoctin Assocs., 1993—. Arbitrator, mediator Ind. Employment Rels. Bd., 1975-83. Author: General Chemistry, 1967, Experiments in General Chemistry, 1968. Bd. dirs. Indpls. Sci. and Engring. Found., 1972-75, 79-82, Westminster Found., Lafayette, Ind., 1972-74, Am. Chem. Soc., 1986-92. With U.S. Army, 1954-56; col. USAR, 1956-84. Grantee NSF, 1959-74; Grantee NIH, 1963-70; Grantee Office Naval Research, 1953 Mem. Ind. Acad. Sci., Am. Chem. Soc. (chmn. sect. 1972, counselor 1973-92). Presbyterian. Home: 2229 Greenpark Dr Richardson TX 75082-4219

NEVILLE, BRUCE DAVID, librarian; b. Painesville, Ohio, June 14, 1955; s. Wayne Foster and Barbara Lee (Naughton) N. BS, U. Miami, 1977; MLS, Fla. State U., 1992. Biologist Gen. Devel. Corp., Miami, 1977-83; assoc. scientist Environ. Sci. & Engring., 1983-86; environ. scientist Kimley-Horn & Assocs., West Palm Beach, Fla., 1986-87, Gaby & Gaby, Inc., South Miami, 1987-90; libr. Terra Inc., Tallahassee, 1990-92, U. Tex., El Paso, 1992-96, U. N.Mex., Albuquerque, 1996—. Co-author: The Wentletrap Book, 1999; contbr. articles to profl. jours. Elected bd. dirs. Tropical Audubon Soc., Miami, 1982-89. Mem. N.Mex. Ornithological Soc. (bd. dirs. 1998—), Fla. Ornithological Soc. (sec. 1985-93), Conchologists of Am., High Desert Shell Club (founder 1998—), Beta Phi Mu, Sigma Xi (outstanding svc. award 1995). Avocation: avid birder and conchologist. Office: Centennial Libr U Nmex Albuquerque NM 87131-1466

NEVILLE, EMILY TAM LIN, writer, educator; b. N.Y.C., Nov. 2, 1944; d. Glenn Thomas and Emily (Cheney) N.; m. Richard Leavitt, Mar. 14, 1970 (div. Sept. 1973); m. Herbert Julian Stern, Apr. 30, 1977; 1 child, Anna Charlotte. BA in Religion, Temple U., 1968; MFA, Vt. Coll., 1989. Creative writing tchg. fellow Butler U., Indpls., 1990-97; part-time faculty Emerson Coll., 2001—. Author: (poetry) Journey Cake, 1998. Avocation: reading. Home: 24 Quincy St Somerville MA 02143-1720 Office: Emerson College Dept English 120 Boylston St Boston MA 02116

NEVILLE, GWEN KENNEDY, anthropology educator; b. Taylor, Tex., Mar. 23, 1938; d. Matthew Ranken and Gwendolyn (Harrison) Kennedy; m. William Gordon Neville (div.); children: Katherine, Mary Grace, William Kennedy; m. Jack Gregory Hunnicutt, Jr., 1975. BA, Mary Baldwin Coll., Staunton, Va., 1959; MA, U. Fla., 1968, PhD, 1971. Asst. prof. Emory U., Atlanta, 1971-78, assoc. prof., 1978-79, Southwestern U., Georgetown, Tex., 1979-84, prof. anthropology, 1984—, Elizabeth Root Paden chairholder, 1979—. Cons. Wenner-Gren Conf., Mt. Kisco, N.Y., 1983; grant holder NEH, Washington, 1972, 89; researcher, writer Lilly Endowment, Indpls., 1988—; bd. dirs. Soc. for Anthropology of Europe, 1988—. Author: Kinship and Pilgrimage, 1987, The Mother Town, 1995; co-author: Generation to Generation, 1973, Learning Through Liturgy, 1978; contbr. articles to profl. jours. Fellow Am. Anthropol. Assn.; mem. Am. Ethnological Soc., Am. Folklore Soc., Soc. for Anthropology of Europe (bd. dirs. 1989-92), Assn. for Scottish Ethnography, Coun. on Anthropology and Edn. (bd. dirs. 1971-74), So. Anthropol. Soc. (editor 1974-77), Phi Beta Kappa. Methodist. Office: Southwestern Univ University Ave at Maple St Dept Anthropolgy Georgetown TX 78626

NEVILLE, JAMES EDWARD, lawyer; b. East St. Louis, Ill., Jan. 1, 1955; s. Hugh Edward and Eugenia Catherine Neville; m. Carol Sullivan; children: Jared, Suzanne, Patrick, Evan. BSBA, St. Louis U., 1977, JD, 1980. Bar: Ill. 1980, U.S. Dist. Ct. (so. and ctrl. dists.) Ill. 1980, U.S. Dist. Ct. (ea. dist.) Mo. 1991, U.S. Ct. Appeals (7th cir.) 1991, Mo. 1992. Atty. Gundlach Lee Eggmann Boyle & Roessler, Belleville, Ill., 1980-94, Neville Richards DeFranco & Wuller, Belleville, 1994—. Spkr. in field. Contbr. articles to profl. jours. Coach Belle Clair Soccer League, Belleville, Ill., 1984—, West End Khoury League, Belleville, 1984-99. Roman Catholic. Avocations: sports, coach, reading. Home: 501 Oak Hill Dr Belleville IL 62223-2258 Office: Neville Richards DeFranco & Wuller #5 Park Pl Profl Ctr Belleville IL 62226 E-mail: jneville@nrdw-law.com.

NEVILLE, JAMES MORTON, retired lawyer, consumer products executive; b. Mpls., May 28, 1939; s. Philip and Maurene (Morton) N.; m. Judie Martha Proctor, Sept. 9, 1961; children: Stephen Warren, Martha Maurene Hereford. BA, U. Minn., JD magna cum laude, 1964. Bar: Minn. 1964, Mo. 1984. Assoc. Neville, Johnson & Thompson, Mpls., 1964-69, ptnr., 1969-70; assoc. counsel Gen. Mills, Inc., 1970-77, sr. assoc. counsel, 1977-83, corp. sec., 1976-83; v.p., sec., asst. gen. counsel Ralston Purina Co., St. Louis, 1983-84, v.p., gen. counsel, sec., 1984-96, v.p., gen. counsel, 1996-2000, v.p., sr. counsel, 2000-01; ret., 2001; chmn. The Thompson Ctr., 2002—. Lectr. bus. law. U. Minn., 1967-71. Named Man of Yr., Edina Jaycees, 1967. Mem. ABA, Mo. Bar Assn., U.S. Supreme Ct. Bar Assn., St. Louis Bar Assn., U. Minn. Law Sch. Alumni Assn., Old Warson Country Club, Ladue Racquet Club, Order of Coif, Phi Delta Phi, Psi Upsilon. Episcopalian. Home: 9810 Log Cabin Ct Saint Louis MO 63124-1133 E-mail: jnev57@aol.com.

NEVILLE, PHOEBE, choreographer, dancer, educator; b. Swarthmore, Pa., Sept. 28, 1941; d. Kennith R. and Marion (Eberbach) Balsley; m. Philip E. Hipwell, June 21, 1969 (dissolved Sept. 1978); m. Philip Corner, Nov. 3, 1996. Student, Wilson Coll., 1959-61. Cert. practitioner body mind centering, registered somatic movement therapist. Instr. Bennington (Vt.) Coll., 1981-84, 87-88; vis. lectr. UCLA, 1984-86. Dancer, choreographer Judson Meml. Ch., N.Y.C., 1966—70, Dance Uptown Series, 1969, Cubiculo Theatre, 1972—75, Delacorte Dance Festival, 1976, Dance Umbrella Series, 1977, Riverside Dance Festival, 1976, 1978, N.Y. Seasons, 1979—, dancer, artistic dir. Phoebe Neville Dance Co., N.Y.C., 1975—, Jacob's Pillow Splash! Festival, 1988—, Dance Theater Workshop Winter Events, 1988—, performances with Philip Corner: Venice, Genoa San Michele al' Adige, 1966—, BBB Festival, Thailand, Genoa, Salso Maggiore, Terme, 1997—, Seoul NY Max Festival, N.Y.C., 1998, Malpartida de Caseras, Spain, Caserano, Italy, 1998, Besancon, France, 1998, Paris, Lyon, 1999, Saluggia, Italy, 1999, Performance Festival, Odense, Denmark, 1999, 2001, Bassano del Grappa, Genoa, Italy, 2000, 2001, 2002. Recipient Creative Artist Public Svc. award, 1975; Nat. Endowment for Arts fellow, 1975, 79, 80, 85-87, 92-94, Choreographic fellow N.Y. Found. for Arts, 1989. Mem.: Internat. Assn. Healthcare Practitioners, Internat. Movement Edn. and Therapy Assn. (registered), Body-Mind Centering Assn. (cert. practitioner and tchr.). Buddhist.

NEVILLE, ROY GERALD, scientist, chemical management and environmental consultant; b. Bournemouth, Dorsetshire, Eng., Oct. 15, 1926; came to U.S., 1951, naturalized, 1957; s. Percy Herbert and Georgina Lallie (Jenkins) N.; m. Jeanne Frances Russ, July 26, 1952; children: Laura Jean, Janet Marilyn. BSc with honors, U. London, 1951; MSc, U. Oreg., 1952, PhD, 1954; FRIC, Royal Inst. Chemistry, London, 1963, DSc (hon.), 1973. Research chemist Monsanto Chem. co., Seattle, 1955-57; sr. chem. engr. Boeing Co., 1957-58; sr. research scientist Lockheed Missiles & Space Co., Palo Alto, Calif., 1958-61; sr. staff scientist Aerospace Corp., El Segundo, 1961-63; prin. scientist Rockwell Internat. Corp., Los Angeles, 1963-67; head dept. materials Scis. Lab., Boeing Sci. Research Labs. Boeing Co., Seattle, 1967-69; sr. environ. engring. specialist Bechtel Corp., San Francisco, 1969-73; pres. Engring. & Tech. Cons., Inc., Redwood City, Calif., 1973—. Contbr. numerous sci. articles on inorganic and organic synthesis, thermally stable polymers, pollution control processes to profl. jours. and books; many U.S. and fgn. patents in field; associateship Southampton U., England, 1951. Fulbright scholar to U.S., 1951; USPHS fellowship, 1951-52, Research Corp. fellow, 1952-54; chartered chemist, London. Fellow Royal Soc. Chemistry (London), Am. Inst. Chemists, AAAS; mem. Am. Chem. Soc., Am. Inst. Chem. Engrs., History Sci. Soc., Soc. Study Early Chemistry, Royal Instn. Great Britain, Research Soc. Am., Soc. Mining Engrs. of AIME, Calif. Mining Assn., Sigma Xi. Office: ETC Inc 1068 Eden Bower Ln Redwood City CA 94061-1806

NEVILLE, THOMAS LEE, food service company executive; b. Columbus, Ind., Jan. 1, 1947; s. Frank Thomas and Esquline Coons (Davis) N.; m. Shavona Rose Lagneau, Aug. 10, 1966; children: Timothy David, Sherry Lynn. AAS, Austin Peay State U., Clarksville, Tenn., 1994. Cert. exec. chef; cert. food exec. Enlisted U.S. Army, 1966, apptd. WO1, 1976, commd. CW3, 1986; food advisor Army Food Rsch., Devel. and Engring. Ctr., Natick, Mass.; ret. U.S. Army, 1990; regional mgr. KCA Corp., Hopkinsville, Ky., 1990—. Mem. Warrant Officers Assn., 1976-90. Mem. Ret. Officers Assn., Am. Soc. Quality Control, Am. Culinary Fedn., Am. Mgmt. Assn., Internat. Food Svc. Execs. Assn., Masons. Home: 1728 Clara Ct Clarksville TN 37040-7823 Office: KCA Corp PO Box 641 Hopkinsville KY 42241-0641 E-mail: tneville@kcacorp.com.

NEVIN, CROCKER, investment banker; b. Tulsa, Mar. 14, 1923; s. Ethelbert Paul and Jennie Crocker (Fassett) N.; m. Mary Elizabeth Sherwin, Apr. 24, 1952 (div. 1984); children: Anne, Paul, Elizabeth, Crocker; m. Marilyn Elizabeth English, Nov. 3, 1984; 1 child, Jennie Fassett. Grad. with high honors, St. Paul's Sch., 1942; AB with high honors, Princeton U., 1946. With Vick Chem. Co., 1949-50, John Roberts Powers Cosmetic Co., 1950-52; with Marine Midland Grace Trust Co. of N.Y., 1952—, exec. v.p., 1964-66, pres., 1966-70, chmn. bd., chief exec. officer, 1968-73; also dir.; vice chmn. bd. Evans Products Co., N.Y.C., 1974-76, Drexel Burnam Lambert Co., investment bankers, N.Y.C., 1976-88; chmn. bd., chief exec. officer CF & I Steel Corp., Pueblo, Colo., 1985-93. Dir. Magnatck, Inc. Chmn. exec. com. ACCION Internat. Lt. (j.g.) AC USN, 1942-46. Mem. Riverside Yacht Club, N.Y. Yacht Club (N.Y.C.), Blind Brook Club. Home: 20 Hope Farm Rd Greenwich CT 06830-3331

NEVIN, DAVID WRIGHT, real estate broker, mortgage broker; b. Culver City, Calif., July 27, 1947; s. Wilbur D. and Anita J. (Hulderman) N.; m. Shirley Grimes, Nov. 12, 1977; children: Jenny, David Wright Jr. BA, Calif. State Poly. U., 1974. Rural manpower asst. employment devel. State Calif., Riverside, 1970-74; pers. mgr. Lindsay Olive Growers, 1974-79; employee rels. mgr. Morton Salt Co., Newark, 1979-80; real estate salesman Valley Realty, Fremont, 1980-85; owner Nevin & Nevin Inc., 1984-88, CitiDesign, Fremont, 1989—. Co-owner Brokers Exch., Inc., 1985-86; dir., officer CitiBrokers Real Estate, Inc., 1986-94; owner Nevin Fin/Mortgage Exchange 1992—; br. mgr. Brandt Property Mgmt. Group, 1994-95; mgr. Internat. Trade Corp., Saigon, Vietnam, 1997. Sustaining mem. Rep. Nat. Com., Washington, 1984; mem. Presdl. Task Force, Washington, 1984, Cornerstone Fellowship. With U.S. Army, 1967-69. Mem. Realtors Nat. Internat. Real Estate Fedn., So. Alameda County Bd. Realtors (local govt. rels. com. 1983-86). Address: 2209 Carol Ann Dr Tracy CA 95377-6614 E-mail: davidwnevin@yahoo.com.

NEVIN, JEAN SHAW, artist; b. Bklyn., Dec. 21, 1934; d. Marshall Robert and Dorothy Frances (Brown) Shaw; m. Robert Stephen Nevin, Dec. 9, 1955. BA in English, SUNY, Albany, 1956. Textbook and freelance editor, 1959-74; printmaker, papermaker Jean Nevin Gaphics, Indpls., 1969-84; owner, mgr., knitwear designer Chameleon, 1985-88; pres., knitwear designer Knitting Machine Shop, Inc., 1988-91; owner Knitwearables, Albuquerque, 1991-97; painter, 1995—. Instr. print and paper making Indpls. Art League, 1974-83, exhibits coord., 1969, 73, edn. coord., 1979-80, editor Artifacts, 1968-69, 72-73; editor, pub. Swatchnotes, 1987-91; owner, gallery dir. Kokopelli Gallery, 2000-01. Exhibited to nat. group shows and galleries prints and handmade paper, 1970-84, garments and jewelry, 1992-97; painter, sculptor, mixed media artist, 1995—. Mem. Soc. Layerists in MultiMedia. Home: 9641 Mendoza Ave NE Albuquerque NM 87109-6614 Studio: Ste B 10753 Prospect Ave NE Albuquerque NM 87112 E-mail: jean@nevinart.com.

NEVIN, JOHN ROBERT, business educator, consultant; b. Joliet, Ill., Jan. 27, 1943; s. Robert Charles and Rita Alice (Roder) N.; m. Jeanne M. Conroy, June 10, 1967; children: Erin, Michael. BS, So. Ill. U., 1965; MS, U. Ill., 1968, PhD, 1972. Asst. prof. bus. U. Wis., Madison, 1970—77, assoc. prof. bus., 1977—83, prof. bus., 1983—, Wis. disting. prof. bus., 1988—89, Grainger Wis. disting. prof. bus., 1989—, exec. dir. Grainger Ctr. for Supply Chain Mgmt., 1992—, assoc. dean masters program, 1999—2002. Mem. investment adv. com. Venture Investors of Wis., Inc., Madison, 1986-99. Author: International Marketing: An Annotated Bibliography, 1983; mem. editl. bd. Jour. of Mtg. Channels, The Haworth Press, Inc., 1991—; contbr. articles to profl. jours. Bd. dirs. Madison civic Ctr., 1983-99. Mem. Am. Mktg. Assn. (bd. dirs. PhD consortium 1979, editorial bd. Jour. of Mktg. Chgo. chpt. 1983-97), Assn. for Consumer Rsch. Avocations: golf, skiing, running. Home: 7514 Red Fox Trl Madison WI 53717-1860 Office: U Wis Grainger Ctr Supply Chain Mgmt 975 University Ave Madison WI 53706-1324 E-mail: jnevin@bus.wisc.edu.

NEVIN, JOSEPH FRANCIS, computer systems engineer; b. Washington, Mar. 20, 1947; s. John Joseph and Mary Frances (O'Donnell) N.; m. Kathleen Cecelia Ridgell, Mar. 16, 1991; children: Christopher, Andrew, Amy, Megan. BA, Georgetown U., 1969; MS, Am. U., 1977. Dir. applications devel. U.S. Dept. HHS/Health Resources and Svc. Adminstrn., Rockville, Md., 1997—. Historian Smithsonian Assocs., Washington, 1982—. Dir. Balt. and Ohio RR Hist. Soc., 1979—, pres., 1982-83, 94-97, v.p., 1984-94. Recipient Adminstrs. award Health Resources and Svcs., 1983; Pub. Health Spl. Recognition award USPHS, 1984. Avocations: railroad and transportation history. Office: 5600 Fishers Ln Rockville MD 20852-1750

NEVIN, PHILLIP, baseball player; b. Fullerton, Calif., Jan. 19, 1971; First baseman San Diego Padres, 1999—, Anaheim Angles, 1998—99, Detroit Tigers, 1995—97, Houston Astros, 1995—95. Office: San Diego Padres Qualcomm Stadium 8880 Rio San Diego Dr San Diego CA 92112-2000*

NEVINNY-STICKEL, HANS BORIS, oncologist; b. Jan. 12, 1927; MD, Leopold Franzen's U., Innsbruck, Austria, 1951; SM in Hygiene, Harvard U., 1961. Rsch. fellow, assoc. Harvard Med. Sch., 1958-70; rsch. assoc. Children's Cancer Rsch. Found. and Peter Bent Brigham Hosp., Boston, 1963-70; clin. asst., assoc. prof. U. Ill., Chgo., 1970-87; assoc. prof. hematology/oncology sect. U. Chgo., 1988-89; dir. Alfred Strauss Tumor Inst. L.A. Weiss Meml. Hosp., Chgo., 1970-89; chief med. oncology Cancer Treatment of Tulsa, 1990—. Contbr. articles to profl. publs. and chpts. to books, including Cancer Rsch., Cancer Chemotherapy Reports, Jour. of AMA,

Am. Jour. Surgery. Bd. dirs. Uptown br. Am. Cancer Soc., 1970-89. Mem. Am. Assn. for Cancer Rsch., Am. Soc. Oncology, Am. Assn. for Cancer Edn. Office: Meml Med Ctr and Cancer Inst 2408 E 81st St Ste 100 Tulsa OK 74137-4222 E-mail: hans.nevinny@ctcoftulsa.com.

NEVINS, ARTHUR GERARD, JR. lawyer; b. Bklyn., Dec. 23, 1948; s. Arthur Gerard Sr. and Gertrude Anna May (Schlueter) N.; m. Reine T. Hughes, June 26, 1982; m. Amanda Mitchell, May 16, 1989. BS, Cornell U., 1971; JD, Fordham U., 1974. Bar: N.Y. 1975, N.J. 1976. Assoc. Lester, Schwab, Katz & Dwer, N.Y.C., 1975-77, Law Offices of Peter De Blasio, N.Y.C., 1977-80, Law Offices of Robert Ginsberg, N.Y.C., 1980-82; pvt. practice, 1982—. Mem. ABA, N.Y. State Bar Assn., N.J. Bar Assn., N.Y. County Bar Assn., Hudson County Bar Assn., Phi Gamma Delta. Roman Catholic. Home: 41 Charlestown Rd Hampton NJ 08827-2781 Office: 138 Central Ave Jersey City NJ 07306-2119 also: 225 Broadway Ste 3111 New York NY 10007-3001

NEVINS, BRYAN DEXTER, integrated circuit design engineer; b. San Francisco, May 16, 1961; s. Oren Sidney and Anna Lucile N.; m. Katarzyna Magdalena Martyka, Dec. 25, 1993. SB in Physics, MIT, 1983; MS in Physics, U. Ill., 1984, PhD in Physics, 1991. Design engr. Stanford Rsch Systems, Sunnyvale, Calif., 1992-93; device modeling engr. Linear Tech. Corp., Milpitas, 1994-98; analog IC design engr. Semtech Corp., Santa Clara, 1998—. Contbr. articles to profl. jours. Mem. Am. Scientific Affiliation. Lutheran. Avocations: bicycling, philosophy. Home: 617 Arcadia Terr #301 Sunnyvale CA 94085 Office: Semtech Corp 1111 Comstock Ave Santa Clara CA 95054 Home Fax: 810-222-5166; Office Fax: 408-727-8994. E-mail: bknevins@pacbell.net., bnevins@semtech.com.

NEVINS, HANK, marketing professional; b. Lockport, N.Y., July 23, 1948; m. Mary Elizabeth Provenzano, May 7, 1977; children: Henry P IV, Maria Luciana. AA, Grahm Coll., 1968; BA, SUNY, 1976. Ops. mgr. Sta. WBEN AM/FM, Buffalo, 1985-91; sr. dir., promotion MusicAmerica, Williamsville, N.Y., 1991-94; ops. mgr. Dame Media, Albany, 1994-96; dir. mktg. and pub. rels. Lockport (N.Y.) Meml. Hosp., 1996-2000; exec. dir. PHWNY Found., Williamsville, N.Y., 2000—. Contbr. Movies and Music, 2000. Bd. dirs. Diocese of Buffalo Media Adv. Bd., 1986-89; mktg. cons. Niagara Labor and Bus. Partnership, Niagara Falls, N.Y., 2000—, People Inc., Williamsville, 1999—. With U.S. Army, 1969-70. Mem. Vietnam Vets. of Am., Planned Giving Consortium (bd. dirs. 2000—). Roman Catholic. Avocations: travel, music, radio, memorabalia. Home: 28 Bonner Dr Lockport NY 14094 Office: Presbyterian Homes of WNY Found 4455 Transit Rd Williamsville NY 14221 Fax: 716-631-5461. E-mail: hnevins@buffnet.net.

NEVINS, LYN (CAROLYN A. NEVINS), educational supervisor, trainer, consultant; b. Chelsea, Mass., June 9, 1948; d. Samuel Joseph and Stella Theresa (Maronski) N.; m. John Edward Herbert, Jr., May 1, 1979; children: Chrissy, Johnny. BA in Sociology, Edn., U. Mass., 1970; MA in Women's Studies, George Washington U., 1975. Cert. tchr., trainer. Tchr. social studies Greenwich (Conn.) Pub. Schs., 1970-74; rschr. career/vocat. edn. Conn. State Dept. Edn., Hartford, 1975-76; rschr., career/vocat. edn. Area Coop. Edn. Svcs., Hamden, Conn., 1976-77; program mgr., trainer career edn. and gender equity Coop. Ednl. Svcs., Norwalk, 1977-83, trainer, mgr., devel., Beginning Educator Support and Tng. program Fairfield, 1987—; state coord. career edn. Conn. State Dept. Edn., Hartford, 1982-83; supr. Sacred Heart U., Fairfield, 1992—. Bias com. Conn. State Dept. Edn., Hartford, 1981—; vision com. Middlesex Mid. Sch., Darien, Conn., 1993-95; mem. ednl. quality and diversity com. Town of Darien, 1993-95; cons., trainer career devel./pre-retirement planning Cohen and Assocs., Fairfield, 1981—, Farren Assocs., Annandale, Va., 1992—, Tracey Robert Assocs., Fairfield, 1994—; freelance cons., trainer, Darien, 1983-87; presenter Nat. Conf. GE, 1980, Career Edn., 1983, Am. Edn. Rsch. Assn., 1991; lectr. in field. Tennis coach Spl. Olympics, 1993—, Darien (Conn.) Girls' Softball League, 1992-96, tennis coord. Spl. Olympics Summer Games, 1997—; mem. bldg. com. Darien (Conn.) High Sch., 1999—. Mem. NOW (founder, state coord. edn. 1972-74), ASCD. Avocations: tennis, running, walking, golf, travel. Home: 4 Hollister Ln Darien CT 06820-5404 Office: Coop Ednl Svcs 25 Oakview Dr Trumbull CT 06611-4723

NEVINS, PATRICK FREDRICK, librarian; b. Oak Park, Ill., Jan. 21, 1950; s. George Howard and Mary Jane Nevins; m. Barbara Ann Borowski, July 30, 1977; children: Kimberly J., Timothy P. BA, U. Ill., Chgo., 1972; MA in Libr. Sci., Rosary Coll., 1976. Libr. student asst. U. Ill., Chgo., 1969-72, math. libr. supr., 1972-76; libr. tech. asst. Northeastern Ill. U., 1972; head libr. Markham (Ill.) Pub. Libr., 1976-78, Grande Prairie Pub. Libr., Hazel Crest, Ill., 1978-79, Richton Park (Ill.) Pub. Libr., 1980—. Adv. com. rep. Suburban Libr. Sys., Burr Ridge, Ill., 1984-84, 97-99; bldg. cons. Homewood (Ill.) Pub. Libr., 1997. Leisure svcs. com. mem. Homewood-Flossmoor (Ill.) Pk. Dist., 1989-92, 93-96, pk. commr., 1997—, v.p., 1999-2002, pres., 2002—; softball and baseball coach Homewood (Ill.) Baseball, 1990-97; vol. Cancer Support Ctr., Homewood, 1997—, bd. mem., 2001-. Named Vol. of Yr., Ill. Assn. Pk. Dists. and Ill. Pk. and Recreation Assn., 1993. Mem. ALA, Ill. Libr. Assn., Ill. Assn. Pk. Dists. Avocations: reading, basketball, storytelling. Home: 1343 187th St Homewood IL 60430-3831 Office: Richton Pk Pub Libr Dist 4045 Sauk Trl Richton Park IL 60471-1239 E-mail: nevinsp@sls.lib.il.us.

NEVINS, WILLIAM J. oil and gas brokerage executive, consultant; b. Yonkers, N.Y., Sept. 16, 1952; s. Francis Robert and Alice Frances (Stager) N.; m. Joan Evelyn Leach, June 8, 1975 (div. June, 1980). BA in English Lit. and Fin., U. Miami, Coral Gables, Fla., 1974; postgrad. studies in Law, Western State U., Fullerton, Calif., 1974-75. CEO Nevins Enterprises Ltd., various cities, U.S., 1976—; CEO, pres. Century 21, Heritage Realty, Inc., North Miami, Fla., 1985-87, N&Z, Heritage Realty, Inc., Miami, 1987-96; sr. assoc., registered rep. Texakoma Fin. Oil and Gas, Dallas, 1996-98; oil and gas broker Western Am. Securities, Reef Exploration, Inc., 1998—; v.p., 1998-2001; sr. v.p., 2001—. V.p., bd. dirs. Pyramid Fin. Svcs., Inc. N. Miami Beach, Fla., 1983-84; cons. Park West Overtown Devel. Com., Miami, Fla., 1984-85, Miami Beach Developers and Investors Conf., 1985-90. Vol. asst. mgr. John V. Lindsay Miami Dem. Primary Campaign. 1972; founder Universal Children's Found. Inc., 1995. Mem. Nat. Assn. Security Dealers (registered rep.). Roman Catholic. Avocations: game fishing, antique autos, coin collecting, travel, yachting. Office: Nevins Enterprises Ltd 13237 Montfort Dr Ste 438 Dallas TX 75240-1117 E-mail: wjnevins@yahoo.com.

NEVLING, HARRY REED, human resources consultant; b. Rochester, Minn., Sept. 15, 1946; s. Edwin Reid and Ruth Margaret (Mulvihill) N.; m. Joanne Carol Meyer, Nov. 26, 1976; 1 son, Terry John. AA, Rochester C.C., 1973; BA cum laude, U. Winona, 1974; MBA, U. Colo., 1990. Pers. rep. Rochester Meth. Hosp., 1974-75; dist. mgr. Internat. Dairy Queen Corp., 1975-76; with David Realty Corp. David Realty Corp., Littleton, Colo., 1976-83, v.p., 1979-83, gen. mgr., 1981-83, Longmont (Colo.) United Hosp., 1977-99, pers. dir., 1977-87, dir. human resources, 1988-95, v.p. human resources, 1995-99; prin. HR Cons., Longmont, 1999—, pres., 1999. Cons. Front Range C.C. Denver, 1983-85; prin. Harry R. Nevling-Broker, 1983-85, 95-97; v.p. Realty Mart Internat., Inc., 1985-93, Dist. chmn. Am. party, 1973-74, St. Vrain Valley Sch. Dist., Health Occupations Adv. Com. 1977—, chmn. 1979-85, Vocat. Edn. Adv. Coun. 1986-91, pres. 1986-91; with Citizen Amb. People to People Program, Hungary, Czech Republic, Germany, 1991; mem. exec. com. Nat. Health Care Skills Stds. Project, 1993-95; spkr., presenter in field. Co-author: Healthcare Reform: The Human Resources Cornerstone to Successful Reform, 1992. Served to capt. U.S. Army, 1965-72; Vietnam. Decorated D.F.C., Bronze Star with oakleaf cluster, Air medal (22, valor device). Recipient Rescue citation for lifesaving Boeing Co., 1969, Helping Hand award United Way, 1974. Outstanding Svc. award, 1979, cert. of appreciation, 1982, Disting. Young Alumni award Winona State U., 1989. Mem. VFW (past post comdr.), Longmont Area Human Resources Assn., 1980-89, Boulder Area Human Resource Assn., 1978-2000, Mountain States VHA (pers. com. 1989-96, chmn. 1989-93), Colo. Healthcare Assn. for Human Resource Mgmt. (sec. 1980, pres. elect 1981, pres. 1981-82, exec. com. 1986-2000), Am. Soc. for Healthcare Human Resources Adminstrn. (ann. meeting chmn. 1985-86, regional dir. 1986-90, legis. and labor liaison 1988-90, chpt. rels. com. 1990-91, pres. elect 1991-92, pres. 1992-93, immediate past pres. 1993-95, exec. com. 1991-95, chmn. nominating com. 1994-95, chmn. conflict of interest com., 1994-95, nat. nominating com. 1996, Bylaws com. 1992-93, 96-99, Disting. Svc. award 1996), Soc. Human Resource Mgmt., Human Resource Cert. Inst. (sr. profl. in human resources), Vietnam Helicopter Pilots Assn.; bd. mem. Bus. Dependent Care Assn., 1995-99, pres. 1996. Home and Office: 1916 Century Hills Dr NE Rochester MN 55906-7623

NEVO, EVIATAR, biology educator; b. Tel Aviv, Israel, Feb. 2, 1929; s. David and Lea (Goldis) Levitas; m. Sarah Schneider, July 1951 (div.); children: Tal (dec.), Orit. MS with spl. distinction, Hebrew U., Jerusalem, 1958; PhD summa cum laude, Hebrew U., 1964. Lectr. biology Oranim Tchrs. state Coll., Israel, 1956-63; fellow in biology Harvard U., 1965-66; rsch. assoc. dept. genetics Hebrew U., Jerusalem, 1967-68, lectr. genetics, 1968-70, sr. lectr., 1970-71; rsch. assoc. Mus. Vertebrate Zoology U. Calif., Berkeley, 1972-73; from assoc. to prof. biology U. Haifa, Israel, 1973—, dir. Inst. Evolution, 1977—, incumbent chair evolutionary biology, 1984—. Vis. prof. zoology U. Tex., 1964-65. Editor: (with S. Karlin) Population Genetics and Ecology, 1976, Evolutionary Processes and Theory, 1986, (with O.A. Reig) Evolution of Subterranean Mammals at the Organismal and Molecular Levels, 1990, Mosaic Evolution of Subterranean Mammals: Regression, Progression, and Global Convergence, 1999; mem. editorial bd.: Theoretical Population Biology, 1975, Evolutionary Theory, 1978—, Israel Jour. Zoology, 1981, Genetique, Selection, Evolution, 1985, Bolletino Zoologico, 1985, Internat. Jour. Glirology, 1991—, Evolutionary Ecology, 1991—, Ecology and Noospherology, 1995—; contbr. over 750 articles to profl. jours., including Israel Jour. Zoology; contbr. 14 books. Fellow Fulbright, 1964, Guggenheim, 1978-80; recipient Decree of Merit, Internat. Biographical Ctr., Cambridge, Eng., 1996, Presdl. Seal of Honor, Am. Biog. Inst., 1996, Disting. Leadership award, Am. Biog. Inst., 1997, Hall of Fame award, Am. Biog. Inst., 1998, 20th Century Achievement award, Am. Biog. Inst., 1998, 2000 Millenium Medal of Honor, Am. Biog. Inst., 1998; named Man of Yr, Am. Biog. Inst., 1997, Man of Yr., Internat. Biog. Ctr., Cambridge, 1998, mem. Leading Intellectuals of the World, Am. Biog. Inst., 1998, mem. Order of Internat. Fellowship, Internat. Biog. Ctr., Cambridge, 1998. Fellow AAAS (fgn. mem.), Linnean Soc. London, N.Y. Acad. Scis. (Charles Darwin Assocs.); mem. NAS (fgn.), Soc. for Study Evolution (v.p. 1978), Am. Soc. Naturalists, Genetics Soc. Am., Genetics Soc. Israel, Zool. Soc. Israel, Ukrainian Bot. Soc. (hon.), Assn. Iberoamericana Biology Evolution (directing coun. 1993—), Human Genome Orgn., Ukraine NAS (fgn.), World Univ. Roundtable (hon. cultural dir.), Linnean Soc. London (fgn. mem.). Avocations: music, theater, arts. Home: 3 Hazaz St Haifa 34996 Israel Office: Inst Evolution Haifa U Mount Carmel 31905 Haifa Israel Fax: 04.8246554. E-mail: nevo@research.haifa.ac.il.

NEVOLA, ROGER, lawyer; b. N.Y.C., Apr. 30, 1947; m. Molly Cagle; children: Adrienne L., Jake F. Student, U. Notre Dame, 1964-66; BSME, Stanford U., 1968; JD, U. Tex., 1974. Bar: Tex. 1974. Assoc. Vinson & Elkins, Houston, 1974-79, Austin, 1979-81, ptnr., 1981-95; pvt. practice, 1995—. Fellow Tex. Bar Found. (life). Home: 4304 Benedict Ln Austin TX 78746-1940 Office: PO Box 2103 Austin TX 78768-2103 E-mail: roger@nevola.com.

NEW, ANNE LATROBE, public relations, fund raising executive; b. Evanston, Ill., May 10, 1910; d. Charles Edward and Agnes (Bateman) N.; m. John C. Timmerman, Sept. 30, 1933; 1 child, Jan LaTrobe. AB, U. S.C., 1930; postgrad., Hunter Coll., 1930-31, NYU, 1932-33. APR (Accredited Pub. Relations Practitioner). Editl. asst. Pictorial Review Mag., N.Y.C., 1930-32; copy asst. J. Walter Thompson Co., 1932-33; sub editor Cosmopolitan Mag., 1933-37, with Girl Scouts of the U.S., 1937-57, chief pub. rels. officer, 1945-57; dir. pub. info. edn. Nat. Recreation and Park Assn., 1957-66; special asst. gen. dir. Internat. Social Svc. Am. Branch, N.Y.C., 1966-68; dir. devel. Nat. Accreditation Coun. for Agys. Serving Blind and Visually Handicapped, 1969-78; pres. Timmerman & New Inc., Mamaroneck, N.Y., 1980-2001. Cons. dept. pub. adminstrn. Baruch Coll., CUNY, 1987-94, Sch. Pub. Affairs, 1994-99. Author: Service For Givers, The Story of the National Information Bureau, 1983, Raise More Money for Your Nonprofit Organization, 1991; contbr. articles to profl. jours. Bd. dirs. Mamaroneck (N.Y.) United Fund, 1963-64; chair nominating com. LWV, Mamaroneck, 1988; warden emerita St. Thomas' Episc. Ch., Mamaroneck. Recipient Marzella Garland award for outstanding achievement in promotion of improved housing conditions in Mamaroneck Village, 1995. Mem. Pub. Rels. Soc. Am. (bd. dirs. N.Y. chpt. 1958-72), Women Execs. Pub. Rels. (sec. 1962-63), Assn. Fundraising Profls. (bd. dirs. Greater N.Y. chpt. 1978-84), Phi Beta Kappa. Democrat. E-mail: annetimmerman@aol.com.

NEW, CLAUDIA MOSS, hospice social worker; b. Mexia, Tex., Oct. 17, 1941; d. William Thomas and Viola (Reynolds) Moss; m. Noah Edward New Jr., Sept. 22, 1963; 1 child, Courtney Page. AA, Coll. of the Mainland, 1969; BS in Psychology, U. Md., 1984; MS in Social Svc. Work, U. Tex., Arlington, 1991. Lic. master social worker, Tex. Vol. caseworker ARC, Seoul, Korea, 1984-85; exec. dir. DeSoto (Tex.) Community Outreach, 1987-90. Mem. NASW, Bus. and Profl. Women (pres.), DeSoto Jr. Svc. League, LaMarque Jaycee-ettes (pres.), Pilot Club, Alpha Delta Mu. Democrat. Methodist. Avocations: sketching, collecting seashells, reading mysteries. Home: 136 Highridge Dr De Soto TX 75115-6222 Office: Vis Nurse Assn 211 W Mulberry St Kaufman TX 75142-1940

NEW, ROSETTA HOLBROCK, home economics educator, nutrition consultant; b. Hamilton, Ohio, Aug. 26, 1921; d. Edward F. and Mabel (Kohler) Holbrock; m. John Lorton New, Sept. 3, 1943; 1 child, John Lorton Jr. BS, Miami U., Oxford, Ohio, 1943; MA, U. No. Colo., 1971; PhD, The Ohio State U., 1974; student Kantcentrum, Brugge, Belgium, 1992, Lesage Sch. Embroidery, Paris, 1995, Kent State U., 1998. Cert. tchr., Colo. Tchr. English and sci. Monahans (Tex.) H.S., 1943-45; emergency war food asst. U.S. Dept. Agr., College Station, Tex., 1945-46; dept. chmn. home econs., adult edn. Hamilton (Ohio) Pub. Schs., 1946-47; tchr., dept. chmn. home econs. East H.S., Denver, 1948-59, Thomas Jefferson H.S., Denver, 1959-83; mem. exec. bd. Denver Pub. Schs.; also lectr.; exec. dir. Ctr. Nutrition Info. U.S. Office of Edn. grantee Ohio State U., 1971-73. Mem. Cin. Art Mus., Nat. Trust for Historic Preservation. Mem. Am. Home Econs. Assn., Am. Vocat. Assn., Embroiders Guild Am., Hamilton Hist. Soc., Internat. Old Lacers, Ohio State U. Assn., Ohio State Home Econs. Alumni Assn., Fairfield (Ohio) Hist. Soc., Republican Club of Denver, Internat. Platform Assn., Phi Upsilon Omicron. Presbyterian. Lodges: Masons, Daughters of the Nile, Order of Eastern Star, Order White Shrine of Jerusalem. Home and Office: 615 Crescent Rd Hamilton OH 45013-3432

NEW, THOMAS L. public affairs, consultant; b. Greenfield, Ind., Apr. 4, 1951; m. Deborah R. New; 1 child, Emily R. BA cum laude, Harvard U., 1973; MAT, U. Chgo., 1974; M of Pub. Policy, Harvard U., 1984. Tchr. social scis. and humanities Maine Twp. H.S. South, Park Ridge, Ill., 1974-81; spl. asst. U.S. Senator Alan J. Dixon, Washington, 1982; tchg. fellow Johns F. Kennedy Sch. Govt./Harvard U., Cambridge, Mass., 1983-84; fiscal policy adivosr Ind. Senate Dem. Caucus, Indpls., 1984-88; exec. asst. for policy devel. Office of Lt. Gov. of Ind., 1989-92, chief of staff, 1992-95, Office of Gov. of Ind., Indpls., 1997—2000; exec. dir. govt. affairs Krieg DeVault LLP, 2000—. Dem. candidate Ind. State Treas., 1997—2000; campaign mgr. Gov. Frank O'Bannon, 1996, 2000.

NEW, WILLIAM NEIL, physician, retired naval officer; b. Atoka, Okla., Oct. 24, 1908; s. Robert Calvin and Nommar Bell (Willmore) N.; m. Ruth Anderson Pride, Mar. 30, 1940. BA, Central State Tchrs. Coll., Edmond, Okla., 1931; BS in Medicine, U. Okla., 1932, MD, 1934; postgrad., Northwestern U. Med. Sch., 1947-48. Diplomate: Am. Bd. Dermatology and Syphilology. Intern So. Pacific R.R. Hosp., San Francisco, 1934-35; commd. lt. (j.g.), M.C. U.S. Navy, 1935, advanced through grades to rear adm., 1963; resident dermatology and syphilology Naval Hosp., Phila., 1946-47; med. officer on gunboat and USMC Hosp., Shanghai, 1937-39; regtl. surgeon 7th Marines in Guadalcanal; later div. surgeon 5th Marine Div. (Japanese occupation), 1945; established Naval Med. Field Research Lab., Camp Lejeune, 1943; chief dermatology services naval hosps. Great Lakes, Ill., 1948-51, Phila., 1951-53, San Diego, 1956-59; force surgeon Fleet Marine Force, Pacific, 1954-56; comdg. officer U.S. Naval Hosp., Yokusuka, Japan, 1959-62; dir. staff Office Dep. Asst. Sec. Def. for Health and Med., 1962-66; pvt. practice dermatology Dallas Med. and Surg. clinic, 1968-91; ret., 1991. Clin. assoc. prof. dermatology Southwestern Med. Sch., U. Tex., Dallas, 1966-92. Mem. ACP (life), Am. Acad. Dermatology (life), Pacific Dermatol. Assn. (life), Assn. Mil. Dermatologists (past pres.), N.Am. Clin. Dermatol. Soc. (co-founder, life), Space Dermatol. Found. (co-founder), Cutaneous Therapy Soc. (co-founder, life). Home: 3310 Fairmount St Apt 17C Dallas TX 75201-1241 *Love and live today as we plan a rewarding tomorrow.*

NEWACHECK, DAVID JOHN, lawyer, writer; b. San Francisco, Dec. 8, 1953; s. John Elmer and Estere Ruth Sybil (Nelson) N.; m. Dorothea Quandt, June 2, 1990. AB in English, U. Calif., Berkeley, 1976; JD, Pepperdine U., 1979; MBA, Calif. State U., Hayward, 1982; LLM in Tax, Golden Gate U., 1987. Bar: Calif. 1979, D.C. 1985, N.Y. 1987, U.S. Dist. Ct. (no. dist.) Calif. 1979, U.S. Ct. Appeals (9th cir.) 1979, U.S. Supreme Ct. 1984. Tax cons. Pannell, Kerr and Forster, San Francisco, 1982-83; lawyer, writer, editor Matthew Bender and Co., 1983—. Instr. taxation wills and trusts Oakland (Calif.) Coll. of Law, 1993—; lawyer, tax cons., fin. planner San Leandro, Calif., 1983—; bd. dirs. Aztec Custom Co., Orinda, Calif., 1983—; cons. software Collier Bankruptcy Filing Sys., 1984. Author/editor: (treatises) Ill. Tax Service, 1985, Ohio State Taxation, 1985, N.J. Tax Service, 1986, Pa. Tax Service, 1986, Calif. Closely Held Corps., 1987, Texas Tax Service, 1988; author: (software) Tax Source 1040 Tax Preparation, 1987, Texas Tax Service 1988, California Taxation, 1989, 2d edit., 1990, Bender's Federal Tax Service, 1989, Texas Litigation Guide, 1993, Family Law: Texas Practice & Procedure, 1993, Texas Transaction Guide, 1994, Ohio Corporation Law, 1994, Michigan Corporation Law, 1994, Massachusetts Corporation Law, 1994. Mem. youth com. Shepherd of the Valley Luth. Ch., Orinda, 1980-85, ch. coun., 1980-82; bd. dirs. Oakland Coll. Law, treas., CFO, 1997—. Mem. ABA, Internat. Platform Assn., State Bar Assn. Calif., Alameda County Bar Assn., U. Calif. Alumni Assn., U. Calif. Band Alumni Assn., Kiwanis Club San Leandro (bd. dirs. 1998—, v.p. 1999-2000, pres. elect 2000-01, pres. 2001—), Commonwealth Club (San Francisco chpt.), Mensa. Republican. Avocations: music, competitive running, sports. Home: 5141 Vannoy Ave Castro Valley CA 94546-2558 Office: 220 Juana Ave San Leandro CA 94577-4839 E-mail: dnewacheck@abanet.or.

NEWBAUER, JOHN ARTHUR, editor; b. Newport, R.I., Apr. 24, 1928; s. John Arthur and Theo Caroline (Trewhella) N.; m. Marilyn Mahler, Oct. 14, 1956; children: April, Dana, Miranda. BA, U. Calif., Berkeley, 1951. Sr. editor and writer sci. and engring., rocket devel. dept. U.S. Naval Ordnance Test Sta., China Lake, Calif., 1951-56; editor in chief Astronautics and Aeronautics jour., N.Y.C., 1963-83; adminstr. sci. publs. AIAA, 1983-91, cons. editor, 1991—; editor in chief Aerospace Am., 1983-87, aquisitions editor, 1987-89. Fellow AIAA (assoc.), Brit. Interplanetary Soc. Home: 356 Bay Ridge Ave Brooklyn NY 11220-5315

NEWBERG, AARON NELSON, physician, pediatrician; b. Phila., Mar. 30, 1936; s. Samuel Aaron and Lillian B. Newberg; m. Gail Susan Snyderman, Aug. 9, 1964; children: Alison, Heather. BA, U. Pa., 1957; MD, Hahnemann Med. Coll., 1961. Diplomate Am. Bd. Pediats. Intern Albert Einstein Med. Ctr., Phila., 1961-62; resident in pediatrics Jefferson Hosp., 1962-64; attending physician Elkins Park (Pa.) Hosp., 1964—, Albert Einstein Med. Ctr., Phila., 1964—; clin. affil. pediats. Children's Hosp. Phila., 1968—, St. Christopher's Hosp. Phila., 1968—. Capt. U.S. Army, 1966-68. Mem. AMA, Pa. Med. Soc., Phila. County Med. Soc., Phila. Pediat. Soc. Avocation: physical fitness. Office: Tri-County Pediats Inc 9150 Marshall St Ste 14 Philadelphia PA 19114-2217 E-mail: DocofKids@comcast.net.

NEWBERG, ANDREW B. neuroscientist; b. Phila., Aug. 18, 1966; married. MD, U. Pa. Diplomate Am. Bd. Internal Medicine, Am. Bd. Nuclear Medicine, Am. Bd. Nuclear Cardiology. Asst. prof. U. Pa., Phila., 1998—. Bd. dirs. Phila. Ctr. for Religion and Sci., Phila., Inst. for Religion in an Age of Sci., Inst. for the Sci. Study Meditation, Phila. Author: The Mystical Mind: Probing the Biology of Religious Experience, 1999 (CTNS award , 2000), Why God Won't Go Away: Brain Science and the Biology of Belief, 2001. Mem.: AMA, Internat. Soc. for Neuroimaging in Psychiatry, Am. Soc. Nuclear Cardiology, Soc. Nuclear Medicine. Office: Univ Pa 110 Donner Bldg 3400 Spruce St Philadelphia PA 19104

NEWBERG, DOROTHY BECK (MRS. WILLIAM C. NEWBERG), portrait artist; b. Detroit, May 30, 1919; d. Charles William and Mary (Labedz) Beck; student Detroit Conservatory Music, 1938; m. William C. Newberg, Nov. 3, 1939; children: Judith Bookwalter Bracken, Robert Charles, James William, William Charles. Trustee Detroit Adventure, 1967-71, originator A Drop in Bucket Program for artistically talented inner-city children. Cmty. outreach coord. Reno Police Dept.; bd. dirs. Bloomfield Art Assn., 1960-62, trustee 1965-67; bd. dirs. Your Heritage House, 1972-75, Franklin Wright Settlement, 1972-75, Meadowbrook Art Gallery, Oakland U., 1973-75, Sierra Nevada Mus. Art, 1978-80, NCCJ; mem. adv. bd. Gang Alternatives Partnership Adv. Bd. Recipient Heart of Gold award, 1969; Mich. vol. leadership award, 1969, Outstanding Vol. award City of Reno, 1989-90. Mem. Nevada Mus. Art, No. Nev. Black Cultural Awareness Soc. (bd. dirs.), Hispanic 500 C. of C. No. Nev. Roman Catholic. Home: 2000 Dant Blvd Reno NV 89509-5193

NEWBERG, WILLIAM CHARLES, stock broker, real estate broker, automotive engineer; b. Seattle, Dec. 17, 1910; s. Charles John and Anna Elizabeth (Anderson) N.; BSME, U. Wash., 1933; MME, Chrysler Inst. Engring., 1935; LLB (hon.), Parsons Coll., 1958; m. Dorothy Beck, Nov. 3, 1939; children: Judith N. Newberg Bookwalter, Robert Charles, James William, William Charles. Salesman, Am. Auto Co., Seattle, 1932-33; student engr. Chrysler Corp., Detroit, 1933-35, exptl. engr., 1935-42, chief engr. Chgo. plant, 1942-45, mem. subs. ops. staff, Detroit, 1945-47, pres. airtemp. divsn., Dayton, Ohio, 1947-50, v.p., dir. Dodge divsn., Detroit, 1950-51, pres. Dodge divsn., 1951-56, group v.p., Detroit, 1956-58, exec. v.p., 1958-60, pres., 1960; corp. dir. Detroit Bank & Trust, Detroit, 1955-60; corp. cons., Detroit, 1960-76; realtor Myers Realty, Inc., Reno, 1976-79; owner Bill Newberg Realty, 1979— ; account exec. Allied Capital Corp., Reno, 1980— ; chmn. Newberg Corp., 1982; treas. Perfect "10" Industries. Elder, St. John's Presbyn. Ch., Reno, 1976— ; mem. exec. bd. Detroit Area coun. Boy Scouts Am., 1955-74, Nev. Area coun. Boy Scouts Am., 1976— ; Mich. state chmn. March of Dimes. 1967-68. Mem. Soc. Automotive Engrs., Am. Def. Preparedness Assn. (life), Automotive Orgn. Team (life), U. Wash. Alumni Assn. (life), Newcomen Soc., Franklin Inst., Alpha Tau Omega. Clubs: Prospectors, Harley Owners Group. Home: 1520 Sky Valley Dr Ste 204 Reno NV 89503

NEWBERG, WILLIAM CHARLES , JR. company executive; b. Pontiac, Mich., Dec. 27, 1964; s. William Charles and Dorothy (Beck) N.; m. Kari Ann Moyle, Nov. 21, 1992; children: Benjamin William, Kaisa Ann. BS in Bus. Mgmt., U. Nev., 1988, MBA, 1992. Contr., CFO, Grove-Madsen Industries, Reno, 1989-99, v.p., 1999—, also bd. dirs. Chmn. fiscal and efficiency group Regional Law Enforcement Task Force, Reno, 1995—96; mem. Regional Governing Bd., 1996—99, Dist. Bd. Health, Reno, 1998—2000; trustee Airport Authority of Washoe County, 2001—; councilman City of Reno, 1996—2000. Recipient meritorious svc. and leadership award Nev. chpt. Am. Planning Assn., 1995. Mem. Prospectors Club. Avocations: skiing, hiking, golf. Fax: 775-322-3995.

NEWBERN, WILLIAM DAVID, retired state supreme court justice; b. Oklahoma City, May 28, 1937; s. Charles Banks and Mary Frances (Harding) N.; m. Barbara Lee Rigsby, Aug. 19, 1961 (div. 1968); 1 child, Laura Harding; m. Carolyn Lewis, July 30, 1970; 1 child, Alistair Elizabeth. BA, U. Ark., 1959, JD, 1961; LL.M., George Washington U., 1963; MA, Tufts U., 1967. Bar: Ark. 1961, U.S. Dist. Ct. (we. dist.) Ark. 1961, U.S. Supreme Ct. 1968, U.S. Ct. Appeals (8th cir.) 1983. Commd. 1st lt. advanced to maj. U.S. Army JAGC, 1961-70; Prof. law U. Ark., Fayetteville, 1970-84; adminstr. Ozark Folk Ctr., Mountain View, Ark., 1973; judge Ark. Ct. Appeals, Little Rock, 1979-80; assoc. justice Ark. Supreme Ct., 1985-99. Mem. faculty sr. appellate judges seminar NYU, 1987-91; panel chmn. com. on profl. conduct Ark. Supreme Ct., 2001—. Editor Ark. Law Rev., 1961; author: Arkansas Civil Practice and Procedure, 1985, 2d edit., 1993. Mem. Fayetteville Bd. Adjustment, 1972-79; bd. dirs. Decision Point, Inc., Springdale, Ark., 1980-85, Hot Springs Music Festival, 2000—; bd. dirs. Little Rock Wind Symphony, 1993-2001, pres. 1993-95. Fellow Ark. Bar Found.; mem. Ark. Bar Assn., Am. Judicature Soc. (bd. dirs. 1985-89), Inst. Jud. Adminstrn., Ark. IOLTA Found. (bd. dirs. 1985-87). Democrat. Avocation: string band-guitar, mandolin, banjo and brass quintet-tuba. E-mail: dnewbern@aristotle.net.

NEWBERRY, CONRAD FLOYDE, aerospace engineering educator; b. Neodesha, Kans., Nov. 10, 1931; s. Ragan McGregor and Audra Anitia (Newmaster) N.; m. Sarah Louise Thonn, Jan. 26, 1958; children: Conrad Floyde Jr., Thomas Edwin, Susan Louise. AA, Independence Jr. Coll., 1951; BEME with aero. sequence, U. So. Calif., 1957; MSME, Calif. State U., Los Angeles, 1971, MA in Edn., 1974; D.Environ. Sci. and Engring., UCLA, 1985. Registered profl. engr., Calif., Kans., N.C., Tex.; chartered engr., U.K. Mathematician L.A. divsn. N.Am. Aviation Inc., 1951-53, jr. engr., 1953-54, engr., 1954-57, sr. engr., 1957-64; asst. prof. aerospace engring. Calif. State Poly. U., Pomona, 1964-70, assoc. prof. aerospace engring., 1970-75, prof. aerospace engring., 1975-90, prof. emeritus, 1990—; staff engr. EPA, 1980-82; engring. specialist space transp. systems div. Rockwell Internat. Corp., 1984-90; prof. aeronautics and astronautics Naval Postgrad. Sch., Monterey, Calif., 1990—2002, prof. emeritus, 2002—, acad. assoc. space systems engring., 1992-94. Recipient John Leland Atwood award as outstanding aerospace engring. educator AIAA/Am. Soc. Engring. Edn., 1986, Fred Merryfield Design award ASEE, 1997. Fellow: Brit. Interplanetary Soc., Inst. Advancement Engring., AIAA (dep. dir. edn. region VI 1976—79, dep. dir. career enhancement 1982—91, chmn. L.A. sect. 1989—90, chmn. acad. affairs com. 1990—93, dir.tech. aircraft sys. 1990—93, chmn. Point Lobos sect. 1999—2001); mem.: Planetary Soc., SID, SAFE, Am. Soc. Naval Engrs., Nat. Assn. Environ. Profls., Calif. Water Pollution Control Assn., Assn. Unmanned Vehicle Sys. Internat., Soc. Allied Weight Engrs., Soc. Automotive Engr., Water Environ. Fedn., Exptl. Aircraft Assn., Inst. Environ. Scis., Air and Waste Mgmt. Assn., Soc. Naval Architects and Marine Engrs., Am. Helicopter Soc., U.S. Naval Inst., Am. Meteorol. Soc., Am. Soc. Pub. Adminstrn., Am. Soc. Engring. Edn. (divsn. exec. com. 1976—80, chmn. aerospace divsn. 1979—80, exec. com. ocean, marine engring. divsn. 1982—85, newsletter editor 1982—87, divsn. exec. com. 1989—94, exec. com. ocean, marine engring. divsn. 1990—97, program chmn. 1991—93, chmn. 1993—95, chmn. Profl Interest Coun. 1995—97, bd. dirs. 1995—97, trustee 1999—2002), Am. Acad. Environ. Engrs. (cert. air pollution control engr.), Calif. Soc. Profl. Engrs., Royal Aero. Soc., NSPE, ASME, AAAS, IEEE, Kappa Delta Pi, Sigma Gamma Tau, Tau Beta Pi. Democrat. Mem. Christian Ch. (Disciples Of Christ). Achievements include research on aircraft, spacecraft, missiles, and engine design, waveriders, aircrew centered system design and related impacts on exergy, quality, concurrent engineering, cost and environmental controls. Home: 9463 Willow Oak Rd Salinas CA 93907-1037 Office: Naval Postgrad Sch Dept Aeronautics Astronautics AA/Ne 699 Dyer Rd Monterey CA 93943-5106

NEWBERRY, ELIZABETH CARTER, greenhouse and floral company owner; b. Blackwell, Tex., Nov. 25, 1921; m. Weldon Omar Newberry, Sept. 24, 1950 (dec. Nov. 1984); 1 child. Student Hardin Simmons U., 1938-39. Office mgr. F. W. Woolworth, Abilene, Tex., 1939-50; acct. Western Devel. & Investment Corp., Englewood, Colo., 1968-72; owner, operator Newberry Bros. Greenhouse and Florist, Denver, 1972—; bd. dirs. Western Devel. and Investment Corp. Englewood, Colo., 1979-87. Pres. Ellsworth Elem. Sch. PTA, Denver, 1961-62; v.p. Hill Jr. High Sch. PTA, Denver. Home: 201 Monroe St Denver CO 80206-5505 Office: Newberry Bros Greenhouse 201 Garfield St Denver CO 80206-5518

NEWBERRY, JAMES HENRY, JR. lawyer; b. Glasgow, Ky., Dec. 16, 1956; s. James H. Sr. and Carrie (Walker) N.; m. Cheryl Ann Harlow, Dec. 29, 1979. BA, U. Ky., 1978, JD, 1981. Bar: Ky. 1981, U.S. Dist. Ct. (ea. dist.) Ky. 1981. Gen. counsel Airdrie Stud, Inc., Midway, Ky., 1984-88; exec. officer Office Lt. Gov. State of Ky., Frankfort, 1987-89; ptnr., shareholder Newberry, Hargrove & Rambicure, PSC, Lexington, Ky., 1990-98; counsel, ptnr. Wyatt, Tarrant & Combs, 1998—, ptnr.-in-charge Lexington office, 2002—. Acting sec. Ky. Natural Resources and Environ. Protection Cabinet, Frankfort, 1991-92; deacon Calvary Bapt. Ch., Lexington, 1986-89, 92-95; bd. dirs. Blue Grass Cmty. Found., 2000--, v.p., 2001--; mem. Bluegrass regional bd. dirs. Nat. Conf. for Cmtys. and Justice, 2001--. Mem. Ky. Bar Assn. (sec.-treas. corp. house counsel sect. 1987-88), Fayette County Bar Assn., U. Ky. Nat. Alumni Assn. (bd. dirs. 1987-88), Phi Beta Kappa, Sigma Nu, Omicron Delta Kappa (Nat. scholar 1979). Democrat. Avocations: tennis, reading. Home: 744 Cottage Grove Ln Lexington KY 40502 Office: 250 W Main St Ste 1600 Lexington KY 40507-1714 E-mail: jnewberry@wyattfirm.com.

NEWBERY, ILSE SOFIE MAGDALENE, German language educator; b. Darmstadt, Germany, Nov. 15, 1928; came to U.S., 1965; d. Otto and Charlotte (Brill) Brusius; m. A.C.R. Newbery, Dec. 28, 1954; children: Martin Roger, Frances Janet. Diplom akad. gepr. Übersetzer, U. Mainz, Germany, 1949; Staatsexamen Höh. Lehrfach, U. Frankfurt, Germany, 1954; PhD, U. B.C., Vancouver, Can., 1964. Part-time lectr. Queen's U., Belfast, Ireland, 1955-56; grad. asst. U. B.C., 1958-62; lectr. U. Calgary, Can., 1964-65; asst. prof. Georgetown (Ky.) Coll., 1965-67, assoc. prof., 1968-83, prof. German, 1983-94, chair langs. dept., 1989-94, prof. emeritus, 1994—. Examiner Goethe Inst., 1983-87; oral proficiency tester ACTFL, 1985-87; rsch. in German exile lit. Author software in field, 1989—. Founding mem. internat. folk ensemble Singing Hons, Lexington, 1977—. Recipient KCTFL Project award, Ky. Coun., 1994, Rollie Graves Tech. Excellence award, 1993. Mem. Am. Assn. Tchrs. German (v.p. Ky. chpt. 1979-81, pres. 1981-83), Am. Coun. Tchrs. Fgn. Langs., Ky. Coun. Tchrs. Fgn. Langs. (bd. dirs. 1979-83). Avocations: music, tennis, squash, skiing, climbing.

NEWBILL, KAREN MARGARET, elementary school educator, education educator; b. East Orange, N.J., Oct. 6, 1945; d. Richard Oliver and Edna Mae (Crook) Jacobson; m. Gary C. Newbill, Aug. 18, 1965; children: Kari L., Erick D. BA, Seattle Pacific U., 1968; MEd, City U., Bellevue, Wash., 1993. Cert. tchr., Wash. Tchr. Shoreline Pub. Schs., Seattle, 1969-71, Northshore Sch. Dist., Bothell, Wash., 1971-74; tutor, substitute tchr. Issaquah (Wash.) Sch. Dist., 1980-89, tchr., 1989—, tech. and curriculum integration cons., 1991—. Adj. prof. N.W. Coll., Kirkland, Wash., 1994—, mem. prof. edn. adv. bd., 1994—; adj. prof. Seattle Pacific U., 1994—; student tchr. supr. U. Wash., Seattle, 1991—, guest lectr., 1996—98, City U., 1998—; presenter Nat. Brain Expo, 2000—02. Mem. ASCD, NEA, Wash. Edn. Assn., Nat. Coun. Tchrs. Math., Internat. Reading Assn. Avocations: decorative painting, reading, traveling, music. Home: 420 Kalmia Pl NW Issaquah WA 98027-2619 Office: Issaquah Sch Dist 565 NW Holly St Issaquah WA 98027-2899 E-mail: newbillk@aol.com.

NEWBLATT, STEWART ALBERT, federal judge; b. Detroit, Dec. 23, 1927; s. Robert Abraham and Fanny Ida (Grinberg) N.; m. Flora Irene Sandweiss, Mar. 5, 1965; children: David Jacob, Robert Abraham, Joshua Isaac. BA with distinction, U. Mich., 1950, JD with distinction, 1952. Bar: Mich. 1953. Ptnr. White & Newblatt, Flint, Mich., 1953-62; judge 7th Jud. Cir. Mich., 1962-70; ptnr. Newblatt & Grossman (and predecessor), Flint, 1970-79; judge U.S. Dist. Ct. (ea. dist.) Mich., 1979-93, sr. judge, 1993—. Adj. instr. U. Mich.-Flint, 1977-78, 86. Mem. Internat. Bridge Authority Mich., 1960-62. Served with AUS, 1946-47. Mem. Fed. Bar Assn., State Bar Mich., Dist. Judges Assn. 6th Circuit. Jewish. Office: PO Box 522 Glen Arbor MI 49636-0522

NEWBOLD, BENJAMIN MILLARD, JR. library manager, education consultant; b. La Grange, Ga., June 20, 1941; s. Benjamin Millard and Zeppa (Dasher) N.; married, 1968 (div. 1977); 2 children. BA in Sociology, Roger Williams Coll., 1970; MEd in Spl. Edn., Mid. Tenn. State U., 1975; MLS, U. So. Fla., 1985. Cert. tchr., Tenn., Fla., Ga., S.C., La. Tchr. psychotic, emotionally disturbed, mentally retarded Montanari Clin. Sch., Hialeah, Fla., 1970-72, 76-77; tchr. educatable mentally retarded Colleton County Bd. Edn., Walterboro, S.C., 1972-73, John Coleman Sch., Smyrna, Tenn., 1973-76, Hahnville H.S., Boutte, La., 1978-79, Gulf Comprehensive H.S., New Port Richie, Fla., 1979-80; tchr. severely mentally retarded, psychology supr. Sunniland Tng. Ctr., Ft. Myers, 1983-84; grad. asst. U. So. Fla., Tampa, 1984-85; adult reference libr. Houston Pub. Libr., 1986-89, libr. br. mgr., 1989-94, collection devel. mgr. Scenic Woods Regional Cluster, 1994; geneal. researcher Clayton Libr./Ctr. for Geneal. Rsch., 1994—. Pilot project tchr. Garrison Environ. Model, Rutherford County Bd. Edn., Murfreesboro, 1973-76; county coord. Spl. Edn. Grad. Credit, Murfreesboro, 1973-76; supr., adminstr., cons. pub. schs., pub. and pvt. facilities, librs.; active community pub. rels. P.T.A., sch. dists., librs.; ind. distbr. Enviro-tech Internat., Family of Eagles; ptnr. Bus. Leadership Inst. Vol. tchr. ESL Houston Pub. Libr., 1996—; active CONNECTEXAS, Austin, Fonwood P.T.A., Houston, Fontaine-Scenic Woods Civic Club, Houston, positive interaction program Houston Police Dept.; past mem. exec. bd. Houston Pub. Libr. Staff Assn. Recipient Spirit award Wall St.-The Club, 1991. Republican. Avocations: education, art, writing, politics, acting. Office: Clayton Libr Ctr Gen Rsch 5300 Caroline St Houston TX 77004-6803 Address: PO Box 324 Clallam Bay WA 98326-0324

NEWBOLD, HERBERT LEON, JR. psychiatrist, writer; b. High Point, N.C., Nov. 3, 1921; s. Herbert Leon and Mary Temperance (Sherrod) N.; m. Susan Deena Hecht; children: Lucile, Susan. Student, U. Chgo., 1941, Coll. William and Mary, 1941; BS, MD, Duke U., 1945; postgrad., Northwestern U., 1951, New Sch. Social Research, 1960-61. Intern U. Chgo. Clinics, 1945-46, U. Minn., 1949-50; resident Woodlawn Hosp., Chgo., 1946; resident in internal medicine Vanderbilt U. and associated VA Hosp., Nashville, 1946-47; resident in psychiatry U. Ill. and associated VA Hosp., Hines, Ill., 1955-58; practice medicine specializing in internal medicine Newton, N.C., 1947-48; practice medicine specializing in psychiatry Chgo., 1950-55, 1958-60; Asheville, N.C., 1961-70; N.Y.C., 1970—; pvt. practice specializing in psychiatry and neurology, 1976—; instr. neurology and psychiatry Sch. Medicine, Northwestern U., Chgo., 1958-61. Freelance writer, 1950—. Author: (novels) 1/3 of an Inch of French Bread, 1961, Long John, 1979, Dr. Cox's Couch, 1979, others under pseudonym, 1950-60; (sci. books) Psychiatric Programming of People, 1972, Mega-Nutrients for Your Nerves, 1975, Doctor Newbold's Revolutionary New Discoveries about Weight Loss, How to master hidden allergies that make you fat, 1977, Physicians Handbook on Orthomolecular Medicine, 1977, Vitamin C Against Cancer, 1979, Mega-Nutrients, 1987, Dr. Newbold's Type A/Type B Weight Loss Book, 1991, Dr. Newbold's Nutrition for Your Nerves, 1993, Dr. Newbold's Diet To Cure Incurable Diseases, 1994; (with others) The New Chemotherapy in Mental Illness, 1958; contbr. articles to profl. jours.; numerous appearances radio and TV. Served with U.S. Army, 1943-45, 46-47. Mem. AMA. Address: 21 E 10th St Apt 10C New York NY 10003-5922 *There are only two horses that win. One is called luck and the other persistence, and you can't count on the one called luck.*

NEWBOLD, JOHN LOWE, banker, financial consultant; b. Washington, Dec. 26, 1935; s. John Lowe and Katharine Emily (Wilkins) N.; m. Judith Allen Bourne, June 20, 1959; children: Jennifer Hathaway, Timothy Bourne, Michael Fleming. BS, Yale U., 1957; MBA, NYU, 1963; sr. execs. program cert., MIT, 1970. Asst. v.p., credit instr. Citibank, N.A., N.Y.C., 1968-69, v.p. retail trade unit, 1969-70, v.p. info. svcs. dept., 1970-72, v.p., corp. bank head Tokyo, 1972-73, v.p., country head Singapore, 1974-76, sr. v.p., shipping dept. head N.Y.C., 1976-85, divsn. exec., Global Shipping Divsn., 1985-89, divsn. exec., Global Transp. Divsn., 1989-97; ret., 1997; chmn., dir. Mchts. Fund, Inc., Bethesda, Md., 1981—. Bd. dirs. Timex N.V., Grupo Transportacion Maritima Mexicana, Mex., Chartering Solutions, Castalia Ptnrs. Ltd., One Fifth Ave. Corp. Trustee Reeves Reed Arboretum, Summit, N.J., 1999-2002, Summit Area Cmty. Coun., 1983-86, United Way, Summit, 1984-92; pres. PTA Presidents' Coun., Summit, 1981-83; dir. One Fifth Ave. Apt. Corp., 2001—. Served as lt. (j.g.) USNR, 1957-63. Mem. Yale Club of Ctrl. N.J. (trustee 1980-85). Home: 1 Fifth Ave 11J New York NY 10003 E-mail: jocknewb@aol.com.

NEWBORG, GERALD GORDON, state archives administrator; b. Ada, Minn., Dec. 13, 1942; s. George Harold and Olea (Halstad) N.; m. Jean Annette Gruhl, Aug. 14, 1964; children: Erica, Annette. BA, Concordia Coll., Moorhead, Minn., 1964; MA, U. N.D., 1969; MBA, Ohio State U., 1978. Cert. archivist. Tutor, preceptor Parsons Coll., Fairfield, Iowa, 1964-67; state archivist Ohio Hist. Soc., Columbus, 1968-76; v.p. Archival Systems Inc., 1978-81; state archivist State Hist. Soc. of N.D., Bismarck, 1981—. Instr. Franklin U., Columbus, 1974; adj. prof. Bismarck State Coll., 1985-86. Co-author: North Dakota: A Pictorial History, 1988. Recipient Resolution of Commendation Ohio Ho. of Reps., Columbus, 1976. Mem. Soc. Am. Archivists, Nat. Assn. Govt. Archives & Records Adminstrs. (bd. dirs. 1984-86, sec. 1994-99), Midwest Archives Conf., N.D. Libr. Assn. (exec. bd. 1985-86). Home: 1327 N 18th St Bismarck ND 58501-2827 Office: State Hist Soc 612 E Boulevard Ave Bismarck ND 58505-0660

NEWBORN, JUD, anthropologist, writer, curator, educator; b. N.Y.C., Nov. 8, 1952; s. Solomon and Rita (Cohen) N. BA magna cum laude in Anthropology and English, NYU, 1974; postgrad., Clare Hall, Cambridge U., 1974-75; MA in Anthropology, U. Chgo., 1977, PhD with distinction, 1994. Free-lance writer, N.Y.C., Munich, Chgo., 1974—; publicist Oxford U. Press, N.Y.C., 1975-76; founding historian Mus. Jewish Heritage (N.Y. Holocaust Meml. Commn.), 1986-92, 96-00. Pub. rels. cons.; cons., spkr., lectr. in field. Author: Shattering the German Night: The Story of the White Rose Anti-Nazi Resistance, 1986; contbg. editor Diplomatic World Obs., UN, 1999-2000; freelance writer, lyricist. Fulbright fellow, 1980-82; Newcombe fellow, 1984-85. Mem. ASCAP, Am. Anthrop. Assn., The Am. Hist. Assn., Authors Guild, Assn. Holocaust Orgns., N.Y. Old Growth Forest Survey, Phi Beta Kappa.

NEWBURGER, BETH WEINSTEIN, medical telecommunications company executive; b. Schenectady, July 8, 1937; d. H. Edward and Shirley (Diamond) Weinstein; m. Alan C. Newburger, Jan. 23, 1963 (dec. Oct. 1980); children: Mark, Lori, Eric, Jill; m. Richard Schwartz, May 26, 1989. BA, Cornell U., 1959. Dir. advt. New Republic, Washington, 1974-77; mktg. mgr. Washington Post, 1977-84; pres. Owlcat/Digital Rsch., Inc., Monterey, Calif., 1984-86; pres., CEO Corabi Internat. Telemetrics, Inc., Alexandria, Va., 1986-95; assoc. adminstr. Gen. Svcs. Adminstrn., Washington, 1996—2001; dir. comm. Nat. Trust for Hist. Preservation, 2001—. Chmn. bd. Health Street, Inc., Bethesda, Md., 1985—95; mem. NASA adv. coun. Tech. Commercialization Adv. Com., 1995—98; co-chmn. President's Comm. on Celebration of Women in Am. History, 1998—2000; commr., exec. dir. Women's Progress Commemorative Commn., 2000—01; bd. dirs. Nat. Women's History Project, 2000—; adv. bd. Eleanor Roosevelt Papers, 2000—; bd. dirs. Nat. Women's Hall of Fame, 2001—. Chmn. bd. Capital Children's Mus., Washington, 1994—98, trustee, 1984—; bd. dirs. Arena Stage , Washington, 1993—, BOAT/U.S., 1990—, Nat. Women's Hall of Fame, 2001—. Named Woman of Yr., Svc. Guild, Washington, l972, 73. Mem. Women in Advt. and Mktg. (bd. dirs. 1986-89). Home: 1401 N Oak St Arlington VA 22209-3648

NEWBURGER, CARYN LASON, English educator; b. Chgo., Aug. 28, 1960; d. Marvin Mitchell and Sandra Woolman Lason; m. Manuel Harry Newburger, Aug. 14, 1983; children: Michael Jonathon, Joshua Ian. BA in English, U. Tex., 1982, postgrad., 1996-97, MEd in Ednl. Psychology, 1989. Cert. counselor; cert. tchr. Tex. Tchr. lang. arts Bastrop (Tex.) Ind. Sch. Dist., 1982-89; assoc. prof. Austin C.C., 2001—. Adj. instr., writing Austin C.C., 1989-2001, assoc. prof. devel. writing, 2001—; adj. rep. Austin C.C., Austin, 1996-2001; ednl. cons., writer Comms. Cons., Norman, Okla., 1989—. Student coun. advisor Bastrop Ind. Sch. Dist., 1983-86, mid. sch. gifted program coord., 1988-89; room parent St. Francis Sch., Austin, 1998-2000; ballet docent Ballet Austin, 1989-90. Recipient Tchg. Excellence award Nat. Inst. for Staff and Orgnl. Devel., 2000. Mem. MLA, Nat. Coun. of Tchrs. of English. Avocations: ballet dancing, writing, gardening. Office: Austin CC 5930 Middle Fiskville Rd Austin TX 78752-4341 E-mail: carynn@austin.cc.tx.us.

NEWBURGER, HOWARD MARTIN, psychoanalyst; b. N.Y.C., May 16, 1924; s. Bernhard and Bertha (Travers) N.; m. Doris Schekter, July 3, 1949; children: Amy, Barry, Cary. BA, NYU, 1948, MA, 1950, PhD, 1952; tng. in Jungian, Neo-Freudian and Horneyian psychoanalysis. Cert. in group psychotherapy and psychodrama. Rotating intern N.J. Dept. Instns. and Agys., 1948-49; chief psychologist N.J. State Instn., Annandale, 1949-52; dir. psychoanalysis Div. Social Def. UN, 1952; pvt. practice in psychoanalysis and group psychotherapy, 1952—; dir. rsch. HEW, 1958; rsch. assoc. Beth Israel Hosp., 1958-69. Staff mem. St. Agnes Hosp., White Plains, 1991—; lectr., adj. assoc. prof. NYU, 1951-60, chmn. dept. exceptional child and youth, 1954-62; chmn. faculty and supr. treatment Inst. Applied Human Dynamics, 1960—; lectr., cons. in field; prelect prof. psychology John Jay Coll. Criminal Justice, 1969-72; chmn. bd. dirs. Inst. Applied Human Dynamics, N.Y.C. and Westchester, N.Y., 1960-81, exec. v.p., 1983-85; cons. Police Dept., Harrison, N.Y., 1970—, dean faculty IAHD, 1999-2002. Co-author: Winners and Losers. Assoc. editor: Excerpta Medica, 1951-62. Contbr. articles and papers to tech. jours. Trustee Acad. Jewish Religion, 1991-96. Served with AUS, World War II, ETO; with AUS, MTO. Recipient Outstanding Service to Humanity award Inst. Applied Human Dynamics for Handicapped, 1970 Mem. Am. Psychol. Assn., Am. Soc. Group Psychotherapy and Psychodrama (sec.-treas. 1954-55). Office: 4 Timber Trl Rye NY 10580-1935 *Our country affords tremendous opportunity. Through the development of our inner resources, and their assertion, we can all have happy and effective lives.*

NEWBY, EARL FERNANDO, educator; b. Louisville, Apr. 14, 1948; BS, Tenn. State U., 1970; MA, U. Louisville, 1972; EdD, Spalding U., 1998. Cons., tchr. edn. Ky. Dept. Edn., Frankfort, 1970; tchr., prin. Jefferson County Schs., Louisville, 1971-75, Greater Clark County Schs., Jeffersonville, Ind., 1975-98; cons., computer tech. Newby & Assocs., Louisville, 1996—; asst. prof. Morehead (Ky.) State U., 1998—. Adj. prof. Western Ky. U., Bowling Green, 1998; prof. Eastern Ky. U., 1999-2001; presenter in field. Contbr. articles to profl. publs. Named to Order Ky. Cols. Mem. Am. Assn. Sch. Adminstrs. (presenter ann. internat. conf. Orlando, Fla. 2001), NAESP (presenter ann. internat. conf. San Diego, Calif. 2001), So. Regional Coun. Ednl. Adminstrs., Nat. Coun. Profs. Ednl. Adminstrn. (presenter nat. conf. Houston 2001), Nat. Assn. Black Sch. Educators, Ky. Assn. Sch. Adminstrs., Ky. Assn. Black Sch. Educators, Lexington Assn. Black Sch. Educators, Kappa Alpha Psi, Phi Delta Kappa, Pi Lambda Theta (presenter profl. assn. in edn. ann. conf. Mpls. 2001), Sigma Rho Sigma. Democrat. Methodist. Avocations: tennis, basketball, reading, bowling, golf. Home: PO Box 211 Harrods Creek KY 40027-0211 Office: Eastern Ky U/Coll Edn Dept Counseling & Edn 521 Lancaster Ave Richmond KY 40475-3100 Fax: 859-622-1126.

NEWBY, ELIZABETH ANN, elementary education educator; b. Greensburg, Ky. BS, U. Louisville, 1974, M in Edn., 1980. Cert. elem. tchr., Ky., supr. instrn., elem. sch. prin., endorsement for kindergarten, adminstrn. and supervision. Tchr. Jefferson County Pub. Schs., Louisville, 1974-90, tchr., acting prin. Zachary Taylor, 1990-95, Ky. resource tchr. Zachary Taylor, 1995-96, prin. intern Fern Creek and Tully Schs., 1996-97, tchr. Dunn Elem. Sch., 1997—; prin. for Tomorrow Jefferson County Schs. and U. Louisville, 1994-95. Coord. Jr. Achievers, Louisville, 1996-97; scorer Sch. Leaders Licensure Test, 2000; presenter in field. Advisor jr. usher bd. Quinn Chapel Ch., Louisville, 1985—, treas. usher bd., 1997—, asst. dir. young people dept., 1998—; mem. Missionary Soc., Louisville, 1990—. Mem. NEA, Ky. Edn. Assn., U. Louisville Alumni, Phi Delta Kappa, Delta Sigma Theta, Pi Lambda Theta. E-mail: fernearlfol.aol.com. Home: 7005 Bridgepointe Prospect KY 40059 Office: Jefferson County Pub Sch PO Box 34020 Louisville KY 40232-4020

NEWBY, JOHN ROBERT, metallurgical engineer; b. Kansas City, Mo., Nov. 17, 1923; s. Merritt Owen and Gladys Mary (McCleery) N.; m. Audry Marie Loniker, Sept. 21, 1963 (div. 1980); children: Deborah A., Walter J., William F., Matthew O., Robert J. BA, U. Mo., Kansas City, 1947; BS in Metall. Engring., Colo. Sch. Mines, 1949; MS, U. Cin., 1963. Cert. profl. engr. Chemist Bar Rusto Plating Corp., Kansas City, 1949; supr. United Chromium, Ferndale, Mich., 1949-52; prin. rsch. metallurgist Armco Inc., Middletown, Ohio, 1952-85; prin. John Newby Cons., 1985—. Cons. Phoenix Cons., Inc., Cin., 1988—. Author, editor: Formability 2000, 1982, Metallic Materials, 1978, Sheet Metal Forming, 1976; editor: Mechanical Testing, Vol. 8, 9th edit., 1985. Scoutmaster Boy Scouts Am., Middletown, 1952-86, now asst. dist. commr.; chmn. Safety Coun., Middletown, 1978-80. Staff sgt. USAF, 1943-46, PTO. Fellow ASTM (chmn. 1963—, chmn. E-28 com. on mech. testing 1998-2002, Award of Merit 1984), ASM (sustaining mem., chpt. chmn. 1970, Award of Merit 1980); mem. SAE (sect. chmn. 1984). Democrat. Achievements include patent for high strength formable steel sheet; development of interstitial free steel, strain analysis process for metallic sheet formability. Home and Office: 100 Marymont Ct Middletown OH 45042-3735

NEWCOM, JENNINGS JAY, lawyer; b. St. Joseph, Mo., Oct. 18, 1941; s. Arden Henderson and Loyal Beatrice (Winans) N.; m. Cherry Ann Phelps, Apr. 4, 1964; children: Shandra Karine, J. Derek Arden. BA, Graceland U., Lamoni, Iowa, 1964; JD, Harvard U., 1968; LLD (hon.), Graceland U., 1999. Bar: Ill. 1968, Calif. 1973, Mo. 1979, Kans. 1981, Colo. 1999. Atty. McDermott, Will & Emery, Chgo., 1968-73; ptnr. Rifkind, Sterling & Lockwood, Beverly Hills, Calif., 1973-79, Shook, Hardy & Bacon L.L.P., Kansas City, Mo., 1979-99, Davis, Graham & Stubbs, LLP, Denver, 1999—; gen. counsel Putnam, Lovell Capital Ptnrs., Inc., L.A., 1999—; dir. Stein Roe Investment Counsel, Chicago, Skillpath Seminars, Overland Park, Kans. Trustee Hubbard Found., Linde Found., Graceland U. Mem. Denver Bar Assn., State Bar Assn. Calif. Office: Davis Graham & Stubbs LLP 1550 17th St Ste 500 Denver CO 80202-1500

NEWCOMB, BRUCE, state legislator, farmer, rancher; b. Burley, Idaho, Mar. 2, 1940; m. Celia Gould; 5 children. Student, N.W. Christian Coll., Stanford; BS, U. Oreg. Mem. Idaho Ho. of Reps., Boise, 1987, past majority leader, caucus chmn., house spkr., 1999—. Methodist. Avocations: fly fishing, hunting, family. Office: State Capitol Boise ID 83720-0001 Fax: 208-334-2491. E-mail: infocenter@lso.state.id.us.*

NEWCOMB, CAROLYN JEANNE, special education educator; b. St. Louis, June 12, 1936; d. John Mason and Dorothy Marie (Bayley) Seamans; m. Harris Denman Newcomb, Nov. 30, 1957 (dec.); children: Pamela Jeanne, Kristina Lynne, Keith Daniel. BS in Elem. Edn., Cen. Mo. State Coll., 1958; MA in Edn., Lindenwood Coll., 1978. Cert. elem. tchr., emotionally disturbed, learning disability, mentally retarded edn., Mo. Tchr. 1st grade Ferguson/Florissant (Mo.) Sch. Dist., 1959-61, Riverview Gardens Sch. Dist., St. Louis County, Mo., 1961-62; tchr. 1st, 2d and 3d grades St. Charles (Mo.) Sch. Dist., 1963-75, tchr. emotionally disturbed, 1975-85, tchr. mentally retarded and autistic, 1985-93; homebound tchr., 1993-99. Supervising tchr. Lindenwood Coll., St. Charles, 1965-93, U. Mo., St. Louis, 1965-93; spkr. on ind. behavior mgmt. St. Charles Sch. Dist., 1967-74, head coach Spl. Olympics, 1989-96. Treas. PTA, 1964; tchr. adult class St. Charles Presbyn. Ch., 1986-92, Stephen min., 1993—, 2001-, congregational care, 1997—; asst. minister, 2002-. Named Tchr. of Yr. Monroe Sch., 1974, Benton Sch., 1984; recipient awards St. Charles Sch. Dist., 1985, 86, 91, 92. Mem. Coun. for Exceptional Children (sec. 1985, v.p. 1986, pres. 1987, Chpt. 212 Tchr. of Yr. award 1987), St. Charles Edn. Assn. (v.p. 1974, pres. 1975). Avocations: piano, gardening, travel, needlework. Home: 13 Ashland Pl Saint Charles MO 63301-4605 Office: St Charles Presbyn Ch 131 Gamble St Saint Charles MO 63301-1601

NEWCOMB, ELDON HENRY, retired botany educator; b. Columbia, Mo., Jan. 19, 1919; s. Ernest Henry and Ruby Josephine (Anderson) N.; m. Joyce Bright Rieling, June 21, 1949; children— Norman Robert, Barbara Pauline, Cynthia Irma. Student, U. Kansas City, 1936-38; AB, U. Mo., 1940, A.M., 1942; PhD, U. Wis., 1949; DS honoris causa, U. Mo., Columbia, 1993. Asst. prof. botany U. Wis.-Madison, 1949-54, assoc. prof., 1954-58, prof., 1958-90, prof. emeritus, 1990—; dir. Inst. Plant Devel., 1979-88; chmn. dept. botany U. Wis.-Madison, 1982-88, Folke Skoog prof. botany, 1987—. Cons. Shell Devel. Co., 1954-59 Sr. author: Plants in Perspective, 1963; mng. editor Protoplasma, 1969-73; mem. editorial bd. Ann. Rev. Plant Physiology, 1965-69, Protoplasma, 1973-99, Planta, 1981-90; contbr. articles to profl. jours. Served with AUS, 1942-45. NRC predoctoral fellow U. Wis., 1946-49; Guggenheim Found. fellow U. Calif. at Berkeley, 1951-52; Sci. Faculty fellow Harvard, 1963-64; Fulbright Sr. Research scholar Australian Nat. U., Canberra, 1976 Mem. NAS, Am. Soc. Cell Biologists, Am. Acad. Arts and Scis., Bot. Soc. Am., Am. Soc. Plant Physiologists, Soc. Devel. Biology, Phi Beta Kappa (pres. Wis. Alpha chpt. 1978-79), Sigma Xi. Achievements include being a mem. expdn. to Great Barrier Reef, 1973. Home: 52 Oak Creek Trl Madison WI 53717-1510 E-mail: enewcomb@facstaff.wisc.edu.

NEWCOMB, ROBERT CARL, retired naval officer, real estate broker; b. Woburn, Mass., Apr. 14, 1926; s. Horace Irving and Hester Elizabeth (Fuller) N.; m. Elizabeth Canaday, Oct. l2, 1952; children: Janet E., Glenn R., Mark H., Carl A. BA, Tufts Coll., 1947; cert., Grad. Realtors Inst. Commd. ensign USN, 1947, advanced through grades to capt., 1968, comdg. officer USS Pigeon, 1954-55, comdg. officer USS Nicholas, 1964-65, ret., 1973; realtor Merkli-McGuire Realty, Alexandria, Va., 1973-80; broker, owner Parkway Realty, Inc., 1980-2000; assoc. broker Jobin Realty, Va., 2001—. Pres. Gunston Manor Property Owners Assn., Lorton, Va., 1975. Decorated Bronze Star;

Newcomb Bay named in his honor, Antarctica, 1955. Mem. Nat. Assn. Realtors, U.S. Naval Inst. (life), Antarctican Soc., Glacier Soc., Masons, Ruritans. Republican. Methodist. Avocation: photography.

NEWCOMB, ROBERT DOUGLAS, optometrist, clinician, educator; b. Middletown, Ohio, Jan. 8, 1947; s. Huber Charles and Betty Marie (Martz) N.; m. Pamela Kristine Yerian, June 16, 1984; 1 child, Nicholas Scott. BS in Physiol. Optics, Ohio State U., 1970, OD, 1971; MPH, U. Ala., Birmingham, 1975. Diplomate Nat. Bd. Examiners in Optometry; lic. optometrist, Ohio, Fla. Chief optometry svc. VA Med. Ctr., Birmingham, Ala., 1976-80, VA Outpatient Clinic, Columbus, Ohio, 1980-97; assoc. prof. optometry U. Ala., Birmingham, 1976-80; clin. prof. optometry, endowed chair Vision Svc. Plan Ohio State U., Columbus, 1997—. Cons. Nat. Bd. Examiners in Optometry, 1981-89, Ohio State Bd. Optometry, Coun. on Optometric Edn., Coun. on Clin. Optometric Care; invited lectr. profl. orgns. in field. Co-editor: (textbook) Public Health and Community Optometry, 1980, 2d edit., 1990; contbr. articles to profl. jours. Fellow Am. Acad. Optometry (program com. 1982-86, exec. coun. 1986—); mem. APHA (Outstanding Paper/Project award 1982), Am. Optometric Assn. (editl. bd. 1977-83, Optometric Recognition award 1980), Nat. Assn. VA Optometrists (treas. 1976-87, prs. 1976-83), Ohio Optometric Assn. (chair continuing edn. 1992-98, chair new technology 1995-97), Assn. Mil. Surgeons U.S. (Outstanding Svc. and Recognition award 1997), Nat. Acad. Practice Optometry (chair 2001—). Republican. Avocations: tennis, music. E-mail: newcomb.2@osu.edu.

NEWCOMB, ROBERT WAYNE, electrical engineer educator; b. Glendale, Calif., June 27, 1933; s. Robert Dobson and Dorothy Opal (Bissinger) N.; m. Sarah Eleanor Fritz, May 22, 1954; children: Gail E., Robert. W. BSEE, Purdue U., 1955; MS, Stanford U., 1957; PhD, U. Calif., Berkeley, 1960. Registered profl. engr., Calif. Rsch. intern Stanford Rsch. Inst., Menlo Park, Calif., 1957-60; tchg. assoc. U. Calif., Berkeley, 1957-60; asst. and assoc. prof. Stanford U., 1960-70; prof. elec. engring. U. Md., College Park, 1970—. Bd. dirs. PARCOR Rsch. program, Universidad Politecnica de Madrid, Spain. Author: Linear Multisport Synthesis, 1966, Active Integrated Circuit Synthesis, 1968, Concepts of Linear Systems and Control, 1968, Network Theory, 1967; editor: Neurocomputing Letters, 2002—. Recipient IEEE CAS Edn. awrd, 2001; Fulbright fellow, 1963; Fulbright-Hays fellow, 1976; Robert Wayne Newcomb Lab. opened at U. Politecnica Madrid, 1995. Fellow IEEE (life, golden jubilee medal 1999); mem. Soc. Indsl. and Applied Math., Math. Assn. Am., Acad. Am. Poets. Avocations: film, literature, poetry. Home: 13120 Two Farm Dr Silver Spring MD 20904-3418 Office: U Md Microsystems Lab Elec/Computer Engring College Park MD 20742-0001 E-mail: newcomb@eng.umd.edu.

NEWCOMBE, HOWARD BORDEN, biologist, consultant; b. Kentville, N.S., Can., Sept. 19, 1914; s. Edward Borden and Mabel Elsie (Outerbridge) N.; m. Beryl Honor Callaway, Feb. 14, 1942; children— Kenneth Donald, Charles Philip, Richard William B.Sc., Acadia U., Wolfville, N.S., 1935; Assoc., Imperial Coll. Tropical Agr., Trinidad, 1938; PhD, McGill U., Montreal, P.Q., Can., 1939; D.Sc. (hon.), McGill U., 1966, Acadia U., 1970. Sci. officer Brit. Ministry of Supply, London, 1940-41; research assoc. Carnegie Instn. Washington, 1946-47; research sci. Atomic Energy of Can. Ltd., Chalk River, Ont., 1947-79, head biology br., 1949-70, head population research br., 1970-79. Vis. prof. genetics Ind. U., Bloomington, 1963; mem. Internat. Commn. on Radiol. Protection, 1965-77, chmn. com. on biol. effects, 1965-72 Contbr. articles to profl. jours. Served to lt. Brit. Royal Naval Vol. Res., 1941-46 Fellow Royal Soc. Can.; mem. Genetics Soc. Am. (sec. 1956-58), Am. Soc. Human Genetics (pres. 1965), Genetics Soc. Can. (pres. 1964-65) Home: 67 Hillcrest Ave PO Box 135 Deep River ON Canada K0J 1P0

NEWCOMBE, JOANNE PAULINE, educational administrator; b. Chicopee, Mass., July 10, 1947; d. Eugene L. and Veronica Rita Maciolek Galuska; m. Randall William Helweg, Aug. 29, 1970 (div.); m. Edward Jeffrey Newcombe, Oct. 9, 1982. BA, U. Mass., 1969; MEd, U. Lowell, 1975; EdD, Northeastern U., 1985. Cert. tchr., adminstr., Mass., Mich., Conn., N.H., Maine. Tchr. Ellsworth Sch., Windsor, Conn., 1969-70, Muraco Sch., Winchester, Mass., 1970-75; asst. prin. Londonderry (N.H.) Jr. H.S., 1975-78; prin. South Sch., Londonderry, 1978-80, Birch Hill Sch., Nashua, N.H., 1980-84; dir. instructional svcs. Ludington (Mich.) Area Schs., 1984-86; supt. schs. Auburn, Mass., 1986-90, Kittery, Maine, 1990-92; prof. Bridgewater (Mass.) State Coll., 1992—, acting dean, 1995-97; prof. Harvard U., 1999—2001. Mem. faculty Lesley Coll., Cambridge, Mass., 1971-74, Worcester (Mass.) State Coll., 1987-90; mem. The Adminstrv. Search Consortium, 1999—; with Wessex Assocs., London, 2000—, Newcombe Cons., 1995—; spkr. at nat. convs. on ednl. adminstrn. Mem. Nashua Assn. Sch. Prins. (pres. 1983-84), N.H. Coalition Ednl. Leaders (pres. 1980-82), N.H. Assn. Sch. Prins. (exec. bd. 1982-84, regional pres. 1980-82), Am. Assn. Sch. Adminstrs., Mass. Assn. Sch. Supts., Maine Sch. Supt. Assn., ASCD, Mass. Assn. Supervision and Curriculum Devel. (sec. 1989-90), Worcester County Supts. Assn. (treas. 1989-90), N.E. Coalition Ednl. Leaders, Nat. Supts. Acad. (cert. of excellence 1986), Rotary, Phi Delta Kappa, Kappa Delta Pi, Delta Kappa Gamma. Democrat. Roman Catholic. E-mail: jnewcombe@bridgew.edu' jnewcome@ma.ultranet.com. Home: 25 Old Meetinghouse Rd Auburn MA 01501-3312 Office: 25 Hart Hall Bridgewater MA 02325

NEWCOMER, CLARENCE CHARLES, federal judge; b. Mount Joy, Pa., Jan. 18, 1923; s. Clarence S. and Marion Clara (Charles) N.; m. Jane Moyer Martin, Oct. 2, 1948; children: Judy (Mrs. Kenneth N. Birkett Jr.), Nancy Jane Newcomer (Mrs. Edward H. Vick), Peggy Jo Pollack (dec.). AB, Franklin and Marshall Coll., 1944; LL.B., Dickinson Sch. Law, 1948. Bar: Pa. 1950, U.S. Dist. Ct. Pa., U.S. Ct. Appeals (3rd cir.), U.S. Supreme Ct. Pvt. practice, Lancaster, 1950-52; spl. dep. atty. gen. Dept. Justice, Commonwealth of Pa., 1952-54; partner firm Rohrer, Honaman, Newcomer & Musser, Lancaster, 1957-60; with Office of Dist. Atty., 1960-64, 1st asst. dist. atty., 1964-68, dist. atty., 1968-72; partner Newcomer, Roda & Morgan, 1968-72; fed. dist. judge Eastern Dist. Pa., Phila., 1972-88, sr. judge, 1988—. Served to lt. (j.g.) USNR, 1943-46, PTO. Office: US Dist Ct 13614 US Courthouse 601 Market St Philadelphia PA 19106-1713

NEWCOMER, JAMES HENRY, federal agency administrator; b. Waterloo, Iowa, Sept. 11, 1920; s. Henry Raymond and Nettie (Logston) Newcomer; m. Esther Laura Reinhardt, July 29, 1941; children: James Ralph, Edward Reinhardt, Henry Lewis, Carolyn Ruth. Warehouseman Cutler Wholesale Hardware, Waterloo, 1939-42; electrician Cedar Falls (Iowa) Electric & Hardware, 1946-51; quality assurance rep. Def. Contract Adminstrn. Svcs., St. Louis, 1951-78; trail ranger Black Hawk County Conservation Bd., Cedar Falls, 1990-96; tchr. computers Waterloo Sr. Activity Ctr., 1996. Compiler geneology: Newcomer and Related Families. With U.S. Army, 1942—46, ETO. Decorated Purple Heart, Bronze Star; recipient Disting. Career award, Dept. Def., 1978, cert. of Appreciation, Hawkeye Valley Area Agy. Aging, 1996, Gov.'s Vol. award, 1997. Mem.: VFW, DAV, Am. Legion. Republican. Presbyterian. Avocations: photography, boating, woodworking, metalworking, cooking. Home: 5051 Foulk Rd Waterloo IA 50702-4825 E-mail: jhander@mchsi.com.

NEWCOMER, JANET ANN, family physician; b. Lower Burrell, Pa., June 6, 1963; d. Francis Joseph and Margaret Louise (Fuhrman) Strellec; m. Raymond John Newcomer, June 29, 1985. BS, U. Pitts., 1985, MD, 1989. Diplomate Am. Bd. Family Practice. Resident in family practice St. Margaret Meml. Hosp., Pitts., 1989-92; pvt. practice, 1992—. Mem. Am. Acad. Family Physicians. Democrat. Roman Catholic. Office: Penn Plum Family Medicine 100 Delafield Rd Ste 101 Pittsburgh PA 15215-3247

NEWCOMER, JOHN WHITNEY, psychiatrist, educator; b. Subic Bay Naval Base, Philippines; s. John L. and Barbara L. Newcomer; m. Barbara L. Freedman, Aug. 4, 2001; children: Leah Eliza, Adam Samuel. AB, Brown U., 1981; postgrad., U. Calif., San Francisco, 1984, Yale U., 1984; MD, Wayne State U., 1985. Diplomate Nat. Bd. Med. Examiners, Am. Bd. Psychiatry and Neurology with added qualification in Geriatric Psychiatry. Intern in internal medicine Sinai Hosp., Detroit, 1985—86; resident in psychiatry Stanford (Calif.) U. Sch. Medicine, 1986—89; rsch. fellow in psychiatry Dept. Vets. Affairs Med. Ctr. Stanford U. Sch. Medicine, Palo Alto, 1988—90; instr. dept. psychiatry Washington U. Sch. medicine, St. Louis, 1990—92, asst. prof. psychiatry, 1992—2000, adj. asst. prof. psychology, 1997—, assoc. prof. psychiatry, 2000—; dir. rsch. Malcolm Bliss Mental Health Ctr., 1990—95. Chmn. drug utilization rev. bd. Mo. Dept. Social Svcs., Divsn. Med. Svc., 1997—; mem. study sect., spl. emphasis panels, ad hoc mem. treatment assessment sect. NIMH, 1998—; rsch. complaince med. officer Gen. Clin. Rsch. Ctr., 2001—; lectr. in field.; outpatient psychotherapy group co-leader Stanford Adult Outpatient Psychiatry Clinic, 1989—90; rsch. psychiatrist Malcolm Bliss Mental Health Ctr., St. Louis, 1990—95; mem. med. staff Barnes Hosp., St. Louis, 1990—94, Jewish Hosp., St. Louis, 1990—94, Barnes/Jewish Hosps., St. Louis, 1994—; instr. Mo. Dept. Mental Health Tng. Program, 1991; cons. in field. Contbr. numerous articles, abstracts to profl. publs. Recipient Scientist Devel. award, NIMH, 1992—97, Ind. Scientist award, 1997—, Zeneca Pharms. Group; grantee, Nat. Inst. Drug Abuse, 1998—, NIMH, 2001—, NIH, 1999—, Pfizer Inc., 1997—, Janssen Pharmaceutica, 2000—, Eli Lilly, 1997—, McDonnell Ctr. for Higher Brain Function. Mem.: AMA, AAAS, Am. Diabetes Assn., Am. Coll. Psychiatrists, Internat. Soc. Psychoneuroendocrinology, Soc. for Neurosci., Am. Pschopathol. Assn., Ea. Mo. Psychiat. Soc., Am. Psychiat. Assn., Am. Coll. Neuropsychopharmacology, Alpha Omega Alpha, Sigma Xi, Phi Beta Kappa. Office: Washington U Sch Medicine Dept Psychiatry 660 S Euclid Ave Campus Box 8134 Saint Louis MO 63110

NEWELL, CLAYTON COKE, media professional, writer; b. Denver, May 16, 1958; s. John William and Suzann Allison (Boardman) N.; m. Cindy Jo Gehrig, Aug. 18, 1981; 7 children. BA in Journalism, Colo. State U., 1990. Media rels. officer Ch. of Jesus Christ of Latter-Day Saints, Salt Lake City, 1993—. Author: Dying Words—Colombian Journalists and the Cocaine Warlords, 1990, Cowchips Aren't for Dippin'—A Guide to Life in the New Wild West, 1996, Latter Days—A Guided Tour Through Six Billion Years of Mormonism, 2000; contbr.: The Mission: Inside the Church of Jesus Christ of Latter-Day Saints, 1996; editor, co-author: (CD ROM) Faith in Every Footstep, 1997; contbr. articles to profl. publs. Dir. Utah Home Edn. Assn., 1995-99. Recipient Bronze Anvil award Pub. Rels. Soc. Am., 1998; Scripps Howard scholar, 1988, 89, 90; Reader's Digest rsch. grantee Reader's Digest Edn. Found., 1989-90. Mem. Am. Soc. Journalists and Authors, Soc. Profl. Journalists (profl. mem.), Phi Beta Kappa, Phi Kappa Phi. Avocations: traveling, guitar, children. Office: Ch of Jesus Christ of Latter-day Saints 15 E South Temple Salt Lake City UT 84150-9701 E-mail: newellcc@ldschurch.org.

NEWELL, ERIC JAMES, financial planner, tax consultant, former insurance executive; b. Toronto, Ont., Can., Sept. 24, 1930; came to U.S., 1959, naturalized, 1970; s. James and Anne (Brown) N.; m. Essie Miskelly, Sept. 30, 1950; 1 son, Eric Wayne. Student, U. Toronto, 1951-53. Pub. acct. W.J. Wilcox & Co., Toronto, 1949-53; chief acct. Toronto Mut. Life Ins. Co., 1953-57; asst. sec. Holland Life Ins. Co., Toronto, 1957-59; with Penn Mut. Life Ins. Co., Phila., 1959-86, assoc. controller, 1965-70, 2d v.p., controller, 1970-84, v.p., controller, 1984-86, ret., 1986; fin., tax cons., 1986—; dir. Hotel Brunswick, Lancaster, Pa., 1982-85. Mem. Traffic and Transp. Bd., Cherry Hill, N.J., 1971-73, Zoning Bd., 1975-78; vice chmn. Cherry Hill Econ. Devel. Bd., 1973-75; pres. Greater Kingston Civic Assn., Cherry Hill, 1970-76; Democratic committeeman, Camden County, 1976-79; vice chmn. Dem. Party, Cherry Hill, 1976. Fellow Life Mgmt. Inst., Royal Commonwealth Soc.; mem. Fin. Execs. Inst., Am. Inst. Corp. Contrs., N.Y. Ins. Accts. Club (chmn. 1984), Nat. Soc. Tax Profls., Royal Black Knights of Ireland, Loyal Orange Assn. (past master), Scotch-Irish Soc. of U.S. (mem. coun., pres. 1999), Am. Legion. Presbyterian (deacon 1969—). Home and Office: 137 E Partridge Ln Cherry Hill NJ 08003-4407

NEWELL, KATHERINE CLAIBORNE, librarian; b. Columbia, Mo., Aug. 1, 1957; d. Jerry David and Anna Faye (Hooks) Claiborne; children: David, Danny. Student, U. Neuchâtel, Switzerland, 1977-78; BA in History and French, U. Del., 1979; MS in Libr. Sci. and Info. Studies, Drexel U., Phila., 1994. Mgmt. trainee, supr. C&P Telephone Co., Washington, 1979-80; office mgr. Bus. & Ins. Mgmt., Bethesda, Md., 1980-81, Gauge Corp., Wilmington, Del., 1981-82; exec. asst. Med. Soc. Del., 1982-89; spl. collections asst. Langston Hughes Meml. Libr., Lincoln University, Pa., 1989-92, interlibr. loan libr., 1992-95, spl. collections libr., 1995-98; rsch. libr. Hagley Mus. and Libr., Wilmington, Del., 1998—2002; dir. J. Lewis Crozer Libr., Chester, Pa., 2002—. Mem. ALA, AAUP, AAUW, Spl. Librs. Assn., Assn. Coll. and Rsch. Librs., Beta Phi Mu, Phi Alpha Theta, Pi Delta Phi. Office: J Lewis Crozer Libr 620 Engle St Chester PA 19013 E-mail: crozerlibrary@delco.lib.pa.us.

NEWELL, MICHAEL ALFRED, electrical engineer; b. L.A., May 26, 1963; s. Paul Eugene and Clare Fritzsche Newell; m. Thuy Lam Newell. BSEE, Calif. Poly. State U., 1990. Electronics design engr. Space Payloads Group, Pasadena, Calif., 1983—86; software engr. Qualitel Svcs., Pomona, 1986—88; sr. mem. tech. staff Jet Propulsion Lab., Pasadena, 1988—. ASIC designer Cassini Spacecraft Jet Propulsion Lab., Pasadena, 1992—94, electronics lead APEX reconfigurable hardware Flight Experiment, Pasadena , 1994—97, Muses CN electronics cognizant engr., Pasadena, 1998—2001, Deep Impact avionics lead, 2001—; Gilgamesh Supercomputer electronics cognizant engr. Caltech, Pasadena, 2000—; task mgr. extreme electronics, Electronics Parts Program NASA, Pasadena, 2001—. Contbr. articles to profl. jours.; patentee in field. Exec. advisor JPL Explorer Post, Pasadena, 1993—2001. Mem.: IEEE. Avocations: bicycling, reading. Home: 3545 N Glenrose Ave Altadena CA 91001 Office: Jet Propulsion Lab 4800 Oak Grove Dr Pasadena CA 91109 Personal E-mail: mikenewell@earthlink.net. Business E-Mail: Michael.A.Newell@jpl.nasa.gov.

NEWELL, MICHAEL STEPHEN, finance company executive, international finance, protective services consultant; b. Denver, Dec. 22, 1949; s. Henry Michael and Marlene (McRae) N.; m. Linda Margaret Wolfe, Sept. 19, 1987; children: Katherine Margaret, Brittany Nicole; children from previous marriage: Troy, Angela, Michael, Jennifer. Grad., Denver Police Acad., 1972; CO Real Estate Lic., Real Estate Prep., 1977; HHD (hon.), Am. Acad. Inst. Pub. Theology, 1997. Cert. peace officer, Colo. Police officer Denver Police Dept., 1972-79; prin. Michael Newell & Assocs., Denver, 1979-82; sr. account exec. Am. Protection Industries, Los Angeles, 1982-84; chief exec. officer Newco Fin., Huntington Beach, Calif., 1984—. Chmn. The Newco Internat. Group/Newco Fin., Huntington Beach; with VALUES Self Improvement Program, Fountain Valley; bd. dirs. Lifesong Self-Esteem workshops, Huntington Beach.; expert witness stalking crimes and preador control techniques; condr. seminars on stalker suppression, stalking survival, threat mgmt. in the workplace. Author: The Security Manual, 1995, Stalker Suppression, 1996, (novel and screenplay) Balanger, TMC, Stalking Rescue, The Book of F.A.T.E. (From Abuse to Empowerment), (video prodns.) The Personal Protection Technique, 1995, Stalking Survival, 1995; author, facilitator: Your Paradigm Shift. Founder, bd. dirs. Law Enforcement Support Assn., Denver, 1981; bd. dirs. Axis Intervention and Tng. Inst./Stalking Rescue. With U.S. Army, 1968-71, Viet Nam. Decorated Bronze Star, Viet Svc. medal with clusters; recipient Pres.'s Nat. Patriotism medal Am. Police Hall of Fame, Nat. Assn. Chiefs Police, 1996, Knight Chevalier The Venerable Order of Michael the Archangel, others; named "The Real Life Equalizer", CBS News/48 Hours. Republican. Mem. Religious Sci. Ch. Avocations: music, photography, travel. Office: Internat Risk Cons PO Box 558 Littleton CO 80160-0558 E-mail: stalkthestalker@worldnet.att.net.

NEWELL, NORMAN DENNIS, paleontologist, geologist, museum curator, educator; b. Chgo., Jan. 27, 1909; s. Virgil Bingham and Nellie (Clark) N.; m. Valerie Zirkle, Feb. 25, 1928 (dec. 1972); m. Gillian Wendy Wormall, Apr. 28, 1973 BS, U. Kans., 1929, MA, 1931; PhD in Geology, Yale U., 1933. Faculty mem. U. Kans., Lawrence, 1934-37; assoc. prof. geology U. Wis.-Madison, 1937-45; prof. geology Columbia U., N.Y.C., 1945-77, prof. emeritus, 1977—; curator Am. Mus. Nat. History, 1945-77, curator emeritus, 1977—. Geologist Kans. Geol. Survey, Lawrence, 1929-37; cons. on petroleum geology Peruvian Govt., 1942-45 Author: Permian Reef Complex of the Guadalupe Mountains Region, Texas and New Mexico, 1953, Creation and Evolution: Myth or Reality?, 1982, also numerous sci. articles and papers. Recipient Disting. Svc. Alumni award Kans. U., 1961, Hayden award Phila. Acad. Sci., 1965, Verrill medal Yale U., 1966, Gold medal for achievment in sci. Am. Mus. Natural History, 1978, Raymond C. Moore medal Soc. Econ. Paleontologists and Mineralogists, 1980, Scientific Freedom and Responsibility award AAAS, 1987, Geol. Soc. Peru medal, 1997, Internat. Symposium on the Paleobiology and Evolution of the Bivalvia Festschrift, 1998, The Royal Tyrrell Mus. Palaeontology, Drumheller. Mem. Nat. Acad. Scis. (Mary Clark Thompson medal 1960), Am. Philos. Soc., Am. Acad. Arts and Scis., Am. Assn. Petroleum Geolologists (spl. award 1996), Geol. Soc. Am. (Penrose medal 1990), Soc. Study Evolution (pres. 1949), Soc. Systematic Zoology (pres. 1972-73), Paleontol. Soc. (pres. 1960-61, medal 1979), Can. Soc. Petroleum Geologists (hon.). Avocation: geologic field expeditions. Home: 135 Knapp Ter Leonia NJ 07605-1216 Office: Am Mus Natural History Central Park W and 79 St New York NY 10024 E-mail: newell@amnh.org.

NEWELL, PAUL HAYNES, JR. engineering educator, former college president; b. Nashville, July 1, 1933; s. Paul Haynes Newell; m. Martha A. Newell; children: Paul Haynes III, Mike, Nan. B.M.E., U. Tenn., 1958, M.M.E., 1961; Mech.E., Mass. Inst. Tech., 1964, PhD, 1966. Registered profl. engr., Ala., Tenn., Tex., N.J. Student asst. mech. engring. U. Tenn., 1957, instr. mech. engring., 1958-62; NSF Sci. faculty fellow Mass. Inst. Tech., 1962-65; asso. prof. mech. engring. U. Ala. Coll. Engring., 1966-69; prof. mech. engring. Tex. A. and M. U., 1969-72, asso. dean engring., 1972; prof. biomed. engring., dept. phys. medicine Baylor Coll. Medicine, 1969-74, prof. biomed. engring., dept. physiology, 1970-74, prof. biomed. engring., dept. community medicine, 1972-74, prof. biomed. engring., dept. rehab., 1972—, mem. grad. faculty, 1970-74; prof., head indsl. engring. dept. Tex. A. & M. U., 1972-74, prof., head combined programs of behavioral engring., bioengring., cybernetic engring., hygiene and safety engring., indsl. engring., 1972-74; pres., prof. Newark Coll. Engring., N.J. Inst. Tech., 1974-78; prof. Adminstrn. Prosthetics Ctr., N.Y., 1973-75, VA Hosp., Houston, 1972-75, Baylor Coll. Medicine, Houston, from 1971; pres. Newell Engring., Greenbrier, Tenn., 1979—. Dir. N.J. Bell Telephone Co., Mid Atlantic Nat. Bank, Thomas-Betts Corp. Contbr. articles to profl. jours., chpts. to books. Mem. NSF liaison com., Newark Transp. Council, N.J. Safety Council; sec. exec. com. council Boy Scouts Am., Birmingham, Ala., 1966-68; bd. dirs. N.J. State Opera, United Hosps. Newark. Served with USMCR, Korean Conflict. Recipient NSF Sci. Faculty fellowship. Mem. Am. Soc. Tool and Mfg. Engrs., N.Y., Ala. acads. scis., AAAS, Am. Congress Rehab. Medicine, Am. Heart Assn., Am. Inst. Indsl. Engrs., Am. Soc. Artificial Internal Organs, Am. Soc. Engring. Edn., ASME, Biomed. Engring. Soc., Inst. Engring. Deans, Internat. Soc. Prosthetics and Orthotics, Nat. Soc. Profl. Engrs., Soc. Advanced Med. Systems, Soc. Engring. Sci., Pres.'s Assn., Am. Fluid Power Soc., N.J. Soc. Engrs., Sigma Xi, Tau Beta Pi, Phi Kappa Phi, Pi Tau Sigma. Clubs: Rotary. Address: 1855 Lake Rd Greenbrier TN 37073-4619 Office: Newell Engring Greenbrier TN 37073-4619

NEWELL, REGINALD EDWARD, physics educator; b. Peterborough, Eng., Apr. 9, 1931; came to U.S., 1954, naturalized, 1969; s. Harold Aubrey and Edith (Swiffin) N.; m. Maireen W. Lees, Sept. 6, 1954; children: Madeleine, Elizabeth, Oliver, Nicholas. BS in Physics, U. Birmingham, Eng., 1954; MS, Mass. Inst. Tech., 1956, Sc.D., 1960. With Brit. Meteorol. Office, 1947-50; successively research staff asst., asst. prof., asso. prof., prof. MIT, Cambridge, 1954—; mem IUGG Internat. Commn. Meteorology Upper Atmosphere, 1967-75; mem. Internat. Commn. Atmospheric Chemistry and Global Pollution, 1971-83; pres. Internat. Commn. on Climate, 1977-83. Joint author: The General Circulation of the Tropical Atmosphere, Vol. I, 1972, Vol. 2, 1974, Global Ocean Surface Temperature Atlas, 1990; contbr. articles to profl. jours. Served with RAF, 1950-51. Fellow Royal Meteorol. Soc., Am. Meteorol. Soc.; mem. Am. Geophys. Union. Home: 45 Jason St Arlington MA 02476-6446 Office: MIT 54-1824 77 Massachusetts Ave Cambridge MA 02139-4307

NEWELL, RUSSELL ANDERSON, financial planner; b. N.Y.C., Mar. 16, 1921; s. William Anderson and Ethel Rogers N.; m. Carol Byrnes, July 29, 1943; 1 child, Karen Newell Tiburzl. BSME, Rennselaer Poly Tech Inst., 1949; MS, MIT, 1957. CFP; comml. pilot. Design engr. Eastman Kodak Co., Rochester, N.Y., 1949-52; engring. mgr., chief engr., project mgr. RCA, Moorestown, N.J., 1952-67; exec. v.p. United tech. Norden Group, Norwalk, Conn., 1967-69; pres. Ranco Co., Haddonfield, N.J., 1969-76; 1st v.p. Smith Barney, Phila., 1976-97; retired. Fin. advisor Smith Barney, Phila., 1977-97; pres. Buy & Sell Mag., Westmont, N.J., 1972-75, Ranco Co., Haddonfield, N.J., 1970—. Chmn. West Jersey Health & Hosp. Found., Vorhees, N.J., 1986-97; mem., pres. Wedgewood Swim Club, Haddonfield, 1951-57. 1st lt. U.S. Army Air Corps, 1942-46; pilot instr. Aircorp. Sloan fellow MIT, 1957. Mem. Jonanthan's Landing Golf Club, Palm Valley Country Club, Tavistock County Country Club, Sigma Xi, Pi Tau Sigma, Tau Beta Pi. Avocations: gardening, travel, computers, financial and management. Home: 425 Queensboro Ln Haddonfield NJ 08033-4014

NEWELL, WILLIAM HENRY, interdisciplinary studies educator; b. Springfield, Vt., Nov. 27, 1943; s. Maurice Clayton and Grace Mildred (White) N.; children: Silvia, W. James. AB in Philosophy, Amherst Coll., 1965; PhD in Econs., U. Pa., 1971. Teaching asst. econs. U. Pa., Phila., 1969; instr. econs. Temple U., 1969-70; asst. prof. econs. St. Olaf Coll., Northfield, Minn., 1970-74; tutor in social scis. The Paracoll., 1970-74; asst. prof. interdisciplinary studies Miami U., Oxford, Ohio, 1974-77, assoc. prof. interdisciplinary studies, 1977-83, prof. interdisciplinary studies, 1983—; dir. Inst. in Integrative Studies, 1992—. Founding pres. Assn. for Integrative Studies, 1979-80, sec.-treas., newsletter editor, 1983—, exec. dir., 1991—; cons., external evaluator interdisciplinary programs for more than 85 colls. and univs., 1985—; charter faculty mem. Sch. Interdisciplinary Studies, Miami U., 1974. Author: Interdisciplinarity: Essays from the Literature, 1998, Interdisciplinary Undergraduate Programs, 1986, Population Change and Agricultural Development in 19th Century France, 1977; contbr. articles to profl. jours. Avocations: backpacking, canoeing, squash. Home: 8650 Long Ln Cincinnati OH 45231-5019 Office: Sch Interdisciplinary Study Miami U Oxford OH 45056

NEWELL, WILLIAM JAMES, sign language educator; b. Port Jefferson, N.Y., Sept. 13, 1947; s. William James and Mary Louise (Pinder) N.; m. Beverly Jo Beller, June 18, 1971; children: Eric James, Christopher Ian. BA, St. Edwards U., Austin, Tex., 1970; MS, St. Cloud State U., 1977; PhD, Greenwich U., 1994. Cert. tchr. Am. Sign Lang.; cert. Coun. on Edn. of the Deaf. Houseparent, tchr. aide Tex. Sch. for the Deaf, Austin, 1969-70; tchr. of the deaf Harris County Pub. Schs., Houston, 1970-72, Dade County Pub. Schs., Miami, Fla., 1972-74; supervising tchr. of the deaf Hennepin Tech. Ctrs., Mpls., 1974-78; instr. Am. Sign Lang. Rochester (N.Y.) Inst. Tech., 1978-81; chairperson sign communication dept. Nat. Tech. Inst. for the Deaf, Rochester, 1981-91, rsch. assoc., 1991-96, prof. Am. sign lang. and deaf studies, 1996—. Proprietor Sign Lang. Consulting Svcs., Ednl. Cons., Adult Edn. Resource. Co-developer: Sign Communication Proficiency Interview, 1981—; author: Basic Sign Communication, 1983. Recipient Outstanding Svc. award Sign Instrs. Guidance Network, Silver Spring, Md. Mem. Am. Sign Lang. Tchrs. Assn. (pres. 1986-90, chairperson evaluation and cert. com. 1990—, Veditz award 1996, 2000), Conv. of Am. Instrs. for the Deaf. Avocations: home brewing, walking for fitness, backyard birdfeeding. Home: 5259 Lower Egypt Rd Canandaigua NY 14424-8850 Office: Nat Tech Inst for the Deaf 52 Lomb Memorial Dr Rochester NY 14623-5604

NEWELL, WILLIAM KEITH, neurobiological researcher; b. Buffalo, Oct. 12, 1954; s. Frederick Dwelley Newell and Dian Sloan Randel; m. Joanne Marrie Hatch, Dec. 1979 (div. July 1983); 1 child, Arian Justine. BA in Psychology, SUNY, Binghamton, 1985. Rschr. assoc. U. Pitts., 1986-90, rsch. specialist, lab. mgr. dept. neurosci., 1990-95, rsch. specialist MRI rsch., MRI rsch. machinist, 1995-98. Democrat. Avocations: mural art, electronics.

NEWELL, WILLIAM TALMAN, JR. hospital administrator; b. Newport News, Va., Apr. 4, 1932; s. William Talman and Helen Louise (Woolfolk) N.; m. Mary Hill Chilton, Feb. 11, 1956; children— William Talman III, John Chilton, Anne Caroline BS in Hotel Adminstrn., Cornell U., 1954; MBA in Health Care Adminstrn., George Washington U., 1967. Asst. mgr. Dayton (Ohio) Biltmore Hotel, 1956-57; restaurant mgr. Marriott Corp., Washington, 1957-60; food service mgr. The Fairfax Hosp., Falls Church, Va., 1960-63, asst. dir. gen. services div., 1963-64, dir. gen. services div., 1964-66, asst. to the adminstr., 1966-67; asst. dir. Yale-New Haven (Conn.) Hosp., 1967-70, assoc. dir., 1970-75; chief exec. officer U. Miss. Hosp., 1975-83; exec. dir. Univ. Hosp., SUNY, Stony Brook, 1983-94, ret., 1994. Lectr. Sch. Epidemiology and Pub. Health, Yale U. Sch. Medicine, 1969-75; dir. Miss. Blue Cross & Blue Shield, 1979-83; mem. Appalachian Council Teaching Hosps., 1979;

mem. Miss. Gov.'s Health Care Task Force on Children and Youth, 1982-83 Chmn. bd. Vocat. Rehab. Ctr. for Blind, Jackson, Miss.; adminstrv. bd. Nassau-Suffolk Hosp. Council Bd.; v.p. ops. Suffolk County council Boy Scouts Am.; bd. dirs. U. Hosp. Consortium; pres. bd. dirs. Miss. Blood Services, 1977-83; bd. dirs. Hosp. Assn. N.Y. Served to 1st lt. U.S. Army, 1954-56 Mem. Am. Coll. Health Care Adminstrs. Episcopalian.

NEWETT, EDWARD J., JR. accountant; b. Phila., Mar. 6, 1949; s. Edward Joseph and Teresa (Gallardo) N.; m. Sue M. Homa, Nov. 9, 1974; children: Edward III, Kathleen. AA in Bus. Adminstrn., Bucks County C.C., Newtown, Pa., 1977; BS in Commerce, Rider Coll., Lawrenceville, N.J., 1980. CPA, Pa. Bus. mgr., ptnr. Newtt's Decorators, Trevose, Pa., 1971-77; auditor N.J. State Dept. Treasury, Trenton, 1977-79, N.J. State Dept. Health, Trenton, 1979-82, analyst, 1982-85; CFO diversified health svcs. Camden Co. Health Svcs. Ctr., Camden, N.J., 1985-93; CFO Cedarbrook Nursing Home, Allentown, Pa., 1993-99, Fair Acres Geriatric Ctr., Lima, 1993—2001. Chmn. Pa. Assn. of County Homes Fiscal Mgmt. Com., Harrisburg, 1993—. Mem. AICPAs, Pa. Inst. CPAs (long term healthcare com. 1993—, legis. com. 1989—), Healthcare Fin. Mgmt. Assn., Inst. Mgmt. Accts., Phi Theta Kappa. Republican. Roman Catholic. Avocations: golf, tennis, swimming, reading. Home: 4743 Hale Ln Emmaus PA 18049-4944 Office: Fair Acres Geriatric Ctr Rt 352 Glen Riddle Lima PA 19037

NEWGENT, REBECCA ANN, counselor, educator; b. Ohio; BA in Psychology, Kent (Ohio) State U., Kent, OH, 1986; MEd in Cmty. Counseling, Kent (Ohio) State U., 1993; PhD in Guidance and Counseling, U. Akron, 2001. Cert. family and divorce mediator. Case mgr. II/counselor trainee Cmty. Support Svcs., Inc., Akron, Ohio, 1988—93; counselor, family life edn. coord., vol. coord., divorce mediator Jewish Family Svc., 1993—95; counselor Cath. Svc. League, 1995—96; divorce mediator Domestic Rels. Divsn. Summit County Ct. Common Pleas, 1995—99; pvt. practice counselor, divorce mediator Akron Psychol. Assocs., 1995—98; counselor, sch.-based counselor, divorce mediator Cath. Social Svcs. of Summit County, Inc., 1997—99; emergency clinician Portage Path Behavioral Health-Psychiat. Emergency Svcs., 1997—2000; grad. asst. dept. counseling and spl. edn. U. Akron, 1998—2000, mem. adj. faculty dept. ednl. founds. and leadership, 2000, mem. ad hoc temporary grad. faculty, doctoral intern dept. counseling and spl. edn., 2000—01; asst. prof. counselor edn. U. Ark., Fayetteville, 2001—. Bd. advisors The Clinic for Child Study and Family Therapy U. Akron, 1998—2001. Mem. mental health trauma action team Summit County Red Cross Disaster Svcs., Akron, 1998—2000. Mem.: Ark. Assn. Assessment in Counseling, Ark. Assn. Counselor Edn. and Supervision, Ark. Counseling Assn., Assn. for Advancement of Ednl. Rsch., Assn. Counselor Edn. and Supervision, Am. Counseling Assn., Chi Sigma Iota (Outstanding Doctoral Student award 2001). Office: U Ark 236 Graduate Education Bldg Fayetteville AR 72701 Office Fax: 479-575-2492. Business E-Mail: rnewgent@uark.edu.

NEWHALL, DAVID, III, former government official; b. Phila., Dec. 6, 1937; s. David Jr. and Jane Martyn (Dunn) N. AB in Politics, Princeton U., 1961. Mgr. Bell Tel. Co. of Pa., Norristown, 1961-63; adminstrv. asst. U.S. Rep. R.S. Schweiker, Washington, 1963-69; chief of staff U.S. Senator R.S. Schweiker, 1969-81, HHS, Washington, 1981-83; pres. Marmion Plantation Co., King George, VA., 1983-91; prin. dep. asst. sec. def.(health affairs) U.S. Dept. Def., Washington, 1985-90, acting asst. sec. def. (health affairs), 1989-90; gen. ptnr. Marmion Partnership Restorations, 1990—. Bd. dirs. Western Healthcare Alliance, Phoenix, 1995-97, Nat. Hotline Svcs., Inc., Fredericksburg, Va., 1998—; chmn. compliance com. and lead dir. TrailBlazer Health Enterprises, LLC, Dallas, 1997—; mem. nat. adv. bd. Am. Compliance Inst., Alexandria, Va. Mem. Princeton Tower Club. Republican. Episcopalian. Avocation: beef cow-calf operation. Home and Office: 7382M Marmion Ln King George VA 22485-7300

NEWHALL, EDITH ALLERTON, writer; b. Phila., Feb. 13, 1951; d. John Allerton and Dorothy (Todd) N.; m. David Walters, May 29, 1988. BA in Art History, Moore Coll., 1973; MFA, Art Inst. Chgo., 1979. Asst. editor Phila. Bulletin, 1974-76, Harry N. Abrams Publ., N.Y.C., 1979-81; writer N.Y. Mag., 1981—.

NEWHALL, ERIC LUTHER, American literature educator; b. Reno, July 3, 1945; s. David Havens and Geraldine (Gilbert) N.; m. Sylvia Kurtovich, July 21, 1971 (div. June 1988); children: David K., Katherine H.; m. Jaclyn Toni Rodriguez, Apr. 7, 1990; chldren: Andrea Rodriguez-Scheel, Amanda Rodriguez-Newhall. BA, Occidental Coll., L.A., 1967; PhD, UCLA, 1975. Prof. Am. lit. Occidental Coll., L.A., 1975—. Contbr. articles to profl. jours. Liaison Hispanic Urban Ctr./Occidental Coll., 1976-82; mem. Learn coun. Eagle Rock Elem. Sch., L.A., 1998-2000. Recipient Oreg. Peace award Coun. of Chs., Portland, 1971, Loftsgordon award for outstanding tchg., 1979, 85, 93, 99, 2000; Danforth Assoc., 1981-85. Mem. MLA (regional del.), Am. Studies Assn., Phi Beta Kappa. Democrat. Avocations: tennis, chess. Home: 2037 Escarpa Dr Los Angeles CA 90041-3016 Office: Occidental Coll 1600 Campus Rd Los Angeles CA 90041-3314 E-mail: newhall@oxy.edu.

NEWHALL, JOHN HARRISON, non profit company executive; b. Phila., Sept. 29, 1933; s. Blackwell and Mary Large (Harrison) N.; m. Jane Carol Ward, July 15, 1961; children: Carol Newhall Neilson, Thomas Blackwell, Daniel Ward. BA, Williams Coll., 1955; MBA, Harvard U., 1960. Product advt. mgr., product mktg. mgr. Pepperidge Farm subs. Campbell Soup Co., Camden, NJ, 1960—67; product group mgr. Gen. Foods Corp. (now Kraft Corp.), White Plains, NY, 1967—70; dir. corp. planning, gen. mgr. Europe H.J. Heinz Co., Pitts., 1970—77; v.p. mktg. Sunoco Corp., Phila., 1977—81; chmn., CEO Aitkin-Kynett Co. (subs. Foote Cone & Belding), 1981—84; mng. dir., exec. v.p. Campbell-Ewald Co., N.Y.C., 1984—86; prin. mgmt. cons. SRI Internat., Menlo Park, Calif., 1987—90; mng. dir. Strategic Directions, Narberth, Pa., 1990—99; pres. Advanced Promotion Techs., Deerfield Beach, Fla., 1992—93; CEO The Newcomen Soc. of the U.S., Exton, Pa., 1999—. Mem. devel. council Williams Coll., Williamstown, Mass., 1977-87, Reg. v. chmn. Capital Campaign, 1991-93; mem. Com. of 70, Phila., 1981-84; bd. dirs. Bryn Mawr (Pa.) Hosp., 1982-88, The Haverford (Pa.) Sch., 1980-86, Headmaster sel. comm., 1992, Strategic Planning Comm., 1994, World Affairs Council, Phila., 1982-86, Found. for Vascular Hypertension Research, Phila., 1982—, chmn., 1987, Jr. Achievement, Phila., 1977-81, vice chmn., 1981, SE chpt. ARC, Phila., 1981-84, Pa. Economy League, 1981-84; vestryman, lay reader Episcopal Ch., 1964-70, chmn. ann. campaign, 1992, vice chmn. capital campaign, 1994. Lt. USN, 1955-58. Recipient Cert. of Merit Chapel of Four Chaplains, 1983, 85; named to Hospitality Hall of Fame, 2000. Mem. Assn. Nat. Advertisers (exec. com. 1977-81), Harvard Bus. Sch. Club Phila. (pres. 1994-96, vice chmn. 1996-97, chmn. 1998). Clubs: Union League (Phila.); Merion Cricket (Haverford); Gulph Mills (Pa.) Golf; Harbor (Seal Harbor, Maine). Republican. Episcopalian. Avocations: skiing, tennis, sailing. Home: 414 Righters Mill Rd Narberth PA 19072-1423 Office: The Newcomen Soc of the US 412 Newcomen Rd Exton PA 19341-1934 E-mail: info@newcomen.org.

NEWHART, BOB, entertainer; b. Oak Park, Ill., Sept. 5, 1929; m. Virginia Quinn, Jan. 12, 1963; 4 children. BS, Loyola U., Chgo., 1952. Acct. U.S. Gypsum Co.; copywriter Fred Niles Film Co.; appeared on Jack Paar Show, 1960; TV performer numerous guest appearances, 1961—; star TV series Newhart, 1982-90, The Bob Newhart Show, 1972—78. Rec. artist (album) The Button Down Mind of Bob Newhart; royal command performance, London, 1964, appeared in films Hell is for Heroes, 1962, Hot Millions, 1968, Catch 22, 1970, On a clear Day You Can See Forever, 1970, Cold Turkey, 1971, First Family, 1980, Little Miss Marker, 1980; TV films include Thursday's Game, 1974, Marathon, 1980, In and Out, 1997. Grand marshall Tournament Roses Parade, 1991. With U.S. Army, 1952-54. Recipient Emmy award, 1961, Peabody award, 1961, Sword of Loyola award, 1976, Legend to Legend award, 1993, three Grammy awards 1960, The Sports Pages/How Doc Waddems Finally Broke 100, 2001; named to Acad. Hall of Fame, 1993. Office: c/o Capell Duitch Franklin 11601 Wilshire Blvd Ste 2350 Los Angeles CA 90025-1759

NEWHOUSE, ALAN RUSSELL, retired federal government executive; b. N.Y.C., Feb. 27, 1938; s. Russell Conwell and Clara Lucille (Scovell) N.; m. Margo Stiles Hicks, Feb. 3, 1960; children: Daryl, Jeffrey, William. BEE, Cornell U., 1960. Engr. Bur. of Ships, Washington, 1964-66; nuclear power engr., chief West Milton field office AEC, Schenectady, N.Y., 1966-69; sr. exec. AEC, ERDA, U.S. Dept. Energy, Washington, 1969-92; dep. asst. sec. Space and Def. Power Systems Office Nuclear Energy, 1992-93; dir. Office Space and Def. Power Systems, 1993-95; retired, 1995; ind. cons., 1995—. Cons. Energy Conversion Techs. Composer numerous musical works. Bd. trustees River Road Unitarian Ch., Bethesda, Md., 1973-75; mem. Cmty. Orchestra So. Md. in Concert, Friday Morning Music Club. Lt. USN, 1960-64. Mem.: AIAA, IEEE, Am. Soc. Naval Engrs., Am. Nuc. Soc. Unitarian Universalist. Home and Office: 24670 Greenview Dr Hollywood MD 20636-4823 E-mail: Newhouse@ieee.org.

NEWHOUSE, Mrs. EDWARD See DELAY, DOROTHY

NEWHOUSE, JOSEPH PAUL, economist, educator; b. Waterloo, Iowa, Feb. 24, 1942; s. Joseph Alexander and Ruth Linnea (Johnson) Newhouse; m. Margaret Louise Locke, June 22, 1968; children: Eric Joseph, David Locke. BA, Harvard U., 1963, PhD, 1969; postgrad (Fulbright scholar), Goethe U., Frankfort, Germany, 1963—64. Staff economist Rand Corp., Santa Monica, Calif., 1968—72, dep. program mgr., health and biosci. rsch., 1971—88, sr. staff economist, 1972—81, head econs. dept., 1981—85, sr. corp. fellow, 1985—; John D. MacArthur prof. health policy and mgmt., dir. div. Health Policy Rsch. and Edn., Harvard U., 1988—. Lectr. UCLA, 1970—83, adj. prof., 1983—88; mem. faculty Rand Grad. Sch., 1972—88; dir. Rand-UCLA Ctr. for Study Health Care Fin. Policy, 1984—88, co-dir., 1988—92; prin. investigator health ins. study grant HHS, 1971—86; chmn. health svcs. rsch. study sect. HHS-Agy. for Health Care Policy and Rsch., 1989—93; mem. Nat. Commn. Cost Med. Care, 1976—77; mem. health svcs. devel. grants study sect. HEW, 1978—82, Inst. Medicine of NAS, 1978—, mem. coun., 1991—97; mem. Physician Payment Rev. Commn., 1993—96; chmn. Prospective Payment Assessment Com., 1996—97; vice chair Medicare Payment Assessment Commn., 1997—; bd. regents Nat. Libr. Medicine, 1999—; bd. dirs. Aetna, ABT Assocs. Author: The Economics of Medical Care, 1978, The Cost of Poor Health Habits, 1991, A Measure of Malpractice, 1993, Free for All?, 1993, Pricing the Priceless, 2002; editor: Jour. Health Econs., 1981—; assoc. editor: Jour. Econ. Perspectives, 1992—98; contbr. articles to profl. jours. Recipient David Kershaw award and prize, Assn. Pub. Policy and Mgmt., 1983, Baxter Am. Found. prize, 1988, Adminstr.'s citation, Health Care Fin. Adminstrn., 1988, Hans Sigrist Found. prize, 1995, Elizur Wright award, 1995, Zvi Griliches award, 2000, Kenneth Arrow award, 2001. Fellow: Am. Acad. Arts and Scis.; mem.: Internat. Health Econs. Assn. (bd. dirs. 1996—, pres. 1996—98), Econometric Soc., Royal Econ. Soc., Am. Econ. Assn., Assn. for Health Svcs. Rsch. (bd. dirs. 1991—, pres. 1993—94, Article of Yr. award 1989). Office: Harvard U Health Policy Rsch and Edn 180 Longwood Ave Boston MA 02115-5821

NEWHOUSE, MARK WILLIAM, publishing executive; b. N.Y.C., Oct. 14, 1948; s. Norman Nathan and Alice (Gross) N.; m. Lorry A. Whitehead, June 1, 1974; children: Jesse Louis, Charlotte Ann. BA, Yale U., 1969. V.p., gen. mgr. The Star-Ledger, Newark, 1980—. Bd. dirs. N.Y.C. Opera, 1992—, pres., 1993—; bd. dirs. Audit Bur. of Circulations, 1995—, Glimmerglass Opera, 1997—. Office: Newark Morning Star Ledger Co One Star Ledger Plz Newark NJ 07102-1200

NEWHOUSE, MATTHEW, journalist; b. Oklahoma City, Sept. 16, 1965; s. Bill Newhouse and Grace Dougherty. A, St. Gregory's Coll., Shawnee, Okla., 1985; BA in History, Kans. Newman Coll., 1987. Editor Vantage, Wichita, Kans., 1986—87, Clearwater (Kans.) Times, 1987; reporter Marion (Kans.) County Record, 1988—96, news editor, 1996—. Bd. dirs. Hoch Pub., Inc., Marion, 1999—. Founding mem. Chingawassa Days Festival, Marion, 1996, bd. dirs., 1998—; chmn. Leadership Marion County, 2000—01. Mem.: U.S. Cavalry Assn., Kiwanis (sec., past pres. Marion chpt.). Office: Hoch Pub Inc 117 S 3d St Marion KS 66861-0278

NEWHOUSE, NANCY RILEY, newspaper editor; b. Bellingham, Wash. d. Fenwick Charles and Elizabeth (Grace) Riley; m. John Newhouse, Sept. 27, 1961 (div. 1970); m. Michael Iovenko, Mar. 6, 1983. BA, Vassar Coll., 1958. Sr. editor N.Y. Mag., N.Y.C., 1970-75, House & Garden Mag., N.Y.C., 1976; successively home editor, style editor and travel editor N.Y. Times, 1976—. Editor: Hers: Through Women's Eyes, 1985; editor Hers column N.Y. Times, 1976-92; mem. adv. bd. Vassar Quar., Poughkeepsie, N.Y., 1985—. Decorated chevalier Nat. Order Merit; recipient Penney-Mo. Newspaper award U. Mo. Sch. Journalism, 1982-83. Mem. The Century Assn., Women's Forum N.Y. Office: NY Times Co 229 W 43rd St New York NY 10036-3959

NEWHOUSE, QUENTIN, JR. social psychologist, educator, researcher; b. Washington, Oct. 20, 1949; s. Quentin Sr. and Berlene Delois (Byrd) N.; m. Brenda Joice Washington, Feb. 17, 1973 (div. Mar. 1984); m. Debra Ann Carter, July 7, 1984 (div. Mar. 2000); 1 child, Alyse Elizabeth Belinda. BA in Psychology, Marietta (Ohio) Coll., 1971; MS in Psychology, Howard U., 1974, PhD in Psychology, 1980. Asst. prof. Antioch U., Balt., 1976-79; pres. Quentin Newhouse Jr. and Assocs., Inc., Washington, 1981-84; computer systems analyst U.S. Army, 1984, 85; asst. prof. Howard U., 1982-88; adj. prof. U. D.C., 1984, 91—, Bowie State U., 1982-86, 91—; mentor Prince George's Community Coll., Largo, Md., 1986-89; computer specialist Bur. of the Census, Ctr. for Survey Methods Rsch., Suitland, 1988-91, social sci. statistician, 1991-93; dir. mktg. analyst Safeway Inc., Lanham, Mo., 1994; job developer Prince George's Pvt. Industry Coun., Largo, Md., 1994-95; asst. prof., interim chair dept. behaviour and human svcs. Bowie (Md.) State U., 1995—98; adj. prof. U. Mo., 1999—. Tenn. State U., 2001—, Middle Tenn. Sch. Anes., 2001—; asst. dir. EMIT, 2002—. V.p. Bureautots, Inc., Largo, 1989-91. Commr. Prince George's County Children and Youth, Upper Marlboro, Md., 1991, Prince George's County Commn. for Children, Youth and Families, 1992-95; bd. dirs. Prepare Our Youth, Inc., Tacoma Park, Md., Shiloh Bapt. Ch. Nursery, Washington, 1988-90; mem. State of Md. Adv. Com. for Children, Youth and Families, 1992-93, regional coun. Prince George's United Way, 1994-96; bd. dirs. Met. Boys and Girls Clubs, 1995—, Mental Health Assn. of Prince George's County, 1994-95. Recipient Cmty. Svc. award U. D.C., 1982, 84, Gov.'s cert. of svc. State of Md., 1993, Appreciation cert. Prince George's County, 1995, 96; named Outstanding Young Man of Am., 1982, 86. Mem. APA, Social Sci. Computing Assn., Census SAS Users Group (co-chair 1991-93), Tau Epsilon Phi (life). Democrat. Avocations: walking, reading, working with computers. Office: Bowie State U MLK 201 Dept Behavioral Scis & Human Svcs Bowie MD 20715

NEWICK, CRAIG DAVID, architect; b. Orange, N.J., Feb. 14, 1960; s. Russel Forester and Helen (Welch) N.; m. Linda Hammer Lindroth, June 6, 1987; 1 child, Zachary Eran. BA in Architecture, Lehigh U., 1982; MArch, Yale U., 1987. Registered architect, Conn. Designer, draftsman The Archtl. Studio, Easton, Pa., 1983-84; job capt., project designer Svigals & Assocs., New Haven, 1985; designer, draftsman Centerbrook (Conn.) Architects, 1986; job capt., project designer Allan Dehar Assocs., Architects & Planners, New Haven, 1988-90; ptnr. Lindroth & Newick, 1991—; designer Cesar Pelli & Assocs., Inc., 1992; project arch. Tai Soo Kim Ptnrs., Hartford, 1995—2001; prin. Newick Archs., New Haven, 2001—. Vis. faculty Vis. Critics Studio, Lehigh U., 1993; vis. critic Wesleyan U., 1990-93, R.I. Sch. Design, 1988; faculty Creative Arts Workshop, New Haven, 1991, 92. Exhibitions include Out Of Bounds; author: Simultaneous Space (first prize artists books, 1994). Recipient 1st place award Am. Visionary Set Design Competition, 1989, 3d place award Astronauts Meml. Design Competition, 1988, ID Mag. Ann. Design Rev. award, 1990, 2d prize African Burial Ground Competition Mcpl. Arts Soc. N.Y., 1994, 1st place drawing award Conn. Soc. Architects, 1997, AIA Conn. honor award, 2000; grantee New Eng. Found. for Arts, 1992, NEA Interarts grantee Rockefeller Found., 1989-90, Found. for Contemporary Performance Art, 1989, 90, Humanities Coun. of Fairfield U., 1995; New Eng. Found. for Arts Regional fellow, 1993, Conn. Commn. on the Arts fellow, 1998, others. Mem. Architecture League N.Y. (young architects forum 1991, emerging voices, 1996). Office: Newick Archs 85 Willow St New Haven CT 06511

NEWILL, JAMES WAGNER, accounting executive; b. Greensburg, Pa., Dec. 22, 1934; s. James Meyers and Ruth Elizabeth (Wagner) N.; m. Helene Margaret Dolibois, Feb. 18, 1957; 1 child, J. Eric. BBA, St. Vincent Coll., Latrobe, Pa., 1962. CPA, Pa., Ohio, Fla. Staff acct. George Conti & Co., CPA, Greensburg, 1962-65; internal auditor Duquesne Light Co., Pitts., 1965-67; supr. accounts payable and gen. ledger Kennametal, Inc., Latrobe, 1967-71; asst. controller Glosser Stores, Inc., Johnstown, Pa., 1971-73; controller, asst. treas. Meridian Plastics, Inc., Byesville, Ohio, 1973-76; regional controller Friendly Ice Cream Corp., Wilbraham, Mass., 1976-79; pres. J.W. Newill Co., Troy, Ohio, 1979-92; pvt. practice Fla., 1993—. Bd. dirs. S.W. Nat. Bank, Greensburg, 1st Commonwealth Fin. Corp., Indiana, Pa. V.p., bd. dirs. Troy-Hayner Cultural Ctr., 1982-85. Served to staff sgt. USAF, 1954-58. Mem. AICPA, Pa. Inst. CPAs, Ohio Soc. CPAs, Fla. Inst. CPAs, Nat. Assn. Accts., Sea Ranch Club Boca (bd. dirs. 1999—), Masons, Shriners, Scottish Rite, Rotary (chmn. com., Paul Harris fellow), Elks. Republican. Presbyterian. Avocations: travel, tennis, theater.

NEWIRTH, RICHARD SCOTT, cultural organization administrator; b. N.Y.C. BA in Maths. magna cum laude, Brown U., 1980; MBA, U. Calif., Berkeley, 1990. Dividend analyst, actuarial asst. Met. Life Ins. Co., San Francisco, 1980-83, sr. underwriter, 1983-85, mgr. renewal svcs., 1985-87, dir. fin. analysis, 1988; benefits and ins. adminstr. San Francisco Symphony, 1990-92; asst. dir. San Francisco Art Commn., 1993-95, dir. cultural affairs, 1995—. Cons. Berkeley (Calif.) Repertory Theatre, 1990; spkr. Nat. Conf. State Legislators, 1997, Far W. Region Cultural Tourism Leadership Forum, 1997; dist. chair Calif. Assembly of Local Arts Agys.; v.p. Urban Arts Fedn., 1998-99, pres., 2000. Mem. mktg. com., vol. Under One Roof. Recipient Pub. Managerial Excellence award, 2001, CA AAS Coun. Exemplary Leadership award, 2001. Office: City San Francisco San Francisco Art Commn 25 Van Ness Ave Ste 240 San Francisco CA 94102-6053 Fax: 415-252-2595.

NEWITT, JOHN GARWOOD, JR. lawyer; b. Charlotte, N.C., Apr. 9, 1941; s. John Garwood and Sarah Elizabeth (Stratford) N.; m. Catherine Elizabeth Hubbard, Aug. 28, 1965; children: Catherine Stratford, Elizabeth Blake. BA, Wake Forest U., 1963, JD, 1965; postgrad., U. Va., 1966-68; CBA in Bus. Mgmt., C.P.C.C., 2001. Bar: N.C. 1965, U.S. Ct. Mil. Appeals 1965, U.S. Dist. Ct. (we. dist.) N.C. 1968, U.S. Ct. Claims 1968, U.S. Tax. Ct. 1968, U.S. Ct. Appeals (4th cir.) 1984. Ptnr. Newitt & Newitt, Charlotte, 1968-73; sr. ptnr. Newitt & Bruny, 1973—. Lectr. The Judge Advocate Gen.'s Sch., 1965-68, United Way Vol. Leadership Devel. Program, 1986-93. Contbr. articles to profl. jours. Chmn. Bd. Zoning Adjustment, 1971-77; bd. dirs. Carolina Group Homes, 1992-95. Recipient awards ASCAP. Mem. N.C. Bar Assn., Mecklenburg County Bar Assn., N.C. Coll. Advocacy (cert. competency), Charlotte Econs. Club, Myers Park Country Club (past pres.), bd. dirs.), Selwyn Men's Fellowship (past pres.), Good Fellows, Phi Delta Phi (past sec.). Republican. Presbyterian. Avocations: jogging, golf. Home: 3216 Ferncliff Rd Charlotte NC 28211-3259 Office: Newitt & Bruny 417 East Blvd Ste 104 Charlotte NC 28203-5163 E-mail: johnnewitt@cs.com., newittbru@cs.com.

NEWKIRK, ISAAC L. communications executive; b. Pahokee, Fla., Apr. 7, 1950; s. Isaac L. and Alice L. (Davis) N.; m. Paula L. Hyman, Dec. 19, 1951; children: Kajuansa, Qiana, Isaac IV, Brittany. BA in German, BS in Physics, Morehouse Coll., 1973. News editor, anchorman Sta. WQXI AM-FM, Atlanta, 1972-74, supr. tng. and devel., 1976-80, producer pub. affairs show, 1976—, moderator Open Line Talk Show, 1976—, broadcast book reviewer, 1976—; English and Math. instr. Boyd Elem. Sch., 1973-74; moderator, producer Community Watch, AIB Cable Channel, 1983-84, moderator, producer Wednesday Morning Dialogue, 1986—; dir. pub. affairs WQXI AM/FM Radio, 1979—; program dir. WQXI/AM, 1992—. Chmn. Hungry Club Pub. Affairs Forum, Atlanta, 1980-83, Met. Atlanta Drug Abuse Community Adv. Coun., 1983-86; chmn. pub. awareness com. Ga. Commn. on Children and Youth, v.p., 1990-91; chmn. bd. dirs. Coun. for Children, Atlanta, 1986—; mem. Ga. Juvenile Justice Coordinating Coun. Recipient Meritorious Achievements in Broadcasting award Nat. Assn. Media Women, 1979, Abraham Lincoln award for Disting. Broadcasters, So. Bapt. Conv., 1982, J.C. Penney Golden Rule award for Outstanding Vol. Service, 1983; named Young Person of Yr., Y's Men Internat. Mem. Nat. Broadcast Assn. for Community Affairs (bd. dirs. Boston 1980-86, editor newsletter 1980-86, chmn. nat. ann. conf. 1984), Atlanta Interfaith Broadcasters (chmn. bd. dirs. 1979-84). Avocation: softball umpire. Office: Sta WQXI-AM-FM 3350 Peachtree Rd NE Atlanta GA 30326-1040

NEWKIRK, JOHN BURT, metallurgical engineer, administrator; b. Mpls., Mar. 24, 1920; s. Burt Leroy and Mary Louise (Leavenworth) N.; m. Carolyn Mae Jordan, Aug. 4, 1951; children: Jeffrey Burt (dec.), John Jordan, Victoria Louise Lierheimer, Christina Newkirk Seldomridge. B. Metall. Engring, Rensselaer Poly. Inst., Troy, N.Y., 1941; MS, Carnegie Inst. Tech., 1947, Sc.D., 1950. Metall. investigator Bethlehem Steel Co., Pa., 1941-42; Fulbright postdoctoral fellow Cambridge (Eng.) U., 1950-51; research metallurgist research lab. Gen. Electric Co., Schenectady, 1951-59; prof. Cornell U., 1959-65; Phillipson prof. U. Denver, 1965-74, prof. phys. chemistry, 1975-84, Phillipson prof. emeritus, 1984—; pres. Denver Biomaterials, Inc., 1969-86, Colo. Biomed., Inc., 1987-2000, ret. Editor Rews. on High Temperature Materials, 1973-78; co-editor: 16 ann. volumes Advances in X-Ray Analysis; contbr. over 75 articles profl. jours. Lt. USNR, 1942-46. Fellow Am. Soc. Metals (life); mem. Sigma Xi, Tau Beta Pi, Phi Kappa Phi, Alpha Sigma Mu (internat. pres. 1950), Alpha Tau Omega. Republican. Baptist. E-mail: meadows@purplemountain.net.

NEWKIRK, PEGGY ROSE WILLS, civic volunteer; b. Middletown, Ohio, Oct. 8, 1936; d. Hurby and Mirl Daisy (Amburgey) Wills; m. Raymond Daniel Spencer (div. 1972); children: Debra, Raymond II, Stephany; m. Donald Richard Newkirk, Dec. 9, 1976. BS in Edn., Ohio State U., 1984. Cert. tchr., Ohio. Exec. sec. Ohio Dominican Coll., Columbus, 1971-74; exec. asst. Ctrl. Ohio Reg. Coun. on Alcoholism, 1974-76, Ohio Hosp. Assn., Columbus, 1976-77; cons. Mercy Hosp., 1984; dir. human resources Hosp. Choice Health Plan, 1984-86. Author: Wills Ancestry in America (From England to New Jersey, Kentucky, Ohio, California), 1997, Wills Ancestry in America From England To New Jersey and Migration Throughout the United States, 2d edit., 2001; contbr. articles to mags. Vol. Willowbrook Christian Nursing Home, Columbus, 1987; mem. Ohio Hist. Soc., Ky. Hist. Soc. Mem. DAR (vice regent 1992-94, regent 1994-96, chmn. mag. and advt. 1996-98, yearbook editor 1998—, Excellence in Cmty. Svc. award 2001), Internat. Soc. for Brit. Genealogy and Family History, Nat. Soc. Colonial Dames XVII Century, Nat. Soc. Descendants of Early Quakers, 1999, Worthington Hist. Soc. (yearbook editor 1993—), Worthington Art Study (yearbook editor 1995—), Worthington Women's Club. Republican. Avocations: genealogy research, writing, flower gardening, music. Home: 7185 Cypress Dr Westerville OH 43082-8111

NEWKIRK, THOMAS CHARLES, lawyer; b. N.Y.C., June 6, 1942; s. Rudolph H. and Ruth H. (Wilson) N.; m. Nancy W., Dec. 23, 1965; children: Jennifer L., Christopher T. BA, Cornell U., 1964, LLB with distinction, 1966. Bar: N.Y. 1966, D.C. 1976, U.S. Ct. Appeals (2d cir.) 1968, U.S. Ct. Appeals (D.C. cir.) 1974. Assoc. Donovan Leisure Newton & Irvine, N.Y., 1966-72; asst. chief counsel Securities Industry Study, U.S. Senate, Washington, 1972; assoc. Donovan Leisure Newton & Irvine, 1973-75; sr. atty. Office of Legal Counsel, Dept. Justice, 1975-78; asst. gen. counsel Dept. Energy, 1978-79, dep. gen. counsel, 1979-85, chief counsel for jud. litigation, 1985; chief litigation counsel SEC, 1986-93, assoc. dir. div. of enforcement, 1993—. Lectr. in field. Contbr. articles to profl. jours. Recipient Presdl. Meritorious Exec. award Pres. of U.S., 1980, 92, Exceptional Svc. award Sec. of Energy, 1985, Outstanding Svc. medal Sec. of Energy, 1981. Mem. ABA, Assn. Bar City of N.Y. Office: SEC 450 5th St NW Washington DC 20549-0801 E-mail: newkirkt@sec.gov.

NEWKIRK, TRIXIE DARNELL, family nurse practitioner; b. Sault St. Marie, Mich., July 22, 1964; d. Mitchell and Lois I. (Johnston) Darnell; m. Shane P. Newkirk, July 19, 1986; 1 child, Breana Alysha. BSN, Southwestern Okla. State U., 1986; MS, Tex. Woman's U., 1994, cert. family nurse practitioner, 1997. RN, Okla., Tex.; cert. nurse practitioner, Tex.; cert. BCLS, instr. ACLS, CCRN, FNP. Staff nurse St. Francis Hosp., Tulsa; asst. nurse mgr. CCU Humana MCD Hosp., Dallas; staff nurse Baylor U. Med. Ctr., supr. nurse educator critical care unit, 1991-95; clin. nurse specialist for cardiovasc. svcs., 1995-98; family nurse practitioner BG Mills Clinic Assn., Mesquite, Tex., 1997-98; nurse practitioner Heart Place Cardiology, Dallas, 1998-2000, St. Paul Med. Ctr.'s Cardiovasc. Inst., Dallas, 2000—. Mem. ANA, Am. Assn. Nurse Practitioners, Am. Diabetes Assn., Am. Acad. Nurse Practitioners, Tex. Nurses Assn., AACN, Sigma Theta Tau. Home: PO Box 465 Scurry TX 75158 E-mail: Trixie.Newkirk@swmc.org.

NEWLAND, CHESTER ALBERT, public administration educator; b. Kansas City, Kans., June 18, 1930; s. Guy Wesley and Mary Virginia (Yoakum) N. BA, U. N. Tex., Denton, 1954; MA, U. Kans., 1955, PhD, 1958. Social Sci. Rsch. Coun. fellow U. Wis. and U.S. Supreme Ct., 1958-59; instr. polit. sci. Idaho State U., Pocatello, 1959-60; mem. faculty U. North Tex., Denton, 1960-66, prof. govt., 1963-66, dir. dept. govt., 1963-66; prof. polit. sci. U. Houston, 1967-68; dir. Lyndon Baines Johnson Libr., Austin, Tex., 1968-70; prof. pub. adminstrn. U. So. Calif., 1966-67, 68-71, 76-82, 84-92, Duggan disting. prof. pub. adminstrn., 1992—; prof. George Mason U., Fairfax, Va., 1982-84. Mem. faculty Fed. Exec. Inst., 1971-76, dir. 1973-76, 80-81; mgr. task force on fed. labor-mgmt. rels. U.S. Pers. Mgmt. Project, Pres.'s Reorgn., Washington, 1977-78. Editor in chief Pub. Adminstrn. Rev., 1984-90; contbr. articles to profl. jours. Chmn. Mcpl. Rsch. Coun., Denton, 1963-64; city councilman, Denton, 1964-66; mem. Pub. Sector Commn. on Productivity and Work Quality, 1974-78; trustee Sacramento (Calif.) Mus. History, Sci. and Tech., 1993-95; mem. UN Devel. Program Kazakhstan, 1997-2000, strategy review program, 2002, Moldova, 1994, Kuwait, 1991, 95-96; cons. Poland, 1990-91, Hungary, 1991, Czech and Slovak Republics, 1992, Bank of Greece, 1999-2002, Taiwan, 2001. Recipient Van Ryer Pub. Adminstrn. award, 2002. Mem. Nat. Acad. Pub. Adminstrn., Southwestern Social Sci. Assn. (chmn. govt. sect. 1964-65), Am. Soc. Pub. Adminstrn. (pres. Dallas-Ft. Worth chpt. 1964-65, nat. coun. 1976, 78-81, editorial bd. jour. 1972-76, chmn. publ. com. 1975-79, program chmn. 1977, nat. pres. 1981-82, Dimock award 1984, Van Riper award 2002), Am. Polit. Sci. Assn., Internat. Pers. Mgmt. Assn. (program chmn. 1978, Stockberger award 1979), Am. Acad. Polit. and Social Sci., Internat. City Mgmt. Assn. (hon.), Nat. Assn. Schs Pub. Affairs and Adminstrn. (Staats Pub. Svc. award 1989). Office: Univ Southern California 1800 I St Sacramento CA 95814-3004

NEWLAND, HILLARY REID, pathologist; b. Wilmington, N.C., July 3, 1940; s. Hillery Reid and Annie Mae (Bowden) N.; m. Eleanor Milner, Aug. 25, 1963; children: Benjamin Reid, Sarah O'Beirne, Emily Cobb. BS, Davidson (N.C.) Coll., 1962; MD, Med. Coll. Ga., 1968. Diplomate Am. Bd. Pathology. Intern in internal medicine New Eng. Med. Ctr. Hosps., Boston, 1968-69; resident in pathology Med. Coll. Ga. Hosps., Augusta, 1969-70, Madigan Army Med. Ctr., Tacoma, 1970-72; asst. prof. medicine U. Alta., Edmonton, Can., 1974-75; clin. instr. U. Vt. Med. Sch., Burlington, 1975-77; pathologist diagnostic svcs. Lancaster, N.H., 1975-77; pathologist Athens (Ga.) Regional Med. Ctr., Athens, Ga., 1979-2000, Wentworth-Douglass Hosp., Dover, N.H., 1978-79; pvt. practice North Ga. Pathology/Cytology, Athens, 2000—; med. dir. Integrated Regional Labs. Ga., Snellville, 2001—. Pres. Athens Rsch. and Tech., Inc., 1985—; adj. faculty mem. dept. cell biology U. Ga., Athens, 1988-2000. Contbr. articles to profl. publs. Maj. USAR, 1970-74. Fellow ACP, Coll. Am. Pathologists, Am. Soc. Clin. Pathologists, Am. Coll. Quality Assurance Physicians; mem. Athens C. of C. (bd. dirs. 1990-92), Med. Assn. Ga. (chmn. continuing med. edn. 1989—). Democrat. Avocations: tennis, walking. Office: North Ga Pathology/Cytology 1010 Prince Ave Athens GA 30606-5811 Business E-Mail: hrnewland@worldnet.att.net.

NEWLAND, JANE LOU, nursing educator; b. Toledo, July 18, 1931; d. Clarence Charles Meinen and Bernice Isabell (Floyd) Scott; m. Byron Merle Newland, Aug. 4, 1962; children: Jeffrey Bruce, Brian James. Diploma in nursing, Lima (Ohio) Meml. Hosp., 1952; BSN, Ohio State U., 1959; M Vocat. Edn., U. South Fla., 1983, EdS in Vocat. Edn., 1989. RN, Ohio, Fla.; cert. tchr., Fla. Stewardess nurse Balt. & Ohio R.R., Cin., 1953-56; dir. nursing Lima State Hosp., 1960-67, dir. nursing edn., 1967-72; renal nurse children's svc. Health and Rehabilitative Svcs. Fla., Ft. Myers, 1975-78; practical nursing instr. Lee High-Tech. Ctr. Ctrl., 1979—. Adv. bd. Practical Nurse Assn., Lima, 1966-71. Mem., sec. St. James City Civic Assn., 1973-76; den leader Boy Scouts Am., St. James City, 1970-76; treas. PTA Pine Island Elem. Sch., Pine Island Center, Fla., 1973-75; bd. dirs. Railroad Mus. South Fla. Recipient Assoc. Master Tchr. award Fla. State Bd. Edn., 1986. Mem.: Lee County (Fla.) Soc., Health Occupation Educators Assn. Fla., Fla. Vocat. Assn., Lee County Vocat. Assn. (Outstanding Health Occupation Tchr. award 1985, Outstanding Vocat. Edn. Tchr. award 1990), Nat. Assn. Health Occupations Tchrs., Assn. Practical Nurse Educators Fla., Mus. of Island (Pine Island, Fla.), Ladies Aux. VFW (trustee), Alumnae Panhellenic of Lee County, St. James City Hobby Club (editor), Niobians of Cape Coral (Fla.), Order Ea. Star, Ladies Oriental Shrine, Phi Kappa Phi, Kappa Delta (v.p. 1983—85, pres. 1993—97, treas. 1997—). Lutheran. Avocations: crafts, stamp collecting, history. Home: 2261 Carambola Ln Saint James City FL 33956-2018 Office: Lee County High Tech Ctr 3800 Michigan Ave Fort Myers FL 33916-2204

NEWLAND, RUTH LAURA, small business owner; b. Ellensburg, Wash., June 4, 1949; d. George J. and Ruth Marjorie (Porter) N. BA, Cen. Wash. State Coll., 1970, MEd, 1972; EdS, Vanderbilt U., 1973; PhD, Columbia Pacific U., 1981. Tchr. Union Gap (Wash.) Sch., 1970-71; owner Newland Ranch Gravel Co., Yakima, Wash., 1998; ptnr. Arnold Artificial Limb, 1981-86, owner, pres. Yakima and Richland, Wash., 1986—. Owner Newland Ranch, Yakima, 1969—. Contbg. mem. Nat. Dem. Com., Irish Nat. Caucus Found.; mem. Pub. Citizen, We The People, Nat. Humane Edn. Soc.; charter mem. Nat. Mus. Am. Indian. George Washington scholar Masons, Yakima, 1967. Mem. NAFE, NOW, Am. Orthotic and Prosthetic Assn., Internat. Platform Assn., Nat. Antivisection Soc. (life), Vanderbilt U. Alumni Assn., Peabody Coll. Alumni Assn., Columbia Pacific U. Alumni Assn., World Wildlife Fund, Nat. Audubon Soc., Greenpeace, Mus. Fine Arts, Humane Soc. U.S., Wilderness Soc., Nature Conservancy, People for Ethical Treatment of Animals, Amnesty Internat., The Windstar Found., Rodale Inst., Sierra Club (life), Emily's List. Democrat. Avocations: reading, gardening, sewing, handcrafts, people. Home: 2004 Riverside Rd Yakima WA 98901-8540 Office: Arnold Artificial Limb 9 S 12th Ave Yakima WA 98902-3106 *Personal philosophy: God first. Then be politically and socially conservative but liberal in your concern for others.*

NEWLANDS, SHEILA ANN, consumer products company executive; b. Worcester, Mass., Mar. 8, 1953; d. Joseph and Doris Edna (Bachand) N.; m. Domenic V. Testa Jr., Oct. 2, 1976 (div. 1983). BA summa cum laude, Worcester State Coll., 1975; cert. interior design, Bunkerhill Community Coll., 1976; MS, Simmons Coll., 1976; MBA, Suffolk U., 1983. Cert. real estate broker, Mass.; CPA, Wash. Dir. health scis. library Lynn Hosp., Mass., 1976-78, Mt. Auburn Hosp., Cambridge, 1978-81; assoc. fin. analyst Data Gen., Westboro, Mass., 1981-82, fin. analyst, 1982-84, sr. fin. analyst, 1984; fin. analyst Stimson Lane Vineyards and Estates, Woodinville, Wash., 1985-86, dir. fin., 1986-91, v.p., contr., 1991-97, sr. v.p., contr., 1998—, sr. v.p. contr., 1998-2000, exec. v.p., CFO, 2000—. Guest lectr. Simmons Coll. Sch. Library Sci., Boston, 1980-81. Mem. Fin. Mgmt. Honor Soc., Phi Alpha Theta. Avocations: hiking, running. Home: PO Box 514 Issaquah WA 98027-0020 Office: Stimson Lane Wine & Spirits One Stimson Ln Woodinville WA 98072

NEWLER, JEROME MARC, accountant; b. Irvington, N.J., Dec. 3, 1947; s. Leon and Lola Lee (Warner) N.; m. Holly Ann Ogust, Mar. 13, 1977 (div.); children: Jonathan Lane, Andrea Meryl. BBA, Marquette U., 1969; postgrad., NYU, 1970-74. CPA, N.J. Fgn. tax specialist, supr. ops. Bankers Trust Co., N.Y.C., 1970-74; pub. acct. Howard Kuperman, Newler & Tracy Co., East Orange, N.J., 1974-77; ptnr. Newler & Co. CPAs, Union, 1977-84; owner J.M. Newler & Co CPAs, Springfield, 1984—; prin., dir. litig. support svcs. Zeller, Weiss & Kahn LLP CPAs, Mountainside, 1998-2000. Ind. trustee First Fidelity Bank Collective Investment Trust, 1987-90; treas., instr. N.J. Chung Do Kwan Inc., 1997—; lectr. N.J. Jud. Coll., Adminstrv. Office of Supreme Ct., N.J. Inst. for Legal Edn., others; cons. N.Y. Minority Enterprises. With Army N.G., 1969-75. Mem. AICPA, N.J. Soc. CPAs (com. to confer with bench and bar, chmn. com. matrimonial acctg., chmn. jud. edn., profl. conduct com., chmn. Union County chpt. com. to confer with bench and bar, trustee Union County chpt.), Nat. Soc. Pub. Accts., Inst. Bus. Appraisers, Marquette U. Alumni Assn. (alumni admissions asst., class agt.), B'nai B'rith, Alpha Epsilon Pi. Avocation: Chung Do Kwan Tae Kwan Do (black belt 1st degree). Home: 580 Patten Ave unit 77 Long Branch NJ 07740-7881 Office: JM Newler & Co PO Box 522 Springfield NJ 07081-0522

NEWLIN, DOUGLAS RANDAL, lead information engineer; b. Denver, Mar. 26, 1940; s. Loren Randall and Nola Berniece (Paris) N.; m. Sandra Temple, June 22, 1968; children: Jason Britt, Jeremy Owen. BS in Journalism, U. Colo., 1968. Advt. prodn. mgr. Am. Sheep Producers Council, Denver, 1968-70; promotion dir. Sta. KLZ-AM-FM, 1970-71; account mgr. Curran-Morton Advt., 1971-72; advt. and sales promotion specialist Gates Rubber Co., 1972-78; mktg. communications mgr. Hewlett Packard Co., Ft. Collins, Colo., 1978-90; lead learning products engr., 1990—. Vis. lectr. U. Colo., Boulder, 1972-73, statis. quality control course George Washington U., Washington, 1984; web page designer. Author hardware and software catalogs, 1984-90, UNIX Tech. Documentation, 1990-99, Hewlett-Packard Visualize Worksta. User Documentation, 1999—; U.S. newsletter editor Ted Heath Music Appreciation Soc. of U.K. (Eng.); contbr. articles to profl. jours. Pres. Lake Sherwood Homeowners Assn., Ft. Collins, 1982; treas. Lake Sherwood Lake Com., Ft. Collins, 1983-85. Served with U.S. Army, 1959-61. Recipient Gold Key award Bus. and Profl. Advt. Assn., 1976. Mem. Big Bands Internat. Republican. Avocation: bicycling, teaching swing dancing. Home: 4112 Mt Vernon Ct Fort Collins CO 80525-3335 Office: Hewlett Packard Co 3404 E Harmony Rd Fort Collins CO 80528-9599

NEWLIN, GEORGE CHRISTIAN, writer; b. Bklyn., Feb. 14, 1931; s. Albert Chauncey and Janet Bethell Newlin; m. Janine Jordan, Dec. 23, 1967 (div. Apr. 1991); children: Jennifer Williams, Pamela Bowen, Ian Williams, Elizabeth Coker, Colin. AB, Princeton U., 1952; postgrad., Salzburg Mozarteum, 1954, Vienna Acad. Music, 1955-56; LLB, Yale U., 1955; MA in History, Trinity U., San Antonio, 1958. Legal assoc. Milbank, Tweed, Hadley & McCloy, N.Y.C., 1958-65; vp. corp. fin. Dominick & Dominick, Inc., 1965-71; v.p. corp. fin. G. H. Walker & Co. Inc., 1971-72; v.p., gen. counsel Faxon Comm. Inc., White Plains, N.Y., 1972-76; pres. Braintree Mgmt. Ltd., N.Y.C., 1976-88, Windows into Fiction, Somers, N.Y., 1988—. Presenter, lectr. in field English lit., U.S., Can., Eng.; vis. lectr. Lucyle Hook series Barnard Coll., Calif. State U., Fullerton; lectr. Dickens Conf., U. Calif., Santa Cruz. Author, editor: (anthologies) Everyone in Dickens, 3 vols., 1995, Every Thing in Dickens, 1996, (textbooks) Understanding A Tale of Two Cities, 1998, Understanding Great Expectations, 2000, (collections) The Book of Our History, 2002, Fifty Years at Home and Abroad, 2002; concert pianist N.Y. met. area; stage actor; trained with Shakespeare & Co., Lenox, Mass.; interviewee Can. Pub. Radio, ABC Radio, N.Y.; appeared in spl. TV broadcast on Great Expectations, Learning Channel. Past mem. planning bd., past chmn. conservation bd., New Castle, N.Y.; founder New Castle Glazier Arboretum; treas., bd. dirs. Koussevitzky Found. for Music, Robert Miller Fund for Music; past pres., past chmn. bd. dirs. Westchester Conservatory of Music; trustee, mem. fin. com. Bagby Found. for Music; founding pres. then chmn. Coun. for Arts in Westchester (now Westchester Arts Coun.); trustee, asst. treas. Composers Conf. Wellesley Coll. Mem. The Century Assn. N.Y.C. Home and Office: 428 Heritage Hls Unit A Somers NY 10589-1919 E-mail: gcnewlin@aol.com.

NEWLIN, KIMREY DAYTON, international trade consultant, political consultant, personal computer analyst; b. Greensboro, N.C., Jan. 27, 1944; s. Dayton Gilbert and Pearl (Kimrey) N.; m. Beverly Jane Agnew, Mar. 9, 1968; children: Kim, Jr., Stephanie, Laurie. BS in Physics, Guilford Coll., 1966; MS in Agrl. Econs., Clemson U., 1969; MEd in Indls. Engring., Texas A&M U., 1970. Cert. Prof. Logistician, Cost Analyst, Profl. Estimator. Gen. engr., lifetime staff and faculty mem. Army Logistics Mgmt. Coll./Darcom/Dept. of Def., Ft. Lee, Va., 1968-71; economist Army Procurement Rsch. Office/Army Logistics Mgmt. Coll./Darcom/Dept. of Def., 1971-75, ops. rsch. analyst, 1975-78; statistician fisheries mgmt. S.E. Fisheries Ctr./Nat. Marines Fisheries Svc./Nat. Oceanographic Atmospheric Adminstrn./Dept. Commerce, Miami, 1978—, environ. compliance officer fisheries mgmt., 1992—98. Author: Treatment of Textile Waste, 1971, How to Run Successful Projects, 1976—90, Handbook for Chapter Plan Guide, 1976—90, DT LCC, Logistics Spectrum, 1978, 64 seafood dealer directories, 2002; contbr. articles to profl. jours. Trustee Fla. Sci. Senate Found., 2001—; presdl. advisor Fla. Jaycees Act Team, 1983—89, Fla. Jaycees Lakeland, 1985—86; sec. Friendship JCS, 1990—; v.p. Va. Jaycees, Roanoke, 1978—79, community devel., life mem., 1977—; life mem., col. Fla. Gator Corps, 1993—; ctr. rep. SEFSC So. Fla. Fed. Exec. Bd., 1986—, chairperson steering com., 1999—2000, mem. policy bd., 2001—02; set up charitable remainder trust for the Lord homeless hosps./med. rsch. and scholarships, 25 var. charities, 1997; logistics chmn. U.S. JCI Senate, 1992; chief of staff Coconut Grove Jaycees, Fla., 1979—90; adminstrv. v.p., treas. Fla. JCI Senate, Lakeland, 1988—90, reg. dir., 2001—02. Recipient Outstanding Svc. plaque as Adminstr. V.P., Fla. JCI Senate, 1990, Coconut Grove Jaycees Palm award for Outstanding Svc. for Last 10 Yrs., 1989, Hommer Shepard Meml. award, Fla. JCI Senate, 1989, Presdl. award of Honor Plaque for Outstanding Svc., Coconut Grove Jaycees, 1981—87, Henry Colona award, Fla. Jaycees, 1986, 1982, Logistics Cert., Miami Fed. Volunteerism Cert. Exec. Bd., 1991—97, Get Up Off That Thing plaque, Coconut Grove JCS, 1993, Champions of the Heart Legacy award, Am. Heart Assn., 1998, Founders Soc. Alzheimer's Assn., 1997, Lifetime Giving Soc., N.C. State U. Found., 1997, Heritage League award, Am. Cancer Soc., 1997, Heritage Soc. award, Diabetes Rsch. Inst. Found., 1997, Guilford Coll., 1997, Amb. award, Mercy Found., 1997, Forsyth Soc., Texas A & M U., 2001. Fellow Soc. Logistics Engrs. (life, corp.); mem. Fla. JCI Senate (life), AARP, NARFE (life). Republican. Presbyterian. Avocations: woodworking, flea markets, personal computers, travel, yard sales. Home: 755 Allendale Rd Miami FL 33149-2402

NEWLIN, LYMAN WILBUR, bookseller, consultant; b. Buda, Ill., May 26, 1910; s. Fred Matheny and Maude Lillian (Potter) N.; m. Evy Ottonia Magnusson, 1966; children: Fred M. II, Erik B.M. Student, Coll. Emporia, Kans., 1928-30, U. Chgo., 1930-32. Buyer, bus. mgr. Follett Book Co., Chgo., 1934-44; mgr. Minn. Book Store and Macalester Coll. Book Store, Mpls. and St. Paul, 1944-48; co-owner Broadwater Lodge, Hackensack, Minn., 1948-65; founder, owner Broadwater Books, Lewiston, N.Y., 1948—; buyer, dept. mgr. Kroch's & Brentano's Book Store, Chgo., 1951-65; regional mgr. Richard Abel and Co., Portland, Oreg. and Zion, Ill., 1966-69, asst. to pres., 1969-75; founder, prin. counselor Lyman W. Newlin Book Trade Counsellors, Lewiston, N.Y., 1975—; mdse. mgr. Coutts Library Services, Inc., 1976-90; pub. rels. advisor The Charleston (Coll. Libr.) Conf., 1985—; pub. liaison Book News, Inc., Portland, 1989—. Program coord. Acad. of Scholarly Pub. seminar Coll. of Charleston, 1995—; cons. Rutgers U. Press, New Brunswick, N.J., 1975-81; panelist and lectr. to acad. librs. and schs., booksellers. Pub. Rev. Index Quar. Guide to Profl. Revs., 1941-43; co-editor: Scholarly Publishing, Books, Journals, Publishers and Libraries in the Twentieth Century, 2002; pub. rels. advisor, contbr. Bi-Monthly Publ. Against the Grain, 1985—; contbr. articles to profl. jours. Founder, 1st pres. Boy River Chain of Lakes Improvement Assn., Cass County, Minn., 1961-65, Concerned Parents Orgn., Freehold, 1976-79; trustee, v.p., sec., chmn. new libr. bldg. com. Lewiston Pub. Libr., 1985-98, pres. bd. trustees, 1998-2002; committeeman Niagara County Dem. Party, 1987—, sec., 1988-90; mem. coun. Luth. Ch. Messiah, Lewiston, 1982-93, deacon, 1992-97; mem. Town of Lewiston Sr. Citizens Adv. Bd., 1992—; mem., com. person Zion Luth. Ch., Niagara Falls, N.Y., 1995—. Mem. ALA, Assn. Book Travelers (50 Yr. award 1984), Am. Booksellers Assn. (50 yr. bronze plaque 1998), Soc. Scholarly Pub. (program com. 1985), Am. Assn. Pubs. (emeritus), Pi Kappa Delta. Lutheran. Democrat. Avocations: amateur ornithology, Am. folk music, New Orleans jazz, book collecting. Office: PO Box 278 Lewiston NY 14092-0278 *If the Golden Rule is truly one's rule in living, no other rule is needed.*

NEWLIN, WILLIAM RANKIN, lawyer; b. Pitts., Dec. 1, 1940; s. Theodore F. Newlin and Elizabeth Crooks; m. Ann Kleinschmidt, Aug. 25, 1962; children: Steffler Ann, Shelley Kay, William Rankin II. AB, Princeton U., 1962; JD, U. Pitts., 1965; DBA (hon.), Robert Morris Coll., 1997. Bar: Pa. 1965. Assoc. Buchanan Ingersoll, Pitts., 1965-71, ptnr., 1971—, mng. dir., 1980—; mng. gen. ptnr. CEO Venture Fund, 1985—; chmn. bd. Kennametal Inc., Latrobe, Pa., 1996—. Bd. dirs. bd. Nat. City Bank Pa., Pitts., Parker/Hunter, Pitts., Black Box Corp., Pitts., Pitts. Regional Alliance, (hon.) British Consul, Pitts. Editor in chief U. Pitts. Law Rev., 1963; contbr. articles to profl. jours. Chmn., Gov. Thornburgh's Corp. Adv. Com., 1980-82; bd. dirs. Mfr. Studies Bd. nat. Rsch. Coun., Washington, 1988-89, Pitts. High Tech. Coun., 1982—, Pa. Tech. Coun. Recipient Entrepreneur of Yr. award Ernst & Young, Inc. Mag./ Merrill Lynch, 1991. Fellow Am. Bar Found., Pa. Bar Found.; mem. ABA (corp. banking, bus. law sect.), Pa. Bar Assn. (mem. coun. corp. banking and bus. law sect. 1973-82, chmn. sect. 1979-81, Spl. Achievement award 1982), Allegheny County Bar Assn., Assn. of Bar of City of N.Y., Am. Law Inst., Pa. S.W. Assn. (trustee), Greater Pitts. C. of C. (bd. dirs.), Duquesne Club (dir. 1982-85), Rivers Club (bd. dirs. 1983—), Laurel Valley Golf Club, Allegheny Country Club (bd. dirs. 1988—). Office: Buchanan Ingersoll One Oxford Centre 301 Grant St Fl 20 Pittsburgh PA 15219-1410 E-mail: newlinwr@bipc.com.

NEWMAN, ALEXANDRA M. operations research educator; b. Urbana, Ill., July 14, 1972; d. John Kevin and Frances Marilyn Stickney Newman. BS, U. Chgo., 1993; MS, U. Calif., Berkeley, 1994; PhD, U. Calif., 1998. Rsch. asst. prof. Naval Postgrad. Sch., Monterey, Calif., 1998-2000; asst. prof. Colo. Sch. Mines, Golden, 2000—. Contbr. articles to profl. jours., chpt. to book. Named Female Athlete of Yr. NCAA/U. Chgo., 1993. Mem. Inst. Ops. Rsch. and Mgmt. Sci., Phi Beta Kappa, Sigma Xi. Avocation: distance running. Office: Colo Sch Mines Divsn Econs and Bus Golden CO 80401 E-mail: newman@mines.edu.

NEWMAN, ANDREW EDISON, restaurant executive; b. St. Louis, Aug. 14, 1944; s. Eric Pfeiffer and Evelyn Frances (Edison) N.; m. Peggy Gregory, Feb. 14, 1984; children: Daniel Mark, Anthony Edison. BA, Harvard U., 1966, MBA, 1968. With Office of Sec. Def., Washington, 1968-70; with Edison Bros. Stores, Inc., St. Louis, 1970-95, v.p. ops. and adminstrn., 1975-80, dir., 1978-96, exec. v.p., 1980-86, chmn., 1987-95; chmn., CEO Race Rock Internat., 1995—. Bd. dirs. Sigma-Aldrich Corp., St. Louis, Lee Enterprises, Davenport, Iowa. Trustee Washington U. Office: 8000 Maryland Ave Saint Louis MO 63105-3752

NEWMAN, ANITA NADINE, surgeon; b. Honolulu, June 13, 1949; d. William Reece Elton and Margie Ruth (Pollard) Newman; m. Frank E.X. Ward, Sept. 9, 1995; children: Justin Ellis, Chelsea Newman, Andrew Frank, Tyler William. BA, Stanford U., 1971; MD, Dartmouth Coll., 1975. Diplomate Am. Bd. Otolaryngology. From intern to resident in gen. surgery Northwestern Meml. Hosp., Chgo., 1975-77, resident in otolaryngology, 1977-78; resident UCLA Hosp. and Clinics, 1979-82; assoc. prof. UCLA, 1982-96; rsch. fellow in neurotology, 1984-88; surgeon USC Head and Neck Group, 1997-2000; staff surgeon Wadsworth VA Hosp., L.A., 1982-84; pvt. practice, 2000—. Contbr. articles to profl. jours. Mem. alumni admissions support com. Dartmouth Med. Sch. Alumni Coun., 1983-87. Fellow ACS; mem. Am. Acad. Otolaryngology, Am. Med. Women's Assn., L.A. County Med. Women's Assn., Assn. Rsch. Otolaryngology, Stanford Women's Honor Soc. Democrat. Office: 8631 W 3d St Ste 625E Los Angeles CA 90048 E-mail: entdoc49@aol.com.

NEWMAN, ARNOLD, photographer; b. N.Y.C., Mar. 3, 1918; s. Isidore and Freda (Perell) N.; m. Augusta Rubenstein, Mar. 6, 1949; children— Eric Allan, David Saul. Student, U. Miami, Coral Gables, Fla., 1937-38, DFA (hon.), 1981; HHD (hon.), Art Ctr. Coll. Design, Pasadena, Calif., 1985; hon. univ. doctorate, U. Bradford, Eng., 1989; DFA (hon.), New Sch. Social Rsch./Parson Sch. Design, 1990. Began photography, 1938; exptl. portraiture, 1941; opened N.Y.C. studio, 1946; adj. prof. photography Cooper Union, N.Y.C., 1968-75. Resident dir.s visitor/lectr. Inst. for Advanced Study, Princeton, N.J., 1991; lectr. U.S. and abroad. Exhibited and represented in collections, Mus. Modern Art, N.Y.C., Met. Mus. Art, N.Y.C., Art Inst. Chgo., Smithsonian Instn., Washington, Phila. Mus. Art, Internat. Mus. Photography at George Eastman House, Rochester, N.Y., Photography Gallery, London, Israel Mus., Jerusalem, Victoria and Albert Mus., London, Moderna Museet, Stockholm, Australian Nat. Gallery, Camberra, Nat. Portrait Gallery, London, Nihon U. Coll. Art, Tokyo, Odakyu Gallery, Tokyo, Japan, others; traveling retrospective exhbn., Arnold Newman-Five Decades, Mus. of Photographic Arts, San, Diego, 1986, Art Inst. of Chgo., 1986, Mpls. Inst. Art, 1987, Norton Gallery & Sch. Art, MIT Mus., Cambridge, 1988, Modern Art Mus., Ft. Worth, 1988-89, Cin. Art Mus., 1989, De Nieuwe Kerk, Amsterdam, The Netherlands, 1989, The Joan Miró Fedn., Barcelona, Spain, 1990, Frankfurter Kunstverein, Germany, Musee de l'Elysee, Lausanne, Switzerland, 1992, Mus. Modern Art, Oxford, England, 1992, Arnold Newman's Ams., Nat. Portrait Gallery, Washington, 1992; author: Bravo Stravinsky, 1967, One Mind's Eye: The Portraits and Other Photographs of Arnold Newman, 1974, Faces USA, 1978, The Great British, 1979, Artists: Portraits from Four Decades, 1980, I Grandi Fotografi Arnold Newman, 1983, Arnold Newman-Five Decades, 1986, Arnold Newman in Florida, 1987, Arnold Newman's Americans, Portrait Gallery, Washington, 1992, The Detroit Inst. Arts, 1993, LBJ Libr. & Mus., Austin, Tex., 1993, Columbus (Ga.) Mus. Art, 1993-94, Greenville (S.C.) County Mus. Art, 1994, Worcester (Mass.) Art Mus., 1994, Arnold Newman's Gift, George Eastman House, Rochester, N.Y., 1994; contbr. to Travel and Leisure, Life, Look, Holiday, Fortune, Esquire, Town & Country, Vanity Fair, 1946—; subject of Nebr. Ednl. TV program The Image Makers: The Environment of Arnold Newman, 1977; invited exhbn. and lecture tour throughout country Czechoslovakian govt., 1989, Mus. Contemporary History, Budapest, Hungary, 1990. Recipient Photokina award, Cologne, Germany 1951, Newhouse citation Syracuse (N.Y.) U. 1961, Gold medal 4th Biennale Internazionale della Fotagrafic, Venice, Italy 1963, Andy award Advt. Club N.Y., 1983, Mo. Honor medal for journalism U. Mo., 1985, Medal of Merit, 1986, Medal of Merit Lotos Club, 1986, Lifetime Achievement in Photography award Photographic Adminstrs., 1989, others; named Hon. Fellow of Israel Mus. of Jerusalem, 1986, Commemorative medal in hon. 150th anniversary photography Ministry of Culture Czechoslovakia, 1989, Disting. Alumnus award U. Miami, 1993; named N.Y. Alumnus of Yr. U. Miami, 1993; The Arnold Newman Scholarship Fund named in honor Parsons Sch. Design, N.Y.C., 1993. Mem. Am. Soc. Mag. Photographers (Life Achievement in Photography award 1975), Inst. for Advanced Study (bd. dirs. visitor Princeton chpt. 1991). Office: 39 W 67th St New York NY 10023-6244

NEWMAN, BARBARA MAE, retired special education educator; b. Rockford, Ill., July 16, 1932; d. Greene Adam and Emma Lorene (Fields) N. BS Edn., No. Ill. U., 1973. Cert. elem. edn. K-8 tchr., spl. edn. (blind and p.s.) K-12 tchr. Exec. sec. Rockford Art Assn., 1961-70; tchr. Title 1 Rockford Pub. Sch. Dist. #205, 1975-76, tchr. vision impaired, 1977-91. Feature editor (Rock Valley Coll. newpaper) The Valley Forge, 1970; contbg. writer (Rockford Coll. history) A Retrospective Look, 1980. St. Bernadette adult choir, 1958-95, Cathedral Chorale, 1995—; holder 5 offices Am. Bus. Women's Assn., Forest City chpt., 1963-70; vol. Winnebago Ctr. for the Blind, Rockford, 1965-70; mem. Rockford Diocesan Chorale, 1969—. Named Woman of Yr., Am. Bus. Women's Assn., Forest City chpt., Rockford, 1966; scholar Ill. State Scholarship Commn., No. Ill. U., 1970-73. Mem. Ill. Ret. Tchrs. Assn., Cath. Woman's League. Roman Catholic. Avocations: writing, swimming.

NEWMAN, BARBARA MILLER, psychologist, educator; b. Chgo., Sept. 6, 1944; d. Irving George and Florence (Levy) Miller; m. Philip r. Newman, June 12, 1966; children: Samuel Asher, Abraham Levy, Rachel Florence. Student, Bryn Mawr Coll.; AB with honors in Psychology, U. Mich., 1966, PhD in Devel. Psychology, 1971. Undergrad. research asst. in psychology U. Mich., 1963-64, research asst. in psychology, 1964-69, teaching fellow, 1965-71, asst. project dir. Inst. for Social Research, 1971-72, univ. lectr. in psychology and research assoc., 1971-72; asst. prof. psychology Russell Sage Coll., 1972-76, assoc. prof., 1977-78; assoc. prof. dept. family rels. and human devel. Ohio State U., 1978-83, prof., 1983-86, assoc. provost for faculty recruitment and devel., 1987-92, prof., 1992-2000; prof. and chair dept. human devel. and family studies U. R.I., 2000—. Author (with P. Newman): Living: The Process of Adjustment, 1981; author: Understanding Adulthood, 1983, Adolescent Development, 1986, Development Through Life, 1975, 7th edit., 1999, When Kids Go to College, 1992, Childhood and Adolescence, 1997. Mem. AAAS, APA, Soc. Rsch. in Child Devel., Am. Psychol. Soc., Nat. Coun. Family Rels., Groves Conf. on Marriage and Family, Soc. for Rsch. on Adolescence, Am. Assn. Family and Consumer Scis. Author books including: (with P. Newman) Living: The Process of Adjustment, 1981; Development Through Life, 1995, 7th edit., 1999; Understanding Adulthood, 1983; Adolescent Development, 1986; When Kids Go to College, 1997; contbr. articles to profl. publs. Office: U RI Human Devel and Family Studies 112 Transition Ctr Kingston RI 02881 E-mail: bnewman@uri.edu.

NEWMAN, BARNEY DAVID, medical administrator, internist; b. East Liverpool, Ohio, July 27, 1950; s. Maurice J. and Esther G. (Solomon) N.; m. Jean M. Wester, Aug. 5, 1973 (div.); children: Jeremy, Gabriel, Caitlin; m. Carrie Hoodkiss, Mar. 13, 2000. BA, U. Pa., 1972; MD, Pa. State U., 1977. Diplomate Am. Bd. Internists. Resident in internal medicine Montefiore Hosp., Bronx, N.Y., 1977-80; staff internist Westchester Cmty. Health Plan,

White Plains, 1980-83, chief medicine, 1983-85; physician-in-chief Kaiser Permanente, 1985-88, group med. dir., 1988-94, assoc. regional med. dir., 1994-99; pvt. practice West Chester, 1999—; med. dir. Westchester Med. Group, PC, White Plains, 1999—. Pres., bd. dirs. N.E. Permanente Med. Group, White Plains, 1986-99; bd. dirs. N.E. Permanente Mgmt. Corp., Farmington, Conn.; bd. dirs. Westchester Med. Group, P.C., 1999—; clin. asst. prof. medicine Weill Med. Coll.; adj. clin. asst. prof. N.Y. Med. Coll. Mem. editl. bd. Permanente Jour.; managed care editor Medscape. Bd. dirs. The Lord's Pantry, White Plains, 1992—. Mem. ACP, Am. Coll. Physician Execs. Avocations: skiing, running, tennis. Office: Westchester Med Group PC 210 Westchester Ave White Plains NY 10604-2901

NEWMAN, BARRY INGALLS, retired banker, lawyer; b. N.Y.C., Mar. 19, 1932; s. M.A. and T.C. (Weitman) N.; m. Jean Short, Mar. 6, 1965; children: Suzanne, Cathy, David. BA, Alfred U., 1952; JD, NYU, 1955. Bar: N.Y. 1957, Ohio 1958, U.S. Supreme Ct. 1967, Calif. 1990; practice in N.Y.C., 1957. Assoc., then ptnr. firm Shapiro Persky Marken & Newman, Cleve., 1957-63; asst. v.p. Meinhard & Co. (now Meinhard Comml. Corp.), N.Y.C., 1963-65; v.p. Amsterdam Overseas Corp., 1966-68; pres. No. Fin. Corp., L.A., 1968-72; sr. v.p. Aetna Bus. Credit, Inc., Hartford, Conn., 1972-78; exec. v.p. Security Pacific Fin. Group, San Diego, 1978-81, chmn., pres., CEO, 1981-82; sr. exec. v.p. Gt. Am. First Savs. Bank, 1982-88, ret., 1988. Chmn. bd. dirs. San Diego County Capital Asset Leasing Corp., 1984-2000. Past pres. U. Club of San Diego; past chmn. bd. trustees Calif. Ctr. for the Arts, Escondido; past pres. San Diego County Taxpayers Assn.; dep. foreman San Diego County Grand Jury, 1999-2000; chmn. San Diego County Treasury Oversight com., 1995—; mem. bd. govs. San Diego Found.; commr. San Diego County Civil Svc. Commn.; treas. The Episcopal Diocese of San Diego, 1993-2001. Recipient Disting. Svc. award Cleve. Jr. C. of C., 1961. Mem. ABA, N.Y. State Bar Assn., Ohio Bar Assn., Calif. Bar Assn., San Diego Bar Assn., Masons. Republican. Home: 3308 Avenida Sierra Escondido CA 92029-7937 E-mail: BNewmanlaw@aol.com.

NEWMAN, BARRY MARC, pediatric surgeon; b. N.Y.C., Dec. 13, 1951; s. Sheldon and Miriam (Jasphy) N.; m. Jane Post, July 2, 1989; 1 child, Alexander Ross. BA, U. Pa., 1973; MD, SUNY, Stony Brook, 1976. Diplomate Nat. Bd. Med. Examiners, Am. Bd. Surgery, Am. Bd. Pediatric Surgery. Resident in surgery N.Y. Med. Coll., N.Y.C., 1976-78; sr. resident in surgery SUNY, Stony Brook, 1978-81; chief resident pediatric surgery Childrens Hosp. of Buffalo, 1981-83, fellow pediatric surgery and gastroenterology, 1983-84; asst. prof. surgery U. Va., Charlottesville, 1984-88, U. Ill., Chgo., 1988-93; dir. pediatric surgery Luth. Gen. Children's Hosp., Park Ridge, Ill., 1991-96; clin. assoc. prof. surgery U. Chgo., 1993-95; dir. pediatric surg. svcs. Loyola U. Med. Ctr., Maywood, Ill., 1996—, co-dir. surg. laparoscopy lab., 1996-97, assoc. prof. surgery and pediatrics, 1996—. Instr. Adv. Trauma and Life Support, ACS, Chgo., 1984—. Contbr. articles to profl. jours., chpts. to books. NIH grantee, 1982-83, 87-88. Fellow ACS, Am. Coll. Chest Physicians, Am. Acad. Pediatrics; mem. Am. Gastroenterol. Assn., Am. Pediatric Surg. Assn., Am. Coll. Physician Execs. Democrat. Jewish. Avocations: wine collecting, scuba diving, underwater photography, personal computing. Office: Loyola U Med Ctr Dept Surgery 2160 S 1st Ave Dept Surgery Maywood IL 60153-3304

NEWMAN, BRUCE MURRAY, antiques dealer; b. N.Y.C., Jan. 27, 1930; s. Meyer and Evelyn (Kantor) Newman; m. Judith S Brandus, June 26, 1965; 1 child Emily Rachel. BA, Pratt Inst., 1953, BFA (hon.), 1998. Pres. Newel Art Galleries Inc., N.Y.C., 1975—. Lectr mus and univs; mem regional adv bd Chase Manhattan Bank; mem regional adv bd J P Morgan Chase Bank. Author: (book) Fantasy Furniture, 1989; featured numerous TV & radio programs, mags, and other publs, guest CBS Morning Show, 1988. Assoc mem Mt Sinia Med Ctr, 1988—; bd dirs New York City Ctr, 1988—90; trustee Pratt Inst, Brooklyn, NY, 1983—. Named Man of the Yr, Pratt Inst, 1993; recipient Designer Award, Art Dirs Club, 1984. Mem.: Victorian Soc Am, Am Soc Interior Designers (bd dirs 1989—). Avocations: golf, reading, jogging, travel.

NEWMAN, CAROL L. lawyer; b. Yonkers, N.Y., Aug. 7, 1949; d. Richard J. and Pauline Frances (Stoll) N. AB/MA summa cum laude, Brown U., 1971; postgrad., Harvard U. Law Sch., 1972-73; JD cum laude, George Washington U., 1977. Bar: D.C. 1977, Calif. 1979. With antitrust divsn. U.S. Dept. Justice, Washington and L.A., 1977-80; assoc. Alschuler, Grossman & Pines, L.A., 1980-82, Costello & Walcher, L.A., 1982-85, Rosen, Wachtell & Gilbert, L.A., 1985-88, ptnr., 1988-90, Keck, Mahin & Cate, L.A., 1990-94; pvt. practice, 1994—. Adj. prof. Sch. Bus., Golden Gate U., spring 1982. Commr. L.A. Bd. Transp. Commrs., 1993—98, v.p., 1995—96; pres. Bd. Taxicab Commrs., 1999—2001; candidate for State Atty. Gen., 1986; bd. dirs. Women's Progress Alliance, 1996—98. Mem. ABA, State Bar Calif., L.A. County Bar Assn., L.A. Lawyers for Human Rights (co pres. 1991-92), Log Cabin (bd. dirs. 1992-97, pres. 1996-97), Calif. Women Lawyers (bd. govs. 1991-94), Order of Coif, Phi Beta Kappa. E-mail: cnewman540@aol.com.

NEWMAN, CHARLES A. lawyer; b. L.A., Mar. 18, 1949; s. Arthur and Gladys Newman; children: Anne R., Elyse S. BA magna cum laude, U. Calif., 1970; JD, Washington U., 1973. Bar: Mo. 1973, U.S. Dist. Ct. (ea. dist.) Mo. 1973, U.S. Ct. Appeals (8th cir.) 1975, U.S. Supreme Ct. 1976, D.C. 1981, U.S. Tax Ct. 1981, U.S. Claims Ct. 1981, U.S. Ct. Appeals (11th cir.) 1994, U.S. Ct. Appeals (9th cir.) 1995, U.S. Dist. Ct. (ctrl. dist.) 1996, U.S. Ct. Appeals (3d, 5th, 7th and 10th cirs.) 1996, U.S. Ct. Appeals (6th cir.) 1997. From assoc. to ptnr. Thompson & Mitchell, St. Louis, 1973-96; ptnr. Thompson Coburn, 1996-97, Bryan Cave LLP, St. Louis, 1997—. Lectr. law Washington U., St. Louis, 1976-78. Bd. dirs. Hawthorn Found., 1997-2000; trustee Mo. Bar Found., 1990-96, mem. Mo. Bar Bd. Govs, 1980-84; bd. dirs. United Israel Appeal, N.Y.C., 1990-93, Coun. Jewish Fedns., N.Y.C., 1992-95, United Jewish Appeal Young Leadership Cabinet, N.Y.C., 1985-88, Ctr. for Study of Dispute Resolution, 1985-88, Legal Svcs. Ea. Mo., 1985-94, St. Louis Community Found., 1992-2001, vice-chmn. 1997-99, St. Louis chpt. Young Audiences 1993-95, Planned Parenthood St. Louis, 1986-89, Jewish Fedn., St. Louis, 1986-98, asst. treas., 1989-90, v.p. fin. planning, 1990-93, asst. sec., 1994-95; v.p. Repertory Theatre, St. Louis, 1986-89, sr. v.p., 1990-91; pres. St. Louis Opportunity Clearinghouse, 1974-78. Recipient Lon O. Hocker Meml. Trial award Mo. Bar Found., 1984. Mem. Bar Assn. Met. St. Louis (Merit award 1976). Democrat. Avocations: golf, reading, music, sailing. Office: Bryan Cave LLP One Metropolitan Square Saint Louis MO 63102-2750

NEWMAN, CLAIRE POE, private investor; b. Jacksonville, Fla., Dec. 12, 1926; d. Leslie Ralph and Gertrude (Criswell) Poe; m. Robert Jacob Newman, July 3, 1948 (dec. 1994); children: Leslie Claire, Robert, Christopher David. Student, Fla. State Coll. for Women, 1944-45, Tulane U., 1971-73. Co-owner Vineyards in Burgundy, France. Com. mem. New Orleans Mus. Art; women's com. New Orleans Philharmonic Symphony Assn., 1961—, chmn. orch. rels. com., 1961-63; chmn. New Orleans Easter Seal Drive, 1963; La. trustee Nat. Soc. Crippled Children and Adults, 1963-65. Featured on cover of Life mag., Sept. 25, 1944. Mem. Women's Aus. C. of C., New Orleans Soc. Archeol., Inst. Am. (v.p. 1972-74), Confrèrie des Chevaliers du Tastevin, Sigma Kappa, Eichenheim Golf Club, Golden Skibook Club (Austria), Ski Club (Arlberg), Eichenheim Golf and Country Club. Address: Timberg 6370 Kitzbuehel Austria

NEWMAN, CONSTANCE BERRY, federal agency administrator; b. Chgo., July 8, 1935; d. Joseph Alonzo and Ernestine (Siggers) B.; m. Theodore Roosevelt Newman, July 25, 1959 (div. 1980). AB, Bates Coll., 1956; BSL, U. Minn., 1959; JD (hon.), Bates Coll., 1972, Amherst Coll., 1980; LHD (hon.), Central State U., 1991. Dir. VISTA, Washington, 1971-73; commr. Consumer Product Safety Commn., 1973-76; asst. sec. U.S. HUD, 1976-77; pres. The Newman & Hermanson Co., 1977-82; cons. Govt. of Lesotho, 1987-88; dir. nat. voter coalition Bush-Quayle '88, Washington, 1988; dir. Office Pers. Mgmt., 1989-92; under sec. Smithsonian Instn., 1992-2000; vice chair D.C. Fin. Responsiblity and Mgmt. Assistance Authority, 1995—; ptnr. Upstart Ptnrs., 2000—; asst. adminr. bur. for africa USAID, Washington, 2001—. Mem. adj. faculty John F. Kennedy Sch. Govt., Harvard U., Cambridge, Mass., 1979-82. Contbr. articles to profl. jours. Mem. Adminstrn. Conf. U.S., Washington, 1973-76, 1989—; commr. M.L. King Fed. Holiday Commn., Washington, 1989; chmn. Def. Adv. Com. on Women in the Svcs., Washington, 1985-86; trustee Community Coll. Balt., 1985-89; adv. to chmn. 1988 Rep. Nat. Conv., New Orleans, 1988; bd. overseers Morehouse Coll. Sch. Medicine, Atlanta, 1976-77; bd. dirs. Brookings Instn., Aspen Inst., Coun. for Excellence in Govt. Recipient Pub. Svc. award Ohio State U., 1991. Mem. NAACP, Exec. Women in Govt. (founding mem.). Avocation: photography. Office: USAID Bur for Africa RRB 1300 Pennsylvania Ave NW Washington DC 20523-4600 Office Fax: 202-216-3008. E-mail: newmancb@visto.com.*

NEWMAN, CORY FRANK, clinical psychologist; b. Phila., Jan. 20, 1960; BA, U. Pa., 1981; MA, SUNY, Stony Brook, 1983, PhD, 1987. Lic. psychologist, Pa.; diplomate in behavioral psychology, Am. Bd. Profl. Psychology. Postdoctoral fellow Ctr. for Cognitive Therapy, Phila., 1987-88, assoc. dir. edn., 1988-90, clin. dir., 1990—, asst. prof. psychology, 1991-2000, assoc. prof., 2000—. Nat. and internat. lectr. in field. Composer: Rhapsody on a Thematic Mirage, chamber music, 1981; co-author: Cognitive Therapy of Borderline Personality Disorder, 1993, Cognitive Therapy of Substance Abuse, 1993, Choosing To Live: How To Defeat Suicide Through Cognitive Therapy, 1996, Bipolar Disorder: A Cognitive Therapy Approach, 2001; mem. numerous editl. bds.; contbr. articles to profl. jours. Named One of Best Therapists in Phila. Area, Phila. mag.; grad. Coun. fellow SUNY, 1981; rsch. grantee Sigma Xi, 1985. Fellow Acad. Cognitive Therapy (founding); mem. APA, Internat. Assn. Cognitive Psychotherapy, Assn. for Advancement Behavior Therapy, Phi Beta Kappa. Avocations: classical piano, composing, tennis, ice hockey. Office: U Pa Ctr for Cognitive Therapy 3535 Market St Fl 2 Philadelphia PA 19104-3309 E-mail: Newcory@landru.cpr.upenn.edu.

NEWMAN, CRAIG ALAN, lawyer; b. Detroit, June 29, 1957; s. Norman and Ruth (Chodoroff) N.; m. Susan Marcie Lipton, Mar. 22, 1987; children: Rachel Ariel, Jonathan Ross. BS, Ariz. State U., 1979; MA, U. Mo., 1981; JD, U. Detroit, 1984. Law clk. to Chief U.S. Dist. Judge Philip Pratt U.S. Dist. Ct. (ea. dist.) Mich., 1984-86; assoc. Cahill Gordon & Reindel, N.Y.C., 1986-89; ptnr. Arnold & Porter, 1989-95, 99—; sr. v.p., gen. counsel Americast, L.A. and N.Y.C., 1996-99. Editor-in-chief U. Detroit Law Rev., 1983-84; contbr. articles to profl. publs. Recipient Nathan Burkam award ASCAP, 1984, Clarence Burton scholarship U. Detroit, 1983-84, Outstanding Grad. in Journalism Soc. Profl. Journalists, 1979. Mem. N.Y. State Bar Assn., D.C. Bar Assn., Mich. Bar Assn. Office: Arnold & Porter 399 Park Ave Fl 35 New York NY 10022-4690 E-mail: craig_newman@aporter.com.

NEWMAN, DAVID WHEELER, lawyer; b. Salt Lake City, Apr. 5, 1952; s. Donnell and Vera Mae (Siratt) N.; m. Mahnaz Navai, Mar. 14, 1981; 1 child, Anthony Dara. BA cum laude, Claremont Men's Coll., 1973; JD, UCLA, 1977; LLM in Taxation, NYU, 1979. Bar: Calif. 1978, U.S. Dist. Ct. Calif. 1978, U.S. Tax Ct. 1979. Tax ptnr. Mitchell, Silberberg & Knupp, L.A., 1982—. Mem. exec. com. tax sect. L.A. County Bar, 1991-2000. Trustee New Visions Found., 1995—; trustee, pres. New Rds. Sch., 2000—. Mem. Calif. Club, Men's Garden Club L.A. (dir. 2000—). Avocations: tennis, skiing, gardening. Office: Mitchell Silberberg & Knupp 11377 W Olympic Blvd Los Angeles CA 90064-1625

NEWMAN, DIANA S. development consultant; b. Toledo, June 15, 1943; d. Fred Andrew and Thelma Elizabeth (Hewitt) Smith; m. Dennis Ryan Newman, Feb. 15, 1964; children: Barbara Lynn Newman LaBine, John Ryan, Elizabeth Anne. Student, Oberlin Coll., 1961-64. Asst. treas. Marble Cliff Quarries Co., 1964-68; community vol., 1968-83; dir. Ohio Hist. Found., Columbus, 1983-90; v.p. advancement The Columbus (Ohio) Found., 1990-95; pres. Philanthropic Resource Group, Columbus, 1995—. Author: Opening Doors: Pathways to Diverse Donors, 2002. Chair governing com. First Cmty. Ch., 1983-88; bd. dirs. LWV, 1968-72, Ohio Mus. Assn., 1985-90, Nat. Soc. Fundraising Execs. Cen. Ohio chpt., Columbus, 1983—, Crittenton Family Svcs., Columbus, 1992-95, Nat. Com. on Planned Giving, 1999-2002.; founder Franklin County Com. on Criminal Justice, Columbus, 1972; past pres. Jr. League Columbus. Mem. Ctrl. Ohio Planned Giving Coun. (bd. dirs. 1990—, pres. 1998), Columbus Female Benevolent Soc. (bd. dirs. 1984—). Home: 1944 Chatfield Rd Columbus OH 43221-3702 Office: Philanthropic Resource Group 1944 Chatfield Rd Columbus OH 43221-3702

NEWMAN, DONALD JOHN, marketing executive; b. Chgo., Dec. 22, 1939; s. William Francis and Dorothy Isabel (Asay) N.; m. Arlene Louise Neustadt, Apr. 4, 1964; children: Nancy, Julie. BA in Polit. Sci., St. Ambrose U., 1961. Br. mgr. Dun & Bradstreet, Inc., Chgo., 1962-68; mktg. mgr. 3M Co., St. Paul, 1968-87; v.p. mktg. Oce Industries, Inc., Chgo., 1987-88; v.p. mktg. and product devel. Bell & Howell Document Mgmt. Products Co., 1988-91; v.p. mktg. Bankers Systems, Inc., St. Cloud, Minn., 1991-95; v.p., COO Gen. Pump, Inc., Mendota Heights, 1996-99; pres. DNA (Don Newman Assocs.), Sauk Rapids, 2000-01; COO, Nahan Printing, Inc., St. Cloud, 2001—. Keynote speaker Info. and Image Mgmt. Congress conf. and exposition, Sydney, Astralia, 1990. Contbr. articles to profl. jours. Program chmn. Internat. Info. and Image Mgmt. Congress, Vienna, Austria, 1987. With U.S. Army Res. 1961-67. Recipient Smithsonian award for innovative use of technology. Mem. Assn. Info. and Image Mgmt. (bd. dirs. 1990-93), Internat. Image Mgmt. Congress (bd. dirs. 1989-92). Democrat. Roman Catholic. Avocations: auto enthusiast, golf, fishing. Home and Office: 29 Portage Trail Sauk Rapids MN 56379-1157 E-mail: dnewmanandassoc@aol.com., don.newman@nahan.com.

NEWMAN, ELSIE LOUISE, mathematics educator; b. Bowling Green, Ohio, Mar. 25, 1943; d. Carroll E. and Grace G. (Underwood) Frank; m. Lawrence J. Newman, Sept. 15, 1962; children: Timothy, Jennifer. BS cum laude, Bowling Green (Ohio) State U., 1968; MEd, U. Toledo, 1992. Study supr. After Sch. Study Tutorial Program, Bowling Green, 1983-85; prof. Owens C.C., Toledo, 1987—. Office mgr. K.C. Ins. Co., Bowling Green, 1984; tutor in maths. Bowling Green City Schs., 1984-88, Bur. of Vocat. Rehab., Oregon, Ohio, 1988-91. Co-editor Jour. Tchg. and Learning, 1998—; contbr. articles to profl. jours. Advisor 4H Club, Bowling Green, 1985-98; asst. Christmas Clearing bur. Voluntary Action Ctr., United Way, Bowling Green, 1982-86, residential crusade chmn. Am. Cancer Soc., Bowling Green, 1981-82. Bowling Green U. scholar, 1966-68. Mem. Nat. Coun. Tchrs. of Math., Am. Math. Assn. Two Yr. Colls., Ohio Assn. Devel. Edn., Owens Faculty Assn. (treas. 1998-2000), Phi Kappa Phi, Kappa Delta Pi, Pi Lambda Theta. Home: 328 S Summit St Bowling Green OH 43402-3017

NEWMAN, ESTHER B, foundation administrator; b. Washington, Nov. 26, 1944; d. Sol and Gussie Berlin; m. Stuart L. Newman, Jun. 15, 1962; children: Keith Newman, Lisa Newman Loring. AA Mental Health, Montgomery Coll., 1975; BA Human Svcs. Adminstrn., Antioch U., 1978; MS Applied Behavioral Sci., Johns Hopkins U., 1984. Founder, exec. dir. Family Life Ctr. of Montgomery County, Olney, Md., 1976-79; publ. rels. cons. Montgomery Gen. Hosp., 1975-81; cmty. corr. The Courier/Gazette Newspapers, 1978-84; prog. dir. YWCA of Montgomery County, Silver Spring, 1983-85; exec. dir. Montgomery County C. of C., Rockville, 1986-88; founder, exec. dir. Leadership Montgomery, 1988—. Pres. Montgomery Coll. alumni bd., Rockville, MD, 1989-2002; founding bd. mem. Leadership Maryland, Annapolis, 1992-99; conf. chair MD Assn. Leadership Orgns., Rockville, MD, 1997-99; bd. mem. Montgomery Coll. Humanities Inst., Rockville, 1999—. Comm. chair County Exec.'s Ball for the Arts, Rockville, MD, 1986—. Recipient Preceptor award Natl. Assn. for Comm. Leadership, Indianapolis, IN, 1998; named Woman of the Year Mid-Montgomery Bus. and Profl. Women, 1986, Outstanding Mental Health Assoc. of the Yr., Montgomery Coll., 1975. Mem. Greater Washington Soc. Assn. Execs., Women of Washington. Avocations: boating, travel. Office: Leadership Montgomery 5705 Arundel Ave Ste 200 Rockville MD 20852-1811 E-mail: LeaderMont@aol.com.

NEWMAN, FREDERICK J. writer; b. St. Stephen, N.B., Can., Aug. 15, 1955; s. Everette E. and Virginia R. Newman; m. Eileen D. Newman, Aug. 27, 1973 (div. Sept. 5, 2000); children: Frederick J. II, Jeremy A., Daniel E. Student, Calais Vocat. Tech. Sch. Asst. cook Seamans Inn, Mystic, Conn.; carpenter C & D Builders, Woodland, Maine; equipment operator Ga. Pacific Corp.; finishing rm. operator Domtar. Author: Images, 2000; contbr. poetry to lit. publs. Shop steward, v.p., pres. U.P.I.U. Local 27, Woodland; pension trustee Joint E.J.P.T., 1982—88. Recipient Best Poem award, Nat. Libr. Poetry, 1995, Hon. Mention, 1996. Mailing: PO Box 718 Princeton ME 04668-0718

NEWMAN, FREDRIC ALAN, plastic surgeon, educator; b. Bklyn., Aug. 16, 1948; s. Harold Louis and Isabel (Seltzer) Newman; m. Stacey Hope Clarfield, Nov. 27, 1983; children: Benjamin, Marissa, Alexandra. BA, Yale Coll., 1970; MD summa cum laude, SUNY Downstate, Bklyn., 1974. Diplomate Am Bd Plastic Surgery, Am Bd Surgery. Resident gen. surgery Beth Israel Hosp., Boston, 1974-77; resident and chief gen. surgery SUNY Downstate, Bklyn., 1977-79; fellow plastic surgery NYU/Inst. Reconstrv. Plastic Surgery, N.Y.C., 1979-81; fellow facial reconstruction Jackson Meml. Hosp., Miami, Fla., 1981-82; asst. clin. prof. dept. plastic surgery N.Y. Med. Coll., West, 1984-95, Columbia Coll. Physicians and Surgeons, N.Y.C., 1995—. Chmn bd dirs, CEO, pres Edno Surg Devices, Inc, Del., 1998—. Author: (book) Aesthetic Plastic Surgery, 1984, Plastic Surgery, 1985; contbr. articles to profl jours. Fellow: ACS, Int Col Surgeons; mem.: NY State Med Soc, Am Cleft Palate Asn, Am Soc Aesthetic Plastic Surg, Am Soc Plastic and Reconstructive Surgeons. Avocations: sailing, skiing, reading, computers. Office: 722 Post Rd Darien CT 06820 E-mail: drnewman@snet.net.

NEWMAN, FREDRIC SAMUEL, lawyer, business executive; b. York, Pa., June 22, 1945; s. Nat. Howard and Josephine (Farkas) N.; m. Mary E. Kiley, May 19, 1973; children: Lydia Ann, Anne Marie, Pauline. AB cum laude, Harvard U., 1967; JD, Columbia U., 1970; cert. the exec. program, U. Va., 1984. Bar: N.Y. 1971, U.S. Dist. Ct. (so. and ea. dists.) N.Y. 1972, U.S. Ct. Appeals (2d cir.) 1974, U.S. Ct. Claims 1993. Assoc. White & Case, N.Y.C., 1970-80; asst. gen. counsel Philip Morris Cos., 1981-87; gen. counsel, v.p., sec. Philip Morris, Inc., 1987-90; chief exec. officer TeamTennis, Inc., 1991; prin. Law Office of Fredric S. Newman, N.Y.C., 1992-95; founding ptnr. Hoguet Newman & Regal, LLP, 1996—; pres., CEO, Pathe Comm. Corp., N.Y.C., 1993-97. Bd. dirs. Exel Ins. Co., Bermuda. Trustee Calhoun Sch., N.Y.C., 1985-88; bd. dirs. N.Y. Fire Safety Found., N.Y.C., 1985-88. Fellow Am. Bar Found. Office: 10 E 40th St New York NY 10016-0200

NEWMAN, GERALDINE ANNE, advertising executive, inventor; b. Boston, Apr. 01; d. Joseph M. and Clara (Bistry) N. BS, UCLA; postgrad., Alliance Francaise, Paris, Los Angeles Sch. Fine Arts, NYU. Writer Tinker Dodge and Delano, N.Y.C., 1970-72, Ketchum Advt., N.Y.C., 1972-75, Advt. to Women, N.Y.C., 1975-78; v.p., creative supr. Young and Rubicam, 1978-83; v.p., assoc. creative dir. Backer Spielvogel Bates Worldwide Internat. Div., 1983-90; pres. Geraldine Newman Comm., Inc., 1990—. County committeewoman Dem. Party, N.Y.C., 1972; advt. adviser Youth at Risk, Breakthrough Found., Food Bank, Food for All, Gifts that Give Back. Featured in Adweek mag., 1986; winner Andy award 1975, 78, 82, 84, Clio award 1982, ERA award, 1998, numerous others. Mem. Ad-net (bd. dirs. 1984-89, creative dir. 1986-89, Pres.'s award 1988), Electronic Retailing Assn., Ad Club N.Y. Avocations: painting, travel. Home and Office: 315 E 72nd St New York NY 10021-4625

NEWMAN, HOWARD NEAL, lawyer, educator; b. N.Y.C., June 11, 1935; s. Herman and Sarah (Steinsaltz) N.; m. Carol Redstone, Dec. 25, 1960; children: Leslie, Amy. AB, Dartmouth Coll., 1956, MBA, 1957; MS, Columbia U., 1959; JD, Temple U., 1970. Trainee to asst. v.p. Roosevelt Hosp., N.Y.C., 1957-65; assoc. adminstr. Pa. Hosp., Phila., 1965-70; commr. Med. Services Adminstrn., Washington, 1970-74; pres. Dartmouth-Hitchcock Med. Center, Hanover, N.H., 1974-80; adminstr. Health Care Financing Adminstr., Dept. Health and Human Services, Washington, 1980-81; ptnr. Memel, Jacobs, Pierno & Gersh, 1982-86, Powell, Goldstein, Frazer & Murphy, Washington, 1986-88; dean, prof. health policy and mgmt. NYU, 1988-94, prof. health policy and mgmt., 1994—. Served with USAR, 1959-65. White House fellow, 1967-68 Mem. Nat. Inst. for Dispute Resolution, D.C. Bar Assn. Jewish. Office: 4 Washington Sq N New York NY 10003-6671 E-mail: howard.newman@nyu.edu.

NEWMAN, J. KEVIN, broadcast journalist; b. Toronto, Ont., Can., June 2, 1959; came to U.S., 1994; s. George Edmund and Sheila Lorraine (Stevenson) N.; m. Catharine Erica Kearns, June 15, 1985; children: John Alexander, Erica Louise. BA, U. Western Ont., 1981. Atlantic bur. chief CTV Nat. News, Halifax, N.S., Can., 1987, parliament reporter Ottawa, Ont., Can., 1987-89, CBC Nat. News, Ottawa, 1990-92; anchor CBC Midday, Toronto, 1992-94, ABC World News This Morning, N.Y.C., 1994-96; news anchor Good Morning America, 1996-98; corr. ABC World News Tonight, 1996—; co-host Good Morning Am., 1998—. Instr. in journalism Ryerson U., Toronto, 1992-94. Avocations: skiing, canoeing, camping. Office: ABC News 47 W 66th St Rm 800 New York NY 10023-6290

NEWMAN, JAMES MICHAEL, judge, lawyer; b. Bklyn., Apr. 3, 1946; s. Sheldon and Ethel (Silverman) Newman; m. Lee Galen; children: Danielle Cari, Matthew Evan, Merrie Lee, Cindy Joy, Bradley Curtis. BA, Queens Coll., 1966; JD, NYU, 1969, LLM, 1975. Bar: NY 1970, NJ 1977, cert.: N.J. (matrimonial atty.). Assoc. Kramer, Marx, Greenlee & Backus, N.Y.C., 1970-73, Forsyth, Decker, Murray & Broderick, N.Y.C., 1973-74; ptnr. Tommaney & Newman, 1975-82, Goldzweig, Reilly, Grossman & Newman, Marlboro, N.J., 1978-79, Canarick & Newman, Freehold, 1979-97, Newman, Scarola & Assocs., Freehold, 1998—2001, Newman Scarola & Schneider, Freehold, 2001—; pub. defender Marlboro Twp. (N.J.), 1984-86; judge Marlboro Twp., 1986—, Englishtown Borough, 1990—, Farmingdale Borough, 1991—, Manalapan Township, 1993—, Borough Fair Haven, 1996—. Dep mayor Marlboro Twp, 1975—79, dir econ develop, 1975—79, dir commuter affairs, 1974; interim comnr Monmouth Utilities Authority, 1977; mem Cent NJ Transp Bd, 1974—76. Mem.: Am Judges Asn, Monmouth County Judges Asn (pres 1995), Monmouth County Bar Asn (co-chairperson family law comt 1996—98, trustee 1999—2002), NJ Bar Asn, Masons. Jewish. Office: 64 W Main St Freehold NJ 07728-2142 E-mail: jnewman@monmouthlaw.com.

NEWMAN, JAMES WILSON, business executive; b. Clemson, S.C., Nov. 3, 1909; s. Charles Carter and Grace (Strode) N.; m. Clara Collier, July 1934; children: Clare Adelaide, Mildred Bledsoe, James Wilson, Charles Carter II. BS, Clemson U., 1931, also LL.D. (hon.); student, Am. Inst. Banking, 1931-32; JD, N.Y. U., 1937. Bar: N.Y. bar 1937. Reporter R.G. Dun & Co., 1931-46; v.p. Dun & Bradstreet, Inc., 1946-52, pres., chief exec. officer, 1952-60, chmn., chief exec. officer, 1960-68, chmn. finance com., 1968-80, dir., to 1980. Adv. bd. Chem. Bank, Gen. Foods Corp., 1963-81, Internat. Paper Co., until 1982; trustee Atlantic Mut. Ins. Co., Mut. Life Ins. Co. Am., until 1982; chmn. spl. rev. com. Lockheed Corp., 1976-78 Chmn. Pres.'s Task Force on Small Bus., 1969; mem. Commn. on Bankruptcy Laws U.S., 1970-73; chmn. Nat. Bur. Econ. Rsch., 1974-78; trustee Com. Econ. Devel., Va. Mus. Fine Arts, 1978-94; mem. coun. Miller Ctr. Pub. Affairs, U. Va., 1983-94; mem. Price Commn., 1971-72; chmn. Sweet Briar Coll., 1963-69. Mem. ABA, Farmington Country Club (Va.), Phi Delta Phi. Home: 500 Crestwood Dr Apt 2606 Charlottesville VA 22903-4884 Office: 503 Falconer Dr Madison Park Suite 4A Charlottesville VA 22903

NEWMAN, JAY HARTLEY, financial company executive; b. N.Y.C., Dec. 20, 1951; children: David Timothy, Daniel James. BA, Yale U., 1973; JD, Columbia U., 1976; LLM, NYU, 1981. Bar: N.J. 1976, N.Y. 1977, D.C. 1978. Assoc. Cravath Swaine & Moore, N.Y.C., 1977-79, Hughes Hubbard & Reed, N.Y.C., 1979-83; v.p. Lehman Bros., 1983-85; sr. v.p. Shearson Lehman Hutton, Inc., 1985-88, mng. dir., 1988—89, Dillon Read & Co., 1989—90, Morgan Stanley & Co., Inc., N.Y. C., 1990-93, Emerging Market Strategies, Inc., N.Y.C., 1993-98; vice chmn. Lease Holding B.V., Amsterdam, The Netherlands, 1996-98. Sr. portfolio mgr. Elliot Assocs., LP, N.Y.C., 1996—. Editor notes and comments Columbia Law Rev., 1974-76. Trustee N.Y.C. Police Foun., 1997—, coun. fgn. rels., 2000—.

NEWMAN, JOAN MESKIEL, lawyer; b. Youngstown, Ohio, Dec. 12, 1947; d. John F. and Rosemary (Scarmuzzi) Meskiel; children: Anne R., Elyse S. BA in Polit. Sci., Case-Western Reserve U., 1969; JD, Washington U., St. Louis, 1972, LLM in Taxation, 1973. Bar: Mo. 1972. Assoc. Lewis & Rice, St. Louis, 1973-80, ptnr., 1981-90, Thompson Coburn, St. Louis, 1990—. Adj. prof. law Washington U. Sch. Law, St. Louis, 1975-92; past pres. St. Louis chpt., mem. Midwest Pension Conf. Mem. nat. coun. Washington U. Sch. Law, 1988—91; chmn. bd. dir. Great St. Louis coun. Girl Scouts USA, 1975—92, officer, 1978—92; mem. cmty. wide youth svcs. panel United Way Greater St. Louis, 1992—96; fin. futures task force Kiwanis Camp Wyman, 1992—93; chmn. staff blue ribbon fin. com. Sch. Dist. , Clayton, 1986—87; vol. Women's Self Help Ctr.; bd. dir., exec. com. Girl Scouts USA, 1993—99, nat. treas.,

1996—99; bd. dirs. Met. Employment and Rehab. Svcs., 1980—2001, chmn. bd. dir., 1994—96; bd. dirs. Jewish Ctr. Aged, 1990—92, bd. dir., 1999—2001, Jewish Fedn. St. Louis, 1991—96, City Mus., 1998—2001, Parents as Tchrs., 2000—; chmn. bd. dir. Women of Achievement, 1993—96; bd. dir. United Way Greater St. Louis, 2000—, Oasis, 1999—2001; bd. dirs. MERS/Goodwill Industries, 2001—, Walker Scottish Rite Ctr., 2002—. Named Woman of Achievement St. Louis, 1991. Mem. Mo. Bar Assn. (staff pension and benefits com. 1991—), Bar Met. St. Louis (past chmn. taxation sect.), St. Louis Forum, Order of Coif (hon.). Office: Thompson Coburn LLP US Bank Plz Ste 3300 Saint Louis MO 63101-1643

NEWMAN, JOANN, occupational therapist, educator; b. Lamesa, Tex., Jan. 18, 1932; d. Burey Burton and Willie Leone B.; m. Travis Ryan White, Aug. 6, 1949 (div. Nov. 1962); children: Constance Spickelmier, Elaine Spong, Terry White, Cynthia Rae Gough (dec.); m. Quilla Joe Newman, Jan. 1, 1971; 1 child, Jonathan. BS, Tex. Woman's U., 1974, MA, 1981. Registered occupl. therapist Nat. Bd. Certification Occupl. Therapy. Occupl. therapist Meth. Hosp., Lubbock, Tex., 1964-71, Helping Hand Devel. Ctr., Irving, 1974-75; rehab. coord. Good Samaritan Village, Denton, 1976-84; pres. Elder Care, Inc., 1984-90; dir. The Home Place, The Day Home, 1984-90; asst. clin. prof. Tex. Woman's U., 1992—. Cons. various retirement villages, nursing homes, Denton, Tex., 1984-91. Mem. Elderly Svc. Providers, Denton, Tex., 1980—; member, past v.p. Denton County Alliance for Mentally Ill, 1989—; bd. dirs. Adult Day Care North Tex., Inc. Mem. Am. Occupl. Therapy Assn., Tex. Occupl. Therapy Assn. Baptist. Avocations: music, writing poetry, walking, travel, gardening. E-mail: jnewman@twu.edu.

NEWMAN, JOHN HENRY, university administrator; b. Chgo. s. Richard August and Nancy Jane Newman. BA, Allegheny Coll.; PhD, Pa. State U. Acad. advisor Pa. State U., University Park, 1988-90; asst. prof. Mt. St. Mary's Coll., Emmitsburg, Md., 1990-96; rsch. fellow U. So. Calif., L.A., 1996-99; head rsch. and evaluation Searle Ctr. for Tchg. Excellence, Northwestern U., Evanston, Ill., 1999-2000; assoc. dir. for assessment and evaluation MIT, Cambridge, Mass., 2001—. Mem. faculty for the 21st century Project Kaleidoscope, 1994—; councilor Coun. on Undergrad. Rsch., 1995-98. Recipient Presdl. citation APA, 2000. Avocations: fencing, photography. Office: MIT Tchg and Learning Lab 5-122 77 Massachusetts Ave Cambridge MA 02139 E-mail: jnewman@mit.edu.

NEWMAN, JOHN KEVIN, classics educator; b. Bradford, Yorkshire, Eng., Aug. 17, 1928; came to U.S., 1969, naturalized, 1984; s. Willie and Agnes (Shee) N.; m. Frances M. Stickney, Sept. 8, 1970; children: Alexandra, John, Victoria. BA in Lit.-Humaniores, Exeter Coll., Oxford U., 1950, BA in Russian, 1952, MA, 1953; PhD, Bristol U., 1967. Classics master St. Francis Xavier Coll., Liverpool, Eng., 1952-54, Downside Sch., Somerset, Eng., 1955-69; mem. faculty U. Ill., Urbana, 1969—, prof. classics, 1980—, chmn. dept., 1981-85. Author: Augustus and the New Poetry, 1967, Latin Compositions, 1976, Pindar's Art, 1984, The Classical Epic Tradition, 1986, Roman Catullus, 1990, Lelio Guidiccioni, Latin Poems, 1992, Augustan Propertius, 1997; co-author: (with A.V. Carozzi) Horace-Benedict de Saussure, 1995; editor: Ill. Classical Studies, 1982-87; contbr. The New Princeton Encyclopedia of Poetry and Poetics, 1993. Mem. sr. common room Corpus Christi Coll., Oxford U., 1985-86 Recipient silver medals Vatican, Rome, 1960, 62, 65, 97. Roman Catholic. Home: 703 W Delaware Ave Urbana IL 61801-4806 Office: Dept Classics U Ill 4090 Fgn Lang Bldg 707 S Mathews Ave Urbana IL 61801-3625 E-mail: j-newman@uiuc.edu.

NEWMAN, JOHN M., JR. lawyer; b. Youngstown, Ohio, Aug. 15, 1944; BA, Georgetown U., 1966; JD, Harvard U., 1969. BAr: Ill. 1970, Calif. 1972, Ohio 1976. Law clerk ctrl. dist. U.S. Dist. Ct., Calif., 1969-70, asst. U.S. Atty. ctrl. dist., 1970-75; ptnr. Jones, Day, Reavis & Pogue, Cleve. Fellow Am. Coll. Trial Lawyers; mem. Phi Beta Kappa. Office: Jones Day Reavis & Pogue North Point 901 Lakeside Ave E Cleveland OH 44114-1190 E-mail: jmnewman@jonesday.com.

NEWMAN, JOHN MERLE, lawyer; b. Cleve., June 25, 1934; s. Emanuel Robert and Theresa Esther (Dreissinger) N.; 1 child, Thomas Edward; m. Thelma Aitken, July 10, 1992; 1 child, Jennifer Ann Newman-Brazil. AB, Miami U., Oxford, Ohio, 1957; LLB, Cornell U., 1957. Bar: N.J. 1971, U.S. Ct. Appeals (3d cir.) 1961, U.S. Dist. Ct. N.J. 1983, U.S. Dist. Ct. (so. and ea. dists.) N.Y. 1983; cert. civil atty. Supreme Ct. of N.J. Assoc. Bertram Polow, Morristown, N.J., 1960-62; ptnr. Porzio Bromberg & Newman P.C., 1962-76, 80—; presiding judge chancery/family divsn. Superior Ct. of N.J., 1976-80. Trustee, officer Cmty. Med. Ctr., Randolph Libr., Morristown, 1970-74, Hist. Speedwell Mus., Morristown, 1991—, Family Svc., Morristown, 1988-91; trustee Occupational Tng. Ctr., Morristown, 1965-69. Recipient Cert. of Acad. Performance U. Edinburgh, Scotland, 1956, Trial Bar award N.J. Trial Lawyers Assn., 1997, various certs. for bar and cmty. svcs. Fellow Internat. Soc. Barristers; mem. ABA (litigation sect., environ. subcom., environ. law sect. corp. counsel subcom., vice chair various coms.), N.J. State Bar Assn., Morris County Bar Assn., Omicron Delta Kappa. Avocations: cycling, tennis. Office: Porzio Bromberg & Newman 163 Madison Ave Ste 6 Morristown NJ 07960-7323

NEWMAN, JOHN NICHOLAS, naval architect educator; b. New Haven, Mar. 10, 1935; s. Richard and Daisy (Neumann) N.; m. Kathleen Smedley Kirk, June 16, 1956; children— James Bartram, Nancy Kirk, Carol Ann. BS Mass. Inst. Tech, 1956, MS, 1957, Sc.D., 1960; postgrad., Cambridge (Eng.) U., 1958-59; D Technicae honoris causa, U. Trondheim, Norway, 1992. Research naval architect David Taylor Model Basin, Navy Dept., Washington, 1959-67; assoc. prof. naval architecture MIT, Cambridge, 1967-70, prof., 1970—, prof. emeritus. Vis. prof. U. New South Wales, Australia, 1973, U. Adelaide, Australia, 1974, Tech. U. Norway, 1981-82; cons. Navy Dept., Dept. Justice, pvt. firms. Author: Marine Hydrodynamics, 1977; Contbr.: articles to profl. jours., including Sci. Am. Recipient prize Am. Bur. Shipping, 1956; Walter Atkinson prize Royal Instn. Naval Architects, 1973, also Bronze medal, 1976; Guggenheim fellow, 1973-74; research grantee Office Naval Research; NSF. Mem. AAAS, NAE, Soc. Naval Architects and Marine Engrs. (Davidson medal 1988), Norwegian Acad. Sci. Home: 1 Bowditch Rd Woods Hole MA 02543-1201 Office: MIT Dept Ocean Engring Cambridge MA 02139 E-mail: jnn@mit.edu.

NEWMAN, JOHN SCOTT, chemical engineer, educator; b. Richmond, Va., Nov. 17, 1938; s. Clarence William and Marjorie Lenore (Saucerman) Newman; m. Nguyen Thanh Lan, June 30, 1973; children: Natalie Diane, Michael Alexander. BS, Northwestern U., 1960; MS, U. Calif., Berkeley, 1962, PhD, 1963. Asst. prof. chem. engring. U. Calif., Berkeley, 1963-67, assoc. prof., 1967-70, prof., 1970—; prin. investigator environ. energy tech. divsn. Lawrence Berkeley Nat. Lab., 1963—. Vis. prof. U. Wis., Madison, 1973; Onsager prof. Norwegian U. Sci. and Tech., 2002; summer participant Oak Ridge Nat. Lab., 1965, 66. Author: (book) Electrochemical Systems, 1973, Electrochemical Systems, rev. edit., 1991; editor (assoc. editor): Jour. Electrochem. Soc., 1990—2000; contbr. articles to profl. jours. Fellow: Electrochem. Soc. (Young Author's prize 1966, 1969, David C. Grahame award 1985, Henry B. Linford award 1990, Olin Palladium medal 1991); mem.: AIChE (Excellence in Indsl. Rsch. award No. Calif. sect. 2000), NAE. Home: 114 York Ave Kensington CA 94708-1045 Office: U Calif Dept Chem Engring Berkeley CA 94720-1462 E-mail: newman@newman.cchem.berkeley.edu.

NEWMAN, JON O. federal judge; b. N.Y.C., May 2, 1932; s. Harold W. Jr. and Estelle L. (Ormond) Newman; m. Martha G. Silberman, June 19, 1953; children: Leigh, Scott, David. Grad., Hotchkiss Sch., 1949; AB magna cum laude, Princeton U., 1953; LLB, Yale U., 1956; LLD (hon.) , U. Hartford, 1975, U. Bridgeport, 1980, Bklyn. Law Sch., 1995, N.Y. Law Sch., 1996. Bar: Conn. 1956, D.C. 1956. Law clk. to Hon. George T. Washington U.S. Ct. Appeals, 1956—57; sr. law clk. to Hon. Earl Warren U.S. Supreme Ct., 1957—58; ptnr. Ritter, Satter & Newman, Hartford, Conn., 1958—60; counsel to majority Conn. Gen. Assembly, 1959; spl. counsel to gov. Conn., 1959—61; asst. to sec. HEW, 1961—62; adminstrv. asst. to U.S. senator, 1963—64; U.S. atty. Dist. of Conn., 1964—69, U.S. dist. judge, 1972—79; pvt. practice, 1969—71; U.S. cir. judge Hartford, 1979—93; chief judge U.S. Ct. of Appeals 2d Cir., 1993—97, sr. judge, 1997—. Co-author: Politics: The American Way, 1964. With USAR, 1954—62. Recipient Learned Hand medal, Fed. Bar Coun., 1987. Fellow: Am. Bar Found.; mem.: ABA, Am. Judicature Soc., Conn. Bar Assn., Am. Law Inst. Democrat. Office: US Ct Appeals 2d Cir 450 Main St Hartford CT 06103-3022

NEWMAN, JOSEPH HERZL, advertising consultant; b. N.Y.C., Dec. 1, 1928; s. Max A. and Tillie C. (Weitzman) N.; m. Ruth Zita Marcus, Dec. 19, 1954 (div. Feb. 1987); children: Deborah Lynn, David Alan, Mark Jonathan; m. Nancy Kramer Deutschman, Aug. 19, 1990; stepchildren: Pamela Sue Deutschman, Douglas Hayes Deutschman, Cindi Elaine Deutschman. AB, Bethany Coll., W.Va., 1949; MS Grad. Sch. Bus., Columbia U., 1956. With 20th Century Fox Film Corp., NYC, 1949—53; media supr. Fred Wittner Advt. Agy. (now Hammond Farrell Inc.), 1953—56; media dir. O.S. Tyson & Co. (now Poppe Tyson, Inc.), 1956—64; v.p., media dir. Marsteller Inc. (now Lord, Dentsu and Ptnrs.), 1965—85; v.p., assoc. media dir. HBM/Creamer, 1985—87, Della Femina, McNamee, Inc., NYC, 1987—89; pres. Newman And Assocs., Cleve., 1989—. Mem. faculty Advt. Age Media Workshop, 1972; past chmn. media mgrs. adv. com. Bus. Publs. Audit of Circulation Inc., N.Y.C.; condr. profl. media planning seminars, 1989-99. Contbr. articles to profl. jours. Past chmn. bus.-to-bus. media com. Am. Assn. Advt. Agys.; vice chmn. tax incentive rev. coun. City of Mayfield Heights, Ohio, 1994-97, chmn., 1997—. With U.S. Army, 1950-52. Mem. Bus. Mktg. Assn. (past mem. media comparability coun., media data form com. and rsch. resource com., Agy. Exec. of Yr., N.Y. chpt. 1960, 66, 71, 73, cert. bus. communicator). Home and Office: 6338 Woodhawk Dr Mayfield Heights OH 44124-4153 E-mail: nknewmansion@aol.com.

NEWMAN, JOYCE A. obstetrician/gynecologist; b. N.Y.C., 1940; MD, NYU, 1975. Diplomate Am. Bd. Ob/gyn. Resident in ob/gyn. Mt. Sinai Hosp., N.Y.C., 1975-79; asst. attendant Beth. Israel Hosp., 1980—, N.Y. Downtown Hosp.; pvt. practice N.Y.C.; instr. Mt. Sinai Med. Sch. Fellow Am. Coll. Ob/gyn.; mem. N.Y. Med. Soc. Home: 5261 Fieldston Rd Bronx NY 10471-2911 Office: 233 E 69th St New York NY 10021-5414

NEWMAN, JUDITH ALICE, education educator, educator; b. Preston, Eng., May 9, 1950; d. Ellis Edward and Alice Dorothy Elizabeth (Herringshaw) N.; m. Ian William Revie, Oct. 10, 1978; 1 child, James Michael Edward. MA in English, U. Edinburgh, Scotland, 1972, MA in French, 1974; PhD, U. Cambridge, Eng., 1982. Lectr. U. Metz, France, 1973-74, U. Newcastle, Eng., 1976-90, reader Eng., 1990-95, prof. Am. and postcolonial lit. Eng., 1995-2000; prof. Am. studies U. Nottingham, Eng., 2000—. Author: Saul Bellow and History, 1984, John Updike, 1988, Nadine Gordimer, 1988, H.B. Stowe, Dred: A Tale of the Great Dismal Swamp, 1992, The Ballistic Bard: Postcolonial Fictions, 1994, Alison Lurie: A Critical Study, 2000. Recipient Arthur Miller prize U. East Anglia, 1993. Mem. British Assn. Am. Studies (sec. 1993-95, chair 1995-98, chair rsch. assessment panel Am. studies 1999—). Mem. Labour Party. Avocations: family, gardening. Office: U Nottingham Sch Am Studies Nottingham NG7 2RI Scotland E-mail: Judith.Newman@nottingham.ac.uk.

NEWMAN, LARRY, music educator; b. Chambersburg, Pa., Jan. 21, 1959; s. Lawrence Leroy and Elizabeth Lucille Newman; m. Susie Sugerman, Aug. 13, 1989; children: Brandon, Tyler. MusB Edn. (cum laude), Temple U., Phila., 1982; MusM in Trumpet Performance, Ea. Ill. U., Charleston, 1985; Post Grad. Studies in Music Edn., U. So. Calif., L.A., 1993—94. Cert. Tchr. Calif., 1985. Music educator Phila. Sch. Dist., 1982; trumpet player Glenn Miller Orch., N.Y.C., 1983—84; grad. tchg. asst. jazz studies Ea. Ill. U., Charleston, 1984—85; trumpet player S/S Norway Cruise Ship, Miami, Fla., 1985—86; instrumental music instr. LA Unifed Sch. Dist., 1986—92; music dir. Malibu (Calif.) H.S., Calif., 1992—94; trumpet instr. Glendale (Calif.) Coll., 1992—94; exec. dir. Children's Music Workshop, LA, Inc., Los Angeles, Calif., 1994—. Author: (instruction book) Recorder Fun Book for Young Students, 1997. Mem.: So. Calif. Sch. Band and Orch. Assn., LA County Music Educators Assn., LA City Elem. Sch. Music Assn. (clinician 1999—2002), Calif. Music Educators Assn., Nat. Assn. Music Edn. Personal E-mail: newman@childrensmusicworkshop.com.

NEWMAN, LAWRENCE WALKER, lawyer; b. Boston, July 1, 1935; s. Leon Bettoney and Hazel W. (Walker) N.; children: Timothy D., Isabel B., Thomas H. AB, Harvard U., 1957, LL.B., 1960. Bar: D.C. 1961, N.Y. 1965. Atty. U.S. Dept. Justice, 1960-61, Spl. Study of Securities Markets and Office Spl. Counsel on Investment Co. Act Matters; U.S. SEC, 1961-64; asst. U.S. atty. So. Dist. N.Y., 1964-69; assoc. Baker & McKenzie, N.Y.C., 1969-71, ptnr., 1971—. Mem. internat. adv. coun. World Arbitration Inst., 1984-87; mem. adv. com. Asia Pacific Ctr. for Resolution of Internat. Trade Disputes, 1987—; mem. adv. bd. Inst. for Transnational Arbitration, 1988—; chmn. U.S. Iranian Claimants Com., 1982—; mem. adv. bd. World Arbitration and Mediation Report, 1993—; mem. bd. adv. to Corporate Counsel's Internat. Adviser, 1995—. Co-author: The Practice of Internat. Litigation, 1992, 93, 2nd edit. 1998, Litigating Internat. Commercial Disputes, 1996; columnist N.Y. Law Jour., 1982—; adv. bd. World Arbitration and Mediation Report; bd. advisors Corp. Counsel's Internat. Adviser; contbr. articles to profl. jours. and books on litigation and internat. arbitration; editor: Enforcement of Money Judgments, Attachment of Assets; chmn. editl. bd. Juris Pub., Inc.; co-editor: Revolutionary Days: The Iran Hostage Crisis and the Hague Claims Tribunal, A Look Back, 1999. Mem. ABA (internat. litigation com., internat. arbitration com.), Internat. Bar Assn. (com. dispute resolution, com. constrn. litigation), Inter-Am. Bar Assn., Fed. Bar Coun., Am. Fgn. Law Assn., Maritime Law Assn. U.S., Assn. Bar City N.Y. (com. on arbitration & alternative dispute resolution 1991-94), Am. Arbitration Assn. (corp. counsel com. 1987—, panel comml. arbitrators), U.S. Coun. Internat. Bus., Ct. Arbitration of Polish Chamber Fgn. Trade (panel of arbitrators), Brit. Col. Internat. Comml. Arbitration Ctr., Am. Law Inst., Bar Assn. City N.Y. (inaugural mem. com. on internat. dispute resolution). E-mail: lwn@ bakernet.com. Office: Baker & McKenzie 805 3rd Ave New York NY 10022-7513

NEWMAN, LAWRENCE WILLIAM, financial executive; b. Chgo., Jan. 14, 1939; s. Eskil William and Adele Diane (Lawnicki) N.; m. Christine Harriet Jaronski, Sept. 22, 1962; children: Paul, Scott, Ron. BBS, U. Ill., 1965; MBA, Northwestern U., 1970. CPA, Ill. Auditor Price Waterhouse, Chgo., 1965-66; controller ECM Corp., Schaumburg, Ill., 1966-70, Nachman Corp., Des Plaines, 1970-76, v.p., treas., controller, 1976-79; v.p. fin. P & S Mgmt. Inc., Schiller Park, 1979-83; controller Underwriters Labs., Northbrook, 1983-86, asst. treas., 1986-89, v.p., 1990-98, treas., 1990-97; CFO, 1997—; sr. v.p. Underwriters Labs., Northbrook, 1998—. Mem. Fin. Execs. Inst., Am. Inst. CPA's. Clubs: Exec. of Chgo. Office: Underwriters Labs 333 Pfingsten Rd Northbrook IL 60062-2002

NEWMAN, LEONARD JAY, retail jewel merchant, gemologist; b. Milw., Oct. 25, 1927; s. David and Pia Goldie (Smith) N.; m. Louise Shainberg, Jan. 14, 1951; children: Shelley, Marty, Alan, Heidi, Dee. BS, Purdue U.; postgrad., Washington U., St. Louis. Owner, mgr. Newman's Diamond Ctr., Jasper, Ind., 1951—; tchr. The Jasper Ctr., 1970-80. Bd. dirs. Sta. WFIU Pub. Radio, VUJC Found., State Bd. Health Systems Agy., sub area Health Systems Agy., Internat. Harp Competition, Bloomington United Way, Ind. U. Hillel Found.; consellor Sr. corps Re. Execs.; 1st v.p. Vincennes Univ. Found.; past pres. Jasper Community Arts Commn.; pres. Friends of Arts; commnr. Boy Scouts Am.; mem. Dubois County Mental Health Assn.; lay adv. bd. Convent Immaculate Conception Sisters of St. Benedict, Ferdinand, Ind,; adv. bd. Jasper Hist. Soc., German Club, Young Abe Lincoln Soc., WFIU pub. radio; bd. dirs. Dubois County Crippled Children's Soc., Bloomington (Ind.) Symphony, Patoka Valley Vocat. Coop., Patoka Valley Rehab., Beth Shalom, Monroe County Purdue Alumni, Camerata Orch., Ind. U. Friends of Music, Ind. Jewish Hist. Soc., Hillel Found.; pres. Jasper Edn. Fund; mem., chmn. nominee com. Raintree Coun. Girl Scouts U.S.A., bd. dirs.; Midwest bd. dirs. Anti-Defamation League. Recipient Outstanding Citizenship award Purdue U. Alumni Assn., 1980 Outstanding Alumni award Jasper High Sch., Outstanding Community Svc. award Bloomington, Ind. C. of C., 2000, 01, Gov.'s award Sagamore of the Wabash, 2001. Mem. Nat. Assn. Jewelry Appraisers (sr.), Ind. Jewelers Orgn. Am., Retail Jewelers Am., Jasper C. of C., Jaycees (Rooster, past pres., past nat. bd. dirs., Disting. Svc. award 1957), Monroe County Purdue Alumni Club (bd. dirs.), Nat. Soc. Arts and Letters (bd. mem.), Svc. Corp. Ret. Execs. (pres.), Purdue Agrl. Alumni Assn. (hon.), Skull and Crescent (hon.), Hadassah, Sigma Alpha Mu, Alpha Phi Omega, Lions, Masons, Shriners (past pres.), B'nai Brith, Temple Beth Shalom (pres.). Home: 2344 Linden Hill Dr Bloomington IN 47401-8179 Office: Newman's Diamond Ctr 3 D Pl Jasper IN 47546 E-mail: lnewman320@aol.com.

NEWMAN, LOIS MAE, marketing executive; b. Phoenix, Aug. 16, 1942; d. Harold Orville and Agnes Louise (Rindos) Little; children: Annette Horning, Tyler Katonak. BA, Hamilton Coll., Utica, N.Y., 1964; MA, Hamilton Coll., 1968; postgrad., U. Ariz., 1969, Ariz. State U., 1970. Office mgr. Dunes Hotel and Country Club, Phoenix, 1962-83; prin., treas. Sincere Press, Inc., 1982-90; pres., CEO Euneek, 1983—; staff Ridd Assocs., Inc., 1986-89; reg. mktg. exec. Golden Nugget, 1988-89; adminstr. James F. O'Toole Co., Inc., 1991-94, Western Promotions, Inc., Phoenix, 1994—. Bd. dirs. Sincere Press, Inc., Internat. Wines & Spirits Ltd., Encino, Calif., Euneek, Inc. Bd. dirs. Sml. Bus. Coun., Phoenix, Congl. Action Com., Phoenix, Israel Bonds, Phoenix; active Better Bus. Bur., Arizonians for Jobs & Energy, Valley Leadership, others; chmn. Phoenix Childrens Hosp. Peregrinations; original founder, endorser Maimonides Day Sch.; chmn. Anti-Defamation League; adv. com. vice chmn. Nat. Coun. Christians and Jews; arrangements chmn. City of Hope. Mem. Phoenix Met. C. of C., Ariz. World Trade Assn., Internat. Wine and Food Soc. of Scottsdale (bd. dirs. local chpt., founder). Home: 6808 N 26th St Phoenix AZ 85016-1208 Office: Euneek 3104 E Camelback Rd Phoenix AZ 85016-4502

NEWMAN, MALCOLM, mechanical and civil engineering consultant; b. N.Y.C., June 29, 1931; m. Estelle Ruth Glotzer, June 11, 1955. BSCE, CCNY, 1952; MSCE, Columbia U., 1957; D in Engring. Sci., NYU, 1962. Registered profl. engr., N.Y. Chief structural mechanics Republic-Fairchild Hiller Corp., Farmingdale, N.Y., 1962-65, staff cons., 1970-71; dir. structural mechanics Harry Belock Assocs. Inc., Great Neck, 1965-69; dir. structural mechanics and design Analytical Mechanics Assn., Jericho, 1969-70; prof. mech. engring. Tel Aviv U., 1972-75; pres., tech. dir. Inter-City Testing and Cons., Mineola, N.Y., 1976—. Pres. Athletic Safety Products Inc., Mineola, 1985—; adj. prof. engring. Cooper Union. Contbr. over 80 articles to profl. jours.; patentee in field. Bd. dirs. Cinema Arts Ctr., Huntington, N.Y., 1989—. Mem. NSPE, Am. Soc. Safety Engrs., Nat. Assn. Profl. Accident Reconstruction Specialists, Soc. Automotive Engrs., System Safety Soc. (pres. 1983-85). Office: Inter-City Testing & Cons 167 Willis Ave Ste 2 Mineola NY 11501-2680

NEWMAN, MARC ALAN, electrical engineer; b. Jasper, Ind., Nov. 21, 1955; s. Leonard Jay and P. Louise (Shainberg) N.; m. Shelley Jane Martin, Aug. 13, 1977; 1 child, Kelsey Renée. BSEE, Purdue U., 1977, MSEE, 1979. Sr. elec. engr. Sperry Corp. Flight Systems, Phoenix, 1979-85; staff engr. Motorola Inc., Tempe, 1985-88, Quincy St. Corp., Phoenix, 1988-89; prin. staff scientist Motorola Inc., Chandler, 1989-91, Scottsdale, 1991—2001, Gen. Dynamics, Scottsdale, 2001—. Prolog and artificial intelligence expert Motorola Inc., Tempe, Chandler and Scottsdale, 1985—2001. Patentee in field. Mem. IEEE, The Assn. for Logic Programming (London), Am. Assn. Artificial Intelligence, Ariz. Artificial Intelligence Assn. (founder), Phi Sigma Kappa, Eta Kappa Nu. Achievements include patent combining expert system with artificial neural network, a patent for cell phone security device, a patent for evaluating patents for legal errors; patent for interfacing cellular telephones to personal computers. Avocations: fine music, photography, astronomy, mountain bicycling, travel. Home: 7411 S Rita Ln Estate 110 Tempe AZ 85283-4790 Office: Gen Dynamics 8220 E Roosevelt St Scottsdale AZ 85257 E-mail: Alan.Newman@gd-decisionsystems.com.

NEWMAN, MARY CATHERINE, psychologist, educator, researcher; b. Bklyn., Apr. 23, 1949; children: Kate, Eric, Becky. BA, U. Ariz., 1986, PhD, 1995. Postdoctoral fellow U. Ariz., Tucson, 1995-2000; asst. prof. S.W. Mo. State U., Springfield, 2000—. Mem. grant rev. com. Alzheimer's Assn., 2000-02; mem. exec. bd. Parkinson's Disease Group Ozarks, Springfield, Mo., 2000-02; internal rev. bd. Walnut Grove (Mo.) Sch. Dist., 2000-02; mem. Cmty. Alliance Compassionate Care End life, Springfield, 2001-02. Scholar U. Ariz., 1993; Grad. fellow Flinn Found., 1993-95. Mem. APA (Dissertation Rsch. award 1993, Postdoctoral Rsch. award 1996, 97, 98), Internat. Neuropsychological Assn., Ariz. Alzheimer's Rsch. Ctr. Office: SW Mo State U Dept Psychology 901 S National Springfield MO 65804 E-mail: marynewman@smsu.edu.

NEWMAN, MARY LYNN CANMANN, lawyer, retired; b. Highland Park, Ill. d. Harry Louis and Elizabeth (Gwinn) C; m. Brian Newman, Nov. 9, 1996. BA, U. Mich., 1986; JD, U. Colo., 1991. Bar: Colo. 1991, Ill. 1992, Nev. 1992, U.S. Dist. Ct. Nev. 1992, U.S. Dist. Ct. Colo. 1994, U.S. Ct. Appeals (9th cir.), Ind. 1998. With No. Trust Bank, Chgo., 1986-88; law clk. to Judge Adams, 2d Jud. Dist. Ct., Reno, 1991-92; assoc. Jones, Jones, Close & Brown, 1992-93, Hartman & Armstrong, Reno, 1994-96; ptnr. Dordick, Hopkins & Canmann, Boulder, Colo., 1993-94; assoc. gen. coun. Nev. Indsl. Ins. Systems, Carson City, 1996-98; v.p., assoc. gen. counsel Conseco Svcs., LLC, Carmel, Ind., 1998-2001, ret., 2001. Mng. editor Colo. Jour. Internat. Environ. Law and Policy, 1990-91. Mem. ABA (young lawyers divsn.), ATLA, Nev. Trial Lawyers Assn., No. Nev. Bankruptcy Bar. Avocations: skiing, tennis, hiking.

NEWMAN, MICHAEL RODNEY, lawyer; b. N.Y.C., Oct. 2, 1945; s. Morris and Helen Gloria (Hendler) N.; m. Cheryl Jeanne Anker, June 11, 1967; children: Hillary Abra, Nicole Brooke. Student NASA Inst. Space Physics, Columbia U., 1964; BA, U. Denver, 1967; JD, U. Chgo., 1970. Bar: Calif. 1971, U.S. Dist. Ct. (cen. dist.) Calif. 1972, U.S. Ct. Appeals (9th cir.) 1974, U.S. Dist. Ct. (no. dist.) Calif. 1975, U.S. Supreme Ct. 1978, U.S. Dist. Ct. (so. dist.) Calif. 1979, U.S. Tax Ct. 1979, U.S. Dist. Ct. (ea. dist.) Calif. 1983. Assoc. David Daar, 1971-76; ptnr. Daar & Newman, 1976-78, Miller & Daar, 1978-88, Miller, Daar & Newman, 1988-89, Daar & Newman, 1989—; judge pro-tem L.A. Mcpl. Ct., 1982—, L.A. Superior Ct., 1988—. Vice chmn., bd. dirs. German-Am. C. of C.; bd. govs. U. Haifa, Israel, mem. fin. and phys. devel. com.; bd. dirs. Consulegis EEIG; mem. bd. dirs. Ctr. Study Emeritus Markets (Grad. Coll. Bus. and Econs. Calif. State U. Fullerton); founder, facilitator First, Second and Third Ann. German-Am. Strategic Partnership Conf.; lectr. Ea. Claims COnf., Ea. Life Claims Conf., Nat. Health Care Anti-Fraud Assn., AIA Conf. on Ins. Fraud, Consulegis A.G.M.'s Paris, 1997, Madrid, 1998, Dublin, 1999. Mem. L.A. Citizens Organizing Com. for Olympic Summer Games, 1984, mem. govtl. liaison adv. commn., 1984; mem. So. Calif. Com. for Olympic Summer Games, 1984; cert. ofcl. Athletics Congress of U.S., co-chmn. legal com. S.P.A.-T.A.C., chief finish judge; trustee Massada lodge B'nai Brith; bd. dirs. Ctr. for the Study of Emerging Markets, Calif. State U. Fullerton Grad. Sch. Bus. and Econs. Recipient NYU Bronze medal in Physics, 1962, Maths. award USN Sci., 1963. Mem.: TAC (bd. dirs., Disting. Svc. award 1988), ABA (multi-dist. litigation subcom., com. on class actions), German Am. C. of C. (vice chmn.), So. Pacific Assn., Conf. Ins. Counsel, Los Angeles County Bar Assn. (chmn. attys. errors and omissions prevention com., mem. cts. com., mem. internat. law com., state cts. coord. com. litigation sect.), City Club on Bunker Hill, Breakfast Club, Porter Valley Country Club. Office: 865 S Figueroa St Ste 2300 Los Angeles CA 90017-2567

NEWMAN, MONROE, retired economist, educator; b. Bklyn., Jan. 31, 1929; s. David A. and Ida Mary (Leight) N.; m. Ruth Zielinski, Feb. 6, 1951. BA, Antioch Coll., 1950; MA, U. Ill., 1953, PhD, 1954. Mem. rsch. staff AFL, 1947-48; examiner NLRB, 1949-50; asst. rsch. analyst U. Ill., 1950-54; research analyst Assn. Casualty and Surety Cos., 1954-55; mem. faculty Pa. State U., University Park, 1955-86, prof. econs., 1961-86, prof. emeritus, 1986—, head dept., 1958-62, 78-85, chmn. grad. program regional planning, 1971-72, dir. Ctr. for Study of Environ. Policy, 1972-73. Vis. rsch. prof. econs. U. Pitts., 1964-65; economist Appalachian Regional Commn., Washington, 1964-65, rsch. dir., 1965-66, spl. cons., 1966-86, sr. econ. advisor, 1986-93. Co-author: Insurance and Risk, 1964, Acid Mine Drainage in Appalachia, 1969, Experiment in Appalachia, 1973; author: Political Economy of Appalachia, 1972, also articles. Mem. So. Regional Sci. Assn. (pres.), Am. Econ. Assn., Regional Sci. Assn. Home: 4101 Cathedral Ave NW Washington DC 20016-3585

NEWMAN, MORRIS, mathematician, educator; b. N.Y.C., Feb. 25, 1924; s. Isaac and Sarah (Cohen) N.; m. Mary Aileen Lenk, Sept. 18, 1948; children: Sally Ann, Carl Lenk. AB, N.Y.U., 1945; MA, Columbia U., 1946; PhD, U. Pa., 1952. Mathematician applied math Div. Nat. Bur. Standards, Washington, 1951-63, chief numerical analysis sect., 1963-70, sr. rsch. mathematician, 1970-76; prof. math. U. Calif., Santa Barbara, 1976-94, prof. emeritus,

1994—; dir. Inst. Interdisciplinary Applications of Algebra and Combinatorics, 1976-80. Lectr. U. B.C., 1960, U. Calif.-Santa Barbara, 1965, Am. U., Cath. U., U. Md. Author: Matrix Representations of Groups, 1968, Integral Matrices, 1972; editor: Jour. Research Nat. Bur. Standards, 1966-76, Math. of Computation, 1975-86; assoc. editor: Jour. Linear and Multilinear Algebra, 1973— , Letters in Linear Algebra, 1979— ; contbr. articles to profl. jours. Recipient Gold medal U.S. Dept. Commerce, 1966 Mem. Am. Math. Soc. (council 1980-86), London Math. Soc., Math. Assn. Am., Washington Acad. Scis., AAAS, sigma Xi Home: 1050 Las Alturas Rd Santa Barbara CA 93103-1608 Office: U Calif Dept Math Santa Barbara CA 93106 E-mail: newman@math.ucsb.edu.

NEWMAN, MORTON B. psychoanalyst, psychiatrist; BA magna cum laude, Harvard Coll., 1952; MD, Boston U., 1956. Diplomate in psychiatry Am. Bd. Psychiatry and Neurology; cert. in child psychiatry Am. Bd. Psychiatry and Neurology; cert. Nat. Bd. Med. Examiners. Intern Mass. Meml. Hosps., 1956-57; resident Boston State Hosp., 1957-59; fellow in child psychiatry Douglas A. Thom Clinic for Children, 1961-63; pvt. practice child and adult psychotherapy Mass., 1963—. Dir., clin. dir. Mystic Valley Comprehensive Cmty. Mental Health Ctr., Lexington, 1963-79; faculty, co-chmn. extension divsn. Boston Psychoanalytic Soc. and Inst. Inc.; assoc. med. dir. mental health Pvt. Health Care Svcs., Inc., 1993-2001. Capt. U.S. Army, 1959-61. Fellow Am. Psychiat. Assn. (life); mem. Am. Psychoanalytic Assn., Mass. Psychiat. Soc., Inc., Mass. Med. Soc. (Suffolk dist. br.), Boston Psychoanalytic Soc. and Inst. Inc., New Eng. Coun. Child and Adolescent Psychiatry, Alpha Omega Alpha, Begg Soc. Home: 121 Intervale Rd Chestnut Hill MA 02467-1166 Office: 121 Intervale Rd Chestnut Hill MA 02467-1166

NEWMAN, MURIEL KALLIS STEINBERG, art collector; b. Chgo., Feb. 25, 1914; d. Maurice and Ida (Nudelman) Kallis; m. Albert H. Newman, May 14, 1955; 1 son by previous marriage, Glenn D. Steinberg. Student, Art Inst. Chgo., 1932-36, Ill. Inst. Tech., 1947-50, U. Chgo., 1958-65. Hon. life trustee, benefactor Met. Mus. Art, N.Y.C., vis. com. dept. 20th Century Art, acquisitions com., 1981—, decorative arts com., 1989; also Costume Inst. Dir., 20th Century Painting and Sculpture Com., Art Inst. Chgo., 1955-80, governing mem. inst., 1955—, disting. benefactor, 1979—; pioneer collector Am. abstract expressionist art, 1949—, major show of collection, Met. Mus. Art, N.Y.C., 1981, personal collection of costumes and jewelry, 1981. Bd. govs. Landmarks Preservation Council, Chgo., 1966-78; woman's bd. U. Chgo., 1960-81, Art Inst. Chgo., 1953—, 20th century com., Asian com.; trustee Mus. Contemporary Art, 1970, benefactor, 1970; trustee Chgo. Sch. of Architecture Found., 1971, Archives Am. Art, 1976; bd. dirs. Bright New City Urban Affairs Lecture Series, 1966—. Recipient Scroll Recognition of Pub. Svc., U.S. Dept. State, 1958; named Disting. Benefactor, Art Inst. Chgo., 1998. Mem. Antiquarian Soc. of Art Inst. Chgo., Chgo. Hist. Soc. (mem. guild 1958—), Arts Club Chgo., Casino Club Chgo. Clubs: Arts (Chgo.), Casino (Chgo.). *Searching for truth is a given for a life of value. For me visual art ontologically reveals the truth of the search. Striving for excellence is the spearhead with which to proceed.*

NEWMAN, MURRAY ARTHUR, aquarium administrator; b. Chgo., Mar. 6, 1924; emigrated to Can., 1953, naturalized, 1970; s. Paul Jones and Virginia (Murray) N.; m. Katherine Greene Rose, Aug. 8, 1952; 1 child, Susan. B.Sc., U. Chgo., 1949; postgrad., U. Hawaii, 1950; MA, U. Calif., Berkeley, 1951; PhD, U. B.C. (Can.), Vancouver, 1960. Curator fisheries UCLA, 1951-53, Ichthyology Museum, U. B.C., 1953-56; curator Vancouver Public Aquarium, 1956-66, dir., 1966-93; pres. Mana Aquarium Cons. Fgn. adv. Nat. Mus./Aquarium Project, Taiwan; past chmn. adv. com. Western Can. Univs. Marine Biol. Soc.; co-chmn. Enoshima (Japan) Internat. Aquarium Symposium, 1997; spl. advisor Enoshima Aquarium, 1998, Port of Nagoya Pub. Aquarium, 1999, 2000; hon. com. Fifth Internat. Congress, Monaco, 2000. Author: Life in a Fishbowl: Confessions of an Aquarium Director, 1994. Served with USN, 1943-46. Decorated Order of Can.; recipient Man of Yr. award City of Vancouver, 1964; Centennial award Govt. Can., 1967, cert. of merit, 1988; Harold J. Merilees award Vancouver Visitors Bur., 1976, 75 Achievers award, 1987, Silver Bravery medal Royal Soc. Canada, 1992, Canada 125 medal, 1992. Mem. Am. Assn. Zool. Parks and Aquariums, Internat. Union Dirs. Zool. Gardens, Can. Assn. Zool. Parks and Aquariums (pres. 1978-79), Vancouver Club, Round Table Club. Office: Vancouver Pub Aquarium PO Box 3232 Vancouver BC Canada V6B 3X8

NEWMAN, OSCAR (BOUNDING WARRIOR), architect, city planner, sculptor; b. Montreal, Sept. 30, 1935; m. Irene Kopper; children: Paul, Jon, Hinde. BArch, McGill U., Montreal, 1959. Cert. arch., city planner. Assoc. prof. arch., city planning Washington U., St. Louis, 1964-68, Columbia U., N.Y.C., 1968-70, NYU, 1970-72, dir. Inst. Planning and Housing, 1970-72; exec. dir., founder Inst. Cmty. Design Analysis, N.Y.C., 1972—. Keynote spkr. Internat. Crime Prevention Conf., New Zealand, Australia, 2001, Environ. Design Rsch. Conf. Harvard U., 1995; participant numerous confs.; feature writer The Mountain Eagle, 2000; spkr. in field. Author: Defensible Space, 1972, Community of Interest, 1976, Unmasking a King, 1981, Issues in Housing Discrimination, 1985, Creating Defensible Space, 1996, Visualizing Myth, 1999; contbr. articles to profl. jours.; sculptor Native Am. masks, totem poles; work featured in documentary; featured in Nat. Pub. Radio NBC Nightly News, Dateline NBC TV, other radio and tv shows; subject of articles in Miami Herald, Time, U.S. News and World Report, Readers Digest, Chgo. Tribune, N.Y. Times, The Oregonian, Newsweek, San Francisco Examiner, L.A. Times, numerous other publs. Exec. dir. Interdenominational Housing Program, N.Y., 1978—; mem. bd. rev., bd. dirs. Greene Co. Coun. on the Arts, 1998—; fed. ct. master Yonkers (N.Y.) housing discrimination case, 1986-94 Named Man of Yr. Law Enforcement News, 1995; recipient Achievement award Environ. Design Rsch. Conf., 1997, Annual Award of Achievement Environ. Design Rsch. Assn., 1998. Office: Inst Cmty Design Analysis 672 Round Hill Rd Hensonville NY 12439

NEWMAN, PAULINE, judge; b. N.Y.C., N.Y., June 20, 1927; d. Maxwell Henry and Rosella Newman. BA, Vassar Coll., 1947; MA, Columbia U., 1948; PhD, Yale U., 1952; LLB, NYU, 1958. Bar: N.Y. 1958, U.S. Supreme Ct. 1972, U.S. Ct. Customs and Patent Appeals 1978, Pa. 1979, U.S. Ct. Appeals (3d cir.) 1981, U.S. Ct. Appeals (fed. cir.) 1982. Research chemist Am. Cyanamid Co., Bound Brook, NJ, 1951—54; mem. patent staff FMC Corp., N.Y.C., 1954—75, Phila., 1975—84, dir. dept. patent and licensing, 1969—84; judge U.S. Ct. Appeals (fed. cir.), Washington, 1984—; Disting. prof. George Mason Law Sch., 1995—. Program specialist Dept. Natural Scis. UNESCO, Paris, 1961—62; mem. State Dept. Adv. Com. on Internat. Indsl. Property, 1974—84; lectr. in field. Contbr. articles to profl. jours. Trustee Phila. Coll. Pharmacy and Sci., 1983—84; bd. dirs. Med. Coll. Pa., 1975—84, Midgard Found., 1973—84. Mem.: ABA (coun. sect. patent trademark and copyright 1983—84), Coun. Fgn. Rels., U.S. Trademark Assn. (bd. dirs. 1975—79, v.p. 1978—79), Pacific Indsl. Property Assn. (pres. 1979—80), Am. Inst. Chemists (bd. dirs. 1960—66, 1970—76), Am. Chem. Soc. (bd. dirs. 1972—81), Am. Patent Law Assn. (bd. dirs. 1981—84), Yale Club, Vassar Club, Cosmos Club. Office: US Ct Appeals Nat Cts Bldg 717 Madison Pl Washington DC 20439-0002

NEWMAN, PHILIP ROBERT, psychologist; b. Dec. 17, 1942; s. Samuel M. and Sara Rose (Dumain) N.; m. Barbara Miller, June 12, 1966; children: Samuel Asher, Abraham Levy, Rachel Florence. AB with high distinction, U. Mich., 1964, PhD, 1971. Asst. prof. psychology U. Mich., Ann Arbor, 1971-72, Union Coll., Schenectady, N.Y., 1972-76; dir. human behavior curriculum project APA, Washington, 1977-81; pvt. practice psychology Columbus, Ohio, 1978-2000, South Kingston, R.I., 2000—. Adj. prof., sr. rschr. young scholars program Ohio State U., 1990-98; adj. prof. human devel. and family studies U. R.I., 2000—; cons. Agy. Instrnl. TV, 1979. Author: (with B. Newman) Development through Life: A Psychosocial Approach, 1975, 7th edit., 1999; Infancy and Childhood Development and Its Context, 1978, An Introduction to the Psychology of Adolescence, 1979, Personality Development through the Life Span, 1980, Living: The Process of Adjustment, 1981, Understanding Adulthood, 1983, Principles of Psychology, 1983, Adolescent Development, 1986, When Kids Go to College: A Parents Guide to Changing Relationships, 1992, Childhood and Adolescence, 1997, (with B. Newman, L. Landry-Meyer, and B. Lohman) LIfe Span Development: A Case Book, 2003; editor: (with B. Newman) Development Through Life: A Case Study Approach, 1976. Woodrow Wilson fellow U. Mich., 1964, Univ. fellow, 1964-66, Horace H. Rackham Rsch. scholar, 1969-71. Mem. APA, APHA, Internat. Assn. Applied Psychology, Internat. Sociol. Assn., Soc. Psychol. Study Social Issues, Am. Sociol. Assn., Nat. Coun. Family Rels., Groves Conf. Marriage and Family, Ea. Psychol. Assn., Midwestern Psychol. Assn., Western Psychol. Assn., N.Y. Acad. Sci., Gerontol. Soc. Am., Am. Orthopsychiat. Assn., Am. Statis. Assn., Soc. for Rsch. on Child Devel., Soc. for Rsch. on Adolescence, Phi Beta Kappa, Sigma Xi, Phi Kappa Phi. Home and Office: 240 Broad Rock Rd Wakefield RI 02879 E-mail: prn10@yahoo.com.

NEWMAN, RACHEL, magazine editor; b. Malden, Mass., May 1, 1938; d. Maurice and Edythe Brenda (Tichell) N.; m. Herbert Bleiweiss, Apr. 6, 1973 (div. Apr. 1989). BA, Pa. State U., 1960; cert., N.Y. Sch. Interior Design, 1963. Accessories editor Women's Wear Daily, N.Y.C., 1964-65; designer, publicist Grandoe Glove Corp., 1965-67; assoc. editor McCall's Sportswear and Dress Merchandiser mag., 1967; mng. editor McCall's You-Do-It Home Decorating, 1968-70, Ladies Home Jour. Needle and Craft mag., N.Y.C., 1970-72; editor-in-chief Am. Home Crafts mag., 1972-77; fashion dir. Good Housekeeping mag., 1977-78, home bldg. and decorating dir., 1978-82; editor-in-chief Country Living mag., 1978-98; founding editor Country Cooking mag., 1985-90, Dream Homes mag., 1989-2000, Country Kitchens mag., 1990-93, Country Living Gardener Mag., 1993-2000, Healthy Living mag., 1996-2000. Bd. dirs. Mothers & Others for a Livable Planet. Pa. State U. Alumni fellow, 1986; recipient Cir. of Excellence award Internat. Furnishings and Design Assn., 1992, YMCA Hall of Fame, 1992; named Disting. Alumna, Pa. State U., 1988. Mem. N.Y. Fashion Group, Nat. Home Fashions League, Am. Soc. Interior Designers, Am. Soc. Mag. Editors. E-mail: Rachelsfree@aol.com.

NEWMAN, RANDY, singer, songwriter, musician; b. Los Angeles, Calif., Nov. 28, 1943; s. Irving and Adele N.; m. Gretchen Newman; children: Amos, Eric, John, Patrick, Alice. Degree, U. Calif. Arranger, singer, songwriter, musician various record firms; singer-composer: (albums) including Randy Newman, 1968, Twelve Songs, 1969, Live, 1971, Sail Away, 1972, Good Old Boys, 1974, Little Criminals, 1977, Born Again, 1979, Trouble In Paradise, 1983, Land of Dreams, 1988, Bad Love, 1999; (with others) Randy Newman's Faust, 1995; appeared in film: Ragtime, 1981; also TV and concert engagements; music composer for films: Performance, 1970, Pursuit of Happiness, 1971, Cold Turkey, 1971, Ragtime, 1981, The Natural, 1984, Three Amigos (also co-wrote screenplay), 1986, Parenthood, 1989, Avalon, 1990, Awakenings, 1990, Toy Story, 1995 (Acad. award nominee for best original score 1996, Acad. award nominee for best original song 1996); composer (films) Michael, 1996, James and the Giant Peach, 1996 (Acad. award nomination), Cat's Don't Dance, 1997, A Bug's Life, 1998, Pleasantville, 1998, Toy Story 2, 1999 (Best Song Written for a Motion Picture, TV or other Visual Media Grammy award 2001), Meet the Parents, 2000 (nominee Best Music Acad. award 2001), Monsters, Inc., 2001 (Top Box Office Film ASCAP award 2001, Best Music Acad. award 2002); recorded 30 Years of Randy Newman (4 CD set), 1998. Recipient Grammy award for best instrumental composition, 1984 Office: care Cathy Kerr Mgmt 9079 Nemo St Los Angeles CA 90069-5511*

NEWMAN, RAYMOND MELVIN, biologist, educator; b. New Castle, Pa., June 10, 1956; s. Raymond Melvin and Sarah L. (Lawton) N.; m. Patricia Ann Scott, Nov. 22, 1989. BS in Biology, Slippery Rock (Pa.) U., 1978; MS, U. Minn., 1982, PhD in Fisheries, 1985. Grad. asst. U. Minn., St. Paul, 1979-84, rsch. specialist forest resources, 1985-86, asst. prof. fisheries, 1988-94, assoc. prof. fisheries, 1995—2002, prof. fisheries, 2002—; fellow natural resources U. Conn., Storrs, 1986-88; investigator U. Mich. Biol. Sta., Pellston, 1987-88. Exotics task force Nat. Sea Grant, Silver Spring, Md., 1991; mem. interagy. exotic species com. Minn. Dept. Natural Resources, St. Paul, 1992—; vis. scientist Inst. for Freshwater Ecology, River Lab., Dorset, U.K.; guest scientist Max Planck Inst. Chem. Ecology, Jena, Germany, 2002. Assoc. editor Jour. N.Am. Biol. Soc., 1994-98; mem. editl. bd. Ecology Freshwater Fish, 1992—; contbr. articles to profl. jours., chpts. to books. Bd. dirs. Twin Cities Trout Unltd., Mpls., 1982-87. Fellow Am. Inst. Fishery Rsch. Biologists; mem. Am. Fisheries Soc. (exec. com. Minn. chpt. 1992, 96), Ecol. Soc. Am., N.Am. Benthological Soc. Achievements include rsch. in chemical defense from herbivory by aquatic plants, control of exotic weed by native insects. Office: U Minn Fisheries Wildlife 1980 Folwell Ave Saint Paul MN 55108-1037 E-mail: rmn@fw.umn.edu.

NEWMAN, RICHARD ALAN, publisher, editor and consultant; b. Watertown, N.Y., Mar. 30, 1930; s. Gordon Leon and Belle (Burton) N.; m. Ann Cowan Meredith, 1955 (div. 1960); m. Peggy J. Hoyt, 1964 (div. 1978); m. Belynda Blair Bady, 1996. BA, Maryville Coll., 1952; M.Div., Union Theol. Sem., 1955; postgrad., Syracuse U., 1959-61, Harvard U., 1966. Ordained to ministry Presbyn. Ch., 1955, demitted, 1977; minister Westminster Presbyn. Ch., Syracuse, N.Y., 1955-59; instr. religion Vassar Coll., Poughkeepsie, 1962-63; prof., chmn. dept. social scis. Boston U., 1964-73; sr. editor G.K. Hall Co., Boston, 1973-79; exec. editor Garland Pub. Co., N.Y.C., 1978-81; mgr. publs. N.Y. Pub. Libr., 1981-92. Cons. Columbia U., N.Y.C., 1992-93; publs. officer, mng. editor The Harvard Guide to African-Am. History, W.E.B. DuBois Inst., Harvard U., 1993-95, fellows officer, 1995—, rsch. officer, 1997—. Author: Black Index, 1981, Bless All Thy Creatures, Lord, 1982, Lemuel Haynes, 1984, Afro-American Education, 1984, Black Access: A Bibliography, 1984, Black Power and Black Religion, 1987, Words Like Freedom, 1989, Black Preacher to White America, 1990; editor: Treasures From the New York Public Library, 1985, This Far By Faith, 1996, Everybody Say Freedom, 1996, Go Down, Moses, 1997, African-American Quotations, 1998; contbr. articles to profl. jours. Dem. candidate for N.Y. State Assembly from Onondaga County, 1960. Mem. New Eng. Hist. Genealogical Soc., Friends of Union Sem. Libr., Boston Athenaeum, Studio Mus. in Harlem, Friends of Amistad Rsch. Ctr., Schomburg Commn. for Preservation of Black Culture. Home: 160 Commonwealth Ave Apt 614 Boston MA 02116-2744 E-mail: rnewman@fas.harvard.edu.

NEWMAN, RICHARD AUGUST, psychiatrist, educator; b. Oak Park, Ill., May 27, 1931; s. Henry Adolph and Mildred Kathyn (Haaker) N.; m. Nancy Jane Werdelin, Aug. 28, 1954; children: John Henry, Kurt Alan, Richard Steven, Scott David. BS, U. Ill., 1953, MD, 1956. Diplomate Am. Bd. Psychiatry and Neurology. Intern Swedish-Am. Hosp., Rockford, Ill., 1956-57; resident in psychiatry Walter Reed Gen. Hosp., Washington, 1958-61; rschr. Walter Reed Army Inst., 1961; chief psychiat. svc. Valley Forge Gen. Hosp., Phoenixville, Pa., 1962-64, also asst. chief dept. psychiatry and neurology, 1962-64; practice medicine, specializing in psychiatry Paoli, 1962-96; dir. milieu therapy Phila. Gen. Hosp., 1968-69; dir. residency tng., dept. mental health scis. Hahnemann Med. Coll., 1969-73, assoc. prof., 1970-79; prof. psychiatry Med. Coll. Pa., Phila., 1979—. Dir. continuing mental health edn., 1983—87, 1983—87; dir. continuing med. edn., 1985—87; regional med. dir. for mental health Intracorp/Cigna, 1989—93; assoc. med. dir. for mental health U.S. Healthcare, 1993—95; prof. psychiat. Hahnemann U., Phila., 1995—; vis. prof. psychiatry U. Alta., 1975; chief cons. psychotherapy Chester County Cmty. Mental Health Clinic, 1967—68; psychiatrist Chester County Commr.'s Bd. for Mental Health/Mental Retardation, 1971—77; instr. Phila. Psychoanalytic Soc. Extension Sch., 1972—90; mem. faculty Inst. of Phila. Psychoanalytic Soc. ; chmn. psychiatric sect. Paoli Meml. Hosp., 1974—83, med. dir. psychiatry svc., 1977—83; psychiat. cons. St. Judes Hosp., St. Lucia, West Indies, 1983—89, St. Jones Ctr. for Behavioral Health, 1999, Kent Gen. Hosp., Dover, Del., 1999, Fairbanks (Alaska) Health Ctr., Alaska, 1999—2000; interim med. dir. Connections CSP, Wilmington, Del., 1995—96; staff psychiatrist Philhaven Hosp., Mt. Gretna, Pa., 1996—97; cons. St. Joseph's Hosp., Reading, Pa., 2000—. Contbr. articles to profl. jours. Maj. M.C., AUS, 1958-64. Fellow APA (life), Pa. Psychiat. Assn. (chmn. ethics com.); mem. AMA, Phila. Psychoanlaytic Soc., Am. Psychoanalytic Assn. (cert. psychoanalyst), Christian Med. Soc., Soc. Med. Coll. Dirs. Continuing Med. Edn., Pa., Chester County Med. Socs., Dirs. of Residency Tng. in Psychiatry of Del. Valley (past pres.). Lutheran. Home: 600 Nancy Jane Ln Downingtown PA 19335-1670

NEWMAN, ROBERT C. urologist, educator; b. Shattuck, Okla., Mar. 7, 1950; s. Floyd Smith and Erwina (Schollenbarger) N.; m. Lynn Schneider, Aug. 8, 1981. BS, Okla. U., 1972, MD, 1976; MS in Health Adminstrn., U. Colo., 1990. Resident in urology Okla. U., Okla. City, 1976-81; staff urologist Newman Med. Ctr., Shattuck, Okla., 1981-84; fellow in urology U. Fla., Gainesville, 1984-85, asst. prof., 1985-88, assoc. prof. urology/surgery Coll. of Medicine, 1988-98, prof. urology/surgery Coll. of Medicine, 1998—, also dir. compliance. Contbr. articles to profl. jours. Mem. AMA, Am. Urol. Assn., Endourology Soc. Avocations: cooking, reading, antiques. Home: 214 NE 9th Ave Gainesville FL 32601-4377 Office: U Fla Coll Medicine Box 100247 1600 Archer Rd Gainesville FL 32610-0247

NEWMAN, ROBERT GABRIEL, physician; b. The Netherlands, Oct. 26, 1937; came to U.S., 1939; s. Randolph H. and Eva E. (Feilchenfeld) N.; m. Seiko Kusuba, Oct. 26, 1968; children— Henry Seiji, Hana Marie. BA, NYU, 1958; MD with honors, U. Rochester, 1963; MPH, U. Calif.-Berkeley, 1969. Intern and resident in surgery Univ. Hosps., Cleve., 1963-65; dist. health officer N.Y.C. Health Dept., 1968; dir. Nat. Nutrition Survey of N.Y.C., 1969-70; asst. commr. N.Y.C. Health Dept., 1970-74; health cons., 1974-76; assoc. gen. dir. Beth Israel Med. Ctr., N.Y.C., 1976-78, CEO, pres., 1978-97; prof. dept. community medicine Mt. Sinai Sch. Medicine, N.Y.C., 1982-94; prof. depts. epidemiology and social medicine/psychiatry Albert Einstein Coll. of Medicine, 1994—; CEO, pres. Continuum Health Ptnrs. Inc. (formerly Greater Met. Health), N.Y.C., 1997—2000; dir. Baron Edmond de Rothschild Chem. Dependency Inst., 2000—. Cons. addiction problems Govt. of Hong Kong, 1975-85 Author book in field of methadone treatment; contbr. articles to profl. jours. Trustee U. Rochester, NY, 1994—2002. With USAF, 1965—67. WHO fellow, 1972 Fellow N.Y. Acad. Medicine, Am. Coll. Preventive Medicine; mem. Public Health Assn. N.Y.C., Hosp. Assn. N.Y. State (past chmn. 1992), Greater N.Y. Hosp. Assn. (past chmn. bd.), Am. Public Health Assn. Office: Continuum Health Ptnrs Inc 555 W 57th St Fl 18 New York NY 10019-2925 E-mail: rgnewmanmd@thomail.com.

NEWMAN, RUTH TANTLINGER, artist; b. Hooker, Okla., May 28, 1910; d. Walter Warren and Jean Louise (Hayward) Tantlinger; m. John Vincent Newman; children: Peter Vincent, Michael John. Student, Pomona Coll; BFA, UCLA, 1932; postgrad., Instituto Allende, U. Guanajuato, Mex. Art tchr. Santa Ana (Calif.) Schs., 1933-34, Santa Ana Adult Edn., 1934-40; watercolor tchr. Ventura (Calif.) Recreation Ctr., 1941-50; pvt. tchr. watercolor Calif., 1950-85. One-woman shows include Ventura County Mus. History and Art, 1993, Santa Barbara Art Assn., Ojai Art Ctr., Ventura Art Club, Oxnard (Calif.) Art Club, Art Club of Westlake Village, Thousand Oaks (Calif.) Art Club, others; commd. to paint 12 Calif. Missions, 1958, watercolors at San Juan Bautista Retreat House, Calif., oils at Ch. of San Bernardino, Mallorca, Spain; book featuring reproductions of selected works, Ruth Newman: A Lifetime of Art, introduced at her solo show in Ventura Mus., 1993. Mem. Westlake Village Art Guild, Thousand Oaks Art Club, Buena Ventura Art Club (charter). Home: 32120 Oakshore Dr Thousand Oaks CA 91361-3808

NEWMAN, RYAN, race car driver; b. South Bend, Ind. Degree in vehicle structure engring., Purdue U., 2001. Racecar driver Penske Racing, 2001—. Named winner, All-Am. Midget Series, 1993, Rookie of the Yr., USAC Nat. Midget Series, 1995, USAC Silver Crown Series, 1996, Sprint Car, 1999, winner, USAC Coors Light Silver Bullet Series, 1999, Pepsi Automobile Racing Club Am. 200, 2000, Automobile Racing Club Am. Ky. Speedway, 2000, Automobile Racing Club Am. Lowe's Motor Speedway, 2000; scholar Rich Vogler Meml. scholar, 2001. Office: c/o Penske Racing 136 Knob Hill Rd Mooresville NC 28117*

NEWMAN, SAMUEL, trust company executive; b. N.Y.C., Mar. 12, 1938; s. Aaron and Rachel (Hershkowitz) N.; m. Carolyn Gropper, Oct. 27, 1963; children: Marci Ann, Jodi Robin, Michael David. BBA, CUNY, 1971; grad. Advanced Mgmt. Program, Harvard U., 1982. Methods analyst Bankers Trust Co., N.Y.C., 1960-67; project leader Clark O'Neill SVC Corp., Fairview, N.J., 1967-68; sr. v.p. Irving Trust Co., N.Y.C., 1968-85; sr. v.p., gen. mgr. trade svcs. and GEOSERVE legal and regulatory support Mfrs. Hanover Trust (merger with Chem. Bank 1992), 1985-92; sr. v.p., gen. mgr. funds transfer and trade svcs. Chem. Bank, 1992-93; sr. v.p and bus. head payment products First Fidelity Bank NA, Newark, 1993-95; head dept. project support Fleet Pa. Svcs. Inc., Scranton, Pa., 1995-98; dir. new bus. devel., mgr. customer svc., internat. fin. instns. Fleet Bank, N.Y.C., 1998—2001; dir. float mgmt. Fleet Nat. Bank, Melville, NY, 2001—. Past chmn. bd. dirs. S.W.I.F.T. Terminal Svcs.; past chmn. N.Y. Clearing House funds transfer com.; speaker industry confs. Contbr. articles to profl. jours. Advisor Nat. Conf. of Commrs. on Uniform State Laws; former mem. U.S. coun. Internat. Banking Exec. Com., U.S. del. to Uncitral Working Group on Internat. Payments; former chief U.S. del. to tech. com. 168 Internat. Standards Orgn. Mem. Soc. Worldwide Fin. Telecom. (bd. dirs. 1978-92, dep. chmn 1989-92), Internat. Fin. Svcs. Assn. (bd. dirs. 2001—). Avocations: numismatics, collecting Hummel figurines. Office: Fleet Nat Bank MS NYEH 32904B 300 Broad Hollow Rd Melville NY 11747 E-mail: samuel_newman@fleet.com.

NEWMAN, SANDRA SCHULTZ, state supreme court justice; BS, Drexel U., 1959; MA, Temple U., 1969; JD, Villanova U., 1972; D (hon.) (hon.) , Gannon U., 1996, Widener U., 1996, Clarion U., 2000. Bar: Pa., U.S. Dist. Ct. (ea. dist.) Pa., U.S. Ct. Appeals (3d cir.), U.S. Supreme Ct. Asst. dist. atty. Montgomery County, Pa.; pvt. practice; judge Commonwealth Ct. of Pa., 1993—95; justice Supreme Ct. of Pa., 1995—. Past chair bd. consultors Villanova U. Law Sch.; mem. jud. coun. Supreme Ct. of Pa., liaison to the 3rd cir. task force on mgmt. of death penalty litigation, liaison to Pa. lawyers fund for client security bd., liaison to domestic rels. procedural rules com.; liaison Pa. Bar Inst.; jud. work group HHS; mem. adv. com. Nat. Ctr. for State Cts., Am. Law Inst.; mem. Drexel U. Coll. Bus. and Adminstrn.; lectr. and spkr. in field. Author: Alimony, Child Support and Counsel Fees, 1988; contbr. Named named Disting. Daughter of Pa.; recipient Phila. award for Super Achiever, Pediatric Juvenile Colitis Found. Jefferson Med. Coll. and Hosp, 1979, award for Dedicated Leadership and Outstanding Contbns. to the Cmty. and Law Employment , Drexel 100 award, Police Chiefs Assn. of Southeastern Pa., 1993, Medallion of Achievement award, Villanova U., 1993, Susan B. Anthony award, Women's Bar Assn. Western Pa., 1996, award, Justinian Soc., 1996, Tau Epsilon Law Soc., 1996, Legion of Honor Gold Medallion award, Chapel of Four Chaplain, 1997, honored by, Women of Greater Phila., 1996. Fellow: Pa. Bar Found., Am. Bar Found.; mem.: Montgomery Bar Assn., Nat. Assn. Women Judges, Am. Law Inst. Office: Supreme Ct Pa Ste 400 100 Four Falls Corporate Ctr West Conshohocken PA 19428-2950*

NEWMAN, SHARON LYNN, elementary education educator; b. Lewisburg, Tenn., Jan. 9, 1946; d. Hermit Taft and Martha Elizabeth (Pardue) Simmons; m. George Wynne Newman Sr., June 11, 1967; 1 child, George Wynne Jr. BS in Edn., Athens State Coll., 1979; MEd, Cumberland U., 2001. From substitute tchr. to chpt. 1 reading tchr. Giles County Bd. Edn., Pulaski, Tenn., 1979—2002, chpt. I reading tchr., 2002—. Chpt. 1 coord. Elkton (Tenn.) Elem. Sch., 1989—02, mem. steering com., 1989—, chair math. dept., 1993-95, chpt. title I com., 1995—, site dir. title I, 1996—, mem. disaster preparedness team, student learning com., 2002-. Ch. libr. Elkton (Tenn.) Bapt. Ch., 1992—; vol. Giles County Hist. Soc. Libr. and Mus., 1995—. Mem. NEA, Nat. Coun. Tchrs. Math., Giles County Edn. Assn. (rsch. chairperson 1993-95, IPD com. 1999—, sch. membership rep. 2002-). Home: 1758 Old Stage Rd Ardmore TN 38449-5308 Office: Elkton Elem Sch Elkton TN 38455

NEWMAN, SLATER EDMUND, psychologist, educator; b. Boston, Sept. 8, 1924; s. Max and Gertrude (Raphael) N.; m. Corrine Lois Silfen, June 18, 1950 (div. 1968); children— Kurt Douglas, Jonathan Mark, Eric Bruce; m. Patricia Ellen Christopher Thomas, July 2, 1969; 1 stepchild, Arthur C. Thomas III. BS, U. Pa., 1947; MA, Boston U., 1948; PhD, Northwestern U., 1951. Research psychologist U.S. Air Force, 1951-57; mem. faculty N.C. State U., Raleigh, 1957—, now prof. psychology. Vis. fgn. mem. Exptl. Psychology Soc. U.K., 1973-74, 82-83, 90. Contbr. chpts. to books, articles to profl. publs. Bd. dirs. ACLU, 1992-97, mem. biennial conf. com., 1994-97, mem. task force internat. human rights, 1994—, mem. spl. nominating com. 1996, mem. constn. com., 1996-97, youth affairs com., 1997, mem. nat. adv. coun., 1998—; pres. N.C. Civil Liberties Union, 1980-82, organizing com., 1965, exec. com., 1986-87, bd. dirs., 1969-73, 76-82, 84-90, 91-97; chmn. com. on Internat. Human Rights, 1988—; chair founding com. Wake County Chpt. ACLU, 1969, pres., 1969-72, 84-86, bd. dirs., 1969-73, 76-82, 84-90, 91-97, 99—; mem. steering com. ACLU-Affiliate Leadership Network, 1991-95; founding mem. North Carolinians Against the Death Penalty, 1967, bd. govs., 1967-73; mem. Mayor's Com. UN Week, Raleigh, 1986-95; active Amnesty Internat.; co-founder, coord. Com. to Reverse Arms Race, 1982—; co-founder, mem. steering com. North Carolinians Against Apartheid, 1985-87; mem. Wake County Com. Bicentennial U.S. Constn., 1987-89; co-founder, co-chair

N.C. Com. for Celebration of Human Rights, 1989-97; mem. Human Rights Week Com. N.C. State U., 1993-99, founder, 1993, chair, 1993-96; co-founder, co-chmn. Human Rights Coalition N.C., 1997—; co-founder North Carolinians for Ratification, Conv. on Elimination of All Forms of Discrimination Against Women, 1997, chmn., 1998—; mem. civil rights adv. bd. N.C. Mus. History, 2001—. 2d lt. USAF, 1943-46, 52-53. USPHS spl. rsch. fellow U. Calif.-Berkeley, 1965-66; U. London hon. rsch. fellow, 1973-74, 82-83, 90; recipient W.W. Finlator award ACLU of Wake County, 1997, Norman Smith award ACLU of N.C., 1998. Fellow AAAS, APA, Am. Psychol. Soc.; mem. Psychonomic Soc., UN Assn. (bd. dirs. Wake County chpt. 1991-95), So. Soc. Philosophy and Psychology, Cognitive Sci. Soc., Southeastern Workers in Memory (founder 1969), Southeastern Psychol. Assn. (exec. com. 2001—), mem. Comm. Profl. Paper Award (chmn. 2002-), N.C. Cognition Group (founder 1972), Ea. Psychol. Assn., AAUP (pres. N.C. State U. chpt. 1968-69), N.C. Acad. Sci., Carolinas Conf. for Undergrad. Rsch. in Psychology (co-founder 1976), Sigma Xi, Psi Chi (v.p. southeastern region 1990-94, nat. pres.-elect. 1996-97, mem. nat. coun. 1990-94, 96-99, nat. pres. 1997-98, nat. past pres. 1998-99), liason to APA comm. on internat. relations in psychol. Home: 315 Shepherd St Raleigh NC 27607-4031 Office: NC State U Dept Psychology Raleigh NC 27695-7801

NEWMAN, STACEY CLARFIELD, artist, curator; b. N.Y.C., July 21, 1956; d. Wallace J. Clarfield and Elinor (Kandel) Clarfield-Toberoff; m. Fredric Alan Newman, Nov. 27, 1983; children: Benjamin Clarfield, Marissa Paige, Alexandra Brooke. Student, Franklin & Marshall, 1974-76; BS in Labor Rels. and Mgmt., U. Bridgeport, 1978. Dir. ops. Nat. Rec. and Video Studios, N.Y.C., 1978-80; dir. tech. ops. VCA/Teletronics, 1980-82, cons., client rep./MTV, 1981-83, exec. prodr., 1982-85; artist, art curator Stacey Clarfield Newman Studios, Scarsdale, N.Y., 1986—. Merchandise cons. Tahari Fashions, N.Y.C., 1985-86; artist mem., jury com. You Gotta Have Art program White Plains Hosp. Ctr., 1990-92; art tchr. collage Scarsdale (N.Y.) Adult Edn. Program, 1993-95; artist in residence Scarsdale Elem. Schs., 1995-97; art cons., curator Manhattan Transfer, Inc., N.Y.C., 1997-2000. One-person shows include Quogue (N.Y.) Gallery, 1986, Ch. St. Gallery, White Plains, N.Y., 1987, Greenburgh Nature Ctr., N.Y., 1988, Grinton I. Will Libr. Gallery, Yonkers, N.Y., 1988, Scarsdale (N.Y.) Nat. Bank Gallery, 1989, Bronxville (N.Y.) Libr. Gallery, 1991, Piermont (N.Y.) Fine Arts Gallery, 1997-98, Manhattan Transfer, Inc., 1997, Piermont Fine Arts Gallery, 2001, J&W Gallery, New Hope, Pa., 1999, Studio 4 West, 1999, 93 South Gallery, 2000, Adele Greenberg Salon, Cambridge, Mass., 2000, Amb. Galleries, Palm Beach, Fla., 2001, Viridian Gallery, N.Y.C., 2001, Piermont Fine Arts Gallery, 2001, Viridian Gallery @ Chelsea, 2002; exhibited in juried group shows: Piermont Fine Art Gallery, 1995, 96, 98, 2000, 01, Anaya Gallery, Scarsdale, 1986, Katonah (N.Y.) Gallery, 1986, Gallery at Jamaica, Stratton Mountain, Vt., 1987, CDS Contemporary Art, Albuquerque, 1989, Mari Galleries, Mamaroneck, N.Y., 1992, Manhattan Transfer, Inc., 1993, 98, 93 South Gallery, Nyack, N.Y., 1998-99, Bibro Fine Arts Gallery, Chelsea, N.Y., 1998, Weber Fine Art, Scarsdale, N.Y., 1998, 2000, 93 South Gallery, Nyack, N.Y., 1998, J&W Gallery, New Hope, Pa., 1998, 99, 2001, Studio 4 West, Piermont, N.Y., 1999, Hewlett Mus., 2000, Ambassador Gallery, Palm Beach, Fla., 2000, Viridian Gallery, N.Y.C., 2000, 01, 02, Adele Greenberg Salon, 2000, 01, A Pirate Space, Denver, 2001, Contemporary Art Oasis, Denver, 2001, J&W Gallery, 2001, 2002, Manhattanville Coll. Gallery, 2002; commd. Am. Soc. Plastic and Reconstructive Surgeons, L.A. Conv. Ctr., 1988, White Plains Hosp. Ctr., 1989, 90, Cystic Fibrosis Found., N.Y.C., 1990, Joan Kroc Found., Calif., 1989-91. 1st v.p., bd. dirs. Internat. Coll. Surgeons aux., Chgo., 1988—90; mem. Juvenile Diabetes Found., Gala, 2000; Regional v.p. Am. Cancer soc., White Plains, 1986—88; bd. dirs. White Plains Hosp. Ctr. Aux., 1995—; fund raiser, event planner Holocaust Commn., N.Y.C., 1998; mem. Hewlett Mus., 2000, J&W Gallery, 2000—, Viridian Artists, Inc., 2001—; active Scarsdale Tremont Synagogue Gala, 2001, 2002. Mem. Internat. Platform Assn., Nat. Mus. Women in Contemporary Arts, Nat. Assn. Women Artists, Inc., Nat. Arts Club, Penumbra Soc. (artist mem.), Katonah Mus., Piermont Fine Arts Gallery (publicity chair), Nat. Mus. Women in the Arts (artist mem.). Avocations: piano, photography, tennis, kayaking, skiing. Studio: 21 Wayside Ln Scarsdale NY 10583-2911 E-mail: StaceySCN21@aol.com.

NEWMAN, STANLEY RAY, oil refining company executive; b. Milo, Idaho, Mar. 5, 1923; s. Franklin Hughes and Ethel Amelda (Crowley) N.; m. Rosa Klein, May 27, 1961 (div. Mar. 1980); children: Trudy Lynn, Susan Louise, Karen Elizabeth, Paul Daniel, Phillip John; m. Madelyn Wycherly, Jan. 10, 1991; children: Heidi, Heather, Amy. Student, Tex A&M U., 1944-45; BS, U. Utah, 1947; PhD, 1952. With Texaco Rsch. Ctr., Beacon, N.Y., 1951-82; technologist, 1973-77; sr. techonolgist rsch. mfg.-fuels, 1977-82; profl. cons. on fuels and chems., 1983-91. Chmn. Planning Bd., Village of Fishkill, N.Y., 1973-77; village trustee, 1990-92; mem. Dutchess County Solid Waste Mgmt. Bd., 1974-76. Patentee in field. With inf. Signal Corps U.S. Army, 1944-46. Mem. AAAS, N.Y. Acad. Scis., Dutchess County Geneal. Soc. (pres. 1981-87, exec. v.p. 1987-88), N.Y. Fruit Testing Assn., Sigma Xi (pres. Texaco Rsch. Ctr. br. 1980-81). Republican. Mem. Lds Ch. Home: 285 Plantation Cir Idaho Falls ID 83404-7990 E-mail: stamad39@cs.com. *I was born of humble parents in Idaho. Life was hard and difficult so early in my life at considerable sacrifice I went the extra distance to go to a good high school to prepare for college. By working at night and weekends, I was able to complete college with a Ph.D. Blessed with an inquiring mind, a strong will to work, and a desire to learn, I moved to the east coast, worked hard both at my job and in the community, always retaining the honesty, integrity and strong religious values taught by my humble parents. At retirement, I had numerous patents, publications, and had world wide responsibility for fuels for Texaco.*

NEWMAN, STEPHEN MICHAEL, lawyer; b. Buffalo, Jan. 12, 1945; s. Howard A. and Mildred (Ballow) N.; m. Gayle Mallon, May 24, 1969; children: Holly, Deborah. AB, Princeton U., 1966; JD, U. Mich., 1969. Bar: N.Y. 1969, Fla. 1976. Assoc. Hodgson, Russ, Andrews, Woods & Goodyear, Buffalo, 1969-73; ptnr. Hodgson Russ, LLP (formerly Hodgson, Russ, Andrews, Woods &, 1973—. Lectr. in field. Bd. dirs. Leukemia Soc., United Jewish Fedn. Buffalo Inc., Jewish Ctr. Greater Buffalo Inc., Temple Beth Zion; bd. dirs., chpt. chmn., exec. com. Am. Jewish Com., Buffalo chpt.; active Vol. Action Ctr. United Way of Buffalo and Erie County. Fellow Am. Coll. Trusts and Estates Coun.; mem. ABA (personal svc. corps. com. tax sect.), N.Y. State Bar Assn. (chair trusts and estates law sect. 2001), Princeton Club of Western N.Y. (sch. com.). Office: Hodgson Russ LLP 2000 1 M&T Plz Buffalo NY 14203 E-mail: snewman@hodgsonruss.com.

NEWMAN, STEPHEN ALEXANDER, chemical engineer, thermodynamicist; b. Auburn, N.Y., Apr. 12, 1938; s. Solomon and Anna (Reich) N.; m. Mary Ellen Lassow, July 26, 1964; children: Sharon Rose, Lori Suzanne. *Daughter Sharon Rose, BA University of Pennsylvania, PhD Columbia University, MD Columbia College of Physicians and Surgeons. She is currently physician and Instructor in Clinical Pediatrics at New York-Presbyterian Hospital, New York City. Daughter Lori Suzanne, BA Princeton, PhD Rockefeller University, MD Cornell University Medical College. She is currently physician at Brigham & Women's Hospital and Instructor of Internal Medicine at Harvard Medical School, Boston.* BSChemE, Rensselaer Poly. Inst., 1960; MSChemE, MIT, 1962; PhD, Rutgers U., 1976. Registered profl. engr., N.J. Rsch. engr. M.W. Kellogg Co., Piscataway, N.J., 1962-67; tech. mgr. Foster Wheeler Energy Corp., Clinton, 1967-96; cons. engr. Kvaerner Process, Bridgewater, 1996-2000; clients include ABB Lummus Global, Bloomfield, 2000-01, Kvaerner Process, Bridgewater. Frequent speaker nat. and internat. sci. meetings; organizer, conf./symposium chmn. Nat. Thermodynamics Conf., 1978, World Congress Chem. Engring., Montreal, 1981, CODATA Congress, Jerusalem, 1984; panel NAS, 1980-82; cons. Nat. Bur. Standards, Washington, 1979; chmn. various project coms. U.S. Dept. Energy, 1977-84. Editor: Thermodynamics of Aqueous Systems with Industrial Applications, 1980, Chemical Engineering Thermodynamics, 1983, Shale Oil Upgrading and Refining, 1983, Acid and Sour Gas Treating Processes, 1985; book and article reviewer Chem. Engring. mag., Gulf Publs., 1980—; contbr. numerous articles to profl. jours. Pres. Mens' Club Temple Israel, Union, N.J., 1980-81. AEC fellow, 1961-62; grantee NSF, 1978, 84. Fellow AIChE (chmn. nat. rsch. com. 1984-85, co-founder Design Inst. Phys. Property Data 1977, vice chmn. 1979-85, award 1989); mem. Am. Petroleum Inst. (chair contractors com. on tech. data 1978-96), Gas Processors Assn. (project monitor 1976-85, tech. com.), Am. Assn. Engring. Socs. Jewish. Home: 941 Douglas Ter Union NJ 07083-6523

NEWMAN, STEVEN E. neurologist; b. Detroit, July 1, 1945; children: Nathan, Rachel, Emily, Benjamin, Daniel. BA, Albion Coll., 1966; MD, U. Mich., 1970. Diplomate Am. Bd. Psychiatry & Neurology, Am. Bd. Forensic Examiners, Am. Bd. Forensic Medicine, Am. Bd. of Clin. Neurophysiology, Am. Bd. of EEG. With dept. neurology Dept. Internal Medicine, Dept. Psychiatry U. Mich., 1971-77; with NIH, 1977-79, Detroit Inst. PM&R, 1979—. Mem. Mich. Spinal Cord/Traumatic Brain Injury Adv. Com., 1994-97; mem. State of Mich. Adv. Coun. Traumatic Brain Injury Grant Com., 1999—; med. dir. Fedn. for Spinal Cord Injury Prevention; bd. dirs. Mich. Neurol. Assn. Author: Legal Medicine, 1995; contbr. articles to profl. jours. Fellow Am. Acad. Neurology; mem. Am. Coll. of Forensic Examiners, Mich. State Med. Soc. (bd. dirs.), Oakland County Med. Soc. (pres. 2000-2001), Nat. Assn. Disability Evaluating Physicians, Am. Acad. Clin. Neurophysiology. Office: Detroit Inst Phys Med & Rehab 25811 W 12 Mile Rd Southfield MI 48034-1896

NEWMAN, STEVEN HARVEY, insurance company executive, director; b. Bklyn., Apr. 26, 1943; s. Charlotte Newman Bart; m. Lenore Blaustein, June 14, 1964; children: Richard, Michael, Stephanie. BS, Bklyn. Coll., 1963. Actuarial asst. Royal Globe Ins. Co., N.Y.C., 1963-65; asst. sec. Ins. Rating Bd., 1965-69; v.p., sr. casualty actuary Am. Internat. Group, 1969-82; exec. v.p. Home Ins. Co., 1982-85, pres., 1985-86, also bd. dirs.; chmn., CEO Underwriters Reinsurance Co., Woodland Hills, Calif., 1987—2001; now chmn. Platinum Underwriters Holdings, Ltd., Bermuda, 2002—. Chmn. GCR Holdings, 1993-97, Reins. Assn. Am., 1995-96. Fellow Casualty Actuarial Soc. (pres. 1981-82); mem. Am. Acad. Actuaries, Internat. Actuarial Assn.

NEWMAN, SUZANNE DINKES, web site development executive; b. Bklyn., Apr. 28, 1949; d. Philip and Natalie (Hollander) Dinkes; m. Ralph Michael Newman, Mar. 9, 1975. Student, Cooper Union, 1967-71, Sch. Visual Arts, N.Y.C., 1971-72. Asst. art dir. Lincoln Ctr. Art Progs., N.Y.C., 1973-74; art dir. BimBamBoom Mag., Yonkers, NY, 1974; with Fairfax Advtg., N.Y.C., 1974-75; dir. ops. TBE Advtg., 1975-87, ceo Yonkers, NY, 1987-94; art dir. Timer Barrier Express, 1975-80; CEO R.S. Newman Assocs., 1994-98; ptnr. WWW.Dott-Comm.com, 1997—. Concert coord. Classic Harmony Prodns., N.Y.C., 1975; apl. event planner, The Left Bank, Mt. Vernon, N.Y., 1980-81; apl. event cons. Glen Island Casino, New Rochelle, N.Y., 1984-85; event coord., Top Brass, Yonkers, 1986-87; art dir., cons. various music publs., 1974-80, dir. comms., Yonkers C. of C., 1998—. Editor: Rockin' in the Fourth Estate, 1979-80, Chamber News, 1998—. Art dir.: White and Still All Right!, 1977, Sun Records, 1980, The Buddy Holly Story, 1979. Mem. Yonkers Citizen's Adv. Grp., Yonkers Mayorial Transition Com., 1991-92, Alliance Devel. Com., Yonkers Sch. and Bus. Alliance, 1991-94, prog. com., 1991-94; mem. Yonkers Coun. Pres.'s Citizens Adv, Grp., 1992, Yonkers Dem. Com., dist. leader, 1991-93; jour. chair gala com. Hudson River Mus., 1992; mem. Yonkers Local Bus. Adv. Coun., 1992-94; mem. Yonkers Pvt. Industry Coun., 1992-94, sec. 1993-94; promotion chair Yonkers Hudson Riverfest, 1992-93; bus. adv. com. Yonkers Econ. Devel. Zone, 1993-94; active Yonkers Waterfront Task Force, 1993-94; bd. dirs. Youth Theater Interaction, 1994—; bd. dirs. Westchester divsn. Jewish Guild for Blind, 1994-97, gala chair, 1994; events coord. Mayor's Inaugural Ball, 1996; leader Jr. Girl Scouts, Southwest Yonkers, 1996—. Recipient Disting. Leadership and Svc. Awd., Westchester County C. of C., 1985, Westchester Awd., Westchester Small Bus. Counc., 1989, Outstanding Leader award Girl Scouts U.S., 2000. Mem. Westchester Small Bus. COun. (comms. chmn. 1984-85, Westchester winner, 1989), Yonkers C. of C. (bd. dirs. 1996-98, 2001—, comm. chair 1996-97), Coun. for Arts Westchester. Democrat. Jewish. Avocations: reading, antiques, gardening. E-mail: snewman@dott-comm.com.

NEWMAN, TERRIE LYNNE, advertising and marketing executive; b. Boston; d. Joseph and Clara (Bistry) N.; m. Fredric Aron Kerstein, June 18, 1978. BA in English, U. Mass., Boston, 1973. Copywriter Vanda Beauty Counselor, Inc., N.Y.C., 1973-75, creative dir., 1975-76; sr. writer Avon Products, Inc., N.Y.C., 1976-79; copywriter Hume, Smith, Mickelberry Advt., Inc., Miami, Fla., 1979-80, Beber, Silverstein & Ptnrs., Advt., Miami, 1980-81; pres., creative dir. Terrie Lynne Newman, Inc., 1981-92, Terrie Newman Communs., Miami, 1992—. Recipient Internat. Gold Echo award Direct Mktg. Assn., 1987, 88, Internat. Bronze Echo award, 1987, Gold Award for Excellence in Mktg., Gold Coast chpt. Am. Mktg. Assn., 1987, First Place Gold medallion Broadcast Promotion & Mktg. Execs., 1986, Clio award, 1981, Emmy award, 1981, others. Home: 6970 SW 125th St Miami FL 33156-6240

NEWMAN, THEODORE ROOSEVELT, JR. judge; b. Birmingham, Ala., July 5, 1934; s. Theodore R. and Ruth L. (Oliver) N. AB, Brown U., 1955, LL.D., 1980; JD, Harvard U., 1958. Bar: D.C. 1958, Ala. 1959. Atty. civil rights div. Dept. Justice, Washington, 1961-62; practiced law in, 1962-70; assoc. judge D.C. Superior Ct., 1970-76; judge D.C. Ct. Appeals, 1976-91, chief judge, 1976-84, sr. judge, 1991—; bd. dirs. Nat. Center for State Cts., v.p., 1980-81, pres., 1981-82. Trustee Brown U. With USAF, 1958-61. Fellow Am. Bar Found.; mem. Nat. Bar Assn. (past pres. jud. coun., C. Francis Stradford award 1984, William H. Hastie award 1988). E-mail. E-mail: tnewman@dcca.state.dc.us.

NEWMAN, THOMAS DANIEL, minister, school administrator; b. London, Eng., May 12, 1922; s. Frederick and Margaret (O'Leary) N.; m. Louise Johannah Albertano, Apr. 1, 1963; 1 dau., Susan (Mrs. Alan J. Rennie). Student, Glasgow Sch. Accounting, 1946, Unity Sch. Christianity, 1962-66, Harvard Div. Sch., 1967—; DSc, Alma Coll., 1975. Ordained to ministry Ch. of Christ, 1966. Mng. dir. Thomas Newman (Printers) Ltd., 1945-49; mng. dir. H. & M.J. Pubs. Ltd., 1947-49, Forget-Me-Not Greeting Cards Ltd., 1949-61, Diplomat Greetings Ltd., 1957-61, Nevill's Ltd., 1955-57; pastor Christ's Ch., Springfield, Mo., 1966-67, Longwood, Brookline, Mass., 1967-99; adminstrv. dir. Am. Schs. Oriental Rsch., 1968, treas., 1970—, trustee, 1972—. Pastor Jefferson (N.H.) Cmty. Chapel, 2000—; founder Carthage Rsch. Inst., Kheredine, Tunisia, 1975, Cyprus Archaeol. Rsch. Inst., Nicosia, 1977; cons. Joint Archeol. Expdns. to, Ai, 1969-73, to; Tell-El-Hesi, 1970-73, to, Idalion, 1970-73; mem. Joint Archeol. Expdn. to, Caesarea Maritima, 1971, to; Carthage, 1975; dir. Logistics Survey Qu'Rayyah, Saudi Arabia, 1973; pub. cons. (Dead Sea Scrolls Com.), 1968-73; Trustee Allbright Inst. Archeol. Rsch., Jerusalem.; Am. Center Oriental Rsch., Amman, Jordan. Served with RAF, 1940-45. Mem. Archeol. Inst. Am., Soc. Bibl. Lit., Soc. O.T. Studies, Masons, Harvard Faculty Club, Univ. Club Boston. Clubs: Mason, Harvard Faculty; University (Boston) (Sarasota). Home: PO Box 375 Lancaster NH 03584-0375 Office: Jefferson Cmty Chapel Rte 2 Jefferson NH 03583 E-mail: revtomn@bestnetpc.com., revtomn@ncia.net.

NEWMAN, WILLIAM BERNARD, JR. consultant; b. Providence, Nov. 16, 1950; s. William Bernard and Virginia (Crosby) N.; m. Karen O'Connor, Jan. 11, 1951. BA, Ohio Wesleyan U., 1972; JD, George Mason U., Arlington, Va., 1977; postgrad., Harvard U., 1987. Bar: Va. 1977, D.C. 1978. Atty. com. energy Ho. of Reps., Washington, 1978-81; v.p., Washington counsel Consol. Rail Corp. Dept. Govt. Affairs, 1981-98; cons., 1999—. Bd. dirs. Nat. Coun. for Adoption, 1994-98. Mem. Va. Bar Assn., D.C. Bar Assn. Home: 1009 Priory Pl Mc Lean VA 22101-2134

NEWMAN, WILLIAM GUY, producer, director, consultant; b. Neptune, N.J., May 2, 1952; s. Oscar Newman and Gwen Ruth (Hall) Evans; m. Sally Ann Aurnhammer, Sept. 20, 1991; 1 child, William Duncan. Student, Brookdale Coll., 1970-72, New Sch., 1974-76. Co-owner Creative Film Co., Spring Lake, N.J., 1974-79; prodn. coord. MSW Studios, N.Y.C., 1979-82; dir. photography, asst. dir. New Venture Media, Neptune, 1983-85; prodn. mgr., writer Bill Quinn Prodns., Asbury Park, N.J., 1985-93; ind. prodr., dir., cons., 1993—; co-owner Newman/Arneth Prodns., 1994—; co-creator, co-writer, dir. (radio comedy) The Snappy Pickles Show, 1998—. Comedy writer Smittee (MTV's mascot), Asbury Park, 1986—, road mgr.; co-owner U & B Industries. Co-author: (TV pilot) The Future of TV, 1985; author: (radio comedy series) SPACE: 1888, 1987; writer and editor promotional trailer for Time Out; writer, filmed and editor numerous indsl. and comml. videos; co-prodr., cameraman (documentary interview) Without a Condo, 1994; co-prodr., dir. (t.v. series) On The Edge, 1995—. Fundraiser Greenpeace, Washington, 1985—; mem. Citizens Against Unjust & Severe Enforcement, Environ. Def. Fund. Recipient Telly awards, 1990, 91. Mem. Am. Film Inst., Soc. Associated Performers (v.p. 1990-94), Internat. Platform Assn., Manasquan Beach Communal Block Soc. (v.p. 1977-82, author, editor newsletter 1975-82). Democrat. Avocation: bicycling. E-mail: williamnewman@hotmail.com.

NEWMAN, WILLIAM MARK, real estate broker, real estate appraiser; b. Newburgh, N.Y., Feb. 9, 1943; s. Thomas Leonard and Muriel (Delit) N.; m. Susan Smith, 1969 (div. 1976); 1 child, Victoria L.; m. Frances Boudreau, 1978 (div. 1995); m. Sylvia Anderson Marks, 1999. BA, Syracuse U., 1965, MS, 1967; PhD, New Sch. for Social Rsch., N.Y.C., 1970. Prof. sociology U. Conn., Storrs, 1969-97, emeritus prof. sociology, 1997—; ptnr. Conn. Comml. Realty, New London, Conn., 1990-98, pres., 1999—. Author: American Pluralism, 1973; co-author: Atlas of Religious Change in America, 1952-90, 1993, Understanding Social Life, 1993, Atlas of American Religion, 1776-1990, 2000. Fellow Soc. Sci. Study of Religion; mem. Assn. Sociology of Religion, Religion Rsch. Assn., Appraisal Inst. (assoc.), Nat. Assn. Realtors. Home: PO Box 2089 New London CT 06320-2089 E-mail: ccrsales@aol.com.

NEWMARK, EMANUEL, ophthalmologist; b. Newark, May 25, 1936; s. Charles Meyer and Bella (Yoskowitz) Newmark; m. Tina Steinberg, Aug. 25, 1957; children: Karen Beth, Heidi Ellen, Stuart Jeffrey. BS in Pharmacy, Rutgers U., 1959; postgrad., U. Amsterdam, The Netherlands, 1960-63, Armed Forces Inst. Pathology, Washington, 1971; MD, Duke U., 1966; postgrad., Harvard U., 1967. Diplomate Am. Bd. Ophthalmology. Intern George Washington U. Hosp., Washington, 1966; trainee NIH rsch. U. Fla., Gainesville, 1967-70; resident ophthalmology U. Fla. Hosp., 1967-70; instr. dept. ophthalmology U. Fla., 1970; cons. ophthalmology Gainesville VA Hosp., 1970; clin. instr. ophthalmology U. Tex. Med. Sch., San Antonio, 1971-72; cons. ophthalmology Kerrville (Tex.) VA Hosp., 1971-72; asst. chief ophthalmology svc. Brooke Army Gen. Hosp., Fort Sam, Tex., 1971-72. Clin. asst. prof. ophthalmology Bexar County Hosp. and Clinics, San Antonio, 1971—72; tchg. faculty Joint Com. Allied Health Pers. Ophthalmology; sec., treas. Palm Beach Eye Assocs., Atlantis, 1973—98; pharm. adv. com. Agy. for Health Care Adminstrn. Bd. Optometry, 1991—; mem. adv. bd. Fla. east coast chpt. Nat. Sjorgren's Syndrome. *Dr. Newmark's research fellowship at the University of Florida led to the discovery of a cure for fungal corneal ulcers. He has special interest in corneal transplantation surgery and was trained by Professor Herbert Kaufman. During his United States Army service he received the coveted army commendation medal for his excellence as a teacher, surgeon and clinician. Dr. Newmark is committed to education of allied health personnel and is the editor of Refinements, published by the American Academy of Ophthalmology. Dr. Newmark was listed amongst the best physicians in South Florida as published in the October 1998 issue of the Miami Metro Magazine.* Contbr. chapters to books, articles to profl. jours. Alumni assoc. Rutgers Coll. Pharmacy, 1990—, chmn. reunion, 1986, 2001, Duke U. Med. Alumni Assn., NC, 1967—; centurian Davison Club-Duke U. Med. Sch., 1982—; campaign chmn., nat. vice chmn. Israel Bonds, Palm Beach County, Fla., 1988—; participant charitable orgns.; v.p. Palm Beach Liturgical Culture Found., 1994—2000, pres., 2000—01. Decorated Lion of Judea State of Israel; recipient Gates of Jerusalem medal, 1991, Jerusalem medal, 1996, Recognition award, Joint Commn. Allied Health Personnel in Ophthalmology, 2001. Fellow: ACS, Am. Acad. Ophthalmology (del. to coun. 1996—2001, editor Refinements 1998—2000, Fla. state chmn. ednl. trust, allied health edn. com., Achievement award 2001, Councillors award 2001); mem.: AMA, Fla. Soc. Ophthalmology (ethics chmn. 1985—90, pres. 1990—91, James W. Clower Jr. Cmty. Svc. award 1995), Palm Beach County Ophthal. Soc. (pres. 1984—85), Palm Beach County Med. Soc. (chair ethics com. 1997—2000, vice chair ethics com. 2002), Fla. Med. Assn. (ho. dels. 1993—95, 2001—02), Am. Orgn. for Rehab. Through Tng. Fedn. (nat. exec. com.-campaign cabinet 1987, pres. 1987—90, Palm Beach Men's Achievement award 1988, Pres. award 1989), Internat. Platform Assn., Founder's Soc. Duke U. Jewish. Avocations: travel, organizational business, teaching. Home: 180 Palm Cir Atlantis FL 33462-6627 Office: Regional Eye Inst 1920 Palm Beach Lakes Blvd West Palm Beach FL 33409-3512

NEWMARK, HAROLD LEON, biochemist, researcher, educator; b. N.Y.C., July 21, 1918; s. Abraham and Mollie W. (Wolf) N.; m. Helen Rosenberg, Mar. 13, 1949 (dec. Aug. 1985); children: Jonathan, Robin L.; m. Phyllis Klein, Sept. 6, 1987. BS, CCNY, 1939; MS, N.Y. Poly. U., 1950; DSc, Rutgers U., 1998. Chemist Chem. Spec. of N.J.-Syntex, Newark, 1939-41, Intramed Co., N.Y.C., 1946-49, Chase Chem. Co., Newark, 1949-50, Vitarine Co., N.Y.C., 1950-59, Hoffmann LaRoche, Inc., Nutley, N.J., 1959-81, dir. food, agrl. products, 1966-81; chemist Ludwig Inst. for Cancer Rsch., Toronto, Ont., Can., 1981-84; biochem. rschr. Sloan-Kettering Inst., N.Y.C., 1984-95; rsch. scientist Strang Cancer Prevention Ctr. Rockefeller U., 1996-99. Adj. prof. lab. cancer rsch. Coll. Pharmacy, Rutgers U., Pisacataway, N.J., 1987—; assoc. mem. Cancer Inst. N.J., 1994—. Author, editor: Calcium, Vitamin D and Colon Cancer, 1991; contbr. more than 145 articles to sci. publs. Cpl. USAAF, 1942-46. Mem. AAAS, Am. Chem. Soc., Am. Assn. Cancer Rsch., Am. Soc. Clin. Nutrition, N.Y. Acad. Scis. Achievements include more than 20 patents for pharmaceuticals. Home: 11 Carmer Dr Maplewood NJ 07040-2119

NEWMARK, HARRIS, III, diagnostic radiologist; b. L.A., Feb. 11, 1942; Office: 227 Toyopa Dr Pacific Palisades CA 90272-4463

NEWMARK, LEONARD DANIEL, linguistics educator; b. Attica, Ind., Apr. 8, 1929; s. Max Jacob and Sophie (Glusker) N.; m. Ruth Broessler, Sept. 16, 1951; children: Katya, Mark. AB, U. Chgo., 1947; MA, Ind. U., 1951, PhD, 1955. Instr. English U. Ill., Urbana, 1951; vis. asst. prof. linguistics U. Mich., Ann Arbor, 1961; assoc. prof. English Ohio State U., 1954-62; assoc. prof. linguistics Ind. U., Bloomington, 1962-63; prof. linguistics U. Calif., San Diego, 1963-91, prof. emeritus, 1992—, chmn. dept., 1963-71, 79-85, head program in Am. lang. and culture, 1979-84, rsch. linguist Ctr. for Rsch. in Lang., 1992—. Author: Linguistic History of English, 1963, Spoken Albanian, 1997, Standard Albanian, 1982, Albanian-English Dictionary, 1998, Albanian Handbook, 1999; inventor memory aid device. Mem. Linguistics Soc. Am., Dictionary Soc. N.Am., Phi Beta Kappa. Home: 2643 St Tropez Pl La Jolla CA 92037-3541 Office: U Calif San Diego Dept Linguistics La Jolla CA 92093 E-mail: ldnewmark@ucsd.edu.

NEWMARK, MARILYN, sculptor; b. N.Y.C., July 20, 1928; d. Edward Ellis and Mabel (Davies) Newmark; m. Leonard J. Meiselman, Mar. 15, 1952. Student, Adelphi Coll., 1945-47, Alfred U., 1949. Sculpture specializing in horses, equestrian figures, dogs, foxes. Exhibited in group shows; sculpture exhbn. Ky. Derby Mus., Fleischer Mus., Scottsdale, Leigh Yawkey Woodson Art Mus., Wis., Bennington Ctr. for Arts, Vt., Calif. Acad. Sci., NAD, N.Y.C., Nat. Arts Club, N.Y.C., Nat. Art Mus. Sport, N.Y.C., James Ford Bell Mus., Wis., Smithsonian Instn., Washington, Mus. of Horse, Ky., Phila. Acad. Natural Scis., Port of History Mus., Pa., Marietta/Cobb Mus. Art, Wildlife Experience, Denver, Brookgreen Gardens, S.C.; represented in permanent collections Nat. Mus. Racing, Saratoga, N.Y., Internat. Mus. Horse, Ky. Horse Park, also in pvt. collections. Recipient Anna Hyatt Huntington award, 1970, 71, 72, 75, 78, 80, 81, 82, 83, 86, 88, 90, 97, gold medal, 1973, award Coun. Am. Artists Socs., 1972, 73, 79, 80, Hudson Valley John Newington award, 1973, 77, gold medal, 1979, Elliot Liskin Meml. award, 1989, 96, Academician Nat. Acad. Design Ellin P. Speyer award, 1974, 93, 99, Artist Fund award, 1982. Fellow Nat. Sculpture Soc. (coun. 1973-75, rec. sec. 1976, sec. 1977-79, coun. 1981-83, 92-97, Bronze medal 1986, Mildred Victor Meml. award 1996), Audubon Artists (Elliott Liskin Meml. award 2000), Am. Artists Profl. League (Gold medal 1974, 77, medal of hon. 1987), Allied Artists Am. (Gold medal 1981, 93, In Memorium award 1994), Pen & Brush Club (Gold medal 1977, Salmagundi Club award 1982, 83, 91, C. Dunwiddie Meml. award 1999), Soc. Animal Artists (jury of admissions 1972-75, 90—, bd. dirs. 1991—, v.p. 1998—, Legacy award 2002), Am. Acad. Equine Art (founding mem., dir. sculpture 1980—), Nassau Suffolk Horsemans Assn. (dir. 1968-82), Catherine Lorillard Wolfe Art Club, Smithtown Hunt Club, Meadowbrook Hunt Club. Address: 22 Woodhollow Rd Roslyn Heights NY 11577-2217

NEWMARK, MARIS S. interior designer, consultant; b. Bklyn., May 1, 1943; d. Louis G. and Pauline (Cantor) Levine; m. Alan Robert Newmark, Nov. 23, 1961; children— Jeffrey Todd, Kerri Gay. Student Bklyn. Coll., Moore Coll. Art; cert. Phila. Coll. Art, 1984. Mdse. mgr. J.C. Penney Co.,

Audubon and Voorhees, N.J., 1973-80; sr. dist. designer Phila. and N.J. dists. Cort Furniture Rental, Maple Shade, N.J., 1980-83; pres. Maris Newmark Interior Design, Inc., Cherry Hill, N.J., 1983— . Vol. charity orgns., Cherry Hill, 1976— ; leader Girl Scouts U.S.A., Cherry Hill, 1974-75; pres., founder Deborah Hosp. Charity chpt., Bklyn., 1962-63. Mem. Nat. Home Fashion League, Nat. Assn. Female Execs., South Jersey Builders League. Democrat. Jewish. Avocations: travel; yoga; photography; art. Home and Office: 41 Strathmore Dr Cherry Hill NJ 08003-1720

NEWMARK, RICHARD ALAN, chemist; b. Urbana, Ill., Nov. 11, 1940; s. Nathan M. and Anne Mae (Cohen) N.; m. Joan Friedman, July 4, 1965; children: David, Merel. AB, Harvard Coll., 1961; PhD, U. Calif., Berkeley, 1964. Postgrad. fellow Mass. Inst. Tech., Cambridge, 1964-66; asst. prof. U. Colo., Boulder, 1966-69; rsch. chemist 3M, St. Paul, 1969-72, rsch. specialist, 1972-76, sr. rsch. specialist, 1976-81, staff scientist, 1981-92, corp. scientist, 1992—2001; ret., 2002—. Councilor Minn. section Am. Chem. Soc., Washington, 1992-94. Contbr. articles to profl. jours. Chair Dist. 1 Community Coun., St. Paul, 1984-88; co-chair St. Paul Sch. Bd. Commn. of Gifted and Talented, 1986-88. Recipient award 3M Carlton Soc., 1993, Minn. award Am. Chem. Soc., 2000. Mem. Phi Beta Kappa, Sigma Xi. Jewish. Avocations: skiing, bicycling. Office: 3M 201-bs 05 Saint Paul MN 55144-0001

NEWMEYER, FREDERICK JARET, linguist, educator; b. Phila., Jan. 30, 1944; s. Alvin S. and Fritzie B. (Nisenson) N.; m. Carolyn V. Platt, Apr. 28, 1968 (div. 1974); m. Marilyn M. Goebel, Dec. 25, 1993. BA, U. Rochester, 1965, MA, 1967; PhD, U. Ill., 1969. Asst. prof. linguistics U. Wash., Seattle, 1969-75, assoc. prof., 1975-81, prof., 1981—, chair, 1990-2000. Vis. prof. U. London, 1979, Cornell U., 1981, U. Md., 1982, UCLA, 1982-83, La Trobe U., Australia, 1987. Author: English Aspectual Verbs, 1975, Linguistic Theory in America, 1980, Grammatical Theory, 1983, Politics of Linguistics, 1986, Generative Linguistics, 1995, Language Form and Language Function, 1998; editor: Linguistics: The Cambridge Survey, 1988, Natural Language and Linguistic Theory, 1987—; assoc. editor: Language, 1980-85. NEH fellow, 1973-74. Mem. Linguistic Soc. Am. (sec.-treas. 1989-94, v.p. 2001, pres. 2002). Avocations: gardening. Home: 4621 NE 107th St Seattle WA 98125-6947 Office: U Wash Dept Linguistics Seattle WA 98195-4340

NEWMILLER, WILLIAM ERNEST, English educator; b. Chgo., Dec. 6, 1947; s. Walter George and Gladys Marie (Anderson) N.; m. Gloria Louise Freehling, June 24, 1967; children: Tracy Lippard, Todd Newmiller, Joel Newmiller. BA, Mich. State U., 1969; MA, U. Mich., 1977; BS, Chapman U., 1993. Tchr. Reeths-Puffer H.S., Muskegon, Mich., 1969-70; commd. 2d lt. USAF, 1970, advanced through grades to lt. col., 1987; ret., 1993; unit chief FBI, Washington, 1993-94; prof. English, USAF Acad., Colorado Springs, 1994—. Bd. dirs. Bioconnect, Inc., 1998—. Editor electronic pub. War, Lit. and the Arts, 1998—. Mem. bd. edn. St. Paul Sch., Wichita Falls, Tex., 1975-76, Redeemer Luth. Sch., Colorado Springs, 1988-92, Amazing Grace Luth. Sch., Seattle, 1982-84. Mem. Alliance for Computers and Writing. Avocations: hiking. Home: 7645 Hickorywood Dr Colorado Springs CO 80920-6617 Office: USAF Acad Dept English 2354 Fairchild Dr Ste 6d35 U S A F Academy CO 80840-6299 E-mail: bill@newmiller.com.

NEWPORT, L. JOAN, clinical social worker, retired psychotherapist; b. Newkirk, Okla., July 5, 1932; d. Crawford Earl and Lillian Pearl (Peden) Irvine; m. Don E. Newport, July 9, 1954 (div. 1971, dec. 1999); children: Alan Keith, Lili Kim. BA cum laude, Wichita State U., 1955; MSW, U. Okla., 1977. Bd. cert. diplomate in clin. social work Acad. Cert. Social Workers; lic. social worker, Okla. Dir. children's work Wesley United Meth. Ch., Oklahoma City, 1969-71; social worker Dept. Human Svcs., Newkirk, Okla., 1972-77; in-sch. suspension counselor Kay County Youth Svcs., Ponca City, 1977; med. social worker St. Joseph Med. Ctr., 1977-78, dir. social work, 1978-83; pvt. practice, 1979-97; med. social worker Healthcare Svcs., 1983-84; pvt. practice home studies, cons., supervision, Newkirk, 1997—. Cons. Blackwell, Perry, Pawhuska, O'Keene Hosps., 1978-85; cons. social work Bass Meml. Hosp., Enid, Okla., 1985; sponsor, organizer Kay County Parents Anonymous, Ponca City, 1976-83; vice chair Okla. State Bd. Lic. Social Workers, Oklahoma City, 1988-90; presentor, lectr. in field; supr. students Okla. U. Sch. Social Work, Okla. State U., No. Okla. Coll., Okla. Christian Coll., 1977-85; supr. for clin. social workers working toward lic. in Okla., 1985—. Mem. Okla. Women's Network, 1989-96; mem. adv. bd. Displaced Homemakers, Ponca City, 1985-89; mem. adv. bd. Kay County Home Health, 1979-83, chair, 1979-81; Sunday sch. tchr. Newkirk United Meth. Ch.; mem. Newkirk Main St., 1999-2000. Named Hon. State Life Mem. Burbank PTA, Oklahoma City, 1971; scholar Wichita (Kans.) Press and Radio Women, 1953, Conoco, Inc., Houston, 1951-54. Mem. NASW (Okla. del. Del. Assembly Washington 1987, chmn. vendorship com. 1985-87, pres. Okla. chpt. 1988-90, Social Worker of Yr. 1987), Child Abuse Prevention Task Force (pres. dist. 17 1986-88, mem. grant evaluation com. 1986-96), Zeta Phi Eta. Democrat. Methodist. Home: 109 N Walnut Ave Newkirk OK 74647-2036 Office: PO Box 74 Newkirk OK 74647-0074

NEWSOM, BARRY DOUGLAS, cardiovascular and thoracic surgeon; b. Tucson, Sept. 27, 1953; s. Douglas Lee and Annie Laura (Tribble) N.; m. Nancy Macfarlan Irby, Feb. 11, 1978; children: Lori Anne, Julia Caroline, Ellen Brown, Jonathan David. MD, U. Miss., Jackson, 1978. Diplomate Am. Bd. Surgery, Am. Bd. Thoracic Surgery. Intern in gen. surgery U. Miss., 1978-79, resident in gen. surgery, 1979-83, fellow in vascular surgery, 1983-84, resident thoracic surgery, 1984-86; pvt. practice, Tuscaloosa, Ala., 1986—. Contbr. articles to profl. jours. Fellow ACS; mem. AMA, Soc. Thoracic Surgeons, So. Thoracic Surg. Assn., Alpha Omega Alpha. Avocations: radiocontrol model aircraft, violin. Office: Thoracic and Cv Assocs 701 University Blvd E Tuscaloosa AL 35401-2086

NEWSOM, CAROLYN CARDALL, management consultant; b. South Weymouth, Mass., Feb. 27, 1941; d. Alfred James and Bertha Virginia (Roy) Cardall; m. John Harlan Newsom, Feb. 4, 1967; children: John Cardall, James Harlan. AB, Brown U., 1962; MBA, Wharton Sch., 1978; PhD, U. Pa., 1985. Systems engr. IBM, Seattle, 1964-70, Newsom S.E. Services, Seattle, 1970-76; instr. U. Pa. Wharton Sch., Phila., 1978-81; v.p., prin. sr. cons. PA Cons. Group, Princeton, N.J., 1981-88; pres. Newsom Assocs., Yardley, Pa., 1988; ptnr. Bus. Strategy Implementation, Princeton, N.J., 1989-90; pres. Strategy Implementation Solutions, Yardley, Pa., 1990—. Examiner, sr. examiner, instr. N.J. Gov.'s Performance Excellence Award, 1993-2002. Bd. dirs. Chandler Hall, 1980-87; trustee St. Mary Hosp., Langhorne, Pa., 1986-94; sec. bd. dirs. Gordonstown Am. Found., 1999—. Mem. Acad. Mgmt., Am. Soc. for Quality, Brown Alumni Assn. (pres.-elect 1993-95, pres. 1995-97), Quality N.J. (vice chair 1998-99). Office: Strategy Implementation Solutions 1588 Woodside Rd Yardley PA 19067-2611

NEWSOM, DAVID DUNLOP, foreign service officer, educator; b. Richmond, Calif., Jan. 6, 1918; s. Fred Stoddard and Ivy Elizabeth (Dunlop) N.; m. Jean Frances Craig, Nov. 17, 1942; children: John, Daniel, Nancy, David, Catherine. AB, U. Calif., 1938; MS, Columbia U., 1940; LLD, U. Pacific, 1979. Pulitzer traveling scholar, 1940-41; pub. Walnut Creek (Calif.) Courier-Jour., 1946-47; 3d sec., info. officer Am. embassy, Karachi, Pakistan, 1948-50; 2d sec., vice consul Oslo, 1950-51; pub. affairs officer Baghdad, Iraq, 1952-55; officer-in-charge Arabian peninsula affairs Dept. State, Washington, 1955-59; with Nat. War Coll., 1959-60; 1st sec. Am. embassy, London, 1960-62; dep. dir. Office No. African Affairs, Dept. State, Washington, 1962-63, dir., 1963-65; U.S. ambassador Libya, 1965-69; asst. sec. state for African affairs, 1969-74; U.S. ambassador Indonesia, 1974-77, Philippines, 1977-78; under-sec. state of polit. affairs Washington, 1978-81; dir. Inst. Study of Diplomacy, Sch. Fgn. Svc., Georgetown U., 1981-90, Marshall Coyne rsch. prof. diplomacy, 1989-91; interim dean Sch. Fgn. Svc. Georgetown U., 1995-96; Cumming Meml. prof. internat. rels. U. Va., 1991-98; spl. adviser U.S. del. UN Gen. Assembly, 1972, 78, 79, 80. Sr. fellow The Miller Ctr., U. Va., 1999-2001; mem. com. on sci., tech. and health aspects of fgn. policy Nat. Rsch. Coun., 1999. Served to lt. USNR, 1942-46. Recipient Commendable Service award USIS, 1955; Dept. State Meritorious Service award, 1958; Nat. Civil Service League award, 1972; Rockefeller Pub. Service award, 1973; Lifetime award Am. Fgn. Svc. Assn., 2000. Mem. U.S. Fgn. Svc. Assn., Coun. Fgn. Rels., Cosmos Club. Presbyterian. Home: 2409 Angus Rd Charlottesville VA 22901-2631

NEWSOM, GERALD HIGLEY, astronomy educator; b. Albuquerque, Feb. 11, 1939; s. Carroll Vincent and Frances Jeanne (Higley) N.; m. Ann Catherine Bricker, June 17, 1972; children: Christine Ann, Elizabeth Ann. BA, U. Mich., 1961; MA, Harvard U., 1963, PhD, 1968. Research asst. McMath-Hulbert Obs., Pontiac, Mich., summers 1959, 61; research asst. astronomy dept. U. Mich., Ann Arbor, 1959-61; research asst. Shock Tube Lab. Harvard U., Cambridge, Mass., 1962, 64-68; research asst. dept. physics Imperial Coll., London, 1968-69; asst. prof. astronomy Ohio State U., Columbus, 1969-73, assoc. prof., 1973-82, prof., 1982—, acting chmn. dept. astronomy, 1991-93, vice chmn. dept. astronomy, 1993—, acting asst. dean, 1985-86; sr. post-doctoral research asst. Physikalisches Institut, Bonn, Fed. Republic of Germany, 1978. Author: Astronomy, 1976, Exploring the Universe, 1979; contbr. articles to profl. and scholarly jours. Fellow Woodrow Wilson Found., 1961-62, NSF, 1961-63; grantee Noble Found., 1961-64. Mem. Internat. Astron. Union, Am. Astron. Soc. Home: 46 W Weisheimer Rd Columbus OH 43214-2545 Office: Ohio State U Dept Astronomy 140 W 18th Ave Columbus OH 43210-1173

NEWSOM, HOLLY ANN, management consultant; b. Plattsburgh, N.Y., Mar. 27, 1962; BBA in Acctg., Tex. Christian U., 1984, MBA in Fin., 1990. CPA, Tex. Auditor Coopers & Lybrand, Ft. Worth, 1984-86; sr. auditor McCaslin Wright & Greenwood, 1986-88; sr. cons. Andersen Consulting, Dallas, 1990-93; prin. Booz Allen & Hamilton, 1993—. Mem. AICPA, Tex. Soc. CPAs. Avocations: reading, biking, horseback riding, piano. Office: Booz Allen and Hamilton 901 Main St Ste 6500 Dallas TX 75202-8298 Fax: 214-712-6660.

NEWSOM, JAMES THOMAS, lawyer; b. Carrollton, Mo., Oct. 6, 1944; s. Thomas Edward and Hazel Love (Mitchell) N.; m. Sherry Elaine Retzloff, Aug. 9, 1986; stepchildren: Benjamin A. Bawden, Holly K. Bawden. AB, U. Mo., 1966, JD, 1968. Bar: Mo. 1968, U.S. Supreme Ct. 1971. Assoc. Shook, Hardy & Bacon, London and Kansas City, Mo., 1972, ptnr., 1976—. Mem. Mo. Law Rev., 1966-68. Lt. comdr. JAGC, USNR, 1968-72. Mem. ABA, Kansas City Met. Bar Assn., U. Mo. Law Sch. Law Soc., U. Mo. Jefferson Club, Order of Coif, Perry (Kans.) Yacht Club, Stone Horse Yacht Club (Harwich Port, Mass.). Avocations: skiing, sailing, car racing. Office: Shook Hardy & Bacon One Kansas City Pl 1200 Main St Ste 3100 Kansas City MO 64105-2139 E-mail: jnewsom@shb.com.

NEWSOM, JOHN HARLAN, family physician; b. Worland, Wyo., May 6, 1940; s. John Cecil and Arlene Zelda (Finch) N.; m. Carolyn Cardall, Feb. 4, 1967; children: John Cardall, James Harlan. BS, U.S. Naval Acad., 1963; MD, U. Wash., 1971. Diplomate Am. Bd. Family Practice. Intern Doctors Hosp., Seattle, 1971-72; physician in pvt. practice, Newport, Oreg., 1972-73; physician Group Health, Seattle, 1973-74; physician in solo pvt. practice, Yardley, Pa., 1974—; mem. med. staff St. Mary Med. Ctr., 1974—, chmn. family practice dept., 1978-80, pres. med. staff, 1980-81, v.p. med. affairs, 1983-85, 99—. Trustee St. Mary Hosp., Langhorne, Pa., 1981-83; bd. dirs. Pennswood Village, Newtown, Pa., 1978-81; clin. asst. prof. Temple U. Sch. Medicine, 1978-91; clin. instr. Pa. State Med. Sch., 2000-01. Contbr. articles to profl. jours. Pres. Parents at Lawrenceville, N.J., 1989-90. Lt. USN, 1963-67. Decorated Bronze Star. Fellow Am. Acad. Family Physicians; mem. U. Washington Alumni Assn. (pres. Del. Valley chpt. 1989-90), Pa. Med. Soc. (del. 1985), Bucks County Med. Soc. (pres. 1985). Office: 1588 Woodside Rd Yardley PA 19067-2611

NEWSOM, MELVIN MAX, retired research company executive; b. El Paso, Tex., Dec. 27, 1931; s. Melvin William and Dorthy Maxine (Kinnison) N.; m. Rose Marie Neill, June 5, 1953; children— Terri Laine, Cherri Leigh, Michael Dirk, Thomas Cody. BS in Elec. Engring, Tex. A. and M. U., 1955, MS in Elec. Engring. (Tex. Power & Light fellow), 1956. Mem. tech. staff Sandia Lab., Albuquerque, 1956—, sect. supr., 1961-64, div. supr., 1964-77, dept. mgr., 1977-92, dir. Ctr. for Applied Def. Tech., 1992-94. Cons. Dept. Energy; mem. U.S. group on petroleum tech. Joint U.S./USSR Energy Program; participant several programs Nat. Acad. Engring. Contbr. numerous articles to profl. jours. Dist. chmn. Rep. Party, 1960-61, asst., 1963-64; pres. Scenic Hills Cmty. Assn., 2000—. With USN, 1951-53. Decorated Am. Spirit Honor medal; Dept. Energy grantee. Mem. Am. Inst. Mining Engrs., Am. Rose Soc., Tau Beta Pi, Eta Kappa Nu. Clubs: Coronado (chmn. bd. 1965-66, 69-70, 73-74, 76-79, dir.). Presbyterian. Achievements include research in improved drilling tech. for petroleum, geothermal and sci. drilling, and on high temperature well logging. Home: 3628 Scenic Dr Cibolo TX 78108-2227 E-mail: mnewsom53@aol.com.

NEWSOME, ELIZABETH ANN, art historian, educator; b. Athens, Ga., Sept. 10, 1960; d. George Lane Jr. and Martha Newsome. BFA, U. Ga., 1982; MA, U. Tex., 1985, PhD, 1991. Prof. U. Wis., Eau Claire, 1992—96, U. Calif., San Diego, 1996—. Author: Trees of Paradise and Pillars of the World, 2001. Fellow rsch., Dumbarton Oaks Rsch Libr., Washington, 1995, Hellman Found., 1999, NEH, 2001. Mem.: Soc. Am. Archaeology, Am. Anthropol. Assn., Coll. Art Assn. Office: U Calif-San Diego 9500 Gilman Dr La Jolla CA 92093-0084

NEWSOME, HEBER H. academic administrator; Dean Va. Commonwealth U. Med. Coll., 2000—. Office: Deans Office PO Box 980565 Sanger Hall Richmond VA 23298*

NEWSOME, JAMES E. federal agency administrator; m. Margaret Pomeroy. BS in Econ., U. Fla., 1982; MS in Agrl., Miss. State U., 1985. Commr. U.S. Commodity Futures Trading Commn., Washington, 1998-01; chmn. Commodity Futures Trading Comn., 2001—. Exec. v.p. Miss. Cattlemen's Assn. and Beef Coun., chmn. Miss. Agribus. Coun., mem. Gov's. Task Force on Future Miss. Agrl., pres. Fla. Future Farmers Am., pres. U. Fla. Agrl. Coun. Mem. Assn. Miss. Agrl. Orgns. (pres.). Office: Commodity Futures Trading Comn The Comn 3 Lafayette Centre 1155 21st St NW Washington DC 20581 Office Fax: 202-418-5533.*

NEWSOME, KATHY NOEL, accountant; b. Lexington Park, Md., Mar. 29, 1941; d. William Clement Sr. and Myrtle Sarah (Harris) Butler; m. Walter Burch Noel Jr., July 13, 1957 (div.); 1 child, Walter B. Noel III; m. Billy Gene Newsome, Oct. 30, 1966 (div.); 1 child, Adrienne Y. BS in Acctg. magna cum laude, Meyers Coll., 1984. Cert. govt. fin. mgr., cert. dept. of def. logistics auditor. Agt. IRS, 1984-85; auditor Navy Internal Rev., Patuxent River, Md., 1985-87, AF Audit Agy., Wright-Patterson AFB, Ohio, 1987-88; fin. ops. supr. 375 Combat-Support Group, Scott AFB, Ill., 1988-90; NAF fin. mgmt. officer AFE 7276 AB6, Crete, Greece, 1990-92; auditor AF Audit Agy., Eglin AFB, Fla., 1992-94, audit mgr. Wright Patterson AFB, 1994—. Mem. Am. Soc. Mil. Contrs., Federally Employed Women. Democrat. Avocations: music, movies, games, exercise, fashion. Office: Air Force Audit Agy 4170 Hebble Creek Rd Ste 1 Wright Patterson AFB OH 45433-5653

NEWSOME, MOSES, social work educator; b. Charleston, W.Va., Sept. 6, 1944; s. Moses and Ruth Newsome; m. Barbara Love; children: Ayanna, Mariana. BA in Sociology and Pschology, U. Toledo, 1966; MS in Group Work and Comty. Orgn., U. Mich., 1970; PhD in Social Welfare Policy, U. Wis., 1976. Program cons. Dane County Spl. Planning Agy., Madison, Wis., 1972-73; asst. prof. Howard U., Washington, 1973-78, assoc. prof., asst. dir., 1978-84, asst. dean, dir DSW program, 1980-84; dean Norfolk (Va.) State U., 1984-99; vis. prof. Jackson (Miss.) State U., 2000, Rutgers U., N.J., 2000-01; v.p. rsch., planning, cmty. and econ. devel. Miss. Valley State U., 2001—. Bd. dirs. Child Abuse Ctr., Hampton Rds., Norfolk, 1984—, United Way S. Hampton Rds., Norfolk, 1989—, Child and Family Svcs., Norfolk, 1993—; mem. adv. bd. Ea. Va. Med. Coll. Area Health Ednl. Ctr., Norfolk, 1984—. Co-author: (book) Human Behavior Social Environment, 1998; contbr. articles to Jour. of Baccalaureate Social Work, 1995, Social Work Edn. Reporter, 1997, 98. Bd. dirs. Norfolk Planning Coun., 1988—; state liaison Nat. Ctr. for Social Policy and Practice, Washington, 1993-95; pres. Coun. on Social Work Edn., 1995-98. Named Disting. Scholar Social Work, Albany (Ga.) State Coll., 1995; recipient Outstanding Social Work Edn. award, Va. Social Work Edn. Consortium, Hampton, Va., 1996; invited Commencement Speaker, Va. Commonwealth U., Richmond, 1997, Catholic U., 1998, Columbia U., 1998. Mem.: Leflore County C. of C. Avocations: tennis, golf, jogging, karate. Home: PO Box 924 Itta Bena MS 38941-0924

NEWSOME, RANDALL JACKSON, judge; b. Dayton, Ohio, July 13, 1950; s. Harold I. and Sultana S. (Stony) N. BA summa cum laude, Boston U., 1972; JD, U. Cin., 1975. Bar: Ohio 1975, U.S. Dist. Ct. (so. dist.) Ohio 1977, U.S. Ct. Appeals (6th cir.) 1979, U.S. Supreme Ct. 1981. Law clk. to chief judge U.S. Dist. Ct. (so. dist.) Ohio, 1975-77; assoc. Dinsmore & Shohl, Cin., 1978-82; judge U.S. Bankruptcy Ct. (so. dist.) Ohio, 1982-88, U.S. Bankruptcy Ct. (no. dist.) Calif., Oakland, 1988—. Faculty mem. Fed. Jud. Ctr., ALI-ABA, 1987—; mem. Nat. Conf. of Bankruptcy Judges, 1983—, mem. bd. govs., 1987-88, pres., 1998-99. Contbg. author: Chapter 11 Theory and Practice, 1994—, Collier on Bankruptcy, 1997—. Fellow Am. Coll. Bankruptcy; mem. Am. Law Inst., Phi Beta Kappa. Democrat. Office: US Bankruptcy Ct PO Box 2070 Oakland CA 94604-2070

NEWSOME, VERONICA KIM, rheumatologist; b. June 17, 1969; BS, Walsh Coll., 1991; DO, Ohio U., 1995. Diplomate Am. Bd. Internal Medicine, Am. Bd. Rheumatology. Intern Grandview Hosp./Ohio U. Coll. Osteo. Medicine, Dayton, 1995-96, resident in internal medicine, 1996-99; rheumatology Ind. U. Sch. Medicine, Indpls., 1999-2001. Co-chief internal medicine resident Grandview Hosp., 1998-99, treas. internal medicine residents, 1997-99; rep. Ctrs. for Osteo. Regional Edn., Ohio, 1997-99. Home: 26 Bluegrass Rd Pataskala OH 43062-7851 Office: 2131 Beacon Hill Rd Ste 180 Columbus OH 43228

NEWTH, REBECCA, writer; b. Lansing, Mich., Sept. 21, 1940; d. William Arthur Newth and Catherine Lois Messenger; m. John Arthur Harrison, Dec. 16, 1961; children: John William, Olivia Catherine. BA, Mich. State U., 1962; MA, U. Ark., 1988. Libr. tech. Harvard Sch. Edn., Cambridge, 1962-65; instr. creative writing Guilford (Conn.) Handicraft Ctr., 1971-75; instr. creative writing continuing edn. U. Ark., Fayetteville, 1984-85, prodr. NPR Radio, 1990-98; founder, dir. Will Hall, Inc., 1994—. Assoc. artist, writer Atlantic Ctr. Arts, New Smyrna Beach, Fla., 1988; guest instr. Patagonia (Ariz.) Arts Assn., 2001. Author: (poems) Finding the Lamb, 1983, Great North Woods, 1994; (prose) Milk Horses, A Memoir, 1998; (children's book) Antonia Quail, 2000. Bd. dirs., treas. Fayetteville Sister Cities, Inc., 1999—. Recipient Lit. Anthology prize Nat. Endowment Arts, 1971; fellow Ark. Arts Coun., 2000. Office: 611 Oliver Ave Fayetteville AR 72701

NEWTON, ALEXANDER WORTHY, lawyer; b. Birmingham, Ala., June 19, 1930; s. Jeff H. and Annis Lillian (Kelly) N.; m. Sue Aldridge, Dec. 22, 1952; children: Lamar Aldridge Newton, Kelly McClure Newton Hammond, Jane Worthy Newton, Robins Jeffry Newton. BS, U. Ala., 1952, JD, 1957. Bar: Ala. 1957. Pvt. practice law, Birmingham; assoc. Hare, Wynn & Newell, 1957; ptnr. Hare, Wynn, Newell & Newton, 1961—. Del. U.S. Ct. Appeals (11th cir.) Jud. Conf., 1988, 89, 90, 91; mem. Jefferson County Jud. Nominating Com., 1983-89; mem. Birmingham Airport Authority, 1991—; founding dir. First Comm. Bank. Co-author: (with others) Federal Appellate Procedure, 11th Circuit, 1996. Vice chmn. Birmingham Racing Commn., 1984-87; v.p. U. Ala. Law Sch. Found., 1978-79, pres., 1980-82, exec. com., 1987—; mem. Leadership Ala. Class IV; trustee Ala. Trust Fund; bd. dirs. St. Vincent Hosp. Found. Capt. inf. U.S. Army, 1952-54. Recipient Disting. Alumnus award Farrah Law Soc. U. Ala., 1982, Sam W. Pipes Disting. Alumnus award 1982. Fellow Am. Coll. Trial Lawyers (state chmn. 1983-84, regents' nominatin com. 1984-85), Internat. Soc. Barristers (bd. dirs. 1974-75, sec.-treas. 1976-77, v.p. 1977-78, pres. 1979-80), Internat. Acad. Trial Lawyers (bd. dirs. 1998—); mem. ABA, ATLA, Am. Bar Found., Ala. State Bar (chmn. practices and procedures subsect. 1965, governance com. and pres.'s task force 1984-86, pres.'s com. 1987-88), Birmingham Bar Assn. (exec. com. 1967), Ala. Trial Lawyers Assn. (sec.-treas. 1958-65), Am. Judicature Soc., 11th Cir. His. Soc. (trustee 1988—), Sigma Chi. Clubs: Shoal Creek, Birmingham Country (Birmingham); Capital City (Atlanta); Garden of the God (Colorado Springs, Colo.); University Club (New York). Democrat. Presbyterian. Home: 2837 Canoe Brook Ln Birmingham AL 35243-5908 Office: Hare Wynn Newell & Newton 800 Massey Bldg 2025 3d Ave N Birmingham AL 35203-3330

NEWTON, BALDWIN CHARLES, artist, educator; b. Lucknow, India, Jan. 24, 1936; came to U.S., 1986; s. Harry Charles and Kathren Georgina (Gardner) N.; m. Shirley Hatfield (dec. Sept. 23, 1992); children: Beverly, Richard, Michelle, Dawn. Diploma in fine arts, Coll. Arts, India, 1962; BA, Meerut U., India, 1971. Art tchr. Woodstock Sch., Mussoorie, India, 1962; art tchr. Mil. Sch., Tilya Dam, India, 1963-64, Wynberg Allen Sch., India, 1965-74, Mt. Hermon Coll., Darjeeling, India, 1977-78, Barnes Sch., Develali, India, 1978-86, Sr. Cityzen, Batavia, Ohio, 1993, New Creative Enterprice, Milford, 1999—2002. One-man show at Carnegie Visual Art Ctr., Ky., 1999 (award), Exposition of 20th Century Art Consortium, 2000; works include Roller Coaster, a painting for Louisville Art Assn., 1996 (merit award 1997), Hidden Odyssey, a painting for Arts Consortium, 1996 (merit award 1996), Master Works 53, a painting for Cin. Art Club, 1995 (1st pl. award 1995). Recipient Manhattan Internat. award of excellence, 1995, honorable mention Can. Water Color Soc., Courtnay, B.C., 1996, Art Crowd Internat. award, 2001, Norman Kohlhepp award, 2001. Mem. Umoja. Home: 320 Hanna Ave Bldg 2 Apt 11 Loveland OH 45140-3074 E-mail: bnewton6@earthlink.net.

NEWTON, BARBARA BENEDETTI, artist, educator, writer; b. Puyallup, Wash., Oct. 25, 1943; d. Andrew Joseph and Ethel Vivian (Heimsoth) Benedetti; m. Charles William Iles, Jr., June 26, 1965 (div. 1983); children: Tobin William Iles, Andrea Iles Foster; m. Jay Newton, Apr. 25, 1987. Grad., Burnley Art Sch., Seattle, 1966. Owner Bina Designs, Renton, Wash., 1988—. Instr., owner Colored Pencil Workshops, Renton, Wash., 1993—. Editor Colored Pencil Soc. Am. DC207 newsletter, 1991-2000, Women Painters of Washington newsletter, 1998—; artwork published in all edits. of: Best of Colored Pencil series (5 books), Creative Colored Pencil, 1996, The Best of Flower Painting, I and II, 1997, 99, Exploring Colored Pencil, 1999; co-author: Colored Pencil Solution Book, 2000; contbr. articles to Artist's Mag., Am. Artist Mag., Internat. Artist Mag.; one-woman shows include Renton (Wash.) Arts Commn. Closing Artist, 1995, Kent Arts Commn. Opening Artist, 1995, PACCAR Inc., Bellevue, Wash., 1994, Auburn Arts Commn. Visual Arts Exhbn., Wash., 1993; exhibited in group shows at Catharine Lorillard Wolfe Art Club, N.Y.C., 1996, Bellevue Art Mus., 1996, Realism, 1996-98, Parkersburg (W.Va.) Art Ctr., 1996, Oreg. State U., 1996, Internat. Colored Pencil Exhbn., Oreg., 1994, Ohio, 1995, Calif., 1996, Ill., 1997, Washington, 1998, Mich., 2000, Gango Gallery, Portland, 1994-96, Sidney Gallery, Port Orchard, Wash., 1996, Sitka Art Invitational, Portland, 1996, 97, 98, 99, 2000, Sidney Gallery, Port Orchard, 1995, Artsplash, Redmond, Wash., 1995—, Eastside Assn. Fine Arts, 1994-95, 97, 98, Western Wash. State Fair Art Show, 1992. Recipient Ridgewood Art Inst. award, 1996, Best of Show award Eastside Assn. Fine arts, 1994-95. Colored Pencil Soc. Am. (charter mem. 1990, signature mem., 1996, nat. membership dir. 1993-94, pres. 1994-95, advisor to bd. 1995-96), Catherine Lorillard Wolfe Art Club, Allied Artists of Am. (assoc.), Eastside Assn. Fine Arts, Women Painters of Wash. E-mail: bbnewton@mindspring.com.

NEWTON, DALE ALAN, pediatrician, educator; b. Oct. 25, 1946; BS, N.C. State U., 1969; MD, U. N.C., 1973. Intern, resident N.C. Meml. Hosp., Chapel Hill, N.C., 1973-77; head sect. acad. gen. pediats. East Carolina U. Sch. Medicine, Greenville, prof. pediats., adj. assoc. prof. medicine, dir. combined internal medicine/pediats. residency program. Editor: Primary Care Clinics, 1996. Mem. AMA, APA, N.C. Med. Soc., N.C. Pediat. Soc., Soc. Gen. Internal Medicine, So. Soc. Pediat. Rsch., Am. Acad. Pediat., Med./Pediat. Dirs. Assn. Office: East Carolina U Sch Medicine Dept Pediatrics 3E139 Brody Med Sci Bldg Greenville NC 27858 E-mail: newtond@mail.edu.edu.

NEWTON, DARRELL MOTTLEY, communication educator; b. Memphis, Apr. 23, 1954; s. Charles and Grace Marie (Newton). MA in English, U Wis. Milwaukee, 1981; MA in Comm., U Wis. Madison, 1995; PhD, U. Wis. Madison, 2002. Customer svc. mgr. Atlanta Blueprint, 1986-90; news writer WITI TV, Milwaukee, 1990-91; resident dir. U. Wis., Platteville, 1995-96; lectr. Milwaukee Tech. Coll., Milwaukee, 1993-95, Madison Tech. Coll., 1993-96, U. Wis., Madison, 1998-99, Whitewater, 1991—. Cons. U. Wis. Sys., Madison, Multicultural Ctr. Mem. Internat. Commn. Assn., Nat. Comm. Assn., Pub. Relations Soc. Am., 100 Black Men Madison, 100 Milwaukee Men

Milwaukee, Alpha Phi Alpha. Avocations: creative writing, photography, film production, videography. Office: U Wis 450 Heide Hall Whitewater WI 53190 Home: 610 59th St Kenosha WI 53140-4121 E-mail: newtond@mail.uww.edu.

NEWTON, DAVID TRAVIS, alcohol/drug abuse services professional; b. Atlanta, Aug. 14, 1969; s. Alan Blair and Elizabeth (McCannon) N. BS, Ga. State U., Atlanta, 1991; MA, Pepperdine U., L.A., 1995. Lic. profl. counselor, Ga.; cert. HIV counselor Ga. Dept. Human Resources; cert counselor Nat. Bd. Cert. Counselors. Case mgr. HIV AID Atlanta, 1991-93; counseling intern HIV and substance abuse AIDS Project L.A., 1994-95; counselor young adult HIV and addictions Walden Ho., San Francisco, 1995-96; clin. coord. family assessment CHRIS Homes, Atlanta, 1997-98; coord. addictions program DeKalb Addiction Clinic, 1998—. Youth advocate GLBT Youth Pride, Inc., Atlanta, 1997—. Mem. Psi Chi. Office: DeKalb Addiction Clinic 455 Winn Way Decatur GA 30030 E-mail: DavidN@dekcsb.org.

NEWTON, DON ALLEN, real estate broker, economic development consultant; b. Laurel, Miss., Oct. 19, 1934; s. Wilfred L. and Mary (McMullan) N.; m. Coleta Farrell, Oct. 11, 1958; children: Don Jr., Coleta Midge Rast. AA, Meridian C.C., 1954; BA in Journalism, U. Ala., 1956; postgrad. assn. mgmt., U. N.C.; postgrad. econ. devel., U. Okla. Asst. mgr. Meridian C. of C., Miss., 1956; mgr. Winston County C. of C., Louisville, 1960-61; asst. dir. Delta Council Indsl. and Community Devel. Bd., Stoneville, 1961-62; dir. Delta Coun. Indsl. and Cmty. Devel. Bd., 1963-70; exec. v.p. Met. Devel. Bd., Birmingham, Ala., 1970-74, Birmingham Area C. of C., 1974—99; pres. Birmingham Area C. of C. Found., Inc., 1988-99; ret., 1999; pres. Devel. Assocs. Real Estate, Econ. Devel. and Pub. Cons., 1999—. Pub. Birmingham Mag., Birmingham Bus. Mag., ret. 1999. Contbr. articles to profl. jours., newspapers. Former appointee Ala. Export Coun.; bd. dirs. Birmingham Met. Devel. Bd., Ala. Sports Found., Birmingham Festival Arts. Lt. USNR, 1957-60. Named Ala. Mktg. Man of Yr., 1972. Mem. Ala. C. of C. Execs., Econ. Devel. Assn. Ala., Am. C. of C. Execs., U. Ala. Commerce Execs. Soc., Sigma Chi. Home: 2541 Canterbury Rd Birmingham AL 35223-1909 Office: Development Assocs PO Box 530093 Birmingham AL 35253-0093

NEWTON, FRANK GEORGE, bank executive; b. Bklyn., Oct. 2, 1936; s. Anthony and Hedwig (Borak) N.; m. Mary Soto Newton, Apr. 20, 1963; children: Kevin Francis, Andrew Francis. BS, CCNY, 1958; MA, Alexander Hamilton Inst., N.Y.C., 1960. V.p., sec. Long Island City Savings Bank, N.Y.C., 1960-75; exec. v.p. Bay Ridge Savings Bank, Bklyn., 1975-81; pvt. investor; owner Gables Inn. Bd. incorporators Lee Bank, Mass., 1999—; bd. regents Long Island Coll. Hosp., Bklyn., 1977-80; pres. Queens County Bankers, N.Y., 1972. Pres. Lenox C. of C., Mass., 1990-95; treas. Lenox Rep. Party, Mass., 1995-2000. With U.S. Army, 1959-61. Mem. Lenox Club, Montauk Club. Roman Catholic. Avocation: collecting art and music. Home: 17 Main St Lenox MA 01240 Office: The Gables Inn 81 Walker St Lenox MA 01240

NEWTON, GLORIA JONES, accountant, feminist activist; b. Gary, Tex., Feb. 3, 1960; d. Jessie Wyatt and Vera Mae (Jackson) Jones; m. Larry Donell Newton, Aug. 20, 1979 (div. Oct. 1988); 1 child, Jasmine Tiffany. Student, Kilgore (Tex.) Jr. Coll., 1978-79; BBA, Jarvis Christian Coll., 1982; postgrad., U. Houston, 1983-85. Lic. ins. agt., Tex. Database rschr. GTE, Baytown, Tex., summer 1981; clerical asst. Social Security Adminstrn., Tyler, summer 1982; sales mgr. Revelation Shoes, Baytown, 1982; warehouse acct. Universal Terminal Warehouse, Houston, 1982-83; sr. acct. Bayer, 1984-90, fixed asset acct., 1990-95. Author: (autobiography) In My Father's House. Mem. Tex. Dem. Caucus, Houston, 1995; vol., mem. spkr.'s bur., hotline advocate Houston Area Women Ctr., 1994—; lobbyist Planned Parenthood; pres., chmn. Jr. Achievement, Tex., 1993. Mem. NOW (activist 1994—). Democrat. Avocations: traveling, reading, singing, writing, gardening. Home: PO Box 300812 Houston TX 77230-0812

NEWTON, GWENDOLYN STEWART, elementary school educator; b. Opelika, Ala., Dec. 6, 1946; d. William Thomas and Mildred Lena (Vinson) Stewart; m. Rickey Lane Newton, Aug. 26, 1972; children: Thomas Lane, Richard Stewart. BS in Elem. Edn. with honors, Huntington Coll., 1969; MEd in Elem. EDn. with honors, Auburn U., 1970; 6 Yr. Splst. Degree in Elem. Edn. with honors, Troy State U., 1994. Early childhood tchr. Clubview Elem., Columbus, Ga., 1970-75, Cussetta Rd. Elem., Columbus, 1976-78, Double Churches Sch., Columbus, 1978—, lead tchr., 1995—. Mentor for new tchrs. Double Churches and Muscogee Counties, Columbus, Ga., 1996—; rep. math. collaborative dept. Columbus Coll., 1995—, pres. Rock Eagle for Family Math Columbus State U., 1995-96, instr. Smart Camp, 1997, 98, 99, 2000. Vol. Morningside Bapt. Ch., Columbus, Ga., 1995—, Columbus Olympics, 1996 Named first runner up Reader's Choice Columbus Ledger, 1994, Tchr. of Yr. Muscogee County, 1997-98. Mem.: Profl. Assn. of Ga. Educators, Internat. Reading Assn., Kappa Delta Pi. Democrat. Baptist. Avocations: reading, cooking, aerobics. Home: 3 Treetop Ct Columbus GA 31909-4825 Office: 1213 Double Churches Rd Columbus GA 31904-2406 E-mail: gwen.newton@knology.net.

NEWTON, HERBERT BRUCE, neuro-oncologist; b. San Diego, Nov. 8, 1956; s. Jefferson Frederick and Leona Maxine (Reese) N.; m. Cheryl Lynn Donaldson, Jul. 6, 1991; children: Alexander James, Ashley Rene. BA, SUNY, 1979, MS, 1980, MD, 1984. Diplomate Am. Bd. Psych. & Neurology. Internship SUNY Buffalo Affiliated Hosp., Buffalo, 1984-85; residency U. Mich. Medical Ctr., Ann Arbor, Mich., 1985-88; fellowship neuro oncology Meml. Sloan-Kettering Cancer Ctr., N.Y., 1988-90; asst. prof., dir. div. neuro-oncology The Ohio State U., Columbus, 1990-96, assoc. prof., dir. neuro-oncology, 1996—; grad. faculty Neuroscience Grad. Studies Program, Ohio, 1991—; staff physician sec. neurology dept. pediatrics Children's Hosp., 1991—. Adv. profl. edn. com., Am. Cancer Soc., Columbus, 1991—; cons. Cen. Ohio Brain Tumor Support group, Columbus, 1990—. Contbr. articles to profl. jours. Recipient rsch. grant for treatment of malignant glioma, Amgen, 1994. Fellow Am. Acad. Neurology; mem. Am. Acad. Neurology, Internat. Soc. Analytical Cytology, Am. Assn. Cancer Rsch., Ctrl. Soc. Neurol. Rsch. Avocations: basketball, reading sci. fiction, music, art. Office: Ohio State U dept Neurology 1654 Upham Dr 465 Means Hall Columbus OH 43210 Office Fax: 614-293-6111. E-mail: newton.12@osu.edu.

NEWTON, HUGH C. public relations executive; b. N.Y.C., Oct. 17, 1930; s. Avery Curtis and Ruth (Juster) N.; m. Charlotte Eloise Wallin, Nov. 3, 1956 (div. 1968); 1 child, Margaret Wren Newton Rossello; m. Joanne Elaine Harding, Dec. 27, 1969; children: Matthew Curtis, Christopher Stuart, Kimberly Kelly. BA, Washington & Lee U., 1952. Reporter Danville (Va.) Bee, 1955; mgr. news Carnegie Inst. Tech., Pitts., 1956-57; staff writer Westinghouse Elec., 1957; acct. exec. Burson Marsteller Assocs., 1958-59; asst. dir. pub. rels. Rockwell Mfg., 1959-61; mgr. spl. projects Reynolds Metals Co., Richmond, Va., 1961-64; dir. pub. rels. Nat. Right to Work Com., Washington, 1964-67, Air Transport Assn., Washington, 1967-68; pres. Hugh C. Newton & Assocs., 1968—. Mem. Interstate Commn. on Potomac River Basin, Washington, 1982-89. Contbr. to Lesly's Public Relations Handbook, 1991. Bd. dirs. Friends of the Torpedo Factory Art Ctr., Alexandria, Va., 1987-91. Recipient Silver Anvil award Pub. Rels. Soc. Am., 1966, 85. Mem. Soc. Profl. Journalists, Nat. Press Club, Capitol Hill Club. Episcopalian. Avocations: skiing, boating, stamp collecting. Home: 629 S Fairfax St Alexandria VA 22314-3833 Office: Hugh C Newton & Assocs 108 N Washington St Alexandria VA 22314

NEWTON, JAMES QUIGG, JR. lawyer; b. Denver, 1911; s. James Quigg and Nelle (Singleton) N.; m. Virginia Shafroth, June 6, 1942; children: Nancy Grusin, Nelle Grainger, Abby Hornung, Virginia Rice. AB, Yale U., 1933, LLB, 1936, MA (hon.), 1951; DPS (hon.), U. Denver, 1952; LLD, Adams State Coll., 1960, Colo. Coll., 1962, U. Colo., 1975. Bar: Colo. 1938. Legal sec. to W.O. Douglas SEC, 1936-37; practiced in Denver, 1938-42, 46-47; lectr. U. Denver, 1938-41; with Ford Found., N.Y.C., 1955-56, v.p., 1956; pres. U. Colo., 1956-63, Commonwealth Fund, N.Y.C., 1963-75, vice chmn., 1975-76, dir., 1951-55, 57-78; sr. cons. Henry J. Kaiser Family Found., Menlo Park, Calif., 1978-80; of counsel firm Davis, Graham & Stubbs, 1981—. Dir. N.Y. Life Fund, 1972-95, Kaiser Found. Hosps./Health Plan, 1972-80; trustee Dry Dock Savs. Bank; mem. Yale Corp., 1951-55, Western Interstate Com. Higher Edn., 1957-63; mem. nat. adv. mental health coun. NIH, 1964-68; mem. Inst. Medicine, Nat. Acad. Scis., 1972—, VA Spl. Med. Adv. Group, 1968-74; fellow Ctr. for Advanced Study in Behavioral Scis., 1977-78. Mayor, City and County of Denver, 1947-55; Sec. bd. trustees U. Denver, 1938-42, pres., 1946-47; pub. trustee Nutrition Found.; chmn. bd. YMCA Greater N.Y., 1976-77. Served with USNR, 1942-46. Fellow Acad. Arts and Scis.; mem. Am. Municipal Assn. (pres. 1950), Am. Council Edn. (dir. 1959-62), Am. Arbitration Assn. (dir., exec. com.), Fgn. Bondholders Protective Council (dir. 1975—), Phi Delta Phi, Alpha Delta Phi. Home: 2552 E Alameda Ave #85 Denver CO 80209-3320

NEWTON, JOHN MILTON, academic administrator, psychology educator; b. Schenectady, Feb. 25, 1929; s. Harry Hazleton and Bertha A. (Lehmann) N.; m. Elizabeth Ann Slattery, Sept. 11, 1954; children: Patricia, Peter, Christopher. BS, Union Coll., Schenectady, 1951; MA, Ohio State U., 1952, PhD, 1955. Lic. psychologist, Nebr. Rsch. psychologist Electric Boat divsn. Gen. Dynamics Corp., Groton, Conn., 1957-60; mem. faculty U. Nebr., Omaha, 1960—, prof. psychology, 1966-99, chmn. dept., 1967-74, acting vice chancellor acad. affairs, 1994-95, prof. emeritus, 1999—, dean Coll. Arts and Scis., 1974-94, dean emeritus, 1999—. Cons. in field, 1960-72 Author research papers in field. Served to 1st lt. Med. Service Corps, AUS, 1955-57. Mem. Am. Psychol. Assn., Psychonomic Soc., Midwestern Psychol. Assn. Home: 5611 Jones St Omaha NE 68106-1232 Office: Univ of Nebr-Omaha Dept Psychology Omaha NE 68182-0001 E-mail: jnewton@mail.unomaha.edu.

NEWTON, JOHN WHARTON, III, lawyer; b. Beaumont, Tex., Feb. 18, 1953; s. John Wharton and Katherine (King) N.; children: Martha Garrison, John Wharton IV, Stephen King. BA, U. Tex., 1975; JD, U. Houston, 1978. Bar: Tex. 1979, U.S. Dist. Ct. (ea. dist.) Tex. 1979, U.S. Ct. Appeals (5th cir.) 1981, U.S. Dist. Ct. (so. dist.) Tex. 1987. Ptnr. Orgain, Bell & Tucker, Beaumont, 1984—. Mem. ABA, Tex. State Bar Assn., Tex. Assn. Def. Counsel, Jefferson County Bar Assn., Coll. of State Bar of Tex., Beaumont Club (pres. 1988-89). Episcopalian. Office: Orgain Bell & Tucker 470 Orleans St Ste 400 Beaumont TX 77701-3076

NEWTON, KENNETH KURT, physician, educator, administrator; b. Landsberg, Germany, May 18, 1927; came to U.S., 1946; s. Arthur Neuweg and Margaret Joan (Blume) Newton. BA, U. Buffalo, 1951; MD, Western Res. U., 1955; honor grad., U.S. Army Command/Gen. Staff Coll., Ft. Leavenworth, Kans., 1972; flight surgeon tng., U.S. Army Aviation Sch., Ft. Rucker, Ala., 1974. Med. lic. Ohio, Mich. Advanced through ranks to col. U. S. Army, 1946-97; intern Henry Ford Hosp., Detroit, 1955-56, resident in internal medicine, phys. medicine and rehab., 1956-60; preceptor, dept. family medicine Wayne State U., Mich. State U., U. Mich., 1960—; clin. assoc. prof. medicine Wayne State U., Detroit, 1995—; dir. med. edn. Holy Cross Hosp., 1976-88, chief dept. medicine, 1977-79, 91, pres. of staff, 1982-83; departmental surgeon Reserve Officers Assn. of Mich., 1988-98; pres. EKG Assocs., P.C., 1990—. Med. officer 107th med. battalion, Mich. Army N.G., 1955-57, divsn. artillery surgeon, 46th inf. divsn., 1957-59, command surgeon, 1959-75, state surgeon, 1975-85, post surgeon Camp Atterbury Res. Forces Tng. Area, 1985-89, divsn. surgeon 70th divsn., Livonia, Mich., 1989-92, flight surgeon U.S. Army 1993; instr., course dir. ACLS, Am. Heart Assn., 1977—, Acad. Health Scis., U.S. Army, Ft. Sam Houston, Tex., 1992—; mem. governing bd. Holy Cross Hosp. 1988-92, pres. 1990; tchr. U. Buffalo, N.Y., 1950-51, preceptor U. Essen, Germany, 1980, U. Göttingen, Germany, 1993, U. München, Germany, 1993, Humboldt U., Berlin, 1994; med. advisor to Selective Svcs. Sys., Washington, 1968-76; mem. ad hoc med. panel to Res. Forces Policy Bd., Dept. Army, Washington, 1972; mem. adv. group for Aerospace R&D, NATO, 1978; mem. med. evaluation bds. State of Mich., Lansing, 1975-85. Decorated Legion of Merit, 1977, 97; recipient cert. of pub. svc. State of N.Y., 1958, Disting. Svc. medal State of Mich. 1985, Spl. tribute State of Mich. Senate, 1985, Invitation Governing Mayor of Berlin, 1990, Conspicuous Svc. order, State of N.Y., 1997. Mem. (life) Sr. Army Reserve Comdrs. Assn., (life) Reserve Officers Assn. (nat. surgeon 1993), (life) Nat. Guard Assn. (dir. 1979-82), Am. Heart Assn. (course dir. 1980—), Soc. of Med. Consultants to the Armed Forces, Confedn. Interalliée des Officiers de Reserve NATO (del. 1973—, vice chief del. 1986). Avocations: travel, photography, music and the arts, national security. Office: 15252 Gratiot Ave Detroit MI 48205-1327 E-mail: kennethknewtonmd@aol.com.

NEWTON, LISA HAENLEIN, philosophy educator; b. Orange, N.J., Sept. 17, 1939; d. Wallen Joseph and Carol Bigelow (Cypiot) Haenlein; m. Victor Joseph Newton, June 3, 1972; children: Tracey, Kit, Cynthia Perkins, Daniel Perkins, Laura Perkins. Student, Swarthmore Coll., 1957-59; BS in Philosophy with honors, Columbia U., 1962, PhD, 1967. Asst. prof. philosophy Hofstra U., Hempstead, N.Y., 1967-69, Fairfield U., Conn., 1969-73, assoc. prof., 1973-78, prof., 1978—, dir. program in applied ethics, 1983—, dir. program in environ. studies, 1986—; lectr. in medicine Yale U., 1984—. Lectr., cons. in field Author: Ethics in America, Ethics and Sustainablility; co-author: Watersheds, 1994, 3d edit., 2001, Wake-Up Calls, 1996; co-editor: Taking Sides: Controversial Issues Business Ethics, 7th edit., 2002; contbr. articles to profl. jours.; author: (novels) Ethics & Sustainability, 2002. Mem. exec. bd. Conn. Humanities Council, 1979-83. Mem. Am. Soc. Value Inquiry (past pres.), Am. Philos. Assn., Am. Soc. Polit. and Legal Philosophy, Soc. Ethics Across Curriculum (exec. bd.), Am. Soc. Bioethics and Humanities, Soc. Bus. Ethics (past pres.), Phi Beta Kappa (local sec.). Assoc. Prac. Prof. Ethics (exec. bd.) Home: 4042 Congress St Fairfield CT 06324 Office: Fairfield U Program Applied Ethics Fairfield CT 06324 E-mail: ihnewton@fair1.fairfield.edu.

NEWTON, RHONWEN LEONARD, writer, microcomputer consultant; b. Lexington, N.C., Nov. 13, 1940; d. Jacob Calvin and Mary Louise (Moffitt) Leonard; children: Blair Armistead Newton Jones, Allison Page, William Brockenbrough III. AB, Duke U., 1962; MS in Edn., Old Dominion U., 1968. French tchr. Hampton (Va.) Pub. Schs., 1962-65, Va. Beach (Va.) Pub. Schs., 1965-66; instr. foreign lang. various colls. and univs., 1967-75; foreign lang. cons. Portsmouth (Va.) Pub. Schs., 1973-75; dir. The Computer Inst., Inc., Columbia, S.C., 1983; pres., founder The Computer Experience, Inc., 1983-88, RN Enterprises, Columbia, 1991—. Author: WordPerfect, 1988, All About Computers, 1989, Microsoft Excel for the Mac, 1989, Introduction to the Mac, 1989, Introduction to DOS, 1989, Introduction to Lotus 1-2-3, 1989, Advanced Lotus 1-2-3, 1989, Introduction to WordPerfect, 1989, Advanced WordPerfect, 1989, Introduction to Display/Write 4, 1989, WordPerfect for the Mac, 1989, Introduction to Microsoft Works for the Mac, 1990, Accountant, Inc for the Mac, 1992, Introduction to Filemaker Pro, 1992, Quicken for the MAC, 1993, Quicken for Windows, 1993, WordPerfect for Windows, 1993, Advanced WordPerfect for Windows, 1993, Lotus 1-2-3 for Windows, 1993, Introduction to Quick Books, 1994, Quick Book for Windows, 1994, Introduction to Word for Windows, 1995, Introduction to File Maker Pro 4.0, 1998, Introduction to Microsoft Word, 1999, Introduction to Microsoft Excel, 1999, Introduction to AOL, 1999, Introduction to Excel, 1999, Using America OnLine, 1999. Mem. Columbia Planning Commn., 1980-87; bd. dirs. United Way Midlands, Columbia, 1983-86, Assn. Jr. Leagues, N.Y.C., 1980-82, S.C. Wildlife Fedn., 1997-98 ; trustee Heathwood Hall Episcopal Sch., Columbia, 1979-85; mem. S.C. Episcopal Home Bd., 1999—, chmn., 2001—; vestry Trinity Cathedral, 1999—; mem. S.C. Real Estate Appraisers Bd., 2000. Mem. Investment Club (pres. 1995-97, regional coun.), Nat. Assn. Investors Corp. (dir. S.C. Midlands regional coun. 1998—). Republican. Episcopalian. Avocations: golf, walking. Home and Office: 1635 Kathwood Dr Columbia SC 29206-4509 E-mail: rnewton@sc.rr.com.

NEWTON, ROGER GERHARD, educator, physicist; b. Landsberg, Germany, Nov. 30, 1924; came to U.S., 1946, naturalized, 1949; s. Arthur and Margaret (Blume) Neuweg; m. Ruth Gordon, June 18, 1953; children: Rachel, Julie, Paul. Student, U. Berlin, Germany; AB summa cum laude, Harvard, 1949, MA, 1950, PhD, 1953. Teaching fellow Harvard, 1951-52; mem. Inst. Advanced Study, Princeton, 1953-55, 79; mem. faculty Ind. U., 1955-, prof. physics, 1960-78, disting. prof. physics, 1978—, chmn. dept., 1973-80, chmn. math. physics program, 1965-86, dir. Inst. for Advanced Study, 1982-86. Vis. prof. U. Rome, Italy, 1962-63, U. Montpellier, France, 1971-72 Author: Scattering Theory of Waves and Particles, 1966, 2d edit., 1982, The Complex j-Plane, 1964, Inverse Schrödinger Scattering in Three Dimension, 1989; assoc. editor: Jour. Math. Physics, 1967-70, 73-76, 83-86, Inverse Problems, 1985-90 (internat. adv. panel 1991—), Am. Jour. Physics, 1986-88; contbr. articles to sci. publs. Pres. Bloomington Civil Liberties Union, 1968. Served with AUS, 1946-47. Recipient Bowdoin prize Harvard, 1948; Jewett fellow, 1953-55; NSF sr. postdoctoral fellow, 1962-63; C.N.R.S. fellow U. Montpellier, France, 1971-72 Fellow AAAS (coun. 1987-89), Am. Phys. Soc. (chmn. Heinemann prize com. 1991-92); mem. AAUP, N.Y. Acad. Scis., Fedn. Am. Scientists, Phi Beta Kappa (pres. Gamma chpt. 1991-92), Sigma Xi.

NEWTON, WILLIAM ALLEN, JR. pediatric pathologist; b. Traverse City, Mich., May 19, 1923; s. William Allen and Florence Emma (Brown) N.; m. Helen Patricia Goodrich, Apr. 21, 1945; children: Katherine Germain, Elizabeth Gale, William Allen, Nancy Anne. B.Sc. cum laude, Alma (Mich.) Coll., 1943; MD, U. Mich., 1946. Diplomate: Am. Bd. Pathology, Am. Bd. Pediatrics. Intern Wayne County Gen. Hosp., Detroit, 1947; resident in pediatric pathology/pathology/hematology Children's Hosp. Mich., 1948-50; res. in pediatrics Children's Hosp. Phila., 1950; dir. labs. Children's Hosp. Columbus, Ohio, 1952-88, rsch. pathologist, 1989—; mem. faculty Coll. Medicine, Ohio State U., 1952—, prof., 1965—, chief pediatric pathology, 1952-89, chief div. pediatric hematology, 1952-88, prof. emeritus, 1989—. Chmn. pathology com. Children's Cancer Study Group, 1965-91; chmn. Pathology Com. Intergroup Rhabdomyosarcoma Study Group; chmn. pathology com. Late Effects Study Group. Contbr. articles to med. jours. Trustee, mem. exec. com. Am. Cancer Soc., Ohio div., 1972-86; mem. adv. com. on childhood cancer Am. Cancer Soc.; chmn. exec. com. Consortium for Cancer Control of Ohio, 1982-86; mem. sci. adv. com. Armed Forces Inst. Pathology; pres. Internat. Conf. for Cure of Childhood Cancer in China, 2000—. Served to capt. M.C. U.S. Army, 1950-52, brig. gen. Res. ret. Mem. Ohio State Med. Assn. (com. on cancer), Midwest Soc. Pediatric Research (mem. council 1960-63, pres. 1964-65), Soc. Pediatric Research, Am. Pediatric Soc., Pediatric Pathology Club (pres. 1968-69), Am. Soc. Clin. Oncology, Internat. Soc. Pediatric Oncology, Sigma Xi, Phi Sigma Pi. Republican. Baptist. Home: 2500 Harrison Rd Johnstown OH 43031-9540 Office: 700 Childrens Dr Columbus OH 43205-2664 E-mail: wnewton@chi.osu.edu.

NEXSEN, JULIAN JACOBS, lawyer; b. Kingstree, S.C., Apr. 14, 1924; s. William Ivey and Barbara (Jacobs) N.; m. Mary Elizabeth McIntosh, Jan. 28, 1948; children: Louise Ivey (Mrs. Heyward Harles Bouknight, Jr.), Julian Jacobs Jr. Student, The Citadel, 1941-43; BS magna cum laude, U. S.C., 1948, JD magna cum laude, 1950. Bar: S.C. 1950, U.S. Supreme Ct. 1960. Partner firm Nexsen Pruet Jacobs & Pollard, Columbia, S.C. Trustee Richland County Pub. Libr., chmn., 1976-77; trustee Providence Hosp., chmn., 1984-86; trustee Providence Found., Providence Ministries, Sisters of Charity of St. Augustine Health Sys.; past bd. dirs. Columbia Music Festival Assn., ARC Richland-Lexington Counties, Ctrl. Carolina Cmty. Found.; mem. U.S.C. Law Sch. partnership bd.; elder Presbyn. Ch., trustee Congaree Presbytery, 1967-87, Synod, S.C., 1969-74, mem. Trinity Presbytery Coun., 1991-95. Lt. inf. AUS, 1943-46, ETO, capt., 1950-51, Korea. Decorated Bronze Star with oak leaf cluster; recipient Compleat Lawyer award U. S.C. Sch. Law. Mem. ABA, S.C. Bar (treas., bd. govs. 1974-79, ho. of dels. 1980-92), Richland County Bar Assn. (pres. 1974-75, Disting. Svc. award 1987), Am. Bar Found., S.C. Bar Found. (pres. 1971-72), S.C. Law Inst. (coun., exec. com. 1986—), Am. Law Inst., Am. Coll. Trust and Estate Counsel (regent 1973-82), Am. Judicature Soc., Forest Lake Country Club, Palmetto Club, Kiwanis (bd. dirs. 1972-74, 77-79), Phi Beta Kappa. Home: 2840 Sheffield Rd Columbia SC 29204-2332 Office: Nexsen Pruet Jacobs & Pollard Drawer 2426 1441 Main St Columbia SC 29202-2848 E-mail: jjn@npjp.com.

NEXSEN, JULIAN JACOBS, JR. lawyer; b. Columbia, S.C., Sept. 22, 1954; s. Julian J. and Mary Elizabeth (McIntosh) N.; m. Christine Spigner Johnston, Feb. 25, 1984; children: Elizabeth Kincaid, Julian J. III, Sarah Ivey. BA, Washington and Lee U., 1976; JD, U. S.C., 1979. Bar: S.C. 1979, U.S. Ct. Appeals (4th cir.) 1982. Assoc. Nexsen, Pruet, Jacobs & Pollard, Columbia, S.C., 1979-84; assoc. in house counsel, asst. sec. Greenwood (S.C.) Mills, Inc., 1984-95, exec. v.p., 1999—2001; exec. v.p., COO Greenwood Devel. Corp., 1995-99, pres., CEO, 1999—. Bd. dirs. The County Bank, Greenwood Devel. Corp., Ctrl. Trust Co., SC Biotech. Incubation Program, Partnership for a Greater Greenwood. Bd. visitors Lander Coll., 1985-87; bd. dirs. Edn. Enrichment Found., 1986-89, Greenwood United Way, 1989-92, Greenwood Community Theatre, 1989-93, Greenwood Uptown Devel. Corp., 1991-93; bd. deacons 1st Presbyn. Ch., 1990-93, session, 1993-96; trustee Self Meml. Hosp., 1992-98, Self Family Found., Self Regional Healthcare Ctr.; bd. dirs. Greenwood County Econ. Alliance, 1999-2001. Mem. ABA, Am. Corp. Counsel Assn., S.C. Bar Assn., Forest Lake Club, Greenwood Country Club, S.C. C. of C. (bd. dirs. 1990-93). Presbyterian. Home: 512 E Henrietta Ave Greenwood SC 29649-3142 Office: Greenwood Devel Corp PO Box 1546 Greenwood SC 29648-1546 E-mail: jnexsen@greenwooddevelopment.com.

NEY, JUDY LARSON, lawyer, sociology educator; b. St. Louis, Mar. 4, 1951; d. Robert Israel and Annette (Palan) Larson; m. Leo E. Ney Jr., May 25, 1975; 1 child, Leo E. IV. BA, Bradley U., 1973; MA, MSW, U. Mo., St. Louis, 1975; JD, S. Tex. Coll., 1982. Bar: Tex. 1983, U.S. Dist. Ct. (so. dist.) Tex. 1983. Project controls supr., planner Brown & Root Inc., Houston, 1974—83; pvt. practice, 1983—2001; state govt. atty. Tex. Worker's Compensation Commn., 2001—. Instr. sociology ITT Tech. Inst., 1993—2000, lectr. on alcohol, drugs and the law, 1984. Info. and referral counselor Mental Health Assn., 1990-95; religious sch. instr. Congregation Emanu El, 1990--. Named Vol. of Yr., Mental Health Assn., 1994. Mem.: ABA (Tex. ho. of dels. 1997—98), Houston Bar Assn. (minority opp. com., law day chair 1997, continuing edn. commn.), Tex. Bar Assn., Biographical Inst., South Tex. Coll. Law Alumni, U. Mo.-St Louis Alumni Assn., Bradley U. Alumni Assn., Phi Alpha Delta. Republican. Jewish. Avocations: travel, politics, reading. Home: 12242 Brookvalley Dr Houston TX 77071-2722 Office: Tex Worker's Compensation Commn 8485 Gulf Fwy Ste B Houston TX 77017-5001 Fax: 713-723-5380. E-mail: judylneyjd@aol.com.

NEY, MICHAEL VINCENT, university administrator; b. Indpls., Nov. 19, 1947; s. Marshal M. and Delphine M (Deitrick) N.; m. Marietta J. Anderson, Dec. 19, 1997. Student, U. Hawaii, 1966; BS, Butler U., Indpls., 1972; MHA, Ind. U.-Purdue U., Indpls., 1990. EDP operator L.S. Ayres & Co., Indpls., 1963-65; city surveyor, 1969; with Am. Fletcher Nat. Bank, 1970-74; credit adjuster Am. States Ins. Co., 1974; adminstr. asst. to dean Sch. Medicine Ind. U., 1974-80, asst. dir. fiscal affairs, 1980-83, asst. to chmn. opthalmology, 1983-85, adminstr. dept. surgery, 1985-95, dir. adminstrn. & info., 1995—. Bd. dirs., treas. Ind. Mems. Credit Union; adj. faculty Schs. Pub. and Environ. Affairs, 1991; pres., CEO Cyberhelp, Inc., 1996— 2nd v.p. United Cerebral Palsy Cen. Ind., Indpls. 1983-85, bd. dirs., 1978-80; pres. United Cerebral Palsy Cen. Ind. Found. Inc., Indpls. 1987; v.p. United Cerebral Palsy Ind., Indpls., 1985-87; treas. Collaboration 2000, Inc., 1996-98; pres. Ind. Cmty. Network Assn.; treas. Whispering Pine Homeowners Assn., 1998-2001; mem. Ind. Transp. Mus.. With U.S. Army, 1965-69, Vietnam, capt. USAR, 1990; lt. col., govt. rels. advisor Ind. Wing Civil Air Patrol. Decorated Vietnam Svc. medal, Vietnam Camp medal, Commendation medal USNG, 1981; recipient Mktg. cert. Ford Mktg. Corp., Dearborn, Mich., 1971, Samuel H. Hopper award for Acad. Achievement, Sch. Pub. and Environ. Affairs, 1990. Mem. ALA, Am. Coll. Healthcare Execs., Am. Med. Colls. Assn., Am. Med. Info. Assn., Assn. Acad. Surg. Adminstrs., Med. Group Mgmt. Assn., Group on Bus. Affairs, Am. Soc. for Info. Sci., Healthcare Info. Mgmt. Systems Soc., Libr. and Info. Tech. Assn., Ind. Fedn. Rsch. Adminstrs., Ind. Forum for Rsch. Adminstrs. (bd. dirs.), Collaboration 2000, Ind. Health Sci. Librs. Assn., Am. Legion (comdr. 1980-85), Lions, Kiwanis. Republican. Lutheran. Avocations: aerobics, baseball, computers, softball, volleyball. Home: 10233 Whispering Way Indianapolis IN 46239-9675 Office: 545 Barnhill Dr # 203 Indianapolis IN 46202-5112 E-mail: mney@iupui.edu., mney@comcast.net.

NEY, ROBERT W. congressman; b. Wheeling, W. Va., July 5, 1954; m. Candy (div.); children: Bobby, Kayla Marie. BS in Edn., Ohio State U., 1976. Am. Embassy tchr., supr. affiliate school of Shiraz (Iran), 1978; health and edn. program mgr. Ohio Office of Appalachia, 1979; safety dir. City of Bellaire, Ohio, until 1980; mem. Ohio Ho. of Reps., 1980-84, Ohio Senate, 1984-94, U.S. Congress from 18th Ohio dist., 1995—; mem. fin. svcs. com., transp. and infrastructure com., mem. adminstrn. com. Mem. Kiwanis, Elks, Lions, Sportsmen clubs, NRA. Office: US House of Reps 1024 Longworth Ho Office Bldg Washington DC 20515-3518 also: 3201 Belmont St Ste 604 Bellaire OH 43906-1547*

NEYER, JEROME CHARLES, consulting civil engineer; b. Cin., July 15, 1938; s. Urban Charles and Marie Helen (Hemsteger) N.; m. Judy Ann Drolet, June 17, 1961; children: Janet, Karen. BCE, U. Detroit, 1961; MCE, U. Wash., 1963. Registered profl. engr. 16 states. Facilities engr. Boeing Co., Seattle, 1961-62; found. engr. Metro Engrs., 1962-65; project engr. Hugo N. Helpert Assocs., Detroit, 1965-70; pres. NTH Cons. Ltd., Farmington Hills, Mich., 1970—. Adj. prof. U. Detroit, 1973-79. Contbr. articles to profl. jours. Mem. mineral well adv. bd., Lansing, Mich., 1975, mem. constrn. safety stds. bd., 1982; chmn. bldg. appeals bd. City of Farmington Hills, 1983. Mem. ASTM, ASCE (br. pres. 1973-74), Engring. Soc. Dtroit, Cons. Engrs. Mich. (pres. 1981), Mich. Soc. Profl. Engrs. (bd. dirs. 1980), Assn. Engring. Firms Practicing in the Geoscis. (pres. 1991). Roman Catholic. Avocations: golfing, tennis. Home: 26478 Ballantrae Ct Farmington Hills MI 48331-3528 Office: NTH Consultants Ltd 38955 Hills Tech Dr Farmington MI 48331-3434 E-mail: jneyer@nthconsultants.com.

NEYLAN, JOHN FRANCIS, III, nephrologist, educator, scientist; b. Chgo., Feb. 20, 1953; s. John Francis and Mary Alice (Coogan) N.; m. Cynthia Barnes, May 17, 1980; children: John Francis IV, Elizabeth Marie, James Christopher. BS, Duke U., 1975; MD, Rush Med. Coll., Chgo., 1979. Intern in medicine Vanderbilt U., Nashville, 1979-80, resident, 1980-82; fellow in nephrology Brigham and Women's Hosp., Boston, 1983-84; fellow in immunogenetics Harvard U. Med. Sch., 1984-86, clin. preceptor, 1986; asst. prof. medicine U. Calif., Davis, 1986-88, Emory U., Atlanta, 1988-93, assoc. prof., 1993-98, prof. medicine, 1998-2000, med. dir. renal transplantation, 1988-2000; v.p. clin. rsch. and devel. Wyeth Rsch., Collegeville, Pa., 2000—. Vis. cons. Wanless Hosp., Miraj, India, 1982-83; assoc. med. dir. Lifelink of Ga. Organ Procurement Orgn., Atlanta, 1989-2000; bd. govs. Lifelink Found., Tampa, Fla., 1988-2000. Editor: Am. Soc. Transplantation Newsletter, 1994-98; contbr. articles and abstracts to med. jours., chpts. to books. Vol. Nat. Kidney Found., N.Y.C., 1990—, ARC, Atlanta, 1991, Spl. Olympics, Atlanta, 1991—, Habitat for Humanity, 1993—; chmn. Nat. Kidney Found. Coun. on Transplantation, 1995-98; bd. dirs. United Network for Organ Sharing. Recipient Physician's Recognition award AMA, 1989. Mem. ACP, Am. Fedn. Clin. Rsch. (councillor 1988), Am. Soc. Transplantation (co-chmn. patient care com. 1988-90, chmn. 1991-93, councillor-at-large exec. coun. 1993-96, sec.-treas. 1996-97, pres.-elect 1997-98, pres. 1998-99, editor newsletter), Am. Soc. Nephrology, Internat. Soc. Nephrology, Transplantation Soc., United Network for Organ Sharing, Circumnavigator Club, Alpha Omega Alpha. Avocations: bicycling, tennis, windsurfing. Office: Wyeth Rsch 500 Arcola Rd Collegeville PA 19426 E-mail: neylanj@war.wyeth.com.

NEYLAND, MALCOLM, priest, curator; Ordained priest Roman Catholic. Ch. Dir. Vatican Mus. Exhbn. Office: 2220 Broadway Lubbock TX 79401 Fax: 806-749-2350.

NEYMAN, JAMES NELSON, computer systems analyst, nuclear engineer; b. West Grove, Pa., Aug. 11, 1945; s. William Nelson and Margaret Louise (Cockerham) N. BS, Pa. State U., 1972, MS, 1978. Registered profl. engr., Calif., Ariz. Nuclear engr. Bechtel Bower Corp., Norwalk, Calif., 1974; reactor engr. Sacramento (Calif.) Mcpl. Utility Dist., 1974-78; computer engr. Gen. Pub. Utilities Svc. Corp., Parsippany, N.J., 1978-79; systems programmer Honeywell Process Mgmt. Systems Div., Phoenix, 1979-83; reactor engr. Fla. Power Corp., Crystal River, Fla., 1983-84; simulator software engr. Gen. Pub. Utilities Nuclear Corp., Middletown, Pa., 1984-87; computer systems analyst Yankee Atomic Electric Co., Bolton, Mass., 1987—. Sgt. USAF, 1964-68. Mem. ASME, Am. Nuclear Soc., Soc. for Computer Simulation. Home: 39 Village Xing Fitchburg MA 01420-1341 Office: Yankee Atomic Electric Co 19 Midstate Dr # 200-210 Auburn MA 01501-1858

NEYMAN, JOSEPH DAVID, JR. lawyer; b. Memphis, Feb. 4, 1971; s. Joseph David Sr. and Linda Vaughn Neyman; m. Mary Phillips Johnson, May 17, 1997. BPA cum laude, U. Miss., 1993, JD, 1996. Bar: Miss. 1996, U.S. Dist. Ct. (no. and so. dists.) Miss. 1996, U.S. Ct. Appeals (5th cir.) 1996, Tenn. 1997. Law clk. NLRB, Memphis, 1995; assoc. Walker, Brown & Brown, P.A., Hernando, Miss., 1996—. Participant Leadership DeSoto, Hernando, 1997. Mem. ATLA, Miss. Trial Lawyers Assn., Tenn. Bar Assn., Miss. Bar Assn., DeSoto County Bar Assn., DeSoto County Young Lawyers Assn. (pres. 1998), Optimist Club (v.p./pres. 1997-99). Presbyterian. Avocations: hunting, reading history, shooting, following college athletics. Office: Walker Brown & Brown PA PO Box 276 Hernando MS 38632-0276

NEYMEYER-TYNKOV, VALERIE R. patent lawyer; b. Clinton, Iowa, Nov. 24, 1969; d. Calvin Eugene and Carol Dean N. BA with honors, U. Iowa, 1991, MS, 1995; postgrad., Chgo-Kent Coll. Law, 1998-2001. Bar: U.S. Patent and Trademark Office 2000, Ill. 2001. Scientist Bio-Rsch. Products, Inc., Coralville, Iowa, 1996-97; rsch. assoc. II Chiron Corp., Emeryville, Calif., 1997-98. Mem. AAAS, ABA. E-mail: ValerieN@aol.com.

NEZHMETDINOV, ISKANDER RASHIDOVICH, mathematics educator; b. Kazan', Tatarstan, Russia, Mar. 3, 1954; s. Rashid Gibyatovich and Tamara Ivanovna (Kislyakova) N.; m. Guzel' Il'gamovna Ganeeva, Apr. 30, 1982; 1 child, Timur. Diploma, Kazan (Russia) State U., 1976, candidate in science degree, 1979. Asst. Kazan State U., 1979-85, assoc. prof. math., 1985—. Vis. prof. Indian Inst. Tech.-Madras, 1999-2000. Reviewer Math. Revs., Providence, 1992—, Zentralblatt Mathematik, Karlsruhe, 1998—; contbr. articles to profl. publs. Brit. Coun. study fellow, 1989. Mem. London Math. Soc., Am. Math. Soc. Avocation: farming. Home: Flat 18 76 Bauman St Kazan 420111 Russia Office: Lehigh University Christmas-Saucon Hall 14 E Packer Av Bethlehem PA 18015-3174 also: Kazan State U 18 Kremlevskaya St Kazan 420008 Russia E-mail: nezh@ksu.ru.

NEZU, ARTHUR MAGUTH, psychologist, educator; b. N.Y.C., Nov. 24, 1952; s. Tetsuo and Mary N.; m. Christine Maguth Nezu, June 1983; stepchildren: Frank, Alice, Linda. BA (N.Y. State Regents scholar 1970-74), SUNY, Stony Brook, 1974, MA, 1976, PhD, 1979. Clin. intern Norwich (Conn.) Hosp., 1977-78; asst. dir., coordinator tng. Psychol. Services div. Fairleigh Dickinson U., Teaneck, N.J., 1978-85, clin. asst. prof. dept. community dentistry, 1981-88, clin. asst. prof. dept. psychology, 1982-84, clin. assoc. prof., 1984-85, assoc. prof. psychology, 1985-88, co-dir. behavioral scis. sect. dept. community dentistry, 1983-88, co-dir. readjustment counseling program for Vietnam vets., 1983-85, adj. prof., 1988—; chief psychologist Beth Israel Med. Ctr., N.Y.C., 1988—, dir. research dept. psychiatry ; assoc. prof. psychiatry Mt. Sinai Sch. Med., 1988—; instr. dept. psychology SUNY-Stony Brook, 1976-77; adj. faculty Ramapo Coll. N.J., 1980. Author (with Christine Nezu, Michael Perri) Problem-Solving Therapy for Depression: Theory, Research, and Clinical Guidelines, 1988; contbr. articles to profl. jours. Mem. Am. Psychol. Assn., Eastern Psychol. Assn., Assn. Advancement Behavior Therapy, Soc. Behavioral Medicine, Assn. Children with Down's Syndrome, Am. Assn. Mental Deficiency, AAAS, Am. Assn. Dental Schs., Phi Beta Kappa. Contbr. articles to profl. jours. Home: 1060 Windsor Rd Teaneck NJ 07666-2746

NG, CHI-SING, pathologist, consultant; b. Hong Kong; s. Pang and Yee (Chan) Ng; m. Yuen-Wah Yvonne Chan, Nov. 23, 1992; children: Pok-Hym, Paul. MBBS, U. Hong Kong, 1979. Resident Queen Elizabeth Hosp., Hong Kong, 1981-83, Prince of Wales Hosp., Hong Kong, 1983-86, cons., 1986-87, Caritas Med. Ctr., 1987—. Chief of svc. Caritas Med. Ctr., Hong Kong, 1991—; dir. Lion's Eye Bank, Hong Kong, 1995—; examiner Hong Kong Coll. of Pathologists, 1995—; lab. inspector Hong Kong Coll. of Pathologists, 1996—. Author: (book) Diagnostic Histopathology of Tumors, 1995; contbr. articles to profl. jours. Fellow Royal Coll. Pathologists, Hong Kong Coll. Pathologists, Hong Kong Acad. Medicine. Office: Caritas Med Ctr 111 Wing Hong St Kowloon Shamshuipo Hong Kong China E-mail: ngcs@ha.org.hk.

NG, HELEN M. financier, civil engineer; b. Santa Ana, Calif., July 27, 1965; d. Steve K. and Evelyna H. (Hung) N. AB in Internat. Rels., BSCE, Stanford (Calif.) U., 1988; MBA Sloan Sch. Mgmt., MIT, Cambridge, 1995. Reg. profl. engr., Calif. Civil engr. Morrison-Knudsen Engrs., San Francisco, 1989-91, Deleuw-Cather & Co., San Francisco, 1991-92; trans. industry analyst Fed. R.R. Adminstrn., U.S. Dept. Transp., Washington, 1995-96; assoc. project fin. BZW/Barclays Bank PLC, N.Y., 1996-98; asst. v.p. telecom./media fin. Dresdner Kleinwort Benson, N.Y.C., 1998—. Lectr. in field. Author: (nat. policy draft for high-speed ground transp.) Fed. Railroad Adminstrn., Dept. Transp., Washington D.C., 1995-96; donor: Salon de Virtuosi. Named Amb. of Goodwill Rotary Internat. to Russia, 1992-93, Rimsky-Korsakoff Conservatoire. Avocation: classical piano. Home: The Ansonia # 7-104 2109 Broadway New York NY 10023-2106 Office: Dresdner Kleinwort Benson 75 Wall St New York NY 10005-2833

NG, KWOK-WAI, physics educator; b. Hong Kong, Aug. 15, 1958; came to U.S., 1981; s. Wan-Fu and Kam-Har (Sin) N.; m. Grace Mun Yan, Dec. 28, 1987; 1 child, Nelson Eukai. BSc, U. Hong Kong, 1981; PhD, Iowa State U., 1986. Postdoctoral fellow U. Tex., Austin, 1986-88; asst. prof. physics U. Ky., Lexington, 1988-94, assoc. prof., 1994-2000, prof., 2000—. Contbr. articles to Phys. Rev. Letter, Phys. Rev. B, Japanese Jour. Applied Physics. Mem. IEEE, Am. Phys. Soc., Phi Kappa Phi. Achievements include gap anisotropy of high Tc superconductors; superconducting tunneling spectroscopy. Office: Univ Ky Dept Physics Astronomy Lexington KY 40506-0001 E-mail: kwng@pop.uky.edu.

NG, LAWRENCE MING-LOY, pediatrician; b. Hong Kong, Mar. 21, 1940; came to U.S., 1967, naturalized, 1977; s. John Iu-cheung and Mary Wing (Wong) N.; m. Bella May Ha Kan, June 25, 1971; children: Jennifer Wing-mui, Jessica Wing-yee. B in Medicine, U. Hong Kong, 1965; B in Surgery, 1965. Diplomate Am. Bd. Pediatrics. House physician Queen Elizabeth Hosp., Hong Kong, 1965-66, med. officer Hong Kong, 1966-67; resident physician Children's Hosp. of Los Angeles, 1967-68, Children's Hosp. Med. Ctr., Oakland, Calif., 1968-70; fellow in pediatric cardiology, 1970-72; now mem. teaching staff; practice medicine specializing in pediatrics and pediatric cardiology, San Leandro, Calif., 1972—, Oakland, 1982—; mng. ptnr. Pediatric Med. Assocs. of East Bay, 1990—. Chief of pediatrics Oakland Hosp., 1974-77; chief of pediatrics Vesper Meml. Hosp., 1977-79, sec. staff, 1984, v.p. staff, 1985; chief pediatrics Meml. Hosp., San Leandro, 1986-88; founder Pediatric Assocs. of East Bay, 1990. Active Republican Party. Fellow: Am. Acad. Pediatrics; mem.: AMA, Chancellor's Assocs. U. Calif. at Berkeley, Children's First Healthcare Network (bd. dirs. 1997—), Oakland Chinatown C. of C. (bd. dirs. 1986—91, adv. bd. 1992—, bd. dirs. 1986—91), Ethnic Health Inst. (bd. dirs. 1998—), Fedn. Chinese Med. Socs. (dir. 1998—), Chinese-Am. Physicians Soc. (sec. 1980, pres. 1983, exec. dir. 1997—2001), Chinese-Am. POlit. Assn. (life), Orgn. Chinese Ams. (chpt. pres. 1984), Smithsonian Assocs., L.A. Pediat. Soc., Alameda County Assn. Primary Care Practitioners (membership chmn. 1993—97, sec.-treas. 1994—97), Am. Heart Assn., Calif. Med. Assn., Hong Kong U. Alumni Assn. (sec. No. Calif. chpt. 1992—96, pres. 1997—2000, chair 2001—), Friends of Hong Kong U. (bd. dirs. 2001—), Consumer's Union (life), Stanford U. Alumni Assn. (life), Oakland Asian Cultural Ctr. (dir. 1996—99, treas. 1996—99), No. Calif. Golf Assn., San Leandro Golf Club, U.S. Golf Assn. (life), Commonwealth Club. Buddhist. Office: 345 9th St Ste 204 Oakland CA 94607-4206 also: 101 Callan Ave Ste 401 San Leandro CA 94577-4523

NG, MALEN, utilities executive; From dir. fin. planning and reporting to v.p. corp. fin. Hydro One Networks, Inc., Toronto, Canada, 1994—97, pres., CEO Canada, 1997—. Office: Hydro One Networks Inc 483 Bay St 10th Fl Toronto M5G 2P5 Canada

NG, WING CHIU, accountant, computer software consultant, educator, activist, lawyer; b. Hong Kong, Hong Kong, Oct. 14, 1947; came to U.S., 1966; s. Bing Nuen and Oi Ying (Lee) Ng. BS, MS, Yale U., 1969; PhD, NYU, 1972; JD, U. Hawaii, 2000. CPA, Hawaii. Rsch. assoc. SUNY, Stony Brook, 1972-74; asst. prof. U. Md., College Park, 1974-76; rsch. physicist U. Bonn, Fed. Republic of Germany, 1976-78; chartered acct. Richter, Usher & Vineberg, Montreal, Can., 1978-80; pvt. practice Honolulu, 1980—; pres. Bowen, Ng & Co., 1983-84, Asia-Am. Investment, Inc., Honolulu, 1983—, Mathematica Pacific, Inc., Honolulu, 1984—. Part-time prof. U. Hawaii, Honolulu, 1982—; ptnr. Advance Realty Investment, Honolulu, 1980—; dir. S & L Internat., Inc., Honolulu, 1987—. Creator: (computer software) Time Billing, 1984, Dbase General Ledger, 1987, Dbase Payroll, 1987, Dbase Accounts Receivable, 1989; co-author: Draft Constitution of the Federal Republic of China, 1994. Dir. Orgn. of Chinese Ams., Honolulu, 1984-86, Fedn. for a Dem. China, Honolulu, 1990—, Hong Kong, 1991—; dir. Alliance Hong Kong Chinese in U.S., 1995—. Included in Prominent People of Hawaii, Delta Pub. Co., 1988. Mem. AICPA, Hong Kong Soc. Accts., Hawaiian Trail & Mountain Club (auditor 1987—). Democrat. Buddhist. Avocations: hiking, the internet. Office: 1149 Bethel St Ste 306 Honolulu HI 96813-2210

NG, WOON LAM, artist, educator; b. Kluang, Johor, Malaysia, Apr. 17, 1971; MSc in Math. English and Sci., Nat.U. of Singapore, 1999. Exhibited in group shows at Trafalgar Square, 2000 (Selected by NWS for the 80th International Juried Show, 2000), Old Man, 2000 (Pat Brentnall's Sponsor Award, 2000). Recipient First Prize, Daler Rowney The Art Paper Summer Frontpage Competition, 2001, Award of Excellence, Western Fedn. of Watercolor Socs., 2001, Pat Brentnall's Sponsor award, San Diego Watercolor Soc., 2000. Mem.: Fedn. Canadian Artists (Linda Lando Fine Arts award 2001), Singapore Watercolour Soc. (Outstanding Watercolor Painting award 2001), Nat. Soc. and Canadian Soc. Painters in Water Colou, Victorian Watercolour Soc., Australia (hon.). Personal E-mail: woonlam@yahoo.com.

NGO, TUNG THANH, writer, photographer; b. Soctrang, Vietnam, May 18, 1936; came to U.S., 1975; s. Lung The Ngo and Thui Thi Lam; m. Lan My Vu, Jan. 12, 1962; children: Peter, Vincent, Mike, Vinh. B of Law, U. Saigon, Vietnam, 1964; M of Pub. Affairs, U. Pitts., 1970. Judge advocate, corps II South Vietnam Armed Forces, Pleiku, 1964—66; assemblyman, gen. sec. Nat. Constituent Assembly, Saigon, Vietnam, 1966—67; dean, prof. Hoa-Hao U., Long Xuyen, Vietnam, 1970—75; sch. tchr. Garden Grove (Calif.) Sch. Dist., 1978—86; computer operator Alta Bates Med. Ctr., Berkeley, 1987—2001; writer, photography instr. Vietnamese Photoraphy Assn., Calif., 1981—. Author: (in Vietnamese) Visiting California, 1995, Entering Photography I, 1999, Entering Photography II, 2000; editor: Vietnam's Traditional Angling, 1977, Dr. Cung or Boat People, 1987, Selection of Photgraphs, 2001. Grantee The Ford Found., 1975; hon. fellowship The Hong Kong Photography Club of L.A., 2000, The Vietnamese Artists Photography Assn., 2000. The Vietnamese Artistic Photography Assn. (v.p. 1981—, hon. fellowship 2000), The Vietnamese Artistic Photography Assn. in No. Calif. (chpt. pres.). Home: 49 Killybegs Rd Alameda CA 94502

NGUYEN, ALEX THINH, internet company executive, aerospace engineer, consultant; b. Saigon, Vietnam, Nov. 25, 1974; came to U.S., 1980; s. Chien Van Nguyen and Bich-dao Thi Trinh. BS in Aerospace Engring., U. Md., 1996, postgrad.; MS sys. engring., Univ. MD, 2001. Systems programming coord. U. Md., College Park, 1992-98; aerospace systems engr. Analytical Graphics, Inc., Lanham, Md., 1998-00; dir. bus. devel. Wonderclick.com, Inc., Washington, 1999—; v.p. bus. devel. AboveCable.com, Inc., 1999—; founder, pres. Concepts Beyond, Inc.; mng. dir. AboveCable India Pvt. Ltd., 2000—. Cons. Analytical Graphics, Inc., Lanham, 2000—. Pres. Vietnamese Cultural Soc., Falls Church, Va., 1998-99, bd. dirs. 2000—; mem. Asian Am. LEAD, Washington, 1998—. Mem.: Asia Soc., Vietnamese Cultural Soc., Nat. Air and Space Mus., Balt. Coun. for Fgn. Affairs, Omicron Delta Kappa, Sigma Gamma Tau (pres. 1995). Avocations: skiing, camping, mountain biking, photography. Office: AboveCable 2400 N St NW Washington DC 20037

NGUYEN, AN DUC, industrial development, consultant; b. Hai-Hung, Vietnam, Feb. 27, 1930; came to U.S., 1983; s. Giat Duc and Bien Thi (Pham) N.; m. Thuoc Thi Bui, Dec. 21, 1948; children: Tuan, Khoi, Thang, Phuong Nguyen Khanh Nguyen, Long Nguyen Kein Nguyen. BA, U. Hanoi, Vietnam, 1952. Custom officer Directorate of Vietnam Customs, Haiphong, Saigon, Vietnam, 1952-63; dist. mgr. Royal Dutch Shell, Saigon, Vietnam, 1964-75; pres. Windeco World Industrial Devel., Inc., Houston, Hanoi, 1990—. Pres. Lion Internat., Saigon, 1970-71; coord. United Medical Found., 1992. Decorated Economic medal Minister of Econ., Saigon, 1974. Avocations: sports, music, gardening.

NGUYEN, ANN CAC KHUE, pharmaceutical and medicinal chemist; b. Kieu Moc, Sontay, Vietnam, Nov. 12, 1949; d. Nguyen Van Soan and Luu Thi Hieu. BS, U. Saigon, 1973; MS, San Francisco State U., 1978; PhD, U. Calif., San Francisco, 1983. Teaching and research asst. U. Calif., San Francisco, 1978-83, postdoctoral fellow, 1983-86, research scientist, 1987—. Contbr. articles to profl. jours. Recipient Nat. Research Service award, NIH, 1981-83; Regents fellow U. Calif., San Francisco, 1978-81. Mem. AAAS, Am. Chem. Soc., N.Y. Acad. Scis., Bay Area Enzyme Mechanism Group, Am. Assn. Pharm. Scientists. Roman Catholic. Home: 1488 Portola Dr San Francisco CA 94127-1409 Office: U Calif PO Box 446 San Francisco CA 94143-0001 E-mail: cackhue@itsa.ucsf.edu.

NGUYEN, CHARLES CUONG, engineering educator, researcher; b. Danang, Vietnam, Jan. 1, 1956; came to U.S., 1978, naturalized, 1948; s. Buoi and Tinh Thi Nguyen; m. Kim-Bang Pham, Aug. 5, 1989; children: Carissa Kim Thuy Duong, Olivia Quynh Duong, Dylan Nhat Khang, Parker Duy Khang. Diplom ing., Konstanz U., Fed. Rep. Germany, 1978; MS with distinction, George Washington U., 1980, DSc with superiour performance, 1982. Engr. Siemens Corp., Erlangen, Fed. Rep. Germany, 1977-78; lectr. George Washington U., Washington, 1978-82; asst. prof. engring. Cath. U. Am., 1982-85, assoc. prof. elec. engring., 1985-92, prof., 1992—, chmn. dept. elec. engring. and computer sci., 1997-2001, dean Sch. Engring., 2001—. Cons. Mitre Corp., Meridian Corp., Jet Propulsion Lab., others; dir. Ctr. for Artificial Intelligence and Robotics, 1985—; mem. organizing coms. for various robotics confs.; sr. rsch. assoc. NAS, 1990-; program v.p. IEEE; program vice chair IEE-Internat. Conf. on Robotics 2d Automation, 1997, Internat. Symposium and Robotic Automation (ICRA 97); chmn. organizing com. Robotics Internat., Internat. Symposium Robotics and Mfg. Founding editor, editor-in-chief Jour. Intelligent Automation and Soft Computing; editor: Robotics and Manufacturing, Vol. 5, 1994, Intelligent Automation and Soft Computing, Vol. 1, 1994, Vol. 2, 1994; mem. editl. bd. Jour. Intelligent and Fuzzy Sys., Engring. Design and Automation; contbr. numerous papers IEEE Transaction of Automatic Control, Internat. Jour. Control, Jour. Robotics and Autonomous Sys., Jour. Robotic Sys., Jour. Intelligent Robotic Sys.; assoc. editor Computers and Elec. Engring.: An Internat. Jour., 1992—; guest editor Jour. Robotic Sys. Recipient Rsch. Initiation award Engring. Found., 1985, Rsch. Excellence award Cath. U. Am., 1989; fellow NASA-Am. Soc. Elec. Engrs., 1985, 86; NASA-ASEE summer fellow Goddard Space Flight Ctr., 1994; Disting. Alumni scholar George Washington U., 2001-02. Mem. IEEE (sr., v.p. Washington chpt.), Internat. Soc. Mini-and Microcomputers, Soc. Mfg. Engrs. (sr. Robotics Internat.), Sigma Xi, Tau Beta Pi (faculty advisor). Roman Catholic. Avocations: guitar, singing, tennis, skiing, ping pong. E-mail: nguyen@cua.edu.

NGUYEN, CLIFFORD HAM-THIEM, telecommunications engineer; b. Saigon, Vietnam, Nov. 7, 1962; came to U.S., 1982; s. Nghi Duc Nguyen and Lien Kim Hoang; m. Julie Thach Pham. BSEE, Poly. U., 1988, MSEE, 1989; MA in Stats., Columbia U., 1998. Electronics engr. DoD-ARDEC, Dover, N.J., 1989-91; switch engr. Bell Atlantic/NYNEX, N.Y.C., 1991-96, sr. engr., 1996-99, sr. specialist, 1999, Lucent, 1999-2000; ops. mgr. Bell Labs, 2000—, mem. tech. staff. E-mail: cliffnguyen@lucent.com.

NGUYEN, DUC THAI, civil engineering educator; b. July 19, 1952; s. Dac Khac and Thinh Thai; m. Hang N. Nguyen, July 31, 1956; children: Eric, Don. BSCE, Northeastern U., 1975; PhD in Civil Engring., U. Iowa, 1982. Asst. prof. Old Dominion U., Norfolk, Va., 1985-90, assoc. prof., 1990-96, prof., 1996—. Presenter in field. Contbr. articles to profl. jours. Recipient Giga Flop Internat. award Gray Rsch. Co., Nev., 1989, NASA Tech. Brief award NASA Langley, Hampton, Va., 1993. Office: Old Dominion Univ 135 KAUF Norfolk VA 23529

NGUYEN, DUNG DANG, physician; Diplomate Am. Bd. Internal Medicine, Am. Bd. Nephrology. Attending physician NYU Downtown Hosp. Fellow ACP, Am. Soc. Nephrology; mem. Renal Physicians Assn. Office: 254 Canal St Rm 5001A New York NY 10013-3501

NGUYEN, GIANG DAI, artist, sculptor, graphic artist, muralist; b. Hanoi, Vietnam, May 21, 1944; came to U.S., 1992; s. Bui Dinh and Luan Thi (Le) N.; m. Thuy Bich Cao, Dec. 1976 (div. May 1985); children: Anh Nhat, Lan Thuy; m. Nguyen Tuoi Thi, Oct. 24, 1998. Grad. Sch. Art, Hanoi, 1965; AA, Coll. Art, Hanoi, 1968; BA, Coll. Art, Moscow, 1974. Supervisory artist advtg. and exhibiting co., Hanoi, 1975-78; lectr. Coll. Art, 1978-80; polit. prisoner, 1980-87; polit. refugee Hong Kong, 1988-91; artist Seattle, 1992—. Pvt. collections in U.S., Japan, Can., Hong Kong, France; collection in Mus. of Art, Voronezh, Russia; murals include USA Today, Seattle, 1995, American Jazz, Seattle, 1994, Traditions of Vietnamese Culture, Seattle, 1992, Old Medicine of the Philippines, Battayon, 1991; exhbns. include Chinese Galley: Asian artists group show, Seattle, 1996, University Friends Ctr., Seattle, 1994, solo show at Pillar Point, Hong Kong, 1991, internat. group show at mus., Sophia, Bulgaria, 1977, group show Moscow, 1972; inventor of Upside Down art; author: Manifesto of Upside-Downism. Named Most Talented Artist of the World in internat. competition Stockholm, 1997; winner 3rd prize 1st Internat. Drawing Contest World of Art, 1997, 3rd prize Internat. Competition, Stockholm, 1997, 3rd prize Wash. State Conv. Ctr. group show, 1993, Best Contemporary Art CD-ROM--juried collection, 1996. Mem. Vietnamese Artist Assn. of N.W. U.S.A., S.E. Effective Devel., Inc. Home: 7165 Holly Park Dr S Seattle WA 98118-3527

NGUYEN, HAN VAN, mechanical engineer; b. Danang, Vietnam, June 10, 1956; came to U.S., 1974; s. Tien Van and Dieu Anh (Khoa) N.; m. Thien-Tam Trang, Jan. 7, 1995; children: Huy, Minh. BSME with distinction, Iowa State U., 1979; MSME, Purdue U., 1981, PhD, 1986. Registered profl. engr., Calif., Wash. Grad. rsch. asst. Purdue U., West Lafayette, 1979—83; sr. engr. Westinghouse Electric Corp., Sunnyvale, Calif., 1983—87; mem. tech. staff The Boeing Co., Huntington Beach, 1987—91, engring. specialist, 1991—96, sr. engring. specialist, 1996—2000, prin. engr./scientist, 2000—02, assoc. tech. fellow, 2002—. Mem. adj. faculty Calif. State Poly. U., Pomona, 1995-97. Contbr. articles to profl. jours. Bd. dirs. L.A. Coun. Engrs. and Scientists, 2000-01. Recipient Cert. of Appreciation, Rockwell Internat. Corp., 1989, 94, Instant Compensation award Rockwell Internat. Corp., 1992, 94, NASA Group Achievement award, 1992; Iowa State U. scholar; Purdue U. fellow Fellow AIAA (assoc., liquid propulsion tech. com., 2000-, conf. session chmn., 2002), Inst. Advancement Engring.; mem. Boeing Asian Am. Profl. Assn., Golden Key, Sigma Xi, Phi Kappa Phi, Tau Beta Pi, Pi Tau Sigma, Eta Kappa Nu, Pi Mu Epsilon, Phi Eta Sigma. Achievements include development of numerous thermo-fluid models to evaluate the design and predict the performance of launch vehicle propulsion systems, and publications in space propulsion. Office: The Boeing Co MC H012-B201 5301 Bolsa Ave Huntington Beach CA 92647-2048

NGUYEN, KAREN NGOC-KHANH, pharmacist; b. Saigon, Vietnam, Feb. 16, 1962; came to U.S., 1991; d. Tien Minh Nguyen and Hoa Thi Huynh. BS in Chem. Engring., Poly. U., Saigon, 1985; pre-pharmacy, Montgomery Coll., 1993; PharmD, U. Md., Balt., 1997. Registered pharmacist, Md., Va., Fla., Calif. Biol. aid Nat. Cancer Inst., Bethesda, 1991-93, summer 1994, 95; pharmacy technician Johns Hopkins Hosp., Balt., 1995-96, Giant Pharmacy, Gaithersburg, Md., 1996-97; intern Rite Aid Pharmacy, Alexandria, Va., 1996-97, pharmacist Herndon, 1997-98, So. Md. Hosp. Ctr., Clinton, 1998—, IHS Infusion Svcs., Rockville, Md., 1998-99, Giant Pharmacy, Germantown, 1999—. Mem. Am. Pharm. Assn., Am. Soc. Health Sys. Pharmacists, Md. Soc., Health Sys. Pharmacists, Alpha Zeta Omega. Avocations: traveling, reading, drawing, music, photography.

NGUYEN, KY DUC, electrical engineer; b. Saigon, Vietnam, July 31, 1959; came to U.S., 1979; s. Trinh Duc and Mo Thi (Tran) N.; m. Oanh Hoang, Jan. 17, 1987; children: Khue-Nghi, Huan Quoc. BSEE, Ariz. State U., 1986; MBA, U. Phoenix, 1996. Registered profl. engr., Calif, Ariz. Engr. ABB Combustion Engring., Windsor, Conn., 1986-88, Underwriters Labs., Inc., Santa Clara, Calif., 1988-89; sr. engr. Palo Verde Nuclear Sta., Tonopah, Ariz., 1989-97; design engr. Edison Internat., San Clemente, Calif., 1997—. Mem. Elec. Power Rsch. Inst., Palo Alto, 1993-94. Mem. IEEE, Am. Nuclear Soc. Home: 1906 Teresita Ln Newport Beach CA 92660-4443 Office: Edison Internat 5000 Pacific Coast Hwy San Clemente CA 92674 E-mail: nguyenkd@songs.sce.com., kdnguyen@yahoo.com.

NGUYEN, LUU THANH, engineering executive; b. Saigon, Vietnam, Oct. 11, 1954; s. Luong Thanh Nguyen and Cuc Bach Tran; m. Van D. Do; children: Kevin, Scott children: Kelly. PhD, MIT, 1984. Mem. rsch. staff IBM Rsch. Labs, Yorktown Heights, NY, 1984—88; sr. rsch. scientist Phillips Rsch. Labs, Sunnyvale, Calif., 1988—91; sr. engring. mgr. Nat. Semiconductor

Corp., Santa Clara, 1991—. Named Fulbright/Nokia Fellow, 2002. Fellow: IEEE. Office: Nat Semiconductor Corp PO Box 58090 Mail Stop 19-100 Santa Clara CA 95052-8090 Office Fax: 408-746-2007. Business E-Mail: luu.nguyen@nsc.com.

NGUYEN, MAI (MAI TUYET NGUYEN), writer; b. Saigon, Vietnam, Nov. 18, 1936; arrived in U.S.A., 1983; d. Tu Van Mai and Hiep Thi Doan; m. Tony Tung Quoc, Sept. 30, 1967; 1 child Kevin Duy. Degree, Dai Hoc Van Khoa, Saigon, Vietnam, 1960. Sec. Soc. Gen. de Surveillance, Belgium Consulate, Saigon, Vietnam, 1954—57; adminstrv. mgr. Connell Bros. Co., 1959—75; adminstrv. asst. Tandon Corp., Calif., 1983—86; freelance writer, 1986—. Author: God's Will, 1996, Little Daisy, 1998, 10 books, 1996—2001, Shadow of Hapiness, 2002. Mem.: Independent Scholars Asia, Nat. Writers Assn. Avocations: reading, art, music, travel, landscaping.

NGUYEN, NGAN-LIEN THI, internist, surgeon; b. Mytho, Vietnam, Mar. 11, 1957; came to U.S., 1975; d. Nhac D. Nguyen and Bich Du Ho; m. Kinh D. Pham, June 8, 1985; children: Larissa, Galen. BS in Biochemistry, Portland (Oreg.) State U., 1979; MD, Oreg. Health Scis. U., 1984. Diplomate Am. Bd. Internal Medicine. Rsch. asst. Portland State U., 1979-80; chem. engr. Tektronix, Beaverton, Oreg., 1980; intern in internal medicine Oreg. Health Scis. U., Portland, 1984-85, resident, 1985-87; pvt. practice, 1987—. Recipient Clyde Johnson award Am. Inst. of Chemists, 1979. Mem. AMA, ACP. Buddhist. Avocations: gardening, travel, collecting antiques, orchids. Home: 10929 SW 11th Dr Portland OR 97219-6471 Office: Portland Adventist Med Grp Internal Medicine Assocs 10201 SE Main St Ste 12 Portland OR 97216-2937

NGUYEN, PAUL DUNG QUOC, lawyer; b. Hung Yen, Vietnam, Feb. 2, 1943; came to U.S., 1975; s. Trac Trong and Do Thi (Vu) N.; m. Kim-Dung T. Dang, Dec. 26, 1967; children: Theresa Thu, Catherine Bao-Chau, Jonathan Hung. LLB, Hue Law Sch., Vietnam, 1965; MA in Pub. Policy Adminstrn., U. Wis., 1973. Bar: N.Y. 1979, U.S. Dist. Ct. (so. and ea. dists.) N.Y. 1979, U.S. Tax Ct. 1979. Prof. law Hue & Can Tho Law Schs., Vietnam, 1973-75; assoc. Proskauer, Rose, Getz & Mendelsohn, N.Y.C., 1979-80; pvt. practice, 1980-81; corp. law specialist Office of Corp. Counsel, City of N.Y., 1981-94; counsel, country rep. Hanoi Rep. Office White & Case, Vietnam, 1994-95; counsel Port Authority of N.Y. and N.J., N.Y.C., 1995—. Adj. asst. prof. NYU, 1998—. Bd. dirs. N.Y.C. Indochinese Refugees; hon. chmn. lawyers com. for human rights Vietnamese Legal Protection Fund, 1990-94; legal advisor Indochina Resource Action Ctr., 1990-94; dir. S.E. Asia Resource Action Ctr., 1995-98. Recipient Nat. Legion Honor award Office of Pres., Saigon, 1970. Mem. ABA, Assn. of Bar of City of N.Y. (Outstanding Performance award com. on mcpl. affairs 1986), Asian Am. Bar Assn. N.Y. (pres. 2000-01, bd. dirs. 1993—), Nat. Asian Pacific Am. Bar Assn. (N.E. regional gov. 1998-2000). Avocations: tennis, reading, classical music.

NGUYEN, PHU THIEN, obstetrician-gynecologist; b. Quang Duc, Vietnam, Mar. 7, 1963; s. Khoi Nguyen and Phan Vu; m. Julie Hwynn, Feb. 18, 1996; 1 child Jett. BSChemE, Calif. Inst. Tech., 1984; DO, Western U., 1992. Diplomate Am. Bd. Ob-Gyns. Advanced head vacuum process engr. IBM, San Jose, Calif., 1984-87; intern Coast Plaza Doctors Hosp., Norwalk, 1992-93; resident Cook County Hosp., Chgo., 1993-97; staff physician Roseland Cmty. Hosp., 1997-2000; pvt. practice Garden Grove, Calif., 2000—. Interim dept. chmn. Roseland Cmty. Hosp., 1998-99, co-chmn., 1999-2000. Recipient scholarship Calif. Inst. Tech., 1984, acad. award Long Beach Lions Club, 1983, medal Math. Assn. Am., 1980, Intern Yr. award Coast Plaza Drs. Hosp., 1993, First Place Rsch. award Cook County Hosp., 1997. Fellow ACOG; mem. AMA, Am. Coll. Ob-Gyn., Primary Care Network, Am. Acad. Ambulatory Care, Calif. Med. Assn., Orange County Med. Assn.. Avocations: tennis, swimming, music, guitar.

NGUYEN, QUOC, mechanical engineer; b. Saigon, Vietnam, Jan. 10, 1953; came to U.S. 1976; s. Thinh V. and Oanh (Le) N.; children: Jenifer, Michelle. BSME, West Coast U., 1978. Mech. engr. Jaras, Baum & Bolles, L.A., 1976-80, asst. office mgr., 1980-83; project mgr. Store, Matakovich & Wolfberg, San Gabriel, Calif., 1983-86, v.p. El Monte, 1986-93, sr. v.p., 1993—, also dir., 1986—; prin. Antieri & Assocs., Cons. Engrs., Inc., L.A., 1998-99; pres. East West Cons. Svcs., Pomona, Calif., 1999—. Mem. ASHRAE.

NGUYEN, RU, entomologist; b. Nhatrang, Khanh Hoa, Vietnam, Dec. 12, 1944; s. Tam Nguyen and Van Thi Le; m. Kim-Dung Thi Nguyen, Jan. 28, 1981; 1 child Kim-Anh. BS, Coll. Agr., Saigon, Vietnam, 1966; PhD, U. Fla., 1975. Asst. entomologist U. Fla., Gainesville, 1976—78; rsch. fellow Alexander von Humboldt-Stiftung/U. Bonn, Germany, 1978—79; rsch. entomologist, leader USDA-APHIS-PPQ, Ft. Lauderdale, Fla., 1980—82; rsch. entomologist divsn. plant industry Fla. Dept. Agr., Gainesville, 1982—. Mem. Caribbean fruit fly tech. com. Fla. Dept. Agr., 1983—; mem. citrus leafminer task force U. Fla., Gainesville, 1994—98; mem. nat. genetic resources adv. coun. USDA, Washington, 2000—. Contbr. articles to profl. jours.; author: (book) Catalog of Aleyrodidae on Citrus and Their Natural Enemies, 1993. Recipient Disting. Svc. to Agr. award, Gamma Sigma Delta, 1995, Outstanding Achievement award in developing Fly Free Zone, Fla. Dept. Agr. and Consumer Svcs., 1984. Mem.: Fla. Entomol. Soc. (Team Rsch. award 1997, Achievement award for rsch. 2002), Internat. Orgn. for Biol. Control, Entomol. Soc. Am. Home: 6625 NW 57th Way Gainesville FL 32653 Office: Divsn Plant Industry PO Box 147100 Gainesville FL 32614 Office Fax: 352-372-3505. E-mail: nguyenr@doacs.state.fl.us.

NGUYEN, SAM (VAN NGUYEN), economist, researcher; b. Vinhthanh, Vietnam, Aug. 7, 1928; s. Phuoc Van and Mai thi Nguyen; m. Diem Tonnu, Jan. 25, 1958; children: hang, Huy, Khoi, binh, Trang, Loan. BA in Law, Saigon U., 1957, MS in Econs., 1961; AA, Ohlone Coll., 1995. Officer Nat. Bank of Vietnam, Saigon, 1959-75; econs. rschr. Calif., 1990—. Author: Eph Pha Tha, 1998. Home: 2075 Springwater Dr Fremont CA 94539 E-mail: Sam_Nguyen@yahoo.com.

NGUYEN, TAI QUYEN, neurosurgery educator; b. Saigon, Vietnam, Dec. 26, 1944; came to U.S., 1974; s. Bau Quyen and Loi Le N.; m. Trinh Ngoc Pham, Oct. 1973; children: Trang, Tri, Trac. MD, Saigon U., 1972. Diplomate Am. Bd. Neurosurgery. Intern in gen. surgery Yale-New Haven Hosp., 1975-76; resident in neurosurgery Yale-New Haven Hosp., Hartford (Conn.) Hosp., 1976-79; instr. neurosurgery Saigon U. Sch. Medicine, 1972-74; asst. prof. neurosurgery U. Fla. Coll. Medicine, Jacksonville, 1980-86, assoc. prof., 1986—, assoc. chmn. dept., 1986—; chmn. dept. neurosurgery Univ. Med. Ctr., 1986—. Contbr. articles to med. jours. Fellow ACS; mem. Am. Assn. Neurol. Surgeons, Congress Neurol. Surgeons, Vietnamese Med. Assn. Fla. (chmn 1988-90). Office: U Fla Health Sci Ctr 653 8th St Jacksonville FL 32209-6511

NGUYEN, THACH NGOC, cardiologist; b. Feb. 2, 1953; s. Sau Ngoc Nguyen and Hanh Hong Tran. Resident internal medicine Bklyn. Hosp., 1982-85, fellow cardiology, 1985-87; clin. asst. prof. medicine Ind. U. Sch. Medicine, 1992—; dir. cardiovascular rsch. St. Mary Med. Ctr., Hobart, Ind., 1997—, pres. med. staff, 2002—; pvt. practice. Dir. Interventional Cardiology, St. Mary Med. Ctr., Hobart, Ind.; chmn. Internat. Continuing Med. Edn. Com., 1995—; course dir. Cardiology Update, Siriraj Hosp., Bangkok, 1999; chmn. sci. com. 11th and 12th Great Wall Internat. Congress of Cardiology, Beijing, 2000; edit. cons. Jour. of Interventional Cardiology , 1998, Vietnamese Med. Jour., 2001. Editor: Cardiology Today, 1995, Advances and Challenges in Today's Cardiology, 1997, Management of Complex Cardiovascular Problems: The Consultant's Approach, 1999, Management of Complex Cardiovascular Problems: The Consultant's Approach, 2d edit., 2001, Management of Complex Cardiovascular Problems: The Consultant's Approach, Spanish edit., 2000, Management of Complex Cardiovascular Problems: The Consultant's Approach, Vietnamese edit., 2000, Practical Handbook of Advanced Interventional Cardiology, 2000, Management of Complex Cardiovascular Problems: The Consultant's Approach, Vietnamese edit., 2001. Fellow ACP, Am. Coll. Cardiology, Soc. Cardiovascular Angiography and Intervention. Roman Catholic. Address: 200 E 86th Pl Merrillville IN 46410-6258 Fax: 219-756-1410. E-mail: thachnguyen2000@yahoo.com.

NGUYEN, THINH VAN, internist; b. Vietnam, Apr. 16, 1948; came to U.S., 1971; s. Thao Van and Phuong Thi (Tran) N.; m. Phi Thi Ho, Jan. 2, 1973; children: Anh-Quan, Andrew. BS, U. Saigon, 1970; MS, U. Mo., 1973; MD, U. Tex., 1982. Diplomate Am. Bd. Internal Medicine, Am. Acad. Pain Mgmt., Fed. Lic. Examination. Rsch. asst. U. Tex. Med. Sch., Dallas, 1974-78; intern U. Tex. Med. Br., Galveston, 1982-83, resident, 1983-85; internist Family Health Plan, Inc., Long Beach, Calif., 1985-88, internist, area chief, 1988-89; pvt. practice San Jose, 1990—; chmn. quality assurance/UM com. Premier Care of No. Calif. Med. Group, Inc., 1996-99, also bd. dirs.; chief medical officer Healthglobe, Inc., 2000—. Chmn. interdisciplinary com. Charter Cmty. Hosp., Hawaiian Gardens, Calif., 1988-89, San Jose Med. Ctr., 1993—. Fellow ACP-Am. Soc. Internal Medicine, Am. Acad. Otolaryngic Allergy (affiliate), Am. Soc. Laser Med. Surgery, 1998—; mem. AMA, Am. Acad. Pain Mgmt., Calif. Assn. Med. Dirs. (bd. dirs. 1988-92), Calif. Med. Assn., Santa Clara County Med. Assn. Office: 2470 Alvin Ave Ste 5 San Jose CA 95121-1664

NGUYEN, TUAN D. director, researcher; arrived in U.S., 1962; s. Dinh Gia and Thuy Thi (Tran) Nguyen; m. Thien-Kim Pham, July 15, 1995; children: Andy, Vince; m. Michele Lee McColm, May 9, 1967 (div. June 10, 1994). BA in Philosophy, Lycee Yersin, Dalat, Vietnam, 1961; BA in Econ., San Diego State Coll., 1965; MA in Learning Theories, San Diego State U., 1971; PhD in Social-Personality, Purdue U., 1975. MIS mgr. mental health divsn. Dept. Public Health, San Francisco, 1981—92; dir. rsch. evaluation and planning MHMRA of Harris County, Houston, 1992—. Assoc. dir. program evaluation dist. 5 CMHC, San Francisco; adj. assoc. prof. U. Calif. , San Francisco, 1977—94, U. Tex. Sch. Pub. Health, Houston, 1995; instr. U. Calif., Berkeley, 1985—86; cons., lectr. in field. Contbr. articles to profl. jours. Scholar AID scholar, 1962. Avocations: gardening, poetry, song writing. Home: 614 White Wing Ln Houston TX 77079 Office: MH/MR Authority--Harris County PO Box 25381 1502 Taub Loop Houston TX 77265-2538 Office Fax: 713-970-7106. Business E-Mail: tuan.nguyen@mhmraharris.org.

NGUYEN, TUAN HUY, internist; b. Saigon, Vietnam, Feb. 26, 1965; MD, U. Utah, 1991. Diplomate Am. Bd. Internal Medicine. Intern Kaiser Permanent Med. Ctr., Santa Clara, Calif., 1991-92, resident in internal medicine, 1992-94; pvt. practice, Torrance, 1994—. Mem. staff Torrance Meml. Med. Ctr., 1994—. Mem. AMA. Office: Healthcare Ptnrs Med Group 3565 Del Amo Blvd Torrance CA 90503-1637

NGUYEN, VO D. physician; b. Hung Yen, Vietnam, Mar. 5, 1953; s. Hau V. and Kim T. (Dang) N.; m. Sonia Lim; children: Mai L., Aimee L. MD, U. de Liege, 1978. Cert. Am. Bd. Internal Medicine and Nephrology. Lectr. in medicine U. Mich., Ann Arbor, 1986-87; asst. prof. of medicine Jefferson Coll. of Medicine, Phila., 1987-89; pvt. practice Tri-State Nephrology, Cin., 1989-91, Meml. Clin., Olympia, Wash., 1991—. Office: Meml Nephrology Assocs 500 Lilly Rd NE Olympia WA 98506-5102 E-mail: vdnguyen9@pol.net.

NGUYEN-DINH, THANH, internist, geriatrician, acupuncturist; b. Saigon, Vietnam; s. Bam and Chanh (Thi Duong) Nguyen-Dinh; m. Kim-Chi Nguyen-Dinh; children: Trung, Kim-Trang, Kim-Trinh, Trong. MD, Free U. Brussels, 1974; Tropical MD, Antwerp Tropical Med. Inst., 1975. Diplomate Am. Bd. Internal Medicine, Am. Bd. Geriat. Medicine, Am. Bd. Forensic Examiners, Am. Bd. Forensic Medicine, Coll. Acupuncture and Neuromuscular Therapy, Am. Assn. Integrative Medicine. Asst. prof. medicine Howard Med. Svc., Washington, 1981—; physician dir. St. Elizabeth Unit, D.C. Gen. Hosp., 1983-94. Co-dir. Howard U. Md. Clinics, D.C. Gen. Hosp., 1990-96. Contbr. articles to profl. jours. Fellow ACP, Am. Assn. Integrative Medicine (diplomate). Avocations: chess, swimming. Office: 611 S Carlin Springs Rd Ste 211 Arlington VA 22204-1078 E-mail: tnguyendinh@netscape.net.

NGUYEN-ELY, DARLENE, sculptor; b. Saigon, Vietnam, May 27, 1968; came to U.S., 1975; d. Hue Thi Tran; m. Paul Ely, May 22, 1992. BFA, Calif. State U., Long Beach, 1992. One-woman shows include Long Beach Pub. Main Libr., Calif., 1992, 1993, Acme Art Co., Columbus, Ohio, 1984, Creative Arts Ctr. Mcpl. Gallery, Burbank, Calif., 1994, FireHouse Gallery Rogue C.C., Grants Pass, Oreg., 1995, Sinclair C.C., Dayton, Ohio, 1995, U. Pacific, Stockton, Calif., 1995, Chico Art Ctr., Calif., 1995, Bachman Gallery, Munster, Ind., 1995, U. Ala., Huntsville, 1996, Sun Cities Mus. of Art, Phoenix, 1997, Diane Farris Gallery, Vancouver, B.C., Can., 1997, King County Art Gallery, Seattle, 1998, Diane Farris Gallery, Vancouver, B.C., Can., 1999, Sonia Zaks Gallery, Chgo., 1999, Lane C.C. Art Gallery, Eugene, Oreg., 2000, Washington Sq. Gallery, San Francisco, 2000, Precious Metal Gallery, Boulder, 2000, Charleston Height Arts Ctr., Las Vegas, 2001, Sonia Zaks Gallery, Chgo., 2001, Diane Farris Gallery, Vancouver, B.C., Can., 2001, Artswest, Seattle, 2002, Ill. Cen. Coll., Peoria, 2002, exhibited in group shows at Spring Street Gallery, L.A., 1995, Hunsaker Schlesinger Gallery, Santa Monica, Calif., 1996, Ariana Gallery, Royal Oak, Mich., 1996, Orlando Gallery, Sherman Oaks, Calif., 1996, Sonia Zaks Gallery, Chgo., 1996, Site Gallery, L.A., 1997, Diane Farris Gallery, Vancouver, B.C., Can., 1997, 1998, 1999, Art Forum Berlin, 1999, Gary Snyder Fine Art, N.Y.C., 2000, Artcore Gallery, Toronto, Ont., Can., 2000, Vancouver Art Gallery, 2000, Pa. Acad. Fine Arts, Phila., 2001, Bellevue (Wash.) Art Mus., 2002, numerous others, Represented in permanent collections Rockwell Internat. World Hdqrs., L.A.; contbr. articles. Recipient award The Drawing Room Studios and Gallery, 1993, Assn. Viet Arts, 1993, Creative Arts Ctr. 1993, 94, 95, Calif. Discovery Gold award, 1993, Gallery 57, 1994, Calif. Works, 1994, Thousand Oaks Art Assn., 1994, Riviera Fine Arts Ctr., 1994, Baystreet Galleria, 1995, Michael Levy Gallery, 1996; (honorarium paid) Sinclair C.C., 1995, Rogue C.C., 1995, Ryals Gallery, 1995, Assn. for Viet Arts, 1995, Chico Art Ctr., 1995, U. Ala., 1996, Palos Verdes Art Ctr., Mcpl. Art Ctr., 1996; Individual Artist fellow, 1996-97; grantee Pollock-Krasner Found., 1994-95, 98—, Ruth Chenven Found., 1995-96, Elizabeth Greenshield Found., 1996-97, 99, 2000, Artist Trust, 1998. Avocations: listening to classical music, travel, biking, hiking. Studio: DNE Studio 15698 168th Ave SE Monroe WA 98272-2695

NI, LUQUN, research scientist; b. Shanghai, China, May 15, 1942; parent Shenzong and Huizhen Ni; m. Huili Zhang. Cert. for study in math., U. Calif., Santa Barbara, 1981. Asst. rschr. Inst. Math. Academia Sinica, Beijing, 1977—83; vis. scholar Stanford U., Calif., 1986—87; assoc. prof. Inst. Math. Academia Sinica, Beijing, 1983—92; vis. scholar U. Calif., Santa Barbara, 1979—83, San Diego, 1988—96, assoc. rsch. scientist, 1997—; guest prof. Lab Nonlinear Mechanics of Continous Media, Inst. Mechanics, Academia Sinica, Beijing, 1994—99. Author: (research article) Journal of Mathematical Analysis & Applications, 1982, Quarterly Applied Mathmatics, 1984, The International Journal of Robotics Research, 1990, Journal of the Mechanics and Physics of Solids, 1990, European Journal of Applied Mathematics, 1994, Mechanics of Materials, 1996, Philosophical magazine, 2000, Journal of Applied Mechanics, 2001, SIAM Journal of Applied Mathematics. Personal E-mail: niluqun@hotmail.com. Business E-Mail: lni@ucsd.edu.

NI, SHAWN, economics educator; b. Beijing, Sept. 4, 1962; came to U.S., 1985; s. Daxin Ni and Guangmei Zhang; m. Xi Tao, Sept. 21, 1985; children: Daniel, Alan. BS, Tsinghua U., Beijing, 1985; PhD, U. Minn., 1991. From asst. to assoc. prof. U. Mo., Columbia, 1990—. Contbr. articles to profl. jours. including Econ. Theory, Can. Jour. Econ., Rev. Econ. and Stats., Jour. Monetary Econ. Grantee U. Mo., 1996-99. Mem. Am. Econ. Assn. E-mail: nix@missouri.edu.

NIBECK, SUSAN NELSON, real estate sales agent; b. St. Louis, July 17, 1938; d. Maurice Hughes and Susan Jeanette (Steuber) Nelson; m. James I. Nibeck, Jan. 31, 1959; children: Christopher Robert, Kimberly Sue. AB, Washington U., St. Louis, 1960. Cert. tchr., Mo. Sales assoc. Realty World Porterfield, Hinsdale, Ill., 1977-1982, ERA-Jensen & Feinstein Realtors and predecessors, Hinsdale, 1982—. Coord. and founder Widowed Persons of Western Suburbs, 1990—; sec. Hinsdale Caucus, 1989-93. Mem. DAR, AAUW (chmn. study group 1990—), Hinsdale C. of C. (coord. farmers market 1977—), Kappa Kappa Gamma (pres. and other offices). Mem. Congregational Ch. Home: 122 N Monroe St Hinsdale IL 60521-3145 Office: ERA-Jensen & Feinstein LLC 19 W Chicago Ave Hinsdale IL 60521-3461

NIBLACK, NANCY LEE PARHAM, insurance agent, financial consultant, social worker; b. Martin, Tenn., Jan. 24, 1941; d. Thomas Anderson Jr. and Helen Rose (Hilliard) Parham; m. John Cumming Watkins Jr., Sept. 26, 1964 (div. Oct. 1971); 1 child, Scott Christopher Watkins Niblack; m. James Frederick Niblack, June 7, 1981 (div. Oct. 1990). AA, St. Johns River Jr. Coll., 1961; BA, U. Fla., 1963; MSW, U. Ala., 1969. CLU, ChFC. Psychiat. social worker Bryce Hosp., Tuscaloosa, Ala., 1965-69; asst. prof. Inst. Contemporary Corrections & Behavioral Sci. Sam Houston State Univ., Huntsville, 1969-70; clin. social worker Comprehensive Care Ctr., Lexington, Ky., 1971-79, Mental Health Svcs., Inc., Gainesville, Fla., 1979-80; spl. agt. Prudential Preferred Fin. Svcs., 1980-96; life specialist Allstate Life, 1996-99; evaluation counselor, LCSW, Shands at Vista, 1999—. Part time lectr. Univ. Ky., Lexington, 1971-79. Elder, treas. Grace Presbyn. Ch., 1987-90. Fellow Life Underwriting Tng. Coun.; mem. NASW, Acad. Cert. Social Workers, Soc. Fin. Svc. Profls., Gainesville Assn. Ins. and Fin. Advisors (pres. 1988-89, Key Man award 1988, Agt. of Yr. award 1992), Estate Planning Coun. Gainesville, Hon. Order Ky. Cols. (treas. Gator chpt. 1988-94), Kiwanis, Alpha Omicron Pi (corp. treas. 1986-95). Democrat. Avocations: swimming, hiking, white water rafting, kayaking, Koi pond. Office: Shands at Vista 4101 NW 89th Blvd Gainesville FL 32606 E-mail: niblale@shands.ufl.edu.

NIBLEY, ANDREW MATHEWS, editorial executive; b. Maxwell AFB, Ala., May 25, 1951; s. Owen Smoot and Frances Elizabeth (Browder) N.; m. Mary Elizabeth Michael, Nov. 24, 1984; children: Kevin Mathews, Carlyle Gower, Leath Michael. Attended, Montgomery Coll, Rockville, Md., 1970-72, Univ. Md., 1973. Legis. corr. UPI, Hartford, Conn., 1975-78, bur. chief Concord, N.H., 1979, Treasury corr. Washington, 1980, Reuters N.Am., Washington, 1980-82, editor-in-charge, 1982, news editor, 1982-85, N.Y.C., 1985-87; news editor Europe Reuters Holdings, London, 1987-89; editor, America Reuters America Inc., N.Y.C., 1989-94, sr. v.p., news and TV, 1993-94; editor, exec. v.p., bd. dirs. Reuters New Media Inc., N.Y.C., 1994-97; pres. Digest and Media Publishing Reuters Group PLC, 1998-99; exec. v.p. Reuters Am. Holdings Plc.; pres. Reuters TV Am., Inc., 1998-99; pres., CEO Get Music LLC, 1999—2001. Mem. Knight-Bagehot editl. panel Columbia U., 1995-99; bd. dirs. Sportsline USA, Inc., iMediation SA, Kinecta Corp.; bd. advisors Red Herring Mag., Nervestruck Media, Xlantic LLC; exec. mgmt. com. Reuters Am. Holdings, Inc., 1994-99; bd. dirs. New Directions for News, Overseas Press Club Found. Mem. Gov.'s Coun. on Alcoholism and Drug Abuse, mem. media subcom., 1991-92; trustee N.J. Ctr. for Family Studies; bd. advisors Grad. Sch. Journalism U. Calif., Berkeley, 1993-98; patron: Birds of Vt. Mus. Recipient Meritorious Service award Nat. Press Club. Mem. Am. Soc. Newspaper Editors (editl. bd. 1992-93), Overseas Press Club (program vice chmn. 1990-93, bd. govs. 1993-96, treas. 1996-2000), Fgn. Press Assn., Internat. Platform Assn., N.Y. New Media Assn., Triathlon Fedn. Am., Montclair Golf Club (Verona, N.J.), Essex Running Club, The Athletic and Swim Club (N.Y.C.). Avocations: golf, tennis, jogging, racquetball, triathlons.

NICASTRO, DAVID HARLAN, forensic engineer, consultant, author; b. L.A., Mar. 12, 1961; s. Leo and Ruth Elizabeth (Moody) N. BA, Pomona Coll., 1983; MS, U. Tex., 1985. Registered profl. engr., Tex. Staff engr. Law Engring. Inc., Houston, 1985-86, project engr., 1986-90, sr. engr., 1990-91; prin. engr., 1992-94; pres. Engring. Diagnostics, Inc., 1994-2000, CEO, 2000—. Contbr. articles to profl. jours. Recipient Tileston prize Pomona Coll., 1983. Mem. ASCE (chmn. materials divsn. Houston chpt. 1989, tech. coun. for forensic engring., chmn. com. on dissemination of failure info., 1991—), ASTM (chmn. com. C24). Democrat. Mem. Christian Ch. Achievements include development of taxonomy for failure classification, matrix method of objective failure mechanism evaluation. Office: Engring Diagnostics Inc 106 E 6th St Ste 620 Austin TX 78701-3638

NICASTRO, FRANCIS EFISIO, defense electronics and retailing executive; b. N.Y.C., Apr. 21, 1942; s. Louis and Janet Amaloa (Onnis) N.; m. Rosalind Piperno, Nov. 22, 1972 (div. Aug. 1995); 1 child, Jason. BS in Econs., U. Pa., 1964. Audit analyst ops., coordinator audit and procedures S.H. Kress and Co., N.Y.C., 1967-68; mgr. audit and acctg. Singer Co., 1968-76, dir. acctg. and budgets, 1976-77, dir. cons. acctg., 1977-79, dir. domestic treasury ops. Stamford, Conn., 1979-80, asst. treas., 1980-86, treas., 1986-89; corp. v.p., treas. Grand Union Co., Wayne, N.J., 1989-2000; restructuring specialist FTI Policano and Manzo, Saddlebrook, 2000—. Served to 1st lt. U.S. Army, 1964-66. Republican. Home: 61 Rowayton Woods Dr Norwalk CT 06854-3907 E-mail: fnicastro@aol.com.

NICASTRO-DOHERTY, CYNTHIA MARIE, systems director; b. Quincy, Mass., Mar. 8, 1958; d. John Joseph and Gina (Roffo) Nicastro; m. Michael Francis Doherty, July 21, 1989; 1 child, Rebecca. BS with honors, Am. Internat. Coll., 1980. Programmer Evans Corp., Braintree, Mass., 1982-83; programmer, analyst Comml. Union Ins., Boston, 1983-84, John Hancock Property & Casualty, Boston, 1984-85, project leader, 1985-87, systems mgr., 1987-93; dir. quality assurance Edn. Loan Svcs., Inc., Braintree, Mass., 1993-94, dir. info. design and delivery, 1994—. Vol. Boston Marathon, 1986-91; co. rep. United Way, Boston, 1990. Mem. High Performance Profls., Franklin Country Club. Avocations: cross country skiing, crafts, interior design, stock market. Office: Edn Loan Svcs Inc 25 Braintree Hill Office Park Braintree MA 02184-8702

NICCOLI, ANNE MARIE, social sciences educator; b. Hartford, Conn., Sept. 22, 1952; d. Alfred Joseph and Angeline P. (Thibodeau) Lizotte; m. Arthur Peter Niccoli, Mar. 11, 1972; 1 child, Eric Andrew. BS in Bus., Psychology, Sociology, Nathaniel Hawthorne, 1980; MA in Psychology and Counseling, Rivier Coll., 1987; hon. diploma, Oglala Lakota Coll., 1997. Cert. counselor educator, N.H. Test examiner RGI, San Diego, 1991, Office Pers. Mgmt. U.S. Govt., Boston, 1992—; adj. faculty Franklin Pierce Coll, Nashua, N.H., sr. adj. instr. Grad. and Profl. Studies Divsn. NH, 1995—2002. Mem. PTK adv. force Hesser Coll., Manchester, 1991, adj. faculty 1991-98; team mem. for integrating online instrn. Franklin Pierce Coll., Rindge, N.H., 1995-2002; master lectr. faculty Daniel Webster Coll., Nashua, 1996—; faculty tchg. internats. N.H. Coll., Manchest r, 1996—; workshop leader Castle Coll., Windham, N.H., 1997; developer on-line courses. Mem. ptnrs. coun. Habitat for Humanity, Atlanta, 1999. With USAF, 1971-73. Named Hon. Citizen, Boys Town. Mem. Amnesty Internat., Southern Poverty Law Ctr., Concord Coalition, Ctr. for Sci. Pub. Interest, Union Concerned Scientists, The Carter Ctr., The Wilson Ctr., Rivier Coll. Alumni Assn., The Ctr. Civic Life. Avocations: camping and outdoor activities, museums, reading, music. Home: 2 Nakomo Dr Litchfield NH 03052-2417

NICCOLINI, DIANORA, photographer; b. Florence, Italy, Oct. 3, 1936; came to the U.S., 1945, naturalized, 1960; d. George and Elaine (Augsbury) N. Student, Hunter Coll., 1955-62, Art Students League, 1960, Germain Sch. Photography, 1962; BA magna cum laude, Marymount Manhattan Coll., 1995. Med. photographer Manhattan Eye, Ear and Throat Hosp., 1963-65; organizer med. photography dept. Lenox Hill Hosp., 1965-67, 1st chief med. photographer, 1965-67; organizer, head dept. med. and audio visual edn. St. Clare's Hosp., N.Y.C., 1967-76; mem. Third Eye Gallery, 1974-76; owner Dianora Niccolini Creations, 1976—. Instr. photography Camera Club N.Y., 1978-79, Germain Sch. Photography, 1978-79, N.Y. Inst. Photography, 1981-83; instr. comml. photography N.Y. Inst. Tech., 1996-97. One-woman shows include 209 Photo Gallery, Top of the Stairs Gallery, Third Eye Gallery, 1974, 75, 77, Photographics Unltd. Gallery, N.Y.C., 1981, West Broadway Gallery, N.Y.C., 1981, Camera Club N.Y., 1982, Overseas Presss Club, N.Y.C., 1983, Impulse Gallery, Provincetown, Mass., 1992, Throckmorton Fine Art Gallery, N.Y.C., 1998, 2001; exhibited in group shows at Photography Over 65, N.Y.C., 1978, Jacob Javits Fed. Bldg., N.Y.C., 1992, Neikrug Gallery, N.Y.C., 1993, Ward-Nasse Gallery, N.Y.C., 1996, Internat. Salon, N.Y.C., 1996, Curcio-Spector Gallery, N.Y.C., 1996, Throckmorton Fine Art, Inc., 1997, 2001; pub. portfolios; author: Women of Vision, 1982, Men in Focus, 1983, Big Fun with Billy, 2001; editor: P.W.P. Times, 1981-82; contbr. to photog. books, 1979, 80; designer greeting cards Flashcards, Inc., 1988-90; contbg. editor Functional Photography, 1979-80, N.Y. Photo Dist. News, 1980; listed in numerous anthologies. Mem. Women Photographers N.Y. (founder 1974), Biol. Photog. Assn., Internat. Ctr. Photography, Am. Soc. Mag. Photographers, Am. Soc. Picture Profls., Profl. Women Photographers (pres. 1980-84). Home: 356 E 78th St New York NY 10021-2239 E-mail: dianoran@aol.com.

NICCOLINI, DREW GEORGE, gastroenterologist; b. Rockville Center, N.Y., July 27, 1945; s. George D and Elaine A (Augsbury) Niccolini; children: Alyssa, Rachael, Lesley, Matthew, Adam. BA, Johns Hopkins U., 1967; MD, Tufts U., 1971. Diplomate Am Bd Internal Med, Am Bd Gastroenterology.

Intern St. Elizabeth Hosp., Boston, 1971-72, resident, 1972-74, gastrointestinal fellow, 1974-75, Faulkner Hosp., Boston, 1975-76; clinician Pentucket Med. Assocs., Haverhill, Mass., 1976—; staff physician Hale Hosp., 1976—, Lawrence (Mass.) Gen. Hosp., 1976—. Consult Holy Family Hosp, Methuen, Mass., 1976—; chief med Hale Hosp, Haverhill, Mass., 1987—88. Capt U.S. Army, 1971—77. Fellow: Am Col Gastroenterology; mem.: AMA, ACP, Am Soc Gastroenterology Endoscopy, New Eng Endoscopy Soc (trustee 1997—, bd dirs), Alpha Omega Alpha. Avocations: skiing, tennis. Office: One Parkway Haverhill MA 01830

NICE, CARTER, conductor, music director; b. Jacksonville, Fla., Apr. 5, 1940; s. Clarence Carter and Elizabeth Jane (Hintermister) N.; m. Jennifer Charlotte Smith, Apr. 4, 1983; children: Danielle, Christian, Olivia. MusB, Eastman Sch. Music, 1962; MusM, Manhattan Sch. Music, 1964. Asst. condr., concert master New Orleans Philharm., 1967-79; condr., music dir. Sacramento Symphony, 1979-92; music dir., condr. Bear Valley Music Fest., 1985—. Office: 7729 Rio Barco Way Sacramento CA 95831-4458 E-mail: ccniii@aol.com.

NICE, PAMELA MICHELE, theatre director; b. Mpls., Apr. 24, 1949; d. Charles Monroe and Mary Ellen (Cranmer) N.; 1 child, Nicole Michele. BA, U. Minn., 1972, MA, 1980, PhD, 1984. Cert. in Acting, London Acad. Music and Dramatic Art. Actress Rochester (N.Y.) Shakespeare Theatre, 1973-74, GEVA Repertory Theatre, Rochester, 1974-75; reporter Capitol Hill News Svc., Washington, 1975; theatre dir. Mpls., St. Paul, 1976—; artistic dir. Paul Bunyan Playhouse, Bemidji, Minn., 1987-90; asst. prof. theatre Gustavus Adolphus Coll., St. Peter, 1981-85; vis. instr. Macalester Coll., St. Paul, 1992, 95; assoc. dir. faculty devel. U. St. Thomas, 1990—; artistic dir. Lagniappe Theatre, 1993—. Adj. instr. Theatre, English and Honors Symposia U. St. Thomas. Dir. numerous prodns., including (opera) Flying Dutchman, 1992, (flamenco ballets) Flor, 1990, Sadja, 1996, Garden of Names, 1996, Virtud Negra, 2000—, (plays) Wild Honey, Romeo and Juliet, Good, The Real Thing, Fair Country, As You Like It; video direction and writing: Opening Doors, 1994, Interview with Frida Kahlo, 1996, Hermes Web, 1997; dir., writer (film) Let Her, 2001. Recipient Best Dir. award Minn. One-Act Play Festival, 1991, 93; Fulbright fellow, 1972-73, Malone fellow Nat. Coun. U.S./Arab Rels., 2000; grantee Paul Bunyan Playhouse, 1989, Lagniappe Theatre, MRAC, 1994, 95, 96, 97, 99, Upper Midwest Assn. Internat. Edn. travel grant to Egypt, 1998, Jerome study and travel grant to Egypt, 2000. Mem. Actors' Equity Assn., Mid. Ea. Studies Assn., Theatre Comm. Group, Profl. and Orgn. Devel. Network, Collaboration for Advancement of Teaching and Learning; book and film reviewer Al Jadid, 1999—. Avocations: music, flamenco dancing, political activity, Arabic language, history, literature and arts. Home: 2008 Brewster St Apt 301 Saint Paul MN 55108-2014 Office: U St Thomas 2115 Summit Ave Saint Paul MN 55105-1048 E-mail: pmnice@stthomas.edu.

NICELY, ANDREW ABBOTT, lawyer; b. Rochester, N.Y. s. William Abbott and Linda Brunjes Nicely. BA in Psychology, Bates Coll., 1990; MA in Clin. Psychology, SUNY, Buffalo, 1994; JD, U. Pa., 1997. Bar: Va. 1997, U.S. Ct. Appeals (4th cir.), 1997, D.C. 1998, Ill. 1998, U.S. Dist. Ct. (ea. dist.) Va. 1998, U.S. Dist. Ct. D.C. 1998, U.S. Ct. Appeals (6th, 8th and D.C. cirs.) 1998, U.S. Bankruptcy Ct. (ea. dist.) Va. 1999, U.S. Supreme Ct. 2001. Program counselor Alternatives Unlimited, Inc., Whitinsville, Mass., 1990-91; program mgr. Waltham (Mass.) Com., 1991-92; law clk. Office of Disciplinary Counsel, Phila., 1996-97; assoc. Mayer, Brown & Platt, Washington, 1997—. Mem. Va. Sta Bar Assn., D.C. Bar Assn., Ill. State Bar Assn., Order of Coif. Avocation: aviculture. Office: Mayer Brown Rowe & Maw 1909 K St NW Washington DC 20006-1152

NICELY, CONSTANCE MARIE, career consultant, physician recruiter; b. St. Louis, Sept. 30, 1955; d. Austin and Gertrude Carol (Hogenmiller) N. AA, St. Louis Community Coll., 1989; BA in Polit. Sci., Webster U., St. Louis, 1991. Cert. paralegal; lic. cosmetologist. Cosmetologist Headquarters, Ltd., St. Louis, 1974-75, Eastside/Westside, St. Louis, 1975-79, Joseph Kemble's, Houston, 1980-84, Bushwackers, Houston, 1979-80, Ta Da Hair Salon, St. Louis, 1984—; paralegal Legal Assistance of St. Louis, 1990-91, Snyder, Weir, Shaller, Bachman, St. Louis, 1991, Dubail Judge, P.C., St. Louis, 1992-93, Brown & Crouppen, P.C., 1992-93, Rosen Law Firm, 1993; fin. planner Mut. of N.Y., Clayton, Mo., 1993-94, Mass. Mut., Chesterfield, 1995-96; physician recruiter, career cons. exec. mgmt. Physician Opportunities Network, Inc., Wildwood, 1996—. Mem. NAFE, Assn. Gateway Human Resources Assn., Internat. Assn. Career Mgmt., Nat. Abortion Rights Action League, Ct. Appointed Advocate for Abused and Neglected Children. Democrat. Avocations: singing, ballet, theatre, dance. Home and Office: Omni Network Opportunities 2703 Mars Ln Maryland Heights MO 63043-1942

NICELY, ROBERT FRANCIS, JR. education educator, administrator; b. Greensburg, Pa., Jan. 10, 1940; s. Robert Francis and Jean Isabelle (Baird) N.; m. Donna Comnale, Dec. 29, 1962; children: Lisa Ann, Scott Alan. BS, Pa. State U., 1961; MEd, Indiana U. Pa., 1965; PhD, U. Pitts., 1970. Cert. tchr. math and sci., Pa. Tchr. math. and chemistry Norwin and Gateway Schs., 1961-67; instrnl. cons. Pitts. Sch. Dist., 1967-68; lectr, asst. prof., rsch. assoc. U. Pitts., 1968-72; asst. prof. edn. Pa. State U., University Park, 1972-76, assoc. prof., 1976-86, prof. curriculum supervision ednl. adminstrn., 1986—, also asst. dean, 1987-90, coll. coord. outreach, 1979—87, acting dean, 1989, assoc. dean edn., 1990-98, prof. in charge grad. program curriculum and supervision, 1999-2000, dir. Internship Program in Ednl. Adminstrn., 1999—, coord. grad. studies in curriculum and instrn., 2000-2001. Contbr. articles to profl. jours.; spkr. in field. Mem. ASCD (bd. dirs. 1981-85, 95-99, chair nominating com. 1986-87, chair conf. com. 1990, exec. coun. 2001—, assoc. editor, co-editor, mem. editl. bd. Jour. Curriculum and Supervision 1985-92, Outstanding Affiliate Newsletter and Jour. awards 1993, 94, 96, 98, 2000), Pa. ASCD (pres. 1982-84, exec. bd. 1978—, editor PASCD Update and Pa. Ednl. Leadership, Outstanding Rsch. and Pub. award 1985, 99, Disting. Svc. award 1986, Spl. Leadership award 1990, 97), Cen. Pa. ASCD, Coun. Profs. Instrnl. Supervision, Nat. Coun. Tchrs. Math. (chair instrnl. issues adv. com. 1992-94), Pa. Coun. Tchrs. Math. (pres. 1988-90, Outstanding Leadership and Svc. award 1983, Outstanding Contbns. to Math. Edn. award, 1991, co-editor 4 PCTM Yearbooks), Pa. Edn. Rsch. Assn. (pres. 1987-88, 94-95, editor Pera-Scope 1985-95), Phi Delta Kappa (pres. Pa. state chpt. 1984-85). Avocations: aerobic conditioning, golf, landscape design and construction, genealogy. Home: 2266 Sagamore Dr State College PA 16803-2420 Office: Pa State U 314 Rackley University Park PA 16802-7023 E-mail: bobnicely@psu.edu.

NICHOL, MICHAEL BRUCE, pharmacy educator; b. Encino, Calif., Dec. 15, 1952; s. Monte Bruce and Patricia Carlton N.; m. Shirlynn Irene Spacapan, Aug. 18, 1974 (dec. July 1995); m. Jane Margolies, Apr. 13, 1997; 1 child, Riley. BA in Polit. Sci., U. Tulsa, 1974; MS in Pub. Affairs, U. Oreg., 1983; PhD in Pub. Adminstrn., U. So. Calif., 1987. Health planner Oreg. State Health Planning Devel. Agy., Salem, 1974-77; health planning assoc. Western Oreg. Health Sys. Agy., Eugene, 1977-79, asst. dir. planning, 1979-81, planning, rev. mgr., 1981-83, exec. dir., 1983-84; instr. U. Oreg., 1984; rsch. asst. U. So. Calif., L.A., 1984-87, from lectr. to assoc. prof., 1986-1993, assoc. prof., 1993—, sr. rsch. assoc., 1988—, chair dept. pharm. econs. policy, 1998—. Quantum sufficit ad Centurion prof., 1999. Pharmacoeconomic adv. bd. Amgen, 1993-96; grad. rsch. com. Am. Acad. Coll. Pharmacy, 1998, nat. depression adv. bd. Eli Lilly and Co., 1998; cons., presenter in field. Co-author: (chpt.) California Policy Choices for Long-Term Care, 1990, Annual Review of Gerontology and Geriatrics: Volume 12, 1992, The Health Economics of Depression, 1993; mem. editl. bd. Annals Pharmacotherapy; reviewer JAMA, Pharm. Rsch., PharmacoEconomics, Med. Care, Van Nostrand Reinhold, Annals Pharmacotherapy, Jour. Pharmacy Tech., Jour. Social Adminstrv. Pharmacy; contbr. articles to profl. jours. Bd. dirs. Pub. Health Found. L.A. County, 1992-96, Vis. Nurses Assn., East San Gabriel Valley, 1993-96. Recipient Third Place Faculty Mentor award Searle Fellowship Pharmacy, 1990, 91, Second Place, 1992, Faculty Achievement award Burlington Resources Found., 1992; co-recipient Drug Therapy Rsch. award Am. Soc. Hosp. Pharmacists Rsch. Edn. Found., 1993; Scapa Praetors Student fellow, 1984-86; grantee Eli Lilly, 1989, 95-96, Beohringer-Ingelheim, 1989-90, Kaiser-Permanente Med. Care Program, 1992-95, Upjohn, 1993-94, Astra Merck Group, 1994-95, 95, 97—, Prescription Solutions, 1998, Janssen Pharms., 1999, others. Mem. Internat. Soc. Pharmacoeconomics Outcomes Rsch., Internat. Soc. Quality Life Rsch., Am. Pharm. Assn. (econ. social adminstrv. sci. sect., reviewer), Am. Pub. Health Assn. (drug policy pharmacy svcs. com., med. care sect., reviewer), Am. Assn. Coll. Pharmacy, Assn. Health Svcs. Rsch., Assn. Pub. Policy Mgmt., Pi Alpha Alpha, Phi Lambda Sigma. Office: 1540 Alcazar St # St140 Los Angeles CA 90089-0103 Fax: 323-442-1462. E-mail: mnichol@hsc.usc.edu.

NICHOL, NORMAN J. manufacturing executive; b. East Cleveland, Ohio, Feb. 12, 1944; s. Norman George and Irene Josephine (Peters) N.; m. Janice E. Nichol, Oct. 19, 1968; children: Gerard, Katherine. BBA, Kent State U. Mktg. trainee A.B. Dick Co., Chgo., 1968, sales rep., supr.-spl. markets mgr., 1971-75, br. mgr. Indpls. and Chgo., 1975-80, dir.-gen. mgr. internat., 1980-82, pres., 1982—; pres., CEO Rycoline Products Co., 1982—; pres. Sun Graphic Inc., Rogersol Inc. With U.S. Army, 1968-70. Home: 1021 Dover Ct Libertyville IL 60048-3509 Office: Rycoline Products Inc 5540 N Northwest Hwy Chicago IL 60630-1134 E-mail: njnsplace@aol.com., norm.nichol@rycoline.com.

NICHOLAS, ARTHUR SOTERIOS, manufacturing company executive; b. Grand Rapids, Mich., Mar. 6, 1930; s. Samuel D. and Penelope A. (Kalapodes) N.; m. Bessie Zazanis, Aug. 25, 1957; children: Niki Stephanie, Arthur S., Thomas. BS in Chem. Engrng, U. Mich., 1953; BA in Indsl. Mgmt, Wayne State U., 1957. Registered profl. engr., Mich. Project engr. B.F. Goodrich Co., 1953-54; plant mgr. Cadillac Plastics and Chem. Co., 1954-69; pres., chief exec. officer Leon Chem. and Plastics, Inc., Grand Rapids, 1960-69; with U.S. Industries, Inc., 1969-73, pres., chief operating officer, 1973; now pres. The Antech Group. Bd. dirs. ERO Industries, Inc. Patentee in field. Judge Jr. Achievement, Chgo. Served with USNR, 1948-49. Recipient Distinguished Alumni award Grand Rapids Jr. Coll., 1970 Mem. Young Pres. Orgn., Soc. Plastic Engrs., Mich. Acad. Sci., Arts and Letters, Chgo. Coun. on Fgn. Rels., Pres.' Assn. Mem. Greek Orthodox Ch. Clubs: Chgo. Athletic Assn. (Chgo.), Executives (Chgo.). Home: 655 Oak Rd Barrington IL 60010-3135 Office: 2300 Barrington Rd # 411 Hoffman Estates IL 60195-2082

NICHOLAS, DAVID ROBERT, minister, college president; b. L.A., May 10, 1941; s. Robert Grant and Pearl Elizabeth (Pickard) N.; m. Donna Lynn Roberts, June 28, 1969; children: Joy Lynn, Faith Elizabeth. AB, Azusa Pacific U., 1963; MS, U. So. Calif., 1967; MDiv., L.A. Bapt. Theol. Sem., 1966; ThM, Talbot Theol. Sem., 1971; ThD, Grace Theol. Seminary, 1982. Ordained to ministry Gen. Assn. Regular Bapt. Chs., 1970. Dir. admissions, mem. faculty L.A. Bapt. Coll., Newhall, Calif., 1966-71; dean, pres. Van Nuys (Calif.) Christian Coll., 1972-76; pastor Tri-Lakes Bapt. Ch., Columbia City, Ind., 1977-78; acad. dean, assoc. prof. Southwestern Coll., Phoenix, 1978-80; sr. pastor, acad. supt. Grace Bapt. Ch., Yuba City, 1980-82; sr. pastor Placerita Bapt. Ch., Newhall, 1982-84; pres., prof. theology Shasta Bible Coll., Redding, Calif., 1985—. Chmn. Greater Redding Area Christian Edn. Conv., 1988—; mem. accreditation commn. Transnat. Assn. Christian Colls. and Schs., 1994—; trustee Regular Bapt. Conf. So. Calif., 1983-85, pres., 1963-65; dir. Bapt. Youth Assn., So. Calif., 1969-71. Author: Foundations of Biblical Inerrancy, 1978, What's A Woman to Do ... In the Church?, 1979, Church Discipline: Option or Obligation, 1991, Biblical Judgments, Dictionary of Pre-Millenial Theology, 1996; contbr. articles to religious jours.; recordings include Trombone Testimonies, 1990; Bible tchr. broadcast program Truth for Today, 1988—, Bible Answer Man, 1978-80. Trustee Christian Heritage Coll., El Cajon, Calif., 1981-85; mem. steering com. Calif. Activists Network, Los Altos, Calif., 1991; del. Conf. on the Preservation of the Family, 1991; gov. Am. Coalition for Trad. Values, Washington, 1984; chaplain Los Angeles County Bd. Suprs., 1984. Recipient Svc. award Am. Legion, 1955. Mem. Evang. Theol. Soc., Creation Rsch. Soc., Shasta County Evang. Ministerial Assn. (pres. 1992-95), Kappa Tau Epsilon. Republican. Home: 8264 Taylor Ln Redding CA 96001-9530 Office: Shasta Bible Coll 2951 Goodwater Ave Redding CA 96002-1544

NICHOLAS, FAYARD ANTONIO, dancer, actor, entertainer; b. Mobile, Ala., Oct. 20, 1914; s. Ulysses Domonick and Viola (Harden) N.; m. Geraldine Pate (div. 1955); children: Anthony Fayard, Paul Didier; m. Barbara January, Sept. 17, 1967. Pvt. ed. in, high sch. and coll. related courses. Owner, dancer Cotton Club, Phila., from 1932. Guest lectr. San Francisco State U., UCLA, U. So. Calif., U. Hawaii. Appeared in films Kid Millions, 1934, The Big Broadcast, 1936, Down Argentine Way, 1940, Tin Pan Alley, 1940, The Great American Broadcast, 1941, Sun Valley Serenade, 1941, Orchestra Wives, 1942, Stormy Weather, 1943, The Pirate, 1948, others; Broadway shows include Ziegfield Follies, 1936, Babes in Arms, 1937, St. Louis Woman, 1946; actor The Liberation of L.B. Jones, 1970; choreographer Broadway musical Black and Blue (Tony award), 1989; starred in ballet Nutcracker, San Diego Ballet Co., 1990; commd. Japan Satellite Broadcasting Co., 1991; performer maj. TV shows; entertainer (with Bob Hope) troops in Vietnam. Supporter numerous charity events including Danny Thomas-St. Jude Hosp., Jerry Lewis Telethon, Negro Coll. Fund, Drug Abuse, Spl. Concern with the Plights of Homeless. With U.S. Army, 1943-44. Recipient Emmy award, 1965, Bumps Blackwell Life Achievement award, 1980, Ellie award Nat. Film Soc., 1984, City of L.A. award, 1984, resolution, 1991, City of Hope award, 1986, Golden Angel award, 1986, Josephine Baker award, 1986, Ebony Life Achievement award, 1987, Jeanne Golden Halo award, 1988, Tony award, 1989, Lafayette Players West award, 1991, Paul Robeson award Black Am. Cinema Soc., 1992, Dance Mag. award, 1995, numerous others; named to Black Filmmakers Hall of Fame, 1989; with brother Harold honored at White House and Kennedy Ctr., 1991; honored TV Documentary, 1992; honored Lincoln Ctr., N.Y.C., 1993. Mem. Acad. Arts and Sci. (life), Dance Gallery, Friars Club (life), San Fernando Valley Art Coun. Home: 23388 Mulholland Dr Woodland Hills CA 91364-2733

NICHOLAS, FREDERICK M. lawyer; b. N.Y.C., May 30, 1920; s. Benjamin L. and Rose F. (Nechols) N.; m. Eleanore Berman, Sept. 2, 1951 (div. 1963); children: Deborah, Jan, Tony; m. Joan Fields, Jan. 2, 1983. AB, U. So. Calif., 1947; postgrad., U. Chgo., 1949-50; JD, U. So. Calif., 1952. Bar: Calif. 1952, U.S. Dist. Ct. Calif. 1952, U.S. Ct. Appeals (9th cir.) 1952. Assoc. Loeb & Loeb, L.A., 1952-56; ptnr. Swerdlow, Glikbarg & Nicholas, Beverly Hills, Calif., 1956-62; pvt. practice, 1962-80; pres., atty. Hapsmith Co., 1980—. Bd. dirs. Malibu Grand Prix, L.A., 1982-90; gen. counsel Beverly Hills Realty Bd., 1971-79; founder, pres. Pub. Counsel, L.A., 1970-73. Author: Setting Up a Shopping Center, 1960, Commercial Real Property Lease Practice, 1976. Chmn. Mus. Contemporary Art, L.A., 1987-93, chmn. com. Walt Disney Concert Hall, L.A., 1987-95; trustee Music Ctr. L.A. County, 1987-95, L.A. Philharm. Assn., 1987-95, Mus. of Flying, Santa Monica, Calif., 1991--; chmn. Calif. Pub. Broadcasting Commn., Sacramento, 1972-78; pres. Maple Ctr., 1977-79; co-developer Ronald Reagan Bldg., Washington, 1998; adminstr. Estate of Sam Francis, 1996—; trustee Pitzer coll., 1992-95; hon. trustee Art Ctr. Coll. of Design, 2001—. Recipient Citizen of Yr. award Beverly Hills Bd. Realtors, 1978, Man of Yr. award Maple Ctr., 1980, Pub. Svc. award Coro Found., 1988, The Medici award L.A. C. of C., 1990, Founders award Pub. Counsel, 1990, Trustees award Calif. Inst. Arts, 1993, City of Angels award L.A. Ctrl. Bus. Assn.; named Outstanding Founder in Philanthropy, Nat. Philanthropy Day Com., 1990, Disting. Svc. award U. So. CAlif. Law Sch., 2002. Mem. Beverly Hills Bar Assn. (bd. govs. 1970-76, Disting. Svc. award 1974, 81, Exceptional Svc. award 1986), Beverly Hills C. of C. (Man of Yr. 1983). Home: 1001 Maybrook Dr Beverly Hills CA 90210-2715 Office: Hapsmith Co 5440 McConnell Ave Los Angeles CA 90066

NICHOLAS, HENRY THOMPSON, III, communications engineering executive; BSEE, MSEE, PhD in EE, UCLA. With TRW; dir. microelectronics PairGain Techs.; pres., CEO Broadcom Corp., Irvine, Calif., 1991—. Named one of Top 20 Entrepreneurs, 1997 Red Herring, 1997, World's Top Cyber Elite, 1997 Time Digital Mag., 1997; recipient Engrepreneur of the Yr. award, Ernst & Young, 1996. Office: Broadcom Corp PO Box 57013 Irvine CA 92619-7013 Office Fax: 949-450-8715.

NICHOLAS, JAMES A. surgeon, consultant, educator; b. Portsmouth, Va., Apr. 15, 1921; s. Harry and Julie N.; m. Kiki Chris, June 14, 1952; children: Philip Duncan, Stephen James, Nicole Hambro. BA, NYU, 1942; MD, Downstate Med. Ctr., 1945. Diplomte Am. Bd. Orthop. Surgery. Resident various hosps., N.Y.C., 1946-52; asst. dir. rsch. Hosp. Spl. Surgery, 1952-60; dir. dept. orthop. surgery Lenox Hill Hosp., 1970—, dir. emeritus, 1995—; founding dir. Nicholas Inst. Sports Medicine, 1973—; dir. Inst. Sports Medicine & Athletic Trauma, 1973-99, dir. emeritus, 1999—; dir. Gulf & Western Corp., 1983-93, Paramount Comm., Inc., N.Y.C. Orthopaedic cons. NFL, N.Y.C., 1968—97; mem. Presdl. Coun. Phys. Fitness in Sports, Washington, 1979—82, cons., 1993—98; prof. orthopaedic surgery Cornell Med. Coll., N.Y.C., 1970—2001. Editor 15 books including: Injuries to the Spine and Lower Extremity in Sports Medicine, 1986, 2nd edit., 1995, the Upper Extremity in Sports Medicine, 1990, 2nd edit., 1996; patentee manual muscle tester. Trustee ctr. coun. Cornell U. Med. Ctr. N.Y. Hosp., 1986—94; trustee Am. Jour. of Sports Medicine, 1980—2002. Capt. U.S. Army, 1945—46, capt. U.S. Army, 1952—53. Recipient Frank Babbott Disting. Alumnus award, 1985, Royal Order of Phoenix, Greek Govt. Svc., 1970, David D. Moyer award Ea. Athletic Tng. Assn., 1997; named Health Am. Fitness Leader, Jaycees, 1982; Spingold Found. grantee in sports medicine, 1976—. Fellow ACS, Am. Orthop. Assn.; mem. Orthop. Rsch. Soc. (sec. treas. 1968-69), Am. Orthop. Soc. for Sports Medicine (pres. 1980, named Mr. Sports Medicine 1982, 86), N.Y. Acad. Medicine (pres. 1974), Acad. Orthop. Soc., Greek Orthodox, Mill Reef Club (Antigua, West indies), Hellenic Univ. Club, Westchester Country Club. Avocations: astronomy, golf, piano, synthesizer. Home: 22 Cayuga Rd Scarsdale NY 10583-6940 Office: 130 E 77th St New York NY 10021-1851 E-mail: jnismat@aol.com.

NICHOLAS, LAWRENCE BRUCE, advisory company executive; b. Dallas, Nov. 9, 1945; s. J. W. and Helen Elouise (Whiteacre) N.; m. Virginia Pearl Farmer, Aug. 5, 1967; children: Helen Brooke, John Lawrence, Alexis Bradlee. BBA, So. Meth. U., 1968. Mem. sales staff Nicholas Machinery Co., Dallas, 1963-69; sales mgr. Indsl. and Comml. Rsch. Corp., 1969-74; v.p. Precision Concepts Corp., 1974-76, gen. mgr., 1976-78, pres. Addison, Tex., 1978-86, dir., 1974-86; pres. INCOR Inc., 1974-91, dir., 1972—; pres. INCOR Internat., Dallas, 1981-91. Pres., dir. Multiple Axis Machine Corp., 1981-96, Investment Svcs. Corp., 1991-93; mem. adv. bd. Consultores Patrimoniales, Mex. City, 1992—; pres. Equity Capital Interests, Inc., San Antonio, Tex., 1993—; chmn. bd. dirs. Cross Securities Internat. Corp., San Antonio, 1993-94; pres. Worldwide Exec. Aviation, 1996—. Served as officer Ordnance Corps, U.S. Army, 1968, N.G., 1968-74. Mem. NRA, Soc. Mfg. Engrs., Nat. Shooting Sports Found., Safari Club Internat.

NICHOLAS, LYNN HOLMAN, historian, researcher, writer; b. New London, Conn., Nov. 11, 1939; d. William Grizzard Holman and Carol (Ackiss) Wakelin; m. Robert Carter Nicholas III, Dec. 20, 1965; children: William C., R. Carter, Philip H. Student, Radcliffe Coll., 1957-59; diploma, U. Madrid, 1960; BA, Oxford (Eng.) U., 1964. Mem. adv. panel Presdl. Commn. on Holocaust Assets in the U.S., 1999. Author: The Rape of Europa, 1994 (Nat. Book Critics Circle award 1995). Recipient Chevalier Légion d'Honneur, France, 1999. E-mail: lynnick105@aol.com.

NICHOLAS, NICKIE LEE, retired industrial hygienist; b. Lake Charles, La., Jan. 19, 1938; d. Clyde Lee and Jessie Mae (Lyons) N. BS, U. Houston, 1960, MS, 1966. Tchr. sci. Pasadena (Tex.) Ind. Sch. Dist., 1960-61; chemist FDA, Dallas, 1961-62, VA Hosp., Houston, 1962-66; chief biochemist Baylor U. Coll. Medicine, 1966-68; cheist NASA Johnson Spacecraft Ctr., 1968-73; analytical chemist TVA, Muscle Shoals, Ala., 1973-75; indsl. hygienist, compliance officer OSHA, Dept. Labor, Houston, 1975-79, area dir. Tulsa, 1979-82, mgr. Austin, Tex., 1982-96, ret., 1996. Mem. faculty VA Sch. Med. Tech., Houston, 1963-66. Recipient award for outstanding achievement German Embassy, 1958, Suggestion award VA, 1968, Group Achievement award Skylab Med. Team, NASA, 1974, Personal Achievement award Dept. Labor Fed. Women's Program, 1984, Career Achievement award Federally Employed Women, Inc., 1988, Meritorious Performance award DOL-OSHA, 1990, Disting. Career Svc. award Det. Labor, 1991, Sec.'s Exceptional Achievement award Dept. Labor, 1991, Cert. Appreciation, Osha, 1991, Asst. Sec.'s Leadership award DOL-OSHA, 1992, 96. Mem. Am. Chem. Soc. (dir. analytical group Southeastern Tex. and Brazosport sects. 1971, chmn. elect 1973), Am. Assn. Clin. Chemists, Am. Conf. Govtl. Indsl. Hygienists, Am. Indsl. Hygiene Assn., Am. Soc. Safety Engrs., Am. Harp Soc., Fed. Exec. Assn. (pres. 1984-85), Order Eastern Star, Kappa Epsilon. Home: 1002 Sundance Dr Dripping Springs TX 78620-9501

NICHOLAS, PETER M. medical products executive; married; 3 children. BS, Duke U.; MS, U. Pa. Chmn., CEO Boston Sci., Natick, Mass., 1979—99, co-founder, chmn. bd. dirs., 1999—. Office: Boston Sci 1 Boston Sci Pl Natick MA 01760-1537

NICHOLAS, RALPH WALLACE, anthropologist, educator; b. Dallas, Nov. 28, 1934; s. Ralph Wendell and Ruth Elizabeth (Oury) N.; m. Marta Ruth Weinstock, June 13, 1963. BA, Wayne U., 1957; MA, U. Chgo., 1958, PhD, 1962. From asst. prof. to prof. Mich. State U., East Lansing, 1964-71; prof. anthropology U. Chgo., 1971—, chmn. dept., 1981-82, dep. provost, 1982-87, dean of coll., 1987-92, dir. Ctr. Internat. Studies, 1984-95, William Rainey Harper prof. anthropology and social scis., 1992-2000, William Rainey Harper prof. emeritus, 2000—; pres. Internat. House of Chgo., 1993-2000. Cons. Ford Found., Dhaka, Bangladesh, 1973 Author: (with others) Kinship Bengali Culture, 1977; editor: Jour. Asian Studies, 1975-78. V.p. Am. Inst. Indian Studies, 1974-76, treas., 1993-2001, pres.-elect 2001-2002, pres. 2002—; trustee Bangladesh Found. Ford Found. fgn. area tng. fellow, India, 1960-61; Sch. Oriental and African Studies research fellow, London, 1962-63; sr. Fulbright fellow, West Bengal, India, 1968-69 Fellow AAAS, Am. Anthrop. Assn., Royal Anthrop. Inst. (Eng.); mem. Assn. Asian Studies, India League of Am. Found. (trustee). Office: U Chgo Dept Anthropology 1126 E 59th St Chicago IL 60637-1580

NICHOLAS, RONALD WAYDE, business consultant; b. Dallas, July 29, 1938; s. J.W. Nicholas and Helen Eloise Whiteacre Duniven; m. Wanda Elaine Hagen, Aug. 27, 1960; children: Charles Wayde, Laurence Eliot. BBA, U. Tex., 1960. Dir. instnl. sales Anderson Clayton Foods, Dallas and Sherman, Tex., 1962-84; comml. dir. Anderson, Clayton S.A. de C.V., Mexico City, 1984-86; ptnr., operator 2 retail businesses, Pittsburg, Tex., 1986-87; assoc. gen. dir. Pilgrim's Pride, S.A. de C.V., Mexico City, 1987-97; bus. cons. Ray & Berndtson, 1997—. Cmty. advisor Jr. League of Mexico City, 1996—. Co-founder, bd. dirs. Am. Charities, A.C., Mexico City, 1996—; co-founder, chair Am. Charities Golf and Tennis Classic, 1996—; bd. mem. Tex./Mexico Bus. Coun., 2000—. Capt. U.S. Army, 1960-62. Mem. Am. C. of C. (bd. dirs. 1993-94, procedures auditor 1995-96), U.S./Mex. C. of C. (chair agr. com., bi-nat. bd., Mexico City bd. 1992—), VFW, Am. Soc. of Mex. (bd. dirs., pres.), Am. Benevolent Soc. (sec., bd. dirs., pres.), U. Tex. Ex Students Assn. (bd. dirs., v.p.), Phi Sigma Kappa (treas., pres.). Avocations: golf, stamp collecting, cooking. Office: Ray & Berndtson Palo Santo 6 Col Lomas Alta Mexico City Mexico 11950 E-mail: ronwan@aol.com.

NICHOLAS, S. SCOTT, allergist; b. Des Moines, Dec. 23, 1936; s. Sydney S. and Dorothea (McCallom) N.; children: Mark A., Kim L., Gregory S.; m. Roslynn Robarge, June 14, 1975. BA cum laude, U. Minn., 1958, BS, MD, U. Minn., 1961; MS, U. Mich., 1966; mgmt. for physicians cert., St. Thomas U., 1997. Diplomate Am. Bd. Allergy and Immunology. Practice medicine specializing in allergy, Mpls., 1966—; clin. assoc. prof. internal medicine U. Minn., 1967-81, clin. prof., 1981—. Contbr. articles to profl. jours. Mem. ad hoc com. Minn. Relative Value Index, Mpls., 1971-73. Fellow Am. Coll. Allergy and Immunology (mem. program com. 1986-87, bd. regents 1987-90), Am. Acad. Allergy and Immunology, Am. Coll. Chest Physicians; mem. AMA, Minn. State Med. Assn., Mpls. Acad. Medicine (exec. council 1979-86, recorder 1981-83, v.p. 1983-84, pres. 1984-85), N. Cen. Allergy Soc. (pres. 1977), Minn. Allergy Soc. (pres. 1976-77), Twin City Allergy Soc. (pres. 1970-71), Rotary. Clubs: Minikahda. Lutheran. Avocations: skiing, golf, biking. Home: 2110 W Lake Of The Isles Pky Minneapolis MN 55405-2425 Office: 221 Medical Arts Bldg Minneapolis MN 55402

NICHOLAS, WILLADENE LOUISE, artist; b. Streator, Ill., Mar. 21, 1910; d. Almyron Clarence and Etta Helen (Dunbar) Kelly; m. Ray Thomas Nicholas, Dec. 25, 1932 (dec. 1992); children: Sally Jo, Gayle Dene, Ray Thomas Jr. Student, Monmouth Coll., 1926-27, U. Ill., 1928-29. Art tchr. in pvt. practice, Grayslake, Ill., 1945-60; tchr. adult art Grayslake H.S., 1960's. Author (poetry book) Angel Children, 1994, 3d edit. 1999, (non-fiction) Leo & His Rainbow Brush, 1995, Stories of a Railroad Child, 1995, (children's fiction) Minnie the Sunflower, 1995; creator spl. series of wren birdhouses. Charter mem. United Protestant Ch. Grayslake. Named Top Homemaker Grayslake, Grayslake Times, 1962; recipient Blue Ribbon awards State

Garden Clubs Ill. Inc., 1996. Mem. Soc. Mayflower Descendants, Grayslake Woman's Club (publicity dir. 1995-97), Grayslake Hist. Soc., Old Plank Rd. Questers, Grayslake Greenery Garden Club (founder, bd. dirs.). Republican. Avocations: experimental research in horticulture, pure translucent watercolorist, ancient Chinese art. Home: 275 S Slusser St Grayslake IL 60030-2356

NICHOLAS, WILLIAM RICHARD, lawyer; b. Pontiac, Mich., June 19, 1934; s. Reginald and Edna Irene (Bartlett) N.; m. Diana Lee Johnson, Aug. 20, 1960; children: Susan Lee, William Richard Jr. BS in Bus., U. Idaho, 1956; JD, U. Mich., 1962. Bar: 1963. Of counsel Latham & Watkins, Los Angeles, 1962-96. Contbr. numerous articles on taxation. Lt. (j.g.) USN, 1956-59. Mem. Calif. Bar Assn., Los Angeles County Bar Assn., Am. Coll. Tax Counsel. Home: 1808 Old Ranch Rd Los Angeles CA 90049-2207 Office: Latham & Watkins 633 W 5th St Ste 4000 Los Angeles CA 90071-2005

NICHOLAS, (RICHARD G. SMISKO), bishop; b. Perth Amboy, N.J., Feb. 23, 1936; s. Andrew and Anna (Totin) S. Grad., Christ the Saviour Sem., Johnstown, Pa., 1959; student, Patriarchal Theol. Acad., Istanbul, Turkey; BA, U. Youngstown, 1961; BTh, U. Pitts. Ordained priest Am. Carpatho-Russian Orthodox Greek Cath. Diocese, 1959. Pastor Sts. Peter and Paul Ch., Windber, 1959-62; prefect of discipline, tchr. Christ the Saviour Sem., Johnstown, 1963-65; pastor Sts. Peter and Paul Ch., Homer City, 1965-71, St. Michael's Ch., Clymer, 1971-72, St. Nicholas Ch., N.Y.C., 1972-78; elevated to archimandrite Am. Carpatho-Russian Orthodox Greek Cath. Diocese, 1976; abbot Monastery of Annunciation, Tuxedo Park, N.Y., 1978-82; elected titular bishop of Amissos, aux. bishop Ukrainian Orthodox Diocese of Ecumenical Patriarchate, 1983; consecrated bishop Am. Carpatho-Russian Orthodox Greek Cath. Diocese, 1985, bishop, 1985—. Asst. Christ the Saviour Cathedral, 1963-65; chmn. XIV Diocesan Coun., New Brunswick, N.J., 1985, XV Diocesan Coun., Pitts., 1991, elevated to Met., 1998. Office: 312 Garfield St Johnstown PA 15906-2122

NICHOLERIS, CAROL ANGELA, music educator, composer, conductor; b. Cambridge, Mass., Oct. 15, 1955; d. Menelaus and Sophia (Flecca) N. BMusic, Boston U., 1977, D in Mus. Arts, 1997; MAT, Bridgewater State Coll., 1983, CAGS Edn. Adminstrn., 1991. Cert. music specialist, supr./dir. music edn. Dir. music Hingham Congl. Ch., 1976-95; tchr. music Silver Lake Regional H.S., Kingston, Mass., 1977-79, Hingham (Mass.) Pub. Schs., 1982, Whitman (Mass.) Pub. Schs., 1982-88; asst. prof. elem. music edn. Bridgewater (Mass.) State Coll. Lab. Sch., 1988-98, asst. prof. music composition and gen. studies, 1998-2000, assoc. prof. music composition & gen. studies, 2000—. Asst. condr. Harbour Chora Arts Soc., Hanover, Mass., 1988—93; music dir. Braintree Choral Soc., 1998—2001, Bridgewater State Coll. Alumni Chamber Choir, 2000—. Pub. composer of choral music. Mem. NEA, Am. Choral Dirs. Assn. (life), Music Educators Nat. Conf., Pi Kappa Lambda (life). Avocations: winter mountaineering, hiking, fishing, skiing. Office: Bridgewater State Coll Music Dept Maxwell Libr Bridgewater MA 02325-0001 E-mail: cnicholeris@bridgew.edu.

NICHOLLS, CHRISTINE STEPHANIE, writer, editor; b. Bury, Lancashire, Eng., Jan. 23, 1943; d. Christopher James and Olive (Kennedy) Metcalfe; m. Anthony James Nicholls, Mar. 12, 1966; children: Alexander, Caroline, Isabel. BA, Oxford (Eng.) U., 1964, MA, DPhil, Oxford (Eng.) U., 1968. Rsch. fellow London U., 1968-69; freelance writer BBC, London, 1970-74; rsch. asst. Oxford U., 1975-76; joint editor Dictionary of Nat. Biography, Oxford, 1977-89, editor, 1989-95, Hutchinson Ency. of Biography, 1995—. Author: The Swahili Coast, 1971, (with P. Awdry) Cataract, 1985; author, editor: The Dictionary of National Biography, 4 vols., 1981, 86, 90, 93, 96, Power: A Political History, 1990, David Livingstone, 1998, A History of St. Antony's College, Oxford 1950-2000, 2000. Avocation: playing the flute. Home: 27 Davenant Rd Oxford OX2 8BU England E-mail: christine.nicholls@lineone.net.

NICHOLLS, ETHAN ADOLPHUS, anesthesiologist, educator; b. San Nicholas, Aruba, Nov. 29, 1958; s. Clayton A. and Sheila G. Nicholls; m. Kristina H. Austin, June 4, 1988; children: Olivia, Julia. AB, Harvard U., 1980; MD, Stanford U., 1988. Cert. in anesthesiology. Intern Kaiser Permanente Med. Ctr., Santa Clara, Calif., 1988-89; resident U. Calif., San Francisco, 1989-92, fellow, 1992; staff anesthesiologist, pain mgmt. cons. El Camino Hosp., Mountain View, Calif., 1993—, chief dept. anesthesiology, 1999-2000; asst. prof. anesthesiology and pain mgmt., asst. clin. prof. U. Calif., San Francisco, 1993—. Bd. dirs. El Camino Surgery Ctr., Mountain View; chmn. ethics com. El Camino Hosp., Mountain View, 1996-97, mem. fin. com., 2001--; lectr. in field. Mentor student alumni program Stanford (Calif.) U., 1991—. Mem. Internat. Anesthesia Rsch. Soc., Am. Soc. Anesthesiology, Calif. Soc. Anesthesiology (del. dist. 4 2001—), South Peninsula Anesthesia Assn., Inc. (v.p. 1997-98). Office: El Camino Hosp Dept Anesthesiology 2500 Grant Rd Dept Mountain View CA 94040-4378

NICHOLLS, RICHARD ALLEN, middle school social studies educator; b. Chgo., Sept. 1, 1944; s. Harry Allen and Rita Mae (O'Connell) N.; m. Linda Lee Soderberg, Mar. 27, 1969 (div. 1979). AA, Lincoln Coll., 1964; BA, MacMurray Coll., 1966; postgrad., Loyola U., 1967; MA, Nat. Lewis U., 1991. Cert. volleyball coach. 6th grade tchr. Chgo. Pub. Schs., 1966-67; 7th & 8th grades tchr. Palos Sch. Dist. 118, Palos Park, Ill., 1967—. Sponsor student govt. Palos Sch. Dist. 118, 1971-73, sponsor pompon squad, 1971-73, mem. curriculum devel. com., 1970-72; writer (with others) curriculum for devel. of thematic units for transition of Palos South Jr. H.S. to Palos Mid. Sch., summer 1995; volleyball coach Palos South Jr. H.S. (now Palos South Mid. Sch.), 1977-90, Victor J. Andrew H.S., 1981-84, Carl Sandburg H.S., 1985-91; mem. Ill. Goals Assessment Program com. for sch. stds., 1992-93. Mem. NEA, Ill. Edn. Assn., U.S. Volleyball Assn., Palos Edn. Assn., Am. Athletic Union (volleyball coach, nat. champions 1981, 82, 95, finalists 1984, 85, 87 jr. Olympics Nat. Tournament, 5th pl. jr. Nats., 1994) Am. Legion (Citizenship award 1964), Phi Theta Kappa. Avocations: coaching volleyball, sponsoring school trips, personal training for physical fitness. Office: Palos Sch Dist 118 8800 W 119th St Ste 1 Palos Park IL 60464-1099

NICHOLLS, RICHARD AURELIUS, obstetrician, gynecologist; b. Norfolk, Va., Aug. 12, 1941; s. Richard Beddoe and Aurelia (Gill) N.; m. Geri Bowden, Feb. 24, 1986. BS in Biology, Stetson U., 1963; MD, Med. Coll. Va., 1967. Diplomate Am. Bd. Ob-Gyn. Intern, Charity Hosp., Tulane div., New Orleans, 1967-68, resident in ob-gyn, 1968-71; asst. prof. ob-gyn Tulane Med. Sch., New Orleans, 1973-74, clin. asst. prof., 1974-83; practice medicine specializing in ob-gyn, Pascagoula, Miss., 1974-89; pvt. practice medicine, Ocean Spring, Miss., 1989—; mem. staff Singing River Hosp., chmn. surg. and ob-gyn depts., 1979-80, chmn. Ob-Gyn Dept., 1984, mem. staff Ocean Springs Hosp., laser com., pharmacy com., and theraputics com., chmn. OB-Gyn dept., mem. exec. bd., 1990-91; sec., treas. staff Ocean Springs Hosp., 1991-92, exec. bd., 1991-92, chief of staff elect, 1992-93, chief of staff, 1993-94; bd. dirs. Singing River Hosp. System, 1993-94. Bd. dirs. Miss. Racing Assn. Maj. US. Army, 1971-73. Fellow Am. Coll. Ob-Gyn, ACS; mem. Miss. State Med. Soc., Singing River Med. Soc., Am. Fertility Soc., Am. Assn. Gynecol. Laparoscopists, Am. Med. Soc., So. Med. Soc., New Orleans Grad. Med. Assembly, New Orleans Ob-Gyn Soc., Gulf Coast Ob-Gyn Soc., Conrad Collins Ob-Gyn Soc., Am. Venereal Disease Soc., Am. Cancer Soc. (bd. dirs Jackson County Br.). Contbr. articles to med. jours.

NICHOLLS, RICHARD H. lawyer; b. Toronto, Ont., Can., Oct. 27, 1938; s. Richard S. and Roberta T. Nicholls; m. Judy Carter, Apr. 15, 1963; children: Christopher T., Jamie C.; m. Anne Delaney, June 10, 1978. BA cum laude, Amherst Coll., 1960; LLB, Stamford U., 1963; LLM, NYU, 1964. Bar: Calif. 1964, N.Y. 1965, D.C. Assoc. Mudge Rose Guthrie, Alexander & Ferdon and predecessor, N.Y.C., 1964-70, ptnr., 1971-94; of counsel Orrick, Herrington & Sutcliffe, N.Y., 1995—. Mem. ABA, N.Y. State Bar Assn., Nat. Assn. Bond Lawyers, Stamford Yacht Club. Home: 159 Ocean Dr W Stamford CT 06902-8004 Office: Orrick Herrington & Sutcliffe 666 5th Ave Rm 203 New York NY 10103-1798 E-mail: rnicholls@orrick.com.

NICHOLLS, ROBERT LEE, civil engineer, educator; b. Lincoln, Nebr., June 11, 1929; s. Carroll C. and Claire (McDermet) N.; m. Ruth Ann Allen, Aug. 30, 1958; children: David, Jonathan, Carol. BSCE with high honors, U. Colo., 1951; MSCE, Iowa State U., 1952, PhD, 1957. Registered profl. engr., Del., Pa., Iowa, Md. Design engr., constrn. supr. U.S. Army Corps Engrs., Japan, Korea, 1953-55; chief materials engr. and hwy. design engr. Gannett & Fleming, Harrisburg, Pa., 1957-59; prof. civil engring. U. Del., Newark, 1959-93. Geotech. engring. and constrn. materials cons. DuPont, Hercules, Thiokol, others. Author: Composite Construction Materials, 1976; co-author: Civil Engineering Systems, 1972 (also Polish and Spanish edits.); author, editor: ASCE Structural Plastics Selection Manual, 1984; also articles; 7 patents in field. Dist. advance chmn. Boy Scouts Am. Fellow ASCE (pres. Del. sect. 1974-75, recipient nat. citation for sect. activities 1975), Ops. Rsch. Soc. Am., Internat. Soc. Soil Mechanics, Transp. Rsch. Bd., Am. Concrete Inst.

NICHOLLS, STEPHEN CHARLES, surgeon, educator; b. New Zealand, Oct. 8, 1950; came to U.S., 1976; BS, U. Auckland, New Zealand, MD, 1975. Diplomate Am. Bd. Surgery, Am. Bd. Vascular Surgery. Intern Auckland Pub. Hosp., 1975; resident in surgery Albert Einstein Med. Ctr., N.Y.C., 1976-77, Mt. Sinai Hosp., N.Y.C., 1979-83, fellow vascular surgery, 1985-86; fellow clin. rsch. U. Wash., Seattle, 1983-85, surgeon, 1986—; chief vascular surgery, dir. vascular lab. Harborview Med. Ctr.; assoc. prof. U. Wash., 1986—. Fellow AHA Stroke Coun., Wellcare Networks; mem. Internat. Soc. Cardiovascular Surgery, Soc. Vascular Surgery. Home: 726 12th Ave E Seattle WA 98102-4622 Office: U Wash Dept Surgery 359796 325 9th Ave Seattle WA 98104-2499

NICHOLLS, THOMAS MAURICE, business owner; b. Hancock, Mich., June 22, 1960; s. David and Ericka (Weiss) N.; m. Mary Ann Erspamer, Apr. 30, 1983; 1 child, Michael. Owner Northland Svcs., Hurley, Wis., 1983—; gen. mgr. K & L Enterprises, Marquette, Mich., 1985-91; exec. mgr. S & S Inc., Sun Prairie, Wis., 1991-94; owner Northern Venture, Hurley, 1992—, Venture Express, Hurley, 1999—. Mem. Just Say No, Ironwood, Mich., 1992. With USN, 1979-83. Mem. Jaycees (v.p. 1986, Presdl. award of Honor 1986, Jaycee of Yr., Mich. 1986). Avocations: photography, woodworking, hunting. Home and Office: Northern Venture 502 Poplar St Hurley WI 54534-1169

NICHOLS, ALBERT MYRON, retired minister; b. Creston, Iowa, Oct. 17, 1914; s. Albert Maurice and Lou (Myers) N.; m. Phyllis Cochran, June 28, 1939; children: Byron Albert, Phillip Garrett. AB, UCLA, 1936; BS, San Francisco Theol. Sem., 1940; DD, Occidental Coll., 1952. Ordained to ministry United Presbyn. Ch. in U.S.A., 1940. Pastor chs., North Hollywood, Calif., 1940-43; assoc. pastor Pasadena (Calif.) Presbyn. Ch., 1943-57; pastor 1st Presbyn. Ch., Pendleton, Oreg., 1957-82, ret., 1982. Chmn. gen. assembly com. on responsible marriage and parenthood United Presbyn. Ch. in U.S.A., 1959-62, mem. Bd. Christian Edn., 1969-72; mem. 1st coun. Synod of Pacific; moderator Oreg. Synod, 1968, 69; stated clk. Ea. Oreg. Presbytery, 1975-99. Pres. Pasadena Child Guidance Clinic, 1955-57; trustee San Francisco Theol. Sem., 1963-84; life trustee Lewis and Clark Coll., Portland, Oreg.; mem. Pendleton City Recreation Commn., 1965-2001; founding bd. dirs. Presbyn. Intercommunity Hosp., Whittier, Calif.; mem. State of Oreg. Health Coun., 1985-88, State Trauma Adv. Bd., 1987-91; chmn. City of Pendleton Capital Improvements Commn., 1983-2001; treas., Glen Eddy Resident Assn., 2001. Named 1st Citizen of Pendleton, 1984. Home: 114 Glen Eddy Dr Niskayuna NY 12309

NICHOLS, ALLEN BRYANT, physician, cardiologist; b. Cleve., Aug. 8, 1945; s. Frederick Doveton and Jane (Root) N.; m. Lois Mann, July 7, 1979; children: Bryant, Catherine, Stafford, Elizabeth. BA, Yale U., 1967; MD, U. Va., 1971. Clin. rsch. fellow in cardiology Mass. Gen. Hosp.-Harvard Med. Sch., Boston, 1976-78; resident in medicine U. Mich., Ann Arbor, 1971-74, fellow in cardiology, 1974-76; asst. prof. medicine Columbia Presbyn. Med. Ctr., N.Y.C., 1978-85, assoc. prof. clin. medicine, 1985-88; pvt. practice in cardiology Riverside Med. Ctr., 1988—, Mary Immaculate Hosp., Newport News, Va., 1988—, chmn. dept. medicine, 1996-98, asst. chief of staff, 1998—, chief of staff, 2000—02; pvt. practice in cardiology Williamsburg (Va.) Cmty. Hosp., 1988—. Contbr. more than 40 articles to profl. jours. Grantee N.Y. Heart Assn., 1981. Fellow ACP, Am. Coll. Cardiology; mem. Am. Heart Assn. (coun. clin. cardiology). Office: 12720 Mcmanus Blvd Ste 201 Newport News VA 23602-4414

NICHOLS, C. WALTER, III, retired trust company executive; b. N.Y.C., Aug. 25, 1937; s. Charles Walter and Marjorie (Jones) N.; m. Anne Sharp, Aug. 8, 1959 (dec. Nov. 1996); children: Blair, Sandra, Walter, Hope. V.p. Citibank, N.Y.C., 1962-78, J.P. Morgan & Co., N.Y.C., 1979-93; 1st v.p. Republic Nat. Bank N.Y., 1994. Bd. dirs. Nichols Found., Inc., 1965—, Greenwich House, 1969-94, pres., 1984-90; trustee Choate Rosemary Hall, 1972-77, 82-89, Westover Sch., 1979-81, ea. N.Y. chpt. Nature Conservancy, 1978-87; Caramoor Music Festival, 1980-90, John Jay Homestead, 1980-2000, Nat. Audubon Soc., 1983-87; mem. adv. bd. Wildlife Conservation Soc. (Bronx Zoo), 1987-94. Served to 1st lt. U.S. Army, 1960-62. Decorated Army Commendation medal. Mem. Naturist Soc., Nat. Assn. Railroad Passengers (bd. dirs. 1996-98), Am. Assn. for Nude Recreation, Pilgrims of U.S., Yale (N.Y.C.) Club. Home: 1 Bent Oak Run Westport MA 02790-5179

NICHOLS, CARL MICHAEL, venture capital executive; b. Springfield, Mass., Sept. 19, 1961; BS, Brown U., 1983; MBA, Harvard U., 1987. Mgr. Aarhus Olrefabrik, Aarhus, Denmark, 1983; project mgr. Booz Allen & Hamilton, San Francisco, 1983-85, 87-91; mgr. AT&T Internat., Morristown, N.J., 1986; v.p. strategic bus. mgmt. Scrivner Inc., Oklahoma City, 1991-94; asst. v.p. Pacific Telesis, San Francisco, 1994-96; mng. ptnr. Minds Ventures, 1996—; COO Internet Fin. Network Corp., 1996-97; v.p. bus. devel. Net Channel, Inc., 1996-97; COO Epicentric Inc., 1998-99. Editor: Technology in Business, 1983 (award 1984). Cons. Jr. Achievement, Edmond, Okla., 1991-93; vol. Okla. Sch. Sci. and Math., Oklahoma City, 1992-94; bd. dirs. San Francisco Edn. Fund, 1996-97. Mem. Sigma Xi. Avocations: tennis, skiing, sailing.

NICHOLS, CARL WHEELER, retired advertising agency executive; b. Ottawa, Kans., Oct. 9, 1923; s. Carl Wheeler and Cora Merle (Hanks) N.; children: Christine, Carl Wheeler, Nancy, Matthew; m. Anna Norris, Apr. 18, 1992. Student, Baker U., 1940-41, U. Mo., 1941-43; BA, U. Mich., 1944. Research analyst Cunningham & Walsh, Inc. (advt. agy.), N.Y.C., 1946-49, copywriter, 1949-58, co-creative dir., v.p., 1958-59, dir. account mgmt., 1959-61, pres., 1961-69, chmn., chief exec. officer, 1969-85, chmn. emeritus, 1986. Trustee Ctr. for the Arts, Vero Beach, Fla., 1996. Capt. USMCR, 1943-46, 50-52, Korea. Named to Advt. Hall of Fame, 1986. Mem. N.Y. Advt. Coun. (bd. dirs. 1974-85), Am. Advt. Fedn. (dir. 1972—, chmn. 1975-76), Advt. Ednl. Found. (bd. dirs., sec., treas. 1983-91), Woodway Country Club, John's Island Club, Sigma Xi. Presbyterian (elder). Home: 241 Island Creek Dr Vero Beach FL 32963-3304

NICHOLS, CAROL D. real estate professional; BA, U. Pitts., 1964; cert. in advanced mgmt., U. Chgo. From mgmt. trainee to buyer May Dept. Stores Co., Pitts., 1964-70; various mgmt. positions, then mng. dir. mortgage/real estate Tchrs. Ins. and Annuity Assn. Am., N.Y.C., 1970-97; sr. mng. dir. Insignia/ESG Capital Advisors, 1997—. Instr. real estate div. continuing edn. Marymount Manhattan Coll., N.Y.C., 1975-76, Woman's Sch. Adult Edn. Ctr., N.Y.C., 1976-77; Real Estate Bd. N.Y., past chmn. fin. com. Recipient Nat. Humanitarian award, Arthur B. Lorber award Nat. Jewish Med. and Rsch. Ctr., Nat. Brotherhood award NCCJ. Mem. Assn. Real Estate Women (past pres.), Urban Land Inst. (trustee, past chmn. urban devel. and mixed use coun., past chmn. awards for excellence jury). Home: 165 Winfield St Norwalk CT 06855-1622 Office: Insignia/ESG Capital Advisors 200 Park Ave New York NY 10166-0005 E-mail: carol.nichols@iesg.com.

NICHOLS, CAROLYN FAYE, scriptwriter; b. Shreveport, La, July 11, 1954; d. Leo and Helen Brown Nichols. Student, La. State U., 1999—2003. Screenwriter Diamond Star Literary Agy., Shreveport, 1986—2002. Pub. rels. profls. Diamond Star Literary Agy., Shreveport. Author: (screenplays) Desperadoes Of The San Joaquin, 2002, Young Man From Manhattan, God's Spokesman, Nero, Elizabeth Barrett Browning, 1963, Hubble's Constant, Edgar Allan Poe, Rumors Of Peace I and II, Belteshazzar, (novels) Last Days On Planet Earth, (poetry collection) Heart and Soul; contbr. music soundtrack. Pub. rels. profl. Bluegrass Festivals, Shreveport, 1986—2003. Sr. airman USAFR, 1977—80. Named Quarter Finalist for Young Man From Manhattan, Chesterfield Film Co., 1999. Mem.: Am. Film Inst. Avocation: singing and playing the fiddle. Home: L-26 8525 Chalmette Dr Shreveport LA 71115 Personal E-mail: cnichols@studentmail.lsus.edu.

NICHOLS, CHERIE L. art publishing executive, artist representative; b. Portsmouth, Va., Apr. 4, 1955; d. Conley Ray and Ann Lanease (Holderfield) Edwards; m. Harold Eugene Nichols, 1971 (div. 1975); life partner Chloe S. Burke. Art sales Poster Art-N-Graphics, Tarzana, Calif., 82-84; art cons. Martin Lawrence Galleries, L.A., 1984-86; print rm. mgr. Circle Fine Art Corp., 1986-93; driver United Cerebral Palsy, Sacramento, 1997-98; owner Morning Dove Pub., 1997—. Art dir. Lavender Libr., Archives and Cultural Exch., Sacramento, 1999-2002; artist, rep. and product devel. plush toys Milk Buds, 1999; assoc. Frames Unlimited, Mich., Ohio, Ind. Avocations: music, guitar, drums, golf, yardwork. E-mail: cnik55@yahoo.com.

NICHOLS, CLYDE RICHARD, clergyman, company executive; b. N.Y.C., Apr. 15, 1945; s. William and Novella Nichols; m. Marsha A. Wade, Oct. 11, 1986; 1 child, Forest. BS, Met. State Coll., Denver, 1985; ThD, Berean Bible Coll., Dallas, 1994. Ordained pastor and bishop Fellowship of Deliverance Chs., Inc. Correction officer City and County Denver, 1981-92; sr. pastor Redeeming Love Ch., Denver; sr. dir. M&C Enterprises, Inc. Dir. membership Greater Metro Denver Ministers Alliance Orgn., Denver, 1997-99. Bd. dirs. Denver Opportunities for Outreach and Reflection (D.O.O.R.), 2000—. Recipient award for outstanding cmty. work Cheyenne (Wyo.) br. NAACP, 1982, award for outstanding cmty. activities 24th Syl Morgan Acad. Arts, Denver, 1992, Juanita Gray award. Avocations: travel, reading, computers. Home and Office: PO Box 31092 Aurora CO 80041-0092 E-mail: rev98crn@aol.com., mcenterpr31092@aol.com.

NICHOLS, DONALD ARTHUR, economist, educator; b. Madison, Conn., Dec. 20, 1940; s. Edward Charles and Ruth (Nilson) Nichols; m. Linda Powley, Aug. 19, 1962 (dec. Oct. 1982); children: Charles Spencer, Elizabeth Clarke; m. Barbara Jakubowski Noel, May 22, 1983 (dec. Dec. 26, 2000); m. Jane Bartels, Sept. 26, 2001. BA, Yale U., 1962, MA, 1963, PhD, 1968. Mem. faculty dept. econs. U. Wis., Madison, 1966—, prof., 1977—, chmn. dept. econs., 1983-86, 88-90, mem. exec. com. faculty senate, 1987-90, chmn., 1989-90, dir. Robert M. LaFollette Sch. Pub. Affairs, 2002—; lectr. Yale U., 1970—71; sr. economist Senate Budget Com., Washington, 1975—76; dep. asst. sec. for econ. policy and rsch. Dept. Labor, 1977-79; dir. Ctr. for Rsch. on Wis. Economy. Econ. advisor to gov. State of Wis., 1983—86; exec. sec. Gov.'s Coun. Econ. Advisors, 1983—86; mem. Gov.'s Export Strategy Commn., 1994—95; bd. dirs. Thompson, Plumb Funds, 1987—, Sustainable Woods Co-operative, 2001; cons. in field; dir. Ctr. for World Affairs and Global Economy, 1995—2000; affiliate Christensen Assocs., Madison, 1999—. Author: (with Clark Reynolds) Principles of Economics, 1970, Dollars and Sense, 1994; contbr. articles to profl. jours. Trustee U. Wis. Bookstore, 1990-95; bd. advisors Am. Players Theatre, Spring Green, Wis., 1993-2001. NSF fellow, 1963-66, 70-72; Nat. Commn. Employment Policy rsch. grantee, 1980-82; recipient William H. Kiekhofer Meml. Teaching prize U. Wis., 1973 Mem. Am. Econ. Assn., Econometric Soc., Royal Econ. Soc. Office: U Wis 1225 Observatory Dr Madison WI 53706

NICHOLS, DONNA MARDELL, nurse anesthetist; b. Mpls., Mar. 24, 1936; d. Donald Burma and Lucille Elvera Nichols. Diploma, Northwestern Hosp. Sch. Nursing, Mpls., 1957, Mpls. Sch. Anesthesia, 1959; BS in Nurse Anesthesia, U. Minn., 1977. RN Minn., 1957. Nurse anesthetist Hennepin County Med. Ctr., Mpls., 1959—60, Eden Twp. Hosp., Castro Valley, Calif., 1960—63, Bethesda Hosp., St. Paul, 1963—64, Meml. Bapt. Hosp., Houston, 1964—67, St. Joseph's Hosp., St. Paul, 1967—95; ret., 1995. Mem.: Minn. Assn. Nurse Anesthetists (bd. dirs. 1975—77), Am. Assn. Nurse Anesthetists (emeritus, cert. anesthetists). Avocations: golf, gardening, antiques. Home: 3958 Palisade Way Eagan MN 55122

NICHOLS, EDIE DIANE, executive recruiter; b. Grahamstown, Eastern Cape Province, Republic of South Africa, Mar. 28, 1939; arrived in U.S., 1963; d. Cyril Doughtry and Dorothy Ethel (Nottingham) Tyson; m. John F. Nichols, Dec. 16, 1962 (div. Dec. 1978); 1 child, Ian Tyson. Adminstrv. asst. Am. Acad. Medicine, N.Y.C., 1963-64, Jack Lenor Larsen, Inc., N.Y.C., 1964-70; v.p. John Scott Fones, Inc., 1971-76, Howard J. Rubenstein Assocs. Inc., N.Y.C., 1976-80; dir. comm. Carl Byoir & Assocs., 1981-83; account supr. Hill and Knowlton, 1983-85; broker Cross & Brown Co., 1986-88; v.p. Marc Nichols Assocs., Inc., 1989-95; mng. ptnr. Nichols Brown Internat., 1995—. Trustee Ctrl. Pk. Hist. Soc., N.Y.C., 1978-80. Mem. NOW, Internat. Assn. Corp. and Profl. Recruitment, N.Y. Women in Comm. (pub. rels. chair 1980-81, v.p., programs bd. dirs. 1985-87), Fin. Women's Assn. of N.Y. (bd. dirs. 1997-98), City Club of N.Y. (trustee, v.p., fin. and devel. 1987-89). Democrat. Episcopalian. Office: Nichols Brown Internat 155 W 20th Ste 2J New York NY 10011-3612 Home: 16 Stuyvesant Oval Apt 10F New York NY 10009

NICHOLS, EDITH ROTHMAN, publications director, editor; b. Bklyn., July 26, 1938; d. Louis and Selma (Kaplowitz) Rothman; m. Monroe Karetzky, Mar. 12, 1961 (div. Dec. 1971); children: Laura, Sarah; m. Stephen George Nichols, Mar. 23, 1972. BS, Buffalo State, 1959; MS, Bklyn. Coll., 1962. Elem. sch. tchr. N.Y.C. and N.Y. State Schs., 1960-66; dir. pub. rels. & mktg. Woodland Mus., Cooperstown, N.Y., 1966-67; pub. info. coord. Dept. Psychiatry Dartmouth Med. Sch., Hanover, N.H., 1974-77; dir. pub. info. West Ctrl. N.H. Cmty. Mental Health, 1977-85; editor house organ U. Pa. Med. Ctr., Phila., 1986-92; assoc. dir. pub. affairs Johns Hopkins Medicine, Balt., 1992-93, dir. publs., 1993—; editor Hopkins Med. News. Cons. Med. U. of S.C., Johns Hopkins Sch. of Public Health. Recipient Gold touchstone Am. Hosp. Assn., 1987. Mem. Assn. Am. Med. Colls. (award of excellence external publs. 1995, individual publs. 2000, award of distinction external publs. 1997, 99, 2000), Premier Performance, Coun. for Advancement and Support of Edn. (gold medal internal audience publs. 1991, 98, silver medal 1992, bronze medal spl. audience mags. 1994, 95, 2001, silver medal 1997, 2000, 01, silver medal external audience newsletters 2000, judge 1991, 97, 2001). Home: 5 St Martins Rd Baltimore MD 21218-1815 Office: Johns Hopkins Medicine 550 N Broadway Fl 11 Baltimore MD 21205-2020 E-mail: enichols@jhmi.edu.

NICHOLS, EUGENE DOUGLAS, mathematics educator; b. Rovno, Poland, Feb. 6, 1923; came to U.S., 1946, naturalized, 1951; s. Alex and Anna (Radchuk) Nichiporuk; m. Alice Bissell, Mar. 31, 1951. BS, U. Chgo., 1949, postgrad., 1949-51; MEd, U. Ill., 1953, MA, 1954, PhD, 1956. Instr. math. Roberts Wesleyan Coll., North Chili, N.Y., 1950-51, U. Ill., 1951-56; assoc. prof. math. edn. Fla. State U., 1956-61, prof., head dept., 1961-73; dir. Project for Mathematical Devel. of Children, 1973-77; dir. math program NSF, 1958-61; dir. Math. Inst. Elem. Tchrs., 1961-70; pres. Nichols Schwartz Pub., 1992—; prof. math. edn. Fla. State U., 1974-90. Chmn. U. Ill. Com. on Sch. Math., 1954-55; cons. editor math McGraw-Hill Book Co., summer 1956 Co-author: Modern Elementary Algebra, 1961, Introduction to Sets, 1962, Arithmetic of Directed Numbers, 1962, Introduction to Equations and Inequalities, 1963, Introduction to Coordinate Geometry, 1963, Introduction to Exponents, 1964, Understanding Arithmetic, 1965, Elementary Mathematics Patterns and Structure, 1966, Algebra, 1966, Modern Geometry, 1968, Modern Trigonometry, 1968, Modern Intermediate Algebra, 1969, Analytic Geometry, 1973, Holt Algebra 1, 1974, 78, 82, 86, 92, Holt Algebra 2, 1974, 78, 82, 86, 92, Holt Geometry, 1974, 78, 82, 86, Holt School Mathematics, 1974, 78, 81, Holt Pre-Algebra Mathematics, 1980, 86, Holt Mathematics, 1981, 85, Elementary School Mathematics and How to Teach It, 1982, Geometry, 1991, Holt Pre-Algebra, 1992, Mathematics Dictionary and Handbook, 1993, 95, 98, 99; author: Pre-Algebra Mathematics, 1970, Introductory Algebra for College Students, 1971, Mathematics for the Elementary School Teacher, 1971, College Mathematics, 1975, College Mathematics for General Education, rev. edit., 1975. Named Fla. State U. Disting. Prof., 1968-69; recipient Disting. Alumni award U. Ill. Coll. Edn., 1970. Mem. Am. Math. Soc., Math. Assn. Am., Sch. Sci. and Math. Assn., Nat. Coun. Tchrs. Math., Coun. Basic Edn., Text and Acad. Authors Assn., Pi Mu Epsilon, Phi Delta Kappa. Home: 3386 W Lakeshore Dr Tallahassee FL 32312-1305 E-mail: enichols@mailer.fsu.edu. *Do not look for a career--look for opportunities to do kind things for others. Be honest with yourself and with those around you.*

NICHOLS, GEORGE LEON, JR. minister; b. Phila., Mar. 7, 1938; s. George Leon Sr. and Elva Grace (Berger) N.; m. K. Diane Hunt, Sept. 21, 1963; children: Katherine J., Stephen J. BS in Bible, Phila. Coll. Bible, 1961; postgrad., Reformed Episcopal Sem., Phila., 1961-63; DD, Fla. Bible Coll, Hollywood, 1976; D of Ministry, Luther Rice Sem., Jacksonville, Fla., 1979; MA, Liberty U., 1988. Ordained to ministry Bapt. Ch., 1961; cert. Christian counselor. Pastor Nicetown Bapt. Ch., Phila., 1961-64, 1st Bapt. Ch., Elmer, N.J., 1964-67; sr. pastor Pennsville Bapt. Ch., Mt. Pleasant, Pa., 1967-87, Faith Bapt. Ch., Wilmington, Del., 1987—. Trustee Phila. Biblical U., Langhorne, Pa., 1987; trustee, v.p. Out-island Ministries, St. Petersburg, Fla., 1973; bd. dirs. Mil. Evangelism, Aberdeen, Md., Sandy Cove Ministries, N.E. Md. Mem. Am. Assn. Christian Counselors, United Assn. Christian Counselors (bd. dirs., pres. Harrisburg, Pa.), Bibl. Archeol. Soc., Evang. Theol. Soc. Home: 2707 Burnley Rd Wilmington DE 19808-3623 Office: Faith Bapt Ch 4210 Limestone Rd Wilmington DE 19808-2099 E-mail: fbc@dpnet.net. *To enjoy life we must have a theology that is practical and practiced.*

NICHOLS, GERALD, counselor, hypnotist; b. L.A., Dec. 30, 1934; s. Clyde William and Iva Margaret Nichols. AA, L.A. City Coll., 1968; BA, Calif. State U., L.A., 1970. Cert. profl. hypnotist. Counselor, v.p. Nat. League for Social Understanding, L.A. Cons. Internat. Gay and Lesbian Archives, L.A., Leathermasters Internat., L.A.; instr. UCLA; spkr. in field. Mem. Stonewall Dem. Club, L.A., 1989—; Rev., life mem. Universal Ch. of the Master, 1969-99. Mem.: Wagner Soc., L.A. Opera League. Avocation: selling collectibles. Office: Nat League for Social Understanding Ste 293 4470 Sunset Blvd Los Angeles CA 90027-6305 E-mail: jeromestevens1@excite.com.

NICHOLS, GREG MARK, systems analyst; b. Elgin, Ill., Nov. 25, 1967; s. Grace (Ipema) N. A in Data Processing, Blackhawk Tech.; student, U. Wis., Whitewater. Cert. assoc. computer profl. Analyst Ameritech Svcs., Milw., 1988—, analyst, LAN adminstr., 1990—. Pres. Nichols Consulting, Delavan, Wis., 1991—. Sunday sch. tchr. Delavan Christian Ch., 1990; cadet leader Ch. Boys Club, Delavan, 1990-91; speaker Boy Scouts Am., Milw., 1991—. Avocations: sports, farming. Home: N4070 Westwood Dr Delavan WI 53115-2832

NICHOLS, GUY WARREN, retired institute executive, utilities executive; b. Colchester, Vt., Oct. 27, 1925; s. Guy W. and Gladys (Tomlinson) N.; m. Shirley Hibbard, June 21, 1947; children: Pamela, Gail, Sally. BSCE, U. Vt., 1947; postgrad., Worcester Poly. Inst. Sch. Indsl. Mgmt., 1953-56; MS in Bus. Adminstrn., MIT, 1961. With New. Eng. Electric System, Westborough, Mass., 1947-84, exec. v.p., 1968-70, pres., 1970-84, chief exec. officer, 1972-84, chmn. bd., 1978-84. Bd. dirs. Amoresco Inc. Chmn., trustee Woods Hole Oceanographic Instn., 1985-95; trustee Worcester Found. Biomed. Rsch., Vt. Hist. Soc. Sloan fellow, MIT, 1961. Fellow Am. Acad. Arts and Scis. Office: 25 Research Dr Westborough MA 01582-0001 E-mail: looncall00@aol.com.

NICHOLS, HAROLD JAMES, university dean; b. Mitchell Field, N.Y., July 27, 1945; s. Harold J. and Ruth (McCain) N.; m. Mary Frances Lutes, Nov. 25, 1967 (div. 1992); children: Ruth, David, Debra; m. Anna Marie Douet, July 4, 1992. BS, Iowa State U., 1967; MA, Ind. U., 1969, PhD, 1971. Assoc. instr. Ind. U., Bloomington, 1970-71; asst. prof. Kans. State U., Manhattan, 1971-75, assoc. prof., 1975-81, prof., 1981-84, prof., head speech dept., 1985-93; dean Coll. Fine Arts and Humanities, U. Nebr., Kearney, 1993-97; dean Sch. Arts and Scis., Ga. Southwestern State U., Americus, GA, 1997—. Guest scholar DePauw U. Undergrad. Honors Conf., Greencastle, Ind., 1988; cons. Commonwealth of Va. Dept. Edn., 1988, Nebr. Wesleyan U., Lincoln, 1989, So. Ill. U., 1989, U. Va., 1992, U. No. Iowa, 1992. Co-editor: Status of Theatre Research-1984, 1986; contbr. articles to profl. jours. Named Outstanding Coll. Tchr., Kans. Speech Communications Assn., 1985. Mem. Assn. Theatre in Higher Edn. (pres. 1987-88), Am. Coll. Theatre Festival (region chair 1987-88, Kennedy Ctr. medallion 1990), Mid-Am. Theatre Conf. (chief regional officer 1978-81). Home: 1923 Rose Ave Americus GA 31709-4721 Office: Ga Southwestern State Univ Sch Arts and Scis 800 Wheatley St Americus GA 31709-4376 E-mail: hjn@canes.gsw.edu.

NICHOLS, HENRY ELIOT, lawyer, savings and loan executive; b. N.Y.C. m. Frances Griffin Morrison, Aug. 12, 1950 (dec. July 1978); children: Clyde Whitney, Diane Spencer; m. Mary ann Wall, May 31, 1987. BA, Yale U., 1946; JD, U. Va., 1948. Bar: D.C. 1950, U.S. Dist. Ct. 1950, U.S. Ct. Appeals 1952, U.S. Supreme Ct. 1969. Assoc. Frederick W. Berens, Washington, 1950-52; sole practice, 1952—. Real estate columnist Washington Star, 1966-81; pres., gen. counsel Hamilton Fed. Savs. & Loan Assn., 1971-74; vice chmn. bd. Columbia 1st Bank (formerly Columbia 1st Fed. Savs. & Loan Assn.), Washington, 1974-90, bd. dirs.; pres. Century Fin. Corp., 1971-90; regional v.p. Preview, Inc., 1972-78; bd. dirs., exec. com. Columbia Real Estate Title Ins. Co., Washington, 1968-78. Contbr. articles to profl. jours.; patentee med. inventions. Nat. adv. bd. Harker Prep. Sch., 1975-80; exec. com. Father Walter E. Schmitz Meml. Fund, Cath. U., 1982-83; bd. dirs. Vincent T. Lombardi Cancer Rsch. Ctr., 1979-84; del. Pres. Johnson's Conf. LAw and Poverty, 1967; vice chmn. Mayor's Ad Hoc Com. Housing Code Problems, Washington, 1968-71; mem. Commn. Landlord-Tenant Affairs Washington City Coun., 1970-71; vice chmn. Washington Area Realtors Coun., 1970; exec. com., dir. Downtown Progress, 1970; bd. dirs. Washington Mental Health Assn., 1973, Washington Med. Ctr., 1975. Capt. USAAF, 1942-46. Mem. Am. Land Devel. Assn., Nat. Assn. Real Estate Editors, Washington Bd. Realtors (pres. 1970, Realtor of Yr. 1970, Martin Isen award 1981), Greater Met. Washington Bs. Trade (bd. dirs. 1974-80), U.S. League Savs. Assns. (attys. com. 1971-80), Washington Savs. and Loan League, ABA, D.C. Bar Assn., Internat. Real Estate Fedn., Yale Club, Cosmos Club, Rolls Royce Club, Antique Auto Club, St. Elmo Club, Omega Tau Rho. Episcoppalian. Home: 1 Kittery Ct Bethesda MD 20817-2137 Office: 1112 16th St NW Washington DC 20036-4823

NICHOLS, HENRY LOUIS, lawyer; b. Collin County, Tex., Nov. 7, 1916; s. Jesse Cleveland and Leva (Stiff) N.; m. Elaine Guentherman, May 17, 1949; children: David Michael, Martha Marie. LL.B., So. Meth. U., 1940. Bar: Tex. 1939. Asst. city atty., Dallas, 1946-50; sole practice, 1951—. Mem. adv. bd. Ctr. for Legal Mcpl. Studies. Served to lt. col. AUS, 1941-46; col. USAR ret. Rsch. fellow Southwestern Legal Found., 1964. Fellow Am. Bar Found.; mem. ABA, Dallas Bar Assn. (pres. 1963-64), State Bar Tex., Tex. Bar Found. (charter) Clubs: Lakewood Country. Home: 3131 Maple Ave Apt 13H Dallas TX 75201-1206 Office: 1800 Lincoln St Dallas TX 75226-2248 *As a night-school graduate (Law School), I believe the opportunities in America are unlimited for anyone willing to work. Nowhere in the world are such opportunities available. We who live in the U.S.A. are blessed and the most fortunate of all people. We should strive to maintain that which our fathers preserved for us.*

NICHOLS, IRIS JEAN, illustrator; b. Yakima, Wash., Aug. 2, 1938; d. Charles Frederick and Velma Irene (Hacker) Beisner; (div. June 1963); children: Reid William, Amy Jo; m. David Gary Nichols, Sept. 21, 1966. BFA in Art, U. Wash., 1978. Freelance illustrator, graphic designer, Seattle, 1966—; med. illustrator, head dept. illustration Swedish Hosp. Med. Ctr., 1981-86; owner, med. and scientific illustrator Art for Medicine, 1986—. Part-time med. illustrator U. Wash., Seattle, 1966-67; part-time med. illustrator, graphic coord. dept. art The Mason Clinic, 1968-78; instr. advanced illustration Cornish Coll. Arts, Seattle, 1988-90; organized, coordinated and gifted the artwork of Prof. Glen E. Alps after his death in 1966. Illustrator various books including Bryophytes of Pacific Northwest, 1966, Microbiology, 1973, 78, 82, 94, 98, Introduction to Human Physiology, 1980, Understanding Human Anatomy and Physiology, 1983, Human Anatomy, 1984 Regional Anesthesia, 1990, many other med. and sci. books, and children's books on various subjects; exhibited in group shows at Seattle Pacific Sci. Ctr., summer 1979, 82, Am. Coll. Surgeons (1st prize 1974), N.W. Urology Conf. (1st prize 1974, 76, 2d prize 1975); pub. illustrations Constellation Pk. and Marine Res., City Seattle Pk., 1999. Pres. ArtsWest (formerly West Seattle Arts Coun.), 1983; active Seattle Art Mus. Named to West Seattle H.S. Alumni Hall of Fame, 1986, Matrix Table, 1986-96. Mem. Assn. Med. Illustrators (Murial McLatchie Fine Arts award 1981), Nat. Mus. Women in the Arts (Wash. state com., bd. dirs. 1987-95, pres. 1993-94), Women Painters of Wash. (pres. 1987-89), U. Wash. Alumni Assn., Lambda Rho (pres. 1995-98). Avocations: artwork, printmaking, small books, entering juried art exhibitions. E-mail: artformed@aol.com.

NICHOLS, J. HUGH, economic development consultant; b. Sprott, Ala., Nov. 27, 1930; s. Joseph Gordon and Mary Roberta (Stone) N.; m. Annie Sue Ratliff, Dec. 30, 1948; children: Duane A., Sharon K., Gerald Hugh, Jonathan G.; 1 foster child, John Dorsey. AB, U. Ala., 1957; MA, The Am. U., 1967. Sr. scientist Dunlap & Assocs., Washington, 1963-67; dir. plans and programming Informatics, Inc., Bethesda, Md., 1967-73; dir. pub. affairs Ocean Data Systems, Inc., Rockville, 1973-77; asst. budget sec. State of Md., Annapolis, 1977-78; county exec. Howard County Md., Ellicott City, 1978-86; dir. econ. devel. Entergy Corp., New Orleans, 1986-93; prin. ICA, Maplesville, Ala., 1993—. Cons. NSF, Washington, 1972-78. Contbr. articles to profl. jours. Charter mem., bd. dirs. Howard County, 1966-68, mem. county coun., 1969-70; mem. state legislature Md. Ho. of Dels., Annapolis, 1970-77; mem. Howard County Exec., 1978-86. Served with U.S. Army, 1948-54, ETO. Mem. AAAS (life), VFW (life), Acad. Polit. Sci. (life), Nat. Acad. Scis. (Space Application Bd. 1983-86), Nat. Rifle Assn. (life), Am. Legion (life), Mensa, Phi Beta Kappa, Phi Alpha Theta, Pi Sigma Alpha. Lodges: Alcazar Temple, Patmos. Republican. Methodist. Avocations: writing, flying, boating, traveling. Home: 318 Chilton Rd 214 Maplesville AL 36750 Office: ICA PO Box 223 Maplesville AL 36750-0223

NICHOLS, JACK EDWARD, JR. educational administrator; b. Huntington, W.Va., Feb. 3, 1948; s. Jack Edward and Elizabeth A. (Arrington) N.; B.A., Marshall U., 1970, M.A., 1972; Ph.D., Ohio U., 1980; m. Sue Ellen Ferguson, Dec. 22, 1973; 1 child, Heather Beth. Tchr. Cox's Landing Elem. Sch., Cabell County, W.Va., 1970-76; prin. Greenbottom Elem. Sch., Cabell County, 1977; asst. prin. Milton Elem. Sch., Cabell County, 1978; prin. Harveytown Elem. Sch., Huntington, W.Va., 1979-81, Jefferson Elem. Sch., Huntington, 1981-83, Culloden Elem. Sch., 1983-88, Altizer Elem. Sch., Huntington, 1988—. Active Big Bros. Am.; coach Boys' Club. Hershel C. Price Ednl. Found. scholar, 1976-79. Mem. NEA, Cabell County Elem. Prins. Assn., Phi Delta Kappa. Republican. Methodist. Club: Esquire Country. Home: 819 Big Bend Rd Barboursville WV 25504-9795

NICHOLS, JAMES LEE, advertising executive; b. Parkersburg, W. Va., Apr. 30, 1929; s. James L. and Eleanor (Kidd) N.; m. Shirley Chelsted, June 18, 1952; children: Keith David (dec.), Cheryl Lee, Eric Daniel. , Carnegie Inst. Tech., 1952; BS, U. Pitts., 1953. Salesman Mt. Lebanon Hardware Co., Pitts., 1948-53; advt. account exec. Ketchum MacLeod & Grove, Inc., 1953-55; dir. advt. (sales promotion) N.Y.C., 1955-82; with Univac div. Sperry Rand Corp., communications planning mgr. Phila., 1982-84; pres. Nichols Advt. Inc., Blue Bell, Pa., 1984—. Instr. advt. courses Bucks Community Coll. Contbr. articles to profl. jours. Dir. music, Presbyn. Ch., 1953—, campaign dir. indsl. div., Community Chest-United Fund, Pitts., 1954-55; with USNR, 1946-48. Mem. Nat. Wild Life Assn., Assn. Indsl. Advertisers, Nat. Audio-Visual Assn., Sales Exec. Office: 1166 Dekalb Pike Ste 104 Blue Bell PA 19422-1844 E-mail: jlnichol272@yahoo.com.

NICHOLS, JAMES RAYMOND, JR. civil engineer; b. Holyoke, Mass., Mar. 14, 1966; s. James Raymond and Donna Jean (Riley) N. BSCE, Northeastern U., 1989; MS in Environ. Engring., U. Conn., 1994. Registered profl. engr., Wash. Staff engr. N.L. Jacobson & Assocs., Chester, Conn., 1989-95; project engr. II City of Olympia (Wash.) Pub. Works Dept., 1995-97; program coord., instr. South Puget Sound C.C., Olympia, 1997-2000; quality control mgr. Triton Marine Constrn., Bremerton, Wash., 1997-99; pub. works dir., city engr. City of Chehalis (Wash.) Pub. Works Dept., 1999—. Spkr. Am. Filtration & Separations Soc. conf., Nashville, 1995, Impervious Surface Reduction Rsch. Symposium, Olympia, Wash., 1996, Western Regional Urban Streams Conf., Arcata, Calif., 1996, Water/Wastewater Operators Workshop, Ocean Shores, Wash., 1999. Contbr. articles to profl. jours. Active Chester Inland Wetlands Commn., 1993-95. Mem.: APWA, ASCE, City Engrs. Assn. Wash. (sec.-treas. 2002—). Achievements include research in recirculating sand filters for wastewater treatment. Home: 5500 Park Place Loop SE Lacey WA 98503-4339 Office: City of Chehalis PO Box 871 Chehalis WA 98532-0871 E-mail: chehalispw@localaccess.com.

NICHOLS, JAMES RICHARD, civil engineer, consultant; b. Amarillo, Tex., June 29, 1923; s. Marvin Curtis and Ethel (Nichols) N.; m. Billie Louise Smith, Dec. 24, 1944; children: Judith Ann, James Richard Jr., John M. BS in Civil Engring., Tex. A&M U., 1949, MS in Civil Engring., 1950. Registered profl. engr., Tex., Okla., N.Mex. Ptnr. Freese & Nichols, Inc., Cons. Engrs., Fort Worth, 1950-76, pres., 1977-88, chmn., 1988—. Chmn. Tex. Bd. Profl. Engrs. Former chmn. Ft. Worth Conv. and Visitors Bur.; bd. dirs. Pub. Comm. Found. North Tex., Tex. A&M Rsch. Found., Tex. Wesleyan U. With U.S. Army, 1943-46. Fellow Am. Cons. Engrs. Coun.; mem. NSPE, Tex. Water Conservation Assn., Ft. Worth C. of C. (bd. dirs., adv. coun.), Exch. Club, Ft. Worth Club, Rotary. Methodist. Home: 4821 Overton Woods Dr Fort Worth TX 76109-2429 Office: Freese & Nichols Inc 4055 Internat Plz Ste 200 Fort Worth TX 76109-4895 E-mail: jrn@freese.com.

NICHOLS, JEFFREY NORMAN, geriatrician; b. Ithaca, N.Y., Aug. 22, 1947; s. Benjamin and Ethel G. Nichols; m. Arlene Ellen Katz, June 4, 1967; children: Daniel, Sara, Gabriel. BA, Columbia U., 1968; MD, Cornell U., 1976. Diplomate Am. Bd. Internal Medicine, Am. Bd. Geriatrics, Am. Bd. Hospice and Palliative Care. Dir. profl. affairs Elderplan, Bklyn., 1986-87; med. dir. Frances Schervier Home and Hosp., Bronx, 1987-94; med. dir., chmn. ethics com. Cabrini Ctr. for Nursing and Rehab., N.Y.C., 1994—; chief geriat. Cabrini Med. Ctr., 1994—; assoc. med. dir. Cabrini Hospice, 1998—. Cons. med. affairs Franciscan Sisters of Poor Found., N.Y.C., 1989—, bd. dirs. 1998—; ; bd. dirs. St. Cabrini Nursing Home, Dobbs Ferry, N.Y. Pres. Svc. Program for Older People, N.Y.C., 1991—; bd. dirs. N.Y. Coalition Against Hunger, N.Y.C., 1993—, treas., 1997—; co-chmn. social action com. Congregation Ansche Chesed, N.Y.C., 1990-97. Mem. N.Y. Med. Dirs. Assn. (bd. dirs. 1988—, v.p. 1997—), Met. Area Geriatrics Soc. (bd. dirs. 1988-92, 95-97). Democrat. Jewish. Office: Cabrini Medical Center 227 E 19th St Rm C440 New York NY 10003-2602 E-mail: jnichols@ccnr.cabrininy.org.

NICHOLS, JOHN DAVID, insurance broker, entrepreneur; b. Walton/Oneonta, N.Y., Mar. 18, 1948; s. Sidney Newton and Emily Matilda (Clark) N.; m. Annemarie Margaret Meinke, June 24, 1978; children: David Sean, Christine Marie, James Edmund. BA, Muskingum Coll., 1971; postgrad., Am. Coll. Lic. ins. broker, CPCU, 1992. Underwriter trainee U.S. Fidelity & Guaranty, Scranton, Pa., 1972-73, underwriter Balt., 1973-76, supervising underwriter Toledo, 1976-77; sr. casualty underwriter The Hartford Ins. Group, Mt. Kisco, N.Y., 1977-81; assoc. account exec. Murray, Schoen & Homer, Inc., Bronxville, 1981-84; sr. casualty underwriter N.Am. mgrs. Am. Internat. Group, N.Y.C., 1984-85; assoc. acct. exec. A. Matarasso & Co., Inc., White Plains, N.Y., 1985-88; acct. exec. Walter Kaye Assocs., Inc., N.Y.C., 1988-90; analyst Interstate Risk Mgmt. Corp., Bedford, N.Y., 1990-92; mgr. dirs. and officers liability ins. dept. Interstate Risk Placements, Inc., Interstate Coverage Corp., 1990-92; with Prudential Ins. Co., Yorktown Hghts., 1992-93; ins. broker, 1993—; comml. underwriter Utica First Ins. Co., Peekskill, N.Y., 1994-96; prin. Bus. Ins. and Risk Mgmt. Svcs., 1994—2000; underwriter, broker Sieger & Smith, Inc., Scarsdale, N.Y., 1996; ins. broker, 1996. Gen. contractor most trades, 1997—2001; ins. broker Pond Ins. agy., Delhi, NY, 2001—. Life Underwriter Tng. Coun. Fellow, 1994. Mem. CPCU Soc., Soc. Fin. Svc. Profls., Masons, Rotary. Republican. Episcopalian. Avocations: family activities, outdoor sports, home projects, music, church activities.

NICHOLS, JOHN DOANE, diversified manufacturing corporation executive; b. Shanghai, China, 1930; m. Alexandra M. Curran, Dec. 4, 1971; children: Kendra E., John D. III. BA, Harvard U., 1953, MBA, 1955. Various operating positions Ford Motor Corp., 1958-68; dir. fin. controls ITT Corp., 1968-69; exec. v.p., COO Aerojet-Gen. Corp., 1969-79, Ill. Tool Works Inc., Chgo., 1980-81, CEO, dir., 1982-95, chmn., 1986-96; pres., CEO Marmon Group Inc., Chgo., 2002. Bd. dirs. Household Internat., Philip Morris Cos., Inc., Rockwell Internat.; overseer Harvard U., 1994-99, vis. com. Sch. Edn., com. athletics, com. univ. resources. Trustee U. Chgo., 1987-93, Lyric Opera Chgo., Mus. Sci. and Industry, Jr. Achievement Chgo., Chgo. Commerce Club Civic Com.; life trustee Chgo. Symphony Orch.; bd. dirs. Art Inst. Chgo., past chmn.; mem. bd. govs. Argonne (Ill.) Nat. Lab., 1988-93; vice chmn. exec. com. Chgo. Cmty. Trust, 1997—. Mem. Harvard Club (N.Y., Chgo.), Indian Hill Club (Winnetka, Ill.), Chgo. Club, Comml. Club, Econ. Club Chgo. Office: Marmon Group Inc 225 W Washington St Chicago IL 60606

NICHOLS, KAREN, academic administrator; b. Ind. m. Jim Nichols. DO, U. Health Scis., Coll. Osteo. Medicine, Kansas City. Intern and resident in internal medicine Okla. Osteo. Hosp., Tulsa; asst. dean grad. med. edn. Ariz. Coll. Osteo. Medicine; dean Chgo. Coll. Osteo. Medicine, 2002—. Contbr. articles to profl. jours. Bd. trustees Mut. Ins. Co. of Ariz.; with Mesa Symphony, Mesa United Way, Central Christian Ch. Recipient Physician of Yr., Ariz. Osteo. Med. Assn., 1996, Educator of Yr., Mesa Gen. Hosp. Mem.: Am. Osteo. Assn. (chair bur. state and govt. affairs, mem. health related and fed. health policies coms., chair adv. com. of end-of-life care). Office: Chgo Coll Osteo Medicine Midwestern U 555 31st St Downers Grove IL 60515*

NICHOLS, KATIE, investment company executive; b. Des Moines, May 19, 1940; d. Gardner "Mike" and Lois (Thornburg) Cowles; m. Julian Strauss, June 11, 1960 (div. 1971); children: Elizabeth Lois Strauss Grossi, Gwen Beatrix Strauss Jenkins, Kate Anne Strauss Long; m. Roger Marvin Nichols, Sept. 1, 1973 (div. 1981); m. H.E. Rummel, Mar. 27, 1983 (div. 1994). Student, Cornell U., 1957-61. Ptnr., v.p. The Rummel Group, Inc., St. Petersburg, Fla., 1985—. Trustee Cowles Charitable Trust, N.Y.C., 1985—. Vol. Hosp. Albert Schweitzer, Deschapelles, Haiti, 1961-63; vice chmn. Fla. Human Rels. Commn., Tallahassee, 1974-75 (award of honor 1985); Dem. candidate Fla. Pub. Svc. Commn., 1976; commr. Fla. Pub. Svc. Commn., 1981-89, chmn., 1987-89; vice chmn. Fla. Corrections Commn., 1994-98; bd. dirs. Nat. Coun. on Crime and Delinquency, San Francisco, 1990—, chmn. 1997-98; bd. dirs. HAS2000 Campaign for Hosp. Albert Schweitzer, Haiti; trustee Cowles Charitable Trust, 1985—. Mem. NOW, Emily's List, League of Women Voters of Fla. Democrat. Episcopalian. Avocations: reading, needlepoint. Home: 1682 Oceanview Dr Tierra Verde FL 33715-2500 Office: The Rummel Group Inc 1641 1st Ave N Saint Petersburg FL 33713-8935

NICHOLS, LEE ANN, library media specialist; b. Denver, Apr. 27, 1946; d. Bernard Anthony and Margaret Mary (Pughes) Wilhelm; m. Robert Joseph Nichols, July 12, 1975; children: Rachel, Steven, Sarah. BS in Edn., St. Mary of the Plains, Dodge City, Kans., 1968; MA in Edn., Colo. U., 1978. Cert. type B profl. tchr., Colo. Tchr. So. Tama Sch. Dist. Montour, Iowa, Iowa, 1968-70, Strasburg (Colo.) Sch. Dist., 1970-73; svc. rep. Montain Bell, Denver, 1973-75; libr., tchr. Simla (Colo). Sch. Dist., 1976-78; dir. Simla Br. Libr., 1978-81; dir. Christian edn. St. Anthony's Ch/, Sterling, Colo., 1983-84; libr. cons. Rel Valley Sch., Iliff, 1984-98, Plateau Sch. Dist., Peetz, 1986-99; dir. Fleming Cmty. Libr., 1997—. Mem. Colo. Coun. for Libr. Devel., Denver, 1986-92, chmn. 1991; instr. Northeastern Jr. Coll., Sterling; del. Gov.'s Conf. on Libr. and Info. Scis., 1990. Contbr. articles to profl. jours. Active Sterling Arts Coun., sec., 1982-85, v.p., 1985, pres., 1986-87; chair Northeastern Jr. Coll. Found., Sterling, 1983-87, mem. 1981-91; mem. community adv. coun. Northeastern Jr. Coll., 1991-93, chair, 1993; bd. dirs. Wagon Wheel chpt. Girl Scouts Am., 1975-78. Mem. ALA, Am. Assn. Sch. Librs., Assn. Libr. Svcs. to Children, Colo. Ednl. Media Assn., Colo. Libr. Coun., Internat. Reading Assn. (Colo. Coun.). Avocations: reading, sewing. Home: 12288 County Road 370 Sterling CO 80751-8494 Office: Fleming Cmty Libr 506 N Fremont Ave Fleming CO 80728-9520

NICHOLS, MARCI LYNNE, gifted education coordinator, educator, consultant; b. Cin., July 7, 1948; m. James G. Nichols, June 19, 1970; children: Lisa, Jeannette. B in Arts and Sci., Miami U., Oxford, Ohio, 1970, MEd, 1990, PhD, 1997. Cert. Secondary English, elem. gifted edn., computer edn., Ohio. Secondary English tchr. West Clermont Local Schs., Cin., 1970-71; coord. gifted edn. and tchr. Batavia (Ohio) Local Schs., 1981—. Spkr., cons. Local Gifted Orgns., Cin., 1988—; vis. instr. dept. ednl. psychology Miami U., Oxford, Ohio, 1991-98, assoc./adj. prof. 1998—; presenter Nat. Rsch. Symposium on Talent Devel., 1991. Author, presenter: (videotape series) Parenting the Gifted Parts I and II, 1992; columnist, contbr. Resources for Everyday Living; contbr. articles to profl. jours; creator attitude assessment instrument. Speaker Christian Women's Club, Ohio, Ind., Ky., W.Va., 1981—; deacon First Presbyn. Ch. of Batavia, Ohio, 1986-88; bd. trustee Super Saturday program gifted edn. com. Miami U., 1995—. Recipient Douglas Miller Rsch. award Miami U., 1991. Mem. ASCD, Am. Ednl. Rsch. Assn. (presenter 1997, 98), Nat. Assn. for Gifted Children, Consortium Ohio Coords. of Gifted, Parents Assn. for Gifted Edn. (trustee 1997), Midwest Ednl. Rsch. Assn. (presenter), Internat. Platform Assn., Mensa (ann. gathering presenter 1998), Phi Kappa Phi. Home: 110 Wood St Batavia OH 45103-2923 Office: Batavia Local Schs 800 Bauer Ave Batavia OH 45103-2837

NICHOLS, MARGARET FOSTER, librarian; b. South Weymouth, Mass., May 31, 1956; d. John Alden and Barbara Tuttle Nichols. BA, Oberlin Coll., 1977; MA, Cornell U., 1980, PhD, 1983; MLS, Syracuse U., 1990. Vis. asst. prof. St. John Fisher Coll., Rochester, N.Y., 1982-83; instr. Northea. U., Boston, 1983-84; sr. spl. collections asst. Cornell U. Libr., Ithaca, N.Y., 1985-87, adminstrv. supr., 1987-92, asst. rare book libr., 1992-97, tech. svcs. coord., 1997-99, head tech. svcs., 1999—. Contbr. articles to profl. jours. Vis. tutor Literacy Volunteers, Ithaca, 1997-99. Mem. MLA, Am. Libr. Assn., Soc. for History of Authorship, Reading, and Publishing. Democrat. Avocations: chorus, piano, walking, reading. Office: Cornell U Libr Divsn Rare/Manuscript Colls 2B Kroch Library Ithaca NY 14853

NICHOLS, M(ARIAN) THERESA, radio station executive; b. Bowman, S.C., Feb. 15, 1947; d. Marion Carvin and Jessie Mae (Robinson) Day; m. Bobby Bernard Nichols, Aug. 2, 1969; 1 child, Yvette Rochelle. BA, S.C. State Coll., 1968; MA, Atlanta U., 1971; PhD, U. S.C., 1977. Cert. mediator, assessor, S.C. Assoc. prof. English, S.C. State Coll., Orangeburg, 1969-88; copy editor, asst. slot editor The State, Columbia, S.C., 1988-90; edn. program cons. S.C. Dept. Edn., 1990, coord. edn. project, 1990-97; media dir., cmty. affairs coord. Sta. WIIZ-FM, Barnwell, S.C., 1997—. Reading cons. Dorchester Sch. Dist. 4, St. George, S.C., 1971; grammar cons. S.C. State Coll., Orangeburg, 1972-82, The State, 1988; workshop presenter, motivational speaker, 1989—; cons. race/sex equity, 1990—; mem. S.C. Black History Curriculum Com. Co-editor coll. catalog, coll. self-study. Mem. Multicultural Forum, U. S.C., 1992-97; mem. multicultural/gender equity task force S.C. Dept. Edn., 1992-97, mem. civil rights compliance MOA task force, 1991-97, sch. safety task force, 1993-97; active Dem. Party, Balt., 1966-67; vol. Am. Cancer Soc., Orangeburg, 1985, Leukemia Soc. Am., 1989, The Male's Place, 1991-92. Nat. Fellowship for Black Ams. fellow, 1976. Mem. NAFE, Ga. Assn. Broadcasters, Phi Delta Kappa, Kappa Delta Pi, Sigma Tau Delta, Alpha Kappa Alpha, Alpha Kappa Mu. Methodist. Avocations: reading, travel, fashion, interior decorating, architectural design. Home: 375 Woodlawn Dr NE Orangeburg SC 29115-2755 Office: WIIZ Radio WIZ Plz 8968 Marlboro Ave Barnwell SC 29812 E-mail: wiizard@ntinet.com., wiizard@aol.com.

NICHOLS, MARK EDWARD, aerospace engineer; b. Schenectady, N.Y., Sept. 3, 1950; s. John Burton and Betty Jane (Paulsen) N.; m. Cornelia Rocas. BS in Engring. Physics, U. Calif., Berkeley, 1972; MS in Sci. and Engring. Mgmt., West Coast U., 1984; postgrad., Ind. Coll. Armed Forces, 1977. Cert. in Nat. Security Mgmt. Inst. and mech. technician Wetzel-Moreau Engring. Co., Inglewood, Calif., 1970-71; sales engr., supr. United Tech. Industries/Turbocooler Divsn., Manhattan Beach, 1972-73; wind tunnel test engr. Space Divsn. Rockwell Internat., Downey, 1973-76, flight and sys. engr. Space Sys. Divsn. Palmdale, 1976-78, aero. test engr. Space Sys. Divsn. Downey, 1980-85, project engr. payloads-cargo integration Aerospace Divsn., 1985-96; flight test integration engr. Gen. Dynamics/Convair, San Diego, 1978-80; project engr. mission/manifest integration requirements Boeing Space Sys. Divsn., 1996-99; lead flight interface engr. Boeing Reusable Space Systems, 1999-2001; sr. lead flight integration engr., reconfiguration engring. Boeing Human Space Flight and Exploration. Instr. Aerodynamics and Aeronautics, Adv. Career Tng., Downey, 1986—; instrnl. aide, lectr. Discover-E, Downey, 1992—. Columnist, Long Beach Press-Telegram, 1987-90. With USN, 1968-69. Judge L.A. County and Calif. State Sci. and Engring. Fairs, 1987—. Recipient Achievement award Bank of Am., 1968, Silver Snoopy Achievement award NASA, 1978; Gov.'s scholar, 1968. Mem. ASME, AIAA, Nat. Mgmt. Assn., Am. Legion #270, Planetary Soc., Moose #1739, Los Amigos Men's Club. Republican. Avocations: golf, skiing, sailing, travel, motorcycling. Home: 11682 Lakewood Blvd Downey CA 90241-5272 Office: Boeing Human Space Flight & Exploration Divsn 5301 Bolsa Ave Huntington Beach CA 92647

NICHOLS, MICHAEL WHITMAN, lawyer; b. Munfordville, Ky., June 4, 1962; s. Clem and Dianne Nichols; m. Stacey Tharp, Aug. 17, 1965; children: Forrest, Stuart, Olivia. Bar: Ky., 1987. Atty. Hart County Attys. Office, Munfordville, Ky., 1987—. Capt., judge advocate USAR, 1993—. Mem. Ky. Bar Assn. Office: Hart County Attys Office PO Box 838 Munfordville KY 42765-0838

NICHOLS, MYRNA BULLOCK, real estate broker; b. Dallas, May 7, 1937; d. Ollie O. and Patty Lou (Sutherland) Bulloch; children— Susan Janice Nichols Walton, Jere Blake Nichols. Student McMurry Coll., 1955-56, U. Tex.-Arlington, 1957, Stephen F. Austin State U., 1958. Licensed real estate broker, Tex. Documentation engr. Sci. Control Corp., Carrollton, Tex., 1967-69; asst. to v.p. Electronic Data Systems, Dallas, 1969-73; mktg./leasing agt. Vantage Companies, Dallas, 1973-76; comml. broker Cushman & Wakefield of Texas, Inc., Dallas, 1979— . Named 1984 Broker of the Year, Cushman & Wakefield; recipient 1984 Outstanding Achievement award, Comml. Real Estate Women. Mem. Tex. Assn. Realtors, Nat. Assn. Realtors, Women in Indsl. Real Estate, Comml. Real Estate Women (pres. 1985, treas. 1984), Greater Dallas Bd. Realtors (comml. investment div.). Methodist. Republican. Home: 1114 Lake Cross Rd Lindale TX 75771-5157

NICHOLS, RALPH ARTHUR, lawyer; b. Clinton, N.Y., Jan. 27, 1919; s. Arthur Britcher and Carrie Lena (Pitcher) N.; m. Pamela Crow Bermingham, May 3, 1947 (dec. Feb. 1980); children: Jeremy Nichols Pierce, Ralph A. Jr., Melinda Nichols Mayer; m. Victoria Requa Lalli, Sept. 5, 1981. AB, Hamilton Coll., 1940; LLB, Yale U., 1947. Bar: Conn. 1949, N.Y. 1947, U.S. Dist. Ct. (so. dist.) N.Y. 1949, U.S. Dist. Ct. Conn. 1950, U.S. Supreme Ct. 1959. Assoc. Burke & Burke, N.Y.C., 1947-49, Maguire, Walker & Middleton, Stamford, Ct., 1949-54; assoc., then ptnr. Cummings & Lockwood, 1954—. Founder, former bd. dirs. Stamford Land Conservation Trust; former bd. dirs. Conservationists Stamford, Inc., Stamford YMCA; former bd. dirs., sec. Stamford Area Commerce and Industry; trustee Stamford YMCA. Lt. USNR, 1942-46, ETO, PTO. Fellow Am. Coll. Trust and Estate Counsel; mem. ABA, Woodway Country Club (Darien, Conn.), Yale Club (N.Y.C.), Phi Delta Phi. Republican. Episcopalian. Home: 656 Den Rd Stamford CT 06903-3824 Office: Cummings & Lockwood PO Box 120 4 Stamford Plz Stamford CT 06902-3834 E-mail: rnicho@cl-law.com.

NICHOLS, RICHARD ALAN, ecologist; b. L.A., Apr. 18, 1951; s. Harry Alfred and Sheila Helen (Davidson) N. BA in Biol. Scis., Calif. State U., Chico, 1978; MS in Range Mgmt., U. Calif., Davis, 1983. Cert. rangeland mgr., Calif.; cert. profl. in erosion and sediment control, Internat. Erosion Control Assn. Botanist U.S. Forest Svc., Yreka, Canby, Calif., 1981-82; postgrad. rsch. asst. U. Calif., Davis, 1983-84; range conservationist U.S. Dept. Interior Bur. Land Mgmt., Caliente, Nev., 1984-86, 1st Strategic Aerospace Divsn., Vandenberg AFB, Calif., 1986-87, natural resources planner, 1987-88; sr. botanist Western Ecol. Svcs. Co., Novato, 1988-91; sr. program mgr. Fugro Inc., Roseville, 1991-95; dir. natural resources EIP Assocs., San Francisco, 1995-2001; prin. biologist Levine-Fricke Inc., 2001—. Cons. to Delta in-channel island group San Frncsico Estuary Project, Sacramento, 1996—. Contbr. articles to profl. jours. Recipient Sustained Superior Performance award USAF, 1990-91. Mem. Calif. Native Grass Assn. (bd. dirs. 1997—, treas. 1999-2000, pres.-elect 2001, instr. Habitat Restoration Workshop 1999—), Soc. Ecol. Restoration, Calif. Native Plant Soc., Soc. Range Mgmt., Constrn. Materials Assn. Calif. (environ. com. 1998). Episcopalian. Achievements include successful application of biotech. bank stabilization on a major California river; founder mitigation com. and chief California coastal dune restoration planner for Peace Keeper/Rail Garrison Project; developed several successful habitat restoratio projects in California and Nevada. Home: 550 Battery St Apt 1114 San Francisco CA 94111-2325 Office: LFR 1900 Powell St 12th Fl Emeryville CA 94608 E-mail: richard.nichols@lfr.com.

NICHOLS, ROBERT LEIGHTON, civil engineer; b. Amarillo, Tex., June 24, 1926; s. Marvin Curtis and Ethel Nichols; m. Frances Hardison, June 8, 1948; children: Eileen, William C., Michael L. BSC.E., Tex. A&M U., 1947, MSC.E., 1948. Grad. asst., instr. Tex. A&M U., 1947-48; assoc. Freese & Nichols (and predecessors), Ft. Worth, 1948-50, partner, 1950-77, v.p., 1977-88, pres., 1988-91, vice chmn., 1991-92, pres. emeritus, 1992—. Mem. Bldg. Stds. Commn., 1956—62. Chmn. Horn Frog dist. Boy Scouts Am., pres. Longhorn coun., 1990—93, Ozark Trails coun., 1998—99. Mem.: NSPE (pres. 1977—78), ASCE, Nat. Inst. Engring. Ethics (pres. 1995—97), Tex. Pub. Works Assn., Tex. Water Utilities Assn., Am. Pub. Works Assn., Water Environ. Assn. Tex. (pres. 1962—63), Water Environ. Fedn., Tex. Water Conservation Assn., Am. Water Works Assn., Tex. Soc. Profl. Engrs. (pres. 1965—66), C. of C. Webb City, Mo. (exec. dir. 1997—2001), Masons, Chi Epsilon, Tau Beta Pi. Methodist. Office: 1 S Main St Ste 102 Webb City MO 64870-2325 E-mail: rnl@freese.com.

NICHOLS, ROBERT LYMAN, retired foreign service officer, lecturer; b. Milw. s. Malcolm Strong and Ruth Mary (Lyman) N.; m. Virginia Lee Straghan, Sept. 7, 1947 (dec. 1989); children: Robert Gibbs, Nancy Lee, Peter Lyman. Student, Swarthmore Coll., 1942-43; BA, Tufts U., 1949; MA, Fletcher Sch. Law & Diplomacy, Medford, Mass., 1950; diploma, U.S. Army War Coll., Carlisle, Pa., 1969. Fgn. svc. officer U.S. Dept. State, The Philippines, 1951-53, USIA, Italy, 1954—56, Holland, 1956—58, Taiwan, 1959—61, Taiwan, 1969—71, Hong Kong, 1961—65, Singapore, 1971—74; dir. Chinese divsn. Voice of America, 1966-69; dep. dir. East Asia Cultural Afairs U.S. Dept. State, Washington, 1974-76; dep. dir. East Asia USIA, 1977-79; ret., 1979; part-time faculty Cape Cod C.C., Barnstable, Mass., 1981—2002; tchr. of Chinese Light House Charter Sch., Orleans, 1997. Chinese lang. officer USIA and Dept. State, 1959—79; China tour leader Chinese Ednl. Travel, Nat. Com. US-China Rels. and Smithsonian, 1980—95, 1999; lectr. on China and U.S. China rels., 1980—2002. Contbr. feature articles and Op-Ed pieces to internat. newspapers and jours. Mem. bd. Cape Cod Human Svcs., Hyannis, Mass., 1987-2001, chmn., 1990-91. Quartermaster 1st class, USN, 1943-46, Pacific. Episcopalian. Avocations: boating, fishing, theater acting. Home: 248 Kates Path Yarmouth Port MA 02675-1451 E-mail: rlnichols@attbi.com.

NICHOLS, ROCKY, state representative, non-profit consultant; b. Topeka, Sept. 4, 1969; s. Kenneth Leroy and Rita Ann Nichols. BA in Polit. Sci., Washburn U., 1993. Lic. Nat. Soc. Fund Raising Execs. Legis. aide State of Kans., Topeka, 1991-92; state legislator 58th dist. State Ho. of Reps., 1992—; owner P.M. Consulting, 1993-97; dir. of devel. Family Svc. & Guidance Ctr., 1995-98; owner Fund Consulting, 1997—. Dir. Inst. for Comty. Partnerships, Washburn U., Topeka, 1995-97; mem. adv. bd. Pres.'s Com. on Mental Retardation, Washington, 1997-99; mem. adv. com. Capper Found., Topeka, 1995—; bd. dirs. Kans. Film Commn.; com. mem. Coun. of State Govt., Washington, 1997—. Plenary lectr. Pres.'s Com. on Mental Retardation, Washington, 1997; bd. dirs. Friends of Topeka Zoo, 1995—; Big Brother, Big Bros./Big Sisters Topeka, 1993-2000. Named Outstanding Pub. Ofcl. of Yr., Kans. Assn. of Mental Health Ctrs., 1996, Frank A. Hines Legislator of Yr., Kans. Chiropractic Assn., 1996, Legislator of Yr., Kans. Assn. Pub. Employees, 1994, 96, 97; BILLD fellow La Follette Inst. Pub. Affairs, Wis., 1997. Mem. ETAP (bd. dirs.), Highland Park Optimist Club (pres. 1997-98), Shawnee Heights Optimists Club, Highland Park Alumni Assn. (bd. dirs.). Democrat. Baptist. Avocations: exercise, computers. Home: 2329 SE Virginia Ave Topeka KS 66605-1358 Office: State Ho of Reps State Capitol Topeka KS 66612

NICHOLS, RONALD LEE, surgeon, educator; b. Chgo., June 25, 1941; s. Peter Raymond and Jane Eleanor (Johnson) N.; m. Elsa Elaine Johnson, Dec. 4, 1964; children: Kimberly Jane, Matthew Bennett. MD, U. Ill., 1966, MS, 1970. Diplomate Am. Bd. Surgery (assoc. cert. examiner, New Orleans, 1991), Nat. Bd. Med. Examiners. Intern U. Ill. Hosp., Chgo., 1966-67, resident in surgery, 1967-72, instr. surgery, 1970-72, asst. prof. surgery, 1972-74; assoc. prof. surgery U. Health Scis. Chgo. Med. Sch., 1975-77, dir. surg. edn., 1975-77; William Henderson prof. surgery Tulane U. Sch. Medicine, New Orleans, 1977—, vice chmn. dept. surgery, 1982-91, staff surgeon, 1977—, prof. microbiology, immunology and surgery, 1979—. Cons. surgeon VA Hosp., Alexandria, La., 1978-93, Huey P. Long Hosp., Pineville, La., 1978—, Lallie Kemp Charity Hosp., Independence, La., 1977-85, Touro Infirmary, New Orleans, Monmouth Med. Ctr., Long Branch, N.J., 1979-88; mem. VA Coop. Study Rev. Bd., 1978-81, VA Merit Rev. Bd. in Surgery, 1979-82; mem. sci. program com. 3d Internat. Conf. Nosocomial Infections, Ctr. Disease Control, mem. sci. program and fundraising com. 4th Internat. Conf.; bd. dirs. Nat. Found. Infectious Diseases, 1989—, v.p., 1994-97, pres.-elect., 1997-99, pres., 1999-2001, past pres., 2001—; hon. fellow faculty Kasr El Aini Cairo U. Sch. Medicine, 1989; mem. adv. com. on infection control Ctrs. for Disease Control, 1991-97; disting. guest, vis. prof. Royal Coll. Surgeons Thailand 14th Ann. Clin. Congress, 1989, 17th Ann. Clin. Congress, 1992; mem. infectious diseases adv. bd. Roche Labs., 1988-95, Abbott Labs., 1990-92, Kimberly Clark Corp., 1990-99, SmithKline Beecham Labs., 1990-95, Fujisawa Pharm., chmn., 1990-99, Bayer Pharm., 1994-2001, Merck Sharpe Dohme, 1996, Depotech, 1996, Zeneca Pharm., 1997—, Rhone-Poulenc Rorer, 1997-99, Wyeth-Ayrest Labs., 1998—, Pfizer Pharm., 1999, Searle Pharm., 1999—, GlaxoWellcome, 1999, Aventis, 1999-2000, others; mem. study group Prophylaxis Antibiotic Project La. Health Care Rev., Inc., 1995-2000, Nat. Com. Study Blood Borne Disease Transmission make Nat. Policy, The Rockefeller Brothers Fund, 2001—; lectr. Royal Coll. Physicians and Surgeons Can., 1998, Internat. Infectious Disease Soc. Ob-gyn., 1998, 20th N.Y. State Surg. Symposium, 1998, dept. surgery Dept. U. Ark., 1998; apptd. by gov. La. commn. HIV and AIDS, 1999—. Author: (with Gorbach, Bartlett and Nichols) Manual of Surgical Infection, 1984; author, guest editor: (with Nichols, Hyslop Jr. and Bartlett) Decision Mking in Surgical Sepsis, 1991; guest editor, author: Surgical Sepsis and Beyond, 1993; mem. editl. bd. Current Surgery, 1977—, Hosp. Physician, 1980—, Infection Control, 1980-86, Guidelines to Antibiotic Therapy, 1976-81, Am. Jour. Infection Control, 1981-99, Internat. Medicine, 1983—, Confronting Infection, 1983-86, Current Concepts in Clin. Surgery, 1984—, Fact Line, 1984-91, Host/Pathogen News, 1984—, Infectious Diseases in Clin. Practice, 1991—, surg. sect. editor, 1992—, Surg. Infections: Index and Revs., 1991—, So. Med. Jour., 1992-97, ANAEROBE, 1994—, Surg. Infections, 1998—, Clin. Infectious Diseases, 1999—; editl. adv. bd. MD Consult Infectious Diseases, 2002-; mem. adv. bd. Physician News Network, 1991-95; patentee (with S.G. schoenberger and W.R. Rank) Helical-Tipped Lesion Localization Needle Device; patentee in field. Elected faculty sponsor graduating class Tulane Med. Sch., 1979-80, 83, 85, 87, 88, 91-92. Maj. USAR, 1972-75. Recipient House Staff tchg. award U. Ill. Coll. Medicine, 1973, Rsch. award Bd. Trustees U. Health Scis.-Chgo. Med. Sch., 1977, Owl Club Tchg. award, 1980-86, 90; named Clin. Prof. of Yr. U. Health Scis., Chgo. Med. Sch., 1977, Clin. Prof. of Yr., Tulane U. Sch. Medicine, 1979; Douglas Stubbs Lectr. award Surg. Sect. Nat. Med. Assn., 1987, Prix d'Elegance award Men of Fashion, New Orleans, 1993, Annual La. Laureate Emeritus lectureship, 2002; named Brit. Jour. of Surgery Lectr., 1997, 1st Annual Warren Cole lectr., 2001, 2d Annual La. Laureate Emeritus lectr., 2002. Fellow Infectious Disease Soc. Am. (mem. FDA subcom. to develop guidelines in surg. prophylaxis 1989-93, co-recipient Joseph Susman Meml. award 1990), Am. Acad. Microbiology, Internat. Soc. Univ. Colon and Rectal Surgeons, ACS (mem. operating rm. environ. com. 1978-80, vice chair operating rm. environ. com. 1980-81, chmn. operating rm. environ. com. 1981-83, sr. mem. operating rm. environ. com. 1983-87, mem. internat. rels. com. 1987-93, sr. mem. internat. rels. com. 1993-97); mem. AMA, Nat. Found. for Infectious Diseases (bd. dirs.), Joint Commn. on Accreditation of Health Care Orgn. (Infection Control adv. group, 1988-98, sci. program com. 3d internat. conf. nosocomial infections CDC/Nat. Found. Infectious Diseases 1990, FDA Subcom. to Develop Guidelines in Surg. Prophylaxis, 1989-93; prophylactic antibiotic study group La. Health Care Rev. Inc. 1996-2000, clin. advisor, mem., 2001—, AIDS commr. State of La. 1992-94, mem., La. Commn. HIV and AIDS, 1999—), 5th Nat. Forum on AIDS (sci. program com.), U.S. Pharmacopeial Convention Inc. (adv. panel surg. drugs and devices 1995-2000, nominating com. The Heinz Awards 1995-96), Assn. Practitioners in Infection Control (physician adv. coun. 1991-98), Internat. Soc. Anaerobic Bacteria, So. Med. Assn. (vice chmn. sect. surgery 1980-81, chmn. 1982-83), Assn. Acad. Surgery, N.Y. Acad. Sci., Warren H. Cole Soc. (pres.-elect 1988, pres. 1989-90), Assn. VA Surgeons, Soc. Surgery Alimentary Tract, Inst. Medicine Chgo., Midwest Surg. Assn., Cen. Surg. Assn., Ill. Surg. Soc., European Soc. Surg. Rsch., Collegium Internationale Chirugiae Digestivae, Chgo. Surg. Soc. (hon.), New Orleans Surg. Soc. (bd. dirs. 1983-87), Soc. Univ. Surgeons, Surg. Soc. La., Southeastern Surg. Soc., Phoenix Surg. Soc. (hon.), Hellenic Surg. Soc. (hon.), Cen. N.Y. Surg. Soc. (hon.), Tulane Surg. Soc., Alton Ochsner Surg. Soc., Am. Soc. Microbiology, Soc. Internat. de Chirugie, Surg. Infection Soc. (sci. study com. 1982-83, fellowship com. 1985-87, ad hoc sci. liaison com. 1986-89, program com. 1986-87, chmn. ad hoc com. rels. with industry 1990-93, mem. sci. liaison com. 1995-96), Soc. for Intestinal Microbial Ecology and Disease, Soc. Critical Care Medicine, Am. Surg. Assn., Kansas City Surg. Soc., Bay Surg. Soc. (hon.), Cuban Surg. Soc. (hon.), Panhellenic Surg. Soc. (hon.), Tacoma Surg. Club (hon.), Sigma Xi, Alpha Omega Alpha. Episcopalian. Home: 1521 7th St New Orleans LA 70115-3322 Office: 1430 Tulane Ave New Orleans LA 70112-2699 E-mail: RLNMD@yahoo.com.

NICHOLS, SANDRA LEE, community health nurse; b. Sanford, Maine, Mar. 5, 1949; d. Earl John and Lorraine (Beaulieu) Johnstone; m. Arland C. Nichols, May 5, 1978; 1 child, Anne Cathleen. Diploma, N.H. Hosp., 1970; BA, New Eng. Coll., 1975; MEd, Incarnate Word Coll., 1986. RN, Tex. Staff nurse psychiat. unit Santa Rose Hosp., San Antonio, 1977-78; staff nurse San Antonio State Sch. and Hosp., 1978-83; sch. nurse San Antonio Ind. Sch. Dist., 1983-86; infection control nurse, in-svc. edn. coord. Lubbock (Tex.) State Sch., 1986-88; sch. nurse Lubbock Ind. Sch. Dist., 1988—. Recipient award N.H. Dept. Health and Welfare Adv. Bd.

NICHOLS, STEVEN PARKS, mechanical engineer, lawyer, educator; b. Cody, Wyo., July 1, 1950; s. Rufus Parks Nichols and Gwen Sena (Frank) Keyes; m. Mary Ruth Barrow, Aug. 5, 1990; 1 child, Nicholas Barrow Nichols. PhD, U. Tex., Austin, 1975, JD, 1983. Assoc. dir. Tex. Space Grant Consortium, Austin, 1989-91, dir. Design Projects Program, 1989—; dep. dir. Ctr. for Energy Studies, U. Tex., 1988-91, dir. of Ctr., 1991-99, acting dir. Ctr. for Electromechanics, 1994-99, assoc. prof. mech. enging., 1996—, assoc. chair dept. mech. enging., 1999—2001, dir. Ctr. for Energy and Environ. Resources, 1998—, dir. Chair of Free Enterprise, 2001—, assoc. v.p. rsch., 2002—. Bd. dirs. Assn. Mfg. Excellence; chmn. Nat. Coun. Space Grant Dirs., NASA, 1989-92; bd. dirs. So. Coalition for Advanced Transp., 1994-99, chair elect 1998-99, chair 1998-2000; bd. dirs. Nat. Inst. for Engring. Ethics, 1996-2001; chmn. mgmt. divsn. ASME Internat., 1999-2001. Patentee (with others) pulsed welding techniques, railgun igniter, inert burner, rail thruster, other patents pending. Fellow ASME; mem. NSPE, ABA, Am. Soc. Engring. Edn. (Fred Merryfield Design award 2001), Nat. Inst. Engring. Ethics (bd. govs. 1987-93, 96-2001), N.Y. Acad. Scis. Home: 1400 Lorrain St Austin TX 78703-4023 Office: U Tex Dept Mech Engring Austin TX 78712

NICHOLS, TRENT WILLIAM, JR. physician, gastroenterologist; b. Colorado Springs, Oct. 22, 1943; s. Trent William Nichols and Muriel Vesta Reich; m. Susan Crawford, June 18, 1966 (div. 1990); 1 child, Trent William III; m. Sharon Ann Minch, Nov. 24, 1990. BS, U. Denver, 1965; MD, Northwestern U., 1969. Diplomate Am. Bd. Internal Medicine, Am. Bd. Gastroenterology. Intern U.S. Naval Hosp., Great Lakes, Ill., 1969-70; resident in internal medicine Evanston (Ill.) Hosp., 1974-76; fellow in gastroenterology Northwestern U., 1976-78; physician Hanover, Pa., 1978—; CEO Ctr. for Nutrition and Digestive Disorders, 1995—, Advanced Magnetic Rsch. Inst. Pa., 1999—; v.p. Advanced Magnetic Rsch. Insts. Internat., 2001. Adv. bd. Inst. of Functional Medicine, Gig Harbor, Wash., 1998—2001; rsch. bd. Health Commn., Gig Harbor, 1996—2001; adv. bd. Great Smokies Diagnostic Lab., 2001—. Co-editor, author: Optimal Digestion, 1999. Lt. comdr. USN, 1969-74. Fellow ACP, Am. Coll. of Gastroenterology, Am. Coll. of Nutrition; mem. AMA, N.Am. Acad. of Magnetic Therapy (v.p. 2001-), Pa. Soc. of Gastroenterology. Avocations: bicycling, magnetic research, ancient Chinese art. Home: 724 High Rock Rd Hanover PA 17331-7997 Office: CNDD 195 Stock St Ste 211 Hanover PA 17331-2266 E-mail: twnichol@blazenet.net.

NICHOLS, VICKI ANNE, financial consultant, librarian; b. Denver, June 10, 1949; d. Glenn Warner and Loretta Irene (Chalender) Adams; m. Robert H. Nichols, Oct. 28, 1972 (div.); children: Christopher Travis, Lindsay Meredith. BA, Colo. Coll., 1972; postgrad., U. Denver, 1976-77. Treas., controller, dir. Polaris Resources, Inc., Denver, 1972-86; controller InterCap Devel. Corp., 1986-87; treas., controller, dir. Transnat. Cons., Ltd., 1986-91; web coord. Jefferson County (Colo.) Pub. Libr., 1986—. Dir., owner Nichols Bus. Services. Home: 4305 Brentwood St Wheat Ridge CO 80033-4412 Office: 10200 W 20th Ave Lakewood CO 80215 E-mail: vnichols@jefferson.lib.co.us.

NICHOLS, WILLIAM CURTIS, psychologist, family therapist, consultant; b. Fayette, Ala., Apr. 16, 1929; s. William Curtis and Eva (Hargett) N.; m. Alice Louise Mancill, May 29, 1954 (dec. 1990); children: Alice Camille, William Mancill, David Paul; m. Mary Anne Pace, Feb. 29, 1992. AB, U. Ala., 1953; EdD, Columbia U., 1960. Diplomate Am. Bd. Profl. Psychology. Asst. prof. sociology U. Ala., Birmingham, 1960-63; postdoctoral fellow Merrill-Palmer Inst., 1963-64, mem. psychotherapy faculty, 1965-69; prof. sociology Samford U., Birmingham, Ala., 1963-65; pvt. practice clin. psychology and marital and family therapy Grosse Pointe, Mich., 1969-73, 76-87; pvt. practice psychology, marital and family therapy Birmingham, 1976-87; prof. home and family life, dir. marriage and family counseling Fla. State U., 1973-76; exec. dir. Gov.'s Constituency Children, Fla., 1987-89; pvt. practice marital and family therapy S.E. Family Inst., 1989-90; pres. William Nichols Assocs., Organizational Cons., 1990-91; cons., marital and family therapist Atlanta, 1992—97; cons. in field, 1997-98; with The Nichols Group, Inc., 1998. Adj. prof. clin. psychology U. Detroit, 1976-83; adj. prof. family therapy Fla. State U., 1990-91; adj. prof., grad. faculty child and family devel. dept. U. Ga., 1992—, founder, chair adv. com. Family Therapy Archives, 1993—, The Nichols Group, Inc., 1998-99. Author: Treating People in Families: An Integrative Framework, 1997, Marital Therapy: An Integrative Approach, 1988, Treating Adult Survivors of Childhood Sexual Abuse, 1992, The AAMFT: Fifty Years of Marital and Family Therapy, 1992; co-author: Systematic Family Therapy, 1986; editor: (with others) Handbook of Family Development and Intervention, 2000; editor The Family Coord., 1970-75, Jour. Marriage and Family Counseling, 1974-76, Contemporary Family Therapy: An Internat. Jour., 1986—, Family Therapy News, 1986-91, The Internat. Connection, 1996-99; mem. editl. bd. Internat. Jour. Family Therapy, 1977-85, Jour. Divorce and Remarriage, 1976-83, 85—, Sage Family Studies Abstracts, 1977—, Family Systems Medicine, 1982-96, Jour. Marital and Family Therapy, 1984—, Jour. Family Psychotherapy, 1990—, Jour. Family Psychology, 1986-90. Mem. mental health and health coms. Mayor's Commn. on Children and Youth, 1966-69; bd. dirs. Family and Children's Svc., Oakland, Mich., 1977-87, chmn., 1984-86, dir. emeritus, 1987—. With C.E., U.S. Army, 1948-49. Recipient Svc. award Ala. Assn. for Mental Health, 1962, Spl. award for Outstanding Contbns. Fla. Assn. Marriage and Family Therapy, 1977, 82, 90; NSF fellow U. Colo., 1963, Disting. Svc. to families award Southeastern Coun. on Family Rels., 1996. Fellow: Am. Assn. Marriage and Family Therapy (dir. 1969—72, founding editor Jour. Marital and Family Therapy 1974—76, co-chmn. Atlanta Multiregional Conf. 1975, chmn. accreditation com. 1976—77, co-chmn. Atlanta Multiregional Conf. 1977, pres.-elect 1979—80, dir. 1979—83, pres. 1981—82, Spl. awards 1976, 1978, Disting. Leadership awards 1982, 1983, Disting. Leadership award 1991, Orgnl. Contbns. award 1992), Am. Psychol. Soc., APA; mem.: Internat. Family Therapy Assn. (bd. dirs. ex-officio 1996—98, charter, editor Internat. Connections 1996—99, pres.-elect 1998—99, pres. 2000—01), Ga. Assn. for Marriage and Family Therapy (pres.-elect 1994—95, pres. 1996, 1999—2001), Mich. Bd. Marriage Counselors (chmn. 1980—87), Nat. Coun. on Family Rels. (dir. and mem. exec. com. 1969—78, pres. 1976—77), Mich. Assn. Marriage Counselors (pres. 1969—71, chmn. profl. liaison com. 1972—73), Mich. Inter-Profl. Assn. on Marriage, Divorce and Family (com. chmn. 1968—71, 1976—86, trustee 1977—80, Orgnl. Contbn. award 1992), Assn. Marital and Family therapy Regulation Bds. (mem. MFT examination adv. bd. 1989—92), Am. Assn. Marriage and Family therapy Edn. and Rsch. Found. (trustee 1992—94). Home: 1041 Ferncreek Dr Watkinsville GA 30677-4212 Fax: 770-725-7984. E-mail: nicholsw@aol.com.

NICHOLS, WILLIAM FORD, JR. foundation executive, business executive; b. Palo Alto, Calif., July 4, 1934; s. William Ford and Elizabeth (Woodyatt) N.; m. Rosemary Peterson, 1988; children: Deborah, John, Andrew. AB, Stanford U., 1956, MBA, 1958. CPA, Calif. With Price Waterhouse, San Francisco, 1958-69, Price Waterhouse & Co., Sydney, Australia, 1966; asst. contr. Saga Corp., Menlo Park, Calif., 1969-72, contr., 1972—, asst. treas., 1981-83; assoc. prof. San Jose State U., 1983-88; treas. William and Flora Hewlett Found., Menlo Park, 1985-2000. Trustee Investment Fund for Founds., 1991-2001. Bd. dirs. Lucile Packard Found. for Children's Health, Palo Alto, Calif., 1999—. Mem. AICPA, Calif. Soc. CPA's, Inst. Mgmt. Accts. (nat. v.p. 1974-75, bd. dirs.), Fin. Execs. Inst. (pres. Santa Clara Valley chpt. 1979-80). Home: 330 August Cir Menlo Park CA 94025-5829

NICHOLS, WILLIAM J. film studies educator; b. N.Y.C., Aug. 19, 1942; s. James William and Nellie Mae Nichols; m. Catherine M. Soussloff, June 24, 1994; 1 child, Eugenia Clark. BA, Duke U., 1964; MA, UCLA, 1972, PhD, 1978. Prof. Queen's U., Kingston, Ont., Can., 1978-87, chair Can., 1976-85, San Francisco State U., 1987-90, prof., 1987-2001; prof. art history, Frances Knapp Allen chair of art history U. Rochester, 2001—. Vis. assoc. scholar U. Calif., Santa Cruz, 1990-93; legal cons., L.A. and San Francisco, 1991—; critic Sta. KUSP-NPR Radio, Santa Cruz, 1990-2001. Author: Movies and Methods, 2 vols., 1985, Representing Reality, 1991, Blurred Boundaries, 1994 (Critic's Choice award, 1994), Introduction to Documentary, 2001, Maya Deren and the American Avant-Garde, 2001. Getty rsch. assoc. Getty Mus., L.A., 1999-00. Office: Dept Art & Art History U Rochester 424 Morey Hall Rochester NY 14627 E-mail: wnichols@sfsu.edu.

NICHOLSON, BRADLEY JAMES, lawyer, court staff; b. Montebello, Calif., Sept. 22, 1958; s. Thomas Edwin and Charlotte Elizabeth (Knight) N.; m. Anne Marie Dooley, Oct. 6, 1990. BA, Reed Coll., 1983; JD, U. Pa., 1990. Bar: Calif. 1990, Nev. 1998, Oreg. 2001. Atty. Wilson, Sonsini, Goodrich & Rosati, Palo Alto, Calif., 1990-91; law clk. to Hon. Morris S. Arnold U.S. Dist. Ct., Ft. Smith, Ark., 1991-92; atty. Coudert Bros., San Jose, Calif., 1992-94; law clerk to Hon. Morris S. Arnold U.S. Cir. Ct., Little Rock, 1994-96; atty. Brown & Bain, Palo Alto, Calif., 1997-98; staff atty. ctrl. legal staff Nev. Supreme Ct., Carson City, 1998-99, prin. staff atty., ctrl. legal staff, 1999-2000; appellate staff atty. Oreg. Supreme Ct., Salem, Oreg., 2000—. Contbr. articles to profl. jours. Mem. Federalist Soc.(vice chmn. publications Litigation practice group, 1997-98, pres. Little Rock lawyers chpt. 1995-96). Avocations: golf, fishing, music. Office: Oreg Supreme Ct 1163 State St Salem OR 97301-2563

NICHOLSON, DOUGLAS ROBERT, accountant; b. Avon, N.Y., Dec. 4, 1921; s. Robert William and Ruth (Neff) N.; m. Gertrude Jane Scott, Apr. 24, 1944; children— Laurie, Scott, Susan, Steven. AB, U. Rochester, 1942, MS, 1948. Baseball player St. Louis Cardinal Farm Teams, 1942, 46; staff acct. Oliver & Clapp, 1948-49; sr. acct. Charles L. Clapp & Co., 1949-51; tchr. income taxes U. Rochester, 1950-61; office mgr. Williams, Clapp & Co., 1951-53, ptnr., 1953-56; prin. Haskins & Sells, CPA's, Rochester, N.Y., 1956-59, ptnr., 1959-67, ptnr.-in-charge Rochester office, 1967-82. Author: After Reagan-Bish is it Too Late, 2002. Pres. Estate Planning Coun. Rochester; team capt. YMCA capital fund dr., 1961, Rochester Inst. Tech. new campus fund dr., 1964; chmn. spl. gifts com. U. Rochester, 1965, group leader 38 million capital fund campaign, 1966; mem. acctg. adv. bd. Syracuse U., 1968; adv. com. M.S. program Rochester Inst. Tech. Bd. Dirs.; treas. Highland Hosp., Rochester; bd. dirs. Hosp. Computer Ctr. Rochester, Rochester Regional Rsch. Libr. Coun.; mem. deferred giving adv. coun. Rochester Inst. Tech.; mem. N.Y. State Bd. Pub. Accountancy, 1977-82. Lt. USN, 1942-45, WWII. Recipient Gannett Newspapers award, 1956, SUNY Empire Stae Medal for Philanthropy, 1999. Mem. AICPA, N.Y. State Soc. CPAs (past pres. Rochester), Nat. Assn. Accts., Am. Acctg. Assn., Am. Mgmt. Assn., Rochester C. of C., Beta Alpha Psi. Democrat. Unitarian (trustee). Clubs: Oak Hill Country, University, Genesee Valley. Home and Office: 663 Lake Rd Webster NY 14580-1552

NICHOLSON, ELEANOR ANN, educator; b. Chgo., July 15, 1930; d. Louis Earl and Viola F. (Gaffner) Kuester; m. Thomas Laurence Nicholson, Sept. 11, 1954; children: Anne Nicholson Weber, John C., Sarah S., Martha Nicholson. BA in English, Carleton Coll., Northfield, Minn., 1952; MA in Ednl. Adminstrn., U. Chgo., 1981, postgrad., 1952-54; PhD, Loyola U., Chgo., 1995. Tchr., adminstr. The Lab. Schs., Chgo., 1969-75; dir. Ancona Sch., 1975-86; head upper sch. The Latin Sch., 1986-89; dir. Forest Ridge Acad., Schererville, Ind., 1990-93. Mem. bd. Ind. Schs. Assn. Ctrl. States, 1980-85; pres. Ind. Sch. Assn. Greater Chgo., 1982-85; adj. prof. Erikson Inst., Chgo., 1997—. Community rep. Local Sch. Coun. Shoesmith Sch., Chgo., 1989-97; mem. women's bd. U. Chgo. Recipient Anne Tyskling award Ind. Schs. Assn. Greater Chgo., 1989. Mem. ASCD, Nat. Mid. Schs. Assn., Communal Studies Assn., Soc. Utopian Studies, The Friday Club, The Fortnightly, Quadrangle Club. Avocations: violin, gardening, tennis, cross-country skiing. Home: 600 Barton Ave Evanston IL 60202 E-mail: halsbarn@aol.com.

NICHOLSON, ELLEN ELLIS, clinical social worker; b. Boston, Apr. 1, 1940; d. George Letham and Mary Stirling (Money) McIver; divorced; 1 child, Matthew Norman Ellis. Dental Hygienist, Forsyth Coll., 1959; BS, Northeastern U., 1973, MEd in Counseling, 1974; MSW, Boston U., 1984. Registered dental hygienist, Mass. Dental hygienist, 1959-66; clin. coord., pvt. dental practice Forsyth Dental Ctr., Boston, 1966-70; dir. vol. counseling Solomon Mental Health Ctr., Lowell, Mass., 1974-75; social worker East Boston Social Ctrs., Inc., 1976-77, dir. youth family counseling, 1977-79; supr. family svc. Boston Housing Authority, 1979-81; social worker Mass. Soc. Prevention Cruelty to Children, Hyannis, 1984-86, supr., 1986-93, clinic dir., 1993-95; dir. profl. svcs. Child and Family Svc. of Cape Cod, 1995-98, dir., 1998—, dir. Abuse Prevention Svcs., 1995-96, dir., 1995—. Psychotherapist Riverview Sch., Sandwich, Mass., 1989-93. Advisor youth group Christ Episcopal Ch., Needham, Mass., 1960-64, St. Paul's Ch., Newburyport, Mass., 1964-65; vol. counselor Solomon Mental Health Ctr., Lowell, 1972-74; chair Barnstable County Children's Task Force, 1994-96; chmn. adv. com. Barnstable County Sexual Abuse Intervention Network, 1994-96; mem. task force Barnstable County Juvenile Firesetters, 1995-96, mem. steering com., 1996—; mem. adv. bd. Cape and Islands Child Advocacy Ctr.; mem. Cape & Islands Domestic Violence Coun. Bd., 1998—. Mem. NASW, Am. Profl. Soc. on Abuse of Children, Assn. for Treatment of Sexual Abusers, Sigma Phi Alpha, Sigma Epsilon Rho, Kappa Delta Pi. Avocations: travel, ballroom dancing, skiing. Office: Child and Family Svc of Cape Cod 1019 Route 132 Hyannis MA 02601-1839

NICHOLSON, GERALD LEE, air transportation executive; b. Belleville, Ill., Dec. 30, 1944; s. Chester Lee and Bette Joan (Tarr) N.; m. Cathy Ann Sammons, May 3, 1975; children: Laura, Brianna. BA in Sociology, So. Ill. U., 1974, BS in Math., MBA, So. Ill. U., 1976. Bus. mgr. Northland Orthopedic Group, St. Louis, 1976-78; cons. AMA, Chgo., 1978-80; cons. pvt. practice Evansville, Ind., 1981-85; adminstr. Mo. Eye Inst., St. Louis, 1985-91; regional v.p. Co-Care Eye Cts., 1985-91; adminstr. Orthopaedic Assoc., P.C., Cape Girardeau, 1992—2001; gen. mgr. Mt. Vernon (Ill.) Airport. Tax preparer Nicholson Cons., St. Louis, 1990-92. Mem. Citizen Interaction Com., Chesterfield, Mo., 1989, Leadership Cape, 1992. Capt. USMC, 1966-72, Vietnam. Mem.: Am. Assn. Airport Execs., Aircraft Owners and Pilots Assn, Exptl. Aircraft Assn., Little Egypt Bicycle Club, Elks, Rotary Internat. (pres. local chpt.). Avocations: running, flying. Home: 3010 Jamison Mount Vernon IL 62864 Office: Mt Vernon Airport 100 Aviation Dr Mount Vernon IL 62864

NICHOLSON, HENRY HALE, JR. surgeon; b. Statesville, N.C., June 22, 1922; s. Henry Hale and Martha Haseltine (Miller) N.; m. Freda Hyams, Sept. 24, 1956; children: Henry Hale III, Thomas Dalton Miller, John Christie, Michael Witherspoon, Freda Amanda, W. Stuart Cooper. BA in Chemistry, Duke U., 1944, MD, 1947; grad., USAF Sch. Aviation Medicine, 1952. Diplomate Am. Bd. Gen. Surgery, Am. Bd. Colon and Rectal Surgery. Rotating intern U. Wis. Gen. Hosp., Madison, 1947-48; resident in gen. surgery Med. Coll. Va., Richmond, 1948-49, Alton Ochsner Hosp. and Clinic, New Orleans, 1949-51, 53-55, inaugeral resident in colon and rectal surgery, 1955-56; resident in gen. surgery Tulane U., La. Charity Hosp., 1949-51, 53-55; pvt. practice gen., colon and rectal surgery, aerospace medicine Charlotte, N.C., 1956—; sr. surg. staff mem. Carolinas Med. Ctr. and Mercy Hosp. Sr. active staff Presbyn. Hosp., Charlotte; sr. active teaching staff Carolinas Med. Ctr., 1956-85, cons. staff, 1985—. Mem. Airport Authority Charlotte/Douglas Internat. Airport, 1992—; mem. Mayor's Com. of 100 to study regional transp. and make appropriate recommendations, 1993-94; sr. examiner FAA, 1952—; mem. athletic-med. bd. N.C. Shrine Bowl, 1980—. With U.S. Army, 1943-46; flight surgeon USAF, 1951-53, Korea; col. USAFR, 1961-82; 1st air surgeon N.C. (command) Air. NG, 1970-82, surg. cons. Surgeon Gen. USAF, 1971-82, command flight surgeon 1981 (award) U.S. Air NG, 1st alternate flight surgeon 1982 (award) USAF. Decorated Legion of Merit; recipient Disting. Svc. medal N.C. Fellow ACS, Am. Soc. Colon and Rectal Surgeons; mem. Mecklenberg County Med. Soc. (pres. 1972), Charlotte Surg. Soc. (pres. 1987), Shriners (Scottish Rite), Masons (32 degree), Jesters, Alton Ochsner Surg. Soc., Hazel Creek Trout Club, Robert Burns Soc., St. Andrews Soc. of Carolina, Air Force Assn., Hound Ears Club (Blowing Rock, N.C.), Charlotte Country Club, Alpha Tau Omega, Phi Chi, Omicron Delta Kappa. Methodist. Avocations: golf, snow skiing, fly fishing, travel, painting. Home: 3933 Fellsway Dr Charlotte NC 28209-3417

NICHOLSON, JOSEPH BRUCE, real estate developer; b. San Jose, Calif., Jan. 21, 1940; s. Wilmot Joseph and Ruth (Russell) N.; m. Susan Knight, Nov. 1963 (div. 1972); children: Kelsey Erin, Craig Wilmot; m. Linda Mirassou, Aug. 1992. BArch, U. Oreg., 1963. Exec. v.p. Nicholson-Brown Inc., Santa Clara, Calif., 1967-80; prin. Nicholson Assocs., Aptos, 1977—; v.p., gen. mgr. Nicholson-Wilson Co., Santa Clara, 1980-83; prin. The Nicholson Co., Campbell, Calif., 1984—; v.p. Pacific Property Ventures Inc., 1988—; pres. Nicholson Constrn. Inc., 1989—; v.p. Nicholson Property Mgmt. Inc., 1989—; pres. The Nicholson Family Found., 1996—. Bd. dirs. Transmetrics Inc., San Jose. Bd. dirs. Triton Mus., Santa Clara, 1979, Hope Rehab. Svc., San Jose, 1979, United Way Ctrl. Area, San Jose, 1991. Devel. Engring. Rsch. Inst., Carmel, Calif., 1999—; pres. adv. bd. de Saisset Mus., Santa Clara U., 1991; trustee Mus. of Art and History, Santa Cruz, 1993. Lt. USN, 1963-67. Mem. Rotary, Commonwealth Club (San Francisco), World Trade Club (San Francisco), Santa Cruz Yacht Club, Tennis Club Rio Del Mar. Republican. Avocations: travel, reading, art collecting, cooking, tennis. Home: 218 Shoreview Dr Aptos CA 95003-4621 Office: The Nicholson Co 75 Cristich Ln Campbell CA 95008-5403 E-mail: brucenicholson@thenicholsonco.com.

NICHOLSON, JUNE C. DANIELS, retired speech pathologist; b. Augusta, Maine, Dec. 28, 1938; d. Sumner T. and Bernadette (Dulac) Daniels; m. Kenneth E. Nicholson, June 27, 1964; children: Jeffrey Scott, Daren Patrick. BS, Abilene Christian U., 1963; MS, U. Vt., 1980. Cert. ASHA CCC, Vt. Dept. Edn.; cert. tchr., Vt. Speech pathologist grades K-12 Arlington (Vt.) Pub. Sch.; ret. Vol. Peace Corp., Shumen, Bulgaria. Mem. NEA, Ret. Tchrs. Assn. of NEA, Am. Speech/Hearing Assn., Vt. Speech/Hearing Assn., Vt. Edn. Assn., Vt. Ret. Tchrs. Assn., Delta Kappa Gamma.

NICHOLSON, LELAND ROSS, retired utilities company executive, energy consultant; b. Carrington, N.D., Feb. 21, 1924; s. Malcom and Lena May (Kerlin) N.; m. Virginia E. Blair, Mar. 16, 1946; children: Heather Le Nicholson Studebaker, Leland B., Holly Kay. Student, Northwestern U., 1940-41; BSEE, U. N.D., 1949; postgrad. in utility mgmt., U. Minn., 1952. Planning and mktg. engr. Minkota Power Coop., Grand Forks, N.D., 1949-54; dir. new bus. Kans. Power & Light Co., Topeka, 1954-64, v.p. mktg., 1964-76, sr. v.p., 1976-80, exec. v.p., 1980-83, also bd. dirs.; pres. Kans. Power & Light Gas Service, 1985-88, ret., 1988; pres., chief operating officer The Gas Service Co., Kansas City, Mo., 1983-85. Pres. Indsl. Devel. Corp., Topeka; chmn. Kans. Council on Electricity and Environment; exec. com. Kansas City Labor Mgmt. Council, 1986-89; mem. Mktg. Execs. Conf.; bd. dirs. Gas Service Energy Corp., Kansas City, Merchants Nat. Bank, Topeka. Idea innovator heat pump water heater, photo cell controlled yard light, electric grill. Bd. dirs., area relations com. Kansas City (Mo.) Area Econ. Devel. Council, 1983-89; bd. dirs. Kansas City Pvt. Industry Council, 1986-89, Kansas City Downtown Council; trustee U. Mo., Kansas City, 1984-91; mktg. chmn. Kansas City Full Employment Council; past chmn., mem. Topeka-Shawnee County Planning Commn.; adult adv. com. Sea Scouts. Served to master sgt. USMC, 1942-46. Mem. Am. Gas Assn., Midwest Gas Assn. (bd. dirs. 1985-89), Mo. Valley Electric Assn. (chmn. 1979-81), Edison Electric Inst. (mktg. chmn. 1978-80), Assoc. Industries of Mo., Kans. Assn. Commerce and Industry, Greater Kansas City (Mo.) C. of C. (bd. dirs. 1979-82), Shawnee Yacht Club (Topeka) (commodore 1972-74), Lake Gaston Assn. (pres. 1993-97), Kansas City Club, Rotary. Republican. Congregationalist. Avocations: sailing, canoeing, fishing, reading, electronics.

NICHOLSON, MICHAEL, lawyer; b. Alexandroupolis, Greece, Nov. 26, 1936; m. Diana Long, June 21, 1964. BSCE, Northwestern U., 1961; MSCE, Columbia U., 1963; JD, St. John's U., 1970. Bar: N.Y. 1971, U.S. Dist. Ct. (ea. dist.) N.Y. 1979, U.S. Ct. Appeals (2d cir.) 1990. Counsel George A. Fuller Co., N.Y.C., 1970-72, Leonard Wegman Cons. Engrs., N.Y.C., 1972-73; sr. ptnr. Corner, Finn, Nicholson & Charles, Bklyn., 1978—. Contbr. articles to profl. jours. Bd. dirs. Bklyn. Nephrology Found., 1979, Pelham Bay Gen. Hosp., 1979. Mem. ABA, NSPE, Am. Arbitration Assn., N.Y. State Bar Assn., N.Y. State Soc. Profl. Engrs., Mcpl. Engrs. City N.Y. (award 1972). Office: 75 Livingston St 29th Fl Brooklyn NY 11201-5054

NICHOLSON, NORMAN EUGENE, artist, illustrator, educator; b. San Francisco, Oct. 15, 1931; s. Eugene H. and Myrtle A. N.; m. Barbara (dec. July 1981). BA with distinction, Art Ctr. Coll. Design, 1958. Owner Norman Nicholson Illustration, San Francisco, 1960-90, Norman Nicholson Fine Arts, Alamo, Calif., 1990—. Instr., chair illustration program Calif. Coll. Arts and Crafts, Oakland, 1977-90; tchr. painting Acad. Art Coll., San Francisco, San Jose State U. Illustrator: corps., design firms, publishers, advtsg. agys., wine labels, books and posters; one man exhibns. in Calif. and throughout the U.S.; group exhibns include Soc. Illustrators N.Y., L.A., San Francisco, pvt. galleries in the West, Smithsonian, The White House, Nat. Park Hqrs., W.Va., Sec. of Interior Office, Calif. State Capitol Bldg.; commd. by U.S. Nat. Park Svc. Mem. San Francisco Soc. Illustrator (charter, pres. 1967-68). Avocations: travel, writing. Office: Norman Nicholson Studio 132 Leona Ct Alamo CA 94507-2441

NICHOLSON, R. STEPHEN, organization administrator; b. Radford, Va., Mar. 4, 1926; s. Roy S. and Ethel Dovie (Macy) Nicholson; m. Carol Peterson; 1 child Suzanne Carpenter. AB, Marion Coll., 1950; MA, Syracuse U., 1956; PhD, Mich. State U., 1971. Pres. Daley Coll., Chgo., 1969-71; prof. Lansing (Mich.) Community Coll., 1963-66, Acad. dean, 1966-69; pres. Clark County Community Coll., 1971-76; chancellor Oakland Community Coll., 1985-90; vice chancellor Higher Colls. of Tech., United Arab Emirates, 1990-92; CEO Internat. Christian Leadership, 1992-93; pres. emeritus Mt. Hood Coll., 1993-94; pres. Mt. Hood CC Dist., 1976-85; CEO Mercy Corps Internat., 1994—99, chmn. bd. dirs., 1997-2000. Pres. Creative Futures; bd. dirs. MCI. Sr. fellow for higher edn. M.J. Murdock Trust, 1993—95, 1996—99; chair bd. dirs. N.W. Autism Found., 2000—02. Mem.: World Affairs Coun., Am. Acad. Polit. and Social Scis., Am. Sociology Assn., Am. Sch. Adminstrs. Assn., N.W. Assn. Cmty. and Jr. Coll.s (pres. 1976), Am. Assn. Cmty. and Jr. Colls. (pres. Pres.'s Acad. 1982, bd. dirs. 1985—87), Am. Futuristic Soc., Japan-Am. Soc., Gresham C. of C. (dir. 1977—79), Rotary Club (pres. 1983, Paul Harris fellow 1986), Phi Delta Kappa. Home: 9685 Irvine Bay Ct Las Vegas NV 89147-8365

NICHOLSON, RICHARD JOSEPH, trust banking executive; b. N.Y.C., Feb. 19, 1932; s. Robert William and Mary Elizabeth (McShane) N.; m. Barbara Helen Malisky, Oct. 15, 1955; 1 child, Richard Jr. BS in Social Sci., Georgetown U., 1952; MBA, NYU, 1957. Asst. cashier Citibank Trust Divsn., N.Y.C., 1952-66; sr. v.p. 1st Fidelity Bank, Newark, 1966-90, ret., 1990. Mem. exec. com. N.J. Bankers Assn. Trust Divsn., Princeton, 1983-85. Bd. dirs. Family Svc. Bur. of Newark, 1976-2001; mem. coun. Newark Mus., 1979-90. Republican. Roman Catholic. Avocations: travel, history.

NICHOLSON, RICHARD SELINDH, educational association administrator; b. Des Moines, Apr. 5, 1938; s. George Eugene and Margaret (Selindh) N.; m. Mary Lou Weisbrod, Aug. 1, 1958 (div. 1971) 1 child, Jeffrey Richard; m. Lois Ann Karls, Aug. 15, 1976; 1 child, Gregory Michael. BS, Iowa State U., 1960; PhD, U. Wis., 1964; LHD (hon.), CUNY, 1994, CUNY-Mt. Sinai Med. Ctr., 1994. Rsch. assoc. U. Wis., Madison, 1963-64; asst. prof. Mich. State U., East Lansing, 1964-67, assoc. prof., 1967-70; program dir. NSF, Washington, 1970-77, div. dir., 1977-82, chief of staff, 1983-85, asst. dir., 1985-89; exec. dir. Nat. Sci. Bd. Commn., 1982-83; exec. officer, pub. Science AAAS, 1989—. Cons. on sci. affairs Pres. of U.S., Washington, 1978-79; exec. sec. Pres.' Com. on Nat. Medal Sci., Washington, 1976-84; mem. Pres.' Nat. Commn. on Superconductivity, 1989; vice chair Commn. on Phys. Scis., Math and Resources NRC, 1989—, Edn. Coordinating Coun., 1991—, com. on environ. rsch., 1991-92, co-chair coun. on competitiveness, 1993—; mem. statutory vis. com. Nat. Inst. of Stds. and Tech., 1990-93; vis. com. chemistry dept. Harvard U., 1989—; bd. dirs. Quality Edn. for Minorities Network, 1989—; trustee Gordon Rsch. Conf., 1989—; sci. policy adv. com. com. space, sci. and tech. U.S. Ho. Reps., 1992—; co-chair Coun. on Competitiveness, 1993—, Dept. of Energy Panel on Basic Rsch., 1995—; chmn. edn. adv. com. Genentech, 1993—. Mem. editorial bd. Analytical Chemistry, 1980-82, Chem. and Engring. News, 1985-88; contbr. articles to profl. jours. and chpts. to books. Served as seaman USN, 1956-63. Recipient Presdl. Disitng. Ranking, Pres. Reagan, 1982, Alumni Citation Merit award Iowa State U., 1983. Fellow AAAS; mem. Am. Chem. Soc. (chmn. Mich. State U. sect. 1968-70), Chem. Soc. Washington (nominations com. 1977), Cosmos Club, Nat. Press Club. Avocations: sports, tennis, reading. Home: 1020 Union Church Rd Mc Lean VA 22102-1115 Office: AAAS 1200 New York Ave NW Ste 100 Washington DC 20005-3941

NICHOLSON, ROBERT ARTHUR, college president; b. Pepin, Wis., Oct. 13, 1923; s. Arthur W. and Ethel (Weeden) N.; m. Dorothy Nelis, June 17, 1944; children: Paul, Gary. BS, Anderson U., Ind., 1944; MA, NYU, 1946, PhD, 1953. With Anderson U., 1945-90, successively instr., asst. prof., assoc. prof. music, chmn. dept., asst. to dean, 1945-58, dean, 1958-83, v.p., 1964-83, pres., 1983-90, pres. emeritus, 1990—. Author: Handbook to the Hymnal of the Church of God, 1953; Editor: Hymnal of the Church of God, 1953, 71. Interim CEO Ch. of God Ministries, Inc., 1998, cons., 1997-99; interim exec. pastor, Park Place Ch. of God, 1995; interim min. of music, 1999-2002; mem. pub. bd. Ch. of God, 1955-80, chmn. commn. higher edn., 1963-70, 83-86, vice chmn., 1970-83, cons., 1990-96; cons. Warner Pacific Coll., Oreg., 1990-98, N.Ind. United Meth. Found., Inc., 1992-95, Anderson Pub. Libr., 1994-95, United Faith Housing Corp., 1994, Hopewell Ctr., 1996, Alexandria Cmty. Ctr., Inc., 1997, Family Network Agy., Inc., 1997-2000, Wilson Boys and Girls Club, 1997, Cmty. Found. Grant County, 1998, United Way Anderson and Madison County, Ind., 1998, 2000, Anderson Area C. of C., 1998, 2001, Christian Ctr., 2001; bd. dirs. Anderson Symphony Orch., 1974-87, 93-94, United Way Madison County, 1985-89, 91-94, Minnetrista Cultural Found., 1988-2002; bd. dirs., v.p. Anderson Internat., 1990-93; bd. dirs. Cmty. Hosp. Madison County, 1986-95, vice chmn., 1988-94, interim pres., CEO, 1991; mem. Madison County Cmty. Found., Inc., 1991—, pres., 1991-97. Mem. Associated Colls. of Ind., Ind. Colls. and Univs. of Ind. (chmn. 1988-89), Anderson Area C. of C. (bd. dirs. 1985-90, vice chmn. and chmn. elect 1988, chmn. 1989). Home: 721 Maplewood Ave Anderson IN 46012-3028

NICHOLSON, ROBERT D. manufacturing executive; b. Milton, Mass., Feb. 7, 1942; s. Nelson D. and Ruth V. (Simpson) N.; m. Priscilla A. Johnson, May 8, 1963 (dec. July 2000); children: Lea, Dana. Student, USAF Acad., 1959; BS in mech. engring., Northeastern U., 1964; MS, MIT, 1969; MBA, U. Detroit, 1974. Lic. profl. engr., Mich. Project engr. Pegasus, Troy, Mich., 1969-72, engring. mgr., 1972-80, Cadillac Gage, Warren, Mich., 1980-82; pres. Nicholson Engring. Co., Birmingham, 1982—. Holder 11 U.S. patents. Chair Birmingham Mich. Democratic Club, 1995-98, 2000-02; mem. Bd. Canvassers, Birmingham, 1997—. Mem. ASME, Soc. Automotive Engrs. Office: Nicholson Engring Co 563 Wellesley St Birmingham MI 48009-1518 E-mail: bob.nicholson@alum.mit.edu.

NICHOLSON, SHELIA ELAINE, senior print production manager; b. Bklyn., Jan. 20, 1963; d. Emmett Sr. and Louise (Ashford) Caldwell; m. Gerard Nicholson, Aug. 2, 1986. BS, Hampton U., 1985. Cert. in CPR. Adminstrv. asst. Lazar Mgmt. Techs. Inc., N.Y.C., 1985-86; mgr. print prodn. The Wessel Co./Horah Graphics, 1986-87, 88-96; acctg. clk. The Howard Marlboro Group, 1987-88; community relations coord. The Nurturing Ctr., Columbia, SC, 1996-97; sen. print production mgr. The Horah Group, New York, 1997—. Ind. beauty cons. Mary Kay Cosmetics, Inc., 1993—. Democrat. Baptist. Avocations: weight lifting, volleyball, bassoonist. Home: 9518 Sea View Ct Brooklyn NY 11236-5434 Office: The Horah Group 49 W 37th St Fl 13 New York NY 10018-8308 E-mail: scn12063@aol.com., Shelia@Horah.com.

NICHOLSON, TOM COTTON, school district administrator; b. Kewanee, Ill., Oct. 28, 1945; s. Dale Willard Thomas and Berniece Pearl (Cotton) N.; m. Carol Gail Colvin, June 24, 1967; children: John, Benjamin, Thomas, Lindsey. BS, Ill. State U., 1967; MEd, U. Ill., 1968. Cert. tchr., supr. Ill. Dir. career edn. Orion (Ill.) Cmty. Sch. Dist. 223, 1968—2002. Vis. prof. So. Ill. U., Carbondale, 1975; adv. bd. juvenile justice rev. Ill. 14th Jud. Cir., 1996—. Chmn. Henry County Bd., Ill., 1988—; chmn. Congrl. Acad. Appt. Bd., 17th U.S. Congrl. Dist. Ill., 1984—; trustee Lynn Twp., Henry County, 1981—. Named Adminstr. of Yr. Assn. of Ill. Rural and Small Schs., 1992, Ill. Vocat. Assn., 1984, Tchr. of Yr. Ill. Office of Edn., 1975. Mem.: Nat. Assn. State Tchrs. of Yr., Twp. Offcls. of Ill., Ill. Edn. Assn. (Outstanding Educator 1974), Ill. Coun. Vocational Adminstrs. (pres. 1979—80), Ruffed Grouse Soc. Democrat. Presbyterian. Avocations: opera, fishing, hunting, antiques. Home: 11500 E 250th St Lynn Center IL 61262-9542 Office: Office of Chmn Henry County Bd 307 W Ctr St Cambridge IL 61238 E-mail: tomcnicholson@yahoo.com.

NICHOLSON, WILL FAUST, JR. bank holding company executive; b. Colorado Springs, Colo., Feb. 8, 1929; s. Will Faust and Gladys Olivia (Burns) N.; m. Shirley Ann Baker, Nov. 26, 1955; children: Ann Louise Nicholson Naughton, Will Faust III. S.B., M.I.T., 1950; MBA, U. Denver, 1956. V.p. Van Schaack & Co., Denver, 1954-66; pntr. N. G. Petry Constrn. Co., 1966-70; sr. v.p. Colo. Nat. Bankshares, Inc., 1970-75, pres., 1975-95, chmn. bd., chief exec. officer, 1985-95; chmn. Rocky Mountain Bankcard Sys., Denver, 1995—2001. Bd. dirs. Boys and Girls Clubs of Metro Denver; active Downtown Denver, Inc., Colo. Assn. of Commerce and Industry, chmn. 1990-91, Denver Urban Renewal Authority, 1958-59, Denver Bd. Water Commrs., 1959-65, pres. 1964, 65; Nat. Western Stock Show; bd. Health One. With USAF, 1950-53. Mem. Assn. Bank Holding Cos. (bd. dirs. 1979-87, 89-91, exec. com. 1980-85, vice chmn. 1981-82, chmn. 1983-84), U.S. C. of C. (bd. dirs. 1990—, chmn. 1999-2000), U.S. Golf Assn. (exec. com. 1974-82, v.p. 1978, 79, pres. 1980, 81), Denver Country Club, Univ. Club Colo., Univ. Club N.Y., Castle Pine Golf Club, Royal and Ancient Golf Club (St. Andrews, Scotland), Augusta (Ga.) Nat. Golf Club. Republican. Episcopalian. Home: 37 Polo Club Cir Denver CO 80209-3307 Office: Rocky Mountain BankCard Sys Inc PO Box 5168 Denver CO 80217-5168

NICHOLSON, WILLIAM JOSEPH, forest products company executive; b. Tacoma, Aug. 24, 1938; s. Ferris Frank and Athyleen Myrtle (Fesenmaier) N.; m. Carland Elaine Crook, Oct. 10, 1964; children: Courtney, Brian, Kay, Benjamin. SB in ChemE, MIT, 1960, SM in ChemE Practice, 1961; PhD in ChemE, Cornell U., 1965; MBA, Pacific Luth. U., 1969. Registered profl. chem. engr., Wash. Sr. devel. engr. Hooker Chem. Co., Tacoma, 1964-69, Battelle N.W., Richland, Wash., 1969-70; planning assoc. Potlatch Corp., San Francisco, 1970-75, mgr. corp. energy service, 1976-94, dir. corp. energy and environ. svcs., 1994—; chair energy coun. Am. Forest and Paper Assn., Washington, 1998—. Chmn. electricity com. Am. Forest and Paper Assn., 1977-98, mem. solid waste task force, 1988-91, air quality com., 1989—, mem. regulatory policy com., 1994—, vice-chmn. life cycle analysis work group, 1994-2000, chmn. wood products environ. task force, 1994-99; U.S. expert on environ. labelling to Internat. Stds. Orgn., 1994-2000; chmn. Forest Products Lab., U. Calif., Richmond, 1993-95, mem. adv. bd. 1992—; mem. adv. bd. Coll. of Natural Resources, U. Calif., Berkeley, 1993-95; mem. adv. com. Fed. Biomass, 2000—. Mem. AAAS, AIChE (assoc.), TAPPI, Am. Chem. Soc., Commonwealth Club (San Francisco), Sigma Xi. Republican. Avocation: industrial history. Home: PO Box 1114 Ross CA 94957-1114 Office: Potlatch Corp 244 California St Ste 610 San Francisco CA 94111-4351

NICHOLSON, WILLIAM NOEL, clinical neuropsychologist; b. Detroit, Dec. 24, 1936; s. James Eardly and Hazel A. (Wagner) N.; m. Nancy Ann Marshall, June 15, 1957; children: Anne Marie, Kristin, Scott. AB, Wittenberg U., 1959; MDiv, Luth. Theol. Sem., Phila., 1962; PhD, Mich. State U., 1972. Diplomate Am. Bd. Forensic Examiners, Am. Bd. Med. Psychotherapists; lic. clin. psychologist, Mich.; ordained to ministry Luth. Ch., 1962; cert. Nat. Register health Care Providers in Psychology. Parish pastor Our Saviour Luth. Ch., Saginaw, Mich., 1962-69; intern in psychology Ingham Mental Health Bd., 1971-72; resident in psychology Bay-Arenac Mental Health Bd., 1972-74; dir., psychologist Riverside Ctr., Bay City, Mich., 1974-75; pastor, psychologist Psych Studies & Clergy Consultation of Mich., 1989—. Pres. Bay Psychol. Assocs., P.C., Bay City, 1975— ; cons. Gov.'s Office of Drug Abuse, 1972-74. Author: A Guttman Facet Analysis of Attitude-Behaviors Toward Drug Users by Heroin Addicts and Mental Health Therapists, 1972, An Episcopalian Guide to the Augsburg Confession, 1997; contbr. articles to profl. jours. Mem. APA, Mich. Psychol. Assn., Mental Health Assn. (pres. Bay-ARenac chpt. 1981), Bay City Yacht Club. Office: Behavioral Med Ctr 3442 Wilder Rd Bay City MI 48706-2331 E-mail: fatherbill36@hotmail.com.

NICHOLSON-GUTHRIE, CATHERINE S. See GUTHRIE, CATHERINE

NICHTER, LARRY STEVEN, medical educator, plastic surgeon; b. Nov. 12, 1951; BA, Boston U., 1973, MD, 1978; MS in Surgery, U. Va., 1983. Diplomate Am. Bd. Surgery, Am. Bd. Plastic Surgery. Intern UCLA Med. Ctr., 1978, chief resident dept. surgery, 1982; fellow in hand surgery U. Va., 1983, chief resident plastic surgery, 1983; clin. prof. plastic surgery U. So. Calif. Med. Ctr., 1993—; pres. Pacific Ctr. for Plastic Surgery. Pres., founder Plasticos Found.; examiner Am. Bd. Plastic Surgery. Office: 7677 Center Ave Ste 401 Huntington Beach CA 92647-3098 also: 1441 Avocado Ave Ste 808 Newport Beach CA 92660

NICKEL, ALBERT GEORGE, advertising agency executive; b. Pitts., July 12, 1943; s. Frank George and Dorothy (Wiefling) N.; m. Dana Cooper; children: Mark, Grace, Olivia. AB, Washington and Jefferson Coll., 1965; MBA, Ind. U., 1967. Mktg. rsch. anlyst Pfizer, Inc., N.Y.C., 1967, prof. svc. rep., 1967-68, mktg. rsch. mgr., 1968-69, product mgr., 1969-70; profduct mgr. USV Internat., Tuckahoe, N.Y., 1970-71; account supr. Sudler & Hennessey, N.Y.C., 1973-77; sr. v.p. mgmt. group supr. Young and Rubicam, 1977-79; chmn., pres., COO Dorritie Lyons & Nickel, Inc.; chmn., pres., CEO HMC Group Omnicom, Inc., 1999—; pres., chmn., CEO Lyons, Lavey, Nickel, Swift, Inc., 2000—. Trustee Wilton YMCA, Five Town Found.; bd. dirs., exec. com. Wilton LaCrosse Assn.; bd. trustees Dominican Coll., Healthcare Businesswoman's Assn., Wilton H.S. Long Range Planning Team, Am. Coun. on Sci. and Health; co-chmn. TBWA WorldHealth. Capt. USAF, 1969. Recipient Ellis Island medal of honor, 2002. Mem. Pharm. Rsch. and Mfrs. Assn. (bd. dirs.), Healthcare Mktg. and Comm. Coun. (bd. dirs.), Vis. Nurses Assn. (mem. found. bd.), Midwest Healthcare Mktg. Assn., Wilton Riding Club (pres.), Shore and Country Club, Silver Spring Country Club. Home: 65 Keelers Ridge Rd Wilton CT 06897-1608

NICKEL, ALLAN EUGENE, physician, educator; b. Portsmouth, Ohio, June 2, 1949; s. James Harold and Virginia Marie Nickel; m. Susan Mary Pohlman, Sept. 23, 1978; children: Erin, Laura, Brian. BS in Zoology, Ohio State U., 1971, MD, 1975. Diplomate Am. Bd. Internal Medicine, Am. Bd. Nephrology. Resident in internal medicine U. Tex. Southwestern, Dallas, 1975-78; fellow in nephrology U. Tex., San Antonio, 1978-80; staff nephrologist Trouer Clinic, Madisonville, Ky., 1980-83, Scott & White Clinic, Temple, Tex., 1983-2001; assoc. prof. nephrology Tex. A&M U., 1983-2001. Mem. Phi Beta Kappa, Alpha Omega Alpha. Roman Catholic. Avocations: hiking, swimming. Office: Scott & White Clinic 2901 S 31st St Temple TX 76508-0001

NICKEL, JAMES ALVIN, mathematician, educator, consultant; b. Grants Pass, Oreg., Sept. 27, 1925; s. Jacob Alexander and Gladys I. Beakley (Gilson) Nickel; m. Jerri Lou Sullivan, Apr. 23, 1999; m. Byrl Ray Udvardi, Sept. 6, 1952 (dec. May 1998); children: Jay Bruce, Ron Bradley, Mark Blair. BA/BS, Willamette U., 1949; MS, Oreg. State U., 1951, PhD, 1957. Mem. faculty math. Willamette U., Salem, Oreg., 1953—59; chmn. math. Okla. City U., Okla. City, Okla., 1959—67; sr. rsch. math. Dykewood Corp., Albuquerque, 1967—69; prin. rsch. math. Tech. Inc., San Antonio, 1967—71; scientific programming specialist Lockheed Electronics, Tuscon, Ariz., 1971—72; prof. math. & computer sci. U. Tex. Permian Basin, Odessa, Tex., 1972—93, prof. emeritus, 1993—. Rsch. assoc. Okla. U. Rsch. Inst., Normon, Okla., 1960—67; statistician Oreg. State Hwy. Dept., Salem, Oreg., 1954—59; adj. prof. elec. engring. U. N.Mex., Albuquerque, 1969; conf. statistician N.Mex. Annual Conf., Albuquerque, 1988—92. Cpl. U.S. Army, 1944—46. Recipient Francis Asbury award, United Meth. Ch., 1994. Mem.: Am. Statistical Assn., Am. Math. Soc., Math. Assn. Am. Methodist. Avocation: Boy Scouts Am.. Home: 3942 Monclair Ave Odessa TX 79762-7207

NICKEL, JANET MARLENE MILTON, geriatrics nurse; b. Manitowoc, Wis., June 9, 1940; d. Ashley and Pearl Milton; m. Curtis A. Nickel, July 29, 1961; children: Cassie, Debra, Susan. Diploma, Milw. Inst., 1961; ADN, N.D. State U., 1988. Nurse Milw. VA, Wood, Wis., 1961-62; supervising nurse Park

Lawn Convalescent Hosp., Manitowoc, 1964-65; newsletter editor Fargo (N.D.) Model Cities Program, 1970-73; supervising night nurse Rosewood on Broadway, Luth. Hosps. and Homes, Fargo, 1973-92; assoc. dir. nursing Elim Care Ctr., 1992-94, night nurse, 1994—. Mem. Phi Eta Sigma. Home: 225 19th Ave N Fargo ND 58102-2352 Office: 3534 S University Dr Fargo ND 58104-6228

NICKEL, MELVIN EDWIN, metallurgical engineer; b. St. Louis, Aug. 24, 1915; s. Jacob William and Mary Anna Nickel; m. Mary Louise Breuer, Sept. 12, 1942; children: Elizabeth Ann Nickel Overleas, Mary Patricia Nickel Hepburn, Sheila Breuer Nickel Stojak, William Louis. BS in Metall. Engring., U. Mo., Rolla, 1938, Profl. Degree of Metall. Engring., 1967. Mgmt. trainee Bethlehem (Pa.) Steel Corp., 1938-39; asst. to supt. blast furnaces Wis. Steel div. Internat. Harvester Co., Chgo., 1939-43, gen. foreman furnaces, blast furnaces, 1943-48, asst. supt. blast furnaces, 1948-49, supt. open hearths, 1949-61, supt. basic oxygen furnaces, mgr. steel prodn., 1961-68, mgr. primary ops., 1968-77; mgr. facilities planning and appropriations, works mgr. Envirodyne Industries, Inc., Wis. Steel Corp., 1977-80; pres. Melvin E. Nickel & Assocs., Inc., Chgo., 1980—. Contbr. articles to profl. jours.; developer early practices for prodn. of spl. bar quality and alloy steel in top blown basic oxygen furnace, 1962-64. Bd. trustees Iron and Steel Soc. Found., Warrensdale, Pa., 1980-91. Recipient Disting. Merit award U. Mo.-Rolla, 1960, Benjamin F. Fairless award Iron and Steel Soc., 2001; inducted Mo. Sch. Mines/U. Mo.-Rolla Athletic Hall of Fame, 1993. Mem. AIME (hon., nat. v.p., dir. 1974-76, Hon. Membership award 1978), Iron and Steel Soc. of AIME (nat. pres. 1974-75, elected disting. mem. 1975), Metall. Soc. of AIME (nat. chmn. iron and steel divsn. 1972-74), Assn. of Iron and Steel Engrs., Western States Blast Furnaces and Coke Assn., U. Mo., Rolla Alumni Assn. (pres. 1956-59, bd. dirs.), Triangle Fraternity, Jackson Hole Wildlife Soc., Acad. Sch. Mines and Metallurgy, U. Mo.-Rolla (elected 1998), Ridge Country Club of Chgo., Beverly Hills Univ. Club. Republican. Roman Catholic. Avocations: hunting, fishing, carpentry, mineral collecting, boating. Home and Office: 10601 S Hamilton Ave Chicago IL 60643-3127

NICKELL, CHRISTOPHER SHEA, lawyer; b. Paducah, Ky., Mar. 21, 1959; s. Carl Duane and Anna June (Starrett) N. BA, DePauw U., 1981; JD, U. Ky., 1984. Bar: Ky. 1984, U.S. Dist. Ct. (ea. dist.) Ky., 1985, U.S. Dist. Ct. (we. dist.) Ky. 1989. Assoc. Truman L. Dehner, Morehead, Ky., 1984-87; asst. commonwealth atty. 21st Jud. Dist. Ky., 1986-87; assoc. Boehl, Stopher, Graves & Deindoerfer, Paducah, 1989-91, Saladino Law Firm, Paducah, Ky., 1991-97, Nickell Law Firm, Paducah, 1997—. Vis. lectr. U. N.C., Chapel Hill, 1987-88; adj. prof. Murray State U., 1989-91. Trustee DePauw U., Greencastle, 1981-84; bd. dirs. N.E. Ky. Legal Svcs., Inc., Morehead, 1985-87, Western Ky. Easter Seal Soc., 1993-99. Named to Hon. Order Ky. Cols., 1981. Mem. ABA, Ky. Bar Assn. (Ky. Outstanding Young Lawyer award 1995), McCracken County Bar Assn., Ky. Acad. Trial Attys., Masons (32 deg.) Paducah Lions Club (bd. dirs., chmn. Easter Seals telethon, pres., vice dist. gov., dist. gov.), Delta Theta Phi. Democrat. Office: Nickell Law Firm Old Courthouse Sta 634 Kentucky Ave Paducah KY 42003-1720 E-mail: shea@paducahattorney.com.

NICKELL, JOE HERMAN, paranormal expert; b. Lexington, Ky., Dec. 1, 1944; s. James Wendell and Ella Kathleen (Turner) N. BA, U. Ky., 1967, MA, 1982, PhD, 1987. Profl. stage magician, Toronto, Ont., Can., 1968-73; pvt. investigator, 1973-75; mus. exhibit designer Dawson City (Yukon) Mus., 1975-76; freelance investigative writer, 1976—; tchg. asst. U. Ky., Lexington, 1980-87, instr., 1987-95; sr. rsch. fellow Com. for the Sci. Investigation of Claims of the Paranormal, Amherst, N.Y., 1995—. *Joe Nickell has been an artist and poet, inventor, and civil rights activist. He augmented his professional career with stints as a blackjack dealer, riverboat manager, carnival pitchman, movie extra, and other "roles" (including undercover jobs as a detective). Although best know as a paranormal investigator, (traveling the world to examine crop circles, "weeping" icons, allegedly haunted places, monster claims, and many other mysteries), he also has an avocation as a historical-document consultant. As such, he has exposed numerous sensational forgeries (such as the reputed Jack the Ripper diary) as well as authenticating many other rare documents and texts.* Author: Inquest on the Shroud of Turin, 1983, Secrets of the Supernatural, 1988, The Magic Detectives, 1989, Wonder-workers, 1991, Mysterious Realms, 1992, Looking for a Miracle, 1993, Camera Clues, 1994, Entities, 1995, Detecting Forgery, 1996, (with John F. Fischer) Crime Science, 1999, Pen, Ink & Evidence, 2000, Real-Life X-Files, 2001; mem. editl. bd. Skeptical Inquirer, 1993—, columnist, 1995—. Fellow Com. for the Sci. Investigation of Claims of the Paranormal. Home: 1992 Sheridan Dr Apt 6 Buffalo NY 14223-1249 Office: Ctr for Inquiry 3965 Rensch Rd Amherst NY 14228-2743

NICKELS, GREG, mayor; b. Chicago, Ill., Aug. 7, 1955; s. Bob and Kathie Nickels; m. Sharon Nickels; children: Jacob, Carey. Legis. asst. to Councilmember Norm Rice City of Seattle, 1979—87; mem. King County Coun., 1987—2002; mayor City of Seattle, 2002—. Chair Seattle/King County Bd. Health; mem. exec. com. & bd. dirs. Dirs. of Sound Transit. Office: Office of the Mayor 600 4th Ave 12th Fl Seattle WA 98104 E-mail: Mayors.Office@ci.seattle.wa.us.*

NICKELS, JOHN L. retired state supreme court justice; m. Merita Nickels; 7 children. Bachelor's degree, No. Ill. U.; law degree, DePaul U. Pvt. practice, 20 yrs; judge Appellate Ct.; cir. judge 16th Jud. Cir.; supreme ct. justice State of Ill., 1992-98; ret., 1998. Bd. dirs. Kane County Bank & Trust Co. Bd. trustees Waubonsee Coll.; mem. adv. coun. and found. Kaneland Sch. Dist.; mem. Kane County Planning Commn., Zoning Bd. Appeals; mem. St. Gall's Parish, Elburn. Home: 17901 Owens Rd. Maple Park IL 60151*

NICKELS, MAVIS LANORE, secondary education educator, farmer; b. Okeene, Okla., May 19, 1939; d. E. E. and Eleanor (Bingo) Woodson; m. J.D. Nickels, Sept. 27, 1958 (dec. May 1996); children: Kevin, Kyle, Kent, Allison. Student, Okla. State U., 1956-59; BS, Phillips U., 1966; postgrad., U. Okla., Oklahoma City, 1968-70, U. Oreg., Portland, 1970-72. Tchr. Moore (Okla.) Pub. Schs., 1966-68; contractor Nickels Constrn., Battle Ground, Wash., 1972-76; tchr. Battle Ground Pub. Schs., 1976-00; farmer Battle Ground, 1976—; adj. prof. Concordia U., Portland, 2000—. Mem., writer Wash. Commn. Student Learning, Olympia, 1994-99; presiding co-chair Program Delivery Coun., Brush Prairie, Wash., 1997-99; assessment coord. Prairie H.S., Brush Prairie, 1998-00; cons. Everett (Wash.) Pub. Schs., 2000. Fellow Okla. U. Sch. Medicine, 1968-70, U. Oreg. Sch. Medicine, 1970-72. Mem. AAUW (treas. Hudson's Bay Br.), NEA, Nat. Coun. Tchrs. Math., Wash. State Coun. Math Tchrs., Battle Ground Edn. Assn. (pres., sec.). Avocations: oil painting, gardening, sewing, crocheting, reading.

NICKELS, THOM, writer, journalist; b. Darby, Pa., Oct. 12, 1947; s. Thomas Clavey Nickels and Teresa Marie Muldoon. Diploma in journalism, Charles Morris Price Sch. Advt.and Journalism, 1967; BA, Eastern Coll., Batl., 1968. Ordained priest Anglican Cath. Byzantine Orthodox Ch., 2001. Station editor TV Guide, 1978; editor Soc. Hill Towers Newsletter, Phila., 1981—83; gay issues columnist Welcomat, 1983—94; resume and grant writer, 1990—94; commetary columnist Phila. Inquirer, 1998—2001; newspaper columnist, feature writer Weekly/Univ. City Press, 1999—. Book reviewer Lambda Books Report, Washington, 1996—; commentary columnist Phila. Daily News, 1999—2001; feature writer Philly Style Mag., Phila., 2000—01; weekly issues columnist PrideVisionTV, Toronto, Que., Canada, 2001—; freelance arts and entertainment writer, reviewer TPI Metro, Phila., 2001—. Author: (plays) Z for Shelter, 1967 (Hon. Mention Samuel French Young Playwrights Contest, 1968), (novels) The Cliffs of Aries, 1988, Two Novellas: Walking Water & After All This, 1989 (Nominated for a Hugo award and a Lambda Literary award), (book) Manayunk, 2001, Gay and Lesbian Philadelphia, 2002, Tropic of Libra, 2002, (anthology) The Boy on the Bicycle, 1992, The Boy on the Bicycle (reissue), 1993; contbr. (anthology) Superstars, 2000, 2001, 2002, Tough Guys, 2002. Vol. Lyndon B. Johnsom Presdl. Campaign, West Chester, Pa., 1964; founder Coalition Phila. Art, 1998—2002; mem. Boston Gay Liberation Front, 1968—69. Mem.: Nat. Lesbian and Gay Journalist Assn. Home and Office: 2643 Mercer St Philadelphia PA 19125

NICKELSON, KIM RENÉ, internist; b. Chgo., Feb. 13, 1956; d. Robert William and Carolynn Lucille (Marts) N.; m. Louis Peter Sguros; children: Brian Louis, Justin Robert Peter. BS in Chemistry, U. Ill., 1978; MD, Loyola U., Maywood, Ill., 1981. Diplomate Am. Bd. Internal Medicine. Intern and resident in internal medicine Luth. Gen. Hosp., Park Ridge, Ill., 1981-84; pvt. practice Oakbrook, 1984-87, Plantation, Fla., 1987—. Adj. attending staff Rush-Presbyn. St. Luke's Med. Ctr., Chgo., 1984-87; assoc. attending staff Hinsdale (Ill.) Hosp., 1984-87, Westside Regional Med. Ctr., Plantation, Plantation Gen. Hosp., Fla. Med. Ctr., Lauderhill, Fla. Musician Elk Grove (Ill.) Community Band, 1978-87, Hollywood (Fla.) Symphony Orch., 1987—, Sunrise (Fla.) Pops Symphony, 1987—, Deerfield (Fla.) Community Band, 1987—. Mem. ACP, Internat. Horn Soc. Office: Internal Medicine Assocs 499 NW 70th Ave Ste 200 Plantation FL 33317-7578

NICKENS, CATHERINE ARLENE, retired nurse, freelance writer; b. Litchfield, Ill., Oct. 30, 1932; d. Harley Lloyd Moore and Ida Mae Reynolds; m. Carl Roland Nickens, Sept. 4, 1954 (div. Apr. 1975); children: Linda Dianne, Carl Roland Jr., Karen Patricia, Eric Moore. Nursing diploma, St. Joseph's Hosp., 1954. RN, Calif. Staff nurse St. Joseph's Hosp., Alton, Ill., 1954-55, St. Mary's Hosp., Streator, 1962-68, supr., acting dir., 1968-70; nursing supr. Illini Hosp., Silvis, 1970-74; office nurse pediatrician's office, 1974-75; staff nurse telemetry/drug abuse North Miami Gen. Hosp., Miami, Fla., 1975-80; staff nurse, relief supr. Petaluma (Calif.) Valley Hosp., 1981-97. Participant women's health study Brigham and Women's Hosp., Boston, 1994—. Author: (hist. fiction) The Thoroughly Compromised Bride, 1991 (award 1992), The Highwayman, 1993 (award 1994). Mem. ACLU, N.Y.C., 1995, Parents, Families and Friends of Lesbians and Gays, Washington, 1994-99, Nat. Mus. of Am. Indian/Smithsonian Instn., Washington, 1996-97; friend of the quilt NAMES Project Meml. Quilt, San Francisco, 1992-99; mem. friendship cir. Am. Found. for AIDS Rsch., Washington, 1994—; vol. Santa Rosa Police Dept., 1997-2000. Mem. Romance Writers of Am. (mentor to unpublished writers 1995-99). Avocations: reading, traveling, needlework, doll-making. Home and Office: 105 Olive St Santa Rosa CA 95401-6241

NICKERSON, BEE DAVIS, social services executive, volunteer; b. Balt., Mar. 27, 1933; d. Edward Hollister and Liselotte (Heise) Davis; m. Edward Ashton Nickerson, Sept. 16, 1955; children: Louisa Talcott, Matthew Ashton. BA, Goucher Coll., 1955; M in Social Svcs., Adelphi Coll., 1959; PhD, U. Del., 1981. Caseworker Balt. Dept. Pub. Welfare, 1955-56, Cmty. Svc. Soc., N.Y.C., 1959-61; cons. Barlow Sch., Amenia, N.Y., 1962-64; caseworker Vander Heyden Hall, Troy, 1964-67, Family and Children's Svcs., Troy, 1967-70; exec. dir. Del. chpt. NASW, Wilmington, 1982-83; assoc. exec. dir. Geriatric Svcs. of Del., 1982-83, exec. dir., 1983-91; ret., 1991. Vol. cons. West Side Model Cities Neighborhood Coun., Wilmington, 1970-72; mem., chair Task Force on Child Protective Svcs., Coun. Family Svcs., 1975-78, Com. on Permanency Planning, Inter-Agy. Child Care Coun., 1980-82; mem. Title XX rev. com. divsn. social svcs. State of Del., 1975-78; vol. cons., v.p. Parents Anonymous of Del., 1980-82. Author: Welfare Handbook, 1972. Rsch. vol. Del. Cmty. Found., Wilmington, 1992; mem. adv. bd. Primary Health Care Network, Sharon, Conn., 1994-95; bd. dirs. Housatonic Ctr. for Mental Health, Lakeville, Conn., 1993-96, Geer Nursing and Rehab. Ctr., Caanan, Conn., 1997-98. Mem. Litchfield County Univ. Club. Avocations: micro-economics, nonfiction writing, walking, swimming. Home: 63 Belgo Rd Lakeville CT 06039-1002

NICKERSON, BRUCE DONALD, medical services administrator; b. Poughkeepsie, N.Y., Feb. 9, 1957; s. Donald W. and Joyce (Smith) N.; m. Aline A. Becker, Oct. 11, 1992; 1 child, Mark. BS, Nasson Coll., 1983, MBA, 1989; ADN, So. Maine Tech. Coll., 1993. RN, LPN. Caretaker Quiet Meadows Farms, Hopewell Junction, N.Y., 1970-75; stock control engr. LeMar Pharmacy, Wappingers Falls, 1975-77; staff nurse VA Med. Ctr. Castle Point, 1977-80, 83-86; adminstrv. asst. to pres. Nasson Coll., Springvale, Maine, 1980-83; staff nurse So. Maine Med. Ctr., Biddeford, 1986-93; DON York Manor, 1993, dir. residential care, 1994-96; case mgmt. supr. Concentra Managed Care Inc., Falmouth, Maine, 1996-99; v.p. ops. Med. Case Mgmt. Group, Gray, 2001—; cons. Crawford & Co. Med. Svcs., 1999—2001. Mem. quality assurance rev. com. So. Maine Area Agy. on Aging, Portland, 1994-95; mem. product evaluation com. So. Maine Med. Ctr., Biddeford, 1990-93. Vestry mem. St. George's Episcopal Ch., Sanford, 1994-98, acolyte master, 1993-96. Mem. Case Mgmt. Soc. Am., Acad. Cert. Case Mgrs. (cert.), Order of St. Vincent (chpt. warden 1993-96), Order of DeMolay (life, sec.-treas. 1973-78, chevalier 1975). Avocations: model railroading, gardening. Office: Medical Case Mgmt Group PO Box 938 Gray ME 04039

NICKERSON, GARY LEE, secondary education educator; b. Cleve., Nov. 7, 1942; s. Alto Lee and Louise Evelyn (Watson) N.; m. Barbara Marie Butler, Aug. 17, 1968; 1 child, L'Oreal. BS, Ohio U., 1966; MA, Atlanta U., 1971. Cert. secondary tchr., Ohio. With Cleve. Pub. Schs., 1966-98; sci. dept. chmn. John F. Kennedy High Sch., Cleve., 1985-98; youth edn. coord. Cleve. Bot. Garden, 1999—. Physics instr. Case Western Res. U., Cleve., summer 1988; sci. instr. Std. Oil Elem. Teaching Retraining Program summer 1986; mem. adv. panel Ednl. Devel. Ctr., Inc., Newton, Mass., 1989-98; sci. instr. Cleve. Ednl. Found. Elem. Teaching Retraining Program, 1990—, Baldwin Wallace U. Upward Bound Program, 1992; engring. project instr. MEIOP Summer Program Case Western Res. U., 1991; tchr. trainer Kent State U. Trivet program, 1991-98; sci. tchr. Gov.'s Inst. for Gifted and Talented, Cleve. State U., 1992-98. Co-author curriculum guides. Trustee N.E. Ohio Sci. and Engring. Fair, 2001—. Recipient Cert. of Excellence in Teaching Rotary, 1990. Mem. NAACP, Urban League, Cleve. Regional Coun. Sci. Tchrs. (bd. dirs. 1986-87, pres. 2002--), Metrocabse Assn., Nat. Sci. Tcrhrs. Assn., Sci. Edn. Coun. Ohio, Kappa Alpha Psi. Democrat. Baptist. Avocations: ice skating, tennis, swimming, singing, weight lifting. Home: 5871 White Pine Dr Cleveland OH 44146-3075 Office: Cleve Bot Garden 11030 East Blvd Cleveland OH 44106-1706

NICKERSON, HARDY OTTO, football player; b. Compton, Calif., Sept. 1, 1965; m. Amy Nickerson; children: Ashleigh, Hardy, Haleigh. Degree in sociology, U. Calif. Linebacker Pitts. Steelers, 1987-92, Tampa Bay Buccaneers, 1993-98, Jacksonvilel Jaguars, 1998—2001, Green Bay Packers, 2002—. Named to 1st Team All-Pro by AP and the Sporting News, 1993, Pro Bowl, 1996. Office: 1265 Lombardi Ave Green Bay WI 54304*

NICKERSON, JAMES FINDLEY, retired educator; b. Gretna, Nebr., Dec. 16, 1910; s. Elmer Samuel and Lulu Perkins (Patterson) N.; m. Juanita M. Bolin, Mar. 3, 1934; children: Ann Rogers Nickerson Lueck, Maria De Miranda. BS, Nebr. Wesleyan U., 1932; MA, Columbia Tchrs. Coll., 1940; PhD, U. Minn., 1948; ScD (hon.), Yankton (S.D.) Coll., 1971. Tchr. pub. schs., Giltner, Nebr., 1932-35; sch. music supr. Gordon, 1936-38, Bayshore, L.I., 1939-41, Grand Island, Nebr., 1941-42; instr. Coll. Edn., music supr. high sch. U. Minn., 1942-46, vis. prof. Coll. Edn., summer 1948; asst. prof. music edn. U. Kans., 1946-48, assoc. prof., 1948-53. Rsch. assoc. dept. psychology U. So. Calif., assigned human factors div. U.S. Navy Electronics Lab., San Diego, 1953-54; dean edn., dir. summer quar., prof. psychology Mont. State U., 1954-64, head dept. psychology, 1954-56, rsch. assoc. Electronics Rsch. Lab, 1958-64; v.p. acad. affairs N.D. State U., Fargo, 1964-66; pres. Minn. State U., Mankato, 1966-73, then pres. emeritus, disting. svc. prof., 1973-76; dir. Svc. Mems. Opportunity Colls., Am. Assn. State Colls. and Univs., Washington, 1973-81; dir. Northwestern Nat. Bank, Mankato, 1967-69; cons. publ. edn. Office Gov. Wash., 1964; exec. sec., study dir. interim com. edn. Wash. Legislature, 1959-60; chmn. regional conf. womanpower Nat. Manpower Coun. and Mont. State Coll., 1957; mem. steering com. Pacific N.W. Con. Higher Edn., 1962; mem. nat. adv. com. sci. edn. NSF, 1968-71, chmn., 1970-71; mem. vis. com. Harvard Grad. Sch. Edn., 1970-76, Schola Cantorum, N.Y.C., 1938-39, Choral Arts Soc., Washington, 1969-71. Stringbass Mont. State Coll. Symphonette, 1959-63, Mankato Symphony Orch., 1967-73, 83-93, bd. dirs., 1987-90. Recipient citation interim study Wash. Legislature and Gov., 1960, Outstanding Achievement award Bd. Regents U. Minn., 1968, Alumni award Nebr. Wesleyan U., 1968; Sec. Def. medal for outstanding pub. svc., 1981, citation Am. Coun. Edn., 1981; James F. Nickerson Medal of Merit for outstanding svc. to mil. edn. created by Am. Assn. Sr. Colls. and Univs., 1981; Danforth Found. adminstrn. grantee, 1969; named to Internat. Adult & Continuing Edn. Hall of Fame, 1999. Mem. Nat. Assn. State Univs. and Land Grant Colls. (senate, chmn. div. tchr. edn. 1962-65, sec. coun. acad. officers 1965), Am. Assn. State Colls. and State Univs. (bd. dirs. 1966-71), Am. Assn. Colls. Tchr. Edn. (bd. dirs. 1969-71), Am. Assn. Higher Edn. (chmn. resolutions com. 1974), Assn. Minn. Colls. (pres. 1972), Edn. Commn. States (commr. 1967-73, mem. task force on coordination, governance and structure postsecondary edn. 1973), Sigma Xi, Phi Mu Alpha Sinfonia. Home and Office: 301 S 5th St Apt 220 Mankato MN 56001-4580

NICKERSON, JOHN HENRY, artist, sculptor, designer; b. Mpsl., May 15, 1939; s. John and Lucile Ruth (Jones) Scott; m. Margie Lynette Hay, Sept. 9, 1962 (div. June 1970); 1 child, Shae Mikell Nickerson Elliott. BA, Mont. State U., 1964; MFA, Alfred (N.Y.) U., 1969. Ceramic designer Pacific Stoneware, Inc., Portland, Oreg., 1964; indsl. design sculptor GM Styling Staff, Warren, Mich., 1965-66; staff designer Shuron-Continental, Div. Textron Corp., Rochester, N.Y., 1967; asst. prof. ceramics and design Colo. State U., Ft. Collins, 1969-70; designer in residence Blenko Glass Co., Inc., Milton, W.Va., 1970-74; assoc. master design, drawing, sculpture, ceramics and glass Georgian Coll. Art and Technol., Barrie, Ont., Can., 1976-77; artist in residence Kanawha County Continuing Edn. Program, Charleston, W.Va., 1976-77; artist Cleve. Inst. Art Summer Sessions, 1989, 97. Guest lectr. Cleve. Inst. Art, 1995-97. Numerous exhbtns. include Corning (N.Y.) Mus., 1979, Woodson Mus. Art, Wausaw, Wis., 1984, C. Corcoran Gallery, Muskegan, Mich., 1988, 89, Cartons, Cans, and Other Containers, Salem (Oreg.) Art Assn., 1989, Glassworks I Joan Robery Gallery, Denver, 1989, Sculptural Glass, Grohe Glass Gallery, Hyannis, Mass., 1990; permanent collections include Corning Mus., Del. Art Mus., Wilmington, Denver Art Mus., Muskegan (Mich.) Mus. Art, Musée des Arts Décortifs, Lausanne, Switzerland. Nat. Endowment for the Arts craftsman's fellow, 1981, creative fellow, 1986; Colo. Gov.;s Awards Commn., 1986. Home and Office: Ste 8 Glass 182 Richland St Waynesville NC 28786-3792

NICKERSON, JOHN MITCHELL, political science educator; b. Lewiston, Maine, July 1, 1937; s. Elmer Winfield and Marion Gertrude (Howard) N. BA, U. Maine, 1959; MA, Wash. State U., 1966; PhD, U. Idaho, 1971. Commd. 2d lt. U.S. Army, 1959, advanced through grades to capt., resigned, 1967; rsch. assoc. Bur. Pub. Adminstrn. U. Maine, Orono, 1967-68, mem. grad. faculty, 1970-88, asst. prof. to assoc. prof. polit. sci. Augusta, 1970-81, prof., 1981—, developer 9 baccalaureate degrees in pub. adminstrn.; dir. New Eng. Govtl. Research Inst., Inc., Waterville, Maine, 1971. Lectr. Colby Coll., Waterville, Maine, 1979, Maine State Dedimus Justice; cons. in field Author: The Control of Civil Disturbances, 1968, Municipal Police in Maine - A Study of Selected Personnel Practices with Emphasis on Recruit Selection and Training, 1969, (with others) A Study of Policy-Making: The Dynamics and Adaptability of the U.S. Federal System, 1971; editor, author foreward: Is the Municipality Liable for Insufficiently Trained Police? (James P. Murphy), 1968; contbr. articles to profl. jours. Mem. Maine State Police Planning Adv. Group, 1984-87, Maine State Bd. Assessment Rev., 1981-84, Maine Hwy. Safety Com., 1984-87; vice chmn. adv. bd. Salvation Army, Augusta, 1980-85; trustee, treas. Lithgow Library, 1980-85; incorporator Kennebec Valley Med. Ctr., Augusta, 1980-97. Dept. Justice grantee, 1967. Mem. Am. Polit. Sci. Assn., New Eng. Polit. Sci. Assn., Northeastern Polit. Sci. Assn., Acad. Polit. Sci. (life), Am. Acad. Polit. and Social Sci. (life), Am. Soc. for Pub. Adminstrn., ACLU (life), Kennebec Hist. Soc. (life), Kennebec Valley Humane Soc. (life), Maine Civil Liberties Union (life, legis. com.), Pi Sigma Alpha, Pi Alpha Alpha. Home: 192 Capitol St Augusta ME 04330-6237 Office: U Maine at Augusta 46 University Dr Augusta ME 04330 E-mail: john.nickerson@maine.edu.

NICKERSON, RICHARD G. conductor, educator; b. Newcastle, New Brunswick, Canada, Feb. 20, 1963; s. Ralph Theodore and Janice Marie Nickerson; children: Ariana Vera, Sarah Nadezhda. BME Vocal Music Edn., U. Maine, Orono, ME, 1986, MM Choral Conducting, 1999; DMA Choral Conducting, U. Mo., Kansas City, 2002. Teaching Certificate Maine. Chous master Portland Opera Repertory Theatre, Portland, Maine, 1994—96; condr. So. Maine Youth Chorale, Gorham, 1997—99; sr. choir dir. Hope Luth. Ch., Shawnee, Kans., 1999—2001; artistic dir. / condr. Boy Singers Maine, Portland, Maine, 2001—; music educator Windham H.S., Windham, 1987—. Condr. US Youth Chorale, Palmer, Mass., 1997—. Conductor of numerous choirs; composer: (piano work) The Lord Bless You and Keep You, Singin' Halleluja, The Holly and the Ivy. Recipient Invitational Performance, Maine Music Educators Conf., 1999, Acad. Award, Maine State Sch. for the Performing Arts, 1997, Invitational Performance, Congl. Ball, White Ho., 1996, Prize of Vienna, Internat. Youth and Music Festival, 1996; grantee Grad. Tchg. Assistantship, U. Mo., 1999-2001. Mem.: Music Educators Nat. Conf. (choral v.p. 1989—94), Am. Choral Directors Assn. (pres. (maine) 1997—99). Avocations: baseball, reading. Home: 1500 Forest Ave Apt8A Portland ME 04103 Home Fax: 207-892-1826. Personal E-mail: richardns@aol.com.

NICKERSON, RICHARD GORHAM, research company executive; b. Harwich, Mass., Nov. 20, 1927; s. Ephriam Gorham and Elizabeth (Wardle) N.; m. Eileen Florence Tressler, June 7, 1957 (dec. Apr. 1994); children: Holly Anne, Wendy Elyse, Susan Denise; m. Barbara Bernice Bagster Harper-Schofield, Aug. 14, 1999. BS cum laude, U. Mass., 1950; PhD, Northwestern U., 1955; postgrad., Poly. Inst. Bklyn., 1955-57; MBA cum laude, Boston U., 1983. Rsch. chemist DuPont, Cellophane Tech. Sect., Richmond, Va., 1954-55; rsch. chemist Dewey & Almy divsn. W.R. Grace Corp., Cambridge, Mass., 1957-60; v.p. R & D Electronautics Corp., Maynard, 1960-61, pres., 1961-63; project leader Polyco Borden Chem. divsn. Borden, Inc., Leominster, Mass., 1963-65, group leader, 1965-67, devel. mgr., 1967-81, lab. mgr., 1981-87; pres., mng. dir. Boston Profls. Internat., Inc., Hopkinton, 1987—. Patentee in field; designer, developer of water based polymers to meet specific performance requirement. With Chem. Corps, U.S. Army, 1955-57. Mem. Am. Chem. Soc., Soc. Plastics Engrs., Sigma Xi, Phi Lambda Upsilon, Alpha Chi Sigma. Avocations: sailing, photography, antique autos, classical music, dancing. Home: 9 Lyford Rd Hopkinton MA 01748-1581

NICKERSON, RONALD GEORGE, recreation and parks educator; b. Nov. 12, 1956; BA, Lemoyne Coll., 1978; MS, U. Minn., 1994, PhD, 1998. Tchr. social studies Cathedral Sch., V.I., 1979-80; bus. mgr., pers. aide Minn. Dept. Natural Resources, St. Paul, 1980-87, park planner, 1991-99; fiscal analyst Minn. Ho. of Reps., 1987-91; asst. prof. dept. recreation, parks and leisure svcs. Minn. State U., Mankato, 1999—. Office: Minn State U Dept Rec Pks Leisure Svcs 213 Highland Ctr N Mankato MN 56001-6038 E-mail: ronald.nickerson@mankato.msus.edu.

NICKFORD, JUAN, sculptor, educator; b. Havana, Cuba, Aug. 8, 1925; s. Basil and Maria (Hoshko) N.; m. Jene Rashkind, Aug. 16, 1952; children—Dena, Marc. M.F.A., Bellas Artes, Havana, 1945; postgrad., U. Havana, 1944-46. Head welding dept. Sculpture Center of N.Y., 1955-62; vis. artist Vasar Coll., 1962-63, Smith Coll., 1966-67, U. Hartford, 1965-66, Bklyn. Mus. Art Sch., 1968-70, Finch Coll., San Marino, 1975; prof. art CCNY, 1975-91, prof. emeritus, from 1991. One man shows, Leonard Gallery, Woodstock, N.Y., 1981, Emanuel Coll. Gallery, Boston, 1977, Sculpture Center, 1974, Art Glass Gallery, Toronto, Ont., Can., 1985, numerous others; retrospective Hopper House, Nyack, N.Y., 1986; group shows include, Thorpe Intermedia Gallery, Sparkill, N.Y., 1974, Hopper House, Nyack, N.Y., 1978, Sculpture Center, N.Y.C., 1978, Sculpture Gallery, Palo Alto, Calif., 1981, numerous museums; represented in permanent collection, Newberger Coll., N.Y., numerous pvt. collections. Cintas Found. grantee, 1970-71, CUNY Faculty Research Found. grantee, 1982-83; recipient Bronze medal N.Y. State Expn., 1964 Mem. Sculptors Guild. Home: Tappan, NY. Died Aug. 22, 2001.

NICKISCH, WILLARD WAYNE, funeral director; b. Bismarck, N.D., July 23, 1939; s. Elmo and Frieda (Moser) N.; m. Jeanette Ruff, Sept. 4, 1960 (div.); m. Eileen Lawlar, June 12, 1993; children: Daphne D., Dirk D. AA, Cin. Coll. of Mortuary Sci., 1959. Lic. mortician, N.D., S.D., Minn. Mortician, funeral dir. Nickisch Funeral Home, Wishek, N.D., 1960-72; funeral dir., pres. Nickisch-Ressler Funeral Home, Bismarck, 1972-91, Boelter Funeral Home, Bismarck, 1981-91; regional sales mgr. United Family Life Ins., St. Charles, Mo., 1991-96; dir. regional sales Columbian Fin. Group, 1996-98; mktg. mgr. CNA Life, 1998-2000; agt. N.Y. Life Ins. Co., 2000—. Mem. lay bd. St. Alexius Med. Ctr., Bismarck, 1976-91, pres. 1984; pres. S.W. region Luth. Social Svcs. N.D., 1987-91. Mem. N.D. Funeral Dirs. Assn. (pres. 1978-79), Nat. Funeral Dirs. Assn. (dist. gov. 1980-83), Nat. Selected Morticians, Luth. Brotherhood (publicity counselor Bismarck br. 1986-88), Bismarck State Coll. Found. Bd., Masons, Shriners (pres. Mo. orgn. 1988-89), Kiwanis. Republican. Lutheran. Avocation: flying. Home: 2840 La Brea Dr Saint Charles MO 63303-9008

NICKLAS, ROBERT BRUCE, cell biologist, educator; b. Lakewood, Ohio, May 29, 1932; s. Ford Adelbert and Marthabelle (Beckett) N.; m. Sheila Jean Counce, Sept. 17, 1960. BA, Bowling Green State U., 1954; MA (Eugene Higgins fellow), Columbia U., 1956, PhD, 1958. Instr. in zoology Yale U., 1958-61, asst. prof. zoology, 1961-64, assoc. prof., 1964-65; asso. prof. Duke U., 1965-71, prof., 1971-99, chair dept., 1983-86, A.S. Pearse prof., 1999—. Mem. NSF Postdoctoral Fellowship Panel, 1969-71, Am. Cancer Soc. Sci. Adv. Com. for Virology and Cell Biology, 1975-78; mem. adv. bd. 12th Internat. Chromosome Conf., 1994. Contbr. numerous articles to profl. publs.; mem. editorial bd. Chromosoma, 1966-83, Jour. Exptl. Zoology, 1970-72, Jour. Cell Biology, 1980-81, Jour. Cell Sci., 1984-91, European Jour. Cell Biology, 1985-89. Recipient award for disting. tchg. Duke Alumni, 1975; Yale fellow in scis., 1963-64; John Simon Guggenheim fellow, 1972-73, E.B. Wilson medal Am. Soc. Cell Biology, 1995, Inst. Gen. Med. Scis. USPHS grantee, 1960—. Fellow AAAS; mem. Am. Soc. Cell Biology (exec. com. 1976-78, coun. 1975-78, E.B. Wilson medal 1995), Am. Soc. Naturalists, Genetics Soc. Am., Sigma Xi. Home: 3101 Camelot Ct Durham NC 27705-5405

NICKLE, DENNIS EDWIN, electronics engineering consultant, church deacon; b. Sioux City, Iowa, Jan. 30, 1936; s. Harold Bateman and Helen Cecilia (Killackey) H. BS in Math., Fla. State U., 1961. Ordained deacon Roman Cath. Ch., 1979. Reliability mathematician Pratt & Whitney Aircraft Co., West Palm Beach, Fla., 1961-63; br. supr. Melpar Inc., Falls Church, Va., 1963-66; prin. mem. tech. staff Xerox Data Sys., Rockville, Md., 1966-70; sr. tech. officer WHO, Washington, 1970-76; software tech. mgr. Melpar divsn. E-Sys., Inc., Falls Church, 1976-95; software process improvement mgr. Bell Atlantic, Arlington, Va., 1996-97; sr. software mgr. Litton Denro, Gaithersburg, Md., 1997—2001; cons., 2001—. Lectr. in field; coord. D.C. Software Process Improvement Network, 1995—2001, chair, 1997—2002. Author: Stress in Adolescents, 1986; co-author: Handbook for Handling Non-Productive Stress in Adolescence, Standard for Software Life Cycle Processes, IMPEESA Junior Leader Training Guide, Standard for Software Quality Assurance, 1984-91, Standard for Developing Software Life Cycle Processes, Configuration Management Procedures, Software Quality Assurance Procedures, Software Development Procedures; contbr. to profl. jours. Chief judge for computers Fairfax County Regional Sci. Fair, 1964-88; scoutmaster, commr. Boy Scouts Am., 1957-92; youth custodian Fairfax County Juvenile Ct., 1973-87; chaplain No. Va. Regional Juvenile Detention Home, 1978-88; moderator Nocturnal Adoration Soc.; parochial St. Michael's Ch., Annandale, Va., 1979-89, Christ the Redeemer, Sterling, Va., 1990-93. With U.S. Army, 1958-60. Recipient Eagle award, Silver award, Silver Beaver award, other awards Boy Scouts Am.; Ad Altare Dei, St. George Emblem, Diocese of Richmond. Mem. Assn. Computing Machinery, Computer Soc., Am. Soc. for Quality Control, CODSIA (chmn. working groups), ORLANDO II (Govt./industry working group), Old Crows Assn., Rolm Mil-Spec Computer Users Group (internat. pres.), San Antonio I (select industry coord. group), Nat. Security Indsl. Assn. (conv. com. 1985-96, software quality assurance subcom., regional membership chmn. 1981-89, nat. exec. vice-chmn. 1989-94, chmn. 1994-96), Am. Security Coun., IEEE (sr., stds. working group in computers 1983—. Outstanding Vol. award 1993, Golden Core 1996), Def. Software Devel. Stds. Adv. Bd. (chmn. 1991-96), Soc. Software Quality, Hewlett-Packard Users Group, Smithsonian Assn., Internat. Platform Assn., NRA (endowment), Nat. Eagle Scout Assn. (life), KC (4 deg.), Alpha Phi Omega (life), Sigma Phi Epsilon.

NICKLES, DON (DONALD NICKLES), senator; b. Ponca City, Okla., Dec. 6, 1948; s. Robert C. and Coeweene (Bryan) N.; m. Linda L. Morrison, Sept. 5, 1968; children— Donald Lee II, Jennifer Lynn, Kim Elizabeth, Robyn Leigh. BA in Bus. Adminstrn., Okla. State U., 1971. Owner, operator Don Nickles Profl. Cleaning Svc., Stillwater, Okla., 1968-71; v.p., gen. mgr. Nickles Machine Corp., Ponca City, 1972—; mem. Okla. Senate, 1979-80, U.S. Senate from Okla., 1981—. Asst. majority whip, 1996—; chmn. Senate Rep. policy com., mem. com. on energy and natural resources, com. on rules and adminstrn., com. on budget fin., budget com., mem. arms control observer group, rural health caucus, world climate conv. observer group, Rep. task force on nat. security and regulatory reform; passed legislation to provide for econ. and employment impact statement for all new laws and regulations. Chmn. platform com. Rep. Nat. Conv., 1992; bd. dirs. Ponca City United Way; bd. advisors Close Up Found.; mem. Kay Coun. for Retarded Children, Ponca City, St. Mary's Roman Cath. Parish Coun.; mem. adv. bd. Salvation Army, Ponca City. With USNG, 1970-76. Named one of Outstanding Young Men of Am., U.S. Jaycees, 1983. Mem. Fellowship Christian Athletes, Ponca City C. of C. Clubs: Rotary. Republican. Office: US Senate 133 Hart Senate Office Bldg Washington DC 20510-0001*

NICKLES, I. MACARTHUR, librarian; b. Pittsfield, Mass., Feb. 5, 1944; s. Irving J. and Elsie (Hutchinson) N.; m. Rosalie M. Cangialose, Jan. 14, 1978; 1 child, Vincent Charles Nickles. BA, SUNY, Albany, 1965, MA, 1968, MLS, 1971. Asst. libr. SUNY Coll. at Oneonta, 1971-77; jr. libr. Passaic (N.J.) Pub. Libr., 1978; dir. Garfield (N.J.) Pub. Libr., 1979—. Pres. Bergen County Coop. Libr. System, Hackensack, N.J., 1993. Gate attendant Tanglewood, Lenox, Mass., 1965—; mem. Garfield Sta. N.J. Transit Arts Com., 1999—. With U.S. Army, 1969-70. Mem. ALA, N.J. Libr. Assn., Garfield Rotary (pres. 1981-82, 2001-02, Paul Harris fellow 1992), Garfield C. of C., N.J. Transit Arts Com. Garfield Sta. Avocations: reading, classical music. Office: Garfield Pub Libr 500 Midland Ave Garfield NJ 07026-1606 E-mail: mac@bccls.org.

NICKLOW, JOHN WILLIAM, civil engineer, educator; BS in Civil Engring., MS in Civil Engring., Bucknell U., 1993; PhD, Ariz. State U., 1998. Engring. officer USPHS, Casa Grande, Ariz., 1993-97; grad. assoc. Ariz. State U., Tempe, 1997-98; asst. prof. So. Ill. U., Carbondale, 1998—. Mem. Internat. Assn. Hydraulic Rsch., Internat. Water Resources Assn., Am. Soc. Civil Engrs. Office: So Ill Univ Dept Civil Engring Carbondale IL 62901

NICKON, ALEX, chemist, educator; b. Poland, Oct. 6, 1927; came to U.S., 1955, naturalized, 1961; s. Steve and Maria (Nickon); m. Beulah Monica Godby, Aug. 22, 1950; children— Dale Beverly, Linda Cheryl, Leanne Marie. B.Sc., U. Alta., 1949; MA, Harvard U., 1951, PhD, 1953. Vis. lectr. Bryn Mawr Coll., 1953; postdoctoral fellow Birkbeck Coll., U. London, Eng., 1953-54, NRC, Ottawa, Can., 1954-55; NSF sr. fellow; Imperial Coll., London, 1963-64; U. Munich, Germany, 1971-72; mem. faculty Johns Hopkins, 1955—, prof. chemistry, 1964-94, Vernon K. Krieble prof. chemistry, 1975-94, prof. emeritus, 1994—. Vis. assoc. Am. Chem. Soc. on Profl. Tng., 1975-95; mem. medicinal chem. panel NIH, 1966-70; postdoctoral panel NRC, 1968-69. Sr. editor Jour. Organic Chemistry, 1965-71; Am. exec. editor: Tetrahedron Reports, 1978-96. Recipient Md. Chemist award, 1990; Sloan Found. fellow, 1957-61 Fellow N.Y. Acad. Scis.; mem. Am. Chem. Soc. (nat. awards com. 1974-76), Brit. Chem. Soc. Home: 1009 Painters Ln Cockeysville Hunt Valley MD 21030-1729 Office: Dept Chemistry Johns Hopkins U Baltimore MD 21218-2685

NICODEMUS, CHRISTOPHER FARLEY, biotechnology educator, physician, researcher; b. N.Y.C., June 12, 1957; s. Richard Townsend and Elisabeth (Marchet) N.; m. Elizabeth Ping Chow, June 16, 1984. AB, Harvard U., 1979; MD, SUNY, Syracuse, 1984. Diplomate Am. Bd. Internal Medicine, Am. Bd. Allergy and Immunology. Resident in medicine New Eng. Deaconess Hosp./Harvard U., Boston, 1984-87; fellow in allergy clin. immunology Brigham & Women's Hosp./Harvard U., 1987-89; instr./letr. Harvard Med. Sch., 1998-2000; assoc. med. dir., sr. assoc. Pfizer, Inc., N.Y.C., 1990-93; sr. dir. med. affairs ImmuLogic Pharm. Corp., Waltham, Mass., 1993-94, v.p. med. affairs, 1994-97; v.p. clin. ops. Diatide, Inc., Londonderry, N.H., 1997-99; sr. v.p. clin. rsch., devel. chief med. officer AltaRex Corp., Waltham, Mass., 1999—. Career counselor Harvard U., Cambridge, Mass., 1993—. NIH grantee, 1987-89. Mem. ACP, AMA, AAAS, Am. Acad. Allergy Asthma Immunology, Mass. Med. Soc. Office: AltaRex Corp 610 Lincoln St Ste 125 Waltham MA 02451-1217

NICOL, DOMINIK, writer, photographer; b. nr. Oltenia, Romania, Sept. 25, 1930; came to U.S., 1969, naturalized, 1976; s. Dumitru and Valentina (Sandulescu) Nicolaescu-Stroe. Diploma in Chemistry and Tech. of Antibiotics, The Tech. Sch., Bucharest, Romania, 1954. Photo-reporter Agerpress, Bucharest, 1950-51; med. photographer Cantacuzino Hosp., 1955-68; ret., 1995. Author, editor: Self Encounter, 1979, Ten Oneiric Sketches, 1980, Rendes-Vous sau Intalnire cu mine insumi, 1987; (play) Vacuum (Colocviu de abis), 1979, Vacuum-Void, 1988, Pe portativul vietii, 1992. Home: 334 W 49th St Apt 4FE New York NY 10019-7308

NICOL, JESSIE THOMPSON, librarian; b. Cleveland, Tenn., Dec. 26, 1931; d. Franklin Monroe and Lucile Geneva (Bagby) Thompson; m. Andrew Emerson Helms, July 30, 1953 (div. 1970); children: Diana Sue, Arthur William; m. William Kennedy Nicol, Jan. 1974 (dec. 1990). BFA, U. Houston, 1972; MLS, U. Tex., 1975; postgrad., U. Tenn., 1985-87. Cert. libr., Va. Libr., archivist Am. Nat. Ins. Co., Galveston, Tex., 1973-77; libr., head acquisitions U. Tenn., Chattanooga, 1977-87, Va. Poly. Inst. and State U., Blacksburg, 1987-91; libr., cons. Info. Emporium, Cleveland, 1991—. Libr. Davis Conservation Libr., League City, Tex., 1972-73; substitute tchr. La Marque Ind. Sch. Dist., 1968-73; women's editor Tex. City Sun, 1962. Contbr. articles to profl. jours. Active La Marque PTA, 1957-68, Tex. City Art League, Boy Scouts Am., Little League Am.; vol. Galveston County Hosp. Aux.; asst. leader Girl Scouts Am.; mem. Chattanooga Symphony and Opera Guild, 1993—. Mem. ALA (LAMA fiscal and bus. officers discussion group 1985-89), Southeastern Libr. Assn. (legis. com. 1987-88, 89-90, interstate cooperative com. 1987-88), DAR, AAUW (v.p. Chattanooga chpt. 2000-01). Methodist. Avocations: sculpture, printmaking, drawing, woodworking, handwork. Home and Office: 471 Weatherly Switch Rd SE Cleveland TN 37323-9203 E-mail: jfthnicol@aol.com.

NICOL, MALCOLM F. physical chemistry educator; b. N.Y.C., Sept. 13, 1939; s. John and Hilda E. (Foertner) N.; m. Ann Carolyn Tryon, Aug. 25, 1963 (div. May 1990); children: Barbara, Katherine, Virginia. BA, Amherst Coll., 1960; PhD, U. Calif., Berkeley, 1963. Postdoctoral chemist UCLA, 1963-64, asst. prof. phys. chemistry, 1965-70, assoc. prof., 1970-75, prof., 1975-99; vis. prof. chemistry and physics U. Nev., Las Vegas, 1998—, exec. dir. High Pressure Sci. and Engring. Ctr., 1998—. Cons. Lawrence Livermore (Calif.) Nat. Lab., 1985—, Los Alamos Nat. Lab., 1990—. Assoc. editor Jour. Phys. Chemistry, 1981-90, sr. editor, 1991-98; contbr. over 100 articles on chemistry, physics and geophysics to sci. jours. Fellow Alfred P. Sloan Found., 1973-77. Fellow AAAS, Am. Phys. Soc.; mem. Am. Chem. Soc. (councilor 1986-88, 91-95), Internat. Assn. for the Advancement of High Pressure Rsch. and Tech. (treas. 1999—), Am. Geophys. Union. Home: 1663 Gabriel Dr Las Vegas NV 89119 Office: U Nev Las Vegas Dept Physics Box 454002 Las Vegas NV 89154-4002

NICOLADIS, MICHAEL F. engineering company executive; b. New Orleans, Aug. 15, 1960; s. Frank and Peggy (Yemelos) N. B in Engring. magna cum laude, Vanderbilt U., 1982; MBA, Duke U., 1984. Assoc. N-Y Assocs., Inc., Metairie, La., 1984-85, v.p., 1985-97, COO, sr. v.p., 1997—. Mem. Holy Trinity Greek Orthodox Cathedral, New Orleans. Fuqua scholar, Conoco scholar Duke U. Mem. ASCE, Am. Cons. Engrs. Coun., Soc. Am. Mil. Engrs., Tau Beta Pi, Chi Epsilon. Avocations: tennis, reading, travel. Office: N Y Assocs Inc 2750 Lake Villa Dr Metairie LA 70002-6786

NICOLAI, EUGENE RALPH, public relations consultant, editor, writer; b. Renton, Wash., June 26, 1911; s. Eugene George and Josephine (Heidinger) N.; student U. Wash., 1929, Whitman Coll., 1929-30; B.A., U. Wash., 1934; postgrad. Am. U., 1942; M.A., George Washington U., 1965; m. Helen Margaret Manogue, June 5, 1935; 1 son, Paul Eugene. Editor, U. Wash. Daily, Seattle, 1934; asst. city editor, writer, nat. def. editor Seattle Times, 1934-41; writer Sta. KJR, Seattle, 1937-39; writer, editor, safety edn. officer Bur. Mines, Washington, 1941-45; news dir. Grand Coulee Dam and Columbia Basin Project, Washington, 1945-50; regional info. dir. Bur. Mines, Denver and Pitts., 1950-55, asst. chief mineral reports, Washington, 1955-61, news dir. office of oil and gas, 1956-57; sr. info. officer, later sr. public info. officer Office Sec. Interior, Washington, 1961-71, staff White House Nat. Conf. on Natural Beauty, spl. detail to White House, 1971, ret.; now public relations cons., tech. editor, writer. Formerly safety policy adviser Interior Dept.; com. mem. Internat. Cooperation Year, State Dept., 1971. With George Washington U. Alumni Found.; founder, mng. dir. Josephine Nature Preserve; pres. Media Assocs. Bd. dirs. Wash. State Council on Alcoholism; adviser Pierce Transit Authority, Pierce County Growth Mgmt., Pierce County Ethics Commn. Named Disting. Alumnus, recipient Penrose award, both Whitman Coll., 1979. Mem. Nature Conservancy, Wash. Environ. Council, Nat. Audubon Soc. (Am. Belgian Tervuren dist. rep.), Crook County (Oreg.) Hist. Soc., Washington State Hist. Soc., Emerald Shores Assn, Sigma Delta Chi, Pi Kappa Alpha. Presbyn. Clubs: George Washington U., Purdy (pres.). Lodge: Masons. Author: The Middle East Emergency Committee; editor: Fed. Conservation Yearbooks. Home: 9809 N Seminole Dr Spokane WA 99208-8608

NICOLAÏ, JUDITHE, international business trade executive; b. Lawrence, Mass., Dec. 15, 1945; d. Victor and Evelyn (Otash) Abisalih; children: Michelle Marie, Monique Therese. Student in photography, L.A. City Coll., 1967, UCLA, 1971; AA in Fgn. Langs., Coll. of Marin, 1983; hon. degree, Culinary Inst., San Francisco, 1981; AS with hon. in Photography, San Francisco City Coll., 2002. Photographer Scott Paper Co., N.Y.C., 1975; owner, operator restaurant The Raincheck Room, West Hollywood, Calif., 1976; prin., pres., chief exec. officer, photographer fashion Photographie sub. Nicolaï Internat. Svcs., Nice, France, 1977—; prin., pres., chief exec. officer, instr. catering and cooking Back to Basics sub. Nicolaï Internat. Svcs., San Francisco, 1980—; chief photographer exhibit and trade show, chief of staff food div. Agri-Bus. U.S.A., Moscow and Washington, 1983; head transp. U.S. Summer Olympics, L.A., 1984, interpreter for Spanish, French, Portuguese, and Italian, 1985; prin., pres., chief exec. officer, interpreter Intertrans subs. (Nicolaï Internat. Svcs.), San Francisco, 1985—; founder, pres. Nicolaï Internat. Svcs., 1985—; pres., CEO Cyprus Personal Care Products, Inc., 1994—. Mem. Internat. Diplomacy Coun., 1997—. Contbr. column on food and nutrition to jour., 1983-84. Mem. NAFE, Internat. Diplomacy Coun., Alpha Gamma Sigma. Avocations: cooking, fencing, archery, golf, photography. Office: Nicolai Internat Svcs 1686 Union St Ste 203 PMB San Francisco CA 94123-4509 Address: 2269 Chestnut St PMB 237 San Francisco CA 94123-2600

NICOLAI, PAUL PETER, lawyer; b. Trenton, N.J., Jan. 22, 1953; s. Ernest and Preziosa E. (Cattani) N.; m. Anne Marie Elizabeth LaRochelle, May 14, 1976; children: Caroline Emma, Peter Ernest, Margaret Elizabeth, Alexandra Marie, Elizabeth Anne. BA, Am. Internat. Coll., 1975; JD, Western New Eng. Coll., 1979. Bar: Mass. 1979, U.S. Dist. Ct. Mass. 1980, U.S. Ct. Appeals (1st cir.) 1983, U.S. Supreme Ct. 1984, N.Y. 1987, Washington 1987, U.S. Ct. Appeals (Fed. cir.) 1990, U.S. Tax Ct. 1991. Legal asst. Friendly Ice Cream Corp., Wilbraham, Mass., 1976-79, staff counsel, 1979-81, co. counsel, 1981-88; pres. Nicolai Law Group, P.C., Springfield, 1990—. Pres., dir., chair bus. plan rev. com. WMV Forums, Inc., 2000—. Bd. dirs. Citizens for Ltd. Taxation, Mass., 1981-84, chmn., 1984-97; mem. we. Mass. exec. com. NCCJ, mem. we. Mass. and Conn. devel. com. 1995-99, nat. trustee, 1991-99; corporator Springfield Day Nursery, Inc., 1995—, mem. mktg. com., 1995-96, Springfield Libr. Mus. Assn., Inc., 1985—; bd. dirs. Pioneer Valley Montessori Soc., Inc., Springfield, 1985-93, v.p., 1988-92, pres., 1992-93; bd. dirs., chmn. Citizens Econs. Rsch. Found., Inc., Boston, 1984-97; mem. adv. bd. Springfield Enterprise Ctr., 1998—. Mem. ABA, Am. Arbitration Assn. (arbitration panel 1992—), Mass. Bar Assn. (fee arbitration bd. 2000—, fee arbitration panel 1997-2002, arbitration and mediation panel 1999—, fee arbitration bd. 2000—), Hampden County Bar Assn. (arbitration and mediation panel 1998—), Boston Bar Assn., Assn. Bar City N.Y., D.C. Bar Assn., Fed. Cir. Ct. Appeals Bar Assn., Am. Internat. Coll. Corp. (reunion com., 2000, nat. bd. dirs., v.p. 1989-90, pres. 1990-91, corporator 2000—), Soc. Everett Barney Inc. (treas., clk. 1995-99, dir. 1995-2002, sec. 1996-99), Western Mass. Tech. Bus. Coun. (bd. dirs. 2001—), Western Mass. Software Assn. (bd. dirs. 1998-2001, treas. 2000-01). Roman Catholic. Avocation: reading. Home: 24 Venture Dr Springfield MA 01119-2727 Office: Nicolai Law Group PC 146 Chestnut St Ste 501 Springfield MA 01103-1539 E-mail: paul.nicolai@niclawgrp.com.

NICOLAIDES, NICOLAOS, legal advocate, consultant; b. Limassol, Cyprus, Apr. 4, 1968; s. Christodoulos and Marianna (Nicolaidou) N. Higher Diploma in Law, Frederic Poly. U., Limassol, 1989; LLB (hon.), U. Wales, Aberystwyth, 1991, LLM, 1993. Bar: Cyprus. Adv., legal cons. Crysses Demetriades & Co., Limassol, 1994-96, Christos Pourgourides & Co., Limassol, 1996, C.P. Erotocritou & Co., Limassol, 1996-97, Andreas Sophocleous & Co., Limassol, 1997-98, Nicolaos Chr. Nicolaides Law Office, Limassol, 1998—, Counsil of Europe Com. of Human Rights, Strasbourg, France, 1993. With Cyprus army, 1985-87. Mem. Cyprus Bar Assn., Limassol Bar Assn. Greek Christian Orthodox. Avocations: philosophy, chess, cinema, karate, body building. Home: 7 Alkiviades St CY-3066 Limassol Cyprus Office: 6 Steliou Kyriakides St CY-3080 Limassol Cyprus also: PO Box 53900 CY-3318 Limassol Cyprus Fax: 05-385067.

NICOLAS, CARL-RICHARD, commodities trading company executive, translator; b. Port-Au-Prince, Haiti, June 21, 1966; came to U.S., 1982; s. Carl-Michel and Maggalie (Joseph) N.; m. Ana-Maria Guidoni, June 21, 1989 (div. 1991). BBA, Fla. Atlantic U., 1992. Sales supr. Food & Import-Export, Miami, Fla., 1986-90; sales mgr., customer svc. supr. Inter-Continents Trading Corp., Hollywood, 1990-93; dir. internat. dept. Clear Comm., 1993-95; pub. rels. dir. P3 Exec. Svcs., Miami, 1995-97; cert. interpreter Broward Ct. House, Fort Lauderdale, 1995-96; CEO Inter-Continents World of Products Commodities, Hollywood, Fla., 1995-97, Agro-Trades Internat., Pembroke Pines, 1997—. Pres., adv. bds. Clear Comm., Hollywood, 1993-95. Author: (poetry) Dreaming in Metaphors, 1997; contbr. poems to anthologies. State rep. assisting Haitian refugess, Miami Herald, 1993. Home: 6610 Forrest St Hollywood FL 33024-2941

NICOLAS, KENNETH LEE, international financial business executive; b. San Francisco, Feb. 7, 1944; s. Norman L. and Bernice L. (Hameister) N.; m. Anne Vanderwielen, July 5, 1992 (dec.); children: Juliana M., Camille G. BA in Polit. Sci., Calif. State U., Fullerton, 1968; MA in Legis. Affairs/Econs., George Washington U., 1975. Exec. asst. Congressman Richard T. Hanna, Washington, 1970-72; sr. staff assoc. Nat. Assn. Ednl. Broadcasters, 1972-74; founder, pres. Nicolas Assocs. Internat., Inc., 1972; exec. dir. Am. Coll. Nuclear Physicians, Washington, 1974-77; aide to the Pres. White House, 1977-80; v.p. McSweeney & Co. Consulting, Newport Beach, Calif., 1980-83, L.E. Peterson & Co. Investment Banking, Costa Mesa, 1983-85; founder, pres. Fin. Strategies Group, Inc., Newport Beach, 1985—; CEO Tradex Internat., Inc., 1988-94; founder, CEO Trade Access Group, Inc., 1994—. Adj. prof. Orange Coast Coll., Costa Mesa, 1983-97, internat. MBA program U. So. Calif., 1989-90, Thunderbird Sch. Internat. Bus., Orange County, 1990-92, U. Calif., Riverside and Irvine, 1996-98; adj. prof. internat. bus. MBA program Webster U., 1998—. Author: (article series) Business to Business Mag., 1984-87 (Excellence award 1984-87). Bd. dirs., v.p. Leukemia Soc. Am., Orange County, Calif., 1982-88; chmn. Holiday Project, 1992-94; mem. bd. mgrs., chmn. capital devel. com. Orange County YMCA, 2001—. With U.S. Army, 1968-70, Vietnam. Recipient Outstanding Svc. award Nat. Holiday Project, 1993, Nat. Svc. Appreciation award Pres. Jimmy Carter, 1980, Excellence award Leukemia Soc. Am., 1988. Mem. Japan Am. Soc. (Orange County chpt. chmn. bd. dirs. 1997—), Japan Am. Soc. So. Calif. (exec. bd. 1996-98). Avocations: Karate, sailing, travel, chess, swimming. E-mail: finadvisor@earthlink.net.

NICOLETTI, PAUL LEE, veterinarian, educator; b. Goodman, Mo., Oct. 26, 1932; s. Felix and Clarice N.; m. Earline Blackburn, June 6, 1954; children: Diana, Julie, Nancy. BS in Agr., DVM, U. Mo., 1956; MS, U. Wis., 1962. Diplomate Am. Coll. Vet. Preventative Medicine. Veterinarian U.S. Dept. Agriculture, Mo., Wis., N.Y., 1956-68, UN Food and Agr. Orgn., Tehran, Iran, 1968-72, U.S. Dept. Agriculture, Jackson, Miss., 1972-75, Gainesville, Fla., 1973-78; prof. veterinary medicine U. Fla., 1978—. Recipient awards from Fla. Cattleman's Assn., 1978, Dairy Farmers, Inc., 1978, Borden award, 1979, Gold Star award Fla. Veterinary Medicine Assoc., 1981, 86, U. Austral, Chile, 1981, P.R. Dairy Assn., 1978, faculty alumni award U. Mo., 1987; named Basic Scis. Tchr. of Yr. Nat. Student Am. Veterinary Med. Assn., 1994, Alumnus of Yr. award, U. Mo., 2000. Mem. Am. Veterinary Medicine Assn. (internat. prize 1991), Fla. Veterinary Medicine Assn. (pres. 1995-96, veterinarian of yr. 1994, Disting. Svc. award 1999), Am. Coll. Veterinary Preventive Medicine (pres. 1997-98), Phi Zeta (nat. pres. 1997-99). Home: 2552 SW 14th Dr Gainesville FL 32608-2042 Office: Univ of Fla Coll Vet Medicine PO Box 110880 Gainesville FL 32611-0880 E-mail: nicolettip@mail.vetmed.ufl.edu.

NICOLL, DANIEL JULES, internist, insurance company executive; b. Bklyn., Apr. 30, 1948; s. Jacob and Eva N.; m. Rachelle Nicoll, Apr. 1, 1971; children: James Howard, Linda Melanie. BA, NYU, 1968; MD, SUNY, Bklyn., 1972; MPH, Columbia U., 1987. Diplomate Am. Bd. Internal Medicine. Pvt. practice, Roslyn, N.Y., 1975-92; med. dir. Local 32 B-J Health Ctr., N.Y.C., 1992-94, Aetna U.S. Healthcare, Uniondale, N.Y., 1994-97; COO Univ. Physician Group, S.I., 1997-99; regional med. dir. for provider partnerships CIGNA Healthcare, N.Y.C., 1999—. Co-chair peer rev. com. Nassau Cmty. Med. Soc., Garden City, N.Y., 1991—; mem. exec. com. Nassau Cmty. Med. Soc., Garden City, 1992—. Fellow: ACP, Am. Coll. Physician Execs.; mem.: Nassau County Med. Soc. (pres. 2001—02). Office: CIGNA Healthcare 499 Washington Blvd # 526 Jersey City NJ 07310-1995

NICOLOSI, JOSEPH, psychologist, writer, researcher; b. N.Y.C. BA, L.I. U., 1970; MA in Psychology, New Sch. for Social Rsch., 1971; PhD, Calif. Sch. Profl. Psychiatry, 1975. Clin. dir. Thomas Aquinas Psychol. Clinic, Encino, Calif., 1980—. Author: (books) Reparative Therapy of Male Homosexuality: A New Clinical Approach, 1991, Healing Homosexuality: Case Stories of Reparative Therapy, 1993, Preventing Homosexuality: A Parent's Guide, 2002; contbr. articles to profl. jours. Mem. Nat. Assn. for Rsch. and Therapy of Homosexuality (pres. 2000—). Office: Thomas Aquinas Psychol Clinic 16633 Ventura Blvd Encino CA 91436-1801

NICOLS, ANGELA C. software engineer, computer consultant; b. Jamaica, N.Y., Apr. 15, 1940; d. Henry Ralph and Josephine Sadie (Zarcone) Grieco; m. Otto John Nicols, May 21, 1960; children: Annemarie Nicols-Grinenko, Elizabeth Marie, John Joseph, William Joseph, Richard Joseph. BS in Math., Hofstra U., 1979; MS in Math. and Computer Sci., Adelphi U., 1985. Supr. programs/project leader Book Clubs Info. Sys. Doubleday and Co. Inc., Garden City, N.Y., 1979-87; mgr. software engring. Martin Marietta Info. Sys., Orlando, Fla., 1987-94; chmn. tech. and grants Apopka (Fla.) Hist. Soc./Mus. of the Apopkans, 1994—; computer cons. and trainer, owner Nicols Cons., Apopka, 1995—. Vol. Apopka H.S. Adv. Coun., 1994-97; sec. Bd. Edn.: Bishop Moore H.S., Orlando, 1995-98. Chmn. respite St. Francis Disabilities Com., 1995—; mem. pastoral coun. St. Francis of Assisi Ch., mem. social action commn., 2000—. Mem. AAUW, IEEE Computer Soc., Assn. for Computing Machinery, Math. Assn. Am., Nat. Assn. Women in Computing, Am. Math. Soc., Apopka Hist. Soc., Coun. Cath. Women, Gray Panthers, Foliage Garden Club of Apopka (2d v.p. 1996—), Errol Estates Country Club (comms. com. 1998-2000), Golfside Village Homeowners Assn. (exec. v.p. 1999--), Kappa Mu Epsilon. E-mail: angenic@cfl.rr.com.

NICOSIA, SANTO V. pathologist, educator; b. Catania, Italy, Dec. 12, 1943; m. Louise Mary Pineider, Sept. 3, 1969; children: Lydia Mary, Lara Ann, Nocole Claudia. MD, Cath. U. Sacred Heart, Rome, 1967; MS in Pathology, U. Ill., Chgo., 1971. Chmn. dept. pathology U. South Fla. Coll. Medicine, Tampa, 1995—; dir. divsn. cytopathology H. Lee Moffitt Cancer Ctr. and Rsch. Inst., Fla., 1986—97, chief pathology svcs., 1989—2001, dir. pathology core facilities, 1997—2002, prof. dept. interdisciplinary occ., 2001—. Cons. J.A. Haley VA Hosp., Tampa, 1988—; residency reveiw com. U. So. Fla. Coll. Medicine, Tampa, 1990—; pathology program leader H. Lee Moffitt Cancer Ctr., Tampa, 2000—01. Author: (chpts.) Elsevier-North Holland Biomedical Press, 1980. Mem.: U.S. Can. Acad. Pathology, Internat. Soc. Gynel. Pathologists, Am. Soc. Cytopathology (sec./treas. 1982—). Achievements include patents in field. Office: U So Fla Coll Medicine MDC11 12901 Bruce B Downs Blvd Tampa FL 33612

NICULESCU, FLORIN IOAN, immunology and rheumatology researcher, educator; b. Blaj, Alba, Romania, Feb. 4, 1955; came to U.S., 1990; s. Ionel and Iuliana Niculescu; m. Daniela Niculescu; 1 child, Linda. MD, U. Med. Sch., Cluj, Romania, 1981, PhD, 1992. Diplomate in internal medicine and rheumatology Am. Bd. Internal Medicine. Intern, fellow in clin. immunology Med. Clinic, Cluj, 1981-85; clin. rschr. Cantacuzino Inst., Bucharest, 1985-90; fellow in immunology U. Md., Balt., 1990-92, immunology instr., 1993, asst. prof., 1994—. Assoc. editor Jour. Immunology, 1999—; contbr. more than 65 articles to profl. jours., 5 chts. to med. textbooks; inventor in field. Recipient Fogarty Internat. award NIH, 1991, Complement Internat. award, 1992. Mem.

AMA, ACP, AAAS, Am. Assn. Immunologists, Am. Coll. Rheumatology, Romanian Acad. Scis. Avocations: medical research, classical music, literature, painting. E-mial. E-mail: fnicules@umaryland.edu.

NIDETZ, MYRON PHILIP, health care delivery systems consultant; b. Chgo., Dec. 29, 1935; s. David J. and Rose Y. (Yudell) N.; m. Linda Freeman, Dec. 18, 1960; children: Julia, Allison. BS, U. Ill., 1958; M in Bus. and Commerce, Hamilton Inst., Phila., 1972; MPA, Roosevelt U., 1981. Diplomate Am. Acad. Med. Adminstrs. Dir. Union Coop. Eye Care Ctr., Chgo., 1961-65; dir. med. admistrv. svcs. Michael Reese Hosp. and Med. Ctr., 1965-75; assoc. dir. program to imrpove med. care and health svcs. AMA, 1975-79; exec. dir. North Ctrl. Dialysis Ctrs., 1979-92; pres. Myron P. Nidetz & Assocs., Inc., 1992—. Disting. adj. prof. health care adminstrn. Roosevelt U., Chgo.; Nat. Inst. Corrections tech. cons. U.S. Dept. Justice, 1978-90; adj. prof., program chair Calumet Coll., St. Joseph U., Whiting, Ind., 1997—; bd. govs. Roosevelt U., 1992—, pres. pub. adminstrn. coun., 1993—, mem. curriculum rev. com. pub. adminstrn., 1992-97, chair admissions com., 1992-94, chair coun. and chpt. leadership com., 1998—. Active Health Planning Facilities Bd., Ill., 1979-93, Ill. Dept. Pub. Aid, 1992-99, Ill. Dept. Aging, 1992-99; mem. adv. bd. Am. Kidney Fund, chmn. Midwest core group, 1979-92; mem. adv. bd. Nat. Kidney Found., 1992-99, Inst. of Medicine, 1979—; Met. area satellite group, state legis. com. 1992-99, cmty. coord. Am. Assn. Ret. Persons, 1992-98; pres. bd. dirs., Suburban Area Agy. on Aging, 1997-99, sr. adv. cons. 1999—; counselor Svc. Core of Ret. Execs., 1992—; bd. dirs. Aetive Srs. Found., 1999—, chair bd. devel. com. With U.S. Army, 1959-60. Fellow: APHA, Am. Acad. Med. Adminstrs., Royal Soc. Health; mem.: AMA, Ind. Pub. Health Assn., Ill. Pub. Health Assn., Am. Mgmt. Assn., Assn. U. Programs Health Adminstrn., Gerontol. Soc., Inst. Soc. Ethics and Life Scis., Am. Mgmt. Assn., Am. Hosp. Assn., Am. Geriatrics Soc., Am. Acad. Polit. and Social Sci., Nat. Renal Adminstrs. Assn. (govt. affairs com.), Am. Assn. Kidney Patients, Nat. Dialysis Assn. (sec.), Assn. Hosp. Med. Edn., Ind. U. Northwest Cultural Discovery & Learning Group (bd. dir.), Ind. U. Northwest Theatre Patron, Ind. U. Northwest (bd. dir.), Books, Brushes & Bands (bd. dir.), Munster Ednl. Found. (bd. dir.), Hammond Cmty. Concerts Assn. Soc., Hammond Cmty. Concerts Assn., No. Ind. Arts Assn. (bd. dir., devel. com.), Lyric Opera Chpt., Auditorium Bldg. Soc., NW Ind. Excellence in Theatre Found. (bd. dir.), Ridgewood Arts Found., Ill. Theatre Ctr. Guild (chmn. 1990—91), Ill. Theatre Ctr., Northwest Ind. Symphony Soc., No. Ind. Arts Assn. (bd.dir.). Home and Office: 8650 Beech Ave Munster IN 46321-2605

NIE, GUOJUN, research scientist; b. Huangmei, Hubie, China, Apr. 12, 1963; parents Songshan Nie and Shuie Yan; m. Jinghua Feng, July 7, 1987; children: Pingting, George F., Derek H. BS, Hubei Normal U., Huanghsi, China, 1984; MS, Chinese Acad. Scis., Changchun, Jilin, 1987; PhD, Utah State U., Logan, 1999. Asst. prof. Wuhan Inst. Chem. Tech., Hubei, 1987—94; rsch. scientist U. Kans. Med. Ctr., Kansas City, 1999—2001, Baxter Biosci., Columbia, Md., 2001—. Contbr. articles to profl. jours. Scholar E.L. and Inez Waldron Biotech. Endowment Fund Biotech. Ctr. Utah State U. Mem. ACS, Am. Soc. Biochemistry and Molecular Biology, Chinese Student and Scholar Assn. Achievements include invention of WZ-2 reducing agent for fuel oil viscosity, WZ-1 emulsifier for heavy fuel oil. Avocations: basketball, tennis, soccer, fishing. Home: 6351 Rowanberry Dr Elkridge MD 21075 Office: Baxter Biosci 1015 Old Columbia Rd Columbia MD 21046

NIED, THOMAS H. media company executive; b. Queens, N.Y., May 4, 1942; s. Herman Joseph and Margaret (Jos) N.; m. Carol J. Thomas, June 6, 1964; children: Stacey, Allison. BA, Rutgers U., 1964, LLB, 1967; LLM in Taxation, NYU, 1972. CPA, N.J., Ga. Tax mgr. Ernst & Young, N.Y.C., Atlanta, Newark and Trenton, N.J., 1968-77; v.p. taxation N.Y. Times Co., N.Y.C., 1977-97; v.p. fed. tax Universal Music Group (formerly Polygram Holding Inc.), 1997—. Founder Media Tax Group, 1979, mem., 1979-99. Mem. ABA, AICPA, Tax Execs. Inst. (bd. dirs. 1986-2001, pres. N.Y. chpt. 1991-92, exec. com. 1992-93), Newspaper Assn. of Am. (chmn. tax com. 1995-97, chmn. ind. contractor task force 1995-97, mem. pub. policy com. 1995-97). Avocations: travel, reading, philately, birding, investing. Home: 31 Vreeland Ct Princeton NJ 08540-6760 E-mail: thomas.Nied@Groupvu.com.

NIEDERHUBER, JOHN EDWARD, surgical oncologist and molecular immunologist, university educator and administrator; b. Steubenville, Ohio, June 21, 1938; s. William Henry and Helen (Smittle) N.; m. Tracey J. Williamson; children: Elizabeth Ann, Matthew John. BS, Bethany Coll., 1960; MD, Ohio State U., 1964. Diplomate Am. Bd. Surgery. Internship, surgery Ohio State U. Hosp., Columbus, 1964-65; resident, surgery U. Mich. Med. Ctr., Ann Arbor, 1967-69, NIH acad. trainee in surgery, 1969-71, resident, surgery, 1971-72, chief resident surgery, 1972-73, asst. prof. surgery and asst. prof. microbiology, 1973-77, dir. transplantation program, 1975-76, assoc. prof. surgery and assoc. prof. microbiology, 1977-80, chief divsn. surg. oncology and transplantation, sect. gen. surgery, 1979-82, sr. assoc. dean med. sch., 1983-86, assoc. dean rsch., 1982-86, chief divsn. surg. oncology sect. gen. surgery, 1982-86, prof. surgery, prof. microbiology and immunology, 1980-87; cons. Wayne County Gen. Hosp., Mich., 1973-84; cons. surgery Ann Arbor VA Hosp., 1973-87; prof. surgery, oncology, molecular biology and genetics The Johns Hopkins U. Sch. Med., Baltimore, 1987-91; Emile Holman prof. surgery, chair, dept. surgery, head sect. surgical scis. Stanford (Calif.) U. Sch. Medicine., 1991-95, prof. microbiology and immunology, 1991-97; chief of surgery Stanford (Calif.) U. Hosp., 1991-95; dir. planning Comp. Cancer Ctr. Stanford (Calif.) Med. Ctr., 1991-95; prof. surgery and oncology Sch. Medicine, asst. dean oncology, dir. Comprehensive Cancer Ctr. U. Wis., Madison, 1997—. Vis. prof. Howard Hughes Med. Inst. Dept. Molecular Biology and Genetics The Johns Hopkins U. Sch. Medicine, Baltimore, 1986-87; cons. in field. Authored books on cancer and surgery; mem. editl. bd. Jour. Immunology, 1981-85, Jour. Surg. Res., 1989-95, Current Opinion in Oncology, 1989—, Annals of Surgery, 1991—, Surg. Oncology, 1991—, Jour. Clin. Oncology, 1993, Annals of Surg. Oncology, 1993—, Jour. Am. Coll. Surgeons, 1994—, The Oncologist, 1995—, Surgery, 1999—; contbr. articles to profl. jours. Active NCI divsn. Cancer Treatment Bd. Scientific Councilors, 1986-91, chmn., 1987-91, Gen. Motors Cancer Rsch. Found. Awards Assembly, 1988-92, 98—. Served to capt. U.S. Army, 1965-67 Recipient USPHS Rsch. Career Devel. award Nat. Inst. Allergy and Infectious Disease, 1974-79, Disting. Faculty Svc. award U. Mich., 1978, Alumni Achievement award Ohio State U. Coll. Medicine, 1989, Alumni Achievement award in Medicine Bethany Coll., 1995; vis. rsch. fellow divsn. immunobiology Karolinska Inst., Stockholm, 1970-71, Am. Cancer Soc. Jr. Faculty Clin. fellow, 1977-79. Fellow ACS; mem. Am. Soc. Transplant Surgeons, Transplantation Soc., Am. Surg. Assn., Am. Assn. Immunologists, Am. Assn. Cancer Insts. (v.p. 1999—), Coller Surg. Soc., Soc. Univ. Surgeons, Assn. Acad. Surgeons, Soc. Surg. Oncology (v.p. 1999-2001, pres. 2001—), Ctrl. Surg. Soc., Am. Assn. Cancer Rsch., Am. Soc. Clin. Oncology, Soc. Clin. Surgery, Biology Club II, Robert M. Zollinger-Ohio State U. Surg. Soc., Pacific Coast Surg. Assn., Soc. Surgery of the Alimentary Tract, Soc. Surg. Oncology (v.p. 1999—). Avocations: golf, gardening. Office: U Wis Dir Comprehensive Cancer Ctr 600 Highland Ave Madison WI 53792-0001*

NIEDERMAN, JAMES CORSON, physician, educator; b. Hamilton, Ohio, Nov. 27, 1924; s. Clifford Frederick and Henrietta (Corson) N.; m. Miriam Camp, Dec. 12, 1951; children— Timothy Porter, Derrick Corson, Eliza Orton, Caroline Noble. Student, Kenyon Coll., 1942-45, D.Sc. (hon.), 1981; MD, Johns Hopkins U., 1949. Intern Osler Svc. Johns Hopkins Hosp., Balt., 1949-50; asst. resident in medicine Yale-New Haven Med. Center, 1950-51, assoc. resident, 1953-55; med. ctr. practice specializing in internal medicine, infectious disease and clin. epidemiology New Haven, 1955-97; instr. Yale U., 1955-58, asst. prof., 1958-66, assoc. prof., 1966-76, clin. prof. medicine and epidemiology, 1976-97, emeritus clin. prof. medicine and epidemiology, 1997—, clin. prof. emeritus epidemiology and pub. health, 1998; mem. Nat. Coun. for Johns Hopkins Medicine. Trustee Kenyon Coll., 1974-97, trustee emeritus, 1997—; bd. counselors Smith Coll., 1970-77. Served to 1st lt. M.C. U.S. Army, 1951-53. Fellow Silliman Coll., Yale U. Fellow Am. Coll. Epidemiology; mem. Infectious Diseases Soc. Am., Am. Epidemiol. Soc., Johns Hopkins Med. and Surg. Assn.; trustee Assocs. of Cushing Whitney Med. Libr.; mem. The Kenyon Rev. Bd. Trustees, Conn. Soc. Arts and Scis. Clubs: Yale (N.Y.C.); New Haven Lawn. Democrat. Episcopalian. Achievements include research in clin. epidemiology of Epstein Barr virus infections and its causal relationship of infectious mononucleosis. Home: 429 Sperry Rd Bethany CT 06524-3544 Office: 60 College St New Haven CT 06510-3210 Fax: 203-393-1902. E-mail: dr.j.@cshore.com.

NIEFELD, JAYE SUTTER, advertising executive; b. Mpls., May 27, 1924; s. Julius and Sophia (Rosenfeld) N.; m. Piri Elizabeth Von Zabrana-Szilagy, July 5, 1947; 1 child, Peter Wendell. Cert., London U., 1945; BA, U. Minn., 1948; BS, Georgetown U., 1949; PhD, U. Vienna, 1951. Project dir. Bur. Social Sci. Research, Washington, 1952-54; research dir. McCann-Erickson, Inc., N.Y.C., 1954-57; v.p., dir. mktg. Keyes, Madden & Jones, Chgo., 1957-60; pres., dir. Niefeld, Paley & Kuhn, Inc., 1961-71; exec. v.p. Bozell, Inc., 1971-89; pres. The Georgetown Group, Inc., 1991—. Cons. U.S. Dept. State, Commerce, HEW, also others; lectr. Columbia U., Northwestern U., U. Chgo., 1989-94; chmn. Ctr. Advanced Comm. Rsch.; owner Glencoe Angus Farms, Glencoe Arabians; comm. adv. com. Arabian Horse Registry Am.; ptnr. Sunny Valley Farm, Talcott-Fromkin Freehold Assocs., Neptune Realty, J&J Enterprises; bd. dirs. Mktg. Decisions, Inc., E. Morris Comms., Inc. Author: The Making of an Advertising Campaign, 1989; (with others) Marketing's Role in Scientific Management, 1957, Advertising and Marketing to Young People, 1965, The Ultimate Overseas Business Guide for Growing Companies, 1990; contbr. articles to profl. jours. Mem. adv. bd. Glencoe Family Svc.; bd. dirs. Big Bros. Met. Chgo.; exec. v.p. City of Hope; mem. Theodore Thomas Soc. Chgo. Symphony Orch., Overture Soc. Lyric Opera Chgo. Capt. AUS, 1942-46. Decorated Bronze Star. Mem. Am. Assn. Pub. Opinion Rsch., Am. Film Inst., Am. Mktg. Assn., Am. Sociol. Assn., Smithsonian Instn., Internat. Arabian Horse Assn., Arabian Horse Registry (comm. com.), The Caxton Club, Chgo. Horticultural Soc. (governing bd.), Chgo. Coun. on Fgn. Rels. Home: 1011 Bluff St Glencoe IL 60022-1120 E-mail: Jaye8@msn.com.

NIEFORTH, KARL ALLEN, university dean, educator, retired; b. Melrose, Mass., July 7, 1936; s. Reginald Lemuel and Mabel (Zeimetz) N.; children from previous marriage: Scott, Keith, Karla, Kraig; m. Joan Carolyn Whitney, Feb. 14, 1989. BS, Mass. Coll. Pharmacy, 1957; MS in Med. Chemistry, Purdue U., 1959, PhD, 1961. Lic. pharmacist, Conn., Mass. Asst. prof. med. chemistry Sch. Pharmacy, U. Conn., Storrs, 1961-68, assoc. prof., 1968-75, prof., 1975—, asst. dean, 1967-76, assoc. dean, 1976-81, dean, 1981-93, dept. head, dept. pharm. sci., 1997-98, ret., 2000. Lectr. psychiatry Yale U., 1970-76; mem. evaluation panels NSF, 1974-76, NIH, 1972-75; bd. dirs. Ctr. Drug and Alcohol Studies, Farmington, Conn., 1976-78; mem. pharmacy educators com. Nat. Assn. Chain Drugstores, 1988-93. Mem. adv. com. Conn. Dept. Mental Health, 1972-75; bd. dirs. Ea. Conn. Drug Action Program, 1970-72; mem. pharm. tripartite com. Conn. Dept. Consumer Protection, 1979-82, 89-95. Mem. Am. Found. Pharm. Edn. (Charles Lynn Fellow 1960-61), Am. Chem. Soc., Am. Pharm. Assn., Am. Assn. Colls. Pharmacy, Conn. Pharm. Assn., Conn. Soc. Hosp. Pharmacists, Acad. Pharm. Scis., Sigma Xi, Kappa Psi, Phi Lambda Sigma, Phi Lambda Upsilon, Rho Chi, Phi Kappa Phi. Republican. Office: U Conn, Office of the Pres. Gulley Hall, Storrs Campus 352 Mansfield Rd, Unit 2048 Storrs Mansfield CT 06269-2048

NIEHAUS, DEBORAH ANN, peri-anesthesia/perioperative care nurse; b. Hillsboro, Ohio, Sept. 17, 1949; d. Francis E. and Eleanor M. (Rosselott) Stephens; m. Raymond R. Niehaus, Nov. 28, 1970; children: Tiffany Renata, Ryan Robert. Diploma, Bethesda Hosp. Sch. Nursing, Cin., 1970; BS in Nursing/Mgmt. cum laude, Coll. Mt. St. Joseph, Cin., 1989. Cert. perianesthesia nurse. Staff nurse med./surg. Highland Dist. Hosp., Hillsboro, Ohio; splty. team leader, relief charge nurse, pediatric, ICU Bethesda Oak Hosp., Cin., staff nurse surg., pain mgmt. nurse PACU; staff clin. nurse III Bethesda North Ambulatory Surg. Ctr. LLC. Speaker in field. Contbr., contbg. editor Perianesthesia and Ambulatory Surgery Nursing textbooks. Past pres., officer cmty. and philanthropic orgns., Cin. and Anderson Twp. Mem. Am. Soc. Perianesthesia Nurses (pres. 1990-91, treas. 1985-89), Assn. Oper. Rm. Nurses, Am. Pain Mgmt. Nurses (pres. 1982-83), Ohio Perianesthesia Nurses Assn., Cin. Area Perianesthesia Nurse Assn. (prs. 1982-83).

NIEHAUS, SHERRY M. social welfare administrator; b. Heber Springs, Ark., Dec. 12, 1946; d. Ewing W. and Fay D. Mays; m. Joseph T. Niehaus, May 27, 1972 (div.); children: Vicent E., Jessica F.; m. Stephen P. Mers, April 30, 1992. Tabulating clk. Dover Elevator, Cin., 1968-71; data machine operator Little Rock Water Works, 1971-76; acctg. clk. Mays Mission for the Handicapped, Heber Springs, Ark., 1978-85, exec. dir., 1985-95, pres., 1995—. Bd. dirs. Ark. State Rehab. Coun., Little Rock, 1999—. Bd. sec. Cmty. Sch. Cleburne County, Heber Springs, 1987—; vol. Vol. Tax Income Assistance, Heber Springs, 1978. Mem. Rotary Club of Cleburne County (bulletin editor 1995—, sec. 2000-01). Avocations: horses, reading, genealogy, computers, martial arts. Home: 176 Wolf Branch Rd Greenbrier AR 72058 Office: Mays Mission for the Handicapped 604 Colonial Dr Heber Springs AR 72543 E-mail: sniehaus@maysmission.org.

NIEHAUS-KLEINMAN, AGNES, pianist, educator; b. St. Louis, Sept. 21, 1925; d. Aaron Niehaus and Clarice (Weisman) Sachs; m. Raymond Bowman, Aug. 1944 (div. 1947); m. Ira Kleinman, Dec. 27, 1952; children: Ronald, Judy, Michael, Debbie. Student, Phila. Conservatory Music, 1943-44; diploma in Piano, Julliard Sch. Music, 1945, postgrad., 1945-47; BA, Los Angeles State Coll., 1951. Accompanist Marina Koshetz, Calif. and Can., 1948-60; ind. pianist and tchr., 1960—. Debut recital Hollywood (Calif.) Assistance League Playhouse, 1941; performed with various groups including Evenings on the Roof, Los Angeles, 1950. Recipient 1st prize San Francisco World's Fair Competition, 1940, 1st prize Chopin Inter-Am. Piano Contest, 1946, 1st prize Gainsborough Contest, 1947, 1st prize Young Artists Competition, 1947, 48; scholar Phila. Conservatory Music, 1944, Julliard Sch. Music, 1945. Mem. Am. Fedn. Musicians. Democrat. Jewish. Home and Office: 6508 Petit Ave Van Nuys CA 91406-5623

NIEHM, BERNARD FRANK, mental health center administrator, retired; b. Sandusky, Ohio, Feb. 7, 1923; s. Bernard Frank and Hedwick (Panzer) N.; m. Eunice M. Patterson, Oct. 4, 1924; children— Julie, Patti, Bernie. BA, Ohio State U., 1951, MA, 1955, PhD in Ednl. Exceptional Children, Guidance and Couseling, Psychology, 1968. Tchr. pub. schs., Sandusky, 1951-57; chief ednl., vocat. and occupational therapy svcs. Vineland (N.J.) Tng. Sch., 1957-61; exec. dir. Franklin County Coun. Retarded Children, Columbus, Ohio, 1962-64; dir. Ohio Sheltered Workshop Planning Project Mental Retardation, 1964-66, coordinator mental retardation planning, 1966-68; project dir. Ohio Gov.'s Citizen Com. on Mental Retardation Planning, 1966-68; adminstr. Franklin County Program for Mentally Retarded, 1968-70; supt. Gallipolis (Ohio) State Inst., 1970-76; tchr. spl. edn. Ohio U., Columbus, 1975-77, dir. consultation and edn., 1977-79, dir., 1978-95; exec. dir. Woodland Ctrs. Inc., Gallipolis, 1995; ret. Woodland Farm, 1995. Pres. Gallco, 1989-90. Contbr. articles to profl. jours. Active Foster Grandparents Adv. Coun., Gallia County, 1974-76, Gallipolis State Inst. Parent Vol. Assn., 1970-76, Franklin County Bd. Mental Retardation, 1967-68; chmn. MGM dist. Tri-State Boy Scout Coun.; chmn. Meigs, Gallia, Mason Counties Boy Scout Dist., 1972-94; pres. Gallipolis Girls Athletic Assn. Booster Club, 1976—, Gallia County Arthritis Unit, 1986-96, Galleo Industries Bd. to Serve Handicapped Adults, 1987-94; pres. bd. dirs. Outreach Ctr. Gallia County, 1997-99; mem. Ch. Coun., St. Paul Luth. Ch., 1994-99, pres.; bd. dirs. United Cerebral Palsy, Columbus, 1968-70; mem. United Way Gallia County. With U.S. Army, 1943-46. Mem. Am. Assn. Mental Deficiency (past chmn. Ohio chpt., chmn. Great Lakes region), Am. Mental Health Adminstrs. (nat., Ohio chpts.), Nat. Rehab. Assn., Ohio Rehab. Assn., Ohio Assn. Retarded Children (2d v.p. 1974-76, dir.), Vocat. Rehab. Assn., Ohio Coun. Community Mental Health Ctrs., Gallia County Arthritis Assn. (pres. 1991—), Gallipolis Area C. of C., Gallipolis Rotary. Lutheran. Home: 1525 Mill Creek Rd Gallipolis OH 45631-8616 Office: Woodland Ctr Inc 3086 State Route 160 Gallipolis OH 45631-8418

NIEHOFF, ARTHUR HERMAN, publishing executive; b. Indianapolis, Ind., Dec. 30, 1921; s. Bernard and Marie Niehoff; m. Juanita Hobbs Niehoff (div.); m. Carol Khudson (div.); children: Justin. BA, Ind. U., Bloomington, IN, 1948; PhD, Columbia U., New York, 1957. Curator Milw. Pub. Mus., Milwaukee, Wis., 1951—59; staff Agy. Intern Devel. Dept. State, Laos, 1959—61; asst. prof. anthropology U. Wis., Milwaukee, Wis., 1962—63; prof. anthropology George Wash. U., Washington, 1963—68, Calif. State U., Los Angeles, Calif., 1969—89; husbandman San Diego, 1990—; pub. www.hominidpress.com, 1994—. Author: (book) Factory Workers in India, Takeover: How Euroman Changed the World, On Being a Conceptual Animal, An Anthropologist Under the Bed, Bicycling for Life, Stroke, East Indians in the West Indies, Cultural Reality and Technical Change, Introducing Social Change, A Casebook of Social Change, Planned Change in Agrarian Countries, Case Histories in Technical Assistance, Another Side of History, On Becoming Human; contbr. articles to profl. jours. Cpl. AC, 2002—02. Avocations: gardening, bicycling. Home: 31765 Rockinghorse Road Escondido CA 92026 Personal E-mail: niehoff@tfb.com.

NIEHOFF, KARL RICHARD BESUDEN, financial executive; b. Cin., May 11, 1943; s. Karl George and Jean (Besuden) N.; children: K. Richard B. Jr., Kelly B. BA, U. Cin., 1967. Corp. trust ops. officer 5th-3d Union Trust, Cin., 1968-74; v.p., gen. mgr. Sabina (Ohio) Water Co., 1974-76; v.p., sec. Weil, Roth and Irving, Inc., 1974-76; co-mgr., mcpl. fin. dept. Thomson McKinnon Securities, Cin. and N.Y.C., 1976-79; exch. rep. Consol. Quote, Consol. Tape Oper. Coms., 1979-90, alt., 1991-92; pres. Fin. Instruments Svcs. Corp., Cin., Chgo., London, 1985-90; v.p. Trading Svcs. NASDAQ, Inc., 1990—92, D.E. Shaw Securities, LLC, N.Y.C., 1992—94, D.E. Shaw & Co., N.Y.C., 1992-94; pres., mng. ptnr. Niehoff and Assocs., 1994-99; mng. dir., chief of party OTC Capital Mkt. Devel. Project, Warsaw, 1994—96; dep. advisor Ministry Mass Privatization, Republic of Poland, 1994-96; v.p., dir. Third Market Trading Corp., Chicago, 1994-98; pres., dir. SBX Inc., Cin., Princeton, N.J., 1997-2000, VSX Techs. Inc., N.Y.C., Indpls., 1999—2000; pres., CEO Webix, Inc., N.Y.C., 2000—02; chmn. X-Change Corp., 2002—; pres. X-Change Tech. Corp., 2002—, Mark Securities, Inc., Boston, 2002—. Witness U.S. Ho. Reps. Consumers Protection and Fin. Com., 1977—, other gen. oversight, gen. acctg. office and GAO com. panels and inquiries, 1987-94; v.p. Wit Capital Corp., New York, 1998-99, trustee Cin. Stock Exch., 1974-90, chmn. bd. trustees, 1978-79; voting mem. Inter-Market Trading Com., 1980-90, Stock Exch. Chief Execs. Com., 1988-90; mem. Cin. Stock Exch., 1974-89, P.B.W. Stock Exch., Phila., 1975-77, GLOBEX Task Force Com., 1988-89, Easdaq, Brussels, Belgium, 1995-96; vis. lectr. U. Cin. Coll. Bus. Adminstrn., Xavier U. Bus. Adminstrn. Coll., Cin.; long-term planning com. Chgo. Bd. Options Exch., 1987-88; pres. Digital Stock Market, N.Y.C., 1998-99; vis. com. U.S. Info. Agy., N.Y.C., 1992-95; mng. dir. trading and tech. Unified Mgmt. Corp., Inc., Indpls. and N.Y.C., 1999-2000; dir., sec. Schuyler Park Manor Co-op, Pelham Manor, N.Y., 2000—. Trustee, sec. Contemporary Arts Ctr., Cin., 1975-83; mem. Young Mens Mercantile Libr. Assn., 1974-90, adv. com., 1974-77; mem. devel. com. Tangeman Gallery of Art, 1981-82; pres., dir. Bermuda Condominium High Assn., Delray Beach, Fla., 1999— Mem.: Internat. Ops. Divsn. (N.Y.), Securities Traders Assn. N.Y. (chmn. listed trading com. 1993, OTC Bulletin Bd. com. 2002—), Nat. Acad. Design, India House, Keeneland Assn. (Lexington, Ky.), Queen City Mcpl. Bond Club (trustee 1974—80), NYAC Yacht Club (Pelham Manor, N.Y.), N.Y. Stock Exch. Luncheon Club, Univ. Club (Cin.), N.Y. Athletic Club, Cin. Stock and Bond Club (trustee and 1st v.p. 1974—90), Nat. Arts Club (N.Y.C.), Phi Alpha Theta. Office: 36 W 44th St Ste 1201 New York NY 10036-8102

NIEHOFF, LEONARD MARVIN, lawyer; b. St. Louis, Dec. 2, 1957; s. Leonard Marvin and May (Gordon) Niehoff. BA with high distinction, U. Mich., 1981, JD, postgrad., U. Mich., 1984. Bar: Mich. 1984, U.S. Dist. Ct. (ea. dist.) Mich., 1985, U.S. Dist. Ct. (we. dist.) Mich. 1985, U.S. Ct. Appeals (6th cir.) 1985, U.S. Supreme Ct. 1988. Research asst. U. Mich. Law Sch., Ann Arbor, 1983; shareholder Butzel Long, Detroit, 1984—. Adj. prof. law U. Detroit Law Sch., 1988—, Wayne State U. Law Sch., 1989—. Editor U. Mich. Jour. Law Reform, 1983-84. Bd. advisors C.S. Mott Children's Hosp.; bd. dirs. Mich. Theatre Found. Named to 40 Under 40, Crain's Detroit Bus., 1996. Mem. ABA (forum com. on comms. law 1985—), Fed. Bar Assn. (exec. bd. 1995—), State Bar Mich. (chmn. constl. law com., mem. law and media com., bar jour. adv. bd.), Detroit Bar Assn., Washtenaw Bar Assn. (chmn. trial practice sect.), U. Musical Soc. (bd. dirs.), Mich. Theater Found. (bd. dirs.), CS Mott Children's Hosp. (bd. dirs.). Avocations: music, film, art. Office: 350 S Main St Ste 300 Ann Arbor MI 48104-2131

NIEHOFF, PHILIP JOHN, lawyer; b. Beaver Dam, Wis., Dec. 31, 1959; s. John Henry and Muriel Jean (Moore) N. BBA with distinction, U. Wis., 1982, JD cum laude, 1985; LLM in Securities Regulation, Georgetown U., 1988. Bar: Wis. 1985, U.S. Dist. Ct. (we. dist.) Wis. 1985, Ill. 1991. Atty. SEC, Washington, 1985-90; assoc. Mayer, Brown & Platt, Chgo., 1990-95, ptnr., 1996—. Co-author: Current Law of Insider Trading, 1990, Public Offerings, securities law handbook, 1997; contbg. author: Securitization of Financial Assets, 1991. Fed. Bar Assn. scholar, 1988. Mem. ABA, State Bar Wis., State Bar Ill., Chgo. Bar Assn., Order of Coif, Golden Key Honor Soc., Beta Gamma Sigma, Phi Kappa Phi, Phi Eta Sigma. Republican. Lutheran. Avocations: fishing, computers, reading, travel. Home: 2800 N Lake Shore Dr Apt 2416 Chicago IL 60657-6248 Office: Mayer Brown & Platt 190 S La Salle St Ste 3100 Chicago IL 60603-3441

NIEHUSS, JOHN MARVIN, lawyer; b. Ann Arbor, Mich., Mar. 7, 1937; s. Marvin Lemmon Niehuss and Lois Celicia Markham; m. Rosemary Juliette Neaher, June 30, 1973 (div. Mar. 1991); children: Juliette, John. BA, Amherst Coll., 1958; JD, U. Mich., 1962. Assoc. atty. Sullivan & Cromwell, N.Y.C., 1966-69; legal advisor Govt. of Zambia, Lusaka, 1969-71; loan officer, dir. World Bank, Washington, 1971-73, 90-91; dep. asst. sec. U.S. Treasury Dept., 1974-77, 89-90; v.p. Merrill Lynch, N.Y.C., 1977-89; gen. counsel Inter-Am. Devel. Bank, Washington, 1992-99, Export-Import Bank U.S., Washington, 1999-2001. Mem. adv. bd. Internat. Law Inst., Washington, 1977—. Mem. Coun. Fgn. Rels., Met. Club. Avocations: golf, hiking, fly fishing. Home: 3019 45th St NW Washington DC 20016-3523

NIELSEN, CHRISTIAN BAYARD, lawyer; b. San Jose, Calif., May 10, 1954; s. Bayard R. and June (Morgan) N.; m. Kathleen Dearden, Oct. 25, 1980; children: Bayard Douglas, Chandler Kathleen. BA, U. Pacific, Stockton, Calif., 1976; JD, Pepperdine U., 1979. Cert.: Nat. Bd. Trial Advocacy (civil trial advocate), bar: Calif. 1979, U.S. Dist. Ct. (no. and ea. dists.) Calif. 1979. Sr. ptnr. Robinson & Wood, Inc., San Jose, Calif., 1979—. Arbitrator Fed. Panel and State Panel, 1982—; lectr. Calif. Continuing Edn. of the Bar, 1989—. Mem.: ABA, Santa Clara County Bar Assn., Internat. Assn. Ins. Counsel, Def. Rsch. Inst., Am. Bd. Trial Advocates, Assn. Def. Counsel of No. Calif. (lectr. 1988—). Republican. Methodist. Office: Robinson & Wood Inc 227 N 1st St Fl 2 San Jose CA 95113-1000 E-mail: cbn@r-winc.com.

NIELSEN, ELOISE WILMA SOULE, elementary education educator; b. Sanilac County, Mich., Apr. 24, 1923; d. Stanley and Jessie Christina (Hacker) Soule; m. Harald Christian Nielsen, Dec. 19, 1953; children: Brenda Mae Nielsen Stone, Judy Ann (dec.), Paul Eric, Gloria Lynn Nielsen Iannucci. Student, Cen. Mich. U., Mt. Pleasant, 1942, BS, 1946; MA, Mich. State, 1953; postgrad., Bradley U I.S.U., U. Ill. Cert. Mich. perman, Ill. all grades, Jr. Coll. Ill. spl. edn., learning disabilities, behavior disorder. Tchr. Appin Rural Sch., Ubly, Mich., 1942-44, Mt. Pleasant (Mich.) Pub. Schs., 1944-46, Mt. Clemens Pub. Schs., Dickinson and Grant, 1946-52; social worker, psychologist, remedial reading Lansing (Mich.) Pub. Schs., 1953-57; spl. edn. programmer Dist. 150, Peoria, Ill., 1967-87; pioneered learning disability and behavior disorder, 1988—. Organizer: (booklet for tchrs.) Day Brighteners, 1989; editor ann. Soule-Nielsen Notebook, 1984-99. Mem. NEA, Coun. for Exceptional Children, Alpha Delta Kappa (pres.). Democrat. Lutheran. Avocations: music, crafts, genealogy, square dance, camping, touring. Home: 2318 N Gale Ave Peoria IL 61604-3229

NIELSEN, ERLAND KOLDING, library director; b. Frederiksberg, Denmark, Jan. 13, 1947; s. Olav and Anna (Kolding) N.; m. Anne Birthe van Holck, 1969 (div. 1981); children: Gudrun, Jens Christian; m. Inger SØrensen, 1982. MA in History, PhD, U. Copenhagen, 1973. Lectr. Royal Sch. Librarianship U. Copenhagen, 1971-80, asst. prof. Inst Contemporary History, 1973-83, head dept. humanities and social scis., 1980-86, head Edn. Research Librarians and Documentalists Royal Sch. Librarianship, 1984-86; dir. gen. Royal Libr., Copenhagen, 1986—. Bd. dirs. Electronic Rsch. Libr. of Denmark; mem. Nat. Coun. of Librs., 1998—; mem., chair evaluation coms. for appt. of nat. librarians and libr. dirs. in Scandinavia. Author, editor 12 books in history and library sci.; contbr. articles to profl. jours. Mem. Internat. Fedn. Libr. Assns. and Instns. (sec. standing commn. for nat. librs., 1990-98, chmn. gen. rsch. librs. div., mem. profl. bd. 1991-93), Rsch. Librarian's Council (sec. 1975-79, chmn. 1979-82), Danish Rsch. Libraries Assn. (bd. dirs. 1987—, vice chair 1996-98, chair 1998-2002), Danish Libr. Assn. (mem. bd. dirs. 1990—), Adv. Coun. Rsch. Libraries (bd. dirs. 1987—), Conf. Dirs.

Nat. Libraries, Nat. Libr. Policy Bd., Conf. European Nat. Librs., Liber (exec. bd. dirs. 1994—, vice-chair 1999—), Arbeitsgemeinschaft Bibliotheca Baltica (bd. dirs. 1994-98), Arnamagnean Commn., Commn. Literary Sources Danish History (chair 1990—), Electronic Rsch. Libr. Denmark (bd. dirs. 1998—), Nat. Commn. on Export of Cultural Assets (chair 1995—). Home: Egholmsvej 1 DK-2830 Virum Denmark Office: Det Kongelige Bibliotek Postboks 2149 DK 1016 Copenhagen Denmark E-mail: ekn@kb.dk.

NIELSEN, FORREST HAROLD, research nutritionist; b. Dancy, Wis., Oct. 26, 1941; s. George Adolph and Sylvia Viola (Blood) N.; m. Emily Joanne Currie, June 13, 1964; children: Forrest Erik, Kistin Emily. BS, U. Wis., 1963, MS, 1966, PhD, 1967. NIH grad. fellow, dept. biochemistry U. Wis., Madison, 1963-67; rsch. chemist, Human Nutrition Rsch. Inst. USDA, Beltsville, Md., 1969-70, rsch. chemist Human Nutrition Rsch. Ctr. Grand Forks, N.D., 1970-86, ctr. dir. and rsch. nutritionist, 1986-2001, rsch. nutritionist, 2001—. Adj. prof. dept. biochemistry and molecular biology, U. N.D., Grand Forks, 1971—, speaker in field. Assoc. editor Magnesium and Trace Elements Jour., 1990-93; mem. editl. bd. Jour. Trace Elements in Exptl. Medicine, 1988—, Biol. Trace Element Rsch. Jour., 1979—, Jour. Nutrition, 1984-88, Biofactors, 1997—; contbr. articles to profl. jours. Capt. U.S. Army, 1967-69. Recipient Klaus Schwarz Commemorative medal and award Internat. Assn. of Bioinorganic Scientists; named Scientist of Yr. U.S. Dept. Agrl., 1993. Mem. Internat. Soc. Trace Element Rsch. in Humans (gov. bd. 1989—, pres. 1992-95), Soc. for Exptl. Biology and Medicine, Am. Soc. for Nutritional Scis., N.D. Acad. Sci. (pres. 1988-89), Internat. Bone and Mineral Soc., Sigma Xi (pres. U. N.D. chpt. 1976-77). Lutheran. Achievements include patent for use of Boron Supplements to Increase in Vivo Production of Hydroxylated Steroids; discovery of the nutritional essentiality of the trace elements boron and nickel. Office: USDA ARS GFHNRC PO Box 9034 Grand Forks ND 58202-9034 E-mail: fnielsen@gfhnrc.ars.usda.gov.

NIELSEN, GEORGE LEE, architect; b. Ames, Iowa, Dec. 12, 1937; s. Verner Henry and Verba Lucile (Smith) N.; m. Karen Wall, Feb. 28, 1959; children: David Stuart, Kristina, Melissa. B.Arch., Iowa State U., 1961; M.Arch., M.I.T., 1962. Registered arch., Mass., Ohio, N.Y., Ill., Ind., Nat. Coun. Archtl. Registration Bds. Designer Perry, Shaw, Hepburn & Dean, Boston, 1961-64, F.A. Stahl & Assos., Cambridge, Mass., 1964-65; project architect Peirce & Pierce, Boston, 1965-70; project mgr. A.M. Kinney Assos., Cin., 1970—, partner, 1978—; sec. A.M. Kinney Assocs., Inc., Ill., 1993—, also dir.; v.p. A.M. Kinney Inc., 1992-94, pres., 1994-99, also dir.; sr. prin. A.M. Kinney Inc. Assocs., 1999—. Architect assoc. with major projects for Avco Rsch. Lab., Children's Hosp. Med. Ctr., Square D. Corp., Nalco Chem. Co., Olin Corp., Mead Johnson/Bristol Myers Squib, Cin. Gas and Elec. Co., Sandoz Pharm. Corp., Hoechst Celanese, Hoechst Marion Roussel, Witco Corp., Sotheby's, Shell Chem. Co., Bayer Corp., Univ. Ky., Purdue U., Wright Patterson and Edwards AFB. Served with U.S. Army, 1962-64. Mem. AIA (design awards 1970-71, 74, 78, 81, 91, 94, 95). Episcopalian. Home: 3419 Ault View Ave Cincinnati OH 45208-2518 Office: A M Kinney Inc 150 E 4th St Fl 6 Cincinnati OH 45202-4131 E-mail: nielsengl@amkinney.com.

NIELSEN, GREG ROSS, lawyer; b. Provo, Utah, Sept. 24, 1947; s. Ross T. and Carma (Peterson) N.; m. Jo Rita Beer, Sept. 3, 1971; children: Jennifer, Jerilyn, Eric Michael, Brittany Anne. BA in Polit. Sci. magna cum laude, Brigham Young U., 1971; JD cum laude, Harvard U., 1975. Bar: Ariz. 1975, U.S. Dist. Ct. Ariz. 1975, U.S. Ct. Appeals (9th cir.) 1977, Utah 1990. Assoc. Snell & Wilmer, Phoenix, 1975-80, ptnr., 1981-91, mng. ptnr. Salt Lake City, 1991—2002, adminstrv. coord. real estate practice group Phoenix, 1988-90. Mem. dist. com. Theodore Roosevelt coun. Boy Scouts Am., 1988-90, Valley Partnership, Phoenix, 1989-90; trustee Utah Heritage Found., 1998-2000, Swaner Nature Preserve, 2002—. Hinckley scholar Brigham Young U., 1970; fellow Ford Found., 1970. Mem. ABA, State Bar Ariz., Utah Bar Assn. Republican. Mem. Lds Ch. Office: Snell & Wilmer 15 West South Temple Ste 1200 Salt Lake City UT 84101 E-mail: gnielsen@swlaw.com.

NIELSEN, HARALD CHRISTIAN, retired chemist, researcher; b. Chgo., Apr. 18, 1930; s. Svend Aage and Seena (Hansen) N.; m. Eloise Wilma Soule, Dec. 19, 1953; children— Brenda Mae, Paul Erick, Gloria Lynn, Judy Ann. BA, St. Olaf Coll., 1952; PhD, Mich. State U., 1957. Cereal grain protein chemist Nat. Ctr. for Agrl. Utilization Rsch. (formerly No. Regional Research Ctr.), Agrl. Research Service, USDA, Peoria, Ill., 1957-87. Contbr. articles to profl. jours. Mem. Peoria Area Combined Fed. Campaign Coord. Com., 1980—87; pres. local 3247 Am. Fedn. Govt. Employees, AFL-CIO, 1977—86; active Peoria Prostrate Cancer Support Group, 1996—, editor newsletter, 2000—. Mem.: Nat. Assn. Ret. Fed. Employees (officer chpt. 268 1989—92, pres. chpt. 268 1991, editor chpt. newsletter 1999—), Am. Assn. Cereal Chemists. Democrat. Lutheran. Home: 2318 N Gale Ave Peoria IL 61604-3229 E-mail: nielsen425@yahoo.com. *What useful thing have I accomplished this day? What did I learn today? These two questions I ask myself at the end of each day.*

NIELSEN, JAKOB, computer interface engineer; b. Copenhagen, Oct. 5, 1957; came to U.S., 1990; s. Gerhard and Helle (Hopfner) N.; m. Hannah Kain, Feb. 18, 1984. MS in Computer Sci., Aarhus (Denmark) U., 1983; PhD in Computer Sci., T.U. of Denmark, 1988. Rsch. fellow Aarhus U., 1983-84; vis. scientist IBM User Interface Inst., Yorktown Heights, N.Y., 1985; adj. asst. prof. T.U. Denmark, Lyngby, 1986-90; mem. rsch. staff Bell Comm. Rsch., Morristown, N.J., 1990-94; disting. engr. Sun Microsystems, Mountain View, Calif., 1994-98; principal Nielsen Norman Group, CA, 1998—. Author: Hypertext and Hypermedia, 1990, Usability Engineering, 1993, Multimedia and Hypertext: The Internet and Beyond, 1995, Designing Web Usability: The Practice of Simplicity, 2000, Homepage Usability: 50 Websites Deconstructed, 2001; editor: Coordinating User Interfaces for Consistency, 1989, Designing User Interfaces for International Use, 1990, Usability Inspection Methods, 1994, International User Interfaces, 1996; mem. editl. bd.: Behavior and Info. Tech., 1989—, mem. editl. bd.: Hypermedia Jour., 1989—95, mem. editl. bd.: Interacting with Computers, 1989—, mem. editl. bd.: Internat. Jour. Human-Computer Interaction, 1989—, mem. editl. bd.: Internat. Jour. Man-Machine Studies, 1991—94, mem. editl. bd.: ACM Networker, 1997—2000, mem. editl. bd.: Personal Technologies, 1997—; contbr. Mem.: Assn. for Computing Machinery (papers co-chair internat. conf. 1993, editl. bd. Networker 1997—2000, spl. interest group on computer human interaction). Achievements include patents for holder 63 patents in field; founding of discount usability engineering approach; invention (with R. Molich) of heuristic evaluation method for cost-effective improvement of user interfaces; demonstration (with T.K. Landauer) that user testing and heuristic evaluation both follow same mathematical model; definition of the parallel design method for rapidly exploring user interface alternatives.

NIELSEN, JENNIFER LEE, molecular ecologist, researcher; b. Balt., Mar. 21, 1946; d. Leo Jay and Mary Marriott (Mules) N.; divorced; children: Nadja Ochs, Allisha Ochs. MFA, Ecole des Beaux Arts, Paris, 1968; BS, Evergreen State Coll., 1987; MS, U. Calif., Berkeley, 1990, PhD, 1994. Artist, Seattle, 1969-78; fish biologist Weyerhaeuser Co., Tacoma, 1978-89; resource cons. Berkeley, 1989-90; rsch. biologist USDA-Forest Svc., Albany, Calif., 1990-99; vis. scientist Stanford U., Pacific Grove, 1994-99; supr. fisheries Alaska Biol. Sci. Ctr., Anchorage, 1999—. Rsch. assoc. Calif. State U. Mosslanding Marie Sta., 1995-99; adj. prof. integrated biology U. Calif., Berkeley, 1998; adj. prof. U. Alaska, Fairbanks, 1999—; supervisory rsch. fishery biologist U.S. Geol. Svc., Biol. Resources Divsn., Alaska Biol. Sci. Ctr., Anchorage, 1999—. Editor-in-chief: Reviews in Fish Biology and Fisheries, 1999—; editor: Evolution and the Aquatic Ecosystem, 1995, Environ. Biology of Fishes, 1998—; contbr. over 50 articles to profl. jours.; paintings exhibited at Metro. Mus. Modern Art, 1966; represented in numerous pvt. collections, U.S. and Europe. Mem. Am. Fisheries Soc. (pres. chpt. 1993-94, genetics sect. pres. 1999—), Molecular Marine Biology and Biotech. (regional editor 1995), Animal Behaviour Soc. (policy com. 1993-94). Avocations: painting, cooking, gardening, rock climbing, sailing. Office: USGS/BRD Alaska Biol Sci Ctr 1011 E Tudor Rd Anchorage AK 99503-6119

NIELSEN, JENS EVALD, retired engineer; b. Langå, Denmark, Oct. 1, 1930; s. Ingvard and Edith Sofie (Nielsen) N.; m. Gunhild Slot (dec. 1980); 1 child, Sussi. BS in Engring., Teknikum U., Copenhagen, 1956. Sales engr. Poul Klinge A/S, Copenhagen, 1956-60, H. Meisner Jensen A/S, Copenhagen, 1960-61, Islef & Hagen, Copenhagen, 1961-63, chief engr., 1963-70, divsn. mgr., 1970-86; mng. dir. Gri Europe AS, Kokkedal, 1987-98. Patentee position sensors. Avocations: films, editing videos. Home: Randager No 86 DK-2620 Copenhagen Denmark

NIELSEN, KENNETH ANDREW, chemical engineer; b. Berwyn, Ill., Oct. 10, 1949; s. Howard Andrew and La Verne Alma (Wentzer) N.; m. Linda Kay Miller, Aug. 22, 1970; children: Annette Marie, Kirsten Viola. BS in Chem. Engring., Iowa State U., 1971, MS in Chem. Engring., 1974, PhD in Chem. Engring., 1977. Sr. engr. Union Carbide Corp., Charleston, W.Va., 1976-80, project scientist, 1980-87, rsch. scientist, 1987-94, sr. rsch. scientist, 1994—. Contbr. articles to profl. jours. Co-founder Forest Hills Asns., Charleston, 1981; advisor Boy Scout Explorer Post, Charleston, 1992. Recipient Fellowships NDEA Title IV, Procter and Gamble Co., Am. Oil Co., Elias Singer award Troy Chem. Co., 1990, Kirkpatrick Chem. Engring. Achievement award Chem. Engring. mag., 1991, Profl. Progress in Engring. award Coll. Engring. Iowa State U., 1992. Mem. AIChE, Soc. Rheology, Inst. Liquid Atomization and Spraying Sys. Achievements include invention of UNICARB system for spray coating, a recognized major new pollution-prevention tech.; co-inventor of SERT process for applying mold release agents in polyurethane foam manufacture; discovery of fundamentally new type of spray atomization, known as a decompressive spray; 30 U.S. patents and 5 U.S. patents pending, also foreign patents. Home: 108 Stratford Pl South Charleston WV 25303-2819 Office: Union Carbide Corp PO Box 8361 South Charleston WV 25303

NIELSEN, KENNETH RAY, academic administrator; b. Oct. 15, 1941; s. Frank and Elinor (Hansen) N.; children: Elizabeth, Mary. BEd, U. Wis., Whitewater, 1965; MS, U. Wis., Stout, 1966; EdD, U. Wyo., 1968. Dir. student activities Cornell U., Ithaca, N.Y., 1968-72; adminstr., prof. Tchr. Tng. Coll., San Juan, P.R., 1974-77; v.p. student affairs Northland Coll., Ashland, Wis., 1972-77; v.p. student life Seattle U., 1977-84; pres. Coll. St. Mary, Omaha, 1984-96, Woodbury U., Burbank, Calif., 1996—. Bd. dirs. Boy Scouts Am., Girl Scouts U.S.A., Nat. Coun. Christians and Jews, Providence Hosp. Found.; chmn. edn. sect. United Way Bd.; mem. Gov.'s Community Svcs. and Continuing Edn. Mem. Am. Coun. Edn., Am. Assn. Higher Edn., Am. Assn. Univ. Adminstrs., Coun. Ind. Colls. Roman Catholic. Avocations: reading, exercising. Office: Woodbury U 7500 N Glenoaks Blvd Burbank CA 91504-1099

NIELSEN, LINDA MILLER, city councilwoman; b. Cedar Falls, Iowa, Apr. 13, 1948; d. Donald Hugh and Mary I. (Hansen) Miller; m. Kenneth Andrew Nielsen, Aug. 22, 1970; children: Annette Marie, Kirsten Viola. BS in Home Econs., Iowa State U., 1970, MS in Food Sci., 1972. Rsch. asst. Iowa State U., Ames, 1970-72, rsch. assoc., 1972-74, instr., 1975-76; city councilwoman City of Charleston, W.Va., 1988—; asst. dir. continuing edn. and cmty. svc. W.Va. State Cmty. and Tech. Coll., 1998—. Leader Girl Scouts U.S.A., 1978-96; chair environ. and recycling com. of Charleston, 1991—, chair realignment com. of Charleston, 1992-94, mem. planning com., 1988—, fin. com., 1995—, storm water com., 1997-99, parks and recreation com., 1988-95; classroom vol. Kanawha County Schs., Charleston, 1978-90; mem., officer Forest Hills Comm. Assn., Charleston, 1983-87. Contbr. articles to profl. publs. Mem. Nat. Inst. for Chem. Studies (bd. dirs. 1994—), Sigma Xi, Iota Sigma Pi, Omicron Nu. Republican. Avocations: hiking, camping, reading, sewing, cooking. E-mail: nielsenl@mail.wvsc.edu.

NIELSEN, LYNN CAROL, lawyer, educational consultant; b. Perth Amboy, N.J., Jan. 11, 1950; d. Hans and Esther (Pucker) N.; m. Russell F. Baldwin, Nov. 22, 1980; 1 child, Blake Nielsen Baldwin. BS, Millersville U., 1972; MA, NYU, 1979; JD, Rutgers U., 1984. Bar: N.J. 1984; cert. tchr. handicapped, reading specialist, learning disability tchr. cons., elem. edn. supr. Instr. Woodbridge (N.J.) Twp. Bd. Edn., 1972-83; legal intern appellate sect. divsn. criminal justice Atty. Gen. State N.J., Trenton, 1983, dep. atty. gen. divsn. civil law, 1985; assoc. Kantor & Kusic, Keyport, N.J., 1984-86, Kantor & Linderoth, Keyport, 1986-92. Officer Fords (N.J.) Sch. # 14 PTO, 1974-75; elder First Presbyn. Ch. Avenel, N.J., 1985-88, Flemington (N.J.) Presbyn. Ch., 1997-99; bd. dirs. New Beginnings Nursery Sch., Woodbridge, 1989-90, Flemington Presbyn. Nursery Sch., 1991-93; elder Flemington Presbyn. Ch., 1997-99; bd. mem. Woodside Farms Homeowners Assn., 1996-99. Mem. ABA, N.J. Bar Assn., Monmouth County Bar Assn., Hunterdon County Bar Assn. Avocations: reading, skiing, sailing. Home and Office: 3 Buchannan Way Flemington NJ 08822-3205

NIELSEN, NIELS CHRISTIAN, JR. theology educator; b. Long Beach, Calif., June 2, 1921; s. Niels Hansen and Frances (Nofziger) N.; m. Erika Kreuth, May 10, 1958; children— Camilla Regina, Niels Albrecht. BA, George Pepperdine Coll., L.A., 1942; BD, Yale U., 1946, PhD, 1951. Ordained to ministry Meth. Ch., 1946. Pastor Woodbury (Conn.) Meth. Ch., 1944-46; instr. religion Yale U., New Haven, 1948-51; faculty Rice U., Houston, 1951—, J. Newton Rayzor prof. religious studies., prof. emeritus, 1991—; Amax presdl. prof. humanities Colo. Sch. Mines, Golden, 1982-83. Author: Philosophy and Religion in Contemporary Japan, 1957, Geistige Landerkunde USA, 1960, A Layman Looks at World Religions, 1962, God in Education, 1966, Solzhenitsyn's Religion, 1975, The Religion of Jimmy Carter, 1977, The Crisis of Human Rights, 1978, Religions of the World, 1982, Revolutions in Eastern Europe: The Religious Roots, 1991, Fundamentalism, Mythos and World Religions, 1993; editor: Religion After Communism in Russia, 1994; contbr. articles to profl. jours. Mem. Am. Acad. Religion, Am. Philos. Soc., Am. Soc. Study Religion (sec. 1977-89), Soc. European Culture, Soc. for Values in Higher Edn. Democrat. Home: 2424 Swift Blvd Houston TX 77030-1806 E-mail: niels@ruf.rice.edu.

NIELSEN, PAMELA JEANNE, artist, writer; b. Austin, Tex., Mar. 15, 1953; d. Robert Allen and Marjorie Lenore (Peterson) Newstrom. Student, U. Md., Heidelberg, Germany, 1976-77, U. Tex., El Paso, 1979-80, Otis Parsons Sch. Design, L.A., 1985-86. Pvt. tchr. art, Long Beach, Calif., 1988—. One-woman show Long Beach Cmty. Players Gallery, 1991, Gaga's, Long Beach, 1991, Omellete Inn, 1998; exhibited in group shows Long Beach Arts, 1992, 98, Long Beach City Coll., 1993, Lance Green Arts, Long Beach, 2000; rec. artist Disclosure-Voices of Women, New Alliance Records, 1992; writer, performer Royal Theater, Queen Mary, Long Beach, 1993; contbr. poetry to various publs. Juvenile counselor Los Padrinos Prison, Downey, Calif., 1989; spkr. high schs., Long Beach, 1993—; mem. arts and cultural edn. subcom. City of Long Beach, 1994; asst. to gen. dir. Long Beach Opera, 1998—. Scholar and grantee Otis Parsons Sch. Design, 1985-86. Mem. Long Beach Arts, Sierra Club. Avocations: photography, reading, animals and nature, psychology, art therapy. Home: # 208 4045 E 3d St Long Beach CA 90814

NIELSEN, PAUL DOUGLAS, Air Force officer, engineering manager; b. New Orleans, Apr. 18, 1951; s. Jack Alton and Shirley Mae (Gillette) N.; m. Dorothy Webb Spragins, May 3, 1975; children: Eric Douglas, Kristin Echols, Steven Spragins. BS, USAF Acad., 1972; MS, U. Calif., Davis, 1973, PhD, 1981; MBA, U. N.Mex., 1977; postgrad., Nat. War Coll., 1988-89. Mil. asst., col. Office of Asst. Sec. Def., Washington, 1989-92; comdr. Rome Lab., Griffiss AFB, N.Y., 1992-95; command dir. Cheyenne Mountain Ops. Ctr., Cheyenne Mountain Air Sta, Colo., 1995-96, chief ops., 1996-97; brig. gen., dir. plans N.Am. Aerospace Def. Command, Peterson AFB, Colo., 1997-99; vice comdr. Aero. Systems Ctr., Wright-Patterson AFB, Ohio, 1999-2000; maj. gen. Air Force Rsch. Lab., 2000—. Fellow Hertz Found., Livermore, Calif., 1972-73, 78-81. Fellow AIAA (assoc., Hap Arnold award 2002), Armed Forces Comm. and Electronics Assn., Air Force Assn. Home: 516 Metzger Dr Dayton OH 45433-1133 Office: AFRL/CC 1864 4th St Ste 1 Wright Patterson AFB OH 45433-7130 E-mail: paul.nielsen@wpafb.af.mil.

NIELSEN, PHILIP EDWARD, physicist, research manager; b. Chgo., July 18, 1944; s. John Edward and Doris Anne (Roessler) N.; m. Mary Jane Hill, Aug. 21, 1971; children: Aaron P., June E., David C. BS in Physics, Ill. Inst. Tech., 1966; MS in Physics, Case Western Reserve U., 1968, PhD, 1970. Commd. 2d lt. USAF, 1970, advanced through ranks to col., 1988; ret., 1996; chief, interaction physics group AF Weapons Lab., Kirtland AFB, N.Mex., 1970-74; assoc. prof. physics AF Inst. Tech., Wright-Patterson AFB, Ohio, 1974-79; dep. dir. Directorate of Aerospace Studies, Kirtland AFB, 1980-84; dep. chief, missile divsn. AF Studies and Analyses, Pentagon, Washington, 1984-86, chief, force analyses divsn., 1986-87; dir. tech. Fgn. Tech. Divsn., Wright-Patterson AFB, 1988-92; chief, tech. requirements HQ AF Materiel Command, 1992-96; dir. tech. ctr. MacAulay-Brown, Inc., Dayton, Ohio, 1996—. Author: Effects of Directed Energy Weapons, 2000. Pres. Shadowbrook Homeowners Assn., Mt. Vernon, Va., 1986-87. Recipient USAF R & D award, 1975, Supr. Rsch. award Air Command and Staff Coll., Montgomery, Ala., 1980, Disting. Govt. Svc. award Albuquerque-Santa Fe Fed. Exec. Bd., 1983, Devel. Planning cert. of merit AF Systems Command, Washington, 1983. Mem. AAAS, Am. Phys. Soc., Inst. Ops. Rsch. and Mgmt. Sci., Mil. Ops. Rsch. Soc. Achievements include co-discovery (with P.L. Taylor) of an effect in the low-temperature thermoelectric power of metals and alloys now known as the "Nielsen-Taylor" or "N-T" effect; resolution of many puzzling results in the laser-induced breakdown thresholds of clean and aerosol-laden atmospheres; analysis of solid response to laser radiation which provided insights needed to extrapolate small scale experiments to large scale applications. Home: 9138 Payne Farm Ln Dayton OH 45458-9388 Office: MacAulay-Brown Inc 4021 Executive Dr Dayton OH 45430-1062 E-mail: phil.nielsen@macb.com.

NIELSEN-JONES, IAN RICHARD, lottery and gaming executive, financial consultant; b. Winchester, England, Jan. 24, 1950; arrived in Can., 1950; came to U.S., 1995; s. Richard and Jean-Marie (Edwards) Nielsen-J.; m. Linda Ann George, June 10, 1972; children: Christopher James, Alison Leigh, Eric Philip. BA in Econs., Loyola Coll., 1971; MA in Econs., McMaster U., 1972. From investigator to dep. dir. investigation & rsch. Competition Bur., Ottawa, Ontario, Canada, 1972-89; pres. Ont. Lottery Corp., Toronto, Sault Ste. Marie, Can., 1989-93; mng. dir. nat. lottery Rank Orgn. Plc, London, 1993-94; pres. gaming and recreation Rank Canada Ltd., Toronto, 1994-95; pres., chief operating officer CUE Network Corp., Irvine, Calif., 1995-97; pres., CEO Online Internat. Corp., Smithtown, N.Y., 1997-99, Gaming Mgmt. Corp., Del., 1999-2000, Entertainment Mgmt. Group Ltd., British Virgin Islands, 2001—. Bd. dirs. Lotto4U.com, Calif., Computer Radio Network, Ltd., Toronto, LotCo Plc, London, Gamex Corp., Nev., Gaming Mgmt. Corp., Del. Hon. bd. dirs. Bushplane Mus., Sault Ste. Marie, Ont.; bd. dirs. Econ. Devel. Corp., Sault Ste. Marie, 1992-93, United Way, 1990-93, Plummer Hosp., 1991-93, Algoma Univ. Coll., 1991-93. Named newsmaker of yr. Gaming and Wagering Mag., 1992. Avocations: writing, music, running, coin collecting, traveling. Home: 1100 Queens Ave Unit 15 Oakville ON Canada L6H 2B5 E-mail: iannielsenjones@sympatico.ca.

NIELSON, ALYCE MAE, poet; b. Saugerties, N.Y., Feb. 27, 1943; d. George John Wodischeck and Martha Elizabeth Casler; m. David Bruce Nielson, Oct. 5, 1963; children: Kenneth David, Nancy Lynn Nielson Nowicki. AS in Food, SUNY, Cobleskill, N.Y., 1963. Sch. lunch mgr. Bklyn. Pub. Sch. #61, 1963-64; clk. stock and bond dividend dept. First Nat. City Bank, N.Y.C., 1966-79; lectr., trainee, group leader, ctr. mgr. Weight Watchers, N.Y.C., Bklyn., S.I., 1979-97. Contbr. poetry to anthologies. Vol. Warm up Am., Kingston, N.Y., 1999-2002. Named to Internat. Poetry Hall of Fame, 1996; recipient numerous Editors Choice awards, 1995-99. Mem. Internat. Soc. of Poets. Avocations: Tae Kwon Do (2d degree black belt), Tai Chi, music, needlework, cooking.

NIEMANN, JODY MARIE, occupational therapist; b. Dell Rapids, S.D., Dec. 21, 1969; d. Robert Wayne and Roxanne Marie (Unger) Ellis; m. Tracy Joe Niemann, Aug. 24, 1996. BS, S.D. State U., 1992; MS in Occupl. Therapy, U. S.D., 1994. Registered Nat. Bd. Cert. in Occupl. Therapy, lic. occupl. therapist S.D. Staff therapist Jenkins Living Ctr., Watertown, S.D., 2000—. Supr level II occupl. therapy students U. S.D., Vermillion, 1996—2000; interim instr. occupl. therapy asst. program Lake Area Tech. Inst., 2000. Mem.: S.D. Occupl. Therapy Assn. (chmn. fundraising com. 1996—97, chmn. strategic planning com. 1998—2000, pres. 1998—2000, chmn. reimbursement com. 2000—02), Am. Occupl. Therapy Assn. Roman Catholic. Avocation: Avocations: baking jogging, pets. Address: 905 N Maple Watertown SD 57201-3943 E-mail: jody@dakota.net.

NIEMANN, NICHOLAS KENT, lawyer; b. Quincy, Ill., May 2, 1956; s. Ferd E. and Rita M. (Jochem) N.; m. Ann Marie Forbes, June 14, 1980; children: Katie, Becky, Christine, David, Lisa, Trish. BSBA summa cum laude, Creighton U., 1978, JD magna cum laude, 1981. Bar: Nebr. 1981, U.S. Dist. Ct. Nebr. 1981, U.S. Ct. Appeals (8th cir) 1981, U.S Tax Ct. 1981, U.S. Claims Ct. 1985; CPA, Nebr. Assoc. McGill, Koley, Parsonage & Lanphier, P.C., Omaha, 1981-83, McGrath, North, Mullin & Kratz, P.C., Omaha, 1983-85, ptnr., 1985—. Mem. Nebr. tax rsch. coun., Nebr. tax forum; adj. faculty Creighton Law Sch., Creighton U., 1993-98. Mem. AICPA (taxation sect. 1984—), Nebr. Bar Assn., Omaha Bar Assn., (pub. svc. com. 1983-84, Nebr. Soc. CPAs (taxation com. 1983-90, vice chmn. 1987-88, chmn. 1988-89, small bus. com. 1989-92, vice chmn. 1989-90, chmn. 1990-91)), Omaha C. of C. (pres. club. 1986-90, exec. dialogue 1986-93, taxation com. 1988—), Nebr. Tax Forum, Nebr. C. of C. and Industry (taxation coun. 1989—), Kiwanis (membership com. Omaha club 1986), Optimists (bd. dirs. 1987-89), Alpha Sigma Nu (exec. com. 1985—, sec. 1986-87, treas. 1990, pres. 1992), Beta Gamma Sigma. Roman Catholic. Avocations: golf, tennis, riding horses, travel, baseball. Home: 1537 N 131st Ave Omaha NE 68154-3619 Office: McGrath North Mullin & Kratz 1 Central Park Plz Ste 1400 Omaha NE 68102-1638

NIEMANN, YOLANDA FLORES, humanities educator; b. Chgo., Jan. 28, 1954; d. Candor Tovar and Eva Flores Benavidez; m. Barry Alan Niemann, July 24, 1976; children: Russell Flores, Mychaelanne Flores. MEd in Counseling, U. Houston, 1989, MA in Psychology, 1991, PhD in Psychology, 1992. Asst. prof. U. Houston, 1992-96; asst. prof. ethinic studies and psychology Wash. State U., Pullman, 1996-2000, assoc. prof., 2000—, asst. to provost, 2000—, dir. Latina/o Outreach, 2001—. Mem. adv. com. Wash. State Divsn. Alcohol and Substance Abuse. Contbr. articles to profl. publs. Grantee NSF, 1990, Nat. Inst. Drug Abuse, 1998, Wash. State U. Alcohol and Drug Abuse Ctr., 1998. Mem. APA, Nat. Assn. Chicana and Chicano Studies. Avocations: golf, mystery novels. Office: Wash State U Dept CAC 2710 Univ Dr Richland WA 99352-1671

NIEMELÄ, MIKA RISTO, neurosurgeon; b. Oulu, Finland, Jan. 23, 1964; s. Eino and Toini (Taskinen) Niemelä. MD, Helsinki U., 1989, PhD, 2000. Bd. cert. neurosurgeon. Resident dept. of neurosurgery Helsinki U. Hosp., 1997, cons. in neurosurgery, 1997—; asst. prof. neurosurgery Helsinki U., 2000—; vis. prof. dept. neurosurgery Brigham and Women's Hosp., Harvard Med. Sch., Boston, 2001—. Vis. prof. Harvard Med. Sch., Boston, 2001—02. Contbr. articles to profl. jours. 2d lt. Finnish Army, 1992—93. Mem.: Scandinavian Neurosurg. Soc. (bd. dirs. 2001—), Finnish Neurosurg. Soc., Finnish Med. Assn., Am. Assn. Neurol. Surgeons (assoc.). Achievements include research in in hemangioblastomas of CNS and Retina; impact of von Hippel-Landau disease, gliomas, subarachnoid hemorrhage. Avocations: golf, skiing, fly fishing, windsurfing. Office: Dept Neurosurg Helsinki U Topeliuksenkatu 5 00260 Helsinki Finland Fax: 358-9-47187560. E-mail: mika.niemela@hus.fi.

NIEMETH, CHARLES FREDERICK, lawyer; b. Lorain, Ohio, Nov. 25, 1939; s. Charles Ambrose and Christine Cameron (Mollison) N.; m. Anne Marie Meckes, Oct. 12, 1968. BA, Harvard U., 1962; JD, U. Mich., 1965. Bar: Calif. 1966, N.Y. 1984. Assoc. O'Melveny & Myers, Los Angeles, 1965-72, ptnr., 1973—. Mem. leadership com. Consol. Corp. Fund of Lincoln Ctr. Mem. nat. com. Mich. Law Sch. Fund; trustee Challengers Boys and Girls Club, 1968-83; mem. bus. adv. coun. UCLA, 1979-83; mem. exec. com. Internat. Student Ctr., 1979-83; bd. dirs. Olympic Tower Condominium, 1986-92; bd. visitors Mich. Law Sch., mem. Tri-Bar Opinion Com. Mem. Riviera Tennis Club, Regency Club, N.Y. Athletic Club, Field Club (Greenwich, Conn.), Bel-Air Bay Club. Democrat. Roman Catholic. Home: 10660 Bellagio Rd Los Angeles CA 90077-3713 also: 70 Oneida Dr Greenwich CT 06830-7131 Office: O'Melveny & Myers 1999 Avenue Of The Stars Los Angeles CA 90067-6035 also: 153 E 53rd St Fl 54 New York NY 10022-4611 E-mail: cniemeth@omm.com.

NIEMEYER, ANTONIO BILISOLY, JR. school system administrator; b. Norfolk, Va., Apr. 13, 1928; s. Antonio Bilisoly Niemeyer and Lutie Stuart Spotts; m. Alice Virginia Berry, Nov. 20, 1965; children: William Frederic, Frank Berry, John Stuart. BS, Va. Mil. Inst., 1949; MEd, U. Va., 1955; cert. advanced study, Old Dominion U., 1973. Asst. prin. Portsmouth (Va.) Schs., 1966-67, supr. sci., 1967-77, prin. Churchland Jr., 1977-78, prin. Manor H.S., 1978-80, 86-88, dir. secondary edn., 1980-86, dir. personnel, 1988-91. Dir. Va. Jr. Acad. Sci., 1979-81. Cons. Science Far and Near, Tchrs. edit., 1973. Pres.

Tidewater Heart Assn., 1968. Recipient Disting. Svc. award Jr. C. of C., 1957; named Sci. Educator of Yr., Tidewater Sci. Congress, 1975; fellow Va. Acad. Sci. Mem. SAR. Episcopalian. Avocation: historical studies. Home: 4324 Greendell Rd Chesapeake VA 23321-5504 E-mail: niemeyer@gateway.net.

NIEMEYER, ERIN JANICE, insurance sales representative, journalist, editor; b. Torrance, Calif., July 5, 1974; d. Robert Frederick and Patricia Ann Niemeyer. BA magna cum laude, U. Nev., Las Vegas, 1998. Freelance writer-editor, Las Vegas, 1997—; substitute tchr. Clark County Sch. Dist., 1998—; individual ins. sales rep. UNUMProvident, 1998—. Vol. Juvenile Diabetes Found., Las Vegas, 1992-95, Big Bros. and Big Sisters, Las Vegas, 1996-97. Mem. Soc. Profl. Journalists, Phi Kappa Phi, Phi Alpha Delta, Alpha Gamma Delta. Republican. Christian. Avocations: writing, reading nonfiction, exercising, teaching, motivational speaking. Office: UNUMProvident 3960 Howard Hughes Pkwy Ste 430 Las Vegas NV 89109-5980 E-mail: ejniemeyer@unum.com.

NIEMEYER, JANICE MARIE, social worker; b. Kansas City, Mo., July 1, 1933; d. Louis Frederick and Loretta (Halloran) N. BA, U. San Francisco, 1966; MSW, Loyola U., Chgo., 1968. Primary sch. tchr. St. Theresa's Sch., New Orleans, 1953-56; group mother emotionally disturbed students Mt. St. Joseph's Sch., San Francisco, 1956-61; tchr., intermediate coord., spl. edn. tchr. Marillac Sch., Kansas City, 1961-66; designer, implementer sch. social work program Cath. Charities, San Francisco, 1968-70; social work adminstr. Guardian Angel Settlement, St. Louis, 1970-74; dir. infant program, dir. St. Jude Baby Village St. Vincent Infant Home, New Orleans, 1974-79; asst., maternity counselor Marywood Maternity and Adoption Svc., Austin, Tex., 1979-88; dir. social svcs. Marillac Social Ctr., Dallas, 1988—. Mem. Nat. Assn. Social Workers. Roman Catholic. Avocation: crafts. Office: Marillac Social Ctr 2827 Lapsley St Dallas TX 75212-4421 E-mail: janicl@juno.com.

NIEMEYER, PAUL VICTOR, federal judge; b. Princeton, N.J., Apr. 5, 1941; s. Gerhart and Lucie (Lenzer) Niemeyer; m. Susan Kinley, Aug. 24, 1963; children: Jonathan K., Peter E., Christopher J. AB, Kenyon Coll., 1962; student, U. Munich, Federal Republic of Germany, 1962—63; JD, U. Notre Dame, 1966. Bar: Md. 1966, U.S. Dist. Ct. Md. 1967, U.S. Ct. Appeals (4th cir.) 1968, U.S. Supreme Ct. 1970, U.S. Dist. Ct. (so. dist.) Tex. 1977, U.S. Ct. Appeals (5th cir.) 1978, U.S. Ct. Appeals (3d cir.) 1980. Assoc. Piper & Marbury, Balt., 1966—74, ptnr., 1974—88; U.S. dist. judge U.S. Dist. Ct. Md., 1988—90; fed. judge U.S. Ct. Appeals (4th cir.), 1990—. Lectr. advanced bus. law Johns Hopkins U., Balt., 1971—75; lectr. Md. Jud. Conf., Md. Ct. Clks. Assn.; sr. lecturing fellow in appellate advocacy Duke U. Sch. of Law, 1994—; mem. standing com. on rules of practice and procedure cts. appeals, 1973—88; atty. grievance com.-hearing panel, 1978—81; select com.-profl. conduct, 1983—85; adv. com. on Fed. Rules of Civil Procedure, 1993—2000; chmn., 1996—2000. Co-author: Maryland Rules Commentary, 1984, Maryland Rules Commentary supplement, 1988, Maryland Rules Commentary, 2d. edit., 1992; contbr. articles to profl. jours. Recipient Spl. Merit citation, Am. Judicature Soc., 1987. Fellow: Am. Law Inst., Md. Bar Assn. (Disting. Svc. award litigation sect. 1981), Md. Bar Found., Am. Bar Found., Am. Coll. Trial Lawyers; mem.: Lawyers' Round Table, Wednesday Law Club. Republican. Episcopalian. Office: US Cir Ct Md US Courthouse 101 W Lombard St Ste 910 Baltimore MD 21201-2611

NIEMI, BEATRICE NEAL, social services professional; b. Fitchburg, Mass., July 23, 1923; d. Albert G. and Florence E. (Copeland) Neal; m. Walter V. Niemi, Oct. 21, 1944 (div. 1970); children: Karen Smith-Gary, Gail Niemi Shaw. AS, Colby-Sawyer Coll., 1942; BS in Psychology, Northeastern U., 1972; MA in Counseling Psychology, Assumption Coll., 1974. Diplomate in psychotherapy Am. Psychotherapy Assn. Dir. homemaker svcs. Children's Aid and Family Svcs., Inc., Fitchburg, 1965-73; founder, exec. dir. Home Health Aide Svc. of North Cen. Mass., Inc., 1973-85, Ctr. for Well Being, Inc., Fitchburg, 1985—; instr. Touch for Health Found., Pasadena, Calif., 1977—; tchr., 7th degree master The Radiance Technique Assn. Internat., St. Petersburg, Fla., 1986—; Outreach trainer The Monroe Inst., Faber, Va., 1990—. V.p. Mass. Coun. for Homemaker-Home Health Aide Svcs., Inc., 1973-81. Pres. Children's Aid and Family Svcs., Inc., Fitchburg, 1964-65; bd. dirs. United Way of Greater Fitchburg, Inc., 1964-70, Leominster (Mass.) Vis. Nursing Assn, 1972-78; chmn. adv. bd. Salvation Army, Fitchburg, 1970-72; v.p. Fitchburg Coun. of Girl Scouts. Mem. ACA, Am. Psychotherapy Assn. (diplomate), Assn. Comprehensive Energy Psychology, Am. Mental Health Counselors Assn., Am. Holistic Health Assn., Am. Holistic Med. Found., Mass. Assn. Cmty. Health Agys. (bd. dirs. 1970-83), Mass. Mental Health Counselors Assn., Assn. for Transpersonal Psychology, Nat. Guild Hypnotists, N.E. Holistic Counselors Assn., Touch For Health Kinesiology Assn., others. Avocations: Yoga, meditation, travel. Office: Ctr for Well Being Inc 70 Bond St Fitchburg MA 01420-2251

NIEMI, JANICE, retired lawyer, former state legislator; b. Flint, Mich., Sept. 18, 1928; d. Richard Jesse and Norma (Bell) Bailey; m. Preston Niemi, Feb. 4, 1953 (div. 1987); children: Ries, Patricia. BA, U. Wash., 1950, LLB, 1967; postgrad., U. Mich., 1950-52; cert., Hague Acad. Internat. Law, The Netherlands, 1954. Bar: Wash. 1968. Assoc. firm Powell, Livengood, Dunlap & Silverdale, Kirkland, Wash., 1968; staff atty. Legal Svc. Ctr., Seattle, 1968-70; judge Seattle Dist. Ct., 1971-72, King County Superior Ct., Seattle, 1973-78; acting gen. counsel, dep. gen. counsel SBA, Washington, 1979-81; mem. Wash. State Ho. of Reps., Olympia, 1983-87, chmn. com. on state govt., 1984; mem. Wash. State Senate, 1987-95; sole practice Seattle, 1981-94; superior ct. judge King County, 1995-2000; chief criminal judge, 1997-2000; ret., 2000; mem. Wash. State Gambling Commn., 2002—. Mem. White House Fellows Regional Selection Panel, Seattle, 1974-77, chmn., 1976, 77; incorporator Sound Savs. & Loan, Seattle, 1975; bd. dirs. Artists Trust. Bd. visitors dept. psychology U. Wash., Seattle, 1983—87, bd. visitors dept. sociology, 1988—98; mem. adv. bd. Tacoma Art Mus., 1987—; mem. Wash. State Gender and Justice Commn., 1987—89; Bd. dirs. Allied Arts, Seattle, 1971—78, Ctr. Contemporary Art, Seattle, 1981—83, Women's Network, Seattle, 1981—84, Pub. Defender Assn., Seattle, 1982—84, Artist's Trust, 2002—. Named Woman of Yr. in Law, Past Pres.'s Assn., Seattle, 1971, Woman of Yr., Matrix Table, Seattle, 1973, Capitol Hill Bus. and Profl. Women, 1975. Mem. Wash. State Bar Assn., Wash. Women Lawyers. Democrat. Home: PO Box 20516 Seattle WA 98102-1516

NIEMI, RICHARD GENE, political science educator; b. Green Bay, Wis., Jan. 10, 1941; s. Eugene H. and Dorothy M. (Stevens) N.; m. Shirley A. Gill, Aug. 4, 1962; children: Nancy, Patricia, Jennifer, Julie. BA, Lawrence Coll., 1962; PhD, U. Mich., 1967. Asst. prof. polit. sci. U. Rochester, N.Y., 1967-71, assoc. prof., 1971-75, prof., 1975—, disting. grad. tchg. prof., 1983-86, chmn. dept. polit. sci., 1979-83, assoc. dean, 1986-89, sr. assoc. dean, 1989-91, Watson prof., 1999—. Vis. prof. U. Lund, Sweden, 1974, 81, U. Iowa, 1985; vis. rschr. Kobe U., Japan, 1991. Co-author (with M. Kent Jennings): (poliical science book) The Political Character of Adolescence, 1974; author: Generations and Politics, 1981, How Generations Perceive Each Other, 1974; co-author (with others): Minority Representation and the Quest for Voting Equality, 1992; co-author: (with Jane Junn) (Education Book) Civic Education: What Makes Students Learn, 1998; co-author: (with others) (Political Science Book) Term Limits in the States, 1999; co-editor (with Harold Stanley): (Polit. Sci. Book) Vital Statistics on American Politics, 1988, 8th edit.; co-editor: (with Herbert Weisberg) (Politic. Sci. Book) Controversies in Voting Behavior, 2001; co-editor: (Polit. Sci. Book) Comparing Democracies, 1996; co-author: Trends in Public Opinion; co-editor: Comparing Democracies, 2002. Fellow, Guggenheim Found., 1983—84, Ctr. for Advanced Study in Behavioral Sci., 1989; grantee, NIMH, 1969—70, Ford Found., 1972—73, NSF, 1974—77, 1980—86, 1994—, Am. Ednl. Rsch. Assn., 1997—98, U.S. Dept. Edn., 1997—99, 2001—02. Mem. Am. Polit. Sci. Assn., Phi Beta Kappa. Lutheran. Home: 45 Boniface Dr Rochester NY 14620-3333 Office: U Rochester Dept Polit Sci Rochester NY 14627-0146 E-mail: niemi@rochester.edu.

NIEMIEC, DAVID WALLACE, investment managment executive; b. Midland, Mich., Dec. 17, 1949; s. George G. and Eleanor (Yack) N.; m. Melanie Taveau Mason, Oct. 4, 1975; children: Elizabeth Street, Margaret Johnson AB, Harvard U., 1972, MBA, 1974. Assoc. Dillon, Read & Co., Inc., N.Y.C., 1974-78, v.p., 1979-81, sr. v.p., chief adminstrv. officer, 1982-83, mng. dir., chief adminstrv. officer, 1984-97, vice chmn., 1991-97; mng. dir. Saratoga Ptnrs., 1998—2001, adv., 2001—. Bd. dirs. Emeritus Corp., Seattle. Trustee Nightingale-Bamford Sch., N.Y.C., 1993—; bd. govs. The Mannes Coll. of Music, N.Y.C., 1996—. Mem. Union Club N.Y.C. Republican. Unitarian Universalist. Office: Saratoga Ptnrs 535 Madison Ave New York NY 10022-4212

NIEMIEC, EDWARD WALTER, professional association executive; b. Detroit, Nov. 1, 1936; s. Walter A. and Mary N.; m. Nancy M. Bennett, Aug. 25, 1962; children: Lisa, Julie, Brenda. BS, U. Detroit, 1959, MBA, 1961. With Paine Webber Jackson & Curtis, N.Y.C., 1959-80, exec. v.p., dir. adminstrv. div., to 1980; v.p., bd. dirs. Moseley, Hallgarten, Estabrook, Weeden, Inc., 1980-82; also bd. dirs. Moseley, Hallgarten, Estabrook & Weeden Holding Corp.; pres., chief exec. officer, dir., mem. exec. com. Securities Settlement Corp. (subs. The Travelers 1982), N.Y.C., 1980-87; pres., dir. Inc Trading Co. subs. Instinet Corp., 1988-89; chief oper. officer Instinet Corp. subs. Reuters Holdings Plc., 1988-89; group v.p. AICPA, N.Y.C., 1989—2001. Served with U.S. Army. Roman Catholic. Office: AICPA Harborside Fin Ctr 201 Plaza Three Jersey City NJ 07311-3881

NIENHUIS, ARTHUR WESLEY, physician, researcher; b. Hudsonville, Mich., Aug. 9, 1941; s. Willard M. and Grace (Prince) Nienhuis; children: Carol Elizabeth, cragi Wesley, Kevin Robert, Heather Grae, Carol Elizabeth, Craig Wesley, Kevin Robert, Heather Grace. Student, Cornell Coll., 1959-61; MD, UCLA, 1963-68. Am. Bd. Internal Medicine, Am. Bd. Hematology. Intern Mass. Gen. Hosp., Boston, 1968-69, asst. resident, 1969-70; clin. assoc. NHLBI, NIH, Bethesda, Md., 1970-72; clin. fellow hematology Children's Hosp., Boston, 1972-73; chief. clin. svc. Molecular Hematology NIH, Bethesda, Md., 1973-77; dept. clin. dir. NHLBI, NIH, 1976-93, chief clin. Hematology Branch, 1976-93; dir. St. Jude Children's Rsch. Hosp., Memphis, 1993—. Editor BLOOD-J Am. Soc. Hematology, Bethesda, Md., 1988-92; chmn. Hematology Bd. Am. Bd. Internal Med., Phila., 1988-92. Editor: Molecular Basis of Blood Diseases, 1986, 93. Mem. Am. Soc. Hematology (pres. 1994), Am. Soc. Clin. Investigation, Assn. Am. Physicians, Nat. Cancer Adv. Bd. Office: St Jude Children's Rsch Hosp 332 N Lauderdale St Memphis TN 38105-2729 E-mail: Arthur.Nienhuis@stjude.org.

NIENOW, BETH MARIE, librarian; b. Rochester, Minn., Jan. 22, 1961; d. Duane Reuben and Elaine Nienow. BA, Hamline U., St. Paul, 1983; MLS, U. Wis., 1984; MA, Mankato (Minn.) State U., 1998. Libr. U. N.D., Grand Forks, 1984-89, U. Tenn., Chattanooga, 1989-91; grad. asst. Mankato State U., 1991-93; libr. Rochester Pub. Libr., 1994—. Lutheran. Home: 2303 Fisher Ct NW Rochester MN 55901-8084 Office: Rochester Pub Libr 101 2d St SE Rochester MN 55904

NIER, HARRY KAUFMAN, lawyer; b. N.Y.C., Aug. 13, 1925; s. Harry K. Sr. and May O. Nier. LLB, U. Colo., 1950. Bar: Miss., Colo., U.S. Ct. Appeals, U.S. Supreme Ct. Pvt. practice, Denver, 1952—. Chmn. Denver-Havana Friendship Sister Cities Project, 1990—. Mem.: Denver Bar Assn., Colo. Bar Assn., Nat. Lawyers Guild. Avocation: mountaineering. Home: 1470 S Quebec Way Apt 81 Denver CO 80231-2657 Office: 1700 Lincoln St Ste 3901 Denver CO 80203-4539

NIERENBERG, NORMAN, urban land economist, retired state official; b. Chgo., May 8, 1919; s. Isadore Isaac and Sadie Sarah (Dorfman) N.; m. Nanette Joyce Fortgang, Feb. 9, 1950; children: Andrew Paul, Claudia Robin. AA, U. Chgo., 1939; AB, Calif. State Coll., L.A., 1952; MA, U. So. Calif., 1956. Lic. real estate broker, Calif.; cert. supr. and coll. instr., Calif. Right-of-way agt. Calif. Dept. Transp., L.A., 1951-61, 85-90, sr. agt. San Francisco, 1988-89; instr. UCLA, 1960-61, 67-75, 81-85; coord. continuing edn. in real estate U. Calif., Berkeley, 1961-64. Coord. econ. benefits study Salton Sea, Calif. Dept. Water Resources, L.A., 1968-69; regional economist L.A. dist. CE, 1970-75, chief economist, 1981-85; regional economist Bd. Engrs. for Rivers and Harbors, Ft. Belvoir, Va., 1975-81; faculty resource person Oakland Project, Ford Found., U. Calif., Berkeley, 1962-64; project reviewer EPA, Washington, 1972-73. Editor: History of 82d Fighter Control Squadron, 1945; assoc. editor Right of Way Nat. Mag., 1952-55. Capt. USAAF, 1942-46, ETO, Lt. Col. USAFR ret. Mem.: NEA, L.A. Coll. Tchrs. Assn., Calif. Tchrs. Assn., Ret. Officers Assn., Omicron Delta Epsilon. Democrat. Jewish. Home: Unit 4 21931 Burbank Blvd Woodland Hills CA 91367-6456 *Personal philosophy: Strive for excellence. Honorable in all endeavors.*

NIERENGARTEN, ROGER JOSEPH, judge; b. St. Cloud, Minn., Nov. 19, 1925; s. Henry Clarence and Rose (Josephine) N.; m. Dolores Rosalind Lehman, Oct. 4, 1954; children: Therese, Catherine, Mary, Carolyn. BA, St. John's U., Collegeville, Minn., 1948; JD, Marquette U., 1951. Bar: Minn. 1951, U.S. Dist. Ct. Minn. 1951, U.S. Claims Ct., U.S. Supreme Ct. Adminstv. asst. to mayor City of St. Cloud, 1954-56; pvt. practice St. Cloud, 1956-84; judge Minn. Ct. Appeals, St. Paul, 1984-89; sr. ptnr. Hall, Byers, Hanson, Steil & Weinberger Law Offices, St. Cloud, 1989-92; pvt. practice, 1992—. Stearns County atty., St. Cloud, 1962-66. Spl. asst. atty. gen. State of Minn., 1967-71; chmn. Minn. Cath. Conf. Bd. Edn., St. Paul, 1979-83, Cen. Minn. Coun. for Pub. Radio, 1984-87; trustee Minn. Pub. Radio, St. Paul, 1984-87; mem. Minn. Higher Edn. Coordinating Bd., 1989-91. With U.S. Army, 1943-46, 50-51. Mem. ABA, Minn. Bar Assn., Fed. Bar Assn., Assn. Trial Lawyers Am., Minn. Trial Lawyers Assn. Democrat. Roman Catholic. Avocation: reading, writing. E-mail: nlo.cloudnet.com. Office: Ste 106 600 25th Ave S Saint Cloud MN 56301-4820

NIERMAN, LYNDY ANN, human resources executive; b. Chgo., May 28, 1947; d. Henry J. and Laverne C. (Murray) N. BA, Coll. of Racine, 1969; postgrad., Northeastern Ill. State U., 1971-75. Tchr. Prospect Heights (Ill.) Sch. Dist., 1969-77; sr. account exec. Interviewing Dynamics, Chgo., 1977-80; sr. human resource cons. Costello & Co., Boston, 1980-1985, v.p., mgr. of the Midwest region, 1985-89; pres. Nierman & Assocs. Ltd., Chgo., 1989—. Speaker in field; bd. dirs. Nierman Printing Co. Mem. Employment Mgrs. Assn., Soc. Human Resources Mgmt., High Tech. Forum (bd. dirs. 1985—), Electronics Pers. Assn., Soc. Human Resource Profls. (pres. 1990, bd. dirs. 1987—, regional dir. Execll Net 1991—). also: 120 S Riverside Plz Chicago IL 60606-3913

NIERSTE, JOSEPH PAUL, software engineer; b. Marion, Ind., Feb. 20, 1952; s. Louis Lemuel and Mary Catherine (Dragstrem) N.; m. Deborah Mae Goble, Sept. 20, 1986. BA Applied Piano, Bob Jones U., 1975; MM in Musical Performance, Ball State U., 1977, MS in Computer Sci., 1984. Instr. Marion Coll., 1983-84, Ball State U., Muncie, Ind., 1983-84; software engr. Tokheim Corp., Ft. Wayne, 1984, Delco Electronics, Kokomo, 1984-98, Delphi Delco Electronics Sys., Kokomo, 1998—. Mem. Pi Kappa Lambda. Republican. Baptist. Avocations: sports, music, computers. Home: 3508 Melody Ln W Kokomo IN 46902-7514 Office: Delphi Delco Electronics Systems CT-40-C PO Box 9005 Kokomo IN 46904-9005 E-mail: c2xjpn@eng.delcoelect.com.

NIESEN, JAMES LOUIS, theater director; b. St. Louis, Feb. 15, 1946; s. James Louis and Emily Elise (Brennecke) N. BFA, Ill. Wesleyan U., 1968; MFA, Ohio U., 1974. Actor Stage South, Columbia, S.C., 1974-75, Long Wharf Theatre, New Haven, 1977-78, Geva Theater, Rochester, N.Y., 1978-79; freelance dir., 1980-83; stage mgr. Roundabout Theater, N.Y., 1982-83; artistic dir. Irondale Ensemble Project, 1983—. Panelist N.Y. Found. on the Arts, N.Y., 1988-89. Author: (book) Game Guide, 1988; contbr. articles to profl. jours.; dir. (play) St. Joan of the Stockyards, 1993, Danton's Death, 1994, You Can't Win, 1994, Andrew Carnegie Presands the Jew of Malta, 1996, The Mother, 1997, Degenerate Art, 1998, The Murals of Rockefeller Center, 1999, The Pope and the Witch, 2000, Brecht on Brecht, 2000, Jungle of Cities, 2001, Peter Pan, 2001. Mem. Actor's Equity Assn. Avocations: folk music, country music, tennis. Home: 419 Pacific St Brooklyn NY 11217-2204 Office: Irondale Ensemble Project PO Box 150604 Brooklyn NY 11215-0604

NIESZ, GEORGE MELVIN, tool and die company executive; b. Norwood, Ohio, Aug. 6, 1926; s. George John and Anita Agnes Lucille (Chialastri) N.; student pub. schs., Norwood and Deer Park; m. Evelyn Catherine Rayburn, Oct. 18, 1946; children— Nancy L., George J., Jr. Profl. baseball player St. Louis Cardinals Orgn., 1944-45; tool and die maker Steelcraft Mfg. Co., Cin., 1946-51; supt., mgr. Abco Tool & Die Co., 1951-70; founder, pres. Niesz Tool & Die Co., Cin., 1970-85; officer, dir. Pvt. Investment Co., 1985—. State dir., v.p. Sycamore-Deer Park Jr. C. of C., 1956-59. Ky. Col. Mem. Am. Soc. Metals, Soc. Mfg. Engring., Cin. C. of C., Anderson Twp. C. of C. Republican. Clubs: Masons (32 deg); Shriners. Patentee portable tool attachment; chess champion. Home: 4171 Winesap Ct Cincinnati OH 45236-1735 Office: DPHS Alumni Assn 8351 Plainfield Rd Cincinnati OH 45236-2445

NIETO, JOHN WESLEY, artist; b. Denver, Aug. 6, 1936; s. Simon and Natalia (Venegas) N.; m. Renay Hagin, Nov. 15, 1974; children: John Arthur, Laura Elizabeth, Anaya, Quint. Student, Pan Am. U., 1955-56, So. Meth. U., 1957-59. Artist: work has been reproduced in numerous publications including Tucson Mag., Austin (Tex.) Mag., Scottsdale Mag., Ariz. Daily Star, Art in the West, 1988, Nat. Geographic, 1990, New Mex. Mag., Horizon Mag., The Art Experience; featured on radio and TV shows including Japan Nat. TV, 1989, ABC TV Network, 1984, Nat. Pub. Radio, Washington, 1982, Voice of Am., 1981. Mem. adv. bd. Wheelwright Mus., Santa Fe, New Mex., 1985-86; trustee Meadow Sch. of Arts So. Meth. U., Dallas, 1993-94, So. Meth. U., 1993-94; vol. lectr. Recipient Gov.'s award, New Mex., 1994.

NIETO, JUAN MANUEL, emergency medicine physician; b. Alpine, Tex., Sept. 24, 1949; s. Edmundo Miguel and Socorro (Herrera) N.; children: Ana Raquel, Cristina Marie. BS, U. Notre Dame, 1970; MD, U. Colo., 1974. Intern L.A. County, U. So. Calif. Med. Ctr., 1974-75; physician Cmty. Health Found., L.A., 1975-77, Emergency Dept. Physicians Med. Group, Marina Del Ray, Calif., 1977-78; resident in emergency medicine Denver Gen.-St. Anthony Hosp. Sys., 1978-80; mem. staff North Colo. Med. Ctr., Greeley, 1980-83; emergency physician, med. dir. emergency dept. Brackenridge Hosp., Austin, Tex., 1984-85; practice medicine, 1983—. Emergency physician Emergency Physicians Affiliates, 1986-89; asst. prof. U. Tex. Health Sci. Ctr., San Antonio, 1994—; mem. planning com. Starflight Helicopter Air Transport, 1985; instr. advanced cardiac life support, 1977; bd. dirs. Nat. Chicano Health Orgn., 1971-74; advisor East Los Angeles Hypertension Screening Program, 1978; med. advisor Weld County Ambulance Service, 1980-83; med. dir. Air Life, 1980-83; med. dir. Alamo Heights Emergency Med. Svc., 1988-90, med. dir. AMR Ambulance, 1991-98. Del. Colo. Med. Soc., 1983. Fellow: NHMA, Am. Acad. Emergency Medicine, Am. Coll. Emergency Physicians, NYU Wagner Sch. (leadership fellow 2001); mem.: APHA, Physicians for a Nat. Healthcare Program, Nat. Hispanic Med. Assn., Travis County Med. Soc., Tex. Med. Assn., Nat. Hispanic Med. Assn. (leadership fellow 2001—), Amnesty Internat.

NIEUWSMA, MILTON JOHN, writer, journalist; b. Sioux Falls, S.D., Sept. 5, 1941; s. John and Jean (Potter) N.; BA, Hope Coll., Holland, Mich., 1963; postgrad. Wayne State U., 1963-65; MA, U. Ill., 1978; m. Marilee Gordon, Feb. 1, 1964; children: Jonathan, Gregory, Elizabeth. Pres. Trans Am. Syndicate, Inc., Chgo., 1988-97; vis. prof. Rutgers U., New Brunswick, N.J., 1990-95, St. Xavier U., Chgo., 1996-97. Author: Kinderlager, 1998; contbg. editor Chgo. Tribune, L.A. Times, others. Home: 2421 Central-Idlewood Beach Holland MI 49424-2277

NIEVES, ALVARO LEZCANO, sociology educator; b. N.Y.C., Mar. 7, 1944; s. Alvaro and Julia N.; m. Leslie Anne Dugdale, Oct. 3, 1964; children: Wanda, Julia, Waleska, Tyron, Antonio, Ramon. PhD, Va. Polytech. Inst. & State U., 1980. Sr. rsch. scientist Battelle Pacific Northwest Labs., Richland, Wash., 1978-83; prof. sociology Wheaton (Ill.) Coll., 1983—. Cons. Argonne (Ill.) Nat. Lab., 1990—. Author: Ethnic Minorities in Evangelical Christian College, 1990. Lay leadership roles United Meth. Ch., Aurora, Ill., 1999-2001. With U.S. Army, 1964-67. NIMH fellow, 1969-71. Mem. Am. Sociol. Assn. Office: Wheaton Coll Dept Sociology 501 E College Ave Wheaton IL 60187 E-mail: alvaro.l.nieves@wheaton.edu.

NIEVES, ANGEL L., JR. humanities educator; b. San Juan, Puerto Rico, Aug. 28, 1947; s. Angel L. Nieves Sr., Justina Morales; life ptnr. Patricia A. Eaton; children: Julie A., Rebecca F., Meghann E. BS in History, Fitchburg State Coll., 1994. ESL tchr. Gardner (Mass.) Sch. Sys., 1977—78; Spanish tchr. Fitchburg (Mass.) Sch. Sys., 1978—79; correctional counselor Dept. Corrections, MCI Lancater, 1979—85; logistics analyst Digital Equipment Corp., Maynard, 1985—90; ESL tchr. Lowell (Mass.) Sch. Sys., 1992—94; history tchr. Worcester (Mas.) Pub. Sch. Sys., 1994—. Recreation dir. Town of Clinton, 1976—77, Town of Townsend, Mass., 1980—81. Home: PO Box Sutton MA 01590 Home Fax: 508-865-3689. Personal E-mail: wechonieves@aol.com.

NIEVES, JOESPHINE, federal agency administrator; BBA, CUNY; MS, Columbia U.; PhD, Union Grad. Sch. Assoc. asst. sec. employment and tng. Dept. of Labor, 1994-96; exec. dir. Nat. Assn. Social Workers, 1996-01. Recipient Lifetime Achievement award Nat. P.R. Forum, Disting. Achievement Human Svcs. award Boricua Coll., Martin Luther Jr. medal Freedom; named Acad. Women Achievers YWCA, N.Y.C. Home: 1400 E West Hwy Silver Spring MD 20910-3230 E-mail: josephinenieves@msn.com.

NIEWIAROSKI, TRUDI OSMERS (GERTRUDE NIEWIAROSKI), social studies educator; b. Jersey City, Apr. 30, 1935; d. Albert John and Margaret (Niemeyer) Osmers; m. Donald H. Niewiaroski, June 8, 1957; children: Donald H., Donna, Margaret Anne, Nancy Noel. AB in History and German, Upsala Coll., East Orange, N.J., 1957; MEd, Montgomery County Pub. Schs., Rockville, Md., 1992. Cert. tchr., Md. Tchr. geography Colego Americano, Quito, Ecuador, 1964-66; bd. dirs. Cotopaxi Acad., 1964-65; tchr. speed reading Escuela Lincoln, Buenos Aires, Argentina, 1966-67; substitute thcr. Montgomery County Pub. Schs., Rockville, 1978-83, tchr. social studies, 1984—. Del. Eisenhower People to People Educators' Del. Vietnam, 1993; pres. Fulbright Meml. Fund Program, 1997; resident tchg. fellow Russia-Ukraine Excellence in Tchg. Program, 1997; resident scholar in Korea, The Korea Soc., 1999. Author curricula; contbr. chpts. to books, articles to profl. jours.; lectr. at workshops. Bd. dirs. Cotopaxi Acad., Quito, 1964-65; pres. Citizens Assn., Potomac, Md., 1977-81; leader Girl Scouts U.S., 1975-76; adv. coun. Milken Found; pres. Fulbright Meml. Fund Program Japan Alumni, 1999—, Summer Fellowship Korean Studies Program, 1999, Fulbright fellow for study in South Africa, 2001. Recipient Md. Tchr. of Yr. award State of Md. Edn. Dept., 1993, finalist nat. Tchr. of Yr., 1993, Disting. Alumni award Upsala Coll., 1993, Nat. Educator award Milken Found., 1994; Fulbright fellow, India, 1985, China, 1990, Japan Keizai Koho Ctr. fellow, 1992, Fulbright Meml. Fund Tchr. Program fellow, Japan, 1997, Fulbright fellow, South Africa, 2001; UMBC-U. Mex. Art and Culture scholar, 1995. Mem. AAUW, ASCD, Nat. Coun. Social Studies, Md. Coun. for Social Studies, Asia Soc., Smithsonian Instn., Montgomery County Hist. Soc., Spl. Interest Groups-China, Japan and Korea, Md. Bus. Roundtable for Edn., Nat. Social Studies Suprs. Assn., Kappa Delta Pi. Avocations: cake and cookie decorating, travel. Office: R Montgomery High Sch Rockville MD 20852 E-mail: trudi_niewiaroski@fc.meps.kil.md.us.

NIFFENEGGER, AUDREY ANNE, artist; b. June 13, 1963; BFA, Sch. of the Art Inst. of Chgo., 1985; MFA, Northwestern U., Evanston, Ill., 1991. Asst. prof. Columbia Coll. Chgo. Ctr. for Book and Paper Arts, 1995—. E-mail: aniffenegger@popmail.colum.edu.

NIGG, CLAUDIO RENATO, science educator; b. Samedan, Graubuenden, Switzerland, Mar. 30, 1970; s. Benno and Margareta Nigg; m. Patricia Jordan; 1 child Zoe. PhD, U. R.I., 1999. Asst. prof. rsch. U. R.I., Kingston, 1999—2001; asst. prof. U. Hawaii-Manoa, Honolulu, 2001—. Author rev. articles and book chpts. Recipient Validating the stages of change for phys. activity, Robert Wood Johnson Found., 2002, Dissertation award, APA Divsn. 47 (Sport and Exercise Psychology), 2000. Mem.: Am. Coll. of Sports Medicine, Soc. Behavioral Medicine. Avocations: beach volleyball, skiing, hockey, travel. Office: U Hawaii Dept Pub Health Sci 1960 East-West Rd Honolulu HI 96822 Office Fax: 808-956-6041. Business E-Mail: cnigg@hawaii.edu.

NIGH, JAY JACKSON CASEY, investment analyst; b. Omaha, Jan. 21, 1965; s. Leon Jackson and Norma Jean (Proplesch) N. BS, U. Nebr., Kearney, 1987; MBA, U. Nebr., Omaha, 1991. Chartered fin. analyst; registered rep.; registered gen. prin.; registered options prin.; registered mcpl. prin.; cert. mgmt. acct. Mgmt. trainee, rep. First Investors Corp., Omaha, 1987-88; sr./investment analyst Securities Am., Inc., 1989-95; chief portfolio mgr. Maestro Investment Mgmt., 1994-95; CFO, treas. Calif. Med. Transport, Mountain View, Calif., 1994-97; sr. fin. specialist No. Plains Natural Gas Co., Omaha, 1995—; reg. rep. Securities Am., Inc., 1995-97; pres. Nigh & Assocs.,

1997—. Fin. advisor Omaha Cath. Archdiocese Tax Sheltered Annuity Com., Omaha, 1992-96. Mem. socially responsible investment task force Omaha Cath. Archdiocese, 1993-95. U. Nebr. at Kearney Coop. scholar, 1983-87; Beta Sigma Psi Edn. Found. scholar, 1986. Mem. Nat. Assn. Securities Dealers, Internat. Soc. Fin. Analysts, Assn. for Investment Mgmt. and Rsch., Omaha/Lincoln Soc. Fin. Analysts, Inter Frat. Coun., Inst. Mgmt. Accts., Am. Soc. Appraisers (candidate), Beta Sigma Psi (treas., pres., scholastic chmn., chaplain). Republican. Lutheran. Avocations: powerlifting, hunting, fishing, music. Office: No Plains Natural Gas Co PO Box 3330 Omaha NE 68103-0330

NIGH, ROBERT RUSSELL, JR. lawyer; b. Enid, Okla., Nov. 1, 1959; s. Robert Russell and Helen Louise (Russell) N.; m. Susan Althadene Placek, Oct. 1, 1989. BA, William Jewell Coll., 1982; JD, U. Okla., 1986. Assoc. Jones, Bryant & Nigh, Enid, 1986-89; asst. pub. defender Tulsa County, Office of Pub. Defender, 1989-92; asst. fed. defender Fed. Pub. Defender's Office, Tulsa, 1992-94, Lincoln, Nebr., 1994-96; pvt. practice Tulsa, 1996-2000; atty. Brewster and De Angelis, 2001—. Mem. Nat. Assn. Criminal Def. Lawyers, Okla. Criminal Def. Lawyers Assn. (bd. dirs. 1991-94), Tulsa County Bar Assn. Avocations: hunting, fishing, basketball. Office: 2617 E 21st St Tulsa OK 74114

NIGHTINGALE, CHARLES H. hospital administrator, researcher; b. N.Y.C., June 14, 1939; BS, Fordham U., Bronx, N.Y., 1961; MS, St. John's U., Jamaica, N.Y., 1966; PhD, SUNY, Buffalo, 1970. Prof. rsch. U. Conn., Storrs; v.p. rsch. Hartford (Conn.) Hosp., 2002—. Office: Hartford Hosp 80 Seymour St Hartford CT 06112

NIGHTINGALE, DEBORAH SEIFERT, systems engineer, consultant; b. Dayton, Ohio, Sept. 10, 1949; m. Tom Seifert, 1971; children: Jessica, Danielle, Jordan. BS, U. Dayton, 1970; MS, Ohio State U., 1975, PhD, 1979. Programmer U. Dayton Rsch. Inst., 1968-71; sr. engring. scientist Wright Patterson AFB, 1971-79; project leader Allied Signal Engines, 1979-80; mgr. facility planning, factory modernization, Corp CIM Com., 1980-84, mfg. sys. engr., indsl. engr., ops. support, chmn., 1984-87, sr. project mgr. mktg. svc., dir. strategic planning, 1987-96; cons. Paradise Valley, Ariz., 1996—; prof., focus lead, Lean Enterprise Team & Lean Aerospace Initiative Dept. of Aerospace & Aeronautics, MIT, Cambridge, Mass., 1997—. Contbr. articles to profl. jours. Mem. NAE (4th decade com. 1993—), Inst. Indsl. Engrs. (pres. elect 1994—), Soc. Mfg. Engrs., Computer and Automated Sys. Assn. Home: 43 Canterbury St Andover MA 01810-2850 Office: Dept Aerospace & Aeronautics MIT Rm E10-105a 77 Mass Ave Cambridge MA 02139

NIGHTINGALE, EDMUND JOSEPH, clinical psychologist, educator; b. St. Paul, Jan. 10, 1941; s. Edmund Anthony and Lauretta Alexandria (Horejs) N.; m. Marie Arcara, Apr. 9, 1978 (dec. April 1992); one child: Edmund Bernard. Student, Nazareth Hall Prep. Sem., 1959-61; AB, St. Paul Sem., 1963; AB magna cum laude, Catholic U. of Louvain, Belgium, 1965; MA, S.T.B. cum laude, , 1967; postgrad., U. Minn., 1971; MA, Loyola U., Chgo., 1973; PhD in Clin. Psych., 1975. Lic. clin. psychologist, Ill., Minn., cert. Nat. Registry of Health Svc. Providers in Psychology; diplomate clin. psychology Am. Bd. Profl. Psychology. With Cath. Archdiocese of St. Paul and Mpls., 1967-73; int. in clin. psychology Michael Reese Hosp. and Med. Ctr., Chgo., 1973-74; with W. Side VA Hosp., 1974-75; staff psychologist Student Counseling Ctr., Loyola Univ., 1975; staff psychologist, clin. coord. inpatient unit Drug Dependency Treatment Ctr., 1975—80; chief psychology VA Med. Ctr., Danville, IL, 1980-86, VA Med. Ctr. Mpls., 1986—. Mem. personnel bd. Archdiocese of St. Paul and Mpls., 1968-70; lectr. psychology, Loyola U., Chgo., 1975; asst. professorial lectr. psychology, St. Paul Xavier Coll., Chgo., 1975-78; adj. asst. prof. psychology in psych., Abraham Lincoln Sch. Med., Med. Ctr. U. Ill., Chgo., 1977-82; adj. prof. psychology, Purdue Univ., 1981-87; asst. prof. psych. Med. Sch., U. Minn., 1987—, clin. assoc. prof. psychology Coll. Liberal Arts, 1986-90; adj. asst. prof., 1990—; clin. asst. prof. U. Ill. Sch. Med., Urbana/Champaign, 1982-87; mem. grad. fac. in counseling psychology Ind. State U., Terre Haute, 1983-86. Founding editor: Louvain Studies, 1966; editor: VA Dir. of Psychology Staffing and Svcs., 1982, 83, 84, 85, 87. Bd. dirs. Inst. Postgrad. Studies, Ill. Psychol. Assn. Recipient Outstanding Leadership awd., Assn. VA Chief Psychologists, 1992. Fellow APA (clin. psychology, pub. svc., psychol. hypnosis, sec. treas. pub. svc. 1990-91, coun. reps. 1999—); mem. AAAS, Am. Psychol. Soc., Assn. for Advancement of Psychology, Ill. Psychol. Assn. (clin. psychology and acad. sects., sec. 1982-83, pres.-elect 1983-84, pres. 1984-85), Am. Group Psychotherapy Assn., Am. Soc. Clin. Hypnosis, Minn. Psychol. Assn. (pub. svc.- pres. 1997-99), Eagle Scout, Assn. VA Chief Psychologists (sec., treas. 1987-90, pres.-elect 1990-91, pres. 1991-92, past pres. 1992-93), Minn. Soc. of Clin. Hypnosis (bd. dirs. 1999-2001). Home: 2281 Ocala Ct Mendota Heights MN 55120-1646 Office: VA Med Ctr Minneapolis MN 55417

NIGHTINGALE, ELENA OTTOLENGHI, geneticist, physician, administrator; b. Livorno, Italy, Nov. 1, 1932; arrived in U.S., 1939, naturalized; d. Mario Lazzaro and Elisa Vittoria (Levi) Ottolenghi; m. Suart L. Nightingale, July 1, 1965; children: Elizabeth, Marisa. AB summa cum laude, Barnard Coll., 1954; PhD, Rockefeller U., 1961; MD, NYU, 1964. Asst. prof. Cornell U. Med. Coll., N.Y.C., 1965-70, Johns Hopkins U., Balt., 1970-73; fellow in clin. genetics and pediatrics Georgetown U. Hosp., Washington, 1973-74; sr. staff officer NAS, 1975-79, sr. program officer Inst. Medicine, 1979-82, sr. scholar in residence, 1982-83; spl. advisor to pres. Carnegie Corp. N.Y., N.Y.C., 1983-94, sr. program officer, 1989-94; scholar-in-residence Nat. Acad. Scis., Washington, 1995—. Vis. assoc. prof. Harvard Med. Sch., Boston, 1980—84, vis. lectr., 1984—95; adj. prof. pediatrics Georgetown U. Med. Ctr., 1984—, George Washington U. Med. Ctr., 1994—; mem. recombinant DNA adv. com. NIH, Bethesda, Md., 1979—83. Editor: The Breaking of Bodies and Minds: Torture, Psychiatric Abuses and the Health Professions, 1985, Prenatal Screening, Policies and Values: The Example of Neural Tube Defects , 1987, Promoting the Health of Adolescents: New Directions for the 21st Century, 1993, Adolescent Risk and Vulnerability: Concepts and Measurement, 2001; co-author: Before Birth: Prenatal Screening for Genetic Disease, 1990; contbr. Bd. dirs. Amnesty Internat., U.S.A., Washington, 1989—91, Ctr. for Youth Svcs., Washington, 1980—84, Sci. Svc., Inc., Washington, 1985—96. Fellow: AAAS (chmn. com. on sci. freedom and responsibility 1985—88), Royal Soc. Med., N.Y. Acad. Scis.; mem.: Inst. Medicine of NAS (chmn. com. on health and human rights 1987—90), Genetics Soc. Am., Am. Soc. Human Genetics (social issues com. 1982—85), Am. Soc. Microbiology, Harvey Soc., Sigma Xi, Phi Beta Kappa. Office: Nat Acad Scis 2101 Constitution Ave NW Washington DC 20418-0007

NIGHTINGALE, STUART LESTER, physician, public health officer; b. N.Y.C., Jan. 26, 1938; s. Lester M. Nightingale and Beatrice L. N. (Liebowitz) Helpern; m. Elena Ottolenghi, July 1, 1965; children: Elizabeth S., Marisa O. BA, Yale U., 1959; MD, NYU, 1964. Diplomate Am. Bd. Internal Medicine. Intern in medicine and surgery Montefiore Hosp. and Med. Ctr., Bronx, N.Y., 1964-65, resident in internal medicine, fellow in adolescent medicine, 1965-66, 67-69, asst. attending physician, 1969-70; resident in anatomical pathology NYU Sch. Medicine, 1966-67; med. dir. drug abuse adminstrn. Dept. Health and Mental Hygiene State of Md., Balt., 1971-72; chief treatment and rehab., office of programs, spl. action office for drug abuse prevention Exec. Office of Pres., Washington, 1972-74, chief office treatment and rehab., spl. action office for drug abuse prevention, 1974-75; dir. divsn. resource devel. Nat. Inst. on Drug Abuse, Rockville, Md., 1974-76; asst. to dir. Bur. Drugs, Food and Drug Adminstrn., 1976-79; dep. assoc. commr. for health affairs FDA, 1979-82, acting assoc. commr. for health affairs, 1979-82, assoc. commr. for health affairs, 1982-2000; sr. med. adv. to asst. sec. for planning and evaluation and dir. global health affairs Office of the Sec. Dept. of Health and Human Svcs., Washington, 2000—. Vis. physician Balt. City Hosps., 1970-72; clin. instr. dept. medicine Coll. Medicine SUNY, Bklyn., 1970; asst. physician outpatient dept., instr. dept. medicine Johns Hopkins U. Sch. Medicine, Balt., 1970-72, med. dir. drug abuse ctr., 1970-71, instr. dept. med. care and hosps. Sch. Hygiene and Pub. Health, 1971-74, rsch. program mgr. health svcs. rsch. and devel. ctr., 1970-71; chmn. rsch. involving human subjects com. FDA, 1979-84; liaison mem. Commn. on Fed. Drug Approval Process, U.S. Congress, 1980-81; mem.-at-large U.S. Pharmacopeial Conv., Inc., 1985-95; bd. trustees The Milton Helpern Libr. of Legal Medicine, N.Y.C., 1982-2000; bd. dirs. Nat. Coun. on Patient Info. and Edn., Washington; mem. forum on drug devel. and regulation Inst. Medicine, NAS, Washington, 1986-2000. Contbg. author Jour. AMA, 1985-99, Am. Family Physician, 1986-99. Capt. med. corps USAR, 1966-72; with USPHS. Recipient Disting. Svc. Spl. Action Office for Drug Abuse Prevention award Exec. Office of Pres., 1975, Pub. Health Superior Svc. award, 1983, Disting. Contbn. award Nat. Coun. Patient Info. and Edn., 1987, Achievement award Am. Assn. Physicians for Human Rights, 1990, Presdl. Meritorious Exec. Rank award, 1990, Pub. Health Svc. Spl. Recognition award, 1993, Sec.'s Recognition award Dept. HHS, 1999. Fellow ACP; mem. AMA, APHA, Sr. Execs. Assn., Cosmos Club. Office: Dept Health and Human Svcs 200 Independence Ave SW Washington DC 20201-0004

NIGHTINGALE, TRACY IRENE, lawyer; b. Bloomer, Wis., May 16, 1966; d. Russell L. and Dorothy I. (Bluem) Pederson; m. Brian J. Nightingale, July 16, 1990; children: Austin M., Carson D., Sierra C. BA, U. Wis., Eau Claire, 1988; JD, Hamline U., 1991. Bar: Minn. 1992, U.S. Dist. Minn. 1993, Wis. 1994. Pvt. practice, Mpls., 1991-98; atty. Legal Legacy, Ltd., St. Louis Park, Minn., 1996-98; exec. dir. Nat. Assn. Debt Mgrs., 1997-98; atty. Hurwitz Law Firm, 1998-2000; pvt. practice Nightingale Law Office, Mpls., 2000—. Mediator West Suburban Mediation Ctr., Hopkins, Minn., 1992-2001. Author: Trust and Estate Planner, 1996. Mem. ABA, Minn. Bar Assn., Wis. Bar Assn., Hennepin County Bar Assn. Office: Nightingale Law Office Ste 700 5775 Waysata Blvd St Louis Park MN 55416 E-mail: nightingale-law@justice.com.

NIGHTINGALE, WILLIAM JOSLYN, management consultant; b. Mpls., Sept. 16, 1929; s. William Isaac and Gladys (Joslyn) N.; children: Paul, Sara, William Joslyn, Margaret. BA, Bowdoin Coll., 1951; MBA, Harvard U., 1953. Mktg. mgr. Gen. Mills. Inc., Mpls., 1957-66; sr. assoc. Booz, Allen & Hamilton Inc., N.Y.C., 1966-68; v.p. fin. Hanes Corp., Winston-Salem, N.C., 1969; pres. Bali Co. Inc., N.Y.C., 1970—95; sr. advisor Nightingale & Assocs. Inc., Stamford, Conn., 1975—. Bd. dirs. Ring's End Inc.; trustee Naragansett Tax Free Bond Fund, Churchill Tax Free Bd. Fund. Active numerous charitable orgns.; vestryman St. Luke's Episcopal Ch., 1975-78, sr. warden, 1989-91; mem. Darien Representative Town Meeting, 1971-74. Lt. (j.g.) USNR, 1953-57. Mem. Wee Burn Country Club, Noroton (Conn.) Yacht Club, Harvard Club (N.Y.C.). Republican. Home: 195 Rowayton Ave Norwalk CT 06853-1237 Office: Soundview Plz 1266 E Main St Stamford CT 06902-3546

NIGRO, RUSSELL M. state supreme court justice; b. Mar. 23, 1946; Assoc. justice Pa. Supreme Ct., Phila., 1996—. Office: Pa Supreme Ct 1818 Market St Ste 3730 Philadelphia PA 19103-3639*

NIHART, FRANKLIN BROOKE, museum consultant , editor, writer, marine officer; b. L.A., Mar. 16, 1919; s. Claude Eugene and Vera Howard (Brooke) N.; m. Mary Helen Brosius, Feb. 11, 1945; children: Mary Catherine, Virginia Brooke Nihart. BA, Occidental Coll., 1940. Commd. 2nd lt. USMC, 1940, advanced through grades to col., 1957, dep. dir. Marine Corps. History and Mus., 1973-92. Fellow, past gov., pres. Co. Mil. Historians, 1967-71; founder Marine Corps Hist. Found., 1979. Decorated Navy Cross, Bronze Star with one gold star; named to Order del Mar Oceano; recipient Disting. Svc. award Co. Mil. Historians, 1982, Disting. Svc. award Marine Corps. Hist. Found., 1992. Mem. Am. Assn. Mus., Internat. Coun. Mus., Freedom Mus. (bd. advisors), Va. Mus. Mil. Vehicles (bd. dirs.), Cold War Mus. (mem. bd. advisors, bd. dirs.), Internat. Assn. Mus. Arms and Mil. History (hon. life), Orgn. Mil. Mus. Can. (hon. life), Washington Naval Corrs. Circle, Army and Navy Club, Mil. Order of Carabao (Disting. Svc. award 1987), Ends of the Earth Club, Order of St. Crispins. Republican. Presbyterian. Avocations: history, politics, travel, shooting, writing.

NIHILL, KAREN BAILEY, nursing home executive, nurse clinician; b. Erie, Pa., Mar. 15, 1947; d. William C. and Eleanor (Danielson) Bailey; 1 son, Liam H. RN, Hamot Med. Ctr., Erie, 1968; postgrad., SUNY, Gannon U., U. S.C., U. Pa., 1974—. RN, Pa. Critical care nurse Hamot Med. Ctr., 1968-71, VA Hosp., Phila., 1974-77; dir. nursing Chapel Manor and Nursing Home, 1977—, also Phila. Protestant Home and Elmira Jeffries Nursing Home; critical care nurse coord., supr. Millcreek Community Hosp., Erie, Pa., 1991—. Active Lutheran Ch. Women's Orgn. Served to lt. Nurse Corps, USN, 1971-73. VA grantee, 1974. Mem. ACLS, Am. Assn. Critical Care Nurses, Pa. Nurses Assn. Republican. Home: 5316 Bryant St Erie PA 16509-2404

NIHISER, DENNIS EDWARD, aeronautical engineer; b. Decatur, Ill., June 13, 1954; m. Patricia Mae Rund; children: Pamela, Christopher. AAS in Avionics Instrument Sys., C.C. of Air Force, 1980; BS in Aero/Astronautical Engring., U.of Ill., 1984; MS in Sys. Engring., Air Force Inst.of Tech., 1988; PhD in Mgmt., Hamilton U., 1999. Mgr. strategic missile devel. analysis Ballistic Missile Orgn., Norton AFB, Calif., 1982—89; dir. spl. programs Nat. Test Facility, Schriever AFB, Colo., 1992—93; sys. engr. TRW Strategic Sys. Divsn., Albuquerque, N.Mex., 1993—94; from asst. dir. threat sys. engring. to asst. dep. engring. Ballistic Missile Def. Orgn., Washington, 1999—2001, asst. dep. engring., 2001—. Capt. USAF, 1973—93. Home: 7403 Ni River Landing Fredericksburg VA 22407-2502 Office: Ballistic Missile Defense Organization 7100 Defense Pentagon, FOB#2 Washington DC 20301-7100 Office Fax: 703-695-5836. Personal E-mail: Dennis_Nihiser@msn.com. Business E-Mail: Dennis.Nihiser@bmdo.osd.mil.

NIJENHUIS, ALBERT, mathematician, educator; b. Eindhoven, Netherlands, Nov. 21, 1926; came to U.S., 1952, naturalized, 1959; s. Hendrik and Lijdia (Koornneef) N.; m. Marianne Dannhauser, Aug. 14, 1955; children: Erika, Karin, Sabien, Alaine. Candidaat, U. Amsterdam, Netherlands, 1947, Doctorandus, 1950, Doctor cum laude, 1952. Assoc. Math. Ctr., Amsterdam, Netherlands, 1951-52; asst. Inst. Advanced Study, Princeton, N.J., 1955, mem., 1953-55, 61-62; instr., rsch. assoc. U. Chgo., 1955-56; faculty U. Wash., Seattle, 1956-63, prof., 1961-63, affiliate prof., 1988—; prof. math. U. Pa., Phila., 1963-87, prof. emeritus, 1987—; Fulbright lectr. U. Amsterdam, 1963-64; vis. prof. U. Geneva, Switzerland, 1967-68, Dartmouth Coll., 1977-78. Researcher and author publs. on subjects including differential geometry, deformation theory in algebra, combinatorics, especially tensors, holonomy groups, graded lie algebras, algorithms. Co-author: Combinatorial Algorithms, 1975, 78; editor: Jour. Algorithms, Jour. Differential Geometry Conidin. Postdoctoral fellow Princeton, 1952-53; Fulbright grantee, 1952-53, 63-64; Guggenheim fellow, 1961-62 Mem. Am. Math. Soc., Math. Assn. Am., Netherlands Math. Soc., AAUP, Royal Netherlands Acad. Scis. (corr.) Office: U Wash Dept Math PO Box 354350 Seattle WA 98195-4350 E-mail: nijenhuis@math.washington.edu.

NIJENSOHN, DANIEL EDGARDO, neurosurgeon; b. Mendoza, Argentina, Nov. 8, 1946; s. Leon and Mary Bekerman N.; m. Goldie L., June 25, 1972; children; Zev D., Samuel E. BA, Nat. Coll. Mendoza, Argentina, 1962; MD summa cum laude, Nat. U. Cuyo Med. Sch., Argentina, 1970; MS in Neurosurgery, U. Minn., 1976; PhD in Neuroanatomy, Nat. U. Cuyo, 1976. Rsch. asst. dept. physiology U. Cuyo, 1964-66; intern U. Buenos Aires, 1969-70, Baylor Coll. Medicine Affiliated Hosps., Tex. Med. Ctr., Houston, 1970-71; resident Mayo Clinic, U. Minn. Sch. Medicine, 1971-76; staff mem. Gamma Knife Ctr. Yale-New Haven (Conn.) Health; courtesy staff Griffin Hosp., Derby, Conn.; sr. attending staff Bridgeport (Conn.) Hosp.; chief divsn. neurosurgery St. Vincent's Med. Ctr., Bridgeport; assoc. clin. prof. neurol. surgery Yale U. Sch. Medicine. Presenter in field. Contbr. articles to profl. jours. Recipient Myrtle Wreath award Conn. Region Hadassah, 1981; Med. Sch. scholar. Fellow Am. Coll. Surgeons, Am. Coll. Neurosurgeons, Am. Heart Assn., Argentine Coll. Neurosurgeons; mem. AMA, Am. Assn. Neurol. Surgeons, L.Am. Neurol. Fedn. (founding), New England Neurol. Soc. (trustee), Conn. Med. Soc., Conn. Soc. Neurol. Surgeons (pres. 1997-99), Fairfield County Med. Assn., Greater Bridgeport Med. Soc., Congress Neurol. Surgeons, Interam. Coll. Physicians & Surgeons, Mayo Alumni Assn., Mayo Alumni Neurol. Soc. Office: Neurol Surgeons 340 Capitol Ave Bridgeport CT 06606-5445 Fax: 203-336-5802. E-mail: nijensohn@aol.com.

NIJINSKY, TAMARA, actress, puppeteer, author, librarian, educator; b. Vienna; came to U.S., 1961; d. Waslaw and Romola (de Pulszky) N.; widowed; 1 child, Kinga Maria Szakats-Gaspers. ed. in Europe, postgrad. studies in U.S. Mem., actress Nat. Theater of Budapest; owner, tchr. Tamara Nijinsky Performing Art Studio, Montreal; tchr. speech/drama, French and German, libr. Cath. H.S., Phoenix; established non-profit internat. orgn. The Waslaw and Romola Nijinsky Found., Inc., 1991, exec. dir., 1991—. Lectr. on Nijinsky, U.S., Can. and Europe. Author: Nijinsky and Romola, 1991. Decorated Chevalier de l'Ordre des Arts et des Lettres, France, 1995, Officier de l'Ordre des Arts et des Lettres, 2000; recipient Nijinsky medal, Pagart, Poland, Polish Order of Arts and Letters, 1997. Roman Catholic. Avocations: reading, computer, swimming. Office: Nijinsky Foundation Inc PO Box # 15981 Phoenix AZ 85060-5981 Fax: (602) 952-7149, 602-840-9605.

NIKAIDO, HIROSHI, microbiologist; b. Tokyo, Mar. 26, 1932; came to U.S., 1962; s. Tatsuya and Ryo N.; m. Kishiko Jokura, March 11, 1963; children: Michio, George. MD, Keio U., Tokyo, 1955, D in Med. Sci., 1961. Assoc. in bacteriology Harvard Med. Sch., Boston, 1963-64, asst. prof., 1965-69; assoc. prof. U. Calif., Berkeley, 1969-71, prof., 1971—. Sci. adv. Essential Therapeutics, Mountain View, Calif., 1992—. Co-author: Microbial Biotechnology, 1995; contbr. articles to profl. jours. Recipient Paul Ehrlich award Paul Ehrlich Found., 1969. Fellow Am. Acad. Microbiology; mem. Am. Soc. Microbiology (editor Jour. Bacteriology 1998-2002, Hoechst-Roussel award 1984), Am. Soc. Biochemistry and Molecular Biology.

NIKAIN, REZA, civil engineer; b. Tehran, Iran, Sept. 26, 1962; came to U.S., 1978; s. Heshmatalah and Maryam N.; m. Denise Maroon; children: Cyrus A., Aaron D. BSCE, Rutgers U., 1985, MS, 1988. Registered profl. engr., N.J., Pa., Del., Ky., Fla., Ohio, Kans., Utah, N.Y.; cert. project mgmt. profl. Asst. supt. Lefrak Orgn., New Brunswick, N.J., 1981-86; project mgr. N.J. Transit Corp., Newark, 1986-88; exec. v.p. The Nielsen-Wurster Group, Inc., Princeton, N.J., 1988—. Mem. ASCE, NSPE, Am. Concrete Inst., Soc. Am. Value Engrs., Nat. Acad. Experts. Achievements include development of a computerized program for schedule delays analysis; methods to evaluate construction schedules and delays on construction projects. Office: The Nielsen-Wurster GroupInc 345 Wall St Princeton NJ 08540-1518

NIKAS, RICHARD JOHN, lawyer; b. Long Beach, Calif., Sept. 9, 1968; s. John Nikolas and Dorothy (Bernardo) N. BA in Internat. Rels., U. So. Calif., 1991, JD, 1995. Bar: Calif. Spl. projects coord. Vessel Assist Assn. Am., Newport Beach, Calif., 1989-94; lawyer Williams Woolley Cogswell Nakazawa & Russell, Long Beach, 1994—. Guest lectr. maritime law U. So. Calif., L.A., 1998—; lectr. admiralty and maritime law Calif. Maritime Acad., Vallejo; chmn. USCG Working Group on Nat. Maritime Incident Reporting Sys., Washington, 1997—. Author: Benedict on Admiralty, 1998, Moore's Federal Practice, 1998, The Last Yankee, 1999, Recreational Boating Law, 2000, Admiralty Practice and Procedure, 2000. Head football coach Ocean View H.S., Long Beach, 1995; mentor Long Beach Unified Sch. Dist., 1997—; pitcher Greek Olympic Baseball Team, Atlantic City Surf Profl. Baseball Club; bd. govs. The Am. Mariner, Loyola U., 1999. Recipient Best Oralist award Spong Nat. Invitational Moot Ct., Williamsburg, Va., 1995, Meritorious Pub. Svc. medal USCG. Mem. Calif. State Bar Assn., Maritime Law Assn., Soc. of Naval Architects and Marine Engrs. (chmn. panel 0-38). Avocation: baseball. Address: 17652 Wrightwood Ln Huntington Beach CA 92649-4969

NIKISCHER, FRANK WILLIAM, SR. retired restaurant owner and operator; b. Fullerton, Pa., Sept. 26, 1931; s. Frank and Theresa (Steiner) N.; m. Ruth Reese, Aug. 27, 1955 (dec. July 1983); children: Frank William, David, Wendy; m. Judith Savitz Mohr, Jan. 1, 1986. BS in Hotel Adminstrn., Pa. State U., 1953. Commd. ensign USN, 1953; advanced through grades to lt. comdr. USNR, 1963, ret., 1976; gen. mgr. Walp's Restaurant, Allentown, Pa., 1956-86; owner, operator Walp's Restaurant and Guest House, 1986-98; pres., chief exec. officer Double N., Inc., 1986-98; ret., 1999. Recipient Allentown/Lehigh County C. of C. Small Bus. Coun. Excellence in Bus. award, 1991. Mem. Retired Officers Assn., Naval Res. Assn., Navy League of U.S., Nat. Restaurant Assn., Jr. Hotelmen Am., Pa. State U. Alumni Assn., VFW, Am. Legion, Quarter Deck Soc., Consistory Valley of Allentown (32 degree), Masons, Shriners, Alpha Phi Omega, Sigma Eta Alpha. Republican. Avocations: gardening, sports, music. Home: care The Barrton Unit 6-E 555 SE 6th Ave Delray Beach FL 33483-5251 also: RR #1 Box 1912 Kunkletown PA 18058-9763 E-mail: DBLE-N@webtv.net.

NIKOLAI, LOREN ALFRED, accounting educator, writer; b. Northfield, Minn., Dec. 14, 1943; s. Roman Peter and Loyola (Gertrude) N.; m. Anita Carol Baker, Jan. 15, 1966; children: Trishia, Jay. BA, St. Cloud State U., 1966, MBA, 1967; PhD, U. Minn., 1973. CPA, Mo. Asst. prof. U. N.C., Chapel Hill, 1973-76; assoc. prof. U. Mo., Columbia, 1976-80, prof., 1980-82, Ernst & Young Disting. prof. Sch. Accountancy, 1982—, dir. masters programs, 2002—. Author: Financial Accounting: Concepts and Uses, 1988, 3d edit., 1995, Intermediate Accounting, 1980, 8th edit., 2000, Accounting Information for Business Decisions, 1st edit., 2000. Recipient Faculty award of merit Fedn. Schs. of Accountancy, 1989, Disting. Alumni award St. Cloud U., 1990, Coll. of Bus. Faculty Mem. of Yr. award, 1991, Mo. Outstanding Acctg. Educators award, 1993; Kemper fellow U. Mo., 1992, Alumni award MU Faculty, 1996, UM Presdl. awd. for Outstanding Teaching, 1999; Coll. of Bus. Teacher of the Yr., 1999. Mem. AICPA, Am. Acctg. Assn., Mo. Soc. CPAs, Fedn. Schs. of Acctg. (pres. 1994). Office: U Mo Sch Accountancy 303 Cornell Hall Columbia MO 65211-0001

NIKOLAY, FRANK LAWRENCE, lawyer; b. Marathon County, Wis., Sept. 1, 1922; s. Jacob and Anna Bertha (Illig) N.; m. Mary Elizabeth Gisvold, Aug. 3, 1958. LLB, U. Wis., 1948. Bar: Wis. 1948, U.S. Dist. Ct. (we. dist.) Wis. 1948, U.S. Supreme Ct. 1961. Dist. counsel Office Price Stabilization, Green Bay, Wis., 1951-52; asst. U.S. atty. U.S. Dist. Ct. (we. dist.) Wis., 1952-53, U.S. atty., 1953-54; mem. assembly State of Wis., 1959-70; ptnr. Nikolay Law Offices, Colby, 1970—. Mem. bd. regents U. Wis., Madison, 1983-90; mem. Clark County (Wis.) Bd. Suprs., 1949—. Col. U.S. Army, 1948-74. Mem. ABA, Wis. Bar Assn., Am. Legion (post comdr. 1975—), Lions (sec. 1978). Democrat. Roman Catholic. Office: Nikolay Law Offices PO Box 465 Colby WI 54421-0465 Office Fax: 715-223-8834.

NIKOLIC, JEAN GREAVES DAVIS, artist; b. Jackson, Miss., Sept. 6, 1932; d. John Dan and Delia Fondren (Greaves) Davis; m. Nikola Nikolic, July 2, 1960; children: Nikola Andrew, Carolina Greaves. Student, La. State U., 1952-55; BFA with tchrs. license, Miss. U. for Women, 1957; cert., Mus. Modern Art, 1958; postgrad., Columbia U., 1959. Asst. to the dir. Martha Jackson Gallery, N.Y.C., 1961-62; dir. Gallery of Modern Art, Fredericksburg, Va., 1976-77. Group exhbns. include Children's Art Ctr., Norfolk, Va., 1979, The Sydney and Frances Lewis Contemporary Art Coll., Va. Mus. Fine Arts, Richmond, 1979, Ctrl. Rappahannock Regional Libr., Fredericksburg, Va., 1979, Longwood Coll., Farmville, Va., 1979, First & Merchants' Ctr. Gallery, Richmond, Va., 1982, United Va. Bank Gallery, Richmond, 1984, 87, Printed Matter, N.Y.C., 1985, Eric Schindler Gallery, Richmond, 1986, Henry St. Gallery, Richmond, 1987, Crestar Bank Gallery, Richmond, 1989, James Ctr. Gallery, Richmond, 1990, Richmond Pub. Libr., 1992, 93, many others; represented in permanent collections The Sydney and Frances Lewis Contemporary Art Collection, Va. Mus. Fine Arts, Richmond, Grey Art Collection, NYU, N.Y.C., Quad-Graphics Collection, Milw., La. State U., Baton Rouge, Miss. U. For Women, Columbus, First & Merchants' Nat. Bank, Richmond, numerous pvt. collections. Mem. Nat. Mus. Women in the Arts (charter), Washington Project for the Arts, Richmond Artists' Assn., Va. Mus. Fine Arts, Eyeclopes Gallery. Home: 12 Winston Pl Fredericksburg VA 22405-3053

NIKOUI, HOSSEIN REZA, quality assurance professional; b. Tehran, Iran, Feb. 4, 1949; came to U.S., 1977; s. Gholam Reza and Monireh (Jahanshahi) N.; m. Niki Forouzi, Oct. 25, 1983; children: Neda Lili, Amir Reza. BSChemE, Arya-Mehr Univ., Tehran, 1971; Diploma in Ops. Rsch., U. Toronto, 1981; cert. in quality assurance, Ryerson Univ., Toronto, 1983; cert. sys. approach/quality improvement, Madonna U., Livonia, Mich., 1996; MSBA in Quality and Ops. Mgmt., Madonna U., 1998. Registered profl. engr.; cert. quality engr., quality auditor, quality systems lead auditor, quality mgr.; cert. lean manufacturing, U. Mich., 2001. Quality engr. Gen. Motors, Tehran, 1971-72, supt. supplier quality assurance, 1973-74, mgr. quality assurance, 1975-78, resident materials mgr. Oshawa, Ont., Can., 1978-79; mgr. quality control G.S. Woolley, Toronto, 1979-82, mgr. quality assurance, 1982-85; dir. corp. quality assurance The Progressive/Woolley Group, 1985-88, Manchester Plastics, Troy, Mich., 1988-97; dir. quality assurance Collins & Aikman Plastics, Manchester, 1997-99; dir. corp. quality assurance Oakwood Group, Dearborn, 1999-2000, dir. ops., 2000-01; lean mfg. coach Ford Motor Co., 2001—. Instr. Centenial Coll., Toronto, 1984-88; cons. Can. Post Corp., Toronto, 1985-86. Contbr. articles to profl. jours. Fellow Am. Soc. for Quality; mem. ASTM, Soc. Plastic Engrs., Am. Inst. Indsl. Engrs., Soc. Automotive

Engrs., Engring. Soc. Detroit, Inst. of Quality Assurance. Avocations: collecting stamps and coins, tennis, reading, classical music. Home: 5539 Pinecrest Estates Dr Ann Arbor MI 48105-9351 Fax: 734-668-6883. E-mail: hnikoui@cs.com.

NIKS, INESSA, piano teacher; b. St. Petersburg, Russia, Nov. 6, 1938; came to U.S., 1979; d. Cesar Tuman and Gertrude Slutskaya; m. Mikhail Niks, Aug. 1967 (dec. 1996); children: Dimitri, Marina. MusM with distinction, St. Petersburg Conservatory, 1961. Tchr. Music Coll. Novgorod, Russia, 1962-65, Spl. Music Sch., Leningrad, Russia, 1966-76; head musicology dept. Music Coll., Pskov, Russia, 1976-79; pvt. tchr. piano and musicology Redlands, Calif., 1983—; founder Niks' Hands Retraining Ctr., 1992—. Creator, mfr. Hand Guide device for pianists, 1991—, also co-author manual Play Without Tension supplement to the device 1998); author: Type Without Tension, 1999; contbr. articles to California Music Teacher mag. Recipient Silver medal Internat. Piano Rec. Competition, 1983, Bronze medal, 1984. Mem.: European Piano Tchrs. Assn., Music Tchrs. Assn. Calif., Nat. League Am. Pen Women. Achievements include research in vocal art, lecturing; breakthrough in acoustics of piano sound, revealed in recording of the lecture-recital Mystery of Singing Tone, 1997. Home and Office: Niks' Hands Retraining Ctr 1434 Fulbright Ave Redlands CA 92373-4938 E-mail: Driks@citrus.UCR.Edu.

NILES, BARBARA ELLIOTT, psychoanalyst; b. Boston, Jan. 31, 1939; d. Byron Kauffman and Helen Alice (Heissler) Elliott; m. John Denison, June 25, 1960 (div. 1981); children: Catherine Elliott, Andrew Elliott. AA, Briarcliff Coll., 1958; BA, SUNY, 1984; MSW, Hunter Coll., 1986. Cert. psychotherapy and psychoanalysis Inst Contemporary Psychotherapy; social worker. Exec. com. Legal Aid Soc. Women's Aux., N.Y.C., 1965-67; sec. Water Quality Task Force Scientists' Com. for Pub. Info., 1973-74; founding dir., sec. Consumer Action Now Inc., 1970-77; dir. devel. Consumer Action Now's Council Environ., 1976-77; dir. 170 Tenants Corp., 1979-81; mem. pub. interest com. Cosmopolitan Club, 1979-82; dir. INFORM Inc., 1978-84; pvt. practice psychotherapy and psychoanalysis, 1986—. Mem. adj. faculty metro ctr. Empire State Coll., N.Y.C., NY, 1987—97. Editor: (biography) Off the Beaten Track, 1984. Bd. trustees The Salisbury Assn., 2001—; mem. Land Trust Bd., 2001—, Salisbury Housing Trust, 2001—. Mem.: NASW, St Botolph Club (Boston), Vincent Club (Boston), Cosmopolitan Club (N.Y.C.). Avocations: wilderness camping, travel, literature. Office: c/o Arnold Rosen MD 200 E 78th St New York NY 10021-2004

NILES, GEDDES LEROY, private investigator; b. Haines, Alaska, Oct. 31, 1926; s. Geddes William and Gladys Bell (McCormack) N.; m. Aline Terii Tehei, June 17, 1960; children: Diana Mareva Niles-Hansen, Stephen Lloyd Teva. BA, U. Calif., Berkeley, 1949. Investigator and hearing officer U.S. Civil Service Commn., San Francisco, 1955-62, Honolulu, 1962-78; pres. Niles Realty Ltd., 1979—; dir. The Niles Agy., 1983—. Mem. Neighborhood Bd., Kailua, Hawaii, 1979-80. Mem.: Iaorana Tahiti (Honolulu) (treas. 1985-89). Avocation: mystery writer. Office: 350 Ward Ave Ste 106 Honolulu HI 96814-4004

NILES, JOHN SOUTHWORTH, III, counselor, farmer; b. Carbondale, Pa., Dec. 3, 1933; s. John S. Jr. and Helen Hemelright Niles; m. Elsie E. Axford (div. 1969); children: John S. IV, David A., Elizabeth C.; m. Dorothy L. Keill, June 12, 1999. BA, Yale U., 1956. Cert. addictions counselor, Pa. Roughneck Mim Oil Drilling Co., Victoria, Tex., 1959; mfg. mgr. KVP-Sutherland Paper Co., Kalamazoo, 1960-67; mgr. Cold Springs Farms, Pleasant Mount, Pa., 1968-79, Baccus Farms, Minneapolis, Kans., 1979-82; counselor Marworth Treatment Ctr., Waverly, Pa., 1982-93, ret., 1993. 1st lt. USMC, 1956-58. Mem. NRA, Marine Corps Assn., Countryside Convervancy, Delta Kappa Epsilon. Republican. Avocations: hunting, fishing, horses, reading, sports. Home: Crystal Lake RR 1 Box 1106 Carbondale PA 18407-9015 E-mail: jsniles@webtv.net.

NILES, JUDITH F. librarian; b. Temple, Tex., Mar. 18, 1944; d. Fern Fredrickson Niles, John Loraine Niles. BA, U. N.D., 1966; MA, U. Wis., 1968; MLS, Ind. U., 1973. Serials libr. U. Tex., San Antonio, 1974—77; head tech. svcs. Laredo (Tex.) State U., 1977—81; head acquisitions Rice U., Houston, 1981—85; dir. libr. tech. svcs. U. Louisville, 1986—91, dir. libr. collection mgmt., 1991—. Contbr. articles to profl. jours. Grantee Fulbright Grant, U.S. Dept. State, 1966—67. Mem.: AAUP, ALA, N.Am. Serials Interest Group, Assn. for Libr. Collections and Tech. Svcs. (chair budget and fin. com. 2001—02), Beta Phi Mu, Phi Beta Kappa. Presbyterian. Avocation: travel. Office: Univ Louisville Ekstrom Libr LL41 2301 S 3rd St Louisville KY 40292

NILES, THOMAS MICHAEL TOLLIVER, business association executive; b. Lexington, Ky., Sept. 22, 1939; s. John Jacob and Rena (Lipetz) N.; m. Carroll C. Ehringhaus, July 22, 1967; children: John Thomas, Mary Chapman. BA, Harvard U., 1960; MA, U. Ky., 1962. Commd. fgn. service officer Dept. State, Washington, 1962, U.S. ambassador to Can., 1985-1989; then permanent rep. EEC, Brussels; asst. sec. of state Europe and Can., 1991-93; amb. to Greece Athens, 1993-97; v.p. Nat. Def. U., 1997-98; pres. U.S. Coun. Internat. Bus., 1999. Recipient Superior Honor award Dept. State, 1982, 85, Presdl. award, 1988, 89, 94. Mem. Phi Beta Kappa Office: USCIB 1212 Ave of Ams New York NY 10036

NILLES, JOHN MATHIAS (JACK NILLES), futurist; b. Evanston, Ill., Aug. 25, 1932; s. Elmer Edward and Hazel Evelyn Nilles; m. Laila Padorr, July 8, 1957. BA magna cum laude, Lawrence Coll., 1954; MS in Engring., UCLA, Los Angeles, 1964. Sr. engr. Raytheon Mfg. Co., Santa Barbara, Calif., 1956-58; section head. Ramo-Woodridge Corp., L.A., 1958-59; project engr. Space Technology Lab., 1960; dir. The Aerospace Corp., 1961-67; sr. systems engr. TRW Systems, 1967-69; assoc. group dir. The Aerospace Corp., 1969-72; dir. interdisciplinary programs U. So. Calif., 1972-81, dir. info. technology program, 1981-89; pres. JALA Internat. Inc., 1980—. Coord. EC Telework Forum, Madrid, 1992—; dir. Internat. Telework Assocs., & Coun., 1991-97, pres., 1993-94; chmn. Telecommuting Rsch. Inst., Inc., L.A., 1990—. Author: The Telecommunications Transportation Tradeoff, 1976, Japanese edit., 1977, Exploring the World of the Personal Computer, 1982, French edit., 1985, Micros and Modems, 1983, French edit., 1986, Making Telecommuting Happen, 1994, Portuguese edit., 1997, Managing Telework, 1998; mem. editl. bd. Revista Portuguesa de Gestao, 2000—. Capt. USAF, 1954-56. Recipient Rod Rose award Soc. Rsch. Adminstrs., 1976, Environ. Pride award L.A. Mag., 1993, Environ. Achievement award Renew Am., 1994-96, Commendation, L.A. County Bd. Suprs., 1997; inducted into Telework Hall of Fame, 1998. Mem. IEEE, IEEE Computer Soc., AAAS, Assn. Computing Machinery, Inst. Ops. Rsch. and Mgmt. Scis., World Future Soc., Calif. Yacht Club. Avocations: sailing, photography. Office: JALA Internat Inc 971 Stonehill Ln Los Angeles CA 90049-1412 E-mail: jnilles@jala.com.

NILLES, JOHN MICHAEL, lawyer; b. Langdon, N.D., Aug. 20, 1930; s. John Joseph and Isabel Mary (O'Neil) N.; m. Barbara Ann Cook, June 22, 1957; children: Terese M., Daniel J., Marcia L., Thomas M., Margaret J. BA cum laude, St. Johns U., 1955; JD cum laude with distinction, U. N.D., 1958. Bar: N.D. 1958, U.S. Dist. Ct. N.D. 1958, U.S. Ct. Appeals (8th cir.) 1958, Minn. 1991. Shareholder, dir., pres. Nilles, Hansen and Davies, Ltd., Fargo, N.D., 1958-90, of counsel, 1990-95; exec. v.p., gen. counsel Met. Fin. Corp., Mpls., 1990-95, First Bank F.S.B., Mpls., 1995; ret., 1996. Pres., bd. dirs. Legal Aid Soc. N.D., Fargo, 1970-76, Red River Estate Planning Coun., 1980-87; vice-chmn. disciplinary bd. Supreme Ct. N.D., 1984-90. Bd. editors N.D. Law Rev., 1957-58. Mem. exec. bd. Red River Valley coun. Boy Scouts Am., 1959-70; bd. regents U. Mary, Bismarck, N.D., 1967-77; pres., bd. dirs. Cath. Charities, Fargo, 1959-65, Southeast Mental Health Ctr., Fargo, 1972-80. Staff sgt. USAF, 1951-54. Fellow Am. Coll. Trust and Estate Counsel (state dir. 1979-90); mem. ABA, State Bar Assn. N.D., Minn. Bar Assn., Order of Coif. Republican. Roman Catholic. Avocations: tennis, downhill skiing, cross-country skiing, hunting, gun collecting. Home: 10412 Fawns Way Eden Prairie MN 55347-5117

NILLES, KATHLEEN MARY, lawyer; b. Fargo, N.D., May 27, 1951; d. J. Gerald and Barbara L. (Accornero) N. BA, U. Santa Clara, 1973; MA, Yale U., 1976; JD, U. Va., 1985; LLM in Taxation, Georgetown U., 1992. Bar: D.C. 1985, U.S. Tax Ct. 1987. Assoc. Patton & Boggs, Washington, 1985-88, Groom & Nordberg, Washington, 1988-90; tax counsel ways and means com. U.S. Ho. of Reps., 1991-95; ptnr. Gardner, Carton & Douglas, 1995—. Mem. steering com. D.C. Bar Tax Sect., Washington, 1995-97. Co-author: Tax-Exempt Status of Health Care Organizations, 1996. Co-chair fed. club steering com. Human Rights Campaign, Washington, 1997-2000. Avocation: golf, biking. Office: 1301 K St NW Ste 900 East Tower Washington DC 20005

NILLES, LAILA PADORR, musician, record producer; b. Chgo., July 25, 1929; d. Abraham Leonard Ginsburg and Jeanette Padorr; m. Jack Mathias Nilles, July 8, 1957. MusB, B of Music Edn., Northwestern U., 1947, M of Music, 1949; postgrad., Julliard Sch. Music, 1950, 51, Ecoles d'Art Am. Fontainebleau, France, 1953. Founder, dir. Padorr Trio, Chgo. and Los Angeles, 1951-55, 56-72; dir. Concerts at the Mt., Los Angeles, 1958-60; mgr., dir. Concerts West, 1965-75; freelance musician, 1975-77; asst. dir. Protone Records, 1977-82, assoc. dir., 1982—; v.p. Jala Internat., Inc., 1982—. Dir. design for Sharing UCLA, L.A., 1984-89, Friends of Music U. So. Calif., 1984-90, Am. Youth Symphony, 1981-88. Soloist on record: Music for Flute and Piano by Four Americans, 1976; co-prodr.: 42 records, cassettes and compact discs, 1977—2001; freelance A&R/prodr. :. Recipient First prize Coleman Auditions, 1956, Young Artists League, 1956. Mem. Audio Engring. Soc., Nat. Acad. Recording Arts and Scis., Musicians Union Local 47. Clubs: Calif. Yacht (Marina Del Ray). Avocations: photography, sailing, astronomy. Home and Office: 971 Stonehill Ln Los Angeles CA 90049-1412 E-mail: lnilles@jala.com.

NILSEN, LAURANCE BECKWITH, retired endocrinologist; b. Toledo, Aug. 8, 1936; BA, Williams Coll., Williamstown, Mass., 1958; MD, Cornell U. Med. Sch., N.Y.C., 1962. Med. diplomate Am. Bd. Internal Medicine, 1969, 1977, Am. Bd. Internal Medicine, Endocrinology and Metabolism, 1972. Internship Strong Meml. Hosp., U. Rochester Sch. Medicine and Dentistry, 1962-63, asst. resident internal medicine, 1963-64; sr. asst. resident internal medicine Duke U. Med. Ctr., Durham, N.C., 1966-67; sr. asst. surgeon L.A. County Hosp., 1964-66; chief endocrinology St. Joseph's Hosp. and Med. Ctr., 1987-94; part-time pvt. practice, Phoenix, 2000—. Pres. Ariz. Soc. Internal Medicine, 1976-78, Maricopa Found. for Med. Care, 1978-80, v.p., dir. 1981-94; bd. dirs. Mut. Ins. Co. Ariz. Contbr. numerous articles to profl. jours. Bd. dirs. Greater Phoenix Ariz. Affordable Health Care Found., 1983-95. Mem. Am. Coll. Endocrinology, Am. Diabetes Assn., Maricopa County Med. Soc. (bd. dirs. 1976-78). Office: Endocrinology Assocs PA 3522 N 3d Ave Phoenix AZ 85013-3989

NILSON, ERIC GAWAIN, systems analyst, consultant; b. Madison, Wis., June 26, 1947; s. Gunnar N. and Nell (Barnitz) N.; m. Hisako Natori. AA in Math., St. Petersburg Jr. Coll.; BS in Math., U. Fla., 1969. Computer specialist ICC, 1976-82; system adminstr. UNIX Adminstrv. Office U.S. Cts., Washington, 1982-86, application programmer, 1986-90, team leader, 1990-93, chief br. software engring., 1993-94; EDI software cons. Paper Free Systems Corp., 1994-2000, v.p. software engring. Vienna, 1995—. Cons. Trans Systems Corp., 1985-87, Advanced Systems Devel., 1987-88, Paper Free Systems, 1988-90. With USN, 1969-72. Mem. IEEE, Phi Kappa Phi. Home: 6813 Crossman St Annandale VA 22003-3406

NILSON, LINDA BURZOTTA, academic administrator; b. Chgo., June 26, 1949; d. Frank S. and Florence M. (Jelke) Burzotta; m. Gregory Bauernfeind. BA in Sociology, U. Calif. Berkeley, 1970; MS in Sociology, U. Wis., 1972, PhD in Sociology, 1974. Prof. sociology UCLA, 1975-85; bus. editor Inland Empire Mag., Riverside, Calif., 1986-88; owner, mgr. Impressive Resumes, Redlands, Riverside, 1985-89; dir. tchr. devel. program U. Calif., Riverside, 1989-93; dir. Ctr. for Teaching Vanderbilt U., Nashville, 1993-98, dir. office tchg. effectiveness and innovation, 1998—. Rsch. assoc. Inst. for Social Sci. Rsch., UCLA, 1977-78, Social Rsch. Advisory, Redlands, Calif., 1980-86, Policy Rsch. Ctr., Redlands, 1980-83; chair So. Regional Faculty & Instrnl. Devel. Consortium, 1995-98. Author: (book) The TA Handbook: Teaching Techniques and Self-Improvement Strategies, 1981, Teaching Techniques, 1990, Teaching at Its Best, 1998. Del. Dem. Nat. Conv., N.Y.C., 1976; club v.p. pub. rels. Nashville Toastmasters, 1993-94, club pres., 1994-95. Named Leader of Yr., Leads Club, 1987. Mem. So. Regional Faculty and Instrnl. Devel. Consortium (chair 1995-98, Profl. and Orgnl. Devel. Network in Higher Edn. (Bright Idea award 2000), Toastmasters Internat. (Humorous speech contest winner 1995), Pub. Rels. Soc. Am. (Pub. Rels. award 1988). Avocations: running, yoga, drawing, hiking, travel. Home: 101 Sunrise Harbor Dr Anderson SC 29621-2464 Office: Clemson U 445 Brackett Hl Clemson SC 29634-0001

NILSON, PATRICIA, clinical psychologist; b. Boulder, Colo., Oct. 22, 1929; d. James William and Vera Maude (Peacock) Broxon; m. Eric Walter Nilson, Dec. 23, 1950; children: Stephen Daniel, Eric Jon, Christopher Lawrence. Registered Phys. Therapist, Med. Coll. Va., 1951; MA in Clin. Psychology, L.I. U., 1972, PhD, 1973. Cert. psychologist N.Y. Clin. psychologist Court Cons. Unit, Hauppauge, N.Y., 1972-92, Three Village Counseling Svc., Setauket, 1974-75, Farmingville (N.Y.) Mental Health Ctr., 1992-95; pvt. practice Commack, 1975—. Adj. asst. prof. C.W. Post Coll., Brookdale, 1974-80; cons., supr. psychologist Wayside Sch. for Girls, Valley Stream, 1975-85; cons. L.I. Lighting Co., 1980; lectr. in field. Author children's therapeutic stories; author therapeutic games: The Road to Problem Mastery; contbr. articles to profl. jours. Mem. APA, Suffolk County Psychol. Assn., Nat. Register Health Svc. Providers in Psychology, Soc. for Clin. and Exptl. Hypnosis (life). Office: 11 Montrose Dr Commack NY 11725-1312 E-mail: drpat11@netzero.net.

NILSSON, EDWARD OLOF, architect; b. Queens, N.Y., Nov. 10, 1947; s. Gerhard Eugene and Selma Kristina (Landy) N.; m. Frances Britton Stith, Apr. 27, 1974; children: Anders, Peter. BArch, The Cooper Union, 1970; MArch, Harvard U., 1971; MBA, Babson Coll., 1997. Registered architect, Mass. Architect The Architects Collaborative, Cambridge, Mass., 1971-77, Anderson Notter Finegold, Inc., Boston, 1977-80; prin. Nilsson Assocs., Marblehead, Mass., 1981-92, Nilsson & Siden Assocs., Inc., Marblehead, 1992—. Author: architect AIA Conf. on Bldg. Redesign and Energy Challenges, 1984; prin. works include Rivervision 2020, Boston, also instnl., comml. and residential projects. Mem. Watertown (Mass.) Planning Bd., 1981-83, Marblehead Planning Bd., 1985-91, chmn., 1986-90; mem. Episcopal Times Editl. Bd., Boston, 1986-88, bd. dirs. Gen. Theol. Libr., Boston, 1986-88. Mem. AIA, Boston Soc. Architects, Rotary. Democrat. Home: 28 Naugus Ave Marblehead MA 01945-1551

NILSSON, MARY ANN, music educator; b. N.Y.C., Jan. 5, 1944; d. Gerhard Eugene and Selma Christine (Landy) N.; m. June 19, 1988. BS with honors, New Paltz State U., 1965; MA, NYU, 1983; MM, Meredith Coll., 2000. LPN, N.Y. Piano tchr. New Paltz (N.Y.) State U. Coll., 1983-85, Ulster County C.C., Stone Ridge, N.Y., 1983-85; music instr. Piedmont C.C., Roxboro, N.C., 1999, Durham Tech. Coll., 1999, Durham (N.C.) C.C., 2000. Music history tchr. Family of Ellenville, N.Y., 1990-91; tchr. music appreciation Long Meml. Music Acad., Roxboro, N.C., 2001, tchr. music course continuing edn. , 2001; music instr. Mt. Olive Coll., Research Triangle Park, N.C., 2002. Musician (Performances): New Paltz State U., 1992, Town of Lumberland, N.Y., 1993, Lunch & Listen series, 1994, Hudson Valley Sr. Residence, 1995, South Winds Sr. Residence, 1995, Forest at Duke, 1997, Long Meml. Ch., 1997; musician: (pianist competition) Meredith Coll., 1999; musician: (master class) Walter Hautzig Meredith Coll., 1999; musician: (recital) Meredith Coll., Durham Regents, 2001, Forest at Duke, Carolina House, 2001; contbr. Choir dir., organist First Presbyn. Ch., Monticello, N.Y., 1985-86; vol. Durham (N.C.) Hosp., 1996—. Grantee, Ulster County Office of Aging, 1983, Sullivan County Office of Aging, Nat. Music Tchrs. Assn., 2001, Music Tchrs. Nat. Assn., 2001. Mem. Nat. Guild Piano Tchrs. (adjudicator 1983—, chmn. piano audition ctr. 1988-95), Durham Music Tchrs. Assn., Pi Kappa Lambda. Avocations: reading German, walking, fitness. Home and Office: 214 Equestrian Chase Rougemont NC 27572-9351

NIMER, STEPHEN, physician, leukemia researcher; b. Chgo., May 20, 1954; m. Georgia Takigawa, Oct. 18, 1987. BS, MIT, 1975; MD, U. Chgo., 1979. Diplomate Am. Bd. Internal Medicine, Am. Bd. Hematology, Am. Bd. Med. Oncology. Asst. prof. medicine UCLA Sch. Medicine, 1987-92; dir. transplantation biology Jonsson Compr. Cancer Ctr., L.A., 1991-92; assoc. mem. Sloan-Kettering Inst., N.Y.C., 1993-99, mem., 1999—; chief hematology svc. Meml. Hosp., 1993—; head, divsn. hematologic oncology Meml. Sloan-Kettering Cancer Ctr., 1996—; prof. medicine Weill Medical Coll., 2000—. Mem. editl. bd.: Blood, 1997—; co-editor: Hematologic Complications of Cancer, 1996; contbr. over 100 sci. articles to profl. jours. Chmn. med. adv. bd. G&P Charitable Found., N.Y.C., 1998—. Recipient Irma T. Hirschl Career Scientist award Cornell U. Med. Sch., 1995, Investigator award NIH, 1990, 96. Fellow ACP; mem. Am. Soc. for Clin. Investigation, Am. Soc. for Hematology, Am. Soc. of Clin. Oncology, Am. Assn. for Cancer Rsch., Am. Assn. of Blood Banks, Leukemia Soc. of Am. (bd. trustees 1998—), Aplastic Anemia Found. of Am. (bd. med. dirs. 1996—), Alpha Omega Alpha. Avocations: tennis, photography, gardening. Office: Meml Sloan Kettering Cancer Ctr Box 575 1275 York Ave New York NY 10021-6094

NIMETZ, GLORIA LORCH, real estate broker, photographer; b. N.Y.C., May 25, 1944; d. Joseph and Claire (Weil) Lorch; m. Matthew Nimetz, June 24, 1975; children: Alexandra, Lloyd. BA, Wheaton Coll., 1966; MBA, Am. U., Washington, 1980. Dir. Brown, Harris Stevens LLC, N.Y.C., 1990—. Works collected in Bklyn. Mus. Art, 1997, N.Y. Pub. Libr., 1997, Dorsky Mus., 1997, Mus. Fine Arts, Houston. Recipient J&J Purchase award Printmaking Coun. N.J., 1996, Personal Statement 1st prize Golden Lights Awards, 1997. Office: 655 Madison Ave Fl 3 New York NY 10021-8043

NIMETZ, MATTHEW, investment company executive; b. Bklyn., June 17, 1939; s. Joseph L. and Elsie (Botwinik) N.; m. Gloria S. Lorch, June 24, 1975; children: Alexandra Elise, Lloyd. BA, Williams Coll., 1960, LL.D. (hon.), 1979; BA (Rhodes scholar), Balliol Coll., Oxford (Eng.) U., 1962, MA, 1966; LL.B., Harvard U., 1965. Bar: N.Y. 1966, D.C. 1968. Law clk. to Justice John M. Harlan, U.S. Supreme Ct., 1965-67; staff asst. to Pres. Johnson, 1967-69; asso. firm Simpson Thacher & Bartlett, N.Y.C., 1969-74, ptnr., 1974-77; counselor Dept. of State, Washington, 1977-80, acting coord. refugee affairs, 1979-80, under sec. of state for security assistance, sci. and tech., 1980; ptnr. firm Paul, Weiss, Rifkind, Wharton & Garrison, N.Y.C., 1981-2000; ptnr., mng. mem. Gen. Atlantic Ptnrs. LLC, Greenwich, Conn., 2000—. Commr. Port Authority N.Y. and N.J., 1975-77; dir. World Resources Inst., chmn., 1982-94; mem. N.Y. State Adv. Coun. on State Productivity, 1990-92; presdl. envoy Greece-Macedonian Negotiations, 1994-95, spl. rep. UN Sec. Gen., 1999—. Trustee William Coll., 1981-96; chmn. UN Devel. Corp., 1986-94; bd. dirs. Charles H. Revson Found., 1990-98, N.Y. State Nature Conservancy, 1997—; chmn. Carnegie Forum in U.S., Greece and Turkey, 1996-98; chmn. Ctr. for Democracy and Reconciliation in S.E. Europe, 1998—; dir. Inst. Pub. Adminstrn., 1999—; mem. internat. adv. com. Ctrl. European U., Budapest, Hungary, 1998—. Mem. Assn. of Bar of City of N.Y., Coun. on Fgn. Rels. Clubs: Harvard (N.Y.C.). Office: Gen Atlantic Ptnrs LLC 3 Pickwick Plz Greenwich CT 06830-5538 E-mail: mnimetz@gapartners.com.

NIMIROWSKI, RAMONA FURPHY, legal administrator; b. Manchester, Conn., Mar. 10, 1952; d. John Edward and Madeline Raymond F.; m. Peter John Nimirowski, Aug. 7, 1971 (div. Jan. 1986); children: Todd Justin, Teresa Rose. Degree in acctg. and bus. adminstrn., Manchester (Conn.) C.C., 1980; BS in Bus., U. Hartford, 1987. Paralegal, clerk Travelers Ind. Co., Hartford, 1981-90, mgr., 1987-87, asst. dir. corp. law, 1990-98, 2d v.p., 1998—. Mem. Eta Mu Lambda. Home: 102 Wetherell St Unit 102 Manchester CT 06040 Office: Travelers Ins Co 1 Tower Sq Hartford CT 06183 E-mail: ramona.f.nimirowski@travelers.com.

NIMKIN, BERNARD WILLIAM, retired lawyer; b. N.Y.C., Apr. 15, 1923; s. Myron Benjamin and Anabel (Davidow) N.; m. Jean Horowitz, Feb. 9, 1947; children— David Andrew, Margaret Lee, Katherine. BS cum laude, Harvard U., 1943, LL.B. cum laude, 1949. Bar: N.Y. State bar 1949, U.S. Supreme Ct., 1999. Asso. firm Carter, Ledyard & Milburn, N.Y.C., 1949-58; asso. and partner firm Kaye Scholer, LLP, 1958-91. Lectr. Practising Law Inst., Banking Law Inst.; Mem. Am. Law Inst.; vis. com. U. Miami Law Sch.; mem. adv. bd. Rev. of Securities Regulation. Contbr. articles to profl. jours. Mem. Conservation Commn., Town of Mamaroneck, N.Y., 1970-74; bd. dirs., sec. United Way of Tri-State, 1985-91. Served to 1st lt. U.S. Army, 1943-46. Mem. ABA (mem. fed. regulation of securities com. 1975—, corp. laws com. 1984-92, legal opinions com. 1989—), N.Y. State Bar Assn. (chmn. sect. banking corp. and bus. law 1979-81, ho. of dels. 1981-84, chmn. corp. law com. 1976-79), Assn. Bar City of N.Y. (chmn. uniform state laws com. 1962-65), Tribar Opinion Com. Democrat. Jewish. Home: 116 E 63rd St New York NY 10021-7325 Office: Kaye Scholer LLP 425 Park Ave New York NY 10022-3506 E-mail: bandjnimkin@earthlink.net.

NIMMAGADDA, RAO RAJAGOPALA, materials scientist, researcher; b. Donepudi, Andhra Pradesh, India, July 1, 1944; came to U.S., 1967; s. Suryaprakasa Rao and Bullemma (Venigalla) N.; m. Usha Rani Chava, Nov. 7, 1965 (div. Nov. 1980); children: Sandhya Rani, Pramada Shree; m. Jhansi Rani Talluri, Dec. 18, 1980; children: Sai Chandra and Sri Spandana. B Tech. with honors, Indian Inst. Tech., Bombay, 1965; MS, Mich. Tech. U., 1970; PhD, UCLA, 1975. Jr. sci. officer Def. Metall. Rsch. Labs., Hyderabad, India, 1965-67; postdoctoral scholar UCLA, 1975-78, rsch. engr., 1978-81; rsch. scientist Smith Tool, Irvine, Calif., 1981-83, Burroughs, Westlake Village, 1983-84; rsch. engr. Memorex Corp., Santa Clara, 1984-86; staff scientist Lockheed Missiles & Space Co., Palo Alto, 1986-93; sect. head Akashic Memories Corp., San Jose, 1993-98; sputter process engr. IBM, 1998—. Contbr. articles to profl. jours. Pres. Telugu Assn. So. Calif., 1977, dir. Hindu Temple Soc. So. Calif., 1977-80, pres., 1980. Recipient of Outstanding Tech. Achievement award Strategic Def. Initiative Orgn., Washington, 1989. Mem Am. Vacuum Soc., Materials Rsch. Soc. Republican. Hindu. Achievements include patents for titanium nitride coatings to improve wear resistance of oil drilling bit components, dual squeeze seal gland for oil drilling bits, wear resistant coatings for o-ring seals of oil drilling bits. Home: 120 Gilbert Ave Santa Clara CA 95051-6705 Office: IBM Corp 5600 Cottle Rd San Jose CA 95193-0001 E-mail: nimm@us.ibm.com., raonimm@aol.com.

NIMOITYN, PHILIP, cardiologist; b. Phila., Mar. 6, 1951; s. Benjamin Solomon and Edith (Ornstein) N.; m. Hillary Rachel Saul, June 11, 1989. BS in Biology with distinction, Phila. Coll. Pharmacy and Sci., 1972; MD, Thomas Jefferson U., 1976. Cert. Nat. Bd. Med. Examiners, Am. Bd. Internal Medicine, Am. Bd. Cardiovascular Disease. Intern Hahnemann U. Hosp., Phila., 1976-77; resident in internal medicine Thomas Jefferson U. Hosp., 1977-79, cardiovascular disease fellow, 1979-81, instr. medicine, 1981-90, clin. asst. prof., 1990—; attending physician Pa. Hosp., 1995—; cons. physician Wills Eye Hosp., 1981—; attending physician Penn. Hosp., 1995—. Author: (with others) Artificial Cardiac Pacing, 1984, Quick Reference to Cardiovascular Disease, 1987, Cardiac Emergency Care, 1991; contbr. articles to profl. jours. Recipient Cert. of Merit for Sci. Exhibits AMA, 1974, 2d prize for sci. exhibits Ind. State Med. Assn., 1974. Fellow Am. Coll. Cardiology; mem. AMA, Pa. Med. Soc., Phila. County Med. Soc. Office: 1128 Walnut St Ste 401 Philadelphia PA 19107-5568

NIMS, DONNA LEE KILKER, educator, special education educator; b. Marshalltown, Iowa, Dec. 13, 1940; d. Donald and Mary Ann (McKinney) Kilker; div. Mar. 1993; children: Craig, Rebecca, Stephanie, Stacey. BS, Drake U., 1974, MS, 1981, postgrad., 1991, Grandview Coll., 1995-98. Cert. nurse's aid, tchr. Iowa. Substitute tchr. Des Moines Schs.; spl. edn. tchr. woodward Acad., 1995, Quakerdale Sch., 1996, Four Oaks Phase Sch., 1997—. Mem. AAUW (v.p. 1981-86), Assn. Nat. Assn. Edn. Young Children. Avocation: dancing, reading, crafts, music. Home: 4336 NW Country Club Dr Urbandale IA 50322-1515

NINE, JOHN EDWARD, pharmaceutical company executive; b. Warsaw, Apr. 22, 1936; s. Ira Cecil and Mary (Bidelman) N.; m. Janet Elizabeth Allen, Aug. 8, 1966; children: Jenna Elizabeth, Janelle Elise. BS in Pharmacy, Purdue U., W. Lafayette, Ind., 1963; DSc (hon.), Purdue U., 1983; DSc (hon.) Pharmacy, L.I. U., 1993. Registered pharmacist. Dir. prodn. Ciba Geigy, Union, N.J., 1968-76; v.p. mfg. Schering-Plough, Kenilworth, 1976-80, sr. v.p. tech., 1980-86, pres. tech. ops., 1985-86, pres. SPKK Japan, 1986—, sr. v.p. group C Kenilworth, 1988-90, pres. tech. ops. U.S., 1990-96, corp. v.p., pres. tech. ops., 1996—. Pres. bd. health, Pompton Lakes, N.J., 1965. With U.S. Army, 1959-62. Republican. Avocation: golf.

NING, TAK HUNG, physicist, microelectronic technologist; b. Canton, China, Nov. 14, 1943; came to U.S., 1964; s. Hong and Kwai-Chan (Lee) N.; m. Yin Ngao Fan; children: Adrienne, Brenda. BA in Physics, Reed Coll., 1967; MS in Physics, U. Ill., 1968, PhD in Physics, 1971. IBM Rsch. Div., Yorktown Heights, N.Y., 1973-78, mgr. bipolar devices and cirs., 1978-82, mgr. Advanced Silicon Technology Lab., 1982-83, mgr. silicon devices and technology, 1983-90, mgr. VLSI design and tech., 1990-91; IBM fellow, 1991—. Patentee in field. Fellow IEEE (assoc. editor Trans. on Electron Devices 1988-90, J.J. Ebers award 1989, Jack a. Morton award 1991), Am. Phys. Soc.; mem. NAE (Pan Wen-Yuan award 1998). Home: 3085 Weston Ln Yorktown Heights NY 10598-1962 Office: IBM T J Watson Research Ct Yorktown Heights NY 10598

NING, XUE-HAN (HSUEH-HAN NING), physiologist, researcher; b. Peng-Lai, Shandong, People's Republic of China, Apr. 15, 1936; came to U.S., 1984; s. Yi-Xing and Liu Ning; m. Jian-Xin Fan, May 28, 1967; 1 child, Di Fan. MD, Shanghai 1st Med. Coll., People's Republic of China, 1960. Rsch. fellow Shanghai Inst. Physiology, 1960-72, leader cardiovasc. rsch. group, 1973-83, head, assoc. prof. cardiovasc. rsch. unit, 1984-87, prof. and chair hypoxia dept., 1988-90, vice chairperson academic com., 1988-90; NIH internat. rsch. fellow U. Mich., Ann Arbor, 1984-87, vis. prof., hon. prof., rsch. investigator, 1990-95; prof. and dir. Hypoxia Physiology Lab. Academia Sinica, Shanghai, 1989-90. Acting leader, High Altitude Physiology Group, Chinese mountaineering and sci. expdn. team to Mt. Everest, 1975; leader High Altitude Physiology Group, Dept. Metall. Industry of China and Ry. Engring. Corps, 1979; vis. prof. dept. physiology Mich. State U., East Lansing, 1989-90; vis. prof. dept. pediat. U. Wash., Seattle, 1994-97; affiliate prof., U. Wash., 1997—; rsch. scientist Children's Hosp. and Regional Med. Ctr., Seattle, 1997—. Author: High Altitude Physiology and Medicine, 1981, Reports on Scientific Expedition to Mt. Qomolungma, High Altitude Physiology, 1980, Environment and Ecology of Qinghai-Xizang (Tibet) Plateau, 1982; mem. editl. bd. Chinese Jour. Applied Physiology, 1984—, Acta Physiologica, 1988-90; contbr. articles to profl. jours. Recipient Merit award Shanghai Sci. Congress, 1977, All-China Sci. Congress, Beijing, 1978, Super Class award Academia Sinica, Beijing, 1986, 1st Class award Nat. Natural Scis., Beijing, 1987, # 1 Best Article award Tzu-Chi Med. Jour., Taiwan, 1995. Mem. Am. Physiol. Soc., Am. Heart Assn., Internat. Soc. Heart Rsch., Royal Soc. Medicine, Shanghai Assn. Physiol. (bd. dirs. 1988-91), Chinese Assn. Physiol. (com. applied physiology 1984-93, com. blood, cardiovascular, respiratory and renal physiology 1988-93), Chinese Soc. Medicine, Chinese Soc. Biomed. Engring. Achievements include research in predictive evaluation of mountaineering performance, paradox phenomenon of cardiac pump function injury after climbing or giving oxygen, blood flow-metabolism-function relationship of heart during hypoxia and ischemia, effect of medicinal herbs on cardiac performance, cardiovascular adaptation and resistance to hypoxia and ischemia, Hypothermic adaptation protects heart from subsequent ischemia and hypoxia; the critical temperature 30 degrees celsius "temperature threshold" for modulating myocardial energy, metabolism and gene expression to resist ischemia and hypoxia, hypothermia preserves signaling for mitochondrial biogenesis, triggers stress pathways and inactivates apoptosis in hypoxic myocardium; first electrocardiograph recording at summit of Mt. Everest. Home: 7033 43rd Ave NE Seattle WA 98115-6015 Office: U Wash Dept Pediatrics Box 356320 1959 NE Pacific St Seattle WA 98195-0001

NINNEMANN, THOMAS GEORGE, secondary education educator; b. Chgo., Apr. 13, 1950; s. Milton Charles and Bernice Helen (Sharp) N.; m. Nancy Gail Rogers, Aug. 12, 1972; children: Stephanie Christine, Peter Christopher. BA, U. No. Colo., 1972. Dir. news. Sta. KGLN, Glenwood Springs, Colo., 1972-73; program mgr. Sta. KKEP, Estes Park, 1973-74; ops. mgr. Sta. WMST-AM-FM, Mt. Sterling, Ky., 1974-75; dir. news Sta. KPIK-AM-FM, Colorado Springs, Colo., 1975-77; news stringer AP, UPI, various stas., 1977-78; mgr. driver edn., safety dept. Am. Automobile Assn., Denver, 1978-81; pres. mkt. rschr. Rampart Range Broadcasting Inc., Castle Rock, Colo., 1981-83; news editor Sta. KDEN, Denver, 1983-84; dir. news Stas. KSGT and KMTN-FM, Jackson, Wyo., 1984-94; instr. TV/prodr. dist. TV programming Teton County Sch. Dist., 1989—. Panelist Yellowstone Fire Rev., Yellowstone Nat. Pk., 1989; contract spokesperson on fire safety Bridger-Teton Nat. Forest, Jackson, 1990-97; seasonal pub. affairs specialist Grand Teton Nat. Park, summers 1995-2001; mem. broadcast curriculum adv. com. Ctrl. Wyo. Coll., 1995—. Asst. scoutmaster, then scoutmaster Boy Scouts Am., Castle Rock, Colo., 1979-84, mem. dist. com., 1984-93, 2001—; vice chair Teton County Centennial Com., Jackson, 1989; co-founder Jackson Hole Cmty. Band, 1989—; charter mem. Shepherd of the Mountains Luth. Ch., 1985-2000; active Jackson Hole Brass Quintet, 1985—; mem. local com. Christian Ministry in Nat. Parks, 1988-96; mem. pub. adv. com. Wyo. Pub. Radio, 1990—; com. mem. Jackson divsn. Am. Heart Assn., 1994-95; bd. dirs. Jackson Hole Crimestoppers, 1996—. Recipient Tony Bevinette Friend of Wyo. Tourism award Wyo. Travel Commn., 1993, Bronze Smokey award U.S. Forest Svc., 1998; co-recipient Wyo. News Station of Yr. award AP, 1990; named Colo. Broadcast Newsman of Yr. AP, 1976. Mem.: Broadcast Edn. Assn. Avocations: instrumental music, camping, furniture refinishing, local history. office e-mail. Home: PO Box 1050 Jackson WY 83001-1050 Office: Jackson Hole HS PO Box 568 Jackson WY 83001-0568 E-mail: tninn@aol.com., tninnemann@teton1.k12.wy.us.

NINOS, NICHOLAS PETER, retired career officer, physician; b. Chgo., May 11, 1936; s. Peter Spiros and Ann (Lesczynsky) N. BA in Art, Bradley U., 1958, BS in Chemistry, 1959; MD, U. Ill., Chgo., 1963. Diplomate Am. Bd. Internal Med., Am. Bd. Cardiology. Intern Cook County Hosp., Chgo., 1963-64, resident in internal medicine, 1964-67, fellow in cardiology, 1967-68; commd. capt. U.S. Army, 1968, advanced through grades to col., 1979, chief dept. medicine U.S. Army Community Hosp. Fed. Republic Germany, 1968-69, Wurzberg, Fed. Republic Germany, 1969-72; chief critical care Letterman Army Med. Ctr., San Francisco, 1976-91; dep. comdr. San Francisco med. command Letterman Army Med. Ctr./Naval Hosp. of Oakland, San Francisco and Oakland, Calif., 1988-90; ret., 1991. Assoc. prof. medicine and surgery Uniformed Svcs. U. Health Scis., Bethesda, Md., 1981-91; critical care medicine cons. to U.S. Army Surgeon Gen., 1981-91; lectr. in field. Author: (jour.) Ethics, 1988; co-editor: Nutrition, 1988, Problems in Critical Care, Nutrition Support; mem. editl. bd. Jour. Critical Care Medicine, 1988-91; illustrator: Medical Decision Making, 1988. 2d v.p. Twin Springs Condominium Homeowners Assn., Palm Springs, Calif., 1993-94, sec., 1994-96, v.p., 1999—; ch. bd. councilman St. George Orthodox Ch. of the Desert, Palm Desert, Calif., 1993-95; active Palm Springs Comm., 1993—; bd. dirs. Mizell Sr. Ctr., Palm Springs, 1996—, 1st v.p., 1997-2001, exec. v.p. 2001—. Decorated Legion of Merit, Meritorious Svc. medal with oak leaf cluster. Fellow Am. Coll. Critical Care Medicine (mem. bd. regents 1989-94, chmn. 1989-91); mem. AMA, Soc. Critical Care Medicine (pres. uniformed svcs. sect. 1987-90, Shubin/Weil award 1988), Soc. Med. Cons. to Armed Forces (assoc.), Inst. Critical Care Medicine (exec. v.p. 1991-92), Toastmasters Internat. (sec.-treas. Palm Springs chpt. 1993-94, pres. 1994, gov. area D-3 1994-95, divsn. D dist. 12 gov. 1995-96, spkrs. bur. dist. 12 1994-96), Am. Legion. Avocations: art, skiing, jogging, traveling, music.

NIPERT, DONNA ANN See BARRETT, JESSICA

NIPPER, PATRICIA DIANE, accounting and economics educator; b. Halifax, Va., July 3, 1956; d. Malcolm Bruce and Barbara Jean (Overby) Henderson; m. Jack Jefferson Nipper, Jr., Aug. 27, 1977; 1 child, Megan Brooke. BS, Va. Poly. Inst. and State U., 1977; MBA, Va. Commonwealth U., 1983. CPA, Va. Mktg. analyst Md. Nat. Bank, Balt., 1977-78; credit analyst Ctrl. Fidelity Bank, Richmond, 1978; staff supr. C&P Telephone Co.-Va.; staff mgr. fin. analysis C&P Telephone Cos., Washington, 1983-85, staff mgr. corp. budgets, fin. planning, 1985-88, program mgr. competitive pricing Silver Spring, Md., 1988; assoc. prof. acctg., econs. Southside Va. C.C., Keysville, 1989—. Author: (instructor's manual) Economics, 1998, 2001; contbr. article to profl. jour. Treas., edn. chairperson Fuqua Sch. PTSA, Farmville, Va., 1998-2001. Recipient Master Tchr. Excellence award Nat. Inst. Staff Org. Devel., 1994. Mem. Va. Bus. Educators Assn., Va. Collegiate Honors Coun., Va. C.C. Assn. (Faculty Showcase award 1999), Phi Theta Kappa (advisor 1992-98, Horizon award 1992, Paragon Advisor award 1996), Alpha Delta Kappa. Baptist. Avocations: needlework, photography, scuba diving, reading, singing. Home: 2036 Salishan Dr Halifax VA 24558-3307 Office: Southside Va C C 200 Daniel Rd Keysville VA 23947-3559 E-mail: diane.nipper@sv.vccs.edu.

NIRENBERG, LOUIS, mathematician, educator; b. Hamilton, Ont., Can., Feb. 28, 1925; arrived in U.S., 1945, naturalized, 1954; s. Zuzie and Bina (Katz) Nirenberg; m. Susan Blank, Jan. 25, 1948; children: Marc, Lisa. BSc, McGill U., Montreal, 1945, DSc (hon.) , 1986; MS, NYU, 1947, PhD, 1949; DSc (hon.) , U. Pisa, Italy, 1990, U. Paris Dauphine, 1990, McMaster U., Can., 2000. Mem. faculty NYU, 1949—, prof. math., 1957—, dir. Courant Inst., 1970—72. Visitor Inst. Advanced Study, 1958; hon. prof. Nannkai U., Zhejiang U. Author rsch. articles. Recipient Crafoord prize, Royal Swedish Acad., 1982, Nat. medal of Sci., 1995; fellow NRC, 1951—52, Sloan Found., 1958—60, Guggenheim Found., 1966—67, 1975—76, Fulbright, 1965. Mem.: NAS, Ukrainian Acad. Sci. (fgn.), Accademia de Scienze e Lettere (fgn.), Istituto Lombardo, Accademia dei Lincei (fgn.), French Acad. Scis. (fgn.), Am. Philos. Soc., Am. Math. Soc. (v.p. 1976—78, M. Bocher prize 1959, L.P. Steele prize 1994), Am. Acad. Arts and Scis. Home: 221 W 82nd St New York NY 10024-5406 Office: Courant Inst 251 Mercer St New York NY 10012-1185

NIRENBERG, MARSHALL WARREN, biochemist; b. N.Y.C., N.Y., Apr. 10, 1927; s. Harry Edward and Minerva (Bykowsky) Nirenberg; m. Perola Zaltzman, July 14, 1961. BS in Zoology, U. Fla., 1948, MS, 1952; PhD in Biochemistry, U. Mich., 1957. Postdoctoral fellow Am. Cancer Soc. at NIH, 1957—59; postdoctoral fellow USPHS at NIH, 1959—60; 60mem. staff NIH, 1960—; research biochemist, chief lab. biochem. genetics Nat. Heart, Lung and Blood Inst., 1962—. Co-recipient Louisa Gross Horowitz prize Columbia, 1968, Nobel prize in medicine and physiology, 1968; recipient Molecular Biology award, NAS, 1962, award in biol. scis., Washington Acad. Scis., 1962, medal, HEW, 1964, Modern Medicine award, 1963, Harrison Howe award, Am. Chem. Soc., 1964, Nat. Medal Sci., Pres. Johnson, 1965, Hildebrand award, Am. Chem. Soc., 1966, Research Corp. award, 1966, A.C.P. award, 1967, award merit, Gairdner Found., Can, 1967, Prix Charles Leopold Meyer, French Acad. Scis., 1967, Franklin medal, Franklin Inst., 1968, Albert Lasker Med. Research award, 1968, Priestly award, 1968. Fellow: AAAS, N.Y. Acad. Scis.; mem.: NAS, Pontificial Acad. Scis., Leopoldina Deutsche Akademie der Naturforscher, Soc. Devel. Biology, Soc. for Study Devel. and Growth, Washingon Acad. Scis., Harvey Soc. (hon.), Biophys. Soc., Am. Acad. Arts and Scis., Am. Chem. Soc. (Paul Lewis award enzyme chemistry 1964), Am. Soc. Biol. Chemists. Achievements include research in mechanism protein synthesis, genetic code, nucleic acids, regulatory mechanisms in synthesis macromolecules, and neurobiology.*

NIRENSTEIN, JACK, writer; b. Poland, Dec. 25, 1928; came to U.S., 1931; s. Hyman and Frieda N.; divorced; children: Michael, Debby Bloom. Owner advt. co. Virtu Assocs., N.Y.C., 1965-86. Author: Guided Muscles for Winning Sports, 2000. With U.S. Army, 1947-49. Avocations: running, sports, computer graphics, photography. Home: # 50A 623 Canterbury Dr Myrtle Beach SC 29579 E-mail: pro8form@aol.com.

NIRO, CHERYL, lawyer; b. Feb. 19, 1950; d. Samuel James and Nancy (Canezaro) Ippolito; m. William Luciano Niro, July 1, 1979; children: Christopher William, Melissa Leigh. BS with highest honors, U. Ill., 1972; JD, No. Ill. U., 1980. Bar: Ill. 1981, U.S. Dist. Ct. (no. dist.) Ill. 1981, U.S. Ct. Appeals (7th cir.) 1990, U.S. Supreme Ct. 1999, cert.: negotiator, mediator, facilitator. Assoc. Pope Ballard Sheppard & Fowle, Chgo., 1980-81; ptnr. Partridge and Niro PC; now ptnr. Quinlan & Carroll, Chgo. Spec counsel to atty gen Office Ill. Atty. Gen., 1996—99; consult Ill Office Educ, 1975; conflict resolution program develop US Atty Gen; pres Assocs in Dispute Resolution Inc; exec dir Comt to Commerorate US Constituion in Ill, 1985—86; creator Bicentennial Law Sch Program; tchg asst program instrn lawyers mediation and negotiation worshops; guest lectr Harvard Univ; mem appt panel US Ct Appeals (7th cir). Chmn Task Force on Children; co-chair Ill. Conclave on Legal Edn.; bd dirs Univ Chicago Lying-In Hosp, 1982—. Named one of Ten Most Influential Women Lawyers in Ill, Am Lawyer Media, 2000; named to Today's Chgo. Woman Mag. Hall of Fame, 2002. Mem.: ATLA, ABA (comn multijurisdictional practice, standing comt bar servs, dispute resolution sect coun, house delegs), Internat. Bar Assn., Ill Bar Asn (mem assembly 1993, bd govs 1994—97, treas 1995—96, 2d vpres 1997—98, pres 1999—2000, pres. 1999—2000, standing comt legal-related educ pub), Ill Trial Lawyers Asn. Home: 633 N East Ave Oak Park IL 60302-1715 Office: Quinlan & Carroll 30 N Lasalle St Ste 2900 Chicago IL 60602-2590 Business E-Mail: cniro@qclaw.com.

NIRSCHL, ROBERT PHILLIP, orthopedic surgeon; b. South Milwaukee, Wis., Aug. 28, 1933; s. Boyd A. and Helen (Wozny) N.; m. Mary Ann Oleniczak, June 21, 1958; children: Suzanne, Robert C., Julie. Student, Coll. Holy Cross, 1951-53, Marquette U., 1953-54; MD, Med. Coll. Wis./Marquette U., 1958; MS, U. Minn., 1965. Diplomate Am. Bd. Orthop. Surgery. Intern St. Mary's Hosp., Duluth, Minn., 1958-59; resident in orthop. Mayo Clinic, Rochester, 1959-63; lt. comdr. USN, Washington, 1963-65; pvt. practice Arlington, Va., 1965—. Attending orthop. surgeon Arlington (Va.) Hosp., v.p. med. staff, 1980-83, dir. Hand Surgery Svc., 1975-85; chief orthop. surgery No. Va. Cmty. Hosp., 1971-82; founding dir. Nirschl Orthop. Sports Medicine Clinic, Va. Sports Medicine Inst., 1974—, Nirschl Orthop. Sports Med. Clinic Orthop. Sports Medicine Fellowship Program Arlington Hosp., 1987—; mem. clin. faculty Georgetown U. Med. Ctr., 1965—; orthop. cons. Pres.'s Coun. Phys. Fitness, Washington, 1981-87; mem. sports sci. com. USTA, N.Y.C., 1987-94; course dir. numerous symposia in field. Author: Arm Care, 1981, rev. edit., 1996, Isoflex Exercise System, 1983; chief med. editor Orthop. Today, 1983-93; mem. editl. bd. The Physician and Sportsmedicine, 1992—, The Med. Sentinel, 1996—; creator 6 video programs; contbr. chpts. to books and over 100 articles to profl. publs.; patentee in field. Chmn. Jeffersonian Health Policy Found., Williamsburg, Va., 1994-97; mem. Va. Bd. Medicine, 2000—. Grantee Pfizer Inc., 1992-93, Sano Corp, 1993-94, Iomed Corp., 1999—. Mem. AMA, ACS, Am. Acad. Orthop. Surgery (health fin. com. 1994-2000, bd. counselors 2000—, comm. and state soc. coms. bd. of counselors 2000—), Am. Orthop. Sports Medicine Soc. (ethics com. 1992-97), Soc. Tennis Medicine and Sci. (exec. com.), Ea. Orthop. Assn., Washington Orthop. Soc., Va. Orthop. Soc. (pres. 1998-99), Med. Soc. Va. (chmn. sports medicine com. 1973-84, trustee polit. action com. 1990—, legis. com. 1995—), Arlington County Med. Soc. (pres. 1977, chmn. legis. com. 1987—, Welburn award 1995), Washington Golf and Country Club. Republican. Roman Catholic. Avocations: fitness activities. Office: Nirschl Orthop Sports Medicine Clinic 1715 N George Mason Dr Ste 504 Arlington VA 22205-3670 E-mail: nirschl@erols.com.

NISBET, JOHN STIRLING, electrical engineering educator; b. Darval, Scotland, Dec. 10, 1927; s. Robert George Jackson and Kathleen Agnes (Young) N.; m. J. Valerie Payne, Jan. 10, 1953; children: Robert John, Alexander Stevens. BS, London U., 1950; MS, Pa. State U., 1957, PhD, 1960. Trainee, engr. Nash & Thompson Ltd., Surbiton, Eng., 1944-51; engr. Decca Radar Ltd., 1951-53, Can. Westinghouse, Hamilton, Ont., 1953-55; research assoc. electric engring. dept. Pa. State U., University Park, 1955-60, prof., 1960—, Disting. Alumni prof. elec. engring., 1985-90, Disting. Alumni prof. elec. engring. emeritus, 1990—, dir. Ionosphere Rsch. Lab., 1971-84, dir. Communications and Space Scis. Lab., 1984-86. Author numerous sci. papers; mem. editorial bd.: Jour. Atmospheric and Terrestrial Physics. NSF sr. postdoctoral fellow Brussels, 1965; Fulbright Hays lectr. Council Internat. Exchange Scholars, USSR, 1979; NRC-Nat. Acad. Sci. fellow Goddard Space Flight Ctr., 1980 Sr. mem. IEEE, Am. Geophys. Union, Sigma Xi, Phi Kappa Phi Unitarian Universalist. Home: 618 Glenn Rd State College PA 16803-3474 Office: Communications & Space Scis Lab 316 Electrical Eng University Park PA 16802

NISBET, THOMAS K. architect; b. Richland Center, Wis., Jan. 9, 1931; s. Thomas Kenneth and Eva Louise (Klein) N.; m. Lynnette Patricia MacIntyre, Aug. 27, 1954; children: Bruce W., Jay T., Christopher W. Student, Columbia Coll., 1949-51; BArch, Columbia U., 1955. Registered arch., N.Y., Wis. Apprentice arch. Albert M. Skinner AIA, Watertown, N.Y., 1946-49; asst. editl. Archtl. Record, N.Y.C., 1950-51; draftsman Weiler/Strang, Madison, Wis., 1952-55; arch. H.C. Montgomery AIA, Watertown, 1958-61; arch./assoc. Flad & Assocs., Madison, 1961-83; prin. Nisbet/Archs., 1983—. Mem. Wis. Examining Bd., 1982-83, Nat. Coun. Archs. Registration Bd., 1983. Works include co-designer Sentry Ins. home office, 1975 (honor award 1975), Wis. Telephone/ASC/WARF, 1970-75 (merit awards 1970-75), U. Wis. Libr./Vilas Hall (merit award 1974); awarded commission for Tri State Vets. Meml. with Severson/Schultz Sculptors. Deacon Westminster Presbyn. Ch., Madison, 1964; v.p., bd. dirs. Nakoma Golf Club, Madison, 1976-82. Recipient Columbia U. traveling fellowship Europe, 1957-58. Mem. AIA, Wis. Archs. Found. (pres. 1981-85). Avocations: art, photography. Office: Nisbet/Architects 4340 Hillcrest Cir Madison WI 53705-5017 E-mail: tknisbet@chorus.net.

NISBETT, DOROTHEA JO, retired nursing educator; b. Lodi, Tex., May 16, 1940; d. Cecil Robey and Lola Ruby (Pippin) Lovett; m. Leonce Paul Lanoux Jr., June 10, 1966 (div. July 1984); 1 child, Cecil Lance Lanoux; m. James Harris Nisbett, May 12, 1990. Diploma in nursing, Tex. Ea. Sch. Nursing, 1963; BSN, Tex. Christian U., 1965; MS, Tex. Woman's U., 1977. RN, Tex. Asst. charge nurse med./surg. unit Med. Ctr. Hosp., Tyler, Tex., 1963-64, asst. dir. nursing, 1967; instr. nursing Tex. Ea. Sch. Nursing, 1965-66; head nurse med./surg. unit Providence Hosp., Waco, Tex., 1966-67; dir. nursing Laird Meml. Hosp., Kilgore, 1967-69; instr. nursing Kilgore Coll., 1969-73, McLennan C.C., Waco, 1973-96, ret., 1996; asst. prof. U. Tex. Health Sci. Ctr., San Antonio, 1996-98; ret., 1998; ind. beauty cons. Mary Kay Cosmetics, 1997—. Charter sec. Am. Heart Assn., Kilgore, 1968-69; bd. dirs. Heart of Tex. Soccer Assn., Waco, 1982-85. Mem. Nat. Orgn. Assoc. Degree Nursing, Tex. Jr. Coll. Tchr. Assn., Assn. Profl. and Staff Devel., Beta Sigma Phi (Outstanding Young Woman of Yr. 1981, 98, Sweetheart 1970, 82, 91, Woman of Yr. 1990, 98, 99, Order of the Rose 1980, Silver Cir. award 1990). Methodist. Avocations: golf, arts and crafts.

NISBETT, RICHARD EUGENE, psychology educator; b. Littlefield, Tex., June 1, 1941; s. R. Wayne and Helen (King) N.; m. Susan Ellen Isaacs, June 29, 1969; children: Matthew, Sarah. AB summa cum laude, Tufts U., 1962; PhD, Columbia U., 1966. Asst. prof. psychology Yale U., New Haven, 1966-71; assoc. prof. psychology U. Mich., Ann Arbor, 1971-77, prof., 1977—, Theodore M. Newcomb prof. psychology, 1989-92, Theodore M. Newcomb disting. univ. prof. of psychology, 1992—. Author: (with others) Attribution: Perceiving the Causes of Behavior, 1972, Induction: Processes of Inference, Learning and Discovery, 1986, Rules for Reasoning, 1992, (with L. Ross) Human Inference: Strategies and Shortcomings of Social Judgment, 1980, The Person and the Situation, 1991, (with D. Cohen) Culture of Honor, 1996. Recipient Donald T. Campbell award for disting. rsch. in social psychology APA, 1982, Disting. Sci. Contbn. award APA, 1991, Am. Acad. Arts & Sci., 1992, Disting. Sr. Scientist award Soc. Exptl. Social Psychology, 1995, J. McKeen Cattell award, 1998; fellow Ctr. for Advanced Studies in Behavioral Scis., William James award Am. Psychol. Soc., 1995, John Simon Guggenheim fellow, 2001; Russell Sage Found. scholar, 2001, Nat. Acad. Sci., 2002. Office: U Mich 5261 ISR Rsch Ctr Group Dynamics Ann Arbor MI 48106

NISENHOLTZ, MARTIN ABRAM, telecommunications executive, educator; b. Phila., Apr. 1, 1955; s. Louis William and Rhoda Greta (Koenig) N.; m. Anne Ermine Stockler, July 26, 1987; children: Johanna, Marjorie. BA, U. Pa., 1977, MA, 1979. Research scientist NYU, N.Y.C., 1979-83; mgr. Ogilvy & Mather, 1983-84, v.p., 1984-89, sr. v.p., 1989-94; dir. content strategy Ameritech Corp., Chgo., 1994-95; pres. N.Y. Times Electronic Media Co., 1995-99; CEO N.Y. Times Digital, 1999—. Mem. oper. Ogilvy & Mather Direct, 1992—94; adj. assoc. prof. NYU, 1983—; bd. dirs. internet advtsg. bur. Ctr. for Comm., 1999. Mem. Annenberg Sch. Alumni Bd., 1996—. Recipient Merrill Panott Citizenship award, 1997; grantee Nat. Endowment Arts, 1981. Mem.: Online Pubs. Assn. (founding chmn. 2001—), Interactive Svcs. Assn. (dir. 1985—94, chmn. 1991, Disting. Svc. award 1994). Office: NY Times Digital 500 7th Ave New York NY 10000-6700 E-mail: martin@nytimes.com.

NISENOFF, MARTIN, physicist; b. N.Y.C. s. Louis and Ruth Nisenoff; m. Phyllis B. Simon, 1994; three children. BS, Worcester Poly. Inst., 1950; MS, Purdue U., 1952, PhD, 1960. Rsch. assoc. Purdue U., West Lafayette, Ind., 1960-61; physicist Ford Sci. Lab., Dearborn, Mich., 1961-70; low temperature physicist Stanford Rsch. Inst., Menlo Park, Calif., 1970-72; rsch. physicist U.S. Naval Rsch. Lab., Washington, 1972-99; physicist M. Nisenoff Assocs., North Bethesda, Md., 1999—. Fellow IEEE; mem. Am. Phys. Soc., Applied Superconductivity Conf. Inc. (bd. dirs. 1982-88, 90-96, 98—). E-mail: m.nisenoff@ieee.org.

NISHI, JIN, lawyer; b. Torrance, Calif., Mar. 28, 1965; s. Katsuhisa and Kikuko Nishi. BA, UCLA, 1987; JD, U. San Francisco, 1992. Bar: Calif. 1992, Hawaii 1994, U.S. Dist. Ct. (cen. dist.) Calif. 1993, U.S. Dist. Ct. (no. dist.) Calif. 1997. Pvt. practice, Gardena, Calif., 1992-93; assooc. Liddi & Rose, Long Beach, 1993-96; assoc. Erickson Arbuthnot Kilduff Day & Lindstrom, Oakland, 1996—. Mem. Japanese Bar Assn. (bd. govs. 1993-96). Office: Ericksen Arbuthnot Kilduff Day & Lindstrom 530 Water St # 720 Oakland CA 94607-3746

NISHIKIDA, KOICHI, research scientist; b. Osaka City, Japan, Nov. 12, 1938; s. Naokazu and Yukie (Tanaka) N.; m. Michiko Kobayashi, Jan. 15, 1968; 1 child, Kaori. BS, Osaka U., Japan, 1961, MA, 1963, DSc, 1967. Rsch. scientist Shionogi Pharm. Co., Osaka City, Osaka, Japan, 1963-72; rsch. assoc. U. Tenn., Knoxville, 1972-75, U. Utah, Salt Lake City, 1975-77; dir. R&D Union Giken Co., Hirakata, Osaka, 1977-78, Perkin-Elmer Japan Co., Yokohama, Japan, 1979-91; sr. staff scientist Perkin-Elmer Instruments, Norwalk, Conn., 1991-2000; sr. scientist Thermo Spectra-Tech, Shelton, 2001—02; principal scientist Thermo Nicolet, Madison, Wis., 2002—. Author: (in Japanese) Material Characterization by Infrared Spectroscopy, 1988, FT-IR Spctroscopy, 1990; (in English) Selected Applications of Modern FT-IR Techniques, 1995; contbr. articles to profl. jours. Mem. Japan Soc. Fairfield County (bd. dirs. 1993-97, v.p. 1998-2000), Soc. Applied Spectroscopy (Gold Medal award N.Y. sect. 1997). Office: Thermo Spectra-Tech 5225 Verona Rd Madison WI 53711

NISHIMURA, JOSEPH YO, retired retail executive, accountant; b. Berkeley, Calif., Nov. 4, 1933; s. Masamoto and Kimiko (Ishihara) N.; m. Joyce Toshiye Mori, Sept. 1, 1956; children: Brenda Joyce, Stephen Lloyd. AB cum laude, Princeton U., 1956; MBA, Stanford U., 1961. CPA, Calif., N.Y.; cert. Employee Benefit Specialist. Audit supr. Touche Ross & Co., San Francisco, 1961-66; contr. Scott Co. of Calif., Oakland, 1966-67, Purity Stores, Inc., Burlingame, Calif., 1967-69; pres. Cubit Sys. Corp., 1969-72; sr. v.p. Golden West Fin. Corp., Oakland, 1972-73; exec. v.p. Victory Mkts., Inc., Norwich, N.Y., 1973-90; gen. ptnr. Mori Enterprises, 1994—. Dir. Carl's Drug Co., Rome, N.Y., 1988-90, mem. site devel. com., Wakefern Food Corp., Edison, N.J., 1996—. V.p., bd. dirs. Chenango Meml. Hosp., Norwich, 1981-87; bd. dirs. United Fund, Norwich, 1984-90, N.Y. State Food Mchts. Assn., 1988-90, Binghamton (N.Y.) Philharmonic, 1988-98, treas., 1990-93. Served to lt. (j.g.) USN, 1956-59; Japan. Mem. AICPA, N.Y. State Soc. CPA's, Calif. Soc. CPA's, Marbella Country Club, Princeton (N.Y.C.) Club. Democrat. Presbyterian.

NISHIMURA, KOICHI, electronics manufacturing company executive; B Elec. Engring., M Elec. Engring., San Jose State U.; D Materials Sci. and Engring., Stanford U. Mgr. disk film design, tech. and mfg. divsns. IBM; COO Solectron, Milpitas, Calif., 1988-90, pres., COO, 1990-92, co-CEO, pres., pres., CEO, 1992—, chmn. bd., 1996—. Chmn. bd. Santa Clara Valley Mfg. Groups; mem. bds. Merix Corp., Ctr. Quality Mgmt.; mem. adv. bd. Santa Clara U. Tearney Sch. Bus. Past bd. mem. Tech. Mus. Innovation, San Jose, Calif.; active Japanese Western U.S. Assn., Ku-Ai Kai Sr. Cmty. Ctr., San Jose. Recipient Malcolm Baldrige Nat. Quality award, 1991, 97. Mem. IEEE, Soc. Mfg. Engrs. Office: Solectron 777 Gibraltar Dr Bldg 5 Milpitas CA 95035-6332*

NISHIMURA, PETE HIDEO, oral surgeon; b. Hilo, Hawaii, Aug. 7, 1922; s. Hideichi and Satsuki N.; m. Tomoe Nishimura, June, 1949; children—Dennis Dean, Grant Neil, Dawn Naomi. Student, U. Hawaii, 1940-44; D.D.S., U. Mo., 1947; MSD., Northwestern U., 1949. Practice dentistry specializing in oral surgery, Honolulu, 1952—; pres. Oral Surgery Group, 1978—. Mem. coun. Nat. Bd. Dental Examination; dir. Hawaii Dental Svc., 1962-85, pres., 1970-72, 76-78; pres. State Bd. Dental Examiners, Delta Sigma Delta, Fedn. Dentaire Internat. Served with U.S. Army, 1952-54. Fellow Am. Coll. Dentists, Internat. Coll. Dentists; mem. Hawaii Dental Assn. (past pres.), Delta Dental Plans Assn. (dir.), Honolulu County Dental Soc., ADA, Hawaii Soc. Oral Surgeons, Am. Assn. Oral and Maxillofacial Surgeons, Western Soc. Oral and Maxillofacial Surgeons, Am. Assn. Dental Examiners, Pierre Fauchard

Acad. (citation for oustanding contbn. to arts and sci. of dentistry 1987). Democrat. Home: 494 Halemaumau St Honolulu HI 96821-2135 Office: 848 S Beretania St Honolulu HI 96813-2551 E-mail: hilopete@aol.com.

NISHITANI, MARTHA, dancer; b. Seattle, Feb. 27, 1920; d. Denjiro and Jin (Aoto) N. BA in Comparative Arts, U. Wash., 1958; studied with, Eleanor King, Mary Ann Wells, Perry Mansfield, Cornish Sch., Conn. Coll. Sch. Dance, Long Beach State U. Founder, dir. Martha Nishitani Modern Dance Sch. and Co., Seattle, 1950—; dance dir. Helen Bush Sch. and Central YWCA, 1951-54; choreographer U. Wash. Opera Theater, 1955-65, Intiman Theater, 1972—; dance instr. Elementary and Secondary Edn. Act Program, 1966; dance specialist spl. edn. program Shoreline Pub. Schs., 1970-72; condr. workshops and concerts King County Youth Correctional Instns., 1972-73. Dance adv. counsel Wash. Cultural Enrichment Program; dance adv. bd. Seattle Parks and Recreation; mem. multimedia Japanese-Am. legacy project to capture history and testimony of Japanese Americans, 1999. Dancer Eleanor King Co., Seattle, 1946-50, dance films, 1946-51, Channel 9, Ednl. TV, 1967-68; lectr. demonstrator numerous colls., festivals, convs., childrens theater.; author articles on dance; one of the subjects: A Celebration of 100 Years of Dance in Washington, 1989. Trustee Allied Arts Seattle, 1967. Recipient Theta Sigma Phi Matrix Table award, 1968, Asian Am. Living Treasure award Northwest Asian Am. Theater, 1984, Small Bus. award Seattle Mayor, 1998; listed Dance Archives, N.Y.C. Libr., 1991, N.Y.C. Lincoln Ctr. Dance Archives, 1991, U. Wash. Libr. Archives, 1993, exhibit of Japanese Am. Women of Achievement, Burke Mus., 1997, Ploudit award nat. Dance Assn., 1999, 50th Anniversary of Martha Nishitani Modern Dance Sch. and Creative Dance for Children in Sch., 2000; selected for DENSHO-the Japanese-Am. Legacy Project, 1998. Mem. Am. Dance Guild (exec. com. 1961-63), Com. Research in Dance, Seattle Art Mus., Internat. Dance Alliance (adv. council 1984), Smithsonian Assos., Progressive Animal Welfare Soc. Address: 4205 University Way NE PO Box 45264 Seattle WA 98145-0264 *Until a few years ago a compelling force within me would let nothing interfere with performing, teaching, and directing dance. My belief: "I must be selfish about that which means most to me." This dedication was in constant battle with loneliness, frugality and neglect of loved ones. My first solo dance was Credo in Conflict. I have earned a degree of success, satisfaction, joy and recognition. My thoughts are now that I have learned to pursue a balance in life as I battle. The scars of selfishness persist but the broader view brings validity to my beliefs.*

NISHIWAKI, TAKEO, structural engineering educator; b. Nakatsugawa, Gifu-Pref, Japan, Jan. 20, 1927; s. Isehiko and Mae (Endo) N.; m. Ayako Watabe, Nov. 17, 1955; children: Sachiko Ogura, Yukiko Mabe. Assoc. of Engring., Nagoya (Japan) Inst. Tech., 1949; D of Engring., Tokyo (Japan) U., 1969. Rsch. assoc. Tokyo (Japan) U., 1949-59; assoc. prof. Musashi Inst. Tech., Tokyo, Japan, 1959-69, prof., 1969-97, prof. emeritus, 1997—. Mem. Cons. Com. for Seto-Bridge, Japan, 1959-70, Cons. Com. for Ohnaruto-Bridge, Japan, 1961-65; chmn. Rsch. Com. for High-Strength Bolted Joints, 1990-94. Recipient Tanaka award Soc. Civil Engrs., Japan, 1991. Avocations: gardening, photography. Home: 2-81-11 Kotake-cho Nerimaku Tokyo 176-0004 Japan Office: Musashi Inst Tech 1-28-1 Tamazutsumi Setagaya 158 Tokyo Japan E-mail: tnisiwa@eng.musahi-tech.ac.jp.

NISHIYAMA, CHIAKI, economist, educator; b. Fukuoka-ken, Japan, Aug. 9, 1924; s. Michiki and Teruko (Tsuji) N.; m. Shigeko Okabe, June 9, 1957; children: Keita, Mikiko. BA in Econs., Rikkyo U., Tokyo, 1950; MA in Polit. Sci., U. Chgo., 1952, PhD in Social Thought, 1960, postgrad. in econs., 1959-60. Lectr. U. Chgo., 1957-61; assoc. prof. Rikkyo U., 1962-64, prof. econs., 1964-90, prof. emeritus, 1990—. Sr. rsch. fellow Hoover Instn., Stanford U., 1977—; prof. econs. Grad. Sch. Internat. Mgmt., U. Japan, 1994-97; lectr. Tng. Inst., Min. Trade and Industry, Japanese Govt., 1964-66, Gakushuin U., 1970-71, Waseda U., 1972-74; exec. dir. Assembly on U.S.-Japan Econ. Policy, 1972-76; prime minister's spl. envoy to White House, 1971, 75; specialist counselor Japan Employers' Assn., 1975-85; del. European Assembly, Strasbourg, France, 1982; world travel for Japanese Min. Fgn. Affairs, Japan External Trade Orgn., 1968-82; lectr. various univs., U.S. and Europe, 1976-94; mem. Am. Citizen to Citizen Econ. and Fin. Mgmt. Del. to the USSR, 1991; spl. envoy of Japan to Czechoslovakia, Hungary, Bulgaria, Ukraine, Russia, 1991. Author numerous books including: Lecture on Modern Economics, 1964, Free Economy, Its Policies and Principles, 1974, The Price for Prosperity, 1974, A Monetary History and Analysis of the Japanese Economy, 1968-70, 74, Reflection on Japanese Economy, 1976, Monetarism, 1976, The Last Chance for Creativity, Liberty and Prosperity, 1981, Human Capitalism, 1982, The Fourth Philosophy, Vol. I, 1982, Vol. II, 1983, No Limits to Growth, 1984, The Essence of Hayek, 1984, The Japanese Economy, 1987, Paradigm Shift, 1987, Japanese Economy and Life Tomorrow, 1988, A New Economics Under a New Paradigm, 1991, The End of Recession, 1994, Depression or New Prosperity, 1998, Market Economy: New Way, 1999; editl. bd. Jour. Internat. Money and Fin., 1981—. Hon. fellow Inst. Econ. Affairs, London, 1976—; mem. adv. bd. Econ. Inst. Paris, 1984-86, Carl Menger Inst., Wien, 1984; councilor The Daiwa Welfare Found., 1994—. Recipient Japan Econ. Lit. award Japan Econ. Jour., 1974; Earhart fellow, 1967-61, E.C. Nef fellow, 1958-59, Woodrow Wilson Internat. Ctr. for Scholars fellow, 1976-77; grantee Relm, 1964-67, Ford, 1965-66, Lilly, 1966-67, Bank of Japan, Bankers Assn. Japan, other fin. orgns., 1978-83. Mem. Am. Enterprise Inst. (adj. scholar), Am. Econ. Assn., Econometric Soc., Theoretical Econs. Assn., Internat. Econ. Assn., Statis. Soc., Mont Pelerin Soc. (pres. 1980-82, sr. v.p. 1982-85, hon. v.p. 1986-88), Japan Econ. Rsch. Ctr. (spl. mem. 1964). Episcopalian. Office: Nishiyama-Kenkyushitsu 5-15-18 Kamiuma Setagaya-ku 154-0011 Tokyo Japan

NISKANEN, WILLIAM ARTHUR, JR. economist, think-tank executive; b. Bend, Oreg., Mar. 13, 1933; s. William Arthur and Nina Elizabeth (McCord) Niskanen; m. Kathryn Washburn; children: Lia, Pamela, Jaime. BA, Harvard U., 1954; MA, U. Chgo., 1955, PhD, 1962. Staff economist RAND Corp., Santa Monica, Calif., 1957—62; staff dir. U.S. Dept. Def., Washington, 1962—64; divsn. dir. Inst. Def. Analyses, 1964—70; asst. dir. Office of Mgmt. and Budget, 1970—72; prof. U. Calif., Berkeley, 1972—75; chief economist Ford Motor Co., Dearborn, Mich., 1975—80; prof. UCLA, 1980—81; mem. Coun. Econ. Advisers, Washington, 1981—85; chmn. CATO Inst., 1985—. Author: Bureaucracy and Representative Goverment, 1971, Reaganomics, 1988, Policy Analysis and Public Choic, 1998, Going Digital, 1998; editor: Regulation mag., 1990—96. Founder Nat. Tax Limitation Com. Mem.: Atlantic Econ. Assn. (past pres.), Pub. Choice Soc. (past pres.), Am. Econ. Assn. Republican. Office: Cato Inst 1000 Massachusetts Ave NW Washington DC 20001-5400 E-mail: wniskan@cato.org.

NISLY, L. LAMAR, literature educator; BA, Messiah Coll., 1990; MA, PhD, U. Del., 1993. Asst. prof. English Bluffton (Ohio) Coll., 1996—2000, assoc. prof. English, 2000—. Author: (book) Impossible to Say: Representing Religious Mystery in Fiction by Malamud, Percy, Ozick, and O'Connor, 2002; contbr. articles to profl. jours. Grantee, Bluffton Coll., 1999. Mem.: MLA, Christianity and Lit. Office: Bluffton Coll 280 W College Ave Bluffton OH 45817 Business E-Mail: nislyl@bluffton.edu.

NISLY, LORETTA LYNN, medical and surgical nurse, geriatrics nurse; b. Cheverly, Md., Jan. 26, 1967; d. Mart and Mary (Miller) Overholt; m. Timothy Daniel Nisly, July 18, 1987. AD, Germanna Community Coll., Locust Grove, Va., 1994; LPN, Piedmont Tech. Edn. Ctr., Culpeper, Va., 1989. LPN, RN, Va. Med.-surg. charge nurse Culpeper Regional Hosp., 1989—90, 1995—2002; RN Family Birth Ctr./Culpeper Regional Hosp., 2002—; charge nurse Mt. View Nursing Home, Aroda, Va., 1990-92, Orange County Nursing Home, Orange, 1992-94. Recipient Florence Nightengale award Germanna Cmty. Coll., 1995. Mem. Mennonite. Avocations: horseback riding, reading, sports. Home: HC 5 Box 128 Aroda VA 22709-9703

NISSEN, BRUCE ALLEN, labor studies educator; b. Ames, Iowa, Jan. 20, 1948; s. Raymond A. and Irene A. Nissen; m. Karen L. Lieberman, Apr. 26, 1978; children: Jared A., Leif A. BA, Grinnell Coll., 1970; PhD, Columbia U., 1975. Prof. labor studies Ind. U. N.W., Gary, 1985-97, Fla. Internat. U., Miami, 1997—. Editor: Theories of the Labor Movement, 1987, Unions and Workplace Reorganization, 1997, Which Direction for Organized Labor?, 1999, Unions in a Globalized Environment, 2002; author: Fighting for Jobs, 1995. Office: Ctr Labor Rsch and Studies Fla Internat U University Park Miami FL 33199-0001

NISSENSON, ALLEN RICHARD, physician, educator; b. Chgo., Dec. 10, 1946; s. Harry and Sylvia Lillian (Chapnitsky) N.; m. Charna H. Karp, May 28, 1978; 1 child, Ariel Rose. BS in Medicine, Northwestern U., 1967, MD, 1971. Diplomate Am. Bd. Internal Medicine, bd. cert. internal medicine and nephrology. Intern in medicine Michael Reese Hosp. and Med. Ctr., Chgo., 1971-72, resident in internal medicine, 1972-74; fellowship in nephrology Northwestern U., 1974-76; assoc. medicine Northwestern U. Med. Sch., 1976-77; asst. prof. medicine UCLA Sch. Medicine, 1977-82, assoc. prof. medicine, 1982-88, prof. medicine, 1988—; dir. dialysis program UCLA Ctr. for the Health Scis., 1977—, med. dir. renal mgmt. strategies. Adj. attending physician Northwestern Meml. Hosp., Chgo., 1976-77; asst. attending physician UCLA Ctr. for Health Scis., 1977-82, assoc. attending physician, 1988—; attending physician nephrology Wadsworth VA Hosp., 1978—; cons. on peritoneal dialysis Baxter-Travenol Labs., 1981—; mem. nephrology adv. com. Nephrology Nursing Edn. Grant, Calif. State U., 1983-90; vice chmn. Forum of End Stage Renal Disease Networks, 1988-91; mem. sci. adv. bd. Nat. Kidney Found., 1989-91, chmn. coun. on clin. nephrology, dialysis and transplantation, 1989-91; cons. on End Stage Renal Disease reimbursement Rand Corp., 1990—, others. Editor-in-chief Advances in Renal Replacement Therapy, 1993—; mem. editl. bd. Dialysis and Transplantation, 1978—, UCLA Health Insights, 1981-89, Perspectives in Peritoneal Dialysis, 1983—, Internat. Jour. Artificial Organs, 1984—, Seminars in Dialysis, 1987—, Am. Jour. Nephrology, 1989—, Am. Jour. Kidney Diseases, 1989—, Geriat. Nephrology and Urology Jour., 1989—; mem. editl. adv. bd. Contemporary Dialysis, 1983—, Nephrology Practice Today, 1989—, Hematopoietic Therapy Index and Revs., 1993—, Primary Care Reports, 1994—; editl. cons. Am. Jour. Nephrology, 1981-88; contbr. chpts. to books, abstracts and articles to profl. publs. Recipient Nat. Kidney Found. So. Calif. Cmty. Svc. award, 1981; Robert Wood Johnson policy fellow Office of Sen. Paul Wellstone, 1994-95. Fellow ACP; mem. Am. Soc. for Artifical Internal Organs, Am. Fedn. for Clin. Rsch., Am. Soc. Nephrology, Internat. Soc. Nephrology, Internat. Soc. Artificial Organs, Western Soc. for Clin. Investigation, European Dialysis and Transplant Assn., N.Am. Soc. for Dialysis and Transplantation, Renal Physicians' Assn. (bd. dirs. 1993—, sec. bd. dirs. 1994—, pres. 1999-2001), Calif. Renal Physicians (bd. dirs. 1987—). Office: UCLA Med Ctr Dialysis Ctr Ste 565-59 200 Medical Plaza Los Angeles CA 90024-6945 E-mail: anissenson@mednet.ucla.edu.

NISSINEN, MIKKO, performing company executive; b. Helsinki, Finland; Student, Finnish Nat. Ballet Sch., 1973—77, Kirov Ballet Sch., 1979. Dancer Dutch Nat. Ballet, Basel Ballet; prin. dancer San Francisco Ballet; artistic dir. Marin Ballet, San Rafael, Calif., 1996—98, Alberta Ballet, Calgary, Canada, 1998, Boston Ballet, Boston, 2001—. Office: Boston Ballet 19 Clarendon St Boston MA 02116-6100*

NISSINEN, MIKKO PEKKA, dancer; b. Helsinki, Finland, Mar. 4, 1962; came to U.S., 1987; s. Pekka and Pirkko (Pulkkinen) N. Grad., Finnish Nat. Ballet Sch., 1977; postgrad., Leningrad Acad. Ballet Sch., 1979-80. Mem. corps de ballet Finnish Nat. Ballet, Helsinki, 1977-79, soloist, 1980-82; grand sujete Dutch Nat. Ballet, Amsterdam, The Netherlands, 1982-84; soloist Basel (Switzerland) Ballet, 1984-87, San Francisco Ballet, 1987-88, prin. dancer, 1988-96; artistic dir. Marin Ballet, 1996-97, Alberta Ballet, Calgary, Canada, 1998—2002, Boston Ballet, 2001—. Guest artist La Bayadere, Nat. Ballet Can., 1989, Oberlin Dance Collective, 1993; bd. dirs. Le Don Des Etoiles, 1989—; guest tchr. Royal Acad. of Dancing, 1993, Kennedy Ctr. Ednl. Program, 1994, Nat. Ballet Sch., Toronto, 1994; lectr. on dance history and state of dance today Stanord U., Leathbridge U., St. Mary's Coll., Christensen Soc. Repertoire as dancer includes (with San Francisco Ballet) The Sleeping Beauty, Swan Lake, Bizet Pas de Deux, Handel-a Celebration, Haffner Symphony, Con Brio, Ballet d'Isoline, Giuliani: Variations on a Theme, Tchaikovsky Pas de Deux, Symphony in C, Theme and Variations, Ballo della Regina, The Nutcracker, Airs de Ballet, Variations de Ballet, Rodin, Rodeo, Maelstrom, Dark Elegies, Harvest Moon, Napoli, Job, The Wanderer Fantasy, In the middle, somewhat elevated, Calcium Light Night, Le Corsaire Pas de Deux, Dreams of Harmony, Pulcinella, The Dream; (with other cos.) Don Quixote, Giselle, A Midsummer Night's Dream, Les Biches, Sleeping Beauty, Pyrrich Dances, Masse, Le Tombeau de Couperin, Symphony in C, The Four Temperaments, The Prodigal Son, Rodin, Pierrot Lunaire, La Fille mal gardée, Swan Lake, Henze, Five Tangos, In and Out, Bits and Pieces, Jeu de Cartes; appeared in the Gala Des Etoiles Canadian Internat. Ballet Gala, 1989, 90, 91, 92, 93, 94, 95, Reykjavik Arts Festival, 1990, Internat. Ballet Gala, Kuodio, Finland, 1992, Internat. Ballet Gala, Vail, Colo., 1993, Night of Stars Ballet Gala, Helsinki, 1993; profiled in nat. and internat. radio and TV programs, including CNN Worldwide Report, 1992; featured on cover of Dance Mag., 1992; choreographer Full Evening Nutcracker, Marin Ballet, 1996, Alta. Ballet, 2000. Recipient 1st prize 1st Nat. Dance Competition Kuopio, Finland, 1978. Office: Boston Ballet 19 Clarendon St Boston MA 02116-6100 E-mail: mikkoN@albertaballet.com., Mikko403@aol.com.

NISSMAN, BONNIE O'BRIAN, library services supervisor; b. Great Bend, Kans., Oct. 19, 1940; d. Claude Marion and Mildred Geraldine (Schmaider) Baker; m. Patrick Gilbert Gibson (div.); 1 child, Debra Kathleen; m. John Robinson O'Brian, Nov. 2, 1968 (dec.); m. Edward S. Nissman, Mar. 11, 2000. BS, UCLA, 1961; MS, Calif. State U., Northridge, 1977; Credential in Libr. Media Svcs., Calif. State U., Long Beach, 1978. Libr. L.A. Unified Sch. Dist., Northridge, 1978-84, supr. chpt. 2 L.A., 1984, coord. field libr., 1984-87, supr. libr. svcs., 1987—. Asst. prof. libr. sci. Calif. State U., L.A.; condr. workshops in field. Pub. Focus on Books CD-ROM, 1998-2000. Recipient N.W. Valley Parent Tchr. Student award 1978, San Fernando Valley Reading Assn. Myrtle Shirley Reading Motivation award 1986. Mem. ALA, Am. Assn. Sch. Librs., Calif. Sch. Libr. Assn. (pres.), So. Calif. Coun. on Lit. for Children and Young People, White House Conf. on Libr. and Info. Svcs. Republican. Office: Los Angeles Unifed Sch Dist 1320 W 3rd St Los Angeles CA 90017-1410

NISWENDER, GORDON DEAN, physiologist, educator; b. Gillette, Wyo., Apr. 21, 1940; s. Rex Lel and Inez Irene (Dillinger) N.; m. Joy Dean Thayer, June 14, 1964; children: Kevin Dean, Kory Dean. BS, U. Wyo., 1962; MS, U. Nebr., 1964; PhD, U. Ill., 1967. NIH postdoctoral fellow U. Mich., 1967-68, asst. prof. physiology, 1968-72; mem. faculty Colo. State U., Ft. Collins, 1972—, prof. physiology, 1975—; assoc. dean research Coll. Veterinary Medicine and Biomed. Scis., 1982-95, dir. animal reproduction and biotech. lab., 1986—, disting. prof., 1987—. Mem. rev. panels NIH; cons. FDA. Recipient Merit award NIH, 1988-99, grantee, 1968—. Mem.: Soc. Study Reprodn. (treas. 1972-75, pres. 1981-82, editor-in-chief Biology of Reprodn. 1995—99, Rsch. award 1988, Disting. Svc. award, 2001), Am. Assn. Animal Scientists (Outstanding Young Scientist award western sect., 1974, animal Physiology and Endocrinology award 1983). Office: Colo State U Animal Reprod & Biotech Lab College Of Veterinary Med Fort Collins CO 80523-1683

NITECKI, JOSEPH ZBIGNIEW, librarian; b. Dabrowa Górnicza, Poland, Jan. 31, 1922; came to U.S., 1951, naturalized, 1956; s. Henryk W. and Antonina S. N.; m. Sophie V. Zboinski, June 17, 1945; children: Zbigniew H., Danuta A. BA in Philosophy, Wayne State U., 1955; MA, Roosevelt U., 1959; MA in L.S., U. Chgo., 1963. Various profl. and adminstrv. positions in libraries U. Chgo., 1961-63, Chgo. City Coll., 1963-66, U. Wis., Milw., 1967-70, Temple U., Phila., 1970-78; prof., exec. dir. libraries U. Wis., Oshkosh, 1978-80; dir. libraries SUNY, Albany, 1980-88, prof. Sch. Info Sci. and Policy, 1988-90, prof. emeritus, 1990—. Cons. library issues. Author, editor compiler and reviewer in field; ref. and manuscript reader. Served with Polish Armed Forces under Brit. command, 1939-48. Mem. ALA, Beta Phi Mu. Home: 430 Coburg Village Way Rexford NY 12148-1461 E-mail: jzn@albany.edu., jznitecki@thebiz.net.

NITIKMAN, FRANKLIN W. lawyer; b. Davenport, Iowa, Oct. 26, 1940; s. David A. and Janette (Gordon) N.; m. Adrienne C. Drell, Nov. 28, 1972. BA, Northwestern U., 1963; LLB, Yale U., 1966. Bar: Ill. 1966, U.S. Dist. Ct. (no. dist.) Ill. 1967, U.S. Tax Ct. 1972, Fla. 1977, D.C. 1981. Assoc. McDermott, Will & Emery, Chgo., 1966-72, ptnr., 1973—. Co-author: Drafting Wills and Trust Agreements, 1990. Bd. dirs. Owen Coon Found., Glenview, Ill., 1985—, Jewish United Fund, Jewish Fedn. Met. Chgo., 1994—; bd. dirs. Spertus Inst. Jewish Studies, Chgo., 1991—, chmn. bd., 1999—. Fellow Am. Coll. Trust and Estate Coun., Am. Bar Found.; mem. Standard Club, Arts Club (Chgo.). Home: 365 Lakeside Pl Highland Park IL 60035-5371 Office: McDermott Will & Emery 227 W Monroe St Ste 4700 Chicago IL 60606-5096 E-mail: fnitikman@mwe.com.

NITSCH, BARBARA ANN, radiologist; b. Toronto, Ontario, Can., Aug. 16, 1954; came to U.S., 1992, naturalized, 1998; BSc with hons., York U., Toronto, Ontario, Can., 1978; MD, McMaster U., Hamilton, Ontario, Can., 1984. Diplomate Am. Bd. Diagnostic Radiology with Spl. Competence in Nuclear Medicine.. Radiologist Toronto Gen. Hosp., 1990-92, Wellington (Fla.) Regional Med. Ctr., 1992-95, Midtown Imaging, West Palm Beach, Fla., 1992—. Med. rschr. Princess Margaret Hosp., Toronto, 1978-80 Mem. Wellington (Fla.) Equestrian Alliance, 1997. Fellow Royal Coll. Physicians and Surgeons, Royal Coll. Physicians; mem. Radiol. Soc. N. Am., Soc. Nuclear Medicine, Palm Beach County Radiol. Soc. Avocations: riding, tennis, golf, skiing.

NITTA, DOUGLAS, family practice physician; b. Seattle, Mar. 30, 1954; s. Susumu and Donna (Tokuda) N. BA in Chemistry magna cum laude, U. Wash., 1976, MD, 1980. Diplomate Am. Bd. Family Practice. Internship, resident Irvine Med. Ctr. U. Calif., 1980-83; mem. active staff St. Jude Med. Ctr., Fullerton, Calif., 1982—, chmn. dept. family practice, 1989—. V.p., bd. dirs. St. Jude Med. Group, Inc., Fullerton, Calif., 1996—; mem. adv. bd. St. Jude Heritage Health Found., 1997-99; chmn. primary care dept. St. Jude Med. Ctr., 1999. Fellow Am. Acad. Family Physicians; mem. Calif. Med. Assn., Phi Beta Kappa. Office: 301 W Bastanchury Rd Ste 155 Fullerton CA 92835-3477

NITTOLY, PAUL GERARD, lawyer; b. Bklyn., July 13, 1948; s. Edward Joseph and Philomena (Lorenzo) N.; m. Maryann Racioppi, May 31, 1970; children: Melissa Beth, Matthew Edward. AB, Rutgers U., 1970; JD, N.Y. Law Sch., 1973. Bar: NJ, U.S. Dist. Ct. NJ 1973, U.S. Ct. Appeals (3d cir.) 1990, U.S. Dist. Ct. (so. and ea. dist.) NY 1998, U.S. Supreme Ct. 1979, cert.: NJ Supreme Ct. (trial atty. civil and criminal law). Asst. prosecutor, sr. trial atty. Essex County Prosecutor's Office, Newark, 1974-79; ptnr. Shanley & Fisher, P.C., Morristown, N.J., 1979-99, Drinker Biddle & Shanley LLP, Florham Park, 1999—. Moot trial ct. judge Seton Hall Law Sch., Newark, 1982—; lectr. symposium on perinatal malpractice Am. Coll. Ob-Gyn and Rutgers U. Med. Sch., Morristown, N.J., 1984; mem. practitioner's adv. group to U.S. Sentencing Commn., 1992—. Author: Readings in White Collar Crime, 1991; mem. editl. adv. bd. Corporate Criminal Liability Reporter; contbr. chpts. to books. Past pres., master C. Willard Heckel Am. Inn of Ct.; del. adv. Am. Bd. Trial Advs.; bd. trustees Pub. Interest Law Ctr. N.J., 1998—. Capt. U.S. Army, 1972. Mem. ABA, N.J. Bar Assn., Essex County Bar Assn. (pres. 1998-99), Morris County Bar Assn., Nat. Assn. Criminal Def. Lawyers, Assn. Criminal Def. Attys. N.J., Trial Attys. N.J. (v.p.), Assn. Fed. Bar State N.J. (trustee 2000—), Park Ave. Club (Morristown), Delta Upsilon. Roman Catholic. Home: 275 Meetinghouse Ln Mountainside NJ 07092-1305 Office: Drinker Biddle & Shanley LLP 500 Campus Dr Fl 4 Florham Park NJ 07932-1047 E-mail: pnittoly@dbr.com.

NITZ, FREDERIC WILLIAM, electronics company executive; b. St. Louis, June 22, 1943; s. Arthur Carl Paul and Dorothy Louise (Kahm) N.; m. Kathleen Sue Rapp, June 8, 1968; children: Frederic Theodore, Anna Louise. AS, Coll. Marin, 1970; BS in Electronics, Calif. Poly. State U., San Luis Obispo, 1972. Electronic engr. Sierra Electronics, Menlo Park, Calif., 1973-77, RCA, Somerville, N.J., 1977-79; engring. mgr. EGG-Geometrics, Sunnyvale, Calif., 1979-83; v.p. engring. Basic Measuring Insts., Foster City, 1983-91; exec. v.p. Reliable Power Meters, Los Gatos, 1991—. Cons. in field, Boulder Creek, Calif., 1978—. Patentee in field. Bd. dirs. San Lorenzo Valley Water Dist., Boulder Creek, 1983—, Water Policy Task Force, Santa Cruz County, Calif., 1983-84. With U.S. Army, 1965-67. Democrat. Lutheran. Home: 499 Navarra Dr Scotts Valley CA 95066-3748 Office: Reliable Power Meters 400 Blossom Hill Rd Los Gatos CA 95032-4511 E-mail: fnitz@reliablemeters.com.

NITZE, WILLIAM ALBERT, government official, lawyer, not-for-profit developer; b. N.Y.C., Sept. 27, 1942; s. Paul Henry and Phyllis (Pratt) N.; m. Ann Kendall Richards, June 5, 1971; children: Paul Kendall, Charles Richards. BA, Harvard U., 1964, JD, 1969; BA, Oxford U., 1966. Bar: N.Y. 1970, U.S. Supreme Ct. 1987. Assoc. Sullivan and Cromwell, N.Y.C., 1970-72; v.p. London Arts, Inc., 1972-73; counsel Mobil South, Inc., 1974-76; gen. counsel Mobil Oil Japan, Tokyo, 1976-80; asst. gen. counsel exploration and producing divsn. Mobil Oil Corp., N.Y.C., 1980-87; dep asst. sec. for environment, health and natural resources U.S. Dept. State, Washington, 1987-90; pres. Alliance to Save Energy, 1990-94; asst. adminstr. for internat. activities U.S. EPA, 1994-2001; pres. Gemstar Group, 2001—. Mem. adv. com. Sch. Advanced Internat. Studies, Washington, 1982-95, professorial lectr., 1993-94, 2001-02; vis. scholar Environ. Law Inst., Washington, 1990; dir. Charles A. Lindbergh Fund, Mpls., 1990-94, Nat. Symphony Orch. Assn., Washington, 1990—, Atlantic Coun. U.S., Washington, 2002, Charles Darwin Found., Inc., Falls Church, Va., 2002—. Trustee Aspen Inst., Queenstown, Md., 1988—, Krasnow Inst., Fairfax, Va., 1996-2002; co-chmn. Climate Inst., Washington, 2001—; dir. Atlantic Coun. of the U.S., 2002--. Mem.: Coun. on Fgn. Rels., Assn. Bar City NY, Links Club, Cosmos Club, Met. Club. Republican. Episcopalian. Avocations: running, piano, collecting art. Home: 1537 28th St NW Washington DC 20007-3059 Office: Gemstar Group 910 17th St NW Ste 1110 Washington DC 20006 E-mail: wanitze@aol.com.

NIU, GUOFU, electrical engineer, educator; b. Anyang, China, Dec. 17, 1971; s. Pinzhang Niu and Xuehua Feng; m. Ying Li, Aug. 8, 2000. BS, Fudan U., Shanghai, 1992, PhD, 1997. Rsch. assoc. City U. Hong Kong, 1995-97; postdoctoral rsch. assoc. Auburn (Ala.) U., 1997-2000, assoc. prof. elec. and computer engring., 2000—. Mem.: IEEE (sr.). Office: Auburn U 200 Broun Hall Auburn AL 36849 E-mail: guofu@eng.auburn.edu.

NIU, WEIHUA, psychologist, educator; b. Beijing, Jan. 10, 1967; d. Kuanxin Wang; m. Youjun Guo. BE, Beijing Normal U., 1989; MS, Chinese Acad. Scis., Beijing, 1995; MPhil, Yale U., 2001. Rsch. asst. Inst. Psychology Chinese Acad. Scis., Beijing, 1989—94, asst. prof., 1989—98; rsch. fellow dept. psychology Yale U., New Haven, 1999—. Contbr. articles to profl. jours. Fellow, Yale U., 1998—2002, 2002; grantee, Coun. E. Asian Studies, Yale U., 2001. Mem.: APA. Office: Yale Univ 2 Hillhouse Ave New Haven CT 06520 E-mail: weihua.niu@yale.edu.

NIVARTHI, RAJU NAGA, anesthesiology educator; b. Nandyal, India, June 16, 1964; came to U.S., 1993; s. Kameswara Sarma and Suseelamma Nivarthi; m. Aparna Nagaraju Nivarthi; children: Nidhi, Aditya. BSc with Chemistry, Zoology and Botany, Sri Venkateswara U., Tirupati, India, 1984; MSc in Biochemistry, Sri Kirshnadevaraya U., Anantapur, India, 1986; PhD, U. Hyderabad, 1996. Fellow Sch. Life Scis., U. Hyderabad, India, 1987-93; rsch. asst. prof. dept. anesthesiology NYU Med. Ctr., N.Y.C., 1996, scientist, 1996-99, Wyeth-Ayerst Rsch., Pearl River, N.Y., 1999-2001; sr. scientist, mgr. analytical biochemistry Bristol-Meyer Squibb, Syracuse, NY, 2001—. Contbr. articles to profl. jours. Jr. Rsch. fellow Coun. Sci. and Indsl. Rsch., India, 1987, Sr. Rsch. fellow Coun. Sci. and Indsl. Rsch., 1990, Postdoctoral fellow NIH, 1998; recipient cert. of merit Pharmacia & Biotech Prize for Young Scientists, 1997, named 2000 Outstanding Scientist of 20th Century, 1998, Internat. Biographical Ctr. Mem. AAAS, Acad. Med. Cmty., Am. Chem. Soc., Am. Soc. Anesthesiologists, Am. Soc. Biochemistry and Molecular Biology, Internat. Anesthesia Rsch. Soc., Internat. Soc. for Study of Xenobiotics, Nat. Geographic Soc., N.Y. Acad. Scis. Office: Bristol-Myer Squibb 6000 Thompson Rd East Syracuse NY 13057-5050 Home: 161 North Way Camillus NY 13031-1253 E-mail: rnivarthi@yahoo.com.

NIVISON, DAVID SHEPHERD, Chinese and philosophy educator; b. Farmingdale, Maine, Jan. 17, 1923; s. William and Ruth (Robinson) N.; m. Cornelia Green, Sept. 11, 1944; children— Louise, Helen Thom, David Gregory, James Nicholas. AB summa cum laude, Harvard U., 1946, MA, 1948, PhD, 1953. Instr. Chinese Stanford U., 1948-52, Ford Found. faculty fellow, 1952-53, instr. Chinese and philosophy, 1953-54; Fulbright research scholar Kyoto, Japan, 1954-55; lectr. philosophy Stanford U., 1955-58, asst. prof. Chinese and philosophy, 1958-59, assoc. prof., 1959-66, prof., 1966-88, Walter Y. Evans-Wentz prof. Oriental Philosophies, Religions and Ethics, 1983-88, chmn. dept. philosophy, 1969-72, 75-76, acting chmn. dept. Asian langs., 1985-86, emeritus, 1988—. Author: The Life and Thought of Chang

Hsüeh-ch'eng, 1738-1801, 1966, The Ways of Confucianism: Investigations in Chinese Philosophy, 1996; co-author: Chinese Language, Thought and Culture: Nivison and His Critics, 1996; editor, co-compiler: Stanford Chinese Concordance Series, 1979; co-editor: Confucianism in Action, 1959, Studies on the Modern Text of the Bamboo Annals (in Chinese), 2002; contbr. articles to profl. jours. and encys. Served with AUS, 1943-46. Recipient Prix Stanislas-Julien Inst. de France, 1967; Am. Council Learned Socs. fellow, 1973; John Simon Guggenheim fellow, 1973-74 Mem. Assn. Asian Studies, Am. Philos. Assn. (v.p. Pacific div. 1978-79, pres. 1979-80), Am. Oriental Soc. (Western br. v.p. 1964-65, sec. 1965-70, pres. 1971-72), AAUP (pres. No. Calif. Conf. 1964-66), Internat. Acad. Chinese Culture (Beijing, Peoples Republic of China), Phi Beta Kappa. Home: 1169 Russell Ave Los Altos CA 94024-5066 E-mail: dnivison@stanford.edu.

NIX, BARBARA LOIS, real estate broker; b. Sept. 25, 1929; d. Martin Clayton and Norma (Gunter) Westfield; m. B. H. Nix, July 12, 1968; children: William Martin Dahl, Theresa Irene Dahl; stepchildren: Dennis Leon, Denise Lynn. Student, St. Elizabeths Sch. Nursing, Yakima, Wash., 1949-50; AA, Sierra Coll., 1978; student, Calif. State U., Sacramento, 1984. Bookkeeper, office mgr. Lakeport (Calif.) Tire Svc., 1966-69, Dr. K. J. Absher, Grass Valley, Calif., 1972-75; real estate sales and office mgr. Rough and Ready Land Co., Penn Valley, 1976-77, co-owner, v.p., sec., 1978—, Wildwood West Real Estate, Gateway Real Estate. Co-owner Nix's Antiques, 1996—. Youth and welfare chmn. Yakima Federated Jr. Women's Club, 1957; den mother Cub Scouts, 1959-60; leader Girl Scouts, 1961-62; mem. Friends of Hospice; mem. Sierra, Nev. Meml. Hosp. Found.; adv. bd. dirs., v.p. Roots and Wings Ednl. Found., 1991-95; mem. Nevada County Sch. Dist. Redistricting Bd. Recipient Pres.'s award Sierra Coll., 1973, others. Mem. Lake Wildwood Women's Club, Penn Valley (founder, pres. 1978), Sierra Nevada Meml. Hosp. Aux., Job's Daus. (life). Republican. Roman Catholic. Home: 19365 Wildflower Dr Penn Valley CA 95946-9735 Office: PO Box 191 Rough And Ready CA 95975-0191

NIX, DARRELL EUGENE, auditor; b. Farmville, Va., Dec. 20, 1946; s. Paul Oliver and Amy Leona (Locke) Nix; divorced; children: Darren, Deana. BS, N.C. State U., 1969; MBA, James Madison U., 1979. Indsl. engr. Collins & Aikman, Siler City, NC, 1971—75; prodn. supr. Frank Ix & Sons, Charlottesville, 1975—78, adminstrv. mgr., 1978—80; mgmt. engr. N.C. Dept. Adminstrn., Raleigh, 1980—86; revenue field auditor N.C. Dept. Revenue, Rocky Mt., NC, 1987—. Lyricist:. Active Sunset Ave. Bapt. Ch., Rocky Mt., NC, 1988—. With U.S. Army, 1969—71. Decorated Nat. Def. medal; recipient Spoke award, U.S. Jaycees, 1973; scholar Talent for Svc. scholarship, N.C. State, 1965. Mem.: NRA, Assn. of MBA Execs., Rocky Mount Shag Club (treas.), Elks Club, Am. Legion. Avocations: song writing, dancing, firearms. Home: 1452 Brookmeade Ct Rocky Mount NC 27804-9192 Office: NC Dept Revenue 239 Station Sq Rocky Mount NC 27804

NIX, DENISE ELAINE, accountant; b. Atlanta, Feb. 29, 1960; d. Ben A. and Hazel G. (Ingram) Ward; m. James C. Nix, Feb. 14, 1981; children: Jessica E., J. Levi. BS in Bus. Adminstrn. and Acctg. cum laude, Brenau U., 1993. Bookkeeper Lanier Pk. Hosp., Gainesville, Ga., 1981-84; asst. controller, consolidation acct. Protein Foods, 1984-93; asst. controller Turbo Transport, 1993—. Mem. Inst. Mgmt. Accts. Baptist. Avocations: camping, swimming, art, reading, youth group activities.

NIX, EDMUND ALFRED, lawyer; b. Eau Claire, Wis., May 24, 1929; s. Sebastian and Kathryn (Keirnan) N.; m. Mary Kathryn Nagle Daley, Apr. 27, 1968; children: Kim, Mary Kay, Norbert, Edmund Alfred, Michael. BS, Wis. State U., 1951; LL.B., U. Wis., 1954, postgrad. in speech, 1956-57. Bar: Wis. 1954. Practice in Eau Claire, 1954-65; dist. atty. Eau Claire County, 1958-64; U.S. atty. Western Dist. Wis., Eau Claire, 1965-69, U.S. magistrate, 1969-70; dist. atty. La Crosse County, Wis., 1975-77; mcpl. judge City of La Crosse, 1992—. Co-chmn. United Fund, Eau Claire, 1958; Pres. Young Democrats Wis., 1951-53; mem. adminstrv. bd. Wis. Dem. party, 1953-54; chmn. 10th Congl. dist., 1965; sec. Kennedy for Pres. Club Wis., 1959-60. Served with AUS, 1954-56. Mem. Fed. Bar Assn., Wis. Bar Assn. (state chmn. crime prevention and control com.), La Crosse County Bar Assn. (pres.), Nat. Dist. Attys. Assn., KC. Roman Catholic. Office: 123 4th St N La Crosse WI 54601-3235 E-mail: nixe@ffax.net.

NIX, JAMES RAYFORD, nuclear physicist, consultant; b. Natchitoches, La., Feb. 18, 1938; s. Joe Ebbin and Edna (Guin) N.; m. Sally Ann Wood, Aug. 19, 1961; children: Patricia Lynne, David Allen. BS in Physics, Carnegie Inst. Tech., 1960; PhD in Physics, U. Calif., Berkeley, 1964. Summer physicist Lawrence Livermore Nat. Lab., Livermore, Calif., 1961; rsch. asst. Lawrence Berkeley Lab., Berkeley, 1961-64, postdoctoral physicist, 1966-68; NATO postdoctoral fellow Niels Bohr Inst., Copenhagen, 1964-65; mem. staff Los Alamos Nat. Lab., 1968-77, 89-94, group leader, 1977-89, fellow, 1994-98, sci. cons., 1998—. Vis. prof. Centro Brasileiro de Pesquisas Fisicas, Rio de Janeiro, 1974; cons. Calif. Inst. Tech., Pasadena, 1976, 79; chmn. Gordon Research Conf. Nuclear Chemistry, New London, NH, 1976; chmn. physics divsn. adv. com. Oak Ridge Nat. Lab., 1976, 97; chmn. nuclear sci. divsn. vis. com. Lawrence Berkeley Lab., 1979—80. Contbr. articles to numerous publs. Recipient Alexander von Humboldt Sr. U.S. Scientist award, Univ. Munich and Max-Planck Inst. for Nuclear Physics, 1980—81; fellow, Phi Kappa Phi, Berkeley, Calif., 1960—61; scholar, Alfred P. Sloan Found., Pitts., 1956—60. Fellow: Am. Phys. Soc. (exec. com. 1973—75); mem.: AAAS, Phi Kappa Phi, Sigma Xi. Democrat. Home and Office: 12 Los Pueblos Los Alamos NM 87544-2659 E-mail: j.nix@starband.net.

NIX, KATHERINE JEAN, medical case manager; d. Samuel Watson and Dorothy Lee (Woods) Lewis; m. Robert Milton Nix, May 5, 1963 (div. Feb. 1988); children: Araina Catrice, Cynthia Lathier. AA in Safety and Health, Merritt Coll., 1976; AA in Nursing, Chabot Coll., 1974; BSN, U. San Francisco, 1979. RN Calif. Staff nurse Highland Hosp., Oakland, Calif., 1961-73; nurse cmty. health Alameda County, 1973-75; nurse occupational health Caterpiller Tractor Co., San Leandro, 1975-77, inspector safety hygiene, 1981-84; nurse cons. occupational health Intel Corp., Livermore, 1981-84; cons. health & safety Quaker Oats Co., Oakland, 1984-86; nurse cons. occupational health Rawson Drug & Sundry Co., San Leandro, 1986-89; rehab. nurse Continental Rehab. Resources, Pleasanton, Calif., 1989-91; rehab. nurse cons. GAB, Campbell, 1991-93; med. case mgr. Conservco Travelers Ins. Co., Walnut Creek, 1993-95, Olsten Kimberly Quality Care, San Leandro, 1995—. Health advisor Black Women Organized for Polit. Action, Oakland, 1979—, Alemeda (Calif.) Coll., 1982-86. Fellow Nat. Safety Coun., Rehab. Nurses Group. Democrat. Avocations: skiing, reading, stage plays. Home: PO Box 5834 Oakland CA 94605-0834 Office: St Marys Hosp 450 Stanyan St San Francisco CA 94117-1079

NIX, LINDA ANNE BEAN, public relations executive; b. Sept. 20, 1943; d. Norman Arthur and Gladys Mae (Charlton) Bean, Jr.; m. Henry Taylor Betts, Jr., Sept. 5, 1964 (div. 1970); m. John Asa Nix, Nov. 24, 1971 (div. 1990). Student, Syracuse U., 1961-64; BA, Scarritt Coll., 1965; postgrad., Middle Tenn. State U., 9171-73. Mobile coord. Children's Mus., Nashville, 1967-69; promotion dir. Sta. WDCN-TV/8, 1969-82; dir. pub. info. Sta. WYES-TV/12, New Orleans, 1982—; mktg. dir. Sta. KOFY-TV Radio San Francisco, 1989-91, Sta. KUSI-TV, San Diego, 1992-93; self-employed in pub. rels., 1992—. Mem. pub. info. adv. com. Pub. Broadcasting Service, Washington, 1977-80, chmn. 1979-80, mem. festival task force, 1979-80. Author, editor: (tchr. workbook) Yellow Submarine, 1968; contbr. Great Chefs, 2001—; contbr. articles to profl. jours. Bd. dirs. Nashville League for Hearing Impaired, 1973-76, Tennessee Williams/New Orleans Literacy Festival, 1995—; chmn. membership com. Coun. Cmty. Svcs., Nashville, 1978-80; mem. allocation panel United Way Greater Nashville, 1979-81, United Way Greater New Orleans, 1982-86. Mem. Pub. Rels. Soc. Am. (chmn. accreditation com. 1985, pres. New Orleans chpt. 1988), Broadcast Promotion and Mktg. Execs., Inc. (Promax) (bd. dirs. 1982-91, pres. 1989-90). Avocations: flying (multi-engine, commercial), sewing. Home and Office: PO Box 7068 Metairie LA 70010-7068 E-mail: lagator@mindspring.com.

NIX, MARTIN EUGENE, engineer; b. Winston-Salem, N.C., Sept. 26, 1951; s. Richard Nix and Margaret Searborn-Collins. B, U. N.Mex., 1973, postgrad., 1980. Engr. Boeing, Seattle, 1980—. Chief exec. officer Solarshack, Seattle, 1989—.

NIX, ROBERT ROYAL, II, lawyer; b. Detroit, Mar. 27, 1947; s. Robert R. and Betty Virginia (Karicofe) N.; m. Suzanne Martha Turner, July 11, 1970; children: Christian Michael, Heather Michele. BS, Ea. Mich. U., 1968; JD cum laude, Wayne State U., 1971. Bar: Mich. 1971, U.S. Dist. Ct. (ea. dist.) Mich. 1971, U.S. Ct. Appeals (6th cir.) 1976. Rsch. atty. Mich. Ct. Appeals, Lansing, 1971-72, law clk. to Hon. Charles L. Levin, 1971, law clk. to Hon. S. Jerome Bronson, 1972-73; ptnr. Kerr, Russell and Weber, 1973—. Lectr. in field. Contrb. articles to Michigan Real Property Law Review. Mem. Mich. Land Title Stds. Com., 1990—. Fellow Mich. State Bar Found.; mem. ABA (partnership com. real property, probate and trust law sect., mortgages and secured financing com. corp., banking and bus. law sect., forum constrn. industry sect.), State Bar Mich. (chmn. real property law sect. 1994-95, coun. vice-chmn. 1992-93, chmn. com. on mortgage related financing devices, 1984-87, mem. sect., 1973—, partnership com. 1982—), Oakland County Bar Assn., Detroit Bar Assn., Am. Coll. Real Estate Lawyers, Am. Coll. Mortgage Attys. Republican. Methodist. Office: Kerr Russell and Weber Detroit Ctr Ste 2500 Detroit MI 48226 E-mail: rrn@krwplc.com.

NIXON, AGNES ECKHARDT, television writer, producer; m. Robert Nixon (dec.); 4 children. Student, Sch. Speech, Northwestern U. Writer for radio and TV; freelance writer for: TV programs Hallmark Hall of Fame, Robert Montgomery Presents, Studio One; creator, packager, head writer: daytime TV series All My Children; creator nightime mini-series The Manions of America; creator, packager daytime TV series One Life to Live; creator, packager: daytime TV series Loving; co-creator: daytime TV series As The World Turns; formerly head writer, The Guiding Light, daytime TV series Another World; creator, story cons. The City. Recipient Trustees award Nat. Acad. TV Arts and Sci., 1981, Super Achiever award Jr. Diabetes Found., 1981, Wilmer Eye Inst. award, 1981, Communicator award Am. Women in Radio & TV, 1984, Gold Plate award Am. Acad. Achievement, 1993, Popular Culture Lifetime Achievement award Popular Culture Assn., 1995, Pub. Svc. award Johns Hopkins Hosp., 1995, Humanitarian award Nat. Osteoporosis Found., 1996; inducted into TV Hall of Fame, 1993. Mem. Internat. Radio and TV Soc. Nat. Acad. TV Arts and Scis., Harvard Found. (bd. dirs.), Mus. TV and Radio (bd. dirs.), The Friars Club. Address: All My Children 320 W 66th St New York NY 10023-6304

NIXON, ARLIE JAMES, gas and oil company executive; b. Ralston, Okla., May 22, 1914; s. James Gordon and Wella May (Platt) N.; m. Wylie Elizabeth Jones, Apr. 21, 1939 (div May 1950); children: Cole Jay, Kathleen (Mrs. S. Brent Joyce); m. Lisa Marie Grant, Dec. 7, 1981 (div. June 1989). BS, Okla. State U., 1935. Airline capt. Trans World Airlines, N.Y.C., 1939-74; pres. Crystal Gas Co., Jennings, Okla., 1960—, Blackburn Gas Co., Jennings, 1964—, Blackberry Oil Co., Jennings, 1969—. Represented U.S. in several ofcl. dels. to internat. aviation tech. meetings, also represented Internat. Fedn. Air Line Pilots Assns. at internat. confs. Lt. (j.g.) USNR, 1935-63. Mem. Internat. Fedn. Air Line Pilots Assn. (regional v.p. 1972), Internat. Platform Assn., Wings Club. Democrat. Home: RR 2 Box 8651 Jennings OK 74038-9324 Office: PO Box 68 Jennings OK 74038-0068

NIXON, CHARLES WILLIAM, acoustician; b. Wellsburg, W.Va., Aug. 15, 1929; s. William E. and Lenora S. (Treiber) Nixon; m. Barbara Irene Hunter, May 19, 1956; children: Timothy C., Tracy Scott. BS, Ohio State U., 1952, MS, 1953, PhD, 1960. Tchr. spl. edn. Ohio and W.Va. Pub. Schs., Wheeling, 1954—56; rsch. audiologist Aeromed Lab., Wright Patterson AFB, Ohio, 1956—67; supervisory rsch. audiologist Armstrong Lab., 1967—96, Veridian, Dayton, 1996—. Chair W4 Am. Nat. Stds. Inst., N.Y.C., 1968—96; U.S. rep. hearing protection Internat. Stds. Orgn., Geneva, 1968—96; USAF rep. NRC-NAS Hearing Com., Washington, 1976—94; chair robotics panel Joint Dirs. Labs., Washington, 1987—88. Author: reports and book chpts. Cpl. U.S. Army, 1953—55. Recipient Meritorious Svc. medal, U.S. Dept. Def., Dayton, Ohio, 1986, Outstanding Civilian Svc. award, 1996. Fellow: Acoustical Soc. Am.; mem.: Rsch. Soc. Am. Achievements include research in noise exposure, voice communications, hearing protection, sonic boom, active noise reduction, 3-D audio displays, others. Home: 4316 Sillman Pl Dayton OH 45440-1141 E-mail: cwnixon@woh.rr.com.

NIXON, DANIEL WALKER, oncologist, researcher; b. Brunswick, Ga., Sept. 8, 1943; s. Marvin Elesberry and Mildred Anita (Whitehead) N.; m. Sandra Gayle Brakefield, July 18, 1970; children: William B., Marvin A. BS, U. Ga., 1965, MD, 1969. Diplomate Am. Bd. Internal Medicine, Am. Bd. Med. Oncology; lic. physician, Ga., S.C. Asst. prof. Med. Coll. Ga., Augusta, 1973-75; from assoc. prof. to prof. Emory U., Atlanta, 1975-87; assoc. dir. divsn. cancer prevention and control, Nat. Cancer Inst. NIH, Bethesda, Md., 1987-89; v.p., prof. edn. Am. Cancer Soc., Atlanta, 1989-94; Folk prof., assoc. dir. prevention and control Hollings Cancer Ctr., Med. U. S.C., Charleston, 1994—. Mem. sci. bd. Cancer Treatment Rsch. Found., 1996; bd. dirs. Kincaid Found., Washington. Author: Cancer Recovery Eating Plan, 1994; editor: Cancer Chemoprevention, 1994; editor-in-chief: (jour.) Cancer Prevention Internat., 1994—; contbr. more than 100 articles to med. jours. Capt. USNR, 1987—. Recipient several found. awards; grantee NIH, 1975—. Mem. Nutrition Oncology Adjuvant Therapy Soc. (pres. 1996), Army and Navy Club, Druid Hills Country Club, Country Club of Charleston. Achievements include research in cancer prevention and nutrition; chemoprevention and cancer metabolism. Avocations: golf, fishing. Office: Med Univ S C 171 Ashley Ave Charleston SC 29425-0001

NIXON, DAVID, dancer; b. Windsor, Ont., Can. Student, The Nat. Ballet Sch. With Nat. Ballet of Can., 1978-84, 1st soloist, 1982-84, prin. dancer, 1988-90; prin. dancer Berlin Opera Ballet, 1985-90, Bayerisches Staatsoper Ballet Munich, 1990-91; prin. dancer and 1st Ballet master Deutsche Opera Ballet Berlin, 1994-95; various guest appearances including Alexander Godunov and Stars, summer 1982, Milw. Ballet, 1984, Sydney Ballet Australia, 1984, World Ballet Festival Tokyo, 1985, 88, Hamburg Ballet, 1988, 89, Staatsoper Berlin, 1988-91, Bayerisches Staatsballet, 1988-90, Komische Opera Berlin, 1990-93; prodr. David Nixon's Dance Theatre, Hebbel Theatre, Berlin, 1990, 91; prodr., artistic dir. BalletMet, 1995-2001; choreographer Butterfly, 1983, La Follia, 1984, Dangerous Liaisons, 1990, 96, African Fantasy, 1990, Celebrate Mozart, 1991, Sudden Impulse, 1994, A Summer's Nights Reflections, 1995, Full-Length Nutcracker, 1995, Butterfly, 1996, Beauty and the Beast, 1997, Carmen, 1997, Romeo and Juliet, 1998, Swan Lake, 1998, Dracula, 1999, A Midsummer Nights Dream, 2000, A Celebration of Dance with Music by Gershwin, 2001; artistic dir. Northern Ballet Theatre, Eng., 2001—.

NIXON, DAVID L. lawyer; b. Concord, Mass., Mar. 19, 1932; s. Louis Gerard and Patricia (Williams) N.; m. Joanne P. Nixon; children: Leslie C., Melanie D., Wendy W.N. Branch, Amy W., David Lee Jr., Louis Gerard II. BA cum laude, Wesleyan U., Middletown, Conn., 1953; LLB, U. Mich., 1958. Bar: N.H. 1958, U.S. Dist. Ct. N.H. 1959, U.S. Ct. Appeals (1st cir.) 1961, U.S. Supreme Ct. 1968. Assoc. McLane Carleton Graf Greene & Brown, Manchester, N.H., 1958-61; ptnr. King & Nixon, 1961-69, Nixon, Christy & Tessier, Manchester, 1969-76; dir. Brown & Nixon P.A., 1976-88; pres. Nixon, Hall & Hess P.A., 1988-93, of counsel, 1993-94; pres., dir. Nixon, Raiche, Manning & Casinghino P.A., 1994—. Mem. N.H. Supreme Ct. Accreditation Commn., 1985—, N.H. Jud. Coun., 1980-83, 93—. Rep. N.H. Legis., Concord, 1969-74, senate pres., 1973-74; moderator Town of New Boston, N.H., 1964-92. With U.S. Army, 1953-55. Named Trial Lawyer of the Decade, N.H. Trial Lawyers Assn., 1988. Mem. ABA (ho. of dels. 1970-72), Manchester Bar Assn. (pres. 1973-74, named Manchester Lawyer of the Yr. 1995), N.H. Bar Assn. (pres. 1980-81, Disting. Svc. award 1982, award for Professionalism 1993), New Eng. Bar Assn. (pres. 1970-72), Internat. Soc. Barristers (pres. 1996-97), Inner Circle Advs., Manchester Crimeline, Inc. (dir., legal counsel), Hillsborough County law Enforcement Assn. (chmn. scholarship com.), DAV (life), Am. Legion (judge adv. Post 2). Office: Nixon Raiche Manning & Casinghino PA 77 Central St Manchester NH 03101-2423 Home: 77 Central St Manchester NH 03101-2423

NIXON, DAVID MICHAEL, poet; b. Batavia, N.Y., Jan. 21, 1945; s. Duncan Alfred and Esther Maria (Gillard) N.; m. Barbara Anne Fisher, June 11, 1978; stepchildren: Robert Byrnes Jr., Marjorie Byrnes, Timothy Byrnes. BA in English, Hobart Coll., 1967. Housecleaner, yardworker, Rochester, Naples, N.Y., 1972—. Tchr. poetry Poetry Workshop Rochester, 1969-84, Green Turtle Poetry Project, South Bristol, N.Y., Writers and Books, Rochester, 1998—. Numerous poetry readings in N.Y. State, including Cayuga C.C.; author: (poetry chapbooks) You See Me in the Trees, 1979, Blue Water Line Blues, 1988, Hunting the World, 1989, (poetry) Season of the Totem, 1997, 99; contbr. over 200 poems to mags., anthologies, lit. revs. LIFT grantee Ontario County Arts Coun., South Bristol, 1990. Mem. Golden Link Folk Singing Soc., Metro Justice, War Resisters League, Writers and Books. Avocations: a cappella folk singing, basketball playing, reading. Address: 140-1 Lake Vista Ct Rochester NY 14612-5332 also: 140-1 Lake Vista Ct Rochester NY 14612-5332

NIXON, DAVID PATRICK, public relations executive; b. 1965; With N. Amer. Network , Washington, 1986—89; founder, pres. The Nixon Group, Miami, 1989—2002; exec. V.P., managing dir. Golin Harris Int., Miami , 2002—. Office: Golin Harris Int Penthouse 4500 Biscayne Blvd Miami FL 33137*

NIXON, EMILY, art advisor, curator; b. San Angelo, Tex., May 8, 1951; d. Stanley W. and Grace Louise Nixon; m. Dean A. Langworthy, Dec. 19, 1995. BA, Wheaton Coll., 1973; MFA, U. Ariz., 1977; cert. collection care mgmt., Art Inst. Chgo., 1975-77. Lectr. U. Ariz., Tucson, 1977-79; asst. prof. Lawrence U., Appleton, Wis., 1979-87; assoc. curator Continental Bank, Chgo., 1987-99; art advisor, pres. Nixon Art Assocs., 1987—. Recipient scholarship U. Ariz., 1977. Mem. Assn. Profl. Art Advisors (bd. dirs. 1991-92), Nat. Assn. Corp. Art Mgrs., Assn. Corp. Art Curators (pres. 1984-87, 94–2002), Arts Club, Tavern Club. Avocations: music, golf. Office: Nixon Art Assocs 333 N Michigan Chicago IL 60601-3901 E-mail: nixonart@prodigy.net.

NIXON, EUGENE RAY, chemist, educator; b. Mt. Pleasant, Mich., Apr. 14, 1919; s. William S. and Grace (Brookens) N.; m. Phyllis R. Jones, June 10, 1945; children— Cynthia L., Emily E. Sc.B. summa cum laude, Alma Coll., 1941; PhD, Brown U., 1947. Research chemist Manhattan Project, 1942-46; instr. chemistry Brown U., 1947-49; mem. faculty U. Pa., Phila., 1949-85, prof. chemistry, 1965-85, vice dean grad. sch., 1958-62, acting chmn. dept. chemistry, 1965-66, dir. materials research lab., 1969-72, prof. emeritus, 1985—. Vis. prof. U. London, 1963-64; vis. lectr. Bryn Mawr Coll., 1957-58 Mem. Am. Chem. Soc., Am. Phys. Soc., Soc. Applied Spectroscopy (Jour. award 1965, Spectroscopist of Yr. award Del. Valley sect. 1988), Coblentz Soc. (bd. mgrs.), Sigma Xi. Research, publs. on phys. chemistry, molecular structure and molecular spectroscopy, properties of crystals, intermolecular interactions, laser spectroscopy and laser chemistry. Home: 35 Julio Dr Apt 106 Shrewsbury MA 01545-3049

NIXON, JAMES GREGORY, economic development consultant; b. Kansas City, Mo., Dec. 7, 1962; s. Gerald Glen and Jane Ardis (Mountain) N.; m. Carol Ann Lake, June 21, 1986; 1 child, Kathryn Grace. BBA, U. Okla., 1985; MBA, Okla. State U., 1992. Cert. econ. developer. Govt. rels. aide Pub. Svc. Okla., Oklahoma City, 1985-86, info. analyst Tulsa, 1986-87, econ. devel. cons., 1987-97; with CSW Energy Svcs., 1997—. Mem. Am. Econ. Devel. Coun., So. Indsl. Devel. Coun. (alt. dir. 1986—), Order of Arrow (Vigil honor mem.). Republican. Mem. Christian Ch. (Disciples Of Christ). Avocations: sailing, golf, water skiing, snow skiing, music. Office: CSW Energy Svcs 2 W 2nd St Tulsa OK 74103-3123

NIXON, JEREMIAH W. (JAY NIXON), state attorney general; b. DeSoto, Mo., Feb. 13, 1956; s. Jeremiah and Betty (Lea) Nixon; m. Georganne Nixon; children: Jeremiah, Will. BS in Polit. Sci., U. Mo., 1978, JD, 1981. Ptnr. Nixon, Nixon, Breeze & Roberts, Jefferson County, Mo., 1981—86; mem. Mo. State Senate from Dist 22, 1986—93; atty. gen. State of Mo., 1992—. Chmn. select com. ins. reform; creator video internat. devel. and edn. opportunity program. Named Outstanding Young Missourian, Jaycees, 1994, Outstanding Young Lawyer, Barrister's Mag., 1993; recipient Conservation Fedn. Mo award, 1992. Mem.: Mo. Assn. Trial Attys., Midwest Assn. Attys. Gen., Nat. Assn. Attys. Gen. Democrat. Methodist. Office: Atty Gen Office PO Box 899 Jefferson City MO 65102-0899*

NIXON, JOHN HARMON, retired economist; b. Mpls., Apr. 7, 1915; s. Justin Wroe and Ida Elisabeth (Wickenden) N. AB, Swarthmore Coll., 1935; AM, Harvard U., 1949, PhD, 1953. Analyst U.S. R.R. Retirement Bd., Washington, 1938-41; economist U.S. Office of Price Adminstrn., 1941-46; teaching fellow, sr. tutor Harvard Coll., Cambridge, Mass., 1947-50; asst. prof. econs. CCNY, 1953-56; dir. econ. devel. N.Y. State Dept. Commerce, Albany, 1956-59; dir. area devel. Com. for Econ. Devel., N.Y.C., 1959-65; dir. tech. assistance U.S. Econ. Devel. Adminstrn., Washington, 1966-67; urban economist U.S. AID, Saigon, Vietnam, 1967; economist Ralph M. Parsons Co., Washington, 1968-70, chief economist/systems Pasadena, Calif., 1971-82. Mem. adv. bd. U.S. Area Devel. Adminstrn., Washington, 1963-65. Co-author, editor: Community Economic Development Efforts, 1964, Living Without Water (Cairo), 1980. Vice chmn. Mayor's Com. on Econ. Devel., L.A., 1974-75; pres. Pasadena Devel. Corp., 1982-84. Mem. Plato Soc. UCLA, Phi Beta Kappa. Democrat. Presbyterian. Office: PO Box 76267 Los Angeles CA 90076-0267

NIXON, JOHN TRICE, judge; b. New Orleans, Jan. 9, 1933; s. H. C. and Anne (Trice) N.; children: Mignon Elizabeth, Anne Trice. AB cum laude, Harvard Coll., 1955; LL.B., Vanderbilt U., 1960. Bar: Ala. bar 1960, Tenn. bar 1972. Individual practice law, Anniston, Ala., 1960-62; city atty., 1962-64; trial atty. Civil Rights Div., Dept. Justice, Washington, 1964-69; staff atty., comptroller of Treasury State of Tenn., 1971-76; pvt. practice law Nashville, 1976-77; cir. judge, 1977-78; gen. sessions judge, 1978-80; judge U.S. Dist. Ct. (mid. dist.) Tenn., Nashville, 1980—, sr. judge, 1998—. Served with U.S. Army, 1958. Mem. Fly Club (Cambridge), Harvard-Radcliffe Club (Nashville). Democrat. Methodist. Office: US Dist Ct 745 US Courthouse Nashville TN 37203

NIXON, JUDITH MAY, librarian; b. Gary, Ind., June 14, 1945; d. Louis Robert Sr. and Mable Sophia (Reiner) Vician; m. Cleon Robert Nixon III, Aug. 20, 1967; 1 child, Elizabeth Marie. BS in Edn., Valparaiso U., 1967; MA in LS, U. Iowa, 1974. Tchr. U.S. Peace Corps, Kingdom of Tonga, 1968-69; popular books libr. Lincoln Libr., Springfield, Ill., 1971-73; reference libr. Cedar Rapids (Iowa) Pub. Libr., 1974-76; reference coord. U. Wis., Platteville, 1976-82; bus. libr. U. Ariz., Tucson, 1982-84; consumer and family sci. libr. Purdue U., West Lafayette, La., 1984-93, Krannert mgmt. and econs. libr., 1993—. Editor: Industry and Company Information, 1991, Organization Charts, 1992, 2d edit., 1996, Hotel and Restaurant Industries, 1993; editor quar. serial Lodging and Restaurant Index, 1985-93. Leader Girl Scouts U.S., Lafayette, 1985—. Recipient John H. Moriarty award Purdue U. Librs., 1989. Mem. ALA (chairperson bus. reference and svcs. sect. 1995-96, GALE Rsch. award for excellence in bus. librarianship 1994). Home: 2375 N 23rd St Lafayette IN 47904-1242 Office: Purdue U Mgmt and Econs Libr Krannert Grad Sch Mgmt West Lafayette IN 47907 E-mail: nixon@mgmt.purdue.edu.

NIXON, MARNI, singer; b. Altadena, Calif., Feb. 22, 1930; d. Charles and Margaret (Wittke) McEathron; m. Ernest Gold, May 22, 1950 (div. 1969); children: Andrew Maurice, Martha Alice, Melani Christine; m. Lajos Frederick Fenster, July 23, 1971 (div. July 1975); m. Albert David Block, Apr. 11, 1983. Student, L.A. City Coll., UCLA, U. So. Calif., Tanglewood, Mass. Dir. vocal faculty Calif. Inst. Arts, Valencia, 1970-72; pvt. tchr., vocal coacn, condr. master classes, 1970—; pvt. voice tchr., coach, condr. master classes, 1970—; head apprentice divsn. Santa Barbara Music Acad. of West, 1980; formerly dir. opera workshop Cornish Inst. Arts, Seattle. Tchr. in field; judge Met. Opera Internat. Am. Music Awards, Nat. Inst. Music Theatre, 1984-87; panelist New Music, Nat. Assn. Tchrs. Singing, pres., N.Y. chpt., 1994—; dialect dir., opera recs. Actress Pasadena (Calif.) Playhouse, 1940-45, soloist Roger Wagner chorale, 1947-53, appeared with New Eng. Opera Co., L.A. Opera Co., Ford Found. TV Opera, 1948-63, San Francisco Spring Opera, 1966, Seattle Opera, 1971-73; classical recitals and appearances with symphony orchs. throughout U.S., Can., also Eng., Israel, Ireland; in motion pictures as Sister Sophia in Sound of Music, 1964, Aunt Alice in I Think I Do, 1996; appeared on (TV) Boomerang, from 1975; Broadway and off-Broadway shows: Eliza Doolittle in My Fair Lady, 1964, Edna in Taking My Turn, 1983, Sadie in Opal, 1992-94, Fraulein Schneider in Cabaret, 1998, Mrs. Willson in Ballymore, 1999, Heidi Schiller in Follies, 2001, Aunt Kate in James Joyce's The Dead, 1999-2001; taped for Great Performances PBS-TV Role of Edna, 1994; voice dubbed for film My Fair Lady, The King and I, An Affair to Remember, West Side Story, Disney's Mulan, others; rec. artist for Columbia, Mus. Heritage

Records, Capital, RCA Victor, Ednl. Records, Reference Recs., Varese-Sarabande, Nonesuch. Recipient 4 Emmy awards for best actress, 2 Action for Childrens TV awards, 1977; nominee Drama Desk award; recipient Chgo. Film Festival award, 1977, 2 Gold Records for Songs from Mary Poppins and Mulan, 2 time Grammy award nominee Nat. Acad. Rec. Arts and Scis. (1st rec. Cabaret Songs and Early Songs by Arnold Schoenberg, RCA, 1977 and 1st rec. Emily Dickinson Songs by Aaron Copland, Reference Recs., 1988). Mem. Nat. Assn. Tchrs. Singing (pres. N.Y. chpt. 1994-97). E-mail: singermarnix@aol.com.

NIXON, MARY LEE, accountant, auditor; b. Crossett, Ark., July 8, 1953; d. James Thomas and Kathryn (Martin) D.; children: Donna, Lamar, Miriah. BS in Acctg., Avila Coll., 1982. Bookeeper, acct. Jen-Sal Corp., Kansas City, Mo., 1973-76; bookkeeper II Kansas City Govt., 1976-80; acctg. aide Dept. of Treasury, Kansas City, 1980-85, tax technician, 1985-94, revenue agt. Independence, Mo., 1994—. Bd. dirs. Tremont Redevelopment, 1999, treas., sec., 1999—. Mem. Assn. for Improvement of Minorities (treas. 1999, instr., cons. 1999—). Avocations: writing, reading, motivational speaking, bowling. Home: PO Box 1574 Blue Springs MO 64015-7710

NIXON, ROBERT OBEY, SR. business educator; b. Pitts., Feb. 14, 1922; s. Frank Obey and Margurite (Van Buren) N.; m. Marilyn Cavanagh, Oct. 25, 1944 (dec. 1990); children: Nan Nixon Friend, Robert Obey, Jr., Dwight Cavanagh. BS in bus. adminstrn., U. Pitts., 1948; MS, Ohio State U., 1964; MBA, U. Phoenix, 1984. Commd. 2d lt. USAF, 1943, advanced through grades to col., 1970, master navigator WWII, Korea, Vietnam; sales, adminstrn. U.S. Rubber Corp., Pitts., 1940-41; asst. engr. Am. Bridge Corp., 1941-42; underwriter, sales Penn Mutual Life Ins. Corp., 1945-50; capt., nav. instr. USAF Reserves, 1945-50; ret. USAF Col., divsn. chief Joint Chiefs of Staff, 1973; educator, cons. U. Ariz., 1973-79; bus. dept. chmn., coord., founder weekend coll. Pima C.C., Tucson, 1979-90, prof. mgmt., 1991-98, coord. weekend coll. program, 1991—. Adj. faculty Pima C.C., 1998—; founder, pres. Multiple Adv. Group ednl. cons., Tucson, 1978—. Author: Source Document: On Accelerated Courses and Programs at Accredited Two- and Four-Year Colleges and Universities, 1996; contbr. articles to profl. jours. Mem. Soc. Logistics Engrs. (sr., charter mem.), Phi Delta Theta. Presbyterian. Avocations: tennis, hiking, swimming. Home: 1824 S Regina Cleri Dr Tucson AZ 85710-8664 Fax: 520-885-2378. E-mail: eb58271@goodnet.com., bnixon@pimacc.pima.edu.

NIXON, SANDRA L. retired registrar; b. Kansas City, Mo., Feb. 23, 1944; d. C. Harold and Anna Pearl Scott-Mann; m. Hiram Luttmers, Mar. 6, 1965 (div. Aug. 1973); children: Hiram Charles, Gerald Lee; m. Douglas L. Nixon, July 16, 1976; children: Karen, Katherine, Raymond, Hiram Charles, Gerald. Student, Cen. Mo. State U., 1962-63, Nat. Coll., 1991-93. Credit clk. Harzfeld's, Kansas City, Mo., 1963-65; typist/receptionist Powers Regulator Co., Overland Park, Kans., 1965-69; ins. typist Comml. Union Ins. Co., Kansas City, Mo., 1969-73; typist Social Security Admin., 1973-78; dir. of Mothers Day Out Birchwood Bapt. Ch., Independence, 1978-80; accompanist K.C. Mo. Sch. Dist., Kansas City, 1979-81; registrar Northeast Mid. Sch., 1981-2000. Mem. ABWA (pres. 1990-91, Woman of Yr. 1992-93), VFW Aux. Post 4242 (sr. v.p. 2000-01, pres. 2001—). Baptist. Avocations: piano, ceramics, Precious Moments. E-mail: sandynixon@fellowship.net.

NIXON, SCOTT SHERMAN, lawyer; b. Grosse Pointe, Mich., Feb. 7, 1959; s. Floyd Sherman and Marjorie Jane (Quermann) N.; m. Cathryn Lynn Starnes, Aug. 27, 1983; children: Jeffry Sherman, Kelsy Jane, James Robert. BABA, Mich. State U., 1981; JD, U. Denver, 1984. Bar: Colo. 1984, U.S. Dist. Ct. Colo. 1984, U.S. Ct. Appeals (10th cir.) 1984. Assoc. Pryor, Carney & Johnson, P.C., Englewood, Colo., 1984-89, shareholder, 1990-95; pres., shareholder Pryor, Johnson, Montoya, Carney & Karr, P.C., 1995—. Officer, bd. dirs. Luth. Brotherhood Br. 8856, Denver, 1993-99, Mark K. Ulmer Meml. Native Am. Scholarship Found., Denver, 1994—; officer, mem. coun. Bethan Luth Ch., Englewood, 1993-95. Mem. ABA, Colo. Bar Assn., Denver Bar Assn., Colo. Def. Lawyers Assn. Avocations: music performance, physical fitness, carpentry/construction. Home: 6984 S Pontiac Ct Englewood CO 80112-1127 Office: Pryor Johnson Montoya Carney & Karr PC Ste 1313 6400 S Fiddlers Green Cir Englewood CO 80111-4939 E-mail: snixon@pjmck.com.

NIXON, SCOTT WEST, oceanography science educator; b. Phila., Aug. 24, 1943; s. Robert Scott West and Elizabeth (Wright) West Nixon; m. Pendleton Hall, (div.); children: Carter Hall, Elizabeth Pendleton; m. Virginia Lee. BA, U. Del., 1965; PhD, U. N.C., 1970. Prof. oceanography U. R.I., Kingston, 1970—, dir. sea grant coll. program, 1983-2000. Mem. ocean studies bd. NRC, 1999—. Author: (with others) A Coastal Marine Ecosystem, 1978, The New England High Salt Marshes, 1982; editor-in-chief Estuaries, 1988—; also articles. Recipient Ketchum award Woods Hole Oceanographic Inst., 1992, Achievement award New Eng. Estuarine Rsch. Soc., 2000, Achievement award Nat. Sea Grant Assn., 2001; grantee NSF, NOAA, EPA, Office Water Resources Rsch., State of R.I. Mem. Am. Soc. Limnology and Oceanography (governing bd. 1984-87), Estuarine Rsch. Fedn., Am. Soc. for Environ. History. Office: Univ of RI Dept Of Oceanography Kingston RI 02881 E-mail: swn@gso.uri.edu.

NIXON, TRACEY ELIZABETH, urban planner; b. N.Y.C., 1967; d. Ralph Ferrara and Anne Moehle-Ferrara; m. William A. Nixon. BA in Econs., SUNY, Buffalo, 1989; M Urban Planning, NYU, 1991. Planner Parsons Brinckerhoff, Indpls., 1998—. Mem. Am. Inst. Cert. Planners. Office: Parsons Brinckerhoff 47 S Pennsylvania St Indianapolis IN 46204-3678

NIXON, WAYNE ROBERT, engineering manager; b. Chgo., Apr. 5, 1932; s. Edwin Marlow and Mildred Ingebord Elvira (Myhrman) N.; m. Lorraine Ina Johnson, Sept. 1, 1956; children: Lynn Marie Cooney, Jill Kerry Anderson. BSMechE, U. Ill., 1953. Design engr. Danly Machine Specialties, Cicero, Ill., 1953-60; rsch. engr., supr, supervising mgr. in corp. devel. Am. Can Co., Barrington/Greenwich, Ill./Conn., 1960-83; mgr. project planning The Stolle Corp. divsn. Alcoa, Sidney, Ohio, 1983-86; project mgr. R&D Quaker Oats Co., Barrington, 1986-89; owner, prin. Pal-Craft, Palatine, Ill., 1989-98. Mem. patent com. Am. Can Co., Greenwich, 1978-80; profl. recruiting mgr. The Stolle Corp. divsn. Alcoa, Sidney, 1982-83. Patentee material for can making. Active Cultural Heritage Found., Rockford, Ill., Swedish Am. Mus. Ctr., Chgo.; alumni advisor mech. engrng. dept. U. Ill., Champaign-Urbana, 1961-67. With U.S. Army, 1954-56. Scholar U. Ill., 1953. Mem. ASME (assoc.), Am. Union Swedish Singers, Ind. Order Suithoid (chmn. lodge # 1 1990-98, dir. 1991-2001), Swedish Glee Club Waukegan (trustee 1993-2002), Chgo. Swedish Male Chorus, Suncoast Swedish Vets. Chorus, Am. Legion, Pi Tau Sigma, Sigma Iota Epsilon, Sigma Tau. Avocations: wood working, photography, music, golf, travel. Home: 10479 137th Ln N Largo FL 33774 E-mail: wayniixo@aol.com.

NIZAMI, IFTIKHAR RIAZ, research scientist; b. Clitheroe, Lancashire, Eng., Mar. 17, 1959; m. Claire Shelley Barnes, Aug. 19, 1997. BSc, U. Toronto, 1982, MSc, 1988, PhD, 1999. With Boys Town Nat. Rsch. Hosp., Omaha. Contbr. articles to profl. jours.; patentee in field. Mem. AAAS, Soc. Neurosci., Assn. Rsch. Otolaryngology, Acoustical Soc. Am., N.Y. Acad.Sci., Sigma Xi (grantee 1994). Office: Boys Town Nat Rsch Hosp 555 N 30th St Omaha NE 68131 E-mail: nizami@boystown.org.

NIZAMI, TARIQ AHMED, investment company executive; b. Karachi, Pakistan, Aug. 23, 1958; s. Zilley Ahmad and Birgis (Talat) N.; m. Yasmin Nizami, 1995. BS in Bus. Adminstrn., Calif. State U., L.A., 1981, MBA in Mktg., 1983. Product mgr. Cal Switch, Gardena, Calif., 1980-82; ops. mgr. Computer Valley, Walnut, 1982-84; prin., dir. Computerland, Diamond Bar, 1984—. Pres. Ampak Investments, Brea, Calif.; CEO Pakistan Northern Ins. Co. Ltd., Tryintr.net. Recipient Gold medal U.S. Pres., 1989. Republican. Moslem. Avocations: computer games, exotic cars. E-mail: tanizami@la.com.

NIZIN, LESLIE STEPHEN, lawyer; b. N.Y.C., Nov. 21, 1939; s. Albert and Bertha D. Nizin; m. Gail L. Gordon. BA, Queens Coll., 1961; LLB, Bklyn. Law Sch., 1964, JD, 1967. Bar: N.Y. 1964. Atty. Sturim & Nizin, Kew Gardens, N.Y., 1969—. Pres. sch. bd. Half Hollow Hills, Huntington, N.Y., 1977-92. Mem.: Network Bar Leaders (pres.), Queens County Bar Assn. (bd. mgrs., v.p., past pres.). Office: 12510 Queens Blvd Kew Gardens NY 11415-1519 E-mail: lnasjm@aol.com.

NIZZE, JUDITH ANNE, retired physician assistant; b. L.A., Nov. 1, 1942; d. Robert George and Charlotte Ann (Wise) Swan; m. Norbert Adolph Otto Paul Nizze, Dec. 31, 1966 (dec. Sept. 2000). BA, UCLA, 1966, postgrad., 1966-76; grad. physician asst. tng. program, Charles R. Drew Sch. Postgrad., L.A., 1979; BS, Calif. State U., Dominguez, 1980. Cert. physician asst., Calif. Staff rsch. assoc. I-II Wadsworth Vet. Hosp., L.A., 1965-71; staff rsch. assoc. III-IV John Wayne Clinic Jonsson Comprehensive Cancer Ctr., UCLA, 1971-78; clin. asst. Robert S. Ozeran, Gardena, Calif., 1978; physician asst. family practice Fred Chasan, Torrance, 1980-82; sr. physician asst. Donald L. Morton prof., chief surg. oncology Jonsson Comprehensive Cancer Ctr., UCLA, 1983-91; administrv. dir. immunotherapy John Wayne Cancer Inst., Santa Monica, Calif., 1991-98; ret. Cons. clin. rsch. orgn. devel. John Wayne Cancer Inst., 1998—, spl. rsch. projects coord., 2001—. Contbr. articles to profl. jours. Fellow Am. Acad. Physician Assts., Am. Assn. Surgeons Assts., Calif. Acad. Physician Assts.; mem. Assn. Physician Assts. in Oncology. Republican. Presbyterian. Avocations: sailing, tennis, skiing, securities trading, computers. Home: 13243 Fiji Way Unit J Marina Del Rey CA 90292

NJIE, VERONICA P.S. nursing educator, clinical nurse; b. Banjul, Gambia, Nov. 15, 1963; d. Edward G. Njie and Grace B.S. Daniels-Njie. BSN, Howard U., Washington, 1992; MSN, The Cath. U. Am., Washington, 1996. RN Washington, clin. specialist in med.-surg. nursing. Tchr. Dept. Edn., Banjul, The Gambia, 1980—82; state registered nurse (SRN) Royal Victoria Hosp., Banjul , 1985—86; rsch./field asst. Med. Rsch. Coun., Fajara, 1986—87; nurse technician Howard U. Hosp., Washington, 1988—90, clin. nurse II, 1990—96; clin. nurse N.W. Health Care Ctr. Beverly Enterprise, 1990—98; clin. instr. Montgomery Coll., Tacoma Park, Md., 1996; asst. prof. nursing Balt. City C. C., Balt., 1997. Contbr. articles. Recipient Intramural Rsch. Tng. award, NIH, 2000. Mem.: Md. Assn. Higher Edn., ANA, Assn. Faculties Advnacement C.C.'s, Nat. League Nursing, Sigma Theta Tau. Democrat. Roman Catholic. Avocations: reading, travel, theater , dancing, movies. Office: Balt City C C 2901 Liberty Heights Ave Baltimore MD 21215 Office Fax: 410-462-7785. Personal E-mail: vnjie@bccc.state.md.us. Business E-Mail: vnjie@bccc.state.md.us. E-mail: vpnjie@aol.com.

NJOKU, ATHAN ONWUSAKA, economist, educator; BA, St. Edwards U., 1964; MS, Oreg. State U., 1966; PhD, U. Ill., 1971. Prof. Benedict Coll., Columbia, SC, 1971. Home: 627 Glenthorne Rd Columbia SC 29203-3630

NJOKU, ENI GERALD, research scientist; b. Ibadan, Nigeria, May 13, 1950; arrived in U.S., 1972; s. Eni and Winifred Olive Njoku; m. Mary Kathleen Brand; 1 child Eni William. BA, Cambridge (Eng.) U., 1972; MS, MIT, 1974, PhD, 1976. Scientist Jet Propulsion Lab., Pasadena, Calif., 1977—84, rsch. scientist, 1990—; assoc. prof. Harvey Mudd Coll., Claremont, 1984—86; discipline scientist NASA, Washington, 1986—90. Vis. prof. MIT, 2001—02. Fellow: IEEE; mem.: AAAS, Am. Geophys. Union, Sigma Xi. Office: Jet Propulsion Lab 4800 Oak Grove Dr Pasadena CA 91109 Personal E-mail: njoku@alum.mit.edu. Business E-Mail: eni.g.njoku@jpl.nasa.gov.

NNADOZIE, EMMANUEL UZOMA A. economist, educator; b. NSU, IMO, Nigeria, July 2, 1956; came to U.S., 1989; s. Martin A. and Susanna Adamma (Egerue) N.; 1 child, Adaeze Sonia. BS with honors, U. Nigeria, 1980, MS, 1983; D.E.A., Sorbonne, Paris, France, 1985; PhD, U. Paris, Sorbonne, 1987. Projects officer Nigerian Agrl. and Coope Bank, Kaduna, Nigeria, 1979; planning officer Ogun State Agrl. Devel. Corp., Abeokuta, Nigeria, 1980-81; acting chief planning officer World Bank Agrl. Devel. Program, Bauchi, Nigeria; asst. lectr. Inst. for Rural Devel. and Coop., U. Nigeria, Nsukka, Nigeria, 1981-82; technical econ. exec. Soc. de Commercialization de Materiel Lourd, Paris, France, 1987-88; cons. Inst. de Recherche et Applications de Methodes du Devel., France; asst. prof. econs. N.E. Mo. State U., Kirksville, Mo., 1989—; dir. program for minorities (summer) Inst. de Recherche et Applications de Methodes du Devel.; pres. African Profiles Internat. mag., 1992—; dir. McNair Post-Baccalaureate Achievement, 1992—. Cons., researcher, I.R.A.M., Paris, 1983; guest lectr. U. N.C. at Charlotte, 1989. Editor: (book) Economics, 1990; author: (books) Chad, Oil in Nigeria. Grantee ELF Aquitaine, Paris, France, 1986, French Govt., 1988, N.E. Mo. State U., 1990. Mem. Congress of Polit. Economists (founding mem.), Am. Econ. Assn., African Studies Assn., African Fin. and Econ. Assn., Nigerian Assn. Agrl. Economists, S.E. Africanists Assn., Club Franco-Nigerian. Avocations: reading, soccer, music, travel. Office: NE Mo State Univ Normal St Kirksville MO 63501-4200

NOACK, HAROLD QUINCY, JR. lawyer; b. San Francisco, May 1, 1931; m. Ann Crosby, Nov. 1952 (div. Sept. 1974); children: Stephen Tracy, Peter Quincy, Andrew Crosby; m. Susan K. Sherwood, Dec. 1975 (div. Jan. 1983); m. Penny Jo Orth, Apr. 2, 1988 (div. May 1989); m. Linda F. Killeen, Mar. 15, 1994 (div. May 1996). BA, U. Calif., Berkeley, 1953; LLB, U. Calif., San Francisco, 1959. Bar: Calif. 1960, Idaho 1969, U.S. Dist. Ct. Idaho 1969. Assoc. Fernoff & Wolfe, Oakland, Calif., 1959-64, Cooley, Crowley, Gaither, Godward, Castro & Huddleson, San Francisco, 1964-65; pvt. practice Oakland, 1965-66; ptnr. Oliphant, Hopper, Stribling & Noack, 1966-69; assoc. Eberle, Berlin, Kading & Turnbow, Boise, Idaho, 1969-70; pvt. practice, 1970-83, 85-88; assoc. Anthony Parks, 1970-75; ptnr. Noack & Korn, 1970-75, Noack & Hawley, Boise, 1983-85, Lyons & Noack, Boise, 1988-89; pvt. practice law, 1989—. Contbr. articles to profl. jours. Bd. dirs., pres. Idaho Planned Parenthood, Boise, 1970-72; bd. dirs. Idaho Heart Assn., Boise, 1975. 2d lt. U.S. Army, 1954-55. Mem. ABA, Calif. Bar Assn., Idaho Bar Assn. (fee grievance com. 1986—), Boise Bar Assn., Rotary (bd. dirs. Boise club 1980). Avocations: running, walking, fishing, cooking. Home: PO Box 875 1915 N 24th St Boise ID 83702-0204 Office: 733 N 7th St Boise ID 83702-5500

NOAH, JULIA JEANINE, retired librarian; b. Craig, Mo., July 14, 1932; d. Hiram Curtis and Eloise Julia (Puckett) True; m. Raymond Laverne Noah, Sept. 5, 1954; children: David Scott, Danny Ray, Deborah Jill, Douglas True. BS, U. Ill., 1953; MA in Library Sci., U. South Fla., 1983. Asst. rsch. librarian Parke, Davis & Co., Detroit, 1953-55; cataloging librarian U. Mo., Columbia, 1955-57; sch. librarian High Point Elem. Sch., Clearwater, Fla., 1968; library aide Clearwater High Sch., 1973-78; reference asst. Dunedin (Fla.) Pub. Library, 1978-84, dir. info. svcs., 1984-88, library dir., 1988-94; ret. Mem. ALA, DAR, Fla. Libr. Assn., Pinellas Genealogy Soc., Questers, Phi Kappa Phi, Beta Phi Mu. Republican. Presbyterian. Avocations: antiques, genealogy.

NOAH, PAUL RANDALL, lawyer; b. Hastings, Mich., Oct. 24, 1961; s. Melvin Laverne and Ellen Kay (Catchick) N.; m. Chen Yin Chow, Aug. 6, 1988; children: Sean, Kelly. BA, Mich. State U., 1983; JD, U. Mich., 1986. Assoc. Catchick & Dodge, Grand Rapids, Mich., 1986-88, Knapp & Vernon, Palo Alto, Calif., 1988-89, Bledsoe, Cathcart, Leahy, Star, San Francisco, 1989-90, Wilson, Sher, Marshall & Peterson, Oakland, Calif., 1990-91; pvt. practice Walnut Creek, 1991-92; ptnr. Noah & Nerland, 1992-95; pvt. practice Orinda, Calif., 1996—. Office: 8 Camino Encinas Ste 220 Orinda CA 94563-3350 E-mail: pnoah@ix.netcom.com.

NOAKES, BETTY LAVONNE, retired elementary school educator; b. Oklahoma City, Aug. 28, 1938; d. Webster L. and Willie Ruth (Johnson) Hawkins; m. Richard E. Noakes, Apr. 22, 1962 (dec.); 1 child, Michele Monique. Student, Oklahoma City U., MEd, 1971; BS, Cen. State U., 1962; postgrad., Cen. State U., Okla. State U. Elem. tchr. Merced (Calif.) Pub. Schs., 1966-67, Oklahoma City Schs., 1971-73, Mid-Del Schs., Midwest City, Okla., 1973-95; founder, owner Noakes-I Care Day Care, 1995—2002. 2d v.p. PTA, Pleasant Hill, 1991, cert. recognition, 1992-93; active Nat. PTA, 1991-92; charter mem. Nat. Mus. of Am. Indian-Smithsonian Instn.; chmn. Internat. Fashion Show, Quayle U. Meth. Ch., 1997—, chmn. stewardship com. 1998—, mem. Wesley Found. bd. Langston U.; mem. Urban League, Urban League Guild, YWCA. Recipient Cert. Appreciation YMCA, 1992-92, Disting. Svc. award Mid-Del PTA, 1992. Mem. NEA, AAUW, NAACP, NAFE, Nat. Therapeutic Recreation Assn., Okla. Edn. Assn., Nat. Ret. Tchrs. Assn., Okla. Ret. Tchrs. Assn., Smithsonian Instn., Oklahoma City U. Alumni Assn., United Meth. Women Assn. (chair membership nurture and outreach), Ctrl. State U. Alumni Assn., Okla. Ea. Star, Order of the Golden Cir. (aux. of Great We. Consistory # 34 Dorcas-LL Inter-gard assembly # 41), Daus. of Isis, Phi Delta Kappa (sgt.-at-arms), Zeta Phi Beta (1st v.p.). Avocations: aerobics, singing, piano, clarinet, folk dancing. Home: 5956 N Coltrane Rd Oklahoma City OK 73121-3409 E-mail: nblnzeta@aol.com.

NOAM, ELI MICHAEL, telecommunications educator; b. Jerusalem, Aug. 22, 1946; came to U.S., 1963; s. Ernst and Lotte (Dahn) N.; m. Nadine Strossen, 1980. AB, Harvard U., 1970, AM, 1972, PhD in Econs., JD, Harvard U., 1975. Bar: N.Y. 1996, D.C. 1997. Asst. prof. Princeton (N.J.) U., 1975-76, Columbia Bus. Sch., N.Y.C., 1981-84, prof. finance and econ., 1984—; commr. N.Y. State Pub. Svc. Commn., 1987-90. Dir. Columbia Inst. for Tele-Info., N.Y.C., 1983-87, 1990—. Author or editor: Telecommunications Regulation: Today and Tomorrow, 1982, Video Media Competition, 1985, Law of International Telecommunications in the United States, 1988, The Cost of Libel, 1989, Television in Europe, 1991, Telecommunications in Europe, 1991, Telecommunications in Western Asia, 1997, Telecommunications in Latin America, 1998. Telecommunications in Africa, 1998.. Bd. dirs. IRS Computer Modernization, Washington, D.C., 1988-89, Fed. Telecom System FTS-2000 Selection, Washington, 1990—. With Israel Air Force, 1967, 73. Grantee NSF, 1982, 85, 86; fellow German Marshall Fund U.S., 1983-84, 1966-68, Mideast Wars; Fellow Freedom Forum Media Center, 1996. Mem. Coun. on Fgn. REls., Phi Beta Kappa. Jewish. Avocations: flying, skiing, diving. Office: Columbia U Inst Tele-Info 809 Uris Hall New York NY 10027

NOAR, MARK DAVID, internist, gastroenterologist, therapeutic endoscopist, consultant, inventor; b. Boston, Sept. 10, 1953; s. Myron Theodore and Phyllis (Krinsky) N.; m. Martine Denise Motard, May 15, 1983; children: Emmanuelle, Ariane, Jean-Claude. BS in Biology, Ursinus Coll., Collegeville, Pa., 1975; MPH in Internat. Health, Tulane U., 1977; MD, U. Cen. del Este, Dominican Republic, 1980. Intern 5th Pathway program Coll. Medicine and Dentistry N.J.-Newark Beth Israel Hosp., 1980-81; resident in internal medicine U. Nebr. Med. Ctr., Omaha, 1981-84; fellow in gastroenterology SUNY Downstate Med. Ctr., Bklyn., 1984-86; fellow in therapeutic and surg. endoscopy, vis. staff Univ. Hosp. Hamburg, Germany, 1986-87; pvt. practice, Balt., 1988—; pres., CEO Md. Gastrenterology Network, Inc., 1993—. Bd. dirs. 3CPM Co., Inc., Americas Bank; clin. cons. in therapeutic endoscopy Bklyn. VA Med. Ctr., 1987; dir. project devel., v.p. med. devel. Ixion, Inc., Seattle, 1987—96; staff physician dept. gastroenterology St. Joseph Hosp., Balt., Franklin Square Hosp., Balt.; bd. dirs., dir. ops. Disaster Support Network, Balt., 1990—95; session co-chmn. World Congress Gastroenterology, Sydney, Australia, 1990, IX European Workshop on Therapeutic Digestive Endoscopy, Brussels, 1991; CEO, med. dir. The Endoscopy Ctr., Inc., Balt., 1990—; CEO, bd. dirs. Md. Gastroenterology Network, Inc., The Endoscopy Ctr.; course dir. internat. hands-on ERCP Conf., Balt., 1994, Balt., 95; founder, dir. Internat. ERCP Edn. Found., 1994—; founder CEO Digestive Health Edn. Found.; dir. The Hepatitis Study Ctr. Author: (with N. Soehendra and H. Grimm) A Compendium of Therapeutic Endoscopy for the General Practitioner, 1991; editor-in-chief Internat. Video Jour. Therapeutic and Diagnostic Endoscopy; assoc. editor Endoscopy Rev.; contbr. articles and abstracts to med. jours., chpts. to books; inventor robotic interactive endoscopy simulation, precurved papillotome and ERCP catheters, "Noar pump" for disinfection and cleaning of endoscopes. Pub. lectr. Am. Cancer Soc., Balt., 1988—; physician educator Doctor and Lawyer Coalition Against Drugs, Balt., 1991-92. Fellow Royal Soc. Tropical Medicine and Hygiene; mem. ACP, AMA, Am. Coll. Gastroenterology, Am. Soc. Gastrointestinal Endoscopy (instr. regional advanced endoscopy 1993—, award for achievement and edn. in diagnostic/therapeutic biliary and pancreatic endoscopy 1992), Baltimore County Med. Soc., Md. Ambulatory Surgery Assn. (legis. chmn., bd. dirs. 1995—), Sigma Xi. Avocations: guitar, banjo, sailing, orchid culture, gourmet cooking. Office: Endoscopic Microsurgery Assocs 7402 York Rd Ste 100 Baltimore MD 21204-7532

NOBACK, RICHARDSON KILBOURNE, medical educator; b. Richmond, Va., Nov. 7, 1923; s. Gustav Joseph and Hazel (Kilborn) N.; m. Nan Jean Gates, Apr. 5, 1947; children: Carl R., Robert K., Catherine E. MD, Cornell U., 1947; BA, Columbia U., 1993. Diplomate Am. Bd. Internal Medicine. Intern N.Y. Hosp., 1947-48; asst. resident Cornell Med. div. Bellevue Hosp., N.Y.C., 1958-50, chief resident, 1950-52; instr. medicine Cornell U., 1950-53; asst. prof. medicine SUNY Upstate Med. Ctr., Syracuse, 1955-56; assoc. prof. medicine U. Ky. Med. Ctr., Lexington, 1956-64; exec. dir. Kansas City (Mo.) Gen. Hosp. and Med. Ctr., 1964-69; assoc. dean, prof. medicine U. Mo. Sch. Medicine, Columbia, 1964-69, founding dean Kansas City, 1969-78, prof. medicine, 1969-90, prof. and dean emeritus, 1990—. Cons. U. Tenn., U. Mich., U. Del., Northeastern Ohio Group, U. Mo., Eastern Va. Med. Sch., Tex. Tech. U. Contbr. numerous articles to profl. jours. Bd. dirs. Kansas City Gen. Hosp., Truman Med. Ctr., Wayne Miner Health Ctr., Jackson County Med. Soc., The Shepherd's Ctr., Am. Fedn. Aging Rsch., Mo. Gerontol. Inst., The Shepherd's Ctrs. of Am.; dir. Mo. Geriatric Edn. Ctr., 1985-88. Capt. USAF Med. Svcs. 1953-55. Recipient medal of honor Avila Coll., Kansas City, 1968, merit award Met. Med. Soc., 1991, recognition award Mo. Soc. Internal Medicine, 1993. Mem. AMA, Mo. Med. Assn. (former mem. ho. of dels., v.p. 1992), Am. Geriatric Soc., Alpha Omega Alpha, Phi Kappa Phi. Avocations: photography, writing, travel. Home: 2912 Abercorn Dr Las Vegas NV 89134-7440 E-mail: Nanori@aol.com.

NOBBS, ZANE ROBERT, economist, consultant; b. Saginaw, Mich., Apr. 5, 1963; s. Robert Marion and Alice Marie Nobbs. AAS, Delta Coll. U. Ctr., Bay City, Mich., 1985; BSBA, Ctrl. Mich. U., 1987, M, 1989. Economist UN, N.Y.C., 1988-94; equity rschr. CS First Boston, 1992-93; project mgr. Ziff-Davis Pub. Co., 1995-96; rsch. mgr. ICM Conf., Chgo., 1997-98; economist Gene Kaufman, Archs., N.Y.C., 1998-99; mng. dir. Unism Found., 1994—; sr. cons. Unism, Inc., 1994—. Mem. China External Trade Coun., N.Y.C., 1994-2001; bus. advisor Creative Artists Lab., N.Y.C., 1998-99. Author: Getting to Know Your Computer, 1995; contbr. to profl. mags. incl. World Investment Report and World Investment Directory. Trainer ARC, Coleman, 1982. Mich. Competitive scholar State Mich., 1987; fellow UN, 1989-2001. Mem. Japan Soc., Alpha Kappa Psi (chaplain 1986-87). Republican. Methodist. Avocations: music, linguistics, modelling, history. Office: Unism Inc 765 United Nations Plz 2 G New York NY 10017 E-mail: Zanenobbs@worldnet.att.net.

NOBE, KEN, chemical engineering educator; b. Berkeley, Calif., Aug. 26, 1925; s. Sidney and Kiyo (Uyeyama) N.; m. Mary Tagami, Aug. 31, 1957; children: Steven Andrew, Keven Gibbs, Brian Kelvin. BS, U. Calif., Berkeley, 1951; PhD, UCLA, 1956. Jr. chem. engr. Air Reduction Co., Murray Hill, N.J., 1951-52; asst. prof. chem. engrng. UCLA, 1957-62, assoc. prof., 1962-68, prof., 1968—, chmn. dept. chem., nuclear and thermal engrng., 1978-83, founding chmn. chem. engrng., 1983-84. Mem. tech. staff Ramo-Wooldridge Corp., El Segundo, Calif., 1958-59. Div. editor: Jour. Electrochem. Soc, 1967-91, Electrochimica Acta, 1977-85 Served with U.S. Army, 1944-46. Mem. Electrochem. Soc. (Henry B. Linford award 1992), Am. Chem. Soc., Nat. Assn. Corrosion Engrs., Internat. Soc. Electrochemistry, Sigma Xi. Office: UCLA Dept Chemical Engring Los Angeles CA 90095-1592

NOBE, KENNETH CHARLES, international agricultural and water resource economics consultant; b. Venedy, Ill., Oct. 26, 1930; s. Elmer F. and Alvina (Froekhe) N.; m. Hazel Leona McCullough, Oct. 22, 1949; children—Sandra, Jeffrey, Michael. BS, So. Ill. U., 1953; MS, Cornell U., 1954, PhD, 1959. Mktg. agt. USDA, Ithaca, N.Y., 1954-55; instr. Cornell U., 1955-56; economist USDA, Washington, 1958-61, USPHS, Denver, 1961-63, U.S. Dept. Interior, Washington, 1963-64; econ. cons. Harza Engring. Co. Internat., Lahore, West Pakistan, 1964-65; assoc. prof. econs. Colo. State U., Ft. Collins, 1966-69, prof. econs., chmn. econs. dept., 1969-83, prof. agrl. econs., chmn. dept. agr. and resource econs., 1984-87, emeritus prof., 1987—; exec. v.p. RAD Internat. Inc., Ft. Collins, 1987—2002; chmn. exec. council Environ. Resources Center, 1970-71; dir. Internat. Sch. Econ. Devel. Studies, 1980-83; exec. dir. Internat. Sch. Agr. and Resource Devel., 1983-85; sr. ptnr. Nobe Econ. Cons., 2002—. Econ. advisor to dir. West Pakistan Water and Power Devel. Authority, 1964-65; cons. U.S. Dept. State, AID, 1966, 76-92, Ford Found., India, 1980, World Bank, 1984-88, 94-96, FAO, UN, 1988-90, Philippines Dept. Agr., 1977, U.N. Devel. Program, Viet Nam, 1993, Viet Name Dept. Agr. and Rural Devel., 1998; Asian Devel. Bank, Pakistan, 2001; chmn. Western Agr. Econs. Coun., 1976-78. Served with USAF, 1948-50. Recipient Ill. State Farmer award Future Farmers Am., 1947, Disting. Service award Colo. State U., 1979 Mem. Omicron Delta Epsilon. Home: 579 Bighorn Cir Silverthorne CO 80498-9216

NOBEL, GLENN LLOYD, investment group director, arbitrator, mediator; b. Perth Amboy, N.J., Mar. 23, 1957; s. Irving Robert and Karen Zelda (Rosenfeld) N.; m. Karen Lynne Fuchs, June 17, 1957. BA in Cmty. Devel., Rutgers U., 1979. Sub. tchr. New Brunswick (N.J.) Bd. Edn., 1980-81; trader B. Weisenfeld and Co., Phila., 1981-82, Bess and Co., Phila., 1982; gen. ptnr., trader Nobel Securities, 1983—; dir. bus. devel. TFM Investment Group. Arbitrator FDIC/Resolution Trust Corp., Washington, 1994—, Nat. Futures Assn., EEOC, U.S. Postal Svc. (REDRESS); mem. panel Am. Stock Exch., Adminstrv. Conf. of the U.S., Coffee Sugar & Cocoa Exch., Chgo. Bd. Options Exch. Comex, Mpcl. Rulemaking Bd., Phila. Stock Exch., Phila. Stock Exch. Disciplinary Rev. Bd., N.Y. Stock Exch.; mediator U.S. Bankruptcy Ct., Dept. Justice, 1996; mem. adjudication com. N.Y. Mercantile Exch. Youth aid panelist, officer Bucks County Youth Aid Panel, Middletown, Pa., 1993-95, Newtown, Pa., 1995. Mem. ABA (assoc.), Soc. Profls. in Dispute Resolution (assoc.), Am. Arbitration Assn. (cert. arbitrator, mediator 1987—), Nat. Futures Assn., Nat. Assn. Securities Dealers (arbitrator, mediator 1993—), Nat. Adoption Ctr. (bd. dirs., corp. com. 1986-94, Recognition award 1993), Pa. Coun. Mediators. Jewish. Avocations: sailing, wreck diving, gliding. Office: TFM Investment Group Ste 616 1900 Market St Philadelphia PA 19103-3513 E-mail: gnobel@tfminvestmentgroup.com.

NOBEL, JOEL J. biomedical researcher; b. Phila., Dec. 8, 1934; s. Bernard D. and Golda R. (Nobel) Judovich; m. Bonnie Sue Goldberg, June 19, 1960 (div.); children: Erika, Joshua; m. Loretta Schwartz, Oct. 28, 1979; 1 child, Adam. AB, Haverford Coll., 1956; MA, U. Pa., 1958; MD, Thomas Jefferson Med. Coll., Phila., 1963. Intern Presbyn. Hosp., Phila., 1963-64; resident in surgery Pa. Hosp., 1964-65; resident in neurosurgery U. Pa. Hosp., 1965-66; practice medicine specializing in biomed. engrng. rsch. and healthcare tech. assessment, hosp. planning and mgmt., Phila., 1968—; dir. research Emergency Care Research Inst., Plymouth Meeting, 1968-71, dir., pres., 1971—2001; pres. Plymouth Inst., 1979—2002; founder and pres. emeritus ECRI, 2001—; founder, pres. ECRI Bhd, Malaysia, 2001—; CEO The Nobel Group, 2002—. Cons. in field; bd. dirs. Consumers Union, 1976-79, 1980—, chmn. tech. policy com., exec. bd. Publisher Health Devices, 1971-2001, Health Devices Alerts, 1977-2001; contbr. articles to profl. jours. Served with USNR, 1966-68. Smith, Kline & French fgn. fellow, 1962; grantee HEW, 1968-72; grantee Am. Heart Assn., 1965-66 Mem. AMA, APHA, Assn. Advancement Med. Instrumentation, Critical Care Med. Soc., Pa. Med. Assn., Navy League, U.S. Naval Inst., Sunday Breakfast Club, Brit. Officers Club of Phila. Home: 1434 Monk Rd Gladwyne PA 19035-1315 Office: ECRI 5200 Butler Pike Plymouth Meeting PA 19462-1298 E-mail: jnobel@ecri.org.

NOBIL, JAMES HOWARD, JR. real estate investor, developer, consultant, broker; b. Columbus, Ohio, Mar. 21, 1955; s. James Howard Nobil and Carol Mae (Wiesenberger) Greenbaum; m. Elizabeth Ann Corro, Apr. 16, 1983 (div. 1998); children: Jonathan James Michael, Jennifer Carrie Lee. BA in Polit. Sci., Tufts U., 1973-75; postgrad., George Washington U., 1978-80. Lic. real estate broker Md., Va., D.C., Fla.; cert. leasing specialist ICSC. Account exec. Riviere Securities Corp., Washington, 1977-78; v.p. ops. Fed. Realty Investment Trust, Bethesda, Md., 1978-83; mng. gen. ptnr. NRW Devel. Co., Vienna, 1983-84; v.p. acquisitions Oxford Nat. Properties Corp., Bethesda, 1984-85; 1st v.p. Washington Real Estate Investment Trust, 1985-86; pres. Washington Comml. Properties, Inc., McLean, Va., 1986—, Rent Verification Svcs. (subs. of Washington Comml. Properties, Inc.), McLean, 1986—. Mem. Internat. Coun. Shopping Ctrs., Nat. Assn. Realtors, D.C. Assn. Realtors, Area Comml. Brokers Coun. Avocations: running, boating, skiing, tennis. Office: Washington Comml Properties Inc 1443 Dolley Madison Blvd Mc Lean VA 22101

NOBLE, CHERYL A. library director; b. Kansas City, Mo., May 12, 1959; d. Louis A. and JoAnn (Nash) Lang; m. Steven E. Meyer, Jan. 6, 1979 (div. 1993); m. J. Randall Noble, Oct. 14, 1994 (div. 1999); children: Steven N., Cameron A., Cara D., Eric M., Laura E. A.Office Mgmt., Longview C.C., Lee's Summit, Mo., 1986; BBA, Webster U., St. Louis, 1994; MLA, Emporia (Kans.) State U., 1998. Corp. sec. Charles Paint Rsch., Inc., Kansas City, 1976-89; exec. asst. St. Luke's Health Sys., 1989-96; dir. Carnegie Pub. Libr., Albany, Mo., 1997—. Troop leader Girl Scouts U.S., Albany, 1996-99, Overland Park, Kans., 1990-96. Mem. ALA, Mo. Libr. Assn., Pub. Libr. Assn. Avocations: family camping, genealogy. Home: 101 Fourth St Darlington MO 64438-9700 Office: Carnegie Public Libr 101 W Clay St Albany MO 64402-1601

NOBLE, DOUGLAS ROSS, museum administrator; b. Sturgis, Ky., Jan. 19, 1945; s. Roscoe and Robbie Rae (Martin) N.; m. Catherine Ann Richardson, Nov. 3, 1973; children: Kate Faxon, Jennifer Martin. BS, Okla. State U., 1967; MSA, Ga. Coll., 1978; D Pub. Adminstrn., U. Ga., 1987. Asst. to dir. Savannah (Ga.) Sci. Mus., 1971-73; exec. dir. Mus. Arts and Scis., Macon, Ga., 1973-80; dir. museums Memphis Mus. Sys., 1980-2001; CEO Ind. State Mus., Indpls., 2001—. Mem. mus. assessment program Inst. of Mus. Services, Washington, 1982—, grant reviewer, 1983—; cons. Mus. Mgmt. Program, Sarasota, Fla., 1985. Contbr. articles to profl. jours. Grad., Leadership Memphis, 1984; bd. dirs. Memphis in May Internat. Festival. 1st lt. U.S. Army, 1968-70, Vietnam. Decorated Bronze Star. Mem. Natural Sci. for Youth Found. (trustee 1980-87, Naumburg award 1978), Am. Assn. Museums (S.E. rep. 1984-87, chmn. mus. assessment program adv. com. 1987-89, treas., v.p. fin. 1990-92, bd. dirs. 1997-2000, chmn. nature ctr. accreditation com. 1985), Southeastern Museums Conf. (pres. 1982-84, James R. Short Lifetime Achievement award 2000), Memphis Museums Roundtable (co-founder 1984, Thomas W. Briggs Cmty. Svc. award 2000). Episcopalian. Home: 310 E Ohio St Indianapolis IN 46204 Office: Ind State Mus 650 W Washington St Indianapolis IN 46204

NOBLE, ERNEST PASCAL, pharmacologist, biochemist, educator; b. Baghdad, Iraq, Apr. 2, 1929; came to U.S., 1946; s. Noble Babik and Barkev Grace (Kasparian) Babikian; m. Inga Birgitta Kilstromer, May 19, 1956; children— Lorna, Katharine, Erik BS in Chemistry, U. Calif.-Berkeley, 1951; PhD in Biochemistry, Oreg. State U., 1955; MD, Case Western Res. U., 1962. Diplomate Nat. Bd. Med. Examiners. Sr. instr. biochemistry Western Res. U., Cleve., 1957-62; intern Stanford Med. Ctr., Calif., 1962-63, resident in psychiatry, 1963-66, research assoc., asst. prof., 1965-69; assoc. prof. psychiatry, psychobiology and pharmacology U. Calif.-Irvine, 1969-71, prof., chief neurochemistry, 1971-76, 79-81; dir. Nat. Inst. Alcohol Abuse and Alcoholism HEW, 1976-78, assoc. adminstr. sci., alcohol, drug abuse and mental health, 1978-79; Pike prof. alcohol studies, dir. Alcohol Research Ctr. UCLA Sch. of Medicine, 1981—. Mem. various med./sci. jour. editorial bds.; contbr. numerous articles to profl. jours., chpts. to books V.p. Nat. Coun. on Alcoholism 1981-84; pres. Internat. Commn. for the Prevention of Alcoholism and Drug Dependency, 1988. Fulbright scholar, 1955-56; Guggenheim fellow, 1974-75; Sr. Fulbright scholar, 1984-85; recipient Career Devel. award NIMH, HEW, 1966-69 Fellow Am. Coll. Neuropsychopharmacology; mem. Internat. Soc. Neurochemistry, Am. Soc. Pharmacology and Exptl. Therapeutics, Research Soc. on Alcoholism. Office: UCLA 760 Westwood Plz Los Angeles CA 90095-8353

NOBLE, JAMES WILKES, actor; b. Dallas, Mar. 5, 1922; s. Ralph Byrne and Lois Frances (Wilkes) N.; m. Carolyn Owen Coates, May 19, 1956; 1 child: Jessica Katherine. Student, North Tex. Coll., Arlington, 1939-41, So. Methodist U., Dallas, 1941-43, 1946-47. Lectr. acting and mime Am. Acad. Dramatic Art, 1956-59. Mem. Lydia Tarnower Modern Dance Co., 1937-39; title role in 1st TV drama, The Egoist on Dumont TV, 1943; 1st N.Y. Stage appearance Helena's Room, 1947; 1st Broadway appearance: The Big Knife, 1949; others include: The Velvet Glove, 1949; Medea, 1951; Come of Age, 1952; A Far Country, 1961; Strange Interlude, 1963; 1776, 1971; The Runner Stumbles, 1976; mem. Am. Mime Theatre, 1952-59; appeared in numerous TV dramas and soap operas; appeared in more than 200 plays in theatres throughout the world most recent: Stratford Characters in Stratford-Upon-Avon, England, T.S. Eliot in The Poet's Theatre, Cambridge, Mass., 1996, Out of Order, Calgary, Alta., Can., 1997, Moon Over Buffalo, Edmonton, Alta., 1998; TV appearances include the role of the Governor on Benson, ABC-TV, 1979-86, series First Impressions, CBS-TV, 1987, series Archies, NBC-TV, 1990, Law and Order, 1991; movies include: Dragonfly, 1965; The Sporting Club, 1967; 1776, 1972; Promises in the Dark, 1978; Ten, 1979; Being There, 1979; Airplane II, 1983; You Talkin' To Me?, 1986; Tiger's Tale, 1987, Chances Are, 1988, Absent Minded Professor, 1989, Law and Order, 1991, All My Children, 1992; numerous other appearances. Author jour. article on Am. mime. Served as lt. USNR, 1943-46, P.T.O. Named Hon. Gov., N.J., N.Y., 1982; appreciation award Am. Heart Assn., 1983. Mem. Actors Studio (life), Actors Equity, SAG, AFTRA. Democrat. Roman Catholic. Avocation: Photography. Office: Paradigm Agy 10100 Santa Monica Blvd Los Angeles CA 90067-4003

NOBLE, JOSEPH VEACH, fine arts administrator; b. Phila., Apr. 3, 1920; s. Joseph Haderman and Helen Elizabeth (Veach) N.; m. Olive Ashley Mooney, June 21, 1941 (dec. Sept. 1978); children: Josette, Ashley, Laurence; m. Lois Cook Cartwright, Oct. 27, 1979. Student, U. Pa., 1942. Cameraman, dir. DeFrenes and Co. Studios, Phila., 1939-41; studio mgr. WPTZ, Philco TV Sta., 1941-42, DeFrenes and Co. Studios, 1946-49; gen. mgr. Murphy-Lillis Prodns., N.Y.C., 1949-50; exec. v.p. Film Counselors, Inc., 1950-56, dir., 1950-82; operating adminstr. Met. Mus. Art, 1956-67, vice dir. adminstrn., 1967-70; dir. Mus. City N.Y., 1970-85; exec. dir. Soc. Medalists, 1985-95. Photog. salon exhibitor, from 1936; lectr. CCNY, 1949-51 Author: The Techniques of Painted Attic Pottery, 1965, The Historical Murals of Maplewood, 1961, Forgery of the Etruscan Terracotta Warriors, 1961; Contbr.: Ency. Brit, 1970. Trustee Corning Mus. of Glass, 1970—; mem. Morrow Meth. Ch., pres. trustees, 1972-77; chmn. N.Y. State Bd. Hist. Preservation 1972-76; co-chmn. Save Venice, Inc., 1972; trustee Brookgreen Gardens, 1971—, pres., 1976-90, chmn., 1990-95, chmn. emeritus, 1995—. With AUS, 1942-46. Recipient Venice Film Festival medal for photography in sci., 1948, Sigma Xi award 1963, Maple Leaf award Maplewood, N.J., 1966, 87, Gold medal for The Big Apple N.Y. Film Festival, 1979, Disting. Svc. award Maplewood C. of C., 1987. Fellow Soc. Antiquaries London, Am. Numismatic Soc.; mem. N.Y. State Assn. Museums (pres. 1970-72), NAD (medal 1976), Nat. Sculpture Soc. (medal 1978, 91), Artists' Fellowship (medal 1978), Archeol. Inst. Am. (treas. 1963-70), Museums Council N.Y.C. (chmn. 1965-67), Am. Assn. Museums (pres. 1975-78, Disting. Svc. Awd., 1991), Cultural Instns. Group N.Y.C. (chmn. 1984-85), Soc. Promotion Hellenic Studies; Am. Watercolor Soc. (medal 1982). Clubs: Maplewood Country; Explorers (N.Y.C.), Century Assn. (N.Y.C.). Home: 107 Durand Rd Maplewood NJ 07040-2103 Office: Brookgreen Gardens PO Box 3368 Pawleys Island SC 29585-3368 *As a classical archaeologist I always have been guided by the ancient saying, "Let the light of the past illumine a pathway to the future."*.

NOBLE, LAWRENCE ALAN, artist; b. Tampa, Fla., Nov. 11, 1948; s. Clymer Marlay and Mary Alice (Cortes) N.; m. Elizabeth Wearden, May 22, 1982; children: Casey Josephine, John Marlay. Student, Tex. Acad. Art, 1969, Houston Mus. Fine Art Sch., 1974-75. Illustrator U.S. Army, Ft. Sheridan, Ill., 1970, San Francisco, 1971; staff artist, promotion dept. The Houston Chronicle, Houston, 1972; art dir., designer, illustrator Middaugh Assocs., 1973; freelance illustrator Noble Studio, 1973-88, designer, sculptor Crestline, Calif., 1988—. Sculptor, com. mem. San Bernardino County Peace Officers Meml. Com., San Bernardino, 1995—, designer sculptor Victor Salmones galleries, 1995—, sculptor, com. mem. Jack Benny Meml. Com., 1992-93, Ft. Sheridan Centennial Com., 1989-90. Sculptor, designer various art galleries. Hon. firefighter City of Redlands Fire Dept., 1997; marshall 4th July Parade Crestline Resorts C. of C., 1996, vol. McGovern for Pres., Dem. party, 1972. With U.S. Army, 1969-71. Recipient 4th U.S. Army Leadership and Integrity medal, 1986. Mem. Nat. Sculptors Soc., Internat. Sculpture Ctr., Calif. Profl. Firefighters, Star Wars Fan Club, Star Trek Fan Club. Republican. Roman Catholic. Avocations: surfing, reading, history. Office: Noble Studio PO Box 2229 Crestline CA 92325-2229

NOBLE, LAWRENCE MARK, lawyer, association administrator; b. N.Y.C., Mar. 30, 1952; s. Hyman S. and Jeanette (Lapides) N.; m. Patricia Fay Bak, Mar. 28, 1981; children: Jonathan, David. BA, Syracuse U., 1973; JD, George Washington U., 1976; Program for Sr. Mgrs. in Govt., John F. Kennedy Sch. Govt., Boston, 1991. Bar: D.C. 1976, U.S. Dist. Ct. 1977, U.S. Ct. Appeals (D.C. cir.) 1977, U.S. Supreme Ct. 1980, U.S. Ct. Appeals (4th cir.) 1989, U.S. Ct. Appeals (5th cir.), 1992. Atty. Aviation Consumer Action Project, Washington, 1976-77; litigation atty. Fed. Election Commn., 1977-79, asst. gen. counsel for litigation, 1979-83, dep. gen. counsel, 1983-87, gen. counsel, 1987-2000; exec. dir., gen. counsel Ctr. Responsive Politics, 2001; adj. prof. law George Washington U. Law Sch., 1999—. Mem. ABA election law commn., 1988-93; mem. adminstrv. conf. U.S., Washington, 1987-96. Contbr. articles to profl. jours.; lectr., spkr. in field. Mem. Coun. on Govt. Ethics Laws (pres. 1997-98), D.C. Bar Assn. Avocations: computer graphics, photography, writing. Home: 9438 Sunnyfield Ct Potomac MD 20854-2090 Office: Ctr Responsive Politics 1101 14th St NW Ste 1030 Washington DC 20005 E-mail: lnoble@crp.org.

NOBLE, LINDA MARIAN, psychology educator; b. Miami, Fla., July 16, 1958; d. George Lindsay and Jean Louise Noble. BA in Psychology, Ga. Coll., 1980; MS in Psychology, U. Ga., 1983, PhD in Psychology, 1985. Asst. prof. psychology Kennesaw (Ga.) State U., 1985-91, assoc. prof. psychology, 1991-97, prof. psychology, 1997—, chmn. dept. psychology, 1994-98, dean Coll. Humanities and Social Scis., 1998—. Sect. editor jour. Methods and Techniques in Tchg. of Psychology, 1996-99. Mem. APA (divsn. sec. 1996-99, pres.-elect divsn. 2, 2002), Assn. Am. Colls. and Univs., Am. Assn. Higher Edn., Coun. Colls. of Arts and Scis. Home: 705 E Ponce de Leon Ave Decatur GA 30030 Office: 1000 Chastain Rd NW Kennesaw GA 30144-5588 E-mail: lnoble@kennesaw.edu.

NOBLE, MARION ELLEN, retired home economist; b. Blanchardville, Wis., Feb. 18, 1914; d. Dwight Eldridge and Doris Edna (Parkinson) Baker; m. B. Frank Smyth (dec. 1979); children: William, Ann Smyth Marris, Robert (dec. 1998), Larry, Margaret Smyth Decker; m. George C. Noble, 1981 (dec. 2001). BS, U. Wis., Madison, 1936. V.p. Smyth Bus Systems, Canton, Ohio, 1950; womens editor Radio Station WFAH, Alliance, 1952-58; home economist extension svc. Stark County, Ohio State U., Canton, 1961-70. Contbr. articles to profl. jours. Named Woman of the Year Urban League, Canton, 1964. Mem. AAUW, Nat. Assn. Extension Home Economists, Pacific Pioneer Broadcasters, Home Econs. Club, Thimble Collectors Internat., Thimble Collectors San Diego, Ladies Oriental Shrine N.Am., Phi Upsilon Omicron, Epsilon Sigma Phi. Republican. Methodist. Avocations: needlework, collecting thimbles and antique sewing items. Home: 3240 San Amadeo Unit A Laguna Beach CA 92653-0667

NOBLE, MERRILL EMMETT, retired psychology educator, psychologist; b. Las Vegas, N.Mex., July 25, 1923; s. Merrill Emmett and Martha (Van Petten) N.; m. Joy Lind, July 18, 1953; children: Margaret Lind, Eric Severin. BA, N.Mex. Highlands U., 1947; MA, Ohio State U., 1949, PhD, 1951. Research asso. Ohio State U., 1951-54, summers 1956, 58; mem. faculty Kans. State U., 1954-67, prof. psychology, 1961-67, chmn. dept., 1962-67; prof. psychology Pa. State U., 1967-89, chmn. dept., 1967-77, ret., 1989. Vis. scientist Inst. for Perception TNO, Soesterberg, Netherlands, 1973-74, 77-78, 80, also NATO vis. lectr. several univs. Mem. editorial bd. Psychol. Bull., 1963-64, Jour. Exptl. Psychology, 1967-78, Acta Psychologica, 1978-82, Human Performance, 1987-92. Fellow APA (com. on adv. svcs. for edn. and tng. 1967-70, accreditation com. 1979-82), AAAS, Psychonomic Soc., Midwestern Psychol. Assn. (mem. coun. 1967-70), Sigma Xi. Home: 2562 Calle Delfino Santa Fe NM 87505-6488

NOBLE, MILDRED M. retired social worker; b. Ont., Can., July 13, 1925; d. Edward Paibomasai and Mary Baids; 1 child, Carol Mills. BA, Boston Coll., 1984; MS, MIT, 1988. Cert. in alcohol counseling Boston Med. Ctr. Lectr. Harvard U., Cambridge, Mass., Radcliffe Coll., U. Mass., Amherts, Boston Coll., Wheelock Coll., Wellesley (Mass.) Coll., 1997—, R.I. Mus., Providence, 1997. Author: Sweet Grass, 1998; prodr., dir. video Clan Women in the 90s, 1990 (Thanks Be to Grandmother Winifred Found. grantee). Advocate Native Am. Cmtys. in New Eng. Region, Boston Indian Coun., 1972—; cultural coord. Children's Mus., Boston, 1978; bd. dirs. Native Am. Ctr. of Boston, 1972—, Boston Writer's Room, 1997. Recipient Cert. of Recognition, Mass. Ctr. for Native Am. Awareness, Inc., 1994. Home: 255 Massachusetts Ave Boston MA 02115-3505

NOBLE, PAUL RONALD, TV film director; b. N.Y.C., Dec. 6, 1935; s. H. Robert and Sylvia (Ide) N.; m. Paulette Cooper, May 17, 1988. AB, Cornell U., 1957; MS, Boston U., 1958. Producer, dir. Sta. WGBH-TV, Cambridge, Mass., 1957-61; exec. producer Sta. WNYW-TV (formerly Sta. WNEW-TV), N.Y.C., 1961-91. Producer TV programs including S.O.S. Save Our Schools, 1977 (Emmy award 1977), Mrs. Eleanor Roosevelt: Prospects of Mankind, Invitation to Art, Filmmakers Showcase, Forever Yesterday, 1982 (Emmy award 1982), The Alan Burke Show, The Bishop Sheen Program, Midday, 1971-86 (Emmy award 1983), Movie Greats, The Cost of Crime, The Princess Marries a Soldier, The Future of Black America, Big Apple Minutes, The Channel 5 Movie Club; host Fox Five Movie Club, In Full Effect (Emmy award 1991); co-author (books) Reward, 1994, 277 Secrets Your Dog Wants You To Know, 1995, The Top 100 Psychics in America, 1996; v.p. film acquisitions and scheduling Lifetime TV, 1993—. Mem. NATAS (N.Y. chpt. pres. 1989-93, bd. trustees, chmn. pub. rels. com.).

NOBLE, RICHARD LLOYD, lawyer; b. Oklahoma City, Oct. 11, 1939; s. Samuel Lloyd and Eloise Joyce (Millard) N. AB with distinction, Stanford, 1961, LLB, 1964. Bar: Calif. 1964. Assoc. firm Cooper, White & Cooper, San Francisco, 1965-67; assoc., ptnr. firm Voegelin, Barton, Harris & Callister, Los Angeles, 1967-70; ptnr. Noble & Campbell, Los Angeles, San Francisco, 1970—. Dir. Langdale Corp., L.A., Gt. Pacific Fin. Co., Sacramento; lectr. Tax Inst. U. So. Calif., 1970; mem. bd. law and bus. program Stanford Law Sch. Contbr. articles to legal jours. Bd. govs. St. Thomas Aquinas Coll. Recipient Hilmer Dehlman Jr. award Stanford Law Sch., 1962; Benjamin Harrison fellow Stanford U., 1967. Mem. ABA, State Bar Calif., L.A. Bar Assn., San Francisco Bar Assn., Commercial Club (San Francisco), Petroleum Club (L.A.), Capitol Hill Club (Washington), Pi Sigma Alpha. Republican. Home: 355 S Grand Ave Ste 2600 Los Angeles CA 90071-1505 Address: 355 S Grand Ave Ste 2600 Los Angeles CA 90071-1505

NOBLE, STEPHEN LLOYD, information scientist; b. Louisville, July 5, 1960; s. Charles Francis and Joyce N.; m. Joann Vance, Feb. 23, 1979; children: Jennifer Marie, Sharon Rose, Anna MaRose, Adam Titus. BA, U. Louisville, 1996, MPA, 1998. Coord. media svcs. U. Louisville, 1991-98; mgr. product devel. Recording for Blind and Dyslexic, Princeton, 1998-2000; policy analyst Ky. Assistive Tech. Svc. Network, 2000—. Vice chair Ky. Assistive Tech. Svcs. Network, Louisville, 1995-99. Contbg. editor Info. Tech. and Disabilities, 1994—; contbr. articles to profl. jours. Deacon Manslick Rd. Ch. of Christ, Louisville, 1996-99; chair knowledge resource com. United Way, Louisville, 1997-99. Mem. Assn. Coll. and Resource Librs., Am. Assn. Higher Edn., Am. Soc. Pub. Adminstrn., Phi Kappa Phi, Pi Alpha Alpha, Golden Key. Avocations: fencing, amateur astronomy. Office: KATS Network 8412 Westport Rd Louisville KY 40242-3044 E-mail: steve.noble@mail.state.ky.us.

NOBLE, TIMOTHY PETER, business executive; b. Gerrards Cross, Eng., Dec. 21, 1943; s. Andrew Napier and Sigrid (Michelet) N.; m. Elizabeth Mary Aitken, Dec. 18, 1976; children: Sasha, Lorne, Andrew. MA in Law, Oxford U., 1965; MBA, INSEAD, Fontainebleau, France, 1970. Barrister; fin. securities lic. Exec. Kleinwort Benson Ltd., London, 1966-68, E.E.D. SA, Paris, 1968-69, Gen. Telephone & Electronics, Brussels, 1970—73; dir. Lyle Shipping Plc, Glasgow, 1976—80, chief exec., 1980-84, Noble Group Ltd., Edinburgh, 1984-2000, chmn., 2000—. Chmn. Palmaris Capital Plc, Edinburgh, 2000—, Darnaway Venture Capital Plc, Edinburgh, 1995—; bd. dirs. Murray Global Return Trust Plc, Glasgow, Scottish Friendly Assurance Soc., , Glasgow. Chmn. Bus. Archives Coun. Scotland, Glasgow, 1986-95, Royal Scottish Nat. Orch. Trust, Edinburgh, 1994-2000; chmn. Brit. Ski Acad., Chamonix, 1997—. Mem. Brit. Ski and Snowboarding Fedn. (dir. 1993-98). Avocations: skiing, tennis, bridge, wine, astronomy. Office: Noble Group Ltd 76 George St Edinburgh EH2 3BU Scotland

NOBLE, WILLIAM PARKER, writer, educator; b. N.Y.C., Jan. 25, 1932; s. William Parker and Ethel Kathryn (Karsch) N.; m. Madeline Ann Carman, Sept. 18, 1954 (div. Sept. 1969); children: William III, John Alden; m. June Solveig Brogger, Sept. 26, 1969 (dec. June 1984); m. Angela Elizabeth Warner Whitehill, December 27, 1998. BA, Lehigh U., 1954; JD, U. Pa., 1961. Bar: Pa. 1961, Supreme Ct. Pa. 1961. Prodn. asst. Columbia Broadcasting Sys., N.Y.C., 1958; atty. Townsend, Elliott & Munson, Phila., 1961-62; corp. atty. Armstrong World Industries, Lancaster, Pa., 1962-68; dir. model cities program City of Lancaster, 1968-69; freelance writer, lectr. and cons. Salisbury, Vt., 1969—. Instr. creative and fiction writing C.C. of Vt., Rutland, 1986—; Vt. humanities scholar Vt. Coun. on Humanities, Morrisville, 1991—; writing assessment mentor C.C. Vt., Rutland, 1993-99; lectr. and instr. lit. and mystery writing Ocean County Coll., N.J., 1999-2001; lectr. nonfiction writing Georgian Ct. Coll., Lakewood, NJ, 2002-. Author: Shut Up! He Explained, 1987, Make That Scene, 1988, Bookbanning in America, 1990, Show Don't Tell, 1991, The Twenty-Eight Biggest Writing Blunders, 1992, Conflict, Action & Suspense, 1994, Three Rules for Writing a Novel, 1997, Writing Dramatic Nonfiction, 2000; co-author: (with J. Noble) The Custody Trap, 1975, How to Live With Other People's Children, 1978, The Private Me, 1980, The Psychiatric Fix, 1981, Steal This Plot, 1985, (with A. Whitehill) Parent's Book of Ballet, 1988, Young Professional's Book of Ballet, 1990, The Dancer's Book of Ballet, 2000, Ballet Magic, 2001. Chmn. bd. Econ. Inc., Lancaster, 1968-69; bd. mem. Lancaster Anti-Poverty Agy., 1968-69; chmn. Avalon (N.J.) Zoning Bd., 1973-76; bd. dirs. Vt. Ballet Theatre, Burlington, 1985-89; polit. cons. Small is Beautiful Party, New Haven, 1988-93. Lt. (j.g.) USCG, 1954-57. Mem. The Authors Guild. Avocations: reading, theatre, sports, dance, education. Home and Office: PO Box 187 Island Heights NJ 08732-0187 E-mail: wllmnob@aol.com.

NOBLES, DANNY GENE, army officer; b. Florence, Ala., May 10, 1956; s. Oscar Sherrill and Mary Christine (Davis) N.; m. Connie Sue Bradshaw, May 14, 1976; children: Coral, Heidi. AA, Wichita State U., 1987; BS, SUNY, Albany, 1987; MSW, Syracuse U., 1994; M of Strategic Studies, U.S. Army War Coll., 2001. Enlisted U.S. Army, advanced through grades to lt. col., 1999; staff engr. 89th ARCOM, Wichita, 1985-87; engr. ops. officer 98th Divsn., Rochester, N.Y., 1987-91; chief plans & ops. divsn. U.S. Army Engr. Ctr., Ft. Leonard Wood, Mo., 1993-95; ops. officer 412th Engr. Command, Heidelberg, Germany, 1995-97; installation plans officer Headquarters Dept. Army, Washington, 1997-99, dep. garrison comdr. Ft. Hood, Tex., 1999-2000; joint engr. plans officer Joint Staff, Washington, 2001—. Mem. Soc. Am. Mil. Engrs., U.S. Army Engrs. Assn. Mem. Ch. of Christ. Home: 7932 Tower Court Rd Severn MD 21144

NOBLES, LAURENCE HEWIT, retired geology educator; b. Spokane, Sept. 28, 1927; s. Harry and Florence (Giffin) N.; m. Barbara Joanne Smith, Aug. 28, 1948; children: Heather C., Laurence F. BS, MS, Calif. Inst. Tech., 1949; PhD, Harvard, 1952. Instr. geology Northwestern U., 1952-55, asst. prof., 1955-61, assoc. prof., 1961-67, prof., 1967-90, prof. emeritus, 1990—; also asst. dean Northwestern U. (Coll. Arts and Scis.), 1966-67, assoc. dean, 1968-70, acting dean, 1970-72, dean adminstrn., 1972-81, v.p. adminstrn. and fin. planning, 1981-86. Trustee Adler Planetarium, 1980-86; faculty rep. Big Ten Conf., 1976-81; trustee Chgo. Acad. Scis., 1967-87, pres., 1973-78, hon. trustee, 1987—. Mem. Am. Geophys. Union, Geol. Soc. Am.

NOBLIT, BETTY JEAN, publishing technician; b. St. Elmo, Ill., June 12, 1948; d. Clyde W. and Lucille M. (Haggard) N. Grad. in restaurant and club food mgmt., LaSalle U., 1973; grad., Am. Sch. Travel, 1975. Teletype puncher Sarasota (Fla.) Herald-Tribune, 1968-70, Pueblo Chieftain, 1970—; unified composer; DTI pagination operator Star Jour. Pub. Co., Pueblo, Colo. Personal corr. Prime Min. Indira Gandhi. Active Mahatma Gandhi Ctr. for Peace and Nonviolence, Pueblo, Colo. Mem. Nat. Geog. Soc., Colo. Hist. Soc., Gandhi Ctr. Peace and Nonviolence Pueblo. Home: 1 Cambridge Ave Apt 4B Pueblo CO 81005-2024

NOBLITT, HARDING COOLIDGE, political scientist, educator; b. Marion, N.C., Oct. 31, 1920; s. Walter Tate and Nellie Mae (Horton) N.; m. Louise Hope Lester, July 3, 1943; 1 son, Walter Thomas. BA, Berea Coll., 1942; MA, U. Chgo., 1947, PhD, 1955. Mem. faculty Concordia Coll., Moorhead, Minn., 1950-90, prof. polit. sci., 1956-90, Wije Disting. prof., 1979-82, chmn. dept., 1964-72, prof. emeritus, 1990. Mem. editorial bd.: Discourse: A Review of the Liberal Arts, 1957-67, acting editor, 1959-60. Democratic candidate Congress, 1962; del. Dem. Nat. Conv., 1964; chmn. Profs. for Johnson-Humphrey, Minn., 1964; chmn. platform com. Dem. State Conv., 1968; mem. Gov's Citizens Council on Aging, 1963-68; mem. City Charter Commn., Moorhead, 1985— ; mem. Minn. Higher Edn. Coordinating Bd., 1971-81, sec., 1974-75, pres., 1979-80. Served with AUS, 1943-46, ETO. Recipient 1st ann. Great Tchr. award Concordia Coll., 1960; recipient Flaat Disting. Service award Concordia Coll., 1982 Mem. Am. Polit. Sci. Assn., Am.

Legion, Phi Kappa Phi, Pi Gamma Mu, Tau Kappa Alpha, Pi Kappa Delta Presbyterian (elder). Home: 2014 4th St S Moorhead MN 56560-4131 Office: Concordia Coll Dept Polit Sci Moorhead MN 56560

NOBLITT, NANCY ANNE, aerospace engineer; b. Roanoke, Va., Aug. 14, 1959; d. Jerry Spencer and Mary Louise (Jerrell) N. BA, Mills Coll., Oakland, Calif., 1982; MS in Indsl. Engring., Northeastern U., 1990. Data red specialist Universal Energy Sys., Beaver Creek, Ohio, 1981; aerospace engr. turbine engine divsn. components br. turbine group aero-propulsion lab. Wright-Patterson AFB, 1982-84, engine assessment br. spl. engines group, 1984-87; lead analyst cycle methods computer aided engr. GE, Lynn, Mass., 1987-90, Lynn PACES project coord., 1990-91; software sys. analyst Sci. Applications Internat. Corp., with artificial intelligence Va., 1991-92, software engring. mgr., intelligence applications integration Hampton, 1992-93, mgr. test engring. and sys. support, 1993-94, mgr. configuration mgmt., 1994, mgmt. asst. to TBMCS program mgr., 1994-95; sr. simulation engr. Chem Demil, 1995-98; supervisory engr. Analytical Mechanics Assocs., Hampton, 1998-99; sr. project engr. Newport News (Va.) Shipbuilding Inc., 1999-00, Coll. William and Mary Law Sch., Williamsburg, Va., 2000—. Tutor math. and sci. Centerville Sch. Bd., Ohio, 1982-86; tutor math. and physics Marblehead Sch. Bd., Mass., 1988-90; tutor math., chemistry and physics Poquoson Sch. Bd., Va., 1994—; rep. alumnae admissions Boston area Mills Coll., 1987-91, trustee, bd. govs., 1995-98; mem. Citizens for Hilton Area Revitalization, 1994—. Math. and sci. tutor Centerville Sch. Bd., Ohio, 1982-86, math. and physics tutor Marblehead (Mass.) Sch. Bd., 1988-90; tutor math., chemistry and physics Poquoson Sch. Bd., Va., 1994—; rep. alumnae admissions Mills Coll., Boston area, 1987-91, trustee/bd. govs., 1995-98; mem. Citizens for Hilton Area Revitalization, 1994—. Recipient Notable Achievement award USAF, 1984, Spl. award Fed. Lab. Consortium, 1987. Mem. Soc. Mfg. Engrs., Sports and Entertainment Law Soc., Phi Alpha Delta. Avocation: book collecting. Home: 58 Hopkins St Newport News VA 23601-4034 Office: Newport News Shipbuilding Newport News VA 23607

NOBREGA, FRED THOMAS, medical society executive; b. Kansas City, Mo., May 11, 1935; s. Ferdinand Baptiste and Mary Helen (Bowes) N.; children: Thomas P., John M., Paul E. BS cum laude, Rockhurst Coll., 1956; MD, U. Kans., 1960; grad., USN Sch. Aviation Medicine, 1963; MPH, Johns Hopkins U., 1965; Cert. Med. Mgmt., U. N.C., 1996. Diplomate Am. Bd. Preventive Medicine; cert. aviation med. examiner. Intern St. Francis Hosp., Wichita, Kans., 1960-61; resident in internal medicine Mayo Grad. Sch. Medicine, Rochester, Minn., 1961-62; rsch. assoc. dept. med. stats. Epedemiology and population genetics Mayo Clinic, 1965-67; resident in internal medicine Mayo Grad. Sch. Medicine, 1967-69; staff St. Mary's Hosp., 1969-92, Rochester Meth. Hosp., 1969-92; prof. preventive medicine Mayo Med. Sch., 1985-92; v.p. med. affairs St. Joseph Mercy Hosp., Pontiac, Mich., 1992-93; v.p. med. edn. Grant/Riverside Meth. Hosp., Columbus, Ohio, 1993-2000; exec. dir. Zumbro Valley Med. Soc., 2001—. Co-investigator Program Project Grant, Rochester Olmsted County, 1966-74; cons. divsn. preventive medicine, dept. internatl medicine Mayo Clinic, 1969-92, chair sect. health svcs. evaluation, 1973-88; lectr. in field. Contbr. articles to profl. jours. Capt., naval flight surgeon USNR, 1962-64. With USN, 1965—92. Recipient Letter of Appreciation (Apollo Project), 1964. Fellow: ACP, Am. Coll. Preventive Medicine (Disting. Svc. award 1993); mem.: ACP/Am. Soc. Internal Medicine, AMA, Minn. Med. Assn., Am. Coll. Physicians Execs., Alpha Sigma Nu. E-mail: fnobrega@ohiohealth.com.

NOCE, DAVID D. federal magistrate judge; b. 1944; AB, St. Louis U., 1966; JD, U. Mo., 1969. Bar: Mo. Law clk. to Hon. H. Kenneth Wangelin U.S. Dist. Ct. (ea. and we. dists.) Mo., 1972-73; law clk. to Hon. John F. Nangle U.S. Dist. Ct. (ea. dist.) Mo., 1973-75; asst. U.S. atty. Eastern Dist. Mo., St. Louis, 1975-76; magistrate judge U.S. Dist. Ct. (ea. dist.) Mo., 1976—. Adj. prof. law St. Louis U. Sch. Law, Washington U. Sch. Law, St. Louis. Author: Jury Instructions Drafting Workbook West, 1999. Served with U.S. Army, 1970-72. Mem. ABA, Mo. Bar, Bar Assn. Met. St. Louis, Fed. Magistrate Judges Assn. Office: US Courthouse 17th Flr N 111 S 10th St Saint Louis MO 63102

NOCERA, JOHN ANTHONY, lawyer; b. Bklyn., June 15, 1952; s. Anthony Carmine and Louise Margaret (Retta) N.; m. Debralee Marilyn Miller, Sept. 25, 1987. BA, Fordham U., 1974; JD, St. John's U., N.Y.C., 1978. Bar: N.Y. 1979, U.S. Dist. Ct. (so. and ea. dists.) N.Y. 1980, N.J. 1985, U.S. Dist. Ct. N.J. 1985, Pa. 1989, U.S. Ct. Appeals (2nd cir.) 1989. Assoc. Hendler and Murray, N.Y.C., 1978-82, ptnr., 1982-85, Rosner and Nocera, N.Y.C., 1985—. Sr. mem. St. John's Law Rev., 1976-77; contbr. articles to profl. jours. V.p. Parkview Condominium Assn., 1982. St. Thomas Moore scholar, 1976-78. Mem. ABA, N.Y. Bar Assn. Avocations: numismatics, skiing. Office: Rosner and Nocera 90 Washington St New York NY 10006-2214

NOCHIMSON, DAVID, lawyer; b. Paterson, N.J., June 19, 1943; s. Samuel S. and Mildred (Singer) N.; m. Roberta Maizel, June 5, 1966 (div. 1972); m. Gail Burgess, May 26, 1978. BA, Yale U., 1965; LLB, Columbia U., 1968; LLM, Australian Nat. U., Canberra, 1969. Bar: N.Y. 1970, Calif. 1977. Assoc. Paul, Weiss, Rifkind, Wharton and Garrison, N.Y.C., 1970-72; sr. v.p. Comprop Equities Corp., 1972-76; assoc. Mitchell, Silberberg and Knupp, L.A., 1977-80, ptnr., 1980-83, Ziffren, Brittenham, Branca & Fischer, L.A., 1983—. Adv. com. UCLA Entertainment Symposium, 1979-99, co-chmn., 1981-82. Contbr. articles to Encyclopedia of Investments, 1982, profl. jours. Pres. Friends of the L.A. Free Clinic, 1994-96; trustee Santa Monica (Calif.) Mus. of Art, 1995—. Fulbright scholar, Australia, 1968-69. Mem. ABA (forum com. on entertainment and sports industries 1982—, editor The Entertainment and Sports Lawyer 1982-89, chmn. 1989-92), Internat. Bar Assn. (Vice chmn. entertainment com. 1986-90), Am. Bar Found., Beverly Hills Bar Assn. Democrat. Jewish. Avocations: tennis, racquetball, playing piano, hiking. Office: Ziffren Brittenham Branca & Fischer 1801 Century Park W Los Angeles CA 90067-6406

NOCHMAN, LOIS WOOD KIVI (MRS. MARVIN NOCHMAN), retired educator; b. Detroit, Nov. 5, 1924; d. Peter K. and Annetta Lois (Wood) Kivi; m. Harold I. Pitchford, Sept. 6, 1944 (div. May 1949); children: Jean Wood Pitchford Scott, Joyce Lynn Pitchford Undiano; m. Marvin A. Nochman, Aug. 15, 1953; 1 child Joseph Asa. AB, U. Mich., 1946, AM, 1949. Tchr. adult edn., Honolulu, 1947, Ypsilanti (Mich.) H.S., 1951-52; spl. instr. English Wayne State U., Detroit, 1953, 54; tchr. Highland Park (Mich.) Coll., 1950-51, instr. English, 1954-83; ret., 1983. Mem. exec. bd. Highland Park Fedn. Tchrs., 1963—66, 1973, del. to nat. conv., 64, 1971—74; rep. higher edn. Mich. Fedn. Tchrs. Exec. Com., 1972—76; mem. faculty adv. com. Gov's Commn. Higher Edn., 1973—. Contbr. articles to profl. jours. Tchr. Baha'i Schs., Davison, Mich., 1954—55, 1958—59, 1963—66, Beaulac, Canada, 1960, Greenacre, Maine, 1965; sec. local spiritual assembly Baha'is, Ann Arbor, Mich., 1953, sec. Detriot, 1954, chmn., 1955; mem. nat. com. Baha'is U.S., 1955—58; sec. com. and coun. Baha'i Schs., Davison, Mich., 1956, 1958, 1963—68; Baha'i lectr. subject of local TV show Senior Focus, 1992. Named one of 10 Best of 1995, Swim Mag., 2000; recipient Women's Movement plaque, Women Lawyers Assn. Mich., 1975, Lawrence award, Mich. Masters Swimming, 1991, 6 World Master Records in Age Group short course meters, 1994—95, 5 records in Long Course Meters, 1995, 23 Nat. Masters Records, 1994—96, 6 Nat. YMCA records, 1995, 2 U.S. Nat. Sr. Sports Classic Records, 1995, 2 World Sr. Games Records, 1993, All-Am. award, 1990—2001, U.S. Long Distance All Star, 1995—2001, U.S. MS Finals All Star, 1995, 2000, 8 Huntsman World Sr. Games Records, 1998, 5 Huntsman Masters World Records short course meters, 1999, 9 Huntsman World Games Records in age group 75-79, 1999. Mem.: MLA, NOW, Nat. Soc. Lit. and Arts, Am. Fedn. Tchrs., Mich. Coll. English Assn., Nat. Coun. Tchrs. English, Women's Equity and Action League (sec. Mich. chpt. 1975—79), Alpha Gamma Delta, Alpha Lambda Delta. Avocation: U.S. Swimming Master Champion.

NOCK, STEFFEN R. science administrator; b. Karlsruhe, Germany, Feb. 23, 1967; came to U.S., 1996; s. Albrecht and Heidemarie Nock; m. Silke R. Doerfler, July 31, 1999. PhD, U. Bayreuth, Germany, 1996. Founder, dir. biochemistry Zyomyx Inc., Hayward, Calif., 1998-2000, founder, sr. dir. biochemistry, 2000—01, v.p. biochemistry, 2002—. Rsch. fellow Stanford (Calif.) U., 1996-98. Fellow German Rsch. Commn., 1997. Office Fax: 510-784-2569. E-mail: steffennock@hotmail.com., snock@zyomyx.com.

NOCKLER, LINDA A. financial consultant; d. Erich Nockler and Sandra Anne Griffith; m. Michael R. Samis, June 10, 1995. B in Commerce, U. Cape Town, South Africa, 1987, U. Cape Town, 1988; MPhil in Internat. Rels.International Economics), Cambridge (Eng.) U., 1992. CFA Level 1. Analyst Union Bank of Switzerland, Zurich, 1989—91; mgmt. program Anglo Am. Corp., Johannesburg, 1993—95; product devel. cons. Phillips, Hager & North, Vancouver, Canada, 1995—97; v.p., dir. content mgmt. Greenwich Associates , Greenwich, Conn., 1998—. Scholar, Std. Bank South Africa, 1985, IBM Corp., 1987. Buddhist. Avocations: art, theater , travel, yoga. Office: Greenwich Assocs 8 Greenwich Office Park Greenwich CT 06831-5195

NOCKS, JASON YVES, software engineer, telecommunications specialist; b. Springfield, Pa., Feb. 21, 1971; s. James J. and Ellen J. (Leblang) N. BSEE, U. Del., 1993. Cons. Starnet, West Chester, Pa., 1993, software engr., 1994-95, sr. software engr., 1996—. Inventor in field. Mem. Soc. Am. Magicians. Avocations: magic, skiing. Home: 1149 Broad Run Rd Coatesville PA 19320-4833 Office: Starnet PO Box 2651 West Chester PA 19380-0901

NODA, TAKAYO, artist; b. Tokyo, Sept. 20, 1934; came to U.S., 1961; d. Jun and Hide Tatebe; 1 child, Ken. Student, Gakushuin U., Tokyo, 1953-55, Art Students League, N.Y.C., 1979-83. Freelance craft deisgner Woman's Day Mag., N.Y.C., 1969-72. One-woman shows include Wenninger Graphics, Boston, 1988, 1989, 1990, Pen and Brush, N.Y.C., 1992, InterChurch Ctr., 1994, Tiffany Windows, 1995, Van Eck Global, 1997, Port Washington (N.Y.) Pub. Libr., 1998, Nat. Arts Club, 2002, exhibitions include Butler Inst. Am. Art, Jan Voorhees Zimmerli Art Mus., New Brunswick, N.J., Mus. Provincetown (Mass.) Art Assn., Portland (Oreg.) Art Mus., Nat. Acad. Design, N.Y.C., Alexandria (La.) Mus. Art, Silvermine Guild Arts Ctr., New Canaan, Conn., Honolulu Acad. Arts, Ringling Sch. Art, Sarasota, Fla., Taller Galeria Fort, Barcelona, La. State U., Boston U., Columbia U., U. Alaska, La. State U., Print Ctr., Phila., Newark Mus., Bergen Mus. Art and Sci., Paramus, N.J., U. Hawaii, Hilo, Fairfield (Conn.) U., Bristol (R.I.) Art Mus., UBS Pain Webber Art Gallery, N.Y.C., Caracas, London and Bhopal, India. Mem.: Authors Guild, The Acad. of Am. Poet, Allied Artists Am., Inc., Nat. Assn. Women Artists, Boston Printmakers, Soc. Am. Graphic Artists (coun. mem. 1999—), Audubon Artists, Nat. Arts Club, Lotos Club. Avocations: listening to music and opera, reading, making jewelry, walking. Home: 5 Charles St Apt 2R New York NY 10014-3039 E-mail: takayonoda@cs.com.

NODDINGS, NEL, education educator, writer; b. Irvington, N.J., Jan. 19, 1929; d. Edward A. Rieth and Nellie A. (Connors) Walter; m. James A. Noddings, Aug. 20, 1949; children: Chris, Howard, Laurie, James, Nancy, William, Sharon, Edward, Vicky, Timothy. BA in Math., Montclair State Coll., 1949; MA in Math., Rutgers U., 1964; PhD in Edn., Stanford U., 1973; PhD (hon.), Columbia Coll., S.C., 1995. Cert. tchr., Calif., N.J. Tchr. Woodbury (N.J.) Publ Schs., 1949-52; tchr. math. dept. Matawan (N.J.) High Sch., 1958-62, chair, asst. prin., 1964-69; curriculum supr. Montgomery Twp. Pub. Schs., Skillman, N.J., 1970-72; dir. precollegiate edn. U. Chgo., 1975-76; asst. prof. Pa. State U., State College, 1973; from asst. prof. to assoc. prof. Stanford (Calif.) U., 1977-86, prof., 1986—, assoc. dean, 1990-92, acting dean, 1992-94, Lee L. Jacks prof. child edn., 1992-98, prof. emeritus, 1998—; prof. philosophy and edn. Columbia U., N.Y.C., 1998—. Bd. dirs. Ctr. for Human Caring Sch. Nursing, Denver, 1986-92; cons. NIE, NSF and various other sch. dists. Author: Caring: A Feminine Approach to Ethics and Moral Education, 1984, Women and Evil, 1989; author: (with W. Paul Shore)) Awakening the Inner Eye: Intuition in Education, 1984; author: (with Carol Witherell)) Stories Lives Tell, 1991; author: The Challenge to Care in Schools, 1992, Educating for Intelligent Belief or Unbelief, 1993, Philosophy of Education, 1995; author: (with Suzanne Gordon and Patricia Benner)) Caregiving, 1996; author: (with Michael Katz and Kenneth Strike) Justice and Caring, 1999; author: Starting at Home: Caring and Social Policy, 2002, Educating Moral People, 2002. Mem. disting. women's adv. bd. Coll. St. Catherine. Recipient Anne Roe award for Contbns. to Profl. devel. of Women, Harvard Grad. Sch. Edn., 1993, medal for disting. svc. Tchrs. Coll. Columbia, 1994, Willystine Goodsell award, 1997, Laureate chpt. Kappa Delta Pi, Pi Lambda Theta award, 1999; Spencer Mentor grantee, Spencer Found., 1995-97. Fellow Philosophy of Edn. Soc. (pres. 1991-92); mem. Am. Ednl. Rsch. Assn. (Div B, 2000, Lifetime achievment award), Am. Philos. Assn., Nat. Acad. Edn. (pres. 2001—), John Dewey Soc. (pres. 1994-96), Phi Beta Kappa (vis. scholar). Avocation: gardening. E-mail: noddings@stanford.edu.

NODDINGS, SARAH ELLEN, lawyer; b. Matawan, N.J. d. William Clayton and Sarah Stephenson (Cox) Noddings; children: Christopher, Aaron. BA in Math., Rutgers U., New Brunswick, N.J., 1965, MSW, 1968; JD cum laude, Seton Hall U., Newark, 1975; postgrad., UCLA, 1979. Bar: Calif. 1976, Nev. 1976, N.J. 1975, U.S. Dist. Ct. (ctrl. dist.) Calif. 1976, U.S. Dist. Ct. N.J. 1975. Social worker Carteret (N.J.) Bd. Edn., 1970-75; law clk. Hon. Howard W. Babcock, 8th Jud. Dist. Ct., Las Vegas, Nev., 1975-76; assoc. O'Melveny & Myers, L.A., 1976-78; atty. Internat. Creative Mgmt., Beverly Hills, Calif., 1978-81, Russell & Glickman, Century City, 1981-83, Lorimar Prodns., Culver City and Burbank, 1983-87, v.p., 1987-93; atty. Warner Bros. TV, Burbank, 1993-2001, v.p., 1993-2001, sr. atty., 1999-2001; pvt. practice , 2001—. Dir. county youth program, rsch. analyst Sonoma County People for Econ. Opportunity, Santa Rosa, Calif., 1968-69; VISTA vol. Kings County Cmty. Action Orgn., Hanford, Calif., 1965-66; officer, PTA bd. West H.S., Casimir Mid. Sch. and Arlington Elem. Sch. Mem. Acad. TV Arts and Scis. (nat. awards com. 1994-96), L.A. Copyright Soc. (trustee 1990-91), Women in Film, L.A. County Bar Assn. (intellectual property sect.), Women Entertainment Lawyers, Media Dist. Intellectual Propr. Bar Assn. (bd. dirs. 1999-2001). Avocations: travel, tennis, skiing, bicycling, swimming.

NODEEN, JANEY PRICE, company executive; b. Scotland Neck, N.C., Nov. 7, 1959; d. Wade Hampton and Joyce Ann (Councill) P.; m. Thomas Nodeen. BS in Info. Sci., Christopher Newport Coll., 1987; grad., Def. Sys. Mgmt. Coll., 1994; grad. advanced mgmt. program, Nat. Def. U., 1995. Engring. analyst Newport News (Va.) Shipbldg., 1978-86; mgr. submarine info. resources and computer ops. Dept. of the Navy, Washington, 1986-93, mem. exec. devel. program, 1993-96, sr. staff Navy Acquisition Reform Exec., 1995, dep. program exec. officer Submarines for Acquisition, 1996-97; prin. Burke Consortium, Inc., Springfield, Va., 1997—. Mil. legis. fellow for Congressman Sam Gejdenson, 1994; sr. exec. fellow John F. Kennedy Sch. Govt. Harvard U., class officer, 1994. Home: 6915 Ashbury Dr Springfield VA 22152-3221 Office: Burke Consortium Inc Ste 510 5500 Cherokee Ave Alexandria VA 22312 Office Fax: 703-941-0704.

NODELMAN, NANCY ZIEGLER, sculptor, designer; b. Scranton, Pa., Apr. 23, 1937; d. Alvin and Gertrude (Friedman) Ziegler; m. Jared Nodelman, Aug. 31, 1958 (div. Dec. 17, 1993); children: Seth, Ilisa. BS, Ohio State U., 1957, postgrad., 1958; sculpture student, San Francisco Art Inst., 1986-87. Founder Fiber Dimensions, Kentfield, Calif., 1990; co-dir. Atrium Gallery, Greenbrae, Calif., 1992—. Exhbns. include Regional Ctr. Arts Biennials, 1991, 93, Convergence Internat. Biennial, 1992 (Hon. Mention), Calif. Contemporary Design Biennial, 1992, Md. Park Commn. and Catalog, 1994, Internat. Miniature Textiles Biennial, Catalog, 1996, Gallery Strasse Hyogo, Japan, 1997, SOFA98NYC, 1998, Calif. Design 2000, Fiberarts Design Book Six; work featured in Fiber Arts mag., 1992; represented in permanent collections Szombathely Keptár Mus., Bank of Am. Marathon Plaza, Marin Gen. Hosp. Mem. humanities coun. bd. Marin Gen. Hosp., Greenbrae, Calif., 1992—; trustee Isaac Ziegler Trust, Scranton, Pa., 1996—. Recipient Hon. Mention Handweavers Am., 1992. Mem. Internat. Wine and Food Soc., Fiber Art Internat., Soc. Encouragement of Contemporary Art. Avocations: architectural, landscape and furniture design, paper toy collecting, consulting.

NOE, ELNORA (ELLIE NOE), retired chemical company executive; b. Evansville, Ind., Aug. 23, 1928; d. Thomas Noe and Evelyn (West) Dieter. Student, Ind. U.-Purdue U., Indpls. Sec. Pitman Moore Co., Indpls., 1946—60; with Dow Chem. Co., 1960-90, pub. rels. asst. then mgr. employee comm., 1970-87, mgr. cmty. rels., 1987-90, DowBrands, Inc., Indpls., 1986-90, vice chmn. corp. affairs discussion group, 1988-90, chmn., 1989-90; mem. steering com. Learn About Bus. Mem. steering com. Learn About Bus. Recipient 2d pl. award as Businesswoman of Yr., Indpls. Bus. and Profl. Women's Assn., 1980, Indpls. Profl. Woman of Yr. award Zonta, Altrusa, Soroptimist & Pilot Svc. Clubs, 1985, DowBrands Great Things Cmty. Svc. award, 1991. Mem. Am. Bus. Women Assn. (Woman of Yr. award 1965, past pres.), Ind. Assn. Bus. Communicators (hon., Communicator of Yr. 1977), Assn. Women in Comm. (Louise Eleanor Kleinhenz award 1984), Zonta (dist. pub. rels. chmn. 1978-80, area dir. 1980-82, pres. Indpls. chpt. 1977-79, bd. dirs. 1993-95, 2000—), Dow Retiree Club (pres. 1995—). E-mail: elenoe@aol.com.

NOE, GUY, retired social services administrator; b. Brussels, Jan. 28, 1934; came to U.S., 1955, naturalized, 1961; s. Marinus Cornelis and Johana Dorothea (Beijne) N.; 1 child, Jeanette Sue. BS, Regional Agrl. Sch., Loiret, France, 1954. Social worker State of Wyo., Casper, 1962-66; dir. Natrona County (Wyo.) Dept. Public Assistance, 1966-79, Wyo. Div. Mental Health, Cheyenne, 1979-82, asst. adminstr. Divsn. of Youth Svcs., 1992-95; former mgr. Platte County Office Pub. Assistance and Social Svcs., Wheatland, Wyo., dir. low income energy assistance programs, 1994-95. Lectr. in field. V.p. Wyo. chpt. Big Bros., 1976-77; chmn. adv. coun. social svcs. State of Wyo., 1969-79; bd. dirs. Casper United Way, 1970—, Casper Salvation Army, 1970—, Casper chpt. ARC, 1977—; mem. Gov.'s Drug Abuse Adv. Bd., 1992—; pres. State Employees Assn. Named Outstanding Adminstr. State of Wyo., 1976 ; recipient Youth Svcs. award Wyo. Human Resources Confederation, 1988. Mem. ASPA, Am. Public Welfare Assn. (Wyo. membership chmn.), Wyo. State Employees Assn. (pres. 1996-97), Toastmasters. Democrat. Home: 2731 Deming Blvd Cheyenne WY 82001-5709

NOE, JAMES KIRBY, computer consultant; b. Denver, June 21, 1951; s. George F. and Fern D. (Wilterdink) N. BSBA in Mgmt. Info., U. No. Colo., 1983. Cert. data processor, systems profl. Systems supr. USN Tactical Support Ctr., Sigonella, Sicily, Italy, 1978-79; tech. mgr. Empire Dispatch of No. Colo., Greeley, 1979-80; cons. Greeley C. of C., 1983; project mgr. software devel. Microhealth Systems Corp., Denver, 1983-84; database analyst Manville Corp., Littleton, 1984; leader project devel. Citicorp Diners Club, Englewood, 1985; cons. Mountain Bell Telephone, Denver, 1985-86; computer programmer Colo. Dept. Revenue, 1986-87; cons. DST Systems, Inc., Kansas City, Mo., 1987-91, Broadcast Data Systems, Kansas City, 1991-92, U.S. Sprint, Kansas City, 1992—2001. Pres. Pine Tree Players, Brunswick, Maine, 1976-77, Sigonella Theatre Co., 1978; bd. dirs. Theatre Assocs. Group, Inc., Denver, 1985-86, v.p., 1987. Recipient Eagle Scout award Boy Scouts Am., 1964, bronze palm, 1965, 5-Yr. Svc. award Am. Cancer Soc., Brunswick, 1977; named Outstanding Vol. Theatre Assocs. Group, Inc., 1987. Mem. Assn. for Computing Machinery (com. mem. 1984-98, chmn. Denver chpt. 1987), Data Processing Mgmt. Assn. (com. mem. 1984-98). Republican. Presbyterian. Avocations: gemology, theater. Home: 600 E 8th St Apt 813 Kansas City MO 64106-1621

NOE, KENNETH WILLIAM, historian, educator; b. Richmond, Va., Nov. 9, 1957; s. Kenneth Elmo and Betty Lou (Handelman) N.; m. Nancy Jean Wahlbrink, June 22, 1985; 1 child, Jesse B. BA in Edn., Emory & Henry Coll., 1979; MA in History, Va. Poly. Inst., 1981; MLS, U. Ky., 1983; PhD in History, U. Ill., 1990. Librarian Blue Ridge Regional Libr., Martinsville, Va., 1983-85, Berea (Ky.) Coll., 1987-88; archivist Ill. Hist. Survey, Urbana, 1988-90; prof. history State U. West Ga., Carrollton, 1990-2000, Auburn (Ala.) U., 2000—. Author: Southwest Virginia's Railroad, 1994, Perryville: This Grand Havoc of Battle, 2001 (Peter Seaborg Book award 2002); editor: A Southern Boy in Blue, 1996 (Tenn. History Book award 1996); co-editor: The Civil War in Appalachia, 1997; contbr. articles to profl. jours. Mem. Ala. Assn. Historians, Ala. Historical Assn., Appalachian Studies Assn. (program com. 1987-88), Org. Am. Historians, So. Hist. Assn. (membership com. 1994-95), Soc. Civil War Historians, Phi Alpha Theta, Beta Phi Mu, Phi Kappa Phi. Democrat. Lutheran. Avocations: gardening, model aircraft, traveling, hiking. Home: 117 Carter St Auburn AL 36830 Office: Dept History Auburn Univ 310 Thach Hall Auburn AL 36849 E-mail: noekenn@auburn.edu.

NOE, SAMUEL VANARSDALE, JR. retired urban planning educator; b. Louisville, May 16, 1933; s. Samuel VanArsdale and Elizabeth (McDonald) N.; m. Lynn Clifford, Sept. 8, 1956; children: Stephen V., David C. AB, Princeton U., 1954; BArch, N.C. State U., 1959; MArch in Urban Design, Harvard U., 1963. Cert. Nat. Coun. Archtl. Registration Bds. Draftsman Geodesics, Inc., Raleigh, N.C., 1957-59; arch. Boileau-Labourdette, Paris, 1959, Fry, Drew & Ptnrs., London, 1960, McCullough & Bickel, Louisville, 1960-62; prof. urban planning U. Cin., 1963-96; ret., 1996. Urban planning cons., Cin., 1963-68, 83-96; ptnr. Hayden B. May & Samuel V. Noe, Urban Design, Cin., 1970-82; chief planning advisor P.T. Bumi Serpong Damai, Jakarta, Indonesia, 1985; planning advisor Municipality of Istanbul, Turkey, 1988; Fulbright lectr. Mid. East Tech. U., Ankara, Turkey, 1968-69; vis. rsch. prof. Nat. Coll. Art, Lahore, Pakistan, 1976-77, Sch. Architecture and Planning, Delhi, India, 1979-80, Istanbul Tech. U., 1983-84, Anna U., Madras, India, 1991-92. Contbg. author: Delhi Through the Ages, 1986, Urban Development in the Muslim World, 1993; book rev. editor Studies in Comparative Internat. Devel., 1983-86. Mem. various comms. and task forces on urban planning City of Cin., 1972-83, mem. Cin. City Planning Commn., 1996-98; mem. Select Com. on Urban Character, Collier County, Naples, Fla., 1999—; mem. City of Naples Planning Adv. Bd., 2002—. 1st lt. U.S. Army, 1954-56. Fulbright-Hays fellow, Turkey, 1968, Pakistan, 1976, India, 1991, fellow Indo-U.S. Commn. on Edn. and Culture, India, 1979, Kingdom of Saudi Arabia, 1980. Mem. Am. Inst. Cert. Planners (charter). Avocation: sailing. Home: 4451 Gulf Shore Blvd N Apt 405 Naples FL 34103-2640

NOEHREN, ROBERT, organist, organ builder; b. Buffalo, Dec. 16, 1910; s. Alfred H. and Juliet (Egelhoff) N.; m. Eloise Southern, Aug. 27, 1938; children: Judith, Arthur. Student, Inst. Mus. Art, N.Y.C., 1929-30, Curtis Inst. Music, Phila., 1930-31; BMus, U. Mich., 1948; DMus (hon.), Davidson Coll., 1957. Instr. Davidson Coll., 1946-49; prof., univ. organist U. Mich., 1949-77, prof. emeritus, 1977—. Vis. prof. Eastman Sch. Music, 1967, U. Kans., 1975; organ builder; important instruments include organ in St. John's Roman Cath. Cathedral, Milw., 1st Unitarian Ch., San Francisco, 1st Presbyn. Ch., Buffalo, St. Andrew's Episc. Ch., Newport News, Va., Calvary Episc. Ch., Rochester, Minn.; designer, cons., 1954—; concert tours of Europe, 1948—; soloist Phila. Orch., Philharmonia Hungarica, New Sinfonia; rec. artist Lyrichord, Urania, Orion, Delos records; spl. research old organs Europe, 17th and 18th century organs in France. Author: An Organist's Reader, 1999; contbr. articles to profl. jours.; composer pieces for organ, piano, and voice; patentee combination action for organs. Recipient Grande Prix du Disque. Home: 17605 Drayton Hall Way San Diego CA 92128-2057

NOEL, CHERYL ELAINE, artist, poet; b. Syracuse, N.Y., Oct. 1, 1954; d. Arthur Raymond and Alice Thane N.. BA in Philosophy, Randolph-Macon Women's Coll., 1978; postgrad., Lynchburg Coll. Rehab. counselor Hudson House, Lynchburg, Va.; waitress The Ground Round; tchr. modern dance Campbell County Dept. Recreation; asst. mgr. Burgerette, Inc.; staff counselor Camp Zarahemela, Clintwood; inventory counter GE, Lynchburg, copper plating processor. Author: poems; dancer traveling dance theater, Randolph-Macon; exhibitions include Leagett at Randolph-Macon, featured.

NOEL, DON OBERT, JR. retired newspaper columnist; b. Elizabeth, N.J., Nov. 27, 1931; s. Don O. and Catherine (Pyle) N.; m. Elizabeth Bradford Foulds, Aug. 29, 1953; 1 child, Emily Rebecca. BA in Am. Studies, Cornell U., 1954. Reporter Hartford (Conn.) Times, 1958-68, asst. mng. editor, 1968-69, editorial page editor, 1969-74, editor in chief, 1974-75; sr. corr. WFSB-TV, host Face the State Post-Newsweek Stas., 1975-84; polit. columnist op-ed page Hartford Courant, 1984-97, ret., 1997. Bd. sec. Blue Hills Civic Assn., Hartford, 1988—. Served alt. mil. duty Am. Friends Svc. Com., Tokyo, 1954-56. Recipient Sevellon Brown Meml. award New England AP, 1964, Nat. Journalism award AMA, 1972, Nat. Journalism award Am. Soc. Planning Officials, 1972, 74; fellow Alicia Patterson Found., 1966-67; finalist Pulitzer Prize for non-deadline reporting, 1964. Mem. Soc. Of Friends. Avocations: gardening, birdwatching, language study. Home: 141 Ridgefield St Hartford CT 06112-1837 E-mail: dononoel@cs.com.

NOEL, EDWIN LAWRENCE, lawyer; b. St. Louis, July 11, 1946; s. Thomas Currie and Christine (Jones) N.; m. Nancy Carter Simpson, Feb. 7, 1970; children: Caroline, Edwin C. BA, Brown U., 1968; JD cum laude, St. Louis U., 1974. Bar: Mo. 1974, U.S. Dist. Ct. (ea. dist.) Mo. 1974, U.S. Ct. Appeals (8th cir.) 1974, U.S. Ct. Appeals (6th cir.) 1978, U.S. Ct. Appeals (7th cir.) 1994, U.S. Supreme Ct. 1986. Ptnr. Armstrong, Teasdale, Schlafly & Davis, St. Louis, 1974—, mng. ptnr., 1993-97. Bd. dirs. Corley Printing Co., Elcom Industries, St. Louis, Home Fed. Savs. Bank of Mo., 1988-93. Bd. dirs.

Edgewood Children's Ctr., St. Louis, 1982-92, St. Louis Assn. for Retarded Citizens, 1984-87, Churchill Sch., 1988-94, Whitfield Sch., 1991-95; chmn. Mo. Clean Water Com., Jefferson City, 1982-86; chmn. environ. com. St. Louis Regional Commerce and Growth Assn., 1982-88. Mem. Mo. Bar Assn., Bar Assn. Met. St. Louis, Attys. Liability Assurance Soc. (bd. dirs. 1995—). Republican. Episcopalian. Home: 301 S Mcknight Rd Saint Louis MO 63124-1884 Office: Armstrong Teasdale LLP 1 Metropolitan Sq Ste 2600 Saint Louis MO 63102-2740 E-mail: enoel@armstrongteasdale.com.

NOEL, FRANKLIN LINWOOD, judge; b. N.Y.C., N.Y., Dec. 7, 1951; s. Charles Alexander and Mayme (Loth) N.; m. Ellen Barbara Perl, Sept. 15, 1979; children: Kate Alexandra, Charles David. BA, SUNY, Binghamton, 1974; JD, Georgetown U., 1977. Bar: D.C. 1977, U. S. Dist. Ct. D.C. 1978, U.S. Ct. Appeals (D.C. cir.) 1978, Pa. 1979, Minn. 1983, U.S. Ct. Appeals (8th cir.) 1983, U.S. Dist. Ct. Minn. 1984. Assoc. Arnold & Porter, Washington, 1977-79; asst. dist. atty. Phila. Dist. Attys. Office, 1979-83; asst. U.S. atty. U.S. Attys. Office, Mpls., 1983-89; U.S. magistrate judge U.S. Dist. Ct., 1989—. Legal writing instr. U. Minn., Mpls., 1989-92, adj. prof. Law Sch., 1996—. Mem. League of Am. Wheelman, Phi Beta Kappa. Episcopalian. Avocation: bicycling. Office: US Dist Ct 300 S 4th St Minneapolis MN 55415-1320

NOEL, HANS CHRISTOPHER, political scientist; b. Portland, Oreg., Nov. 3, 1971; s. Grant Ellsworth Noel and Bonnielou Siedelman. BS in Journalism, Northwestern U., Evanston, Ill., 1994; MA in Polit. Sci., UCLA, 1999, PhD in Polit. Sci., 2002. Editor, designer Virginian-Pilot, Norfolk, Va., 1994-97; rsch. asst., tchg. asst. UCLA, 1998—. Dir. Possessed Pictures, Chgo., 2000. Dir.(films): The Rest of Your Life, 2000; co-author: Beating Reform: The Resurgence of Party in Presidential Nominations. Dr. J.A.C. Grant Found. fellow, 1997, Hoffenberg Stern fellow, 2000. Avocations: sailing, karate. also: UCLA Bunche Hall 2165 Los Angeles CA 90095 E-mail: hnoel@ucla.edu.

NOEL, MARY MARGARET, nutritionist, educator; b. Tacoma, July 13, 1948; d. Webster Young and Mary Leize Barth; m. George W. Noel, June 30, 1973; children: Katherine Mary, Joseph William. BS in Dietetics, Mich. State U., 1969; MPH, U. Mich., 1973; PhD in Family Ecology, Mich. Sate U., 1988. Registered dietician. Intern in dietetics Barnes Med. Ctr., St. Louis, 1970; nutrition cons. Vis. Nurse Assn., 1970-72; clin. nutritionist U. Mich., Ann Arbor, 1973-76; instr. dietetics Mich. State U., East Lansing, 1975-76; cons. in nutrition, 1976-86; exec. dir. Dairy Coun. of Mich., Okemos, 1986-88; asst. prof. dept. family practice, Coll. Human Medicine Mich. State U., East Lansing, 1988-93, assoc. prof., 1993—2000, prof., 2000—, assoc. chair dept., 1997—. Vol. Neighborhood Assn., East Lansing, 1983-97; bd. dirs., treas. Downtown Devel. Authority, East Lansing, 1986-96; vol. East Lansing Pub. Schs., 1982-98. Grantee NIH, 1997—. Mem. Am. Dietetic Assn. (sect. sec. 1970—), Mich. Dietetic Assn. (parliamentarian 1972—, nominating com., Recognized Young Dietitian 1977), Soc. for Nutrition Edn., Soc. for Tchrs. of Family Medicine, Vis. Nurses of Lansing (vice chair, then chair 1987-91). Office: Mich State U Dept Family Practice Coll Human Medicin B101 Clin Ctr East Lansing MI 48824 E-mail: noel@msu.edu.

NOEL, NICHOLAS, III, lawyer; b. Pottstown, Pa., June 5, 1952; s. Nicholas Jr. and Elaine (Buckwalter) N.; m. Karen Bean Schomp, Oct. 28, 1978; children: Carol Elaine, Nicholas IV. BA magna cum laude, Lehigh U., 1974; JD, U. Detroit, 1977. Bar: Pa. 1977, U.S. Dist. Ct. (ea. dist.) Pa. 1979, U.S. Ct. Appeals (3rd cir.) 1980, U.S. Supreme Ct. 1986, U.S. Dist. Ct. (mid. dist.) Pa. 1989. Assoc. Hahalis Law Office, Bethlehem, Pa., 1977-84; assoc. Teel, Stettz, Shimer & DiGiacomo, Easton, 1984-87; ptnr. Teel, Stettz, PC, 1987-2000, sr. litigation ptnr., 1989-2000, v.p., 1998-2000, pres., 2000, Noel & Kovacs, P.C., Easton, 2000—. Adj. prof. Northampton County C.C., Bethlehem, 1990, 97, 2000; solicitor Chiefs of Police Assn. of Mid. Ea. Pa., 1977—, Palmer Twp. Zoning Hearing Bd. solicitor, Easton, 1989—; arbitrator Am. Arbitration Assn., 1986—; lectr. Pa. Bar Inst., 2001. Contbr. to several books. Trustee Palmer Twp. Moravian Ch., 1985-97, 99—, pres., 1986-92, sec. bldg. expansion com., 1998-2001; mem. Moravian Ch. No. Province Ch. and Soc. Com., 1990—, Palmer Moravian Day Sch. bd., 1991-94, 99-2000. Named Outstanding Young Man Am., 1974. Fellow Pa. Bar Found.; mem. ABA, Pa. Bar Assn. (civil rights chair 1989-92, vice-chmn. legal edn. com. 1992, profl. stds. com. 1983, ho. of dels. 1998-2001), Northampton County Bar Assn. (legal ethics and responsibility com. 1987-94, bd. govs. 1991-99, treas. 1995, v.p. 1996, pres.-elect 1997, pres. 1998, past pres. 1999), Clinton Budd Palmer Inn of Ct. (1995-2000), Pa. Ho. Dels. (1998—). Avocations: most athletic events, swimming, hiking. Home: 2840 Green Pond Rd Easton PA 18045-2504 Office: 400 S Greenwood Ave Ste 300 Easton PA 18045-3776 E-mail: nn6552@aol.com.

NOEL, THOMAS J. humanities educator, writer; b. Cambridge, Mass., May 6, 1945; s. Dix Webster and Louise Jacob N.; m. Violet Sumiko Kamiya. MA in Libr. Sci., U. Denver, 1969; MA in History, U. Colo., 1976, PhD in History, 1978. Lang. arts tchr. 7th grade Hillel Hebrew Acad., Denver, 1969-72; tour leader Smithsonian Instn., 1982—; dir. pub. history and preservation U. Colo., Denver, 1984—, chair history dept., 1992-96, prof. history, 1986—. Tavern tours Colo. Hist. Soc., Denver, 1985—; cemetery tours Denver Mus. Natural History, 1991—. Author: Buildings of Colorado, 1997, Colorado: A Liquid History and Tavern Guide, 1998; co-author: Denver: Mining Camp to Metropolis, 1996, Historical Atlas of Colorado, 1993; mem. editl. bd. Western History Assn., 1990; commentator in field. Review bd. dirs. Nat. Register of Hist. Places, 1995—; commr., chair Denver Landmark Preservation Commn., 1983-93; posse mem., sheriff Denver Posse Westerners, 1984—. Democrat. Roman Catholic. Avocations: gardening, book collecting, hiking, swimming, beaching. Home: 1245 Newport St Denver CO 80220-2910 Office: U Colo 1200 Larimer St Denver CO 80204-5310

NOËLDECHEN, JOAN MARGUERITE, writer; b. West Islip, N.Y., May 20, 1963; d. Warren G. Noëldechen and Joan Marguerite Walter. BA in English and Drama, Flagler Coll., St. Augustine, Fla., 1985. Author: (novel) Dreamers Out of Step, 1995, (poetry) Ashes and Embers, 1996, (poetry) Following Angels and Wolves, 1997, (novella) Eve's Song, 1997, (anthologies) Bedside Prayers, 1997, Bless the Day, 1998, Trinity Poems, 1999, Takoma Poems, 2001. Mem. Thomas Wolfe Soc. Avocations: reading, cooking, gardening, hiking, photography.

NOELKEN, MILTON EDWARD, biochemistry educator, researcher; b. St. Louis, Dec. 5, 1935; s. William Henry Noelken and Agnes (Westbrook) Burkemper; m. Carol Ann Agne, June 9, 1962. BA in Chemistry, Washington U., St. Louis, 1957, PhD in Chemistry, 1962. Rsch. chemist Ea. Regional Rsch., Dept. Agr., Phila., 1964-67; asst. prof. dept. biochemistry U. Kans. Med. Ctr., Kansas City, 1967-71, assoc. prof., 1971-81, acting chmn., 1973-74, prof., 1981—, interim chmn., 1993-94. Vis. prof. Fed. U. Minas Gerais, Brazil, 1978. Contbr. articles to profl. jours. Recipient Scholastic Achievement award Am. Inst. Chemists, Washington U., 1957; NSF fellow, Washington U., 1959. Mem. Am. Chem. Soc., Am. Soc. for Biochemistry and Molecular Biology, Biophysical Soc., Sigma Xi. Achievements include research in properties of antibody molecules related to antigen binding, stucture of collagen of basement membranes, and stability of proteins. Office: U Kans Med Ctr Dept Biochemistry 39th And Rainbow Blvd Kansas City KS 66160-7421 E-mail: mnoelken@kumc.edu.

NOERDLINGER, PETER DAVID, astrophysicist, educator; b. N.Y.C., May 3, 1935; s. Julius Peter and Helen Caroline (Jacobs) N.; m. Carol Anne White, June 1957 (div. 1962); 1 dau., Lucy Anne; m. Judy Anne Nau, Nov. 4, 1964 (dec. 1986); children: Henry Clifford, Frederick Nicholas, Rachel Holly, Victor David. AB magna cum laude (Harvard Coll. Hon. fellow), Harvard Coll., 1956; PhD (U.S. Steel Found. fellow 1958-59, Howard Hughes fellow 1959-60, NSF fellow 1959), Calif. Inst. Tech., 1960. Instr. U. Chgo., 1960-63, asst. prof., 1963-66; assoc. prof. U. Iowa, 1966-68; asso. prof. N.Mex. Inst. Mining and Tech., 1968-69, prof., 1969-71; vis. prof. U. Calif., Santa Cruz, 1971; prof. astronomy and astrophysics Mich. State U., 1971—, acting chmn. dept. astronomy and astrophysics, 1974-75; NSF sr. resident research assoc. NASA, Ames Research Center, Moffett Field, Calif., summers 1974-75, NRC sr. resident research assoc., 1979-80; prin. research analyst Solar Energy Research Inst., 1981-82; staff mem. Los Alamos Nat. Lab., 1982—. NASA-Stanford U. summer fellow, 1969-70, NRC sr. postdoctoral research assoc., summer 1971; vis. scientist Smithsonian Astrophys. Obs., Harvard U., summer 1973, High Altitude Obs., Boulder, Colo., 1977-78; sr. research assoc. Astron. Inst., U. Amsterdam, summer 1976; vis. research assoc. U. Colo., 1977-78; disting. lectr. U. N.Mex., 1978 Contbr. articles to sci. jours. Active Council for a Livable World, 1963-66; campus rep. Fedn. Am. Scientists, 1973-77; mem. adv. bd. Am. Friends Service Com., Chgo., 1963-66, Lansing, Mich., 1972-75. Recipient hon. mention Gravity Research Found., 1971; NSF research grantee, 1977-79 Fellow Am. Phys. Soc., Royal Astron. Soc.; mem. Am. Astron. Soc., AAAS, Am. Assn. Physics Tchrs., Fedn. Am. Scientists, Internat. Astron. Union, Am. Geophys. Union, Phi Beta Kappa, Sigma Xi (award for meritorious research 1974) Mem. Soc. Of Friends. Home: 8805 Montpelier Dr Laurel MD 20708-2410 Office: Microcosm Inc 401 Coral Cir El Segundo CA 90245-4622

NOETH, LOUISE ANN, journalist; b. Evergreen Park, Ill., Nov. 17, 1954; d. Cy John and Alice Rose (Bobrovich) N.; m. Michael T. Lanigan, Aug. 29, 1992. Editor Petersen Pub. Co., Inc., Calif., 1980; assoc. pub., editor Autoscene Mag., Westlake Village, 1981; investigative editor Four Wheeler Mag., Canoga Park, 1982—; owner, founder Landspeed Prodns., 1984; automotive writer, columnist Press-Courier Newspaper, Oxnard, Calif., 1992-94, Ventura County Newspapers, 1994-95, L.A. Times, 1995; Car Craft Mag., 1994—; with EG&G, Inc., 1992; auto writer, columnist Ventura County Newspapers, 1994-95; adminstr. Spirit of Am. World Land Speed Record Team, 1996—; team mem. Team Vesco, 1999—. Cons. Spirit Am. World Speed Record Team, Pontiac Motor divsn. Land Rover N.Am, others; mem. Green Mamba Racing Team, Reseda, Calif., 1978—; graphic art commns. for Wallenius Lines, Radisson Hotels, GTE, Ferro Corp, SEA, Sailing; publicist TEAMVesco Racing, 1999. Author: Ventura County Destination Guide: Channel Islands Harbor Retrospect, Bonneville Salt Flats, Hot Rod Performance and Custon, 1979; prodr.: Renewing Pride, Schoolroom in Paradise, Heritage Square; contbr. articles; photographer (exhibitions) Ventura Village Art Gallery, 1994, Ventura County Mus. History and Art, 1991, Ventura County Nat. Bank, 1990, Ventura County Fair, 1990 (spl. non-competition award profl. category), Internet Cafe, 1996—. Mem. project R.A.F.T. Russians and Ams. for Teamwork, Buffalo Bill's West Show; mem. bd. dirs., pub. chair Carnegie Art Mus., 1995-97. Recipient Moto award in investigative news category, Automotive Journalism Conference, 1983-84, 96, Silver Medallion feature writing mag., 1997, 98, 99, 2000, pub. rels., 1996, photography, 1998; named Historian of Yr. Dry Lakes Racing Hall of Fame, 2001. Mem. Tallship Californian Quarter deck Comm., Oxnard C. of C., Edn. Comm. Youth Edn. Motivation Program, Internat. Motor Press Assn. (sec. 1986—), Specialty Equipment Market Assn. (pub. relations com. 1983, suspension and tire com. 1984-85), Am. Auto Racing Writers and Broadcasters Assn., Soc. Automotive Engrs. E-mail: lanspeed@west.net.

NOETHER, EMILIANA PASCA, historian, educator; b. Naples, Italy; came to U.S., 1919; d. Guglielmo and Bianca (Dramis) Pasca; m. Gottfried E. Noether, Aug. 1, 1942; 1 dau., Monica Gail. AB, Hunter Coll., N.Y.C., 1943; MA, Columbia U., 1944, PhD, 1948. From instr. to asst. prof. history Douglass Coll., Rutgers U., 1947-52; rsch. assoc. Center Internat. Studies, Mass. Inst. Tech., 1952-54; from lectr. to prof. history Regis Coll., Weston., Mass., 1959-66; prof. history Simmons Coll., Boston, 1966-68, U. Conn., Storrs, 1968-87. Editor: Italian sect. Am. Hist. Rev, 1958-75, Recently Published Articles, 1976-90, Garland Modern History Dissertation Series (Italy), 1989—; author: Seeds of Italian Nationalism, 2d edit, 1969, also articles.; co-editor, contbr.: Modern Italy: A Topical History Since 1861, 1974; contbg. editor: The American Constitution as a Symbol and Reality for Italy, 1989. AAUW fellow, 1946-47, 62-63; Bunting Inst. fellow, 1961-62; sr. Fulbright scholar Florence, Italy, 1965-66; Rome, 1982; Rsch. grantee Am. Philos. Soc., summer 1970; U. Conn. Research Found., 1969-71, 73-77, 81-86 Mem. Am. Hist. Assn. (council 1975-78, chmn. com. women historians 1976), Soc. Italian Studies (chmn. prize award and citation com. 1968-69, adv. council 1979-82, adv. council v.p. 1981-83, pres. 1983-85), Berkshire Conf. Women Historians (sec. 1962-64, pres. 1967-71), Coordinating Com. on Women in Hist. Profession, AAUW, Phi Beta Kappa, Pi Gamma Mu., Phi Kappa Phi Home: 1010 Waltham St #B-346 Lexington MA 02421 E-mail: epnoether@mindspring.com.

NOETHLING, VICTORIA ANN, delivery service executive; b. Pitts., Jan. 8, 1958; d. James Ralph and Elizabeth Mary Sage; m. Robert August Noethling, June 23, 1979; children: Samantha, Rebecca. Bus. cert., Bradford Bus. Sch., Pitts. Adminstrv. asst. Grant Thornton, Pitts., 1977-86, Margolis Wine & Spirits, Pitts., 1986-87; supr., adminstr. Arby's, Inc., Atlanta, 1987-91, UPS Hdqs., Atlanta, 1991-93, supr. customer info. mgmt., 1993—3003; supr. shared svcs. Retail Technology Group, 2002—. Mentor Girl Scouts Am., 2000, assoc. Boys & Girls Club Met. Atlanta, 1993—, torchbearer 1996 Olympics, Atlanta. Recipient Ember award Camp Fire Girls, Atlanta, 1998--. Mem. NAFE, Toastmasters Internat. (pres., v.p. edn., sec. 1998-2000, Competent Toastmaster award 1998, Advanced Toastmaster Bronze award 2001). Roman Catholic. Avocations: reading, water skiing, crafts, cooking. Office: UPS 55 Glenlake Pkwy NE Atlanta GA 30328-3474 E-mail: vnoethling@ups.com.

NOETZEL, ARTHUR JEROME, business administration educator, management consultant; b. East Cleveland, Ohio, July 2, 1916; s. Arthur John and Margaret (Weinfurtner) N.; m. Dorothy Elizabeth McKeon, Oct. 23, 1945 (dec. March 1988); children: Catherine Ellen Noetzel Levitt, Gretchen Marie Noetzel Walsh. BSBA, John Carroll U., 1938; MBA, Northwestern U., 1940; PhD, U. Mich., 1955; LittD (hon.), John Carroll U., 1985. Instr. John Carroll U., Cleve., 1941-42, asst. prof., 1942-46, prof. bus. adminstrn., 1955—; asst. dean Sch. Bus. John Carroll U., 1945-56, dean, 1956-70, academic v.p., 1970-84. Bd. dirs. Ctr. for Family Bus., Cleve., Ohio Coll. Podiatric Medicine, Cleve. Contbr. articles and book reviews to profl. jours. Bd. dirs. St. Vincent Charity Hosp., Cleve., 1970-82, Borromeo Coll., Wickliffe, 1978-84; chmn. Communication and Devel. Commn., Univ. Heights, Ohio, 1980—. Named Citizen of Yr., City of Univ. Heights, Ohio, 1983; recipient Alumni award John Carroll U., 1984, Cert. of Merit, Minority Developers Council, Cleve., 1985, You're The Top award, Golden Age Ctrs. of Cleve., 1997; Danforth Found. fellow, 1956. Roman Catholic. Avocation: reading. Home: 2405 Fenwood Rd Cleveland OH 44118-3805 Office: John Carroll U University Hts Cleveland OH 44106

NOFER, GEORGE HANCOCK, lawyer; b. Phila., June 14, 1926; BA, Haverford Coll., 1949; JD, Yale U., 1952. Bar: Pa. 1953. Pvt. practice, Phila., 1953—; ret. ptnr. Schnader, Harrison, Segal & Lewis, 1961-91, sr. counsel, 1992—. Pres. bd. sch. dirs. Upper Moreland Twp., Pa., 1965—73; trustee Beaver Coll., Glenside, 1969—76; co-trustee, exec. dir. Oberkotter Found., 1985—; elder, trustee, deacon Abington (Pa.) Presbyn. Ch., 1956—2000; bd. dirs. Fox Chase Cancer Ctr., Phila., 1989—94; bd. dirs. Phila. Presbyn. Homes, Inc., 1983—98, A.G. Bell Assn. for Deaf, Washington, 1992—98. Fellow Am. Coll. Trust and Estate Counsel (regent 1975— , pres. 1983-84, chmn. Pa. 1973-78), Am. Law Inst., Am. Bar Found.; mem. ABA (standing com. on specialization 1980-86, chmn. 1983-86), Pa. Bar Assn., Phila. Bar Assn., Internat. Acad. Estate and Trust Law, Phi Beta Kappa, Phi Delta Phi Home: 108 Quail Ln Radnor PA 19087-2729 Office: Schnader Harrison Segal & Lewis 1600 Market St Ste 3600 Philadelphia PA 19103-7287 E-mail: gnofer@schnader.com., ghnofer@aol.com.

NOFFKE, JANE BUNGE, sculptor; b. Madison, Wis., Oct. 28, 1957; d. William Wheeler and Elizabeth Ann (Carpenter) Bunge; m. Stephen Henry Noffke, Apr. 25, 1991; children: Payvand, Aaron, Anne Rose. BS with honors, U. Wis., 1987; postgrad., Ea. Mich. U., Ypsilanti, 1989—91. Artist, 1980—; pvt. sculpture tchr. Ann Arbor, 1996—; author/lectr., 1995—; tchr./sculpture juror U. Mich., Ann Arbor, 1994-98; mentor/tchr. U. Mich./Eaton Acad., Detroit, 1998; art tchr. Crane Correctional Instn. for Women, Women Caucus for the Arts, 1997-98. Exhbns. include photographs at UN, 1996-2000, bronze sculpture at Smithsonian Art Inst., 1994—, commd. bronze at the White House, photographs at Nat. Mus. of Women, 1995—, gallery bronzes at Toledo Mus. Art, 1992—, gallery bronzes at Galerie Alain Daune, Paris, 1995-98, Swords Into Plowshares UN Global Focus, 1997; contbr. articles to profl. jours. Recipient Dick Blick award for Artistic Excellence, 1992, Transforming Visions award Swords Into Plowshares Gallery, Detroit, 1993, 1997, Outstanding Achievement award Washtenaw Coun. for the Artists, 1997, 1998, Ethel Odegard scholarship for Artistic Excellence U. Wis., 1987, Outstanding Artistic Citation U. Wis., 1986, Gov.'s award for Outstanding Citizenship & Achievement, 1985, Outstanding Artistic Excellence award Internat. Exhbn., Russia, 1985, Nat. Endowment for the Arts grant Milw. Found., 1982; work selected to go on world tour UN Beijing Women's Conf., 1995-96. Mem. Nat. Sculpture Soc., Nat. Women's Caucus for the Arts, Chgo. Coalition of Artists, Detroit Artists Market. Avocations: photography, gardening. Studio: Technology Ctr Noffke Studio 410 W Washington St # 20 Ann Arbor MI 48103-4230 E-mail: jbnoffke@peoplepc.com.

NOFSINGER, JOHN, finance educator, consultant; b. Hampton, Va., Nov. 25, 1965; m. Suzzanna Frenier. BSEE, PhD in Fin., Wash. State U.; MBA, Chapman U. Engr. Pacific Gas , San Francisco, 1988—89; fin. prof. Marquette U., Milw., Wash. State U., Pullman. Cons. N.Y. Stock Exch., Assn. for Investment Mgmt. Rsch. Author: Investment Madness, 2001, Investment Blunders, 2002; contbr. articles to profl. jours. Capt. USAF, 1989—92. Named winner acad. paper competition, Chgo. Quantitative Alliance, 1997. Mem.: Fin. Mgmt. Assn. (Best of the Best Paper award 1997, Best Paper in Investments award 1997), Am. Fin. Assn. Office: Wash State Univ Dept Fin/Coll Bus Pullman WA 99164-4746 Business E-Mail: john_nofsinger@wsu.edu.

NOGEE, JEFFREY LAURENCE, lawyer; b. Schenectady, N.Y., Oct. 31, 1952; s. Rodney and Shirley Ruth (Mannes) N.; m. Freda Carolyn Wartel, Aug. 31, 1980; children: Rori Caitlen, Amara Sonia, Jaden Gwynn. BA cum laude, Bucknell U., 1974; JD, Boston U., 1977. Bar: N.Y. 1978, U.S. Dist. Ct. (so. and ea. dists.) N.Y. 1978. Assoc. Hale Russell & Gray, N.Y.C., 1977-83; sr. atty. Ebasco Services Inc., 1984-88, dir. Countertrade unit, 1985-88; sr. ptnr. Fogh & Nogee Assocs., 1988; ptnr. Brauner, Baron, Rosenzweig, Bauman & Klein, N.Y.C., 1988-90; sr. ptnr. Nogee & Wartel, Westbury, N.Y., 1990—. Pvt. counsellor for internat. bus. firms, 1987—. Prin. bassoonist, bd. dirs. The Band of L.I., 1997—, sec., 1997-99, pres., 1999—; prin. bassoonist Rockway-Five Towns Symphony Orch., 1998-99, Lawrence Philharm., 2000—. Trustee Temple Emanu-el of East Meadow, 1995-99, v.p., 1996-97. Mem. ABA, Am. Arbitration Assn., Assn. of Bar of City of N.Y., Nassau County Bar Assn., Internat. Platform Assn., N.Y. New Media Assn., Phi Beta Kappa, Pi Sigma Alpha. Avocations: fencing, bassoon and saxophone music, racquet sports, hiking, bicycling. Office: Ste 211 900 Merchants Concourse Westbury NY 11590-5114 E-mail: jnogee@nogeelaw.com.

NOGINOV, MIKHAIL A. physicist, researcher, educator; b. Dolgoprudnyi, Russia, May 28, 1962; came to U.S., 1991; s. Anatolii M. and Lidia V. (Platonova) N.; m. Natalia E. Chernova, July 3, 1982; children: Maxim M., Julia M. MS, Moscow Inst. Physics and Tech., 1985; PhD in Physics and Math., USSR Acad. Scis., Moscow, 1990. Engr., from jr. rsch. staff to rsch. staff Gen. Physics Inst. of USSR Acad. Scis., 1985-91; postdoctoral rsch. assoc. MIT, Cambridge, Mass., 1991-93; from asst. to assoc. rsch. prof dep. physics Ala. Agrl. Mech. U., Huntsville, 1993-97; assoc. rsch. prof. Ctr. for Materials Rsch., Norfolk (Va.) State U., 1997—. Reviewer sci. jours.; presenter in field. Contbr. more than 50 articles to profl. jours. Mem. IEEE, Optical Soc. Am., N.Y. Acad. Scis., Sigma Xi. Achievements include research in spectroscopy of laser-released solid-state materials; energy transfer upconversion in laser materials; solid-state lasers; nonlinear optics. Avocations: travel, windsurfing.

NOGUCHI, THOMAS TSUNETOMI, author, forensic pathologist; b. Fukuoka, Japan, Jan. 4, 1927; came to U.S., 1952; s. Wataru and Tomika Narahashi N. D of Medicine, Nippon Med. Sch., Tokyo, 1951; prof. honoris causa, U. Braz Cubas Fedn. Faculties Mogi Das Cruzes, Sao Paolo, Brazil, 1980; DSc (hon.), Worcester State Coll., 1985. Dep. med. examiner Los Angeles County Dept. Chief Med. Examiner, L.A., 1961-67, coroner, 1967-82; prof. forensic pathology U. So. Calif. Med. Sch., 1982-99, prof. emeritus forensic pathology, 1999—. Author: Coroner, 1983 (N.Y. Times Bestseller 1984), Coroner At Large, 1985; (fiction) Unnatural Causes, 1988, Physical Evidence, 1990. Recipient Imperial medal Order of Sacred Treasure, His Majesty the Emperor of Japan, 1999. Fellow Am. Acad. Forensic Sci. (chmn. sect. 1966); mem. AMA, Am. Coll. Legal Medicine, Am. Soc. Law, Medicine and Ethics, Internat. Acad. Legal and Social Medicine, Nat. Assn. Med. Examiners (pres. 1983), Calif. State Coroners Assn. (pres. 1974), World Assn. Med. Law (v.p.). Republican. Avocations: fine arts, gourmet Oriental cooking, painting stills and abstracts. Office: U So Calif Med Ctr 1200 N State St Rm 2520 Los Angeles CA 90033-1029 Fax: 323-733-9860. Business E-Mail: noguchi@hsc.usc.edu.

NOH, JUN-YONG, computer scientist, researcher; b. Seoul, Republic of Korea, Feb. 14, 1971; s. Hae-Kyu Noh and Yoo-im Bang. Bachelor magna cum laude, U. So. Calif., 1994, Master, 1996, PhD, 2002. Rschr. on brain-like computer Info. Scis. Inst., Marina del Rey, Calif., 1997; rschr. facial animation U. So. Calif., L.A., 1998—. CEO Digital Clone Lab., L.A., 2002—. Pvt., 1999, Seoul. Achievements include patent for expression cloning. Avocations: scuba diving, travel.

NOHE, RICHARD EDGAR, telecommunications executive; b. Greenville, S.C., June 9, 1963; s. Richard E. and Catherine D. (Cashin) N. BA, Augusta (Ga.) Coll., 1986; M in Profl. Studies, NYU, 1989; JD, N.Y. Law Sch., 1996. News dir. WRDW-TV CBS, Augusta, 1983-87; rschr. Columbia U., Ctr. Telecomm. and Info. Studies (name changed to Columbia Inst. Tele-Info.), N.Y.C., 1989-90; mgr. NTT Am., 1990-93, sr. mgr., 1993-95, dir., 1995-97, v.p. corp. strategy, gen. mgr. Washington, 1997—. Congl. fellow subcom. on oversight, ways and means com. U.S. Ho. of Reps., 1996. Contbr. articles to profl. publs. Congl. fellow Brookings Instn., 1996. Mem. ABA, Brookings Instn. (congressional fellow 1996), Washington Export Coun. Avocations: golf, tennis, reading, films, writing. Address: NTT Am 101 Park Ave Fl 41 New York NY 10178-4199 Office: 1300 Pennsylvinia Ave NW Ste 450 North Washington DC 20004

NOHRDEN, PATRICK THOMAS, lawyer; b. Santa Cruz, Calif., Mar. 7, 1956; s. Thomas Allen and Roberta Eugenia (Brydon) Nohrden; children: Steven, Laura, Maranda, Patricia. AS, Excelsior Coll., Albany, 1980; BA in English with great distinction, San Jose State U., 1984; JD, U. Akron, 1992. Bar: Nev. 1993, U.S. Dist. Ct. Nev. 1993. Regional dir. CareerPro, Inc., Roseville, Calif., 1984-91; cons. Patrick T. Nohrden & Assocs., Youngstown, Ohio, 1991-93; pvt. practice, Las Vegas, Nev., 1993—. Exec. dir. Geisa Project; bd. dirs. Profl. Resume Svc., Inc., Las Vegas, Las Vegas Diamondbacks, Inc., Clark County Pro Bono Project, Maui Land Devel. Co., Inc., World Internat. Intelligence Bur., Inc.; adj. prof. C.C. So. Nev.; CEO World Microbes, Inc. Sgt. U.S. Army, 1975-81. Recipient 2 Spirit of Pro Bono awards, Meritorious Svc. award. Mem. ATLA, ABA (family law sect.), Fed. Bar Assn., Nev. Trial Lawyers Assn., State Bar Nev. (family law and bankruptcy sects.), Clark County Bar Assn., Phi Kappa Phi. Republican. Roman Catholic. Office: 6312 W Cheyenne Ave Ste A Las Vegas NV 89108 E-mail: nohrden@lvcm.com.

NOHRNBERG, JAMES CARSON, English language educator; b. Berkeley, Calif., Mar. 19, 1941; s. Carson and Geneva Gertrude (Gibbs) N.; m. Stephanie Payson Lamport, June 14, 1964; children: Gabrielle L., Peter Carson L. Student, Kenyon Coll., 1958-60; BA, Harvard Coll., 1962, postgrad., 1965-68; PhD, U. Toronto, 1970. Tchg. fellow dept. English U. Coll., U. Toronto, 1963-64; jr. fellow Soc. of Fellows Harvard U., 1965-68; acting instr. dept. English Yale U., New Haven, 1968-69, lectr., 1969-70, asst. prof., 1970-75, assoc. prof., 1975; prof. English U. Va., Charlottesville, 1975—. Adj. instr. English Harvard U. , Cambridge, 1967; Gauss Seminars in Criticism lectr. Princeton U., 1987; lectr. various univs., 1974—2002. Author: The Analogy of The Faerie Queene, 1976, 80, Like Unto Moses: The Constituting of an Interruption, 1995; mem. editl. bd. Spenser Ency., 1977-90, Spenser Studies, 1977—; contbr. articles to profl. jours. and editor vols. on allegory, Bible, Homer, Dante, Boiardo, Spenser, Milton, Thomas Pynchon, Northrop Frye, among others. Recipient Am. Acad. Poets prize Harvard U., 1962; Woodrow Wilson fellow, 1962, jr. fellow Harvard U., 1965-68, Morse fellow Yale U., 1974-75, U. Va. Ctr. for Advanced Studies fellow, 1975-78, Guggenheim fellow, 1981-82, Ind. U. Inst. for Advanced Studies fellow, 1991. Mem.: MLA, Spenser Soc., Phi Beta Kappa. Presbyterian. Avocations: writing poetry, collecting books and records. Home: 1874 Wayside Pl Charlottesville VA 22903-1631 Office: U Va Dept English Bryan Hall Charlottesville VA 22903 E-mail: jcn@virginia.edu.

NOIA, ALAN JAMES, utility company executive; b. Selbitz, Germany, Feb. 18, 1947; came to U.S., 1949; s. Franz and Anneliese (Gossler) N.; m. Cynthia Dee Rathman BSEE, U. Va., Charlottesville, 1969. Engr. Potomac Edison Co., Hagerstown, Md., 1969-72, database adminstr., 1972-73; data base adminstr., supr. tech. svcs. Allegheny Power Svc. Corp., Greensburg, Pa., 1973-75, staff asst. N.Y.C., 1975-79; asst. v.p., treas. Allegheny Power System, 1979-80, treas., 1980-82, v.p., treas., 1983-84; v.p. bulk power supply, CFO Allegheny Power System, Inc. and Allegheny Power Svc. Corp., 1984-87; pres. Potomac Edison Co., Hagerstown, Md., 1990-94; pres., COO Allegheny Power, 1994—; chmn., pres., CEO Allegheny Energy. Bd. dirs. Allegheny Power Svc. Corp., Monongahela Power Co., Potomac Edison Co., West Penn Power Co., Allegheny Generating Co.; mem. Md. Econ. Devel. Com. Trustee East Ctrl. Nuclear Group, N.Y.C., 1979—; bd. dirs. Md. Symphony Orch., Southeastern Elec. Exch., Inc. Mem. Phi Eta Sigma, Eta Kappa Nu, Tau Beta Pi. Roman Catholic. Home: 9532 Childacrest Rd Boonsboro MD 21713-1507 Office: Allegheny Energy 10435 Downsville Pike Hagerstown MD 21740-1732*

NOKES, JOHN RICHARD, retired newspaper editor, writer; b. Portland, Oreg., Feb. 23, 1915; s. James Abraham and Bernice Alfaretta (Bailey) N.; m. Evelyn Junkin, Sept. 13, 1936; children: Richard Gregory, William G., Gail (Mrs. William M. Hulden), Douglas J., Kathy E. BS, Linfield Coll., 1936, LHD (hon.), 1988. With The Oregonian, Portland, 1936-82, city editor, 1950-65, asst. mng. editor, 1965-71, mng. editor, 1971-75, editor, 1975-82; disting. vis. prof. journalism Linfield Coll., 1982-85. Cons. editor The Hong Kong Standard, 1994. Author: American Form of Government, 1939, Columbia's River: The Voyages of Robert Gray 1787-1793, 1991, Almost a Hero: The Voyages of John Meares to China, Hawaii and the Pacific Northwest, 1998; editor Oreg. Edn. Jour., 1944. Bd. dirs. Portland U.S.O., 1968-72, U.S. Coast Guard Acad. Found., 1972-74, Portland Opera Assn., 1976-78; trustee Linfield Coll., 1977-93; v.p. Oreg. UN Assn., 1983-85, chmn. Oreg. UN Day, 1983. Lt. (j.g.) USNR, 1944-46; comdr. Res. (ret.). Mem. Navy League U.S. (pres. Portland coun. 1969-71), Linfield Coll. Alumni Assn. (pres. 1940), World Affairs Coun. Oreg. (pres. 1973-74), AP Mng. Editors Assn. (dir. 1973-80), Am. Soc. Newspaper Editors, N.W. China Coun., Sigma Delta Chi (pres. Willamette Valley chpt. 1975-76) Clubs: Multnomah Athletic (Portland). Republican. Methodist. Home: 11789 SW Queen Elizabeth Portland OR 97224-2601

NOLAN, ALAN TUCKER, retired lawyer, labor arbitrator, writer; b. Evansville, Ind., Jan. 19, 1923; s. Val and Jeannette (Covert) N.; m. Elizabeth Clare Titsworth, Aug. 26, 1947 (dec. Nov. 1967); children: Patrick A., Thomas C., Mary F., Elizabeth T., John V.; m. Jane Ransel DeVoe, Feb. 7, 1970; adopted children: John C. DeVoe, Ellen R. DeVoe, Thomas R. DeVoe. AB in Govt., Ind. U., 1944, LHD (hon.), 1993; LLB, Harvard U., 1947. Bar: Ind. 1947. Law clk. U.S. Ct. Appeals (7th Cir.), Chgo., 1947-48; assoc. Ice, Miller, Donadio & Ryan, Indpls., 1948-58, ptnr., 1958-93, ret., 1993—. Chmn. Disciplinary Commn. Supreme Ct. Ind., Indpls., 1966-73. Author: The Iron Brigade, 1961, As Sounding Brass, 1964, Lee Considered, 1991; editor (with S. Vipond) Giants in Tall Black Hats, 1998, (with Gary Gallagher) The Myth of the Lost Cause and Civil War History, 2000, Rally Once Again, 2000; contbg. editor The Civil War, 1985-89; contbr. numerous articles to profl. jours. Life mem. NAACP Indpls., v.p., 1950-54; bd. dirs., founder Ind. Civil Liberties Union, Indpls., 1953-60; bd. dirs. Indpls. Art League, 1981-87; chmn., bd. trustees Ind. Hist. Soc., Indpls., 1986-93; trustee Eiteljorg Mus., Indpls., 1987-93. Fellow Co. Mil. Historians, Am. Bar Found., State Hist. Soc. Wis.; mem. ABA, Ind. Bar Assn., Indpls. Bar Assn. (bd. mgrs. 1958-60, chmn. Grievance Com. 1960-64), Indpls. Civil War Round Table, Ensemble Music Soc. (bd. dirs. 1999—). Democrat. Roman Catholic. Avocations: travel, gardening, reading. Home and Office: 4118 N Pennsylvania St Indianapolis IN 46205-2611 E-mail: indynolan@aol.com.

NOLAN, BENJAMIN BURKE, retired civil engineer; b. Detroit, Oct. 6, 1931; s. Benjamin Augustus and Helen Louise (Boughey) N.; m. Katherine Mary Zeman, may 14, 1961. BSCE, U. Calif., Berkeley, 1958. Registered civil engr., Calif. City engr. City of Newport Beach, Calif., 1965-78, pub. works dir., 1978-94. Mem. Orange County Transp. Authority, Calif., 1978-94, Transp. Corridor Agys., Orange County, 1984-94; active City Engrs. Assn., Orange County, 1965-94. With USAF, 1951-53, France. Mem. ASCE (life), Am. Pub. Works Assn. Achievements include participation in creation of Orange County Transp. Corridor Agys.; beach erosion solutions; hwy. and bridge constrn. and widening; coastal estuary restoration; harbor facilities and ocean pier improvements; water supply, sanitary sewerage, and storm drainage improvements; and publ. parks and bldgs. constrn. Home: 614 Hassett St Brookings OR 97415-8206

NOLAN, CATHAL J. historian; b. Dublin, Ireland, Aug. 2, 1956; came to the U.S., 1995; m. Valerie E. Duff, Sept. 7, 1985; children: Ryan Casey, Genevieve Michelle. BA in History, U. Alta., Edmonton, Can., 1978; MA in History, U. Toronto, Can., 1982, PhD in Polit. Sci., 1989; diploma in human rights, Can. Human Rights Found., 1984. CUSO vol., English and social studies instr. Govt. Secondary Sch., Kazaure, Kano, Nigeria, 1978-80, head of arts, 1979-80; contract rschr., writer Wandel Ltd., Toronto, 1982-83; cons. policy devel. and rsch. divsn. Can. Internat. Devel. Agy., Govt. Can., Ottawa, 1985-86; editl. intern Can. Jour. Polit. Sci., 1987-88; asst. prof. polit. sci. St. Francis Xavier U., 1989-90; asst. prof. internat. rels. Miami U., Oxford, Ohio, 1990-91; asst. prof. polit. sci. U. B.C., Vancouver, 1991-95, rsch. assoc. Inst. Internat. Rels., 1993-94; rsch. assoc. prof. internat. rels. Boston U., 1995-99, asst. to pres./chancellor, 1995-99, assoc. prof. history and politics, 1999—, exec. dir. Internat. History Inst., 1999—. Lectr. in field. Author: Principled Diplomacy: Security and Rights in U.S. Foreign Policy, 1993, The Longman Guide to World Affairs, 1995, Maailma Poliitika Leksikon, 1995, Greenwood Encyclopedia of International Relations, 4 vols., 2002; editor: Ethics and Statecraft: The Moral Dimension of International Affairs, 1995, Notable U.S. Ambassadors Since 1775, 1997; founding editor (book series) Humanistic Perspectives on International Relations, 1998—; co-editor: Shepherd of Democracy? America and Germany in the 20th Century, 1992; founding co-editor: (book series) International History, 1999—; contbr. chpts. to books and articles to profl. jours. Connaught Found. Project Devel./SSHRC Project grantee, 1986, rsch. grantee Ctr. for Internat. Studies, 1986, U. Toronto, 1986, St. Francis Xavier, 1990, Consortium for the Study of Intelligence, 1990, Alumni Assn. Miami, 1990, Humanities and Social Sci., 1992, Carnegie Coun. on Ethics and Internat. Affairs, 1992, 93, 98, Cooperative Security Program, 1995, Robert R. McCormick Tribune Found., 1999, 2001; Barton fellow in peace and security, 1993. Mem. Hist. Soc., Soc. for Historians Am. Fgn. Rels., Planetary Soc. Office: Internat History Inst Boston Univ 725 Commonwealth Ave Boston MA 02215 E-mail: cnolan@bu.edu.

NOLAN, CHRISTOPHER ALOYSIUS, III, real estate developer, architect; b. Boston, July 17, 1950; s. Christopher Aloysius Nolan Jr. and Gladys Edna (Kiely) McMakin; m. Deborah Ellen Barham, July 22, 1982 (dec. Feb. 1999). BA, U. Toronto, 1972; MArch, Harvard, 1979; student, Sch. of Museum of Fine Arts, Boston, 1972-75. Registered architect, N.Y., N.J., Conn. Grad. architect Hugh Adams Russell Architects, Cambridge, 1977-79; architect Eli Attia and Assocs., N.Y.C., 1979-80, Haines Lundberg Waehler, N.Y.C., 1980-81, Castro-Blanco Piscioneri Feder, N.Y.C., 1981-84; chief architect Howco Investment Corp., Livingston, N.J., 1984-88; devel. mgr. Hirschfeld Realty, N.Y.C., 1988; exec. v.p., chief oper. officer Hilton Devel. Co., Inc., N.Y.C. and Parsippany, N.J., 1988-96; project exec. AJ Contracting Co., Inc., N.Y.C., 1996-2000; dir. devel. LCOR Inc., 2000—. Mem. planning bd. Clermont, N.Y.; mem. adv. bd. Madison Sq. Boys and Girls Clubs, N.Y. Mem. AIA, Harvard Club. Avocations: yoga, swimming, agriculture. Office: LCOR Inc 1 Penn Plz Ste 3310 New York NY 10119-3310 E-mail: cnolan@world.std.com., cnolan@lcor-ny.com.

NOLAN, DAVID BRIAN, lawyer; b. Washington, Jan. 1, 1951; s. John Joseph and Mary Jane Nolan; m. Cheryl Ann Cottle, June 30, 1979; children: John Joseph II, David Brian II, Christopher Dalton. BA, Duke U., 1973; MPA, Am. U., 1975; JD, U. La Verne, 1978; postgrad., Georgetown U., 1981-89. Bar: Calif. 1978, U.S. Dist. Ct. (cen. dist.) Calif. 1979, U.S. Ct. Claims 1981, U.S. Tax Ct. 1981, U.S. Ct. Appeals (D.C. cir.) 1984, U.S. Supreme Ct. 2000. Intern Congressman Joel Broyhill, 1971; asst. dir. rsch. Younger-Curb Campaign, L.A., 1978; assoc. L. Rob Werner Law Offices, Encino, Calif., 1979-80; atty. conflicts Office of Pres. Elect, Washington, 1980-81; staff atty. Office of counsel to the Pres. White House, 1981; staff asst. office of sec. U.S. Dept. Treasury, 1981-85; spl. asst. office gen. counsel U.S. Dept. Energy, 1985-90, atty. advisor enforcement div. Office of Nuclear Safety, 1990-91, trial atty. adminstrv. litigation div. Econ. Regulatory Adminstrn., 1991-95, trial atty. Office of Gen. Counsel, 1995-2001; pvt. law practice, 2001—. Bd. dirs., treas. Energy Fed. Credit Union. Mem. editl. bd. New Guard Mag., 1983-85. Steering com. L.A. Reps., 1979-80, Reagan for Pres., L.A., 1980; chmn. 39th Assembly, Rep. Ctrl. Com., 1979-80; alt. del. 1972 Rep. Nat. Conv.; pres. N.C. Coll. Rep. Com., 1972-73; nat. treas., bd. dirs. Young Amers. for Freedom, Sterling, Va., 1983-85; corp. dir. Am. Sovereignty Task Force, Vienna, Va., 1984—, State Dept. Watch Ltd., Vienna, 1984—. Charles Edison Youth Found. scholar, 1971; named one of Outstanding Young Men in Am., Jaycees, 1976-86; recipient Mgr. of Yr. honor Dept. Energy Women's Adv. Coun., 1988, Achievement in Equal Opportunity Deptl. award, 1988. Mem. Fed. Bar Assn., Bar Assn. of D.C. (chmn. ethics com. young lawyers div. 1985-87), D.C. Bar, Calif. Bar, U.S. Supreme Ct. Soc., Federalist Soc., U.S. Justice Found. (co-founder, of counsel 1979-80), Conservative Network Club, Whistle Blowers Ave Patriots (co-founder 1999). Home: 8310 Wagon Wheel Rd Alexandria VA 22309-2175 Office: David B Nolan & Assocs Box 23019 Washington DC 20026-1864 E-mail: dbnesq1@aol.com.

NOLAN, DAVID CHARLES, lawyer, mediator; b. San Mateo, Calif., Oct. 12, 1940; s. Clarence Charles and Leona Henrietta (Lindeman) N.; m. Cynthia Ann James, Feb. 20, 1971; children: Matthew, John, Scott. AB, Stanford U., 1962; JD, U. Calif., Berkeley, 1965. Bar: Calif. 1966, U.S. Ct. Appeals (9th cir.) 1971, U.S. Ct. Appeals (D.C. cir.) 1975, U.S. Dist. Ct. (no. dist.) Calif. 1969, U.S. Dist. Ct. (D.C. cir.) 1970, U.S. Tax Ct., U.S. Supreme Ct. 1972. Ptnr. Graham & James, San Francisco, 1968-93; sole practitioner Walnut Creek, Calif., 1993—. Bd. dirs., officer Family Homes for Retarded, Belmont, Calif., 1978-81; founding dir. Orinda (Calif.) Baseball Assn., 1982-86; commr. Diablo Valley Baseball League, Martinez, Calif., 1983-90. Lt. comdr. USCG, 1965-68. Mem. ABA, Calif. Bar Assn., Contra Costa County Bar Assn., No. Calif. Mediation Assn., Assn. Transp. Practitioners, Commonwealth Club, Maritime Law Assn., Order of Coif. Home: 12 E Altarinda Dr Orinda CA 94563-2406 Office: 1990 N California Blvd Walnut Creek CA 94596-3742 Fax: 925-937-5442.

NOLAN, DAVID JOSEPH, author, historian; b. Cambridge, Mass., June 27, 1946; s. Joseph Thomas and Virginia Theodate (Tappin) N.; children: Sudie Ariyoshi, Hamilton Joseph. Student, U. Va., 1963-65. Field sec. Va. Students' Civil Rights Com., Lawrenceville, 1965-66; editor New South Student mag., Nashville, 1966-69; freelance writer, lectr., 1969—. Author: Fifty Feet in Paradise, 1984 (Author's award Coun. for Fla. Librs.), The Houses of St. Augustine, 1995; contbr.: The Book Lover's Guide to Florida, 1992. Pres. Marjorie Kinnan Rawlings Soc., 1993-95; trustee Ft. Mose Hist. Soc., 1996-99. Mem. Friends of St. Augustine Architecture. Avocations: reading, photography. Home: 30 Park Terrace Dr Saint Augustine FL 32080-5334

NOLAN, EDITH ELLEN, research scientist, psychology educator; b. Brooklyn, N.Y., Sept. 21, 1951; d. Anthony Vincent and Sheila Frances (Whelan) Ventrice; m. Mark William Nolan jr., May 28, 1970 (div. May 1975); 1 child, Mark William; m. Gerard Michael Damm, Aug. 9, 1987. BA in psychology, SUNY, Stony Brook, 1981; PhD, 1988; MA in Exptl. Psychology, L.I. U.-C.W. Post, 1984. Clinician's asst. psychiatry dept. SUNY, Stony Brook, 1986, field coord. Medication Evaluations Program, 1986-90, sr. rsch. scientist, 1991—; field observer Devel. Disabilities Clinic, 1987. Adj. instr. L.I. U., Brookville, 1985-89, SUNY, Stony Brook, 1988, St. Joseph's Coll., Patchogue, N.Y., 1988-90; adj. asst. prof. Dowling Coll., Oakdale, N.Y., 1987—; behavioral intervention cons., Maryhaven Therapeutic Presch., Port Jefferson, N.Y., 1983-85; speaker in field. Mem. Brookhaven Village Assn., 1994. Rsch. grantee NIMH, 1994. Mem. APS, Sigma Xi. Achievements include field-testing modification of and extensive research with procedure for conducting school-based medication evaluations for hyperactive children, procedure for toilet training developmentally disabled children. Office: Dept Psychiatry Putnam Hall S Campus Stony Brook NY 11794-0001

NOLAN, EDMUND FRANCIS, management consultant; b. Buffalo, June 9, 1931; s. James Paul and Isabel Jane (Curry) N.; m. Chloe Dandison Nolan, Dec. 19, 1959 (div. Aug. 1979); children: Andrew Dandison, Jeffrey Stewart; m. Ann Hopkins Chadbourne, Aug. 18, 1979; stepchildren: Gay Chadbourne Canepa, Scott Holt Chadbourne. BA, Cornell U., 1953; MBA, Columbia U., 1957. Sales and mktg. staff Armstrong World Industries, Lancaster, Pa., 1957-63; mgmt. cons. Hay Group, Phila., 1963-72; dir. compensation and benefits Nashua (N.H.) Corp., 1972-76; sr. mgmt. cons. Coopers & Lybrand, N.Y.C., 1976-83; dir. compensation and benefits Svc. Systems Corp., Buffalo, 1983-87; mgmt. cons. Nolan Consulting, Falmouth, Mass., 1987—97; substance abuse counselor Miller House men's residential program Goshold Treatment Ctr., 1997—. Bd. dirs. J R Hess & Co., Inc., Cranston, R.I.; mem. adv. bd. L F Giampietro, PC, Falmouth. Del. Rep. state conv., Boston, 1990, Econ. Devel. Com. Town of Falmouth, 1993—; mem. Bikeways Com., Town of Falmouth, 1990—; trustee Falmouth Pub. Libr., 1994—. 1st lt. U.S. Army, 1953-55, Korea. Mem. Cape Cod Cornellians (pres. 1987-89), Falmouth Sports Ctr., Woods Hole Theatre Co. (pres. 1990-95), Delta Phi (v.p. 1950—). Congregationalist. Avocations: teaching, acting, tennis, skiing, biking, running (6 marathons). Office: Miller House 165 Woods Hole Rd Falmouth MA 02540

NOLAN, JAMES PAUL, medical educator, scientist; b. Buffalo, June 21, 1929; s. James Paul and Isabel (Curry) N.; m. Christa Paul, July 23, 1956; children— Lisa, James, Christopher, Thomas. BA, Yale U., 1951, MD cum laude, 1955. Diplomate Am. Bd. Internal Medicine. Instr. in medicine Yale U., New Haven, 1961-63; intern Grace-New Haven Hosp., 1955-56, resident, 1958-60, chief med. resident, 1961-62, assoc. physician, 1962-63; asst. prof. medicine SUNY, Buffalo, 1963-67, asso. prof., 1967-69, prof., 1969—, vice-chmn. dept. medicine, 1973-77, acting chmn. dept., 1978-79, chmn. dept., 1979-95, disting. svc. prof., 1996—; chief of medicine Buffalo Gen. Hosp., 1969-80, attending, 1969—; asso. attending Edward J. Meyer Meml. Hosp., Buffalo, 1963-68, attending, 1968-71, cons., 1971—; cons. physician Millard Fillmore Hosp., 1981—, Deaconess Hosp., 1973—. Attending Buffalo VA Hosp., Children's Hosp. Buffalo; cons. Roswell Park Meml. Inst., 1970— ; acting dir. dept. medicine Erie County Med. Center, 1978-80, dir. dept., 1980— ; Trustee Buffalo Gen. Hosp., 1974— Editorial adv. bd. Jour. Medicine Exptl. and Clin, 1971— ; reviewer: Gastroenterology, 1973— ; contbr. numerous articles to med. and sci. jours. Served to lt. comdr., M.C. USN, 1956-58. NIH grantee, 1979-86; Hartford Found. grantee, 1981 Mem. ACP (master, chair bd. regents 1994-95), Am. Fedn. Clin. Rsch., AAAS, Am. Gastroent. Assn. (procedures com.), Am. Assn. Study of Liver Disease, Reticuloendothelial Soc., N.Y. Acad. Sci., Am. Clin. and Climatol. Assn., Interurban Club, Ctrl. Soc. Clin. Rsch., Internat. Assn. Study of Liver, Assn. Am. Physicians, Assn. Profs. Medicine (pres. 1993-94), Phi Beta Kappa, Alpha Omega Alpha. Office: 462 Grider St Buffalo NY 14215-3021 Address: 213 Burbank Dr Snyder NY 14226-3938 E-mail: jpnolanmd@yahoo.com.

NOLAN, JANIECE SIMMONS, health care company executive; b. Ft. Worth; d. James Coleman and Berenice Johnson Simmons; m. Robert L. Nolan; children: Douglas, Patricia, Nancy, Margaret, Sheffield, Gemini Janiece. BA, U. Tex., 1961, MA, 1963; PhD, Tulane U., 1968; MPH, U. Calif., Berkeley, 1975. Diplomate Am. Coll. Healthcare Execs. Rsch. scientist Tex. Nuc. (Nuc. Chgo.), Austin, 1963-65; head cell biology Gulf South Rsch. Inst., New Orleans, 1968-70; postdoctoral fellow dept. physiology/anatomy U. Calif., Berkeley, 1970-72; rsch. physiologist, acting assoc. chief of staff for rsch. VA Hosp., Martinez, Calif., 1970-75; COO, v.p. adminstrn. John Muir Med. Ctr., Walnut Creek, 1977-97; pres., CEO John Muir/Mt. Diablo Health Network, 1997—. Mem. med. adv. commn. Contra Costa County, Martinez, 1996, East Bay chpt. Amigos de la Americas, Orinda, 1997; commr. State Commn. Emergency Svcs., Sacramento, 1997; Bd, dirs. Calif. Healthcare Assn. Polit. Action, 1996. Capt. USNR, (ret.). Woodrow Wilson fellow, 1960; named Woman of Yr., Women Health Care Execs., San Francisco, 1989; recipient Navy Commendation medals (3), Humanitarian Svc. medal, 2 Armed Forces Res. medals (2). Mem.: Ind. Physician Assn., Med. Group Mgmt. Assn., Am. Mil. Surgeons of the U.S., Assn. Integrated Health Delivery Systems, Rotary (Paul Harris fellow). Avocations: international travel, genealogy research. Office: John Muir/Mt Diablo Health Network 1400 Treat Blvd Walnut Creek CA 94596-2142 E-mail: Janiece.Nolan@jmmdhs.com.

NOLAN, JOHN BLANCHARD, lawyer; b. Providence, Aug. 30, 1943; s. John O'Leary and Elizabeth Rita (Blanchard) Nolan; m. Marguerite Ruth Hartley, Mar. 1, 1969 (dec. Aug. 1988); children: Suzanne, Caroline, Danielle; m. Lillian B. Prestley, 1989. AB, Brown U., 1965; JD, Georgetown U., 1968. Bar: Conn. 1968, U.S. Dist. Ct. Conn. 1969, U.S. Ct. Appeals (2d cir.) 1969, U.S. Dist. Ct. (so. dist.) N.Y. 1973, N.Y. 1974, U.S. Cat. Appeals (1st cir.) 1991, U.S. Dist. Ct. Ariz. 1994, U.S. Supreme Ct. 1995. Assoc. Day, Berry & Howard, Hartford, Conn., 1969-76, ptnr., 1976—. Bd. dirs. Spiritus Wines, Inc.; chmn. local rules practice adv. com. U.S. Bankruptcy Ct., 1981—. Corporator St. Francis Hosp. Med. Ctr., Hartford, 1982—; bd. dirs. Greater Hartford Arts Coun., Inc., 1993—, v.p., mem. exec. com.; mem. parish coun. Ch. St. Timothy; trustee St. Mary Home Found., 1983—, U. Hartford Art Sch., 1988—94. Fellow: Conn. Bar Found.; mem.: ABA, Insolvency Internat., Hartford County Bar Assn., Conn. Bar Assn., Am. Bankruptcy Inst., Loomis Chaffee Sch. Alumni Assn. (bd. dirs. 1996—98), Hartford Golf Club (bd. dirs. 2000—). Democrat. Roman Catholic. Avocations: golf, skiing, travel, wines. Home: 34 Northmoor Rd West Hartford CT 06117-1709 Office: Day Berry & Howard 185 City Place Hartford CT 06103-3499

NOLAN, JOHN EDWARD, lawyer; b. Mpls., July 11, 1927; s. John E. and Teresa (Franey) N.; m. Joan Dobbins, June 3, 1950; children: Carol N. Klatt, John Edward III (dec.), Kelly N. Spencer, Richard Clark, Patricia N. McNeill. BS, U.S. Naval Acad., 1950; JD, Georgetown U., 1955. Bar: D.C. 1955, U.S. Supreme Ct. 1959, Md. 1961. Law clk. to Justice Clark U.S. Supreme Ct., 1955-56; adminstrv. asst. to Atty. Gen. Robert F. Kennedy, 1963-64; assoc. Steptoe & Johnson, Washington, 1956-62, ptnr., 1962-63, 65—. Assoc. counsel Cuban families com. Cuban Prisoners Exch., Havana, 1962-63; spl. counsel refugee subcom. Senate Jud. Com., Vietnam, 1967-68; mem. CPR Panel of Disting. Neutrals, Washington, U.S. Ct. Appeals mediator D.C. cir.; mem. exec. com. Lawyers Com. for Civil Rights Under Law; bd. dirs. Hooper Holmes, Inc., Iomega, Inc.; vis. fellow Wolfson Coll., Cambridge (Eng.) U., 1987, 92. Trustee Robert F. Kennedy Meml., 1969—; bd. dirs. Fund Dem. Majority; moderator Aspen Inst., 1980—. 2d. Lt. to Capt. USMC, 1950-54, Korea. Decorated Silver Star, Bronze Star with Combat V, Purple Heart. Mem. ABA, D.C. Bar Assn. (gov.), Am. Law Inst., Met. Club (Washington), Congl. Club, Univ. Club (N.Y.C.). Democrat. Roman Catholic. Office: 1330 Connecticut Ave NW Washington DC 20036-1704 E-mail: jnolan@steptoe.com.

NOLAN, JOHN EDWARD, retired electrical corporation executive; b. Bklyn., Apr. 15, 1925; s. John C. and Elizabeth (Reighton) N.; m. Dorothea Scheuermann, Aug. 23, 1952; children: Kathleen, Elizabeth, John Edward, James, Michael, Patricia, Maureen. BEE, Cooper Union, 1950; MSEE, U. Pitts., 1955. With Westinghouse Electric Corp., 1950-90, mem. staff Bettis Atomic Power Lab., 1951-69, with Advanced Reactors div., 1969-79, dir. Hanford Engring. Devel. Lab., 1980-87, pres. Westinghouse Hanford Co., 1988-90; ret., 1990. With U.S. Army, 1943-46, ETO. Mem. IEEE, ASME, Am. Nuclear Soc. Home: 411 Snyder St Richland WA 99352-1945

NOLAN, JOHN JOSEPH, law educator, lawyer; b. Derby, Conn., Nov. 1, 1928; s. Vincent J. and Edna M. (Coté) N.; m. Louise M. McLaughlin, Jan. 18, 1958 (div. Oct. 1974); children: John J., Brian V., Scott R.; m. Adrienne Constance, Aug. 14, 1976; children: Evan G., Alysson C. BS, Holy Cross Coll., 1950; JD, Suffolk U., 1955; LLM, Harvard U., 1962. Assoc. William D. Harlow, Esq., Milford, Conn., 1955-56, Goldstein & Goldstein, Boston, 1956-57; from asst. to full prof. Law Sch. Suffolk U., 1956-62, prof., 1962—75, 1978—2001, prof. emeritus, 2001—; ptnr. Vinci & Nolan, Boston, 1975-78; lectr. Boston U., 1977. Fellow Ford Found., 1961-62. Republican. Roman Catholic. Avocations: skiing, reading, home maintenance and improvement, travel, swimming. Office: Suffolk U Law Sch 120 Tremont St Boston MA 02108-4977 E-mail: jjnolan@acad.suffolk.edu.

NOLAN, JOHN MICHAEL, lawyer; b. Conway, Ark., June 21, 1948; s. Paul Thomas and Peggy (Hime) N. BA, U. Tex., 1970, JD, 1973; LLM in Taxation, George Washington U., 1976. Bar: Tex. 1973, D.C. 1975, U.S. Ct. Mil. Appeals 1973, U.S. Ct. Appeals (D.C. cir.) 1975, U.S. Tax Ct. 1975, U.S. Supreme Ct. 1975. Chief counsel to chief judge U.S. Ct. Mil. Appeals, Washington, 1976-77; assoc. Winstead, McGuire, Sechrest & Minick PC, Dallas, 1977-81; shareholder Winstead Sechrest & Minick PC, 1981—. Editor in Chief The Advocate, 1973-76. Capt. JAGC, U.S. Army, 1973-76. Named one of Outstanding Young Men in Am., U.S. Jaycess, 1976. Mem. ABA (real property, probate and trust sect., real property com., partnerships, joint ventrues, and other investment vehicles), Tex. Bar Assn. (real property, probate and trust sect.), D.C. Bar Assn., Dallas Bar Assn. (real estate group), Tex. Coll. Real Estate Lawyers, Coll. State Bar Tex., Real Estate Coun., Salesmanship Club Dallas, Royal Oaks Country Club. Presbyterian. Home: 6681 Crest Way Ct Dallas TX 75230-2868 Office: Winstead Sechrest & Minick 5400 Renaissance Tower 1201 Elm St Ste 5400 Dallas TX 75270-2199

NOLAN, JOHN THOMAS, JR. retired oil industry administrator; b. Boston, Apr. 15, 1930; s. John T. Sr. and Margaret M. (Craig) N.; m. Mary Sharkey, May 7, 1955; children: Anne, Margaret, John T. III, Stephen, Michael. AB, Cath. U. Am., 1951; PhD, MIT, 1955. Chemist Texaco, Inc., Beacon, N.Y., 1955-59, group leader, 1959-69, supr., 1969-79, asst. mgr., 1979-82, assoc. dir., 1982-87, dir. strategic rsch., 1987-92. Contbr. over 5 articles to profl. jours. Bd. dirs. Cmty. Coll. Found., 1987—, chmn. 1989-92, chmn. planning com. 1992—. Mem. Am. Chem. Soc., Sigma Xi, Phi Beta Kappa. Achievements include patents in field. Home: 18 Relyea Ter Wappingers Falls NY 12590-5824

NOLAN, JOSEPH THOMAS, journalism educator, communications consultant; b. Waterbury, Conn., Apr. 11, 1920; s. Thomas Francis and Mary Margaret (Gaffney) N.; m. Virginia Theodate Tappin, May 6, 1943; children—Carol Nolan Rigolot, David J. AB, Holy Cross Coll., 1942; MA in English Lit., Boston U., 1945; PhD in Econs, NYU, 1973. Washington corr. UPI, 1943-49; writer, copy editor N.Y. Times, N.Y.C., 1949-55; mgr. editorial and press services RCA Corp., 1955-62; sr. v.p. corporate communications Chase Manhattan Bank, 1962-74; prof. journalism and pub. affairs U. S.C., Columbia, 1974-76; v.p. pub. affairs Monsanto Co., St. Louis, 1976-85; Gannett vis. prof. communications U. Fla., 1985-86; prof. communications U. North Fla., Jacksonville, 1986-92; adj. prof. bus. and comm. Flagler Coll., St. Augustine, Fla., 1985—95. Contbr. articles to various mags. Fellow Pub. Rels. Soc. Am. Roman Catholic. Home: 30 Park Terrace Dr Saint Augustine FL 32080-5334

NOLAN, MELISSA, writer, educator; b. Newport News, Va., Mar. 28, 1974; d. Lynn Del and Knstie Klemme Ridley. Bachelor of the arts, William & Mary, Williamsburg, Va, 1997. French, spanish, reading & writing tchg Richmaond Pub. Schs, Richmond, Va., 2000—02; french tchr. Wash. D.c. schools, Washington, 1999—2000; french english tchr. Nottaway county schools, Npttaway, Va., 1997—99. Mem. Modern Lang. Assoc, Nottaway, Va., Albania, 1997—2002, Am, Coun. For Teachers For Lang., Nottoway, Va., 1997—2002, Am. Ass. For Teachers Of French, Nottoway, Va., 1997—2002. Volounteer Maymont Pk., Richmond, va, Va., 2001—02; vol. Avalon Chatlered Women's Shelter, Williamsburg, 1994—96; coach City Intramureal Field League, 1995. Recipient Who's Who In Amercian Educators, Marquis Who's Who, 2001, Whos Who In Am. Coll. Students, 1993; scholar Scholarship To Mla/actfl Conf., for languages assoc. of VA., 1998. Roman Catholic. Achievements include Co-Founder Of C.S. Lewis Club On Yahoo!. Avocations: writing, rugby , singing, travel,reserch. Home: 2000 Lakeview Ave Aptc Richmond VA 23220 Personal E-mail: simonebeauvair@yahoo.com.

NOLAN, OWEN, professional hockey player; b. Belfast, Northern Ireland, Feb. 12, 1972; Selected 1st round NHL entry draft Que. Nordiques, 190, right wing, 1990-96, San Jose Sharks, 1996—. Named to OHL All-Star 1st team, 1989-90; played in NHL All-Star Game 1992, 96. Recipient Emms Family award, 1988-89, Jim Mahon Meml. Trophy, 1989-90. Office: c/o San Jose Sharks 525 W Santa Clara St San Jose CA 95113-1520*

NOLAN, PATRICK BATES, museum director; b. Mpls., Feb. 4, 1942; s. Thomas James and Cecile (Helbling) N.; m. Bobbe Shapiro, Mar. 16, 1963; 1 child, Philip George. BA, U. Minn., 1964, MA, 1967, PhD, 1972. Prof. history U. Wis., River Falls, 1971-73; dir. archives Wright State U., Dayton, Ohio, 1973-88; exec. adminstr. Hagley Mus., Wilmington, Del., 1988-92; program officer Nat. Endowment, Washington, 1985-86; dir. Sam Houston Mus., Huntsville, Tex., 1992—. Cons. Aviation Trail Inc., Dayton, 1973-88, B&O R.R. Mus., Balt., 1991; mem. coun. Tex. Coun. Humanities, Austin, 1998—. Author: Early Flight 1899-1911, 1984, Vigilantes on the Border, 1985, Keeping the Promise, 1988, Kitty Hawk and Beyond, 1990. Vestryman St. Stephens Ch., Huntsville, 1996-97. Fellow Nat. Endowment, 1991, J.J. Hill Reference Libr., St. Paul, 1991, Rockefeller Archives, Tarrytown, N.Y., 1992, Minn. Hist. Soc., St. Paul, 1992. Mem. Rotary (bd. dirs. Huntsville 1995-98).

Avocations: hiking, camping, riding railroads. Home: 3348 Winter Way Huntsville TX 77340 Office: Sam Houston Museum Box 2057 SHSU Huntsville TX 77341 E-mail: smm_pbn@shsu.edu.

NOLAN, PATRICK JOSEPH, screenwriter, playwright, educator; b. Jan. 2, 1933; children: Patrick, Christian, Mark. BA, Villanova U., 1955; MA, U. Detroit, 1961; PhD, Bryn Mawr Coll., 1973. Teaching fellow and mem. faculty dept. English U. Detroit, 1959-62; instr. English Villanova (Pa.) U., 1962-80, prof., 1980—. Playwright: Chameleons, 1980, Midnight Rainbows, 1991; TV screenwriter: The Jericho Mile, 1979 (Emmy award). Vol. dir. devel. Daemion House Cmty. Counseling Ctr. Served to lt. (j.g.) USNR, 1955-59, PTO. Recipient teaching excellence award Philadelphia mag., 1980, Alumni Medallion award Villanova U., 1986. Mem. Writers Guild Am. (West chpt.), Dramatists Guild. Roman Catholic. Avocations: swimming, biking.

NOLAN, PETER JOHN, physics educator; b. N.Y.C., Mar. 25, 1934; s. Peter John and Nora (Gleeson) Nolan; m. Barbara Nolan, 2000; children from previous marriage: Thomas, James, John, Kevin. BS in Physics, Manhattan Coll., 1956; cert. in meteorology, UCLA, 1958; MS in Physics, Adelphi U., 1966, PhD in Physics, 1974. Engr. various corps., N.J., N.Y., 1956-63; systems analysis engr. on lunar module Gruman Aircraft Engring. Corp., Bethpage, N.Y., 1963-66; asst. prof. Physics SUNY, Farmingdale, 1966-68, assoc. prof. Physics, 1968-71, prof. Physics, 1971—. Chmn physics dept SUNY, Farmingdale, 1970—77. Author: Experiments in Physics, 1982, 2d edit., 1995, Electromagnetic Theory for Electrical Technology Students, 1995, Fundamentals of College Physics, 1993, Italian Version, Fundementi Di Fisica, 1996. Mem.: Am Asn Physics Teachers. Home: 47 Fairdale Dr Brentwood NY 11717-1337 Office: SUNY Dept Physics Farmingdale NY 11735 E-mail: nolanpj@farmingdale.edu., peter.nolan@farmingdale.edu.

NOLAN, RICHARD ANTHONY, political scientist, educator; b. Louisville, June 9, 1953; s. Robert William and Elizabeth Maxine Nolan; m. Kim Bernhard Nolan, Feb. 4, 1984; children: Christopher, Kelly. BA, U. Ga., 1975, MA, 1981; PhD, U. Fla., 1994. Libr. asst. U. Colo., Denver, 1983—85; grad. tchg. asst. U. Fla., Gainesville, 1985—93, adj. lectr., 1994—95, 2000—, vis. asst. prof., 1995—2000, vis. lectr. Assoc. dir. Fla. Consortium for Polit. Rsch., Gainesville, 1986—88. Vol. Habitat for Humanity, Gainesville, 1996—, St. Francis House Homeless Shelter, Gainesville, 2000—; coach Pop Warner Youth Football, 1998. Mem.: Internat. Studies Assn., Am. Polit. Sci. Assn. Office: U Fla Dept Polit Sci PO Box 117325 Gainesville FL 32611

NOLAN, RICHARD THOMAS, clergyman, educator; b. Waltham, Mass., May 30, 1937; s. Thomas Michael and Elizabeth Louise (Leishman) N.; life ptnr. Robert C. Pingpank, Sept. 14, 1955. BA, Trinity Coll., 1960; cert. in clin. pastoral edn., Conn. Valley Hosp., 1962; diploma, Berkeley Divinity Sch., 1962; MDiv., Hartford Sem. Found., 1963; postgrad., Union Theol. Sem., N.Y.C., 1963; MA in Religion, Yale U., 1967; PhD, NYU, 1973; postgrad., Ctr. Career Devel. and Ministry, Newton Center, Mass., 1987, Harvard U., 1991. Ordained deacon Episcopal Ch., 1963, priest, 1965; cert. in death, dying and bereavement Waterbury Hosp. Health Ctr., Conn., 1977; notary pub., Fla. Instr. Latin and English Watkinson (Conn.) Sch., 1961-62; instr. math. Choir Sch. of Cathedral of St. John the Divine, N.Y.C., 1962-64; instr. math. and religion, assoc. chaplain Cheshire (Conn.) Acad., 1965-67; instr. Hartford (Conn.) Sem. Found., 1967-68, asst. acad. dean, lectr. philosophy and edn., 1968-70; instr. Mattatuck C.C., Waterbury, Conn., 1969-70, asst. prof. philosophy and history, 1970-74, assoc. prof., 1974-78, prof. philosophy and social sci., 1978-92, prof. emeritus, 1992—; vicar St. Paul's Parish, Bantam, 1974-88, pastor emeritus, 1988—; pres. Litchfield Inst., Conn. and Fla., 1984-96; adj. lectr. in philosophy Palm Beach C. C., Fla., 2000—02. Mem. ethics com. Waterbury Hosp. Health Ctr., 1984—88; vis. and adj. prof. philosophy, theology and religious studies Trinity Coll., Conn., L.I. U., U. Miami, St. Joseph Coll., Conn., Pace U., Teikyo Post U., U. Conn., Hartford Grad. Ctr., Ctrl. Conn. State U., 1964—95, Broward C.C., Fla.; lectr. philosophy and theology Barry U., Fla., 1973, Fla., 1989—92, Fla., 1997—98; adj. assoc. in continuing edn. Berkeley Div. Sch. Yale U., 1987—89; Rabbi Harry Halpern Meml. lectr., Southbury, Conn., 1987; adj. prof. philosophy Fla. Atlantic U., 1999; adj. prof. The Union Inst., Fla., 1999; guest spkr various chs. and orgns.; mem. faculty of cons. examiners Charter Oak State Coll., Conn., 1990—93; assoc. for edn. Christ Ch. Cathedral, Hartford, Conn., 1988—94, hon. canon, Conn., 1991—; cons. Dept. Def. Activity Non-Traditional Ednl. Support, Ednl. Testing Svc., Princeton, NJ, 1990; vis. scholar Coll. Preachers, Washington Nat. Cathedral, 1994; supply priest Episcopal Diocese of S.E. Fla., 1994—2002; ret. priest-in-residence St. Andrew's Ch., Lake Worth, Fla., 2002—. Author: (with H. Titus and M. Smith) Living Issues in Philosophy, 7th edit., 1979, Indonesian edit., 1984, 8th edit., 1986, 9th edit., 1995, (with F. Kirkpatrick) Living Issues in Ethics, 1982, 2d edit., 2000, Chinese edit., 1988 (Honored Author for Books Exceeding 100,000 Copies award 1986); editor, contbr. Diaconate Now, 1968; host Conversations with ..., 1987-89; editor website www.philosophy-religion.org. Rsch. fellow Yale U., 1978, 87; recipient Founder's Day award NYU, 1973. Mem. Am. Acad. Religion, Am. Philos. Assn., Authors Guild, Hemlock Soc. Fla. (adv. bd. 1998—), Interfaith Alliance, Integrity, Boston Latin Sch. Alumni Assn., Tabor Acad. Alumni Assn., McCook Fellows Soc. Trinity Coll., Cavalier King Charles Spaniel Club, Am. Friends of Anglican Centre in Rome, Anglican Assn. Bibl. Scholars, Phi Delta Kappa. Avocation: Cavalier King Charles Spaniels. Home: 2527 Egret Lake Dr West Palm Beach FL 33413-2161 E-mail: canon@rtnolan.com. *Who am I? By baptism I am a resurrected child of God born to love and be loved; my pilgrimage among others is lived within this baptismal identity, more enduring than any achievement.*

NOLAN, STANTON PEELLE, surgeon, educator; b. Washington, May 29, 1933; s. James Parker and Ellen Dubose (Peelle) N.; m. Marion Faro, June 16, 1955; children: Stanton Peelle Jr., Tiphanie Ravenel Clarke. BA, Princeton U., 1955; MD, U. Va., 1959, MS, 1962. Cert. Am. Bd. Surgery, Am. Bd. Thoracic Surgery. Intern U. Va. Med. Ctr., Charlottesville, 1959-60, asst. resident gen. surgery, 1960-61, research fellow surgery, 1961-62, sr. asst. resident gen. surgery, 1962-64, chief resident gen. surgery, 1964-65, chief resident thoracic cardiovascular surgery, 1965-66; sr. rsch. assoc. Clinic of Surgery Nat. Heart Inst., NIH, Bethesda, Md., 1966-68; asst. prof. surgery U. Va. Med. Ctr., Charlottesville, 1968-70, assoc. prof. surgery, 1970-74, surgeon in charge div. thoracic cardiovascular surgery, 1970-93, prof. surgery, 1974-81, Claude A. Jessup prof. surgery, 1981-98, clin. prof. surgery, 1998—, med. dir. Thoracic Cardiovascular post-operative unit, 1989-93. Established investigator Am. Heart Assn., 1969-74; mem. surgery A study sect. NIH, Washington, 1972-76, surgery and bioengring. study sect. 1984-87, chmn. 1985-87; cons. thoracic cardiovascular surgery VA Hosp., Salem, Va., 1968-98, Am. Bd. Surgery cons. to qualifying examination com., 1988-91; surg. cons. Bur. Crippled Children, Charlottesville, 1968-93; vis. cons. cardiothoracic surgery Aga Khan U., Karachi, Pakistan, 1995. Mem. editl. bd. Jour. Surg. Rsch., 1973-79, Annals of Thoracic Surgery, 1979-88; mem. sci. adv. bd. Jour. for Heart Valve Disease, 1993—; mem. editl. adv. bd. ECRI Operating Rm. Risk Mgmt., 1992—; co-editor: Comprehensive Thoracic Surgery Curriculum, TSDA, 1995; contbr. numerous articles to profl. jours., chpts. to books. Bd. mgrs. Ctrl. Va. Health Network, 2000—. Recipient John Horsley Meml. prize U. Va. Med. Sch., 1962; Merit award Research Forum of Am. Coll. Chest Physicians, 1968; research fellow Va. Heart Assn., 1961-62, Am. Cancer Soc., 1963-64; grantee NIH, 1968-84, Am. Heart Assn., 1970-73, Medtronic Corp., 1975-81 Fellow ACS (com. allied health pers. 1996—, exec. com. 1997-2000, vice chair, exec. com. rep. to Am. Acad. Physician Assts. 1997—), Am. Coll. Cardiology, Am. Surg. Assn.; mem. Am. Assn. Thoracic Surgery (rep. to Assn. Am. Med. Colls., Am. Bd. Cardiovascular Perfusion, Am. Soc. Extracorporeal Tech., others), Am. Heart Assn. (coun. on cardiovascular surgery 1969-99, anesthesiology, radiology and surgery study com. 1991-94), Andrew G. Morrow Soc., Assn. Acad. Surgery, Assn. Advancement of Med. Instrumentation (chair 1998-2000, chair-elect 1996, co-chmn. cardiac valve prostheses stds. com. 1974—, mem. internat. stds. com. 1989—, bd. dirs. 1990-2000, stds. bd. 1991—, edn. com. 1992-93, nominating com. 1996-2000, chair 1998-2000, exec. com. 1996-2000, govt. rels. com. 1996-2000), Internat. Stds. Orgn. (chmn. subcom. on cardiovascular surg. implants 1982—), Assn. Clin. Cardiac Surgeons, Halsted Soc. (exec. com. 1985-89), Coord. Com. on Perfusion Affairs (chmn. 1990-2000), Internat. Assn. Cardiac Biol. Implants (sci. com. 1994), Am. Assn. for Vascular Surgery, Muller Surg. Soc. (pres. 1979), Soc. Internat. de Cirurgie, Soc. Vascular Surgery, Soc. Thoracic Surgeons (ad hoc com. on industry rels. 1992-97, stds. and ethics com. 1993-95, 98-2001, edn. and resources com. 1996-97), Soc. Univ. Surgeons, Southeastern Surg. Congress, So. Surg. Assn. (2d v.p. 1982), Thoracic Surgery Found. Rsch. and Edn. (chair New Century Soc. com. 1997-2000), Va. Surg. Soc. (v.p. 1980-83, pres. 1984), Va. Vascular Soc. (exec. coun. 1985-86), Soc. Critical Care Medicine, Raven Soc., Assn. Am. Med. Colls. (rep. coun. acad. socs. 1992-01), Alpha Omega Alpha, Omicron Delta Kappa. Clubs: Chevy Chase (Md.); Farmington Country (Va.); Princeton (N.Y.C.). Office: U Va TCV Surgery PO Box 800679 Charlottesville VA 22908-0679 E-mail: snolan@virginia.edu.

NOLAN, VAL, JR. biologist, lawyer; b. Evansville, Ind., Apr. 28, 1920; s. Val and Jeannette (Covert) N.; m. Susanne Howe, Dec. 23, 1946 (div. Aug. 29, 1980); children: Val, Ann Clare, William Alan; m. Ellen D. Ketterson, Oct. 17, 1980. AB, Ind. U., 1941, JD, 1949. Bar: Ind. 1949. Dep. U.S. marshal, 1941; agt. White House Detail, U.S. Secret Service, 1942; asst. prof. law Ind. U., 1949-52, assoc. prof., 1952-56, prof., 1956-85, prof. emeritus, 1985—, research scholar in zoology, 1957-68, prof. zoology, 1968-77, prof. biology, 1977-85; prof. emeritus, 1985—; acting dean Sch. Law, 1976, 80. Author: (with F.E. Horack, Jr.) Land Use Controls, 1955, Ecology and Behavior of the Prairie Warbler, 1978; editor Ind. Law Jour., 1945-46, Jour. Avian Biology, 1998—; co-editor Current Ornithology, 1994—. Served with USNR, 1942-46. Guggenheim fellow, 1957; recipient Ind. U. Disting. Alumni Svc. award, 1987; named to Acad. Law Alumni Fellows, Ind. U., 1988. Fellow AAAS, Am. Ornithologists Union (v.p. 1989-90, Brewster Meml. award 1986); mem. Brit. Ornithologists Union, Cooper Ornithol. Soc., Wilson Ornithol. Soc. (co-recipient Margaret M. Nice award 1998), Assn. Field Ornithologists, Ecol. Soc. Am., Am. Soc. Naturalists, Animal Behavior Soc., Deutsche Ornithologen-Gesellschaft, Nederlandse Ornithologische Unie, Soc. for Study of Reprodn., Phi Beta Kappa, Sigma Xi. Democrat. Home: 4675 E Heritage Woods Rd Bloomington IN 47401-9312

NOLAN, VICTORIA, theater director; b. Portland, Maine, June 15, 1952; d. Herbert Wallace and Diane Katharine (Kremm) N.; m. Clarkson Newell Crolius, Aug. 30, 1980; children: Covey Emmeline, Wilhelmina Adams. BA magna cum laude, U. Maine, 1976. Publicity asst. Loeb Drama Ctr. Harvard U., Cambridge, Mass., 1975; pub. rels. asst. to dir. Sch. for Arts Boston U., 1975-76; mgmt. asst. TAG Found., N.Y.C., 1976-77; mng. dir. Ram Island Dance Co., Portland, 1977-78; dir. devel. Ctr. Stage, Balt., 1979-81, assoc. mng. dir., 1981-87; mng. dir. Ind. Repertory Theatre, Indpls., 1988-93; dep. dean, mng. dir., prof. Yale Sch. Drama, Yale Repertory Theatre, New Haven, 1993—. Program evaluator Nat. Endowment for Arts, Washington, 1988—, panelist, 1991—; mem. Indpls. Cultural Consortium, v.p., 1991-93; bd. dirs. Greater Indpls. Progress Com., Indpls. Urban League, Arts Coun. Indpls.; mem. nat. bd. Theatre Comm. Group, N.Y.C., treas., 1995-99; bd. dirs. New Haven Arts Industry Coalition, co-chair, 1997-99, treas., 1999—. Mem. exec. com. League Resident Profl. Theatres. Nat. Performing Arts Mgmt. fellow Exxon, Doner Fedn. and NEA, 1978; Elizabeth L. Mahaffey arts adminstrn. fellow Conn. Commn. on the Arts, 2000. Home: 120 Rimmon Rd Woodbridge CT 06525-1915 Office: Yale Repertory Theater PO Box 208244 Yale Station 222 York St New Haven CT 06520-8244

NOLAN, WILLIAM JOSEPH, III, banker; b. N.Y.C., Apr. 6, 1947; s. William J. Jr. and Alice Nettleton (Edwards) N.; m. Wendy Collison French, Mar. 21, 1981; children: William J. IV, Anina Chrysler. Student, Hackley Sch., Tarrytown, N.Y., 1958-65; E.S.U. scholar, Eastbourne Coll., U.K., 1966; BA, Colgate U., 1970; MBA, Stanford U., 1973. V.p. Bankers Trust Co., N.Y.C., 1973-83; mng. dir. Becker-Paribas, 1983-84; exec. v.p., treas. PaineWebber, 1984-2001. Bd. trustees Adirondack Mus. (Blue Mountain), 1996—, (treas. 2000—). Mem. Pub. Securities Assn. (money market exec. com. 1985-89, chmn. 1987, bd. dirs. 1988-91, treas. 1990), Adirondack League, Piping Rock Club, Union Club of N.Y.C. Home: 1088 Park Ave New York NY 10128-1132 E-mail: billnolan1088@aol.com.

NOLAND, CHARLES DONALD, lawyer, educator; b. Tulsa, July 31, 1946; s. Clyde Earl and Birdeen Elizabeth (White) N.; m. Elisabeth Hooper Reynolds, June 27, 1987; 1 stepchild, Richard G. Reynolds. BA in Journalism, U. N.Mex., 1972, JD, 1978. Bar: N.Mex. 1978, U.S. Dist. Ct. N.Mex. 1979, U.S. Ct. Appeals (10th cir.) 1991, U.S. Supreme Ct. 1991. Reporter, copy editor New Mexican, Santa Fe, 1968, 69; newsman AP, Des Moines, 1969-71, Albuquerque, 1968-69, 73-74; editor programmed instrn. materials Systema Corp., 1974-75; pvt. practice, 1978-79; from asst. gen. counsel to gen. counsel N.Mex. Dept. Edn., Santa Fe, 1979-83; asst. atty. gen. State of N.Mex., 1984-85; pvt. practice, 1985-95; dep. gen. counsel N.Mex. Dept. Corrections, 1995-97; legal counsel Spl. Edn. Office N.Mex. Dept. Edn., 1997—. Adj. prof. U. N.Mex. Grad. Sch. Edn., 1981, 92, 98, N.Mex. Highlands U. Grad. Sch. Edn., 1985, Coll. Santa Fe, 1984-89; pvt. practice, of counsel Simons, Cuddy & Friedman, Santa Fe, 1985-95; hearing officer tchr. termination appeals N.Mex. Bd. Edn., 1980, 81; presenter N.Mex. Sch. Bds., Assn. Law Conf., 1980-95, 98, 2002; panelist pub. sch. reduction in force Nat. Sch. Bds. Assn. Conv., Dallas, 1981; participant Lawyers Adv. Opinion Project, N.Mex. Ct. Appeals, 1986-87. Contbr. articles to profl. jours. Founding bd. dirs. Santa Fe Symphony Orch., 1984-85, corp. sec., 1985-88; community musician Santa Fe Concert Band, Santa Fe Brass Ensemble, 1983-89; mem. audit com. Christ the King Episc. Mission, 1996, chair 1997, treas., 1998; mem. Holy Faith Episc. Ch., 1998—, mem. choir, 1999— Mem. State Bar N.Mex. (pub. advocacy sect., alt. dispute resolution), N.Mex. Assn. Sch. Bd. Attys. (treas. 1980-83, pres. 1987-88, 90-93). Avocation: trombone. Home: 2 Pino Pl Santa Fe NM 87508-8750 Office: NMex Dept Edn Spl Edn Office 300 Don Gaspar Ave Santa Fe NM 87501-2786 E-mail: cnoland@sde.state.nm.us.

NOLAND, KENNETH CLIFTON, artist; b. Asheville, N.C., Apr. 10, 1924; s. Harry C. and Bessie (Elkins) N.; m. Cornelia Langer (div.); children: Cady, William L., Lyndon; m. Stephanie Gordon, 1967 (div.); m. Peggy Schiffer; children: Samuel Jesse (div.); m. Paige Rense, 1994. Student, Ozzip Zadkine, Paris, 1948-49; studied, Black Mountain Coll., N.C., summers, 1950, 51. Tchr. Inst. Contemporary Arts, 1950-52, Cath. U., 1951-60. One man shows include Galerie Creuze, Paris, 1949, Tibor de Nagy Gallery, N.Y.C., 1957, 58, Jefferson Pl. Gallery, 1958, French & Co., N.Y.C., 1959, Bennington Coll., 1961, Andre Emmerich Gallery, N.Y.C., 15 shows from 1960-83, Andre Emmerich Gallery, Zurich, Switzerland, 1973, 76, 79, 82, David Mirvish Gallery, Toronto, Can., 1965, 67, 74, 76, Jewish Mus., 1965, Salander O'Reilly Galleries, N.Y.C., 1989, Leo Castelli Gallery, N.Y., 1995, Gana Art Gallery, Seoul, 1995-96, also other galleries in Milan, Italy, Paris, Zurich, Dusseldorf, Hamburg and Cologne, Fed. Republic Germany, London, Montreal and Toronto, Can.; retrospective show Guggenheim Mus., N.Y.C., 1977; group shows include Kootz Gallery, N.Y.C., 1954, Norman Mackenzie Art Gallery, Regina, Sask., Can., 1963, Corcoran Gallery, Washington, 1956, 59, 63, 64, 67, 70, 75, Corcoran Gallery Biennial in Italy, 1964, Fogg Art Mus., Cambridge, Mass., 1965, 72, Mus. Modern Art, N.Y.C., 1965, 68, Nat. Gallery, Washington, 1968, U.S. Pavilion Expo 67, Montreal, Art Inst. Chgo., 1962, 70, 72, 76, Balt. Mus., 1957, 70, 77, Jewish Mus., 1963, Tate Gallery, London, 1964, 74, Guggenheim Mus., 1961, 66, 70, 73-74, 76-77, L.A. County Mus., 1964, Inst. Contemporary Art, Boston, 1964, 65, 67, Whitney Mus., N.Y.C., 1961-67, 69-73, 76, Met. Mus. N.Y.C., 1968, 70, Mus. Fine Arts, Boston, 1972, Albright-Knox Gallery, Buffalo, 1978, 80, Ameringer Howard Fine Art, NY, 99; Meredith Long Gall., Houston ,Tex., 99; Andre Emmerich, CLosing Exhibition of Gall., NY, 99; CHAC-Mool Gall., CA, 99, Ameringer/Howard Gall., N.Y.C, 1999-2001, Farnsworth Mus. Art, Maine, 2002, Naples (Fla.) Mus., 2002; represented in permanent collections Salander O'Reily Galleries, N.Y.C., Mus. of Fine Arts, Houston, 1994, Ft. Lauderdale, 1994; Arte Metro Roma, Rome Colosseum Ctrl. Subway Mosaic Installed, 1995. Trustee Bennington (Vt.) Coll. Recipient 1st prize Premio Nacional Internat., Inst. Torcuato de Tella, Buenos Aires, 1964, Creative Arts award Brandeis U., 1965, 4th prize Corcoran Biennale, 1967; recipient The N.C. Award/medal of arts, 1995.

NOLAND, MARCUS, economist, educator; b. Greensboro, N.C., Mar. 29, 1959; BA, Swarthmore Coll., 1981; PhD, Johns Hopkins U., 1985. Sr. fellow Inst. for Internat. Econs., Washington, 1985—; asst. prof. U. So. Calif., L.A., 1990-91; sr. economist Coun. Econ. Advisers, Washington, 1993-94. Vis. prof. Saitama U., Urawa, Japan, 1988—89; vis. scholar Korea Devel. Inst., Seoul, 1991; vis. assoc. prof. Johns Hopkins U., Balt., 1991—98; vis. prof. Tokyo U., 1996, U. Ghana, 1997; cons. Internat. Food Policy Rsch. Inst., 1999—; POSCO vis. fellow East-West Ctr., Honolulu, 2000. Author: Pacific Basin Developing Countries, 1991, Avoiding the Apocalypse: The Future of the Two Koreas, 2000; editor: Economic Integration on the Korean Penninsula, 1998; co-author: Japan in the World Economy, 1988, Reconcilable Differences?, 1993, Global Effects of the Asian Currency Devaluations, 1998; co-editor: Pacific Economic Dynamism, 1993; co-author: No More Bashings: Building A New Japan-U.S. Economic Relationship, 2001. Recipient Ohira Meml. prize, 2002; Japan Soc. for Promotion of Sci. fellow, 1988, Internat. Affairs fellow Coun. on Fgn. Rels., 1993, Coun. for Internat. Exch. of Scholars fellow, 1997. Mem. Coun. on Fgn. Rels. Office: Inst for Internat Econs 1750 Massachusetts Ave NW Washington DC 20036-1207 E-mail: mnoland@iie.com.

NOLAND, MARIAM CHARL, foundation executive; b. Parkersburg, W.Va., Mar. 29, 1947; d. Lloyd Henry and Ethel May (Beare) Noland; m. James Arthur Kelly, June 13, 1981. BS, Case Western Res. U., 1969; M in Edn., Harvard U., 1975. Asst. dir admissions, fin. aid Baldwin-Wallace Coll., Berea, Ohio, 1969-72; asst. dir. admissions Davidson (N.C.) Coll., 1972-74; case writer Inst. Edn. Mgmt., Cambridge, Mass., 1975; sec., treas., program officer The Cleve. Found., 1975-81; v.p. The St. Paul Found., 1981-85; pres. Community Found. for S.E. Mich., 1985—. Bd. trustees Coun. Mich. Founds., 1988-98, Coun. on Founds., 1994-99, Henry Ford Health System, 1994—, Alma Coll., 1994—; commr. Detroit 300, 2000-01. Office: Community Found Southeastern Mich 333 W Fort St Ste 2010 Detroit MI 48226-3134 Business E-Mail: mnoland@voager.net.

NOLAND, ROYCE PAUL, association executive, physical therapist; b. Walla Walla, Wash., Dec. 6, 1928; s. Homer Vernon and Mildred Bessie (Royce) N.; m. April Lynn Hawkes, Feb. 10, 1979; children— Royce Paul, Richard Mitchell BA, Whitman Coll., Walla Walla, Wash., 1951; Cert. in phys. therapy, Stanford U., 1952. Pvt. practice in phys. therapy, Santa Cruz, Calif., 1961-68; exec. dir. Calif. chpt. Am. Phys. Therapy Assn., 1965-69, exec. dir. Washington, 1969-87; pres., chief exec. officer Inst. Profl. Health Service Adminstrs., Alexandria, 1988-91; exec. dir., CEO Fedn. of State Bds. of Phys. Therapy, Va., 1992-97; CEO. Nat. Phys. Rehab. Networks, Inc., 1997-2000; ret., 2000. Co-inventor phys. therapy device; contbr. articles to profl. publs. Mem. Am. Soc. Assn. Execs. (cert.), Presdl. Commn. Employment of Handicapped, Am. Pub. Health Assn. Clubs: Belle Haven Country (Alexandria). Republican. Avocation: golf. Home: 2302 Popkins Ln Alexandria VA 22306-2443

NOLD, AURORA R. business and economics educator; b. Honolulu, Apr. 21, 1958; m. Allan Jeffrey Nold, Aug. 1, 1995. BSBA cum laude, St. Louis U., 1969, MS in Bus. Adminstrn. magna cum laude, 1975, PhD, 1986. Exch. prof., dept. chairperson mgmt. St. Louis U., Baguio City, Philippines, 1980-86; rsch. asst. East/West Ctr. for Am. Studies, Honolulu, 1986-87; dir. Am. studies United State Info. Svcs., Washington, 1987-89; fin. cons. Shadow Hill Samaritan, Long Beach, Calif., 1989-93; dir. A&A Edu Care Consultancy Programs, Inc., Las Vegas, Nev., 1993—. Bd. advisors Am. Biog. Inst., Raleigh, N.C., 1995—, Internat. Biog. Ctr., Cambridge, Eng., 1995—; rschr. S.H.S. Inc., Las Vegas, 1995—; prof. econs., bus and mgmt. C.C. So. Nev.; prof. stats. U. Nev., Las Vegas; tutor C.C. So. Nev. Author: Business Education in the Philippines, 1986; contbr. articles to profl. jours. Pres. Rep. Presdl. Task Force, Las Vegas, 1995—. Cultural Exch. grant Fulbright Am. Studies, 1987, scholarship grant St. Louis U., 1979-86; recipient Appreciation award Nat. Humane Edn. Soc., 1996, Nat. Park Trust, 1996, Nat. Law Enforcement Officers Meml. Fund, 1997, Oustanding Cmty. and Profl. Achievement Commemorative medal Am. Biog. Inst., 1997, internat. cultural diploma of honor, 2000. Mem. AAUW, NAFE, Asian Am. Studies Assn., U.S. Profl. Bookkeepers Assn., Nev. Faculty Alliance. Republican. Mem. Lds Ch. Avocations: collecting rare coins, writing, reading, music and coin collecting. Office: A&A Edu Care Consultancy Programs Unit 657-10 7812 Clarkdale Dr Las Vegas NV 89128-3866 E-mail: auroranold@cs.com.

NOLEN, CRYSTAL ME'KELLE, poet, educator; b. Lexinton Park, Md., July 2, 1972; d. A. Jay, Jr. and Carolyn L. Nolen; children: Stanley, Garney. BA in English, Norfolk State U., 1999. Teacher's asst., sch. cmty. trainer Norfolk (Va.) Pub. Sch. Sys., 1993—. Coord. Million Woman Mar. Bus Trip, Norfolk, 1997. Actor: (plays) Summers in Suffolk, 2000. Home: PO Box 367 Portsmouth VA 23705 Personal E-mail: Cryswrites2000@aol.com.

NOLEN, ROY LEMUEL, b. Montgomery, Ala., Nov. 29, 1937; s. Roy Lemuel Jr. and Elizabeth (Larkin) N.; m. Evelyn McNeill Thomas, Aug. 28, 1965; 1 child, Rives Rutledge. BArch, Rice U., 1961; LLB, Harvard U., 1967. Bar: Tex. 1968, U.S. Ct. Appeals (5th cir.) 1969. Law clk. to sr. judge U.S. Ct. Appeals (5th cir.), 1967-68; assoc. Baker Botts LLP, Houston, 1968-75, ptnr., 1976-2000; co-head Corp. Dept., 1985-90; mem. exec. com., 1988-91; adminstrv. ptnr., 1997-2000; ret., 2000. Cmty. rep. instnl. animal care and use com. M.D. Anderson Cancer Ctr., 2001—. Bd. dirs. Houston Ballet Found., 1980-92, Rice Design Alliance, 1995-96; exec. com. Contemporary Arts Mus., 1990-96, 97—; exec. com. Houston Symphony Soc., 1994-99, gen. counsel, 1994-98; bd. dirs. Menil Found. (Menil Collection), 1999—, sr. warden Christ Ch. Cathedral, 1991-92; chmn. Houston area devel. initiative Episcopal Diocese of Tex., 1997. 1st lt. USMC, 1961-64. Mem. State Bar of Tex., Coronado Club, Allegro, Paul Jones Dancing Club. Episcopalian. Office: Baker Botts LLP One Shell Plz 910 Louisiana St Houston TX 77002-4995

NOLEN, SUSAN CARDILLO, insurance executive, lawyer; b. Rochester, N.Y., July 21, 1960; d. Arnold Edwin and Mary Louise Cardillo; m. Raymond Joseph Nolen, III, Dec. 10, 1988; children: Katherine, Raymond IV, Laura. BA, Bucknell U., 1982; JD, Case Western Res. U., 1985. Bar: Pa. 1986, N.J. 1986. Assoc. Griffith & Burr, PC, Phila., 1985-86; house counsel Physicians Ins. Co., Plymouth Meeting, Pa., 1986-89; asst. v.p., assoc. gen. counsel, asst. sec. Gen. Accident Ins., Phila., 1989-94, v.p. human resources, 1994-97, corp. sr. v.p. bus. svcs., 1997-98; corp. sr. v.p. CGU Ins., 1998-99. Adult edn. instr. St. Francis De Sales, Aston, Pa., 1996—; parent vol. Indian Lane Elem. Sch., Media, Pa., 1998, 99, Girl Scouts of Am., Media, 1998, 99. Mem. ABA, Phila. Bar Assn., Ins. Soc. Phila. (adv. bd. corp. career opportunity program 1994-97), Omicron Delta Kappa, Phi Delta Phi. Republican. Roman Catholic. Avocations: golf, running, photography, music. Home: 380 Olde House Ln Media PA 19063-5320

NOLEN, WILLIAM GILES, lawyer, accountant; b. Fayetteville, Ark., Aug. 4, 1931; s. William Jefferson and Marie (Giles) N.; m. Carole Turner, Aug. 25, 1957; children: Kathy, Thomas (dec.). BSBA, U. Ark., 1960; JD, U. Houston, 1980. Bar: Tex. 1980; CPA, Tex. Auditor Arthur Andersen & Co., Houston, 1960-66; sec., treas. Brown & Root (U.K.) Ltd., London, 1966-69; v.p. Highlands Ins. Co., Houston, 1969-73, sr. v.p., 1973-80, dir., 1973-88; v.p. Halliburton Co., Dallas, 1980-82; sr. v.p. Brown & Root, Inc., Houston, 1982-86; exec. v.p. Highlands Ins. Co., 1986-88; of counsel Whitmore, Sheppard & Pollicoff, 1988-92, Policoff, Smith & Myres LLP, Houston, 1992-95, Policoff, Smith, Myres & Remels LLP, Houston, 1995-2000, Pollicoff, Smith & Remels, Houston, 2000—. Maj. USAF, 1951-56. Mem. Am. Assn. Atty. CPAs (past pres., bd. dirs.), Tex. Soc. CPAs (Tex. CPA of Yr. 1961), Mensa. Presbyterian.

NOLF, DAVID M. financial consultant; b. Hartford, Conn., Nov. 25, 1942; s. Richard A. and Erreld I. (Manstan) N.; m. Linda J. Anderson, June 20, 1964; 1 child, Cristina E. BSChemE, Lafayette Coll., 1964; MBA, U. Conn., 1968. Prodn. engr. Am. Cyanamid, Wallingford, Conn., 1664-66; adminstrn. supr. Electric Boat Div. Gen. Dynamics, Groton, 1966-71; chief fin. and adminstrv. officer, corp. sec. Analysis and Tech. Inc., North Stonington, 1971—99; cons., 2001—. Bd. dirs. Analysis and Tech., Inc., North Stonington, Conn., 1978—99. Chmn. Ch. Fin. Com., Westerly, R.I., 2002—; trustee Westerly Hosp., 1993—, vice-chmn. 2002—; bd. dirs. The Day Newspaper, 1997—, bd. dirs. Mem.: Beta Gamma Sigme, Tau Beta Pi. Avocations: fishing, golf. Home: 347 Lantern Hill Rd Mystic CT 06355-3623

NOLFI, EDWARD ANTHONY, lawyer; b. Warren, Ohio, Sept. 30, 1958; s. Eugene Vincent Sr. and Margaret Joyce (Futey) N.; m. Sheri Ann Loue, June 5, 1982. AB, Brown U., 1980; JD, U. Akron, 1983. Bar: Ohio 1983, N.Y. 1986, U.S. Dist. Ct. (no. dist.) Ohio 1987, U.S. Tax Ct. 1987, U.S. Ct. Appeals (6th cir. 1989), U.S. Supreme Ct. 1989. Juggler Miracle Sta., Warren, 1976; instr. Sch. One, Providence, 1980; tech. writer Doctors' Hosp., Massillon, Ohio, 1982; pvt. practice Warren, 1983-84; assoc. editor Lawyers Coop. Pub. Co., Rochester, N.Y., 1985-87; pvt. practice Akron, Ohio, 1987—. Prof. Acad. Ct. Reporting, Akron, 1988-91; prof. Kent State U., 1993, Mt. Aloysius Coll., Cresson, Pa., 1996; product developer and lead sr. case law editor LexisNexis,

Miamisburg, Ohio, 1999—. Author: The Master Juggler, 1980, Basic Legal Research, 1993, Basic Wills, Trusts, and Estates, 1995; articles editor Am. Law Reports, Fed., 1986-87. Mem. ABA. Roman Catholic. Avocation: juggling. Home: 1101 E Archwood Ave Akron OH 44306-2857 E-mail: nolfi@netzero.net.

NOLL, RICHARD DEAN, JR. psychologist, educator and historian; b. Detroit, Oct. 27, 1959; s. Richard Dean and Betty Ann (Adamczak) Noll; m. Mary Beth McAndrews, Apr. 27, 1986 (div. 1993); m. Susan J. Naylor, May 13, 1994 (div. 2002); 1 child Wolfgang Naylor ;1 child Dylan James Patterson. BA, U. Ariz., 1979; MA, New Sch. for Social Rsch., 1982; PhD, New Sch. for Rsch., 1992. Lic. clin. psychologist, Pa. Staff clin. psychologist Ancora Psychiat. Hosp., Hammonton, N.J., 1985-88; clin. psychologist in pvt. practice Phila., 1988-92; instr. dept. psychology West Chester (Pa.) U., 1992-94; postdoctoral fellow Harvard U., Cambridge, Mass., 1994-96, Lectr. in History of Sci., 1997-98; resident fellow Dibner Inst. History of Sci. and Tech. MIT, 1995-96; asst. prof. psychology De Sales Univ., Center Valley, Pa., 2000—. Invited lectr. Acad. Scis., Budapest, Hungary, 1991, Warsaw U., 1991, Chinese Acad. Scis., Beijing, 1994; vis. scholar MIT, 1995-96. Author: The Encyclopedia of Schizophrenia and the Psychotic Disorders, 1992, 2d rev. edit., 2000, Vampires, Werewolves and Demons: Twentieth Century Case Reports in the Psychiatric Literature, 1992, The Jung Cult, 1994 (named best book in psychology Assn. Am. Publishers 1994), The Aryan Christ, 1997, Encyclopedia of Schizophrenia and Other Psychotic Disorders, rev. 2d edit., 2000; contbr. articles to profl. jours. Wenner-Gren Found. for Anthropol. Rsch. grantee, 1993. Mem. APA, History of Sci. Soc., Soc. for Sci. of Clin. Psychology. E-mail: richard.noll@desales.edu.

NOLL, ROGER GORDON, economist, educator; b. Monterey Park, Calif., Mar. 13, 1940; s. Cecil Ray and Hjordis Alberta (Westover) Noll; m. Robyn Schreiber, Aug. 25, 1962 (dec. Jan. 2000); 1 child Kimberlee Elizabeth ; m. Ann Seminara, Dec. 2, 2001. BS, Calif. Inst. Tech., 1962; AM, Harvard U., 1965, PhD in Econs, 1967. Mem. social sci. faculty Calif. Inst. Tech., 1965-84, prof., 1973-82, inst. prof., 1982-84, chmn. div. humanities and social scis., 1978-82; prof. econs. Stanford U., 1984—, Morris M. Doyle centennial prof. of pub. policy, 1990—2002, dir. pub. policy program, 1986—2002, dir. Ctr. Rsch. Econ. Devel. and Policy Reform, 2002—; Jean Monnet prof. European U. Inst., 1991; vis. fellow Brookings Instn., 1995-96, non-resident sr. fellow, 1996—2000, dir. Am. Studies Program, 2001—01. Sr. staff economist Coun. Econ. Advisors, Washington, 1967—69; sr. fellow Brookings Instn., Washington, 1970—73; mem. tech. adv. bd. Com. Econ. Devel., 1978—82; mem. adv. coun. NSF, 1978—89, NASA, 1978—81, SERI, 1982—90; mem. Pres.'s Commn. Nat. Agenda for Eighties, 1980; chmn. L.A. Sch. Monitoring Com., 1978—79; mem. Commn. Behavioral Social Scis. and Edn. NAS, 1984—90, mem. bd. sci., tech. and econ. policy, 2000—; mem. energy rsch. adv. bd. Dept. Energy, 1986—89; mem. Sec. Energy Adv. Bd., 1990—94, Calif. Coun. Sci. and Tech., 1995—2000. Author: (book) Reforming Regulation, 1971, The Economics and Politics of Deregulation, 1991, The Economics and Politics of the Slowdown in Regulatory Reform, 1999; co-author: Economic Aspects of Television Regulation, 1973, The Political Economy of Deregulation, 1983, The Technology Pork Barrel, 1991; editor: Government and the Sports Business, 1974, Regulatory Policy and the Social Sciences, 1985, Challenges to Research Universities, 1998; co-editor: Constitutional Reform in California, 1995, Sports, Jobs and Taxes, 1997, A Communications Cornucopia, 1998; supervisory editor: Info. Econs. and Policy Jour., 1984—92. Recipient 1st ann. book award, Nat. Assn. Ednl. Broadcasters, 1974; fellow Guggenheim, 1983—84; grantee NSF, 1973—82. Mem.: Am. Econ. Assn. Democrat. Home: 4153 Hubbartt Dr Palo Alto CA 94306-3834 Office: Stanford U Dept Econs Stanford CA 94305

NOLLAU, LEE GORDON, lawyer; b. Balt., Feb. 6, 1950; s. E. Wilson and Carolyn G. (Blass) N.; m. Carol A. Haughney, Aug. 12, 1978; children: Ann G., Catherine E., Margaret C. BA, Juniata Coll., 1972; MAS, Johns Hopkins U., 1975; JD, Dickinson Sch. Law, 1976. Bar: Pa. 1976, U.S. Dist. Ct. (mid. dist.) 1982, U.S. Dist. Ct. (we. dist.) 1988, U.S. Ct. Appeals (3d cir.) 1980, U.S. Supreme Ct. 1982. Instr. Juniata Coll., Huntingdon, Pa., 1976-78; asst. dist. atty. Centre County, Bellefonte, 1978-80, dist. atty., 1981; assoc. Litke, Lee, Martin, Grine & Green, 1981-83, Jubelirer & Assocs., State College, Pa., 1983-87; ptnr. Jubelirer, Nollau, Young & Blanarik, Inc., 1988-89, Jubelirer, Rayback, Nollau, Walsh, Young & Blanarik, Inc., State College, 1989-94, Nollau & Young, State Coll., Pa., 1994—. Mental health rev. officer Centre County, Bellefonte, 1982—; instr. Pa. State U. Smeal Coll. Bus. Adminstrn., 1995—; lectr., author Pa. Bar Inst., 1995—. Author: Trial Tactics: Ten Tips for Direct Examination. Mem. ABA, Pa. Bar Assn., Centre Co. Bar, Pa. Assn. Criminal Def. Lawyers. Presbyterian. Office: Nollau & Young 2153 E College Ave State College PA 16801-7204

NOLLETTI, JAMES JOSEPH, lawyer; b. Portchester, N.Y., Sept. 20, 1953; s. James Louis and Anne Marie (Mandracchia) N.; children: Jay, Justin, Jamie-Lynn, Jeff. BA, Villanova U., 1975; JD, Fordham U., 1978. Bar: N.Y. 1979, U.S. Dist. Ct. (so. dist.) N.Y., U.S. Supreme Ct. Asst. dist. atty. Westchester County Dist. Atty.'s Office, White Plains, N.Y., 1978-81; assoc. Sirlin & Sirlin, Mamaroneck, 1981-84; ptnr. Sirlin, Sirlin & Nolletti, 1984-99, Pirro, Collier, Cohen & Halpern LLP, White Plains, N.Y.C., 1999-2000, Collier, Halpern, Newberg, Nolletti & Bock, LLP, White Plains, N.Y.C., 2000—. Village atty. Village of Mamaroneck, 1985-99; mem. adv. bd. Westchester Abstract Co., White Plains, 1985-88; bd. dirs., legal advisor Orienta Beach Club, Inc., Mamaroneck, 1986-90. Commr. ABC bd. Westchester County, White Plains, 1984-88, Westchester County Pub. Employees Rels. Bd., 1986-88. Mem. ATLA, ABA, N.Y. State Bar Assn., Westchester County Bar Assn., Westchester County Col. Lawyers Bar Assn. (bd. dirs., v.p. 1989-93). Office: Collier Halpern Newberg Nolletti & Bock LLP One North Lexington Ave White Plains NY 10601 also: Collier Halpern Newberg Nolletti & Bock LLP 99 Park Ave New York NY 10016-1601 Fax: 914-684-6986; 212-696-4064. E-mail: jnolletti@chnnb.com.

NOLLY, ROBERT J. hospital administrator, pharmaceutical science educator; b. Amsterdam, N.Y., Jan. 8, 1947; m. Diera R. Lehtonen, June 21, 1969; children: Shelby Alexandra, Kirby Alycia, Kendall Alexis. BS in Pharmacy with honor, Albany Coll. Pharmacy, 1970; MSc in Hosp. Pharmacy, Ohio State U., 1979. Pharmacy extern Matt Pharmacy, Canajoharie, N.Y., 1967-70; pharmacy intern Park Row Drugs, 1970-71, asst. mgr., 1971-72; staff pharmacist Mary Imogene Bassett Hosp., Cooperstown, N.Y., 1972-74, 75-77; med. svc. rep. Dista Products Co., Eli Lilly and Co., Indpls., 1974-75; resident hosp. pharmacy Grant Hosp., Columbus, Ohio, 1977-79; asst. dir. pharmacy svcs. City of Memphis Hosp., 1979-81, U. Tenn. Bowld Hosp., Memphis, 1980-82, dir. pharmacy svcs. and materials mgmt., 1982-85, asst. adminstr. pharmacy svcs. and materials mgmt., 1985-91, adminstr. ops., 1991—, exec. dir., 1999—. Asst. prof. dept. pharmacy practice Coll. Pharmacy U. Tenn., Memphis, 1979-83, asst. prof. dept. health sci. adminstrn. dept. pharmaceutics, 1983-92, assoc. prof. dept. clin. pharmacy divsn. pharmacy adminstrn., 1992-96, assoc. prof. dept. pharm. scis., 1992—, assoc. prof. Dept. Pharmacy Practice and Pharmacoeconomics, 1996—; attended confs., mgmt. tng. programs in field; lectr. Columbus Tech. Inst., 1978-79, City of Memphis Hosp., 1980-81; trustee Diversified Svcs., Inc., Tenn. Hosp. Assn., 1990-96, mem. pharmacy adv. com., 1990; bd. dirs. Ava Marie Nursing Home, chmn. nom. com., 1988, 89, mem. long-range planning com., 1989, 90, mem. constn. and by-laws com., 1990, mem. govtl. rels. com., 1991-93; presenter in field. Editor U. Tenn. Bowld Hosp. Pharmacy Newsletter, 1987-91; mem. editl. bd. Drug and Therapeutics Newsletter, U. Tenn. Coll. Pharmacy, 1989, 90. Usher Ch. of Holy Spirit, 1988-96; mem. Am. Cancer Soc. Recipient Order of Sword award Am. Cancer Soc., 1992. Mem. Am. Soc. hosp. Pharmacists, Tenn. Soc. Hosp. Pharmacists (mem. com. 1980, constn. and by-laws com. 1985, 88, 89, 90, chmn. nominating com. 1989, orgn. and goals com. 1991, strategic planning com. 1992), Tenn. Pharmacists Assn. (pharmacy tech. task force 1988, 89, 90, ho. dels. 1988, 89, 90, 91, 92, 94, chmn. tech. curriculum com. 1991, tech. edn. accreditation com. 1991, 92, 94), Memphis Area Soc. Hosp. Pharmacists (pres.-elect 1984, pres. 1985, past pres. 1986, chmn. nominating com. 1991), Tenn. Hosp. Assn. (liaison Tenn. Med. Assn. com. 1991), Mid-South Healthcare Materials Mgmt. Assn. (co-chmn. founding orgnl. com. 1991), Kappa Psi, Rho Chi. Home: 2927 Mikeyair Dr Germantown TN 38138-7148 E-mail: rnolly@utmem.edu.

NOLPH, GEORGIA BOWER, physician; b. Appleton, Minn., Jan. 26, 1938; d. Clarence Walter and Gladys Mae (Hanson) Bower; m. Karl David Nolph, July 26, 1961; children: Erika Lynn, Kristoper Karl. BA, St. Olaf Coll., 1960; MD, Woman's Med. Coll. Pa., 1964. Pvt. practice with G.H. Ferguson MD, Bala-Cynwyd, Pa., 1965-67; civil service Walter Reed Army Med. Ctr., Washington, 1967-69; instr. community health and med. practice U. Mo., Columbia, 1969-70; asst. prof. U. Mo. Med. Sch., 1970-77, assoc. prof. family and community medicine, 1977—. Acting med. dir. Family Med. Care Ctr., U. Mo. Hosp. and Clinics, Columbia, 1980—87; med. dir. NBA Lenoir Retirement Cmty., 1987—99, bd. dirs., 2000—, v.p., 2001—. Assoc. editor. (profl. jour.) Continuing Education for the Family Physician, 1972-73. V.p. Parents for Drug Free Youth, Columbia, Mo., 1985-86, 86-87, pres. 1987-88, 88-89. Mem.: Boone County Med. Soc., Mo. State Med. Assn., Am. Bus. Women's Assn., Am. Med. Women's Assn. (state dir. 1975—, region VII gov. 1996—), Am. Legion Aux. Republican. Methodist. Avocations: music, reading, travel, needlework. Home: 908 Hickory Hill Dr Columbia MO 65203-2320 Office: U Mo Med Sch Dept Family and Cmty Medicine 1 Hospital Dr Columbia MO 65201-5276

NOLTE, CLAIRE ELAINE, history educator; b. Woodbury, N.J., Feb. 8, 1946; d. Carl Tobias and Clara Bertha Nolte; m. Carl Blass, Nov. 11, 1981. BA, Douglass Coll., 1968; MA, Columbia U., 1972, PhD, 1990. Instr. N.Y. Inst. Tech., 1974-82; adj. asst. prof. C.C. Phila., 1984-90, Drexel U., 1990-91; Mellon postdoctoral fellow Washington U., St. Louis, 1991-92; vis. asst. prof. Bucknell U., Lewisburg, Pa., 1992-93; asst. prof. Manhattan Coll., Riverdale, N.Y., 1993-97; assoc. prof., 1997—; dir. program in internat. studies Manhattan Coll., 1996-2000, chair, dept. history, 2001—, prof., 2002—. Author: The Sokol in the Czech Lands to 1914: Training for the Nation; contbr. articles to profl. jours. Recipient Fulbright award, 1968, 78; rsch. grantee Woodrow Wilson Ctr. Advanced Internat. Study, 1992. Mem. Assn. Women Slavic Studies (Heldt prize 1994), Am. Assn. Advancement Slavic Studies, Am. Hist. Assn. (Bernadotte E. Schmitt grantee 1995), Internat. Soc. Study Phys. Edn. and Sport, The Historical Soc. Czechoslovak History Conf. (officer-at-large 1992-94, v.p. 1998-2000, Stanley Z. Pech prize 1995), Phi Beta Kappa (officer Upsilon of N.Y. chpt.). Office: Manhattan Coll Dept History Riverdale NY 10471

NOLTE, HENRY R., JR. lawyer, former automobile company executive; b. N.Y.C., Mar. 3, 1924; s. Henry R. and Emily A. (Eisele) Nolte; m. Frances Messner, May 19, 1951; children: Gwynne Conn, Henry Reed III, Jennifer Stevens, Suzanne Saunders. BA, Duke U., 1947; LLB, U. Pa., 1949. Bar: N.Y. 1950, Mich. 1967. Assoc. Cravath, Swaine & Moore, N.Y.C., 1951-61; assoc. counsel Ford Motor Co., Dearborn, Mich., 1961, asst. gen. counsel, 1964-71, assoc. gen. counsel, 1971-74, v.p., gen. counsel, 1974-89, Philco-Ford Corp., Phila., 1961-64; v.p., gen. counsel, sec. Ford of Europe Inc., Warley, Essex, Eng., 1967-69; gen. counsel fin. and ins. subs. Ford Motor Co., 1974-89; sr. ptnr. Miller, Canfield, Paddock & Stone, Detroit, 1989-93, of counsel, 1993—. Dir. emeritus Charter One Fin., Inc. Formerly vice chmn. and trustee Cranbrook Ednl. Cmty.; mem. Internat. and Comparative Law Ctr. of Southwestern Legal Found.; bd. dirs. Detroit Symphony Orch.; trustee Beaumont Hosp. Lt. USNR, 1943-46, PTO. Mem. ABA (past chmn. corp. law depts.), Mich. Bar Assn., Assn. Bar City N.Y., Assn. Gen. Counsel, Orchard Lake Country Club, Bloomfield Hills Country Club, Everglades Club (Fla.), Gulfstream Golf Club (Fla.), Ocean Club (Fla.). Episcopalian. Office: Miller Canfield Paddock & Stone 840 W Long Lake Rd Troy MI 48098-6356

NOLTE, JACQUELINE, accountant; b. Clinton, Iowa, Jan. 27, 1965; d. Ronald Frances and Linda Sue (Adams) N. ABA with high honors, Highland C.C., Freeport, Ill., 1986; BA magna cum laude, Mt. St. Clare Coll., 1998. CPA Ill.; CMA. Loan officer, supr. loan dept. Blackhawk Area Credit Union, Savanna, Ill., 1986-95; title policy mgr. Northwestern Title Co., Morrison, 1996-98; sales and use tax analyst Bandag, Inc., Muscatine, Iowa, 1998-99; asst. contr. Happy Joe's Pizza and Ice Cream Parlor, Inc., Bettendorf, 1999—2000; audit supr. Anderson, Gabelmann, Lower, Whitlow, P.C., 2000—. Mem. AICPA, Ill. CPA Soc., Iowa Soc. CPAs, Inst. Cert. Mgmt. Accts., Cornbelt Running Club. Avocations: running, bicycling, gardening, crocheting, reading. Home: 3440 Jersey Ridge Rd Apt 22 Davenport IA 52807-2083 Office: Anderson Gabelmann Lower Whitlow PC 852 Middle Rd Ste 100 Bettendorf IA 52722

NOLTE, NICK, actor; b. Omaha, 1941; m. Rebecca Linger, Feb. 19, 1984 (div. 1995); 1 child, Brawley King. Student, Pasadena City Coll., Phoenix City Coll.; studies with, John Paul, Allen Dutton. Actor: (play) The Last Pad, 1973, (TV movies) Winter Kill, 1974, The California Kid, 1974, Death Sentence, 1974, Adams of Eagle Lake, 1975, The Treasure Chest Murder, 1975, The Runaways, 1975, (mini-series) Rich Man, Poor Man, 1976; (films) The Deep, 1977, Return to Macon County, 1975, Who'll Stop the Rain, 1978, North Dallas Forty, 1979, Heart Beat, 1980, Cannery Row, 1982, 48 Hours, 1982, Under Fire, 1983, The Ultimate Solution of Grace Quigley, 1984, Teachers, 1984, Down and Out in Beverly Hills, 1986, Weeds, 1987, Extreme Prejudice, 1987, Farewell to the King, 1988, Three Fugitives, 1988, New York Stories, 1989, Everybody Wins, 1989, Q & A, 1990, Another 48 Hours, 1990, Prince of Tides, 1991, Cape Fear, 1991, Lorenzo's Oil, 1992, The Player, 1992, Blue Chips, 1994, I'll Do Anything, 1994, I Love Trouble, 1994, Jefferson in Paris, 1995, Mulholland Falls, 1996, Mother Night, 1996, Nightwatch, 1997, Afterglow, 1997, U-Turn, 1997, Affliction, 1998, Thin Red Line, 1998, The Best of Enemies, 1999, Breakfast of Champions, 1999, The Golden Bowl, 2000, Trixie, 2000.

NOLTE, RICHARD HENRY, political science researcher, consultant; b. Duluth, Minn., Dec. 27, 1920; s. Julius Mosher and Mildred (Miller) N.; m. Jeanne McQuarrie, Mar. 27, 1945; children: Charles McQuarrie, Roger Reed, Douglas Mitchell, Jameson Jay. AB, Yale U., 1943, MA, 1947; BA (Rhodes scholar), Oxford (Eng.) U., 1950, MA, 1954, Inst. Current World Affairs fellow, 1948-54; DSc (hon.), U. Wis., Milw., 1979. Assoc. on Middle East Am. Univs. Field Staff, 1953-58; asst. dir. humanities Rockefeller Found., Inc., N.Y.C., 1958-59; exec. dir. Inst. Current World Affairs, 1959-78, Alicia Patterson Found., N.Y.C., 1965-78; exec. v.p. Hamilton, Johnston & Co., Inc., 1978-81; cons. Middle East Dillon, Read & Co., Inc., 1981-82; assoc. for Middle East HME Internat. Adv. Assocs., Inc., 1982-90; gen. ptnr. Washburn Island Res. Ltd. Partnership, East Falmouth, Mass., 1981-89; pres. Near East Found., N.Y.C., 1984—87, trustee emeritus; ambassador to Egypt Cairo, 1967. Editor: The Modern Middle East, 1963. Co-chmn. Amb.'s Round Table Stamford Forum for World Affairs, 1991-2001; bd. dirs. Pro Bono, Inc., 1994-99; hon. trustee Inst. Current World Affairs, 1995—. Pilot USNR, 1943-45. Mem. Am. Geog. Soc. (pres. 1973-80, now chmn. emeritus bd.), Nat. Aphasia Assn. (bd. dirs. 1990-99, bd. dirs. Fund for Peace 1993-96), Coun. on Fgn. Rels., World Acad. Art and Sci., Yale Club, Mid-Atlantic Club, Phi Beta Kappa. Home and Office: 80 Lyme Rd #213 Hanover NH 03755 E-mail: rhnolte@webtv.net.

NOLTING, EARL, retired academic administrator; b. Columbus, Ind., July 24, 1937; s. Earl Seeger and Gladys Marie (Veale) N.; m. Judith Lynn Tegeler, June 18, 1961; children: Susan, Matthew, David. BSBA, Ind. U., 1959, MS in Edn., 1961; PhD in Psychology, U. Minn., 1967. Lic. psychologist Minn. Counselor, asst. prof. U. Minn., Mpls., 1966-68; assoc. dir. U. Wis., Madison, 1968-72, assoc. dean, assoc. vice-chancellor, 1970-74; assoc. prof. edn. Kans. State U., Manhattan, 1974-86, dean of students, 1974-86; dir. dept. counseling, Univ. Coll. U. Minn., Mpls., 1986-97, dir. student support svcs., Univ. Coll., 1997-2000; ret., 2000. Cons. psychologist Alberg and Assocs., Shoreview, Minn., 1989—. Contbr. articles to profl. publs. Exec. bd. Adult Learner Svcs. Network, St. Paul, 1989-90. 1st lt. U.S. Army, 1961-62. Mem. APA, Minn. Psychol. Assn., Am. Coll. Pers. Assn. (news editor 1977-82, sen. 1982-85, Presdl. award 1982), Am. Coll. Counseling Assn., Acad. of Family Mediators, Assn. for Conflict Resolution. Avocations: canoeing, gardening, reading. Home: 3336 Lake Johanna Blvd Saint Paul MN 55112-7942 Office: 470 Highway 96 W Ste 280 Shoreview MN 55126-1956

NOME, WILLIAM ANDREAS, lawyer; b. Springfield, Ohio, May 21, 1951; s. Reidar Andreas and Nancy Louisa (Smith) N.; m. Carolyn Ruth Johnson, Feb. 7, 1981. BA, Akron U., 1973; JD, Cleve. State U., 1976. Bar: Ohio 1976, U.S. Dist. Ct. (no. dist.) Ohio 1977, U.S. Ct. Appeals (6th cir.) 1985, U.S. Supreme Ct. 1987. Asst. prosecutor Portage County Prosecutor's Office, Ravenna, Ohio, 1977; pvt. practice, 1977-82; assoc. Arthur & Clegg, Kent, Ohio, 1982-85; ptnr. Arthur, Nome & Assocs., 1985-96, Arthur, Nome, Can, Szymanski & Clinard, Kent, Cuyahoga Falls, 1996-97, Arthur, Nome, Can & Szymanski, Kent, Cuyahoga Falls, 1997-98, Arthur, Nome and Szymanski, Kent, 1998—2002, Arthur Nome and Assocs., 2002—. Legal advisor Portage Area Regional Transit Authority, Kent, 1986—. Chmn. Highland Home Health Care, Ravenna, 1980, Kent Bd. Bldg. Appeals, 1987, Portage County Mental Health Bd., 1988; trustee Kevin Coleman Mental Health Ctr., 1989-93, pres., 1991-93; pres. Force Investment Club, 1999-2002. Col. Ohio Mil. Res., 1986—. Recipient Cert. of Achievement, Emergency Mgmt. Inst., Fed. Emergency Mgmt. Agy., 1987, 93, 95. Mem. Ohio Bar Assn., Akron Bar Assn., Portage County Bar Assn. (sec.-treas. 1982-85, 98-2000, v.p. 2000-2001, pres. 2001-02), Portage County Estate Planning Coun., Delta Theta Phi. Republican. Lutheran. Avocations: gardening, cooking, target shooting, reading. Office: Arthur Nome & Assocs 1325 S Water St Kent OH 44240-3851 E-mail: anslawyers@aol.com.

NOMICOS, NICHOLAS EUGENE, emergency medicine physician; b. Memphis, May 22, 1962; s. Eugene Nicolas and Melva Ann (Adams) N. BS, Coll. of Idaho, 1983; MD, Am. U. of the Caribbean, 1987. Rsch. assoc. Harbor UCLA Med. Ctr., Torrance, Calif., 1987-89; cert. family life educator Harbor Free Clinic, San Pedro, 1987-89; intern/resident St. Joseph Mercy Hosp., Pontiac, Mich., 1989-91; ind. emergency physician Coldwater, 1991—; med. dir. Br. County Med. Control Authority, 1994-2000; emergency dir. Duane Waters Hosp., Jackson, 2000—; asst. emergency dir. Doctors Hosp., 2000—. Resident educator, instr. Cmty. Health Ctr. of Br. County, 1994-2000; ATLS instr., 1995—, ACLS instr., 2001; bd. county rep. S.W. Mich. Trauma Coalition, Kalamazoo, 1994-2000; emergency dir. Cmty. Hosp., Watervliet, Mich., 1992; presenter in field. Author, photographer: Expedition: Bikini Atoll Diving Ground Zero of Operation Crossroads, 1997; contbr. articles to profl. jours. Fellow Assn. Emergency Physicians; mem. AMA (Physicians Recognition award 1994, 97), Am. Assn. Physician Specialists, Am. Coll. Physician Execs., Masons. Republican. Greek Orthodox. Avocations: concert violinist, master scuba diver/underwater photographer, travel, sports, fine arts. Office: Emergency Med Cons 109 N Elm Jackson MI 49202

NOMPLEGGI, DOMINIC J. gastroenterologist, medical educator; b. Boston, May 1, 1950; AB, Georgetown U., 1972, PhD, 1977, MD, 1982. Intern Harvard Med. Sch./New Eng. Deaconness Hosp., Boston, 1982—83, resident, 1983—85, chief resident, 1985—86; fellow in gastroenterology Brigham & Women's Hosp., 1988-91; clin. chief gastroenterology divsn. U. Mass. Med. Ctr., Worcester, 2000—; asst. prof. medicine and surgery U. Mass. Med. Sch., 1991-98, assoc. prof. medicine and surgery, 1998—; dir. adult nutrition support svc. U. Mass. Med. Ctr., 1992—. Author: Intensive Care Medicine, 1999; contbr. articles to profl. jours. Recipient James L. Tullis Lectureship award for disting. study New Eng. Deaconess Hosp./Harvard Med. Sch., 1995. Mem. Am. Gastroenterol. Assn. (Rsch. Scholar award 1992-95), Am. Coll. Gastroenterology, Am. Soc. Parenteral and Enteral Nutrition. Office: U Mass Meml Health Care 55 Lake Ave Worcester MA 01655 Fax: 508-856-3981. E-mail: nomplegd@ummhc.org.

NOMURA, MASAYASU, biological chemistry educator; b. Hyogo-Ken, Japan, Apr. 27, 1927; s. Hiromichi and Yaeko N.; m. Junko Hamashima, Feb. 10, 1957; children— Keiko, Toshiyasu. PhD, U. Tokyo, 1957. Asst. prof. Inst. Protein Research, Osaka (Japan) U., 1960-63; assoc. prof. genetics U. Wis., Madison, 1963-66, prof., 1966-70, Conrad Elvehjem prof. in Life Sci. genetics and biochemistry, 1970-84, co-dir. Inst. for Enzyme Research, 1970-84; prof. biol. chemistry, Grace Bell chair U. Calif., Irvine, 1984—. Recipient U.S. Steel award in molecular biology Nat. Acad. Scis., 1971, Acad. award Japanese Acad. Arts and Sci., 1972, Abbot-ASM Lifetime Acheivement award Am. Soc. Microbiology, 2002. Mem. Am. Acad. Arts and Scis., Nat. Acad. Scis., Royal Danish Acad. Scis. and Letters, Royal Netherlands Acad. Arts and Scis., Japanese Biochem. Soc. Home: 74 Whitman Ct Irvine CA 92612-4066 Office: U Calif Dept Biol Chemistry 240D Med Sci I Dept Irvine CA 92697-1700 E-mail: mnomura@uci.edu.

NONDORF, JANICE KATHRYN, special education educator; b. Hoisington, Kans., Oct. 30, 1956; d. Francis Joseph and Evelyn Helen (Huschka) Behr; m. John Raymond Nondorf, Aug. 3, 1979; children: AdreAnne Claire, Allyson Kate. BS in Edn., Ft. Hays State U., Hays, Kans., 1978; MS in Spl. Edn., Ft. Hays State U., 1982. Early childhood handicapped tchr. Early Childhood Developmental Ctr., Hays, 1979-82, Russell Child Devel. Ctr./High Plains Ednl. Coop., Liberal, Kans., 1982-85, Russell Child Devel. Ctr., USD # 457, Garden City, 1985-91; family svcs. coord. Parents and Children Together, Inc., 1992—. Dem. precinct committeewoman, Liberal, 1988; Internat. Pancake Day Race contestant, 1989, 90; mem. Internat. Pancake Day bd. execs., 1990—, gen. chmn. Internat. Pancake Day 2000; bd. dirs. Liberal Latchkey, 1996—, pres. 2002. Named an Outstanding Young Woman in Am., 1982. Mem. Ft. Hays U. Alumni Assn. Roman Catholic. Avocations: philately, needlecraft.

NONNA, JOHN MICHAEL, lawyer; b. N.Y.C., July 8, 1948; s. Angelo and Josephine (Visconti) N.; m. Jean Wanda Cleary, June 9, 1973; children: Elizabeth, Caroline, Marianne, Timothy. AB, Princeton U., 1970; JD, NYU, 1975. Bar: N.Y. 1976, U.S. Dist. Ct. (so. dist.) N.Y. 1978, U.S. Ct. Appeals (2d cir.) 1978, U.S. Ct. Appeals (9th cir.) 1980, U.S. Ct. Appeals (5th cir.) 1997, U.S. Dist. Ct. Conn. 1988, U.S. Supreme Ct. 1998. Law asst. to Hon. D.L. Gabrielli N.Y. Ct. Appeals, Albany, 1975-77; assoc. Reid & Priest, N.Y.C., 1977-84; ptnr. Werner & Kennedy, 1984-99, LeBoeuf, Lamb, Greene & MacRae, 1999—. Contbr. articles to profl. jours. Dep. mayor, trustee Village of Pleasantville, N.Y., 1990-95, mayor, 1995—, acting justice, 1983-89. With USNR, 1970-75. U.S. Olympic Team, Munich, 1972, Moscow, 1980. Fellow Am. Bar Found. (life); mem. ABA (torts and ins. practice sect. com. chair 1986-87, 92-93), N.Y. State Bar Assn. (chair comml. and fed. litigation sect. 1998-99, co-editor in chief 2000), Assn. Bar City N.Y., N.Y. Fencers Club (pres. 1990-93). Avocations: fencing, running, piano. Office: LeBoeuf Lamb Greene & MacRae 125 W 55th St New York NY 10019-5369 E-mail: jnonna@llgm.com.

NOOIJEN, MARCEL A. chemist; b. Veghel, Brabant, Netherlands, June 2, 1963; s. Harrie M. and Gerda A. (van Os) Nooijen. BA, Vrije U., Amsterdam, 1987, PhD, 1992; Kandidaats, Tech. U., Eindhoven, Netherlands, 1985. Postdoctoral assoc. U. Fla., Gainesville, 1993—97; asst. prof. Princeton (N.J.) U., 1997. Mem.: Am. Chem. Soc. Office: Princeton U Washington St Princeton NJ 08544 Business E-Mail: nooijen@princeton.edu.

NOOLAN, JULIE ANNE CARROLL, management consultant; b. Adelaide, South Australia, Australia, June 14, 1944; came to U.S., 1966; d. Archibald Henry and Norma Mae (Gillett) Noolan; m. Daniel Thuering Carroll, Aug. 20, 1977. MA, U. Chgo., 1968, PhD, 1974, Exec. MBA, 1983. With State Library of South Australia, 1962-63, Repatriation Dept. South Australia, 1962-66; asst. librarian U. Chgo. Libraries, 1966-68; dir. edn. Med. Library Assn., Chgo., 1972-77; exec. dir. Assn. Coll. and Research Libraries, 1977-84; COO Carroll Group, Inc., 1984-95; pres. COO Carroll Group, Inc., 1995—. Mem. faculty U. Chgo., 1968-89, Am. U., 1995—. Author: Libraries and Accreditation in Higher Education; contbr. articles to jours. U. Chgo. fellow, 1967-68, Higher Edn. Act fellow, 1969-72; Nat. Library of Medicine grantee, 1967-69; named Outstanding Young U.S. Leader 1985 Coun. on the U.S., Mem. ALA, Am. Soc. Assn. Execs., Am. Mgmt. Assn., Spol. Librs. Assn., Am. Soc. for Info. Scis. (past pres., doctoral award, Watson Davis award), ASTD, Nat. Tng. Labs. (bd. dirs. 1990-94), Orgn. Devel. Network, Internat. Assn. Neuro-Linguistic Programming (bd.dirs. 1990-93), Internat. Plant Genetic Resources Inst. (Rome, bd. dirs. 1991-98), Internat. Ctr. Agrl. Rsch. in Dry Areas (Syris, bd. dirs. 1992-98), Planning Forum, Beta Phi Mu.

NOONAN, CHARLES THOMAS, lawyer; b. Ashland, Ky., May 27, 1924; s. Arthur Kelly and Tina May (Beam) N.; m. Constance Charlotte Snelling, Nov. 10, 1945; children: Thomas, Susan, Karl, James, Todd. AB magna cum laude, Harvard Coll., 1945, JD, 1949. Bar: Pa., U.S. Supreme Ct. English and lit. tchr. Harwich (Mass.) H.S., 1945-46; pvt. practice Allentown, Pa., 1950-52; ptnr. Donecker & Noonan, 1952-89, Noonan and Prokup, Allentown, 1989—. Dir., legal counsel Mchts. Bank Allentown, 1974-91; assoc. Cedar Crest Coll., 1986, trustee, 1994, chmn. bd., 1997. Dir., treas., pres. East Pa. Union Sch. Dist., Emmaus, 1954-59; deacon Solomons Ch., Macungie, Pa., 1959-60; dir., pres. Allentown Jr. C. of C., 1950-60; chmn. Lehigh County Pub. Solicitations Bd., Allentown, 1955-57. Recipient Disting. Svc. award

Allentown Jr. C. of C., 1958; named Col. Order of Ky. Cols., Louisville, 1966. Mem. ABA, Pa. Bar Assn., Lehigh County Bar Assn., Phi Beta Kappa. Republican. Avocations: skiing, tennis, water skiing, music, reading. Home: 3817 Larkspur Dr Allentown PA 18103-9740 Office: Noonan and Prokup 526 W Walnut St Allentown PA 18101-2322

NOONAN, DANIEL CHRISTOPHER, consultant; b. Conn., Dec. 17, 1950; s. Daniel Alexander and Eleanor Noonan; children: Erin, Teresa, Sean, Beth. Student, Loyola U., L.A., 1971. Project mgr. Loyola U., L.A., 1968-71; prin. CBIS, 1969-71; dir. Continental Airlines, 1971-82; sr. mgr. Coopers & Lybrand, 1982-84; sr. v.p. Security Pacific Corp., Denver and San Diego, 1984-90; chief info. officer Com Systems, L.A., 1991; exec. cons. The Genessee Group, Thousand Oaks, Calif., 1991—. Address: 1144 El Monte Dr Thousand Oaks CA 91362-2117

NOONAN, JAMES C. lawyer, mediator-arbitrator; b. Chgo., July 16, 1928; s. T. Clifford and Ethel (Jennett) N.; m. Carol Colbert, Nov. 24, 1954 (div. June 1975); children: James, Christopher, Mary, Anne, Catherine; m. Ardis Niemann, May 24, 1986. AB, U. Notre Dame, 1953, MA in Criminology, 1954; JD, William Mitchell Coll. Law, St. Paul, 1962. Bar: Minn. 1962, U.S. Dist. Ct. Minn. 1963, U.S. Ct. Appeals (8th cir.) 1971, U.S. Supreme Ct. 1969. Probation officer Ramsey County Juvenile Ct., St. Paul, 1954-57; supt. Woodview Detention Home, 1957-63; assoc. Firestone, Fink, Krawetz, Miley, O'Neill, 1963-67; ptnr. Firestone Fink, Krawetz, Miley, Maas and Noonan, 1967-70, Magistad & Noonan, St. Paul, 1971-75; owner James C. Noonan and Assocs., 1975—. Mem. adv. bd. Home of Good Shepherd, St. Paul, 1958-74; mem. citizen adv. bd. Detention and Corrections Authority, St. Paul, 1966-80. Mem. ABA, Minn. State Bar Assn., Ramsey County Bar Assn., St. Paul Amateur Radio Club, Am. Radio Relay League. Roman Catholic. Avocation: amateur radio (W90SN). Home and Office: 339 Summit Ave Saint Paul MN 55102-2176 Fax: (651) 222-3340. E-mail: nnn.nnn@juno.com., W90SN@arrl.net.

NOONAN, JOHN T., JR. judge, law educator; b. Boston, Oct. 24, 1926; s. John T. and Marie (Shea) Noonan; m. Mary Lee Bennett, Dec. 27, 1967; children: John Kenneth, Rebecca Lee, Susanna Bain. BA, Harvard U., 1946, LL.B., 1954; student, Cambridge U., 1946—47; MA, Cath. U. Am., 1949, PhD, 1951, LHD, 1980; LL.D., U. Santa Clara, 1974, U. Notre Dame, 1976, Loyola U. South, 1978; LHD, Holy Cross Coll., 1980; LL.D., St. Louis U., 1981, U. San Francisco, 1985; student, Cath. U. Am., 1980, Gonzaga U., 1986, U. San Francisco, 1986; LLD, Duquesne U., 1995, Valparaiso U., 1996, U. San Diego, 1999; LHD, Loyola U., Chgo., 1999. Bar: Mass. 1954, U.S. Supreme Ct. 1971. Mem. spl. staff Nat. Security Council, 1954-55; pvt. practice Herrick & Smith, Boston, 1955-60; prof. law U. Notre Dame, 1961-66, U. Calif., Berkeley, 1967-86, chmn. religious studies, 1970-73, chmn. medieval studies, 1978-79; judge U.S. Ct. Appeals (9th cir.), San Francisco, 1985-96, sr. judge, 1996—. Oliver Wendell Holmes, Jr. lectr. Harvard U. Law Sch., 1972; Pope John XXIII lectr. Cath. U. Law Sch., 1973; Cardinal Bellarmine lectr. St. Louis U. Div. Sch., 1973; Ernest Messenger lectr. Cornell U., 1982; John Dewey Meml. lectr. U. Minn., 1986; Baum lectr. U. Ill., 1988; Strassberger lectr. U. Tex., 1989; chmn. bd. Games Rsch., Inc., 1961—76; overseer Harvard U., 1991—. Author: The Scholastic Analysis of Usury, 1957, Contraception: A History of Its Treatment by the Catholic Theologians and Canonists, 1965, Power to Dissolve, 1972, Persons and Masks of the Law, 1976, The Antelope, 1977, A Private Choice, 1979, Bribes, 1984, The Responsible Judge, 1993, Professional and Personal Responsibilities of the Lawyer, 1997, The Lustre of Our Country, 1998; editor: Natural Law Forum, 1961—70, Am. Jour. Jurisprudence, 1970, The Morality of Abortion, 1970; author: Canons and Canonists in Context, 1997, Narrowing the Nation's Power, 2002. Chmn. Brookline Redevel. Authority , Mass., 1958—62; cons. Papal Commn. on Family, 1965—66, Ford Found., Indonesian Legal Program, 1968, NIH, 1973, 1974; expert Presdl. Commn. on Population and Am. Future, 1971; pres. Thomas More-Jacques Maritain Inst., 1977—; trustee Population Coun., 1969—76, Phi Kappa Found., 1970—76, U. San Francisco, 1971—75; mem. com. theol. edn. Yale U., 1972—77; cons. U.S. Cath. Conf., 1979—86; sec., treas. Inst. for Rsch. in Medieval Canon Law, 1970—88; trustee Grad. Theol. Union, 1970—73; exec. com. Cath. Commn. Intellectual and Cultural Affairs, 1972—75; bd. dirs. Ctr. for Human Values in the Health Scis., 1969—71, S.W. Intergroup Rels. Coun., 1970—72, Inst. for Study Ethical Issues, 1971—73. Recipient St. Thomas More award, U. San Francisco, 1974, Christian Culture medal, 1975, Laetare medal, U. Notre Dame, 1984, Campion medal, Cath. Book Club, 1987, Alemany medal, Western Dominican Province, 1988; fellow Guggenheim fellow, 1965—66, 1979—80, Ctr. for Advanced STudies in Behavioral Scis. fellow, 1973—74, Wilson Ctr. fellow, 1979—80, Kluge fellow, Libr. Congress Ctr. for Scholars, 2002—. Fellow: Am. Acad. Arts and Scis., Am. Soc. Legal Historians (hon.); mem.: Am. Law Inst., Canon Law Soc. Am. (gov. 1970—72), Am. Soc. Polit. and Legal Philosophy (v.p. 1964), Phi Beta Kappa (senator United chpts. 1970—72, pres. Alpha of Calif. chpt. 1972—73). Office: US Ct Appeals 9th Cir PO Box 193939 San Francisco CA 94119-3939

NOONAN, PATRICK FRANCIS, conservation executive; b. St. Petersburg, Fla., Dec. 2, 1942; s. Francis Patrick and Henrietta (Donovan) N.; m. Nancy Elizabeth Peck, Aug. 15, 1964; children: Karen Elizabeth, Dawn Wiley. AB, Gettysburg Coll., 1961-65; M.City and Regional Planning, Catholic U. Am., 1967; MBA, Am. U., 1971. Pres. The Nature Conservancy, 1973-80; chmn. The Conservation Fund, 1985—, Am. Farmland Trust, 1991-97. Trustee Nat. Geog. Soc., 1990, Nat. Geog. Edn. Found., 1995—, Gettysburg Coll., 1978—91, Duke U. Sch. Environment, 1979—, Ind. Sector, 1984—91, Am. Conservation Assn., 1986—, Natural Resources Coun. Am., 1996—; dir. Ashland, 1991—, Internat. Paper, 1993—, Saul Ctrs., 1993—; mem. Pres.' Commn. on Am. Outdoors, 1985—87, Pres.' Commn. on Environ. Quality, 1991—93, Pres.' commn. on White House Fellows, 2001—. MacArthur Found. fellow, 1985-90. Home: 11901 Glen Mill Rd Potomac MD 20854-1920

NOONAN, ROBERT HARRY, art educator, music educator; b. Mpls., Sept. 18, 1924; s. William Earl and Nellie Morene Noonan; BS in Chemistry, Northwestern State Coll., 1948; MusB in Music Edn., Centenary Coll., 1963. Cert. tchr. music, chemistry, sci., math., visually talented and musically talented La. Sr. chemist Ark. Fuel Oil Co., Shreveport, La., 1948-53; grad. asst. U. Wyo., Laramie, 1953-54; asst. chief chemist Atlas Processing Co., Shreveport, 1955-58; Frenh horn player Shreveport Symphony Orch., 1948-72; sch. sys. employee East Baton Rouge Sch. Sys., Baton Rouge, 1972-81; pub. sch. tchr. Ascension Parish Schs., Donaldsonville, 1981-95; tchr. visually talented St. James Parish Schs., Lutcher, 1997—2001. Composer, arranger: music One Step from the Edge, 1999—2000, composer, arranger: music I Am Your Child, 2000—01, composer, arranger: music Finding My Way, 2001—02;one-man shows include Jones Creek Libr., Baton Rouge, 1993, Donaldsonville (La.) H.S., 1994, Galvez (La.) Libr., 1994, Westbank Libr., Harvey, La., 1995, Bruno Gallery, New Orleans, 1997, exhibited in group shows, Baton Rouge, Jackson, Plaquemine, Morgan City, numerous others, Represented in permanent collections , La., Tex., Miss., Ala., Okla., others. Chmn. La. Sch. Employees Coun.l, 1977—81. With Air Corps U.S. Army, 1943—46. Grantee Goals 2000, State of La., 1995—96, Spl. Arts, 1997—99. Mem.: Jefferson Art Guild, St. Bernard Art Guild (pres. 1999—2001), New Orleans Art Assn. (v.p. 1998—2000), Am. Chem. Soc. (sr. grade chemist 1948—58), La. Partnership for the Arts. Avocations: outdoor painting, writing article for newspapers. Home: 11254 E Lanoux PO Box 713 Gonzales LA 70707-0713

NOONAN, WILLIAM DONALD, lawyer, physician; b. Kansas City, Mo., Oct. 18, 1955; s. Robert Owen and Patricia Ruth Noonan. AB, Princeton (N.J.) U., 1977; JD, U. Mo., Kansas City, 1980; postgrad., Tulane U., 1981-83; MD magna cum laude, Oreg. Health Scis. U., 1991. Bar: Mo. 1980, U.S. Ct. Appeals (5th cir.) 1982, U.S. Patent & Trademark Office 1982, U.S. Ct. Appeals (D.C. cir.) 1984, Oreg. 1985, U.S. Ct. Appeals (9th Cir.) 1985. Assoc. Shurgue, Mion, Zinn, Washington, 1983-84, Keaty & Keaty, New Orleans, 1984-85; ptnr. Klarquist, Sparkman, Portland, Oreg., 1985—; intern in internal medicine Portland Providence Med. Ctr., 1993-94; resident in ophthalmology Casey Eye Inst., Portland, 1994-95. Adj. prof. patent law Tulane U., New Orleans, 1984-85, U. Oreg., 1992-93. Casenotes editor U. Mo. Law Rev., 1979. Nat. Merit scholar. Mem. ABA, AMA (Leadership award 1994), Alpha Omega Alpha (pres. Oreg. chpt. 1990-91). Republican. Avocation: raising horses, mountain climbing, hiking. Office: 1600 World Trade Ctr 121 SW Salmon St Portland OR 97204-2901

NOONE, KATHLEEN MARY, art educator; b. Wynnewood, Pa., Mar. 16, 1971; d. John Francis and Mary Louise (McCahon) N. BS, Kutztown U., 1993. Art educator Villa Maria Acad., Malvern, Pa., 1994—, cons. fine arts ctr., 1995-97, dept. chair visual arts, 1996-97. Art tchr. summer enrichment program Archbishop John Carroll H.S., Radnor, Pa., summers 1996, 97. Bd. dirs. Archdiocesan Curriculum Com. for Fine Arts, Phila., 1996—; vol. tchr. aide GED course Ardmore Libr., 1995. Recipient Connelly Art Connection award Connelly Found., Mus. Am. Art, 1997. Mem. NEA, Nat. Art Edn. Assn., Pa. Art Edn. Assn., Am. Crafts Coun., Phila. Mus. Art, Main Line Art Ctr. Roman Catholic. Avocations: coaching field hockey. Home: 316 E Athens Ave Ardmore PA 19003-3108

NOONE, PALMER, academic administrator; Doctorate in higher edn. adminstrn., Union Insit.; JD, MBA, U. Iowa; BBA, U. Dubuque. Pres. U. Phoenix, 2002—, provost, sr. v.p. acad. affairs, dir. acad affairs, faculty; atty gen. civil practice Iowa, Ariz.; judge City of Chandler. Office: U Phoenix 3201 E Elwood St Phoenix AZ 85034*

NOONE, R. BARRETT, plastic surgeon; b. Scranton, Pa., Oct. 30, 1939; s. Robert Patrick and Margaret Ann (Barrett) N.; m. Barbara Ellen Atkins, May 29, 1965; children: Robert B. Jr., Megan J., Genevieve C., Rebecca B., Theresa Ann. BS, U. Scranton, 1961; MD, U. Pa., 1965. Diplomate Am. Bd. Surgery, Am. Bd. Plastic Surgery. Rotating intern Hosp. of U. Pa., Phila., 1965-66, resident in surgery, 1966-71, resident in plastic surgery, 1971-73; asst. prof. surgery Sch. Medicine, U. Pa., 1974-83, clin. assoc. prof. surgery, 1983-89, clin. prof. surgery, 1989—; head sect. on plastic surgery Pa. Hosp., Phila., 1974-80; chief svc. plastic surgery Bryn Mawr (Pa.) Hosp., 1977—, Lankenau Hosp., Phila., 1980-91; chmn. dept. surgery Bryn Mawr (Pa.) Hosp., 1991—; exec. dir. Am. Bd. Plastic Surgery, 1997—. Bd. dirs. Am. Bd. Plastic Surgery, Phila., 1987-94, vice chmn. 1993-94; bd. dirs. Plastic Surgery Ednl. Found., Chgo., 1981-91, pres. 1989-90. Contbr. articles to profl. jours. Bd. dirs., trustee Rosemont (Pa.) Sch. of the Holy Child, 1983-87, U. Scranton, 1998—. Capt. USAF, 1967-69. Recipient Frank J. O'Hara Disting. Alumnus award U. Scranton, 1986. Fellow Am. Coll. Surgeons (bd. govs. 1994-98); mem. AMA (del. plastic surgery 1986-88), Am. Soc. Plastic and Reconstructive Surgery (bd. dirs. 1989-90, 92-95, chmn. bd. trustees 1994-95), Am. Assn. Plastic Surgeons (sec. 1995-98, v.p. 1998-99, pres.-elect 1999-2000, pres. 2000—), Northeastern Soc. Plastic Surgeons (pres. 1985-86), Robert H. Ivy Soc. (pres. 1982-83), Merion Cricket Club, Phila. Country Club. Republican. Roman Catholic. Avocations: golf, tennis, photography, swimming, travel, reading. Home: 234 Cheswold Hill Rd Haverford PA 19041-1814 Office: Plastic & Reconstructive Surg Assocs 888 Glenbrook Ave Bryn Mawr PA 19010-2506

NOONKESTER, JAMES RALPH, retired college president; b. Flatridge, Va., June 10, 1924; s. Reggie L. and Arcie (Parks) N.; m. Naomi Hopkins, June 10, 1947; children: Myron Craig, Lila. BA, U. Richmond, 1944, LLD, 1968; ThM, So. Bapt. Theol. Sem., 1947, PhD, 1949; LHD (hon.), Blue Mountain Coll., 1982; postgrad., Harvard U., 1980. Minister edn. 1st Bapt. Ch., Charlottesville, Va., 1950-52; prof., head div. religion and philosophy William Carey Coll., Hattiesburg, Miss., 1952-53, acad. dean, 1953-56, pres., 1956-89, pres. emeritus, 1989—. Pres. Miss. Found. Ind. Colls.; mem. Edn. commn. So. Bapt. Conv., chmn., 1983; bd. dirs. Miss. Sch. Bds. Assn. Workers Compensation Trust, 1993-95, chmn., 1994. Chmn. bd. dirs. Am. Cancer Soc., Miss. divsn., 1966; campaign chmn. United Givers Fund, 1975-76, pres. 1976-77; coun. chmn. Boy Scouts Am., dir. Planned Giving Pine Burr Area Boy Scouts Am., 1990-93; trustee Hattiesburg Pub. Schs., 1990-95, pres. bd. trustees, 1992-95. Recipient award Outstanding Grad. English U. Richmond, 1944; named Hattiesburg's Outstanding Young Man of 1956.; recipient Silver Beaver award Boy Scouts Am., 1981, HUB award, 1983; named Sales and Mktg. Execs. Man of Yr., 1983 Mem. NEA, Miss. Edn. Assn., Hattiesburg Concert Assn. (bd. dir.), So. Assn. Bapt. Colls. and Schs. (pres.), Miss. Assn. Colls. (pres.), Hattiesburg C. of C. (pres. 1966), Phi Beta Kappa, Phi Delta Kappa, Chi Beta Phi, Omicron Delta Kappa. Clubs: Kiwanian. Home: 100 Lesley Ln Hattiesburg MS 39402-2922

NOORDERGRAAF, ABRAHAM, biophysics educator; b. Utrecht, Netherlands, Aug. 7, 1929; s. Leendert and Johanna (Kool) N.; m. Geertruida Alida Van Nee, Sept. 6, 1956 (div. Jan. 2001); children: Annemiek (Mrs. James A. Young), Gerrit Jan, Jeske Inette, Alexander Abraham. B.Sc., U. Utrecht, 1953, MS, 1955, PhD, 1956; MA (hon.), U. Pa., 1971. Teaching asst. U. Utrecht, 1949-50, asst. dept. physics, 1951-53, research asst. dept. med. physics, 1953-55, research fellow dept. med. physics, 1956-58, sr. research fellow dept. med. physics, 1959-65; tchr. math. and physics Vereniging Nijverheidsonderwijs, Utrecht, 1951; research asst. U. Amsterdam, Netherlands, 1952; vis. fellow dept. therapeutic research U. Pa., Phila., 1957-58; assoc. prof. biomed. engring. Moore Sch. Elec. Engring., U. Pa., 1964-70, acting head electromed. div., 1968-69, prof. biomed. engring., 1970-97, assoc. dir. biomed. engring. tng. program, 1971-76, asso. dir. sch., 1972-74, chmn. grad. group in biomed. electronic engring., 1973-75, chmn. dept. bioengring., 1973-76, chmn. grad. group bioengring., 1975-76, dir. systems and integrative biology tng. program, 1979-84; prof. physiology Sch. Vet. Medicine U. Pa., 1976-97, prof. Dutch culture Sch. Arts and Scis., 1983-97, prof. anesthesia Med. Sch., 1990-97, prof. emeritus, 1997—. Vis. prof. biomed. engring. U. Miami, 1970-79, Erasmus U. Med. Sch., Rotterdam, The Netherlands, 1970-71, Tech. U., Delft, 1970-71, Polish Acad. Scis., Warsaw, 1975; hon. vis. prof. physiology U. Ljubljana, 1994—; mem. cardiovasc. study sect. NIH, 1985-89, temp. mem., 1998-2000; cons. sci. affairs divsn. NATO, 1973—; participant numerous internat. confs. in field. Author: (with I. Starr) Ballistocardiography in Cardiovascular Research, 1967, Circulatory System Dynamics, 1978; contbg. author: Biological Engineering, 1969; Editor: (with G.N. Jager and N. Westerhof) Circulatory Analog Computers, 1963, (with G.H. Pollack) Ballistocardiography and Cardiac Performance, 1967, (with E. Kresch) The Venous System: Characteristics and Function, 1969, (with J. Baan and J. Raines) Cardiovascular System Dynamics, 1978, (with Reichenbach-Consten) Two Hundred Years of Netherlands-American Interaction; sci. editor Biophysics and Bioengring. Series, 1976-94; contbr. numerous articles to profl. jours.; Referee: Biophys. Jour., 1968—, Physics in Medicine and Biology, 1969— , Bull. Math. Biophysics, 1972-84, Circulation Research, 1977— ; mem. editorial adv. bd.: Jour. Biomechanics, 1969-84; assoc. editor: Bull. Math. Biology, 1973-84. Vice pres. Haverford Friends Sch. PTA, 1968-70. Recipient S. Reid Warren Jr. award U. Pa. Sch. Engring. and Applied Sci., 1986, Christian and Mary Lindback award U. Pa., 1988, Lifetime Achievement award, 2001. Fellow IEEE (mem. adminstrv. com. engring. in medicine and biology group 1967-70, mem. edn. com. group biomed. engring. 1968-70, sec. Phila. chpt. 1974-75, mem. regional council profl. group engring. in medicine and biology 1974-77), N.Y. Acad. Scis., AAAS, Explorers Club, Coll. Physicians Phila., Am. Coll. Cardiology, Royal Soc. Medicine London; mem. Nederlandse Natuurkundige Vereniging, Ballistocardiograph Research Soc. U.S.A. (sec.-treas. 1965-67, pres. 1968-70), Biophys. Soc. (charter), European Soc. for Noninvasive Cardiovascular Research (co-founder 1960, sec.-treas. 1960-61, mem. com. on nomenclature 1960-61, officer 1961-62, Herman C. Burger award 1978, Disting. Rsch. Award, 1993), Cardiovascular System Dynamics Soc. (co-founder 1976, pres. 1976-80, hon. life 1986), Franklin Inst., John Morgan Soc., Biomed. Engring. Soc. (founding mem., chmn. membership com. 1978-79, dir. 1972-75), Am. Heart Assn., Instrument Soc. Am. (sr. mem.), Soc. Math. Biology (charter mem.), Am. Physiol. Soc., Microcirculatory Soc., Am. Assn. Med. Systems and Informatics, Pa. Acad. Sci., Sigma Xi, Phi Zeta. Presbyterian. Achievements include discovery (with Maximilian Moser) of impedance-defined flow, generalizing William Harvey's 1628 theory of blood circulation. Home: 620 Haydock Ln Haverford PA 19041-1208 Office: U Pa 101 Hayden Hall Philadelphia PA 19104-6392 E-mail: anoor@seas.upenn.edu.

NOORI, MOHAMMAD NOORI, mechanical engineering educator; b. Tehran, Iran, Dec. 24, 1952; m. Nahid Bozorgi; children: Haeman, Hooman, Naudereh. BS, U. Ill., 1977; MS, Okla. State U., 1980; PhD, U. Va., 1984. Surveyor dept. civil engring. U. Ill., Urbana, 1975-77; instr. dept. civil engring. Okla. State U., Stillwater, 1977-79; civil engr. Urban Devel., Iran, 1979-80; rsch. asst. civil engring. dept. U. Va., Charlottesville, 1980-84; asst. prof. mech. and mfg. engring. Worcester (Mass.) Poly. Inst., 1984-90, assoc. prof. mech. and mfg. engring., 1998-92, prof., head mech. and aerospace engring. dept., 1991-99, John Woodman Higgins prof., 1998—2000, dir. Ctr. Loss prevention and Structural Integrity, 1998—; prof., head mech. engring. dept. North Carolina U., 1999—. Mem. editl. bd.: 5 internat. jours.; contbr. over 150 articles to profl. jours., chpt. to book. Fellow: ASME (chair profl. devel. com. 1988—, invitee presdl. commn. on civil infrastructures, fellow various awards 1988—), Japan Soc. Promotion of Sci.; mem.: ASCE (mem. com. 1991—), AIAA, Soc. Engring. Sci., Am. Soc. Engring. Edn. Achievements include patent pending for vibration absorber for offshore platforms, SMA Mechanism for Seismic Isolation. Avocations: woodworking, reading, computers, hiking, biking. Office: Mech & Aerospace Engring Dept North Carolina State U Raleigh NC 27695 E-mail: mnoori@eos.ncsu.edu.

NOPAR, ALAN SCOTT, lawyer; s. Myron E. and Evelyn M. Nopar; m. Angela P. Yancey, Aug. 26, 2000. BS, U. Ill., 1976; JD, Stanford U., 1979. Bar: Ariz. 1979, U.S. Dist. Ct. Ariz. 1980, U.S. Ct. Appeals (9th cir.) 1980, U.S. Supreme Ct. 1982, Calif. 1989; CPA, Ill. Assoc. O'Connor, Cavanagh, Anderson, Westover, Killingsworth & Beshears P.A., Phoenix, 1979-85, ptnr., 1985-87; of counsel Tower, Byrne & Beaugureau, 1987-88; ptnr. Minutillo & Gorman, San Jose, Calif., 1989-91, Bosco, Blau, Ward & Nopar, San Jose, 1991-96; exec. v.p., gen. counsel, dir. AmeriNet Fin. Systems, Inc., Ontario, Calif., 1996-97; sole practice law Palo Alto, 1998-99; ptnr. Bosco, Ward & Nopar, 2000—. Mem. Ariz. Rep. Caucus, Phoenix, 1984-88. Mem. AICPA, ABA (bus. law and law practice mgmt. sects., mem. forum com. on franchising), Ariz. Bar Assn. (bus. law sect.), Calif. State Bar Assn. (bus. law sect.). Avocations: golf, skiing, tennis. Office: 425 Sherman Ave Ste 100 Palo Alto CA 94306-1849

NOPLIS, LINDA SHOCKEY, elementary school educator; b. Hazard, Ky., Feb. 28, 1948; d. Manuel Shockey and Pauline Smith; children from previous marriage: Kandace Marie Hunt, Charles R. II. B, U. Ky., 1970; M, Eastern Ky. U. Tchr. 3rd grade Mary Ford Elem. Sch., Charleston, SC, 1970—76, Perry County Schs.-RW Combs, Hazard, Ky., 1976—77, Hazard Ind. Schs., Hazard, 1977—. Fellow mem. Sch. Site Based Com., Hazard, Ky., 1998—99; elected mem. Supt. Search Com., Hazard, Ky., 2001; tchr. rep. Tchrs. Rights Com., Hazard, Ky., 2001—02; after sch. tutor ESS Hazard Ind. Schs., Hazard, Ky., 1990—. Registered vol. Spruce Abuse Ctr., Hazard, Ky., 2000—; Sunday sch. tchr. First Bapt. Ch., 1995—. Fellow: Nat. Edn. Assn., Hazard Edn. Assn. (sch. rep.), Ky. Edn. Assn. Democrat. Avocations: walking, reading, gardening, reading and studying the Bible, writing. Home: 74 Meadow Brook Terr Hazard KY 41701-6823 Office: Walkertown Primary Sch 325 School St Hazard KY 41701

NORA, AUDREY HART, physician; b. Picayune, Miss., Dec. 5, 1936; d. Allen Joshua and Vera Lee (Ballard) H.; m. James Jackson Nora, Apr. 9, 1966; children: James Jackson Jr., Elizabeth Hart. BS, U. Miss., 1958, MD, 1961; MPH, U. Calif., 1978. Diplomate Am. Bd. Pediatrics, Am. Bd. Hematology and Oncology. Resident in pediatrics U. Wis. Hosp., Madison, 1961-64; fellow in hematology/oncology Baylor U., Tex. Childrens Hosp., Houston, 1964-66, asst. prof. pediatrics, 1966-70; assoc. clin. prof. pediatrics U. Colo. Sch. Medicine, Denver, 1970—; dir. genetics Denver Childrens Hosp., 1970-78; cons. maternal and child health USPHS, Denver, 1978-83, asst. surgeon gen. regional health adminstr., 1983-92, dir. maternal & child health bur., health resources and svc. adminstrn., 1992-99, commd. med. officer, 1978, advanced through grades to asst. surgeon gen., 1983. Adv. com. NIH, Bethesda, 1975-77; adv. bd. Metronet Health, Inc., Denver, 1986—, Colo. Assn. Commerce and Industry, Denver, 1985—. Author: (with J.J. Nora) Genetics and Counseling in Cardiovascular Diseases, 1978, (with others) Blakiston's Medical Dictionary, 1980, Birth Defects Encyclopedia, 1990, (with J.J. Nora and K. Berg) Cardiovascular Diseases: Genetics, Epidemiology and Prevention, 1991; contbr. articles to profl. jours. Recipient Virginia Apgar award Nat. Found., 1976. Fellow Am. Acad. Pediatrics; mem. Am. Pub. Health Assn. (governing coun. 1990-92, coun. mem. maternal and child health 1990—), Commd. Officers Assn., Am. Soc. Human Genetics, Teratology Soc., Western Soc. Pediatric Rsch. Presbyterian. Avocations: quilting, cooking, hiking. Office: 1973 S Kenton Ct Aurora CO 80014-4709

NORA, HOPE, healthcare consultant; b. Laredo, Tex., June 4, 1949; d. Felix C. and Esperanza (Coronado) Rocha; m. Amaury Nora, June 19, 1971; children: Amaury E., Araceli E. BS, U. Houston, 1971; MS, Tex. A&I U., 1972; PhD, U. Houston, 1986. Staff psychologist, counselor Tex. Commn. for Vocat. Rehabv., Laredo, Tex., 1973-78; dir. programs Laredo State Ctr. for Human Devel., 1978-82; dir. clin. programming Los Encinas Hosp., Pasadena, Calif., 1987-89; dir. clin./support svcs. Woodland Hosp., Hoffman Estates, Ill., 1989-92; quality mgr. Ill. Dept. Mental Health and Developmental Disabilities, 1992-96; ind. healthcare cons. Houston, 1996—. Mem. Am. Soc. for Quality. Mem. Tex. Psychol. Assn. (cert.). Democrat. Avocations: reading, music. Home: 2001 Holcombe #803 Houston TX 77030 Office: Unit 803 2001 Holcombe Blvd Houston TX 77030-4214 E-mail: hopenora@hotmail.com

NORA, JAMES JACKSON, physician, writer, educator; b. Chgo., June 26, 1928; s. Joseph James and Mae Henrietta (Jackson) N.; m. Barbara June Fluhrer, Sept. 7, 1949 (div. 1963); children: Wendy Alison, Penelope Welbon, Marianne Leslie; m. Audrey Faye Hart, Apr. 9, 1966; children: James Jackson Jr., Elizabeth Hart Nora. AB, Harvard U., 1950; MD, Yale U., 1954; MPH, U. Calif., Berkeley, 1978. Diplomate Am. Bd. Pediatrics, Am. Bd. Cardiology, Am. Bd. Med. Genetics. Intern Detroit Receiving Hosp., 1954-55; resident in pediatrics U. Wis. Hosps., Madison, 1959-61, fellow in cardiology, 1962-64; fellow in genetics McGill U. Children's Hosp., Montreal, Can., 1964-65; assoc. prof. pediatrics Baylor Coll. Medicine, Houston, 1965-71; prof. genetics, preventive medicine and pediatrics U. Colo. Med. Sch., Denver, 1971—, prof. emeritus, 1986. Dir. genetics Rose Med. Ctr., Denver, 1980—; dir. pediatric cardiology and cardiovascular tng. U. Colo. Sch. Medicine, 1971-78; mem. task force Nat. Heart and Lung Program, Bethesda, Md., 1973; cons. WHO, Geneva, 1983—; mem. U.S.-U.S.S.R. Exchange Program on Heart Disease, Moscow and Leningrad, 1975. Author: The Whole Heart Book, 1980, 2d rev. edit., 1989; author: (with F.C. Fraser) Medical Genetics, 4th Rev. edit., 1994; author: Genetics of Man, 2d rev. edit., 1986, Cardiovascular Diseases: Genetics, Epidemiology and Prevention, 1991; author: (novels) The Upstart Spring, 1989; author: The Psi Delegation, 1989, The Hemingway Sabbatical, 1996; author: (poetry) Songs from a Brazen Bull, 2001. Com. mem. March of Dimes, Am. Heart Assn., Boy Scouts Am. Served to 2ndlt. USAAC, 1945-47. Grantee Nat. Heart, Lung and Blood Inst., Nat. Inst. Child Health and Human Devel., Am. Heart Assn., NIH; recipient Virginia Apgar Meml. award. Fellow Am. Coll. Cardiology, Am. Acad. Pediatrics, Am. Coll. Med. Genetics; mem. Am. Pediatric Soc., Soc. Pediatric Rsch., Am. Heart Assn., Teratology Soc., Transplantation Soc., Am. Soc. Human Genetics, Authors Guild, Authors League, Acad. Am. Poets, Mystery Writers Am., Rocky Mountain Harvard Club. Democrat. Presbyterian. Avocations: writing fiction, poetry.

NORA, LOIS MARGARET, dean; BS in Biology with honors, U. Ill., 1976; MD, Rush Med. Coll., Chgo., 1979; JD, U. Chgo., 1987. Diplomate Am. Bd. Neurology, Am. Bd. Electrodiagnostic Medicine; bar: Ill. 1988, D.C. 1988. Intern in family medicine Cmty. Meml. Gen. Hosp., LaGrange, Ill., 1980; resident in neurology Rush-Presbyn.-St. Luke's Med. Ctr., Chgo., 1981-84, chief resident in neurology, 1983-84, fellow electromyography and neuromuscular disease, 1984-85; asst. prof. dept. neurology, asst. dean clin. curriculum Rush Med. Coll., 1987-94, assoc. prof. dept. neurology, 1994-95; fellow Ctr. for Clin. Med. Ethics U. Chgo., 1993-95; assoc. dean acad. affairs, assoc. prof. dept. neurology U. Ky. Coll. Medicine, 1995—2002; prof. neurology U. Ky. Coll. Law, 1996—2002; dean Northwestern Ohio Univ. Coll. of Med., 2002—. Spkr. in field. Contbr. articles to profl. jours., chpts. to books. Vice chair Epilepsy Found. of Greater Chgo., 1988-90, chair, 1991, chair strategic planning com. 1990-91, bd. dirs., 1987-94; bd. dirs. Epilepsy Found. of Am., 1992-95, co-chair quality standards com. 1992-94; mem. needs assessment com. United Way of Chgo., 1989-90; camp physician children's summer camp program Muscular Dystrophy Assn., 1984-86; vol. tchr. Christ the King Elem. Sch., 1996—. Mem. AMA (mem. dean's com. on family violence curriculum 1993, mem. report and resolutions subcom. for reference com. C 1997), Am. Acad. Neurology (mem. ethics com. 1997—), Am. Assn. Electrodiagnostic Medicine (chair profl. practice com. 1991—, mem. ethics com. 1992—, mem.

grievance subcom. 1992—), Am. Coll. Physician Execs., Soc. Clin. Neurologists, Ky. Med. Assn. (mem. membership task force 1997, mem. edn. com. 1997), Fayette County Med. Soc. Office: Northeastern Univ. College of Medicine 4209 St., Rt. 44, PO Box 95 Rootstown OH 44272*

NORA, WENDY ALISON, lawyer; b. New Haven, Feb. 14, 1951; d. James Jackson Nora and Barbara June (Fluhrer) P.; m. Jay Robert Vercauteren, Aug. 21, 1973 (div. Nov. 1981); children: Lucas Jay, Eric Robert. BA, U. Wis., 1971, JD, 1975. Bar: Wis. 1975, U.S. Dist. Ct. (we. dist.) Wis. 1975, Minn. 1985, U.S. Dist. Ct. Minn. 1985, U.S. Supreme Ct. 1986. Pvt. practice, Cross Plains, Wis., 1975-81, Madison, 1981-84, Mpls., 1986-90, Madison, Wis., 1991—; developer, incorporator, pres. Cmty. Investment Credit Corp., 1997—. Atty. State of Wis., 1977-81, asst. pub. defender, 1983-84. Fellow U. Minn. Mem. ABA (vice-chmn. adminstrv. law sect., criminal law and juvenile justice com. 1982—). Home: 6931 Old Sauk Rd Madison WI 53717-1122 Office: 6515 Grand Teton Plz Ste 135 Madison WI 53719-1048

NORAAS, DIANE RICE, computer scientist, educator; b. Kansas City, Mo., Feb. 20, 1948; d. Ray R. and Nellie Lu (Clark) Rice; m. Dennis P. Tihansky, Feb. 20, 1971 (div. June 1983); children: Suzanne Marie Landsparger, John Raymond Tihansky; m. William C. Noraas, May 25, 2001. BS, Marygrove Coll., Detroit, 1969; MS, Harvard U., 1972. Computer programmer I City of Alexandria, Va., 1972; computer programmer U.S. Dept. Treasury, Washington, 1972—74; computer specialist, rsch. asst. Resources for the Future, 1976; instr. Fla. Internat. U., Miami, 1977—78; asst. prof. and chair dept. math. and computer sci. St. Mary's Coll., Orchard Lake, Mich., 1983—89; infrastructure analyst EDS, Troy, 1989—99; adj. faculty Baker Coll., Clinton Twp., 2001—. Asst. leader Girl Scouts U.S., Cambridge, Mass., 1981—82; treas. PTA, Miami, Fla., 1980—81. Mem.: Ridgedale Players (bd. dirs. 1997—), Avon Players (Stoney award 1999, 2001), Kappa Gamma Pi. Republican. Roman Catholic. Avocations: reading, needlecrafts, puzzles, community theater. Home: 23375 Crystal Dr Clinton Township MI 48036-1285

NORBACK, CRAIG THOMAS, writer; b. Pitts., Nov. 14, 1943; s. Howard George and Maybelle Veronica Montaigne (Cosse) N.; m. Judith Carol Shaul, Oct. 12, 1976. BS, Washington U., St. Louis, 1967; postgrad., Drew U., 1986—. Author, co-author, compiler, producer over 150 books, including: The Misspeller's Dictionary, 1972, Everything You Can Get from the Government for Free or Almost for Free, 1975, The Dream Machine: The Golden Age of American Automobiles 1946-65, 1976, Great Songs of Madison Avenue, 1976, Great North American Indians, 1977, The Health Care Directory, 1977, The Older American's Handbook, 1977, The Educational Marketplace, 1978, Famous American Admirals, 1978, Newsweek Travel Guide to the U.S., 1978, The Dow Jones-Irwin Guide to Franchising, 1979, The Horseman's Catalog, 1979, The Must Words, 1979, The Practical Inventor's Handbook, 1979, ABC Complete Book of Sports Facts, 1980, ABC Monday Night Football, 1980-81, 1980, The Bible Almanac, 1980, Check Yourself Out, 1980, The Signet Book of World Winners, 1980, The TV Guide Almanac, 1980, The World's Great News Photos (1840-1980), 1980, The Allergy Encyclopedia, 1981, American Expressions, 1981, The Computer Invasion, 1981, The Consumer's Energy Handbook, 1981, 500 Questions New Parents Ask, 1982, Business Week Almanac, 1982, The International Yellow Pages, 1982, The Puzzle King's Bafflers, 1982, The Associated Press Sunday Crossword Puzzle Book, 1983, Chilton's Job Textbook Series: Advertising Management, 1983, Office Management, 1983, It's a Fact, 1983, National Education Association Parent and Child Success Library: Helping Your Child Read, 1983, How Letters Make Words, 1983, How to Prepare Your Child for School, 1983, Learning the Alphabet, 1983, Learning to Add, 1983, The Ultimate Toy Catalog, 1983, U.S. Publicity Directory, various years, Advertising and Promotion Management, 1983, America Wants to Know, 1983, Certified Professional Secretary modules I through VI, 1984, East Coast Publicity Directory, 1984, Human Resources Yearbook, 1987, 88, 89, 90, Princeton Area Job Finder, 1986-87, Career Encyclopedia, 1987, Travel Publicity Directory, 1987, 88, 89, 90, Arthur Young Guide to Venture Capital, 1987, Hazardous Chemicals on File, 1988, Joint Ventures, 1992. Home: 3112 Kaitlyn Ct Princeton Junction NJ 08550-5349

NORBECK, JANE S. nursing educator; b. Redfield, S.D., Feb. 20, 1942; d. Sterling M. and Helen L. (Williamson) N.; m. Paul J. Gorman, June 28, 1970. BA in Psychology, BSN, U. Minn., 1965; MS, U. Calif., San Francisco, 1971, DNSc, 1975. Psychiat. nurse Colo. Psychiat. Hosp., Denver, 1965-66, Langley Porter Hosp., San Francisco, 1966-67; pub. health nurse San Francisco Health Dept., 1968-69; prof. U. Calif. Sch. of Nursing, San Francisco, 1975—, dept. chair, 1984-89, dean, 1989-99. Chair study sect. Nat. Inst. of Nursing Rsch., 1990-93, mem. editl. bd. Archives of Psychiat. Nursing, 1985-95, Rsch. in Nursing and Health, 1987—, Western Jour. of Medicine. Co-editor: Annual Review of Nursing Research, 1996-97; contbr. articles to profl. jours. Mem. ANA, Am. Acad. Nursing, Inst. of Medicine, Sigma Theta Tau. Office: U Calif Sch Nursing 521 Parnassus Ave San Francisco CA 94143-0001

NORBERG, ARTHUR LAWRENCE, JR. historian, physicist educator; b. Providence, Apr. 13, 1938; s. Arthur Lawrence Sr. and Margaret Helen (Riley) N. BS in Physics, Providence Coll., 1959; MS in Physics, U. Vt., 1962; PhD in History of Sci., U. Wis., 1974. Asst. prof. physics St. Michael's Coll., Winooski, Vt., 1961-63, 64-68; assoc. scientist Westinghouse Electric Co., Pitts., 1963-64; instr. in physics U. Wis., Whitewater, 1968-71; rsch. historian U. Calif., Berkeley, 1973-79; program mgr. NSF, Washington, 1979-81; dir. Charles Babbage Inst. for History of Info. Processing U. Minn., Mpls., 1981-93, 99—, prof. history of sci. and tech., 1995—, assoc. prof. computer sci., 1981-95, prof. computer sci., 1995—. Del. Am. Coun. Learned Socs., N.Y.C., 1981-87; mem. adv. coun. NASA, Washington, 1988-93; endowed ERA Land Grant chair U. Minn., 1989-93, 99—. Editor: Annals of the History of Computing, 1982-93; adv. editor Tech. and Culture, 1985-92, (book) Transforming Computer Technology: Information Processing for the Pentagon; contbr. articles to profl. jours. Founding pres. City Works-A Tech. Ctr., Mpls., 1987-90; exec. dir. Charles Babbage Found., 1984-94; trustee Charles Babbage Found., 1993-96. Fellow AAAS; mem. History of Sci. Soc. (treas. 1975-80), Brit. Soc. for History of Sci., Soc. for History of Tech., Sigma Xi. Office: U Minn Dept Computer Sci 4-192 EE/CS Bldg Minneapolis MN 55455-0290 E-mail: norberg@cs.umn.edu.

NORBY, A. PAUL, urban planner; b. Jamestown, N.D., Dec. 15, 1950; s. Allen Paul and Jean Hansberger Norby; m. Karen Lee Norby, Dec. 30, 1972; children: Aric, Jennifer. BA in Geography, Valparaiso U., 1972; MS in City and Regional Planning, So. Ill. U., 1974. Planner I, planner II, sr. planner Augusta (Ga.)-Richmond County Planning Commn., 1974-77; dir. current planning, dir. planning Dept. Cmty. Devel. and Planning, Ft. Wayne, Ind., 1977-80; asst. planning dir., planning dir., asst. city mgr. City Durham, N.C., 1980-88; dir. Durham City-County Planning Dept., 1988-99, City-County Planning Bd., Winston-Salem, N.C., 1999—. Guest lectr. Duke U.-Fuqua Sch. Bus., Durham, U. N.C., Chapel Hill, N.C. State U., Raleigh. Pres. congregation Grace Luth. Ch., Durham, 1987-89, 97-99. Mem. Am. Inst. Cert. Planners (cert., charter), Am. Planning Assn. Avocations: golf, travel. Office: City County Planning Bd PO Box 2511 Winston Salem NC 27102 E-mail: pauln@ci.winston-salem.nc.us.

NORCEL, JACQUELINE JOYCE CASALE, educational administrator; b. Nov. 19, 1940; d. Frederick and Josephine Jeanette (Bestafka) Casale; m. Edward John Norcel, Feb. 24, 1962. BS, Fordham U., 1961; MS, Bklyn. Coll., 1966; 6th yr. cert., So. Conn. State U., 1980; postgrad., Bridgeport U. Elem. tchr. pub. schs., N.Y.C., 1961-80; prin. Coventry (Conn.) Schs., 1980-84, Trumbull (Conn.) Schs., 1984—. Guest lectr. So. Conn. State U., 1980; cons. Monson (Mass.) Schs., 1984; mem. Conn. State Prin. Acad. Adv. Bd., 1986-88; mem. adj. faculty Sacred Heart U., Fairfield, Conn., 1985—, So. Conn. State U., summer 1991; fed. rels. coord. Nat. Assn. Elem. Sch. Prins., Conn., 1999—. Editor: Best of the Decade, 1980; mem. editl. adv. bd. Principal Matters; contbr. articles to profl. jours. Chmn. bldg. com. Trumbull Bd. Edn., 1978-80; chmn. Sch. Benefit Com., Trumbull, 1985-86; catechist Bridgeport Diocese, Roman Cath. Ch., Conn., 1975-85, youth min., 1979-84, coord., evaluator leadership tng. workshops for teens and adults, 1979-84; mem. St. Stephen's Parish Coun., 1993-97, trustee, 1997—; Eucharist minister, 1999—; com. mem. New Sch. Bldg. Town of Trumbull, 2001—. Recipient Town of Trumbull Svc. award, 1982, Nat. Disting. Prin. award, 1988, Joseph Formica Disting. Svc. award EMSPAC, 1994. Mem.: ASCD, Assoc. Tchrs. Math. in Conn., New Eng. Coalition Ednl. Leaders, Ea. Conn. Coun. Internat. Reading Assn., Conn. Assn. Elem. Sch. Prins., Trumbull Adminstrs. Assn. (pres.-elect 1989—91, pres. 1991—93, 2002—), Conn. Assn. Supervision and Curriculum Devel., Nat. Assn. Elem. Sch. Prins. (del. to gen. assemblies 1984—90, zone I dir. 1987—90, del. to gen. assemblies 1999—), Hartford Area Prins. and Suprs. Assn. (local pres. 1981—82), Conn. Assn. Schs. (bd. mem. 2000—), Adminstrn. and Supervision Assn. (sec. 1980—81, pres. 1981—82, exec. bd. 1982—93), Elem. Mid. Sch. Prins. Assn. (pres. 1985—86, state elected rep. 1989—90, fed. rels. coord. 1990—94, dists. 1, 2 and 3 dir. 1995—, commr. 1997—2000, fed. rels. coord. 1999—2002, Citizen of Yr. award 1991, Pres.'s award 1981—85), N.E. Regional Elem. Prins. Assn. (rep. 1984—86, sec. 1986—87), Delta Kappa Gamma (v.p. 1996—2000), Pi Lambda Theta, Phi Delta Kappa (v.p. rsch. and projects 1993—95, Disting. Fellow award 1992). Home: 5240 Madison Ave Trumbull CT 06611-1016 Office: Tashua Sch 401 Stonehouse Rd Trumbull CT 06611-1651 E-mail: norcelJ98@Yahoo.com.

NORCIA, STEPHEN WILLIAM, advertising and internet advertising executive, consultant; b. N.Y.C., Jan. 21, 1941; s. William Matthew and Amelia (Marrone) N.; m. Martha Elizabeth Whelan, Apr. 22, 1978; children: Matthew F., Daniel P., Anne E. BA, U. Conn., 1962. Media planner and buyer SSC&B, N.Y.C., 1965-66; account exec. McCann-Erickson Co., Chgo., 1966-68, v.p., dep. mgr. Milw., 1971-72, v.p., mgmt. supr. N.Y.C., 1972-74, sr. v.p., gen. mgr. Atlanta, 1974-78, exec. v.p., gen. mgr. N.Y.C., 1978-81; exec. v.p., mem. exec. policy com., mem. mgmt. com. Lintas, 1981-94, exec. v.p., 1989-91, world wide client dir., dir. bus. devel., 1991-94, also bd. dirs.; mng. ptnr. Earle Palmer Brown, 1994-96; dir. global account DDB Needham, 1996-99, mng. dir., 1998-2000; v.p. bus. devel. Agency.com, 2000—; owner cons. co. Norcia Group, 2002—. Account exec. Needham, Harper & Steers, Chgo., 1968-70; dir. mktg. product devel. workshop Interpub., N.Y.C., 1970-71; bd. dirs. Communication Counselors Network; adj. prof. Fordham U. Bd. dirs. U. Ga. Master of Br. Mgmt. Program, 1985, 86, 87, Advt. Edn. Found., 1999—. 1st lt. U.S. Army, 1962-65. Recipient Robert E. Healy award Interpub. Group Cos., 1975, Effie award Am. Mktg. Assn., 1985, Grand Effie award Am. Mktg. Assn., 1984. Mem. Am. Assn. Advt. Agys., Advt. Club N.Y., Am. Yacht Club. Republican. Roman Catholic. Avocations: tennis, boating, skiing, bicycling. Home: 1 Topsail Ln Rye NY 10580-3116 Office: Norcia Group 1 Topsail Ln Rye NY 10580-3116 E-mail: steve@norciagroup.com.

NORCOTT, FLEMMING L., JR. state supreme court justice; b. New Haven, Oct. 11, 1943; BA, Columbia U., 1965, JD, 1968. Bar: Conn. 1968. Peace corps vol. U. East Africa, Nairobi, Kenya; legal staff Bedford-Stuyvesant Restoration Corp.; asst. atty. gen. Office Atty. Gen., V.I.; judge Superior Ct., 1979-87, Appellate Ct., 1987-92; assoc. justice Conn. Supreme Ct., Hartford, 1992—. Hearing examiner Conn. Commn. Human Rights and Opportunities; co-founder, exec. dir. Ctr. Advocacy, Rsch. and Planning, Ind., New Haven; lectr. Yale U. Bd. govs. U. New Haven; bd. dirs. Dixwell Community House, Ea. Collegiate Football Ofcls. Assn., New Haven Football Ofcls. Assn., Long Wharf Theatre; assoc. fellow Calhoun Coll., Yale U.; bd. trustees Yale-New Haven Hosp. Mem. Omega Psi Phi Office: PO Box N Hartford CT 06126-1898*

NORCROSS, ALVIN WATT, retired personnel administrator, consultant; b. Buffalo, Sept. 21, 1918; s. William Watt and Nettie Anne (Alexander) Norcross; m. Charlotte Anne Guptill, Oct. 23, 1948; children: David Lichty, Nancy Dayna. BA, Baldwin-Wallace Coll., 1940; MPA, Harvard U., 1948. Employment mgr. Nat. Screw & Mfg. Co., Cleve., 1941-43; spl. asst. to dir. civilian pers. Dept. of the Air Force, Washington, 1954-58; chief of employment Gen. Svcs. Adminstrn., 1959-61; asst. dir. pers. U.S. Treasury Dept., 1961-67; dep. dir. Bur. Pers. Mgmt. Evaluation U.S. Civil Svc. Commn., 1967-73; project mgr., pub. adminstrn. advisor UN, Kubul, Afghanistan, 1975-80, chief tech. advisor Male, Republic of Maldives, 1982-84; ret., 1984. Pers. expert, cons. Agy. for Internat. Devel., Washington, 1974-75; cons. on exec. pay Orgn. Resource Counselors, Inc., N.Y.C., 1975; prin. assoc., cons. Exec. Mgmt. Svcs., Inc., Arlington, Va., 1981. Author of pamphlets. Councilman Town of Vienna, Va., 1959-65; mem. Svc. Corps of Ret. Execs., New Bedford, Mass., 1984-87, Recycling/Solid Waste Com., Westport, Mass., 1986-94; mem. citizen advd. com. Mass. Dept. Mental Health, 1989-97. 1st lt. USAF, 1943-46; lt . col. USAFR, 1946-72, ret. Mem. ASPA, Old Dartmouth Hist. Soc., Westport Hist. Soc., Westport River Watershed Alliance (bd. dirs. 1989-98), Harvard Club Greater New Bedford (adv. bd. mem. 1997-98), YMCA Greater New Bedford. Avocations: travel, tennis, drama, walking. Home: 36 Shirley St Westport MA 02790-1333

NORCROSS, MARVIN AUGUSTUS, veterinarian, retired government agency official; b. Tansboro, N.J., Feb. 8, 1931; s. Marvin A. and Katherine V. (McGuigan) N.; m. Diane L. Tuttle, Nov. 22, 1956 (div. 1991); children: James, Janet. Student, Rutgers U., 1954-55; VMD, U. Pa., 1959, PhD, 1966. Pathologist Merck Sharp & Dohme Rsch. Labs., Rahway, N.J., 1966-69, dir. clin. research, 1969-72, sr. dir. domestic vet. research, 1972-75; dir. div. vet. med. rsch. Ctr. Vet. Medicine, FDA, Rockville, Md., 1975-78, assoc. dir. for rsch., 1978-82, assoc. dir. for human food safety, 1982-84, assoc. dir. for new animal drug evaluation, 1984-87; asst. dep. adminstr., then dep. adminstr. Sci. and Tech., Food Safety and Inspection Svc. USDA, Washington, 1987-93, exec. asst. to the adminstr., 1993-94; U.S. coord. for Codex Alimentarius USDA, 1994-96, sr. sci. advisor to adminstr., 1996; cons. vet. medicine and food safety, 1996—. Adj. prof. faculty Va.-Md. Regional Coll. Vet. Medicine, Blacksburg, Va., 1980-85. Contbr. articles to profl. jours. Trustee Scotch Plains (N.J.) Community Fund, 1969-72. Served to lt. AUS, 1952-54; col. Res., 1954-83 (ret.). Recipient FDA Merit award, 1978, Meritorious Presdl. Rank award, 1989; named to Artillery OCS Hall of Fame, 2000. Mem. AVMA, AAAS, Am. Assn. Avian Pathologists, Assn. Mil. Surgeons U.S., Civil Affairs Assn., Inst. Food Technologists, Nat. Assn. Fed. Veterinarians, N.J. Acad. Sci., N.Y. Acad. Scis., Res. Officers Assn., Soc. Toxicologic Pathologists, Sigma Xi. Home and Office: 14304 Brickhowe Ct Germantown MD 20874-3431 E-mail: mjnorcross@bww.com.

NORCROSS-MEHLMAN, KARYL, neurologist, educator; b. Joliet, Ill. d. Anthony S. Music and Mary Anne Music-Ressler; m. Dan Nechay, Aug. 8, 1988 (dec. Dec. 1990); m. Myron A. Mehlman, Apr. 14, 1999. BA, Northwestern U., 1973, MD, PhD, 1978. Intern in general medicine Northwestern Meml. Hosps., Chgo., 1978-79, resident in neurology, 1979-82; asst. prof. neurology U. Tex. Med. Br., Galveston, 1982-87, assoc. prof neurology, 1987-2000, clin. prof. neurology, 2000—, dir. electroencephalography-evoked potential dept., 1982-2000, dir. EEG-evoked potential and intracoop. monitoring dept., 1982-2000, adj. prof. pediat., 1985-2000, assoc. prof. pharmacology, 1991-2000, assoc. prof. anesthesiology, 1996-2000; pres. Med. Neuro. Tox., RLLP, Princeton, N.J., 2000—; mem. med. staff Med. Ctr. Princeton, 2000—. Cons., advisor, reviewer BlueCross BlueShield of Tex., Richardson. Contbr. articles to profl. jours. Panel mem. diving adv. bd. Tex. A&M U., Galveston, 1984—. Mem. AMA, Tex. Neurol. Soc. (v.p. 1989), N. Am. Spine Soc., 1998—. Avocations: open water diving (cert.), computer graphics. Home: 7 Bouvant Dr Princeton NJ 08540-1208 Office: U Tex Med Br EEG/EP Dept 300 University Blvd Galveston TX 77555-0595 also: Med Neuro Tox RLLP 7 Bonvant Dr Princeton NJ 08540 Fax: (609) 683-0838. E-mail: mehlman@rcn.com.

NORD, ERIC THOMAS, retired manufacturing executive; b. Amherst, Ohio, Nov. 8, 1917; s. Walter G. and Virginia C. (Greive) N.; m. Jane H. Baker; children: Virginia, Emily, Carlotte, Richard. BS in Mech. Engring., Case Inst. Tech., 1939. Pres., chief exec. officer Nordson Corp., Amherst, Ohio, 1954-73, chmn., 1973-97. Also bd. dirs. Pres. Oberlin (Ohio) Bd. Edn., 1965; chmn. Oberlin City Council, 1959; bd. trustees Oberlin Coll., 1977—.

NORD, H. JUERGEN, gastroenterologist; b. Arolsen, Germany, Oct. 25, 1936; s. Rudolf and Elisabeth Nord; m. Linda M. Nord, Dec. 30, 1967; children: Dorothy, Christoph. MD, U. Frankfurt, 1964. Intern hosps., Kassel, Germany, 1964-66; resident Ind. U., Indpls., 1966-67; fellow Washington U., St. Louis, 1967-68, Ind. U., 1968-69; resident, rsch. assoc. Gutenberg U., Mainz, Germany, 1969-73; from asst. prof. to prof. medicine U. South Fla., Tampa, 1973—. Dir. divsn. digestive diseases and nutrition U. South Fla., 1990—2000. Author: Critical Care Gastroenterology, 1982, Colonoscopy: Principles and Technique, 1995. Scholar Fulbright scholar, 1963—69. Fellow: ACP, Fla. Soc. Gastrointestinal Endoscopy, Am. Soc. Gastrointestinal Endoscopy (pres. 1998—99, 1981—82), Fla. Gastroenterol. Soc. (pres. 1996—97), Am. Coll. Gastroenterology (bd. govs. 1988—92). Office: U So Fla Coll Med 4 Columbia Dr Ste 630 Tampa FL 33606-3568

NORD, HENRY J. transportation executive; b. Berlin, May 1, 1917; came to U.S., 1937, naturalized, 1943; s. Walter and Herta (Riess) N.; children: Stephen, Philip. Student, U. Oxford, Eng., 1934, Northwestern U., 1938-40, Ill. Inst. Tech., 1942; JD, De Paul U., 1949. CPA, Ill. Apprentice in export, Hamburg, Germany, 1935- 37; with GATX Corp., Chgo., 1938-85, comptroller, 1961-67, v.p., 1967-71, exec. v.p., 1971-78, sr. v.p., 1978-80, v.p., 1980-82, cons., 1982-84, fin. cons., 1982—, dir., 1964-78. Dir. Planned Lighting, Inc. to 1988. Trustee DePaul U. Served to 1st lt. AUS, 1943—46. Mem. Internat. Law Assn. Clubs: Tavern (Chgo.). Home: 1000 N Lake Shore Pl Chicago IL 60611-1308 Office: 55 W Monroe St Ste 500 Chicago IL 60603-5003

NORD, ROBERT EAMOR, lawyer; b. Ogden, Utah, Apr. 11, 1945; s. Eamor Carroll and Ella Carol (Winkler) N.; m. Sherryl Anne Smith, May 15, 1969; children: Kimberly, P. Ryan, Debra, Heather, Andrew, Elizabeth. BS, Brigham Young U., 1969; JD, U. Chgo., 1972. Bar: Ill. 1972, U.S. Dist. Ct. (no. dist.) Ill. 1972, U.S. Ct. Appeals (D.C. cir.) 1974, U.S. Dist. Ct. (mid. dist.) Fla. 1976, U.S. Ct. Appeals (7th cir.) 1977, U.S. Dist. Ct. (no. dist.) Ind. 1978, U.S. Dist. Ct. (no. dist.) Fla. 1979, U.S. Supreme Ct. 1981, U.S. Dist. Ct. (ea. dist.) Mich. 1984, U.S. Ct. Appeals (11th cir.) 1985, U.S. Ct. Appeals (3d cir.) 1996. Assoc. Chadwell & Kayser, Chgo., 1972-75; from assoc. to ptnr. Hinshaw & Culbertson, 1975—. Republican. Mem. Lds Ch. E-mail: rnord@hinshawculber+son.com. Home: 481 Woodlawn Ave Glencoe IL 60022-2175 Office: Hinshaw & Culbertson 222 N La Salle St Ste 300 Chicago IL 60601-1081 E-mail: rnord@hinshawlaw.com.

NORD, WALTER ROBERT, business administration educator, researcher, consultant; b. Mt. Kisco, N.Y., July 2, 1939; s. Arthur William and Elizabeth (Reimstedt) N.; m. Ann Feagan, June 10, 1967. BA in Econs., Williams Coll., 1961; MS in Organizational Behavior, Cornell U., 1963; PhD in Social Psychology, Washington U., St. Louis, 1967. Asst. prof. organizational psychology Washington U., 1967-70, assoc. prof., 1970-73, prof., 1973-89; prof. mgmt. U. South Fla., 1989—, Disting. Univ. prof., 2001; vis. prof. faculty commerce Northwestern U., 1981, U. B.C. (Can.), Vancouver, 1975-76. Author: (with S. Tucker) Implementing Routine and Radical Innovations, 1987; editor: Concepts and Controversy in Organizational Behavior, 1972, rev. edit, 1976; (with P. Frost and V. Mitchell) Organizational Reality, 1978, rev. edit., 1982, 86, 92; (with H. Meltzer) Making Organizations Humane and Productive, 1982; (with P. Frost and V. Mitchell) Managerial Reality, 1989, HRM Reality, 1992; (with A. Brief) Meanings of Occupational Work, 1990, (with S. Clegg and C. Hardy) Handbook of Organization Studies, 1996 (George Terry Book award 1997). Fellow APA; mem. Acad. Mgmt. Home: 6004 Pratt St Tampa FL 33647-1043 Office: U South Fla Sch Bus Tampa FL 33620-5500 E-mail: wnord@coba.usf.edu.

NORD, WARREN ALLEN, university official; b. Breckenridge, Minn., Dec. 7, 1946; m. Nancy Elizabeth Ehle; 1 child, Jeremy. BA, U. Minn., Morris, 1967; PhD, U. N.C., 1978. Dir. program humanities and human values U. N.C., Chapel Hill, 1979—. Author: Religion and American Education: Rethinking a National Dilemma, 1995; co-author: Taking Religion Seriously Across the Curriculum, 1998. Office: U NC Campus Box 3425 Chapel Hill NC 27599 Office Fax: 919-962-4318. E-mail: wnord@email.unc.edu.

NORDBERG, JOHN ALBERT, federal judge; b. Evanston, Ill., June 18, 1926; s. Carl Albert and Judith Ranghild (Carlson) N.; m. Jane Spaulding, June 18, 1947; children: Carol, Mary, Janet, John. Student, Carleton Coll., 1943—44, student, 1946—47; JD, U. Mich., 1950. Bar: Ill. 1950, U.S. Dist. Ct. (no. dist.) Ill. 1957, U.S. Ct. Appeals (7th cir.) 1961. Assoc. Pope & Ballard, Chgo., 1950-57; ptnr. Pope, Ballard, Shepard & Fowle, 1957-76; judge Cir. Ct. of Cook County, Ill., 1976-82, U.S. Dist. Ct. (no. dist.) Ill., Chgo., 1982-95, sr. judge, 1995—. Editor-in-chief, bd. editors Chgo. Bar Record, 1966-74 Magistrate of Cir. Ct. and justice of peace Ill., 1957-65. Served with USN, 1944-46; PTO Mem. ABA, Chgo. Bar Assn., Am. Judicature Soc., Law Club Chgo., Legal Club Chgo., Union League Club of Chgo., Order of Coif. Office: US Dist Ct #1886 219 S Dearborn St Chicago IL 60604-1706

NORDBY, EUGENE JORGEN, orthopedic surgeon; b. Abbotsford, Wis., Apr. 30, 1918; s. Herman Preus and Lucille Violet (Korsrud) N.; m. Olive Marie Jensen, June 21, 1941; 1 child, Jon Jorgen BA, Luther Coll., Decorah, Iowa, 1939; MD, U. Wis., 1943. Diplomate Am. Bd. Orthopedic Surgery. Intern Madison Gen. Hosp., Wis., 1943-44, asst. in orthopedic surgery, 1944-48; practice medicine specializing in orthopedic surgery Madison, 1948—. Pres. Bone and Joint Surgery Assocs., S.C., 1969—91; chief staff Madison Gen. Hosp., 1957—63; assoc. clin. prof. U. Wis. Med. Sch., 1961—; bd. dirs. Wis. Physicians Svcs., 1958—, chmn., 1979—; dir. Wis. Regional Med. Program, Chgo. Madison and No. R.R.; bd. govs. Wils Health Care Liability Ins. Plan; chmn. trustees S.M.S. Realty Corp.; mem. bd. attys. Profl. Responsibility of Wis. Supreme Ct., 1992—. Assoc. editor Clin. Orthopaedics and Related Research, 1964—; mem. adv. edtl. bd. Spine, 1994-2000. Pres. Vesterheim Norwegian Am. Mus., Decorah, Iowa, 1968-97, pres. emeritus, 1997—. Served to capt. M.C., AUS, 1944-46 Decorated Knight 1st class Royal Norwegian Order St. Olav; named Notable Norwegian Dane County Norwegian-Am. Fest, 1995; recipient Disting. Svc. award Internat. Rotary,1 987, Den Hoyeste Aere award Vesterheim, 1993, Eugene J. Nordby Rsch. award established Internat. Intradiscal Therapy Soc., 1993, Lyman Smith, M.D. and Eugene J. Nordby, M.D. award for minimally invasive spine surgery established N.Am. Spine Soc., 1998, The Nordby Bldg. designated Wis. Phys. Svc. Health Ins. Co., 1998, Disting. Eagle Scout award, 2000. Fellow Wisdom Hall of Fame; mem. Acad. Orthopaedic Surgeons (bd. dirs. 1972-73), Clin. Orthopaedic Soc., Assn. Bone and Joint Surgeons (pres. 1973), Internat. Soc. Study Lumbar Spine, State Med. Soc. Wis. (chmn. 1968-76, treas. 1976-97, Coun. award 1976), Am. Orthopaedic Assn., N.Am. Spine Soc., Internat. Intradiscal Therapy Soc. (sec. 1987-99, exec. dir. 1996—), Wis. Orthopaedic Soc., Dane County Med. Soc. (pres. 1957), Nat. Exch. Club, Madison Torske Klubben (founder, pres. 1978-98, pres. emeritus 1998—), Norwegian-Am. Orthopaedic Soc., Am. Acad. Orthopedic Surgeons, Am. Orthopedic Assn., Phi Chi. Lutheran. Home: 7824 Courtyard Dr Madison WI 53719 Office: 2704 Marshall Ct Madison WI 53705-2256 *We must remember no matter how dedicated we are to the accumulation of knowledge, it isn't always what you know that matters but what you can think of in time.*

NORDEL, PATRICIA A. OLMSTEAD, medical/surgical, critical care, and obstetrical nurse; b. New Britain, Conn., Jan. 19, 1965; d. Lester B. and Patricia (Tufts) Olmstead; m. David R. Nordel; children: David M., Dominic X. BSN, U. Conn., 1987. Cert. med.-surg. nurse. Commd. 2d lt. USAF, 1987, advanced through grades to capt., 1991, staff nurse med.-surg. Ill., Travis AFB, Calif., charge nurse outpatient RAF Greenham Common, Eng., staff nurse obstetrics RAF Upper Heyford, Eng., 1987-94; staff nurse Travel Nurse Broker Svc., Napa, Calif., 1994-95; RN Profl. Nursing Svcs., Suisun City, 1995-96; staff nurse Lake Meade Med. Ctr., Las Vegas, 1996-98; substitute tchr., sch. nurse DODDS, 2001—; sales assoc. AAFES, RAF Fairford, England, 2000—01; substitute tchr. DODDS, Yokota AB, Japan, 2001—.

NORDELL, HANS RODERICK, journalist, retired editor; b. Alexandria, Minn., June 26, 1925; s. Wilbur Eric and Amelia (Jasperson) N.; m. Joan Projansky, Apr. 30, 1955; children: Eric Peter, John Roderick, Elizabeth Sabin. AB magna cum laude, Harvard U., 1948; B Litt, U. Dublin, 1951. Exec. editor World Monitor: The Christian Science Monitor Monthly; with Christian Sci. Monitor, Boston, 1948-93, arts editor, 1968-73, asst. chief editorial writer, 1973-83, home forum editor, 1983-85, feature editor, 1985-87; exec. editor World Monitor: The Christian Science Monitor Monthly, 1988-93. Bd. dirs. Cmty. Music Ctr., Boston, 1970-94, corp. chair, 1994—; bd. dirs. Young Audiences, 1970-88; mem. Com. for Harvard Theatre Collection, 1977-91; trustee Berklee Coll. Music, 1970-97, trustee emeritus, 1997—. With USMCR, 1943-46. Fellowship Rotary Found., 1950-51. Mem. St. Botolph Club, Phi Beta Kappa. Christian Scientist. Home: 25 Meadow Way Cambridge MA 02138-4635 E-mail: rnordell@attbi.com.

NORDENBERG, MARK ALAN, law educator, university official; b. Duluth, Minn., July 12, 1948; s. John Clemens and Shirley Mae (Tappen) N.; m. Nikki Patricia Pirillo, Dec. 26, 1970; children: Erin, Carl, Michael. BA, Thiel Coll., 1970; JD, U. Wis., 1973. Bar: Wis. 1973, Minn. 1974, U.S. Supreme Ct. 1976, Pa. 1985. Atty. Gray, Plant, Mooty & Anderson, Mpls., 1973-75; prof. law Capital U. Law Ctr., Columbus, Ohio, 1975-77, U. Pitts., 1977—, acting dean Sch. Law, 1985-87, dean Sch. Law, 1987-93, interim univ. sr. vice chancellor and provost, 1993-94, Univ. Disting. Svc. prof., 1994—, interim univ. chancellor, 1995-96, univ. chancellor, 1996—. Mem. U.S. Supreme Ct. Adv. Com. on Civil Rules, Washington, 1988-93, Pa. Supreme Ct. Civil Procedure Rules Com., Phila., 1986-92; reporter civil justice adv. group U.S. Dist. Ct., Pitts., 1991-96; bd. dirs. Mellon Fin. Corp. Author: Modern Pennsylvania Civil Practice, 1985, 2d edit., 1995. Trustee Thiel Coll., Greenville, Pa., 1987-97; bd. dirs. Inst. for Shipboard Edn. Found., Pitts. Tech. Coun., Pitts. Regional Alliance, Pitts. Digital Greenhouse, Pitts. Life Scis. Greenhouse, Urban League of Pitts., United Way of Allegheny County, World Affairs Coun. of Pitts., The Carnegie Mus., Pitts., Allegheny Conf. on Cmty. Devel., Pitts., Pitts. Coun. on Higher Edn., Pa. Assn. Colls. and Univs. Named Vectors Pitts. Person of Yr. in Edn., 1996, Person of Yr., 1997, Pitts. Mag. Person of Yr., 2001. Fellow Am. Bar Found.; mem. ABA, AAU, Pa. Bar Assn., Allegheny County Bar Assn., Pitts. Athletic Assn., Law Club Pitts., Univ. Club, Duquesne Club, Wildwood Golf Club, Pitts. Golf Club. Office: U Pitts Cathedral of Learning Pittsburgh PA 15221-3662

NORDGREN, RONALD PAUL, engineering educator, researcher; b. Munising, Mich., Apr. 3, 1936; s. Paul A. and Martha M. N.; m. Joan E. McAfee, Sept 12, 1959; children: Sonia, Paul. BS in Engring., U. Mich., 1957, MS in Engring., 1958; PhD, U. Calif., Berkeley, 1962. Rsch. asst. U. Calif., Berkeley, 1959-62; mathematician Shell Devel. Co., Houston, 1963-68, staff rsch. engr., 1968-74, sr. staff rsch. engr., 1974-80, rsch. assoc., 1980-90; Brown prof. civil and mech. engring. Rice U., 1989-2000, rsch. prof., 2001—. U.S. nat. com. on theoretical and applied mechanics NRC, 1984-86, U.S. nat. com. for rock mechanics, 1991-95. Contbr. articles to profl. jours.; assoc. editor Jour. Applied Mechanics, 1972-76, 81-85; patentee in field. Fellow: ASME; mem.: NAE, Soc. Engring. Sci., Sigma Xi. Office: Rice U PO Box 1892 Houston TX 77251-1892 E-mail: nordgren@rice.edu.

NORDGREN, WILLIAM BENNETT, engineering executive; b. Salt Lake City, Mar. 5, 1960; s. Kent Widstoe and Eliza (Schmuhl) N.; m. Carolyn B. Erickson, June 26, 1981; children: William Tyson, Cameron Lynn, Cassy Erin. BS, Brigham Young U., 1986, MS, 1989. Engr. Boeing Airplanes Co., Seattle, 1986-88; pres. CIM Engring. Assocs., Orem, Utah, 1988-89; v.p. engring. Prodn. Modeling Corp., 1989-93; pres. F & H Simulations, Inc., 1993—. Developer, polar coordinant mill. Mem. Soc. Mfg. Engrs., Inst. Indsl. Engrs. Republican. Mem. Lds Ch. Avocations: fishing, camping, sports. Office: PO Box 658 Orem UT 84059-0658

NORDGULEN, ROY E. psychotherapist; b. Havre, Mont., Nov. 27, 1935; s. Roy Wolford and Joyce Nordgulen; m. Doris Nordgulen, June 15, 1961 (div. June 1988); children: Suzan Nuquist, Sandee Wurtz; m. Vicki Nordgulen, Mar. 10, 1997. AA, No. Mont. Coll., 1960; BA, U. Colo., 1980, MA, 1994. Police officer Colorado Springs Police Dept., 1960-88; instr. criminal justice Pikes Peak C.C., Colorado Springs, 1967-94; chief judge City of Havre, 1996-98; psychotherapist Lic. Profl. Counseling Assocs., 1996-98; psychotherapist, owner Another Path Counseling, Kerrville, Tex., 1998—. Grad. rsch. asst. U. Colo., 1994; co-presenter Cmty. Seminar on Couples Commn., Colorado Springs, 1995. Founding mem. Colo. Coun. on Law Enforcement, Denver, 1979, Colo. Crime Prevention Assn., Denver, 1980, Colo. Crime Stoppers, 1983; founding mem., sgt.-at-arms Colorado Springs Police Protective Assn., 1972; bd. advisors Pikes Peak C.C., 1970-92, Domestic Violence, 1979-83; accreditation officer Colo. Bd. Higher Edn. Accreditation Panel for Pikes Peak C.C.; singer Ballhook Bottoms Barber Shop Chorus, 1996-98. Mem. Nat. Assn. Forensic Counselors (cert., master addiction counselor), Am. Counseling Assn. Avocations: golf, swimming, acting. Home: PO Box 569 Ingram TX 78025-0569 Office: 310 Hwy 27 W Ingram TX 78025 E-mail: thebear@hctc.com.

NORDHAGEN, HALLIE HUERTH, nursing home administrator; b. Sarona, Wis., Apr. 2, 1914; d. Mathias James and Ethel Elizabeth (Fann) Huerth; B.Ed., U. Wis., Superior, 1938, M.A., 1949; m. Carl E. Nordhagen, May 24, 1947; children: Bruce Carl, Brian Keith. Prin., tchr. Wis. Public Schs., 1932-46; supervising tchr. Wis. Community Coll., 1946-48; psychiat. adminstr. Trempealeau County Health Care Center, psychiat. nursing home, Whitehall, Wis., 1959— ; mem. Wis. Nursing Home Adminstrs. Examining Bd.; fellow Menninger Clinic, Topeka, 1979-81; cons. to the bishop Evangelical Lutheran Ch., Western Wis. Synod. Chairperson BRAD Assn./Acohol & Drug Abuse, mem. Trampealeau County Alliance Drug Free Youth; mem. com. cons. to bishop Evang. Luth. Ch. Am., 1995, 96. Recipient Disting. Service award in edn. and hosp. adminstrn., London, 1967, award for services to human services programs Wis. Assn. Human Services, 1972, award for outstanding services to exceptional children Assn. Retarded Children, 1978, award for accomplishments in human resources Trempealeau County Conservation Service, 1981; Wis. State Senate citation, 1983; citation Wis. Gov., 1984; Women Of Leadership, elta Kappa Gamma Alpha Kappa Chptr. Jackson Counties, Wis., 2000. Mem. Wis. Assn. County Homes, Wis. Edn. Assn., Wis. Assn. Human Services Programs, Internat. Platform Assn., Am. Lutheran Ch. Women. Clubs: Whitehall Country, Women's. Author: Wisconsin Indians, 1966. Home: 35681 Claire St Whitehall WI 54773-8430

NORDHAUS, ROBERT RIGGS, lawyer; b. Albuquerque, Mar. 27, 1937; s. Robert J. and Virginia (Riggs) N.; m. Jean Friedberg, June 27, 1964; children: Ronald E., Hannah E. BA, Stanford U., 1960; LLB, Yale U., 1963. Bar: N.Mex. 1963, D.C. 1981, U.S. Supreme Ct. 1982. Asst. counsel U.S. House Reps., Washington, 1963-74, counsel interstate and fgn. commerce com., 1975-76; asst. adminstr. FEA, 1977; gen. counsel Fed. Energy Regulatory Commn., 1977-80; ptnr. Van Ness, Feldman & Curtis, 1981-93; gen. counsel Dept. of Energy, 1993-97; ptnr. Van Ness Feldman, 1997—. Adj. prof. Georgetown U. Law Ctr., Washington, 1980-85. 2d. lt. U.S. Army, 1960. Mem. Fed. Energy Bar Assn. (bd. dirs. 1989-92). Office: Van Ness Feldman Ste 700 1050 Thomas Jefferson St NW Washington DC 20007-3877

NORDIN, ERIC STANLEY, physician; b. May 11, 1961; BS, U. Cin., 1984; DO, Ohio U., 1992. Fellow in sports medicine St. Elizabeth Sports Medicine Ctr., Dayton, Ohio, 1995-96; asst. team physician U. Dayton, 1995—; family physician, sports medicine Family Practice Group, Dayton, 1996—; sch. sys. physician Northridge Schs., 1996—. Home: 243 Lairwood Dr Dayton OH 45458-9443

NORDIN, JOHN ALGOT, economist, educator; b. Mpls., Mar. 18, 1916; s. John A. and Beda (Nelson) N.; m. Agnes June Leith, Apr. 8, 1944 (dec. June 1969); children: Karen Frances, Margaret Lynn Nordin Ragle, Barbara Jean; m. Margaret N. Lahey, Mar. 30, 1970. BA, U. Minn., 1935, MA, 1937, PhD, 1941. Mem. faculty Iowa State U., 1941-61, successively asst. prof. econs., assoc. prof., 1941-56, prof. charge instrn., 1956-61; prof. dept. econs. Kans. State U., 1961-84, prof. emeritus, 1984—. Author: (with Virgil Salera) Elementary Economics, 1954; contbr. articles to profl. jours. Served with USNR, 1942-45. Mem. Phi Beta Kappa Episcopalian. Home: Apt E563 14515 W Granite Valley Dr Sun City West AZ 85375-6024

NORDIN, PHYLLIS ECK, sculptor, painter, consultant; b. Chgo. Student, Beloit Coll., Wayne State U.; BS, U. Toledo, 1963, BA cum laude, 1972, MLS, 1992. Instr. Lourdes Coll., Sylvania, Ohio, 1986-89, U. Toledo, 1986-89. Prin. works include large bronze sculptures Lucas County Main Libr., Toledo, Christ figure St. Joan of Arc Ch., Maumee, Ohio, Ronald McDonald House, Toledo, First English Evangel. Luth. Ch., Grosse Pointe Woods, Mich., Christ Presbyn. Ch., Covenant Presbyn. Ch., Toledo, Toledo Hosp., Reynolds Br. Libr., Toledo, Port Clinton and Defiance (Ohio) Librs., stone wall mural Epworth United Meth. Ch., Toledo, Beloit Coll., Wis., bronze fountain U. Toledo, bronze life-size children Treasure Coast Mall, Stuart, Fla., Kingston, Tenn. Pub. Libr., welded steel sculpture Town Ctr. Mall, Port Charlotte, Fla., Carey (Ohio) Bank, Toledo Bank, Bi-Centennial Park, Toledo, wood wall carvings 1st Meth. Ch., LaGrange, Ill., ferro-cement abstract Flower Hosp., Sylvania, Ohio, Rossford (Ohio) Meth. Ch., 12 stained glass windows Lucas County Courthouse, Toledo, 2 stained glass panels 1st Bapt. Ch., Holland, Ohio; numerous others; exhibited Allied Artists Am., Salmagundi Club, Audubon artists, Ohio Watercolor Soc., N.Am. Sculpture exhibit, numerous others; represented by Collectors Corner Toledo Mus. Art, 1970—, Am. Gallery, Sylvania. Recipient Alpha award Foothills Art Ctr., 1983, 1st prize Ann. Nat. Art Exhbn., 1978, numerous others; named to Lyons Twp. H.S. Hall of Fame, 1996. Mem. N.W. Ohio Watercolor Soc., Athena Art Soc., Toledo Artists Club (bd. dirs.), Phi Kappa Phi (hon.). Home: 4035 Tan Tara Dr Toledo OH 43623-3311

NORDLAND, GERALD, art museum administrator, historian, consultant; b. Los Angeles; AB, JD, U. So. Calif. Dean of faculty Chouinard Art Sch., L.A., 1960-64; dir. Washington Gallery of Modern Art, 1964-66, San Francisco Mus. Art, 1966-72, Frederick S. Wight Art Galleries, UCLA, 1973-77, Milw. Art Mus., 1977-85; ind. curator, author, editor Chgo., 1985—. Author: Paul Jenkins, 1972, Gaston Lachaise/The Man and His Work, 1974, Richard Diebenkorn , 1987, rev. and expanded 2d edit. , 2001, Frank Lloyd Wright: In the Realm of Ideas, 1988, Zhou Brothers, 1994, Ynez Johnston, 1996, Lev Syrkin, 1998, Twentieth Century American Drawings, 1998. Gaston Lachaise Found. grantee, 1973-74; John Simon Guggenheim Found. fellow, 1985-86. Home and Office: 645 W Sheridan Rd Chicago IL 60613-3316

NORDLAND, RODNEY LEE, news correspondent; b. Phila., Mar. 17, 1959; s. Lorine Elizabeth (Myers) Nordland; m. Sheila Caroline Webb, May 17, 1991; children: Samantha Lorine Webb, Johanna Joyce Webb, Jake Peter Webb. BS, Pa. State U., 1972—72. Fgn. corr. Asia Phila. Inquirer, Bangkok, 1978—82, fgn. corr. Ctrl. Am. San Salvador, El Salvador, 1982—84; fgn. corr., Mideast bur. chief Newsweek Mag., Beirut, 1984—85, Cairo, 1985—86, dep. fgn. editor, sr. writer N.Y.C., 1987—88, bur. chief, fgn. corr. Rome, 1989—92, Balkans bur. chief, fgn. corr. Sarajevo, Bosnia-Herzegovina, 1992—95, corr.-at-large London, 1995—. Editor: (book) The Watergate Files, 1972. Co-recipient Pulitzer prize, 1978; recipient George Polk award, 1981; fellow, Brit. Am. Soc., Johns Hopkins Sch. Advanced Internat. Studies, 1989, Neiman, Harvard U., 1988—89. Mem.: Soc. Profl. Journalists, Fgn. Press Assn. Britain, Fgn. Corrs. Club Thailand, Associazione della Stampa Estera in Italia, Investigative Reporters & Editors, Oversees Press Club, Nat. Press Club. Office: Newsweek Mag 18 Park St London 10019W1K 2HQ England Business E-Mail: rod@nordland.com.

NORDLANDER, PETER JAN ARNE, physics educator, researcher; b. Stockholm, Nov. 21, 1955; came to U.S., 1985; s. Arne Nils Ludwig and Blenda Mimmi (Sjosell) N.; m. Nancy Jean Halas, Aug. 1, 1990. MSc in Engring. Physics, Chalmers U., Sweden, 1980, PhD, 1985. Postdoctoral fellow rsch. divsn. IBM, Yorktown Heights, N.Y., 1985-86; rsch. asst. prof. Vanderbilt U., Nashville, 1987-88, adjoint asst. prof., 1988-91; sr. postdoctoral fellow Rutgers U., Piscataway, N.J., 1988-89; asst. prof. physics Rice U., Houston, 1989-93, assoc. prof., 1993-97, prof., 1997—. Cons. AT&T Bell Labs., N.Y., 1987-89; docent Chalmers U., 1991; dir. Rice quantum Inst., 2000—. Editor: Procs. Inelastic Ion Surface Collisions-10, 1994, Inelastic Ion Surface Collisions-12, 1999. 2d lt. cav. Swedish Army, 1976-77. Recipient Charles Duncan award, 1999. Mem. Am. Phys. Soc., Am. Chem. Soc. Office: Rice U Dept Physics 6100 Main St Houston TX 77005-1827 E-mail: nordland@rice.edu.

NORDLEY, GERALD DAVID, writer, investor; b. Mpls., May 22, 1947; s. V. Gerald and Evelyn May (Whitesel) N.; (div. 1973); 1 child, Sharon; m. Gayle Ann Wiesner, May 9, 1976; children: Jeffrey Goldberg, Andrew Nordley. BA in Physics, Macalester Coll., 1969; MS in System Mgmt., U. So. Calif., L.A., 1980. Enlisted USAF, 1969, commd. 2nd lt., 1970, advanced through grades to maj., 1982; inter-range ops. officer Network Ops. Div., Sunnyvale AFB, Calif., 1973-76; chief orbital ops. br. Def. Satellite Communications Directorate, L.A. AFB, 1976-81; chief spacecraft engr. br. DSCS III Program Office, 1981-82; battle dir. Mangilsan Liason Annex, Mang Il San, South Korea, 1983; chief advanced propulsion br. A.F. Rocket Propulsion Lab., Edwards AFB, Calif., 1984-86; rsch. staff mgr. ARIES office Astronautics Lab., 1986-89; ret. USAF, 1989; writer, pvt. investor Sunnyvale, 1990—. Mem. dir. Macalester Coll. Rep. Club, St. Paul, 1967-68; pres. Park Knowles Estates Property Owners Assn., Boron, Calif., 1988; co-chair Silicon Valley Writers Workshop, Cupertino, Calif., 1992, 93; treas. Contact: Cultures of the Imagination, 1997-99. Decorated Air Force Commendation medal with 4 oak leaf clusters, Meritorious Svc. medal with 1 oak leaf cluster; recipient Anlab award Analog Mag., 1992, 93, 2000. Fellow Brit. Interplanetary Soc.; mem. AIAA (elec. propulsion com. 1984-86), Air Force Assn., Sci. Fiction Writers Am., Whensday People Writers Group, Ft. Mason's Officers Club, Am. Legion. Unitarian Universalist. Avocation: amateur astronomy. E-mail: gdnordley@aol.com.

NORDLIE, ROBERT CONRAD, biochemistry educator; b. Willmar, Minn., June 11, 1930; s. Peder Conrad and Myrtle (Spindler) N.; m. Sally Ann Christianson, Aug. 23, 1959; children: Margaret, Melissa, John. BS St. Cloud State Coll., Minn., 1952; MS, U. N.D., 1957, PhD, 1960. Tchg., rsch. asst. biochemistry U. N.D. Med. Sch., Grand Forks, 1955-60, rsch. prof. biochemistry, 1962-74, Chester Fritz disting. prof. biochemistry, 1974—, Cornatzer prof., chmn. dept. biochemistry and molecular biology, 1983-2000; Chesiter Fritz disting. emeritus prof., 2000—. Hon. prof. San Marcos U., Lima, Peru, 1981, 82—; emeritus prof., 2000-; NIH fellow Inst. Enzyme Rsch., U. Wis., 1960-61; mem. biochemistry study sect. NIH; merit rev. com. VA, 1994—; cons. enzymology Oak Ridge, 1961—; vis. prof. Tokyo Biomed. Inst., 1984; mem. predoctoral fellowship rev. group Howard Hughes Inst., 1990-93. Mem. editorial bd.: Jour. Biol. Chemistry, Biochimca et Biophysica Acta. Research publs. on enzymology relating to metabolism of various carbohydrates in mammalian livers, regulation blood sugar levels. Served with AUS, 1953-55. Recipient Disting. Alumnus award St. Cloud State U., 1983; recipient Sigma Xi Rsch. award, 1969, Golden Apple award U. N.D., 1968, Edgar Dale award U. N.D., 1983, Burlington No. Faculty Scholar award, 1987, Thomas J. Clifford Faculty Achievement award for excellence in rsch. U. N.D. Found., 1993. Mem. AAAS, Am. Soc. Biol. Chemistry and Molecular Biology, Am. Chem. Soc., Internat. Union Biochemists, Soc. Exptl. Biology and Medicine, Am. Inst. Nutrition, Sigma Xi, Alpha Omega Alpha. Home: 162 Columbia Ct Grand Forks ND 58203-2947 E-mail: rnordlie@medicine.nodak.edu .

NORDLING, BERNARD ERICK, lawyer; b. Nekoma, Kans., June 14, 1921; s. Carl Ruben Ebben and Edith Elveda (Freeburg) N.; m. Barbara Ann Burkholder, Mar. 26, 1949. Student, George Washington U., 1941-43; AB, McPherson Coll., 1947; JD, U. Kans., 1949. Bar: Kans. 1949, U.S. Dist. Ct. Kans. 1949, U.S. Ct. Appeals (10th cir.) 1970. Pvt. practice, Hugoton, Kans., 1949—; ptnr. Kramer, Nordling & Nordling, 1950-99; mem. Kramer, Nordling & Nordling, LLC, 1999—; city atty. City of Hugoton, 1951-87; county atty. Stevens County, Kans., 1957-63. Kans. mem. legal com. Interstate Oil Compact Commn., 1969-93; mem. supply tech. adv. com. nat. gas survey FPC, 1975-77. Editor U. Kans. Law Rev., 1949. Mem. Hugoton Sch. Bds., 1954-68, pres. grade sch. bd., 1957-63; trustee McPherson Coll., 1971-81, mem. exec. com., 1975-81; mem. Kans. Energy Adv. Coun., 1975-78, mem. exec. com., 1976-78. With AUS, 1944-46. Recipient Citation of Merit, McPherson Coll., 1987, Disting. Alumnus award, Kans. U. Law Sch., 1993, Lifetime Achievement award, Hugoton Kans. Area C. of C., 1994, James Wood Green medallion, Kans. U. Law Sch., 2001. Fellow: Am. Bar Found. (Kans.); mem.: ABA, S.W. Kans. Royalty Owners Assn. (exec. sec. 1968—94, asst. exec. sec. 1994—), Nat. Assn. Royalty Owners (bd. govs. 1980—99), City Attys. Assn. Kans. (exec. com. 1975—83, pres. 1982—83), Am. Judicature Soc., S.W. Kans. Bar Assn., Kans. Bar Assn., Kans. U. Alumni Assn. (bd. dirs. 1992—97, Fred Ellsworth medallion 1997, James Woods Green medallion 2001), Kans. U. Endowment Assn. (trustee 1989—), U. Kans. Law Soc. (bd. govs. 1984—87), Phi Alpha Delta, Order of Coif. Address: 4404 Nicklaus Dr Lawrence KS 66047 E-mail: benordling@sunflower.com.

NORDLINGER, GERSON, investor; b. Washington, Feb. 2, 1916; s. Gerson and Camille (Bensinger) N. BA, George Washington U., 1935; BCS, Benjamin Franklin U., 1939. Head Navy Dept. Bur. Aeros. Budget, 1946-50; pres. Nordlinger Investment Corp., Washington, 1955—; trustee Washington Real Estate Investment Trust, 1961-98. Chmn. D.C. Arts Commn., 1965-67; v.p. Nat. Symphony Assn., 1953-59, Nat. Ballet, 1966-70, Alliance Francaise, 1980-97; pres. Prevention of Blindness Soc., 1960-67; treas. Friendship House, 1951-69; vice chmn. D.C. Recreation Bd., 1960-67; trustee Washington Performing Arts Soc., Mt. Vernon Coll., Washington Opera, Cathedral Choral Soc., Phillips Collection (Angel of Arts award 2001); mem. state com. Republican Party, 1952-64. Lt. comdr. Supply Corps, USNR, 1941-46, PTO. Mem. D.C. Inst. CPAs, Cosmos Club, Met. Club. Home: 2700 Calvert St NW # 515 Washington DC 20008-2621 also: 3900 Galt Ocean Dr Fort Lauderdale FL 33308-6631 E-mail: gersonn@aol.com.

NORDLINGER, STEPHANIE G. lawyer; b. L.A., 1940; BA, UCLA, 1961, MA, 1969, U. Calif., Berkeley, 1962; JD, Loyola U., 1975. Bar: Calif. 1975, U.S. Dist. Ct. (ctrl. dist.) Calif. 1976, U.S. Ct. Appeals (9th cir.) 1976, U.S. Supreme Ct. 1992. Pvt. practice, L.A., 1976-77, 89—; dep. pub. defender L.A. County, 1977-79; adj. prof. Calif. State U., Northridge, 1979; pvt. practice Santa Monica, Encino, Calif., 1979-83; assoc. Baltaxe, Rutkin & Levin, Beverly Hills, 1983-84; pvt. practice Marina del Rey, 1984-87; exec. dir. Westside Legal Svcs., Santa Monica, 1988. Mem. adv. com. U.S. Ct. Appeals (9th cir.), San Francisco, 1987-90; dir. Joseph Beggs Found., Redlands, Calif., 1992-95. Cons.: (book) CEB California Civil Writ Practice, 1987; editor User Friendly, 1997-98. Bd. dirs. Beverly Hills-Westwood chpt. pres. ACLU, 1973-74; pres. Westwood Dem. Club, L.A., 1993-95; mem. state ctrl. com. Calif. Dems., 1995-96. Mem. RAND Alumni Assn., L.A. Computer Soc. (pres. 1994, 2000-01, dir., editor), Sierra Club. Avocations: genealogy, gardening, travel. Office: PO Box 78757 Los Angeles CA 90016-0757 E-mail: snordlinge@aol.com.

NORDLUND, DONALD CRAIG, lawyer; b. Chgo., May 23, 1949; s. Donald E. and Jane (Houston) N.; m. Sally Baum, Sept. 7, 1975; children: Courtney Elizabeth, Michael Andrew, Laurie Katherine. AB, Stanford U., 1971; JD, Vanderbilt U., 1974. Assoc. Ware & Freidenrich, Palo Alto, Calif., 1974-77; atty. Hewlett-Packard Co., 1977-87, assoc. gen. counsel, sec., 1987-99; sr. v.p., gen. counsel, sec. Agilent Technologies, Inc., 1999—. Sec. Agilent Tech. Found. and various Agilent Tech. subsidiaries, 1999—; panelist ann. disclosure doc. seminar Practicing Law Inst., 1982—2001, co-chmn., 2002; bd. dirs. Addison Ave. Fed. Credit Union, 2002—. Chmn., bd. dirs. Santa Clara County chpt. Jr. Achievement, 1995-97. Mem.: Am. Corp. Counsel Assn. (bd. dirs. San Francisco chpt. 1984—2000, pres. 1989—90, nat. bd. dirs. 1995—2001), Am. Soc. Corp. Secs. Inc. (pres. San Francisco region 1986—88, bd. dirs. 1987—90, mem. exec. com. 1988—89, chmn. securities law com. 1995—98, nat. chmn. 1999—2000), Foothills Tennis and Swimming Club. Avocations: tennis, skiing, sailing, golf. Office: Agilent Technologies Inc 395 Page Mill Rd Palo Alto CA 94306-2024

NORDLUND, DONALD ELMER, manufacturing company executive; b. Stromsburg, Nebr., Mar. 1, 1922; s. E.C. and Edith O. (Peterson) N.; m. Mary Jane Houston, June 5, 1948; children: Donald Craig, William Chalmers, Sarah, James. AB, Midland Coll., 1943; JD, U. Mich., 1948. Bar: Ill. 1949. With Stevenson, Conaghan, Hackbert, Rooks and Pitts, Chgo., 1948-55, A.E. Staley Mfg. Co., Decatur, Ill., 1956-85, v.p., dir., mem. exec. com., 1958-65, pres., chief operating officer, 1965-80, dir., mem. exec. com., 1965-85, also chmn., 1975-85; chief exec. officer Staley Continental, Inc., Rolling Meadows, Ill., 1985-88, chmn. and chief exec. officer, 1985-88. Past chmn. bd. trustees Millikin U., now hon. trustee; trustee Mus. Sci. and Industry, Chgo., Rush-Presbyn. St. Lukes Med. Ctr., Chgo.; bd. dirs. Lyric Opera Chgo.; mem. grad. dirs. coun. Decatur Meml. Hosp. Mem. ABA, Chgo. Bar Assn., Corn Refiners Assn. (bd. dirs., past chmn., now hon. dir.), Legal Club, Comml. Club, Chgo. Club, Tavern Club, Barrington Hills Club, Phi Alpha Delta.

NORDLUND, WILLIAM CHALMERS, lawyer; b. Chgo., Aug. 29, 1954; s. Donald E. and Jane H. (Houston) N.; m. Elizabeth Apell, Oct. 1, 1983; children: William Chalmers Jr., Scott Donald. BA, Vanderbilt U., 1976; JD, Duke U., 1979; MM, Northwestern U., 1990. Bar: Ill. 1979, Md. 1991, Mich. 1992. Assoc. Winston & Strawn, Chgo., 1979-87, ptnr., 1987-90; atty. Constellation Holdings, Inc., 1990-91; v.p., sec., gen. counsel The Oxford Energy Co., Dearborn, Mich., 1991-92, sr. v.p., sec., gen. counsel, 1992-93; gen. counsel Panda Energy Corp., Dallas, 1993-94, v.p. and gen. counsel, 1994-95; v.p., gen. counsel Panda Energy Internat., Inc., 1995-96, sr. v.p., gen. counsel, 1996-97, exec. v.p. of fin., 1997-98; prin. Twinbridge Capital Holdings, LLC, New Canaan, Conn., 1999-2000; mng. dir. Dolphin Networks, Ltd., Morristown, N.J., 2000-01, pres., COO, 2001—. Bd. dirs. Orch. of Ill., Chgo., 1983-85; bd. dirs., sec. Literacy Vols. of Am.-Ill., Chgo., 1985-88, treas., 1988-90. Avocations: golf, tennis, skiing. Office: Dolphin Networks Ltd Ste 1419 89 Headquarters Plz N #1419 Morristown NJ 07960 E-mail: wnordlund@dolphin-networks.com.

NORDMAN, CHRISTER ERIC, chemistry educator; b. Helsinki, Finland, Jan. 23, 1925; came to U.S., 1948, naturalized, 1960; s. Eric Johan and Gertrud (Nordgren) N.; m. Barbara Lorraine Neal, Nov. 28, 1952 (div. 1993); children: Christina, Aleta, Eric, Carl; m. Outi Marttila, Dec. 28, 1994. Dipl. Ing., Finnish Inst. Tech., Helsinki, 1949; PhD, U. Minn., 1953. Research asso. Inst. Cancer Research, Phila., 1953-55; mem. faculty U. Mich., Ann Arbor, 1955—, prof. chemistry, 1964-95; prof. emeritus, 1995—. Mem. U.S. Nat. Com. Crystallography, 1970-72. Served with Finnish Army, 1943-44. NIH spl. fellow, 1971-72; recipient A.L. Patterson award, 1997. Fellow AAAS; mem. Am. Chem. Soc., Am. Phys. Soc., Am. Crystallographic Assn., Finnish Soc. Scis. and Letters. Home: 27 Haverhill Ct Ann Arbor MI 48105-1406 Office: Univ Mich Dept Chemistry Ann Arbor MI 48109

NORDMAN, OETHER, security firm executive; b. Scio, Oreg., May 28, 1950; Grad. h.s., Sacramento. Author: (poem) Dreamscape, 2000 (Editor's Choice award, 2000). Staff Sgt. U.S. Army, 1968—88. Recipient Cert. Appreciation, Am. Soc. for Indsl. Security, 2001. Baptist. Avocations: camping, writing, working on house. Home: 4637 Raley Blvd Sacramento CA 95838 Office: Securitas Inc Ste 250 1620 E Roseville Pkwy Roseville CA 95661

NORDMAN, OLLI, optical engineer; b. Finland; s. Helvi and Vilho Salminen; m. Nina Nordman. PhD, U. Joensuu, Finland. Docent U. Joensuu. Contbr. articles. Mem.: OSA. Office: Univ Ariz Optical Sci 1630 E University Blvd Tucson AZ 85721 Business E-Mail: onordman@u.arizona.edu.

NORDMARK, GLENN EVERETT, civil engineer; b. Sioux City, Iowa, Jan. 12, 1929; s. Klas Everett and Laura Evangeline (Medalen) N.; m. Mary Lou Scott, Aug. 23, 1952; children: Bruce Scott, Craig Eric, Scott Douglas. BSCE, S.D. State U., 1951; MSCE, U. Ill., 1955. Registered profl. engr., Pa. From rsch. engr. to tech. specialist Alcoa Tech. Ctr., Alcoa Center, Pa., 1955-93. Author: (Book) Fatigue Design of Aluminum Components and Structures; contbr. articles to profl. jours. Scoutmaster Boy Scouts Am., Lower Burrell, Pa., 1957-90. Capt. USAF, 1951-53. Mem. ASCE (fatigue com. 1958-62, 73-78), SAE (fatigue design evaluation com.), Toastmasters (pres. 1980-90, Outstanding Club Pres. 1980), Am. Welding Soc., Sigma Xi. Presbyterian. Home: 331 Claremont Dr Lower Burrell PA 15068-2413 Office: 331 Claremont Dr Lower Burrell PA 15068-2413

NORDQUIST, STEPHEN GLOS, lawyer; b. Mpls., May 13, 1936; s. Oscar Alvin Nordquist and Georgiana (Glos) Ruplin; m. Cynthia Alexandra Turner, Aug. 16, 1958 (div. Aug. 1967); children: Darcy Alden Sullivan, Timothy Turner; m. Regina Frances Stanton, Nov. 1, 1969 (div. May 1996); 1 child, Nicholas Alden; m. Sandra Schnitzer Stern, Sept. 2, 1999. BA cum laude, U. Minn., 1958, LL.B cum laude, 1961. Bar: Minn. 1961, N.Y. 1962. Assoc. Dewey, Ballantine, Bushby, Palmer & Wood, N.Y.C., 1961-69, ptnr., 1969-85; sr. v.p. W.P. Carey & Co., Inc., 1985-86, exec v.p., sec., 1986-87; ptnr. Cole & Deitz (now Winston & Strawn), 1988-89; of counsel Dreyer and Traub, 1990-91; mem. Nordquist & Stern PLLC, 1996—. Pres., bd. dirs. Carey Corp. Property, Inc., Carey-Longmont Inc., Carey-Longmont Real Property, Inc., N.Y.C., 1985-87, 520 East 86th Street, Inc. Commr. N.Y. Law Revision Commn., 1999—. Mem.: Knickerbocker Club (house com.). Republican. Congregationalist. Home: 211 E 53d St Apt 7D New York NY 10022-4805 also: 10791 & 10817 Rognaldson Rd Brainerd MN 56401-8444 Office: 509 Madison Ave Ste 612 New York NY 10022-5501 E-mail: SGNLAW@aol.com.

NORDQVIST, ERIK ASKBO, shipping company executive; b. Copenhagen, Aug. 8, 1943; s. Joergen and Lissie (Moeller) A.; m. Kirsten Vibeke Kenholt, Sept. 17, 1970; children: Ken-Martin, Alexander. Student, Danish Comml. Coll. Commerce, London, 1963-64, U. S.C., 1964-65. Vice pres. Import Center W.S., L.A., 1964-65; mgr. Denning Freight Forwarders Ltd., Toronto, Ont., Can., 1965-66; sales dir. overseas Samson Transp. Co., Copenhagen, 1967-68; mng. dir., pres. Seair AS, 1969-71, Nordbird Group, Vedbaek,

Denmark, 1971—, Nordbird AS, 1971—; chmn. European Steamship Line, Vedbaek, 1995—, European Airline Sys., Vedbaek, 1995—. Also Nordbird Oil, Nordbird Fin., Copenhagen, Nordbird Internat. Financing Ltd., Toronto, Ont.; v.p. N. Sea Products Inc., High Point, N.C., 1980—; bd. dirs. Fino Travel, Odense, Denmark, Annex Furniture Galleries, European Broadcast Comm., Vedbaek, On Holding Ltd., Gibraltar, Olsen & Nordqvist Holding, Holbaek, Denmark, pres., 1986—, NQ-Byg Aps, Holbaek, Auto Dan-Am., Holbaek, Autotel Internat., Roskilde, On Holding APS, Vedbaek Dansk-Fransk Osters Aps, 3 Danish Open, U.S., Gt. Britain, Japan,, Tins and Cans, Denmark; chmn. European Broadcast Comm., Charlottenlund, Denmark, London, European Aid Found., Vedbaek, Denmark, Lac, Albanien; cons. Frederikshavns. Skibsvaerf AS, Copenhagen Cmty. Chmn. European Broadcast Comm., Copenhagen and London, 1992—, European Aid Found., Copenhagen and N.Y.C.; del. Internat. Red Cross, Copenhagen, 1994—. Recipient Devel. honor for shipping City of Le Havre, France, 1971. Mem. Det Udenrigspolitiske Selskab, Funen Soc. (founder, past pres.). Conservative. Lutheran. Office: EAS/ESL/RSD 35 Flintemarken 2950 Vedbaek Denmark E-mail: enq@sol.dk.

NORDSTROM, BLAKE W. retail executive; Pres. Nordstrom, Inc., Seattle. Office: Nordstrom Inc 1617 Sixth Ave Seattle WA 98101-1742*

NORDT, SEAN PATRICK, clinical toxicologist; b. Port Jefferson, N.Y., Nov. 6, 1967; s. Kenneth Albert and Mary Anne (Ryan) N.; m. Lisa Elaine Vivero, Feb. 2, 1997. BS, St. John's U., Jamaica, N.Y., 1993, DPharm, 1995. Lic. pharmacist Calif., N.Y., Fla.; diplomate Am. Bd. Applied Toxicology. Asst. dir. San Diego divsn. Calif. Poison Control Sys., 1995—; asst. clin. prof. U. Calif., San Diego. Cons. San Diego Zoo, 1995—, Sea World San Diego, 1995—, 3E Co., San Diego, 1995—. Contbr. chpts. to books. Texaco Postdoctoral fellow Am. Acad. Clin. Toxicology, 1996. Mem. Am. Acad. Clin. Toxicology, Am. Assn. Poison Control Ctrs., Am. Coll. Clin. Pharmacy, Nat. Assn. Against Health Fraud. Achievements include pharmacokinetic analysis of medications, laboratory interactions and assays, toxicity case reports and research. Office: Calif Poison Control System 200 W Arbor Dr San Diego CA 92103-9000

NORDYKE, ELEANOR COLE, population researcher, public health nurse; b. Los Angeles, June 15, 1927; d. Ralph G. and Louise Noble (Carter) Cole; m. Robert Allan Nordyke, June 18, 1950; children: Mary Ellen Nordyke-Grace, Carolyn Nordyke-Cozzette, Thomas A., Susan E., Gretchen Nordyke Worthington. BS, Stanford U., 1950; P.H.N. accreditation, U. Calif.-Berkeley, 1952; MPH, U. Hawaii, 1969. RN. Pub. health nurse San Francisco Dept. Health, 1950-52; nurse-tchr. Punahou Sch., Honolulu, 1966-67; clinic coordinator East-West Population Inst., East-West Ctr., 1969-75, population rschr., 1975-82, rsch. fellow, 1982-92. Cons. Hawaii Commn. on Population, Honolulu, 1970-83; mem. Hawaii Policy Action Group for Family Planning, Honolulu, 1971-89, chmn., 1976-77; nurse-cons. vol. Straub Clinic and HOsp., 2001--. Author: The Peopling of Hawaii, 1977, 2d rev. edit., 1989, A Profile of Hawaii's Elderly Population, 1984; author: (with Robert Gardner) The Demographic Situation in Hawaii, 1974; author: Pacific Images Views from Cook's Third Voyage, 1999, I'm Third-An American Boy of Depression Years, 2002; mem. editl. bd. Hawaiian Jour. History, 1980—; contbr. articles to profl. jours. Bd. dirs. YMCA, Honolulu, 1970-85, YMCA Camp Erdman Br., 1985—, vice-chmn. 1978-79, chmn. YMCA Camp Erdman, 1989-92; bd. dirs. Hawaii Planned Parenthood, 1974-78, Friends of Libr. of Hawaii, 1985-87, 2002—; trustee Hawaiian Hist. Soc., 1978-82, Arcadia Retirement Residence, Honolulu, 1978-87; mem. liberal arts coun. Hawaii Pacific U., 1988—. Mem. Population Reference Bur., Am. Statis. Assn., Hawaii Econ. Assn., Hawaiian Hist. Soc., Friends of East-West Ctr., Friends of Univ. Hawaii Sch. Medicine, Stanford Nurses Alumni Assn., Stanford Alumni Assn. (bd. dirs. Hawaii chpt.), U. Hawaii Sch. Pub. Health Alumni Assn. (life), Gen. Fed. Women's History Club, Adventurers' Club of Honolulu, Book Reading Club, Outrigger Canoe Club, Morning Music Club, Caledonian Soc., NAIC Wiki Kala Investment Club, Phi Beta Kappa. Democrat. Congregationalist. Avocations: music, art, swimming, birds, travel. Home: 2013 Kakela Dr Honolulu HI 96822-2158 E-mail: rnordyke@aol.com.

NORDYKE, ROBYN LEE, primary school educator; b. Dodge City, Kans., Aug. 20, 1948; d. Donald L. and Lois O. (Blattner) Dansel; m. Rod E. Nordyke, July 11, 1970; children: Alisha, Kelsey, Gina. AA, Dodge City C.S., 1968; BS in Edn., Fort Hays State U., 1970. First grade tchr. Unified Sch. Dist. #214, Ulysses, Kans., 1970-76, kindergarten tchr., 1976-79, 92—; dir., owner Robyn's Nest Pre-Sch., 1980-92. Cons. Discovery Toys, Livermore, Calif., 1984-90. 4-H project leader, 1988—, cmty. leader, 1999—; bd. mem. Unified Sch. Dist. #214 Bd. Edn., Ulysses, 1981-85; bd. mem., treas. and chmn., sec. libr. bd. Grant County, Ulysses, 1986-95, mem. extension exec. bd., 1997-98; mem. Grant County 4-H Program Devel. Com., 1997-98; mem. adv. bd. Parents as Tchrs., 1998—. Avocations: skiing, walking, reading. Home: 109 S Durham St Ulysses KS 67880-2307

NOREIKA, JOSEPH CASIMIR, ophthalmologist; b. Scranton, Pa., Aug. 21, 1950; s. Joseph C. and Joan (Stirna) N.; m. Joanne Elizabeth Keane, May l4, 1977; children: Sarah, Michael, Katya, Mathew. BS, U. Scranton, 1972; MD, Jefferson Med. Coll., l976; MBA, Case Western Res. U., l988. Diplomate Am. Bd. of Opthalmology. Intern Dartmouth Hosps., Hanover, N.H., 1976-77; resident in ophthalmology U. Pitts., 1977-80, assoc. clin. prof., l98l-83; fellow U. Calif., San Francisco, 1980-8l; pvt. practice Medina, Ohio, 1983—. Founding mem. Physician Resources Group, 1995, bd. dirs., mem. nominating com., chmn. compensation com., 1995, chmn. practice mgmt. physician adv. bd.; adj. cl in. staff Cleve. Clinic Found., 1980-92. Editl. advisor The Argus; sect. contbr.: Ocular Surgery News, editl. bd., Adminstrv. Ophthalmology; editl. bd. Eye World News Svc.; contbr. articles to profl. jours. Bd. dirs. Physician Resource Group. Recipient Shoemaker award Pa. Acad. Ophthalmology, 1979; Heed Found. fellow, l980. Mem. AMA (Physician Recognition award 1984-96), Am. Acad. Ophthalmology (chmn. computerized patient record task force 1994-95, chair practice mgmt. com. 1997, managed care adv. com. 1994-95, Honor award 1996, chair e-practice task force, cons. practice mgmt. com. 2001), Am. Soc. Cataract and Refractive Surgeons (sci. adv. bd. rep., rep. to AMA CPT adv. com., govt. rels. com.), Am. Soc. Ophthalmology Adminstrs. (editl. bd. Adminstrv. Ophthalmology, Ohio State Med. Assn., Ohio Ophthalmology Soc. (editor Managed Care-n Focus, chmn. managed care com.), Medina County Med. Soc. (past pres., program chmn.), Cleve. Ophthalmology Soc. (past pres.), Alpha Sigma Nu, Beta Gamma Sigma. Avocations: computers, collecting toy trains. Office: Eye Care Medina Inc Reserve Commons Dr Medina OH 44256-8155

NORELID, JAN A. construction materials company executive; b. Sweden, 1953; , naturalized; married; 2 children. Grad., Stockholm Sch. Econs. Various fin. and mgmt. positions various multinat. corps.; CFO U.S. oper. subs. of Swedish med. equipment mfr.; owner printing co.; v.p., CFO Devcon Internat. Corp., Deerfield Beach, Fla., 1997—. Office: Ste 201 1350 E Newport Center Dr Deerfield Beach FL 33442

NORELL, MARK ALLEN, paleontology educator; b. St. Paul, July 26, 1957; s. Albert Donald Norell and Helen Louise Soltau; m. Vivian Pan, Nov. 1, 1991; 1 chld, Inga Pan. BS, Long Beach State U., 1980; MS, San Diego State U., 1983; PhD, Yale U., 1988. Assoc. curator Am. Mus., N.Y.C., 1989-99, chmn. dept., 1996—, divsn. chmn., curator, 1999—. Adj. assoc. prof. dept. biology Yale U., New Haven, 1991—. Author: All You Need to Know About Dinosaurs, 1991, Discovering Dinosaurs, 1995, 2d edit., 2000, Searching for Velociraptor, 1996, A Dinosaur and Its Nest, 1999. Named Disting. Alumnus, Long Beach State U., 2000. Fellow: Willi Hennig Soc.; mem.: Soc. Vertebrate Paleontology (Romer prize 1987). Office: Am Museum of Natural History 79th at Central Park W New York NY 10024-5192 E-mail: norell@amnh.org.

NOREM, RICHARD FREDERICK, SR. musician, music educator; b. Joliet, Ill., June 28, 1931; s. Oscar Lewis and Mabel Vera (Meyer) N.; m. Sally Lou Jarvis, July 24, 1954; 1 son, Richard Frederick II. Mus.B., U. Rochester, 1953, Mus.M., 1958; postgrad., Guildhall Sch., London, 1974. Instr. Joliet Musical Coll., Ill., 1951-53; tchr. Rochester Pub. Schs., N.Y., 1956-57; mem. faculty La. State U., Baton Rouge, 1957-95, prof., asst. dean music, 1969-84, prof. emeritus, 1995. Dir., sec.-treas. Bank Commerce, 1983-97; bd. dirs., sec.-treas. NBC Fin. Corp., 1988-97; mem. adv. bd. dirs. First Am. Tenn. Bank., 1997-99, AmSouth Bank, 1999-2002. Mem. Baton Rouge Symphony Orch., 1957—, Timm Woodwind Quintet, 1957-95; founder La. State U. Faculty Brass Quintet (now named Norem Brass Quintet of La. State U.), 1999. With USMC Band, 1953-56. Mem. Am. Legion (past post comdr.), Rolls-Royce Owners Club (sec.-treas. So. Delta region 1982-98, regional chmn. 1997-99), Norwegian Club Baton Rouge, La. State U. Faculty Club, Baton Rouge Model R.R. Club, Rotary. Republican. Episcopalian. Home: 4821 Sweetbriar St Baton Rouge LA 70808-8660 Office: La State U Sch Music Baton Rouge LA 70803-0001 *I have been blessed by the divine creator with an artistic talent in music to which I have dedicated my life. Early during my performing career I knew I must share with others the knowledge I had obtained in music; consequently my goals have been to train and educate the hundreds of music students I have taught during my teaching career. I have also tried to continue to bring beauty to our world in my own way as an active performing musician in the Baton Rouge Symphony Orchestra.*

NORFLEET, SCOTT ALAN, software engineer; b. Claremore, Okla., Jan. 18, 1959; s. Stan Edward and Gayle Patrick (Raulston) Norfleet. BSEE, Okla. State U., 1982. Sr. software engr. ABB Automation, Bartlesville, Okla., 1982—. Mem. com. United Way, Bartlesville, 1998; mem. Energy Mgmt. Com., Bartlesville, 1994-98; vice chmn. Green Country Ind. Living Ctr., Bartlesville, 1994-98. Mem. Jaycees (Okla. state treas. 1992-95, gov. 1991, Bartlesville local dir. 1987-98, Project Chmn. of Yr. 1998). Avocation: flying. Home: 4908 Baylor Dr Bartlesville OK 74006-8507 Office: 7051 Industrial Blvd Bartlesville OK 74006-6036 Fax: 509 693-8767. E-mail: scotnor@swbell.net.

NORFOLK, WILLIAM RAY, lawyer; b. Huron, S.D., Mar. 15, 1941; s. James W. and Helen F. (Thompson) N.; m. Marilyn E. Meadors; children: Stephanie G., Allison T., Meredith H. BA, Miami U., Oxford, Ohio, 1963; student, U. London, 1963-64; LLB, Duke U., 1967. Bar: N.Y. 1968, U.S. Dist. Ct. (so. and ea. dists.) N.Y. 1969, U.S. Ct. Appeals (2d cir.) 1969, U.S. Ct. Appeals (9th cir.) 1977, U.S. Ct. Appeals (5th cir.) 1979, U.S. Ct. Appeals (3d and 11th cirs.) 1981, U.S. Dist. Ct. (ea. dist.) Mich. 1986, U.S. Ct. Appeals (6th and 8th cirs.) 1986, U.S. Ct. Appeals (Fed. cir.) 1990, U.S. Ct. Internat. Trade 1990, U.S. Dist. Ct. (we. dist.) Mich. 1992. Assoc. Sullivan & Cromwell, N.Y.C., 1967-74, ptnr., 1974—. Trustee N.Y. Meth. Hosp. Mem. ABA, N.Y. State Bar Assn., Assn. of the Bar of the City of N.Y. Office: Sullivan & Cromwell 125 Broad St Fl 28 New York NY 10004-2489

NORGAARD, RICHARD BRUCE, economist, educator, consultant; b. Washington, Aug. 18, 1943; s. John Trout and Marva Dawn (Andersen) N.; m. Marida Jane Fowle, June 19, 1965 (div.); children: Kari Marie, Marc Anders; m. Nancy A. Rader, June 5, 1993; children: Addie Nelle, Mathiesen Rader. BA in Econs., U. Calif., Berkeley, 1965; MS in Agrl. Econs., Oreg. State U., 1967; PhD in Econs., U. Chgo., 1971. Instr. Oreg. Coll. Edn., 1967-68; asst. prof. agrl. and resource econs. U. Calif., Berkeley, 1970-76, assoc. prof., 1976-77, 80-87, assoc. prof. energy and resources, 1987-92, prof. energy and resources, 1992—. Project specialist Ford Found., Brazil, 1978-79; environ. cons. to internat. devel. agencies; mem. sci. com. on problems of the environment U.S. Nat. Rsch. Coun.; chmn. bd. Redefining Progress, 1993-97; mem. sci. adv. com. U.S. EPA, 2000-. Author: Development Betrayed: The End of Progress and a Coevolutionary Revisioning of the Future, 1994; contbr. numerous articles to acad. jours. Active civil rights, environ., and peace orgns. Mem. AAAS, Am. Econs. Assn., Internat. Soc. Ecol. Econs. (pres. 1998-2001, past pres. 2002-), Fedn. Am. Scientists, Assn. Environ. and Resource Econs., Am. Inst. Biol. Scis. (bd. dirs. 2000-). Home: 1198 Keith Ave Berkeley CA 94708-1607 Office: U Calif Energy & Resources Program 310 Barrows Hall Berkeley CA 94720-3050

NORGREN, WILLIAM ANDREW, retired religious denomination administrator; b. Frostburg, Md., May 5, 1927; s. William Andrew and Martha Elizabeth Leona (Richardson) N. BA, Coll. William and Mary, 1948; STB, now STM, Gen. Theol. Sem., N.Y.C., 1953; LittB, Oxford (Eng.) U., 1959; DD (hon.), Gen. Theol. Sem., N.Y.C., 1984, Berkeley Div. Sch. at Yale, 1995. Ordained to ministry Episcopal Ch., 1953. Chaplain Christ Ch. Cathedral, Oxford, 1955-59; exec. dir. Commn. on Faith and Order Nat. Coun. Chs. of Christ in U.S.A., N.Y.C., 1959-71, mem. gen. bd., 1979-95; pastoral asst. Trinity Ch., 1972-74; assoc. ecumenical officer Episcopal Ch., 1975-79, ecumenical officer, 1979-94, theol. cons., 1995-2000. Observer 2d Vatican Coun., Roman Cath. Ch., Vatican City, 1963-65; mem. assemblies World Co. Chs., various cities, 1961, 68, 83, 91. Editor: Living Room Dialogues, 1965, Implications of the Gospel, 1988, Toward Full Communion and Concordat of Agreement, 1991; author: Commentary on Called to Common Mission, 1999. Fellow Gen. Theol. Sem., 1953-55. Democrat. Avocations: art, music, theatre, walking.

NORI, DATTATREYUDU, oncologist, researcher; b. Vallur, India, Oct. 18, 1947; came to U.S., 1976; s. Satyanarayana and Kanakadurgamba Nori; m. Mar. 9, 1974; children: Sateesh, Priya. B of Medicine and Surgery, Kwinool Med. Coll., India, 1971; MD, Osmnonia Med. Coll., India, 1975. Diplomate Am. Bd. Radiology. Fellow Meml. Sloan Kettering Cancer Ctr.; chief brachytherapy Sloan-Kettering Meml. Hosp., N.Y.C., 1986-89; dir. oncology The N.Y. Hosp., Queens, 1989-94; chmn. dept. radiation oncology Booth Meml. Med. Ctr., N.Y.C., 1989—; prof., chmn. dept. radiation oncology The N.Y. Hosp. Cornell Med. Ctr., 1994—; chmn. dept. radiation oncology The N.Y. Presbyn. Hosp., 1995—; dir. Cancer Ctr. The N.Y. Hosp. Author: Textbook of Gynecological Radiation, 1988, (with Hilaris) Atlas of Brachytherapy, 1991, (with Anderson) Principles of Brachytherapy, 1989; contbr. 200 aricles to profl. jours. Fellow Am. Coll. Radiology. Achievements include introduction of many new cancer treatments using brochytherapy. Office: 525 E 68th St New York NY 10021 Address: 2 High Point Ter Scarsdale NY 10583-3128 E-mail: dnori@nyp.org.

NORIEGA, CAROLOS I. astronaut; b. Lima, Peru, Oct. 8, 1959; s. Rodolfo and Nora Noriega; m. Wendy L. Thatcher; 5 children. BS in Computer Sci., U. So. Calif., 1981; MS in Computer Sci., MS in Space Systems Ops., Naval Postgrad. Sch., 1990. Commd. 2d lt. USMC, 1981, advanced through grades to lt. col.; helicopter pilot Marine Corps Air Sta., Kaneohe Bay, Hawaii; base ops. officer Marine Air Base Squadron 24; aviation safety officer, instr. pilot MCAS, Tustin, Calif.; with U.S. Space Command, Colorado Springs, Colo., comdr. Space Surveillance Ctr.; staff 1st Marine Aircraft Wing, Okinawa, Japan; astronaut NASA, Houston, 1994—, mission specialist, 1996. Decorated Air medal with Combat Disting. Device, Air medal, Navy Achievement medal. Achievements include logged 461 hours in space; 19 EVA hours in 3 space walks; mem. crew on STS-84 (1997) and STS-97 (2000). Office: Astronaut Office/CB NASA Johnson Space Ctr Houston TX 77058*

NORINS, ARTHUR LEONARD, physician, educator; b. Chgo., Dec. 2, 1928; s. Russell Joseph and Elsie (Lindemann) N.; m. Mona Lisa Wetzer, Sept. 12, 1954; children: Catherine, Nan, Jane, Arthur. BS in Chem. Engring, Northwestern U., 1951, MS in Physiology, 1953, MD, 1955. Diplomate: Am. Bd. Dermatology; subcert. in dermatopathology. Intern U. Mich., Ann Arbor, 1955-56; resident in dermatology Northwestern U., Chgo., 1956-59; asst. prof. Stanford U., 1961-64; prof., chmn. dept. dermatology, prof. pathology Ind. U. Sch. Medicine, Indpls., 1964-93, prof. emeritus, 1993—. Mem. staff Riley Children's Hosp., Univ. Hosp., Wishard Hosp.; cons. VA Hosp. Contbr. articles to profl. jours. Capt. M.C. U.S. Army, 1959-61. Recipient Pres.' award Ind. U., 1979 Fellow ACP; mem. Am. Acad. Dermatology (bd. dirs.), Am. Dermatol. Assn., Soc. Pediatric Dermatology (founder, past pres.), Am. Soc. Dermatopathology, Am. Soc. Photobiology (founder), Soc. Investigative Dermatology. Home: 10100 Torre Ave Apt 211 Cupertino CA 95014-2168 Office: 550 University Blvd Ste 3240 Indianapolis IN 46202-5149

NORIS, PETER DANA, financial services executive; b. Dec. 5, 1955; BS in Econs., U. Pa., 1978; MBA in Fin., NYU, 1984. CFA. Portfolio mgr. Continental Asset Mgmt., N.Y.C., 1983-84; prin. Morgan Stanley, 1984-92; v.p. Salomon Bros., 1992-95; exec. v.p., chief investment officer Axa Fin./Equitable, 1995—. Bd. dirs. Alliance Capital Mgmt., N.Y.C. Trustee EQ Advisors Trust, N.Y.C., Axa Premier V.I.P. Trust. Office: Axa Fin./Equitable Equitable 1290 Ave of Americas New York NY 10104

NORKIN, CYNTHIA CLAIR, retired physical therapist; b. Boston, May 6, 1932; d. Miles Nelson and Carolyn (Green) Clair; m. Stanislav A Norkin, Feb. 19, 1955 (dec. 1970); 1 child Alexandra. BS in Edn., Tufts U., 1954; cert. phys. therapist, Bouve Boston Coll., 1954; MS, Boston U., 1973, EdD, 1984. Instr. Bouve Boston Coll., 1954-55; staff phys. therapist New Eng. Med. Ctr., Boston, 1954-55, Abington (Pa.) Meml. Hosp., 1965-70, Ea. Montgomery Country Vis. Nurse Assn., 1970-72; asst. prof. phys. therapy Sargent Coll./Boston U., 1973-84; assoc. prof. phys. therapy, dir., founder Ohio U. Sch. Phys. Therapy, Athens, 1984-95, ret., 1995. Consult Boston Ctr Independent Living, Cambridge Vis Nurse Asn, Mass Medicaid Cost Effectiveness Project, 1978; secy Health Planning Coun Greater Boston, 1976—78; book, manuscript reviewer F A Davis Co, 1986—; arthritis adv comt Ohio Dept Health. Author (with P Levangie and C Norkin): (book) Joint Structure and Function: A Comprehensive Analysis, 1983, Joint Structure and Function: A Comprehensive Analysis, 3d ed, 2001; author: (with D J White) Joint Measurement: A Guide to Goniometry, 1985, Joint Measurement: A Guide to Goniometry, 2d ed, 1995. Trustee Brimmer and May Sch, 1980. Mem.: APHA, AAAS, Athens County Vis Nurse Asn (secy adv coun 1984—95), Mass Asn Mental health, Mass Physical Therapy Asn (chair quality assurance comt 1980—83), Am Physical Therapy Asn (on site evaluator comn on accreditation 1986—95). Episcopalian.

NORLAND, DONALD RICHARD, retired foreign service officer; b. Laurens, Iowa, June 14, 1924; s. Norman and Aletta (Brunsvold) N.; m. Patricia Bamman, Dec. 13, 1952; children: Richard Boyce, David, Patricia D. Student, Iowa State Tchrs. Coll., 1941-43, N.W. Mo. State Tchrs. Coll., 1943-44; BA, U. Minn., 1948, MS, 1950; postgrad., U. Mich., 1951-52, Grenoble (France) U., 1948-49. Instr. history and polit. sci. U. No. Iowa, 1949-51; teaching fellow U. Mich., 1951-52; with Fgn. Svc., U.S. Dept. State, 1952-81; posts include Rabat, Morocco, 1952-56, Washington, 1956-58, Abidjan, Ivory Coast, 1958-60; mem. NATO del., Paris, 1961-63, NATO delegation, The Hague, The Netherlands, 1964-69; dep. chief mission Conakry, Guinea, 1970-72; U.S. Dept. State fellow Stanford (Calif.) U., 1969-70; dep. dir. Office Mil. Assistance and Sales, Bur. Politico-Mil. Affairs, Dept. State, Washington, 1972-73, chief polit. officers counseling br. Office Pers., 1973-75; dep. dir. Office Mgmt. Ops., 1975-76; amb. to Botswana, Lesotho and Swaziland Gaborone, Botswana, 1976-79; amb. to Chad, 1979-81; ret. Fgn. Svc., U.S. Dept. State, 1981; lectr. African affairs; internat. cons., specialist econ. devel. Chmn. African studies Fgn. Svc. Inst. of U.S. Dept. of State, Washington, 1987-89; program dir. Ctr. for Internat. Pvt. Enterprise affiliate U.S. C. of C., Washington, 1990-91; sr. cons. World Space, Inc., 1995, sr. policy advisor, 1996—. Bd. dirs. Calvert New Africa Fund, 1995. Lt. (j.g.) USNR, 1943-46. Mem. Am. Fgn. Svc. Assn. (v.p. for retirees 1993-95, sec. 1995-97, mem. editl. bd. Fgn. Svc. Jour. 1992-95), World Space Found. (pres. 1997-98). Home: 4000 Cathedral Ave NW Apt 636B Washington DC 20016-5286

NORLIN, CHARLES, JR. (CHUCK NORLIN), pediatrician; b. Miami, Oct. 29, 1949; s. Ernest Charles and Mary Virginia Norlin. BA, Emory U., 1971; MD, N.Y. Med. Coll., 1976. Diplomate Am. Bd. Pediatrics. Pediatrician FHP of Utah, Salt Lake City, 1980-82; pediatrician, owner Westside Pediatrics, W. Valley City, UT, 1983-90; asst. med. dir. Primary Children's Med. Ctr., Salt Lake City, 1993-98; assoc. prof. pediatrics U. Utah, 1990—, divsn. chief gen. pediatrics, 1993—. Bd. trustees Pioneer Valley Hosp., W. Valley City, Utah, 1985—87; pres. med. staff Primary Children's Med. Ctr., Salt Lake City, 1989; mem. exec. com. Faculty Practice Orgn. U. Utah Health Scis., 1994—2000; med. dir. Pediat. Clinic U. Utah Hosp., 2001; co-dir. Med. Home Devel. Project, 2001—; dir. Inter Mountain Consortium ChildHealth Svcs. Rsch., 2001. Editor: Handbook of Attention Deficit Disorder, 1987; contbr. articles to profl. jours. Fellow: Am. Acad. Pediats.; mem.: Ut. Med. Assn., Ambulatory Pediat. Assn., Intermountain Pediat. Soc. Office: U Utah 50 N Medical Dr Salt Lake City UT 84132-0001 E-mail: chuck.norlin@hsc.utah.edu.

NORLING, BERNARD, retired history educator; b. Hunters, Wash., Feb. 23, 1924; s. Thomas Frederick and Catherine (Lucey) N.; m. Mary Theresa Norling, Jan. 30, 1948. BA, Gonzaga U., Spokane, Wash., 1948; MA, U. Notre Dame, 1949, PhD, 1955. Instr. history U. Notre Dame, Ind., 1950-52, asst. prof. history, 1952-60, assoc. prof., 1960-70, prof. history, 1970-85, prof. emeritus history, 1985—. Author: Towards a Better Understanding of History, 1960, Timeless Problems in History, 1970, Understanding History Through American Experience, 1976, Return to Freedom, 1983, Behind Japanese Lines, 1986, Nazi Impact on a German Village, 1993, Lapham's Raiders, 1996, Intrepid Guerrillas of North Luzon, 1999. Sgt. U.S. Army, 1943-46. Avocations: reading, golf, travel, softball, volleyball. Home: 504 E Pokagon St South Bend IN 46617-1326

NORLING, IRWIN DENISON, retired measurement specialist, photographer; b. Mpls., June 8, 1916; s. Carl Oscar and Harriet (Denison) N.; m. June Rose Mills, Aug. 28, 1943; children: Patricia June Erwin, Michael Carlos, David Irwin. Student, U. Minn., 1936, 43, 44. Machine operator Electric Machinery Co., Mpls., 1935-37; salesman Minn. Mut. Life Ins. Co., 1938-39; draftsman No. Pump Co., 1939; machine operator V.A. Boker & Sons, 1939-40; measurement specialist Honeywell, Inc., 1940-79; photographer Richfield (Minn.) Police Dept., Fire Dept., 1953-75, Bloomington (Minn.) Police and Fire Dept., 1953-75. Staff photographer Bloomington Sun Weekly Newspaper, 1954-65; cons., designer of measuring devices for several mfrs., 1989-95. Contbr. photographs to numerous publs. Dir. Emergency Mgmt. Communications Divsn., Bloomington, Minn., 1964-72, 79-86; mem. Bloomington Sch. Bd. Adv. Commn., 1973-79. Mem. Soc. Mfg. Engrs. (life), Am. Assn. Retired Persons (pres. Bloomington chpt. #1328 1989-90, bd. dirs. 1991-97, sec. 1996, asst. sec. 1997—), Bloomington Citizens Crime Prevention Assn. (bd. dirs. 1983-90, sec. 1987-91, hon. bd. mem. 1992—, life mem.), Bloomington Lions (pres. 1966-67). Republican. Episcopalian. Avocations: music, electronics, computers, travel, genealogy. Home: Brightondale Apt 320 2700 Rice Creek Rd New Brighton MN 55112-5377

NORLING, RICHARD ARTHUR, health care executive; b. Waterbury, Conn., Dec. 9, 1945; s. Arthur and Alice Norling; m. Jeanne Marie Bone, Oct. 1, 1946; children: Jennifer, Stephanie. BS in Math., Tufts U., 1967; MS in Systems Engring., U. Ariz., 1969; MHA, U. Minn., 1975. Systems analyst Univ. Hosp., Tucson, 1969-70, mgr. systems engring., 1970-72, asst. to adminstr., 1972-73; adminstrv. resident Presbyn. Hosp. Ctr., Albuquerque, 1974-75; asst. dir. Calif. Med. Ctr., Los Angeles, 1975-77, assoc. dir., 1977-79, pres., exec. dir., 1979-86; exec. v.p. LHS Corp., from 1986; former pres., CEO Fairview Hosp. and Healthcare Svcs., Mpls.; now chmn., CEO Premier Inc. , San Diego. Mem. Joint Commn. on Accreditation of Healthcare Orgn.'s Adv. Group, 1993; chmn., Foun. for the Malcolm Balridge Nat. Quality Award, 2001-. Bd. mem. Am. Healthcare Systems, 1989, Augsburg Coll., 1992, Benefit Panel Svcs., 1991, Express Scripts, Inc., 1992, Hosp. Edn. and Rsch. Found., 1989, Minn. Bus. Partnerships, Inc., 1991. Kings Fund fellow, 1984-90; named Emerging Health Care Leader Assn. of Western Hosps. Mem. Am. Hosp. Assn. (chmn. various coms., coun. on fin. 1980-83), Am. Coll. Healthcare Execs., Edina Country Club, Mpls. Club. Congregationalist. Avocations: golfing, gardening, raquetball. Office: Premier Inc 12225 El Camino Real San Diego CA 92130*

NORMAN, ALBERT GEORGE, JR. lawyer; b. Birmingham, Ala., May 29, 1929; s. Albert G. and Ila Mae (Carroll) N.; m. Catherine Marshall DeShazo, Sept. 3, 1955; children: Catherine Marshall, Albert George III. BA, Auburn U., 1953; LLB, Emory U., 1958; MA, U. N.C., 1960. Bar: Ga. 1957. Assoc. Moise, Post & Gardner, Atlanta, 1958-60, ptnr., 1960-62, Hansell & Post, Atlanta, 1962-86, Long, Aldridge & Norman, Atlanta, 1986-2000. Dir. Atlanta Gas Light Co., 1976-2000. Served with USAF, 1946-49. Mem. ABA, Ga. Bar Assn., Atlanta Bar Assn., Lawyers Club Atlanta (pres. 1973-74), Am. Law Inst., Am. Judicature Soc. (dir. 1975-78), Old War Horse Lawyers Club, (pres. 1991-92), Cherokee Town and Country Club. Episcopalian. E-mail: almarnorman@mingspring.com.

NORMAN, ARLENE PHYLLIS, principal; b. Seattle; d. Samuel Edward and Connie Solveig (Jorgensen) Hendricksen; m. Charles Edward Norman; children: Tamara, Mark, Todd, Lisa. BA, Wash. State U.; MAT, Lewis and Clark Coll., 1980; postgrad., Portland State U. Tchr. Salem (Oreg.) Sch. Dist., 1956, Beaverton (Oreg.) Sch. Dist., 1973-83, prin. Terra Linda Sch., 1984-94; prin. Aloha Park Sch., 1994. Prof. Portland State U.; presenter children's seminar Nat. Coun. Tchrs. Eng. Confs. Contbr. articles to mags. Mem. selection com. Associated Oreg. Industries, 1994, 95. Named Prin. of

Excellence, Assoc. Oreg. Industries, 1991, sch. named Sch. of Excellence, 1991. Mem. NASEP, N.W. Women in Ednl. Adminstrn., Profl. Assistance Com. for State of Oreg., Toastmasters (pres.), Phi Delta Kappa, Pi Lambda Theta (pres.).

NORMAN, ARNOLD MCCALLUM, JR. engineer; b. Little Rock, May 1, 1940; s. Arnold McCallum and Ann Carolyn (Gibson) N.; m. Sylvia Burton, July 1, 1962 (div. 1967); m. Marisha Irene Malin, June 7, 1969); children: Frank Lee, Paul James. BS in Physics, Ga. Inst. Tech., 1962. Test engr. Rocketdyne div. Rockwell Internat., Canoga Park, Calif., 1962-64, engr. in charge of various programs, 1964-75, engr. in charge, project engr. large chem. lasers, 1975-85, project engr. space sta. propulsion system, 1985-87, project engr. nat. launch system health mgmt. systems, 1987-92, project engr. kinetic energy weapons, 1993-94; project engr. advanced propulsion systems Rockwell Internat., 1994-95, sr. engring. specialist, 1995-96; health mgmt. sys. team head, x-33 Aerospike rocket engine Boeing-N.Am. Rocketdyne Divsn., 1996-97; cons. rocket propulsion sys., ops. and health mgmt., 1997—. Mem. ops. com. health mgmt. ctr. U. Cin., 1988-94; mem. program com. Ann. Internat. Conf. on Engring. Applications of Artificial Intelligence, 1988-90; presenter in field. Mem. editorial bd. Jour. Applied Intelligence, 1990-94; author numerous papers in field. Bd. dirs. Sebastopol Ctr. for Arts, 2000—. Fellow AIAA (assoc., sect. chair sr. adv. com. 1991-93, San Fernando Valley sect., chmn. 1989-90, sys. effectiveness & safety com. 1995-97), Inst. Advancement Engring; mem. Tau Beta Pi. Home: 4053 Bones Rd Sebastopol CA 95472-9756

NORMAN, BILL, information technology executive; married; 3 children. MBA, Northeastern U. Various mgmt. positions Digital Equipment Corp., 1976—94; from mem. staff to corp. v.p. Microsoft, Redmond, Wash., 1994, corp. v.p. Avocations: golf, time with family. Office: One Microsoft Way Redmond WA 98052-6399*

NORMAN, BOBBY DON, artist; b. Dallas, June 5, 1933; s. Reuben Ray Norman and Bessie Mae Norman-Gregory; m. Mae Pearl Delley (div. Sept. 11, 1966); 1 child Parette Michelle. Cert. grad.(hon.) , S.W. Sch. Bus. Adminstrn., 1959. Mgr. Mile High Club, Dallas, 1955—57; city distbn. clk. U.S. Post Office, 1956—66; office mgr., co-dir. So. Christian Leadership Conf., 1969—73; cmty. liaison dir. Planned Parenthood N.E. Tex., 1974—76; exec. v.p., gen. mgr. Davis Norman & Zanders, Inc., 1977—78; house mgr., supr. Fed. Bur. Prisons, 1982—83; supr. Halfway House Tex. Dept. Corrections, 1983—84; artist, writer, scientist, 1955—. Founder, pres. Assn. Advancing Artists and Writers, Inc., Dallas, 1969—72; active Internat. Platform Assn. Pub. Spkrs., Dallas, 1977—78. Author: Artistic Theological Science, 1998, Biblical Geology, 1998. Bd. mem. Greater Dallas Cmty. Rels. Commn., 1970—72, Greater Dallas Coun. Chs., 1970—71; organizer, tactical negotiator Dallas-Ft. Worth Coalition for the Free Flow of Info. , 1970—72. Cpl. USAF, 1951—55, Korea. Recipient Tng. award, So. Christian Leadership Conf., 1969, Svc. award, Greater Dallas Cmty. Rels. Commn., 1972, Art award, Black C. of C., 1973. Baptist. Avocation: fishing. Office: Art Religious PO Box 191904 Dallas TX 75219-8509

NORMAN, COLIN ARTHUR, astrophysics educator; b. Melbourne, Australia, May 3, 1948; came to U.S., 1984; s. Howard Arthur Norman and Jean Olice (Macgregor) Downing; m. Wen Shen, June 2, 1988; children: Alexandra Jean, Arthur Shen, Victoria Amelia. BE with honours, U. Melbourne, 1969; DPhil, Oxford U., 1973. Rsch. fellow Magdalen Coll., Oxford (Eng.) U., 1973-77, U. Calif., Berkeley, 1975-77; asst. prof. U. Leiden (Netherlands), 1977-84; prof. physics and astronomy Johns Hopkins U., Balt., 1984—, head acad. affairs div. Space Telescope Sci. Inst., 1987-91, head Hubble Fellow program Space Telescope Sci. Inst., 1991-94. Sr. rsch. fellow Inst. Astronomy, Cambridge, Eng., 1981-84, European So. Obs., Munich, 1983-84; vis. prof. U. Paris, 1983; Melbourne. Sackler Lecture Cambridge IL. 1995, Astor Lecture, Oxford U. 2002. Editor: Stellar Populations, 1987, Quasar Absorption Lines, 1988, Massive Stars and Star Formations, 1991; contbr. articles to astrophysics jours. Rhodes scholar, 1970-73. Fellow Royal Astron. Soc.; mem. Am. Phys. Soc., Am. Astron. Soc., Amnesty Internat., Greenpeace, Johns Hopkins Club, Hamilton St. Club. Office: Johns Hopkins U Dept Physics and Astronomy Baltimore MD 21218

NORMAN, DENNIS KEITH, psychologist, educator; b. Oklahoma City, Aug. 31, 1949; s. B.J. and Gertrud (Thuringer) N.; m. Wendy McNeal (div. Mar. 1973); children: Tamsen, Jakob; m. Carol Goodwin Taylor, Apr. 21, 1978; children: Ross, Jessie. BS in Psychology, U. Oregon, 1971; MEd in Allied Health Edn., U. Houston, 1975; MA in Child Psychology, Tufts U., 1978; EdD Human Devel. & Counseling Psychology, Harvard U., 1981. Diplomate Am. Bd. Profl. Psychology; lic. psychologist, Mass.; diplomate in clin. psychology Am. Bd. Profl. Psychology; cert. health care provider in psychology, Mass. Chief psychologist child psychiatry svc. Mass. Gen. Hosp., Boston, 1985—, dir. psychology tng., 1989—, chief of psychology, 1990—; asst. prof. psychology Harvard Med. Sch., 1986-95, assoc. prof. psychology, 1995—. Chmn. Bd. Registration of Psychology, Boston, 1997-98. Contbr. over 50 articles to profl. jours. Jessie Noyes scholar Baylor Coll. Medicine, 1975. Fellow APA, Mass. Psychol. Assn., Soc. Personality Rsch., Acad. Clin. Psychology, Soc. for Clin. Psychology. Home: 10 Fieldstone Way Boxford MA 01921-1639 Office: Mass Gen Hosp Psychology Dept 5 Emerson Pl Ste 105 Boston MA 02114-2240

NORMAN, DONALD ARTHUR, cognitive scientist; b. N.Y.C., Dec. 25, 1935; s. Noah N. and Miriam F. N.; m. Martha Karpati (dec.); children—Cynthia, Michael; m. Julie Jacobsen; 1 child, Eric BSEE, MIT, 1957; MSEE, U. Pa., 1959, PhD in Psychology, 1962; degree in psychology (hon.), U. Padua, Italy, 1995. Lectr. Harvard U., 1962-66; prof. dept. psychology U. Calif.-San Diego, La Jolla, 1966-92, prof. emeritus, 1992—, prof., chair dept. cognitive sci., 1988-92, chair dept. psychology, 1974-78; Apple fellow Apple Computer Inc., Cupertino, Calif., 1993-97, v.p. advanced tech., 1995-97; exec. info. appliances Hewlett Packard, Palo Alto, 1997-98; co-founder, prin. Nielsen Norman Group, Mountain View, 1998—; pres. learning sys. UNext, 1999—2001; prof. dept. computer sci. Northwestern U., 2001—. Cons. to industry on human computer interaction and user-centered design. Author: Human Information Processing, 2d edit., 1977, Learning and Memory, 1982, User Centered System Design, 1986, The Psychology of Everyday Things, 1988, The Design of Everyday Things, 1989, Turn Signals Are the Facial Expressions of Automobiles, 1992, Things That Make Us Smart, 1993, The Invisible Computer, 1998. Recipient Excellence in Rsch. award, U. Calif., 1983. Fellow: Assn. Computing Machines, Human Factors & Ergonomics Soc., Am. Acad. Arts and Scis., Am. Psychol. Soc.; mem.: Inst. Design, IIT Chicago (trustee), Cognitive Sci. Soc. (chmn., founding mem.). E-mail: norman@nngroup.com.

NORMAN, DOUGLAS JAMES, physician; b. Seattle, Mar. 6, 1946; s. James Carroll and Pearl Barbara N.; Jennie Sage Norman, Nov. 23, 1977; children: Alex Jameson, Lauren Sage. BA, Stanford U., 1968; MD, U. Washington, 1972. Cert. Nat. Bd. Med. Examiners, 1973; Am. Bd. Internal Medicine, 1976; Am. Bd. Internal Medicine/Nephrology, 1978; Am. Bd. Histocompatibility/Immunogenetics, 1994. Med. intern San Francisco Gen. Hosp., 1972-73; asst resident medicine U. Calif., San Francisco, 1973-74; ships physician Scripps Inst. Oceanography, 1974-75; sr. resident medicine Beth Israel Hosp., Boston, 1975-76; clin. fellow neph. Brigham and Women's Hosp., 1976-77, Childrens Hosp. M.C., Boston, 1977; rsch. fellow transplantation, immunology, immunogentics Brigham and Women's Hosp., 1977-79; med. dir. ESRD Program Oregon Health Sci. U., Portland, Oreg., 1979; dir. lab immunogenetics, transplantation Oreg. Health Sci. U., 1979, chief hemodialysis unit, 1982-84, dir. transplantation medicine, 1986—. Pres. United Network Organ Sharing, Richmond, Va., 1993—94. Editor: ASTP Primer on Transplantation, 1997, 2001. Mem. Am. Soc. Transplantation (pres. 1995-96), Am. Soc. Nephrology, Am. Soc. Histocompatitbility and Immunogenetics, Am. Assn. for the Advancement of Sci., Pacific Northwest Transplant Soc. (pres., 1988-90), Am. Coll. Physicians. Office: Oregon Health Sci U 3181 Sam Jackson Park Rd MQ 360 Portland OR 97201 E-mail: normand@ohsu.edu.

NORMAN, E. GLADYS, business computer educator, consultant; b. Oklahoma City, June 13, 1933; d. Joseph Eldon and Mildred Lou (Truitt) Biggs; m. Joseph R.R. Radeck, Mar. 1, 1953 (div. Aug. 1962); children: Jody Norman, Ray Norman, Warren Norman (dec. May 1993), Dana Norman; m. Leslie P. Norman, Aug. 26, 1963 (dec. Feb. 1994); 1 child, Elayne Pearce. Student, Fresno (Calif.) State Coll., 1951-52, UCLA, 1956-59, Linfield Coll., 1986-95. Math. aid U.S. Naval Weapons Ctr., China Lake, Calif., 1952-56, computing systems specialist, 1957-68; systems programmer Oreg. Motor Vehicles Dept., Salem, 1968-69; instr. in data processing, dir. Computer Programming Ctr., 1969-72; instr. in data processing Merritt-Davis Bus. Coll., 1972-73; sr. programmer, analyst Teledyne Wah Chang, Albany, Oreg., 1973-79; sr. systems analyst Oreg. Dept. Vets. Affairs, 1979-80; instr. in bus. computers Linn-Benton C.C., 1980-95; ret., 1995. Computer cons. for LBCC Ret. Sr. Vol. Program, 1995—; presenter computer software seminars State of Oreg., 1991-93, Oreg. Credit Assoc. Conf., 1991, Oreg. Regional Users Group Conf., 1992; computer tchr. Linn-Benton C.C., 1999-2001; computer cons. Oremet-Wah Chang, 1996—, Oreg. State Yr. 2000 Project, 1997-98; adj. prof. Cheneketa C.C., 2000-2002; computer cons. in field. Mem.: Assn. Info. Tech. Profls. (region treas. 1999, region sec. 2000—02), Data Processing Mgmt. Assn. (bd. dirs. 1977—84, 1989—95, region sec. 1995—96, assoc. v.p. 1988, Diamond Individual Performance award 1985). Democrat. Avocations: drawing, painting, sewing. E-mail: gladys_norman@juno.com., gladys33@quik.com.

NORMAN, FORREST ALONZO, lawyer; b. Renton, Pa., Nov. 21, 1929; s. Forrest Alonzo and Nellie Corley Norman; m. Christine Dende Norman, July 5, 1954; children: Sally, Forrest III, William. BBA, Western Res. U., 1952, LLB, 1954. Bar: Ohio 1954, U.S. Dist. Ct. (no. dist.) Ohio 1956, U.S. Supreme Ct. 1980. Assoc. Hauxhurst, Inglis, Sharp and Cull, Cleve., 1956-64; ptnr. Hauxhurst, Sharp, Mollison & Gallagher, 1964-76, Gallagher, Sharp, Fulton and Norman, Cleve., 1976—. Pres. Fed. Ins. and Corp. Counsel, Walpole, Mass., 1981-82. Contbr. articles to profl. jours. Gen. chmn. Case Western Res. U. Ann. Fund, 1990-91. With USNR, 1947-52, U.S. Army, 1954-56. Recipient Disting. Svc. award Def. Rsch. Inst., 1979, 83, Centennial medal Case Western Res. U., 1995. Fellow Am. Coll. of Trial Lawyers, Ohio State Bar Found., Nat. Assn. R.R. Trial Counsel (bd. dirs. 1986—); mem. Order of Coif, Internat. Soc. Barristers, Am. Bd. Trial Advocates. Republican. Avocations: golf, gardening, reading. Home: 2977 Courtland Blvd Shaker Hts OH 44122-2803 Office: Gallagher Sharp Fulton & Norman 1501 Euclid Ave Ste 700 Cleveland OH 44115-2108 E-mail: fan@gsfn.com.

NORMAN, GEORGE BUFORD, JR. foreign language educator; b. Columbus, Miss., July 26, 1945; s. G. Buford and Patricia (Franklin) N.; 1 child, Phillip. AB, Davidson Coll., 1967; MPhil, Yale U., 1970, PhD, 1971. Asst. prof., assoc. prof. Iowa State U., Ames, 1971-80; assoc. prof. dept. fgn. langs. and lits. U. S.C., Columbia, 1980, prof. dept. French and Classics, 1989—, chmn., 1990-93, Jessie Chapman Alcorn meml. prof. fng. langs., 2000—. Co-author: The Wordworthy Computer, 1987; editor: Philippe Quinault, livrets d'opera, 1999; co-editor: Philippe Quinault Alceste, 1994; author: Portraits of Thought, 1988, Touched by the Graces, 2001; contbr. articles to profl. jours. NEH fellow, 1994, Chevalier dans l'Ordre des Palmes Académiques. Mem. MLA, N.Am. Soc. for 17th Century French Lit., Internat. Ctr. for 17th Century Rsch., Am. Assn. Tchrs. French. Avocations: music, tennis. Home: 9 Cassia Ct Columbia SC 29209-4226 Office: U SC Dept Langs Lits and Cultures Columbia SC 29208-0001 E-mail: norman-buford@sc.edu.

NORMAN, JOHN BARSTOW, JR. designer, educator; b. Paola, Kans., Feb. 5, 1940; s. John B. and Ruby Maxine (Johnson) N.; m. Roberta Jeanne Martin, June 6, 1967; children: John Barstow III, Elizabeth Jeanne. BFA, U. Kans., 1962, MFA, 1966. Designer and illustrator Advt. Design, Kansas City, Mo., 1962-64; asst. instr. U. Kans., Lawrence, 1964-66; art dir. Hallmark Cards, Inc., Kansas City, 1966-69; instr. dept. art U. Denver, 1969-73, asst. prof., 1973-78, assoc. prof., 1978-93, disting. prof., 1980-93, prof. emeritus, 1993—; sr. designer Mo. Coun. Arts & Humanities, 1966-67; cons. designer Rocky Mt. Bank Note Corp., Denver, 1971—. Cons. designer Signage identity System, U. Denver; bd. dirs. comm. U. Denver; tech. cons. Denver Art Mus., 1974—, designed exhbns, 1974-75; adv. cons. Jefferson County (Colo.) Sch. System, 1976—; chmn. Design and Sculpture Exhbn., Colo. Celebration of the Arts, 1975-76. One-man shows include GalleryCortina, Aspen, Colo., 1983; commd. works include Jedda, Saudi Arabia, Synegistics Corp., Denver; represented in permanent collections Pasadena Ctr. for Arts, N.Y. Arts Dirs. Club, Calif. State U./Fiber Collection, Pasadena Ctr. Arts, N.Y. Art Dirs. Club, Midland Art Coun./Fiber Collection, Geologic Soc. Am.; represented in traveling exhbns. L.A. Art Dirs. Show and N.Y. Art Dirs. Show, U.S., Europe, Japan, 1985; featured in Denver Post, 1984, Post Electric City Mag., 1984, Rocky Mt. News, 1984, Douglas County Press, 1984, Mile High Cable Vision, 1985, Sta. KWGN-TV, 1985, Les Krantz's Am. Artists, 1988; illustrated Survey of Leading Contemporaries, 1988, U.S. Surface Design Jour., 1988; co-work represented in film collectin Mus. Modern Art, N.Y.C.; selected fashion show designs displayed Sister City dels., Denver, 1987. Recipient Silver medal award N.Y. Internat. Film and Video Competition, 1976, Design awards Coun. ADvancement and Support Edn., 1969, 71, 73, 76, Honor Mention award L.A. Art Dirs. Club, 1984, Honor Mention award N.Y. ARt Dirs. Club, 1984, Native Am. Wearable Art Competition, 1985, 5th pl. Nat. Wind Sail Am. Banners Competition, Midland, Mich., 1985, also awards for surface designs in Colo. Ctr. for Arts Wearable ARt Competition, 1984-85, Foothills Art Gallery Nat. Wearable Competition, 1984-85, Fashion Group Denver Competition, 1984-85. Mem. Art Dirs. Club Denver (Gold medals 1974-82, Best of Show Gold medal 1983, Honor Mentin award 1984, 3 gold medals 1989), Univ. Dirs. Assn. Home: PO Box 507 Lake George CO 80827-0507

NORMAN, JOHN EDWARD, petroleum landman; b. Denver, May 22, 1922; s. John Edward and Ella (Warren) N.; m. Hope Sabin, Sept. 5, 1946; children— J. Thomas, Gerould W., Nancy E., Susan G., Douglas E. BSBA, U. Denver, 1949, MBA, 1972. Clk., bookkeeper Capitol Life Ins. Co., Denver, 1940-42, 45-46; salesman Security Life and Accident Co., Denver, 1947; bookkeeper Central Bank and Trust Co., Denver, 1947-50; automobile salesman H.A. Hennies, Denver, 1950; petroleum landman Continental Oil Co. (name changed to Conoco Inc. 1979), Denver, 1950-85; ind. petroleum landman, 1985; ind. investor 1985—. Lectr. pub. lands Colo. Sch. Mines, 1968-85; lectr. mineral titles and landmen's role in oil industry Casper Coll., 1969-71. Mem. Casper Mcpl. Band Commn., 1965-71, mem. band, 1961-71, mgr., 1968-71; former musician, bd. dirs. Casper Civic Symphony; former bd. dirs. Jefferson Symphony, performing mem., 1972-75. Served with AUS, World War II. Mem. Am. Assn. Petroleum Landmen (dir. at large, chmn. publs. for regional dir.), Wyo. Assn. Petroleum Landmen (pres.), Denver Assn. Petroleum Landmen, Rocky Mountain Oil and Gas Assn. (pub. lands com. 1981-85), Rocky Mountain Petroleum Pioneers. Episcopalian (mem. choir, vestryman, past dir. acolytes). Club: Elks. Home and Office: 2710 S Jay St Denver CO 80227-3856

NORMAN, LALANDER STADIG, insurance company executive; b. Binford, N.D., Apr. 10, 1912; s. John and Corinne (Stadig) N.; m. Garnet Johnston, Nov. 8, 1941; children: Eric John, Martha Mary Norman Neely, Carol Jean Norman Wellborn, Shirley Ann Norman Cook. AB, U. Mich., 1935, MBA, 1937. Actuarial asst. Central Life Ins. Co. of Ill., Chgo., 1937-40, mgr. Eastern dept., 1940-41; actuary Mich. Life Ins. Co., Detroit, 1941-43; asst. actuary Guarantee Mut. Life Co., Omaha, 1946-49; asso. actuary Am. United Life Ins. Co., Indpls., 1949, actuary, 1950-77, dir., 1959-77, v.p., 1962-69, sr. v.p., 1969-77; ret., 1977. Bd. mgrs. AUL Fund B, 1969-84, chmn., 1973-84; actuary Ind. Dept. Ins., 1977-79 Bd. dirs. Cyprus Village Assn., 1981, 1983—85. Served with USNR, 1943—46. Recipient Navy Commendation award, 1946, Theta Xi Distinguished Service award, 1958. Fellow Soc. Actuaries; mem. Am. Acad. Actuaries, Indpls. Actuarial Club (past pres.), Woodland Country Club (Carmel), Sugarmill Woods Golf and Racquet Club, So. Woods Golf Club, Phi Beta Kappa, Theta Xi (regional dir. 1953-59), Phi Kappa Phi, Beta Gamma Sigma. Republican. Home: Sugarmill Woods 21 Graytwig Ct W Homosassa FL 34446-4727 Office: 1 American Sq Indianapolis IN 46282-0020

NORMAN, MARY MARSHALL, educator, counselor, therapist; b. Auburn, N.Y., Jan. 10, 1937; d. Anthony John and Zita Norman. BS cum laude, LeMoyne Coll., 1958; MA, Marquette U., 1960; EdD, Pa. State U., 1971. Cert. alcoholism counselor. Tchr. St. Cecilia's Elem. Sch., Theinsville, Wis., 1959-60; vocat. counselor Marquette U., Milw., 1959-60; dir. testing and counseling U. Rochester (N.Y.), N.Y., 1960-62; dir. testing and counseling, dean women, assoc. dean coll. Corning (N.Y.) C.C., Corning (N.Y.) C.C., 1962-68, asst. dean students, dir. student activities, asst. prof. ps University Park, 1962-68; rsch. asst. Ctr. for Study Higher Edn. Pa. State U., Pa., 1969-71; dean faculty South Campus C.C. Allegheny County, West Mifflin, 1971-72, campus pres., coll. v.p., 1972-82; pres. Orange County C.C., 1982-86; alcohol counselor Sullivan County Alcohol Drug Abuse Svc., 1985-90; sr. counselor Horton Family Program, 1990-96, ednl. cons., writer, 1996—. Cons. Boricua Coll., N.Y.C., 1976-77; reader NSF, 1977-78; mem. govtl. commn. com. Am. Assn. Cmty. and Jr. Colls., 1976-79, bd. dirs., 1982—; mem. and chmn. various middle state accreditation teams. Contbr. articles to profl. jours. Mem. Econ. Devel. Seneca County, Seneca County Tourism Bd.; active St. Patrick's Ch.; bd. dirs. Orange County United Way; bd. dirs. Orange County Alcoholism and Drug Abuse Coun., 1993—96; bd. dirs. Seneca County Hist. Soc. , 1997—, Guild and Altar Soc., 1999. Mem. Nat. Women's Hall of Fame. Mem.: Pa. Coun. on Higher Edn., Nat. Am. Coun. on Edn. (Pa. rep. identification women for adminstrn. 1978—82, bd. dirs., pres. 1980—96), Pitts. Coun. Women Execs. (charter), Pa. Assn. Acad. Deans, Pa. Assn. Two-Yr. Colls., Am. Assn. Women in Cmty. and Jr. Colls. (charter, Woman of the Yr. 1981), Nat. Assn. Women Deans and Counselors, Am. Assn. Higher Edn., Seneca County C. of C. (bd. dirs., mem. tourism com.), Orange County C. of C. (bd. dirs.), Amnesty Internat. (charter mem. women's coun. 2000—), Concerned Citizens for Good Govt. (charter), Kiwanis (bd. dirs. Seneca Falls), Gamma Pi Epsilon. Home: 9 S Park St Seneca Falls NY 13148-1423

NORMAN, MATTHEW WEST, psychiatrist; b. Winston-Salem, N.C., Feb. 19, 1969; s. James Theron and Jewel Anita (West) N.; m. English Stewart Johnson, Aug. 31, 1991. BA in Psychology, U. Va., 1991; MD, Mercer U., 1997. Health svc. technician Ga. Mental Health Inst., Atlanta, 1989; mental health assoc. G. Werber Bryan Psychiat. Hosp., Columbia, S.C., 1990; mental health asst. Psychiat. Inst. of Atlanta, 1992-93; psychiat. resident physician Emory U. Sch. Medicine, Atlanta, 1997—2002. Author: Colonel Burton's Spiller and Burr Revolver, 1996. Fellow, APA-Glaxo Wellcome, 1999—2001. Mem. AMA, So. Hist. Assn., Ga. Hist. Soc., Soc. for the History of Tech., Harpers Ferry Hist. Assn., Am. Psychiat. Assn., Ga. Psychiat. Physicians Assn., Atlanta Hist. Soc. Democrat. Avocation: home repair.

NORMAN, PARALEE FRANCES, English language educator, researcher; b. Lubbock, Tex., Jan. 2, 1932; d. Hugh Redlingshafer and Hazel Irene (Brinegar) N. AB, U. Mo., 1954; MA, Drake U., 1959; PhD, U. Iowa, 1978. Cert. permanent prof., Iowa. Instr. English Mitchell Coll., New London, Conn., 1960-62; asst. prof. English W.Va. Weslyan U., Buckhannon, 1967-69, Marycrest Coll., Davenport, Iowa, 1969-70; instr. English Muscatine (Iowa) Community Coll., 1970-71; asst. prof. English Upper Iowa U., Fayette, 1978-79; prof. English Ft. Polk campus Northwestern State U. La., Leesville, 1979—, mem. grad faculty, 1991—. Cons. La. Com. for Humanities: Readings Am. Themes, Leesville-DeRidder, La., 1984; presenter 3d Internat. Short Story Conf., U. No. Iowa. Author: Marmion Wilme Savage 1804-1872: Dublin's Victorian Satirist, 2000; editor LCTE Coun. Notes, 1998—; contbr. articles and revs. to scholarly jours. Recipient Invitational Conf. award NEH and Vanderbilt, Phoenix, 1984, Cert. Appreciation Dept. Army, 1985, Officers' Wives Club, Ft. Polk, 1988, 91, commendations 5th Div. Tank Unit, Ft. Polk, 1989; grantee LEH, NEH, BESE for summer Tchrs. Inst., 1993, 2000. Mem. Irish-Am. Cultural Inst., La. Coun. Thcrs. English (sec., exec. com. 1990-92), La. Coun. Tchrs. English (1st v.p. 1992-94, pres. 1994-96), Victorian Soc. Office: Northwestern State U 3329 University Pkwy Leesville LA 71446-9041 E-mail: normanp@alpha.nsula.edu.

NORMAN, PETER MINERT, fundraising consulting company executive; b. Rochester, N.Y., Mar. 23, 1932; s. Jesse George and Doris (Colony) N.; m. Janet G. Wasson, Sept. 6, 1952; children: Susan Jane, Paula Lea, Christa MacLeod, Peter Minert II. BA, Trinity Coll., Hartford, Conn., 1954; MDiv, Yale U., 1957. Ordained priest Episcopal Ch., 1957; lic. nursing home adminstr. Curate St. Stephen's Episc. Ch., Rochester, 1957-60; rector Zion Episc. Ch., Avon, N.Y., 1960-68; cons. Health and housing programs, Rochester and Washington, 1968-73; dir. Ward, Dreshman, Reinhardt, Worthington, Ohio, 1973-77; v.p. Seabury Western Sem., Evanston, Ill., 1977-80; exec. dir. Cathedral Found., Jacksonville, Fla., 1980-82; chmn. CEO Ward, Dreshman & Reinhardt, Worthington, 1982-92, WDR Community Svcs., Worthington, 1990-92; exec. v.p. Goettler Assocs., Columbus, Ohio, 1992-93; corp. v.p. of devel. svcs. St. Francis Acad., Salina, Kans., 1993-94; exec. officer devel. Episcopal Retirement House, Cin., 1994—. Pres. Clan MacLeod Soc. U.S.A., 1988-89; chmn. Dunvegan Fund, N.Y./Edinburgh, 1988; chmn. World Fundraising Counsel, Amsterdam, 1990-92. Author: How to Assure Successful Every Member Canvass, 1979, Hospital Prayer Book, 1958. Mem. Worthington Hills Country Club, Am. Assn. Fundraising Counsel (treas. 1989-90, vice-chmn. 1990-91), Phi Beta Kappa, Pi Gamma Mu. Republican. Home: 1308 Clubview Blvd S Columbus OH 43235-1643 Office: Episcopal Retirement Homes 3870 Virginia Ave Ste 3 Cincinnati OH 45227-3427

NORMAN, PHILIP SIDNEY, physician; b. Pittsburg, Kans., Aug. 4, 1924; s. P. Sidney and Mildred A. (Lawyer) N.; m. Marion Birmingham, Apr. 15, 1955; children: Margaret Reynolds, Meredith Andrew, Helen Elizabeth. AB, Kans. State Coll., 1947; MD cum laude, Washington U., St. Louis, 1951. Intern Barnes Hosp., St. Louis, 1951-52; resident Vanderbilt U. Hosp., Nashville, 1952-54; fellow Rockefeller Inst., 1954-56; instr. medicine Johns Hopkins U. Sch. Medicine, Balt., 1956-59, asst. prof., 1959-64, assoc. prof., 1964-75, prof., 1975—, chief allergy and immunology div., 1971-91. Editor Jour. of Allergy and Clin. Immunology, 1993-98; contbr. chpt. to books, articles to profl. jours. Served with USAAF, 1943-46; Served with USPHS, 1954-56. Fellow Am. Acad. Allergy (pres. 1975); mem. Am. Fedn. Clin. Research, Am. Assn. Immunologists, Am. Soc. Clin. Investigation, Am. Assn. Physicians, N.Y. Acad. Scis., Soc. Exptl. Biology and Medicine, Am. Thoracic Soc., Am. Clin. and Climatol. Assn., Johns Hopkins Med. Soc., Alpha Omega Alpha. Episcopalian. Office: Johns Hopkins U Asthma and Allergy Ctr 5501 Hopkins Bayview Cir Baltimore MD 21224-6821 E-mail: pnorman@jhmi.edu.

NORMAN, RALPH LOUIS, physicist, consultant; b. Kingston, Tenn., Mar. 25, 1933; s. Walter Hugh and Helen Irene (Smith) N.; m. Agnes Irene Pickel, Sept. 5, 1964; children: Mark Alan, Max Alvin. BS, U. Tenn., 1959; LL.B., Blackstone Sch. Law, 1967, JD, 1971; certificate, Indsl. Coll. Armed Forces, 1969; MA in Pub. Adminstrn, U. Okla., 1971; D.Sci. (hon.), Apollo Research Inst., 1976. Engr. Chrysler Corp. Missile Div., Huntsville, Ala., 1959-60; physicist Army Rocket & Guided Missile Agy., Redstone Arsenal, 1960-61; asst. project mgr. Army Missile Command, 1961-62, project mgr., 1962-89, ret., 1989; cons. to several def. contractors, 1989—; faculty Athens (Ala.) Coll., 1970-71, Calhoun Jr. Coll., Decatur, Ala., 1971-74, 85-90, U. Montevallo, 1973-74, U. Ala. at Huntsville, 1976-77, Columbia (Mo.) Coll., 1977-79. Cons. firm Bishop and Sexton, 1973— , Athens (Ala.) State Coll.; reviewer NSF, 1974-76; FAA examiner. Contbr. articles profl. jours. Served with USN, 1951-55. Recipient Dept. Def. commendations, 1961, 65, Dept. Army commendation, 1972 Mem. N.Y. Acad. Scis., Assn. U.S. Army. Home: 102 Nobleton Ln NW Huntsville AL 35806-4014 *I strive to make the knowledge gained through my research benefit all mankind.*

NORMAN, SHERI HANNA, artist, educator, cartographer; b. Chgo., Dec. 15, 1940; d. L. J. and Margaret Maxine (Kuyper Fleischer) Hanna; m. Donald Lloyd Norman, Feb. 28, 1963 (div. 1996); 1 child Ronald Wayne. BA, U. Wyo., Laramie, 1963; postgrad., Dayton Art Inst., 1975; MFA, San Francisco Art Inst., 1993. Substitute tchr. Arlington, Va. and Yellow Springs, Ohio Pub. Sch. Dists., 1965-71; tech. illustrator, draftsperson U. Tex. Austin, Geotek, Inc., Denver, 1976-85; cartographer British Petroleum, San Francisco, 1985-87; draftsperson Earth Scis. Assocs., Palo Alto, 1988-92; intern, printmaking asst. Crown Point Press, San Francisco, 1991-92; freelance cartographer, 1993—; educator pub. printmaking & papermaking workshops, 1995-96, Napa, 1997—; pub. printmaking demonstrations San Francisco Women Artists Gallery, 1995; book-arts workshops Calistoga, San Francisco, 1999; tchr. Napa Valley Adult Sch., Napa, 1999-2001. Leader pub. nature/women's ceremony-ritual, San Francisco, 1991—93; artist in residence Villa Montalvo Ctr. Arts, Saratoga, Calif., 1996, Dorland Mountain Arts Colony, Temecula, Calif., 1996; vis. faculty Art Inst. Boston, 2002. Book, , , ; curatore, participating book artist A Display of Contemporary Book Arts, Napa, 2000. Mem. Arts Coun. Napa Valley, Land Trust Napa County. Mem.: Calif. Coun.

Adult Edn. (grantee North Coast chpt. 2002), Calif. Soc. Printmakers (exhbn. com. 1995). Avocations: ongoing nature studies and nature advocacy, early mythologies and meditative practice. Home: 423 Cross St Napa CA 94559-3335 E-mail: inklings@napanet.net.

NORMAN, STEPHEN PECKHAM, financial services company executive; b. Norwich, Conn., May 20, 1942; s. Richard Leonard and Mary Ellen (Carr) N.; m. Jacqueline Mary Batten, June 29, 1968; children— Adrian Gates, Hilary Batten, Philip Douglas, Matthew Jeremy Mitchell. BA, Yale U., 1964; JD, U. Pa., 1967. Bar: Conn. 1967, N.Y. 1972. Atty. Am. Express Co., N.Y.C., 1970-78, v.p. corp. office, 1978-82, sec., 1982—. Mem. bd. editors Corp. Governance. Served to sgt. U.S. Army, 1968-70; Vietnam Mem. Am. Soc. Corp. Secs. (past chmn.). Clubs: Am. Yacht (Rye). Republican. Episcopalian. Home: 6 Highland Park Pl Rye NY 10580-1736 Office: Am Express Co 90 Hudson St Jersey City NJ 07302 E-mail: stephen.p.norman@aexp.com.

NORMAN, T. GAIL, family practice physician; b. San Diego, July 20, 1958; d. William Robert and Joan Louise (Elms) Arnold; m. James G. Norman Jr., Feb. 28, 1986; children: Alexandra Nicole, Joshua Andrew. BS, Oral Roberts U., 1980, MD, 1984. Diplomate Am. Bd. Family Practice. Resident in family practice Oru City of Faith, 1984-86, Bayfront Hosp., St. Petersburg, Fla., 1986-87; pvt. practice Tampa, 1987—. Fellow Am. Acad. Family Practice; mem. AMA, Fla. Acad. Family Practice. Avocations: running, reading, travel, triathalons. Office: 3000 E Fletcher Ave Ste 300 Tampa FL 33613-4645

NORMAN, WILLIAM STANLEY, travel and tourism executive; b. Roper, N.C., Apr. 27, 1938; s. James Colbitt and Josephine Cleo (Woods) N.; m. Elizabeth Patricia Patterson, May 31, 1969; children: Lisa Renée, William Stanley II. BS, West Va. Wesleyan U., 1960; MA, Am. U., 1967; exec. program, Stanford U., 1976. Math. tchr. Washington High Sch., Norfolk, 1961; commd. USN, 1962; advanced through grades to comdr., 1973; naval flight officer Airborne Early Warning Squadron Eleven, 1962-65; asst. combat info. ctr. officer U.S.S. Constellation, 1965; staff officer air weapons systems analysis Office Chief Naval Ops., Pentagon, Washington, 1965-66; history and fgn. affairs instr. U.S. Naval Acad., 1967-69; social aide The White House, 1967-69; carrier div. staff officer SE Asia, 1969-70; spl. asst. to Chief Naval Ops. for Minority Affairs, 1970-72; asst. to Chief Naval Ops. for Spl. Projects, 1972-73; dir. corp. action Cummins Engine Co. Inc., Columbus, Ind., 1973-74, exec. dir. corp. responsibility, 1974-76; exec. mktg. mgr., 1976-77; exec. dir. distbn. mktg. Cummins Engine Co. Inc., Columbus, Ind., 1977-78; v.p. eastern divsn., 1978-79; v.p. sales and mktg. Amtrak, Washington, 1979-81, group v.p., 1981-84, exec. v.p., 1984-94; pres., CEO Travel Industry Assn. of Am., 1994—. Bd. dirs. Bestfoods Inc., Englewood Cliffs, N.J., Corn Products Internat., Bedford Park, Ill., Logistics Mgmt. Inst., McLean,Va. Bd. dirs. USN Meml. Found., Washington, 1980—, Internat. Consortium on Health Effects of Radiation, 1993—, An-Bryce Found., 1993—; bd. visitors Am. U. Kogod Sch. of Bus.; bd. overseers Hospitality Industry Hall of Honor and Archives, 1995—; bd. trustees W.Va. Wesleyan Coll., Buckhannon. Capt. USNR. Mem. Travel Industry Assn. Am. (bd. dirs. 1980—, chmn. bd. 1987-89, chmn. bd. dirs. of found. 1990-92), UN Assn. U.S. (bd. dirs. 1983—, bd. govs. 1985—), Coun. on Fgn. Rels., United Nations Assn. of U.S. (mem. nat. coun.), Travel and Tourism Govt. Affairs Coun. (bd. dirs. 1988—). Democrat. Episcopalian. Avocations: golf, tennis, jogging, walking, cycling. Home: 1308 Timberly Ln Mc Lean VA 22102-2504 Office: Travel Industry Assn of Am Ste 450 1100 New York Ave NW Washington DC 20005-3934

NORMAN, WYATT THOMAS, III, landman, consultant; b. Austin, Tex., Dec. 30, 1952; s. Wyatt Thomas Jr. and Frances Claire (Bliss) N. BS in Agronomy, Tex. A&M U., 1975. Cert. profl. landman, environ. site assessor. Mgr. farm and ranch Bennett Bros., Inc., Pearsall, Tex., 1975-78; landman Corpus Christi, 1978—. Mem. Flour Bluff (Tex.) Vol. Fire Dept., 1984-90. Mem. Am. Assn. Profl. Landmen, Soc. for Creative Anachronism, Assn. Former Students, Century Club, Padre Isles Property Owners Assn., Internat. Game Fish Assn., Corpus Christi Town Club, Single Action Shooting Soc., Coastal Conservation Assn., Tex. Riviera Pistoleros. mem. Exec. Com. for Corpus Christi Assn. Profl. Landmen. Republican. Presbyterian. Avocations: hunting, fishing, skiing. Home: 13946 Man O'War Ct Corpus Christi TX 78418-6340 Office: 615 Leopard St Ste 434 Corpus Christi TX 78476-2225 E-mail: WTN111@aol.com.

NORMAND, ROBERT, lawyer; b. Montreal, Que., Can., Sept. 24, 1936; s. Lucien and Eva (Rochon) N.; m. Madeleine Scott, Sept. 16, 1961; children: Eric, Yves, Genevieve. BA, U. Montreal, 1956; LLL, U. Sherbrooke, Que., 1960; diploma, Inst. d'etudes politiques, Paris, 1962. Bar: Que. 1960. Legal adviser Nat. Assembly, Quebec City, 1962-67, law clk., 1967-71; asst. dep. min. justice Que. Govt., 1970-71, dep. min. justice, 1971-77, dep. min. intergovtl. affairs, 1977-82, dep. min. fin., 1982-87; pres., pub. Le Soleil (Hollinger), 1987-93; v.p. corp. affairs UniMedia Inc., 1993-94, dep. min. internat. affairs, 1994-96; pres., dir. gen. Télé-Québec, 1996-99. Sec. Study Com. on Expropriation 1965-67; guest prof. legis. law faculty Laval U., Ottawa U., 1971; pres. Que. Police Inst., 1974; chmn. Com. Supervising Olympic Security, 1974-76; chmn. Uniform Law Conf. Can.; dir. Caisse de Dèpot et Placement du Quèbec, 1982-87; v.p. Can. del. Diplomatic Conf. on travel contracts, Brussels, 1970; pres. Can. del. at convs. Internat. Inst. French Lang. law, 1974, 76. V.p. Hosp. du Saint-Sacrement, Quebec City, 1988-94; vice chmn. Inst. Rsch. on Pub. Policy, Montreal, 1988-94; pres. Que. Symphony Orch., Quebec City, 1989-92; consul gen. Sweden, Quebec City, 1989-94; co-pres. United Way Campaign Greater Quebec Region, 1989, hon. chmn. Telethon for Cerebral Palsy, 1990; mem. Citizens Forum, Spicer Commn., 1990-91; chmn. Ec. Nat. de l'Humour, 1997-99. Capt. Can. Army, 1954-60. Named Queen's Counsel, 1971, Comdr., Royal Order of the Polar Star, Sweden, Chevalier de la Legion d'honneur, France; recipient Pub. Adminstrn. award of excellence Nat. Sch. Pub. Adminstrn. Alumni, Quebec City, 1986. Mem. Investment Dealers Assn. Can. (dir. 1989-94), Que. Garrison Club (dir. 1991-96), Profl. Liability Ins. of Que. Bar (dir. 1991-94), Que. Bar (supervisory com. 1988-93), La Commanderie de Bordeaux. Roman Catholic. Avocations: fishing, hunting. Home: 2750 de L'Anse Sainte Foy QC Canada G1W 2G5

NORMANDEAU, ANDRE GABRIEL, criminologist, educator; b. Montreal, Que., Can., May 4, 1942; s. Gabriel E. and Laurette D. (Sauve) N.; m. Pierrette La Pointe, Aug. 14, 1965; children: Alain, Louis, Jean. MA in Criminology, U. Pa., 1965, PhD in Sociology, 1968. Asst. prof. criminology U. Montreal, 1968-71, assoc. prof., 1971-76, prof., 1976—, chmn. dept. criminology, 1970-80, dir. Internat. Ctr. Comparative Criminology, 1983-89, dir. Rsch. Inst. on Police, 1990—. Author: Public Attitudes and Crime, 1970, The Measurement of Crime, 1975, Patterns of Robbery, 1980, Crimes of Violence, 1985, A Vision of the Police, 1990, Crime Prevention, 1993, Justice and Minorities, 1995, Community Policing, 1998, Death Penalty, 2002. Woodrow Wilson fellow, 1964-68 Mem. Internat. Soc. Criminology, Am. Soc. Criminology, Am. Sociol. Assn., Can. Criminal Justice Assn. Roman Catholic. Home: 3150 Ave Kent Montreal QC Canada H3S 1N1 Office: Dept Criminology U Montreal Montreal QC Canada H3C 3J7 *Happiness is achieved by working for it, not by waiting for it to come to you.*

NORMENT, ERIC STUART, newspaper editor; b. Butler, Pa., July 26, 1956; s. Hillyer Gavin and Reva Lucille (Shepherd) N.; m. Ann Hobin, Aug. 22, 1987; chldren: Timothy Hobin, Peter John, Laura Mary, Daniel Hillyer. BA, U. Chgo., 1979; MS, Northwestern U., Evanston, Ill., 1980. Reporter Paddock Publs., Arlington Heights, Ill., 1980-83; asst. night editor Cape Cod Times, Hyannis, Mass., 1983; copy editor The Boston Herald, 1983-85, copy desk chief/news, 1985-87, features prodn. editor, 1987-88, asst. Sunday editor, 1988-94, Sunday editor, 1994—. Instr. journalism Northeastern U., Boston, 1984. Recipient Peter Lisagor Pub. Svc. award Chgo. Headline Club, 1981, Edn. Reporting award Ill. Press Assn., 1981. Office: 1 Herald St Boston MA 02118-2200 E-mail: enorment@bostonherald.com.

NORQUIST, JOHN OLAF, mayor; b. Princeton, N.J., Oct. 22, 1949; s. Ernest O. and Jeannette (Nelson) N.; m. Susan R. Mudd, Dec. 1986; children: Benjamin Edward, Katherine Elisabeth. Student, Augustana Coll., Rock Island, Ill., 1967-69; BS, U. Wis., 1971, MPA, 1988. Assemblyman Wis. State Assembly, Madison, 1974-82, co-chmn. state joint com. fin., 1980-81; mem. Wis. State Senate, 82-88, asst. majority leader, 1984-85, 87; mayor City of Milw., 1988—. Bd. dirs. Congress for the New Urbanism. Sgt. USAR, 1971-77. Mem. Wis. Alliance of Cities, Congress for New Urbanism (bd. dirs.). Democrat. Presbyterian. Avocation: map collecting. Office: Office of Mayor City Hall 200 E Wells St Rm 201 Milwaukee WI 53202-3515

NORRBY, KLAS CARL VILHELM, pathology educator; b. Shanghai, China, Jan. 8, 1937; s. Åke Vilhelm and Ingrid Maria (Wedblad) N.; m. Ulla Margareta Hjort, June 17, 1961; children: Katarina, Cecilia, Jacob. BSc, Uppsala (Sweden) U., 1957; MB, Göteborg (Sweden) U., 1959, MD, 1964, PhD, 1970. Asst. prof. pathology Göteborg U., 1967-71; sr. lectr. in pathology Linköping U., 1972-84, chmn. Inst. Med. Microbiology and Pathology, 1980-84; prof. pathology, regal chair Göteborg U., 1985—; vis. prof. in cell biology Harvard Med. Sch., Boston, 1989-90; chmn. Inst. Labor Medicine Sahlgrenska U. Hosp., Göteborg, 1997-2000. Author over 200 articles to profl. jours. Sub.-lt. Royal Swedish Navy Med. Corps, 1972-86. Office: Sahlgrenska U Hosp Dept Pathology SE-41345 Göteborg Sweden

NORRELL, MARY PATRICIA, nursing educator; b. Seymour, Ind., Jan. 03; d. William C. and Mary Elizabeth (Elkins) Ulrey; m. Robert Gerald Norrell, Aug. 17, 1974; children: Shannan, Richard, Trisha. BSN, Ball State U., 1971; MS, Ind. U., 1996. Cert. inpatient obstetrics, TB and CPR instr. Team leader Mt. Sinai Med. Ctr., Miami Beach, Fla., 1971-73; charge nurse Jackson County Schneck Meml. Hosp., Seymour, 1971, 73-74; nurse Camp Matoaka, Oakland, Maine, 1973; prof. Ivy Tech. State Coll., Columbus, Ind., 1974—. Item writer Nat. Coun. Licensure Exam. for Practical Nurses, 1992; participant Acad. for Instrl. Excellecne, Ivy Tech. Coll., 2001-02. Home: 572 Shawnee Ct Seymour IN 47274-1956

NORRID, HENRY GAIL, osteopathic physician and surgeon, biologist, researcher, human anatomy and physiology educator; b. Amarillo, Tex., June 4, 1940; s. Henry Horatio and Johnnie Belle (Combs, Cummins) N.; m. Andreia Maybeth Hudson, Jan. 29, 1966 (dec. 1988); children: Joshua Andrew, Noah Adam; m. Cheryll Diane Payne, Mar. 19, 1989 (div. Aug. 2000); stepchildren: Kim Sheri Payne, Matthew Dominic Payne; m. Carolyn A. Layton, June 8, 2002; stepchildren: Crissey Ann Elizabeth Bruce, David Randall Marshall Bruce. AA, Amarillo Coll., 1963; BA, U. Tex., 1966; MS, W. Tex. State U., 1967; DO, Kirksville Coll., 1973. Diplomate Bd. Osteo. Physicians and Surgeons, Nat. Bd. Examiners Osteo. Physicians and Surgeons; cert. basic sci. tchr. Iowa, Tex., Colo. Intern Interboro Gen. Hosp., Bklyn., 1973-74; attending physician dept. gen. practice Osteo. Hosp. and Clinic N.Y., N.Y.C., 1974-77; gen. practice medicine specializing in osteo. Amarillo, Tex., 1978—; emergency care physician Amarillo Emergency Receiving Ctr. Amarillo Hosp. Dist., 1978-79, Ready Care Emergency Ctr., Arlington and Bedford, Tex., 1990-92, St. Anthony Hosp., Amarillo, 1992. Emeritus mem. consulting staff physician dept. family practice Northwest Tex. Hosp., Amarillo, 1995; emergency/trauma physician Tex. EM Care, 1995—; mem. mass casualty nat. disaster response team ARC, 1995; contract staff physician Tex. Tech. Univ. Sch. Medicine and Health Scis. Ctr., med. dept. and infirmary Tex. Dept. Corrections, Tex. Dept. Criminal Justice, 1992-94; med. cons. rehab. medicine vocat rehab. divsn. Tex. Rehab. Commn., Plano, 1992-94; cattleman, ranch owner, Van Zandt County, Tex.; lectr. osteo. prins. and practice, The Osteo. Hosp. and Clinic N.Y., 1974-77, mem. credentials com., 1975-76; mem. exec. com. Southwest Osteo. Hosp., Amarillo, 1983-84, chief of staff, 1984-85; sec. dept. family practice Northwest Tex. Hosp., Amarillo, 1981-82, mem. credentials com., 1984-85, joint practice com. dept. family practice, 1986-87; mem. orgnl. com. for devel. of dept. osteo. prins. and practices, chmn. N.Y.C. group N.Y. Coll. Osteo. Med., 1977; mem. founding com. N.Y. Coll. Osteo. Medicine, N.Y. Inst. Tech., Old Westbury L.I., 1976-77; mem. North Tex. Support Group, Dallas; instr. human anatomy and physiology dept. biol. scis. Amarillo Coll., 1998—. Contbr. articles to Tex. Jour. Sci., other publs. Scout physician Llano Estecato council Boy Scouts Am., Tex., 1978-85. Served to E-4 U.S. Army, 1956-63. Recipient William M. Giltner Meml. Fund award 1972, Humanitarian award Am. Cath. Conf., 1979, Century award Boy Scouts Am., 1982, Pfizer Sr. Med. Student award, 1973; Maxwell D. Warmer Meml. scholar 1973; scholar Kirksville Coll. Osteo. Medicine, 1970; Tex. Legislature scholar, 1969-73; named to Eminent Soc. Border Legionaires, 11th Armored Cavalry Regiment, Germany, 1958. Mem. Am. Coll. Gen. Practitioners, Tex. Osteo. Med. Assn. (pres. dist. I, mem. ho. of dels. 1981-82, 95), Tex. C.C. Tchrs. Assn., SAR, The Sons of Republic of Tex., Am. Congress Rehab. Medicine, Am. Osteo. Assn., World Future Soc. (profl.), Gen. Soc. War of 1812, Tex. & Southwest Cattle Raisers Assn., N.Y. Acad. Scis., Ex-Student's Assn. of The Univ. Tex. (life), 11th Armored Cavalry Regiment Assn., 36th (Tex.) Inf. Divsn. Assn. (life), Baron of the Magna Charta (Somerset chpt. Magna Charta Barrons 1994—), Masons, Am. Legion, Beta Beta Beta, Sigma Sigma Phi (pres. 1972), Alpha Phi Omega, Psi Sigma Alpha, Theta Psi, Theta Psi Clowns (1969-73). Avocations: astronomy, short wave listening, camping, fishing, anthropology. Office: 1422 S Tyler St Ste 102 Amarillo TX 79101-4238

NORRIS, ALAN EUGENE, federal judge; b. Columbus, Ohio, Aug. 15, 1935; s. J. Russell and Dorothy A. (Shrader) N.; m. Nancy Jean Myers, Apr. 15, 1962 (dec. Jan. 1986); children: Tom Edward Jackson, Tracy Elaine; m. Carol Lynn Spohn, Nov. 10, 1990. BA, Otterbein Coll., 1957, HLD (hon.), 1991; cert., U. Paris, 1956; LLB, NYU, 1960; LLM, U. Va., 1986; HLD, Capital U. Law Sch., 2001. Bar: Ohio 1960, U.S. Dist. Ct. (so. dist) Ohio 1962, U.S. Dist. Ct. (no. dist) Ohio 1964. Law clk. to judge Ohio Supreme Ct., Columbus, 1960-61; assoc. Vorys, Sater, Seymour & Pease, 1961-62; ptnr. Metz, Bailey, Norris & Spicer, Westerville, Ohio, 1962-80; judge Ohio Ct. Appeals (10th dist.), Columbus, 1981-86, U.S. Ct. Appeals (6th cir.), Columbus, 1986—. Contbr. articles to profl. jours. Mem. Ohio Ho. of Reps., Columbus, 1967-80. Named Outstanding Young Man, Westerville Jaycees, 1971; recipient Legislator of Yr. award Ohio Acad. Trial Lawyers, Columbus, 1972. Mem. Ohio Bar Assn., Columbus Bar Assn. Lodges: Masons (master 1966-67). Republican. Methodist. Office: US Ct Appeals 328 US Courthouse 85 Marconi Blvd Columbus OH 43215-2823

NORRIS, ALBERT STANLEY, psychiatrist, educator; b. Sudbury, Ont., Can., July 14, 1926; s. William and Mary (Zell) N.; m. Dorothy James, Sept. 2, 1950; children: Barbara Ellen, Robert Edward, Kimberly Ann. MD, U. Western Ont., 1951. Intern Ottawa (Ont.) Civic Hosp., 1951-52; resident in psychiatry U. Iowa, Psychopathic Hosp., Iowa City, 1953-55, Boston City Hosp., 1955-56; practice medicine Kingston, Ont., Can., 1956-57; instr. Queen's U., 1956-57; asst. prof. psychiatry U. Iowa, 1957-62, asso. prof., 1962-64, 1965-66, prof., 1966-72; asso. prof. U. Oreg., 1964-65; prof. So. Ill. U. Sch. Medicine, Springfield, 1972-84, chmn. dept. psychiatry, 1972-82; prof. emeritus, 1984—; practice medicine specializing in psychiatry Cedar Rapids, Iowa, 1984—. Vis. prof. U. Auckland, N.Z., U. Otago, New Zealand, U. Liverpool. Contbr. chpts. to books, articles to med. jours. Fellow Am. Psychiat. Soc. (life); mem. AMA, Am. Psychopath. Assn., Soc. Biol. Psychiatry, Can. Psychiat. Soc., Am. Soc. Psychosomatic Ob-Gyn, Royal Soc. Medicine. Republican. Presbyterian. Home: 5 Penfro Dr Iowa City IA 52246-4927 Office: PO Box 1408 Cedar Rapids IA 52406-1408 *A life is only fulfilled by a quest, a vision of the future and a commitment to a greater value than one's self. A flickering candle is poor light, unless there is no other.*

NORRIS, ANDREA SPAULDING, art museum director; b. Apr. 2, 1945; d. Edwin Baker and Mary Gretchen (Brendle) Spaulding. BA, Wellesley Coll., 1967; MA, NYU, 1969, PhD, 1977. Intern dept. western European arts Met. Mus. Art, N.Y.C., 1970, 72; rsch. and editorial asst. Inst. Fine Arts NYU, 1971, lectr. Washington Sq. Coll., 1976-77; lectr. Queens Coll. CUNY, 1973-74; asst. to dir. Art Gallery Yale U., New Haven, 1977-80, lectr. art history, 1979-80; chief curator Archer M. Huntington Art Gallery, Austin, Tex., 1980-88; lectr. art history Dept. Art U. Tex., 1984-88; dir. Spencer Mus. Art U. Kans., Lawrence, 1988—. Co-author: (catalogue) Medals and Plaquettes from the Molinari Collection at Bowdoin College, 1976; author: (exhbn. catalogues) Jackson Pollock: New-Found Works, 1978; exhbn. The Sforza Court: Milan in the Renaissance 1450-1535, 1988-89. Mem.: Assn. Art Mus. Dir., Coll. Art Assn. (bd. dir. 2000—, v.p. for coms. 2002—), Renaissance Soc. Am., Phi Beta Kappa. Office: Spencer Mus Art U Kans 1301 Mississippi St Lawrence KS 66045-7500

NORRIS, CHARLES HEAD, manufacturing executive; b. Boston, Sept. 14, 1940; s. Charles Head and Martha Marie N.; m. Diana D. Strawbridge, July 27, 1974 (div. 1994); 1 child, Margaret Dorrance; m. Ceil T. Walner, Oct. 13, 2001. BA, U. Pa., 1963; JD, 1968; MA, U. Wash., 1965. Mem. Morgan, Lewis & Bockius, Phila., 1968-77; pres., chief exec. Artemis Corp., 1978-79; chmn. bd., chief exec., 1979-91; chmn. exec. com., vice-chmn. bd. Remington Rand Corp., 1979-81; ptnr. Artemis Energy Co., 1980-92; chmn., CEO Norris Investment Co., 1992—. Chmn. Norris Mfg. Co., 1994—, Garret Precision Products, 1996—; chmn., CEO AmTech Engring. Co., 1996—; trustee maj. stockholders' voting trust Campbell Soup Co., 1987-90; bd. dirs. SBSF Funds, Inc., 1988-91, Del. Trust, 1987-91. Mem. Harvard U. Overseas Com. to Visit Libr., 1989—; mem. Pa. Commn. to Crime and Delinquency, 1980-84; mem. Thouron Award Selection Com., 1985-90; mem. Pa. Electoral Coll., 1980; mem. West Pikeland Twp. Suprs., 1969-72; mem. bd. visitors Carnegie Mellon U. Sch. Urban and Pub. Affairs, 1988-90; corp. mem. Belmont Hill Sch., 1990—. Served with USAF, 1960. Mem. ABA, Pa. Bar Assn., Am. Econ. Assn., Phila., Knickerbocker, Vicmead Hunt, Everglades (bd. dirs. 1986-91, Bath and Tennis Club (treas., bd. dirs. 1985-91), Sunningdale Golf (Eng.), The Country (Brookline), Coral Beach and Tennis Club (Bermuda), Mid Ocean Club (Bermuda). Office: PO Box 112 Boston MA 02117-0112

NORRIS, CHARLES MORGAN, laryngologist, educator; b. New Milford, Pa., Aug. 17, 1915; s. Ben Clark and Emma (Morgan) N.; m. Sarah Wistar Harwood, Nov. 6, 1948; children— Charles Morgan, Stephen Harwood. BS, Pa. State Coll., 1935; MD, Temple U., 1939; MS, 1944. Intern Temple U. Hosp, 1939-41, resident otolaryngology and broncho-esophagology, 1941-44; mem. faculty Med. Sch., 1944—, prof., chmn. dept. laryngology and broncho-esophagology, 1961-85. Recipient Alumni award Temple U., 1954 Mem. Am. Broncho-Esophalogical Assn. (pres. 1964-65), Pan. Am. Assn. Oto-Rhino-Laryngology and Broncho-Esophagology (sec. 1961-66), Internat. Bronchoesophagological Soc. (sec. 1961-83), Am. Laryngol. Assn. (pres. 1976-77), ACS, Am. Acad. Opthalomology and Otolaryngology, Am. Soc. Head and Neck Surgery (pres. 1973-74), Am. Laryngol., Rhinol. and Otol. Soc. (v.p. 1973-74), Am. Coll. Chest Physicians, Cricket Club. Home: 8007 Navajo St Philadelphia PA 19118-3926 Office: Chevalier Jackson Norris Clin 3401 N Broad St Philadelphia PA 19140-5103

NORRIS, CHUCK (CARLOS RAY), actor; b. Ryan, Okla., Mar. 10, 1940; m. Dianne Norris (div.); m. Gena O. Norris; children: Mike, Eric, Dina; stepchildren: Kelley, Tim. Appeared in films The Wrecking Crew, 1969, Return of the Dragon, 1972, Breaker, Breaker, 1976, Good Guys Wear Black, 1977, Force of One, 1978, The Octagon, 1979, An Eye for an Eye, 1980, Silent Rage, 1981, Forced Vengeance, 1981, Lone Wolf McQuade, 1982, Missing in Action, 1984, Missing in Action II-The Beginning, 1985, Code of Silence, 1985, (co-screenwriter) Invasion, U.S.A., 1985, Delta Force, 1986, Firewalker, 1986, (co-screenwriter) Braddock: Missing in Action III, 1987, Hero and the Terror, 1988, Delta Force 2: Operation Stranglehold, 1990, The Hitman, 1991, (co-exec. prodr.) Sidekicks, 1993, Top Dog, 1994, Forrest Warrior, 1995; TV films Logan's War: Bound by Honor, 1998, The President's Man, 2000, The President's Man: A Line in the Sand, 2002, TV series Walker: Texas Ranger, 1993-2001; author: The Secret Power Within Zen Solutions to Real Problems, 1996; (with Joe Hyams) The Secret of Inner Strength: My Story, 1988; host: The Ultimate Stuntman: A Tribute to Dar Robinson. Founder, pres. United Fighting Arts Fedn.; founder, chmn. Kick Drugs Out of Am. Profl. world middleweight karate champion, 1968-74*

NORRIS, CURTIS BIRD, writer, journalist; b. Quincy, Mass., July 14, 1927; s. Lowell Ames and Helen (Curtis) N.; m. Eileen Patricia Schindler, Mar. 23, 1959; children: Katharine Eileen, Helen Carolyn, Suzanne Elizabeth. AB, Middlebury Coll., 1951; postgrad., Bridgewater (Mass.) State Coll., 1986-95. Free-lance writer, 1945—; writer Sikorsky Aircraft Co., Stratford, Conn., 1957-59, N.Am. Aviation, Downey, Calif., 1959-61; editor Hughes Aircraft Co., Fullerton, 1961-62, Whitman (Mass.) News, 1962-65; sci. writer U. Vt., 1965-66; editor Wareham (Mass.) Courier, 1966-69; med. sci. editor Brown U., Providence, 1969-77; dir. pub. affairs Stonehill Coll., North Easton, Mass., 1977-83; staff columnist Quincy (Mass.) Patriot Ledger, 1982-99; news dir. Bridgewater State Coll., 1985-87; indsl. rels. dir. Morgan Meml. Goodwill Industries, Boston, 1987-89; instr. Stonehill Coll., North Easton, 1991—; columnist Attleboro (Mass.) Sun Chronicle, 1999—, Foxboro (Mass.) Reporter, 1999—. Lectr., feature writer Boston Sunday Herald-Traveler, 1963-76, Yankee mag., 1963—; staff investigative reporter Globe Communications, Montreal, Can., 1973—; bd. dirs. pub. rels. programs Composite Tech. Alloys Co., Attleboro, Mass., 1975—; coord. Ea. Writers Conf., Salem, Mass., 1982; cons. pub. rels., 1983—; instr. Stonehill Coll., 1991. Author: Seldom Heard Tales of New England, 1964, American Holocaust, 1975, Phantom P-40, 1981, Little Known Mysteries of New England, 1992, Ghosts I Have Known, 1993, The Boston Bogeyman, 1995, The Man Who Talked to Trees, 1995, Clue of the Talking Potato - And More of Connecticut's Forgotten Crimes, 1996, Horror on the Midnight Bus, and Other Massachusetts True Crime Mysteries, 1997, Mr. Spooner's in the Well, 1997, Depression Kid, 1999; assoc. editor: Stonehill Alumni News, 1977-81; editor: Stonehill Rev., 1977-83; originator (TV programs) Health Call, Science Call, Providence; prodr.: (cable TV program) Seldom Heard Tales of New Eng., 1986-88; represented in anthologies including Yankees Under Steam, 1970, Mysterious New England, 1971, Danger, Disaster and Horrid Deeds, 1974, Best Detective Cases, 1975-77, True Police Yearbook, 1975, 77, Startling Detective Yearbook, 1975-77, The World Wars Remembered, 1979, Best of Old Farmers Almanac, 1991; author manuscripts in Norris Collection, Brown U.; contbr. numerous stories to mags., TV Unsolved Mysteries, 1989. Chmn. publicity Wareham chpt. Am. Cancer Soc., 1966, cmty. chmn., 1967-69; assoc. mem. Federated Ea. Indian League; bd. dirs. Opera New Eng. of Greater Brookton, Norton Land Preservation Com., 1999. With USAAF, 1945-47; maj. Mass. N.G. Recipient Grand award Coun. Advancement and Support of Edn., 1976-77, Philippine Liberation medal Philippine Govt., 1994, Philippine Independence medal, W.W.II victory ribbon, China War medal (Chinese Govt.), 2000. Mem. New Eng. Press Assn., Am. Defenders of Bataan and Corregidor, Am. Med. Writers Assn., Assn. Am. Med. Colls., Mystery Writers Am., State Def. Force Assn. of U.S., Ret. Officers Assn., U.S. Coast Guard Aux. Flotilla 1108, Mass. Soc. Mayflower Descs., Kappa Delta Rho. Unitarian Universalist. Home: 166 E Main St Norton MA 02766-2328 *Life can be like a jaunt thru a candy store, full of tasty morsels for the creative and adventurous to grasp. Always observe nobless oblige and the ten commandments - you will be rewarded severalfold. My most useful knowledge? High school Latin. Regrets? Unable to return to Bataan or to visit English roots.*

NORRIS, CYNTHIA JEANETTE, education educator; b. Chattanooga, July 7, 1937; d. David Leigh and Mary Juanita (Morgan) Hudson; m. Joseph Leon Norris, June 2, 1956 (div. Aug. 1984); children— Sherry Lynne Norris Hutsell, Dayna Karen. B.S., Tenn. Wesleyan U., 1967; M.S., U. Tenn., 1975, Ed.D., 1984. Tchr. Chattanooga City Schs., 1969-70; tchr. Athens City Schs., Tenn., 1964-74, spl. edn. dir., 1974-84, prin. Westside Sch., Athens, 1984-86; adj. prof. U. Tenn., Chattanooga, 1982-86; asst. prof. U. Houston, 1986-91, assoc. prof., 1992-96; sr. nat. lectr. Nova Southeastern U., 1995—; facilitator Danforth Prin. Preparation Program, 1989-95; exec. dir. Metro Houston Prin. Assessment Ctr (NASSP), 1986-94; cons. Tenn. elem. sch. com. So. Assn. Colls. and Schs., 1983-86; sr. lectr. Nova Southeastern U., Ft. Lauderdale, 1995-96. Mem. ASCD, Tenn. Assn. for Gifted (treas. 1978-80), Nat. Assn. Secondary Sch. Principles, Phi Delta Kappa (Knoxville chpt. outstanding research award 1984), Phi Kappa Phi. Avocations: music, dancing, poetry. Office: Univ Houston Dept Ednl Leadership Houston TX 77004

NORRIS, DARELL FOREST, retired insurance company executive; b. Pontiac, Mich., Oct. 19, 1928; s. Forest Ellis and Mabel Marie (Smith) N.; m. Thordis Marie Johansen, Aug. 21, 1955; children: Dara Lee, Jennifer, Lisa, Nancy. BS, U. Kans., 1950. CLU; ChFC. Reporter, mem. sports staff Kansas City (Mo.) Star, 1950-51; pilot TWA, 1955-58; divsn. agy. mgr. Merced (Calif.) region Farmers Group, Inc., 1959-62, sales rep. Colorado Springs (Colo.) region, 1962-64, regional agy. mgr. Ill., 1964-66, regional sales mgr. Santa Ana, Calif., 1966-69, mem. mgmt. tng. program staff, dir. agys. L.A., 11969-71, regional mgr. Austin, Tex., 1971-73, v.p. sales L.A., 1973-76, v.p. field ops. midwestern zone, 1976-79, v.p. field ops. western zone, 1979—. Pres. Farmers New World Mgmt. Co., 1977-81, v.p. staff ops., 1981-85, sr. v.p. life co. ops. and staff support svcs., 1985-90, farmers cons., 1990-93; gen. ins. cons., 1993—. Bd. dirs. Northridge Hosp. Med. Found.; chmn. bd. deacons 1st Bapt. Ch., Granada Hills, Calif., 1977-89; sustaining mem. Rep. Nat. Com. Capt. USAF, 1951-55. Mem. Am. Soc. CLUs, ChFC, Ins. Edn. Assn. (trustee 1982-84). E-mail: DNorris268@aol.com.

NORRIS, DAVID RANDOLPH, recording artist, philanthropist; b. Oakland, Calif., Sept. 19, 1952; s. Joseph Lloyd and Corene (Keenom) N. AA, Gulf Coast Community Coll., Panama City, Fla., 1974. Touring/recording artist, worldwide. Cons. accoustic and electric 12-string guitar. Artist: (records recorded in 1990) Cindy, Loosing You, Why Is She Cruel, Alone, Just An Old Sargent, Carolina, VA Two Step, Establishment Ties, No More, Hoot Owl Trail, Blond Child. Carpenter/contractor Pres. Carter's Habitat for Humanity, project team leader, 1990. With USAF, 1972-73, Vietnam. Decorated Silver Star, Bronze Star with clusters, purple Heart with clusters; pub. svc. honoree Rep. Party/NRA, Washington, 1970-90, honored by Pres. Reagan at White House, 1988. Mem. NRA (life mem.), Calif. Rifle and Pistol Assn. (Pub. Svc. award 1988). Republican. Avocations: carpenter, trap shooter, fisherman, philanthropist. Home: PO Box 5488 Santa Monica CA 90409-5488

NORRIS, DOROTHY MARIE, interior designer, consultant; b. Chgo., Aug. 19; children: William, Rebecca. Cert., Harrington Inst. Interior Design, 1965; B of Gen. Studies, Roosevelt U., 1972. Interior design coordinator Sears, Roebuck and Co., Chgo., 1965-69; display coordinator Laura Ashley, Inc., 1981-84, regional interior design consultant, mgr. asst., 1984—. Mem. Nat. Assn. Female Execs., Inc. Office: Laura Ashley 272 Market Sq Lake Forest IL 60045-5503

NORRIS, E. ELIZABETH, music educator; b. Bklyn., Jan. 15, 1951; d. Eva Poppendieck and John William Brabant; m. Kristan Troy Norris, July 9, 1962; children: Peter Brabant, Adam Brabant, Kathleen, Keith. MusB, Ill. State U., 1975; MusM, Ind. U., 1979; D in Musical Arts, U. Kans., 1990. Coord. voice dept. Meredith Coll., Raleigh, NC, 1991—92; asst. prof. William Jewell Coll., Liberty, Mo., 1992—97; instr. music & the humanities Lincoln County Campus of FVCC, Libby, Mont., 1997—2002; asst. prof. Lyndon State Coll., Lyndonville, Vt., 2002—. Faculty advisor Sigma Alpha Iota, Raleigh, 1991—92, Liberty, Mo., 1993—97; founder, condr. Lincoln County Ensemble, Libby, 1997—2002; artistic dir. Kootenai Heritage Coun., Libby, 1997—98. Prodr.: Cmty. Concerts, 1997. Episcopalian. Avocations: quilting, writing, gardening. Home: 921 Greer's Ferry Rd Libby MT 59923

NORRIS, FLOYD HAMILTON, financial journalist; b. L.A., Sept. 6, 1947; s. Floyd H. and Martha Leota (Buntin) N.; m. Mary Christine Bockelmann, Oct. 5, 1984; 1 child, John Buntin. Student, U. Calif., Irvine, 1965-68; MBA, Columbia U., 1982. Reporter Coll. Press Svc., Washington, 1969-70, Manchester (N.H.) Am., 1970-72, Concord (N.H.) Monitor, 1972-74, UPI, Vt. and Ala., 1974-77; press sec. Sen. John Durkin, Washington, 1977-78; fin. writer AP, N.Y.C., 1978-81; columnist Barron's, 1982-88; fin. columnist N.Y. Times, 1988-98, mem. editl. bd., 1998-99, chief fin. corr., 1999—. Recipient Gerald Loeb award for fin. journalism commentary. Office: N Y Times 229 W 43rd St New York NY 10036-3959 E-mail: norris@nytimes.com.

NORRIS, FRANKLIN GRAY, thoracic and cardiovascular surgeon; b. Washington, June 30, 1923; s. Franklin Gray and Ellie Narcissus (Story) N.; m. Sara Kathryn Green, Aug. 12, 1945; children: Gloria Norris Sales, F. Gray III. BS, Duke U., 1947; MD, Harvard U., 1951. Diplomate Am. Bd. Surgery, Am. Bd. Thoracic and Cardiovasc. Surgery, Am. Bd. Gen. Vascular Surgery. Resident Peter Bent Brigham Hosp., Boston, 1951-54, Bowman Gray Sch. Medicine, 1954-57, practice medicine specializing in thoracic and cardiovascular, 1957—. Prof. anatomy and physiology, Valencia C.C., Orlando, Fla., 1995—; pres. Norris Assocs., Orlando, 1985—; mem. staff Brevard Meml. Hosp., Melbourne, Fla., Waterman Meml. Hosp., Eustis, Fla., West Orange Meml. Hosp., Winter Garden, Fla., Orlando Regional Med. Ctr., Fla. Hosp., Lucerne Hosp., Arnold Palmer Children Hosp., Princeton, Fla. Hosp. N.E. and South (all Orlando). Bd. dirs. Orange County Cancer Soc., 1958-64, Ctrl. Fla. Respiratory Disease Assn., 1958-65. Capt. USAAF, 1943-45. Decorated Air medal with 3 oak leaf clusters. Mem. ACS, Fla. Heart Assn. (dir. 1958—), Orange County Med. Soc. (exec. com. 1964-75, pres. 1971-75), Ctrl. Fla. Hosp. Assn. (bd. dirs. 1980-85), Soc. Thoracic Surgeons, So. Thoracic Surg. Assn., Am. Coll. Chest Physicians, Fla. Soc. Thoracic Surgeons (pres. 1981-82), Am. Coll. Cardiology, So. Assn. Vascular Surgeons, Fla. Vascular Soc., Citrus Club, Orlando Country Club, Phi Kappa Psi. Presbyterian. (elder). Home: 1801 Bimini Dr Orlando FL 32806-1515 Office: Norris Assocs 1801 Bimini Dr Orlando FL 32806-1515 Fax: 407-894-4977. E-mail: fnorris8@hotmail.com.

NORRIS, GEOFFREY, geology educator, consultant; b. Romford, Essex, Eng., Aug. 6, 1937; came to Can., 1964; s. Alfred Frederick Henry and Winifred Lucy (Camps) N.; m. Anne Frances Facer, Sept. 20, 1958; children—Grant, Theresa, Brett, Sonia BA, Cambridge U., Eng., 1959, MA, 1962, PhD, 1964. Sci. officer N.Z. Geol. Survey, Lower Hutt, 1961-64; postdoctoral fellow McMaster U. Hamilton, Ont., Can., 1965; rsch. scientist Pan Am. Petroleum, Tulsa, Okla., 1965-67; prof. U. Toronto, Ont., Can., 1967—, chmn. dept. geology Can., 1980-90; rsch. assoc. Royal Ont. Mus., Toronto, 1967—; A.V. Humboldt fellow Cologne U., W.Ger., 1976. Ptnr. Austin and Cumming Exploration, Calgary, Alta., Can., 1980-87; vis. scientist Fla. Marine Research Lab., St. Petersburg, 1986, Fla. Mus. Natural History, U. Fla., Gainesville, 1994; mem. Univ. Coll., 1993—; pres. Rosalex, Inc., 1996—. Contbr. articles to profl. jours. Pres. White Light Hospice Found., Toronto, 1987-96; dir. Metro Toronto Residents Action Com. for Rail Safety, 1980-95; bd. dirs. Can. Geol. Found., 1997—. Recipient numerous operating, equipment and travel grants, Nat. Scis. and Engring. Research Council of Can., 1967— Fellow Am. Assn. Stratigraphic Palynologists (pres. 1972), Royal Soc. Can. (sec. divsn. earth, ocean and atmospheric scis. 1990-92, dir. 1993-96), Geol. Assn. Can. (councilor 1987-90), Geol. Soc. Am.; mem. Can. Assn. Palynologists (pres. 1982), Internat. Commn. Palynology (sec.-treas. 1975-80), Internat. Union Geol. Scis. (Can. nat. com. 1990-98). Office: U Toronto Dept Geology Toronto ON Canada M5S 3B1 E-mail: rosalex@interlog.com.

NORRIS, GLENN L. lawyer; b. Clarinda, Iowa, Sept. 25, 1946; s. Harold E. and Darlene Louise (Crane) N.; m. Dale Bailey, Jan. 28, 1967 (div. June 1990); m. Tiffinny C. Sparks, Nov. 14, 1998; children: Christopher Steven, Catherine Beth, Glenn Leonard Jr., Janet Darlene. BA, Simpson Coll., 1968; JD, U. Iowa, 1971. Bar: Iowa 1971, So. Dist. Iowa 1971, U.S. Dist. Ct., no. dist., Iowa, 8th circuit, 1972, U.S. Supreme Ct., 1976. Law clerk U.S. Dist. Judge Hanson, Ft. Dodge, Iowa, 1971-73; assoc. Hawkins, Hedberg & Ward, Des Moines, 1973-78; ptnr. Hawkins & Norris, P.C., 1978—. Editor: Iowa Academy of Trial Lawyers Handbook, 3d edit., 1999. Mem. tech. com. Iowa Supreme Ct. Commn. for Planning for 21st Century, 1996-98, Iowa Supreme Ct. Budget Adv. Com., 1997—; dir. men's chorus Sacred Heart Knights of Columbus. Recipient St. George award for Disting. Svc. to Cath. Scouting, Boy Scouts Am. Fellow Iowa Acad. Trial Lawyers; master C. Edwin Moore Am. Inn of Ct. (pres. 1998-2000); mem. Am. Bd. Trial Advs. (cert. civil trial advocate 2000—), Iowa State Bar Assn. (mem. fed. practice com. 1999—), Iowa Assn. Trial Lawyers (bd. govs. 1987-98). Roman Catholic. Home: 6205 Oakwood Hills Dr Johnston IA 50131-1962 Office: Hawkins & Norris PC 2501 Grand Ave Ste C Des Moines IA 50312-5311 E-mail: gnorrislaw@hotmail.com.

NORRIS, JAMES HAROLD, lawyer; b. New Kensington, Pa., Sept. 18, 1953; s. J. Harold and Eleanore Rose (Arch) N.; m. Ann Marie Annase, Nov. 25, 1988; children: Ryan, Scott, Nicholas. BA, Washington Jefferson Coll., 1975; JD, Duquesne U., 1978. Bar: Pa. 1978, U.S. Dist. Ct. (we. dist.) Pa. 1978, U.S. Ct. Appeals (3d cir.) 1994, U.S. Dist. Ct. (no. dist.) W.Va. 1996. Assoc. Ruffin Hazlett Snyder Brown & Stabile, Pitts., 1979-83; ptnr. Eckert Seamans Cherin & Mellott, 1983—; exec. v.p., gen. counsel Academy System; adj. prof. U. Pitts. Sch. Law. Chief counsel Allegheny Regional Asset Dist.; bd. dirs. Epilepsy Found. Western Pa., Western Pa. Growth Fedn. Mem. bd. regents La Roche Coll., 1997. Mem. Allegheny County Bar Assn., Pa. Bar Assn. (chmn. adminstrv. law sect. 1992-94, spl. achievement award 1993). Home: 2545 Country Side Ln Wexford PA 15090-7941 Office: Eckert Seamans Cherin & Mellott 600 Grant St Pittsburgh PA 15219-2702

NORRIS, JAMES ARNOLD, federal agency administrator, consultant; b. Fargo, N.D., May 26, 1937; s. Cecril Leon and Gladys Louise (Arnold) N.; m. Catherine Anne Wright, Mar. 2, 1963; children: Suzanne, Erica, James. SB, MIT, 1959, SM, 1965; PhD, U. Calif., 1963. Economist US AID, Tunis, Tunisia, 1966-71, Jakarta, Indonesia, 1971-76, Cairo, 1976-80, dir. Bangladesh-India office Washington, 1980-82, mission dir. Dhaka, Bangladesh, 1982-84, Islamabad, Pakistan, 1988-92, Moscow, 1992-96, counselor to agy. Washington, 1984-85, dep. adminstr. Asia and Near East, 1985-88; project dir. Ralph M. Parsons Co., St. Petersburg, Russia, 1996-98; assoc. asst. adminstr. USAID, Washington, 1999; chief of party Chemonics Internat., Cairo, Egypt, 1999—. Recipient Presdl. Meritorious Svc. award President U.S., 1984, 87, Presdl. Disting. Svc. award President U.S., 1989. Address: Abdel Kader Hamza St #9 Garden City Cairo Egypt

NORRIS, JOAN CLAFETTE HAGOOD, educational administrator; b. Pelzer, S.C., June 26, 1951; d. William Emerson and Sarah (Thompson) Hagood; divorced; 1 child, Javiere Sajorah. BA in History and Secondary Edn., Spelman Coll., 1973; MA in Teaching in Edn., Northwestern U., 1974; MA in Adminstrn. and Supervision, Furman U., 1984. Cert. elem. edn. tchr., elem. prin., social studies tchr., elem. supr., S.C.; notary pub., S.C. Clk. typist Fiber Industry, Greenville, S.C., 1970, Spelman Coll. Alumni Office, Atlanta, 1970-73; tchr. Chgo. Bd. Edn., 1973-74, Greenville County Pub. Schs., Greenville, S.C., 1974-97, Hollis Acad., Greenville, 1996-97; asst. prin. Nevitt Forest Elem. Sch., Anderson, 1997—, after sch. site dir. SC, 2000—01. Dir. elem. summer sch. Anderson Sch. Dist. 5, 1998, asst. prin. acad., 2001—02; mem. steering com. N.W. area Greenville County Sch. Dist., 1994—95, chmn. elem. steering com., 1996, participant Curriculum Leadership I, 96, participant potential adminstrs. internship program, 1997—; participant Asst. Prins. Inst. Furman U., summer, 1999; flagship status application reader S.C. Sch., 2000. Contbr. articles to profl. jour. Active NAACP, Greenville, 1989—92; dir. Anderson County Elem. Sch. Dist. 5 summer sch. program, 1998, mem. staff devel. com., 2000—; active Girl Scouts of Old 96 Coun. Inc., 2001—; sec. Webette's Temple 1312, Greenville, 1985, parliamentarian, 1986; bus. ptnr. contact person Nevitt Forest Elem. Sch., 1997—2000, comm. contact person, 1997—2000. Selected to Potential Adminstrs. Acad., Furman U., 1991; named Tchr. of Yr., Armstrong Elem. Sch., 1982, 91; grantee Alliance of Quality Edn., 1989-90, 97-98, Chick-A-Fil-A extended day program in math and reading, 1998; grantee Publix Charities Media Ctr. Books, 2000. Mem. NEA, AAUW (exec. bd. cmty. rep. Greenville br. 1993-94, v.p. programs 1994-96, pres.-elect. 1996-97, pres. 1997-98, nominating com., gift honoree, 5 Star Recognition award 1998), S.C. Assn. Sch. Adminstrs. (nom. Disting. Asst. Prin. 2000, Sch. of Promise application reader 2000), S.C. Assn. Curriculum Devel. (nat. mem.), Spelman Alumni Assn., Northwestern Alumni Assn., S.C. Coun. Sci., Phi Kappa Delta (sec. chpt. 1993-94), Phi Delta Kappa (chpt. alt. del. 1992-93, v.p. membership 1996-97). Democrat. Baptist. Avocations: reading, talking to older people, listening to blues music, travel, playing basketball. Home: 219 Barrett Dr Mauldin SC 29662-2030 E-mail: jhagoodnorris@hotmail.com.

NORRIS, JOHN ANTHONY, health sciences executive, lawyer, educator; b. Buffalo, Dec. 27, 1946; s. Joseph D. and Maria L. (Suite) N.; m. Kathleen E. Mullen, July 13, 1969; children: Patricia Marie, John Anthony II, Joseph Mullen, Mary Kathleen, Elizabeth Mary. BA, U. Rochester, 1968; JD, MBA with honors, Cornell U., 1973; cert., Harvard U., 1986. Bar: Mass. 1973. Assoc. Peabody, Brown, Boston, 1973-75; from assoc. to ptnr., exec. com., v.p., dir. Powers Hall, 1975-80; chmn. bd., pres., CEO, founder Norris & Norris, 1980-85; dep. commr., COO FDA, Washington, 1985-88, chmn. action planning and cap coms., 1985-88, chmn. reye syndrome com., 1985-87, chmn. trade legis. com., 1987-88; corp. exec. v.p. Hill & Knowlton, Inc., N.Y.C., 1988-93; worldwide dir. Health Scis. Cons. Group., 1988-93; chmn. health scis. policy coun. Health Scis. Cons. Group, 1989-93; chmn. bd., pres., CEO, founder John A. Norris, Esq., PC, Boston, 1993—; pres., CEO Nat. Pharm. Coun., Reston, Va., 1995-96. Faculty Tufts Dental Sch., 1974-79, Boston Coll. Law Sch., 1976-80, Boston U. Law Sch., 1979-83, Harvard U. Pub. Health Sch., 1988—; mem. bd. editors FDA Drug Bull. and FDA Consumer Report, 1985-88; bd. dirs. Summit Tech., Inc., Cytologics, Inc., Horus Therapeutics Inc., Nat. Applied Scis., Med. Knowledge Processing, Inc. Founder, faculty editor-in-chief Am. Jour. Law and Medicine, 1973-81; editor-in-chief Cornell Internat. Law Jour., 1971-73; reviewer New Eng. Jour. Medicine Law-Medicine Notes, 1980-81; assoc. editor Medicolegal News, 1973-75. Chmn. U.S. Del. to Japan, Austria, Saudi Arabia, 1987, Finland, Denmark, Italy, 1986; chmn. Mass. Statuatory Adv. Com. on Regulation of Clin. Labs., 1977-83; chmn. Boston Alumni and Scholarship Com., U. Rochester, 1979-85; mem. trustees coun. U. Rochester, 1979-85; exec. com. Cornell Law Sch. Assn., 1982-85; mem. Mass. Gov.'s Blue Ribbon Task Force on Hosp. Determination of Need DON, 1979-80, bd. trustees Jordan Hosp., 1978-80, exec. com., 1979-80, chmn., CEO search com., 1980; chmn. Joseph D. Norris, Esq. Health Law and Pub. Policy Fund., 1979—; chmn. bd. Boston Holiday Project, 1981-83; mem. U.S. Pres. Chernobyl Task Force, 1986, vice-chmn. health affects sub.-com.; mem. U.S. Intra-Govtl. AIDS Task Force, 1987; mem. IOM Drug Devel. Forum, 1986-88, co-chmn. end points sub-com., 1987-88, Fed. Pain Commn., 1984-85; bd. dirs. Mass. 4-H Found., 1982—, vice-chmn. bd. 1996—. With U.S. Army, 1972-73. Fed. Comprehensive Health Planning fellow, 1970-73; recipient Kansas City Hon. Key award, 1988, Nat. Health Fraud Conf. award, 1988, FDA Award of Merit, 1987-88, PHS award, 1987, HHS Sec. award, 1988; named one of Ten Outstanding Young Leaders award, 1982. Mem. ABA (vice-chmn. medicine and law com. 1977-80), Mass. Bar Assn., Am. Soc. Hosp. Attys., Nat. Health Lawyers, Am. Soc. Law and Medicine (1st v.p. 1975-80, chmn. bd. 1981-84, life mem. award 1981), Soc. Computer Applications to Med. Care (bd. dirs. 1984-85), Internat. Coun. for Global Health Progress (bd. dirs. 1989-95), Phi Kappa Phi. Home: 531 W Washington St Hanson MA 02341-1067

NORRIS, JOHN HART, lawyer, director; b. New Bedford, Mass., Aug. 4, 1942; s. Edwin Arter and Harriet Joan (Winter) N.; m. Anne Kiley Monaghan, June 10, 1967; children: Kiley Anne, Amy O'Shea. BA, Ind. U., 1964; JD, U. Mich., 1967. Bar: Mich. 1968, U.S. Ct. Claims 1975, U.S. Tax Ct. 1979, U.S. Ct. Mil. Appeals 1969, U.S. Supreme Ct. 1974. From assoc. to ptnr. Monaghan, Campbell, LoPrete, McDonald and Norris, 1970-83; of counsel Dickinson, Wright, Moon, Van Dusen & Freeman, 1983-84, ptnr., 1985—; dep. asst. atty. gen. State of Mich., 1997—. Natural gas law counsel to claims mediator Columbia Gas Transmission Corp.; chpt. 11 bankruptcy procs. in Wilmington, Del. Bankruptcy Ct., 1992—; dep. asst. atty. gen. State Mich., 1997—; bd. dirs. Prime Securities Corp., Ray M. Whyte Co., Ward-Williston Drilling Co., One Stop Cap. Shop. Contbr. articles to profl. jours. Mem. Rep. State Fin. Com.; founder, co-chmn. Rep. Majority Club; bd. trustees Boys and Girls Clubs of Southeastern Mich., 1979—, Mich. Wildlife Habitat Found., Mercy Coll., Detroit, Detroit Hist. Soc., 1984—; bd. trustees, bd. dirs. African Wildlife Found.; trustee, 1st vice chmn. Salk Inst., dir. One Stop Capital Shop, Detroit, 1999—. Recipient numerous civic and non-profit assn. awards. Fellow Mich. State Bar Found.; mem. ABA (litigation and natural resources sects.), Mich. Oil and Gas Assn. (legal and legis. com.), State Bar Mich. (chmn. environ. law sect. 1982-83, probate and trust law sect., energy conservation task force, oil and gas com.), Oakland County Bar Assn., Detroit Bar Assn. (pub. adv. com.), Am. Arbitration Assn., Fin. and Estate Planning Coun. of Detroit, Def. Orientation Conf. Assn., Detroit Zool. Soc., Blue Key Nat. Hon. Fraternity, Phi Delta Phi. Clubs: Bloomfield Hills Country, Thomas M. Cooley, Detroit Athletic, Econ. (Detroit), Hundred, Prismatic, Turtle Lake, Yondotega. Roman Catholic. Home: 1325 Buckingham Ave Birmingham MI 48009-5881 Office: Dickinson Wright 38525 N Woodward Ave Bloomfield Hills MI 48304-2971

NORRIS, JOHN STEVEN, healthcare company executive; b. Chgo., Apr. 25, 1943; s. Norris Dale and Olive (Grissinger) N.; m. Susan Jean Armstrong, May 3, 1975; children: Lindsey Jean, Whitney Ann, John Scott. BA, U. Ariz., 1967; B in Fgn. Trade, Thunderbird, The Am. Grad Sch. Internat. Mgmt., 1968; MPH, U. Ariz., 1995. Diplomate Am. Coll. Healthcare Execs.; lic. nursing home adminstr., gen. contractor, real estate broker. Inspection officer Citicorp, Brazil, Columbia, Mex., 1968—73, asst. cashier N.Y.C., 1973—74; pres., gen. mgr. Phoenix Athletic Club, 1974-76; bus. mgr. Phoenix Pub. Inc., 1976-77; project mgr. Environ. Constn. Co., Phoenix, 1977-79; pres. AGN Devel. Corp., 1979—, Valley View Realty, Inc., Phoenix, 1981-87; exec. v.p., sec., pres. RGW Constrn. Co., Inc.; pres. Norris/Roberts Group, Inc., Phoenix, 1987-90; CEO Christian Care Cos., Inc., 1990—. Chmn. Covenant Health Network, 2001--. Ex officio bd. dirs. Christian Care Inc.; elder 1st Christian Ch., bd. dirs. Promise Endowment; bd. dirs., v.p. region 1 Area Agy. Aging. Recipient award of honor Ariz. Assn. Homes and Svcs. for Aging, 1999. Fellow: Am. Coll. Healthcare Adminstrs.; mem.: Am. Assn. Home Svcs. Aging, Moon Valley Country Club, Rotary Internat. (treas., past pres. Phoenix club, treas. Dist. 5490, Jim Graham--Service Above Self award 2002, Paul Harris fellow), Phi Delta Theta. Republican. Avocations: golf, skiing, racquetball. Home: 111 W Tam O'Shanter Dr Phoenix AZ 85023-6241 Office: Christian Care Cos 2002 W Sunnyside Dr Phoenix AZ 85029-3534 E-mail: jnorris@christiancare.org.

NORRIS, KATHARINE EILEEN, communications professional, educator; b. Norwalk, Calif., Feb. 2, 1960; d. Curtis Bird and Eileen Patricia N. BA, Salem State Coll., 1982; MA, Brown U., 1987. Feature writer The Enterprise newspaper, Brockton, Mass., 1984, 87-88; editor Assoc. Newspapers, Stoughton, 1987-88, Mansfield (Mass.) News, 1988-89; instr. comm. Bristol C.C., Fall River, Mass., 1989—; instr. Mt. Ida Coll., Newton Centre, 1990-95, Bridgewater (Mass.) State Coll., 1991-96; radio talk host WPEP, Taunton, Mass., 1991-99; dir. mktg. and pub. rels. Zeiterion Theatre, New Bedford, 1995—. Asst. editor: The Guide for Students and Parents to 101 of the Best Values in America's Colleges and Universities, 1993. Active Taunton Animal Care Adv. Bd., Cape Cod Civil War Round Table, Friends of Taunton Animal Care Facility, 2000. Avocations: study of czarist Russia, collecting old New England post cards.

NORRIS, KENNETH MICHAEL, lawyer; b. Ludlow, Mass., Jan. 22, 1952; s. Kenneth Richard and Santa (LiAntonio) N. BS in Nuclear Engring., USCG Acad., 1973; MSChemE, Purdue U., 1977; MBA, U. Md., 1979; JD, George Washington U., 1983. Bar: D.C. 1984, Tex. 1988, Calif. 1992, Wash. 1998; registered profl. engr., Tex. Marine engr. USCG, Seattle, 1973-75, chem. engr. Washington, 1977-82; del. Internat. Maritime Orgn., London, 1978-82, UN Com. on Trade and Devel., Geneva, 1979-82; resigned USCG, 1984; patent atty. Sandler & Greenblum, P.C., Arlington, Va., 1984-85; sr. cons. Booz, Allen & Hamilton, Inc., Washington, 1985-86; corp. counsel Resource Engring., Inc., Houston, 1986-88; environ. atty. Butler & Binion, 1988-90; ptnr., dir. environ. law dept. Norton & Blair, 1990-91; environ. atty. Morgan, Lewis & Bockius, L.A., 1991-93; sr. environ. counsel Chem. Waste Mgmt., Houston, 1993-96; sr. counsel Fluor Hanford, Inc., Richland, Wash., 1997—. Rep. Am. Nat. Standards Inst. Com. N-14 and Com. N-522; adj. prof. environ. law U. Houston Law Ctr., 1989-97; faculty Columbia Basin Coll., 1999—; mil. aide to Pres. Carter, Pres. Reagan, 1978-82. Contbr. articles to profl. publs. Treas. Westchester Found., Arlington, 1982-86; atty. Arlington Coun. on Fin., 1984; pres. Wroxton Owners Assn.; v.p. Benton Franklin Dispute Resolution Ctr., 1999-2000, bd. dirs., 1999-2002; bd. dirs. Willobrook Cmty. Assn., 2002—; bd. dirs. Neurol. Ctr., 1998—, pres., 1999—. With USCG, 1969-84, capt. USCGR, 1984-96. Mem. ABA, AAAS, D.C. Bar, Tex. Bar, Calif. Bar, Wash. Bar Assn., Am. Chem. Soc., Am. Nuc. Soc., Neurol. Ctr. (bd. dirs. 1999—, pres. 2000—), Houston Striker Rugby Club, West Potomac Rugby Club (Washington) (pres.), Masons. Republican. Avocation: rugby. Home: 227 Sitka Ct Richland WA 99352 E-mail: Kenneth-M-Ken-norris@rl.gov.

NORRIS, LOIS ANN, elementary school educator; b. Detroit, May 13, 1937; d. Joseph Peter and Marguerite Iola (Gourley) Giroux; m. Max Norris, Feb. 9, 1962 (div. 1981); children: John Henry, Jeanne Marie, Joseph Peter. BS in Social Sci., MA, Ea. Mich. U., 1960; cert. adminstr., Calif. State U., Bakersfield, 1983. Kindergarten tchr. Norwalk-LaMirada Unified Sch. Dist., 1960-62; tchr. various grades Rialto Unified Sch. Dist., 1962-66; kindergarten tchr. Inyokern (Calif.) Sch., 1969-82; 1st grade tchr. Vieweg Basic Sch, 1982-92, kindergarten tchr., 1992-96; retired, 1996. Head tchr. Sierra Sands Elem. Summer Sch.; adminstrv. intern Sierra Sands Adult Sch., master tchr., head tchr., counselor. Ofcl. scorekeeper, team mother, snack bar coord. China Lake Little League; team mother, statistician Indian Wells Valley Youth Football; bd. mem. PTA; pres. Sch. Site Coun.; treas. Inyokern Parents Club; run coord. City of Hope; timekeeper, coord. Jr. Olympics; mem. planning com. Sunshine Festival; active Burros Booster Club; docent Maturango Mus.; mem. Pink Lady orgn. Ridgecrest Regional Hosp.; mem. Women's Aux. for Commd. Officers Mess. Recipient Hon. Svc. award PTA, 1994. Mem. NEA, AAUW, Calif. Tchrs. Assn., Desert Area Tchrs. Assn., Assn. Calif. Sch. Adminstrs., Inyokern C. of C. (sec.), Am. Motorcycle Assn., NRA, Bakersfield Coll. Diamond Club, Inyokern Rotary, Beta Sigma Phi. Republican. Mem. Lds Ch. Avocations: swimming, physical fitness, music, American history, gardening. Home: PO Box 163 201 N Brown Rd Inyokern CA 93527 E-mail: anorris@iwvisp.com.

NORRIS, LONNIE HAROLD, dean; b. Houston, Nov. 22, 1942; s. Mary Ethel (Jacobs) King; m. Donna M. Farmer, June 18, 1966; children: Marlaina M., Michael A. BA in Chemistry, Fisk U., 1964; DMD, Harvard U., 1976, MPH, 1977. Asst. prof. oral & maxillofacial surgery Tufts U. Sch. Dental Medicine, Boston, 1981-88, assoc. prof., 1988-95, prof., 1995—, interim dean, 1995-96, dean, 1996—. Mem. com. on dental accreditation. Mem. Gov.'s Commn. to Study the Oral Health Status and Accessibility of Dental Care Svcs. for Residents of the Commonwealth of Mass. Named Disting. Practitioner Nat. Acads. of Practice, Dentist of Yr., New England chpt. Pierre Fauchard Acad. Fellow Am. Acad. Dental Sci., Am. Coll. Dentists, Am. Assn. Oral/Maxillofacial Surgeons, Am. Bd. Oral/Maxillofacial Surgery, Internat. Coll. Dentists, Phi Beta Kappa, Omicron Kappa Upsilon. Avocations: travel, family. Office: Tufts U Sch Dental Medicine 1 Kneeland St Boston MA 02111-1527

NORRIS, MACKIE LYVONNE HARPER, registered nurse, health care consultant; b. Bivins, Tex., Dec. 10, 1940; d. McNoble and Corine Rosetta (Collins) Harper; m. Alfred L. Norris Sr., Sept. 9, 1961; children: Alfred, Lisa, Tyrone, Angela. BSN, Dillard U., 1960; MN, Emory U., 1971, PhD, 1996. RN, N.Mex., La., Ga. Asst. prof. Dillard U., New Orleans, 1977-84; assoc. prof. Woodruff Sch. Nursing Emory U., Atlanta, 1985-92. Cons. Aftercare, Ltd., Atlanta, 1991-92, United Meth. Ch., N.Y.C., 1996—, Not Even One Project, N.Mex., 1997; mem. faculty U. Phoenix Nursing Dept. Mem. Presbyn. Hosp. IRB, Albuquerque, 1993—; treas. N.Mex. Sickle Cell Coun., Albuquerque, 1994—. Mem. ANA, APHA, Nat. League Nursing, N.Mex. Pub. Health Assn., Omichron Delta Kappa, Sigma Theta Tau.

NORRIS, MEGAN PINNEY, lawyer; b. Mpls., May 20, 1961; d. Rollin Bradford and Margo Pinney N.; m. Howard William Trevor Matthew, May 27, 1989; 1 child, Taylor Norris Matthew. BA, Wesleyan U., 1983; JD, U. Mich., 1986. Bar: Mich. 1986, U.S. Dist. Ct. (ea. dist.) Mich. 1986, U.S. Dist. Ct. (we. dist.) Mich. 1989, U.S. Ct. Appeals (6th cir.) 1998. Assoc. Miller, Confield, Paddock and Stone, P.L.C., Detroit, 1986-94, prin., 1995—99, sr. prin., 2000—. Bd. dirs. Detroit Metropolitan Bar Assn., 1995—, pres.-elect, 2001—, pres., 2002—; adv. bd. Inst. Continuing Legal Edn., Ann Arbor, Mich., 1997—. Co-author: Michigan Public Employee Labor Relations Manual, 1994, Employment Discrimination Law Supplement, 1998, 2000; contbr. articles to profl. jours. Pres., bd. trustees Deaf, Hearing & Speech Ctr., Detroit, 1996-98, Wayne State Episcopal Chaplaincy, Detroit, 1993-98; pres., bd. dirs. Whittaker Sch. Theology, Detroit, 1993-94; mem. City of Detroit Bd. Police Commnrs., 2001—, vice chair, 2001—; mem. bd. trustees Wesleyan U., 2001—. Recipient Leadership Detroit award Detroit C. of C., 1996. Mem. Detroit Barristers Assn. (pres. 1994-95), Wesleyan U. bd. trustees nominating com. (1995-97), Episcopal Diocese Mich., Christ Ch. Detroit (sr. warden 1994). Democrat. Avocations: biking, cooking. Office: Miller Canfield Paddock and Stone PLC 150 W Jefferson Ave Ste 2500 Detroit MI 48226-4416 E-mail: norris@millercanfield.com.

NORRIS, MELVIN, lawyer; b. Cambridge, Mass., Aug. 17, 1931; BA, Northeastern U., Boston, 1954; JD, Boston Coll., 1959. Bar: Mass. 1959, U.S. Supreme Ct. 1965. Atty. FTC, Boston, 1960-62; pvt. practice Boston, 1962-76; ptnr. Norris, Kozodoy, Krasnoo & Fong, 1976-90, Norris, Kozodoy & Fong, Boston, 1991-96; pvt. practice Newton, Mass., 1997—. Ethics com. for govt. lawyers Supreme Jud. Ct. Mass., 1999-2000. Bd. editors Mass. Lawyers Weekly, 1984-93. Vice-chmn. Newton Crime Commn., 1966-67; mem. Newton Bldg. Code Revision Com., 1972-73; chmn. bd. dirs., pres. Waterville Estates Assn., Campton, N.H., 1992-94. With USCG, 1954-56. Mem. Fed. Bar Assn. (pres. Boston chpt. 1977-78, v.p. 1st circuit 1978-99, exec. com. 1982-83, Cert. Appreciation 1996, Mass. chpt. Outstanding Leadership award 1999), Mass. Bar Assn. Office: 260 Boston Post Rd Ste 9 Wayland MA 01778

NORRIS, NEAL ALBERT, financial and business consultant; b. Elyria, Ohio, Mar. 7, 1951; s. Roy Albert and Alice May (Joviak) N.; m. Diane Lynn Dobney, Aug. 4, 1973; children: Kerri, Kristine. BA, Miami U., Oxford, Ohio, 1973; MEd, U. Mass., 1977, EdD, 1982. Coordinator curriculum and profl. devel. Reading (Pa.) Area Community Coll., 1983-86; personal fin. planner IDS-Am. Express, Reading, 1987-88; mgr. tng. and devel. Berk-Tek, New

Holland, Pa., 1988-89; mgr. personnel devel. RAM Motors & Controls, Reading, 1989-91; account exec. Lincoln Investment Planning, 1991-92; dist. rep. Aid Assn. for Luths., 1992-93; dir. corp. and found. rels. Muhlenberg Coll., Allentown, Pa., 1994—. Futures cons. Adminstrn. Action Newsletter, Stillwater, Okla., 1988—. Editor/author: Community College Futures: From Rhetoric to Reality, 1989. Mem. ch. coun., mem. endowment fund and stewardship coms. Atonement Luth. Ch., Wyomissing, Pa., 1987-89; mem. blue ribbon panel N.Mex. Systematic Sci. Initiative, 1992-93. Recipient Individual Merit award, Nat. Coun. for Staff, Prog. and Orgnl. Devel., 1986. Mem. Coun. for Advancement and Support of Edn., Nat. Soc. for Fund-Raising Execs., World Future Soc., Nat. Coun. for Staff Program and Orgnl. Devel. (chmn. future trends commn. 1986). Home: 2224 Heatherwood Dr Findlay OH 45840

NORRIS, RICHARD ANTHONY, accountant, waste systems company executive; b. Birmingham, Eng., July 6, 1943; s. Albert Edward and Audrey (Rowley) N.; m. Geri M., Jan. 20, 1947; 1 child, Karen Louise. BA, U. Leeds, York, Eng., 1966. Chartered acct., Can. Auditor Price Waterhouse & Co., Bristol, Eng., 1966-70, mgr. Montreal, Que., Can., 1970-78; from mgr. corp. acctg. to controller Can. Pacific Enterprises, Montreal and Calgary, Alta., Can., 1978-85; v.p. fin. U.S. Ops. Laidlaw Waste Systems Inc., North Richland Hills, Tex., 1986-96; v.p., CFO, Nexcycle, Inc., Dallas, 1997-2000; sr. v.p., CFO Casella Waste Systems Inc., Rutland, Vt., 2000—. Home: 448 Curtis Brook Rd Rutland VT 05701 Office: Casella Waste Sys Inc 25 Greens Hill Ln Rutland VT 05701 also: Casella Waste Sys Inc 25 Greens Hill Ln Rutland VT 05701-3804 E-mail: Richard.Norris@casella.com.

NORRIS, RICHARD PATRICK, museum director, history educator; b. Galveston, Tex., May 21, 1944; s. William Gerard and Iris Elsa (Allington) N.; m. Therese Louise Aalid, July 27, 1974; children: William Gerard, John Patrick. BA, Ohio State U., 1966; MA, SUNY, Binghamton, 1968; PhD, U. Minn., 1976. Instr. U. Minn., Mpls., 1970-76; lectr. U. Md., Europe/Asia, 1976-78; dir. Chippewa Valley Mus., Eau Claire, Wis., 1978-80, Kalamazoo Valley Mus., 1985—; curator of history Mus. Sci. & Hist., Fort Worth, 1980-85. Lectr. Tex. Christian U., Fort Worth, Tex., 1981—85; cons. Am. Assn. Mus., Washington, 1979—, NEH, Washington, 1989; adj. prof. We. Mich. U., Kalamazoo, 1986—. Author: History by Design, 1984; book reviewer Mus. News, History News; contbr. articles to profl. jours. Mem.: Assn. Midwest Mus., Internat. Coun. Mus., Am. Assn. State and Local History, Am. Assn. Mus., Rotary (dir. Kalamazoo club 1991—93, pres. 1999—2000). Office: Kalamazoo Valley Museum PO Box 4070 Kalamazoo MI 49003-4070 E-mail: pnorris@kvcc.edu.

NORRIS, ROBERT WHEELER, military officer; b. Birmingham, Ala., May 22, 1932; s. Hubert Lee and Georgia Irene (Parker) N.; m. Martha Katherine Cummins, Feb. 19, 1955; children— Lisha Katherine Norris Utt, Nathan Robert BA in Bus. Adminstrn., U. Ala., 1954, LL.B., 1955; LL.M., George Washington U., 1979; postgrad., Air Command & Staff Coll., 1968, Nat. War Coll., 1975. Commd. 2d lt. USAF, advanced through grades to maj. gen., dep. judge advocate gen., 1983-85, judge advocate gen., 1985-88; gen. counsel Ala. Bar Assn., Montgomery, 1988-95; ptnr. London & Yancey, Birmingham, Ala., 1995—. Decorated D.S.M., Legion of Merit, Meritorious Svc. medal. Mem. ABA. Methodist. Office: London & Yancey 2001 Park Pl Ste 400 Birmingham AL 35203-2787

NORRIS, STEVEN J. elementary school educator; b. Huntingdon, Pa., July 4, 1952; s. Joseph Eugene and Patricia Louise Norris; m. Wendy Lou Norris, Nov. 23, 1979; children: Ian Thomas, Justin Wade, Brea Lynn. BA in Elem. Edn., Juniata Coll., 1975; M of Elem. Edn., Edinboro (Pa.) U., 1985. Activity dir. Cmty. Ctr. Huntingdon C.C., 1970—75; dir. camp edn. James Creek (Pa.) YCC, 1975; tchr. elem. edn. Warren County Sch. Dist., Pa., 1975—. Head basketball coach, asst. Warren County Sch. Dist., 1975—, head football coach, asst., 1979—99, head track coach, asst., 1981—. Columnist: Valley Voice newspaper, 1979—81. Named Body Bldg. Champion, Tri-State - Drug Free, 1994, Lake Ont. Internat. Marathon Champion, 1981, Kane Marathon Champion (record holder), 1981. Mem.: Elks. Lutheran. Avocations: body building, running, reading, being a parent. Home: 125 N Irvine St Warren PA 16365

NORRIS, SUSAN ELIZABETH, social worker; b. Lubbock, Tex., Oct. 8, 1952; d. William Oxford and Katherine Burton (Sydnor) N. BA, U. Tex., Arlington, 1974; MSW, U. Conn., 1987. Child protective svcs. social worker Tex. Dept. Human Resources, Ft. Worth, 1978-82; temp. word processor various cos., 1983-85; rsch. cons. Hartford, Conn., 1986-89; dir. child care svcs. United Way Conn., 1987-92, dir. program svcs., 1992-93; faculty/assoc. dir. child and family studies, pediatrics U. Conn. Health Ctr., Farmington, 1993-94, dir., 1994-96; program mgr. Work/Family Directions, Boston, 1996-97; dir. child care svcs. Maximus, 1997-98, deputy project mgr., 1998-2000, project mgr., 2000—02, dir., 2002—. Mem. adj. faculty sch. social work U. Conn., 2000—. Bd. dirs., sec. Hartford Interval House, 1989-93; pres. bd. dirs. Hartford Area Child Collaborative, 1992-94. Democrat. Avocations: travel, reading, exercise. Office: 11419 Sunset Hills Rd Reston VA 20190-

NORRIS, TRACY HOPKINS, retired public relations executive; b. Ainsworth, Iowa, Nov. 1, 1927; s. Lee E. and Ruth C. (Simpson) N.; m. Emilie Lathrop, Nov. 11, 1956; 1 child, Shawn Tracy. BA, Cornell Coll., Mt. Vernon, Iowa, 1952; MA, U. Iowa, 1957. Admissions counselor Cornell Coll., Mt. Vernon, 1952-54; dir. news bur. Wittenberg U., Springfield, Ohio, 1956-70; exec. dir. univ. relations and communications Ball State U., Muncie, Ind., 1970-88. Active United Way Springfield, Ohio, Muncie, 1965—. Served with USN, 1945-48. Recipient Silver Anvil award Pub. Relations Soc. Am., 1967. Mem. Council for Advancement and Support Edn., Exchange Club. Lutheran. Avocations: golf, travel, lawn and garden activities. Home: PO Box 2329 Muncie IN 47307 E-mail: tnorris629@aol.com.

NORSKOG, EUGENIA FOLK, elementary education educator; b. Staunton, Va., Mar. 23, 1937; d. Ernest and Edna Virginia (Jordan) Folk; m. Russell Carl Norskog, Nov. 25, 1967; children: Cynthia, Carl, Roberta, Eric. BA, King Coll., 1958; MEd, George Mason U., 1977. Cert. tchr., Va. Tchr. elem. Bristol (Va.) Pub. Schs., 1958-61, 62-65, Staunton (Va.) Pub. Schs., 1961-62, Fairfax (Va.) County Pub. Schs., 1965-68; with Project 100,000, USAFI, Fort Ord, Calif., 1969; tchr. elem. Monterey (Calif.) Peninsula Sch. Div., 1970-71, Prince William County Schs., Manassas, Va., 1972-2001, ret., 2001; Va. rehab. sch. Prince William County, Richmond, 1979-82. V.p. Fauquier Gymnastics, Warrenton, Va., 1982-83, pres., 1983-85; coach, bd. dirs., referee Warrenton Soccer Assn., 1980-88; soccer referee Piedmont Referee Assn., Manassas, 1990-95. Mem. NEA, Va. Edn. Assn. Prince William Edn. Assn. (bd. dirs. 1974-77). Home: 7160 Airlie Rd RR 8 Box 398 Warrenton VA 20187-9448

NORSTRAND, HANS PETER, lawyer, real estate investment company executive; b. Cambridge, Mass., Aug. 1, 1940; s. Hans Donald and Marion (Hardy) N.; m. Janet Hoover, Dec. 30, 1967 (div.); children: Rachel Bell, Hans Christopher; m. Katherine Tallman, Feb. 5, 1994. AB, Dartmouth Coll., 1963; JD, Boston Coll., 1966. Bar: Mass., 1966; U.S. Supreme Ct., 1994. Asst. atty. gen., Mass., 1966-69; assoc. Sullivan & Worcester, Boston, 1969-74; v.p., gen. csl Kuras & Co., Inc., 1974-76; pvt. practice, 1977-80; v.p., gen. counsel Boston Co. Real Estate Counsel, Inc., 1980-81; prin. Aldrich, Eastman & Waltch, Boston, 1981-91; mng. dir. Sun Capital Adv.,Inc., 1991-93; prin. State St. Global Advs., 1994-99; v.p. ASB Capital Mgmt., Inc., 1999; pvt. practice Brookline, Mass., 2000; dir. real estate Commonwealth of Mass. Divsn. Capital Asset Mgmt., Boston, 2000; dir. real estate, dep. commr, divsn. capital asset mgmt. Commonwealth of Mass., 2001—. Office: 1 Ashburton Pl 15th Fl Boston MA 02108 E-mail: ksthpn@aol.com., HPeter.Norstrand@state.ma.us.

NORSTRAND, IRIS FLETCHER, psychiatrist, neurologist, educator; b. Bklyn., Nov. 21, 1915; d. Matthew Emerson and Violet Marie (Anderson) Fletcher; m. Severin Anton Norstrand, May 20, 1941; children: Virginia Helene Norstrand Villano, Thomas Fletcher, Lucille Joyce. BA, Bklyn. Coll., 1937, MA in Biochemistry, 1965, PhD in Biochemistry, 1972; MD, L.I. Coll. Medicine, 1941. Diplomate Am. Bd. Psychiatry and Neurology, cert. geriat. psychiatry. Intern Montefiore Hosp., Bronx, N.Y., 1941-42; asst. resident in neurology N.Y. Neurol. Inst.-Columbia-Presbyn. Med. Ctr., N.Y.C., 1944-45; pvt. practice Bklyn., 1947-52; resident in psychiatry Bklyn. VA Med. Ctr., 1952-54, resident in neurology, 1954-55, staff neurologist, 1955-81, asst. chief neurol. svc., 1981-91, staff psychiatrist, 1991-95. Neurol. cons. Indsl. Home for Blind, Bklyn., 1948-51; clin. prof. neurology SUNY Health Sci. Ctr., Bklyn., 1981—; attending neurologist Kings County Hosp., Bklyn., State U. Hosp., Bklyn.; cons. in field. Contbr. articles to profl. jours. Mem. Nat. Rep. Congl. Com., Rep. Senatorial Inner Circle. Recipient Spl. plaque Mil. Order Purple Heart, 1986, Spl. Achievement award PhD Alumni Assn. of CUNY, 1993, Lifetime Achievement award Bklyn. Coll., 1995, others. Fellow Am. Psychiat. Assn., Am. Acad. Neurology, Internat. Soc. Neurochemistry, Am. Assn. U. Profs. Neurology, Am. Med. EEG Soc. (pres. 1987-88), Nat. Assn. VA Physicians (pres. 1989-91, James O'Connor award 1987), N.Y. Acad. Scis., Sigma Xi. Republican. Presbyterian. Avocations: writing, piano, travel, reading. Home: 7624 10th Ave Brooklyn NY 11228-2309

NORSWORTHY, ELIZABETH KRASSOVSKY, lawyer; b. N.Y.C., Feb. 26, 1943; d. Leonid Alexander and Wilma (Hudgens) Krassovsky; m. John Randolph Norsworthy, June 24, 1961 (div. 1962), m. Nov. 26, 1977 (div. 1984); 1 child, Alexander. AB magna cum laude, CUNY, 1965; MA, U. N.C., 1966; JD, Stanford U., 1977. Bar: D.C. 1978, Mass. 1992, Vt. 1998, U.S. Ct. Appeals (D.C. cir.) 1979. Atty. applications, disclosure rev. and investment adviser regulation, divsn. investment mgmt. SEC, Washington, 1978-79, 80-82, atty. operating brs. and disclosure policy divsn. corp. fin., 1979-80, chief, spl. counsel office of regulatory policy divsn. investment mgmt., 1983-86; assoc. Kirkpatrick & Lockhart, 1986-90; ptnr. Sullivan & Worcester, Boston, 1990-92; pvt. practice Norfolk, Mass., 1992-95, Concord, Vt., 1996—. Pub. arbitrator, chairperson NASD; mediator, facilitator Cmty. Justice Ctr., St. Johnsbury. Mem. North Country Chorus, Wells River; chair investment com. North Congl. Ch., St. Johnsbury; mem. adv. bd. Natural Resources, Concord. Mem.: Vt. Coverts, Vt. Grass Farmers, Am. Farmland Trust, Jacob Sheep Breed Assn., Am. Livestock Breed Conservancy, Vt. Bar Assn. (ADR com., family law com.), College Club (St. Johnsbury), Athenaeum (St. Johnsbury), Catamount Arts Club (St. Johnsbury), Phi Alpha Theta, Phi Beta Kappa. Democrat. Mem. United Church of Christ. Avocations: farming, swimming, singing, environmental protection. Office: Winterbrook Farm 1342 Woodward Rd Concord VT 05824-9620 Fax: 802-695-2516. E-mail: ekn@kingcon.com.

NORSWORTHY, JOHN RANDOLPH, economist, educator; b. Norfolk, Va., Aug. 26, 1939; s. John Tignor and Annie Vivian (Smith) N.; m. Elizabeth Krassovsky, June 24, 1961 (div. 1962); 1 child, Leonid Alexander; m. Susan Foster, Aug. 15, 1964 (div. 1971); 1 child, Ann Randolph; m. Irene Jacobsohn, June 19, 1991. BA with distinction, U. Va., 1961, PhD in Econs., 1966. Asst. prof. econs. U. Ill., Chgo., 1966-68; asst., then assoc. prof. Temple U., Phila., 1968-71; chief applied econs. divsn. Office of Emergency Preparedness, Exec. Office Pres., Washington, 1971-73; chief productivity rsch. divsn. Bur. Labor Stats., 1973-82; chief ctr. for econ. studies Bur. Census, U.S. Dept. Commerce, 1982-85; cons. economist, 1985-86; prof. econ. and mgmt. Rensselaer Poly. Inst., 1986—. Mem. Brookings Panel on Econ. Activity, 1979; dir. Ctr. Sci. and Tech. Policy, 1990-92; cons. in telecom. and productivity AT&T, 1995-97. Author: (with S.L. Jang) Pub. Analysis of Technological Change and Productivity: Applications in High Technology and Service Industries, 1992, (with D.H. Tsai) The Macroeconomic Environment as Implicit Industrial Policy, 1997, (with Ivan L. Pitt) Technological Change and Productivity in U.S. Commercial Airlines, 1999; contbr. articles to profl. jours. Recipient Disting. Achievement award for Rsch., U.S. Dept. Labor, 1980, Lawrence R. Gordon award for Grad. Tchg. and Rsch. in Econs., Rensselaer Poly. Inst., 1988; NDEA fellow, U. Va., 1961-65, postdoctoral fellow econs. U. Chgo., 1965-66, NSF/Am. Statis. Assn. fellow U.S. Bur. Census, 1990-91. Mem. Am. Econ. Assn., Am. Statis. Assn., Econometric Soc., Am. Fin. Assn., Fin. Mgmt. Assn. Internat., Conf. on Rsch. in Income and Wealth (exec. com. 1981-85), Phi Beta Kappa, Phi Eta Sigma, Tau Kappa Epsilon.

NORSWORTHY, LEONID A. bank executive, educator; b. N.Y.C., Jan. 15, 1962; s. John Randolph and Elizabeth Krassovsky N.; m. Valentina Alekhina, Dec. 7, 1995; children: Alexandra, Elizabeth, Paul, Julia, Margaret. BA, Am. U., 1984, MA, 1986, PhD, 1989; MBA, Georgetown U., 1999. Asst. dir. devel. Am. U., Washington, 1984-88; mgr. mktg. rsch. Am. Enterprise Inst., 1988; dir. devel. svcs. Cath. U., 1988-91; dir. fgn. and fin. policy studies Daiwa Group, 1991-95; mgr., cons. World Bank Group, 1995—. Prof. lectr. Am. U., 1988—96; adj. prof. Syracuse U., 2001. Co-author, editor: Rural Development Natural Resources, 2000, Russian Views of Transition, 2000; co-author: The Clinton Revolution, 1993, Dawn of a New Era, 1992; editl. adv. bd. Taft Group FRI, Rockville, Md., 1992-93. Pers. coord. Conservative Fund, 1984; copy writer, cons. Advance Mktg., 1986. Mem. Am. Polit. Sci. Assn., Internat. Studies Assn., Am. Econ. Assn., Alpha Delta Phi, Phi Kappa Phi, Beta Gamma Sigma. Avocations: writing, horseback riding, guitar. Home: 5018 N 25th Place Arlington VA 22207 Office: World Bank Group 1818 H St NW Washington DC 20433 E-mail: l_a_norsworthy@hotmail.com.

NORTELL, BRUCE, lawyer; b. Nov. 19, 1946; s. Joseph and Dorothy Nortell; children: Adam, Daniel, Anthony. AB, Boston U., 1968; JD, U. Chgo., 1971. Bar: Ill. 1971, U.S. Dist. Ct. (no. dist.) Ill. 1971, U.S. Supreme Ct. 1979. Sole practice, Chgo., 1971—74; asst. dir. legal affairs AMA, 1974—81, counsel, sec. jud. coun., 1976—81; dir. tax and fin. planning Loyola U., 1981—88, North Ctrl. Coll., Naperville, 1988—. Contbr. articles to profl. jours.; , author two books novels. Mem.: ABA, Chgo. Bar Assn., Ill. Bar Assn. (Lincoln award 1975), Phi Beta Kappa (bd.). Home: 1124 Dickens Ln Naperville IL 60563-4301 Office: 30 N Brainard St Naperville IL 60540-4607

NORTH, A. FREDERICK, physician; b. Milw., July 3, 1931; s. Alexander F. and Florence (Reineking) N.; m. Jane Whittlesey, Dec. 18, 1954; children: Lindsay Elizabeth, Robert Whittlesey, Wendy Katherine. Student, Yale Coll., 1953; MD, Yale U., 1956. Intern Strong Meml. Hosp., Rochester, N.Y., 1956-58, resident pediatrics, 1960-62; instr. pediatrics U. Rochester, 1962-66; sr. pediatrician Project Head Start, Washington, 1966-68; assoc. prof. pediatrics George Washington U., 1968-72; assoc. med. dir. Children's Hosp. of D.C., 1968-72; vis. prof. pediatrics, pub. health U. Pitts., 1972-79; physician for retarded persons Govt. of D.C., Washington, 1978-88; pvt. practice in pediat. Rockville, Md., 1988—. Cons. various locations, 1966-88. Author: Infant Care, 1980; contbr. articles to pubs. Lt. USNR, 1958-60. Fellow Acad. of Pediatrics, Am. Pub. Health Assn.; mem. Am. Pediatric Soc., Ambulatory Pediatric Assn. (pres. 1966-67), Chevy Chase Club. Republican. Episcopalian. Home: 5703 Overlea Rd Bethesda MD 20816-1918 E-mail: afnorth@msn.com.

NORTH, ANITA, secondary education educator; b. Chgo., Apr. 21, 1963; d. William Denson and Carol (Linden) N. BA, Ind. U., 1985; MS in Edn., Northwestern U., 1987. Cert. tchr., Ill. High sch. social studies and English tchr. Lake Park High Sch., Roselle, Ill., 1987-89; high sch. social studies tchr. West Leyden High Sch., Northlake, 1989—. Exch. program coord. West Leyden High Sch., 1989-98, head coach boys' tennis team, 1989-97, asst. coach girls' tennis team, 1994-2000, asst. speech coach, 1992-93; adj. prof. Orgnl. Mgmt. program Concordia U., River Forest, Ill., 2000—. Docent, Chgo. Architecture Found., 2000—. Humanities fellow Nat. Coun. Humanities, 1995; recipient Fern Fine Tchg. award West Leyden H.S., 1992. Mem. Nat. Coun. for Social Studies, Ill. Coun. for Social Studies, Orgn. Am. Historians, Ill. Tennis Coaches Assn., Phi Delta Kappa. Christian. Avocations: wilderness backpacking, tennis, orienteering, gardening, antique books and maps.

NORTH, CAROL SUE, psychiatrist, educator; b. Keokuk, Iowa, May 6, 1954; d. Ray Stemen and Doris Ethelyn (Wood) N. BS in Gen. Sci., U. Iowa, 1976; MD, Wash. U., St. Louis, 1983, M in Psychiatric Epidemiology, 1993. Resident in psychiatry Barnes Hosp., Washington U. Med. Sch., St. Louis, 1983-87; rsch. fellow dept psychiatry Washington U., 1987-90, instr. dept. psychiatry, 1987-89, asst. prof. dept. psychiatry, 1989-97, assoc. prof. psychiatry, 1997-2001, prof., 2001—; staff psychiatrist Grace Hill Neighborhood Health Ctr., 1987-96, Midwest Psychiatry, 1993-95, Adapt of Am., 1995—. Author: Welcome, Silence, 1987, Multiple Personalities, Multiple Disorders: Psychiatric Classification and Media Influence, 1993; contbr. articles to profl. jours. Bd. Dirs. St. Louis Met. Alliance for the Mentally Ill, 1992-2000; trustee Rosati Stblzn. Ctr. for Homeless and Mentally Ill, 1992-94; bd. med. advisors Grace Hill Neighborhood Health Ctr., 1997—. Nat. Inst. Alcoholism and Alcohol Abuse grantee, 1988-93, Nat. Hazards Rsch. Applications Info. Ctr. grantee, 1987-88, NIMH grantee, 1991-95, 97-98, Ctr. Substance Abuse Treatment grantee, 1997—, Nat. Inst. on Drug Abuse grantee, 1998—. Fellow Am. Psychiat. Assn., Am. Psychopathol. Assn.; mem. AMA, Life History Rsch. Soc., Ea. Mo. Psychiat. Soc. (exec. coun. and pres. 1996-98), Internat. Soc. Traumatic Stress Studies, Am. Acad. Clin. Psychiatrists (bd. dirs. 1999-2001), Nat. Alliance for Mentally Ill, Am. Assn. Cmty. Psychiatrists, St. Louis Track Club. Presbyterian. Avocations: distance running, oil painting, historic home rehabilitation. Office: Washington U Sch Medicine Dept Psychiatry 4940 Childrens Pl Saint Louis MO 63110-1002

NORTH, CHARLES LAURENCE, poet, educator; b. N.Y.C., June 9, 1941; s. Monroe Daniel and Viola Utstein North; m. Paula De Pillis, June 2, 1963; children: Jill, Michael. BA magna cum laude, Tufts U., 1962; MA with honors, Columbia U., 1964. Poet-in-residence Pace U., N.Y.C., 1982—. Author: (books of poems) Leap Year, 1978, The Year of the Olive Oil, 1989, New and Selected Poems, 1999, The Nearness of the Way You Look Tonight, 2000; (essays) No Other Way, 1998; editor: (with J. Schuyler) Broadway, 1979, Broadway 2, 1989. Mem. poetry project St. Mark's Ch. Recipient Poets Found. award Poets Found., N.Y.C., 1972, Fund for Poetry award Fund for Poetry, N.Y.C., 1987, 89, 98; Creative Writing fellow Nat. Endowment for the Arts, Washington, 1980, 2001. Mem. PEN, Poetry Soc. Am., Poets House, Phi Beta Kappa. Office: Pace Univ Dept English 1 Pace Plz Dept English New York NY 10038-1598

NORTH, DORIS GRIFFIN, retired physician, educator; b. Washington, Nov. 30, 1916; d. Edward Lawrence and Ruth Gladys (Spray) Griffin; m. Victor North, Nov. 2, 1940 (dec. 1984); children: James, Daniel, Frederick. BA, U. Kans., 1938, MT, 1939; MD, Kans. U., 1947. Med. tech. Ralph G. Ball, M.D., Manhattan, Kans., 1939-40, St. Francis Hosp., Pitts., 1940-41, John Minor, M.D., Washington, 1941-43; intern Wesly Hosp., Wichita, Kans., 1947-48; resident in pediat. and internal medicine Sedgwick Hosp., 1948-49; pvt. practice family physician Kans., 1951-96; ret., 1996. Clin. asst. prof. medicine Kans. U. Sch. Medicine, Wichita, 1974-96. Mem. AMA, Am. Acad. Family Practice, Kans. Med. Soc., Med. Soc. Sedgwick County, Phi Beta Kappa, Alpha Omega Alpha. Home: 1000 S Woodlawn St Apt 408 Wichita KS 67218-3641

NORTH, DOUGLAS MCKAY, academic administrator; b. Albany, N.Y., Oct. 14, 1940; s. Henry Saxe and Elsie (Sewell) N.; m. Ellen Cole, Dec. 10, 1975; children: Jeffrey, Lisa, Anton, Gabriel. BA, Yale U., 1962; MA, Syracuse U., 1964; PhD, U. Va., 1970. Asst. prof. SUNY, New Paltz, 1964-67, Wesleyan U., Middletown, Conn., 1970-71; prof. Goddard Coll., Plainfield, Vt., 1973-81, dir. devel., 1982-89; pres. Prescott (Ariz.) Coll., 1989—94; prof., pres. Alaska Pacific U., 1995—. Contbr. articles to profl. jours. Dept. Edn. grantee, Washington, 1988-91. Mem. Nat. Consortium Single Parent Educators (bd. dirs. 1988—). Office: Office of Pres 4101 University Dr Anchorage AK 99508 E-mail: dnorth@alaskpacific.edu.*

NORTH, DOUGLASS CECIL, economist, educator; b. Cambridge, Mass., Nov. 5, 1920; s. Henry Emerson and Edith (Saitta) North; m. Elisabeth Willard Case, Sept. 28, 1972; children from previous marriage: Douglass Alan, Christopher, Malcolm Peter. BA, U. Calif., Berkeley, 1942, PhD, 1952; D in Natural Scis. (hon.) , U. of Cologne, Federal Republic of Germany, 1988, U. Zurich, Switzerland, 1993, Stockholm Sch. of Econs., Sweden, 1994, Prague Sch. Econs., 1995. Asst. prof. econs. U. Wash., 1950—56, assoc. prof., 1957—60, prof., 1960—83, prof. emeritus, 1983—, chmn. dept., 1967—79; dir. Inst. Econ. Research, 1960—66, Nat. Bur. Econ. Research, 1967—87; Spencer T. Olin prof. in arts and scis. Washington U., St. Louis, 1983—. Pitt prof. Am. history and instns. Cambridge U., 1981—82; fellow Ctr. for Advanced Study on Behavioral Scis., 1987—88. Author: The Economic Growth of the U.S. 1790-1860, 1961, Growth and Welfare in the American Past, 1966; author: (with L. Davis) Institutional Change and American Economic Growth, 1971; author: (with R. Miller) The Economics of Public Issues, 1971, 1974, 1976, 1978, 1980; author: (with R. Thomas) The Rise of the Western World, 1973; author: Structure and Change in Economic History, 1981, Institutions, Institutional Change and Economic Performance, 1990. Recipient Nobel Prize in Econ. Sci., Nobel Found., 1993; fellow, Guggenheim, 1972—73; grantee, Social Sci. Rsch. Coun., 1962, Rockefeller Found., 1960—63, Ford Found., 1961, 1966, NSF, 1967—73, Bradley Found., 1986—. Fellow: Am. Acad. Arts and Scis.; mem.: Econ. History Assn., The Brit. Acad. (corr.), Am. Econ. Assn. Office: PO Box 1208 Saint Louis MO 63188-1208

NORTH, E(DWARD) LEE, author, former aerospace company professional; b. Englewood, N.J., June 2, 1924; s. Edward Louis North and Genevieve Jean (Smith) North Francais; m. Florence Kirkland Hennen, Aug. 29, 1945; children: Patrick Lee, Diane North Goncalves. BA, Washington & Jefferson Coll., 1946. Sports editor Washington (Pa.) Reporter, 1947-49; publicity dir. Washington and Jefferson Coll., 1949-51; writer, editor Grumman Aerospace Corp., Bethpage, N.Y., 1951-78, proposal mgr., 1978-89. Hon. consul Free Polish Govt., London, 1980-95. Author: For this One Hour, 1970, Redcoats, Redskins, and Red-Eyed Monsters: A human-interest history of West Virginia, 1979, Battling the Indians, Panthers and Nittany Lions, 1991, Chris the Rhode Island Wonder Dog, 1993, The 55 West Virginias, 1998, Mark of the White Wolf, 2000, Snowflakes on the Don, 2001. Chmn. Good Govt. Party, Suffolk County, NY, 1956—57; bd. of policy Liberty Lobby, Washington, 1975—2001; chmn. Islip Town (NY) Conservative Party, 1970s; hist. Brightwaters Village, 1990—. Recipient Gold Cross of Merit Free Poland Govt., 1985. Mem.: Phi Kappa Psi, The Authors Guild, Football Writers of Am., Am. Edn. Assn. (bd. dirs. 1992—). Episcopalian. Avocations: tennis, golf, bridge, scrabble, study of wolves. Home: 55 Woodland Dr Brightwaters NY 11718 E-mail: north444@aol.com.

NORTH, GERALD DAVID WILLIAM, lawyer; b. N.Y.C., Feb. 15, 1951; s. David North and Isabella (Leonard) Cadgene; m. Jeanne Curtis, Nov. 1970 (div. 1977); m. Carmela Benvenuto, Feb. 21, 1980; 1 child, David II. BA (hon.) with distinction, U. Iowa, 1972, JD with high distinction, 1975; postgrad., Oxford (Eng.) U., 1975-76. Bar: Iowa 1975, Ill. 1977, U.S. Dist. Ct. (no. dist.) Ill. 1977, U.S. Supreme Ct. 1982, U.S. Dist. Ct. (no. dist. trial bar) Ill. 1983, U.S. Ct. Appeals (fed. cir.) 1984, Ariz. 1985, U.S. Dist. Ct. Ariz. 1985, U.S. Ct. Appeals (9th cir.) 1985. Assoc. Sidley & Austin, Chgo., 1976-81; ptnr. Brace & North, 1981-82; v.p., gen. counsel Trans-Global Group, 1983-84; of counsel McCabe, Polese, Pietzsch, Phoenix, 1984-87; founder, shareholder North & Barron, 1987-92; sr. shareholder North & Vaira, Phila., Phoenix, 1992-93; prin. counsel IMPRA, Inc., Phoenix, 1984-93; chmn. bd. Fibrin Techs., Inc., Wilmington, Del., 1993-97; prin. counsel MinTec, Inc., Freeport, Bahamas, 1995-96; bd. dirs. Fenders Auto Leasing Inc., Vancouver, Can., 1996-97; asst. sec. Summit Spirits, Ltd., Grand Cayman, Cayman Islands, 1998—. Contbg. author: European Investment in U.S. and Canadian Real Estate, 1990, Directory of Asian High Tech Companies in the U.S., 1991. Fellow Ariz. Bar Found.; past mem. ABA (antitrust sec. 1975-93) Am. Intellectual Property Law Assn., Assn. Trial Lawyers Am., Fed. Cir. Bar Assn., Univ. Club (Chgo.), United Oxford and Cambridge Club (London), Legal Club (Chgo.); mem. National Club (Moscow), Order of Coif, Monte Carlo Country Club, Phi Beta Kappa, Omicron Delta Kappa. Avocations: skiing, sailing, tennis. Home: 3977 E Paradise View Dr Paradise Valley AZ 85253-3808

NORTH, HELEN FLORENCE, classicist, educator; b. Utica, N.Y. d. James H. and Catherine (Debbold) N. AB, Cornell U., 1942, MA, 1943, PhD, 1945; LLD (hon.), Rosary Coll., 1982; DLitt (hon.), Trinity Coll., Dublin, 1984, Fordham U., 1999; LHD (hon.), La Salle U., 1985, Yale U., 1986. Instr. classical lang. Rosary Coll., River Forest, Ill., 1946-48; mem. faculty Swarthmore Coll., 1948-91, prof. classics, 1961-91, chmn. dept., 1959-91, emerita, 1991—, Centennial prof. classics, 1966-73, 78-91, Kenan prof., 1973-78. Vis. asst. prof. Cornell U., summer 1952—; vis. assoc. prof. Barnard Coll., 1954-55; vis. prof. LaSalle Coll., Phila., 1965, Am. Sch. Classical Studies, Athens, 1975, 87; Blegen disting. vis. rsch. prof. Vassar Coll., 1979. Author: Sophrosyne: Self-Knowledge and Self-Restraint in Greek Literature, 1966, From Myth to Icon: Reflections of Greek Ethical Doctrine in Literature and Art, 1979, (with Mary C. North) The West of Ireland: A Megalithic Primer, 1999; translator: John Milton's Second Defense of the English People, 1966; editor: Interpretations of Plato: A Swarthmore Symposium, 1977; co-editor: Of Eloquence, 1970; editor: Jour. History of Ideas; mem. editorial bd.: Catalogus Translationum et Commentariorum, 1979— . Bd. dirs. Am. Coun. Learned Socs., 1977-85; chmn. bd. trustees LaSalle U., 1991-93; trustee King's Coll., Am. Acad. in Rome; chmn. com. on Classical Sch. Recipient

Harbison prize Danforth Found., 1969; named Distinguished Daughter of Pa., 1989, del. of Am. Philological Assn. to Am. Coun. Learned Socs., 1991-95 ; grantee Am. Coun. Learned Socs., 1943-45, 73, fellow, 1971-72, 87-88; Mary Isabel Sibley fellow Phi Beta Kappa Found., 1945-46, Ford Fund Advancement Edn. fellow, also Fulbright fellow Rome, 1953-54; grantee Danforth Found., 1962, Lindbach Found., 1966; fellow AAUW, 1963-64; NEH sr. fellow, 1967-68; NEH Coll. Tchrs. fellow, 1983-84; Martin classical lectr. Oberlin Coll., 1972; Guggenheim fellow, 1958-59, 75-76; Centennial medal Am. Acad. Rome, 1995. Mem. Am. Philol. Assn. (dir. 1968— , pres. 1976— , Charles J. Goodwin award of merit 1969, Disting. Svc. medal 1996), Classical Assn. Atlantic States, Catholic Commn. Intellectual and Cultural Affairs (chmn. 1968-69), Am. Acad. Arts and Scis., Am. Philos. Soc., Soc. Religion Higher Edn., Phi Beta Kappa (bd. vis. scholars 1975-76, senate 1991—), Phi Kappa Phi. Home: 604 Ogden Ave Swarthmore PA 19081-1131 E-mail: hnorth1@swarthmore.edu.

NORTH, JAMES LITTLE, b. Anniston, Ala., Oct. 10, 1936; s. John Pelham and Winnie (Little) N.; m. Lettie Lane Hurlbert, Sept. 5, 1959; 1 child, James Little, Jr. BS, U. Ala., 1958; JD, U. Va., 1964. Law clk. U.S. Supreme Ct., Washington, 1964-65; from assoc. to ptnr. Bradley, Arant, Rose & White, Birmingham, Ala., 1965-73; ptnr. North, Haskell, Slaughter & Young, 1973-85, James L. North & Assocs., Birmingham, 1985—. Bd. dirs., gen. counsel Adtran, Inc. Lt. U.S. Army, 1959-61. Recipient commendation medal U.S. Army, 1961. Fellow Am. Bar Found. (life), Internat. Soc. Barristers; mem. ABA (ho. dels. 1986-88), Ala. Law Inst. (coun.), Ala. State Bar (pres. 1985-86, award of merit), Eleventh Cir. Hist. Soc. (trustee). Trustee Dem. Nat. Com.; chmn. fin. Clinton-Gore campaign, Ala., 1992, 96; bd. trustees Presbyn. Home for Children, Talladega, Ala.; bd. dirs. Pub. Affairs Rsch. Coun., Birmingham. Home: 4008 Lenox Rd Birmingham AL 35213 Office: 300 21st St N 700 Title Bld Birmingham AL 35203

NORTH, JOHN ADNA, JR. accountant, real estate appraiser; b. Atlanta, Oct. 20, 1944; s. John Adna and Julia Osborn (Napier) N.; m. Alexa Ruth Bryans, Mar. 20, 1976; 1 child, William Bryans. BA in Econs., U. Ga., 1966; M of Profl. Accountancy, Ga. State U., 1977, M of Taxation, 1980; JD, Woodrow Wilson Coll. Law, Atlanta, 1980. CPA, Ga.; cert. real estate appraiser. Trust adminstr. Trust Co. Bank, Atlanta, 1968-71; fin. produce sales exec. Dean Witter Reynolds Inc., 1971-73; with acctg. firm and in pvt. practice, 1973-80; multi-state tax, staff, gen. tax counsel Texaco Inc., White Plains, N.Y., 1980-87; mgr. multi-state tax Price Waterhouse, Atlanta, 1987-88; dir. various corps. MacMillan Bloedel (USA) Inc., Wilmington, Del., 1988-91; pres. Cobb Svc. Assocs. Inc., Marietta, Ga., 1991—. Chmn. supervisory com. Texaco Fed. Credit Union, Atlanta, 1980-88; bd. dirs., treas. Atlanta Credit Union League, 1986-87; v.p. The Planning Forum, Atlanta, 1984-85. Alumni trustee The Lovett Sch., Atlanta, 1985-89. Capt. U.S. Army, 1966-68. Mem. Nat. Soc. Scabbard and Blade, Mil. Order of Stars and Bars, Beta Alpha Psi. Anglican. Avocations: personal computers, building custom fly fishing rods, genealogy.

NORTH, KATHRYN E. KEESEY (MRS. EUGENE C. NORTH), retired educator; b. Columbia, Pa., Jan. 25, 1916; d. Isaac and Elizabeth (French) Keesey; B.S., Ithaca Coll., 1938; M.A., N.Y. U., 1950; m. Eugene C. North, Aug. 18, 1938. Dir. music Cairo (N.Y.) Central Sch. Dist., 1938; music edn. cons. Argyle (N.Y.) Central Sch. Dist., 1939; dir. gen. music curriculum Hartford (N.Y.) Central Sch. Dist., 1939; mem. staff Del. Dept. Pub. Instrn., Dover, 1943; dir. music edn. Herricks (N.Y.) Pub. Schs., 1944-71; ret., 1971. Vis. lectr. Ithaca Coll., summers 1959, 60, 62-65, Fairleigh-Dickinson U., Rutherford, N.J., summer 1966, Albertus Magnus Coll., New Haven, summer 1968; instr. Adelphi Coll., 1954-55, Sch. Edn., N.Y.U., 1964-65. Mem. Music Educators Nat. Conf., N.E.A., N.Y. State Sch. Music Assn., N.Y. State Tchrs. Assn., Nassau Music Educators Assn. (exec. bd. 1947-58), N.Y. State Council Adminstrs. Music Edn. (chpt. v.p. 1967-68), Herricks Tchrs. Assn. (pres. 1948), Sigma Alpha Iota. Mem. Order Eastern Star. Home: 1645 Calle Camille La Jolla CA 92037-7107

NORTH, MARJORIE MARY, columnist; b. Mt. Clemens, Mich., Oct. 21, 1945; d. Robert Haller and Hilla Beryl (Willard) Wright; m. William B. Hirons; children: Laura, Christina, Angela. Student, Wayne State U., 1963-65. Features editor Elizabeth City (N.C.) Daily Advance, 1966-69; news/mng. editor Brandon (Fla.) News, 1977-78; city editor Leesburg (Fla.) Daily Comml., 1978-79; metro editor Sarasota (Fla.) Herald Tribune, 1979-80, Fla. West editor, 1980-85, daily columnist, 1985—. Host Weekly Interview Show, SNN-TV, 1997—. Author: Sarasota: A City For All Seasons, 1994, (plays) With the Best Intentions, 1994, Back in the Game, 1998. Recipient Layout, Creativity and Overall Publ. awards Fla. Press Assn., numerous comty. awards and citations; winner Fla. shorts competition Fla. Studio Theater New Play Festival, 1994, 98; Paul Harris fellow, 1994. Avocations: tennis, entertaining, theater. Office: Sarasota Herald-Tribune PO Box 1719 Sarasota FL 34230-1719 E-mail: m.north@juno.com.

NORTH, PERCY, art historian, educator; b. Balt., June 22, 1945; d. William Randolph and Leona Elizabeth (Kappler) N. BA in English, Radford Coll., 1966; MA in Art History, Pa. State U., 1968; PhD in Art History, U. Del., 1974. Asst. prof. Mary Washington Coll., Fred, Va., 1972-74; vis. asst. prof. U. Minn., Mpls., 1975; asst. prof. George Mason U., Fairfax, Va., 1976-84; lectr., adj. prof. Art History Georgetown U., Washington, 1984—; prof. Art History, coord. Art History Montgomery Coll., Rockville, Md., 1989—. Guest curator U. Minn. gallery Mpls., 1977, The Jewish Mus., N.Y.C., 1981-82, The High Mus., Atlanta, 1989-91; vis. asst. prof. Art History James Madison U., Harrisonburg, Va., 1985-86, Emory U., Atlanta, 1986-88, Vanderbilt U., Nashville, 1988-89; Fulbright prof. U. Lyon (France), 1978-79. Author: Max Weber: The Cubist Decade (1910-1920), 1991, Bernhard Gutmann: American Impressionist, 1995; numerous monographs, catalogues with essays; lectr. in field; contbr. articles to profl. jours. Smithsonian fellow, 1970-71, Royal Oak fellow, Eng., 1981. Mem.: Artable, Am. Studies Assn., Coll. Art Assn., Washington Biography Group. Home: 1916 Greenspring Valley Rd Stevenson MD 21153-0649

NORTH, ROBERT CARVER, political science educator; b. Walton, N.Y., Nov. 17, 1914; s. Arthur W. and Irene (Davenport) N.; m. Dorothy Anderson, Mar. 12, 1977; children by previous marriage: Woesha Kristina, Mary Davenport, Elizabeth Katrynka, Robert Cloud, Renya Catarina. AB, Union Coll., 1936; MA, Stanford U., 1948, PhD, 1957. Tchr. English, History Milford (Conn.) Sch., 1939-42; research asst. Hoover Instn., Stanford, Calif., 1948-50, research assoc., 1950-57; assoc. prof. polit. sci. Stanford (Calif.) U., 1957-62, prof., 1962-85, prof. emeritus, from 1985. Author: Revolt in San Marcos, 1941 (Commonwealth Gold medal), Moscow and Chinese Communists, 1952, The World That Could Be, 1976, (with Nazli Choucri) Nations in Conflict, 1975, War, Peace, Survival, 1990, (with Nazli Choucri and Susumu Yamakage) The Challenge of Japan: Before World War II and After, 1992. Served to capt. USAAF, 1942-46. Recipient Prix Mondial, U. Geneva, Hautes Etudes Internats., 1998. Mem. Am. Polit. Sci. Assn. (Conflicts Processes Sect. Lifetime Achievement award 1993), Internat. Studies Assn. (Disting. scholar award in fgn. policy analysis, pres. 1970-71), Internat. Peace-Sci. Assn., Explorers Club Democrat. Unitarian Universalist. Home: Woodside, Calif. Died July 15, 2002.

NORTH, STEVEN EDWARD, lawyer, educator; b. Oct. 16, 1941; s. Irving J. and Barbara (Grubman) N.; m. Sue J. Buznitsky, Dec. 24, 1966; children: Jennifer, Samantha. BA, CCNY, 1963; JD, Bklyn. Law Sch., 1966; LLM, NYU, 1967. Bar: N.Y. 1967, U.S. Dist. Ct. (so. and ea. dists.) N.Y. 1970, U.S. Supreme Ct. 1971. Asst. dist. atty. homicide bur. N.Y. County Dist. Attys. Office, N.Y.C., 1967-71; spl. asst. atty. gen., bur. chief N.Y. State Atty. Gen.'s Office, 1972-75; pvt. practice 1975—. Mem. adv. com. Ann. Civil Litigation Inst., Practicing Law Inst., 1996; chmn. Assn. Bar Subcom. on Investigation into Imposition of Legis. Limits on Awards for Non-Econ. Damages, 1995; mediator U.S. Dist. Ct. (so. dist.) N.Y., 1994—, apptd. jud. screening program; mem. adv. coms. solo law practice Practicing Law Inst., 1991, adv. bd. tort litigation, 1989—; vis. faculty Sch. Law, NYU, faculty workshop Cardozo Sch. Law, judge appellate argument, alumni advisor; faculty advisor Trial of Breast Cancer Case, Law Jour. Seminars, 2000; lectr. in field. Author: Prevention and Detection of Fraud in Industry, 1973, Controlling the Deposition: Winning Your Case Before Trial, 1978, Deposition Strategy, Law and Forms, vol. 1 (Introduction and Law), vol. 5 (Medical Malpractice), vol. 8 (Personal Injury), 1981, (course handbooks) Trial Mechanics, Personal Injury Desbook, 1983, Trial Mechanics and Discovery, 1985, 86, Medical Malpractice Litigation, 1988, Managing the Multi-Million Dollar Case, 1990, Objectifying Brain Damage in Closed Head Injury, 1990, Fundamentals of Medical Malpractice Litigation, 1991, Damage Update, 1992, 93, 94, 95, 96, 97—, Proving & Defending Damages, 1993, Conducting & Defending Depositions, 1993; contbr. chpts. to books; editor: Cancer Litigation Bull., 1994—, Fear of Developing Cancer; contbg. editor: Law and Order mag.; med.-legal editor Perinatology, 1983; contbr. articles to legal jours.; commentator Eyewitness News, 1994, Court TV, 1994-98, Talk News TV, 1996. Mem. leadership coun. So. Poverty Law Ctr. Mem. ATLA, NCCJ (lawyers divsn., ann. dinner com.), NOW (benefits com.), U.S. Holocaust Mus. (charter mem.), Am. Bd. Trial Advs., Soc. Med. Jurisprudence, N.Y. State Bar Assn. (faculty), N.Y. State Trial Lawyers Assn. (bd. dirs. 1990—, faculty chmn. Depositions in Action 2000, North's Ninety-Nine Pointers on Advanced Deposition Practices 1999), Lotos Club, Nat. Eagle Scout Assn., State Trial Lawyers Assn. (bd. dirs. 1990—, seminar faculty chmn. 1993, faculty decisions program 1991—, Law Day dinner com.), N.Y. County Lawyers Assn. (exec. com. med. malpractice sect., exec. com. gen. tort law sect.), Assn. Bar of City of N.Y. (civil ct. com. 1980-83, legal and continuing edn. com. 1983—, legal referral svc. com., med. malpractice mediator 1994—, chmn. subcom. on imposition of legis. limits to awards for non-econ. damages), Vol. Lawyers for the Arts, Million Dollar Advs. Forum, Vol. Lawyers for the Arts, N.Y. County Supreme Ct. Com. Med. Malpractice Litigation, N.Y. Soc. Anesthesiologist (speaker), N.Y. State Bar Assn. Home: 148 E 74th St New York NY 10021 Office: 148 E 74th St New York NY 10021-3542

NORTH, TERESA LYNN, student services administrator; b. Huntsville, Ala., Dec. 17, 1956; d. Richard E. and Marian M. (Wood) N. BS in Animal Sci., U. Calif., Davis, 1978, MS in Animal Sci., 1979, PhD in Nutrition, 1984. Cert. livestock mgr., Ill. Grad. tchg. asst. U. Calif. Dept Animal Sci., Davis, 1981-82, assoc. tchg. asst., 1983, Rosenburg Rsch. assoc., 1983-84; asst. prof. Western Ill. U. Dept. Agrl., Macomb, 1984-87, chairperson, 1986, beef herd feedlot mgr., 1987-99, assoc. prof., 1987-99, beef evaluation sta. dir., 1990-98, asst. to v.p. student svcs., 1999—. Advisor Sigma Alpha Sorority, Macomb, Ill., 1991-99. Spring Lake Watershed Agrl. Mgr., Macomb, Ill., 1994-99. Grantee Ill. Coun. Agrl. Rsch., 1996,97. Mem. Nat. Assn. Student Pers. Adminstrs., Am. Coll. Pers. Assn., Ill. Coll. Pers. Assn., Ill. St. Acad. Sci. (publ. editor), Alpha Zeta Agrl. Avocations: travel, camping, reading, landscaping. Home: 1713 W Adams St Macomb IL 61455-1203 Office: W Ill VP Student Svcs 1 University Cir Macomb IL 61455-1367 Fax: 309-298-2558. E-mail: tln1ltj2@macomb.com., teresa_north@ccmail.wiu.edu.

NORTH, TERRY CLAIRE, clinical psychologist; b. Brunswick, Ga., Apr. 8, 1959; d. Henry Carlton Jr. and Jimmie Claire (Copeland) North; m. Scott Alan Yonker, Sept. 21, 1991. BA, Auburn U., 1982; MA, U. S.D., 1986, PhD, 1989. Lic. psychologist, Nebr. Neuropsychologist Immanuel Med. Ctr., Omaha, 1989-90, St. Joseph Ctr. for Mental Health, Omaha, 1990-91; psychologist in pvt. practice Heartland Psychotherapy Assocs., Papillion, Nebr., 1991-95; dir. post-traumatic stress disorder clinic Omaha VA Med. Ctr., 1995—. Clin. asst. prof. adj. faculty dept. psychiatry U. Nebr. Med. Ctr., 2000—; adj. asst. prof. dept. psychology U. SD Vermillion, 1998—; asst. clin. prof. dept. psychiatry Creighton U., 2001—. Mem.: Internat. Soc. for Traumatic Stress Studies. Avocation: dressage. Office: Omaha VA Med Ctr 1401 Woolworth Ave Omaha NE 68105

NORTH, TRICIA A. librarian; b. Hays, Kans., Mar. 22, 1973; d. Daryl A. and Linda K. North. BA in English and History, Ft. Hays State U., 1996; MA in History, Emporia (Kans.) State U., 1998. Summer sch. tchr.'s asst. St. Teresa's Home for Children, Ft. Worth, 1995; grad. tchg. asst. Dept. Social Scis. Emporia State U., 1996—98; mus. coord. Korean War Vets. Nat. Mus. and Libr., Tuscola, Ill., 1998—99; serials libr. asst. Forsyth Libr. Ft. Hays State U., Hays, 1999—2001, libr. asst. II, 2001—. Apprentice Ellis County Hist. Soc., Hays, 1995; intern Nat. Archives and Records Adminstrn., Kansas City, Mo., 1998; guest lectr., commentator Dept. Social Scis. Emporia State U., 1998. Author: (video script) Remembering the Forgotten War: The Korean War in American History, 1998. Mem.: Kans. Libr. Operation Assocs., Kans. Libr. Assn.

NORTH, WARREN JAMES, government official; b. Winchester, Ill., Apr. 28, 1922; s. Clyde James and Lucille Adele (Bishop) N.; m. Mary Strother; children— James Warren, Mary Kay, Susan Lee, Diane. BS in Engring, Purdue U., 1947; MS, Case Inst. Tech., 1954, Princeton, 1956. Engr. and test pilot NACA, Cleve., 1947-55, asst. chief aerodynamics br., 1955-59; chief manned satellites NASA, Washington, 1959-62; chief flight crew support div. NASA (Manned Spacecraft Center), Houston, 1962-71; asst. dir. space shuttle NASA (Flight Ops. Directorate), 1972-85; pres. Spalding Edn. Found., Glendale, Ariz., 1986—. Contbr. articles to profl. jours. Served with USAAF, 1943-45. Recipient DeFlorez tng. award, 1966; NASA award for exceptional service, 1968, 69 Mem. Am. Inst. Aero. and Astronautics (asso. fellow 1955), Tau Beta Pi, Pi Tau Sigma. Clubs: Mason. Home: 6933 W Kimberly Way Glendale AZ 85308-5757 Office: Spalding Edn Found 2814 W Bell Rd Ste 1405 Phoenix AZ 85053-7531

NORTH, WHEELER JAMES, marine ecologist, educator; b. San Francisco, Jan. 2, 1922; s. Wheeler Orrin and Florence Julia (Ross) N.; m. Barbara Alice Best, Apr. 25, 1964; children: Hannah Catherine, Wheeler Orrin. BS in Engring, Calif. Inst. Tech., 1944, BS in Biology, 1949; MS in Oceanography, U. Calif. at San Diego, 1953; PhD, 1953. NSF postdoctoral fellow Cambridge (Eng.) U.; Electronics engr. U.S. Navy Electronics Lab., Point Loma, Calif., 1947-48; asst. research biologist Scripps Inst. Oceanography, U. Calif. at San Diego, 1953, Rockefeller postdoctoral fellow, 1955-56; asst. research biologist Inst. Marine Resources Scripps Inst. Oceanography, 1956-63; assoc. prof. Calif. Inst. Tech., Pasadena, 1963-70, prof., 1970-92, prof. emeritus, 1992—. Cons. marine biology U.S. Govt., State of Calif., San Francisco, Los Angeles, San Diego, numerous industries, 1957— ; Phi Beta Kappa vis. scholar, 1973-74; mem. Calif. Adv. Commn., 1972-73, Nav. and Ocean Devel. Commn., 1973-76; dir. Marine Biol. Cons. Contbr. articles to profl. jours. Recipient NOGI award Underwater Soc. Am., 1975, John Olguin Marine Environ. award, 1999, Lifetime Achievement award Am. Acad. Underwater Sci., 2001. Mem. Am. Littoral Soc. (James Duggan award), AAAS, Am. Soc. Limnology and Oceanography, Am. Soc. Zoology, Soc. Gen. Physiology, Calif. Acad. Sci., Fish Protective Assn. (dir.), N.Y. Acad. Sci., Am. Geophys. Union, Smithsonian Instn., Am. San Diego museums, Marine Tech. Soc., Western Soc. Naturalists, Calif. Soc. Profl. Engrs., Am. Zoomalac Soc., Internat. Oceanographic Found., Sigma Xi. Home: 387 W Bay St Apt 17 Costa Mesa CA 92627-2049 Office: Calif Inst Tech Divsn Enging Applied Sci Pasadena CA 91125-0001

NORTH, WILLIAM HAVEN, foreign service officer; b. Summit, N.J., Aug. 17, 1926; s. Eric M. and Gladys (Haven) N.; m. Jeanne Foote, Sept. 2, 1950; children: Jeannette Haven, William Ashby, Charles Eric. BA in History with honors, Wesleyan U., Middletown, Conn., 1949; MA in History, Columbia, 1951. Program officer ICA, Ethiopia, 1953-57; then dep. chief program div. ICA (African-European Regional Office), Washington; asst. dir. for program Lagos, Nigeria, AID, until 1965; dir. Ctrl. and Western African affairs AID, Washington, 1966-70, U.S. AID mission to Ghana, 1970-76; dep. asst. adminstr. Africa Bur. AID, 1976-82, spl. asst. Office of the Adminstr., 1982-83, assoc. asst. adminstr. Ctr. Devel. Info. and Evaluation, 1983-89, ret.; pvt. cons. Internat. Devel. for World Bank, 1989—, UN Devel. Program USAID, 1989—; coord. Evaluation of Global Environ. Facility, 1993, Evaluation Spl. Porgram of Asst. to Africa, 1997-98, Evaluation DAC/OECD Eval. Group, 1998; evaluator UNDP Aid Coordination, 1998—. Evaluator UNDB Global Program for HIV/AIDS, 2000, African Governance Capacity Bldg, UNDP; fellow Ctr. for Internat. Affairs, Harvard U., 1965-66; chmn. experts group on evaluation Devel. Assistance Commn., OECD, 1985-88; vice-chmn. editl. bd. Fgn. Svc. Jour., 1983-86; mem. adv. panel on evaluation Inter-Am. Devel. Bank, 1993-94; prin. evaluator Internat. Fin. Corp.; program dir. U.S. Fgn. Assistance Oral History Program, 1995—; cons. UN Devel. Coop. Political Branch, 2000-02. Served with AUS, 1944-46. Recipient Meritorious Svc. award for exemplary achievement in pub. adminstrn., W.A. Jump Honor cert., Superior Honor award for Nigerian Relief Adminstrn., Equal Employment Opportunity award, Disting. Honor award AID, Presdl. Meritorious Svc. medal, Adminstrs. Career Svc. award. Mem. Soc. for Internat. Devel., African Studies Assn., Assn. Diplomatic Studies and Tng., Am. Evaluation Assn., Applachian Mountain Club. Methodist. Home and Office: Internat Development 6748 Brigadoon Dr Bethesda MD 20817-5436

NORTHCUTT, CLARENCE DEWEY, lawyer; b. Guin, Ala., July 7, 1916; s. Walter G. and Nancy E. (Homer) Northcutt; m. Ruth Eleanor Storms, May 25, 1941. AB, U. Okla., 1939, LL.B., 1938. Bar: Okla. 1938. Pvt. practice, Ponca City, 1938—. Mem. bd. visitors U. Okla. Served with AUS, 1941-46. Decorated Bronze Star, Air medal with oak leaf cluster., Order St. John of Jerusalem; named Outstanding Citizen of Ponca City, 1982; inducted to Okla. Hall of Fame, 2001. Fellow Am. Coll. Trial Lawyers, Am. Coll. Trust and Estate Attys., Am. Bar Found.; mem. Acad. Univ. Fellows, Internat. Soc. Barristers, Am. Bd. Advocacy, Internat. Acad. Trial Lawyers, Okla. Bar Assn. (pres. 1975, bd. govs.), Ponca City C. of C. (past pres.). Clubs: Mason, Kiwanian. Democrat. Baptist. Home: 132 Whitworth Ave Ponca City OK 74601-3438 Office: PO Box 1669 Ponca City OK 74602-1669 E-mail: cdnorth@northcuttlawfirm.com.

NORTHCUTT, KATHRYN ANN, elementary school and gifted-talented educator, reading recovery educator; b. Ft. Worth, Nov. 11, 1953; d. Lawrence William and Eva Jo (McCormick) Lloyd; m. Frank E. Northcutt, Aug. 28, 1980; 1 child, Matthew Adam. Student, North Tex. State U., 1972-75; BS in Edn., U. Tex., Tyler, 1980, MEd, 1986. Cert. elem. educator, music educator, supr. K-8; cert. curriculum and instrn. supr. Tchr. grade 1 Longview (Tex.) Ind. Sch. Dist., Longview, 1980-87, tchr. gifted and talented reading, 1990-92, tchr. 3d grade, 1992-93, tchr. 4th grade, 1993-95, reading recovery tchr., 1995—; tchr. 1st grade Pine Tree Ind. Sch. Dist., 1987-90. Mem. Gregg County Hist. Soc., Longview Opera Guild (pres.). Mem. ASCD, Nat. Coun. Tchrs. Math., Assn. Tex. Profl. Educators, Reading Recovery Coun. N.Am., Jr. League of Longview (sustaining), Phi Beta Kappa, Sigma Alpha Iota. Home: 1206 Rosewood Ct Longview TX 75604-2872 Office: Longview Ind Sch Dist PO Box 3268 Longview TX 75606-3268

NORTHCUTT, MARIE ROSE, educator; b. White Plains, N.Y., Feb. 2, 1950; d. Carlo and Marcelline Marie Rose (Benoit) DeMarco; m. Kenneth Walter Northcutt, Mar. 17, 1984; children: James Lee, Thomas Joseph. BA, Lynchburg Coll., 1972; MA, Columbia U., 1977. Cert. elem. and secondary tchr., N.Y. Tchr. Petersburg (Va.) Pub. Schs., 1972-74; asst. relocation mgr. Ticor Co., White Plains, 1974-75; 3d grade tchr. Resurrection Sch., Rye, N.Y., 1975-76; 6th grade tchr. Harrison (N.Y.) Cen. Sch. Dist., 1976-78, learning disabilities specialist, 1981—; tchr. of emotionally handicapped N.Y.C. Schs., 1978-80; learning evaluator Empire State Coll., White Plains, 1981-82. Ind. evaluation cons., White Plains, 1981—; chair Mid. States Sub-com. Active Harrison H.S. PTA. Mem. Assn. for Children with Learning Disabilities, Westchester County Assn. for Children with Learning Disabilities, Spl. Edn. Parents Tchrs. Assn., Orton Soc., Phi Delta Kappa. Roman Catholic. Avocations: reading, cooking. Home: 81 Griffin Pl White Plains NY 10603-3609 Office: Harrison Cen Sch Dist Union Ave Harrison NY 10528-2108

NORTHCUTT, WAYNE, history educator; b. New Orleans, July 5, 1944; s. Bernard Duke and Clara Lenore Northcutt. BA in History, Calif. State U., Long Beach, 1966, MA in History, 1968; PhD in European History, U. Calif., Irvine, 1974; postgrad., Ecole Partique des Hautes, Etudes, Paris, 1978. Asst. prof. of history and head western European area study Monterey (Calif.) Inst. of Internat. Studies, 1975-78; lectr. in history and internat. rels. Schiller Coll., Paris, 1978; tchg. assoc. U. Calif., Irvine, 1979-80; fgn. expert Chinese People's U., Beijing, 1983; coord. internat. studies program Niagara (N.Y.) Univ., 1985—, prof. of history, 1980—. Author: The Regions of France, 1996, Mitterand: A Political Biography, 1992, Historical Dictionary of the French Fourth and Fifth Republic, 1946-1991, 1992, The French Socialist and Communist Party Under the Fifth Republic, 1958-1981, 1985. Office: Dept History Niagara U Niagara University NY 14109 E-mail: northcutt@niagara.edu.

NORTHEN, HELEN E(STHER), retired social work educator, consultant; b. Butte, Mont. d. John Alfred and Amelia Sigred (Anderson) N. BA, U. Wash., 1939; MSW, U. Pitts., 1944; PhD, Bryn Mawr Coll., 1953. Lic. social worker, Calif. Field instr. YWCAl-U. Pitts., 1945-49; rsch. asst. Bryn Mawr (Pa.) Coll., 1949-51; assoc. prof. U. Hawaii, Honolulu, 1951-53, U. So. Calif., L.A., 1953-59, prof. social work, 1959-86, prof. emerita, 1986—, disting. prof. emerita, 1999—. Cons. to numerous local and nat. social welfare orgns. Author: Clinical Social Work, 1982, 2d edit., 1995, Social Work With Groups, 1969, 2d edit., 1988, 3d edit., 2001; co-author: Child, Family, Neighborhood, 1982, Families and Health Care, 1990; co-editor: Theories of Social Work With Groups, 1976; mem. editorial bds. several profl. jours., 1985-88; cons. editor Jour. Social Work Edn., 1989—; contbr. articles to profl. jours. Mem. nat. bd. Camp Fire Girls, Inc., N.Y.C., 1961-70; bd. dirs. Portals House, L.A., 1968-76. Mem. Nat. Acads. Practice (Disting. Practitioner award 1983), NASW (Nat. Coun. on Clin. Social Work 1987—, award for Outstanding Achievement in Health/Mental Health Policy 1998), Assn. for Advancement Social Work with Groups (exec. com. 1985-88, cert. honor 1979), Coun. on Social Work Edn., Am. Friends of London Sch. Econs., AAUP, AAUW, LWV, Phi Kappa Phi. Democrat. Avocations: travel, contemporary literature, beach combing. Home: 1942 Westlake Ave Apt 2316 Seattle WA 98101 E-mail: hnorthen@earthlink.net.

NORTHRIP, ROBERT EARL, lawyer; b. Sleeper, Mo., May 8, 1939; s. Novel and Jessie (Burch) N.; m. Linda Kay Francis, June 15, 1968; children: Robert E. Jr., William F., Darryl F., David F. BA, Southwest Mo. State, 1960; MA, U. N.C., 1965; JD, U. Mo., 1968. Bar: Mo. 1968, U.S. Dist. Ct. (we. dist.) Mo. 1968, U.S. Ct. Appeals (10th cir.) 1976, U.S. Ct. Appeals (8th cir.) 1980, U.S. Ct. Appeals (9th cir.) 1983, U.S. Ct. Appeals (3d cir.) 1987, U.S. Supreme Ct. 1978. Ptnr. Shook, Hardy & Bacon, Kansas City, Mo., 1968—. Active Nelson Art Gallery, Soc. of Fellows, Kans. City, Mo. 1st lt. US Army, 1963-65. Mem. ABA, Mo. Bar Assn., Lawyers Assn. Kansas City, Mo. Orgn. Def. Lawyers, Kansas City Met. Bar Assn., U. Mo. Alumni Assn. (past pres. Kansas City chpt.), Nat. Soc. Arts and Letters. Republican. Avocations: baseball, football. Office: Shook Hardy & Bacon 25 Cannon St London EC4M 5SE England E-mail: rnorthrip@shb.com.

NORTHROP, EDWARD SKOTTOWE, federal judge; b. Chevy Chase, Md., June 12, 1911; s. Claudian Bellinger and Eleanor Smythe (Grimke) N.; m. Barbara Middleton Burdette, Apr. 22, 1939; children: Edward M., St. Julien (Mrs. Kevin Butler), Peter. LLB, George Washington U., 1937. Bar: Md. 1937, D.C. 1937. Village mgr., Chevy Chase, Md., 1934-41; pvt. practice, Rockville, Washington, 1937-61; mem. Md. Senate, 1954-61, chmn. fin. com., joint com. taxation fiscal affairs, majority leader, 1959-61; judge U.S. Dist. Ct. Md., Balt., 1961-70; chief judge U.S. Dist. Ct. of Md., 1970-81, sr. judge, 1981—. Mem. Met. Chief Judges Conf., 1970-81; mem. Jud. Conf. Com. on Adminstrn. of Probation System, 1973-79, Adv. Corrections Council U.S., 1976— , Jud. Panel on Multidist. Litigation, 1979— ; judge U.S. Fgn. Intelligence Surveillance Ct. of Rev., 1985— Trustee Woodberry Forest Sch.; founder Washington Met. Area Coun. Govts. & Mass Transp. Agy. Served to comdr. USNR, 1941-45. Decorated Army commendation medal, Navy commendation medal; recipient Profl. Achievement award George Washington U., 1975, Disting. Citizen award State of Md., 1981, Spl. Merit citation Am. Judicature Soc., 1982. Mem. ABA, Md. Bar Assn. (Disting. Svc. award 1982), D.C. Bar Assn., Montgomery County Bar Assn., Barristers, Washington Ctr. Met. Studies. Clubs: Chevy Chase (Md.). Lodges: Rotary. Democrat. Episcopalian. Office: US Dist Ct 101 W Lombard St Ste 8A Baltimore MD 21201-2903

NORTHROP, MARY RUTH, retired nurse; b. Washington, June 5, 1919; d. William Arthur and Emma Aurelia (Kaech) N. Diploma in nursing, Georgetown U., 1951, BS in Nursing cum laude, 1952; MS, U. Md., 1958; MA in Anthropology, U. Va., 1970. RN, Va. Asst. dir. nursing U. Md. Hosp., Balt., 1958-60; dir. nursing Georgetown U. Hosp., Washington, 1961; nursing rep. ARC, Pa., 1962, regional dir. nursing, 1963-68; pediatric nursing cons. Va. Dept. Health, Richmond, 1971-84; clin. nursing specialist Va. Dept. Mental Health and Mental Retardation, Petersburg, Va., 1988-99. Adj. asst./assoc. prof. U. Md. Sch. Nursing, Balt., 1958-60. Author: Matthew Ryan and Mary Schmitz of North Star Township, Brown County, Minnesota, 1998; editor Lively Experiment, 2001—. Nursing fellow rsch. HEW, U. Md., Bethesda, 1957-68, nursing fellow anthropology U. Va., 1968-70; recipient Recognition Georgetown U. Alumni Assn., Richmond, 1987. Mem. ANA, Va. Nursing Assn., DAR (chpt. regent 1983-86, dist. treas. 1992-95), Nat. Soc. Women

Descendants Ancient and Hon. Arty. Co. (treas. Va. chpt. 1995—), Daus. of Founders and Patriots of Am. (registrar Va. 1997—), Order of First Families of R.I. and Providence Plantation (charter), Sons and Daus. of Colonial and Antebellum Bench and Bar (charter), Soc. First Families of Minn., Mensa, Sigma Theta Tau. Republican. Roman Catholic. Avocations: genealogy, reading, travel. Home: 300 W Franklin St Apt 401E Richmond VA 23220-4967

NORTHRUP, HERBERT ROOF, economist, business executive; b. Irvington, N.J., Mar. 6, 1918; m. Eleanor Pearson, June 3, 1944; children: James Pearson, Nancy Warren, Jonathan Peter, David Oliver, Philip Wilson. AB, Duke U., 1939; A.M., Harvard U., 1941, PhD, 1942. Instr. econs. Cornell U., 1942-43; sr. hearing officer Nat. War Labor Bd., 1943-45; asst. prof. econs. Columbia U., 1945-49; labor economist Nat. Indsl. Conf. Bd., 1949-52; indsl. relations cons. Ebasco Services, 1952-55; v.p. indsl. relations Penn-Texas Corp., N.Y.C., 1955-58; employee relations mgr. Gen. Electric Co., 1958-61; prof. industry Wharton Sch., U. Pa., Phila., 1961-88; prof. emeritus Wharton Sch. U. Pa., 1988—; chmn. dept. industry Wharton Sch., U. Pa., 1964-69, dir. indsl. research unit, 1964-88, chmn. Labor Relations Council, 1968-85. Cons. and expert witness on manpower, pers. and labor rels. problems for many cos.; arbitrator in labor rels. disputes. Author: Organized Labor and the Negro, 1944, Unionization of Professional Engineers and Chemists, 1946, Economics of Labor Relations, 1950, 9th edit., 1981, Government and Labor, 1963, Readings in Labor Economics, 1963, Boulwarism: Labor Policies of General Electric Company, 1964, Negro and Employment Opportunity, 1965, Hours of Labor, 1965, Compulsory Arbitration and Government Intervention in Labor Disputes, 1966, Restrictive Labor Practices in Supermarket Industry, 1967, Negro in the Automobile Industry, 1968, Negro in the Aerospace Industry, 1968, Negro in the Rubber Tire Industry, 1969, Negro in Paper Industry, 1969, Negro in the Tobacco Industry, 1970, Negro Employment in Basic Industry, 1970, Negro Employment in Southern Industry, 1970, Negro Employment in Land and Air Transport, 1971, Impact of Government Manpower Programs, 1975, Open Shop Construction, 1975, The Impact of OSHA, 1978, Objective Selection of Supervisors, 1978, Black and Other Minority Participation in the All-Volunteer Navy and Marine Corps, 1979, Manpower in the Retail Pharmacy Industry, 1979, The Impact of the ATT-EEO Consent Decree, 1979, Multinational Collective Bargaining Attempts, 1979, Multinational Union Organizations in the Manufacturing Industries, 1980, Employee Relations and Regulations in the 80s, 1982, Internat. Transport Workers' Federation and Flag of Convenience Shipping, 1983, Open Shop Construction Revisited, 1984, Personnel Policies for Engineers and Scientists, 1985, Doublebreasted Operations and Pre-Hire Agreements in Construction: The Facts and the Law, 1987, The Federal Government as Employer: The Federal Labor Relations Authority and the PATCO Challenge, 1988, The Changing Role of Women in Research and Development, 1988, Government Protection of Employees in Mergers and Acquisitions, 1989, The Railway Labor Act, 1990, Union Corporate Campaigns and Inside Games as a Strike Form, 1994, Union violence: The Record and the Response by Courts, Legislatures, and the NLRB, rev. edit., 1999, Construction Union Tactics to Regain Jobs and Public Policy, 2002, The Impact of Union-Management Relations on Urban Industrial Employment, 2000, The Great Paper Strike and Its Aftermath: International Paper vs. the United Paperworkers, 2002, also over 300 articles in field. Mem. Am. Econ. Assn., Indsl. Relations Research Assn., Am. Arbitration Assn., Phi Beta Kappa. Clubs: Harvard (N.Y.C.); Harvard-Radcliffe (Phila.); University (Washington), Faculty (U. Pa.). Home and Office: 205 Avon Rd Haverford PA 19041-1612

NORTHUP, ANNE MEAGHER, congresswoman; b. Louisville, Jan. 22, 1948; d. James L. and Floy Gates (Terstegge) Meagher; m. Robert Wood Northup, Apr. 12, 1969; children: David, Katherine, Joshua, Kevin, Erin, Mark. BA in Econs. and Bus., St. Mary's Coll. Notre Dame, South Bend, Ind., 1970. Mem. Ky. Ho. of Reps., Frankfort, 1987-96, U.S. Congress from 3d Ky. Dist., 1997—; mem. house appropriations com.; founder House Reading Caucus, 1998; mem. speaker's drug free task force, 1998; chair speaker's task force on education, 1998; mem. World Trade Org. congl. advisory group, 1999, free trade working group, 2000, comm. on educational accountability, 1993—95, economic development task force, 1991—92, task force to study highway needs, 1990—91, state debt capacity task force. Mem. fin. adv. bd. EPA, 1989-93; mem. home econs. adv. bd. U. Ky. Coll. Agr., 1992— Appeared on Meet the Press, Fox News Sunday, Larry King Live, CNN & Co., Hardball with Chris Matthews. Mem. exec. com. Partnership Ky. Sch. Reform, 1990—; bd. dirs. Greater Louisville Pub. Radio, 1993—, Hospice Louisville, 1994—, Ky. Cancer Consortium, 1992—; mem. cmty. adv. bd. Jr. League Louisville, 1993—; active Holy Spirit Cath. Ch. Named Outstanding Woman of Achievement St. Matthews BPW, 1990; recipient Cath. Schs. Disting. Alumni award, 1991, U. Notre Dame award of the yr. Ky. Alumni Assn., 1991, Clearing the Air award Am. Lung Assn. of Ky., 1991, Svc. Above Self award St. Matthews Rotary Club, 1992, Pub. Svc. award Am. Heart Assn., 1992, Sacred Heart Acad. Alumna award, 1994, Nat. Fedn. of Ind. Bus./Guardian of Small Bus. award, 1996, 97, 98, Legislator of Yr. award Environ. Industry Assn., 1997, Outstanding Freshman Mem. of Congress award Nat. Industries for Blind, 1997, Spirit of Enterprise award U.S. C. of C., 1997, Bulldog award Watchdogs of Treasury, 1998, Jefferson award Citizens for Sound Economy, 1998, Outstanding Support award Am. Printing House for Blind, 1998, Legislator of Yr. award Assn. Equipment Distbrs., 1999, Cmty. Healthcare Champion award Nat. Assn. Cmty. Health Ctrs., Inc., 1999, Spirit of Enterprise award C. of C., 1999, Susan B. Anthony Congl. award, 1999, Pub. Policy Adv. of Yr. award Nat. Assn. Women Bus. Owners, 1999, Honor Roll of Legis. Achievement in Econ. Devel. award So. Econ. Devel. Coun., Inc., 1999, Legislator of Yr. award Nat. Beer Whoesalers Assn., 1999. Mem. Nat. Order Women Legislators, Nat. Conf. State Legislators, Nat. Rep. Legis. Conf., Inst. Rep. Women, So. Legis. Conf. (alternate from Ky. to fiscal affairs and govtl. com.), Nat. Fedn. Ind. Bus. Roman Catholic. Home: 3340 Lexington Rd Louisville KY 40206-3050 Office: US Ho Reps 1004 Longworth House Office Bl Washington DC 20515-0001*

NORTHWAY, WANDA I. real estate company executive; b. Columbia, Mo., July 11, 1942; d. Herman W. and Goldie M. (Wood) Proctor; m. Donald H. Northway, June 12, 1965; 1 child, Michelle D. Student U. Mo., 1966. Lic. real estate agt., Mo.; grad. Realtors Inst. Realtor, assoc. Gentry Real Estate Co., Columbia, 1969-80; realtor Griffin Real Estate Co., 1980-81; pres., realtor, ptnr. House of Brokers Realty, Inc., Columbia, 1981— ; pres., organizer Realtor-Assoc. Sales Club, Columbia, 1975; pres. Columbia Bd. Realtors, 1982. Contbr. articles to realty mags. Sunday sch. tchr., girls' aux. leader Baptist Ch.; vol. ARS, local hosp; campaign worker for Columbia legislators; mem. allocation com. United Way; active vol. Am. Cancer Soc. and Heart Assn. Named Realtor Assoc. of Yr., Columbia Bd. Realtors, 1974, Realtor of Yr., 1980. Mem. Mo. Assn. Realtors (state dir. 1974-77, Realtor Assoc. of Yr. award 1977), Realtors Nat. Mktg. Inst. (cert. residential specialist 1978), Nat. Assn. Realtors, (nat. dir. 1977), Epsilon Sigma Alpha (state corr. sec., local pres.). Republican. Baptist. Clubs: Million Dollar (life); Federation of Women's (pres. Mo. 1980). Office: House of Brokers Realty Inc 1515 Chapel Hill Rd Columbia MO 65203-5457

NORTMAN, M. JUDITH HAWORTH, geriatrics nurse; b. Milw., Mar. 11, 1959; d. Daniel T. and Mary (Hormuth) Haworth. BSN, Marquette U., 1981; MS in Gerontology, U. Wis., 1985, MS in Healthcare Adminstrn., 1989. RN, Wis.; cert. gerontol. nursing and nursing adminstrn. ANA. Supr. Milw. Cath. Home for Aged, 1981-85; project asst. St. John's Home for Aged, Milw., 1985; rsch. asst. Ctr. Nursing Rsch. and Evaluation U. Wis., 1985-86; nurse gerontologist community outreach nursing program St. Mary's Hosp., 1986-92; pvt. geriatric care mgmt. nurse Whitefish Bay, Wis., 1992; asst. dir. nursing Roseville East Nursing Home, Milw., 1992-94; mgr. Westside Sr. Day Ctr., 1994—. Presenter in field. Contbr. articles to profl. jours. Mem. adv. bd. SDC; adv. com. Guardianship Tng. Program. Mem.: Marquette U. Coll. Nursing Alumni Assn. (past bd. dirs.), Nat. Coun. on Aging, Nat. Gerontol. Nursing Assn. (mem. social devel. commn. aging bd., Innovations to Nursing Practice award 2001), Mid-Am. Congress on Aging, Sigma Theta Tau (treas. Eta Nu chpt., past treas. fin. com. Eta Nu chpt., Rsch. award). Home: 4647 N Sheffield Ave Whitefish Bay WI 53211-1107 Office: Westside Sr Day Ctr 5920 W Center St Milwaukee WI 53210-2258 E-mail: jnortman@mcfi.net.

NORTON, ANDRE ALICE, author; b. Cleve., Feb. 17, 1912; d. Adalbert and Bertha Stemm N. Librarian Cleve. Pub. Libr., until 1951; dir. High Hallack Genre Writers' Rsch. Libr., Murfreesboro, Tenn. Author (140 books including): The Sword is Drawn, 1944 (Dutch Gov. award, 1946); author: Sword in Sheath, 1949 (Ohioana Juvenile award Honor Book, 1950), Starhunter, 1961 (Hugo award nomination World Sci. Fiction Conv., 1962), Witch World, 1963 (Hugo award nomination World Sci. Fiction Conv., 1964), Night of Masks, 1964 (Boy's Club of Am. Cert. of Merit, 1965), (series include) Swords Trilogy, Star Ka'at Sci. Fiction series, Witch World Fantasy series, Solar Queen series, Oak series, Elvenbane series (1st vol. Science Fiction Book Club Choice for Book of Yr., 1991). Bd. dirs. High Hallack Genre Writers Rsch. Libr., 1999. Recipient Invisible Little Man award Westercon XVI, 1963, Phoenix award 1976, Gandalf Master Fantasy award World Sci. Fiction Convention, 1977, Andre Norton award Women Writers of Sci. Fiction, 1978, Balrog Fantasy award 1979, Ohioana award, 1980, Fritz Leiber award, 1983, E.E. Smith award, 1983, Nebula Grand Master award Sci. Fiction Writers of Am., 1984, Jules Verne award, 1984, Second Stage Lensman award, 1987, Favorite Book of Yr. award Sci. Fiction Book Clubs, 1991; named to Ohio Hall of Fame, 1981; named to Sci. Fiction Writers Hall of Fame, 1996. Mem. Sci. Fiction Writers Am.

NORTON, CLIFFORD M., JR. minister; b. Farmington, Maine, July 27, 1957; s. Clifford M. and Evie A. Norton; m. Karen J. Moyer, July 23, 1983; children: Rebecca J., Amanda J., Nathaniel B., Karyssa J., Caleb M. BA, Southeastern Bible Coll., 1986; MMin, Internat. Sem., Plymouth, Fla., 1991; MA, postgrad., Trinity Theol. Sem., 2002—. Ordained min. Bapt. Ch., 1993. Pastor First Bapt. Ch., Winter Harbor, Maine, 1988-94, Bucks Harbor Bapt. Ch., Machiasport, 1999—; adminstr. Transport for Christ, Denver, 1994-96, BCM Internat., Upper Darby, 1995-97; interim pastor Grace Fellowship, Ephrata, 1997-98. Leadership instr. Walk Thru the Bible, Atlanta, 1998—; behavioral cons. Inst. for Motivational Living, New Castle, Pa., 1997—. With USN, 1975-79. Avocations: piano, computer, gardening, wood working. Office: HC 70 Box 510 Machiasport ME 04655-9618

NORTON, DELMAR LYNN, candy company executive; b. Vernal, Utah, Sept. 6, 1944; s. La Mar and Velma (Hullinger) N.; m. Connie Jean Bryan, Mar. 10, 1967; children: Bryan Lynn, Christopher Max, Wendy, Nicholas Delmar. Student, U. Utah, 1962-63, Famous Artists Sch., 1966-69. Nat. sales mgr. Maxfield Candy Co., Salt Lake City, 1965-72; sec.-treas. Ice Cream & Candy Shops, 1972-73; pres., gen. mgr. Ostlers' Candy Co., 1973—; chmn. bd. Nat. Mktg. Co., 1974—; pres., gen. mgr. Rent-A-Flick, Inc., Salt Lake City.; v.p. Redi-Therm Insulation, Inc., 1991-94; nat. sales mgr. Uphill Down U.S.A., 1994—. Mem. Ch. Jesus Christ of Latter-Day Saints (missionary). Home: 4240 S 1650 E Salt Lake City UT 84124-2556 Office: PO Box 71470 Salt Lake City UT 84171-0470

NORTON, DONALD ALAN, retired adult education educator; b. Mt. Kisco, N.Y., Mar. 15, 1920; s. Arthur Alonzo and Anne Bertha Norton; m. Jane Louise Lemke, 1948; children: Anne Louise, Janet Marie. BS, Harvard U., 1941; PhD, U. Wis., 1949. Maj. U.S. Army, 1942—45. Home: 34481 Creeksedge Rd Davis CA 95616

NORTON, DOROTHA OLIVER, speech educator; b. Rutherford, Tenn. d. Lacey A. and Pearl (Cunningham) Oliver; m. Robert Marion Norton, Aug. 17, 1958; children: Robbie Jean Norton Eddings, Robert Marion II. BA, Union U., Jackson, Tenn., 1959; MA, Memphis State U., 1961, Murray (Ky.) State U., 1974. Cert. speech, English and bus. tchr., guidance counselor, Tenn. Tchr. Enlgish, shorthand, guidance counselor Kenton (Tenn.) H.S., 1958-66; instr., asst. prof. English and speech U. Tenn., Martin, 1966-77, assoc. prof. speech, 1977-91, prof. speech, 1991—. Author: Kenton: Folklore and Fact, 1972; contbr. articles to profl. jours. Tchr. Sunday Sch. 1st Bapt. Ch., Kenton, 1984-94, 97—, also narrator Christmas cantata; spkr. Kenton XYZ Sr. Citizens Club, Dyer (Tenn.) Golden Agers Sr. Citizens. Named Woman of Yr., Kenton Jaycees, 1973, Tchr. of Yr., The Pacer, U. Tenn., 1991; nominated for Coffey Outstanding Tchg. award Coll. of Humanities and Fine Arts, U. Tenn., 2001. Mem. NEA, Nat. Comm. Assn., (panelist various dates), Ctrl. State Comm. Assn. (panelist various dates), So. States Comm. Assn. (panelist various dates), Tenn. Comm. Assn. (pres. 1990-91, exec. dir. 2000—, panelist various dates, Educator of Yr. award 1992), Tenn. Edn. Assn., Gen. Fedn. Women's Clubs, Tenn. Fedn. Women's Club (dist. pres. 1978-80), Kenton Women's Club (past pres.), Phi Kappa Phi (pres. 2000-01). Avocations: visiting senior citizens, reading, travel, picnicking. Home: 528 S Poplar St Kenton TN 38233-3624 Office: U Tenn 305 Gooch Hl Martin TN 38238-0001 E-mail: dnorton@utm.edu.

NORTON, DOUGLAS EVATT, mathematician, educator; b. Danville, Ill., Aug. 2, 1957; s. Luther Hooper and Lucy Evatt N.; m. Kathryn Ann Friggle, Sept. 15, 1979; children: Hannah, Jacob. BS, Wake Forest U., 1979; MA, U. Wis., 1984; PhD, U. Minn., 1989. Asst. prof. math. scis. Villanova (Pa.) U., 1989-96, assoc. prof. math. scis., 1996—. Fulbright lectr., rsch. scholar U. Botswana, 1996-97. Contbr. articles to profl. jours. Co-pres. Haverford H.S. Parent-Tchr. Student Assn., Havertown, Pa., 1999-2000. Rotary fellow 1979-80. Mem. AAAS, AAUP, Am. Math. Soc., Math. Assn. Am., Soc. for Indsl. and Applied Math., Assn. for Women in Math., Nat. Coun. Tchrs. Math., Pa. Acad. Sci., Phi Beta Kappa, Omicron Delta Kappa, Phi Kappa Phi, Sigma Xi. Home: 12 Llandaff Rd Havertown PA 19083 Office: Villanova U Dept Math Scis 800 Lancaster Ave Villanova PA 19085 Fax: 610-519-6928. E-mail: douglas.norton@villanova.edu.

NORTON, DOUGLAS RAY, former auditor general; b. Portales, N.Mex., Mar. 23, 1933; s. Clayton G. and Lillian W. (Powers) N.; m. Wanda Jones, May 23, 1951 (div. July 1979); children: Debbie Norton Goodman, Vicki Norton Hulet, Denise Norton Jolley; m. Robertta J. Andersen, July 31, 1998. BS, U. Ariz., 1963. CPA, Ariz. Staff acct., audit supr. Ernst & Ernst, Tucson, 1963-67; ptnr. Baker, Price & Norton, Prescott, 1968-75, Lester Witte & Co., Prescott, 1975-76; auditor gen. State of Ariz., Phoenix, 1976-99; ret., 1999. Former mem. Profl. Adv. Bd. Sch. Acctg. Ariz. State U., Tempe; former mem. acctg. bd. advisors U. Ariz. Pres. Prescott Bd. Edn., 1976. Served with U.S. Army, 1953-55. Mem. AICPA, Ariz. Soc. CPAs, Nat. Assn. State Auditors, Comptrollers and Treasurers (pres. 1993-94), Nat. State Auditors Assn. (pres. 1982-83), Lions (pres. Prescott chpt. 1973-74). Home: PO Box 10130 Glendale AZ 85318-0130

NORTON, DUNBAR SUTTON, economic developer; b. Hoquiam, Wash., Jan. 30, 1926; s. Percy Dunbar and Anna Fedelia (Sutton) N.; m. Kathleen Margaret Mullarky, Dec. 21, 1948 (dec. Apr. 1994); children: Priscilla K., Rebecca C., Jennifer A., Douglas S.; m. Mary Ethel Wolff, May 25, 1996. Student, U. Oreg., 1946-48; diploma, U.S. Army Command & Gen. Staff, 1964. Enlisted U.S. Army, 1944, commd. 2d lt., 1948, advanced through grades to lt. col., ret., 1974; dir. econ. devel. dept. Yuma (Ariz.) County C. of C., 1974-83; exec. v.p. Lakin Enterprises, Yuma, 1983-87; owner Norton Cons., 1987—; dir. Lower Colo. River Rsch. Ctr., Ariz. West Coll./No. Ariz. U., 1998-2000. Corp. mem. Greater Yuma Econ. Devel. Corp., 1984-96, vice chmn., 1993-95. Mem. Yuma County Indsl. Devel. Authority, 1984-90, 92—, pres., 1992—; chmn. fundraising com. Yuma Cross Park Coun., 1984-88, sec., 1988-90, v.p., 1990-92, bd. dirs., 1982-96; bd. dirs. Yuma Leadership, 1984-93, Yuma Youth Leadership, 1993-96; chmn. devel. com. Yuma County Airport Authority, 1985-92, v.p., 1992—; vice chmn. Yuma Main St. Bd., 1988-90, Yuma County Geog. Info. Sys. Task Force, 1991-95, Yuma Kids Voting, 1990-91, bd. dirs. Ariz. Partnership Air Transp., 1990-96, v.p. 1993-95; bd. dirs. Yuma County Civic Trusteeship, 1993-95, Ariz. Western Coll. Found. Bd., 2000-02, chmn. scholar awards commn., 2000-02; chmn. The Southwest Inst., 1995-96, What's Best for Our Kids, 1995-96, Yuma Sch. Dist. No. 1 New Elem. Sch. Planning Com., 1996-97; mem. bd. trustees Yuma county Libr., 1996-02; chmn. Yuma County Complete Count com. U.S. Census, 1990, 95, 2000; co-chmn. maintain the level budget override com., Yuma Sch. Dist. 1, 1999-2001. Decorated Legion of Merit with oak leaf cluster, Bronze Star, Meritorious Svc. and Army Commendation Medal with Oak Leaf Cluster. Mem. Ariz. Assn. for Econ. Devel. (bd. dirs. 1975-82, pres. 1982-83, legis. affairs com. 1987—, Developer of Yr. 1978, William W. Lampkin award 2001), Yuma Execs. Assn. (sec.-treas., exec. dir. 1987—). Republican. Episcopalian. Avocations: golf, swimming, singing. Home and Office: 12267 E Del Norte Yuma AZ 85367-7356 E-mail: yumexec@mindspring.com.

NORTON, EDWARD, actor; b. Boston, Aug. 18, 1969; Motion picture and stage actor. Film appearances include Everone Says I Love You, 1996 (L.A. Film Critics Assn. award 1996), Primal Fear, 1996 (nominee Best Supporting Actor Oscar 1996, Chgo. Film Critics Assn. award 1997, Golden Globe award 1996, Nat. Bd. Rev. award 1996), The People vs. Larry Flynt, 1996, Rounders, 1998, Am. History X, 1998 (nominee Best Actor Oscar 1999, Chgo. Film Critics Assn. award 1999, Golden Satellite award 1999), Fight Club, 1999, The Score, 2001, Death to Smoochy, 2002, Red Dragon, 2002, Frida, 2002, 25th Hour, 2002; dir., prodr. Keeping the Faith, 2000. Office: Endeavor Talent Agy 9701 Wilshire Blvd Fl 10 Beverly Hills CA 90212-2010

NORTON, ELEANOR HOLMES, congresswoman, lawyer, educator; b. Washington, June 13, 1937; d. Coleman and Vela (Lynch) Holmes; m. Edward W. Norton (div.); children: Katherine Felicia, John Holmes. BA, Antioch Coll., 1960; MA in Am. Studies, Yale U., 1963, LLB, 1964. Bar: Pa., 1965, U.S. Supreme Ct., 1968. Law clk. to Judge A. Leon Higgonbotham Fed. Dist. Ct., 1964-65; asst. legal dir. ACLU, 1965-70; exec. asst. to mayor City of N.Y., 1971-74; chmn. N.Y.C. Commn. on Human Rights, 1970-77, EEOC, Washington, 1977-81; sr. fellow Urban Inst., 1981-82; prof. law Georgetown U., 1982—; del. U.S. Congress from D.C. , 1990—; mem. coms. on govt. reform and transp./infrastructure. Office: US Ho of Reps 2136 RayburnHo Office Bldg Washington DC 20515-0001*

NORTON, ELIZABETH WYCHGEL, lawyer; b. Cleve., Mar. 25, 1933; d. James Nicolas and Ruth Elizabeth (Cannell) Wychgel; m. Henry Wacks Norton Jr., July 16, 1954 (div. 1971); children: James, Henry, Peter, Fred; m. James Cory Ferguson, Dec. 14, 1985 (div. Apr. 1988). BA in Math., Wellesley Coll., 1954; JD cum laude, U. Minn., 1974. Bar: Minn. 1974. Summer intern Minn. Atty. Gen.'s Office, St. Paul, 1972; with U.S. Dept. Treasury, 1973; assoc. Gray, Plant, Mooty, Mooty & Bennett, P.A., Mpls., 1974-79, prin., 1980-94, of counsel, 1995-96. Mem. Minn. Lawyers Bd. Profl. Responsibility, 1984-89; mem. U. Minn. Law Sch. Bd. Visitors, 1987-92. Trustee YWCA, Mpls., 1979-84, 89-91, co-chmn. deferred giving com., 1980-81, chmn. by-laws com., bd. dirs., 1976-77, lectr.; treas. Minn. Women's Campaign Fund, 1985, guarantor, 1982-83, budget and fin. com. bd. dirs., 1984-87; trustee Ripley Meml. Found., 1980-84; treas. Jones-Harrison Home, 1967, bd. dirs., 1962-69, 2d v.p., chmn. fin., 1968-69; mem. Sen. David Durenberger's Women's Network, 1983-88. Durant scholar. Fellow Am. Bar Found.; mem. ABA (mediation task force family law sect. 1983-84), Minn. Bar Assn. (human rights com. family law sect., task force uniform marital property act 1984-85), Minn. Bar Found. (dir. 1991-94), Hennepin County Bar Assn. (pres. 1987-88, chmn. task force on pub. edn. 1984, chmn., mem. exec. com. family law sect. 1979-94), Minn. Inst. Legal Edn., Minn. Women's Lawyers (exec. com.), Hemlock Soc. (co-chmn. 1999-2001), U. Minn. Law Sch. Alumni Assn. (dir. 1975-81, exec. com. 1981-83), Wellesley Club, Phi Beta Kappa. Home: 26 Water Oaks Way Naples FL 34105-7157

NORTON, FLOYD LIGON, IV, lawyer; b. Shreveport, La., Oct. 23, 1950; s. Floyd Ligon III and Grace Louise (Julian) N.; m. Kathleen Fair Patterson, Nov. 24, 1979; children: Caroline, Elizabeth. BA with honors, U. Va., 1972, JD, 1975. Bar: Va. 1975, D.C. 1975. Assoc. Reid & Priest, Washington, 1975-83, ptnr., 1983-95, Morgan Lewis & Bockius, 1995—. Mem. ABA, Fed. Energy Bar Assn. Episcopalian. Home: 4107 Bradley Ln Bethesda MD 20815-5236 Office: Morgan Lewis & Bockius 1111 Pennsylvania Ave NW Washington DC 20004-5802 E-mail: fnorton@morganlewis.com.

NORTON, GALE ANN, secretary of the interior; b. Wichita, Mar. 11, 1954; d. Dale Bentsen and Anna Jacqueline (Lansdowne) N.; m. John Goethe Hughes, Mar. 26, 1990. BA, U. Denver, 1975, JD, 1978. Bar: Colo. 1978, U.S. Supreme Ct. 1981. Jud. clk. Colo. Ct. of Appeals, Denver, 1978-79; sr. atty. Mountain States Legal Found., 1979-83; nat. fellow Hoover Instn. Stanford (Calif.) U., 1983-84; asst. to dep. sec. USDA, Washington, 1984-85; assoc. solicitor U.S. Dept. of Interior, 1985-87; pvt. practice law Denver, 1987-90; atty. gen. State of Colo., 1991-99; atty. Brownstein, Hyatt & Farber, P.C., sr. counsel, 1999-2000; sec. U.S. Dept. Interior, Washington, 2001—. Lectr. U. Denver Law Sch., 1989; transp. law program dir. U. Denver, 1978-79. Contbr. chpts. to books, articles to profl. jours. Past chair Nat. Assn. Attys. Gen. Environ. Com.; co-chair Nat. Policy Forum Environ. Coun.; candidate for 1996 election to U.S. Senate; chair environ. commn. Rep. Nat. Lawyers Assn. Named Young Career Woman Bus. and Profl. Wome, 1981, Young Lawyer of Yr., 1991, Mary Lathrop Trailblazer award Colo. Women's Bar Assn., 1999. Mem. Federalist Soc., Colo. Women's Forum, Order of St. Ives. Republican. Methodist. Avocation: skiing. Office: Dept of the Interior Office of the Sec 1849 C St NW Washington DC 20240

NORTON, GERALD PATRICK, lawyer; b. West Roxbury, Mass., Jan. 25, 1940; s. Thomas W. and Genevieve (Sweeny) N.; m. Judith C. Ralphs, Apr. 24, 1965 (dec. Oct. 1969); children: Jeremy, Elizabeth; m. Amanda B. Norton, Sept. 25, 1971; 1 child, Adam. AB magna cum laude, Princeton U., 1961; LLB magna cum laude, Columbia U., 1964. Bar: N.Y. 1964, D.C. 1966. Law clk. to judge U.S. Ct. Appeals (2d cir.), N.Y.C., 1964-65; assoc. Covington & Burling, Washington, 1965-73; asst. to solicitor gen. Dept. Justice, 1973-75; dep. gen. counsel FTC, 1975-79; ptnr. Pepper Hamilton & Scheetz, 1979-92, Harkins Cunningham, Washington, 1992—. Mng. and research editor Columbia U. Law Rev., 1963-64; contbr. articles to profl. jours. Bd. dirs. Washington Lawyer Com. for Civil Rights & Urban Affairs, 1984—; 1st v.p., bd. dirs. Washington Met. Planning and Housing Assn., 1969-70; vol. atty. ACLU, Washington. Recipient Arthur E. Flemming award Jaycees of Nat. Capital Area, 1979; named Grad. of Yr., Province I Phi Delta Phi, 1964. Mem.: Supreme Ct. Moot Ct. Panel, Nat. Assn. Attys. Gen., DC Bar (spl. com. on govt. lawyers and the model rules of profl. conduct 1986—88, legal ethics com. 1989—95, com. on rev. of rules and profl. conduct 1995—2001). Democrat. Office: Harkins Cunningham 801 Penn Ave NW Washington DC 20004-2615 E-mail: gnorton@harkinscunningham.com.

NORTON, GOLDY See GOLDSTEIN, NORTON MAURICE

NORTON, HOLLY LOUISE, English literature educator; b. Redondo Beach, Calif., Apr. 27, 1968; d. Frank Richard and Lorna May (Rodine) N. BA, Luther Coll., Decorah, Iowa, 1990; MA, Iowa State U., 1992; PhD, Bowling Green State U., 1996. Tchr. asst. in English Iowa State U., Ames, 1991-92; sr. lectr. in English Tiffin (Ohio) U., 1996—, Northwestern Coll., Lima, Ohio, 1999—. Contbr. works to The Flannery O'Connor Bull., The Ency. of Multiculturism, The Sixties in America. Mem. AAUW (chair lit. group 1995—, publicity chair 1997—), Flannery O'Connor Soc., Emily Dickinson Internat. Soc. Avocations: reading, playing violin, writing poetry and essays. Home: 1212 Bellefontaine Ave Apt 7 Lima OH 45804-3167 Office: U Northwestern Ohio 1441 N Cable Rd Lima OH 45805-1409 E-mail: hnorton@unoh.edu.

NORTON, JAY LEWIS, lawyer, recording company executive; b. Olathe, Kans., Nov. 26, 1968; s. Joseph Lewis and Jane Marie (Bushfield) N.; m. Katherine Lucy Rampton, Dec. 30, 1993. BA, U. Kans., 1991, JD, 1994. Assoc. Moriarty, Erker & Moore, Overland Park, Kans., 1994-96; ptnr. Erker & Moore, Olathe, 1996-98; pres. Iconoclastic Pop Records, Lawrence, Kans., 1993—; ptnr. Erker, Norton & Hare, Olathe, 1999—. Author: Art of War for Criminal Defense Attorneys, 1997. Coach Nat. Mock Jury competition, Shawnee Mission, Kans., 1997. Named one of Kansas City's 29 most influential people under age 30, Kansas City mag., 1996. Mem. Nat. Coll. of DUI Def., Kans. Assn. Criminal Def. Lawyers, Kans. Bar Assn. Libertarian. Avocations: guitar playing, painting, writing. Home: 3727 Pennsylvania Ave Kansas City MO 64111-1616 Office: Erker Norton & Hare 130 N Cherry St Ste 203 Olathe KS 66061-3460

NORTON, JODY (JOHN DOUGLAS NORTON), English language and women's studies educator; b. Princeton, N.J., Nov. 13, 1943; s. Paul Foote and Alison Edmunds (Stuart) N.; m. Alexandra Holt Morey, Aug. 20, 1977; children: Joselle, Jackson, Tayo. BA, U. Mass., Amherst, 1966; MA, U. Calif., Berkeley, 1981, PhD, 1988. Vis. asst. prof. Rice U., Houston, 1988-89, Albion (Mich.) Coll., 1989-94; lectr. Ea. Mich. U., Ypsilanti, 1994—. Author: Narcissus Sous Rature: Male Subjectivity in Contemporary American Poetry, 2000; contbr. articles to profl. jours. Fellow U. Calif., 1979-80, 80-81, 84-85, 87-88, Yale U., 1966-67; faculty rsch. grantee Albion Coll., 1992, 93, 94. Mem. MLA, Midwest MLA, Soc. for Critical Exch., Popular Culture Assn., Phi Beta Kappa, Phi Kappa Phi. Avocations: tennis, mountain climbing, camping, playing electric bass, blues and country western music. Home: 2820 Kimberley Rd Ann Arbor MI 48104-6455 Office: Eastern Mich U Dept English Lang & Lit Ypsilanti MI 48197 E-mail: eng_norton@online.umich.edu.

NORTON, JOHN HISE, lawyer; b. Kansas City, Mo., Oct. 18, 1952; s. William Harrison and Helen (Gosslee) N.; children: Elijah Hise, Hunter Jackson, Robbie Norfleet. AB, U. Mo., 1974; JD with distinction, Thomas M. Cooley Law Sch., Lansing, Mich., 1978. Bar: Mo. 1978, U.S. Dist. Ct. (we. dist.) Mo. 1978, U.S. Ct. Appeals (8th cir.) 1978. Pntr. Norton, Pollard & Norton, Kansas City, 1978-89, Norton, White & Norton, Kansas City, 1989-90, Norton & Norton, PC, Kansas City, 1990-96, Norton, Norton & Noland PC, Kansas City, 1996—. Bd. dirs. Lawson (Mo.) Bank; mem. 7th Jud. Commn. Mo., 1989-96; frequent lectr. at profl. litigation sems.; presenter in field. Contbr. articles to law jours., chpt. to book. Recipient Lon O. Hocker Meml. Trial Lawyers award Mo. Bar Found., 1988. Mem. ATLA (state del. 1989-95), Mo. Bar Assn., Mo. Assn. Trial Attys. (bd. govs. 1986—, exec. bd., past v.p. and pres.), Clay County Bar Assn. (past pres.), Kansas City Met. Bar Assn. Democrat. Episcopalian. Avocations: golf, flying. Office: Norton Norton & Noland PC 6000 N Oak Trfy Ste 201 Kansas City MO 64118-5176 Fax: 816-454-5016. E-mail: jhnlaw@aol.com.

NORTON, KAREN ANN, accountant; b. Nov. 1, 1950; d. Dale Francis and Ruby Grace (Gehlhar) N. BA, U. Minn., 1972; postgrad., U. Md., 1978; MBA, Calif. State Poly. U., Pomona, 1989. CPA, Md. Securities transactions analyst Bur. of Pub. Debt, Washington, 1972-79, internal auditor, 1979-81, IRS, Washington, 1981; sr. acct. World Vision Internat., Monrovia, Calif., 1981-83, acctg. supr., 1983-87; sr. sys. liaison coord. Home Savs. Am. (name changed to Washington Mut.), 1987-97, sys. auditor, 1997-2000, sect. mgr., 2000—. Cons. (vol.) info. systems John M. Perkins Found., Pasadena, Calif., 1985-86. Author: (poetry) Ode to Joyce, 1985 (Golden Poet award 1985). 2d v.p. chpt. Nat. Treasury Employees Union, Washington, 1978, editor chpt. newsletter; mem. M-2 Prisoners Sponsorship Program, Chino, Calif., 1984-86. Recipient Spl. Achievement award Dept. Treasury, 1976, Superior Performance award Dept. Treasury, 1977-78; Charles and Ellora Alliss scholar, 1968. Mem. Angel Flight, Flying Samaritans. Avocations: flying, chess, racquetball, whitewater rafting.

NORTON, KAREN INA, pediatric radiologist; b. Bronx, N.Y. AB, Bryn Mawr Coll., 1976; MD, Mt. Sinai Sch. Medicine, 1980. Diplomate Am. Coll. Radiology. Asst. prof. radiology Mt. Sinai Sch. Medicine, N.Y.C., 1985-92, assoc. prof. pediat., 1995—, assoc. prof. radiology, 1992—. Cons. Englewood (N.J.) Hosp. and Med. Ctr., 1997—; dir. divsn. pediat. radiology Mt. Sinai Hosp. Dept. Radiology, 1985—. Mem. Am. Roentgen Ray Soc., Am. Coll. Radiology, Soc. Pediat. Radiology, Radiol. Soc. N.Am. Office: Mt Sinai Hosp Dept Radiology Box 1234 New York NY 10029 E-mail: karen_norton@smtplink.mssm.edu.

NORTON, KENNETH FREDERICK, music educator; b. Orlando, Fla., May 12, 1952; s. Forrest Walter and Marion Blanche Norton; m. Linda Sue Brubaker; children: Rebekkah, Keven, Marianne, Jonathan. MusB in Edn., U. Tampa, 1974; M of Ednl. Leadership, St. Leo U., 1999. Cert. profl. tchg. Tchr. Bayshore Christian Sch., Tampa, 1975—78; band dir. Plant City (Fla.) H.S., 1978—98, Van Buren Mid. Sch., Tampa, 1998—99, Robinson H.S., Tampa, 1999—2001, Alonso H.S., Tampa, 2001—. Ch. music dir. Kings Way Worship Ctr., Seffner, FLA., 1988—95; ch. orch. dir. Southside Assembly of God, Lakeland, FLA., 1995—97. Mem.: Nat. Band Assn., Am. Sch. Band Dirs. Assn., Fla. Bandmasters Assn. (dist. chmn. 1988—94), Fla. Music Educators Conf., Music Educators Nat. Conf. Home: Apt 205 12404 Plantation Pine Ln Tampa FL 33635 Office: Alonso HS 8302 Montague St Tampa FL 33635 Office Fax: 813-356-1529. Personal E-mail: kenfnorton10@hotmail.com. Business E-Mail: kenfnorton10@hotmail.com.

NORTON, KURT MATTHEW, printing company executive; b. Phoenix, Sept. 2, 1964; s. Sue Ann and Robert Eugene Norton. Student, San Francisco State U., 1983—88, credential in secondary tchg., 1992. Fin. analyst West Pub., San Francisco, 1992—97; bus. mgr. Thomson Learning, Belmont, 1997—. Democrat. Office: Thomson Learning 10 Davis Dr Belmont CA 94002 Personal E-mail: kmnorton@hotmail.com.

NORTON, LILBURN LAFAYETTE, chemist, consultant; b. Lenoir City, Tenn., Jan. 2, 1927; s. William Clyde and Eula Comfort (Tate) Norton; m. Wilma Virginia Parrish, Dec. 23, 1946 (dec. Feb. 1984); m. Barbara Hill Sampson, July 11, 1986; children: David Michael, Nancy Camille, Gary Lynn, Lee Anne. BS, Carson-Newman Coll., Jefferson City, Tenn., 1949; MS, Northwestern U., Evanston, Ill., 1951; PhD, U. Tenn., Knoxville, 1954. Rsch. chemist Fibers dept. DuPont Co., Chattanooga, 1954—59, rsch. supr. Seaford, Del., 1959—66, rsch. assoc., 1966—89, rsch. fellow, 1989—91; ret., 1991; ind. tech. cons. Nortech, Inc., Seaford, 1991—. Contbr. Mem.: Del. Acad. Sci., Am. Chem. . Republican. Baptist. Achievements include patents for in field. Avocations: camping, woodworking, travel, fishing. Home and Office: Nortech Inc 95 Rivers End Dr Seaford DE 19973

NORTON, LINDA LEE, pharmacist, educator; b. Vallejo, Calif., Aug. 12, 1953; d. Don Leroy and Pearl Etta (Cain) Hartzell; m. Lawrence Henry Norton, Aug. 19, 1972; children: Joshua David, Gabriel Aaron. PharmD, U. Pacific, 1991. Lic. pharmacist, Calif., Nev. Pharmacy resident St. Joseph's Med. Ctr., Stockton, Calif., 1991-92, U. Ariz., Tucson, 1992-93; fellow in pain rsch. and drug info. U. of Pacific and Am. Acad. Pain Mgmt., Stockton, 1993-95; asst. prof. pharmacy practice U. of Pacific, 1995-99, assoc. coord. postgrad. profl. edn., 1995-99, assoc. prof., dir. postgrad. profl. edn., 1999—. Mng. editor Enjoying Good Health, 1997-99; contbr. articles to profl. jours. Bd. dirs. SMART Coalition, Sacramento, 1998—. Mem. shared governance com. Liberty Union H.S., Brentwood, Calif., 1995-97, health careers acad. com., 1995-97. Recipient Award for outstanding article in pain mgmt. Am. Jour. Pain Mgmt., 1997; grantee Valley Mountain Reg. Ctr., 1998—, Diagnostek, 1994; Thomas J. Long Faculty fellow, 1997, 98. Mem. Am. Assn. Colls. Pharmacy, Am. Soc. Health-Sys. Pharmacists, Calif. Soc. Health-Sys. Pharmacists (co-chair C.E. Focus '98), Rho Chi. Avocations: small-scale farming and ranching, horse shoe pitching, fishing. Office: Univ of the Pacific Sch of Pharmacy 751 Brookside Rd Stockton CA 95211-0001

NORTON, MARY BETH, history educator, author; b. Ann Arbor, Mich., Mar. 25, 1943; d. Clark Frederic and Mary Elizabeth (Lunny) N. BA, U. Mich., 1964; MA, Harvard U., 1965, PhD, 1969; DHL (hon.), Siena Coll., 1983, Marymount Manhattan Coll., 1984, De Pauw U., 1989; DLitt (hon.), Ill. Wesleyan U., 1992. Asst. prof. history U. Conn., Storrs, 1969-71; from asst. prof. to prof. Cornell U., Ithaca, N.Y., 1971-87, Mary Donlon Alger prof. Am. history, 1987—. Author: The British-Americans: The Loyalist Exiles in England, 1774-1789, 1972, Liberty's Daughters: The Revolutionary Experience of American Women, 1750-1800, 1980 (Berkshire prize for Best Book Woman Historian 1980), Founding Mothers and Fathers: Gendered Power and the Forming of American Society, 1996 (finalist Pulitzer prize in history 1997); co-author: A People and A Nation, 1982, 6th rev. edit., 2001; editor: AHA Guide to Historical Literature, 3d rev. edit., 1995; co-editor: Women of America: A History, 1979, To Toil the Livelong Day: America's Women at Work, 1790-1980, 1987, Major Problems in American Women's History, 1989, 2nd rev. edit., 1995; contbr. articles to profl. jours. Trustee Cornell U., 1973-75, 83-88; mem. Nat. Coun. Humanities, Washington, 1979-84. Woodrow Wilson Found. fellow, 1964-65, NEH fellow, 1974-75, Shelby Cullom Davis Ctr. fellow Princeton U., 1977-78, Rockefeller Found. fellow, 1986-87, Soc. for Humanities fellow Cornell U., 1989-90, John Simon Guggenheim Meml. Found. fellow, 1993-94, Starr Found. fellow Lady Margaret Hall, Oxford U., 2000, Mellon postdoctoral fellow Huntington Libr., 2001. Fellow Soc. Am. Historians (exec. bd. 1974-87, Allan Nevins prize 1970); mem. Am. Hist. Assn. (v.p. for rsch. 1985-87), Am. Acad. Arts and Scis., Orgn. Am. Historians (exec. bd. 1983-86), Berkshire Conf. Women Historians (pres. 1983-85) Democrat. Methodist. Office: Cornell U Dept History 325 Mcgraw Hall Ithaca NY 14853-4601 E-mail: mbn1@cornell.edu.

NORTON, NATHANIEL GOODWIN, marketing executive; b. Chgo., Jan. 7, 1948; s. Wilbur H. and Eva (Geneen) N.; m. Ariel Taylor, Nov. 15, 1980 (div. July 1987). BA, U. N.C., 1969. Mktg. mgr. Canteen Corp., Chgo., 1971-74; sr. v.p. Mathieu, Gerfen & Bresner, N.Y.C., 1974-83; pres., ptnr. Rand Pub. Rels., 1983-89; ind. marketing cons. North Hampton, N.H., 1989—.

NORTON, NORMAN JAMES, retired exploration geologist, educator; b. Du Quoin, Ill., Apr. 26, 1933; s. James Harlan Norton and Helen Jane (Riley) Norton Rosen; m. Bettie Jean Greer, July 7, 1955; children— Matthew James, Jane Alison BS, So. Ill. U., 1958; MS, U. Minn., 1960, PhD, 1963. From asst. to prof. biology Hope Coll., Holland, Mich., 1964-74; prof., chmn. dept. biology Ball State U., Munice, Ind., 1974-78, acting v.p. acad. affairs, 1978-79; acting dean Ball State U. Coll. Arts and Scis., 1979-81; provost, v.p. acad. affairs Ind. U. Pa., 1981-83; cons. geologist Gulf Oil Corp., Houston, 1970-83; sr. staff geologist Gulf Oil Exploration and Prodn. Co., 1983-85; biostratigrapher, stratigraphic services, exploration Chevron Overseas Petroleum Inc., San Ramon, Calif., 1985-91; supr. biostratigraphy sect. Chevron U.S.A., Inc., Houston, 1991-93; acting divsn. geologist Chevron U.S.A. Inc., 1993-95, divsn. geologist, 1995—, geol. cons., 1997-98, ret., 1998. Contbr. articles to profl. jours. With USAF, 1952-56. Recipient Outstanding Tchr. Educator award Sr. Class of Hope Coll., 1969, acad. citation for disting. achievement Mich. Acad. Scis., Art and Letters, 1969, Outstanding Achievement award Chevron Overseas Petroleum Inc., 1990. Mem. Am. Assn. Stratigraphic Palynologists (Disting. Svc. award 1978, chmn. bd. trustees found., archives com. 1970—, constrn. revision com.). Home: 514 Ruddy Turnstone Johns Island SC 29455

NORTON, ROBERT HOWARD, entertainer, musical arranger, author; b. N.Y.C., July 19, 1946; s. Howard R. and Lena (Triano) N.; m. Eileen Williams, Sept. 29, 1966 (div. 1976); children: Brian, Lelania. Student, Broward C.C., Ft. Lauderdale, Fla., 1970-75; community antenna TV engr. cert., Nat. Cable TV Inst., 1976. Rec. session artist Motown and various other recording labels, 1964—; entertainer various concerts, 1964—; systems technician Selkirk Communications, Ft. Lauderdale, Fla., 1979-81; cable TV engr. Gen. Instrument Corp., Hatboro, Pa., 1981-84; entertainer (with Leilani Chandler) The Sophisticats, Ft. Pierce, Fla., 1984—; owner, author, software writer Norton Music, 1990—. Author: The Artist's and Entertainer's Tax Bible, 1990, Entertainer's Guide to Cruising, 1991—; writer mus. software: 350 User Styles, 1991—, writer mus. software: Band-in-a-Box Supercharger, 1993—, writer mus. software: 22 Band-in-a-Box Fake Disks, 1994—, writer mus. software: 13 Band-in-a-Box User Style Disks, 1993—, software 475+: Gen. MIDI Sequences, 1993—; composer: numerous songs, —; : arranger of more then 400 songs, —. Mem. Internat. Wind Synthesis Assn. Home and Office: Norton Music PO Box 13149 Fort Pierce FL 34979-3149 E-mail: norton@nortonmusic.com.

NORTON, ROBERT MICHAEL, mathematician, educator, statistician; b. Richmond Heights, Mo., July 1, 1946; s. Robert and Eunice Louise Ethel (Hoffman) N.; m. Elizabeth Ferry, Aug. 6, 1972; children: Andrew Robert, Susan Hall. BS, BS in Edn., N.E. Mo. State U., 1968; MS in Math., Okla. State U., 1971, PhD in Math., 1974. Asst. prof. math. Coll. of Charleston, S.C., 1974-79, assoc. prof., 1979-86, prof., 1986—. Bd. examiners Nat. Coun. for Accreditation of Tchr. Edn., 1990-93; dir. MS program in math. U. Charleston, 1994-98, dir. EdM in sci. and math., 1997-2002; expert witness in stats.; stats. quality control cons. Contbr. articles to profl. jours. Dir. region III H.S. wrestling ofcls. S.C. H.S. League, 1989-96. With U.S. Army, 1969-70, Vietnam. Named S.C. Wrestling Referee of the Yr., S.C. H.S. League, Columbia, 1997. Mem. Am. Statis. Assn. (pres. S.C. chpt. 1979-80), Math. Assn. Am., Am. Soc. for Quality (sect. chair 2000-01), VFW (life). Avocation: high school and college wrestling official.

NORTON, RUTH ANN, education educator; b. Sioux City, Iowa, Mar. 7, 1947; d. Burton Ellwood and Mildred Ruth (Schneider) N.; m. Jack William Moskal, May 30, 1985. BA, U. No. Iowa, 1969; MS, Syracuse U., 1984, EdD, 1985. Cert. tchr., Iowa, Vt. Tchr. Cedar Falls (Iowa) Unified Sch. Dist., 1969-79; asst. didr. Area 7 Tchr. Ctr., Waterloo, Iowa, 1979-80; tchr. Moretown (Vt.) Elem. Sch., 1980-81; doctoral candidate Syracuse (N.Y.) U., 1981-85; prof. Calif. State U., San Bernardino, 1985—, dir. student teaching, 1989-95, coord. elem. intern program, 1996-99, dir. elem. edn. program, 1999—. Cons. tech. tng. inst. Calif. State U., San Bernardino, Constl. Heritage Inst.; trainer supervision workshops Calif. State U., San Bernardino; cons. Lime St. Elem. Sch., Hesperia, Calif.; bd. dirs. Redlands Ednl. Partnership Found.; chairperson Reflections Com. for Redlands PTA Coun. Contbr. articles to profl. jours. Recipient Affirmative Action Faculty Devel. grant Calif. State U., 1986, Profl. Devel. Monetary grant Calif. State U., 1987, Meritorious Performance & Profl. Promise award Calif. State U., 1988. Mem. ASCD, Am. Ednl. Rsch. Assn., Assn. Tchr. Educators, Calif. Assn. for Supervision and Curriculum Devel., Calif. Coun. for Social Studies, Nat. Coun. for Social Studies, So. Calif. Assn. Tchr. Educators, Phi Delta Kappa. Avocations: gardening, camping, swimming, needlework, reading. Office: Calif State U 5500 University Pkwy San Bernardino CA 92407-2318 E-mail: rnorton@csusb.edu.

NORTON, STEPHEN ALLEN, geological sciences educator; b. Newton, Mass., May 21, 1940; m. Anne Peer, Apr. 25, 1970; children: David S., Lisa A., Stephen A. BA, Princeton U., 1962; MA, Harvard U., 1963, PhD, 1967. Prof. geol. scis. U. Maine, Orono, 1978—, chmn. dept., 1978-82, 93-99, dean arts and scis., 1984-86. Fellow Geol. Soc. Am.; mem. Am. Soc. Limnology and Oceanography. Office: U Maine Dept Geol Scis Bryand Ctr Orono ME 04469-5790

NORTON, WAYNE ANDERSON, retired journalism educator, public relations specialist; b. Memphis; BS, Memphis State U., 1961; MS, Ohio U., 1963; PhD, U. So. Miss., 1993. Dir. pub. rels. W.Va. Inst. Tech., Montgomery, 1962-63, Findlay (Ohio) Coll., 1963-66; dir. pub. info. Murray (Ky.) State U., 1966-68; dir. news svcs. S.E. Mo. State U., Cape Girardeau, 1968-84, asst. prof. mass comm., 1984-92, Fla. So. Coll., Lakeland, 1992-96; adj. asst. prof. journalism U. Ark., Little Rock, 1996-98; asst. prof. journalism Bowling Green (Ohio) State U., 1998—2002.

NORTON, WILLIAM ALAN, lawyer; b. Garretsville, Ohio, Apr. 26, 1951; s. Hugh Delbert and Tommie (Leet) N.; m. Denise Ann, May 2, 1991; children: Rachel, Sarah Megan, William Tucker. AA, U. Fla., 1972, BS, 1973, JD, 1976. Bar: Fla. 1977, U.S. Dist. Ct. (so. and mid. dist.) Fla. 1995. Assoc. Law Office of David Paul Horan, Key West, Fla., 1978-79; asst. pub. defender 16th Jud. Cir., Monroe County, 1979-81, 1st Jud. Cir., Ft. Walton Beach, 1981-85; assoc. Jones & Foster, P.A., West Palm Beach, 1985-88, Montgomery Searcy & Denney, West Palm Beach, 1988-89, Searcy Denney Scarola Barnhart & Shipley, P.A., 1989-93, atty./shareholder, 1989—, shareholder. Lectr. in civil trial and securities litigation. Mem. Fla. Bar Assn. (cert. civil trial litigation), Pub. Investors Arbitration Bar Assn., Palm Beach County Bar Assn., Acad. Fla. Trial Lawyers. Home: 12710 Drake Ln Palm Beach Gardens FL 33410 Office: Searcy Denney Scarola et al 2139 Palm Beach Lakes Blvd West Palm Beach FL 33409-6601

NORTWEN, PATRICIA HARMAN, music educator; b. New Ulm, Minn., Mar. 6, 1930; d. Joseph Absolom and Viola Maureen (Stroud) Harman; m. Dallas Ernest Andrew Nortwen, Dec. 22, 1956; children: Laura Lee, Daniel Harman. BA magna cum laude, U. Minn., 1952, BS in Edn., MA, U. Minn., 1956. Tchr. music N.W. Sch., U. Minn., Crookston, 1952-54; instr. music S.D. State U., Brookings, 1954-56; tchr. music Robbinsdale (Minn.) Jr. H.S., 1956-57; music dir. Bethlehem Luth. Ch., Mpls., 1957-67; instr. music Golden Valley Luth. Coll., 1967-85; ind. music tchr., 1957—. Performer Early Music Consort, also others; prodr. (cable TV series) Women/Music, 1984-85; author, mng. editor: Music Theory Workbook, Vols. 1-6, 1993-96. Bd. dirs., sec., pres. Civic Orch. Mpls., 1989-94; cmty. adv. bd. U. Minn. Sch. Music, 1998—. Mem.: Thursday Mus. (pres. 1988—92, various offices 1992—97, devel. chair 1997—), Young Peoples Symphony Concert Assn. (v.p. 1992—2000), U. Minn. Sch. Music Alumni Coun. (chair 1997—99), Minn. Music Tchrs. Assn. (chair edn. found. 1995—97, pres.-elect 1997—99, pres. 1999—2001, found. bd. dirs. 2000—, found. treas. 2002—), Frederic Chopin Soc. (sec. 1992—96, bd. dirs. 1992—), Music Tchrs. Nat. Assn., Phi Beta Kappa, Sigma Alpha Iota (nat. dir. 1975—89, 1998—, province officer, Nat. Leadership award 1952, Ring of Excellence award 1990). Avocations: reading, singing, hiking, fishing. Home: 210 W Grant St Apt 313 Minneapolis MN 55403-2244 E-mail: pdnortwen@juno.com.

NORWALK, KELLI CURRAN, retail executive, entrepreneur; b. Cleve., Sept. 25, 1949; d. Paul Joseph and Ella (Eylar) Curran; m. Keith Otto Norwalk, Apr. 3, 1970; children: Keith Curran, Alyssa Barr. BA, Butler U., 1978. Exec. dir. Heritage Place, Indpls., 1975-77; social worker Americana Health Care, 1978-81; pres., prin. Down By the Ducks, Inc., 1982-85; chief exec. officer, prin. The Tarkington Tweed, Inc., 1985—. Mem. Butler Tarkington Neithborhood Assn., Indpls., 1978—, Arts, Ind. Finalist Entrepreneur of Yr. award Ernst and Young Ind. Heartland, 1998. Mem. 500 Festival Assocs., Indpls. C. of C. Democrat. Roman Catholic. Avocations: painting, theatre, travel. Home: 5534 Bay Landing Ct Indianapolis IN 46254-9564 Office: The Tarkington Tweed Inc 5631 N Illinois St Indianapolis IN 46208-1554

NORWICK, BRAHAM, textile specialist, consultant, columnist; b. N.Y.C., July 6, 1916; s. Mark and Rose (Ungar) N.; m. Thérèse Thoisy, May 7, 1939; 1 child, Noel Alex. BS in Chemistry, Rensselaer Polytech. Inst., 1938; cert. d' Etudes, U. de Besançon, France, 1945. Tech. dir. Beaunit Mills, N.Y.C., 1938-78; v.p. Joseph Bancroft & Sons Co., Wilmington, Del., 1973-78; expert witness TAG, N.Y.C., 1980—; columnist Maschen Industrie, Bamberg, Fed. Republic of Germany, 1983—. Vis. prof. Cornell U., Ithaca, N.Y., 1982; lectr. in Tibetan studies. Author: Locating Tibet - The Maps, 1988, Why Tibet Disappeared from Scientific 16th -17th Century European Maps, 1992, Modern Mapping of Tibet, A Cautionary Tale, 1994, William Woodville Rockhill: The First American Fluent in Tibetan, 2002, (mag.) Indsl. & Engring. Chemistry, 1942; contbg. author: Developments in Applied Spectroscopy, 1968, Analytical Methods for a Textile Laboratory, 1968, 84; columnist Daily News Record Newspaper, 1979-86. Cons. Jacques Marchais Mus., S.I., 1975—. With U.S. Army, 1943-46, ETO. Recipient Bronze medal Am. Assn. Textile Techs., 1977. Fellow ASTM (spokesman Internat. Standardization Orgn. 1960—, Gold Harold de Witt Smith medal, 1984), Am. Soc. for Quality Control; mem. Am. Chem. Soc. (life), Am. Assn. Textile Chemists and Colorists, N.Y. Acad. Scis., Chemists Club. Achievements include first to make heat set nylon parachutes; first characterization and standardization of dyestuffs for industrial computerized dyeing; development of wash and wear finishes; utilization of small sample statistical methods and rare events statistics in textile processing, chromatographic methods; employment of infrared methods in textile chemicals analysis. Home: 200 E 57th St New York NY 10022-2860 E-mail: bnorwick@worldnet.att.net.

NORWOOD, BERNARD, economist; b. Boston, Nov. 21, 1922; s. Hyman and Rose (Fink) N.; m. Janet Lippe, June 25, 1943; children: Stephen Harlan, Peter Carlton. BA, Boston U., 1947; MA, Fletcher Sch. Law and Diplomacy, 1948, PhD, 1957. Internat. economist State Dept., 1949-58; joined U.S. Fgn. Svc., 1955; 1st. sec. U.S. mission to European Communities, Brussels, Belgium, 1958-62; asst. chief comml. policy and treaties divsn. Dept. State, 1962; chmn. trade staff com. Office Spl. Rep. for Trade Negotiations, Exec. Office Pres., 1963-67; assigned The Nat. War Coll., 1967-68; advisor divsn. internat. fin. bd. govs. Fed. Res. Sys., 1968-75; prin. assoc., sr. cons. Nathan Assocs., Inc., 1975-94. Mem. U.S. del. to negotiations and confs. GATT, Geneva, 1953-67. Served with AUS, 1943-46. Home and Office: 5610 Wisconsin Ave # 21D Chevy Chase MD 20815-4415

NORWOOD, B.J. SCOTT, business and management educator, Russian studies, pro bono public service; b. San Diego, June 24, 1926; s. Guy Johns and Louise Elizabeth Norwood; m. Barbara Ann Norwood, Jan. 28, 1956; children: Jonathan Scott, Beverly Norwood Dulaney. AA, UCLA, 1947, BS, 1949; MBA, Harvard U., 1951. Asst. prof. San Jose (Calif.) State U., 1955-58, assoc. prof., 1958-62, prof., 1962—. Chmn. bd. dirs. Radiation Detection Co., Sunnyvale, Calif., 1972-83; mgmt. cons., rschr., educator, Calif., 1960-83, U.S. Govt., 1973-98; econ. transition advisor various govt. entities, Russia, Belarus, Mongolia, 1990-95. Founding editor Vectors, 1989-98; contbr. to profl. publs. Commr. County of Santa Clara-Moscow Region Sister County Commn., 1995—. With USNR, 1944-46, PTO. Named Outstanding Prof., San Jose State U., 1976; recipient Outstanding Svc. award, Air Force ROTC, 1982, medal for superior pub. svc., Sec. of Navy, 1988, Jefferson award, FBI, Washington, 1993. Mem.: Navy League U.S. (state pres. 1986—87, region v.p.-at-large 1995—97, nat. dir., 11 awards 1990—98), Assn. U.S. Army (state pres. and regional exec. v.p. 1988—90, regional exec. v.p. 1995—96, 7 awards 1994—98), Air Force Assn. (state chmn. bd. 1982—84, state pres., 10 awards 1981—89), Propeller Club (mem. nat. bd. govs. 2002—, pres. San Francisco Bay Region 2002—), Knights Hospitaller (chevalier), Sovereign Order of John, Sovereign Mil. Order Temple of Jerusalem (knight comdr. 1995, grand officer 1999, chevalier). Avocations: Russian language, travel in Russia.

NORWOOD, CAROLYN VIRGINIA, business educator; b. Florence, S.C., Dec. 11; d. James Henry and Mildred (Jones) N. BS, N.C. A&T State U., 1956; MA, Columbia U., 1959; postgrad., Seton Hall U., Temple U.; cert. scholarly distinction, Nat. Acad. Paralegal Studies, 1991. Instr. Gibbs. Jr. Coll., St. Petersburg, Fla., Fayetteville State U., N.C.; asst. prof. C.C. Phila.; prof. Essex County Coll., Newark, 1968—. Cons. Mercer County Coll., Trenton, N.J.; mem. assessment team Lehman Coll., Bronx, N.Y., Mid.-States Comm., Phila., 1980—; vol. tutor Newark Literacy Campaign, 1998—. Co-author: Alphabetic Indexing, 6th edit., 1999. Mem. Nat. Coun. on Black Am. Affairs, AACC; vol. tutor Newark Literacy Campaign. Recipient EDDY award Gregg/McGraw-Hill Co., N.Y.C., 1986, cert. of recognition of outstanding and dedicated svc. Mid. States Assn. Colls. and Schs., Commn. on Higher Edn., 1994; profiled in NBEA Yearbook chpt. on Leadership in Bus. Edn., 1993; postdoctoral fellow Temple U., 1977-78. Mem. AAUW, NAACP, Nat. Coun. Black Am. Affairs, Nat. Bus. Edn. Assn. (bd. dirs. 1982-85), Ea. Bus. Edn. Assn. (pres. 1986-87, membership dir. 1976-85, Educator of the Yr. 1994), Nat. Coun. Negro Women, N.J. Bus. Edn. Assn., Alpha Kappa Alpha, Phi Delta Kappa, Delta Pi Epsilon. Avocations: bowling, photography. Office: Essex County Coll 303 University Ave Newark NJ 07102-1719

NORWOOD, CHARLES W., JR. congressman; b. Valdosta, Ga., July 27, 1941; m. Gloria Norwood; 2 children. BS, Ga. So. U., 1964; DDS, Georgetown U., 1967. Pvt. practice, Augusta, Ga., 1969-94; owner Norwood Tree Nursery, 1984—; mem. U.S. Congress from 10th Ga. dist., 1995—, mem. commerce, edn. and the workforce coms., vchmn. health subcom., chmn. workforce protection com.; pres. Georgia Dental Assoc., 1983. Capt. U.S. Army, 1967-69, Vietnam. Decorated Combat Medic badge, Bronze Star for Meritorious Svc., Bronze Star for Meritorious Achievement. Mem. Ga. Dental Assn. Republican. Methodist. Office: US Ho of Reps 1707 Longworth Hob Washington DC 20515-1010*

NORWOOD, DEBORAH ANNE, law librarian; b. Honolulu, Nov. 12, 1950; d. Alfred Freeman and Helen G. (Papsch) N.; 1 child, Nicholas. BA, U. Wash., 1972; JD, Willamette U., 1974; M in Law Librarianship, U. Wash., 1979. Bar: Wash., U.S. Dist. Ct. (we. dist.) 1975, U.S. Ct. Appeals (9th cir.) 1980. Ptnr. Evans and Norwood, Seattle, 1975-79; law librarian U.S. Courts Library, 1980-89; state law librarian Wash. State Law Libr., Olympia, 1989—2002, reporter of decisions, 1994-2001; asst. dir. pub. svcs. Jacob Burns Law Libr. George Washington U., Washington, 2002—. Mem. ALA, Spl. Librs. Assn., Am. Assn. Law Librs. (chmn. state, ct. and county spl. interest section 1995-96, chair legal info. svcs. to pub. spl. interest sect. 2001—). Office: Jacob Burns Law Libr George Washington U 716-20th St NW Washington DC 20052 E-mail: dnorwood@burns.nlc.gw.edu.

NORWOOD, JANET LIPPE, economist; b. Newark, Dec. 11, 1923; d. M. Turner and Thelma (Levinson) Lippe; m. Bernard Norwood, June 25, 1943; children: Stephen Harlan, Peter Carlton. BA, Douglass Coll., 1945; MA, Tufts U., 1946; PhD, Fletcher Sch. Law and Diplomacy, 1949; LLD (hon.), Fla. Internat. U., 1979, Carnegie Mellon U., 1984, Harvard U., 1997. Instr. Wellesley Coll., 1948-49; economist William L. Clayton Ctr., Tufts U., 1953-58; with Bur. Labor Stats., U.S. Dept. Labor, Washington, 1963-91; dep. commr., then acting commr. Bur. Labor Stats. Dept. Labor, 1975-79, commr. labor stats., 1979-92; sr. fellow The Urban Inst., 1992-99; counselor, sr. fellow N.Y. Conf. Bd., 2001—. Dir. Mid Atlantic Med. Svcs., Inc., Nat. Opinion Rsch. Ctr., chair adv. coun. unemployment compensation, 1993—96; dir. Inst. Global Ethics; chair panel to rev. 2000 census NAS, mem. divsn. engring. and phys. scis.; mem. adv. bd. Bur. Transp. Stats.; mem. adv. coun. Schl. Pub. Affairs Am. UAW, 2001—; pres. COSSA, 2001—. Author: Organizing to Count: Change in the Federal Statistical System, 1995; contbr. Named Hall Disting. Alumni, Rutgers U., 1987; recipient Disting. Achievement award, Dept. Labor, 1972, Spl. Commendation award, 1977, Philip Arnow award, 1979, Elmer Staats award, 1982, Pub. Svc. award, 1984, Presdl. Disting. Exec. Rank, 1988, Elizabeth Scott award, Com. Pres.'s Statis. Assns., 2002. Fellow: AAAS (Founder's award 1997), Nat. Assn. Bus. Economists, Royal Statis. Soc., Am. Statis. Assn. (pres. 1989); mem.: Nat. Inst. Statis. Sci. (bd. trustees 1991—2000), Nat. Acad. Pub. Adminstrn., Am. Econ. Assn., Internat. Assn. Ofcls. Stats., Internat. Statis. Inst., Douglass Coll. Soc. Disting. Achievement, Cosmos Club (pres. 1995—96). Home: 5610 Wisconsin Ave Ph 21-d Chevy Chase MD 20815-4444 E-mail: janetnor@aol.com.

NORWOOD, SAMUEL WILKINS, III, financial consultant; b. Chgo., Apr. 6, 1941; s. Samuel Wilkins and Miriam Lois (Cary) N.; m. Julianne Parker Jones, Jun. 15, 1962 (div. Sept. 1981); children: Samuel Parker, Elizabeth Cary; m. Alice Ann Lynch, Jan. 13, 2000. Student, Vanderbilt U., 1959-61; BA, Tulane U., 1964; MBA, U. Chgo., 1965. Supr. spl. studies Allied Corp., N.Y.C., 1965-67; mgr. analysis and planning ITT Semiconductors Corp., West Palm Beach, Fla., 1967-69; dir. fin. planning Fuqua Industries, Atlanta, 1969-73, v.p. planning, 1976-81, v.p. corp devel., exec. asst. to chmn., 1981-89; pres., CEO, dir. Vista Resources, Inc., 1991-95; ptnr. Tatum CFO Ptnrs., LLP, 1997—. Cons., Atlanta, 1973-76. Founder N. Atlanta Mediation Ctr., 1972. Mem. Planning Execs. Inst. (bd. dirs. 1979-85, chmn. 1984-85, pres. Atlanta chpt. 1976-77), The Planning Forum (bd. dirs. 1985-87), Atlanta Yacht Club (bd. govs. 1984-87, commodore 1989), Allatoona Canoe and Sailing Club (commodore 1988-89), Assn. for Corp. Growth, Soc. Internat. Bus. Fellows (bd. dirs. 1996-99, exec. com. bd. 1998-99). Avocations: competitive sailing, skiing, mountain climbing/hiking. Home: 42 Camden Rd NE Atlanta GA 30309-1508 E-mail: snorwood@tatumcfo.com., snorwood@mindspring.com.

NOSANOW, BARBARA SHISSLER, art association administrator; b. Roanoke, Va. d. Willis Morton and Kathryn Sabin (Bradford) Johnson; m. John Lewis Shissler Jr., July 28, 1957 (dec. May 1972); children: John Lewis Shissler III, Ada Holland Shissler; m. Lewis Harold Nosanow, Oct. 15, 1973. AB, Smith Coll., 1957; MA, Case Western Res. U., 1958. Asst. mng. editor Jour. Aesthetics and Art Criticism, Cleve. Mus. Art, 1958-63; dir. publs. and rsch. Mpls. Inst. Arts, 1963-72; dir. U. Minn. Art Mus., Mpls., 1972-76; dir. exhbns. and edn. Nat. Archives, Washington, 1976-79; curator Smithsonian Instn., 1979-82; asst. dir. Nat. Mus. Am. Art, Smithsonian Instn., 1982-88; dir. Portland (Maine) Mus. Art, 1988-93, Art Spaces, 1993—; study leader, lecturer Smithsonian Study Tours of France and Russia. Lectr. art history, also author. Past mem. various rev. panels NEH, Washington. Bd. dirs. Md. Com. for Humanities, Balt., 1980-83. Mem. Internat. Women's Forum. Avocation: travel. Office: Art Spaces 3386 Piperfife Ct Keswick VA 22947-9142 Fax: 434-923-0031. E-mail: bnosanow@att.com.

NOSEK, FRANCIS JOHN, lawyer, diplomat; b. Evanston, Ill., Apr. 13, 1934; s. Francis J. and Loretto (Brannan) N.; m. Janet Child, Dec. 30, 1964; children: Francis J. III, Peter C. BA in Polit. Sci., U. Idaho, 1956, JD, 1960. Bar: Calif. 1961, U.S. Dist. Ct. (no. dist.) Calif. 1961, U.S. Ct. Appeals (9th cir.) 1961, Alaska 1962, U.S. Dist. Ct. Alaska 1962, D.C. 1978. Pvt. practice, Anchorage, 1960-67, 75—; assoc. Bell, Sanders & Tallman, 1961-62; sr. ptnr. Nosek, Bradberry, Wolf and Schlossberg, 1967-75; hon. consul Czech Republic. Adj. prof. U. Alaska, Mat-Su C.C., Anchorage, 1976-82; lectr. Anchorage C.C., 1979-83, SBA, 1975-97; editor State of Alaska Real Estate Commn., Anchorage, 1983; presenter in field; bd. of dirs. on real estate and bus. topics. Author: Alaska Mortgage Law, How to Buy and Sell a Business; contbr. articles to law jours. Chmn. Anchorage Parks and Recreation, 1968-83, IIHF World Jr. Championships, Anchorage, 1988; named hon. Consul for Czech Republic. Mem. Am. Coll. Real Estate Lawyers, Alaska Bar Assn. (chmn. real estate law 1978, mem. internat. law exec. com. 1991-95), Calif. Bar Assn. (real estate law coms.), D.C. Bar Assn. (internat. law com.), Anchorage Bar Assn. Avocations: mountain climbing, ice hockey, antique cars. Office: 310 K St Ste 601 Anchorage AK 99501-2041

NOSHER, JOHN LOUIS, radiologist; b. East Orange, N.J., Jan. 31, 1946; s. Louis P. and Pauline Nosher; m. Marjorie Theresa Dolan, 1970; children: John Christopher, Todd Matthew, Brittany Paige. BS, St. Joseph's Coll., 1967; MD, Jefferson Med. Coll., 1971. Diplomate Am. Bd. Radiology, cert. Added Qualification, vascular/interventional radiology. Intern Jefferson Med. Coll., Phila., 1971-72; resident Columbia-Presbyn. Med. Ctr., N.Y.C., 1972-75; radiologist U. Radiology Group (formerly Radiology Group New Brunswick), East Brunswick, N.J., 1975—; program dir. diagnostic radiology residency program Robert Wood Johnson Med. Sch. U. Medicine and Dentistry of N.J., New Brunswick, 1985-87, program dir. vascular/interventional fellowship program RWJ Med. Sch., 1985—, chmn. dept. radiology Robert Wood Johnson Med. Sch., 1987—, clin. prof. radiology, 1989—. Chief radiology svcs. Robert Wood Johnson U. Hosp., New Brunswick, 1985—, divsn. vascular/interventional radiology dept. radiology RWJ U. Hosp., 1985—; attending radiologist, RWJ U. Hosp., St. Peter's U. Hosp., 1975—; exec. coun. U. Medicine and Denstistry-Robert Wood Johnson Med. Sch., Ctr. Biomed. Imaging; clin. com. chmn. Robert Wood Johnson Med. Sch., Robert Wood Johnson U. Hosp., med. bd.; mem. com. Vascular Ctr. N.J.; bd. dirs. U. Radiology Group. Author: Angiography & Interventional Radiology, 1991; co-author: Interventional Radiology-A Multimedia Approach (textbook, CD-ROMS), 2000; (with others): Atlas of Radiologic Imaging, 1989, Genitourinary Radiology: A Multimodality Approach, 1990, Invasive Diagnostic Procedures, 1994, Atlas of Diseases of the Kidney, 1998. Named one of N.J.'s finest physicians N.J. Monthly, 1998. Mem. Am. Coll. Radiology, Assn. Univ. Radiologists, Soc. Chmn. Acad. Radiology Depts., Soc. Cardiovascular and Interventional Radiology, N.J. Radiol. Soc., Middlesex County Med. Soc., Assn. Program Dirs. Radiology, Roxiticus Country Club, Seaside Park Yacht Club (fleet surgeon). Avocations: skiing, surfing, sailing, golfing, gardening. Office: UMDNJ Robert Wood Johnson Med Sch PO Box 19 1 Robert Wood Johnson Pl New Brunswick NJ 08903 E-mail: nosher@umdnj.edu.

NOSHI, MOHAMMED SALAH-ELDIN, physician, consultant; b. Cairo, Egypt, June 13, 1965; came to U.S., 1992 MD with honors, Cairo U., 1988. Diplomate Am. Bd. Internal Medicine, Am. Bd. Hosp. Physicians, Am. Bd. Ethical Physicians, cert. Bd. for Nutrition Specialists. Intern, resident Cairo U. Hosps., 1989-90; rsch. asst. Nat. Rsch. Inst. Ophthalmology, Cairo, 1990-91; clin. instr. Cairo U. Sch. Medicine, 1992-93; resident physician in internal medicine Nassau County Med. Ctr./SUNY Stony Brook, East Meadow, N.Y., 1993-96; attending physician in internal medicine Imperial Point Med. Ctr., Ft. Lauderdale, Fla., 1996—, Broward Gen. Med. Ctr., Ft. Lauderdale, 1996—, Holy Cross Hosp., Ft. Lauderdale, 1996—; acute care hospitalist North Broward Med. Ctr., 2002. Cons. Eli Lilly Pharm., Ft. Lauderdale, 1997—, Novartis Pharms.; prin. investigator Bristol Myers. Author and speaker in field. Vol. Salvation Army Clinic for Homeless and Indigent Population, Broward County, Fla. Recipient Physician Recognition award AMA. Fellow ACP, Am. Bd. Hosp. Physicians; mem. AMA, Fla. Med. Assn., Am. Soc. Internal Medicine, Am. Coll. Nutrition. Avocations: running, swimming, scuba diving, soccer, hiking.

NOSIKOVA, KSENIA, musician, educator; b. Moscow, Feb. 24, 1966; came to the U.S., 1991; d. Alexander Nosikov and Tatiana Lebedeva. MusB, Moscow Conservatory, 1985, MusM, 1989; D in Musical Arts, U. Colo., 1997. Adj. piano faculty mem. Moscow Sch. of the Arts, 1983-89; tchg. asst. Moscow Conservatory, 1983-89; tchg. asst. U. Colo., Boulder, 1993-97, adj. instr., 1998; chamber music faculty Young Musical Artists Assn., Lawrence, Kans., 1996; asst. prof. U. Iowa, Iowa City, 1998—; mem. piano trio Moscow State Tchaikovsky Conservatory, 1986-89; artist-in-residence Congress of the European Assns. of the Conservatories, Rovin, Yugoslavia, 1987; solo pianist USSR Ministry Culture, 1989-91; accompanist internat. vocal competitions Internat. Vocal Competitions, Hertogenbosch, The Netherlands, 1990, Stuttgart Internat. Voice Competition, Germany, 1990; rehearsal pianist Colo. Ballet Co., 1991-93, Opera Colo. Co., 1991--93; accompanist Opera Colo. Co. Outreach Program, 1992, 93; opera coach, accompanist Aspen (Colo.) Music Festival, 1994; sr. music editor Soviet Composer Pub. House, Moscow, 1989-91; jury mem. piano competitions, 1998-99. Musician: Moscow Conservatory Orch. USA Tour, 1988, Festival of Soviet Music, 1988, Jefferson Symphony Orch. , 1995, U. Colo. Symphony Orch., 1995, La. Symphony Orch., 1996, Carnegie Recital Hall, 1996, 2001, Donnell Auditorium, 1997, Ctr. for New Music East Coast Tour, 1998, Ibla-Ragusa, 1998, U. Iowa Symphony and S.E. Iowa Symphony. Finalist William Byrd Young Artist Competition, 1995, St. Charles Internat. Piano Competition, 1995, Joanna Hodges Internat. Piano Competition, 1997; prize winner Moscow Conservatory Contemporary Music Competition, 1983, Ala. Internat. Piano Competition, 1996, Frinna Awerbuch Internat. Piano Competition, N.Y.C., 1996, Ibla Internat. Piano Competition, Italy, 1998. Mem. Ibla Internat., Music Tchr. Nat. Assn., Coll. Music Soc. Office: U Iowa Sch Music 1006 Voxman Music Bldg Iowa City IA 52242 also: 1829 Gryn Dr Iowa City IA 52246-4406

NOSKIN, GARY ALAN, physician; b. Ft. Knox, Ky., Feb. 5, 1959; s. Gerald Martin and Shari C. N.; m. Cori Ann Levinson, Nov. 7, 1993; children: Jeremy Michael, Matthew Jacob. BA, Washington U., 1981; MD, Chgo. Med. Sch., 1986. Diplomate Am. Bd. Internal Medicine and Infectious Diseases. Intern dept. medicine Northwestern U., 1986-87, resident dept. medicien, 1987-89, fellow divsn. infectious diseases, 1989-91; asst. prof. medicine Northwestern U. Med. Sch., Chgo., 1991-97, assoc. prof. medicine, 1997—; med. dir. infection control and prevention Northwestern Meml. Hosp., 1997—, healthcare epidemiologist, 1997—. Contbr. over 80 articles to profl. jours., chpts. to books. Mem. Am. Soc. Microbiology, Ctr. Soc. Clin. Rsch., Infectious Diseases Soc. Am., Soc. Healthcare Epidemioloyg of Am. Office: Northwestern Meml Hosp 251 E Huron St Chicago IL 60611-2908

NOSKO, MICHAEL GERRIK, neurosurgeon, educator; b. Montreal, Feb. 24, 1957; came to U.S., 1991; s. Joseph John and June Elizabeth (Salter) N.; m. Deborah Anne Branciere, May 23, 1981; children: Douglas Joseph, Denise Elizabeth, Keith Michael. BS, McMaster U., 1978; MD, U. Toronto, 1982; PhD, U. Alberta, 1986. Intern U. Toronto (Ont., Can.) Gen. Hosp., 1982-83; resident U. Alberta Hosps., Edmonton, Can., 1986-91; assoc. prof. neurosurgery Robert Wood Johnson Med. Sch., New Brunswick, N.J., 1991—, chief, divsn. neurosurgery, 1991—. Cons. and presenter in field. Contbr. articles to profl. jours., chpts. to books. Rsch. fellow Alberta Heritage Found., 1983-86; Chancellor' scholar McMaster U., 1975, Univ. scholar, 1976, Edwin Marwin Dalley Meml. scholar, 1977; recipient Acad. award Am. Acad. Neurol. Surgery, 1986. Fellow Am. Coll. Surgeons (Resident Rsch. award 1986), Royal Coll. Surgeons Can., Acad. Medicine N.J.; mem. AMA, Am. Assn. Neurol. Surgeons, Can. Neurosurg. Soc., N.J. Neurosurg. Soc., N.Y. Acad. Scis., Middlesex County Med. Soc., Soc. Critical Care Medicine, Congress Neurol. Surgeons, Alpha Omega Alpha. Anglican. Avocations: aircraft/helicopter pilot/instructor, fishing. Office: Divsn Neurosurgery 125 Paterson St Ste 2100 New Brunswick NJ 08901-1962 E-mail: nosko@umdnj.edu.

NOSLER, ROBERT AMOS, sports company executive; b. Ashland, Oreg., Apr. 21, 1946; s. John Amos and Louise (Booz) N.; m. Joan Kathleen Hilliard, July 15, 1967; children: Christie Lynn, Jill Ann, John Robert. Student, U. Oreg., 1965. V.p., gen. mgr. Nosler Bullets, Inc., Bend, Oreg., 1974-88, pres., chief exec. officer, 1988-90; pres., CEO Nosler, Inc., Bend, 1990—. Regional bd. dirs. US Bank. Editor: Nosler Reloading Manual #1, 1976. Bd. dirs. Bend C. of C., 1984-88, treas., 1988; chmn. Central Oreg. Welcome Ctr. Steering Com., 1988. With USN, 1966-70; trustee Ctrl. Oreg. Community Coll. Found., 1992-98; trustee Nat. Rifle Assn. Found., 1997—. Recipient Pres.' award Bend C. of C., 1984, 87, 88. Mem. Nat. Reloading Mfrs. Assn. (bd. dirs. 1982-86, 90-93, pres. 1984-86), Greater Bend Rotary (dir. 1989-91). Republican. Lutheran. Avocations: hunting, outdoors, sports. Office: Nosler Inc 107 SW Columbia St Bend OR 97702-1014

NOSRATINIA, ARIA, engineering educator, researcher; b. Tehran, Iran, June 8, 1965; s. Youssef Nosratinia and Farkhondeh Hashemi-Vaziri; m. Alexandra Jessica Parkin, July 1, 2000. PhD, U. Ill., Urbana-Champaign, 1996. Vis. scholar Princeton (N.J.) U., 1995-96; vis. prof., faculty fellow Rice U., Houston, 1996-99; asst. prof. U. Tex. at Dallas, Richardson, 1999—. Contbr. chpt.: Applied and Computational Control, Signals and Systems; assoc. editor IEEE Transactions on Image Processing; contbr. articles to profl. jours. Recipient Career award NSF, 2000, Advanced Rsch. program award Tex. Higher Edn. Coordinating Bd., 1999. Mem. IEEE Signal Processing Soc. (program chair Dallas chpt. 2000—). Office: U of Tex at Dallas Dept Elec Engring 2601 N Floyd Rd Richardson TX 75080

NOSSAMAN, MARIAN ALECIA, manufacturing engineering executive; b. Kansas City, Mo., Apr. 26, 1961; d. M.A. and Ellen Ardena (Hume) Nossaman; m. Michael Keith Taylor, July 26, 1986 (div.); children: Alecia Ellen, Nathaniel Alexander. AA, Johnson County C.C., 1989; BSME, BS in Bus., U. Kans., 1993. Dental asst. SE Brotherson DDS, Kansas City, Kans., 1983-85; dental instr. Kansas City Coll. of Med. and Dental Careers, Overland Park, 1985-86; math tutor, 1988-91; tech. writer ArComm, Lenexa, Kans., 1991-92; total quality mgmt. rschr. U. Kans., Lawrence, 1992-93; process engr. Symbios Logic Inc., Ft. Collins, Colo., 1993-95; mfg. devel. engr. Hewlett Packard, Loveland, 1995-97, mech. engring. mgr., 1998-99, support engring. sect. mgr., 1999—2001, strategic support program mgr. Roseville, Calif., 2001—02, customer adv., mktg., 2002—; owner Alyse Sagen, Antelope. Sec. Hilltop Child Devel. Ctr., Lawrence, 1991-93. Contbr. articles to profl. jours. Student senator U. Kans. Student Senate, Lawrence, 1992-93; com. mem. Kans. U. Child Care Com., Lawrence, 1991-93, work and family com., 1991-92; mem. libr. bd. City of Loveland, 1999—. Recipient U. Kans. Hilltopper award, 1993. Mem. ASME (treas. 1992-93), Oaks Nontraditional Students Orgn. (pres. 1991-92, treas. 1990-91, editor 1990-92), Tau Beta Pi, Pi Tau Sigma. Avocations: reading, sports events, music, hiking, puzzles. Home: 4705 Majister Ct Antelope CA 95843 Office: Hewlett Packard Loveland Mfg Ctr 815 14th St SW Loveland CO 80537-6330

NOSTRAND, HOWARD LEE, retired humanities educator; b. N.Y.C., Nov. 16, 1910; s. Elijah H. and Ida Josephine (Maeder) N.; m. Frances Anne Levering, June 23, 1933 (div. Aug. 1967); children: David L., Richard L., Robert M.; m. Frances Helen Brewer, Aug. 9, 1967. BA, Amherst Coll., 1932; MA, Harvard U., 1933; D, l'Université de Paris, 1934. Tchr. U. Buffalo, 1934-36, U.S. Naval Acad., 1936-38, Brown U., 1938-39; prof. romance langs. U. Wash., Seattle, 1939-81, chmn. dept., 1939-64, prof. emeritus, 1981—. Vis. prof. Coll. de France, 1975, Simon Fraser U., 1982.; Fulbright lectr., France, 1970-71; Nostrand vs. Balmer, Wash. State loyalty oath annulled by U.S. Supreme Ct., 1964; cons. Am. Coun. on Teaching Fgn. Langs., 1982, chair Nat. Commn. on Ethnography, 1974-80; Am. Assn. of Tchr. of French (pres.1960-62); Nat. Commn. Profl. Stds., 1986-88; mem. Nat. Commn. on Profiency, 1986-93, mem., chair Nat. Commn. on Telematics, 1990-92; co-chair Nat. Commn. on Cultural Competence, 1992-96; mem. Nat. Commn. Student Stds., 1993-95; cons. Ednl. Testing Svc., 1988-90. Author: Le Theatre Antique, 1934, Ortega y Gasset's Mission of the University, 1944, The Cultural Attaché, 1947, Research on Language Teaching...International Bibliography, 1962, 2d edit., 1965, The University and Human Understanding, 1963, Film-Recital of French Poems and Cultural Commentary, 1964, Background Data for the Teaching of French, 1967; (with others) La France en mutation, 1979, Savoir vivre en français, 1988, Databases: Our Third Technical Revolution, 1991, Acquiring Cross-Cultural Competence, 1996; assoc. editor Modern Lang. Quar., 1940-44; contbr. articles to profl. jours. Bd. mem. Seattle Nantes Sister City Assn., 1980-90, pres., 1987-89; bd. mem. U.S. Com. for a Cmty. Democracies, 1983-92, hon. chair, Seattle, 1986-92. Guggenheim fellow, 1953-54; named Order of Sun Peru, 1947, French Govt. Palmes Académiques, 1950, Chevalier, Legion d'Honneur, 1962, Officer, 1994; recipient Pro Lingua award Wash. Assn. Fgn. Lang. Tchrs., 1977, award for leadership N.E. Conf. on Teaching Fgn. Langs., 1978, Nelson Brooks award Am. Coun. Teaching Fgn. Langs., 1980, Outstanding Pub. Svc. award U. Wash. Alumni, 1980, award for vision and leadership Bonjour Seattle Festival, 1979-80, Alliance Française Seattle award, 1990. Mem. Assn. pour la recherche interculturelle (hon.). Democrat. Unitarian Universalist. E-mail: nostrand@u.washington.edu.

NOTA, KENNETH JOSEPH, lawyer; b. Providence, Mar. 9, 1962; s. Albert J. and Jean M. (Lepre) N.; m. Patricia A. Matyia, Sept. 16, 1989; children: Adam Edward, Christopher Paul, Matthew Thomas. BA, R.I. Coll., 1985; JD with honors, U. Conn., 1988. Bar: R.I. 1988, Mass. 1989. Paralegal Roberts, Carroll, Feldstein & Peirce, Providence, 1983-85; assoc. Edwards & Angell, 1988-90; v.p., gen. counsel Dryvit Systems, Inc., West Warwick, 1990—. Mem. R.I. Bar Assn. (continuing legal edn. com.), Mass. Bar Assn. Avocations: golf, softball, wood-working. Office: Dryvit Systems Inc 1 Energy Way West Warwick RI 02893-2322

NOTARBARTOLO, ALBERT, artist; b. N.Y.C., Jan. 12, 1934; m. Valerie Cervelli, June 1, 1962. Student (scholar), Nat. Acad. Fine Arts, 1950; apprentice to mural painter, Ignacio LaRussa, 1951-53. Tchr., 1967—. Represented in permanent collections, Smithsonian Instn., Washington, Mus. Modern Art, N.Y.C.; one-man shows include Hemisphere Gallery of Time-Life Inc., 1973, U. P.R., 1966, David Gavin Gallery, Millerton, N.Y., 1993; exhibited group shows, Tate Gallery, London, 1965, Corcoran Gallery Art, Washington, 1968, Del. Art Mus., Wilmington, 1970, Mus. Modern Art, N.Y.C., 1971, 74, 76, Nat. Gallery Art, Washington, 1976, Smithsonian Instn., Washington, 1976, Santa Barbara (Calif.) Mus. Art, 1976, Taft Mus., Cin., Bell Gallery, Greenwich, Conn., 1977, Huntsville (Ala.) Mus. Art, 1978, Hokin Gallery, Palm Beach, Fla., 1982, Drawing Ctr., N.Y.C., 2001. Served with AUS, 1957-59. Recipient Nat. Community Art Competition award HUD, 1973; U.S. Bicentennial Flag Competition award, A Flag for the Moon, 1976. Mem. Nat. Soc. Lit. and the Arts. Home: 99 Battery Pl Apt 27H New York NY 10280-1329 *When I turned thirteen my Aunt Rosa Pucci gave me a gift— a small packet of reproductions of Raphael's paintings. On the overleaf she inscribed, "Art does affect the lives of men; it moves to ecstasy, thus giving colour and movement to what be otherwise a rather grey and trivial affair." The intonation of this phrase today makes me believe that an act of art echoes on, invoking a continuing music, a vitality for the future while all else turns into the dust of history.*

NOTARI, PAUL CELESTIN, communications executive; b. Chgo., Sept. 8, 1926; s. Peter and Mae Rose (Luvisi) N.; m. Marlene Fineman, Feb. 21, 1969; children: Cathy Notari Davidson, Kenneth, Sharon Notari Christian, Mindy Nielsen, Debbie McGrath. BS in Physics, DePaul U., 1952; MS in Comml. Sci., Rollins Coll., 1968. Mgr. publs. and tng. Motorola Inc., Chgo., 1952-65; supr., publs. engr. Martin Co., Orlando, Fla., 1966-67; dir. comm. Bus. Equipment Mfrs. Assn., N.Y.C., 1967-70; dir. publs., pub. jour. Am. Water Works Assn., Denver, 1971-79; mgr. tech. info. Solar Energy Research Inst., 1979-91; pres. SciTech Comm., Inc., 1992—. Lectr. bus. communications Northwestern U. Served with USNR, 1944-46. Mem. Assn. Computer Programmers and Analysts (founding pres. 1970-73), Soc. Tech. Writers and Pubs. (chmn. chpt. 1965-66), Am. Solar Energy Soc. (nat. chmn. 1990-91). Office: 1000 Monaco Pkwy Ste 77 Denver CO 80220-4649 E-mail: paulnotari@cs.com. *In this complex world we live in, a nation lives or dies by its technological achievements, made possible by a steady flow of information between scientists, engineers, technicians and producers. I believe I have made a significant contribution on this behalf.*

NOTARO, ANTHONY, computer engineer; b. Queens County, NY, Sept. 13, 1956; s. Ignatius and Ida Notaro. AA, Nassau C.C., Garden City, NY, 1976; BS in Computer Sci., Hofstra U., 1978. Data analyst Hofstra U., Hempstead, NY, 1978; programmer Sperry Corp., Great Neck, 1978—80; sys. designer L.I. Lighting Co., Hicksville, 1980—84; sr. sys. analyst Grumman Corp., Bethpage, 1984—85; self-employed cons. West Hempstead, 1985—90; engr. Keyspan Energy Corp., Hicksville, 1990—. Plant engr. Shoreham (NY) Nuclear Power Sta., 1990—94; elec. supervising svc. operator Hewlett (NY) Elec. Ops., 1994—97. Contbr. articles on martial arts to profl. publs. Vol. Fedn. United Martial Arts, NJ, 1986—89, Fedn. Practicing Ju Jitsus, 1982—. Recipient Ismael Quiles award, South Bronx Cmty., 1988. Mem.: IEEE, Assn. Computing Machinery, Amred Forces Comms. Electronics Assn., Am. JuJitsu Assn., U.S. Navy Seals Mus. Assn. (life). Republican. Roman Catholic. Avocation: martial arts. Home: 319 Garfield Ave Hempstead NY 11552 Office: Key Span Energy Corp 175 E Oco Country Rd Hicksville NY 11801

NOTEBAERT, RICHARD C. telecommunications industry executive; b. 1947; married. With Wisconsin Bell, 1969-83; v.p. marketing and operations Ameritech, Chicago, 1983-86; pres. Ameritech Mobile Comm., 1986-89, Indiana Bell Telephone Co., 1989-92, Ameritech Services, 1992-93, pres., COO, 1993-94; chmn., pres., CEO Ameritech Corp., Chicago, 1994—99; pres., CEO Tellabs, 2000—02; chmn., CEO Qwest Commn. Internat. , Denver, 2002—. Office: Qwest Commn Internat 1801 California St Denver CO 80202*

NOTESS, GREG RALPH, librarian; b. Buffalo, Mar. 18, 1962; s. Charles B. Notess and Shirley (Harrington) Neupert; m. Cecelia Marie Zalewski, Oct. 24, 1987; children: Laura Elizabeth, Mary Frances. BM, Univ. Cin., 1983, M in music, 1987; M in librarianship, Univ. Wash., 1990. Seasonal park svc. ranger Glacier Nat. Park, West Glacier, Mont., 1986-90; third horn Lexington (Ky.) Philharmonic Orchestra, 1985-88; reference libr. Montana State Univ. Libr., Bozeman, Mont., 1990—. Writer, speaker, cons. on internet search engines, Bozeman, 1992—. Author: Internet Access Providers: An International Resource Directory, 1994, Government Information on the Internet, 1997, 98, 2000; contbr. articles to profl. jours. Roman Catholic. Avocations: hiking, climbing. Office: Montana State Univ Libr PO Box 173320 Bozeman MT 59717-3320 Fax: 253-390-7391. E-mail: greg@notess.com.

NOTHAFT, FRANK EMILE, economist; b. Jersey City, Apr. 10, 1956; s. Frank Emil and Rita Johanna (Laer) N.; m. Lisa Beth Greenfield, June 13, 1981; children: Frank Austin, Daniel Blake, John Paul. BA, N.Y.U., 1976; MA, Columbia U., 1977, MPhil, 1979, PhD, 1986. Economist Bd. Govs. Fed. Reserve System, Washington, 1983-86; sr. economist Freddie Mac, McLean, Va., 1986-88, dep. chief economist, 1988-90, dir., office of chief economist, 1990—, chief economist, 2001—. Contbr. articles to profl. jours. Sec., bd. dirs. Falls Church Housing Corp., Va., 1988-91. Sloan Found. grantee, 1982; Columbia U. fellow, 1976-79; recipient Founders' Day award, N.Y.U., 1976. Mem. Am. Econ. Assn., Am. Real Estate Urban Econs. Assn. (bd. dirs. 1990-92), Fin. Mgmt. Assn. Office: Freddie Mac 8200 Jones Branch Dr Mc Lean VA 22102-3110

NOTHERN, MARJORIE CAROL, nursing administrator; b. Bonners Ferry, Idaho, June 23, 1936; d. Carl John and Ione Faye (Hobson) Frank; m. Abbott Burton Squire, Dec. 15, 1956 (div. Aug. 1972); m. William Thomas Nothern, Aug. 5, 1972. Diploma, Deaconess Hosp. Sch. Nursing, Spokane, Wash., 1956; BA, Stephens Coll., Columbia, Mo., 1981; MBA, Golden Gate U., San Francisco, 1987. Cert. nursing adminstrn. advanced ANCC. Relief head nurse Deaconess Hosp., Spokane, Wash., 1956-57; staff nurse Kadlec Meth. Hosp., Richland, 1957-58, Southern Pacific Hosp., San Francisco, 1958-59; relief evening supr. The Gen. Hosp., Eureka, Calif., 1959-60; med. office nurse Eley & Davis, 1960-66; head nurse Redbud Cmty. Hosp., Clear Lake, 1968-72, dir. nurses, 1972-77; supr. Hosp. Nursing Kaiser Found. Hosp., Martinez, 1977-78; dir. med. ctr. nursing Kaiser Permanente Med. Ctr., Richmond, 1978-80; asst. hosp. administr. Kaiser Found. Hosp., Hayward, 1980-94; assoc. M2, Inc., San Francisco, 1996—; nurse evaluator II, Calif. Dept. Health Svcs., 1996-99, assoc. govt. program analyst, 2000—. Mem. health sci. adv. commn. Ohlone Coll., Freemont, Calif., 1980—94; mem. med. aux. and nursing adv. com. Chabot Coll., Hayward, 1980—94; mem. Grad. Coll. Nursing adv. bd. San Francisco State U., 1986—96; mem. Calif. State U., Hayward Sch. Sci. Adv. coun., Stephens Coll. Alumnae Bd., 1996—2002. Recipient Leadership award Sigma Theta Tau, Alpha Gamma, San Jose State U., 1990. Mem. ANA-Calif., Calif. Assn. Nurse Leaders, East Bay Assn. Nurse Leaders, Assistance League Diablo Valley, Blackhawk Country Club, Blackhawk Bus. Women, Sigma Theta Tau., Alpha Gamma, Nu Xi. Democrat. Avocations: philately, gardening. Home: 363 Jacaranda Dr Danville CA 94506-2124 E-mail: carolnorthern@yahoo.com.

NOTHWANGER, ROSEMARY WOOD, artist, geological illustrator; b. Marton-in-Cleveland, Yorkshire, Eng., Dec. 1, 1927; came to the U.S., 1958; d. Robert Morgan and Margery Florence (Wood) Raikes; m. Robert C. Nothwanger, Apr. 17, 1952; children: Caroline Ann, Candace Jane. Student, Heatherley's, London, 1951; AA, George Washington U., 1977; BSc in Geomorphology, Md. U., 1980. Illustrator Bell Advt. Agy., Buenos Aires, 1956-58; geol. illustrator Smithsonian Instn., Washington, 1981-88, Geol. Survey, Reston, Va., 1983-88, Woods Hole (Mass.) Oceanog., 1988. Geol. illustrator U.S. State Dept., Washington, 1982. Exhbns. include Air & Space Mus. Smithsonian Inst., 1985, Nat. History Mus., 1985, 87, 92, 95, Ga. Watercolor Soc., 1988-90, Balt. Watercolor Soc. Mid-atlantic Regional, 1988, 90, 92, 96, 97, 98, Wildlife Fedn., 1991-93, Arts for Pks., 1993, Strathmore Hall, Rockville, Md., 1994, 98, 99 (award 1999), So. Watercolor Soc., 1996,

NIH Fed. Res. Bldg., 1997. Artist-in-residence various elem. schs., Montgomery County, Md., 1983. Mem. Assn. Am. Geographers (newsletter editor 1981-84), Guild Natural Sci. Illustrators (jour. editor 1985), Ga. Watercolor Soc. (signature mem., Moore award 1988), Balt. Watercolor Assn. (signature mem.), Washington Watercolor Assn. (mem.-at-large 1987-97), Potomac Valley Watercolorists (mailing com. 1995-97, 1st place in design MD and DC Informational Graphics award 1995-96). Avocations: landscape gardening, interior desiging, hiking, Plein Air painting.

NOTKIN, LEONARD SHELDON, architect; b. N.Y.C., Apr. 1, 1931; s. Murry and Evelyn (Mofshatz) N.; m. Ann Mathilda Stefanko, Nov. 24, 1956; children: Jennifer, Mead. BArch, U. Pa., 1954. Registered architect, N.Y., Mass., Ohio, Pa., Nat. Coun. Archtl. Registration Bds. Architect, Percival Goodman (Architect), N.Y.C., 1956-58; Architect Bloch and Hesse (Architects), 1958-59, Resnick and Green (Architects), N.Y.C., 1959-60; architect, prin., v.p. The Architects Collaborative, Inc., Cambridge, Mass., 1960-95; chief design critic Boston Archtl. Center, 1964-69; mem. Lexington (Mass.) Design Adv. Com., 1970-73, chmn., 1972; profl. studio critic Harvard Grad. Sch. Design, 1974-76; pres. Boston Design Assocs., Inc., Waltham, Mass., 1995—. Major recent works include Intermediate Sch. 137, Bronx, N.Y., 1976, Visual Arts Instructional Facility SUNY, Purchase, 1976, Lahey Clinic Med. Ctr., Burlington, Mass., 1976—, W. Penn Hosp., Pitts., 1977, St. Francis/St. George Hosp., Cin., 1978, Blue Cross/Blue Shield of Conn. Hdqrs., North Haven, Temple U. Hosp., Phila., composite hosp. Loring AFB, Limestone, Maine, Med. Facilities, Fort Drum, N.Y., Health Care Internat. Ltd., Glasgow, Scotland, Intensive Care Hosp. and Hotel, Univ. Ky. Cancer Rsch. Ctr., Children's Hosp. Med. Ctr. Rsch. Lab., Cin., new main entrance, lobby and admissions facilities Hosp. of U. Pa., Phila., Childrens Hosp., Kuwait, 1996, Health Facilities, Algiers, Algeria, 1996, Office Building/Auburn, Mass., Greenfield Comty. Coll., Mass. Served with U.S. Army, 1954-56. Recipient Design award for IBM Hdqrs., Gaithersburg, Md. Progressive Architecture mag., 1964; 1st pl. award for Worcester (Mass.) Community Center AIA, 1966; Design award for Worcester Found. Exptl. Biology bldg. Mass. chpt. AIA, 1968; Design award NIH Research Lab., Bethesda, Md. GSA, 1972; Best Bldg. of Yr. award for Norwalk (Conn.) High Sch. Assn. for Better Community Design, 1972; Honor award Conn. Soc. Architects AIA, 1974 Mem. AIA, Mass. State Assn. Architects, Boston Soc. Architects (dir. 1976-79, spl. design citation 1993). Office: Boston Design Assocs Inc 393 Totten Pond Rd Waltham MA 02451-2003

NOTLEY, THELMA A. retired librarian and educator; b. Ogbomosho, Nigeria, Feb. 7, 1928; came to U.S., 1931; d. John Spurgeon and Della (Black) Richardson; m. Loren Spencer Notley, June 16, 1946 (dec.); children: Dan, Kathleen, R. Steven, Laura. BS in Lang. Arts, Okla. State U., Stillwater, 1961; MS in LS, Okla. U., 1972. Tchr. English, Helena (Okla.) Pub. Schs., 1962-64, Skiatook (Okla.) Pub. Schs., 1964-66, Tulsa Pub. Schs., 1966-67, sch. libr., 1967-86; tchr. ESL Dongbi U. Fin. and Edn., Dalian, China, 1988-90; tchr. English, libr. Anglican Internat. Sch., Jerusalem, Israel, 1994-96. Author: China Bound, 1999; contbr. articles to profl. jours. Republican. Episcopalian. Avocations: writing, quilting, travel. Home: RR 2 Box 1920 Adair OK 74330-9438 E-mail: tnotley@rectec.net.

NOTO, GLEN A. educator; b. N.Y.C., May 18, 1953; s. Joseph A. and Marion N.; m. Mary E. Velez, May 31, 1993; children: Christina Maria, Maria Christiana. BA in History, Glassboro State Coll., 1975; MA in History, Montclair State Coll., 1988. Cert. tchr. social studies, K-12, N.J., N.Y. Tchr. social studies Park Ridge (N.J.) H.S., 1977—, athletic dir., 1985—, coach football, softball, baseball, basketball, wrestling, 1977—. Chmn. disputes and countroversies com. Bergen County Scholastic League, N.J., 1985-97, v.p., 1995-97, pres., 1998-98. Founder New Lisbon Hist. Soc., N.Y., 1999—. Mem.: Bergen County Football Coaches Assn., Bergen County Coaches Assn. (Spl. Svcs. award 2001, Asst. Coach of Yr. 2000), N.Y. State Hist. Soc., Orgn. Am. Historians. Roman Catholic. Avocations: semi-pro baseball player, 1975-99. Home: 197 Merritt Ave Bergenfield NJ 07621 Office: Park Ridge High Sch 2 Park Ave Park Ridge NJ 07656

NOTO, LUCIO A. gas and oil industry executive; b. Apr. 24, 1939; BS in Physics, U. Notre Dame; MBA, Cornell U.; Woodrow Wilson Fell., U. Notre Dame; Bache Fell., Cornell U. With Mobil Corp., 1962—2002; pres. Mobil Saudi Arabia, 1981-85, chmn., 1985-86; v.p. planning and econs. Mobil Corp./Mobil Oil Corp. (now Exxon Mobil Corp.), 1986-88, CFO, 1989-93, pres., 1993—2002, chmn. bd., CEO, COO, 1994-99, vice chmn., 1999-2001; ret. Internat. Business Machines Corp. (dir.), Amer. petroleum Inst. Public Policy Committee, The Business Council, The Council on Foreign Relations & Business Roundtable. Office: Exxon Mobil Corp 5959 Las Colinas Blvd Irving TX 75039-2298

NOTTI, DONNA BETTS, special education educator; b. Manassas, Va., Sept. 4, 1968; d. William Jackson and Christine Joan (Fant) B.; m. David L. Notti, Oct. 14, 1995. BS in Spl. Edn., Old Dominion U., 1990. Tchr., counselor Southeastern Cooperative Ednl. Programs, Norfolk, Va., 1991—; vol. tutor Tonelson Teaching and Learning Ctr., 1989. Mem. Coun. for Exceptional Children (v.p. 1989-90), Coun. for Children With Behavior Disorders, Coun. for Exceptional Children-Mental Retardation, Am. Re-ED Assn. Lutheran. Office: 861 Glenrock Rd Norfolk VA 23502-3720

NOTTINGHAM, EDGAR JAMESON, IV, clinical psychologist; b. Richmond, Va., Nov. 11, 1951; s. Edgar Jameson, III and Anna Sue (Springfield) N.; B.A., Randolph-Macon Coll., 1974; M.S. in Clin. Psychology, Va. Poly. Inst. and State U., 1976, Ph.D., 1979. Diplomate Am. Bd. Profl. Psychology. Approved supr. rational-emotive therapy. Staff psychologist, coordinator treatment, acting dir. forensic unit Southwestern State Hosp., Marion, Va., 1977-78; intern clin. psychology U. Tenn. Center Health Scis., Memphis, 1978-79; clin. psychologist, dir. and coordinator tng. in psychology Memphis Mental Health Inst., 1979-81; cons. psychologist Lakeside Hosp., 1981-86; partner East Memphis Psychol. Assocs., 1979—, Germantown Psychol. Assocs., 1984—; clin. exec. dir. Germantown Psychol. Assocs., 1986-93, dir. psychol. services Parkwood Hosp., 1987-93; clin. asst. prof. U. Tenn. Ctr. Health Scis., 1981—; mem. adj. faculty Memphis State U., 1980—. Fellow Acad. Clin. Psychology; mem. APA, Inst. Advanced Study in Rational Psychotherapy (profl. mem.), Southeastern Psychol. Assn., Tenn. Psychol. Assn., Memphis Area Psychol. Assn., Assn. Advancement in Behavior Therapy, Am. Assn. Marriage and Family Therapy (clin. mem.), Am. Group Psychotherapy Assn. (clin. mem.), Phi Kappa Phi, Psi Chi, Omicron Delta Kappa, Pi Gamma Mu, Sigma Phi Epsilon. Author: It's Not As Bad As It Seems: A Thinking Straight Approach to Happiness; co-author manual; contbr. articles profl. jours. Office: 7516 Enterprise Ave Ste 1 Germantown TN 38138-3802

NOTTINGHAM, EDWARD WILLIS, JR. federal judge; b. Denver, Jan. 9, 1948; s. Edward Willis and Willie Newton (Gullett) N.; m. Cheryl Ann Card, June 6, 1970 (div. Feb. 1981); children: Amelia Charlene, Edward Willis III; m. Janis Ellen Chapman, Aug. 18, 1984 (div. Dec. 1998); 1 child, Spencer Chapman. AB, Cornell U., 1969; JD, U. Colo., 1972. Bar: Colo. 1972, U.S. Dist. Ct. Colo. 1972, U.S. Ct. Appeals (10th cir.) 1973. Law clk. to presiding judge U.S. Dist. Ct. Colo., Denver, 1972-73; assoc. Sherman & Howard, 1973-76, 78-80, ptnr., 1980-87, Beckner & Nottingham, Grand Junction, Colo., 1987-89; asst. U.S. atty. U.S. Dept. Justice, Denver, 1976-78; U.S. dist. judge Dist. of Colo., 1989—. Mem. Jud. Conf. of the U.S. Com. on Automation and Tech., 1994-2000, chmn., 1997-2000. Bd. dirs. Beaver Creek Met. Dist., Avon, Colo., 1980-88, Justice Info. Ctr., Denver, 1985-87, 21st Jud. Dist. Victim Compensation Fund, Grand Junction, Colo., 1987-89. Mem. ABA, Colo. Bar Assn. (chmn. criminal law sect. 1983-85, chmn. ethics com. 1988-89), Order of Coif, Denver Athletic Club, Delta Sigma Rho, Tau Kappa Alpha. Episcopalian. Office: US Dist Ct 1929 Stout St Denver CO 80294-1929 E-mail: Edward_W._Nottingham@cod.uscourts.gov.

NOTTINGHAM, JAMES (LEROY NOTTINGHAM), retired protective services official, professional society administrator; b. Ft. Myers, Fla., Sept. 6, 1937; s. George M. and Josephine E. (Holcomb) N.; m. Bonita Jean Hager, Sept. 2, 1957; children: James Jr., Mark, Dale, Valarie. Student, Fla. State Fire Coll., 1964—, St. Pete Jr. Coll., 1966—. Cert. firefighter, Fla., cert. EMT, cert. real estate agt., ins. salesman, notary; instr., Fla.; security lic.; bus. agt. permit, Fla. Firefighter, engr., capt. Ft. Myers Fire Dept., 1963-94. Negotiator Ft. Myers Firefighters L. 1826, 1971—; instr. Fla. Standard Firefighters, Fla. State, 1973—, mem. and chmn., 1981-94; chmn. MDA, 12th Dist. IAFF, N.C., S.C., Ga., Fla., V.I., 1986—. Mem. Civil Svc. Bd. Ft. Myers City, 1968-71; pres. N. Ft. Myers Little League, 1971-76, N. Ft. Myers Pop Warner, 1973, Peace River Conf., 1974; head coach N. Ft. Myers Babe Ruth 16-18, 85-85, state champions, 1978, 81; fire commr. N. Ft. Myers Fire and Rescue, 1993. Named Firefighter of Yr., City of Ft. Myers, 1992, Fla. State Cabinet and Fla. Profl. Firefighters, 1993; recipient Good Neighbor award TV Sta. 20, NBC, Ft. Myers, 1993. Mem. Nat. Fire Protection Assn., Ft. Myers and S.W. Fla. Profl. Firefighters (pres. 1970—), Fla. Profl. Firefighters (lobbyist 1970—, dist. v.p. 1978—), Masons (32 deg.), Shriners. Democrat. Baptist. Avocations: golf, scuba diving, fishing, RV camping. Home: 53 Victoria Dr Fort Myers FL 33917-4103 Office: SW Fla Profl Firefighters 1601 Lee St Ste 100 Fort Myers FL 33901-2953

NOTTINGHAM, WILLIAM JESSE, retired church mission executive, minister; b. Sharon, Pa., Nov. 22, 1927; s. Jess William and Alice May (Green) Nottingham; m. Patricia Clutts, Feb. 1, 1949; children: Theodore Jess, Deborah Joan Selke, Nancy Alice, Gregory Philip. BA, Bethany Coll., W.Va., 1949, DD (hon.), 1987; BD, Union Theol. Sem., N.Y.C., 1953; PhD, Columbia U., 1962; DD (hon.), Christian Theol. Sem., Indpls., 1984. Ordained to ministry Christian Ch. (Disciples of Christ), 1945. Machinist apprentice Westinghouse, 1943—45; pastor Ch. of Christ, Canoe Camp and Covington, Pa., 1949-50; field worker Ch. of the Master, N.Y.C., 1950-53; assoc. min. Nat. City Christian Ch., Washington, 1954-58; fraternal worker Coun. on Christian Unity, France, 1958-65; with CIMADE and Centre de Glay; with youth dept. World Coun. of Chs., Geneva, 1965-68; exec. sec. for Latin Am. and Caribbean Christian Ch. (Disciples of Christ) and United Ch. Christ, Indpls., 1968-76; exec. sec. East Asia and Pacific Divsn. Overseas Ministries, Christian Ch. (Disciples of Christ), 1976-83; pres., exec. sec. Europe divsn. Overseas Ministries Christian Ch. (Disciples of Christ), Indpls., 1984-94; affiliate prof. mission Christian Theol. Sem., 1995—; ret., 1994. Author: Christian Faith and Secular Action: An Introduction to the Life and Thought of Jacques Maritain, 1968, The Practice and Preaching of Liberation, 1986, The Social Ethics of Martin Bucer 1491-1551, 1962; translator: God's Underground, 1970, Prayer at the Heart of Life, 1975, Materialist Approaches to the Bible, 1985, Madeleine Barot, 1991; contbr. articles to theol. jours. Mem. Ind. Faith and Labor Network. Chaplain USNR, 1954—64. Recipient Eagle Scout award, Boy Scouts Am., 1946, Disting. Alumnus award, Union Theol. Sem., 1999, Fulbright scholarship, Strasbourg, France, 1953—54. Mem.: Disciples Justice Action Network, United Christian Missionary Soc., Am. Maritain Assn., Christians Associated for Rels. with Ea. Europe, Assn. Disciples for Theol. Discussion, Nat. Coun. Chs. of Christ in USA (gen. bd.). Democrat. E-mail: patn@mibor.net., bnottingham@cts.edu.

NOTTO, ROBERT VINCENT, music educator; b. Brooklyn, Ny, Dec. 3, 1953; s. Vincent J. and Marion T. Notto; children: Brynn E. BS Music Edn., Hofstra U., Hempstead, NY, 1978; MS Music, Aaron Copland Sch. of Music, Queens Coll., Queens, NY, 1983. Teacher-band/orch. Baldwin Harbor Elem. Sch., Baldwin, NY, 1978—82, Milburn Elem. Sch., Baldwin, 1978—82, Meadow Elem. Sch., Baldwin, 1980—81, Baldwin H.S., Baldwin, 1978—83, Plz. Elem. Sch., Baldwin, 1981—83; teacher-concert band, marching band, jazz emsemble Baldwin Mid. Sch., 1983—. Mem. Baldwin MS Adv. Com., Baldwin, NY, 1992—, mentor-new teachers, NY, 1999—; union rep. Baldwin Schools, Baldwin, NY, 1999—2000. Recipient Helen Slonim Meml. award, PTA Baldwin Mid. Sch., 1993, Recognition Of Excellence Award, Baldwin Schools, 1995, 96, 97, 99; grantee Music Libr., Baldwin Found. for Edn., 2001. Mem.: NY State United Teachers, Nassau Music Educator Assn., Music Educators Nat. Conf. Home: 8 Meadow Rd Massapequa Park NY 11762

NOTZ, JOHN KRANZ, JR. arbitrator and mediator, retired lawyer; b. Chgo., Jan. 5, 1932; s. John Kranz and Elinor (Trostel) N.; m. Janis Wellin, Apr. 23, 1966; children: Jane Elinor Notz (Mrs. Ian H. Watson), John Wellin. BA, Williams Coll., 1953; JD, Northwestern U., 1956. Bar: Ill. 1956, Fla. 1957, Wis. 1989, U.S. Supreme Ct. 1960. Assoc. 1st Nat. Bank Chgo., 1954, 1956; from assoc. to ptnr. Gardner, Carton & Douglas, Chgo., 1960-95, of counsel, 1990-95; ret., 1996. Arbitrator, mediator Am. Arbitration Assn., Chgo. Internat. Dispute Resolution Assn., NASD Dispute Resolution Inc., Nat. Futures Assn., N.Y. Stock Exch., Am. Stock Exch. Contbr. articles to profl. jours. Sec. State Corp. Acts Adv. Com., 1982-95, chmn., 1987-89; pres. Chgo. Lit. Club, 1996-97, Ill. Inst. Continuing Legal Edn., 1980-91, chmn., 1990-91; bd. dirs., pres. Black Point Historic Preserve, Inc.; trustee Graceland Cemetery; former trustee Beloit Coll. 1st lt. USAF, 1957-60. Recipient Svc. award Northwestern U., 1978 Fellow Am. Bar Found. (life), Ill. Bar Found. (life), Chgo. Bar Found. (life); mem. Am. Law Inst., Ill. State Bar Assn., Chgo. Bar Assn., Wis. State Bar, Lawyers Club City Chgo., Racquet Club Chgo., Lake Geneva (Wis.) Country Club, Mid-Day Club (Chgo.), Literary Club (Chgo.), Caxton Club (Chgo.), The Cliff Dwellers (Chgo.), Soc. of Archtl. Historians (treas.). Office: care Gardner Carton & Douglas 3100 Quaker Tower 321 N Clark St Chicago IL 60610-4795 E-mail: jnotz@gcd.com.

NOUR, BAKR M. surgeon, health facility administrator; s. Mohamed Mahmoud Nour and Fatheya A. Hussein; m. Sohair A. Kheir, Dec. 23, 1976; children: May, Mohamed. MD, U. Alexandria, 1974, M in Surgery, 1978, D in Surgery, 1986. Diplomate Bd. Gen. Surgery, Egypt. Intern U. Alexandria, Egypt, 1975-76, resident in gen. & pediatric surgery Egypt, 1976-79, instr. surgery Egypt, 1979, asst. lectr. pediatric surgery Egypt, 1979-82, sr. asst. lectr. pediatric surgery Egypt, 1984-86, asst. prof. pediatric surgery Egypt, 1987-89; clin./rsch. fellow, vis. asst. prof. surgery dept. pediatric surgery U. Pitts. Med. Ctr., Children's Hosp. Pitts., 1982-84, 90; clin. fellow U. Pitts. Med. Ctr., Transplantation Inst., 1990-92, asst. prof. surgery, 1992-94; chief pediatric liver transplantation, adult liver transplant surgeon Okla. Transplantation Inst., Bapt. Med. Ctr., Oklahoma City, 1994-97; chief abdominal transplantation Okla. Transplantation Inst., Integris Bapt. Med. Ctr., 1997-98, dir. abdominal organ transplant divsn., 1998-99, interim dir., 1999-2000, dir., chmn., 2000—. Past mem. staff Presbyn. U. Hosp. Pitts., Montefiore Hosp., Pitts.; mem. human rights com. Children's Hosp. Pitts., 1993-94; mem. libr. com. Bapt. Med. Ctr. Okla. Contbr. articles to profl. jours. Founding mem. Innocent Childhood Benevolent Charity Assn., Alexandria; mem Islamic Charity Assn. Recipient World Cmty. award Results, 1998. Mem. AMA, ACS, Arab Am. Med. Assn., Am. Coll. Physician Execs., Am. Assn. Study of Liver Disease, Am. Soc. Transplant Surgeons, Egyptian Physician's Syndicate, Egyptian Med. Assn., Egyptian Soc. Surgeons, Egyptian Assn. Pediatric Surgeons, Alexandria Med. Assn., Brit. Assn. Pediatric Surgeons, Okla. State Med. Assn., Okla. County Med. Soc., Internat. Coll. Surgeons, Internat. Gastro-Surg. Club, Internat. Liver Transplantation Soc., Tex. Transplant Soc., Soc. Surgery Alimentary Tract, Alexandria Sporting Club, Oklahoma City Golf and Country Club. Moslem. Achievements include research in cell model to study bacterial translocation in transplanted small bowel, FK506 as immunosuppressive agent, small bowel transplantation, causes of anemia in transplant patients, Alpha interferon therapy, for viral hepatitis. Home: 14409 Rosebay Pl Oklahoma City OK 73142 Office: Okla Transplantation Inst Nazih Zuhdi 3300 NW Expressway Oklahoma City OK 73112-4418 E-mail: NourBM@Integris-Health.com.

NOURI, KEYVAN, dermatologic surgeon; b. Tehran, Iran, Sept. 21, 1967; s. Ali and Zohreh (Khajavi) N. MD summa cum laude with distinction, Boston U., 1993. Diplomate Nat. Bd. Med. Examiners. Dir. mohs, dermatol. and laser surgery Sch. Medicine U. Miami, Fla., 1999—, dir. surg. tng., asst. prof. dermatol. and cutaneous surgery, 1999—. Editor Internat. Jour. Dermatology, 2002; contbg. editor Dermatologic Surgery Jour., 1999—; contbr. articles to profl. pubs., including Jour. Am. Acad. Gaumont Skin Cancer Found. scholar Skin Cancer Found., 1997. Fellow Am. Acad. Dermatology (European Acad. Dermatology scholar 1999, 19th World Congress Dermatology scholar 1997); Am. Soc. Laser Medicine and Surgery, Internat. Soc. Dermatologic Surgery; mem. AMA (liaison Boston U. chpt. 1990-91), Am. Coll. Mohs Micrographic Surgery and Cutaneous Oncology, Primary Care Soc. (so-task force leader for family practice 1989-91), Soc. Investigative Dermatology (Kligman fellow 996), Mass. Med. Soc. (liaison Boston U. chpt. 1990-91), Golden Key, Phi Beta Kappa, Phi Beta Delta (v.p. 1989-92), Phi Delta Epsilon (pres. 1990-91). Avocations: travel, art, music, swimming, tennis. Office: Univ Miami Sch Medicine 1475 NW 12th Ave Ste 2175 Miami FL 33136 Fax: 305-243-4184. E-mail: KNouri@med.miami.edu.

NOVA, CRAIG, writer; b. Los Angeles, July 5, 1945; s. Karl and Elizabeth (Sinclair) N.; m. Christina Barnes, July 2, 1977; children: Abigail, Tate. BA, U. Calif.-Berkeley, 1967; M.F.A., Columbia U., 1969. Author: Turkey Hash, 1972, The Geek, 1975, Incandescence, 1978, The Good Son, 1982, The Congressman's Daughter, 1986, Tornado Alley, 1989, Trombone, 1992, The Book of Dreams, 1994, The Universal Door, 1997, Brook Trout and the Writing life, 1999, Wetware, 2001. Recipient Harper-Saxton prize Harper and Row, Pubs., 1972; recipient award in lit. Am. Acad. and Inst. Arts and Letters; Guggenheim Found. fellow, 1977; fellow Nat. Endowment for Arts, 1973, Nat. Endowment for Arts, 1975, Creative Artists Pub. Service, 1976; NEA fellow, 1985; story included in Best Am. Short Stories, 1987.

NOVACK, ALVIN JOHN, physician; b. Red Lodge, Mont., Mar. 11, 1925; s. John and Anna Geraldine (Maddio) N.; m. Betty P. Novack, Jan. 10, 1952; children— Vance, Deborah, Michelle, Mitchel, Craig, Brad, Mary Ellen, Garth. MD, U. Wash., 1952. Intern Harper Hosp., Detroit, 1952, resident in surgery, 1953; resident in otolaryngology Johns Hopkins U., 1954-57; resident in surgery Columbia-Presbyn. Med. Center, N.Y.C., 1957-60, fellow head and neck surgery, 1957-60; dir. head and neck surgery Swedish Hosp., Seattle, 1960-91; dir. otolaryngology Children's Orthopedic Hosp., 1965-78; ret., 1991. Contbr. articles to med. jours. Served to lt. AUS, 1940-43. Nat. Cancer Inst. fellow, 1957-60 Fellow A.C.S.; mem. AMA, Am. Acad. Otolaryngology and Head and Neck Surgery, Soc. Head and Neck Surgeons, North Pacific Surg. Assn., Pacific Coast Surg. Assn., Seattle Surg. Soc.

NOVACK, SANDY ALISSA, social worker; b. Springfield, Mass., May 6, 1958; d. Joseph and Naomi Samuella Novack. Student, Brandeis U., 1976-78; BA, Tufts U., 1980; MSW, Boston U., 1982; MBA, Northeastern U., 1986. Lic. ind. clin. social worker, Mass. Fin. analyst Burroughs Corp., Woburn, Mass., 1985; dir. tenant assistance Jewish Cmty. Housing for the Elderly, Brighton, 1986—2002. Adv. bd. Commn. on Affairs of the Elder, Boston City Hall, 1993—; mem. Com. for the Study and Prevention of Violence Against Social Workers, Boston, 1995—; chairperson bus. devel. com. Social Work Symposia, Boston, 1998—; tel. counselor Ceridian Performance Ptnrs., Boston, 1998-99; cons. Social Work Bd. Dirs. Fin. Com., 2000-2002. Editor: Nine Quills and a Red Pencil, 1989. Alumni interviewer Tufts U., Medford, Mass., 1988—. Recipient Pioneer citation Citizens' Housing and Planning Assn., Mass., 1995, Best Practices in Health Promotion and Aging award Health Promotion Inst., Nat. Coun. on Aging, 1999, Golden Trowel Merit award Garden Design Mag., 2000. Mem. NASW (treas. Mass. chpt. 2002—), Acad. Cert. Social Workers.

NOVACK, TEVOR D. surgeon, consultant; b. Boston, Sept. 6, 1928; MD, Harvard Med. Sch., 1954. Diplomate Am. Bd. Surgery. Intern Beth Israel Hosp., Boston, 1954-55; resident in surgery Beth Isreal Hosp., 1955-56; resident in gen. surgery Letterman Gen. Hosp., San Francisco, 1957-59; resident in thoracic surgery Walter Reed Gen. Hosp., Washington, 1966-68; staff Meth. Hosps., Gary and Merrillville, Ind., St. Anthony Med. Ctr., Crown Point; med. dir. Gary works U.S. Steel, 1979-94; cons. in occupl. medicine, 1995—; clin. asst. prof. surgery N.W. Ctr. for Med. Edn., Ind. U. Med. Sch., 1982—. Col. U.S. Army, 1956-79. Fellow Am. Coll. Surgeons, Am. Coll. Occupl. and Environ. Medicine; mem. AMA.

NOVAK, ALAN LEE, retired pharmaceutical company executive; b. Chgo., Oct. 25, 1928; s. Samuel Adolph and Tina Lillian (Oris) N.; m. Delores Jane Tonkel, Dec. 17, 1950; children: Shaya Ray, G. Alexander, Cheryl Lynn. BS, Fla. So. Coll., 1951. Cert. purchasing mgr. Police officer Lakeland (Fla.) Police Dept., 1952-53; sales rep. Sinclair Refining Co., Tampa, Fla., 1954-58; prin. Novak's Texaco s/s and Fuel Co., 1958-62; sales rep. Burroughs Wellcome Co., Columbus, Ohio, 1962-70, purchasing agt. Research Triangle Park, N.C., 1970-74, dir. purchasing, 1974-94. Bd. dirs. Eastern N.C. Better Bus. Bur., 1989-96. Mem. N.C. Coun. on the Holocaust, 1996—; vol. Friends Helping Friends Vet. Sch., N.C. State U., 1994—; records dept. Raleigh Polic Dept., 1994—; mem. area contact Am. Israel Polit. Affairs Coun., Raleigh, 1984—86; fin. sec. Temple Beth Or, 1975—77, treas., 1996—97; pres. Raleigh Chpt. B'nai B'rith, 1999—2000. With U.S. Army, 1946—47, Japan. Mem. Am. Legion Jewish War Vets. 1st Cav. Divsn. Assn., Drug, Chem., and Allied Trades Assn. (area rep. 1975-78, bd. dirs. 1978-84, treas. 1985, v.p. 1986, pres. 1987-88), Nat. Assn. Purchasing Mgmt., Purchasing Mgmt. Assn. Carolinas-Va., Triangle Purchasing Assn., Raleigh C. of C., Burroughs Wellcome Retirees Club (pres.), Tau Kappa Epsilon, Omicron Delta Kappa. Lodges: B'nai B'rith (Double Chai award 1985-87), AMRAN Shrine Temple (charter). Republican. Jewish. Avocations: hunting, fishing. E-mail: zayden@intrex.net.

NOVAK, ALAN P. political organization administrator; Chair Pa. State Rep. Party, Harrisburg, 1996—. Office: 112 State St Harrisburg PA 17101-1024*

NOVAK, BARBARA, art history educator; b. N.Y.C. d. Joseph and Sadie (Kaufman) N.; m. Brian O'Doherty, July 5, 1960. BA, Barnard Coll., 1951; MA, Radcliffe Coll., 1953, PhD, 1957. TV instr. Mus. Fine Arts, Boston, 1957-58; mem. faculty Barnard Coll., Columbia U., N.Y.C., 1958-98, prof. art history, 1970—, Helen G. Altschul prof., 1984-98, prof. emeritus, 1998—. Adv. council Archives of Am. Art, NAD Author: American Painting of the 19th Century, 1969, Nature and Culture, 1980, rev. edit., 1995, The Thyssen-Bornemisza Collection 19th Century American Painting, 1986, Alice's Neck, 1987, The Ape and the Whale, 1995, (play) The Ape and the Whale: Darwin and Melville in Their Own Words, 1987 (performed at Symphony Space 1987), Dreams and Shadows: Thomas H. Hotchkiss in 19th Century Italy, 1993; co-editor: Next to Nature, 1980; mem. editorial bd. Am. Art Jour. Chair commn. Nat. Portrait Gallery. Fulbright fellow Belgium, 1953-54; Guggenheim fellow, 1974; Nat. Book Critics nominee, 1980; L.A. Times Book Award nominee, 1980; Am. Book Award paperback nominee, 1981; recipient disting. tchg. award Coll. Art Assn., 1997, Lawrence Fleishman award for outstanding scholarship Archives Am. Art, 1999, medal of distinction, Barnard Coll., 2002. Fellow Soc. Am. Historians, Phila. Atheneum; mem. Soc. Am. Historians, Am. Antiquarian Soc., Coll. Art Assn. (dir. 1974-77, Disting. Tchg. of Art History award 1997), PEN.

NOVAK, DAVID, Judaic studies educator, rabbi; b. Chgo., Aug. 19, 1941; s. Syd and Sylvia (Wien) N.; m. Melva Ziman, July 3, 1963; children: Marianne, Jacob George. AB in Classics and Ancient History, U. Chgo., 1961; M in Hebrew Lit., Jewish Theol. Sem. Am., 1964; PhD, Georgetown U., 1971. Ordained rabbi, 1966. Rabbi Shaare Tikvah Congregation, 1966-69; dir. Jewish chaplaincy St. Elizabeth's Hosp., 1966-69; rabbi Emanuel Synagogue, Oklahoma City, 1969-72, Beth Tfiloh Congregation, Balt., 1972-77, Congregation Beth El, Norfolk, Va., 1977-81, Congregation Darchay Noam, Far Rockaway, N.Y., 1981-89; Edgar M. Bronfman prof. modern Judaic studies U. Va., Charlottesville, 1989-97; J. Richard and Dorothy Shiff chair of Jewish studies U. Toronto, 1997—. Lectr. philosophy Oklahoma City U., 1969-72, New Sch. for Social Rsch., 1982-84; lectr. Jewish studies Balt. Hebrew Coll., 1972-77; adj. asst. prof. philosophy Old Dominion U., 1977-81; vis. assoc. prof. Talmud Jewish Theol. Sem. Am., 1986-88; adj. assoc. prof. Baruch Coll., CUNY, 1984-88, adj. prof., 1989; founder, v.p., coord. panel Halakhic Inquiry Union Traditional Judaism/Inst. Traditional Judaism; disting. vis. prof. religion and corp. ethics Drew U., 1995; Yarnton/Lancaster lectr. Oxford U., 1996. Contbg. editor First Things. Sec.-treas. Inst. on Religion and Pub. Life. Essay winner Hyman G. Enelow prize Jewish Theol. Sem. Am., 1975; recipient Rabbi Jacob B. Augus award Jewish Theol. Sem. Am., 1984; Woodrow Wilson Internat. Ctr. for Scholars fellow, 1992-93. Fellow Acad. for Jewish Philosophy, Am. Acad. for Jewish Rsch.; mem. Am. Theol. Soc., Assn. for Jewish Studies, Am. Acad. Religion, Jewish Law Assn., Am. Acad. for Jewish Rsch. Office: Univ Coll 15 King's College Cir Toronto ON Canada M5S 3H7

NOVAK, DAVID C. restaurant company executive; Formerly with PepsiCo., Kentucky Fried Chicken, Pizza Hut, 1977-97; vice-chmn., pres. Tricon Global Restaurants, Inc., Louisville, 1997-2000, CEO, chmn., 2000—. Office: Tricon Global Restaurants 1441 Gardiner Ln Louisville KY 40213-1914*

NOVAK, DENNIS E. family practice physician; b. East Liverpool, Ohio, Jan. 5, 1946; BA, Bklyn. Coll., 1966; Lic. in Med. Scis., U. Brussels, 1972; MD, Rutgers U., 1974. Diplomate Am. Bd. Family Practice, Nat. Bd. Med. Examiners. Resident in family practice Monmouth Med. Ctr., Long Branch, N.J., 1974-77; clin. instr. to clin. asst. prof. Robert Wood Johnson Med. Sch.,

1977—; chmn. dept. family practice, mem. med. exec. com. Cmty. Med. Ctr., 1990—; pvt. practice specializing in family medicine, 1977-96; group practice, exec. com. Cmty. Health Assocs. of St. Barnabas Health Care Sys., 1996-2000; pvt. practice, 2001—. Attending physician utilization rev. com. Cmty. Meml. Hosp., 1987-88, quality assurance com., 1988, dept. family practice quality assurance com.; physician reviewer, quality assurance Health-South Rehab. Hosp. Mem. exec. adv. bd. Ocean County coun. Boy Scouts Am., asst. scoutmaster Ocean Coun., 1997-2002, com. chair Troop 165, 2000—; trustee United Way Ocean County., Area VII Physician Rev. Org., 1983-86. Named to list of top doctors in N.Y. Metro. Area, Castle-Connolly, one of Top Docs in N.J. Fellow Am. Acad. Family Practice; mem. Ocean County Acad. Family Practice (v.p. 1983), Ocean County Med. Soc. (bd. trustees 1983-87). Avocations: photography, scuba, guitar. Address: PO Box 780 1001 Lacey Rd Forked River NJ 08731-1042

NOVAK, GORDON S., JR. computer scientist, educator; b. Colo., 1947; m. Susan Raye Strawn, May 7, 1977; children: Genevieve, Courtney. BSEE, U. Tex., 1969, MA in Computer Sci., 1971, PhD in Computer Sci., 1976. Mgr. sys. programming Tracor Inc., Austin, Tex., 1966-76; instr. U. Tex., 1976-77, asst. prof., 1978-81, 83-84, assoc. prof., 1984-98; prof., 1998—; dir. Artificial Intelligence Lab. U. Tex., Austin, 1984-99; computer sci. SRI Internat., Menlo Park, Calif., 1977-78. Vis. asst. prof. Stanford (Calif.) U., 1981-83. Contbr. articles to profl. jours. Office: U Tex Dept Computer Sci Austin TX 78712

NOVAK, GREGORY, marketing professional; b. Johnstown, Pa., Oct. 19, 1949; s. Eugene F. and Joan (Tross) N.; m. Naomi Sosia Wall; children: Rebecca, Jeffrey, Jacqueline. BA, U. Vt., 1971. Project dir. Dun & Bradstreet, N.Y.C., 1973-74; sr. analyst Colgate Palmolive, 1974-76; mgr. brand rsch. R.J. Reynolds, Winston-Salem, N.C., 1976-77, mgr. group new brand rsch., 1977-80, dir. new bus., 1980-81, dir. group mktg., 1981-84; nat. dir. mktg. Deloitte Haskins & Sells, N.Y.C., 1984-90; pres. Novak Mktg. Inc., 1990—. Office: Novak Mktg Inc 29 Brandon Dr Mount Kisco NY 10549-3720 E-mail: NovMkt@aol.com.

NOVAK, HARRY R. investment banking executive; b. Chgo., Sept. 30, 1951; s. Edward M. and Rose (Loncar) N.; m. Shawn Sternquist, Sept. 7, 1975; children: Andrea, Jacob, Bethany. BS in Econs., MacMurray Coll., Jacksonville, Ill., 1973; MBA in Fin., DePaul U., 1977. Ops. mgr. to v.p., regional mgr. Heller Fin. Inc., Chgo., 1974-87; v.p. Golenberg & Assocs., Cleve., 1987-88; from sr. v.p., CFO to pres., COO Gibson-Homans Co., Twinsburg, Ohio, 1988-2000; exec. v.p. Laux & Co., Medina, 2000—. Congregation pres. First Luth. Ch., Strongsville, Ohio, 1987-92; founder Strongsville Area Youth Group, 1992; mem. Strongsville Choral Boosters, 1991-99. Mem. Cleve. Growth Assn., Sr. Exec. Network. Avocations: chess, golf, pocket billards, computers. Office: Laux & Co 672 W Liberty St Medina OH 44256-2285 E-mail: hnovak@lauxco.com.

NOVAK, JO-ANN STOUT, chemical engineer; b. Glen Ridge, N.J., June 25, 1956; d. Herbert Austin and Anna (Messina) Stout; m. John Robert Novak Jr., Oct. 30, 1976. B in Chem. Engring., Ga. Inst. Tech., 1977; MBA, Oakland U., 1984. Cert. engr.-in-tng., Ga.; registered profl. engr., Mich. Trainee AC Spark Plug divsn. GM, Flint, Mich., 1977-78, chemist, 1978-79, exptl. chemist, 1979-81, mfg. engr., 1981-84, sr. mfg. engr., 1984-87; sr. mfg. project engr., 1987-89; mgr. bus. and engring. processes, 1989-90; program planning mgr., 1990-92; supr. engring.-info. and sys., 1992-94; staff engr. chem. and metall. processes, 1994—; advanced mfg. engr., 2001—. Mem. AIChE, NSPE, Am. Electroplaters Soc. (dir. Saginaw Valley br. 1981-83, ednl. chmn. 1984-85, sec.-treas. 1984-86, 2d v.p. 1986-87, 1st v.p. 1987-88, pres. 1988-89), Soc. Mfg. Engrs., Engring. Soc. Detroit. Office: Delphi Auto Sys 1300 N Dort Hwy Flint MI 48506-3956

NOVAK, JOE, artist; b. Springfield, Mass., Oct. 15, 1930; s. Benjamin D. and Mae (Lavitt) N. BA, Dartmouth Coll., 1952; JD, Harvard U., 1955. Solo exhbns. include Vered Gallery, East Hampton, N.Y., 1985, 87, 88, Milari Ltd., N.Y.C., 1989, Light Emanations, Tesuque, N.Mex., 1992, The Bank of Santa Fe, 1996, Davidson & Daughters, Portland, Maine, 1997, McKesson Plz., San Francisco, 1998, Sirius Art Gallery, Santa Fe, 2000, Circle Elephant Art, L.A., 2001, Evo Gallery, Santa Fe, 200-02, Hood Mus. Art, Dartmouth Coll., 2002; exhibited in group shows at Parrish Art Mus., Southampton, N.Y., Guild Hall Mus., Vered Gallery, Milari, Ltd., Olaf Clasen Gallery, Cologne, Germany, Lewallen Gallery, Santa Fe, Circle Elephant Art, L.A., Anderson Contemporary Art, Santa Fe, numerous others; works in pub. collections include Boston Mus. Fine Arts, Guild Hall Mus., U. Tex.-Pan Am., Mus. Fine Arts, Santa Fe, Mus. Art, Ft. Lauderdale, Fla., Hood Mus. Art, Dartmouth Coll., U. Calif.-Berkeley Art Mus., Art Mus. Fla. Internat. U., Miami; subject of articles. Lt. USN, 1955-58. Recipient awards for art. Home: PO Box 393 Tesuque NM 87574-0393 E-mail: Kiva1@ix.netcom.com.

NOVAK, JOHN ALFRED, mechanical engineer; b. Pitts., Jan. 26, 1954; s. Alfred John and Rita Rose N.; m. Mary Elizabeth Oliverio, Aug. 8, 1979; 1 child, Melody Joy. AS in Gen. Studies, C.C. Pitts., Pitts., 1975; AS in Indsl. Design and Art Tech., Community Coll., Pitts., 1978; BS, Point Pk. Coll., Pitts., 1984. Registered profl. engr., Pa. Draftsmen trainee Heppenstall, Pitts., 1978-79; product drafsman Mesta Machine, West Homestead, Pa., 1979-83; designer Sun Industries, Pitts., 1983-85; devel. engr. J.D. Hollingsworth, Greenville, S.C., 1985-87; chief engr. Blaw Knox, Pitts., 1987-93; design engr., chief engr. Voest Alpine, 1993—. Author: (computer programs) Grip Force, 1984, Center of Gravity C-Hook, 1985, Balance C-Hook, 1985, Double Pivot Tong, 1985. 3rd class petty officer USN, 1975-77, Norfolk. Mem. NSPE, ASME, DAV. Republican. Presbyterian. Avocations: computer programming, gardening, volunteer for church functions. E-mail: jnovak6204@aol.com.

NOVAK, JOSEPH ANTHONY, law librarian; b. Detroit; s. Thomas Paul and Mary Cecilia N. AA, Macomb C.C., Warren, Mich., 1984; BA, Oakland U., 1986; JD, Mich. State U., 1991; M Libr. and Info. Sci., Wayne State U., 1998. Intern Wayne County Pub. Defender's Office, Detroit, 1986; intern Office of Jud. Assistance 3d Jud. Cir. Ct. Mich., 1993, law clk. to Hon. Diane M. Hathaway, intern, 1996; law libr. St. Louis Correctional Facility, 2000—01, Mid-Mich. Correctional Facility, 2001—. Vol., Vol. Income Tax Assistance Program, Detroit, 1995-2001. Recipient Outstanding Vol. Volunteer Income Tax Assistance Program, 1995, 96, 98, 99, 2000, The Spirit of Am. Is In the Heart of Its Volunteers IRS, 1995, 96, 97, 99. Mem. Am. Assn. Law Librs., Spl. Librs. Assn., Acctg. Aid Soc., Coun. of State Agy. Librs., Mich. Corrections Assn. Democrat. Roman Catholic. Avocations: coin and stamp collecting, water skiing, walking. Home and Office: PO Box 12 Saint Louis MI 48880-0012

NOVAK, JOSEPH ANTHONY, physician, pathologist; b. Cleve., Mar. 20, 1960; s. Joseph Zvonimir and Sally Ann N.; m. Marjeta Zobec Novak, Aug. 5, 1989; children: Ana, Katarina. BS, Ohio State U., 1981; MD, U. Ljubljana, Slovenia, 1990. Diplomate Am. Bd. Pathology, Am. Bd. Anatomic Pathology, Am. Bd. Clin. Pathology, Am. Bd. Cytopathology. Resident Mt. Sinai Med. Ctr., Cleve., 1991-96; fellow U. Fla., Jacksonville, 1996-97; asst. prof. Med. Coll. Wis., Milw., 1997—. Dir. dept. lab. medicine Columbia Hosp., 2000—; med. dir. sect. microbiology Columbia Hosp., Milw., 1997—, mem. infection control com., 1997—. Contbr. articles to profl. jours. Fellow Coll. Am. Pathologists; mem. Soc. Slovene Studies. Home: 4901 N Newhall St Whitefish Bay WI 53217-6049 Office: Columbia Hosp Dept Labs 2025 E Newport Ave Milwaukee WI 53211-2990

NOVAK, JOSEPH DONALD, science educator, knowledge studies specialist; b. Mpls., Dec. 2, 1930; s. Joseph Daniel and Anna (Podany) N.; m. Joan Owen, July 18, 1953; children: Joseph Mark, Barbara Joan, William John BS, U. Minn., 1952, MA, 1954, PhD, 1958; Doctorate (hon.) , U. Comanhue, Neuquen, Argentina, 1998, Pub. U. Navarra, 2002. Teaching asst. U. Minn., Mpls., 1952-56, instr., 1956-57; asst. prof. Kans. State Tchrs. Coll., 1957-59, Purdue U., West Lafayette, Ind., 1959-62, assoc. prof., 1962-67; prof. Cornell U., Ithaca, N.Y., 1967-95, prof. emeritus, 1995—; pres. Joseph D. Novak Knowledge Consultants, Inc.; sr. rsch. scientist U. West Fla. Knowledge constrn. and orgn. cons. to Procter & Gamble and other cos.; cons. to over 400 schs. and colls., 1975—; vis. fellow Harvard U., 1965-66; disting. vis. prof. U. N.C., Wilmington, 1980, U. Western Fla., 1987-88, vis. sr. rsch. scientist, 1996—; vis. prof. U. South Fla., 1995. Author: Learning How to Learn, 1984, in 10 langs. 1984-96, Educational Psychology: A Cognitive View, 1978, A Theory of Education, 1977, Aprendizaje Significativo: Techieas y Aplicaciones, 1997, Learning, Creating, and Using Knowledge: Concept Maps as Facilitative Tools for Schools and Corporations, 1998, Teaching Science for Understanding, 1998, Assessing Science Understanding, 2000, Una aportacion a la mejora de la calidad de la docentia universitaria: Los mapas Conceptuales, 2000, Errores Conceptuales: Diagnosis, Tratamientoy Reflexiones, 2001, 15 others; contbr. over 100 articles to profl. jours. Fellow Tozer Found., Lydia Anderson, 1955-56; research assoc. Harvard U., 1965-66; Fulbright-Hayes Sr. Scholar, Australia, 1980 Fellow AAAS (sec. sect. Q); mem. NSTA, Nat. Assn. Rsch. in Sci. Tchr. (Outstanding Contbns. Sci. Tchg. Through Rsch. award 1990), Nat. Assn. Biology Tchrs. (hon.), Assn. for Edn. of Tchrs. of Sci., Am. Ednl. Rsch. Assn., Coun. Sci. Soc. Pres.'s (1st hon. award for rsch. in sci. edn. 1998), Sigma Xi. Avocations: hiking, swimming, dancing, music. Home: 90 Highland Ave S Club 3 Unit 302 Tarpon Springs FL 34689 Office: Cornell U Dept Edn Kennedy Hall Ithaca NY 14853 Home (Summer): 77 Alcott Cir Taunton MA 02780-1056 E-mail: jdn2@cornell.edu.

NOVAK, KIM (MARILYN NOVAK), actress; b. Chgo., Feb. 13, 1933; d. Joseph A. and Blanche (Kral) N.; m. Richard Johnson, April 1965 (div.); m. Robert Malloy, Jan. 1977. Student, Wright Jr. College, Chgo.; AA, Los Angeles City College, 1958. Appeared in: (films) The French Line, 1953, Pushover, 1954, Phffft, 1954, Five Against the House, 1955, Son of Sinbad, 1955, Picnic, 1955, The Man with the Golden Arm, 1956, The Eddie Duchin Story, 1956, Jeanne Eagles, 1957, Pal Joey, 1958, Vertigo, 1958, Bell, Book and Candle, 1958, Middle of the Night, 1959, Strangers When We Meet, 1960, Pépé, 1960, Boys' Night Out, 1962, The Notorious Landlady, 1962, Of Human Bondage, 1964, Kiss Me Stupid, 1964, The Amorous Adventures of Moll Flanders, 1965, The Legend of Lylah Clare, 1968, The Great Bank Robbery, 1969, Tales That Witness Madness, 1973, The White Buffalo, 1977, Just a Gigolo, 1979, The Mirror Crack'd, 1980, The Children, 1990, Liebestraum, 1991; (TV movies) Third Girl from the Left, 1974, Satan's Triangle, 1975, Malibu, 1983; (TV series) Falcon Crest, 1986-87, Alfred Hitchcock Presents, 1985, Liebestraum, 1989. Named one of 10 most popular movie stars by Box-Office mag. 1956, All-Am. Favorite 1961, Brussels World Fair poll as favorite all-time actress in world 1958. Office: William Morris Agency care Norman Brokaw 151 S El Camino Dr Beverly Hills CA 90212-2775

NOVAK, LAURA J. secondary school educator; b. Bismarck, N.D., Apr. 7, 1969; d. John and Ann (Hruby) N. BA in English Edn., N.D. State U., 1991; MEd in Ednl. Adminstrn., U. N.D., 1998. Cert. tchr., N.D., secondary principal, N.D. English educator Simle Jr. H.S., Bismarck, 1991-93; English tchr. Mandan (N.D.) H.S., 1991—, French tchr., 1992-96, chair English dept., 1996—, dir. alternative edn., 1998—. Mem. faculty adv. com. Mandan H.S., 1996—, adminstrv. intern, 1997—; adj. faculty English Bismarck State Coll., 2000-. Mem. NEA, N.D. Edn. Assn., Mandan Edn. Assn., Phi Delta Kappa (rsch. rep. 1996-98, treas. 1998—), Delta Kappa Gamma. Avocations: travel, reading, tennis. Office: Mandan HS 905 8th Ave NW Mandan ND 58554-2457

NOVAK, MARK, lawyer; b. Buffalo, Jan. 28, 1952; s. Eugene Francis and Joan (Tross) N.; m. Charlene Mary Ingoglia, Sept. 2, 1972; children: Jason Charles, Jennifer Rose. BA, U. Rochester, 1974; JD, Loyola U., Chgo., 1977. Bar: Ill. 1977, U.S. Dist. Ct. (no. dist.) Ill. 1977, U.S. Ct. Appeals (7th cir.) 1978. Assoc. Anesi, Ozmon & Lewin, Ltd., Chgo., 1977-83; ptnr. Anesi, Ozmon, Rodin, Novak & Kohen, Ltd., 1983—. Fundraiser Christmas is for Kids Charity, Chgo., 1992—. Mem. ATLA (product liability sect. 1985—), ABA, Ill. Trial Lawyers Assn., Trial Lawyers for Pub. Justice, Chgo. Bar Assn. (jud. evaluation com. 1995—). Avocations: painting, gardening, traveling. Home: 1212 N Lake Shore Dr Chicago IL 60610-2371 Office: Anesi Ozmon Rodin Novak & Kohen Ltd 161 N Clark St Fl 21 Chicago IL 60601-3206

NOVAK, MARLENA, artist, educator, writer, curator; b. Brownsville, Pa., Mar. 6, 1957; d. Anthony Edward and Mary Margaret (Shader) N.; m. Jay Alan Yim, June 28, 1990. BFA in Painting, Carnegie-Mellon U., 1982; MFA in Art Theory and Practice (Painting), Northwestern U., 1986. Tchr. art, Northwestern U., Evanston, Ill., 1985, 89, 96-00, De Paul U., Chgo., 1986-92, 94, 96-99, Amsterdams Inst. voor Schilderkunst, The Netherlands, 1996; asst. prof. U. N.Mex., Albuquerque, 1992-93. One person shows include Handled With Care Gallery, Provincetown, Mass., 1983, Dittmar Gallery, Evanston, 1986, Carson Street Gallery, Pitts., 1989, C.G. Jung Inst. Chgo., Evanston, 1990, Wabash Coll., Crawfordsville, Ind., 1990, Esther Saks Gallery, Chgo., 1991, MC Gallery, Mpls., 1992, Ruschman Gallery, Indpls., 1993, Kay Garvey Gallery, Chgo., 1994, 95, Three Ill. Ctr., Chgo., 1994, Galerie Vromans, Amsterdam, 1995, Galerie Waszkowiak, Berlin, 1997; Galerie Ucher, Cologne, 1998, Roy Boyd Gallery, Chgo., 1999; exhibited in group shows at Harrisburg (Pa.) Mus., 1984, Govt. Ctr., Boston, 1984, Univ. Kobe (Japan), 1985, Union Art Gallery, Milw., 1986, Rockford (Ill.) Mus., 1986, Gracie Mansion Gallery Mus. Store, N.Y.C., 1987, George Walter Vincent Smith Art Mus., Springfield, Mass., 1988, East West Contemporary Art Gallery, Chgo., 1989, Provincetown Art Assn. and Mus., 1989, 94, Eve Mannes Gallery, Atlanta, 1990, Mary and Leigh Block Gallery, Northwestern U., Ill., 1990, Deson-Saunders Gallery, Chgo., 1990, Chgo. Cultural Ctr., 1990, Art Inst. Chgo., 1990, Esther Saks Fine Art, Chgo., 1991, 92, DePaul U. Art Gallery, Chgo., 1992, Ruschman Gallery, 1992, 94, MC Gallery, 1992, Lowe Gallery, Atlanta, 1992, Kay Garvey Gallery, 1992, 93, 95, Charlotte Jackson Fine Art, Santa Fe, 1993, John Sommers Gallery, 1993, CWCA, Chgo., 1993, Klein Art Works, 1993, Greenpeace Fund Benefit, Chgo., 1994, Bethany Coll. Fine Art Ctr., Mankato, Minn., 1994, Galerie Vromans, 1994, 95, Wabash Coll., 1994, Global Focus, Beijing, 1995, Stichting Amazone, Amsterdam, 1995, Galerie Beeld & Ambeeld, Enschede, The Netherlands, 1996, Galerie Waszkowiak, Berlin, 1996, Mindy Oh Gallery, N.Y., 1997, Barnes Inst., Stuttgart, 1997; Roy Boyd Gallery, Chicago, 1998, Mary and Leigh Block Mus., Evenston, Ill., 1998; Gallery 312, 'Chicago Artists,' Chicago, 1998, Klein Art Works, Abstract, Chgo., 1998, Roy Boyd Gallerym 1999, UNESCO-ICSU Conf. on Sci. Exhbn., 1999, Galerie Beeld and Aabeold, Enschede, Netherlands, 1999, Margin Gallery, Chgo., 1999, N.Y. Polish Consulate, 1999, Galerie Ucher, Köln, Germany, 1999; contbr. articles to various publs. Avocations: travelling, sailing, contemporary music festivals and concerts. Home: 835 N Wood St Apt 102 Chicago IL 60622-5044

NOVAK, MAXIMILLIAN ERWIN, English language educator; b. N.Y.C., Mar. 26, 1930; s. George and Elsie (Loewy) N.; m. Estelle Gershgoren, Aug. 21, 1966; children: Ralph, Daniel, Rachel. PhD, UCLA, 1958; D.Phil., St. John's Coll., Oxford U., Eng., 1961. Asst. prof. English, U. Mich., Ann Arbor, 1958-62; prof. English, UCLA, 1962—2001, Clark Library prof., 1973-74, prof. emeritus, 2001—. Author: Economics and the Fiction of Daniel Defoe, 1962, Defoe and the Nature of Man, 1963, Congreve, 1971, The Wild Man Within, 1972, English Literature in the Age of Disguise, 1977, Realism, Myth and History in the Fiction of Daniel Defoe, 1983, Eighteenth-Century English Literature, 1983, Passionate Encounters, 2000, Daniel Defoe Master of Fictions, 2001; editor: Augustan Reprint Soc. Dryden: Works, vol. 10, 1970, vol. 13, 1984, Southerne, Oroonoko, 1976, Collected Writings of Daniel Defoe, 1999—. Fulbright fellow, 1955-57, Guggenheim fellow, 1965-66, 85-86, Am. Philos. Soc. fellow, 1979, NEH fellow, 1980-81, Beinecke Libr. fellow, 1991, Pres.' fellow U. Calif., 1991—, Huntington Libr. fellow, 1991—. Mem. MLA, Am. Soc. 18th Century Studies, Johnson Soc. So. Calif., Western Soc. Eighteenth Century Studies. Democrat. Jewish. Home: 451 S El Camino Dr Beverly Hills CA 90212-4221 E-mail: novak@humnet.ucla.edu.

NOVAK, MICHAEL (MICHAEL JOHN NOVAK), religion educator, author, editor; b. Johnstown, Pa., Sept. 9, 1933; s. Michael John and Irene (Sakmar) N.; m. Karen Ruth Laub, June 29, 1963; children: Richard, Tanya, Jana. AB summa cum laude, Stonehill Coll., North Easton, Mass., 1956; BT cum laude, Gregorian U., Rome, 1958; MA, Harvard U., 1966; LLD, Keuka (N.Y.) Coll., 1970, Stonehill Coll., Mass., 1977, Thomas More Coll., 1992; LHD, Davis and Elkins (W.Va.) Coll., 1971, LeMoyne (N.Y.) Coll., 1976, Sacred Heart U., 1977, Muhlenberg Coll., 1979, D'Youville Coll., 1981, Boston U., 1981, New Eng. Coll., 1983, Rivier Coll., 1984, Marquette U., 1987; D en Ciencias Sociales, U. Francisco Marroquin, Guatemala, 1993, Jacksonville U., 1994; HHD, Saint Xavier U., 1995. Teaching fellow Harvard U., 1961-63; asst. prof. Stanford U., 1965-68; assoc. prof. philosophy and religious studies State U. N.Y., Old Westbury, 1968-71; assoc. dir. humanities Rockefeller Found., N.Y.C., 1973-75; provost Disciplines Coll., SUNY, Old Westbury, 1969-71; vis. prof. Jan. session Carleton Coll., Northfield, Minn., 1970, Immaculate Heart Coll., Hollywood, Calif., 1971, U. Calif., Santa Barbara, 1972, Riverside, 1975; Ledden-Watson disting. prof. religion Syracuse U., 1977-79; journalist nat. elections Newsday, 1972; writer in residence The Washington Star, 1976, syndicated columnist, 1976-80, 84-89; columnist Forbes Mag., 1989—; George Frederick Jewett chair pub. policy and religion Am. Enterprise Inst., Washington, 1983—, dir. social and polit. studies, 1987—; chmn. working seminar on family and Am. welfare policy Ind., 1986; faculty U. Notre Dame, 1986-87, vis. W. Harold and Martha Welch Prof. Am. Studies, 1987, 88. Judge Nat. Book awards, 1971, DuPont Broadcast Journalism awards, 1971-80; speechwriter nat. polit. campaigns, 1970, 72; mem. Bd. Internat. Broadcasting, 1983—; mem. Presdl. Task Force Project Econ. Justice, 1985-87, Council Scholars Library of Congress, 1986—; mem. monitoring panel UNESCO, 1984; vice chmn. Lay Commn. Cath. Social Teaching and U.S. Economy, 1984-86; U.S. Ambassador to Experts Meeting on Human Contacts of the Conf. On Security and Cooperation in Europe, Bern, Switzerland, 1986; U.S. rep. to human rights commn. UN, 1981-83; hon. prof. U. Cuyo, Argentina, 1992. Author: novel The Tiber was Silver, 1961, A New Generation, 1964, The Experience of Marriage, 1964, The Open Church, 1964, Belief and Unbelief, 1965, 3d edit., 1994, A Time to Build, 1967, A Theology for Radical Politics, 1969, American Philosophy and the Future, 1968, Story in Politics, 1970, (with Brown and Herschel) Vietnam: Crisis of Conscience, 1967, Naked I Leave, 1970; Politics: Realism & Imagination, 1971, Ascent of the Mountain, Flight of the Dove, 1971, A Book of Elements, 1972, All the Catholic People, 1971, novel Naked I Leave, 1970, The Experience of Nothingness, 1970, The Rise of the Unmeltable Ethnics, 1972, Choosing Our King, 1974, The Joy of Sports, 1976, The Guns of Lattimer, 1978, The American Vision, 1978, Rethinking Human Rights I and II, 1981, 82, The Spirit of Democratic Capitalism, 1982, Confession of a Catholic, 1983, Moral Clarity in the Nuclear Age, 1983, Freedom with Justice, 1984, Human Rights and the New Realism, 1986, Will It Liberate? Questions About Liberation Theology, 1986, Character and Crime, 1986, The New Consensus on Family and Welfare, 1987, Taking Glasnost Seriously: Toward an Open Soviet Union, 1988, Free Persons and the Common Good, 1989, This Hemisphere of Liberty, 1990, The Spirit of Democratic Capitalism, 1991 (Anthony Fisher award 1992), Choosing Presidents, 1992, The Catholic Ethic and the Spirit of Capitalism, 1993, Awakening from Nihilism, Joy of Sports, rev. 1995; Belief and Unbelief, rev, 1995; Business as a Calling, 1996, The Fire of Invention, 1997, with daughter Jana Novak, Tell Me Why: A Father Answers His Daughter's Questions About God, 1998, On Cultivating Liberty, 1999, To Empower People, anniv. ed, 1995, A Free Society Reader ed, 2000, Three in One, 2001 (essays on Dem. Capitalism 1976-2000), On Two Wings, 2001; numerous other articles and books transl. into all maj. langs.; assoc. editor Commonweal mag., 1966-69; contbg. editor Christian Century, 1967-80, Christianity and Crisis, 1968-76, Jour. Ecumenical Studies, 1967—, This World, 1982-89, First Things, 1990—; religion editor Nat. Rev., 1979-86; founder, pub. Crisis, 1982—, editor-in-chief, 1993-95. Decorated K.M.G., Soverign Mil. Order of Malta, 1987, Order of the Byzantine Cross Republic of Slovakia, 1996; Kent fellow, 1961—; fellow Hastings Inst., 1970-76; named Most Influential Prof. Sr. Class Stanford U., 1967, 68; Man of Yr. Johnstown, Pa., 1978; recipient Faith and Freedom award Religious Heritage Am., 1978, HIAS Liberty award, 1981, Friend of Freedom award, 1981; Newman Alumni award CCNY, 1984; George Washington Honor medal, 1984; award of Excellence, Religion in Media, 8th annual Angel Awards, 1985, Ellis Island Honor medal, 1986, Anthony Fisher award, 1992, Wilhelm Weber Prize, 1993, One Million Dollar Templeton prize for progress in religion, 1994, Internat. prize Inst. World Capitalism, 1994, Award for the Arts City of Bratislava, 1998, Gold Medal Slovak Acad. Scis., 2000, Masaryk award Czech Republic, 2000, IDI Award for Econs., Fondazione Istituto Dirigenti, Rome, 2000, Cezanne medal Mayor of Aix-en-Provence, 1998, Boyer award Am. Enterprise Inst., 1999, Internat. Prize for Cath. Culture, Italy, 1999, Gold medal Pa. Soc., 2001; diploma as vis. prof. U. Francisco Marroquin, 1985; named acad. corr. mem. from U.S., Argentina Nat. Acad. Scis., Morals & Politics, 1985, others. Mem. Soc. Religion in Higher Edn. (ctrl. com. 1970-73), Am. Acad. Religion (prog. dir. 1968-72), Coun. Fgn. Rels., Cath. Theol. Soc., Soc. Christian Ethics, Inst. Religion and Democracy (dir. 1981—), Nat. Ctr. Urban and Ethnic Affairs (dir. 1982-86). Office: Am Enterprise Inst 1150 17th St NW Washington DC 20036-4603 E-mail: mnovak@aei.org. *Many persons have found a certain emptiness at the heart of human life — an experience of nothingness. Hidden in it, implicit in it, are prior commitments to honesty, courage, freedom, community. To increase the frequency of such acts in our lives is to grow, and to feel them diminish is to wither.*

NOVAK, MICHAEL JOHN, computer specialist; b. Traverse City, Mich., Mar. 24, 1948; s. Theodore and Stella Constance (Poplawski) N.; m. Eiko Teramoto, Dec. 23, 1980; children: Michael J. Jr., Jennifer A. BS, U.S. Naval Acad., 1970; BA, U. Md., 1977, M Gen. Adminstrn., 1981. Commd. ensign USN, 1970, advanced through grades to comdr., 1988, served in various locations, transerred to Naval Res., 1981; quality assurance mgr. R.C. Warren & Co., Inc., Traverse City, 1981-83; staff specialist, software quality assurance Def. Logistics Agy., Detroit, 1983—. Mem. IEEE, Am. Soc. Quality Control, Assn. Asian Studies, U.S. Naval Inst. Roman Catholic. Avocations: hunting, fishing. Home: 4701 Hopkins Dr Dumfries VA 22026-1357 Office: Def Logistics Agy 477 Michigan Ave Detroit MI 48226-2523

NOVAK, MICHAEL PAUL, English language educator; b. July 6, 1935; BA, Cath. U. of Am., 1957; MFA, U. Iowa, 1962. Instr. English Ill. State U., Bloomington, 1961-63; assoc. prof. English St. Mary Coll., Leavenworth, Kans., 1963-2001, prof. emeritus, 2001. Office: 700 Garfield St Leavenworth KS 66048-3772 E-mail: novakm@hub.smcks.edu.

NOVAK, RAYMOND FRANCIS, environmental health/toxicology research institute director, pharmacology educator; b. St. Louis, July 26, 1946; s. Joseph Raymond and Margaret A. (Cerutti) N.; m. Frances C. Holy, Apr. 12, 1969; children: Jennifer, Jessica, Janelle, Joanna. BS in Chemistry, U. Mo., St. Louis, 1968; PhD in Phys. Chemistry, Case Western Res. U., 1973. Assoc. in pharmacology Northwestern U. Med. Sch., Chgo., 1976-77, asst. prof. pharmacology, 1977-81, assoc. prof., 1981-86, prof., 1986-88; prof. pharmacology Wayne State U. Sch. Medicine, Detroit, 1988—; dir. Inst. Environ. Health Scis. Wayne State U., 1988—, dir. NIEHS Ctr. in Molecular and Cellular Toxicology with Human Application, 1994—. Mem. toxicology study sect. NIH, Bethesda, Md., 1984-88; adj. sci. Inhalation Toxicology Rsch. Inst., Lovelace Biomed. and Environ. Rsch. Inst., 1991-98; program leader Epidemiology and Environ. Carcinogenesis, Karmanos Cancer Inst. and Comprehensive Cancer Ctr., 1996-98. Assoc. editor Toxicol. Applied Pharmacology, 1992-96; editor Drug Metabolism and Disposition, 1994-2000; mem. editorial bd. Jour. Toxicology and Environ. Health, 19 87-92, In Vivo, 1986—, Toxic Substances Jour., 1993-98; mem. bd. pub. trustees Am. Soc. Pharmacology and Experimental Therapeutics, 1994-2000; contbr. articles to profl. jours. Recipient Disting. Alumni award U. Mo., St. Louis, 1988; grantee Nat. Inst. Environ. Health Sci., 1979—, Gen. Medicine sect. NIH, 1979-82, 89-94. Mem. Am. Soc. for Biochem. and Molecular Biology, Soc. Toxicology (councilor 1996-98, chmn. cont. edn. com. 1995-96), Am. Assn. for Cancer Rsch., Am. Soc. for Pharmacology and Exptl. Therapeutics (bd. publ. trustees 1994-99), Am. Soc. Hematology, Internat. Soc. for Study Xenobiotics. Office: Wayne State U Inst Environ Health Scis 2727 2nd Ave Rm 4000 Detroit MI 48201-2671 E-mail: R.Novak@wayne.edu.

NOVAK, ROBERT DAVID SANDERS, newspaper columnist, television commentator; b. Joliet, Ill., Feb. 26, 1931; s. Maurice Pall and Jane Anne (Sanders) N.; m. Geraldine Williams, Nov. 10, 1962; children: Zelda, Alexander. AB, U. Ill., 1952; LLD (hon.), Kenyon Coll., 1987; LittD (hon.), U. Ill., 1998. Reporter Joliet (Ill.) Herald-News, 1947-51, Champaign-Urbana (Ill.) Courier, 1951-52, AP, Omaha, Lincoln, Nebr., Indpls. and Washington, 1954-58, Wall St. Jour., Washington, 1958-63; syndicated columnist N.Y. Herald-Tribune, 1963-66; commentator Corinthian Broadcasting, 1963-65, Metromedia, Washington, 1966-76, RKO-Features, Washington, 1976-78; syndicated columnist Chgo. Sun-Times, 1966—; commentator Cable News Network, 1980—, Am. Voice, 1993—. Pub. Evans-Novak Polit. Report, Washington, 1967—, Evans-Novak Tax Report, Washington, 1985-92, Evans-Novak Japan Report, Washington, 1989-92; contbg. editor Readers Digest, 1979—. Author: Completing the Revolution, 2000; co-author: (with Rowland Evans) The Agency of the GOP, 1965, Lyndon B. Johnson: The Exercise of Power, 1967, Nixon In The White House, 1971, The Reagan Revolution, 1981. Trustee Bullis Sch., Potomac, Md., 1987-98, Phillips Found., 1991—, Children Charities Found., 1994—. 1st lt. U.S. Army, 1952-54. Recipient ACE award Cable Broadcasting Industry, 1990, Laureate Order of Lincoln, Lincoln

Acad. Ill., 1999. Mem. Soc. Profl. Journalists, Washington Gridiron Club, Nat. Press Club, Army and Navy Club. Home: 801 Pennsylvania Ave NW Washington DC 20004-2615 Office: Ste 1203 1750 Pennsylvania Ave NW Washington DC 20006-4501

NOVAK, ROBERT J. science educator; b. Pueblo, Co., June 5, 1947; s. John M. and Alice M. Novak; m. Loraine J. Krane Novak, Sept. 2, 1972; children: Lisa J., Karen S. BS in Liberal Arts & Sciences, U. S. Co., 1969; MS, U. Utah, 1971; PhD, U. Ill., 1976. NIH post-doctoral fellow U. Notre Dame, 1976—78; rsch. entomologist CDC, Atlanta, 1978—80, San Juan, PR, 1980—88; prof. scientist Ill. Nat. Hist. Survey, Champaign, 1988—; prof. U. Ill., Urbana, 1990—. Pres. Am. Mosquito Control Assn., Rutgers, NJ, 1996—97; tech. mem. WHO Vector Biology, Geneva, 1998—; cons. USAID/ Environ. Health, Arlington, Va., 1999—. Contbr. chapters to books, scientific papers. Fellow: Am. Mosquito Control Assn. (v.p., pres. 1994—99); mem.: Soc. Vector Ecology, Am Soc. Tropical Med. & Hygiene. Office: Illinois Natural History Survey 607 E Peabody Champaign IL 61820

NOVAK, ROBERT LOUIS, civil engineer, pavement management consultant; b. Chgo., Feb. 29, 1928; s. Louis and Frances (Kucera) N.; m. Virginia Staas, Jan. 22, 1955 (div. 1962); children: Susan Grace, Nina Louise; m. Joyce Eloise Keen, May 7, 1966; stepchildren: Robert John Moore, William Keen Moore, Marilyn Joyce Moore, James Clifford Moore. BCE, Ga. Inst. Tech., 1948. With Am. Bridge Co., 1948-49; soils engr. Soil Testing Svc., Chgo., 1952-54; chief materials engr. Skidmore Ownings and Merrill USAF Acad., Colorado Springs, 1954, dir. field invest; asst. dir. engring. O'Hare field constrn. Naess & Murphy, Chgo., 1958-60; pres. Novak, Dempsey & Assocs., Palatine, Ill., 1960-85; ptnr. Infrastructure Mgmt. Svcs., Arlington Heights, 1985-89, cons., 1989—. Contbr. articles to profl. jours. With U.S. Army, 1950-52. Mem. ASTM, Am. Pub. Works Assn. (life; Meritorious Svc. award 1990), Transp. Rsch. Bd. Achievements include a pioneer in field of pavement mgmt. and development of one of the first pavement management computer software programs. Home: 1066 Truman St Nokomis FL 34275-4401

NOVAK, STEPHEN BRUCE, endocrinologist; b. Springfield, Mass., July 24, 1946; s. Paul and Bernice Florence (Cohen) N.; m. Mary M. Milewski, Apr. 17, 1994. BA, Clark U., 1968; MD, Tufts U., 1972. Diplomate Am. Bd. Internal Medicine, Am. Bd. Endocrinology and Metabolism. Intern, then resident U. Miami (Fla.) Affiliated Hosp., 1972-76, chief resident, 1976-77, fellow in endocrinology, 1977-79; pvt. practice Hollywood, Fla., 1979—. Fellow Am. Assn. Clin. Endocrinologists; mem. Endocrine Soc. Avocations: sports, traveling. Office: 1150 N 35th Ave Ste 590 Hollywood FL 33021-5468

NOVAK, TERRY LEE, public administration educator; b. Chamberlain, S.D., Sept. 1, 1940; s. Warren F. and Elaine M. N.; m. Barbara Hosea, Aug. 29, 1981; 1 child, David. B.Sc., S.D. State U., 1962; postgrad. (Rotary fellow), U. Paris, 1962-63; M.P.A., Colo. U., 1965, PhD, 1970. Asst. city mgr. City of Anchorage, 1966-68; city mgr. City of Hopkins, Minn., 1968-74, City of Columbia, Mo., 1974-78, City of Spokane, Wash., 1978-91; v.p. bus. and fin. Ea. Wash. U., Cheney, 1991-92, prof. public adminstrn., 1992—, dir. grad. program pub. adminstrn., 1994-95; dir. Spokane Joint Ctr. for Higher Edn., 1995-98; bus. mgr. Riverpoint campus Wash. State U., 1998-99; prof pub. adminstrn. Eastern Wash. U., 1999—. Asst. adj. prof. U. Mo., Columbia, 1975, 77; adj. instr. Gonzaga U., Spokane, 1986-88; mem. nat. adv. coun. on environ. policy and tech. EPA. Author: Special Assessment Financing in American Cities, 1970; contbr. articles to profl. jours. Mem. ASPA, Internat. Pers. Mgmt. Assn., Internat. City Mgrs. Assn. (Acad. Profl. Devel.). Episcopalian. Office: 668 N Riverpoint Blvd Spokane WA 99202-1677 E-mail: tnovak@terrynovak.net.

NOVAK-LYSSAND, RANDI RUTH, engineer, computer scientist; b. Chgo., July 10, 1954; d. Bernard Richard and Shirley Ann (Fiedorczyk) Novak; children: Rona Rachel, Bonnie Shaina. BS in Math., BA in Econs. with honors, U. Calif., Santa Cruz, 1976; postgrad., U. Rochester, 1976-78. Rsch. asst. U. Calif., Santa Cruz, 1974-76; Russian translator U. Chgo., 1977-78; intern economist Congl. Budget Office, Washington, 1977; engr. Lockheed MSC, Sunnyvale, Calif., 1978-82; software engr. contractor Silicon Valley Systems, Belmont, 1982, 83-84, Data Encore (subs. of Verbatim), Sunnyvale, 1982-83; systems programmer CompuPro/Viasyn Corp., Hayward, Calif., 1984-87; mem. tech. staff Network Equipment Techs., Redwood City, 1987-89; v.p. engring., founder Segue Setups, Burlingame, 1989-92, ptnr., 1992—; sr. mem. tech. staff NEC Am., San Jose, 1992-94; sr. systems engr. Hitachi Computer Products, Santa Clara, 1994-96; prin. engr. Rapid-City Comms./Bay Networks/Nortel Networks, 1996—. Fellow Dept. Treasury, 1974-76, NSF, 1977-78, U. Rochester, Rush Rhees fellow. Mem. IEEE Computer Soc., Am. Math. Assn., Computer Profls. for Social Responsibility, Soc. for Computing and Info. Processing, Internat. Platform Assn., Calif. Scholarship Fedn. (life). Avocations: piano, oboe, music, photography, mathematics. Home: 4166 School St Pleasanton CA 94566-6218

NOVAKOV, GEORGE JOHN, JR. gifted and talented educator, consultant; b. New Orleans, Apr. 1, 1945; s. George John Novakov Sr. and Gloria (Edwards) Frost; m. Ann Marie Mariano, Dec. 27, 1969; children: Jay, Jaime. BA, U. New Orleans, 1967, MEd, 1970, postgrad., 1985, Tulane U., Loyola U., 1985. Tchr. New Orleans Pub. Schs., 1967—, adminstrv. asst., dir. admission Edna Karr Secondary Sch., 1994—, student data mgr. Edna Karr Secondary Sch., 1994—. Grant writer asst. Edna Karr Secondary Sch., New Orleans Pub. Libr., 1987-99. Author: (play) The Christmas Caper, 1980. Ind. Study Humanities fellow, 1991. Mem. La. Assn. of Computer Using Educators (assoc. editor newsletter, 1992), Greater New Orleans Coun. of Tchrs. of English. Democrat. Roman Catholic. Avocations: opera, science fiction, computers. Home: 7340 Edward St New Orleans LA 70126-2012 Office: Edna Karr Secondary Sch 3332 Huntlee Dr New Orleans LA 70131-7046 E-mail: george_novakov@mops_k12_la.us.

NOVALES, RONALD RICHARDS, zoologist, educator; b. San Francisco, Apr. 24, 1928; s. William Henry and Dorothy (Richards) N.; m. Barbara Jean Martin, Dec. 19, 1953; children: Nancy Ann, Mary Elizabeth. BA, U. Calif., Berkeley, 1950, MA, 1953, PhD, 1958; postgrad., U. Calif., Los Angeles, 1951-52. Asst. prof. biol. scis. Northwestern U., Evanston, Ill., 1958-64, assoc. prof., 1964-70, prof., 1970-80, prof. neurobiology and physiology, 1981-93, emeritus prof. neurobiology and physiology, 1993—. Cons. A.J. Nystrom Co., 1969 Mem. editorial bd.: The American Zoologist, 1969-73; Contbr.: articles to profl. jours. Ency. Brit. Book of Year. Served with U.S. Army, 1953-55. NSF research grantee, 1959-73, 75-78 Fellow AAAS. Unitarian Universalist. Home: 2008 Mcdaniel Ave Evanston IL 60201-2125 *Remember not to "die on the barbed wire" of all the conflicting demands of your work. It is possible for you to cut through the individual strands and to make a successful rush for the enemy's trench.*

NOVALES FLAMARIQUE, IÑIGO, biophysicist; b. Bilbao, Vizcaya, Spain, Aug. 18, 1966; Canadian citizen; BS in Physics, McGill U., Montreal, 1988, BS in Biology, 1990; MS in Biology, U. Victoria, B.C., 1993, PhD in Biology, 1997. Cert. scuba rescue diver, NAUI, PADI. Postdoctoral fellow Marine Biol. Lab., Woods Hole, Mass., 1997—; asst. prof. dept. biol. scis. Simon Fraser U., Burnaby, B.C., Can., 2001—. Grant rev. NSERC, Canada, 1996—, CUNY, 1997—; jour. rev. Biol. Bulletin, Mass., 1996—, Jour. Exptl. Biology, Cambridge. Author: (book) Victoria's Shore Dives, 1995 (Gov. Gen. Gold medal, 1997); contbr. articles to profl. jours. including Visual Neurosci., Jour. Exptl. Biology, Jour. Optical Soc. Am., Comp. Physiol. A, Vision Rsch. Asst. contbr. Am. Soc. Zoologists Symposia, Victoria, 1991, 96; singer U. Victoria Choir, 1993-97; asst. organizer Garden City Al- & Marathon, Victoria, 1994-97, others. Mem. Victoria Conservation Soc., Sigma Xi. Achievements include discovery of a mechanism for the detection of polarized light by fishes, of the first invertebrate polarization detection visual system based on 2 visual pigments; identification of neural elements in the processing of ultraviolet and polarized light in the central nervous system of fishes; proved the role of polarization vision in fishes in the detection of prey, established the salmonid visual system as a vertebrate model for study of neuronal death and regeneration. Avocations: soccer, hiking, guitar, photography. Home: 3125 Fendall St Montreal QC Canada H3T IN3 Office: Simon Fraser U Dept Biol Sc 8888 University Dr Burnaby BC Canada V5A 1S6 E-mail: inigo@sfu.ca.

NOVARA, MICHAEL J. lawyer; b. N.Y.C., May 9, 1960; BA in Politics, Cath. U. Am., 1982; JD cum laude, Bklyn. Law Sch., 1987. Bar: N.Y. 1989, Pa. 1992, U.S. Dist. Ct. (ea. and so. dists.) N.Y. 1989, U.S. Dist. Ct. (we. dist.) Pa. 1992, U.S. Ct. Appeals (3rd cir.) 1994. Intern U.S. Justice Dept., N.Y.C., 1986; law clerk Hon. Gustave Diamond, Pitts., 1987-89, 92-93; assoc. Cahill Gordon & Reindel, N.Y.C., 1989-92; investigator Fed. Pub. Defenders Office, Pitts., 1993, asst. fed. pub. defender, 1993—. Co-founder, chmn. bd. dirs. Pitts. Cares, Pitts., 1992-97. Office: Fed Pub Defenders Office 1450 Liberty Ctr 1001 Liberty Ave Pittsburgh PA 15222-3714

NOVAS, JOSEPH, JR. advertising agency executive; b. Bueu, Pontevedra, Spain, Sept. 21, 1921; came to U.S., 1928; s. Joseph and Josephine (Regueira) N.; m. Carmen Ramos, Feb. 9, 1989; children by previous marriage: Stephen, Robert, Paul, Patricia. AB, Brown U., 1946; postgrad., Columbia U., 1948-49. Asst. advt. mgr. Colgate-Palmolive, Jersey City, 1946-49; internat. advt. mgr. The Gillette Co., Boston, 1949-53; founder, pres. Laradiotel, C.A., Havana, Caracas, Mexico, San Juan, N.Y.C., 1953-58; founder Telefilms, C.A., Venezuela, 1955; founder, pres. Novas-Criswell Advt., Caracas, Mexico City, Madrid, Bogota, Sao Paulo, San Juan, Buenos Aires, 1958-74; chmn. and mem. exec. com. Leo Burnett Co., Inc., Spain, Portugal, 1974-77, sr. v.p., 1977-83, also bd. dirs.; chmn. Leo Burnett Europe/ME Ltd., London, 1983-86. Cons. CMQ-TV, Havana, Cuba, 1953-54, Channel 2, Caracas, Venezuela, 1951-58, Heinz Co., Europe, 1985-87, Leo Burnett, 1986-93; lectr. Caracas Central U., Caracas Andres Bello U., Mich. State U., Ohio U., Eastern Ill. U., McGill U., Montreal, Can. Served to lt. (j.g.) USN, 1942-46. Named Advt. Man of Yr., Venezuela Mem. Internat. Advt. Assn. (world pres. 1974-76), Sales and Mktg. Execs. (pres. Venezuela chpt. 1962-64), Broken Sound Club (Boca Raton) E-mail: josephnovas@aol.com. *Frankness, forthrightness—always with the cards on the table. You lose some but you win most, and you always look in the mirror with pride and self respect.*

NOVELLO, ANTONIA COELLO, state health commissioner, former surgeon general; b. Fajardo, P.R., Aug. 23, 1944; d. Antonio and Ana D. (Flores) Coello; m. Joseph R. Novello, May 30, 1970. BS, U. P.R., Rio Piedras, 1965; MD, U. P.R., San Juan, 1970; MPH, Johns Hopkins Sch. Hygiene, 1982; DSc (hon.), Med. Coll. Ohio, 1990, U. Ctrl. Caribe, Cayey, P.R., 1990, Lehigh U., 1992, Hood Coll., 1992, U. Notre Dame, Ind., 1991, N.Y. Med. Coll., 1992, U. Mass., 1992, Fla. Internat. U., 1992, Cath. U., 1993, Washington Coll., 1993, St. Mary's Coll., 1993, Ea. Va. Med. Sch., 1993, Ctrl. Conn. State U., 1993, Georgetown U., 1993, U. Mich., 1994, Mt. Sinai Sch. Medicine, 1995; LHD (hon.), Alvernia Coll., 1996; HHD (hon.), Kings Coll., 1996; D in Health Sci. (hon.), Ponce Sch. of Medicine, 1996; D in Law (hon.), Gannon U., 1997; LHD (hon.), Loyola U., 1997. Diplomate Am. Bd. Pediatrics. Intern in pediatrics U. Mich. Med. Ctr., Ann Arbor, 1970-71, resident in pediatrics, 1971-73, pediatric nephrology fellow, 1973-74, Georgetown U. Hosp., Washington, 1974-75; project officer Nat. Inst. Arthritis, Metabolism and Digestive Diseases NIH, Bethesda, Md., 1978-79, staff physician, 1979-80; exec. sec. gen. medicine B study sect., div. of rsch. grants NIH, 1981-86; dep. dir. Nat. Inst. Child Health & Human Devel., NIH, 1986-90; surgeon gen. HHS, Washington, 1990-93; spl. rep. for health and nutrition UNICEF, N.Y.C., 1993—96; commr. of health New York, 1999—. Clin. prof. pediatrics Georgetown U. Hosp., Washington, 1986, 89, Uniformed Svcs. U. of Health Scis., 1989; adj. prof. pediatrics and communicable diseases U. Mich. Med. Sch., 1993; adj. prof. internat. health Sch. Hygiene and Pub. Health, Johns Hopkins U., Balt.; mem. Georgetown Med. Ctr. Interdepartmental Rsch. Group, 1984—; legis. fellow U.S. Senate Com. on Labor and Human Resources, Washington, 1982-83; mem. Com. on Rsch. in Pediatric Nephrology, Washington, 1981—; participant grants assoc. program seminars Nat. Inst. Arthritis, Diabetes and Digestive and Kidney Diseases, NIH, Bethesda, 1980-81; pediatric cons. Adolescent Medicine Svc., Psychiat. Inst., Washington, 1979-83; nephrology cons. Met. Washington Renal Dialysis Ctr. affiliate Georgetown U. Hosp., Washington, 1975-78; phys. diagnosis class instr. U. Mich. Med. Ctr., Ann Arbor, 1973-74; chair Sec.'s Work Group on Pediatric HIV Infection and Diseases, DHHS, 1988; cons. WHO, Geneva, 1989; mem. Johns Hopkins Soc. Scholars, 1991. Contbr. numerous articles to profl. jours. and chpts. to books in field; mem. editorial bd. Internat. Jour Artificial Organs, Jour. Mexican Nephrology. Served to capt. USPHS, 1978—. Recipient Intern of Yr. award U. Mich. Dept. Pediatrics, 1971, Woman of Yr. award Disting. Grads. Pub. Sch. Systems, San Juan, 1980, PHS Commendation medal HHS, 1983, PHS Citation award HHS, 1984, Cert. of Recognition, Divsn. Rsch. Grants, NIH, 1985, PHS Outstanding medal HHS, 1988, PHS Unit Commendation, 1988, PHS Surgeon Gen.'s Exemplary Svc. medal, 1989, PHS Outstanding Unit citation, 1989, DHHS Asst. Sec. for Health Cert. of Commendation, 1989, Surgeon Gen. Medallion award, 1990, Alumni award U. Mich. Med. Ctr., 1991, Elizabeth Blackwell award, 1991, Woodrow Wilson award for disting. govt. svc., 1991, Congl. Hispanic Caucus medal, 1991, Order of Mil. Med. Merit, 1992, Washington Times Freedom award, 1992, Charles C. Shepard Sci. award, 1992, Golden Plate award, 1992, Elizabeth Ann Seton award, 1992, Ellis Island Congl. Medal of Honor, 1993, Legion of Merit medal, 1993, Athena award Alumnae Coun., 1993, Nat. Citation award Mortar Bd., 1993, Disting. Pub. Svc. award, 1993, Healthy Am. Fitness Leaders award, 1994, Pub. Leadership Edn. Network Mentor award, 1994, Disting. Svc. award Nat. Coun. Cath. Women, 1995, James E. Van Zandt Citizenship award, 1995, Ronald McDonald Children's Charities Excellence award, 1995, Hispanic Heritage Leadership award, 1998, Disting. Alumnus award Am. Assn. of State Colls. and Univs., 1997; named Health Leader of Yr., COA, 1992; inductee Nat. Women's Hall of Fame, 1994, Internat. Pediatric Hall of Fame Miami Children's Hosp., 1996. Fellow Am. Acad. Pediatrics (Excellence Pub. Svc. award 1993); mem. AMA (Nathan Davis award 1993, Meritorious Svc. award 1993), Inst. Medicine, Internat. Soc. Nephrology, Am. Soc. Nephrology, Latin Am. Soc. Nephrology, Soc. for Pediatric Rsch., Am. Pediatric Soc., Assn. Mil. Surgeons U.S., Am. Soc. Pediatric Nephrology, Pan Am. Med. and Dental Soc. (pres.-elect, sec. 1984), D.C. Med. Soc. (assoc.), Johns Hopkins U. Soc. Scholars, Alpha Omega Alpha. Avocation: collecting antique furniture. Office: N.Y. State Health Commr. Corning Tower Empire State Plaza Albany NY 12237*

NOVESKE, FRANCIS GREGORY, psychiatrist; b. Elyria, Ohio, Mar. 8, 1948; s. Walter John and Lucille (Tarnowski) N.; m. Janet Deborah Wood, June 13, 1970; children: Katherine, Peter, Julia. BS cum laude in chemistry, John Carroll U., 1970; MD, Ohio State U., 1974. Diplomate Am. Bd. Psychiatry and Neurology, Am. Bd. Child Psychiatry and Neurology. Child psychiatrist Akron (Ohio) Child Guidance Ctr., 1979-81; child psychiatrist Portage Path Child Guidance Ctr., Kent, Ohio, 1980-81; psychiatrist Guthria Clinic Ltd., Sayre, Pa., 1981-92; pvt. practice Westlake, Ohio, 1993—. Cons. Medina County Cath. Social Svcs., Medina, Ohio, 1995—, Lorain County Cath. Social Svcs., Elyria, 1996—, Lighthouse Family Svcs., 2000—, Cuyahoga County Cath. Social Svcs., Cleve., 2002--; med. dir. Columbia St. John Westshore Hosp., Westlake, 1994-2002, chmn. dept. psychiatry, 1999—; clin. asst. prof. Northeastern Ohio U. Coll. Medicine, Rootstown, 1980-81, asst. prof., 1981; clin. asst. prof. SUNY Binghampton, 1983-93; clin. instr. Case Western Res. U., Cleve., 1994—. Mem. Am. Psychiat. Assn., Ohio Psychiat. Assn., Cleve. Psychiat. Soc. Roman Catholic. Avocations: chess, music, reading. Office: 29101 Health Campus Dr Westlake OH 44145-5270

NOVETZKE, SALLY JOHNSON, former ambassador; b. Stillwater, Minn., Jan. 12, 1932; married; 4 children. Student, Carleton Coll., 1950-52; PhD (hon.), Mt. Mercy Coll., 1991. Amb. to Malta, Am. Embassy, Valletta, 1989-93. Past mem., legis. rep. Nat. Coun. on Vocat. Edn.; past mem. adv. coun. for career edn., past mem. planning coun. Kirkwood C.C.; bd. dirs., life trustee Cedar Rapids (Iowa) Cmty. Theater, Cedar Rapids; past bd. dirs. James Baker III Pub. Policy Inst., Rice U.; past trustee, v.p. bd. dirs. Shattuck-St. Mary's Sch., Faribault, Minn., Mt. Mercy Coll., Cedar Rapids; vice chmn., life trustee, mem. exec. com. Hoover Presdl. Libr., 1982—, v.p. Hoover trustees; mem. Coun. Am. Ambs.; trustee 4-Oaks Juvenile Facility; chmn. Nat. Coun. Youth Leadership; trustee Am. U., Rome, 2001—; state chmn.. Iowa Rep. Ctrl. Com., 1984—86; co-chair rep. Ctrl. Com.; chmn. Linn County Rep. Com., 1980—83; mem. adv. bd. Iowa Redn. Rep. Women, 1987—89; co-chmn. V.P. Bush Inauguration, 1980; Iowa co-chmn. George Bush for Pres.; trustee Am. U. in Rome, 2001—; bd. dirs. Ambs. Forum. Decorated dame Order of Knights of Malta; recipient Disting. Alumnus award Stillwater High Sch., 1991; Disting. Alumni award for outstanding achievement Carleton Coll., 1994. Home: 4747 Mount Vernon Rd SE Cedar Rapids IA 52403-3941

NOVICK, ANDREW CARL, urologist; b. Montreal, Apr. 5, 1948; came to U.S., 1974; s. David and Rose (Ortenberg) N.; m. Thelma Silver, June 29, 1969 (div. Dec. 1983); 1 child, Lorne J.; m. Linda Friedman, May 24, 1992; children: Rachel H., Eric D. BSc, McGill U., Montreal, 1968, MD, CM, 1972. Diplomate Am. Bd. Urology. Resident in surgery Royal Victoria Hosp., Montreal, 1972-74; resident in urology Cleve. Clinic Found., 1974-77, staff dept. urology, 1977—, head sect. renal transplant, 1977—, chmn. dept. urology, 1985—, chmn. Organ Transplant Ctr., 1985—. Trustee Am. Bd. Urology, 1995—2001, Urology Residence Rev. Com., 1997—. Editor: Vascular Problems in Urology, 1982, Stewart's Operative Urology, 1989, Renal Vascular Disease, 1995, Innovations in Urologic Surgery, 1997; contbr. more than 500 articles to profl. jours. Fellow ACS, Med. Coun. Can.; mem. Am. Urol. Assn., Am. Assn. Genito-Urinary Surgeons, Clin. Soc. Genito-Urinary Surgeons. Home: 22325 Canterbury Ln Cleveland OH 44122-3901 Office: Cleve Clinic Found 9500 Euclid Ave A100 Cleveland OH 44195-0001

NOVICK, IVAN JAY, real estate executive; b. Butler, Pa., Apr. 5, 1927; s. Harry Novick and Sadye Breman; m. Natalie Eger, Aug. 27, 1950 (dec. July 1982); m. Mary Biscay, Dec. 14, 1986; children: Howard Alan, William Eger, Phyllis Susan Silverman. Student, John Hopkins U., 1944, Va. Polytech. Inst., 1945; degree econs. and polit. sci., U. Pitts., 1949. Real estate broker John Whiteman Co., Pitts., 1950-54; gen. ptnr. Whiteman Ins. Agy., 1954-57; pres. San Toy Mining Co., 1957-58; exec. v.p. Apollo Industries Inc., 1958-64; pres. J.J. Gumberg Devel. Co., 1961-64; ptnr. West Penn Realty Co., 1965-85; mng. gen. ptnr. Nobil Novick Assocs., Boca Raton, Fla., 1978-91; pres. NN & Assocs. Inc., Pitts., 1989—; chmn. Nat. Common Life Cmtys., Ltd. , Phila. and Pitts., 2002—. Chmn. Oakmont Realty Ptnrs. Inc., Pitts., 1992—, Internat. Sr. Devel., Phila., 1996—, Four Rivers Software Systems, Inc., Pitts., 1991—; mem. Greater Pitts. Bd. of Realtors, Assisted Living Fedn. of Am. Author: (booklet) The Caesarea Process: An American Zionist Perspective, 1983. Exec. com. Nat. Rep. Coalition, Washington, 1978—; mem. Pitts. High Tech. Coun.; past. cmn. Am. Friends of Tel Aviv U. Recipient Israel Svc. award Zionist Orgn. of Am., Justice Louis D. Brandeis award, Jabotinsky award Jabotinsky Found., 1980, Israel Knesset medal Govt. of Israel, 1982. Mem. Nat. Assn. Realtors, Internat. Coun. Shopping Ctrs. (chmn. econ. issues govt. rels. com. internat. coun.), Assisted Living Fedn. Am., Grtr. Pitts. Bd. Realtors, Zionist Orgn. Am. (past nat. pres.), Rivers Club, Concordia Club. Office: NN & Assocs Inc Fort Pittcommons 445 Fort Pitt Blvd LL-300 Pittsburgh PA 15219-1318

NOVICK, JULIUS LERNER, theater critic, educator; b. N.Y.C., Jan. 31, 1939; s. Solomon Joseph and Ethel (Lerner) N.; m. Phyllis Belle Spaeth, May 27, 1983; 1 child, Ilana BA, Harvard U., 1960; D.F.A., Yale U., 1966. Theatre critic WNDT-TV, Channel 13, N.Y.C., 1968-70; asst. prof. English NYU, 1969-72; assoc. prof. lit. SUNY-Purchase, 1972-80, prof., 1980—2001, prof. emeritus, 2002—; theatre critic The Village Voice, N.Y.C., 1958-89, The N.Y. Observer, N.Y.C., 1987-91, Newsday, N.Y.C., 1992-94, Kempner Disting. prof., 1997-99. Vis. lectr. drama div. Juilliard Sch., N.Y.C., 1968-71; dramaturg The Acting Co., N.Y.C., 1971-73; vis. critic Dartmouth Summer Repertory Co., Hanover, N.H., 1976, 79, 80, 82, 83, 84; master critic Nat. Critics Inst., Waterford, Conn., 1971— Author: Beyond Broadway, 1968. Fulbright scholar, 1960-61; Woodrow Wilson fellow, 1961-62; Guggenheim fellow, 1977; recipient George Jean Nathan award for dramatic criticism, 1981-82 Mem.: Am. Theatre and Drama Soc., Assn. for Theatre in Higher Edn., Assn. for Jewish Studies, Am. Theatre Critics Assn., Am. Soc. for Theatre Rsch. Jewish.

NOVICK, MARVIN, investment company executive, former automotive supplier executive, accountant; b. N.Y.C., July 16, 1931; s. Joseph and Anna Novick; m. Margaret A. Blau, Apr. 9, 1960; children: Jeffrey, Stuart, Barry. BBA, CCNY, 1952; MBA, NYU, 1955, postgrad., 1955-58. CPA, N.Y., Mich., La., N.C. Sr. v.p. Mich. Blue Cross/Blue Shield, Detroit, 1961-70; v.p., dir. fin. Meadowbrook Ins., Southfield, Mich., 1970-72; ptnr. Touche Ross and Co., Detroit, 1972-84; vice chmn. Dura Corp., Southfield, 1984-87, Wesnovtek Corp., Birmingham, Mich., 1987-91; pres. R&M Resources Inc., 1991—; advisor Meadowbrook Ins. Group, Southfield, Mich., 1995—. Chmn. Oak Park-Huntington Woods-Pleasant Ridge (Mich.) Dem. Orgn., 1970-72, 18th Dem. Congl. Dist., 1972-74; trustee Mich. Assn. for Emotional Children, 1965—, also past pres.; trustee Providence Hosp., Southfield, 1975-83, also past chmn., trustee bldg. bd., 1982-89; trustee Oak Park (Mich.) Bd. Edn., 1964-71, also past pres.; trustee Temple Beth El, Birmingham, Mich., 1968—, also past pres.; trustee, vice chmn. Union of Am. Hebrew Congregation, 1981—; chmn. fin. com., fin. sec. World for Prog. Judaism-Internat., 1985-99; chmn. pers. com. Jewish Welfare Found., 1987-91, assoc. chmn. cultural and edn. fedn. com., 1984-97, chmn. subcom. Israel and Overseas Com., 1988-99; mem. com. Jewish Agy. in Israel, 1987-99; vice chmn. fin. com., trustee Sinai Hosp., 1988-92, mem. audit com., 1995-97; trustee, treas. Mariners Inn, 1996-2000, Karmanos Cancer Inst.; bd. dirs. B'nai B'rith Centennial Lodge, 1970-79, past v.p.; trustee, mem. exec. com. Rose Hill Ctr., Inc., 1992—; mem. com. Hillel Ctr., U. Mich.; mem. various coms. Jewish Welfare Fedn. Recipient Honor and Service cert. Oak Park Bd. Edn., 1972, Past Pres. award Mich. Assn. Emotionally Disturbed Children, 1986; named one of Outstanding Young Men of Am., Outstanding Am. Found., 1968. Mem. Am. Inst. CPA's, Mich. Assn. CPA's, N.Y. State Assn. CPA's. Home: 12820 Burton St Oak Park MI 48237-1679

NOVICK, NELSON LEE, dermatologist, internist, writer, consultant, dermatological surgeon; b. Bklyn., June 27, 1949; s. Benjamin and Vivian (Meltzer) N.; m. Meryl Sohnis, June 20, 1971; children: Yonatan, Yoel, Ariel, Daniel, Avraham, Shmuel. BA in Biology magna cum laude, Bklyn. Coll., 1971; MD, Mt. Sinai Sch. Medicine, 1975. Diplomate Am. Bd. Internal Medicine, Am. Bd. Dermatology, Am. Bd. Med. Examiners. Resident in internal medicine Mt. Sinai Med. Ctr., N.Y.C., 1975-78, assoc. attending, 1980—, postgrad. preceptee, 1980-83, outpatient dept. clinic chief, dermatology svc., 1983—; resident Skin and Cancer Unit NYU Med. Ctr., 1978-80; assoc. clin. prof. Mt. Sinai Sch. Medicine, 1980—. Cons. Westwood-Squibb Skin Care Info. Ctr., Vaseline Intensive Care Rsch., Bausch & Lomb, Schering-Plough, Sandoz Internat., Procter & Gamble, Lever-2000, Novartis, Bradley Pharms., Merz Pharms., Inst. for Med. Info., Collagenesis Corp., PediFix, others. Author: Saving Face, Skin Care for Teens, Super Skin, Baby Skin, You Can Do Something About Your Allergies, You Can Look Younger at Any Age, Diseases of the Mucus Membranes, (novel) In the Path of the Wolf, (audiotape series) Keeping That Baby Skin Look, Healthier and Younger-Looking Skin, Lunchtime Beauty Fixes for a Prettier Face, Breathing Easier, Fido, Food and Fumes; co-author: The External Ear; reviewer Annals Internal Medicine, Jour. Am. Acad. Dermatology, Jour. Dermatol. Surgery, Internat. Jour. Dermatology; editl. advisor Exec. Health's Good Health Report, Snyder Comm., Your Baby Wallboard Program; former med. editor Current Podiatric Medicine, Jour. Am. Angalgesia Soc.; contbr. articles to profl. jours. Regent's Coll. scholar, 1971, Max and Leah Strauss Fund scholar, 1971, Grand St. Found. scholar, 1971; recipient Dept. Dermatology award, 2000-01. Fellow ACP (direct election), Am. Acad. Dermatology, Am. Soc. Dermatol. Surgery, Am. Acad. Cosmetic Surgery, Skin Cancer Found. (hon.); mem. AMA, AAAS, Soc. Investigative Dermatology, Skin Phototrauma Found., Internat. Soc. for Androgenic Disorders, Skin Cancer Found. (charter), N.Y. Acad. Scis., N.Y. County Med. Soc., Am. Soc. Dermatologic Surgery, Am. Analgesia Soc. (past bd. dirs.), Am. Soc. Cosmetic Dermatology & Aesthetic Surgery (charter), Nature Conservancy, Audubon Soc., Nat. Geog. Found., N.Y. Zool. Soc., Am. Mus. Natural History, Smithsonian Instn., Nat. Wildlife Fedn., The Wilderness Soc., Author's Guild, Author's League Am., Phi Beta Kappa. Jewish. Office: 328 E 75th St New York NY 10021-3317 *The true measure of a person's success in life is not how much he accomplished, but how much of his God-given potential he has used.*

NOVICK, STUART ALLAN, owner business consulting firm; b. Savannah, Ga., Aug. 21, 1944; s. Jehiel and Dorothy Ruth (Selicovitz) N.; m. Francesca Julita Lim, June 22, 1986 (div. Mar. 1993); 1 child, Casey Adam. Grad., Stanford U., 1967. Mgr. Chico-San, Inc., Seattle, 1969-72; bus. mgr. Seventh Inn, Boston, 1972-74; owner, mgr. Simulsense, Seattle, 1974-77, More Time! Good Time!, Honolulu, 1977-80; pres. Foodpower, 1980-83, Profitability Cons., Honolulu, 1983-88, Novick and Einstein Advt., Honolulu, 1988-96; owner Profitability World, 1996—. Pub. Hawaii Environ. Gazette, 1994-95. Coord. Gov.'s Energy Awards Program, 1991; chmn. Hunger Project Found.,

Honolulu, 1977-80; coord. Pau Hunger Found., Honolulu, 1980-81; co-founder, coord. Partnership for the Environment, 1992-95. Mem. Exch. Club (coord. Hilo 1990-91). Avocations: photography, running, writing, cooking, speaking.

NOVICKI, DONALD EDWARD, urologic surgeon; b. Balt., Jan. 31, 1942; s. Vernon Joseph and Gertrude Margaret N.; m. Barbara Ann Block, June 7, 1967; 1 child, Philip Brian. BS, Mt. St. Mary's Coll., Emmitsburg, Md., 1963; MD, U. Md., 1967. Diplomate Am. Bd. Urology. Intern Malcom Grow USAF Med. Ctr., Andrews AFB, Md., 1967-68; resident Wilford Hall USAF Med. Ctr., Lackland AFB, Tex., 1972-76; commd. officer USAF, 1967, advanced through grades to col., 1980, ret., 1986; chmn. dept. urology and residency program dir. Wilford Hall USAF Med Ctr., 1978-86; assoc. prof. surgery, urology U. Tex. Health Svc. Ctr., San Antonio, 1986-89; urologist Alamo Urol. Assocs., 1989-93; cons. in urology, assoc. prof. urology Mayo Med. Sch., Rochester, Minn., 1993-2000, prof. urology, 2000—. Mil. cons. to Air Force Surgeon Gen. in urology, 1979-86. Contbr. numerous articles and book chpts. to profl. jours. and sci. books., 1976—; asst. editor Am. Urol. Assn. Update Series, 1979—2002; mem. editl. bd. Jour. Urology, 1999—. Bd. govs., pres. Soc. Airforce Clin. Surgeons, 1980-85; bd. dirs. S. Tex. Organ Bank, San Antonio, 1983-86. Mem. Am. Urol. Assn. (we. sect. 1993—, Harry Spence Pyelogram award S. Ctrl. Sect. 1986), Soc. Univ. Urologists, Soc. Govt. Svc. Urologists (pres. 1980, Col. John F. Patton award 1984, GU oncology award 1984), Phoenix Urol. Soc., 1993. Avocations: golf, sports cars, gardening, med. history, profl. sports. Office: Mayo Clinic Scottsdale 13500 E Shea Blvd Scottsdale AZ 85259 Personal E-mail: barbnovicki@cox.net. E-mail: novicki.donald@mayo.edu.

NOVIK, YELENA, oncologist, hematologist; b. June 29, 1959; MD, Sch. Medicine and Dentistry, Moscow, 1988. Asst. prof. medicine Albert Einstein Coll. Medicine, N.Y.C., 1996—, N.Y. Med. Coll., N.Y.C., 1998-2000; attending phys. Comprehensive Cancer Ctr., 1998-2000; attending physician Beth Israel Cancer Ctr., 2001—. Mem. Ea. Coop. Oncology Group. Contbr. articles to med. jours. Fellow ACP; mem. Am. Cancer Soc., Am. Soc. Clin. Oncology, Am. Soc. Hematology. Office: Beth Israel Med Ctr Cancer Ctr 10 Union Sq E Ste 4E13 New York NY 10003

NOVIKOFF, HAROLD STEPHEN, lawyer; b. N.Y.C., Apr. 5, 1951; s. Eugene Benjamin and Vivian (Hirsch) N.; m. Amy Pearl, Aug. 20, 1972; children: Sara Heather, Elyse Fana. AB, Cornell U., 1972; JD, Columbia U., 1975. Bar: N.Y. 1976, U.S. Dist. Ct. (so. dist.) N.Y. 1976. Ptnr. Wachtell, Lipton, Rosen & Katz, N.Y.C., 1975—. Mem. ABA, N.Y. State Bar Assn., Assn. Bar City N.Y. (bankruptcy and reorgn. com. 1995-99, chair 1999—), Nat. Bankruptcy Conf. Office: Wachtell Lipton Rosen Katz 51 W 52nd St Fl 29 New York NY 10019-6150 Business E-Mail: hsnovikoff@wlrk.com.

NOVITCH, MARK, physician, retired pharmaceutical executive; b. New London, Conn., Apr. 23, 1932; s. Charles Weinger and Mary (Margolick) N.; m. Katherine Louise Henderson, Oct. 9, 1971; 1 dau., Julia Drummond. AB, Yale U., 1954; MD, N.Y. Med. Coll., 1958. Intern, asst. resident in medicine Boston City Hosp., 1958-60; rsch. fellow Harvard Med. Sch., 1960-62, asst. in medicine, 1962-64, instr. medicine, 1964-67; mem. med. staff Peter Bent Brigham Hosp., Boston, 1962-67; asst. physician Univ. Health Svcs., Harvard U., 1961-67; asst. to dep. asst. sec. for health and sci. affairs HEW, Washington, 1967-71; dep. assoc. commr. for med. affairs FDA, 1971-78, assoc. commr. for health affairs, 1978-81; dep. commr. food and drugs HHS, 1981-85; corp. v.p. The Upjohn Co., Kalamazoo, 1985-86, sr. v.p. sci. adminstrn., 1986-88, exec. v.p., 1989-90, vice-chmn. bd. dirs., 1991-93; prof. health scis. George Washington U., Washington, 1994-97. Adj. prof. George Washington U., 1997—2001; bd. dirs. Guidant Corp., Calypte Biomed., Inc., Neurogen Corp., Kos Pharms., Inc., Alteon, Inc.; chmn. bd. dirs. Food and Drug Law Inst.; trustee U.S. Pharmacopeial Conv. Inc., 1999—2000, pres., 1990—95. Bd. dirs. Nat. Fund Med. Edn. USPHS fellow, 1960-62; Brookings Instn. fed. exec. fellow, 1970-71 Mem. Mass. Med. Soc., Am. Soc. Clin. Pharmacology and Therapeutics, Nat. Acad. Social Ins. Home: 3558 Albemarle St NW Washington DC 20008-4214

NOVITSKI, CHARLES EDWARD, biology educator; b. Rochester, N.Y., Oct. 3, 1946; s. Edward and Esther Ellen (Rudkin) N.; m. Margaret Thornton Sime, June 15, 1968; children: Nancy Ellen, Linda Nicole, Elise Michelle. BA in Biology, Columbia Coll., 1969; PhD in Biophysics, Calif. Inst. Tech., 1979. Rsch. fellow and assoc. City of Hope Nat. Med. Ctr., Duarte, Calif., 1977-80; sr. tutor in biochemistry Monash U., Victoria, Australia, 1980-82, lectr. in biochemistry Australia, 1982-84; program leader and rsch. scientist in nematode control Agrigenetics Advanced Sci. Co., Madison, Wis., 1985-88; assoc. prof. molecular biology Cen. Mich. U., Mt. Pleasant, 1989—. Assoc. editor Jour. Nematology, 1994-97; contbr. articles to various profl. jours. Mem. Soc. of Nematologists, Internat. Soc. of Plant Molecular Biology. Achievements include patent for Nematode Control; research in the molecular genetics of mitochondria and of nematodes. Home: 1208 E Preston Rd Mount Pleasant MI 48858-3927 Office: Cen Mich U Dept Biology Mount Pleasant MI 48859-0001

NOVITZ, CHARLES RICHARD, television executive; b. Chgo., Oct. 25, 1934; m. Eve Krzyzanowski, Feb. 11, 1988; 1 child, Alexandra Maris. BS in Journalism, U. Ill., Champaign-Urbana, 1956; MS, Columbia U., 1960; MPA, NYU, 1971. Reporter, writer, editor City News Bur., Chgo., 1956-57, UPI, Chgo., 1957-59; editor, writer, field producer NBC News, N.Y.C. and Chgo., 1959-60; with ABC News, 1960-79; mgr. ABC News (TV network syndication), 1973-79; mng. dir. Ind. TV News Assn., N.Y.C., 1979-81; producer, exec. NBC News, 1982-85, 87; assoc. Rowan & Blewitt, Inc./Exec. TV Workshop, 1985-95; pres. NovaNews Comm. Cons., 1994—. On-air talent Money Call News, 1988; freelance TV producer, cable and pub. TV series, 1985—; adj. instr. LIU, 1967-69, NYU, 1969-70; asst. adj. prof. Lehman Coll., 1970-71; adj. prof., producer interactive televised course CUNY, 1972-75 Mem. Silurians, Broadcast Pioneers, Radio TV News Dirs. Assn., Alumni Assn. Columbia Grad. Sch. Journalism (pres. 1979), Deadline Club N.Y.C. (pres. 1969), Deadline Club Found. (pres. 1999—), Soc. Profl. Journalists-Sigma Delta Chi (pres. 1981-82). Office: 160 West End Ave Apt 29D New York NY 10023-5616 also: 392 Moonstone Beach Rd Wakefield RI 02879-5102 E-mail: evevideo@earthlink.net.

NOVKOV, JULIE LAVONNE, political scientist; b. Cleve., Oct. 4, 1966; d. Raymond Eugene and Diane Lavonne Novkov; m. Joel David Bloom, Aug. 11, 1996; children: Asher Moses Novkov-Bloom, Shira Rena Novkov-Bloom AB, Harvard-Radcliffe, 1989; JD, NYU, 1992; MA, U. Mich., 1994, PhD, 1998. Asst. prof. U. Oreg., Eugene, 1996—2002, assoc. prof., 2002—. Author: (book) Constituting Workers, Protecting Women, 2001; contbr. articles to profl. jours. Mem. Western Polit. Sci. Assn., Am. Polit. Sci. Assn., Law and Soc. Assn., Law and History Assn. Democrat. Jewish. Office: U Oreg Dept Polit Sci Eugene OR 97403 E-mail: novkov@oregon.uoregon.edu.

NOVOA, YANIRA, diplomat; b. San Salvador, El Salvador, Mar. 5, 1956; arrived in U.S., 1977; d. Numa Pompilio and Donna Rodriguez Novoa. BA, Mount Marty Coll., Yankton, S.D. Min. counselor Min. Fgn. Affairs, El Salvador, coun. gen. El Salvador, free trade agreement investment chpt. mem. El Salvador. Recipient Mother Jerome scholarship, Mount Marty Coll. Mem.: Internat. Ct. Justice. Home: 7345 Pioneers Blvd Apt 106 Lincoln NE 68506-4694 Address: 4800 N 15th Apt 211 Lincoln NE 68521-5605

NOVOA DE ARMAS, HECTOR, scientific researcher; b. Havana, Cuba, Nov. 16, 1968; s. Hector German Novoa Blanco and Perfecta Olga de Armas Reyes. Lic., U. Havana, 1991, MSc, 1996; postgrad., Katholieke U., Leuven, Belgium, 1998-2000. Assoc. rschr. Ctr. Pharm. Chemistry, Havana, 1991-99; rschr. Katholieke U., Leuven, 1998—. Cons. Forensic Lab., Havana, 1996-98. Contbr. articles to profl. jours. Fellow Third World Acad. Scis.; mem. Am. Crystallographic Assn., Nederlandse Vereniging voor Kristallografie, Internat. Ctr. for Diffraction Data, Sociedad Mejicana de Cristalografia. Avocations: music, reading, computers, sports, photography. Office: Katholieke U Lab An Chem Van Everstraat 4 3000 Leuven Belgium Fax: 32 16 323469. E-mail: hector.novoa@farm.kuleuven.ac.be.

NOVOGROD, NANCY GERSTEIN, editor; b. N.Y.C., Jan. 30, 1949; d. Max and Hilda (Kirschbaum) Gerstein; m. John Campner Novogrod, Nov. 7, 1976; children: James Campner, Caroline Anne. AB, Mt. Holyoke Coll., 1971. Sec. fiction dept. The New Yorker, N.Y.C., 1971-73, reader, 1973-76; asst. editor Clarkson N. Potter, Inc., 1977-78, assoc. editor, 1978-80, editor, 1980-83, sr. editor, 1984-86, exec. editor, 1987; sr. editor HG (House and Garden mag.), 1987-88, editor-in-chief, 1988-93, Travel & Leisure, N.Y.C., 1993—; editl. dir. Am. Express Pub., 2000—. Bd. dirs. N.Y. Bot. Garden, 1991—; exec. com., bd. dirs. Mount Holyoke Coll., 1992—97; adv. bd. Breast Cancer Rsch. Found., 1993. Office: Travel & Leisure 1120 Avenue Of The Americas New York NY 10036-6700 E-mail: nnovogrod@travelandleisure.com.

NOVOTNEY, DONALD FRANCIS, superintendent of schools; b. Streator, Ill., July 10, 1947; s. Andrew Stephen and Irene Marie (Lux) Novotney; m. Jane Francis Loeffelholz, June 3, 1973; children: Nicole, Tara, Thomas, Michael, Theresa. BA, Loras Coll., 1969; MS in Tchg., U. Wis., Platteville, 1973; MS, U. Dayton, 1985. Cert. tchr., Wis.; cert. tchr. and adminstr., Ohio. Prin. Holy Ghost Sch., Dickeyville, Wis., 1969-75, St. John Sch., Green Bay, 1975-76, Beaver Dam (Wis.) Cath. Schs., 1976-83; coord. Jordan Cath. Schs., Rock Island, Wis., 1983-85; supt. schs. Diocese of Fargo, N.D., 1985-86, Diocese of La Crosse, Wis., 1987—. Mem. Nat. Cath. Edn. Assn. (del. to nat. congress for cath. schs.). Republican. Roman Catholic. Avocations: athletics, travel. Home: 3314 33rd St S La Crosse WI 54601-7706 Office: Diocese of La Crosse 3710 East Ave S La Crosse WI 54601-7215

NOVOTNY, DEBORAH A. management consultant; b. Oak Lawn, Ill., Sept. 23, 1964; d. Russell Anthony and Barbara J. Novotny. BA in Econs., Northwestern U., 1986; postgrad., U. Minn., 1988-91; Masters cert. in project mgmt., George Washington U., 2000. Series 7 lic. mutual fund mktg. analyst, cert. project mgr., QMS coord., auditor, PowerBuilder developer-profl., instr., PowerSoft divsn. Sybase, Inc., 1993. Mgr. lab., cons. Northwestern U., Evanston, Ill., 1983-86; asst. mgr. microcomputer services Sara Lee Corp., Chgo., 1986; sr. cons. Lante Corp., 1987-88; fin. exec., Series 7 lic. mutual fund mktg. analyst, nat. non-bank banking sys. coord., credit dept. mgr. IDS Fin. Svcs., Inc., Mpls., 1988-91; fin. system coord. Met. Water Reclamation Dist. of Greater Chgo., Chgo., 1991-92; mgmt. systems cons., pres., CEO Deborah A. Novotny, Inc., 1992—; various consulting, mgmt. positions Sybase, Inc., 1993—, area project mgmt. office mgr., 1999—. Invited spkr., instr. ann. Powersoft User Conf., Comdex Trade Show, homeless and underprivileged families Christmas gift program, 1994—. Active teen retreat team St. Michael's Ch., Orland Park, Ill., 1978-84; vol. Greater Chgo. Food Repository, 1997—; vol. Cath. Charities, 1990—0; vice chmn., chair fin. com. Mount Assisi Acad. Bd. of Dirs., 1997-99. Ill. State scholar. Mem. MacIntosh Users Group, Chi Omega Rho (charter, chmn. housing assn. 1986-91). Avocations: piloting aircraft, photography, travel, reading, writing.

NOVOTNY, DONALD WAYNE, electrical engineering educator; b. Chgo., Dec. 15, 1934; s. Adolph and Margaret Novotny; m. Louise J. Eenigenburg, June 26, 1954; children: Donna Jo Kopp, Cynthia Mason. BEE, Ill. Inst. Tech., 1956, MS, 1957; PhD, U. Wis., 1961. Registered profl. engr., Wis. Instr. Ill. Inst. Tech., 1957-58; mem. faculty U. Wis., Madison, 1958—, prof. elec. engring., 1969-96, chmn. dept. elec. and computer engring., 1976-80, Grainger prof. power electronics, 1990—, prof. emeritus, 1996—. Vis. prof. Mont. State U., 1966, Eindhoven (The Netherlands) Tech. U., 1974, Tech. U. Louvain, Belgium, 1986; Fulbright lectr. Tech. U. Ghent, Belgium, 1981; dir. Wis. Elec. Machines and Power Electronics Consortium, 1981—; assoc. dir. Univ.-Industry Rsch. Program, 1982-93; chmn. elec. engring. program Nat. Technol. U., 1989—; cons. to industry. Author: Introductory Electromechanics, 1965, Vector Control and Dynamics of AC Drives, 1996; also rsch. papers; assoc. editor: Electric Machines and Power Systems, 1976—. Recipient Kiekhofer tchg. award U. Wis., 1964, Benjamin Smith Reynolds tchg. award, 1984, Holdridge tchg. award, 1995, Nat. Technol. U. Outstanding Instr. award, 1996-2001, IEEE-IAS Outstanding Achievement award, 1998; Outstanding paper award Engring. Inst. Can., 1966; named IEEE-IAS Disting. Lectr., 1995; fellow GE, 1956, Ford Found., 1960; grantee numerous industries and govt. agys. Fellow IEEE (prize paper awards 1983, 84, 86, 87, 90, 91, 93, 94, 3d Millennium Medal 2000); mem. Am. Soc. Engring. Edn., Sigma Xi, Tau Beta Pi, Eta Kappa Nu. Lodges: Rotary. Congregationalist. Home: 1421 E Skyline Dr Madison WI 53705-1132 Office: U Wis Dept Elec and Computer Engring 1415 Engineering Dr Madison WI 53706-1607 E-mail: novotny@engr.wisc.edu.

NOVOTNY, PATRICIA SUSAN, lawyer, educator; b. Omaha, Nov. 22, 1953; d. John Albert and Lauretta Lee (Waters) N. BA, Reed Coll., 1976; JD, U. Wash., 1983. Bar: Wash. 1983, U.S. Supreme Ct. 1995. Staff atty. Wash. Appellate Defender Assn., Seattle, 1989-91, 92-95, asst. dir., 1994-95; spl. counsel Wash. Defender Assn., 1991-92; pvt. practice, 1986-89, 95—. Lectr. U. Wash. Sch. Law, U. Wash. Women Studies, Seattle, 1996—; mem. legal com. N.W. Women's Law Ctr., Seattle, 1990—, chmn., 1995-97. Contbr. articles to profl. jours. Recipient Individual Artist award Seattle Arts Commn., 1990. Mem.: Wash. Appellate Lawyers Assn., Wash. Assn. Criminal Def. Lawyers. Avocations: creative writing, birdwatching, gardening, hiking, jazz. Office: 3418 NE 65th St Ste A Seattle WA 98115-7341

NOVOTNY, VLADIMIR, educator, consultant; b. Olomouc, Czech Rep., Aug. 30, 1938; came to U.S., 1969, naturalized, 1983; s. Vladimir and Frantiska (Havrankova) N.; m. Lynn Emily Braasch, June 14, 1975; children: Paul Martin, Eric Vladimir. Diploma in Engring., Tech. U., Brno, Czech Rep., 1963, degree in Sci., 1968; PhD, Vanderbilt U., 1971. Rsch. engr. Water Mgmt. Inst., Brno, Czech Rep., 1962-69; rsch. assoc. Vanderbilt U., Nashville, 1969-71; project engr. Aware, Inc., 1970-73; pres. Aquanova Internat., Ltd., Mequon, Wis., 1989—; prof. Marquette U., Milw., 1973—2002; CDM chair, prof. Northeastern U., Boston, 2002—. Dir. Inst. Urban Environ. Risk Mgmt. Marquette U., Milw., 1998—; dir. workshop NATO, Viena, 1994; expert pollution abatement Venezia Nuova, Venice, 1989-2001. Author: Handbook of Nonpoint Pollution, 1981, Water Quality, 1994, 2002; editor: Management of Degraded River Basins, 1995. Rsch. grantee Water Environ. Rsch. Found., Alexandria, Va., 1992, 95, U.S. EPA, Washington, 1993, 97, Ill. EPA, 2000—. Mem. Internat. Water Assn. (chmn. com. 1993-98, chair internat. conf., Chgo., 1993, Edinburgh, 1998, Milw. 2001), Internat. Water Resource Assn., Am. Water Resources Assn. (dir. 1985-89), Water Environ. Fedn. Home: 305 Beacon St Boston MA 02116 Office: Northeastern U 360 Huntington Ave Boston MA 02115- E-mail: novotny@coeneu.edu.

NOWACKI, JAMES NELSON, lawyer; b. Columbus, Ohio, Sept. 12, 1947; s. Louis James and Betty Jane (Nelson) N.; m. Catherine Ann Holden, Aug. 1, 1970; children: Carrie, Anastasia, Emma. AB, Princeton U., 1969; JD, Yale U., 1973. Bar: Ill. 1973, N.Y. 1982, U.S. dist. Ct. (no. dist.) Ill. 1973, U.S. Ct. Appeals (7th cir.) 1978, U.S. Ct. Appeals (6th cir.) 1987, U.S. Supreme Ct. 1992. Assoc. Isham, Lincoln & Beale, Chgo., 1976-79; ptnr. Kirkland & Ellis, 1980—. Mem. Winnetka Sch. Bd. Dist. 36, Ill. 1983-91, bd. pres., 1989-91; mem. New Trier Sch. Bd., 1997-99, pres., 1997-98. Harlan Fiske Stone prize Yale U., 1972. Mem. ABA (forum com. on constrn. industry, litigation sect.), Mid-Am. Club, Skokie Country Club. Home: 708 Prospect Ave Winnetka IL 60093-2320 Office: Kirkland & Ellis 200 E Randolph St Fl 60 Chicago IL 60601-6636

NOWAK, CAROL ANN, city official; b. Buffalo, Mar. 5, 1950; d. Walter S. and Stella M. (Gurowski) N. AAS in Bus. Adminstrn., Erie Community Coll., Buffalo, 1986; BS in Bus. Mgmt., SUNY, Buffalo, 1991. With Liberty Nat. Bank/Norstar, Buffalo, 1968-70, City of Buffalo, 1970-74, asst. adminstrn. and fin., 1974-82, pension clk., adminstr. city police and fire pension fund, city clk., 1982-90, sr. coun. clk., city clk., 1990—. Artist, designer holiday greeting cards, 1984—. Mem. Nat. Notary Assn., SUNY Alumni Assn., Golden Key, Alpha Sigma Lambda. Avocations: fashion design, art, writing. Home: 422 Dingens St Buffalo NY 14206-2321

NOWAK, GREGORY JOSEPH, lawyer, educator; b. Phila., Aug. 5, 1959; s. Joseph Michael and Mary Anne N.; m. Denise Marie Maggetti, May 25, 1985. BA, La Salle U., 1981; JD, Cornell U., 1984; LLM, NYU, 1988. Bar: Pa. 1984, N.J. 1984, U.S. Dist. Ct. (ea. dist.) Pa. 1984, U.S. Dist. Ct. N.J. 1984, U.S. Tax Ct. 1985. Assoc. Stradley, Ronon, Stevens & Young, Phila., 1984-92, ptnr., 1993-99; exec. v.p. for mergers and acquisitions and product devel. Villanova Capital, Conshohocken, Pa., 1999—. Instr. Inst. for Paralegal Edn., Phila., 1986-89; bd. dirs. Marian Juniata Fed. Credit Union, Phila., 1978-99. Contbr. articles to popular mags. Bd. dirs. Holy Redeemer Found. Christian Bros. scholar, 1978-81, Lindback scholar, 1981. Mem. ABA (chmn. regulated investment cos. com.), Phila. Bar Assn. (chmn. exempt orgn. com. 1997-99), Pa. Econ. League. Avocations: golf, running. Office: Villanova Capital 1200 River Rd Conshohocken PA 19428-2436

NOWAK, JACQUELYN LOUISE, state agency administrator, realtor, consultant; b. Harrisburg, Pa., Sept. 2, 1937; d. John Henry and Irene Louise (Clark) Snyder: children: Andrew Alfred IV, Deirdre Anne. Student, Pa. State U., 1973-74; BA, Lycoming Coll., 1975. Editl. writer Patriot News Co., Harrisburg, 1957-58; dir. West Shore Sr. Citizens Ctr., New Cumberland, Pa., 1969-72; exec. dir. Cumberland County Office Aging, Carlisle, 1972-80; bur. dir. Bur. Advocacy/Pa. Dept. Aging, Harrisburg, 1980-88; exec. asst. to Senator John D. Hopper Senate Com. on Aging and Youth, Pa., 1989; assoc. Century 21 Piscioneri Realty, Inc., Camp Hill, 1989-94; adminstrv. officer Am. Trauma Soc., 1994-2000; exec. asst. to dep. sec. pub. health programs Pa. Dept. Health, 2000—. Owner D&J Prodns./Art and Handcrafted Teddy Bears, 1986, Ted E. Bear's Emporium, Harrisburg, 1988-92; adminstr. Country Meadows West Shore II, Mechanicsburg, Pa., 1993-94; recorder Pa. Gov's Coun. Aging Cen. Region, 1972-74, chmn. pub. rels., 1973-74; state planning com. Pa. State conf. Aging, 1974, panelist, 1975-78; mem. state bd. Pa. Coun. Homemakers-Home Health Aide Svcs., 1972-80, v.p., 1975, chmn. ann. meeting, 1973-75; sr. citizens subcom. chmn. Pa. Atty. Gens. Commn. to Prevent Shoplifting, 1983. Spl. projects coord. Pa. divsn. Am. Trauma Soc., 1991-93; adv. com. Tri-County Ret. Sr. Vol. Program, 1972-74; bd. dirs. Coun. Human Svcs. Cumberland, Dauphin, and Perry Counties, 1973-74, Cumberland County Unit Am. Cancer Soc., 1964-76, state del., 1964-66, chmn. county pub. rels., 1965-66, cancer crusade chmn., 1964; svc. com. Family and Children's Svc. Harrisburg, 1970-74, policy com. 1973-74 Recipient Herman Melitzer award Pa. Conf. Aging, 1978; named Woman of Yr. Sta. WIOO Radio, Carlisle, Pa., 1979. Mem. Nat. Assn. Area Ags. on Aging (bd. dirs. 1975-80, pres. 1976-77, sec. 1978-79), Nat. Soc. Decorative Painters (bd. dirs. Penns Woods Painters chpt. 1995—, sec. 1996-97, v.p. 1998-99, pres. 2000-2001), Pa. Watercolor Soc., Harrisburg Art Assn., Mechanicsburg Art Ctr. (pres. 1987-90, bd. dirs. 1984-95), Am. Trauma Soc. (state bd. Pa. divsn. 1985-88), Older Womens League (founder chpt.), Lycoming Coll. Alumni Assn. (exec. bd. 1987-89), Pa. Fedn. Womens Club (divsn. chmn. 1972-76), Torch Club (pres. 1987-88, 2d v.p. 1985-86), Zonta Internat. (sec. 1986-89). Home: 15 Paddock Ln Camp Hill PA 17011-1268

NOWAK, JAN ZDZISLAW, writer, consultant; b. Warsaw, Poland, May 15, 1913; came to U.S., 1977; s. Waclaw Adam and Elisabeth (Piotrowski) Jezioranski; m. Jadwiga Zaleski, Sept. 7, 1944. MS, U. Poznan, Poland, 1936; Doctorate honoris causa, U. Poznan, U. Wroclaw, 1999, U. Cracow, 2000. Sr. researcher U. Poznan, 1937-39; emissary Polish resistance movement, 1941-45; editor BBC, London, 1947-51; dir. Polish Service Radio Free Europe, Munich, Fed. Republic of Germany, 1951-76; v.p., nat. dir. Polish Am. Congress, Washington, 1979-96. Cons. Nat. Security Coun., 1979-92. Author: Courier from Warsaw, 1982, War on Airways, 1985, Poland From Afar, 1988; contbr. articles to mags. Served to maj. Polish Army, 1939-45. Decorated Virtuti Militari; decorated Cross of Valour, King's medal for Courage, Order of White Eagle, Poland, gt. ribbon Polonia Restituta, Comdrs. Cross of Merit with star (Poland), Order of Grand Duke Gedyminas (Lithuania), Presdl. Medal of Freedom, 1996. Roman Catholic. Home: 3815 Forest Grove Dr Annandale VA 22003-1959

NOWAK, JERZY MIECZYSLAW, cultural organization administrator; b. Poznan, Poland, Jan. 4, 1924; s. Tadeusz and Helena (Bakalarczyk) N.; m. Anna Konieczna, June 23, 1979. MSc in Econs., Adam Mickiewicz U., Poznan, 1946; MSc, U. Poznan, 1950. Asst. Acad. Trade, Poznan, 1950-52; dep. dir. Bldg. Joinery Factory, Wolomin, 1952-54; dep. mgr. Bldg. Joinery Co., Warsaw, 1957-60, gen. mgr., 1960-72; vice dir. dept. fins. Ministry of Housing, 1955-56; exec. dir., head Office Bldg. Info. Inst. Econ. and Orgn., 1973-82. Chmn. Union Managerial Info. in Poland; first v.p., dep. dir., initiator of Confederation of Polish Employers, 1989. Mem. Assn. Polish Employers (pres.), Internat. Union Bldg. Ctrs., Polish Chamber Fgn. Trade, Polish Acad. Sci. Investment (dir. 1982-91), Yacht Club.

NOWAK, JOHN E. law educator; b. Chgo., Jan. 2, 1947; s. George Edward and Evelyn (Bucci) N.; m. Judith Johnson, June 1, 1968; children: John Edwin, Jeffrey Edward. AB, Marquette U., 1968; JD, U. Ill., 1971. Law clk. Supreme Ct. of Ill., Chgo., 1971-72; asst. prof. U. Ill., Urbana, 1972-75, assoc. prof., 1975-87, law prof., 1978—, grad. coll. faculty, 1982—, Baum Prof. Law, 1993—. Chmn. Constl. Law Sch. Sect.; faculty rep. Big Ten Intercollegiate Conf., Schaumburg, Ill., 1981-91; vis. prof. law U. Mich., Ann Arbor, 1985; Lee Disting. vis. prof. Coll. William and Mary, 1993. Co-author: Constitutional Law, 6th edit. 2000, Treatise on Constitutional Law, 1986, 3d edit., 1999, Story's Commentaries on the Constitution, 1987. Scholar-in-Residence, U. of Ariz., Tucson, 1985, 87. Mem. Assn. of Am. Law Schs. (chm. constl. law sect., accreditation com. 1980-88), Nat. Collegiate Athletic Assn. (mem. infractions com. 1987—), Am. Law Inst., Am. Bar Assn., Ill. Bar Assn., Order of the Coif (Triennial Book award com.). Roman Catholic. Home: 1701 Mayfair Rd Champaign IL 61821-5522 Office: U Ill Coll Law 504 E Pennsylvania Ave Champaign IL 61820-6909

NOWAK, JOHN MICHAEL, retired air force officer, company executive; b. Grand Rapids, Mich., Dec. 17, 1941; s. John F. and Dorothy F. (Smigiel) N.; m. Maureen K. Henry, Apr. 20, 1963; children: Kimberly, Susan, John, Michael, Lynn. BA in Sociology and Polit. Sci., Aquinas Coll., Mich., 1963; M in Mgmt., U. So.Calif., 1973. Commd. 2d lt. U.S. Air Force, 1963, advanced through grades to lt. gen., 1993; dir. maintenance Ogden Air Logistics Ctr., Hill AFB, Utah, 1984-86; dep. chief staff for maintenance Air Force Logistics Command, Wright-Patterson AFB, Ohio, 1986-89; dep. chief staff for logistics and engring. Hdqrs. Mil. Airlift Command, Scott AFB, Ill., 1989-92; dep. chief staff for logistics Hdqrs. Air Mobility Command, 1992; dir. of supply Hdqrs. U.S. Air Force, Washington, 1992-93, dep. chief for logistics, 1993-1995; pres., CEO Logtec, Fairborn, OH, 1995—. Decorated DSM, Legion of Merit, Bronze Star medal, Meritorious Svc. medal with 3 oak leaf clusters, Air Force Commendation medal; named Entrepreneur of Yr.for So. Ohio and Ky. region Ernst & Young, 2002. Avocations: golf, boating, fishing. Office: LOGTEC Inc 2900 Presidential Dr Ste 130 Fairborn OH 45324-6292 E-mail: nowakj@logtec.com.

NOWAK, JUDITH ANN, psychiatrist; b. Albany, N.Y., Feb. 18, 1948; d. Jacob Frank and Anne Patricia Nowak. BA, Cornell U., Ithaca, N.Y., 1970, MD, 1974. Bd. cert. Psychiatry. Resident U. Va. Hosp., Charlottesville, 1974-77; fellow in psychiatry Westchester divsn. Cornell U. Med. Coll. Westchester Div., White Plains, N.Y., 1977-78; clin. affiliate Cornell U. Med. Coll., 1978-79; staff psychiatrist Chestnut Lodge Hosp., Rockville, Md., 1979-81; med. officer in psychiatry St. Elizabeths Hosp., Washington, 1981; pvt. practice Washington, 1981—. Clin. asst. prof. of psychiatry, George Washington U., Washington, 1981-89; clin. assoc. prof. psychiatry, George Washington U. 1989-94, clin. prof. psychiatry, 1994—. Mem. Am. Psychiat. Soc. (pub. affairs rep. 1995), Am. Psychoanalytic Soc., Washington Psychiat. Soc. (sec. 1989-90, 2001—, pres. 1991-92), D.C. Med. Soc. (speaker ho. of dels. 1996-98, chair coun. med. specialty socs. 1998-2000). Office: 908 New Hampshire Ave NW Washington DC 20037-2049

NOWAK, LISA M. astronaut, military officer; b. Washington, May 10, 1963; m. Richard T. Nowak; 3 children. BS in Aerospace Engring., USN Acad. Annapolis, Md., 1985; MS in Aeronautical Engring., MS in Aeronautical Engring., USN Postgrad. Sch., Monterey, Calif. , 1992. Commd. ensign U.S. Navy, Annapolis, 1985, advanced through grades to cmmdr.; Temporary duty NASA Johnson Space Ctr., Houston, 1985; student pilot USN Flight Sch., 1986; trainee Electronic Warfare Sch., Corry Sta. , Fla., 1988; pilot Electronic Warfare Aggressor Squadron 34, Point Magu, Calif., 1989—90; grad. student USN Postgrad. Sch., Monterey, 1990—92; engr. Systems Engring. Test Directorate, Pauxent River, Md., 1993; student test pilot U.S. Navy Test Pilot Sch. , 1993—94; aircraft systems project officer Strike Aircraft Test Squadron, 1994—95; acquistion project USN Air Systems Command, 1995—96; astronaut NASA Johnson Space Ctr., Houston, 1996—. Mem.: AIAA, USN Acad. Alumni Assn., Tau Beta Pi. Achievements include 0ver 1,100 flight hours using 30 different aircraft. Avocations: bicycling, crossword puzzles, gourmet cooking, running, rubber stamps. Office: Astronaut Office/CB Johnson Space Ctr Houston TX 77058

NOWAK, PATRICIA ROSE, advertising executive; b. Toledo, Nov. 29, 1946; d. Robert Joseph and Hedwig Rose (Rutkowski) Stack; m. Casimir Robert Nowak Jr., June 3, 1967 (dec.); children: Martin Robert, Laura Kristen. Student, Bowling Green State U., 1964-67. Events dir. Sta. WTTO, Toledo, 1967-68; dir. spl. events Tiedtke's, 1968-72; dir. fashion and pub. rels. Lion Store, 1980-86; owner, mgr. Pat Nowak & Assocs., Sylvania, Ohio, 1986-90; dir. pub. rels., consumer affairs Seaway Foodtown Stores, Maamee, 1990—. Bd. dirs. State of Ohio Workforce Devel. Com. Contbr. articles to local newspaper. Auction chair Toledo Opera, 1978, 86-87, bd. dirs., 1998; bridge chair Toledo Symphony, 1987; gifts chair St. Johns H.S., Toledo, 1988-89; chair holiday parade Citifest, Toledo, 1988-89, Sapphire Ball, 1996; dir. opening ceremonies World Cup, Toledo, 1988-90; bd. dirs. Am. Heart Assn., Toledo Repertoire Theatre, Pvt. Industry Coun., Toledo Mus. Art, 1998; active Boy Scouts Am., Gov.'s Workforce Devel. Com. Recipient salute Old Newsboys, 1997. Mem. Toledo C. of C. (solicitation com., vol. award 1989), Jr. League Toledo (pub. rels. com. 1984-85). Roman Catholic. Home: 8130 Hidden Harbour Dr W Holland OH 43528-9398 Office: 1020 Ford St Maumee OH 43537-1820

NOWAK, ROBERT MICHAEL, chemist; b. South Milwaukee, Wis., Oct. 28, 1930; s. Casimer M. and Anita Marie (Anderson) N.; m. Susan Lora Boyd, Oct. 12, 1957; children: Karen Sue Nowak Sapsford, Janet Lynn Nowak McMorris. Student, U. Wis., Racine, 1949-51; BS, U. Wis., Madison, 1953; PhD, U. Ill., 1956. Rsch. chemist Phys. Rsch. Lab., Dow Chem. Co., Midland, Mich., 1956-64, from group leader to asst. lab dir., 1964-72; dir. rsch. and devel. plastics dept. Dow Chem. Co., 1972-73, dir. rsch. and devel. Olefin and Styrene plastics depts., 1973-78, dir. rsch. and devel. plastics dept., 1978-83, dir. cen. rsch., 1983-90, chief scientist, dir. cen. rsch. and devel., 1990-94; pres., CEO Mich. Molecular Inst., 1994—. Contbr. articles to profl. jours.; patentee organic reaction mechanisms and reinforced plastics. Mem. NAE, AIChE, Am. Chem. Soc. Office: MI Molecular Inst 1910 W Saint Andrews Rd Midland MI 48640-2657 E-mail: nowak@mmi.org.

NOWELL, GLENNA GREELY, librarian, consultant, city manager; b. Gardiner, Maine, Apr. 15, 1937; d. Bion Mellon and Faith Louise (Hutchings) Greely; m. Dana Richard Nowell, Sept. 1, 1956 (div. 1971); children: Dana A., Mark R., Dean E. BA in English, U. Maine, 1986. Dir. Gardiner Pub. Libr., 1974-97; city mgr. Gardiner, 1997-00. Bd. dirs. Gardiner Bd. Trade; mem. Maine Libr. Commn., 1980-88, Gov.'s Commn. Employment of Handicapped, 1978-81; mem. adv. bd. Gardiner Savs. Bank, 1986—; trustee J. Walter Robinson Welfare Trust, 1986—. Creator, editor Who Reads What publ., 1988—. Mem. Gardiner Econ. Devel. Com., 1989-98; interim city mgr. City of Gardiner, 1991; bd. dirs. Kennebec Valley Mental Health, 1995-97; trustee Maine Criminal Justice Acad., 1998-99; mem. State Ct. Libr. Com., 1996-99; mem. Maine Real Estate Commn., 2000—. Recipient Hugh Hefner 1st Amendment award Playboy Found., 1987, Outstanding Libr. award Maine Libr. Assn., 1993, Cmty. Svc. award Kennebec Valley C. of C., 1993. Mem. Rotary (pres. Gardiner chpt. 1993-94). Office: RR 5 Box 1910 Gardiner ME 04345-9738 E-mail: nowell@adelphia.net.

NOWELL, LINDA GAIL, organization executive; b. Ft. Worth, Apr. 24, 1949; d. Jesse Wayne and Bennie Dale (Flint) Stallings. BA in English, North Tex. State U., 1970. Cert. secondary edn. tchr., Tex. Ind. sales rep. Jostens Printing & Pub. Div., Owatona, Minn., 1980-84; v.p. Nowell Equipment Co., Cranfills Gap, Tex., 1984-89; edn. coord. Tex. Farm Bur., Waco, 1987-90; account exec. MAC Printing, Las Vegas, 1991-94; mgr. frontier health outreach program Nev. Rural Health Ctrs., Inc., 1994-97; state coord. Nev. 5-A-Day Coalition, 1995-96; exec. dir. No To Abuse, Pahrump, Nev., 1999—. Grant writer, editor (health newsletter) Ridin' the Circuit. Participant Landmark Edn., Inc. Mem. NAFE, United Way Pioneer Territory (bd. dirs.), Fam/Fam Connection (adv. bd.). Home: PO Box 790 Pahrump NV 89041-0790

NOWELL, PETER CAREY, pathologist, educator; b. Phila., Feb. 8, 1928; s. Foster and Margaret (Matlack) Nowell; m. Helen Worst, Sept. 9, 1950; children: Sharon, Timothy, Karen, Kristin, Michael. BA, Wesleyan U., Middletown, Conn., 1948; MD, U. Pa., 1952. Intern Phila. Gen. Hosp., 1952—53; resident pathology Presbyn. Hosp., Phila., 1953—54; med.-teaching, research specializing in cancer, 1956—; from instr. to prof. pathology Sch. Medicine U. Pa., 1956—, chmn. dept. pathology, 1967—73; dir. (Cancer Center), 1973—75. Lt. M.C. USNR, 1954—56. Recipient Rsch. Career award, USPHS, 1964—67, Parke-Davis award, 1965, Lindback Disting. Tchg. award, 1967, Passano award, 1984, Rous-Whipple award, Am. Assn. Pathology, 1986, de Villers award, Leukemia Soc. Am., 1987, Mott prize, GM Cancer Rsch. Found., 1989, 3M award, FASEB, 1993, Lasker Found. award, 1998. Home: 345 Mount Alverno Rd Media PA 19063-5313 Office: U Pa Sch Medicine Dept Pathology & Lab Medicine Philadelphia PA 19104-6082 E-mail: nowell@mail.med.upenn.edu.

NOWICK, ARTHUR STANLEY, metallurgy and materials science educator; b. N.Y.C., Aug. 29, 1923; s. Hyman and Clara (Sperling) N.; m. Joan Franzblau, Oct. 30, 1949; children: Jonathan, Steven, Alan, James. AB, Bklyn. Coll., 1943; A.M., Columbia U., 1948, PhD, 1950. Physicist NACA, Cleve., 1944-46; instr. U. Chgo., 1949-51; asst. prof., then assoc. prof. metallurgy Yale U., 1951-57; mgr. metallurgy research IBM Corp Research Center, Yorktown Heights, N.Y., 1957-66; prof. metallurgy Columbia U., 1966-90, Henry Marion Howe prof. metallurgy and materials sci., 1990-95, prof. emeritus, 1996—. Adj. prof. CBEMS dept., U. Calif., Irvine, 2001; A. Frank Golick lectr. U. Mo., 1970; vis. prof. Technion, Haifa, Israel, 1973; co-chmn. Internat. Conf. Internal Friction, 1961, 69; cons. in field. Author: Crystal Properties Via Group Theory, 1995; co-author: Anelastic Relaxation in Crystalline Solids, 1972; co-editor: Diffusion in Solids, 1975, Diffusion in Crystalline Solids, 1984; contbr. articles to profl. jours. Named David Turnbull lecturer Materials Rsch. Soc., 1994. Fellow AIME, Am. Phys. Soc.; mem. Materials Rsch. Soc. (Turnbull lectr. 1994), Sigma Xi (pres. Kappa chpt. 1983-85). Home: 24 Hillsdale Dr Newport Beach CA 92660-4234 Office: U Calif Irvine 916 Engineering Tower Irvine CA 92697-2575 E-mail: anowick@uci.edu.

NOWICKI, GEORGE LUCIAN, retired chemical company executive; b. Rutherford, N.J., Dec. 4, 1926; s. Justin Nowicki; m. Mary Elisabeth Baker, Aug. 30, 1947; children: Barbara, Peter, Paul, James. BSChemE, CCNY, 1949; MSChemE, NYU, 1956. Registered profl. engr., N.Y., Pa. Chemist Ideal Toy Co., N.Y.C., 1949; chem. engr. Bklyn. Union Gas Co., 1949-50, Sonotone Corp., Elmsford, N.Y., 1950-52; dept. head Burroughs Wellcome Co., Tuckahoe, 1952-70; v.p. mfg. Quaker Chem. Corp., Conshohocken, Pa., 1970-79, v.p. domestic ops., 1984-89, ret., 1989; pres. Selby Batersby Co., Phila., 1979-81; mng. dir. Quaker Chem. Holland BV, Uithoorn, The Netherlands, 1981-84. Chmn. bd. Overdale Corp., Alsip, Ill., 1987-89, Quaker Chem. Can. Ltd., Toronto, 1985-89. Pres. Ctrl. Sch. Dist. 7, Hartsdale, N.Y., 1960-69, Westchester County Sch. Bds. Assn., White Plains, N.Y., 1965; bd. dirs. Suburban Gen. Hosp., Norristown, Pa., 1986; mem. governing bd. Vt. Common Cause, 1993—; bd. dirs. Martha Canfield Libr., Arlington, Vt., 1994-2000; counselor Svc. Corps Ret. Execs., 1993-95. Mem. Am. Inst. Chem. Engrs., Mfrs. Assn. Del. Valley (bd. dirs. 1987-89). Avocations: swimming, skiing, video photography, stamps. Home: 1268 Berwal Rd Arlington VT 05250-8821

NOWIK, DOROTHY ADAM, medical equipment company executive; b. Chgo., July 25, 1944; d. Adam Harry and Helen (Kichkaylo) Wanaski; m. Eugene Nicholas Nowik, Aug. 9, 1978; children: George Eugene, Helen Eugene. A.A., Columbia Coll., 1980. Cert. lactation counselor, lactation educator, lactation cons. Sec., adminstrv. asst. to pres. Zenco Engring Corp., Chgo., 1970-71; sales rep. Medizenco USA Ltd., Chgo., 1971-73; ptnr. Pacific Med. Systems, Inc., Bellevue, Wash., 1973-76, pres., 1976—. Mem. NAFE, Pacific Mothers Support, Inc. (pres. 1991), Wash. Assn. Lactation Cons. (treas. 1994—). Mem. Orthodox Ch. Am. Home: 303 126th Ave NE Bellevue WA 98005-3217 Office: 1407 132nd Ave NE # 10 Bellevue WA 98005-2259

NOWIK, HENRY IAN, marketing executive, consultant; b. Posen, Poland, Feb. 3, 1917; came to U.S., 1979; s. Alexander Joseph and Elizabeth Augusta (von Kuhn) N.; m. Evelyn Phyllis Barnard, Sept. 17, 1949 (dec. 1992); m. Kathleen Yvonne Jones, May 12, 1995. BS in Econs., London U., 1949; PhD, U. Lyon, 1948. Student advisor U. London, 1948-52; export mktg. exec. Parke Davis Ltd., Eng., 1952-54; mgr. market rsch. Mather & Crowther, Eng., 1954-56; mgr. new products Hoover Ltd., Eng., 1956-58; mgr. market rsch. Petfoods Ltd. div. Mars, Inc., Eng., 1958-64; v.p. mktg., sales Uncle Ben's, Australia, 1964-68, gen. mgr., mng. dir. Australia, 1968-78; v.p. mktg. Mars, Inc., U.S., 1979-80, group pres. U.S., 1980-84; cons. mktg., 1984—; sr. cons. Food System Assocs., Washington, 1985—. Prof., lectr. Georgetown U., Washington, 1984—. Author: Disciplined Entrepreneur, 1976, Research in Marketing, 1964, (with others) Product and Process Development in the Food Industry, 1985; contbr. articles to profl. jours. Justice of Peace, Sydney, Australia, 1973; bd. dirs. Australian Ballet Found., Melbourne, 1975; trustee World Wildlife Fund, Australia, 1976; chmn. Decentralization Adv. Bd., Canberra, Australia, 1977-78. Served with RAF, 1939-45. Decorated Officer of Most Excellent Order Brit. Empire, Officer of Order of Australia, Comdr. with Star of Polonia Restituta, Polish Gold Cross of Merit, Knight Supreme Mil. Order Temple Jerusalem. Fellow Royal Statis. Soc., Brit. Inst. Mgmt., Australian Inst. Mgmt., Advt. Inst. Australia, Inst. Dirs. Australia; mem. Internat. Law Assn., Acad. Polit. Sci. (life), Lloyds of London (underwriting), Market Rsch. Soc., Chartered Inst. of Mktg., Am. Mgmt. Assn., N.Y. Acad. Sci., London Reform Club, Georgetown Club (Washington), Royal Yacht Squadron Club (Sydney, Australia). Roman Catholic. Avocations: collecting coins, stamps and first edition books.

NOWITZKE, GARY EARL, investment company executive; b. Trenton, Mich., Feb. 2, 1955; s. Robert E. and Janice E. (Sims) N.; m. Marguerite M. Twombly, July 20, 1956; children: Katherine, Brian, Bradley. BA, Ea. Mich. U., 1977, MS, 1980; EdD, U. Toledo, 1988. Owner Lotus Fin. Svcs., Monroe, Mich., 1983—. Cons. in field. Football, basketball official. Home and Office: 4252 Bluebush Rd Monroe MI 48162-9428 E-mail: gnowitzke@yahoo.com.

NOWLAN, DANIEL RALPH, engineering executive; b. Hammond, Ind., Feb. 23, 1947; s. Kenneth Edwin and Patricia Jane (Prendergast) N.; m. Sharon Louise Greichunos, Sept. 7, 1968; children: Daniel Ralph Jr., Kevin Anthony, Cynthia Ann. BSEE, MSEE, Purdue U., 1969. Engr./scientist McDonnell Douglas Astronautics Co, Santa Monica, Calif., 1969-75; engring. mgr. McDonnell Douglas Aerospace-West, Huntington Beach, 1975-96. Tax preparer Tax Corp. of Am., Montrose, Calif., 1975-76; cons. in field; MDC fellow McDonnell Douglas Aerospace-West, 1996-97; sr. mgr., Boeing tech. fellow Boeing Co., 1997—. Eucharistic minister to convalescent homes St. Vincent De Paul Soc., Huntington Beach, 1993—; youth soccer coach Am. Youth Soccer Orgn., Westminster and Huntington Beach, 1975-82; bldg. fund dr. capt. St. Vincent De Paul Cath. Ch., Huntington Beach, 1979, 82, 97. Recipient Popular Sci. Achievement award, 1993, Space Frontier award, 1994, Engring. Project Achievement award, L.A. & Orange County Engring. Coun., 1994. Fellow AIAA (assoc.); mem. IEEE, Phi Kappa Theta, Tau Beta Pi, Eta Kappa Nu, Phi Eta Sigma. Roman Catholic. Avocations: arranging music for piano and keyboard, study of modern physics, study of philosophy. Home: 15931 Diamond St Westminster CA 92683-7203 Office: The Boeing Co M/C:HO13-C318 5301 Bolsa Ave Huntington Beach CA 92647-2048

NOWLAND, JAMES FERRELL, lawyer; b. Talladega, Ala., Dec. 7, 1942; s. James Franklin and Wilma Delene (Dean) N.; m. Faye Roberts, Aug. 28, 1964; children: Angela Roschelle, James Ferrell II. BS, Jacksonville (Ala.) State U., 1967; BS in Med. Technology, U. Ark., 1972; grad., U. Ark. Med. Ctr., 1974; JD, Oglethorpe U., 1983. Bar: Ga. 1984, U.S. Dist. Ct. (no. dist.) Ga. 1984, U.S. Ct. Appeals (11th cir.) 1984, U.S. Supreme Ct. 1988. Chemist U.S. Army C.E., Marietta, Ga., 1972-97; pvt. practice Cobb County, 1984—. Capt. USAF, 1967-72. Mem. ABA, Ga. Bar Assn., Cobb County Bar Assn. Home: 50 Mt Calvary Rd Marietta GA 30064-1918 Office: PO Box 1847 Marietta GA 30061-1847

NOWLIN, JAMES ROBERTSON, federal judge; b. San Antonio, Nov. 21, 1937; s. William Forney and Jeannette (Robertson) N. BA, Trinity U., 1959, MA, 1962; JD, U. Tex., Austin, 1963. Bar: Tex. 1963, Colo. 1993, U.S. Dist. Ct. D.C. 1966, U.S. Ct. Claims 1969, U.S. Supreme Ct. 1969, U.S. Dist. Ct. (we. dist.) Tex. 1971. Assoc. Kelso, Locke, & King, San Antonio, 1963-65; assoc. Kelso, Locke & Lepick, 1966-69; legal counsel U.S. Senate, Washington, 1965-66; propr. Law Offices James R. Nowlin, San Antonio, 1969-81; mem. Tex. Ho. of Reps., Austin, 1967-71, 73-81; judge U.S. Dist. Ct. for Western Dist. Tex., 1981-99, chief judge, 2000—. Instr. Am. govt. and history San Antonio Coll., 1964-65, 71-73. Capt. U.S. Army, 1959-60, USAR, 1960-68. Fellow State Bar Found (life); mem. San Antonio Bar Assn., Colo. Bar Assn. Republican. Presbyterian. Avocations: pilot, skiing, hiking, jogging. Office: US Courthouse 200 W 8th St Austin TX 78701-2325 Fax: 512-916-5680.

NOWLIN, SUSAN RAE, social service administrator; b. Cleve., Oct. 12, 1944; d. S. Steele and Betty Marie (Hirchert) N. BA, Kent State U., 1967; MSW, U. Denver, 1974. Lic. ind. social worker, Ohio. Social worker Lorain County Children Svcs., Elyria, Ohio, 1967-68, 69-78; social worker, parent coord. Lorain County Head Start, 1968-69; supr. Lorain County Children Svcs., 1978-89, asst. dir. social svcs., 1989-96, dir. social svcs., 1996—. Bd. dirs. Ctr. for Children and Youth Svcs., Elyria, 1990-96, pres. bd., 1995-96; vol. Lorain County Free Clinic, 1986—, pres. bd. dirs., 1999-2001. Mem. NASW, Am. Humane Assn.

NOWOSATKO, JEROME RAYMOND, software engineer; b. Detroit, Apr. 30, 1965; s. Raymond Peter and Sophie Helen (Pendzik) N. AA in Computer Sci., BS in Info. Systems, U. Md., Naples, Italy, 1989; MS in Software Engring., Colo. Tech., 1996. Cert. data processor, sys. profl., computing profl. Commd. E-4 U.S. Army, 1984; software engr. Compuware Corp., Detroit, 1990-91, Columbus, Ohio, 1991-92, Colorado Springs, 1992-97; pres., owner NOVUS Profl. Svcs. Inc., 1997—. Mem. Data Processing Mgmt. Assn., Inst. for Certification of Computing Profls., Project Mgmt. Inst., Buckley Sch. Forensic Soc. Republican. Roman Catholic. Avocations: hiking, scuba diving, reading, mountain biking, skiing. Home: 7215 Big Valley Ct Colorado Springs CO 80919-1035 Office: NOVUS Profl Svcs 7215 Big Valley Ct Colorado Springs CO 80919-1035

NOWSTRUP, ELDON INOR, physicist, consultant, retired; b. Alexander, N.D., Aug. 13, 1924; s. Peter and Anna C. (Larson) Nowstrup; m. Catherine Gall, July 12, 1949; children: Dennis, Sandra, Karen. PhB, U. N.D., 1950, MS, 1951; postgrad., Oak Ridge Sch. Reactor Tech., 1955-56. Lic. nuc. reactor operator. Physicist U.S. Naval Rsch. Lab., Eniwetok Atoll, 1951-52, nuclear reactor physicist, 1952-54, sr. nuclear reactor physicist, 1954-57, nuclear reactor mgr. Washington, 1957-65; sr. reactor safety splst. U.S. Atomic Energy Commn., 1965-75; dep. chief nuclear and indsl. safety and fire protection br. Energy Rsch. and Devel. Adminstrn., 1975-77; chief nuclear safety stds. and metrication br. USDOE, 1977-79; cons. Walkersville, Md., 1980-93; ret., 1993. Metric coord. U.S. Atomic Energy Commn., Energy Rsch. and Devel. Adminstrn., USDOE, Washington, 1971—79; invited lectr. Summer Sci. Inst. U. N.D., Grand Forks, 1958; nuc. cons. USN, Antarctica, 1971; del. UK Study Mission London Am. Nat. Metric Coun., 1976; first chmn. metrication operating com. U.S. Fed. Interagency Coun., 1976—79; chmn. metric stds. subcom. U.S. Fed. Interagency Com. Stds. Policy, 1978—79. Contbr. articles to profl. jours. Recipient award for Outstanding Contributions to the U.S. Metric Program, U.S. Metric Bd., 1980. Mem.: U.S. Metric Assn., Nat. Assn. Ret. Fed. Employees, Am. Nat. Metric Coun., Damascus Travel Club, Inc., Delta Tau Delta, Sigma Xi. Home: 217 Oakmanor Way Walkersville MD 21793-8135

NOYES, H(ENRY) PIERRE, physicist; b. Paris, Dec. 10, 1923; s. William Albert and Katharine Haworth (Macy) N.; m. Mary Wilson, Dec. 20, 1947; children— David Brian, Alan Guinn, Katharine Hope. AB magna cum laude, Harvard U., 1943; PhD, U. Calif., Berkeley, 1950. Physicist MIT, 1943-44, U. Calif., Berkeley, 1949-50; Fulbright fellow U. Birmingham, Eng., 1950-51; asst. prof. U. Rochester, N.Y., 1951-55; group leader Lawrence Livermore Lab., 1955-62; Leverhulme lectr. U. Liverpool, Eng., 1957-58; adminstrv. head theory sect. Stanford Linear Accelerator Center, 1962-69; asso. prof. Stanford U., 1962-67, prof., 1967-2000, prof. emeritus, 2000—. Vis. scholar Center Advanced Study Behavioral Scis., Stanford, 1968-69; cons. in field. Author papers in field. Chmn. Com. for Direct Attack on Legality of Vietnam War, 1969-72; mem. steering com. Faculty Political Action Group, Stanford U., 1970-72; mem. policy com. U.S. People's Com. on Iran, 1977-79. Served with USNR, 1944-46. Fellow NSF, 1962; Fellow Nat. Humanities Faculty, 1970; recipient Alexander von Humboldt U.S. Sr. Scientist award, 1979. Mem. Alternative Natural Philosophy Assn. (pres. 1979-87, 1st alternative natural philosopher award 1989), Am. Phys. Soc., AAAS, Sigma Xi. E-mail: noyes@slac.stanford.edu. *What success I may have had has come because I have tried to bring together my physics and politics and family to serve the people. I aim to achieve a unified materialist philosophy that might help others to greater success than my own. I sum up this philosophy as "fixed past - uncertain future".*

NOYES, JUDITH GIBSON, library director; b. N.Y.C., Apr. 19, 1941; d. Charles II and Alice (Klauss) Gibson; m. Paul V. Noyes, June 1, 1991; children from previous marriage: Andrea Elizabeth Green, Michael Charles Green. BA, Carleton Coll., 1962; MLS, U. Western Ont., London, Can., 1972. Libr. edn. U. New Brunswick, 1972-86; libr. Can. Inst. Sci. and Tech. Info., Ottawa, Ont., Can., 1975-86; librarian Colgate U., Hamilton, N.Y., 1986—. Mem. Online Computer Libr. Ctr. Adv. Com. on Coll. and Univ. Librs., 1991-94; pres. bd. trustees Ctrl. N.Y. Libr. Resources Coun., 1992-96; bd. dirs. Heritage Farm, 1997—, Oneida Cmty. Mansion House Svcs. Bd., 1995-98. Dir. Heritage Farm Bd., 1997—; bd. dirs. Oneida Cmty. Mansion House Svc., 1995-98. Mem. ALA, Am. Coll. and Rsch. Librs. (nominating com. 1988-89, 92-93, legis. com. coll. libr. sect. liaison 1989-91, chair task force on intellectual freedom, 1992-94), Internat. Stds. Orgn. (tech. com. 46, 1981-89), N.Y. Libr. Assn. (acad. and spl. libr. bd. dirs. 1996—). Office: Colgate U Everett Needham Case Libr 13 Oak Dr Hamilton NY 13346-1383

NOYES, RICHARD HALL, bookseller; b. Evanston, Ill., Feb. 12, 1930; s. George Frederick and Dorothy (Hall) N.; m. Judith Claire Mitchell, Oct. 10, 1953; children— Catherine, Stephanie, Matthew. BA, Wesleyan U., 1952. Tng. program, elementary-high sch. salesman Rand McNally & Co., Colo., Utah, Idaho, Wyo., 1955-59; founder, owner, mgr. The Chinook Bookshop, Colorado Springs, Colo., 1959—. Contbr. to A Manual on Bookselling, 1974, The Business of Book Publishing, 1984; contbr. articles to newspapers and trade jours. Co-chmn. Colo. Media Coalition, 1974—; bd. dirs. Colorado Springs Fine Arts Ctr., 1977-81, Citizens Goals for Colorado Springs, 1976-88; trustee Fountain Valley Sch., 1979-81; vice chmn. Colorado Springs Charter Rev. Commn., 1991-92; mem. adv. com. U. Colo., Colorado Springs, 1997—, Downtown Partnership, 1998—. Served with AUS, 1952-54. Recipient Intellectual Freedom award Mountain Plains Librs. Assn., 1977, Disting. Svc. award U. Colo., 1980, Recognition award Pikes Peak Arts Coun., 1989, Charles S. Haslam award, 1990), Entrepreneur of Yr. award U. Colo., 1992, Gordon Saull award for outstanding bookseller Mountains and Plains Booksellers Assn., 1996. Mem. Am. Booksellers Assn. (pres., dir.) Home: 1601 Constellation Dr Colorado Springs CO 80906-1609 Office: The Chinook Bookshop Inc 210 N Tejon St Colorado Springs CO 80903-1385

NOYES, ROBERT EDWIN, publisher, writer; b. N.Y.C., June 22, 1925; s. Clarence A. and Edith (LaDomus) N.; m. Janet Brown, Mar. 24, 1952 (div. June 1963); children— Keith, Steven, Mark, Geoffrey; m. Mariel Jones, July 24, 1964; children— Rebecca, Robert. BS in Chem. Engring, Northwestern U., 1945. Chem. engr. Am. Cyanamid Co., Pearl River, N.Y., 1947; sales exec. Titanium Pigment Corp., N.Y.C., 1948-55; market research mgr. U.S. Indsl. Chem. Co., 1956-58; sales mgr. atomic energy Curtiss Wright Export, 1958-60; founder, pres., chmn. bd. Noyes Data Corp., Westwood, N.J., 1960-99; pub. Noyes Press, Noyes Publs., 1961-99, Noyes Strategic Pubs., Saddle River, N.J., 1999—. Author numerous books in fields of internat. fin., devel., tech., space, military. Served to lt. (j.g.) USNR, 1945-47. Mem.: AIAA, Am. Inst. Chem. Engrs., Am. Chem. Soc., N.Y. Yacht Club. Episcopalian. Home: 224 W Saddle River Rd Saddle River NJ 07458-2620

NOYES, STANLEY TINNING, writer, educator, arts administrator; b. San Francisco, Apr. 7, 1924; s. James Goodman and Winifred (Tinning) N.; m. Nancy Black, Mar. 9, 1949; children: Frank Garnis II, Charles de St. Maurice, Julie Hoyt. AB, U. Calif., Berkeley, 1950, MA, 1951. Instr. U. Calif. Berkeley Extension Divsn., 1954, 55, Calif. Coll. Arts and Crafts, 1958, asst. prof. humanities, dean of men, 1961; lectr. humanities Coll. Santa Fe, 1965-71; lit. arts coord. N.Mex. Arts Divsn., 1972-86; writer, 1986—. Vis. lectr. U. N.Mex., 1976; part time poetry editor N.Mex. Mag., 1973-77. Author: (novels) No Flowers for a Clown, 1961, Shadowbox, 1972, (poetry) Faces and Spirits, 1974, Beyond the Mountains, 1979, The Commander of Dead Leaves, 1984, (history) Los Comanches: The Horse People, 1751-1845, 1993, Comanches in the New West, 1895-1908, 1999; editor: (with Gene Frumkin) The Indian Rio Grande: Recent Poems from 3 Cultures, 1977. Bd. dirs. No. N.Mex. chpt. ACLU, Santa Fe, 1972-74, Friends of the Santa Fe Pub. Libr., 1975. Served with U.S. Army, 1943-46. Decorated Bronze Star; MacDowell fellow, 1967. Mem. PEN Am. Ctr., Santa Fe County C. of C. Avocations: hiking in the mountains, skiing, cross-country skiing, snowshoeing. Home and Office: 634 Garcia St Santa Fe NM 87505-2858

NOYES, WALTER OMAR, writer, tree surgeon; b. Brookton, Maine, Aug. 4, 1929; s. Vinal Lloyd and Gladys May (Craig) N.; m. Anne Elizabeth Prout; children: Andrew W., Cynthia A.; m. Lorraine Gillespie, June 18, 1983. Grad. high sch., Lee, Maine. Tree climber Bartlett Tree Expert Co., Washington, 1949-50, R.E. Tillgren Tree Co., Brockton, Mass., 1953-55, Internat. Paper Co., Mattawamkeag, Maine, 1955-59, Great No. Paper Co., East Millinocket, 1959-62, with, 1958-62; tree climber Hartney Tree Co., Dedham, Mass., 1962-64, Town of Bridgewater, 1964-69; tree climber, foreman Davey Tree Expert Co., Las Vegas, 1969-70, Maltby Tree Co., Stoughton, Mass., 1970-79; tree lift operator Asplundh Tree Expert Co., Brockton, 1979-93; freelance writer, 1984—. Devel. tng. and safety manual for entry-level jobs in field; cons. U.S. Dept. Labor. Contbr. articles to profl. jours. and poems in various anthologies, including The Best Poems of the '90's, also Best Poems and Poets of the 20th Century, 2000, The Best Poems and Poets of 2002. Cpl. U.S. Army, 1951-53. Avocations: writing poetry, philosophy. Home: 71 Maplewood Ave Holbrook MA 02343-1067 E-mail: china_gal_3174@prodigy.net.

NOZISKA, CHARLES BRANT, lawyer; b. Oakland, Calif., Aug. 28, 1953; s. Charles Richard and Shirley Ann (Orme) N. BA, Colo. Coll., 1975; JD magna cum laude, U. San Diego, 1982. Bar: Calif. 1982, U.S. Dist. Ct. (so. dist.) Calif. 1982. Ptnr. Thorsnes, Bartolotta, McGuire & Padilla, San Diego, 1982—. Co-author: Landslide and Subsidence Liability, 1988. Mem. Assn. Trial Lawyers Am., Calif. Trial Lawyers Assn., San Diego Trial Lawyers Assn., San Diego County Bar Assn. Democrat. Avocations: ocean sports. Office: Thorsnes Bartolotta McGuire & Padilla 2550 5th Ave Ste 11 San Diego CA 92103-6612

NOZZI, DOM, urban planner; b. New Britain, Conn., Feb. 15, 1960; s. Albert M. and Sara (Lupia) N. BA in Environ. Sci., SUNY, Plattsburgh, 1983; MS in Urban and Regional Planning, Fla. State U., 1985. Environ. specialist Fla. Dept. Environ. Protection, Tallahassee, 1984-85; growth mgmt. specialist City of Boulder, Colo., 1996-97; from assoc. to sr. long-range planner City of Gainesville, Fla., 1986-96, sr. urban design planner, 1997—. Presenter in field. Author, editor: A Decade of Growth and Change in Alachua County, 1992; editor: Gainesville Development Guide. Bd. dirs. Gainesville chpt. ACLU, 1995; advisor, mem. Alachua Greenway Alliance, Gainesville, 1994-95; pres. Duckpond Neighborhood Assn., 1999—. Mem. Am. Planning Assn., Am. Inst. Cert. Planners, Congress for New Urbanism. Avocations: bicycling, kayaking, hiking, beer making, scuba diving. Office: City of Gainesville PO Box 490 Gainesville FL 32602-0490 E-mail: nozzidj@ci.gainesville.fl.us.

NRIAGU, JEROME OKON, environmental geochemist; b. Ora-eri Town, Anambra, Nigeria, Oct. 24, 1942; came to U.S., 1993; s. Martin and Helena (Anaekwe) N.; children: Chinedu Delbert, Uzoma Vivian, Osita Jide. BSc with honors, U. Ibadan, Nigeria, 1965, DSc, 1987; MS, U. Wis., 1967; PhD, U. Toronto, Ont., 1970. Rsch. scientist Environment Can., Burlington, Ont., 1970-93; prof. environ. chem. sch. of pub. health U. Mich., Ann Arbor, 1993—; dir. environ. health scis. program, 1996-99; rsch. scientist Ctr. for Human Growth and Devel., U. Mich., 1997—. Adj. prof. U. Waterloo, Ont., 1985—96; vis. scientist NOAA, Ann Arbor, 1992; bd. dirs. Ecology Ctr. Mich., Alliance to End Childhood Lead Poisoning, Washington, 1998—. Author: Lead and Lead Poisoning in Antiquity, 1983; editor: (book series) Advances in Environmental Science and Technology, 1982—, Trace Metals in the Environment, 1996—, 29 books on various environ. topics, 1979—, Sci. of the Total Environment, 1983—; mem. editl. bds.: 9 jours.; contbr. articles to profl. jours. Recipient Rigler medal, Can. Soc. Limnologists, 1988; grantee Fulbright sr. fellowship, 2002. Fellow Royal Soc. Can. (Romanowski medal

1999); mem. Am. Pub. Health Assn., Geochem. Soc. Roman Catholic. Avocations: photography, reading (African authors), travel. Office: Univ of Michigan Environ/Indsl Health 109 Observatory St Ann Arbor MI 48109-2029 E-mail: jnriagu@sph.umich.edu.

NUBEL, MARIANNE KUNZ, cultural administrator, writer, composer; b. Cin., Sept. 14, 1966; d. Walter Charles and Marjorie (Larson) Kunz; m. Christopher Robert Nubel, Aug. 12, 1989. BS in Cmty. Arts Mgmt., East Carolina U., 1989. Exec. dir. Cmty. Arts Ctr., Wilmington, N.C., 1989-94; dir. film and media svcs. and cultural arts coord. City of Wilmington, 1994—. Founding mem., v.p. 5 & Dime Cultural Prodns., Wilmington, 1992-96,Big Dawg Productions, 1995; bd. dirs. Arts Coun. of the Lower Cape Fear, Wilmington, 1991-95, sec., 1994-95; pres. prodn. bd. Cape Fear Shakespeare, Wilmington, 1994—, music dir., coord., 1994—; pres. adv. bd. Journey Prodn. Performance Edn. Theatre, 2000—; mem. adv. bd. Big Dawg Theatre Co, 2001—. Composer for children's theatre. Music dir. Pied Piper Theatre, Jr. League, Wilmington, 1989-95; mem. co. Bessie's Underground Mole Players, Wilmington, 1995-99; mem. Arts Coun. Lower Cape Fear, Opera House Theatre Co. Recipient Arts and Humanities award N.C. Recreation and Parks Soc., 1993, 94, Cmty. Svc. award Thalian Assn. Cmty. Theatre, 1993, 94. Mem. Theatre N.O.W., Blues Soc. of the Lower Cape Fear (bd. dirs. 1990-92, 1st woman dir.), Big Dawg Theatre Co., Lower Cape Fear Hist. Soc., Opera House Theater Co., Wilmington Choral Soc. Avocations: writing, composing, community theatre, children's theatre, travel. Office: City of Wilmington Pub Svcs and Facilities PO Box 1810 Wilmington NC 28402-1810 E-mail: Marianne.Nubel@ci.wilmington.nc.us.

NUCCIARONE, A. PATRICK, lawyer; b. Denville, N.J., Aug. 29, 1947; s. H. Joseph and Alice Marie (McGuirk) N. BA, U. So. Calif., 1969; JD, George Washington U., 1973. Bar: N.J. 1973, N.Y. 1981, Vt. 1984, U.S. Dist. Ct. N.J. 1973, U.S. Dist. Ct. (no. dist.) Ohio 1986, U.S. Ct. Appeals (3d cir.) 1976, U.S. Supreme Ct. 1995. Com. staff asst. U.S. House of Reps., Washington, 1971-72; staff asst. Exec. Office of Pres. of U.S., 1972-73; asst. U.S. Atty. Office of U.S. Atty., Newark, 1974-83, chief environ. sect., 1978-83; spl. asst. Atty. Gen. Office of Atty. Gen., Montpelier, Vt., 1984; ptnr. Hannoch Weisman, Roseland, N.J., 1984-91, Dechert, Price & Rhoads, Princeton, 1991-95. Co-chmn. N.J. Hazardous Task Force, Trenton, 1978-83; supr. Rutgers U. Environ. Law Clinic, Newark, 1978-83; mem. Environ. Expn. Adv. Bd., Trenton, 1985-90; chmn. ann. seminar on impacts of environ. law bus. trans. Practicing Law Inst., 1986-92, mem. adv. com. on environ. law, 1986—; mem. faculty NYU Summer Inst. on Environ. Law, 1991-94. Contbr. articles to profl. jours. Recipient Outstanding Service award U.S. Dept. Justice, Washington, 1980, Spl. Achievement awards U.S. Dept. Justice, 1978, 79, Presdl. Citation for Excellent Performance Exec. Office of Pres., Washington, 1973. Mem. ABA (vice chmn. sect. on natural resources, energy and environ. law 1987-93), N.J. State Bar Assn. (bd. dirs. environ. law sect. 1985-89), Monmouth County Bar Assn. Office: 1540 Hwy 138 Ste 107 Wall NJ 07719-3766

NUCCIO, PAUL VINCENT, lawyer; b. Bklyn., Jan. 10, 1965; s. Paul Lewis and Lucille (Visceglia) N. BBA, Pace U., 1987; JD, Touro Law Sch., 1993. Bar: N.Y. 1994, Pa. 1993, U.S. Dist. Ct. (ea. and so. dists.) N.Y. 1994. Ptnr. Gilberto, Guastaferri & Nuccio LLP. Mem. Columbian Lawyers of Brooklyn, Arbitrator's Asns. N.Y.C. Democrat. Roman Catholic. Office: 32 Court St Ste 1104 Brooklyn NY 11201-4404

NUCHO, AINA OZOLINS, social worker, art therapist; b. Riga, Latvia; came to U.S., 1949; d. Janis Alfreds and Austra (Babulis) Ozolins; m. Fuad Nucho (dec.). Student, U. Tuebingen, Germany, 1945-49; BA, St. Olaf Coll., 1950; MSS, Bryn Mawr Coll., 1957; PhD, Bryn Mawr Coll., 1966. Bd. Cert. Diplomate in Clin. Social Work; cert. clin. social worker, Md.; registered art therapist; cert. eidetic psychotherapist. Psychiat. caseworker Lankenau Hosp., Phila., 1957-59, Norristown (Pa.) State Hosp., 1952-59; psychotherapist pvt. practice Balt., 1972—; asst. prof. U. Md., 1966-69, assoc. prof., 1969-91, prof., 1991—2001, prof. emeritus, 2001—. Author: The Psychocybernetic Model of Art Therapy, 1987, Stress Management: The Quest for Zest, 1988, Spontaneous Creative Imagery, 1995, also four books in Latvian. Recipient Travel grant Luth. World Fedn., 1950, Internat. Rsch. and Exchs. Bd., Washington, 1994, 95. Mem. NASW, AAUP, Am. Art Therapy Assn. (various coms. and task forces 1972—), Am. Soc. for Study of Psychopathology of Expression (bd. dirs. 1972—, Disting. Fellow 1993, Ernst Kris award 2000), Coun. on Social Work Edn., Md. Art Therapy Assn. (pres. 1972-74). Lutheran. Avocation: Alpine skiing. Office: U Maryland 525 W Redwood St Baltimore MD 21201-1705

NUCKOLLS, JOHN HOPKINS, physicist, researcher; b. Chgo., Nov. 17, 1930; s. Asa Hopkins and Helen (Gates) N.; m. Ruth Munsterman, Apr. 21, 1952 (div. 1983); children: Helen Marie, Robert David; m. Amelia Aphrodite Liaskas, July 29, 1983 BS, Wheaton Coll., 1953; MA, Columbia U., 1955; D.Sc. (hon), Fla. Inst. Tech., 1977. Physicist U. Calif., Lawrence Livermore Nat. Lab., 1955—, assoc. leader thermonuclear design div., 1965-80, assoc. leader laser fusion program, 1975-83, div. leader, 1980-83, assoc. dir. physics, 1983-88, dir., 1988-94, assoc. dir. at large, 1994-97, dir. emeritus, 1997—. Mem. U.S. Strategic Command Strategic adv. group; tech. adv. bd. Network Physics, Inc.; cons. def. sci. bd. Dept. Def. Recipient E.O. Lawrence award Pres. and AEC, 1969, Fusion Leadership award, 1983, Edward Teller medal Internat. Workshop Laser Interaction and Related Plasma Phenomena, 1991, Resolution of Appreciation, U. Calif. Regents, 1994, Sec. of Def. Outstanding Pub. Svc. medal, 1996, Disting. Assoc. award U.S. Dept. Energy, 1996, Career Achievement award Fusion Power Assocs., 1996. Fellow AAAS, Am. Phys. Soc. (J.C. Maxwell prize 1981); mem. NAE. Office: Lawrence Livermore Nat Lab PO Box 808 Livermore CA 94551-0808

NUCKOLS, FRANK JOSEPH, psychiatrist; b. Akron, Ohio, Apr. 7, 1926; s. William Alexander Jr. and Jean (Harrison) N.; m. Jane Fleetwood McIntosh, June 16, 1948; children: Claud Alexander, John Andrew. BA, U. Louisville, 1946; MD, U. Ala., 1951. Diplomate Am. Bd. Psychiatry and Neurology. Intern Holy Name Jesus Hosp., Gadsden, Ala., 1951; ward physician Ala. State Hosp., Tuscaloosa, 1951-52; resident U. Louisville, USPHS Hosp., Lexington, Ky., 1953-56; mem. faculty dept. psychiatry U. Ala. Med. Ctr., Birmingham, 1958-68, dir. tng. psychiat. residents, 1964-68, head div. community psychiatry, 1964-68, head continuing psychiat. edn. for physicians, 1964-68; chief psychiat. staff in-patient svc. U. Hosp., 1966-68; dir. tng. Hill Crest Hosp., 1975-79; pvt. practice, 1968-93; cons. Ala. Div. Disability Determinations, 1993—. Staff Med. Ctr. East Hosp., Birmingham, Bapt. Med. Ctr. Montclair, Birmingham; cons. staff St. Vincent's Hosp., Birmingham, Lloyd Noland Hosp., Birmingham, South Highland Hosp., Birmingham; vis. faculty, mem. interuniv. forum in cmty. psychiatry Harvard U., Boston, 1963-66; vis. faculty Baylor U. Med. Sch., Houston, 1967-71. Ensign USNR, 1941-43; sr. surgeon USPHS, 1956—. Fellow Am. Psychiat. Assn. (life), So. Psychiat. Assn.; mem. Med. Assn. Ala., So. Med. Assn., Jefferson County Mental Health Assn. (v.p. 1960), Jefferson County Med. Soc., Mental Health Assn. State Ala. (chmn. profl. adv. com. 1961), Nat. Assn. Disability Examiners, Phi Beta Pi, Tau Kappa Epsilon. Home and Office: Kalinka Farm 272 Valley View Ln Pelham AL 35124-3635

NUCKOLS, WILLIAM MARSHALL, electrical goods manufacturing executive; b. Washington, Nov. 1, 1939; s. Edgar Marshall Jr. and Helen Abigail (Potter) N.; m. Margaret Louise Beebe, July 9, 1963 (div. 1980); children: Teryl K., Kerena A.; m. Maureen Joy Ryan, July 18, 1981 (div. 1990); children: Lauren E., Lindsay A.; m. Tuula Elina Renko, June 8, 1991; children: Wilson M., Julia A. BEE, Cornell U., 1962; MS in Indsl. Mgmt., MIT, 1965. Ops. and fin. analyst Ebasco Industries, N.Y.C., 1965-69; mktg. mgr. Gen. Cable Corp., 1970-73, dir. corp. planning Greenwich, Conn., 1974, group v.p., 1975-81; v.p. ops. devel. Penn Ctrl. Corp., 1982-83; group v.p. electronics Burndy Corp., Norwalk, Conn., 1984-89; dir. bus. devel. Uponor Group, Helsinki, 1990-91; chmn., pres., CEO, Pass & Seymour/Legrand, Syracuse, N.Y., 1991-98, chmn., 1999, cons., 1999—. Bd. dirs. Ortronics, Inc., Pass & Seymour Can., Inc., The Watt Stopper, Inc.; v.p. Legrand Holding, Inc., 1991-99. Dir. Hiawatha coun. Boy Scouts Am., Syracuse, 1992-99. Mem. IEEE, Elec. Mfrs. Club, Am. Electronics Assn. (dir. 1985-88), Mfrs. Assn. Ctrl. N.Y. (dir. 1993-99). Avocations: sailing, skiing, genealogy, shop, computers. Home: Viputie 4A 02940 Espoo Finland

NUECHTERLAIN, JAMES HOWARD, music educator; b. Frankenmuth, Mich., Sept. 14, 1953; s. Howard and Erema Nuechterlain; m. Donna Sue Nuechterlain, June 23, 2001; children: Patrick, Joshua. MM Music Edn., Mich. State U., East Lansing, Michigan, 1988; BME, Grand Valley State U., Allendale, Michigan, 1980; BS Bus. Adminstrn., Ferris State U., Big Rapids, Michigan, 1975. Band and orch. dir. Monroe Pub. Schools, Monroe, Mich., 1988—; band dir. Marcellus Cmty. Schools, Marcellus, 1984—88, Vicksburg Cmty. Schools, Vicksburg, 1980—81; dept. head JC Penny Co., Battle Creek, 1975—76. Mem.: Mich. Sch. Band and Orch. Assn., Nat. Edn. Music Conf. Office: Monroe High School 901 Herr Road Monroe MI 48161 E-mail: nuechten@monroe.k12.mi.us.

NUECHTERLEIN, DONALD EDWIN, political scientist, educator, writer; b. Saginaw, Mich., June 20, 1925; s. Edwin W. and Laura A. Nuechterlein; m. Mildred U., July 16, 1948.; children: Jan L. Steiert, Jill E. Vosburg, Jeffrey D., Jonathan E. BA, U. Mich., 1948, MA, 1949, PhD, 1959. Staff officer USN, Bainbridge, Md., 1945—, Bremerhauen, Germany, 1946; staff writer U.S. Office Mil. Govt., Berlin, 1946-47; rsch. officer U.S. Dept. State, Washington, 1952-54; info. officer U.S. Embassy, Reykjavik, Iceland, 1954-56; staff officer U.S. Info. Agy., Washington, 1957-60; cultural attache U.S. Embassy, Bangkok, 1961-63; sr. staff officer Naval Ops., 1964-65, Office Sec. Def., Washington, 1965-68; prof. Fed. Exec. Inst., Charlottesville, Va., 1968-88; vis. prof. Queen's U., Ontario, Can., 1989-90, 92-93, U. Kaiserslautern, Germany, 1991-92, 94-95. Lectr. internat. rels. U.S. fgn. policy. Author: God's Country and Mine: Denmark and America, 1951, Iceland Reluctant Ally, 1961, Thailand and the Struggle for Southeast Asia, 1965, U.S. National Interests in a Changing World, 1973, National Interests and Presidential Leadership, 1978, America Overcommitted: U.S. National Interests in the 1980s, 1985, America Recommitted: U.S. National Interests in a Restructured World, 1991, A Cold War Odyssey, 1997, America Recommitted: A Superpower Assesses Its Role in a Turbulent World, 2d edit., 2000; columnist: fgn. policy for several Va. daily newspapers. With U.S. Navy, 1943-46; commd. ensign USNR, 1945; retired lt. comdr. USNR, 1968. Recipient Fulbright-Hays award U. Wales, Aberystwyth, U.K., 1976; rsch. fellow Rockefeller Found. U. Calif., Berkeley, 1963-64, Australian Nat. U., Canberra, Australia, 1990; vis. scholar St. Anthony's Coll. Oxford U., U.K., 1982. Mem. Charlottesville Com. Fgn. Rels., Retired Officers Assn. Charlottesville, Charlottesville Rotary Club.

NUERNBERG, WILLIAM R(ICHARD), lawyer; b. Pitts., July 7, 1946; s. William W. and Frances (Hubler) N. BA cum laude, Denison U., 1968; JD cum laude, U. Mich., 1971. Bar: Pa. 1971, U.S. Dist.Ct. (we. dist.) Pa. 1971, Fla. 1995. Mem. Eckert Seamans Cherin & Mellott LLC, 1981-98; ptnr. Duane Morris LLP, Miami, 1999—. Bd. govs. Big Bros. Big Sisters Greater Miami. Pitt fellow U. Pitts. Sch. Bus., 1987-88. Mem. ABA, Pa. Bar Assn., Fla. Bar Assn., Miami City Club. Office: Duane Morris LLP 200 S Biscayne Blvd Ste 3400 Miami FL 33131-2318

NUESSLE, WILLIAM RAYMOND, surgeon; b. Bismarck, N.D., Sept. 17, 1951; s. Robert Frederick and Margaret Elizabeth (Bergeson) N.; m. Anna Maria Marlow, June 26, 1982; children: Aaron, Alexa, Matthew. BS, U. N.D., 1973, BS Medicine, 1975; MD, U. Ala., 1977. Diplomate Am. Bd. Surgery and Colon and Rectal Surgery. Resident gen. surgery Ochsner Found., New Orleans, 1977-1982; resident colon and rectal surgery U. La., Shreveport, 1982-83; colon and rectal surgeon Quain and Ramstat Clinic, Bismarck, N.D., 1983-90, Clinic for Colon & Rectal Surgery, Huntsville, Ala., 1990—, Huntsville (Ala.) Hosp., 1990—, Crestwood Hosp., Huntsville, 1990—. Fellow ACS, Am. Soc. Colon and Rectal Surgeons; mem. SAGES. Avocations: tennis, fishing, music. Office: Clinic for CRS 115 Manning Dr SW Ste D101 Huntsville AL 35801-4341 E-mail: wrn@hiwaay.net.

NUFFER, DAVID O. former federal judge; b. 1952; BA, JD, Brigham Young U. Magistrate judge U.S. Dist. Ct. Utah, St. George. Office: 192 E 200 N Fl 3 Saint George UT 84770-2866

NUGENT, CHARLES ARTER, internist, educator; b. Denver, Nov. 18, 1924; s. Charles Arter and Florence (Cohn) N.; m. Margaret Flint, Aug. 30, 1950; children— Stephen, Sara, Daniel (dec.). Student, U. Chgo., 1941-43, Ill. Inst. Tech., 1943, U. Minn., 1944, U. S.D., 1945-46; MD, Yale U., 1951. Intern, asst. resident New Haven Hosp., 1951-53; resident Salt Lake County Gen. Hosp., Salt Lake City, 1954-56; mem. faculty U. Utah Coll. Medicine, 1956-67, assoc. prof. medicine, 1965-67; prof. dept. internal medicine U. Hawaii Med. Sch., 1967-70; prof. sect. endocrinology dept. internal medicine U. Ariz. Coll. Medicine, Tucson, 1970-98, prof. emeritus, 1998—. Contbr. articles to profl. jours. Served with U.S. Army, 1943-46, 53. James Hudson Brown Meml. fellow, 1949-50 Mem. AAUP, Endocrine Soc., Western Assn. Physicians, Physicians Forum, Am. Soc. Clinical Investigation. Home: 3242 E 5th St Tucson AZ 85716-4902 Office: PO Box 245021 1501 N Campbell Ave Tucson AZ 85724-0001 E-mail: nugent@u.arizona.edu.

NUGENT, CONNIE, elementary education educator; b. Lawrence, Kans., July 3, 1948; m. Kenneth M. Nugent, Aug. 3, 1968; children: Rebecca, Michael. BA, U. Iowa, 1972; MLS, U. Md., 1973; Tchg. Cert., U. Tex., Tyler, 1986. Reporter, photographer County Newspapers, Richmond/Rosenberg, Tex., summers 1967-68; sec., med. libr. Sch. Medicine, Washington U., St. Louis, 1968-69, asst. cataloger, med. libr., 1969-71; cataloger med. libr. Nat. Children's Hosp., Washington, 1973; ref. libr. Nat. VA Hosp., 1974; patients' libr. vol. U. of Iowa Hosp. and Clinics, Iowa City, 1979-84; libr. dept. ob-gyn U. Iowa Hosp. and Clinics, 1979-84; elem. tchr. English, tchr. gifted and talented reading Lubbock (Tex.) Ind. Sch. Dist., 1987—. WRITE trainer Lubbock Ind. Sch. Dist., 1988—; coach Tex. Future Problem Solving Program, Austin, 1989—, evaluator, trainer, 1990—; textbook cons. 1999—; pre-AP cons. Coll. Bd.; presenter in field. Author: (curriculum guides) WRITE Guides, 1990—, Novel Units, 1989—; co-author: Credit by Exam Writing Course, 1998; contbr: Tex. FPS activity packets. Mem. Tex. Assn. for Gifted and Talented (bd. dirs.), Tex. Coun. Tchrs. English, Internat. Reading Assn., Beta Phi Mu, Delta Kappa Gamma. Avocations: reading, writing. Office: Hardwick Elem Sch 1420 Chicago Ave Lubbock TX 79416-5426

NUGENT, DENISE, holistic nurse consultant and educator; b. Winston Salem, N.C., July 27, 1959; d. Richard Delane and Betty Jean (Williams) Smith; m. Francis Barney William Nugent Jr., Sept. 19, 1980. RN, Cabarrus Hosp. Sch. Nursing, Concord, N.C., 1980; cert., Internat. Inst. Reflexology, St. Petersburg, Fla., 1990, cert. in reflexology, 1996. RN, N.C., Va., Pa., Mass., Ariz., Calif. Staff nurse oncology dept. Bapt. Hosp., Winston Salem, 1980-82; staff nurse diabetes dept. Lehigh Valley Hosp., Allentown, Pa., 1982-83; staff nurse home health Berks Vis. Nurse Assn., Reading, 1983-85; staff nurse diabetic educator Moses Taylor Hosp., Scranton, 1990-93; staff nurse, supr. In Home Health, San Mateo, Calif., 1993-94; holistic nurse, cons. in pvt. practice Foster City, 1995—. Dir. profl. svcs. in Olsten Health Care, Scranton, 1992—93; cons., 1995—; tchr. Reiki, 1995—; homeopathy practitioner, 2001—. Mem. San Mateo adv. bd. Arthritis Found. Mem. Am. Holistic Nurses Assn. (cert. program holistic nursing, bd. cert. holistic nurse). Avocations: mind-body practices, healthy couple relationships, prosperity consciousness, mentorship programs. Home: 44 Rock Harbor Ln Foster City CA 94404-3565 Office: 969G Edgewater Blvd Ste 764 Foster City CA 94404-3760

NUGENT, GEORGE ROBERT, neurosurgeon; b. Yonkers, N.Y., Feb. 6, 1921; s. George Fitzsimmons and Alberta Belle (Wolven) N.; m. Virginia Ellen Hayes, July 3, 1947; children: Dana A., Robert W., Leslie Ellen, Barnes L., Courtney A. BA, Kenyon Coll., 1950; MD, U. Cinn., 1953. Diplomate Am. Bd. Neurol. Surgery. Resident Duke U. Med. Ctr., Durham, 1958, instr. of neurosurgery, 1957-58; asst. dir. Divsn. Neurosurgery U. Cinn. Coll. Medicine, 1958-61; asst. prof. neurosurgery to prof. neurosurgery W. Va. U. Med. Ctr., Morgantown, 1961—, chmn. dept. neurosurgery, 1970-85, prof. neurosurgery, 1985—. Cons. VA Hosp., Clarksburg, W.Va., 1961-93, Pa. Trauma Found., Pittsburgh, 1991-92; participant seminars in field; guest prof. various univs. Exhibitor various sci. exhibits, 1973-79; contbr. articles to profl. jours. and publs. Team physician W. Va. U. Mountaineers, Morgantown, 1966—. Lt. (j.g.) U.S. Maritime Svc., 1943-45. Fellow Am. Bd. Neurol. Surgery; mem. Am. Assn. Neurol. Surgeons, Congress Neurol. Surgeons, So. Neurosurg. Soc. (v.p. 1970-96), Soc. Neurol. Surgeons. Democrat. Avocations: tennis, woodworking, travel, cooking, reading. Office: Robert Byrd Health Scis Ctr Morgantown WV 26506 Fax: 304-292-4944. E-mail: nugent@labyrinth.net.

NUGENT, HELEN JEAN, history educator; b. Indpls., Oct. 14, 1934; d. John Isaac and Ruth Augusta (Mather) McClelland; m. Paul Thomas Nugent, Aug. 19, 1935; children: Paula Jean Nugent Barickman, Thomas J. II, Ruth E. B. Nugent Simard. BA, Franklin Coll., 1956; MA, U. Ill., 1965, Ind. U., 1971; PhD, Mich. State U., 1983. Lifetime cert. in secondary edn., Ind. Tchr. grades 9-12 Union City (Ind.) H.S., 1956-57, Seven Mile (Ohio) H.S., 1957-58; tchr. history St. Rose Acad., Vincennes, Ind., 1962-64; instr. history Margaret Hall Sch., Versailes, Ky., 1964-66; lectr. history Ind.U./Purdue U., Columbus, 1976-82; vis. lectr. Ind. U./Purdue U., 2001; dir. Can. studies Franklin (Ind.) Coll., 1984-95, chair dept. history, 1996-99, prof. emerita history, dir. emerita Can. studies, 1999—. Contbr. numerous articles, papers to profl. jours., chpts. to books. Recipient Alumni award Franklin Coll., 1997. Mem. AAUP, Mid West Assn. Can. Studies (v.p. 1990-92, exec. coun. 1992-94), Assn. Can. Studies U.S. (exec. bd. 1993-97), Phi Alpha Theta, Theta Alpha Phi, Delta Kappa Gamma, Phi Kappa Phi. Roman Catholic. E-mail: hnugent@franklincollege.edu.

NUGENT, JOHN HILLIARD, communications executive; b. Paterson, N.J., Aug. 20, 1944; s. James Joseph and Jacqueline Ann (Storms) N.; m. Mary Elizabeth Maher, June 3, 1967; 1 child, Jill Frances. BA, Columbia U., 1970; MSA, Southeastern U., 1978; DBA, Bus. Sch. of Lausanne, Switzerland, 1989. Adminstr. Chase Manhattan Bank, N.Y.C., 1970-71; analyst U.S. Dept. of Army, Washington, 1971-72; chmn. Strategic Planning & Rsch. Corp., Dallas, 1977-95; pres. AT&T Aviation Tech. and Sys., Ltd., Arlington, Va., Hong Kong, Beijing, 1993; exec. CDX, Inc., Dallas, 1995; pres., bd. dirs. SA Telecomm., Inc., Richardson, Tex., 1996-97, also bd. dirs., pres., 1996; mng. dir. Cordoba Capital, Southport, Conn., 1998-99. V.p., fin. acct. AdCon Inc./Internat. Bank, Reston, Va., 1971-79; CFO HDS, Inc., Reston, 1979-82; pres. Group L Corp., Herndon, Va., 1983-85; pres., bd. dirs. AT&T/Datotek, Dallas, 1985-92; asst. prof. telecomms. Grad. Sch. Mgmt. U. Dallas, 1999—. Author: Corporate Decline: Causes, Symptoms, and Prescriptions for a Turnaround, 1989, Plan to Win: Analytical and Operational Tools-Gaining Competitive Advantage, 2002. Cpl. USMC, 1962-66. Mem. AICPAs, D.C. Inst. CPAs, Tex. Soc. CPAs, Nat. Assn. Accts., Dallas Com. on Fgn. Rels., Columbia Club of N.Y. Republican. Avocation: reading. E-mail: (home) (bus.). Office: Grad Sch Mgmt U Dallas Irving TX 75062-4736 Address: 2469 County Road 855 Mc Kinney TX 75071 E-mail: jnugent@texoma.net, jnugent@gsm.udallas.edu.

NUGENT, LORI S. lawyer; b. Peoria, Ill., Apr. 24, 1962; d. Walter Leonard and Margery (Frost) Meyer; m. Shane Vincent Nugent, June 14, 1986; children: Justine Nicole, Cole Tyler. BA in Polit. Sci. cum laude, Knox Coll., 1984; JD, Northwestern U., Chgo., 1987. Bar: Ill. 1987, U.S. Dist. Ct. (no. dist.) Ill. 1988, U.S. Ct. Appeals (7th cir.) 1995. Assoc. Peterson & Ross, Chgo., 1987-94, Blatt, Hammesfahr & Eaton, Chgo., 1994, ptnr., 1994-2000, Cozen O'Connor, Chgo., 2000—. Co-author: Punitive Damages: A Guide to the Insurability of Punitive Damages in the United States and Its Territories, 1988, Punitive Damages: A State-by-State Guide to Law and Practice, 1991, 2d edit., 2002, Japanese edit., 1995; contbr. articles to law jours. Office: Cozen O'Connor Ste 1500 222 S Riverside Plz Chicago IL 60606-6000 E-mail: lnugent@cozen.com.

NUGENT, NELLE, theater, film and television producer; b. Jersey City, May 24, 1939; d. John Patrick and Evelyn Adelaide (Stern) N.; m. Donald G. Baker, June 6, 1960 (div. 1962); m. Benjamin Janney, June 22, 1969 (div. Apr., 1980); m. Jolyon Fox Stern, Apr. 7, 1982; 1 child, Alexandra Fox Stern. BS, Skidmore Coll., 1960, DHL (hon.), 1981. Chmn. bd. McCann & Nugent, Prodns. Inc., N.Y.C., 1976-86; pres. Foxboro Prodns., Inc., 1985-94; pres., CEO Foxboro Entertainment, 1990-94; pres. The Foxboro Co., Inc.; co-prin. Golden Fox Films, Inc. Stage mgr. various off-Broadway shows, 1960-64; prodn. asst.: Broadways plays Any Wednesday, 1963-64, Dylan, 1964, Ben Franklin in Paris, 1964-65; stage mgr. Broadway shows, 1964-68; prodn. supr., then gen. mgr., 1969-76, assoc. mng. dir. Nederlander Corp., operating theaters and producing plays in, N.Y.C. and on tour, 1970-76; prodr.: Dracula, 1977 (Tony award), The Gin Game (Tony nom.), The Elephant Man, 1978 (Tony award, Drama Critics award), Morning's at Seven, 1980 (Tony award), Home, 1980 (Tony nomination), Amadeus, 1981 (Tony award); also produced: Rose and Piaf, 1980, Otherwise Engaged, The Life and Adventures of Nicholas Nickleby, 1981 (Tony award, Drama Critics award), The Dresser (Tony award nominee), 1981, Mass Appeal, 1981; The Lady & The Clarinet, 1982; The Glass Menagerie (revival), 1983; Painting Churches (Obie award), 1983; Total Abandon, 1983; All's Well That End's Well, 1983 (Tony nominee); Pilobolus Dance Company, 1983; Pacific Overtures (revival), 1984; Much Ado about Nothing/Cyrano de Bergerac (repertory) (Tony award nominees), 1984; Leader of the Pack (Tony award nominee), 1985, The Life and Adventures of Nicholas Nickleby (revival) (Tony award nominee), 1986; prodr.: TV spls.; Morning's At Seven, Piaf; Pilobolus; prodr. A Fighting Choice, 1986-88, A Conspiracy of Love, 1987, The Final Verdict, 1990 (Cable Ace award nominee Best Picture); exec. prodr. (TV pilot) Morning Maggie, 1987, Dick Clark Prodns., 1988-90, (feature films) Student Body, 1993, Getting In, 1994, Jane Doe, 1996; (TV films) In the Presence of Mine Enemies, 1995-96 (Houston Festival Silver Star award), A Town Has Turned to Dust, 1997 (World Festival Silver medal 1998), After the Storm (Best Feature Film N.Y. Internat. Independent Film & Video Festival, 2000), Angelciti Festival (Best Feature 2001), Houston Worldfest (Platinum award, Best Film Made for TV 2001), (Broadway prodn.) The Smell of the Kill, 2002. Mem.: Prodr.'s Guild of Am. (co-chair East Coast chpt.), Am. Women's Econ. Devel. Corp. (bd. dirs.). Office: Foxboro Co Inc 133 E 58th St Ste 301 New York NY 10022-1236

NUGENT, SHANE VINCENT, lawyer; b. Bozeman, Mont., July 14, 1962; s. John Vincent Nugent and Marilyn Jean (Piotrowski) Cloven; m. Lori Sue Meyer, June 14, 1986; children: Justine Nicole, Cole Tyler. BA, Knox Coll., 1984; JD, Northwestern U., 1987. Bar: Ill. 1987. Assoc. Lord, Bissell & Brook, Chgo., 1987-93; pvt. practice Barrington, Ill., 1993-94; of counsel Blatt Hammesfahr & Eaton, Chgo., 1994-96; pvt. practice Barrington, 1996-98; exec. v.p., COO Intelligent Learning Sys., Inc., Austin, Tex., 1998—. Contbr. articles to profl. jours. Recipient NASA Space Act award, 2000; named one of Outstanding Young Men Am., 1987. Mem. Chgo. Bar Assn., Beta Theta Pi (Ray M. Arnold prize Xi chpt. 1984, chpt. advisor 1987-92, asst. gen. sec. 1992-97), Xi Alumni (pres. 1992—).

NUGENT, WALTER TERRY KING, historian; b. Watertown, N.Y., Jan. 11, 1935; s. Clarence A. and Florence (King) N.; children from previous marriage: Katherine, Rachel, David, Douglas, Terry, Mary; m. Suellen Hoy, 1986. AB, St. Benedict's Coll., 1954, DLitt, 1968; MA, Georgetown U., 1956; PhD, U. Chgo., 1961. Instr. history Washburn U., 1957-58; asst. prof. Kans. State U., 1961-63; asst. prof. history Ind. U., 1963-64, assoc. prof., 1964-68, prof., 1968-84, assoc. dean Coll. Arts and Scis., 1967-71, dir. overseas study, 1967-76, chmn. history dept., 1974-77; Andrew V. Tackes prof. history U. Notre Dame, 1984-00, Andrew V. Tackes prof. emeritus, 2000—. Paley lectr., Fulbright vis. prof. Hebrew U., Jerusalem, 1978-79; vis. prof. U. Hamburg, 1980, U. Warsaw, 1982; Mary Ball Washington Fulbright prof. U. Coll., Dublin, 1991-92; summer seminar dir. NEH, 1979, 84, 86; bd. mem. U.S.-Israel Edn. Found., 1985-89; USIA acad. specialist, lectr., Brazil, 1996. Author: The Tolerant Populists, 1963, Creative History, 1967, The Money Question During Reconstruction, 1967, Money and American Society 1865-1880, 1968, Modern America, 1973, From Centennial to World War: American Society 1876-1917, 1977, Structures of American Social History, 1981, Crossings: The Great Transatlantic Migrations 1870-1914, 1992, (with Martin Ridge) The American West: The Reader, 1999, Into the West: The Story of Its People, 1999 (Caughey award 2000). Newberry Libr. fellow, 1962, Guggenheim fellow, 1964-65, Huntington Libr. fellow, 1979, 85, Beinecke fellow Yale U., 1990. Mem. Western Hist. Assn., Soc. Am. Historians, Soc. of Historians of the Gilded Age and Progressive Era (pres. 2000—). Democrat. Roman Catholic. E-mail: walter.nugent.1@nd.edu.

NUGTEREN, CORNELIUS, air force officer; b. Colton, S.D., Feb. 7, 1928; s. Adrian Joe and Marie Johanna N.; m. Liane Albrecht, Sept. 22, 1956; children: Cecile, Aneli. BA, Central Coll., Pella, Iowa, 1951. Commd. 2d lt. USAF, 1953, advanced through grades to maj. gen., 1980; advisor Vietnam Air Force, 1970-71; served in Germany, 1971-77; vice comdr. (Air Logistics Center), Utah, 1977-79; comdr. (Aerospace Rescue and Recovery Service), Scott AFB, Ill., 1979-81; chief (Joint U.S. Mil. Aid Group), Greece, 1981-82;

comdr. Air Logistics Ctr., Robins AFB, Ga, 1983-88; ret.; cons. for def. industries Warner Robins, Ga., 1988-94; v.p. Chem. Tech. Internat., Mercer U. Engring. Rsch. Ctr., Warner Robins, 1996—. Decorated D.S.M., Legion of Merit, Bronze Star, Superior Service medal; recipient USAF EEO award, 1979 Mem. Air Force Assn., Order Daedalians, Internat. Order Hansen, Order of the Sword. Office: 114 Holly Dr Warner Robins GA 31088-6615 E-mail: gennewt@aol.com. *Service to one's country is not just a job...it's a calling. Integrity to and within the institution to which you belong is an absolute necessity. Loyalty to peers and subordinates is equally important as loyalty to your superiors. Attitude toward life, humankind and profession is key determinant to success. Goals should be set high enough so as to be unattainable. Standard of conduct must always include duty, honor, country.*

NUHN, CHARLES KELSEY, advertising executive; b. Ivoryton, Conn., Aug. 6, 1925; s. George Leonard and Marian (Kelsey) N.; m. Ruth Irene Maynard (div. 1979); children: Peter W., Catherine A., James K, John M. ARTP, Yale U., 1951; student, NYU, 1969, Hartford (Conn.) Art Sch., Wadsworth Athenaeum, Hartford. Owner/pres. Nuhn Printing Co., Old Saybrook, Conn., 1953-62; pres. Nuhn Advt., Inc., Old Saybrook and Madison, 1963-89, Charles Kelsey Nuhn Advt. Inc., Madison, 1990; with Retired Advt. Exec. Recruiting Vols., Old Lyme, Conn., 1991—. Artist Old Lyme and Madison, 1987—; design artist "Benefit for Hunger Relief Share Our Strengths", Am. Express, Taste of the Nation, 1992; publicity chmn. for Billy Graham Crusade, New Haven, 1983; v.p. New Horizons Adult Care Ctr., Inc., 1997—. Mem. Lyme Acad. of Fine Arts, 1992—; mem. commn. on aging Town of Old Lyme, 1997—; assoc. mem. Lyme Art Assn., 1991—; mem. bd. dirs. Found. Fighting Blindness Conn. affiliate. With U.S. Army, 1945. Mem. Old Saybrook Art Assn. (v.p. 1988-89). Republican. Episcopalian. Home and Office: RAER Vols 249 Boston Post Rd Apt 15 Old Lyme CT 06371-1317

NULAND, SHERWIN, surgeon, author; b. N.Y.C., Dec. 8, 1930; s. Meyer and Violet (Lutsky) N.; m. Sarah Peterson, May 29, 1977; children: Victoria Jane, Andrew Meyer, William Peterson, Amelia Rose. BA, NYU, 1951; MD, Yale U., 1955. Surgeon Yale-New Haven Hosp. (Conn.), 1962-91; clin. prof. surgery Yale Sch. Medicine, New Haven, 1962—. Contbg. editor: The New Republic, The American Scholar. Author: The Origins of Anesthesia, 1983, Doctors: the Biography of Medicine, 1988, Medicine: The Art of Healing, 1991, How We Die: Reflections on Life's Final Chapter, 1994 (Nat. Book award for non-fiction 1994, Pulitzer prize finalist 1995), The Wisdom of the Body: How We Live, 1997, The Mysteries Within: A Surgeon Reflects on Medical Myths, 2000, Leonardo da Vinci, 2000. Pres. med. com. Jewish Home Aged, New Haven, 1985-87; v.p. Conn. Hospice, New Haven, 1978-80. Fellow AAAS, ACS, Yale Inst. Social & Policy Studies; mem. New Eng. Surg. Soc., Assocs. of Yale Med. Sch. Libr. (chmn. 1982-94), Yale-China Assn. (chmn. med. 1988-93), History of Medicine and Allied Scis. (chmn. bd. jour. 1979—). Democrat. Jewish. Avocation: tennis. Home: 29 Old Hartford Tpke Hamden CT 06517-3523 Office: PO Box 6356 Hamden CT 06517-0356 E-mail: snuland@rcn.com.

NULL, ELISABETH HIGGINS, librarian, writer; b. Worcester, Mass., Dec. 1, 1942; d. Carter Chapin Higgins and Katharine Huntington (Bigelow) Doman; m. Henry Harrison Null IV, July 13, 1963 (div. 1970); children: John Higgins, Jacob Van Vechten. BA, Sarah Lawrence Coll., Bronxville, N.Y., 1983; MA, Yale U., 1985, MPhil in Am. History, 1989; MA in Folklore, U. Pa., 1987; M Libr. and Info. Sci., Cath. U. Am., 1995. V.p. Abington Pub. Co., Clark's Summit, Pa., 1966-70; CEO Green Linnet Records, Danbury, Conn., 1971-81; vis. lectr. Am. Musical Life, Georgetown U., 1991-98; libr. and conversion specialist nat. digital libr. program Libr. of Congress, Washington, 1996-98, expert cons., 1995; writer on edn. issues Rural Sch. and Cmty. Trust, 1999—. Bd. dirs. Maine Folklife Ctr., 2001-; Horizon Internat., New Haven, 1978—; program chair Folklore Soc. Greater Washington, 1993-94; humanities scholar-in-residence Conn. Coun. for Humanities and Conn. Dept. for the Arts, Waterbury, Conn., 1986-87; program co-chair Washington Folk Festival, 1999-2000; fieldworker in folklore Waterbury Ethnic Music Project, 1986-87. Singer 2 recordings: The Feathered Malden, 1977, American Primitive, 1981; performance career with guitarist Bill Shute included 6 appearances with Garrison Keillor's A Prairie Home Companion; major venues include Phila. Folk Festival, Bklyn. Mus., Mus. Natural History. Incorporator John Woodman Higgins Armory, Worcester, Mass., 1966—; sec. Stanton Park Neighborhood Assn., Washington, 1990; bd. dirs. John and Clara Higgins Found., 1999—; mem. adv. bd. Maine Folklife Ctr., 2001--. Folger Shakespeare Libr. Seminar fellow, 1989-91. Mem. ALA, Am. Folklore Soc., Soc. for History of Early Am. Rep., Folklore Soc. Greater Washington (bd. dirs., program dir., festival com.). Democrat. Episcopalian. Avocations: folk music performer, song writer. Home and Office: 706 Bonifant St Silver Spring MD 20910-5534 E-mail: elisabeth.null@tcs.wap.org.

NULL, JAMES WESLEY, educator; b. Memphis, Jan. 8, 1973; s. Ronnie Hugh and Jeannine Ross N.; m. Dana Renee George, Mar. 11, 1995. BS magna cum laude, Eastern N.Mex. U., 1995, MEd, 1998. Tchr. sci. Artesia (N.Mex.) Intermediate Sch., 1995-96, tchr. gifted & talented, 1996-97; tchr. sci. Pflugerville (Tex.) Mid. Sch., 1997-99, tchr. social studies, 1998-99; grad. tchg. asst. U. Tex., Austin, 1999—; asst. prof. sch. edn. Baylor U. Presenter in field. Named to Blue Key Honor Soc. Mem.: ASCD, Soc. Philosophy and History Edn., Nat. Soc. SAR, History Edn. Soc., Midwest History Edn. Soc., Soc. Study Curriculum History, Nat. Soc. Study Edn., Am. Fedn. Tchrs., Am. Assn. Teaching & Curriculum, Kappa Delta Pi. Methodist. E-mail: wesley_null@baylor.edu.

NULL, MICHAEL ELLIOT, lawyer; b. Chgo., Feb. 14, 1947; s. Samuel Joseph and Rose (Baren) N.; m. Eugenia Irene Frack, Dec. 21, 1969; children: Jennifer Susan, Emily Lauren. B.S. in Psychology, U. Ill., 1969; J.D., Ill. Inst. Tech. Chgo. Kent Law Sch., 1974. Bar: Ill. 1974, U.S. Dist. Ct. (no. dist.) Ill. 1974, U.S. Dist. Ct. (ea. dist.) Mich., 1985, U.S. Dist. Ct. (ea. dist.) Wis., 1986, U.S. Ct. Appeals (7th cir.) 1981, U.S. Ct. Appeals (6th cir.) 1985, U.S. Supreme Ct., 1985. Prin. Michael Null And Assocs., Chgo., 1977—. Author: Truths: A Guide to Practical Metaphysics; composer musical selections. Mem. ABA, 1st Amendment Lawyers Assn. Office: 155 N Michigan Ave Chicago IL 60601-7511

NULL, PAUL BRYAN, minister; b. Oakland, Calif., May 7, 1944; s. Carleton Elliot and Dorothy Irene (Bryan) N.; m. Renee Yvonne Howell, Aug. 23, 1969; children: Bryan Joseph, Kara Renee. BS, Western Bapt. Coll., 1973; MDiv, Western Conservative Bapt. Sem., 1979; DMin, Trinity Theol. Sem., 1994. Ordained to ministry Bapt. Ch., 1982. Asst. pastor Bethel Bapt. Ch., Aumsville, Oreg., 1972-74, sr. pastor, 1974-87, The Calvary Congregation, Stockton, Calif., 1987-94; pastor Sierra Comty. Ch., South Lake Tahoe, 1994-98; exec. pastor Dayspring Fellowship, Salem, Oreg., 1998—. Trustee Conservative Bapt. Assn. of Oreg., 1982-85, mem. Ch. extension com., 1975-85. Radio show commentator Food for Thought, 1987. Panel mem. Presdl. Anti-Drug Campaign, 1984; vice chmn. bd. Western Bapt. Coll., Salem, Oreg., 1998—. Served with U.S. Army, 1965-67. Named Outstanding Young Man Am., 1979. Mem. Conservative Bapt. Assn. of Am., No. Calif. Conservative Bapt. Assn. (pres. 1992-93), Delta Epsilon Chi. Avocations: weight training, aerobics, writing, hiking, cross-country skiing. Home: 575 Belmont St NE Salem OR 97301-1255 Office: Dayspring Fellowship 1755 Lockhaven Dr NE Keizer OR 97303-2071 E-mail: paul_null@yahoo.com.

NULTON, WILLIAM CLEMENTS, retired lawyer; b. Pittsburg, Kans., Feb. 22, 1931; s. Perley Edgar and Mary Celia (Anderson) N.; m. Vicki Smith, Aug. 20, 1956; children: Carnie, Erica. BA, Kans. U., 1953, LLB with honors, 1958; postgrad., NYU, 1953-54. Bar: Kans. 1958, Mo. 1959. Sr. atty. Great Lakes Pipe Line Co., Kansas City, Mo., 1958-66, asst. sec., 1961-66; assoc. Blackwell, Sanders, Matheny, Weary & Lombardi, 1966-68, ptnr., 1968-81; assoc. Shughart Thomson & Kilroy, 1981-83, ptnr., 1983-94. Contbr. articles to profl. jours. Bd. dirs. Corinth Hills Home Assn., Shawnee Mission, 1974-76, Faith Friends, 1999—, Front Porch Alliance, 1999—; pres. Beta Theta Pi Kansas City Alumni Assn., 1977; mem., elder Village United Presbyn. Ch., Prairie Village, Kans., 1976—, trustee, 1992-94, mem. found. bd., 1997—; bd. dirs. Prairie Village Mcpl. Found., 1987—, pres., 2002—; bd. dirs. Kansas City Civil Rights Consortium, 1993—, Marillac Acad., 1994-99; mem. Kans. adv. com. U.S. Civil Rights Commn., 1994—, acting chmn., 1998; mem. Shawnee Mission Unified Bd. Edn., 1969-73, v.p., 1973; pres. Corinth Elem. Bd. Edn., Johnson County, Kans., 1969; chmn. Full Employment Task Group on Employment Disabled, Kansas City, 1987. Summerfield scholar Kans. U., 1949-53, Root-Tilden scholar NYU, 1953-54. Mem. ABA (mgmt. chmn. labor and employment law sect., com. on arbitration and collective bargaining 1989-92), Am. Acad. Hosp. Attys. (co-chmn. task group on bylaws for small rural hosps. 1992-93), Mo. Bar Assn. (chmn. labor law com. 1982), Nat. Health Lawyers Assn. (co-chmn. task group on alternative dispute resolution in health care field 1990-91), Phi Beta Kappa, Order of Coif. Republican. Home: 7908 El Monte St Shawnee Mission KS 66208-5047

NULTY, MARY ANNE, clinical social worker; b. Salt Lake City, June 9, 1946; d. Leo C. and Dorothy Caroline (Boyer) N.; married June 7, 1969 (div. 1974); 1 child, John Christopher Levtov. BS, George Mason U., 1974; MSW, Va. Commonweath U., 1980. Lic. clin. social worker. Social worker Fairfax (Va.) County Family Svcs., 1977—79, United Community Ministries, Alexandria, Va., 1975-77; probation counselor 31st Dist. Family Ct. Svc. Unit, Manassas, 1981-83; intake counselor 18th Dist. Family Ct. Svc. Unit, Alexandria, 1983-84; family counselor 19th Dist. Family Ct. Svc. Unit, Fairfax, 1988-93, 15th Dist. Family Ct. Svc. Unit, Fredericksburg, Va., 1984-88; pvt. practice, 1990—. Pres., founder Va. Assn. Ct. Family Counselors, 1990—; mem. PrivatePractice.Com, 2002—. Chair Human Rels. Com., Fairfax, 1982-84; mem. Madison H.S. Booster Club, Vienna, Va., 1986-88; v.p., pres.-elect Old Dominion U. Parent Assn., 1990. Mem. NASW (del. assembly, sec. Va. chpt. 2000-02, bd. mem., 1998-2000), Brent Soc., Nat. Assn. Forensic Social Workers. Roman Catholic. Avocations: biking, rollerblading, crafts, gardening, gourmet cooking. Office: 200 Little Falls St Falls Church VA 22046-4302

NUMATA, NOBUO, software company executive, consultant, engineer; b. Ashiya, Hyogo, Japan, Mar. 5, 1954; came to U.S., 1964; s. Jack Tetsuya and Tomoko (Noguchi) N. BEE, Princeton U., 1976; M in Computer Sci., Columbia U., 1979. Analyst Impex (Japan) Ltd., Tokyo, 1976-78, mgr., 1978-80, v.p., 1980-82, pres., 1982—, Tecnopac Inc., N.Y.C., 1988-97. V.p. Am. Tech. Group, Palo Alto, Calif., 1984-86. Contbr. articles to profl. jours. Trustee Princeton-in-Asia, 1979-93. Mem. Tokyo Am. Club, Tokyo Lawn and Tennis Club, Internat. House Japan, Princeton Club Japan, Tokyo Club. Avocations: photography, cooking, golf, woodworking, surfing. Home: 3899 Waakaula Pl Kihei HI 96753-8407

NUMBERE, DAOPU THOMPSON, petroleum engineer, educator; b. Buguma, Nigeria, Mar. 30, 1951; came to the U.S., 1975; s. Thompson and Norah (West) N.; m. Tonye Eugenia Higgwe, Dec. 29, 1987. BS in Mech. Engring., U. Coll. Swansea, 1975; MS in Petroleum Engring., Stanford U., 1977; PhD, U. Okla., 1982. Asst. prof. U. Mo., Rolla, 1982-88, assoc. prof., 1988-96, prof., 1996—, head dept. petroleum engring., 1996-2000. Cons. Sigma Cons., Mattoon, Ill., 1987-93, Marathon Oil Co., 1998; chmn. Mo. Oil and Gas Coun., 1996-2000. Author: Petroleum Reservoir Class Manual, 1991, Principles of Waterflooding, 1998. Recipient Shell-BP award, 1971-75, Selwyn Caswell prize U. Coll. Seansea, 1975, Okla. Rsch. award Okla Rsch. Coun., 1981. Mem. ASME, Internat. Soc. for Computer Methods and Adv. in Geomechanics, Soc. Petroleum Engrs., Sigma Xi. Achievements include development of an innovative method for streamline generation for oil recovery prediction, simultaneous prediction of oil recovery and water influx for oil and gas reservoirs. Office: U Mo Rolla 119 Mcnutt Hall Rolla MO 65401

NUMMINEN, TEPPO, professional hockey player; b. July 3, 1968; With Winnipeg Jets/Phoenix Coyotes, 1998—. Played in NHL All Star Game, 1999 & 2000. Achievements include winning a silver and bronze medal with the Finnish Olympic team. Office: America West Arena/Cellular One Ice Den 9375 E Bell Rd Scottsdale AZ 85260*

NUNEMACHER, STEPHEN C. (STEVE BLAZE), musician, writer; b. New Orleans; s. Dennis Emile and Judith Ann (Hautot) Nunemacher; m. Melissa McCurdy, Jan. 12, 1984 (div. June 1985); 1 child Brittany. Student, La. State U., Baton Rouge, Loyola U., New Orleans. Recording artist MCA Records, L.A., 1990—94, I.R.S. Records, L.A., 1994—99, Z Records, London, 1999—2001; sales mgr. Newton & Assocs., Kenner, La.; recording artist Noiselab Records, New Orleans, 2001—. Tchr. guitar, New Orleans, 1993—98. Producer, artist, writer: albums. Recipient scoring championship, Metaire Basketball Assn., 1999—2001. Achievements include Sold 750000 albums worldwide. Toured the world for 15 years. Hundreds of print, radio, internet features and interviews. Avocations: basketball, acting, Tae Kwon Do, weightlifting. Fax: 504-466-6131. E-mail: stevblaze@aol.com.

NUNES, JUDY OMAI, artist; b. San Mateo, Calif., Dec. 1, 1951; d. Noboru and Misaye Yamanaka Omai; m. Manuel Edwin Nunes, Nov. 1, 1975. BA, Calif. State U., San Jose, 1975. Exhibited in group shows at City Gallery, Sacramento, 1986, Judith Weintraub Gallery, 1990—92, Elliott Fouts Gallery, 2001, Represented in permanent collections Weintraub, Genshiea and Sproul, Sacramento, Sutter Club, Wilke, Fleury, Hoffet, Gould and Birney, Sacramento. Recipient Crocker-Kingsley award Crocker Mus., 1989, award Discovery 1993, Stockton Art League, 1999, 2000. Home: 827 Caroline Ave Galt CA 95632-2001

NUNES, MORRIS A. lawyer; b. Oceanside, N.Y., Apr. 9, 1949; s. Myron A. and Betty Ann (Ecoff) N.; m. Jane S. Chargar, Aug. 30, 1970 (dec. Aug. 2002); 2 children. BA, BS, U. Pa., 1970; JD, Georgetown U., 1975. Bar: Va. 1975, D.C. 1976. Auditor Arthur Young & Co. CPAs, Boston, 1970; controller Sanitary Group, Inc., West Haven, Conn., 1970-72; securities analyst Donatelli, Rudolph & Schoen, Washington, 1972-74; group controller Potomac Electric Power Co., 1974-77; pvt. practice Falls Church, Va., 1977—. Adj. prof. Cath. U. Law Sch., 1991—, Georgetown U. Law Sch., 1999—, Georgetown MBA program, 2001—; arbitrator Am. Arbitration Assn., Washington, 1980-97; bus. appraiser, pres. Net Worth, Inc., 1988—; hearing officer Va. Supreme Ct., 1996-2000; bus. adv. bd. James Monroe Bank, 1998-2001. Author: Operational Cash Flow, 1982, Balance Sheet Mgmt., 1987, The Right Price for Your Business, 1988; co-author: Property Logbook, 1985, Basic Legal Forms for Business, 1989; producer, host TV show Gen. Counsel, 1985-87; contbr. articles to profl. jours. Appointed mem. Va. State Bd. Prof. & Occup. Regulation, 1995—, chmn., 1997—; mem. Fairfax County Edn. Adv. Bd., Va., 1983-87; del. Rep. State Conv., 1993, 94. Mem. Va. State Bar Assn., D.C. Bar Assn., Washington Ind. Writers, Am. Soc. Appraisers, Nat. Assn. Corp. Dirs., Nat. Fedn. Ind. Bus., Internat. Churchill Soc., Wharton Club of D.C., Alpha Lit. and Philosophy Soc., Sigma Chi. Republican. Avocations: racquetball, chess, wargames, music appreciation, squash. Office: 7247 Lee Hwy Falls Church VA 22046-3710 E-mail: manapc@cox.rr.net.

NUNES-DÜBY, SIMONE EDITH, molecular biology researcher; b. Bern, Switzerland, June 26, 1942; came to U.S., 1970; d. Hans and Edith Düby; m. Anthony Charles Nunes, Oct. 27, 1972; children: Christopher C., Benjamin P. MD, U. Bern Med. Sch., 1968, Dr.Med. in Immunology, 1973. Resident in anesthesiology ob/gyn., Bern, 1968-69; clin. rsch. assoc. Brookhaven Nat. Lab., L.I., 1970-72; resident physician Inst. Pathology U. Bern, 1973; postdoctoral rsch. assoc. molecular biology Brown U., Providence, 1984-89, asst. prof., 1989-98, assoc. prof., 1999—. Vis. scientist Inst. Cell Biology ETH, Zurich, Switzerland, 1984, Nat. Inst. Standards and Tech., Md., 1994-95. Contbr. articles to profl. jours. Bd. dirs., chair corp. sponsorship com. Chorus of Westerly, R.I., 1990-94, 96—, singing mem., 1978—. Mem. AAAS, Verbindung der Schweizer Aertzte, Phi Kappa Phi. Avocations: singing, aerobics, drawing. Office: Brown U Bio Med 69 Brown St Box G-J361 Providence RI 02906-1224 E-mail: Simone_Nunes-Duby@brown.edu.

NUNEZ, ERNEST VINCENT, social worker; b. Rock Springs, Wyo. AS, Utah Tech. Coll., 1978; BS, Weber State Coll., 1983; MSW, U. Utah, 1985. Adolescent counselor Esperanza Para Mañana, Salt Lake City, 1983-84; therapist Human Affairs Internat., 1984-85; adolescent counselor Decker Lake Youth Ctr., 1985; mental health specialist Dept. Mental Health, 1984-85; child welfare worker Dept. Adoptions, Los Angeles, 1985-86; psychiat. social worker Dept. Mental Health, 1986—. Com. chmn. Cub Scouts, Ogden, Utah, 1982; mem. Chicano Scholarship Com., Salt Lake City, 1985; com. mem. Community Improvement Council, Ogden, 1982; v.p. Spanish Speaking Community Orgn., Ogden, 1981. Gov.'s Vocat. scholar, Utah Tech. Coll., Salt Lake City, 1976, Ethnic Minority scholar Weber State Coll., Ogden, 1982, 83, Chicano scholar, Salt Lake City, 1984, Nat. Hispanic scholar, San Francisco, 1985. Mem. Nat. Assn. Social Workers, East Los Angeles Jaycees. Roman Catholic. Avocations: basketball, tennis, softball, weightlifting, poetry writing.

NUNEZ, PAUL LEE, biomedical engineer, physicist; b. Miami Beach, Fla., Jan. 29, 1940; BS, MS, U. Fla., Gainesville, 1963; phD, U. Calif.-San Diego, La Jolla, 1969. Rsch. engr. Gen. Dynamics, San Diego, 1963—65; scientist KMS Tech. Ctr., 1969—70, Sci. Applications, La Jolla, 1970—71; rsch. neuroscientist U. Calif.-San Diego, 1971—80; assoc. prof. elec. and computer engring. San Diego State U., 1981—85; prof. biomed. engring. Tulane U., New Orleans, 1985—. Vis. rsch. scientist Brain Scis. Inst., Melbourne, Victoria, Australia, 1998—2000. Author: (book) Electric Fields of the Brain: The Neurophysics of EEG, 1981, Neocortical Dynamics and Human EEG Rhythms, 1995.

NUNEZ, VICTOR, film director, producer, writer; Director, cinematographer, writer: Gal Young 'Un, 1979, A Flash of Green, 1984; director, writer: Ruby in Paradise, 1993 (nominated Ind. Spirit award best dir. 1993, best screenplay 1993, Grand Jury prize Sundance Film Festival dramatic category 1993), Ulee's Gold, 1997 (nominated 1st prize Mystfest, 1997, nominated Ind. Spirit award best dir., best screenplay 1998, nom. Grand Spl. prize Deauville Film Festival 1997); cinematographer: Without Evidence, 1995; prodr.: Gal Young 'Un, 1979; actor: Squeeze, 1997. Recipient Outstanding Achievement in Film award Fla. Film Critics Circle, 1998. Office: c/o DGA 7920 W Sunset Blvd Los Angeles CA 90046-3300*

NUÑEZ DE VILLAVICENCIO, MARIA IRENE, small business owner, consultant; b. Caibarien, Cuba, Jan. 19, 1940; came to U.S., 1956; d. Candido Gregorio and Sofia Irene Diaz; m. Antonio Luis Nuñez de Villavicencio, July 15, 1960; children; Ana Maria, Jacqueline, Mark Allan, Paul Anthony, Jennifer Susan. Student, Marsh Bus. Sch., Atlanta, 1960, Bentley Coll., 1989. With accounts receivable dept. GE Credit Corp., Atlanta, 1960-62; cashier Digital Equipment Corp., Marlboro, Mass., 1981-83, auditor, 1983-87, with profit and loss statements dept. Maynard, 1987-92; owner, v.p. ops., cons. AMN Assocs., Westboro, 1991-94; with AMN Enterprises, 1994—, Hobe Sound, Fla., 1996—. Roman Catholic. Avocations: investing, reading, travel, swimming, trap shooting. Address: PO Box 1476 Hobe Sound FL 33475-1476 Home and Office: Apt 1403 5049 N Highway A1A Fort Pierce FL 34949-8289

NUNEZ-LAWTON, MIGUEL G. international finance specialist; b. Havana, Cuba, Feb. 8, 1949; came to U.S., 1964; s. Miguel Nunez-Cancio and Silvia Lawton-Alfonso. BSBA, Georgetown U., 1971, postgrad. in Econs., 1973. Asst. treas. Deltec Securities Corp., N.Y.C., 1971; debt specialist internat. econs. dept. World Bank, Washington, 1973-95; internat. cons. Miami, Fla., 1996—. UN Conf. in Trade and Devel. cons. Nat. Bank Angola, Luanda, 2000; UNCTAD chief tech. adviser Bur. Treasury, Manila, 1989—90. Bd. dirs., treas. Friends of Art Mus. of the Americas, OAS, Washington, 1988-90; bd. dirs. Friends of Peru, 1991—; panel mem. The Lawrenceville Sch., 1992; mem. Presdl. Inaugural Com., Washington, 1997. Roman Catholic. Avocations: art collecting, genealogy. Home: 8860 SW 123rd Ct Apt K106 Miami FL 33186-4152 E-mail: mnlawton@hotmail.com.

NUNEZ-PORTUONDO, RICARDO, investment company executive; b. N.Y.C., June 9, 1933; s. Emilio and Maria (Garcia) N-P.; m. Dolores Maldonado, Sept. 7, 1963; children— Ricardo Jose, Emilio Manuel, Eduardo Javier. LL.D., U. Havana, Cuba; postdoctoral in law, U. Fla., 1975. Bar: Cuba, Fla. Editor Latin Am. div. USIA, Miami, Fla., 1961-71, editor Washington, 1961-71; nat. dir. Cuban Refugee Program, 1975-77; pres. Cultural Pub., Inc., Miami, 1994—, Central Investment Trust, Coral Gables, Fla., 1977—; chmn. bd. Interstate Bank of Commerce, Miami, 1986-88; v.p. Century 21, Coral Gables, 1989—. Author: A Critique on the Linowitz Report, 1975, Cuba: La Otra Imagen, 1994, Un Procer Cubano, 1994, Cuban Refugee Program, The Early Years, 1995. Dir. Nat. Hispanic Scholarship Fund, San Francisco, 1978— ; dir. COSSMHO, Washington, 1980—; trustee emeritus Fla. Internat. U., 1984— ; pres. Mercy Hosp. Found., Miami, 1985—; bd. dirs. ARC, Greater Miami. Recipient numerous awards for civic contbns. including day named in honor Ricardo Nunez Day, Miami, 1975. Mem. Cuban Lawyers Assn., Cuban Acad. History, Metro. Club, Lyford Cay Club, Ocean Reef Club, Key Biscayne Yacht Club, Big Five Club, 200 Club. Republican. Roman Catholic. Home: 4651 W Flagler St Apt 9 Miami FL 33134-1532 Office: PO Box 141720 Coral Gables FL 33114-1720

NUNLEY, CHARLES ARTHUR, language educator; b. Topeka, Sept. 22, 1959; s. Harold C. and Ruth G. (Gelinas) N.; m. Gayle Roof, June 22, 1991. BA, Middlebury Coll., 1982, MA, 1985, Princeton U., 1986, PhD, 1993. Assoc. prof. Middlebury Coll., Middlebury, Vt., 1988—. Grantee Am. Philos. Soc., 1994-95; rsch. grantee Govt. France, 1986-87. Mem. MLA, AAUP, Am. Assn. Tchrs. French, Am. Coun. Tchg. Fgn. Langs., Northeast Modern Lang. Assn., 19th Century Studies Assn., Interdisciplinary Nineteenth-Century Studies. Office: Middlebury Coll Dept French Middlebury VT 05753

NUNN, CHARLES BURGESS, religious organization executive; b. Richmond, Va., May 1, 1931; s. Charles Burgess Sr. and Virginia Atkinson (Goode) N.; m. Helen Agnes Parker, Sept. 1, 1957; children: Patsy Virginia, Catherine Louise, Stephen Charles, Stewart Gavin. BA in Econs., Randolph Macon Coll., 1953; BD, Southwestern Bapt. Theol. Sem., 1959, MDiv, 1969; DMin, Pitts. Theol. Sem., 1979. Ordained to Gospel ministry, 1954. Pastor Warwick Rd. Bapt. Chapel, Richmond, Va., 1952-53, Garrett's Bluff Bapt. Ch., Arthur City, Tex., 1954-56, Plymouth Haven Bapt. Ch., Alexandria, Va., 1959-68, First Bapt. Ch., Bluefield, W.Va., 1968-77; exec. dir. missions Richmond (Va.) Bapt. Assn., 1977-97; adminstr., treas. So. Bapt. Conf./Assoc. Dirs. Missions, 1997—. Trustee Bluefield (W.Va.) Coll., 1972-82, U. Richmond, Va., 1989-93; first v.p. Va. Bapt. Gen. Bd., Richmond, 1974-75; dir. Home Mission Bd., So. Bapt. Conv., Atlanta, 1976-84. Author: (children's book) Following Jesus, 1968. Commr. Bluefield (W.Va.) Urban Renewal Authority, 1971-74; chmn. Bluefield (W.Va.) Beautification Commn., 1972-73; pres. North Chamberlayne Civic Assn., Richmond, 1989-91. Recipient Disting. Svc. award City of Bluefield, 1970, Disting. Alumnus award Alumni Soc. Randolph Macon, Ashland, Va., 1992, Vol. Missions award Richmond Regional Devel. Coun. of the Fgn. Mission Bd., So. Bapt. Conv., 1995. Mem. Richmond Rotary Club (bd. dirs. 1990-92), Sandston Rotary Club, Omicron Delta Kappa. Avocations: traveling, fishing, photography, baseball. E-mail: sbcadom@aol.com.

NUNN, GRADY HARRISON, political science educator emeritus; b. Arlington, Tex., Apr. 12, 1918; s. William Roy and Floy Brooke (Dugan) N.; m. Ann Torrey Welsh, June 15, 1951 (dec. 1980); 1 child, Therese von Hohoff.; m. Virginia Cotton Chivington, Dec. 18, 1982. BA, U. Okla., 1939, MA, 1941; PhD (Penfield fellow), N.Y.U., 1961. Instr. N.Y.U., 1946-49; from instr. to asso. prof. U. Ala., Tuscaloosa, 1949-65, prof., chmn. dept. polit. sci. Birmingham, 1969-83, prof. emeritus, 1983—; vis. asst. prof. Ind. U., 1960-61; asst. prof., asso. prof. U. Pitts. at Ahmadu Bello U., Nigeria, 1964-68; assoc. prof. U. Pitts., 1968, Auburn U., 1968-69. Bd. dirs. Unitarian Universalist Service Com., 1978-84, v.p., 1981-82 Assoc. editor: Background on World Politics, 1957-62; Contbr. to: Readings in Government in American Society, 1949, Federalism in the Commonwealth, 1963, The Politics and Administration of Nigerian Government, 1965; editorial bd.: Jour. of Politics, 1971-74. Mem. Birmingham Regional Planning Commn., 1995-2000. Capt. F.A., AUS, 1942-46. Ford Found. Fgn. Area fellow, 1956-57 Mem. Am. Polit. Sci. Assn., So. Polit. Sci. Assn. (exec. council 1974-77), Royal African Soc., AAUP (pres. Ala. conf.), Phi Beta Kappa, Pi Sigma Alpha, Phi Eta Sigma, Alpha Tau Omega, Omicron Delta Kappa. Unitarian Universalist. Home: 805 Rockhurst Ln Birmingham AL 35209 E-mail: ghnunn@aol.com.

NUNN, ROBERT WILLIAM, protective services official; b. Greensboro, N.C., June 7, 1962; s. Lester G. and Pauline B. Nunn. BS in Social Work, U. N.C., Greensboro, 1995, MA in Pub. Affairs, 2000. Sentencing specialist One Step Further, Inc., Greensboro, 1993—. Vol. mediator Mediation Svcs. Guilford, Greensboro, 1997—; human rels. commr. City of Greensboro. Scholar, Cemela Found., 1999—2000. Mem.: Nat. Assn. Sentencing Adv. Avocations: tennis, travel, swimming. Home: 4300 Triston Dr Greensboro NC 27407 Office: One Step Further Inc 621 Eugene Ct Ste 101 Greensboro NC 27401 Home Fax: 336-378-0959; Office Fax: 336-378-0959.

NUNNALLY, STEPHENS WATSON, civil engineer; b. Gadsden, Ala., Nov. 30, 1927; s. John Marshall and Mae Louise (Watson) N.; m. Joan Marie Arel, May 29, 1957; children: Stephens Jr., Janine, John. BS, U.S. Mil. Acad., 1949; MS, Northwestern U., 1958, PhD, 1966. Cert. profl. engr. Fla., Ala. Commd. lt. U.S. Army, 1949, advanced through grades to lt. col., retired, 1970; asst. prof. U. Fla., Gainesville, 1971-75; prof. N.C. State U., Raleigh, 1975-84; freelance cons. Satellite Beach, Fla., 1984--. Author: Managing Construction Equipment, 1977, Construction Methods and Management, 1980, 87, 93, 98; co-author: Residential and Light Building Construction, 1990. Recipient Outstanding Extension Svc. award N.C. State U. 1982. Fellow ASCE (exec. com. Cclo. div. 1990—), Am. Soc. for Engring. Edn. (com. chmn. 1980-81). Republican. Episcopaian. Home: 474 Saint Lucia Ct Satellite Beach FL 32937-3842

NUNZ, GREGORY JOSEPH, aerospace engineer, program manager, educator, entrepreneur; b. Batavia, N.Y., May 28, 1934; s. Sylvester Joseph and Elizabeth Marie (Loesell) N.; m. Georgia Monyea Costas, Mar. 30, 1958; children: Karen, John, Rebecca, Deirdre, Jaimie, Marta. BSChemE, Cooper Union, 1955; postgrad., U. So. Calif., Calif. State U.; MS in Applied Math., Columbia Pacific U., 1991, PhD in Mgmt. Sci., 1993. Adv. design staff, propulsion mgr. U.K. project Rocketdyne div. Rockwell, Canoga Park, Calif., 1955-65; mem. tech. staff Aerospace Corp., El Segundo, 1965-70; mem. tech. staff propulsion div. Jet Propulsion Lab., Pasadena, 1970-72; chief. monoprop. engring. Bell Aerospace Corp., Buffalo, 1972-74; group supr. comb. devices Jet Propulsion Lab., Pasadena, 1974-76; dep. group leader, asst. div. leader, program mgr. internat. HDR geothermal energy program, program mgr. space-related projects Los Alamos (N.Mex.) Nat. Lab., 1977—. Assoc. prof. electronics L.A. Pierce Coll., Woodland Hills, Calif., 1961-72; instr. No. N.Mex. C. C., Los Alamos, 1978-80, div. head scis., 1980-92; adj. prof. math. U. N.Mex., Los Alamos, 1980—; sr. mgmt. rep. Excel Telecom., Inc., 1995-98. Author: Electronics Lab Manual I, 1964, Electronics in Our World, 1972; co-author: Electronics Mathematics, vol. I, II, 1967, Imotep to Khufu: How It Can Be Done, 2001; contbg. author Prentice-Hall Textbook of Cosmetology, 1975, Alternative Energy Sources VII, 1987; contbr. articles to profl. jours.; inventor smallest catalytic liquid N2H4 rocket thrustor, co-inventor first monoprop/biprop bimodal rocket engine, tech. advisor internat. multi-prize winning documentary film One With the Earth. Mem. Aerial Phenomena Research Orgn., L.A., 1975. Fellow AIAA (assoc., liquid propellants com. on stds.); mem. ARISTA, Math. Assn. Am. Avocations: travel, archaeology, foreign languages, golf. Office: Los Alamos Nat Lab PO Box 1663 Los Alamos NM 87545-0001 also: U NMex Los Alamos Br 4000 University Dr Los Alamos NM 87544-2233 E-mail: grunz@lanl.gov.

NURENBERG, DAVID, retired oil company executive; b. N.Y.C., Mar. 25, 1939; s. Abraham S. and Katherine G. N.; m. Brenda G. Schwait, Sept. 1963; children— Jill Suzanne, Brian Michael. BS in Marine Engring, U.S. Mcht. Marine Acad., 1960; MS in Indsl. Mgmt, Columbia U., 1963, PhD in Mgmt. Sci, 1965. With Exxon Corp., 1963-67; employee relations mgr. Esso Pappas, Athens, Greece, 1968-72; labor relations and compensation mgr. Esso Europe, London, 1972-77; corp. sec. Esso Eastern Inc., Houston, 1977-82; mgr. exec. compensation Exxon Corp., N.Y.C., 1982-90, mgr. compensation and exec. programs Irving, Tex., 1990-98; ret. Past mem. coun. exec. compensation Conf. Bd., past chmn.; adj. prof. Union Inst. Past mem. exec. edn. adv. bd. Wharton Sch., U. Pa.; past mem. adv. bd. Ctr. for Effective Orgns., U. So. Calif. Mem. Am. Compensation Assn. (bd. dirs., chmn., exec. comp. coun., bd. steering com.).

NURHUSSEIN, MOHAMMED ALAMIN, internist, geriatrician, educator; b. Adwa, Ethiopia, Apr. 4, 1942; came to U.S., 1972; s. Hagos and Teberih (Yusuf) N.; m. Zahra Said, June 10, 1972; children: Nadia, Siham, Safy. BS, Haile Selasie Mil. Acad., Harar, Ethiopia, 1961; MD, Zagreb (Yugoslavia) U., 1968. Intern, resident, then fellow Bklyn.-Cumberland Med. ctr., 1972-77; emergency rm. physician Cumberland Hosp., Bklyn., 1977-79; attending physician in medicine Kings County Hosp. Ctr., 1979—; faculty practice medicine, geriatrics SUNY Univ. Hosp., 1983—. Instr., then asst. prof. SUNY Health Sci. Ctr., bklyn., 1979—; med. cons., dir. drug abuse treatment Coney Island Hosp., Bklyn., 1982-84; adv. bd. Bklyn. Alzheimer's Disease Assistance Ctr., 1992—. Fellow ACP; mem. Am. Geriatric Soc., Am. Lung Assn., N.Y. Acad. Scis., Amnesty Internat., Physicians for Human Rights. Democrat. Moslem. Office: SUNY Health Sci Ctr 450 Clarkson Ave Brooklyn NY 11203-2056

NURKSE, DENNIS, writer, poet; b. N.Y.C., Dec. 13, 1949; s. Ragnar and Henriette Nurkse; m. Lucy Cobb, 1982 (div. 1994); 1 child, Sonia. BA magna cum laude, Harvard U., 1970. Lectr. Wagner Coll., S.I., N.Y., 1988; program officer Def. for Children USA, N.Y.C., 1987-92; mem. faculty The Writer's Voice, 1997-2000; lectr. New Sch. U., 1996—. Author: Shadow Wars, 1988, Staggered Lights, 1990, Voice Over Water, 1993, rev. edit., 1996, Leaving Xaia, 2000, The Rules of Paradise, 2001, The Fall, 2002. Vol. Amnesty Internat., 1973—. Recipient Poetry award Whiting Found., 1990, Tanne Found., 2000; poetry fellow N.Y. Found. for the Arts, 1999, 2000, NEA, 1984, 95. Mem. PEN. E-mail: dnurkse@hotmail.com.

NURNBERG, CHARLES GORDON, publishing company marketing executive; b. Newark, Nov. 16, 1947; s. Max and Eleanor (Gordon) N.; m. Barbara Ann Goldstein, Dec. 20, 1970; children: Jeremy, Peter, David. BA, Syracuse U., 1969. Proofreader Frederick Fell Pub., Inc., N.Y.C., 1969, editor, 1970-72, sales, 1972-74, sales mgr., 1974-75, v.p. sales, 1975-77, exec. v.p., 1977-78, pub., 1978; pub. paperbacks Sterling Pub. Co., Inc., 1978-80, v.p., dir. mktg., 1980-82, sr. v.p., 1982-89, exec. v.p., 1990—. Mem. Book Industry Study Group com., 1992-95. Mem. Assn. Am. Pubs. (mem. mktg. com. 1970-73, chmn. pubs. forum com. 1973-79), Marlboro Soccer Assn. (bd. dirs., coach 1974, boys travel team). Avocations: writing, travel, fitness. Home: 25 Whitman Rd Morganville NJ 07751-1442 Office: 387 Park Ave S New York NY 10016-8810 E-mail: cnurnberg@sterlingpub.com.

NURNBERGER, RALPH D. public affairs executive; b. N.Y.C., July 10, 1946; BA, Queens Coll., 1967; MA, Columbia U., 1968; PhD, Georgetown U., 1975. Fgn. policy staff mem. Senator James Pearson, Washington, 1976-78; profl. staff mem. Senate Fgn. Rels. Com., 1978-79; sr. fellow Ctr. Strategic Studies, 1979-81; legis. liason Am. Israel Pub. Affairs Com., 1981-89; dir. congl. rels. Dept. Commerce, 1989-90; v.p. Conkling Fiskum McCormick, 1990-94; sr. ptnr. Nurnberger & Assocs., 1994-99; govtl. affairs counselor Preston Gates Ellis Rouvelas Meeds, 1999—. Adj. prof. Georgetown U., Washington, 1975—. Sr. counsel Builders for Peace, Washington, 1993-97. Office: Preston Gates Ellis & Rouvelas Meeds, LLP and predecessor 1735 New York Ave NW Washington DC 20006-5209 Fax: (202) 331-1024. E-mail: ralphn@prestongates.com.

NURSE, SIR PAUL M. cancer researcher; Dir. gen. (sci.) Cancer Rsch. U.K., London. Recipient Nobel Prize in Physiology or Med., The Nobel Found., 2001, Royal medal Royal Soc., 1995, H. P. Heineken prize for biochemistry and biophysics Royal Netherlands Acad. Arts and Scis., 1996, Dr. Josef Steiner prize, Cancer Found., Bern, Switzerland, 1996, Alfred P. Sloan Jr. prize and medal, GM Cancer Rsch. Found., 1997, Albert Lasker award USA, 1998, Berkan Judd award, 1998. Office: Cancer Rsch UK PO Box 123 Lincoln Inn Fields London England WC2A3PX E-mail: paul.nurse@cancer.org.uk.

NUSBACHER, GLORIA WEINBERG, lawyer; b. N.Y.C., July 22, 1951; d. Murray and Doris (Togman) Weinberg; m. Burton Nusbacher, Aug. 4, 1974; 1 child, Shoshana. BA, Barnard Coll., 1972; JD, Columbia U., 1975. Bar: N.Y. 1976. Assoc. Hughes Hubbard & Reed LLP, N.Y.C., 1975-83, counsel, 1983-91, ptnr., 1991—. Lectr. in field. Contbr. articles to profl. jours.; mem. Columbia Law Rev. Troop leader, leader trainer Girl Scouts USA, 1991-97. Mem. ABA (employee benefits and exec. compensation com. 1987—, fed. regulation securities com., subcom. employee benefits, exec. compensation and sect. 16, 1983—, task force Sect. 16, 1991-97, vice-chair com. employee benefits and exec. compensation, 2001—, chair subcom. fed. and state securities laws of com. employee benefits and exec. compensation 1994-2001, task force exec. compensation 1992-94), Phi Beta Kappa. Office: Hughes Hubbard & Reed LLP 1 Battery Park Plz New York NY 10004-1482

NUSBAUM, GEOFFREY DEAN, psychotherapist; b. Berkeley, Calif., Apr. 1, 1946; s. Wayne Dale and Jeanne (Hankins) N.; m. Barbara Ann Pierfy, June 1, 1986; 1 child, Michael Wayne. BA, Washington U., St. Louis, 1967; MA, Hartford Sem. Fdn. Consortium, 1971, PhD, 1978. Diplomate Am. Bd. Med. Psychotherapy; cert. therapist Am. Assn. for Marriage and Family Therapy; lic. therapist, N.J. Pvt. practice, Marlton, N.J. and Phila., 1972—; cons. N.Y. Fertility Rsch. Found., N.Y.C., 1978-83, Bancroft Sch., Haddonfield, N.J., 1983-87. Fellow Internat. Coun. Sex. Edn. and Parenthood Am. U. Author: Community, Self Identity, 1978; peer manuscript reviewer to sci. jours. Bd. dirs. Calcutta House AIDS Hospice. Mem. Am. Soc. for Reproductive Medicine, Am. Soc. for Psychosomatic Ob-Gyn., N.Y. Acad. Scis.

NUSBAUM, MURRAY L. obstetrician-gynecologist; b. Utica, N.Y., Feb. 22, 1922; s. Morris and Anna Gertrude Nusbaum; m. Bridgetta A. Nusbaum, July 31, 1949; children: Devra L., Korrine P. AB, Antioch Coll., 1946; MD, Case Western Res. U., 1947. Diplomate Am. Bd. Ob-Gyn. Rotating intern No. Permanente Hosp., Vancouver, Wash., 1947-48; resident in ob-gyn. and pathologoy Dr.'s Hosp., Cleve., 1948-50; surg. resident Woman's Hosp., Detroit, 1950, 53; sr. resident in ob-gyn. Florence Crittenden Hosp., 1953-54; clin. asst. prof. SUNY, Syracuse, 1974-80, assoc. prof., 1980-83, prof., 1983-94; pvt. practice Utica, 1954-94; ret., 1994. Med. dir. Ferre Inst., Utica, 1975—, Planned Parenthood of Mohawk Valley, Utica, 1966-83; hon. staff Faxton Hosp., utica, St. Elizabeth Hosp., Utica, St. Luke's Meml. Hosp. Ctr., Utica; cons. Masonic Home, Utica; mem. adj. staff State Univ. Hosp., Syracuse. Contbr. articles to profl. jours. Bd. dirs. Utica Coll. of Syracuse U., 1972-81, mem. emeritus, 1982—; bd. dirs. Temple Emanuel, Utica, Family Svcs. of Greater Utica, 1962-64; past pres., bd. dirs. Jewish Social Svcs., utica. With USN, 1942-45, 50-52. Fellow Am. Coll. Ob-Gyn. (life, med. advisor, exec. com. local dist. 1988—, grievance com. 1996—, internat. affairs com., nominations com., Pres.'s Cmty. Svc. award 1995, Outstanding Dist. Svc. award 1988); mem. AMA, Med. Soc. N.Y. (com. on state legislation 1988—), Am. Acad. Medicine and Sci. (bd. dirs. 1993—), Am. Soc. Reproductive Medicine (life), Ctrl. N.Y. Acad. Medicine (past pres., Scroll award 1984, 97), Ctrl. N.Y. Assn. Gynecologists and Obstetricians (past pres.), Fertility Soc. of Upstate N.Y., Am. Assn. Gynecol. Laparoscopists, Soc. Reproductive Surgeons, Fallopius Internat. Soc. Avocations: skiing, gardening. E-mail: MLNusbaum@aol.com.

NUSHOLTZ, GUY SAMUEL, research engineer; b. Detroit, Nov. 4, 1948; s. Phillip and Shirley Fern (Altschuler) Nusholtz; m. Pat S. Kaiker, June 5, 1988. BS, Antioch Coll., 1972; MS, U. Mich., 1974. Fire chief Antioch Coll. Fire Dept., Yellow Springs, Ohio, 1970-72; rsch. assoc. U. Mich., Ann Arbor, 1974-81, rsch. scientist, 1981-88; rsch. engr. Chrysler, Auburn Hill, Mich., 1988—; bio-engring. Wayne State U., Detroit, 1993—. Cons. mech. engring. U. Va., Charlottesville, 1989—; mem. adv. bd. STAPP, Warrendale, Mich., 1991—, Motor Vehicle Rsch. Adv. Com., Washington, 1991—; mem. bioengring. adv. bd. Wayne State U., 1994. Mem. AAAS, Soc. Exptl. Mechanics, Soc. Automobile Engrs., Sigma Xi. Achievements include development of motion-tracking system using linear accelerometers, x-ray cinematographic, crash impact signal processing procedures, non linar shift varient filters, air bag gas jet model, fire fighting procedures using high pressure fog. Office: Chrysler CIMS 483-05-10 800 Chrysler Dr Auburn Hills MI 48326-2757

NUSIM, STANLEY HERBERT, chemical engineer, consultant; b. N.Y.C., Oct. 2, 1935; s. Seymour and Ranna T. (Weiner) N.; m. Marcia Anne Borsig, Feb. 21, 1960; children: David Mark, Jill Wendi. BChemE, CCNY, 1957; MChemE, N.Y. U., 1960, PhD, 1967. Rsch. engr. Battelle Meml. Inst., Columbus, Ohio, 1956; researcher, chem. engring. rsch. and devel. Merck Rsch. Labs. Div., Rahway, N.J., 1957-68, sect. mgr., 1968-70; tech. svcs. mgr. Merck Chem. Mfg. Div., 1970-73, mfg. mgr., 1973-80; dir. subsidiary projects Merck Internat. Div., 1981-82, exec. dir. Latin Am., Far East, Near East ops., 1982-88; exec. dir. licensee, Latin Am., Far East, Asia ops. Merck Pharm. Mfg. Div., 1989-92; exec. dir. licensee ops. worldwide Merck Mfg. Divsn. Merck & Co. Inc., Whitehouse Station, NJ, 1992-94; v.p. mfg. and ops. Therics Inc., Princeton, 1994-97; pres. S.H. Nusim Assocs., Inc., Aventura, Fla., 1994—. Mem. adv. bd. CCNY Sch. Engring., 1982—; bd. dirs. AGI Dermatics Inc., Freeport, NY. Author: Kinetic Studies on C4 Hydrocarbon Systems, 1967. V.p. men's club Temple Beth Shalom, Livingston, N.J., 1975-78; rep. to bd. edn. Livingston Home and Sch. Assn., 1982-83; bd. govs. Turnberry Isle Yacht and Racquet Club, Aventura, Fla., 1992-94. Mem. Am. Inst. Chem. Engrs. (bd. dir. N. Jersey sect. 1968-71, scholarship award 1955), Am. Chem. Soc., Tau Beta Pi, Garden State Yacht Club (bd. govs. 1987-88). Achievements include U.S. and foreign patents on the continuous manufacture of halogenated acetone, development of "clean room" concepts for pharmachemical manufacturing, development of sophisticated training techniques for sterile pharmaceutical manufacturing. Home: 19355 Turnberry Way Apt 4L Aventura FL 33180-2532

NUSINOVICH, GREGORY SEMEON, physicist, researcher; b. Berdichev, Russia, July 18, 1946; arrived in U.S., 1991; s. Semeon and Esther (Burdo) Nusinovich; m. Yelena Naydich, July 2, 1968; children: Maria, Liza, Paulina. MSc, Gorky (Russia) State U., 1968, PhD, 1975. Rsch. scientist Radiophys. Rsch. Inst., Gorky, 1968-77; sr. rsch. scientist, group leader Inst. Applied Physics, Acad. Scis. of Russia, 1977-90; sr. rsch. scientist Inst. for Rsch. Electronics and Applied Physics, U. Md., College Park, 1991—. Mem. sci. coun. phys. electronics Acad. Scis. Russia, 1981—90; cons. Phys. Scis., Inc., Alexandria, Va., 1991—, Sci. Applications Internat. Corp., McLean, Va., 1991—93, McLean, 2000—, Omega-P, New Haven, 1995—2000. Co-editor: (book) Gyrotrons, 1980, Gyrotron, 1981, Gyrotrons, 1989; guest editor spl. issues: IEEE-PS on high-power microwaves; guest editor spl. issues IEEE-PS on cyclotron resonance masers and gyrotrons; contbr. chapters to books. Fellow: IEEE, Am. Phys. Soc. Achievements include development of of the theory of multimode gyrotrons; the nonlinear theory of relativistic gyrodevices; theory of gyroamplifiers and the gyrotron producing 100 KW power at the frequency of 500 GHZ. Office: U Md Inst Rsch Electronics and Appli Physics College Park MD 20742-3511 E-mail: gregoryn@glue.umd.edu.

NUSS, BARBARA GOUGH, artist; b. Washington, Apr. 11, 1939; d. Gaines Homer Gough and Edwerta Barbara (Beyer) Barber; m. Frederick A. Johnson, Sept. 30, 1968 (div. 1975); 1 child, Mark Eugene; m. Fred Dean Nuss, Dec. 18, 1982. BFA, Syracuse U., 1960; postgrad., Schuler Sch. Fine Arts, Balt., 1986-87. Art dir. Chappell's Dept. Store, Syracuse, N.Y., 1960-62, 66; mgr., illustrator Holman Anderson & Moore, Washington, 1967-70; art dir., advt. mgr. Ad-Media & Howard Advt. Assocs., Columbia, Md., 1970-75; acct. exec. Graphic Arts Inc., Alexandria, Va., 1975-77; sales mgr. The Jour. Newspapers, Washington, 1977-82; tchr., adult edn. Montgomery Coll., Rockville, Md., 1984-85; pvt. tchr. fine arts, Woodbine, 1982-96. Chmn. Montgomery County Juried Art Exhibit, Rockville, 1988; pres. Nuss Fine Arts, Inc., 1992—; chmn. Mid-Atlantic Regional Watercolor Exhibit, 1998, 99. One-woman shows include Pa. State U., 1986, NIH, Bethesda, Md., 1989, 1990, Md. Nat. Capital Pk. and Planning Commn., 1991, Art League Gallery, Alexandria, Va., 1992, Bendann Art Galleries, Towson, Md., 1999, 2000, exhibited in group shows at Art League at the Torpedo Factory, 1987—92, Heritage Gallery Classical Realism, 1989—90, Art Barn Gallery, Washington, 1990, Carmen's Gallery, 1991—2000, Bendann's Art Gallery, Towson, 1997—2002, Art Showcase 100 Md. Artists, 1991—92, Assn. pour la Promotion du Patrimoine Artistique Francais, Galerie Jean Lammelin, Argenteuil, France, 1991, Salmagundi Club 14th Ann. Exhbn., 1991, 18th Ann. Exhbn., 1995, Atrium Gallery Georgetown U., Washington, 1991, Strathmore Hall, Bethesda, 1995, Mid-Atlantic Regional Watercolor Exhbn., 1989 (Holbein award), 1990, 1996, State House, Annapolis, 1996, World Trade Ctr., Balt., 1996, Principle Gallery, Alexandria, Va., 1998—2002, Miniature Painters, Sculptors and Gravers Soc. Washington, 1999, Miniature Art Soc. Fla., 2000, Oil Painters Am., 2000, 2001, Addison/Ripley Fine Art Gallery, Washington, 1999, Main St. Gallery, Annapolis, 1999, 2000, Troika Gallery, Easton, 2001, 2002, Rock Creek Gallery, Washington, 1999, 2001, Washington County Arts Coun. Gallery, Hagerstown, 2001, Represented in permanent collections Nat. Park Found., NIH, Am. Coun. Edn., NIH, Bell Atlantic, Kiplinger Washington Editors, Fairhaven Retirement Cmty., Md. State Treas.'s Office. Finalist still life competition, Artist's mag., 1996; recipient 1st prize for watercolor, C&O Canal Show, 1987, 1st prize for oil painting, Rockville Art League, 1987, Montgomery County Art Assn., 1983, 1989, Gaithersburg Fine Arts Assn., 1983, 1989, grand champion award for oil painting, Howard County Fair, 1989, one of Top 100 award for oil painting, Nat. Arts for Parks, 1989, 1991, 1992, 2001, Top 200, 1990, 1993, 1996, Best in Show award, Nat. League Am. Pen Women, Md. Biennial Conv., 1999. Mem. Nat. League Am. Pen Women (sec. Bethesda, Md. 1989, treas. 2000-02), Balt. Watercolor Soc. (bd. dirs. 1997-99), Washington Soc. Landscape Painters (sec. 1999, pres. 2000-02, Baustian award for Excellence 1999), Salmagundi Club (N.Y.C.), Oil Painters Am. Avocations: quilting, crossword puzzles. Home: 3132 Cabin Run Woodbine MD 21797-7933

NUSS, JOANNE RUTH, sculptor, artist; b. Gt. Bend, Kans., May 2, 1951; d. Melvin Oliver and Ruth Helen (Brauer) N. Student, Valparaiso U., 1969-71, U. Kans., 1972-73, U. Copenhagen, 1974; BA, Ft. Hays State U., 1975; MFA, Santa Fe Inst. Fine Arts, 1991. Lectr. Noon Edition Sta. KCMO-TV, Kansas City, 1981, Menoriah Hosp., Brookridge Elem. Sch., The Jill Shurin Show Telecable 10, Kansas City, 1982, Barton County C.C., Gt. Bend, Nelson-Atkins Mus., Kansas City, Mo., 1984; artist-in-residence Helen Wurlitzer Found., Taos, N.Mex., 1984, 90. One-woman shows include Bette Moses Gallery, Great Bend, 1980, Art Expo Ctr., San Francisco, 1981, Univ. Gall., Ft. Hays State U., 1985, Am. Legation Mus., Tangiers, Morocco, 1986, Inma Gallery, Dhahran, Saudi Arabia, 1994, Bab Rouah Gallery, Rabat, Morocco, 1996, Agora Gallery, Soho, New York, 2001, others, exhibited in group shows at Second Internat. Sculpture Fair, Boston, 1980, Joan Cooke Gallery, Kansas City, Mo., 1983, The Batz Lawrence Gallery, Kansas City, 1984, Galerie de Rond Point des Champs Elyssees, Paris, 1989, Tetouan & La Kabila Gallery, Tetouan, Morocco, 1991, N.Mex. Sculptors Guild, Fuller Lodge Art Gallery, Los Alamos, 1992, Hermosas Fine Arts Gallery, Durango, Colo., 1995, Tanjah Flandria Art Gallery, Tangiers, 1997—99, Shidoni Gallery, Tesuque, N.Mex., 1999—2002, Birger Sandzen Gallery, Lindsborg, Kans., 2000, Nat. Assn. Women Artists, Sarasota Visual Arts Ctr., 2000, U. No. Iowa, Cedar Falls, 2001 (1st pl., 2001), Coplan Gallery, Boca Raton, Fla., 2002, Attleboro (Mass.) Mus., 2002, Jeanette Hare Art Gallery, West Palm Beach, Fla., 2002; featured artist Artist Spectrum Mag. Recipient 1st Kans. Artist Purchase award Ft. Hays State U., 1985, Best 3-D Works award Wichita Art Assn., 1983; 1st female fgn. artist commd. for archtl. major project, Tangiers, 1988-90. Mem. Nat. Assn. Women Artists, Nat. Sculpture Soc., Nat. Mus. of Women in the Arts, Internat. Sculpture Ctr., Kans. Sculptor's Assn., Internat. Platform Assn. Achievements include listed in Dictionary of American Sculptors, 1984; listed in Kansas City Single Professionals. Avocations: traveling, working with other artists, gardening.

NUSS, ROBERT CONRAD, oncologist; b. Boyertown, Pa., Sept. 11, 1937; s. Raymond W and Elsie (Conrad) Nuss; m. Ann L. Harwood, Sept. 21, 1984; children: Pamela S., Robin L., Jennifer D. BS, Muhlenberg Coll., 1958; MD, Jefferson Med. Coll., 1962. Diplomate Am. Bd. Ob-Gyn, Am. Bd. Med. Examiners. Rotating intern Naval Hosp., Phila., 1962-63, resident in ob-gyn., 1964-67; fellow gynecologic oncology Hahnemann Med. Coll. and Hosp., 1970-72, instr. dept. ob-gyn., 1970-72; dir., div. gynecologic oncology Jacksonville (Fla.) Health Edn. Program, Univ. Hosp., 1972-94, assoc. prof., 1972-87, prof., 1987, assoc. chmn., 1986-94; assoc. dean for clin. affairs U. Fla. Coll. Medicine, Jacksonville, 1994—; pres., CEO U. Fla. Jacksonville Healthcare, 1994—; sr. v.p. med. affairs Shands Jacksonville Med. Ctr., 1999—. Chmn. numerous coms. in field; mem. U. Hosp. Exec. Faculty, 1983—; trustee Faculty Clinic, Inc.; presenter in field. Author (numerous publs. in field). With USMC, with USN, 1962—70, with USNR, 1970—93, rear adm. USNR, 1985—93. Recipient Ob-Gyn prize, Jefferson Med. Coll., 1962, Physician Recognition award, AMA, 1983—85, 1985—88, Outstanding Tchg. award Jacksonville Health Edn. Program, Ob-Gyn Alumni Assn., 1981, 1997. Fellow: Am. Coll. Ob-Gyn; mem.: Am. Cancer Soc., Jacksonville Soc. Oncology, Jacksonville Ob-Gyn Soc., Duval County Med. Soc., Fla. Med. Assn. (Continuing Med. Edn. award 1985—88), Fla. Ob-Gyn Soc., South Atlantic Assn. Ob-Gyn, Soc. Gynecologic Oncologists, Am. Soc. Clin. Oncology, Am. Soc. Colposcopy and Cervical Pathology. Republican. Avocation: Avocations: fishing, tennis, gardening. Home: 8151 Blue Jay Ln Jacksonville FL 32256-7201 Office: 653 W 8th St Jacksonville FL 32209-6511 also: U Fla Coll Med 653-1 W 8th St Jacksonville FL 32209-6511 E-mail: Robert.Nuss@jax.ufl.edu.

NUSS, SHIRLEY ANN, computer coordinator, educator; b. Madison, Min., Oct. 22, 1946; d. Woodland Henry and Aileen Thelma (Mattox) Cover; divorced; 1 child, Melissa Ann. BEd, Trinity U., Washburn U., 1969; MA, Mich. State U., 1982, PhD, 1990. 3d grade tchr. Topeka Pub. Schs. System, 1969-70; 6th grade tchr. McCune (Kans.) Middle Sch., 1970-72; 7th grade English tchr. Muskego (Wis.) Norway Sch. Dist., 1972-78; intermediate level. tchr. Gibson Sch. for Gifted Children, Redford, Mich., 1979-82; 3d grade tchr. Cranbrook Edn. Community, Bloomfield Hills, 1982-89, multi media/computer coord., instr., 1989—. Adj. prof. ednl. tech. cert. program Mich. State U., 2000-01; ednl. adv. bd. Henry Ford Mus. and Greenfield Village, Dearborn, 1988-91; Renaissance Outreach for Detroit Area Schs; task force Mich. Coun. for the Humanities, Lansing, 1991-92; speaker, presenter on tech. Mich. Sci. Tchr. Assn., Lansing, 1992-96, Mich. Assn. Computer Users in Learning, Ind. Sch. Assn. Ctrl. States; tchr. adv. bd. Teaching and Computer Magazine, 1988-90; developer grades 1-5 multimedia/computer curriculum Brookside Sch., Cranbrook, 1995-96. Author: (museum activities) Henry Ford Museum, Greenfield Village, 1991. Space camp fellowship Mary Bramson award Huntsville, Ala., 1992; Detroit Edison Conservation grantee Detroit Edison, 1992, ROADS Mimi grant Mich. Coun. for Humanities, Lansing, 1993. Mem. Cranbrook Schs. Faculty Coun. (pres., v.p. 1993-95). Republican. Presbyterian. Avocations: antique collecting, reading, gardening, computers and technology. Home: 1715 Shankin Dr Walled Lake MI 48390-2446 Office: Cranbrook Schs Brookside 550 Cranbrook Rd # 801 Bloomfield Hills MI 48301 E-mail: snuss@cranbrook.edu., drnuss@aol.com.

NUSS, WILLIAM MARTIN (BILL NUSS), television producer, writer; b. Lawrence, N.Y., Mar. 29, 1954; s. David Bernard and Nadia Sybil (Messing) N. BS, Northwestern U., 1976. Freelance TV writer James at 15, Eight is Enough, Good Times, Welcome Back Kotter, Fernwood Tonite, Hollywood, Calif., 1976-78; v.p. NBC Entertainment, Burbank, 1978-82; writer Metromedia Producers Corp., 1982-84; producer, story editor, writer Riptide, The A-Team Stephen J. Cannell Prodns., Hollywood, 1985-90, exec. producer 21 Jump Street, Booker, 1985-90. Exec. producer Hat Squad, 1992, Renegade, 1993-95; creator, exec. producer, Pacific Blue, 1997-2000; prodr., writer Hunter: Everyone Walks in L.A., 1995. Recipient NAACP award, Asian-Am. award, Newman Found. award, NCCJ Imagen award, Media Access award. Mem. Nat. Acad. TV Arts and Scis., Hollywood Radio and TV Soc.

NUSSBAUM, A(DOLF) EDWARD, mathematician, educator; b. Rheydt, Fed. Republic Germany, Germany, Jan. 10, 1925; came to U.S., 1947; s. Karl and Franziska (Scheye) N.; m. Anne Ebbin, Sept. 1, 1957; children: Karl, Franziska. MA, Columbia U., 1950, PhD, 1957. Mem. staff electronic computer project Inst. Advanced Study, Princeton, N.J., 1952-53, mem., 1962-63; instr. math U. Conn., Storrs, 1953-55; asst. prof. Rensselaer Poly. Inst., Troy, N.Y., 1956-58; vis. scholar Stanford U., Calif., 1967-68; asst. prof., then assoc. prof. Washington U., St. Louis, 1958-66, prof., 1966-95, prof. emeritus, 1995—. Contbr. articles to profl. jours. Grantee NSF, 1960-79 Mem. Am. Math. Soc. Home: 8050 Watkins Dr Saint Louis MO 63105-2517 Office: Washington U Dept Math Saint Louis MO 63130 E-mail: addi@math.wustl.edu.

NUSSBAUM, BERNARD J. lawyer; b. Berlin, Mar. 11, 1931; came to U.S., 1936; s. William and Lotte (Frankfurther) N.; m. Jean Beverly Enzer, Sept. 4, 1956; children— Charles, Peter, Andrew AB, Knox Coll., 1948-52; JD, U. Chgo., 1955. Assoc. Proskauer Rose Goetz & Mendelsohn, N.Y.C., 1955-56; assoc. Sonnenschein Nath & Rosenthal, Chgo., 1959-65, sr. ptnr., 1965—. Master bencher Am. Inns of Ct., 1986—; appointed to com. on civility 7th cir. U.S. Ct. Appeals, 1989-92. Editor U. Chgo. Law Rev., 1954-55; mem. nat. adv. bd. BNA Civil Trial Man., 1985— ; contbr. articles to profl. jours. Mem. vis. com. U. Chgo. Law Sch., 1977-83. Served to capt. U.S. Army, 1956-59 Fellow Am. Bar Found., Ill. Bar Found. (charter); mem. ABA, Chgo. Bar Assn. (chmn. com. on fed. civil procedure 1968-69, mem. com. on judiciary 1970-76), Ill. Bar Assn. (council Antitrust sect. 1971-73, assembly del. 1972-80), U. Chgo. Law Sch. Nat. Alumni Assn. (pres. 1981-83), Law Club Chgo., Legal Club Chgo. Avocations: skiing; cycling. Office: Sonnenschein Nath & Rosenthal 8000 Sears Tower 233 S Wacker Dr Ste 8000 Chicago IL 60606-6491

NUSSBAUM, JAY, writer, educator; b. N.Y.C., Jan. 30, 1960; s. J. Herbert and Alice Nussbaum; m. Betty Garcia, Sept. 3, 1995; children: Taylor J., Brian Isiah. BA, Brandeis U., 1982; JD Boston U., 1985. Bar: NY. Sr. v.p., gen.

counsel Mercury Capital Corp., N.Y.C., 1993—96; editor-in-chief Miller Freeman Pub. Co., 1996—2000; legal editor Brownstone Pubs., 2001—. Martial arts instr. NY Sports Club, N.Y.C., 1992—96; adj. prof. Eastern philosophy and martial arts Cornell U., Ithaca, NY, 1997—2000. Author: Blue Road to Atlantis, 2002; editor: (legal newsletter) Cmty. Assn. Mgmt. Insider, 2001—02. Mem. Lustgarten Found. for Pancreatic Cancer Rsch., Roslyn, NY, 2001—. Mem.: Internat. Uechi-ryu Karate Fedn. (4th degree black belt 1999), NY Uechi-ryu Karate Club (sr. bd. dirs. 1992—). Office: Brownstone Pubs 149 Fifth Ave New York NY 10010 Office Fax: 631-737-5386.

NUSSBAUM, JEFFREY JOSEPH, musician; b. N.Y.C., July 7, 1952; s. Eli and Dorothy (Wolkowitz) N.; m. Alison Knopf (div. 1984); m. Joan Feigenbaum, April 5, 1990; 1 child, Samuel Leonard Baum. BA in Music, Hunter Coll., N.Y., 1977; MA in Edn., Bklyn. Coll., 1987; MFA in Early Music, Sarah Lawrence Coll., Bronxville, Tex., 1989. Cert. N.Y.S., N.Y.C. Freelance musician (trumpet, cornetto, natural trumpet), 1979—; tchr. music Park West H.S., N.Y., 1984—. Pres., founder Historic Brass Soc., N.Y., 1989—; dir. Manhattan Early Wind Ensemble, N.Y., 1992—, Pan Brass Quintet, N.Y., 1978-84; organized Internat. Hist. Brass Symposium, Amherst, Mass., 1995; organizer Early Brass Colloquium, Royal Acad. Music, London, 1997, Internat. Hist. Brass Symposium, co-sponsored by Cité de la Musique, Paris, 1999, Internat. Symposium co-sponsored with Stimu, Utrecht, Germany, 2000, HBS Cornetto Symposium, Bate Coll., Oxford U.; co-organizer Toronto 2000: Musical Intersections, 2000. Author: Brass Teaching and Learning: History, Development and Technology of Brass Instruments, 1998; contbr. articles to jours. in field. Mem. Am. Fedn. Musicians, Am. Musicological Soc., Internat. Trumpet Guild, Galpin Soc. Home: 148 W 23rd St Apt 2A New York NY 10011-2447 E-mail: president@historicbrass.org.

NUSSBAUM, LAUREEN, retired foreign language educator; b. Frankfurt, Germany, Aug. 3, 1927; came to the U.S., 1957; d. Edmund Joseph and Marianne Felicitas (Blumenthal) Klein; m. Rudi H. Nussbaum, Oct. 15, 1947; children: Ralph E., Fred D., Elka N. BA, Portland State U., 1962; MA, U. Wash., 1966, PhD, 1977. Instr. Portland (Oreg.) State U., 1962-77, asst. prof., 1978-81, assoc. prof., 1981-86, full prof., 1987-88, prof. emerita, 1989—. Author: (yearbook) Exilforschung 5 & 11, 1987, 93, (anthologies) Women Writing in Dutch, 1994, Children in the Holocaust—Children in Exile, Children Under Fascism, 1998, Anne Frank: Reflections on Her Life and Legacy, 2000, (handbook) Yale Companion to Jewish Writing and Thought in German Culture, 1997, (reference companion) Bertolt Brecht, 1997, (handbook) Shedding Light on the Darkness: A Guide to Teaching the Holocaust, 2000; editor: Unvorhanden und Stumm, 1991. Recipient Mosser award Oreg. State Bd. Higher Edn., 1967; Rsch. and Pub. grantee Portland State U., 1983; Visitor's fellow Netherlands Orgn. for Pure Rsch., Leiden, 1985. Mem. Am. Assn. Netherlandic Studies, Am. Assn. Tchrs. German, Internat. Brecht Soc. (exec. com. 1980-82), Soc. for Exile Studies, Assn. for German Studies, Women in German, Am. Friends Svc. Com., Women's Internat. League for Peace and Freedom. Avocations: hiking, swimming, sailing, grandparenting, supporting husband's research. Office: Portland State Univ Dept FLL Box 751 Portland OR 97207 E-mail: d4rn@odin.pdx.edu.

NUSSBAUM, LEO LESTER, retired college president, consultant; b. Berne, Ind., June 27, 1918; s. Samuel D. and Margaret (Mazelin) N.; m. Janet Nell Gladfelter, Nov. 25, 1942; children: Felicity Ann, Luther James, Margaret Sue. BS, Ball State U., 1942, MA, 1949; PhD, Northwestern U., 1952; postgrad., U. Mich., 1963. Tchr. Monmouth H.S., Decatur, Ind., 1946-48; dean men, asst. prof. bus. Huntington (Ind.) Coll., (Ind.), 1948-51; dean coll. liberal arts, assoc. prof. edn. and psychology U. Dubuque, Iowa, 1952-60; dean coll., prof. edn. and psychology Austin Coll., 1960-67; dean coll., prof. psychology Coe Coll., 1967-82, pres., 1970-82, pres. emeritus, 1982—; dir. Acad. Sr. Profls. Eckerd Coll., 1983-87; dir. PEL-ASPEC Project, 1988-95; coord. faculty ASPEC Colleagues, St. Petersburg, 1992-97. Cons. pvt. practice St. Petersburg, Fla., 1982—; Fulbright lectr. U. Mysore, India, 1958-59; cons., evaluator So. Assn. Colls. and Schs., Atlanta, 1963-67, North Cen. Assn. Colls. and Schs., 1959-60, 67-82, dir. I.E. Industries and Iowa Electric Light and Power Co., Cedar Rapids, 1982-91, dir. emeritus, 1991-92. Contbr. articles to profl. jours. Bd. dirs. Cedar Rapids Symphony, 1968-70; mem. cabinet Cedar Rapids United Way, 1980-82; elder Presbyn. Ch., moderator Presbytery of S.W. Fla., 1989. Sgt. U.S. Army, 1942-46. Recipient Disting. Alumnus award Ball State U., 1976, Alumni Merit award Northwestern U., 1977. Mem. Assn. Colls. Midwest (chmn. 1975-77), Iowa Assn. Ind. Colls. and Univs. (chmn. 1976-77), Danforth Assocs., Rotary (Cedar Rapids pres. 1975-76), Phi Delta Kappa, Blue Key, Pi Gamma Mu Home: 6909 9th St S Apt 336 Saint Petersburg FL 33705-6207

NUSSBAUM, MICHEL ERNEST, physician; b. L.A., Nov. 7, 1947; s. Schymen and Jeannette Eleanor (Pequignot) N.; m. Joyce Wendy Laudon, Nov. 1, 1981; children: Eleanor, Anna. BA, Cornell U., 1969; MD, Free U. Brussels, 1977. Intern internal medicine N.Y. Hosp. Med. Ctr. of Queens, Flushing, 1977-78, resident, 1978-80, fellow gastroenterology, 1980-82, attending physician N.Y., 1982—; physician pvt. practice, 1982—; attending physician Flushing Hosp. Med. Ctr., 1987—; clin. instr. medicine Cornell U. Med. Coll., N.Y.C., 1994-98, clin. asst. prof. medicine, 1998—; med. dir. Franklin Ctr. for Nursing and Rehab., Flushing, 1995-99. Physician in charge endoscopic svcs. N.Y. Hosp. Med. Ctr. of Queens, 1990—, asst. dir. gastroenterology, 1998—, pres. med. staff soc., 1992-96, chmn. med. bd., 1997—, bd. trustees, 1998—. Fellow ACP, Am. Coll. Gastroenterology. Office: 142-43 Booth Memorial Ave Flushing NY 11355-5343

NUSSBAUM, PAUL A. retired hospitality executive; Ret. chmn., CEO Wyndhaur Internat.; chmn. Panco Svcs., Inc., Dallas. Office: # 250 3100 Monticello Ave Dallas TX 75205-3442

NUSSBAUM DRILL, SHEILA, gallery director and owner; b. Phila., Mar. 9, 1940; m. Richard Drill, Nov. 1, 1992; children: Jim, Andrew. Student, U. Pa., NYU, New Sch. for Social Rsch., N.Y. Sch. Interior Design. Founder, dir. and owner Sheila Nussbaum Gallery, Millburn, N.J., 1982—. Guest lectr. Colo. Artist-Craftsmen, Denver, Washington Guild of Goldsmiths, Washington; guest appearances on N.J. Network's TV series "State of the Arts", 1985, 86, 88, 92, 95, Parsons Sch. Design, N.Y.; bus. cons. New Philharmonic of N.J.; jury invitations include Morristown (N.J.) Craft Show, N.J. Designer Craftsmen Show, Madison, N.J., 1991, 6th Biennial Washington Guild of Goldsmiths Exhbn., Alexandria, Va., 1991, 18th Ann. Tenn. Craft Fair, Nashville, 1989, many others. Lectr. to sch. and charitable groups for benefit of N.J. Designer Craftsmen, Albert Einstein Med. Coll., The Hospice Inc. of Montclair, Brandeis U., Parsons Sch. of Design. Trustee Montclair, N.J., Art Mus.; dir. Mental Health Assn. Essex County (N.J.); mem. dean's adv. coun. Mason Gross Sch. Art, Rutgers U.; juror N.J. State Crafts Festival. Recipient "Bus. Watch '88" award Bus. Jour. N.J.; named 1987 Woman of the Yr., Bus. and Profl. Women of Millburn-Short Hills, Inc. Mem. Soc. of Jewelry Historians. Avocations: tennis, classical music. Office: Sheila Nussbaum Gallery 325 Ravine Dr South Orange NJ 07079-1644

NUSSENBAUM, SIEGFRIED FRED, chemistry educator; b. Vienna, Austria, Nov. 21, 1919; came to U.S., 1939; s. Marcus and Susan Sara (Rothenberg) N.; m. Celia Womark, Feb. 20, 1951; children: Deborah M., Evelyn R. BS in Chemistry, U. Calif., Berkeley, 1941, MS in Food Tech., 1948, PhD in Comparative Biochemistry, 1951. Analytical chemist Panam. Engring. Co., Berkeley, 1942-43; asst. chief chemist Manganese Ore Co., Las Vegas, 1943-45; rsch. assoc. U. Calif., Berkeley, 1951-52, dir. master clin. lab. sci. program San Francisco, 1969-87; from instr. to prof. Calif. State U., Sacramento, 1952-90, chair dept. chemistry, 1958-65. Cons. biochemist Sacramento County Hosp., 1958-70; lectr. U. Calif. Davis Med. Ctr., 1970-93, guest lectr., 1993-95. Author: Organic Chem-Principles and Applications, 1963; contbr. articles to profl. jours. Sgt. U.S. Army, 1945-47. Fellow AAAS; mem. Am. Chem. Soc., Am. Assn. Clin. Chemistry (Outstanding Contbn. in Edn. award no. sect. 1991), Nat. Acad. Clin. Biochemistry. Achievements include research in pectic enzymes, mechanism of amylopectin formation and differentiation from amylose, phenotyping of lipemias. Home: 2900 Latham Dr Sacramento CA 95864-5644

NUSSLE, JAMES ALLEN, congressman; b. Des Moines, June 27, 1960; s. Mark S. and Lorna Kay (Fisher) N.; m. Leslie J. Harbison, Aug. 23, 1986. BA, Luther Coll., Decorah, Iowa, 1983; JD, Drake U., 1985. Bar: Iowa 1985. Pvt. practice law, Manchester, Iowa, 1986; states atty. Delaware County Atty., 1986-90; mem. U.S. Congress from 2d Iowa dist., Washington, 1991—, mem. house ways and means com., chmn. house budget com. Lutheran. Avocation: guitar. Office: US Ho of Reps 303 Cannon Hob Washington DC 20515-0001

NÜSSLEIN-VOLHARD, CHRISTIANE, medical researcher; b. Magdeburg, Germany, Oct. 20, 1942; d. Rolf Volhard and Brigitte (Haas) Volhard. Diploma in Biochemistry, U. Tübingen, 1968, PhD, 1973; ScD (hon.), Yale U. Rsch. assoc. lab. of Dr. Schaller Max-Planck Inst. for Devel. Biology, Tübingen, 1972-74; postdoctoral fellow lab. of Dr. W. Gehring, Biozentrum, Basel, Switzerland, 1975-76; postdoctoral fellow lab of Dr. K. Sander U. Freiburg, 1977; head rsch. group European Molecular Biology Lab., Heidelberg, 1978-80; rsch. group leader Friedrich-Miescher Lab. Max-Planck-Gesellschaft, Tübingen, 1981-85; sci. mem. Max-Planck Assn., dir. Max-Planck Inst. for Devel. Biology, 1985-90, dir. genetics dept., 1990—. Hon. prof. U. Tübingen. Contbr. numerous articles to profl. jours. Recipient Albert Lasker Basic Med. Rsch. award Albert and Mary Lasker Found., 1991, Louisa Gross Horowitz prize Columbia U., 1992, Forderpreis award Deutschen Forschungsgemeinschaft, 1986, Franz Vogt prize U. Giessen, 1986, Carus medal German Acad. Leopoldine, 1989, Rosenstiel medal Brandeis U., Nobel Prize in Medicine, 1995; Schering prize, Berlin, 1993. Mem. European Molecular Biology Orgn., Berlin Brandenburgische Acad., Am. Philosophical Soc. Achievements include rsch. in using embryos, created a series of genetic screens that led to the identification of most of the genes responsible for the organism's body segment development, establishing that genes encode signaling molecules that tell cells where they are in the organism's overall structure and what their function is to be. Office: Max Planck Inst Entwicklung Sbiologie Spemannstr 35 D-72076 Tübingen Germany*

NUSZ, PHYLLIS JANE, not-for-profit fundraiser, consultant, educational consultant; b. Lodi, Calif., Dec. 16, 1941; d. Fred Henry and Esther Emma (Enzminger) Nusz. BA, U. Pacific, 1963, MA, 1965; EdD, Nova Southeastern U., 1987. Cert. fund raising exec. Prof. speech comm. Bakersfield (Calif.) Coll., 1965-86; from asst. dir. student activites to found. exec. dir. Bakersfield (Calif) Coll., 1965-86; mgmt. seminar dir. Delta Kappa Gamma Soc. Internat., Austin, 1983-86; loaned exec. United Way San Joaquin County, Stockton, Calif., 1990; fundraising and edn. cons. PJ Enterprises, Lodi, 1987—. Bd. dirs. U. Calif. Sch. Medicine Surg. Found., San Francisco, 1989—92; mem. Heritage Cir. and Chancellor's Assn. U. Calif., 1987—. Recipient Archives award of merit, Evang. Luth Ch. Am., 1988; fellow, Calif. Luth. U., 1985—. Mem.: NEA, Nat. Assn. Parliamentarians, Nat. Soc. Fund Raising Execs. (bd. dir. 1988—91, chmn. mentor program Calif. Capital chpt. 1991, chmn. acad. fund raising 1991, chmn. mentor program Golden Gate chpt. 1991, founding pres. San Joaquin chpt. 1992—93, Pres.'s award for Meritorious Svc., Golden Gate chpt. 1991), Rotary Internat. (North Stockton bd. dir. 1993—99, treas. 1994—96, pres.-elect 1996—97, pres. 1997—98, dist. 5220 membership devel. com. 1997—98, immediate past pres. 1998—99, membership task force 1998—99, dist. membership chmn. 1999—2000, dist. gov. elect 2000—01, dist. gov. 2001—02, mem. Afghan refugee relief coun. 2001—02, Zone 24 promotion coord. 2002—, mem. avoidable blindness task force 2002—, Zone 24 coord., Zone 23 & 24 leadership devel. task force 2001—, multiple Paul Harris fellow, RI Found. Bequest Soc., RI Found. benefactor), U. Pacific Alumni Assn. (bd. dir. 1974—82), Delta Kappa Gamma (chpt. pres. 1976—78, Chi State parliamentarian 1979—81, chair Internat. Golden Gift Fund 1982—86, sec. 1985—87). Republican. Lutheran. Avocations: photography, travel, swimming, walking, fishing. Office: PJ Enterprises 1300 W Lodi Ave Ste A11 Lodi CA 95242-3000 E-mail: pjnursz@aol.com.

NUTTALL, FRANK QUENTIN, physician, researcher; b. Utah, May 8, 1929; m. Barbara Nuttall; children: Maureen, Greg, Bryan, Jennifer. MD, U. Utah, 1955; PhD, U. Minn., 1970. Intern Mpls. Med. Gen. Hosp., 1955-56; resident U. Minn., 1956-57, 59-60, 1960-61; chief resident St. Paul Ramsey Hosp., 1960-61; dir. admissions Mpls. VA Med. Ctr., 1961-63, dir. clin. chemistry, 1963-69, dir. endocrine sect., 1970—. Office: Mpls VA Med Ctr One Veterans Dr Minneapolis MN 55417

NUTTALL, RICHARD NORRIS, management consultant, physician; b. Hamilton, Ont., Can., Feb. 7, 1940; s. James William and Margaret Gay (Walsh) N.; m. Ethel Jane Pickering, July 9, 1977; children: Andrew Richard, John Patrick. BSA, U. Toronto, 1961; MPA, Harvard U., 1964; MB, BS, U. London, Eng., 1974. Cert. Coll. Family Physicians Can., Mgmt. Cons. Zone dir. Health and Welfare Can., Prince Rupert, B.C., 1977-79, regional dir. Edmonton, Alta., 1980-82; pres. Rutland Consulting Group, Ltd., Vancouver, B.C., 1982-87, Richmond Assocs. Internat., Vancouver, 1988-90; med. health officer Govt. N.W. Ters., Yellowknife, B.C., 1990-93, Regina Health Dist., 1993-97; pres. Anjohn Med. Svcs., Inc., Victoria, 1997—. Staff physician Royal Jubilee Hosp., Victoria Gen. Hosp. Fellow Am. Coll. Preventive Medicine, Am. Coll. Healthcare Execs., Can. Coll. Health Svc. Execs.; mem. Can. Pub. Health Assn. (bd. dirs. 1991-93). Office: 1494 Fairfield Rd Victoria BC Canada V8S 1E8

NUTTER, DAVID GEORGE, urban planner; b. Manchester, Conn., Nov. 25, 1939; s. George Huitt and Catherine Lavina (Casey) N.; m. Ellen Marie Manfredonia, Sept. 7, 1968; children: Susan Katharine, Anne Amelia. BA in English cum laude, Tufts U., 1961; MS in Urban Planning, Columbia U., 1967. City planner Balt. City Planning Commn., 1967-69; dir. planning Charles Ctr.- Inner Harbor Mgmt., Inc., Balt., 1969-72, v.p., 1972-76; pvt. cons., 1976-83; dir. downtown mall mgmt. dist. Denver Partnership, Inc., 1983-85; exec. dir. Rochester (N.Y.) Downtown Devel. Corp., 1985-87; prin. Nutter Assocs., Rochester, 1987-2000; dir. Salisbury-Wiconico Planning and Zoning Commn., 2000—. Author: Selecting a Developer, 1983. Bd. dirs. Soc. Preservation of Fed. Hill, Balt., 1969-73, Arts for Greater Rochester, 1986-90, Nabb Rsch. Ctr. for Delmarva, History and Culture, Salisbury (Md.) U., 1998—, Lower Eastern Shore Heritage Com., 2000—; chmn. Town of Brighton (N.Y.) Conservation Bd., 1992-95. Sgt. U.S. Army, 1962-65. William F. Kinne fellow for travel in Europe, Columbia U., 1967. Mem. Am. Inst. Cert. Planners, Am. Planning Assn., Urban Land Inst. (assoc.), Canal Soc. of N.Y. State. Avocations: historical map and atlas collecting, American and English history, computer mapping, hiking, history of settlement and urbanism. E-mails: (bus.) (personal). Home: 507C South Blvd Salisbury MD 21801 E-mail: dnutter@wicomico.org., dnutter@aol.com.

NUTTER, FRANKLIN WINSTON, lawyer; b. Charleston, W.Va., Apr. 17, 1946; s. Frank Hamilton and Marie Agnes (Pyles) N.; m. Linda Jean Davis, Sept. 2, 1972; children: Alycia Marie, Aaron Davis. BBA in Econs., U. Cin., 1968; JD, Georgetown U., 1974. Bar: D.C., Va., U.S. Dist. Ct. (no. dist.) Va., U.S. Ct. Appeals (9th and D.C. cirs.), U.S. Supreme Ct. 1993. Gen. counsel Nat. Flood Ins. Assn., Washington, 1975-78, Reins. Assn. Am., Washington, 1978-81, pres., 1981-84, 91—, Alliance Am. Insurers, Schaumburg, Ill., 1984-91, Property Loss Research Bur., Schaumburg, 1984-91. Bd. overseers Inst. Civil Justice subs. Rand Corp., 1984-91; chair Natural Disaster Coalition. Bd. dirs. Advs. for Hwy. and Auto Safety, 1989-91; trustee Nat. Commn. Against Drunk Driving. Lt. (j.g.) USN, 1968-72. Mem. ABA (torts and injury practice sect., past chmn. internat. ins. law, excess and surplus lines and reins. com., coun. tort and ins. practice sect.), Va. Bar Assn., Ins. Inst. Hwy. Safety (bd. dirs. 1984-91), Workers' Compensation Rsch. Inst., Industry Sector Adv. Coun. on Svcs. Home: 8458 Portland Pl Mc Lean VA 22102-1708 Office: 1301 Pennsylvania Ave NW Washington DC 20004-1701

NUTTER, JAMES RANDALL, management educator; b. Stephenville, Tex., Nov. 11, 1945; s. Coleman Evan and Mary Frances (Jay) N.; m. Marilyn Grace Marotta, Aug. 23, 1969; children: Heather Elizabeth, Susan Mary, Katherine Grace. BS, No. Ill. U., 1968, MEd, 1969; DSc, Nova U., 1991; DBA, Nova S.E. U., 1995. Tchr. social studies Hinsdale (Ill.) South H.S., 1968-69, Govt. U.S. V.I., St. Thomas, 1969-71; dir. employee rels. Shuron divsn. Textron Corp., Rochester, N.Y., 1971-73; dir. corp. tng. Sybron Corp., 1973-75; dir. human resources Red Wing Co., Fredonia, N.Y., 1975-82; assoc. prof., dept. chair Liberty U., Lynchburg, Va., 1982-92; prof., chair bus. dept., dir. grad. bus. studies Geneva Coll., Beaver Falls, Pa., 1992—. Pres. Nutter/Forbus Group, Inc., Lynchburg, 1982-92; mem. adv. bd. U.S. Rep. Ronald Klink, Cranberry, Pa., 1995-2000, Riverside Sch. Dist., North Sewickley, Pa., 1994-97; bd. dirs. Lynchburg Preheater Inc.; commr. Assn. Collegiate Bus. Schs. and Programs, 1998—; mem. acad. adv. coun. Pacific Inst. for Bus. Mgmt.; vis. prof. Peoples Republic of China, Fgn. Experts Bur., N.W. Nazarene U. MBA Mex. Program. Treas. Fine Arts Boosters, New Brighton, Pa., 1995—. Mem. Am. Mgmt. Assn., Soc. Strategic Mgmt., Acad. Mgmt., Soc. Human Resource Mgmt. (faculty advisor 1972—), Christian Bus. Faculty Assn. Republican. Avocations: fishing, travel, reading. Home: 108 Dana Dr Monaca PA 15061-2871 E-mail: jrn@geneva.edu.

NUTTER, ZOE DELL LANTIS, retired public relations executive; b. Yamhill, Oreg., June 14, 1915; d. Arthur Lee Lantis and Olive Adelaide (Reed) Lantis-Hilton; m. Richard S. West, Apr. 30, 1941 (div. Nov. 1964); m. Ervin John Nutter, Dec. 30, 1965. Assoc. in Bus., Santa Ana Jr. Coll., 1944. Cert. spl. emergency secondary tchr., Calif.; FAA cert. lic. commercial, instrument, single/multi engine land airplanes pilot. Promoter World's Fair & Comml. Airlines Golden Gate Internat. Expn., San Francisco, 1937-39; pirate theme girl, official hostess Treasure Island's World Fair, 1939-40; prin. dancer San Francisco Ballet, 1937-41; artist, 1941-45; program dir. Glenn County H.S., Willows, Calif., 1952-58; pub. rels. Monarch Piper Aviation Co., Monterey, 1963-65; pilot, pub. rels. Elano Corp., Xenia, Ohio, 1968-85. Bd. dirs. Nat. Aviation Hall of Fame, Dayton, Ohio, pres., chmn., 1989-92, bd. trustees, 1976—, chmn. bd. nominations, 1992—; bd. trustees Ford's Theatre, Washington, Treasure Island Mus., San Francisco; charter mem. Friends of First Ladies, Smithsonian, Washington, 1990-93. Assoc. editor KYH mag. of Shikar Safari Internat., 1985-87; contbg. columnist Scripps Howard San Francisco News, 1938. Bd. dirs. Cin. May Festival, 1976-80; cen. com. Glenn County Rep. Party, Willows, 1960-64; state cen. com. Rep. Party, 1962-64; adv. bd. Women's Air & Space Mus., Dayton, 1987-94. Warrant officer, Civil Air Patrol, 1967-69. Recipient Civic Contbn. Honor award Big Brothers/Big Sisters, 1991, John Collier Nat. award Camp Fire Girls & Boys, 1988, Tambourine award Salvation Army, 1982, State of Ohio Gov.'s award for Volunteerism, 1992, Spirit of Innovation award Wright State U., 2001, Amb. award Wright Bros. Heritage Benefit, 2001; named Most Photographed Girl in World, News Burs. & Clipping Svcs., 1938-39. Mem., founder Dancers Over 40, NYC; Fellow Pres.'s Club U. Ky., Ohio State U., Wright State U.; mem. 99's Internat. Women Pilots Orgn. (life, hospitality chmn. 1968), Monterey Bay Chapter 99's (mem. chmn. 1964-65), Walnut Grove Country Club, Rotary (Paul Harris fellow 1987), Shikar Safari Internat. (host com. 1976), Country Club of the North. Avocations: flying, horseback riding, hunting, shooting, fashion. Home: 986 Trebein Rd Xenia OH 45385-9534

NUTTING, MAUREEN MURPHY, historian, educator; b. N.Y.C. d. Patrick Joseph and Marie (Clarke) Murphy; m. Theodore Michael Nutting, May 3 1975; children: Teresa, Andrew, Stephen, Eileen. BA in History, Fordham U., Bronx, N.Y., 1968; MA in Am. Studies, U. Notre Dame, Ind., 1969, PhD in History, 1975. Asst. prof. history Humboldt State U., Arcata, Calif., 1972-75, Chaminade U., Honolulu, 1975-77; asst. dir. minorities & women's scholarly & profl. interests Am. Hist. Assn., Washington, 1979-81; asst. prof. history U. Miami, Coral Gables, Fla., 1987-90, Seattle U., 1990-91; instr. history Seattle Ctrl. C.C., 1992-96; prof. history, chair North Seattle C.C., 1996—. Vol. Seattle Pub. Sch. Dist., 1982—86, 1990—98; chair local draft bd. U.S. Selective Svc., Seattle, 1998—, mem. local draft bd., 1992—; vol. homeless ministry St. James Cathedral, 1994—. Recipient rsch. travel grants Asian Studies Devel. Program, East-West Ctr., China, 1996, India, 1995, Summer Inst. grants NEH, Hawaii, 1994, Brazil, 1998, Guatemala, Honduras and Mex., 2002, trustees' lifetime learning award Seattle C.C. Dist., 1999; selected rsch. seminar Libr. of Congress, Am. Hist. Assn., C.C. Humanities Assn., Washington, 1999. Mem.: Cmty. Coll. Humanities Assn., Coordinating Coun. for Women's History, Western Assn. Women Historians, Immigration and Ethnic History Soc. (program com. 1999—), C.C. Humanities Assn. (chair nat. conf. program 2001), Orgn. Am. Historians, Am. Hist. Assn. (mem. coun. 2001—, mem. task force on pub. history 2001—). Roman Catholic. Office: North Seattle CC 9600 College Way N Seattle WA 98103-3514 E-mail: mnutting@sccd.ctc.edu.

NUTTING, PAUL JOHN, city manager; b. Oswego, N.Y., July 6, 1952; s. Robert Truman and Joan Violet (Joyce) N. BA, SUNY, Oswego, 1974; MPA, SUNY, Albany, 1977. Adminstrv. asst. City of League City, Tex., 1978-79, acting city adminstr., 1979-80, 81, asst. city adminstr., 1980-81, exec. asst. to mayor, 1981-82, city adminstr., 1982-95; city mgr. City of Springfield, Tenn., 1995—. Bd. dirs. Tenn. Energy Acquisition Corp., Five Rivers Resource Conservation and Devel. Coun. Bd. dirs. League City Family Welfare Coun., 1978-89, United Way, Robertson County; mem. exec. bd. Mainland Communities United Way, Texas City, Tex., 1991-94; adv. dir. League City Mchts. and Bus. Assn., 1989-95, North Galveston County C. of C., Dickinson, Tex., 1989-95. Mem. Internat. City and County Mgmt. Assn., Tenn. City Mgmt. Assn., Texas City Mgmt. Assn., Am. Soc. for Pub. Adminstrn. (pres. Houston area chpt. 1991-93, dir. 1990-91, 93-95), Springfield-Robertson County C. of C., League City Rotary Club (pres. 1985-86, 93-94), Rotary. Roman Catholic. Avocations: golf, tennis. Home: 130 Pepper Grove Cv Springfield TN 37172-2125 Office: City of Springfield 405 N Main St Springfield TN 37172-2408

NUTTING, WALLACE HALL, army officer; b. Newton, Mass., June 3, 1928; s. Gerry B. and Ethel M. (Hall) N.; m. Jane Anne Walker, June 17, 1950; children: Elizabeth J., John T., Katherine A., Sally W. BS, U.S. Mil. Acad., 1950; MA in Internat. Affairs, George Washington U., 1963; postgrad., Naval War Coll., 1963, Nat. War Coll., 1968; D of Mil. Arts & Scis. (hon.), Norwich U., 1984. Commd. cavalry officer/platoon ldr. U.S. Army 2nd Infantry Divsn., Republic of Korea, 1950-52; comdr. 1st Squadron 10th Cavalry, Vietnam, 1966-67; advanced through grades to gen. U.S. Army; asst. dir. plans Dept. Army, Washington, 1968-70, dep. dir. plans, 1973-74; comdr. 11th Armored Cavalry Regiment, Vietnam, 1970-71; dep. comdr. ops. 1st brigade 5th Inf. Div., Vietnam, 1971; Army mem. chmn.'s staff group Orgn. Joint Chiefs of Staff, Washington, 1971-73; comdg. gen. 1st Inf. div. forward, Fed. Republic Germany, 1974-75; dir. strategy plans and policy Dept. Army, 1975-77; comdg. gen. 3d Armored div., Fed. Republic Germany, 1977-79; comdr. in chief U.S. So. Command, Quarry Heights, Panama, 1979-83; comdr.-in chief U.S. Readiness Command, dir. Joint Deployment Agy., MacDill AFB, Fla., 1983-85; assoc. fellow Ctr. for Internat. Affairs, Harvard U., 1986; sr. fellow Inst. Higher Def. Studies, Nat. Def. U., Washington, 1986-96. Mem. exec. bd. Trans-Atlantic coun. Boy Scouts Am., 1977-79, Panama Canal coun., 1979-83; mem. Gulf Ridge coun. Boy Scouts Am., 1983-85, dist. chmn. Pine Tree coun., 2002.. Decorated Defense D.S.M. with oak leaf cluster, Silver Star, Legion of Merit with 2 oak leaf clusters, Soldier's medal, Bronze Star with oak leaf cluster, Air medal (7), Purple Heart with oak leaf cluster, Army Commendation medal with oak leaf cluster, Presdl. Unit citation, Korean Svc. medal with 5 stars, Vietnam Svc. medal with 4 stars, U.N. Svc. medal, JCS Identification badge, Gen. staff Identification badge, Vietnamese Cross of Gallantry with palm and silver star, Brazilian Order Mil. Merit, Order Mil. Merit Dominican Republic, Cross of Venezuelan Armed Forces, Mil. Star Armed Forces Chile, Cross Armed Force Republic of Honduras, Order Mil. Merit in grade grand officer (Argentina), Order Mil. Merit (Panama), Korea Campaign medal, Vietnamese Campaign medal; recipient Silver Beaver award, Living Legacy award So. Maine Agy. on Aging, 2000. Mem. U.S. Armor Assn., Assn. U.S. Army (Lyman L. Lemnitzer award 1996), Coun. on Fgn. Rels. Congregationalist. Home: PO Box 96 Biddeford Pool ME 04006-0096 Office: Dept of Army Gen Officer Mgmt Ofc Washington DC 20310-0001

NUTZLE, FUTZIE (BRUCE JOHN KLEINSMITH), artist, writer, cartoonist; b. Lakewood, Ohio, Feb. 21, 1942; s. Adrian Ralph and Naomi Irene (Rupert) Kleinsmith; children: Adrian David, Arielle Justine and Tess Alexandra (twins); m. Halina Renatta Kleinsmith. Author: Modern Loafer, Thames and Hudson, 1981, (authiobiography) Futzie Nutzle, 1983, Earthquake, 1989, Run the World: 50 Cents Chronicle Books, 1991; illustrator: The Armies Encamped Beyond Unfinished Avenues (Morton Marcus), 1977, Box of Nothing, 1982, The Duke of Chemical Birds (Howard McCord), 1989, Book of Solutions, 1990, Fact and Friction, 1990, Managing for the 90s, 1992, Soundbites for Success, 1994; feature cartoonist Rolling Stone, N.Y.C., 1975-80, The Japan Times, Tokyo and L.A., 1986—, The Prague Post, Czechoslovakia, 1991-92; contbr. exhbns. include Inaugural, 1966, Cupola, 1967, Rolling Renaissance, San Francisco, 1968, 100 Acres, O.K. Harris 1971, N.Y.C., San Francisco Mus. Art, 1972, Indpls. and Cin. Mus. Art, 1975, Leica, L.A., 1978, Santa Barbara Mus. Annex, Calif., 1978, Swope, Santa Monica, West Beach Cafe, Venice, Calif., 1985, Les Oranges, Santa Monica, Correspondence Sch., 1970-78, 1st Ann. Art-A-Thon, N.Y.C., 1985, Am. Epiphany with Phillip Hefferton, 1986, Polit. Cartoon Show, Braunstein, San Francisco,

Komsomolskaya Pravda, 1988, retrospective Eloise Packard Smith, 1990, exemplary contemporary, Cowell, U. Calif. Santa Cruz, 1991, Silicon Graphics Inc., Computer Graphics for NAB, Las Vegas, 1993, Prague Eco-Fair, 1991; represented in pvt. and pub. collections (complete archives) Spl. Collections, McHenry Libr., U. Calif., Santa Cruz, Mus. Modern Art, N.Y.C., San Francisco Mus. Modern Art, Oakland Mus., San Francisco Mus. Cartoon Art, Whitney Mus. Am. Art, N.Y.C. regular contbr. The Japan Times. Ltd., Tokyo. Address: PO Box 325 Aromas CA 95004-0325 also: Fools Gold 34A Polk St San Juan Bautista CA 95045

NUWER, HENRY JOSEPH (HANK NUWER), journalist, educator; b. Buffalo, Aug. 19, 1946; s. Henry Robert and Teresa (Lysiak) N.; m. Alice May Cerniglia, Dec. 28, 1968 (div. Mar. 1980); 1 child, Henry Christian; m. Jenine Howard, Apr. 9, 1982; 1 child, Adam. BS in English, SUCNY, Buffalo, 1968; MA in English, N.Mex. Highlands U., 1971; PhD equivalency, Ball State U., 1987. Freelance author, journalist, 1969—; asst. prof. Clemson (S.C.) U., 1982-83; assoc. prof. Ball State U., Muncie, Ind., 1985-89; sr. editor Rodale Press, Emmaus, Pa., 1990-91; editor in chief Arts Ind. Mag., Indpls., 1993-95; assoc. prof. journalism U. Richmond, Va., 1995-97. Hazing expert-lectr., 1990—; Hazing cons. NBC Movie-of-the-Week Moment of Truth: Broken Pledges, Indpls., 1994; adj. prof. journalism Ind. U. Sch. Journalism, Indpls., 1995—, Anderson U., 1998-2002; asst. prof. journalism Franklin (Ind.) Coll., 2002—; nat. advisor/NCAA study and survey on hazing in coll. athletic groups Alfred U., 1999. Author: Steroids, 1990, Broken Pledges: The Deadly Rite of Hazing, 1990, How to Write Like an Expert, 1995, The Legend of Jesse Owens, 1998, Wrongs of Passage, 1999, revised edit., 2002, High School Hazing, 2000, To the Young Writer, 2002; mem. editl. staff Chic Mag., 1976-77; contbr. articles to profl. jours. Grantee Nat. Endowment for the Arts, 1976, Idaho Humanities Coun., 1985, Gannett Found., 1988; named New Mag. Adviser of Yr., Coll. Media Advisers, 1988, Disting. Alumnus, Buffalo State Coll., 1999. Mem. Soc. Profl. Journalists (3rd. pl. Best Bus. Article Ind. competion 2002), Investigative Reporters and Editors. Democrat. Roman Catholic. Office: Franklin Coll Journalism Dept 501 E Monroe St Franklin IN 46131-2598 E-mail: hnuwer@hanknuwer.com.

NUZUM, JOHN M., JR. banker; b. Milw., Dec. 22, 1939; s. John M. and Helen (Ollis) N.; m. Margaret Bolway, Feb. 25, 1967 (div. 1999); children: Kimberly, Courtney, Leah, Jonathan. AB, Princeton U., 1962; MBA, U. Pa., 1964. Sr. v.p. J.P. Morgan, Chase & Co., N.Y.C., 1965—. Dir. Chase Manhattan Bank USA, NA, Wilmington, Del., 1995—; mem. governing bd. Credit Rsch. Ctr., Georgetown U., Washington, 1995-97. Project Reach Youth, Bklyn., 1977—, Park Slope Family Ctr., Bklyn., 1984-95. Mem. Risk Mgmt. Assn. (bd. dirs. 2000—), Montauk Club (bd. dirs. 1985-94), Princeton Club. Office: One Chase Manhattan Plz New York NY 10081-2014

NUZUM, ROBERT WESTON, lawyer; b. Evanston, Ill., Dec. 11, 1952; s. John Weston and Janet Marie (Talbot) N.; m. Julia Ann Abadie, Sept. 16, 1983. BS in Fin., La. State U., 1974, JD, 1977; LLM in Taxation, N.Y.U., 1978. Bar: La. 1977, D.C. 1979. Assoc. Office Chief Counsel, Washington, 1978-81, Jones, Walker, Waechter, Poitevent, Carrere & Denegre, New Orleans, 1981-85; ptnr. Jones, Walker, Waechter, Potevent, Carrere & Denegre, 1985-88, Deutsch, Kerrigan & Stiles, New Orleans, 1988-89, Phelps Dunbar, L.L.P. and predecessor firm, New Orleans, 1989—. Prof. law, state and local taxation Tulane U. Sch. Law, New Orleans, 1998—. Editor La. Law Rev., 1977; contbr. articles to profl. jours. Wallace scholar N.Y.U., 1978. Mem.: Tulane Tax Inst. (planning com. 1993—, tax specialization adv. commn.), New Orleans Bar Assn. (chmn. tax sect. 2001—), La. Bar Assn. (program chmn. tax sect. 1992—93, sec.-treas. 1993—94, vice chmn. 1994—95, chmn. 1995—96), Order of Coif. Republican. Roman Catholic. Avocations: golf, reading, fishing. Office: Phelps Dunbar LLP 365 Canal St Ste 2100 New Orleans LA 70130-1133 E-mail: nuzumb@phelps.com.

NUZZO, ANTHONY GERALD, services executive; b. New Haven, Aug. 9, 1951; s. Michael Anthony and Theresa Mary (Aitro) N.; m. Julie Nuzzo, Mar. 22, 1975; children: Beth, Michael, Cortney. BA, Boston Coll., 1973; MBA, Columbia U., 1975. CLU. Brand asst. Procter & Gamble, Cin., 1975-76, sales rep. Cinn., 1976, asst. brand mgr., 1976-77; asst. product dir. Johnson & Johnson, New Brunswick, N.J., 1977-78, spl. project dir., 1978-79, product dir. Milltown, 1979-82, group product dir., 1982-84; v.p. Am. Express Travel Related Services, New York, 1984-87; v.p., exec. com. Am. Express Can., Inc., Markham, Ont., 1987-88; v.p. internat. mktg. Am. Express, N.Y., 1988; v.p. Chemical Bank, N.Y.C., 1988-90, sr. v.p., 1990-91; pres., CEO Chemical Bank Del., Wilmington, 1991-92; pres., founder Advanced Mktg. Assocs., Inc., East Brunswick, N.J., 1992-93; pres., CEO Fidelity Trust Co., Salt Lake City, 1993-98, chmn., 1998-99; pres., CEO Fidelity TempWorks/TempSource, Boston, 1998-99; chmn., pres., CEO @Bank, Framingham, 1999-2000; pres., CEO Engage, Andover, 2000—01; pres., CEO, founder The Nuzzo Group, Inc., Wellesley, 2001—. Mem. Visa Mktg. Advisors, 1989-92, 93-98. Editor: Physiology, 1984. Dir., co-chair, co-founder Citizens Against UnSafe Environments, East Brunswick, N.J., 1981-93; bd. dirs. Utah Bd. Fin. Instns., 1995-98. Named to PS&D Merchandising Hall of Fame Procter & Gamble, Cin., 1977, named Scholar of the Coll., Boston Coll., 1973; recipient Bus. Sch. Service award Columbia U., 1975, Excellence award Package Designer Coun., N.Y.C., 1980, Clio Creative Excellence award Clio Adv. Body, N.Y.C., 1981, Effie award, N.Y.C., 1989. Mem. Boston Coll. Alumni Assn., Columbia Bus. Sch. Alumni Assn. (dir. N.Y. club 1975), Utah Bankers Assn. (bd. dirs. 1996-98), Utah Assn. Fin. Svcs. (bd. dirs. 1993-98, treas. 1995-96). Avocations: golf, skiing, baseball coaching, hockey managing, reading. E-mail: agnuzzo@aol.com.

NUZZO, SALVATORE JOSEPH, defense/electronics company executive; b. Norwalk, Conn., Aug. 6, 1931; s. Rocco and Angelina (Renzull) N.; m. Lucille Cocco, Oct. 3, 1953; children: James, David, Thomas, Dana. BS in Elec. Engring, Yale U., 1953; MS in Bus, Columbia U., 1974. With Hazeltine Corp., Greenlawn, N.Y., 1953-88, v.p. govt. products and mktg., 1969-73, v.p. govt. products div., 1973-74, sr. v.p. ops., 1974-76, exec. v.p., chief oper. officer, 1976, pres., chief oper. officer, 1977-88, chief exec. officer, 1980-87, chmn., 1986-88, ret., 1988; chmn., Technautics Corp., Cleve., 1991-94; chmn. Marine Mech. Corp., 1994—. Bd. mem. Avnet Inc.; chmn., CEO, bd. dirs. Datron, Inc., 1996—. Fellow Poly. Inst. N.Y. Mem. Yale Sci. and Engring. Assn. (former pres.). Home: 118 Saint Mellions Pinehurst NC 28374-8104 also: 1101 Waterfront on 800 Ocean Dr Juno Beach FL 33408-1715

NWAGBARAOCHA, JOEL ONUKWUGHA, academic administrator, educator; b. Victoria, Cameroons, Nov. 21, 1942; came to U.S., 1964; naturalized, 1974; s. John O. and Christiana (Ihejeihu) N.; m. Patsy Coleman, Aug. 27, 1977; children: Jason, Jonathan, John, Eric. BS in Math., cert. in physics, Norfolk State U., 1969; EdM, Harvard U., 1970, EdD (Univ. fellow), 1972. Tchr. math. and physics Emmanuel Coll., Owerri, Nigeria, 1960-64; asst. dir. Manpower Rsch. Inst./Norfolk (Va.) State Coll., 1969-70; rsch. assoc. Harvard U. Grad. Sch. Edn., 1969-72; assoc. dir. co-op acad. planning program Inst. for Svcs. to Edn., Washington, 1972-74, dir. instnl. planning and mgmt. program, 1974-76, dir. divsn. acad. planning and faculty devel., 1976-78; assoc. prof. edn., v.p. planning and ops. analysis Morgan State U., Balt., 1978-87; v.p. acad. affairs Voorhees Coll., Denmark, S.C., 1987-80; pres. Barber-Scotia Coll., Concord, N.C., 1990-94; prof. edn., bus. adminstrn. Strayer U., Washingtn, 1994—, dir. grad. studies, 2000—. Dean Tacoma Park Campus, Strayer Coll., Washington; cons. in higher edn. planning and evaluation system devel., 1972—. Co-author: Operational Manual for ollege Planning Development, 1977, Planning Management and Evaluation System, 1979; mem. edit. bd. Spartan Echo, 1967-69; contbr. articles to profl. jours. Mem. AAAS, Am. Coun. on Edn., Nat. Coun. on Social Studies, Am. Assn. for Higher Edn., Am. Humanist Assn., Soc. for Coll. and Univ. Planning, Am. Assn. Univ. Adminstrs., Am. Mgmt. Assn., Higher Edn. Group of Washington, Smithsonian Nat. Assoc., Alpha Kappa Mu, Phi Beta Sigma, Beta Kappa Chi, Phi Delta Kappa. Home: 10928 Battersea Ln Columbia MD 21044-2701 Office: Strayer Univ Washington DC Campus 1025 15th St NW Washington DC 20005-2601

NWANGWU, JOHN TOCHUKWU, epidemiologist, public health educator; b. Ogidi, Anambra, Nigeria, Apr. 16, 1952; came to U.S., 1973; s. Sidney N. and Phoebe Nwangwu; m. Chioma Ugonwa Nwokolo, Sept. 3, 1988; children: Nmadinobi, Tobenna, Kamsiyo. MB, U. Nebr., Omaha, 1979; MPH, Loma Linda U., 1981; PhD, Columbia U., 1988; postgrad., Erasmus U., Rotterdam, The Netherlands, 1991. Cons. WHO, 1982-87; instr. Columbia U., N.Y.C., 1983-85, St. Joseph's Coll. Hosp., Bklyn., 1986-88; asst. prof. SUNY, 1988-89; chief epidemiologist Kern County Health Dept., Bakersfield, Calif., 1989-90, dir. epidemiology and data mgmt., 1990; assoc. prof. pub. health Conn. State U., New Haven, 1991-95, prof. pub. health, 1995—. Vis. prof. Calif. State U., Bakersfield, 1990, Yale U., New Haven, 1992, adj. prof. epidemiology Sch. Medicine, 1995—; epidemiologist/rsch. affiliate faculty Yale U. Sch. Medicine, 1993—; cons. Hosp. of St. Raphael, New Haven, 1995—; cons. to fgn. countries, 1982—; presenter in field; adj. prof. cmty. medicine Sch. Medicine U. Conn., 1995—; vis. prof. Harvard Sch. Pub. Health, 1998; vis. scholar Dana-Farber Cancer Inst., Harvard U., Boston; cons. in infectious disease VA Hosp., Rocky Hill, Conn., 1998. Contbr. articles to profl. publs. Erasmus U. fellow, 1991. Fellow Royal Soc. Medicine, Am. Coll. Epidemiology; mem. APHA, Internat. Epidemiol. Assn., N.Y. Acad. Scis., Assn. Tchrs. Preventive Medicine. Avocations: badminton, squash, reading. Home: 898 Greenway Rd Woodbridge CT 06525-2413 Office: Conn State U Dept Pub Health 144 Farnham Ave Dept Pub New Haven CT 06515-1202 also: Yale U Sch Medicine Dept Epidemiology and Pub Health 60 College St New Haven CT 06510-3210 E-mail: Nwangwu@scsu.ctstateu.edu.

NWANKWO, EMEKA OBIOMA, chemical engineer, educator, entrepreneur; b. Emekuku, Imo, Nigeria, June 9, 1967; s. Ochia Christian and Bridget Chikere (Akwada) N. BSc with honors, U. Ife, Nigeria, 1987; MS, U. Rochester, N.Y., 1992; D Engring. Sci., Columbia U., 1996. Indsl. engr. Michelin (Nigeria) Ltd., Port Harcourt, 1987-88; instr. Columbia U., N.Y.C., 1991-94; vis. scientist DuPont Ctrl. Rsch. & Devel., Wilmington, Del., 1993-94, rsch. engr. process synthesis and fundamentals, 1994-96, rsch. engr. advanced process control and optimization, 1996—. Chmn. bd. dirs., CEO Group E Broadcasting, Aba, Nigeria, 1996—, VendCorp. Ltd., Digital Threshold Ltd.; CEO Q Corp Ltd., Nigeria; chmn., CO Aquada Devel. Corp., Nigeria; adj. assoc. prof. dept. math. scis. U. Del., Newark. Contbr. articles to profl. jours. Trustee St. Bridget's Coll., Aba, 1995, St. Bridget's Primary Sch., Aba, 1987—. Recipient honors fellowship U. Rochester, 1989, Alumni prize in engring. econs. U. Ife, Ile-Ife, 1987, Nat. Process Plant Design prize Nigerian Soc. Chem. Engrs., Lagos, 1988. Mem. AIChE, Am. Soc. Engring. Edn., Inst. Chem. Engrs. (Eng.), Am. Chem. Soc., Internat. Soc. African Scientists (project dir. 1995—), N.Y. Acad. Scis., Sigma Xi. Achievements include development of high-performance computing environments for chemical process synthesis and design, co-development of a high-precision analytical technique for high-speed (ultrasonic) characterization of linear viscoelastic polymers, an efficient technique for calibration of gel-permeation chromatographic devices. Avocations: tennis, fishing, ham radio, flying, saxophone. Home: PO Box 561 Montchanin DE 19710-0561 Office: E I duPont de Nemours Inc DuPont Exptl Sat PO Box 80101 Wilmington DE 19880-0101 also: PO Box E Umuahia Abia Nigeria

NWEEIA, MARTIN THOMAS, dentist, musician, composer, anthropologist; b. New Britain, Conn., Apr. 15, 1954; s. Alexander and Nellie (Lazar) N. BA in English and Biology, Trinity Coll., Hartford, Conn., 1977; DDS, Case Western Res. U., 1984; cert., Brånemark Clinic, Göteborg, Sweden, 1989. Pvt. practice, Honolulu, 1984—95, Sharon, Conn., 1995—; clin. faculty Harvard Sch. Dental Medicine, 2002—. Dental corr. Sta. KGMB-TV, 1988—92; dental columnist Honolulu Star-Bull., Gannett-USA Today, 1988—95; attending cons. Sharon Hosp., 1995—; internat. dir. World Dental Network; leader expdn. to study adult tooth morphology of living Ticuna Indians of Colombian Amazon, 1978; leader expdn. to study childhood dental diseases of Micronesia Ulithi Atoll, Yap State, 83; expert witness for dental malpractice MedQuest, 1998—; faculty restrative dentistry Harvard Sch. Dental Medicine, 2002—. Author: (pamphlet) Baby-Bottle Tooth Decay, 1989, The Whole Tooth, Answers to Questions You Always Wanted to Ask Your Dentist, 1999; editor Hawaii Dental Jour., 19990-94 (Golden Pen award 1994); contbr. articles to profl. jours. including Am. Jour. Dental Rsch., Internat. Jour. Dental Rsch., Am. Jour. Phys. Anthropology; music dir. As One Hawaii, 1992, Do It Together, Honolulu, 1993, Cool Notes, Hawaii Dept. Edn., 1994; PBS documentaries including; Light in Art, 1988, Facets, 1989 (Kona Gold, Blue Ribbon Am. Film and Video Assn.), Dark After Daylight, Taiwan, 1990, Dialog, 1994, to debut video for Waikiki Aquarium Jellyfish (Bronze award N.Y. Internat. Film Festival, Cine Golden Eagle 1994). Constrn. worker rep. United Ch. Fedn., Tarsus, Turkey, 1972. Rsch. grantee in anthropology Explorers Club N.Y., Colombian Amazon, 1978; Joseph Silber fellow Am. Cancer Soc., 1982-83, grad. student rsch. fellow Smithsonian Instn., 1981. Fellow Amer. Col. of Dentists, Acad. Gen. Dentistry (Editl. award of excellence 1999), Acad. Dentistry Internat. (hon.), Internat. Coll. Dentists (hon.), Pierre Fauchard Acad. (hon.), Explorers Club (nat.); mem. Hawaii Dental Assn. (trustee 1993-95), Hawaii Acad. Gen. Dentistry (pub. info. award 1990-93, pres. 1993-95, nat. award for cmty. involvement 1990, nat. award for media rels. 1992, nat. award for editorials, 1999). Republican. Mem. United Ch. of Christ. Avocations: documentary composer and arranger, anthropologist, windsurfing, skiing, tennis and squash. Home: 16 Grandview Ln Sharon CT 06069-2040 also: 358 Kupaua Pl Honolulu HI 96821-2152 Office: 6 New St Sharon CT 06069-2077 E-mail: boo@snet.net.

NWOKEAFOR, COSMAS UCHENNA, communications educator; b. Portharcourt, Rivers, Nigeria, Sept. 26, 1955; s. Oliver Ibekwe and Josephine A. (Ejekwu) N.; m. Catherine Adaku Anyanwu, Dec. 21, 1985; children; Uchenna, Nneka, Chinwendu, Chinedu. NCE, Alvan Ikoku Coll. Edn., Owerri, Nigeria, 1983; BA, Howard U., 1986, MA, 1990, PhD, 1992. Grad. tchg./rsch. asst. Howard U., Washington, 1990-92; asst. prof. Bowie (Md.) State U., 1992—. Adj. prof. Bowie State U., 1990-92, George Mason U., Fairfax, Va., 1993—; editl. coord. Bowie State U. newspaper (Spectrum), 1996—. Contbg. author: (books) Press and Politics in Africa, 1997, Sustainable Democratization Through Emerging Communications Media, 1997; contbr. chpt. to book. Recipient Poynter Inst. Fellowship award Poynter Inst. for Media Studies, St. Petersburg, 1995, API Fellowship award Am. Press Inst., Reston, Va., 1995; named All-Am. Scholar, U.S. Achievement Acad., 1990. Mem. Nat. Comm. Assn., Assn. for Edn. in Journalism and Mass Comms., Pub. Rels. Student Soc. of Am. (faculty advisor 1993—), Ea. Comm. Assn., Internat. Comm. Assn., African Coun. for Comm. Edn., KC. Roman Catholic. Avocations: swimming, soccer, readins. Home: 12703 Sutters Ln Bowie MD 20720-4636 Office: Bowie State U 14000 Jericho Park Rd Bowie MD 20715-3319 E-mail: cnwokeafor@bowie.state.edu.

NWOKOGBA, ISAAC, financial analyst; b. Etche, Rivers State, Nigeria, June 5, 1957; s. Nwokogba Nwezi and Jenny Nwokogba. BBA, S.W. Tex. State U., San Marcos, 1985. Sr. rate analyst Pub. Utility Commn. Tex., Austin, 1989—97; rate analyst Edison Source, Industry, Calif., 1997—2000; fin. analyst pricing design and tariffs Regulatory Policy & Affairs, So. Calif. Edison, Rosemead, 1999—. Author: (books and articles) America, Here I Come: A Spiritual Journey, 2001, (book) Seeds of Luck: The ABCs of Creating Your Heart's Desires, 2001; featured on cover: Kiplinger's Personal Finance Mag. Avocations: reading, writing, travel, performing arts. Home: PO Box 4023 Long Beach CA 90804 Personal E-mail: seedsofluck@yahoo.com.

NWOKOYE, PATRICK IKECHUKWU, priest, researcher; b. Amawbia, Nigeria, Mar. 25, 1970; arrived in U.S., 1997; s. Anizoba and Nwakaego Nwokoye. BA, Lateran U., Rome, 1992, MA in Philosophy, 1994, PhD, 1997; MA, MDiv, Kenrick Sch. Theology, 2002. Clergy Diocese of Springfield-Cape Girardeau, Mo., 1997—. Tchr. Notre Dame H.S., Mo., 1999—2000; co-host talk show Raidue, Rome, 1995—96. Youth dir. St. Mary Cathedral, Cape Girardeau, Mo., 1999—2000. Mem.: Internat. Lateran Assn., World Phenomenology Inst., Fellowship of Cath. Scholars. Roman Catholic. Avocations: soccer, ping pong, basketball, ballet, hockey. E-mail: pul1997@hotmail.com.

NWOYE, JOSEPH, educator; b. Nawfia, Anambra, Nigeria, Apr. 10, 1959; s. Emmanual Okeke Nwoye, Josephine Mgboye Nwoye; m. Melinda Dawn Beck; children: Uchenna, Bernadette, Chioma. Ed.D, Indiana University of Pennsylvania, Indiana, Pennsylvania, 1992—97, M.Ed, 1992—95; MBA, Bowie State University, Bowie, Maryland, 1989—91; B.Sc. Marketing, Indiana University of Pennsylvania, Indiana, Pennsylvania, 1983—87. Assistant District Manager Kinney Shoes, Wheaton, MD, 1989—91; Executive Director/Founder CNIA Inc., Atlanta, 1996—92; Teacher/Activities Leader Nicholas Oriem Middle School, Prince George's, MD, 1990—92; Instructor Indiana University of Pennsylvania, Indiana, PA, 1995—97; Assistant Professor West Liberty State College, West Liberty, WV, 1997—99, Illinois State University, Normal, IL, 1999—2002. Diversity Consultant Chicago School District, Chicago, IL, 2000—02. Author: (book) Multi-Cultural Education, 1999; editor: (Book) Multicultural Education: Diverse Perspectives, 2001; author: (Article) Journal of Philosophy and History of Education, 1999, Illinois Schools Journal, 2002, Journal of Philosophy and History of Education, 2000. Bylaw Committee Member Association of Teacher Educators, Fall Church, VA, 1995—2002; Member National Association for Multicultural Education, 1998—2002, Society of Philosophy and History of Education, Norma, OK, 1999—2002; Area Coordinator National Association of African American Studies, Houston, 1999—2002. Mem.: Association of Teacher Educators (Bylaw Committee Member 1995—2002). Home: 402 Stanhope Lane Normal IL 61761 Office: Illinois State University Normal IL Business E-Mail: jinwoye@ilstu.edu.

NYBERG, DONALD ARVID, oil company executive; b. Ridgewood, N.J., Aug. 23, 1951; s. Arvid H. and Rita T. (Tenwick) N.; m. Susan Radis, Feb. 16, 1985; children: Matthew D., Ryan T. BA, St. Lawrence U., 1973; MBA, Harvard U., 1975. Mgr. marine ops. Standard Oil, L.A., 1982-83, mgr. ops. planning Cleve., 1984-85, dir. strategic studies, 1986; divsn. mgr. Brit. Petroleum, Ltd., London, 1987-88; v.p., gen. mgr. U.S. gas bus. BP Exploration, Houston, 1989, v.p., gen. mgr. tech., 1990, with, 1991-94; pres., CEO BP Pipelines, Anchorage, 1991-94; pres. Marya Resources, Houston, 1994—; v.p. MAPCO, Tulsa, 1996; pres. Tesoro Marine Svcs., Houston, 1996—. Mem. devel. coun. Tex. Children's Hosp.; bd. dirs. Boys and Girls Country Houston. Mem. Forest Club, Bentwater Country Club. Avocations: running, weight lifting, reading. Office: 9426 Telephone Rd Houston TX 77075-2020 E-mail: dnyberg@tesoropetroleum.com.

NYBERG, LARS, electronics company executive; b. Sweden; married; four children. BS in bus. adminstrn., U. Stockholm, 1974. With Philips Electronics NV, U.K., The Netherlands, Sweden, chmn., CEO comm. sys. divsn.; chmn., CEO AT&T Global Info. Solutions, mem. mgmt. exec. com., 1995-96; chmn., pres. and CEO NCR Corp., 1997—. Office: NCR Corp 1700 S Patterson Blvd Dayton OH 45479-0002*

NYBERG, STANLEY ERIC, cognitive scientist; b. Boston, Jan. 30, 1948; s. Leroy Milton and Anna Maria (Olson) N. PhD, SUNY, Stony Brook, 1975; M of Pub. and Pvt. Mgmt., Yale U., 1984. Postdoctoral fellowship U. Calif., Berkeley, 1975-76; asst. prof. North Pk. Coll., Chgo., 1976-79, Barnard Coll., Columbia U., N.Y.C., 1979-82; sys. mgmt. Interactive Data Corp., Lexington, Mass., 1984-88, Dept. of Revenue, Commonwealth of Mass., Boston, 1988-2000; with Dept. of Environ. Protection, Commonwealth of Mass., 2000—01; registrar vital records and stats. Commonwealth of Mass., 2001—. Co-author: Human Memory: An Introduction to Research and Theory, 1982. Bd. dirs. Childrens Home of Cromwell, Conn., 1988-94, Decade Fund, Yale U. Sch. Mgmt., 1984-85, Scandinavian Charitable Soc. of Greater Boston; ch. coun. Luth. Ch. of Redeemer, Woburn, Mass., 1991-97, West Roxbury Rugby Football Club, 1984-87; v.p., sec. L Street Running Club, South Boston, 1987—; mem. divsn. ecumenism New Eng. Synod, Evang. Luth. Ch. in Am., 1997—; bd. dirs. Scandinavian Charitable Soc. Greater Boston, 2000—. Fellow Am. Psychol. Soc.; mem. Soc. for Applied Rsch. in Memory and Cognition, Eastern Psychol. Assn., Midwestern Psychol. Assn., Am. Psychol. Assn. Home: PO Box 1849 Boston MA 02205-1849 E-mail: snyberg@aol.com.

NYBORG, KARINE, economist, researcher; b. Oslo, June 12, 1962; d. Per Nyborg and Anne Alvik; m. Jan-Erik Støstad; children: Mads, Hanna, Morten. Cand. oecon., U. Oslo, 1988, D Politics, 1996. Vis. scholar dept. econs. Stanford (Calif.) U., 1996-97; rsch. economist Stats. Norway, Oslo, 1989-96, rsch. fellow, 1997-99, sr. rsch. fellow, 2000—01; rschr. Ragnar Frisch Centre for Econ. Rsch., 2001—. Mem. Commn. for Cost Calculations, 1994-99, Petroleum Tax Commn., 1999-2000. Editor Sosialøkonomen, 2000—; contbr. articles to profl. jours., including Jour. Pub. Econs., Rev. Income and Wealth, Jour. Econs., Pub. Choice, Jour. Consumer Policy, Nordic Jour. Polit. Economy, Jour. Econ. Behavior and Orgn., Ecol. Econs., Environ. and Resource Econs., Ecol. Econs., Økonomiske Analyser, Sosialøkonomen, also newspapers; contbr. chpts. to books, including Approaches to Environomental Accounting, 1993. Mem. Am. Econ. Assn., European Assn. for Environ. and Resource Econs., Internat. Soc. for New Instnl. Econs., Norwegian Economists Assn. Home: Tjernsrud Plass 6 N-1358 Jar Norway Office: The Ragnar Frisch Centre for Econ Rsch Gaustadalleen 21 N-0349 Oslo Norway Fax: +4722 95 8825. E-mail: karine.nyborg@frisch.uio.no.

NYBORG, KENNETH WAYNE, retired social sciences educator, small business owner; b. Mountain Lake, Minn., May 27, 1939; s. Lester C. and Clara E. Nyborg; m. Carol E. Nyborg; children: Glen, David, Solveig Kruse. BA, St. Olaf Coll., 1961; MSEd, Winona State U., 1970. Cert. life gen. secondary tchr. Calif. Tchr. Barstow (Calif.) Unified Sch. Dist., 1964—2002; bus. co-owner Nyborg's Music, 1979—91. Dist. tech. lead Barstow Unified Sch. Dist., 1992—96; tech. lead Barstow H.S., 1994—98, dept. chair social studies, 1997—2001, co-chair WASC accreditation com., 1999—2001. Mem. Barstow C. of C., 1979—91. Named Small Bus. of Yr., Barstow C. of C., 1988, Tchr. of Yr., Barstow H.S., 2001. Mem.: Calif. Ret. Tchrs. Assn. (newsletter co-editor 2001—02). Lutheran. Avocations: reading, travel, golf, church choir, computers. Home: 921 Windy Pass Barstow CA 92311 Personal E-mail: knyb@hotmail.com.

NYBORG, WESLEY LEMARS, physics educator; b. Ruthven, Iowa, May 15, 1917; s. Isaac and Leva (Larson) N.; m. Beth Woolsey, Sept. 8, 1945; 1 dau., Elsa Beth. BA, Luther Coll., 1941; MS, Pa. State U., 1944, PhD, 1947. Asst. prof. physics Pa. State U., Univ. Park, 1948-50; asst. prof. Brown U., Providence, 1950-54, assoc. prof., 1954-60; prof. U. Vt., Burlington, 1960-86, acting chmn. physics dept., 1978-79, prof. emeritus, 1986—. Vis. scientist Oxford (Eng.) U., 1960-61, Univ. Coll., Cardiff, Wales, 1969, U. of Rochester, 1987; Exec. council Am. Inst. Ultrasound in Medicine, 1972-74, 76-78, chmn. bioeffects com., 1976-78; adv. bd. Bur. Radiol. Health, 1972-75; cons. FDA, 1976— ; chmn. sci. com. 66 Nat. Council Radiation Protection and Measurements, 1980— ; mem. working group on biol. effects ultrasound, WHO, 1982, 85, 88; mem. study sect. diagnostic radiology NIH, 1982-85; adv. mem. Rochester Ctr. for Biomed. Ultrasound, 1986. Author: Intermediate Biophysical Mechanics, 1975; co-editor: Biological Effects of Ultrasound, 1985; Editorial bd.: Ultrasound in Medicine and Biology, Clinics in Diagnostic Ultrasound; internat. adv. editor: Ultrasonics; co-editor Proc. Symposium on Safety and Standardization in Med. Ultrasound, 2d World Fedn. Ultrasound in Medicine and Biology, 1989; contbr. to profl. jours. Recipient Presdl. recognition award Am. Inst. Ultrasound in Medicine, 1977, Univ. scholar award in phys. scis. U. Vt., 1984, Disting. Svc. award Luther Coll., 1996, Vt. Acad. Sci. and Engring., 1997, Lauriston S. Taylor Lectr. award 2001; USPHS fellow MIT, 1956-57; research grantee NIH, 1955—. Fellow AAAS, Acoustical Soc. Am. (exec. coun. 1965-68, Silver medal 1990), Am. Inst. Ultrasound in Medicine (Joseph H. Holmes award 1985, W.J. Fry Lecture award 1990), Ultrasonic Soc. India (hon.); mem. NAE, Am. Phys. Soc., Biophys. Soc., Am. Assn. Physics Tchrs., Sigma Xi, Sigma Pi Sigma. Home: 2 Stirling Pl Burlington VT 05401-2634 E-mail: wnyborg@zoo.uvm.edu.

NYCE, DAVID SCOTT, electronics company executive; b. Norristown, Pa., Jan. 25, 1952; s. Jonathan J. and Emma R. (Dusza) N.; m. Gwen Ann Gordon, Apr. 26, 1975; children: Timothy S., Christopher D., Megan S. BSEE, Temple U., 1973; MBA, Concordia Coll., 2001. Cert. pvt. pilot, helicopter pilot; cert. firearms instr. N.C. Project engr. Robinson-Halpern Co., Plymouth Meeting, Pa., 1973-77; sr. devel. engr. Honeywell, Ft. Washington, 1977-78; chief engr. Chatlos Systems, Inc., Whippany, N.J., 1978-79; mgr. engring. Environ. Tectonics Corp., Southampton, Pa., 1979-80; v.p., dir. engring. Neutronics, Inc., Exton, 1980-90; dir. tech. MTS Systems Corp., Research Triangle Park , NC, 1990—. Cons. in field; proprietor Nyce Sporting Equipment, Apex, N.C., 1985—, Nyce Sounds, Trappe, Pa., 1987-90. Contbr. chapters to books. Tchr. aerodynamics and rocketry Apex Sch. System, 1990—; merit badge counselor Boy Scouts Am. Recipient Vaaler award Chem. Engring. Mag., 1988. Mem. AAAS, Aircraft Owners and Pilots Assn., Instrument Soc. Am. (sr.), NRA (life, cert. instr., sharpshooter), Lower Providence Rod and Gun Club (capt. pistol team 1987-89, high on team 1988-89), U.S. Hang Gliding Assn., U.S. Parachute Assn., U.S. Judo Assn. (brown belt), Nat. Assn. Rocketry, Nat. Trappers Assn., Acad. Model Aero., The Planetary Soc., Tripoli Rocketry Assn. Achievements include patents for low power magnetostriction, threshold compensating detector, bandwidth limiting, densimeter, pulse detector, fluid level and density; magnetostrictive sensor with waveguide referenced to tip, magnetostrictive transducer for a shock absorber, Electromagnetic liquid level monitor. Office: MTS Systems Corp Sensors Divsn 3001 Sheldon Dr Cary NC 27513-2006 E-mail: David.Nyce@mts.com .

NYCKLEMOE, GLENN WINSTON, bishop; b. Fergus Falls, Minn., Dec. 8, 1936; s. Melvin and Bertha (Sumstad) N.; m. Ann Elizabeth Olson, May 28, 1960; children: Peter Glenn, John Winston, Daniel Thomas. BA, St. Olaf Coll., 1958; MDiv, Luther Theol. Sem., St. Paul, 1962; D of Ministry, Luth. Sch. Theology, Chgo., 1977. Ordained to ministry Am. Luth. Ch., 1962. Assoc. pastor Our Savior's Luth. Ch., Valley City, N.D., 1962-64, Milw., 1964-67, co-pastor, 1967-73, sr. pastor Beloit, 1973-82, St. Olaf Luth. Ch., Austin, Minn., 1982-88; bishop Southeastern Minn. Synod, Evang. Luth. Ch. in Am., Rochester, 1988—2001. Bd. dirs. Luth. Social Svcs. of Minn., Mpls., Bd. of Social Ministries, St. Paul, Minn. Coun. Chs., Mpls. Mem. bd. regents St. Olaf Coll., Northfield, Minn., 1988—. Avocations: skiing, trap shooting, golf.

NYCUM, DEBRA WETZEL, English language educator; b. Cumberland, Md., Feb. 8, 1953; d. Robert Lee and Pauline Elizabeth (Walker) Wetzel; m. David Lloyd Nycum, Oct. 7, 1989. BA, James Madison U., 1975; Master's equivalency, Hood Coll./Frostburg State U., 1982. Std. profl. cert., Md. Tchr. English Broad Run H.S., Leesburg, Va., 1975-80, North Hagerstown H.S., Hagerstown, Md., 1980-92; tchr. English summer sch., 1981-90; fitness instr. Hagerstown YMCA, 1982-92; English instr. Hagerstown C.C., 1991-94; writing resource tchr. Washington County Bd. Edn., Hagerstown, 1992-95; tchr. English Williamsport (Md.) H.S., 1995—; English instr. Hagerstown Bus. Coll., 2000—. Chair English dept. North Hagerstown H.S., 1989-92; com. mem. Essential Curriculum for Washington County. Pub. rels. co-chair State Del. Campaign, Hagerstown, 1986, 88; sec. staff parish rels. Mt. Nebo United Meth. Ch. (sec. 1999-2001, chair 2001, fin. com., worship com. 2001, communion steward 2000—). Recipient Gov.'s Fitness Participation award State of Md. Mem. NEA, Nat. Coun. Tchrs. of English, Washington County Tchrs. Assn. (bd. dirs., Tchr. Appreciation award 1987), Self-Help and Resource Exch. (co-coord. 1994-97), Md. State Tchrs. Assn., Sigma chpt. Alpha Delta Kappa (scholarship com. 1994-95, ways and means com. 1995-97). Republican. Methodist. Avocations: reading, flower gardening, rubber stamping, exercising. Office: Williamsport H S 5 S Clifton Dr Williamsport MD 21795-1124 E-mail: Nycumdeb@wcboe.k12.ed.md.us.

NYCUM, SUSAN HUBBELL, lawyer; BA, Ohio Wesleyan U., 1956; JD, Duquesne U., 1960; postgrad., Stanford U. Bar: Pa. 1962, U.S. Supreme Ct. 1967, Calif. 1974. Sole practice law, Pitts., 1962-65; designer, adminstr. legal rsch. sys. U. Pitts., Aspen Sys. Corp., 1965-68; mgr. ops. Computer Ctr., Carnegie Mellon U., 1968-69; dir. computer facility Computer Ctr., Stanford U., Calif., 1969-72, Stanford Law and Computer fellow, 1972-73; cons. in computers and law, 1973-74; sr. assoc. MacLeod, Fuller, Muir & Godwin, Los Altos, Los Angeles and London, 1974-75; ptnr. Chickering & Gregory, San Francisco, 1975-80; ptnr.-in-charge high tech. group Gaston Snow & Ely Bartlett, Boston, NYC, Phoenix, San Francisco, Calif., 1980-86; mng. ptnr. Palo Alto office Kadison, Pfaelzer, Woodard, Quinn & Rossi, Los Angeles, Washington, Newport Beach, Palo Alto, 1986-87; sr. ptnr., chmn. U.S. intellectual property/info. tech. practice group Baker & McKenzie, Palo Alto, 1987—, mem. U.S. leadership team, 1987-97, mem. Asia Pacific regional coun., 1995—. Trustee EDUCOM, 1978-81; mem. adv. com. for high tech. Ariz. State U. Law Sch., Santa Clara U. Law Sch., Stanford Law Sch., U. So. Calif. Law Ctr., law sch. Harvard U., U. Calif.; U.S. State Dept. del. OECD Conf. on Nat. Vulnerabilities, Spain, 1981; invited speaker Telecom, Geneva, 1983; lectr. N.Y. Law Jour., 1975—, Law & Bus., 1975—, Practicing Law Inst., 1975—; chmn. Office of Tech. Assessment Task Force on Nat. Info. Sys., 1979-80. Author:(with Bigelow) Your Computer and the Law, 1975, (with Bosworth) Legal Protection for Software, 1985, (with Collins and Gilbert) Women Leading, 1987; contbr. monographs, articles to profl. publs. Fellow Am. Bar Found.; mem. Town of Portola Valley Open Space Acquisition Com., Calif., 1977; mem. Jr. League of Palo Alto, chmn. evening div., 1975-76 NSF and Dept. Justice grantee for studies on computer abuse, 1972— Fellow Assn. Computer Machinery (mem. at large of coun. 1976-80, nat. lectr. 1977—, chmn. standing com. on legal issues 1975—, mem. blue ribbon com. on rationalization of internat. propr. rights protection on info. processing devel. in the '90s 1990—), Coll. Law Practice Mgmt.; mem. ABA (chmn. sect. on sci. and tech. 1979-80), Internat. Bar Assn. (U.S. mem. computer com. of corps. sect.), Computer Law Assn. (v.p. 1983-85, pres. 1986—, bd. dirs. 1975—), Calif. State Bar Assn. (founder first chmn. econs. of law sect., vice chmn. law and computers com.), Nat. Conf. Lawyers and Scientists (rep. ABA), Strategic Forum on Intellectual Property Issues in Software of NAS, Internat. Coun. for Computer Comm. (gov. 1998). Home: 35 Granada Ct Portola Valley CA 94028-7736 Office: Baker & McKenzie PO Box 60309 Palo Alto CA 94306-0309

NYDEGGER, RICK D. lawyer; b. Salt Lake City, Apr. 24, 1949; s. A. Don and Jean Virginia (Hansen) N.; m. Denise Winegar, Oct. 22, 1970; children: Dan L., Chad E., Kurt D., Brittney, Trent R. BSEE cum laude, Brigham Young U., 1974, JD cum laude, 1977. Bar: Utah 1977, U.S. Dist Ct. (ctrl. dist.) Utah 1977, U.S. Patent Office 1977, U.S. Ct. Appeals (5th and 10th cirs.) 1980, U.S. Supreme Ct. 1990, U.S. Ct. Appeals (fed. cir.) 1994. Assoc. Fox, Edwards, & Gardiner, 1977-81, shareholder, dir., 1981-84; founding shareholder, dir., officer Workman, Nydegger & Seeley, Salt Lake City, 1984—. Adj. prof. U. Utah Coll. Law, 1988-89, Brigham Young U. Coll. Law, 1998—. Contbr. articles to profl. jours. Bd. dirs. Nat. Inventors Hall of Fame, 2000—, bd. dirs. found., 1998—; trustee Am. Intellectual Property Law Assn. Found., 2001—. Fellow Am. Intellectual Property Law Assn. (founding mem., chmn. electronic computer law com. 1990-93, bd. dirs. 1993-96, editl. bd. quar. jour., vice-chmn. ad hoc com. PCT practice, 1994-98, nominations com. 1997, chmn. mid-winter Inst. 2000 planning com., 2d v.p. 2000-01, 1st v.p. 2001—); mem. ABA, Utah State Bar (chmn. patent, trademark, copyright sect. 1985-87), Fed. Cir. Bar Assn., U.S. Supreme Ct. Hist. Soc. (10th cir. rep. 1993-94, Utah rep. 1992-93), Nat. Coun. Intellectual Property Law Assn. (chmn. 2000-01). Office: Workman Nydegger & Seeley 60 E South Temple Ste 1000 Salt Lake City UT 84111-1011

NYE, DANIEL WILLIAM, retired elementary school educator; b. Harrisburg, Pa., Apr. 14, 1942; s. Daniel J. and Clarice L. (Stonesifer) N.; m. Carol A. Stewart, Aug. 10, 1968; 1 child, Michael S. BS in Health Edn., West Chester (Pa.) U., 1964; MEd in Elem. Edn., Towson (Md.) U., 1970. Cert. tchr., Md. Tchr. phys. edn. elem. sch. Harford County Pub. Schs., Bel Air, Md., 1964-72, tchr. phys. edn. mid. sch., 1972-73, tchr. phys. edn. elem. sch., 1974-2000, ret., 2000. Rep. United Rep. Life Ins. Co., Harrisburg, Pa., 1981-85. Mem. AAHPERD, NEA, Md. State Tchrs. Assn., Harford County Edn. Assn., Md. chpt. AAHPERD. Republican. Avocations: avid golfer, antique car collector and restorer, stamp collector. Home: 1119 Carrs Mill Rd Bel Air MD 21014-2414 Office: Harford County Pub Schs 45 E Gordon St Bel Air MD 21014-2915

NYE, ERIC WILLIAM, English language and literature educator; b. Omaha, July 31, 1952; s. William Frank and Mary Roberta (Lueder) N.; m. Carol Denison Frost, Dec. 21, 1980; children: Charles William, Ellen Mary. BA, St. Olaf Coll., 1974; MA, U. Chgo., 1976, PhD, 1983; postgrad., Queens' Coll., Cambridge, England, 1979-82. Tutor in coll. writing com. U. Chgo., 1976-79, tchg. intern, 1978; tutor Am. lit. Cambridge (Eng.) U., 1979-82; asst. prof. English, Religious Studies U. Wyo., Laramie, 1983-89, assoc. prof., 1989—. V.p., bd. dirs. Plainview Tel. Co., Nebr.; hon. vis. fellow U. Edinburgh (Scotland) Inst. for Advanced Studies in the Humanities, 1987; guest lectr. NEH summer Inst., Laramie, Wyo., 1985, Carlyle Soc. of Edinburgh, 1987, Wordsworth summer Conf., Grasmere, Eng., 1988, cons. NEH. Contbr. articles and reviews to profl. jours. Mem. Am. Friends of Cambridge U., Friends of Cambridge U. Libr. (life), Gen. Soc. Mayflower Descendants; elected mem. Wyo. Coun. for Humanities, 1992-96, mem. exec. com., 1993-94; mem. adv. bd. Wyo. Ctr. for the Book, 1995—; leader Boy Scouts Am. Named Nat. Merit Scholar St. Olaf Coll., 1970-74; recipient Amb. Fellowship, Rotary Found., 1979-80, grant Am. Coun. of Learned Socs., 1988, Disting. Alumnus award, Lincoln (Neb.) E. High Sch., 1986. Mem.: MLA (del. assembly 1991—93), Bibliog. Soc. London (hon. sec.-treas. for N.Am. 2002—), Soc. History of Authorship, Reading, and Pub., Assn. Lit. and Linguistic Computing, Assn. Computers and the Humanities, Assn. Literary Scholars and Critics (life), Queens' Coll. Club (Cambridge), Wyo. State Hist. Soc. (life), Jane Austen Soc. N.Am. (life), Coleridge Soc. (life), Friends of Dove Cottage (life), Carlyle Soc. (life), Tennyson Soc. (life), Penn Club (London), Royal Oak Found., Charles Lamb Soc., The Victorian Inst., Phi Beta Kappa (pres., v.p., sec. Wyo. chpt. 1988—). Home: 1495 Apache Dr Laramie WY 82072-6966 Office: U Wyo Dept English PO Box 3353 Laramie WY 82071-3353

NYE, ERLE ALLEN, electric power industry executive, lawyer; b. Ft. Worth, June 23, 1937; s. Ira Benjamen N.; m. Alice Ann Grove, June 5, 1959; children: Elizabeth Nye Janzen, Pamela Nye Schneider, Erle Allen Jr., Edward Kyle, Johnson Scott. BEE, Tex. A&M U., 1959; JD, So. Meth. U., 1965. With Dallas Power & Light Co., 1960-75, v.p., 1975-80, Tex. Utilities Co. (dba TXU Corp.), Dallas, 1980, exec. v.p., 1980-87, pres., 1987-95, pres., CEO, 1995-97, chmn., CEO, 1997—. TU Svcs., 1982-97, chmn., CEO, 1997—, Tex. Utilities Properties Inc., 1994, Tex. Utilities Commn., Dallas, 1995-97, chmn., CEO, 1997—; pres. Tex. Utilities Fuel Co., 1982-97, chmn., CEO, 1997—; chmn. Tex. Utilities Australia Pty., Ltd., 1996—, chmn. and CEO ENSERCH Corp., Enserch Devel. Corp., Dallas, 1997—, chmn. Enserch Energy Svcs. Inc., 1997—; dir. The Energy Group PLC, London, 1998—; chmn. and CEO Tex. Energy Industries Inc., Dallas, 1997—, Southwestern Electric Svc. Co., 1997—, chmn. Lufkin-Conroe Comm. Co., 1997—, chmn. bd., CEO Tex. Utilities Integrated Solutions Inc., 1997—. Bd. dirs. Dallas Bar Found., 1980-83, Dallas Cen. Bus. Plan Com., 1980-83, Inroads/Dallas-Ft. Worth Inc., 1984-88, trustee Baylor Dental Coll., Dallas, 1985-94; mem. Dallas Together Forum, 1989—, Dallas Com. Fgn. Rels., 1991—, Bd. of Boys & Girls Clubs of Am., 1991—; The Dallas Found., 1994—; The Science Pl., Dallas, 1995-99; The Salvation Army's Dallas County Adv. Bd., 1995-99. Mem. ABA, Dallas Bar Assn., Tex. State Bar Assn., Dallas C. of C. (bd. dirs. 1991-95, vice chmn. 1992-95). Clubs: Engineers (pres. 1982-83), Northwood (Dallas). Methodist. Home: 6924 Desco Dallas TX 75225 Office: TXU Corp 1601 Bryan St Fl 41 Dallas TX 75201-3411*

NYE, GENE WARREN, retired art educator; b. Sacramento, July 3, 1939; s. Charles Frederick and Dorthy Dell Nye; m. Alena Mae Nye, Sept. 20, 1974; children: Dirk, Ronni, Anthony, Timothy. AA, American River Coll., Sacramento, 1962; AB, Sacramento State U., 1964; cert. Secondary Art Tchr., U. Calif., Berkeley, 1966. Printer Roseville (Calif.) Press Tribune, 1957-60; typographer Oakland (Calif.) Tribune, 1960-65; tchr. art Long Beach (Calif.) Unified Sch. Dist., 1965-67; tchr., chair art dept. Woodland (Calif.) Unified Sch. Dist., 1967-98; retired, 1998. Freelance artist Wildcat Art, Sacramento, 1985—; cons. in field; workshop presenter, including Nat. Assn. Student Couns., Calif. Assn. Dir. of Activities, Nat. Assn. Secondary Sch. Prins., others. Author: (workbook set and video) Posters Made EZ, 1990; (interactive CD) Posters Made EZ, 2001, How to Create Successful Posters, on CD, 2001. Mem. task force Constn. Revision of CADA, L.A., 1988-89. Named to Calif. Assn. Dirs. of Activities Hall of Fame, 1992. Mem. NEA (life), Calif. Tchrs. Assn., Calif. Retired Tchrs. Assn., Woodland Edn. Assn. (v.p. 1971-72), Calif. Art Edn. Assn., Nat. Art Edn. Assn., Calif. League Mid. Schs., U. Calif.-Berkeley Alumni Assn. (life). Home: 2200 Eastern Ave Sacramento CA 95864-0805

NYE, JOHN ROBERT, furniture company executive, transportation consultant; b. Phila., Apr. 18, 1947; s. William E. and Mary B. (Brick) N.; m. Judy Burris, May 31, 1969 (div. Dec. 1977); children: Keith, Lanny, John; m. Grace M. Adams, Feb. 28, 1981 (div. Aug. 1993); children: Annette, Mark. BA, N.C. State U., Raleigh, 1969. Prodn. mgr. Highland House, Hickory, N.C., 1969-79; distbn. mgr. Hickory Chair Co., 1979-97; mgr. Tydings House, Hickory, 1983—; distbn. mgr. Baker Furniture, 1998—. Owner J.R. Investments, 1989. Mem. Catawba Valley Traffic Club; vice-chmn. Catawba County Mayors Com. for Handicapped, 1987-89. Mem. Met. Planning Assn. Republican. Lutheran. Home: PO Box 3136 Hickory NC 28603-3136

NYE, W. MARCUS W. lawyer; b. N.Y.C., Aug. 3, 1945; s. Walter R. and Nora (McLaren) N.; m. Eva Johnson; children: Robbie, Stephanie, Philip, Jennifer. BA, Harvard U., 1967; JD, U. Idaho, 1974. Bar: Idaho 1974, U.S. Dist. Ct. Idaho 1974, U.S. Ct. Appeals (9th cir.) 1980; lic. pilot. Ptnr. Racine, Olson, Nye, Budge & Bailey, Pocatello, Idaho, 1974—. Vis. prof. law U. Idaho, Moscow, 1984; adj. prof. Coll. Engring. Idaho State U., 1993—; pres.-elect Idaho State U. Found., U. Idaho Coll. Law Found. Commr., Idaho State Centennial Found., 1985-90. Recipient Alumni Svc. award U. Idaho, 1988. Fellow ABA (bd. govs. 1997-2000), Am. Bar Found. (stat. chmn. 1992-95); mem. Am. Bd. Trial Advs. (nat. bd. dirs.), Am. Coll. Trial Lawyers, Idaho State Bar Assn. (pres. 1987-88), Idaho Def. Counsel Assn. (pres. 1982), 6th Dist. Bar Assn. (pres. 1982). Avocation: flying. Home: 173 S 15th Ave Pocatello ID 83201-4056 Office: Racine Olson Nye Budge & Bailey PO Box 1391 Pocatello ID 83204-1391

NYE, WILLIAM ROGER, psychologist; b. Haverhill, Mass., Oct. 23, 1940; s. Kenneth Enoch and Virginia Pauline (Cook) N.; children: Michael Shepherd Abowitz Nye; 1 stepson, Christopher J. Wells; domestic ptnr.: Donald W. Ashley. BA, Yale U., 1962; MDiv, Union Theol. Sem., N.Y.C., 1965; PhD, Adelphi U., Garden City, N.Y., 1981. Lic. psychologist, N.Y. Pastor Ch. of the Evangel, Bklyn., 1965-77; asst. minister Plymouth Ch. of the Pilgrims, 1977-82; pastor All Souls Universalist Ch., 1983—; exec. dir. Blanton-Peale Counseling Ctrs., Forest Hills, N.Y., 1983—. Past pres. Met. Assn. of N.Y. Conf. of United Ch. of Christ, 1969-73. Pres. Pastoral and Ednl. Svcs., Bklyn., 1983-87, The Vinmont Found., N.Y.C., 1988—. Mem. Am. Psychol. Assn. Democrat. United Ch. of Christ. Home: 888 E 19th St Brooklyn NY 11230-3108 E-mail: realbilnye@aol.com.

NYENHUIS, JACOB EUGENE, college official; b. Mille Lacs County, Minn., Mar. 25, 1935; s. Egbert Peter and Rosa (Walburg) N.; m. Leona Mae Van Duyn, June 6, 1956; children: Karen Joy, Kathy Jean, Lorna Jane, Sarah Van Duyn. AB in Greek, Calvin Coll., 1956; AM in Classics, Stanford U., 1961, PhD in Classics, 1963; LittD (hon.), Hope Coll., 2001. Asst. in classical langs. Calvin Coll., Grand Rapids, Mich., 1957-59; acting instr. Stanford (Calif.) U., 1962; from asst. prof. to prof. Wayne State U., Detroit, 1962-75, dir. honors program, 1964-75, chmn. Greek and Latin dept., 1965-75; prof. classics, dean for humanities Hope Coll., Holland, 1975-78, dean for arts and humanities, 1978-84, provost, 1984—2001, prof. and provost emeritus, 2001—; sr. rsch. fellow A.C. Van Raalte Inst., 2001—02, dir., 2002—. Cons. Mich. Dept. Edn., Lansing, 1971-72, Gustavus Adolphus Coll., St. Peter, Minn., 1974, Northwestern Coll., Orange City, Iowa, 1983, Whitworth Coll., Spokane, Wash., 1987, The Daedalus Project, 1988; reviewer NEH, Washington, 1986-87, panelist, 1991; reviewer Lilly Endowment, Indpls., 1987-89, U.S. Dept. Edn., 1993, Mich. Humanities Coun., 1999-2001; vis. assoc. prof. U. Calif., Santa Barbara, 1967-68, Ohio State U., Columbus, 1972; vis. rsch. prof. Am. Sch. Classical Studies, Athens, Greece, 1973-74, also mem. mng. com.; vis. scholar Green Coll. Oxford U., 1989; mem. editl. adv. bd. Christianity and The Arts, 1998, chmn., 1999-2001. Co-author: Latin Via Ovid, 1977, rev. edit., 1982, A Dream Fulfilled: The Van Raalte Sculpture in Centennial Park, 1997; editor: Petronius: Cena Trimalchionis, 1970, Plautus: Amphitruo, 1970, Centennial History of 14th Street Christian Reformed Church, Holland, Michigan, 2002, Myth and the Creative Process: Michael Ayrton and the Myth of Daedalus, the Maze Maker, 2002; authors articles in field. Elder Christian Ref. Ch., Palo Alto, Calif., 1960—62, elder, clk. Grosse Pointe, Mich., 1964—67, Holland, 1976—85, v.p., 1988—91, mem. exec. com., 1994—95; bd. trustees Calvin Theol. Sem., 2001—; chmn. human rels. coun. Open Housing Com., Grosse Pointe, 1971—73. Mem. Am. Philol. Assn., Danforth Assocs. (chmn. regional com. 1975-77), Mich. Coun. for Humanities (bd. dirs., 1976-84, 88-92, chmn. 1980-82, 96-99, Disting. Svc. award 1984), Nat. Fedn. State Humanities Couns. (bd. dirs. 1979-84, pres. 1981-83), Gt. Lakes Colls. Assn. (bd. dirs. 1991-93), Coun. on Undergrad. Rsch. (councilor-at-large 1993-99), Green Coll. Soc. (Oxford U.), Mortar Bd. (hon.), Eta Sigma Phi (hon.). Democrat. Avocations: photography, carpentry. Home: 51 E 8th St Ste 200 Holland MI 49423-3501 Office: Hope Coll Van Raalte Inst PO Box 9000 Holland MI 49422-9000

NYERGES, ALEXANDER LEE, museum director; b. Rochester, N.Y., Feb. 27, 1957; s. Sandor Elek and Lena (Angeline) N.; m. Kathryn Gray; 1 child, Robert Angeline. BA, George Washington U., 1979, MA, 1981. Intern The Octagon, Washington, 1976-79; archeol. asst. Smithsonian Instn., 1977; curatorial intern Nat. Mus. Am. History, 1978-79; adminstrv. asst. George Washington U., Washington, 1979-81; exec. dir. DeLand Mus. Art, Fla., 1981-85, Miss. Mus. Art, Jackson, 1985-92; dir. Dayton (Ohio) Art Inst., 1992—. Mem. grants panel Nat. Endowment for the Arts, 1988—; field surveyor Inst. Mus. Svcs., Washington, 1985-88, nat. review panel, 1990-92; treas., bd. dirs. Volusia County Arts Coun., Daytona Beach, Fla., 1983-85. Author: Selections from the Permanent Collection, 1999, In Praise of Nature: Ansel Adams and Photographers of the American West; contbr. articles to profl. jours. Bd. dirs. West Volusia Hist. Soc., 1984-85; pres. Miss. Inst. Arts and Letters, 1987-88; trustee Cultural Arts Ctr., DeLand, 1984-85, Miami Valley Cultural Alliance, 1993-95, Intermus. Conservation Lab., 1993-99, Montgomery County Arts and Culture Dist., 1994—; bd. trustees Montgomery Co. Convention and Vis. Bureau. U.S. Dept. Edn. scholar, 1973. Mem. DeLand Area C. of C. (bd. dirs., tourist adv. com. 1984-85), Assn. Art Mus. Dirs., Am. Assn. Mus. (S.E. regional rep. to non-print media com. 1983-85, nat. legis. com. 1986-93), Miss. Mus. Assn., Assn. Art Mus. Dirs., Southeastern Mus. Conf. (bd. dirs. 1991-92), Fla. Mus. Assn., Fla. Art Mus. Dirs. Assn., Cultural Roundtable (pres. 1993-95), Ohio Mus. Assn. (trustee 1993-98) Phi Beta Kappa. Avocations: photography, gardening, music, writing, sports, scuba diving. Home: 229 Volusia Ave Dayton OH 45409-2226 Office: Dayton Art Inst 456 Belmonte Park N Dayton OH 45405-4700 E-mail: anyerges@daytonartinstitute.org.

NYERGES, GEORGE LADISLAUS, lawyer; b. Cleve., Aug. 27, 1925; s. Constantine L. and Irene (Schneider) N.; m. Joanne Mayo, Aug. 2, 1958; children: James George, Susan Joanne. BS, Case Western Reserve U., 1946; LLB, Cleveland-Marshall Law Sch., 1951, LLM, 1956; JD, Cleve. State U., 1969. Bar: Ohio 1951, U.S. Dist. Ct. (no. dist.) Ohio 1954, U.S. Ct. Appeals (6th cir.) 1985, U.S. Supreme Ct. 1991; lic. USCG. Lawyer, sole practice, Cleve., 1951—. Lectr. legal and med. ethics Cuyahoga C.C., Cleve., 1989; pvt. and ct. interpreter Hungarian lang., 1955—; ind. real estate broker, Ohio, 1960—; cons. to various religious groups, 1985—. Mem. Magyar Club of Cleve., 1952—, sec., 1954-57, pres. 1958; mem. "Night in Budapest Com." in Cleve., 1958-65, Vermilion (Ohio) Yacht Club, 1973—, sec., 1974-76; coach girls baseball Summer Recreational Jr. Girls Baseball, Westlake, Ohio, 1980, coach boys football Fall Recreational Jr. Boys Football, Westlake, 1980-82; former precinct committeeman Dem. Party, Westlake, 1990. Recipient Cert., Am. Judicature Soc., 1961, Plaque Am. Arbitration Assn., 1970, Cert. of Appreciation, Cleve. Bar Assn., 1987-88. Mem. ATLA, ABA, FBA, Ohio State Bar Assn. (Cert. of Appreciation 1991), Phi Gamma Delta. Democrat. Presbyterian. Avocations: former comdr., including lesser chairs and charter mem. of Rocky River Power Squadron. Office: United Office Bldg 2012 W 25th St Ste 803 Cleveland OH 44113-4127 Home: 26865 Sleepy Hollow Dr Westlake OH 44145-3238

NYGAARD, LANCE COREY, nurse, data processing consultant; b. Casper, Wyo., June 21, 1952; s. Miles Adolph and Jenile Hansine (Mosman) N.; m. Susan Leigh Wilson, May 8, 1995; 1 child from previous marriage, Kari Melissa. AA in Nursing, U. S.D., 1980; BS in Chemistry, 1974; MLS, U. Ill., 1975. Libr. asst. Brookings Pub. Libr., S.D., 1971-75, asst. dir., 1975-77; emergency med. technician Brookings Hosp., 1976-78; sr. emergency med. technician Vermillion Ambulance, S.D., 1978-80; nurse McKennan Hosp., Sioux Falls, S.D., 1980-91, VA Hosp., 1991-96, Sioux Valley Hosp., 1996—, cardiovasc. data sys. coord., 1997—; owner operator Data Processing Svcs., Sioux Falls, 1983—; applications cons. Computer Dimensions, Sioux Falls, 1984-85. Fin. sec., mem. ch. coun. Holy Cross Luth. Ch., Sioux Falls, S.D., 1986-91, info. resources coord., 1991-92; troop leader Minn-Ia-Kota coun. Girl Scouts U.S., 1989—, region troop supr., 1991-95. Mem. Vermillion Chemistry Club (pres. 1973-74), Sioux Valley Rose Soc. (v.p. 1988-89, pres. 1989-90), Sons of Norway (guard 1976-77). Republican. Lutheran. Avocations: World War II military history, photography, amateur radio. Home: 3500 S Grace Cir Sioux Falls SD 57103-7226 Office: Sioux Valley Hosp 1100 S Euclid Ave Sioux Falls SD 57105-0496

NYGAARD, MARY PAYNE, primary school education; b. Rome, Dec. 27, 1948; d. Julian Wesley and Mary Kate Payne; m. Steven Jay Nygaard, Apr. 5, 1975; children: Mandy Lee Nygaard Herreid, Carrie Ann Nygaard Wells. BA, Berry Coll., 1969; M in Ednl. Leadership, U. Portland, 1994. Lifetime tchg. cert. Wash. First grade tchr. Goldendale (Wash.) Primary Sch., 1969-73, kindergarten tchr., 1973-76; sch. bd. mem. Goldendale (Wash.) Christian Sch., 1981-82, kindergarten tchr., 1982-86, tchr. grades 1-3, 1986-87; home sch. tchr. grades 4 and 6 Goldendale, 1987-88; substitute tchr. grades K-8 Centerville Sch. Goldendale (Wash.) Primary Sch., 1988-90, tchr. grade 1, 1990-94, title I coord., 1994-97, tchr. kindergarten support svcs. Early Childhood Ctr., 1997-99, kindergarten tchr., Early Childhood Ctr. tchr., 1999-2000, 2d grade tchr., 2001, kindergarten tchr., 2001—. Mem. Delta Kappa Gamma (pres. 1992-94). Baptist. Avocation: collecting dolls. Office: Goldendale Primary Sch 820 S Schuster Ave Goldendale WA 98620-9297

NYGAARD, RICHARD LOWELL, federal judge; b. Thief River Falls, MN, 1940; BS cum laude, U. So. Calif., 1969; JD, U. Mich., 1971. Mem. Orton, Nygaard & Dunlevy, 1972—80; judge Ct. Common Pleas, 6th Dist. Pa., Erie, 1981—88, U.S. Ct. Appeals (3d cir.), Erie, 1988—. Councilman Erie County, Pa., 1977—81. With USNR, 1958—64. Mem.: ABA, Erie County Bar Assn., Pa. Bar Assn. Office: 500 First Nat Bank Bldg 717 State St Ste 500 Erie PA 16501 also: James A Byrne Courthouse 601 Market St Rm 2100 Philadelphia PA 19106*

NYGREN, MALCOLM ERNEST, minister; b. Portsmouth, Ohio, Sept. 12, 1925; s. Gustav Henning and Alma Marie (Viberg) N.; m. Betty Sue Perry, May 14, 1950 (dec. Oct. 1996); children: Melinda (Mrs. Robert Pierce), Nancy; m. Mimi Cozad, Oct. 12, 1999. AB, Hanover Coll., 1949; BD, McCormick Theol. Sem., 1952; STD, San Francisco Theol. Sem., 1980. Ordained to ministry Presbyn. Ch. (USA), 1952. Sr. pastor 1st Presbyn. Ch., Champaign, Ill., 1959-90; ret., 1990. Author: Lord of the Four Seasons, 1986; syndicated columnist Champaign News Gazette, Wabash Valley Morning News, others; contbr. religious and humorous articles to periodicals. Bd. dirs. Kemmerer Village, Assumption, Ill., 1976-82; pres., fellow Charles W. Christie Found., Champaign, 1975-86; mem. instl. rev. bd. U. Ill., Urbana-Champaign, 1991-97. With inf. U.S. Army, 1943-46, ETO. Mem. Rotary. E-mail: nygrenme@home.com. *We are all citizens of two worlds-and the world we can't see is more significant than the one we do.*

NYHAN, WILLIAM LEO, pediatrician, educator; b. Boston, Mar. 13, 1926; s. W. Leo and Mary N.; m. Christine Murphy, Nov. 20, 1948; children: Christopher, Abigail. Student, Harvard U., 1943-45; MD, Columbia U., 1949; MS, U. Ill., 1956, PhD, 1958; hon. doctorate, Tokushima U., Japan, 1981. Intern Yale U.-Grace-New Haven Hosp., 1949-50, resident, 1950-51, 53-55; asst. prof. pediatrics Johns Hopkins U., 1958-61, assoc. prof., 1961-63; prof. pediatrics, biochemistry U. Miami, 1963-69, chmn. dept. pediatrics, 1963-69; prof. U. Calif., San Diego, 1969—, chmn. dept. pediatrics, 1969-86. Mem. FDA adv. com. on Teratogenic Effects of Certain Drugs, 1964-70; mem. pediatric panel AMA Council on Drugs, 1964-70; mem. Nat. Adv. Child Health and Human Devel. Council, 1967-71; mem. research adv. com. Calif. Dept. Mental Hygiene, 1969-72; mem. med. and sci. adv. com. Leukemia Soc. Am., Inc., 1968-72; mem. basic adv. com. Nat. Found. March of Dimes, 1973-81; mem. Basil O'Connor Starter grants com., 1973-93; mem. clin. cancer program project rev. com. Nat. Cancer Inst., 1977-81; vis. prof. extraordinario U. del Salvador (Argentina), 1982 Author (with E. Edelson): The Heredity Factor, Genes, Chromosomes and You, 1976; author: Genetic & Malformation Syndromes in Clinical Medicine, 1976, Abnormalities in Amino Acid Metabolism in Clinical Medicine, 1984, Diagnostic Recognition of Genetic Diseases, 1987; author: (with P. Ozand) Atlas of Metabolic Disease, 1998; author: (with G.F. Hofmmann, J. Zsclocke, S.G. Kuleler and E. Mayatep) Invented Metabolic Diseases, 2001; editor: Amino Acid Metabolism and Genetic Variation, 1967, Heritable Disorders of Amino Acid Metabolism, 1974; mem. editl. bd.: Jour. Pediat., 1964—78, mem. editl. bd.: Western Jour. Medicine, 1974—86, mem. editl. bd.: King Faisal Hosp. Med. Jour., 1981—85, mem. editl. bd.: Annals of Saudi Medicine, 1985—87, mem. editl. com.: Ann. Rev. Nutrition, 1982—86, mem. editl. staff: Med. and Pediat. Oncology, 1975—83; editor: (with G. Hoffmann, J. Zschocke, S. Kahler and E. Mayatenek) Inherited Metabolic Diseases, 2002. Served with U.S. Navy, 1944-46; U.S. Army, 1951-53. Nat. Found. Infantile Paralysis fellow, 1955-58; recipient Commemorative medallion Columbia U. Coll. Physicians and Surgeons, 1967, Guthrie award Am. Assn. Mental Retardation, 1998, Pool of

Bethesda award Bethesda Luth. Homes and Svcs., 1999. Fellow: Am. Acad. Pediat. (Borden award 1980, Lifetime Achievement award 1999); mem.: AAAS, Inst. Medicine of Nat. Acad. Scis., Biochem. Soc., Am. Coll. Med. Genetics, Am. Assn. Clin. Chemists, Am. Soc. Human Genetics (dir. 1978—81), Am. Soc. Clin. Investigation, Soc. Exptl. Biology and Medicine, Am. Inst. Biol. Scis., Am. Pediatric Soc., South African Human Genetics (hon.), Inst. Investigaciones Citologicas (Spain) (corr.), Soc. Francaise de Pediatrie (corr.), N.Y. Acad. Sci., Western Soc. Pediatric Rsch. (pres. 1976—77), Am. Soc. Pharmacology and Exptl. Therepautics, Am. Assn. Cancer Rsch., Soc. Pediatric Rsch. (pres. 1970—71), Am. Chem. Soc., Am. Fedn. Clin. Rsch., Alpha Omega Alpha, Sigma Xi. Office: U Calif San Diego Dept Pediatrics # 0830 9500 Gilman Dr La Jolla CA 92093-0830

NYHUS, LLOYD MILTON, surgeon, educator; b. Mt. Vernon, Wash., June 24, 1923; s. Lewis Guttorm and Mary (Shervem) N.; m. Margaret Goldie Sheldon, Nov. 25, 1949; children: Sheila Margaret, Leif Torger. BS, Pacific Luth. Coll., 1945; MD, Med. Coll. Ala., 1947; Doctor honoris causa, Aristotelian U., Thessalonika, Greece, 1968, Uppsala U., Sweden, 1974, U. Chihuahua, Mex., 1975, Jagallonian U., Cracow, Poland, 1980, U. Gama Filho, Rio de Janeiro, 1983, U. Louis Pasteur, Strasbourg, France, 1984, U. Athens, 1989. Diplomate Am. Bd. Surgery (chmn. 1974-76). Intern King County Hosp., Seattle, 1947-48, resident in surgery, 1948-55; practice medicine specializing in surgery Seattle, 1956-67, Chgo., 1967—; instr. surgery U. Wash., Seattle, 1954-56, asst. prof., 1956-59, assoc. prof., 1959-64, prof., 1964-67; Warren H. Cole prof., head dept. surgery U. Ill. Coll. Medicine, 1967-89, emeritus head, 1989—, prof. emeritus, 1993. Emeritus surgeon-in-chief U. Ill. Hosp.; sr. cons. surgeon Cook County, West Side VA, Hines (Ill.) VA hosps.; cons. to Surgeon Gen. NIH, 1965-69. Author: Surgery of the Stomach and Duodenum, 1962, 4th edit., 1986, named changed to Surgery of the Esophagus, Stomach and Small Intestine, 5th edit., 1995, Hernia, 1964, (book name change) Nyhus and Condon's Hernia, 5th edit., 2002, Abdominal Pain: A Guide to Rapid Diagnosis, 1969, 95, Spanish edit., 1996, Russian edit., 2001, Manual of Surgical Therapeutics, 1969, latest rev. edit., 1996, Mastery of Surgery, 1984, 3d edit., 1997, Spanish edit., 1999, Surgery Ann., 1970-95, Treatment of Shock, 1970, 2d rev. edit., 1986, Surgery of the Small Intestine, 1987; editor-in-chief Rev. of Surgery, 1967-77, Current Surgery, 1978-90, emeritus editor, 1991—; assoc. editor Quar. Rev. Surgery, 1958-61; editl. bd. Am. Jour. Digestive Diseases, 1961-67, Scandinavian Jour. Gastroenterology, 1966-97, Am. Surgeon, 1967-89, Jour. Surg. Oncology, 1969-99, Archives of Surgery, 1977-86, World Jour. Surgery, 1977-95; contbr. articles to profl. jours. Served to lt. M.C. USNR, 1943-46, 50-52. Decorated Order of Merit (Poland); postdoctoral fellow USPHS, 1952-53; recipient M. Shipley award So. Surg. Assn., 1967, Rovsing medal Danish Surg. Soc., 1973; Disting. Faculty award U. Ill Coll. Medicine, 1983, Disting. Alumnus award Med. Coll. Ala., 1984, Disting. Alumnus award U. Wash., 1993, 99; Guggenheim fellow, 1955-56. Fellow ACS (1st v.p. 1987-88), Assn. Surgeons Gt. Brit. and Ireland (hon.), Royal Coll. Surgeons Eng. (hon.), Royal Coll. Surgeons Ireland (hon.), Royal Coll. Surgeons Edinburgh (hon.), Royal Coll. Physicians and Surgeons Glasgow (hon.), Internat. Soc. Surgery Found. (hon., sec.-treas. 1992-2001); mem . Am. Gastroent. Assn., Am. Physiol. Soc., Pacific Coast Surg. Assn., Am. Surg. Assn. (recorder 1976-81, 1st v.p. 1989-90), Western Surg. Assn., Ctrl. Soc. Clin. Rsch., Chgo. Surg. Soc. (pres. 1974), Ctrl. Surg. Assn. (pres. 1984), Seattle Surg. Soc., St. Paul Surg. Soc. (hon.), Kansas City Surg. Soc. (hon.), Inst. Medicine Chgo., Internat. Soc. Surgery (hon. fellow 2001, pres. U.S. sect. 1986-88, pres. 34th World Congress 1991, internat. pres. 1991-93), Internat. Soc. for Digestive Surgery (pres. III world congress Chgo. 1974, internat. pres. 1978-84), Soc. for Surgery Alimentary Tract (sec. 1969-73, pres. 1974), Soc. Clin. Surgery, Soc. Surg. Chmn., Soc. U. Surgeons (pres. 1967), Duetschen Gesellschaft für Chirurgie (corr.), Polish Assn. Surgeons (hon.), L'Academie de Chirurgie (France) (corr.), Nat. Acad. of Medicine (France, Argentina and Brazil, hon.), Swiss Surg. Soc. (hon.), Brazilian Coll. Surgeons (hon.), Surg. Biology Club, Warren H. Cole Soc. (pres. 1981), Japan Surg. Soc. (hon.), Assn. Gen. Surgeons of Mex. (hon.), Columbian Surg. Soc. (hon.), Costa Rican Coll. Medicine & Surgery (hon.), Assn. Surgeons Costa Rica (hon.), Internat. Fedn. Surg. Colls. (hon. treas. 1992-99), Sigma Xi, Alpha Omega Alpha, Phi Beta Pi. Home: 310 Maple Row Winnetka IL 60093-1036 Office: U Ill Coll Medicine Dept Surgery MC 958 840 S Wood St Chicago IL 60612-7322

NYIRJESY, ISTVAN, obstetrician, gynecologist; b. Budapest, Hungary, Nov. 14, 1929; came to U.S., 1954, naturalized, 1960; s. Sandor D. and Margit (Bertalan) N.; m. Michelle Shoepp, June 16, 1956; children— Francis, Paul, Christine. MD, Catholic U. Louvain, Belgium, 1955. Diplomate: Am. Bd. Ob-Gyn. Intern Cath. U. Louvain and Little Co. Mary Hosp., Evergeen Park, Ill., 1954-55; resident in gynecology obstetrics, 1960-63; chief obstetrical research Nat. Naval Med. Center, Bethesda, Md., 1966-68; ret., 1968; practice medicine specializing in Ob-Gyn Bethesda, 1968—. Clin. prof. Ob-Gyn Georgetown U., 1968—; cons. NIH, 1974—. FDA, 1977-88. Lit. editor Breast Disease: contbr. articles to med. jours.; author: Prevention and Detection of Gynecologic and Breast Cancer, 1994. Pres., Internat. Found. for Gynecol. Cancer Detection and Prevention, 1993—. Officer M.C. USN, 1956-68; advanced through grades to comdr. Recipient Sword of Hope pin Am. Cancer Soc., 1973, Vicennial medal Georgetown U., 1988. Fellow ACOG (Host award 1964), Hungarian Gynecologic Soc. (hon.), Internat. Coll. Surgeons; mem. Montgomery County (Md.) Med. Soc. (chmn. profl. edn. com. 1971-72), Am. Soc. of Breast Disease (past pres.), Assn. Profs. Ob-Gyn., Am. Soc. Reproductive Medicine, Washington Gynecol. Soc. (v.p. 1993-94, 1st v.p. 1994-95, pres. 1996-97). Office: 5301 Westbard Cir Ste 5 Bethesda MD 20816-1429

NYKIEL, KAREN ANN, development administrator; b. Chgo., July 27, 1945; d. John Marion and Dorothy Ann (Lasko) N. BA, Coll. St. Benedict, St. Joseph, Minn., 1969; MSNS, Seattle U., 1975; MA, Mundelein Coll., Chgo., 1989. Tchr. science Benet Acad., Lisle, Ill., 1969-73; adult edn. coord. St. Joan of Arc Ch., 1973-77; adj. faculty chemistry Coll. DuPage, Glen Ellyn, Ill., 1975—; campus min. Diocese of Joliet, 1982-92; adminstr. Queen of Peace Ctr., Lisle, 1992-97; devel. dir. St. Mary of Providence, Chgo., 1998—. Cons. Nat. Fusion Co., Plainfield, Ill., 1980-82; mem. Benedictine Sisters Sacred Heart, Lisle, 1965—, bd. dirs., 1980-92; state coord. Pax Christi Ill., 1994—; pres. Queen of Peace Ctr., Inc., Lisle, 1992-97; adj. faculty religious studies Coll. DuPage, Benedictine U., Coll. St. Francis; mem. med. team Republic of the Congo, 1996. Mem. C. of C., Lisle, 1992—. Grantee NSF, 1971, 72, 73, 74. Mem. Am. Chemical Soc., Assn. Sr. Svc. Providers, Rotary Internat. (Lisle chpt. chair internat. com., pres. 1997-98). Democrat. Roman Catholic. Avocations: playing guitar, reading, lecturing. Home and Office: Sacred Heart Monastery 1910 Maple Ave Lisle IL 60532-2164

NYKOLYN, IRMA M. product manager; b. N.Y.C., Nov. 17, 1960; d. Wilfredo Arroyo and Ambrosia Rosado; m. Dennis J. Nykolyn, Aug. 13, 1988; 1 child, Miranda. BA, SUNY, Albany, 1986; Cert. in Corps. Law, Adelphi U., 1986; MA, NYU, 1997. Cert. in corps. law. Product mgr. Symantec Corp., Melville, N.Y., 1998-2000; product mktg. mgr. VIGILANTe, 2000—. Regents scholar N.Y. Regents, 1978. Mem. Assn. for Ednl. Comm. and Tech., Phi Beta Kappa. Democrat. Roman Catholic. Avocation: travel. Office: VIGILANTe 290 Broadhollow Rd Melville NY 11747 E-mail: irma.nykolyn@vigilante.com., irmoi@hotmail.com.

NYKROG, PER, French literature educator; b. Copenhagen, Nov. 1, 1925; came to U.S., 1979; s. Kai S. Nathanson and Karen E. (Olsen) Nykrog; m. Vibeke H. Rasmussen, 1951 (dec. 1977); children: Thomas, Jakob; m. Usha Saksena Nilsson, Jan. 2, 1981. Grad., U. Copenhagen, 1952; PhD, U. Aarhus, Denmark, 1957. Asst. prof. U. Aarhus, 1953-57, prof., 1957-79; prof. French lang. and lit. Harvard U., Cambridge, Mass., 1979-98. Author: Les Fabliaux, 1957, La Pensée de Balzac, 1965, L'Amour et la Rose, 1986, La Recherche du Don perdu, 1987, Chrétien de Troyes romancier discutable, 1995. Mem. Royal Soc. Scis. Denmark. Home: 243 Concord Ave Cambridge MA 02138-1360 Office: Harvard U Dept Romance Langs Boylston Hall Cambridge MA 02138

NYLANDER, JANE LOUISE, museum director; b. Cleve., Jan. 27, 1938; d. James Merritt and Jeannette Cayford; m. Daniel Harris Giffen, 1963 (div. 1970); children: Sarah Louise, Thomas Harris; m. Richard Conrad Nylander, 1972: 1 child, Timothy Frost. AB, Brown U., 1959; MA, U. Del., 1961; postgrad., Attingham (Eng.) Summer Sch., 1970; PhD (hon.), New England Coll., 1994. Curator Hist. Soc. York (Pa.) County, 1961-62, N.H. Hist. Soc., Concord, 1962-69; instr. New England Coll., Henniker, N.H., 1964-65, Monadnock Community Coll., Peterborough, 1966-69; curator of textiles and ceramics Old Sturbridge (Mass.) Village, 1969-85; adj. assoc. prof. Boston U., 1978-85; sr. curator Old Sturbridge Vill., 1985-86; dir. Strawbery Banke Mus., Portsmouth, N.H., 1986-92, Soc. Preservation New England Antiquities, Boston, 1992-93; pres. Soc. for Preservation of New Eng. Antiquities, 1993—2002, pres. emerita, 2002—. Adj. prof. art history and Am. studies Boston U., 1993-96; trustee Worcester (Mass.) Hist. Mus., 1978-84, Hist. Deerfield (Mass.), Inc., 1981-94, hon. trustee, 1994—, Hist. Mass. Inc., 1991-93, Decorative Arts Trust, 1991-, Portsmouth Athenaeum, 1988-90, Japan Soc. N.H., 1988-92, Fort Ticonderoga, 2000-; mem. adv. bd. Concord (Mass.) Mus., 1986-94, Wentworth-Coolidge Commn., 1991-96; mem. adv. bd. John Nicholas Brown Ctr. for Am. Studies, Providence, 1995—; mem. adv. com. Wentworth-Coolidge, 1996—; mem. adv. bd. dept. Am. decorative arts Mus. Fine Arts, Boston, 1971-99, Art of the Ams., 1999-2000; mem. coun. Colonial Soc. Mass., 1993-96; cons. in field. Author: Fabrics for Historic Buildings, 4th edit., 1990, Our Own Snug Fireside: Images of the New England Home 1760-1860, 1993, paperback edit., 1994, Windows on the Past, 2000, The Art of Family, 2002; mem. editl. bd.: Hist. N.H., 1993—2000, mem. editl. bd.: The Dublin Seminar, 1984—; contbr. Mem. adv. bd. New Eng. Heritage Ctr., 1993—; active State House Adv. Com., Boston, 1984-85, Gov.'s Coun. for Wentworth Coolidge Mansion, Concord, 1964-66; mem. Com. for Preservation of N.H. State Flags, 1989-92; mem. H.F. duPont award com. Winterthur Mus., 1993-2001, Mt. Vernon adv. com. for 1999, 1996-99, collections com. N.J. Hist. Soc., 1994-96; designator The Henderson Found., 1992—. Recipient Charles F. Montgomery Prize Decorative Arts Soc., 1985, (with Richard C. Nylander) The Anne and Roger Webb award Historic Massachusetts, Inc., 1996. Mem.: N.H. Hist. Soc., Costume Soc. Am. (bd. dirs. 1977—83), New Eng. Hist. Geneal. Soc., N.H. Humanities Coun., Soc. Preservation of N.H. Forests, Historic Mass., Soc. Winterthur Fellows, Trustees of Reservations, Mass. Hist. Soc., New Eng. Mus. Assn., Portsmouth Athenaeum, Royal Oak Assn., Nat. Trust for Historic Preservation, Am. Assn. for State and Local History (Cert. of Commendation 2001), Am. Antiquarian Soc., Nat. Soc. Colonial Dames in Mass. (courtesy), Friends of Hist. Deerfield, Nat. Soc. Colonial Dames in N.H. (bd. dirs. 1967—73), Colonial Soc. Mass., St. Botolph Club, Brown Club N.H. (trustee 1988—93). Episcopalian. Home: 17 Franklin St Portsmouth NH 03801-4501

NYMAN, CARL JOHN, JR. university dean and official; b. New Orleans, Oct. 21, 1924; s. Carl John Sr. and Dorothy (Kraft) N.; m. Betty Spiegelberg, July 15, 1950; children: Gail Katherine, John Victor, Nancy Kraft. BS, Tulane U., 1944, MS, 1945; PhD, U. Ill., 1948. Jr. technologist Shell Oil Co., Wilmington, Cal., 1944; instr. chemistry U. Ill., 1948, Wash. State U., Pullman, 1948-50, asst. prof., 1950-55, assoc. prof., 1955-61, prof., 1961-88, prof. emeritus, 1988—, vice provost for rsch., 1981-86, acting dean grad. sch., 1968-69; dean, 1969-87; dean and vice provost emeritus for rsch. grad. sch. Wash. State U., 1988—. Vis. asst. prof. Tulane U., summer, 1950, adj. prof., 1986-87; vis. fellow Cornell U., 1959-60, Imperial Coll. Sci. and Tech., 1966-67; vis. fellow Swiss Fed. Inst. Tech., Zurich, 1973; chmn. Acad. Coun. Ctr. Grad. Study, Richland, Wash., 1968-70, N.W. Assn. Colls. and Univs. for Sci., 1969; mem. Gov.'s Adv. Coun. on Nuclear Energy, 1968-70, Washington State High Tech. Coord. Bd., 1984-86; mem. exec. com., coun. on rsch. policy and grad. edn. Nat. Assn. State Univs. and Land Grant Colls., 1972-75; bd. dirs. Coun. of Grad. Schs. in U.S., 1977-80. Author: (with G. B. King and J. A. Weyh) Problems for General Chemistry and Qualitative Analysis, 4th edit., 1980, (with R. E. Hamm) Chemical Equilibrium, 1967, (with W. E. Newton) Procs. of the 1st Internat. Conf. Nitrogen Fixation; contbr. articles to profl. jours. Mem. Am. Chem. Soc. (chmn. Wash.-Idaho border sect. 1961-62), AAAS, Sigma Xi, Phi Lambda Upsilon, Alpha Chi Sigma, Omicron Delta Kappa. Home: 1419 E Cambridge Ln Spokane WA 99203-3962

NYMAN, DAVID HAROLD, retired nuclear engineer; b. Aberdeen, Wash., May 21, 1938; s. Carl Victor and Elsie Ingagord (Laaksonen) N. Assoc., Grays Harbor Coll., 1958; BSMetE, U. Wash., 1961, MSMetE, 1963. Engr. GE Co., Richland, Wash., 1963-68; engring. specialist United Nuclear Corp., New Haven, 1968-73; mgr. Westinghouse Hanford subs. Westinghouse Corp., Richland, 1973-96; ret., 1996. Contbr. articles to profl. jours. Mem. Robotics Internat. of Soc. Mfg. Engrs. (div. chmn. 1985-86, tech. v.p. 1986-88, Pres.'s award 1989), Robots West Conf. (adv. com. 1984, vice-chmn. 1986), Am. Nuclear Soc. (chmn. meetings, proceedings, and transactions com. 1992-96), Am. Soc. Metals., Inst. Nuclear Materials Mgmt., Columbia Basin Dog Tng. Club (pres. 1982-84), Richland Kennel Club, West Highland White Terrier Club of Puget Sound, West Highland White Terrier Club Am. (obedience com. 1982-88), Am. Kennel Club (judge tracking dog excellent tests), Tri Cities Enological Soc. Republican. Lutheran. E-mail: nymandave@aol.com.

NYMAN, GEORGIANNA BEATRICE, painter; b. Arlington, Mass., June 11, 1930; d. Daniel Eugene Nyman and Irene Krans (Müller) Lombardi; m. David Aronson, June 10, 1956; children: Judith, Benjamin, Abigail. Diploma, Boston Mus. Sch. Art., 1952, student, 1952-54; postgrad., Longy Sch. Music, Cambridge, Mass., 1965-73. Portraits displayed in Inst. Critical Care Medicine, U. Pitts., McClosky Inst. Voice Therapy, Boston, U.S. Supreme Ct., Washington, New Eng. Sch. of Law, Boston, 1991, Milton (Mass.) Acad., Boston Acad. Music; group exhbns. include Shore Studio Gallery, Boston, 1960,61, Lee Nordness Gallery, N.Y.C., 1963, Copley Soc., Boston, 1980, Nat. Acad. Design, N.Y.C., 1990, Alter and Gil Gallery, Beverly Hills, Calif., 1999; solo exhbns. include Nancy Lincoln Gallery, Brookline, 1990; represented in permanent collections Rose Art Mus., Brandeis U., U. Pitts. Sch. Medicine, New Eng. Sch. Law, Boston; commd. portraits include Justice Sandra Day O'Connor, Mr. and Mrs. Pieh--headmaster Milton Acad., 1992, Justice Harry A. Blackmun, 1993, Julie Harris Am. actress, 1994, Hon. James R. Lawton, 1994, Richard Conrad, opera singer, dir. Boston Acad. Music, 1994, Justice Clarence Thomas, 1995, David Leisner, 1995, Lincoln Almond, Gov. of R.I., 2002. Jurist Art and Mental Illness--An Itinerary Boston U., 1989; active in LeMoyne Found., Fla., 1989; elected mem., bd. dirs. Boston Acad. Music, 1994. Recipient Boit prize, 1951, cert. of merit NAD, 1992; Kate Morse fellow Boston Mus. Fine Arts, 1953. Mem. Women's Indsl. Inst. (life), Mass. Soc. Mayflower Descendants. Avocations: music, vocal recitals. Home: 137 Brimstone Ln Sudbury MA 01776-3200 also: RR 2 Cornwall PE Canada C0A 1HO

NYMANN, P. L. lawyer; b. Clermont, Iowa, May 18, 1924; s. Jens Christian and Minnie Amalia (Osmundson) N.; m. Charmaine Ann Petersen, Dec. 2, 1951 (div. 1979); children: Michel, Candace, Kimberly, Christopher, Jon (dec.); m. Anne Barrett McDermott, Feb. 15, 1992. BA, U. Iowa, 1949, JD, 1951. Bar: Iowa 1951. Assoc. Louis S. Goldberg, Sioux City, Iowa, 1951-57; ptnr. Goldberg, Nymann & Probasco, 1957-64; v.p., gen. counsel IBP, Inc., Dakota City, Nebr., 1964-72; pvt. practice Sioux City, 1972-74, 83-87; ptnr. Jacobs, Gaul, Nymann & Green, 1974-83, Nymann & Kohl, Sioux City, 1987—. Chmn., Civil Svc. Commn., 1977-79; bd. dirs. United Way Siouxland, 1979-85. With AUS, 1943-46. Mem. ABA, Iowa Bar Assn., Am. Arbitration Assn., Rotary Club. Republican. Avocations: travel, boating, music. Home: 9364 Decatur Plz Omaha NE 68114-1225 Office: Nymann & Kohl 383390 Orpheum Electric Sioux City IA 51101

NYQUIST, JOHN DAVIS, retired radio manufacturing company executive; b. Peoria, Ill., May 28, 1918; s. Eliud and Linnea (Widen) N.; m. Alice Schmidt, June 5, 1942; 1 child, Sarah Lynn. BS in Mech. Engring, U. Ill., 1941. With Collins Radio Co., Cedar Rapids, Iowa, 1941—, v.p., gen. mgr. Iowa region, 1965-69, v.p. operations, 1969-70, sr. v.p., 1970-73, also dir.; ret., 1973; cons. Rockwell-Collins. Dir. Norwest Bank Iowa N.A. (formerly Peoples Bank & Trust Co.), Cedar Rapids. Bd. dirs. Am. Cancer Soc., YMCA, St. Lukes Hosp. Recipient award for outstanding achievement Am. Inst. Indsl. Engrs., 1966, Indsl. Engring. award, 1969, Coll. Engring. Alumni Honor award, 1977; both U. Ill.). Mem. Iowa Mfrs. Assn., Am. Mgmt. Assn., Am. Inst. Indsl. Engrs., IEEE, Cedar Rapids C. of C. (dir.) Clubs: Cedar Rapids Country. Home: 3279 Jordans Grove Rd Springville IA 52336-9786

NYQUIST, MAURICE OTTO, federal agency administrator, scientist; b. Fairmont, Minn., May 30, 1944; s. Carl Arther and Wilda Yvette (Freitag) N.; m. Mary Maud Magee, Aug. 8, 1977; children: Gretchen, Beth. BS in Biology, Hamline U., 1966; MA in Biology, Mankato State U., 1968; PhD in Zoology, Wash. State U., 1973. Asst. prof. zoology Wash. State U., Pullman, 1973-74; scientist Nat. Park Svc., Lakewood, Colo., 1974-76, mgr., 1979-93; mgr., scientist Nat. Biol. Svc., Denver, 1993-96, USGS, Denver, 1996—; coord. The Aurora Partnership, 1999—. Affiliate faculty Sch. Natural Resources, Colo. State U., Ft. Collins; mem. peer rev. coms. for academia, govt. and pvt. industry; agy. rep. Fed. Geographic Data Com., chair biol. data working group, mem. standards working group and coordination group. Dir. prodn. interactive computer exhibit on remote sensing for Denver Mus. Nat. History; contbr. sci. articles to profl. jours. Bd. dirs. Nat. Park Service Equal Employment Opportunity Com., Denver, 1981, chmn., 1982. Recipient Mgrs. award Nat. Park Service, Lakewood, 1981, Performance Commendation award, 1988, Excellence of Svc. Team awrd U.S Dept. Interior, 1999; NRA rsch. grantee, 1972. Fellow Am. Soc. Potogrammetry and Remote Sensing (exec. com., bd. dirs. 1988-90, v.p. 1992, pres.-elect 1993, pres. 1994, dir. remote sensing applications divsn. 1987-89); mem. Am. Congress on Surveying and Mapping (joint satellite mapping and remote sensing com.), The Wildlife Soc., GRASS Users Group (steering com. 1986—, treas. 1987—), ELAS Users Group (co-chmn. 1985-86, chmn. 1986-87), Sigma Xi. Avocations: tennis, skiing, soccer. E-mail: maury_nyquist@usgs.gov. *Personal philosophy: We need to view the land as a community to which we all belong, instead of a commodity for individual gain. (adopted from Aldo Leopold's A Sand County Almanac, 1949).*

NYQUIST, THOMAS EUGENE, consulting business executive, mayor; b. Froid, Mont., June 20, 1931; s. Richard Theodore and Lydia (Baker) N.; m. Corinne Elaine Johnson, Dec. 22, 1956; children: Jonathan Eugene, Lynn Marie Nyquist Bergstrausser. BA, Macalester Coll., 1956; MA, U. Mont., 1958; PhD, Northwestern U., 1966. Prof. SUNY, New Paltz, 1968-76, adminstr. cen. div. Albany, 1976-90; pres. Nyquist Assocs., New Paltz, N.Y., 1991—. Mem. adv. bd. George Washington's Hdqrs., Newburgh, N.Y., 1980-92; acad. dir. N.Y. Edn. Dept., Kenya, 1982; head del. House of Peace and Friendship/Village of New Paltz delegation, St. Petersburg, Russia, 1992; mem. Japan Com., 1997-99; co-chair Scenic Byways Com, 2002—; chmn. Regatta Com., 2000—. Author: (monograph) Urban Africans in South Africa, 1977, (book) African Middle Class Elite, 1983. Mem. Ulster County Legislature, 1976-79; dep. mayor Village of New Paltz, 1983-87, mayor, 1987—, mem. exec. bd., N.Y. Conf. Mayors, 2000—; chmn. New Paltz Centennial Com., 1986-87; bd. dirs. Ulster Region Credit Union, Kingston, N.Y., 1976-87, Ulster Performing Arts Ctr., 1978-82, Friends of Cuttington Coll., Liberia, 1994-98; bd. dirs. Partnership in Svc. Learning, 1985—, mem. exec. bd., 1998—; treas. Lower Hudson Conf., 1988, 89-90, 91-92. With U.S. Army, 1952-54. Fellow SUNY, South Africa, 1975; Ford Found. grantee, 1986. Mem. African Studies Assn., N.Y. African Studies Assn. (exec. bd. dirs. 1973—, co-editor newsletter 1974—), Am. Polit. Sci. Assn. Democrat. Avocations: hiking, cross county skiing. Home: 140 Huguenot St New Paltz NY 12561-1018 Office: Office of Mayor Village Hall 25 Plattekill Ave New Paltz NY 12561-1918 E-mail: nyq@hvi.net.

NYREN, NEIL SEBASTIAN, publisher, editor; b. Boston, June 13, 1948; s. Karl Edwin and Dorothy Elizabeth (Smith) N.; m. Lois Miriam Sharfman, Oct. 11, 1970; 1 child, Alexander BA, Brandeis U. V.p. G.P. Putnam's Sons Pub., N.Y.C., 1997—; editor Random House Pubs., 1974-77, Arbor House Pubs., N.Y.C., 1977-78; exec. editor Atheneum Pubs., 1978-84; sr. editor G.P. Putnam's Sons Pub., 1984-86, editor-in-chief, 1986—, pub., 1989—, sr. v.p., 1997—. Democrat. Jewish. Office: GP Putnam's Sons 375 Hudson St New York NY 10014-3658 E-mail: nnyren@penguinputnam.com.

NYROP, DONALD WILLIAM, airline executive; b. Elgin, Nebr., Apr. 1, 1912; s. William A. and Nellie (Wylie) N.; m. Grace Cary, Apr. 19, 1941; children: Nancy, William, Karen, Kathryn. AB, Doane Coll., 1934; LL.B., George Washington U., 1939. Bar: D.C. 1938. Atty. Gen. Counsel's Office, CAA, Washington, 1939-41; exec. officer to chmn. CAB, 1942, chmn., 1952; rep. U.S. airlines; mem. ofcl. U.S. delegations Internat. Civil Aviation Orgn. Assemblies, 1946, 47; dep. adminstr. for ops. CAA, 1948-50, adminstr., 1950-51; chmn. CAB, 1951-52; pres. Northwest Airlines, Inc., 1954-78. Served with Air Transport Command USAAF, 1942-46. Decorated Legion of Merit. Mem.: Minneapolis, Minnesota. Home: 4505 Golf Ter Minneapolis MN 55424-1510

NYS, JOHN NIKKI, lawyer; b. Duluth, Minn., May 3, 1948; s. Leslie Leo and Kathleen Cecilia (Beaudin) N.; m. Sandra Ann Stephenson, Aug. 20, 1977; 1 child, John Stephenson. BA, Dartmouth Coll., 1970; JD, Stanford U., 1973. Bar: Minn. 1973, U.S. Dist. Ct. Minn. 1973, U.S. Ct. Appeals (8th cir.) 1984, U.S. Dist. Ct. (we. dist.) Wis. 1985, Wis. 1986. Ptnr. Johnson, Killen, Thibodeau & Seiler, Duluth, 1973—. Pres., treas., bd. dirs. Duluth Regional Care Ctr., 1979-85; v.p., bd. dirs. Western Community Coun., 1980-86; cubmaster Lake Superior coun. Boy Scouts Am., 1987-90; mem. state cen. com. Dem. Farmer Labor Party, 1976-78; pres., bd. dirs. Morgan Park Smithville Community Club, 1978-85. Mem. ABA, Duluth Young Lawyers (pres. 1974-75), Minn. State Bar Assn. (chmn. lawyers referral com. 1986-88, bd. govs. 1990-98, pres. 1996-97), 11th Dist. Bar Assn. (pres. 1989-90). Lutheran. Office: Johnson Killen Thibodeau & Seiler 811 Norwest Ctr Duluth MN 55808 E-mail: jnys@duluthlaw.com.

NYS, PAULINE S. health facility adminstrator, educator; b. Zhitomir, Ukraine, Russia, Oct. 4, 1937; d. Simon P. and Genia I. (Fuks) Chuck; m. David A. Nys, July 16, 1959; 1 child, Igor D. M, U. Kazan, Russia, 1960; PhD, Physical Chem. Inst., Moscow, 1968; D in Chem. Scis., Inst. Antibiotics, Moscow, 1984. Postgrad. fellow Inst. Antibiotics, Moscow, 1962-67, jr. rschr., 1968-71, sr. rschr., 1971-84, chief rschr., 1985-92; chief lab. Ctr. for Antibiotics, 1993—. Full prof. Inst. Antibiotics, Moscow. Contbr. articles to profl. jours. Recipient State prize of Russia, 1984. Mem. N.Y. Acad. Scis. Avocations: literature, painting, architecture, journey. Home: Rechnikov st 26-2-66 115407 Moscow Russia Office: Nat Rsch Ctr Antibiotics Nagatinskaya St 3A 113105 Moscow Russia E-mail: davidnys@writeme.com.

NYSTROM, LORNE, member of parliament; B in Polit. Sci., U. Saskatchewan, Can. Cert. tchr. Can. Mem. 37th parliament House of Commons, Ottawa, Canada, 1968—; owner consulting firm, 1993—97. Mem. privy coun. House of Commons, 1992, critic for fin. and Dem. reform, dep. house leader; spkr. in field. Author: Just Making Change, 2002. Mem. New Dem. Party, 1975—95, chair task force employment and parliamentary reform. Recipient l'Ordre de la Pléiade, French Rep. Office: House of Commons 710 Justice Bldg Ottawa ON K1A 0A6 Canada also: 1059 Albert St Regina SK S4R 2P9 Canada*

NYSTROM, PAUL CLIFDON, business educator; b. St. Paul, June 23, 1940; s. Donald Theodore and Thelma Irene (Searle) N.; m. Carol Jean Lewis, Jan. 20, 1962; children: Leigh Erik, Joy Beth Nystrom Mast. BSE, U. Minn., 1962, MA in Pub. Adminstrn., 1966, PhD, 1970. Budget analyst Sec. of Def., Washington, 1963-64; pers. analyst Gen. Mills, Inc., Mpls., 1965; instr. U. Minn., 1965-68; orgnl. planner ADM Co., 1966-67; asst. prof. U. Wis.-Milw., 1969-74, assoc. prof., 1974-78, prof. bus. adminstrn., 1978—. Co-editor: Handbook of Organizational Design, 1981 (named Acad. of Mgmt. Best Book 1983); contbr. articles to profl. jours. Named Manegold Professorship, U. Wis.-Milw. Found., 1996-99; recipient Tchg. award SBA Bus. Adv. Coun., 1982, 90, Rsch. Professorship, U. Wis., 1985-96, Educator award Orgnl. Behavior Tchg. Soc., 1994. Mem. Acad. of Mgmt., Soc. for Indsl. and Orgnl. Psychology, Inst. for Ops. Rsch. and Mgmt. Sci., Am. Psychol. Soc. (charter). Avocations: photography, European history. Office: 3202 N Maryland Ave Milwaukee WI 53211-3164

NYUNT, ZARNI, politician, writer; b. Rangoon, Burma, July 17, 1956; arrived in U.S., 1987, naturalized; d. Aung and Daw Khin-Saw (Than) Nyunt; m. Hla K-Khine; children: Rupa, Thelma. R.A.S.U., Rangoon, Burma; BSc, Acctg. Sch., Rangoon, Burma; attended, Inya Lake Hotel, Rangoon, Burma. Cert. in hotel and restaurant mgmt. Atlanta, Ga. . Writer Zarni Pub. Co., Rangoon, 1974—79; mgr. The Dynamites Band, 1974—79, Silver Beach Restaurant-Bar St., Rangoon, 1978—; contractor-merchant, 1980—87; seaman, supply officer cook, 1981—87; mgr. Aung Social Svc., Alhambra, Calif., 1990; rep. all Burma students Dem. Front, 1990—93; gen. sec. Fed. Freedom Front, 1991—; state advisor Senate Republican Nat. Com., 1994—. Author: Civil War and Air Support , 1974. Calif. state advisor Senate Rep. Nat. Com., Calif., 1994—2002; rep. All Burma Students Dem. Front, 1990—93; gen. sec. Fed. Freedom Front (Burma), 1991—2002. Achievements include Vol. Force idea in Gulf War 1991 helping immigration reform; idea for billions of money for I.N.S. and others. Home: 18519 Marimba St Rowland Heights CA 91748

NYWEIDE, JEFFREY O. management and business executive; b. Chgo., Feb. 8, 1956; s. Lysle John and Marion (Ottmuller) N. BS in Econs., Northwestern U., 1978. Product specialist Service Bur. Co., Chgo., 1978-79, account exec., 1980-81, sales and service mgr., 1981-82; cons. Control Data Bus. Ctrs., Atlanta, 1982-84, product sales mgr. Greenwich, Conn., 1984-85, nat. product mgr., 1985-87; mng. ptnr. Quantum Mgmt., Inc., 1987-88; exec. v.p., pres., COO Dataware Technologies, Inc., Boston, 1988-2000, also bd. dirs.; venture ptnr., sr. advisor, entrepreneur in residence Millennium Tech. Ventures LP, N.Y.C., 2001—. Contbr. articles to profl. jours. Mem. ADAPSO, Am. Mgmt. Assn., Human Resources System Profls., Am. Payroll Assn., Phi Gamma Delta. Clubs: Norwalk Yacht. Avocations: sailing, swimming, music. Home: PO Box 1426 Manchester Center VT 05255 Office: 350 Park Ave New York NY 10022-6022

NZELIBEJ, JOSEPH OKECHUKU, retired writer, researcher; b. Ihiala, Anambra, Nigeria 05/10/29; s. Novaku Nzelibe and Mary Nwagbaghalie Nzelibe; m. Faith Karola Nzelibe, June 18, 1966; children: Adaora Nzelibe, Jide Nzelibe, Chika Nzelibe, Sobechi Nzelibe. BA Economics, Oberlin, Oberlin, Ohio, 1959—63; MA Economics, Howard, Washington, DC, 1963—65; MA Internat. Studies, Am. U., Washington, DC, 1972—73; PhD Pub. Adminstrn., Century U., New Mexico, 1989—91. Author: (book) Toward a Dynamic Social Development, Philosophy of Balanced Reasoning, Nigeria As I See It. Avocations: christian fellowship groups, singing in choir, men's groups, bible study. Home: 2626 Kirkwood Place #203 Hyattsville MD 20782

OAK, CLAIRE MORISSET, artist, educator; b. St. Georges, Quebec, Can., May 31, 1921; came to U.S., 1945; d. Louis and Bernadette (Coulombe) Morisset; m. Alan Ben Oak, July 2, 1947. Student, Ecole des Beaux Arts, 1938-42, Parsons Sch. Design, N.Y.C., 1945, Art Students League, 1945-46. Staff artist Henry Morgan & R. Simpson, Montreal, 1942-45; artist illustrator W.B. Golovin Advt. Agy., N.Y.C., 1947-49; freelance illustrator Arnold Constable & Advt. Agy., 1948-50, Le Jardin des Modes, Paris, 1950-51, May & Co., L.A., 1956, Katten & Marengo Advt., Stockton, Calif., 1962-84; pvt. practice illustrator, designer San Joaquin Valley, 1984-92; art instr. San Joaquin Delta Coll., Stockton, 1973—. Owner Fashion Illustrator's Workshop, N.Y.C., 1953-54; instr. Bauder Coll., Sacramento, 1975-76; painting workshop leader Lodi Art Ctr., 1991—; watercolor workshop leader D'Pharr Painting Adventures, Virginia City, Nev., 1992; on-going watercolor workshop Galerie Iona, Stockton, Calif., 1993—. Named S.B. Anthony Woman of Achievement in the Arts, U. Pacific, 1982. Mem. Stockton Art League, Lodi Art Ctr., Ctrl. Calif. Art League, The League of Carmichael Artists, Delta Watercolor Soc. (bd. mem. 1988—). Avocations: outdoor painting, drawing from a model. Home: 2140 Waudman Ave Stockton CA 95209-1755 *You are a success in the visual arts if you teach others how to see.*

OAK, JEFFREY CHARLES, ethicist; b. Weymouth, Mass., July 1, 1959; s. Wayne LeRoy and Myrna Eloise (Noble) O.; m. Carol Pinkham, Oct. 11, 1986; children: Nathaniel Charles, Julia Elizabeth. BA, Gettysburg (Pa.) Coll., 1981; MDiv, Yale U., 1985, STM, 1986, PhD, 1996. Ordained Methodist Church. Clergyman United Meth. Conf. Ea. Pa., Valley Forge, 1986-87, United Meth. Conf. N.Y., White Plains, 1987-91; lectr., tchg. asst. Yale U., New Haven, 1991-96; healthcare ethicist Arden Hill Health Care, Goshen, N.Y., 1996-98; v.p. corp. integrity and ethics Arden Hill Sr. Health System, 1998-99; sr. v.p. Coun. of Ethical Orgns., Alexandria, Va., 1999-2001; chief ethics and compliance officer Vets. Health Adminstrn., Washington, 2001—. Chmn. U.S. code of ethics Health Care Compliance, Phila., 1998-99, chmn. nat. edn. com., 1998-99. Editor Pastin Report on Healthcare Compliance, 2000; assoc. editor Report on Healthcare Compliance, 1999—; contbr. articles to profl. jours. Trustee, vice chair Arden Hill Health System, Goshen, 1993-96; chmn. ethics com. Arden Hill Hosp., Goshen, 1990-99, Hospice of Orange County, Middletown, N.Y., 1996-99; mem. steering com. Hudson Valley Healthcare Ethics Network, Bronx, 1993-97; trustee Health Care Compliance Assn., 2001-, Southold Yacht club, 2001-. Recipient Keith Pappas award Gettysburg Coll., 1981, Disting. Alumni award Manheim Twp. H.S., 1998; John Wesley fellow Found. for Theol. Edn., 1992-95, Yale U. fellow, 1994. Avocations: sailing, woodworking, jogging, kayaking, Nordic skiing. Office: Vets Health Adminstn Office Compliance (10B3) 810 Vermont Ave NW Washington DC 20420 E-mail: jcoak@att.net.

OAKES, CLAUDIA, museum administrator; Asst. dir. pub. programs Utah Mus. Nat. History, Salt Lake City; asst. dir. exhibits & ops. Utah Mus. Natural History & Hansen Planetarium, assoc. dir. mus. affairs; v.p. pub. programs Milw. Pub. Mus., Milw.; assoc. curator, acting aeronautics dept. chmn. Smithsonian Inst. Nat. Air & Space Mus., Washington. MAP III surveyor; reviewer IMLS-GOS. Mem.: Am. Assn. Mus. (v.chmn.), Nat Assn. Mus. Exhib. (bd. dir.), We. Mus. Assn. (bd. dir.). Office: Utah Museum Natural History 1390 E Presidents Circle Salt Lake City UT 84112-0050*

OAKES, DAVID, statistician; b. Stockport, England, May 8, 1947; came to U.S., 1983; s. Norman Edward and Kathleen O.; m. Peggy Foster, Apr. 23, 1977; 1 child, William Foster. MA, U. Cambridge, 1972; PhD, London U., 1972. Asst. prof. Harvard U., Cambridge, Mass., 1977; sr. lectr. London Sch. Hygiene & Tropical Medicine, 1977-83; from assoc. prof. to prof. statistics & biostatistics U. Rochester, N.Y., 1983—. Chair dept. statistics U. Rochester, 1989-95, chair dept. biostatistics, 1995—. Co-author: Analysis of Survival Data, 1984; contbr. articles to profl. jours. Fellow Am. Statistical Assn., Internat. Statistical Inst. Office: U Rochester Dept Biostatistics 601 Elmwood Ave Rochester NY 14642-0001

OAKES, DAVID DUANE, medical educator; b. LaPorte, Ind., Mar. 14, 1941; m. Donna Gottdiener, June 26, 1966 (dec. 1990); children: Daniel A., Daryl A.; m. Sheila R. Botein, Aug. 19, 2000. BA in European History magna cum laude, Harvard Coll., 1963; MD, Harvard Med. Sch., 1968. Diplomate Am. Bd. Surgery, Am. Bd. Thoracic Surgery. Intern in surgery Peter Bent Brigham Hosp., Boston, 1968-69, jr. asst. resident, 1969-71, sr. asst. resident, 1972-74; chief resident in surgery W. Roxbury (Mass.) VA Hosp., 1974-75; assoc. chief gen. surgery Santa Clara Valley Med. Ctr., San Jose, Calif., 1977-80, chief divsn. gen. thoracic surgery, 1980-89, dir. trauma svcs., 1984-87; from asst. prof. to prof. surgery Stanford (Calif.) U. Sch. Medicine, 1977-98, prof. surgery, 1998—. Chmn. tumor bd. Santa Clara VAlley Med. Ctr., San Jose, 1977—; adv. com. No. Calif. Regional Spinal Injury Sys., 1982-87; mem. adminstrv. panel for protection of human subjects in med. rsch. Stanford U., 1977-92, 98—, chmn., 1987-92, 98—. Contbr. articles to profl. jours. Maj. U.S. Army Med. Corps., 1975-77. Fiske scholar Trinity Coll., 1963-64, Harvard Nat. scholar, 1964-68; grantee Montreal Gen. Hosp., 1971-72. Fellow ACS (cancer liaison physician 1977—), Am. Assn. Surgery Trauma, No. Calif. Chpt. ACS (trauma com.); mem. Assn. Acad. Surgery, Calif. Med. Assn., Am. Assn. Thoracic Surgery, Santa Clara County Med. Assn., Santa Clara County Surg. Soc. (pres. 1983), San Jose Surg. Soc., Home: 149 Greenoaks Dr Atherton CA 94027-2159 Fax: 408 885 6054.

OAKES, DUWAYNE EARL, retired principal; b. Fillmore, N.D., May 28, 1926; s. Ralph William Oakes and Ella Catherine (Anderson) Baril; m. Elva Jean Jacobsen, Nov. 6, 1948; children: Jon, Robert, Kathleen, Mary. BA in Edn., Pacific Luth. U., 1952, MA, 1972. Tchr. DuPont Ft. Lewis Sch. Dist., Wash., 1952-59, prin., 1959, Clover Park Sch. Dist., Lakewood, Wash., 1959-71. Author: God's Call to Communion, 1982; contbr.: National Poetry Library Anthology, 1995-96, God's Plan, 1999; inventor fishing rod socket. Inductee Internat. Poetry Hall of Fame, 1996. Mem. Norwegian Lodge, Eagles Club. Christian Socialist. Lutheran. Avocations: singing in church choir, normanna Chorus. Home: 8515 94th St SW Lakewood WA 98498-4527

OAKES, ELLEN RUTH, psychotherapist, health institute administrator; b. Bartlesville, Okla., Aug. 19, 1919; d. John Isaac and Eva Ruth (Engle) Harboldt; m. Paul Otis Oakes Sr., June 12, 1937 (div. April 1974); children: Paul Otis Jr., Deborah Ellen, Nancy Elaine Masters; m. Siegmar Johann Knopp, Nov. 24, 1975 (div. Feb. 1998). BA in Sociology, Psychology summa cum laude, Oklahoma City U., 1961; MS in Clin. Psychology, U. Okla., 1963, PhD, 1967. Lic. clin. psychologist, Okla. Chief psychometrist Okla. U. Guidance Ctr., Norman, 1962; psychology trainee VA Hosp., Oklahoma City, 1962-64, Cerebral Palsy Ctr., Norman, Okla., 1964-65; psychology intern Guidance Service, 1965-66, staff psychologist, 1966-67; asst. prof. psychology Okla. U. Med. Sch., Oklahoma City, 1967-70; supr. psychology interns Okla. Univ. Health Scis. Ctr., 1967-80; founder, dir. Timberridge Inst., Oklahoma City, 1970-90, pres., 1980-90; pvt. practice clin. psychologist, 1970-92. Instr. Okla. U. extension course, Tinker AFB, Oklahoma City, 1963, U. Okla., 1965-66; discussion leader Inst. for Tchrs. of Disadvantaged Child Oklahoma City Sch. System, 1966; leader group therapy sessions Asbury Meth. and Westminster Presbyn. Chs., Oklahoma City, 1966; mem. psychology team confs. for hearing disorders, Okla. U. Med. Sch., 1967-70; cons. Oklahoma City Pub. Schs., 1970-72; cons., group leader halfway house, 1972; lectr. chs., PTAs, hosps.; reviewer Am. Psychol. Assn. Civilian Health and Med. Program of the Uniformed Svcs., 1978-89. Workshop conductor on Shame & Sexuality, Zurick Jungian Inst. winter seminar, 1992; attended Européen Congrés de Gestalt Thérapie in Paris, 1992; contbr. articles to profl. jours. Speaker Okla. County Mental Health Assn. Annual Worry Clinic, St. Luke's Ch., Oklahoma City, 1968-92, psychology dept. Sorosis Club, St. Luke's Ch.; charter mem. English spkg. Christian Congregation mission outreach Pauluskirche, Bochum, Germany, 1993-97, exec. coun., 1996-97. Mem. Am. Psychol. Assn. (peer rev. project with CHAMPUS, 1978-89), Okla. Psychol. Assn. (pres. 1975-76). Avocations: art, travel, poetry, photography, walking.

OAKES, JAMES L. federal judge; b. Springfield, Ill., Feb. 21, 1924; m. Evelena S. Kenworthy, Dec. 29, 1973 (dec. Oct. 1997); m. Mara A. Williams, Jan. 1, 1999; m. Rosalyn Landon, Oct. 2, 1945; 3 children. AB, Harvard Coll., 1945; LLB, Harvard U., 1947; LLD, New Eng. Coll., 1976, Suffolk U., 1980, Vt. Law Sch., 1995. Bar: Calif. 1949, Vt. 1950. Pvt. practice, Brattleboro, Vt.; spl. counsel Vt. Pub. Svc. Commn., 1959—60; counsel Vt. Statutory Revision Commn., 1957—60; mem. Vt. Senate, 1961—65; atty. gen. Vt., 1967—69; U.S. dist. judge, 1970—71; judge U.S. Ct. Appeals 2d Cir., Brattleboro, 1971—, chief judge, 1989—92. Adj. faculty Duke U. Law Sch., 1985—96, Iowa U. Coll. Law, 1993—97. Office: US Ct Appeals PO Box 696 Brattleboro VT 05302-0696

OAKES, JUDY DIANNE, real estate broker; b. Charleston, W.Va., Aug. 14, 1950; d. William E. and Betty A. Hager; m. Gary H. Oakes, Dec. 21, 1968; children: Scott E., Christina D. McDaniel, Brian M. Real estate sales Bishop Realtors, Cleve., 1973-82, Armstrong Realty, Riverside, Calif., 1986-88; real estate broker Remax All Stars, 1988-94, Realty Exec., Riverside, 1994—2001. Named #1 Agt. in Co., Real Estate Sales, 1994-2001. Mem. Cert. Residential Specialist, Magnolia Ave. Bapt. Ch., Inland Valley Assn. Realtors (bd. dirs. 1995). Avocations: reading, rose garden, ocean. E-mail address. Office: Judy Oakes Real Estate Group 8441 Mimosa Tree Riverside CA 92504 E-mail: judy@judyoakes.com.

OAKES, LESTER CORNELIUS, retired electrical engineer, consultant; b. Knoxville, Oct. 11, 1923; s. Charles Vaughn and Maude Cornelia (Harrison) O.; m. Kathleen Clark, Dec. 27, 1947; children: Michael, Richard, Cynthia, Melissa. BS in E.E., U. Tenn., 1949, MS, 1962. Registered profl. engr., Tenn. Engr. Fairchild Engring. and Aircraft, Oak Ridge, 1949-51; engr. I&C div. Oak Ridge Nat. Lab., 1951-68, dep. head I&C div., 1968—, asst. dir. I&C div., 1971-90; cons. Oak Ridge Nat. Lab., electric Power Rsch. Inst., Nuclear Regulatory Commn., 1990—. Contbr. articles to profl. jours.; patentee in field. Served with USAF, 1943-46. Martin Marietta Corp. fellow. Fellow IEEE Presbyterian. Home: 710 Pleasant Hill Rd Maryville TN 37803-7337 E-mail: lesoakes@aol.com.

OAKES, ROBERT JAMES, physics educator; b. Mpls., Jan. 21, 1936; s. Sherman E. and Josephine J. (Olson) O.; children: Cindy L., Lisa A. BS, U. Minn., 1957, MS, 1959, PhD, 1962. NSF fellow Stanford U., 1962-64; asst. prof. physics, 1964-68; assoc. prof. physics Northwestern U., 1968-70, prof. physics, 1970-76, prof. physics and astronomy, 1976—. Vis. staff mem. Los Alamos Sci. Lab., 1971-92; vis. scientist Fermi Nat. Accelerator Lab., 1975—, CERN, 1966-67; mem. Inst. for Advanced Study, Princeton, 1967-68; vis. scientist DESY, 1971-72; faculty assoc. Argonne Nab. Lab., 1982— ; U.S. scientist NSF-Yugoslav joint program, 1982-92; panelist Nat. Rsch. Coun., 1990-98. A.P. Sloan fellow 1965-68; Air Force Office Sci. Rsch. grantee, 1969-71, NSF grantee 1971-87, Dept. Energy grantee, 1987—; named Fulbright-Hays Disting. prof. U. Sarajevo, Yugoslavia, 1979-80; recipient Natural Sci. prize China, 1993. Fellow Am. Phys. Soc., AAAS; mem. N.Y. Acad. Sci., Ill. Acad. Sci., Physics Club (Chgo.), Sigma Xi, Tau Beta Pi. Clubs: Physics (Chgo.). Office: Northwestern U Dept Physics 2145 Sheridan Rd Evanston IL 60208-0834

OAKES, TERRY LOUIS, retail clothing store executive; b. Denver, June 12, 1953; s. Robert Walter and Stella Marie (Ray) O.; m. Cynthia Alison Bailey, Jan. 10, 1981; children: Madeleine Bailey, Robert Alan. BBA, So. Meth. U., 1975. Dept. mgr. Woolf Bros., Dallas, 1975-76; buyer I.K.O. Dry Goods, Denver, 1976-79, gen. sales mgr., 1979-81, exec. v.p., mdse. mgr., 1981-86; nat. sales mgr. Fresh Squeeze div. Bayly Corp., 1986-88; owner, pres. Bolderdash, 1988—. Tchr., mem. adv. bd. fashion mdse. divsn. Colo. Inst. Art., Denver, 1991-98. Bd. dirs. Vail Racquet Club, Vail, Colo. Mem. Vail Racquet Club (bd. dirs.). Democrat. Presbyterian. Home: 5390 S Geneva St Englewood CO 80111-6205 Office: Bolderdash 2721 E 3d Ave Denver CO 80206-4919 E-mail: bolderdash@prodigy.net.

OAKES, THOMAS WYATT, environmental engineer, computer engineer; b. Danville, Va., June 14, 1950; s. Wyatt Johnson and Relia (Sceacre) O.; m. Terry Lynn Jenkins, June 15, 1974; 1 child, Travis Wyatt. BS in Nuclear Engring., Va. Polytechnic U., 1973, MS in Nuclear Engring., 1975; MS in Environ. Engring., U. Tenn., 1981. Ordained deacon Bapt. Ch., 1989. Health physics asst. Va. Polytechnic U., Blacksburg, 1972-74; radiation engr. Babcock and Wilcox Co., Lynchburg, Va., 1974-75; dept. mgr. Oak Ridge (Tenn.) Nat. Lab., 1975-78, environ. mgr., 1978-85; corp. environ. coord. Martin Marietta, Oak Ridge, 1985-87; asst. v.p. Sci. Applications Internat. Corp., 1987-90; environ. mmgr. Westinghouse Environ. and Geotech. Svcs., Knoxville, Tenn., 1990-91; mgr. S.E. region environ. svcs. ATEC & Assocs., Inc., Marietta, Ga., 1991-93; asst. v.p. environ. svcs. Scitek, Ft. Campbell, Ky., 1993-98; ind. sr. cons., 1998—; pres. T30 Nat. Svc. Inc., 1998—. Contbr. over 107 articles to scholarly and profl. jours. Recipient Spl. Recognition award Union Carbide Corp., 1980, Best Paper award Nat. Safety Coun., 1982, Tech. Publs. award Soc. Tech. Communications, 1987. Mem. AAAS, Am. Indsl. Hygiene Assn., N.Y. Acad. Scis., Health Physics Soc. (sec.-treas. environ. sect. 1984-85), Am. Naval Soc., Am. Soc. for Quality Control. Office: 11130 Kingston Pike Ste 1-328 Knoxville TN 37922-2800 E-mail: t30oakes@inetmail.att.net.

OAKES, WALTER JERRY, pediatric neurosurgeon; b. De Soto, Mo., July 10, 1946; s. Marvin Melton and Mildred Florene (Link) O.; m. Linda Helen Maas (div. Jan. 1985); 1 child, Kathleen Suzanne; m. Jean Evans, Dec. 1988; children: Matthew Marvin, Peter Clifford. BA in Chemistry, U. Mo., 1968; MD, Duke U., 1972. Diplomate Am. Bd. Neurol. Surgeons. Neurosurgery resident Duke U., Durham, N.C., 1972-78, asst. prof. neurosurgery, 1979-90, assoc. prof. neurosurgery, 1991—, asst. prof. pediatrics, 1981-92, assoc. prof. pediatrics, 1992; pediatric neurosurgery resident U. Toronto Hosp. for Sick Children, Ont., Can., July-Dec., 1975; registrar pediatric neurosurgery U. London Hosp. for Sick Children, Eng., Sept., 1978-Feb., 1979; prof. neurosurgery and pediatrics U. Ala. Birmingham, 1992—. Fellow ACS. Office: Children's Hosp of Ala 1600 7th Ave S Ste 400 Birmingham AL 35233-1785 E-mail: jerry.oakes@ccc.unb.edu.

OAKFORD, LAWRENCE XAVIER, electron microscopist, laboratory administrator; b. Cleve., Jan. 6, 1953; s. Gerald Frederick and Mary Elizabeth (Pestak) O.; m. Dorothy Jean Savage, Aug. 18, 1985; children: Tony, Jamil. MS, Calif. State Poly. U., 1977; PhD, Wash. State U., 1986. Tchg. asst., technician Calif. State Poly. U., Pomona, 1975-77; rsch. asst. Wash. State U., Pullman, 1977-79, tchg. asst., 1977-82; lab. dir. U. North Tex. Health Sci. Ctr., Ft. Worth, 1982—. Contbr. over 50 articles to profl. jours. Com. chmn. Cowtown Marathon and 10k Run, Ft. Worth, 1984-2001; MSA Certification bd. mem., 1995-2001, tech. forum mem., 1993—; mentor, judge Ft. Worth Ind. Sch. Dist. Adopt-a-Sch. Program, 1984-93; mem. pastoral coun. St. Andrews Cath. Ch., 1993-95, small Christian cmtys. core team, 1995-98; judge Internat. Sci. and Engring. Fair, 1998. Recipient Diatome award, 1997. Mem. AAAS, Microscopy Soc. Am., Societé de Microscopie du Can., Tex. Soc. for Electron Microscopy. Office: UNT Health Sci Ctr Dept Pathology and Anatomy 3500 Camp Bowie Blvd Fort Worth TX 76107-2690 E-mail: loakford@hsc.unt.edu.

OAKLEY, ANDREW ARTHUR, journalist, educator; b. Chgo., Oct. 22, 1958; s. Arthur George and Dolores Margarite (Hernandez) O.; m. Suzanna Pinter, Sept. 7, 1985; children: Glen Matthias, Ryan Arthur. BS in Journalism, Northwestern U., 1980, MS, 1981. Reporter Woodstock (Ill.) Daily Sentinel, 1980-81; police reporter Herald-Palladium, St. Joseph, Mich., 1981-82; city hall reporter Daily Herald, Arlington Heights, Ill., 1982-84; instr. journalism Oakton C.C., Des Plaines, 1984-85; features editor North Shore Mag., Winnetka, 1985-86; news editor City and State, Chgo., 1986-93; journalism editor P.O. Publ. Co., Port Murray, N.J., 1993-2000; newsletter editor All Aboard for Hackettstown, 1996-98. Lectr. Northwestern U., Evanston, Ill., 1990-96; columnist Daily Herald, Arlington Heights, Ill., 1995-96; copy editor Full Time Dads Mag., Clifton, N.J., 1997-2000; corr. Daily Herald, Arlington Heights, 1995—. *Having worked as a newspaper journalist and fiction writer, Andy Oakley has developed a college curriculum that emphasizes literary journalism to his writing students. Both his professional and academic work propound a synthesis between fiction and non-fiction writing. He stresses during his college courses and public speaking engagements that the best writers are masters of both fiction and non-fiction; this is especially necessary due to the upheaval in communication technology that will make some writing forms, including daily newspaper journalism, obsolete. Still, he believes that basic newspaper reporting is a solid foundation for the construction of a writing career.* Author: Eighty-Eight, 1988, Issues Confronting City and State Governments, 1992, Beginning Journalism Packet, 1994; cons. editor P.O. Pub. Co., Skokie, Ill., 1988-92. Lifetime mem. N Club, 1980—; commr. Skokie Human Rels. Commn., 1987-94; co-chmn. Skokie Centennial Events Com., 1987-88; advisor Mcpl. Alliance Lit. Club, 1997-98. Mem. No. Ill. Newspaper Assn. (Pub. Affairs Reporting award 1983), Ill. Press Assn. (Edn. Reporting award 1983), Suburban Press Club Chgo. (Investigative Series award 1984), Soc. Profl. Journalists (Peter Lisagor award 1984), Investigative Reporters and Editors, Assn. for Edn. in Journalism and Mass Comm., Medill Alumni Assn., Evanston Running Club. Methodist. Avocations: coaching youth sports, writing. E-mail: OAKLEYANDY@aol.com.

OAKLEY, CAROLYN COBB, library director, academic administrator; b. Wilson, N.C., Nov. 5, 1946; d. Raymond Earl and Edna Gay (Hardison) Cobb; m. Robert Carroll Oakley, Nov. 25, 1971 (div. Oct. 1988); 1 child, Robert Carroll Oakley, Jr. BS, E. Carolina U., 1969, MEd, 1970; postgrad., U. N.C., 1976-77, N.C. State U., 1986—. Cataloger N.C. Dept. C.C., Raleigh, 1969-70; libr. Vance-Granville C.C., Henderson, N.C., 1970-76, coord. library svcs., 1976-87; dir. Learning Resources Ctr., 1987-88; dept. chair for learning resources Wilson (N.C.) Tech. C.C., 1989-96; dir. Learning Resources Ctr. Cape Fear C.C., Wilmington, N.C., 1996—. Cons. Rose's Stores, Henderson, 1986-87, Ark. Dept. of Higher Edn., Little Rock, Ark., 1994. Author: Index to Doctoral Theses, 1967-85 (N.C. State U.), 1987. Mem. ALA, N.C. Libr. Assn., Am. Assn. Women in Community Colls., SE Libr. Assn., N.C. Cmty. Coll. Learning Resources Assn. Democrat. Baptist. Home: 1221 Buckingham Ave Wilmington NC 28401-7653 Office: Cape Fear CC 411 N Front St Wilmington NC 28401-3993

OAKLEY, DAVID STERLING, physics educator, consultant; b. Denver, Apr. 2, 1958; s. Gary Addison and JoAnn (Winans) O.; m. Barbara JoAnn Quinn, Apr. 5, 1986; children: David Addison, Andrew Timothy, Madeleine. BA, Colo. U., 1981; MA, Tex. U., 1985, PhD, 1987. Rsch. assoc. Colo. U., Boulder, 1987-89; asst. prof. Lewis and Clark Coll., Portland, Oreg., 1989-93; assoc. prof. Colo. Christian U., Lakewood, 1993—. Dir. rsch. Safe Air Monitoring Systems, Inc., Denver, 1989—. Contbr. articles to profl. jours. Youth counselor Young Life, Austin, Tex., 1981-87; mem. So. Utah Wilderness Alliance, Salt Lake City, 1986—, Oreg. Rivers Coun., Portland, 1992—. Mem. Am. Phys. Soc. Presbyterian. Achievements include patent in method for detecting hydrogen containing compounds, detection of natural gas and household radon; research in correlation between solar neutrino flux and solar magnetic fields, in nuclear structure, role of space-time in Christian theology. Office: Colo Christian Univ 180 S Garrison St Lakewood CO 80226-1053

OAKLEY, DIANE, insurance executive, benefit consultant; b. Teaneck, N.J., Dec. 27, 1953; d. Geard Joseph and Joan B. (Peterson) O. BS, Fairfield U., 1975; MBA, Fordham U., 1984. Actuarial asst. TIAA-CREF, N.Y.C., 1975-79, benefit plan counselor, 1979-82, adv. officer, 1982-85, branch mgr., 2nd v.p. Bethesda, Md., 1985-89, v.p., assns. & govt. rels., 1989-95, v.p., 1995—2002, v.p. for spl. cons. svcs., 2002—. Bd. dirs. Nat. Assn. Coll. and Univ. Bus. Officers, 1995-2000; bd. trustees Fairfield U. Mem. Am. Assn. Higher Edn., Am. Assn. Women in C.C.'s, Women in Govt. Rels., Working in Employee Benefits, Secure Retirement Coalition (treas.). Roman Catholic. Home: 4400 E West Hwy Apt 432 Bethesda MD 20814-4504 Office: TIAA-CREF Ste 700 South 55512th St NW Washington DC 20004

OAKLEY, FRANCIS CHRISTOPHER, history educator, former college president; b. Liverpool, Eng., Oct. 6, 1931; came to U.S., 1957, naturalized, 1968; s. Joseph Vincent and Siobean (NiCurean) O.; m. Claire-Ann Lamenzo, Aug. 9, 1958; children: Deirdre, Christopher, Timothy, Brian. BA, Corpus Christi Coll., Oxford U., 1953, MA, 1957; postgrad., Pontifical Inst. Medieval Studies, Toronto, 1953-55; MA, Yale U., 1958, PhD, 1960; LLD, Amherst Coll., 1986, Wesleyan U., 1989; LHD, Northwestern U., 1990, North Adams State Coll., 1993, Bowdoin Coll., 1993; LittD, Williams Coll., 1994. Mem. faculty Yale U., 1959-61, Williams Coll., Williamstown, Mass., 1961—, prof. history, 1970—, dean faculty, 1977-84, Edward Dorr Griffin prof. history of ideas, 1984-85, 94—, pres., 1985-94, pres. emeritus, 1994—; hon. fellow Corpus Christi Coll., Univ. Oxford, 1991—. Vis. lectr. Bennington (Vt.) Coll., 1967, Sir Isaiah Berlin vis. prof. Oxford U., 1999-2000; Merle Curti lectr. U. Wis., Madison, 2001; mem. Inst. Advanced Study Princeton, 1981-82; assoc. Nat. Humanities Ctr., 1991; guest scholar Woodrow Wilson Internat. Ctr. for Scholars, 1994; chair bd. dirs. Am. Coun. Learned Socs., 1993-97; trustee Sterling and Francine Clark Art Inst., 1985—, pres. 1998—; trustee MassMoCA Found., 1995—, Willamstown Art Conservation Ctr., 1995-98, Williamstown Theatre Festival, 1985-93, Nat. Humanities Ctr., 1996—, Lake Forest Coll., 1997-2001; trustee Inst. Advanced Cath. Studies, 1998—, vice chair, 2002--; mem. MassMoCA Cultural Devel. Commn., 1988—; mem. adv. coun. Ctr. for Study of Religion, Princeton U., 1999—. Author: The Political Thought of Pierre d'Ailly: The Voluntarist Tradition, 1964, Kingship and the Gods: The Western Apostasy, 1968, Council over Pope?, Towards a Provisional Ecclesiology, 1969, Medieval Experience: Foundations of Western Cultural Singularity, 1974, rev. England edit., The Crucial Centuries, 1979, Spanish edit., 1980, 95, Medieval Acad. edit., 1988, 93, The Western Church in the Later Middle Ages, 1979, rev. edit., 1985, 88, 91, Natural Law, Conciliarism and Consent in the Late Middle Ages, 1984, Omnipotence, Covenant and Order: An Excursion in the History of Ideas, 1984, Community of Learning: The American College and the Liberal Arts Tradition, 1992, Scholarship and Teaching: A Matter of Mutual Support, 1996, Politics and Eternity: Studies in the History of Medieval and Early Modern Political Thoughts, 1999; editor: (with Daniel O'Connor) Creation: The Impact of an Idea, 1969; contbr. articles to profl. jours. Lt. Brit. Army, 1955-57. Goldsmith's Co. London fellow, 1953-55, Social Sci. Rsch. Coun. fellow, 1963, Am. Coun. Learned Socs. fellow, 1965, 69-70, Weil Inst. fellow, 1965, Folger Shakespeare Libr. fellow, 1974, NEH fellow, 1976, 81-82; recipient Wilbur Lucius Cross medal Yale Grad. Sch., 1997. Fellow Medieval Acad. Am. (pres. fellows 1999-2002), Am. Acad. Arts and Scis.; mem. Am. Hist. Assn., Am. Cath. Hist. Assn., Am. Ch. History Soc., New Eng. Medieval Conf. (pres. 1983-84), Am. Coun. Learned Socs. (chair bd. dirs. 1993-97, interim pres. 2002--), The Century Assn., Am. Cusanus Soc. (adv. bd. 1997—). Democrat. Roman Catholic. Office: Williams Coll Oakley Ctr Humanities & Soc Sci Williamstown MA 01267 E-mail: francis.c.oakley@williams.edu., fcoakley@acls.org.

OAKLEY, JOEL NEESE, lawyer; b. Greensboro, N.C., Jan. 30, 1960; s. Julius H. Oakley and Yvonne P. Berkerly; m. Nancy Calvin, Nov. 25, 1989; 1 child, Erica Danielle. BA, Appalachain State, 1982; JD summa cum laude, N.C. Ctrl. Sch. Law, 1986. Bar: N.C. 1986, U.S. Dist. Ct. (mid. dist.) N.C. 1986. Atty. N.C. Bar, Greensboro, 1986—. Mem. Greensboro Criminal Def. Lawyers Assn. (bd. dirs. 1993—, pres. 1994-95), Guilford Inns Ct., Triad Rugby Dogs. Democrat. Avocation: rugby. Office: 322 S Eugene St Greensboro NC 27401-2322

OAKLEY, JOHN BILYEU, law educator, lawyer, judicial consultant; b. San Francisco, June 18, 1947; s. Samuel Heywood and Elsie-Maye (Bilyeu) O.; m. Fredericka Barvitz, May 25, 1969; children: Adélie, Antonia. BA, U. Calif., Berkeley, 1969; JD, Yale U., 1972. Bar: Calif. 1972, U.S. Dist. Ct. (no. dist.) Calif. 1974, U.S. Dist. Ct. (ctrl. and ea. dists.) Calif. 1975, U.S. Supreme Ct. 1977, U.S. Ct. Appeals (5th cir.) 1979, U.S. Ct. Appeals (9th cir.) 1992. Rsch. atty. chief justice Donald R. Wright Supreme Ct. of Calif., 1972-73, sr. rsch. atty. chief justice Donald R. Wright, 1974-75; sr. law clk. chief judge M. Joseph Blumenfeld U.S. Dist. Ct. Conn., Hartford, 1973-74; acting prof. law U. Calif., Davis, 1975-79, prof. law, 1979—. Reporter Speedy Trial Planning Group, U.S. Dist. Ct., Sacramento, 1977-82, Civil Justice Reform Act Adv. Group, 1991-94, U.S. Jud. Conf. Com. on Fed.-State Jurisdiction, 1991-96, Western Regional Conf. on State-Fed. Jud. Relationships, 1992-93, 2000; scholar-in-residence, sr. trial atty. Civil Rights Divsn., U.S. Dept. Justice, Washington, 1979-80; vis. scholar U. Coll., Oxford (Eng.) U., 1982-83; apptd. counsel death penalty appeal Supreme Ct. Calif., 1984-96; cons. Calif. Jud. Coun. Commn. on the Future of the Cts., 1992-93; vis. prof. U. Calif. Berkeley, 2001, U. Tenn., 2001. Co-author: Law Clerks and the Judicial Process, 1980, An Introduction to the Anglo-American Legal System, 1980, 2d edit., 1988, 3d edit., 2001, Civil Procedure, 1991, 2d edit., 1996, 3d edit., 2001, Federal Courts, 10th edit., 1999; contbr.: Restructuring Justice, 1990. Pub. mem. New Motor Vehicle Bd. Calif., Sacramento, 1976-82, Calif. Jud. Coun. Appellate Process Task Force, 1997-2001; bd. dirs. Fallen Leaf Lake (Calif.) Mutual Water Co., 1980-82, 94—; western regional assoc., field assoc. Duke U. Primate Ctr., 1986-91, bd. visitors, 1997-2000. With U.S. Merchant Marine, 1969, Vietnam. Nat. Merit scholar, 1964. Mem. Am. Law Inst. (reporter Fed. Jud. Code Revision Project 1995—), Assn. Am. Law Schs. (chair sect. on civil procedure 1979-80, 96-97), Am. Judicature Soc. (bd. dirs. 1996-98), Am. Inns of Ct., Phi Beta Kappa. Avocations: aviation, photography, railroads, rugby, running. Office: Univ Calif Sch Law Davis CA 95616

OAKLEY, JOHN HOWARD, humanities educator; b. Elizabeth, N.J., Nov. 6, 1949; s. Howard Thurston and Marjorie Ethel (Deyo) O.; m. Evi Gertrud Hessler, May 8, 1990; children: Nicholas Todd, Jacob Travis. BA, Rutgers U., 1972, MA, 1976, PhD, 1980. Asst. prof. Coll. William and Mary, Williamsburg, Va., 1980-86, assoc. prof., 1986-93, prof. classical studies, 1993—, chancellor prof., 1993—, Forrest D. Murden, Jr. prof. classical studies, 2000—, dept. chair, 2001—. Vis. prof. Canterbury U., Christchurch, N.Z., 1997; Whitehead vis. prof. Am. Sch. Classical Studies, Athens, 1997-98, dir. summer session, 1986, mng. com., 1982—; adv. coun. Am. Acad. in Rome, 1985—; vis. fellow classics dept. Princeton U., 2000-01. Author: The Phiale Painter, 1990, Corpus Vasorum Antiquorum-Baltimore, 1992, The Achilles Painter, 1997, others; co-author: The Wedding in Classical Athens, 1993; editor: Corpus Vasorum Antiquorum, 1985—, Bryn Mawr Electronics Resources Rev., 1997—; adv. bd. Am. Jour. Archaeology, 1992-93; contbr. articles to profl. jours. 1st lt. U.S. Army, 1972-80. Recipient Phi Beta Kappa Award for Advancement of Scholarship, 1990; Alexander von Humboldt Stiftung fellow, 1988-89, 91-92, NEH, 1997-98, Andrew W. Mellon fellow Met. Mus. Art, 2000-2001. Mem. Archaeol. Inst. Am. (pres. Williamsburg soc. 1995-97, travelling lectr. 1989-91, 95—), Am. Philological Assn., Classical Assn. of Mid. West and South. Home: 2864 Hidden Lake Dr Williamsburg VA 23185-8020 Office: College William and Mary Dept Classical Studies Williamsburg VA 23187

OAKLEY, WANDA FAYE, management consultant, educator; b. Durham, N.C., June 27, 1950; d. Joseph Napolian and Doris Gray (Thomas) O. BSBA, U. N.C., 1971, postgrad., 1972-73. CPA, N.C.; cert. fraud examiner, cert. govt. fin. mgr. Acct. Oakley Motors, Durham, 1965-73; controller Airheart Ins. Agy., Inc., 1973-75; controller, owner Quality Car Wash, 1974-83; acct. computer svcs. dept. William H. Mitchell, P.A. and CPAs, 1983-84; mgr. John Anderson & Assocs., Inc., 1984-85; v.p. CMS Svcs., Inc., York, S.C., 1985-86; adminstr. N.C. State U., Raleigh, 1986-89; pvt. practice bus. cons., 1989—. Instr. Wake Tech. Community Coll., Raleigh, 1985—, Small Bus. Ctr., Johnston Community Coll, Smithfield, N.C., 1990—; proctor N.C. State Bd. CPA Examiners, Raleigh, 1986—; bus. cons. in field. Fellow N.C. Assn. CPAs, AICPA; mem. NAFE, Assn. Cert. Fraud Examiners, Exersafety Internat. (master's cert. 1984), Assn. Govt. Accts., U. N.C. Alumni Assn. (life). Home: PO Box 3257 Durham NC 27715-3257 Office: 4404 Ryan St Durham NC 27704-1808

OAKS, B. ANN, retired plant physiologist, educator; b. Winnipeg, Man., Can., June 4, 1929; d. H.A. and Bernice (Farlinger) O. BA with honors, U. Toronto, Ont., Can., 1951; MA, U. Sask., Can., 1954, PhD, 1959. Alexander von Humbolt Rsch. Inst. for Dairying, Freising, Fed. Republic Germany, 1959-60; rsch. assoc. Purdue U., West Lafayette, Ind., 1960-64, Oak Ridge (Tenn.) Nat. Lab., 1964-65; asst. prof. biology McMaster U., Hamilton, Ont., 1965-68, assoc. prof., 1968-74, prof., 1974-89, prof. emeritus, 1989—; prof. U. Guelph, Ont., 1989-98; retired, 1998. Vis. prof. Wash. State U., 1979-80, U. Nancy, France, 1980, Chiba U., Japan, 1984; adj. prof. U. Guelph, 1987-89; affiliated scientist NRC Lab., Saskatoon, Sask., 1988-92. Assoc. editor Biochemistry and Cell Biology, 1988-90; mem. editl. bd. Plant Physiology, 1970-89, Jour. Plant Physiology, 1984-95, Physiologia Plantarium, 1995-96, Plant and Cell Physiology, 1989-93; contbg. author various books; contbr. articles to profl. jours. Rsch. grantee in field. Fellow Royal Soc. Can.; mem. Can. Soc. Plant Physiologists (treas. 1974-76, Gold medal 1989), Am. Soc. Plant Physiologists. Avocations: skiing, hiking, naturalist, writing letters to members of parliament. Address: 1604-685 Woodwich St Guelph ON Canada NIH 8M6

OAKS, LUCY MOBERLEY, retired social worker; b. Lexington, Ky., May 10, 1935; d. Shelton Neville Moberley and Jane Emison (Roberts) Meadors; m. William Bryant Oaks, Nov. 10, 1956; children: Bryant, Michael, Kevin, Richard, Deborah. BA in Social Work, U. Ky., 1957; MA in Counseling Psychology, Bowie (Md.) State Coll., 1979. Cert. mental health counselor, Wash. Youth dir. Calvary Bapt. Ch., Renton, Wash., 1960-64, ch. tng. dir., 1980-87; youth dir. Temple Bapt. Ch., Redlands, Calif., 1965-68, Calvary Bapt. Ch., Morgantown, W.Va., 1971-73; cmty. coll. parent educator Bellevue (Wash.) Cmty. Coll., 1980-89; pvt. counselor Renton, 1980-90; Christians social svcs. dir. Puget Sound Bapt. Assn., Federal Way, Wash., 1984-87; therapeutic program dir. ACAP Child and Family Svcs., Auburn, 1984-93, assoc. dir., 1994-96; retired, 1996. Parent instr. APPLE Parenting, Auburn, 1990-92; seminar presenter, Puget Sound, Wash., 1980-95; dir. social svc. ministries ACAP Child and Family Svcs., 1996-97; cons. Mary Kay Cosmetics, 1996—; file supr. Year 2000 Dept. of Commerce/Census Bur., Bellevue (Wash.) br., 1999-2000. Bd. trustees Valley Cmty. Players , Renton, 1995; featured spkr. parent edn. Puget Sound Area, 1988—96; mem. Census Bur., 1999—2000; bd. dirs. Calvary Bapt. Ch., Renton, 1981—87. Mem. Puget Sound Adlerian Soc. (bd. dirs. 1981-83), Kiwanis (chmn. interclub com., membership chmn. 1994-95). Democrat. Avocations: drama, reading, walking, traveling, bowling. Home: 2218 177th Pl NE Redmond WA 98052-6071

OAKS, MAURICE DAVID, retired pharmaceutical company executive; b. Everett, Pa., Jan. 22, 1934; s. Jacob Garvin and Hannah Alma (Young) O.; m. Judith Ann Rayne; 1 child, Kimberly. BS in Biology, Franklin and Marshall Coll., 1956. Sales rep. Squibb Pharm, Salisbury and Balt., Md., 1959-69; div. sales mgr. Squibb Pharm., Columbus, Ohio, 1969-71, product mgr. Princeton, N.J., 1971-76, group product dir., 1976-78, dir. product planning, U.S., 1979-80, v.p. world wide mktg. devel., 1980-82, v.p. mktg. svcs., 1983-85, pres. Princeton Pharm. Products, 1985-89; exec. v.p. Squibb Pharm. Group U.S., 1989-90; v.p. worldwide ops. planning Bristol-Myers Squibb Pharms. Ops., 1990-92. Bd. dirs. Nat. Pharm. Coun., McLean, Va., 1985-90, mem. exec. com., 1988-90; bd. dirs., mem. audit com., chmn. nominating com. Penn Engrng. Mfg., Danboro, Pa. Mem. coun. Franklin and Marshall Coll. Commn. on Found. and Corp. Support, Lancaster, Pa., 1987-90, ann. fund class capt., 1991-97; mem., pres. Mid-Atlantic regional adv. coun. Franklin and Marshall Coll., also mem. phys. scis. labs. renovation com., 1996-97; bd. dirs. Surf's Edge Condo Assn., Ocean City, Md., 1995-99; active YMCA, Doylestown, Pa. With U.S. Army, 1956-58. Mem. Doylestown (Pa.) Country Club. Republican. Methodist. Avocations: tennis, golf, bicycling.

OATES, CARL EVERETTE, lawyer, director; b. Harlingen, Tex., Apr. 8, 1931; s. Joseph William and Grace (Watson) O.; m. Eileen Noble Hudnall; children: Carl William, Gregory Carl Hudnall, Patricia O. Chase, Matthew Noble Hudnall. BS, U.S. Naval Acad., 1955; LLB, So. Meth. U., 1962. Bar: Tex. 1962, D.C. 1977, Nebr. 1985. Assoc. Akin, Gump, Strauss, Hauer & Feld, Dallas, 1962-64, ptnr., 1965-91. Asst. atty. gen. State of Texas, 1992-94, spl. coun., Tex. Dept. Banking, 1994-95, prin. Carl E. Oates, P.C. Chmn. bd. trustees S.W. Mus. Sci. and Tech., Dallas; v.p. S.W. Sci. Mus. Found., Dallas; bd. dirs. Kiwanis Wesley Dental Ctr., Inc., Dallas; pres. Wesley Dental Found., Dallas. Lt. USN, 1955-59. Mem. ABA, D.C. Bar Assn., Tex. Bar Assn., Dallas Bar Assn., Barristers, Northwood Club, Delta Theta Phi. E-mail: coates00@aol.com.

OATES, CYNTHIA ANNE, public relations executive; b. Clarksburg, W.Va., Oct. 21, 1940; d. John Baptiste and Norma Marie (Hessom) Molle; m. William Robert Oates Sr., Feb. 29, 1964; 1 child, William Robert Jr. BS in Journalism, W.Va. U., 1962. Reporter Clarksburg (W.Va.) Exponent, 1961, Virginian Pilot, Norfolk, 1962; city editor Morning Herald, Hagerstown, Md., 1962-72; pub. rels. cons. Johns Hopkins Rsch. Ctr., 1974-75; info. officer Homewood Retirement Ctrs., Williamsport, Md., 1982-86; sr. staff writer Pa. Electric Co., Johnstown, Pa., 1986-88; mgr. corp. comm. CSX/Sea-Land Intermodal, Balt., 1988-89; dir. pub. info. Johns Hopkins Rsch. Ctr., Hagerstown, 1989; owner Comm. Initiatives, Williamsport, 1990—. Vol., bd. dirs. United Way, Hagerstown; bd. dirs. Easter Seals. Mem. Pub. Rels. Soc. Am. (accredited), Exch. Club. Presbyterian. Avocations: tennis, piano, golf. Home and Office: PO Box 1617 Hedgesville WV 25427 E-mail: caoates@erols.com.

OATES, ELIZABETH WOODS, physician, psychiatrist; b. New Haven, May 3, 1958; d. John Francis and Rosemary (Walsh) O.; m. John Shangkyun Shin, Mar. 24, 1995; children: Catherine, Alexandra. BA cum laude, Duke U., 1980; MD cum laude, Loyola U., Maywood, Ill., 1993. Diplomate in psychiatry Am. Bd. Psychiatry and Neurology. Resident in psychiatry Tripler Army Med. Ctr., Honolulu, 1993-97, chief resident, 1996-97, asst. chief inpatient psychiat. svc., 1997-98; chief Cmty. Mental Health Svcs., Ft. Sill, Okla., 1998—. Contbr. articles to profl. jours. Maj. U.S. Army, 1984—. Recipient Janet M. Glascow Meml. citation Am. Med. Women's Assn., 1993, Physician Recognition award AMA, 1994. Mem. Am. Psychiat. Assn., Alpha Omega Alpha. Democrat. Episcopalian. Office: Cmty Ptnrs in Mental Health Care 1502 W Hwy 54 Durham NC 27707

OATES, JOHN ALEXANDER , III, medical educator; b. Fayetteville, N.C., Apr. 23, 1932; s. John Alexander and Isabelle (Crowder) O.; m. Meredith Stringfield, June 12, 1956; children: David Alexander, Christine Larkin, James Caldwell. BS magna cum laude, Wake Forest Coll., 1953; MD, Bowman Gray Sch. Medicine, 1956. Intern, asst. resident medicine N.Y. Hosp.-Cornell U. Med. Center, N.Y.C., 1956-58, 61-62; from clin. assoc. to sr. investigator Nat. Heart Inst., 1958-63; faculty Vanderbilt U. Sch. Medicine, Nashville, 1963—, prof. medicine and pharmacology, 1969—, Werthan prof. investigative medicine, 1974-84, chmn. dept. medicine, 1983-97, Thomas F. Frist Sr. prof. medicine, 1984—. Drug research bd. Nat. Acad. Scis.-NRC, 1967-71; chmn. pharmacology and toxicology tng. com. Nat. Inst. Gen. Med. Scis., 1969-70; mem . adv. coun. Nat. Heart, Lung and Blood Inst., 1985-89. Master ACP; fellow Am. Acad. Arts and Scis., 1996; mem. Am. Fedn. Clin. Rsch. (pres. 1970-71), Am. Soc. Clin. Investigation (v.p. 1976-77), Assn. Am. Physicians (pres. 1981-82), Am. Soc. Pharmacology and Exptl. Therapeutics (chmn. exec. com. divsn. clin. pharmacology 1967-69), Inst. of Medicine. Achievements include participation in discovery of antihypertensive effect of methyldopa, elucidation of a number of interactions between drugs in man; research on the biochemistry and pathophysiology of eicosanoids. Home: 2032 Sunset Hills Terr Nashville TN 37215 Office: Vanderbilt Med Ctr 536 RRB Nashville TN 37232-0001 E-mail: john.oates@mcmail.vanderbilt.edu.

OATES, JOHN FRANCIS, classics educator; b. Holyoke, Mass., Aug. 7, 1934; s. William Adrian and Lilian (Woods) O.; m. Rosemary Walsh, June 27, 1957; children: Elizabeth, Emily, John Francis, Sarah. BA, Yale U., 1956, MA, 1958, PhD, 1960; postgrad. (Fulbright fellow), Am. Sch. Classical Studies in Athens, Greece, 1956-57. Instr. classics Yale U., 1960-63, asst. prof., 1963-67; asso. prof. ancient history Duke U., 1967-71, prof., 1971—, chmn. dept. classical studies, 1971-80, chmn. humanities coun., 1975-80, dir. database of documentary papyri, 1982—, dir. papyrus catalog project, 1992-95. Hon. rsch. asst. Univ. Coll. London, 1965-66; vis. prof. Smith Coll., Northampton, Mass., 1967, 68; mem. mng. com. Intercollegiate Ctr. Classical Studies in Rome, Italy, 1972-77, Am. Sch. Classical Studies in Athens, 1973—, mem. com. on coms., 1975-77; mem. Coun. for Internat. Exch. of Scholars, 1974-77; v.p., trustee Triangle Univs. Ctr. for Advanced Study, Inc., 1975-90; trustee Nat. Humanities Ctr., 1977-90, trustee emeritus, 1990—; adv. coun. Sch. Classical Studies, Am. Acad. in Rome, 1976—; dir. summer seminar Nat. Endowment Humanities, 1978; dir. Nat. Fedn. State Humanities Couns., 1980-83; mem. N.C. Humanities Com., 1977-83, chmn. 1980-82. Author: The Status Designation, 1963 (with A.E. Samuel and C.B. Welles) Yale Papyri in the Beinecke Library, 1967, A Checklist of Papyrological Editions, 5th edit., 2001, (with Willis) Duke Data Bank of Documentary, Papyri (CD-ROM), 1996, The Basilikos Grammateus, 1995; mem. adv. bd. Greek, Roman and Byzantine Studies, 1977—, Humanities Report, 1981-83. ACLS fellow, 1973-74 Mem. Am. Philol. Assn. (chmn. com. computer activities 1974-75, dir. 1975-78, mem. nominating com. 1980-83), Archaeol. Inst. Am., Am. Hist. Assn., Am. Soc. Papyrologists (v.p. 1971-73, pres. 1976-80, dir.), Assn. Internationale de Papyrologues, Classical Assn. Middle West and South (v.p. 1972-74, pres. So. sect. 1974-76). Home: 843 Inglenook Rd Durham NC 27707-3961 Office: Duke U Dept Classical Studies Durham NC 27708-0103 Fax: 919-681-4262. E-mail: joates@duke.edu.

OATES, JOHNNY LANE, former professional baseball team manager; b. Sylva, N.C., Jan. 21, 1946; BS in Health and Phys. Edn., Va. Tech. U. Player minor league team Chgo. White Sox, 1967, Balt. Orioles, 1967-71, player, 1970, 72, mgr. minor league team, 1988, coach, 1989-91, mgr., 1991-94; player Atlanta Braves, 1973-75, Phila. Phillies, 1975-76, L.A. Dodgers, 1977-79, N.Y. Yankees, 1980, minor league coach, 1981-83; coach Chgo. Cubs, 1984-87; mgr. Texas Rangers, 1994—. Named Internat. League Mgr. of Yr., 1988, coach Am. League All-Star Team, 1993, 95, Am. League Mgr. of the Year by The Sporting News, 1993, 96, co Am. League Mgr. of the Year by Baseball Writers' Assn. of Am., 1996.*

OATES, JOYCE CAROL, author; b. Lockport, N.Y., June 16, 1938; d. Frederic James and Caroline (Bush) O.; m. Raymond Joseph Smith, Jan. 23, 1961. BA, Syracuse U., 1960; MA, U. Wis., 1961. Instr. English U. Detroit, 1961-65, asst. prof., 1965-67; prof. English U. Windsor, Ont., Can., 1967-87; writer-in-residence Princeton (N.J.) U., 1978-81, prof., 1987—. Author: (short story collections) By the North Gate, 1963, Upon the Sweeping Flood, 1966, The Wheel of Love, 1970, Marriages and Infidelities, 1972, The Hungry Ghosts, 1974, The Goddess and Other Women, 1974, Where Are You Going, Where Have You Been?: Stories of Young America, 1974, The Poisoned Kiss and Other Stories From the Portuguese, 1975, The Seduction and Other Stories, 1975, Crossing the Border, 1976, Night-Side, 1977, All the Good People I've Left Behind, 1978, The Lamb of Abyssalia, 1980, A Sentimental Education: Stories, 1981, Last Days: Stories, 1984, Wild Nights, 1985, Raven's Wing: Stories, 1986, The Assignation, 1988, Heat: And Other Stories, 1991, Where is Here?, 1992, Haunted: Tales of the Grotesque, 1994, Will You Always Love Me? and Other Stories, 1995; (novels) With Shuddering Fall, 1964, A Garden of Earthly Delights, 1967 (Nat. Book award nomination 1968), Expensive People, 1967 (Nat. Book award nomination 1969), them, 1969 (Nat. Book award for fiction 1970), Wonderland, 1971, Do With Me What You Will, 1973, The Assassins, 1975, Childwold, 1976, The Triumph of the Spider Monkey, 1976, Son of the Morning, 1978, Unholy Loves, 1979, Cybele, 1979, Bellefleur, 1980 (L.A. Times Book award nomination 1980), A Sentimental Education, 1981, Angel of Light, 1981, A Bloodsmoor Romance, 1982, Mysteries of Winterthurn, 1984, Solstice, 1985, Marya, 1986, You Must Remember This, 1987, (as Rosamond Smith) The Lives of the Twins, 1987, American Appetites, 1989, (as Rosamond Smith) Soul-Mate, 1989, Because It Is Bitter, and Because It Is My Heart, 1990, (as Rosamond Smith) Nemesis, 1990, I Lock My Door Upon Myself, 1990, The Rise of Life on Earth, 1991, Black Water, 1992, (as Rosamond Smith) Snake Eyes, 1992, Foxfire: Confessions of a Girl Gang, 1993, What I Lived For, 1994 (PEN/Faulkner award nomination 1995) The Barrens, 2001, Faithless: Tails of Transgression, 2001, Middle Age: A Romance, 2001, Big Mouth and Ugly Girl, 2002; (poetry collections) Women in Love, 1968, Expensive People, 1968, Anonymous Sins, 1969, Love and Its Derangements, 1970, Angel Fire, 1973, Dreaming America, 1973, The Fabulous Beasts, 1975, Season of Peril, 1977, Women Whose Lives are Food, Men Whose Lives are Money: Poems, 1978, The Stepfather, 1978, Celestial Timepiece, 1981, Invisible Women: New and Selected Poems, 1970-1972, 1982, Luxury of Sin, 1983, The Time Traveller, 1987; (plays) The Sweet Enemy, 1965, Sunday Dinner, 1970, Ontological Proof of My Existence, 1970, Miracle Play, 1974, Three Plays, 1980, Daisy, 1980, Presque Isle, 1984, Triumph of the Spider Monkey, 1985, In Darkest America, 1990, I Stand Before You Naked, 1990, The Perfectionist and Other Plays, 1995; (essays) The Edge of Impossibility, 1972, The Hostile Sun: The Poetry of D.H. Lawrence, 1973, New Heaven, New Earth, 1974, Contraries: Essays, 1981, The Profane Art, 1984, On Boxing, 1987, (Woman) Writer: Occasions and Opportunities, 1988; editor, compiler: Scenes from American Life: Contemporary Short Fiction, 1973, (with Shannon Ravenel) Best American Short Stories of 1979, 1979, Night Walks, 1982, First Person Singular: Writer's on Their Craft, 1983, (with Boyd Litzinger) Story: Fictions Past and Present, 1985, (with Daniel Halpern) Reading and Fights, 1988, The Oxford Book of American Short Stories, 1992, The Sophisticated Cat: An Anthology, 1992; editor (with Raymond Smith) Ontario Rev.; contbr. to nat. mags. including N.Y. Times Book Rev., Mich. Quarterly Rev., Mademoiselle, Vogue, North Am. Rev., Hudson Rev., Paris Rev., Grand Street, Atlantic, Poetry, Esquire. Recipient O. Henry award, 1967, 73, Rosenthal award Nat. Inst. Arts and Letters, 1968, O. Henry Spl. award continuing achievement, 1970, 86, Award of Merit Lotos Club, 1975, St. Louis Lit. award, 1988, Rea award for the Short Story, 1990, Alan Swallow award for fiction, 1990, Nobel Prize in Lit. nomination, 1993; Guggenheim fellow, 1967-68, Nat. Endowment for the Arts grantee, 1966, 68. Mem. Am. Acad. and Inst. Arts and Letters. Office: care John Hawkins 71 W 23rd St Ste 1600 New York NY 10010-4102 also: Princeton U Dept Creative Writing 117 185 Nassau St Princeton NJ 08544-0001*

OATES, JOYCE MARIE, psychiatrist; b. Salt Lake City, Mar. 31, 1948; d. Douglas Francis and Lois Joy (Allgaier) O. BS magna cum laude, U. Utah, 1970, MD, 1974. Diplomate Am. Bd. Psychiatry and Neurology. Intern Pa. Hosp., Phila., 1974-75; resident in psychiatry Inst. of Pa. Hosp., 1975-78; physician Intensive Treatment unit Copper Mountain Community Mental Health Ctr., Salt Lake City, 1978-79; pvt. practice psychiatry, 1980-88; med. dir. psychiatry Yuma (Ariz.) Reg. Med. Ctr., 1988-90; psychiatrist locum tenens CompHealth, Salt Lake City, 1990; pvt. practice psychiatrist Las Vegas, 1990—; med. dir. Cinnamon Hills residential treatment, 1993—; med. dir., part owner Vista Treatment Ctr., St. George, Utah, 1995-96; med. dir. RedRock Canyon Sch., 1999-2000. Mem. Latter Day Saints. Avocations: writing, weaving, spinning.

OATES, MARY ELIZABETH, radiologist; b. Boston, June 20, 1954; d. Robert George Oates and Joan Marie (Artesani) Snelling; m. Donald Edloe Winfrey, Sept. 13, 1981; children: Victoria Joan, Olivia Kathryn, Cecilia Jeanne. AB summa cum laude, Smith Coll., 1976; MD, Boston U., 1985. Diplomate in radiology and nuc. radiology Am. Bd. Radiology. Chief div. nuclear medicine New England Med. Ctr., Boston, 1986—2001; head sect. nuc. radiology Boston Med. Ctr., 2002—. Prof. radiology Tufts U. Sch. Medicine, Boston, 1986-2001, Boston U., 2002–; examiner Am. Bd. Radiology, Louisville, 1995—. Mem. Am. Assn. Women Radiologists, Radiol. Soc. N.Am., Soc. Nuc. Medicine. Office: Boston Med Ctr Nuclear Radiology 88 E Newton St Boston MA 02118 E-mail: elizabeth.oates@bmc.org.

OATES, SHERRY CHARLENE, portraitist, artist, photographer; b. Houston, Sept. 11, 1946; d. Charles Emil and Berniece Faye (Lohse) O. Student, North Tex. State U., 1965-66; student under Martin Kellogg; BA in English, Health and Phys. Edn., Houston Bapt. U., 1968. Cert. art tchr., Tex. Tchr. Jackson Jr. High Sch., Houston, 1968-69, Percy Priest Sch., Nashville, 1969-70, Franklin (Tenn.) High Sch., 1970-84; freelance illustrator Bapt. Sunday Sch. Bd., Nashville, 1978-85, United Meth. Pub. House, Nashville, 1980-85; portraitist in oils, owner Portraits, Ltd., 1984—. Portraits include corp. leaders, educators, politicians, hist. and equestrian subjects, society figures and children; participated in various exhbns. at Bapt. Sunday Sch. Bd. and All State and Ctr. South Exhibits at the Parthenon. Recipient 3d place in graphics Ctrl. South Exhbn. at The Parthenon-Tenn. Art League, 1986. Mem. Tenn. Art League. Republican. Baptist. Avocation: antiques. Studio: 816 Kirkwood Ave Nashville TN 37204-2602

OATES, STEPHEN BAERY, history educator; b. Pampa, Tex., Jan. 5, 1936; s. Steve Theodore and Florence (Baer) O.; divorced; children: Gregory Allen, Stephanie; m. Marie Phillips. BA magna cum laude, U. Tex., 1958, MA, 1960, PhD, 1968; Litt.D. (hon.), Lincoln Coll., 1981. Prof. history U. Mass., Amherst, 1971—, now also Paul Murray Kendall prof. biography, adj. prof. English, 1980—. Author: Confederate Cavalry West of the River, 1961, Rip Ford's Texas, 1963, Republic of Texas, 1968, Visions of Glory, 1970, To Purge This Land With Blood: A Biography of John Brown, 1970, Portrait of America, 2 vols., 1973, rev. edits., 1976, 83, 86, 90, 94, The Fires of Jubilee: Nat Turner's Fierce Rebellion, 1975, With Malice Toward None: The Life of Abraham Lincoln (Christopher award for outstanding lit., Barondess/Lincoln award N.Y. Civil War Round Table 1977), Our Fiery Trial: Abraham Lincoln, John Brown, and the Civil War Era, 1979, Let the Trumpet Sound: The Life of Martin Luther King, Jr., 1982 (Christopher award, Robert F. Kennedy Meml. Book award), Abraham Lincoln, The Man Behind the Myths, 1984, Biography as High Adventure: Life Writers Speak on Their Art, 1986, William Faulkner: The Man and the Artist, 1987, A Woman of Valor: Clara Barton and the Civil War, 1994, The Approaching Fury: Voices of the Storm, 1820-1861, 1997, The Whirlwind of War: Voices of the Storm, 1861-1865, 1998; contbr. articles and essays to periodicals; lectr. Presdl. Writers award, 1985; Master Tchr. award U. Hartford, 1985; Silver Medal award Case Council for Advance and Support of Edn., Prof. of Yr., 1986, 87, Kidger award New Eng. History Tchrs. Assn., Nevins-Freeman award Chgo. Civil War Round Table, 1993; Guggenheim fellow, 1972; sr. summer fellow NEH, 1978. Fellow Tex. State Hist. Assn.; mem. Tex. Inst. Letters, Soc. Am. Historians, Am. Antiquarian Soc., Phi Beta Kappa. Office: U Mass Dept History Amherst MA 01003 E-mail: sbo@history.umass.edu.

OATES, TRICIA B. music educator; b. St. Louis, Mar. 5, 1970; Student, Washington U., St. Louis, 1988-89; MusB, So. Ill. U. of Edwardsville, 1992, MMus, 1994. Ednl. initiatives mgr. KFUO-FM Classic 99, St. Louis, 1995—; organist Florissant Valley Christian Ch., 1992—; pvt. piano tchr. Edwardsville, Ill., 1991-95. Adj. faculty/grad. asst. So. Ill. U., Edwardsville, 1992-94; judge NAACP, Afro-Acad., Cultural, Technol. and Sci. Olympic ACT-SO Competition, St. Louis, 1996; role model, St. Louis Pub. Schs., 1996—. Creator/coord. music edn. materials for youth: Symphony Kids. Pres. bd. dirs. United Christian Found., Edwardsville, 1996-97. Mem. Music Tchrs. Nat. Assn., Edn. Dirs. Arts Round Table, Phi Kappa Phi, Pi Kappa Lambda. Office: KFUO-FM Classic 99 85 Founders Ln Saint Louis MO 63105-3059

OATES, WALLACE EUGENE, economics educator; b. L.A., Mar. 21, 1937; s. Eugene A. and Irene G. (Young) O.; m. Mary Irby, Sept. 6, 1959 (div. 1976); children: Catherine, Christopher, Mary Nora; m. Grace Mary Garry, Jan. 13, 1979. MA, Stanford U., 1959, PhD in Econs., 1965. Asst. prof. econs. Princeton (N.J.) U., 1965-71, assoc. prof. econs., 1971-75, prof. econs., 1975-79, U. Md., College Park, 1979—. Cons. economist European Econ. Community, Brussels, 1976, OECD, Paris, 1982-84, 91-92, Nat. Oceanic and Atmospheric Adminstrn., Washington, 1980-81, NSF, Washington, 1983-84, U.S. EPA, Washington, 1992—. Author: Fiscal Federalism, 1972, Studies in Fiscal Federalism, 1991; co-author: The Theory of Environmental Policy, 1975, Introduction to Econometrics, 1974, Economics, Environmental Policy and the Quality of Life, 1979; editor: The Economics of the Environment, 1992. Lt. USNR, 1959-62, Italy. Sr. Fulbright-Hays rsch. scholar, London, 1974-75, John Simon Guggenheim Fellow, London, 1974-75, scholar-in-residence, Resources for the Future, Washington, 1985-86. Fellow Resources for the Future; mem. Am. Econ. Assn., So. Econ. Assn. (pres. 1993-94), Ea. Econ. Assn. (pres. 1989-90), Royal Econ. Soc. Office: U Md Dept Econs College Park MD 20742-0001

OATES, WILLIAM ARMSTRONG, JR. investment company executive; b. Pitts., July 27, 1942; s. William Armstrong and Margaret (Nichols) O.; m. Elizabeth Dick Macy, Sept. 7, 1968; children: Elizabeth N., Katherine M., Emily E.A. BA, Colby Coll., 1965; MBA, Harvard U., 1972. Asst. treas. Morgan Guaranty Trust, N.Y.C., 1966-70; trustee, dir. Northeast Investors Trust, Boston, 1972—; pres. Northeast Investors Growth Fund, 1980—; ptnr. Guild, Monrad & Oates, Inc., 1984—. Dir. Horn Corp., Ayer, Mass., Furman

Lumber Co., Boston, Clifford Inc., Bethel, Vt. Pres. bd. trustees Groton (Mass.) Sch., 1979; trustee, treas. Roxbury Latin Sch., West Roxbury, Mass., 1975—. Served to 2d lt. Army N.G., 1966-70. Mem.: Harvard (Boston); Brookline Country (Brookline, Mass.); Somerset (Boston). Republican. Episcopalian. Home: 201 Village Ave Dedham MA 02026-4230 Office: Guild, Monrad & Oates Inc 50 Congress St Boston MA 02109-4002

OATWAY, FRANCIS CARLYLE, corporate executive; b. Bermuda, Nov. 29, 1936; s. Charles Y. and Josephine (McLellan) O.; m. Ann Thomason; children— Stephen F., Karen E., Andrew C., Christopher M. BSBA, Boston Coll., 1960. CPA, Mass., N.Y., others. With Deloitte Haskins & Sells, N.Y.C., 1960-80, ptnr., 1970-80; v.p. taxation Continental Group, Inc., Stamford, Conn., 1980-81, v.p. treasury and taxation, 1981-82, v.p. fin., 1982-83, v.p., chief fin. officer, 1983; exec. v.p., pres., dir. Continental Forest Industries, Inc., 1984-85; pres. Hargro Assocs., S. Pomfret, Vt., 1985—; pres., CEO, dir. Hargro Enterprises, Inc., 1985—. Chmn., CEO, bd. dirs. NER Data Products, Glassboro, N.J., 1985—; pres., bd. dirs. Covent Ins. Co. Ltd., Hamilton, Bermuda, 1980-85; chmn. bd., mng. dir. CCC Finanz A.G., Zug, Switzerland, 1980-85; mng. dir. Continental Group Overseas Fin. N.V., Curacao, Netherlands Antilles, 1981-85; bd. dirs. Juecia Ins. Co. Am., Tarrytown, N.Y., chmn. bd. Apple Syndicate Corp., Westport, Conn., 1983-85. Contbg. editor: Federal Income Taxation of Banks and Financial Institutions, 1968, Professional Responsibility in Federal Tax Practice, 1970; contbr. articles to fin. jours. Trustee Convent of Sacred Heart, Greenwich, Conn., 1979-83; mem. acctg. adv. bd. Columbia U. Grad. Sch. Bus., N.Y.C., 1982-86; mem. exec. com. Boston Coll. Wall St. Coun., 1989-2002; trustee Conn. Pub. Expenditure Coun., Inc., Hartford, 1984-85; mem. pres.'s adv. bd. Weston Sch. Theology, Cambridge, 1993-99. Mem. Woodstock Country Club, Orchid Island Golf and Beach Club, Quail Valley Golf Club (Fla.) Roman Catholic. Also: Hargro Assocs PO Box 62 South Pomfret VT 05067-0062

O'BAIRE, MARIKA, pediatrics nurse, educator; b. Manila, The Philippines, Oct. 3, 1947; d. Gerald John and Giovanna (BelForti) Barry; children: Matthew, Alexei, Rita, D. Patrick. Student, U. Conn., 1964-65; diploma, Ellis Hosp. Sch. Nursing, 1977; BSN, Russell Sage Coll., 1980, postgrad., 1983, 94; grad. ontological design, Logonet Inc. ODC-J, 1993; postgrad. in humanities, Calif. State U., Dominguez Hills, 1995—; postgrad., Univ. Dundee, 2000—. RN, N.Y.; lic. Avatar Master/Wizard. English tchr. Lang. Inst., Taipei, Taiwan, 1971-73; team leader, staff nurse in acute psychiatry Samaritan Hosp., Troy, N.Y., 1978-80; staff nurse, pediatric ICU Albany (N.Y.) Med. Ctr., 1980-84, 97—; rsch. nurse Commn. on Quality Care for Mentally Disabled, Albany, 1984; staff nurse Columbia-Greene Med. Ctr., Catskill, N.Y., 1984-89; night charge nurse Conifer Park, Scotia, 1991-92; nursing educator St. Clare's Hosp., Schenectady, 1992-96; adjunct clin. educator Albany Med. Ctr. So. Vt. Coll., Bennington, 1997—2001. Philosophy coaching Cmty. Hospice Saratoga, N.Y., 1998—; founder Future Design: Create What You Prefer, Avatar Tech. & Skills, 2000; Favorite Nurses, Colunie, N.Y., 2002—. : publ., poet, lit. writer, screenwriter, : comml. artist Echo Mag. Vol. curriculum designer in gifted and talented programs; mem. Red Cross Disaster Team. Mem. Amnesty Internat. Childreach Plan Internat., Upstate Independent Filmakers/Screenwriters, Thorobred Toastmasters. Home and Office: PO Box 5102 90 Lincoln Ave Saratoga Springs NY 12866-3505 E-mail: mobaire@earthlink.net.

OBAMOGIE, MERCY A. physician; b. Lagos, Nigeria, Jan. 18, 1954; d. Godwin I and Janet E. (Amiolemen) O.; m. Abiodun O. Odunmbaku, June 20, 1980 (div. 1995); children: Abisola, Adenike, Abiodun. BS, Columbia U., 1980; MD, U. Medicine and Dentistry N.J., Piscataway, 1984; MPH, Johns Hopkins U., 1987; MBA, U. Calif., Irvine, 2000. Diplomate Am. Bd. Family Practice, Nat. Bd. Med. Examiners. Intern in internal medicine Muhlenberg Hosp., Plainfield, N.J., 1984-85; resident in gen. preventive medicine Johns Hopkins U., Balt., 1985-86; resident in family practice Georgetown U./Providence Hosp., Washington, 1986-89; pvt. practice Washington, Greenbelt, Md., 1989—; med. dir. Doctors Slim and Fitness Ctr., Greenbelt, 1996-98. Med. adv. bd. Metra Health Ins. Co., 1992-94; utilization com. Aetna Ins. Co., 1993-95, credentialing com., 1996; med. adv. com. United Health-Care, 1997; mem. planning com. Providence Hosp., Washington, 1996-98; with Prince George's Hosp. Ctr., Cheverly, Md., Howard U. Hosp., Washington, Doctors Cmty. Hosp., Lanham, Md., Providence Hosp., Washington; pres., med. dir. Mercy Med. Ctr., Benin City, Nigeria, 1996—; pres., CEO ASAKI Corp., Greenbelt, Md., 2000—. Contbr. articles to profl. jours. Home: 25 Atwood Ct Silver Spring MD 20906-2089 Office: 7323 Hanover Pkwy Ste A Greenbelt MD 20770-3617 E-mail: aimmercy@aol.com.

O'BANNION, MINDY MARTHA MARTIN, nurse; b. Cushing, Okla., Aug. 19, 1953; d. John William and Martha Florence (Vineyard) Martin; children: Mindi Martha Mae, William Neale Aaron. Student, Okla. State U., 1971-73, Oscar Rose Jr. Coll., 1973; grad., St. Anthony Sch. Nursing, 1975. RN, Tex. Med. clk. Martin Clinic, Cushing, Okla., 1968-72; nursing asst. Cushing Mcpl. Hosp., 1973-75, head nurse surg. fl., 1975-76, charge nurse med. unit, 1978-79, 82-83; staff nurse Met. Hosp., Dallas, 1985; staff nurse med. unit Mesquite (Tex.) Cmty. Hosp., 1985-87; nurse post partum unit, breastfeeding and discharge educator post partum unit Trinity Med. Ctr. Tenet Healthcare System, Carrollton, Tex., 1987—. Ind. beauty cons. Mary Kay Cosmetics, Dallas, Tex., 1993-99. Social com. Royal Haven Bapt. Ch. Women's Missionary Union, Dallas, 1977-78; mem. extension dept. nursery First Bapt. Ch., Cushing, 1979-82, extension dept. presch., 1982-84; mem. extension dept. presch. Royal Haven Bapt. Ch., Dallas, 1986-87; active Montgomery Elem. Sch. PTA, Farmers Branch, Tex., 1986-94, Vivian Field Jr. H.S. PTA, Farmers Branch, 1993-97, Valwood Park Bapt. Ch., Farmers Branch, 1994-2002, R.L. Turner H.S. PTA, R.L. Turner H.S. Orch. Booster Club, 1995-2001, Farmers Branch/Carrollton, 1995-2001, Prestonwood Bapt. Ch., Plano, Tex., 2002-; treas., nominating com. Joyce Harms group Women's Missionary Union; clk., charter mem. Brookhaven Bapt. Ch., Farmers Branch, 1989-92. Mem. Am., Tex., Okla. State Nurses Assns., St. Anthony Hosp. Sch. Nursing Alumnae, Bluebonnet Shelties (founder), Tau Beta Sigma (Alpha chpt.), Alpha Xi Delta (epsilon Omicron chpts. corr. sec. 1973). Baptist. Home: 13505 Onyx Ln Dallas TX 75234-4912

O'BANNON, DEBORAH JEAN, civil engineering educator; b. Nurnburg, Germany, Dec. 4, 1956; came to U.S., 1958; d. William James and Emily Wilhemina (Mead) McKechnie; m. Craig James Mossman, July 16, 1988 (div. May 1995); m. Daniel Patrick O'Bannon, July 20, 1996. BSCE, MIT, 1979; M Engring., Manhattan Coll., 1983; PhD, U. Iowa, 1988. Registered profl. engr., Iowa, Kans., Mo. Jr. sanitary engr. Dept. Environ. Quality Engring., Westborough, Mass., 1979-81, sr. sanitary engr., 1981-83, prin. sanitary engr., 1983-84; asst. prof. U. Mo.-Columbia, Kansas City, 1989-95, assoc. prof., 1995-2000, U. Mo., Kansas City, 2001—. Cons. Fayette (Mo.) Environ. Svcs., 1997-2000. Contbr. articles to profl. jours. Am. fellow AAUW, 1987; recipient Eminent Engr. award Tau Beta Pi, 1996. Fellow: Soc. Women Engrs. (bd. dirs. 1995—97, editl. bd. 2000—); mem.: ASCE, Am. Soc. Engring. Eductators. Libertarian. Avocations: cooking, gardening, sewing, opera, evangelism. Office: U Mo Dept Civil Engring 5100 Rockhill Rd Kansas City MO 64110-2481 E-mail: obannon@alum.mit.edu.

O'BANNON, DON TELLA, JR. lawyer; b. Ft. Eustous, Va., Feb. 16, 1957; s. Don T. and Doris (Salone) O'B.; children: Danielle, Dionne. BA, Dartmouth Coll., 1979; JD, U. Va., 1982. Bar: Tex. 1982, U.S. Dist. Ct. (so. dist.) 1984, (no. dist.) 1987, (we. dist.) 1989, (ea. dist.) 1992, U.S. Ct. Appeals (5th cir.) 1989. Law clk. to hon. Gabrielle K. McDonald, judge U.S. Dist. Ct. (so. dist.) Tex., Houston, 1982-84; assoc. Fulbright & Jaworski, 1984-87; sr. assoc. Bickel & Brewer, Dallas, 1987-88; ptnr. Arter & Hadden, 1988-94; of counsel Robinson & West, 1994-95; divsn. chief bus. litigation Dallas Area Rapid Transit, 1995-97; prin. Bell & Nunnally, PLLC, Dallas, 1997—. Contbr. articles to profl. jours. Treas. Judge Victoria Welcome Re-election campaign, Dallas, 1989-90; bd. dirs. Dallas Park & Recreation, 1992-93; mem. Coun. on Child Abuse and Neglect Prevention, Austin, 1989-93; chmn. Moorland YMCA, 1990-94, Dallas Black Dance Theater, 1990—. Named Vol. of Yr. Moorland YMCA, 1989. Mem. Dallas Bar Assn., State Bar of Tex. Office: Bell & Nunnally PLLC 2504 Aaron Cir Dallas TX 75233-4002

O'BANNON, FRANK LEWIS, governor, lawyer; b. Louisville, Jan. 30, 1930; s. Robert Pressley and Rosella Faith (Dropsey) O'B.; m. Judith Mae Asmus, Aug. 18, 1957; children: Polly, Jennifer, Jonathan. AB, Ind. U., 1952, JD, 1957. Ind. 1957. Pvt. practice, Corydon; ptnr. Hays, O'Bannon & Funk, 1966-80, O'Bannon, Funk & Simpson, Corydon, 1980-88; mem. Ind. Senate, 1970-89, minority floor leader, 1979-89, asst. minority floor leader, 1972-76; lt. gov. State of Ind., 1989-97, gov., 1997—. Chmn., dir. O'Bannon Pub. Co., Inc.; chair Dem. Gov.'s Assn., 1999. Served with USAF, 1952-54. Mem. Ind. Dem. Editorial Assn. (pres. 1961), Am. Judicature Soc., Am. Bar Assn., Ind. Bar Assn. Democrat. Methodist. Office: Office of the Gov State Capitol Rm 206 Indianapolis IN 46204

O'BANNON, JACQUELINE MICHELE, geriatrics and mental health nurse; b. Southampton, N.Y., Feb. 13, 1947; d. John Andrew Koval and Genevieve Cecelia Ryder; children: Christopher, Timothy. AAS in Nursing, SUNY, Farmingdale, 1967; student, Suffolk Community Coll., Brentwood, N.Y., 1990—, Stony Brook (N.Y.) U., 1990, St. Joseph's Sch., Patchogue, N.Y., 1991—. Cert. gerontol. nurse. Pvt. duty nurse Brightman Agy., East Islip, N.Y., 1971-83; charge nurse Kings Park (N.Y.) Psychiat. Ctr., 1983-91; admission acut unit Charter Hosp., Jackson, Miss., 91-94, St. Catherines Village, Madison, 1994-98; charge nurse Bethany Health Care, Framingham, Mass., 1999—. Mem. AIDS curriculum com., sexual abuse prevention com., 1987-91; mem. policy bd. Brentwood Tchr. Ctr., 1987-91; mem. evaluation and accountability com. Brentwood Dist., 1990. Mem. Madison chpt. Am. Cancer Soc., Madison County Ednl. Found. for Excellence. Mem. Nat. Sch. Bd. Assn., N.Y. Sch. Bd. Assn., Kings Park Nurses Assn., Suffolk County Orgn. Promotion Edn. Office: Bethany Health Care 97 Bethany Rd Framingham MA 01702-7237

O'BARR, BOBBY GENE, SR. lawyer; b. Houston, May 5, 1932; s. Walter Morris and Maggie (Whitt) O'B.; children: Morris Clayton, William Clinton, Candace Jean, Bobby G.; m. Jennifer Ryals, Dec. 5, 1984; 1 child, Richard. BA, U. Miss., 1959, JD, 1958. Bar: Miss. 1958, U.S. Dist. Ct. (no. dist.) Miss. 1958, U.S. Dist. Ct. (so. dist.) Miss. 1966, U.S. Ct. Appeals (5th cir.) 1970, U.S. Supreme Ct. 1971. Pvt. practice, Houston, 1958-59; assoc. W.M. O'Barr, Jr., Okolona, Miss., 1959-60; adminstrv. judge Miss. Workmen's Compensation Commn., 1960-65; assoc. Cumbest, Cumbest, O'Barr and Shaddock, Pascagoula, Miss., 1965-68, Hurlbert & O'Barr, O'Barr, Hurlbert and O'Barr, Biloxi, 1968-80; pvt. practice, owner Bobby G. O'Barr, P.A., 1980—. Mem., pres. Biloxi Port Commn., 1975-90; mem. mgmt. coun. Gulf Mex. Fishery, 1979-82. With USAF, 1951-54. Mem. VFW, State Bar Found., Southeastern Admiralty Law Inst., Miss. Trial Lawyers Assn., Am. Legion, Masons, Shriners. Office: PO Box 541 Biloxi MS 39533-0541

OBASEKI, LOVETTE I. consulting company executive, systems analyst; b. July 4, 1953; d. Samson O. Amba A. (Okai) O. BS, Fla. A&M U., 1979, MEd, 1984; diploma in systems analysis, NYU, 1989; cert. in small bus. program, Baruch Coll., 1995. Cert. Novell netware engr. Supr. systems adminstrn. Buccellati Ltd., N.Y.C.; systems mgr. JCCA, 1988-95; cons. Binam Cons. Svcs., 1995—; sr. sys. analyst cons. Paragon, N.J., 1996—. Active numerous ch. groups. Recipient Honors awards Fla. A&M U. Mem. NAFE, NOW, AAUW, Assn. Sys. Mgmt. (bd. dirs. 1989—, v.p. 1992-93, Excellence in Sys. Mgmt. award 1994, Outstanding Svc. award 1992-93, Appreciation cert. 1990-91, Honors award), Data Processing Mgmt. Assn., Am. Mgmt. Assn., DAV Comdrs. Club (Bronze Leader 1995). Democrat. Address: PO Box 901026 Far Rockaway NY 11690-1026

OBEAR, FREDERICK WOODS, academic administrator; b. Malden, Mass., June 9, 1935; s. William Fred and Dorothea Louise (Woods) O.; m. Patricia A. Draper, Aug. 30, 1959 (dec. Dec. 1993); children: Jeffrey Allan, Deborah Anne, James Frederick; m. Ruth Crowley Sundell, Feb. 21, 1998. BS with high honors, U. Mass., Lowell, 1956, LHD, 1985; PhD, U. N.H., 1961. Mem. faculty dept. chemistry Oakland U., Rochester, Mich., 1960-81, prof., 1979-81, v.p. for acad. affairs, provost, 1970-81; chancellor U. Tenn., Chattanooga, 1981-97, univ. prof., chancellor emeritus, 1997—. Mem. nat. adv. panel Nat. Commn. on Higher Edn. Issues, 1981; mem. pres. commn. NCAA, 1991-94. Trustee Marygrove Coll., 1973-79. Am. Council Edn. fellow, 1967-68 Mem. AAAS, Am. Assn. State Colls. and Univs. (bd. dirs. 1992-96, chair 1995), Am. Chem. Soc., Am. Assn. Higher Edn., Sigma Xi. Roman Catholic. Office: 417H Fletcher Hall 615 McCallie Ave Chattanooga TN 37403-2504 E-mail: frederick-obear@utc.edu.

O'BEIL, HEDY, artist; b. Bronx, N.Y. d. Leo Gersten and Viola Cymberg; m. Jerome Liebowitz (div. Sept. 1981); children: S. Jay Liebowitz, Josh E. Liebowitz. Student, Traphagen Sch. Art, 1949, Art Students League, 1953-55, Skowhegan Sch. Art, 1958, Bklkyn Mus. Arts, 1961-64; BS, CUNY, 1974; MFA, Goddard Coll., 1976. Art lectr. Art Ctr. of No. N.J., New Milford, 1976—; curator Soho 20 Gallery, N.Y., 1982, Chuck Levitan Gallery, N.Y.C., 1998, Broom St. Gallery, N.Y.C., 1999. Exhbns. include Hofstra U., Hempstead, N.Y., 1965, Nassau C.C., Garden City, N.Y., 1965, Oswego (N.Y.) State Coll., 1969, Heckscher Mus., Huntington, N.Y., 1970, Jacques Seligman Gallery, N.Y.C., 1973, Landmark Gallery, N.Y., 1979, Barbara Ingber Gallery, 1983, Phila. Mus. Art, 1986, Columbus Mus. of Art, 1986, Elaine Benson Gallery, Bridgehampton, N.Y., 1992, Provincetown (Mass.) Artists Assn., 1992, Arlene Bujese Gallery, East Hampton, N.Y., 1993, Katherina Perlowe Gallery, N.Y.C., 1998, Savannah (Ga.) Coll. Art and Design, 1999, La Mama La Galleria, N.Y.C., 2000, Get Real Art Gallery, N.Y.C., 2000, 01, Gallery 2/20, N.Y.C., 2001, Andre Zarre Gallery, N.Y.C., 2002, A.I.R. Gallery, N.Y.C., 2002; art critic Arts Mag., N.Y.C., 1976-85. Recipient 1st pl. award L.I. Artists, Guild Hall, East Hampton, N.Y., 1971, Pen & Brush-Sussman/Stevenson award, 1997, 99, Outstanding Tchrs. award, Art Ctr. of No. N.J., 2000; fellow Yaddo, 1985; scholar Bob Blackburn Printmaking Workshop, 1991; grantee Richard Florsheim Art Fund, 1999. Mem. AICA, ASCA, CAG, N.Y. Artists Equity. Avocations: voice, guitar, piano. Home: 463 West St Apt A1103 New York NY 10014-2040

OBER, PAUL RUSSELL, lawyer; b. Indiana, Pa., Dec. 23, 1945; s. Paul Leo and Florence Elizabeth (Kenly) O.; m. Mary Jo DeSantis, Oct. 3, 1987; children: Joshua P., Michele, Gretchen L., Karl M. BA, Gannon U., 1968; JD, Dickinson U., 1973. Bar: Pa. 1973, U.S. Dist. Ct. (ea. dist.) Pa. 1973. Assoc. Edelman, Schaeffer, Saylor, Readinger & Poore, Reading, Pa., 1973-77; ptnr. Erickson, Ober & Ober, 1977-87, Paul R. Ober & Assocs., Reading, 1987—. Assoc. editor Law Rev. Nat. Moot Court. Dir. Berks County Conservancy, Reading, 1985-94, Montessori Children's Home, Reading, 1992-88, Tulpehocken Youth Orgn., Inc.; pres., dir. Bernville (Pa.) Area Recreation Assn., 1995—. With U.S. Army, 1969-70. Mem. Pa. Bar Assn. (mineral & natural resources com. 1980—, mcpl. law com. 1976—), Berks County Bar Assn., Ducks Unltd. (pres. Middlecreek chpt. 1978-80), Mid. Atlantic Redsetter Club (pres. 1972-80), Nat Redsetter Field Trail Club (pres. 1978-80), Order of Coif, Order of Barristers. Avocations: breeding, training and competing with bird dogs, breeding Tennessee walking horses. Office: 234 N 6th St Reading PA 19601-3300 E-mail: paul@oberandassociates.com.

OBER, ROBERT FAIRCHILD, JR. college president, retired government official; b. Hartford, Conn., June 8, 1935; s. Robert Fairchild and Celia (Mahoney) F.; m. Elizabeth Ann Stone, Aug. 22, 1959; children: Elise, Abigail, Robert III. AB, Princeton U., 1958; JD, Harvard U., 1961; MA in History, Ind. U., 1969. Fgn. svc. officer U.S. Dept. of State, Washington, 1961-87; econ. counselor Am. Embassy, Moscow, 1985-87; dir. devel., alumni sec. Kent (Conn.) Sch., 1987-98; pres. Internat. Coll., Beirut, Lebanon, 1999-2001. Fgn. svc. included assignments in Hamburg, Warsaw, New Delhi, Athens, Washington, Moscow (3 times). Contbr. articles to mags. and newspapers including Washington Post, Christian Sci. Monitor, Cleve. Plain Dealer, Orbis. Trustee Internat. Coll., Beirut, Lebanon, 1987—. Recipient Superior Honor awards, Dept. State, Washington, 1974, 80; named State Dept. fellow Coun. on Fgn. Rels., 1981-82. Episcopalian. Home: 187 West Woods Rd Sharon CT 06069 Office: Internat Coll 850 3d Ave New York NY 10022 E-mail: oberrl@mohawk.net.

OBER, RUSSELL JOHN, JR. lawyer; b. Pitts., June 26, 1948; s. Russell J. and Marion C. (Hampson) O.; children: Lauren Elizabeth, Russell John III; m. Sandi J. Antill. BA, U. Pitts., 1970, JD, 1973. Bar: Pa. 1973, U.S. Dist. Ct. (we. dist.) Pa. 1973, U.S. Tax Ct. 1982, U.S. Ct. Appeals (4th cir.) 1976, U.S. Ct. Appeals (3d cir.) 1979, U.S. Ct. Appeals (D.C. cir.) 1985, U.S. Ct. Appeals (2d cir.), 1990, U.S. Ct. Appeals (7th cir.) 1993, U.S. Supreme Ct. 1976, U.S. Ct. Appeals (6th cir.) 2000. Asst. dist. atty. Allegheny County, Pitts., 1973-75; ptnr. Wallace Chapas & Ober, 1975-80, Rose, Schmidt, Hasley & DiSalle, Pitts., 1980-92, Meyer, Unkovic & Scott, Pitts., 1992—. Bd. dirs. Parent and Child Guidance Ctr., Pitts., 1983-90, treas., 1985-86, pres., 1986-88; bd. mgmt. South Hills Area YMCA, 1989-91; mem. Mt. Lebanon Traffic Commn., 1976-81; bd. dirs. Whale's Tale Youth Family Counseling Ctr., 1990-95. Mem. ABA (discovery com. litigation sect. 1982-88, ho. of dels. young lawyers div. 1982-83), Pa. Bar Assn. (ho. of dels. 1983—), Allegheny County Bar Assn. (chmn. young lawyers sect. 1983, bd. govs. 1984, fin. com. 1984-88, mem. coun. civil litigation sect. 1991-93), Nat. Bd. Trial Advocacy (diplomate), Acad. Lawyers Allegheny County (fellow 1983—, bd. govs. 1988-90) U. Pitts. Law Alumni Assn. (bd. govs. 1984-89, v.p. 1985-87, pres. 1987-88), Rivers Club. Office: Meyer Unkovic & Scott 1300 Oliver Bldg Pittsburgh PA 15222 E-mail: rjo@muslaw.com.

OBER, STUART ALAN, investment consultant, book publisher; b. N.Y.C., Oct. 2, 1946; s. Paul and Gertrude E. (Stollerman) Ober; m. Joanne Michaels, Sept. 20, 1981 (div. July 1995); 1 child Erik Kenneth Michaels-Ober ; m. Allison Craig, June 23, 2002. BA, Wesleyan U., Middletown, Conn., 1968; postgrad., U. Sorbonne, Paris, 1970, CUNY, 1976-77. Pres., editor-in-chief, chmn. bd. Beekman Pubs. Inc., N.Y.C., 1972—; investment cons., 1972—; expert witness, 1979—; with Loeb, Rhoades & Co., 1976-77; div. dir. tax investment dept. Josephthal & Co., Inc., 1977; mgr. tax investment dept. Bruns, Nordeman, Rea & Co., 1978-80; pres. Ober Investment Cons., 1980—, Securities Investigations, Inc., 1981—; sr. v.p. Cash Franchise Mgmt., Inc., 1988-89. Author: Everybody's Guide to Tax Shelters; editor-in-chief: Ober Income Letter, 1983-88; pub.: Tax Shelter Blue Book, 1983—. Bd. dirs., v.p. Woodstock Playhouse Assn., 1985-87; trustee Maverick Concerts, 1986—; chmn. Woodstock Arts and Cultural Com., 1988. Mem.: Inst. Cert. Fin. Planners (fin. products stds. bd. 1986—90, treas. 1988—90). Office: PO Box 888 Woodstock NY 12498-0888

OBERDANK, LAWRENCE MARK, retired lawyer, arbitrator; b. Cleve., Nov. 1, 1935; s. Leonard John and Mary (Pavelich) O.; m. Arlene C. Baldini, Aug. 25, 1962; 1 child, Karen A. BA, Western Res. U., 1958, JD, 1965. Bar: Ohio 1965, U.S. Dist. Ct. (no. dist.) Ohio 1966, U.S. Ct. Appeals (6th cir.) 1968, U.S. Supreme Ct. 1970. Assoc. Law Offices Mortimer Riemer, Cleve., 1965-69; ptnr. Riemer and Oberdank, 1969-76; prin. Lawrence M. Oberdank Co., L.P.A., 1976-2000. Arbitrator Ohio Employment Rels. Bd., 1985-89, Cleve. Civil Svc. Commn., 1983—, FMHA, 1989—; chmn. mandatory arbitration panel Ct. Common Pleas; mem. Nat. Mediation Bd., 1986—; instr. indsl. rels. law Cleve. State U., 1982-85; instr. labor rels. Cuyahoga C.C., 1983; arbitrator/mediator U.S. Dist. Ct. (no. dist.) Ohio, ea. divsn. fee dispute panel Cleve. Bar Assn.; mem. securities arbitration panel Am. Stock Exch., N.Y. Stock Exch., 1995—. Bd. mediators U.S. EEOC. Mem. ABA (labor and employment sect., labor arbitration, law collective bargaining agreements, alternate dispute resolution sect., fed. ct. annexed/connected programs com., sr. lawyers sect.), Am. Arbitration Assn. (securities arbitrator, nat. labor panel 1973—, comml. arbitration panel, nat. panel of employment arbitrators), Nat. Assn. Securities Dealers, Inc. (bd. mediators), Bar Assn. Greater Cleve. (labor law com.), Cuyahoga County Bar Assn., Am. Judicature Soc., Internat. Soc. Labor Law and Social Legislation, Ohio State Bar Assn. (chmn. labor law sect. 1970-73), Indsl. Rels. Rsch. Assn., Pub. Sector Labor Rels. Assn., Soc. Profls. in Dispute Resolution (bd. dirs. Southwest Ohio chpt.), Nat. Inst. Dispute Resolution (assoc.), Masons, Phi Gamma Delta. Roman Catholic. Avocations: golf, Civil War history. Home: 8051 Lakeview Ct N Royalton OH 44133-1214 Office: 6450 Rockside Woods Blvd S Cleveland OH 44131-2230

OBERDIER, RONALD RAY, lawyer; b. Norwood, Mo., Nov. 11, 1945; s. Albert Jr. and Edith Louise (Vaughn) O.; children: James Myron, Steven Michael; m. Karal Oberdier; children: Jon Ryan Heffernan, Melissa Ann Heffernan. Student, Ohio State U., 1963-64; AA, SUNY, Albany, 1975; BA, Mary Hardin-Baylor U., 1978; JD, U. Tex., 1980. Bar: Fla. 1981, U.S. Dist. Ct. (no., so. and mid. dists.) Fla. 1981, U.S. Ct. Appeals (5th and 11th cirs.) 1981. Enlisted U.S. Army, 1965, electronic intelligence specialist, 1965-77; assoc. Mahoney, Hadlow, Jacksonville, Fla., 1981-82, Coker, Myers & Schickel, Jacksonville, 1982-85; pvt. practice, 1985-86; ptnr. Humphries & Oberdier, 1987—. Mem. FBA, ATLA (assoc.), Jacksonville Claims Assn., Jacksonville Bar Assn., Jacksonville Assn. Def. Counsel (pres. 1993), Nat. Assn. R.R. Trial Lawyers, Fla. Def. Lawyers Assn. Office: 9550 Regency Square Blvd Ste 609 Jacksonville FL 32225-8116

OBERDORFER, LOUIS F. federal judge; b. Birmingham, Ala., Feb. 21, 1919; s. A. Leo and Stella Maud (Falk) O.; m. Elizabeth Weil, July 31, 1941; children: John Louis, Kathryn Lee, Thomas Lee, William L. AB, Dartmouth, 1939; LL.B., Yale, 1946. Bar: Ala. bar 1946, D.C. bar 1949. Law clk. to Justice Hugo L. Black, 1946-47; pvt. practice, 1947-51; mem. firm Wilmer, Cutler, & Pickering (and predecessors), 1951-61, 65-77; asst. atty. gen. tax div. Dept. of Justice, 1961-65; judge, now sr. judge U.S. Dist. Ct. (D.C. dist.), 1977—. Vis. lectr. Yale Law Sch., 1966-71; adv. com. Fed. Rules Civil Procedure, 1962-84; co-chmn. lawyers com. Civil Rights Under Law, 1967-69; adj. prof. law Georgetown U., Washington, 1993—. Editor-in-chief Yale Law Jour., 1941. Served to capt. AUS, 1941-46. Mem. ABA, D.C. Bar Assn. (bd. govs. 1972-77, pres. 1977), Ala. Bar Assns., Am. Law Inst., Yale Law Sch. Assn. (pres. 1971-73) Office: US Dist Ct 333 Constitution Ave NW Washington DC 20001

OBERFIELD, RICHARD ALAN, oncologist; b. N.Y.C., July 29, 1932; s. George B. and Frances Oberfield; m. Valerie I. Oberfield, Feb. 14, 1954 (dec. Jan. 1980); children: Elizabeth A., Alice A.; m. Keren G. Oberfield, July 28, 1988. BA cum laude, Alfred U., 1953; MD, NYU, 1957. Lic. physician, Mass., N.Y.; diplomate Am. Bd. Internal Medicine. Intern Greenwich (Conn.) Hosp., 1957-58; USPHS sr. asst. surgeon venereal disease br. Detroit Receiving Hosp., 1958-60; tng. fellow pathology NYU Med. Ctr., N.Y.C., 1960-61; resident in medicine Dartmouth Med. Ctr. Affiliated Hosps., Hanover, N.H., 1961-63, fellow in hematology and cancer chemotherapy, 1963-65; staff physician sect. med. oncology dept. internal medicine Lahey Clinic Med. Ctr., Burlington, Mass., 1965—, head sect. med. oncology dept. internal medicine, 1969-85. Hosp. appts. include New Eng. Bapt. Hosp., Boston, 1965—80, New Eng. Deaconess Hosp., Boston, 1965—97, Mary and Arthur R. Clapham Hosp., Lahey Clinic Med. Ctr., Burlington, 1980—; chmn. emeritus sect. med. oncology dept. internal medicine Lahey Clinic Med. Ctr., Burlington, 1997—; clin. rsch. cons. dept. rsch., 1997—; clin. instr. medicine Harvard Med. Sch., Boston, 1972—; asst. prof. dept. medicine Tufts U. Sch. Medicine, 2000—. Contbr. numerous articles to profl. publs. Fellow ACP (Meade Johnson postgrad. scholar 1962-63); mem. AMA (Cert. Merit 1966), Internat. Assn. for Study of Lung Cancer (founding mem.), Nat. Bd. Med. Examiners (diplomate), Am. Assn. for Cancer Rsch., Inc., Am. Soc. Clin. Oncology, Am. Assn. for Cancer Edn., Mass. Med. Soc., Mass. Soc. Internal Medicine, New Eng. Cancer Soc., Mass. Soc. Clin. Oncologists. Avocations: piano, writing, running, reading. Office: Lahey Clinic Med Ctr 41 Mall Rd Burlington MA 01805

OBERG, BARBARA BOWEN, historian, educator, scholarly writer; b. Bay City, Mich., Apr. 5, 1942; d. Edward Woodville Bowen and Barbara Shipman Payson; m. Arthur Kenneth Oberg, June 6, 1964 (dec. Feb. 1977); m. John Perry Leavell, Jr., July 24, 1982. AB, Wellesley Coll., 1964; MA, U. Calif., Santa Barbara, 1967, PhD, 1973. Assoc. editor Papers of Philip Mazzei Fairleigh Dickinson U., Madison, N.J., 1978-81; editor Papers of Albert Gallatin Baruch Coll. of CUNY, N.Y.C., 1981-86; editor-in-chief Papers of Benjamin Franklin Yale U., New Haven, 1986-98, sr. rsch. scholar and lectr. history, 1986—; prof., gen. editor Papers of Thomas Jefferson, lectr. Princeton U., 1999—. Chmn. editl. adv. com. Founding Fathers, Inc., 1988-97, 2001—; reviewer, panelist NEH, 1980—; presenter, spkr., lectr. in field. Editor: The Papers of Benjamin Franklin, Vol. 28, 1990, Vol. 29, 1992, Vol. 30, 1993, Vol. 31, 1995, Vol. 32, 1996, Vol. 33, 1997, Vol. 34, 1998, Vol. 35, 1999, The Papers of Albert Gallatin: A Microfilm Supplement, 1985, The Papers of Thomas Jefferson vol. 29, 2002; assoc. editor: Philip Mazzei: The Comprehensive Microform Edition of His Papers, 1982; co-author: (with Doron Ben-Atar) Federalists Reconsidered, 1998, (with Harry S. Stout) Jonathan Edwards, Benjamin Franklin, and the Representation of American Culture, 1993; contbr. and revs. to profl. jours. Rsch. grantee NEH, 1976-78, Am. Hist. Assn. and Am. Polit. Sci. Assn., 1981, Am. Philos. Soc., 1981; rsch. fellow Libr. Co. Phila., 1993, Henry E. Huntington Libr., 1994, Inst. for U.S. Studies, U. London, 2000. Mem.: Pa. Hist. Assn., Soc. for History of Authorship Reading and Pub., Inst. Early Am. History and Culture, Orgn. Am. Historians, Soc. Historians of Early Am. Republic (mem. editl. bd. Jour. Early Republic

1982—87, co-chair program com. 1986, adv. coun. 1987—93, mem. editl. bd. Jour. Early Republic 1997—, mem. editl. bd. The Works of Jonathan Edwards, mem. editl. bd. The Papes of Eleanor Roosevelt, mem. editl. bd. The Papers of Albert Einstein, mem. editl. bd. the Papers of Albert Einstein, mem. editl. bd. The Papers of John Jay), Soc. Textual Scholarship (exec. bd. 1983—88, co-chair program com. 1987, conf., chair conf. sessions 1987, 1989, 1995, exec. bd. 1995—, pres. 2001—), Assn. Documentary Editing (chaired panels or presented papers 1979, 1981, 1984, nominating com. 1984—85, 1986—87, exec. coun. 1988—90, program com. 1989, chaired panels or presented papers 1989, 1990, 1991, exec. coun. 1992—95, pres. 1993—94, fed. policy com. 1999—2002), Mass. Hist. Soc., Am. Philos. Soc., Internat. Ctr. for Jefferson Studies (adv. bd.). Home: 57 Hodge Rd Princeton NJ 08540-3075

OBERG, LARRY REYNOLD, librarian; b. Midvale, Idaho; s. Gustav Wilhelm and Esther Marie (Watkins) O.; m. Marilyn Ann Gow, Jan. 1, 1964 (div. 1985); 1 child, Marc Aurelien. AB in Anthropology, U. Calif., Berkeley, 1977, MLS, 1978. Reference librarian Stanford (Calif.) U., 1979-80, U. Calif., Berkeley, 1981-82; dir. libr. Lewis-Clark State Coll., Lewiston, Idaho, 1984-86; dir. library Albion (Mich.) Coll., 1986-92; univ. libr. Willamette U., Salem, Oreg., 1992—. Author: Human Services in Postrevolutionary Cuba, 1985 (named a Choice Outstanding Acad. Book, Choice Editors 1984-85); mem. adv. bd. Jour. Info. Ethics; contbr. numerous articles to profl. jours. Mem. Am. Library Assn. (chair coll. librs. sect. 1997-98), Oreg. Library Assn., Phi Beta Kappa. Democrat. Office: Willamette U Mark O Hatfield Libr 900 State St Salem OR 97301-3931

O'BERG, ROBERT MYRON, minister; b. Long Beach, Calif., Apr. 21, 1961; s. Robert Ronald and Carolyn Ruth (Smith) O'B.; m. Kristen Johnson, Mar. 22, 1986; children: Erin Kristine, Robert William. BA, U. Calif., Riverside, 1983, MA, Claremont Grad. Sch., 1990; MDiv, Pacific Luth. Theol. Sem., 1991. Ordained to ministry Evang. Luth. Ch. in Am., 1991. Assoc. pastor Trinity Luth. Ch., Fresno, Calif., 1999—. Book reviewer Augsburg Fortress Pub. House; initial interviewer multi-synodical candidacy com. Evang. Luth. Ch. in Am.; relief chaplain Simi Valley Hosp. and Health Care Svcs., 1994-99; convener Simi Valley Ecumenical Coun. (Luth., Episcopal and Roman Cath.), 1993-95. Mem. steering com. Luth. Social Svcs. Cen. Coast, 1993; bd. dirs. Vols. for You, 1997-99. Recipient Disting. Svc. award Luth. Social Svcs., 1993; named Pastor of Day, Sta. KKLA-FM, 1995. Mem. Aid Assn. for Lutherans, Luth. Brotherhood, U. Calif.-Riverside Alumni Assn., Claremont Grad. Sch. Alumni Assn., Pacific Luth. Theol. Sem. Alumni Assn. Democrat. Avocations: writing, reading history and historical fiction, ancient languages, hunting, music. E-mail: www.tlcfresno.com. Home: 722 N Clovis Ave Clovis CA 93611-0360 Office: Trinity Luth Ch 3973 N Cedar Ave Fresno CA 93726-5299

OBERHAUSEN, JOYCE ANN WYNN, aircraft company executive, artist; b. Plain Dealing, La., Nov. 12, 1941; d. George Dewey and Jettie Cleo (Farrington) Wynn; m. James J. Oberhausen, Oct. 15, 1966; children: Georgann, Darla Renee Estein Oberhausen Christopher, Dale Henry Estein Oberhausen. Student, Ayers Bus. Sch., Shreveport, 1962-63; student, U. Ala., 1964-65. Stenographer, sec. Lincoln Nat. Life Co., Shreveport, 1965-66; co-owner Precision Splty. Co., Huntsville, 1966—; internat. art tchr. Ala., 1974—; sec. Baifield Industries, Shreveport, 1975-86. Co-owner Mil. Aircraft, Huntsville, 1979—; pres., owner Wynnson Galleries Pvt. Collections, Florist, Meridianville, 1987; owner North Ala. Wholesale Flowers, 1988—, Wynnson Enterprises Mil. Packaging Co., 1988—. Co-founder Nat. Mus. Women in Arts; judge 20th Biennial Conv. Internat. Porcelain Arts Tchrs., 1998. Mem. NAFE, Internat. Porcelain Guild, People to People, Porcelain Portrait Soc., United Artists Assn., Am. Soc. of Profl. and Exec. Women Hist. Soc., Nat. Trust Hist. Preservation, Internat. Platform Assn., Met. Mus. Art., Smithsonian Assn., Assn. Cmty. Artists, Rep Senatorial Inner Cir., Ala. Sheriffs Assn., C. of C., Better Bus. Bur., Huntsville Art League and Mus. Assocs. Avocations: oil painting, antiques, handcrafts, gourmet cooking, horseback riding. Home: 156 Spencer Dr Meridianville AL 35759-2023 Office: Wynnson Enterprises Inc 12043 Highway 231 431 N Meridianville AL 35759-1201

OBERHELMAN, HARRY ALVIN, JR. surgeon, educator; b. Chgo., Nov. 15, 1923; s. Harry Alvin and Beatrice (Babel) O.; m. Betty Jane Porter, June 12, 1946; children: Harry Alvin III, James I., Robert P., Thomas L., Nancy L. Student, Yale U., 1942-43; BS, U. Chgo., 1946, MD, 1947. Diplomate: Am. Bd. Surgery. Intern U. Chgo. Clinics, 1947-48, resident in surgery, 1948-51, 52-57; asst. prof., then assoc. prof. surgery U. Chgo. Sch. Medicine, 1957-60; mem. faculty Stanford (Calif.) Sch. Medicine, 1960—, prof. surgery, 1964-95, Emer prof. surgery, 1995—. Mem. div. licensing Calif. Bd. Med. Quality Assurance, 1970-82 Author papers in field. Served with USAF, 1951-53. Mem. AMA, Calif. Med. Assn., Soc. Univ. Surgeons, Am., Western, Pacific Coast surg. assns., Soc. Alimentary Tract, Halsted Soc., Fedn. State Med. Bds. U.S. (bd. dirs. 1979-82) Home: 668 Cabrillo St Stanford CA 94305-8404 E-mail: hoberhelman@hotmail.com.

OBERLANDER, HERBERT, retired physiologist; b. Manchester, N.H., Oct. 2, 1939; BA cum laude in Zoology, U. Conn., 1961; PhD in Biology, Western Res. U., 1965. Postdoctoral fellow U. Zurich, Switzerland, 1965-66; asst. prof. Brandeis U., Waltham, Mass., 1966-71; rsch. physiologist USDA, Agrl. Rsch. Svc., Gainesville, Fla., 1971-76, rsch. leader, physiology unit, insect attractants lab, 1976-84, lab dir. insect attractants, behavior/basic biology rsch., 1984-96; dir. Ctr. for Med. Agrl. and Vet. Entomology, 1996—2001; prof. entomology U. Fla., 1979—2001; ret., 2001. Grantee U.S.-Israel BARD, 1989-93; NSF fellow, 1961-65; NIH fellow, 1965-66; NSF rsch. grantee, 1966-71, 83. Fellow Entomol. Soc. Am. (Founders' Meml. award 1995); mem. Tissue Culture Assn., Phi Beta Kappa, Sigma Xi, Phi Kappa Phi. Office: USDA -ARS - CMAVE PO Box 14565 1700 SW 23rd Dr Gainesville FL 32608-1069

OBERLANDER, SAMUEL G. obstetrician/gynecologist; b. Bklyn., 1940; s. Harry L. and Belle R. (Semel) O.; m. Marjorie Oberlander, June 17, 1962 (div. Sept. 1985); children: Lynn, Jill, Bert; m. Monica Hallacy, May 27, 1989; children: Matthew, Andrew, Laura, Jennifer. BS, Hobart Coll., 1961; MD, Harvard U., 1965. Cert. ob/gyn. Intern Bronx Mcpl. Hosp., N.Y.C., 1965-66, resident in ob/gyn., 1966-67, 69-72; attending physician Weiler Hosp./Einstein Coll. Medicine, Bronx, Lawrence Hosp., Bronx; assoc. clin. prof. Albert Einstein Coll. Medicine; pvt. practice Bronx. Pres. divsn. coun. Weiler Hosp., Bronx, 1994-97; pres. med. staff Montfore Hosp., Bronx, 1997-99. Fellow Am. Coll. Ob/gyn. Home: 1254 Central Park Ave Yonkers NY 10704-1059 Office: 1602 Hering Ave Bronx NY 10461-2006

OBERLIES, JOHN WILLIAM, physician organization executive; b. Rochester, N.Y., June 9, 1939; s. Hubert H. and Martha (Voght) O.; m. Mary Teresa Sundholm, Sept. 29, 1962; children: Katie, Daniel. BCE, Villanova U., 1961; MBA, U. Rochester, 1978. From surveyor to purchasing agt. Rochester Gas & Electric Co., 1959-79, gen. mgr., 1979-82, v.p., 1982-87, sr. v.p., 1988-90; chief ops. officer Le Chase Constrn., Inc., Rochester, 1990-95; COO Rochester Individual Practice Assn. Inc., 1995—. Trustee Aquinas Inst., Rochester, 1986-93; bd. dirs. Cath. Charities, Rochester, 1984-85; chmn. bd. Preferred Care, Inc., Rochester, 1986-90; mem. Diocesan Pastoral Coun., Health Futures of Rochester Commn.; bd. dirs. Rochester Area Found., 1984-85, Rochester C. of C., Highland Hosp.; chmn. nominations com. United Way, Rochester; mem. Rochester Housing Partnership Commn., Rochester Health Commn. With U.S. Army, 1961-62. Mem. Rochester C. of C. (chmn. polit. action com. 1987, bd. dirs. 1999—). Republican. Avocation: fishing. Home: 242 Shoreham Dr Rochester NY 14618-4112 Office: Rochester Individual Practice Assn Inc 2000 Winton Rd S Rochester NY 14618-3970

OBERLY, KATHRYN ANNE, lawyer; b. Chgo., May 22, 1950; d. James Richard and Lucille Mary (Kraus) Oberly; 1 child Michael W. Goetzer ; m. Haynes Johnson, June 29, 2002. Student, Vassar Coll., 1967-69; BA, U. Wis., 1971, JD, 1973. Bar: Wis. 1973, D.C. 1981, N.Y. 1995. Law clk. U.S. Ct. Appeals, Omaha, 1973-74; trial atty. U.S. Dept. Justice, Washington, 1974-77, spl. asst., 1977-81, spl. litigation counsel, 1981-82, asst. to Solicitor Gen., 1982-86; ptnr. Mayer, Brown & Platt, 1986-91; assoc. gen. counsel Ernst & Young LLP, 1991-94, vice-chair, gen. counsel N.Y.C., 1994—. Exec. com. CPR Ctr. for Dispute Resolution. Named one of 50 Most Influential Women Lawyers in Am., Nat. Law Jour., 1998. Mem. ABA, Am. Law Inst., Am. Acad. Appellate Lawyers, Wis. Bar Assn., D.C. Bar Assn. Democrat. Office: Ernst & Young LLP 5 Times Sq New York NY 10036 E-mail: kathryn.oberly@ey.com.

OBERMAN, MICHAEL STEWART, lawyer; b. Bklyn., May 21, 1947; s. Hyman Martin and Gertrude O.; m. Sharon Land, Oct. 8, 1975; 1 child, Abigail Land. AB, Columbia U., 1969; JD, Harvard U., 1972. Bar: N.Y. 1973, U.S. Dist. Ct. (so. and ea. dists.) N.Y. 1973, U.S. Ct. Appeals (2d cir.) 1973, U.S. Supreme Ct. 1976, Calif. 1981, U.S. Dist. Ct. (no. dist.) Calif. 1981, U.S. Ct. Appeals (9th cir.) 1981, U.S. Dist. Ct. (so. and cen. dists.) Calif. 1982, U.S. Ct. Appeals (5th cir.) 1989, D.C. 1992, U.S. Ct. Appeals (7th cir.) 1993. Law clk. to Hon. Milton Pollack, U.S. Dist. Ct. (so. dist.) N.Y., 1972-73; assoc. Kramer Levin Naftalis & Frankel LLP, N.Y.C., 1973-79, ptnr., 1980—. Contbr. articles to profl. jours. Recipient Nathan Burkan prize ASCAP, 1973. Mem. N.Y. State Bar Assn. (mem. ho. of dels. 1989-91, exec. com. comml. and fed. litigation sect.). Office: Kramer Levin Naftalis & Frankel LLP 919 3rd Ave New York NY 10022-3902

OBERMAN, SHELDON ARNOLD, writer, educator; b. Winnipeg, Man., Can., May 20, 1949; s. Allan and Dorothy Oberman; m. Lee Anne Block, Sept. 8, 1973 (div. Mar. 9, 1990); children: Adam, Mira; m. Lisa Ann Dveris, Sept. 2, 1990; 1 child: Jesse. BA in English, U. Winnipeg, 1972; BA in English with honors, U. Jerusalem, Israel, 1973; teaching cert., U. Man., 1974. Tchr. W. C. Millar Collegiate, Altona, Man., Can., 1975-76, Joseph Wolinsky Collegiate, Winnipeg, Man., Can., 1976-95. Author: The Folk Festival Book, 1983, Lion in the Lake: A French English Alphabet Book, 1988, Julie Gerond and the Polka Dot Pony, 1988, TV Sal and the Game Show From Outer Space, 1993, This Business With Elijah, 1993, The Always Prayer Shawl, 1994, The White Stone in the Castle Wall, 1995, By the Hannukah Light, 1997, The Shaman's Nephew: A Life in the Far North, 1999, The Wisdom Bird: A Tale of Solomon and Sheba, 2000; co-editor: A Mirror of a People: The Canadian Jewish Experience in Poetry and Prose, 1985 (Sydney Taylor honor 2000, McNalley Robinson Book award 2001) Recipient Parents Choice Silver Honour, 1999, Norma Fleck award for children's non fiction, 1999, Parents Coun. Outstanding Book, 1999, Nat. Jewish Book award Jewish Book Coun., 1995, Sydney Taylor award, 1995, Best Book of the Yr. A Child's Mag., 1994, Pick of the List award Am. Bookseller, 1994, Can. Author Short Story award Canadian Author's Assn., 1987, Bliss Carmen Poetry prize Banff Sch. of Fine Arts, 1980; various writer and film maker grants. Avocations: public address, acting, collage sculptor, canoing. Home: 822 Dorchester Ave Winnipeg MB Canada R3M 0R7 E-mail: sobermon@mts.net.

OBERMAN, STEVEN, lawyer; b. St. Louis, Sept. 21, 1955; s. Albert and Marian (Kleg) O.; m. Evelyn Ann Simpson, Aug. 28, 1977; children: Rachael Diane, Benjamin Scott. BA in Psychology, Auburn U., 1977; JD, U. Tenn., 1980. Bar: Tenn. 1980, Tenn. Supreme Ct. 1980, Tenn. Criminal Ct. Appeals 1980, U.S. Dist. Ct. (ea. dist.) Tenn. 1980, U.S. Ct. Appeals (4th cir.) 1981, U.S. Ct. Appeals (6th cir.) 1983, U.S. Supreme Ct. 1985. Law clk. Daniel, Duncan & Claiborne, Knoxville, Tenn., 1978-80; assoc. Daniel, Claiborne & Lewallen, 1980-82; ptnr. Daniel, Claiborne, Oberman & Buuck, 1983-85, Daniel & Oberman, Knoxville, 1986—. Pres., Project First Offender, Knoxville, 1983-86; bd. dirs. Fed. Defender Svcs. Eastern Tenn., Inc., v.p. 1994-97, pres. 1998-2000; guest instr. U. Tenn. 1988-90; guest lectr. U. Tenn. Law Sch., 1982-88; guest instr. U. Tenn. Grad. Sch. Criminal Justice Program, 1983, 84; guest speaker Ct. Clk's Meeting, Cambridge, Eng., 1984; guest instr. legal clinic , trial advocacy program U. Tenn., 1984—; adj. prof. U. Tenn. Law Sch., 1993— (Forrest W. Lacey award for outstanding faculty contbn. to U. Tenn. Coll. Law Moot Ct. Program, 1993-94; coach U. Tenn. Law Sch. Nat. Trial Team, 1991-96; spl. judge Criminal Divsn. Knox County Gen. Sessions Court; founding mem. Nat. Coll. for DUI Def.; speaker in field. Author: D.U.I.: The Crime and Consequences in Tennessee, 1991, 3d edit., 2002, supplemented annually; co-author: D.W.I. Means Defend With Ingenuity, 1987; contbr. legal articles on drunk driving to profl. jours. Bd. dirs. Knoxville Legal Aid Soc., Inc., 1986-88 (pres. 1990), Arnstein Jewish Community Ctr., 1987-91, pres. 1990; bd. dirs. Knoxville Racquet Club, 1991-93, pres. 1992-93. Col. Aide de Camp Tenn. Gov.'s Staff, 1983, Moot Ct. Bd. Spl. Svc. award, 1995-96. Mem. ATLA, Nat. Assn. Criminal Def. Lawyers (chair/co-chair DUI advocacy com. 1995—), Nat. Coll. DUI Def. (founding, bd. regents 1999—), Tenn. Assn. Criminal Def. Lawyers (bd. dirs. 1983-89), Knoxville Bar Assn. Jewish. Office: Daniel & Oberman 550 W Main St Ste 950 Knoxville TN 37902-2536

OBERMANN, GEORGE, retired engineering executive; b. Grobla, Poland, Aug. 26, 1935; came to U.S. 1950; s. Hugo and Amanda (Merwitz) O.; m. Alice A. Volpel, Oct. 7, 1961; children: Mark George, James Joseph. BS, U. Mass., Lowell, 1959. Design engr. Controls Co. Am., Schiller Park, Ill., 1959-60; project engr. Oak Mfg. Co., Crystal Lake, 1960-62, Controls Co. Am., Shiller Park, 1962-67, engr. supr., 1967-72; prod. engr. mgr. controls div. Singer Co., 1972-76, rsch. devel. engr. mgr. controls div., 1976-82, staff engr. Eaton controls div., 1982-88; engr. mgr. controls div. Eaton Corp., Carol Stream, Ill., 1988-94; project engr. Otto Engring., Carpentersville, 1995, ret., 1995. Coms. mem. Nat. Elec. Mfrs. Assn., Washington, 1972-78, gen. engrs. com., 1978-93. Patentee in field; contbr. article to profl. jours. Lutheran. Home: 6713 W Forest View Ln Niles IL 60714-4405

OBERMANN, RICHARD MICHAEL, governmental technology and policy analyst; b. May 21, 1949; s. Baird J. and Phyllis L. (Weber) Obermann; m. Grace Karaffa. BS of Engring. in Aerospace and Mech. Scis. cum laude, Princeton U., 1971, PhD in Engring., Aerospace and Mech. Scis., 1977; MS of Engring. in Astronautics and Aeros., Stanford U., 1972; postgrad., Va. Poly. Inst. and State U., Am. U. With MITRE Corp., McLean, Va., 1977-88, engr. transp. systems analysis, transp. energy analysis, telecommunications, project leader, mem. tech. staff in communications and system design; sr. staff officer aeros. and space engring. bd. NRC, Washington, 1988-90, study dir. and analyst technol. and policy issues; mem. profl. staff for space subcom. U.S. Ho. of Reps. Com. on Sci., Space and Tech., 1990-95; minority staff dir., space subcom. U.S. House of Reps. Com. on Sci., 1995—. Author tech. papers and presentations. Fellow AIAA (assoc.), Brit. Interplanetary Soc.; mem. IEEE, AAAS, N.Y. Acad. Scis., Japan-Am. Soc., Asia Soc., Am. Astronaut. Soc. (bd. dirs., exec. com.), Nat. Space Club, Pacific Telecomms. Coun., Women in Aerospace (bd. dirs.), Internat. Acad. Astronautics, World Affairs Coun. Avocations: Japanese, Chinese and Spanish langs., sports, trumpet.

OBERMAYER, HERMAN JOSEPH, newspaper publisher; b. Phila., Sept. 19, 1924; s. Leon J. and Julia (Sinsheimer) O.; m. Betty Nan Levy, June 28, 1955; children: Helen O. Levy-Myers, Veronica O. Atnipp, Adele O. Malpass, Elizabeth Rose. Student, U. Geneva, Switzerland, 1946; AB cum laude, Dartmouth U., 1948. Reporter L.I. Daily Press, Jamaica, N.Y., 1950-53; classified advt. mgr. New Orleans Item, 1953-55; asst. to pub. Standard-Times, New Bedford, Mass., 1955-57; editor, pub. Long Branch (N.J.) Daily Record, 1957-71, No. Va. Sun, Arlington, 1963-89; adj. prof. journalism U. Md., 1989-93; vis. lectr. U. West Indies, Jamaica, 1994-95; publ. com. Commentary Mag., 1989—. Pulitizer Prize juror, 1983, 84; lectr. publs. mgmt. seminars, Hungary, Poland, Lithuania, Latvia, Estonia, Ukraine, Moldova, Slovenia, Macedonia, Russia, Croatia, Serbia, 1990-2002, Internat. Ctr. Journalists, 1992—. Contbr. articles to numerous mags. and newspapers. Bd. dirs. Monmouth Med. Ctr., 1958-71; mem. exec. coun. Monmouth Boy Scouts Am., 1958-71, mem. exec. com. Nat. Capital coun., 1971-79, v.p., 1974-77; mem. Va. Legis. Alcohol Beverage Control Study Commn., 1972-74; trustee Arlington (Va.) Bicentennial Commn., Am. Jewish Com. Cmty. Svc. award, 1986, nat. bd. govs., 1989-96, nat. coun., 1996—; trustee Jewish Inst. for Nat. Security Affairs, 1996—. With AUS, 1943-46, ETO. Rhineland Campaign Star; Recipient Silver Beaver award Boy Scouts Am., 1977, Knight Internat. Press fellow, 1994-95. Mem. Am. Soc. Newspaper Editors, So. Newspaper Pubs. Assn. (dir. 1981-84), Soc. Profl. Journalists, Mont Pelerin Soc., Nat. Press Club (Washington), Cosmos Club (Washington), Washington Golf and Country Club (Arlington, Va.), Dartmouth Club (N.Y.C.), Econ. Club (Washington), Sigma Chi. Jewish. Rotarian. Home: 4114 N Ridgeview Rd Arlington VA 22207-4711

OBERMAYER, MICHAEL ERIK MAX, management consultant; b. Stockholm, May 8, 1948; s. Adolf Max and Gerd Sigrid Ulrica (Malm) O.; m. Marianne Linnander, May 2, 1991; children: Anna Catharina, Johan Georg, Marie Louise, Erik Richard. MSChemE, Royal Inst. Tech., Stockholm, 1973; DSc in Biochemistry with honors, Ludwig Maximilians U., Munich, 1976; MBA with honors, European Inst. Adminstrn. Affairs, Fontainebleau, France, 1977. Fellow Max Planck Inst. Biochemistry, Munich, 1974-76; assoc. McKinsey & Co., Copenhagen, 1977-83, prin. Stockholm, 1983-86, prin., head of office Oslo, 1986-90, dir., head of office Stockholm, 1990-93, dir., chmn. Ea. Europe St. Petersburg, Russia, 1993-94, chmn. Ea. Europe Prague, Czech Republic, 1994-96, Moscow, 1996-2000, London, 2000—. Vis. prof. bus. strategy Faculty Econs. Moscow State U., 1996—. Mem. adv. bd. State Hermitage Mus., St. Petersburg, 1994; mem. Mir Iskusstvo/World of Art Found., Moscow, 1997. Lt. C.E., German Army, 1967-68.

OBERMEYER, THERESA NANGLE, sociology educator; b. St. Louis, July 25, 1945; d. James Francis and Harriet Clare (Shafer) Nangle; m. Thomas S Obermeyer, Dec. 23, 1977; children: Thomas Jr, James, Margaret, Matthew. BA, Maryville U., St. Louis, 1967; MEd, St. Louis U., 1970, PhD, 1975. Lic.: Mo. 1990; real estate broker Alaska, cert. Type A teacher Alaska. Dir. student activities Lindenwood Colls., St. Charles, Mo., 1969-70; asst. dean of students Loyola Coll., Balt., 1972-73; asst. dir. student activities St. Louis C.C., 1973-78; dir. student activities U. Alaska, Anchorage, 1978-79; instr. sociology Chapman U., 1981-93; secondary tchr. McLaughlin Youth Ctr. for Juvenile Delinquents, 1984-90. Elected Anchorage Sch Bd, 1990—94, treas, 1993. Contbr. articles to profl jours. Mem Anchorage Munic Health Comn, 1980—81; elected alt coun urban bd educ Nat Sch Bds Asn, 1994; maj party nominee US Senate gen election, 1996; founder, mem Alaska Women's Polit Caucus, 1979—. Recipient Fed Women's Equity Act, US Dept Educ Univ Alaska, 1978—79; fellow Fulbright, Project India, 1974, Project Jordan, 1977; grantee Title I, Univ Md and Loyola Col, 1972—73; scholar NDEA, 1968—70. Mem.: AAUW (bd dirs Anchorage br 1980—81), DAR (regent Col John Mitchell chpt 1992—94), Am Soc Pub Admin (pres, bd dirs south cent chpt 1981). Avocations: athletics, swimming, horseback riding, skiing, running. Home: 3000 Dartmouth Dr Anchorage AK 99508-4413 Fax: 907-278-9455.

OBERNAUER, MARNE, corporate executive; b. Pitts., Mar. 6, 1919; s. Arthur H. and Anna (Somerman) O.; m. Joan Strassburger, Aug. 1, 1941; children: Marne Jr., Wendy Damon. Grad., Cornell U., 1941. Vice chmn. Beverage Distbrs. Corp. and BDH Inc., Aurora, Colo.; pres. Doric Securities Co. Bus. cons., pvt. investor. Pres., bd. dirs. The Obernauer Found., Inc. Served to lt. USNR, 1942-45. Mem. Concordia Club (Pitts.), Century Country Club (Purchase, N.Y.), Banyan Golf Club (Palm Beach, Fla.). Home: 2 North Breakers Row Palm Beach FL 33480 Office: 60 E 42d St Ste 1912 New York NY 10165 Fax: 561-659-2132; Office Fax: 212-681-8618.

OBERNAUER, MARNE, JR. business executive; b. Lakehurst, N.J., July 1, 1943; s. Marne and Joan Carolyn (Strassburger) O.; m. Marion Fleck Gislason, Aug. 22, 1976 (dec. Jan. 1996); children: Matthew Gene, Michael Sidney. BA, Yale U., 1965; MBA, Harvard U., 1972. With First Nat. City Bank (Citibank, N.A.), N.Y.C., 1965-70, Donaldson, Lufkin & Jenrette, N.Y.C., 1972-74, Devon Group, Inc., N.Y.C. and Stamford, Conn., 1974-98, pres., 1978, CEO, 1980-98, chmn. bd., 1986-98; vice chmn. Applied Graphics Technologies, Inc., 1998—, also bd. dirs. Chmn. bd. dirs. Beverage Distbrs. Co. Trustee The Trinity Sch., The Obernauer Found., Inc.; bd. dirs. Com. for Responsible Fed. Budget. Mem.: Am. Bus. Conf. Found. for Econ. Growth (chmn.), Am. Bus. Conf. (bd. dirs.), Assn. Yale Alumni (bd. govs.), Century Country Club, Yale Club N.Y.C. Office: Ste 1912 60 E 42d St New York NY 10165

OBERNDORF, MEYERA E. mayor; m. Roger L. Oberndorf; children: Marcie, Heide. BS in Elem. Edn., Old Dominion U., 1964. Broadcaster Sta. WNIS, Norfolk, Va.; mem. city coun. City of Virginia Beach, 1976—, vice-mayor, 1986, mayor, 1988—. Mem. exec. bd. Tidewater coun. Boys Scouts Am.; bd. dirs. Virginia Beach Pub. Libr., 1966-76, chmn. bd., 1967-76. Mem. AAUW, U.S. Conf. Mayors, Va. Mcpl. League (exec. bd.), Nat. League Cities (vice-chmn.), Princess Anne Women's Club. Jewish. Home: 5404 Challedon Dr Virginia Beach VA 23462-4112 Office: Office of the Mayor Municipal Ctr Bldg 1 Virginia Beach VA 23456-9115*

O'BERRY, CARL GERALD, former career officer, electrical engineer; b. Lansing, Mich., Apr. 11, 1936; s. Gerald Ray and Edith Lenore (Watson) O'B.; m. Charlene Marice Bussche, June 21, 1958; children: Brian, Eileen, Kevin, Bradley, Kathleen. BSEE, N.Mex. State U., 1972; MS in Systems Mgmt., Air Force Inst. Tech., 1977. Commd. 2d lt. USAF, 1961, advanced through grades to lt. gen., 1993; comdr. 2019 Communications Squadron, Griffiss AFB, N.Y., 1974-76; project engr. Rome Air Devel. Ctr., 1979-81; asst. dep. chief of staff requirements Air Force Systems Command, Andrews AFB, Md., 1982-84; comdr. Rome Air Devel. Ctr., Griffiss AFB, 1984-86; joint program mgr. WWMCCS info. system Hdqrs. USAF, Washington, 1986-88; dir. command, control and communications U.S. European Command, Stuttgart, Fed. Republic Germany, 1988-90; dir. command control systems and logistics U.S. Space Command, Peterson AFB, Colo., 1990-92; command control comm. and computers DCS, HQ USAF, Washington, 1992-95; v.p., dir. strategic planning Motorola Space and Sys. Tech. Group, Scottsdale, Ariz., 1995-98; tech. cons. Def. Sci. Bd., Washington, 1998—; v.p., gen. mgr. govt. info. and comms. sys., space group The Boeing Co., Anaheim, Calif., 2000—. Mem. Air Force Assn., Armed Forces Communications-Electronics Assn., Soc. Logistics Engrs. Roman Catholic. Office: The Boeing Co PO Box 4921 3370 Miraloma Ave Anaheim CA 92803

O'BERRY, PHILLIP AARON, veterinarian; b. Tampa, Fla., Feb. 1, 1933; s. Luther Lee and Marjorie Mae (Mahlum) O'B.; m. Terri Martin, July 31, 1960; children: Kelly, Eric, Holly, Danny, Andy, Toby, Michael Asefa. BS in Agr., U. Fla., 1955; DVM, Auburn U., 1960; PhD, Iowa State U., 1967. With Agrl. Rsch. Svc. USDA, 1956—, asst. to dir. vet. scis. rsch. div. Md., 1967-72; asst. dir. Nat. Animal Disease Ctr., Ames, Iowa, 1972-73, dir., 1973-88, nat. tech. transfer coord., 1988—; prin. scientist Office Agr. Biotech., USDA, 1988-90. Adj. prof. Coll. Vet. Medicine, Iowa State U., 1973—; mem. expert panel livestock infertility FAO; sci. adv. com. Pan Am. Zoonosis Ctr., Buenos Aires; mem. Fed. Coun. Sci. and Tech.; mem. com. animal health, world food and nutrition study NRC; cons. Govt. of Italy, Govt. of Mex., USDA; mem. nat needs grad. fellowship rev. panel USDA, 1989-91, cons. agr. biotech. rsch. adv. com.; mem. sci. adv. bd. Biotech. R&D Corp., 1992-2001, sci. review bd. Am. Jour. Vet. Rsch., 1990-92; mem. USDA Patent Review Com., 1988—. Author 27 rsch. publs. Recipient Cert. of Merit, Agrl. Rsch. Svc., 1972, 84, Alumni Merit award Iowa State Club of Chgo., 1982, Cert. Appreciation, 1988, Tech. Transfer award 1989, USDA Disting. Alumnus award Auburn U., 1991; named Hon. Diplomate Am. Coll. of Vet. Microbiologists, 1995, Ames Citizen of the Yr., 2000, Iowa Gov.'s Vol. award, 2001. Mem. APHA, AVMA, AAAS, Nat. Assn. Fed. Vets., Iowa Vet. Med. Assn., N.Y. Acad. Scis., Conf. Rsch. Workers Animal Diseases, Am. Soc. Microbiology, Am. Assn. Lab. Animal Sci., U.S. Animal Health Assn., Am. Assn. Bovine Practitioners, Livestock Cons. Inst., Sigma Xi, Phi Zeta, Phi Kappa Phi, Gamma Sigma Delta (Alumni award Merit 1976), Alpha Zeta, Spades, Blue Key. Democrat. Home: 3319 Woodland St Ames IA 50014-3550 Office: Nat Soil Tilth Lab Rm 114 Ames IA 50011-0001 E-mail: usdaott@iastate.edu.

OBERST, CHARLOTTE L. physical therapist, nurse; b. Owensboro, Ky., May 20, 1921; d. Andrew Albert Oberst and Charlotte Marie Blau. Cert. in dermo-neuro-musculo therapy, U. Minn., 1951; student, Sister Kenny Polio Ctr., 1954; degree in phys. therapy, U. Kans., 1955; cert. in advanced rehab., NYU, 1956. RN. Pvt., gen. duty nurse St. Joseph Infirmary, Louisville, 1943-47; head nurse Our Lady of Mercy Hosp., Owensboro, 1948-51; phys. therapist Jersey City Med. Ctr.; phys. therapist out-patient poliomyelitis, N.Y.C., 1955—57; intern in advanced rehab. NYU, 1956, Haverstraw, N.Y.; founder, dir. phys. therapy Owensboro Daviess County Hosp., 1958-85; pvt. practice Home Health Svc., 1984—2002; phys. therapist cons., 1988—2002. Lectr. in field; sec. State Bd. Phys. Therapy, 1962-64; cons. Mary Kay Skin Care, 1971—, Melaleuca Mktg. Exec., 2000—. Vol. River Park Ctr. for Arts, Owensboro, 1992—. Elizabeth Kenny Found. scholar, 1951; Ednl. grant Elizabeth Kenny Polio Found., 1955; commd. Col. in Hon. Order of Ky. Cols., 1987. Mem.: World Confederation Phys. Therapy, Ky. Phys. Therapy Assn. (life), Am. Phys. Therapy Assn. (life), Lady's Ky. Col. Soc., Optimist Internat. (life; pres., disting. lt. gov. 1995, pres., lt. gov. 1998, pres., Owensboro chpt. pres, inducted into pres. club.), Altrusa Club Owensboro, Owensboro C. of C. (contact club), Beta Sigma Phi (life). Roman Catholic. Avocation: travel. Office: Oberst Phys Therapy PO Box 455 Owensboro KY 42302-0455 E-mail: clo520@hotmail.com.

OBERST, RICHARD B. military officer, hospital administrator; b. Wyo. Bs in Zoology and Physiology, U. Wyo., 1972; MS in Microbiology, U. Pitts., 1975; PhD in Parasitology and Lab. Practices, U. N.C., 1985. Commd. USN, 1975, advanced through grades to capt.; rschr. Malaria br. CDC, Atlanta; head clin. microbiology Naval Regional Med. Ctr., Portsmouth, Va., Oakland; dir. lab. svcs. Navy Environ. Unit 6, Okinawa, Japan, 1977—79; head parasitology Naval Med. Rsch. Unit 2, Manila, Philippines, 1985; naval med. rsch. dir. Naval Med. Rsch. Inst., officer in charge Peru, dep. dir. infectious disease dept., product mgr. pharm. systems divs. Md.; commdg. officer Naval Med. Rsch. Ctr., Silver Spring, 1998—. Decorated Meritorious Svc. medal (2), Navy Commendation medal, Navy Achievement medal. Office: Naval Medical Rsch Ctr 503 Robert Grant Ave Silver Spring MD 20910*

OBERST, ROBERT JOHN, financial analyst; b. Hackensack, N.J., Aug. 20, 1929; s. Bernard and Elsie (Schneider) O.; m. Ingrid Heilbut, Oct. 6, 1956; children: Jeanne, Robert John, Carl Edward. PhD in Fin. Mgmt., Columbia Pacific U., 1984. Cert. fin. planner, registered health underwriter. Spl. agt., mgr. Prudential Ins. Co. Am., Asbury Park, N.J., 1958-68; pres. Robert J. Oberst, Sr. & Assocs., Red Bank, 1969-92, chmn. bd., 1993—. Newspaper columnist Fin. Planning, 1986-87; prodr., host TV show Fin. Planning Today, 1983-93; contbr. articles to profl. jours. Author newspaper column Fin. Planning, 1986-87; producer, host TV show Fin. Planning Today, 1983-93; contbr. articles to profl. jours. Pres. Monmouth-Ocean Devel. Coun., Manasquan, N.J., 1981-83; bd. dirs. Monmouth County coun. Boy Scouts Am., 1986-93; trustee Brookdale Coll. Found., Middletown, N.J., 1986-92. With USN, 1946-50. Recipient Silver Gull Service award Monmouth/Ocean Devel. Council, 1984. Mem. Inst. Cert. Fin. Planners (Fin. Planner of Yr. award 1979), Internat. Assn. Fin. Planning (bd. dirs. 1986-93, chmn. bd. dirs. 1992-93), Estate Planning Coun. (pres. 1971-72), Million Dollar Round Table (life), Nat. Assn. Life Underwriters, Red Bank C. of C. (bd. dirs.), Registry Fin. Planning Practitioners (chmn. 1987-88), N.J. Assn. Life Underwriters (state pres. 1969-70). Republican. Avocations: civil war history, bicycling, gourmet dining, theater, reading. Home: 2 Cottingham Rd Bluffton SC 29910-4714 Office: Robert J Oberst Sr & Assocs 218 Broad St Red Bank NJ 07701-2002 E-mail: rjo33@aol.com.

OBERSTAR, HELEN ELIZABETH, retired cosmetics company executive; b. Ottawa, Ill. d. Milton Edward and Helen (Herrick) Weiss; m. Edward Charles Oberstar, Feb. 3, 1945 (dec. 1984). BS in Chemistry, Monmouth (Ill.) Coll., 1943; postgrad., Northwestern U., Chgo., 1947-49; LLD (hon.), Monmouth Coll., 1987. Asst. food technologist Standard Brands, Inc., Bklyn., 1943-45; chemist Miner Labs., Midwest div., Arthur D. Little, Chgo., 1946-50; rsch. chemist/rsch. supr. Toni Co., div. Gillette Co., 1951-65; group leader rsch. and devel. Shulton, Inc., Clifton, N.J., 1965-72; sect. leader rsch. and devel. Am. Cyanamid, 1972-75; mgr. rsch. and devel. Clairol Bristol Myers Internat., Stamford, Conn., 1975-82; dir. tech. Clairol Bristol Myers Squibb Consumer Products Group Internat., 1982-93; dir. technology internat. group Clairol, Inc. divsn. Bristol-Myers Squibb, 1993-95; ret. Wilton, Conn., 1995. Patentee in field. Recipient Disting. Alumni award Monmouth Coll., 1986, Hall of Achievement award Monmouth Coll., 1995. Mem. Soc. Cosmetic Chemists (house chmn. 1963-64), Cosmetic Toiletries Fragrance Assn. (internat. com. 1985-95). Episcopalian. Avocations: rughooking, gardening, travel. Home and Office: 512 Belden Hill Rd Wilton CT 06897-4221

OBERSTAR, JAMES L. congressman; b. Chisholm, Minn., Sept. 10, 1934; s. Louis and Mary (Grillo) O.; m. Jo Garlick, Oct. 12, 1963 (dec. July 1991); children: Thomas Edward, Katherine Noelle, Anne-Therese, Monica Rose; m. Jean Kurth, Nov. 1993; stepchildren: Corinne Quinlan Kurth, Charles Burke Kurth, Jr. BA summa cum laude, St. Thomas Coll., 1956; postgrad. in French, Laval U., Que., Can.; MS in Govt. (scholar), Coll. Europe, Bruges, Belgium, 1957; postgrad. in govt, Georgetown U. Adminstrv. asst. Congressman John A. Blatnik, 1963-74; adminstr. Pub. Works Com. U.S. Ho. of Reps., 1971-74; mem. 94th-106th Congresses from 8th Minn. Dist., 1975—, ranking minority mem. transp. and infrastructure com. Mem. Am. Polit. Sci. Assn. Office: US Ho of Reps 2365 Rayburn Hob Washington DC 20515-2308

OBERSTEIN, MARYDALE, geriatric specialist; b. Red Wing, Minn., Dec. 30; d. Dale Robert and Jean Ebba-Marie (Holmquist) Johnson; children: Kirk Robert, Mark Paul, MaryJean. Student, U. Oreg., 1961-62, Portland State U., 1962-64, Long Beach State U., 1974-76. Cert. geriatric specialist, Calif. Florist, owner Sunshine Flowers, Santa Ana, Calif., 1982—; pvt. duty nurse Aides in Action, Costa Mesa, 1985-87; owner, activity dir., adminstr. Lovelight Christian Home for the Elderly, Santa Ana, 1987—; activity dir. Bristol Care Nursing Home, 1985-88; evangelist, speaker radio show Sta. KPRZ-FM, Anaheim, Calif., 1985-88; adminstr. Leisure Lodge Resort Care for Elderly in Lake Forest, Lake Forest, 1996—. Nursing home activist in reforming laws to eliminate bad homes, 1984-90; founder, tchr. hugging classes/laughter therapy terminally ill patients, 1987—; founder healing and touch therapy laughter therapy Merry Sunshine, 1991-93; bd. dirs. Performing Arts Ctr.; speaker for enlightenment and healing. Author (rewrite) Title 22 Nursing Home Reform Law, Little Hoover Commn.; model, actress and voiceovers. Bd. dirs. Orange County Coun. on Aging, 1984—; chairperson Helping Hands, 1985—, Pat Robertson Com., 1988, George Bush Presdl. Campaign, Orange County, 1988; bd. dirs., v.p. Women Aglow Orange County, 1985—; evanglist, pub. spkr., v.p. Women Aglow Huntington Beach; active with laughter therapy and hugging classes for terminally ill; helped write AB 180 Nursing Home Reform Bill and revised title 22. Recipient Carnation Silver Bowl, Carnation Svc. Co., 1984-85, Gold medal Pres. Clinton, 1994; named Woman of Yr., Kiwanis, 1985, ABI, 1990, Woman of Decade, Am. Biog. Soc., 1995, Little Hoover Commn., 1995; honored AM L.A. TV Show, Lt. Gov. McCarthy, 1984. Mem. Calif. Assn. Residential Care Homes, Orange County Epilepsy Soc. (bd. dirs. 1986—), Calif. Assn. Long Term Facilities. Home: 2050 Oak St Santa Ana CA 92707-2921

OBERSTEIN, SALLY, entrepreneur, not-for-profit fundraiser; b. Pasadena, Calif., Sept. 9, 1952; d. Gilbert Harrison and Shirley Joyce Oberstein; m. Eric Paul Knudtson, Mar. 18, 1995; children: Alex Oberstein Knudtson. AA, Orange Coast Coll., Costa Mesa, CA, 1972; BA, Humboldt State U., Arcata, CA, 1974. Recreational specialist Municipality Anchorage, Anchorage, 1975—76; musician Self-employed, 1975—87; cmty. sch. coord. Municipality of Anchorage, Anchorage, 1976—81; cmty. sch. supr. Municipality Anchorage, 1981—82; antique dealer Self-employed, Across United States, 1987—91, visual artist Homer, Anchorage, AK & San Francisco, CA, Alaska, 1992—2001; founder& dir. Generous Antiques, Homer, 1999—. Contbr. articles to profl. jours., chapters to books. Fundraiser Students, individuals & local organizations., Homer, Alaska, 1998—2002. Home: 556 Cowles Way Homer AK 99603

OBERT, CHARLES FRANK, retired banker; b. Cleve., Apr. 28, 1937; s. Carl William and Irene Frances (Urban) O.; m. Linda Marie Thoss, June 3, 1961; children— Lisa Marie, Charles David. Student, Ohio State U., 1955-57. With Ameritrust Corp., Cleve., 1958-92, sr. v.p. affiliate bank div., 1975-80, sr. v.p. corp. service div., 1980-87, sr. v.p. br. adminstrn., 1987-92, mgmt. cons., 1993-2000; ret. Acoustical Cleaning Systems Inc., 2000, pres. Mem. Solon (Ohio) Recreation Commn., 1978-94, Solon Bd. Edn., 1986-94. Mem. Am. Inst. Banking, Am. Bankers Assn., Ohio Bankers Assn., Bank Adminstrn. Inst., Internat. Assn. Laryngectomees, Cleve. Hearing and Speech Ctr., Greater Cleve. Growth Assn., Solon C. of C. Home and Office: 8270 Pebble Creek Ct Chagrin Falls OH 44023-4866

OBERT, KEITH DAVID, lawyer; b. Talladega, Ala., Nov. 22, 1962; s. Sam R. and Alice M. Obert; m. Alaine Anderson, Aug. 3, 1991; 1 child, Baylor Anderson. BS in Acctg., U. Ala., 1984; JD, U. Miss., 1988. Bar: Miss. 1988, Tenn. 1988, Ala. 1989. Acct. Challenger Lighting Co. Inc., Olive Branch, Miss., 1984-85; atty. Wells, Moore, Simmons, Stubblefield and Neeld, Jackson, 1988-89, Copeland, Cook, Taylor & Bush, Jackson, 1989-97; shareholder Akers & Obert, P.A., Brandon, 1997—2002, Obert Law Group P.A., Madison, 2002—. Verger, lector, usher, acolyte Chapel of the Cross, Madison, Miss. Mem. ABA, Miss. Bar Assn. (dir. young lawyers divsn., chmn. nomination com., code adv. com., chmn. membership svcs. com. chmn. pub. rels. com., bus. law sect. co-editor newsletter, Outstanding Young Lawyer in Miss. 2001, inducted fellow young lawyer, 2002), Rankin County Bar Assn., Hinds County Bar Assn. (dir., co-chmn. golf tournament com., mem. bench/bar com., newsletter editl. bd.), Tenn. Bar Assn., Ala. State Bar, Bar Assn. of the Fifth Fed. Cir., Miss. Def. Lawyers Assn., Def. Rsch. and Trial Lawyers Assn., Miss. Claims Assn., Jackson Young Lawyers Assn. (pres., v.p., treas., dir., chmn. bench/bar com., chmn. social com., chmn. golf com.), U. Ala. "A" Club, Public Info. Com. (chmn. 2002-03). Avocations: golfing, hunting, skiing. Office: Obert Law Group One Woodgreen Pl Ste 200 Madison MS 39110

OBERT, PAUL RICHARD, manufacturing executive; b. Pitts. s. Edgar F. and Elizabeth T. Obert. BS, Georgetown U., 1950; JD, U. Pitts., 1953. Bar: Pa. 1954, D.C. 1956, Ohio 1972, Ill. 1974, U.S. Supreme Ct. 1970. Sole practice, Pitts., 1954-60; asst. counsel H.K. Porter Co., Inc., 1960-62, sec., gen. counsel, 1962-71, Addressograph-Multigraph Corp., Cleve., 1972-74; v.p. law Marshall Field & Co., Chgo., 1974-82, sec., 1976-82; v.p., gen. counsel, sec. CF Industries, Inc., Long Grove, 1982—, also officer, dir. various subs. Served to lt. col. USAF. Mem. ABA (corp. gen. counsel com.), Pa. Bar Assn., Allegheny County Bar Assn., Ill. Bar Assn., Chgo. Bar Assn., Am. Soc. Corp. Secs., Am. Retail Fedn. (bd. dirs. 1977-80), Georgetown U. Alumni Assn. (bd. govs.), Pitts. Athletic Assn., Univ. Club (Chgo.), Delta Theta Phi. Office: CF Industries Inc 1 Salem Lake Dr Long Grove IL 60047-8401

OBEY, DAVID ROSS, congressman; b. Okmulgee, Okla., Oct. 3, 1938; s. Orville John and Mary Jane (Chellis) O.; m. Joan Therese Lepinski, June 9, 1962; children: Craig David, Douglas David. BS in Polit. Sci, U. Wis., 1960, MA, 1962. Mem. Wis. Gen. Assembly, 1963-69, asst. minority leader, 1967-69; mem. U.S. Congress from 7th Wis. dist., 1969—; ranking minority mem. appropriations com. Mem. adminstrv. com. Wis. Dem. Com., 1960-62 Named Edn. Legislator of Yr., Rural div. NEA, 1968; recipient Legislative Leadership award Eagelton Inst. Politics, 1964, award of merit Nat. Council Sr. Citizens, 1976, citation for legis. statesmanship Council Exceptional Children, 1976. Office: US Ho of Reps 2314 Rayburn HOB Washington DC 20515-4907*

OBIECHINA, EMMANUEL NWANONYE, humanities educator; b. Nkpor, Anambra, Nigeria, Sept. 20, 1933; came to U.S., 1987; s. Obiechina Enyibuaku Olisakwe and Nwayioye Udenweze Obierika; m. Maria Obiageli Enekebe, Apr. 25, 1964; children: Nnonye, Nneka, Ikenna, Chioma, Nkemjika, Joy. BA in English with honors, Univ. Coll., Ibadan, Nigeria, 1961; PhD in English, Cambridge (Eng.) U., 1967. Asst. sec. Ministry Fgn. Affairs, Lagos, Nigeria, 1961-62; lectr. U. Nigeria, Nsukka, 1967-74, prof., 1974, chair dept. English, 1975-78, 80-81, dean grad. sch., 1981-85; dir. Nigerian Univs. office Embassy of Nigeria, Washington, 1987-90; vis. prof. English Hobart & William Smith Colls., Geneva, 1990-92; vis. prof. humanities U. Pitts., Bradford, Pa., 1992-95; Gerry Carruthers chair U. N.Mex., Albuquerque, 1996; Williams/NEH disting. prof. humanities Ferrum (Va.) Coll., 1997—; vis. prof. Eng. and African-Amer. Studies Univ. Kansas, Lawrence, KS, 2000—. Ahiajoku ann. lectr. Imo State Govt. of Nigeria, Owerri, 1994. Author: An African Popular Literature, 1973, Culture, Tradition and Society in the West African Novel, 1975, Language and Theme, 1990; editor: Baldwin's Go Tell It On the Mountain, 1966. Sec. Nat. Guidance Com., Biafra, 1967-70; mem. coun. Nigerian Inst. Internat. Affairs, 1978-84; exec. mem. Assn. Nigerian Authors, 1982-87; mem. Nat. Anthem Com., Nigeria, 1977-78. Commonwealth Academic fellow, Cambridge, 1972-73, Woodrow Wilson fellow, 1979-80, NEH summer fellow, 1991. Mem. MLA, African Lit. Assn., African Studies Assn., Internat. Comparative Lit. Assn., Clare Coll. Assn., Nigerian Inst. Internat. Affairs (life), Internat. Assn. of Univ. Profs. of English, 2000. Roman Catholic. Avocations: gardening, writing, music, tennis. Home: 14125 Parker Farm Way Silver Spring MD 20906-6326 Office: Ferrum Coll Dept Lang Lit & Philosophy Ferrum VA 24088 E-mail: eobiechina@hotmail.com.

OBIORA, CHRIS SUNNY, architect; b. Lagos, Nigeria, Sept. 2, 1954; came to U.S., 1978; s. Patrick M. and Virginia E. Obiora. Diploma in Physics, Chemistry, and Biology, Christ the King Coll., Onitsha, Anambra, 1974; A in Econs. and Current Affairs, Christ the King Coll., 1976; postgrad., Tex. A&M U., 1986, Coll. Profl. Mgmt., Lintas, Lagos, 1992. CFP; cert. tng. adminstr. Accounts clk. Lintas, Ltd., Lagos, 1976-78, media accounts clk., 1977-78; with San Jacinto Jr. Coll., Houston, 1980-81; The Wacherhit Corp., Coral Gables, Fla., 1980-84; gen. merchant Joncod Overseas Ltd., Lagos, 1974—, world trade strategist Houston, 1987—; retail trader Star Liquor Store, Hempstead, Tex., 1987—; owner, prin. Chris & Chris Assocs., 1989. Coord. Jancod/Bexpharm, Houston, 1987-88; cost acct. Jancod Overseas Ltd., Houston, 1980—; founder, pres. Joncod Internat., Inc., 1987—; founder, com. group head Star Liquor Store, Hempstead, 1987—. Active ARC, 1967-70, PTO, also numerous charitable activities, Lagos, 1970-74. Recipient Professionalism Cert. AMA, 1994, Meritorious Svc. award AIA Students, 1985, Recognition award Nat. Fire Protection Assn., 1986. Fellow The Highlanders Club (svcs. prof. 1993—), Nat. Shrine, Oxford Club, Oblates Mission Mary Immaculate; mem. ACLU, NAFE, ATLA, AIChE, N.Y. Acad. Sci., Am. Chem. Soc., Am. Fin. Assn., Nat. Audubon Soc., Internat. Assn. Fin. Planners, Soc. Applied Learning Tech., Assn. Corp. Tech. Computer Profls., Instr. of Profl. Mgmt. and Adminstrn., Internat. Assn. of Account Practitioners, Constrn. Specs. Inst., Nat. Hist. Soc., Nat. Soc. Accts., Sherrifs Assn. Tex., Soc. Human Rels. Mgmt. Avocations: table and lawn tennis, photography, swimming. Office: Joncod Overseas Ltd PO Box 87549 Houston TX 77287-7549

OBLIGACION, FREDDIE RABELAS, sociology educator, researcher; b. Legazpi City, Albay, The Philippines, July 20, 1959; came to U.S., 1988; s. Wilfredo and Lourdes Rances (Rabelas) O. BS magna cum laude, U. Philippines, Quezon City, 1980, MBA, 1981; MA, Ohio State U., 1990, PhD, 1995. Exec. asst. Concrete Aggregates, Quezon City, 1980-82; asst. prof. Bicol U., Legazpi City, 1982-88; rsch. asst. Ohio State U., Columbus, 1988-89, teaching asst., 1989-92; reviewer Academic Text Rev., 1994—; asst. prof. sociology Moorhead (Minn.) State U., 1994-95; with faculty Wyo. Coll. Advanced Studies, 1996—; asst. prof. sociology, distance learning sch. faculty Western New Eng. Coll., Springfield, Mass., 1996-98; asst. prof. sociology Franklin Pierce Coll., Rindge, N.H., 1998-2000, St. Peter's Coll., Jersey City, 2000—02; asst. prof. human svcs. Audrey Cohen Coll., N.Y.C., 2002—. Prof. lectr. Divine Word Grad. Sch. Bus., Legazpi City, 1982-88; mem. faculty Grad. Sch. Aquinas U., Legazpi City, 1982-88. Contbr. essays and articles to profl. jours. Rsch. grantee Soc. for Psychol. Studies and Social Issues, U. Mich., 1992, Ohio State U. Grad. Sch., 1992, summer rsch. award Western New Eng. Coll. Mem. Am. Sociol. Assn., Internat. Inst. Sociology, Soc. for Applied Sociology (cons. 1992—), Soc. for Psychol. Study Social Issues, Assn. for the Sociology of Religion, Assn. Humanist Sociol., Nat. Coun. on Family Rels., Phi Kappa Phi, Phi Beta Delta. Avocations: travel, playing piano and violin.

O'BLOCK, ROBERT, entrepreneur, publishing executive; BS in Sociology, Pittsburg (Kans.) State U., 1972, MS in Sociology, 1973, EdS, 2001; PhD, Kans. State U., 1976; MA in Psychology, Newport U., 1998, PsyD in Psychology, 2000; MDiv, Trinity Coll., 2001, DMin, 2002. Ordained deacon So. Episcopal Ch., 1999; ordained priest Anglican Cath. Ch., 2002. Patrolman Frontenac (Kans.) Police Dept., 1971-73; probation officer Crawford County Juvenile Ct., 1973-74; spr. Children's Ct. Ctr., 1974; adminstrv. asst. to dean student affairs/cmty. svc. Labette Cmty. Jr. Coll., 1976; dir. night sch. Marymount Coll., 1976; asst. prof. dept. adminstrv. justice Wichita State U., 1977-79; assoc. prof. dept. criminal justice/polit. sci. Appalachian State U., Boone, N.C., 1979-89; prof., chair dept. adminstrn. of justice Coll. of Ozarks, Point Lookout, Mo., 1989-93; exec. dir. Am. Coll. Forensic Examiners, Springfield, 1994—. Founder Am. Bd. Forensic Medicine, Am. Bd. Forensic Examiners, Am. Bd. Forensic Psychol. Specializations, Am. Bd. Forensic Dentistry, Am. Bd. Forensic Engrng. and Tech., Am. Bd. Forensic Nursing, Am. Bd. Law Enforcement Experts, Am. Bd. Forensic Acctg., Am. Bd. of Forensic Counselors, Am. Bd. Forensic Social Work; lectr., cons. in field. Author: Criminal Justice Research Sources, 1983, 3d edit., 1992, (with others) Security and Crime Prevention, 2d edit., 1990; founder, pub. The Forensic Examiner, Annals of the Am. Psychotherapy Assn., co-founder E Bus. Techs., contbr. articles to profl. jours., holder 14 U.S. fed. trademarks. Adv. bd. Larnard State Hosp. Grantee Gov.'s Com. on Criminal Adminstrn., 1976-77, 77, others. Mem.: APA, Am. Assn. Integrative Medicine (co-founder, CEO), Am. Coll. Forensic Examiners (founder), Am. Psychotherapy Assn. (founder, chmn., CEO). Home: 1646 S Cobblestone Ct Springfield MO 65809-2314 Office: 2750 E Sunshine St Springfield MO 65804-2047 E-mail: rloblock@aol.com.

O'BLOCK, ROBERT PAUL, management consultant; b. Pitts., Mar. 9, 1943; s. Paul Joseph and Mary Elizabeth (Galicic) O'B.; m. Megan Marie. BSME, Purdue U., 1965; MBA, Harvard U., 1967. Rsch. and tchg. fellow in fin., econs. and urban mgmt. Harvard U., 1967-70; assoc. in real estate mgmt. and fin. McKinsey & Co., Inc., Boston, 1969-78; gen. and mng. ptnr. Freeport Ctr., Clearfield, Utah, 1971—; prin. McKinsey & Co., Inc., Boston, 1979-84, dir., 1984-98. Vis. lectr. urban econs. Yale Law Sch., Princeton U.; cons. Mass., N.J. housing fin. agys., Rockefeller Assn., HUD, 1968-76; chmn. mgmt. com. Snowbird Lodge (Utah), 1974-86. Contbr. articles to profl. jours. Mem. nat. adv. bd. Snowbird Arts Inst., 1977-83; mem. budget com. N.Y. Pub. Libr., 1977-79; mem. adv. bd. Internat. Tennis Hall of Fame, 1986-89, bd. dirs., 1989-95; mem. bd. overseers Boston Symphony Orch., 1988-2000, vice-chmn. bd. overseers, 1992-95, chmn., 1995-2000, trustee, 2000—; trustee U.S. Ski Ednl. Found., 1989-2001, Park Sch., 1997—. Mem. Devon Yacht Club, Maidstone Club, Nat. Golf Links Am., The Country Club (Brookline). Office: 60 Cramond Rd Chestnut Hill MA 02467-2803

OBLOY, LEONARD GERARD, priest; b. Cleve., Sept. 1, 1951; s. Henry Joseph and Ruth Elsie (Walter) Obloy. AB, Borromeo Coll. of Ohio, 1973; MDiv, St. Mary's Seminary, 1977; SSL, Pontifical Biblical Inst., Rome, 1983, postgrad., 1984. Ordained priest Roman Cath. Ch., 1977. Assoc. pastor St. Helen Parish, Newbury, Ohio, 1977-80, St. Rose of Lima Parish, Cleve., 1984-88; vice-rector Mt. St. Mary's Sem., Emmitsburg, Md., 1988-97, asst. prof. sacred scripture and computer sci., 1988-99, dir. aux. svcs., 1997-99; assoc. pastor St. Francis of Assisi Parish, Gates Mills, Ohio, 1999—2002; pastor St. William Parish, Euclid, 2002—. Adj. prof. St. Mary's Sem., Cleve., 1984—88, Cleve., 1999—; tech. com. Cath. Distance U., Hamilton, Va., 1986—2002, dean grad. divsn., Va., 1995—, also bd. dirs., Va.; guest lectr. Our Lady of Holy Cross Coll., New Orleans, 1988—; lectr. in field. Author, narrator pub. TV series And God Said, Witness; author various pamphlets/audio casettes for Cath. Distance U. Mem.: IEEE Computer Soc., Vatican Radio, Sacred Congregation for Doctrine of Faith, Nat. Cath. Edn. Assn., Corp. for Pub. Broadcasting, Cath. Distance U., Cath. Bibl. Fedn., N.Y. Acad. Scis., Assn. for Computing Machinery. Avocations: computers, audio engineering, audio recording, auto mechanics. Office: St William Parish 367 E 260th St Euclid OH 44132 E-mail: lgobloy@aol.com.

OBNINSKY, VICTOR PETER, lawyer; b. San Rafael, Calif., Oct. 12, 1944; s. Peter Victor and Anne Bartholdi (Donston) O.; m Clara Alice Bechtel, June 8, 1969; children: Mari, Warren. BA, Columbia U., 1966; JD, U. Calif., Hastings, 1969. Bar: Calif. 1970. Sole practice, Novato, Calif., 1970-2001, Tiburon, 2001—. Arbitrator Marin County Superior Ct., San Rafael, 1979—; superior ct. judge pro tem, 1979—; lectr. real estate and partnership law. Author: The Russians in Early California, 1966. Bd. dirs. Calif. Young Reps., 1968-69, Richardson Bay San. Dist., 1974-75, Marin County Legal Aid Soc., 1976-78; baseball coach Little League, Babe Ruth League, 1970-84; mem. nat. panel consumer arbitrators Better Bus. Bur., 1974-88; leader Boy Scouts Am., 1970-84; permanent sec. Phillips Acad. Class of 1962, 1987—; mem. Phillips Acad. Alumni Coun., 1991-95; bd. cmty. advisors Buck Ctr. for Rsch. on Aging, 1990-2001. Mem ABA, State Bar Calif., Marin County Bar Assn. (bd. dirs. 1985-91, treas. 1987-88, pres.-elect 1989, pres. 1990), Phi Delta Phi, Phi Gamma Delta. Republican. Russian Orthodox. Office: 6 Mateo Drive Belvedere Tiburon CA 94920-1046 *An all-out intellectual attempt to understand baseball thoroughly may give sufficient insight to understand oneself; the so-called "designated hitter" rule should be abolished immediately.*

OBOH-IKUENOBE, FRANCISCA EMIEDE, geologist, educator, researcher; b. Lagos, Nigeria, Aug. 23, 1962; came to U.S., 1990; d. Joseph and Christiana (Atiomo) O.; m. Thomas Ikuenobe, Nov. 4, 1995; children: Ordia, Aita, Ami. BSc, U. Ife, Nigeria, 1983, MSc, 1986; PhD, U. Cambridge, Eng., 1990. Reg. geologist, Mo. Prodn. geologist Shell Petroleum Co., Lagos, 1983-84, palynologist War, Nigeria, 1984; geologist, palynologist GEOTREX Sys. Ltd., Lagos, 1987; asst. prof. U. Mo., Rolla, 1991-97, assoc. prof., 1997—. Grad. asst. U. Ife, 1985-87, asst. lectr., 1987; demonstrator, supr. U. Cambridge, 1988-90; cons. Mobil Exploration Producing, Dallas, 1991-95, Shell Petroleum Co., Warri, 1992-94; shipboard sedimentologist Ocean Drilling Program, College Sta., Tex., 1995. Contbr. articles to Palaeogeography, Palaeoclimatology, Palaeoecology, Palynology, Jour. Petroleum Geology Palaios, Geol. Soc. Am. Bulletin. Commonwealth scholar, 1987; grantee Am. Chem. Soc., 1992, 99, NSF, 1994, 2000. Mem. NSF, Am. Chem. Soc., Am. Assn. Stratigraphic Palynologists (Best Poster award 1994), Am. Assn. Petroleum Geologists, Geol. Soc. Am., Soc. Sedimentary Geology, Geol. Soc. Am., Mo. Acad. Sci. (sect. chair 1994-98), Optimist Club (bd. dirs. 1995-98), Sigma Xi. Office: U Mo 125 Mcnutt Hl Rolla MO 65409-0001

OBOLENSKY, GEORGES, retired humanities educator; b. Teheran, Iran, Dec. 31, 1920; s. Georges Obolensky and Vera Wladimirovna Nemtchinova; m. Rhoda Francis Wohl, Sept. 11, 1949; children: Michael, Julianne. BA, Lrcee Denice, Nice, France, 1938, Ind. U., Bloomington, IN, 1949. Wine promotor James Henrt Assn., Frankfurt, Germany, 1960—65, Schenley Industries, New York, NY, 1965—71; wine sales promotor Dorchester Inc., Millburn, NJ, 1971—83; wine appreciation educator Various Adult Schools, 1983—91. Wine promotor Sommelier Soc., New York, NY, 1968—68. Author: (book) Cooking with a Pencil. P.o.w. French Army, 1940—45, Germany. Russian Orthodox. Avocations: tennis, bridge, writing non-fiction. Home: SB266 PO Box 025292 Miami FL 33109 Personal E-mail: obelun@costarica.net.

OBOLENSKY, IVAN, investment banker, foundation consultant, writer, publisher; b. London, May 15, 1925; s. Serge and Alice (Astor) O. (parents Am. citizens); m. Claire McGinnis, 1949 (div. 1956); children— Marina Ava, Ivan Serge, David; m. Mary Elizabeth Morris, 1959; 1 child, Serge. AB, Yale U., 1947. Pres. Hotel Investments, Inc., N.Y.C., 1950-58; v.p., treas. Serge Obolensky Assocs., 1952-75; Ivan Obolensky Inc. and Astor Books, pubs. Ivan Obolensky Inc., pubs., 1956-65; dir. Silver Bear Inc., Atlanta; ptnr. A.T. Brod & Co., investment bankers, Dominick & Dominick Inc., investment bankers, 1965-70, Middendorf Colgate, investment bankers, 1970-73; v.p. C.B. Richard, Ellis/Moseley Hallgarten, investment bankers, 1974-81, Sterling Grace & Co., investment bankers, N.Y.C., 1982-87; sr. v.p. Jesup, Josephthal & Co., investment bankers, 1987-90; gen. ptnr. Astor Capital Mgmt. Assocs., 1980—; v.p. Capital Mgmt. Assocs., N.Y.C., 1990—, Shields & Co., N.Y.C., 1990—. Bd. dirs. Gold Canyon Resources, 1996—; cons. and lectr. in field. Author: Rogues' March, 1956, Who; contbr. to Nihon Keizai Shimbun, Tokyo, on precious metals, 1985—, program com. N.Y. Soc. of Security Analysts for pub., aerospace, oil and gas; contbr. articles to profl. publs. Bd. dirs. Police Athletic League, N.Y.C., 1975-85, exec. com., 1980-85, 96—, U.S.O., 1987—, Audubon Canyon Ranch, Calif., 1989—, Tolstoy Found., 1994—, Soldiers', Sailors' and Airmen's Club, 1976—, pres., 1987-2000, chmn.,ceo, 2000—, Russian Nobility Assn. in Am., 1990—, treas., 1991—, v.p., 1995—, Musicians Emergency Fund, 1985-93, pres.1987-92, Children's Blood Found., N.Y. Hosp., 1952—, pres., 1981-95, pres. emeritus, 1995—; pres., dir. Josephine Lawrence Hopkins Found., 1971—, pres. Whitemarsh Found., 1980-90, Masonic Brotherhood Found., 1996—. Lt. (j.g.) USNR, 1943-45, ret., 1980. Published works by James Agee: A Death in the Family and Tad Mosel; All the Way Home, which received Pulitzer prizes, 2 Caldecott awards. Mem. Am. Legion, Mil. Order Loyal Legion U.S. (sr. vice-comdr. 1955, comdr. 1967-70), St. Elmo Soc., Met. Mus. Art (life), Knickerbocker Club, N.Y. Yacht Club, New Eng. Soc. N.Y., St. Georges Soc. N.Y., The Navy League, Army and Navy Club, Explorer's Club, Masons (Holland #8 master 1981, dist. dep. grand master 1st Manhattan 1983-84, grand treas. 1994-96). Office: Shields & Co 140 Broadway New York NY 10005-1101 E-mail: obolensky@aol.com.

OBOLENSKY, MARILYN WALL (MRS. SERGE OBOLENSKY), metals company executive; b. Detroit, Aug. 13, 1929; d. Albert Fraser and Christine (Frischkorn) Wall; m. Serge Obolensky, June 3, 1971. Student, Duschesne Jr. Coll., 1947. Chmn. bd. Wall-Colmondy Corp., Detroit, 1959-61, exec. sec., 1961—. Chmn. bd. Wall-Gases Inc., Morrisville, Pa., 1959-61; pres. Serge Obolensky Assocs. Bd. dirs. Heart and Lung Assn. N.Y.C., 1963— . Mem.: Bathing Corp. (Southampton, N.Y.), Southampton. Republican. Roman Catholic. Address: 45 Preston Pl Grosse Pointe Farms MI 48236-3035

OBOLENSKY, NICHOLAS, entrepreneur; b. Toronto, Can., June 7, 1956; arrived in U.K., 1960; s. Michael Obolensky; m. Charlotte Isabella Sharpe; children: Alexei, Isabella, Larissa. BA with honors, U. Durham, Eng., 1981; MBA, IMD, Switzerland, 1988. Cert. mgmt. cons. Mng. cons. Ernst & Young, Eng., 1988-90; devel. dir. Somerfield, Eng., 1991-93; U.K. mng. ptnr. Vth Divsn., 1995—; CEO Tomorrow's Co., Eng., 1996-2000; assoc. prof. Nyenrode U., The Netherlands, 1998—; CEO Your Release, Eng., 1999—. Vis. prof. INSEAD, France, 2001—; hon. univ. fellow Exeter (Eng.) U., 2002—. Author: Practical Business Re-engineering; co-author: Management Consulting Best Practice Guide, The RSA on Work and Leadership. Served to maj. Lancers Brit. Army, 1976—88. Fellow: CMC, Inst. of Mgmt. Cons., Royal Geog. Soc., Royal Soc. for Encouragement of Arts, Manufacturers and Commerce. Avocations: surfing, skiing, flying. Office: Vth Dimension Ptnrship 18 Avon Rd Keynsham BS31 1LJ England E-mail: nickobolensky@cs.com.

O'BOYLE, MICHAEL WILLIAM, psychology educator; b. Chgo., Mar. 29, 1952; s. Eugene James and Mildred Mable (Swanson) O'B. BS in Psychology, Loyola U. Chgo., 1975; MA in Psychology, U. Nevada, Las Vegas, 1977; PhD in Psychology, U. So. Calif., 1982. Asst. prof. psychology Iowa State U., Ames, 1982-89, assoc. prof. psychology, 1989-98, prof. psychology, 1999—. Ad hoc reviewer Am. Jour. Psychology, Brain and Cognition, Brain and Lang., Devl. Neuropsychol., Jour. Internat. Neuropsychol. Soc., Laterality., Econ. and Social Rsch. Coun. Gt. Britain, James S. McDonnell Found., Nat. Sci. Found.; participant in inaugural James S. McDonnell Found. Summer Inst. in Cognitive Neurosci., Harvard U., Cambridge, Mass., 1988; vis. scholar U. Melbourne, Parkville, Victoria, Australia, 1991-92. Contbr. over 35 articles to profl. jours. including Jour. Psycholinguistic Rsch., Neuropsychologia, Behavioral and Neural Biology, Brain and Cognition, Brain and Lang., Cortex, others; presentations to sci. confs. and meetings; guest editor: spl. issue Devel. Neuropsychology: Intelligence, Learning Disability and Related Brain Characteristics. Recipient Outstanding Educator award Torch chpt. Mortar Board, Iowa State U., 1989; grantee Sigma Xi, 1982, Midwest Transp. Ctr., 1991-92, 94-95, Ricoh Corp., 1989-90, 91-92, 92-93, 93-94, 94-95, 95-96. 96-97. Mem. Internat. Neuropsychol. Soc., Iowa Acad. Sci. (sect. chair psychology 1989-90. 93-94), Midwestern Psychol. Assn., Psychonomic Soc. Democrat. Achievements include contributions to the understanding of the specialized functions of the left and right cerebral hemispheres and how they serve as neurological basis for individual differences in higher-order thinking processes, particularly as they relate to handedness, sex and intellectual giftedness; study of neurologically damaged patients and the study of how their impairments reveal fundamental principles about how perception, memory and language are subserved by, and organized in the human brain. Office: Iowa State U Psychology Dept Ames IA 50011-0001

OBRAMS, GUNTA IRIS, medical officer; b. Düsseldorf, Germany, Sept. 2, 1953; came to U.S., 1961; d. Robert and Olga (Baltins) O.; m. Malcolm DeWitt Patterson, Dec. 22, 1975; 1 child, Andrew McDougal Patterson. BS in Biology cum laude, Rensselaer Poly. Inst., 1977; MD, Union U., Albany, N.Y., 1977; MPH, Johns Hopkins U., 1982, PhD, 1988. Resident in obstetrics and gynecology Ea. Va. Grad. Sch. Medicine, Norfolk, 1977-78; community physician Southampton Meml. Hosp., Franklin, Va., 1978-81; resident in gen. preventive medicine sch. hygiene and pub. health Johns Hopkins U., Balt., 1981-84, project dir., 1983-85, med. dir., 1985-86; med. officer divsn. cancer etiology Nat. Cancer Inst., Bethesda, Md., 1986-89, dep. chief, 1989-90, chief, 1990-96, dir. extramural epidemiology & genetics program, 1996-2001; mgmt. US Coast Guard Health Svcs., 2001—. Editor: (with M. Potter): The Epidemiology and Biology of Multiple Myeloma, 1991; contbr. articles to profl. jours. With USPHS, 1987—. Recipient Nat. Cancer Inst. Nat. Rsch. Svc. award, 1981, Rsch. Career award Nat. Inst. Occupational Safety & Health; scholar Am. Med. Women's Assn., 1977. Mem. Phi Beta Kappa, Delta Omega, Alpha Omega Alpha. Office: Health Svcs Mgmt Dvsn US Coast Guard Hdqts G-WKH-3 2100 Second St SW Washington DC 20593

OBRANT, SUSAN ELIZABETH, artist, illustrator; b. Phila. d. Abraham Joseph and Rae Thelma O.; m. Stephen Meier, Feb. 24, 1968 (div. June 1980); children: Sarah, Danielle; m. Robert David deFreitas, Dec. 21, 2000. Grad., SUNY, Buffalo, 1966, Parson's Sch. Design, N.Y.C., 1968. Illustrator, freelance, N.Y.C., 1968-84; fine artist Susan Obrant Originals, Cortlandt Manor, N.Y., 1976—. Judge Soc. Illustrators, N.Y.C., 1973; artist in residence Mariandale Dominican Sisters of the Poor, Ossining, N.Y., 1995-96, Pace U. Law Sch., White Plains, N.Y., 1996-97, Gallery Obrant, Eastview Tech. Ctr., White Plains, 1996-99. Mus. exhibits Hudson River Mus., Yonkers, N.Y., 1976, Hammond Mus., No. Salem, N.Y., 1997; group exhibits include Graham Gallery, N.Y.C., 1977, Genesis Gallery, N.Y.C., 1980, Petrenko Gallery, N.Y.C., 1982; one woman show Somerstown Studio and Gallery, Somes, N.Y., 1983; permanent collection Palace Mus. Knights of Malta, Friends of Mus. Modern Art, Caracas, Venezuela, Hapsburg Found., Austria, 2000; pub. works include Visions and Voices of Westchester, 1997, Journeys I: The Southwest, 1998, A Visual Suite, 2001; pvt. collections for Sir Rudy Giuliani, former mayor N.Y.C., tribute to 9/11 Father Judge, Countess Ulrike von Heisermann und von de Goltz, Berlin, Germany, Richard L. Ottinger, White Plains, N.Y., Pace U. Law Sch., White Plains, N.Y., Alfred D. DelBello, former lt. gov. N.Y. State. Recipient award of excellence Soc. Illustrators, 1972, 20 Yrs. of award winners Soc. Illustrators, 1979. Avocations: dance, writing, poetry, wearable crochet art, sculpture.

OBRENTZ, PAULINE TROPP, interior designer, consultant; b. New Haven, June 10, 1908; d. Samuel and Tillie (Werebitzik) Tropp; m. Abraham Irving Obrentz, Feb. 22, 1931 (dec. Jan. 1980); children— Hugh Leonard (dec.), Bruce Everett. Student Yale U. Sch. Art, 1925; grad. Conn. State Tchrs. Coll., 1926. Head design dept. Mallary Furniture, White Plains, N.Y., 1939-55; owner Pauline Obrentz Interiors Inc., Belleair, Fla., 1968— ; tchr. interior design N.Y. Inst. Tech., 1966, St. Petersburg Jr. Coll., Clearwater, Fla., 1970. Works include: Shannon Airport Hotel, Ireland; Pepsi Cola offices, Rome; VA Hosp., Westchester County, N.Y.; Cardinal McCluskey Home for Catholic Children, White Plains, Temple Israel, White Plains, Polish Heritage Room, Tampa U., Hebrew Nat. Orphan Home, Yonkers, N.Y., Library at Hebrew Inst., White Plains, numerous others. Mem. Nat. Home Fashion League, Am. Soc. Interior Designers, Antique Club Am., Bus. and Profl. Assn. Belleair, AAUP, Nat. Council Jewish Women. Club: Hadassah. Home: 1712 Belleair Forest Dr Apt B Clearwater FL 33756-7728 Office: Pauline Obrentz Interiors Inc PO Box 1363 Zephyrhills FL 33539-1363

O'BRIEN, ADRIENNE GRATIA, communications educator; b. N.Y.C., Nov. 19, 1935; d. John Robert and Regina C. (Murphy) O'B.; m. David G. Salten, Dec. 21, 1987. AB, Hunter Coll., N.Y.C., 1957; MA, Villanova (Pa.) U., 1964, MA, 1965; PhD, Syracuse U., 1975. Faculty Cabrini Coll., Radnor, Pa., 1962-68, dir. R & D, 1971-72; prof., chair MA program N.Y. Inst. Tech., Old Westbury, 1974-78, dean Sch. Media and Arts, 1979-91, prof. comm. arts, 1992—. Pres. AID Assocs., N.Y.C., 1972-74, Creative Cons., Port Washington, N.Y., 1992—; reviewer Nat. Coun. Humanities, Washington, 1981; pres. Women in Instrnl. Tech., Washington, 1981. Editor: Computer Based Training Today, 1987; prodr., dir. (video program) Then and Now, 1995 (Communicator award, 1996), Legacy of Mother Ursula, 1996 (Communicator award, 1997), Maritime Mus. of L.I., founder, exec. prodr. L.I. News tonight, 1984; reviewer: Jour. Staff Devel., 1990. Mem. project steering com. Where Are the Women?, 2002; bd. dirs. Girl Scouts of Nassau County, 2002. Recipient Instrnl. Nat. Leadership award, Assn. Ednl. Comm. and Tech., Washington, 1989, Comm. award, Maritime Mus. L.I., 2001, L.I. Top 50 Women award, 2002; fellow Edn. Profl. Devel. Act fellow, U. So. Calif., 1969. Mem.: Women on the Job (v.p. 1995—). Avocation: tennis. Office: NY Inst Tech Old Westbury NY 11568 E-mail: aobrien@optonline.net.

O'BRIEN, ANNE THERESE, chemist; b. N.Y.C., Apr. 11, 1936; d. Charles Daniel O'Brien, Margaret Mary FitzGerald; m. Ronald P. Tedesco, Dec. 28, 1974. BS, Marymount Coll., Tarrytown, N.Y., 1957; PhD, Fordham U., Bronx, 1964. Tchr. Marymount Secondary Sch., Tarrytown, 1957—59; instr. to assoc. prof. Marymount Coll., 1962—72; assoc. prof. U. Waterloo, Canada, 1973—76; sr. rsch. info. chemist Am. Cyanamid, Pearl River, NY, 1976—86; group leader Wyeth Labs., 1986—91, mgr. libr. svcs., 1991—2002; ret., 2002. Mem. Westchester Environ. Coun., Westchester County, NY, 1985—, Tarrytown Environ. Adv. Com., 1980—2001. Mem.: Am. Chem. Soc. (bd. dirs. 2001—, mem. budget and fin. com.). Roman Catholic. Home: 15 Crest Dr Tarrytown NY 10591-4305

O'BRIEN, ANNMARIE, education educator, educator; b. N.Y.C., Nov. 10, 1949; d. Hugh and Margaret (Doherty) O'B.; m. William James McGinty, Dec. 30, 1976; children: Michael Hugh, Liam Patrick. BS in Elem. Edn., Boston U., 1971; MS in Early Childhood Edn., Queens Coll., 1976; EdD in Ednl. Leadership, Portland State U., 1994. Tchr. St. Gerard Majella Elem. Sch., Hollis, N.Y., 1972-76, Lower Kuskokwim Sch. Dist., Bethel, Alaska, 1977-85; child sexual abuse prevention coord. Resource Ctr. for Parents and Children, Fairbanks, 1986; grad. asst., project evaluator Portland (Oreg.) State U., 1989-92, student tchr. supr., 1992; prof. edn., rsch. assoc. Inst. Social and Econ. Rsch. U. Alaska, Anchorage, 1993-96; prin. Old Harbor Sch., Kodiak Island Borough Sch. Dist., Kodiak, Alaska, 1996-99; dir. curriculum and instr. Northwest Arctic Borough, Kotzebue, 1999—. Author: A Child Abuse Prevention Training Manual for Educators, 1976; co-author: The Academy for Future Educators Guidebook, 1992. Recipient scholarship Portland State U., 1991. Mem. ASCD, Kappa Delta Pi. Office: NWA BSD PO Box 51 Kotzebue AK 99752-0051 E-mail: aobrien@nwarctic.org.

OBRIEN, BEA JAE, artist; b. Oshkosh, Wis., Dec. 4, 1940; d. Harry A. and Mammie Anna (Smith) Mac Farlane; m. John Walsh O'Brien, July 27, 1965; 1 child, John Christian. BA, U. Wis. Profl. artist B.J.'s Fine Arts, Moraga, Calif. Publs. include The Best of Watercolor, 1996, Painting Texture, 1997, Best of Drawing and Sketching, 1999, Collective Best of Watercolor, 2002; art included in various art publs.; represented in archives at Women in the Arts Mus., Washington, 1997; exhib. include Dennos Mus., Calif. Art & Wine Festival, 2001, Internat. Art Show, 2001, Valley Art Gallery, Calif., 2001, 2002; one-woman shows include: Moraga, Calif., 1996, 97, 98, 99, 2000, 2001. Vol. children's art publ. Moraga Sch. Sys.; vol. organizer Cmty. Art Gallery, Moraga Gallery, 2000, 01. Recipient 1st place award, Calif. Art and Wine Festival, 1999, Bay Area Art Festival, 1999, 2000; Nat. Coll. award, Nat. Coll. Soc., 1999, 98, 97. Mem.: Women in the Arts Mus. (honor roll), Intuitive Layering Art Group, Valley Arts Ctr., Collage Artists Am., Nat. Collage Soc. (signature), Internat. Soc. Exptl. Artists (signature), Lamorinda Arts Alliance, Coll. Art Am. Avocations: reading history, art publs., volunteer work including children's scholarships programs. Office: BJs Fine Arts 34 Sea Pines Moraga CA 94556-1029

O'BRIEN, BEATRICE MARIE, poet, writer; b. Elizabeth, N.J., June 18, 1920; s. William Kahl and Ida Mae Stevens; m. George O'Brien; children: Bonnie, Dennis, Billy, Maureen, Lisa, Lynn. RN, St. Francis Hosp., Jersey City, 1942. Dir. poet's theatre HAAC, Hornell, NY, 1981—2001; workshop leader libs. and schs., 1997—2001. Editor: (anthologies) Words of Wisdom, 2001. Vol. drug and alcohol rehab. facility, Bath, NY; activist Allegheny County, 1995—. Ensign Nurse Corps USN, 1943—45. Mem.: NY Poetry Forum.

O'BRIEN, BETTY ALICE, theological librarian, researcher; b. Kingsburg, Calif., June 12, 1932; d. Robert Herbert and Alice Dorothy (Larson) Peterson; m. Elmer John O'Brien, July 2, 1966. AA, North Pk. Coll., 1952; diploma, North Pk. Theol. Sem., 1954; BA, Northwestern U., 1956; MLS, U. Calif., Berkeley, 1957. Asst. libr. North Pk. Theol. Sem., Chgo., 1957-69; libr. St. Leonard Coll., Dayton, Ohio, 1971-84; rschr. United Theol. Sem., 1986-96, reference coord., 1991-96; libr. Frasier Meadows Manor, 1997—. Editor: Religion Index 2: Festschriften 1960-69, 1980. Resident coun. Frasier Meadows Manor, 2001—, pres., 2002-. Mem. Am. Theol. Libr. Assn. (bd. dirs. 1981-91, editor Summary Proc. 1982-91), Ohio Theol. Libr. Assn. (sec. 1972-76, chairperson 1978-79), Meth. Librs. Fellowship (v.p. 1989-91, pres. 1991-93). Mem. United Meth. Ch. E-mail: Baobrien@aol.com.

O'BRIEN, BRENDAN JAMES, career planning administrator; b. Washington, Oct. 29, 1973; s. James Francis and Margaret Winifred (Bell) O'Brien. BA in English/Spanish, U. Salamanca, Manchester N.H. and Spain, 1995. Health vol. U.S. Peace Corps, Primero de Marzo, Paraguay, 1996—98, recruiter, coord. Boston, 1998—2001; internat. career advisor Middlebury (Vt.) Coll., 2001—. Actor: (numerous shows) , 1995; , translator Spanish/English transl. Liaison Boston Area Returned Peace Corps Vols., 1998—2001. Democrat. Roman Catholic. Avocations: languages, travel, marathons, reading.

O'BRIEN, CATHERINE LOUISE, museum administrator; b. N.Y.C., July 21, 1930; d. Edward Denmark and Cathrine Louise (Browne) O'B.; m. Philip R. James (div.); m. Sterling Noel (div.). BA, Finch Coll., 1952; postgrad. Williams Coll., 1954, Marymount Coll., 1954. Reprodn. mgr. Met. Mus. Art, N.Y.C., 1975—; dir. sales Simon Pearce Gallery. Exhibited in group shows at Parrish Art Mus., Southampton, N.Y., 1965-70, Met. Mus. Art, N.Y.C., 1975-85, Guild Hall Exhibit, East Hampton, N.Y., 1965-85; founding mem. Parrish Art Mus. Players, Southampton, 1958, Williamstown (Mass.) Theater, 1955; mem. John Drew Theater Co., Guild Hall, 1956-59. Mem. aux. Southampton Hosp., 1970-85; founder East Hampton Horse Show, Ladies Village Improvement Soc., East Hampton, 1970—; mem. fair coms. St. James Ch., N.Y.C., St. Luke's Ch., East Hampton, 1970-85; mem. alumnae adv. bd. Marymount Coll., N.Y.C., 1984-86, chmn. alumnae event, 1994; mem. Women's Nat. Rep. Club, N.Y.C.; chmn. Landmark and Tree Planting Com. for Madison Ave. Assn., N.Y.C., 1994—; mem. founding com. Internat. Debutante Ball, Waldorf Astoria, N.Y.C., 1955; founding mem. Williamstown (Mass.) Theater, 1955; founder Parrish Art Mus. Players, Southampton, N.Y., 1955. Recipient Simon Pearce Employee of Yr. award, 2000. Mem. DAR (founding; vice regent East Hampton chpt. 1974-85), Colonial Dames Am. (archives com. 1980-85), Daus. Brit. Empire (historian 1978-85), United Daus. Confederacy (state historian 1970-85), Daus. Colonial Wars (corr. sec. 1983-85), Sons and Daus. of Pilgrims (corr. sec. 1983-85), Victorian Soc., Soc. Mayflower Descs. (life), English Speaking Union, New Eng. Soc. (mem. ball com. 1983-86), Daus. of Cin. (historian 1979-85), Squadron "A", Devon Yacht, Maidstone, Southampton Yacht, Metropolitan Club (women's com., chmn. debutante ball 1980-84), Reciprocal/India House, St. Anthony Union League. Republican. Episopalian. Avocations: show horses, dogs. Home: 605 Park Ave New York NY 10021-7016 also: Seacote PO Box 1488 East Hampton NY 11937-0711 Office: Met Mus of Art 5th Ave New York NY 10028 also: Simon Pierce Gallery 500 Park Ave New York NY 10022-1606

O'BRIEN, CHARLES H. lawyer, retired state supreme court chief justice; b. Orange, N.J., July 30, 1920; s. Herbert Rodgers and Agnes Sidman (Montanya) O'B.; m. Anna Belle Clement, Nov. 9, 1966; children: Merry Diane, Steven Shawn (dec.), Heather Lynn. LLB, Cumberland U., 1947. Rep. Tenn. Legislature, Memphis, 1963-65, senator, 1965-67; assoc. judge Tenn. Ct. Criminal Appeals, Crossville, 1970-87; assoc. justice Tenn. Supreme Ct., 1987-94, chief justice, 1994-95; ret., 1995; pvt. practice, Crossville, 1995—. Bd. dirs. Lake Tansi Village Property Owners Assn., 1984-89, chmn., 1989. With U.S. Army, 1938-45, ETO, 1950, UN Command, Tokyo. Decorated Bronze Star, Purple Heart with oak leaf cluster. Fellow Tenn. Bar Found.; mem. Tenn. Bar Assn., Cumberland County Bar Assn., Am. Legion, Lake Tansi Village Chowder and Marching Soc. (pres.). Democrat. Avocation: outdoor activities.

O'BRIEN, CONAN, writer, performer, talk show host; b. Brookline, Mass., Apr. 18, 1963; BA Am. Hist., Lit., Harvard U., 1981-85. Staff mem. The Harvard Lampoon, 1981-85 (pres. 1983, 84); head Conaco. Stage appearances with: The Groundlings (L.A.) 1985-87; writer, performer The Happy Happy Good Show (L.A., Chgo.) 1988; writer (TV) Not Necessarily the News (HBO) 1985-87, Saturday Night Live, 1988-91 (NBC, Emmy Outstanding Writing in Comedy series 1989), Lookwell (NBC) 1991; writer, prodr. The Simpsons (Fox) 1991-93, The Wilton North Report (syndicated) 1987, Late Night with Conan O'Brien (NBC) 1993— (Best Writing in Comedy/Variety Show Writer's Guild award 1997, TV award Writers Guild Am. 2000), host, Emmy Awards 2002; TV appearances include Mr. Show, The Single Guy, Arli$$, (voice) Dr. Katz, Professional Therapist, Veronica's Closet, Spin City, Late-Line, Space Ghost Coast to Coast, (voice) Futurama, Tomorrow Night, 1998, Barenaked in America, 1999, Saturday Night Live: 25th Anniversary, 1999, (video) Elmopalooza!, 1998. Named one of 25 Most Intriguing People, People Mag., 50 Funniest People Alive, Entertainment Weekly. Office: Late Night with Conan O'Brien NBC 30 Rockefeller Plz New York NY 10112-0002*

O'BRIEN, DANIEL WILLIAM, lumber company executive; b. St. Paul, Jan. 6, 1926; s. Daniel W. and Kathryn (Zenk) O'B.; m. Sarah Ward Stoltze, June 20, 1952; children: Bridget Ann, Daniel William, Kevin Charles, Timothy John. Student, U. Dubuque, 1943, Ill. State U., 1944; BSL, U. Minn., 1948, JD, 1949. Bar: Minn. 1949. Practice in St. Paul, 1950—; partner Randall, Smith & Blomquist, 1955-65; of counsel Doherty, Rumble & Butler, 1965-99; pres. F.H. Stoltze Land & Lumber Co., 1964—, Maple Island, Inc., 1968—. Served to ensign USNR, 1943-46. Mem. Minn., Ramsey County bar assns., World Pres's. Orgn., Chief Execs. Orgn. Office: 2497 7th Ave E Ste 105 North Saint Paul MN 55109-2902 Home: 3951 S Placita De La Moneda Green Valley AZ 85614-5063 E-mail: dwobrien@maple-island.com.

O'BRIEN, DANIEL ROBERT, lawyer; b. Peoria, Ill., May 7, 1951; s. William Patrick and Irene Cornelia O'Brien; m. Eileen Mary Kahn, Aug. 17, 1974; children: Colleen, Patrick, Bridget. BS, No. Ill. U., 1973; JD, Wash. U., St. Louis, 1976. Bar: U.S. Dist. Ct. (so. dist.) Ill. 1977. Ptnr. Smith Moos Schmitt & O'Brien, Peoria, 1976-82, Moos, Schmitt & O'Brien, Peoria, 1982—. Lectr. Peoria County Bar Assn., Ill. Continuing Legal Edn., Springfield. Dem. precinct committeeman Dem. Party, 1986. Named to Greater Peoria Sports Hall of Fame, 2000. Fellow Ill. Bar Found. (charter mem., Leading Ill. Atty. award), Beta Gamma Sigma. Avocations: coaching children's basketball. Office: Moos Schmitt & O'Brien 331 Fulton St Ste 740 Peoria IL 61602-1499

O'BRIEN, DAVID A. lawyer; b. Sioux City, Iowa, Aug. 30, 1958; s. John T. and Doris K. (Reisch) O'B. BA, George Washington U., 1981; JD with distinction, U. Iowa, 1984. Bar: Iowa 1985, U.S. Dist. Ct. (no. dist.) Iowa 1985, Nebr. 1990, U.S. Dist. Ct. Nebr. 1990. Legis. asst. Nat. Transp. Safety Bd., Washington, 1978-81; assoc. O'Brien, Galvin & Kuehl, Sioux City, 1985-88; ptnr. O'Brien, Galvin Moeller & Neary, 1989-94; chair Wage Appeals Bd. & Bd. of Svc. Contract Appeals U.S. Dept. Labor, Washington, 1994-96, acting dir. Office Adminstrv. Appeals, 1995-96, chair adminstrv. review bd., 1996-98; atty. White & Johnson, P.C., Cedar Rapids, Iowa, 1998-2000; ptnr. Willey, O'Brien & Hanrahan, PLC, 2000—. Dem. candidate for Congress, 6th dist. of Iowa, Sioux City, 1988; chmn. Woodbury County Dem. Party, Sioux City, 1992-94, chair Iowa campaign Clinton for Pres., Des Moines, 1992; bd. dirs. Mid-Step Svcs. Inc., Sioux City, 1986-91, Mo. River Hist. Devel., Sioux City, 1989-94. Mem. Nat. Assn. Trial Lawyers, Iowa Trial Lawyers Assn. (bd. govs. 1991-94). Roman Catholic. Avocations: sports, politics. Office: Willey O'Brien & Hanrahan 3519 Center Pointe Rd NE Cedar Rapids IA 52402 Home Fax: 319-378-1413.

O'BRIEN, DAVID PETER, business executive; b. Montreal, Que., Can., Sept. 9, 1941; s. John Lewis and Ethel (Cox) O'B.; m. Gail Baxter Corneil, June 1, 1968; children: Tara, Matthew, Shaun. BA with honors in Econs., Loyola Coll., Montreal, 1962; B.C.L., McGill U., Montreal, 1965. Assoc. and ptnr. Ogilvy, Renault, Montreal, 1967-77; v.p., gen. counsel Petro-Can., Calgary, Alta., 1977-81, sr. v.p., 1982-85, sr. v.p. fin. and planning, 1982-85, exec. v.p., 1985-89; pres., chief exec. officer Noverco Inc., Montreal, 1989; chmn. bd., pres., chief exec. officer PanCan. Petroleum Ltd., Calgary, Alta., Can., 1990-94; pres., COO Can. Pacific Ltd., Montreal, 1995-96, chmn., pres., CEO Calgary, 1996—2001; chmn., CEO PanCan. Energy Corp., 2001—. Bd. dirs. Air Can., Inco Ltd., Royal Bank Can., Conf. Bd. Can., C.D. Howe Inst., Can. Pacific Ltd.; chmn. bd. dirs. PanCan. Petroleum Ltd., Bus. Coun. Nat. Issues; mem. exec. com. Bus. Coun. on Nat. Issues. Bd. govs. U. Calgary. Mem. Quebec Bar Assn., Glencoe Club, Calgary Petroleum Club, Calgary Golf and Country Club. Office: 4460 Bankers Hall W 888 3d St SW Calgary AB Canada T2P 5C5

O'BRIEN, DAVID SHEPARD, radiologist; b. N.Y.C., May 26, 1935; BA in Fgn. Affairs, U. Va., 1958; MD, U. Va. Sch. Medicine, 1963. Diplomate Am. Bd. Radiology. Intern Norfolk (Va.) Gen. Hosp., 1963-64; resident in radiology U. Va. Med. Ctr., 1964-67, fellow in radiology, 1967; radiologist Anne Arundel Gen. Hosp., Annapolis, Md., 1969-81; pvt. practice, 1976—. Maj. U.S. Army, 1967-69. Fellow Am. Coll. Radiology; mem. AMA, Am. Roentgen Ray Soc., Radiol. Soc. N.Am., Am. Inst. Ultrasound in Medicine, So. Med. Assn. Office: Am Radiology Svcs Inc 116 Defense Hwy Ste Ll100 Annapolis MD 21401-7626

O'BRIEN, DONALD EUGENE, federal judge; b. Marcus, Iowa, Sept. 30, 1923; s. Michael John and Myrtle A. (Toomey) O'B.; m. Ruth Mahon, Apr. 15, 1950; children: Teresa, Brien, John, Shuivaun. LL.B., Creighton U., 1948. Bar: Iowa bar 1948, U.S. Supreme Ct. bar 1963. Asst. city atty., Sioux City, Iowa, 1949—54; county atty. Woodbury County, 1955—59; mcpl. judge Sioux City, 1959-60; U.S. atty. No. Iowa, 1961-67; pvt. practice law Sioux City, 1948—61; U.S. Dist. judge, 1978—; chief judge U.S. Dist. Ct. (no. dist.) Iowa, 1985-92, sr. judge, 1992—; pvt. practice law, 1967—78. Rep. 8th cir. dist. ct. judges to Jud. Conf. U.S., 1990-97. Served with USAAF, 1942-45. Decorated D.F.C., air medals. Mem. Woodbury County Bar Assn., Iowa State Bar Assn. Roman Catholic. E-mail: Dan_O'Brien@iand.uscourts.gov. Office: US Dist Ct PO Box 267 Sioux City IA 51102-0267 E-mail: Don_OBrian@iand.uscourts.gov.

O'BRIEN, EDWARD IGNATIUS, private investor, corporation director; b. N.Y.C., Sept. 15, 1928; s. Edward I. and Marguerite (Malone) O'B.; m. Margaret M. Feeney, June 29, 1957; children: Edward Ignatius III, Margaret Mary, Thomas Gerard, John Joseph. AB, Fordham U., 1950; LLB, St. John's U., 1954; grad., Advanced Mgmt. Program, Cornell U., 1965. Bar: N.Y. 1954. With firm Hale, Kay & Brennan, N.Y.C., 1954-55; with Bache & Co., Inc., 1955-74, gen. counsel, 1960, gen. ptnr., 1964, sec., 1968, v.p., 1965-68, sr. v.p., mem. exec. com., 1969, exec. v.p., 1969, chmn. exec. com., 1971-74; pres. Securities Industry Assn., 1974-93; retired, 1993. Bd. dirs. 8 corps.; lectr. Am. Law Inst., Practising Law Inst., Am. Mgmt. Assn.; exch. ofcl. Am. Stock Exch., 1972; mem. adv. bd., mem. exec. com. Securities Regulation Inst., U. Calif., 1975—. Mem. Cardinal's com. Laity Cath. Archdiocese N.Y., mem. Cardinal's com. for edn.; chmn. Fordham U. Coun., 1971-73; bd. dirs. 3 non-profit orgns.; chmn. corp. devel. com. Fordham U.; trustee, chmn. bd. trustees Fordham Prep. Sch., 1975-77, Capt. USAR. Mem. N.Y. State Bar Assn,. Am. Arbitration Assn., Am. Soc. Internat. Law, Guild Cath. Lawyers, Securites Industry Assn. (chmn. publicly owned firms com. 1972), Nat. Assn. Securities Dealers (dist. com. 1973-74), Shenorock Shore Club (Rye, N.Y.), Town Club (Scarsdale, N.Y.), Met. Club (Washington). Home and Office: 12 Woods Ln Scarsdale NY 10583-6408

O'BRIEN, EDWIN FREDERICK, archbishop; b. Bronx, N.Y., Apr. 8, 1939; BA, St. Joseph's Sem., Yonkers, N.Y., 1961, MDiv, 1964, MA, 1965; STD, Algelicum U., Rome, 1976. Ordained priest Roman Cath. Ch., 1965. Parish priest, chaplain U.S. Mil. Acad., West Point, N.Y., 1965-70; commd. 2d lt. U.S. Army, 1970, advanced through grades to capt., 1973, chaplain, 1970-73, 82nd Airborne Divsn., Ft. Bragg, N.C., 1970-71, 173rd Airborne Brigade, 1st Calalry Brigade, Vietnam, 1971-72; post chaplain Ft. Gordon, Ga., 1972-73; assoc. pastor St. Patrick's Cathedral, N.Y.C., 1976-81; vice chancellor Archdiocese N.Y., 1976-81, dir. comm., 1981-83, sec. Cardinals Terence Cooke, John O'Connor, 1983-85; rector St. Joseph's Sem., Dunwoodie, N.Y., 1985-89, Pontifical N. Am. Coll., Rome, Italy, 1990-94, St. Joseph's Sem., Dunwoodie, N.Y., 1994-97; titular bishop Diocese of Tizica, 1996-99; auxillary bishop Diocese of N.Y., 1996-97; archbishop Archdiocese of Mil. Svcs., Washington, 1997—. Trustee St. Joseph's Sem., Pontifical N.Am. Coll., Pontifical Coll. Josephinum; bd. dirs. Nat. Conf. Cath. Bishops, Basilica of the Nat. Shrine of the Immaculate Conception. Mem. Fellowship Cath. Scholars. Office: Mil Archdiocese PO Box 4469 Washington DC 20017-0469 E-mail: archbishop@erols.com.

O'BRIEN, ELMER JOHN, librarian, educator; b. Kemmerer, Wyo., Apr. 8, 1932; s. Ernest and Emily Catherine (Reinhart) O'B.; m. Betty Alice Peterson, July 2, 1966. AB, Birmingham So. Coll., 1954; Th.M., Iliff Sch. Theology, 1957; MA, U. Denver, 1961. Ordained to ministry Methodist Ch., 1957; pastor Meth. Ch., Pagosa Springs, Colo., 1957—60; circulation-reference librarian Boston U. Sch. Theology, 1961—65; asst. librarian Garrett-Evang. Theol. Sem., Evanston, Ill., 1965—69; librarian, prof. United Theol. Sem., Dayton, Ohio, 1969—96, prof. emeritus, 1996—; abstractor Am. Bibliog. Center, 1969—73; dir. Ctr. for Evang. United Brethren Heritage, 1979—96; acting libr. Iliff Sch. Theology, 2000—01. Chmn. div. exec. com. Dayton-Miami Valley Libr. Consortium, 1983-84; rsch. assoc. Am. Antiquarian Soc., 1990. Author: Bibliography of Festschriften in Religion Published Since 1960, 1972, Religion Index Two: Festschriften, 1960-69; contbg. author: Communication and Change in American Religious History, 1993, Essays in Celebration of the First Fifty Years, 1996; pub. Meth. Revs. Index, 1818-1985, 1989-91; contbr. essay to profl. jour. Recipient theol. and scholarship award Assn. Theol. Schs. in U.S. and Can., 1990-91; Assn. Theol. Schs. in U.S. and Can. library staff devel. grantee, 1976-77, United Meth. Ch. Bd. Higher Edn. and Ministry research grantee, 1984-85 Mem. ALA, Acad. Libr. Assn. Ohio, Am. Theol. Libr. Assn. (head bur. personnel and placement 1969-73, dir. 1973-76, v.p. 1977-78, pres. 1978-79), Am. Antiquarian Soc. (rsch. assoc. 1990), Delta Sigma Phi, Omicron Delta Kappa, Eta Sigma Phi, Kappa Phi Kappa. Clubs: Torch Internat. (v.p. Dayton club 1981-82, pres. 1982-83). Home: 4840 Thunderbird Dr Apt 281 Boulder CO 80303-3829 E-mail: Ejobr@aol.com.

O'BRIEN, EVA FROMM, lawyer; b. Herne, Germany, May 6, 1956; came to U.S., 1959; d. Georg and Eva (Aust) F.; m. John J. O'Brien, Feb. 12, 2000. BS in Chem. Engring., Syracuse U., 1978; JD, U. Houston, 1985. Bar: Tex. 1985, U.S. Dist. Ct. (so. dist.) Tex. 1987, U.S. Ct. Appeals (5th cir.) 1997. Engr. Chrysler Corp., Deer Park, Mich., 1978-79; process engr. Mobay Chem. Co., Baytown, Tex., 1980, ETI Engrs. Inc., Houston, 1981-82; engr. Petromas Inc., 1982-83; sr. chem. engr. NUS Corp., 1983-84; briefing clk., assoc. Hill Parker Franklin Cardwell & Jones, 1985-86; assoc. Fulbright & Jaworski LLP, 1986-93, ptnr., 1994—. Author, editor: Texas Environmental Law Handbook, 1989, 5th edit., 2000, (book chpt.) Environmental Aspects of Real Estate Transactions, 2d edit., 1999. Mem. ABA (co-chair real estate and probate sect., underground storage tank and RCRA com. 1994-95), Houston Bar Assn. (co-chair legal line com. 1988-90; sec. environ. law sect. 1991, vice-chair 1992, chair 1993). Home: 19 Serenity Woods Pl Houston TX 77383 Office: Fulbright & Jaworski LLP 1301 Mckinney St Ste 5100 Houston TX 77010-3031

O'BRIEN, FRANCIS ANTHONY, retired lawyer; b. Albany, N.Y., Sept. 23, 1936; s. Francis Joseph and Helen Marie (Smith) O'B.; m. Maryanne Delia Mahoney, May 2, 1964; children— John, Dennis, Kathleen, Eileen AB, Hamilton Coll., 1958; LLB, Cornell U., 1961. Bar: N.Y. 1962, D.C. 1968. Trial atty. FTC, Washington, 1962-68; assoc. Howrey & Simon, 1968-70, ptnr., 1971-86; prin., ret. Francis A. O'Brien & Assocs. Alumni trustee Hamilton Coll., Clinton, N.Y., 1980-84; mem. Chesterbrook Woods Citizen Assn., McLean, Va., 1976— Mem. ABA, Fed. Bar Assn., N.Y. Bar Assn., D.C. Bar Assn. Roman Catholic. Avocations: basketball; soccer; Civil War history. Home: 1600 Forest Ln Mc Lean VA 22101-3314

O'BRIEN, FRANCIS JOSEPH, internet company executive; b. Chgo., Nov. 10, 1963; s. Francis Peter and Patricia Marie O'B. BA, Ill. Benedictine Coll., 1985; MBA, U. Wis., 2000. V.p. Browning-Ferris Ind., Schaumburg, Ill., 1985-92; co-founder, pres. Bio-Sure Environ., Chgo., 1992—. Cons. SBA-U. Wisc.-Whitewater Small Bus. Devel., 1996-2000; dist. mgr. Genuity Inc. Mem. Am. Chemical Soc., Nat. Solid Waste Mgmt. Assn. Avocations: computers, music, outdoor activities, woodworking. Home and Office: W6011 Mariner Hills Trl Elkhorn WI 53121-2544 E-mail: fob63@aol.com.

O'BRIEN, GAYLE ANN, nurse; b. Warren, Ohio, July 11, 1957; d. James Allen Lipscomb and Delores Pauline (Vauple) Swindler; children: Veronica N., Steven J. BSN, Kent State U., 1980, MSN, 1985. Cert. profl. healthcare quality; clin. nurse specialist, APN. Nurse mgmt. critical care Robinson Meml. Hosp., Ravenna, Ohio, 1980—86, clin. mgr. coronary care unit, 1986-88; instr. U. Akron (Ohio), 1988-90; clin. nurse specialist in critical care Akron Gen. Med. Ctr., 1990—, dir. performance improvement, patient safety officer, 1988-90; patient safety officer, 2001—. Mem. Nat. Assn. Healthcare Quality, Am. Coll. Healthcare Execs., Ohio Assn. Nurse Execs. Office: Akron Gen Med Ctr 400 Wabash Ave Akron OH 44307-2463 E-mail: gobrien@agmc.org.

O'BRIEN, GEOFFREY PAUL, editor, writer; b. N.Y.C., May 4, 1948; s. Joseph Aloysius and Margaret Dorothy (Owens) O'B.; m. Carly Francis O'Brien, Mar. 18, 1977; 1 child, Heather. Student, Yale U., 1966-67, SUNY, Stony Brook, 1968-70. Editor Reader's Catalog, N.Y.C., 1987-91; exec. editor Libr. of Am., 1992-97, editor-in-chief, 1998—. Author: Hardboiled America, 1981, Dream Time, 1988, A Book of Maps, 1989, The Phantom Empire, 1993, The Hudson Mystery, 1994, Floating City: Selected Poems, 1978-1995, 1996, The Times Square Story, 1998, Bardic Deadlines: Reviewing Poetry 1984-95, 1998, The Browser's Ecstasy, 2000, Castaways of the Image Planet, 2002; contbr. ; contbg. writer The Village Voice, 1982—90; editor: Frogpond, 1980—81; co-editor: Montemora, 1974—76. Recipient Writing award Whiting Found., 1988; fellow N.Y. Inst. Humanities, 1998—, John Simon Guggenheim Meml. Found., 1999. Office: Libr of Am 14 E 60th St New York NY 10022-1006

O'BRIEN, GEORGE DENNIS, retired university president; b. Chgo., Feb. 21, 1931; s. George Francis and Helen (Fehlandt) O'B.; m. Judith Alyce Johnson, June 21, 1958; children: Elizabeth Belle, Juliana Helen, Victoria Alyce. AB in English, Yale, 1952; PhD in Philosophy, U. Chgo., 1961. Tchr. humanities, Carnegie rsch. fellow U. Chgo., 1956-57; from instr. to asst. prof., asst. dean Princeton (N.J.) U., 1958-65; on leave in Athens, Greece, 1963-64; spl. honors seminars LaSalle Coll., spring 1963, fall 1964, spring 1965; assoc. prof. philosophy Middlebury (Vt.) Coll., 1965-71, prof., 1971-76, dean of men, 1965-67, dean of coll., 1967-74, dean faculty, 1975-76; pres. Bucknell U., 1976-84, U. Rochester, N.Y., 1984-94; ret., 1994. Dir. Salzburg Seminar in Am. Studies. Author: Hegel on Reason in History, 1975, God and the New Haven Railway, 1986, What to Expect from College, 1991, All the Essential Half-Truths About Higher Education, 1997, The Idea of a Catholic University, 2002; contbr. articles to profl. jours. Trustee LaSalle Coll., Phila., 1965—; bd. dirs. Union Theol. Sem., 1985-90, Rsch. Librs. Group, 1994-96 salzburg Seminar; v.p. Commonweal Found., 1994—. Fellow Am. Coun. Learned Socs., London, 1971-72; Nat. Phi Beta Kappa scholar, 1996-97. Mem. Am. Philos. Assn., Phi Beta Kappa. Home: 153 Wildflower Ln Middlebury VT 05753-9172

O'BRIEN, GERALD JAMES, utilities executive; b. St. Paul, May 1, 1923; s. Dewey Joseph and Henrietta Elizabeth O'B.; m. Patricia Margaret McCorison, Feb. 23, 1946; children: Kathleen, Thomas, John, Andrew. Student, St. Thomas Coll., 1940-41, 45-46; B.C.S., Drake U., 1948. Staff acct. Haskins & Sells, Mpls., 1948-50; with Donovan Cos., Inc., St. Paul, 1950-81, sec., asst. treas., 1977-81; utility rate cons., 1981-84. Dir. Alumbaugh Coal Co., Donovan Constrn. Co., So. Tier Gas Corp., Gas Distbrs. Info. Service. Served with U.S. Army, 1942-45. Decorated Purple Heart. Address: 13313 W Meeker Blvd Sun City West AZ 85375-3808

O'BRIEN, HOLLY, accountant; b. Chgo., June 22, 1946; d. Albert and Virginia Marjorie (Pyne) Schelling; m. Robert T. O'Brien (div. 1982); children: Becky Jacques, Donald Baber. Student, U. Wash., 1968. Acct. Am. Express, Phoenix, 1970-75, D.C. Speer Constrn., Phoenix, 1975-82, Swiss Am. Corp., Phoenix, 1982-84; sr. account cons. TRW Info. Systems, Phoenix and Pleasanton, Calif., 1984-88; acct. Carson Messinger Elliott Laughling & Ragan, Phoenix, 1988—. Pres. Neighborhood Coalition Greater Phoenix, 1990—; chair Encanto Village Planning Com., Phoenix, 1991—; mem. Indian Sch. Task Force, Phoenix, 1991; bd. dirs. Valley Partnership, Phoenix, 1992. Mem. Ariz. Rose Soc., Ariz. Common Cause, Paradise Rep. Women. Avocations: gardening, reading, watercolors. Office: Neighborhood Coalition Greater Phoenix PO Box 13057 Phoenix AZ 85002-3057

O'BRIEN, INGE FRANCES RAPSTINE, research scientist, geological and geophysical consultant; b. Amarillo, Tex., Jan. 10, 1952; d. B. Frank and Frances Louise (Schulze) Rapstine; m. Michael Edwin O'Brien, Sept. 21, 1979; children: Bonnie Lou, Abbey Gayle. BS in Geology, West Tex. State U., 1976, MS, 1980. Geophys. technician Oil Devel. Co., Amarillo, 1975-76, jr. geophysicist, 1976-78; geophysicist Santa Fe Energy Co., Amarillo, 1979-81, sr. geophysicist, 1981-83; cons. geologist/geophysicist, Amarillo, 1983—; geophysicist Corlena Oil Co., Amarillo, 1993-95; sr. scientist Battelle, Amarillo, 1995—; pres. Lufrank Corp., Amarillo, 1985-93; mem. geol. acad. adv. bd. West Tex. State U., Canyon, 1988-89; bd. dirs. Inland Prodn. Corp., Amarillo, Amarillo Natural Gas. Mem. Am. Assn. Petroleum Geologists, Panhandle Geol. Soc. (editor, sec., treas. 1980-83), Am. Inst. Profl. Geologists (cert.), Panhandle Prodrs. and Royalty Owners Assn., Intertel, Mensa, Sigma Gamma Epsilon, Chi Omega. Roman Catholic. Office: Pantex PO Box 30020 Amarillo TX 79120-0020

O'BRIEN, J. WILLARD, lawyer, educator; b. N.Y.C., Oct. 19, 1930; s. J. Willard and Anna C. (Carroll) O.'B.; m. Peggy J. O'Brien. BS, Fordham U., 1952, JD, 1957. Bar: N.Y. 1957. Assoc. Cahill, Gordon, Reindel & Ohl, N.Y.C., 1957-62; asst. prof. law Syracuse U. Coll. Law, 1962-65; prof. law Villanova (Pa.) U. Sch. Law, 1965-98, dean, 1972-83, dir. Connelly Inst. Law and Morality, 1983-95, dean and prof. of law emeritus, 1998—. Mem. Pa. Fed. Jud. Nominating Commn., 1977-80, vice chmn., 1978-80; mem. Pa. Law and Justice Inst., 1972-73, chmn. exec. com., 1973-75, pres., 1975-77 Editor-in-chief Fordham Law Rev, 1956-57. Bd. dirs. Nat. Inst. on Holocaust, 1984-85; bd. dirs. Phila. Coordinating Council on the Holocaust, 1983— . Served with USAF, 1952-54; Served with N.Y. Air N.G., 1954-58. Mem. ABA, N.Y. State Bar Assn., Pa. Bar Assn., Canon Law Soc. Am. Roman Catholic.

O'BRIEN, JAMES ALOYSIUS, foreign language educator; b. Cin., Apr. 7, 1936; s. James Aloysius and Frieda (Schirmer) O'B.; m. Rumi Matsumoto, Aug. 26,1961. BA, St. Joseph's Coll., 1958; MA, U. Cin., 1960; PhD, Ind. U., 1969. Instr. English, St. Joseph's Coll., Rensselaer, Ind., 1960-62; asst. prof. Japanese, U. Wis., Madison, 1968-74, assoc. prof., 1974-81, prof., 1981—, chmn. East Asian langs and lit., 1979-80, 82-85, 96—. Author: Dazai Osamu, 1975, Akutagawa and Dazai: Instances of Literary Adaptation, 1988; translator: Selected Stories and Sketches (Dazai Osamu), 1983, Three Works (Muro Saisei), 1985, Crackling Mountain and Other Stories (Dazai Osamu), 1989. Mem. MIddleton City Common Coun., 1996—. Ford Found fellow, 1965-66; Fulbright-Hays and NDEA fellow, 1966-68; Social Sci. Research Council fellow, 1973-74; Japan Found. fellow, 1977-78 Mem. Assn. Asian Studies, Assn. Tchrs. of Japanese (exec. com. 1981-84, dir. devel. 1981-83, pres. 1984-90) Home: 2533 Branch St Middleton WI 53562-2812 Office: U Wis Dept East Asian Langs-Lit 1220 Linden Dr Madison WI 53706-1525

O'BRIEN, JAMES EDMOND, journalist, editor, educator; b. Schenectady, N.Y., June 30, 1952; cre; s. James Joseph and Marie Crooks (Wilkie) O'B.; m. Ronni Michele Rosenberg, Dec. 1, 1996; children: Ariel Melissa, Alex Michael. BA, SUNY, Potsdam, 1974; MA, Binghamton (N.Y.) U., 1976; MBA, N.Y. Inst. Tech., 1999. Freelance journalist Boston Phoenix, The Real Paper, Boston, 1977-81; reporter Globe Comm. Corp., Boca Raton, Fla., 1981-88; staff writer Your Health mag., 1988-97; exec. dir. Unicorn Children's Found., 1998-99; assoc. editor Nat. Enquirer, Lantana, Fla., 1999—; instr. French, ESL The Lang. Exch., Delray Beach, 1988—; pres. Moondance Enterprises, Inc., Fla., 1989—; tchr. French Palm Beach County Schs./Boca Raton Cmty. H.S., 1992—. Author: Garlic and Vinegar, 1989, Lower Cholesterol 30 Points in 30 Days, 1992, Fat Burning Foods, 1994, Herbal Cures for Common Ailments, 1997. Scholar Bryn Mawr Coll., 1976; recipient Excellence in Journalism award Am. Acad. Allergy and Asthma, N.Y.C., 1986. Avocations: fitness activities, computer programming, dog training, yoga, meditation. Home: 6508 Stonehurst Cir Lake Worth FL 33467-7374

O'BRIEN, JAMES JEROME, construction management consultant; b. Phila., Oct. 20, 1929; s. Sylvester Jerome and Emma Belle Filer (Fulforth) O'B.; m. Carmen Hiester, June 10, 1952 (div. Aug. 1, 1984); children: Jessica Susan, Michael, David; m. Rita F. Gibson, Nov. 1, 1984 BCE, Cornell U., 1952; postgrad., U. Houston, 1957-58. Registered profl. engr., N.Y., N.J., Pa., Ga., Conn., Maine. Project engr. Rohm & Haas, Phila. and Tex., 1955-59, RCA Corp., Moorestown, N.J., Greenland and Alaska, 1959-62; cons. Mauchly Assocs., Fort Washington, Pa., 1962-65; founding ptnr., exec. v.p. Meridian Engring. Co., Phila., 1965-68; pres. MDC Systems, Cherry Hill, 1968-72; ptnr. James J. O'Brien P.E., 1972-77; pres. O'Brien-Kreitzberg & Assocs., N.Y.C., Pennsauken, San Francisco, 1977-80, chief exec. officer, 1980-89, chmn. bd. dirs., 1989-93, vice chmn., 1993—. Author: CPM in Construction Management-Scheduling by the Critical Path Method, 1965, CPM in Construction Management-Project Management with CPM, 5th edit., 1999, Management Information Systems-Concepts, Techniques and Applications, 1970, Management with Computers, 1972, Construction Inspection Handbook, 1974, 4th edit., 1997, Value Analysis in Design and Construction, 1976, Construction Delay-Risks, Rsponsibilities and Litigation, 1976, Preconstruction Estimating: Budget to Bid, 1994, Construction Documentation, 3d edit., 1995; co-author: Construction Management: A Professional Approach, 1974; editor: Recollections (L.D. Miles), 1987; author, editor: Scheduling Handbook, 1969, Contractor's Management Handbook, 1971, 2d edit., 1990, Standard Handbook of Heavy Construction, 3d edit., 1996, Construction Change Orders, 1998; contbr. articles to profl. jours. Lt. 1952-55, USN. Recipient Profl. Mgr. award N.Y. chpt. Soc. Advancement Mgmt., 1969 Fellow ASCE (Constrn. Mgmt. award 1976, v.p. 1985, pres. South Jersey br. 1985, Disting. Engr. South Jersey br. 1986, pres. N.J. sect. 1987-89, mem. com. on quality in civil engring. profession 1990-97), Project Mgmt. Inst. (sec. 1971, v.p. 1972, pres. 1973, chmn. bd. 1974-75, award for contbn. to project mgmt. 1983, Fellow award 1989, project mgmt. profl.), Constrn. Mgmt. Assn. Am. (bd. dirs. 1990-92, Fellow award 1993, Constrn. Mgr. of Yr. award N.Y.-N.J. chpt. 1994), Cornell Soc. Engrs. (dean's adv. com. sch. civil and environ. engring. 1986-87); mem. Soc. Am. Value Engrs. (cert. value specialist, v.p. N.E. region 1986-87, Fallon Value-in-Life award 1993), Miles Value Found. (bd. dirs. 1987-90, 99, trustee 1990-99), Tau Beta Pi, Chi Epsilon. Home: 2 Linden Ave Riverton NJ 08077-1124 Office: O'Brien Kreitzberg 8 Penn Ctr 21st Fl 1628 Jfk Blvd Philadelphia PA 19103-2125

O'BRIEN, JAMES PHILLIP, lawyer; b. Monmouth, Ill., Jan. 6, 1949; s. John Matthew and Roberta Helen (Cavanaugh) O'B.; m. Laurene Reason, Aug. 30, 1969 (div. 1980); m. Lynn Florsheim, Sept. 5, 1987. BA, Western Ill. U., 1971; JD, U. Ill., 1974. Bar: Ill. 1974. Asst. atty. gen. State Ill., Springfield, 1974-75; jud. clerk Ill. Appellate Ct., 1975-76; assoc. Graham & Graham, 1976-81; corp. counsel Am. Hosp. Assn., Chgo., 1981-84; ptnr., chmn. health care dept. Katten, Muchin & Zavis, 1984—. Task force med. malpractice reform legislation Am. Hosp. Assn., 1983-84, tax adv. com., 1987-91, tax reporting and compliance com., 1990-91; spkr. in field. Contbr. numerous articles to profl. jours. Recipient cert. recognition Ill. Dept. Children and Family Svcs., 1981; Edward Arthur Mellinger Found. scholar, Western Ill. U. 1971. Mem.: Am. Arbitration Assn. (Task Force Health Care Dispute Resolution 1982—84), Am. Health Lawyers Assn. Office: Katten Muchin & Zavis 525 W Monroe St Ste 1600 Chicago IL 60661-3693

O'BRIEN, JIM, professional basketball coach; m. Sharon O'Brien; children: Jack, Shannon, Caitlyn. B in Mgmt., Mktg., St. Joseph, 1974; MBA, U. Md., 1981. Head coach Wheeling Jesuit Coll. , 1982—87; asst. coach for Pitino N.Y. Knicks, 1987—88; head coach U. Dayton, 1989—94; assoc. coach to Pitino U. Ky., 1994—97; profl. basketball coach Boston Celtics, 2001—. Asst. coach 6 different colls. Named to St. Joseph's Hall of Fame, 1988, Big Five Hall of Fame, 1989. Office: Boston Celtics Lp 151 Merrimac St #1 Boston MA 02114-4714*

O'BRIEN, JOAN SUSAN, lawyer, educator; b. New York, Apr. 14, 1946; d. Edward Vincent O'Brien and Joan Therese (Kramer) Quinn; m. Michael P. Wilpan, May 27, 1979; children: Edward B. Wilpan, Anabel T. Wilpan. BA, NYU, 1967; JD, Georgetown U., 1970. Bar: N.Y. 1971, Mass. 1971, U.S. Dist. Ct. (so. and ea. dist.) N.Y. 1972, U.S. Ct. Appeals (2d cir.) 1971. Law clk. to Hon. Frank J. Murray U.S. Dist. Ct. Mass., Boston, 1970-71; asst. U.S. atty. Office of U.S. Atty. U.S. Dist. Ct. (ea. dist.) N.Y., Bklyn., 1972-76; pvt. practice N.Y.C., 1976-79; trial atty. Mendes & Mount, 1979-84; asst. prof. St. Johns U., Jamaica, N.Y., 1984-90; adminstrv. law judge N.Y. State Workers Compensation Bd., Hempstead, 1990-93; appellate atty. Scheine, Fusco, Brandenstein & Rada, Woodbury, 1993-97; trial atty. Grey & Grey, L.L.P., Farmingdale, 1997—. Editor: Georgetown Law Jour., 1968-70. Pres. Nassau County Dem. Com. Women's Caucus, Westbury, N.Y., 1988-90; leader Girl Scouts Nassau County, 1990-93. Unitarian-Universalist. Office: Grey & Grey LLP 360 Main St Farmingdale NY 11735-3592

O'BRIEN, JOHN GRAHAM, lawyer; b. N.Y.C., May 12, 1948; s. John Edward and Marian Helen (FitzGerald) O'B.; m. Phyllis Mary Eyth, Apr. 10, 1976; children: John Graham Jr., Jennifer A. BS cum laude, Mt. St. Mary's Coll., Emmitsburg, Md., 1970; JD, Am. U., 1973. Bar: N.J. 1974, D.C. 1974, N.Y. 1982, U.S. Supreme Ct. 1982. Law clk. to Hon. F.C. Kentz and J.H. Coleman, Superior Ct. of N.J., Elizabeth, N.J., 1973-74; assoc. Carpenter, Bennett & Morrissey, Newark, 1975-81; sr. counsel GAF Corp., Wayne, N.J., 1981-90; assoc. gen. counsel Keene Corp., N.Y.C., 1990-93, ISS Internat. Svc. Sys., N.Y.C., 1994-95; cons. GE, Fairfield, Conn., 1993-94; mng. ptnr. Atkins O'Brien Ekblom LLP, N.Y.C., 1995-2000; of counsel McGivney, Kluger & Gannon, 2000—01; gen. counsel Brickforce Staffing Inc., Edison, NJ, 2001—. Author: (monograph) Responding to Products Liability Claims, 1986, also supplements; contbg. author: Toxic Torts Practice Guide, 1992. Recipient Disting. Young Alumni award Mt. St. Mary's Coll., 1976. Mem. N.J. Bar Assn., D.C. Bar, Echo Lke Country Club (assoc.), Coll. Mens Club. Roman Catholic. Office: 2 Ethel Rd Ste 204B Edison NJ 08817-2839 E-mail: obriennj2@aol.com.

O'BRIEN, JOHN CONWAY, economist, educator, writer; b. Hamilton, Lanarkshire, Scotland; s. Patrick and Mary (Hunt) O'B.; m. Jane Estelle Judd, Sept. 16, 1966; children: Kellie Marie, Kerry Patrick, Tracy Anne, Kristen Noël. B.Com., U. London, 1952, cert. in German lang., 1954; tchr.'s cert., Scottish Edn. Dept., 1954; AM, U. Notre Dame, 1959, PhD, 1961. Tchr. Scottish High Schs., Lanarkshire, 1952-56; instr. U. B.C., Can., 1961-62; asst. prof. U. Sask., 1962-63, U. Dayton, Ohio, 1963-64; assoc. prof. Wilfrid Laurier U., Ont., Can., 1964-65; from asst. to full prof. Econs. and Ethics Calif. State U., Fresno, 1965—. Vis. prof. U. Pitts., 1969-70, U. Hawaii, Manoa, 1984, U. Queensland, Brisbane, Australia, 1994; keynote speaker Wageningen Agrl. U., The Netherlands, 1987; presenter papers 5th, 6th, 10th World Congress of Economists, Tokyo, 1977, Mexico City, 1980, Moscow, 1992; presenter Schmoller Symposium, Heilbronn am Neckar, Fed. Republic Germany, 1988, paper The China Confucius Found. and "2540" Conf., Beijing, 1989, 6th Internat. Conf. on Cultural Econs., Univ. Umeå, Sweden, 1990, Internat. Soc. Intercommunication New Ideas, Sorbonne, Paris, 1990, European Assn. for Evolutionary Polit. Economy, Vienna, Austria, 1991; active rsch. U. Göttingen, Fed. Republic Germany, 1987; acad. cons. Cath. Inst. Social Ethics, Oxford; presenter in field. Author: Karl Marx: The Social Theorist, 1981, The Economist in Search of Values, 1982, Beyond Marxism, 1985, The Social Economist Hankers After Values, 1992; editor: Internat. Rev. Econs. and Ethics, Internat. Jour. Social Econs., Ethical Values and Social Econs., 1981, Selected Topics in Social Econs., 1982, Festschrift in honor of George Rohrlich, 3 vols., 1984, Social Economics: A Pot=Pourri, 1985, The Social Economist on Nuclear Arms: Crime and Prisons, Health Care, 1986, Festschrift in honor of Anghel N. Rugina, Parts I and II, 1987, Gustav von Schmoller: Social Economist, 1989, The Eternal Path to Communism, 1990, (with Z. Wenxian) Essays from the People's Republic of China, 1991, Festschrift in Honor of John E. Elliott, Parts I and II, 1992, Communism Now and Then, 1993, The Evils of Soviet Communism, 1994, Ruminations on the USSR, 1994, The Future Without Marx, 1995, Essays in Honour of Clement Allan Tisdell, 1996, Essays in Honor of Clement Allan Tisdell, Part I, 1996, Part II and III, 1997, Part IV and V, 1998, Part VI, 1999, Part VII and VIII, 2000, Social Economists at Work, 1999, Our Fragile Civilization, 2001; translator econ. articles from French and German into English; contbr. numerous articles to profl. jours. With British Royal Army Service Corps, 1939-46, ETO, NATOUSA, prisoner of war, Germany. Recipient GE Corp. award Stanford U., 1966, Ludwig Mai Svc. award Assn. for Social Econs., Washington, 1994; named Disting. Fellow of Internat. Soc. for Intercomm. of New Ideas, Paris, 1990. Fellow Internat. Inst. Social Econs. (mem. coun., program dir. 3d World Cong. Social Econs. Fresno Calif. 1983, keynote spkr. 4th conf. Toronto 1986), Internat. Soc. for Intercomm. New Ideas (disting.); mem. Assn. Social Econs. (dir. west region 1977—, pres.-elect 1988-89, program dir. conf. 1989, pres. 1990, presdl. address Washington 1990, Thomas Divine award 1997), Western Econ. Assn. (organizer, presenter 1977-95), History Econs. Soc., Soc. Reduction Human Labor (exec. com.), European Assn. Evolutionary Polit. Econs., Ga. Acad. Econ. Scis. (Republic of Ga. fgn. mem.). Roman Catholic. Avocations: jogging, collecting miniature paintings, soccer, tennis, photography. Home: 2733 W Fir Ave Fresno CA 93711-0315 Office: Calif State U Econs And Ethics Dept Fresno CA 93740-0001 E-mail: john_obrien@csu.fresno.edu.

O'BRIEN, JOHN E. priest, principal; b. Rockville Centre, N.Y., Jan. 4, 1960; s. John E. and Lois O'Brien. BS, Mt. St. Mary's Coll., Emmitsburg, MD, 1982; BST, MDiv., St. Mary's Sem. and U., Balt., 1986; MEd, Loyola Coll., Balt., 2002. Ordained priest Roman Cath. Ch., 1987. Assoc. pastor St. Margaret Ch., Bel Air, Md., 1987—93; religion tchr. John Carroll Sch., 1992—93; assoc. pastor Sacred Heart Ch., Glyndon, 1993—94; assoc. dir. Msgr. O'Dwyer Retreat House, Sparks, 1994—96, dir., 1996—98; chaplain Calvert Hall Coll. H.S., Balt., 1998—2002; prin. Cardinal Gibbons Sch., 2002—. Recipient Medal of Honor, Archiocese Balt. Divsn. Youth and Young Adult Ministry, 1998. Mem.: Nat. Cath. Edn. Assn., Alpha Sigma Nu.

O'BRIEN, JOHN FEIGHAN, investment banker; b. Cleve., Aug. 8, 1936; s. Francis John and Ann (Feighan) O'B.; m. Regina Quaid Harahan, June 27, 1959 (div. 1976); children: Regina, Victoria, Julie, John Jr.; m. Marilyn E. Schreiner. BS, Georgetown U., 1958. Salesman Appliance Mart, Cleve., 1958-59, ptnr., 1960-66; investment broker McDonald & Co. Investments, 1966-71, ptnr., 1971-83, exec. v.p., 1983-88, mng. dir., 1988-91, sr. mng. dir., 1993—. Bd. dirs. Hitchcock House, Cleve., 1978-89, Recovery Resources; chmn. Alcoholism Svcs. of Cleve., 1989-92, Alcohol and Drug-Addiction Svcs. Bd. of Cuyahoga County, 1992-98; trustee St. Edward H.S., Lakewood, Ohio, Alumnus of Yr., 1997,chmn. capital campaign, 1993-95; grand jury foreman Cuyahoga County, 2000. Named Good Fellow of Yr. Irish Good Fellows Club Cleve., 1996. Mem. Leadership Cleve., Greater Cleve. Growth Assn., Georgetown U. Alumni Assn. (alumni bd. senator, John Carrol award 1999), Westwood Country Club, Cleve. Yacht Club. Home: 8 Westhampton Dr Rocky River OH 44116-2300 also: 1800 S Ocean Dr Fort Lauderdale FL 33316-3704 Office: McDonald & Co Investments 18500 Lake Rd Ste 300 Rocky River OH 44116-1744 E-mail: jfeighanob@aol.com.

O'BRIEN, J(OHN) PATRICK, psychiatrist, educator; b. Washington, Aug. 25, 1941; s. John Francis and Gertrude Estelle (Offutt) O'B. BA magna cum laude, Yale U., 1963; MD, Johns Hopkins U., 1968. Diplomate Am. Bd. Psychiatry and Neurology. Intern U. Pa.-Phila. Gen. Hosp., 1970-71; resident Mass. Gen. Hosp., Boston, 1971-74; clin. fellow psychiatry Harvard U., 1971-74, clin. instr. psychiatry, 1974-79, asst. clin. prof. psychiatry, 1979—; asst. in psychiatry Mass. Gen. Hosp., 1974-83, asst. psychiatrist, 1983—. Lectr. Harvard Extension Sch., Boston, 1985-88. Author: The Disorganized Mind, 1978, poems; translator: (jour.) Formations, 1987. Fellow Royal Soc. Medicine; Am. Psychiat. Assn., N.Y. Acad. Scis., Mass. Psychiat. Assn., Yale Club Mass., Phi Beta Kappa. Democrat. Office: Mass Gen Hosp ACC 806C 15 Parkman St Boston MA 02114-3117

O'BRIEN, JOHN STEININGER, clinical psychologist; b. Lewisburg, Pa., June 3, 1936; s. Peck Zanders and Esther (Steininger) O'B.; children: Peck David, Timothy. AB, Pa. State U., 1967; MA, So. Ill. U., 1969; PhD, Boston U., 1980. Diplomate Internat. Acad. Profl. Psychotherapists, Internat. Acad. Behavioral Medicine/Psychotherapy. Asst. tchr. educable retarded children Selin's Grove (Pa.) State Sch., 1964-66; clin. rsch. asst. Pa. State U., State Coll., 1966-67; rsch. technician Anna (Ill.) State Hosp., 1968; intern Boston City Hosp., 1968-69, from coord. alcohol study unit to psychologist, 1969-73; clin. instr. psychiatry Sch. Medicine Tufts U., St. Elizabeth's Hosp., Brighton, Mass., 1973-81; dir. psychol. svcs. Baldpate Hosp., Georgetown, 1981-94, dir. outpatient substance abuse rehab. program, 1991-94; clin. psychologist Brockton (Mass.) Hosp., 1994—. Bio-behavioral cons. Behavioral Medicine Inst., Quincy, Mass., 1985-88; clin. dir. Social Learning Ctr., Quincy, 1971—; behavioral therapist, clin. coord. TAP Boston Childrens Svc., 1973-76; lectr. in psychology Curry Coll., Milton, Mass., 1994—. Author: Moments with Peck, 1982, Peck's Boat; A Duffy & Duffy, 1991; contbr. 45 articles to profl. jours. Mem. APA, Nat. Register Health Svcs. in Psychology, Soc. Study of Addiction, Assn. Advancement Behavioral Therapy, Am. Assn. Clin. Counselors, Biofeedback Soc. Am., Internat. Acad. Profl. Counselors and Psychotherapists. Avocations: ocean cruising, deep sea fishing, photography, gardening. Home and Office: 111 Hillberg Ave Brockton MA 02301

O'BRIEN, JOHN WILFRID, economist, emeritus university president, educator; b. Toronto, Ont., Can., Aug. 4, 1931; s. Wilfred Edmond and Audrey (Swain) O'B.; m. Joyce Helen Bennett, Aug. 4, 1956; children: Margaret Anne, Catherine Audrey. BA, McGill U., 1953, MA, 1955, PhD, 1962, LLD, 1976; postgrad., Inst. Polit. Studies, Paris, 1954; DCL, Bishop's U., 1976. Lectr. econs. Sir George Williams U., Montreal, 1954-57, asst. prof., 1957-61, assoc. prof., 1961-63, asst. dean U., 1961-63, dean arts, 1963-68, vice-prin. acad., 1968-69, prof., 1965-96, prin., vice chancellor, pres., 1969-74; rector, vice chancellor, pres. Concordia U., 1974-84, rector emeritus, 1984—. Provincial ednl. TV com. Dept. Edn. Que., 1962-66, dep. chmn., 1965-66, mem. tchr. tng. planning com., 1964-66; mem. Gauthier Ad Hoc Com., Univ. Operating Budgets, 1965-68, Council Univs., 1969-76; pres. Conf. Rectors and Prins. Que. Univs., 1974-77; mem. council Assn. Commonwealth Univs., 1975-78; bd. dirs. Assn. Univs. and Colls., Can., 1977-79; mem. Conseil Consultatif sur l'Immigration, Que. Gov., 1977-79, Corp. Higher Edn. Forum, 1983-84; bd. govs. YMCA, 1969-89, Vanier Coll., 1975-79, Fraser-Hickson Inst., 1975-2000, pres. 1989-92, Que. div. Can. Mental Health Assn., 1977-79, Montreal World Film Festival, 1985—; sec., treas., Cinematheque Can., 1988-96, bd. dirs.; sec., treas. World Film Fest. Found., 1989-96; exec. mem. Alliance Que., 1989-96, chmn., 1990-96, bd. dirs.; hon. mem. Corp. Higher Edn. Forum, 1984-2000; hon. v.p. Que. Provincial council Boy Scouts Can., 1974-90; hon. councillor Montreal Mus. Fine Arts, 1969—. Author: Canadian Money and Banking, 1964, (with G. Lermer) 2d edit., 1969.

O'BRIEN, KATHLEEN, lawyer; b. Billings, Mont., Mar. 27, 1956; d. James Richmond and Joan Mae (Haiston) O'B. BA, Oreg. State U., 1977; JD, U. Oreg., 1980. Bar: Oreg. 1983, U.S. Dist. Ct. Oreg. 1983. Ptnr. Wittrock & O'Brien, Portland, Oreg., 1983—. Co-author: Oregon Women and the Law, 1997. Mem.: Oreg. State Bar Assn. Office: 300 SE 80th Ave Portland OR 97215

O'BRIEN, KATHLEEN ANN, economist; b. Augusta, Ga., Apr. 25, 1959; d. John Anthony O'Brien and Rita Jennie Dell Veneri. BA in Econs., U. Colo., 1981. Rschr. Internat. Rsch. Ctr. for Energy and Econ. Devel., Boulder, Colo., 1979-87, Bus. Rsch. Divsn., Boulder, 1987-88; com. mem. Bus.-Econ. Outlook Forum, Denver, 1987-99, Colo. State, Denver, 2000—. Chair justice com. LWV, Boulder; bd. U.S.-Internat. Ctr. for People with Disabilites, Boulder. Mem. 501 Club World Trade Orgn. Roman Catholic. Avocations: flying, swimming, knitting, chess. Home: 8989 W 14th Ave Apt 207 Lakewood CO 80215-4838

O'BRIEN, KEVIN CHARLES, business development; b. Pitts., Dec. 30, 1957; s. Charles James and Minerva O'B.; m. Ann M. Poydockm Oct. 8, 1982; children: Michael, Jessica, Kaitlyn. BS in Polymer Engring., Case Western Res. U., 1979, MS in Polymer Engring., 1981, PhD in Polymer Engring., 1984. Postdoctoral assoc. U. Tex., Austin, 1984-85; project leader Dow Chem., Walnut Creek, Calif., 1985-89; sr. scientist Raychem Corp., Menlo Park, 1989-92; dir. sales, dir. clin. rsch. Lander Corp., 1992-97; bus. specialist Lawrence Livermore (Calif.) Nat. Labs., 1998—2001, new bus. devel., 2001—. Biomedical engring. adv. bd. com., U. Pacific, 2000—; Indsl. Partners Consortium Mgmt. Com., 2000—; assoc. dir. Knowledge Transfer: Ctr. for Biophotonics. Contbr. articles to profl. jours. Com. mem. Next Generation Cities, San Francisco, 1998—. Recipient Fed. Lab. Consortium award for excellence in tech. Mem. Assn. Univ. Tech. Mgrs., Lic. Exec. Soc. Avocations: biking, skiing, physical fitness, running, tennis. Home: 375 Cameron Cir San Ramon CA 94583-2553 Office: Lawrence Livermore Nat Labs L-223 PO Box 808 Livermore CA 94551-0808

O'BRIEN, MARGARET ANN, obstetrics nurse, community health nurse; b. Cleve., Mar. 19, 1943; d. Joseph Andrew and Cecelia Marie (Gedeon) Kilburg; m. Francis Maurice O'Brien, Aug. 8, 1967 (div.) Student, St. John's Coll., Cleve., 1961-62; AS, Cuyahoga Community Coll., Cleve., 1967; student, Akron U., 1985-87, Denison U., 1986. Cert. inpatient obstetric nursing NAACOG Certification Corp. Staff nurse obstetrics Grace Hosp., Cleve., 1966-73; instr. Childbirth Educators Inc., 1975-78; staff nurse obstetrics Amherst (Ohio) Hosp., 1978-80, Lamaze childbirth educator, 1987-91; staff nurse labor and delivery St. Joseph Hosp., Lorain, Ohio, 1980-85; staff nurse obstetrics Amherst (Ohio) Hosp., 1985-91; nurse Vis. Nurse Assn. Cleve., 1991—. Tchr. Ctrl. Cath. H.S., Cleve., 1983-94. Author: Prepared Childbirth, 1986, Early Pregnancy, 1990. Instr. Prolife Orgn., Lakewood, Ohio. Mem. NAACOG. Avocations: reading, crocheting, needlepointing, swimming, traveling. Home: 4179 Columbia Rd Ste 314 North Olmsted OH 44070-2084 Office: 2500 E 22d St Cleveland OH 44115-3204

O'BRIEN, MARK STEPHEN, pediatric neurosurgeon; b. West New York, N.J., Jan. 2, 1933; s. Mark Peter and Hannah (Dempsey) O'B.; m. Mary Morris Johnson, June 3, 1961 (div.); children: David, Derek, Marcia; m. Karen-Marie Sampson, June 1, 1984; children: Blythe, Blake, Lauren-Blair, Connor. AB cum laude, Seton Hall U., 1955; MD, St. Louis U., 1959. Diplomate Am. Bd. Neurol. Surgery, Am. Bd. Pediat. Neurol. Surgery. Intern St. John's Hosp., St. Louis, 1959-60, resident in surgery, 1960; resident in neurology Charity Hosp., New Orleans, 1962-63; resident in neurosurgery St. Vincent's Hosp., N.Y.C., 1963-64, resident in surgery, 1965; sr. resident, chief resident Cin. Children's Hosp., U. Cin., 1965-68, research fellow in neurosurgery, 1966-67, 67-68; NIH spl. fellow in neuroradiology Albert Einstein Coll. Medicine, N.Y.C., 1968-69; mem. faculty dept. surgery Emory U. Sch. Medicine, Atlanta, 1969—, prof. surgery, assoc. prof. pediatrics, 1979—; chief neurosurgery Henrietta Egleston Hosp. for Children, Atlanta, 1971—. Trustee Elaine Clark Center for Exceptional Children; mem. med. adv. bd. Nat. Found., March of Dimes; trustee Henrietta Egleston Hosp. for Children; mem. profl. adv. panel Spina Bifida Assn. Am. Editorial bd. Pediatric Neurosurgery; contbr. chpts. to books, articles to med. jours. Served with USNR, 1960-62. Mem. Am. Assn. Neurol. Surgeons, Soc. Neurol. Surgeons, Congress Neurol. Surgeons, Internat. Soc. Pediatric Neurosurgery, Greater Atlanta Pediatric Soc., Med. Soc. Atlanta, AMA, ACS, Ga. Neurosurg. Soc., Am. Acad. Pediatrics, Am. Soc. Pediatric Neurosurgery, Pediatric Oncology Group, Am. Bd. Pediatric Neurol. Surgery (sec.), Acad. Pediatric Neurosurgeons. Home: 889 W Wesley Rd NW Atlanta GA 30327-1306 Office: 1900 Century Blvd NE Ste 4 Atlanta GA 30345-3307

O'BRIEN, MARLYS CAROL HOWE, retired library director; b. St. Paul, Dec. 10, 1937; d. James Melvin and Emma Linda (Luthi) Howe; m. Gerald Thomas O'Brien, Mar. 29, 1970 (dec. Aug. 1993); stepchildren: Michael, David, Joseph, Kristine, Patrick, Colleen. Cert., U. Oslo, Norway, 1958; BA, U. Minn., 1960, MA, 1963. Libr. asst. St. Paul Pub. Libr., 1954-63; pub. libr. cons. Minn. Office of Libr. Devel. and Svc., St. Paul, 1963-65; librarian Cass County Libr., Pine River, Minn., 1965-69; dir. Kitchigami Regional Libr., 1969-99; ret., 1999. Bd. dirs. Minn. Libr. Found., St. Paul, 1983-86. Mem. ALA (pub. libr. assn. cmty. info. sect., pres. 1994), Minn. Libr. Assn. (councilor Minn. chpt. 1974-78, pres. 1982-83, Cert. of Merit award 1967, 91). Lutheran. Avocations: reading, fishing, baking, church bell choir, sign language. Home: Norway Lake 2338 19th St SW Pine River MN 56474-7909

O'BRIEN, MARY DEVON, communications executive, consultant; b. Buenos Aires, Argentina, Feb. 13, 1944; came to U.S., 1949, naturalized, 1962; d. George Earle and Margaret Frances (Richards) Owen; m. Gordon Covert O'Brien, Feb. 16, 1962 (div. Aug. 1982); children: Christopher Covert, Devon Elizabeth; m. Christopher Gerard Smith, May 28, 1983 BA, Rutgers U., 1975, MBA, 1976. Project mgmt. cert., 1989. Contr. manpower Def. Comm. divsn. ITT, Nutley, N.J., 1977-80, adminstr. program, 1977-78, mgr. cost, schedule control, 1978-79, voice processing project, 1979-80; mgr. project Avionics divsn. ITT, 1980-81, sr. mgr. projects, 1981-93, cons. strategic planning, 1983-95; pres. Anamex, Inc., 1995—. Bd. trustees South Mountain Counseling Ctr., 1987-98, chmn. bd. trustees, 1994—; bd. dirs. N.J. Eye Inst.; session leader Internet Conf., Florence, Italy, 1992; session moderator, panel mem. MES Conf., Cairo, Egypt, 1993, spkr., session leader Vancouver, 1994, keynote spkr. New Zealand, 1995; lectr. in field Author: Pace: System Manual, 1979, Voices, 1982; contbr. articles to profl. jours. and Maplewood Community calendar. Chmn. Citizens Budget Adv. Com., Maplewood, N.J., 1984-87, chmn. recreation, libr., pub. svcs., 1982-83, 94-96, chmn. pub. safety, emergency svcs., 1983-84, chmn. schs. and edn., 1984-85, chmn. gen. gov. and fin., 1998-2000; first v.p. Maplewood Civic Assn., 1987-89, pres., 1989-91, 2000—, sec. 1993-94, bd. dirs., officer, 1984—; chmn. Maple Leaf Svc. award Com., 1987-89, 94—, Community Svc. Coun. of Oranges and Maplewood Homelessness, Affordable Housing, Shelter Com., 1988—; chmn. speaker's bur. United Way, 1989-93; bd. trustees United Way Essex and West Hudson Cmty. Svc. Coun., 1988—; v.p. mktg. United Way Community Svc. Coun. of Oranges and Maplewood, 1989-90, v.p. 1994; mem. Maplewood Zoning Bd. of Adjustment, 1983-95; officer, mem. exec. bd. N.J. Project Mgmt. Inst., 1985—, pres., 1987-88, 95-2000, v.p. adminstrn., 1994-95; bd. dirs. Performance Mgmt. Assn.; chmn. Charter Com.; chmn. Internat. Project Mgmt. Inst. Jour. and Membership survey, 1986-87, mktg. com., 1986-89, long range planning and steering com., 1987—; bd. dirs., vice chmn. Coun. Chpt. Pres. Interaction Com., 1986-90, chmn., 1991—, pres. Internat. Project Mgmt. Inst., 1991, chmn., 1992, v.p. Region II, 1989-90; adv. bd. Project Mgmt. Jour., 1987-90, N.J. PMI Ednl., 1987—; liaison officer, PMI internat. liaison to Australian Inst. of Project Mgmt. and Western Australia Project Mgmt. Assn.; apptd. fellow Leadership N.J., 1993—, Internat. Project Mgmt. Inst. and Performance Mgmt. Assocs.; mem. MCA/N.J. Blood Bank Drive; chmn. Maplewood Community Calendar, 1990-98; trustee community svc. coun. and edn. program United Way Essex and West Hudson, 1988—, also, chmn. leadership div., chmn. speakers bur., 1991— and mem. communications com.; pres. N.J. Project Mgmt. Inst., 1995—; chmn. Maplewood Rep. County Com., 1996—; chair, sec. Essex County Rep. County Com. Recipient Spl. commendation for Community Svc. Twp. Maplewood, 1987; First Place award Anti-Shoplifting Program for Distributive Edn. Club Am., 1981, N.J. Fedn. of Women's Clubs, 1981, 82, Retail Mchts. Assn., 1981, 82; Commendation and Merit awards Air Force Inst. Tech., 1981; Pres.'s Safety award ITT, 1983; State award 1st Pl. N.J. Fedn. of Women's Clubs Garden Show, 1982, Outstanding Pres. award Internat. Project Mgmt. Inst., 1988, Outstanding Svc. and Contbrn. award 1986-87; Cert. Spl. Merit award N.J. Fedn. of Women's Clubs, 1982, Disting. Contbn. award United Way, 1990, Pursuit of Exellence Cost Savings Achievement award ITT Avionics, 1990, Meritorious Svc. Recognition award Internat. Project Mgmt. Inst., 1989-90, Maple Leaf award for outstanding community svc., 1992, Phoebe and Benjamin Shackelford award United Way, 1992, U.S. Ho. Reps. citation, 1992, N.H. Gen. Assembly Senate resolution for Community Leadership and Svc., 1992, resolution of Appreciation Township of Maplewood; N.J. Leadership fellow, 1993, awarded fellow of Internat. Project Mgmt. Inst., 1995. Mem. Internat. Platform Speakers Assn., Grand Jury Assn., Telecommunications Group and Aerospace Industries Assn., Women's Career Network Assn., Nat. Security Indsl. Assn., Assn. for Info. and Image Mgmt., Internat. Project Mgmt. Inst. (liaison officer pres. 1991—), Performance Mgmt. Assn, Indsl. Rels. Rsch. Assn., ITT Mgmt. Assn., NAFE, Rutger's Grad. Sch. Bus. Mgmt. Alumni Assn., Maplewood LWV (chair women and family issues com., voter registration bd. dirs.), Maplewood Women's Evening Membership Div. (pres. 1980-82), Lions (Maplewood dir. 1992-95, program chmn. 1991-92, treas. 1994-95, N.J. dist. 16E zone gov., chmn. 1992-93, 95-96, cabinet sec. internat. dist., region chmn. 1993-94, 96—, trustee Eye Bank N.J., internat. dist. 16-E cabinet sec. 1994-95, dist. 16-E chmn. peace poster contest 1995-99, pres. Newark 1995-97, sec. 1997—, N.J. State chmn. youth outreach and quest 1995-98, internat. dist. 16-E gov., 1999—, dist. MD16 treas., 1999—). Home: 594 Valley St Maplewood NJ 07040-2616 Office: 21 Madison Plz Ste 152 Madison NJ 07940-2354

O'BRIEN, MARYANN ANTOINETTE, retired nursing educator; b. Keiser, Pa., Jan. 30, 1938; d. John James and Antoinette Phyllis (St. Mary) Rugalla; m. Vincent Dennis O'Brien, Nov. 15, 1958; children: Vincent, John, Therese, Joseph. Diploma, Temple U. Hosp., 1958; BA in Profl. Arts., St. Joseph's Coll., 1988; postgrad., Nova U., 1990—. Cert. emergency nurse; cert. BCLS; cert. ACLS. Vis. nurse Vis. Nurse Assn. of Jersey City, 1958-59; staff nurse Bayonne (N.J.) Hosp., 1961-66, Alexian Bros. Hosp., Elizabeth, N.J., 1966-76, Clearbrook Adult Community, Cranbury, 1976-78; asst. dir. nursing Cen. Jersey Jewish Home for the Aged, Somerville, 1978-79; surg. nurse S.W. Regional Med. Ctr., Fort Myers, Fla., 1980; staff, asst dir. nursing Cape Coral (Fla.) Hosp., 1980-89; assoc. exec. dir. nursing Humana McFarland Hosp., Lebanon, Tenn., 1989-90; nurse educator James Lorenzo Walker Inst. Tech., Naples, Fla., 1990—2002, mem. CISD team. Mem. sch. adv. com., 1994—98; chair, 1996—97, 1997—98; sec., 1998—99. Reviewer, author: (with others) Practical Nurse Textbook, 1994, ECG Workbook, 1995; item writer NCLEX-PN, 1994, 96; author: (videos) Enteral Nutrition. Recipient Tchr. of Distinction Collier County Edn. Found., 1999, 2000, 02, Golden Apple Tchr. award, 2001. Mem. NEA, Fla. Nurses Assn., Fla. Vocat. Assn., Fla. Teaching Profl. Assn., Collier County Vocat. Adult Assn., Assn. Practical Nurse Educators of Fla., Temple U. Alumni Assn. E-mail: vinman@swfla.rr.com.

O'BRIEN, MICHAEL F. federal agency administrator; m. Patricia O'Brien; children: Kate, Karen, Beth, Timothy. Grad., U. Va.; MS in Physics, Cornell U.; MS in Aeronautical Systems, U. West Fla.; grad., French Ecole Militaire. Advisor to chmn. of Joint Chiefs of Staff concerning political-military policy in Middle East, Africa and Southwest Asia; commanding officer U.S. Naval Station Roosevelt Roads, PR; dep. dir. for rsch. Inst. Nat. Strategic Studies, Washington; dep. assoc. adminstr. for external rels. NASA Office External Rels. Office: NASA Hqtrs Mail Code I 300 E St SW Washington DC 20546*

O'BRIEN, MICHAEL PATRICK, high-tech IT analyst, project manager, emergency volunteer; b. Clearwater, ID, May 8, 1976; s. Valerie L and Joseph M. O'Brien. BS, Computer Info Systems, DeVry, Phoenix, AZ, 1997; MBA, Keller Grad.Sch., Fremont, Calif., 2002. Network Administrator Barrow Neurol. Inst., Phoenix, 1996—97; cons. PC Scottsdale, 1996—97; test engr. Cisco Systems, San Jose, 1997—2000, IT Analyst, Project Mgr. Calif., 2000—01. Office: Cisco Systems 170 W Tasman Dr San Jose CA 95134

O'BRIEN, MORGAN EDWARD, communications executive, lawyer; b. Washington, Dec. 14, 1944; AB Classical with honors, Georgetown U., 1966; JD, Northwestern U., 1969. Bar: Ill. 1969, Washington 1971. Lawyer Mobile Svcs. divsn. Common Carrier Bur. FCC, Washington, 1970-72; asst. bur. chief Spectrum Mgmt. Pvt. Radio Bur. FCC, 1976-87; co-founder, chmn. bd. Nextel Comm., Inc., Reston, Va., 1987-96, vice chmn., 1996—. Ptnr. Jones, Day, Reavis & Pogue, Washington, 1986-90; pvt. practice, 1979-90. Office: Nextel Comm Inc 2001 Edmund Halley Dr Reston VA 20191-3421

O'BRIEN, NANCY A. youth counselor; b. Watertown, Minn., July 4, 1945; d. Julius Vitus and Viola Frances (Rieland) Hardt; m. Robert S. O'Brien, June 8, 1968; children: Sean, Scott. BS, Coll. St. Teresa, Winona, Minn., 1967; MS, Iowa State U., 1978. Lic. tchr., counselor, Iowa. Tchr. Colorado Springs (Colo.) Community Schs., 1967-68; counselor Title 1 Des Moines Pub. Schs., 1978-79, Waukee (Iowa) Community Schs., 1980-85; guidance cons. Heartland Area Edn. Agy., Johnston, Iowa, 1985-88; counselor Des Moines (Iowa) Pub. Schs., 1988—. Conf. coord., trainer, cons. Children's Health Market. Active Honolulu Symphony, Hawaii Assistance League. Mem. Iowa Assn. For Counseling and Devel. (editor newsletter 1981-83, editorial bd. jour. 1983-85, pres. local chpt. 1985, pub. relations com. 1986, sec. 1987-95), Iowa Sch. Counselors Assn. (sen. 1985, del. to nat. conv. 1987), Am. Assn. for Counseling and Devel., Am. Sch. Counselors Assn. Roman Catholic. Avocation: reading. Home: 94-511 Lumiauau St Waipahu HI 96797-5055

O'BRIEN, NANCY PATRICIA, librarian, educator; b. Galesburg, Ill., Mar. 17, 1955; d. Leo Frederick O'Brien and Yvonne Blanche (Uhlmann) O'Brien Tabb; 1 child, Nicole Pamela. AB in English, U. Ill., 1976, MS in LS, 1977. Vis. instr. U. Ill., Urbana, 1977-78, asst. prof. libr. adminstrn., 1978-84, assoc. prof., 1984-91, prof., 1991—, serials bibliographer, 1977-78, social sci. bibliographer collection devel. div., 1979-81, project dir. Title II-C grant, 1987-88, acting libr. and info. sci. libr., 1989-90, head Edn. and Social Sci. Libr., 1994—, coord. social scis. divsn., 1996—, edn. subject specialist, 1981—. Discussion leader Ill. White House Conf. on Libr. and Info. svcs., 1990; mem. nat. adv. bd. Office Ednl. Rsch. and Improvement, U.S. Dept. Edn., 1989-91; grant proposal reviewer NEH, 1991; mem. adv. bd. Ctr. for Children's Books, 1992-97; cons. Ark. Coll., 1989; chmn. rev. team Instrnl. Materials Ctr., U. Wis., Madison, 1989; chair exec. com. Nat. Edn. Network Nat. Libr. Edn. U.S. Dept. Edn., 1998—2001; presenter in field. Author: Test Construction: A Bibliography of Resources, 1988, (with Emily Fabiano) Core List of Books and Journals in Education, 1991; Education: A Guide to Reference and Information Sources, 2d edit., 2000; co-editor Media/Microforms column Series Rev., 1979-82; mem. editl. bd. Bull. Bibliography, 1982-90; asst. editor Libr. Hi Tech., 1983-85; editor EBSS Newsletter, 1990-91; contbr. articles to profl. jours., chpts. to books. Mem. ALA (Whitney-Carnegie grantee 1990-91), Am. Ednl. Rsch. Assn. (spl. interest group on libr. resources and info. tech.), Assn. Coll. and Rsch. Librs. (access policy guidelines task force 1990-95, vice chmn., chmn.-elect edn. and behavioral scis. sect. 1993-94, chmn. 1994-95, acad. status com. 1996—2000, Disting. Edn. and Behavioral Scis. Libr. 1997), Libr. Adminstrn. and Mgmt. Assn. (edn. and tng. com. pub. rels. sect. 1990-95), Resources and Tech. Svcs. Divsn.(micropub. com. 1982-85, chmn. 1983-85, cons. 1985-87). Office: U Ill Edn & Social Sci Libr 100 Main Libr 1408 W Gregory Dr Urbana IL 61801-3607 E-mail: n-obrien@uiuc.edu.

O'BRIEN, ORIN YNEZ, musician, educator; b. Hollywood, Calif., June 7, 1935; d. George Joseph and Marguerite Graham (Churchill) O'Brien. Studied with Frederick Zimmermann , Milton Kestenbaum and Herman Reinshagen; diploma, The Juilliard Sch., 1957. Double bassist N.Y.C. Ballet Orch., Saidenberg Little Symphony Music Aeterna, Am. Symphony (with Stokowski), 1956-66, N.Y. Philharm., N.Y.C., 1966—; faculty Manhattan Sch. Music, 1969—, Mannes Coll. Music, N.Y.C., 1988—, The Julliard Sch., N.Y.C., 1990—, co-chair double bass dept., 1992—2002. Participant numerous chamber music festivals, including Marlboro; featured in 1st performances of Gunther Schuller Quartet for 4 double basses; artist for GM, CBS and RCA Recording cos. Mem.: Internat. Soc. Bassists, Am. Fedn. Musicians, The Bohemians. Avocations: reading, writing, cooking.

O'BRIEN, PAMELA C. communications educator; b. Wilmington, Del., Sept. 27, 1969; d. Bruce Redfearn and Lestina Larsen Colby; m. Sean D. O'Brien, July 9, 1994; 1 child, Eilean Donan. BA with honors, So. Meth. U., 1991; MA in Mass Comm., Ind. U., 1994, PhD candidate in telecomm., 1994-96. Assoc. instr. Ind. U., Bloomington, 1991-96; vis. prof. comm. George Washington U., Washington, 1996-98, asst. prof. comm., 1998—. Co-writer (TV show) A Tribute to Arthur Miller, 1990. Sec. Greenbrook Estates, Greenbelt, Md., 1998-99. Ednl. fellow Nat. Assn. TV Program Execs., 1998. Mem. Broadcast Ednl. Assn., Internat. Comm. Assn., Popular Culture Assn., Soc. Animation Studies. Avocations: animation studies, commercialization of media. Office: George Washington U 812 20th St NW Washington DC 20052-0001 E-mail: pcobrien@gwu.edu.

O'BRIEN, PATRICIA GRACE, psychiatric clinical nurse, health policy advisor; b. Bklyn. Diploma, St. Vincent's Hosp. Sch. Nursing, N.Y.C.; BS, Hunter Coll.; MA, NYU; PhD in Nursing, Adelphi U., Garden City, N.Y. RN, N.Y.; cert. adult psychiat.-mental health clin. specialist, psychiat. nurse practitioner. Staff nurse, head nurse med. and psychiat. St. Vincent's Hosp. and Med. Ctr., N.Y.C.; clin. supr. Payne-Whitney Clinic, N.Y. Hosp.-Cornell Med. Ctr., 1980-83, asst. DON, 1987-95, interim DON, 1995-97; clin. specialist in psychiat. nursing N.Y. Hosp.-Cornell Med. Ctr., 1984-87; sr. advisor regulatory & profl. affairs Greater N.Y. Hosp. Assn., N.Y.C., 1997-2000, assoc. v.p., 2000—02; psychiat. nurse practitioner Bklyn. Psychiat. Assocs., 1998—2002; DON behavioral health Manhattan divsn. St. Vincent's Cath. Med. Ctrs., N.Y.C., 2002—. Presenter in cognitive behavior therapy related to nursing intervention and stress mgmt. Author: (chpt.) Applied Psychiatric-Mental Health Nursing Standards in Clinical Practice, 1988; editor, contbr. Psychiatric Nursing, An Integration of Theory and Practice, 1999. Clin. fellow Inst. Behavior Therapy, N.Y.C., 1979-81. Mem.: NY Orgn. Nurse Execs., Am. Psychiat. Nurses Assn., Sigma Theta Tau. Office: St Vincent's Cath Med Ctr 144 W 12th St New York NY 10011

O'BRIEN, PATRICK KARL, economic history educator; b. London, Aug. 12, 1932; s. William Patrick and Elizabeth (Stockhausen) O'B.; m. Cassy Cobham, Apr. 15, 1959; children: Karen, Helen, Stephen. BSc in Econs., London Sch. Econs., 1958; DPhil, Oxford (Eng.) U., 1966, MA, 1970; PhD (h.c.), U. Carlos III, Madrid, 1999; Doctorate honoris causa, Uppsala (Sweden) U., 2000. Rsch. fellow Sch. Oriental and African Studies, London, 1960-63, lectr., 1964-66, reader, 1966-70; reader, profl. fellow St. Anthony's Coll., Oxford, Eng., 1970-90, lectr., fellow Eng., 1970-83; prof., dir. Inst. Hist. Rsch. London U., 1990-98; Centennial prof. London Sch. Econs., 1999—. Vis. prof. Yale U., European U., Florence, Princeton U., Columbia U., U. Calif., San Diego, Va. U., Carlos III U., Madrid. Author: The Revolution in Egypt's Economic System, 1966, The New Economic History of Railways, 1977, Economic Growth in Britain and France, 1780-1914, 1978, The Industrial Revolution and British Society, 1992. Fellow Royal Hist. Soc., Brit. Acad., Royal Soc. Arts, Econ. History Soc. U.K. (pres. 1997-2000). Home: 66 St Bernards Rd Oxford OX2 6EJ England Office: London U Inst Hist Rsch London Sch Economics Senate House London England

O'BRIEN, PATRICK MICHAEL, library administrator; b. Newport, R.I., Mar. 17, 1943; s. Joseph Xavier and Loretta (DeCotis) O'B.; m. Roberta Luther, Nov. 27, 1977; children— Megan MacRae, Brendan Watters BA in Eng. Lit., Merrimack Coll., North Andover, Mass., 1964; M.L.S., U. R.I., Kingston, 1965; MBA, Case Western Res. U., Cleve., 1983. Reference libr. Newsweek mag., N.Y.C., 1965-72; asst. dir. rsch. FIND/SVP, 1972-74; head cen. libr., cultural ctr. Chgo. Pub. Libr., 1974-79; dir. Cuyahoga County Pub. Libr., Cleve., 1979-84; dir. librs. Dallas Pub. Libr., 1984-92; dir. Alexandria (Va.) Libr., 1992—. Mem. editorial bd. Handel's Nat. Directory for Performing Arts; contbr. articles to profl. jours. Participant, alumnus Leadership Dallas Program, 1984-85, Leadership Cleve. Program, 1981; mem. nat. adv. com. to Libr. of Congress; mem. adv. coun. Tex. State Libr., Libr. Svcs. and Constrn. Act, 1986-89; co-chair, del. selection com. Tex. Conf. on Librs. and Info. Svcs.; mem. com. Goals for Dallas, 1985; mem. exec. bd. univ. librs. So. Meth. U., 1985-93; bd. dirs. Urban Community Sch., Cleve., 1982-84, Mus. African-Am. Life and Culture, 1985-86; mem. client data base com. Dallas Assn. Svcs. to Homeless, 1988-90; mem. Latchkey Children's Task Force, 1985-90. Recipient Servant as Leader award City of Dallas, 1989, Disting. Alumnus award U. R.I. Grad. Sch. Libr. and Info. Studies, 1990. Mem. ALA (coun. mem. 1987-95), Am. Libr. Trustee Assn. (bd. dirs.), Pub. Libr. Assn. (pres. 1985-86), Pub. Libr. Systems Sect (pres. 1983), Tex. Libr. Assn. (legis com. 1986-92), Tex. Women's Univ. Sch. Libr. and Info. Studies Vis. Com., Tex. Ctr. for Book Dallas Pub. Libr., Cleve. Area Met. Libr. Systems (pres. bd. 1980), Chgo. Libr. Club (pres. 1978), D.C. Libr. Assn., Va. Pub. Libr. Dirs. Assn. (bd. dirs. 1994-96), Va. Libr. Assn., Online Computer Libr. Ctr. (bd. trustees 1992-98), The White House Conf. on Librs. and Info. Svcs. (del. 1991), Pub. Lib. Adminstrs. N.Tex. (pres. 1990-91), Dallas 40, Rotary of Alexandria (bd. dirs. 1996-97, pres. 2002—, Rotarian of Yr. 2001), Alexandria Commn. on Info. Tech., Beta Gamma Sigma. Office: Alexandria Libr 5005 Duke St Alexandria VA 22304-2903

O'BRIEN, PATRICK WILLIAM, lawyer; b. Chgo., Dec. 5, 1927; s. Maurice Edward and Ellen (Fitzgerald) O'B.; m. Deborah Bissell, July 2, 1955; children: Kathleen, Mariellen, Patrick, James, Patricia. BS in Mech. Engring., Northwestern U., 1947, JD, 1950. Bar: Ill. 1951, U.S. Dist. Ct. (no. dist.) Ill. 1954, U.S. Dist. Ct. (so. dist.)Ill. 1956, U.S. Ct. Appeals (7th cir.) 1955, U.S. Ct. Appeals (8th cir.) 1972, U.S. Supreme Ct. 1970. Assoc. Bell, Boyd, Marshall & Lloyd, Chgo., 1950—51, Mayer, Brown, Rowe & Maw, Chgo., 1953—62, ptnr., 1962—94, sr. counsel, 1995—. Served to capt. USAF, 1951-53. Fellow Am. Coll. Trial Lawyers; mem. ABA, Ill. Bar Assn., Chgo. Bar Assn. Clubs: Chgo., Mid-Day, University, Westmoreland Country, Cliff Dwellers, Dairymen's Country. Republican. Roman Catholic. Office: Mayer Brown Rowe & Maw 190 S La Salle St Ste 3100 Chicago IL 60603-3441 Home: 2606 Park Pl Evanston IL 60201-1318

O'BRIEN, RAYMOND FRANCIS, transportation executive; b. Atchison, Kans., May 31, 1922; s. James C. and Anna M. (Wagner) O'B.; m. Mary Ann Baugher, Sept. 3, 1947; children: James B., William T., Kathleen A., Christopher R. BS in Bus. Adminstrn., U. Mo., 1948; grad., Advanced Mgmt. Program, Harvard, 1966. Accountant-auditor Peat, Marwick, Mitchell & Co., Kansas City, Mo., 1948-52; contr., treas. Riss & Co., 1952-58; regional contr. Consol. Freightways Corp. of Del., Indpls., also, Akron, Ohio, 1958-61; contr. Consol. Freightways, Inc., San Francisco, 1961—, v.p., treas., 1962-63, bd. dirs., 1966, v.p. fin., 1967-69, exec. v.p., 1969-75, pres., 1975—, chief exec. officer, 1977-88, 90-91, chmn., 1988—; now chmn. emeritus CNF Transportation. Pres. CF Motor Freight subs. Consol. Freightways, Inc., 1973; dir. Transam. Corp., Watkins-Johnson, Inc.; past chmn. WesternHwy. Inst., Champion Road Machinery, Ltd. Former mem. bus. adv. bd. Northwestern U., U. Calif., Berkeley; bd. dirs., regent, former chmn. bd. trustees St. Mary's Coll.; bd. dirs., regent Charles Armstrong Sch., 1991—; mem. Pres.'s Adv. Herbert Hoover Boys and Girls Club; dir. Boy Scouts Am. Bay Area Coun. Served to 1st lt. USAAF, 1942-45. Recipient Disting. Svc. Citation Automotive Hall Fame, 1991; named Outstanding Chief Exec. five times Financial World Mag. Mem. Am. Trucking Assn. (bd. dirs. Found., exec. com.), Pacific Union Club, World Trade Club, Commonwealth Club (San Francisco), Menlo Country Club. Home: 26347 Esperanza Dr Los Altos CA 94022-2601 Office: CNF Transportation Bldg #2 3000 Sand Hill Rd Ste 130 Menlo Park CA 94025-7113

O'BRIEN, RAYMOND VINCENT, JR. banker; b. Bronx, N.Y., Sept. 23, 1927; s. Raymond Vincent and Blanche (Harper) O'B.; m. Theresa Sweeney, Mar. 29, 1952 (dec. June 1981); children: Susan, Raymond, Christopher, Sean, Carol, Nancy Meisenzahl; m. Ellen Boyle, July 24, 1982. AB, Fordham U., 1951, JD, 1958; postgrad., Advanced Mgmt. Program, Harvard U., 1969. With Chase Manhattan Bank (N.A.), N.Y.C., 1953-74; chief exec. officer, chmn. bd. Emigrant Savs. Bank, 1978-92, pres., 1974-77, dir., 1974—. Dir. Internat. Shipholding Corp. Trustee Fordham U., 1979-92; chmn. bd. trustees Regis High Sch., 1988-92; past chmn. Community Bankers Assn., N.Y., Nat. Assn. Community Bankers: Served with AUS, 1946-47, 51-53. Mem. N.Y. State Bar Assn., Guild Cath. Lawyers, Sky Club, Econ. Club, Navesink Country Club (Middletown, N.J.), Plantation Country Club (Ponte Vedra), Knights of Malta, Friendly Sons St. Patrick. Republican. Roman Catholic. Home: 102 Lands End Ponte Vedra Beach FL 32082-3906

O'BRIEN, RICHARD FRANCIS, advertising agency association executive; b. Everett, Mass., Aug. 3, 1942; s. James Raymond and Gertrude Lucille O'B.; m. Clare Lynch, Apr. 7, 1973; children: Catherine Lynch, Miles Edward. AB magna cum laude, Boston Coll., 1964; MA, Ind. U., 1965; MBA, Columbia U., 1967. With Grey Advt. Inc., N.Y.C., 1967-83, v.p., mgmt. supr., 1973-77, sr. v.p., mgmt. rep., 1977-80, exec. v.p., mgmt. rep., 1980-83; exec. v.p., mgmt. dir. Dancer Fitzgerald Sample, Inc. (name changed to Saatchi & Saatchi Advt.), 1983-88; vice chmn. Dancer Fitzgerald Sample, Inc. (became Saatchi & Saatchi Advt.), 1988-97; bd. dirs. Saatchi & Saatchi Advt. Worldwide, 1989-97; exec. v.p. Spl. Olympics Internat., 1997-2000; exec. v.p., dir. govt. rels. Am. Assn. Advt. Agys., Tylo, 2001—. Bd. dirs. Spl. Olympics Internat., 1983-97. Office: Am Assn Advt Agys 1203 19th St NW 4th Fl Washington DC 20036

O'BRIEN, RICHARD ALAN, research scientist; b. Sioux City, Iowa, June 16, 1961; s. Richard Henry O'Brien. BS, S.D. State U., 1985; MS, U. N.D., 1987; PhD, U. Nebr., 1992. Rsch. scientist Rieke Metals, Inc., Lincoln, Nebr., 1992-93, TPL, Inc., Albuquerque, 1993-97, Hexcel Corp., Decatur, Ala., 1997—. Active Decatur Concert Assn., 1997-98. Mem. Am. Chem. Soc. Office: Hexcel Corp 3300 Mallard Fox Dr NW Decatur AL 35601-7575

O'BRIEN, RICHARD L(EE), medical educator, academic administrator, physician, cell biologist; b. Shenandoah, Iowa, Aug. 30, 1934; s. Thomas Lee O'B. and Grace Ellen (Sims) Parish; m. Joan Frances Gurney, June 29, 1957; children: Sheila Marie, Kathleen Therese, Michael James, Patrick Kevin. MS in Physiology, Creighton U., 1958, MD, 1960. Diplomate: Nat. Bd. Med. Examiners. Intern and resident Columbia med. div. Bellevue Hosp., N.Y.C., 1960-62; postdoctoral fellow in biochemistry Inst. for Enzyme Research, U. Wis., 1962-64; asst. prof. to prof. pathology Sch. Medicine, U. So. Calif., L.A., 1966-82, dep. dir. Cancer Ctr., 1975-80, dir. rsch. and edn. Cancer Ctr., 1980-81, dir. Cancer Ctr., 1981-82; dean Sch. Medicine Creighton U., Omaha, 1982-92, acting v.p. health scis., 1984-85, v.p. health scis., 1985-99, prof. health policy and ethics, Univ. prof., 2000—, dir. office of interprofl. edn., 2002—. Vis. prof. molecular biology U. Geneva, 1973-74; cons. in field; mem. cancer control research grants rev. com. NIH, Nat. Cancer Inst.; mem. Cancer Ctr. Support grant rev. com. Nat. Cancer Inst., 1984-88, chmn. 1987-88; co-chmn. United Way/CHAD Pacesetter campaign, 1988, 94. Contbr. articles; editor various profl. jours. Served to capt. U.S. Army, 1964-66. Spl. fellow Nat. Cancer Inst., 1967-69; Combined Health Agys. Drive—Health Citizen of Yr., 1986. Mem. ACP, Am. Assn. Pathologists, Am. Assn. Cancer Rsch., Am. Assn. Cancer Edn., AAAS, Am. Assn. Cancer Insts. (dir. 1982-83), Assn. Am. Med. Colls. (chmn. MCAT evaluation panel 1987-88, liaison com. on med. edn., 1988-93, co-chmn, 1989-93, adv. panel Strategic Planning Health Care Reform 1992-96), Assn. Acad. Health Ctrs. (long-range planning com. 1986, 2000, nominating com. 1987, 96, Task Force Health Care Delivery 1992, mem. task force on leadership and instl. values 1993-99, bd. dirs. 1998-99), Am. Cancer Soc. (adv. com. Inst. rsch. Grants 1977-80, Outstanding Leadership award, dir. Calif. div. 1980-82, dir. Nebr. divsn. 1992-96), Am. Hosp. Assn. (com. on med. edn. 1986-89), Alpha Omega Alpha. Home: 9927 Essex Dr Omaha NE 68114-3873 Office: Creighton Univ California At 24th Omaha NE 68178-0001 E-mail: rlo@creighton.edu.

O'BRIEN, ROBERT BROWNELL, JR. investment banker, consultant, yacht broker, opera company executive; b. N.Y.C., Sept. 6, 1934; s. Robert Brownell and Eloise (Boles) O'B.; m. Sarah Lager, Nov. 28, 1958; children: Robert Brownell III, William Stuart, Jennifer. BA, Lehigh U., 1957; postgrad., NYU, Am. Inst. Banking. Asst. treas., credit officer, br. locations officer Bankers Trust Co., N.Y.C., 1957-63; v.p., dir. bus. devel. George A. Murray Co., gen. contractors, 1964; also v.p. Bowery Savs. Bank, 1964-69; dir., chief exec. officer Fed. Savs. & Loan Ins. Corp., Washington, 1969-71; chmn. exec. com. Fed. Home Loan Bank Bd., 1969-71; v.p. Bowery Savs. Bank, N.Y.C., 1972; exec. v.p. First Fed. Savs. & Loan Assn., 1973-75; chmn., chief exec. officer Carteret Savs. Bank, Morristown, 1975-91, also bd. dirs.; mng. dir. Printon Kane Group Inc., Short Hills, N.J., 1991-94; dir., former chief exec. officer Govs. Bank Corp., West Palm Beach, 1992-94; pres., CEO Hubert Johnson Inc., 1998—. Bd. dirs. Fed. Home Loan Bank N.Y., Govs. Bank Corp.; vice chmn. 1st Mortgage Capital Corp., Vero Beach, Fla.; chmn. Neighborhood Housing Svcs. Am., 1972-91; vice chmn., bd dirs. U.S. League Savs. Instns., Washington, O'Brien Yacht Sales. Contbr. articles to trade mags. Trustee Trinity Pawling Sch., Palm Beach County Housing Partnership, Lehigh U.; chmn. Housing Opportunities Found.; trustee Toms River Seaport Soc., N.J. Mus. Boating; trustee, past chmn. Cmty. Found. of N.J., 1987—; trustee, pres. Bay Head Hist. Soc.; vice chmn., bd. dirs. Dalt Found.; chmn. adv. bd. Palm Beach Maritime Mus., Peanut Island, Fla.; active Nat. Commn. on Neighborhoods; past chmn., exec. dir. N.J. State Opera. Mem. Nat. Coun. Savs. Instns. (past chmn.), Essex County Savs. and Loan League (past chmn.), N.J. Savs. League (past chmn.), N.J. Hist. Soc. (past chmn.), Greater Newark C. of C. (bd. dirs.), N.J. C. of C. (bd. dirs.), Union League Club, Delray Beach Yacht Club (past commodore), New York Yacht Club, Morris County Golf Club, Somerset Hills Golf Club, Palm Beach Yacht Club, Bay Head Yacht Club (past commodore). Republican. Episcopalian. Home: 500 Club Dr Bay Head NJ 08742-5016 E-mail: Bob@Woodenboatsnj.com.

O'BRIEN, ROBERT EMMET, insurance company executive; b. St. Louis, Sept. 13, 1923; s. Algernon Francis Adams and Adeline (von Weisert) O'B.; m. Mary Lou Gallagher, July 20, 1946 (div. 1978); children: Robert Jr., Gardnar, Scott, Derek, Mary Berkeley; m. Marian Strong Achilles, June 30, 1983. BBA, St. Louis U., 1946, MBA, 1947. Prin., ptnr. R. Newman & R. O'Brien, St. Louis, 1946-52; mem. Lloyd's of London, 1952—; dir. Hunter Engring. Co., St. Louis, 1946-72, Atlas Mfg. Co., St. Louis, 1965-80, Narragansett Corp., St. Louis and Moberly, Mo., 1965-80, Mid-America Coffee Co., St. Louis, 1970-75, Golden-Dipt Corp. and DCA (N.Y.), N.Y.C., 1948-1970; cons. internat. ins. The Law Firm of Honorable Wilbur D. Mills and Herman E. Talmadge, Washington, London, 1976—. Pres. North Atlantic Assurance Co. Ltd., London, 1962-75; elected hon. dir. Atlantic Coun. of the U.S. Treas. St. Louis Trust Coun., 1949-65; apptd. to Bd. Life Govs. Royal Hosp. Putney, West Hill, London, 1969; councillor The Athletic Coun. of U.S., Atlantic Coun. of U.S., Carnegie Found.; mem. U.S. Olympics (Ice) Speed Skating Team, 1939; trustee Errol Flynn Estate, Jamaica and London, 1959-64; mem. Hiberian United Svcs. Club, Dublin, Ireland. With AC U.S. Army, 1942-45, ETO, NATOUSA. Decorated DFC (Eng.). Mem. DAV (life), Royal Air Force Soc., Zurich Internat. Insurers (apptd.), Life Underwriters, Million Dollar Round Table (life), Mid-Atlantic Club, Royal Yacht Club Hobart Tasmania, Royal Yacht Club Tasmania, Army and Navy Club Washington (hon.), Devonshire Club (London), Irish Nat. (London), Liberal Club (London), Royal Jamacia Yacht Club (life), Mo. Athletic Club, Royal Yacht of Fiji, Royal Scots Mil. Club (Edinburgh), U.S. SAMOA Soc. So. Pacific. Home: 117 Old Wharf Rd North Chatham MA 02650-1129

O'BRIEN, ROBERT JAMES, financial consultant, business owner; b. Waterbury, Conn., Nov. 22, 1940; s. Stephen Joseph and Ada Florence (Schiaroli) O'B.; m. Janyce Leah Bruni, Sept. 24, 1966; children: Gayle Elizabeth O'Brien Blachura, Julie Maureen O'Brien Orlando. BA, U. Conn., 1964. Registered investment advisor SEC; CFP; registered fin. cons.; CLU. Commd. ensign USN, 1964, advanced through grades to comdr., ret., 1984; fin. cons. Davenport-Dukes Assocs., Virginia Beach, Va., 1984-97, prin., ptnr., 1992-97; prin., mng. ptnr. Fin. Security Group, Inc., 1997—; pres. Fin. Security Adv., Inc., 1997—. Adj. instr. Commonwealth Coll., Virginia Beach, 1988-91. Elder Kempsville Presbyn. Ch., Va. Beach, 1987—; bd. dirs. Edmarc Children's Hospice, Portsmouth, Va., 1988-92, pres. bd. dirs., 1992; bd. dirs. Bethany Christian Svcs., Va. Beach, Dec. 1995-96. Mem. Nat. Assn. Life Underwriters (Million Dollar Round Table 1994, 95, 96, 97, 98, 99, 2000), Internat. Assn. Registered Fin. Cons. Republican. Avocations: golf, reading, chess. Home: 4841 Kempsville Greens Pkwy Virginia Beach VA 23462-6438 Office: Fin Security Group Inc 448 Viking Dr Virginia Beach VA 23452-7331 E-mail: bob@gofsg.com

O'BRIEN, ROBERT JOHN, JR. public relations executive, former government official, air force officer; b. Wheeling, W. Va., Apr. 16, 1935; s. Robert John and Martha Virginia (Hunter) O'B.; m. Margaret Eugenia Schultz BS in Journalism, Northwestern U., 1957; MA in Journalism, U. Wis., 1970; grad., Indsl. Coll. Armed Forces, 1977. Comnd. officer U.S. Air Force, 1957, advanced through grades to col.; dir. pub. affairs N. Am. Air Def. Command, Colorado Springs, Colo., 1977-80, Air Force Systems Command, Camp Springs, Md., 1980-82; dir. def. info. Office Sec. Def., Washington, 1982-83, dep. asst. sec. def., 1983-86; dir. pub. rels., Washington McDonnell Douglas Corp., Arlington, Va., 1986-97; v.p. pub. rels. The Boeing Co., 1997-99. Decorated D.S.M., Legion of Merit, Bronze Star, Air medal, Medal of Honor (Republic Vietnam). Mem. Air Force Assn., Pub. Rels. Soc. Am., Aviation/Space Writers Assn., U.S. Space Found., Ret. Officers Assn., Williamsburg Nat. Golf Club (Williamsburg, Va.), Nat. Press Club. Republican. Methodist. Avocations: golf, stamp collecting, model railroading.

O'BRIEN, ROBERT S. state official; b. Seattle, Sept. 14, 1918; s. Edward R. and Maude (Ransom) O'B.; m. Kathryn E. Arvan, Oct. 18, 1941 (dec. June 1984). Student public schs. With Kaiser Co., 1938-46; restaurant owner, 1946-50; treas. Grant County, Wash., 1950-65, State of Wash., 1965-89; chmn. Wash. State Fin. Com., 1965-89, Wash. Public Deposit Protection Commn., 1969-89, Wash. Public Employees Retirement Bd., 1969-77, Law Enforcement Officers and Firefighters Retirement System, 1971-77, Wash. State Investment Bd., 1981-89; retired, 1989. Mem. Wash. Data Processing Adv. Bd., 1967-73; Gov.'s Exec. Mgmt. and Fiscal Affairs Com., 1978-80, Gov.'s Cabinet Com. on Tax Alternatives, 1978-80; trustee Wash. Tchr.'s Retirement System, 1965-89; bd. dirs. Centennial Bank, Olympia, Wash. Recipient Leadership award Joint Council County and City Employees-Fedn. State Employees, 1970, Eagles Leadership award, 1967 Mem. Nat. Assn. State Auditors, Comptrollers and Treasurers (pres. 1977), Nat. Assn. Mcpl. Fin. Officers, Nat. Assn. State Treasurers, Western State Treasurers Assn. (pres. 1970), Wash. County Treas. Assn. (pres. 1955-56), Wash. Assn. Elected County Ofcls. (pres. 1955-58), Olympia Area C. of C., Soap Lake C. of C. (pres. 1948) Clubs: Elks (hon. life); Moose, Eagles, Lions, Olympia Yacht, Olympia Country and Golf; Empire (Spokane); Wash. Athletic (Seattle). Democrat. Address: 3613 Plummer St SE Olympia WA 98501-2126

O'BRIEN, ROBERT THOMAS, investment company executive; b. Phila., Oct. 7, 1941; s. James Francis Sr. and Mildred Anita (Gomez); m. Aurora Carol Forsthoffer, Nov. 7, 1964; 1 child, Michael Joseph. Cert., N.Y. Inst. Fin., 1963; BS, St. Joseph's U., 1971. Securities trader Brown Bros. Harriman, Phila., 1964-69, portfolio mgr., 1969-77, investment officer, 1977-80, asst. mgr., investment adv., 1980-83; v.p. Newbold's Asset Mgmt., 1983-85, sr. v.p., 1985-93, also bd. dirs., 1990-93; mng. dir. W.H. Newbold's Son & Co., 1993—. Bd. dirs. Cath. Philopatrian Literary Inst., 1973-76, Mary J. Drexel Home, 1992—, treas. 1992—; mem. fin. and investment com. Neumann Coll., 1990—. Served with USAF and Pa. Air N.G., 1960-67. Mem. Phila. Securities Assn., Air Force Assn. (life), Confederate Air Force (life, wing fin. officer 1992). Clubs: Racquet of Phila., Sailing Assn. (commodore 1980-82); Lewes Yacht, Miles River Yacht, Avalon Yacht, Eastport Yacht, Aronimink Golf, Idle Hour Tennis. Republican. Roman Catholic. Avocations: tennis, squash, sailing, golf. Home: 665 Dodds Ln Gladwyne PA 19035-1514 Office: WH Newbold's Son & Co 1500 Walnut St Philadelphia PA 19102-3523

O'BRIEN, SALLY K. secondary school educator, consultant; b. Madison, SD, Apr. 14, 1940; d. James Albert Karley and Aletha Bernetta Johnson; m. Timothy Evan O'Brien, Feb. 19, 1966 (div. Sept. 1992); children: Lyra Dragonchuk, Lael Pecht. BA, Wichita State U., 1962; MA, Northeastern Ill. U., 1972. Vol. Peace Corps, Philippines, 1962—64; tchr. HS Chgo. Pub. Schs., 1964—67, Dist. 214 HS, Wheeling Grove, 1975—85, dist. adminstr., coord. gifted and talented Arlington Heights, 1985—86, tchr. HS Elk Grove Village, 1986—94; instr. U. Hawaii CC, Hilo, 1995—96; pvt. cons. practice, 1986—. Cons., trainer, spkr., Gilberts, Ill., 1986—95; cons., spkr., trainer, writer, 1995—. Author (contbg.): Creative Communicators, 1990, Chicken Soup for the Soul at Work, 1996. Chair membership and social coms. Hawaii C. of C., Hilo, 1999—2000; mem. adv. com. Read to Me Internat., 2002; mayoral candidate Schaumburg, Ill., 1976. Mem.: Nat. Spkrs. Assn., Rotary Internat. Avocations: travel, reading, dancing, photography, singing. Home and Office: 2405 Kalanianaole Ave Apt 405 Hilo HI 96720 Fax: 808-961-2645. E-mail: skobrien@il.hawaii.net.

O'BRIEN, SOLEDAD, newscaster, news anchor; Student, Harvard U. Prodr. Second Opinion, reporter Health Week in Review Sta. KISS-FM, Boston; assoc. prodr., newswriter Sta. WBZ-TV; prodr. NBC News, 1991-93; co-host The Know Zone Discovery Channel; chief East Bay bur. Sta. KRON-TV, San Francisco, reporter, 1993—; co-host The Site, Nightly News, Weekend Today MSNBC. Recipient Emmy. Office: MSNBC NBC/Microsoft Corp. One MSNBC Plaza Secaucus NJ 07094*

O'BRIEN, TERRENCE LEO, federal judge; b. Lincoln, Nebr., Aug. 8, 1943; s. Leo James and Luella Mildred (Benting) O'B.; m. Dorothy Marguerite Driskill, Mar. 30, 1966; children: Sean Brendan, Heather Kathleen. BS in Acctg., U. Wyo., 1965, JD with honors, 1972. Bar: Wyo. 1972, U.S. Dist. Ct. Wyo. 1972, U.S. Ct. Appeals (7th and 10th cirs.) 1972, U.S. Ct. Appeals (8th, 9th and D.C. cirs.) 1973, U.S. Ct. Appeals (2d and 4th cirs.) 1974, U.S. Supreme Ct. 1975. Staff atty. Land and Natural Resources-U.S. Dept. Justice, Washington, 1972-74; ptnr. Omohundro & O'Brien, Buffalo, 1974-80; judge 6th Jud. Dist. Wyo., Gillette, 1980—2001, U.S. Ct. Appeals (10th Cir.), 2002—. Justice of Peace Johnson County, Buffalo, 1975-80. Mem. Wyo. Community Coll. Commn., 1978-80. Capt. U.S. Army, 1966-69. Mem.: Rotary. Republican. Home: 700 Ross Ave Gillette WY 82716-4230 Office: 532 Potter Stewart US Courthouse 100 E 5th St Cincinatti OH 45202-3988*

O'BRIEN, TIMOTHY ANDREW, writer, journalist, lawyer, educator; b. N.Y.C., July 11, 1943; s. Timothy Andrew and Hildegarde J. (Schenkel) O'B.; m. Maria de Guadalupe Margarita Moreno, Jan. 15, 1971; children: Theresa Marie, Tim A. BA in Comm., Mich. State U., 1967; MA in Polit. Sci., U. Md., 1972; postgrad., Tulane U., 1974-75; JD, Loyola U., New Orleans, 1976. Bar: La. 1976, D.C. 1977, U.S. Supreme Ct 1981. News writer, reporter, anchor WKBD-TV, Detroit, 1968-69, WTOP-TV, Washington, 1969-72, WDSU-TV, New Orleans, 1972-74, WVUE-TV, New Orleans, 1974-77; law corr. ABC News, 1977-99; corr. Cable News Network (CNN), 2001—. Leo Goodwin Prof. Law Southeastern U., 1997; disting. prof. law Hofstra U., Sch. Law, 20000. Contbr. articles to profl. jours. Bd. govs. Woodward Acad., College Park, Ga.; bd. visitors Loyola U. Sch. Law., 1997—. Recipient AP award for outstanding reporting of extraordinary event, 1976, New Orleans Press Club award for non-spot news reporting, 1976, Emmy award for documentary on D.C., 1969, ABA awards of merit, 1979 (2), 80, 85, Gavel award for documentary, 1980, Nat. award for human rights reporting Women in Comm., 1981, Disting. Alumnus award Mich. State U., 1996. Mem. Am. Law Inst., Radio-TV Corrs. Assn. Washington, Am. Judicature Soc. (bd. dirs. 1991-97). Office: CNN 820 First St NE Washington DC 20002

O'BRIEN, TIMOTHY JAMES, lawyer; b. Detroit, Nov. 4, 1945; m. Hyon Baek, Jan. 31, 1970; children: Jean, Jane. AB, Yale U., 1967; JD, Harvard U., 1976. Bar: N.Y. 1977, Hong Kong, 1999. Assoc. Cleary, Gottlieb, Steen & Hamilton, N.Y.C., 1976-80; ptnr. Coudert Bros., N.Y.C. and Hong Kong, 1980—. Lectr. symposium on internat. investment Southwestern Law Found., 1995. Mem.: Harvard Law Rev., 1975—76; contbr. articles to profl. jours. Assoc. dir., vol. Peace Corps, Republic of Korea, 1967-73. Mem. ABA (co-chmn. conf. on Korea-U.S. trade and investment 1990-92), Assn. of Bar of City of N.Y. (internat. law com., Asian affairs com. 1989-94), The Korea Soc. (N.Y.)(sec., bd. dirs. 1996—). Office: Coudert Bros Gloucester Tower 11 Pedder St Landmark 39th Fl Central Hong Kong Hong Kong Fax: 852-2868-1417. E-mail: obrient@coudert.com.

O'BRIEN, WALTER JOSEPH, II, lawyer; b. Apr. 22, 1939; s. Walter Joseph O'Brien and Lorayne (Stouffer) Steele; children: Kelly A., Patrick W., Kathleen; m. Sharon Ann Curling, July 8, 1978; 1 child, John Joseph. BBA, U. Notre Dame; JD, Northwestern U. Bar: Ill., U.S. Dist. Ct. (no. dist.) Ill., U.S. Supreme Ct. Assoc. Nicholson, Nisen, Elliott & Meier, Chgo., 1966-70; pres. Capstan Co., 1970-73, Walter J. O'Brien II, Ltd., Oak Brook, Ill., 1973-78, O'Brien & Assocs., P.C., Oakbrook Terrace, 1978—. Chmn., bd. dirs. Atty. Title Guaranty Fund, Inc., Champaign, Ill., 1979—; arbitrator chairperson 18th Judicial Ct., DuPage County, Ill. Contbr. articles to legal jours. Commr. Oak Brook Plan Commn., 1980-85; mem. Oak Brook Zoning Bd. Appeals, 1985-87, Bd. Edn. Elem. Dist. # 53, Oak Brook, 1991-95; commr. Ill. and Mich. Canal, Nat. Heritage Corridor Commn.; v.p. Oak Brook Civic Assn., 1972; trustee St. Isaac Jogues Ch., Hinsdale, Ill., 1975-76. Capt. Q.M.C., U.S. Army, 1964-66. Fellow Ill. Bar Found.; mem. Ill. State Bar Assn. (mem. assembly), DuPage Bar Assn. (bd. dirs. 1987-88, elected Man of Yr. 1988), Am. Inn of Ct. (master DuPage chpt.), Butterfield Country Club (bd. dirs. 1982-88). Roman Catholic. Office: O'Brien & Assocs PC Ste 501 1900 Spring Rd Oak Brook IL 60523

O'BRIEN, WILLIAM J. electrical engineer; b. Hartford, Conn., Feb. 2, 1926; s. William J. O'Brien and Nettie Bell Rossing; m. Janet McCarthy, July 4, 1950; children: William, Kathleen, Thomas, Mary, Nancy. Grad. in Elec. Engring., Internat. Corr. Sch., Scranton, Pa., 1955. Supt. Travelers Ins. Co., Hartford, 1947—62; pres. Bldg. Svc. Corp. Am., 1962—86; chmn. Internat. Econs. Corp., 1986—. Author: Inflation: Cause and Cure, 1982, Haiti: A Plan for a New Age, 1991, Interest Rates and Worldly Mistakes, 1994. Vice chmn. Greater Hartford Cmty. Chest, 1959—60. With USN, 1943—45. Mem.: Inst. Real Estate Mgmt. (pres. 1970—71). Avocations: flying, travel, mathematics, writing, lake activities.

O'BRIEN, WILLIAM J., III, lawyer; BS, Holy Cross Coll., 1965; LLB, Yale U., 1969. Bar: N.Y. 1970, Mich. 1985. With Hughes Hubbard and Reed, N.Y.C. and Paris, 1969-75; asst. gen. counsel Chrysler Corp., Highland Park, 1983, assoc. gen. counsel, 1984, dep. gen. counsel, 1986, v.p., gen. counsel, sec., 1987; sr. v.p., gen. counsel DaimlerChrysler AG, 1998, 2001—. Office: DaimlerChrysler Corp CIMS 485-14-96 1000 Chrysler Dr Auburn Hills MI 48326-2766

O'BRIEN, WILLIAM JEROME, II, lawyer; b. Darby, Pa., Oct. 22, 1954; s. Richard James O'Brien and Margaret (McGill) Hahn. BA in Econ. and Polit. Sci., Merrimack Coll., 1976; JD, Del. Law Sch., 1981. Bar: Pa. 1982, U.S. Dist. Ct. (ea. dist.) Pa. 1983, U.S. Supreme Ct. 1986. Law clk. Commonwealth Ct. of Pa., Harrisburg, 1982-83; assoc. Philips, Curtin and DiGiacomo, Phila., 1983-86, O'Brien & Assocs. PC, Phila., 1986—. Bd. dirs. New Manayunk Corp., Phila. counselor, 1987-98. Bd. dirs. North Light Inc., 1986-94, sec., 1988-90, pres., 1990-92; bd. dirs. Manayunk Cmty. Ctr. for Arts, 1988-90, chmn. Chaminouix Mansion, 1989—, chmn., 1991—; spl. asst. to U.S. Senator H. John Heinz, 1976-78; Rep. candidate for Phila. City Coun., 1991, for Phila. City Contr., 1997; mem. Rep. State Com. Pa., 1998-2000. Mem. Phila. Bar Assn., Pa. Bar Assn., Del. Law Sch. Alumni Assn. (sec. 1985-87), Bus. Assn. Manayunk (bd. dirs. 1987-89), Union League, Racquet Club (mem. com. 1985-87). Roman Catholic. Avocations: squash, court tennis, scuba, golf. Office: O'Brien & Assocs PC 4322 Main St Philadelphia PA 19127-1421

O'BRIEN, WILLIAM JOHN, ecology researcher; b. Summit, N.J., Nov. 30, 1942; m. Mavion Meier, 1964; children: Connor, Shay, Lia BA, Gettysburg Coll., 1965; postgrad., Cornell U., 1965-69; PhD, Mich. State U., 1970. sch. rsch. assoc. Ctr. Northern Studies, 1977; disting. lectr. Kans. Acad. Sci., 1990. From asst. prof. to prof. aquatic ecology U. Kans., Lawrence, 1971—2000, full prof., 1982—, dir. exptl. and applied ecology program, 1994—99, chair dept. sys. and ecology, 1991—96. Rsch. scientist Ecosys. Ctr. Marine Biol. Lab., 1986—. Grantee NSF, 1975—. Mem.: Internat. Assn. Theoretical and Applied Limnology, Am. Fisheries Soc., Am. Soc. Limnology and Oceanography. Office: U NC Dept Biol 310 Eberhart Bldg Greensboro NC 27402

O'BRIENT, DAVID WARREN, sales executive, consultant; b. Toledo, Oct. 2, 1927; s. Earl James and Jessie Carlton (Edwards) O'B.; m. Enid Jo Wynne O'Brient, Feb. 21, 1962 (div. Apr. 1978); 1 child, David Warren Jr. BS in Archtl. Engring., U. Tex., 1949. Registered profl. engr., Tex. Sales engr. Smith Engring. Co., Houston, 1949-53; dist. sales mgr. Dunham-Bush, Inc., Hartford, Conn., 1953-60; sales mgr. W.L. Lashley & Assoc., Houston, 1960-67; pres., owner OJ & C. Co., Inc., 1967-78, exec. v.p., 1980-83; pres., owner O'Brient Engring. Co., 1983-89. Mem., phone solicitor Rep. Party, Houston, 1962—; mem. adminstrv. bd. First United Meth. Ch., Houston, 1969—. With USN, 1945-46, 50-52, PTO, Korea. Mem. ASHRAE, Phi Eta Sigma, Tau Sigma Delta, Tau Beta Pi. Avocations: sports, music. Home and Office: 9550 Ella Lee Ln Apt 811 Houston TX 77063-1238

O'BRYAN, JAMES A. communications specialist; BS, Boston U., 1978. Sen. U.S. V.I., 1985-87; dir. youth prevention program Dept. Human Svcs., V.I., 1987-90; press sec. to gov. of V.I. Office of Gov., 1990-95, asst. to gov. pub. affairs, 1999—, dist. dir. comms. for congresswoman Christian Christensen, 1997. Chmn. Dem. State Party, 1998—. Mem. Assn. State Dem. Chairs. Office: PO Box 501 Saint Thomas VI 00804-0501

O'BRYANT, CATHY, retired social worker; b. Camden, N.J., Jan. 5, 1941; d. James Hearl and Ruth Virginia Jackson; children: Wendell, Penny, Terence, George, Ramona. A.Liberal Arts, Camden County Coll., Blackwood, N.J., 1972; BA in Psychology, Glassboro State Coll., N.J., 1976. Asst. FIPSE student program dir. Beacon Coll., Washington, 1979—80; dir. Nat. Congress of Neighborhoods, 1980—82; fin. mgr. Alternatives for Women Now, Camden, 1983—84; job search counselor Luth. Settlement House, Phila., 1984—87; admissions coord. Job Corps, 1988—89; social worker Dept. Human Svcs., 1989—94; ret., 1994. Internat. housing conf. coord. Alternatives for Women and UN, Camden, 1987; workshop leader Black Women's Health Project, Nairobi, Kenya, 1985; welfare caucuse leader Women, Work and Welfare, Houston, 1978; motivational spkr.; workshop developer. Author: (book) If My People, 1996; editor: (newsletters) Christian Voices/Grassroots Women Speak, 2002—. Asst. state chmn. N.J. Welfare Rights Orgn., Camden, 1974—77; mem. D.C. Women's Polit. Caucus, 1981—82; cert. mem. Juvenile Conf. Com. of Camden County, NJ, 1976—77. Recipient Bronze Star Outstanding Achievement award, Nat. Hook-Up of Black Women, 1992; grantee, D.C. Humanities Found., 1981. Mem.: Poetic Ministries (founder, dir. 1998—), Parade of Poets (founder, coord. 1996—), Mt. Olivet Christian Writers Club (founder, pres. 2001—02). Democrat. Seventh Day Adventist. Avocations: travel, nature walks, logic puzzles. Home: 231 N Evergreen Ave Apt 34B Woodbury NJ 08096

O'BRYANT-SEABROOK, MARLENE LORETTA LINTON, retired educator; b. Newberry, S.C., Aug. 21, 1933; d. Fletcher Arthur and Arabella Greenwood Linton; m. Evans O'Bryant Jr., Apr. 7, 1956 (div. 1968); children: Kim Denise, Evans III, Wayne Anthony, Darryl Fletcher; m. Arthur Herman Seabrook, Feb. 18, 1977. BS, S.C. State U., 1955; MA in Tchg., The Citadel, 1972; PhD, U. S.C., 1975. Cert. elem. edn., learning disabilites, mental retardation, elem. adminstrn., psychology, S.C. Tchr. Columbia (S.C.) Pub. Schs., 1955-57; social investigator Dept. Social Welfare, Bklyn., 1961-62; tchr. Charleston (S.C.) County Schs., 1962-72, dir. diagnostic/prescriptive tchg. program, 1972-75, head spl. edn. H.S., 1980-87; asst. prof. The Citadel, Charleston, 1972-75, 75-80; ret., 1987. Cons. Lake Greenwood Project, Laurens, S.C., 1972-73, Delaware County Intermediate Unit, Media, Pa., 1972-75, State Divsn. Instn., Raleigh, N.C., 1973-77, U. Mass. Spl. Edn. Dept., Amherst, 1975-77, Upward Bound Coll. Charleston, 1978-81, Follow Through program U.S. Office Edn., 1972-74. Pres. Avery Inst. African-Am. History and Culture, Charleston, 1990-94, v.p., 1998-99, pres., 1999-2001; bereavement counselor Hospice of Charleston, 1992—, bd. dirs., 1998—; mem. edn. bd. Gibbles Mus. Art, Charleston, 1997—. Mem. League Allied Arts (pres. 1998—), Alpha Kappa Alpha (Gamma Xi Omega chpt. v.p. 1996-98, pres. 1998-2000, Soror of Yr. 1998, 99). Episcopalian. Avocations: quilting, cross-stitching, smocking, knitting, painting. Home: 939 Rutledge Ave Charleston SC 29403-3205 E-mail: marlobs@awod.com.

O'BRYON, JAMES FREDRICK, defense executive; b. Schenectady, N.Y., Oct. 1, 1941; s. Frederick Stanley and Elizabeth Mary O'B.; m. Margaret Adina Bell, Oct 23, 1965; children: Daniel, Douglas, Cris, Kera. BS in Math., King's Coll., Briarcliff, N.Y., 1964; MSA in Ops. Rsch., George Washington

U., 1973; SM Through Elec. Engring. Dept., MIT, 1975. Mathematician Ballistics Rsch. Lab. Aberdeen (Md.) Proving Ground, 1966-74, asst. to dir. Ballistics Rsch. Lab., 1975-76, ops. rsch. analyst smart munitions group Ballistics Rsch. Lab., 1976-79, chmn. red-on-blue working group Joint Tech. Coord. Group, 1979-85, chief combat survivability and tech. U.S. Army Materiel Systems Analysis Activity, 1985-86; asst. dep. undersec. def. Office Sec. Def., Washington, 1986-88, dir. live-fire testing, 1988-95, dep. dir. operational test and evaluation, 1995—; chmn. The O'Bryon Group, 2001—, Mobius Bus. Solutions, 2002—. Dir. Joint Live Fire Program, Washington, 1986-2001; mem. Conventional Sys. Com., Washington, 1987—; newscaster, radio personality WRBS-FM, Balt., 1965-80; chmn. Mobile Bus. Solutions, 2002—. Recorded albums Until Then, 1968, Portrait of a Man, 1972, My Favorite Song, 1977, Celebration of Praise, 1982; co-author: (manual) Red-on-Blue Weapons, Effects, 1983; contbr. over 75 articles to profl. jours. Active edn. coun. MIT, Cambridge, 1980—; trustee Dettmer Charitable Trust, Conn.; bd. dirs. Internat. Bible Soc. Found., Colo.; mem. adv. bd. N.Y. Theol. Sem. With U.S. Army, 1964-66. Named Outstanding Young Man in Am., Jaycees, 1970, Disting. Lectr., Def. Systems Mgmt. Coll., 1988. Fellow Ctr. Advanced Engring. Study MIT; mem. AIAA, Nat. Def. Indsl. Assn. (chmn. Test and Evaluation divsn.), Internat. Test and Evaluation Assn., Sigma Xi. Home: 1608 S Tollgate Rd Bel Air MD 21015-5825

OBST, NORMAN PHILIP, economist, educator; b. Bklyn., May 25, 1944; s. Joseph J. and Pearl L. (Newmark) O.; m. Barbara E. Brudevold, Dec. 23, 1970; children: Lindora, Jannise, Laara, Benjamin. BA, SUNY, Binghamton, 1965; MS in Econs., Purdue U., 1967, PhD in Econs., 1970. Asst. prof. U. Wash., 1970-73, Mich. State U., East Lansing, 1973-77, assoc. prof., 1977-92, prof. econs., 1992—. Cons. NSF, Social Scis. and Humanities Rsch. Coun. of Can., Mich. Bar Assn., Little, Brown & Co., Prentice-Hall, Scott-Foresman, Times-Mirror Mosby, D.C. Heath & Co., Allyn & Bacon, West Edn. Pub., Dryden Press, John Wiley & Sons, Inc., BS&A Software, Law Offices of Joseph H. Spiegel. Referee Am. Econ. Rev., Internat. Econ. Rev., Jour. of Money, Credit and Banking, Eastern Econ. Jour., Jour. of Econ. Issues, Jour. of Macroeconomics, Jour. of Econs. and Bus., Zentralblatt fur Mathematik; contbr. articles to profl. jours. Supr., assessor Williamstown Twp., 1988—, sec. bd. appeals, 1988—, planning commn. mem. 1974-88, vice chmn. 1985-88; chief adminstrv. officer, Williamstown Twp. Budget, 1989—; cen. adminstr. Williamstown Twp. Sewer System, 1988—; bd. determination Ingham County Drain Commn., 1989; co-chair govt. com. I-96 strategic econ. plan with Lansing area bus. leaders, 1990. Mem. Am. Econ. Assn., Am. Fin. Assn., Midwest Econ. Assn., Mich. Assessors Assn. Avocations: chess, table tennis, financial markets. Office: Mich State U Marshall Hall Dept Econs East Lansing MI 48824-1038 also: Williamstown Twp Hall 4990 Zimmer Rd Williamston MI 48895-8180

OBUCHOWSKI, MICHAEL J. state legislator; b. Bellows Falls, Vt., Feb. 4, 1952; Student, Harvard U. Staff Basketville Inc., Putney, Vt.; mem. Vt. Ho. of Reps., Montpelier, 1973—, spkr., 1995—2001. Former mem. joint energy com., judicial retention com., former chmn. appropriations com., edn. and energy coms., Vt. Ho. of Reps., spkr. of house 1995—; incorporator New Eng. Kurn Hattin Homes; former mem. Vt. Health Policy Corp. Former mem. New Eng. Bd. Higher Edn.; mem. Rockingham and Windham County Dem. Com.; bd. dirs. Rockingham Meml. Hosp. Bd. Mem. Bellows Falls H.S. Alumni Assn. (sec.), Elks. Address: 72 Atkinson St Bellows Falls VT 05101-1321 E-mail: obie@leg.state.vt.us.*

OBUCHOWSKI, RAYMOND JOSEPH, lawyer; b. LaGrange, Ill., Oct. 2, 1955; s. Harry John and Betty Lou (Roux) O.; m. Marie Ann Fowler, May 28, 1983; children: Michael Jozef, Brian Matthew. BS, Western Ill. U., 1976; JD, Vt. Law Sch., 1980. Bar: Ill. 1980, Vt. 1982, U.S. Dist. Ct. Ill., U.S. Dist. Ct. Vt., 1983, U.S. Ct. Appeals (7th cir.) 1982; bd. cert. in bus. and consumer bankruptcy law Am. Bankruptcy Bd. of Cert. State's atty. investigator McDonough County Gen. State Atty.'s Office, Macomb, Ill., 1976-77; asst. atty. gen. revenue litigation Ill. Atty. Gen.'s Office, Springfield, 1981-82; law clk. to Hon. Charles J. Marro U.S. Bankruptcy Ct. Dist. of Vt., Rutland, 1982-83, estate administrator, 1983-84; assoc. Law Office of Jerome Meyers, Springfield, Vt., 1983, Law Office of Joseph C. Palmisano, Barre, 1984-86; pvt. practice S. Royalton, 1986—; ptnr. Mayer, Berk & Obuchowski, 1988-90; pvt. practice Bethel, Vt., 1990-91; ptnr. Obuchowski & Reis, 1992-96; pvt. practice Obuchowski Law Office, 1997—. Co-author: Vermont Collection Law, 1988, Basic Bankruptcy in Vermont, 1989, Sucessful Creditor's Strategies in Bankruptcy in Vermont, 1990, Foreclosure and Repossession in Vermont, 1991. Mem. Ill. Bar Assn., Vt. Bar Assn. (chmn. bankruptcy com. 1997-2000), Nat. Assn. Bankruptcy Trustees, Am. Bankruptcy Inst., Blue Key. Roman Catholic. Avocation: baseball. Home: PO Box 25 South Royalton VT 05068-0025 Office: PO Box 60 Bethel VT 05032-0060 E-mail: obi@sover.net.

OBUCK, JOHN FRANCIS, artist; b. Detroit, Aug. 20, 1946; s. John and Genevieve (Nowaczyk) O. Student, Macomb Coll., 1966-68; BFA, Wayne State U., 1968; MFA, Sch. Art Inst., Chgo., 1972. Vis. artist/lectr. Princeton (N.J.) U., 1989, 92—, Tyler Sch. Art, Phila., 1992, U. Tex., Austin, 1990-91, 88, 86, R.I. Sch. Design, Providence, 1990, 83, U. N.C., Chapel Hill, 1987, Sch. Art Inst. Chgo., 1987, 83, Boston Mus. Sch., 1985, SUNY, Purchase, 1984, Ill. State U., Normal, 1983. One-man shows include Feigensen/Preston Gallery, Birmingham, Mich., 1992, 90, Jack Hanley Gallery, San Francisco, 1991, Am. Acad. Rome, 1989, Hanes Art Ctr., Chapel Hill, N.C., 1987, Young/Hoffman Gallery, Chgo., 1983, 81, 80, Barbara Gladstone Gallery, N.Y.C., 1982, 80, Delahunty Gallery, Dallas, 1981, N.A.M.E. Gallery, Chgo., 1979; numerous group exhibits. Grantee Pollock/Krasner Found., 1992, 2001, Louis Comfort Tiffany Nat. Endowment for Arts, 1987, 80, 79, Art Matters Inc., 1986; recipient Rome prize N.Y. Found. for Arts, 1988. Mem. Am. Abstract Artist Assn., Soc. Fellows, Am. Acad. in Rome. Home and Office: 20 Murray St 5S New York NY 10007 E-mail: jobuck@mindspring.com.

OBUROTA, GOZI, accountant; b. Asaba, Delta, Nigeria, July 7, 1957; came to U.S., 1981; s. Josiah and Biatrice Oburota; m. Mi-Reta R. Oburota, Oct. 14, 1985. BBA, U. Tex., 1985, MBA, 1988. CPA, Md., Calif. Acct. Randy Coleman Homes, Austin, Tex., 1985-88; sr. acct. IBM, San Jose, Calif., 1988-90; pres. GSO Corp., 1991-94; CEO, pres. Gozi Samuel Oburota, CPA, Washington, 1994—. Mem. AICPA, Inst. Mmgt. Accts. (cert.), Assn. Cert. Fraud Examiners (cert.). Republican. Avocations: reading, travel, sports. Office: Gozi Samuel Oburota CPA Corp 601 Pennsylvania Ave NW Ste 900 S Bldg Washington DC 20004 E-mail: gozi@gsocorp.com.

O'BYRNE, ELIZABETH MILIKIN, pharmacologist, researcher, endocrinologist; b. Miami, Fla., May 19, 1944; d. Richard Mershon and Anne (Smith) Milikin; m. Brian Kenneth O'Byrne, July 1, 1972; children: Lucy Milikin, Kenneth Daniel. AB in Chemistry, Emory U., 1965, MS in Biochemistry, 1968; PhD in Biochemistry, N.Y. Med. Coll., 1985. Assoc. scientist Eli Lilly Rsch. Labs., Indpls., 1968-70; sr. rsch. scientist CIBA-GEIGY Pharms., Summit, N.J., 1970-96; rsch. fellow Novartis Pharms., 1997—. Contbr. articles to profl. jours. Mem. AAAS, N.Y. Acad. Sci., Inflammation Rsch. Assn., Osteoarthritis Rsch. Soc. Achievements include isolation, characterization and development of radioimmunoassay for hormone relaxin to monitor production and secretion, of assays of cytokine and enzyme degradation of cartilage in vitro and in vivo, of proton and sodium magnetic resonance properties of cartilage; demonstration of therapeutic efficacy of matrix metalloprotease inhibitors to retard tissue damage in animal models of diseases; investigation of autologous bone marrow-derived mesechymal stem cells to repair osteoarthritic lesions in cartilage and bone, co-founder of CIBA-GEIGY Partnership in Sci. in which scientists work with teachers to bring hands-on experiences in laboratory investigation to high school students. Home: 234 Sagamore Rd Millburn NJ 07041-2136 Office: Novartis Morris Ave Summit NJ 07901 E-mail: elizabeth.obyrne@pharma.novartis.com.

O'CALLAGHAN, JERRY ALEXANDER, government official; b. Klamath Falls, Oreg., Feb. 23, 1922; s. Jeremiah Patrick and Marie Jane (Alexander) O'C.; m. Florence Marie Sheehan, Aug. 6, 1949; children— Jane Mary, Susan Margaret. BS with honors, U. Oreg., 1943, MA with honors, 1947; PhD, Stanford, 1951. Acting instr. history Stanford, 1951-52, U. Wyo., 1952-53; oil editor Tribune-Herald, Casper, Wyo., 1953-55; acting asst. prof. U. Wyo., 1955-56; legis. asst. to Senator Joseph O'Mahoney (Wyo.), 1956-60; exec. asst. to Senator Joseph Hickey(Wyo.), 1961; asst. dir. lands and minerals mgmt. Bur. Land Mgmt., Dept. Interior, 1961-62, asst. dir. plans and legislation, 1962-64, chief legislation and office coop. relations, 1964-69, chief div. coop. relations, 1969-80, chief hist. studies, 1980-82, historian emeritus, 1982—. Author: Disposition of the Public Domain in Oregon, 1960, America 200— The Legacy of Our Lands, 1976. Bd. govs. St. Columba's Episc. Nursery Sch., 1959-71; vestryman Episc. Ch., 1964-68, outreach leader, 1985-90; lay ministry St. Columba's, 1990—. With AUS, 1943-46. Mem. Soc. of Forest History, Fed. Profl. Assn. (pres. 1972), Fossils, Phi Kappa Psi. Home: 5607 Chesterbrook Rd Bethesda MD 20816-1301

OCANSEY, AARON AKROFI, game designer; b. Ada, Ghana, Africa, Sept. 16, 1949; came to U.S., 1969; s. Alfred Natea Ocansey and Grace Tay; m. Shirley Donaldson, Nov. 23, 1974 (div. Aug. 1990); children: Denis, Aba, Daniela; m. Gloria Jean Penrice, Aug. 25, 1992; 1 child, Layo Penrice. Stage III Level Acctg., Royal Inst. Tech., Accra, New Town, 1969. Cert. of Appreciation, Pres. Ronald Reagan, 1988. Acct. London Agy., Westwood, Calif., 1974-76, Kindle Inc., Inglewood, 1984-90, Rotex Exch., Gardena, 1990-92, Trak Auto Corp., Ontario, 1992; officer Advance Tech., Hollywood, 1992—. Game designer Ocansey Ocean Inc., Accra, 1989—. Designer: (bd. games) Elmina Game, 1996, Ghana Empire Game, 1998. Avocation: game designing. Home: 16240 Vaquero Ct Riverside CA 92504-5856 Office: Ocansey Ocean PO Box 6559 Accra Ghana E-mail: aaronocansey@hotmail.com., a.ocansey@worldnet.att.net.

OCASIO, WILLIAM, management consultant, educator; b. Mayaguez, PR, Dec. 17, 1955; s. Willie Ocasio and Isabel Rodriguez de Ocasio. BA, U. PR, Mayaguez, 1976; MBA, Harvard U., Boston, 1984; PhD, Stanford (Calif.)U., 1992. Asst. to the dir. for planning and devel. Ctr. for Energy and Environment Rsch., San Juan, PR, 1979—82; sr. assoc. ICF Inc., Washington, 1984—86; exec. dir. Governor's Econ. Adv. Coun., San Juan, PR, 1986—90; asst. prof. MIT Sloan Sch. of Mgmt., Cambridge, Mass., 1992—95, Kellogg Sch. of Mgmt., Northwestern U., Evanston, Ill., 1995—2001, John L. and Helen Kellog Disting. Prof. Mgmt. and Orgs., 2001—. Editl. bd. Adminstrv. Sci. Quar., Ithaca, NY, 1998—. Author: (jour. article) Am. Jour. Sociology, 1999 (W. Richard Scott Award, Am. Sociol. Assn., 2001). Mem.: Ibero-Am. Acad. of Mgmt., Strategic Mgmt. Soc., Acad. of Mgmt., Am. Sociol. Assn. Roman Catholic. Office: Northwestern Univ 2001 Sheridan Rd Evanston IL 60208 Office Fax: 847-491-8896. E-mail: w-ocasio@kellogg.northwestern.edu.

OCASIO-MELENDEZ, MARCIAL ENRIQUE, history educator; b. San Juan, P.R., Aug. 22, 1942; s. Manuel C. and Amparo (Melendez) Ocasio; m. Mimi Rivera, Apr. 15, 1973 (div. 1976). BA, U. P.R., 1964, MA, 1977; PhD, Mich. State U., 1988. Tchr. sci. P.R. Dept. Edn., San Juan, 1966-67; tchr. sci., history Nyack (N.Y.) Schs., 1967-71; tchr. sci. Robinson Prep. Sch., Condado, P.R., 1971-72; instr. P.R. Jr. Coll., Rio Piedras, 1972-80; teaching asst. Mich. State U., E. Lansing, 1979-83; instr. history Caribbean U., Bayamon, P.R., 1983-85; instr. Inter Am. U., 1985-87, U. P.R., Rio Piedras, 1983-87; vis. asst. prof. Mich. State U., E. Lansing, 1987-88; asst. prof. history U. Mich., Flint, 1988-91; prof. history U. P.R., Rio Piedras, 1991—, dir. grad. program history, 1991-93, assoc. dean acad. affairs Coll. Humanities, 1993-95, dir. internat. rels., 1995—2001; prof. ctr. advanced grad. studies P.R. and The Caribbean. Bd. dirs. Spanish Speaking Info. Ctr., Flint; lectr. Universidad del Valle, Cali, Universidad de Los Andes, Bogota, Universidad Pedagogica Nacional, Tunja, U. del Norte Barranquilla, Colombia; dir. Rockefeller Found. Caribbean 2000 Project, U. P.R., 1994-95, Urban Preservation Project of Rio Piedras, P.R., 1994-95; pres. P.R.'s Bd. Hist. Preservation, 1999—; mem. editl. bd. Caribbean Studies, 1994-99. Author: Rio Piedras Notas, 1985, Las Americas, Su Tierra, Su Gente, 1997, Capitalism and Development, Tampico 1876-1924, 1998. Pres. P.R. Bd. Hist. Preservation, 1999-2002. Mich. State U. scholar 1981, urban affairs grantee, 1982-83; Fulbright scholar (Colombia) 1989, 90, 2001--; NEH fellow, 1973, 78-79, 91. Mem. Social Sci. Studies Assn., Coun. L.Am. History, Am. Hist. Assn., L.Am. Studies Assn., Assn. P.R. Historians (pres. 1995-97), Joint Border Rsch. Inst., Assn. Caribean Historians, Caribbean Studies Assn., Hispanic Coun. on Internat. Rels., Phi Alpha Theta. Office: Univ PR History Dept PO Box 23350 San Juan PR 00931-3350 E-mail: kokoroko9@hotmail.com.

OCCHIATO, MICHAEL ANTHONY, city official; b. Pueblo, Colo. s. Joseph Michael and Joan Occhiato; m. Peggy Ann Stefonowicz, June 27, 1964 (div. Sept. 1983); children: Michael, James, Jennifer. BBA, U. Denver, 1961; MBA, U. Colo., 1984; postgrad., U. So. Colo. Grad. Real Estate Inst. Sales mgr. Tivoli Brewing co., Denver, 1965-67, acting brewmaster, prodn. control mgr., 1967-68, plant mgr., 1968-69; adminstrv. mgr. King Resources Co., 1969-70; ops. mgr. Canners Inc., Pepsi-Cola Bottling Co., Pueblo, 1970-76; pres. Pepsi-Cola Bottling Co., 1978-82; gen. mgr. Pepsi-Cola Bottling Group div. PepsiCo., 1982, area v.p., 1982-83; ind. cons., 1983—; broker assoc. Sound Venture Realty, 1996-98, Jones Healy Better Homes & Gardens, 1998—. V.p. Colo. Soft Drink Assn., 1978, pres., 1979; regional dir. Pepsi Cola Mgmt. Inst. divsn. Pepsi Co., 1979-82; pres. Ethnic Foods Internat. dba Taco Rancho, Pueblo; chmn. Weifang (China) Sister City Del., 1991—; bd. dirs. HMO So. Colo. Health Plan, 1988-93, Pueblo Diversified Industries; rancher, 1976—; land devel. real estate broker assoc., 1996—; real estate designator, GRI. Mem. Pueblo City Coun., 1978—93, 2001—, pres., 1986—87, 1991; mem. Pueblo Bd. Health, 1978—80, Pueblo Regional Planning Commn., 1980—81, Pueblo Action Inc., 1978—80, Pueblo Planing and Zoning Commn., 1985; chmn. Pueblo Area Coun. Govts., 1980—82; mem. Pueblo Econ. Devel. Corp., 1983—91; chmn. fundraising Pueblo chpt. Am. Heart Assn., 1983—; active Earth Wise Pueblo, 1991; pres. Pueblo City Coun., 2002; bd. dirs. Pueblo Crime Stoppers , 2001—, El Pueblo Boys Ranch; v.p. Colo. Soft Drink Assn., 1979—80, pres., 1980—81; del. 1st World Conf. Local Elected Ofcls. to 1st UN Internat. Coun. for Local Environ. Initiative. Lt. USN, 1961—65. Named to board of directors Pueblo Crime Stoppers. Mem. So. Colo. Emergency Med. Technicians Assn. (pres. 1975), Am. Saler Assn., Am. Quarter Horse Assn., Colo. Cattle Assn., Pueblo C. of C., Rotary, Pi Kappa Alpha (v.p. 1960). Home and Office: 11 Harrogate Ter Pueblo CO 81001-1723

OCH, MOHAMAD RACHID, psychiatrist, consultant; b. Damascus, Syria, Apr. 1, 1956; came to U.S., 1981; s. Seifeddine and Souad (Oubari) O.; m. Marianne Noonan, July 24, 1960; children: Seifeddine, Adam. MD, Aleppo (Syria) U., 1980. Psychiat. cons. Human Resource Inst., Brookline, Mass., 1985; med. dir. Spectrum House, Westboro, 1986-87; assoc. med. dir. Boston Rd. Clinic, Shrewsbury, 1985-97, v.p., 1989—; med. dir. mental health unit Holden (Mass.) Hosp., 1988-90; med. dir. Basic Health Mgmt., Worcester, Mass., 1988-90; dir. clin. ops. Capstan, LLC, 1997—, CEO, med. dir., 1999-2000; nat. med. dir. Civigenics, Marlboro, Mass., 2000—; gen. mng. ptnr. Prescott Healthcare, Worcester. Asst. med. dir. Holden Hosp., 1988—, Basic Health Mgmt., Worcester, 1988—; attending psychiatrist, asst. prof. U. Mass. Med. Ctr., Worcester; dir. mental health unit Milford Whitinsville Hosp., 1990-93, chmn. dept. psychiatry, 1991-92; med. dir. Seven Hills Intensive Residential Treatment Program, 1990-93; asst. chief psychiatry St. Vincent's Hosp., 1996-99; mem. adv. bd. Pfeizer, 1996—; med. dir. HMA behavioral health, 1995-99. Mem. Am. Psychiat. Assn., AMA. Moslem. Office: Prescott Health Care LLP 130 Elm St Worcester MA 01609 E-mail: rachidoch@aol.com.

OCHEJ, HELEN WANDA, technologist; b. Treysa, Germany, Oct. 3, 1946; d. Franek Ochej and Luba Kopytko; m. David R. Sutkoff, Aug. 30, 1980; children: Anne Q. Sutkoff. BA, Lycoming Coll., Williamsport, PA, 1968. Rsch. asst. McNeil Labs, Fort Washington, Pa., 1968—72, Max Planck Inst. Brain Rsch., Koln, Germany, 1972—74, U. Rochester Cancer Control, Rochester, NY, 1975—85, supr. facility, 1975—85; contract med. indexer Kessler, Herner, Caelum, Rockville, Md., 1986—95; tech. info. specialist Nat. Libr. Medicine, Bethesda, 1995—. Pres. Grad. Women Sci., Rochester, NY, 1978—78; focus group NLM Exhibit, Md., 2001—01; treas. Am. Soc. Indexers, Md., 2002—. Contbr. articles to profl. jours. V.p. Neighborhood Assn., Rochester, NY, 1978—79; adv. bd. Gifted and Talented Edn., Montgomery County, Md., 1991—95; active Seneca Valley Pony Club, 1996—98. Grantee Rsch. Grant, Max Planck Inst., 1972-1974. Mem.: Am. Med. Writers Assn. Avocations: gardening, tibetan meditation, tibetan meditation, tibetan meditation. Office: National Library of Medicine 8600 Rockville Pike Bethesda MD 20894 E-mail: helen.ochej@nlm.nih.gov.

OCHELTREE, RICHARD LAWRENCE, lawyer, retired forest products company executive; b. Springfield, Ill., Oct. 9, 1931; s. Chalmer Myerly and Helen Margaret (Camm) O.; m. Ann Maureen Washburn, Apr. 11, 1958; children: Kirstin Ann, Lorraine Page, Tracy Lynn. AB, Harvard U., 1953, LL.B., 1958. Bar: Calif. 1959. Sec., gen. counsel Am. Forest Products Corp./Bendix Forest Products Corp., San Francisco, 1961-81; v.p. adminstrn., sec., gen. counsel Am. Forest Products Co., 1981-87. Served with USAF, 1953-55. Mem. Am., San Francisco bar assns. Home: 1446 Floribunda Ave Apt 102 Burlingame CA 94010-3810

OCHMANEK, DAVID ALAN, defense analyst; b. Oak Park, Ill., Apr. 10, 1951; s. Edwin Joseph and Phyllis Jean (Straass) O.; m. Barbara Jane Larson, June 16, 1973; children: James Edwin, Anne Skaaden. BS in Internat. Affairs, Polit. Sci., USAF Acad., 1973; MPA in Pub. Affairs and Internat. Rels., Princeton U., 1980. Fgn. svc. officer U.S. Dept. State, 1980-85; profl. staff The Rand Corp., 1985-93, 95—; dep. asst. sec. of def. for strategy Washington, 1993-95; sr. def. analyst The RAND Corp., 1995—. Author: NATO's Future: Implications for U.S. Military Capabilities and Force Posture, 2000; co-author: (with Edward L. Warner III) Next Moves: An Arms Control Agenda for the 1990's, 1989, (with Christopher Bowie et al) The New Calculus, 1993, (with Zalmay Khalilzad) Strategic Appraisal, 1997, (with Edward Harshberger el at) To Find and Not to Yield, 1998, (with Anthony Lake) The Real and the Ideal, 2001; contbr. articles to profl. jours., chpts. to books. Capt. USAF, 1973-78. Lutheran. Office: The RAND Corp 1200 S Hayes St Arlington VA 22202-5050

OCHOA, EDUARDO MARTIN, economics educator; b. Buenos Aires, Nov. 18, 1950; came to U.S., 1965; s. Ernesto Agustin and Violeta (Kimelman) O.; m. Holly Dawn Byers, Dec. 20, 1970; children: Michael Andrew, Eric Anthony. BA, Reed Coll., Portland, Oreg., 1973; MS, Columbia U., 1976; MA, New Sch. for Social Rsch., 1981, PhD, 1984. Instr. in politics., econs. and soc. program Politics, Econs., Soc. Program, SUNY, Old Westbury, 1980-81; lectr. Calif. State U., Fresno, 1981-84, asst. prof. econs. L.A., 1984-87, assoc. prof., 1987-92, chmn. dept. econs. and stats., 1990-94, prof., 1992—, assoc. dean Sch. Bus. and Econs., 1994—. Cons. City of Pomona, Calif., 1989-90, M & C, Barcelona, Spain, 1990—, Ward Econ. Devel. Corp., L.A., 1990—, City of L.A., 1992—, Lorente & Assocs., 1992—. Contbr. articles to profl. jours. Mem. Am. Econ. Assn. Office: Calif State U Dept Econs And Stats Los Angeles CA 90032

OCHOA, MANUEL, JR. oncologist; b. N.Y.C., Apr. 22, 1930; s. Manuel and Maria (Diaz) O.; m. Suzanne Ellen Recca, Sept. 1, 1956; children: Elizabeth, Suzanne Elise. AB, Columbia Coll., 1951; MD, Columbia U., 1955. Diplomate Am. Bd. Internal Medicine; lic. physician, N.Y., Mass. Asst. in medicine U. Rochester (N.Y.) Med. Sch., 1958-61; instr. medicine, assoc., asst. prof. Columbia U., N.Y.C., 1964-68; attending physician Meml. Sloan-Kettering Cancer Ctr., 1973—. Investigator Marine Biol. Lab., Woods Hole, Mass., 1965; assoc. prof. clin. medicine Cornell U., N.Y.C., 1982-96, prof., 1996—; cons. Harlem Hosp. Ctr., N.Y.C., 1966-68, Kingston (N.Y.) Hosp., 1970-85; vis. prof. U. Hawaii, Honolulu, 1971, U. Mex., Mexico City, 1979. Contbr. articles to profl. jours. Capt. USAF, 1956-58, ETO. Fellow Lalor Found., 1965. Fellow ACP, ACS. Republican. Roman Catholic. Achievements include discovering genetic code and protein synthesis in cancer cells, cancer chemotherapy. Home: 82 E Middle Patent Rd Bedford NY 10506-2106 Office: Meml Sloan-Kettering Cancer Ctr 1271 York Ave New York NY 10021-6007

OCHOA-ZAMORA, ALBERTO, vineyard executive; b. Zamora, Michoacan, Mexico, May 22, 1957; s. Miguel Ochoa-Bautista, Raquel Zamora-Garcia; m. Virginia Adelaide Cabral; children: Emmanuel Alberto Zamora, Vanessa Celeste Zamora. Student, Napa Valley Coll., Napa, Calif., 1992—94. Cert. viticulture and winery technology. Vineyard/property/prodn. mgr. Jarvis Winery, Napa, Calif.; vineyard mgr. Hess Collection Winery, 1999—2001, Simi Winery, Healdsburg, 2001—. Author: Los Poemas de mi Pubertad, 2000. Mem.: ASEV. Roman Catholic. Avocations: reading, music. Home: 4210 Mataro Ct Napa CA 94558 Personal E-mail: ZAMONET@aol.com.

OCHS, CAROL REBECCA, theologian, philosophy and religion educator; b. N.Y.C., May 7, 1939; d. Herman and Clara Florence (Michaels) Blumenthal; m. Michael Ochs, Sept. 27, 1959; children: Elisabeth Amy, Miriam Adina. BA, CUNY, 1960, MA, 1964; PhD, Brandeis U., 1968. Philosophy lectr. CUNY, 1964-65; from asst. prof. to prof. philosophy Simmons Coll., Boston, 1967-92, prof. emerita, 1992—. Adj. faculty Grad. Sch. Union Inst., Cin., 1992—97, Hebrew Union Coll.-Jewish Inst. Religion, N.Y.C., 1994—97, dir. grad. studies, vis. prof. philosophy, 1997—2001, dir. grad. studies, adj. assoc. prof. Jewish Religious Thought, 2001—; cons. Inst. for Svc. to Higher Edn., Chestnut Hill, Mass., 1972, St. Mary's Coll., South Bend, Ind., 1980; scholar-in-residence Hollins Coll., Roanoke, Va., 1987, numerous temples and synagogues; mem. selection com. Kent Postdoctoral Fellowships Bunting Inst., Radcliffe Coll.; lectr. in field. Author: Behind the Sex of God: Toward a New Consciousness Transcending Matriarchy and Patriarchy, 1977, Women and Spirituality, 1983, 2d edit., 1997, An Ascent to Joy: Transforming Deadness of Spirit, 1989, The Noah Paradox: Time as Burden, Time as Blessing, 1991, Song of the Self: Biblical Spirituality and Human Holiness, 1994, Jewish Spiritual Guidance, 1997, Our Lives as Torah: Finding God in Our Own Stories, 2001; contbr. articles to profl. jours. Mem. Jewish-Cath. Dialogue, Boston, 1989-93; mem. Cath.-Jewish com. Archdiocese of Boston, 1989-93. Fellow NEH, 1976, 88, Nat. Humanities Inst., U. Chgo., 1978-79, Danforth Found., 1981-86, Coolidge Rsch., Colloquium, 1985, Resource Theologian, 1995-99. Fellow Soc. for Values in Higher Edn. (bd. dirs. 1982-88, chair ctrl. com. 1985-87), Assn. for Religion and Intellectual Life (mem. editl. bd. 1986—). Office: 1 W 4th St New York NY 10012

OCHS, MICHAEL, editor, librarian, music educator; b. Cologne, Germany, Feb. 1, 1937; came to U.S., 1939, naturalized, 1945; s. Isaac Julius and Claire (Baum) O.; m. Carol Rebecca Blumenthal, Sept. 27, 1959; children— Elisabeth Amy, Miriam Adina BA, CCNY, 1958; MS, Columbia U., 1963; A.M., NYU, 1964; D.A., Simmons Coll., 1975. Cataloguer CCNY, 1963-65, lectr. in music, 1964; music libr. Brandeis U., Waltham, Mass., 1965-68, creative arts libr., 1968-74; asst. prof. libr. sci. Simmons Coll., Boston, 1974-78; libr. Eda Kuhn Loeb Music Libr., Harvard U., Cambridge, Mass., 1978-88, Richard F. French libr., 1988-92; lectr. music Harvard U., Mass., 1978-81, sr. lectr. music, 1981-92, also libr. cons., 1977-78; music editor W. W. Norton and Co., N.Y.C., 1992-2001; editl. cons., 2001—. Libr. cons. Biblioteca Berenson, Florence, Italy, 1983, Columbia U., 1987; project dir. U.S. Répertoire International des Sources Musicales Manuscript Inventory Ctr. at Harvard U., NEH, Cambridge, Mass., 1985-88. Editor Notes, Jour. Music Libr. Assn., 1987-92, Music Librarianship in America, 1991; contbr. articles to profl. jours., 1976—. Mem. Am. Musicol. Soc. (bd. dirs. 2000—), Internat. Assn. Music Librs. (pres. rsch. librs. br. 1987-90), Music Libr. Assn. (chmn. New Eng. chpt. 1968-69, chmn. com. on bibliog. description 1971-73, chmn. music libr. adminstrn. com. 1975-76, chmn. fin. com. 1976-78, bd. dirs. 1976-78, chmn. publs. com. 1983-87, pres. 1993-95). Office: 115 E 87th St Ste 26A New York NY 10128-1171

OCHS, RICHARD WAYNE, artist, gallery owner; b. Newburgh, N.Y., Dec. 26, 1938; s. Harold John Ochs and Gertrude Adelaid Goetchius; m. Cindy Ochs, Apr. 14, 1968. AB in Econs. and Math., Hamilton Coll., 1960; postgrad., SUNY, New Paltz, 1961-70. Cert. secondary tchr., N.Y. Math. tchr. Newburgh Sch. Dist., 1960-92; artist, owner Richard Ochs Gallery, Newburgh, 1993—. Represented by Art Nook Gallery, Newburgh, 1979-93, Gallery Frame Shop, New Paltz, N.Y., 1996-2000, Jordane Artworks, Fort Myers Beach, Fla., 1998-2000, Nadeja Gallery, Newport, R.I., 2001—; mem. Coast Guard Artists' Program. Treas. Newburgh Tchrs.' Assn., 1965; pres. Dutchess County Art Assn., Poughkeepsie, N.Y., 1979, trustee, 1975-76. Staff sgt. N.Y. ARNG, 1963-69. Recipient Grumbacher Gold medal Mt. St. Mary Coll., 1997, 98, George Gray award USCG. Mem. Artist's Fellowship, Hudson Valley Art Assn. (bd. dirs.), Kent Art Assn. (exec. bd. 1996—, 2nd v.p. 1999-2000), Am. Artist's Profl. League, North East Watercolor Soc. (treas. 1984-94, 1st v.p. 1995-97, pres. 1997—, trustee 2001—), Cmty. Arts Assn. (exec. bd. 1996—), Soc. Creative Artists of Newtown, Middletown, N.Y. Artist's Group, Watercolor Soc. Ala., Soc. Marine Artists, Artist's Fellowship, Ctrl. N.Y. Watercolor Soc., Salmagundi Club. Home and Office: 62 Dalfonso Rd Newburgh NY 12550-7203 E-mail: ROchsWcrGallery@aol.com.

OCHS, ROBERT DAVID, history educator; b. Bloomington, Ill., Mar. 27, 1915; s. Herman Solomon and Fannie Leah (Livingston) O. AB, Ill. Wesleyan U., 1936; MA, U. Ill., 1937, PhD, 1939; MA, Oxford U., Eng., 1964. Research dir. Anti-Defamation League, 1939-41; mem. faculty U. S.C., 1946—, prof. history, 1957-76, disting. prof. emeritus, 1976—, chmn. dept., 1960-74; acting dean U. S.C. (Coll. Arts and Sci.), 1970-71; assoc. editor U. S.C. Press, 1950-53; vis. prof. Merton Coll., Oxford U., 1964. Mem. S.C. Archives Commn., 1960-74 U.S. cons.: History of The 20th Century, 1967. Bd. dirs. Columbia Music Festival Assn., 1957-64, 77-85, v.p., 1961-62, pres., 1962-63; dir. Columbia Lyric Opera, Columbia Mus. Art, 1966-69, 74-77, McKissick Mus., 1991-96. Maj. AUS, 1941-46; lt. col. Mem. Am. Hist. Assn., So. Hist. Assn. (exec. council 1973-76), S.C. Hist. Assn. (editor 1947-55, pres. 1956-57), Am. Studies Assn., Orgn. Am. Historians, Southeastern Am. Studies Assn. (pres. 1960-61), Omicron Delta Kappa. Home: # 200 144 Still Hopes Dr West Columbia SC 29169-7151

OCHS, SIDNEY, neurophysiology educator; b. Fall River, Mass., June 30, 1924; s. Nathan and Rose (Kniaz) O.; m. Bess Ratner; children: Rachel F., Raymond S. Susan B. PhD, U. Chgo., 1952. Rsch. assoc. Ill. Neuropsychiat. Inst., Chgo., 1952-54; rsch. fellow Calif. Inst. Tech., Pasadena, 1954-56; asst. prof. dept. physiology U. Tex. Med. Br., Galveston, 1956-58; assoc. prof. dept. physiology Ind. U., Indpls., 1958-61, prof., 1961-94, prof. emeritus, 1994—. Author: Elements of Neurophysiology, 1965, Axoplasmic Transport and Its Relation to Other Nerve Functions, 1982; founding editor, editor-in-chief Jour. Neurobiology, 1969-76, assoc. editor, 1977-86. Served with U.S. Army, 1943-45 Mem. Internat. Brain Rsch. Orgn., Am. Physiol. Soc., Soc. Neurosci., Am. Soc. Neurochemistry, Peripheral Nerve Soc. Democrat. Jewish. Office: Ind U Med Ctr Dept Cellular & Integ Physiology 635 Barnhill Dr Indianapolis IN 46202-5126

OCHS, WALTER J. civil engineer, drainage adviser; b. Springfield, Minn., May 20, 1934; s. Walter Minrod and Cleo (Schultz) O.; m. Connie Mae Strate, Sept. 15, 1956; children: Julie, Brian. BS in Agrl. Engring., South Dakota U., 1957. Registered profl. civil engr., Mich. Engr. in training USDA, Soil Conservation Svc., Watertown, S.D., 1957-58, project engr. Britton, 1958-61, area engr. Sioux Falls, 1961-63, asst. state conservation engr. East Lansing, 1963-66, state conservation engr., 1966-69, asst. state conservationist Saint Paul, Minn., 1969-71, nat. drainage engr. Washington, 1971-86; drainage adviser World Bank, 1986-96; internat. ind. water mgmt. cons., 1996—. Bd. dirs. Internat. Inst. for Land Reclamation and Improvement Postgrad Land Drainage Course, The Netherlands, 1990-98; particpated in project work over 30 countries; mem. Internat. Commn. Irrigation and Drainage. Contbr. to profl. jours. Named Federal Engr. Of The Year, Nat. Soc. Profl. Engrs., 1982; recipient Outstanding Alumnus award South Dakota State Univ., 1977, Outstanding Contributions award Corrugated Plastic Tubing Assn., 1981; named to Internat. Drainage Hall of Fame, 1996. Fellow: Am. Soc. Agrl. Engrs.; mem.: ASCE (chmn. drainage com. 1975—76, Royce J. Tipton award 2001). Office: 6731 Fern Ln Annandale VA 22003-1903

OCHSNER, JOHN LOCKWOOD, thoracic-cardiovascular surgeon; b. Madison, Wis., Feb. 10, 1927; s. Edward William Alton and Isabel (Lockwood) O.; m. Mary Lou Hannon, Mar. 20, 1954; children: John L., Joby Hannon, Katherine Lockwood, Frank Hannon. MD, Tulane U., 1952. Diplomate Am. Bd. Thoracic Surgery (chmn. 1993-95), Am. Bd. Surgery, Am. Bd. Vascular Surgery. Intern Univ. Mich. Hosp., Ann Arbor, 1952-53, resident, 1953-54, Baylor U. Affiliated Hosp., Houston, 1956-58, 1958-59; chief surg. resident Tex. Children's Hosp., 1959-60; instr. Baylor U., Houston, 1960-61; mem. staff Ochsner Clinic, New Orleans, 1961—, chmn. dept. surgery, 1966-87, chmn. emeritus dept surgery, 1987—; clin. asst. prof. Tulane U., 1961-65, clin. assoc. prof., 1965-70, clin. prof. surgery, 1970—. Author: (with others) Coronary Artery Surgery, 1978. Pres. Tennis Patrons Assn. New Orleans, 1972; image amb. City of New Orleans, 1982; bd. dirs. Internat. Trade Mart, New Orleans, 1983. Capt. USAF, 1954-56. Recipient award Life Mag., 1961, Golden Plate Acad. Achievement award, 1962, medal of honor, Ecuador, 1981. Mem. Internat. Soc. Cardiovascular Surgery (pres. N.Am. chpt. 1983-84, internat. pres. 1989-91), Am. Assn. Thoracic Surgery (sec. 1979-83, pres. 1992-93), New Orleans Surg. Soc. (pres. 1977-78), So. Surg. Assn. (pres. 1991), So. Assn. for Vascular Surgery (pres. 1983), Boston Club, La. Club, New Orleans Country Club, City Club, Alpha Omega Alpha. Republican. Home: 84 Audubon Blvd New Orleans LA 70118-5540 Office: Ochsner Clinic & Hosp 1514 Jefferson Hwy New Orleans LA 70121-2483

OCHSNER, OTHON HENRY, II, importer, restaurant critic; b. Chgo., May 19, 1934; s. Othon Henry and Louise Catherine (Schlichenmaier) O. AA, Chgo. City Coll., 1961. Pub. rels. staff Walgreen Co., Chgo., 1961-65; sales mgr. Porsche Car Imports, Northbrook, Ill., 1966-67; nat. sales mgr. Pirelli Tire Corp., N.Y.C., 1968-73; pres., CEO Ochsner Internat., Chgo., 1974—. Bd.dirs., pres. Swiss-U.S.A. Racing Team, Chgo., 1976—. Author: Ochsner Pocket Guide to the Finest Restaurants and Hotels in the World, 12th edit.; author Ochsner Restaurant Newsletters, 1986—. Pres., Louise Catherine Schlichenmaier and Othon Henry Ochsner I Charitable Family Found., 2000—. With U.S. Army, 1957-59. Mem. The Am. Inst. Wine and Food, Am.-Swiss C. of C., Swiss-Am. Hist. Soc., Swiss Gourmet Soc. (pres. U.S. chpt.), Swiss Travel Club, Swiss Club Chgo., The Bagatelle Club, Conf. de la Chaine des Rotisseurs, Ordre des Canariers. Baptist. Avocations: visiting and reviewing world class French and Swiss restaurants worldwide. Home: 701 Bluff Rd Lake Bluff IL 60044-2116 Office: The Ochsner Bldg 246 E Marquardt Dr Wheeling IL 60090-6430

OCHSNER, SEYMOUR FISKE, radiologist, editor; b. Chgo., Nov. 29, 1915; s. Albert Henry Ochsner and Fleda Fiske; m. Helen Keith, Sept. 8, 1945 (dec. Jan. 1976); children: Anne, Diana, Lida; m. Bobbie Sue Mercer, Dec. 31, 1981 (dec. Jan. 1997). AB, Dartmouth Coll., 1937; MD, U. Pa., Phila., 1947. Diplomate Am. Bd. Radiology, 1953. Intern Johnston-Willis Hosp., Richmond, Va., 1949-50; staff radiologist Ochsner Clinic, New Orleans, 1953-90, also chmn. dept., 1969-77; clin. prof. radiology Tulane Med. Sch., 1955-75; editor Orleans Parish Med. Bulletin, 1985-91. Contbr. articles to profl. jours. Pres. PTA, Metairie, La., 1964. Recipient Disting. Svc. medal So. Med. Assn., 1972, Disting. Svc. award AMA, 1993, fellow, Alton Ochsner Med. Found., New Orleans, 1950-53. Mem. Radiol. Soc. La. (pres. 1965), So. Radiol. Conf. (pres. 1968), Am. Coll. Radiology (pres. 1972, Gold medal 1982), Am. Roentgen Ray Soc. (pres. 1975, Gold medal 1986), Rex Orgn., So. Yacht Club, Candlewood Club. Republican. Episcopalian. Avocations: reading, gardening, travel, sailing. Home: 107 Holly Dr Metairie LA 70005-3915

OCKERBLOOM, RICHARD C. newspaper executive; b. Medford, Mass., Dec. 19, 1929; s. Carl F. and Helen C. (Haraden) O.; m. Anne Joan Torpey, Sept. 17, 1955; children: Catherine, Carl, Gail, Mark, John, Peter. BSBA, Northeastern U., 1952; D Pub. Svc. (hon.), Westfield State Coll., 1989; LLD (hon.), Northeastern U., 1995. With Boston Globe, 1948—, salesman, 1955-63, asst. nat. advt. mgr., 1963-70, nat. advt. mgr., 1970-72, asst. advt. dir., 1972-73, advt. dir., 1973-77, v.p. mktg. and sales, 1977-81, exec. v.p., 1981—, gen. mgr., chief operating officer, 1984-86, pres., chief operating officer, 1986-93, vice chmn., 1993-94; ret.; retired; chmn. bd. Met. Sunday Newspapers. Bd. dirs. Greater Boston Conv. and Visitors Bur., Winchester Hosp., United Way Mass. Bay; vice chmn. bd. trustees Northeastern U.; mem. adv. bd. U. Mass., Boston. With U.S. Army, 1952-54. Mem. Algonquin Club (pres.), WInchester Country Club, Phi Kappa Phi. Nat. Honor Soc. Home: 80 Arlington St Winchester MA 01890-3735

OCKERMAN, HERBERT W. agricultural studies educator; b. Chaplin, Ky., Jan. 16, 1932; m. Frances Ockerman (dec.). BS with Distinction, U. Ky., 1954, MS, 1958; PhD, N.C. State U., 1962; postgrad., Air U., 1964-70, Ohio State U., 1974, 83, 87 & 2001. Asst. prof. Ohio State U., Columbus, 1961-66, assoc. prof., 1966-71, prof., 1971—. Former mem. Inst. Nutrition and Food Tech.; judge regional and state h.s. sci. fairs, 1965—, Ham Contest, Ky. State Fair, Sausage and Ham Contest, Ohio Meat Processing Groups; cons. various food companies, 1975—, Am. Meat Inst., 1977-88, USDA, 1977-88, CRC Press, Inc., 1988—; bd. examiners U. Calcutta, 1987-88; examiner U. Mysore, India, 1990-97; expert witness, various firms, 1992—, UN expert 95; presenter in field. Contbr. over 1585 articles and abstracts to profl. jours. and conf. procs., 73 chpts. to books. Comdr, USAF, 1955-58. Fisher Packing scholar; named Highest Individual in Beef Grading, Kansas City Meat Judging Contest, 1952; recipient Cert. of Appreciation, Ohio Assn. Meat Processors, 1987-2000, Profl. Devel. award Cahill faculty, commendation for internat. work in agr. Ohio Ho. of Reps., badge of merit for svc. to agr. Polish Govt., plaque Argentina Nat. Meat Bd., animal sci. award Roussel UCALF, France, U. Assiuit, Egypt, silver platter Nat. Meat Bd., Sec. Agr., Livestock and Fishery, Argentina, Svc. award Coun. Grad. Students, Pomerance Tchg. award, Outstanding Alumni award U. Ky., also named to Hall of Disting. Alumni, 1995, award for outstanding ednl. achievements Argentine Soc. Agr., Coop. award vet. faculty U. Cordoba, Svc. award Panoma Legis. Br., Brazil; veterinary faculty U. Cordoba, Spain, 1982, 94, Nat. Chung-Hsing U., 1982, 95, Vet. Mus. Ciechanowcu, Poland, internat. award Inst. Food Tech., Assn. Nat. Tecnologis en Alimentos de Mexico, Can. Indst. Food Sci. and Tech., 1998, Appreciation plaque Republic of Argentina, 1999, Candle Stick of Knowledge, Ludhiana U., Punjab, India, 1999, internat. award Am. Meat Sci. Assn., 1999, 2000, Appreciation Plaque Am. Coll. Commerce, 1999, Plaque, Selcuk U., Turkey, 1999, Folklore and Cultural memento Sudanese Socs., Sudan U., 1999, Homage and Acknowledgment, Argentine Sec. Agr., 2000, Most Honored Guest, Weifang, China, 2001, World History award Jhadong U. Taiwan, China, 2001, plaque Congress of Hon., Cordoba, Spain, 2001, Light award Polish Acad. Sci. Mem. NAS, NCR, ASTM, Am. Meat Sci. Assn., Am. Soc. Animal Sci. (rsch. award 1987), Reciprocal Meat Conf., European Meeting of Meat Rsch. Workers, Polish Vet. Soc. (hon.), Inst. Food Technologists (nat. and OVS chpts.), Inst. Food Tech. (Internat. award 1998), Can. Meat Sci. Assn., Internat. Congress Meat Sci. and Tech., Rsch. in Basic Sci., Phi Beta Delta (treas. 1987, pres. 1991, internat. scholar award 1991, internat. faculty award 1991, Presdl. medallion award), Gamma Sigma Delta (rsch. award 1977, internat. award of merit 1988), Sigma Xi (outstanding advisor in coll. award 1995), Phi Beta Kappa (Outstanding Tchg. award 1997, Extension Diversity award 1997, Pomerene Tchg. Enhancement award 1997, Outstanding Internat. Faculty award 1997), Internat. Gamma Sigma Delta (Disting. Achievement Nat. award 1998), Phi Kappa Phi. Office: Ohio State U Meat Lab Animal Sci 2029 Fyffe Rd Columbus OH 43210-1007 E-mail: ockerman.2@osu.edu.

OCKEY, RONALD J. lawyer; b. Green River, Wyo., June 12, 1934; s. Theron G. and Ruby O. (Sackett) O.; m. Arline M. Hawkins, Nov. 27, 1957; children: Carolyn S. Ockey Baggett, Deborah K. Ockey Christiansen, David, Kathleen M. Ockey Hellewell, Valerie Ockey Sachs, Robert. BA, U. Utah, 1959, postgrad., 1959-60; JD with honors, George Washington U., 1966. Bar: Colo. 1967, Utah 1968, U.S. Dist. Ct. Colo. 1967, U.S. Dist. Ct. Utah 1968, U.S. Ct. Appeals (10th cir.) 1969, U.S. Ct. Claims 1987. Missionary to France for Mormon Ch., 1954-57; law clk. to judge U.S. Dist. Ct. Colo., 1966-67; assoc. ptnr., shareholder, v.p., treas., dir. Jones, Waldo, Holbrook & McDonough, Salt Lake City, 1967-91; pres. IntelliTrans Internat. Corp., 1992-94; mem. Utah Ho. of Reps., 1988-90, Utah State Senate, 1991-94; of counsel Mackey Price & Williams, Salt Lake City, 1995-98; asst. atty. gen. Utah, 1998—. Trustee SmartUtah, Inc., 1995—, bd. dirs., mem. exec. com., 1995—; trustee Utah Tech. Fin. Corp., 1995-98; lectr. in securities, pub. fin. and bankruptcy law. Mem. editl. bd. Utah Bar Jour., 1973-75; mem. staff and bd. editors George Washington Law Rev., 1964-66; contbr. articles to profl. jours. Stae govtl. affairs chair Utah Jaycees, 1969; del. state Rep. Convs., 1972-74, 76-78, 80-82, 84-86, 94-96, del. Salt Lake County Rep. Conv., 1978-80, 88-92; sec. Wright for Gov. campaign, 1980; legis. dist. chmn. Utah Rep. Party, 1983-87; trustee Food for Poland, 1981-85, pres., trustee Unity to Assist Humanity Alliance, 1992-95; bd. dirs. Utah Opera Co., 1991-94; trustee Utah Info. Tech. Assn., 1991-2000. Lt. U.S. Army, 1960-66, to capt. JAG, USAR, 1966-81. Mem. ABA, Utah State Bar Assn. (various coms.), Nat. Assn. Bond Lawyers (chmn. con. on state legislation 1982-85), George Washington U. Law Alumni Assn. (bd. dirs. 1981-85), Order of Coif, Phi Delta Phi. Home: 4502 Crest Oak Cir Salt Lake City UT 84124-3825 E-mail: rao@netutah.net.

O'CONNELL, ANTHONY J. bishop; b. Lisheen, County Clare, Ireland, May 10, 1938; Ed., Mt. St. Joseph Coll., Cork, Ireland; Mungret Coll., Mangret Coll., Limerick, Ireland; ed., Kenrick Sem., St. Louis. Ordained priest Roman Cath. Ch., 1963. 1st bishop Diocese of Knoxville, 1988-99; 3d bishop Diocese of Palm Beach, Fla., 1999—2002.

O'CONNELL, BRIAN, community organizer, public administrator, writer, educator; b. Worcester, Mass., Jan. 23, 1930; s. Thomas J. and Mary (Carroll) O'C.; m. Ann C. Brown, July 11, 1953; children: Todd, Tracey, Matthew. BA, Tufts Coll., 1953; postgrad., Maxwell Sch. Citizenship and Pub. Adminstrn., 1953-54; also numerous hon. degrees. Field rep. Am. Heart Assn., Pa., 1954-56, exec. dir. Md., 1956-61, Calif., 1961-66, Nat. Assn. Mental Health, 1966-78, dir. emeritus, 1978—; pres. Nat. Council on Philanthropy, 1978-80; exec. dir. Coalition of Nat. Vol. Orgns., 1978-80; pres. Ind. Sector, 1980-95, founding pres., pres. emeritus, 1995—; prof. pub. svc. Tufts U., Medford, Mass., 1995—. Mem. U.S. Pres.'s Com. Employment of Handicapped, 1966-68; chmn. Liaison Group Mental Health, 1969-72. Author: Effective Leadership in Voluntary Organizations, 1976, Finding Values That Work: The Search for Fulfillment, 1977, America's Voluntary Spirit, A Book of Readings, 1983, The Board Members Book, 1985, Philanthropy in Action, 1987, Our Organization, 1987, Volunteers in Action, 1989, People Power: Service Advocacy, Empowerment, 1994, Board Overboard, 1995, Powered By Coalition: The Story of Independent Sector, 1997, Voices from the Heart: In Celebration of America's Volunteers, 1999, Civil Society: The Underpinnings of American Democracy, 1999. Mem. Alumni Coun. Tufts U., 1970-80, trustee, 1988-2000, trustee emeritus, 2000—, chmn. pres. search com., 1992; trustee Points of Light Found., 1989-95; bd. dirs. Hogg Found., 1990-95; chmn. organizing com., 1st chmn. Civicus: World Alliance for Citizen Participation, 1992-96; bd. dirs. E.M. Kaufman Found., 1994—, The BridgeSpan Group, 1999—. Recipient outstanding agy. prof. award United Way Am., 1979, Lincoln Filene Citizenship award, 1985, John W. Gardner Leadership award, 1994, Gold Key award Am. Soc. Assn. Execs., 1994, Chmns. award, NSFRE, 1994, The Tiffany award, 1998. Fellow Am. Pub. Health Assn., Nat. Acad. Pub. Adminstrn. (trustee 1993-2000), Nat. Com. Patients' Rights (chmn. 1975-77). Home: 50 Chase St Chatham MA 02633-2404 Office: Lincoln Filene Ctr Tufts U Medford MA 02155

O'CONNELL, CARMELA DIGRISTINA, appraisal executive, consultant; b. Johnstown, Pa., Nov. 8, 1925; d. Salvatore and Josephine (Riggio) Digristina; m. Maurice F. O'Connell, Sept. 21, 1974 (dec. Feb. 1984); children: Geraldine, John, Bernard. Diploma, Eastern Secretarial Sch., N.Y.C., Sch. Interior Design. From typist to sec.-treas. Philip P. Masterson Co., N.Y.C., 1942-72; exec. v.p., bd. dirs. Masterson & O'Connell Inc., 1972-80, cons., 1981—; founder, pres. N.Y. Appraisal Corp., 1971-80; co-founder, pres. Park Ave. Appraisal, 1981—. Mem. N.Y. Rep. Com., 1974—, Met. Opera Guild, N.Y.C., 1986; chmn. Ch. of Our Saviour, N.Y.C., 1986; mem. Ladies of Charity, Cath. Charities Archdiocese of N.Y., 1990; bd. dirs. 80 Park Avenue Condominiums, 1997—. Recipient Amita award for Bus. Woman of Yr., 1977, Lena Madesin Phillips award N.Y. League/Fortune 500 Bus. and Profl. Women, 1989. Mem. Nat. Fedn. Bus. and Profl. Women's Clubs Inc. (2d v.p. 1964, 1st v.p. 1966). Roman Catholic. Home: 80 Park Ave New York NY 10016-2553

O'CONNELL, DANIEL AUSTIN, association executive, tax accountant; b. N.Y.C., Aug. 10, 1943; S. Daniel Francis and Mary Frances (McHale) O'C.; m. Patricia Louise Ellerman, Oct. 21, 1967; children: Heather Patrice Stevens, Erinbeth Jennifer Massie, Alison Melissa. BS, Georgetown U., 1965; MBA, NYU, 1971. CPA, Md. CFP, Inst. Cert. Fin. Planners; cert. employee benefit specialist, Found. for Employee Benefit Plans. Budget analyst Bankers Trust Co., N.Y.C., 1967-69; sr. fin. analyst Brown Brothers Harriman & Co., 1969-71; audit asst. Alexander Grant & Co., Washington, 1971-72; asst. v.p. acctg. Auto-Train Corp., 1972-77; asst. v.p. fin. U.S. Rlwy. Assn., 1977-81; treas. Deak-Perera, Washington, 1981-83; dir. adminstrn. Distilled Spirits Coun., 1984—97; cons., 1998; treas. Md. Tax Edn. Found., 2002—. Cons. Hubble Space Telescope Sci. Inst., Balt., 1983-84; tax acct., CPA, Rockville, Md., 1987—. Treas., dir., Manor Lake Civic Assn., Rockville, 1986-88. Lt. (j.g.), USN, 1965-67. Mem. AICPA, Am. Soc. Assn. Execs., Greater Washington Inst. of Assn. Execs., Greater Washington Soc. CPAs, Washington Assn. Fin. Mgmt. Roundtable (dir. 1991-93). Avocations: reading, investments, cartoon collectibles.

O'CONNELL, DANIEL CRAIG, psychology educator; b. Sand Springs, Okla., May 20, 1928; s. John Albert and Letitia Rutherford (McGinnis) O'C. BA, St. Louis U., 1951, Ph.L., 1952, MA, 1953, S.T.L., 1960; PhD, U. Ill., 1963. Joined Soc. of Jesus, 1945; asst. prof. psychology St. Louis U., 1964-66, asso. prof., 1966-72, prof., 1972-80, trustee, 1973-78, pres., 1974-78; prof. psychology Loyola U., Chgo., 1980-89, Georgetown U., Washington, 1990-98, emeritus, 1998—, chmn., 1991-96. Vis. prof. U. Melbourne, Australia, 1972, U. Kans., 1978-79, Georgetown U., 1986, Loyola U., Chgo., 1998—; Humboldt fellow Psychol. Inst. Free U. Berlin, 1968; sr. Fulbright lectr. Kassel U., W. Ger., 1979-80. Author: Critical Essays on Language Use and Psychology, 1988; contbr. articles to profl. jours. Recipient Nancy McNeir Ring award for outstanding teaching St. Louis U., 1969; NSF fellow, 1961, 63, 65, 68; Humboldt Found. grantee, 1973; Humboldt fellow Tech. U. of Berlin, 1987. Fellow Am., Mo. psychol. assns., Am. Psychol. Soc.; mem. Midwestern, Southwestern, Eastern psychol. assns., Psychologists Interested in Religious Issues, Psychonomic Soc., Soc. for Scientific Study of Religion, N.Y., Mo. acads. sci., AAUP, AAAS, Phi Beta Kappa. Home and Office: Loyola U Chgo Psychology Dept 6525 N Sheridan Rd Chicago IL 60626-5344 E-mail: doconn1@luc.edu. *Were it over, it would have been more than my expected share already. The challenge of learning to serve others has moved it along at a quick pace, and I am grateful that I have always received more than I've been able to give in return—from the Lord and from many good people.*

O'CONNELL, DANIEL F. lawyer; b. Orange, N.J., May 5, 1943; BS with honors, Villanova U., 1965; JD, Rutgers U., 1968. Bar: N.J. 1968, N.Y. 1980, U.S. Supreme Ct. 1980. Ptnr. Drinker Biddle & Shanley LLP, Florham Park, N.J. Mem. Supreme Ct. N.J. Dist. VII Ethics Com., 1978-83, sec., 1980-83; chmn. N.J. Commn. Legal and Ethical Problems in the Delivery of Health Care, 1986-90. Mem. ABA (labor and employment law sect., antitrust law sect., health law sect. 1977—), N.J. State Bar Assn. (labor law sect., health and hosp. law sect.), Somerset County Bar Assn. (exec. com. 1977-81, pres. 1979), Am. Health Lawyers Assn., Am. Hosp. Assn. Office: Drinker Biddle & Shanley 500 Campus Dr Florham Park NJ 07932-1047 E-mail: doconnell@dbr.com.

O'CONNELL, EDMOND J. chemist, educator, chemist, consultant; b. Providence, Apr. 26, 1939; s. Edmond J. and Katherine G. O'Connell; m. Genevieve S. O'Connell, July 24, 1965; children: Shannon, Edmond, Daniel, Sean, Kevin, Timothy. BS, Providence Coll., 1960; PhD, Yale U., 1964. Sr. rsch. chemist E.I. DuPont Co., Wilmington, Del., 1964—67; chemistry prof. Fairfield (Conn.) U., 1967—, Yale U., New Haven, 1974—. Cons. in field. Contbr. articles to profl. jours. Grantee, Am. Chem. Soc., 1968, Rsch. Corp., 1972, NSF. Mem.: Sigma Xi. Roman Catholic. Avocation: marathon running. Home: 161 Harbor St Branford CT 06405 Office: Chemistry Dept Fairfield Univ Fairfield CT 06430

O'CONNELL, EDWARD JAMES, JR. psychology educator, computer applications and data analysis consultant; b. Sterling, Ill., Aug. 15, 1932; s. Edward James and Elizabeth E. (Clapham) O.; m. Pamelia Canon Floyd, Aug. 21, 1959; children— Edward James III, John Matthew BS in Psychology, Ill. Inst. Tech., 1958; MA in Psychology, Northwestern U., 1961, PhD in Psychology, 1962. NSF postdoctoral fellow Carnegie Inst. Tech., Pitts., 1962-63, asst. prof. psychology, 1963-65; psychology faculty Syracuse (N.Y.) U., N.Y., 1965-93, prof., 1975-93, prof. emeritus, 1993—. Cons. Rand Corp., Santa Monica, Calif., 1962-64, Abt Assocs., Boston, 1970-73, Marcy Psychiat. Hosp., N.Y., 1979-82 Served to cpl. U.S. Army, 1952-54 NSF predoctoral fellow, 1959-62; NSF postdoctoral fellow, 1962-63; Northwestern U. predoctoral fellow, 1958-59 Mem. Sigma Xi. Democrat. Avocations: billiards; computer programming. Address: PO Box 570 Cashiers NC 28717-0570 E-mail: ejoconn@dnet.net.

O'CONNELL, FRANCIS V(INCENT), textile printing company executive; b. Norwich, Conn., July 8, 1903; s. Thomas Francis and Isabelle (Gelino) O'C.; m. Marie Louise Lemoine, Nov. 7, 1940. LLB, Blackstone Coll. Law, 1932, JD, 1940, LLM, 1942. Textile screen printer U.S. Finishing Co., Norwich, 1921-30; foreman Ahern Textile Print Co., 1930-36; pres., owner Hand Craft Textile Print Co., Plainfield, Conn., 1936—. Roman Catholic. Home: PO Box 165 Plainfield CT 06374-0165 Office: Bishop's Crossing Plainfield CT 06374

O'CONNELL, HUGH MELLEN, JR. retired architect; b. Oak Park, Ill., Nov. 29, 1929; s. Hugh M. and Helen Mae (Evans) O'C.; m. Frances Ann Small, Apr. 13, 1957; children: Patricia Lynn, Susan Marie, Jeanette Maureen. Student mech. engring., Purdue U., 1948-50; BS in Archtl. Engring, U. Ill., 1953. Registered architect, Ariz., Calif., La., Nev., Nat. Council Archtl. Registration Bds. Designer John Mackel; structural engr. Los Angeles, 1955-57; architect Harnish & Morgan & Causey, Ontario, Calif., 1957-63; self-employed architect Ventura, 1963-69; architect Andrews/O'Connell, 1970-78; dir. engring. div. Naval Constrn. Bn. Center, Port Hueneme, Calif., 1978-91, supervisory architect, 1991-93; ret., 1993. Mem. tech. adv. com. Ventura Coll., 1965-78; sec. Oxnard Citizens' Adv. Com., 1969-79, v.p., 1970-72, pres., 1972—; chmn. Oxnard Beautification Com., 1969, 74, Oxnard Cmty. Block Grant adv. com., 1975-76; mem. Oxnard Planning Commn., 1976-86, vice chmn., 1978-79, chmn., 1980-81. Mem. Oxnard Art-in-Pub. Places Commn., 1988—. Served with AUS, 1953-55. Mem. AIA (emeritus, pres. Ventura chpt. 1973), Am. Concrete Inst., Soc. Am. Registered Architects (Design award 1968, dir. 1970), Am. Legion, Soc. for Preservation and Encouragement of Barbershop Quartet Singing in Am. (chpt. pres. 1979, chpt. sec. 1980-83), Acad. Model Aeros. (#9190 1948—), Channel Islands Condors Club (treas. 1986-99), Sports Flyers Assn., Internat. Miniature Aircraft Assn., 1985—, Alpha Rho Chi (Anthemios chpt.). Presbyterian (elder 1963, deacon 1967). Lodges: Kiwanis (pres. 1969, div. sec. 1974-75), Elks. Home and Office: 520 Ivywood Dr Oxnard CA 93030-3527 E-mail: hughoarch@earthlink.net.

O'CONNELL, JAMES CHARLES, regional planner; b. Springfield, Mass., Mar. 2, 1951; s. John James and Helen Louise (Ryan) O'C.; m. Anne Marie O'Connell, Sept. 11, 1982; children: Christopher, Charles. BA, Bates Coll., 1973; MA, U. Chgo., 1974, PhD, 1980. Cert. planner Am. Inst. Cert. Planners. Assoc. dir. Springfield (Mass.) Ctrl. Inc., 1977-81; exec. dir. Hampden County Energy Office, Springfield, Mass., 1981-84; dep. commr. Springfield Cmty. Dept., 1984-87; dep. exec. dir. Springfield Redevel. Authority, 1987-89; econ. devel. officer Cape Cod Commn., Barnstable, Mass., 1990-2001; cmty. planner Boston Support Office Nat. Park Svc., 2001—. Author: Inside Guide to Springfield and Pioneer Valley, 1986, Shaping an Urban Image, 1990, Becoming Cape Cod, 2002; editor: The Pioneer Valley Reader, 1995. Mem. Am. Planning Assn. Avocations: writing travel articles, reading. Office: Nat Park Svc Boston MA 15 State St Boston MA 02109 Business E-Mail: jim_o'connell@nps.gov. E-mail: james.c.oconnell@verizon.net.

O'CONNELL, JAMES JOSEPH, port official; b. Lockport, Ill., Feb. 7, 1933; m. Phyllis Ann Berard, Aug. 1, 1953; children: Lynn, Kathryn, Julia. BSBA, Lewis U., 1958. lic. pvt. pilot FAA. Recorder Will County, Joliet, Ill., 1976-88. Dir., treas., corp. sec., v.p. Joliet Regional Port Dist., 1972—; dir. Des Plaines Valley Enterprise Zone, Joliet; reg. lobbyist Ill. Assn. Pt. Dists., Ill. Real Estate Broker, 1959—; real estate cons. O'Connell Enterprises. Nat. dir., nat. U.S. pres. Internat. O'Connell Clan, Kerry County, Ireland, 1996—; precinct committeeman Will County, Joliet, 1962-72, exec. cen. committeeman, 1965-70, dir. Will County Young Reps., Joliet, 1984, sec. Will County Econ. Affairs Commn., Joliet; GOP candidate for Ill. dist. 11, U.S. Congress, 1994.; treas. U.S. Jaycee Found., 1999; treas. Joliet Housing Authority, 2000-2001. With U.S. Army, 1953-54, Korea. Mem. Ill. Assn. Port Dists. (sec., treas. 1982-86), Ill. Jaycees (senate pres. 1972-73, named to Hall of Fame 1993, Disting. Svc. award 1977), Joliet Flying Club (sec.), Joliet Navy League (pres. 1996—), KC (past Grand Knight 1972, 91), Joliet Exch. Club, Three Rivers Mfg. Assn. (pub. affairs com.), Joliet Columbian Club (pres.), Am. Legion (life, former post officer), VFW (life), U.S. Jr. C. of C. (found. trustee 1997-2001). Roman Catholic. Office: 1009 Western Ave Joliet IL 60435-6801

O'CONNELL, JEANNE, financial planner, insurance broker; b. Stoneham, Mass., Dec. 9, 1951; d. Kenneth Edward and Frances Evelyn (Matulewicz) O'C.; 1 child, Ryan Sulloway. Student U. Oreg., 1971-72; BFA cum laude, U. Mass.-Amherst, 1974, U. Calif.-Sacramento, summer 1973; postgrad., Northeastern U., 1975; MBA, Suffolk U., 1984. CPCU, CLU; chartered fin. cons.; assoc. in underwriting; enrolled agt. designation. Ins. clk. S.B. Swaim & Co., Boston, 1969-72, Hollis Perrin & Co., Boston, 1972; underwriting asst. Pub. Svc. Mut. Ins. Co., Newton, Mass., 1974-77; personal lines analyst Comml. Union Ins. Co., Boston, 1977-80, sr. personal lines analyst, 1980-83, tech.

specialist, 1983-88; pvt. practice fin. cons., brokerage, 1988—. Instr. ins. and fin. planning Ins. Libr. Boston, 1988—; speaker in field; ind. tax preparer; pub. arbitrator NASD, BBB, AMEX; founder, dir. Red Dragon Arts Coop., Boston, 1983; potter, artist Radcliffe Pottery Studio, Boston, 1980-85. Mem. exec. student adv. bd. Suffolk U., 1982—83, student liaison mem. between Exec. MBA Program and regular MBA Program and dean's adv. bd., coord. Exec. MBA Program Policy Seminar Weekend, 1983; v.p., trustee Friends Waltham Pub. Libr., 1998, 1999, asst. treas., 2000, 2000—. Fellow Nat. Tax Practice Inst.; mem. Internat. Assn. Fin. Planners, Nat. Soc. Enrolled Agts., Nat. Soc. Accts., Nat. Assn. Tax Preparers, Waltham Garden Club (photographer 1997—), Delta Mu Delta. Avocations: reading books on tape, photography, rubber stamps, gardening. Studio: 229 School St Waltham MA 02451-4546 E-mail: reddragonarts@rcn.com.

O'CONNELL, JEANNE MARIE, music educator; b. Spring Valley, Wis., Mar. 4, 1948; d. Bernard Alphonsus and Isabelle Agatha (Murphy) O'C.; m. Robert Dale Hasewinkle, Sept. 12, 1980. B Music Edn., U. Wis., Eau Claire, 1970; M Music, U. Oregon, 1976. Cert. elem. tchr., Wis., cert. in comprehensive music. Tchr. elem. and jr. high music Prescott (Wis.) Pub. Schs., 1970-73; tchr. elem. music New Richmond (Wis.) Pub. Schs., 1973-78, 79-81, Internat. Sch., Frankfurt, Fed. Republic Germany, 1979; tchr. 2d grade St. Mary's Sch., New Richmond, 1983-86. Mem. choir Minn. Chorale, Mpls., 1976—78, 1981, Oratorio Soc., St. Paul, 1985—; mem. steering com. Wis. Music Edn. Conf., Madison, 1974—76; program dir. New Richmond Fine Arts Ctr., 1976; mem. enrichment com. United Way, New Richmond, 1984—85; mem. Baldwin Pops Band, Musica Sacra Orch.; asst. condr. Musica Sacra Chorale; choir dir. St. Francis Cath. Ch., Ellsworth, Wis., 1972—75. Named one of Outstanding Young Women Am., 1981; named as head of an Outstanding Elem. Music Program Wis. Music Edn. Assn., 1981. Mem.: Am. Harp Soc. (pres. Gulf Coast chpt.), Baldwin County Piano Tchrs. Assn. Roman Catholic. Avocations: needlecrafts, sailing, skiing, performing music. Home: 724 Holly Dr Fairhope AL 36532-2815 Office: Christ the King Sch 1503 Main St Daphne AL 36526

O'CONNELL, JEFFREY, law educator; b. Worcester, Mass., Sept. 28, 1928; s. Thomas Joseph and Mary (Carroll) O'C.; m. Virginia Kearns, Nov. 26, 1960 (dec. 1994); children: Mara, Devin. Grad. cum laude, Phillips Exeter Acad., 1947; AB cum laude, Dartmouth Coll., 1951; JD, Harvard U., 1954. Bar: Mass. 1954, Conn. 1954, Va. 1983, hon. admittance to Ark. and Minn. bar. Instr. speech Tufts U., 1953-54; assoc. Sherburne, Powers & Needham, 1954-57, Hale & Dorr, Boston, 1958-59; asst. prof., then assoc. prof. law U. Iowa Coll. Law, 1959-62; assoc. dir. automobile claims study Harvard Law Sch., 1963-64; assoc. prof. law U. Ill. Coll. Law, 1964-65, prof., 1965-79; prof. law U. Va. Law Sch., 1980-83, John Allan Love prof., 1983-90, Samuel H. McCoy II prof., 1990—, Class of 1948 rsch. prof., 1994-97. Summer vis. prof. Northwestern U., 1963, U. Mich., 1966, 75, So. Meth. U., 1972, U. Tex., 1977, U. Wash., 1979; John Marshall Harlan vis. prof. N.Y. Law Sch., 1991; vis. fellow Centre for Socio-Legal Studies, Wolfson Coll., Oxford (Eng.) U., 1973, 79; Thomas Jefferson vis. fellow Downing Coll. Cambridge U., Eng., 1989; mem. U. Va. Ctr. for Advanced Study, 1980-83. Author: (with R.E. Keeton) Basic Protection for the Traffic Victim, 1965, After Cars Crash: The Need for Legal and Insurance Reform, 1967, (with Arthur Myers) Safety Last: An Indictment of the Auto Industry, 1966, (with R.E. Keeton, John McCord) Crisis in Car Insurance, 1968, (with Wallace Wilson) Car Insurance and Consumer Desires, 1969, The Injury Industry, 1971, (with Rita James Simon) Payment for Pain and Suffering, 1972, Ending Insult to Injury: No-Fault Insurance for Products and Services, 1975, (with Roger Henderson) Tort Law, No-Fault and Beyond, 1975, The Lawsuit Lottery: Only the Lawyers Win, 1979, (with C. Brian Kelly) The Blame Game: Injuries, Insurance and Injustice, 1986, (with Lester Brickman and Michael Horowitz) Rethinking Contingency Fees: A Proposal to Align the Contingency Fee System with its Policy Roots and Ethical Mandates, 1994, (with Peter Bell) Accidental Justice: The Dilemmas of Tort Law, 1997 Mem. Nat. Hwy. Safety Adv. Com., 1967-70; ednl. adv. bd. John Simon Guggenheim Found., 1973-87; bd. dirs. Consumers Union, 1970-76; mem. com. on competitive safeguards and med. aspects of sports NCAA, 1985-87. Served as 1st lt. USAF, 1954-57. Recipient Robert B. McKay award for ins. scholarship Tort and Ins. Practice sect. ABA, 1992; Guggenheim fellow, 1972-73, 79-80. Mem. ABA, Va. Bar Assn., Casque and Gauntlet, Farmington Country Club, Cosmos Club (Washington), Phi Beta Kappa, Psi Upsilon. Democrat. Roman Catholic. Home: 4 Oak Cir Charlottesville VA 22901-3220 Office: U Va Sch Law 580 Massie Rd Charlottesville VA 22903-1738 E-mail: jo@virginia.edu.

O'CONNELL, JOHN F. lawyer, retired law educator; b. Mahanoy City, Pa., Jan. 4, 1919; s. Thomas Vincent O'Connell and Mary Elizabeth Cunningham; m. Rosemary Teresa O'Connell, Jan. 9, 1943 (dec. June 1990); children: Paul, Rosemarie, Dennis, Michael, Patricia, Kevin; m. Yvonne Louise O'Connell, Dec. 2, 1993. BA, La Salle Coll., 1940; JD, Western Reserve U., 1950; MA, U. Md., 1960; PhD, So. Calif. U., 1995. Commd. 2d lt. USAF, 1943, advanced through grades to col., ret., 1968; dean, law prof. Western State U. Coll. Law, Fullerton, Calif., 1975-87; law prof. Am. Coll. Law, Brea, 1987-89; dean So. Calif. Coll. Law, 1989-91, ret., 1991. Author: Remedies in a Nutshell, 1985. Decorated Legion of Merit, Bronze Star, Army Commendation medal, Air Force Commendation medal. Mem. Air Force Office Spl. Agts., Delta Theta Phi. Republican. Roman Catholic. Home: 8764 Captains Pl Las Vegas NV 89117-3516

O'CONNELL, KEVIN, lawyer; b. Boston, Sept. 4, 1933; s. Michael Frederick and Kathryn Agnes (Kelley) O'C.; m. Mary Adams, July 14, 1990; children: Tiffany W., Elizabeth H., Dana A., Liesel E. AB, Harvard, 1955, JD, 1960. Bar: Calif. 1961. Assoc. firm O'Melveny & Myers, L.A., 1960-63; asst. U.S. atty. criminal div. Cen. Dist. Calif., 1963-65; staff counsel Gov. Calif. Commn. to Investigate Watts Riot, 1965-66; ptnr. Tuttle & Taylor, 1966-70, Coleman & O'Connell, L.A., 1971-75; pvt. practice law, 1975-78; of counsel firm Simon & Sheridan, 1978-89; ptnr. Manatt, Phelps & Phillips, 1989—; adj. prof. law U. So. Calif. Law Sch. Adj. prof. antitrust law U. So. Calif. Law Sch., 2002—. Bd. editors: Harvard Law Rev, 1958-60. Mem. Los Angeles County (Calif.) Democratic Central Com., 1973-74; bd. dirs. Calif. Supreme Ct. Hist. Soc. Lt. USMCR, 1955-57. Mem. Am. Law Inst. Home: 426 N Mccadden Pl Los Angeles CA 90004-1026 Office: Manatt Phelps & Phillips Trident Ctr E Tower 11355 W Olympic Blvd Los Angeles CA 90064-1614 E-mail: koconnell@manatt.com.

O'CONNELL, MARY ANN, state legislator, business owner; b. Albuquerque, Aug. 3, 1934; d. James Aubrey and Dorothy Nell (Batsel) Gray; m. Robert Emmett O'Connell, Feb. 21, 1977; children: Jeffery Crampton, Gray Crampton. Student, U. N.Mex., Internat. Coun. Shopping Ctrs. Exec. dir. Blvd. Shopping Ctr., Las Vegas, Nev., 1968-76, Citizen Pvt. Enterprise, Las Vegas, 1976; media supr. Southwest Advt., 1977—; owner, operator Meadows Inn, 1985—99, 3 Christian bookstores, Las Vegas, 1985-99; mem. Nev. State Senate, 1985—, chmn. govtl. affairs com., vice chmn. commerce and labor com. Vice chmn. Legis. Commn., 1985—86, 1995—96, mem. edn. com. to rewrite standards; mem. Edn. Commn. of the States, 1997—; rep. Nat. Conf. State Legislators; past vice chair State Mental Hygiene and Mental Retardation Adv. Bd. Pres. explorer div. Boulder Dam Area coun. Boy Scouts Am., Las Vegas, 1979-80, former mem. exec. bd. mem. adv. bd. Boulder Dam chpt.; pres., bd. dirs. Citizens Pvt. Enterprise, Las Vegas, 1982-84, Secret Witness, Las Vegas, 1981-82; vice chmn. Gov.'s Mental Health-Mental Retardation, Nev., 1983—; past mem. community adv. bd. Care Unit Hosp., Las Vegas; past mem. adv. bd. Kidney Found., Milligan Coll., Charter Hosp.; tchr. Young Adult Sunday Sch.; 1st vice chmn. Clark County Rep. Party, 2001--. Recipient Commendation award Mayor O. Grayson, Las Vegas, 1975, Outstanding Citizenship award Bd. Realtors, 1975, Silver Beaver award Boy Scouts Am., 1980, Free Enterprise award Greater Las Vegas C. of C., Federated Employers Assn., Downtown Breakfast Exch., 1988, Award of Excellence for Women in Politics, 1989, Legislator of Yr. award Bldg. and Trades, 1991, Legislator of Yr. award Nat. ASA Trade Assn., 1991, 94, Guardian of Liberty award Nev. Coalition of Conservative Citizens, 1991, Internat. Maxi Awards Promotional Excellence, Guardian of Small Bus. award Nat. Fedn. Ind. Bus., 1995-96, Atty. Gen. award Women's Role Model for 2002; named Legislator of Yr., Nev. Retail Assn., 1992, New Assn. Bldg. Contractors, 1999, Nev Polit. Med. Action Com., 1999; inducted into Nev. Vets. Citizens Hall of Fame, 1999; Legislator of Yr. award Nev. Med. Polit. Com., 1999, Assoc. Builders and Contractors, New Mortgage Brokers, 2000, Nev. Ind. Check Cashing Assn., 2001, Nev. Phys. Therapists, 2002. Mem. Retail Mchts. Assn. (former pres., bd. dirs.), Taxpayers Assn. (bd. dirs.), Greater Las Vegas C. of C. (past pres., bd. dirs., Woman of Achievement Politics women's coun. 1988). Republican. Mem. Christian Ch. Avocations: china painting, reading. Office: Nev Legislature Senate 401 S Carson St Carson City NV 89701-4747

O'CONNELL, MARY ITA, psychotherapist; b. Balt., July 3, 1929; d. Richard Charles and Ona (Buchness) O'C.; m. Leon Jack Greenbaum, Dec. 28, 1962 (div. Jan. 1986); children: Jessie A., Elizabeth K. BA, U. Md., 1956; postgrad., Am. U., 1960—; M in Creative Arts in Therapy, Hahnemann Med. Coll., 1978. Registered Acad. Dance Therapists. Tchr. Robert Cohan Sch. Dance, Boston, 1958-61; instr., choreographer Wheaton Coll., Norton, Mass., 1959-60, Harvard/Radcliffe Colls., Boston, 1960-62; tchr., performer, choreographer Profl. Studios, Washington, 1962-69; asst. prof., adminstr. Fed. City Coll., 1969-74; movement psychotherapist Woodburn Ctr. for Community Mental Health, Fairfax, Va., 1975-76, Gundry Hosp., Balt., 1976-77, Prince Georges' Community Mental Health Dept., Capitol Heights, Md., 1978-80; lectr. George Washington U., D.C., 1981-85; pvt. practice psychotherapy Silver Spring, Md., 1977—. Sr. movement psychotherapist Regional Inst. for Children and Adolescents, Rockville, Md., 1980-82; movement cons. Ctr. for Youth Svcs., Washington, 1981-83; movement psychotherapist D.C. Mental Health Ctrs., Washington, 1985-87, 90—, Community for Creative Non-Violence Women's Shelter, Washington, 1986, LICSW, Washington, 1989. Choreographer, soloist (dance performance) The Artist: A Theatre Happening, 1963; choreographer, co-dir. (outdoor dance event) Tree Sculpting, 1974; choreographer (dance performance) Excitations, 1967, A Dance Event, 1974; soloist, New England Opera, 1961; performer, choreographer WGBM TV/Laboratory Concert Series, 1961; performer, CBS-TV/Erika Thimey Dance Theatre, 1965; guest artist, Harford Coll. Art Festival, 1967. U. Md. scholar, 1955-56. Mem. Dance Circle of Boston (life, pres. 1959-61), Modern Dance Council of Washington (exec. bd dirs., editor 1965-69), Am. Dance Therapy Assn. (treas. metro chpt. 1977-81), Assn. Humanistic Psychology, Family Therapy Network, Am. Dance Guild, NIH (movement specialist 1978-79). Democrat. Avocations: sailing, lacrosse, stone collecting, collage making. Home and Office: 16 Sussex Rd Silver Spring MD 20910-5435

O'CONNELL, MAURICE DANIEL, lawyer; b. Ticonderoga, N.Y., Nov. 9, 1929; s. Maurice Daniel and Leila (Geraghty) O'C.; m. Joan MacLure Landers, Aug. 2, 1952; children: Mark M., David L., Ann M., Leila K., Ellen A. Grad., Phillips Exeter Acad., 1946; AB, Williams Coll., 1950; LLB, Cornell U., 1956. Bar: Ohio 1956. Since practiced in, Toledo; assoc. Williams, Eversman & Black, 1956-60; ptnr. Robison, Curphey & O'Connell, 1961-95, of counsel, 1996—; spl. hearing officer in conscientious objector cases U.S. Dept. Justice, 1966-68. Mem. complaint rev. bd. Bd. Commrs. on Grievance and Discipline of Supreme Ct. Ohio, 1987. Mem. Ottawa Hills Bd. Edn., 1963-66, pres., 1967-69; former trustee Toledo Soc. for Handicapped; past trustee Woodlawn Cemetery; past trustee Toledo Hearing and Speech Center, Easter Seal Soc.; mem. alumni council Phillips Exeter Acad. Served to 1st lt. USMCR, 1950-53. Fellow Ohio State Bar Found.; mem. NW Ohio Alumni Assn. of Williams Coll. (past pres.), Ohio Bar Assn., Toledo Bar Assn. (chmn. grievance com. 1971-74), Kappa Alpha, Phi Delta Phi. Clubs: Toledo. Home: 3922 W Bancroft St Toledo OH 43606-2533 Office: 9th Flr Four SeaGate Toledo OH 43604

O'CONNELL, MICHAEL ALEXANDER, social worker; b. Dayton, Ohio, May 28, 1948; s. William J. and Aida May (Duncan) O'Co. BS in econ., U. Pa., 1970; MSW, U. Wash., 1977, PhD in Counseling Psychology, 1997. Cert. social worker, Wash. Dir. Second Chance Youth Alcoholism Program, Seattle, 1977-78; social worker Riverton Hosp., Burien, Wash., 1979-80; therapist Robinson William & Assocs., Seattle, 1981-82; therapist & cons. Althean Assocs., 1982-83, Everett/Mill Creek, 1983—. Author: Working With Sex Offenders, 1990. Pres. Wash. State Chpt., Assn. for the Treatment of Sexual Abusers, 1997—. Mem. Acad. Cert. Social Workers, Assn. Treatment of Sexual Abusers, Am. Profl. Soc. on the Abuse of Children. Office: Michael A O'Connell & Assocs 16300 Mill Creek Blvd Ste 202 Mill Creek WA 98012-1286 E-mail: moconnel@halcyon.com.

O'CONNELL, PHILIP EDWARD, retired retail business owner; b. Watertown, Mass., June 1, 1921; s. Edward Cornelius and Elizabeth Gladys (Cormey) O'C.; m. Mary Madeleine O'Brien, Nov. 6, 1948; children: Michael, Anne Marie, James, Daniel, Mary, Elizabeth, Theresa, Patricia, Eileen, David. Diploma, Admiral Billard Acad., New London, Conn., 1941, Army Air Forces Tech. Sch., 1943; student, Mass. State Coll., 1946-47, Boston Coll., 1956-60. Owner, operator Lobster Shellfish Market, 1947-91. Cons., solicitor for radio program Dangers of Apathy-WNAC, Boston, 1950's. Contbr. letters to the editor to various newspapers and periodicals. Participated in Civil Rights March, Washington, 1963; chmn. Weymouth (Mass.) com. Goldwater for Pres., 1964; chmn. Plympton (Mass.) Com. Reagan for Pres., 1980;polit. grassroots activist for George W. Bush and others, 2000; active Operation Rescue, 1988—; mem., chmn. Rep. Town Com., Plympton, Mass., 1974—; distbr. Meals on Wheels, Kingston, Mass., 1986—; mem. Kingston Emergency Mgmt. Agy., 1993—; driver Cura (Visiting Nurses) Plymouth, Mass., 1993—; mem. Support the Irish Am. Partnership, 1996—, Support the Boston Irish Famine Meml., 1997—, Town of Plympton govt. alternative study com., 1999—, St. Joseph Parish Pastoral Com. Kingston, Mass., 1999-2001; mem. Plympton Recycling Com., 2001—; Eucharistic min. St. Joseph Parish, 1993—; mem. Vols. for the Elderly, 2001—. Mem. North and South Rivers Watershed Assn., New England 65 Plus Runners Club, Mass. Citizens for Life, Am. Legion. Republican. Roman Catholic. Avocations: meteorology, history, religion, sailing, skiing. Home: 85 Ring Rd Plympton MA 02367-1406

O'CONNELL, PHILIP RAYMOND, retired lawyer, paper company executive; b. N.Y.C., June 2, 1928; s. Michael Joseph and Ann (Blaney) O'C.; m. Joyce McCabe, July 6, 1957; children: Michael, Kathleen, Jennifer, David. AB, Manhattan Coll., 1949; JD, Columbia U., 1956; grad., Advanced Mgmt. Program, Harvard U., 1967. Bar: N.Y. 1956, U.S. Supreme Ct. 1961, Conn. 1988. Assoc. Dewey, Ballantine, Bushby, Palmer & Wood, N.Y.C., 1956-61, 62-64; gen. counsel, sec. Laurentide Finance Corp., San Francisco, 1961-62; gen. counsel Wallace-Murray Corp., 1964-66, div. mgr., 1966-70; pres., chief exec. officer, dir. Universal Papertech Corp., Hatfield, Pa., 1970-71; sec. Champion Internat. Corp., Stamford, Conn., 1972-90, v.p., 1979-81, sr. v.p., 1981-90. Mem. legal adv. com. N.Y. Stock Exch., 1985-88, corp. governance subcom., legal adv. com., 1985-94; chmn. lawyers steering com. corp. governance task force The Bus. Roundtable, 1981-87, mem., 1981-94. Mem. Champion Internat. Found., 1979-90; mem. bd. visitors Fairfield Univ. Sch. Bus., 1981-93, chmn., 1983-93; bd. dirs. Kearney-Nat. Corp., 1975-78. With USNR, 1951-54. Mem. Am. Soc. Corp. Secs. (hon.; chmn. 1988-89).

O'CONNELL, RALPH ANTHONY, dean, psychiatrist, educator; b. N.Y.C., Jan. 26, 1938; s. Ralph E. and Agnes H. (O'Connell) O'C.; m. Janes Burke, June 15, 1963; children: Ralph E. III, Ellen C., John B. AB cum laude, Coll. of Holy Cross, Worcester, Mass., 1959; MD, Cornell U., 1963. Diplomate Am. Bd. Psychiatry and Neurology. Intern St. Vincent's Hosp. and Med. Ctr. N.Y., N.Y.C., 1963-64, resident, 1964, 67-69, rsch. psychiatrist, 1969-71, chief inpatient dept. psychiatry, 1971-76, clin. dir. and vice chmn. psychiatry, 1974-95; prof. psychiatry N.Y. Med. Coll., Valhalla, 1984—, dean and provost, 1996—. Editor-in-chief Comprehensive Psychiatry, 1983-96. Served to capt. U.S. Army, 1965-66. Fellow Am. Psychiat. Assn., N.Y. Acad. Medicine (trustee 1989—). Clubs: Univ. (N.Y.C.). Roman Catholic. Office: NY Med Coll Valhalla NY 10595*

O'CONNELL, RICHARD J. insurance adviser; b. West Roxbury, Mass., Feb. 13, 1952; s. William T. and Dorothy M. O'Connell; m. Leslie J. Baskind, June 15, 1974; children: Beth, Amy. BA, U. Denver, 1973. LUTCF. Ins. adviser O'Connell Ins. Agy., Denver, 1978. Dir.-at-large Aurora Assn. Ins. Advisors. Fund raiser Arapahoe County Dems., Aurora, 1999—2002. Office: O'Connell Ins Agy #202 1325 S Colorado Blvd Denver CO 80222

O'CONNELL, ROBERT BRENDAN, public relations and editorial consultant; b. N.Y.C., Nov. 30, 1920; s. Arthur Joseph and Isabel Beatrice (McVeigh) O'C.; m. Frances Harriet Wexler, May 27, 1961; 1 child, Alison Jane O'Connell Neumann. AB, Cornell U., 1949; postgrad., Columbia U., 1953-54, NYU, 1962-63. Promotion events asst. N.Y. Daily News, N.Y.C., 1949-53; mgr. corp. news svc. Prudential Ins. Co., Newark, 1954-65; mgr. corp. pub. rels. Canadry Corp., N.Y.C., 1965-67; asst. regional dir. for pub. affairs. HEW, 1967-81; spl. asst. to asst.-sec. pub. affairs HHS, 1981-83; spl. asst. to adminstr. Healthcare Financing Adminstn., Washington, 1992-93; pub. rels. cons., Basking Ridge, N.J., 1983-92, 93—. Vis. lectr. CUNY, 1978; pres. Family Coun., Lyons, N.J., Va. Nursing Home Care Unit, 1999, 2000, 2001. Author, editor Prudential Bull., 1954-57, Merck Continued mag., 1982-91, Lyons Veterans Adminstrn. Nursing Home Care Unit Family Voice; author, contbr. Back in the Bronx, 1996-98. 1st lt. USAAF, 1942-45, USAF, 1950-52, Korea. Decorated DFC, Air medal with oak leaf clusters; recipient Spl. Achievement award, Healthcare Fin. Adminstrn., 1992. Mem. 8th Air Force Assn., Air Force Assn. 486th Bomb Group Assn. (founder, officer, squadron rep. 1981-86, com. chmn., svc. award 1990), Cornell Alumni U. (charter bd. mem. 1968), Am. Dirs. Inst. (charter bd. mem. 1983-84), Ret. Officers Assn. Office: 31 Coppergate Dr Basking Ridge NJ 07920-2209

O'CONNELL, ROBERT FRANCIS, physics educator; b. Athlone, Ireland, Apr. 22, 1933; came to U.S., 1958; s. William and Catherine (O'Reilly) O'C.; m. Josephine Molly Buckley, Aug. 3, 1963; children: Adrienne Molly, Fiona Catherine, Eimear Kathleen. BSc, Nat. U. Ireland, Galway, 1953, DSc, 1975; PhD, U. Notre Dame, 1962. Telecommunications engr. Dept. Posts and Telegraphs, Dublin, Ireland, 1954-58; scholar Inst. Advanced Studies, 1962-63; systems analyst IBM, 1963-64; sr. rsch. assoc. Inst. Space Studies, N.Y.C., 1966-68; asst. prof. physics La. State U., Baton Rouge, 1964-66, assoc. prof., 1966-69, prof., 1969-86, Boyd prof., 1986—. Editor for theoretical physics Hadronic Jour.; bd. mem. Phys. Rev. A; contbr. articles to profl. jours. Named Disting. Rsch. Master, La. State U., 1975; NAS-NRC fellow, 1966-68, Sci. Rsch. Coun. (Eng.) sr. vis. fellow, 1976. Fellow Am. Phys. Soc.; mem. Am. Astron. Soc., Internat. Astronomy Union, Internat. Soc. Gen. Relativity and Gravitation. Republican. Roman Catholic. Avocation: tennis. Home: 522 Bancroft Way Baton Rouge LA 70808-4807 Office: La State Univ Dept Physics And Astronomy Baton Rouge LA 70803-0001

O'CONNELL, ROBERT JOHN, diversified financial services company executive; b. N.Y.C., May 16, 1943; m. Claire M. Costantini; children: Kristin, Jared. BA, Fordham U., 1965; MA, U. Pa., 1966. With N.Y. Life Ins. Co., N.Y.C., 1970-89, v.p., 1983-86, sr. v.p., 1986-89; sr. v.p. group mgmt. divsn. AIG, 1989-91; pres., CEO AIG Life Ins. Cos., 1991-98; also bd. dirs. A.I. Life; pres., CEO Mass. Mutual Life Insurance, Springfield, Mass., 1998-2000, chair., pres., & CEO, 2000—. Bd. dirs. AIG Life Ins. Co., AIG Equity Sales Corp., Delam Life Ins. Co.; mem. adv. com. to Cato Inst. project on Social Security Privatization. Mem. State Dept. Fin. Svcs. Corps Mission to Czechoslovakia. Mem. Am. Coun. Life Ins., Am. Internat. Life Assn. N.Y. (bd. dirs.). Office: Mass Mutual 1295 State St Springfield MA 01111-0001*

O'CONNELL, TAAFFE CANNON, actress, publishing executive; b. Providence; d. Joseph Ceril and Edith Ethelyn (Dent) O'C. BA, MFA, U. Miss. Regional supr. Gloria Marshall Figure Salons, S.C.; v.p., co-founder Doc Sox Inc., Pacific Palisades, Calif., 1988-90; pres., founder Canoco Pub., L.A., 1991—, 1-800-266-DYNE, L.A., 1992-93. Founder Rising Star Distbn., exec. prodr. Beanie/Twigg 1999-, Canoco Prodn., Yes, I Can Actor's Workshops. Appeared in films, including Men Without Dates, Dangerous, Hot Chili, Cheech & Chong Nice Dreams, Rocky II, Galaxy of Terror, New Years Evil, Rich Man Poor Man Book I, Caged Fury; TV appearances include Malubu Branch, General Hospital, Dangerous Women, Dallas, Knight and Daye, The New Gidget, Knight Rider, Three's Company, Dr. Joyce Brothers Show, Blansky's Beauties, Peter Lupus Show, Fix-It City, Happy Days, Laverne & Shirley, Wonder Woman, The Incredible Hulk; theater appearances include Too True to be Good, Damn Yankees, Anastasia, Star Spangled Girl, The Beaux Stratagem, The Canterbury Tales; founder, pub. Astrocaster, 1991, Power Agent, 1993; Jan. founder Rising Star Distbn. and Canoco Prodns., 1999—; exec prodr.: Beanie & Twigg, Paranormal Private Eyes, Inside the Industry, 2000. Mem. Screen Actors' Guild, Am. Fedn. TV Radio Artists, Actor's Equity, Actor's Forum (bd. dirs. 1985-94). Avocations: singing, spinning, sailing, travel. Office: Canoco Pub 11611 Chenault St Ste 118 Los Angeles CA 90049-4574 E-mail: industryedge@earthlink.net.

O'CONNELL, WILLIAM EDWARD, JR. finance educator; b. N.Y.C., Sept. 16, 1937; s. William Edward and Helen Margaret (Brazel) O'Connell; m. Janet Elinor Shields, Aug. 15, 1965; children: William Edward III, Cathleen Anne. AB, Manhattan Coll., 1959; MBA, Columbia U., 1961; D in Bus. Adminstrn. with honors, Ind. U., 1967; JD, Coll. William & Mary, 1974. Fin. analyst Pfizer, Inc., N.Y.C., 1962-64; asst. prof. U. Conn., Storrs, 1967-69; Morris prof. banking U. Va., Charlottesville, 1988; Chessie prof. bus. Coll. William and Mary, Williamsburg, 1969—. Mem. faculty Va. Bankers Sch., Charlottesville, 1975—99, Stonier Grad Sch. Banking, Newark, 1977—91, Bank Adminstrn. Inst., Madison, Wis., 1978—97; bd. dirs. C. & F Fin. Corp., Citizens & Farmers Bank, Citizens & Commerce Bank. Author: (book) Asset & Liability Management, 1979, Advanced Financial Planning, 1984, Financial Planning for Credit Unions, 1989, Strategic Financial Managment for Commercial Banks, 1993. Mem.: Fin. Mgmt. Assn., Am. Fin. Assn., Omicron Delta Epsilon, Beta Gamma Sigma. Roman Catholic. Home: 102 Overlook Dr Williamsburg VA 23185-4434 Office: Coll William & Mary Sch Bus Williamsburg VA 23187-8795 E-mail: william.oconnell@business.wm.edu.

O'CONNELL, WILLIAM RAYMOND, JR. educational consultant; b. Richmond, Va., Jan. 4, 1933; s. William Raymond and Mary Helen (Wenenger) O'C.; m. Peggy Annette Tucker, June 29, 1957; 1 child, William Raymond III. BMusEd, Richmond Profl. Inst., 1955; MA, Columbia U., 1962, EdD, 1969; HLD (hon.), New Eng. Coll., 1995. Asst. to provost Richmond (Va.) Profl. Inst., 1955-57, dean of men, 1957-59, dean of students, dean of men, 1959-61; asst. to provost, dir. student info. ctr. Tchrs. Coll. Columbia U., N.Y.C., 1962-65, rsch. asst. inst. of higher edn. Tchrs. Coll., 1965-66; rsch. assoc. So. Regional Edn. Bd., Atlanta, 1966-69, dir. spl. programs, 1969-73, project dir., undergrad. edn. reform, 1973-79; dir. curriculum and faculty devel. Assn. Am. Colls., Washington, 1979-80, v.p. for programs, 1980-82, v.p., 1982-85; pres. New Eng. Coll., Henniker, N.H., 1985-95; vis. sr. fellow Assn. Am. Colls. and Univs., 1995-96; dir. health edn. and leadership program Nat. Assn. Student Personnel Adminstrs., 1996—. Cons. Coun. for Advancement Small Colls., 1975; mem. adv. com. project on instnl. renewal through improvement of teaching Soc. for Values in Higher Edn., 1975-78; mem., evaluator N.H. Postsecondary Edn. Commn., 1987-95, vice chmn., 1990-92, chmn., 1992-94; evaluator Nat. Ctr. for Rsch. to Improve Postsecondary Teaching and Learning, 1987-90, New Eng. Assn. Schs. and Colls., 1988, 91; mem. higher edn. rev. panel awards for pioneering achievements in higher edn. Charles A Dana Found., 1988, 89. Author, editor articles in field. Pres. Richmond Cmty. Amb. Project, 1958-60, bd. dirs., 1960-61; bd. dirs. Alumni Assn. Acad. divsn. Va. Commonwealth U., 1970-73; trustee Atlanta Boys Choir, Inc., 1978-79, chmn. fundraising com., 1976-77; trustee Atlanta Coun. for Internat. Visitors, 1973-76, 78-79; pres. UN Assn., Atlanta, 1976, 77; mem. steering com. Nat. Coun. chpt. and divsn. pres. UN Assn. U.S., 1977-79, nat. coun., 1980-90; mem. steering com. Leadership Concord, 1992-95, chmn., 1994-95. Named Community Amb. to Sweden Community Amb. Project of the Experiment in Internat. Living, 1956; sr. fellow Assn. Am. Colls. and Univs., 1995-97. Fellow Royal Soc. of the Arts (U.K.); mem. Soc. Values in Higher Edn., N.H. Coun. on World Affairs (bd. dirs. 1993-95), Greater Concord C. of C. (bd. dirs. 1989-93), Coordinating Coun. for Internat. Univs., Phi Delta Kappa. Methodist. Avocations: antiques, travel.

O'CONNER, LORETTA RAE, lawyer; b. Denver, Dec. 23, 1958; d. Ronald Lee and Norma Jareene (Warner) Barkdoll; m. George Ellis Bentley, Dec. 31, 1976 (div. 1979); m. Donald Hugh O'Conner, Feb. 3, 1987; children: Justin Lee, Brandon Craig. AS, Denver Acad. Ct. Reporting, 1983; BA summa cum laude, Regis U., 1992; JD, U. Colo., 1996. Bar: Colo., 1996. Ct. reporter, Denver, 1983-87; dist. ct. reporter Jud. Dept., State of Colo., Pueblo, 1987-91; ct. reporter, 1991-93; student atty. Pueblo County Legal Svcs.; pvt. practice Pueblo, 1997—; contact atty. State of Colo. Contract rep. Jud. Dept., State of Colo. Chief justice Student Govt. Ct., U. So. Colo., Pueblo, 1992; trained facilitator Kettering Found., Pub. Policy Inst., Dayton, Ohio, 1992; sec. So. Colo. Registered Interpretors for Deaf, Pueblo, 1991. President's scholar U. So. Colo., 1991-92, Alumni Assn. scholar, 1991-92; grantee Kettering Found., 1992; Colo. Legislature grantee and scholar Regis U., 1992; Colo. Legislature grantee U. Colo. Sch. Law, 1993-95, Dean's scholar, Dazzo Scholar, King scholar U. Colo. Sch. Law, 1993-96. Mem. ATLA, ABA, Colo. Trial Lawyers Assn., Colo. Bar Assn., Colo. Womens Bar Assn., Pueblo County Bar Assn.,

Golden Key Nat. Honor Soc., Phi Delta Phi (clk. 1994-95). Avocations: reading, writing, community board memberships. Home: 4310 Muirfield Rd Pueblo CO 81001-1167 Office: O'Conner Law Bldg 426 W 10th St Pueblo CO 81003-2922 Fax: (719) 584-2233.

O'CONNOR, ANN RUTH, information systems educator; b. N.Y.C., Aug. 13, 1932; d. Henry F. and Ruth L. (Schrimpf) Vogler; m. Michael J. O'Connor, Oct. 12, 1950; children: Ruth Ann O'Connor Morrish, Michael J. III. AAS in Exec. Secretarial Sci., Nassau Community Coll., 1975; BS in Edn., Hofstra U., 1978; MS in Tng. and Learning Tech., N.Y. Inst. Tech., 1987. Cert. tchr. bus. edn., distributive edn., art., N.Y. Model, 1949-52; prodn., showrm. asst. Rose Cloak and Suit Co., Bklyn., 1953-56; asst. prodn. mgr. Merry Mites, Inc., N.Y.C., 1956-58; tchr. bus. edn. Bus. Careers Sch., Hempstead, N.Y., 1978, Briarcliffe Coll. for Bus., Mineola, 1978-81, assoc. prof. Hicksville, NY, 1987—95; tchr. bus. edn. H. Frank Carey High Sch., Franklin Sq., N.Y., 1981-83. Adj. asst. prof. Nassau Community Coll., Garden City, N.Y., 1981—; cons. Freelance Tng. Office Automation/Info. Systems, Garden City, 1989—. Author: The Systematic Design and Evaluation of Instruction for Mastery of Learning Independently, 1987. Bd. dirs., chair Property Owners Assn., Garden City, 1965-78; sec. adv. com. on edn. PTA; pres., v.p., treas., chair High Ridge Assocs. Inc., Hampton Bays, N.Y., 1972-83. Mem. ASTD (award for Excellence 1987), Nat. Bus. Edn. Assn. Avocation: art. Home and Office: 71 Beech Ln Hicksville NY 11801-4541

O'CONNOR, BERNARD JOSEPH, priest; b. Sydney Mines, N.S., Can., Mar. 13, 1951; s. Cosmas Bernard and Ella Mae (Young) O'C. BA (Hons.) summa cum laude, St. Francis Xavier U., Antigonish, N.S., 1973; STB magna cum laude, St. Paul U., Ottawa, Ont., 1976; M.Canon Law magna cum laude, U. Ottawa, 1977; STL magna cum laude, Gregorian U., Rome, 1983; JCD in Canon Law, ABD Angelicum U., Rome, 1985; STD/PhD magna cum laude, Gregorian U., Rome, 1986; MA in Spirituality magna cum laude, Creighton U., 1992; JD, U. Tenn., 1994. Ordained priest, Roman Cath. Ch.; master scuba diver. Asst. pastor St. Theresa's Parish, Sydney, N.S., 1977-80, St. Ninian's Cathedral, Antigonish, 1980-81; external spiritual dir. Venerable English Coll., N.Am. Coll., Beda Coll., Rome, 1982-86; faculty in theology Josephinum Coll., Ohio, 1986-87; interim pastor St. Francis de Sales Parish, N.S., 1988; defender of Bond for Matrimonial Tribunal Diocese of Little Rock, 1989; resdl. theologian/ethicist Diocese of Knoxville, 1990-93; faculty religious studies dept. Coll. Nursing, U. Tenn., Knoxville, 1990-94; Regents' lectr. Ea. Mich. U., Ypsilanti, 1994-95, spl. asst. to provost, 1996-98, asst. dean Coll. of Arts and Scis., 1998—. Vis. scholar lectureship Soc. of Christ Sem., Poznan, Poland, 1984; vis. faculty Mass. Gen. Hosp. Inst. Health Professions, summers 1995-96; vis. faculty Found. of Meditation curriculum Straus Inst., Pepperdine U. Law Sch., summer 2000; lectr. in field. Author: Confirmation: Age Debate, 3 vols., 1986; contbr. articles to profl. jours.; editl. bd. Healthlaw Online.com, 2000—, Jour. Managerial Communications, Jour. of Acad. for Studies in Bus. Law. Mem. adjucation com. Internat. Commn. for Slection of Tivoli-Europa prize, 2001; founder, chair Internat. Com. to designate award for Excellence in Conflict Resolution Edn., 2001; cons. Nat. Conf. Cmty. and Justice, 2000; judge state and nat. finals of high sch. competition, We the People...The Citizen and the Constn., 1996—; mem. Mich. Bd. Ethics, 2000—, City of Ypsilanti Bd. of Ethics, 2000—; vice chair law sect. Mich. Acad. Sci. and Letters, 2000—; instnl. rep. U.S. Army "Challenge" Academicians' Program, Ft. Knox, Ky., 2000, Ft. Lewis Seattle, 2001—; appt. to nat. R.O.T.C. adv. com., 2002; founder/chair Alternative Dispute Resolution K-12 Ednl. Program, Mich., 2000; chair Emmanuel Ecumenical Mediation Project, Ypsilanti, 1999; bd. dirs. Grad. Theol. Found., 1999—; mem. spl. task force on univ. edn. and civics We the People, 1998—; founder, chair Mich. Mediation Conf. Com., 1998—; project chair Zion Ecumenical Mediation Project, Ann Arbor, 1998; bd. dirs. Washtenaw County Dispute Resolution Assn., 1997—, others. French Embassy scholar, Touraine Inst., 1984, Germany Embassy scholar, Bavaria, 1985; Oxford Found. fellow, 1999; MEEMIC Ednl. grantee, 2000, CTNS Sci. and Religion Program grantee, 2002; recipient Am. Jurisprudence award, U. Tenn., 1994, Vol. Spirit award, 1994, Nat. Disting. Program award Assn. of Continuing Higher Edn., 1997, Excellence award for contbns. to resdl. cmty. Ea. Mich. U. Housing and Dining Svcs., 1998, Templeton award, 1998; Award for Innovative Tchg. in Polit. Sci., Rowman & Littlefield Pubs./Am. Polit. Sci. Assn., 1999, Burning Light Humanitarian award Ea. Mich. U. Hillel/Jewish Cmty., 1999, Mich. Prof. of the Yr. award Carnegie Found./CASE, 1999; resolution Honoring Outstanding Ednl. Achievement, Ea. Mich. U. Bd. Regents, 2000; Spl. Tribute for Tchg. Excellence, Govt. of Mich., 2000; hon. colonelcy ROTC of Ea. Mich. U., 2000, Martin Luther King Jr. Humanitarian Awd. EMU governance dvsns., 2001; doctorate of Humane Letter (honoris causis), Graduate Theological Found., Indiana, 1999; named Carnegie Case Mt. Prof. of Yr., 2001. Mem. Am. Polit. Sci. Assn., Nat. Coll. Advisors Assn., Mich. Acad. on Scholarship, Soc. for Profls. in Dispute Resolution, Can. Numismatic Assn., Nat. Assn. of Adminstrv. Law Judges. Avocations: numismatics (Canadian tokens), scuba, music (piano and organ). Home: K-107 Cornell Ct Ypsilanti MI 48197 Office: Eastern Michigan Univ Politcal Sci Dept 601 Pray-Harrold Ypsilanti MI 48197 E-mail: boconnor@online.emich.edu.

O'CONNOR, BIRGIT CHRISTEL, artist; b. Hamburg, Germany, Oct. 14, 1958; arrived in U.S., 1959; d. Helmut Erwin and Christel Ilona (Kloth) Wiegandt; m. Danial James O'Connor, July 1, 1978; children: James Danial, Nicholas John Francis. Grad. high sch., Mill Valley. Transport aid Marin Gen. Hosp., Greenbrae, Calif., 1977-78; art tchr. Bolinas, 1998—. Represented in collections at Gallery Mack, Palm Desert, Calif., Seattle, Galerie du Monde, Hong Kong; featured in Australian Artist mag., Where mag., Watercolor Magic. Recipient First Pl. Best of Show Calif. State Expo, 1997, First Pl. Napa Town Country Fair, 1997, Best of Show Petaluma Sonoma Marin Fair, 1997, Internat. award of excellence Magnum Opus, 1998, Best of Show Wasco-Aqua Media, 1998, Silver award EWWS, Nat. award, 1998, Corp. award Catherine Wolfe Art Club, 1998, EWWS Merit award, 1999. Mem. Fedn. Can. Artists (award of excellence 2000), Can. Watercolor Assn., La. Watercolor Soc. (1st Pl. internat. 1998, Holbein award 1998), Bolinas Living Artist, Marin Art Coun., Nat. Womans Caucus. Avocation: gardening. Home and Office: PO Box 828 Bolinas CA 94924-0828

O'CONNOR, BRYAN D. astronaut; b. Orange, Calif., Sept. 6, 1946; m. Susie O'Connor; children: Thomas, Kevin. BS in Engring., U.S. Naval Acad., 1968; MS in Aeronautical Systems, U. West Fla., 1970; grad., Naval Postgrad. Sch., Monterey, Calif., 1972, Naval Air Test Ctr., Patuxent River, Md., 1976. Commd. 2d lt. USMC, 1968, advanced through grades to col.; attack pilot; test piot Strike Test Directorate Naval Air Test Ctr., Patuxent River, Md., project officer, 1977—79; dept. program mgr. Naval Air Systems Command, Washington; astronaut NASA, Houston, 1980, aviation safety officer Astronaut Corps, asst. to space shuttle program mgr., chmn. Space Flight Safety Panel, 1988—89, dep. dir. flight crew ops., 1988—91; commdg. officer Marine Aviation Detachment Naval Air Test Ctr., 1991, dep. dir., chief of staff flight test and engring. group; dep. assoc. adminstr. for space flight NASA, dir. space sta. redesign, dir. Space Shuttle Program, 1994—96; aerospace cons., 1996—. Decorated DFC; named Aviation Week and Space Tech. Laureate; recipient Sys. Effectiveness and Safety award, AIAA, Barry M. Goldwater Edn. award. Achievements include logged over 5,000 hours in over 40 types of aircraft; logged over 386 hours in space; pilot STS-61B Atlantis (1985); crew comdr. STS-40 Columbia (1991). Avocations: hiking, scuba diving, music, travel. Office: Astronaut Office/CB NASA Johnson Space Ctr Houston TX 77058*

O'CONNOR, CHARLES EDWARD, JR. state government official, lawyer; b. Philadelphia, PA, Feb. 21, 1960; s. Charles Edward O'Connor, Ruth Pauline Cardamone-O'Connor; m. Lori Marie Ruszkiewicz; children: Charles Henry. Juris Doctor, Widener University School of Law, Wilmington , Delaware, 1985—88; Bachelor of Arts, LaSalle College, Philadelphia, Pa, 1978—82. Election Clerk County Commissioners' Office, Philadelphia, PA, 1978—81; Parcel Post Machine Clerk United States Postal Service, 1982—83, Letter Carrier Abington, 1983—85; Bail Interviewer Superior Court Common Pleas Court of Philadelphia, Philadelphia, 1985—89; Law Clerk to The Honorable John T.J Kelly Jr. Superior Court of Pennsylvania, 1989—92, Chief Law Clerk to The Honorable John T.J. Kelly Jr., 1992—97, Deputy Prothonotary for the Eastern District of Pennsylvania, 1997—2001; Executive Director 2001 Legislative Reapportionment Commission, Harrisburg, 2001—02. Member 2nd District Police Advisory Council, Philadelphia, PA, 1998—2002; Counsel Summerdale Boys Club, Philadelphia, PA, 1993—97; Member 24th Police District Advisory Council, Philadelphia, PA, 1989—92. President Friends of Summerdale Civic Association, Philadelphia, PA, 1999—2002, Counsel & Civic Improvement Chairman, 1995—99; Member 25th Ward Republican Executive Committee, 1988—89, 53rd Ward Republican Executive Committee, Philadelphia, 1978—82. Mem.: Custodes Pacis Lodge#2085, Grand Army of The Republic Museum, Ancient Order of Hiberians Division#87 (First Degree 2000), Pennsylvania Historical Society, Brehon Law Society. Roman Catholic. Avocation: Pennsylvania History, Neighborhood Clean-up/Graffiti Removal , Old Car Repair and Restoration, Urban Affairs. Home: 1253 E. Cheltenham Avenue Philadelphia PA 19124-1031 Office: 2001 Legislative Reapportionment Comm. 325 Forum Bldg. Senate Box 203079 Harrisburg PA 17120-3079 Office Fax: 717-705-9906. Business E-Mail: fsmdcivic@aol.com.

O'CONNOR, CHARLES P. lawyer; b. Boston, Sept. 29, 1940; m. Mary Linda Hogan; children: Jennifer, Amy, Austin, Catherine. Bachelors degree, Holy Cross Coll., Worcester, Mass., 1963; LLB, Boston Coll., 1966. Bar: Mass. 1966, D.C. 1968, U.S. Supreme Ct. 1974. Atty., gen. counsel's office NLRB, Washington, 1966-67; assoc. Morgan, Lewis & Bockius, LLP, 1968-71; ptnr. Morgan, Lewis & Bockius, 1971—, chmn. labor and employment law sect., 1996-99, mng. ptnr. Washington office, 1995-97. Gen. counsel Major League Baseball Player Rels. Com., N.Y.C., 1989-94. Contbr. numerous articles on labor and employment law to law jours. Spl. counsel elections com. U.S. Ho. of Reps., Washington, 1968-69. Fellow Coll. Labor and Employment Lawyers; mem. ABA, D.C. Bar Assn., Met. Club Washington, Belle Haven Country Club, N.Y. Athletic Club, Cape Cod Nat. Golf Club. E-mail: co'connor@morganlewis.com. Home: 6121 Vernon Ter Alexandria VA 22307-1152 Office: Morgan Lewis & Bockius LLP 1111 Pennsulvania Ave NW Washington DC 20004

O'CONNOR, CLINT HAYNIE, electrical engineer; b. Corpus Christi, Tex., June 23, 1955; s. Robert Barnard Jr. and Edith H. (Haynie) O'C.; m. Christine Ann Schroeder, Mar. 30, 1985. BA, Wabash Coll., Crawfordsville, Ind., 1978. Pres., dir. R&D Analytical Engines, Austin, Tex., 1982-86; sr. project engr. Gould Indsl. Automation, Andover, Mass., 1986-88; mgr. elect. engring. Webtron Corp., Fort Lauderdale, Fla., 1988-93; tech. strategist Dell Computer Corp., Austin, 1993—. Chmn. bd. Analytical Engines, 1982-86; cons. Marine Sci. Inst., Galveston, Tex., 1980. Vol. Dolphin Rsch. Ctr., Grassy Key, Fla., 1989-90. Mem. Sigma Xi. Achievements include development of first 68000 co-processor for Apple II, 68010 co-processor for IBM PC; author 68000 Applesoft BASIC compatible interpreter; software development of Gould C986 co-processor, printing press control systems; development of Dell battery gauge, Dell control, Dell PC-card central and utilities for Dell Latitude portables; 11 patents in field. Office: Dell Computer One Dell Way Round Rock TX 78682

O'CONNOR, DANIEL PATRICK, priest; b. Rockford, Ill., May 10, 1958; s. John Patrick and Shirley Jean O'Connor. BA, U. Iowa, 1980; MA, U. La., Monroe, 1984; MDiv, Notre Dame Sem., New Orleans, 1990. Ordained priest Roman Cath. Ch. Asst. sports editor Freeport Jour.-Std., Ill., 1980—81; assoc. pastor Our Lady of Prompt Succor Ch., Alexandria, La., 1990—92; vocation dir. Cath. diocese of Alexandria, 1992—96; pastor Our Lady of Lourdes Cath. Ch., Marksville, La., 1996—99; pastor, campus minister Northwestern State U., Natchitoches, 2000—02; pastor Our Lady of Promp Succor Ch., Alexandria, 2002—. Chmn. Diocesan Priests' Coun., Alexandria, 1999—. Mem.: Kiwanis, Equestrian Order of the Holy Sepulchre of Jerusalem. Roman Catholic. Avocations: reading, sports. Office: Our Lady of Prompt Succor Cath Ch 401 21st St Alexandria LA 71301

O'CONNOR, DANIEL WILLIAM, retired religious studies and classical languages educator; b. Jersey City, Mar. 17, 1925; s. Daniel William and Emma Pauline (Ritz) O'C.; m. Carolyn Lockwood, June 26, 1954; children—Kathlyn Forssell Beal, Daniel William III BA, Dartmouth Coll., 1945; MA, Columbia U., 1956, PhD, 1960; M.Div., Union Theol. Sem., 1950. Ordained to ministry United Ch. of Christ, 1950. Mem. exec. com., bd. home missions Congl. Chs., 1946-51; pastor Paramus Congl. Ch., N.J., 1950-55; assoc. sec. Student Christian Movement YMCA, N.Y., 1947-48; exec. sec. Earl Hall Columbia U., N.Y.C., 1948-50; tutor asst., dept. N.T. Union Theol. Sem., 1958-59; successively asst. prof., assoc. prof., prof. religious studies and classical langs. St. Lawrence U., Canton, N.Y., 1959-67, dir. summer session, 1966, assoc. dean coll., 1967-68, Charles A. Dana prof. religious studies and classical langs., 1967-89, chmn. dept. religious studies and classical langs., 1974-89, Charles A. Dana emeritus prof., 1989—. Lectr. Elderhostels and Sr. insts. Author: Peter in Rome, 1969; contbr. articles to Ency. Britannica and profl. jours., also revs. Trustee Silver Bay Assn. YMCA, N.Y., 1978-86, 86-92, Lit. Vols. Am., St. Lawrence County, N.Y., 1991-94; bd. dirs. U.S. Power Squadron, St. Lawrence Squadron, N.Y., 1972-75. With USNR, 1943-45. Grantee Lilly Found., Columbia U., 1969-70, Mellon Found., Am. Schs. Oriental Research, Jerusalem, 1979 Mem. AAUP, Am. Assn. Ret. Persons, Nat. Assn. Watch and Clock Collectors, Rotary (pres. Canton Club 1972-73, Rotary Found. scholarship selection com. dist. 7040 1983-87, 96-00, dist. gov. 7040 1987-88, dist. 7040 ext. com. 1988-89, youth exch. com. dist. 7040 1990-93, lit. com. 1991-93). Home: 3 Hillside Cir Canton NY 13617-1409 E-mail: timeout@1000islands.net.

O'CONNOR, DENISE LYNN, marketing communications executive; b. West Palm Beach, Fla., Oct. 29, 1958; d. Joseph John and Ada Colleen (Doyle) Fields; m. William York O'Connor, May 31, 1985; 2 children. BS in Bus., Fla. State U., 1979; MBA, Fla. Inst. Tech., 1983, postgrad. in elec. engring., 1984-86. Cons. Small Bus. Inst., Tallahassee, 1979; mgr. select accts. Burroughs, West Palm Beach, 1980-81; mgr. mktg. communications Harris-Satellite Communications, Melbourne, Fla., 1981-84; sect. mgr. mktg. communications Gen. Electric Info. Svcs., Rockville, Md., 1984-86; mgr. pub. rels. Mgmt. Sci. Am., Atlanta, 1986-88; pres., owner Mktg. Comms. Cons., 1988—, Saddle River, N.J., 1995—. Cons. Sci.-Atlanta (Ga.), Inc., 1988—. Author (brochure) Genie, 1986 (Disting. award Soc. for Tech. Communications); editor (brochure) Electronic Data Interchange, 1986 (Excellence Soc. for Tech. Communications). Vol. Atlanta (Ga.) Humane Soc., 1988, (mem. auxiliary, 1989—). Recipient Ross Systems Pres. award, 1991. Mem. AAUW, PEO (v.p. reciprocity 1990-91, pres. evening and weekend reciprocity coun. 1991-92, chmn. Internat. Peace scholarship 1990), Soc. Tech. Comm., Atlanta Lawn and Tennis Assn.(pres. B-5 team 1989), Country Club South, Delta Zeta. Republican. Methodist. Avocations: tennis, golf, swimming, boating, water and snow skiing. Home and Office: Telcom 8 Denison Dr E Saddle River NJ 07458-2807

O'CONNOR, DORIS JULIA, non-profit fundraiser, consultant; b. Apr. 30, 1930; 1 dau., Kim C. BA cum laude in Econs., U. Houston, 1975. Adminstrv. asst. Shell Cos. Found. Inc., N.Y.C., 1966-71, asst. sec. Houston, 1971-73, sec., 1973-76, sr. v.p., dir., mem. exec. com., 1976-93; prin. Doris O'Connor & Co., 1993—. Corp. assoc. United Way of Am., Washington, 1976-93; corp. advisor Bus. Com. of Arts, N.Y.C., 1976-91, del., 1982-87; dir. Ind. Sector, Washington, 1981-89, vice chmn., 1983-87; mem. contbns. coun. Conf. Bd., N.Y.C., 1976-93; advisor Coun. of Better Bus. Burs., Washington, 1975-94, vice chmn., 1983-87; commr. adv. commn. on work-based learning, Dept. Labor, 1991-93; mem. Houston/Harris County Arts Task Force, 1991-93, Houston Ind. Sch. Dist. Task Force, 1991-93; trustee Houston Grand Opera, 1993-99, Houston Symphony Soc., 1993-99, Soc. Performing Arts, 1993-99, Cultural Arts Coun., 1993-96, Greater Houston Coalition Edn. Excellence, 1993-96; mem. adv. bd. Houston Zool. Soc., 1993-99; mem. New Orleans Mus. of Art, Opera Assn. Mem. Houston Com. Fgn. Rels., Houston Philos-.Soc., Plaza Club (bd. givs. 1987-89), Omicron Delta Epsilon.

O'CONNOR, EDWARD CORNELIUS, army officer; b. Middlesex County, Mass., June 22, 1931; s. Edward Denis and Gladys Marie (Devine) O'C.; m. Charlotte Hubble, June 1, 1958. AB, Boston Coll., 1952; MS, U. N.C., 1966; MS George Washington U., 1979. Commd. 2d lt. U.S. Army, 1952, advanced through grades to maj. gen., 1981; asst. for NATO Affairs, Office of Sec. Def., 1970-72; sec. Joint Staff, Vietnam, 1972; chief staff Joint Mil. Commn., Vietnam, 1973; arty. comdr. 1st Armored Div., Europe, 1973-74; Fed. Exec. fellow Brookings Inst., Washington, 1975-76; chief Army Initiatives Group, Army Staff, Pentagon, 1976-77; dep. dir. ops. Nat. Mil. Command Center, Joint Chiefs of Staff, Washington, 1977-78; asst. div. comdr. (maneuver) 1st Armored Div., Europe, 1978-79; chief nuclear activities SHAPE, Belgium, 1979-82; dir. ops., readiness and mobilization ODCSOPS, Dept. Army, 1982-83; comdg. gen. Security Affairs Command Army Material Command, 1983-86; chief exec. officer, pres. Global Mktg. Corp. (doing bus. as GMA Internat., Inc.), 1986—. Chmn. Contraves, Inc., Pitts., 1992-97; mem. policy working group U.S. State Dept. Def. Trade Adv. Group, Washington, 1994—; bd. dirs. Gas Equipment Engring. Corp., Milford, Conn., 1997—; internat. lectr. in field. Author: Performance Appraisal, 1966. Chmn. Harvard U. Grad. Sch. rels. com. Decorated D.S.M., Legion of Merit with 3 oak leaf clusters, Bronze Star, Air medal with 6 oak leaf clusters, Army Commendation medal with V device and 7 oak leaf clusters, Def. Meritorious Service medal, Def. Superior Service medal, Joint Service Commendation with oak leaf cluster, Identification Badges of Sec. Def. Office, Joint Chiefs of Staff and Army Gen. Staff Mem. Harvard U. Alumni Assn. (bd. dirs. 1989-93). Address: 10202 Eagle Landing Ct Burke VA 22015-2524 E-mail: gmaoc@aol.com.

O'CONNOR, EDWARD GEARING, lawyer; b. Pitts., May 5, 1940; s. Timothy R. and Irene B. (Gearing) O'C.; m. Janet M. Showalter, June 17, 1972; children: Mark G., Susan M. BA, Duquesne U., 1962, JD, 1965. Bar: Pa. 1965, U.S. Dist. Ct. (we. dist.) Pa. 1965, U.S. Ct. Appeals (3d cir.) 1968, U.S. Supreme Ct. 1976. Assoc. Eckert, Seamans, Cherin & Mellott, Pitts., 1965-72, ptnr., 1973-99, sr. counsel, 2000—. Mem. adv. com. on appellate ct. rules Supreme Ct. Pa., 1986—92, mem. procedure rules com., 1998—; bd. dirs., mem. audit com. Federated Investors, Inc. Editor Duquesne U. Law Rev., 1964-65. Chmn. Hampton (Pa.) Twp. Planning Commn., 1986-87; mem. Hampton (Pa.) Twp. Zoning Hearing Bd., 1997—; bd. dirs. Duquesne U.; trustee Noble J. Dick Edn. Fund, 1989—. Recipient Disting. Alumni award Duquesne U. Law Rev., 1985, Disting. Law Alumni award Duquesne U. Sch. Law, 1991, Disting. Svc. award Hampton Twp., 1991, McAnurlty Svc. award Duquesne U., 1992; named Century Club Disting. Alumni, Duquesne U., 1985. Fellow: Pa. Bar Found., Am. Bar Found.; mem.: Ally City Bar Found. (chair fellows com. 2000—01), Acad. Trial Lawyers Allegheny County (bd. govs. 1986—89, 1998—), Pa. Bar Assn. (ho. of dels. 1985—90), Pitts. Athletic Assn., Duquesne U. Alumni Assn. (pres. 1980—82, 1988—90, bd. govs. 1982—90, bd. dirs. 1988—89), Duquesne Club. Republican. Roman Catholic. Home: 4288 Green Glade Ct Allison Park PA 15101-1202 Office: Eckert Seamans Cherin & Mellott 600 Grant St Ste 44th Pittsburgh PA 15219-2702 E-mail: ego@escm.com.

O'CONNOR, EDWARD VINCENT, JR. lawyer; b. Yokosuka, Japan, Nov. 9, 1952; s. Edward Vincent and Margaret (Robertson) O'C.; m. Kathy J. Hunt, May 23, 1992. BA, Duke U., 1975; JD, N.Y. Law Sch., 1981. Bar: Va. 1982, D.C. 1983. Assoc. Lewis, Kinsey, Dack & Good, Washington, 1982-87; ptnr. Lewis, Dack, Paradiso & Good, 1988-89, Lewis, Dack, Paradiso, O'Connor & Good, Washington, 1989-94, The Lewis Law Firm, 1994, Byrd, Mische, Bevis, Bowen, Joseph & O'Connor, Fairfax, Va., 1995—. Arbitrator D.C. Superior Ct.; neutral case evaluator and concilliator Fairfax County Cir. Ct.; lectr. Va. Trial Lawyers Assn., Arlington County Bar Assn. Bd. dirs., treas. Potomac Legal Aid Soc., 2001—. Named One of Best 50 Divorce Lawyers Washingtonian mag., 1995, 2000. Mem. Va. State Bar (lectr., spl. com. on access to legal svcs. 1994—, 5th dist. discipline com.), D.C. Bar, Fairfax County Bar Assn. (lectr., vice chair family law sect. 1995-96, continuing edn. com. 1988-95, chair 1995, mem. pub. svc. com. 1995, chair 1996-98, mem. cir. ct. com. 1994-96, 99-2001, judicial selection com., pro bono com., James Keith award for pub. svc. 1999), Legal Svcs. No. Va. (bd. dirs., chmn. pro bono com., sec.-treas. 1998-2002, pres. 2002-, pro bono award for outstanding svc. 1997).

O'CONNOR, EILEEN J. federal agency administrator; Grad., Columbus State U., Cath. U. Ptnr. Office Fed. Tax Svcs. Grant Thornton, 1984—99; officer for tax svcs. Aronson, Fetridge and Weigle; asst. atty. gen. tax divsn. U.S. Dept. Justice, Washington, 2001—. Adj. prof. law George Mason Law Sch., Georgetown U. Law Sch. Office: US Dept Justice Tax Divsn 950 Pennsylvania Ave NW Washington DC 20530-0001*

O'CONNOR, FRANCIS X. financial executive; b. Bklyn., May 7, 1929; s. Richard B. and Mary (McCafferty) O'C.; m. Leona A. Windorf, June 30, 1951; children: Francis X., Edward K., Brendan T., Richard B. III, A. Bruce, Marianne, Margaret, Leona. BS, St. Peter's Coll., 1951. CPA, N.Y., N.J. Audit mgr. Coopers & Lybrand, N.Y.C., 1951-65; controller Ward Foods, Inc., 1965-66, v.p. fin., CFO, 1966-72, also bd. dirs., 1968-73; v.p. fin., CFO UMC Industries, Inc., 1973-76; v.p. fin. and corp. devel., CFO SKF Industries, Inc., King of Prussia, Pa., 1976-87; v.p. corp. fin. Moore & Schley Securities Corp., Morristown, N.J., 1987-89; mng. dir. Sterling Manhattan Corp. Investment Bankers, N.Y.C., 1989-93. Adv. bd. Boyden Cons. Corp. Mem. AICPA, AIM, N.Y. State Soc. CPAs. Fin. Excs. Inst., Nat. Conf. on Power Transmission (trustee), Machinery and Allied Products Inst. Fin. Coun., St. Peter's Coll. Alumni Assn. (trustee, past pres. Monmouth chpt.), Navy League U.S., Spring Lake Golf Club, (past pres., trustee), Seaview Country Club (N.J.), Green Gables Croquet Club (past pres.), Legacy Golf Club (Ft. Pierce, Fla.), Yacht and Country Club (Stuart, Fla.). Home: 2355 NE Ocean Blvd Stuart FL 34996-2945

O'CONNOR, SISTER GEORGE AQUIN (MARGARET M. O'CONNOR), college president, sociology educator; b. Astoria, N.Y., Mar. 5, 1921; d. George M. and Joana T. (Loughlin) O'C. BA, Hunter Coll., 1943; MA, Catholic U. Am., 1947; PhD (NIMH fellow), NYU, 1964; LL.D. Manhattan Coll., 1983; D of Pedagogy (hon.), Dowling Coll., 1997; DHL, St. Francis Coll., 1997, St. Joseph's Coll., 1997. Mem. faculty St. Joseph's Coll., Bklyn., 1946—, prof. sociology and anthropology, 1966—, chmn. social sci. dept., 1966-69, pres., 1969-97; pres. emeritus. Fellow African Studies Assn., Am. Anthrop. Assn.; Bklyn. C. of C. (dir. 1973-97), Alpha Kappa Delta, Delta Epsilon Sigma. Author: The Status and Role of West African Women: A Study in Cultural Change, 1964. Named one of N.Y. State Senate's Women of Distinction. Office: Saint Joseph's Coll 245 Clinton Ave Brooklyn NY 11205-3602

O'CONNOR, G(EORGE) RICHARD, ophthalmologist; b. Cin., Oct. 8, 1928; s. George Leo and Sylvia Johanna (Voss) O'C. AB, Harvard U., 1950; MD, Columbia U., 1954. Resident in ophthalmology Columbia-Presbyn. Med. Center, N.Y.C., 1957-60; research fellow Inst. Biochemistry, U. Uppsala, Sweden, 1960-61, State Serum Inst., Copenhagen, 1961-62; asst. prof. ophthalmology U. Calif., San Francisco, 1962-68, prof., 1972-84; dir. Francis I. Proctor Found. for Research in Ophthalmology, 1970-84. Mem. Nat. Adv. Eye Council NIH, 1974-78 Author: (with G. Smolin) Ocular Immunology, 1981; asso. editor: Am. Jour. Ophthalmology, 1976-81. Served with USPHS, 1955-57. Recipient Janeway prize Coll. of Physicians and Surgeons, Columbia U., 1954; Doyne medal Oxford U., 1984; NIH grantee, 1962-84 Mem. Am. Bd. Ophthalmology (examiner), Assn. for Rsch. in Vision and Ophthalmology (trustee 1979-83, pres. 1982-83, Weisenfeld award 1990), Am. Ophthal. Soc., Calif. Med. Assn., Frederic C. Cordes Eye Soc., Pan Am. Ophthal. Assn. Clubs: Faculty. Republican. Presbyterian. Home: 22 Wray Ave Sausalito CA 94965-1831 Office: U Calif Med Ctr 315 S San Francisco CA 94143-0001 E-mail: rconnor@itsa.ucsf.edu.

O'CONNOR, JAMES JOHN, retired utility company executive; b. Chgo., Mar. 15, 1937; s. Fred James and Helen Elizabeth O'Connor; m. Ellen Louise Lawlor, Nov. 24, 1960; children: Fred, John (dec.), James, Helen Elizabeth. BS, Holy Cross Coll., 1958; MBA, Harvard U., 1960; JD, Georgetown U., 1963. Bar: Ill. 1963. With Commonwealth Edison Co., Chgo., 1963-98, asst. to chmn. exec. com., 1964-65, comml. mgr., 1966, asst. v.p., 1967-70, v.p., 1970-73, exec. v.p., 1973-77, pres., 1977-87, chmn., 1980-98, CEO, also bd. dirs., 1998; chmn., CEO Unicom Corp., 1994-98, ret., 1998. Bd. dirs. Corning, Inc., Tribune Co., United Air Lines, Smurfit-Stone Container Corp. Mem. The Bus. Coun.; bd. dirs. Lyric Opera, Joffrey Ballet, Helen Brach Found.; bd. dirs., trustee Mus. Sci. and Industry, Chgo. Symphony; past chmn. Met. Savs. Bond Campaign; trustee Northwestern U.; bd. dirs., past chmn. Chgo. Urban League, Chicagoland C. of C.; past chmn. bd. trustees Field Mus. Natural History; life trustee Adler Planetarium, Mus. Sci. and Industry; mem. exec. bd. Chgo. Area coun. Boy Scouts Am.; chmn. Cardinal Bernardin's Big Shoulders Fund; exec. v.p. The Hundred Club Cook County; dir., past pres. Cath. Charities; past chmn., hon. dir. Am. Cancer Soc., Chgo. Conv. and Tourism Bur. With USAF, 1960-63. Mem. ABA, Ill. Bar Assn., Chgo. Bar Assn.

O'CONNOR, JAMES T. civil engineering educator; b. Tulsa, Feb. 28, 1956; s. Joseph Walter and Mary Lois (Walker) O'C.; m. Catherine Morris, Jan. 7, 1995; children: Catherine Claire, James Patrick. BS, Okla. State U., 1979;

MArch, U. Ill., 1980; PhD, U. Tex., 1983. Registered profl. engr., Tex. Archtl. engr. intern Murray Jones Murray, 1977-80; prof. U. Tex., Austin, 1984—. Engr. and mgmt. cons. Arco Chem., Dallas Area Rapid Transit, FSB, Inc., City of Austin, U. Tex. Sys., Fla. Power and Light, Cuyahoga County, Ohio. Contbr. articles to profl. jours.; author 5 course manuals in field. With U.S. Army Corp Engrs., 1975-77. Recipient Nat. Value Engring. award Am. Assn. of State Hwy. Tranps. Ofcls., 1997, Tex. Quality Initiative award State of Tex., 1998, Nat. Quality Initiative award Assn. State Hwy. Transp. Ofcls., Fed. Hwy. Adminstrn., 1999. Mem. ASCE (Rowland prize 1995, 97), Tex. Soc. Profl. Engrs., Constrn. Specifications Inst. Roman Catholic. Achievements include research on project constructability and planning from startup. Avocations: tennis, hiking. Home: 1200 Yaupon Valley Rd Austin TX 78746-4331 Office: U Tex Dept Civil Engring ECJ 5 2 Austin TX 78712 E-mail: jtoconnor@mail.utexas.edu.

O'CONNOR, JOHN EDWARD, theater educator, director; b. Chgo., Jan. 25, 1953; s. Theodore J. and Victoria M. (Bien) O'C.; m. Linda F. Davis, July 31, 1977; children: Patrick D., Michael J. BSEd in Theatre and Speech, No. Ill. U., 1975; MA Theatre, Miami U., Oxford, Ohio, 1978; PhD in Drama, U. Wash., 1989. Tchg. asst. U. Wash., Seattle, 1979-82; instr. Columbia Coll., 1984-85, U. Puget Sound, Tacoma, 1986; asst. prof. theater Buena Vista Coll., Storm Lake, Iowa, 1990-92, U. North Ala., Florence, 1992-98, Fairmont (W.Va.) State Coll., 1998—2001, assoc. prof., 2001—. Stage mgr. Gingerbread Theatre, Florence, Ala., 1994, 96, actor, 1993; actor, singer Shoals Chamber Singers, Florence, 1996; actor Segue Theatre Co., Florence, 1997, Town & Gown Players, Fairmont, W.Va. Contbr. articles, papers to profl. publs. Mem. Am. Soc. Theatre Rsch., Assn. for Theatre in Higher Edn., Voice and Speech Trainers Assn., Christians in Theatre Arts, Phi Kappa Phi. Avocations: acting, directing, Christian education. Office: Fairmont State Coll Sch Fine Arts Fairmont WV 26554 E-mail: joconnor@mail.fscwv.edu.

O'CONNOR, JOHN JAY, III, lawyer; b. San Francisco, Jan. 10, 1930; s. John Jay and Sally (Flynn) O'C.; m. Sandra Day, Dec. 20, 1952; children: Scott, Brian, Jay. AB, Stanford U., 1951, LLB, 1953. Bar: Calif. 1953, Ariz. 1957, D.C. 1981. Mem. Fennemore, Craig, von Ammon & Udall, Phoenix, 1957-81, Miller & Chevalier, Washington, 1982-88; ptnr. Bryan Cave, Washington and Phoenix, 1988-99, of counsel, 2000—. Judge pro-tem Superior Ct. State of Ariz., 1979-81. Chmn. Ariz. Crippled Children's Svcs., 1968; Chmn. planning and zoning commn. Town of Paradise Valley, 1967; Chmn. Maricopa County Young Republicans, 1960, Ariz. Young Rep. League, 1962; bd. dirs. Ariz. Tax Rsch. Assn., 1966-81; chmn. bd. dirs. Maricopa County Gen. Hosp., 1967-70; exec. com. bd. visitors Stanford Law Sch., 1976-80; pres. Stanford Law Fund, 1980-82; mem. nat. coun. Salk Inst. Biol. Studies, San Diego, 1977-90; pres. Phoenix-Scottsdale United Way, 1977-79; bd. dirs. World Affairs Coun. of Phoenix, 1970-81, Legal Aid Soc. Phoenix, Maricopa County Mental Health Assn.; trustee Meridian House Internat., Washington, 1982-88; mem. policy devel. com. Phoenix Cmty. Svc. Fund, 1978; mem. exec. com. Valley Leadership, 1979-81; bd. dirs. Trusteeship for St. Luke's Hosp., 1979-81; mem. adv. com. Nat. Postal Mus., Washington, 1992-98. Served to 1st lt. AUS, 1954-57. Mem. ABA, Stanford Assocs., Paradise Valley Country Club, Ariz. Club (pres. 1979-81), Valley Field Riding and Polo Club, Stanford Club of Phoenix (pres.), Iron Springs Club (pres. 1974-76), Bohemian Club, Met. Club, Alfalfa Club, Alibi Club, Delta Upsilon, Phi Delta Phi. Office: Bryan Cave 700 13th St NW Fl 7 Washington DC 20005-5921

O'CONNOR, JOHN JOSEPH, operations executive; b. Smyrna, Tenn., June 1, 1959; s. John O'Connor and Dolores Jane (Bell) Brem; m. Lea Ann Bradford, Sept. 6, 1986; 1 child, Colleen Michelle. BS, Tex. A&M U., 1981. Cert. marine engr. 3rd asst. engr. Marine Engrs. Beneficial Assn., Houston, 1981-84; asst. engr. Biehl Ship Mgmt., 1984; balance technician Hickham Industries, Inc., LaPorte, Tex., 1984-86, prodn. scheduler/Sulzer, 1986-87, project engr./Sulzer, 1987-88, engring. mgr./Sulzer, 1988-89, ops. mgr./Sulzer Huntington Beach, Calif., 1989-93, sr. engr., corp. mergers and acquisitions La Porte, Tex., 1993-94; tech. and field svc. mgr. Sulzer Turbosys. Internat., Houston, 1994-98; engring. projects mgr. Hickham Industries, Inc., LaPorte, Tex., 1998—. Guest speaker Tex. A&M U., Galveston, Tex., College Station, Tex., 1981-89, U. Houston, 1986-89; moderator Power Machinery and Compressor Conf., Houston, 1989. Prin. engr. inventions in field (Achievement awards 1989); author: Steam Turbine Overhaul and Repair Specifications, 1994. Bd. dirs. Cedar Lawn Assn., pres., 1998-2001; bd. dirs. East End Presch., pres., 1998-99; bd. dirs. (pres.) Galveston Alliance of Island Neighborhoods, 1998—; adv. bd. Galveston Hist. Found., 1999. Recipient Outstanding Records in Engring., Gulf Oil Corp., Galveston, 1981. Mem. ASME (guest speaker convs.), Pacific Energy Assn. (guest speaker convs. 1990-92), Assn. of Former Students/Tex. A&M. Avocations: hiking, camping, travel, automotive restoration, litigation.

O'CONNOR, JOHN MORRIS, III, retired philosophy educator; b. Evanston, Ill., Sept. 21, 1937; s. John Morris and Clare Evelyn (Merrick) O'C.; m. Mary Bittner, Dec. 31, 1960 (div.); 1 dau., Emily; m. Miranda E. P. Ind, Aug. 14, 1971 (div.); 1 dau., Amanda. Student, Georgetown U., 1955-56; BA, Cornell U., 1959; MA, Harvard U., 1962, PhD, 1965. Instr. Vassar Coll., 1964-66, asst. prof. philosophy, 1966-68; asst. prof. Case Western Res. U., Cleve., 1968-70, assoc. prof., 1970-77; exec. sec. Am. Philos. Assn. U. Del., Newark, 1977-84, assoc. prof., 1977-83; asst. dir. for programs Nat. Humanities Ctr., Research Triangle Park, N.C., 1983-87; dean Sch. Humanities William Paterson Univ., Wayne, N.J., 1987-91, dean Sch. Humanities, Mgmt. and Social Scis., 1991-92; coord. spl. projects Office of Provost William Paterson Coll., 1992-93, prof. philosophy, 1992-2001. Contbr. articles to profl. jours.; editor: (with others) Introductory Philosophy, 1967, Modern Materialism, 1969, Moral Problems in Medicine, 1976. Woodrow Wilson nat. fellow, 1959-60. Home: 523 Guilford Ave Chambersburg PA 17201

O'CONNOR, JOHN THOMAS, civil engineering educator; b. N.Y.C., Feb. 11, 1933; married, 1966; 2 children. BCE, Cooper Union, 1955; MSCE, N.J. Inst. Tech., 1958; EngD, Johns Hopkins U., 1961. Sanitary engr. Elson T. Killam Sanit & Hydraulic Consulting Engrs., 1955-56; civil engr. George A. Fuller Constrn. Co., N.Y., 1956-57; sanitary engr. Parsons, Brinckerhoff, Quade & Douglas, 1957; from asst. prof. to prof. civil engring. U. Ill., Urbana-Champaign, 1961-75; prof. civil engring. U. Mo., Columbia, 1975-92, chmn. dept., 1975-89; chief Ill. State Water Survey, 1992-95; pres. H2O'C Ltd., 1995—. Mem. ASCE, Am. Chem. Soc., Am. Water Works Assn., Am. Soc. Limnology and Oceanography, Water Environment Fedn. Achievements include research on drinking water treatment processes; removal of arsenic, microorganisms, organic substances, iron and manganese, radionuclides; wastewater treatment and disinfection; solid and hazardous waste site remediation. E-mail. Address: 2401 Tahoe Ct Columbia MO 65203-1444 E-mail: john@h2oc.com.

O'CONNOR, JOSEPH A., JR. lawyer; b. N.Y.C., Aug. 12, 1937; s. Joseph A. and Louise G. (Lucht) O'C.; children: Joseph A. III, Edward W. BA, Yale U., 1959; LLB, Columbia U., 1962. Bar: N.Y. 1963, U.S. Supreme Ct. 1968, Pa. 1973, Fla. 1978. Assoc. Davis, Polk & Wardwell, N.Y.C., 1963-72; ptnr. Morgan, Lewis & Bockius, Phila., 1972—2002, spl. coun., 2002—; exec. dir. E. Rhodes & Leona B. Carpenter Fedn., 2002—. Mem. ABA, N.Y. State Bar Assn., Pa. Bar Assn., Fla. Bar Assn., Phila. Bar Assn., Assn. of Bar of City of N.Y. Clubs: Racquet (Phila.). Roman Catholic. Office: Morgan Lewis & Bockius LLP 1735 Market St Philadelphia PA 19103-2903

O'CONNOR, KAREN, political science educator, researcher, writer; b. Buffalo, Feb. 15, 1952; s. Robert J. and Norma (Wilton) O'C.; m. F. Allen McDonogh, June 7, 1974 (div. 1986). 1 child, Meghan. B.A., SUNY-Buffalo, 1973, J.D., 1977, Ph.D., 1979. Bar: Ga. 1978. Instr. polit. sci. Emory U., 1977-78, asst. prof., 1978-83, assoc. prof., 1983-88; prof., 1988. adj. prof. law, 1980— . Author: Women's Organization's Use of the Courts, 1980; (with N.E. McGlen) Women's Rights, 1983. Mem. editorial bd. Women & Politics, 1980— , Law & Policy, 1982— , Jour. of Politics, 1984—, Am. Politics Quarterly, 1987—. Contbr. articles to profl. jours. Mem. Am. Polit. Sci. Assn. (exec. council 1985-87). Home: 4383 Westover Pl NW Washington DC 20016-5555

O'CONNOR, KARL WILLIAM (GOODYEAR JOHNSON), lawyer; b. Washington, Aug. 1, 1931; s. Hector and Lucile (Johnson) O'C.; m. Sylvia Gasbarri, Mar. 23, 1951 (dec.); m. Judith Ann Byers, July 22, 1972 (div. 1983); m. Eleanor Celler, Aug. 3, 1984 (div. 1986); m. Alma Hepner, Jan. 1, 1987 (div. 1996); children: Blair, Frances, Brian, Brendan; m. Allie O'Connor, Jul. 15, 2000. BA, U. Va., 1952, JD, 1958. Bar: Va. 1958, D.C. 1959, Am. Samoa 1976, Calif. 1977, Oreg. 1993. Law clk. U.S. Dist. Ct. Va., Abingdon, 1958-59; practice law Washington, 1959-61; trial atty. U.S. Dept. Justice, 1961-65; dep. dir. Men's Job Corps OEO, 1965-67; mem. civil rights div. Dept. of Justice, chief criminal sect., prin. dep. asst. atty. gen., 1967-75, spl. counsel for intelligence coordination, 1975; v.p., counsel Assn. of Motion Picture and Television Producers, Hollywood, Calif., 1975-76; assoc. justice Am. Samoa, 1976; chief justice, 1977-78; sr. trial atty. GSA Task Force, Dept. Justice, 1978-81; insp. gen. CSA, 1981-82; spl. counsel Merit Systems Protection Bd., Washington, 1983-86; U.S. atty. for Guam and the No. Marianas, 1986-89; ret.; pvt. practice Medford, Oreg., 1989—; Am. counsel O'Reilly Vernier Ltd., Hong Kong, 1992-93; ptnr. O'Connor & Vernier, Medford, Oreg., 1993-94; pvt. practice, 1994—. Served with USMC, 1952-55. Mem. Oreg. Bar Assn., D.C. Bar Assn., Va. Bar Assn., Calif. Bar Assn., Am. Samoa Bar Assn., Soc. Colonial Wars, Phi Alpha Delta, Sigma Nu. Home: Box 126 6743 Griffin Ln Jacksonville OR 97530 Office: 916 W 10th St Medford OR 97501-3018

O'CONNOR, KATHLEEN MARY, lawyer; b. Camden, Jan. 14, 1949; d. John A. and Marie V. (Flynn) O'C. BA, U. Fla., 1971, JD, 1981. Bar: Fla. 1981, U.S. Ct. Appeals (11th cir.) 1982, U.S. Supreme Ct. 1987. Atty. Walton, Lantaff, Schroeder & Carson, Miami, 1981-84, Thornton, Davis & Murray PA, Miami, 1984-98, Shook, Hardy & Bacon LLP, Miami, 2001—. Exec. editor U. Fla. Law Rev., 1981; contbr. articles to profl. jours. Legal advocate Miami Project to Cure Paralysis, 1992-97. Mem. ABA, Dade County Bar Assn. (vice-chair appellate cts. com. 1981), Def. Rsch. Inst., Fla. Def. Lawyers Assn. Office: Shook Hardy & Bacon LLP Ste 2400 201 S Biscayne Blvd Miami FL 33131-4332 E-mail: koconnor@shb.com.

O'CONNOR, KAY F. state legislator; b. Everett, Wash., Nov. 28, 1941; d. Ernest S. and Dena (Lampers) Wells; m. Arthur J. O'Connor, Sept. 1, 1959; 6 children. Diploma, Lathrop H.S., Fairbanks, Alaska, 1959. Office mgr. Blaylock Chemicals, Bucyrus, Kans., 1981-84; store mgr. Copies Plus, Olathe, 1984-86; acct. Advance Concrete Inc., Spring Hill, 1986-92; mem. Kans. Ho. of Reps. from 14th dist., 1993-2000, Kans. Senate from 9th dist., 2001—. Exec. dir. Parents in Control, Inc.; bd. dirs. Hometel Ltd.; author sch. voucher legis. State of Kans., 1994-2002; corrections and juvenile justice oversight com., judiciary com., fed. and state affairs com., vice chair elections and local govt. com. Kans. Senate, 2001—. Republican. Roman Catholic. Avocations: choir directing, statue renovations, speaking on school vouchers. Home: 1101 N Curtis St Olathe KS 66061-2709 Office: PO Box 2232 Olathe KS 66051-2232 E-mail: kayoisok@comcast.net.

O'CONNOR, KEVIN JOHN, psychologist, educator; b. Jersey City, July 18, 1954; s. John Lanning and Marilyn (Reynolds) O'C.; m. Ryan Michael, Matthew Benham. BA, U. Mich., 1975; PhD, U. Toledo, 1981. Clin. psychologist Blythedale Children's Hosp., Valhalla, N.Y., 1980-83; dir. psychol. svcs. Walworth Barbour Am. Internat. Sch., Kfar Shmaryahu, Israel, 1983-84; adj. asst. prof. dept. psychology Iona Coll., New Rochelle, N.Y., 1984; clin. psychologist No. Westchester Guidance Clinic, Mt. Kisco, 1985; exec. dir., newsletter editor Assn. for Play Therapy, Fresno, Calif., 1982-97; cons. psychologist Fresno (Calif.) Treatment Ctr., 1986-87, Diagnostic Sch. for Neurologically Handicapped Children, Fresno, Calif., 1986-90; adj. faculty Pacific Grad. Sch. of Psychology, Palo Alto, 1987—, Calif. Sch. Profl. Psychology, Berkeley, 1988-89; prof. Alliant Internat. U., Calif. Sch. Profl. Psychology, Fresno, 1985—. Contbr. numerous presentations in field. Named Psychologist of Yr. San Joaquin Psychol. Assn., 1994. Fellow APA; mem. Assn. for Play Therapy. Democrat. Avocations: travel, art, ceramics. Office: Calif Sch Profl Psych Alliant Internat U 5130 E Clinton Way Fresno CA 93727-2014

O'CONNOR, KEVIN THOMAS, religious organization administrator; b. Dubuque, Iowa, Oct. 9, 1950; s. Francis John and Marion Helen (Rhomberg) O'C.; m. Abbie J. O'Connor, July 17, 1993; 1 child, Sean Francis. BS, Regis Coll., Denver, 1973. Spl. agt. Northwestern Mut. Life, Denver, 1973-78; account exec. Blue Cross/Blue Shield of Colo., 1978-82; pres., owner O'Connor Ins. Cons., 1982-92; dir. devel. Archdiocese of Denver, 1992-95, mgr. Cath. appeal, 1995-96; dir. devel. Archdiocese of L.A., 1996—. Chmn. Regis Coll. Telefund, Denver, 1987-88, 90-91; treas., 1st vice chmn. Serra Trust Fund for Vocations, 1988-93, chmn., 1993-96; mem. fin. coun. St. James Parish, 1988-95, chmn. autumn bazaar, 1985, 87, mem. choir, 1993-95; sec. Mother Teresa Com., 1989; co-founder Pueblo Serra Club, 1992, Colorado Springs Serra Club, 1995, Greeley Serra Club, 1996; pres. Denver Serra Club, 1991-92; dist. 6 gov. Serra Internat., 1995-96. Recipient Share Serra Comm. award Serra Internat., 1989, Spl. Project award Dist. 6, 1986, 88, Spl. Recognition award, 1989, Outstanding Serran award, 1995, Jan Berbers award, 1996, Alumni Svc. award Regis Coll., 1990, Disting. Alumnus award Wahlert H.S., 1994. Mem. Serra Club L.A., Serra Internat. (trustee 1997—, sec. bd. 1998-2001, chmn. internat. vocation com. 2000-01, v.p. 2001—). Roman Catholic. Avocations: golf, tennis, mountain climbing, handball, running. Home: 3510 Fallenleaf Pl Glendale CA 91206-4803 Office: Archdiocese LA 3424 Wilshire Blvd Los Angeles CA 90010-2241 E-mail: ktoconnor@la-archdiocese.org., kevinabbie@earthlink.net.

O'CONNOR, KIM CLAIRE, chemical engineering and biotechnology educator; BS magna cum laude, Rice U., Houston, 1982; PhD, Calif. Inst. Tech., Pasadena, 1987. Postdoctoral rsch. fellow chemistry dept. Calif. Inst. Tech., Pasadena, 1987-88; postdoctoral rsch. fellow chem. engring., biochemistry, molecular biology, and cell biology depts. Northwestern U., Evanston, Ill., 1988-90; asst. prof. chem. engring. Tulane U., New Orleans, 1990-96, assoc. prof. chem. engring., 1996—2002, prof. chem. engring., 2002—, faculty molecular and cellular biology grad. program, Newcomb fellow, 1991—, co-dir. molecular and cellular biology grad. program, 1996-99, interim dir. molecular and cellular biology grad. program, 1997. Mem. Tulane Cancer Ctr., 1994—; adj. assoc. prof. dept. surgery Tulane U. Sch. Medicine, 1999—; cons. in field. Contbr. articles and revs. to profl. jours.; patentee in field. Recipient NASA Space Act award, 1994, 95, 96, Outstanding Engring. Student award Tex. Soc. Profl. Engrs., 1982, Tulane award for excellence in undergrad. tchg., 1999, Lee H. Johnson award for excellence in tchg., 2001, Tulane Interdisciplinary Tchg. award, 2001; Robert A. Welch Merit scholar, 1978-82, Brown Engring. Merit scholar, 1980-82, Roy Merit scholar, 1981-82; Weyerhaeuser Co. Found. fellow, 1982-83. Mem.: Tissue Engring. Soc., Soc. Women Engrs., Soc. In Vitro Biology, European Soc. Animal Cell Tech., Am. Soc. Engring. Edn., Am. Inst. Chem. Engrs., Am. Chem. Soc., Am. Assn. for Cancer Rsch., Phi Lambda Upsilon, Tau Beta Pi, Sigma Xi. Achievements include interdisciplinary research in engineering and the biological sciences. Office: Tulane U Dept Chem Engring Lindy Boggs Ctr Rm 300 New Orleans LA 70118 E-mail: koc@tulane.edu.

O'CONNOR, MAUREEN, state official, lawyer; b. Washington, Aug. 7, 1951; d. Patrick and Mary E. O'Connor; children: Alex, Ed. BA, Seton Hill Coll., 1973; postgrad., SUNY, 1975-76; JD, Cleve. State U., 1980. Pvt. practice, 1981-85; referee Probate Ct., 1985-93; judge Common Pleas, 1993-95; prosecutor Summit County, 1995-99; lt. gov., dir. Dept. Pub. Safety State of Ohio, 1999—. Dir. Summit County Child Support Enforcement Agy.; spkr. in field. Parishioner St. Vincent's Ch.; vol. Comty. Drug Bd., Am. Cancer Soc., bd. dirs.; bd. dirs. Victim Assistance, St. Edward Home, Fairlawn, Furnace St. Mission. Recipient MADD Law Enforcement award, 1997, Cleve. State Disting. Alumnae award for Civic Achievement, 1997. Mem. MADD, Nat. Dist. Attys. Assn., Nat. Child Support Enforcement Assn., Nat. Coll. Dist. Attys. Assn., Ohio Prosecuting Attys. Assn. (exec. com.), Ohio Family Support Assn., Atty. Gen.'s Prosecutor Liaison Com., Summit County Police Chiefs Assn., Summit Forum, Summit County Child Mortality. E-mail: ltgov.o'connor@das.state.oh.us. Office: Office of Lt Gov 77 S High St Fl 30 Columbus OH 43215-6108*

O'CONNOR, MICHAEL PATRICK, religious writer, editor; b. Lackawanna, N.Y., Apr. 7, 1950; s. John David and Anna Mariah (Crosta) O'C. AB, U. Notre Dame, 1970; MA, U. British Columbia, 1972, U. Mich., 1974, PhD, 1978. Editor, Ann Arbor, Mich., 1978—. Author: Hebrew Verse Structure, 1980, An Introduction to Biblical Hebrew Syntax, 1990; editor: The Word of the Lord Shall Go Forth: Essays in Honor of David Noel Freedman in Celebration of His Sixtieth Birthday, 1983, The Bible and Its Traditions, 1983, Backgrounds for the Bible, 1987, Agrammatic Aphasia: A Cross-Language Narrative Sourcebook, 1990; contbr. chpts. to books and articles to profl. jours. Mem. Am. Oriental Soc., Soc. Bibl. Lit., Cath. Bibl. Soc. Roman Catholic. Home: 3041 Broadway New York NY 10027-5710

O'CONNOR, MICHOL, lawyer; b. Houston, Nov. 30, 1942; d. Charles Cary O'Connor and Ida Mae (Mueller) Baird; BA, U. Tex., Austin, 1966; JD, U. Houston, 1973; 1 child, Baird James Craft. Admitted to Tex. bar, 1973; bd. cert. appellate law, Tex. Bd. Legal Specialization, 1986. law clk. 1st Ct. Civil Appeals, Houston, 1974-75; asst. dist. atty. Harris County Dist. Attys. Office, Houston, 1975-76; assoc. firm Kronzer, Abraham & Watkins, Houston, 1976-78; asst. U.S. atty. U.S. Atty.'s Office, So. Dist. Tex., Houston, 1978-81; corp. counsel Century Devel. Corp., 1981-82; of counsel Haight, Gardner, Poor & Havens, 1985-86; sole practice, Houston, 1986-88; judge U.S. Ct. Appeals (1st cir.), Houston, 1989—. Recipient award for jour. article Tex. Bar Found., 1978. Mem. ABA, Tex. Bar Assn. (chmn. adminstrn. justice com.), Houston Bar Assn. (dir. 1977-79), Houston Young Lawyers (dir. 1975-76, Outstanding Contbn. award 1975), Order of Barons. Author: O'Connor Texas Rules and Civil Appeals, 1993, O'Connor's Texas Rules and Civil Trials, 1997; contbr. articles to profl. and polit. jours.; lectr. State Bar of Tex., advanced appellate sems., 1985, 87, 88. Office: First Ct Appeals 1307 San Jacinto St Houston TX 77002-7006

O'CONNOR, NAN G. social worker; b. Chgo., Apr. 27, 1952; d. Joseph Daniel and Donna Marguerite (Birmingham) O'C. BSW, U. Ill., 1975, MSW, 1978. Med. social worker Schaumburg (Ill.) Elem. Sch. Dist., 1978-79, Ingalls Meml. Hosp., Harvey, Ill., 1979-84; case mgmt. supr. United Charities of Chgo., 1984-85; social worker Village of Skokie, Ill., 1990-97. Sec. Mental Health Coalition So.-Suburban, Oak Forest, Ill., 1980-83; co-chair Social Workers in Home Care, Chgo., 1981-83; founder, chairperson Niles Twp Inter-Agy. Network, Skokie, 1993-96. Bd. dirs. CEDA/Neighbors at Work, Evanston, Ill., 1995-96. Recipient Timothy J. Nugent award Delta Sigma Omicron, U. Ill., Champaign, 1974. Mem. NASW, Niles Twp. InterAgency Network (chairperson 1993-96). Avocations: writing poetry, short stories. Home: 1747 W Crystal Ln Apt 102 Mount Prospect IL 60056-5439 E-mail: nanoconnor@aol.com.

O'CONNOR, OTIS LESLIE, lawyer, director; b. Charleston, W.Va., July 6, 1935; s. Robert Emmett and Julia Elizabeth (Aultz) O'C.; m. Elizabeth Frances Morris, Aug. 7, 1965; children: Otis Leslie, James M. AB, Princeton U., 1957; JD, Harvard U., 1963; MBA, W.Va. Coll. Grad. Studies, 1979. Bar: W.Va. 1963, U.S. Dist. (so. dist.) W.Va. 1963. Assoc. Steptoe & Johnson, Charleston, 1963-69, ptnr., 1969—. Mem. city council, Charleston, 1971-75; bd. dirs. Daymark, Inc., 1974-84, 94—, pres., 1981-82. Bd. dirs. Union Mission Ministries, Inc., 1986—; Rep. committeeman, 1970-75. Served with USN, 1957-60; served to comdr. JAGC, USNR, 1960-81. Mem. ABA, W.Va. Bar Assn., Kanawha County Bar Assn., Res. Officers Assn., Rotary Internat. Club (Charleston). Presbyterian. Home: 890 Chester Rd Charleston WV 25302-2817

O'CONNOR, PAT, film director; b. Ardmore, Ireland, 1943; BA, UCLA. Motion picture dir. Dir. films Cal, 1984, A Month in the Country, 1978, Stars and Bars, 1988, Jan. Man, 1989, Fools of Fortune, 1990, Circle of Friends, 1995, Inventing the Abbotts, 1997, Dancing at Lughnasa, 1998, Sweet November, 2001, (T.V. movie) Zelda, 1993. Office: c/o Andrew Connava United Talent Agency 9560 Wilshire Blvd Ste 500 Beverly Hills CA 90212-2427*

O'CONNOR, PATRICIA ERYL, telecommunications consultant; b. Kansas City, Mo., Oct. 16, 1945; d. Jesse Edwin O'Connor and Olive Mae (Geagan) Brooks; m. James Harrie Reed, Dec. 18, 1964 (div. July 1972); 1 child, Jana Diann Reed; m. John Robert Morgan, Sept. 27, 1985. AAS, Pima Community Coll., Tucson, 1982. Cert. Nat. Assn. Broadcast Engrs. Radio, radio-telephone lic. gen. class FCC. Comm. technician AT&T, Kansas City, Mo., 1972-79, Tucson, 1979-85, San Francisco, 1985-92, Denver, 1992-99, Conyers, Ga., 1999—; CEO, cons. Profl. Forum Mgmt./MacCircles, Tucson, 1985, Pleasanton, Calif., 1985-92, Denver, 1992-96. Co-adminstr. Mac Symposium, Cupertino, Calif., 1987-93. Editor: (electronic mag.) Handshake, 1985-96. Election judge, Tucson, 1979-81; area v.p. CWA Local 8150, Ariz., N.Mex., 1984-84, exec. v.p., 1984-85. Avocation: property management. Home: 45 Surrey Chase Dr Social Circle GA 30025-4912 E-mail: patoconnor@aol.com.

O'CONNOR, PATRICIA WALKER, education educator; b. Memphis, Apr. 26, 1931; d. Shade Wilson and Lillie (Mullins) Walker; m. David E. O'Connor, Apr. 4, 1953 (div. Dec. 1964); children: Michael, Erin O'Connor Dawson; m. Anthony M. Pasquariello, Feb. 11, 1978. BA in Edn., U. Fla., 1953, MA, 1954, PhD, 1962. From instr. to assoc. prof. U. Cin., 1962-72, prof., 1972-96, Charles Phelps Taft prof., 1996—. Author: Gregorio y Maria M. Sierra: crónica de una colaboración, 1987, Dramaturgas Españolas de hoy, 1989, Antonio Buero Vallejo en sus espejos, 1996; translator: Plays of the New Democratic Spain, 1992, One-Act Spanish Plays by Women About Women, 1998. Advocate for battered women YMCA, Cin., 1990. Named Alumna of Achievement, U. Fla., 1997; recipient Rieveschl award, 1982. Mem. Royal Spanish Acad. Lang. (corres. mem. 1990—). Avocations: tennis, piano. Office: Univ Cin Dept Rom Lang Ml377 Cincinnati OH 45206-0001 E-mail: pat.oconnor@uc.edu.

O'CONNOR, PATRICK J. family physician, researcher; b. Cleve., July 26, 1952; s. Joseph W. and Helen Rita O'Connor; m. Kerin McTeigue, July 26, 1980; children: Daniel, Cassidy, Luke. BS, Boston Coll., 1974; MPH, U. N.C., 1978; MD, Case Western Res. U., 1979. Diplomate Am. Bd. Family Practice. Resident in family medicine Duke U. Med. Ctr., Durham, N.C., 1979-82; assoc. prof. family medicine U. Conn., Farmington, 1985-93; sr. clin. investigator, diabetes rschr. HealthPtnrs. Rsch. Found., Mpls., 1993—. Cons. or advisor to AHRQ, NHLBI, CMS, NCQA, others; mem. rsch. grants rev. com. Agy. Health Care Rsch. quality, Rockville, Md., 1994—; chmn. diabetes adv. com. Minn. Dept. Health, Mpls., 1995—98. Author: (monograph) Clinical Care of Diabetes, 1993, 2d edit., 1998 (transl. into Japanese and Spanish); contbr. over 90 articles to med. jours., including Jour. AMA, Diabetes Care, Am. Jour. Managed Care; mem. editl. bd. 4 jours. Lt. comdr. USPHS, 1982-85. Fellow Am. Acad. Family Physicians; mem. APHA, Am. Diabetes Assn. (profl. practice com. 2001--), Am. Geriatrics Soc. Roman Catholic. Avocations: swimming, camping, bicycle riding, piano, bread baking. Office: Healthptnrs Rsch Found 8100 34th Ave S Minneapolis MN 55440-1524

O'CONNOR, PATRICK JOSEPH, writer, musician, university educator; b. Wichita, Kans., Dec. 27, 1948; s. Rubie Nell Bishop; m. Carolyn Sue Drummond-Hay (div. Apr. 1, 1979); children: Dalton. MA in Comm., Wichita State U., 1989. Lectr. Wichita State U., 1994—; instr. Embry-Riddle U., 1996—98, Friends U., Wichita, 1997—98; artist in residence Wichita Pub. Schs., 1998—99; music reviewer for popular music and soc. Bowling Green (Ohio) State U., 1996—98. Dir. mus. exhibit Traditions of the Blues in Wichita First Nat. Black Hist. Soc. Kans. and Kans. Interpretive Traveling Exhibit, Kans. State Hist.ociety/Kansas Humanities Council/National Endowment for the Humanities, Wichita, Kansas City, 1996—; dir. prodn. dir. prodn. for panel and happening Wichita Art Mus., 1999—99; interviewer/writer Documentary: The Wichita Blues History Project , 1999—; panelist Friends U., Wichita, 2002—. Author: Tales From A Blackout, 1997, Wichita Blues: Discovery, 1998, Moody's Skidrow Beanery, 1999, Delano/ Stories From The Neighborhood, 2001; musician: (cassette tape) Upscale Blues, 1994, (compact disc) Blue Heaven: Bill Garrison with Jimmy D. Lane, 2000; actor: (musical revue) Pump Boys and Dinettes, 1998; contbr. articles to profl. jours.; , author short stories. Grantee Delano Maggard Scholarship grant, Wichita State U., 1989, Profl. Devel. grant, Kans. Arts Commn., 1994, Heritage Program grant, Kans. Humanities Coun.l/NEH, 1996, Rsch. grant, Wichita Cmty. Found., 1996, Multicultural Activity grant, Kans. Arts Commn./Nat. Endowment for the Arts, 1997, Folk Arts Apprenticeship grant, Kans. State Hist. Soc./Nat. Endowment for the Arts, 1997. Mem.: Wichita Blues Soc., Kans. Folklore Soc., Am. Fedn. Musicians Local #297. Personal E-mail: Rowfant@hotmail.com.

O'CONNOR, PAUL DANIEL, lawyer; b. Paterson, N.J., Nov. 24, 1936; s. Paul Daniel and Anne Marie Christopher O'C.; m. Melissa Monson; children: Steven Paul, Sheryl Lynn, Laura Ann. BS in Engring, U.S. Naval Acad., 1959; LLB, U. Va., 1965. Bar: N.Y. 1965, Calif. 1995. Assoc. firm Winthrop, Stimson, Putnam & Roberts, N.Y.C., 1965-72, partner, 1972-80; sr. v.p., gen. counsel Singer Co., Stamford, Conn., 1980-86; chief exec. officer Citation Builders, 1986-95; trustee Valley Trusts, Oakland, Calif., 1986—. 1st lt. USAF, 1959-62. Mem.: Sonoma County Bar Assn., Bar Assn. San Francisco, Assn. Bar City NY, Fairfield County Hunt Club. Home: 1150 Lombard St # 2 San Francisco CA 94109-9103 Office: Valley Trusts 1939 Harrison St Ste 555 Oakland CA 94612-3586 also: 141 North St Healdsburg CA 95448-3821

O'CONNOR, PEGGY LEE, communications manager; b. Chgo., Apr. 20, 1953; BS in Biology, Northeastern Ill. U., 1982; MBA, No. Ill. U., 1985. Emergency med. technologist, 1976-82; instr. Chgo. City Wide Colls., 1976-81; program dir. U. Ill. Hosp., 1979-81, Fermilab, Roselle, Ill., 1978-81; dist. mgr. Decision Data Svc., Schaumburg, 1981-89; gen. mgr. sales svc. Putnam Pub., 1989-91; mgr. fin. and adminstrn. Weyerhaeuser, 1991-93; ops. mgr. Ameritech Cellular, 1993-96, telesales mgr., 1996-98, customer care mgr., 1999; program mgr. ops. mgmt. Verizon Wireless (formerly Ameritech Cellular), 2000—. Program dir. Am. Cellular Women's Adv. Panel. Recipient awrd Summit Club, 1987, 88, 89. Mem. NAFE, NWAAR, Women in Bus., Pres.'s Club, BPA (chmn. bd. dirs.), Chgo. Credit Mgrs. Assn. Avocation: computers. Office: Verizon Wireless 777 Big Timber Rd Elgin IL E-mail: peggy.oconnor@verizonwireless.com.

O'CONNOR, R. D. retired health care executive; BS in Psychology and Sociology, U. So. Miss., 1960, MS Adminstrv. Pers., 1961, PhD Mgmt. and Orgnl. Comm., 1983. Asst. dean student affairs Holmes Jr. Coll., Goodman, Mo., 1961-64; spl. counselor vocat. rehab. divsn. Dept. Edn., Jackson, 1964-65; asst. adminstr. Hinds Gen. Hosp., 1965-68; adminstr. Rankin Gen. Hosp., Brandon, 1968-76; v.p. Human Resources/ Mktg. Delta Mgmt. Systems, Metairie, La., 1976-79; asst. to exec. dir. Bapt. Med. Ctr., Jacksonville, Fla., 1979-82; pres. RiverGroup Riverside Hosp., Rivercorp Inc., Riverside Found., 1982-87; owner O'Connor & Assocs., 1987-91; pres. Fla. 1st: Managed Health Care, Winter Haven, Orlando & Tampa, 1991-94; dir. orgn. devel. Mid Florida Med. Svcs. Inc., Winter Haven, 1994-97. Instr. U. So. Miss., Hattiesburg, Ms.; tchr., lectr. various univs., C.C.s, military acads.; grad. faculty coord. Webster U. Contbr. articles to profl. jours. and books. Commr. Cleary Heights Sewer Dist., 1978-79; pres'. selective task force Induction Procedures, 1969; chmn. personnel com. San Jose Baptist Ch., 1981-86, strategic planning com., 1986-87; gov's. com. Statewide Planning Vocat. Rehab., 1968; bd. dirs. Rankin County C. of C., 1970-73, exec. com., chmn. health affairs com., 1970-72, chmn. highway com. 1970-74, fin. com. 1971-73), Family Blood Assurance Program, 1972-77, v.p. 1977, Vol. Action Coun., 1973-76, United Givers Fund, 1973-76. With Army Security Agy., Air Nat. Guard, Med. Svc. Corps., ret. Fellow Am. Coll. Healthcare Execs. (life); mem. Fla. Hosp. Assn. (com. chmn. 1984), Greater Jacksonville Area Hosp. Coun. (chmn. 1985), Jackson-Vicksburg Hosp. Coun. (chmn. 1974), Nat. Assn. Mental Health (bd. dirs. 1973-74), Miss. Assn. Mental Health (pres. 1972-74), Miss. Hosp. Assn. (bd. dirs .1973-76, exec. devel. com. 1972-75, mgmt. engring. adminstrv. bd. 1973, fin. com. 1972-74, chmn. nominating com. 1971, coord. divsn. profl. practice 1970). Home: 4049 Cypress Landing East Winter Haven FL 33884-2408

O'CONNOR, RALPH STURGES, investment company executive; b. Pasadena, Calif., Aug. 27, 1926; s. Thomas Ireland and Edith Masury (Sturges) O'C.; m. Alice Maconda Brown, Apr. 28, 1950; children— George Rufus, Thomas Ireland III, Nancy Isabel, John Herman. BA, Johns Hopkins U., 1951; postgrad., Harvard U., 1967. With Highland Resources, Inc., Houston, 1951-87, exec. v.p., 1961-64, pres., 1964-87; pres., chief exec. officer Ralph S. O'Connor and Assocs., 1987—. Chmn. bd. Arnaud's Restaurant, New Orleans, Texas Ice, Clear Lake, Tex. Trustee emeritus Rice U., Johns Hopkins U., Houston Oldfields Sch., Glencoe, Md.; pres., The Marian and Speros Martel Found., Houston, 1983—. With USAAF, 1943-46. Mem. NAS (Pres.'s Circle), Am. Assn. Petroleum Landmen, All Am. Wildcatters, Houston Landmen's Assn. (past pres.), The Johns Hopkins Instns., Presdl. Counselors. Clubs: Bayou (Houston), Coronado (Houston), River Oaks Country (Houston), Petroleum (Houston). Home: 5627 Indian Cir Houston TX 77056-1006 Office: Ralph S O'Connor & Assocs 1001 Fannin St Ste 622 Houston TX 77002-6799 E-mail: ralphsoconnor@yahoo.com.

O'CONNOR, ROD, chemist, consultant, inventor; b. Cape Girardeau, Mo., July 4, 1934; s. Jay H. and Flora (Winters) O'C.; m. Shirley Ann Sander, Aug. 7, 1955; children: Mark Alan (dec.), Kara Ann, Shanna Suzanne, Timothy Patrick. BS, S.E. Mo. State Coll., 1955; PhD, U. Calif., Berkeley, 1958. Asst. prof. chemistry U. Omaha, 1958-60, Mont. State Coll., 1960-63; assoc. prof. chemistry Mont. State U., Bozeman, 1963-66; assoc. prof., coordinator gen. chemistry Kent (Ohio) State U., 1966-67; prof., dir. 1st year chemistry U. Ariz., Tucson, 1968-72; staff assoc. Adv. Council on Coll. Chemistry Stanford (Calif.) U., 1967-68; vis. prof. Wash. State U., Pullman, 1972-73; prof. chemistry Tex. A&M, College Station, 1973-86; pres. Texas ROMEC Inc., 1983-98; prof. environ. studies Baylor U., Waco, Tex., 1996-99. Cons. insect venoms Hollister-Stier Labs., Spokane, Wash., 1963-67; lab. separates editor W.H. Freeman Co., 1968-78; ednl. cons. TUCARA-4 Media Resources, Inc., 1971-74; mem. Coll. Chemistry Cons. Service; vis. scientist, tour lectr. Am. Chem. Soc., 1970-86. Author: (with T. Moeller) Ions in Aqueous Systems, 1972, Fundamentals of Chemistry, 1981, (with C. Mickey and A. Hassell) Solving Problems in Chemistry, 1981, (with L. Peck and K. Irgolic) Fundamentals of Chemistry in The Laboratory, 1981, (with T.E. Taylor and P. Glenn) Toward Success in College, 1981, (with A. Hassell and C. Mickey) Advanced Problems in Applied Chemistry, 2000; films Laboratory Safety, 1971; Contbr. articles to profl. jours.; patentee in field Recipient nat. teaching award Mfg. Chemists Assn., 1978; 4 regional teaching awards. Fellow AAAS, Am. Inst. Chemists, Sigma Xi; mem. Internat. Soc. Toxinology, Am. Chem. Soc. Office: Chem Consulting Svcs 1300 Angelina Cir College Station TX 77840-4855 E-mail: docroc34@hotmail.com.

O'CONNOR, SANDRA DAY, United States supreme court justice; b. El Paso, Tex., Mar. 26, 1930; d. Harry A. and Ada Mae (Wilkey) Day; m. John Jay O'Connor, III, Dec. 1952; children: Scott, Brian, Jay. AB in Econs. with great distinction, Stanford U., 1950, LLB, 1952. Bar: Calif., Ariz. Dep. county atty., San Mateo, Calif., 1952—53; civilian atty. Q.M. Market Ctr., Frankfurt am Main, Germany, 1954—57; pvt. practice Phoenix, 1958—65; asst. atty. gen. State of Ariz., 1965—69; state senator Ariz., 1969—75; chmn. com. on state, county and mcpl. affairs, 1972—73; majority leader, 1973—74; judge Maricopa County Superior Ct., 1975—79, Ariz. Ct. Appeals, 1979—81; assoc. justice U.S. Supreme Ct., 1981—. Referee juvenile ct. Maricopa County, 1962—64; chmn. vis. bd. Maricopa County Juvenile Detention Home, 1963—64; mem. Maricopa County Bd. Adjustments and Appeals, 1963—64, Anglo-Am. Legal Exchange, 1980, Maricopa County Superior Ct. Judges Tng. and Edn. Com., 1977—79, Maricopa Ct. Study Com.; chair com. to reorganize lower cts. Ariz. Supreme Ct., 1974—75; faculty Robert A. Taft Inst. Govt.; mem. Ariz. Criminal Code Commn., 1974—76; bd. visitors Ariz. State U. Law Sch., 1981, liaison com. on med. edn., 81. Mem. bd. editors: Stanford (Calif.) U. Law Rev. Mem. Ariz. Pers. Commn., 1968—69, Nat. Def. Adv. Com. on Women in Svcs., 1974—76; trustee Heard Mus., Phoenix, 1968—74, 1976—81, pres., 1980—81; mem. adv. bd. Phoenix Salvation Army, 1975—81; trustee Stanford U., 1976—81, Phoenix County Day Sch.; mem. citizens adv. bd. Blood Svcs., 1975—77; nat. bd. dirs. Smithsonian Assocs., 1981—, Colonial Williamsburg Found., 1988—2000; exec. bd. Ctrl. Eastern European Law Initiative, 1990—; adv. bd., v.p. NCCJ, Maricopa County, 1977—81; bd. dirs., sec. Ariz. Acad, 1969—75, Cathedral chpt. Washington Nat. Cathedral, 1991—99; past Rep. dist. chmn.; bd. dirs. Phoenix Cmty. Coun., 1969—75, Jr. Achievement Ariz., 1975—79, Blue Cross/Blue Shield Ariz., 1975—79, Channel 8, 1975—79, Phoenix Hist. Soc., 1974—78, Maricopa County YMCA, 1978—81, Golden Gate Settlement. Named Woman of Yr., Phoenix Advt. Club, 1972, National Women's Hall of Fame, 1995; recipient Ann. award, NCCJ, 1975, Disting. Achievement award, Ariz. State U., 1980, Sara Lee Frontrunner award, 1997, ABA medal, 1997. Mem.: ABA (select law enforcement revision commn. vice chair 1979—80), Maricopa County Bar Assn. (referral svc. chair 1960—62), Calif. Bar Assn., Ariz. Bar Assn. (legal edn., pub. rels. com., lower ct. reorgn. com.), Soroptimist Club (Phoenix). Office: US Supreme Ct Supreme Ct Bldg 1 First St NE Washington DC 20543*

O'CONNOR, SHEILA ANNE, freelance writer; b. Paisley, Scotland, Jan. 20, 1960; came to the U.S., 1988; d. Brian Aubrey Witham and Margaret Kirk (Reid) Davies; m. Frank Donal O'Connor, Aug. 9, 1986; children: David Michael, Andrew James, Christine Charlotte. BA in French and German, Strathclyde U., 1980, postgrad. diploma in office studies, 1981, MBA, 1992. Office asst. BBC, London, 1982-83; asst. to mng. dir. Unimatic Engrs. Ltd., 1983-84; freelance word processing operator, 1984-88; staff asst. Internat. Monetary Fund, Washington, 1988-94; prin. Internat. Media Assn., 1988—. Co-author: Chocolate for a Woman's Spirit, 1999; contbr. articles to profl. jours. Mem. Am. Mktg. Assn., Bay Area Travel Writers Assn., Calif. Writers Club. Avocations: animals, travel. Home and Office: 1974 46th Ave San Francisco CA 94116-1005 E-mail: sheila.oconnor@juno.com.

O'CONNOR, STEPHEN JAMES, healthcare educator; b. East Orange, N.J., May 1, 1956; s. Richard James O'Connor, Dorothy O'Connor; m. Vicki O'Connor; children: Lauren, Maggie. AAS, C.C. Morris, 1976; BS, Ind. U., 1979, MPA, 1981; MBA, U. Dallas, 1984; PhD, U. Ala., 1988. Asst. prof. St. Louis U., 1988—90; assoc. prof. U. Wis., Milw., 1990—2000; assoc. prof., dir. MS in Health Adminstrn. U. Ala., Birmingham, 2000—. Bd. trustees Village of Fox Point, Fox Point, 1997—2000. Mem.: Acad. Mgmt., Am. Coll. Healthcare Execs. (Health Mgmt. Rsch. award 1998, 2001). Office: U Ala Webb 508 1530 3d Ave S Birmingham AL 35294-3361

O'CONNOR, THOMAS EDWARD, petroleum geologist, management consultant; b. Boston, Dec. 16, 1936; s. John Stephen and Lucille (Arnold) O'C.; m. Jeannette Canuel, June 30, 1962 (dec. Mar. 1976); children: Kevin Patrick, David Andrew, Shelley Elizabeth; m. Moufida Banawi, Apr. 28, 1977; children: Tammer Thomas, Amr Adel Hammouda. BSc, Stanford U., 1958; MSc., U. Colo., 1961. Geologist Amoco Prodn. West, Denver, 1963-67, Amoco Netherlands, Utrecht, 1968-69, Amoco Europe, London, 1969-74; chief geologist Gulf of Suez Petroleum Co., Cairo, 1974-79; geol. mgr. Amoco Africa, Mid East, Houston, 1979-80; v.p. Aminoil, 1980-84; prin. petroleum engr. The World Bank, Washington, 1985-98; internat. petroleum mgmt. cons., 1998—. Presenter numerous sci. confs., seminars, workshops in U.S. and abroad, 1976—. Lt. USNR, 1960-63. Mem. AAAS, Am. Assn. Petroleum Geologists (cert. petroleum geologist), Geol. Soc. Am., Houston Geol. Soc. Moslem. Home and Office: 3637 Winfield Ln NW Washington DC 20007-2350 E-mail: teoconnor@aol.com.

O'CONNOR, TOM, corporate executive, management consultant; b. Boston, June 11, 1942; s. Thomas Henry and Blanche (Cosgrove) O'C.; m. Mary Alice Kelly; 1 child, Michael Kelly O'Connor. BA in econs., U. Mass., 1971; postgrad., U. Wis., Milw., 1971-73, U. Del., 1978, Am. U., 1980. Economist Interstate Commerce Commn., Washington, 1973-74; mgr. planning U.S. Railway Assn., 1974-75; cons. transp. R.L. Banks & Assocs., 1975-77; asst. dir. Conrail, Phila., 1977-79; asst. v.p. econs. Assn. Am. R.R.'s, Washington, 1979-82; v.p. DNS Assocs., Inc., Washington, Lexington (Mass.), 1982-88; v.p., ptnr. Snavely, King, Majoros, O'Connor & Lee, Inc., Washington, 1988—. Chmn. surface freight transport regulation com. Transp. Rsch. Bd., 1994—. Pres. Green Briar Civic Assn., Fairfax, Va., 1985, Greenbriar Dem. Club, Fairfax, 1984-89, Greenbriar Community Ctr., Fairfax, 1984; v.p. Greenbriar West PTA, Fairfax, 1986-88. Sgt. U.S. Army, 1963-66. Mem. Am. Econ. Assn., Am. Statis. Assn., Coun. Logistics Mgmt., Transp. Rsch. Forum (pres. Washington chpt. 1987-89), Nat. Def. Assn. (bd. dirs. 1991-94), Air Force Assn., Phi Beta Kappa, Phi Kappa Phi. Democrat. Roman Catholic. Avocations: camping, reading, counseling. Home: 13222 Point Pleasant Dr Fairfax VA 22033-3515 Office: Snavely King Majoros O'Connor & Lee Inc 1220 L St NW Ste 410 Washington DC 20005-4050 Fax: (202) 842-4966. E-mail: skmoltom1@aol.com.

O'CONNOR, WILLIAM CHARLES, automobile agency finance executive; b. Poplar Bluff, Mo., July 19, 1943; s. Thomas Francis and Luella Darlene (Davis) O'C.; m. Leigh Volkening, Dec. 21, 1975 (div. May 1992); children: Kelli, Megan, Katie. BA in English, Memphis State U., 1966. High rigger Boiler Makers Union, St. Louis, 1968-70; br. mgr. Pub. Fin. Corp., 1970-74; fin. specialist Pat Ryan & Assocs., Chgo., 1974-77; fin. mgr. Drew Ford, La Mesa, Calif., 1978-80; fin. dir. Honda of Pasadena, 1980-89, Goudy Honda, Alhambra, 1989-94, Honda of Pasadena, 1995-99. Cons. Am. Honda Fin. Corp., Torrance, 1987—. Contbr. articles to profl. jours. Mem. Fin. and Ins. Profls., KC, Jr. C. of C., Young Dems. Orgn. (pres. 1968-69). Avocations: L.A. marathon 1987, golf, fishing. Home: 613 E Camellia Dr Covina CA 91723-3608 Office: 1965 E Foothill Blvd Pasadena CA 91107-3218

O'CONNOR, WILLIAM MATTHEW, lawyer; b. Pensacola, Fla., Apr. 5, 1955; s. William Francis and Rosalind (Shea) O'C.; m. Mary Patricia Keepnews, Oct. 13, 1984; children: William Lawrence, Thomas Patrick, Robert Austin. BS in Psychology, Fordham U., 1977, JD, 1980. Bar: N.Y. 1981, N.J. 1987, U.S. Dist. Ct. N.J. 1987, U.S. Dist. Conn. 1988, U.S. Dist. Ct. (so., ea., no. and we. dists.) N.Y., 1981, U.S. Ct. Appeals (2nd cir.) 1983, U.S. Ct. Appeals (3d cir.) 1996. Intern N.Y. Atty. Gen., N.Y.C., 1978-79; legis. intern Am. Lung Assn., 1979; assoc. Keane & Butler, 1979-81, Keane & Beane, White Plains, N.Y., 1981-83, Cooperman, Levitt & Winikoff, P.C., N.Y.C., 1983-86; sr. assoc. Sullivan, Donovan, Hanrahan & Silliere, 1986-87; ptnr. O'Connor Reddy & Seeler, 1987-95, Harris Beach & Wilcox LLP, N.Y.C., 1995-2000, Buchanan Ingersoll PC, N.Y.C., 2000—. Author: Lobbying Guidebook Am. Lung Assn., 1979. Contbr. articles to profl. jours. Legis. com. pub. schs., White Plains, 1981-82; councilman Town of Pelham, N.Y., 1998—. Mem. ABA, Fed. Bar Coun., N.Y. State Bar Assn. (mem. comml. and fed. litigation sect., creditor's rights com. 1989—), Westchester Bar Assn. (editor in chief Jour. 1983-89, mem. labor law com. 1981—, com. on profl. ethics 1989—), Fordham ILJ Alumni Assn. (bd. dirs. 1984—), New Rochelle Bar Assn. Republican. Roman Catholic. Home: 684 Esplanade Pelham NY 10803-2403 Office: Buchanan Ingersoll PC 140 Broadway New York NY 10005 E-mail: oconnorwn@bipc.com.

O'CONNOR, WILLIAM MICHAEL, executive search company executive; b. Chgo., Sept. 28, 1947; s. Maurice Francis and Margaret (Brand) O'C.; m. Karen Jean Gipson, Jan. 30, 1972; children: Sean, Mary, William, David. BA in History, Loyola U., Chgo., 1970. Interviewer Ill. State Employment Svc., Chgo., 1970-73; ins. agt. Equitable Life Assurance Soc., 1973-76; recruiting officer U.S. Army, 1977-78; profl. employment rep. GTE Network Systems, Northlake, Ill., 1978-81; employment mgr. Molex, Inc., Lisle, 1981-85, Rand McNally & Co., Skokie, 1986; v.p. Richards Cons., Ltd., Chgo., 1987-88; v.p., ptnr. Chestnut Hill Ptnrs., Deerfield, Ill., 1988-95; v.p. Kennedy & Co., Chgo., 1995-2001; pres. Edgewood Internat., Woodridge, Ill., 2001—. Mem. Art Inst. Chgo., Smithsonian Inst., Field Mus. Natural History, Rep. Nat. Com., 1984—. Lt. col. USAR, 1971-99. Decorated Chevalier, Sovereign Mil. Order of Temple of Jerusalem, 1998—. Mem. Res. Officers Assn., U.S. Armor Assn. (Order of St. George), Mil. Police Assn., 337th Cavalry Regiment (Order of the Spur), Bus. Mobilized for Loyola U. Roman Catholic. Home: 3018 Edgewood Pky Woodridge IL 60517 Office: Edgewood Internat 3018 Edgewood Pkwy Woodridge IL 60517 E-mail: theheadhuntingone@yahoo.com., wocatedgewood@aol.com.

O'CONNOR, WILLIAM THOMAS, retired surgeon; b. Elizabeth, N.J., Sept. 17, 1925; MB, BChir, Nat. U. Ireland, 1954. Diplomate Am. Bd. Surgery. Intern Jersey City Med. Ctr., 1954-55; resident E. Orange VA Hosp., N.J., 1956-61, Francis Delafield Hosp., N.Y.C., 1957; pvt. practice, 1961—2001; ret., 2001. Fellow ACS; mem. AMA. Address: PO Box 1329 Sykesville MD 21784 E-mail: wiltcon@aol.com.

O'CONNOR QUINN, DEIRDRE, lawyer; b. N.Y.C., Feb. 19, 1966; d. Raymond and Roisin O'Connor; m. Patrick T. Quinn, Sept. 8, 1990; children: Malachy, Oona, Maeve. BS in Commerce, U. Va., 1987; JD, Boston Coll., 1990; LLM in Taxation, NYU, 1994. CPA Va.; bar: N.Y. 1991. Assoc. White & Case, N.Y.C., 1990-95; v.p., corp. counsel tax sect. Prudential Fin., Newark, 1995—. Mem. AICPA, Assn. of Bar of City of N.Y., N.Y. State Bar Assn. Office: Prudential 213 Washington St Newark NJ 07102-2917 E-mail: deirdre.o'connor_quinn@prudential.com.

O'CONNOR TAYLOR, SHERYL ANN, medical services administrator; b. Rome, Jan. 26, 1951; d. Robert W. and Phyllis M. (Lambert) Nippler; 1 child, Ashley. BS, Ea. Mich. U., 1972; LPN, Washtenaw Community Coll., Ann Arbor, Mich., 1976; RN, Santa Ana Coll., 1980; MA Bus. Mgmt., U. Redlands, 1983. Cert. RN, cert. pub. health nurse, lic. healthcare risk mgr., cert. case mgr., cert. quality assurance/utilization mgmt., cert. med. staff coord., cert. provider credentialing specialist, cert. legal nurse cons., registered health information tech. Med.-surg./oncology nurse Western Med. Ctr., Santa Ana, Calif.; community health nurse Vis. Nurse Assn., Orange; hosp. adminstr. USN Med. Svcs. Corps., Jacksonville, Fla., 1985-88; ins. coord. Blue Cross/Blue Shield Fla., Pensacola, 1988-90; ctr. dir. Singleday Surgery, Jacksonville, 1990-91; dir. quality mgmt. Humana Hosp., Orange Park, Fla., 1991-92; dir. med. affairs Humana Health Plans, Maitland, 1992-93; dir. health svcs. PCA/Century Med. Health Plans, Inc., Orlando, 1993-94; dir. nursing Nations Healthcare Inc., Jacksonville, 1994-95; dir. central credentials and privileging dept. USN Healthcare Support Office, 1995-99; corp. risk mgr. Universal Health Svcs. Inc., King of Prussia, Pa., 1999-2001; dir. risk mgmt. Children's Nat. Med. Ctr., Washington, 2001—. Mem. Am. Coll. Healthcare Execs., Am. Bd. Quality Assurance and Utilization Physicians, Naval Res. Assn., Nat. Assn. Med. Staff Svcs., Am. Soc. Healthcare Risk Mgmt., Am. Health Info. Mgmt. Assn. E-mail: meka@pivot.net.

OCRANT, IAN, pediatric endocrinologist; b. Buffalo, Nov. 13, 1954; s. Lawrence and Nancy Jean (Harris) O.; m. Peggy Ann Kondo, Apr. 21, 1978. BA, Univ. Colo., 1975, MD, 1979; MBA with distinction in entrepreneurship, Calif. State U., Fresno, 2002. Diplomate Am. Bd. Pediatrics, Am. Bd. Pediatric Endocrinology. Pediatric residency Stanford (Calif.) Univ., 1979-82; pediatrician U.S. Air Force, 1982-86; pediatric endocrin fellowship Stanford Univ., 1986-89; pediatric endocrinologist Brown Univ., Providence, 1989-93; dir. pediatric endocrine clinic Rhode Island Hosp., 1989-93; pediat. endocrinologist Valley Children's Hosp., Fresno, Calif., 1994—. Contbr. articles to profl. jours. With USAF, 1982-86. Recipient Individual Nat. Rsch. Svc. award Nat. Inst. Health, 1987-89. Fellow Am. Coll. Endocrinology; mem. Endocrine Soc., Lawson Wilkins Pediatric Endocrine Soc., Am. Fedn. Clin. Rsch. Office: Valley Children's Hospital 9300 Valley Childrens Pl Madera CA 93638-8762

O'CROWLEY, JAMES FRANCIS, III, management executive; b. Troy, N.Y., Aug. 13, 1953; s. James Francis Jr. and Mary Ruth (Faubion) O'C.; m. Susan Gail Jordan, May 11, 1985 (div. Dec. 1988). AA, Menlo Coll., 1974; BS, U. Kans., 1976; MBA, Harvard U., 1978. Product controller Internat. Harvester, Chgo., 1978-79, asst. to pres., 1979-80, asst. to sr. v.p., 1980-82, mgr. divestiture, 1982-83, mgr. market research, 1983-85; dir. product devel. Navistar (formerly Internat. Harvester), 1985-87, dir. product cycle time, 1988-89; gen. mgr. Latin Am. & Asian ops. J.I. Case, Racine, Wis., 1990—, dir. ops. and fin. internat. corp., 1992—. Bd. dirs. Coalter Investment, Overland Park, Kans. Active United Way, Chgo., 1982. Mem.: Chgo. Curling; N.Y. Athletic, Harvard (N.Y.C.). Avocations: skiing, sailing, camping, golf. Home: 270 E Highland Ave Apt 623 Milwaukee WI 53202-6606 Office: JI Case 700 State St Racine WI 53404-3392

OCTAVIANI, HECTOR, pediatrician; b. Ponce, P.R., Mar. 6, 1956; s. Hector and Maita (Olivieri) O.; m. Mayda I. Lugo, May 8, 1980; 1 child, Dalimar. MD, U. P.R., 1982. Diplomate Am. Bd. Pediatrics. Staff pediatrician Ctrl. Fla. Family Health Ctr., Sanford, 1985—, med. dir., 1998—. Office: Ctrl Fla Family Health Ctr 2400 State Road 415 Sanford FL 32771-6012 E-mail: octhec@pol.net.

OCVIRK, OTTO GEORGE, artist; b. Detroit, Nov. 13, 1922; s. Joseph and Louise (Ekle) O.; m. Betty Josephine Lebie, June 11, 1949; children: Robert Joseph, Thomas Frederick, Carol Louise. B.F.A., State U. Iowa, 1949, M.F.A., 1950. Advt. artist apprentice Bass-Luckoff Advt. Agy., Detroit, 1941; engring. draftsman Curtiss-Wright Aircraft Corp., Buffalo, 1942; faculty Bowling Green (Ohio) State U., 1950—, assoc. prof., 1960-65, prof. art, 1965-85, prof. emeritus, 1985—. Exhibited in group shows at, Denver Mus. Art, 1949, 50, 53, Detroit Inst. Art, 71948, 49, 50, 53, 56, Dayton (Ohio) Art Inst., 1950, 51, 56, Ohio State U., 1953, Walker Art Center, Mpls., 1948, 49, Library of Congress, Washington, 1949, Bklyn. Mus., 1949, Joslyn Mus., Omaha, 1949, Colorado Springs Fine Arts Center, 1949; represented in permanent collections, Detroit Inst. Arts, Dayton Art Inst., Friends of Am. Art, Grand Rapids, Mich., State U. Iowa, Iowa City, Bowling Green State U.; (Recipient 24 nat., regional juried art exhbn. awards 1947-57, others.); Author: (with R. Stinson, P. Wigg, R. Bone and David Cayton) Art Fundamentals— Theory and Practice, 1960-97, 7th edit., 1994, 8th edit., 1997, 9th edit., 2001. Scoutmaster Toledo Area council Boy Scouts Am., 1960-63, asst. scoutmaster, 1963-74, dist. commr., 1978-80. Served with AUS, 1943-46. Recipient Silver Beaver award Boy Scouts Am., 1976, Magnifico award Medici Circle, Bowling Green State U., 1987. Mem. Delta Phi Delta (hon.) Methodist. Home and Office: 231 Haskins Rd Bowling Green OH 43402-2206 *"Freedom for expression" keys creative thought into a productive whole.*

OCZKOWICZ, EDYTA KATARZYNA, English educator; b. Cracow, Poland, Aug. 30, 1964; came to U.S., 1985; d. Jerzy and Wladyslawa Oczkowicz. BA in English, Albright Coll., 1988; MA in English, Lehigh U., 1990, PhD in English, 1994. Assoc. prof. English, dir. Writing Ctr., chmn. English dept. Salem (N.C.) Coll., 1994—. Translator Wladimir de Terlikowski, 1999; contbr. articles to profl. jours. Lehigh U. scholar, 1988-91, grantee, 1991-94. Mem. MLA, Mulli-Ethnic Lit. in U.S., Nat. Coun. Tchrs. English. Avocations: hiking, sailing, skiing, movies, travel. Home: 1043 Miller St Winston Salem NC 27103-4440 Office: Salem Coll Dept English PO Box 10548 Winston Salem NC 27108-0548 E-mail: Edyta@salem.edu.

O'DAY, ANITA BELLE COLTON, entertainer, singer; b. Chgo., Dec. 18, 1919; d. James and Gladys (Gill) C. Student, Chgo. public schs. Singer and entertainer various Chgo. Music Clubs, 1939-41; singer with Gene Krupa's Orch., 1941-45, Stan Kenton Orch., 1944, Woody Herman Orch., 1945, Benny Goodman Orch., 1959; singing tours in U.S. and abroad, 1947—; rec. artist Polygram, Capitol, Emily Records, Verve, GNP Crescendo, Columbia, London, Signature, DRG, Pablo; million-seller songs include Let Me Off Uptown, 1941, And Her Tears Flowed Like Wine, 1944, Boogie Blues, 1945; appeared in films Gene Krupa Story, 1959, Jazz on a Summer's Day, 1960, Zigzag, 1970, Outfit, 1974; TV shows 60 Minutes, 1980; Tonight Show, Dick Cavett Show, Today Show, Big Band Bash, CBS Sunday Morning, CNN Showbiz Today; inductee Jazz Hall of Fame, Tampa, 1997, Nat. Endowment Fellowship. Author: High Times, Hard Times, 1981, rev. edit., 1989; performed 50 yr. anniversary concert Carnegie Hall, 1985, Avery Fisher Hall, 1989, Tanglewood, 1990, JVC Festival Town Hall, 1993, Rainbow and Stars, 1995, JVC Festival Carnegie Hall, 1996, JVC Festival Avery Fisher Hall, 1999, Hollywood Palladium, 1999, Blue Note, N.Y.C., 2000, Atlas Supper Club, Los Angeles, 2000, Fez, N.Y.C., 2001, Plus Room, San Francisco, 2002; currently touring worldwide; albums include Drummer Man, Kenton Era, Anita, Anita Sings The Most, Pick Yourself Up, Lady is a Tramp, An Evening with Anita O'Day, At Mr. Kelly's, Swings Cole Porter, Travelin' Light, All the Sad Young Men, Waiter Make Mine Blues, With the Three Sounds, I Told Ya I Love Ya Now Get Out, Uptown, My Ship, Live in Tokyo, Anita Sings the Winners, Incomparable, Anita 1975, Live at Mingos, Anita O'Day/The Big Band Sessions, Swings Rodgers and Hart, Time for Two, Tea for Two, In a Mellowtone (Grammy nomination 1990), At Vine St. Live, Mello'Day, Live at the City, Angel Eyes, The Night Has a Thousand Eyes, The Rules of the Road, Jazz Masters, Skylark, Swingtime in Hawaii, SS 'Wonderful (Carnegie Hall), Jazz Past Midnight, Compact Jazz, Let Me Off Uptown, The Complete Verve/Cleff Sessions, Ultimate Anita O'Day, After Midnight, Hi-Ho Trailus Bootwhip, Legends of the Swing Era, The Legacy Lives On, Finest Hour, complete Signature and London Recordings.. Jazz Masters fellow Nat. Endowment for the Arts, 1997. Mem. AFTRA, Screen Actors Guild, BMI. Office: Alan Eichler 6064 Selma Ave Los Angeles CA 90028-6415 *From the time I was twelve or thirteen, my life was music. I never thought about being on top. I only wanted to be a part of the scene.*

O'DAY, DENIS MICHAEL, ophthalmologist, educator; b. Melbourne, Victoria, Australia, Dec. 10, 1935; came to U.S., 1967; s. Kevin John and Bernadette John (Hay) O'D.; m. Ann Georgina Despard, May 28, 1966; children: Luke Gerard, Simon Patrick, Edward Daniel. Diploma, Xavier Coll., 1953; MBBS, Melbourne U., 1960. Diplomate Am. Bd. Ophthalmology. Intern St. Vincent's Hosp./U. Melbourne, 1961; resident in internal medicine

St. Vincent's Hosp., 1962-64, chief resident dept. medicine, 1964, clin. asst. medicine, 1965-66; 3d asst., mem. asst. Royal Victoria Eye & Ear Hosp., Melbourne, 1967-70; resident in ophthalmology U. Calif., San Francisco, 1970; Wellcome rsch. fellow in corneal disease Inst. Opthalmology, London, 1970-72; asst. prof. ophthalmology Vanderbilt U. Sch. Medicine, Nashville, 1972-74, assoc. prof. ophthalmology, 1974-77, prof. ophthalmology, now chmn., 1977-92, chmn. ophthalmology dept., 1992—; exec. dir. Am. Bd. Ophthalmology, Bala Cynwyd. Cons. ophthalmologist Royal Commonwealth Soc. of Blind, Nigeria, 1972; cons. VA Hosp., 1973-74, active staff, 74; mem. active staff Nashville Gen. Hosp., 1974, Park View Hosp., 1980, Vanderbilt Hosp., 1972; mem. cons. staff St. Thomas Hosp.; bd. dirs. Am. Bd. Ophthalmology, Phila., 1988—; proctor lectr. U. Calif., San Francisco, 1993; co-med. dir. Lions Eye Bank and Sight Svc., 1973-86, med. dir. 1986—; bd. dirs. Lions Eye Bank Mid. Tenn., 1987—; ad-hoc mem. NIH Visual Sci. Study Sect., 1977. Author: Management of Functional Impairment due to Cataract, 1993; contbr. numerous articles, abstracts to profl. publs., chpts. to books. Chair ethics com. Cath. Pub. Policy Commn., Nashville, 1991—. Joyn Hayden rsch. fellow, 1965; recipient Felton Bequest and Potter Found. awards, 1967, recognition award Alcon Rsch. Inst., 1983, Sr. Sci. Investigator award Rsch. to Prevent Blindness, 1987, Health Profl. of Yr. award Tenn. chpt. Assn. for Edn. and Rehab. of Blind and Visually Impaired, 1990. Fellow ACS, Royal Australia Coll. Physicians, Royal Soc. Medicine, Am. Acad. Ophthalmology (sec. quality of care com. 1993—, Honor award for Ednl. Contbns. 1981-85, dir. clin. alert program, pub. health com. 1985-88); mem. AMA, AAUP, Am. Ophthalmol. Soc., Assn. for Rsch. in Vision and Ophthalmology, Nashville Acad. Medicine, Nashville Acad. Ophthalmology (v.p. 1980-81), Oxford Ophthalmol. Soc., Royal Australasian Coll. Physicians, Tenn. Acad. Medicine, Tenn. Acad. Ophthalmology. Roman Catholic. Avocation: sailing. Office: Vanderbilt U Med Ctr East Dept Ophthalmology Med Ctr Fl 8 Nashville TN 37232-0001*

O'DAY, JOHN IGNATIUS, retired computer science educator; b. Buffalo, May 30, 1938; s. John Ignatius and Jean Irene (McCarthy) O'D.; m. Giovanna Rose Foderaro, Aug. 24, 1963 (dec. May 1994); children: Domenique, Jeanne d'Arc, John Ignatius III, Cathleen, Frank; m. Theresa Marie Marzec, July 30, 1999. BS, Canisius Coll., 1963. Programmer analyst N.Y. State Civil Svc. Dept., Albany, 1964-66, U. Buffalo, 1966-67, Computer Task Group, Buffalo, 1967-70; info. systems mgr. Erie County Medicaid, 1974-81; v.p. LODOC, Inc., 1981-83; asst. prof. info. systems mgmt. Buffalo State Coll., 1983-88; dir. data processing Erie County, 1988-99, ret., 2000. Cons. in field. Contbr. articles to profl. jours. Active Erie County Dem. Com., Buffalo, 1976-82; zone chmn., 30th Zone City Buffalo, 1978-82. Mem. N.Y. All Campus Computer Procurement Com., Frontier Dems. Club (Buffalo) (chmn. steering com. 1982—). Roman Catholic. Avocations: music, football. Home: 3682 Briarwood Ct Hamburg NY 14075-2247

O'DAY, PAUL THOMAS, trade association executive; b. May 2, 1935; s. James Thomas and Jeannette Irene (Deschenes) O'D.; m. Nancy Frances Eitler, June 16, 1962; children: Kathleen, Maureen, Michael, Ellen. BA, Am. Internat. Coll., Springfield, Mass., 1958; JD, Georgetown U., 1963; MPA, Am. U., 1967; D of Pub. Adminstrn. honoris causa, Am. Internat. Coll., 1997. Bar: D.C. 1964, U.S. Supreme Ct. 1974. Patent examiner U.S. Patent Office, Washington, 1959-62; exec. sec. panel high-speed ground transp., auto. air poll. Dept. Commerce, 1965-66, staff asst. to sec., 1967-69, exec. asst. to sec., 1969-71, dep. dir. bur. domestic commerce, 1972-74; dep. dir. Nat. Bus. Coun. for Consumer Affairs, 1971-72; cons. to Gen. Counsel GE, Fairfield, Conn., 1974-75; asst. trade rep. Exec. Office of the Pres., Washington, 1975-77; dep. asst. sec. U.S. Dept. Commerce, 1978-84; pres. Am. Fiber Mfrs. Assn., 1984—. Chmn. Fiber Econs. Bur., 1984—; pres. Eisenhower World Affairs Inst., 1993-99, exec. com., 2000—. Corporator Am. Internat. Coll., 1974—; mem. governing coun. Shakespeare Theater Guild, 1989-2001. Recipient Constl. Law award Georgetown U. Law Ctr., 1962; Alumni award Am. Internat. Coll., 1970; Pres.'s Meritorious Exec. award., 1984; Nat. Inst. Pub. Affairs fellow Princeton U., 1964 Mem.: AAAS, Am. Chem. Soc., World Econ. Forum, Jussi Bjorling Soc. USA (charter), O'Dea Clan Assn. (Corofin, Ireland), Cosmos Club. Home: 8261 Private Ln Annandale VA 22003-4471 Office: Am Fiber Mfrs Assn 1530 Wilson Blvd Ste 690 Arlington VA 22209

ODDEN, ALLAN ROBERT, education educator; b. Duluth, Minn., Sept. 16, 1943; s. Robert Norman and Mabel Eleanor (Bjornnes) Odden; m. Eleanor Ann Rubottom, May 28, 1966; children: Sarina, Robert. BS, Brown U., 1965; MDiv, Union Theol. Sem., 1969; MA, Columbia U., 1971, PhD, 1975. Tchr. N.Y.C. Pub. Schs., 1967-72; rsch. assoc. Teachers' Coll. Columbia U., 1972-75; dir. policy Edn. Commn. of the States, Denver, 1975-84; prof. U. So. Calif., L.A., 1984-93, U. Wis., Madison, 1993—. Rsch. dir. Sch. Fin. Commns., Conn., 1974—75, SD, 1975—76, Mo., 1975—76, Mo., 1993, Mo., 94, NY, 1978—81, NJ, 1991—92; co-dir. Consortium Policy Rsch. Edn.; cons. Nat. Govs. Assn., Nat. Conf. State Legislatures, U.S. Sec. Edn., U.S. Senate, U.S. Dept. Edn., many state legislatures and govs.; nat. rsch. coun. task force sch. fin. equity adequacy and productivity, 1996—99; ct. master Superior Ct. N.J. in Abbott V. Burke Sch. Fin. Case, 1997—98. Author: (book) Education Leadership for America's Schools, 1995; co-author: Financing Schools for High Performance, 1998, Paying Teachers for What They Know and Do, 1997, Paying Teachers for What They Know and Do, 2d edit., 2002, School Finance: A Policy Perspective, 1992, School Finance: A Policy Perspective, 2d edit., 2000, Reallocating Resources: How to Boost Student Achievement Without Spending More, 2001; editor: Education Policy Implementation, 1991, Rethinking School Finance, 1992, School-Based Financing, 1999; contbr. articles to profl. jours., chapters to books. Mem. L.A. Chamber Edn. and Human Resources Commn., 1986, Gov.'s Sch. Fin. Commn., Calif., 1987, Calif. Assessment Policy Com., Gov.'s Edn. Task Force, Wis., 1996, Carnegie Corp. Task Force Edn. in the Early Yrs., 1994—96; mem. nat. rsch. coun. com. sch. fin. equity, adequcy and productivity, 1996—99; mem. Gov.'s Blue Ribbon Commn. State and Local Partnerships 21st Century, Wis., 2000. Grantee, Dept. Edn., Carnegie Corp., Spencer Found., Ford Found., Atlantic Philanthropic Svcs., Mellon Found., Carnegie Corp., Pew Charitable Trusts. Mem.: Nat. Soc. Study Edn., Politics Edn. Assn., Nat. Tax Assn., Am. Edn. Fin. Assn. (pres. 1979—80), Am. Ednl. Rsch. Assn. Avocations: Lionel training collecting, youth soccer, baseball coach. Home: 3128 Oxford Rd Madison WI 53705-2224 Office: U Wis Sch Edn Wis Ctr Edn Rsch 1025 W Johnson St # 653E Madison WI 53706-1706 E-mail: arodden@facstaff.wisc.edu.

ODDIS, JOSEPH ANTHONY, associations executive; b. Greensburg, Pa., Nov. 5, 1928; s. Giacinto and Felicetta (D'Amico) O.; m. Jeanne Trevena, July 10, 1954; children— Joseph Michael, Marie Theresa/ BS, Duquesne U., 1950; DSc (hon.), Mass. Coll. Pharmacy, 1975, Phila. Coll. Pharmacy and Sci., 1975, Albany Coll. Pharmacy, Union U., 1976, Duquesne U., 1989, Mercer U., 1995; LHD (hon.), L.I. U., 1991. Staff pharmacist Mercy Hosp., Pitts., 1950-51, asst. chief pharmacist, 1953-54; chief pharmacist Western Pa. Hosp., Pitts., 1954-56; staff rep. hosp. pharmacy Am. Hosp. Assn., Chgo., 1956-60; dir. div. hosp. pharmacy Am. Pharm., Washington, 1960-62; exec. v.p. Am. Soc. Health-System Pharmacists, 1960-98. Pres. Am. Soc. Hosp. Pharmacists Research and Edn. Found., 1986-98. Active Boy Scouts Am., Camp Fire Girls; Sec. Am. Soc. Health-System Pharmacists Research and Edn. Found., 1970-86. Served with AUS, 1951-53. Recipient 1st cert. Honor award Duquesne U. Sch. Pharmacy, 1969, named Outstanding Alumnus, 1978; recipient Harvey A.K. Whitney award Am. Soc. Hosp. Pharmacists, 1970, Julius Sturmer Meml. Lecture award Rho Chi soc. Phila., 1971, Howard C. Newton Lecture award 1977, Samuel Melendy Lecture award, 1978, Hugo H. Schaefer award, 1983, Reed and Alice Henninger Lecture award, 1984, Donald E. Francke medal, 1986, Remington medal award, 1990. Fellow AAAS; mem. Am. Pharm. Assn., Am. Soc. Hosp. Pharmacists, Am. Inst. History Pharmacy, Internat. Pharm. Fedn. (pres. hosp. pharmacy sect. 1977-81, v.p. 1984-86, pres. 1986-90), Drug Info. Assn., Am. Soc. Assn. Execs., Can. Soc. Hosp. Pharmacists (hon.), Soc. Hosp. Pharmacists Australia (hon.), Pharm. Soc. Gt. Britain (hon.), Pharm. Soc. Nigeria (hon.), Nat. Coun. Patient Info. and Edn. (sec. 1982-85), Israel Pharm. Soc. (hon.), Rho Chi, Kappa Psi (hon.), Duquesne U. Century Club (charter). Home: 6509 Rockhurst Rd Bethesda MD 20817-1661 Office: Am Soc Health-System Pharmacists 7272 Wisconsin Ave Bethesda MD 20814-4836

ODDSSON, LARS INGIMAR EUGEN, biomedical researcher; b. Reykavik, Iceland, May 7, 1954; came to U.S., 1993; s. Ingimar and Anna-Stina (Johnsson) O.; m. Annette Xenopoulos. Student program for civil engring., Linköping U., 1973-76; BSc, U. Coll. Phys. Edn. and Sports, Stockholm, 1981; D Med. Sci., Karolinska Inst., Stockholm, 1990. Cert. tchr., nat. team coach instr. Tchr., lectr. Sch. Phys. Edn. Karolinska Inst., Stockholm, 1982-93, rsch. engr., 1986-88; postdoctoral fellow NeuroMuscular Rsch. Ctr. Boston U., 1993, rsch. asst. prof., 1994-96, rsch. assoc. prof., 1996—. Head coach Sollentuna VK, Stockholm, 1982-91; asst. nat. team coach, Sweden, 1982-91. Contbr. articles to profl. jours.; inventor. Recipient Leadership in Sports Honor, Swedish Sports Fedn., 1985, Coach of Yr. award Swedish Volleyball Assn., 1989, Rsch. Grant Whitaker Found., 1995. Mem. Scandinavian Physiol. Soc., Internat. Soc. Biomechanics, Internat. Soc. Electrophys. Kinesiology. Avocations: composing, photography, skiing, tennis, volleyball. Home: 905 Beacon St Boston MA 02215-3710 Office: Boston U Neuro Muscular Rsch Ctr 19 Deerfield St Boston MA 02215-1904 E-mail: loddsson@bu.edu.

ODE, CAROL BUA, academic administrator; b. New Haven, Jan. 28, 1956; d. Nicholas Joseph and Frieda Regina (Spengler) Bua; m. Paul Hicks Ode Jr., Aug. 11, 1979; children: Eric Paul Nicholas, Lydia Carol, Jackson Paul Joseph. BA, U. Vt., 1978; JD, Cornell U., 1981. Bar: Vt.; cert. tchr., Vt. Tchr. Colchester (Vt.) Jr. H.S., 1978-79; assoc. Langrock Sperry Parker & Wool PC, Burlington, Vt., 1981-82; prin. Carol Bua Ode Atty.-at-Law, 1982-86; commr. Vt. State Bd. Edn., 1995—, Burlington Sch. Bd., 1991—, chmn., 1993—2000. Bd. dirs. Lund Family Ctr., Burlington, 1988-94; co-vice chair Burlington Dem. Com., 1989-90; officer Ward 4 Dems., Burlington, 1988-89; mem. Burlington Waterfront Bd., 1989-91; ambassador Flynn Theatre, 1990-92. Recipient Susan B. Anthony award for leadership, YWCA, 2000. Mem. Vt. Bar Assn. (chair pub. edn. com. 1990), Vt. Sch. Bds. Assn. (pres. Chittenden and Grand Isle region 1995-97). Democrat. Roman Catholic. Avocations: gardening, singing, drama, hiking, travel.

O'DEA, DENNIS MICHAEL, lawyer; b. Lowell, Mass., Nov. 1, 1946; s. James Lawrence and Carol France (Gibbons) O'D.; m. Mary Gail Frawley; children: Emily C., Dennis C., Daniel P., Mollie G., Sally Igor Ibradzic. BA in Govt., U. Notre Dame, 1968; JD magna cum laude, U. Mich., 1972. Bar: Mass. 1972, D.C. 1980, Ill. 1981, N.Y. 1994. Assoc. Goodwin, Procter & Hoar, Boston, 1972-74, Fine & Ambrogne, Boston, 1974-77; assoc. prof. Syracuse U. Coll. Law, 1977-78; vis. assoc. prof. Nat. Law Ctr., George Washington U., 1978-80; ptnr. Keck Mahin & Cate, N.Y.C., 1980-96; pvt. practice, 1996-97; ptnr. Wolf, Block, Schorr and Solis-Cohen LLP, N.Y.C., 1997—. Co-dir. The Gilmore Inst., 1995—. Mem. Order of the Coif, Chgo. Lit. Club (pres. 1993). Presbyterian. Home: 5 Opal Ct New City NY 10956-7021 Office: Wolf Block Schorr & Solis-Cohen 250 Park Ave Ste 1000 New York NY 10177-0001

ODEGARD, MARK ERIE, geophysicist, consultant; b. Plentywood, Mont., Nov. 1, 1940; s. Harold Theodore and Edna Marcella (Jacobsen) O.; m. Elisabeth Snow, June 17, 1967; 1 child, Liv. AA, Dawson Coll., Glendive, Mont., 1960; BA, U. Mont., 1962; MS, Oreg. State U., 1965; PhD, U. Hawaii, 1975. Asst. prof. Hawaii Inst. Geophysics, Honolulu, 1974-78; dir. geology and geophysics program Office Naval Rsch., Arlington, Va., 1978-81; assoc. prof. N.Mex. State U., Las Cruces, 1981-83; staff rsch. geophysicist Sohio Petroleum Co., Dallas, 1983-86; prin. scientist Basalt Waste Isolation Program, Richland, Wash., 1986-88; rsch. assoc. Unocol Sci. & Tech., Brea, Calif., 1988-93; mgr. Potential Fields Group, Unocal, Sugar Land, Tex., 1993-98; bd. dirs., v.p. U.S. ops. Geophys. Exploration Tech., 1998—. Contbr. over 50 articles to sci. jours. Chmn. San Bernardino County (Calif.) Svc. Area 48 Adv. Com., 1989-91; vice chmn. Chino Hills Planning Commn., 1992-93; mem. Chino Hills (Calif.) Mcpl. Adv. Coun., 1990-91. Recipient Antarctica Svc. medal U.S. Congress, 1966. Mem. Soc. Exploration Geophysicists, Am. Geophys. Union, Sigma Xi, Am. Planning Assn. Avocations: skiing, golf, hunting, fishing, marathon running. Home: 3418 El Dorado Blvd Missouri City TX 77459-2414 Office: Ste 510 12503 Exchange Dr Stafford TX 77477-3607

O'DEL, JOHN NICHOLAS, educator; b. NY, Dec. 14, 1961; PhD, University at Buffalo, Buffalo, New York, 1987—94. Assistant Professor Rhode Island College, Povidence, RI, 199—Pres; Associate Professor Averett College, Vienna, 1995—99. Author: (Manual on obtaining funding) Grants & Grant Writing 3rd edition, 2001 (Grand Prize for Innovation from the Academy of Management, 1995). Office: R I Coll-Sch of Mgmt & Tech Alger Hall 218 (3) 600 Mt Pleasant Ave Providence RI 02908-1991 Office Fax: 401-456-8759. Business E-Mail: jodel@ric.edu.

O'DELL, EDWARD THOMAS, JR. lawyer; b. Lowell, Mass., Nov. 26, 1935; s. Edward Thomas and Helen Louise (Shaw) O'D.; m. Kerstin Lilly Sjoholm, Mar. 18, 1962; children: Edward Thomas III, Brian Patrick, Christine Marie. BA, Brown U., 1957; JD, U. Chgo., 1960. Bar: N.Y. 1961, Mass. 1968, U.S. Dist. Ct. Mass. 1968, U.S. Ct. Appeals (1st cir.) 1968. Ptnr. Goodwin, Procter, LLP, Boston, 1996—2001; ret.; dir. AETNA Mut. Funds, 2002—. Trustee Gov. Dummer Acad., Byfield, Mass, 1982-87. Mem. ABA, Mass. Bar Assn., Internat. Bar Assn. (chmn. investment cos. and mutual funds com. 1994-98). Home: 96 Wildwood Rd Andover MA 01810-5126 Office: Goodwin Procter LLP Exchange Pl Boston MA 02109-2803

ODELL, HERBERT, lawyer; b. Phila., Oct. 20, 1937; s. Samuel and Selma (Kramer) O.; m. Valerie Odell; children: Wesley, Jonathan, James, Sarah, Samuel. BS in Econs., U. Pa., 1959; LLB magna cum laude, U. Miami, 1962; LLM, Harvard U., 1963. Bar: Fla. 1963, Pa. 1968. Trial atty. tax div. U.S. Dept. Justice, Washington, 1963-65; assoc. Walton, Lantaff, Schroeder, Carson & Wahl, Miami, Fla., 1965-67; from assoc. to ptnr. Morgan, Lewis & Bockius, Phila., 1967-89; ptnr. Zapruder & Odell, 1989-98, Odell & Ptnrs., Phila., 1998-99, Miller & Chevalier (PA) LLC, Phila., 2000—. Adj. prof. U. Miami, Villanova U.; lectr. various tax insts. Contbr. articles to profl. jours. Ford fellow, 1962-63. Mem.: ABA, D.C. Bar Assn., Phila. Bar Assn., Pa. Bar Assn., Fla. Bar Assn., Harvard, Harvard Club, Beta Alpha Psi, Omicron Delta Kappa, Phi Kappa Phi. Avocations: sailing, running, tennis, scuba diving, fishing. Office: Miller & Chevalier 401 E City Ave Ste 415 Bala Cynwyd PA 19004-1121 E-mail: hodell@milchev.com.

O'DELL, JOAN ELIZABETH, lawyer, mediator, business executive, educator; b. East Dubuque, Ill., May 3, 1932; d. Peter Emerson and Olive (Bonnet) O'D.; children: Dominique R., Nicole L. BA cum laude, U. Miami, 1956, JD, 1958. Bar: Fla. 1958, DC 1974, Ill. 1978, Va. 1987, U.S. Supreme Ct. 1972; lic. real estate broker Ill., Va., W.Va. Trial atty. SEC, Washington, 1959-60; asst. state atty. Office State Atty., Miami, Fla., 1960-64; asst. county atty. Dade County Atty.'s Office, 1964-70; county atty. Palm Beach County Atty.'s Office, West Palm Beach, Fla., 1970-71; regional gen. counsel Region IV EPA, Atlanta, 1971-73, assoc. gen. counsel Washington, 1973-77; sr. counsel Nalco Chem. Co., Oakbrook, Ill., 1977-78; v.p., gen. counsel Angel Mining, Washington and Tenn., 1979-96; pres. S.W. Land Investments, Miami, 1979-88; v.p. Events U.S.A., Washington, 1990—. Mem. Exec. Women's Coun., Tucson, 1982—85; co-chmn. sch. improvement coun. Harpers Ferry Jr. H.S., 2000—; bd. dirs. Tucson Women's Found., 1982—84, U. Ariz. Bus. and Profl. Women's Club, Tucson, 1981—85, LWV, Tucson, 1981—85, pres., 1984—85; bd. dirs. LWV Ariz., 1984—85, chmn. nat. security study; bd. dirs. LWV, Palm Beach County, Fla., 1990—92. Mem. Fla. Bar Assn., D.C. Bar Assn., Va. State Bar Assn., Ill. Bar Assn. Avocations: camping, hiking, skiing. E-mail: jeod@aol.com.

ODELL, JOHN H. construction company executive; b. Toledo, Oct. 31, 1955; s. John H. and Doris Odell; m. Kathryn Lau, Oct. 1, 1988; children: Ceara, Heather, Victoria. B of Environ. Design, U. Miami, Oxford, Ohio, 1977. Staff architect Richard Halford and Assocs., Santa Fe, 1978-79; ptnr. B.O.A. Constrn., 1980-84; owner John H. Odell Constrn., 1985—; v.p. Los Pintores Inc., 1990-92; pres. Uncle Joey's Food Svcs. Inc., 1991—, John H. Odell Assocs. Inc., Santa Fe, 1995—. Musician Santa Fe Community Orch., 1982, Huntington Community Orch., Huntington, W.Va., 1972-73; mem. citizen rev. com. Santa Fe Sch. Bd., 1999—, mem. bond and mill levy com., 2000—. Recipient Historic Preservation award City of Santa Fe, 1997. Mem. AIA (assoc., treas., bd. dirs. Santa Fe chpt. yearly 1988—, mem. liaison com. on design 1987—, Cmty. Svc. award 1993), Vine and Wine Soc. (N.Mex. No. Rio Grande chpt. pres., bd. dirs., v.p.), Nat. Assn. of Home Builders. Avocations: skiing, scuba, handball, racquetball. Home: PO Box 2967 Santa Fe NM 87504-2967 Office: John H Odell Assn 1523 Taos St Santa Fe NM 87505-3835 E-mail: johnoinc@aol.com.

ODELL, JOHN STEPHEN, political scientist; b. San Antonio, Aug. 25, 1945; s. Earl T. Odell and Jeraldine Busby; m. Margaret Gonder, Jan. 16, 1971. BA, U. Tex., 1967; MA, U. Wis., 1968, PhD, 1976. Asst. prof. dept. govt. Harvard U., Cambridge, Mass., 1976-82; assoc. prof. Sch. Internat. Rels. U. So. Calif., L.A., 1982-90, dir. Ctr. for Internat. Studies, 1989-92, prof. Sch. Internat. Rels., 1990—; dir. L.Am. policy devel. Office of U.S. Trade Rep., Exec. Office of Pres., Washington, 1984-85. Vis. fellow Inst. for Internat. Econs., Washington, 1985-87, Rsch. Inst., Ministry Internat. Trade and Industry, Tokyo, 1989; cons. Inst. Tch. Autonoma Mex., Mexico City, 1991; cons. World Bank, Asia Found., U.S. Dept. State. Author: U.S. International Monetary Policy, 1982; author: (co-author) Anti-Protection: Changing Forces in U.S. Trade Policies, 1987, International Trade Policies: Gains From Exchange Between Economics, 1990, Negotiating the World Economy, 2000; editor: Internat. Orgn., 1992—96. 1st lt. U.S. Army, 1969-71, Vietnam. Rsch. grantee Carnegie Endowment for Internat. Peace, 1975, Ford Found., 1979-82, 89-90; Fellow Coun. on Fgn. Rels., 1984-85, Social Sci. Rsch. Coun., 1987-89. Mem. Am. Polit. Sci. Assn., Coun. on Fgn. Affairs, Pacific Coun. on Internat. Policy. Office: U So Calif Sch Internat Rels Los Angeles CA 90089-0043 Fax: (213) 742-0281. E-mail: odell@usc.edu.

O'DELL, LYNN MARIE LUEGGE (MRS. NORMAN D. O'DELL), librarian; b. Berwyn, Ill., Feb. 24, 1938; d. George Emil and Helen Marie (Pesek) Luegge; m. Norman D. O'Dell, Dec. 14, 1957; children: Jeffrey, Jerry. Student, Lyons Twp. Jr. Coll., La Grange, Ill., 1957, No. Ill., Coll. of Dupage. Sec. Martin Co., Chgo., 1957-59; dir. Carol Stream (Ill.) Pub. Libr., 1964—. Chmn. automation governing com. DuPage Library System, v.p., 1982-85, pres. exec. com. adminstrv. librarians, 1985-86, chair automation search com., 1991-92. Named Woman of Yr., Wheaton Bus. and Profl. Woman's Club, 1968. Mem. ALA, Ill. Libr. Assn., Libr. Adminstrs. Conf. No. Ill., Pub. Libr. Assn. Lutheran. E-mail: lodell@dupagels.lib.il.us. Home: 182 Yuma Ln Carol Stream IL 60188-1917 Office: 616 Hiawatha Dr Carol Stream IL 60188-1634 E-mail: lodell@cslibrary.org.

O'DELL, MARY ERNESTINE, poet, editor, writer; b. Beckley, W.Va., Sept. 8, 1935; d. Ernest Forbis and Doris Mary (Truman) Houck; m. Daniel Moss Beam, Feb. 22, 1958 (div. May 1994); children: Robert Duke, Dorothy Karen Beam Cecil; m. James Roger O'Dell, Aug. 30, 1986 (dec. July 1996). BA, Transylvania U., 1957; MA, Western Ky. U., 1976, postgrad., 1978. Elem. tchr. LaRue County Pub. Schs., Hodgenville, Ky., 1959-86; editor Grex Press, Louisville, 1986—. Author: (poetry) Homefolks, 1983, Blue Air and Wheels, 1984, Bridesongs, 1989, Poems for the Man Who Weighs Light, 1999, Living in the Body, 2002. Grantee Ky. Found. for Women, 1999, Ky. Arts Coun., 1999; Mary Anderson Ctr. scholar Ky. Found. for Women, 1999. Mem. Ky. Poetry Soc. (pres. 1987), Ky. Writers Coalition (bd. dirs. 1986—), Appalachian Writers Assn., Green River Writers (founder, pres. 1984—). Delta Kappa Gamma. Avocations: reading, swimming. Home and Office: 703 Eastbridge Ct Louisville KY 40223-3907 E-mail: mary_odell@ntr.net.

ODELL, MARY JANE, former state official; b. Algona, Iowa, July 28, 1923; d. Eugene and Madge (Lewis) Neville; m. Garry Chinn, 1945 (dec.); m. Jonn Odell, Mar. 3, 1967 (dec.); m. Ralph Sigler, Nov. 22, 1987; children: Brad, Chris. BA, U. Iowa, 1945; hon. doctorate, Simpson Coll., 1982. Host public affairs TV programs, Des Moines and Chgo., 1953-79; with Iowa Public Broadcasting Network, 1975-79, host Assignment Iowa, 1975-78, host Mary Jane Odell Program, 1975-79; sec. of state State of Iowa, 1980-87, ret., 1987—. Tchr. grad. classes in communications Roosevelt U., Chgo., Drake U., Des Moines. Chmn. Iowa Easter Seals campaign, 1979-83; mem. Midwest Com. Future Options; bd. dirs. Iowa Shares; mem. exec. bd. Iowa Peace Inst., 1985-92; chmn. bd. govs. Iowa Easter Seals, 1998—. Recipient Emmy award, 1972, 75; George Washington Carver award, 1978; named to Iowa Women's Hall of Fame, 1979, Hancher medallian U. Iowa, 1976. Republican. Home: 2909 Woodland Ave Apt 919 Des Moines IA 50312-3832

O'DELL, MICHAEL JAMES, social sciences specialist; b. Rhinebeck, N.Y., June 30, 1949; s. Stanley Patrick and Dorothy Marie (Traver) O'D. AA, Dutchess Community Coll., Poughkeepsie, N.Y., 1969; BA, SUNY, Albany, 1971; MA, Cath. U. Am., 1987. Mgr. Brenner's Co., Poughkeepsie, 1972-73; v.p. Brennco, 1973; statistician U.S. Bur. Census, Washington, 1974-80; social scientist program evaluation and methodology div. U.S. GAO, 1980-84, sr. social scientist health edn. & human svcs. divsn., 1984—2002, ret., 2002. Prin. investigator, testifying witness U.S. Senate Spl. Com. on Aging, Washington, 1988. Editor Harbour Square News, 1992-93, 96-97; founder D.C. Coop. Housing News, 1991; editor D.C. Coop. Housing News, 1991-97. Treas. Fairfax Village, Washington, 1977-86; bd. dirs. Harbour Sq. Owners Inc., Washington, 1989-90, asst. treas., 1989-90, treas., 1990-92, dir., 1992-93, sec., 1997-99; pres. Washington Coop. Housing Coalition, 1991-95, asst. treas., 1990, treas., 1991, v.p., 1995, exec. dir., 1996-98, dir. 1998-99, 2002-. Recipient Outstanding Community Svc. award S.E. Neighbors Assn., Washington, 1982. Democrat. Home: 520 N St SW Washington DC 20024-4574

ODELL, PATRICK LOWRY, mathematics educator; b. Watonga, Okla., Nov. 29, 1930; s. Max Vernon and Pamela (Massey) Odell; m. Norma Lou Maddox, Aug. 16, 1958 (dec. May 1980); children: James M., David L., Michael R.L., Julie K., Patricia L., Deborah L.; m. Dovalee Dorsett, Aug. 3, 1985. BS, U. Tex., 1952; postgrad., UCLA, 1953-54; MS, Okla. State U., 1958, PhD, 1962. Mathematician White Sands (N.Mex.) Proving Grounds, 1952-53, Kaman Nuclear, Albuquerque, 1958-59, U.S. Naval Nuclear Ordnance Evaluation Unit, 1959-62, Ling-Temco Vought Aeros., 1962; asst. prof. math. U. Tex., Austin, 1962-66; prof., chmn. dept. math. Tex. Technol. U., Lubbock, 1966-71, coordinator insts., dir. rsch., Coll. Arts and Sci., 1971-72; prof math. scis. and environ. scis. U. Tex., Dallas, 1972-88, prof. emeritus, 1988—; prof. emeritus math. sci. Baylor U., Waco, 1988—2001; exec. dean grad. studies and rsch. U. Tex., Dallas, 1972-75. Assoc. dir. Tex. Ctr. for Rsch., Austin, 1964—66; rsch. scientist Def. Rsch. Lab., 1963—65; cons. math. statistician, 1962—. Capt. USAF, 1953—57. Fellow: Am. Statis. Assn., Tex. Acad. Sci. (Disting. Tex. Scientist award 1994); mem.: Soc. Indsl. and Applied Math. Home: 3200 Windsor Ave Waco TX 76708-3113

ODELL, WILLIAM DOUGLAS, endocrinologist, educator; b. Oakland, Calif., June 11, 1929; s. Ernest A. and Emma L. (Mayer) O.; m. Margaret F. Reilly, Aug. 19, 1950; children: Michael, Timothy, John D., Debbie, Charles. AB, U. Calif., Berkeley, 1952; MD, MS in Physiology, U. Chgo., 1956; PhD in Biochemistry and Physiology, George Washington U., 1965. Intern, resident, chief resident in medicine U. Wash., 1956-60, postdoctoral fellow in endocrinology and metabolism, 1957-58; sr. investigator Nat. Cancer Inst., Bethesda, Md., 1960-65; chief endocrine service NICHD, 1965-66; chief endocrinology Harbor-UCLA Med. Center, Torrance, Calif., 1966-72, chmn. dept. medicine, 1972-79; vis. prof. medicine Auckland Sch. Medicine, New Zealand, 1979-80; prof. medicine and physiology U. Utah Sch. Medicine, Salt Lake City, 1980-99, chmn. dept. internal medicine, 1980-96, prof. medicine and physiology, 1996-99, emeritus prof. medicine and physiology, 1999—. Pres. med. staff U. Utah Sch. Medicine, 1995-96. Mem. editorial bds. med. jours.; author, editor 8 books in field; contbr. over 330 articles to med. jours. With USPHS, 1960-66. Recipient Disting. Svc. award U. Chgo., 1973, Pharmacia award for outstanding contbns. to clin. chemistry, 1977, Gov.'s award State of Utah Sci. and Tech., 1988, also rsch. awards, Mastership award ACP, 1987. Mem.: Soc. Exptl. Biol. Medicine (councillor), Western Soc. Clin. Rsch. (Mayo Soley award), Western Assn. Physicians (pres.), Pacific Coast Fertility Soc. (pres.), Soc. Study of Reprodn. (bd. dirs.), Endocrine Soc. (v.p., Robert Williams award 1991), Am. Soc. Andrology (pres.), Assn. Am. Physicians, Am. Physiol. Soc., Am. Soc. Clin. Investigation, Alpha Omega Alpha. Office: U Utah Med Ctr 50 N Medical Dr Salt Lake City UT 84132-0001 E-mail: owodell@aol.com.

O'DELL, WILLIAM FRANCIS, retired business executive, writer; b. Detroit, Jan. 24, 1909; s. Frank Trevor and Garnett (Aikman) O'C.; m. Bess Baer, June 10, 1933 (dec. July 1986); m. Helen M. Porter, May 16, 1987 (dec. 1997); children: Peggy, David. BS, U. Ill., 1930. With Penton Pub. Co., 1933-37; v.p. Ross Fed. Research Corp., 1937-44; mng. dir. Statis Research Co., 1944-45; pres. Market Facts, Inc., 1946-64, chmn., 1964-74; pres. ROC Internat., 1961-64; mem. census adv. bd. Dept. Commerce, 1963-73; prof. mktg. McIntire Sch. Commerce U. Va., 1965-78. Vis. prof. Chinese U. of Hong Kong, 1969 Author: Marketing Decision, 1968, Marketing Decision Making, 1976, 4th edit., 1988, How to Make Lifetime Friends—With Peers and Parents, 1978, Twelve Families—An American Experience, 1981, Effective Business Decision Making and the Educated Guess, 1991; mem. editorial rev. bd. Jour. Mktg, 1964-73. Recipient Leader in Mktg. award, 1970, Jour. Mktg. Research editorial award, 1979; William F. O'Dell professorship in commerce named in his honor U. Va., 1983; named Pioneer in Mktg. Rsch., 1998. Mem. Am. Mktg. Assn. (pres. 1960-61), Colonnade Club (Charlottesville), Rotary, Delta Upsilon, Beta Gamma Sigma. Home: 5707 Junonia Ct Fort Myers FL 33908-1667

ODEM, JOYCE MARIE, human resources specialist; b. Des Moines, Mar. 21, 1936; d. Robert Gibson and Minnie Anna (Godown) Hague; m. Phillip Wayne Odem, May 23, 1954; children: Vickie, Phillip, Beth, Amy, Keith. Student, Merced C.C., 1976-78. Legal sec. C. Ray Robinson, Merced, Calif., 1959-60; office mgr., legal aid Kane & Canelo, 1960-65; recorder disciplinary control bd. U.S. Army Civil Svc., Okinawa, Japan, 1965-69; legal aid, office mgr. Courtney & Sharrow, Merced, 1969-72; adminstr. USAF Civil Svc., Okinawa, 1972-75; asst. indsl. rels. mgr. Maracay Mills Divsn. Mohasco, Merced, 1975-78; safety dir., personnel mgr. Keller Industries, 1978-83; mgr. employee rels. McLane Pacific, 1983-85; corp. dir. human resources McLane Co., Inc., Temple, Tex., 1983—2002; v.p. people dept. McLane Foodservice, Carrollton, 2002—. Mem. adv. bd. Pvt. Industry Coun., Merced, 1980-85. Mem. Cen. Tex. Human Resource Mgrs. Assn. (adv. coun.), Soc. Human Resource Mgrs. Avocations: sporting clays, golf, hunting. Office: McLean Foodservice Inc 2085 Midway Rd Carrollton TX 75006

ODEN, JEAN PHIFER, special education educator; b. Chgo., May 2, 1936; d. Dillard James and Lena (Conner) Phifer; m. James Edward Oden, Apr. 26, 1959; 1 child, Eric James. BE, Chgo. Tchrs. Coll., 1958; MEd in Learning Disabilities, Chgo. State U., 1973; postgrad., Nat. Coll. Edn., Evanston, Ill., 1986—, cert. advance studies, 1987; EdD, Nat.-Louis U., 1995. Tchr. elem. schs. Chgo., 1958-73, tchr. learning disabilities elem. schs., 1973-81, cons. spl. edn., ind. edn. program facilitator, 1981; learning disability specialist Phillips High Sch., Chgo., 1982-87, Englewood High Sch., Chgo., 1987-94, Harold Washington Elem. Sch., Chgo., 1994-98. Mem. Ill. Guidelines for Learning Disabilities Devel. Com., Springfield, Ill., 1981-82, Com. to Devel. State Test for Learning Disabilities Tchrs., Springfield, 1986—; speaker Who's Who Congress, Cambridge, Eng., 1992; mem. del. to Vietnam, 1993, China, 1994, Oxford U., 1997, South Africa, 2001; mem. African Affairs Adv. Coun. to Chgo. Human Rels. Commn., 1999; chair edn. com. Chgo. Southside Br. NAACP, 2000. Speaker Nat. Urban League N.Y.C. conf., 1980; mem. Congl. Victory Fund, Chgo., 1985, SCLC Met. Chgo., 1979-81, Mayoral Summit Parent-Community Coun. on Edn. Reform, 1987—, Chgo. Mayor's Edn. Summit on Sch. Reform, 1988; charter mem. Rep. Presdl. Adv. Task Force, 1989, Rep. Inner Circle, 1991, Ctr. for Study of the Presidency, 1998; mem. Coalition Black Trade Unionists, 1991—, cons. pool Nat. Juvenile Justice Resource Ctr., 1991—, NAACP; state chair African Am. Econ. Devel. Task Force, Ill. Legis. Black Caucus, 1992—. U.S. Dept. Edn. grantee, 1986; recipient Citizenship award Chgo. mayor, 1984, Cert. merit NAACP South Side Br., 1978; named state advisor U.S. Congl. Adv. Bd., 1985; speaker edn. seminar 19th Congress on Arts and Communicatiion, Cambridge, Eng. Mem. ASCD, LWV, NAACP (chair edn. com. 2000), Minority Mainstream, United Neighborhoods Intertwined for Total Equality (founder, exec. dir., rschr.), Assn. for Citizens with Learning Disabilities, Coun. for Exceptional Children (liaison to state bd. Ill. Divsn. for Citizens with Learning Disabilities 1980), Spl. Edn. Tchrs. Assn. (1st pres., founder), Black Parents United for Edn. and Related Svcs. (founder), Kappa Delta Pi, Lehigh (Fla.) Country Club, Thousand Trails Club (Ottawa, Ill.). Mem. Carter C.M.E. Ch. Avocations: hiking, racketball, traveling, camping. Fax: 773 821-4456. *Personal philosophy: Those of us in society who are fortunate to reach levels of influence should share skills and talents with the less fortunate. A society which maintain masses of people in an undeveloped state is doomed to class conflict and cultural extinction. Those who don't study history are bound to repeat it.*

ODEN, JOHN TINSLEY, engineering educator, mathematician, consultant; b. Alexandria, La., Dec. 25, 1936; s. John James and Sara Elizabeth (Lyles) O.; m. Barbara Clare Smith, Mar. 19, 1965; children: John Walker, Elizabeth Lee. BS, La. State U., 1959; MS, Okla. State U., 1960, PhD, 1962; doctorate in sci. (hon.), Tech. U. Lisbon, Portugal, 1986; Doctorate (hon.), Polytechnique de Mons, Belgium, 2000, Tech. U. Krakow, Poland, 2001. Registered profl. engr., Tex., La. Teaching asst. La. State U., Baton Rouge, 1959; asst. prof. Okla. State U., Stillwater, 1961-63; sr. structures engr. Gen. Dynamics, Fort Worth, 1963-64; prof., head dept. engrng. mechanics U. Ala., Huntsville, 1964-73; prof. U. Tex., Austin, 1973—, Carol and Henry Groppe prof. engring., Ernest and Virginia Cockrell chair in engring., 1987-93, Cockrell Family Regents prof. engrng. 2, 1993—. Prof. Coope U. Fed., Brazil, 1974; dir. Tex. Inst. Computational Mechanics, Austin, 1974-93, Tex. Inst. Computational and Applied Math., Austin, 1993—; Sci. Rsch. Coun. vis. scholar Brunel U., Eng., 1981; mem. com. on computational mechanics NRC; chmn. U.S. Nat. Com. on Theoretical and Applied Mechanics, 1992-94; founder, CEO computational Mechanics Co., Inc., 1982-96. Author, editor 45 books; editor Jour. Computer Methods in Applied Mechanics and Engring., 1980—; contbr. numerous articles to profl. jours. Decorated chevalier Ordre des Palms Academique (France); recipient rsch. award Southeastern Conf. on Theoretical and Applied Mechanics, 1978, Lohmann medal Okla. State U., 1991, Computational Mechanics medal Japan Soc. Mech. Engrs., 1993; elected Nat. Acad. Engring. Brazil, 1998. Fellow ASCE (Outstanding Svc. award 1968, Walter Huber rsch. award 1973, Theodore von Karman medal 1992, Joe J. King Prof. Engring. award 1994), ASME (Worcester Reed Warner medal 1990, Timoshenko medal 1996), NAE, Soc. Engring. Sci. (pres. 1978, Eringen medal 1991, Hocutt Rsch. award, 1992), Am. Acad. Mechanics (pres. 1990-94, Disting. Svc. medal 1995); mem. Soc. Indsl. and Applied Math., Internat. Assn. Computational Mechanics (pres. 1990-94, Congress-Gauss-Newton medal 1994), U.S. Assn. Computational Mechanics (pres. 1990-92, John Von Neumann medal 1993), Soc. Natural Philosophy, Nat. Acad. Engring. Mex., Nat. Acad. Engring. Brazil. Home: 7403 W Rim Dr Austin TX 78731-2044 Office: Univ Tex Austin TICAM Campus Code CO200 Austin TX 78712

ODEN, ROBERT RUDOLPH, surgeon; b. Chgo., Dec. 2, 1922; s. Rudolph J.E. and Olga H. (Wahlquist) O.; m. Nancy Clow; children: Louise, Boyd, Beach, Lisbeth. BS, U. Ill., 1943; MD, MS in Anatomy, Northwestern U., 1947. Intern Augustana Hosp., Chgo., 1947-48, resident in surgery, 1948-49; resident in orthopaedics Hines Vets. Hosp., 1949-51; resident in children's orthopaedics Shriner's Hosp., 1953-54; pvt. practice Chgo., 1954-57, Aspen, Colo., 1957—. Clin. assoc. prof. in orthopaedics U. Colo.; orthopaedic surgeon U.S. Olympic Com., 1960, 72, 76, 80. Assoc. editor: Clin. Orthopaedics and Related Rsch. Trustee U.S. Ski Ednl. Found., 1967-82, Aspen Valley Hosp., 1978-86; founder Aspen Orthopaedic and Sports Medicine Pub. Found., 1985, Aspen Inst. for Theol. Futures, 1978, Great Tchrs. and Preachers Series Christ Episc. Ch., 1989; mem. organizing com. Aspen World Cup, 1976-92; founder, trustee Pitkin County Bank, 1983—; founder Aspen Pitkin Employee Housing, 1975. Recipient Blegan award for most outstanding svc. to U.S. skiing, 1985, Halsted award U.S. Ski Assn., 1987, inducted into Aspen Hall of Fame, 1996; inducted into Colo. Ski Hall of Fame, 2002, inducted into US Ski Hall of Fame, 2002. Mem. Am. Acad. Orthopaedic Surgeons, ACS, Internat. Coll. Surgeons, Western Orthopaedic Assn., SICOT, Am. Assn. Bone & Joint Surgeons, Rocky Mountain Traumatologic Soc., Canadian Orthopaedic Assn., Am. Orthopaedic Soc. for Sports Medicine, Internat. Ski Safety Soc., ACL Study Group, Internat. Soc. Knee, Internat. Knee Inst., Phi Beta Kappa. Home: PO Box 660 Aspen CO 81612-0660 also: PO Box 172 Captiva FL 33924-0172 Office: 100 E Main St Aspen CO 81611-1778

ODEN, WILLIAM BRYANT, bishop, educator; b. McAllen, Tex., Aug. 3, 1935; s. Charles Alva and Evea (Bryant) O.; m. Marilyn Brown, July 12, 1957; children: Danna Lee Oden Bowen, William Dirk, Valerie Lyn, Charles Bryant. BA, Okla. State U., 1958; MDiv, Harvard U., 1961, postgrad., 1964; ThD, Boston U., 1964; DD (hon.), Oklahoma City U., 1980; LHD (hon.), Centenary Coll., 1990. Ordained to ministry Meth. Ch., 1961. Pastor Aldersgate United Meth. Ch., Oklahoma City, 1963-69, St. Stephen's United Meth. Ch., Norman, Okla., 1969-76, Crown Heights United Meth. Ch., Oklahoma City, 1976-83; prof. Phillips Grad. Sem., Enid, 1976-88; pastor 1st United Meth. Ch., 1983-88; bishop United Meth. Ch., Baton Rouge, 1988-96, bishop for the Dallas area, 1996—, Ecumenical del. to Lambeth Conf., 1998. Pres., United Meth. Coun. Bishops, 2000—; pres. SCJ Coll. of Bishops, 1989-90; del. Gen. Conf., 1976, 80, 84, 88; chmn. Okla. Del. to Gen. and Jurisdictional Confs., 1984, 88; Jackson lectr. Perkins Sch. Theology, So. Meth. U., 1975, Wilson lectr. SCJ Bishop's Week, 1989; co-chair World Meth.-Anglican Dialogue, 1991—; bd. dirs. Wesley Works Project; pres. Gen. Bd. Higher Edn. & Ministry, 1996—; pres. Coun. of Bishops, 1999—, United Meth. Comm., 2000—. Author: Oklahoma Methodism in the Twentieth Century, 1968, Liturgy as Life Journey, 1976, Wordeed: Evangelism in Biblical and Wesleyan Perspective, 1978; contbr.: Send Me: The Iteneracy in Crisis, 1991. Trustee Oklahoma City U., 1980-88, Southwestern U., Winfield, Kans., 1983-88, Centenary Coll., 1988—, Dillard U., 1988—, So. Meth. U., 1996—. Mem. Am. Acad. Homiletics. Avocations: writing, reading biographies, mountain climbing, backpacking. Home: PO Box 8127 Dallas TX 75205-0127

ODENWELLER, ROBERT PAUL, philatelist, association executive, retired airline pilot; b. Sept. 19, 1938; s. Charles Joseph and Robina Katharine (Watson) O.; m. Jane Blackstone Rawlings, June 24, 1965; 1 stepchild, Joy McCorriston; 1 child, Liesl Hasbrouck. BS, U.S. Air Force Acad., 1960. Commd. USAF, 1956, advanced through grades to capt., 1963, resigned, 1956-66. Mem. Collectors Club Inc., N.Y.C., 1964—, gov. 1969—, program chmn., 1970-80, mem. editl. bd., 1975—, sec. 1979-82, v.p. 1983-86, pres. 1987-90, trustee, 1992-98; trustee, vice chmn. then chmn. expert com. Philatelic Found., N.Y.C., 1970—. Author: The FIP Guide to Exhibiting and Judging Traditional and Postal History Exhibits, 1993; author, editor: Philatelic Vocabulary in Five Languages, 1978 (Vermeil medal 1979); editor: Opinions VI, 1992 (Gold medal); contbr. articles to profl. pubs. Recipient Grand Prix d'Honneur, Zeapex Orgn., 1980; selected to sign Roll of Disting. Philatelists, Brit. Philatelic Fedn., 1991, Alfred Lichtenstein Meml. award Collectors Club, N.Y., 1993, TWA Flight Ops. Meritorious Achievement award 1995, award of Excellence, 1995, 2000. Fellow Royal Philatelic Soc. London, Royal Philatelic Soc. N.Z.; mem. Fedn. Internat. de Philatelie (pres. commn. traditional philately 1978-96; Grand Prix d'Honneur 1980, Svc. medal 1996), Am. Philatelic Soc. (bd. dirs. 1981-84, 89-90, named Champion of Champions 1973, Luff award), Assn. Internat. Des Experts Philateliques (expert 1980—, bd. dirs. 1987—), Fedn. New Zealand Philatelic Socs., Grand Prix Club Internat. (sec., treas. 1980-89, bd. dirs. 1989-92, 94-00, v.p. 1994-96, pres. 1996-2000), soc. Australasian Specialists (pres. 1969-72), U.S. Chess Fedn. Republican. Episcopalian. Avocations: stamp collecting, photography, languages, chess, bridge. Home: Chalon Round Top Rd Bernardsville NJ 07924 Office: Collector's Club Inc 22 E 35th St New York NY 10016-3806

ODER, BROECK NEWTON, school emergency management consultant; b. Ill. s. Bruce Newton and Mary Louise Oder; m. Jolene Marie Peragine, June 28, 1975 (dec. June 1979). BA in History, U. San Diego, 1974, MA in History, 1975; postgrad., U. N.Mex., 1976-79. Life C.C. teaching credential, Calif. Rsch. asst. to pres. U. San Diego, 1975; grad. asst. U. N.Mex., Albuquerque, 1976-79; tchr. history, chmn. dept. Santa Catalina Sch., Monterey, Calif., 1979—, asst. dean students, 1981-83, dir. ind. study, 1981-95, dean students, 1983-91, dir. emergency planning, 1986—, dean campus affairs, 1991-94, dir. security, 1994—. Disaster preparedness coun. Monterey County Office Edn., 1988-99; chair Diocesan Sch. Emergency Preparedness Coun, 1991-98. Mem. bd. of tchrs. The Concord Rev.; contbr. articles to profl. publs. including American National Biography. Participant Jail and Bail, Am. Cancer Soc., Monterey, 1988, 89; reviewer sch. emergency plans, Monterey, 1989—. Recipient award of merit San Diego Hist. Soc., 1975, Outstanding Tchr. award U. Chgo., 1985, Outstanding Young Educator award Monterey Peninsula Jaycees, 1988, resolution of commendation Calif. Senate Rules Com., 1988, cert. of commendation Calif. Gov.'s Office Emergency Svcs., 1991, nat. cert. of achievement Fed. Emergency Mgmt. Agy., 1991, Outstanding High Sch. Tchr. award Tufts U., 1998, High Sch. Tchr. of Excellence, U. Calif. at San Diego, 1998, Outstanding Tchr. of Am. HIstory award Calif. DAR, 2001-02. Mem. ACLU, NAACP, NRA (life), Am. Hist. Assn., Orgn. Am. Historians, Nat. Coun. on History Edn., Soc. for History Edn., Second Amendment Found., Law Enforcement Alliance Am., Calif. State Sheriffs Assn., Phi Alpha Theta. Avocations: reading, sports, target shooting. Office: Santa Catalina Sch 1500 Mark Thomas Dr Monterey CA 93940-5291

ODER, FREDERIC CARL EMIL, retired aerospace company executive, consultant; b. Los Angeles, Oct. 23, 1919; s. Emil and Katherine Ellis (Pierce) O.; m. Dorothy Gene Brumfield, July 2, 1941; children— Frederic E., Barbara Oder Debes, Richard W. BS, Calif. Inst. Tech., 1940, MS, 1941; PhD, UCLA, 1952. Commd. 2d lt. U.S. Army Air Force, 1941; advanced through grades to col. U.S. Air Force, 1960; ret., 1960; asst. dir. and program mgr. for research and engring. Apparatus and Optical div. Eastman Kodak Co., Rochester, N.Y., 1960-66; with Lockheed Missiles & Space Co., Sunnyvale, Calif., 1966-91, v.p., asst. gen. mgr. div. space systems, 1972-73, v.p., gen. mgr. div. space systems, 1973-84, exec. v.p., 1984—; cons., 1985-91. Mem. Def. Intelligence Agy. Sci. Adv. Com., 1972-76, assoc. mem., 1976-78; mem. Air Force Studies Bd., Assembly Engring., NRC, 1975-79, Def. Sci. Bd. Summer Study, 1975, Rev. Panel, 1979, Space Applications Bd., 1985-88. Contbr. articles to profl. publs. Decorated Legion of Merit; recipient Nat. Reconnaissance Pioneer. Fellow AIAA; mem. NAE, Masons, Sigma Xi. Episcopalian. Home: 224 La Puerta Way Palm Beach FL 33480-3224 E-mail: fceoder@aol.com.

ODERMAN, STUART DOUGLAS, pianist, composer, playwright; b. Elizabeth, N.J., Feb. 7, 1940; s. A. Davis and Helen (Greenwald) O.; m. Janet Sovey, July 18, 1983. BA, Kean Coll., 1961; MA, SUNY, New Paltz, 1967. Silent film pianist Mus. Modern Art, N.Y.C., 1970—, The New Sch. Social Rsch., N.Y.C., 1970—. Guest pianist Eastman House, Rochester, N.Y., Screen Writers Guild, L.A., Am. Film Inst., Washington, Pub. Broadcasting System, N.Y.C., Pub. Theater, N.Y.C., 1987—, Minuteman Mus. of Our Nat. Heritage, Lexington, Mass., 1988, Athens (Greece) Concert Hall, 1994-95, 2001, Symphony Space, N.Y.C., 1998—, Morgan Libr., 1999; The Gish Theatre, Bowling Green (Ohio) State U. Composer, pianist: (TV) The Eternal Tramp, Pub. Broadcasting System, 1965, The Dawn of Laurel and Hardy, 1976, Laurel and Hardy Laughtunes, 1977, Pandora's Box, 1985, Dead Comics Society, 1991, Lumiére, 1997; author: (plays) The Death of Solly's Warren, Omni Theatre, N.Y.C., 1971, The Team, Omni Theatre, 1971, Season of the Carnival, Omni Theatre, 1972, Two Plus One Equals Two, Omni Theatre, 1973; (book) Roscoe "Fatty" Arbuckle, 1994, Lillian Gish, 1999; contbr. articles to profl. jours. Mem. ASCAP, Am. Fedn. Musicians, Bohemians. Clubs: Bohemians. Home: 243 S Harrison St Apt 9H East Orange NJ 07018-1428

ODERMATT, DIANA B. development consultant; b. Hollywood, Calif., Nov. 25, 1938; d. Harold and Mary H. (Wilson) Birtwistle; m. Robert Allen Odermatt, June 9, 1960; children: Kristin Odermatt Lee, Kyle David Odermatt. BA, Mills Coll., 1960. Assoc. dir. admissions Mills Coll., Oakland, Calif., 1978-82, dean admissions and fin. aid, 1982-85; dir. devel. Head-Royce Sch., 1985-91; major gift officer univ. rels. U. Calif., Berkeley, 1992-95, cons. Coll. Environ. Design, 1995-96; dir. devel. Bentley Sch., Oakland, 1996-99. Tchr., trainer Coun. for the Advancement and Support of Edn., Washington, 1980-93; bd. mem. European Coun. Ind. Schs., Washington, 1982-85; cons. The Coll. Bd., N.Y.C., 1985-92. Contbr. articles to profl. jours. Home: 39 Drury Ln Berkeley CA 94705-1615

ODERMATT, ROBERT ALLEN, architect; b. Oakland, Calif., Jan. 3, 1938; s. Clifford Allen and Margaret Louise (Budge) O.; m. Diana Birtwistle, June 9, 1960; children: Kristin Ann, Kyle David. BArch, U. Calif., Berkeley, 1960. Registered architect, Calif., Oreg., Nev., Colo., Hawaii; cert. Nat. Coun. Archtl. Registration Bds. Draftsman Anderson Simonds Dusel Campini, Oakland, 1960-61; architect James R. Lucas, Orinda, Calif., 1961-62, ROMA Architects, San Francisco, 1962-76, architect, pres., 1976-84; prin. ROMA Design Group, San Francisco, 1962-92; pres. The Odermatt Group, Orinda, Calif., 1992—. Prin. speaker Internat. Conf. on Rebuilding Cities, Pitts., 1988; mem. U.S. Design in Am. Program, Sofia, Bulgaria, Armenian Disaster Assn. Team, 1989, NA Collateral Internship Mgmt. Com.; prin. State of Calif. Bay Area Facilities Plan, 1992; princ. Greece Resort Privatization Program, 1993. Prin. designer U.S. Embassy, Bahrain, Grand Canyon Nat. Park, 1977, Yosemite Nat. Park, 1987; prin. planner hotel complex Westin Hotel, Vail, Colo., 1982, Kaanapali Resort, 1987, Las Montanas Resort, San Diego; master plan U. Calif., Berkeley, 1988, Kohanaiki and Mauna Lani resorts, 1989, Calif. State Strategic Real Estate Plan, 1992, Greek Resort/Marina Privatization Program, 1993, Tektronix Strategic Plan, 1994, United Labs, Manila Master Plan, 1995, State of Calif. Reorganization Plan, 1996, Ford Island Pearl Harbor Master Plan, 1996, Pearl Harbor Visitor Ctr. Plan, 1997, Albiano Resort Study, 1998; master plans include Trefethen Vineyards, Bell Garden, Napa Valley Expo, Wheatland Manor. Mem. Santa Cruz Downtown Assessment, Oakland Mayor's Com. on High Density Housing, 1982, Oakland Gen. Plan Congress, 1994, waterfront plan adv. com. City of Oakland, 1996; mem. Eisenhower E. Plan, Alexandria, Va., Upper Potomac W. Plan, Alexandria; bd. dirs. Nat. Archtl. Accrediting Bd. Fellow AIA (dir. East Bay chpt. 1969-71, pres. 1980-81, dir. Calif. coun. 1979-81, Disting. Svc. award 1991, nat. dir. 1983-86, nat. v.p. 1986-87, chair AIA internat. steering com. 1993-94, graphic stds. adv. com. 1991-92, U. Calif. archtl. review commn. 1992-96, exec. com. Coll. Fellows 1996-98, vice chancellor Coll. Fellows 1998, chancellor 2000, East Bay medal 1997), Am. Archtl. Found. (regent).

ODESCALCHI, EDMOND PÉRY, international financial consultant, author; b. Budapest, Hungary, Oct. 11, 1928; came to U.S., 1950; s. Prince Bela and Princess Charlotte (de Bay) O.; m. Esther de Kando, Sept. 30, 1961; children: Daniel, Dominic. Student, Cornell U., 1951, U. Pa., 1956-57; MS in Econs., St. Andrews U., Scotland, 1959. Adminstrv. asst. French Govt., Baden, Fed. Republic Germany, 1948-50; world trade specialist IBM Corp., Poughkeepsie, N.Y., 1952-60, project mgr., 1960-74, devel. mgr. East Fishkill, 1974; pres. Global Tech., Inc., N.Y.C., 1975-91. Internat. fin. cons., 1975-93. Author: The Global Arena, 1973, Faces of Reality, 1975, The Third Crown, 1997, The Evolution of Behavior, 2002; contbr. articles to profl. jours. Mem. Rep. Nat. Com., 1984—. Mem. Bus. Cons. Assn., Am. Mus. Natural History (assoc.), Internat. Platform Assn. Home and Office: 1020 Freedom Rd Pleasant Valley NY 12569-7636

ODGAARD, ANDERS JACOB, civil and environmental engineer, educator; b. Hvidbjerg, Denmark, Aug. 8, 1942; came to U.S., 1977; s. Peter Johannes and Margrethe (Jensen) O.; m. Anna Joyce Rogers, Feb. 18, 1978; children: Peter Jacob, Christel Margrethe. MS in Civil and Structural Engring., Tech. U. Denmark, Lyngby, 1966, PhD in Civil and Structural Engring., 1970. Registered profl. engr., Iowa. Lectr. Tech. U. Denmark, 1969-72; UN cons. U. Minas Gerais, Belo Horizonte, Brazil, 1972-73; postdoctoral scholar U. Cambridge, Eng., 1973-74; sr. rsch. engr. Danish Hydraulic Inst., Hørsholm, Denmark, 1974-77; adj. asst. prof. U. Iowa, Iowa City, 1977-80, from asst. prof. to assoc. prof., 1984-89, prof. civl and environ. engring., 1989—, assoc. dean engring., 1992—. Assoc. rsch. scientist Iowa Inst. Hydraulic Rsch., Iowa City, 1977-80, rsch. engr., 1980—; cons. Bechtel, San Francisco, 1993—, DHV Cons. BV, Amersfoort, The Netherlands, 1993—, Minn. Dept. Transp., Mpls., 1993—, Parsons Engring. Sci., Inc., Norcross, Ga., 1998—. Editor Jour. Hydraulic Engring., 1994-98; contbr. articles to Jour. Hydraulic Engring., Water Resources Rsch., Jour. Hydraulic Rsch.; patentee Iowa Vane: A Submerged Structure for Sediment Control in Rivers. Fellow ASCE (Karl Emil Hilgard Hydraulic prize 1991); mem. Am. Soc. Engring. Edn., Internat. Assn. for Hydraulic Rsch., Sigma Xi, Chi Epsilon. Home: 934 Estron St Iowa City IA 52246-4600 Office: U Iowa Coll Engring Iowa City IA 52242

ODGERS, RICHARD WILLIAM, lawyer; b. Detroit, Dec. 31, 1936; s. Richard Stanley and Elsie Maude (Trevarthen) O.; m. Gail C. Bassett, Aug. 29, 1959; children: Thomas R., Andrew B. AB, U. Mich., 1959, JD, 1961. Bar: Calif. 1962. Assoc. Pillsbury Winthrop, San Francisco, 1961-69, ptnr., 1969-87, 98-2000; exec. v.p., gen. counsel Pacific Telesis Group, 1987-98; ptnr. Pillsbury Winthrop, 2001—. Chmn., bd. dirs. Legal Aid Soc. San Francisco; dir. Legal Cmty. Against Violence; dir., sec./treas. Van Loben Sels Charitable Found.; dir. Immigrant Legal Resource Ctr.; mem. ABA Special com. on Gun Violence. Served with USNR. Fellow Am. Bar Found., Am. Judicature Soc., Am. Coll. Trial Lawyers; mem. ABA, Am. Law Inst., Coll. Law Practice Mgmt. Office: Pillsbury Winthrop 50 Fremont St San Francisco CA 94105-2228 E-mail: rwodgers@pillsburywinthrop.com.

ODHAV, SATISH, rheumatologist; b. Johannesburg, South Africa, Sept. 28, 1955; came to U.S., 1986; s. Kanaiyalal and Deviben (Bowan) O.; m. Hasna Govin, Feb. 13, 1989; children: Ashika, Chirag. BS in Physiology and Biochemistry, U. Newcastle, Newcastle-upon-Tyne, Eng., 1975; MBBCh, U. Witwatersand, Johannesburg, South Africa, 1986. Diplomate Am. Bd. Internal Medicine, Am. Bd. Rheumatology. Resident in internal medicine U. Tenn., Memphis, 1987-90, fellow in rheumatology, 1990-92; with Med. Specialty Clinic, Jackson, 1992—; clin. instr. U. Tenn. Family Practice, 2000—; pres. Med. Specialty Clinic, 2001—. Dir. Tenn. chpt., West Tenn. chpt. Arthritis Found., Memphis, 1996—. Fellow Am. Coll. Rheumatology; mem. ACP, Sr. Citizens Club (dir., mem. adv. com. 1997—).

ODIER, PIERRE ANDRE, retired educator, writer, photographer, artist; b. Lausanne, Switzerland, May 24, 1940; came to U.S., 1959; s. Leon Odier and Gretha (Vesper) Hough; m. Mary Ellen Patton, Apr. 2, 1967 (div. Apr. 1984); children: Yvette, Debbi. BA, U. Puget Sound, 1967; MFA, Calif. State U., L.A., 1974; postgrad., UCLA, 1976-83. Cert. tchr. Calif. Owner restaurant The End, Tacoma, 1961-64; owner gallery Place des Arts, 1964-65; interpreter Weyerhauser Corp., 1964; chairperson dept. fine arts Hoover H.S., Glendale, Calif., 1967—2001; ret., 2001. Author: The Rock, A History of Alcatraz, 1983, Lummis Inside his Habitat, 1977 (State Hist. Soc. award 1981), A Discovery of Age, Students Look at Aging Process, 1992, A Discovery of Destitution, Students Look at Extreme Poverty; editor: Nat. Photographers Assn. quar., 1980-84. Served with U.S. Army, 1959-62. Recipient Tchr. of Yr. award Parent Tchrs. Student Assn., Glendale, Calif., 1979, Tchr. of Yr. award Glendale c. of C., 1983, Hon. Tchr. award Puiching Sch. China, 1994. Mem. Glendale Tchrs. Assn. (contract negotiator 1977), Nat. Photography Instrs. Assn. (chmn. election com., pres. 1980-85, chairperson conv. 1982), China Exploration and Rsch. Soc. (v.p., editor newsletter, expdn. leader China, Mongolia, Siberia, Russia, U.S.A. 1994), NEA, Adventurers Club (pres. 1999-2000), Explorers Club. Democrat. Lutheran. Home: 1255 Hill Dr Los Angeles CA 90041-1610 E-mail: easedo@aol.com.

ODINECS, ALEKSANDRS, biochemist; b. Riga, Latvia, Feb. 26, 1954; s. Henrihs Odinecs and Sofija Odineca; m. Tatjana Odineca, Aug. 5, 1976; children: Linda, Einars. BS in Biochemistry, U. Latvia, Riga, 1979; PhD in Biochemistry, Chem. Pharm. Inst., St. Petersburg, Russia, 1985; MS in Vet. Medicine, U. London, Eng., 1992. Sr. scientist Inst. Organic Synthesis, Riga, 1985-91; rsch. fellow U. London, 1991-92, U. Padua, Italy, 1992-93; rsch. assoc. U. Wash., Seattle, 1993-95; sr. rsch. assoc. Uniformed Svcs. U. Health Scis., Bethesda, Md., 1995-97; sr. scientist Shaman Pharms. Inc., South San Francisco, Calif., 1997-98; sr. staff investigator Vertex Pharms. Inc., Cambridge, Mass., 1998—. Cons. Hoyle Consulting Inc., Frederick, Md., 1997. Contbr. chpts. to books, numerous articles to profl. jours.; patentee in field. Mem. Am. Assn. Pharm. Scientists, Internat. Soc. for Study of Xenobiotics. Home: 99 Beech St Belmont MA 02478-1828 Office: Vertex Pharms Inc 130 Waverly St Cambridge MA 02139-4242

ODINTSOV, BORIS MIKHAILOVICH, physicist, researcher; b. Kazan, Russia, Oct. 28, 1947; came to U.S., 1996; s. Mikhail Grigor'evich Odintsov and Vera Petrovna Samoilova; m. Vera Vladimirovna Lozovaya, Dec. 31, 1970; 1 child, Andrey. PhD in Physics and Math., State U. of Kazan, 1978; D of Physics and Math., State U. of St. Petersburg, Russia, 1993. Dep. head chem.-phys. dept. Zavoisky Phys.-Tech. Inst., Kazan, 1989-95; prof. State Tech. U., 1993-95; rsch. prof. U. Ill., Urbana, 1996—. Dep. gen. dir. Innovation Found. of Republic Tatarstan, Kazan, 1993—95; sci. expert Govtl. Russia-Turkey Commn., Moscow, 1993—95; prin. sec. Kazan Sci. Ctr., 1983—89. Author: Nuclear-Electron Overhauser Effect in Solutions, 1986 (Silver medal 1989). Recipient Computer Networking award, NATO, Brussels, 1999—2000; grantee Fogarty Internat. grantee, NIH, 1998—2001, Internat. Linkage grantee, NATO, Belgium, 1998—2000, Rsch. grantee, Russian Found. Fundamental Rsch., Moscow, 1993—95, Civilian R&D Found., 2002—. Mem.: Presidium of Kazan Sci. Ctr., Internat. Electron Paramagnetic Resonance Soc. Avocations: water skiing, racquetball. Office: U Ill 506 S Mathews Urbana IL 61801 E-mail: bodintso@uiuc.edu.

ODISHOO, SARAH A. English language educator; b. Chgo., July 12, 1939; d. Saul Eshoo and Nanajan Odishoo; divorced; children: Elizabeth, Leslie. BA in English Lit., Ill. Wesleyan U., 1961; MA in Poetry and English Lit., N.E. Ill. U., 1980. Instr. English composition No. Ill. U., 1982-85; prof. English, world lit., mythology and writing Columbia Coll., Chgo., 1985-95, prof. lit., 1992—. Co-dir. freshman writing program, dir. profl. writing program, dir. profl. writing seminars Columbia Coll., 1985-89, pres. faculty orgn., 1990-92, dir. or co-dir. workshops, 1998, guest poet/collaborator CD/sound collaboration, dept. sound, 1999, liaison to bd. trustees, CCFO rep., 1999-2000; mem. faculty adv. coun. Ill. Bd. Higher Edn., 1985-89; coord. PEN Midwest Reading Series, 1988-89; artist in-residence Nitzana (Israel) Ednl. Project, dept. history Ben Gurion U. of Negev, 1993, U. Wyo., 1999, Byrdcliffe Colony, Woodwtock (N.Y.) Guild, 2000; lectr. River Oaks Art Coun., Oak Park, Ill., 2000; mem. archeol. dig for study of mythology of early Jewish and Christian nomadic cultures, Nitzana, 1992. Office: Columbia Coll Chgo 600 S Michigan Ave Chicago IL 60605 E-mail: sodishoo@popmail.colum.edu.

ODLE, ROBERT CHARLES, JR. lawyer; b. Port Huron, Mich., Feb. 15, 1944; s. Robert Charles and Elizabeth Dagmar (Lassen) O.; m. Lydia Ann Karpinol, Aug. 2, 1969. BA, Wayne State U., Detroit, 1966; JD, Detroit Coll. Law, 1969, LLD (hon.), 1992. Staff asst. to pres. of U.S., 1969-71; dir. adminstrn. Com. Re-election of President, 1971-73; dep. asst. sec. HUD, 1973-76; Washington corp. affairs rep. Internat. Paper Co., 1976-81; asst. sect. Dept. Energy, 1981-85; ptnr. Weil, Gotshal & Manges, 1985—. Mem. Mich. Bar Assn., D.C. Bar Assn., Delta Theta Phi. Clubs: University (Washington). Republican. Roman Catholic. Home: 476 S Union St Alexandria VA 22314-3826 Office: Weil Gotshal & Manges 1501 K St NW Ste 100 Washington DC 20005

O'DOHERTY, BRIAN, writer, filmmaker; b. Ballaghadereen, Ireland; came to U.S., 1957; m. Barbara Novak, 1960. MB BCh, Univ. Coll. Dublin, Nat. U. Ireland, 1952, DPH with honors, 1955; MS in Hygiene, Harvard U., 1958. TV host Invitation to Art, Mus. fine Arts, Boston, 1958-61; art critic N.Y. Times, 1961-64; host Dialogue, WNBC, 1961-64; vis. prof. Berkeley U., 1967; dir. visual arts Nat. Endowment for Arts, 1969-76, dir. media arts, 1976-94; dir. Millennium Projects, 1994-96. Art and architecture critic Today Program, 1971-77; adj. prof. Barnard Coll., 1969-96; editor-in-chief Art in Am., 1971-74; Univ. prof. fine arts and media L.I. U.-Southampton Campus, 1997—. Author: (art book) Object and Idea: A New York Art Journal, 1961-67, 1967; editor: (museum study) Museums in Crisis, 1972, (Art Book) American Masters, The Voice and the Myth, 1973, 3d revised edit., 2002, Inside the White Cube, 1986, revised edit., 1999, (novel) The Strange Case of Mile P., 1992 (Saggitaurus award, 1993), (novels) The Deposition of Father McGreevy, 1999 (Booker prize short list, 2000); dir.: (films) Hooper's Silence, 1981; contbr. articles to profl. jours. Recipient Mpls. Citizens award, 1961, Eire Soc. Gold medal for contbns. to culture, 1963, Grand Prix Montreal Internat. Festival of Arts Film award, 1982, Emmy nominations; Smith-Mundt fellow. Mem. Am. Irish Hist. Soc. (bd. dirs.), Whitney Mus. Am. Art (bd. dirs. 1996-2000), Coll. Art Assn. (life; Mather award 1964). Office: 15 W 67th St New York NY 10023-6226

ODOL, MARILYN ELAINE, accountant; b. Bklyn., Apr. 11, 1941; d. Eugene Fenwick and Marguerite Louise (Gadsden) Bennett; m. William Clarence Odol Jr., Jan. 17, 1974; children: Conrad, Corey. BS, SUNY-Empire State, 1981; student, Bklyn. Coll., 1958-64; diploma, Adelphi U., 1986. CFP, enrolled agt., accredited tax advisor, registered investment advisor; ins. agt.-life, accident/health; licensed Security Dealer Series 63, Security Dealer Series 6. Revenue agt. U.S. Treasury Dept.-IRS, Bklyn., 1966-86; acct./cert. fin. planner Massapequa, N.Y., 1986—. Mem. budget com. Amityville (N.Y.) Union Free Sch. Dist., 1989; mem. Carmen Rd. Civic Assn., Massapequa, N.Y., 1980—; com. mem. Cub Scout Troop 317, Copiague, N.Y., 1986-89; trustee Amityville Libr., 1991-96, pres. bd. trustees, 1993-94, also bd. dirs., v.p.; mem. L.I. Ednl. Coalition, 1991-96; mem. Dem. County Com., Town of Oyster Bay-Nassau County; bd. dirs. L.I. Housing Svcs., Victims Info. Bur. Suffolk County. Mem. Internat. Bd. Stds. and Practices for Cert. Fin. Planners, Fin. Planners Assn., L.I. Soc. Insts. Cert. Fin. Planners (bd. dirs. 1988-90), Am. Soc. Women Accts. (bd. dirs. 1984-86), Tax Inst. Sch. Profl. Accountancy C.W. Post Coll., Nat. Soc. Tax Profls., Nat. Assn. Securities Dealers (registered rep.). Democrat. Methodist. Avocations: sewing, theatre, travel. Home and Office: 28 Ford Dr W Massapequa NY 11758-3719 E-mail: modol@suffolk.lib.ny.us.

ODOM, DAVID MALCOLM, anesthesiologist; b. Glendale, Calif., 1943; MD, Baylor U., 1970. Diplomate Am. Bd. Anesthesiology, Am. Bd. Anti-Aging Medicine. Intern L.A. County-U. So. Calif. Med. Ctr., L.A., 1970-71, res. in anesthesiology, 1975-76, White Meml. Med. Ctr., L.A., 1972-73; pvt. practice anesthesiology Fairbanks, Alaska, 1989—. Mem. Am. Soc. Anesthesiologists, Alaska Soc. Anesthesiologists. Office: 1531 20th Ave Fairbanks AK 99701-5906 E-mail: slimtrim@mosquitonet.com.

ODOM, FLOYD CLARK, surgeon; b. Cisco, Tex., 1946; MD, U. Tex., San Antonio, 1972. Diplomate Am. Bd. Colon & Rectal Surgery, Am. Bd. Surgery. Intern Bexar County Hosp., San Antonio, 1972-73, resident in gen. surgery, 1973-77; fellow in colon & rectal surgery Baylor Med. Ctr., Dallas, 1977-78; colorectal surgeon Presbyn. Hosp., 1997—. Fellow ACS, Am. Soc. Colon and Rectal Surgeons. Office: 8220 Walnut Hill Ln Dallas TX 75231-4406

ODOM, JOHN YANCY, human resources specialist, writer; b. Jackson, Miss., Sept. 22, 1948; s. Corey Franklin and Rosa Belle Odom; m. Annie Sue Perkins, Aug. 15, 1970; 1 child Nikki Annette. BA, Lane Coll., 1969; MS, U. Wis., 1973, PhD, 1978. Cert. tchr., supt. Wis. Tchr. English Beloit (Wis.) Pub. Schs., 1969—72; affirmative action officer Madison (Wis.) Schs., 1973—76, dir. human rels., 1976—80, mid. sch. prin., 1980—85; acad. specialist U. Wis., 1985—86; pres. Odom & Assocs., 1985—. Cons. U.S. Dept. Justice, Boulder, Colo., 1989—93; faculty Credit Union Nat. Assn. Mgmt. Sch., 1996—, Nat. Headstart Acad., Albuquerque; dir. Charles Houston Inst., Madison, 2001—. Author: Saving Black America, 2001; editor: Charles Houston Inst. Newsletter, 2002; performer: (opera premiere) Shining Brow, 1993. Mem. NAACP Edn. Task Force, Balt., 2001, Nat. Rsch. Ctr. on English Learning, Wis., 1996—; pres. Madison NAACP, 1990—93, chair edn. com., 1998—; bd. dirs. Children's Theatre, 1994—. Named Humanitarian of Yr., City of Madison, 1992; recipient Outstanding Alumni award, Lane Coll., Jackson, Tenn., 1979, Ednl. Leadership award, Prairie View U., Tex., 1999, Human Rights award, City of Madison, 2002. Mem.: ASTD, Alpha Phi Alpha (founder Mu Eta Lambda chpt. 1976—). Avocations: singing, acting, fishing, writing. Office: Odom & Assocs LLC PO Box 56155 Madison WI 53705

ODOM, JUDY, software company executive; b. 1952; BBA in Acctg., Tex. Tech. U., 1974. CPA. With Coopers & Lybrand, Dallas, 1974-76, Grant Thornton, Dallas, 1976-85; co-founder, owner Software Spectrum, 1983—. Office: Software Spectrum 2140 Merritt Dr Garland TX 75041-6184

ODOM, MARY E. (LIBBY ODOM), musician, educator; b. Mobile, Ala., Dec. 18, 1928; d. Frederick and Bertha (Summers) Yost; m. Gerald Stuart Odom, Sept. 3, 1947 (dec. Oct. 1997); 1 child, Maria Renee. BS cum laude, U. Ala., 1980, MA in Edn., 1982. Voice tchr., accompanist Madame Rose Palmai Studio, Mobile, Ala., 1944-50; voice and piano tchr. Birmingham, 1954-64; music therapist State Sch. for Girls, Springville, 1951-57; voice and theory tchr. Meridian (Miss.) Jr. Coll., 1964-68; voice and piano tchr. Birmingham, 1968-88. Performer Mobile Opera Guild, Mobile Opera Workshop, 1943-53, Carnegie Hall, 1947, Met. Opera, N.Y.C., 1950-52, Boris Goldovsky Opera, W.Va., 1952-53, Town and Gown Little Theatre, Birmingham, 1953-73. Co-founder Mobile Opera Guild, 1943, Birmingham Civic Opera, 1955, Birmingham Civic Chorus, 1964; choir soloist Govt. St. Meth. Ch., Ctrl. Presbyn. Ch., Mobile, 1943-49, choir soloist, children's choir Ind. Presbyn. Ch., Birmingham, 1953-64; soloist, youth choir dir. Mountain Brook Presbyn. Ch., Birmingham, 1968-78; ch. organist Riverchase Presbyn. Ch., Birmingham, 1980-84, co-founder Active Elders, 1983; chmn., v.p. Birmingham Opera Guild, 1958—; mem. Salvation Army Women's Aux., 1989—; chorus dir. Shades Valley Music Club, 1980—. Recipent Cert. Appreciation Presbytery of Sheppards and Lapsley, Presbyn. Ch. USA, 1991, Riverchase Presbyn. Ch., 1999. Mem. AAUW, Ala. Fedn. Music Club (officer 1953—, Odom scholarship 1999, parliamentarian, past state pres.), Shades Valley Music Club (2d v.p. for programs), Birmingham Music Club Guild (publicity chmn., bd. dirs. 1964-68, guest artist 1953—), Delta Omicron, Kappa Delta Pi. Avocations: gardening, reading, programs for senior citizens, cooking. Home: 3804 Briar Oak Dr Birmingham AL 35243-4834

ODOM, PATRICIAN ANN (PATT ODOM), artist, educator; b. Hattiesburg, Miss., Nov. 21, 1942; d. Charles Casey and Catie Clara (Stringer) O.; m. Robert Frank Drake, Aug. 25, 1964 (div. Jan. 1970); children: Robert Charles, Thomas Casey. BS in Drawing and Painting, U. So. Miss., 1964, M in Art Edn., 1975; studied with Hon Chee Hee, U. Hawaii, 1968; studied with Douglas Walton, La. Tech. U., 1982; student, Ringling Sch. Art & Design, 1994; postgrad., U. Tenn., Arrowmont, 1994-96; numerous art workshops, 1987-98; studied with, Wolf Khan. Tchr. art E. Elem. Sch., Ocean Springs, Miss., 1966-67, Pecan Park, Ocean Springs, 1971-75, Ocean Springs H.S., 1975-79; art instr., gallery dir. Gulf Coast C.C., Gautier, Miss., 1980-99. Guest lectr. Hinds C.C., 1997; guest spkr. Miss. Art Mus., Pascagoula Garden Club; panelist spkr. Miss. Assn. Colls. Conf., 1997; motorator Cmty. Bridges Project, Biloxi, Miss., 1997; guest spkr. Ocean Springs Art Assn, 1998; tchr. John Campbell Folk Sch., N.C. Designed logo for Gulf Coast YMCA, Hattiesburg Racquetball and Fitness Ctr.; executed mural at Keesler Air Force Base, 1992; represented in permanent collections 1st Magnolia Bank, Biloxi, Miss., Mobile Mus. Art, Lamar Bank, U. So. Miss., William Carey Coll., Cottonlaudia Mus. Art; prin. works include sculpture Sen. John Stennis, Seabees Base, Gulfport, Miss., 1988; works appear in numerous calendars, (book) In Harmony with Nature, 1989 (Pen and Ink book), Art in Mississippi, 1720-1980. Recipient Nat. Tchrs. Award of Excellence, 1989, Purchase award, Cottonlandia Mus. Art, 1996, 1st place, Miss. Art Colony Traveling Show, 1997, Honored artist and educator of Miss., Nat. Mus. of Women in the Arts, 2001, Merit award, Cottonlandia Mus. Art, 2002, 3d pl. in exhbn., Art Wave, 2002, 3d pl. Geo Ohr Mus. Nat. Show, Pen and Quill, 2001. Mem. South Miss. Art Assn., Art Wave (show chair 1980-99), Miss. Women in Arts, Jackson County Arts Coun., Singing River Art Assn. (show chair 1988), Ocean Springs Art Assn. (bd. dirs. 1986-87, 95-96, 99, pres. 1994, 2002, receiving chair 1988, receiving chair for annual show 1984-86, past v.p. 1980-81), Biloxi Art Assn., Gulf Coast Art Assn., Nart Art Edn. Assn., Miss. C.C. Art Instructors, Kappa Kappa Iota, Delta Psi Omega. Avocations: painting, gardening, commercial art. Home: 306 Porter St Ocean Springs MS 39564-3714 E-mail: patto@ametro.net.

ODOM, SARAH BERNICE, elementary school educator; b. Orange, Tex., Dec. 17, 1965; d. William Ogden and Thelma Louise (Ball) Gilpatrick; m. Armond G. Odom, Jr., Dec. 15, 1978 (div. Oct. 1999); children: Wesley, Clinton, Cody. AS, Panola Jr. Coll., Carthage, Tex., 1989; BS in Edn. cum laude, U. Tex., Tyler, 1990; M in Elem. Edn., Lamar U., 2001. Cert. life elem. self-contained grades 1-8 tchr., life elem. reaing tchr. grades 1-8, life generic spl. edn. tchr. grades PK-12. Tchr. Mauriceville (Tex.) Middle, 1991—95, Little Cypress Jr. High, Orange, 1995—99, Little Cypress Intermediate, Orange, 1999—2001, Little Cypress Jr. High, Orange, 2001—. Nominee Disney's Am. Tchr. award. Avocations: reading, painting, writing, outdoor activities. Home: 502 Camellia Orange TX 77630 Office: Little Cypress Jr High 6765 Fm Rd 1130 Orange TX 77632

ODOM, SUSAN ANN, program analyst; b. Jacksonville, Ill., May 10, 1957; d. Richard Arlington Jr. and Virginia Lea (Quinlan) Osborne; m. David Lee Odom, Aug. 29, 1979; children: Hope Leigh, Quinlan Day. Student, U. Ill., 1976-80, Trinity Coll., Washington, 1984-87. Prin. investigator U.S. Army Corps of Engrs., Champaign, Ill., 1979-84, mgmt. analyst Washington, 1984-87, with Office of Strategic Initiatives, 1988-89, strategic mgmt. analyst Resource Mgmt. Directorate, 1989-91, career program mgr. Directorate of Resource Mgmt., 1991—, career program mgr., 1987-88. V.p. DSH Enterprises, Springfield, Va., 1986—; Army C.E. rep. Tri-svcs. Com., WAshington, 1986—; program mgr. Leadership Conf., 1989, 90, 91; project mgr. Mid. and Sr. Mgmt. Conf.; project mgr. Focus 89, 90, 91. Mem. Automated Data Processing Profls., Nat. Assn. Female Execs. Roman Catholic. Avocations: bridge, pastels.

ODOM, WILLIAM ELDRIDGE, army officer, educator; b. Cookeville, Tenn., June 23, 1932; s. John Albert and Callie Frances (Everhart) O.; m. Anne Weld Curtis, June 9, 1962; 1 child, Mark Weld. BS, U.S. Mil. Acad., 1954; MA, Columbia U., 1962, PhD, 1970; DSc (hon.), Middlebury Coll., 1987. Commd. 2nd lt. U.S. Army, 1954, advanced through grades to lt. gen., 1984; mem. U.S. Mil. Liaison Mission to Soviet Forces, Germany, 1964-66; from asst. prof. to assoc. prof. govt. U.S. Mil. Acad., West Point, 1966-69, 74-76; asst. Army attache U.S. embassy, Moscow, 1972-74; nat. security staff mem. White House, 1977-81; asst. chief of staff for intelligence Dept. Army, Washington, 1981-85; dir. Nat. Security Agy., Fort Meade, Md., 1985-88; dir. nat. security studies Hudson Inst., 1988—. Adj. prof. pol. sci. Yale U., 1989—; chmn. bd. dirs. Am. Sci. and Engring., V-ONE (Virtual Open Network Environs.). Author: The Soviet Volunteers, 1973, On Internal War, 1992, Trial After Triumph, 1992, America's Military Revolution, 1993, (with Robert Dujarric) Commonwealth or Empire? Russia, Central Asia and The Transcaucasus, 1995, The Collapse of the Soviet Military, 1998; contbr. articles to profl. jours. Trustee Middlebury Coll. Bd., 1987-97. Decorated Def. D.S.M. with oak leaf cluster, D.S.M. with oak leaf cluster, Legion of Merit, Nat. Security medal, Nat. Intelligence D.S.M.; grand cross Order of Merit with Star (Fed. Republic Germany); Order Nat. Security Merit (Republic of Korea), officer Nat. Order of Merit (France). Mem. Coun. on Fgn. Rels., Am. Assn. for Advancement of Slavic Studies, Internat. Inst. for Strategic Studies, Am. Polit. Sci. Assn., Acad. Polit. Sci. Congregationalist. Office: Hudson Inst 1015 18th St NW Ste 300 Washington DC 20036-5200

O'DONNELL, ANTHONY JOSEPH, JR. lawyer, educator; b. Miami, Fla., Apr. 13, 1945; s. Anthony Joseph O'Donnell and Margaret S. (Sloan) Blue; m. Gloria Germain Dworet, Aug. 5, 1967 (div. Dec-c 1977); children: Anthony Joseph, William Tyler; m. Sonia Escobio, Apr. 21, 1978; children: Lara Escobio, Robert Anthony. BA in History, Emory U., 1967; MA in History, Princeton U., 1970, PhD in History, 1974; JD, U. Fla., 1977. Bar: Fla. 1977, U.S. Dist. Ct. (so. dist.) Fla. 1985, U.S. Ct. Appeals (11th cir.) 1985, U.S. Supreme Ct. 1988. Pol. Peace Corps, Malaysia, 1968-69; asst. prof. history U. Mo., St. Louis, 1972-75; assoc.c Mershon, Sawyer et al, Miami, 1977-80; assoc., then ptnr. Greenberg, Traurig, Askew et al, 1981-88; ptnr. Akerman, Senterfitt Eidson, 1988-90; of counsel Baker & McKenzie, 1991—2000. Adj. prof. law U. Miami Law Sch., 1983-95. Pro bono legal counsel St. Thomas Episcopal Ch., Miami, 1985-98, Charlee, abused children charity, Miami, 1988-98; trustee Palmer-Trinity Sch., Miami, 1990-99 Mem. Fla. Bar (CLE com. 1988-90, CLE lectr. 1986, 89, 90, lectr. bus. law seminar 1989, environ. seminar 1990), Dade County Bar Assn., Lambda Alpha. Avocations: sailing, musical theater, classical piano. Home: 1129 Palermo Ave Coral Gables FL 33134-6324

O'DONNELL, DANIEL J. lawyer; b. Flushing, N.Y., Nov. 17, 1960; s. Edward J. and Roseann (Murtha) O'D.; life partner John J. Banta. BA in Pub. Affairs, George Washington U., 1982; JD, CUNY, 1987. Bar: N.Y. 1988, U.S. Dist. Ct. (ea. and so. dists.) N.Y., U.S. Ct. Appeals (2d cir.), U.S. Supreme Ct. 1993. Staff atty. Legal Aid Soc., Bklyn., 1987-94; ptnr. Daniel J. O'Donnell, N.Y.C., 1994—. Mem. Cmty. Bd. 9, N.Y.C., 1995—; pres. Broadway Dems., N.Y.C., 1997-98; founding mem. Morningside Heights Hist. Dist. Com., N.Y.C., 1997—. Office: 2109 Broadway Ste 206 New York NY 10023-2106

O'DONNELL, DENISE ELLEN, lawyer; BS in Polit. Sci., Canisius Coll., 1968; MSW, SUNY, Buffalo, 1973, JD summa cum laude, 1982. Bar: NY 1983, U.S. Dist. Ct. (we., no., ea. and so. dists.) NY, U.S. Ct. Appeals (2d cir.), U.S. Supreme Ct. Law clk. Hon. M. Dolores Denman NY Appellate Divsn. 4th Dept., Buffalo, 1982-85; asst. U.S. atty. Western Dist. N.Y., 1985-90, appellate chief, 1990-93, 1st asst. U.S. atty., 1993—97, U.S. atty., 1997-2001; ptnr. Gen. Litigation Practice Group, Hodgson, Russ, LLP, 2001—. Part-time instr. trial technique program SUNY, 1990—; lectr. ethics, evidence and trial practice Office Legal Edn.U.S. Dept. Justice, 1988—2000; lectr. NITA seminar Western NY Trial Acad., 1994, 98; mem. Atty. Gen.'s Adv. Com., 1999—2001, vice-chair, 2000—01. Mem. Vol. Lawyers Program, 1997—2001; bd. dirs. NCCJ, 2000—, Nat. Women's Hall of Fame, 2001—. Mem.: ABA, Nat. Assn. Former U.S. Attys., NY State Bar Assn., Western NY Trial Lawyers Assn., Women's Bar Assn. State NY (founding mem. Western NY chpt. 1985), Bar Assn. Erie County (dep. treas. 1992—93, treas. 1993—94), West Side Rowing Club. Office: Hodgson Russ LLP One M&T Plz Ste 2000 Buffalo NY 14203-2931 E-mail: dodonnel@hodgsonruss.com.

O'DONNELL, DUCK HEE, cellist, music teacher; b. Seoul, Korea, Dec. 30, 1938; came to U.S., 1963; d. Kap Cho and Hei Sun (Kim) Lee; m. Edward O'Donnell, Aug. 31, 1968; children: Edward, Helen, Nancy. BS in Music, Seoul Nat. U., 1960; Diploma, U. Cin., 1968. Cellist Fla. Gulf Coast Symphony Orch., Tampa, 1968-71; pvt. music tchr. Rockville, Md., 1976—; cellist Friday Morning Music Club, Washington, 1976—. Recipient Tchr. of Yr. award Md. String Tchrs. Assn., 1998. Mem. Music Tchrs. Assn. Am., Md. Music Tchrs. Assn., Friday Morning Music Club. Home: 6 Cleveland Ct Rockville MD 20850-3719

O'DONNELL, EDITH J. educational and information technology consultant, writer, musician; b. Proctorville, Ohio, Mar. 26, 1929; d. John Jordan and Florence Amber (Banks) Black; m. Edward Kennedy O'Donnell, Dec. 8, 1950; children: Kathleen Marie, Michael Edward. AA, Cerritos Coll., 1963; BA, Calif. State U., Long Beach, 1965, MA, 1973; MLS, U. So. Calif., 1977, EdD, 1991. Libr., tchr. St. Joseph's H.S., Lakewood, Calif., 1968-72; libr., media dir. Los Altos H.S., Hacienda Heights, 1972-93; faculty libr. info. sci. San Jose State U., Fullerton, 1991-94; ednl. tech. cons., spkr., 1994—. Condr. workshops and cons. in field; instr. North Orange County C.C. Dist., 1988-90; cons., writer Consolidated Program divsn. State of Calif. Dept. Edn., 1981. Author: Integrating Computers Into the Classroom: The Missing Key, Integrating Internet Into the Classroom: The Missing Icon; contbr. articles to profl. publs.; prod. TV ednl. programs. Del. Gov.'s Coun. on Librs. and Info. Sci., White House Conf., 1980; active La Mirada Symphony Orch., La Mirada Pops Orch. City of Buena Park grantee. Mem. DAR, Computer Using Educators, Calif. Tchrs. Assn., Calif. Sch. Assn. (sect. exec. bd. 1980-86), Sons and Daus. Pioneer River Men, Kappa Delta Pi. Methodist. Address: PO Box 2062 Fullerton CA 92837-0062

O'DONNELL, EDWARD FRANCIS, JR. lawyer; b. Waterbury, Conn., May 13, 1950; s. Edward Francis and Dorothy Patricia (Breheny) O'D.; m. Jayne Ann DeSantis, Dec. 29, 1972; children: Ryan Anderson, Brooke Stires. BA, St. Anselm Coll., Manchester, N.H., 1972; JD, U. Conn., 1977. Bar: S.C. 1978, Conn. 1977, U.S. Dist. Ct. S.C. 1978, U.S. Dist. Ct. Conn. 1980, U.S. Ct. Appeals (1st and 2d cirs.) 1980. Assoc. Ogeltree, Deakins, Nash, Smoak & Stewart, Greenville, S.C., 1977-79; ptnr. Siegel, O'Connor, Zagari, O'Donnell & Beck, P.C., Hartford, Conn., 1979—. Contbr. articles to profl. jours. Mem. ABA, Conn. Bar Assn., S.C. Bar Assn., Hartford Bar Assn., Hartford Club, Phi Alpha Theta. Roman Catholic. Office: Siegel O'Connor Zagari O'Donnell & Beck PC 150 Trumbull St Fl 5 Hartford CT 06103-2400

O'DONNELL, EDWARD JOSEPH, bishop, former editor; b. St. Louis, July 4, 1931; s. Edward Joseph and Ruth Mary (Carr) O'Donnell. Student, Cardinal Glennon Coll., 1949-53; postgrad., Kenrick Sem., 1953-57. Ordained priest Roman Cath. Ch., 1957, consecrated bishop, 1984; assoc. pastor in 5 St. Louis parishes, 1957-77; pastor St. Peter's Ch., Kirkwood, Mo., 1977-81; assoc. dir. Archdiocesan Commn. on Human Rights, 1962-70; dir. Archdiocesan Radio-TV Office, 1966-68, Archdiocesan Vocation Council, 1965; editor St. Louis Rev., 1968-81; vicar-gen. Archdiocese of St. Louis, 1981-84, aux. bishop, 1984-94; bishop Diocese of Lafayette, Lafayette, LA, 1994—. Bd dirs Nat Cath Conf Interracial Justice, 1980—85; chmn Interfaith Clergy Coun Greater St Louis, 1963—67; NAACP, 1964—66; bd dirs Urban League St Louis, 1962—68. Named to Golden Dozen, Int Soc Weekly Newspaper Eds, 1970, 1977. Mem.: Nat Asn TV Arts and Scis, Cath Press Asn. Office: PO Box 3387 Lafayette LA 70502-3387

O'DONNELL, F. SCOTT, banker; b. Brownsville, Pa., Sept. 20, 1940; s. Francis Horner and Rebecca (Warren) O'D.; m. Ann Bukmir, Dec. 30, 1976. BA, Grove City (Pa.) Coll., 1962; postgrad., U. Wis. Grad. Sch. Banking, 1970, Internat. Sch. Banking, U. Colo., 1972. Nat. bank examiner Comptroller of Currency, Cleve., 1965-71; supt. of banks State of Ohio, Columbus, 1975-77; sr. v.p. First Nat. Bank, Steubenville, Ohio, 1971-75; exec. v.p. Heritage Bancorp, 1977-80; from v.p. to exec. v.p. Soc. Corp., Cleve., 1980-95; dep. tax commr. State of Ohio, Columbus, 1996-99, supt. fin. instn., 1999—. Mem. state banking bd. Div. of Banks, Columbus, 1979-85, govt. affairs com. Ohio Bankers Assn., 1982-84. Served with USCG, 1963-69. Mem. Columbus Athletic Club, Pitts. Univ. Club, Belmont Hills Country Club, Lakewood Country Club. Avocations: travel, politics, antiques. Home: 31830 Lake Rd Avon Lake OH 44012-2022 Office: Ohio Divsn Fin Instns 77 S High St Fl 21 Columbus OH 43215-6199

O'DONNELL, JAMES FRANCIS, retired health science administrator; b. Cleve., July 22, 1928; s. John Michael and Mary Louise (Hayes) O'D.; m. Winifred Locke, Sept. 10, 1955; children— Anne Catherine, Patrick John, Mary Elizabeth BS in Biology, St. Louis U., 1949; PhD in Biochemistry, U. Chgo., 1957. Asst., then. assoc. prof. biol. chemistry and exptl. medicine Coll. Medicine, U. Cin., 1957-68; grants assoc., div. research grants NIH, Bethesda, Md., 1968-69; program dir. population and reprodn. grants br. Ctr. for Population Research, Nat. Inst. Child Health and Human Devel., NIH, 1969-71; asst. dir. div. research resources NIH, Bethesda, 1971-76, dep. dir. div. research resources, 1976-90, acting dir. div. research resources, 1981-82, dir. Office of Extramural Programs, Office of the Dir., 1990-99; ret., 1999. Served with U.S. Army, 1950-52 Home: 11601 Bunnell Ct S Rockville MD 20854-3603 E-mail: jfwlodonnell@erols.com.

O'DONNELL, JOHN JOSEPH, JR. optometrist; b. Phila., Oct. 26, 1956; s. John Joseph and Mary Agnes (Hungrige) O'D.; m. Jane Susan Betz, June 28, 1980; children: Kathryn Marie, John Joseph III, Michael Charles. BS in Biology, St. Joseph U., 1978; BS in Ocular Sci., Pa. Coll. Optometry, 1981, OD with honors, 1983. Cardio-pulmonary perfusionist Hosp. U. Pa., Phila., 1978-80; staff optometrist Pa. Eye Assocs., Harrisburg, 1983-85; chief optometric svcs. Meml. Eye Inst., 1986-93; optometrist, ptnr. Premier Eye Care Group, 1994—. Trustee Optometric Svc. Corp. Pa., Harrisburg, 1989. Contbr. articles to profl. jours. Fellow Am. Acad. Optometry; mem. Am. Optometric Assn., Pa. Optometric Assn. (trustee 1987-94, pres. 1994), Ctrl. Pa. Optometric Soc. (pres. 1985-86). Republican. Roman Catholic. Avocations: computers, writing, photography, digital imaging processing. Office: Premier Eye Care Group Inc 92 Tuscarora St Harrisburg PA 17104-1691 E-mail: jjodod@aol.com.

O'DONNELL, JOHN LOGAN, lawyer; b. Chgo., Mar. 6, 1914; s. William Joseph and Elizabeth (McLogan) O'D.; m. Mary Ellen Sipe, Sept. 2, 1939 (dec. Dec. 29, 1979); 1 son, John Logan; m. Michele G. Fischer, May 9, 1981. BA, Williams Coll., 1934; JD, Northwestern U., 1937. Bar: Ill. 1937, N.Y. 1943, D.C. 1977. Asso. firm Defrees, Buckingham, Jones and Hoffman, Chgo., 1937-38; staff atty. Office Gen. Counsel, SEC, 1938-41; instr. Cath. U. Law Sch., 1938-41; assoc. Cravath, Swaine & Moore, N.Y.C., 1941-52; ptnr. Olwine, Connelly, Chase, O'Donnell & Weyher, 1952-91, of counsel, 1991, Twomey, Hoppe & Gallanty, N.Y.C., 1991—. Bd. dirs. Near East Found., 1968-84. Fellow Am. Coll. Trial Lawyers; mem. Assn. Bar City N.Y., Am., Fed., bar assns., Beta Theta Pi, Phi Delta Phi. Clubs: Union, Univ., Williams, (N.Y.C.). Roman Catholic. Avocations: piano, sports. Home: 181 E 73rd St New York NY 10021-3549 Office: Twomey Hoppe and Gallanty 757 3rd Ave New York NY 10017-2013

O'DONNELL, JOHN PATRICK, journalist, photographer; b. Bklyn., Mar. 18, 1936; s. Hugh and Anne Gildea O'Donnell; m. Patricia Carter Critchlow, July 4, 1970 (div. June 1976); 1 child, Joy Anne; m. Sharon Leigh Amar, Aug. 6, 1976 (div. July 1982); 1 child, Sean Patrick. BS cum laude, Kensington U., 1984. Writer, editor, reporter various newspapers including Hollywood Citizen-News and L.A. Times, Calif., 1966-84; editor-in-chief Asian News, L.A., 1984-86; freelance journalist various publs. including Time, Cath. Press, Penthouse, 1986—. Media cons. to U.S. govt.; defined toxic cocktail chem. agts. which poisoned Am. troops in Vietnam, 1982. Comm. media cons. cultural svcs. Korean Govt., L.A., 1985; active Fellowship of the Spirit, 1964—. With USMC, 1954—57, with U.S. Merchant Marine, 1966—67. Recipient Best Feature Writing award L.A. Press Club, 1968; nominated Pulitzer Prize, 1968, 69. Roman Catholic. Avocations: people watching, real-life photography, hiking, journaling. Home: 1310 Royal Oaks Dr Apt C-15 Duarte CA 91010

O'DONNELL, JOSEPH MICHAEL, electronics executive; BS, U. Tenn., 1968, MBA, 1970. Sales mgr. telecommunications ITT, Chgo., 1973-75, dir. mktg. communication Hartford, Conn., 1975-77; dir. mktg. Gen. Instrument Corp., N.Y.C., 1977-81, gen. mgr. Post Falls, Idaho, 1981-84; v.p. Conrac Corp., Stamford, Conn., 1984-87; pres. OD & S Ventures, 1987-88; v.p. Handy & Harman, N.Y.C., 1988-89; CEO, GO/DAN Industries, New Haven, 1990-92; pres., CEO Savin Corp., Stamford, Conn., 1993-94; pres., CEO, Artesyn Techs. Inc., Boca Raton, Fla., 1994—. Office: Artesyn Techs Inc 7900 Glades Rd Boca Raton FL 33434-4167

O'DONNELL, KEVIN, retired metal products executive; b. Cleve., June 9, 1925; s. Charles Richard and Ella (Kilbane) O'Donnell; m. Ellen Blydenburgh, Aug. 16, 1965; children: Kevin, Susan, Michael, John, Maura, Neil, Megan, Hugh. AB, Kenyon Coll., Gambier, Ohio, 1947, PhD (hon.) in Law, 1980; MBA, Harvard U., 1947; PhD in Econs. (hon.) , Pusan (Korea) Nat. U., 1970; PhD in Humanities (hon.) , Ohio Wesleyan U., 1972. Gen. sales mgr. Steel Improvement & Forge Co., Cleve., 1947-60; mgmt. cons. Booz, Allen and Hamilton, 1960-62; gen. mgr., dir. Atlas Alloys-Rio Algom Corp., 1963-66; dir. Peace Corps, Seoul, Republic of Korea, 1966-70, dir. adminstrn. and fin., then dep. acting dir., 1970-71; assoc. dir. internat. ops. ACTION, 1971-72; exec. v.p. SIFCO Industries, Inc., Cleve., 1972-75, pres., chief oper. officer, 1976-83, pres., chief exec. officer, 1983-89, chief exec. officer, 1989-90, chmn., exec. comm., 1990-94; ret., 1994. Bd. dirs. Ctrl. Pk. Media Corp., Doyle Pacific Industries, Ltd., Whole Health Mgmt., Inc., Cleve.; adv. dir. Plz. Group, Houston, Capital Strategies, Inc., Cleve. Mem. Washington Inst. Fgn. Affairs, Cleve. Com. Fgn. Rels., chmn., 1979—82, CCWA, 1982—89; pres. Guest Ho., Inc., 1990—92; trustee Alcohol Svcs., Cleve., 1993—, Cleve. Coun. World Affairs, Nat. Peace Corps. Assn. Decorated Order Civil Merit Republic of Korea. Mem.: Harvard Bus. Sch. Alumni Assn. (dir. Boston 1991—94), Army-Navy Club (Washington), Westwood Country Club, Pepper Pike Country Club, Union Club, 50 Club, First Friday Club, Harvard Bus. Sch. Club Cleve., Knights of Malta (master knight). Republican. Roman Catholic. Avocations: golf, reading. E-mail: kevodoncle@aol.com.

O'DONNELL, LAURENCE GERARD, editorial consultant; b. Bklyn., June 30, 1935; s. Thomas Edward and Dorothy (Clark) O'D.; m. Joan M. Coniglio, Jan. 9, 1960; children: Christopher, Carolyn, Jeffrey, Anthony. AB, Holy Cross Coll., 1957. Reporter Wall Street Jour., N.Y.C., 1958-66, chief Detroit Bur., 1966-74, asst. mng. editor, N.Y.C., 1974-77, mng. editor, 1977-83; assoc. editor Dow Jones & Co., Inc., 1983-90, cons., 1991-99. Pres. Dow Jones Newspaper Fund, 1988-93; bd. dirs. Dow Jones Newspaper Fund, Inter Am. Press Assn.; vis. lectr. Queens Coll./CUNY, 1992-99. Trustee Holy Cross Coll., 1982-90; mem. journalism adv. bd. Queens Coll./CUNY, 1989—; juror Pulitzer Prize, 1982, 83. Mem. Am. Soc. Newspaper Editors. Office: Dow Jones Newspaper Fund PO Box 300 Princeton NJ 08543-0300

O'DONNELL, MARK JOSEPH, accountant; b. St. Louis, Mar. 28, 1954; s. William E. and Jeanne M. (Collins) O'D.; m. Jane E. Wismann, Sept. 29, 1973; children: Sean, Mark Jr., Kyle. BSBA magna cum laude, U. Mo., 1977. CPA, Mo. Cost acct. Hunter Engring., St. Louis, 1973-76; acct. Gen. Dynamics, 1976-77, Lester Witte & Co., St. Louis, 1977-80, mgr., 1980-82; ptnr. Bounds, Poger & O'Donnell, 1982-86, mng. ptnr., 1986-94; mng. prin. O'Donnell, Bonebrake & Co., P.C., 1994—. Named one of Outstanding Young Men Am., U.S. Jaycees, 1978. Mem. Am. Inst. CPA's, Mo. Soc. CPA's. Roman Catholic. Avocations: weight lifting, jogging, road cycling. Office: O'Donnell Bonebrake & Co PC 11457 Olde Cabin Rd Ste 310 Saint Louis MO 63141-7172

O'DONNELL, MARY MURPHY, medical/surgical nurse, consultant; b. Lincoln, Ill., Feb. 21, 1918; d. Thomas Edward and Frances Ward (Hayes) Murphy; m. Maurice A. O'Donnell, Jan. 29, 1942. Diploma, St. John's Sch. Nursing, Springfield, Ill., 1939. RN Ill., Fla. Asst. to ear, nose and throat specialist, 1939—42; nurse U.S. Govt. Hosp., 1942—43; asst. to gen. practitioner Springfield, 1943—55; staff nurse City Health Dept., 1955—65; dir. tng. and edn. Springfield and Sangamon County Civil Def. Agy., 1965—66; exec., cons. in charge med. self-help Ill. Dept. Pub. Health, 1966—74; nurse epidemiologist St. Joseph Hosp., Port Charlotte, Fla., 1975—91, part-time epidemiologist, 1992—93; ret., 1993. Cons., 1993—. Mem. AIDS task force Charlotte County Dept. Pub. Health, Fla., pres. epidemiology group, 1991; instr. AIDS Program, 1987—93; v.p. S. Ctrl. Area Ill. Women's Civil Def. Coun.; mem. Civic Def. Coun.; chmn. civil def. activities ARC; v.p., mem. health svcs. adv. com. U.S. Civil Def. Coun.; ofcl. vol. rep. Am. Social Health Assn. Recipient Spl. award, State Dept. Am. Legion Aux., 1954, cert. Honor, Mayor of City of Springfield, 1966, Silver Wing bracelet, Ground Observer Corps, 1959, Pfizer award merit, U.S. Civil Def. Coun., 1969, Presdl. citation, 1972. Mem.: S.W. Regional Infection Control, Assn. Practitioners Infection Control, USAF Air Def. Team (hon.). Republican. Roman Catholic. Avocations: boating, swimming, clog dancing, golf, horses. Home: 819 Napoli Ln Punta Gorda FL 33950-6525 Personal E-mail: modonnell@comcast.net.

O'DONNELL, MICHAEL JAMES, computer scientist; b. Spartanburg, S.C., Apr. 4, 1952; s. William Joseph and Linnie Lucille (Hynds) O'D.; m. Julie Ann Nerini, Feb. 6, 1982; children: Benjamin Michael, Mary Kathleen. BSc, Purdue U., 1972; PhD, Cornell U., 1976. Rsch. assoc. U. Toronto, Ont., Can., 1976-77; asst. prof. Purdue U., West Lafayette, Ind., 1976-81, assoc. prof., 1981-85, Johns Hopkins U., Balt., 1984-85; prof. U. Chgo., 1985—, assoc. chair computer sci., 1986-87, chair computer sci., 1987-90, sr. fellow Computation Inst., 2000—. Pvt. cons., 1999—; vis. prof. U. Iowa, Iowa City, 1996-97; vis. assoc. prof. Johns Hopkins U., Balt., 1983-84; adv. bd. Founds. of Computation Lab., Queensland, Australia, 1989—. Author: Computing in Systems Described by Equations, 1976, Equational Logic as a Programming Language, 1985; co-author: A Programming Logic, 1978; editl. bd. Jour. of Functional and Logic Programming, 1995—, mng. editor Chgo. Jour. of Theoretical Computer Sci., 1994—2000. Grantee NSF, 1989-94. Mem. IEEE Computer Soc., IEEE Signal Processing Soc., Assn. for Computing Machinery (chmn. SIGSound 2001—), Acoustical Soc. of Am., Midwest Soc. for Programming Langs. and Systems (pres. 1987-94). Achievements include invention and first implemention of lazy evaluation for functional programs; discovery of first practical example of Gödel incompleteness. Avocations: barbershop quartet singing, curling. Office: U Chgo 1100 E 58th St Chicago IL 60637-1588 E-mail: michael_odonnell@acm.org.

O'DONNELL, PATRICK ALAN, software development scientist; b. Port Angeles, Wash., Dec. 5, 1958; s. Albert Ray and Harryetta (Ridings) O'D.; m. Teresa Hohol, June 11, 1988; children: Kelly Marie, Tracy Alana. SB, SM, MIT, 1983. Rsch. engr. MIT, Cambridge, 1983-94; devel. scientist Ascent Tech., Inc., 1994—. TeX computer typesetting lang. cons., Cambridge, 1992-94. Co-author: HANDEY: A Robot Task Planner, 1992; inventor in field. Asst. choir dir., cantor St. Theresa's Parish, Billerica, Mass., 1989-95. Mem. IEEE, Assn. for Computing Machinery, Nat. Assn. Pastoral Musicians, KC. Avocations: music, skiing. Home: 16 Margaret Ln Billerica MA 01821-2965 Office: Ascent Tech Inc 64 Sidney St Cambridge MA 02139-4170

O'DONNELL, PIERCE HENRY, lawyer; b. Troy, N.Y., Mar. 5, 1947; s. Harry J. and Mary (Kane) O'Donnell; m. Dawn Donley, Mar. 17, 1995; children: Meghan Maureen, Brendan Casey, Courtney Dawn, Pierce Dublin, Aidan Yeats. BA, Georgetown U., 1969, JD, 1972; LLM, Yale U., 1975. Bar: D.C. 1973, U.S. Supreme Ct. 1975, Calif. 1978. Law clk. to Justice Byron R. White U.S. Supreme Ct.; law clk. to Judge Shirley M. Hutstedler U.S. Ct. Appeals (9th cir.); assoc. Williams & Connolly, Washington, 1975-78; ptnr. Beardsley, Hufstedler & Kemble, L.A., 1978-81, Hufstedler, Miller, Carlson & Beardsley, L.A., 1981-82, O'Donnell & Gordon, L.A., 1982-87, Kaye, Scholer, Fierman, Hays & Handler, L.A., 1988-95, O'Donnell & Shaeffer, L.L.P., L.A., 1996—; pres. Premiere Media, Inc., 1999—. Exec. asst. U.S. Sec. Edn., 1979; spl. counsel Commn. Jud. Performance, San Francisco, 1979; chmn. Nat. Media, Inc., 1984—92. Co-author: (book) Fatal Subtraction: The Inside Story of Buchwald v Paramount, 1992, Toward A Just and Effective Sentencing System: Agenda for Legislative Reform, 1976; author: Dawn's Early Light, 2001; contbr. articles to profl. jours. Chmn. Friends Cal Tech YMCA, 1983—84, Verdugo-San Rafael Urban Mountain Park Fund, 1980—84; bd. dirs. Foothill Family Svc., 1979—85, chmn., 1984—85; bd. dirs. Interfaith Ctr. To Reverse Arms Race, 1984—90, pres., 1987—88; mem. Econ. Round Table of L.A., 1979—, pres., 2000—01; chmn. Calif. Coast Baseball Acad., 2001—; bd. dirs. Firends of Altadena Libr., 1979—81, Pasadena-Foothill Urban League, E. Altadena Little League, 1993—97. Fellow: Internat. Acad. Trial Lawyers; mem.: ABOTA, NAACP, PEN, Am. Bd. Trial Assocs., Cal Tech Assocs., Am. Law Inst., Sierra Club, Calif. Club, Gridiron Club (Georgetown U.), Bel Air Country Club. Roman Catholic. Home: 405 Linda Vista Ave Pasadena CA 91105-1237 Office: O'Donnell & Shaeffer LLP 633 W 5th St Ste 1700 Los Angeles CA 90071-2027 E-mail: podonnell@oslaw.com.

O'DONNELL, ROBERT GEORGE, fine artist; b. Bklyn., Jan. 6, 1938; s. Lester and Isabela (Creen) O'D.; m. Susan Ann Daly, Dec. 3, 1967; children: Tara, Jason, Stephanie. AS, N.Y.S. Regents Coll., Albany, 1976, BA, 1977. Fin. loan officer SBA, N.Y.C., 1976-85; fine artist Yonkers, N.Y., 1962—. One-man show Bronxville (N.Y.) Women's Club, 1998. With USAF, 1955-62, Japan. Mem. Am. Mensa, Ltd. Avocations: chess, weightlifting, writing. Home: 1 Leighton Ave Apt 6E Yonkers NY 10705-3742

O'DONNELL, ROBERT PATRICK, priest; b. Gary, Ind., June 11, 1919; s. Liquori Alphonsus and Carolyn Emily (Senn) O'D. Student, Art Inst., Chgo.; BA, U. Chgo., 1943; MA, Cath. U., 1945; postgrad., Gregorian U., Rome, 1980-81. Ordained priest Roman Cath. Ch., 1949. Asst. Sacred Heart Ch., Russellville, Ky., 1950-52; adminstr. Our Lady of Lourdes Ch., Otway, Ohio, 1953-55; pub. rels. Glenmary Home Missioners, Glendale, 1956-60; chaplain Glenmary Sisters, Fayetteville, 1960-66; pastor Holy Redeemer Ch., Vanceburу, Ky., 1987-94, St. Agnes Ch., Elkton, 1981-87, St. Mary & St. James Ch., Guthrie, St. Francis De Sales Ch., Idabel, Okla., 1987-94; with Glenmary Home Missioners, Cincinnati, 1994—. Editor, photographer, illustrator Glenmary's Challenge, Cin., 1952-80; designer/builder seven chs. in Ky., Ohio, N.C., 1952-64. Founder/designer: Appalachian Studios-resident artist, gen. mgr., 1966-80; composer music, producer: (musical) From Sheeba They Came, 1990; producer: (movie) Glenmary Story, 1958; other. With USN. With maritime svc. USN, 1943, ATO. Recipient Thomas Jefferson award, U.S. Office of Pres., 1979, Four Chaplains Nat. award Office of Four Chaplains Found., Phila., 1981; Art scholar U. chgo. Mem. Rotary (internat. exc. chmn. 1989-91), Phi Kappa Psi (pres. 1943). Home and Office: 100 Compton Rd 5C3 Cincinnati OH 45215-4141

O'DONNELL, ROSIE, television personality, comedienne, actress; b. Commack, N.Y., Mar. 21, 1962; children: Parker Jaren, Chelsea Belle, Blake Christopher. Attended, Dickinson Coll., Boston Univ. Appearances include (TV series) Gimme A Break, 1986-87, Stand By Your Man, 1992, Women Aloud, 1992, Stand-up Spotlight, VH-1 (American Comedy award nomination best female performer in a TV special 1994, Cable ACE award nomination best entertainment host 1994), (TV) host The Rosie O'Donnell Show, 1995-2002 (Daytime Emmy awards 1997, 98, 99, 2000, 2001), (TV movie) The Twilight of the Golds, 1997; (films) A League of Their Own, 1992, Sleepless in Seattle, 1993 (American Comedy award nomination best supporting female in a motion picture 1994), Another Stakeout, 1993 (American Comedy award nomination best actress in a motion picture 1994), Car 54, Where Are You?, 1994, I'll Do Anything, 1994, The Flintstones, 1994, Exit to Eden, 1994, Now and Then, 1995, Beautiful Girls, 1996, Harriet the Spy, 1996, A Very Brady Sequel, 1996 (uncredited), Wide Awake, 1996, Get Bruce, 1999, Jackie's Back, 1999, Tarzan, 1999 (voice), Flinstones in Viva Rock Vegas, 2000; Broadway shows include Grease, 1994, Seussical th eMusical, 2001; author: Find Me, 2002; editor: Rosie mag., 2000-2002.*

O'DONNELL, SCOTT RICHARD, aviation administrator; b. Pitts., Sept. 27, 1950; s. Robert Thomas and Corinne Ann (Phelps) O'D.; m. Patricia Lea Donnelly, Sept. 1, 1978; children: Ronald, Michael, Daniel. BA, Geneva Coll., 1972. Cert. secondary edn. teaching. Tchr. Montour High Sch., McKees Rocks, Pa., 1973-74; project adminstr. Allegheny County Law Dept., Pitts., 1974-76; adminstrv. asst. Allegheny County Police Dept., 1976-77; exec. asst. Allegheny County Commr., 1977-80; dir. adminstrn. Allegheny County, 1980-88, dir. aviation, 1988-93, dir. property assessment appeals, 1993; v.p. airports Lockheed Air Terminals (now Airport Group Internat.), 1994-98; v.p. Sypher, 1998—. Chmn. Higher Edn. Bldg. Authority, Pitts., 1983-90; dir. Allegheny West Authority, Pitts., 1988-94; mem. Mediate, Moon Twp., Pa., 1991-94; pres. Airport Group Can., 1994—, SABSA, 1997; bd. dirs. HIAPL, 1998—. Recipient Disting. Alumni award Geneva Coll., Beaver Falls, Pa., 1988, Disting. Svc. award FAA, Jamaica, N.Y., 1992; named Man of Yr. in Law and Govt., Vectors, Pitts., 1992. Mem. Am. Soc. Pub. Adminstrn. (past pres., exec. bd.), Airport Area C. of C. (exec. bd. 1988-94), Airport Coun. Internat., Am. Assn. Airport Execs. Democrat. Presbyterian. Avocation: golf. Home: 1311 Northview Rd Escondido CA 92029-5631 Office: 220 Laurier Ave West Ste 500 Ottawa ON KIP529 Canada E-mail: sodonnell@sypherintl.com.

O'DONNELL, TERESA HOHOL, software development engineer, antennas engineer; b. Springfield, Mass., Nov. 25, 1963; d. Marion and Lena Hohol; m. Patrick Alan O'Donnell; children: Kelly Marie, Tracy Alana. BS in Computer Engring., BSEE, MIT, 1985, MSEE, MS in Computer Sci., 1986. Rsch. asst. MIT Rsch. Lab for Electronics, Cambridge, 1985-86; lead VHSIC insertion engr. USAF Electronic Systems Divsn., Hanscom AFB, Mass., 1986-88; intelligent antennas engr. USAF Rome Lab., 1988-91; sr. scientist Arcon Corp., Waltham, 1991—. Composer: (choral mass setting) Mass of Rejoicing, 1989; inventor: patentee cab to cap gap filler, weather seal strip, infant stimulus toy. Performer Zbeide's Harem, Tewksbury, Mass., 1986-93; organist/composer St. Theresa's Choir, Billerica, Mass., 1987-95. Maj. USAF and USAFR. Decorated Commendation medal (2), Joint Svc. Achievement medal, Meritorious Svc. medal (2). Mem. IEEE, Nat. Assn. Pastoral Musicians, Am. Guild Organists, Assn. for Computing Machinery, Res. Officers Assn., Sigma Xi, Eta Kappa Nu (v.p. 1985-86). Roman Catholic. Avocations: music, dancing, theater, composing, roller skating. Office: Arcon Corp 260 Bear Hill Rd Ste 5 Waltham MA 02451-1000

O'DONNELL, TERRENCE, lawyer; b. N.Y.C., Mar. 3, 1944; s. Emmett and Lorraine (Muller) O'Donnell; m. Margaret Lynne Kidder; children: Stephanie T., Erin K., Victoria L. BS, U.S. Air Force Acad., 1966; JD, Georgetown Law Sch., 1971. Bar: D.C. 1971, U.S. Ct. Appeals (D.C. cir.) 1978, U.S. Ct. Appeals (4th cir.) 1987, U.S. Dist. Ct. Md. 1986, U.S. Ct. Mil. Appeals 1990, U.S. Ct. Fed. Claims, U.S. Supreme Ct., others. Commd. 2d lt. USAF, 1966, advanced through grades to capt., various positions, 1966-72, resigned, 1972; spl. asst. Pres. of U.S., The White House, Washington, 1972-77; appointments sec. Pres. Ford, Washington, 1974-77; assoc. Williams & Connolly, 1977-82, ptnr., 1982-89; gen. counsel Dept. Def., 1989-92; ptnr. Williams and Connolly, 1992—; exec. v.p., gen. counsel Textron Inc., 2000—. Presdl. appointee to bd. visitors U.S. Air Force Acad., Colorado Springs, 1982-87, chmn., 1985-86; U.S. corr. and rep. UN Program to Prevent Crime, Washington and N.Y.C., 1977-81; bd. dirs. IGI Inc., MLC Holdings. Trustee Gerald R. Ford Found., Grand Rapids, Mich., 1987—; mem. Adminstrv. Conf. U.S., 1991-92; mem. adv. com. U.S. Ct. Fed. Claims; mem. code com. U.S. Ct. of Mil. Appeals for the Armed Forces, 1993-95; bd. dirs. Falcon Found., 1988—. Decorated Bronze star; recipient Disting. Pub. Svc. medal Dept. of Def., 1992, Disting. Svc. award U.S. Atty. Gen., 1992. Mem. ABA, D.C. Bar Assn., Bar of U.S. Supreme Ct., and others. Home: 5133 Yuma St NW Washington DC 20016-4336 Office: Williams and Connolly 725 12th St NW Washington DC 20005-5901 E-mail: todonnell@textron.com, todonnell@wc.com.

O'DONNELL, THOMAS LAWRENCE PATRICK, lawyer; b. Taunton, Mass., Aug. 12, 1926; s. Patrick Francis and Ellen Balfe (Brady) O'D.; m. Carol Hodgdon, Feb. 16, 1952; children— Ellen, Thomas, Janet Gael, Christopher Hodgdon AB magna cum laude, Harvard U., 1947, LL.B., 1949. Bar: Mass. 1950. Assoc. Ropes & Gray, Boston, 1949-52, 54-61, ptnr., 1962-97, chmn., 1984-90, of counsel, 1998—. Dir. Rath & Strong, Inc., 1985-96. Trustee, Trustees of Reservations, 1970—, chmn. bd., 1975-76; bd. dirs. Mass. Land Conservation Trust, 1975—, chmn. bd., 1986—; bd. dirs. Mass. Taxpayers Found., 1972—, chmn. bd., 1977-79, 93-95, mem. exec. com., 1976—; bd. dirs. Boston Mcpl. Rsch. Bur., 1965—, chmn. bd., 1967-72; mem. pub. pension task force Mass. Bus. Roundtable, 1983-86; bd. dirs., sec. Jobs for Mass., Inc., 1981-83; moderator Town of Hingham, 1967—; del. Rep. Nat. Conv., 1972, all Rep. State convs., 1960-94; overseer Harvard U., 1986-92; bd. dirs. United Way Mass. Bay, 1987—, mem. exec. com. 1993—, chmn. bd. 1997-2000. Lt. USNR, 1994-45, 52-54. Recipient Cushing award Labor Guild of Archdiocese Boston, 1973, Humanitarian award The Nat. Conf. Greater Boston, 1997, The Harvard medal, 1997; mem. Knights of Malta, 1983— Fellow Am. Bar Found.; mem. ABA, Mass. Bar Assn., Boston Bar Assn., Am. Arbitration Assn., Indsl. Rels. Rsch. Assn. (pres. Boston chpt. 1980), Harvard Alumni Assn. (bd. dirs. 1978-81; 1st marshal class of 1947). Clubs: Harvard of Boston (bd. govs. 1985-91), Union of Boston; Hingham Yacht, Comml. Roman Catholic. Home: 7 South Ln Hingham MA 02043-2446 Office: Ropes & Gray 1 International Pl Boston MA 02110-2624

O'DONNELL, THOMAS P. mechanical engineer; b. Pitts., Jan. 7, 1963; s. William J. and Joanne M. O'Donnell; m. Patricia A. Pinyot, Nov. 4, 2000. BSME, Pa. State U., 1985; M Engring., Carnegie Mellon U., 1987; PhD in Mech. Engring., U. Pitts., 1994. Registered profl. engr., Pa. Sr. engr. Westinghouse Electric Corp., Pitts., 1987-96; sr. project engr. John J. McCullen and Assocs., 1996-97; sr. engr. Geo-Centers, Inc., 1998—; v.p. O'Donnell Cons. Engrs., Inc., Bethel Park, Pa., 1988—. Cons. Design Analysis Svcs., Inc., Pitts., 1996—, Decamedics, Columbus, Ohio, 1999—; biomed. engr. artificial heart program U. Pitts. Med. Ctr., Pitts., 1991-2001; intra-aortic balloon pump engr. UPMC STAT MedEvac Flight Team, Pitts., 1998; instr. Pa. State U., 1990-2001. Contbr. articles to profl. jours.; author conf. procs. in field. Mem. Nat. Ski Patrol, 1982—85. Keck Bioengring. fellow Keck Found., 1991-92. Mem. ASME, Tau Beta Pi, Pi Tau Sigma. Avocations: skiing, horseback riding, tennis, travel, water sports. Home: 4717 Doverdell Dr Pittsburgh PA 15236 Office: O'Donnell Cons Engrs 2940 S Park Rd Bethel Park PA 15102

O'DONNELL, WALTER J. clinician, educator, medical executive; b. N.Y.C., Mar. 12, 1960; s. Walter Edward and Madeline Mary O'Donnell; m. Mary Anne O'Donnell, July 7, 1984; children: Kathleen, Thomas, Walter, Mary Claire, Robert. AB, Coll. of the Holy Cross, 1982; MD, Cornell U., 1986. Cert. in internal medicine, pulmonary medicine, critical care medicine Am. Bd. Internal Medicine. Med. dir. sys. improvement Brigham & Women's Hosp., Boston, 1995-96, asst. chief medicine, 1996-98; vice chmn. medicine Allegheny Gen. Hosp., Pitts., 1998—2002; clin. dir. Pulmonary and Critical Care Unit Mass. Gen. Hosp., Boston, 2002—. Author: (book chpt.) Textbook of Critical Care, 1998. Fellow Am. Coll. Chest Physicians; mem. ACP, AMA, Am. Thoracic Soc. Office: Mass Gen Hosp Pulmonary and Critical Care Unit 55 Fruit St Boston MA 02114-

O'DONNELL, WILLIAM DAVID, retired construction firm executive; b. Brockton, Mass., Aug. 21, 1926; s. John Frank and Agnes Teresa (Flanagan) O'D.; m. Dixie Lou Anderson, Jan. 31, 1951; children— Craig Patrick, Ginger Lynn BS, U. N.Mex., 1953. Registered profl. engr., Ill., 1958. Engr. State of Ill., 1953-59; with Gregory-Anderson Co., Rockford, Ill., 1959—, gen. mgr., 1960-61, sec., 1961-81, pres., 1981-94; ret. Bd. dirs. Growth Enterprise, Davis Meml. Park, BankOne, Rockford. Dir. St. Anthony Med. Ctr., Youth Svcs. Network, Cath. Conf. of Ill.; bd. dirs. Rockford YMCA, pres., 1984. Served with USN, 1943-47 Recipient Friend of the Boy award Optimist Club, 1966, Excalibur award for cmty. svc. Rockford Register Star, 1971; named Titan of Yr., Boylan H.S., 1974, Papal Knight Order of St. Gregory the Great; fellow Wisdom Hall of Fame. Fellow: NSPE, ASCE, Soc. Am. Mil. Engrs.; mem.: VFW (life), No. Ill. Bldg. Contractors, Amateur Trapshooting Assn., World Future Soc., Aircraft Owners & Pilots Assn., Balloon Fedn. Am., Am. Polar Soc., Nat. Sporting Clays Assn., Old Antarctic Explorers Assn., Forest Hills Country (Rockford), Metropolitan Club (Chgo.); Adventurers (Chgo.), Adventurers Club, Metropolitan Club, Forest Hills Country Club, Rotary (Service Above Self award 1972; v.p. Rockford chpt. 1983, pres. 1984), Rotary (v.p. Rockford chpt. 1983, pres. 1984, Svc. Above Self award 1972), Am. Legion (life), Tau Beta Pi, Chi Epsilon, Sigma Tau. Home: 2004 Bradley Rd Rockford IL 61107-1258 Office: PO Box 900 Rockford IL 61105-0900

O'DONNELL, WILLIAM EDWARD, Spanish language educator; b. Buffalo, Feb. 5, 1970; s. William James and Kathleen (McCarthy) O'D. BA, Canisius Coll., Buffalo, 1992; MA, SUNY, Buffalo, 1997. Cert. tchr., N.Y. Tchr. English Colegio Meres, Asturias, Spain, 1990-91, Palacio de la Ferreria, Asturias, 1991; sales rep./translator Praxair Inc., North Tonawanda, N.Y., 1992-94; asst. dir. Salamanca Program SUNY, Buffalo, 1997, prof. Spanish Fredonia, 1994—. Mem. MLA, N.Y. State Assn. of Fgn. Lang. Tchrs., Spanish Grad. Student Assn. (v.p. 1997—, treas. 1994-95), Grad. Student Employees Union, Sigma Delta Pi, Di Gamma, Sigma Phi Epsilon. Avocations: music, literature, writing. Home: 141 Saint James Pl Buffalo NY 14222-1457

O'DONNELL, WILLIAM JAMES, engineering executive; b. Pitts., June 19, 1935; s. William James and Elizabeth (Rau) O'D.; m. Joanne Mary Kusen, Jan. 31, 1959; children: Suzanne, Janice, William, Thomas, Kerry, Amy. BSM.E., Carnegie Inst. Tech., 1957; MSM.E., U. Pitts., 1959, PhD, 1962. Jr. engr. Westinghouse Research Lab., 1957-58, asso. engr., 1958; with Westinghouse Bettis Atomic Power Lab., West Mifflin, Pa., 1961-70, adv. engr., 1966-70; pres., chmn. bd. O'Donnell & Assos., Inc., Pitts., 1970—. Contbr. numerous articles on engring. and mechanics to profl. jours.; holder patents on processes and devices. Served with C.E. AUS, 1963-64. Recipient Machinery's Achievement award as outstanding mech. designer, 1957, Pi Tau Sigma Gold medal for achievements in engring., 1967, Pressure Vessel and Piping award ASME, 1994, Disting. Alumni award U. Pitts. Sch. Mech. Engring., 1996. Fellow ASME (nat. award for outstanding contbn. to engring. profession 1973, internat. award for best publ. in pressure vessels and piping 1988, Engr. of Yr. award 1988, Pressure Vessel and Piping medal 1994); mem. NSPE, AAAS, ASTM, Soc. Exptl. Mechanics, Am. Nuclear Soc., Am. Soc. Metals Internat., The Minerals, Metals and Materials Soc., Sigma Xi. Home: 3611 Maplevue Dr Bethel Park PA 15102-1423 Office: O'Donnell Consulting Engrs 2940 S Park Rd Ste 400 Bethel Park PA 15102 E-mail: wjo@odonnellconsulting.com.

O'DONNELL, WILLIAM THOMAS, management consultant; b. Latrobe, Pa., Feb. 22, 1939; s. William Regis and Kathryn Ann (Coneff) O'D; m. Judith Koetke, Oct. 1, 1965; children: William Thomas, William Patrick, Allison Rose, Kevin Raymond. Student Ea., N. Mex. U., 1961-65; student in mktg., John Carrol U., 1961-65; student, Inst. Tech., 1965-66; BSBA, U. Phoenix, 1982, MBA with distinction, 1984; PhD applied orgnl. mgmt. personel psychographics, Union Inst., 1999. Various positions Hickok Elec. Instrument Co., Cleveland, 1961-65; with Fairchild Semicondr., Mpls., 1965-67, Transitron Semicondr., Mpls., 1967-69; regional sales mgr. Burroughs Corp., Plainfield, N.J., 1967-71; mktg. mgr. Owens-Ill., Co., 1972-73; v.p. mktg. Pantek Co. subs. Owens-Ill. Co., Lewiston, Pa., 1973-75; v.p. mktg., nat. sales mgr. Toledo, 1975-76; mktg. mgr. Govt. Electronics divsn. group Motorola co., Scottsdale, Ariz., 1976-80, U.S. mktg.mgr. radar positioning syss., 1981; gen. mgr. J.K. Internat., Scottsdale, 1980-81; mgmt. cons., pres. Cambridge Grp., 1987—; v.p. mktg. Pinnacle Surg. Products, 1989, Kroy, Inc., 1992-94; mgmt. cons., 1994; v.p. mktg. and bus. devel. Kroy, inc., 1992. Adj. prof. Union Grad. Sch; Guest lectr. U. Mich. Grad. Sch. Bus. Administrn.; instr. U. Phoenix, 1984-88, chair strategic mgmt. 1988, pres. faculty, 1989—, area chair mktg., 1995—, area chair grad. assessment, 1999; lectr. Scottsdale Community Coll., Paradise Valley Community Coll; talk show host Sta. KFNN, 1992-95; area chmn gen. mgmt. Union Grad. Sch. Maricopa Community Coll., U. Phoenix Chmn., Rep. precinct, Burnsville, Minn., 1968-70; bd. dirs. Pacific Gateway. Chmn. City fin., Burnsville; dir. community devel. U.S. Jaycees, Mpls., 1968-69;mem. Scottsdale 2000 Com. With USAF, 1957-61. Recipient Outstanding Performance award Maricopa Community Coll. System, 1987, Faciliation award, Maricopa Community Coll.; Citation for Faciliation Ability, U. Phoenix, 1986, 90, 93, 99; named Hon. Citizen, Donaldsville, La., 1978. Mem. Am. Mktg. Assn., Afron-Am. Small Bus. Assn), Phoenix Indian Ctr., Inc. (bd. dirs. 1994), Amateur Athletic Union (swimming ofcl. 1980-82), Phoenix Execs. Club, U. Phoenix Faculty Club (bd. dirs., pres., 1988-91 recipient Presdl. Designation award, officer), North Cape Yacht Club, Scottsdale Racquet Club, Toftness country Club. Roman Catholic. Home: 33144 N 72d Way Scottsdale AZ 85262 E-mail: wto@att.net.

O'DONNELL RICH, DOROTHY JUANITA, small business owner; b. Midland, Pa., Aug. 31, 1934; d. William Theodore and Jennie Cecilia (Forrest) Verzella; m. Hugh Terrence O'Donnell, Aug. 9, 1958 (dec. Jan. 1987); children: Kathleen Denise, Suzanne Lynn; m. Hugh B. Rich IV, Nov. 12, 1988. Ch. organist Blessed Virgin Mary Ch., Midland, 1948-59; sec. E.W. Bliss Co., 1952-59; tchr. piano Beaver, Pa., 1962-81; owner, bus. mgr. H.B. Rich, Drexel Hill, 1988—. Counselor Cath. Daughters of Am., Midland, 1952-54; pianist Midland Rotary Club, 1952-58; program chmn. Sr. Cath. Daughters of Am., Beaver, 1958-68; mem. ways and means com. Jr. Women's Club, Midland, 1954-56; mem. Midland Cath. Sodality; mem. Italian Sons and Daughters of Am., Sewickley, Pa., 1954-60. Named Jr. of the Yr., Jr. Cath. Daus., 1948. Mem. NAFE. Roman Catholic. Avocations: piano, walking, reading, chess, bicycling. Office: HB Rich PO Box 310 Drexel Hill PA 19026-0310

O'DONOHUE, WALTER JOHN, JR. medical educator; b. Washington, Sept. 23, 1934; s. Walter John and Mavis Leota (Terry) O'D.; m. Cynthia Ann Halmintoller, Aug. 10, 1957 (div. 1978); 1 child, Diane Louise; m. Maria Theresa Sauer, Nov. 27, 1978; children: Walter John III, Mary Theresa. BA, Va. Mil. Inst., 1957; MD, Med. Coll. Va., 1961. Diplomate Am. Bd. Internal Medicine, Am. Bd. Pulmonary Medicine. Resident internal medicine Med. Coll. Va., Richmond, 1961-63, 65-66, chief med. resident, 1966-67, cardio-pulmonary fellow, 1967-69, asst. prof. medicine, 1968-73, assoc. prof., 1973-77; prof. Creighton U., Omaha, 1977—, chief pulmonary medicine div., 1977—, chmn. dept. medicine, 1985-96, assoc. chair for edn., 1996—, dir. internal medicine residency program, 1985-98, assoc. dean grad. med. edn., 1998—. Editor: Current Advances in Respiratory Care, 1984, Long-term Oxygen Therapy: Scientific Basis and Clinical Application, 1995, Accurate Coding for Critical Care Services and Pulmonary Medicine, 1996-2002; contbr. more than 100 articles to med. jours., 30 chpts. to books. Served to capt. M.C., U.S. Army, 1963-65. Fellow ACP, Am. Coll. Chest PHysicians (regent 1986-88, gov. for Nebr. 1982-88); mem. AMA (CPT adv. com. 1992—, mem. ho. of dels., alt. del. for Am. Coll. Chest Physicians 1998—), Am. Lung Assn. (bd. dirs. 1981-87), Nebr. Lung Assn. (bd. dirs., pres. 1979-81), Am. Assn. Respiratory Care (chmn. bd. med. advisors 1986-87), Nat. Assn. Med. Dirs. for Respiratory Care (pres. 1995-97). Republican. Roman Catholic. Avocations: hunting, fishing. Home: 12773 Izard St Omaha NE 68154-1243 Office: Creighton U Sch Medicine 601 N 30th St Omaha NE 68131-2137 E-mail: wjo@creighton.edu.

O'DONOVAN, LEO JEREMIAH, former university president emeritus, theologian, priest; b. N.Y.C., Apr. 24, 1934; s. Leo J. Jr. O'D. AB, Georgetown U., 1956; Licentiate in Philosophy, Fordham U., 1961; STB, Woodstock Coll., 1966, Licentiate in Sacred Theology, 1967; ThD, U. Münster, Fed. Republic Germany, 1971; LittD (hon.), Sogang U., Seoul, 1993; DHL, Loyola Coll., 1991, Coll. St. Rose, 2000; MD (hon.), Georgetown U., 2001. Joined S.J., 1957, ordained priest Roman Cath. Ch., 1966. Instr. philosophy Loyola Coll., Balt., 1961-63; asst. prof. Woodstock (Md.) Coll., 1971-74; assoc. prof. Weston Sch. Theology, Cambridge, Mass., 1974-81, prof., 1981-89; pres. Georgetown U., Washington, 1989-2001, prof., 2001—. Provincial asst. formation Md. Province S.J., Balt., 1985-88; cons. Nat. Conf. Cath. Bishops, Washington, 1986-89; vis. fellow Woodstock Theol. Ctr.; bd. dirs. The Riggs Nat. Bank, Walt Disney Co., MedStar Health, Inc. Co-editor: The Society of Jesus and Higher Education in America, 1965; (author preface) Faithful Witness: Foundations of Theology for Today's Church, 1989; assoc. editor Jour. Am. Acad. Religion, 1985-89; mem. adv. bd. America mag., 1985-89; contbr. numerous articles to America, Washington Post, Theol. Studies, Communio, Cross Currents. Bd. dirs. U. Detroit Mercy, 1986-95; mem. Consortium of Univs. of Washington Met. Area, 1989-2001, chair, 1994-96; mem. Fed. City Coun., 1993-2001, Bus.-Higher Edn. Forum, 1989-2001, Nat. Coun. on Arts, 1994-98, Campus Compact, 1989-98, bd. dirs. 1992-98; bd. dirs. Nat. Assn. Ind. Colls. and Univs., 1991-94, Consortium on Financing Higher Edn., 1990-98, chmn. 1995-97; Am. Reads Stery Com., 1997—. Recipient Knight Commander's Cross Federal Republic Germany; Fulbright scholar Fulbright Found., U. Lyon, France, 1956-57; Danforth fellow Danforth Found., 1956-71; Assn. Theol. Schs. grantee on teaching, 1978-79. Fellow Soc. for Values in Higher Edn. (bd. dirs. 1989—); mem. Assn. of Jesuit Colls. and Univs. Assn. Cath. Colls. and Univs. (bd. dirs. 1994-2000), Boston Theol. Soc., University Club. Office: Georgetown U 37th and O St NW Washington DC 20057-1789*

O'DOONAN, MICHAEL ROBERT, retired music educator; b. Iowa City, June 29, 1935; s. Russell Franklin and Clara Iola (Rank) Doonan; m. Gladys Mozelle Ewing, Dec. 14, 1956 (dec. Aug. 1995); m. Bonnie Jean Frey Hitz, June 20, 1998. AA, Pueblo Jr. Coll., Colo., 1955; MusB, U. Colo., 1958; MusM, Drake Univ., 1970; Mus D, Ind. U., 1980. Cert. Cert. in comml. art and illustration Famous Artists Sch., Westport, Conn., 1968. Ednl. dir. Temperance League, Mitchell, SD, 1957—58; acting head of music dept., music tchr. Grand Rapids (Mich.) Bapt. Bible Coll. and Theol. Sem., 1959—62; music prof., chmn. music dept. Faith Bapt. Bible Coll., Ankeny, Iowa, 1962—92, Pillsbury Bapt. Bible Coll., Owatonna, Minn., 1992—94. Singer on weekly radio programs local churches, Pueblo, 1951—55; singer for weddings and funerals various states, 1952—90, singer of sacred concerts, soloist for oratorios, 1954—90. Judge of singing auditions Nat. Assn. Tchrs. of Singing, 1969—94, Talents for Christ, 1963—2002; del. Rep. Party, Iowa, 2002. Mem.: Iowa Nut Growers Assn. (pres. 1989—91). Republican. Baptist. Avocation: fruit and nut growing, grafting.

ODOR, RICHARD LANE, mental health administrator, psychologist; b. Oberlin, Ohio, Aug. 11, 1954; s. Frank and Marjorie Ann (Carpenter) O. Student, Moody Bible Inst., 1972-74; BA, Ohio State U., 1977, MA, 1978, PhD, 1986. Counselor children's groups Gladden Community House, Columbus, Ohio, 1978-79; partial hospitalization counselor Columbus Area Community Mental Health Ctr., 1979-81, residential counselor, 1978-82; grad. rsch. assoc. dept. family rels. and human devel. Ohio State U., 1983-85; emergency svcs. counselor S.E. Community Mental Health Ctr., Columbus, 1983-86, dir. emergency svcs., 1986-87; program dir., psychologist Southeast Counseling Svcs., 1987-92; psychologist Psychol. and Counseling Svcs., Reynoldsburg, Ohio, 1989-98, Richard L. Odor, PhD, Inc., Reynoldsburg, 1998—. Psychologist, clin. supr. New Source Counseling Ctrs., Twinsburg, Ohio, 1990-97; psychologist, owner Psychol. and Recovery Svcs., Columbus, 1991-94; employee assistance program affiliate McDonnell Douglas Corp., Columbus, 1992-95; staff Grant Med. Ctr., Columbus, 1995—; mem. profl. adv. com. Mt. Carmel Behavioral Healthcare, 1998-99; pres. Achieve Performance Consultants, Inc., Reynoldsburg, 2002—. Profl. adv. bd. Ctrl. Ohio Chpt. Nat. Multiple Sclerosis Soc., 1995-97. Recipient Silver medal Pan Am. Master's Weightlifting Championships, 1999, Bronze medal Pan Am. Master's Weightlifting Championships, 2000. Mem. APA, Interact Behavioral Healthcare (credentialling com. 1996-98), Ohio Psychol. Assn., U.S. Weightlifting Fedn., Ohio State U. Weightlifting Club (coach 1982-85, faculty advisor 1984-85), Rotary (bd. dirs. Reynoldsburg-Pickerington chpt. 1992-94, Paul Harris fellow), Phi Kappa Phi, Omicron Nu, Phi Upsilon Omicron. Republican. Avocations: skiing, water skiing, competitive weightlifting, sailing. Office: 7664 Slate Ridge Blvd Reynoldsburg OH 43068-8158

O'DOWD, DONALD DAVY, retired university president; b. Manchester, N.H., Jan. 23, 1927; s. Hugh Davy and Laura (Morin) O'D.; m. Janet Louise Fithian, Aug. 23, 1953; children: Daniel D., Diane K., James E., John M. BA summa cum laude, Dartmouth Coll., 1951; postgrad. (Fulbright fellow), U. Edinburgh, Scotland, 1951-52; MA, Harvard U., 1955, PhD, 1957. Instr., asst. prof. psychology, dean freshmen Wesleyan U., Middletown, Conn., 1955-60; assoc. prof., prof. of psychology, dean Univ. Oakland Univ., Rochester, Mich., 1960-65, provost, 1965-70; pres. Oakland U., 1970-80; exec. vice chancellor SUNY, Albany, 1980-84; pres. U. of Alaska Statewide System, 1984-90. Sr. cons. Assn. Governing Bds. Univs. and Colls. Carnegie Corp. fellow, 1965-66 Mem. APA, AAAS, Phi Beta Kappa, Sigma Xi. Home and Office: 1550 La Vista Del Oceano Santa Barbara CA 93109-1739

ODUM, HOWARD THOMAS, emeritus environmental science educator; b. Durham, N.C., Sept. 1, 1924; s. Howard Washington and Anna Louise (Kranz) O.; m. Virginia Millie Wood (dec. Oct. 1973); children: Frances Ann, Mary Louise Odum Logan; m. Elizabeth Chase. AB, U. N.C., 1947; PhD, Yale U., 1951; DSc (hon.), Ohio State U., 1995. Instr. meteorology AAF Tropical Weather Sch., Howard Field, Panama, 1945-46; asst. prof. biology U. Fla., Gainesville, 1950-54; asst. prof. Duke U., Duke Marine Lab., Eniwetok Marine Lab., 1954-56; dir. Inst. Marine Sci., Port Aransas, 1956-63; chief scientist terrestrial ecology Puerto Nuc. Ctr. U. P.R., 1963-66; prof. ecology U. N.C., Chapel Hill, 1966-70; grad. rsch. prof. environ. engring. scis. U. Fla., 1970-96, grad. rsch. prof. emeritus, 1996—. Dir. Ctr. for Wetlands, U. Fla., 1973-91, dir. Ctr. for Environ. Policy, 1991—; Erskine fellow U. Canterbury, Christchurch, New Zealand, 1978; mem. NSF Exch. Program, Canterbury, 1980; rsch. assoc. Internat. Inst. for Applied Systems Analysis, Laxenburg, Austria, 1983; vis. prof. LBJ Sch. Pub. Affairs, U. Tex., Austin, 1985-86. Author: Environment, Power and Society, 1971, Ecological and General Systems: An Introduction to Systems Ecology, 1983, 1994, Environmental Accounting: EMERGY and Decision Making, 1995; co-author (with B.J. Copeland and E.A. McMahan): Coastal Ecological Systems of the United States, 1969; co-author: (with E.C. Odum) Energy Basis for Man and Nature, 1976, rev. edit., 1981; co-author: (with R.J. Beyers) Ecological Microcosms, 1993; co-author: (with E.C. Odum and M.T. Brown) Environment and Society in Florida, 1998; editor: Heavy Metals in the Environment Using Wetlands for Their Removal, 2000; editor: (with R.F. Pigeon) A Tropical Rain Forest, 1970; editor: (with K. Ewel) Cypress Swamps, 1985; editor: (with E.C. Odum) Modeling For All Scales, 2000; editor: (with B. Marino) Biosphere 2, Research Past and Present, 1999; editor: (with E.C. Odum) A Prosperous Way Down, 2001; contbr. articles to profl. jours. 2d lt. USAF, 1943-46. Recipient Edward S. Deevey Jr. award Fla. Lake Mgmt. Soc., Inst. La Vie prize. Fellow: AAAS; mem.: Simulation Soc., Internat. Soc. Ecol. Modelling and Sys. Ecology, Internat. Soc. Tropical Ecology, Internat. Soc. for Sys. Scis. (pres. 1992), Am. Soc. Limnology and Oceanography (George Mercer award), Ecol. Soc. Am., Am. Ecol. Engring. Soc., Am. Inst. Biol. Sci. (Disting. Svc. award), Royal Swedish Acad. Scis. (Crafoord prize), Am. Meteorol. Soc. (profl.), Phi Beta Kappa, Sigma Xi. Home: 2106 NW 9th Ave Gainesville FL 32603-1019 Office: Environ Engring Scis U Fla Gainesville FL 32611-6450

ODUM, JEFFERY NEAL, mechanical engineer; b. Bristol, Tenn., Sept. 11, 1956; s. Herschel S. and Minnie Lee (Carrier) O.; m. Stacy Elaine Ferrell, mar. 18, 1989; 1 child, Charles Wesley Ferrell. BSME, Tenn. Technol. U., 1978; MS in Engring., U. Tenn., 1983. Sr. project engr. TVA, Knoxville, 1978-81; sr. constrn. engr. Stone & Webster Engring. Corp., Boston, 1981-84; div. engr. E.I. DuPont de Nemours & Co., Aiken, S.C., 1984-89; engring. mgr. Flour Daniel, Greenville, 1989-92; mgr. of projects, Pharmaceutical Bus. Group CRS Sirrine Engrs., Inc., Raleigh, N.C., 1992-93; sr. project mgr. Gilbane Bldg. Co., 1993-95; dir. engring. Gilbane Process Group, Vacaville, Calif., 1995-98; biopharm. core team leader Clark, Richardson and Biskup, Cons. Engrs., Cary, N.C., 1998—. Author: Sterile Product Facility Design and Project Management, 1996; contbr. articles to profl. jours. Vol. Spl. Olympics. Recipient DuPont Engring. Achievement award 1986, 88, 89, Nat. Svc. Alumni award Univ. Tenn. Mem. Parenteral Drug Assn., Soc. Mfg. Engrs., Internat. Soc. Pharm. Engrs. (bd. dirs., pres. Carolina chpt. 1996-97, chair N.Am. Chpt. Coun. 1998, chair publs. com. 2000-01, chair chpt. excellence 2000-01, Svc. award 1999), U. Tenn. Nat. Alumni Assn. (pres. Augusta chpt. 1987-89), Order Engr., Kappa Sigma. Republican. Presbyterian. Avocations: sports, biking, cooking, physical fitness, writing. Office: Clark Richardson & Biskkup 1200 Crescent Green Dr Ste 100 Cary NC 27511-8107

O'DWYER, THOMAS STEPHEN, lawyer; b. San Rafael, Calif., Oct. 21, 1949; s. John Stephen and Nora Maria (Costello) O'D.; m. Diane L. Shields, Dec. 23, 1982; 1 child, Keith Thomas. BA, U. Calif., 1972; MS, U. Wash., 1976; JD, New Eng. Sch. Law, 1981. Bar: Idaho 1983, U.S. Patent Office 1985, U.S. Supreme Ct. 1988, D.C. 1989, U.S. Claims Ct. 1989, U.S. Ct. Appeals (fed. cir.) 1989. Gen. engr. Army R&D Command, Natick, Mass., 1979-81; civil engr. Directorate of Engring., Ft. Devens, 1981-84; naval architect Mil. Sealift Command-Pacific, Oakland, Calif., 1984-85; civil engr. Naval Facilities Engring. Command, San Bruno, 1985-86, contract specialist, 1986-87; patent atty. David Taylor Rsch. Ctr., Bethesda, Md., 1987-89, U.S. Dept. Energy, Oakland, Calif., 1989—2001, Nat. Nuclear Security Adminstrn., Oakland, 2001—. Recipient Ofcl. Commendation, U.S. Army, 1984, Tech. Transfer Cert. of Appreciation, Dept. of Energy, 1990. Mem. ABA (chmn. subcom. 105 govt. rels. to patents 1991-92), Am. Intellectual Property Law Assn., Calif. Bar Assn. (assoc., intellectual property law sect.), Idaho Bar Assn., D.C. Bar Assn., Govt. Patent Lawyers Assn. Democrat. Roman Catholic. Avocations: skiing, tennis. E-mail: thomas.o'dwyer@oak.doe.gov.

ODZA, RANDALL M. lawyer; b. Schnectady, May 6, 1942; s. Mitchell and Grace (Mannes) O.; m. Rita Ginness, June 19, 1966; children: Kenneth, Keith. BS in Indsl. and Labor Rels., Cornell U., 1964, LLB, 1967. Bar: N.Y. 1967, U.S. Ct. Appeals (2d cir.) 1970, U.S. Dist. Ct. (so. and ea. dists.) N.Y. 1969, U.S. Dist. Ct. (we. dist.) N.Y. 1970. Assoc. Proskauer, Rose, Goetz & Mandelsohn, N.Y.C., 1967-69, Jaeckle, Fleischmann & Mugel, Buffalo, 1969-72, ptnr., 1972—. Trustee, legal counsel, past treas. Temple Beth Am; bd. dirs. Buffalo Philharm. Orch. Soc. Fellow Coll. Labor & Employment Lawyers; recipient Honow award Western N.Y. Retail Mchts. Assn., 1980. Fellow Coll. Labor and Employment Lawyers; mem. ABA, Indsl. Rels. Rsch. Assn. Western N.Y., Erie County Bar Assn., N.Y. State Bar Assn., Buffalo Philharm. Soc. (bd. dirs.). Office: Jaeckle Fleischmann & Mugel 12 Fountain Plz Rm 700 Buffalo NY 14202-2292

OECHLER, HENRY JOHN, JR. lawyer; b. Charlotte, N.C., Apr. 9, 1946; s. Henry J. and Convere Jones (McAden) O. AB, Princeton U., 1968; JD, Duke U., 1971. Bar: N.Y. 1972, U.S. Ct. Appeals (2d cir.) 1974, U.S. Ct. Appeals (D.C. cir.) 1975, U.S. Ct. Appeals (8th cir.) 1986, U.S. Ct. Appeals (9th cir.) 1995. Assoc. Chadbourne & Parke, N.Y.C., 1971-80, ptnr., 1980—. Avocations: studying airline schedules. Office: Chadbourne & Parke 30 Rockefeller Plz Fl 31 New York NY 10112-0129

OECHSLI, CHRISTOPHER GEORGE, foundation executive, business executive; b. Costa Rica, Dec. 31, 1953; s. L. Paul and Helen (George) O.; m. Julie Ann Dakin; children: Annika, Alexander. AB, Occidental Coll., 1975; MA in Fgn. Affairs, U. Va., 1978, JD, 1981. Assoc. Wickwire, Goldmark & Schorr, Seattle, 1981-85; prof. East China Law Inst., Shanghai, 1985-86; assoc. McCutchen, Doyle, 1987-90; gen. counsel Gen. Atlantic Group, London, 1990—; dir., pres. Gen. Atlantic Corp., 1995—; pres. Atlantic Philanthropic (Seattle), Inc., Bainbridge Island, Wash., 2000—; ptnr. Estancia BuenAventura, Salta, Argentina, 1998—. Avocations: organic farming, guitar. Home: 14930 Sunrise Dr Bainbridge Island WA 98110-1113 Office: Atlantic Philanthropic (Seattle) Inc The Dockside Bldg, Suite 130 203 Parfitt Way SW Brainbridge Island WA 98110

OEFELEIN, WILLIAM A. astronaut, military officer; b. Ft. Belvoir, Va., Mar. 29, 1965; s. Randall W. and Billye N. Oefelein; m. Michaela Davis; 2 children. BS in Elec. Engring., Oreg. State U., Corvallis, 1988; MS in Aviation Systems, U. Tenn. Space Inst., 1998. Commd. ensign USN, Pensacola, Fla., 1988, advanced in grades to lt. cmmdr.; student pilot USN Marine Fighter/Attack Tng. Squadron, El Toro, Calif., 1990—91; fighter pilot USN Strike Fighter Squadron , Naval Air Sta., Lemoore, 1991—95; student test pilot Naval Air Sta., Patuxent River, Md., 1995; test pilot Strike Air Force Test Squadron, 1995—97; test pilot instr. Test Pilot Sch., Patuxent River, 1997—2008; pilor,strike ops. officer Carrier Air Wing 8 Naval Air Sta., Oceana, Va., 1998; astronaut NASA Johnson Space Ctr., Houston, 1998—. Mem.: Aircraft Owners and Pilots Assn., Seaplane Owners Assn. Achievements include 3000 flight hours in more than 50 different aircraft, 200 carrier landings. Avocations: fishing, hiking, skiing, weightlifting, wake boarding. Office: Astronaut Office/CB Johnson Space Ctr Houston TX 77058

OEFFNER, BARBARA DUNNING, biographer, educator, screenwriter; b. Southampton, N.Y., Aug. 25, 1944; d. Walter Arnold and Grace Dominy (Werner) Renkens; m. Michael Arthur Dunning, Oct. 1, 1966 (div. June 1984); children: Brendan, Ania, Amie, Heidi, Matt; m. F. Thomas Oeffner, Oct. 2, 1991. BS in Journalism, Northwestern U., 1966; MLS and Info. Studies, Fla. State U. Film copywriter Ency. Britannica, Chgo., 1966-69; pub. rels. dir. Eldred Auctions, East Dennis, Mass., 1982-85; editor Sandscript, Cummaquid, 1975-95; ins. agt. State Farm Ins., Delray Beach, Fla., 1992-95; biographer Cape Cod Writers, Inc., Cummaquid, 1995—. V.p. Caribbean Coatings Corp., Moore Haven, Fla., 1996—, Native Am. Prodns., Palm Beach, Fla., 1994—; lectr. Glades County Hist. Soc. Author: (screenplay) The Cuban Accident, 1996; co-author: (screenplay) Chief, 1994; author: (book) Chief: Champion of the Everglades, 1995. Tchr. Meth. Bible Sch., Moore Haven, 1997; activities dir. Campers Club Am., Moore Haven, 1996-97. Grantee Mary Roberts Rinehart Found., 1975, Commonwealth of Mass.-Dept. of Arts and Humanities, 1984, Coord. Coun. Lit. Mags., 1976. Mem. DAR. Democrat. Avocations: water aerobics, line dancing, hiking, traveling, gardening. Home: Box 1236 306 Yacht Club Way Moore Haven FL 33471-2809 Office: Belle Glade Libr 530 Main St Belle Glade FL 33430 Fax: (561) 996-2304.

OEHLER, RICHARD DALE, lawyer; b. Iowa City, Dec. 9, 1925; s. Harold Lawrence Oehler and Bernito Babb; m. Rosemary Heineman, July 11, 1952, (div.); m. Maria Luisa Holguin-Zea, June 11, 1962; children: Harold D., Richard L. BA in Med. Scis., U. Calif., Berkeley, 1951; JD, Loyola U., L.A., 1961. Bar: Calif. 1962, Fla. 1968. Sales rep. Abbott Labs., Pasadena, Calif., 1951-63; with claims dept. Allstate Ins., Tampa, 1963-70; pvt. practice, 1970—. Instr. Dale Carnegie Courses West Fla. Inst., Tampa, Scott Hitchcock & Assocs., Tampa, 1969—. Pres. U. South Fla. Parents Assn., Tampa, 1986-87. Mem. Fla. Bar Assn., Hillsborough County Bar Assn., Acad. of Fla. Trial Lawyers, Assn. of Trial Lawyers of Am., Masons (32d degree), Shriners, Phi Beta Kappa. Republican. Presbyterian. Avocations: jogging, road races, target shooting, fishing. Office: 200 N Pierce St Tampa FL 33602-5020 E-mail: doehlr@mindspring.com.

OEHLER, RICHARD WILLIAM, lawyer; b. N.Y.C., Nov. 24, 1950; s. John Montgomery and Florence Mae (Jahn) O.; m. Linda Tyson. BA, Dartmouth Coll., 1972; JD, Harvard U., 1976. Bar: Calif. 1976, Wash. 1987, D.C. 1988, U.S. Dist. Ct. (no. dist.) Calif. 1976, U.S. Dist. Ct. Wash. 1987, U.S. Claims Ct. 1979, U.S. Ct. Appeals (fed. cir.) 1982. Assoc. Pillsbury, Madison & Sutro, San Francisco, 1976-78; trial atty. U.S. Dept. Justice, Washington, 1978-87; of counsel Perkins Coie, Seattle, 1987-90, ptnr., 1990—. Mem. ABA, Nat. Contract Mgmt. Assn. (Spl. Achievement award 1990-92), Wash. State Bar Assn. Office: Perkins Coie 1201 3rd Ave Fl 40 Seattle WA 98101-3029 E-mail: oehlr@perkinscoie.com.

OEHLERT, WILLIAM HERBERT, JR. cardiologist, administrator, educator; b. Murphysboro, Ill., Sept. 11, 1942; s. William Herbert Sr. and Geneva Mae (Roberts) O.; m. L. Keith Brown, Mar. 14, 1976; children: Emily Jane, Amanda Elizabeth. BA, So. Ill. U., 1967; MD, Washington U., St. Louis, 1967; M in Med. Mgmt., Tulane U., 1999. Diplomate Nat. Bd. Med. Examiners, Am. Bd. Internal Medicine, Am. Bd. Cardiovascular Disease, North Am. Soc. Pacing and Electrophysiology. Med. intern Union Meml. Hosp., Balt., 1967-68, resident, 1968-69, U. Iowa, Iowa City, 1969-70, cardiology fellow, 1970-72; asst. prof. medicine, dir. coronary care units U. Okla. Health Sci. Ctr., Oklahoma City, 1972-74, asst. clin. prof. medicine, 1974-82, assoc. clin. prof. medicine, 1982-88, clin. prof. medicine, 1988—; chmn. dept. cardiology Bapt. Med. Ctr., 1992-95; pvt. practice Oklahoma City, 1974—. Med. dir. cardiovasc. svcs. Integris Bapt. Med. Ctr., 1993-98; pres. Cardiovasc. Clinic, Oklahoma City, 1987-91, chmn. exec. com., 1987-91; med. dir. Cardiovasc. Imaging Svcs. Corp., Oklahoma City, 1987-92; v.p. Plaza Med. Group, 1992-93; CEO W.H. Oehlert, MD, P.C., 1993—; prin. clin. coord Okla. Found. Med. Quality, 1998—. Author: Arrhythmias, 1973, Cardiovascular Drugs, 1976; contbr. articles to profl. jours. Fellow Am. Heart Assn. (nat. program com. 1979-82, pres. Okla. affiliate 1985-86, bd. dirs. 1974-88, ACLS nat. affiliate faculty 1987-90, bd. dirs. Oklahoma City 1999—), Am. Coll. Cardiology; mem. AMA, ACP-Am. Soc. Internal Medicine, Nat. Assn. Residents and Interns, Am. Coll. Physician Execs. (cert. 1999), Am. Diabetes Assn. (western coun. 2000—, ea. coun. 2000-01), Okla. County Med. Assn. (chmn. quality of care com. 1990-91), Okla. State Med. Assn. (trustee 2001—), Okla. City Clin. Soc., Okla. Cardiac Soc. (pres. 1978-79), Osler Soc., Soc. Nuclear Medicine, Okla. Found. for Med. Quality (bd. dirs. 1995-98), Wilderness Med. Soc., Stewart Wolf Soc., Phi Eta Sigma, Phi Kappa Phi Home: 3017 Rock Ridge Pl Oklahoma City OK 73120-5713 Office: Okla Found for Med Quality 5801 Broadway Ext Ste 400 Oklahoma City OK 73118-7484 Fax: 405-840-1343. E-mail: okpro.woehlert@sdps.org.

OEHME, FREDERICK WOLFGANG, medical researcher and educator; b. Leipzig, Germany, Oct. 14, 1933; arrived in came to U.S., 1934; s. Friedrich Oswald and Frieda Betha (Wohlgamuth) Oehme; m. Nancy Beth McAdam, Aug. 6, 1960 (div. June 1981); children: Stephen Frederick, Susan Lynn, Deborah Ann, Heidi Beth; m. Pamela Sheryl Ford, Oct. 2, 1981; 1 child April Virginia. BS in Biol. Sci., Cornell U., 1957, DVM, 1958; MS in Toxicology and Medicine, Kans. State U., 1962; DMV in Pathology, Justus Liebig U., Giessen, Germany, 1964; PhD in Toxicology, U. Mo., 1969. Diplomate Am. Bd. Toxicology, Am. Bd. Vet. Toxicology, Acad. Toxicol. Scis. Resident intern, Large Animal and Ambulatory Clinic Cornell U., 1957-58; gen. practice vet. medicine, 1958-59; from asst. to assoc. prof. medicine Coll. Vet. Medicine Kans. State U., 1959-66, 69-73, dir. comparative toxicology labs., 1969—, prof. toxicology, medicine and physiology Coll. Vet. Medicine, 1974-96, prof. toxicology, pathobiology, medicine and physiology, 1996—; postdoctoral research fellow in toxicology, NIH U. Mo., 1966-69. Cons. FDA, Washington, Ctr. for Vet. Medicine , Rockville, Md.; cons. animal care com. U. Kans., Lawrence, 1969—76, Syntex Corp., Palo Alto, Calif., 1976—77; mem. sci. adv. panel on PBB Gov.'s Office, State of MIch., 1976—77; mem. Coun. for Agrl. Sci. and Tech. Task Force on Toxicity, Toxicology and Environ. Hazard, 1976—83; cons., mem. adv. group on pesticides EPA, Cin., 1977—; expert state and fed. witness; advisor WHO, Geneva; presenter numerous papers to profl. meetings. Reviewer: Toxicology and Applied Pharmacology, reviewer: Spectroscopy, reviewer: numerous others. Mem. adv. coun. Cub Scouts Am., Eagle Scouts; mgr., coach Little League Baseball; active PTA; mem. Manhattan Civic Theatre; trustee Manhattan Marlin Swim Team; dir. meet Little Apple Invitational Swim Meet, 1984; mem. coun. Luth. Ch. Am., mem. sr. choir, numerous coms. Recipient Disting. Grad. Faculty award, Kans. State U., 1977—79, Dir.'s Letter of Commendation, FDA, 1983, Kenneth P. DuBois award, Midwest Soc. Toxicology, 1991, Kenneth F. Lampe award, Am. Acad. Toxicology, 1993, John Doull award, Ctrl. States Soc. Toxicology, 1994, medal, Azabu U., 1994, Silver award, Aristotelian U., 1995, others; fellow, Morris Animal Found., 1967—69. Fellow: Am. Acad. Vet. and Comparative Toxicology (past sec.-treas., numerous coms.), Am. Acad. Toxicology (past pres., numerous coms.); mem.: NRC (subcom. on organic contaminants in drinking water, safe drinking water com., adv. ctr. on toxicology assembly life scis. 1976—77, panel on toxicology marine bd., assembly of engring. 1976—79), AVMA (com. on environmentology 1971—73, adv. com. coun. on biol. and therapeutic agts. 1971—74, Samuel Shiedy award 1999), Nat. Ctr. Toxicol. Rsch. (vet. toxicology rep. sci. adv. bd., sci. adv. bd. 1974—77), N.Y. Acad. Scis., Soc. Toxicologic Pathologists, World Fedn. Clin. Toxicology Ctrs. and Poison Control Ctrs. (past pres.), Soc. Toxicology (past pres., numerous coms.), Cornell U. Athletic Assn., Manhattan Square Dance Club, Cornell U. Crew Club, Sigma Xi, Phi Zeta, Omega Tau Sigma. Republican. Avocations: historical readings, scientific writings, nature tours and walks, travel. Home: 148 S Dartmouth Dr Manhattan KS 66503-3079 Office: Kans State Univ Comparative Toxicology Labs 1800 Denison Ave Manhattan KS 66506-5660 E-mail: oehme@vet.ksu.edu.

OEHME, REINHARD, physicist, educator; b. Wiesbaden, Germany, Jan. 26, 1928; came to U.S., 1956; s. Reinhold and Katharina (Kraus) O.; m. Mafalda Pisani, Nov. 5, 1952. Dr. rer. nat., U. Goettingen, Germany, 1951; Diplom Physiker, U. Frankfurt am Main, Germany, 1948. Asst. Max Planck Inst. Physics, Goettingen, 1949-53; research asso. Fermi Inst. Nuclear Studies, U. Chgo., 1954-56; mem. faculty dept. physics and Fermi Inst., 1958—, prof. physics, 1964—; mem. Inst. Advanced Studies, Princeton, 1956-58. Vis. prof. Inst. de Física Teórica, São Paulo, Brazil, 1952-53, U. Md., 1957, U. Vienna, Austria, 1961, Imperial Coll., London, Eng., 1963-64, U. Karlsruhe, Fed. Republic Germany, 1974, 75, 77, U. Tokyo, 1976, 88; vis. scientist Internat. Centre Theoretical Physics, Miramare-Trieste, Italy, Brookhaven Nat. Lab., Lawrence Radiation Lab., U. Calif., Berkeley, CERN, Geneva, Switzerland, Max Planck Inst., Munich, Fed. Republic Germany, Rsch. Inst. for Fundamental Physics, Kyoto (Japan) U. Author articles in field, chpts. in books. Guggenheim fellow, 1963-64; recipient Humboldt award, 1974, Japan Soc. for Promotion of Sci. Fellowship awards, 1976, 88. Fellow Am. Phys. Soc. Office: Univ of Chicago Enrico Fermi Inst 5640 S Ellis Ave Chicago IL 60637-1433 E-mail: oehme@theory.uchicago.edu.

OEHME, WOLFGANG WALTER, landscape architect; b. Chemnitz, Germany, May 18, 1930; came to the U.S., 1957; s. Walter Gustav and Elisabeth Elsa (Neumann) O.; 1 child, Roland. Degree in horticulture, Bitterfeld Trade Sch., 1950; degree in landscape architecture, U. Berlin, 1954. Exch. student Waterer & Sons Nurseries, Bagshot, United Kingdom, 1954-56; landscape architect Baltimore County Planning, Towson, Md., 1958-65, The Rouse Co., Columbia, 1965-66; asst. prof. U. Pa., Phila., 1962-64, U. Ga., Athens, 1965; pvt. practice Balt., 1965-74; CEO Oehme, Van Sweden and Assocs., Inc., Washington, 1974—. Co-author: Bold Romantic Gardens, 1990, Gardening with Water, 1995, Process Architecture, 1996, Gardening with Nature, 1997. Named to Hall of Fame, Towson Devel. Corp., 1995; named Man of Yr., German Soc. Md., 1996. Fellow Am. Soc. Landscape Architects; mem. Perennial Plant Assn. (Disting. Svc. 1988), Garden Writers Assn. (Quill and Trowel award 1991). Home: 511A W Joppa Rd Baltimore MD 21204-3819 Office: 800 G St SE Washington DC 20003-2816 E-mail: oehme@ovsla.com.

OEHRTMANN, CHARLES FREDERICK, music educator; b. Great Lakes, Ill., Apr. 20, 1954; s. Robert Frederick and Elma Irene (Kaasala) O.; m. Deirdre Clark, June 30, 1984. BA in Music Edn., Rowan/Glassboro State U., 1976, MA, 1979. Orch. dir. Metuchen (N.J.) High Sch., 1980-81, Westfield

(N.J.) Sr. High Sch., 1981-83; string specialist Waterville (Maine) Schs., 1983-84; classroom music tchr. Old Orchard (Maine) Schs., 1984; band dir. Deering High Sch., Portland, Maine, 1984-86; with retail ops. Goodyear Tire & Rubber Co., South Portland, 1987-89; string specialist Oxford Hills Sch., South Paris, 1989—. Mem. Music Educators Nat. Conf., Am. String Tchrs. Assn. (newsletter editor 1984-92), Maine Music Edn. Assn. (orch. v.p. 1990—). Democrat. Avocations: square dancing, gardening, house renovation, cooking. Home: 20 Providence Ave South Portland ME 04106-4721 Office: Oxford Hills Jr High Sch 100 Pine St South Paris ME 04281-1599

OELBAUM, HAROLD, lawyer, corporate executive; b. Bklyn., Jan. 9, 1931; s. Max and Betty (Molomet) O.; m. Nancy Rothkopf, June 28, 1968; children— Louise, Andrew, Jennifer. AB, Franklin and Marshall Coll., 1952; JD, Harvard, 1955; LL.M., N.Y. U., 1959. Bar: N.Y. 1955, Mass. 1960. Atty. Hellerstein & Rosier, Esqs., N.Y.C., 1955-59; gen. atty. Raytheon Co., Lexington, Mass., 1959-68; sr. atty. Revlon, Inc., N.Y.C., 1968-72; pres., dir., mem. exec. com. Kane-Miller Corp., Tarrytown, N.Y., 1972—. Office: Kane-Miller Corp 220 White Plains Rd Tarrytown NY 10591-5837

OELBERG, DAVID GEORGE, neonatologist, educator, researcher; b. Waukon, Iowa, May 26, 1952; s. George Robert and Elizabeth Abigail (Kepler) O.; m. Debra Penuel, Aug. 4, 1979; children: Anna Elizabeth, Benjamin George. BS with highest honors, Coll. William and Mary, 1974; MD, U. Md., 1978. Diplomate in pediatrics and in neonatal-perinatal medicine Am. Bd. Pediatrics. Intern U. Tex. Med. Br., Galveston, 1978-79, resident, 1979-81, house pediat. staff, 1978-81; postdoctoral fellow in neonatal Medicine U. Tex. Med. Sch., Houston, 1981-84, asst. prof. dept. pediat., 1984-90, assoc. prof., 1990-93; assoc. prof. pediat., head perinatal rsch. Ctr. Pediat. Rsch., Ea. Va. Med. Sch., 1993-2001, prof., interim chmn. dept. pediats., 2001—; dir. divsn. neonatal-perinatal medicine Ea. Va. Med. Sch. Mem. hosp. staff Hermann Hosp., Houston, 1983-93; physician Crippled Children's Svcs. Program, Houston, 1985-93; mem. hosp. staff Lyndon B. Johnson County Hosp., 1990-93; vis. prof. Wyeth-Ayerst Labs., 1992; med. dir. Office Rsch., Children's Hosp. of King's Daus., 1993—, v.p. for acad. devel., 2001—; med. dirs. Office of Rsch., Sentara-Norfolk Gen. Hos., 1993—. Mem. editl. adv. bd. jour. Neonatal Intensive Care; contbr. articles to profl. jours.; ad hoc reviewer profl. jours.; patentee in field. Physician cons. Parents of Victims of Sudden Infant Death Syndrome, Houston, 1984. Recipient award in analytica chemistry Am. Chem. Soc., 1974, NIH Clin. Investigator award NHLBI, 1989-94; rsch. grantee Am. Lung Assn., 1989-90, NIH, 1989-94. Fellow Am. Acad. Pediat. N.Y. Acad. Scis.; mem. AMA, NAS, Soc. Exptl. Biology and Medicine, So. Soc. Pediat. Rsch. (councilor, pres.), Soc. Pediat. Rsch. Achievements include a method for optical measurement of bilirubin in tissue. Avocations: woodworking, gardening. Home: 1624 W Little Neck Rd Virginia Beach VA 23452-4720 Office: Ea Va Med Sch Ctr Pediatric Rsch 855 W Brambleton Ave Norfolk VA 23510-1005

OELBERG, ROBERT NATHAN, landscape architect; b. Washington, May 7, 1956; s. George Robert and Elizabeth Abigail (Kepler) O. BA in Art magna cum laude, Maharishi Internat. U., Fairfield, Iowa, 1981; M.Landscape Arch., U. Va., 1985. Registered landscape architect, N.C. Landscape architect, sr. project mgr. Land Design Inc., Alexandria, Va., 1985-93; owner Robert N. Oelberg ASLA PA, Boone, N.C., 1994-97, 99—; dir. HMR Land Planning and Landscape Arch., 1997-99. Project landscape architect Heavenly Mountain Resort, Boone, 1994—, mem. archtl. rev. bd. and exec. bd., 1997—. Bd. dirs. Mcoi Devel. Corp., Washington, 1989-91; chmn. Boone Country Dancers. With USMC, 1974-76. DuPont fellow, 1984. Mem. Am. Soc. Landscape Architects. Democrat. Episcopalian. Office: 155 Briar Rose Trl Boone NC 28607-9422 E-mail: rnola@boone.net.

OELGESCHLAGER, GUENTHER KARL, publisher; b. Jersey City, Apr. 19, 1934; s. Herman Wilhelm and Frieda Johanna (Onken) O.; m. Jacqueline L. Braley, July 16, 1962; children: Stacey, Lauren, Amy. BA cum laude, Princeton U., 1958; postgrad., Columbia U., 1959. Nat. sales mgr. Harper & Row Pubs., N.Y.C., 1959-67; dir. coll. div. F.A. Praeger Co., 1968-69; v.p., gen. mgr. D.C. Heath & Co., Lexington, Mass., 1969-72; pres., dir. Ballinger Pub. Co., Cambridge, 1973-78; v.p., dir. J.B. Lippincott Co., Phila., 1973-78; pres. Oelgeschlager, Gunn & Hain, Pubs., Inc., Cambridge, 1979-87; chmn., pres. bd. dirs. Falcon Software Inc., Wellesley, Mass., 1989—. With U.S. Army, 1954-56. Mem. Software Pubs. Assn. Democrat. Episcopalian. Home: 245 Merriam St Weston MA 02493-1350 E-mail: karl@falconsoftware.com.

OELMAN, ROBERT SCHANTZ, retired manufacturing executive; b. Dayton, Ohio, June 9, 1909; s. William Walter and Edith (Schantz) O.; m. Mary Coolidge, Oct. 17, 1936; children: Bradford Coolidge, Robert Schantz, Jr., Kathryn Peirce, Martha Forrer. AB summa cum laude, Dartmouth Coll., 1931, MA, 1963, LL.D. (hon.), 1981; postgrad., U. Vienna, 1931-32; H.H.D. (hon.), U. Dayton, 1959; LL.D. (hon.), Miami U., Oxford, Ohio, 1960, Wright State U., 1976; L.H.D. (hon.), Wilmington Coll. (Ohio), 1965. With NCR Corp., Dayton, 1933-80, asst. to pres., 1942-45, v.p., 1946-50, exec. v.p., 1950-57, pres., 1957-62, chmn., pres., 1962-64, chmn., 1962-74, chmn. exec. com., 1974-80, dir., 1948-80; ret., 1980. Trustee Dartmouth Coll., 1961-76; Mem. Bus. Council, 1965— ; chmn. bd. trustees Wright State U., 1961-76; bd. dirs. Miami Conservancy, 1967-79, pres., 1975-79; chmn. Air Force Mus. Found., Dayton, 1970-80; trustee C.F. Kettering Med. Center, 1971-80; ind. dir. tournament policy bd. PGA Tour, Ponte Vedra, Fla., 1974-83, chmn., 1978-83. Mem. Country Club of Fla., Ocean Club of Fla., Augusta Nat. Club (Ga.), Delray Beach Yacht Club.

OELSCHLAGER, JAMES, investment company executive; married; 2 children. BA in Econs., Denison U., 1964; JD, Northwestern U., 1967; postgrad., U. Chgo., 1968—69. Dir. pension investments, asst. treas. Firestone Tire and Rubber Co., 1969—85; founder Oak Assocs., ltd, Akron, Ohio, 1985, mng. mem., chief investment officer, 1985—, portfolio mgr. White Oak Growth and Pin Oak Aggressive, 1992—, co-portfolio mgr. Red Oak Tech Select fund, 1998—, co-portfolio mgr. Black Oak Emerging Tech fund, 2000—.*

OERDING, JAMES BRYAN, military educator; b. Roseburg, Oreg., June 21, 1935; s. William Arthur and Naomi Eileen (Cobb) O. BS, U.S. Mil. Acad., 1960; MA, U. Fla., 1975-77; candidate in philosophy, U. Calif., Davis, 1978-80. Cert. community coll. tchr., Calif. Commd. 2nd lt. U.S. Army, 1960, advanced through grades to maj., various assignments, officer 7th Spl. Forces Group N.C., 1973-74, research specialist 1st Psychol. Ops. Bn., 1975-78; internat. plans & tng. specialist U.S. Army Western Command Hdqrs., Ft. Shafter, 1980-85; internat. security assistance analyst U.S. Army, Washington, 1985-86, dir. Army sr. fellowship program, 1986-89; comdt. U.S. Army Mgmt. Engring. Coll., Rock Island, Ill., 1989-91, dep. for strategic plans, 1991-92, East Coast regional rep. East Coast D.M.E.C., 1992-94; ret., 1994. Cons. on mgmt. Escapes Unltd., Greencastle, Pa., 1988-94; cruise lectr., 1994—. Regents' fellow U. Calif. at Davis, 1978, Chancellor's fellow, 1980. Mem. Antarctican Soc., Am. Polar Soc., Spl. Forces Assn. (life), Am. Indochina Vets. Legion (N.C. state chmn. 1975-76), VFW, Disabled Am. Vets. Republican. Avocations: stamp collecting, writing. E-mail: escapesunlimited@hotmail.com.

OERTEL, GOETZ KUNO HEINRICH, physicist, professional association administrator; b. Stuhm, Germany, Aug. 24, 1934; came to U.S., 1957; s. Egon F.K. and Margarete W. (Wittek) O.; m. Brigitte Beckmann, June 17, 1960; children: Ines M.H. Oertel Downing, Carsten K.R. Abitur, Robert Mayer, Heilbronn, Fed. Republic Germany, 1953; vordiplom, U. Kiel, Fed. Republic Germany, 1956; PhD, U. Md., 1963. Aerospace engr. Langley Ctr. NASA, Hampton, Va., 1963-68, chief solar physics Washington, 1968-75; analyst Office of Mgmt. and Budget, 1974-75; head astronomy div. Nat. Sci. Found., 1975; dir. def. and civilian nuclear waste programs U.S. Dept. Energy, 1975-83; acting mgr. sav. river ops. office Aiken, S.C., 1983-84; dep. mgr. ops. office Albuquerque, 1984-85; dep. asst. sec. EH Washington, 1985-86; pres., CEO Assn. Univs. for Rsch. in Astronomy, Inc. (AURA, Inc.), 1986-99, also bd. dirs., disting. advisor, 2000—. Cons. Los Alamos Lab., N.Mex., 1987-92, Westinghouse Electric, 1988—, AURA, Inc., Lampadia Found., Fundacion Andes of Santiago de Chile, Vitae Found. Sao Paulo, Brazil; bd. dirs. Inst. for Sci. and Soc., Ellensburg, Wash., IUE Corp.; mem. of the bd. Nat. Rsch. Coun., Internat. Sci. Orgns.; chmn. bd. Sch. of Computational Sci., George Mason U., 2000—; mem. U.S. Com. for CODATA, 1993—, chmn. 1997-2000; U.S. nat. del. CODATA ICSU, 1999—; mem. peer rev. com. ASME, 1996—; cons. conicyt, Govt. of Chile, 2000—. Patentee in field. Bd. dirs. Internat. Scientific Orgns., 2001—; mem. Nat. Rsch. council. Fulbright grantee, 1957. Fellow Am. Assn. Advancement Sci.; mem. Am. Phys. Soc., Am. Astron. Soc., Internat. Astron. Union, N.Y. Acad. Scis., Internat. U. Exch., Inc. (bd. dirs.), Cosmos Club, Sigma Xi. Lutheran. Avocations: fitness, chess, computing, genealogy. Home: 8833 Watts Mine Ter Potomac MD 20854-5439 Office: PO Box 388 Cabin John MD 20818-0388 E-mail: goetz@oertel.org.

OERTEL, YOLANDA CASTILLO, pathologist, educator, diagnostician; b. Lima, Peru, Dec. 14, 1938; came to U.S., 1966; d. Leonardo A. and Dalila (Ramirez) C.; m. James E. Oertel, Sept. 24, 1969. MD, Cayetano Heredia, Lima, 1964; Dr. honoris causa, U. Peruana Cayetano Heredia, 1999. Diplomate Am. Bd. Pathology (mem. test com. for cytopathology 1988-94). Internat. postdoctoral fellowship NIH, Bethesda, Md., 1966-68; asst. prof. pathology Sch. Medicine George Washington U., Washington, 1975-78, assoc. prof., 1978-84, prof., 1984-98, prof. emerita, 1998—. Adj. prof. pathology and lab. medicine MCP Hahnemann U. Sch. Medicine; cons. Registry Cytology Armed Forces Inst. Pathology, Washington, 1981—. Author: Fine Needle Aspiration of the Breast, 1987; contbr. chpts. to books and articles to profl. jours. Decorated comendador de la Orden Cayetano Heredia, 1999; recipient Francisco A. Camino prize Peruvian Med. Assn., 1965, cert. Meritorious Svc. Armed Forces Inst. Pathology, 1974; named Disting. Alumna Cayetano Heredia Med. Sch., 1989. Mem Internat. Acad. Cytology, Assn. Mil. Surgeons (hon), Colombian Soc. Pathology (hon.), Argentinian Soc. Pathology (hon.), Peruvian Soc. Pathologists (hon.), Argentinian Soc. Cytopathology, (hon.), Am. Soc. Cytology, Internat. Acad. Pathology, Soc. Latinoamericana Patologia, Am. Soc. Clin. Pathologists (coun. on cytopathology 1982-88). Avocations: reading, opera. Office: Washington Hosp Ctr Pathology Dept Washington Cancer Inst 110 Irving St NW Washington DC 20010-2975 Fax: (202) 877-0197. E-mail: Yolanda.C.Oertel@medstar.net.

OERTER, CYNTHIA LYNN, medical technologist; b. Waupaca, Wis., Mar. 8, 1948; d. Lavern Charles and Geraldine Mae (Huffcutt) Trinrud; m. Gregory Van Oerter, June 8, 1968; children: Nathan, Justin. BS, U. Wis., Oshkosh, 1971; MS, Cardinal Stritch Coll., 1993. Cert. Am. Soc. Clin. Pathologists. Med. technologist Mercy Med. Ctr., Oshkosh, Wis., 1970-76, Iola (Wis.) Hosp., 1978-86, wellness cons., 1985-86, Riverside Med. Ctr., Waupaca, Wis., 1986-93, med. technologist, hematology supr., insvc. coord., cons., 1987-95; pres. Pro Health Consul, Inc., 1994—; bus. ptnr., adminstr. Garden Park House, 1994—. Tchr. Fox Valley Coll., Appleton, Wis., 1986, 87; organizer Overeaters Anonymous, Iola, 1985-89; owner Green Fountain Inn, 1995—. Mem. parent's com. for gifted and talented Waupaca Sch. Sys., 1984, charter mem. edn. employment coun., 1989-92, mem. adv. com. guidance program K-12, 1992; vol. Nat. Wellness Inst., 1986-97, Am. Lung Assn., 1986-87; tchr. smokeless program Am. Inst. Preventative Medicine, 1988-93; com. mem. Main St. Design, 1999-. Mem. NAFE, Nat. Platform Assn., Am. Sch. Health Assn. (com. mem.), Rotary (sec. 1996-98, bd. dirs. 1995—, pres. elect 1999-2000, pres. 2000-2001). Republican. Lutheran. Avocations: gardening, gourmet cooking, sailing, Bible study, hobby farm. E-mail: greenfountain@gglbbs.com.

OESTERLE, CAROLYN SCHERER, pediatric ophthalmologist; b. Detroit, Apr. 12, 1949; d. Ernest Francis and Margaret (Palm) Scherer; m. Eric Adam Oesterle, Sept. 15, 1973; children: Adam Clark, Allison Margaret. BS in Chemistry with honors, U. Mich., 1971; postgrad., U. Wis., 1971-72; MD with distinction, Northwestern U., Chgo., 1977. Am. Bd. Ophthalmology. Intern Evanston (Ill.) Hosp., 1977-78; resident in ophthalmology U. Ill. Eye and Ear Infirmary, Chgo., 1978-81; fellow in pediat. ophthalmology Childrens Hosp. Nat. Med. Ctr., Washington, 1981-82; ophthalmologist Evanston Ophthalmologists, 1982-83; pediat. ophthalmologist Wheaton (Ill.) Eye Clinic, 1983—; attending physician Ctrl. DuPage Hosp., Winfield, Ill., 1983—; assoc. in ophthalmology Northwestern U. Med. Sch., Chgo., 1984—. Lectr. in organic chemistry U. Mich., 1973. Contbr. articles to profl. jours. James B. Angell scholar, 1969. Fellow Am. Acad. Ophthalmology; mem. AMA, Am. Assn. Pediat. Ophthalmology and Strabismus, Am. Assn. Ophthalmology, DuPage Med. Soc., Ill. Assn. Ophthalmology, Phi Beta Kappa, Phi Lambda Delta, Alpha Omega Alpha. Home: 645 Lake Rd Glen Ellyn IL 60137-4249 Office: Wheaton Eye Clinic 2015 N Main St Wheaton IL 60187-3190

OESTERLE, ERIC ADAM, lawyer; b. Lafayette, Ind., Dec. 2, 1948; s. Eric Clark and Germaine Dora (Seelye) O.; m. Carolyn Anne Scherer, Sept. 16, 1973; children: Adam Clark, Allison Margaret. BS, U. Mich., 1970, JD, 1973. Bar: Ill. 1973, U.S. Dist. Ct. (no. dist.) Ill. 1973, U.S. Ct. Appeals (7th cir.) 1987, U.S. Supreme Ct. 1986. Assoc. Sonnenschein, Carlin, Nath & Rosenthal, Chgo., 1973-80; ptnr. Sonnenschein Nath & Rosenthal, 1980—. Mem. ABA, Ill. Bar Assn., Chgo. Bar Assn. Home: 645 Lake Rd Glen Ellyn IL 60137-4249 Office: Sonnenschein Nath & Rosenthal 8000 Sears Tower 233 S Wacker Dr Ste 8000 Chicago IL 60606-6491 E-mail: eoesterle@sonnenschein.com.

OESTERLING, THOMAS OVID, retired pharmaceutical company executive; b. Butler, Pa., Mar. 6, 1938; s. Victor Kenneth and Marjorie Gertrude (Oswald) O.; m. Janet Westrick, Dec. 30, 1960 (div. 1983); children: Thomas, Jennifer, Daniel; m. Cynthia Adler, 1984 (div. 1987). BS, Ohio State U., 1962, MS, 1964, PhD, 1966. Rsch. assoc., rsch. head Upjohn Co., Kalamazoo, 1966-76; dir. R&D dermatol. divsn. Johnson & Johnson Corp., New Brunswick, N.J., 1976-78, dir. pharm. R&D, 1978-79; v.p. med. products R&D Mallinckrodt, Inc., St. Louis, 1979-83; sr. v.p. R&D Collaborative Rsch. Inc., Bedford, Mass., 1984-86, pres., 1986-89; chmn., pres., CEO Gliatech Inc., Cleve., 1989-2000; ret. Mem. faculty Arden House Conf. on Stability Evaluation Pharm. Dosage Forms, 1979 Contbr. numerous sci. articles to profl. jours.; patentee in field. Recipient Disting. Alumni award Ohio State U. Coll. Pharmacy, 1982; Parke Davis rsch. grantee, 1962-64; Am. Found. for Pharm. Edn. fellow, 1964-66 Mem. Am. Chem. Soc., Soc. Nuclear Medicine, Acad. Pharm. Scis., Soc. for Neurosci.

OESTMANN, IRMA EMMA, minister; b. Auburn, Nebr., May 6, 1930; d. Martin Edward and Magdalene Augusta (Volkman) O.; m. Allister Roland Behrends, July 29, 1948 (div. 1968); children: John, Allan, Patricia, William, Michael, Russell, Kurt. BS in Edn., U. Nebr., 1972. Ordained min. Unity Ch., Unity Village, Mo., 1982. Dairy farm pvt. farmer, Johnson, Nebr., 1948-68; art tchr. Burke High Sch., Omaha, 1972-73, L.A. (Calif.) Pub. Schs., 1974-77; mgr. U-Rent Furniture, Canoga Park, Calif., 1978-80; min. There Is A Way TV Ministry, Palm Springs, 1982-83, Unity Ch. of Truth, Pomona, 1983-85, Unity of Del Ray Beach, Fla., 1986-87, Unity of Jupiter, 1988-90, Unity Ch. of San Gabriel, Calif., 1991-94, United Fellowship of Grants Pass, Oreg., 1994-95; asst. min. Unity Ch., Ventura, Calif., 1995-96; founder, minister The Unity Ctr., Agoura Hills, 1997—; minister Unity Center Ch.-Conejo Valley, Inc., Thousand Oaks. Cert. hypnotist, self-instr., therapist Encino, Calif., 1978-80; pvt. children's art tchr., Upland, Calif., 1986-87; seminar/workshop presenter, 1980. Artist oil and watercolor paintings, 1968—; author, artist: (audio tapes) Methods of Relaxation, 1980, Inner-Space Meditations, 1994; producer, host: (tv panel series) The Truth Is, 1989; contbr. poems and articles to mags. Mem. San Gabriel (Calif.) Cmty. Coun., 1991-93. Avocations: visual arts, singing, hiking, travel, photography. Home: 985 Sunset Garden Ln O Simi Valley CA 93065 E-mail: irmaoestman@msn.com.

OESTREICH, CHARLES HENRY, retired university president; b. Columbus, Ohio, June 8, 1932; s. Henry F. and Martha (Schwartz) O.; m. Rhoda J. Haseley, Aug. 26, 1957; children: Martha, Mary, David. BS, Capital U., 1954; MS, Ohio U., 1956, PhD, 1961; LLD, Capital U., 1986. Instr. chemistry Va. Mil. Inst., 1956-57, Capital U., Columbus, 1960-62, asst. prof., 1962-64, assoc. prof., 1965-69; acad. dean Tex. Luth. U., Seguin, 1969-76, interim pres., 1976-77, pres., 1977-94, pres. emeritus, 1995—. Postdoctoral rsch. fellow Vanderbilt U., 1965-66 Bd. dirs., past pres. Mid-Tex. Symphony. Mem. Rotary (past pres. Seguin). Home and Office: 2269 S Abbey Loop New Braunfels TX 78130-8965 Fax: 830-625-8306. E-mail: charleso@axs4u.net.

OETJEN, DAVID L. (JON DAVID DOUGLAS), writer, film producer; b. Washington, May 23, 1938; s. Walter Theodor Oetjen and Alyce Marie Peterson. BA, U. of Iowa, 1960. Prodr. Home Shopping Network, Clearwater, Fla.; broadcast prodn. dir. Barlow/Johnson Advt., Syracuse, Albany, Buffalo, Springfield, 1969—73; dir. of promotion, advt. mgr. Sta. WTVH-TV, Meredith Corp., Syracuse, NY, 1977—91. Prodr.: (TV series, television) Dari-Lean "Magic", 1971 (Chgo. Film Festival, 1971); author: (novels) Cody, A Boys Odyssey, 2002, The Villages, 1992. Citizen's adv. Bayfront Med. Ctr., St. Petersburg, 1997—99; advisor Office of the Mayor, Syracuse, 1988—91, Syracuse (N.Y.) Symphony, 1988—90; prodr. Bring Them Home Alive-Missing Childrens' Clearing House, Tampa Bay. Recipient Silver Shaker award for Winterfest, CNY-Pub. Rels. Soc. Am., 1989, 1st Pl. TV Promotion award for Gimmie Five!, Syracuse Advt. Club, 1988, 1st Pl. TV Promotion award for Tell 'Em, 1989, Media award, CNY Parks and Recreation Soc., 1985, Award of Appreciation for svc. as dir. of broadcast promotion and publicity, AAU/USA Jr. Olympics, 1987. Mem.: Broadcast Promotion Assn., Village Writers' Group.

OETTGEN, HERBERT FRIEDRICH, physician; b. Cologne, Germany, Nov. 22, 1923; came to U.S., 1958; s. Peter and Minna (Kaul) O.; m. Trudi Hesberg, Feb. 16, 1957; children: Hans Christoph, Joerg Peter, Anne Barbara. MD, U. Cologne, 1951. Diplomate Bd. Internal Medicine, Fed. Republic of Germany. Resident in pathology City Hosp., Cologne, 1952-54, resident in medicine, 1955-58; fellow Meml. Sloan-Kettering Cancer Ctr., N.Y.C., 1958-62, assoc. to assoc. mem., 1963-69, mem., 1972—, attending physician, 1971—; prof. medicine Cornell U. Med. Coll., 1972—. Assoc. dir. Cancer Rsch. Inst., N.Y.C., 1985—. Author over 350 publs. in hematology, cancer rsch., immunology and clin. oncology. Recipient award for cancer rsch. Wilhelm Warner Found., Hamburg, Fed. Republic Germany, 1970, Lisec-Artz award for cancer rsch. Friedrich Wilhelm U., Bonn, Fed. Republic of Germany, 1982. Presbyterian. Avocations: violin, woodworking. Home: 48 Overlook Dr New Canaan CT 06840-6825 Office: Meml Sloan-Kettering Cancer Ctr 1275 York Ave New York NY 10021-6094 E-mail: oettgenh@mskcc.org., hoettgen@licr.org.

OETTING, MILDRED KATHERINE See **SQUAZZO, MILDRED**

OETTINGER, ANTHONY GERVIN, mathematician, educator; b. Nuremberg, Germany, Mar. 29, 1929; came to U.S., 1941, naturalized, 1947; s. Albert and Marguerite (Bing) O.; m. Marilyn Tanner, June 20, 1954; children: Douglas, Marjorie. AB, Harvard U., 1951, PhD, 1954; Henry fellow, U. Cambridge, Eng., 1951-52; Litt.D. (hon.), U. Pitts., 1984. Mem. faculty Harvard, 1955—, asso. prof. applied math., 1960-63, prof. linguistics, 1963-75, Gordon McKay prof. applied math., 1963—, chmn. program on info. resources policy, 1972—, mem. faculty of govt., 1973—, prof. info. resources policy, 1975—. Mem. command control comm. and intelligence bd. Dept. Navy, 1978-83; mem. sci. adv. group Def. Comm. Agy., 1979-90; chmn. bd. visitors Joint Mil. Intelligence Coll., 1986—; chmn., dir. Ctrl. Intelligence Advanced Tech. Panel, 1995—; cons. Arthur D. Little, Inc., 1956-80, Office Sci. and Tech., Exec. Office of Pres., 1960-73, Bellcomm, Inc., 1963-68, Sys. Devel. Corp., 1965-68, Nat. Security Coun., Exec. Office of Pres., 1975-81, Pres.'s Fgn. Intelligence Adv. Bd., 1981-90; chmn. Computer Sci. and Engring. Bd., Nat. Acad. Scis., 1968-73; mem. Mass. Cmty. Antenna TV Commn., 1972-79, chmn., 1975-79; mem. rsch. adv. bd. Com. for Econ. Devel., 1975-79; trustee Babbage Inst., 1991—; panel mem. Naval Studies Bd. NAS/NRC, 1993-95; mem. banking and fin. team Pres.' Commn. on Critical Infrastructure Protection, 1998. Author: A Study for the Design of an Automatic Dictionary, 1954, Automatic Language Translation: Lexical and Technical Aspects, 1960, Run Computer Run: The Mythology of Educational Innovation, 1969, High and Low Politics: Information Resources for the 80s, 1977, Behind the Telephone Debates, 1988, Mastering the Changing Information World, 1993; editor: Proc. of a Symposium on Digital Computers and Their Applications, 1962; contbr. chpts. to The Information Resources Policy Handbook: Research for the Information Age, 1999. Fellow Am. Acad. Arts and Scis., AAAS, IEEE, Assn. Computing Machinery (mem. coun. 1961-68, chmn. com. U.S. Govt. Rels. 1964-66, editor computational linguistics sect. Commn. 1964-66, pres. 1966-68); mem. Soc. Indsl. and Applied Math. (mem. coun. 1963-67), Coun. on Fgn. Rels., Phi Beta Kappa, Sigma Xi. Clubs: Cosmos (Washington); Harvard (N.Y.C.). Home: 65 Elizabeth Rd Belmont MA 02478-3819 Office: Harvard U Maxwell Dworkin 125 33 Oxford St Cambridge MA 02138-2901 E-mail: anthony@deas.harvard.edu.

OETTINGER, KATHLEEN LINDA, artist, writer; b. Jan. 16, 1943; d. Herbert Irving and Aura Orvokki (Lehto) Johnson; m. Frank Frederic Oettinger, Aug. 24, 1963; children: Meredith Laura, Melanie Beth, Megan Michelle. BFA, Pratt Inst., 1965; MA, Regis Coll., 1984; MFA, Catholic U., 1987. Art instr. Dept. Recreation Montgomery County (Md.), 1971-75; adj. faculty Washington Internat. Coll., 1974-82; writer, editor Nat. Inst. for the Family, Washington, 1981-84; mag. columnist, contbg. editor Abbey Press, St. Meinrad, Ind., 1982-84; studio artist Oettinger Studio, Rockville, Md., 1984-96; art editor Visions Internat. Mag., Fredericksburg, Va., 1994-98; adj. faculty Polk C.C., Winter Haven, Fla., 1998—. Nat. Bd. Outline Com. Catholic Engaged Encounter, Del., 1978-79; Nat. bd. mem. Women's Caucus Art, Phila., 1994-97; guest curator, bd. govs. Fed. Res. Bank, Washington, 1995. One-man shows include Window Gallery, Kotka, Finland, 1995; exhibited in group shows at World Trade Ctr., Beijing, 1995, Elite Gallery, Moscow, 1996, Nat. Mus. Women Arts, Washington, 1996. Family Ministry Commn. Archdiocese Washington, 1979-80; rep. NGO Forum 4th UN World Conf. Women, Beijing, 1995; exhbn. designer Explorations V Children's Mus., Lakeland, Fla., 1997-98. Recipient Creativity Svc. Ams. Children award Every Child by Two, Inc., Washington, 1994; named Feature Artist Finnish-Am. Heritage Ctr., Hancock, Mich., 1993, named artist-in-residence Rockville (Md.) Arts Palace, 1993-96. Mem. So. Graphics Coun., Arts on the Park, Lakeland, Women's Caucus Art (chpt. pres. 1994-96), Fla. Printmakers (bd. dirs.). Roman Catholic. Avocations: family ministry, singing, water sports. Home: 3675 Emerald Ln Mulberry FL 33860-7512

OETTINGER, MARGARET ANNE, librarian; b. Port Jefferson, N.Y., Jan. 19, 1943; d. Thaddeus P. and Catherine M. (McQuade) O. BA in Music Edn., Cath. U. of Am., Washington, 1964; MLS, St. John's U., Jamaica, N.Y., 1971. Music tchr. Commack (N.Y.) Pub. Schs., 1964-66, Three Village Ctrl. Schs., Setauket, N.Y., 1966-69; libr. trainee Smithtown (N.Y.) Libr., 1969-70; libr. Oxhead Elm. Sch., Mid. Country Schs., Centereach, N.Y., 1970-85, Centereach H.S., 1985-98. EMT, chmn. bd. dirs. Ctrl. Islip-Hauppauge (N.Y.) Vol. Ambulance, 1981—, past asst. chief; past pres. Port Jefferson Fire Dept. Ladies Aux. Mem. ALA (mem. spl. needs com. Assn. for Libr. Svc. to Children 1994-98, com. chmn., 1997-98, pub. rels. com. libr. instrn. roundtable discussion group 1993-97, intellectual freedom roundtable, libr. instrn. roundtable, com. resolutions 1998—, YALSA intellectual freedoms com. 1998—), AAUW, Assn. Libr. Svcs. to Children, Libr. Congress Assocs., Assn. Libr. Collections and Tech. Svcs., People to People Internat. (delegate to People's Rep. China, 1993), Young Adult Libr. Svcs. Assn., Freedom to Read Found., Port Jefferson Country Club (bd. govs. 1986-87), U.S. Tennis Assn., U.S. Golf Assn., U.S. Field Hockey Assn. Avocations: golf, tennis, travel.

OETZEL, JENNIFER M. finance educator; b. Milw., May 27, 1969; d. Brian K. and Mary E. Oetzel; m. Jorge E. Rivera, Oct. 7, 2000. BA in Econs., U. Tex., 1991, MS in Urban Planning, 1995; PhD in Bus. Strategy, U. N.C., Chapel Hill, 2002. USAID project evaluator Am.-Mideast Edn. and Tng. Svcs., Inc., Tunis, Tunisia, 1994—95; mktg. and rsch. cons. Ctr. for Info. Sys. Mgmt., U. Tex., Austin, 1996; rsch. assoc. IntelliQuest, 1996; rsch. asst. U. N.C., Chapel Hill, 1997—2001; asst. prof. internat. bus. Am. U., Washington, 2002—. Vol. child abuse prevention and after school tutoring programs, Austin and Durham, N.C., 1990—2000. Fellow field rsch. grant fellow, Tinker Found., 1999; grantee doctoral grantee, Fin. Svcs. Exch., 2001—02, rsch. grantee, Cato Ctr. for Applied Bus. Rsch., U. N.C., 1998, Smith Grad. Rsch. Fund, 2000. Mem.: INFORMS, Am. Polit. Sci. Assn., Strategic Mgmt. Soc., Acad. Internat. Bus., Acad. Mgmt. Avocations: hiking, skiing, tennis, foreign languages, travel. Office: Am U 4400 Massachusetts Ave NW Washington DC 20016-8044

OETZEL, JOHN GERARD, communication educator, consultant; b. Cleve., Dec. 8, 1966; s. John T. and Patricia M. Oetzel; m. Keri Bolton, Aug. 10, 1996. BA, U. N.Mex., 1989; MA, U. Iowa, 1990, PhD, 1995. Tchg. asst. U. Iowa, Iowa City, 1989-91; instr. Citrus Coll., Glendora, Calif., 1991-97; assoc. prof. U. N.Mex., Albuquerque, 1997—. Cons. Intel Corp., Chandler, Ariz., 1999, Rio Rancho, N.Mex., 1999—. Author: Managing Intercultural Conflicts Effectively, 2001; contbr. articles to profl. jours. Recipient 2d place paper award Internat. Assn. Bus. Communicators, 1999. Mem. Internat. Comm. Assn. (Top Paper award 1999), Nat. Comm. Assn., Western Comm. Assn. (Top

Paper award 1999), Phi Beta Kappa. Avocations: jogging, tennis, Spanish, golf. Office: Univ New Mexico Comm And Journalism Bldg Albuquerque NM 87131-0001 Fax: 505-277-4206. E-mail: joetzel@unm.edu.

O'FARRELL, MARK THEODORE, religious organization administrator; b. Milw., Apr. 13, 1948; s. Theodore Wolfred and Ernestine (Shelhammer) O.; m. Phillis Gilley, Sept. 18, 1948; children: Gwen, Kevin. BA, Columbia Bible Coll., 1970; DD, Toccan Falls Coll., 1996. Asst. pastor 1st Alliance Ch., Macon, Ga., 1970-71, sr. pastor Port Charlotte, Fla., 1981-86, Belle Glade (Fla.) Alliance Ch., 1971-81; asst. to dist. supt., ext. dir. Southeastern Dist. of Christian and Missionary Alliance, Orlando, Fla., 1986-93, dist. supt., 1993—. Recipient Spiritual Aims award Kiwanis. Home: Christian & Missionary Alliance Southeastern District 2450 Donaldson Dr Orlando FL 32812 Office: PO Box 720430 Orlando FL 32872-0430 E-mail: sedistrict@cmalliance.org.

O'FARRELL, TIMOTHY JAMES, psychologist, educator; b. Lancaster, Ohio, Apr. 22, 1946; s. Robert James and Helen Loretta (Tooill) O'F.; m. Jayne Sara Talmage, May 19, 1973; 1 child, Colin. BA, U. Notre Dame, 1968; PhD in Psychology, Boston U., 1975. Instr. Harvard U. Med. Sch., Boston, 1977-82, asst. prof., 1982-86, assoc. prof., 1986-2000, prof., 2000—. Chief Harvard Families and Addiction Program, 1991—; staff psychologist VA Med. Ctr., Brockton, Mass., 1975-78, dir. Alcoholism Clinic, 1978-83, dir. Counseling for Alcoholics' Marriages Project, 1978—, chief Alcohol and Family Studies Lab., 1981-91; chief, Harvard Families and Addiction Program, 1991—; assoc. chief psychology svc., 1988—; VA predoctoral grantee, 1969-72; rsch. grantee VA, 1978—, Nat. Inst. on Alcohol Abuse and Alcoholism, 1991—, Smithers Found., 1991—, Guggenheim Found., 1993-94. Author: Alcohol and Sexuality, 1983, Treating Alcohol Problems: Marital and Family Interventions, 1993, Accreditation Guide for Substance Abuse Treatment Programs, 1997; editl. bd. numerous scientific jours.; contbr. articles to profl. jours. Fellow APA, Behavior Therapy and Rsch. Soc.; mem. NIAAA (psychosocial rsch. rev. group 1989-93), Assn. Advancement Behavior Therapy, Eastern Psychol. Assn. Home: 14 Wadsworth Ln Duxbury MA 02332-5116 Office: VA Med Ctr 116B1 Brockton MA 02301 E-mail: timothy_ofarrell@hms.harvard.edu.

O'FARRILL, ALAN JOHN, music educator; b. Miami, Fla., Aug. 26, 1951; s. Carmelo and Raquel Olga O'Farrill; m. Marline Elizabeth Stabile, Aug. 18, 1970; children: John, Christopher. MA, Fla. Internat. U., 1990. Cert. tchr. Fla. Freelance musician Local 655, Miami, 1973—83; music tchr. Driftwood Mid. Sch., Hollywood, 1980—91, McArthur HS, Hollywood, 1991—92, Hollywood Hills HS, 1992—2002, Cypress Bay HS, Weston, 2002—. Cons., Fla., 2000—02. With U.S. Army, 1970—73. Mem.: Fla. Bandmasters Assn. (dist. chmn. 2002—). Democrat. Avocation: motorcycling. Home: 15130 Windbluff St Davie FL 33331 Office: Cypress Bay HS 18600 Vista Park Blvd Davie FL 33332 Personal E-mail: aofarrill@aol.com.

OFFEN, RONALD CHARLES, retired school librarian; b. Chgo., Oct. 2, 1930; s. Charles Henry and Ellen (Shirreffs) O.; m. Sharon Rae Nealy, Mar. 17, 1951 (div.); children: Deirdre, Eric; m. Rosine J. Franke, Aug. 20, 1966 (dec. Apr. 21, 2000); children: Michele, Darren P. AA, Wright Jr. Coll., Chgo., 1950; MA, U. Chgo., 1967. Ins. investigator various ins. cos., Chgo., 1952-68; mng. editor Chicagoland Mag., 1968-70; editor Automotive Fleet, Glenview, Ill., 1970-71; freelance editor, writer, author Chgo., 1971-78; sch. libr. Capistrano Unified Sch. Dist., Laguna Niguel, Calif., 1983-98; ret., 1998. Adminstr. theater co. The Peripatetic Task Force, Chgo., 1975-78. Co-editor Odyssey: Explorations in Poetry, 1956-58; exec. editor Lit. Times, 1975-78; co-author: (non-fiction) Dillinger: Dead or Alive?, 1970; author: (biographies) Cagney, 1973, Brando, 1974; (poetry) Poet as Bad Guy, 1963, Instead of Gifts, 1995, Questions, Answers, 1996, God's Haircut (And Other Remembered Dreams), 1999; editor: The Starving Poet's Cookbook, 1994; editor Free Lunch, 1989—. Mem. Acad. Am. Poets (1st prize 1958), Authors Guild. E-mail: ronoffen@yahoo.com.

OFFENBERGER, ALLAN ANTHONY, electrical engineering educator; b. Wadena, Sask., Can., Aug. 11, 1938; s. Ivy Viola (Hagglund) O.; m. Margaret Elizabeth Patterson, Apr. 12, 1963; children: Brian, Gary. BS, U. B.C., 1962, MS, 1963; PhD, MIT, 1968. Asst. prof. U. Alta., Edmonton, Can., 1968-70, assoc. prof. Can., 1970-75, prof. Can., 1975-95, prof. emeritus Can., 1996—. Cons. Lawrence Livermore (Calif.) Nat. Lab., 1996-98; vis. prof. U.K. Atomic Energy Agy., Abingdon, Oxon, Eng., 1975-76; project dir. Laser Fusion Project, Edmonton, 1984-91; mem. strategic adv. com. Nat. Fusion Program, Atomic Energy of Can. Ltd., Chalk River, Ont., 1987-96; vis. prof. U. Oxford, U.K., 1992, U. Osaka, Japan, 2000. Mem. editorial bd. Laser and Particle Beams, 1987—; contbr. over 150 sci. articles on lasers and plasma physics. Killam Rsch. fellow Can. Coun., 1980-82. SERC rsch. fellow, Eng., 1992. Mem. Can. Assn. Physicists (exec. officer, v.p. elect 1987-88, pres. 1989-90), Am. Phys. Soc., Sigma Xi. Home: 412 Lessard Dr Edmonton AB Canada T6M 1A7 Office: U Alta Dept Elec Computer Engring Edmonton AB Canada T6G 2V4

OFFER, STUART JAY, lawyer; b. Seattle, June 2, 1943; m. Judith Spitzer, Aug. 29, 1970; children: Rebecca, Kathryn. BA, U. Wash., 1964; LLB, Columbia U., 1967. Bar: D.C. 1968, U.S. Tax Ct. 1968, Calif. 1972. Atty., advisor U.S. Tax Ct., Washington, 1967-68; assoc. Morrison & Foerster, LLP, San Francisco, 1972-76, ptnr., 1976—. Trustee Am. Tax Policy Inst. Served as capt. U.S. Army, 1968-72. Mem. ABA (chmn. taxation sect., corp. tax com. 1991-92, coun. dir. 1995-98, vice chair adminstrn. 1998-2000), Internat. Fiscal Assn., Am. Coll. Tax Counsel. Office: Morrison & Foerster LLP 425 Market St San Francisco CA 94105-2482 E-mail: soffer@mofo.com.

OFFICER, LAWRENCE HOWARD, economist, educator; b. Montreal, Que., Can., Feb. 27, 1940; s. Joseph and Sylvia Officer; m. Sue Anne Maurer, May 25, 1979 (div. May 1985); 1 child, Jonathan David; m. Sandra Diane Officer, June 29, 1986; 1 child, Ari Joseph. BA, McGill U., 1960; MA, Harvard U., 1962, PhD, 1965. Asst. prof. econs. Harvard U., Cambridge, 1965-70; prof. econs. Mich. State U., East Lansing, 1970-87, U. Ill., Chgo., 1987—, interim dean Coll. Bus. Adminstrn., 1997-98. Author: Purchasing Power Parity, 1982, Between the Dollar-Sterling Gold Points, 1996; editor: International Economics, 1987, Monetary Standards and Exchange Rates, 1997. Recipient Hon. Mention, Coll. and Univ. Divsn. Jt. Coun. on Econ. Edn., 1980. Avocations: science fiction, physical fitness. Office: U Ill Dept Econs 601 S Morgan St Chicago IL 60607-7121 E-mail: LOfficer@uic.edu.

OFFIT, MORRIS WOLF, investment advisory executive; b. Balt., Jan. 22, 1937; s. Michael and Rhea (Wolf) O.; m. Nancy Silverman, Nov. 26, 1959; children: Ned S., Daniel W. BA in History, Johns Hopkins U., 1957, LHD (hon.), 1996; MBA in Fin., U. Pa., 1959. V.p. investment dept. Mercantile Safe Deposit and Trust, Balt., 1960-68; gen. ptnr. Salomon Bros. Inc., N.Y.C., 1968-80; pres. Julius Baer Securities, 1980-82, Offit Assocs. Inc., N.Y.C., 1983—; CEO OffitBank; now CEO Offit Hall Capital Mgmt. LLC. Bd. dirs. Merc. Bancshares Corp., Balt. Trustee, former chmn. bd. trustees Johns Hopkins U.; chmn. adv. coun. Nitze Sch. Advanced Internat. Studies; trustee Jewish Mus., former chmn.; trustee Jewish Theol. Sem., Thirteen-WNET, United Jewish Appeal Fedn. N.Y., Am. Jewish Com. Mem. Coun. on Fgn. Rels. Office: Offit Hall Capital Mgmt LLC 65 E 55th St New York NY 10022

OFFIT, SIDNEY, writer, educator; b. Balt., Oct. 13, 1928; s. Barney and Lillian (Cohen) O.; m. Avodah Crindell Komito, Aug. 8, 1952; children: Kenneth, Michael Robert. BA, Johns Hopkins U., 1950; DHL (hon.), L.I. U., 1999. Editorial staff Mercury Publs., N.Y.C., 1952-53, Macfadden Publs., N.Y.C., 1953-54; contbg. editor Baseball mag., Washington, 1955-58; faculty NYU, 1964—, adj. prof. creative writing, 1977—; assoc. editor Intellectual Digest, 1970-72, sr. editor, 1972-74. Lectr. creative writing New Sch. Social Research, 1965—; curator George Polk Awards for Journalism, 1977—; mem. nat. bd. Nat. Book Com., 1973-75; commentator Channel 5 TV, N.Y.C., 1975-85, Channel 11 TV, 1992. Author: He Had it Made, 1959, The Other Side of the Street, 1962, Soupbone, 1963, Topsy Turvey, 1965, The Adventure of Homer Fink, 1966, The Boy Who Made a Million, 1968; short stories Not All the Girls Have Million Dollar Smiles, 1971; Only a Girl Like You, 1972, What Kind of Guy Do You Think I Am?, 1977, Memoir of the Bookie's Son, 1995; series sports books for boys, 1961-65, also essays, revs., short stories; book editor: Politics Today, 1978-80. Selection com. Dist. Sch. Bd., N.Y.C., 1968; Mem. exec. bd. Lexington Democratic Club, 1957-60, N.Y. Dem. County Com., 1966— ; chmn. 19th Precinct Community Council of N.Y.C., 1964-80. Recipient Disting. Alumni award Valley Forge Mil. Acad., 1961, Otty Community Svc. award, 1975, Teaching Excellence award NYU, 1981, commendation for achievment as teacher, scholar, communicator N.Y. State Legislature, 1983, proclamation for contbns. to city, N.Y.C. Coun., 1983, Police Athletic League citation for svc. to children of N.Y.C., 1991, 96, 2002, Honors Convocation award Marymount Manhattan Coll., 1994, Detlev W. Bronk award Johns Hopkins Alumni Assn., 1994, Disting. Univ. Tchg. award New Sch. U., 2000. Mem. Tudor and Stuart Club, Authors Guild Found. (pres. 1993—), Authors Guild (coun. 1970-77, 79—, v.p. 1993-95), Authors League (nat. coun. 1976), Authors League Fund (v.p. 1998—), Am. Ctr. PEN (exec. com. 1969-96, v.p. 1970-74, internat. del. 1971-72, 74). Clubs: Century Assn. (N.Y.C.), Coffee House (N.Y.C.). Home: 23 E 69th St New York NY 10021-4919 *I have been guided by a strong devotion to my family and friends and moderate ambition. In both these priorities I have been influenced by my parents. With my writing I have tried to fulfill my own needs, and for the most I have been satisfied by the reception. I do not aspire to fame or great fortune, and this leaves me free to enjoy the sharing of experiences with my friends and family. I consider myself a lucky man and this keeps me grateful to whatever forces there are that contrive man's fortune.*

OFFNER, ERIC DELMONTE, lawyer; b. Vienna, Austria, June 23, 1928; came to U.S., 1941, naturalized, 1949; s. Sigmund J. and Kathe (Delmonte) O.; m. Julie Cousins, 1955 (dec. 1959); m. Barbara Ann Shotton, July 2, 1961; 1 son, Gary Douglas; m. Carol Sue Marcus, Jan. 12, 1980 (dec. 1983) BBA, CCNY, 1949; LLB in Internat. Affairs, Cornell U., 1952. Bar: N.Y. 1952. Assoc. Langner, Parry, Card & Langner, N.Y.C., 1952-57; ptnr. Haseltine, Lake, Waters & Offner, 1957-77; sr. ptnr. Offner & Kuhn, 1978-83; pvt. practice N.Y.C., 1983—. Instr. George Washington U. Law Sch., Cornell U. Law Sch.; spl. prof. law Hofstra Law Sch., 1974-92. Author: International Trademark Protection, 1964, Japanese edit., 1977, International Trademark Service, Vols. I-III 1970, Vol. IV, 1972, Vol. V., 1973, Vol. VI, 1976, Vol. VII, 1981, Vols. I-VII, 2d edit., 1981, Legal Training Course on Trademarks, 1982; editor in chief: Cornell Law Forum, 1950-51; mem. editorial bd.: Trademark Reporter, 1961-64, 69-72; book reviewer Jour. Humanism and Ethical Religion; contbr. articles to profl. jours.; prodr. jazz concerts N.Y.C., 1996—, jazz video and jazz CDs. V.p. Riverdale Mental Health Clinic, N.Y.C., 1966-67; pres. Riverdale Mental Health Assn., 1967-69, Ethical Culture Soc., Riverdale-Yonkers, 1964-67, Ethical Cultural Retirement Ctr., 1975-94; trustee Am. Ethical Union, 1967-73, Internat. Alliance of Holistic Lawyers; bd. dirs. Fit Kids; pres. The Sidney Bechet Soc., Ltd., 1997—. Mem. N.Y. Patent Law Assn. (assoc. editor Bull. 1961-66, gov. 1973-76), ABA, City N.Y. Bar Assn. (sec. 1962-64), U.S. Trademark Assn., World Peace Through Law (charter), Trademark Soc. Washington (charter), Inst. Trade Mark Agts. (London), Sidney Bechet Soc. Ltd. (pres. 1997—), Australian Patent Inst., Internat. Assn. Protection Indsl. Property, Nat. Coun. Patent Law Assn., Internat. Patent, Trademark Assn., Phi Alpha Delta. Home: 20 Joy Dr New Hyde Park NY 11040-1109 E-mail: eoffner@optonline.net. *Do unto others so as to elicit the best in them and thereby the best in yourself.*

OFFNER, ROXANE, retired social worker; b. N.Y.C., Nov. 22, 1930; d. Monroe Marc and Dorothy (Leopold) O.; m. Jules Brody, July 26, 1953 (div. June 1978); children: Jeff, David, Jonathan. BA, Oberlin (Ohio) Coll., 1951; MSSW, Columbia U., 1953. Editor, dept. head United Synagogue of Am., N.Y.C., 1954-63; health educator The Arthritis Found., White Plains, N.Y., 1970-73; cmty. liaison Rusk Inst., NYU Med. Ctr., 1973-78; dep. advocate N.Y. State Office of Advocate for the Disabled, N.Y.C., 1978-92; cons. Lighthouse Internat., 1992-2000, ret., 2000. Author: The InSights Manual, 1995; editor newsletters; author (booklet) ADA Accessiblity, 1994. Profl. adv. com. Nat. Easter Seal Soc., Chgo., 1980's; governing coun. Am. Pub. Health Assn., Washington, 1980's; state accessibility officer Nat. Conf. States/Bldg. Codes and Stds., 1988-92; profl. adv. com. Lighthouse Nat. Ctr. for Vision and Aging, N.Y.C., 1985-92. Mem. NASW, Planned Parenthood, Am. Pub. Health Assn., P-Flag, Phi Beta Kappa. Avocations: gardening, theatre, arts, reading. Home: 21 Fairview Ave Apt 624 Tuckahoe NY 10707-4127 E-mail: harox@att.net.

O'FLAHERTY, JAMES DANIEL, council executive; b. Chgo., Nov. 4, 1942; s. James Carneal O'Flaherty and Lucy Maupin Ribble; m. Cynthia Lane Keyworth, May 21, 1971 (div. July 1983); m. Mayra Gazelle Lacayo, Aug. 9, 1984. BA, Williams Coll., 1965; BA, MA (Rhodes scholar) (hon.) , Oxford (Eng.) U., 1967; MA, Harvard U., 1971. Asst. prof. U. of the South, Sewanee, Tenn., 1971-74; profl. staff Senate Select Com. on Intelligence, Washington, 1974-75; sr. assoc. Carnegie Endowment for Internat. Peace, 1975-83; asst. dir. Group of Thirty, N.Y.C., 1983-86; v.p. Nat. Fgn. Trade Coun., Washington, 1987—; exec. dir. U.S.-South Africa Bus. Coun., 1993—. Bd. advisors Patterson Sch. of Diplomacy U. Ky., Lexington, 1987-95; U.S. adv. com. Robert F. Kennedy Ctr. for Human Rights, Durban, South Africa, 2000—. Contbr. articles to profl. jours. Chmn. Alexandria Dem. Party, 1977—80; mem. Va. Dem. Ctrl. Com., 1977—80. Named Rhodes scholar, Oxford U., 1967. Mem. Coun. on Fgn. Rels. Avocations: classical history, chess. Home: 804 Janneys Ln Alexandria VA 22302 Office: Nat Fgn Trade Coun 1625 K St NW #200 Washington DC 20006 E-mail: doflaherty@nftc.org.

OFNER, WILLIAM BERNARD, investor; b. L.A., Aug. 24, 1929; s. Harry D. and Gertrude (Skoss) Offner; m. Florence Ila Maxwell, Apr. 13, 1953 (div. 1956). AA, L.A. City Coll., 1949; BA, Calif. State U., L.A., 1953; LLB, Loyola U., L.A., 1965; postgrad., Sorbonne, 1951; cert. de Langue Francaise, 1987; postgrad., U. So. Calif., 1966, Glendale Community Coll., 1986-92. Bar: Calif. 1966, U.S. Dist. Ct. Calif. 1966, U.S. Supreme Ct. 1972. Assoc. Thomas Moore and Assocs., L.A., 1967-69; pvt. practice, 1969-70, 74—; assoc. Peter Lam, 1981-94, mng. atty., 1993—. Assoc. C.M. Coronel, 1986-87, Jack D. Janofsky, 1987-89, Mario P. Gonzalez, 1990-92, Genaro Legorreta, Jr., 1997-98; lectr. Van Norman U., 1975; property mgr., 1982—; investor 1984—. With USNR, 1947-54. Mem. Toastmasters, Safari Athletic Club, The Claremont Club. Democrat. Avocations: photography, linguistics, tutoring, travel, watercolor. Office: PO Box 163 Chino Hills CA 91709

OFODILE, FERDINAND, plastic surgeon; b. Nnobi, Anambara, Nigeria, Oct. 20, 1941; came to U.S., 1962; s. Julius and Regina (Eruchalu) O.; m. Caroline N. Ofodile, July 15, 1969; children: Uchenna, Ikechukwu, Nnaemeka, Nnamdi. BS, Northwestern U., Evanston, Ill., 1964; MD, Northwestern U., Chgo., 1968. Diplomate Am. Bd. Surgery, Am. Bd. Plastic Surgery. Rotating intern Columbia U./Harlem Hosp. Program, N.Y.C., 1968-69, resident in gen. surgery, 1971-73, resident in plastic surgery, 1973-75; resident in gen. surgery Columbia Presbyn. Hosp., 1969-71; fellow in plastic surgery Mayo Clinic, Rochester, Minn., 1975-76; sr. lectr., cons. in plastic surgery dept. surgery Univ. Coll. Hosp./U. Ibadan, Nigeria, 1977-82; assoc. attending in plastic surgery St. Lukes/Roosevelt Hosps., N.Y.C., 1985—; chmn. plastic surgery residency program Harlem Hosp. Ctr., 1982—, chief plastic surgery svc., 1982—; clin. prof. surgery Columbia U., 1997—. Vis. prof. U. Sokoto, 1993; mem. internat. symposium com. Plastic Ednl. Found., 1989-98; lectr. in field. Contbr. numerous articles to profl. jours. Fellow ACS, West African Coll. Surgeons, Am. Assn. Plastic Surgeons; mem. Am. Soc. Plastic and Reconstructive Surgeons, Assn. Acad. Chmn. Plastic Surgery, Mayo Alumni Soc., N.Y. Regional Soc. Plastic and Reconstructive Surgery (sec. 1996-97), Webster Soc., N.Y. State Med. Soc., N.Y. County Med. Soc., Manhattan Med. Soc. Achievements include design of ofodile nasal implant for rhinoplasty in blacks and Hispanics; determination of serum levels of vitamins E, C and essential elements in ulcer patients; role of thombin in hemostasis in burns; anthropometric measurements of the Black face; elucidation of the anatomy, morphology and surgery of the Black nose; cosmetic and reconstructive surgery of the breast in Blacks. Office: 2590 Frisby Ave Bronx NY 10461

OFOSU, JOSEPH ROCHESTER, pharmacist, educator; b. Aburi, Ghana, Jan. 9, 1955; s. Stephen B.Q. and Kate Oye (Ntow) O.; m. Christiana Ansah Adu, Dec. 26, 1981; children: Nana Oye, Afua Quaye, Kwadwo Ohene Ansah. BS in Pharmacy magna cum laude, Howard U., 1987, D of Pharmacy (valedictorian), 1988. Registered pharmacist, D.C. Tchg. asst. Coll. Pharmacy Howard U., Washington, 1986-88, asst. prof., 1989-95, assoc. prof. dept. pharmacy practice, 1996—, asst. dean Sch. Pharmacy, 1999—. Presenter in field. Contbr. articles, abstracts to profl. publs. Vol. Bread for the City, Washington, D.C. Gen. Hosp., Project-Earth Watch, YMCA Health Fair, Washington, Sr. Citizens Home, Washington; appeared in WTOP Radio Call for Action, Washington. Recipient Prof. Zalucky Achievement award, 1987, Pennhurst Award, 1988, Cert. of Achievement Lemmon Co., 1988, Sandoz Inc. Pharm. award, 1988. Mem. Am. Assn. Colls. Pharmacy, Am. Coll. Clin. Pharmacy, Am. Soc. Health-Sys. Pharmacists (ednl. programming assoc., reviewer, mem. focus group), Am. Heart Assn., Washington Met. Soc. Hosp. Pharmacists, Sigma Xi, Kappa Psi (Scholarship honor award), Rho Chi. Avocations: photography, travel and sightseeing, family, reading. Office: Howard U Coll Pharmacy 2300 4th St NW Washington DC 20059-1220

OFSTAD, EVELYN LARSEN BOYL, retired primary school educator, radio announcer, video producer; b. Laurel, Oreg., Sept. 11, 1918; d. Walter Winfred and Nellie Lyle (Gellatly) Larsen; m. Robert Morris Boyl (dec.); children: Kathleen Roberta, Robert Morris Jr., Shannon Gae, Brian Larsen; m. Olaf Ofstad, Nov. 15, 1988. BS, Oreg. State U., 1940; MS in Tchg., Portland State U., 1968. Cert. learning specialist. Radio announcer Sta. KOAC, Corvallis, Oreg., 1939-40; announcer, script writer Sta. KWIL, Albany, Oreg., 1940-42, operator, announcer, 1941-42; sec. Higgins Ship Bldg., New Orleans, 1943-44; elem. tchr. Portland Pub. Schs., 1968-71; learning specialist North Clackamas Schs., Milw., 1972-85, home instr. Milwaukie, Oreg., 1985-86. Prodr., actor video travelogues on Portland Cable Access, 1987—; mem. Oreg. Sr. Theater, 1987-95; actor plays and mus. prodns. Plaza Players, 1999—. Co-leader Girl Scouts Am., Oak Grove, Oreg., 1954-55, Webelos Boy Scouts Am., 1956-57, 70-71; videographer Ptnrs. of Ams., Oreg. and Costa Rica, 1990-91; head video prodn. Channel 29 In-House TV of Retirement, Holladay Park Plz.; prodr. biweekly travel show, weekly activities show. Mem. AAUW (pres. Albany chpt.). Avocations: painting, video production, bell playing, travel, swimming.

OFSTEDAL, PAUL ESTREM, retired clergy member; b. Fergus Falls, Minn., May 18, 1932; s. Rudolph Anders and Edith Evangeline (Estrem) O.; m. Dorothea Ann Jerdee, June 22, 1957; children: Anne, Daniel, Joseph, Ruth. BA, Luther Coll., 1954; MDiv, Luther Seminary, 1958. Pastor Our Savior's Luth. Ch., Park Falls, Wis., 1958-64, St. Paul's Luth. Ch., Lakota, Iowa, 1964-70, Riverside Luth. Ch., Sioux City, 1970-75; asst. Iowa dist. Am. Luth. Ch., Storm Lake, 1975-81; sr. pastor First Luth. Ch., Williston, N.D., 1982-92, St. Anthony Park Luth. Ch., St. Paul, 1992-2000. Instr. Waldorf Coll., 1969-70; bd. dirs. North Iowa Mental Health, Mason City, 1968-70; chmn. bd. dirs. Okoboji Bible Camp, Milford, Iowa, 1973-75; exec. com. mem. Western N.D. Synod, Evangel. Luth. Ch. Am., Bismarck, N.D., 1990-92; regent, vice-chmn. Concordia Coll., Moorhead, Minn., 1984-97, Presidential Search Commn., Concordia Coll., 1998-99; bd. pres., China Svc. Ventures, 2001-. Author: Called To Give, 1982; editor: Daily Readings from Spiritual Classics, 1990, repub. as These Words Upon Your Heart, 2002; contbr. author: Grab The Blessing, 1993; contbr. articles to profl. jours. Chmn. Heart, Lakota, Iowa, 1968, 69; precinct rep. Rep. Convention, Iowa, 1968; mem. traffic safety coun. City of Williston, N.D., 1990-92. Chaplain USAR, 1956-65. Lutheran. Avocations: photography, wood working, biking, sailing, walking.

OFTE, DONALD, retired environmental executive, consultant; b. N.Y.C., Aug. 23, 1929; s. Sverre and Ingeborg Ofte; m. Margaret Mae McHenney, July 23, 1955; children: Marc Christian, Nancy Carolyn Appleby, Kirk Donald Jr. BA in Chemistry, Dana Coll., 1952; postgrad. study metall. engring., Ohio State U., 1958-60. Jr. chemist Inst. Atomic Research, Ames, Iowa, 1952-53; sr. research chemist Monsanto Research Corp., Miamisburg, Ohio, 1958-66; ops. engr. AEC, 1966-69, br. chief, div. dir. ops. office Albuquerque, 1969-73, mgr. Pinellas area office Largo, Fla., 1973-79; mgr. Rocky Flats area office Dept. Energy, Golden, Colo., 1979-82, asst. mgr. devel. and prodn. Albuquerque, 1982-83, dep. mgr. ops. office, 1983-84; prin. dep. asst. sec. Dept. Energy Defense Programs, Washington, 1984-87; mgr. ops. office Dept. Energy, Idaho Falls, Idaho, 1987-89; mgmt. cons., 1989-92; v.p. govt. ops. United Engrs. & Constructors (Raytheon Engrs. & Constrn.), Denver, 1992-93; v.p. Adv. Scis., Inc., Albuquerque, 1993-94; pres. FERMCO (also known as Fluor Daniel, Fernald), Cin., 1994-96; ret., 1996. V.p. Fluor-Daniel, Inc., 1994-96; affiliate prof. Idaho State U., 1990-92; bd. dirs. Denver Fed. Exec. Bd., 1979-82. Author: (with others) Plutonium 1960, 1965, Physicochemical Methods in Metals Research; contbr. articles to profl. jours. on metallurgy and ceramics. Campaign chmn. United Way Pinellas, St. Petersburg, Fla., 1978; bd. dirs. Bonneville County United Way, Idaho Rsch. Found.; mem. adv. bd. Teton Peaks Council Boy Scouts of Am., 1987-92, Eastern Idaho Tech. Coll.; chmn. Excellence in Edn. Fund Com., 1990-92; vice chmn., bd. dirs. Rio Grande Ch. ARC, Albuquerque, 1982-84; trustee, bd. dirs. Nat. Atomic Mus., 1999—. Served to lt. (j.g.) USN, 1953-57. Recipient citation AEC for Apollo 12 SNAP 27 Radioisotope Generator, 1969, High Quality Performance award AEC, 1968, Group Achievement award NASA, 1972; Meritorious Svc. award Dept. Energy, 1985, Disting. Career Svc. award, 1989. Mem. Am. Chem. Soc., Am. Nuclear Soc., Am. Soc. Metals, Nat. Contract Mgmt. Assn., Am. Soc. Pub. Adminstrs., Suncoast Archeol. Soc., Idaho Falls C. of C. (bd. dirs., cmty. svc. award 1990), Rotary Internat. (Paul Harris fellow). Avocations: reading, bridge, gardening, golf. Home: 1129 Salamanca St NW Albuquerque NM 87107-5643 E-mail: dofte@aol.com.

OFVERSTEDT, MARGARET ELISE, music educator, library and information scientist; b. Blue Earth, Minn., Feb. 15, 1933; d. George Adam and Olivia Elizabeth (Bartel) Hartwick; m. Elviv Harry Ofverstedt, Feb. 15, 1954; children: Rose Marie Ofverstedt Vohland, Karen Cowdry, Laurie Jaafar. Grad., U. Mo., Kansas City, 1976. Cert. music, libr. sci., math., English, elem. tchr. Mo. 7th gr. sci. tchr. St. Ann's Parochial, Prairie Village, Kans.; 3d and 4th gr. tchr. Pleasant Green Cmty. Sch., Kansas City; sci. tchr. Oxford Park Acad.; tchr. Our Lady of the A, Kansas City; libr. Pleasant Green Cmty. Sch.; sub. tchr. Shawnee Mission and Olathe Pub. Schs., 1988—2001. Mem. Mendelsohn Choir, Kansas City, 1967—71, U. Mo. Kansas City Civic Choir, 1972—2000, Kansas City Mus. Club, 1972—2002; mem. staff Queen's Herald, 1990—2002. Home: 9312 Sturgeon Dr Overland Park KS 66212

OGAN, RUSSELL GRIFFITH, business executive, retired air force officer; b. Reading, Pa., Nov. 20, 1923; s. Russell John and Edna Gwendlyn (Griffith) O.; m. Gloria Mae Withers, Oct. 30, 1943; children: Susan Ann (Mrs. Greg Gunn), Russell Lee. Student, Wyomissing Polytech. Inst., 1942, Air Command Staff Coll., 1948, Nat. War Coll., 1963. Enlisted as pvt. U.S. Army, 1942; advanced through grades to brig. gen. USAF, 1970; fighter squadron comdr. Dover AFB, Del., 1951; dir. combat operations (11th Air Div.), Ladd AFB, Alaska, 1951-53; dir. (Combat Operations Center), Hamilton AFB, Calif., 1953-56; with (Hdqrs. Air Def. Command), Ent AFB, Colo., 1956-60; dir. (Aerospace Def. Systems Office, Air Force Ballistic Missile Div.), 1960-62; from dep. dir. plans to comdr. Sector Operation Ctr. NATO, Germany, 1963-66; dep. dir. personnel data and records (USAF Mil. Personnel Center), Randolph AFB, Tex., 1966-68; comdr. 71st Missile Warning Wing, then vice comdr. (14th Aerospace Force), Ent AFB, Colo., 1968-71; dep. dir. personnel programs Hdqrs. USAF, Washington, 1971-72; dir. Prisoner of War and Missing in Action Affairs, Office Sec. Def., 1972-74; former pres. Vacation Interval Mktg.; real estate broker Fishermen's Village, Punta Gorda, Fla. Decorated D.S.M., Legion of Merit with bronze oak leaf cluster, Air medal with 1 silver and 1 bronze oak leaf cluster. Mem. Daedalians, T.R.O.A., Kingsway Country Club. Flew 62 missions as fighter pilot over France and Germany, 1944-45. Home: 12413 SW Kingsway Cir Lake Suzy FL 34269

O'GARA, BARBARA ANN, soap company executive; b. Newark, Aug. 8, 1953; d. Frank Percy and Rose Stevens. AA, Keystone Jr. Coll., 1973; BS, U. Ariz., 1976. Media buyer Wells, Rich, Green/Townsend, Irvine, Calif., 1977-80; dist. sales mgr. Dial Corp., Phoenix, 1980-82; regional sales mgr. Guest Supply, Inc., North Brunswick, N.J., 1982-85; dir. hotel mktg. and sales Neutrogena Corp., L.A., 1985-92, v.p. hotel mktg. and sales, 1992-96; cons. Bath and Body Works; owner O'Gara & Assocs., Ltd., 1996—. Recipient Outstanding Sales Accomplishment award, Armour-Dial, 1981; scholar Keystone Jr. Coll., 1972, Morris County scholar, 1971. Mem.: Network Exec. Women in Hospitality, Am. Hotel and Motel Assn., Am. Mgmt. Assn., Am. Mktg. Assn. Republican. Roman Catholic. Avocation: tennis, reading, yoga, skiing, photography. Home and Office: 1532 Linden Blvd Vineland NJ 08361-6719 E-mail: bogara@earthlink.net.

OGATA, KATSUHIKO, engineering educator; b. Tokyo, Jan. 6, 1925; came to U.S., 1952; s. Fukuhei and Teruko (Yasaki) O.; m. Asako Nakamura, Sept. 6, 1961; 1 son, Takahiko. BS, U. Tokyo, 1947; MS, U. Ill., 1953; PhD, U. Calif., Berkeley, 1956. Research asst. Sci. Research Inst., Tokyo, 1948-51; fuel engr. Nippon Steel Tube Co., 1951-52; mem. faculty U. Minn., 1956—, prof.

mech. engring., 1961—; prof. elec. engring. Yokohama Nat. U., 1960-61, 64-65, 68-69. Author: State Space Analysis of Control Systems, 1967, Modern Control Engineering, 1970, 4th edit., 2001, Dynamic Programming, 1973, Ingenieria de Control Moderna, 1974, Metody Przestrzeni Stanow w Teorii Sterowania, 1974, System Dynamics, 1978; : 3d edit., 1998, Engenharia de Controle Moderno, 1982, 2d edit., 1993, Teknik Kontrol Automatik, 1985, Discrete-Time Control Systems, 1986, 2d edit., 1995, Gendai Seigyo Riron, 1986, Dinamica de Sistemas, 1987, Solving Control Engineering Problems with MATLAB, 1994, Gendai Seigyo Kogaku, 1994, Designing Linear Control Systems with MATLAB, 1994, Kejuruteraan Kawalan Moden, 1996, Sistemas de Control en Tiempo Discreto, 1996, Projeto de Sistemas Lineares de Controle com MATLAB, 1996, Solucao de Problemas de Engenharia de Controle com MATLAB, 1997. Recipient Outstanding Adv. award Inst. of Tech., U. Minn., 1981, John R. Ragazzini Edn. award Am. Automatic Control Coun., 1999. Fellow ASME; mem. Sigma Xi, Pi Tau Sigma. Office: U Minn Dept Mech Engring Minneapolis MN 55455

OGAWA, DENNIS MASAAKI, American studies educator; b. Manzanar, Calif., Sept. 7, 1943; s. Frank M. and Alice T. (Tanaka) O.; m. Amy Ranko, Jan. 1, 1973; children: Quin, Owen, Autumn. BA, UCLA, 1966, MA, 1967, PhD, 1969. Prof. Am. studies U. Hawaii at Manoa, Honolulu, 1969—. Dir. Nippon Golden Network, Honolulu, 1982—. Author: Jan Ken Po, 1973, Kodomo No Tame Ni, 1978; co-author: Ellison Onizuka: Remembrance, 1986. Dir. Japanese Cultural Ctr., Hawaii, 1992-98, Olelo: Corp. Cmty. Television, 1994-98, Hawaii Internat. Film Festival, 1994-97. Danforth Found. assoc., 1975; named Disting. Historian Hawaiian Hist. Soc., 1992; sr. fellow Japan Soc. Promotion of Sci., 1978, East West Ctr., Honolulu, 1979. Democrat. Office: Univ Hawaii Am Studies Dept 1890 E West Rd Honolulu HI 96822-2318

OGAWA, SEIJI, research scientist, biophysicist; b. Tokyo, Jan. 19, 1934; came to U.S., 1962; s. Shimpei and Mitsu O.; m. Kazuko, Mar. 10, 1962; 1 child, Miwako. BS, U. Tokyo, 1957; PhD, Stanford U., 1967. Rsch. assoc. Mellon Inst., Pitts., 1962-64; postdoctoral Stanford U., Calif., 1967-68; disting. mem. tech. staff Bell Labs., Murray Hill, N.J., 1968—. Elected mem. Inst. of Medicine, 2000. Fellow Internat. Soc. Magnetic Resonance (Gold medal 1995); mem. Biophysical Soc., Am. Physical Soc. (Biol. Physics prize 1996), Neurosci. Office: Lucent Tech Bell Labs 600 Mountain Ave Rm 3l-407 New Providence NJ 07974-2008*

OGBAA, KALU, English literature educator; b. Umuchiakuma, Abia, Nigeria, Aug. 21, 1945; came to U.S., 1977; s. Stephen and Ogonna (Uche) O.; m. Clara Nwankwo, Apr. 5, 1975 (div. Mar. 1994); children: Ikenna, Ndubuisi, Emeka, Nneka, Enyinna, Kelechi; m. Glory Eke Uche, Dec. 27, 1996; children: Uchenna, Adanne, Ekeoma. BA in English with honors, U. Nigeria, Nsukka, 1973; MA in Black Studies, Ohio State U., 1977; PhD in English, U. Tex., 1981. Asst. lectr. Alvan Ikoku Coll. Edn., Owerri, Nigeria, 1974-76; teaching assoc. Ohio State U., Columbus, 1977; asst. instr. U. Tex., Austin, 1978-81, lectr. English, 1981; asst. prof. Imo State U., Okigwe, Nigeria, 1982-85, assoc. prof., 1985-89, Oral Roberts U., Tulsa, Okla., 1989-90, Clark Atlanta U., 1990-92, So. Conn. State U., New Haven, 1992-95, prof. English, 1995—. Acting dir. gen. studies program Imo State U., Okigwe, 1987-89. Author: Gods, Oracles and Divination: Folkways in Chinua Achebe's Novels, 1992, Igbo, 1995, Understanding Things Fall Apart, 1999, Century of Nigerian Literature: A Selct Bibliography, 2002; editor: The Gong and the Flute: African Literary Development and Celebration, 1994. Fed. Nigeria scholar Fed. Ministry Edn., 1971-73, 80-81Postgrad. scholar Imo State Ministry Edn., 1980, So. Conn. State U. faculty scholar, 1999. Mem. MLA, CLA, African Lit. Assn., African Studies Assn., Commonwealth Lit. Assn., Imo State U. Faculty Asembly (sec. 1982-89), Phi Kappa Phi. Presbyterian. Avocations: choirmaster, laypreacher. Office: So Conn State U Dept English New Haven CT 06515 Fax: 203-392-6731.

OGBAR, JEFFREY OGBONNA GREEN, history educator; b. June 10, 1969; BA, Morehouse Coll., 1991; MA, Ind. U., 1993, PhD, 1997. Jeffrey Campbell fellow St. Lawrence U., Canton, N.Y., 1996-97; asst. prof. U. Conn., Storrs, 1997—. Rsch. fellow W.E.B. DuBois Ctr. for Afro-Am. Rsch., Harvard U., 1999-2000; fellow Schomburg Ctr. for Rsch. in Black Culture, Scholars-in-Residence Program, N.Y. Pub. Libr., N.Y.C., 2001-2002.

OGBOGU, CECILIA IFY, lawyer; b. Enugu, Nigeria, Sept. 19, 1964; d. Samuel and Cecilia Ogbogu; children: Jason, Osita. BL with honors, Nigerian Law Sch., Lagos, Nigeria, 1986; LLB with honors, Imo State U., Aba, Nigeria, 1985. Bar: Calif. 1996, U.S. Dist. Ct. (ctrl. dist.) Calif. 1996, Nigerian Bar 1986. Staff counsel Cooperative and Commerce, Bank of Nigeria Plc, Enugu, Nigeria, 1988-93; vol. atty. Legal Aid Found. of L.A., 1996, Bet Tzedek Legal Svcs., L.A., 1996; pvt. practice, 1996—. Fellow The Alliance for Children's Rights, L.A., 1998—. Recipient Wiley Manuel award State Bar of Calif., 1997, Merit award Nat. Ctr. for Missing and Exploited Children, 1997. Mem. ABA (Child Advocacy Nat. Cert. Recognition young lawyers divsn. 2000), ATLA, L.A. County Bar Assn. (barristers' com. 1996—). Democrat. Roman Catholic. Avocations: writing, reading, stamp collecting. Office: 315 W 9th St Ste 603 Los Angeles CA 90015-4207 E-mail: ceeogbogu@lawyer.com.

OGBONNAYA, CHUKS ALFRED, entomologist, agronomist, environmentalist; b. Akoli-Imenyi, Abia, Nigeria, June 30, 1953; came to U.S., 1975; s. Alfred Agbaeze and Christy (Agubuche) Ogbonnaya; m. Joyce Elizabeth Belgrave, Mar. 30, 1985; children: Latoya, Oluchi, Kelechi, Chioma. BS, U. Nebr., 1979, PhD, 1985; MS, N.W. Mo. State U., 1981. Cert. profl. crop scientist, profl. agronomist. Lab. asst. U. Nebr., Lincoln, 1976-78, rsch. asst., 1978-80, 82-85, postdoctoral fellow, 1985; asst. prof., postdoctoral fellow Mountain Empire Coll., Big Stone Gap, Va., 1985-90, prof., 1990—, coord., prof. environ. sci. dept., 1986—; prof., 1995. Disting. scholar-in-residence Pa. State U., summer 1990, vis. prof., 1990. Soccer coach Parks and Recreation, Big Stone Gap, 1989; mem. Va. Water Resources Statewide Adv. Bd., govt.-mined land reclamation adv. bd. Recipient Times Teaching award, 1990, Chancellor's Profs. award Va., 1990; Fulbright scholar, 1993-94. Mem. Am. Soc. Agronomy, Crop Sci. Soc. Am., Entomol. Soc., Va. Acad. Sci., Va. Mining Assn. (Outstanding Contbn. to Comty. award 1993), Internat. Platform Assn., Phi Beta Kappa. Methodist. Avocations: tennis, soccer. Home: 520 Bays View Rd Kingsport TN 37660-3202 Office: Mountain Empire Coll PO Box 700 Big Stone Gap VA 24219-0700

OGBUREKE, KALU UGWA EMMANUEL, oral surgeon, oral and maxillofacial pathologist, molecular biologist; b. Dorowa-Babuje, Nigeria, May 30, 1955; came to U.S., 1993; s. Kalu Ugwa and Ihudiya Grace O.; m. Ezinne Ihuoma Enyioma, Aug. 25, 1991; children: Chinasa, Kalu, Erinma. B of Dental Surgery, U. Ibadan, Nigeria, 1986; MSc in Med. Scis., U. Glasgow, Scotland, 1993; DMSc, Harvard Sch. Dental Medicine, 2001; JD, Suffolk U., 2002. Lic. Med. Dental Coun. Nigeria. Accounts clk. Nigerian TV Authority, Aba, 1978-79; house surgeon Ahmadu-Bello U. Tchg. Hosp., Kaduna, Nigeria, 1986-87; vis. registrar oral and maxillofacial surgery Ahmadu-Bello U. Tch. Hosp., 1991; dental surgeon Hebgreen Dental Clinic, Portharcourt, Nigeria, 1987-88, Nigerian Mil. Hosp., Portharcourt, 1988—89; resident oral and maxillofacial surgery, instr. U. Nigeria Tchg. Hosp., Enugu, 1989-91. Contbr. articles to profl. jours. Sec. African and Carribean Christian Fellowship, Glasgow, Great Britain, Ireland, 1992, pres., 1992-93. Recipient Nat. Rsch. Sci. award NIH, 1996-99; Gani Fawehinmi Undergrad. scholar, 1984, Wanda scholar Harvard Com. Gen. Scholarship, 1999; Primary fellow West African Coll. Surgeons, 1990, Postgrad. Tng. fellow U. Nigeria, 1991-93, Rsch. fellow Harvard Sch. Dental Medicine, 1996—, Postdoc. fellow Forsyth Inst., 1998—; grantee NIH, 1999—. Mem. AAAS, Internat. Assn. Oral Maxillofacial Pathologist, Am. Acad. Oral Maxillofacial Pathology. Avocations: sports, traveling. Home: 4 Trowbridge Place 6B Cambridge MA 02138 Office: Harvard Sch Dental Medicine 188 Longwood Ave Boston MA 02115 Fax: (617)262-4021. E-mail: kogbureke@forsyth.org.

OGBURN, HUGH BELL, chemical engineer, consultant; b. Lexington, Va., July 13, 1923; s. Sihon Cicero Jr. and Bettie Mae (Bell) O.; m. Anne Wotherspoon, Mar. 2, 1946 (div.); children: Margaret Mathews Berenson, Scott A.; m. Nancy Wrenn Petersen, Sept. 5, 1974. BS, Princeton U., 1944, MS, 1947, PhD, 1954. Sect. dir. research and devel. dept. Atlantic Refining Co., Phila., 1950-61; mgr. process engring. M.W. Kellogg Co., N.Y.C., London, 1961-67; dir. research and engring. Union Carbide Corp., N.Y.C., 1967-69; dir. new bus. devel. Weyerhaeuser Co., Tacoma, 1969-72; pres. H.B. Ogburn Assoc., Greenwich, Conn. and Honolulu, 1971—; v.p., dir. Incontrade Inc., Stamford, Conn., 1973-78; v.p. Pacific Resources Inc., Honolulu, 1978-83; chmn. Pacific Oasis, Los Angeles, 1983-85. Dir. Danmore Corp., Planning Research Corp.; cons. AEC; prof. chem. engring. Drexel U., Phila., 1951-61 Contbr. articles to profl. jours.; patentee in field. Pres. bd. trustees Woman's Hosp., Phila., 1954-62, Kapiolani Women's and Children's Med. Ctr., 1980-90; mem. adv. bd. Princeton U., 1960-70. Served to lt. j.g. USNR, 1942-46, PTO. Mem. AIChE, Am. Chem. Soc., Research Engrs. Soc., Pacific (Honolulu) Club, Greenwich Field (Conn.) Club, Princeton (N.Y.C.) Club, Phi Beta Kappa, Sigma Xi, Tau Beta Pi. Republican. Presbyterian. Home and Office: 4340 Pahoa Ave Apt 16 A Honolulu HI 96816-5032

OGBURN, NANCY WRENN, civic volunteer; b. Honolulu, Sept. 16, 1926; d. Heaton Luse and Carolene (Cooke) Wrenn; m. Hugh Gerhard Peterson Jr., July 1, 1948 (div. 1972); children: Hugh G. Peterson III, Suzanne Elise Peterson, Monte Cooke Peterson, Alexander Wrenn Peterson; m. Hugh Bell Ogburn, Sept. 5, 1974. BA, Wellesley Coll., 1948. With outside sales dept. Harris Travel, Greenwich, Conn., 1974-78. Guide Hawaiian Mission Children's Soc., Honolulu, 1978-81, Lyon Arboretum; treas. Rep. precinct, Honolulu, 1993. Recipient Carey E. Quinn award Am. Daffodil Soc., 1964, Roberta C. Watrous award, Medal of Merit Garden Club Am., 1966, Corning medal, 1991. Fellow Honolulu Acad. Arts; mem. Greenwich Garden Club (non-resident, Horticultural Com. award (2)), Garden Club Honolulu (chmn. various coms., Horticultural Com. award). Republican. Episcopalian. Avocations: bridge, traveling, grandchildren, hiking. Home: 4340 Pahoa Ave Apt 16A Honolulu HI 96816-5032

OGDEN, ALFRED, lawyer; b. Bklyn., Oct. 14, 1909; s. Alfred Trecartin and Sophronia (Wisner) O.; m. Mary Fell Jordan, June 25, 1938; 1 child, Alfred Trecartin II. Grad., Phillips Acad., 1928; BA, Yale, 1932; LL.B., Harvard, 1935. Bar: N.Y. 1936. Since practiced, N.Y.C.; partner Alexander & Green, 1955-75; of counsel firm Morgan, Lewis & Bockius, 1979-80, c/o Reboul, MacMurray, Hewitt, Maynard & Kristol, 1980—. Pres., dir. C. Tennant, Sons & Co., N.Y.C., 1952-54 Trustee Fay Sch., Southborough, Mass., 1950-70, Population Reference Bur., 1963-68, Daniel and Florence Guggenheim Found., 1972— , Lavenberg Found., 1986—; trustee Mystic Seaport Mus., Mystic, Conn., 1959— , chmn., 1982-83, chmn. emeritus, 1983— ; bd. mgrs., bd. overseers Meml. Sloan Kettering Cancer Ctr., 1959-97; trustee, exec. com. Robert Coll., Istanbul, Turkey, 1952-73, chmn., 1955-63; bd. dirs., v.p. English Speaking Union U.S., 1950-92, acting pres., 1983-84; bd. dirs., mem. exec. com. Winston Churchill Meml. Fund., 1966— ; trustee Planned Parenthood N.Y.C., 1977-83; bd. dirs. Children's Mus. Manhattan, 1985-87, Nat. Trust Historic Presentation, 1998—. Served to lt. col. Gen. Staff Corps AUS, 1942-46. Decorated Legion of Merit. Mem. ABA, Internat. Law Assn., Soc. Colonial Wars, Pilgrims of U.S., Coun. on Fgn. Rels., Century Assn., Yale Club (N.Y.C.), Wadawanuck Club (Stonington, Conn.), Cosmopolitan Club, Thursday Evening Club. Home: 150 E 73rd St New York NY 10021-4362 also: PO Box 214 Stonington CT 06378-0214 Office: 45 Rockefeller Plz Fl 10 New York NY 10111-1099 *There is nothing permanent except change.*

OGDEN, ANITA BUSHEY, nursing educator; b. Malone, N.Y., May 23, 1938; d. John Richard and Eleanor Miriam (Wright) Bushey; m. William Alan Ogden, Dec. 27, 1972. Nursing diploma, N.Y. Med. Coll., 1959; BSN, Columbia U., 1962; MS in Adult Health, SUNY, Buffalo, 1968; PhD, Cornell U., 1984. Faculty Flower-Fifth Ave. Sch. Nursing, N.Y.C., 1959-62, Meth. Hosp., Bklyn. Sch. Nursing, N.Y.C., 1962-66, Hartwick Coll., Oneonta, N.Y., 1968-73; faculty, chair divsn. nursing edn. Corning (N.Y.) C.C., 1973-89; faculty Alfed U., Alfed Station, N.Y., 1984-88; prof., dir. nurse edn. Elmira (N.Y.) Coll., 1989—; clin. staff nurse various orgns., 1959—. Cons. curriculum devel., 1978—. Mem. adv. coun. Alfed U., Alfed Station, 1984-87; mem. bd. dirs. Cmty. Health Svcs. for Elderly, Elmira, 1992—; nursing cons. St. Kitts/Nevis U.S. Aid Ptnrs. Ams., 1986-87. Mem. ANA (various offices), N.Y. State and Dist. Nurses Assn. (various offices), Internat. Resources Instructional Svcs. (faculty 1990—), Nat. League for Nursing (regional bd. dirs. 1973—, ednl. cons. 1982—), LWV (regional coord.), Order Ea. Star (various offices), Delta Kappa Gamma (scholarship award 1981, 83), Delta Kappa Gamma (pres., bd. dirs. 1970), Sigma Theta Tau. Republican. Avocations: bicycling, hand crafts, cats. Home: 104 Fairview Ave Painted Post NY 14870-1215

OGDEN, ANN, writer; b. Kansas City, Mo. d. Audley W. and Leona R. (Locke) Porter; m. Alvin C. Ogden, Apr. 20, 1954; 1 child, Karen. BS in Tech. Journalism, Kans. State U., 1954; MA in Sec. Edn., U. Mo., Kansas City, 1968. Society editor Lyons (Kans.) Daily News, 1954-56; asst. editor Rose Pubs., Shawnee Mission, Kans., 1962-63; instr. developmental reading U. Mo., Kansas City, 1964-67; journalism tchr. Bishop Miege High Sch., Shawnee Mission, 1966-67; asst. editor Kans. Alumni, Lawrence, 1967-68, Vol. Leader and Trustee of Am. Hosp. Assn., Chgo., 1969-72; asst. editor, directory editor Barks Pubs., 1975-81; adj. instr. bus. English Triton Coll., River Grove, Ill., 1981-84; freelance writer, editor, 1973-94. Bd. dirs. Overland Park (Kans.) Heritage Found., 1991—; bd. dirs. Strang hist. display com., 1991—, sec. 1998-99, pres. 2000-; trustee Shawnee Mission Indian Hist. Soc., Inc. Johnson County, 1993—, 1st v.p., 1996-97, pres. 1998-99; mem. exec. bd. Hospitalized Vets. Writing Project, 1979-80, 89—, v.p., 1996-99, pres., 1999—. U. Mo. Kansas City fellow, 1964-65, 65-66. Mem. Alpha Chi Omega (editor Lyre chpt. 1989-91, historian 1991-93, chaplain 1993-95).

OGDEN, BRUCE E. physician, pediatrician; b. Oakland, Calif., Aug. 16, 1948; s. J. Edward Ogden and Betty Rulene (Greenwell) Woster; m. Lynda Dell Simons, Sept. 4, 1970; children: Melanie Lyn Odgen Sorensen, Maren Elizabeth, Lauren Brooke Ogden Wilkins. BS, Brigham Young U., 1972; postgrad., U. Utah, 1973, MD, 1978. Diplomate pediat. and neonatal/perinatal medicine Am. Bd. Pediat. Intern, resident in pediatrics U. Utah Coll. Medicine, Salt Lake City, 1978-80; neonatal-perinatal fellow U. N.Mex. Sch. Medicine, Albuquerque, 1980-82; mem. hosp. staffs in, 1980—82, L.A., 1982—83, Colorado Springs, Colo., 1983—84, Tulsa, 1985—88, Sioux Falls, 1988—90; med. dir. dept. neonatology McKennan Hosp., SD, 1988—90, Women's Hosp., Las Vegas, 1990-94; mem. staff Univ. Med. Ctr., 1992—; staff pediatrician, neonatologist Lake Mead Hosp. Med. Ctr., North Las Vegas, Nev., 1995—; staff pediatrician Valley Hosp. Med. Ctr., Las Vegas, 1995—. Mem. pediat. staff U. Med. Ctr., 1992—, Lake Mead Hosp. Med. Ctr., 1995—, Valley Hosp. Med. Ctr., 1995—, Mountain View Hosp. Med. Ctr., 1997—, Summerlin Hosp. Med. Ctr., 1997—, Desert Springs Hosp., Las Vegas, 2000—. Contbr. Mem.: AMA, Clark County Med. Soc., Nev. State Med. Assn., Am. Thoracic Soc., Nat. Perinatal Assn., Am. Acad. Pediat. Office: Family Med Group 4550 E Charleston Blvd Las Vegas NV 89104-5525

OGDEN, DANIEL MILLER, JR. government official, educator; b. Clarksburg, W.Va., Apr. 28, 1922; s. Daniel Miller and Mary (Maphis) O.; m. Valeria Juan Munson, Dec. 28, 1946; children: Janeth Lee Martin, Patricia Jo Hunter, Daniel Munson. BA in Polit. Sci., Wash. State U., 1944; MA, U. Chgo., 1947, PhD, 1949. From instr. to assoc. prof. Wash. State U., Pullman, 1949-61; staff asst. resources program U.S. Dept. Interior, 1961-64; asst. dir. U.S. Bur. Outdoor Recreation, 1964-67; dir. budget U.S. Dept. Interior, Washington, 1967-68; dean Coll. Humanities and Social Scis. Colo. State U., Ft. Collins, 1968-76; disting. vis. prof. Lewis and Clark Coll. and Portland (Oreg.) State U., 1977-78; dir. Office of Power Mktg. Coordination U.S. Dept. Energy, 1978-84; mgr. Pub. Power Coun., Portland, Oreg., 1984-88, ret., 1988. Mem. profl. staff com. interstate and fgn. commerce U.S. Senate, 1956-57; spl. asst. to chmn. Dem. Nat. Com., 1960-61; lectr. Mgmt. Devel. Ctrs., U.S. Office Pers. Mgmt., 1966—. Co-author: Electing the President, rev. edit., 1968, American National Government, 7th edit., 1970, American State and Local Government, 5th edit., 1972, Washington Politics, 1960, How National Policy is Made, 4th edit., 1999. Committeeman Wash. Dem. Ctrl. Com., 1952-56; chmn. Whitman County Dem. Ctrl. Com., 1958-60; chmn. 49th Legis. Dist. Dem. Com., 1990-94; chmn. Clark County Dem. Ctrl. com., 1994-98, 1999-2000, vice chair, 1998-99. With inf. U.S. Army, 1943-46. Mem. Phi Beta Kappa, Phi Kappa Phi, Pi Sigma Alpha, Sigma Delta Chi. Mem. Unitarian Ch. Home: 3118 NE Royal Oak Dr Vancouver WA 98662-7435

OGDEN, DAVID WILLIAM, lawyer; b. Washington, Nov. 12, 1953; s. Horace Greeley and Elaine Celia (Condrell) O.; m. Wannett Smith, 1988; children: Jonathan Smith, Elaine Smith. BA summa cum laude, U. Pa., 1976; JD magna cum laude, Harvard U., 1981. Bar: D.C. 1983, Va. 1986, U.S. Dist. Ct. D.C. 1984, U.S. Dist. Ct. (ea. dist.) Va. 1988, U.S. Ct. Appeals (D.C. cir.) 1984, U.S. Ct. Appeals (4th cir.) 1986, U.S. Ct. Appeals (1st cir.) 1989, U.S. Ct. Appeals (10th cir.) 1991, U.S. Supreme Ct. 1987, U.S. Ct. Appeals (5th and 9th cirs.) 2000. Law clk. to presiding judge U.S. Dist. Ct. (so. dist.) N.Y., N.Y.C., 1981-82; law clk. to assoc. justice Harry A. Blackmun U.S. Supreme Ct., Washington, 1982-83; assoc. atty. Ennis, Friedman, Bersoff & Ewing, 1983-85; atty., ptnr. Ennis, Friedman & Bersoff, 1986-88, Jenner & Block, Washington, 1988-94; legal counsel, dep. gen. counsel U.S. DOD, 1994-95; assoc. dep. atty. gen. U.S. Dept. Justice, 1995-97, counselor to the atty. gen., 1997-98, chief of staff to atty. gen., 1998-99, acting asst. atty. gen. for civil divsn., 1999-2000, asst. atty. gen. for civil divsn., 2000-2001; ptnr. Wilmer, Cutler & Pickering, 2001—. Adj. prof. law Georgetown U. Law Ctr., 1992-95. Author: (with Jerald A. Jacobs) Legal Risk Management for Associations, 1995. Recipient Disting. Pub. Svc. medal Dept. Def., 1995, Atty. Gen.'s medallion, 1999, Edmund J. Randolph award in recognition of outstanding svc. to Dept. Justice, 2001. Fellow Am. Bar Found.; mem. ABA, D.C. Bar Assn., Phi Beta Kappa. Democrat. Fax: 202 663-6363.

OGDEN, DENISE THERESA, marketing professional, educator; b. L.A., Sept. 17, 1966; d. Diego Sam and Ninfa Maria (Esquibel) Alarid; m. James R. Ogden, Sept. 19, 1989; stepchildren: David, Anne, Kari. BA in Psychology, BSBA in Mktg., Adams State Coll., 1990; MBA, DeSales U., 1996; PhD in Bus. Adminstrn., Temple U., 2002. Pub. info. clk. U.S. Bur. Reclamation, Alamosa, Colo., 1987-89; bus. analyst, sr. team leader, sr. high risk analyst, mgr. customer and instructional svcs., mgr. instrnl. design Dun & Bradstreet Corp., Bethlehem, Pa., 1990-98. Adj. instr. Cedar Crest Coll., Allentown, 1994; cons. Ogden, Latshaw & Assocs., Coopersburg, Pa., 1993—; instr. mktg. and mgmt. Pa. State U., Fogelsville. Co-author: Principles of Marketing CLEP, 1996; contbr. articles to profl. jours. Mem. adv. bd. Students in Free Enterprise, chair adv. bd., 1996—2002. Grad. fellow Temple U., 1998-2001, faculty fellow Temple U., 1999-2001; grantee Paint Consumer Rsch. Program, 2001. Mem. Internat. Soc. Performance Improvement, Assn. Quality and Participation, Hispanic Bus. Coun., Students in Free Enterprise (chair 1996-2000), Toastmasters Internat. (treas. 1990-98), Alpha Kappa Psi (life). Roman Catholic. Avocations: public speaking, science fiction, writing. E-mail: docdeniseogden@enter.net., dto2@psu.edu.

OGDEN, HUGH, English literature educator, poet; b. Erie, Pa., Mar. 11, 1937; s. Harold S. and Ethel (Yokes) O.; m. Ruth Simpson, Mar. 19, 1960 (div. 1975); children: Cynthia, David, Katherine. BA, Haverford Coll., 1959; MA, NYU, 1961; PhD, U. Mich., 1967. Asst. prof. Trinity Coll., Hartford, Conn., 1967-76, assoc. prof., 1976-92, prof. English, 1992—. Author: Two Roads and This Spring, 1991, Looking for History, 1993, Windfalls, 1996, Natural Things, 1998, Gift, 1998. Sec. Glastonbury (Conn.) Land Heritage Coalition, 1990-94. NEA Poetry fellow 1993, Residency fellow UCross Found., 1994, MacDowell Colony, 1995; poetry grant Conn. Commn. on Arts, 1990. Home: 331 Chestnut Hill Rd Glastonbury CT 06033-4103 Office: Trinity Coll Hartford CT 06106

OGDEN, JAMES RUSSELL, marketing educator, consultant, lecturer, writer; b. Paris, Nov. 4, 1954; s. Russell Lee and Marianne (Johnson) O.; children: David James, Anne Marie, Kari Kristine; m. Denise T. Alarid, 1989. B of Bus. Edn., Ea. Mich. U., 1978; MS, Colo. State U., 1981; PhD, U. No. Colo., 1986. With acctg. and fin. dept. Hydra-Matic Divsn. GM Motors, 1978; dir. mktg. Mich. Tech. Inst., 1979; grad. fellow Colo. State U., Ft. Collins, 1979-81, asst. mgr. family housing, 1979-81; placement counselor U. No. Colo., Greeley, 1981-83, mktg. instr., 1982-83; CEO, pres. Ogden, Ogden Latshaw & Assocs., Coopersburg, Pa., 1982—; chair advt. and mktg. dept., assoc. prof. Adams State Coll., Alamosa, Colo., 1983-89; dept. chair, prof. mktg. Coll. Bus., Kutztown (Pa.) U., 1989—, bd. bus. advisors Students in Free Enterprise, 1996—. Interim dir. Small Bus. Devel. Ctr., Adams State Coll., 1988-89; adj. prof. Ctrl. Mich. U., Mt. Pleasant, 1987—, Cedar Crest Coll., Allentown, 1989—, Pa. State U., 1994-95, Nova Southeastern U., doctoral com. chair, Ft. Lauderdale, Fla., 1995—; spkr. in field; mktg. and advt. cons.; corp. trainer; textbook reviewer, editl. cons. Merrill Pub. Co., Allyn & Bacon, Inc., Richard Irwin, Inc., Macmillan Pub., John Wiley & Sons, Inc., Prentice-Hall, Houghton & Mifflin Co., Austen Press, Simon & Schuster; textbook reviewer Fairchild Books and Visuals, Inc.; tech. editor Rsch. and Edn. Assn.; doctoral com. mem. Nova Southeastern U., Drexel U., Phila., Pace U., N.Y.C., Temple U., Phila.; bd. dirs. Z-Coil, Inc., Albuquerque Author: Developing a Creative and Innovative Integrated Marketing Communication Plan, 1998; co-author: The Best Test Preparation for the CLEP College-Level Examination Program Principles of Marketing, 1996; contbg. author, editor: Principles of Business, 1991, Essentials of Advertising, 1992, rev. edit., 1994, Marketing's Powerful Weapon: Point-of-Purchase Advertising, 2001; editor: Essentials of Marketing, 1994; contbr. over 40 articles to profl. jours. Treas. Com. to Elect Jorge Amaya County Commr., Colo., 1985, Bob Pastore for Senate Com.; senator Assoc. Student and Faculty Senate, Adams State Coll., 1984-85; bd. dirs. Am. Advt. Fedn. Acad. Com., 1991-97, Alamosa Personnel Bd., 1986-88, Alamosa County Devel. Corp., 1987-89, Alamosa Tourism Com., 1988-89, trustee bd. dirs. Creede Repertory Theatre, 1987-89; expert witness in tourism and mktg. State of Colo.; advisor student team entries into Nat. Student Advt. Competition, Coll. World Series of Advt., 1989, 90, 93—; trustee Dr. R.L. Ogden Meml. Scholarship, Colo. State U. Found., 1992—; faculty advisor Students in Free Enterprise (SIFE) nat. competition, 1997—; faculty advisor, mem. bus. adv. bd. Kutztown U. chpt. of Students in Free Enterprise (SIFE). Recipient award for Excellence in Econ. Edn., Freedoms Found. Valley Forge, 1986, Capital award for contbn. to edn., Nat. Leadership Coun., 1991-92, Disting. Leadership award for Excellence in Mktg. Edn., Am. Biog. Inst., 1988; named Outstanding Educator of Sch. of Bus., Adams State Coll., 1987-88; Sam Walton fellow Students in Free Enterprise, 1997, 98, Outstanding Educator award, 1998. Fellow Direct Mktg. Assn.; mem. Am. Advt. Fedn. (faculty advisor 1987-89, 90—, bd. dirs. acad. com. 1991-97), Western Mktg. Educators Assn. (paper reviewer), Nat. Guild Hypnotists (cert. hypnotherapist), Acad. Mktg. Sci., Advt. Club N.Y., Point of Purchase Advt. Inst., Am. Collegiate Retailing Assn., Assn. Nat. Advertisers, Nat. Assn. Hispanic Profs. of Bus. Adminstrn. and Econs., New Eng. Bus. Adminstrn. Assn., Ctrl. Pa. Advt. Club, Phi Kappa Phi, Alpha Sigma Alpha (fin. advisor 1992—), Alpha Kappa Psi (dist. dir.). Democrat. Avocations: scuba, music, traveling. Office: Kutztown U Coll Bus Dept Mktg Kutztown PA 19530 E-mail: ogden@kutztown.edu.

OGDEN, MAUREEN BLACK, retired state legislator; b. Vancouver, B.C., Nov. 1, 1928; came to U.S., 1930; d. William Moore and Margaret Hunter (Leitch) Black; m. Robert Moore Ogden, June 23, 1956; children: Thomas, Henry, Peter. BA, Smith Coll., 1950; MA, Columbia U., 1963; M in City and Regional Planning, Rutgers U., 1977. Researcher, staff asst. Ford Found., N.Y.C., 1951-56; staff assoc. Fgn. Policy Assn., 1956-58; mem. Millburn (N.J.) Twp. Com., 1976-81; mayor Twp. of Millburn, N.J., 1979-81; mem. N.J. Gen. Assembly, Trenton, 1982-96. Chmn. Assembly Environment Com., N.J. Gen. Assembly; chmn. Energy and Pub. Utilities Com., Coun. State Govts., 1991-92; mem. adv. bd. Sch. Policy and Planning, Rutgers Univ., New Brunswick, N.J., 1992-96. Author: Natural Resources Inventory, Township of Millburn, 1974. Bd. govs. N.J. Hist. Soc., Newark, 1992-2000; trustee N.J. chpt. The Nature Conservancy, 1994-99; hon. trustee Paper Mill Playhouse, Millburn, 1990—; former trustee St. Barnabas Med. Ctr., Livingston, N.J.; former pres. N.J. Drug Abuse Adv. Coun.; chair Gov.'s Coun. on N.J. Outdoors, 1996-99; mem. Palisades Interstate Park Commn., 1996-99; chair Garden State Preservation Trust, 1999—. Recipient citation Nat. Assn. State Outdoors Recreation Liaison Officers, 1987, cert. appreciation John F. Kennedy Ctr. for the Performing Arts, The Alliance for Art Edn., 1987, disting. svc. award Art Educators N.J., 1987, ann. environ. quality award EPA Region II, 1988, citation Humane Soc. U.S., 1989, award N.J. Hist. Sites Coun., 1989, N.J. Sch. Conservation, 1990, pres.'s award The Nature Conservancy, 1995, pub. policy award Nat. Trust for Hist. Preservation, 1995. Republican. Episcopalian. Home: 59 Lakeview Ave Short Hills NJ 07078-2240 E-mail: mrogden@worldnet.att.net.

OGDEN, PEGGY A. retired personnel director; b. N.Y.C., Mar. 21, 1932; d. Stephen Arnold and Margaret (Stern) O. BA with honors, Brown U., 1953; MA, Trinity Coll., Hartford, Conn., 1955. Asst. dir. YMCA Counseling Svc., Hartford, 1953-55; employment interviewer R.H. Macy & Co., N.Y.C., 1955; asst. pers. dir. Inst. Internat. Edn., 1956-59; pers. advisor Girl Scouts U.S.A., 1959-61; store and pers. mgr. Ohrbachs, Inc., 1961-74; dir. pers. N.Y.C. Coll. Tech. CUNY, Bkyn., 1974-2000, ret., 2000. Arbitrator, mediator Better Bus.

Bur., N.Y.C., 1988—; cons. Girl Scout Coun. N.Y., N.Y.C., 1988-89. Advocate Am. Diabetes Assn., 1999—. Mem APA, AAAS, Am. Assn. U. Adminstrs., Women in Human Resources, N.Y. Pers. Mgmt. Assn. Home: 1100 Park Ave New York NY 10128-1202

OGDEN, TINA L. merchant banking and financial advisory executive; BS, Cornell U., 1980; postgrad., Brown U., 1980; MBA, Columbia U., 1993. Engr. Norman Porter Assocs., N.Y.C., 1981; anaylst Rockwell Internat., Thousand Oaks, Calif., 1981-82; pub. info. officer Indian Point 3 Nuclear Plant, N.Y. Power Authority, Buchanan, 1984-86, tng. engr. White Plains, 1986-89; project mgr. Inst. Nuclear Power Ops., Atlanta, 1989-90; mgmt. assoc. Bank N.Y., 1993-95; cons. First Manhattan Cons. Group, 1995-97; mng. dir. The Ogden Group, 1997—. Trustee Leukemia Soc. Am., 1994-2000, chmn. exec. com. mktg. and comms., 1998, adv. bd., 2001—, Music Conservatory of Westchester, 2001—. Brown U. rsch. grantee, 1980. Mem.: IEEE (sr.), Cornell Coun., Columbia Bus. Sch. Alumni Club (fin. and banking com. 1999—, fin. and banking com.co-chmn 1995—, exec. com.), Cornell U. Alumni Assn. (v.p. Westchester County chpt. 1985—87, bd. dirs. Atlanta chpt. 1990—91), Cornell Soc. Engrs. (bd. dirs. 1999—), Cornell Club N,Y, (profl. and bus. interests com. 1993—95). E-mail: Tinaogden@IEEE.org.

OGDEN, VALERIA MUNSON, management consultant, state representative; b. Okanogan, Wash., Feb. 11, 1924; d. Ivan Bodwell and Pearle (Wilson) Munson; m. Daniel Miller Ogden Jr., Dec. 28, 1946; children: Janeth Lee Ogden Martin, Patricia Jo Ogden Hunter, Daniel Munson Ogden. BA magna cum laude, Wash. State U., 1946. Exec. dir. Potomac Coun. Camp Fire, Washington, 1964-68, Ft. Collins (Colo.) United Way, 1969-73, Designing Tomorrow Today, Ft. Collins, 1973-74, Poudre Valley Community Edn. Assn., Ft. Collins, 1977-78; pres. Valeria M. Ogden, Inc., Kensington, Md., 1978-81; nat. field cons. Camp Fire, Inc., Kansas City, Mo., 1980-81; exec. dir. Nat. Capital Area YWCA, Washington, 1981-84, Clark County YWCA, Vancouver, Wash., 1985-89; pvt. practice mgmt. cons., 1989—; mem. Wash. Ho. of Reps., 1991—2002, spkr. pro tempere, 1999—2002. Mem. adj. faculty pub. adminstrn. program Lewis and Clark Coll., Portland (Oreg.) State U., 1979-94; mem. Pvt. Industry Coun., Vancouver, 1986-95; mem. regional Svcs. Network Bd. Mental Health, 1993—. Author: Camp Fire Membership, 1980. County vice-chair Larimer County Dems., Ft. Collins, 1974-75; mem. precinct com. Clark County Dems., Vancouver, 1986-88; mem. Wash. State Coun. Vol. Action, Olympia, 1986-90; treas. Mortar Bd. Nat. Found., Vancouver, 1987-96; bd. dirs. Clark County Coun. for Homeless, Vancouver, 1989—, chmn., 1994; bd. dirs. Wash. Wil life and Recreation Coalition, 1995—, Human Svcs. Coun., 1996-02, State Legis. Leaders Found., 2001-02; chair arts and tourism com. Nat. Conf. State Legis., 1996-97, exec. com., 2000-02; bd. Wash. State Hist. Soc., 1996—; spkr. pro tem Wash. Ho. of Reps., 1999-2002; pres. Nat. Order of Women, 1999-2001. Named Citizen of Yr. Ft. Collins Bd. of Realtors, 1975, State Legislator of Yr., Wash. State Labor Coun., 2000; recipient Gulick award Camp Fire Inc., 1956, Alumna Achievement award Wash. State U. Alumni Assn., 1988; named YWCA Woman of Achievement, 1991. Mem. Internat. Assn. Vol. Adminstrs. (pres. Boulder 1989-90), Nat. Assn. YWCA Exec. Dirs. (nat. bd. nominating com. 1988-90), Sci. and Soc. Assn. (bd. dirs. 1993-97), Women in Action, Philanthropic and Ednl. Orgn., Phi Beta Kappa. Democrat. Avocation: hiking, travel. Home: 3118 NE Royal Oak Dr Vancouver WA 98662-7435 E-mail: ogden_va@leg.wa.gov.

OGDON, WILBUR (WILL OGDON), composer, music educator; b. Redlands, Calif., Apr. 19, 1921; s. Alfred Benjamin and Ethel (Brooks) O.; m. Beverly Jean Porter, Aug. 22, 1958; children— Bethany, Benjamin, Erica. MusB, U. Wis., 1942; MA, Hamline U., 1947; postgrad., U. Calif., Berkeley, 1949-50; pvt. composition studies with René Leibowitz, Paris, 1952-53; composition studies with Ernst Krenek, composition studies with Roger Sessions; PhD, Ind. U., 1955. Asst. prof. U. Tex., 1947-50; prof. Coll. St. Catherine, St. Paul, 1955-56; assoc. prof. Ill. Wesleyan U., 1956-65; dir. music Pacifica Found., KPFA, Berkeley, Calif., 1962-64; coordinator music programming U. Ill., 1965-66; prof. music U. Calif., San Diego, 1966-91, chmn. dept. music, 1966-71, research fellow Project for Music Expt., 1973-74. Author: (with Krenek and Stewart) Horizons Circled, 1974; mem. editorial bd. Perspective of New Music; composer: Three Sea Choruses, 1960-62, String Quartet, 1960, By the Isar, 1969, Un Tombeau de Cocteau, I, 1964, II, 1972, III, 1975, Sappho, The Awakening (chamber opera), 1976-80, Capriccio and Five Comments for Orch, 1980, Images, A Winter's Calendar (Soprano, piano and 3 winds), 1980, Six Small Trios for trumpet, marimba and piano, 1982, Five Preludes for violin and piano, 1982, Summer Images and Reflections, 1984-85, Five Preludes for Violin and Chamber Orchestra, 1985, Two Serenades for Wind Quintet, 1987, 90-94, Two Sea Chanteys for soprano, baritone and percussion, 1987-88, Seven Piano Pieces, 1987, 7 pieces and a Capriccio for violin and piano, 1988-89, Four D.H. Lawrence Songs for Soprano and Chamber Ensemble, 1989, 13 Expressions for solo violin and chamber ensemble, 1993, Variation Suite for violin and viola, 1995-96, Introduction and Nine Trios for two violins and piano, 1998, String Quartet, 1999, Chamber Suite for wind quintet, string quartet and piano, 2000, others. Bd. dirs. San Diego Opera Inc., 1967-70, La Jolla Civic Orch. and Chorus Assn., 1967-72, 80-82, San Diego Children's Choir, 1990-95; hon. dir. N.C. Gov.'s Bd. Music, 1964— . Served with AUS, 1942-46. Nat. Endowment of Arts fellow, 1975 Mem. Anton Webern Soc. (charter), Music Execs. Calif., Calif. Profl. Music Tchrs. Assn. (hon.) Home: 482 15th St Del Mar CA 92014-2521

O'GEARY, DENNIS TRAYLOR, retired contracting/engineering company executive; b. Waverly, Va., Feb. 20, 1925; s. King William and Mary Virginia (Traylor) O'G.; m. Alice Stuart Baum, Aug. 3, 1947; children: Dennis Patrick, Mary Alice O'Geary Eisenbarth, Elizabeth Christina O'Geary Bernstorf. Surveying degree, Tri-State U., 1943; BS in Civil Engring., Ill. Inst. Tech., 1947. Resident engring trainee Va. Hwy. Dept., Richmond, 1947-50; civil engring. supt. Wiley Jackson Co., Roanoke, Va., 1950-57; engr., asst. estimator, project mgr., v.p. and asst. to area mgr. S.J. Groves & Sons Co., Mpls. and Springfield, Ill., 1957-77, v.p., area mgr., 1978-82, v.p., asst. divsn. mgr., divsn. estimator Atlanta, 1982-84; pres. Peabody S.W., Inc., Houston, 1984-85; v.p. Houston ops. J.D. Abrams, Inc., Austin, Tex., 1985-99; ret., 1999. Cons. J.D. Abrams, Inc. Served with USNR, 1943-46. Mem. ASCE (life), Am. Concrete Inst., Soc. Am. Mil. Engrs. (50 yr. mem.), Nat. Maritime Hist. Soc. Methodist. Home: 15402 Cresent Oaks Ct Houston TX 77068-2079 Office: 111 Congress Ave Austin TX 78701-4050 E-mail: daogeary@aol.com.

OGEDE, ODE, literature educator; b. Uchenyim Igede, Benue, Nigeria, Sept. 16, 1956; came to the U.S., 1994; s. Ogede and Margaret (Ogwuna) Ode; m. Shianyisimi Asabe, Apr. 5, 1986; children: Ochuole, Ogede, Shekwaga. BA in English Lit. with honors, Ahmadu Bello U., Zaria, Nigeria, 1979, MA in African Lit., 1982, PhD in English, 1987. Sr. lectr. in English Ahmadu Bello U., Zaria, 1988-94; Andrew Mellon faculty fellow U. Pa., Phila., 1994-95; vis. prof. Lincoln U., Pa., 1995-96; English prof. N.C. Ctrl. U., Durham, 1996—. Author: Art, Society and Performance, 1997, Ayi Kwei Armah: Radical Iconoclast, Pitting Imaginary Worlds Against the Actual, 1998, Achebe and the Politics of Representation, 2000; editor SAIWA (Roots), 1989-94; mem. editl. bd. Studies of Nigerian Cultures and Society, 1990-94; contbr. articles to profl. jours. Mem. MLA, MLA of Nigeria (v.p. 1989-91), African Lit. Assn. Am. Home: 129 Celeste Cir Chapel Hill NC 27517-8916 Office: NC Central U Comms Bldg Rm 327 Durham NC 27707

OGG, ELTON JERALD, JR. educator, academic administrator; b. Springfield, Mo., Aug. 25, 1955; s. Elton Jerald Sr. and Janett Northam O.; m. Mary Jane Nichols, Dec. 28, 1973; children: Jennifer Lauren, Jana Elizabeth. JD, U. Tenn., 1978; MJ, La. State U., 1987; PhD, So. Ill. U., 1994. Bar: Tenn. 1979, La. 1984. Pvt. practice law, Baton Rouge, 1983-87; asst. prof. comm. U. Tenn., Martin, 1987-97, chmn. dept. comm., 1997-2000; dean Coll. Humanities and Fine Arts, 2000—; prof. Tenn. Govs. Sch. Humanities, Martin, 1991-2000, dir., 2000—. Contbr. articles to profl. jours. Pres. Parent-Tchr. Orgn., Martin, 1989—90; coach Martin Girls Softball Assn., 1993—2001; dir. Lifeline Blood Svcs., Weakley County, Tenn., 1993—2001. Res. judge adv. USAFR, 1983—. Avocations: golf, softball, tennis, reading. Office: U Tenn 225 Humanities Martin TN 38238-0001

OGG, JAMES ELVIS, microbiologist, educator; b. Centralia, Ill., Dec. 24, 1924; m. Betty Jane Ackerson; 2 children. BS, U. Ill., 1949; PhD, Cornell U., 1956. Bacteriologist Biol. Labs., Ft. Detrick, Md., 1950-53, cons., 1953-56, med. bacteriologist, 1956-58; prof. microbiology Colo. State U., Ft. Collins, 1958-85, prof. emeritus, 1985—; asst. dean Grad. Sch., 1965-66, head dept. microbiology, 1967-77. Dir. Advanced Sci. Edn. Program div. grad. edn. in sci. NSF, Washington, 1966-67; Fulbright-Hays sr. lectr. in microbiology, Nepal, 1976-77, 81; acad. adminstrn. advisor Inst. Agr. and Animal Sci., Tribhuvan U., Nepal, 1988-91; cons. NASA, 1968-69, NSF, 1968-73, Martin Marietta Corp., 1970-76; cons.-evaluator North Central Assn. Colls. and Secondary Schs., 1974-89; cons. Consortium for Internat. Devel., 1990-98, Winrock Internat. Inst. for Agrl. Devel., 1992—. Contbr. articles to profl. jours. Served with AUS, 1943—53. Fellow AAAS, Am. Acad. Microbiology; mem. Am. Soc. Microbiology (chmn. pub. service and adult edn. com. 1975-80). Home: 1442 Ivy St Fort Collins CO 80525-2348 E-mail: jeogg@lamar.colostate.edu.

OGG, ROBERT DANFORTH, corporate executive; b. Gardiner, Maine, June 10, 1918; s. James and Eleanor B. (Danforth) O.; m. Nancy Foote, Oct. 21, 1978; children by previous marriage: Richard Aasgaard, Robert Danforth, James Erling. Student, U. Calif., Berkeley, Stanford U. Utilities engr. State of Calif., 1946-48; gen. mgr. Danforth Anchors, Berkeley, 1948-51, prse., CEO, 1951-59; mng. dir. Danforth divsn. The Eastern Co., 1959-79, dir., 1972-80, Hodgdon Bros., East Boothbay, Maine, 1961-65; pres. Brewers Boatyard, West Southport, 1963-65; v.p. Henry R. Hinckley Co., Manset, 1974-79; pres. Ogg Oceans Systems, 1980—; chmn. Alpha Ocean Systems, 1983—. Author: Anchors & Anchorin (8 edits.); contbr. chpts. to books, articles to profl. jours.; patentee in field; inventor The Danforth Anchor, Inertial Altimeter, Digital Depth Sounder, others. Mem. adv. com. U. Calif. Rsch. Expeditions Program, 1979, co-chmn., 1983—; trustee U. Calif.-Berkeley Found., 1981, exec. com., 1983—, chmn. audit com., 1984-89, fellow, 1990, lifetime emeritus trustee; advisor Lawrence Hall Sci.; founder, sr. warden St. Ann's Episcopal Ch., Windham, Maine, 1976-79; life fellow U. Calif., Berkeley; contbr. to ABC and BBC documentaries on Pearl Harbor. With USN Intelligence, 1941-46, lt. comdr. USNR, ret. Recipient Wheeler Oak meritorious award U. Calif., 1987. Fellow Explorers Club (life), Calif. Acad. Scis. (life); mem. Navy League (founder Marin coun.), Soc. Naval Architects & Marine Engrs., Am. Soc. Naval Engrs., Am. Boat & Yacht Coun., Boating Writers Internat., Am. Geophys. Union, IEEE, Chancellors Cir. U. Calif., Sports Adv. Coun. U. Calif., Bodega Marine Lab., U.S. Naval Inst., R.G. Sproul Assocs., Tail Hook Assocs., Woodshole Assocs., Buncke Microsurg. Found. (bd. dirs. 1994—), Sierra Club, U. Calif.-Berkeley Alumni Assn., Engring. Alumni Assn., N.Y. Yacht Club, Pacific Union Club, Elks, Bear Backers Club, U. Calif. Berkeley Chancellor's Cir. Club, U. Calif. San Francisco Heritage Club. Address: 11490 Franz Valley Rd Calistoga CA 94515-9549

OGG, WILSON REID, lawyer, poet, retired judge, lyricist, curator, publisher, educator, philosopher, social scientist, parapsychologist; b. Alhambra, Calif., Feb. 26, 1928; s. James Brooks and Mary (Wilson) Ogg. Student, Pasadena Jr. Coll., 1946; AB, U. Calif., Berkeley, 1949; JD, U. Calif., 1952; Cultural D in Philosophy of Law, World U. Roundtable, 1983. Bar: Calif. 1955. Assoc. trust dept. Wells Fargo Bank, San Francisco, 1954-55; pvt. practice Berkeley, 1955—. Adminstv. law judge, 1974—93; real estate broker, cons., 1974—; curator-in-residence, Pinebrook, 1964—; owner Pinebrook Press, Berkeley, 1988—; rsch. atty., legal editor dept. of continuing edn. bar U. Calif., 1958—63; instr. 25th Sta. Hosp., Taegu, Republic of Korea, 1954, Taegu English Lang. Inst., 1954; trustee World U., 1976—80; dir. admissions internat. Soc. Phil. Enquiry, 1981—84; dep. dir. gen. Internat. Biographical Ctr., England, 1986—; dep. gov. Am. Biographical Inst. Rsch. Assn., 1986—. *Judge Ogg's career combines not only outstanding achievement in the legal profession but also as in science with a major analysis of the problems of distinguishing co-existence from causality in medicine and natural science. He has formulated the unified theory or the two-way flow theory of consciousness and matter published on the internet at wilsonogg.com under which principles of quantum mechanics, black notes, light, expansion and contraction of manifestation, and physical and biological evolutions are derivative from the basic postulates of the theory.* Author: (book) The Unified Theory; contbr. articles to profl. jours., poems to mags. With AUS, 1952—54. Named to Internat. Poetry Hall of Fame, Nat. Libr. Poetry, 1997; recipient Internat. Peace prize, Auth. of United Cultural Conv., U.S., 2002. Mem.: ACLU, ASCAP, ABA, AAAS, VFW, Inst. Noetic Scis., Triple Nine Soc., Intertel, Calif. Soc. Psychical Study (pres., chmn. bd. 1963—65), Am. Arbitration Assn. (nat. panel arbitrators), San Francisco Bar Assn., State Bar Calif., Internat. Soc. Individual Liberty, Internat. Soc. Unified Sci., Internat. Platform Assn., Internat. Soc. Poets (life), Faculty Club of the U. Calif. at Berkeley (emeritus), Men's Inner Cir. Achievement, Wisdom Soc., Amnesty Internat., Marines Meml. Club, Town Hall Club Calif., City Commons Club (Berkeley), Elks, Shriners, Masons, Am. Legion. Unitarian Universalist. Home: Pinebrook 8 Bret Harte Way Berkeley CA 94708-1611 Office: 1104 Keith Ave Berkeley CA 94708-1607 Fax: 510-540-6052. E-mail: wilsonogg@alum.calberkeley.org.

OGIER, WALTER THOMAS, retired physics educator; b. Pasadena, Calif., June 18, 1925; s. Walter Williams and Aileen Vera (Polhamus) O.; m. Mayrene Miriam Gorton, June 27, 1954; children: Walter Charles, Margaret Miriam, Thomas Earl, Kathryn Aileen. BS, Calif. Inst. Tech., 1947, PhD in Physics, 1953. Research fellow Calif. Inst. Tech., 1953; instr. U. Calif. at Riverside, 1954-55, asst. prof. physics, 1955-60, Pomona Coll., Claremont, Calif., 1960-62, assoc. prof., 1962-67, prof. physics, 1967-89, prof. emeritus, 1989—, chmn. dept., 1972-89. Contbr. articles on metals, liquid helium, X-rays and proton produced X-rays to profl. jours. Served with USNR, 1944-46. NSF Sci. Faculty fellow, 1966-67 Mem. Am. Phys. Soc., Am. Assn. Physics Tchrs. (pres. So. Calif. sect. 1967-69), Tau Beta Pi. Home: 8555 San Gabriel Rd Atascadero CA 93422-4928 E-mail: ogierwt@tcsn.net.

OGILBY, BARRY RAY, lawyer; b. dixon, Ky., Jan. 19, 1947; s. Jess Bryan and Ann (Sutton) O; m. Carolyn Cowser, May 30, 1969 (div. 1973); m. Charlene Marie Coehlo, July 2, 1983; children: Kevin Glenn, Brandon Jesse. BS in Geology, U. Ky., 1969; JD, Memphis State U., 1972. Bar: Tenn. 1972, Tex. 1972, Ky. 1973, Calif. 1985, U.S. Dist. Ct. (cen. and no. dists.) Calif. 1987, U.S. Ct. Appeals (9th cir.) 1989. Litigation atty. Exxon U.S.A., Houston, 1972-74, mktg. atty. Memphis, 1975-76, labor, environ. atty. L.A., 1976-78, refinery atty. Benicia, Calif., 1978-81; counsel Exxon Pipeline Co., Houston, 1981-84; assoc. div. atty. Exxon Co. USA, Thousand Oaks, Calif., 1985-86; sole practice Calabasas, 1986-91; gen. counsel Marine Spill Resource Corp., 1991-94; atty. McCutchen, Doyle et al, 1995—. Adj. prof. environ. law La Verne Coll., 1989-90; lectr. Am. Labor Inst.-ABA legal Edn. Seminar, San Francisco, 1980, 82. Contbr. articles to profl. jours. Mem. ABA (nat. resources law com., marine resources com. 1998—). Office: McCutchen Doyle et al 3 Embarcadero Ctr San Francisco CA 94111-4003 E-mail: bogilby@mdbe.com.

OGILVIE, DONALD GORDON, bankers association executive; b. N.Y.C., Apr. 7, 1943; s. John B. and Ann (Stephens) O.; m. Fan Staunton, Apr. 18, 1966; children: Jennifer B., Adam C. BA, Yale U., 1965; MBA, Stanford U., 1967. Systems analyst Dept. of Def., Washington, 1967-68; pres., dir. ICF Inc., 1969-73; dep. assoc. dir. Office of Mgmt. and Budget, 1973-74, assoc. dir., 1974-76; assoc. dean Yale U., New Haven, 1977-80; v.p. Celanese Corp., N.Y.C., 1980-85; exec. v.p. Am. Bankers Assn., Washington, 1985—. Dir. Colonial Bancorp, 1979-85, MacDermid Corp., 1986—, Marine Spill Response Corp., 1991-2002. Bd. dirs. N.Y.C. Ballet, 1981-88, Hospiec Edn. and Rsch., New Haven, 1978-81; mem. adv. bd. Yale Sch. Orgn. and Mgmt., 1992-94. Home: 3133 Connecticut Ave NW Apt 923 Washington DC 20008-5111 Office: Am Bankers Assn 1120 Connecticut Ave NW Washington DC 20036-3902

OGILVIE, KELVIN KENNETH, university president, chemistry educator; b. Windsor, N.S., Can., Nov. 6, 1942; s. Carl Melbourn and Mabel Adelia (Wile) O.; m. Emma Roleen, May 7, 1964; children: Kristine, Kevin. BS with honors, Acadia U., 1964, DSc (hon.), 1983; PhD, Northwestern U., 1968; DSc (hon.), U. N.B., Can., 1991, McGill U., 1998. Assoc. prof. U. Man., Winnipeg, 1968-74; prof. chemistry McGill U., Montreal, 1974-88, Can. Pacific prof. biotech., 1984-87; bd. dirs. Sci. Adv. Bd., Biologicals, Toronto, Ont., 1979-84; dir. Office of Biotech. McGill U., 1984-87; v.p. acad. affairs, prof. chemistry Acadia U., Wolfville, N.S., 1987-93, pres., vice-chancellor, 1993—. Invited lectr. on biotech. Tianjin, People's Republic of China, 1985; Snider lectr. U. Toronto, 1991; Gwen Leslie Meml. lectr., 1991; Centennial Mossman lectr. McGill U., 1998; mem. Nat. Adv. Bd. Sci. and Tech., 1994-95; chair selection com. Indsl. Postgrad. Scholarship program NSERCC, 1994; mem. Coun. N.S. U. Pres. 1993—; mem. Coun. of Applied Sci. and Tech. for N.S., 1988-93; mem. Nat. Biotech. Adv. Com., 1988-99; mem. Fisher (Can.) Biotech. Adv. Ctr., 1989-92; mem. sci. adv. bd. Allelix Biopharms., 1991-93; chair adv. bd. NRC Inst. for Marine Bioscis., 1990-93; mem. steering com. on biotech. labor Can., 1990-92; mem. Atlantic regional com. Prime Min.'s Awards for Tchg. Excellence in Sci., Tech. and Math., 1993—; chair regional planning forum for a pharm. industry, Atlantic, Can., 1993; mem. Atomic Energy Control Bd., Can., 1997-99; chair sci. adv. bd. Quanta Nova Can., 1998-2001; mem. Can. Electronic Bus. Roundtable, 1999—, Can. Global Bus. Dialogue on Electronic Commerce, 1999, Coun. of Ministers Com. on Online Learning, 2000-01. Mem. editorial bd. Nucleosides and Nucleotides, 1981-92; contbr. over 150 articles to profl. jours.; holder 14 patents. Bd. dirs. Plant Biotech. Inst., 1987-90. Decorated Knight of Malta, Order of Can.; named Hon. Col. 14th Air Maintenance Squadron, RCAF, 1995-2000; recipient Commemorative medal for 125th Anniversary of Confedn. Can., 1992, Buck-Whitney medal, 1983, Manning Prin. award, 1992; named to McLean's Honor Roll of Canadians Who Made a Difference, 1988; E.W.R. Steacie Meml. fellow, 1982-84. Fellow Chem. Inst. Can.; mem. Am. Chem. Soc., Ordre des Chemists of Que., Assn. Univs. and Colls. Can. (standing com. on rsch. 1993-2000), Atlantic Univ. Athletic Assn. (pres. 1995-97). Achievements include inventing of BIOLF-62 (ganciclovir), antiviral drug used worldwide; developed general synthesis of RNA; developed original 'gene machine'; developer complete chemical synthesis of large RNA molecules. Home: PO Box 307 Canning NS Canada B0P 1HO Office: Acadia U Office of Pres Wolfville NS Canada B0P 1X0 E-mail: kelvin.ogilvie@acadiau.ca.

OGILVIE, RICHARD IAN, clinical pharmacologist; b. Sudbury, Ont., Can., Oct. 9, 1936; s. Patrick Ian and Gena Hilda (Olson) O.; m. Ernestine Tahedl, Oct. 9, 1965; children— Degen Elisabeth, Lars Ian. MD, U. Toronto, 1960. Intern Toronto (Ont.) Gen. Hosp., 1960-61; resident Montreal Gen. and Univ. Alta. hosps., 1962-66; fellow in clin. pharmacology McGill U., Montreal, 1966-68, asst. prof. medicine, pharmacology and therapeutics, 1968-73, assoc. prof., 1973-78, prof., 1978-83, chmn. dept. pharmacology and therapeutics, 1978-83. Clin. pharmacologist Montreal Gen. Hosp., 1968-83, dir. div. clin. pharmacology, 1976-83; prof. medicine and pharmacology U. Toronto, 1983— ; dir. div. cardiology Toronto Western Hosp., 1983-88, div. clin. pharmacology, 1983-91; mem. pharm. grants com. Med. Research Coun. Can., 1977-82, chmn. 1980-82; mem. med. adv. com. Que. Heart Found., 1976-82, chmn. 1977-81. Editor Hypertension Canada, 1989—. Bd. dirs. PMAC Health Care Found., 1986-92; hon. sec.-treas. Banting Research Found., 1984-87, chmn. grant rev. com., 1985-86 Decorated knight comdr. Sovereign Mil. Order St. John of Jerusalem, Knights of Malta, 1987, nat. chmn., recipient prize in med. ethics, 1988-98, sci. advisor to the prior, 1987—, Knight Grand Cross, 1990; jury mem. Can. Prix Galien, 1994-99; grantee Can. Kidney Found., J.C. Edwards Found., Med. Rsch. Coun., Que. Heart Found., Can. Found. Advancement Therapeutics, Conseil de la recherche en sante du Que. Fellow ACP, Royal Coll. Physicians of Can.; mem. Can. Soc. Clin. Investigation (coun. 1977-80), Can. Hypertension Soc. (bd. dirs. 1979-81, 89-94, 99—, v.p. 1991-92, pres. 1992-93), Can. Found. Advancement Clin. Pharmacology (dir. 1978-86), Canadian Soc. for Clin. Pharmacology (pres. 1979-82, Sr. Investigator award 1993), Internat. Union Pharmacology (coun. mem. clin. pharmacology sect. 1981-84, chmn. 1984-87), Pharm. Soc. Can., Can. Cardiovascular Soc., Am. Soc. Pharmacology and Exptl. Therapeutics, Am. Soc. Clin. Pharm., Am. Fedn. Clin. Rsch., Toronto Hypertension Soc. (pres. 1988-98). Home: 79 Collard Dr King City ON Canada L7B 1E4 Office: Toronto Hosp Western Div 399 Bathurst St Toronto ON Canada M5T 2S8 also: Toronto Western Hosp 399 Bathurst St Toronto ON Canada M5T 2S8 E-mail: ri.ogilvie@utoronto.ca.

OGILVIE, T(HOMAS) FRANCIS, engineer, educator; b. Atlantic City, Sept. 26, 1929; s. Thomas Fleisher and Frances Augusta (Wilson) O.; m. Joan Husselton, Sept. 11, 1950; children: Nancy Louise, Mary Beth, Kenneth Stuart. BA in Physics, Cornell U., 1950; M.Sc. in Aero. Engring., U. Md., 1957; PhD in Engring. Sci., U. Calif., Berkeley, 1960; D in Naval Arch./Marine Engring. (hon.), Nat. Tech. U. Athens, 1996. Physicist, David Taylor Model Basin, Dept. Navy, Bethesda, Md., 1951-62, 64-67; liaison scientist Office of Naval Research, London, 1962-63; asso. prof. naval architecture and marine engring. U. Mich., Ann Arbor, 1967-70, prof. fluid mechanics, 1970-81, chmn. dept. naval architecture and marine engring., 1973-81; prof. ocean engring. MIT, Cambridge, 1982-96, prof. emeritus, 1996—, head dept. 1982-94. Vis. prof. naval architecture Osaka (Japan) U., 1976; vis. prof. math. U. Manchester, Eng., 1976; founding mem. Ariz. Sr. Acad., Tucson, 1997. Contbr. articles to profl. jours. Recipient Meritorious Pub. Svc. award U.S. Dept. of Transp., 1982. Fellow Soc. of Naval Architects and Marine Engrs. (coun. 1977-82, exec. com. 1978-80, 83-84, William H. Webb medal 1989); mem. Sigma Xi, Phi Beta Kappa. Home: 7559 S Eliot Ln Tucson AZ 85747-9627

OGILVY, CHRISTOPHER STANLEY, neurosurgeon, researcher; b. Norwalk, Conn., Aug. 19, 1957; s. Stephen Hunter and Alicia (Vallado) O.; children: Heather, Sedgwick, Benjamin. Grad. magna cum laude, Yale U., 1980; MD, Dartmouth U., 1984. Diplomate Am. Bd. Neurol. Surgery. Asst. vis. neurosurgeon Mass. Gen. Hosp., Boston, 1991-95, 96—, dir. cerebrovascular surgery, 1993, co-dir. Brain Aneurysm/AVM Ctr., 1993—; asst. prof. surgery Harvard Med. Sch., 1991-96, assoc. prof. surgery, 1996—. Rsch. fellow in neurosci. Dana Found., 1987-89, Charles A. Elsberg fellow, 1992; NIH grantee, 1994-99. Mem. Am. Acad. Neurol. Surgery, Am. Assn. Neurol. Surgeons, Congress Neurol. Surgeons (mem. CNS/AANS jt. sect. on cerebrovascular surgery 1993—). Office: Mass Gen Hosp Dept Cerebrovasc Surgery Fruit St Boston MA 02114 Fax: 617-726-7501.

OGIRRI, DENNIS AREKPITA, educator, political/business management consultant; b. July 10, 1949; arrived in U.S., 1981; s. Ogirri Idor and Asimawu (Ekekwe) O.; m. Esther O. Ogirri, Nov. 15, 1978; children: Osi, Aghie, Pita. BS, U. Ibadan, Nigeria, 1974; MURP, U. Pitts., 1983; PhD, W.Va. U., 1991. Exec. officer, sr. adminstrv. officer Bendel State Civil Svc., Nigeria, 1975-81; stenographic/confidential sec., 1964-71; asst. prof. Johnson C. Smith U., Charlotte, NC, 1989—94, assoc. prof., 1995—, head dept., 1994—96, mem. honors coll. core faculty, 1995—. Adj. prof. U. N.C., Charlotte, 1999, Queens Coll., Charlotte, 2000, Montreat Coll., Charlotte Campus, N.C., 1998—, Shaw U., Kannapolis, 1993-97; presenter/lectr. in field. Reviewer, referee for jours. and pubs.; contbr. articles to profl. jours. Mem. scholar Urban Rsch. Group, Charlotte, 1997—; vol. Charlotte-Mecklenburg Schs., Charlotte, 1994-96; TV polit. analyst/panelist, 1991-97, 2001-02. Recipient Par Excellence Teaching award Bank of Am., 2000. Mem. Am. Polit. Sci. Assn. (Outstanding Tchr. 2000), Acad. Polit. Sci., Southeastern Regional Sem. on African Studies, African Studies Acad., Assn. Am. Colls. and Univs., Urban Affairs Assn., N.C. Polit. Sci. Assn. (panel chair, moderator, presenter). Avocations: reading, soccer, organizing/participating in African cultural presentations. Home: PO Box 563132 Charlotte NC 28256 Office: Johnson C Smith U 100 Beatties Ford Rd Charlotte NC 28216 E-mail: dogirri@carolina.rr.com, dogirri@jcsu.edu.

OGLE, DAVID WILLIAM, art educator, sculptor, ceramist, printmaker; b. Richmond, Calif., May 17, 1944; s. Robert Ray Sr. and Dorothy Aileen (Reynolds) O.; m. Carol Jo Gudenkauf, July 7, 1968; 1 child: Ashley Christina. AA in Art, Contra Costa Coll., San Pablo, Calif., 1964; BA in Ceramics, San Jose State U., 1969, MA in Sculpture, 1970; postgrad., San Francisco State U., 1988. Cert. instr. art C.C., Calif. Owner David Ogle Ceramics and Sculpture, Los Gatos, Calif., 1968—; instr., art lab. technician West Valley Coll., Campbell, 1971-72, instr. art, founder ceramics dept. Saratoga, 1973—, chmn. dept. sculpture, 1973—, chmn. dept. art, 1976-78, chmn. ceramics, 1978—. Foundry apprentice San Francisco Art Foundry, 1974-75; lectr. Corcoran Sch. Art, Washington, 1976—, San Jose State U., Calif. 1986—; chmn. Olympiad of Arts Coll. Divsn., Saratoga, 1993-97. Contbg. author Ceramics Monthly Mag., 1985-97; author: Workbook for Ceramics, 1997; one-man shows include San Jose Mus., 1979; exhibited in group shows at San Francisco Mus. Modern Art, Oakland Mus., De Young Mus., Triton Mus., Los Gatos Mus., Crocker Mus., Arts Coun. Gt. Britain-White Chapel Gallery, Musee d'Art Moderne, Paris, France, La Jolla Mus., Palo Alto Cultural Ctr., Esther Robles Gallery, L.A., William Sawyer Gallery, San Francisco, Smith-Anderson Gallery, Palo Alto, Calif., Fendrick Gallery, Washington, Gargoyle Gallery, Aspen, Colo., Jalbert Gallery, Saratoga, The Art Foundry Gallery, Sacramento, The Art Object Gallery, San Jose, Calif.; represented in permanent collections Addison Gallery Am. Art, Brit. Coun. for Arts; prin. works include Figurescapes, Chi the Vital Spirit, Fates and the

Unknown Artist; represented in numerous pvt. collections. Mentor 2+2+2 Off to Coll. program West Valley Coll., 1993—; vol. Young Authors program VanMeter Elem. Sch., Los Gatos, 1990-92; vol. Montalvo Art Assn., Saratoga, 1992; active San Francisco Mus. Modern Art, 1975—. Recipient numerous sculpture awards, Calif., 1970-80; grantee sabbatical West Valley Coll., 1981-82, profl. growth and devel. grantee West Valley Coll., 1996. Mem. Nat. Coun. Edn. for Ceramic Arts, Faculty Assn. C.C., Los Gatos Athletic Club. Avocations: skiing, racquetball, landscaping, writing, home design and construction. Home: 16555 Topping Way Los Gatos CA 95032-5645 Office: West Valley Coll 14000 Fruitvale Ave Saratoga CA 95070-5640 E-mail: brnzpnut@aol.com.

OGLE, EDWARD PROCTOR, JR. investment counseling executive; b. Inglewood, Calif., Dec. 20, 1935; s. Edward Proctor and Allene Emma (Blumenthal) O.; m. Elizabeth Lovejoy Myers, Mar. 28, 1958; children: Kathryn Ogle Nava, Terry Ogle Nelson, Wendy Ogle Reeves. BA, U. So. Calif., 1964; MA, Claremont Grad. Sch., 1980. Cert. fin. planning practitioner. Zone mgr. Investors Diversified Svcs., Pasadena, Calif., 1964-66; asst. mgr. Merrill Lynch Pierce Fenner Smith, 1966-72; mgr. Clark Dodge & Co-Capital Place Dept., L.A., 1972-74; sr. v.p. Security Pacific Bank - Pacific Century Group, 1974-86; sr. v.p., registered prin. Brown Bros. Harriman & Co., 1986—. Author: (booklet) Role of Bank Trust Department, 1981; editor (booklet) Parade Operations Manual, 1992, 93. Com. sec. Tournament of Roses Assn., Pasadena, 1976—; mem. Town Hall of Calif., L.A., 1977—, Orange County World Trade Assn., Rep. Presdl. Task Force, Orange County, Calif., 1984—; elder Presbyn. Ch.; chmn. bd. councilors U. So. Calif., 1998—. Recipient Corp. Fund Raising Cert. United Way, L.A., 1978-80, Exec. Mgmt. Cert. Claremont Grad. Sch., 1979, Mgmt. and Exec. Cert. Security Pacific Bank, L.A., 1981. Mem. Internat. Assn. Fin. Planners, Drucker Ctr. Mgmt. Assn., Claremont Grad. Sch. Alumni Assn. (pres. 1984-86), Pasadena Bond Club, Bond Club L.A., Jonathan Club, City Club. Republican. Avocations: photography, golf, basketball, music, travel. Office: Brown Bros Harriman & Co 355 S Grand Ave Ste 3250 Los Angeles CA 90071-1569

OGLE, ROBBIN SUE, criminal justice educator; b. North Kansas City, Mo., Aug. 28, 1960; d. Robert Lee and Carol Sue (Gray) O. BS, Ctrl. Mo. State U., 1982; MS, U. Mo., 1990; PhD, Pa. State U., 1995. State probation and parole officer Mo. Dept. Corrections, Kansas City, 1982-92; collector J.C. Penney Co., Mission, Kans., 1990-92; instr. U. Mo., Kansas City, 1990-92; grad. lectr. Pa. State U., University Park, 1992-95; prof. criminal justice dept. U. Nebr., Omaha, 1995—. Contbr. articles to profl. jours. Athletic scholar Ctrl. Mo. State U., Warrensburg, 1978-82. Mem. AAUW, ACLU, NOW, Am. Soc. Criminology, Acad. Criminal Justice Scis., Am. Correctional Assn., Phi Kappa Phi. Avocations: reading, watching basketball, walking dog. Office: U Nebr Dept Criminal Justice 1100 Neihardt Lincoln NE 68588-0630 Home: 2410 N 99th St Omaha NE 68134-5642 E-mail: RSOgle@webtv.net.

OGLESBY, ROGER, publishing executive; BJ, U. Mo.; JD, U. Calif. With Knight-Ridder's San Jose (Calif.) Mercury News, Omaha World Herald; CEO, pres. California Community News; editor, v.p. Allentown (Pa.) Morning Call; pres. Los Angeles Times (Orange County edit.); pub., editor Seattle-Post Intelligencer, 2000—. Office: Seattle Post-Intelligencer Hearst Newspapers PO Box 1909 Seattle WA 98111-1909 also: Seattle Post-Intelligencer 101 Elliot Ave W Seattle WA 98119*

OGLIARUSO, MICHAEL ANTHONY, retired chemist, educator, actor; b. Bklyn., Aug. 10, 1938; s. Andrea and Anna (Bianco) O.; m. Basila Gallo, Apr. 2, 1961; 1 child, Michael Dana. BS, Poly. Inst. Bklyn., 1960, PhD, 1965. Postdoctoral research asso. UCLA, 1965-67; asst. prof. chemistry Va. Poly. Inst. and State U., Blacksburg, 1967-72, assoc. prof., 1972-78, prof., 1978-95, assoc. dean Coll. Arts and Scis., 1984-95; ret. Coll. Arts and Scis.; profl. actor. Contbr. articles to profl. jours. Served with C.E. U.S. Army, 1960-61. Mem. Am. Chem. Soc., Va. Acad. Sci., Sigma Xi, Phi Lambda Upsilon. *I have been fortunate to be associated with the most personally rewarding profession available today, the professional education of young men and women. This career is best suited to persons who wish to remain young in spirit, since regardless of your age you are always surrounded with students who are between 18 and 22 years old. This is the best way I know to remain spiritually young.*

OGNIBENE, ANDRE J(OHN), physician, army officer, educator; b. N.Y.C., Nov. 18, 1931; s. Morris S. and Josephine C. (Macaluso) O.; m. Margaret A. Haug, Apr. 21, 1957; children: Judy, Andrea, Adrienne, Marc, Eric. BA cum laude, Columbia U., 1952; MD, NYU, 1956. Diplomate Am. Bd. Internal Medicine, Am. Bd. Geriatrics, Am. Bd. Med. Mgmt. Intern in medicine Bellevue Hosp., N.Y.C., 1956-57, resident in medicine, 1957-59; commd. capt. U.S. Army M.C., 1957, advanced through grades to brig. gen., 1978; resident in medicine Manhattan VA Hosp., N.Y.C. and chief resident in medicine, 1959-60; chief med. service U.S. Army Hosp., Nurnburg, Germany, 1961-62, chief dept. medicine, 1962-64; fellow in cardiology Walter Reed Gen. Hosp., Washington, 1964-65, asst. in cardiology, 1965-66, asst. chief dept. medicine, 1969-72; chief dept. medicine, chief profl. services U.S. Army Hosp., Ft. Meade, Md., 1966-68; cons. in medicine Hdqrs. U.S. Army, Vietnam, 1969; asst. chief dept. medicine Walter Reed Army Med. Ctr., 1970-72; from chief dept. medicine to dir. med. edn. Brooke Army Med. Center, Ft. Sam Houston, Tex., 1972-78, dir. med. edn., 1976-78, dep. comdr. and chief profl. services, 1976-78, comdr., commanding gen., 1978-81; hosp. dir. San Antonio State Chest Hosp., 1981-85; program dir. internal medicine Canton, Ohio, 1985-95; assoc. dean for med. edn., med. dir. Mercy Med. Ctr., 1995-98; prof. medicine N.E. Ohio U., Rootstown, 1985-98, prof. emeritus, 1998—; chmn. dept. medicine, 1989-98; v.p., treas. Majomed Corp., San Antonio, 1999—. Chmn. dept. medicine N.E. Ohio U., 1989-98; instr. medicine NYU, 1960; assoc. clin. prof. Georgetown U., 1970-72; clin. prof. U. Tex. Health Sci. Center, San Antonio, 1973-85, mem. postgrad. adv. com., 1977-78; mem. Instl. Rev. Bd., 1981-85; pres. Bexar Met. unit Am. Cancer Soc., 1984; dir. Eisenhower Nat. Bank; bd. dirs. Cancer Therapy and Research Ctr.; chmn. South Tex. Epilepsy Found., 1985. Contbr. articles to med. publs. and chpts. to books; editor, prin. author Internal Medicine in Vietnam, Vol. II, 1982; editor-in-chief: Internal Medicine in Vietnam, vol. I, 1977. Trustee Regina Health Ctr., 1992-97; mem. med. adv. bd. Access Health Inc., 1998—. Decorated Disting. Service medal, Legion of Merit. Master ACP (laureate, master tchr.); fellow Am. Coll. Physician Execs., Am. Coll. Angiology; mem. N.Y. Acad. Scis., Am. Fedn. Clin. Rsch., Bexar County Med. Soc., Stark County Med. Soc., Assn. Profs. Medicine, Tex. Med. Found., Alpha Omega Alpha. Home and Office: 27671 Ramblewood St San Antonio TX 78261-2013 *Compassion must remain the universal prescription in medical practice. Technology can provide no solutions in the absence of humanity.*

OGNIBENE, PETER JOHN, writer; b. Washington, Dec. 9, 1941; s. Peter Joseph and Dorothea Vita (D'Amico) Ognibene; m. Brigid Ann Selz, Apr. 7, 1984; 1 child Matthew. BS, U.S. Air Force Acad., 1963; MSE in Aerospace Engring., U. Mich., 1965; MA in Govt. and Politics, U. Md., 1967. V.p. Applied Sys. Inst., Washington, 1986-93, Synex Inc., Columbia, Md., 1993-95; pres. Smart Card Devel. Svcs., Silver Spring, 1995—. Author: (book) Scoop: The Life and Politics of Henry M. Jackson, 1975, The Big Byte, 1984. Capt. USAF, 1963—70. Recipient Excellence in Consumer Journalism, Nat. Press Club, 1979, Award of Merit, Soc. Tech. Comm., 1988. Mem.: Washington Ind. Writers (adv. bd. 1981—). Democrat. Roman Catholic. Avocations: skiing, running. Office: Smart Card Devel Svcs PO Box 3013 Silver Spring MD 20918-3013 E-mail: ognibene@erols.com.

OGRA, PEARAY L. physician, educator; b. Srinagar, Kashmir, India, Mar. 19, 1937; came to U.S., 1961, naturalized, 1969; s. Govinda Kaul and Gunvati (Daftari) O.; children: Sanjay, Monica. MB, Christian Med. Coll., Ludhiana, India, 1961. Intern Binghamton (N.Y.) Gen. Hosp., 1962-63; resident U. Chgo., 1963-64, N.Y. U.-Bellevue Med Center, 1964-66, fellow in infectious diseases, 1966-68; asst. prof. pediatrics SUNY, Buffalo, 1968-71, assoc. prof. pediatrics and microbiology, 1972-74, prof., 1974-91; John Sealy disting. chair, prof. U. Tex. Med. Br., Galveston, 1991-2000, chmn. dept. pediatrics, 1991-99; prof. pediatrics Children's Hosp., Buffalo, 2000—. Dir. div. virology Children's Hosp. Buffalo, 1969-81, chief dept. infectious diseases, 1970-91; dir. Clin. Labs. Children's Hosp., 1985-90; mem. study sect. NIH, 1979-85, maternal child health com., 1987-91; mem., chmn. bd. Internat. Pediat. Rsch. Found., Inc., 1984-89, respiratory diseases steering com. WHO. Recipient E. Mead Johnson award for Pediatric Research Am. Acad. Pediatrics, 1978; Kalhana award Kashmir Sci. Culture and Soc., 1984; Stockton Kimball award SUNY, 1985; Buswell fellow, 1968-71. Fellow Royal Soc. Medicine, Assn. Am. Physicians, Am. Acad. Pediatrics, Am. Acad. Microbiology; mem. Am. Soc. Clin. Investigation, Soc. Pediatric Rsch., Infectious Disease Soc. Am., Soc. Exptl. Biology and Medicine, Am. Assn. Immunologists, Am. Soc. Microbiology, AAAS, Am. Fedn. Clin. Rsch., Reticuloendothelial Soc., Am. Soc. Virology. Home: 163 Troy Del Way Williamsville NY 14221-4505 Fax: 716-888-3804. E-mail: pogra@upa.chob.edu.

O'GRADY, BARBARA VINSON, community health nurse, administrator, retired; b. Alhambra, Calif., July 6, 1928; d. Weston Wright and Merdith Alyda (Noble) Vinson; m. Joseph Putnam O'Grady, Oct. 24, 1952; children: Joseph Jr., Jeffrey, Kent, Kimberly, Kathryn; m. John Mark Prebish, June 28, 1997. BS, UCLA, 1951; MS, U. Minn., 1972. Staff public health nurse San Diego Co. Health Dept., 1952; staff nurse U. Minn. Hosp., 1954-56; staff public health nurse Family Nursing Svc., St. Paul, 1972; asst. prof. Gustavus Adolphus Coll., St. Peter, Minn., 1972-77; dir. Ramsey County Public Health Nursing Svc., St. Paul, 1977-88; health staff Senator Dave Durenberger, Mpls., 1988; cons. pvt. practice, Waterville, Minn., 1989-97, ret., 1998. Mem. bd. govs. U. Minn. Hosp. and Clinic, Mpls., 1983-91, chair, 1985-87; clin. faculty Sch. Pub. Health, 1984-88. Author: (with others) Computer Applications in Medical Care, 1982, Nursing and Computers, 1989, NCNIP: Models for the Future of Nursing, 1989, Procs. of Impact of DRG's on Nursing Conf., 1988; mem. editl. bd. Jour. Cmty. Health Nursing, 1984-94. Mem. Mpls. Charter Commn., 1967-72; co-chair Minn. GOP Issues Devel., 1968, Minn. GOP Constn. Com., 1966-70; chair Dick Erdall Campaign Com., 1965-71; bd. dirs. Presbyn. Homes of Minn., St. Paul, 1982-88; bd. dirs. Living at Home/Block Nurse Program, 1986-98, chair external rels. com., 1988-98. Recipient Outstanding Contbn. Midwest Alliance in Nursing, 1984, Outstanding Achievement award Bd, of Ramsey County Commrs., 1987; Annie Yates scholar L.A. County General Hosp. Alumni Assn., 1948; Living At Home grantee The Commonwealth Fund, 1986. Fellow Am. Acad. of Nursing; mem. ANA, APHA, Nat. League for Nursing, Minn. Public Health Assn., Sigma Theta Tau. Republican. Presbyterian. Avocations: swimming, reading, traveling. Home: PO Box 624 Santa Ynez CA 93460-0624 E-mail: jb@syv.com.

O'GRADY, BEVERLY TROXLER, investment executive, counselor; d. Robert Andrew and Beverly Beam (Barrier) Troxler; m. Robert Edward O'Grady, Aug. 6, 1966. BA, St. Mary's Coll., 1963; MA, Columbia U., 1965. Exec. v.p. Wilkinson & Hottinger Inc., N.Y.C., 1973-94, Helvetia Capital Corp., N.Y.C., 1987-94; pres. Wilkinson O'Grady & Co., Inc., 1994—. Mem. adv. bd. Charles Schwab Fin., San Francisco, 1991-93. Active Women's Nat. Rep. Club, N.Y.C., 1991-94; trustee St. Mary's Coll., Notre Dame, Ind., 2002--. Mem. Assn. Investment Mgrs., N.Y. Soc. Security Analysts, Women's Bond Club (pres. 1992-94), Univ. Club. Roman Catholic. Office: Wilkinson O'Grady & Co Inc 520 Madison Ave New York NY 10022-4213

O'GRADY, DENNIS JOSEPH, lawyer; b. Hoboken, N.J., Nov. 16, 1943; s. Joseph A. and Eileen (Broderick) O'Grady; m. Mary Anne Amoruso, Sept. 9, 1966 (div. Apr. 1984); 1 child, Kara Anne. AB, Seton Hall Coll., 1965; MA, U. So. Calif., 1969; JD, Rutgers U., 1973. Bar: N.J. 1973, U.S. Ct. Appeals (3d cir.) 1975, U.S. Dist. Ct. N.J., U.S. Supreme Ct. 2000. Ptnr. Riker, Danzig, Scherer, Hyland & Perretti, Newark, Trenton and Morristown, N.J., 1974—. Adj. asst. prof. of bus. law St. Peter's Coll., Jersey City, 1973—; adj. prof. law Rutgers U. Law Sch., 1997—. Mem. ABA (bus./bankruptcy sect.), N.J. State Bar Assn. (debtor/creditor sect.), Fed. Bar Assn., Am. Bankruptcy Inst. (health car subcom., bd. profl. cert.), Am. Bd. Cert. (faculty subcom.). Democrat. Roman Catholic. Office: Riker Danzig Scherer Hyland & Perretti 1 Speedwell Ave Ste 2 Morristown NJ 07960-6823 E-mail: dogrady@riker.com.

O'GRADY, JOHN JOSEPH, III, lawyer; b. N.Y.C., Mar. 21, 1933; s. John Joseph and Terese (O'Rourke) O'G.; m. Mary E. McHugh, June 28, 1958; children— Glennon, Ellen, Carol, Paul AB, Holy Cross Coll., 1954; JD, Harvard U., 1957. Bar: N.Y. 1958. Assoc. Cadwalader, Wickersham & Taft, N.Y.C., 1958-66, ptnr., 1966-96, counsel, 1997—. Office: Cadwalader Wickersham & Taft 100 Maiden Ln New York NY 10038-4818

O'GRADY, MARY JOSEPHINE, editor, foundation consultant; b. Chgo., Sept. 25, 1951; d. Valentine Michael and Lillian Mary (Quinlan) O'Grady. Student, St. Mary's Coll., Rome, Italy, 1970-71; BFA, Manhattanville Coll., 1973; MA, Georgetown U., 1996. Assoc. editor Magnum Photos, N.Y.C., 1973-76; asst. picture editor Modern Photography Mag., 1976-78; freelance photographer, 1978-80; sr. producer Trans-Atlantic Enterprises, N.Y.C., L.A., 1981-82; dir. pub. info. World Wildlife Fund, Washington, 1983-84; sr. analyst Mead Data Cen., 1985-87; editor photos U.S. News and World Report, 1987-90; program dir. Sacharuna Found., 1990-92; adminstr. Roland Films, 1991-92; assoc. dir. AIDS Control and Prevention Project Family Health Internat., Washington, 1994-97, assoc. dir. Implementing AIDS Prevention and Care Project, 1998—2001. Cons. Time, Inc., N.Y.C., 1981, Exxon Corp., N.Y.C., 1981—82, U.S. News and World Report, Washington, 1987, The German Marshall Fund of U.S., Conservation Internat., Washington, 1992, W. Alton Jones Found., 1993—94, XIV Internat. Conf. on AIDS, 2002, Swedish Internat. Devel. Coop. Agy., 2002; spkr. in field. Prodr.(TV show): A Conversation With..., 1982, The Helen Gurley Brown Show, 1982, Outrageous Opinions, 1982. Recipient Editl. Excellence award, Natural Resources Coun. Am., 1984. Mem.: Internat. Bioethics Orgn. (trustee), Nat. Orgns. Responding to AIDS Internat. Issues Working Group, Monitoring the AIDS Pandemic Network, Worldwide Women in Environment and Devel., Soc. Environ. Journalists. E-mail: maryogrady@aol.com.

OGREAN, DAVID WILLIAM, sports executive; b. New Haven, Feb. 7, 1953; s. Richard Berton and Dorothy (Nystrom) O.; m. Maryellen Harvey, Aug. 10 1974; children: Matthew David, Tracy Erin, Dana Marie. BA in English cum laude, U Conn., 1974; MS in Film, Boston U., 1978. Asa S. Bushnell intern Ea. Coll. Athletic Conf., Centervill, Mass., 1977-78; pub. rels. dir. Amateur Hockey Assn. U.S., Colorado Springs, Colo., 1978-80; mng. editor Am. Hockey and Arena mag., 1979-80; comm. rep. ESPN, Inc., Bristol, Conn., 1980-83, program mgr., 1983-88; asst. exec. dir. for TV Coll. Football Assn., Boulder, Colo., 1988-90; dir. of broadcasting U.S. Olympic Com., Colorado Springs, 1990-93; exec. dir. USA Hockey, 1993-99; chmn. Colorado Springs Sports Corp., 1996-97; dep. exec. dir. mktg. U.S. Olympic Com., Colorado Springs, 1999-2000; pres., CEO Colorado Springs Sports Corp., 2000—. Chmn. legis. com. U.S. Olympic Com., 1997-99. Mem. Country Club Colo., Broadmoor Golf Club. Office: Colorado Springs Sports Corp 219 W Colorado Ave Colorado Springs CO 80903-3338

OGREN, ROBERT EDWARD, biologist, educator; b. Jamestown, N.Y., Feb. 9, 1922; s. David Paul and Mary Gladys (Ahlstrom) O.; m. Jean Blose Jackson, Aug. 28, 1948; children: Paul Robert, Philip Edward. BA, Wheaton Coll., 1947; MS, Northwestern U., 1948; PhD, U. Ill., 1953. Asst. prof. biology Ursinus Coll., Collegeville, Pa., 1953-57, Dickinson Coll., Carlisle, 1957-63; mem. faculty Wilkes Coll., Wilkes-Barre, 1963—, prof. biology, 1981-86, prof. emeritus, 1986—. Author: Meet the Pastors of First Presbyterian Church, Wilkes-Barre, 1770-1996, 1997, The First Presbyterian Church of Wilkes-Barre, Pennsylvania: History of the Sanctuary, Stained Glass Windows and Pipe Organs, 1996-1998, 1998. Bd. dirs. Northeastern Pa. chpt. Am. Heart Assn., 1971-88; chmn. bd. Northeastern Pa. chpt. Am. HeartAssn., 1973-76; bd. dirs. Wyo. Valley West Sch. Dis., 1973-79, pres., 1979. Served with AUS, 1943-46. Recipient Frank B. Shepela Meml. Vol. award Northeastern Pa. Heart Assn., 1977; NSF grantee, 1960, 63, 65 Fellow AAAS; mem. Am. Soc. Zoologists, Am. Soc. Parasitologists, Am. Micros. Soc., Soc. Protzoologists, Electron Micros. Soc. Am., Wyo. Commemorative Assn., Pa. Acad. Sci. (editor procs. 1961-62 Darbaker award 1989), N.Y. Acad. Sci., Ecol. Soc. Am., Western N.Y. Geneol. Soc., Wyo. Hist. and Geol. Soc., Sigma Xi (chpt. pres. 1981-82) Republican. Presbyterian. Home: 88 Lathrop St Kingston PA 18704-4811 Office: Wilkes Univ Dept Biology S Franklin St Wilkes Barre PA 18701-1201 E-mail: reogren@compuserve.com. *To be involved as a citizen in some aspect of community life. To use academe as an opportunity to prepare scholarly works for publication advancing knowledge in your discipline. To work beyond your limitations. To recognize opportunities and use them for making progress. To be positive, honest, creative and persevering. To enjoy the fruits of your labor and the freedom of expression and movement in our great land.*

OGRODNIK, LANA KATHLEEN, real estate broker; d. Alfred and Mary DeSimone; m. Gregory Walter Ogrodnik; children: Sharyn, Gregory Jr. Student, Tunxis C.C., Farmington, Conn., 1971-74; grad., Real Estate Career Inst., 1986, Realtor Inst., 1995; student, Charter Oak Coll., 1999. Real estate agt. Ferraro Realty, Waterbury, Conn., 1986-88; real estate broker, assoc. Advantage Realty Group, Inc., 1988-90, office mgr., 1990-96, real estate broker, affiliate, 1996—. Real estate commr. State Conn. Real Estate Commn., Hartford, 1998—; chmn. legis. and polit. affairs Greater Waterbury Bd. Realtors, 1996-98, co-chmn. housing needs, 1996-99, chairperson foreclosure prevention, 1996-99; mem. state legis. com. Conn. Assn. Realtors, East Hartford, 1997-98; instr. First Time Homebuyers, 1999—. Commr. bd. agts. Silas Bronson Libr., Waterbury, 1996—; commr. Bd. Voter Admissions, Waterbury, 1996-2000; bd. dirs. East End Cmty. Club, Waterbury, 1995—; commr. Waterbury Human Rights Commn., 2000—. Republican. Office: Advantage Realty Group Inc 131 Homer St Waterbury CT 06704-1728 Fax: 203-753-5642. E-mail: ogrodnik4@aol.com.

OGUL, MORRIS SAMUEL, political science educator, consultant; b. Detroit, Apr. 15, 1931; s. Jack and Sarah (Zimmerman) O.; m. Eleanor Simon, Aug. 26, 1954. BA, Wayne State U., 1952; MA, U. Mich., 1953, PhD, 1958. Instr.. polit. sci. U. Pitts., 1957-59, asst. prof., 1959-64, assoc. prof., 1964-67, prof., 1967-98, prof. emeritus, 1998—. Cons. U.S. Ho. of Reps., 1973, 83, U.S. Office Personnel Mgmt., Washington, 1975— , U.S. Senate, 1977 Author: (with William J. Keefe) American Legislative Process, 1964, 7th edit., 1989, 8th edit., 1993, 9th edit., 1997, 10th edit., 2001, Congress Oversees the Bureaucracy, 1976. Carnegie Corp. research grantee, 1965-68 Mem. Am. Polit. Sci. Assn., Midwest Polit. Sci. Assn. (council 1982-84), Pa. Polit. Sci. Assn. Democrat. Home: 1500 Cochran Rd Apt 814 Pittsburgh PA 15243-1068 Office: U Pitts Dept Polit Sci 4N24 Forbes Quadrangle Pittsburgh PA 15260-7454

OGULNICK, KAREN LEE, education educator; b. N.Y.C., Dec. 15, 1960; d. Ozzie and Linda O. BS, Plattsburgh (N.Y.) State U., 1982; MA, Hunter Coll., 1987; PhD, NYU, 1995. Tchr. spl. edn. N.Y.C. Bd. of Edn., 1982-85; tchr. English Japanese Ministry of Edn., Fukui, Japan, 1985-87; instr. ESL NYU, Hunter Coll., LaGuardia C.C., 1987-89; English lectr. So. Ill. U., Niigata, Japan, 1989-90; lectr. English Lehman-Hiroshim (Japan) Coll., 1993; asst. prof. L.I. U., Brookville, N.Y., 1995—. Author: Onna Rashiku (Like a Woman): The Diary of a Language Learner in Japan, 1998; editor: Language Crossings: Negotiating the Self in a Multicultural World, 2000; contbr. articles to profl. publs. Mombusho fellowship Japanese Ministry of Edn., 1985-87; Bilingual Edn. Enhancement grant N.Y.S. Dept. Edn., 1998; Fulbright scholar, Mex., 2002—. Avocations: travel, language learning. Home: 219 East 85th St New York NY 10028 Office: LI U CW Post Northern Blvd Locust Valley NY 11560 E-mail: kogulnic@liu.edu.

OGUNYEMI, YEMI DIPLOMAN, literary philosopher; b. Lagos, Nigeria, Mar. 21, 1950; came to U.S. s. Reuben Ojagbuwa and Matilda A. (Ikuemonisan) Ogunyemi; m. Maria Magdelena Szuts, Mar. 11, 1955; children: Godwin Akintunde, Michael Olukayode, Daniel Adelowale, Julia Bosede;1 child Katharina Omyemi. MA, Webster U., 1982; PhD, Clayton U., 1986, Lajos Kosuth U., Hungary, 1993; DLitt, Avadh U., Faizabad, India, 1994. Assoc. rsch. fellow Harvard U., Cambridge, 1994-95; dir. Inst. of Creative Writing, Vienna, 1983-93, Devel. News, Vienna, Austria, 1983—, Diaspora Press of Am., 1995—, Inst. of Yoruba/African Nar., Philipines, 2000—. Dir. Writers Without Borders, 2000—; cons. Lobbyists for Pvt. U. Nigeria, 1990—; dir. Movement for the Moderinization of Yoruba Rels., 1998—. Author: Love from Nigeria, 1990 (Golden Trophy), The Political Philosophy of Wole Solinka and Other Narratives; author/editor: The African Soul, 1987 (Amb. of Hope 1987). Mem. Yoruba Cmty. of Mass., Boston, 1995, The New Poetry Club, Boston, 1995, Boston Pan African Forum, Boston, 1995. Fellow The Boston Writers Room. Avocations: jogging, tennis, swimming, piano-playing, reading. Office: Inst Yoruba/African Narrative Philoshies PO Box 200981 Boston MA 02120-0018 E-mail: princeyemi36@hotmail.com.

OH, JOHN KIE-CHIANG, political science educator, university official; b. Seoul, Korea, Nov. 1, 1930; came to U.S., 1954, naturalized, 1971; s. Sung-Jun and Duk-Cho (Kim) O.; m. Bonnie Cho, Sept. 5, 1959; children: Jane J., Marie J., James J. BS, Marquette U., 1957; postgrad., Columbia U., 1957-58; PhD, Georgetown U., 1962. Asst. prof. St. Thomas Coll., St. Paul, 1962-66; assoc. prof. polit. sci. Marquette U., Milw., 1967-71, prof., chmn., 1971-77, dean grad. sch., 1977-85; acad. v.p. Cath. U. Am., Washington, 1985-89, Banigan scholar, prof. dept. politics, 1990-2001, prof. emeritus, 2001—. Author: Korea: Democracy on Trial, 1968, (with Peter Cheng et. al.) Emerging Roles of Asian Nations in the 1980's, 1979, Democratization and Economic Development in Korea, 1990, Korean Politics: The Quest for Democratization and Economic Development, 1999; contbr. articles to profl. jours. Chmn. scholarship com. World Affairs Council, 1976-78; mem. Wis. Gov.'s Commn. for UN, Madison, 1971-74; chmn. Korean Studies com., Assn. Asian Studies, 1975-76. Grantee Hill Found., 1963, Relm Found., 1968, Social Sci. Rsch Coun., 1973, Am. Coun. Learned Socs., 1973. Mem. Am. Polit. Sci. Assn., Assn. Asian Studies, Internat. Polit. Sci. Assn., Midwest Conf. Assn. Affairs (pres. 1970-71, nat. chmn. Asian sect.) Fulbright Hays Program, Assn. Cath. Colls. and Univs. (bd. dirs. 1983-87), Indian Spring Country Club (bd. govs. 2000—), adv. Republic of Korea Embassy, 2001-. Roman Catholic. Home: 8807 Maxwell Dr Potomac MD 20854-3123 E-mail: JNBOH@aol.com.

OH, KONGDAN, international policy analyst, consultant; b. Jechon, Korea, July 4, 1949; came to U.S., 1979; d. Chung Do Oh and Mi Ryo Park; m. Ralph Charles Hassig, Nov. 14, 1981. BA, Sogang U., Seoul, South Korea, 1971; MA, Seoul Nat. U., 1974, U. Calif., Berkeley, 1981, PhD, 1986. Acad. program coord. Ctr. for Korean Studies U. Calif., Berkeley, 1986-87; polit. scientist RAND, Santa Monica, Calif., 1987-95; co-prin. Oh & Hassig Pacific Rim cons., Falls Church, Va., 1995-97; mem. rsch. staff Inst. for Def. Analyses, Alexandria, 1997—. Cons. Lawrence Livermore (Calif.) Nat. Lab., 1995-97; lectr. George Mason U., Arlington, Va., 1997—; non-resident sr. fellow Brookings Instn., Washington, 1997—; mem. com. Coun. for Security Coop. in Asia-Pacific. Author: (with Ralph C. Hassig) North Korea through the Looking Glass, 2000; co-editor: Korea Briefing 2000-2001: First Steps Toward Reconciliation and Reunification, 2002; contbr. more than 50 articles to profl. publs. Bd. dirs. Women's Orgn. Reaching Koreans, L.A., 1992-95; mem. Rep. of Korea Presdl. Commn. for a Peaceful Unification of Korea, L.A., 1993-95. Chancellor's Disting. Dissertation fellow U. Calif., Berkeley, 1984-85; book grantee Smith Richardson Found., 1997. Mem. Coun. Fgn. Rels. (life), Pacific Basin Coun., Women in Internat. Security, Coun. U.S.-Korea Security Studies, Korea club (co-founder, co-dir. 1996—). Avocations: snorkeling, scuba diving, swimming, singing, foreign languages. Office: Inst Def Analyses 4850 Mark Ctr Dr Alexandria VA 22311-1882 Fax: 703-845-6650. E-mail: kohassig@ida.org.

OH, MICHAEL YOUNG-SUK, PhD student & researcher, minister & theological seminary president; b. Philadelphia, PA, Apr. 19, 1971; s. Sung Kyu Henry Oh, Young Ie Lee; m. Pearl Kyung Park; children: Hannah. PhD, University of Pennsylvania, Philadelphia, PA, 2005; Master of Arts, Harvard University, Cambridge, MA, 1999—2001; Master of Divinity, Trinity Evangelical Divinity School, Deerfield, IL, 1995—97; Master of Science, University of Pennsylvania, Philadelphia, PA, 1992—93, Bachelor of Arts, 1989—92. Minister Korean United Church of Philadelphia, Philadelphia, PA, 2001—02; Kellogg Penn-Drew Program Coordinator/Researcher University of Pennsylvania, 2001—02; President Nagoya Theological Seminary (NTS inception 2004), Nagoya, Japan, 2001—10; Minister Chita Zion Presbyterian Church, Japan, 1998—99; Director & Teacher Open House English School, Nisshin, Japan, 1998—99; History Teacher Cheltenham School District, Wyncote, 1993—95; US-Japan Center Research Assistant Harvard University, Cambridge, MA, 1999—2000. President TMF, Deerfield, IL, 1996—97; Director Global Ministries Institute, Deerfield, IL, 1996—97. Founder / Board Member Young Republicans - CHS, Berwyn, PA, 1988—89; Volunteer Republican National Committee, Philadelphia, 1988—88. Mem.: American Anthropology Association. Christian. Home: 1820 South Broad Street, 2nd Floor Philadelphia PA 19145 Personal E-mail: ohfamily@post.harvard.edu.

OH, TAI KEUN, business educator; b. Seoul, Korea, Mar. 25, 1934; s. Chin Young and Eui Kyung (Yun) O.; came to U.S., 1958, naturalized, 1969; B.A., Seijo U., 1957; M.A., No. Ill. U., 1961; M.L.S., U. Wis., 1965, Ph.D., 1970; m. Gretchen Brenneke, Dec. 26, 1964; children: Erica, Elizabeth, Emily. Asst. prof. mgmt. Roosevelt U., Chgo., 1969-73; assoc. prof. Calif. State U., Fullerton, 1973-76, prof. mgmt., 1976— ; vis. prof. U. Hawaii, 1983-84, 86; advisor Pacific Asian Mgmt. Inst., U. Hawaii; internat. referee Asia-Pacific Jour. of Mgmt., 1990—; cons. Calty Design Research, Inc. subs. Toyota Motor Corp. The Employers Group; seminar leader and speaker. Named Outstanding Prof., Sch. Bus. Adminstrn. and Econs., Calif. State U., Fullerton, 1976, 78. NSF grantee, 1968-69, recipient Exceptional Merit Service award Calif. State U., 1984, Meritorious Performance and Profl. Promise award Calif. State U., 1987. Mem. Acad. Mgmt., Indsl. Relations Research Assn., Acad. Internat. Bus. Editorial bd. Acad. Mgmt. Rev., 1978-81; contbg. author: Ency. Profl. Mgmt., 1978, Handbook of Management 1985; contbr. articles to profl. jours. Home: 2044 E Eucalyptus Ln Brea CA 92821-5911

OH, WILLIAM, physician; b. The Philippines, May 22, 1931; came to U.S., 1958, naturalized, 1970; s. Bun Kun and Chay Suat (Lim) O.; m. Mary Oh, June 4, 1960; children— Kenneth Albert, Kerstin Amy. MD, U. Santo Tomas, Phillipines, 1958; MA (hon.), Brown U., 1974; DSc (hon.) , R.I. Coll., 1985. Diplomate Am. Bd. Pediatrics, Am. Bd. Neonatal Perinatal Medicine. Intern Deaconess Hosp., Milw., 1958-59; resident in pediatrics Michael Reese Hosp., Chgo., 1959-63; fellow in neonatology Kavolinska Inst., Stockholm, 1963-65; dir. neonatology Michael Reese Hosp., Chgo., 1965-69; dir. neonatology, assoc. prof. pediatrics UCLA, 1969-73, prof., 1973-74; prof. pediatrics and obstetrics Brown U., Providence, 1974-88, Sylvia Kay Hassenfeld prof. pediatrics, chmn. dept., 1989—; pediatrician-in-chief Women and Infants Hosp. of R.I., 1974—89, R.I. Hosp.; prof., chmn. dept. pediatrics Brown U., 1989—. Mem. NIH study sect. on human embryology and devel., chmn., 1985—; mem. pediatric test com. Bd. Med. Exam., 1985-89; mem. sub-bd. of neonatal-perinatal medicine Am. Bd. Pediatrics, 1982-88; chair com. on Fetus and Newborn, Am. Acad. Pediatrics; mem. Nat. Adv. Coun. for Child Health, 1995-99. Author book in field; contbr. chpts. to books, numerous articles to profl. jours.; editor profl. jour. Adv. com. Nat. Found. of March of Dimes. NIH grantee. Mem. Am. Pediatric Soc., Am. Acad. Pediatrics (fetus and newborn com. 1986-90), Soc. Pediatric Research, Perinatal Research Soc. (pres. 1981), Am. Inst. Nutrition, Fedn. Am. Socs. Exptl. Biology. Clubs: University. Roman Catholic. Home: 24 Robbins Dr Barrington RI 02806-2612 Office: 593 Eddy St Providence RI 02903-4923 E-mail: woh@lifespan.org.

O'HAGAN, JAMES JOSEPH, lawyer; b. Chgo., Dec. 29, 1936; s. Francis James and Florence Agnes (Dowgialo) O'H.; m. Suzanne Elizabeth Wiegand, June 28, 1958; children: Timothy, Karen, Peggy, Kevin. B in Commerce, De Paul U., 1958, JD, 1962. Sr. ptnr. O'Hagan, Smith & Amundsen, Chgo., 1997—. Mem. Cook County Pres.'s Com. on the Cts. for the 21st Century, chmn. suburban subcom., 1998—2000; lawyer Chgo. Claim Mgrs. Assn., 1992—; chmn. USLaw Network, Inc., 2001—. Mem. ABA, Ill. Bar Assn. Chgo. Bar Assn., Internat. Assn. Def. Coun., Def. Rsch. Inst., Profl. Liability Underwriters Soc., Trial Lawyers Club. Roman Catholic. Avocations: golf, tennis, physical conditioning, painting, reading. Office: O'Hagan Smith & Amundsen 150 N Michigan Ave Chicago IL 60601-7553 E-mail: johagan@osalaw.com.

O'HAGAN, WILLIAM GORDON, state agency administrator; b. Allentown, N.J., Oct. 12, 1943; s. Forrest Allen and Voncile Arline (Linton) O'H.; m. Marcia Helen Beck, Aug. 12, 1947 (div. Oct. 1985). Grad. high sch., Azusa, Calif., 1962. Owner Richfield Oil Co., Baldwin Park, Calif., 1970-72; mgr. Am. Teaching Aids, Covina, 1972-88; owner Bill's Auto Repair Co., 1988-93; mechanic, 1993-99; supr., foreman Pub. Auction Agy. Calif., 1996—. Mobile automobile mechanic, 2000—. Block commander Neighborhood Watch, Covina. Republican. Baptist. Home and Office: 163 N Marcile Ave Glendora CA 91741-2453 *Personal philosophy: The clock of life is wound but once - don't wait until tommorrow for the hands may be still.*

O'HAGEN, NICOLE MCCAULEY, marketing professional; b. Plainfield, N.J., Nov. 7, 1973; d. Nicholas Patrick and Elizabeth Anne McCauley O'Hagen. BA, Salve Regina U., 1996, MBA, 1997. Ecommerce analyst BankBoston, Providence, 1994—97; bus. sys. analyst MetLife, N.Y.C., 1997—99; dir. mktg. Imagitas, Inc., Waltham, Mass., 1999—. Mem.: USTA, N.Y. Jr. League, Jr. League Boston. Home: 253 Pierce St South Plainfield NJ 07080 Office: Imagitas Inc 48 Woerd Ave Waltham MA 02453 Personal E-mail: nicoleohagen@hotmail.com. E-mail: ohagenn@imagitas.com.

O'HALLERAN, MICHAEL D. insurance company executive; m. Kay; children: Meghan, Connor. Degree in acctg. and fin., U. Wis., Whitewater. Sr. exec. Wausau Ins. Cos., Gen. Reins., Alexander Re; sr. operating positions Aon Corp., Chgo., 1987, pres., COO; also bd. dirs. Bd. dirs. Cardinal Health, Inc., Optimark Techs., Inc.; COO Aon Group Inc. Dir. Spl. Children's Charities, Providence-St. Mel High Sch., Angus Robinson, Jr. Meml. Found.; mem. arts and letters adv. bd. U. Notre Dame; trustee Dublin City U., Ireland, dir. Coll. Ins. Mem. Econ. Club Chgo., Young Pres.'s Orgn. Office: Aon Corp 123 N Wacker Dr Chicago IL 60606-1700

O'HALLORAN, THOMAS ALPHONSUS, JR. physicist, educator; b. Bklyn., Apr. 13, 1931; s. Thomas Alphonsus Sr. and Nora (Sheehan) O'H.; m. Barbara Joyce Hug, June 4, 1954; children: Theresa Joyce, Maureen Ann, Kevin Thomas, Patrick Joseph. Student, San Jose State U., 1948-50; BS in Physics & Math., Oreg. State U., 1953, MS in Physics, 1954; PhD, U. Calif., Berkeley, 1963. Rsch. asst. Lawrence Berkeley Lab., U. Calif., 1963-64; rsch. fellow Harvard U., Cambridge, Mass., 1964-66; asst. prof. physics U. Ill., Urbana, 1966-68, assoc. prof., 1968-70, prof., 1970-93, prof. emeritus, 1993—; vis. scholar U. Utah, Salt Lake City, 1990-93, rsch. prof. physics, 1993-97. Mem. program adv. com. Argonne Nat. Lab., Lemont, Ill., Fermi Lab., Batavia, Ill., Brookhaven Nat. Lab., Upton, L.I.; vis. scientist Lawrence Berkeley Lab., U. Calif., 1979-80. Contbr. numerous articles on elem. particle physics to profl. jours. Lt. USN, 1954-58. Guggenheim fellow, 1979-80. Fellow Am. Phys. Soc. Home: 4614 Ledgemont Dr Salt Lake City UT 84124-4735 E-mail: toh-boh@worldnet.att.net.

O'HANDLEY, DOUGLAS ALEXANDER, astronomer; b. Detroit, May 7, 1937; s. Malcolm Joseph and Georgie Roberta (MacPherson) O'Handley; m. Christine Jeannete Stube, July 20, 1991; 1 child Douglas Alexander. AB, U. Mich., 1960; MS, Yale U., 1964, PhD, 1967. Astronomer U.S. Naval Obs., Washington, 1960-67; scientist Jet Propulsion Lab., Pasadena, Calif., 1967-85; dir. space station Ames Rsch. Ctr., Moffett Field, 1984-86; mgr. TRW Space Tech. Group, Redondo Beach, 1986-88; dep. asst. adminstr. office exploration NASA, Washington, 1988-92; dir. astrobiology acad. Ames Rsch. Ctr., Moffett Field, 1992—, ret., 1999. Chmn. com. for protection of human subjects in med. rsch., 1982—85; lectr. grad. sch. Georgetown U., Washington, 1964—67; adj. prof. physics Santa Clara U., Calif., 1997—; spkr. in field; v.p. Sci. and Tech. Corp., Hampton, Va., 2001—. Contbr. Extraordinary min. Resurrection Cath. Ch.; bd. dirs. Big Bros. Fellow: AAS, ASMA, AIAA (assoc.), Royal Soc. Medicine; mem.: Internat. Acad. Astronautics, Internat. Astron. Union. Home: 1580 Grackle Way Sunnyvale CA 94087-4715

O'HANDLEY, JOHN G. physician; b. Seattle, Nov. 2, 1940; s. John Grenville and Marie Elizabeth (Schermerhorn) O'H.; m. Hannah Jane Ryan, Mar. 9, 1974; children: Kathleen M., John R., Brendan J., Amy E. BA, St. Louis U., 1968; MD, U. Mo., 1972. Intern St. John's Mercy Med. Ctr., St. Louis, 1972-73, resident in family practice, 1973-75; pvt. practice Lancaster, Ohio, 1975-89; chief of staff Lancaster Fairfield Hosp., 1984; mem. faculty Bethesda Hosp., Cin., 1989-95; residency dir. Bethesda Family Practice Residency, 1992-95; program dir. Mt. Carmel Family Practice Residency, Columbus, 1995—2001; med. dir. Mt. Carmel Outreach, 2001—; clin. assoc. prof. dept. family medicine Ohio State Coll. Medicine, 1997—. Contbr. chpts. to books, articles to profl. jours. Chmn. bd. Red Cross of Fairfield County, Ohio, 1985. Mem. Am. Acad. Family Physicians, Ctrl. Ohio Acad. Family Practice (past pres.), Ohio Acad. Family Practice, Soc. Tchrs. Family Medicine. Republican. Roman Catholic. Avocations: tennis, flying, reading. Home: 4161 Goldenseal Way Hilliard OH 43026-3007 Office: Mt Carmel Family Practice 1335 Dublin Rd Columbus OH 43215-1000 E-mail: johandley@mchs.com.

OHANIAN, LEE EDWARD, economist, educator, consultant; b. L.A., Feb. 24, 1957; s. Edward and Martha Loraine (Taylor) O.; m. Nancy Frances Kane, May 28, 1988. BA, U. Calif., Santa Barbara, 1979, MA, 1982; PhD, U. Rochester, 1993. Sr. analyst Continental Airlines, L.A., 1981-82; v.p. Security Pacific Bank, 1982-88; pvt. practice, 1990—; asst. prof. econs. U. Pa., Phila., 1992-95; assoc. prof. econs. U. Minn., Mpls., 1995-99; prof. econs. UCLA, 1999—. Cons. FRS, 1992—. Contbr. articles to profl. jours. W. Allen Wallis fellow U. Rochester, 1988—, fellow Nat. Inst. on Aging, 1983-84, Alfred P. Sloan fellow, 1999-2001. Office: 405 Hilgard Ave Los Angeles CA 90095-9000 E-mail: ohanian@econ.ucla.edu.

OHANIAN, MIHRAN JACOB, nuclear engineering educator, research dean; b. Istanbul, Turkey, Aug. 7, 1933; came to U.S., 1956, naturalized, 1967; s. Mark and Mary Catherine (Sayabalian) O.; m. Sandra Jean Blair, Apr. 22, 1962; children: Heather Jean Allen, Holly Lynn Welty. BSE.E. with high honors, Robert Coll. Engring. Sch., Istanbul, 1956; M.E.E., Rensselaer Poly. Inst., 1960, PhD in Nuclear Engring. and Sci., 1963. Lectr. nuclear engring. Rensselaer Poly. Inst., 1963, instr., 1958-62; asst. prof. nuclear engring. U. Fla., Gainesville, 1964-67, assoc. prof., 1967-70, prof., 1970-2001, prof. emeritus, 2001—; chmn. dept., 1969-79, assoc. dir. Engring. and Indsl. Expt. Sta., 1977-99, assoc. dean for rsch., 1979-90, assoc. dean for adminstrn. and planning, 1990-91, assoc. dean for rsch. and adminstrn., 1991-98, interim v.p. rsch., dean of grad. sch., 1998-99, pres. Rsch. Found., 1998-99, interim dean Coll. of Engr., assoc. v.p. Engring. and Indsl. Experiment Station, 1999-2001; sabbatical leave Inst. Energy Analysis, Oak Ridge, 1976-77, on assignment, 1977-78. Cons. Fla. Power Corp., Batelle Meml. Inst., Fla. Nuclear Assos., Oak Ridge Nat. Lab., Inst. Energy Analysis, Argonne Nat. Lab., Savannah River Lab., U. Va., Tex. Higher Edn. Bd., NSF; U. Fla. rep. U.S. Nuc. Energy Inst., 1972-2001, mem. adv. coun., 1972-80; U. Fla. rep. to Oak Ridge Assoc. Univs., 1972-76; mem. engring. accreditation commn. Accreditation Bd. Engring. and Tech., 1984-88; mem. rev. com. reactor analysis and safety divsn. Argonne Nat. Lab, 1982-88, chmn. 1986-87, mem. rev. com. reactor engring. divsn., 1992-2001; mem. adv. com. Consol. Fuel Reprocessing Program Oak Ridge Nat. Lab., 1982-88; mem. com. on univ. research reactors Energy Engring. Bd., NRC, 1986-88; mem. U.S. Dept. Energy's Adv. Com. on Nuclear Facility Safety (ACNFS), 1988-90; bd. dirs., chmn. Fla. Inst. Phosphate Rsch., 1990-2001. Contbr. articles to profl. jours. Trustee Fla. Defenders of the Environment, 1969-71, treas., 1969-70, mem., 1969—. Recipient valor medal Am. Legion, 1966, Disting. Faculty award Fla. Blue Key, 1984; Alumnus fellow Rensselaer Poly. Inst., 1994. Fellow AAAS, Am. Nuclear Soc. (v.p., pres.-elect 1989-90, pres. 1990-91, bd. dirs. 1974-77, 84-93, vice chmn., chmn. edn. divsn. 1975-76, exec. com. nuclear fuel cycle divsn. 1978-81, mem. profl. devel. and accreditation com., chmn. tech. program of internat. conf. Washington, 1980, mem. nominating com., 1980-81, 87-88, chmn., 1991-92, exec. com., 1986-92, honors and awards com. 1997-2002, Exceptional Svc. award 1980, adv. editor Nuclear Sci. and Engring. Jour. 1989-2002, hon. chmn. ann. conf. 1997), Engrs.'s Coun. Profl. Devel. (dir. 1976-78), Am. Assn. Engring. Socs. (awards com. 1985-86, bd. dirs. 1990-91, exec. com. 1990-95, sec.-treas., 1992, chair-elect 1993, chair 1994, chair nominating com. 1995, chair awards com. 1996), Am. Soc. Engring. Edn. (adv. com. Ford Found. Resident Fellow Program 1971-79, sec.-treas. nuclear engring. divsn. 1981-82, vice chmn. 1982-83, chmn. 1983-84, projects bd. 1981-87, chmn. awards com. 1985-87; mem. Nat. Audubon Soc. (pres. 1965-66), Sigma Xi, Tau Beta Pi (eminent engr.), Alpha Nu Sigma (pres. 1981-83), Eta Kappa Nu, Phi Kappa Phi, Epsilon Lambda Chi, Rotary (Paul Harris fellow). Presbyterian. Home: 6095 Twin Lakes Rd Keystone Heights FL 32656-9728 E-mail: johanian@ufl.edu.

O'HANLON, RICHARD THOMAS, counseling educator; b. Chichester, Eng., Dec. 16, 1956; came to U.S., 1957; s. Thomas Joseph and Agnes Cecilia (Mahoney) O'H. BA in Philosophy, St. Hyacinth Coll., 1974; MS in Pastoral Counseling, Loyola Coll., 1987, cert. in advanced studies, 1988. Tchr. St. Francis H.S., Athol Springs, N.Y., 1974-82, Archbishop Curley H.S., Balt., 1982-84; editor Franciscan Press, 1984-90; counselor Lighthouse, Catonsville, 1986-87, County of Balt., 1987-88, Human Life Internat., Gaithersburg, Md., 1990-91; prof. Washington Theol. Union, 1990-98; eap Bank of Am., 1998—. Dir. Franciscan Bros., Balt., 1985-88; treas. Cupertino Franciscans, Ellicott City, Md., 1988-97; pres. Continuing Edn. Commn., Balt., 1991-94. Named Citizen of the Yr., Union League, 1969. Mem. ACA, APA, Am. Assn. Christian Counselors, Am. Psychol. Soc., Md. Assn. Counseling and Devel., Md. Assn. for Religious and Value Issues in Counseling, Assn. for Religious and Value Issues in Counseling. Avocation: dramatics. Office: Bank of Am 4401 Coastal Hwy Ocean City MD 21842-6800 Home: 119 133rd St Ocean City MD 21842-4503

OHANNESSIAN, HARRY HAROUTUNE, travel agency executive; b. Jerusalem, Jan. 5, 1919; s. Ohannes and Heripsimeh (Soultanian) C.; m. Eva Hamparsoumian, July 7, 1946 (div. Mar. 1978); children: John, Robert; m. Beatriz Araujo, Dec. 19, 1984. Matriculation, Brit. Govt., 1938; grad., London Sch. of Maths., 1940, London Sch. of Econ. Scis., 1942. Pres. Cedars Travel, Inc., N.Y.C., 1963-88; chmn. Wataniyah Corp., 1973-88; v.p. U.S.-Arab C. of C., 1973-88; internat. commerce and bus. cons. to the middle east. Stony Brook, N.Y., 1989—. Cons. in field. Decorated Knight (Order of St. John). Mem. St. George's Golf and Country Club, Stony Brook Club. Republican. Mem. Christian Ch. Avocations: tennis, swimming, gardening, music. Home: 9 Hillside Rd Stony Brook NY 11790-1002 Office: PO Box 120 Stony Brook NY 11790-0120

O'HARA, CYNTHIA O'CONNOR, writer, columnist, food consultant; b. New Hartford, N.Y., Sept. 17, 1963; d. Miles Joseph and Janice Louise O'Connor; m. Michael Timothy O'Hara, June 17, 1989; children: Colleen Meghan, Kelly O'Connor. Grad., Utica Sch. Commerce, 1984. Culinary instr. Bd. of Coop. Ednl. Svcs., New Hartford, 1996—; newspaper columnist Observer-Dispatch (Gannett News Svc.), Utica, N.Y., 1997—; TV personality numerous TV stas., 1997—. Spkr. N.Y.C. pub. librs., orgns., bus.; food demonstrator various stores, N.Y.C. Author: The Harried Housewife's Cookbooks, 1997; contbr. articles to mags. Leader Girl Scouts Am., Utica, N.Y., 1996-97. Mem. Internat. Assn. Culinary Profls., Mohawk Valley Businesswomen's Network. Roman Catholic. Avocations: cooking, gardening, reading. Office: The Harried Housewife PO Box 16 Whitesboro NY 13492-0016 Fax: 315-768-2714. E-mail: harried@borg.com.

O'HARA, DAVID OAKES, software developer; b. Stamford, Conn., Nov. 12, 1950; s. Charles Edward and Theodora (Oakes) O'H.; m. Janet Livingston McIlvain, May 15, 1976; children: Elizabeth, Caroline. BS, Brown U., 1973; MBA, Babson Coll., 1983. Asst. dir. steel services Data Resources Inc., Lexington, Mass., 1973-82, dir. development personal computers, 1983-85; prod. mgr. EPS McGraw-Hill, Inc., 1986—. Mem. Nat. Assn. Bus. Economists, Tau Beta Pi. Clubs: Myopia Hunt (Hamilton, Mass.). Avocations: sailing, golf, restoring old cars. Office: Data Resources 24 Hartwell Ave Lexington MA 02421-3103

O'HARA, DELIA IGLAUER, family nurse practitioner; b. Cin., Feb. 5, 1942; d. Arnold and Virginia (Dunn) Iglauer; children: Robert, Matthew, William; m. Herbert G. Johnson, Sept. 23, 2000. BS, Simmons Coll., 1965; Cert. Nurse Practitioner, George Washington U., 1975; JD, Howard U., 1987. Bar: D.C.; cert. family nurse practitioner. Dir. home care program for cancer patients George Washington U. Med. Ctr., 1975-79; occupational health nurse practitioner Libr. of Congress, Washington, 1979-84; lawyer FTC, 1987-89; dir. student health svcs. Presdl. Classroom for Young Ams., 1987-98; health svcs. mgr. Time-Life Books, Inc., Alexandria, Va., 1990-92; pvt. practice law Washington, 1990-99; occupational health nurse practitioner Washington Hosp. Ctr., 1993-96, nurse practitioner Admissions Testing Ctr., 1996-98; nurse practitioner dept. pre-surgery Kaiser Permanente Med. Ctr., Oakland, Calif., 1998—. Chmn. D.C. Home Care Task Force; vol. Winterhaven Shelter for Homeless Women; mem. Bd. Nursing, Washington; vestrywoman St. John's Episcopal Ch., Montclair, 1999—2001, mentor edn. ministry, 2001—. Recipient Trustee's scholarship Howard U. Fellow Am. Acad. Nurse Practitioners (bd. dirs. region 3 rep. 1991-94, rec. sec. 1994-96, treas. 1996-97), Am. Acad. Nurse Practitioners Found. (bd. dirs. 1996—, pres. 2001), Nurse Practitioner Assn. of D.C. (pres. 1992-95), Capitol Area Network of Nurse Attys. (v.p. 1992-93), Simmons Coll. Alumnae Assn. (class sec. Class of 1964, 1989-94). Home: 2525 Alida St Oakland CA 94602-2503 Office: Kaiser Permanente Med Ctr 280 W Macarthur Blvd Oakland CA 94611-5642 E-mail: oaklandelia@yahoo.com.

O'HARA, DORENE ANNE, anesthesiologist; b. Hollis, N.Y., Aug. 1, 1957; d. William Peter O'Hara and Ann Yolanda Vass; m. David Richard Marsh, May 4, 1984; children: Diana E. Marsh, Christina C. Marsh. BS in Biophysics, BA in English, U. Conn., 1979; MD, Harvard U., 1983; MSE in Bioengring., U. Pa., 1990. Diplomate Am. Bd. Anesthesiology. Rsch. fellow Northwestern U., Chgo., 1984—85, UMDNJ, Newark, 1985—86; instr., asst. prof. anesthesia U. Pa., Phila., 1988—90; asst. prof. anesthesia Robert Wood Johnson Med. Sch., New Brunswick, NJ, 1990—96; med. dir. Becton Dickinson Corp., Franklin Lakes, 1997; assoc. prof. anesthesiologist N.Y. Med. Coll., Valhalla, 1998—2001; anesthesiologist Judah Schorr, P.C., N.Y.C., 2001—. Dir. Pain Clinic Robert W. Johnson Med. Sch., New Brunswick, 1991—92, N.Y. Med. Coll.-Met. Hosp., N.Y.C., 1998—2001; adj. assoc. prof. engring. Rutgers U., Piscataway, NJ, 1996—2001; reviewer grants in engring. NIH, Rockville, Md., 1996. Author: Heal the Pain, Comfort the Spirit, 2002; contbr. chapters to books. Mem. physicians' adv. bd. Nat. Rep. Party, Washington, 2001. Named hon. cons., Oxford (Eng.) U. Anaesthetics, 2000, invited panelist anesthesia, Post Grad. Assn. N.Y., 2001; recipient third prize anesthesia, Midwest Austin Conf., Mpls., 1986. Mem.: N.J. Soc. Anesthesiologists, Internat. Anesthesia Rsch. Soc., Am. Soc. Anesthesiologists. Achievements include research in pivotal clinical trial of new drug Ketorolac (Toradol) for FDA approval; published critical review of computer-controlled drug delivery. Avocations: choral singing, gardening, walking, swimming, embroidery. Office: 385 Main St #5 Metuchen NJ 08840

O'HARA, JOHN PATRICK, lawyer, accountant; b. N.Y.C., Jan. 11, 1930; s. Thomas James and Anne (Henry) O'H.; m. Mary Ann Leavey, Oct. 15, 1955; children: Ann O'Hara Carroll, Kathleen O'Hara Geary, Maureen O'Hara-Padden. BBA, St. John's U., N.Y.C., 1952; JD, U. Balt., 1960. Bar: Md. 1960. Spl. agt. FBI, 1955-62; chief counsel, staff dir. emeritus subcom. on investigations and oversight Com. on Pub. Works and Transp., Ho. of Reps., Washington, 1962-86; dir. corp. security Flying Tiger Ln., L.A., 1986-89; ptnr. Burgess & O'Hara, Upper Marlboro, Md., 1990-91; cons. Legal Svcs. Corp., Washington, 1990-91, pres., 1991-94; cons., 1994—. 1st lt. USMC, 1952-54. Decorated Nat. Def. Svc. medal, UN medal, Korean Svc. medal. Mem. Md. Bar Assn., Bolling AFB Officers Club, Marines Meml. Assn., Am. Legion. Home: 5904 Mount Eagle Dr Apt 911 Alexandria VA 22303-2539 also: 2471 Misty Meadow Ct Spring Hill FL 34606-3287 E-mail: johnpohara@aol.com.

O'HARA, JOHN PAUL, III, orthopaedic surgeon; b. Detroit, June 10, 1946; m. Randy Baird, Mar. 11, 1987; children: Riley Anne, Nolan Baird, Evan John. BA, U. Mich., 1968, MD, 1972. Resident U. Va. Med. Ctr., Charlottesville, 1973-77; fellow Nuffield Orthopedic Ctr., Oxford, Eng., 1977; practice medicine specializing in orthopaedic surgery Southfield, 1978—; staff Providence Hosp., Mich., 1978—, pres. elect med. staff, 1990, pres. med. staff, 1991; sect. chief orthopedics; pres. Porretta Orthopedic Ctr., 1996—, med. dir., 2001—. Pres. Providence Hosp. Med. Staff Research Found., 1984-85, bd. dirs., 1982—; bd. dirs. Mich. Master Health Plan, Southfield, 1982. Contbr. articles to profl. jours. Pres. Birmingham (Mich.) Little League Baseball. Recipient Disting. Alumni award Brother Rice High Sch., 1986. Fellow Am. Acad. Orthopaedic Surgery, Mid Am. Orthopaedic Soc.; mem. Detroit Orthopaedic Soc., Mich. Orthopaedic Soc., Detroit Acad. Orthopaedic Surgeons (past pres.), Oakland Hills Country Club (Birmingham, Mich.), Beverly Hills (Mich.) Club. Avocations: earthwatch vol., travel, sports. Home: 627 Waddington St Bloomfield Hills MI 48301-2346 Office: Porretta Orthopaedic Ctr 22250 Providence Dr Ste 401 Southfield MI 48075-6212

O'HARA, PATRICK JOSEPH, surgeon; b. Youngstown, Ohio, 1947; MD, Boston U., 1971. Cert. in surgery, recert., subspecialty in gen. vascular surgery, recert. Surg. intern Mass. Gen. Hosp.-Harvard, Boston, 1971—72, resident in surgery, 1972—73, 1975—78, fellow in vascular surgery, 1978—79; vascular surgery staff Cleve. Clinic, 1979—. Mem.: ACS, Ctrl. Surg. Assn., Midwestern Vascular Surgery Soc. (pres. 2000—01), Soc. for Vascular Surgery, Internat. Soc. for Cardiovasc. Surgery, Am. Assn. Vascular Surgery. Office: Cleve Clinic Found Desk S61 9500 Euclid Ave Cleveland OH 44195-0001 E-mail: oharap@ccf.org.

O'HARA, PAUL ANTHONY, JR. retired art educator, artist; b. Indiana, Pa., Sept. 16, 1938; s. Paul Anthony and Hilda M. (Henderson) O;H.; m. Barbara Ann Zolock, May 24, 1965; children: Paul Anthony III, Polly Ann, Rebecca, Mark. BS in Art Edn., Edinboro (Pa.) U., 1961; MA in Painting/Sculpture, Pa. State U., 1965; postgrad., U. Pitts., Calif. U. Pa., 1963-64. Cert. tchr. K-12, supr., Pa. Tchr. jr. h.s. art Chartiers Valley Schs., Pitts., 1961-95. Photographer Pa. State U., University Park, 1977-78; instr. ceramics Allegheny C.C., Pitts.; instr. art Everyday Poeple, Monessen and Donora, Pa. Sculptor, printmaker, painter; one-man shows include Calif. U. Pa., 1962-64, Lutheran Assn. State Coll, Pa., 1964, Pitts. Ctr. for Arts, 1964, 68, St. Francis Coll., Ft. Wayne, Ind., 1968, U. Iowa, Iowa City, 1968, U. Pitts., 1969, Pa. State U., University Park, 1972, Pitts. History and Landmarks Mus., Pitts., 1973, 74, Adam's Art, Bellefonte, Pa., 1994, Frank L. Melega Art Mus., Brownsville, Pa., 2000, Fayette Campus Pa. State U., 2001; exhibited in group shows at Erie Mus. Spring Art Show, 1959-60, 89, 93, 95-96, 2000, Soc. Sculptors, Pitts., 1963-66, 68-84, Associated Artists, Pitts., 1962-63, 66-67, 68, 70, 72-73, 75-79, 81, 84, 86, Mini Print Internat., Cadaques, Spain, 1989-2000, 2001, 2002, Mini Print Internat. traveling show Mex., 1989, Spain, 1989-88, Italy, 1989, Colombia, 1989, Cadaques, 1990, 2001, Japan, 1991-92, Eng., 1992-2001, France, 1995-2001, Korea, 1994, Finland, 2000, Wingfield, England, 1992-2001, Bages, France, Spain, 2000-2001, Pa. State U., University Park, Boston Printmakers, Boston, 1969, Vendome Gallery, Pitts., Pratt Internat., 1971, Pratt Internat. Travelling Show, 1971-74, William Penn Mus., Harrisburg, Pa., Pa. State Traveling Show, 1972-74, Ball State U., Muncie, Ind., 1973-74, Delmar Coll., Corpus Christie, Tex., 1973, Three Rivers Art Festival, Pitts., 1961-67, 71, 73-74, 76-78, 80, Pitts. Connection, Dunfermline, Scotland, 1985, Butler Inst. Am. Art, Youngstown, Ohio, 1987, Seton Hill Coll., Greensburg, Pa., 1989, Greensburg Mus. Art, 1989, Pitts. Ctr. Arts, 1962-68, Ann. Holiday Ornaments Exhbn. Palmer Mus. Art, Pa. State U., University Park, 1997-99, Soc. Am. Graphic Artists 67th Nat. Members Exhbn. Prince St. Gallery, N.Y.C., 1999, Stephen Gang Gallery, N.Y.C., 2000, Nemacolin Woodlands Resort, Farmington, Pa., 2000, The 11th Internat. Miniature Print Exhbn., Seoul, 2000, Sept. 11 Meml. Portfolio, Am. Print Alliance, 2002, Iowa Print Internat., U. Iowa Sch. Art & Art History, 2002 Recipient Frick award Frick Found., 1964. Mem.: Am. Print Alliance, Soc. Am. Graphic Artists, Internat. Sculpture Ctr., Internat. Assn. for the Diffusion of Graphic Arts Print Group. Democrat. Roman Catholic. Avocations: landscaping, renovation, genealogy. Home: PO Box 132 Roscoe PA 15477-0132

O'HARA, SABINE U. academic administrator, dean, economist, educator; b. Ludwigsburg, W. Germany, Oct. 29, 1955; d. Wolfgang E. and Margarete Maier; m. R. Philip O'Hara, Mar. 17, 1983; children: Daniel, David, Dennis. Doctorate, U. Gottingen, Germany, 1984. Dir. pub. policy N.Y. State Coun. Chs., Albany, 1990—93; asst. prof. econs. Rensselaer Poly. Inst., Troy, 1994—99, dir. grad. studies in econs., 1996—99; provost and prof. econs. Green Mountain Coll., Poultney, Vt., 1999—2002; v.p. acad. affairs and dean Concordia Coll., Moorhead, Minn., 2002—. Lectr. in field. Author: (books) Economic Theory for Environmentalists, 1996; contbr. articles to profl. jours. Steering com. Downtown Revitalization Initiative, Poultney, 2001—02; bd. dirs. Girls Inc. of the Greater Capital Dist., Albany, NY, 1998—2000, Employee Ownership Project, Albany, 1997—2000; vice chair Schenectady Econ. Devel. Initiative, 1994—97. Recipient Outstanding Paper award for excellence, Internat. Jour. Social Econs., 1996, 2000, Outstanding Svc. award, N.Y. State Coun. Chs., 1997; grantee Rsch. grantee, Hewlett Found., Froehlich Found., Sloan Found. Mem.: Am. Econ. Assn., Internat. Assn. Feminist Econs., Assn. Social Econs., Internat. Soc. Ecol. Econs. Office: Concordia Coll 901 8th St S Moorhead MN 56562 Office Fax: 218-299-4357. E-mail: ohara@cord.edu.

O'HARA, THOMAS PATRICK, managing editor; b. Phila., July 15, 1947; s. Hugh James and Agatha Mary (Gilroy) O'H.; m. Juliet Munro, 1970 (div. 1974); m. Pamela Smith, Oct. 8, 1977; children: Rachel Kathleen, Patrick Graham. BA in English, Rutgers South Jersey, 1972; MA in Communications,

U. Fla., 1974. Sports reporter Gainesville SUN, 1972-74; reporter Orlando (Fla.) Sentinel, 1974-76, Daytona Beach (Fla.) News Jour., 1976-78; various editing and reporting positions Miami (Fla.) Herald, 1978-86, city editor Palm Beach ed., 1985-86; asst. met. editor Palm Beach Post, West Palm Beach, Fla., 1986-87, met. editor, 1987-88, asst. mng. editor, 1988-89, mng. editor, 1989—2000, The Plain Dealer, Cleve., 2000—. Sgt. USAF, 1969-71. Home: 8890 Spring Valley Dr Broadview Heights OH 44147-2573 Office: The Plain Dealer 1801 Superior Ave Cleveland OH 44114 Office Fax: 216-999-6323. E-mail: tohara@plaind.com.

O'HARA, TIMOTHY PATRICK, marketing professional; b. Abington, Pa., July 18, 1970; s. Joseph John and Mary Ellen Francis O'H.; m. Dyan O'Hara, July 3, 1993; 1 child, Kelsey. BS in Acctg., Drexel U., 1992; MBA, Villanova U., 1995. Cost accountant Merck & Co., Inc., West Point, Pa., 1992-94, product cost analyst, 1994-95, sr. fin. analyst, 1995-97, vaccine specialist, 1997-98, mgr. market rsch., 1998-2000, dist. mgr., 2000—. Office: Merck & Co Inc 1902 Woodrose Manor Ct Warrington PA 18976 E-mail: tim_ohara@merck.com.

O'HARE, CHRISTINE MARIE, critical care nurse; b. Chgo., Mar. 16, 1942; d. Albert Anthony and Dorothy Ann (Perry) Uebbing; m. Thomas Patrick O'Hare, Oct. 14, 1967; children: Brian, Carolyn, Michelle. Diploma in nursing, St. Elizabeth's Hosp., Chgo., 1963. CCRN. Staff nurse St. Elizabeth's Hosp., 1963-65, head nurse, 1965, instr. sch. nursing, 1966-68; tchr. Wheaton (Ill.)-Warrenville High Sch. Dist. 200, 1976-78; staff nurse Community Hosp., Geneva, 1978-85, Fairfax Hosp., Falls Church, Va., 1985—. Mem. AACN. Home: 4891 Oakcrest Dr Fairfax VA 22030-4568

O'HARE, DANIEL JOHN, electrical engineer; b. Bay City, Mich., Dec. 17, 1955; s. John William and Vida Flo (Roberts) O'H.; m. Betty Joanne Luczak, May 23, 1979; children: Jennifer Louise, Meghan Elizabeth, Amanda Jayne. BSEE, Mich. Technol. U., 1978; postgrad., U. Minn., 1979-84, SUNY, Binghamton, 1985. Jr. engr. IBM, Rochester, Minn., 1978-79, assoc. engr. hard file integration, 1979-82, sr. assoc. engr. hardfile integration, 1982-85, project engr., mgr. subsystem serviceability, 1985-88, devel. engr., mgr. hardware devel., 1988-91, adv. engr. interdivsnl. project leader, 1991-95; program mgr. storage adapter all IBM server syss., 1995-97; sr. program mgr. AS/400 Asia Pacific Mktg., 1997—2001, exec. project mgr. IBM e server i series, 2001—. Referee Rochester Youth Baseball Assn., 1988, 89, coach, 1992, 93; line judge Rochester Youth Soccer, 1989; vol. tchr. for gifted and talented edn. at local pub. elem. sch., 1989-94; asst. youth competitive cheerleading squad, Rochester Youth Cheerleading Assn., 1995-98, h.s. cheerleading asst. coach, 1999—; judge Destination Imagination, 2001. Roman Catholic. Avocations: model building, computers, photography. Home: 2607 Westview Ln NW Rochester MN 55901-2362 Office: IBM Hwy 52 at 37th St NW Rochester MN 55901 E-mail: djohare@attglobal.net.

O'HARE, DEAN RAYMOND, insurance company executive, director; b. Jersey City, June 21, 1942; s. Francis and Ann O'H.; m. Kathleen T. Walliser, Dec. 2, 1967; Dean, Jason. BS, NYU, 1963; MBA, Pace U., 1968. Trainee Chubb Corp., N.Y.C., 1963-64, tax advisor, 1964-67, asst. v.p., mgr. corp. fin. devel., 1968-72, sr. v.p., mgr. corp. fin. devel. dept., from 1979, chief fin. officer, 1979-94, pres., 1986-88, chmn., CEO, 1988—. Chmn. Chubb Life Ins. Co. N.H., 1981—; chmn., pres. Fed. Ins. Co., 1988—, Vigilant Ins. Co., 1988—; chmn., dir. Bellemead Devel. Corp., 1973— ; chmn. Colonial Life Ins. Co. Am., 1980—, Chubb Life Ins. Co. Am., 1980— ; bd. dirs. Chubb Ins. Co. Can., Fed. Ins. Co., Vigilant Ins. Co. Dir. Coalition Svc. Industries, The N.J. Partnership; trustee com. for econ. devel., WDC. Mem. Am. Ins. Assn., The Links Club (N.Y.C.). Office: Chubb Corp PO Box 1615 Warren NJ 07059-1615*

O'HARE, JAMES RAYMOND, energy company executive; b. Evergreen Park, Ill., July 20, 1938; s. Raymond Clarence and Helen (Nickel) O'H.; m. Nan Jane Raleigh, Sept. 18, 1965; children: Joan, Daniel, Colleen, Patrick. BS, Marquette U., 1960; MBA, U. Calif. at Los Angeles, 1961. C.P.A., Ind., Ill., Ky., Calif., Tex. Mgr. Peat, Marwick, Mitchell & Co., Chgo., 1961-68, South Bend, Ind., 1968-69; controller Essex Internat., Inc., Fort Wayne, 1969-76, Am. Air Filter Co., Inc., Louisville, 1976-80; fin. v.p. and treas. Petrolane Inc., Long Beach, Calif., 1980-85; treas. Tex. Eastern Corp., Houston, 1985-87, v.p., treas., 1987-88; sr. v.p. fin. and adminstrn. Texas Eastern Gas Pipeline Co., 1988-89; v.p., CFO Enclean Inc., 1991-93; fin. cons., 1993-97; v.p., CFO Ascendant Healthcare Group, Inc., Houston, 1997, John March Ptnrs., Inc., Houston, 1998—. Served with USNR, 1962-68. Mem. Evans Scholars, Fin. Execs. Inst., The Woodlands Country Club, Beta Gamma Sigma.

O'HARE, JOHN MICHAEL, religious studies educator; b. Kansas City, Kans., Apr. 20, 1940; s. John Patrick and Catherine Frances O'Hare; m. Miriam Ann Perkins, Apr. 11, 1966; children: Kieran Joel, Sean Patrick. BA in Philosophy, Conception (Mo.) Sem., 1962; MA in Theology, Marquette U., Milw., 1970; postgrad., Fordham U., Bronx, NY, 1967—70. Instr. theology Villa Madonna Coll., Covington, Ky., 1965—67; assoc. prof. religious studies Benedictine Coll., Atchison, Kans., 1971—, dir. acad. computing, 1992—99. Grantwriter Atchison Cmty. Info. Network, 2000—02, bd. dirs., tech. cons., 2000—; calligrapher for various pvt., religious and comml. clients, 1995—2001. Mem. exec. com. Kans. Rsch. and Edn. Network, 1996—2000; organizer AtchiCIN, Atchison, 2000—01. Named Educator of Yr., Benedictine Coll., 1988; recipient summer fellowship, Inst. for Ecumenical and Cultural Rsch., 1975, Mellon fellowship East-West Seminar, U. Kans., Lawrence, 1980. Mem.: Soc. for Calligraphy. Democrat. Roman Catholic. Avocations: rubber stamps, photography, woodworking. Home: 407 Kearney Atchison KS 66002 Office: Benedictine Coll 1020 N 2d St Atchison KS 66002 E-mail: moh@benedictine.edu.

O'HARE, JOSEPH ALOYSIUS, academic administrator, priest; b. N.Y.C., Feb. 12, 1931; s. Joseph Aloysius and Marie Angela (Enright) O'H. AB, Berchmans Coll, Cebu City, Philippines, 1954, MA, 1955; STL, Woodstock Coll., Md., 1962; PhD, Fordham U., 1968; DHL (hon.), Fairfield U., 1980, Rockhurst Coll., Kansas City, Mo., 1984, Ateneo de Manila U., 1990, CUNY, 1991, Coll. of St. Rose, Albany, N.Y., 1995, St. Francis Coll., Bklyn., 1996, St. Peter's Coll., 1997; DLitt (hon.), Coll. of New Rochelle, 1984; D.D. (hon.), Muhlenberg Coll., 1998. Joined S.J., 1948, ordained priest Roman Cath. Ch., 1961. Instr. Ateneo de Manila U., 1955-58, prof. philosophy, 1968-72; assoc. editor Am. Mag., N.Y.C., 1972-75, editor-in-chief, 1975-84; pres. Fordham U., Bronx, N.Y., 1984—. Author weekly column Of Many Things (Best Original Column award Cath. Press Assn. 1976, 78, 81, 84) Chmn. N.Y.C. Campaign Fin. Bd. Office: Fordham U Office of Pres New York NY 10458 also: President's Office Rose Hill Campus, Admin Bldg S, Rm. 107 441 E. Fordham Road Bronx NY 10458 E-mail: johare@fordham.edu.*

O'HARE, MARILYNN RYAN, artist; b. Berkeley, Calif., Aug. 6, 1926; d. Lawrence and Linnie Marie (Ryan) Atkins; m. Lawrence Bernard O'Hare, Sept. 20, 1947; children: Timothy Lawrence, Kevin Roy, Shannon John, Kacey Sophia, Kelly Katherine. Student, Jean Turner Art Sch., San Francisco, 1944, 45, 46. Artist Cherubs children's dept. store, San Francisco, 1946, 47, Emporium Art Dept., San Francisco, 1947-54; freelance artist Capwells-Emporium, Liberty House, San Francisco, Oakland, 1955-64. Artist-in-residence, coord. art program Childrens Fairyland USA, Oakland, 1962—; commissioned painting for Moffit Hosp., San Francisco, 1970, Havens Sch. Libr., Piedmont, Calif., 1975. Painter children's portraits; designer greeting cards; executed murals Children's Fairyland, Oakland, 1965, 66, 73, Kaiser Hosp., Martinez, Calif., 1974. Vol. art tchr. Oakland Pub. Schs., 1958-62; vol. Oak Mus., 1965—, Convelescant Hosp., Berkeley, Calif., 1975-97. Named Mother of Yr., City of Oakland, 1993. Mem. Oakland Art Assn. Democrat. Avocations: reading, craft design, garage sales. Home: Oakland, Calif. Died Jan. 2000.

O'HARE, VIRGINIA LEWIS, human resources administrator; b. Pitts., May 2, 1951; d. Robert Edward and Ellen Marie (Saylor) Lewis; m. John Francis O'Hare, Sept. 17, 1994; 1 child, Merit Elisabeth. BS in Edn., U. Pitts., 1973; MS in Human Resources Mgmt., Laroche Coll., 1984. Legal asst. Meyer, Darragh, Buckler, Bebenek & Eck, Pitts., 1973-85; legal office mgr. Rockwell Internat., 1985-86; pers. mgr. Rose, Schmidt, Hasley & DiSalle, 1986-88; legal adminstr. Duquesne Light Co., 1988-99; mgr. human resources Klett Lieber Rooney & Schorling, 1999—. Mem. Assn. Legal Adminstrs., Pitts. Legal Adminstrn. Assn. (sec. 1989-93, membership chair 1993-97, edn. chair 1997-2000, pres.-elect 2000-2001), Pa. Bar Assn., Allegheny Bar Assn., Pitts. Human Resources Assn. Republican. Avocations: horseback riding, target shooting, walking, biking. Office: Klett Lieber Rooney Lieber & Schorling 40th Fl 1 Oxford Ct Pittsburgh PA 15219-1407

O'HAREN, THOMAS JOSEPH, financial services executive; b. Shenandoah, Pa., Apr. 1, 1934; s. James Francis and Elizabeth Margaret (Sauer) O'H.; m. Virginia Ann Kobylinski, Mar. 4, 1957; children: Michelle, Timothy, Terrence, Anne, David, Mary. BS, Pa. State U., 1956. CLU, CHFC. Sales rep. Conn. Gen., Houston, 1957-62, asst. mgr., 1962-66, mgr. Atlanta, 1966-85, regional v.p., 1985—, Faculty Leadership Inst. Am. Coll., Atlanta, 1990—. Adj. prof. mgmt. Am. Coll., Bryn Mawr, Pa., 1995, chmn. curriculum com., palnned Giving Com. Am. Coll., 1995; mem. pres.'s adv. coun., mentor program. Editor, contbr. Mgrs. Mag., 1987, Gen. Agts. & Mgrs. News, 1987. Fin. chmn. Mattingly Senate Camapign, 1980, Bell Gubernatorial Campaign, 1987; pres. Cobb County C. of C., 1980; co-chmn. Ga. Rep. Found.; chmn. bd. trustees Gama Found., 1990-97, bd. trustees Ga. State U. Ednl. Found., 1996—; Newt Gingrich Fin. Com., 1992-95, Marist Sch., 1995—, Millner Gubernatorial Campaign, 1994, chmn., treas., 1998; mem. bd trustees Am. Coll. Ednl. Found., 1999—, Alpha Sigma Phi Ednl. Found., 1999—; chmn. bd. trustees Am. Coll. Found., 2001—. Lt. (j.g.) USNR, 1956-58. Named to the Gama Hall of Fame, 1992, Cigna Fin. Advisors Hall of Fame, 1995; recipient Gordon Setchel award for Contbn. to Agy. Mgmt., 1994, Fr. James Hartnett award Marist Sch., 1998. Mem. Gen. Agts. and Mgrs. (Master Agy. award 1983-94, John W. Yates Meml. award 1990, chmn. GAMC Found. 1990-97), CLUs, Chartered Fin. Counsellors, Gen. Agts. Assn. (pres. Atlanta, 1976-77, nat. bd. dirs., 1979-84, nat. pres. 1987-88), Advanced Assn. Life Underwriters (polit. involvement com.), Nat. Assn. Life Underwriters, Million Dollar Roundtable (Top of Table 1988), Atlanta Country Club (bd. dirs. 1986-92, pres. 1988-90), Georgian Club (bd. dirs. 1985 pres.), Equestrian Order of the Holy Sepulchre (knight). Republican. Roman Catholic. Avocations: golf, tennis, reading. Home: 280 Pine Valley Rd Marietta GA 30067-4822 Office: Prudential Fin 3495 Piedmont Rd Bldg 10 Ste 200 Atlanta GA 30305

O'HARE-VANMEERBEKE, ANNE MARIE, dietitian; b. S.I., N.Y., Jan. 5, 1960; d. Robert and Ellen O'Hare. BS in Human Ecology, Marywood Coll., Scranton, Pa., 1982. Registered dietitian. Clin. dietitian Custom Mgmt. Corp., Somerset, N.J., 1982-84, food svc. dir. Westfield, 1984-86; cons. Anne O'Hare Cons. Svcs. (Cen. N.J.), 1986; asst. food svc. Marriott Corp., Nyack, N.Y., 1986-87, food svc. dir. Secaucus, N.J., 1987-88, dist. dietitian N.J. and N.Y. area, 1988-90, dir. food svc. Camden, N.J., 1990-92; dir. ctrl. food svc. Columbia-Presbyn. Med. Ctr., N.Y.C., 1992-94; tng. mgr. area 1, Mariott Health Care Svcs., Avon, Conn., 1993-96. Nutrition cons. LEAP and Ocean Inc., Ocean County, N.J., 1995—. Mem. Am. Cancer Soc., Am. Heart Assn. Mem. Am. Dietetic Assn. Roman Catholic. Avocations: racketball, swimming, biking. E-mail: Anne. Office: 11 Copperfield Ct Eatontown NJ 07724-2115 E-mail: AnneVM1@aol.com.

OHASHI, SHOICHI, business administration educator; b. Seto, Aichi, Japan, Mar. 7, 1932; s. Mitsuo and Yoshie Ohashi; m. Kimiko Ohashi, Nov. 20, 1957; 1 child, Reisaku MBA, Kobe (Japan) U., 1957, DBA, 1967. Acad. asst. Kansai U., Suita, Japan, 1957-60, lectr. Japan, 1960-63, assoc. prof. Japan, 1963-70, prof. bus. adminstrn. Japan, 1970-2000, vice dean students div. Japan, 1972-74, vice dean faculty commerce Japan, 1977-78, dean faculty commerce Japan, 1979-80, dean vocat. div. Japan, 1982-86, acad. v.p. Japan, 1986-92, dean of entrance divsn. Japan, 1993-99; prof., dean faculty tourism, acad. v.p. Osaka Meijo U., Kumatori, Japan, 2000—. Lectr. Osaka U. Fgn. Studies, 1968-74, Kobe U., 1971, Ritsumeikan U., Kyoto, Japan, 1971-73, Kwanseigakuin U., Nishinomiya, Japan, 1979-80, 94-97. Author: Theories on Works Community, 1966, Theory of Business Administration, 1992; co-author: Workers' Participation, 1979; co-editor: Information Society Business, 1988, Business Administration, 1991, Lexicon of Business Administration, 1994, An Inquiry into the Japanese Management, 1996. Researcher com. Rsch. Fund Commn. Japan Ministry Edn., 1987-89. Mem. Japan Soc. Bus. Adminstrn. (internat. com. 1980-83, exec. com. 1983-89, 92-95, v.p. 1995-98), Assn. for Comparative Study of Mgmt. (exec.com. 1980-84, pres. 1994-96), Soc. for the History of Mgmt. Theories (exec. com. 1993-96, v.p. 1996-99). Home: 5-40-602 Mukogawacho Takarazuka Hyogo 665-0844 Japan Office: Osaka Meijo U 5-3-1 Okubo-Minami Kumatori Osaka Japan *Books published as author, editor or co-editor since a first book in 1966, a dissertation book, until 1998 are 25. Being engaged these days in research into Japanese management system sponsored by Japan Ministry of Education and Japan Society for the promotion of Science. Recent accomplishments as Dean of Entrance Division include a successful increase of about 10% in applicants for Kansai University in 1997 entrance examination amid overall decrease of the applicable in Japan.*

O'HEARN, JAMES FRANCIS, chemical company executive; b. Fall River, Mass., Nov. 5, 1935; s. Francis Henry and Eileen Eleanor (James) O'H.; m. Sabrina Sieley Hu, Dec. 31, 1966; children: Kevin, Claudine. BS in Edn., Bridgewater Coll., 1960; student, Sofia U., 1962-63. Tchr. Freetown (Mass.) Elem. Sch., 1960-62, Dept. Def., Tokyo, 1962-63; regional mgr. Reynolds Metals Co., Hong Kong, L.A., 1963-69, Uniroyal Chems., Hong Kong, Singapore, 1969-76, Akron, Ohio, 1976-77, dir. mktg. Brussels, 1977-80; pres. Premier Chem. Co., Taipei, Taiwan, 1980—. Dir. USA-ROC Econ. Coun., Taipei, 1991—, chmn. chem. group, 1986—. Mem. Petrochem. Ind. Assn. Taipei (dir. 1981-86), Am. Club in China (pres. 1993-94), Am. C. of C. (pres. 1991, 92), Am. Univ. Club (dir. 1992—). Republican. Roman Catholic. Avocations: golf, tennis, aerobics, mountain climbing. Home: 229 Chung Shan N Rd Sec 7 Taipei Taiwan Office: Premier Chem Co Ltd 205 Tun Hwa N Rd Ste 704 1302 Taipei Taiwan E-mail: taipei@ucctw.com.tw.

O'HEARN, KEVIN THOMAS, civil engineer; b. Scranton, Pa., Oct. 2, 1952; s. Daniel Julius and Lois Ann (Smith) O'H.; m. Kathleen Holmes, July 19, 1980; children: Katherine, Kevin II, Kyle. BArch Engring., Pa. State U., 1975; MPA, Marywood U., 1988. Registered profl. engr., Pa., Calif. Resident engr. U.S. VA Office Constrn., L.A., 1975-78; design engr. G.S.G.S. & D., Clarks Summit, Pa., 1979-80; tech. editor Nat. Edn. Corp., Scranton, 1980-81; asst. chief engr. VA Med. Ctr., Wilkes-Barre, 1982—. Instr. Pa. State U., Scranton, 1987. Author: A Comprehensive Planning Model for Medical Centers, 1991; editor: (textbook) Industrial Pipefitting and Plumbing, 1981. Mem. ASCE. Roman Catholic. Home: 108 Sharon Dr Pittston PA 18641-9521

O'HEARN, MICHAEL JOHN, lawyer; b. Akron, Ohio, Jan. 29, 1952; s. Leo Ambrose and Margaret Elizabeth (Clark) O'H. BA in Econs., UCLA, 1975; postgrad., U. San Diego, 1977; JD, San Fernando Valley Coll. Law, 1979; postgrad., Holy Apostles Sem., 1993-94. Bar: Calif. 1979, U.S. Dist. Ct. (ctrl. dist.) Calif. 1979. Document analyst Mellonics Info. Ctr., Litton Industries, Canoga Park, Calif., 1977-79; pvt. practice Encino, 1979-80; atty. VISTA/Grey Law Inc., L.A., 1980-81; assoc. Donald E. Chadwick & Assocs., Woodland Hills, Calif., 1981-84, Law Offices of Laurence Ring, Beverly Hills, 1984-85; atty., in-house counsel Coastal Ins. Co., Van Nuys, 1985-89; atty. Citrus Glen Apts., Ventura, 1989-92; pvt. practice Ventura County, 1992-2000; arbitrator, 1995—; propr., property mgr. Channel Islands Village Mgmt. Co., 1998-2000. Life mem. Rep. Nat. Com. Recipient Cert. of Appreciation, Agy. for Vol. Svc., 1981, San Fernando Valley Walk for Life, 1988, Cert. of Appreciation, Arbitrator for the Superior and Mcpl. Cts., Ventura County Jud. Dist., 1996. Mem. KC, Ventura County Bar Assn., Ventura County Trial Lawyers Assn., Secular Franciscan Order., Ahern Clan/Family Assn. Republican. Roman Catholic. Avocations: golf, yachting, fishing. Home: 1941 Fisher Dr Apt B Oxnard CA 93035-3022 Office: 3650 Ketch Ave Oxnard CA 93035-3029 E-mail: mohearn_brightstar@yahoo.com.

O'HEARN, ROBERT RAYMOND, stage designer; b. Elkhart, Ind., July 19, 1921; s. Robert Raymond, Sr. and Ella May (Stoldt) O'H. BA, Ind. U., 1939-43; student, Art Students League, 1943-45. Designer Brattle Theatre, Cambridge, Mass., 1948-52; prof. stage design, chmn. design dept. Sch. Music Ind. U., 1989—. Instr. Studio and Forum Scenic Design, 1968-88. Stage designer: Broadway shows The Relapse, 1950, Loves Labor's Lost, 1953, Othello, Festival, 1955, The Apple Cart, Child of Fortune, 1956; asst. designer: Broadway shows Kismet, 1953, Pajama Game, 1955, My Fair Lady, 1956, West Side Story, 1958; designer: for film A Clerical Error, 1955; designer prodns. Central City Opera House, 1959-63, Opera Soc. Washington, 1958-61, L'Elisir D'Amore at Met. Opera House, 1960, Die Meistersinger, 1962, Aida, 1963; stage designer: As You Like It, Stratford, Conn., 1961, Troilus and Cressida, Stratford, 1961, Kiss Me Kate, Los Angeles Civic Light Opera, 1964, N.Y.C. Center, 1965, Samson and Delila, Met. Opera, 1964, La Sylphide, Am. Ballet Theatre, 1964, Italian Symphony, 1971, Adam Cochrane, Broadway, 1964, Pique Dame, Met. Opera, 1965, La Ventana, 1966, Die Frau Ohne Schatten, 1966, Porgy and Bess, Vienna Volksoper, 1965, Bregenzer Festspiele, 1971, Otello, Boston Opera, also Hamburg State Opera, 1967, Hansel and Gretel, Met. Opera, 1967, Nutcracker Ballet, San Francisco Ballet, 1967, L.A. Ballet, 1979, La Traviata, Santa Fe Opera, 1968, Rosalinda, L.A. Civic Light Opera, 1968, Der Rosenkavalier, Met. Opera, 1969, Tallis Fantasia, N.Y.C. Ballet, 1969, Boris Godunov (unproduced), Met. Opera, 1970, Parsifal, Met. Opera, 1970, Porgy and Bess, Bregenz Festspiel, Austria, 1971, Falstaff, Marriage of Figaro, Gianni Schicci, Central City Opera House, 1972, Barber of Seville, 1973, The Enchanted, Kennedy Center, 1973, The Mind with the Dirty Man, Los Angeles, 1973, Midsummer Night's Dream, Central City Opera, 1974, Coppelia, Ballet West, 1974, Carmen, Strasbourg, 1974, The Pearl Fishers, Miami Opera, 1974, N.Y.C. Opera, 1980, Don Pasquale, Miami Opera, 1976, Scipio Africanus, Central City Opera, 1975, Swan Lake, Strasbourg, 1975, Marriage of Figaro, Met. Opera, 1975, Die Meistersinger, Karlsruhe, Germany, 1975, Girl of the Golden West, Houston Opera, 1976, N.Y.C. Opera, 1977, Vienna Staatsoper, 1976, Boris Godunov, Strasbourg, 1976, Der Rosenkavelier, Karlsruhe, 1976, Don Quixote, Ballet West, 1977, Die Meistersinger, Chgo. Lyric Opera, 1977, Adriana Lecouvreur, Miami Opera, 1978, La Boheme, 1978, Coppelia, Pacific N.W. Dance, Seattle, 1978, Andrea Chenier, N.Y.C. Opera, 1978, Der Rosenkavalier, Can. Opera Co., Toronto, 1978, Taming of the Shrew, Pa. State U., 1980, Die Fledermaus, Miami Opera, 1980, Tosca, Miami Opera, 1981, West Side Story, Bregenz Festspiel, Austria, 1981, Mich. Opera Theatre, 1985; Pique Dame, San Francisco Opera, 1982, La Traviata, Miami Opera, 1982, Of Mice and Men, Miami Opera, 1982, Carousel, Annie Get Your Gun, Miami Opera, 1984, Lucia di Lammermoor, 1984, L'Italiana in Algeri, 1985, Porgy and Bess, Met. Opera, 1985, West Side Story, Mich. Opera Theatre, 1985, Aida, Don Giovanni, Opera Colo., 1986, My Fair Lady, Mich. Opera Theatre, 1986, Samson and Delilah, Manon Lescaut Opera Colo., 1987, Annie Get Your Gun, Paper Mill Playhouse, 1987, Peter Grimes, Ind. U., 1987, Madama Butterfly, N.J. State Opera, 1990. Mem. vis. com. Costume Inst., Met. Museum. Mem. United Scenic Artists. Home: 2604 E 2nd St Bloomington IN 47401-5351

OHIRA, KAZUTO, theatre company executive, writer; b. Hiroshima, Japan, Jan. 5, 1933; s. Kitaro and Ryo (Sugimoto) O.; m. Evelyn Lanham, Sept. 3, 1964. BA, Waseda U., Tokyo, 1956. Theatre mgr. Toho's La Brea Theatre, L.A., 1961-63; gen. mgr. Toho Cinema, N.Y.C., 1963-64; publicity mgr. Towa Co., Ltd., Tokyo, 1965-69; rep., dir., mgr. Toho Internat. Inc., N.Y.C., 1969, chief exec. officer, 1988-97; pres. Internat. Cultural Prodn. Inc. Producer (dance performance and drama) Yasuko Nagamine's Musume Dojoji, 1982, Mandara, 1985, (drama) Yukio Ninagawa's Media, 1987, Takarazuka Show at Radio City Music Hall, N.Y., 1989, KanashibetsU: Furano Group at La Mama, Takarazuka Dance Concert at Joyce Theater, 1992, Sotoba Komachi, Yasuko Nagamine and Co., Beauty of Tokyo, Met. Tokyo, City Ctr., N.Y., 1993, Virtue Senpo Sugihara, Danny Kay Theater, N.Y.C., 1997, Gen: Hiroshima Atom Bomb's Kid, Danny Kay Theater, N.Y.C., 1998, The Winds of God, Am. Pl. Theater, N.Y.C., 1999, Rent, Japan, 2000, Boonah, Come Down, N.Y.C., 2000; author: Broadway parts I and II, 1982, 2d edit., 1987, Broadway, Broadway, 1987, Performing Arts of New York, 1989, Haiku Collection: Though The Travel is Short, The Charms of Broadway, 1994, Broadway Criticism, 1995, Japanese translation of Show Business Is No Business by Al Hirshfeld, 1997, Haiku Collection Flower Garden, 2000. Bd. dirs. Japan Musical Award Com. in U.S., 1994—; chair bd. dirs. Saeko Ichinohe Dance Co. Recipient 2d Fumiko Yamaji Cultural award, 1985, 1st Cultural Bridge award, 1998. Mem. UNESCO, Internat. Theatre Critics Assn., Internat. Theatre Inst. Japan, N.Y. Waseda Univ. Alumni Assn. (hon. dir.), Players Club. Avocation: golf. Home: 235 W 48th St 33B New York NY 10036 Office: ICP Inc 162 W 56th St Rm 504 New York NY 10019 E-mail: icp-ny@rcn.com.

OHL, DANA ALAN, urologist, educator; b. Lansing, Mich., July 18, 1958; s. Emerson Balfour and Dorothy Yvonne (Keller) O.; m. Linda Ellen Ginn, Sept. 4, 1983. BS in Biomed. Scis., U. Mich., 1979, MD, 1982. Diplomate Nat. Bd. Med. Examiners, Am. Bd. Urology. Resident surgery Barnes Hosp., St. Louis, 1982-83; resident surgery/urology Med. Sch. U. Mich., Ann Arbor, 1983-87, instr. Med. Sch., 1987-90, dir. electroejaculation svcs. Male Infertility Clinic, 1987—, asst. prof. surgery/urology Med. Sch., 1990-95, assoc. prof. surgery/urology Med. Sch., 1995—. Contbr. articles to profl. jours. Mem. AMA, Am. Fertility Soc., Am. Soc. Andrology, Reed M. Nesbit Urological Soc. Republican. Office: Univ Mich Dept Urology PO Box 0330 Ann Arbor MI 48106-0330

OHL, JOAN E. federal agency administrator; b. Harrisburg, Pa. m. Ronald E. Ohl. Grad., U. Del.; MEd, SUNY, Buffalo; postgrad., Pa. State U. Commr. Adminstrn. on Children, Youth and Families Dept. HSS, Washington; W.Va. cabinet sec., chief adminstr. Dept. Health and Human Resources. Recipient Disting. West Virginian award, Joan E. Ohl Rural Health Leadership award, W.Va. Rural Health Assn. Office: Dept HHS Adminstrn on Children Youth and Families 330 C St SW Washington DC 20447*

OHLANDER, JAN HERBERT, lawyer; b. Rockford, Ill., July 10, 1954; s. Herbert Eugene Ohlander and Elmina Laura Osen; m. Patricia S. Phillips, June 27, 1976; children: J. Scott, Samuel John, Elle Elyse. BS, U. Ill., 1976; JD, Marquette U., 1979. Bar: U.S. Dist. Ct. (no. dist.) Ill. 1979, U.S. Dist. Ct. (we. and ea. dists.) Wis. 1979, U.S. Ct. Appeals (7th cir.) 1988, U.S. Supreme Ct. 1990. Assoc. Reno & Zahm, Rockford, 1979-81, ptnr., 1982—. Bd. dirs. Rockford Area Crime Stoppers, 1988—. Mem. ATLA, Ill. Trial Lawyers Am., Trial Bar No. Dist. Ill. Office: Reno & Zahm 1415 E State St Ste 900 Rockford IL 61104-2394

OHLEMILLER, KEVIN K. Neuroscientist, educator; b. Indianapolis, Ind., Nov. 1, 1956; s. Robert John and Mary Chew O.; m. Melinda Monroe, Sept. 1, 1985; children: Jacob McGrath, Dillon James. BS in Biology, Ind. U., Bloomington, 1983; PhD, Northwestern U., Evanston, Ill., 1990. Postdoctoral fellow Washington U., St. Louis, 1990-93, Cen. Inst. for the Deaf, St. Louis, 1993-95, rsch. scientist, 1995—; assoc. rsch. prof. Washington U., 1995—. Contbr. articles to profl. jours. U.S. Navy, 1975-79. Recipient Deafness Rsch. Found. scholar, Nat. Rsch. Svcs. award, NIH, 1992, grantee, NIH, 1995, 99. Mem. Neurosci. Soc., Assn. Rsch. Otolaryngology, Phi Beta Kappa. Democrat. Unitarian Universalist. Office: Ctrl Inst Deaf 4560 Clayton Rd Saint Louis MO 63110 E-mail: kohlemiller@cid.wustl.edu.

OHLMAN, DOUGLAS RONALD, commodities and securities trader, investment consultant, lawyer; b. Rockville Centre, N.Y., Mar. 25, 1949; s. Maxwell and Miriam (Frucht) O.; m. Elat Menashe, Dec. 4, 1983 (div. Nov. 1996). B.A., Columbia Coll., 1971; J.D., Hofstra U., 1974. Bar: N.Y. 1975, U.S. Dist. Ct. (so. and ea. dists.) N.Y. 1976, (no. and we. dists.) N.Y. 1978, U.S. Tax Ct. 1978, U.S. Supreme Ct. 1978, U.S. Ct. Claims 1978, U.S. Customs Ct. 1978. V.p. Info. & Research Services, Inc., Roslyn, N.Y., 1975-81; assoc. Baer & Marks, N.Y.C., 1974-75, Rains, Pogrebin & Scher, Mineola, N.Y., 1975-76, Weisman, Celler, Spett, Modlin & Wertheimer, N.Y.C., 1976-79, Hoffberg, Gordon, Rabin & Engler, N.Y.C., 1979-80, Bergner & Bergner, Blum & Ruditz, N.Y.C., 1980-81; gen. counsel Greenfield Ptnrs., N.Y.C., 1981-86, gen. ptnr., 1982-86, dep. mng. ptnr., 1984-86, chief operating officer, sr. v.p., sec., dir. V.W. Investors, Inc., J.L. Investors, Inc., N.Y.C., 1985-88; commodities and securities trader for proprietary accts. Highland Beach, Fla., 1988—; dir. Track Data Corp., N.Y.C., 1983-87; allied mem. N.Y. Stock Exchange, Inc., 1982-88, options prin., 1985, 87. Mem. radio news team WKCR-FM, N.Y.C. (Writers Guild award, Peabody nomination 1968); notes and comments editor Hofstra Law Rev., 1973-74. Communications dir., dep. radiol. officer Nassau County Civil Def., Town of Roslyn, N.Y., 1964-74; mem. com. Nassau County Liberal Party, 1982. Mem. ABA, N.Y. State Bar Assn., N.Y. County Lawyers Assn., Assn. of Bar of City of N.Y. Home: 401 NE Mizner Blvd Apt T502 Boca Raton FL 33432-4024

OHLSON, DOUGLAS DEAN, artist, educator; b. Cherokee, Iowa, Nov. 18, 1936; s. Lloyd E. and Effie O. (Johnson) O. BA, U. Minn., 1961. Prof. art Hunter Coll., N.Y.C., 1964—. One man shows include Fischbach Gallery, N.Y.C., 1964, 66-70, 72, Susan Caldwell Gallery, N.Y.C., 1974, 76, 77, 79, 81, 82, 83, Portland (Oreg.) Ctr. for Visual Arts, 1977, Ruth Siegel Gallery,

N.Y.C., 1985, 87, Andre Zarre Gallery, N.Y.C., 1985, 90, 92, 93, 95, 2000, Gallery 99, Miami, Fla., 1986, Nina Freudenheim Gallery, Buffalo, 1986, Jaffe Gallery, Miami, 1989; group shows include Mus. Modern Art, N.Y.C., 1968, Tate Gallery, London, 1969, Whitney Mus., N.Y.C., 1969, 71, Corcoran Gallery, Washington, 1972, 73, UCLA, 1975, Born in Iowa: The Homecoming, 1986-87, Doug Ohlson 20 Years of Painting: 1982-2002, Hunter Coll./Times Sq. Gallery, N.Y.C.; invitational Am. Acad. Arts and Letters, 1992, 94, 97, 2002; represented in permanent collections Met. Mus. Art, N.Y.C., Nat. Gallery Art, Washington, Am. Fedn. Art, Mus. Modern Art, Frankfurt, Fed. Republic Germany, Lowe Art Mus., Miami, Fla., Karl Ernst Osthaus Mus., Hagen, Germany, Mus. Contemporary Art, Helsinki, Mpls. Inst. Art, Dallas Mus., Bklyn. Mus., Whitney Mus., N.Y.C., Harvard Art Mus., Cambridge, Mass. Served with USMC, 1955-58. Guggenheim fellow, 1968; Creative Artists Public Service grantee, 1974; Nat. Endowment for Arts grantee, 1976 Home: 35 Bond St New York NY 10012-2426

OHLY, D. CHRISTOPHER, lawyer; b. N.Y.C., Nov. 7, 1950; s. Bodo Charles and Ellen Charlotte (Nekolla) O.; m. Karen Vanacek; 1 child, Sara Rebecca. AB, Johns Hopkins U., 1972; JD, U. Va., 1975. Bar: Md. 1975, U.S. Dist. Ct. Md. 1975, U.S. Ct. Appeals (1st, 2d and 4th cirs.), U.S. Tax Ct., U.S. Supreme Ct. Asst. U.S. Atty. U.S. Atty.'s Office, Balt., 1978-81; owner Hazel & Thomas, P.C., 1989-94; ptnr. Patton Boggs, LLP, 1994-99, Blank, Rome, Comisky & McCauley LLP, Balt., 1999—. Contbr. articles to profl. jours. Mem. ABA, Md. Bar Assn., Am. Soc. Internat. Law, Phi Beta Kappa, Omicron Delta Kappa, Pi Sigma Alpha. Avocations: skiing, computers, amateur radio. Home: 5714 Saint Albans Way Baltimore MD 21212-2454 also: Village Chalet 5 Middle Ridge Rd South Londonderry VT 05155-9747 E-mail: Ohly@BlankRome.com.

OHM, HERBERT WILLIS, agronomy educator; b. Albert Lea, Minn., Jan. 28, 1945; s. Wilhelm Carl and Lena Ann (Finkbeiner) O.; m. Judy Ann Chrisinger, Aug. 8, 1964; children: Cari Lynn, David William. BS in Agrl. Edn., U. Minn., St. Paul, 1967; MS in Plant Breeding, N.D. State U., 1969; PhD in Plant Genetics and Breeding, Purdue U., 1972. Cert. agronomist. Asst. prof. Purdue U., West Lafayette, Ind., 1972-77, assoc. prof. agronomy, 1977-83, prof., 1983—. Team leader Interdisciplinary Wheat and Oat Genetics and Breeding Program, West Lafayette, 1980—, Interdisciplinary Purdue/AID Devel. Program, Burkina Faso, West Africa, 1983-85; mgr. hard red winter wheat rsch. Pioneer Hi-Bred Internat., Inc., Hutchinson, Kans., 1980. Contbr. book chpts. Recipient Soils and Crops Merit award Ind. Crop Improvement Assn., 1988, Merit award Orgn. of African Unity, 1989, Meritorious Svc. award Sci., Tech. and Rsch. Commn., 1989, Agronomic Acheivement award American Soc. of Agronomy, 1994, Sch. of Agr. Team award, 2000. Fellow: AAAS, Crop Sci. Soc. Am. (chmn. divsn. 1991), Am. Soc. Agronomy; mem.: Am. Registry Cert. Profls. in Agrl. Crops and Soils (cert.), Coun. Agrl. Sci. and Tech., Nat. Oat Improvement Coun. (chmn.), Am. Oat Workers Conf. (chmn.). Avocations: woodworking, music. Office: Purdue U Dept Agronomy Lilly Hall Life Scis West Lafayette IN 47907-1150

OHMAN, FRANKLIN ERIC, ballet educator, choreographer, choreographer; b. L.A., Jan. 7, 1939; s. Eric Ohman and Irene Iris Harsan; m. Gloria Isaksen, June 24, 1978 (div. Aug. 1984); 1 child Johan Eric. Grad. h.s., Ontario, Calif., 1957. Dancer San Francisco Ballet, 1959—62, N.Y.C. Ballet, 1962—84; dir. N.Y. Dance Theatre, 1974—. Artistic dir. N.Y. Dance Theatre, 1974—; choreographer, tchr. Ohman Sch. Ballet, L.I., NY, 1980—; choreographer Boston Ballet, Am. Movie Classics (divsn. Rainbow Cablevision), Broadhollow Players, L.I.; tchr., choreographer Long Lake Performing Arts Camp, NY. Co-author (with Emily Berkowitz): Mr. Balonchine my teacher/my friend. Pvt. U.S. Army, 1961—67. Grantee, NY State Coun. on Arts, Suffolk County Office of Cultural Affairs. Avocations: painting, choreography, writing. Office: Ohman Sch Ballet Calvert Ave Commack NY 11725

ÖHMAN, MIKAEL, management consultant; b. Norsjo, Sweden, Feb. 15, 1970; s. Sven-Erik and Gun-Britt (Lindfors) O. MSc, Uppsala (Sweden) U., 1994, Case Western Res. U., 1994. Asst. Swedish Embassy, Moscow, 1991-92; cons. EDS, Atlanta, 1994-96; assoc. McKinsey & Co., Stockholm, 1996-98, engagement mgr. Atlanta, 1998-2000, assoc. prin., 2000—. Advisor Norsjo County, 1996—. Served with Swedish Army, 1990-91. Avocation: sports. Home: 1417 Tugaloo Dr NE Atlanta GA 30319 Office: 133 Peachtree St NE Ste 4600 Atlanta GA 30303-1808

OHMER, STEVEN RUSSELL, judge; b. St. Louis, Apr. 18, 1954; s. Russell Joseph and Patricia Ann O.; m. Roberta Marie Ohmer, Dec. 29, 1976; children: Rachel Caroline, Rebecca Anne. BS, Fla. State U., 1975; JD, Creighton U., 1979. Bar: Mo. 1979, Ill. 1980. Asst. cir. atty. Cir. Atty. Office for St. Louis, 1979-83, asst. cir. atty., chief warrant officer, 1987-94; atty. Ohmer & Ohmer, P.C., St. Louis, 1983-87; assoc. cir. judge 22nd Jud. Cir. State of Mo., 1994-2000, cir. judge, 2000—. Lectr. St. Louis Police Dept., 1993-95, Mo. Assn. of Prosecuting Attys., 1991-92, Legal Advocates of Abused Women, 1995. Author: Missouri Judges Handbook, 2000; contbr. articles to profl. jours. Pres. St. Pius V Sponsor's Club, St. Louis, 1992-94. Mem. Mo. Bar Assn., Ill. Bar Assn., Bar Assn. of Metro. St. Louis, Lawyers Assn. of St. Louis. Roman Catholic. Avocations: golfing, reading, gardening. Office: Cir Ct City of St Louis 10 N Tucker Div 15 Saint Louis MO 63101 E-mail: steven_ohmer@osca.state.mo.us.

OHNO, KINJI, neurologist, educator; b. Hashima, Japan, June 24, 1958; came to U.S., 1993; s. Yukio and Midori Ohno; m. Noriko Ohno, June 25, 1989; children: Yukina, Tomoaki. PhD, Nagoya U., Japan, 1992, MD, 1983. Diplomate Japanese Bd. Neurology. Intern Nagoya Nat. Hosp., 1983-85, resident in neurology, 1985-87, mem. neurology faculty, 1987-88; rsch. fellow Mayo Found., Rochester, Minn., 1993-96, rsch. assoc., 1996—; asst. prof. Mayo Med. Sch., 1998—. Recipient Neurology Rsch. award Mayo Found., 1995. Mem. Am. Soc. Human Genetics, Soc. Neurosci., Internat. Assn. for Biomed. Scis. Office: Mayo Clinic 200 1st St SW Rochester MN 55905 E-mail: ohnok@mayo.edu.

OHNO, YUTAKA, information sciences educator; b. Tokyo, Aug. 24, 1924; s. Teikichi and Kin Ohno; m. Kyoko Okuno; children: Takashi, Junko. B of Engring., Tokyo U., 1946, DEng, 1962. Rschr. Railway Tech. Rsch. Inst., Japanese Nat. Railway, Tokyo, 1946-72; prof. Kyoto (Japan) U., 1972-88, dir. Ednl. Ctr. Info. Processing, 1978-88, prof. emeritus, 1988—; prof. Koshien U., Takarazuka, Japan, 1988-90, Ritsumeikan U., Kyoto, 1990-95, dean dept. sci. and engring., 1992-94, dir. Integrated Info. Ctr., 1994-95, dir. rsch. ctr. Biwako Kusatsu campus Kusatsu, 1995—. Pres. Kansai Tech. Licensing Orgn. Co., Ltd., 1998—; mem. Coun. Info. Processing Promotion, Ministry of Internat. Trade and Industry, Tokyo, 1985-96. Author numerous rsch. articles on info. sys. and software tech. Recipient Gen. Dir. award Sci. and Tech. Agy., Japanese Govt., 1961, Purple Ribbon medal Japanese Govt., 1971, 2d Order of Sacred Treasure, 1996. Mem. Engring. Acad. Japan, Person Computer User's Applications Tech. Assn. (pres. 1991—), Info. Processing Soc. Japan (hon. life, pres. 1987-89), Assn. Computing Machinery (dir. Japan chpt. 1997-2000), Orgn. for Engring. Adventure Groups Linkage Prog. (pres. linkage program 1991-98). Buddhist. Avocations: game of Go, golfing, reading, calligraphy. Home: 1-14-4 Takadai Kyoto Nagaokakyo 617 0847 Japan Office: Kansai Tech Lic Orgn Co 17 Chudoji minami-machi Shimogyo Kyoto 600 8813 Japan

O'HOLLAREN, PAUL JOSEPH, former international fraternity administrator; b. Portland, Oreg., Dec. 24, 1927; s. Charles Edward and Helen Henrietta (McHugh) O'H.; m. Patricia Marie Foley, June 27, 1953; children: Mark T., Kevin J., Brian T., Patrick S., Kelly P. JD, Northwestern Coll. of Law, 1954. Bar: Oreg., 1954. Atty. Oreg. State Bar, 1954—; mem. supreme coun. Moose Internat., Inc., Mooseheart, Ill., 1968-79; supreme gov. Loyal Order of Moose, 1978-79, dir. gen., 1984-94, retired, 1994; chmn. exec. bd. Moose Internat., Inc., 1994—. With U.S. Army, 1945-46. Named Jr. First Citizen, U.S. Jr. C. of C., Portland, 1959; recipient Oreg. State Bar award of Merit, 1979. Mem. Multnomah Athletic Club, Loyal Order of Moose. Republican. Roman Catholic. Avocation: golf.

O'HOLLAREN, SEAN B. federal agency administrator; BS in Polit. Sci. and Psychology, Willamette U.; completed intensive studies program, Georgetown U. Former dir. Washington affairs-environment subs. Union Pacific Corp., primary co. liaison to U.S. Customs Svc.; legis. asst. to U.S. Sen. Mark Hatfield; asst. sec. govt. affairs U.S. Dept. Transp., Washington, 2002—. Office: US Dept Transp Govtl Affairs 400 7th St SW Washington DC 20590*

OHRENSTEIN, ROMAN ABRAHAM, economics educator, economist, rabbi; b. Slomniki, Poland, June 12, 1920; came to U.S., 1951, naturalized, 1957; s. Joseph Barukh and Gena (Fiefkopf) O.; m. Ruth Silberstein, Aug. 30, 1953; children: Gena Ann, Ilana Rose. MA in Econs., U. Munich, 1948, PhD cum laude in Econs., 1949, postgrad. in medicine, 1949-51; MHL, Jewish Theol. Sem. Am., 1955; postgrad., Columbia U., 1963-64. Ordained rabbi, 1955. Rabbi, Auburn, N.Y., 1955-57, Pittsfield, Mass., 1957-60, Atlanta, 1960-62, N.Y.C., 1962-66; prof. econs. Nassau Coll., SUNY-Garden City, 1964-99, chmn. econs. dept., 1976-78, 82-84, prof. emeritus, 1999—, campus chaplain, 1970—; chaplain Nassau County Civic Preparedness, N.Y., 1965—; prof. econs. Am. Coll. Jerusalem, 1968-73, mem. Coll. Coun., 1967-73. Vis. prof. U. Newcastle, Australia, 1985, vis. rsch. prof., 1989; past chaplain Kiwanis, Police Dept. Cayuga County, N.Y., 1955-57, Mt. Sinai Hosp., N.Y.C., 1963-64; nat. dir. Jewish Rights Coun.; mem. Coun. of Orgns., U.S.A., 1978-85; mem. spl. com. on Jewish law Rabbinical Assembly, 1971; condr. seminars U. Queensland, Sydney U., Nat. Univ., all Australia, 1989, Sorbonne, Paris, 1990; lectr., guest spkr. on radio, TV, Jewish civic and profl. orgns. Author: (series) Economic Thought in Talmudic Literature, 1968, 70, 83, 86, 87, 89, 91-93, 96, 2002, Inventories During Business Fluctuations, 1973, Inventory Control as an Economic Shock Absorber, 1975, Economic Analysis in Talmudic Literature, 1992; contbr. chpt. to anthology: Ancient and Medieval Economic Ideas, 1998; mem. editl. adv. bd. Internat. Rev. Econs. and Ethics; columnist Algemeiner Jour., N.Y.C.; contbr. articles to profl. jours. Mem. nat. exec. comm. Am. Profs. for Peace in the Mid. East, 1971-73; mem. adv. bd. Am. Acad. Alliance for Israel, 1995—. Recipient 1st Faculty Disting. Achievement award Nassau Coll., SUNY, 1992, 95, Citation of Excellence, Anbar Electronic Intelligence, Eng., 1996; SUNY fellow, 1968, 70. Mem. Nat. Assn. Jewish Chaplains, Rabbinical Assembly N.Y. Bd. Rabbis, Am. Econ. Assn., History of Econs. Soc., Assn. Social Econs., Learned Soc., N.Y. Acad. Scis., Internat. Soc. for Intercommunication New Ideas, Literati Club (Eng.). Home: 28-74 208th St Bayside NY 11360-2421 Office: Nassau Coll Dept Econ Stewart Ave Garden City NY 11530 *I kept my faith in God coupled with loyalty to tradition, sharpened my mind while maintaining discipline of the heart; tenacity in the face of adversity, turning stumbling blocks into stepping stones while never losing sight of life's supreme purpose: to leave the world a little better than I found it.*

OHRI, SANGEETA JEAN MARY, social educator; b. Mumbai, India, Sept. 12, 1943; d. Joseph Marshall and Hilda Mary (Varel) D'Aguiar; m. N. Ohri, Nov. 20, 1961 (div. May 1999); children: Sanjay, Sandeep. BA part I, Shrimati Nathibai Damodar Thackersey, Mumbai, 1980. Organiser day sch. Soc. for Edn. of Crippled, Mumbai, 1978-82, acting prin., 1979-81; resource person Indian Assn. Presch. Edn., 1979—, Indian Nat. chpt. Org. Mondiale Edn. Prescolaire (World Body Presch.), Mumbai, 1987-95. Hon. treas. Indian Assn. Presch. Edn., Mumbai, 1979-81, hon. sec., 1981-86; adminstr. Soc. for Edn. Crippled, Mumbai, 1979-93; chairperson Rural Project, Pune, India, 1993-96. Joint hon. sec. Local Gen. Hosp., Santa Cruz, Mumbai, 1987-89; mem. State Commn. for Handicapped, Pune, India, 1996; v.p. All India Balkan-ji-Bari (Pioneer Child Welfare Assn.), Mumbai, 1996—; exec. v.p. Indian Assn. Presch. Edn., Mumbai, 1997; exec. Bombay Vigilance Assn., 1990—; cons. Save the Children, India; active Parent Tchr. Orgn. Recipient Sahyog award for women's welfare and social work, 1999. Mem. Pers. Mgmt. and Tng. Assn. of Indian Women (v.p.). Avocations: creative dramatics, writing, travel, organising welfare activities. Home: A-14 Hill View Residency Baner Road Baner, Pune 411045 India E-mail: sohri@vsnl.com.

OHRN, NILS YNGVE, chemistry and physics educator; b. Avesta, Sweden, June 11, 1934; came to U.S., 1966; s. Nils E. and Gerda M. (Akerlund) O.; m. Ann M.M. Thorsell, Aug. 24, 1957; children: Elisabeth, Maria. MS, Uppsala U., 1958, PhD, 1963, F.D., 1966. Research assoc. Uppsala (Sweden) U., 1963-66; assoc. prof. U. Fla., Gainesville, 1966-70, prof. chemistry and physics, 1971—, assoc. dir. Quantum Theory Project, 1976-77, dir. Quantum Theory Project, 1983-98, chmn. dept. chemistry, 1977-83. Editor: Internat. Jour. Quantum Chemistry, 1970—. Fulbright grantee Com. for Internat. Exchange of Scholars, Washington, 1961-63; recipient Bicentennial Gold medal King of Sweden, 1980; Fla. Acad. Scis. medal, 1984, Fellow Am. Phys. Soc., Chaire Francqui Interuniversitaires Belgium; mem. Am. Chem. Soc. (Fla. award 1997), Royal Acad. Scis. Uppsala Sweden (fgn.), Finnish Acad. Scis. (fgn.), Royal Danish Acad. Scis. (fgn.), Sigma Xi, Phi Beta Kappa. Home: 1823 NW 11th Rd Gainesville FL 32605-5323 Office: U Fla Quantum Theory Project 2301 NPB Bldg # 92 Gainesville FL 32611-8435 E-mail: ohrn@qtp.ufl.edu.

OHS, KARL, lieutenant governor; b. Havre, Mont., Nov. 18, 1946; m. Sherri Ohs; children: Brad, Eric, Brian, Elizabeth. Student in Agrl. Econ., Mont. State U. Founder Mont. Agrl. Producers, Inc., 1988—; rep. Mont. House Rep., 1995; prin., owner AAA Storage, Helena, 1996—; majority whip Mont. House Rep., 1997, 1999; lt. gov. State of Mont., Helena. Prin. negotiator Freeman standoff FBI , Jordan, Mont., 1996. Bd. dir. Harrison Sch. Bd., Mont., 1974—83. Recipient Lou Peters award, FBI, 1998. Office: State Capitol PO Box 200801 Helena MT 59620-0801*

OI, CHIEKO MUNNIE, physician; b. Tokyo, Dec. 22, 1960; arrived in US, 1963; d. Shojo and Kiyono (Okino) Oi; m. Richard Zu-Sheng Lin, May 14, 1988; children: Austine Lin, Shelby Lin, Winston Lin. BS, Stanford U., Palo Alto, Calif., 1983; MD, U. Calif., San Francisco, 1988. Diplomate Am Bd Internal Med. Pvt. practice internal medicine, Milpitas, Calif., 1991-94; internist San Jose Med. Group, 1994-95, Santa Cruz Med. Clinic, 1996; clin. asst. prof. U. Tex. Health Sci. Ctr., San Antonio, 1997—2001. Recipient Dept Honors Biol Scis Award, Stanford Univ, Palo Alto, Calif, 1983. Office: Dept Vets Affairs Med Ctr 79 Middleville Rd Northport NY 11768

OI, WALTER YASUO, economics educator; b. L.A., July 1, 1929; s. Matsunosuke and Toshiko (Kawada) Oi; m. Marjorie Louise Robbins; children: Jessica Sumiye , Eleanor Haruko. BS, UCLA, 1952, MA in Econs., 1954; PhD in Econs., U. Chgo., 1961. Instr. Iowa State Coll. Dept. Econs., Ames, 1957-58; rsch. econs. Northwestern U., Evanston, 1958-62; from assoc. prof. to prof. U. Wash., Seattle, 1962-67; prof. grad. sch. mgmt. U. Rochester, N.Y., 1967-75, prof. dept. econs., 1975—, chmn. dept. econs., 1976-82, 83-84, Elmer B. Milliman prof. Econs., 1978—. Economist Inst. Def. Analyses, Arlington, Va., 1966; dir. econ. analysis sect. Mil. Manpower Policy Study, U.S. Dept. Def., Washington, 1964-65; staff economist Pres.'s Commission on All-Volunteer Force, Washington, 1969-70. Adult co-chmn. Task Force on Draft and Nat. Svc. White House Conf. on Youth, 1970-71; vice chmn. Pres.'s Com. on Employment of People with Disabilities, 1983-89; chmn. N.Y. State Adv. Com. to U.S. Commn. on Civil Rights, 1988—. Named J. Fish Smith Disting. Vis. Prof. Brigham Young U., Provo, 1984; Emma and Carol Disting. Vis. scholar Hoover Inst., Stanford U., 1970-71; Ctr. for Advanced Study in Behavioral Scis. fellow, Stanford, 1988. Republican. Home: 690 Winton Rd S Rochester NY 14618-1514 Office: U Rochester Dept Econs Harkness Hall Rochester NY 14627

OILER, DORILOU WEMLINGER, artist; b. Columbus, Ohio, May 7, 1971; d. Lee Paul and M. Sue Wemlinger; m. Bradley James Oiler, Aug. 19, 1995. BA, Graceland Coll., 1995; MFA, Ft. Hays State U., 1998. Studio asst. Graceland Coll., Lamoni, Iowa, 1993-95; custom framer The Frame Shop, Columbus, 1995-96; studio asst. Ft. Hays (Kans.) State U., 1996-98, crafts instr., 1998-99; studio artist Oiler Studios, Hays, 1998-99; ceramics instr. W.Va. Wesleyan Coll., Buckhannon, 1999—. Lectr., workshop leader Oiler Studios, Hays, 1996-99. Recipient Shimpo award Shimpo Ceramics, Ft. Worth, 1998. Mem. Nat. Coun. on Edn. for the Ceramic Arts, Coll. Art Assn., Kans. Artist Craftman Assn. (bd. mem., sec. 1996-99). Avocations: woodcrafts, rafting, hiking, traveling. Home: PO Box 2483 Buckhannon WV 26201-7483 Office: WVa Wesleyan Coll Buckhannon WV 26201 E-mail: oiler_d@wvwc.edu.

OINAS, FELIX J. retired Slavic language educator; b. Tartu, Estonia, Mar. 6, 1911; m. Lisbet Kõve, July 12, 1937; children: Helina (Mrs. Charles Piano), Valdar. Student in Finno-Ugric and Slavic langs., Budapest (Hungary) U., 1935-36; MA in Finno-Ugric Lang., Tartu U., 1938; student in Slavic and English langs., Heidelberg (Germany) U., 1946-48; PhD in Linguistics and Slavic Lang., Ind. U., 1952; Doctorate (hon.), Tartu U., 1999. Lectr. various univs., 1938-50; lectr. Russian studies Ind. U., Bloomington, 1950-52, instr. Slavic studies, 1952-55, asst. prof., 1955-61, assoc. prof. Slavic langs. and lits., 1961-65, prof., 1965-81, prof. Uralic and Altaic studies, 1965-81, fellow Folklore Inst., 1965-81, prof. emeritus, 1981—. Vis. prof. Slavic and Finnic folklore, U. Calif., Berkeley, spring 1976; lectr. and presenter in field. Author 26 books, including: Truth and Justice of Vargamäe: Essays, 1984, Studies in Finnic Folklore: Homage to the Kalevala, 1985, Essays on Russian Folklore and Mythology, 1985, Immortal Kalevipoeg, 1994, others; editor: How Writers Write Lund, 1978, European Folklore: Readings from the Journal of the Folklore Institute, 1981, others; mem. adv. bd. Russian Lang. Jour., 1976-77; cons. Ency. Am. Popular Beliefs and Superstitions, 1984; mem. editl. com. The Slavic and East European Jour., 1966—; assoc. editor Uralic and Altaic Series, 1960—; contbr. 26 books, 450 articles, 50 notes and comments, 130 book reviews. Recipient Cultural award Found. Estonian Arts and Letters, 1978, Kalevala medal Finnish Govt., 1985, Lauri prize Found. Estonian Culture in U.S., 1985, medal of Kreutzwald's Mus., Võru, 1991, awarded Presdl. Order of the Estonian State Coat of Arms, II Class, 1997; Finno-Ugric, Slavic and Folklore fellow Tartu U., 1942-44; Fulbright grantee for Finland, 1961-62, Guggenheim grantee, 1961-62, 66-67, Fulbright-Hays grantee for Yugoslavia, 1964-65, grantee Am. Philos. Soc., 1966, Ford Found., summer 1967, travel grantee ACLS, 1973, Rsch. grantee NEH, 1974-75; named hon. doctor Thrtu U., 1999. Mem. Estonian Sci. Soc. (hon.), Folklore Fellows Internat. (hon.). Office: Ind U Dept Slavic Langs and Lit 502 Ballantine Rd Bloomington IN 47401-5018 Fax: (812) 855-2107. E-mail: iuslavic@indiana.edu.

OISHI, CALVIN SHIZUO, orthopedic surgeon; b. Honolulu, Mar. 2, 1961; s. Masaichi and Kazumae (Ichiuji) O.; m. Selma Hiroko Yonamine, Feb. 1, 1992; children: Sarah, Nathaniel. BA in Biology, Pomona Coll., 1983; MD, U. Calif., San Diego, 1987. Diplomate Am. Bd. Orthopedic Surgery. Intern in surgery U. Calif., San Francisco, 1987-88, resident in orthop., 1988-92; fellow in total joint replacement Scripps Clinic and Rsch. Found., 1992-93; orthop. surgeon Orthop. Assocs. of Hawaii Inc., Honolulu, 1993—. Asst. clin. prof. orthop. surgery, U. Hawaii, Manoa, 1993—; mem. knee design team Exactech, Gainesville, Fla., 1994—. Contbr. articles to profl. jours. NCAA scholar Pomona Coll., 1983; U. Calif. med. sch. grantee, 1984. Fellow Am. Acad. Orthop. Surgeons; mem. Hawaii Orthop. Assn., Hawaii Med. Assn., Leroy C. Abbott Orthop. Soc. Methodist. Avocations: golf, weightlifting, swimming. Office: Orthop Assocs of Hawaii Inc 1380 Lusitana St Ste 604 Honolulu HI 96813-2449

OISHI, STEPHEN MASATO, physician; b. San Francisco, Mar. 22, 1956; s. Masaichi and Kazumae (Ichiuji) O.; m. Sharon Naomi Oishi. BS in Biology, U. Hawaii, 1978; MS in Physiology, Georgetown U., 1980, MD, 1984. Diplomate Am. Bd. Internal Medicine. Intern Los Angeles County-U. So. Calif. Med. Ctr., L.A., 1984-85; resident LAC-USC Med. Ctr., 1985-87; physician Malad (Idaho) Valley Clinic, 1987-91, Ctrl. Med. Clinic, Honolulu, 1991—; med. dir. CMC Lab., 1996—. Mem. staff Kuakini Med. Ctr., Honolulu, 1995—; advisor Dept. Transp., Honolulu, 1995—, Interim Health Care, Honolulu, 1997—. Mem. Mid Pacific Country Club. Methodist. Avocations: golf, fishing, downhill skiing, bass guitarist-rock. Home: 1433 Kewalo St Ph 14 Honolulu HI 96822-4103 Office: Ctrl Med Clinic 321 N Kuakini St Ste 201 Honolulu HI 96817-2399

O'JACK, HELEN MARGARET, clinical social worker; b. Denver, Jan. 31, 1951; d. Herbert Henry and Lillian Anna (Meyer) Thimm; m. William Schmeling, July 24, 1982 (div. Dec. 1992); children: Dustin William Schmeling, Alexander Thimm Schmeling; m. Stanislav G. O'Jack, June 16, 1995. BA in Psychology, U. Colo., 1973; MSW, U. Denver, 1982. Lic. clin. social worker, Wyo. Peer counselor Met. C.C., Omaha, 1975-76; outreach worker South Omaha Crisis Ctr., 1976-77; child care worker Mt. St. Vincent's Youth Home, Denver, 1978-81; social work intern health scis. ctr. U. Colo., 1981-82; coord. crisis line Vol. Info. Referral Service, Rock Springs, Wyo., 1983-85; clin. social worker, coord. elderly svcs. S.W. Counseling Svc., 1985-92; med. social worker Wyo. Home Health Care, 1986-95; pvt. practice, 1992—. Facilitator Alzheimer's Family Support Group, Rock Springs, 1983-92; social work cons. Castle Rock Convalescent Ctr., Green River, Wyo., 1990, Sage View Care Ctr., 1992-95; sch. social worker Desert View Sch., 1992—. Mem. Pacific Rim Inst. for Devel. and Edn. Mem. NASW (regional rep. on bd. dirs. Wyo. chpt. 1991-92), ACSW, NEA. Democrat. Avocations: racquetball, hiking. Office: Desert View Elem Sweetwater Sch Dist # 1 PO Box 1089 Rock Springs WY 82902-1089

OJALVO, MORRIS, civil engineer, educator; b. N.Y.C., Mar. 4, 1924; s. Nissim and (Fanny) O.; m. Anita Bedein, Dec. 26, 1948; children— Lynne, Joseph, Howard, Isobel. B.C.E., Rensselear Poly. Inst., Troy, N.Y., 1944, M.C.E., 1952; PhD, Lehigh U., Bethlehem, Pa., 1960; JD, Ohio State U., Columbus, 1978. Bar: Ohio bar 1979. Draftsman Am. Bridge Co., Elmira, N.Y., 1946-47; tutor civil engring. CCNY, 1947-49; instr. Rensselear Poly. Inst., 1949-51; asst. prof. Princeton U., 1951-58; research instr. Lehigh U., 1958-60; mem. faculty Ohio State U., 1960—, prof. civil engring., 1964-82, prof. emeritus, 1982—; vis. prof. U. Tex.-Austin, 1982-83. Author: Thin-Walled Bars With Open Profiles, 1990; contbr. papers in field; patentee warp restraining device. Served with USNR, 1944-46. Mem. ASCE, Structural Stability Research Council. Home and Office: 1024 Fairway Ln Estes Park CO 80517-7156

OJARD, BRUCE ALLEN, photographer, educator; b. Duluth, Minn., Dec. 20, 1951; s. Robert Nelson and Theresa Doris (Kurshoff) O.; m. Susan Kathleen van Druten, Aug. 20, 1983. BBA, U. Minn., 1974. Owner Bruce Ojard Photographics, Duluth, Minn., 1974-85; lab. coordinator Duluth Art Inst., 1975—; staff photographer St. Louis County Heritage & Arts Ctr., Duluth, 1975-83; photography instr. Duluth Art Inst., 1976—; staff photographer City Hall Info. Office, Duluth, 1976-78; photography instr. Duluth Sch. Dist. #709, 1979-97; dir., writer, actor Colder by the Lake Theater Co., Duluth, 1983—; owner Digital Audio-Visual Co., 1985—. Video, performance artist, 1984—; tech. dir. Storymakers Theater Co., Duluth, 1983-84, Norshor Theatre in the State, Duluth, 1992-94; cons. Minn. Ballet Co., 1988-90, Duluth Playhouse, 1985—, photographer, 1983—; writer, cons., videographer Dark Horse Theatre Co., Duluth, 1998. Writer, actor video prodn. Academy O'Comedy, 1985 (Silver Addy award 1986); actor movie Iron Will, 1993; photographs published in numerous jours. Advisor Duluth Community Schs., 1984; vol. The Depot Cultural Arts Ctr., 1976. Prodn. grantee Arrowhead Regional Arts Coun., 1985, 89, 91-96, 98, 2001. Mem. Duluth Art Inst., Friends of Feathers, Scrabble Players. Avocations: collecting Star Wars and Simpsons memorabilia, McCoy pottery, Atari video games. Home: 1729 E 8th St Duluth MN 55812-1224 Office: Duluth Art Inst 506 W Michigan St Duluth MN 55802-1505 E-mail: b_ojard@hotmail.com.

OJIMA, IWAO, chemistry educator; b. Yokohama, Japan, June 5, 1945; came to U.S., 1983; s. Masaharu and Sumiko (Takatsuki) O.; m. Yoko Ogino, Apr. 24, 1971. BS, U. Tokyo, 1968, MS, 1970, PhD in Organic Chemistry, 1973. Rsch. fellow Sagami Inst. for Chem. Rsch., Japan, 1970-76, sr. rsch. fellow, group leader Japan, 1976-83; assoc. prof. chemistry SUNY, Stony Brook, 1983-84, prof., 1984-91, leading prof., 1991-95, disting. prof., 1995—, chmn., 1997—. Editor: Catalytic Asymmetric Synthesis, 1993, 2d edit., 2000, Taxane Anticancer Agents, 1994, Biomedical Frontiers of Fluorine Chemistry, 1996, Anticancer Agents-Frontiers in Cancer Chemotherapy, 2001; contbr. numerous articles to profl. jours.; numerous patents in field. Named fellow J.S. Guggenheim Meml. Found., 1995-97. Fellow AAAS, N.Y. Acad. Sci.; mem. Am. Chem. Soc. (editl. adv. bd. 1995-2000, exec. com. divsn. organic chemistry 1998-2000, A.C. Cope Scholar award 1994, E.B. Hershberg award 2001), Chem. Soc. Japan (Nat. Young Investigator award 1976, Disting. Achievement award 1999), N.Y. Acad. Scis., Sigma Xi. Achievements include research in homogenous catalysis of transition metal complexes; asymmetric synthesis; organic synthesis by means of organometallic reagents; peptides and peptide mimetics; beta-lactam chemistry; organo flourine chemistry, medicinal chemistry especially in regard to enzyme inhibitors and taxane anticancer agents. Home: 41 Roslyn Ct Port Jefferson NY 11777-1462 Office: State U New York Dept Chemistry Stony Brook NY 11794-3400 E-mail: iojima@notes.cc.sunysb.edu.

OKA, TAKASHI, journalist, consultant, educator; b. Tokyo, Oct. 21, 1924; s. William Masakazu and Fumiko Mary Oka; m. Hiroko Imai, Sept. 8, 1956; children: Megumi, Sakuya. B in Econs., Rikkyo U., 1947; BA, Principa Coll., 1950; MA, Harvard U., 1954. Asst. to fgn. editor Christian Sci. Monitor, Boston, 1954-59, fgn. corr. Hong Kong, Saigon, Moscow, 1959-68, Paris, London, Beijing, and Tokyo, 1971-92; bur. chief Tokyo office N.Y. Times, 1968-71; staff dir. internat. dept. New Frontier Party, Tokyo, 1994-98; vis. scholar Sigur Ctr. George Washington U., Washington, 1998-99; Washington rep. Liberal Party of Japan, 1999—. Rsch. assoc. Internat. Inst. of Strategic Studies, London, 1976-78; rsch. fellow Carnegie Endowment for Internat. Peace, 1992-95. Author: Prying Open the Door: Foreign Workers in Japan, 1995. Mem. Internat. Inst. for Strategic Studies. Avocation: tennis. Home and Office: 2555 Pennsylvania Ave NW Washington DC 20037-1614

OKA, TAKESHI, physicist, chemist, astronomer, educator; b. Tokyo, June 10, 1932; arrived in Can., 1963, naturalized, 1973; s. Shumpei and Chiyoko O.; m. Keiko Nukui, Oct. 24, 1960; children: Ritsuko, Noriko, Kentaro, Yujiro. B.Sc., U. Tokyo, 1955, PhD, 1960; PhD (hon.), U. Waterloo, 2001. Rsch. assoc. U. Tokyo, 1960-63; fellow NRC Can., Ottawa, Ont., 1963-65, asst., 1965-68, assoc., 1968-71, sr. rsch. physicist, 1971-80; prof. U. Chgo., 1981—; Robert A. Millikan disting. prof., 1989—; prof. Enrico Fermi inst., 1993—. Mem. editorial bd. Chem. Physics, 1972-92, Jour. Molecular Spectroscopy, 1973—, Jour. Chem. Physics, 1975-77. Recipient Steacie prize, 1972; Earle K. Plyler prize, 1982. Fellow Royal Soc. Can., Royal Soc. London, Am. Phys. Soc., Optical Soc. Am. (William F. Meggers award 1997, Ellis R. Lippincott award 1998), Am. Acad. Scis. and Arts; mem. Am. Astron. Soc; Am. Chem. Soc. (E. Bright Wilson award, 2002). Office: U Chgo Dept Chemistry Astronomy & Astrophysics Chicago IL 60637 E-mail: t_oka@uchicago.edu.

OKADA, GEOFFREY TOSHIO, endodontist; b. Honolulu, June 21, 1955; m. Stella Yan Lau. BA, UCLA, 1978; DDS cum laude, Loyola U., Chgo., 1983; cert in endodontics, Loma Linda U., 1998, MS in Endodontics, 2000. Pvt. practice, L.A., 1984—; instr. dept. oral diagnosis, radiology and pathology Loma Linda (Calif.) U. Sch. Dentistry, 1997-99; asst. prof. dept. endodontics Loma Linda U. Sch. Dentistry, 1999—. Instr. dept. radiation oncology City of Hope Med. Ctr., Duarte, Calif., 1995, 96. Contbr. articles to med. jours. Grantee Am. Assn. Endodontists Found., 1997, 98. Mem. ADA, Am. Assn. Endodontists, Calif. Dental Assn., So. Calif. Acad. Endodontists, San Fernando Valley Dental Soc., Japanese-Am. Dental Soc.

OKADA, ROBERT DEAN, cardiologist; b. Seattle, Sept. 18, 1947; m. Carolyn Okada. BA summa cum laude, U. Wash., 1969; MD, U. Pa., 1973. Intern U. Ariz. Health Scis. Ctr., Tucson, 1973-74, resident in internal medicine, 1974-76, clin. fellow in cardiology, 1976-78; clin. and rsch. fellow in medicine Mass. Gen. Hosp., Boston, 1978-79; fellow in medicine Harvard Med. Sch., 1978-79, instr., 1979-81, asst. prof., 1981-85; prof. U. Okla. Med. Sch., 1985—. Staff cardiologist St. Francis Hosp., Tulsa, 1985—; asst. in medicine Mass. Gen. Hosp., 1982-86, cons. in nuclear medicine, 1981—, sr. staff cardiac catheterization lab., 1979-86, clin. asst. in medicine, 1979-85, dir. cardiac magnetic resonance imaging; prof. Tulsa Med. Coll., 1985—; dir. cardiac magnetic resonance imaging and nuclear cardiology, dir. Warren Med. Rsch. Inst. Contbr. articles to profl. jours. Recipient Am. Legion award U. Wash., 1966, Neisei Vets. award, 1966. Fellow ACP, Am. Coll. Cardiology, Am. Coll. Chest Physicians, N.Y. Acad. Scis., Am. Heart Assn. Coun. Clin. Cardiology; mem. Am. Fedn. for Clin. Rsch., Paul Dudley White Soc., Soc. Nuclear Medicine, Am. Heart Assn. Coun. Clin. Cardiology, Soc. Magnetic Resonance in Medicine, AAAS, Soc. for Magnetic Resonance Imaging, Okla. State Med. Soc., AMA, Am. Soc. Internal Medicine, AAUP, Phi Beta Kappa, Alpha Xi Sigma. Office: Cardiology of Tulsa Inc 6151 S Yale Ave Ste 400 Tulsa OK 74136-1933

OKADA, RYOZO, educator, clinician and researcher; b. Kiryu, Gummaken, Japan, July 20, 1931; s. Kenji and Sachi (Ishihara) O.; m. Shigeko Shindo, May 25, 1958; children: Kyoko, Taro. MD, Tokyo U., 1956, PhD, 1961. Intern then resident; asst. Tokyo U. Sch. Medicine, 1962-63; rsch. fellow Hektoen Inst. Cook County Hosp., Chgo., 1963-66; attending physician Yoikuin Hosp., Tokyo, 1966-68; assoc. prof. Sch. Med. Juntendo U., 1968-83, prof., 1983-97, dir. cardiovascular lab., 1985-97, prof. emeritus, 1997—; rector Gumma Paz Gakuen Coll., Japan, 1998—; dir. Misato Rsch. Inst., Japan, 2000—. Councilor Cardiovasc. Inst. Roppongi, Tokyo, 1990—, Indsl. Medicine Found., 1995—; mem. occupl. diseases com. Min. Health, Welfare and Labor, Japan, 1987—. Contbr. chpts. to books, articles to profl. jours. Bd. dirs. Shirane Kaizen Sch.; Hotaka juridical person, Gumma, Japan. Fellow: Japanese Geriat. Soc., Japanese Angiology Soc., Japanese Circulation Soc., Internat. Union Angiology, Am. Diabetes Assn., Cardiovasc. Pathology, Am. Geriat. Soc., Internat. Electrocardiology, Am. Heart Assn., Coun. Prevention Heart Disease; mem.: Japanese Soc. Medicine. Avocation: travel. Home: 6859-186 Nakayama Takayamamura Agatsumagun Gummaken 377-0702 Japan Office: Gumma Paz Gakuen Coll 6859-251 Nakayama Takayamamura Gummaken 377-0702 Japan E-mail: paz.offi@p.wind.ne.jp.

OKADA, SHIGERU, pathology educator; b. Okayama, Japan, Feb. 15, 1940; s. Keizo and Moyoko (Nishigaki) O.; m. Naoko Kobashi, Nov. 7, 1965; children: Satoru, Rie, Mari. MD, Okayama U., Japan, 1964, PhD, 1969. Chief pathologist Kyoto (Japan) City Hosp., 1977-80; lectr. Sch. Medicine Kyoto U., 1980-90; asst. Med. Sch. Okayama U., 1969-71, lectr., 1971-77; prof. Okayama U. Med. Sch., Japan, 1990; dir. Isotope Ctr. Okayama U., Japan, 1995—2001, advisor to the pres., 1999—2001. Head radiation protection com. Okayama U., 1991-2001. Contbr. articles to profl. jours. Mem. Japan Pathol. Soc. Tokyo, Japan Haematological Soc. Kyoto, Internat. Soc. Hematology, Japanese Cancer Assn. Tokyo, N.Y. Acad. Sci. Office: Okayama U Med Sch 2-5-1 Shikata Okayama 700-8558 Japan

OKAL, EMILE ANDRE, geophysicist, educator; b. Paris, Aug. 7, 1950; came to U.S., 1974; Agrégation, U. Paris, 1971; MS, U. Pierre and Marie Curie, Paris, 1972; PhD, Calif. Inst. Tech., 1978. Asst. prof. Yale U., New Haven, 1978-81, assoc. prof., 1981-83, Northwestern U., Evanston, Ill., 1984-89, prof., 1989—. Editor GRL Am. Geophys. Union, Washington, 1993-96, editor-in-chief, 1996-97. Contbr. over 140 articles to profl. jours. Office: Northwestern U 1847 Sheridan Rd Evanston IL 60208-2150

OKAMOTO, VICKI E. orthodontist; b. Honolulu; BA, U. Hawaii, 1987; DDS, U. Mo., 1992; MS, UCLA, 1994. Cert. in orthodontics, UCLA, 1994. Pvt. practice, L.A., 1994—; lectr. dept. of orthodontics UCLA Sch. of Dentistry, 1995—. Mem. Am. Assn. Orthodontists, ADA, Orange County Dental Soc., Calif. Assn. Orthodontists, Pacific Coast Soc. Orthodontists. Office: 1530 Baker St Ste C Costa Mesa CA 92626-3752

OKAMURA, ARTHUR SHINJI, artist, educator, writer; b. Long Beach, Calif., Feb. 24, 1932; s. Frank Akira and Yuki O.; m. Elizabeth Tuomi, Aug. 7, 1953 (div.); children: Beth, Jonathan, Jane, Ethan; m. Kitty Wong, 1991. Student, Art Inst. of Chgo., 1950-54, U. Chgo., 1951, 52, 57, art seminar Yale, 1954. Faculty Ctrl. YMCA Coll., Chgo., 1956, 57, Evanston (Ill.) Art Center, 1956-57, Art Inst. Chgo., North Shore Art League, Winnetka, Ill., Acad. Art, San Francisco, 1957, Calif. Sch. Fine Arts, 1958, Ox Bow Summer Art Sch., Saugatuck, Mich., 1963, Calif. Coll. Arts and Crafts, Oakland, 1958-59, prof. arts, 1966-97, prof. emeritus, 1997—. Instr. watercolor painting, 1987; dir. San Francisco Studio Art, 1958; tchr. watercolor workshops, Bali, Indonesia, 1989, 92; lectr. in field. Author: (with Robert Creeley) 1, 2, 3, 4, 5, 6, 7, 8, 9, 0, 1971, (with Joel Weishaus) Ox-Herding, 1971, (with Robert Bly) Basho, 1972, Ten Poems by Issa, 1992, (with Steve Kowit) Passionate Journey, 1984, Magic Rabbit, 1995, The Paper Propeller, 2000; one-man shows include Charles Feingarten Galleries, Chgo., 1956, 58, 59, San Francisco, 1957, Santa Barbara Mus. Art, 1958, Oakland Mus. Art, 1959, Legion Honor, San Francisco, 1961, Dallas, 1962, La Jolla (Calif.) Mus., 1963, U. Utah, 1964, San Francisco Mus. Art, 1968, Hanssen Gallery, 1968, 71, Ruth Braunstein, San Francisco, 1981, 82, 84, 86-88, 90, 94, 97, 2000; exhibited in group shows including Pa. Acad. Fine Art, U. Chgo., U. Wash., U. Ill., Art Inst. Chgo., L.A. County Mus., Am. Fedn. Art, Denver Mus., NAD, De Young Mus., San Francisco, Knoedler Gallery, N.Y.C., Feingarten Galleries, Whitney Mus. Art, others; retrospective at Bolinas Mus., 2002, Claudia Chapline Galleries, Stinson Beach, Calif., 1995; represented in permanent collections including Art Inst. Chgo., Borg-Warner Collections, Chgo., Whitney Mus. Art, N.Y.C., Santa Barbara Mus. Art, San Francisco Mus. Art, Ill. State Normal, Corcoran Mus., Nat. Collection Fine Arts, Smithsonian Instn., 1968, many others. Served as pvt. AUS, 1955-56. Recipient 1st prize religious art U. Chgo., 1953; Ryerson travelling fellow, 1954; Martin Cahn award contemporary Am. paintings Art Inst. Chgo., 1957; purchase award U. Ill., 1959; purchase award Nat. Soc. Arts and Letters, N.Y.C., 1960; Neysa McMein purchase award Whitney Mus. Art, 1960; Schwabacher-Frey award 79th Ann. of San Francisco Mus. Art, 1960 Mem.: Commonweal (bd. dirs. 1993—2002). Home: 210 Kale Rd Bolinas CA 94924

OKAMURA, HIDEKI, research scientist, physicist; b. Machida, Tokyo, Japan, Oct. 16, 1964; s. Muneki and Yoko (Kitada) O. BS, U. Tokyo, 1988, MS, 1990, PhD, 1994. Lectr. Japan Optometry and Hygienic Sch., Tokyo, 1988—93; rsch. scientist Inst. Phys. and Chem. Rsch., Saitama, Japan, 1994—2002, sr. rsch. Japan, 2002—. Lectr. in physics Sophia U., Tokyo, 1998—2000; vis. scientist Nat. Rsch. Coun. Can., Ottawa, 2000—01. Contbr. articles to profl. sci. jours. Mem. Atomic Energy Soc. Japan (isotope separation rsch. com. 1996-99), Japan Soc. Applied Physics, Optical Soc. Japan, Optical Soc. Am., Spectroscopical Soc. Japan. Avocations: tennis, flying, swimming, horseback riding. Office: RIKEN Inst Phys Chem Rsch 2-1 Hirosawa Wako Saitama 351-0198 Japan

OKAMURA, HIDEO, manufacturing executive; b. Kochi-City, Japan, May 30, 1943; came to U.S., 1968; s. Junki and Hiroka Okamura; divorced; 1 child, Jennifer H. Prodn. mgr. Power Axle Corp., Compton, Calif., 1984-87; dir. tech. prodn. Dynamic Axle Co., Inc., Long Beach, 1988-90; mng. dir. Aragon Engring., Inc., Rancho Dominguez, 1991-96. Mem. Am. Soc. of Metal, Acad. of Magical Arts, Inc. Avocations: scuba diving, landscaping, photography, golf, travel. Home: 16889 Helena Cir Fountain Valley CA 92708-2815 Office: Transpower Techs Inc 6301 Orangethorpe Ave Buena Park CA 90620-1340

O'KANE, JOHN JOSEPH, special education educator, administrator; b. N.Y.C., July 7, 1947; s. Alexander and Mary Ann O'Kane; m. Susan Elizabeth Harwood, July 10, 1974 (div. Nov. 1988); m. Mary Claire Bell, Dec. 17, 1988; children: Sean Gardner, Erin Gardner, Molly. BA, Union Coll., 1969; MS in Edn., SUNY, Buffalo, 1981. Cert. sch. adminstrn.; cert. spl. edn.; cert. elem. edn. Tchr. Children's Psychiatric Ctr., W. Seneca, N.Y., 1974-82; edn. coord. N.Y. State Divn. Youth, Buffalo, 1982-86; asst. prof. SUNY, Brockport, 1986-90; chairperson com. spl. edn. Rochester (N.Y.) City Sch. Dist., 1988-91; spl. edn. chairperson Penfield (N.Y.) Ctrl. Schs., 1991-2000; dir. pupil pers. svcs. Batavia (N.Y.) City Sch. Dist., 2000—. Adj. instr. SUNY, Brockport, 1986-99; cons. Attica (N.Y.) Ctrl. Schs., 1996; presenter Coun. Exceptional Children. Mem. adv. com. BOCES, Spencerport, N.Y., 1988-90. With U.S. Army, 1971-74. Named Citizen of the Yr. Advocacy Ctr., 1991. Mem. ASCD, Newman Oratory. Roman Catholic. Avocations: baseball, golf, reading, scholarship, community service. Home: 61 South Ave Brockport NY 14420-2009 Office: 39 Washington Ave Batavia NY 14020-2035 E-mail: JohnOKane@aol.com.

O'KANE, MARGARET E. non-profit organization executive; BA in French, Fordham U., 1969; MHS in Health Adminstrn. and Planning, Johns Hopkins U. Sch. Hygiene and Public Health. Second grade tchr. St. Ambrose Sch., Bklyn., 1970-72; neurology rsch. asst. Children's Hosp., Boston, 1972-73; respiratory therapist St. Elizabeth's Hosp., Boston, U. Va. Med. Ctr., Charlottesville, Va., Children's Hosp., Washington, DC, 1973-78; program analyst office of planning, evaluation, legislation health svcs. adminstrn. U.S. Dept. Health and Human Svcs., Washington, 1979-81; rsch. assoc. intergovermental health policy project (IHPP) The George Washington U., 1981-83; public health svc. fellow U.S. Dept. Health and Human Svcs. Nat. Ctr. for Health Svcs. Rsch., 1983-84, special asst. to dir., 1985-86; dir. med. dirs. divsn. Am. Assn. Health Plans (formerly Group Health Assn. of Am., Inc.), 1986-89; dir. quality mgmt. Group Health Assn., Inc., 1989-90; pres. Nat. Com. Quality Assurance, 1990—. Elected mem. Inst. of Medicine, 1999. Named Health Person of Yr. Medicine & Health Jour., 1996; recipient Founder's award Am. Coll. Med. Quality, 1997. Office: Nat Com for Quality Assurance 2000 L St NW Ste 500 Washington DC 20036-4918*

OKAY, JOHN LOUIS, management consultant; b. Emmett, Mich., Mar. 27, 1942; s. Stanley John and Mildred Isabell (Little) O.; m. Judith Ann Gerlach, Aug. 22, 1964; children: Stephen, Christopher, Douglas. BS in Agr., Mich. State U., 1964, MS in Agrl. Econs., 1967, PhD in Resource Econs., 1974. Agrl. economist U.S. Soil Conservation Svc., East Lansing, Mich., 1967-73, program analyst Washington, 1974-83, dir. info. systems, 1983-85; assoc. dir. info. systems USDA, 1985-91, dir. info. systems, 1991-95; dep. commr. Fed. Technology Svc., GSA, Falls Church, Va., 1995-97; sr. v.p. Fed. Sources Inc., McLean, 1997-99; pres. J.L. Okay Cons., Oak Hill, 1999—. Recipient Meritorious Exec. award Pres. of U.S., 1989, 97. Mem. Armed Forces Comm. and Electronics Assn. (bd. dirs. 1994-98), Sr. Execs. Assn. (bd. dirs. 1989-98). Office: 2857 Fox Mill Rd Oak Hill VA 20171-1829 E-mail: john.okay@erols.com.

OKAZAWA-REY, MARGO, social worker, educator; b. Kobe, Japan, Nov. 26, 1949; d. Sidney Mayfield and Kazuko (Okazawa) R. BA, Capital U., 1973; MSW, Boston U., 1974; EdD, Harvard U., 1987. Lic. ind. clin. social worker, Mass. Social worker Hayden Goodwill Inn Sch., Dorchester, Mass., 1975; area drug coord., program dir. Fuller Mental Health Ctr. Drug Program, Roxbury, 1975-79; asst. prof. N.H. Coll., Manchester, 1979-83; founder, tchr. women's ednl. and vocat. enrichment program Women Inc., Roxbury, 1980-83; asst. prof. social work Simmons Coll., Boston, 1984-88, U. Md., Balt., 1988-89; prof., undergrad. program coord. San Francisco State U., 1990—; assoc. fellow Inst. Policy Studies, Washington, 1990—. Head trainer anti-racism tng. group Washington Sch., 1991; Jane Watson Irwin vis. prof. in Women's studies Hamilton Coll., 1999-2000. Author: Women's Lives: Multicultural Perspectives, 1998, Beyond Heroes and Holidys: Anti-Racist K-12 Multicultural Education and Staff Development, 1998, Encyclopedia of African-American Education, 1996; co-editor: Teachers, Teaching, Teacher Education, 1988; peer reviewer Jour. Negro Edn., 1989—, editorial adv. bd., 1991-98, Social Justice, 1999—. Adv. bd. Shanti Project, San Francisco, 1990—; bd. dirs. Afro-Asian Rels. Coun. of Washington, 1990—; co-founder E. Asia-U.S. Women's Network Against Militarism, 1997—. Sara Lawrence Lightfoot fellow Harvard U., 1986; sr. Fulbright scholar, 1994; grantee Hitachi Found., Washington, 1989, Peace Devel. Fund, Amherst, Mass., 1990, Social Sci. Rsch. Coun., 1996. Mem. Coun. on Social Work Edn., Bertha Capen Reynolds Soc. Avocations: long-distance running, tennis. Office: San Francisco State U 1600 Holloway Ave San Francisco CA 94132-1722 E-mail: mor@sfsu.edu.

OKE, FESTUS ERHIURHORE, minister, religious organization administrator; b. Ofoni, Nigeria, Dec. 23, 1938; came to U.S., 1965; d. Ighojigbere Tom and Oghifo Okwede O.; m. Margret A. Ogwilaya, Nov. 7, 1960 (div. 1965); 1 child, Richard; m. Connie J., March 12, 1972; children: Richard, Okwede, Ejenobo, Ojeta, Aweshare. BS, Ind. U., 1969, MS, EdS, 1971, EdD, 1972; MDiv, Bethany Theol. Sem., 1994. Tchg. asst. Ind. U., Bloomington, 1969-72; dept. chair Fla. A&M U., Tallahassee, 1972-74, dir., 1974-76, Ahmadu Bello U., Zaria, Nigeria, 1976-87; machine operator P & H Machine Co., Walkerton, Ind., 1987—90; pastor Turkey Creek Ch. of the Brethren, Nappanee, 1993-94; factory worker Wells Aluminum Corp., Liberty, 1994-95; dir., chaplain Hope Rescue Mission, South Bend, 1995—. Avocations: photography, woodwork. Office: Hope Rescue Mission 532 S Michigan St South Bend IN 46601-2499 E-mail: festus@michiana.org.

O'KEEFE, BEVERLY DISBROW, state official, federal official; b. Wilton, Conn., Sept. 1, 1946; d. Harry Harbs and Jane Corrine (Young) Disbrow; children: Marcia Corrine, Jennifer Lynn; m. John Patrick O'Keefe, Aug. 1981 (div. 1985). AA, Berkshire Community Coll., 1973; BA in Psychology, U. Mass., 1975; MPA, U. S.C., 1979; cert. master gardener, U. R.I., 1999. Lic. social worker, S.C. Statis. clk. U. S.C., Columbia, 1976-78; pub. adminstr. employment and tng. Office of Gov., State of S.C., 1976-78, 88—; project coord. Trident Tech. Coll., Charleston, S.C., 1981-82; office mgr. Med. U. S.C., 1983-85; coord. bus. svcs. AMI East Cooper Community Hosp., Mt. Pleasant, S.C., 1985-87; mktg. rep. R.L. Bryan Co., Columbia, 1987; pub. adminstr. S.C. Dept. Social Svcs., 1988; pub. adminstr., employment and tng. Office Gov. State S.C., 1988-89; mem. employment and tng. staff City of Norfolk (Va.) Div. Soc. Svcs., 1990-91; social sci. analyst Naval Edn. and Tng. Ctr. Family Svc. Ctr., Newport, R.I., 1992-96; program coord. Naval Edn. and Tng. Ctr. Family Svc. Ctr., 1996—; rsch. assoc. U. R.I., Kingston, 1999—; project dir. U. R.I. Family Resource Partnership, Providence, 1999; marine rsch. specialist U. R.I. Narraquansett Bay Campus, 2002—. Editor newsletter Friends of Library, 1982-84. Sec. Friends of Charleston County Libr., 1981-82, pres. 1982-84; bd. dirs. Wando High Sch. Local Adv. Coun., Mt. Pleasant, 1981-84, Newport Armed Svcs. YMCA, 1996-98; pres. Wando High Sch. PTA, 1982-83, editor newsletter, 1982-85; vol. Navy-Marine Corps Relief Soc., 1993-96; mem. Newport County Coun. Cmty. Svcs., 1996-98; publicity chmn. Navy-Marine Corps Relief Soc., Newport, 1993-94; asst. dir., fin. URI RI Sea Grant Program, 2002. Grantee Marine Rsch. Specialist Sea Grant Coll. Program, U. R.I., Narragansett, 2002—. Mem. Am. Counseling Assn., R.I. Counseling Assn., Am. Soc. Pub. Adminstrs., APA, Am. Pub. Welfare Assn., Southeastern Employment and Tng. Assn., Rhode Island Orchid Soc. (sec. 2000). Democrat. Roman Catholic. Avocations: writing fiction, water colors, gardening. Home: 472 Gardiner Rd West Kingston RI 02892-1068 Office: URI Narragansett Bay Campus South Ferry Rd Narragansett RI 02882-1197 E-mail: ladyslip1@mindspring.com.

O'KEEFE, DONALD MARTIN, detective-lieutenant; b. San Francisco, Mar. 30, 1956; s. William J. and Jane T. (English) O'K. Grad., FBI Nat. Acad., Quantico, Va., 1993; BS in Human Svcs., Coll. of Notre Dame, Belmont, Calif., 1995; MPA, U. San Francisco, 1999. Cert. advanced Commn. on Peace Officer Stds. and Tng. (POST), Calif. Dep. sheriff San Mateo County Sheriff's Office, Redwood City, Calif., 1980-88, detective, 1988, sgt., 1988-91, detective sgt., 1991-98, detective lt., 1998—. Recipient commendation for outstanding svc. Am. Legion, Redwood City, 1993, City of East Palo Alto, Calif., 1997. Mem. Calif. Narcotics Officers Assn., Calif. Homicide Officers Assn., Calif. Sexual Assault Officers Assn., Calif. Robbery Investigators Assn., FBI Nat. Acad. Assocs. Republican. Roman Catholic. Avocations: golf, tennis, weight-lifting, skiing. Office: San Mateo County Sheriff's Office 400 County Ctr Ofc Redwood City CA 94063-1662

O'KEEFE, EDWARD FRANKLIN, lawyer; b. S.I., N.Y., June 9, 1937; s. Francis Franklin and Bertha (Hall) O'K.; m. Toni Lynne McGohan; children: Kira Kathleen, Douglas Franklin, Andrew Franklin, Alison Elizabeth, Theadore William, Nigel Francis. AB, U. N.C., 1959; JD, U. Denver, 1961. Bar: Colo. 1962. Law clk. Colo. Supreme Ct., Denver, 1962-63; assoc. gen. counsel Hamilton Mgmt. Corp., 1966-69, sec., 1968-76, v.p. legal, gen. counsel, 1969-76; ptnr. Moye, Giles O'Keefe, Vermeire & Gorrell, Denver, 1976—. Assoc. gen. counsel, sec. ITT Variable Annuity Ins. Co., Denver, 1969, v.p. legal, gen. counsel, 1969-70; sec. Hamilton Funds Inc., Denver, 1968-76 Served with USNR, 1963-66. Mem. Nat. Assn. Security Dealers (dist. conduct com., chmn. 1976), Colo. Assn. Corporate Counsel (pres. 1974-75) also: 2680 Mariners Way SE Southport NC 28461 Office: Moye Giles O'Keefe Vermeire 1225 17th St Fl 29 Denver CO 80202-5534 Home: 2680 Mariners Way SE Southport NC 28461-8512 E-mail: efokeefe@mgovg.com.

O'KEEFE, FREDRICK REA, bishop, consultant, educator, writer; b. Washington, Mar. 26, 1944; s. Roy Fox and Kathryn Isabelle (Rea) O'Keefe; stepson of James Michael O'Keefe. Student, Fordham U., 1970-72; STD (hon.), StarReach Inst., Putnam Valley, N.Y., 1973; student, St. Augustines Sch. Theology, Fla., 1984; HHD (hon.), Trinity Hall Coll. & Sem., Santa Monica, 1987. Mgmt. trainer Sears Roebuck, Peekskill, N.Y., 1971-76, div. mgr., 1970-76; pres. Dreadnought Corp., 1974-76; gen. mgr. R. Shaw Co., Laguna Beach, Calif., 1977, N.D. Burger Co., L.A., 1980-84; mgmt., sales and mktg. trainer, v.p. mktg. Grand Am. Computers and Software Only, Irvine, Calif., 1984-86; tchr. Confraternity Christian Doctrine, Myrtle Beach, S.C., 1967-68; deacon to priest Old Cath. Ch. in N.Am., Peekskill, 1975-82; consecrated bishop Old Episcopal Ch., Scotland, 1982; vicar gen. Lomita, Calif., 1982-83; presiding bishop Redondo Beach, 1983—; archibishop-abbot Incarnation Abbey Found., Order of St. Benedict, 1987—; dir. customer svc. divsn., mgr. MIS networks Peter Lowe Internat. Inc., Tampa, Fla., 1992-94; mgmt. cons. Power Support Engring., Inc., 1997-2000. Dir. Conlegium Spiriti Refulgentis, Redondo Beach, 1975—; exec. dir. Am. Bd. Examiners in Pastoral Counseling, Washington, 1986—, sec., treas., 1982—; exec. dir. Am. Coun. on Schs. and Colls., Washington, 1982—; chmn. Grad. Coll. Theology, L.A., 1983-87; chaplain L.A. Sheriff's Dept., 1983-86; cons. CSR Cons., Clearwater, Fla., 1975-98, CEO, 1984-98, also dir.; dir. customer svc. Peter Lowe Internat., Inc., 1992-94; bd. dirs. Corp. Mgmt. Trust, Advanced Indsl. Techs. Contbr. articles to mags., poetry to collections; assoc. editor, journalist, mng. editor ANCHOR Mag., 1984—. Trustee St. Petersburg (Fla.) Theol. Sem., 1993-95; chmn. Trinity Hall Coll. and Sem., 1998—; bd. dirs. Carrollwood Civic Assn., Fla., 1995-97, Camp Endeavor, 1996—. With USAF, 1964-70. Recipient John Philip Sousa award, 1963. Mem. ASCAP, Am. Ministerial Assn. (sec. 1982-86, bd. dirs. 1985—, internat. pres. 1998—), Nat. Writers Union, Westchase Cmty. Assn. (dir. 1999—), Anglican Soc. N.Am., The Confraternity of the Blessed Sacrament, Silicon Valley Computer Soc., Pinellas IBM-PC Users Group, Inc., Internat. Order of St. Luke the Physician, Soc. of Christian Letters, Soc. Mfg. Engrs., Small Press, Writers and Artists Orgn., Planetary Group Writers Club, Order of the Holy Redeemer, Ecumenical Ch. Fedn., Anglican Inst. Ecumenical Coun. of Cath. and Orthodox Bishops, Tampa Bay Skeptics Soc., Patrons of Husbandry, Carrollwood Sertoma Club. Avocations: composing, carpentry, screenwriting, liturgics. Office: Advanced Indsl Techs #363 N Dale Mabry Hwy Carrollwood FL 33618-2814

O'KEEFE, GARY RAYMOND, actor; b. Riverside, Calif., Oct. 3, 1940; s. Harold Clarence and Geraldine Amelia (Richardson) O'K.; m. Annette Barbara Dimeo, June 2, 1967. Grad. high sch., Santa Monica, Calif. Actor, L.A., 1969—. Appeared in over 200 movies, TV shows and on stage. Chmn. Gower Gulch Neighbor Assn., Hollywood, Calif., 1978-79. Sgt. U.S. Army, 1960-66, Korea, Vietnam. Decorated Purple Heart with oak leaf cluster. Mem. SAG, AFTRA, VFW (life), 28th Inf. Assn. Democrat. Avocation: ironman triathlons (finished 5 times).

O'KEEFE, JOHN DAVID, investment specialist; b. N.Y.C., Nov. 16, 1941; s. Timothy J. and Agnes V. (Timlin) O.; m. Stefanie Carreau Keegan, Jan. 28, 1978; children: Douglas G., Hillary C., John M., Meredith B. BBA, Iona Coll., 1963; MBA, L.I. U., 1968. Analyst L.I. Lighting Co., Mineola, N.Y., 1965-69, Pershing and Co., N.Y.C., 1969-72; mng. dir. Kidder, Peabody and Co., Inc., 1972-89; v.p. Smith Barney, 1989—. Bd. dirs. Heisman Found. Sgt. USMC, 1963-65. Mem.: Securities Industry Assn., Touchdown Club of Am., Inc. (bd. dirs. 2001—), Union Club (N.Y.C.), Downtown Athletic Club (gov. 1986, 1988, chmn. Heisman Trophy com. 1987—88). Republican. Home: 31 Linden Tree Rd Wilton CT 06897-1613 Office: Smith Barney 200 Nyala Farms Rd Westport CT 06880-6267

O'KEEFE, KATHLEEN MARY, state government official; b. Butte, Mont., Mar. 25, 1933; d. Hugh I. and Kathleen Mary (Harris) O'Keefe; m. Nick M. Baker, Sept. 18, 1954 (div. 1970); children: Patrick, Susan, Michael, Cynthia, Hugh, Mardeen. BA in Comm., St. Mary Coll., Xavier, Kans., 1954. Profl. singer, mem. Kathie Baker Quartet, 1962-72; rsch. cons. Wash. Ho. of Reps., Olympia, 1972-73; info. officer Wash. Employment Security Commn., Seattle, 1973-81, dir .pub. affairs, 1981-90, video dir., 1990-95, ret., 1995. Freelance writer, composer, producer, 1973—. Author: Job Finding In the Nineties, The Third Alternative, handbook on TV prodn., (children: So You Want to be President, 1995; composer numerous songs, also writer, dir., prodr. numerous spots. Founder, pres. bd. Eden, Inc., visual and performing arts, 1975—; pub. rels. chmn. Nat. Women's Dem. Conv., Seattle, 1979, Wash. Dem. Women, 1976-85; bd. dirs., composer, prodr., dir. N.Y. Film Festival, 1979; Dem. candidate Wash. State Senate, 1968. Recipient Silver medal Seattle Creative Awards Show for composing, directing and producing Rent A Kid, TV Pub. Svc. spot, 1979. Mem. Wash. Press Women. Roman Catholic. Home: 4426 147th Pl NE # A12 Bellevue WA 98007-7191 Fax: 425-882-8536. E-mail: kathie@nwrain.com.

O'KEEFE, MAURICE TIMOTHY, editor, author, photographer, educator; b. N.Y.C., Mar. 7, 1943; s. Maurice Edward and Jeanne Elizabeth (Murphy) O'K.; 1 child, Timothy Patrick. BA, Washington & Lee U., 1965; MA, U. N.C., 1967, PhD, 1968. From instr. to prof. U. Ctrl. Fla., Orlando, 1968—, head journalism divsn. Nicholson Sch. Comm., 1998—2002. Author: AAA Photo Journey to Central Florida, 1991, Diving to Adventure, 1992, Caribbean Afoot!, A Hiking & Walking Guide to 29 Islands, 1993, 2d edit., 2001, Manatees, Florida's Vanishing Mermaids, 1993, 2d edit., 1995, Hiking Florida, 1993, 2d edit., 2000, Sea Turtles, The Watcher's Guide, 1995, Great Adventures in Florida, 1996, 2d edit., 2000, Seasonal Guide to the Natural Year: Florida and the Alabama and Georgia Coasts, 1996, Caribbean Hiking, 2001; (with Larry Larsen) Fish and Dive the Caribbean, 1991, Fish and Dive

Florida & The Keys, 1992; contbr. photos to newspapers and mags. Past pres. Fla. Outdoor Writers Assn. Recipient of more than 50 regional and nat. awards for writing and photography from 1973-2002, including Best Book (Seasonal Guide to the Natural Year), Best Photojournalism and Best Spl. Interest Publ., Fla. Outdoor Writers Assn., 1997, Best Mag. Photo, Best Article Series (Fla. Fishing) and Best Book (Spicy Camp Cook Book), Fla. Outdoor Writers Assn., 1998, Best Mag. Feature award Fla. Outdoor Writers Assn., 1999, Best Photojournalism award Fla. Outdoor Writers Assn., 1999, Best Mag. Photo award Fla. Outdoor Writers Assn., 1999, Best Travel Destination award Fla. Outdoor Writers Assn., 1999; named Fla.'s Premier Outdoor Photographer and Writer, Tampa Bay Mag. Mem. Nat. Writers Union, Am. Soc. Media Photographers, Soc. Am. Travel Writers. Home: 307 Fox Squirrel Ln Longwood FL 32779-4904

O'KEEFE, MICHAEL DANIEL, lawyer; b. St. Louis, Jan. 3, 1938; s. Daniel Michael and Hanoria (Moriarty) O'K.; m. Bonnie Bowdern, July 11, 1964; children: Collen Coyne, Daniel Michael. AB, LLB, St. Louis U., 1961; postgrad., George Washington U., 1963. Bar: Mo. 1961, U.S. Ct. Appeals (8th cir.) 1961, U.S. Dist. Ct. (ea. dist.) Mo. 1961, Ill. 1975, U.S. Dist. Ct. (so. dist.) Ill. 1975, U.S. Ct. Appeals (5th and 7th cirs.) 1983, (10th cir.) 1995. Asst. atty. U.S. Ct. Appeals, St. Louis, 1962-63, 64-65; pvt. practice, 1964-67; ptnr. Lucas, Murphy & O'Keefe, 1967-74, Thompson & Mitchell, St. Louis, 1974-96. Adj. prof. trial practice Sch. of Law, St. Louis U., 1992—. Editor: American Maritime Cases, 1985—. Active Port Commn., St. Louis; trustee St. Louis U. Capt. USAF, 1962-64. Fellow Am. Coll. Trial Lawyers; mem. Internat. Assn. Def. Counsel, Fedn. Ins. and Corp. Counsel, Maritime Law Assn., USAZ, Nat. Assn. Railroad Trial Counsel, Am. Law Inst. Democrat. Roman Catholic. Avocations: reading, tennis, fencing, archaeology, microbiology. Home: 372 Walton Row Saint Louis MO 63108-1909 Office: Thompson Coburn One Firstar Plz Saint Louis MO 63101-1643

O'KEEFE, ROBERT JAMES, retired banker; b. Boston, Dec. 30, 1926; s. James J. and Irene (Egan) O'K.; m. Mary U. Hughes, Oct. 12, 1951 (dec.); children— Mary F., Robert James; m. Simone A. Charbonneau, Apr. 3, 1976. AB, Boston Coll., 1951. Mem. staff Mass. Inst. Tech., Cambridge, 1951-55; cons. Arthur D. Little, Inc., 1955-58; with Chase Manhattan Bank, N.Y.C., 1958-79, v.p., 1964-69, sr. v.p., 1969-79, Am. Security Bank, Washington, 1979-89; exec. v.p. MNC Info. Svcs., Balt., 1989-90, ret. Trustee Boston Coll., 1974-82, trustee assoc., 1982-86; mem. computer sci. and engring. bd. Nat. Acad. Sci., 1971-73. Served with AUS, 1945-46. Recipient Alumni medal Boston Coll., 1970 Mem. Boston Coll. Alumni Assn. (pres. 1973-74), Country Club at Jacaranda West, Am. Legion, KC. Home: Unit D-2 250 Ridgedale Ave Apt D2 Florham Park NJ 07932-1323

O'KEEFE, SEAN CHARLES, federal agency administrator; b. Monterey, Calif., Jan. 27, 1956; s. Patrick Gordon and Patricia Carlin O'Keefe; m. Laura Jean McCarthy, Oct. 7, 1978; children: Lindsey, Jonathan, Kevin. BA, Loyola U., New Orleans, 1977; MPA, Syracuse U., 1978. Budget analyst U.S. Dept. Def., Washington, comtr., CFO, sec. of the Navy; profl. staff U.S. Senate Appropriations Com., staff dir.; prof. Pa. State U., University Park, Maxwell Sch., Syracuse (N.Y.) U.; adminr. NASA, Washington, 2001—. Bd. dirs. J. Ray McDermott, S.A., New Orleans; trustee CNA Corp., Alexandria, Va.; bd. advisor Pa. State Applied Rsch. Lab., University Park. Editor: Defense Industry in Post Cold War Era, 1998. Staff rep. platform com. Rep. Nat. Com., New Orleans, 1988, advisor, Washington, 1994-97. Fellow Nat. Acad. Pub. Adminstrn.; mem. Bohemian Club San Francisco, Cavalry Club. Republican. Roman Catholic. Avocations: golf, fishing. Office: NASA Adminr Office 300 E St NW Washington DC 20546-0005*

O'KEEFE, THOMAS MICHAEL, academic administrator; b. St. Cloud, Minn., Mar. 25, 1940; s. Thomas William and Genevieve B. (McCormick) O'K.; m. Kathleen Marie Gnifkowski, Aug. 20, 1966; children: Steven Michael, Ann Catherine. Student, Marquette U., 1961-65, BS, 1965; MS in Nuclear Physics, U. Pitts., 1968; DHL, Hamline U., 1989. Dir. edn. planning HEW, Washington, 1969-70, dep. asst. sec., 1977-80; v.p. Carnegie Found. for Advancement of Teaching, 1980-83; pres. Consortium for Advancement Pvt. Higher Edn., 1983-89; exec. v.p. McKnight Found., Mpls., 1989-99; commr. Dept. Human Svcs., State Minn., St. Paul, 1999—2002; pres. Mpls. Coll. Art and Design, 2002—. Dir. Washington internships in edn. George Washington U., 1970-73; dir. policy analysis and evaluation U. Ill., Chgo., 1973-74, assoc. v.p. acad. affairs, 1974-77; head U.S. del. to Orgn. Econ. Coop. and Devel., 1979, 80; mem. Carnegie Forum on Edn. and the Economy, 1985-88; mem. N.J. Commn. on Ind. Higher Edn., 1986-88; mem. task force on ind. higher edn. Edn. Commn. States, 1987-89; co-chair Program on Edn. in a Changing Soc., The Aspen Inst., 1987—. Contbr. articles to profl. jours.; contbg. editor: Change mag., 1985—2001; bd. dirs.: Editl. Project in Edn., 1984—93. Bd. dirs. The Edn. Resources Inst., Boston, 1987-94, Minn. Coun. on Founds., 1994-99, Minn. Pub. Radio, 1999—; trustee Buena Vista Coll., Storm Lake, Iowa, 1984-90; mem. Coun. on Fgn. Rels., 1995-99; bd. regents U. Minn., 1996—. Mem.: Mpls. Club. Democrat. Office: Mpls Coll Art and Design 2501 Stevens Ave S Minneapolis MN 55404

O'KEEFE, VINCENT THOMAS, clergyman, educational administrator; b. Jersey City, Jan. 10, 1920; s. James and Sarah (Allen) O'K. AB, Georgetown U., 1943; MA, Woodstock Coll., 1945, Ph.L., 1944; Th.L., St. Albert de Louvain, Belgium, 1951; student, Muenster (Germany) U., 1951-52; S.T.D., Gregorian U., Rome, 1954. Ordained priest Roman Cath. Ch., 1950. Instr. Latin and math. Regis High Sch., N.Y.C., 1944-47; assoc. prof. fundamental theology Woodstock Coll., 1954-60; acad. v.p. Fordham U., Bronx, N.Y., 1960-62, exec. v.p., 1962-63, pres., 1963-65, rector Jesuit community, 1984-88; gen. asst. to superior gen. Soc. of Jesus, Rome, 1965-83, v.p. spl. projects Jesuit Conf., 1988-90, superior, writer provincial residence, 1990-94; superior Am. House, N.Y.C., 1994-2000. Mem. regents exams. and scholarship center N.Y. State Dept. Edn.; pres., dir., mem. exec. com. Council Higher Ednl. Instns. of N.Y.C. Author: The History and Meaning of Ex Attrito Fit Contritus, 1957; Contbr. articles to religious publs., also book reviews. Dir. N.Y. World's Fair, 1964-65; Corp. Bd. mgrs. New York Bot. Garden; dir., mem. bd. Center Intercultural Formation, Cuernavaca, Mexico; trustee Fordham U. Fellow Royal Soc. Encouragement Arts Mfrs. and Commerce (London); mem. Council Higher Edn. City N.Y., Religion Council Cath. Secondary Schs. Archdiocese of N.Y., Cath. Bibl. Assn., Cath. Theol. Assn. Am., Religion Ednl. Assn., NEA, Jesuit Ednl. Assn., Nat. Cath. Edn. Assn., Internat. Assn. Univs., Soc. Cath. Coll. Tchrs. Sacred Doctrine, Phi Beta Kappa. Office: 106 W 56th St New York NY 10019-3803

O'KEEFFE, CHARLES B. pharmaceutical executive; b. Richmond, Va., Nov. 12, 1939; s. Charles B. and Marie Ellen (McDonough) O'K.; m. Ann Lee Bliley, Jan. 27, 1962; children: Charles B. III, Joan E., Kathleen A., Brian P. MBA, Loyola U., 1978. Pres. Pharm. Svcs., Inc., Richmond, Va., 1968-72, Washington Ref. Labs., Silver Spring, Md., 1972-77; spl. asst. to President The White House, Washington, 1977-80; v.p. govt. affairs Sterling Drug Inc., N.Y.C., 1987-91; exec. v.p. Reckitt & Colman Pharms., Inc., Richmond, 1991-93, pres., CEO, 1993—. Mem. rsch. adv. com. Va. Commonwealth U., Richmond, 1996—. Bd. dirs. St. Joseph's Villa Housing Corp., Richmond, Va., 1996—, March of Dimes, Richmond, 1996-99, Friends of the Nat. Libr. Medicine, 1999—; trustee Commonwealth Cath. Charities, Richmond, 1996—; chmn. pastoral coun. Diocese of Richmond, 1985-95. Mem. Internat. Fedn. Pharm. Mfrs. Assn. (chmn. pub. policy, Geneva 1991-95), Non Prescription Drug Mfg. Assn. (chmn. govt. affairs com. 1988-89), World Fedn. Proprietary Med. Mfrs. (mem. internat. policy com. 1989-91), Va. Commonwealth U. (rsch. adv. com. 1996—). Democrat. Roman Catholic. Home: 12310 Robious Rd Midlothian VA 23113-2229 Office: Reckitt Benckiser Pharm Inc 1909 Huguenot Rd Richmond VA 23235-4314 E-mail: charles.okeeffe@reckitt.com.

O'KELLEY, WILLIAM CLARK, federal judge; b. Atlanta, Jan. 2, 1930; s. Ezra Clark and Theo (Johnson) O'K.; m. Ernestine Allen, Mar. 28, 1953; children: Virginia Leigh O'Kelley Wood, William Clark Jr. AB, Emory U., 1951, LLB, 1953. Bar: Ga. 1952. Pvt. practice, Atlanta, 1957-59; asst. U.S. atty. No. Dist. Ga., 1959-61; partner O'Kelley, Hopkins & Van Gerpen, Atlanta, 1961-70; U.S. dist. judge No. Dist. Ga., 1970—, chief judge, 1988-94. Mem. com. on adminstrn. of criminal law Jud. Conf. U.S., 1979-82, exec. com., 1983-84, subcom. on jury trials in complex criminal cases, 1981-82, dist. judge rep. 11th cir., 1981-84, mem. adv. com. of fed. rules of criminal procedure, 1984-87; bd. dirs. Fed. Jud. Ctr., 1987-91, adv. com. history program, 1989-91, com. on orientation of newly appointed dist. judges, 1985-88; mem. Com. Jud. Resources, 1989-94; mem. Jud. Coun. 11th Cir., 1990-96, exec. com., 1990-96; mem. Fgn. Intelligence Surveillance Ct., 1980-87; mem. Alien Terrorist Removal Ct., 1996—; corp. sec., dir. Gwinnett Bank & Trust Co., Norcross, Ga., 1967-70. Mem. exec. com., gen. counsel Ga. Republican Com., 1968-70; mem. fin. com. Northwest Ga. Girl Scout Coun., 1958-70; trustee Emory U., 1991-97. Served as 1st lt. USAF, 1953-57; capt. USAFR. Mem. Fed. Bar Assn., Ga. State Bar, Atlanta Bar Assn., Dist. Judges Assn. 5th Cir. (sec.-treas. 1976-77, v.p. 1977-78, pres. 1978-80), Lawyers Club Atlanta, Kiwanis (past pres.), Atlanta Athletic Club, Sigma Chi (named Significant Sig 1983), Phi Delta Phi, Omicron Delta Kappa. Baptist. Home: 550 Ridgecrest Dr Norcross GA 30071-2158 Office: US Dist Ct 1942 US Courthouse 75 Spring St SW Atlanta GA 30303-3309

O'KELLY, JAMES BERNARD, elementary school educator; b. N.Y.C., Oct. 9, 1950; s. James and Ann O'Kelly; m. Judith A. Truesdell, July 17, 1976; children: Heather, Erin, James. BA, Rutgers U., Brunswick, N.J., 1973; EdD, Rutgers U., 1999; MA, Kean Coll. of N.J., Union, 1983. Elem. sch. tchr. Sayreville Bd. Edn., NJ, 1973—. Part-time lectr. Rutgers U., New Brunswick, 1991—. Contbr. articles. Recipient Gov.'s Recognition Award for Excellence in Tchg., Sayreville Bd. Edn., 1991, Excellence in Dissertation award, Rutgers Alumni Assn., 2000. Roman Catholic. Mailing: 34 Zaleski Dr Sayreville NJ 08872-1920

OKEN, ROBERT, neuroscientist, researcher, consultant; b. N.Y.C., Oct. 15, 1929; s. Milton and Etta (Weiner) O. BA, NYU, 1949, PhD, 1958. V.p., dir. Oken Fabrics Inc., N.Y.C., 1959-68, 71-73; rschr., cons. U.S. Army, USN, Washington, and Frederick, Md., 1955-56, Teller Environ. Systems, N.Y.C., 1969-70; businessman R.A. Siegel Galleries, 1978-87; cons. to dir. N.Y. State Inst. for Basic Rsch., Staten Island, 1991-93; cons. Gerex Biotech. P.L. McGeer, Vancouver, B.C., Can., 1994-98. Contbr. papers and articles to various profl. jours., including Schizophrenia Bull., Am. Jour. Psychiatry, Annals of Pharmacotherapy, Jour. Dental Rsch., Alzheimer's Disease and Associated Disorders, Medical Hypotheses, Parkinson/Alzheimer Digest, Focus on Parkinson's Disease, Psychiatry Rev. Series. Scientific advisor Lifer Environ. Group, Roxbury, N.J., 1984-87; vol. Dover (N.J.) Gen. Hosp., 1989-90. With U.S. Army. 1955-56. Recipient medal of achievement Dover Gen. Hosp., 1990. Mem. AAAS, Am. Chem. Soc., Am. Philatelic Soc., N.Y. Acad. Scis., N.Y. Neuropsychology Group, Mensa Internat., Intertel, Phi Beta Kappa. Home and Office: PO Box 412 Hopatcong NJ 07843-0412 E-mail: robertjoken@nac.net.

OKERLUND, ARLENE NAYLOR, university official; b. Emmitsburg, Md., Oct. 13, 1938; d. George Wilbur and Ruth Opal (Sensenbaugh) Naylor; m. Michael Dennis Okerlund, June 6, 1959 (div. Apr. 1983); 1 dau., Linda Susan. BA, U. Md., 1960; PhD, U. Calif.-San Diego, 1969. Instr. sci. Mercy Hosp. Nursing Sch., Balt., 1959-63; prof. English San Jose State U., Calif., 1969-80, 94—, dean humanities and arts, 1980-86, acad. v.p., 1986-93. Cons. Ednl. Testing Service, Berkeley, Calif., 1976-80 Editor: San Jose Studies, 1975-80; contbr. articles on the humanities to profl. jours. Bd. dirs. World Forum Silicon Valley, Am. Beethoven Soc.; mem. Peninsula Banjo Band. Grantee NEH, 1979; grantee San Jose State U., 1971-72 Mem. Philol. Assn. Pacific Coast (sec.-treas. 1975-78), MLA (del. to assembly, west coast rep. 1976-77), Internat. Coun. Fine Arts Deans, Calif. Coun. Fine Arts Deans (pres. 1984-86), Am. Beethoven Soc. (bd. dirs.), Peninsula Banjo Band. Democrat. Office: San Jose State U Dept English Washington Sq San Jose CA 95192-0001 E-mail: okerlund@email.sjsu.edu.

OKERSON, ANN SHUMELDA, librarian; b. Austria; d. Jacob and Alexandra Tereshtshenko Shumelda. MLS, U. Calif., 1968. Libr. Simon Fraser U., Vancouver, B.C., Can., 1968-85; dir. libr. svcs. Jerry Alper Inc., Eastchester, N.Y., 1985-90; sr. program officer Assn. of Rsch. Librs., Washington, 1990-95; assoc. dir. librs. Yale U., New Haven, 1995—. Adv. bd. Britannica Online, 1995-98, Acad. Press, 1995-98, Serials Rev., 1995—. Editor numerous books; contbr. articles to profl. publs. Named Alumni of Yr. Mt. View Acad., 1995; recipient Best Article Am. Libr. Assn., 1988, 93, Excellence in Libr. Tech., 1998. Avocations: chocolate, traveling, reading. Office: Yale U Libr PO Box 208240 New Haven CT 06520-8240

OKESON, DOROTHY JEANNE, educational association administrator; b. Garden City, Kans., Aug. 31, 1931; d. Arthur E. and Thelma Lucille (McGraw) Clements-Newman; m. Arnold Leroy Okeson, Dec. 20, 1953; 1 child, Michael Leroy. BA, U. No. Colo., 1961. Cert. jr. high and secondary tchr. Tchr. Weskan (Kans.) Consolidated Sch., 1952-54, Weskan Unified Sch. Dist., 1962-70; corr. sec. Sherman-Wallace Assn. Retarded Children, Goodland, Kans., 1968-95. Mem. Gov.'s Adv. Planning Council, Topeka, 1976-80, Kans. Planning Council Devel. Disabilities, Topeka, 1980-87, chmn., 1985-87. Contbr. articles to Western Times newspaper. Bd. dirs. Assn. Retarded Citizens, Merriam, Kans., 1969-79; asst. campaign mgr. county gubernatorial candidates, Sharon Springs, Kans., 1986; vol. Kans. Spl. Olympics. Mem. NEA (ret. life), AAUW (legis. chmn. 1980-89, pres. 1989-91), Nat. Assn. Devel. Disabilities (chmn. subcom. child devel. 1976-87, mem. coun., by-laws and pub. policy com. 1987). Republican. Lutheran. Avocations: reading, antiques, bird watching. Home: 906 Logan St Apt 106 Atwood KS 67730-1645

OKHAMAFE, IMAFEDIA, English literature and philosophy educator; b. Otuo, Nigeria; s. Obokhe and Olayemi Okhamafe. Double PhD, Purdue U., 1984. Prof. philosophy and English U. Nebr., Omaha, 1993—. Office: U Nebr Annex 26 Omaha NE 68182-0001 also: U Nebr Philosophy Dept Omaha NE 68182-0001 E-mail: imafedia@unomaha.edu.

OKHENDOVSKII, MICHAEL VLADIMIR, lawyer; b. Dubossary, Moldova, Oct. 27, 1973; s. Vladimir Grigorievich Okhendovskii and Maria Safronovna Okhendovskaia; m. Ekaterina Vjacheslavovna Shtefan. M in Law, Kiev (Ukraine) U., 1997. Bar: Kiev region 1999. Lab. asst. Norilsk (Russia) Indsl. Inst., 1991; paralegal Proxen Law Firm, Kiev, 1993—94, lawyer, 1994—98, dep. dir., 1998—. Cons. Verkhovna Rada (Parliament) of Ukraine, Kiev, 1998—. Contbr. books. Mem.: Ukrainian Assn. Internat. Law. Avocations: fitness, travel. Office: Proxen Law Firm 12-a Kibalchicha St Ukraine Kiev 02139 Ukraine Office Fax: +38 (044) 5143305. Business E-Mail: okhendovskii@proxen.kiev.ua.

OKIISHI, THEODORE HISAO, mechanical engineering educator; b. Honolulu, Jan. 15, 1939; s. Clifford Muneo and Dorothy Asako (Tokushima) O.; m. Rae Wiemers, May 28, 1963; children: Christopher Gene, John Clifford, Mark William, Kenneth Edward Student, U. Hawaii, 1956-57; BS, Iowa State U., 1960, MS, 1963, PhD, 1965. Registered profl. engr., Iowa, Ohio. From asst. prof. to assoc. dean coll. engring. Iowa State U., Ames, 1967—. Cons. on fluid dynamics Contbr. articles to profl. jours. Served to capt. C.E., U.S. Army, 1965-67 Decorated Joint Services Commendation award; named Outstanding Prof., Iowa State U. student sect. ASME, 1983, Mech. Engring. Dept. Prof. of Yr., Iowa State U., 1977, 86, 90; recipient award for research NASA, 1975; Ralph R. Teetor award Soc. Automotive Engrs., 1976, Engring. Coll. Superior Teaching award Iowa State U., 1987, Cardinal Key Iowa State U., 1991. Fellow ASME (Melville medal 1989, 98); mem. AIAA, Sigma Xi. Republican. Mem. Ch. of Jesus Christ of Latter-day Saints. Club: Osborn Research Home: 2940 Monroe Dr Ames IA 50010-4362 Office: Iowa State U 104 Marston Hl Ames IA 50011-0001 E-mail: tedo@iastate.edu.

OKIMOTO, GLENN MICHIAKI, state official; b. Honolulu, Mar. 12, 1953; s. Sueo and Matsue (Kojima) O.; m. Hope Kayoko Okabe, Aug. 29, 1981; 1 child, Lauren. BS, U. Hawaii, 1976, MS, 1978, PhD, 1981, Cert. in Pub. Adminstrn., 1983. Economist Dept. of Transp., State of Hawaii, Honolulu, 1981-89, program analysis mgr., 1989-94, dep. dir., 1994—. Rsch. asst. U. Hawaii, Honolulu, 1976-81, lectr., 1987—; mgr. family bus., Honolulu, 1986—. Del. Dem. Party of Hawaii, Honolulu, 1996; speech contest judge Am. Legion, Honolulu. Mem. Govt. Fin. Officers Assn., Gamma Sigma Delta. Avocations: family, golf, tennis. Home: 94-243 Pulelo Pl Waipahu HI 96797-5051 Office: State of Hawaii Dept of Transportation 869 Punchbowl St # 54 Honolulu HI 96813-5036

OKIN, PETER M. internist, educator; b. Bronxville, N.Y., May 16, 1954; married. BS, MIT, 1976; MD, Cornell U., 1980. Diplomate Am. Bd. Internal Medicine, 1983, Cardiovascular Diseases Am. Bd. Internal Medicine, 1985. From asst. prof. medicine to prof. Cornell U. Med. Coll., N.Y.C., 1986—99, prof. medicine, 1999—. Office: Cornell University Medical College 525 East 68th Street New York NY 10021

OKIN, SUSAN MOLLER, political science educator; b. Auckland, New Zealand, July 19, 1946; came to U.S., 1970; d. Erling Leth and Kathleen Marion (Morton) Moller; m. Robert L. Okin, July 29, 1972; children: Laura, Justin. BA, U. Auckland, New Zealand, 1966; MPhil, Oxford U., Eng., 1970; PhD, Harvard U., 1975; PhD (hon.), Mt. Vernon Coll., 1991. Asst. prof. Brandeis U., Waltham, Mass., 1976-81, assoc. prof., 1981-89, prof., 1989-90; Marta Sutton Weeks prof. of ethics in soc., dir. ethics in soc. program Stanford U., Calif., 1990—. Author: Women in Western Political Thought, 1979, Justice, Gender and the Family, 1989; contbr. articles to profl. jours. and chpts. to books. Recipient Bing Tchg. fellowship Stanford U., 1995. Mem. Am. Polit. Sci. Assn. (Victoria Schuck prize 1990), Am. Soc. for Legal and Polit. Philosophy, Conf. for Polit. Thought. Democrat. Avocations: reading, swimming, music, gardening, skiing. Office: Stanford U Dept Polit Sci Stanford CA 94305

OKINAGA, LAWRENCE SHOJI, lawyer; b. Honolulu, July 7, 1941; s. Shohei and Hatsu (Kakimoto) O.; m. Carolyn Hisako Uesugi, Nov. 26, 1966; children: Carrie, Caryn, Laurie. BA, U. Hawaii, 1963; JD, Georgetown U., 1972. Bar: Hawaii 1972, U.S. Dist. Ct. Hawaii 1972, U.S. Ct. Appeals (9th cir.) 1976. Adminstrv. asst. to Congressman Spark Matsunaga, Honolulu, 1964, 65-69; law clk. to chief judge U.S. Dist. Ct. Hawaii, 1972-73; assoc. Carlsmith Ball, 1973-76, ptnr., 1976—. Mem. Gov.'s Citizens Adv. Com. Coastal Zone Mgmt., 1974-79; sec. Hawaii Bicentennial Corp., 1975-77, chmn., 1985-87, vice chmn., 1983-85; mem. Jud. Selection Commn., State of Hawaii, 1979-87, vice chmn., 1986; mem. consumer adv. coun. Fed. Res. Bd., 1984-86; chmn. State of Hawaii Jud. Conduct Commn., 1991-94; apptd. mem. Fed. Savings and Loan Adv. Council, Washington, 1988-89; mem. nat. adv. coun. U.S. Small Bus. Adminstrn., 1994-2000; mem. adv. coun. Fed. Res. Bank of San Francisco, 1995—. Bd. dirs. Moiliili Cmty. Ctr., Honolulu, 1965-68, 73-86, trustee 1993—; bd. visitors Georgetown U. Law Ctr., 1993—; trustee Kuakini Med. Ctr., 1984-88, 89-96. Capt. USAFR, 1964-72, 74-76. Mem. ABA (ho. of dels. 1991-94, standing com. on jud. selection tenure and compensation 1993-96, standing com. on jud. independence 1999—), Hawaii Bar Assn. (sec., bd. dirs. 1981), Am. Judicature Soc. (bd. dirs. 1986, treas. 1995-97, pres. 1997-99), Georgetown U. Law Alumni Assn. (bd. dirs. 1986-91), Omicron Delta Kappa. Office: Carlsmith Ball PO Box 656 Honolulu HI 96809-0656

OKITA, GEORGE TORAO, pharmacologist educator; b. Seattle, Jan. 18, 1922; s. Kazuo and Fusao (Muguruma) O.; m. Fujiko Shimizu, Nov. 29, 1958; children: Ronald Hajime, Sharon Mariko, Glenn Torao. Student, U. Cin., 1943-44; BA, Ohio State U., 1948; PhD, U. Chgo., 1951. Rsch. asst., rsch. assoc., instr., then asst. prof. U. Chgo., 1949-63; assoc. prof. Northwestern U., 1963-66, prof. pharmacology, 1966-90, prof. emeritus, 1990—, acting chmn. dept. Molecular Pharmacology and Biol. Chem., 1968-70, 76-77. Contbr. articles to profl. jours.; Asst. editor: Jour. Pharmacology and Exptl. Therapeutics, 1965-68. Served with AUS, 1944-46. NIH Postdoctoral fellow, 1952 Mem. AAAS, AAUP, Am. Soc. Pharmacology and Exptl. Therapeutics, Internat. Soc. Biochem. Pharmacology, Am. Heart Assn., Cardiac Muscle Soc., Sigma Xi. Achievements include research in med. field. Home: 95-1058 Kihene St Mililani HI 96789 E-mail: gtoki@aol.com.

OKOCHI, CHUX CORNELIUS, minister; b. Ishiagu, Ebonyi , Nigeria, Mar. 18, 1961; s. David Okochi Chukwu, Veronica Ihuoma Chukwu. BA in Philosophy, Urban U., Rome, 1984, BD in Theology, 1988; MA, Duquesne U., 1998. Dir. religious edn. Cath. Diocese Abakaliki, Nigeria, 1989—97; pastor Assumption Cath. Parish, Abina-Ikwo, Nigeria, 1990—97. Primary sch. edn. liaison officer Ikwo Local Govt. Area, Ikwo, Ebonyi, Nigeria, 1991—97. Peace Rreconciliation Ikwo Local Govt. Area, Ikwo, Nigeria, 1995—97. Scholar, Duquesne U., 1997—98. Avocation: Travel and Recreation. Office: St Charles Lwanga Parish 7114 Kelly St Pittsburgh PA 15208 Personal E-mail: kochef@hotmail.com. Business E-Mail: kochef@hotmail.com.

OKOJIE, FELIX A. research administrator; b. Esan, Nigeria, Feb. 13, 1957; s. John and Mary (Elebor) O.; m. Elizabeth Oboh, Dec. 21, 1993; 1 child, Clyde. BS, Auchi Poly. U., 1980; MA, Atlanta U., 1983, EdD, 1985. V.p. Fornafric Group Cos., Nigeria, 1980-82; rsch. assoc. Atlanta U., 1985-87; asst. prof. Jackson (Miss.) State U., 1988-90; dir. ctr. cmty. svc., ednl. technologist Miss. Dept. Edn., Jackson, 1990-93; assoc. prof., to asst. v.p. rsch. & devel. Jackson State U., 1993-99, interim v.p. rsch. & devel., 1999—. Bd. dirs. Hinds Pvt. Industry Coun., Jackson, 1996—; cons. in field; bd. dirs. F&K Group, Jackson. Mem. Am. Statis. Assn., Am. Soc. on Aging, Soc. Rsch. Adminstrn., Jaycees, Alpha Kappa Delta, Phi Delta Kappa. Avocations: table tennis, walking, reading, movies, hiking. Home: 119 Longwood Dr Brandon MS 39042-2800

O'KON, JAMES ALEXANDER, engineering company executive; b. N.Y.C., Aug. 8, 1937; s. A.C. and Rita O'Kon; m. Carol Ann Smith, 1988; children: Sean Fitzgerald, Katherine Shannon. BCE, Ga. Inst. Tech., 1961; MCE, NYU, 1970. Registered profl. engr., Tenn., N.Y., Mo., Conn., Ill., Fla., Tex., Miss., Calif., Ga., Mass., La. N.J., S.C., Ala., Ky., Va., N.C., Kans., Colo., Mich. Hwy. engr. Ga. Hwy. Dept., Atlanta, 1960-62; structural engr. Robert & Co., 1962-64; project coord. So. Design, Spartanburg, S.C., 1964-67; project engr. Crawford-Russell, Stamford, Conn., 1967-68, Farkas Barron Ptnr., N.Y.C., 1968-69; v.p. Lev Zetlin Assocs., N.Y.C., Atlanta, 1969-77; pres. O'Kon and Co. (formerly Lev Zetlin Assocs.), Atlanta, 1977-2000; dir. O'Kon divsn. RBA Group, 2000—. Bd. dirs. Friends of Mexico; mem. bd. constrn. rsch. Ga. Tech. RBA Group. Author: Floating Factory to Produce Precast Concrete Components, 1973, Guidelines for Failure Investigation, 1989, Methodology For The Life Prediction of Buildings, 1989, Floating Factory to Produce Precast Concrete Components, 1973, Methods to Reduce Errors Due to Dependency on Computers, 1994, Bridge From the Past, 1995, Maya Intersite Scabe System, 1997, Error Avoidance in Light Weight Space Frames, 1999, Computer Design of Space Frames, 2000, Seismic Analysis of Large Structures, 2001. Recipient Grand award Builder's Mag., 1983, Archtl. Excellence award Am. Inst. Steel Constructors, 1984, Engring. Excellence award Am. Consulting Engrs. Coun. Ga., 1983, 88, Grand Award for Engring. Excellence, 1988-89, 91-93, USAF Air Mobility award, 1997, Nat. Grand prize Steel Joist Inst., 1999, Grand Nat. Design award Am. Inst. of Steel Constrn., 2000. Fellow Explorer's Club, ASCE (chmn. tech. com. forensic engring.); mem. Am. Inst. Archaeology, Ga. Tech. Bldg. Rsch. Ctr. (Ga. Tech. continuing edn. com.), Bldg. Futures Coun., Soc. Am. Mil. Engrs., Smithsonian Inst., Am. Arbitration Assn. (panel of arbitrators). Democrat. Roman Catholic. Home: 26104 Plantation Dr NE Atlanta GA 30324-2959 Office: O'Kon & Co Inc 1349 W Peachtree St NW Ste 1200 Atlanta GA 30309-2956

OKOSHI-MUKAI, SUMIYE, artist; b. Seattle; One-woman shows include Gallery Internat., N.Y.C., 1970, Miami Mus. Modern Art, 1972, NAS, Washington, DC, Galerie Saison, tokyo, 1982, St. Peter's Ch., Living Room Gallery, N.Y.C., 1987, Viridian Gallery, N.Y.C., 1987, 92, 96, 96, 99, Port Washington Pub. Libr., 1989, NAS, Washington, DC, 1991-92; exhibited in group shows at Bergen Mus. Art and Scis., 1983, Am. Acad. Arts and Scis., 1984, Port Washington Pub. Libr., L.I., N.Y., 1985, Hudson River Mus., 1985, Sao Paulo and N.Y. Culture Exch., 1988, Ctary Snyder Fine Art, N.Y.C., 2002, Hyndai Gallery, Pusan, Korea, 1988; represented in permanent collections at The Mitsui & Co., N.Y., Hotel Nikko, Atlanta, Bank of Nagoya, N.Y., Palace Hotel, Guam Island, Port Washington (N.Y.) Pub. Libr., Lowe Gallery-U. Miami, Miami Mus. Modern Art, Nat. Women's Edn. Ctr., Saitama-ken, Japan, NAS, Washington, DC, Hammond Mus., N.Salem, N.Y., The Jane Voorhees Zimmerli Art Mus., N.J., Asian Traditions Modern Expressions; included in Collage-Techniques, 1994. Mem. Nat. Women Artists Assn. (Belle Cramer award Zluta and Joseph Fund award, Ralph Mayer Meml. award, Doris Kreindler Meml. award 2002), Nat. Mus. Women in the Arts (charter mem. 1994).

OKPALANMA, CHIKA, psychiatrist; b. Owerri, Nigeria, Mar. 30, 1949; MD, St. Georges U., Grenada, 1984. Diplomate Am. Bd. Psychiatry. Intern Bronx (N.Y.) Lebanon Hosp., 1988-89, resident, 1989-91, chief resident, 1991-92, attending psychiatrist, 1992—, unit chief, 1996—. Clin. instr. psychiatry Albert Einstein Coll. Med., N.Y.C., 1992-94, clin. asst. prof. psychiatry, 1994—. Fellow: Am. Coll. Forensic Examiners; mem.: AMA, Black Psychiatrists of Am., Am. Soc. Addiction Medicine, Am. Psychiat. Assn. Office: Bronx Lebanon Hosp Ctr 1276 Fulton Ave Bronx NY 10456-3402 also: 1452 E Gun Hill Rd Ste B Bronx NY 10469-3037 Fax: 718-652-8492. E-mail: cokpalanma@aol.com.

OKRENT, DANIEL, magazine editor, writer; b. Detroit, Apr. 2, 1948; s. Harry and Gizella (Adler) O.; m. Cynthia Jayne Boyer, June 23, 1969 (div. Aug. 1977); m. Rebecca Kathryn Lazear, Aug. 28, 1977. BA, U. Mich., 1969; DHL, North Adams (Mass.) State Coll, 1988. Editor Alfred A. Knopf, Inc., N.Y.C., 1969-73; editorial dir. Grossman Pubs., Inc., 1973-76; editor-in-chief Harcourt Brace Jovanovich, 1976-77; pres. Hilltown Press, Inc., Worthington, Mass., 1978-91, Tex. Monthly Press, Inc., Austin, 1978-83; editor New Eng. Monthly, Northampton, Mass., 1984-89; asst. mng. editor Life mag., N.Y.C., 1991-92, mng. editor, 1992-96; editor new media Time Inc., 1996-99, editor-at-large, 1999-2001. Columnist Esquire mag., N.Y.C., 1985-89. Author: Nine Innings, 1985, The Way We Were: New England Then and Now, 1989; co-author: Baseball Anecdotes, 1989; co-editor: The Ultimate Baseball Book, 1979; appeared in (film) Sweet and Lowdown, 1999. Commr. Nat. Portrait Gallery, 2001—. Mem. Am. Soc. Mag. Editors (bd. dirs. 1987-89), Cuttyhunk Yacht Club, Century Assn. Jewish. Office: Time Inc 1271 6th Ave New York NY 10020-1300

OKRENT, DAVID, engineering educator; b. Passaic, N.J., Apr. 19, 1922; s. Abram and Gussie (Pearlman) O.; m. Rita Gilda Holtzman, Feb. 1, 1948; children: Neil, Nina, Jocelyne. ME, Stevens Inst. Tech., 1943; MA, Harvard, 1948, PhD in Physics, 1951. Mech. engr. NACA, Cleve., 1943-46; sr. physicist Argonne (Ill.) Nat. Lab., 1951-71; regents lectr. UCLA, 1968, prof. engring., 1971-91, prof. emeritus, rsch. prof., 1991—. Vis. prof. U. Wash., Seattle, 1963, U. Ariz., Tucson, 1970-71; Isaac Taylor chair Technion, 1977-78 Author: Fast Reactor Cross Sections, 1960, Computing Methods in Reactor Physics, 1968, Reactivity Coefficients in Large Fast Power Reactors, 1970, Nuclear Reactor Safety, 1981; contbr. articles to profl. jours. Mem. adv. com. on reactor safeguards AEC, 1963-87, also chmn., 1966; sci. sec. to sec. gen. of Geneva Conf., 1958; mem. U.S. del. to all Geneva Atoms for Peace Confs. Guggenheim fellow, 1961-62, 77-78; recipient Disting. Appointment award Argonne Univs. Assn., 1970, Disting. Service award U.S. Nuclear Regulatory Commn., 1985. Fellow Soc. for Risk Analysis, Am. Phys. Soc., Am. Nuclear Soc. (Tommy Thompson award 1980, Glenn Seaborg medal 1987), Nat. Acad. Engring. Home: 439 Veteran Ave Los Angeles CA 90024-1956 E-mail: okrent@ucla.edu.

OKTAVEC, EILEEN M. anthropologist, artist; b. Apr. 9, 1942; d. Albert W. and Margaret (O'Reilley) O. Student, Cooper Union, N.Y.C., 1960-61; BA in Anthropology, SUNY, Stony Brook, 1973; MA in Anthropology, U. Ariz., 1975. Instr. anthropology White Pines Coll., Chester, N.H., 1975-76; art dir. Great Walks, Inc., Goffstown, 1989—. Author: Answered Prayers: Miracles and Milagros Along the Border, 1995; photographs in: Great Walks of Acadia National Park and Mount Desert, 1990, Great Walks of Southern Arizona, 1991, Great Walks of Big Bend National Park, 1991, Great Walks of the Great Smokies, 1992, Great Walks of Yosemite National Park, 1993, Great Walks of Sequoia and Kings Canyon National Parks, 1994, Great Walks of Acadia National Park and Mount Desert Island, 1994, Great Walks of the Olympic Peninsula, 1999, The Woodland Garden, 1996; exhibited in group shows at Rockport (Mass.) Art Festival, 1977, 78, Berkshire Art Assn., Pittsfield, Mass., 1979, The Ogunquit (Maine) Art Ctr., 1982, 83, N.H. Art Assn., Manchester, 1985, Concord (Mass.) Art Assn., 1988, 91, 92, 96-98, Sharon (N.H.) Art Ctr., 1998. Winner Southwest Book award for Answered Prayers, 1997. Mem. Concord Art Assn., Sharon Arts Ctr. Office: Great Walks Inc PO Box 410 Goffstown NH 03045-0410 Home: PO Box 410 Goffstown NH 03045-0410

OKTAY, JULIANNE SHABERMAN, social work educator; b. Detroit, Jan. 4, 1943; d. Harry Louis and Nadine (Lewis) Shaberman; m. Erol Oktay, Aug. 22, 1965; children: Deniz, Liza. BA, Antioch Coll., 1964; MSW, U. Mich., 1966, PhD, 1974. Lic. social worker. Instr. Goucher Coll., Balt., 1971-74; asst. prof. Johns Hopkins U., 1974-78; assoc. prof. U. Md. Sch. Social Work, 1978-92, prof., 1992—. Cons. NIH, Bethesda, Md., 1990-91, Johns Hopkins Ctr. for Health Scis. Rsch., Balt., 1984-86, dept. social work Johns Hopkins Hosp., 1980-86. Author: (book) Breast Cancer in the Life Course: Women's Experiences, 1991, The Chronically Limited Elderly, 1983; contbr. articles to profl. jours. Grantee Designated Rsch. Fund, U. Md., 1990. Mem. NASW, Coun. on Social Work Edn. Office: Univ Md 525 W Redwood St Baltimore MD 21201-1777

OKTEN, GIRAY, mathematician, educator; b. Ankara, Turkey, Sept. 20, 1968; s. Muzaffer and Fikret Hatice Okten; m. Askim Cebeci; children: Arya. BS in Math., Bogazici U., Istanbul, Turkey, 1991; MA in Math., PhD in Math., Claremont U., 1997. Vis. asst. prof. U. Alaska , Fairbanks, 1997—98; asst. prof. math. Ball State U., Muncie, Ind., 1998—. Vis. rsch. scholar Claremont (Calif.) Rsch. Inst. Applied Math. Scis., 2000—01. Author: (book) Contributions to the Theory of Monte Carlo and quasi-Monte Carlo Methods, 1999; contbr. articles to profl. jours. Grantee, Claremont Grad. U., 1996; scholar, Phi Beta Kappa, 1995, Hughes Aircraft Co., 1995. Mem.: Math. Assn. Am., Soc. Indsl. and Applied Math., Am. Math. Soc. Office: Dept Math Scis Ball State Univ Muncie IN 47306 E-mail: gokten@math.bsu.edu.

OKUHARA, TETSU, artist, photographer; b. L.A., Mar. 3, 1940; Student, U. Chgo., 1958-61, The Cooper Union, 1970-71. Lectr., workshop leader Hartwick Coll., Oneonta, N.Y., NYU, Rutgers U., New Brunswick, N.J., Sch. Visual Arts, N.Y.C., New Sch., N.Y.C., Wesleyan U., Middletown, Conn, Cornish Inst., Seattle. Exhibited in one person and group shows at Fotomassan, Goteborg, Sweden, Chgo. Cultural Ctr., 1997, Gotland Konst Mus., Sweden, 1995, San Francisco Camera Work, 1994, Art Inst. Boston, 1994, Artist Space, N.Y.C., 1992, Chgo. Art Inst., 1991-92, Art in General, N.Y.C., 1990, Cleve. Mus. Art, 1978, San Francisco Mus. Modern Art, 1979, Small Works, N.Y. U., 1999, numerous others; represented in permanent collections Mus. Modern Art, N.Y.C., Met. Mus. Art, N.Y.C., ADP, Chgo., Hasselad Collection, Goteborg, Sweden, Tokyo Met. Mus. Photography, Art Inst., Chgo., San Francisco Mus. Modern Art, Los Angeles County Mus., numerous others; contbr. mags., newspapers. Grantee Creative Artist Pub. Svc., 1973-74, 75-76, N.Y. Found. for the Arts, 1988-89, Nat. Endowment for the Arts, 1988-89, La Napoule Found./Nat. Endowment for the Arts, France, 1989, Intercambio, San Juan, P.R., 1991, James P. Phelan Art Award, San Francisco, 1993-94; Guggenheim fellow, 1975-76, N.Y. Found. for Arts fellow, 2000. Home: 202 E 42nd St New York NY 10017-5808

OKUI, KAZUMITSU, biology educator; b. Ohta, Japan, July 8, 1933; s. Sadajiroh and Ume (Tanaka) O.; m. Mizue Aoki Okui, May 6, 1961; children: Teiichiroh, Ari. B Agr., Tokyo U. Agr., 1962, M Agr., 1964, D Agr., 1967. Lectr. biology Denki-Tsushin U., Tokyo, 1968-70, Kitasato U., Sagamihara, Japan, 1970-73, asst. prof. biology Japan, 1973-82, prof. ethology Japan, 1982-2000, prof. emeritus, 2000—, prof. comparative ethology Grad. Sch. Med. Sci., 1998—, dean Ednl. Ctr. of Liberal Arts and Sci. Japan, 1995-98, councilor Japan, 1995-99, prof. comparative ethology Grad. Sch. Med. Sci., 1998-2000, chmn. humanities and social scis., 1998-99, prof. emeritus, 2000; councilor Kitasato Rsch. Ctr. Environ. Sci., 2000—. V.p. Internat. Centre of Wild Silkworm, 1990—; vis. rsch. prof. Waikato U., New Zealand, 1991; mem. book rev. com. Yomiuri Shimbun, Tokyo, 1981-85, Sankei Shimbun, Tokyo, 1990—. Author: Entomology, 1976, Ethology, 1976, General Zoology, 1984, General Zoology, 1985, General Entomology, 1992, Human Ethology, 1992, Essay of Insects, 1993, Textbook For Ethology, 1994, General Zoology, 1997. Mem. Internat. Soc. Wild Silkworm (sec. 1988—, v.p. 1990—), Japan Cosmo-Biol. Soc. (councilor 1987-89), Japan Wild Silkworm Soc. (v.p. 1994—), Sci. Coun. of Japan (mem. rsch. com. 1994—). Home: 3-19-6 Shiroyama Odawara-shi 250-0045 Japan Office: Grad Sch Med Sci Kitasato U 1-15-1 Kitasato Sagamihara Kanagawa 228 Japan

OKUMURA, LYDIA S. painter, sculptor; b. São Paulo, Sept. 4, 1948; d. Takashi and Yaeko (Assahi) O. BFA, Fundacão Armando Alvares, Penteado, 1973; postgrad., Pratt Inst., 1974-77. One woman shows include Varanda Galeria de Arte, São Paulo, 1968, Nobe Gallery, N.Y., 1977, Galeria do SESC, São Paulo, 1977, Cayman Gallery, N.Y., 1978, Nobe Gallery, N.Y., 1978, Guinzakaigakan Gallery, Tokyo, 1979, Utsubo Gallery, Osaka, 1980, 83, Watari Gallery, Tokyo, 1980, Pinacoteca of the State of São Paulo, Brazil, 1981, 95, Condeso/Lawler Gallery, N.Y., 1982, 84, Museu de Arte Moderna, São Paulo, 1984, Galeria São Paulo, 1984, Kate Art Gallery, São Paulo, 1991, Galerie d'art Jean-Claude Bergeron, Ottawa, 1993; exhibited in numerous group shows including Pratt Inst., Bklyn., 1980, Condeso/Lawler Gallery, 1981, Nat. Mus. of Art, Osaka, 1981, Ctrl. Hall Artists Gallery, N.Y., 1982, Ctr. for Interam. Rels., N.Y.C., 1982, Gruenebaum Gallery, N.Y.C., Sande Webster Gallery, Phila., 1983, Equitable Gallery, N.Y., 1983, Internat. House, N.Y.C., 1984, Hara Mus. Contemporary Art, Tokyo, 1985, Forefront Gallery, Long Island City, N.Y., 1986, Galeria Scultura, São Paulo, Rio de Janeiro, Brasilia and Tokyo, 1988, Mus. de Arte de São Paulo, 1989, Museu de Arte Contemporanea, São Paulo, 1990, 95, Discover Mus., Bridgeport, Conn., 1990-91, Housatonic Mus. Art, Bridgeport, 1992, 128 Gallery, N.Y.C., 1996, Museu de Arte Nipo-Brasileiro, São Paulo, 1997, others; represented in numerous permanent collections including Met. Mus. Art, N.Y.C., Mus. Belas Artes, Caracas, Mus. de Arte Moderna, São Paulo, Mus. Arte Moderno, Bogotá, Colombia, Hara Mus. Contemporary Art, Mus. de Arte Brasileira, Contemporary Graphic Art Collection, Fredrikstad, Norway, Pinacoteca do Estado de São Paulo, Museu de Arte Contemporanea da Universidade de São Paulo. Grantee Creative Artists Pub. Svc., 1978; fellow Japan Found., 1979; recipient award São Paulo Internat. Biennial, 1973, 77, acquisition prize Internat. Norway Graphics Biennial, 1978. Office: 32 Union Sq E Ste 513 New York NY 10003-3209

OKUN, DANIEL ALEXANDER, environmental engineering educator; b. N.Y.C., June 19, 1917; s. William Howard and Leah (Seligman) O.; m. Elizabeth Griffin, Jan. 14, 1946; children: Michael Griffin, Tema Jon. BS, Cooper Union, 1937; MS, Calif. Inst. Tech., 1938; ScD, Harvard U., 1948; ScD (hon.), U. N.C., 2000. Registered profl. engr., N.C., N.Y. With USPHS, 1940-42; tchg. fellow Harvard U., 1946-48; with Malcolm Pirnie, N.Y.C., 1948-52; from assoc. prof. dept. environ. scis. and engring. to prof. U. N.C., Chapel Hill, 1952-73, Kenan prof., 1973-82, Kenan prof. emeritus, 1982—, head dept. environ. scis. and engring., 1955-73. Vis. prof. Tech. U. Delft, 1960-61, Univ. Coll., London, 1966-67, 73-75, Tianjin U., 1981; editor environ. scis. series Acad. Press, 1968-75; cons. to industry, cons. engrs., govtl. agys. World Bank, WHO, UNDP, with spl. svc. in Switzerland, Israel, Jordan, Peru, Egypt, Colombia, Brazil, Venezuela, Thailand, Indonesia, Kenya, Zambia, Tunisia, Australia, Taiwan, Bangladesh, Argentina, Chile, New Zealand, Jamaica, Guatemala, Turkey, Finland, Eng., Morocco, China, The Philippines; mem. environ. coun. Rohm & Haas Co., Inc., 1985-92; chmn. expert panel on N.Y.C. water supply EPA, 1992-93. Author: (with Gordon M. Fair and John C. Geyer) Water and Wastewater Engineering, 2 vols., 1966-68, Elements of Water Supply and Wastewater Disposal, 1971; (with George Ponghis) Community Wastewater Collection and Disposal, 1975; Regionalization of Water Management—A Revolution in England and Wales, 1977; editor: (with M.B. Pescod) Water Supply and Wastewater Disposal in Developing Countries, 1971; (with C.R. Schulz) Surface Water Treatment for Communities in Developing Countries, 1984; contbr. to publs. in field. Chmn. Chapel Hill Fellowship for Sch. Integration, 1961-63; mem. adv. bd. Ackland Meml. Art Mus., 1973-78; bd. dirs. Warren Regional Planning Corp., 1971-77, Inter-Faith Coun. Housing Corp., 1975-83, N.C. Water Quality Coun., 1975-77; mem. adv. com. for med. rsch. Pan Am. Health Orgn., 1976-79; chmn. Washington Met. Area Water Supply Study Com., 1976-80, NAS-NRC; mem. bd. sci. and tech. for internat. devel. NRC, 1978-81, vice chmn. environ. studies bd., 1980-83, chmn. water sci. and tech. bd., 1991-94; mem. com. on human rights NAS, 1988-94; pres. Chapel Hill chpt. N.C. Civil Liberties Union, 1991-93. Maj. AUS, 1942-46. Recipient Harrison Prescott Eddy medal for research Water Pollution Control Fedn., 1950, Gordon Maskew Fair award Am. Acad. Environ. Engrs., 1973, Thomas Jefferson award U. N.C. at Chapel Hill, 1973, Gordon Y. Billard award N.Y. Acad. Scis., 1975, 1st Thomas R. Camp Meml. lectr. Boston Soc. Environ. Engrs., Gordon Maskew Fair medal Water Pollution Control Fedn., 1978, First Allen Hazen lectr. New England Water Works Assn., 1990, Donald R. Boyd award Assn. Met. Water Agys., 1993, Jones award Chapel Hill chpt. ACLU N.C., 1998, Gano Dunn award for profl. achievement in sci. and engring. The Cooper Union, 2002; Friendship medal Inst. Water Engrs. and Scientists (Gt. Britain), 1984; NSF fellow, 1960-61; Fed. Water Pollution Control Adminstrn. fellow, 1966-67; Fulbright-Hayes lectr., 1973-74; Daniel A. Okun Disting. Professorship in Environ. Engring. established by U. N.C., 1999. Mem. NAE, AAUP (pres. U. N.C. chpt. 1963-64), ASCE (hon., chmn. environ. engring. divsn. 1967-68, 1st Simon W. Freese award 1977), Am. Water Works Assn. (hon., N.C. Fuller award 1983, Best Paper award ednl. divsn. 1985, Abel Wolman award of Excellence 1991, Best Paper Water Resources Divsn. 1999), Inst. Medicine, Water Environ. Fedn. (hon., chmn. rsch. com. 1961-66, dir.-at-large 1969-72), Am. Acad. Environ. Engring. (pres. 1969-70, hon. diplomate, Kappe lectr. 1995), Assn. Environ. Engring. Profs. (Founders' award 1994), N.C. Pub. Health Assn. (Jarrett award 1994), U. N.C. Order of Golden Fleece), Sigma Xi (pres. U. N.C. chpt. 1968-69). Home: 750 Weaver Dairy Rd Apt 204 Chapel Hill NC 27514-1466 Office: ESE U NC CB 7400 Chapel Hill NC 27599-7400 E-mail: dokun@unc.edu.

OKUN, HERBERT STUART, diplomat, educator; b. N.Y.C., Nov. 27, 1930; s. Irving and Ida Muriel (Levine) O.; m. Lorraine Joan Price, Dec. 5, 1954 (div. 1985); children: Jennifer, Elizabeth, Alexandra; m. Enid Curtis Bok Schoettle, Dec. 27, 1990. AB with gt. distinction, Stanford U., 1951; postgrad., Syracuse U., 1951-52, Princeton U., 1952; Hochschule fuer Politische, Wissenschaft, Munich, Fed. Republic of Germany, 1956-57; MPA, Harvard U., 1959. Mem. U.S. Fgn. Service, 1955-91, vice consul Fed. Republic Germany, 1955-57; with Bur. Intelligence and Rsch., Dept. State Office Soviet Union Affairs, Washington, 1959-61, alt. dir., 1971-73; 2d sec. Am. Embassy, Moscow, 1961-63; consul, prin. officer Am. Consulate, Belo Horizonte, Brazil, 1964-65; 1st sec., prin. officer Am. Embassy, Brasilia, Brazil, 1965-66, counsellor embassy, prin. officer Brazil, 1967-68; assigned to Naval War Coll., 1968-69; spl. asst. to sec. of state Dept. State, Washington, 1969-71, dep. chmn. U.S. Del., U.S.-USSR Talks on Prevention Incidents at Sea, 1971-72; polit. advisor and spl. asst. for internat. affairs to comdr.-in-chief NATO So. Command, Naples, Italy, 1973-74; min.-counsellor, dep. chief mission Am. Embassy, Lisbon, Portugal, 1975-78; dep. chmn. U.S. del. Strategic Arms Limitation Talks with Soviet Union, Geneva, 1978-79; vice chmn. U.S. del. to trilateral U.S.-U.K.-USSR Talks on comprehensive test ban treaty, 1979-80; ambassador to German Democratic Republic East Berlin, 1980-83; amb.-in-residence Aspen Inst., Washington, 1983-85; amb., dep. permanent rep. of U.S. to the UN N.Y.C., 1985-89. Rep. of U.S. to 40th, 41st, 42d and 43d sessions of Gen. Assembly of UN, to UN Security Coun., 1985-89, to 29th and 30th sessions of Com. on Peaceful Uses of Outer Space, 1986, 87, to Disarmament Commn. of UN, 1985-89, to Commn. Human Rights, 1985-89, to 27th and 29th session of com. on program and coordination of Econ. and Social Coun., 1987, 89; amb. in residence Carnegie Corp. of N.Y., 1989-90; U.S. mem. UN Sec. Gen's. Expert Group on Enhancing UN Structure for Drug Abuse Control, 1990; founding exec. dir. Fin. Svcs. Vol. Corps, N.Y.C., 1990-97; vis. lectr. Yale Law Sch., New Haven, 1991—; spl. adviser, dep. personal envoy of the sec. gen. UN, Yugoslavia and Nagorno-Karabakh, 1991-92; spl. adv., dep. co-chmn. Internat. Conf. on former Yugoslavia, 1992-93; UN mediator Dispute between Greece & former Yugoslav Republic of Macedonia, 1993-97; U.S. mem. UN Internat. Narcotics Control Bd., Vienna, Austria, 1992-2002; adv. bd. Chazen Inst. Internat. Bus. Grad. Sch. Bus., Columbia U.; mem. bd. dirs. World Rehab. Fund; mem. adv. bd. Minority Rights Group U.S.A.; spl. advisor Carnegie Commn. on Preventing Deadly Conflict; professorial lectr. in internat. rels., internat. law and instns. Johns Hopkins. U. Sch. Advanced Internat. Studies, Washington, 2002--. Commr. U.S.-Poland Action Commn; mem. Internat. Coun., Found. Inter-Ethnic Rels., The Hague, The Netherlands, 1995—, mem. Adv. Com., Human Rights Watch, N.Y., 1995—; mem. group internat. advisors Internat. Com. Red Cross, Geneva, 1996-2000; bd. overseers Curtis Inst. Music., Phila.; adv. bd. internat. security studies Yale U., New Haven; mem. adv. bd. Portuguese-Am. Leadership Coun. U.S. Served with AUS, 1952-54. Recipient Meritorious Honor award Dept. of State, 1972, Superior Honor award Dept. of State, 1980, Presdl. Meritorious Svc. award, 1983. Mem. Am. Fgn. Svc. Assn., Am. Fgn. Policy (nat. com.), Am. Acad. Diplomacy, Lawyers Alliance World Security (nat. bd. dirs.), Washington Inst. Fgn. Affairs, Phi Beta Kappa. Home: 1133 Park Ave New York NY 10128-1246

OKUN, MAURY, dance company executive; Exec. dir. Eisenhower Dance Ensemble, Troy, Mich., 1996—; co-founder, exec. dir. Detroit Chamber Winds & Strings; exec. dir. Great Lakes Chamber Music Festival. Office: Eisenhower Dance Ensemble Ste 214 755 W Big Beaver Troy MI 48084 also: Detroit Chamber Winds & Strings 17348 W 12 Mile Rd, Suite 102 Southfield MI 48076*

OKUN, MELANIE ANNE, venture capitalist; b. Indpls., May 5, 1959; d. Lawrence and Alegra O. BA in Math., Wesleyan U., 1981; MBA, Stanford Grad. Sch. Bus., Calif., 1983. V.p. BT Capital Corp., N.Y.C., 1983-88; co-founder, gen. ptnr. Triumph Capital, 1988—. Mem. U.S. Tennis Assn. (ranked amateur). Avocations: tennis, teaching, polymer clay jewelry. Office: Triumph Capital 237 Park Ave New York NY 10017-3140

OKUN, NEIL JEFFREY, vitreoretinal surgeon; b. St. Louis, Nov. 21, 1957; s. Edward and Barbara J. (Braham) O.; m. Joan A. Sosnoff, May 19, 1984; children: David E., Sarah E. AB, Dartmouth Coll., 1980; MD, Washington U., 1984. Diplomate Am. Bd. Ophthalmology. Intern internal medicine Jewish Hosp. at Washington U., St. Louis, 1984-85; resident ophthalmology Washington U. Med. Ctr., 1985-88; fellow vitreoretinal Retina Cons., Ltd., Washington U., 1988-89; vitreoretinal surgeon Fla. Retina Inst., Jacksonville, Fla., 1990-91, Retina Assocs. Ctrl. Fla., Orlando, 1991—. Instr. dept. ophthalmology Washington U. Sch. Medicine, St. Louis, 1988-89; clin. asst. prof. dept. ophthalmology U. South Fla., Tampa, 1992—; chmn. dept. ophthalmology Fla. Hosp. Orlando, 1996—. Recipient Upjohn Achievement award for endocrinology and metabolism Washington U. Sch. Medicine, St. Louis, 1984. Fellow ACS, Am. Acad. Ophthalmology; mem. AMA (Physicians's Recognition award for continuing med. edn. 1992—), Assn. for Rsch. in Vision and Ophthalmology, Fla. Med. Assn., Fla. Soc. Ophthalmology, Ctrl. Fla. Soc. Ophthalmology, Orange County Med. Soc., Vitreous Soc., Paul Cibis Club. Avocations: music, art. Office: Retina Assocs Ctrl Fla 2501 N Orange Ave Ste 401 Orlando FL 32804-4644

OKUNEV, YURI BENTSION, scientist, researcher; b. St. Petersburg, Russia, Dec. 31, 1937; came to U.S., 1993; s. Bentsion Okunev and Betty Shmerling; m. Svetlana S. Okuneva, July 4, 1962; children: Irina, Simon. PhD, St. Petersburg State U., 1965. Head, scientific mgr. Digital Comms. Rsch. Lab., St. Petersburg, 1966-93; systems engr. Bell. Lab., Lucent Technologies, Whippany, N.J., 1995-96; sr. scientist PC-Tel, Inc., Waterbury, Conn., 1996—. Author: Phase and Phase-Difference Modulation in Digital Communications, 1997; patentee in field. Mem. IEEE, N.Y. Acad. Sci. Avocations: music, literature. Office: PC Tel Inc 61 Mattatuck Heights Rd Waterbury CT 06705-3839

OKUSANYA, OLUBUKANLA TEJUMOLA, ecologist; b. Ikenne-Remo, Ogun, Nigeria, Aug. 22, 1941; s. Samuel Tayo and Esther Oyeyinka (Bolorunde) O.; m. Iretiola Hope Titilola Omoleye, Sept. 25, 1971; children: Tolulope, Omotayo, Ibukunolu, Olugbenga. BS, U. Ibadan, 1966; MS, U. North Wales, 1970; PhD, U. Lancaster, 1976; MI Biol., Inst. Biology, London, 1971; FLS, Linnean Soc., London, 1977. Tchr. Ijebu-Ode Grammar Sch., Nigeria, 1966-68; asst. prof. U. Lagos, Nigeria, 1971-83, assoc. prof. Nigeria, 1983-85, prof. Nigeria, 1985-92, head of botany dept. Nigeria, 1984-85, dean, Sch. Postgrad. Studies Nigeria, 1986-90. Vis. rsch. prof. Ohio U., Athens, 1985, U. Agr., Abeokuta, Nigeria, 1990-91; adj. lectr. Ocean County Coll., Toms River, N.J., 1992-94, Rider Univ., Lawrenceville, N.J., 1999; cons. Ministry of Sci. and Tech., Lagos, 1989-92. Editorial bd. Nigerian Jour. of Botany, 1993; contbr. articles to profl. jours. Pres. Lagos chpt. Lancaster U. Grad. Assn., 1990-92; commr. Civil Svc., Ogun State, Abeokuta, Nigeria, 1978-80. Fellow Commonwealth Travel fellow, Assn. Commonwealth U., London, 1991, Woodrow Wilson Nat. fellow, Leadership Program for Tchrs., 2001; scholar Commonwealth scholar, Assn. Commonwealth U., London, 1968, 1974, Dodge scholar, 2001. Mem. Bot. Soc. Nigeria (coun. mem. 1986-92), Ecol. Soc. Nigeria (coun. mem. 1989-94), Nigerian Inst. Biology (v.p. 1990-94). Anglican. Achievements include identification of some tropical legumes for growing in saline areas to increase land productivity; salt stress alleviation by mineral nutrients in halophytes is species specific; contrary to exptl. nom, in germination studies, it is necessary to state not only the date of seed collection, but also very important to state prevailing environ. factors - especially temperature and soil characteristics at time of seed prodn. and collection. Home: 869 Astoria Dr Toms River NJ 08753-4462 Fax: 732-506-6520. E-mail: okusanyaNJ@worldnet.att.net.

OLAFSON, FREDERICK ARLAN, philosophy educator; b. Winnipeg, Man., Can., Sept. 1, 1924; s. Kristinn K. and Fredericka (Björnson) O.; m. Allie Lewis, June 20, 1952 (dec.); children— Peter Niel, Christopher Arlan, Thomas Andrew. AB, Harvard U., 1947, MA, 1948, PhD, 1951. Instr. philosophy and gen. edn. Harvard U., 1952-54; asst. prof. philosophy, then assoc. prof. Vassar Coll., 1954-60; assoc. prof. Johns Hopkins U., 1960-64; prof. edn. and philosophy Harvard Grad. Sch. Edn., 1964-71; prof. philosophy U. Calif., San Diego, 1971-91, chmn. dept., 1973-76, assoc. dean grad. studies and research, 1980-85. Author: Principles and Persons, 1967, Ethics and Twentieth Century Thought, 1973, The Dialectic of Action, 1979, Heidegger and the Philosophy of the Mind, 1987, What Is A Human Being?, 1995, Heidegger and the Ground of Ethics, 1998, Naturalism and the Human Condition, 2001. Served to lt. (j.g.) USNR, 1943-46. Mem. Nat. Acad. Edn. Home: 6081 Avenida Chamnez La Jolla CA 92037-7404

OLAGUNJU, AMOS OMOTAYO, computer science educator, consultant; b. Igosun, Kwara, Nigeria, Nov. 27, 1954; came to U.S., 1980; s. Solomon Atoyebi and Ruth Ebun (Adegoke) O.; 1 child, Amanda. EdD, U. N.C., Greensboro, 1987; PhD, Kensington U., 1990; cert. in cryptography and info. systems, MIT, 1996, cert. in design and analysis experiments, cert. in digital comm. networks, MIT, 1999, cert. in bioinformatic principles, 2001. Cert. bioinformatic prins. MIT, 2001. Mgmt. info. system dir. Barber-Scotia Coll., Concord, N.C., 1981-82; lectr. N.C. A&T State U., Greensboro, 1982-87, asst. prof., 1987-90; mem. tech. staff Bell Communications Rsch., Piscataway, N.J., 1986-90; vis. prof. Mich. State U., East Lansing, 1990-91; coord. acad. computing, assoc. prof. Del. State U., 1991-92, prof., chair dept. math. and computer sci., 1992—2001; collegiate prof. UMUC-Asia, 2001—. Cons. NSF, Washington, 1991-93, Edn. Testing Agy., Princeton, N.J., 1995—. Author: Lecture Notes Series in Language C, Systems Programming, Database Systems, Theoretical Aspects of Computing, File Structures, Introduction to Computer Science and Scientific and Engineering Applications of Fortran, 1991-96; contbr. articles to Software Metrics, Automatic Indexing, Perfect Hashing, Number Theory, Efficient Statis. Algorithms, Del. State News. Pres. Ahmadu Bello Assn. Computer Univ. Students, Zaria, Nigeria, 1976, Orgn. United Africans, Concord, N.C., 1982. Recipient Queen's Grad. award Queen's U., Kingston, Ont., 1979; Navy-Am. Soc. for Engring. Edn. fellow, 1997, sr. fellow 1998, 2000. Mem. Assn. for Modelling and Simulation in Enterprises (program chair 1989-90, editor), Assn. for Computing Machinery (reviewer), N.C. Acad. Scis. (program chair 1991—, mem. editl. bd. 1999—), N.Y. Acad. Scis. Achievements include invention of the Bell Communication Rsch. Software Daily Software Report and Analysis Measurement System and Generic Administrative Quantitative Decision Support System. Home: 121 Red Oak Dr Dover DE 19904-2368

OLAH, GEORGE ANDREW, chemist; b. Budapest, Hungary, May 22, 1927; arrived in U.S., 1964, naturalized, 1970; s. Julius and Magda (Krasznai) Olah; m. Judith Agnes Lengyel, July 9, 1949; children: George John, Ronald Peter. PhD, Tech. U. Budapest, 1949, D (hon.) , 1989; DSc (hon.) , U. Durham, 1988, U. Munich, 1990, U. Crete, Greece, 1994, U. Szeged, Hungary, 1995, U. Veszprem, 1995, Case Western Res. U., 1995, U. So. Calif., 1995, U. Montpellier, 1996, SUNY, 1998, U. Pecs, Hungary, 2001. Mem. faculty Tech. U. Budapest, 1949—54; assoc. dir. Ctrl. Chem. Rsch. Inst., Hungarian Acad. Scis., 1954—56; rsch. scientist Dow Chem. Can. Ltd., 1957—64, Dow Chem. Co., Framingham, Mass., 1964—65; prof. chemistry Case Western Res. U., Cleve., 1965—69, C.F. Mabery prof. rsch., 1969—77; Donald P. and Katherine B. Loker disting. prof. chemistry, dir. Hydrocarbon Rsch. Inst., U. So. Calif., L.A., 1977—. Vis. prof. chemistry Ohio State U., 1963, U. Heidelberg, Germany, U. Colo., 1969, Swiss Fed. Inst. Tech., 1972, U.

Munich, 1973, U. London, 1973—79, Louis Pasteur U., Strasbourg, 1974, U. Paris, 1981; hon. vis. lectr. U. London, 1981—95; cons. to industry. Author: Friedel-Crafts Reactions, Vols. I-IV, 1963—64; author: (with P. Schleyer) Carbonium Ions, Vols. I-V, 1969—76; author: Friedel-Crafts Chemistry, 1973, Carbocations and Electrophilic Reactions, 1973, Halonium Ions, 1975; author: (with G.K.S. Prakash and J. Somer) Superacids, 1984; author: (with Prakash, R.E. Williams, L.D. Field and K. Wade) Hypercarbon Chemistry, 1987; author: (with R. Malthotra and S.C. Narang) Nitration, 1989; author: Cage Hydrocarbons, 1990; author: (with Wade and Williams) Electron Deficient Boron and Carbon Clusters, 1991; author: (with Chambers and Prakash) Synthetic Fluorine Chemistry, 1992; author: (with Molnar) Hydrocarbon Chemistry, 1995; author: (with Laali, Wang, Prakash) Onium Ions, 1998; author: A Life of Magic Chemistry, 2001; chpts. to books, numerous papers to profls. jours., patentee in field. Recipient Alexander von Humboldt Sr. U.S. Scientist award, 1979, Calif. Scientist of Yr. award, 1989, Pioneer of Chemistry award, Am. Inst. Chemists, 1993, Mendeleev medal, Russian Acad. Scis., 1992, Kapitsa medal, Russian Acad. Natural Scis., 1995, Order of the Hungarian Corvin-Chain, 2001, Albert Einstein medal; fellow Guggenheim, 1972, 1988. Fellow: AAAS, Chem. Inst. Can., Brit. Chem. Soc. (hon. Centenary lectr. 1978); mem.: NAS, Chem. Soc. Japan, Am. Acad. Arts and Scis., Am. Philos. Soc., Am. Chem. Soc. (award petroleum chemistry 1964, Leo Hendrik Baekeland award N.J. sect. 1966, Morley medal Cleve. sect. 1970, award Synthetic Organic Chemistry 1979, Roger Adams award in organic chemistry 1989, Arthur C. Cope award 2001), Hungarian Acad. Sci. (hon.), Royal Chem. Soc. (hon.), Italy Chem. Soc. (hon.), Chem. Soc. Japan (hon.), European Acad. Arts, Scis. and Humanities, Royal Soc. London (fgn. mem.), Italian Nat. Acad. Sci. Lincei. Home: 2252 Gloaming Way Beverly Hills CA 90210-1717 Office: U So Calif Labor Hydrocarbon Rsch Inst Los Angeles CA 90007 E-mail: olah@usc.edu. *America still is offering a new home and nearly unlimited possibilities to the newcomer who is willing to work hard for it. It is also where the "main action" in science and technology remains.*

OLANDER, RAY GUNNAR, retired lawyer; b. Buhl, Minn., May 15, 1926; s. Olof Gunnar and Margaret Esther (Meisner) O.; m. Audrey Joan Greenlaw, Aug. 1, 1959; children: Paul Robert, Mary Beth. BEE, BBA, U. Minn., 1949; JD cum laude, Harvard U., 1959. Bar: Minn. 1959, Wis. 1962, U.S. Patent Office 1968. Elec. engr. M. A. Hanna Co., Hibbing, Minn., 1950-56; assoc. Leonard, Street & Deinard, Mpls., 1959-61; comml. atty. Bucyrus Internat. Inc., South Milwaukee, Wis., 1961-70, dir. contracts, 1970-76, v.p. comml., 1976-88, gen. atty., 1978-80, corp. sec., 1978-88, gen. counsel, 1980-88, vice chmn., dir., 1988-92; ret. Bd. dirs. Ballet Found. Milw., Inc., 1978-92, Pub. Expenditure Rsch. Found., Inc., Madison, Wis., 1978-94, Pub. Expenditure Survey Wis., Madison, 1978-82. With USN, 1944-46. Mem. ABA, Wis. Bar Assn., Wis. Intellectual Property Law Assn., Am. Soc. Corp. Secs., Inc., Am. Corp. Counsel Assn., VFW, Harvard Club (N.Y.C.), Harvard of Wis. Club, Bonita Bay Club. Republican. Roman Catholic. Home: 3708 Woodlake Dr Bonita Springs FL 34134-8605 E-mail: rogunnarna@aol.com. *Strive for success in whatever you endeavor in every honorable way. Respect the dignity and rights of all persons with whom you come in contact, irrespective of their station in life. Recognize your own shortcomings and allow for those of others.*

O'LAUGHLIN, FRANCIS MICHAEL, III, management consultant; b. Norfolk, Va., Sept. 9, 1946; s. Francis Michael and Margaret Mae (White) O'L.; m. Marilyn Ann Huggins, July 3, 1968; children: Michelle Yvonne, Francis Michael IV. BS in Chemistry, Tex. A&I U., 1969; AA in Quality Control, DeAnza Coll., 1977; MS in Systems Mgmt., U. So. Calif., 1979; MBA in Internat. Bus., U. Houston, 1984; grad., Naval War Coll., 1994. Document control supr. Nat. Semicondr., Santa Clara, Calif., 1973-75; quality engring. mgr. Memorex Corp., 1975-79; quality/reliability mgr. Basic Four Corp., Houston, 1979-80; quality assurance mgr. Dresser Magcobar Data, 1980-82; group mgr. product engring. N.L. McCullough, 1982-87; mgr. integrated logistics support Boeing Petroleum Svcs., New Orleans, 1987-92; dir. quality assurance Source Prodn. and Equipment Co., 1992-93; pres. European Quality Connection, Houston, 1993—. Instr. DeAnza Coll., Cupertino, Calif., 1977-79; seminar lectr. Calif. Inst. Quality Tech., Cupertino, 1979-83; cons., Houston, 1979—. Mem. editl. rev. bd. Quality Mag., 1979-83. Capt. USNR 1969—. Mem. Am. Soc. Quality Control (chmn. 1989-91), Am. Mgmt. Assn., Naval Res. Assn. (chmn. 1992-93), Soc. Logistics Engrs. (chmn. 1990-93). Democrat. Roman Catholic. Home and Office: 3106 Indian Wells Ct Missouri City TX 77459-3461

OLAYAN, SULIMAN SALEH, finance company executive; b. Onaiza, Saudi Arabia, Nov. 5, 1918; s. Saleh and Heya (Al Ghanem) O.; m. Mary Perdikis, Feb. 22, 1974; children: Khaled, Hayat, Hutham, Lubna. Student, Pub. Schs., Bahrain Islands. Rsch. specialist Arabian Am. Oil Co., Saudi Arabia, 1937-47; founder, chmn. The Olayan Group, Saudi Arabia, from 1947. Included in Olayan Group: Olayan Investments Co. Establishment, Olayan Europe Ltd., Olayan Devel. Corp., Ltd., Olayan Am. Corp., Crescent Holding GmbH, Olayan Financing Co.; founding chmn., 1977-89, The Saudi Brit. Bank, Riyadh, Saudi Arabia; bd. dirs. Inst. for Internat. Econs., Washington, 1987—; mem. internat. adv. bd. Am. Internat. Group, 1982-99; mem. internat. coun. J.P. Morgan & Co., Inc., N.Y., 1979-90; internat. councillor, mem. adv. bd. Ctr. for Strategic and Internat. Studies, Washington, 1977-95; bd. dirs. CS First Boston, Inc., 1988-95. Mem. internat. adv. coun. SRI Internat., Menlo Park, Calif., 1965—; alumnus mem. The Rockefeller U. Coun., N.Y.C., 1978—; trustee Am. U. of Beirut, 1979-84; co-chmn. U.S.-Saudi Arabian Business-men's Dialogue under the U.S.-Saudi Arabian Joint Commn. on Econ. Cooperation, 1980-92. Decorated Knight Comdr. Brit. Empire, 1987, comdr. 1st class Royal Order of the Polar Star (Sweden), 1988; recipient Great Cross of the Order of Merit (Spain), 1984, medal of honor Madrid C. of C., 1985. Mem. Internat. Indsl. Conf., San Francisco (internat. chmn. 1985), The Conf. Bd. N.Y. (internat. counselor emeritus), Riyadh Handicapped Children Assn. (vice chmn. 1983-88), Equestrian Club (Riyadh), Knickerbocker Club (N.Y.C.), N.Y. Athletic Club (N.Y.C.), Pacific Union and Bohemian Clubs (San Francisco). Died July 4, 2002.

OLBERT, STANISLAW, physicist; b. Lwow, Poland, May 9, 1923; m. Norma Louise DeVivo, 1954; children: Elizabeth, Thomas. Student, U. Munich, 1946-49; PhD, MIT, 1953. Rsch. scientist divsn. sponsored rsch. MIT, Cambridge, Mass., 1953-57, from asst. prof. to prof. emeritus, 1957-88, prof. emeritus, 1988—, cons. ctr. ednl. computing initiatives, 1999—. Vis. prof. U. Rome, 1986, 87, U. Florence, 1986, 87, Inst. Cosmic Studies, Warsaw, Poland, 1991. Co-author: Introduction to the Physics of Space, 1970; contbr. articles to profl. jours. Office: MIT Ctr Space Rsch 77 Massachusetts Ave Cambridge MA 02139

OLBRICK, VALERIE LYN, management consultant, information technologist; b. Pitts., Feb. 9, 1959; d. Kenneth Donald and LaVerne Estelle (Aiken) O. BS, Grove City Coll., 1981. Sr. telecomm. analyst Timken Co., Canton, Ohio, 1981-85; network planning mgr. Leaseway Transp. Inc., Cleve., 1985-87; group mgr. Network Strategies, Fairfax, Va., 1987-88; sr. mgr. Ernst & Young, L.A., 1988-95, prin. N.Y.C., 1995, dir. tech. planning and deployment Internat. divsn., 1995—. Avocations: sailing, skiing, bicycling, gardening, reading. Office: Ernst & Young Internat 787 7th Ave Fl 14 New York NY 10019-6085

OLCOTT, JOHN WHITING, aviation executive; b. Orange, N.J., Oct. 20, 1936; s. Egbert Whiting and Marion Richmond (Braillard) O.; m. Hope Bennett Phillips, May 14, 1966 (div. Feb. 1987); children: David Whiting, Bradley Phillips, Carter Howell; m. Isobel Waxman Ritter, Nov. 25, 1989. BS in Aero. Engring., Princeton U., 1960, MS in Aero. Engring., 1964; MBA in Gen. Mgmt., Rutgers U., 1970. V.p. Linden (N.J.) Flight Svc., 1960-66; flight rsch. specialist Princeton (N.J.) U., 1966-68; v.p. corp. devel., sr. cons. Aero. Rsch. Assocs. Princeton, Inc., 1968-74; v.p., group pub., editorial dir. McGraw-Hill Aviation Week Group, Rye Brook, N.Y., 1973-92; pres. Nat. Bus. Aviation Assn., Inc., 1992—. Rsch. engring. and devel. adv. com. FAA, 1990—; mem. bd. govs. Flight Safety Found., 1992—; bd. dirs. ARINC, Inc., Annapolis, Md., Nat. Aeronautics and Space Adminstrn., Aerospace Tech. Adv. Com., co-chair FAA Safer Skies Program, 1999—. Crew chief, mem. New Vernon (N.J.) Vol. First Aid Squad, 1974-92; bd. dirs. Aviation Rsch. and Edn. Found., Washington, 1988-92; mem. bd. visitors Aircraft Owner anbd Pilots Assn. Air Safety Found., Frederick, Md., 1988-93; trustee Embry-Riddle Aero. U., Daytona Beach, Fla., 1988-93, 95-97; chmn. panel on gen. aviation and commuter tech. NASA, Washington, 1974-86; chmn. panel gen. aviation safety FAA, Washington, 1983-88. Recipient Meritorious Svc. award Flight Safety Found., 1983, Dir.'s award FAA Ctral Region, 1984, Commendation cert. FAA, 1984, Gill Robb Wilson award Embry-Riddle Aero. U., 1986, Journalism award Helicopter Assn. Internat., 1990; inducted N.J. Aviation Hall of Fame, 2001. Republican. Presbyterian. Office: NBAA 1200 18th St NW Washington DC 20036-2506 also: 3808 N Richmond St Arlington VA 22207-4571 E-mail: jolcott@nbaa.org.

OLCOTT, WILLIAM ALFRED, magazine editor; b. Bklyn., June 29, 1931; s. W. Alfred and Margaret Mary (Carr) O.; m. Anne Maria Gorman, Sept. 7, 1963; children: Christopher, James, Katharine, William, Terence. BA in Philosophy, Mary Immaculate Sem. and Coll., Northampton, Pa., 1956; postgrad., Columbia U. Reporter, writer AP, 1960-66; with McGraw-Hill Publs. Co., 1966-80, 81-84, chmn. editorial bd., 1976-77, editor in chief 26 Plus mag., 1973-77, editor in chief Nat. Petroleum News mag., 1977-81, editor in chief Office Adminstrn. and Automation mag., 1984; editor in chief Fund Raising Mgmt. mag., Garden City, N.Y., 1985-96; publs. exec. editor Hoke Communications, 1989-96. Mem. adv. com. Garden City Bd. Edn., N.Y., 1976—; prin. religious edn. home program St. Joseph's Roman Cath. Ch., Garden City, 1976—, mem. pastoral coun., 1990-94. Recipient Jesse H. Neal Editorial Achievement award Am. Bus. Press, 1974, 80, Golden Mike award Nat. Religious Broadcasters, 1989. Home and Office: 3089 W 102d St Apt 3F New York NY 10025

OLCZAK, PAUL VINCENT, psychology educator; b. Buffalo, May 25, 1943; s. Vincent Henry and Helen (Babula) O.; m. Marie Rose Oliveri, Oct. 20, 1973; children: Paul V. II, Patrick J., Drew M. MA, No. Ill. U., 1969, PhD, 1972. Clin. psychologist Family Ct. Psychiat. Clinic, Buffalo, 1975-77, cons. supervisory psychologist, 1977—; supr. psychol. svcs. Hopevale, Inc., Hamburg, N.Y., 1977-89; clin. psychologist Amherst (N.Y.) Police Dept., 1989—; asst. prof. psychology SUNY, Geneseo, 1977-83, assoc. prof. psychology, 1983-90, prof. psychology, 1990—, chairperson, 1999—; clin. psychologist child and adolescent psychiatry Niagara Falls Meml. Hosp., 1996—. Co-editor: Community Mediation, 1991; contbg. author: The POI in Clinical Situations: A Review, 1991, Self-actualization-Polemics Surrounding Its Use, 1991; contbr. articles to profl. jours./publs. Mem. APA, Ea. Psychol. Assn., Midwestern Psychol. Assn., Psychonomic Soc., Soc. Exptl. Social Psychology, Internat. Assn. for Conflict Mgmt., Psi Chi, Sigma Xi. Home: 150 Briarhill Rd Buffalo NY 14221-1811 Office: SUNY Dept Psychology Geneseo NY 14454 E-mail: olczak@geneseo.edu.

OLD, BRUCE SCOTT, chemical and metallurgical engineer; b. Norfolk, Va., Oct. 21, 1913; s. Edward H.H. and Eugenia (Smith) O.; m. Katharine G. Day, Oct. 7, 1939; children: Edward H., Randolph B., Lansing G., Ashlee Virginia, Barbara Stuart. BS, U. N.C., 1935; ScD, MIT, 1938. Research engr. devel. and research dept. Bethlehem Steel Corp., 1938-41; with Arthur D. Little, Inc., Cambridge, Mass., 1946-78, v.p., 1950-60, sr. v.p., 1960-78; pres. Bruce S. Old Assos., Inc., 1979—. Pres., chmn. Cambridge Corp., 1952-53; pres. Nuclear Metals, Inc., 1954-57; dir. Mass. Investors Trust and 13 other mut. funds in MFS group, 1973-85; chief metallurgy and materials br., div. research AEC, 1947-49; mem. Sci. Adv. Com. to Pres., 1952-56 Co-author: The Game of Singles in Tennis, 1962, Stroke Production in the Game of Tennis, 1971, The Game of Doubles in Tennis, 1956, Tennis Tactics, 1983; Contbr. articles to profl. publs.; patentee in field. Comdr. USNR, 1941-46. Fellow AAAS, Am Soc. Metals, Am. Inst. Chemists; mem. N.Y. Acad. Scis., NAE, Sigma Xi, Tau Beta Pi. Address: 20 Longwood Dr Apt 381 Westwood MA 02090-1149

OLD, HUGHES OLIPHANT, research theologian, clergyman; b. Redondo Beach, Calif., Apr. 13, 1933; s. Shadburne Edward and Emma Coulter (Oliphant) O.; m. Mary Chase McCaw, June 12, 1982; children: Hannah Chase, Isaac Houghton Chambers. BA, Centre Coll., 1955; BD, Princeton Theol. Sem., 1958; postgrad., U. Tubingen, 1964-66; ThD, U. Neuchatel, 1971. Ordained to ministry Presbyn. Ch., 1959. Minister Presbyn. Ch., Atglen, Pa., 1959-64, Faith Presbyn. Ch., West Lafayette, Ind., 1972-85; mem. Ctr. for Theol. Inquiry, Princeton, N.J., 1985—. Lectr. Princeton Theol. Sem., 1998—. Author: Patristic Roots of Reformed Worship, 1975, Worship, 1984, enlarged edit. 2002, Shaping of the Reformed Baptismal Rite, 1992, Leading in Prayer, 1995, Themes and Variations for A Christian Doxology, 1992, The Reading and Preaching of Scripture in the Worship of the Christian Church, Vols. I and II, 1998, Vol. III, 1999, vol. IV, 2002; contbr. numerous articles to scholarly jours. Fellow N.Am. Acad. Liturgy; mem. Union League Phila. Republican. Avocations: painting, music. Home: 818 Lower Ferry Rd Trenton NJ 08628-3501

OLD, MARNIE LORRAINE, food service executive, consultant; b. Evanston, Ill., Dec. 10, 1969; d. Daniel James Old and Margaret Doreen Phimister. Cert. advanced sommelier Ct. of Master Sommeliers. Sommelier, capt. Chanterelles Restaurant, Phila., 1994—96; sommelier Striped Bass Restaurant, 1996—98; beverage dir. Meal Ticket Inc., 1996—2001; wine educator, cons. Old Wines LLC, 2001—. Author: (wine column) Real Philly Mag., 2001. Named Best Sommelier, Phila. Mag., 2001. Mem.: Am. Sommelier Assn. (founding bd. mem. and edn. chair 1997—). Office: Old Wines 710 Chestnut St #3 Philadelphia PA 19106

OLDAKER, BRUCE GORDON, physicist, military officer; b. Albuquerque, June 3, 1950; s. Marion Joseph and Minerva Rae (Rogers) O.; m. Patricia Rose Cooney, Feb. 17, 1973; children: Ian Joseph, Kathleen Marie. B Math., U. Minn., 1972; MS, U. Colo., 1981; PhD, MIT, 1990. Commd. 2d lt. U.S. Army, 1972, advanced through grades to col., 1996, asst. prof., now assoc. prof. physics U.S. Mil. Acad. N.Y., 1981—; dir. Photonics Rsch. Ctr. U.S. Mil. Acad., 1990-94, program dir., advanced physics courses, 1994—. Contbr. articles to profl. jours. Hertz Found. fellow, 1985-89. Mem. Am. Assn. Physics Tchrs., Sigma Xi, Phi Kappa Phi. Achievements include rsch. in momentum distribution of atoms after interaction with a photon field can be used to study properties of the photon field. Office: US Mil Acad Dept Physics West Point NY 10996

OLDEN, KENNETH, science administrator, researcher; b. Parrottsville, Tenn., July 22, 1938; s. Mack L. and Augusta (Christmas) Olden; m. Sandra L. White; children: Rosalind, Kenneth, Stephen, Heather. BS, Knoxville Coll., 1960; MS, U. Mich., 1964; PhD, Temple U., 1970. Rsch. fellow, physiology instr. Harvard U., Cambridge, Mass., 1970—74; sr. staff fellow NIH, Nat. Cancer Inst., Bethesda, Md., 1974—77, biochemistry expert, 1977—78, rsch. biologist, 1978—79; assoc. dir. rsch. Howard U. Med. Sch. Cancer Ctr., Washington, 1979—82, dep. dir., 1982—85, dir., 1985—91; dir. Nat. Inst. Environ. Health Scis. and Nat. Toxicology Program NIH, Rsch. Triangle Park, NC, 1991—. Author numerous books, assoc. editor Cancer Rsch., 1990—2000, Jour. Nat. Cancer Inst., 1990—, Molecular Biology of the Cell, 1991—93, Environ. Health Perspectives, 1992—; contbr. articles to profl. jours. Mem. awards bd. GM Cancer Rsch. Found., Detroit, 1992—96. Recipient Disting. Svc. award, DHHS Sec., 1995, Am. Coll. Toxicology, 1995, Presdl. Meritorious and Disting. Exec. Rank awards, Pres. Clinton, 1996, 1997, City of Medicine award, Durham, N.C., 1996; fellow Porter Devel. postdoctoral, NIH, 1970—73, Macy Faculty, Macy Found., 1973—74. Mem.: Internat. Soc. Study Comparative Oncology, Inst. Medicine NAS, Metastasis Rsch. Soc., So. Biol. Response Modifiers, Am. Soc. Biol. Chemistry, Am. Soc. Cell Biology. Baptist. Avocations: tennis, hiking, cycling, cooking. Home: 19 Quail Ridge Rd Durham NC 27705-1871 Office: Nat Inst Environ Health Scis & Nat Toxicology Prog PO Box 12233 Research Triangle Park NC 27709 E-mail: olden@niehs.nih.gov.

OLDENBURG, CLAES THURE, artist; b. Stockholm, Sweden, Jan. 28, 1929; s. Gosta and Sigrid Elisabeth (Lindforss) O.; m. Patricia Joan Muschinski, Apr. 13, 1960 (div. Apr. 1970); m. Coosje van Bruggen, July 22, 1977. BA, Yale, 1951; student, Art Inst., Chgo., 1952-54. One-man shows include Reuben Gallery, N.Y.C., 1960, Green Gallery, N.Y.C., 1962, Sidney Janis Gallery, N.Y.C., 1964-70, Galerie Ileana Sonnabend, Paris, 1964, Robert Fraser Gallery, London, 1966, Moderna Museet, Stockholm, 1966, 77, Mus. Contemporary Art, Chgo., 1967, 77, Irving Blum Gallery, L.A., 1968, Mus. Modern Art, N.Y.C., 1969, Stedelijk Mus., Amsterdam, 1970, 77, Tate Gallery, London, 1970, Pasadena Art Mus., 1971, Nelson-Atkins Mus., Kansas City, 1972, Art Inst. Chgo., 1973, Leo Castelli Gallery, N.Y.C., 1974, 76, 80, 90, Margo Leavin Gallery, L.A., 1975-76, 78, 88-89, Walker Art Ctr., Mpls., 1975, 92, Art Gallery Ont., Toronto, 1976, Centre Georges Pompidou, Paris, 1977, Rijksmus. Kröller-Muller Otterlo, 1979, Mus. Ludwig, Cologne, 1979, Wave Hill, Bronx, N.Y., 1984, Solomon R. Guggenheim Mus., N.Y.C., 1986, 95, Mus. Haus Esters Krefeld, Germany, 1987, Kunstmuseum, Basel, 1992, Pace Gallery, 1992, 94, Nat. Gallery Art, Washington, 1995, Mus. Contemporary Art, L.A., 1995, Kunst und Ausstellungshalle der Bundersrepublik Deutschland, Bonn, 1996, Hayward Gallery, London, 1996, Whitney Mus. Am. Art, N.Y.C., 2002; group shows include Martha Jackson Gallery, N.Y.C., 1960-61, Dallas Mus. Contemporary Art, 1962, Sidney Janis Gallery, N.Y.C., 1962, 64, Inst. Contemporary Arts, London, 1963, Art Inst. Chgo., 1962-63, Mus. Modern Art, N.Y.C., 1963, 88, 90-91, Washington Gallery Modern Art, 1963, Am. Pavilion, Venice, 1964, 68, Moderna Museet, Stockholm, 1964, Whitney Mus. Am. Art, N.Y.C., 1964-66, 68, 70, 74, 81, 84, 99, Solomon R. Guggenheim Mus., N.Y.C., 1965, 93, Inst. Contemporary Art, Boston, 1966, Mus. Fridericianum, Kassel, 1968, 72, 77, 82, Richard Feigen Gallery, Chgo., 1968-69, Minami Gallery, Tokyo, 1975, Mus. Contemporary Art, Chgo., 1980, Art Gallery NSW, Sydney, 1985, Mus. Ludwig Cologne, 1986, U. Calif. Art Mus., Berkeley, 1987, Westfalisches Landesmus. for Kunst und Kulturgeschichte, Munster, 1987, 97, Mus. Nat. Modern Art, Centre Georges Pompidou, Paris, 1989, La Grande Halle-La Villette, Paris, 1989, Royal Acad. Arts, London, 1991, Mus. Contemporary Art, L.A., 1992, Nat. Gallery, London, 2000, others; represented in permanent collections Solmon R. Guggenheim Mus., N.Y.C., Mus. Modern Art, Albright-Knox Art Gallery, Buffalo, Centre Georges Pompidou, Stedelijk Mus., Tate Gallery, Mus. Ludwig, Moderna Museet, Rose Art Mus. Brandeis U., Waltham, Mass., Oberlin Coll., Nat. Gallery Art, Canberra, Art Gallery Ont., Art Inst. Chgo., Hirshorn Gallery and Sculpture Garden, Whitney Mus. Am. Art, N.Y.C., Mus. Contemporary Art, L.A., others; author: Store Days, 1967, Notes in Hand, 1971, Raw Notes, 1973, Multiples in Retrospect, 1991; co-author: (with Coosje van Bruggen) Claes Oldenburg: Sketches and Blottings Toward the European Dest Top, 1990, Large-Scale Projects, 1994, Claes OldenburgCoosje van Bruggen, 1999, Down Liquidambar Lane: Sculpture in the Park, 2001. Recipient Sculpture award Brandeis U., 1971, Am. Ann., Chgo. Art Inst. 1976, Skowhegan Sculpture medal, 1972, AIA medal, 1977, Wilhelm-Lehmbruck prize, Germany, 1981, Wolf Found. prize, 1989, Creative Arts award Brendeis U., Jack I. and Lillian Poses medal, 1993, Lifetime Achievement award Internat. Sculpture Ctr., 1994, Distinction in Sculpture award Sculpture Ctr., N.Y.C., 1994, Rolf Schock Found., Stockholm, 1995, Nathaniel S. Saltonstall award ICA, Boston, 1996, Nat. Medal Arts, Washington, 2000. Mem.: Am. Acad. Arts and Scis., Am. Acad. Inst. Arts & Letters. E-mail: studio@oldenburgvanbruggen.com.

OLDENBURG, RICHARD ERIK, auction house executive; b. Stockholm, Sept. 21, 1933; came to U.S., 1936, naturalized, 1959; s. Gösta and Sigrid Elisabeth (Lindforss) O.; m. Harriet Lisa Turnure, Dec. 17, 1960 (dec. Apr. 1998). AB, Harvard U., 1954. Mgr. design dept. Doubleday & Co., Inc., N.Y.C., 1958-61; mng. editor trade div. Macmillan Co., Inc., 1961-69; dir. publs. Mus. Modern Art, 1969-72, dir., 1972-94, dir. emeritus, hon. trustee, 1995—; chmn. Sotheby's North and South America, 1995-2000, hon. chmn., 2000—. Served with AUS, 1956-58. Home: 447 E 57th St New York NY 10022-3064 Office: Sotheby's Inc 1134 York Ave New York NY 10021-8300

OLDENBURG, RONALD TROY, lawyer; b. Eldora, Iowa, June 2, 1935; s. Lorenz Frank and Bess Louise (Lewis) O.; m. Vickie Yu; children: John, Keith, Mark. BA, U. N.C., 1957; postgrad., Brunnsvik Folkhogskola, Sorvik, Sweden, 1957-58; JD, U. Miss., 1961. Bar: Miss. 1961, Hawaii 1975. Mgr. Continental Travel Svc., Chapel Hill, N.C., 1956-57, Meridian Travel Svc., Raleigh, 1961, Linmark Internat. Devel., Seoul, 1972-74; fgn. atty. Li Chun Law Office, Taipei, Taiwan, 1965-67; pvt. practice, 1967-72, Honolulu, 1975—. Adj. prof. immigration law U. Hawaii Sch. Law, 1985—97. Compiler: International Directory of Birth, Death, Marriage and Divorce Records, 1985; contbr. articles on immigration law to legal jours. Capt. JAGC, USAF, 1962-65. Mem. Am. Immigration Lawyers Assn. E-mail:. Office: 700 Bishop St Ste 2100 Honolulu HI 96813-3215 Also: 94-229 Waipahu Depot Rd Ste 204 Waipahu HI 96797 E-mail: rtoibm@attglobal.net.

OLDENBURG, WARNER ANDREW, vascular surgeon; b. Cleve., Apr. 22, 1953; MD, Case Western Res. U., 1980. Diplomate Am. Bd. Surgery. Intern Mayo Clinic, Rochester, Minn., 1980-81, resident in surgery, 1981-85, fellow in vasc. surgery, 1985-86; staff St. Luke's Hosp., Jacksonville, Fla. Asst. prof. surgery Mayo Grad. Sch. Mem. Fla. Med. Assn., Internat. Soc. Cardiovasc. Surgery, Peripheral Vascular Soc., Priestly Soc., So. Assn. Vasc. Surgery. Home: Mayo Clinic 4500 San Pablo Rd Jacksonville FL 32224 E-mail: oldenburg.warner@mayo.edu.

OLDENBURGER, NORMA JANE, medical/surgical nurse; b. Carrington, N.D., Oct. 13, 1947; d. Joseph and Edna J. (Larson) Hoggarth; 1 child, Kristen Nicole. Diploma, St. Luke's Hosp. Sch. Nursing, Fargo, N.D., 1968; BSN, Mary Coll., Bismarck, N.D., 1978. RN, N.D.; CCRN; cert. pediatric advanced life support. Staff nurse ICU St. Luke's Hosp., Fargo, insvc. instr. ICU; flight staff nurse ICU St. Alexius Hosp., Bismarck, 1975-98. Instr. ACLS, TNCC. 1st lt. USAR, 1975-77. Mem. ANA, AACN, Emergency Nurses Assn., Sigma Theta Tau. Home: 3000 N 4th St Bismarck ND 58503-0451

OLDENHAGE, IRENE DOROTHY, elementary education educator; b. Jersey City, May 9, 1941; d. Herman Albert and Emma Rose (Scozzafava) Hespos; divorced; 1 child, David George. BA in Elem. Edn., Paterson State Coll., 1962; postgrad., Seton Hall U., 1986; Master's Equivalency, St. Peter's U., Jersey City, 1996; postgrad., U. San Francisco, 1976, St. Peter's U., 1990-91. Elem. tchr. Fairview (N.J.) Bd. Edn., 1962-67, Bogota (N.J.) Bd. Edn., 1969—2002; ret., 2002. Rep. Bogota Libr. Bd., 1984-85; vol. Hands Across Am., Bogota, 1986, Ithaca Coll., 1982. Recipient Gov.'s Tchr. Recognition award State of N.J., 1989. Mem. NEA, N.J. Edn. Assn., Bergen County Edn. Assn., Bogota Edn. Assn. (bldg. rep. 1982—, Svc. to Youth award 1996). Lutheran. Avocations: crafts, reading. Home: 98 Palisade Ave Bogota NJ 07603-1724 Office: Main St Bogota NJ 07603-1308

OLDER, JAY JUSTIN, ophthalmic plastic surgeon; b. Jersey City, Feb. 7, 1940; m. Lois Rosner; children: Benjamin, Jessica. AB, Rutgers U., 1961; MD, Stanford U., 1966. Diplomate Am. Bd. Ophthalmology. Intern, resident in internal medicine Cornell U./Bellevue Hosp. Ctr., N.Y.C., 1968; resident in ophthalmology Stanford (Calif.) U., 1973; fellow in ophthalmic plastic and reconstructive surgery Stanford U., San Francisco, 1974; pvt. practice Tampa, Fla., 1974—. Clin. prof. ophthalmology U. South Fla. Coll. Medicine, Tampa, 1975—, dir. oculoplastic svc., 1974—99. Author: Eyelid Tumors: Clinical Diagnosis and Surgical Treatment, 1987. Fellow Am. Acad. Ophthalmology (Sr. Honor award 1995), Am. Soc. Ophthalmic Plastic and Reconstructive Surgery (pres. 1987, sec. 1983-84), ACS; mem. Phi Beta Kappa (v.p. Greater Tampa Bay Assn. 1995-96). Office: Contemporary Eye Care Specialists 4444 E Fletcher Ave Ste D Tampa FL 33613-4937

OLDER, RICHARD SAMUEL, elementary school music educator; b. Cuba, N.Y., Aug. 10, 1947; s. Laurence Charles and Ann Nell (Reese) O.; m. Helen Mary DiOrio, Nov. 8, 1986; 1 child, Michelle Ann. B in Music Edn., Westminster Choir Coll., 1971. Cert. tchr. of music, N.J. Tchr. 8th grade vocal and gen. music Columbia Jr. H.S., Berkeley Heights, N.J., 1971-81; tchr. vocal and gen. music Woodruff and Mountain Park elem. schs., 1981-88, Woodruff and T.P. Hughes schs., Berkeley Heights, 1988—. Recipient 20 Yrs. of Svc. award PTA Woodruff Sch., 1990. Mem. N.J. Edn. Assn. (local rep. 1986-87), Foxhollow Golf Club. Republican. Presbyterian. Avocations: golf, bowling, swimming, piano, guitar. Home: 43 River Bend Rd Berkeley Heights NJ 07922-1812 Office: TP Hughes Elem Sch Snyder Ave Berkeley Heights NJ 07922 E-mail: olderrj@comcast.net.

OLDERMAN, GERALD, retired medical device company executive; b. N.Y.C., July 16, 1933; s. Cass and Hilda (Klein) O.; m. Myrna Ruth Schwartz, Aug. 3, 1958; children: Sharon, Neil, Lisa. BS in Chemistry, Rensselaer Poly Inst., 1958; MS Phys. Chemistry, Seton Hall U., 1971, PhD, 1972. Rsch. chemist Nat. Cash Register, Dayton, Ohio, 1958-61; tech. mgmt. positions Johnson & Johnson, New Brunswick, N.J., 1961-75, dir. R & D, bd. dirs. surg. products hosp. divsn., 1972-75, v.p. R & D, Surgikos divsn., 1975-78; v.p. R & D, bd. dirs. Am. Convertors divsn. Am. Hosp. Supply corp., Evanston, Ill., 1978-85; v.p. internat. R & D Pharmaseal divsn. Baxter Healthcare Corp., Valencia, Calif., 1985-91; v.p R & D, bd. dirs. cardiopulmonary divsn. C.R. Bard, 1991-96, ret., 1996; cons. R.F. Caffrey & Assoc., Inc., Brownsville, Vt., 1996—; v.p. R & D, mem. bd. dirs. Quick-Med Techs., Inc., Wilmington, Del., 1998—; also bd. dirs. With USMC, 1954-56. Recipient Robert Wood Johnson medal Johnson & Johnson, 1969. Fellow Am. Inst. Chemists; mem. Assn. Advancement Med. Instrumentation, INDA, Assn. Nonwovens Industry (bd. dirs., corp. rep. 1986, 87), Nat. Fire Protection Assn. (industry rep.), Am. Soc. Artificial Internat. Organs. Home: 17 Pickman Dr Bedford MA 01730-1009 Office: RF Caffrey & Assoc Inc PO Box 319 Brownsville VT 05037-0319 also: Quick Med Techs Inc 401 NE 25th Terr Boca Raton FL 33431 E-mail: jolderman@aol.com.

OLDERMAN, MURRAY, columnist, cartoonist; b. N.Y.C., Mar. 27, 1922; s. Max and Jennie (Steinberg) O.; m. Nancy J. Calhoun, Feb. 28, 1945; children: Lorraine Imlay, Marcia Lynn, Mark. BJ, U. Mo., 1943; BS in Humanities, Stanford U., 1944; MJ, Northwestern U., 1947. Sports editor Rockland Leader, Spring Valley, N.Y., 1938-40; cartoonist, writer McClatchy Newspapers, Sacramento, 1947-51, Mpls. Star-Tribune, 1951-52; cartoonist, writer, exec. editor Newspaper Enterprise Assn., N.Y.C., 1952-87; asst. prof. San Francisco State U., 1974-80, U. Redlands, Calif., 1987, U. Oreg., Eugene, 1991-97; sr. editor Palm Springs (Calif.) Life, 1995—. Project dir. Hall of Fame, Oakland (Calif.) Raiders, 1995-99. Author: (books) The Pro Quarterback, 1966, The Running Back, 1969, The Defenders, 1972, Tennis Clinic, 1979, Super: "Just Win, Baby", 1984, Starr, 1987, Mingling with Lions, 2002; (book series) My Best Year, 1969-71. Pres. Calif. Alliance for Mentally Ill, Sacramento, 1994-95. Lt. M.I., U.S. Army, 1944-45, ETO. Recipient Bert McGrane award Football Writers Assn. Am., 1991; named to Nat. Sportswriters and Sportscasters Hall of Fame, Salisbury, N.C., 1993, Internat. Jewish Sports Hall of Fame, Netanya, Israel, 1997. Mem. Nat. Cartoonists Soc. (Best Sports Cartoonist 1973, 78), Golf Writers Assn. Am. (Best Feature 1982), Pro Football Writers Assn. (Dick McCann award 1979, Best Feature 1983), Baseball Writers of Am., Basketball Writers of Am. (Best Feature 1959), Football Writers Assn. Am. (pres. 1960-61), Phi Beta Kappa. Democrat. Avocations: tennis, photography. Home: 832 Inverness Dr Rancho Mirage CA 92270-1451 E-mail: molde55574@aol.com.

OLDERSHAW, LOUIS FREDERICK, lawyer; b. New Britain, Conn., Aug. 30, 1917; s. Louis A. and Annie Louise (Bold) O.; m. Virginia Wakelin, Nov. 30, 1940; children: Peter W., Robert J., David L. AB, Dartmouth Coll., 1939; LL.B., Yale U., 1942. Bar: Mass. 1946, Fed. 1947. Mem. legal staff Army Ordnance Dist., Springfield, Mass., 1942-43; with firm Lyon, Green, Whitmore, Doran & Brooks, Holyoke, 1947-49; partner firm Davenport, Millane & Oldershaw, 1949-64; treas. Nat. Blank Book Co., Inc., 1964-65, pres., 1965-78, chmn. bd., 1978-83; group v.p., dir. Dennison Mfg. Co., Framingham, Mass., 1967-82; counsel Bulkley, Richardson & Gelinas, Springfield, 1983—. Mem. editorial bd.: Yale Law Jour, 1941-42. Trustee Mt. Holyoke Coll., 1966-76, Greater Holyoke YMCA; bd. dirs. emeritus Holyoke C.C. Found., Sta. WGBY-TV. Lt. USNR, 1943-47. Mem.: Rotary, Mill Reef Club (Antigua), Colony Club (Springfield, Mass.), Longmeadow (Mass.) Country Club. Republican. Mem. United Congl. Ch. Home: 1 Brookwood Rd Holyoke MA 01040-9510 Office: Baybank Tower 1500 Main St Ste 2700 Springfield MA 01115-0001 E-mail: loldershaw@bulkley.com.

OLDFIELD, BARNEY, entertainment executive; b. Boston, June 28, 1956; s. Wilbur Joseph and Thelma Florence (Coombs) O. AB, Harvard U., 1979, Cert. Advanced Studies, 1981; Cert. Bus. Entertainment, NYU, 1996. Editor Musicians, 1979-83; copy editor Social Register Assocs., N.Y.C., 1983-87; advt. dir. Local Listings, 1987-89; mkt. rep. Societa Italiana Lavor Oro, 1989-90; bus. mgr. Al-Bab Internat., 1990-92, McKenzie Internat., N.Y.C., 1992-96; gen. mgr. Angelika Entertainment, 1996—; CEO Angelika Releasing, 1999—, Angelika.Com, 1999—; pres. Angelika TV.com, 2000—. Bd. dirs. Anthology Film Archives, N.Y.C., 1995—, Havana Film Festival in N.Y.; chair bd., coord. Harvard Ind. Film Group; mem. adv. com. Internat. Film and TV Exch., exec. prodr. New Filmmakers Series; exec. prodr. Metro Angelika Film Festival. Prodr.: Too Much Sleep, Zero Day; columnist: So. Voice newspaper, 1976—79; editor: Harvard Today, 1997—. Mem. Soc. Calif. Pioneers, San Francisco, 1981—. Mem. Friars Club of Calif., Harvard Club of N.Y., Harvard Club of Boston, Harvard Club of So. Calif., Harvard Faculty Club, Union League Club N.Y. Republican. Anglican. Avocations: squash, tennis. Office: PO Box 4956 New York NY 10185-4956 Fax: (212) 876-4365. E-mail: barney@angelikafilm.com.

OLDFIELD, E. LAWRENCE, lawyer; b. Lake Forest, Ill., Dec. 21, 1944; s. W. Ernest and Evelyn Charlotte (Gyllenberg) O.; m. Kaaren Elaine Sabey, Aug. 24, 1974; 1 stepchild, Kimberly Jo; 1 child, Lauren Elizabeth. Student, L.I. U., 1961-62, Wheaton Coll., 1962-64, Near East Sch. Archeology, Jordan, 1964; BA in Polit. Sci., No. Ill. U., 1969; JD, DePaul U., 1973. Bar: Ill. 1973, U.S. Dist. Ct. (no. dist.) Ill. 1973, U.S. Ct. Appeals (7th cir.) 1974, U.S. Supreme Ct. 1979, U.S. Ct. Appeals (3d cir.) 1985, U.S. Ct. Appeals (10th cir.) 1986, U.S. Ct. Appeals (8th cir.) 1990. Fed. agt. Dept. HUD, 1969-70; assoc. Ruff & Grotefeld Ltd., Chgo., 1973-77; gen. counsel livestock dept. Hartford Fire Ins. Co., 1977-87; prin. E. Lawrence Oldfield & Assocs., Oak Brook, 1987-2000, Oldfield & Fox, P.C., Oak Brook, 2000—. Mediator, arbitrator U.S. Arbitration and Mediation, 1994-97, Resolute Systems, Inc., 1997—. Dir. Edgewater Cmty. Coun., 1973-74; precinct capt. 50th Ward Dems., 1974-77; trustee North Shore Bapt. Ch., 1974-77, chmn. constn. com., 1976-77; dir. Chgo. Bapt. Assn., 1974-77, treas., 1976-77; dir. Ctrl. Bapt. Children's Home, 1978-81, chmn. personel com., 1980-81, deacon, 1981-83, chmn. bd. deacons, 1983, First Presbyn. Ch. Glen Ellen, 1983-84; dir. Chgo. Bible Soc., 1980-84; v.p., 1983-84; trustee Village of Glen Ellyn, 1981-85; committeeman Milton Twp., DuPage County Reps., Wheaton, Ill., 1985-88; publicity chmn. Milton Twp. Reps., Wheaton, 1986-88; mem. Dist. 41 Sch. Bd., 1991-95; elder Christ Ch. of Oak Brook, 1993-2000; bd. govs. Execs. Breakfast Club of Oak Brook 1993—, 1st v.p., 1997-99, pres., 1999-2001. Served in U.S. Army, 1964-67. Mem. ABA, Ill. State Bar Assn., Chgo. Bar Assn., DuPage County Bar Assn., West Suburban Bar Assn., Ill. Trial Lawyers' Assn., Assn. Trial Lawyers Am., U.S. Golf Assn., Safari Club Internat., Wheaton Cmty. Radio Amateurs, Am. Legion, VFW, Kiwanis, Moose, Masons, Shriners (mem. sec. 1998-2001), Jesters, Elks. Avocations: fishing, hunting, golf, amateur radio, chess. Home: 1050 Crescent Blvd Glen Ellyn IL 60137-4276 Office: Oldfield & Fox PC 2021 Midwest Rd Ste 201 Oak Brook IL 60523-1367 also: 30 N Lasalle St Ste 1524 Chicago IL 60602-2502 also: 1622 W Colonial Pkwy Palatine IL 60067-4795 E-mail: eloesq@oldfieldfox.com.

OLDFIELD, EDWARD HUDSON, neurosurgeon, researcher; b. Mount Sterling, Ky., Nov. 22, 1947; s. Ellis Hudson Oldfield and Amanda Caroline Miller; m. Susan Shawler Wachs Oldfield, June 8, 1974; 1 child Caroline Talbott. BA in Physics, U. Ky., 1969, MD, 1973. Diplomate Am. Bd. Neurol. Surgery. Pvt. practice, Lexington, Ky., 1980—81; senior staff fellow NIH, Bethesda, Md., 1981—83, dep. chief clin. neurol., 1983—84, chief clin. neurol., 1984—. Med. dir. VHL disease Family Alliance, 1993—; editl. bd. Jour. Neurosurgery, 1994—; adv. bd. brain cancer McDonnell Found., 1997—. Recipient The Grass Award, Soc. Neurol. Surg., 1995, Farber Award, Am. Assn. Neurol. Surg., 1999. Achievements include patents in field of convective-enhanced drug distribution to the Central Nervous System. Home: PO Box 309 Philomont VA 20131 Office: National Institutes of Health NINDS/SNB 10 Center Dr Room 5D37 Bethesda MD 20892

OLDFIELD, KAREN, transportation executive; Pres., CEO Halifax Port Authority, Canada. Office: Halifax Port Authority PO Box 336 Halifax NS Canada B3J 2P6

OLDHAM, CHRISTOPHER RUSSELL, communications executive; b. Basingstoke, U.K., Sept. 18, 1946; came to U.S., 1986; s. Henry Russell Oldham and Esme Grace (Craufurd) Anderson; m. Elizabeth Jacoba Graham, Jan. 9, 1971 (div. 1978); children: Justin, Mark; m. Janet Patricia Gough, Dec. 9, 1978; children: Carro, Nicholas. Student, Rugby Sch., U.K., 1965, Madrid U., 1967, London Bus. Sch., 1972. Mgmt. exec. Guthrie & Co. (U.K.) Ltd., London and Singapore, 1973-74, mktg. dir. London, 1974-75; mng. dir. William Armes & Son, Sudbury, U.K., 1975-76; chmn. Transmarine Air Holdings Ltd., Luton, U.K., 1976-80; pres., owner S.C.E.A. Du Chateau De Lacaze, Gabarret, France, 1980-87; corp. devel. dir. Chateaux Shippers Ltd., London, 1984-95; pres. Wine Link Inc., San Diego, 1987-95; pres., CEO Global Link Corp., 1999—. Cons. Transmarine Holdings Ltd., London, 1980-97; chmn. Internat. Wine Consortium, 1995-99. Author: Armagnac and Eaux-De-Vie, 1986; author, editor (bi-monthly pub.) Wine Line, 1990-98; contbr. articles to profl. jours. Hist. rsch. Societe Borda, Pau, France, 1981-87; mem. Worshipful Co. of Glaziers, City of London, Liveryman; bd. trustees New Hampton Sch., N.H., 1994-97. Capt. U.K. Cavalry, 1967-71. Recipient Freedom of City of London by Lord Mayor of London, 1975. Mem. British Inst. of Mgmt., Confrerie Cadets de Gascogne, Cavalry Club London, Southwestern Yacht Club (San Diego). Avocations: ocean sailing, wine collecting, golf, computing, literature.

OLDHAM, DARIUS DUDLEY, lawyer; b. Beaumont, Tex., July 6, 1941; s. Darius Saran and Mary Francis (Carraway) O.; m. Judy J. White, Jan. 23, 1965; children: Steven, Michael BA, U. Tex., Austin, 1964; JD, U. Tex., 1966. Bar: Tex. 1966, U.S. Dist. Ct. (so., no., ea. and we. dists.) Tex. 1966, U.S. Supreme Ct. 1974, U.S. Ct. Appeals (3rd and 11th cirs.) 1968; cert. arbitrator and mediator. Assoc. Fulbright & Jaworski, Houston, 1966-74, ptnr., 1974—, mem. policy com., 1980—97, 2001—, mem. exec. com., former chmn. litigation mgmt. com., mem. litigation mgmt. com., 1997—. Mem. faculty grad. litigation program U. Houston; lectr. on corp. def. ins. and product liability. Mem. bd. editors Aviation Litigation Reporter, Personal Injury Def. Reporter; country corr. Internat. Ins. Law Rev.; contbr. articles to profl. jours. Mem. Nat. Jud. Coll. Adv. Coun.; bd. dirs. FICC Found.; past bd. dirs. Houston Pops Orch.; mem. liberal arts adv. coun. U. Tex. Fellow Am. Coll. Trial Lawyers (complex litigation and judicial relations com.), Tex. Bar Found. (life), Am. Bar Found. (life), Houston Bar Found. (life), Am. Bd. Trial Advs. (pres. Houston chpt. 1999); mem. ABA (mem. ho. of dels. 1996-98, chair tort and ins. practice sect. 1994-95, mem. coun. tort and ins. practice sect. 1988-98, chmn. presdl. emissary 1993-95, chmn. Standing Com. on Independence of the Judiciary 2001—, chmn. Commn. on Jud. Campaign Fin. 2000-01), Tex. Bar Assn. (chmn. liaison fed. jud. com. 1989-90, pattern jury charges Vol. IV com. 1988-92), Tex. Young Lawyers Assn. (bd. dirs., chmn.), Fed. Ins. and Corp. Counsel (pres. 1989-90, chmn. bd. 1990-91, exec. com. 1988-91), Tex. Assn. Def. Counsel, Maritime Law Assn. U.S., Am. Counsel Assn. (bd. dirs. 1982-83, 89-94), Def. Rsch. Inst. (chmn. aerospace com. 1984-87, Presdl. Achievement award 1987, bd. dirs. 1989-92, exec. com. 1991-92), Lawyers for Civil Justice (bd. dirs. 1988-98, chmn. 1998, exec. com. 1990-98, pres. 1997), River Oaks Country Club, Houston Ctr. Club, Sigma Chi, Phi Delta Phi. Office: Fulbright & Jaworski 1301 Mckinney St 51st Fl Houston TX 77010-3031 E-mail: doldham@fulbright.com.

OLDHAM, J. THOMAS, lawyer, educator; b. Cleve., Jan. 20, 1948; s. Vern Lawrence and Pauline Adams (Drake) O.; m. Chaille Linn Cooper, Feb. 4, 1995. BA, Denison U., 1970; JD, UCLA, 1974. Bar: Calif. 1974, D.C. 1977, Tex. 1983. Pvt. practice, Beverly Hills, Calif., 1974-81; prof. law U. Houston, 1981—. Vis. prof. law U. Colo., 1984, George Washington U., 1988-89, Cambridge (Eng.) U., 1992, U. of Copenhagen, 1999. Author: Divorce Separation and the Distribution of Property, 1987, Texas Homestead Law, 1991, Texas Marital Property Rights, 1996, Family Law Cases and Materials, 1998, Child Support: The Next Frontier, 2000; mem. bd. editors Family Law Quar., Family and Children's Law Abstracts. Pres. Mus. Area Mcpl. Assn., 1986-90; bd. dirs. Main St. Theater, Houston, 1991-97. Mem. Houston Bar Assn. Office: U Houston Law Sch 4800 Calhoun St Houston TX 77204-0001 E-mail: TOldham@central.uh.edu.

OLDHAM, JOHN MICHAEL, physician, psychiatrist, educator; b. Muskogee, Okla., Sept. 6, 1940; s. Henry Newland and Alice Gray (Ewton) O.; m. Karen Joan Pacella, Apr. 24, 1971; children: Madeleine Marie, Michael Clark. BS in Engring., Duke U., 1962; MS in Neuroendocrinology, Baylor U., 1966, MD, 1967. Licensed physician N.Y., N.J., Tex.; diplomate in psychiat. Am. Bd. Psychiatry and Neurology. Intern pediatrics St. Luke's Hosp., N.Y.C., 1967-68; resident psychiat. Columbia U. Dept. Psychiat., N.Y.S. Psychiatric Inst., 1968-70, chief resident in psychiat., 1970-71; candidate Columbia Psychoanalytic Ctr., 1969-77; dir. psychiatric emergency svcs. Roosevelt Hosp., 1973-74, dir. residency tng. dept. psychiat., 1974-77; dir. short term diagnostic and treatment unit N.Y. Hosp. Westchester Divsn., White Plains, N.Y., 1977-80, dir. divsn. acute treatment svcs., 1980-84; deputy dir. N.Y. State Psychiatric Inst., N.Y.C., 1984-89, acting dir., 1989-90, dir., 1990—; assoc. chmn. dept. psychiatry Columbia U. Coll. Physicians & Surgeons, 1986-96, vice chmn., 1996-2000, acting chmn., 2000—; chief med. officer N.Y. State Office Mental Health, Albany, 1989—. Instr. clin. psychiat. Columbia U. Coll. Physicians & Surgeons, 1974-76, assoc. clin. psychiat., 1976-77, lectr. psychiat., 1977-84, assoc. prof. clin. psychiat., 1984-88, prof. clin. psychiat., 1988-96, Elizabeth K. Dollard profl. clin. psychiatry medicine & law, 1996—; asst. prof. psychiat. Cornell U. Med. Coll., N.Y.C., 1977-83, assoc. prof. clin. psychiat., 1983-84; attending staff dept. psychiat. Roosevelt Hosp., N.Y.C., 1973-77; assoc. attending psychiat., N.Y. Hosp., 1977-84, Presbyn Hosp., N.Y.C., 1984-88, attending pyschiat., 1988—; tng., supervising psychoanalyst Columbia Psychoanalytic Ctr., N.Y.C., 1983—; coord. med. student edn., Cornell U. Med. Coll. Dept. Psychiat., Westchester Divsn., White Plains, N.Y., 1977-84; coord. clin. clerkships in psychiat. Roosevelt Hosp., Columbia U. Coll. Physicians & Surgeons, N.Y.C., 1974-77; mem. acad. adv. com. Pfizer vis. professorship program in psychiat., 1990-92; mem. Sandoz Clozaril nat. adv. bd; spl. adv. bd. Freedom From Fear, Inc.; examiner Am. Bd. Psychiatry and Neurology; chmn. acute divisin rsch. group, Westchester Divsn., N.Y. Hosp., 1981-84, co-project dir. borderline rsch. group, 1982-84, co-prin. investigator familial transmission DSM III personality disorders, 1982-84; prin. investigator personality disorders in bulimia, N.Y.S. Psychiatric Inst., 1985-90, structured DSM III assessment psychoanalytic patients, Columbia Psychoanalytic Ctr., 1986-91; co-prin. investigator validity DSM III R personality disorders, N.Y. State Psychiatric Inst., 1987-94; co=investigator NIMH, 1996—. Author: (with L.B. Morris) The Personality Self-Portrait, 1990; editor Jour. Psychia. Practice; contbg. editor Jour. Personality Disorders; sect. editor Psychiatry; mem. editl. adv. bd. Am. Psychiat. Press, Inc.; mem. exec. editl. bd. Psychiat. Quar.; reviewer Psychiat. Svcs., Jour. of Neuropsychiatry; contbr. numerous articles to profl. jours.; more than 100 presentations in field. Recipient John J. Weber prize Excellence in Psychoanalytic Rsch. Columbia Psychoanalytic Ctr., 1990. Fellow Am. Coll. Psychiatrists, Am. Psychiat. Assn. (chmn. com. psychoanalytic liaison N.Y. County dist. br. 1986-87, pres. 1989-90, com. rsch. psychiat. treatment 1987-93, coun. rsch., steering com. practice guidelines, chmn. sci. program com. 1992-95, cons. 1991-92, 95-96), Am. Psychopath. Assn., N.Y. Acad. Medicine;mem. Am. Psychoanalytic Assn. (cert.), Assn. Psychoanalytic Medicine (pres. 1989-91), Internat. Psychoanalytical Assn., N.Y. Acad. Sci., N.Y. State Med. Soc., Assn. Rsch. Personality Disorders (bd. dirs.), Internat. Soc. for Study of Personality Disorders (pres. 2000—). Office: NY State Psychiatric Inst 1051 Riverside Dr New York NY 10032-1013

OLDHAM, KEITH T. surgeon; b. St. Louis, Aug. 24, 1950; s. Richard Thomas and Gladys (Althen) O.; m. Karen Sue Guice, May 9, 1981; children: Christian, Brian. BA, U. N.C., Chapel Hill, 1971; MD, Med. Coll. Va., 1976. Diplomate Am. Bd. Surgery with subspecialty in surg. critical care and pediat. surgery. Intern U. Wash., Seattle, 1976-77, resident in gen. surgery, 1977-81; fellow in pediat. surgery U. Cin. Children's Hosp., 1981-83; asst. prof. surgery U. Tex. Med. Br., Galveston, 1983-85; asst. prof./assoc. prof. surgery U. Mich., Ann Arbor, 1985-91; prof. and chief divsn. pediat. surgery Duke U. Med. Ctr., Durham, N.C., 1991-98; prof., chief divsn. pediat. surgery Med. Coll. Wis., 1998—; surgeon-in-chief Children's Hosp. of Wis., Milw., 1998—. Author/editor: Surgery of Infants and Children, 1997, Surgery: Principles and Practice, 2001; contbr. numerous articles to profl. jours.; editl. bd. Jour. Surg. Rsch., 1995. Trustee Am. Pediat. Surgery Assn. Found., 1997—. Mem. ACS,, Am. Acad. Pediat. Surgery, Am. Surg. Assn., Am. Pediat. Surg. Assn. (sec. 1997—), Soc. Univ. Surgeons, N.C. Med. Soc. (adv. coun. 1995-97, liaison com. 1994-97). Office: Childrens Hosp of Wis PO Box 1997 Milwaukee WI 53201-1997 E-mail: koldham@mcw.edu.

OLDHAM, MAXINE JERNIGAN, real estate broker; b. Whittier, Calif., Oct. 13, 1923; d. John K. and Lela Hessie (Mears) Jernigan; m. Laurance Montgomery Oldham, Oct. 28, 1941; 1 child, John Laurence. AA, San Diego City Coll., 1973; student Western State U. Law, San Diego, 1976-77, LaSalle U., 1977-78; grad. Realtors Inst., Sacramento, 1978. Mgr. Edin Harig Realty, LaMesa, Calif., 1966-70; tchr. Bd. Edn., San Diego, 1959-66; mgr. Julia Cave Real Estate, San Diego, 1970-73; salesman Computer Realty, San Diego, 1973-74; owner Shelter Island Realty, San Diego, 1974—. Author: Jernigan History, 1982, Mears Geneology, 1985, Fustons of Colonial America, 1988, Sissoms. Mem. Civil Svc. Commn., San Diego, 1957-58. Recipient Outstanding Speaker award Dale Carnegie. Mem. Nat. Assn. Realtors, Calif. Assn. Realtors, San Diego Bd. Realtors, San Diego Apt. Assn., Internationale des Professions Immobilieres (internat. platform speaker), DAR (vice regent Linares chpt.), Colonial Dames 17th Century, Internat. Fedn. Univ. Women. Republican. Roman Catholic. Avocations: music, theater, painting, genealogy, continuing edn. Home: 3348 Lowell St San Diego CA 92106-1713 Office: Shelter Island Realty 2810 Lytton St San Diego CA 92110-4810

OLDKNOW, CONSTANTINA, art historian; b. L.A., June 10, 1955; d. William Henry and Constantina (Skouras) O.; m. Peter Jansen Herzberg, June 9, 1984. BA in Art History, UCLA, 1978; MA in Art History, U. Pa., 1982. Photo archivist J. Paul Getty Mus., Malibu, Calif., 1978-79; curatorial asst. Southwest Mus., L.A., 1981-82; assoc. curator ancient and Islamic art L.A. County Mus. Art, 1982-89; devel. assoc. Henry Art Gallery, U. Wash., Seattle, 1990-91; dir. Donald Young Gallery, 1991-96; writer/ind. curator, 1996-00; curator 20th-century glass Corning (N.Y.) Mus. Glass, 2000—. Curatorial cons. Seattle Art Mus., 1990-99, Tacoma (Wash.) Art Mus., 1996-99 Author: Pilchuck: A Glass School, 1996, Chihuly: Persians, 1997, Richard Marquis Objects, 1997, Dante Marioni: Blown Glass, 2000; editor: Glass Art Soc. Jour., 1996—2002. Mem. gifts and deaccession panel Seattle Arts Commn., 1994-99. Mem. Glass Art Soc., Internat. Assn. for History of Glass, Archaeol. Inst. Am., ArtTable. Office: Corning Mus Glass 1 Corning Glass Ctr Corning NY 14830-2253 E-mail: oldknowt@cmog.org.

OLDLAND, KEVIN BRADLEY, architect; b. Uniontown, Pa., Sept. 20, 1964; s. Paul Richard and Martha Louise (Newcomer) O.; m. Karen Evans Oldland, May 11, 1991; children: Matthew Stephen, Kelsey Lynne. BA, U. N.C., Charlotte, 1989, BArch, 1992. Registered profl. arch., N.C., Del., N.J., Md. Designer, intern Edwin Bouldin Arch., P.A., Winston-Salem, N.C., 1985, 86; project designer, mgr., intern Thomas H. Hughes and Assocs., 1988-91; prin. designer Kevin B. Oldland, Residential Designer, Clemmons, 1992-95; prodn. supr. W.R. Watkins Arch., Winston-Salem, 1992-95; prin. arch. Kevin B. Oldland Arch., Lewisville, N.C., 1995-98; project arch. W.R. Watkins Arch., Winston-Salem, 1995-99; prin. arch. Oldland Archtl. Studio, Lewisville, 1999-00; assoc. Design Exchange Arch., Inc., Lewes, Del., 2000—01; sr. project mgr. Design Exchange Arch., Inc./Tetra Tech. Inc., 2001—. Sports dir. Lewisville Civic Club, 1998—2000; mem. Zoning Com., Town of Georgetown, 2002; dist. insp. U.S. Lighthouse Soc., 2001—; mem. Del. River and Bay Lighthouse Found., 2000—; newsletter editor Luth. Ch. of the Epiphany, Winston-Salem, 1995—2000, min. for congl. life, 1993—95, archtl. liaison needs assessment com. and bldg. com., 1998—2000; mem. Downtown Master Plan Com., Town of Lewisville, 1999; mem. planning bd. Town of Lewisville, 2000. Mem. Nat. Coun. Archtl. Registration Bds., Constrn. Specifications Inst. (cert. constrn. documents technologist), Lewes C. of C., Rehoboth Beach C. of C., Alpha Rho Chi (leadership medal 1992). Republican. Lutheran. Avocations: travel, motorboating, deep sea fishing, painting, photography. Office: Design Exchange Architects Inc 115 W Market St Lewes DE 19958-1357 E-mail: kevin.oldland@tetratech.com.

OLDMAN, ALFRED MAURICE, accountant, management consultant; b. London, May 12, 1948; s. Joseph and Dorothy O.; m. Marilyn Spiro, Jan. 16, 1983. MSc in Mgmt. Studies, U. Bradford, Eng., 1972; DBA, Henley Mgmt. Coll., 1997. Chartered acct., England. Gen. mgr. Europe The Torrington Co., Paris, 1983-87; dir. AMO Cons., Bath, Eng., 1987—. European contr. Measurex Corp., Datchet, Eng., 1979-82; asst. contr. North Europe, Norton Co., Welwyn Garden City, Eng., 1977-79; sr. corp. auditor Am. Express Co., N.Y.C. Editor: Handbook of Cost Management, 1998; author: Cost Management and its Interplay with Business Strategy and Context, 1999. Fellow Inst. Chartered Accts. in Eng. and Wales. Jewish. Avocations: music, antiques, mountain climbing, jogging. E-mail: dramoldman@aol.com.

OLDMAN, GARY, actor; b. London, Mar. 21, 1958; m. Lesley Manville (div.); m. Uma Thurman (div.). BA, Rose Buford Coll. Speech and Drama, 1979. Appearances include (TV movies) Remembrance, 1982, Meantime, 1984, Honest, Decent and True, 1985, Fallen Angels: Dead End for Delia, 1993 (Cable Ace award, Actor in a Dramatic Series); (video) Since I Don't Have You by Guns n' Roses, 1994; (film) Sid and Nancy, 1986, Prick Up Your Ears, 1987 (Brit. Acad. Film and TV Arts nomination 1988), Track 29, 1988, We Think the World of You, 1988, Criminal Law, 1988, Paris by Night, 1989, Chattahoochee, 1990, State of Grace, 1990, Rosencrantz and Guildenstern Are Dead, 1991, JFK, 1991, Bram Stoker's Dracula, 1992, True Romance, 1993, Romeo is Bleeding, 1994, The Professional, 1994, Immortal Beloved, 1994, Murder in the First, 1995, The Scarlet Letter, 1995, Basquiat, 1996, The Fifth Element, 1997, Air Force One, 1997, Lost in Space, 1998, Nil By Mouth, 1998 (also dir., author), The Contender (also exec. prodr.), Anasazie Moon, 1999 (also prodr.); (theatre) Massacre at Paris, 1980, Chinchilla, 1980, Desperado Corner, 1980, A Waste of Time, 1980, Summit Conference, 1982, Rat in the Skull, 1984, The Pope's Wedding, 1984 (Drama Mag. Best Actor award 1985, Fringe Best Newcomer award 1985-86), The War Plays, 1985, The Desert Air, 1985, Women Beware Women, 1986, Real Dreams, 1986, Serious Money, 1987. Recipient Outstanding Brit. Film award Brit. Acad., Best Screenplay award Brit. Acad., Dirs. prize Edinburgh Festival Channel Four, Best Dir. prize Cannes Film Festival, Best Actor and Best Newcomer, Brit. Ind. Film Awards Best Actors. Office: c/o Douglas J Urbanski Douglas Mgmt Inc 515 N Robertson Blvd Los Angeles CA 90048-1730

OLDS, JACQUELINE, psychiatrist, educator; b. Springfield, Mass., Jan. 4, 1947; d. James and Marianne (Ejier) O.; m. Richard Stanton Schwartz, Aug. 26, 1978; children: Nathaniel Leland, Sarah Elizabeth. BA, Radcliffe Coll., 1967; MD, Tufts U., 1971. Diplomate Am. Bd. Psychiatry and Neurology. Resident in adult psychiatry Mass. Mental Health Ctr., Boston, 1974; resident in child psychiatry McLean Hosp., Belmont, Mass., 1976, assoc. attending child psychiatrist, 1979—; psychiatrist-in-charge inpatient unit McLean Hall-Mercer Children's Ctr., 1976-79; assoc. child psychiatry Beth Israel Hosp., Boston, 1979—; cons. in child psychiatry Mass. Gen. Hosp., 1994—. Instr. psychiatry Harvard U. Med. Sch, Boston, 1976-86; asst. prof. clin. psychiatry, 1986-2000, assoc. clin. prof. psychiatry, 2000—; cons. North Shore Mental Health Ctr., Salem, 1981-82. Author: Overcoming Loneliness in Every Day Life , 1996, Marriage in Motion, 2000, editor Clin. Challenges column in Harvard Rev. of Psychiatry; contbr. articles to profl. jours. Recipient Mentoring award Mass. Gen. Hosp. Dept. Child Psychiatry, 1998. Fellow Am. Psychiat. Assn.; mem. Mass. Psychiat. Soc. (ethics com. 1988-93, mem. pub. affairs com. 1992—), Am. Acad. Child Psychiatry, Am. Psychoanalytic Assn., New England Coun. Child and Adolescent Psychiatry (bd. dirs.). Democrat. Avocations: piano, writing, cooking, watercolors.

OLDS, JOHN THEODORE, banker; b. N.Y.C., Dec. 24, 1943; s. Richard J. and Barbara (Moses) O.; m. Candace Rose; children: Richard W., Samantha. Grad., Hill Sch., 1961; BA, U. Pa., 1965. Mng. dir. J.P. Morgan & Co., N.Y.C., 1972-97; vice chmn., CEO Devel. Bank Singapore, 1997-2001, advisor to chmn., 2001—. Trustee Singapore Civil Svc. Coll., Calif. Hist. Soc.; bd. dirs. Internat. Monetary Conf. Mem. Bedford Golf and Tennis Club, Mid-Ocean Club, Knickerbocker Club. Episcopalian. Home: 2450 Steiner St San Francisco CA 94115-1715 Office: DBS Bank 6 Shenton Way DBS Bldg Tower 1 Singapore 068809 Singapore

OLDS, WILLIAM BELLAMY, physician; b. Scotland Neck, N.C., July 28, 1946; s. Hiawatha and Mary Lee (Lamberson) O.; m. Gloria Sonja Grant, Feb. 22, 1975; children: Grant Kandia, Rena Barika. BS, N.C. A&T State U., 1968; MD, U. N.C., 1981. Diplomate Am. Bd. Family Physicians. Rsch. technician N.C. Meml. Hosp., Chapel Hill, 1975-77; physician Person Family Med. Ctr., Roxboro, N.C., 1984-91; pvt. practice, 1991—. Capt. USAF, 1968-75. Mem. Old North State Med. Soc. (asst. treas., Dr. of Yr., 1994), Nat. Med. Assn., Am. Acad. Family Physicians, N.C. Acad. Family Physicians. Avocations: tennis, listening to music. Home and Office: PO Box 1738 Roxboro NC 27573-1738

OLDSHUE, JAMES Y. chemical engineering consultant; b. Chgo., Apr. 18, 1925; s. James and Louise (Young) O.; m. Betty Ann Wiersema, June 14, 1947; children: Paul, Richard, Robert. BS in Chem. Engring., Ill. Inst. Tech., 1947, MS, 1949, PhD in Chem. Engring., 1951. Registered engr., N.Y. Chem. engr. Manhattan Project, Los Alamos, N.Mex., 1945-46; With Mixing Equipment Co., Rochester, N.Y., 1950-92, dir. research, 1960-63, tech. dir., 1963-70, v.p. mixing tech., 1970-92; pres. Oldshue Techs. Internat., NY, 1992—; tchr. Sarasota (Fla.) Sch. Dist. Adj. prof. chem. engring. Beijing U. Chem. Tech., 1992—. Author: Fluid Mixing Technology, 1983; contbr. chpts. and articles to books and jours. Chmn. budget com. Internat. div. YMCA; bd. dirs. Rochester YMCA. Served with AUS, 1945-47. Recipient 1st Disting. Svc. award N.E. YMCA Internat. Com., 1979, J.E. Purkynse medal Czech Republic Acad. Sci.;

named Rochester Engr. of Yr., 1980. Fellow AIChE (pres. 1979, treas. 1983-89, chmn. internat. activities com. 1989-92, Founders award 1981, Eminent Chem. Engr. award 1983, Svc. to Soc. award 1989, F.J. and Dorothy van Antwerpen award for Svc. to the Inst. 1999, centennial com. 2001—); mem. NAE, Am. Assn. Engring. Socs. (chmn. 1985, K.A. Roe award 1987), Am. Chem. Soc., Czech Soc. Chem. Engring. (hon.), World Congress Chem. Engrs. (v.p. 1986, pres. 1992-96), N.Am. Mixing Forum (chmn. 1990-93, Mixing Achievement rsch. award 1992), Interam. Confedn. Chem. Engrs. (sec. gen. 1991-93, v.p. 1993-95, pres. 1995-96), Victor Marquez award 1983), Rochester Engring. Soc. (pres. 1992-93, Rochester Engr. of Yr. 1980), UN Assn. of Rochester (pres. 2001—). Mem. Reformed Ch. in Am. (gen. program coun.). Achievements include design and scale-up procedures in field of fluid mixing. Home and Office: 141 Tyringham Rd Rochester NY 14617-2522 E-mail: smithbev@frontiernet.net.

OLDWINE, BARBARA H. retired social worker, retired association executive; b. Binghamton, N.Y., Feb. 8, 1923; d. William Armstead and Mary Eliza Penrose (Harris) Harris; m. Cornelius V. Oldwine, June 6, 1944; children: B. Eilene Oldwine Carter, Valerie O. Barnes. BA, Fisk U., 1944; advanced mgmt. cert., Syracuse U., 1980. Supr. medicaid and food stamps, caseworker pub. adminstr. Broome County Social Svc., Binghamton, N.Y., 1946-81. Lectr. Broome Community Coll., Binghamton, 1980-85. Author: (booklet) Black Americans Who Made America What It Is, 1989, 28 TV vignettes, 1976 (N.Y. State Broadcasters award-Sta. WBNG). Bd. dirs. Opportunities for Broome, Binghamton, 1970s, Nat. Bd. YWCA of U.S.A., 1981; pres. Broome County Urban League Guild, Binghamton, 1981; trustee Sta. WSKG-PBS, Binghamton, 1990-99; pres. bd. dirs. Am. Cancer Soc., 1993-95, YWCA Broome County, 1973; tchr. All Sts. Episcopal Ch., Johnson City, N.Y., 1990—; apptd. to cmty. adv. com. City of Binghamton, 1993—. Named Bicentennial Women of Yr., Binghamton County, 1976, Citizen of Yr., So. Tier Divsn. NASW, 1989, African Am. Distinction Citizen, Gov. Cuomo N.Y., 1993; recipient Svc. to Mankind award, Sertoma Club, Binghamton, 1981, Pres.'s award, Delta Sigma Theta, 1985, St. George medal, Nat. Am. Cancer Soc., 1989, Nation Gold award, 1992, Lifetime Human Rights award on 50th Anniversary of Universal Declaration of Human Rights, 1998, Whitney M. Young Jr. Svc. award, Boy Scouts Am., 1999, Liberty Bell award, Broome County Bar Assn., 2000, Cmty. Svc. Crystal citation, Broome County Coun. Chs., 2001, Sigma award, Binghamton U., 2002, Dorothy Frederick So. NY Rsch. and Projects grant in her honor, AAUW Found., 2002. Mem.: AAUW (hon. life mem.), Daus. Isis (Ill. commandress Aleppo Ct. # 140 1987—88, dep. imperial directress pub. rels. 1989—). Episcopalian. Avocation: TV program host. Home: 24 Gaylord St Binghamton NY 13904-1608

OLEARCHYK, ANDREW, cardiothoracic surgeon, educator; b. Peremyshl, Ukraine, Dec. 3, 1935; s. Symon and Anna (Kravéts) O.; m. Renata M. Sharan, June 26, 1971; children: Christina N., Roman A., Adrian S. Grad., Med. Acad., Warsaw, Poland, 1961; grad., U. Pa., 1970. Diplomate Am. Bd. Surgery, Am. Bd. Thoracic Surgery. Chief divsn. anesthesiology, asst. dept. surgery Provincial Hosp., Kielce, Poland, 1963-66; resident in gen. surgery Geisinger Med. Ctr., Danville, Pa., 1968-73; resident in thoracic, cardiac surgery Allegheny Gen. Hosp., Pitts., 1980-82; pvt. practice medicine specializing in cardiac, thoracic and vascular surgery Phila. and Camden, N.J., 1982—. Contbr. articles to profl. jours. Achievements include internal repair of the coronary sinus (Valsalva) aneurysm; grating of the internal thoracic to coronary arteries without touching the atherosclerotic ascending aorta, on cardiopulmonary bypass with a beating, warm and vented heart and bradycardia induced by beta-blocker; design of double occlusion clamps for the ascending aorta, Olearchyk R Triple Ringed Cannula Spring Clip to secure vein grafts over blunted cannulas in coronary artery bypass surgery; demonstration of safety of simultaneous use of fluothane and curare as gen. anesthesia; intro. of endarterectomy and external prosthetic grafting of ascending and transverse aorta under hypothermic circulatory arrest; pioneering promotion of grafting of the left anterior descending coronary artery sys. during resection of cardiac aneurysms, and of diffusely diseased coronary arteries with the internal thoracic artery; first to combine insertion of the inferior vena cava filter with iliofemoral venous thrombectomy; combined right femoral and iliac retroperitoneal surgical approach to remove retained intraaortal balloon device; applied a technique for early antegrade flow from an axillary to main graft during replacement of the ascending aorta in proximal aortic dissection. Address: 129 Walt Whitman Blvd Cherry Hill NJ 08003-3746

O'LEARY, BRIAN MICHAEL, lawyer; b. Winchester, Mass., Nov. 12, 1960; s. Daniel James Jr. and Helen O'Leary. BSFS, Georgetown U., 1982; JD, New Eng. Sch. Law, 1985; cert. in govt. program, Harvard U., 2001. Bar: Mass. 1985, Fla. 1986. Trial atty. immigration and naturalization svc. U.S. Dept. Justice, Miami, Fla., 1985-86, spl. asst. U.S. atty., 1986-88, asst. gen. counsel Washington, 1988-89, spl. asst. U.S. atty. Alexandria, Va., 1989—90, dep. assoc. gen. counsel Washington, 1990-93, assoc. gen. counsel, 1993-94, asst. chief immigration judge exec. office immigration rev. Falls Church, Va., 1994—2000, 2001—, acting dep. chief immigration judge exec. office immigration rev., 2000—01. Fellow Nat. Ctr. for State Cts. Inst. for Ct. Mgmt., Ct. Exec. Develop. Program; mem. Fla. Bar Assn., Mass. Bar Assn. Democrat. Irish Catholic. Home: Unit B-1 1411 Belle View Blvd Alexandria VA 22307

O'LEARY, DANIEL FRANCIS, academic administrator; b. Boston, Apr. 17, 1923; s. Dennis Joseph and Catherine Mary (O'Connell) O'L. BA, Oblate Coll., 1950; EdM, U. Buffalo, 1953, EdD, 1956. Tchr. gen. sci., biology Bishop Fallon High Sch., Buffalo, 1951-62, asst. prin., 1962-65; dir. edn. Oblate Fathers, Washington, 1963-68; prin. Bishop Fallon H.S., Buffalo, 1968-74; dir. spl. programs Niagara (N.Y.) U., 1974-77, dean spl. programs, 1977-81, prof. edn., 1982—, dean edn. and continuing studies, 1982-88, prof., dean Coll. Edn., 1982-98, assoc. v.p. acad. affairs, 1998—. Adj. prof. Mt. St. Joseph's Tchrs. Coll., Buffalo, 1956-64, edn. evaluator reading clinic, 1956-64. Asst. dir. family life dept. Diocese of Buffalo, 1953-64. Mem. AAUP, ASCD, Assn. Tchr. Educators, Am. Assn. Sch. Adminstrs., Nat. Coun. for Adminstrn. Tech. Edn., Nat. Coun. for Accreditation of Tchr. Edn., N.Y. State Assn. Tchr. Educators, Am. Assn. Colls. for Tchr. Edn., Phi Delta Kappa. Roman Catholic. Office: Niagara U Assoc VP Acad Affairs Alumni Hall Niagara University NY 14109 Fax: (716) 286-8349. E-mail: dfo@niagara.edu.

O'LEARY, DANIEL VINCENT, JR. lawyer; b. Bklyn., May 26, 1942; s. Daniel Vincent and Mary (Maxwell) O'L.; m. Marilyn Irene Gavigan, June 1, 1968; children: Daniel, Katherine, Molly, James. AB cum laude, Georgetown U., 1963; LLB, Yale U., 1966. Bar: Ill. 1967. Assoc. Wilson & Mc Ilvaine, Chgo., 1967—75, ptnr., 1975—87, Peterson & Ross, Chgo., 1987—94, Schwartz & Freeman, Chgo., 1994—95; of counsel Mandell, Menkes & Surdyk, LLC, 1995—. Pres., bd. dirs. Jim's Cayman Co., Ltd.; pres. TV and Radio Purchasing Group Inc.; asst. sec. L.M.C. Ins. Co. Bermuda, 1990—; pres. Wagering Ins. N.Am. Purchasing Group Inc., 1997—. Lt. comdr. USNR, ret. Mem. Kenilworth Sailing Club (commodore 1985-87). Roman Catholic. Avocations: fishing, scuba diving. Office: Mandel Menkes & Surdyk LLC Ste 300 333 W Wacker Dr Chicago IL 60606 E-mail: doleary@mms-law.net.

O'LEARY, DAVID MICHAEL, priest, educator; b. Lynn, Mass., Mar. 11, 1958; s. Edward William and Kathryn O'L. BA, St. John's Sem., Boston, 1981, MDiv, 1984; MEd, Boston Coll., 1986; STL, Weston Sch. of Theology, 1990. Ordained priest Roman Catholic Ch., 1986; cert. alcohol counselor. Deacon intern Immaculate Conception Parish, Malden, Mass., 1984-86, parochial vicar Everett, 1986-91, St. Augustine's Parish, South Boston, 1991-93; priest St. Theresa's Ch., North Reading, Mass., 1993-95; prof. St. Mary's Sem. and U., Balt., 1995—. Spl. edn. tchr., 1977-81, coll. dir. St. John's spl. edn. program, 1980-81, rschr., writer, film editor Office Religious Edn., Boston diocese, Brighton, Mass., 1981-82; group therpy leader, case worker Brigham and Women's Hosp., Kenmore Sq. De-Tox, 1982-83; substance abuse counselor St. John/ St. Hugh Parish, Roxbury, Mass., 1983-84; lectr. Pro-Life Archdiocese of Boston, 1986—, Basic Tchr. and Intermediate Tchr Trainer and Cert., 1987; vis. lectr. coll. level, 1991, 92; cons. in counseling. Contbr. articles to religious and other pubs. Counselor Camp Fatima Exceptional Citizens Week, 1978-90, asst. resident dir., 1991, resident dir., 1992; founding mem. Everett Ltd. Equity Coop. Project, 1988; mem. steering com., synthesizer and co-editor report to Nat. Conf. Cath. Bishops on Women's Pastoral, 1989; active mem. South Boston Pastoral Com., 1991; mem. Instn. Rev. Bd. Human Subjects Com., U. Mass., 1992; founder spiritual support group for AIDS victims and families, 1992. Mem. KC (life). Democrat. Avocation: long distance running. Home and Office: St Mary's Sem and U 38 Boston Ave Medford MA 02155-6722

O'LEARY, DENIS JOSEPH, retired physician, insurance company executive; b. Ireland, Feb. 5, 1924; came to U.S., 1949, naturalized, 1954; s. Joseph and Mary Christine (Dennis) O'L.; m. Audrey Mary Ryan, Nov. 26, 1952; children: Michael, Brian, Denis, Kevin. MD, Nat. U. Ireland, Cork, 1947. Intern St. Michael's Hosp., Toronto, Ont., Can., 1947-48, resident, 1948-49, St. Vincent's Hosp., N.Y.C., 1949-50, Triboro Hosp., Jamaica, N.Y., 1950-51; with N.Y. Life Ins. Co., N.Y.C., 1952-88, med. dir. employees' health, 1961-70, v.p., 1970-82, sr. v.p., 1982-88; asst. attending physician Bellevue Hosp., N.Y.C., 1955-69, assoc. attending physician, 1969-77, attending physician, 1977-84, sr. attending physician, 1984-87. Instr. medicine, Columbia U., 1958-63, assoc. in medicine, 1963-68; asst. prof. clin. medicine NYU, 1968-86; sec. N.Y. Lung Assn., 1962-67, 69-71, v.p., 1967-69, dir., 1961-86, pres.-elect, 1983, pres., 1985-86. Bd. dirs. Nat. Council on Alcoholism, N.Y.C., 1979-86, pres., 1984-86. Served as capt. M.C. AUS, 1953-55. Fellow Am. Coll. Chest Physicians, Am. Occupational Med. Assn., Am. Pub. Health Assn.; mem. AMA, N.Y. State, New York County med. socs., Am. Thoracic Assn., Soc. Alumni Bellevue Hosp., N.Y. Occupational Med. Assn. (exec. com. 1967—, pres. 1973-74). Clubs: Scarsdale (N.Y.) Golf (gov. 1981-84), Country Club Rancho Bernardo.

O'LEARY, DENNIS SOPHIAN, medical organization executive; b. Kansas City, Mo., Jan. 28, 1938; s. Theodore Morgan and Emily (Sophian) O'L.; m. Margaret Rose Wiedman, Mar. 29, 1980; children: Margaret Rose, Theodore Morgan. BA, Harvard U., 1960; MD, Cornell U., 1964. Diplomate Am. Bd. Internal Medicine, Am. Bd. Hematology. Intern U. Minn. Hosp., Mpls., 1964-65, resident, 1965-66, Strong Meml. Hosp., Rochester, N.Y., 1966-68; asst. prof. medicine and pathology George Washington U. Med. Ctr., Washington, 1971-73, assoc. prof., 1973-80, prof. medicine, 1980-86, assoc. dean grad. med. edn., 1973-77, dean clin. affairs, 1977-86; pres. Joint Commn. on Accreditation Healthcare Orgns., Oakbrook Terrace, Ill., 1986—. Med. dir. George Washington U. Hosp., 1974-85, v.p. Univ. Health Plan, 1977-85; pres. D.C. Med. Soc., 1983. Chmn. editl. bd. Med. Staff News, 1985-86; contbr. articles to profl. jours. Founding mem. Nat. Capital Area Health Care Coalition, Washington, 1982; trustee James S. Brady Found., Washington, 1982-87; bd. dirs. D.C. Polit. Action Com., 1982-84. Maj. U.S. Army, 1968-71. Recipient Community Service award D.C. Med. Soc., 1981, Key to the City, Mayor of Kansas City, Mo., 1982. Fellow Am. Coll. Physician Execs., ACP-Am. Soc. Internal Medicine; mem. AMA (resolution commendation 1981), Soc. Med. Adminstrs., Am. Hosp. Assn. (del. 1984-86, resolution commendation 1981), Internat. Club (Chgo.). Avocation: tennis.

O'LEARY, JOHN CLARENCE, retired radiologist; b. Washington, Nov. 16, 1922; MD, U. Tex., 1946. Diplomate Am. Bd. Radiology. Intern U.S. Naval Hosp., Long Beach, 1946-47; resident in internal medicine Scott-White Meml. Hosp., Temple, Tex., 1949-52; resident in radiology U.S. Naval Hosp., Bethesda, Md., 1956-59; resident in radiol. therapy Walter Reed Army Med. Ctr., Washington, 1959-60; mem. staff Brazosport Meml. Hosp., Lake Jackson, Tex., 1960-92, ret., 1992. Mem. AMA, Am. Coll. Radiology, Am. Inst. Ultrasound Medicine.

O'LEARY, JOSEPH EVANS, lawyer; b. Newton, Mass., Sept. 17, 1945; s. Cornelius Joseph and Dorothy Mary (Evans) O'L.; m. Carolyn Brady, Aug. 16, 1969; children: Caryn, Kevin, David, Catherine. AB, Boston Coll., 1967, JD, 1970; LLM, Georgetown U., 1974. Bar: Mass. 1970, Ill. 1974, N.Y. 1979. Assoc. Seyfarth, Shaw, Fairweather & Geraldson, Chgo., 1974-78, ptnr. N.Y.C., 1978-82; of counsel Choate, Hall & Stewart, Boston, 1982-83, ptnr., 1983-99, McDermott, Will, Emery, Boston, 1999—. Lt. USN, 1971-74. Mem. ABA, Mass. Bar Assn., Boston Bar Assn. Home: 5 Penobscot St Medfield MA 02052-3008 Office: McDermott Will Emery 28 State St Boston MA 02109-1775

O'LEARY, MARION HUGH, university dean, chemist; b. Quincy, Ill., Mar. 24, 1941; s. J. Gilbert and Ruth Elizabeth (Kerr) O'L.; m. Sandra E. Eisemann, Sept. 5, 1964 (div. 1979); children— Catherine, Randall, Jessica; m. Elizabeth M. Kean, Jan. 24, 1981. BS, U. Ill., 1963; PhD, MIT, 1966. Asst. prof. chemistry U. Wis., Madison, 1967-73, assoc. prof., 1973-78, prof. chemistry and biochemistry, 1978-89; prof. and head dept. biochemistry U. Nebr., Lincoln, 1989-96; dean Coll. Natural Scis. and Math., Calif. State U., Sacramento, 1996—. Cons. Institut Pertanian Bogor, Indonesia, 1983-84; vis. prof. Universitas Andalas, Padang, Indonesia, 1984-85, Australian Nat. U., 1982-83. Author: Contemporary Organic Chemistry, 1976. Editor: Isotope Effects on Enzyme-Catalyzed Reactions, 1977. Contbr. articles to sci. publs. Grantee, NSF, U.S. Dept. Agr., Dept. Energy, NIH; Guggenheim Found. fellow, 1982-83; Sloan Found. fellow, 1972-74. Fellow AAAS; mem. Am. Chem. Soc., Am. Soc. Biochemistry and Molecular Biology. Home: 6428 Orange Hill Ln Carmichael CA 95608-4580 Office: Calif State U Coll Natural Scis Math 6000 J St Sacramento CA 95819-6123 E-mail: moleary@csus.edu.

O'LEARY, MARY LOUISE, television producer, educator; b. Providence, Aug. 29, 1955; d. Vincent Christopher and Mary Elizabeth (Bryon) O'L. BA, R.I. Coll., 1977. Assoc. prodr. Guiding Light, CBS-TV, N.Y.C., 1984-95; coordinating prodr. Another World, NBC-TV, 1995-96; prodr. One Live To Live, ABC-TV, 1998-2000, prodr. Gen. Hosp. L.A., 2000—. Guest lectr. at colls. and univs. Alumni-theatre honoree R.I. Coll., 1998. Mem. NATAS, N.Y. Women in Film and TV. Office: General Hospital ABC-TV One Live To Live 4151 Prospect Ave Los Angeles CA 90027

O'LEARY, MICHAEL PHILIP, urologic surgeon; b. Framingham, Mass., May 10, 1952; s. James Joseph and Jacqueline Anne (Hope) O'L.; m. Kathleen J. Welch, Sept. 17, 1983; children: Jacqueline Grace, James Joseph. AB, Harvard U., 1974, MPH, 1980; MD, George Washington, 1980. Diplomate Am. Bd. Urology. Surg. resident New England Med. Ctr., Boston, 1980-82; urology resident Mass. Gen. Hosp., 1982-87; asst. prof. urology Sch. Medicine Tufts U., 1989-93; asst. prof. surgery Harvard Med. Sch., 1993-98, assoc. prof. surgery, 1998—. Vis. scholar Bus. Sch. Stanford (Calif.) U., 1987-89; presenter in field. Contbr. numerous articles to profl. jours. Chmn. Bd. Health, Dedham, Mass., 1994. Robert Wood Johnson scholar U. Calif., San Francisco, 1987-89. Fellow ACS; mem. AMA, AAAS, Am. Urol. Assn. (exec. com. New England sect.), Am. Fertility Soc., Mass. Med. Soc. (house dels. 1995). Home: 62 Channing Rd Dedham MA 02026-5605 Office: Brigham & Women's Hosp 45 Francis St Boston MA 02115-6105 E-mail: moleary1@partners.org.

O'LEARY, PATSY BAKER, writer, educator; b. Greenville, N.C., Sept. 23, 1937; d. Alton Proctor Baker and Ethel (Leary) Baker Williams; m. Denis Louis O'Leary, Aug. 26, 1962 (div. Aug. 1979); 1 child, Linda Jeanette. BS, East Carolina Coll., 1959; MA, Calif. State U., Northridge, 1979. Sec. ABC-TV, L.A., 1959-60; creative devel., prodn. sec. various TV series, 1960-66; asst. to prodr. Get Smart TV series, 1966-70; lectr. English East Carolina U., Greenville, 1980-81, lectr. comm., 1990-95; tchr. creative writing Pitt C.C., 1980—. Author: With Wings as Eagles, 1997. Mem. adminstrv. bd. St. James United Meth. Ch., Greenville, 1996-97. Recipient various awards for poetry, journalism, novel Coun. of Authors and Journalists, 1980-87. Mem. Nat. Writers Union, Ga. Writers, Inc., N.C. Writers Network, Southeastern Writers Assn. Methodist. Avocations: reading, antiques, crafts, auctions.

O'LEARY, PAUL GERARD, investment executive; b. Boston, June 22, 1935; s. Gerard Paul and Marie Agnes (Hennessey) O'Leary; m. Elizabeth Jane Pollins, Oct. 14, 1961; children: Paul Hennessey, William Gerard, Mary Elizabeth, James Daniel. AB cum laude, Harvard U., 1956; MBA, U. Pa., 1958. Alumni dir. Wharton Grad. Sch., U. Pa., Phila., 1958-60; asst. sec. Empire Trust Co., N.Y.C., 1960-65; sr. investment analyst Blyth & Co., Inc., 1965-70; v.p. William D. Witter, Inc., 1970-76, also bd. dirs.; investment sr. v.p. Prudential Ins. Corp. Am., Newark, 1977—2002; retired. Instr fin Univ Pa, 1957—60. V.p. Prudential Found., Newark, 1986—96. Mem.: Boston Latin Sch. Alumni Assn., N.Y. Soc. Security Analysts, N.Y. Property Ins. Underwriting Assn. (mem. investment com. 1994—2002), Ins. Inst. Hwy. Safety (mem. investment com. 1983—2002), Assn. Ins. and Fin. Analysis (pres. 1973—74), Am. Nuc. Insurers (chmn. investment com. West Hartford, Conn. 1989—96), Inst. Chartered Fin. Analysts, Upper Ridgewood Tennis Club, Indian Trail Club (Franklin Lakes, N.J.), Harvard Club N.J. (pres. 1983—84). Roman Catholic. Avocations: tennis, squash, philately, cartography, history. Home: 719 Belmont Rd Ridgewood NJ 07450-1300

O'LEARY, PEGGY RENÉ, accountant; b. Billings, Mont., Dec. 6, 1951; d. Paul Eugene and Norma Dean (Metcalf) O'L.; m. Kim Patric Johnson, Mar. 19, 1983. BS, Mont. State U., 1976. CPA, Mont. Staff acct. Peat Marwick Main, Billings, 1976-80; dir. fin. Billings Clinic, 1980-95; chief ops. officer Billings Sch. Dist. 2, 1996—. Div. leader youth support campaign YMCA, Billings, 1987-88, 92-93, bd. dirs., 1988-94, sec. bd., 1989-94; vol. Big Brother and Sister, 1995—. Mem. Billings C. of C. (sch. tax com. 1982-88), Pink Chips Investment Club (treas. 1987-88). Republican. Roman Catholic. Avocations: running, golf, swimming, bicycling. Home: 4565 Pine Cove Rd Billings MT 59106-1332 Office: Billings Sch Dist 2 415 N 30th St Billings MT 59101-1298

O'LEARY, ROSEMARY, law educator; b. Kansas City, Mo., Jan. 26, 1955; d. Franklin Hayes and Mary Jane (Kelly) O'L; m. Larry Dale Schroeder; 1 child, Meghan Schroeder O'Leary. BA, U. Kans., 1978, JD, 1981, MPA, 1982; PhD, Syracuse U., 1988. Bar: Kans. 1981. Gov.'s fellow Office of Gov., Topeka, 1981-82; asst. gen. counsel kans. Corp. Com., 1982-83; dir. policy, lawyer Kans. Dept. Health and Environment, 1983-85; asst. prof. Ind. u., Bloomington, 1988-90; assoc. prof. Ind. U., 1994—; asst. prof. Syracuse (N.Y.) U., 1990-94. Author: Environmental Change: Federal Courts and the EPA, 1993, Public Administration and the Law, 2d edit., 1996; contbr. more than 50 articles to profl. jours. Bd. govs. U. Kans. Sch. Law, Lawrence, 1980-82, devel. bd., 1981-85; bd. dirs. League Women Voters Syracuse, 1986-88; vol. Habitat for Humanity, Mex., 1990; cons. NSF, 1990; panel mem. Nat. Acad. Scis., Washington, 1990-96. Recipient Outstanding Rsch. award Lily Found., 1992, Best Article award PAR, 1993, 94, Prof. of Yr. award NASPAA, 1996. Mem. ABA (editorial bd. Natural Resources and Environment jour. 1989-95, Award for Excellence 1981), ASPA (exec. com. law and environ. sects., chair environment sect., Rsch. award 1991, Best Conf. Paper award 1991), Am. Polit. Sci. Assn. (nat. chair pub. adminstrn. sect., exec. com. sect. publ.), Acad. Mgmt., Law and Soc. Assn., Assn. Pub. Policy Analysis and Mgmt. Avocations: kayaking, hiking, swimming, canoeing. Office: Ind U SPEA 410J Bloomington IN 47405

O'LEARY, TERESA, controller; b. N.Y.C., Jan. 21, 1960; d. Donald James and Frances W. (McGowan) O'L. BS, N.Y. Inst. Tech., 1981; JD, N.Y. Law Sch., 1994. Lic. fin. and ops. prin. Sr. compliance examiner Nat. Assn. Securities Dealers, N.Y.C., 1982-85; asst. v.p., sr. compliance officer Ryan, Beck & Co., West Orange, N.J., 1985-89; v.p., contr. Chapdelaine & Co., N.Y.C., 1989—. Avocations: boating, travel. Office: Chapdelaine & Co 199 Water St Fl 17 New York NY 10038-3529

O'LEARY, THOMAS MICHAEL, lawyer; b. N.Y.C., Aug. 16, 1948; s. James and Julia Ann (Connolly) O'L.; m. Luise Ann Williams, Jan. 13, 1978; 1 child, Richard Meridith. BA, CUNY, 1974; JD, Seattle U., 1977. Bar: Wash. 1977, U.S. Ct. Mil. Appeals 1978, U.S. Ct. Appeals (9th cir.), U.S. Supreme Ct. 1983. Dep. pros. atty. Pierce County, Tacoma, 1978; commd. 1st lt. U.S. Army, 1978, advanced through grades to capt., 1978; chief trial counsel Office of Staff Judge Adv., Ft. Polk, La., 1978-79, trial def. counsel, trial def. svc., 1979-81; chief legal advisor Office Insp. Gen., Heidelberg, Fed. Republic of Germany, 1981-82; sr. def. counsel Trial Def. Svc., Giessen, Fed. Republic of Germany, 1982-84; asst. chief adminstrv. law U.S. Army Armor Ctr., Ft. Knox, Ky., 1984-85, chief adminstrv. law, 1985, chief legal asst., 1985-86; ret. U.S. Army, 1996; sr. trial atty. Immigration and naturalization Svc., Phoenix, 1987; sector counsel, spl. asst. U.S. atty., U.S. Border Patrol, Tucson, 1987-90; enforcement counsel U.S. Immigration and Naturalization Svc., 1990-95, asst. dist. counsel Phoenix litigation, 1995-97. Apptd. U.S. Immigration Judge, U.S. Immigration Ct., Imperial, Calif., 1997-2000, apptd. sr. U.S. Immigration Judge, Tucson, 2000—; adj. prof. Embry-Riddle Aero. U., Tucson, 2002-. Decorated Purple Heart, Cross of Gallantry (Vietnam). Mem. Judge Advs Assn., Wash. State Bar Assn. E-mail: Thomas.O'Leary@usdoj.gov. Home: 9080 E 25th St Tucson AZ 85710-8675 Office: US Immigration Ct 1705 E Hanna Rd Ste 366 Eloy AZ 85231-9612

O'LEARY, TIMOTHY JOSEPH, pathologist; b. Birmingham, Ala., July 14, 1952; s. Timothy Joseph and Kathleen Ann O'L.; m. Dianne Marie Prost, June 28, 1975; children: Theresa, Thomas, Brendan. BS, Purdue U., 1972; PhD, Stanford U., 1976; MD, U. Mich., 1979. Diplomate Am. Bd. Pathology, Nat. Bd. Med. Examiners. Rsch. assoc. dept. physiology U. Mich., Ann Arbor, 1976-77; resident Lab. of Pathology Nat. Cancer Inst., Bethesda, Md., 1979-81, fellow in anatomic pathology, 1981-82; med. staff fellow Nat. Inst. of Diabetes and Digestive and Kidney Diseases, 1982-86, FDA, Bethesda, 1986-87; chmn. dept. cellular pathology Armed Forces Inst. of Pathology, Washington, 1987—. Cons. FDA, 1987—; subcom. chmn. Nat. Com. on Clin. Lab. Stds., Lancaster, Pa.; chair hematology and pathology devices adv. panel, FDA, 1996—; adj. assoc. prof. of pathology, Uniformed Svcs. U. of the Health Scis., Bethesda. Editl. bd. Pathology Rsch. and Practice, Stutgart, Ga., 1991—, Cell Vision, New Brunswick, Ga., 1993—; editor: (book) Pediatric Molecular Pathology, Pediatric Molecular Pathology: Quantitative Aspects; contbr. more than 90 articles to profl. jours./publs. Surgeon USPHS, 1979-82. Fellow Coll. of Am. Pathologists; mem. Biophys. Soc., Am. Chem. Soc., U.S. Can. Acad. of Pathology. Office: Armed Forces Inst Pathology Dept Cullular Pathology Washington DC 20306-0001

O'LEARY, TIMOTHY MICHAEL, real estate corporation officer; b. Savanna, Ill., Mar. 24, 1946; s. John Patrick and Hazel O'Leary; m. Patricia Ann Woosnam; children: Kevin, Kathleen, Maureen, Mary Margaret, Michael, John. Student, Loras Coll., 1964-68; BS, No. Ill. U., 1970, MSBA, 1974. Systems programmer Newel Co., Freeport, Ill., 1970-71, acting mgr. accounts receivable, 1971-73; v.p., treas. HTO Real Estate Svcs., Chgo., Des Plaines, 1974-90, pres., treas. Northbrook, 1990-94; sr. v.p. Anderson Schroud Group, Schaumburg, 1994-96; pres. O'Leary Realty Corp., 1996—. Chmn. profl. stds. com. Chgo. Bd. Realtors, 1984-85; treas. The Real Estate Consortium, 1993, v.p., 1994-95. Mem. sch. bd. St. Luke Sch., River Forest, Ill., 1985-88, chmn. 1987-88; mem. troop com. Boy Scouts Am., 2000—. Mem. Soc. Indsl. and Office Realtors (vice chmn. regional seminar edn. 1984-87, exec. com. Chgo. chpt. 1987-91, nat. bd. dirs. 1987-90, treas. 1988, sec. 1989, v.p. 1990, pres. 1991), Oak Park Jaycees (past pres.), Realtors Nat. Mktg. Inst. (bd. dirs. Ill. chpt. cert. comml. investment 1988-89), Ill. Assn. Realtors (chmn. comml. indsl. subcom. 1990-91, chmn. CI com. 1991-92, Presdl. award 1991), Am. Soc. Real Estate Counselors, No. Ill. Comml. Assn. of Realtors (bd. dirs. 2001—), Realtors 40 Club (clk. 1985-86, cashier 1989-90, chmn. 1992), KC (dep. grand knight Queen of Peace coun. 2001-02, grand knight 2002—). Roman Catholic. E-mail: tim@olearyrealty.com.

OLECHNO-HUSZCZA, CZESLAW, retired translator and educator; b. Estate Zadworze Wilno, Poland, Aug. 6, 1918; came to U.S., 1952; s. Vincent and Pelagia Olechno-Huszcza; m. Ethel Gillian Taylor, Aug. 25, 1951; 1 child, William Vincent. BA in Latin, U. London, 1950; diploma in edn., U. Leeds, Eng.; MA, U. So. Calif., 1958; postgrad., UCLA, 1960-65. Tchr. langs. Morningside H.S., Inglewood, Calif., 1958-80; head lang. dept., asst. tennis coach. Grad. lang. examiner UCLA, 1964-70; lectr. Polish lang. Loyola Marymont U., L.A., 1976-77; translator books and articles in Latin, Russian, Polish. Translator: The Warsaw Ghetto, 1970, Warsaw Aflame, 1970. Officer Polish Am. Hist. Assn., 1978; chmn. scholarship com. Polish Univ. Club L.A., Inc., 1947-99. Flying officer RAF, 1942-50. Decorated War medal, Air Force medal, Order Knights of Cross of Republic of Poland. Mem. Am. Translators Assn. (founder So. Calif. chpt. 1960), Polish Univ. Club. Democrat. Roman Catholic. Avocations: bridge, tennis, philately. Home: 1841 Saint John Rd Seal Beach CA 90740-4380 E-mail: jillret@mailstation.com.

OLECHNOWICZ FRIDMAN, ELIAS, civil engineer; b. Mexico City, Mex., June 10, 1955; s. Miguel and Bertha (Fridman) O. Degree in Civil Engring., Iberoamericana U., Mexico City, 1978; postgrad., Autonomous Nat. U. Mex., 1993—. Engr.'s asst. Constrns. ARA Co., Mexico City, 1976; schemer engr. AIN SA Co., 1977-78; resident engr. Las Aguilas Constrn. Co., 1978-79, Fernandez and Fridman Constrn. Co., Mexico City, 1980-83; constrn. supt. J.G.I. Constrn., 1983-84; assoc. founder, pres., tech. dir., gen. dir. Promotion and Performance of Constrns. SA de CV, 1984-92; pvt. practice engr., rschr., 1993—. With Mex. Army, 1971-72. Mem. ASCE (affiliate), AAAS, Civil Engrs. Coll. Mex. (affiliate), Mex. Soc. Soil Mechanics. Jewish. Home and Office: Fuente Del Pescador No 22 Lomas de Tecamachalco 53950 Mexico City Mexico

OLEJNICZAK, BERNARD CHARLES, education educator; b. Green Bay, Wis., Aug. 23, 1930; s. Bernard Clement and Helen Josephine (LeClair) Olejniczak; m. Mary Jean Barrett-Terry, Oct. 13, 1956 (div. Dec. 1979); children: Ann Marie, Mary Rose, Patrick James, Thomas Bernard; m. Margaret Jean Olson, Sept. 19, 1980. BA in Philosophy, St. Norbert Coll., 1953; MA in Counseling, U. Wis., 1966. Tchr. in Latin, French and journalism Pulaski (Wis.) H.S., 1957—71; adminstr. Pulaski Elem. Schs., 1971—92; pvt. cons., 1993—96; tech. lectr. U. Wis., Oshkosh, 1996—. Chmn. spirituality curriculum U. Wis. Learning in Retirement, 1997—. Editor (newsletter): Polish Heritage, 1993—, Wisconsin Counselor, 1995—. Pres. Village Bd., Pulaski, 1965—70; v.p. Bd. Edn., 1992—96; sec. Pulaski C. of C., 1958—64; pres. Brown County Libr. Bd., Green Bay, 1985—96, Nicolet Fed. Libr., Green Bay, 1987—92. Named Trustee of Yr., Wis. Libr. Assn., 1997; recipient Profl. Writing award, Wis. Counselors Assn., 1999. Mem.: Lions Club (newsletter editor, sec. 1993—), Phi Delta Kappa. Democrat. Roman Catholic. Avocations: reading, computers. Home: 1625 Graber St Oshkosh WI 54901 Office: Univ Wis Coll Edn 800 Algoma Blvd Oshkosh WI 54901 Fax: 920-235-9377. E-mail: olejnicz@uwosh.edu.

OLEK, MICHAEL JOSEPH, medical educator; b. Camden, N.J., Aug. 31, 1963; m. Elizabeth Ann Olek. BS, N.Y. Inst. of Tech., 1985; DO, Phila. Coll., 1989. Osteopathic intern Wyckoff Heights Med. Ctr., Bklyn., 1989-90; intern neurology Med. Coll. of Va., Richmond, 1990-91, neurology resident, 1991-94; clin. neuroimmunology fellow Brigham and Women's Hosp., 1994-96, attending physician, 1996—; clin. instr. Harvard Med. Sch., Boston, 1996—; clin. assoc. Mass. Gen. Hosp., 1997—. Clin. cons. BWH/Harvard Sch. of Public Health Dietary Etiologies of Multiple Sclerosis and Parkinson's; co-founder Multiple Sclerosis Clinic at the Med. Coll. of Va. Hosps., 1992-94; attending physician Brigham and Women's Hosp., Boston, 1996—; clin. assoc. Mass. Gen. Hosp., Boston, 1997—; presenter, lectr. in field. Contbr. articles to profl. jours. Mem. Am. Acad. of Neurology, Nat. Multiple Sclerosis Soc., Mass. Med. Soc. Home: 1518 Valencia Newport Beach CA 92660-3276 Office: U Calif Irvine Med Ctr Gottschalk Med Plaza Irvine CA 92697-6250

OLEN, MILTON WILLIAM, JR. marketing executive; b. Providence, Sept. 15, 1950; s. Milton William and Elizabeth Amanda (Goodrich) O.; m. Kathleen A. Windridge, June 15, 2001. Student, Fla. So. Coll., 1969-72; BS in Behavioral Scis. magna cum laude, Nova U., 1978. Lic. comml. pilot, USCG capt.; lic. residential contractor, Fla. Mfr.'s rep. for Fla., The Siemens Corp., Ft. Lauderdale, Fla., 1972-77; product mgr., exec. salesman, sales mgr. The Ritter Dental Co., Romulus, Mich., 1977-85; gen. mgr., exec. salesman Olen Homes Internat. Inc., Fort Lauderdale, Fla., 1981—; gen. mgr. Windridge Yacht Charters. Mem. Nat. Assn. Home Builders, C. of C. Miami Beach, Better Bus. Bur. Roman Catholic. Avocation: boating, travel. Office: PO Box 70156 Fort Lauderdale FL 33307-0156

OLENDER, JACK HARVEY, lawyer; b. McKeesport, Pa., Sept. 8, 1935; m. Lovell Olender. BA, U. Pitts., 1957, JD, 1960; LLM, George Washington U., 1961. Bar: D.C. 1961, U.S. Supreme Ct. 1965, Md. 1966, Pa. 1985; diplomate Am. Bd. Trial Advocates,Inner Cir. Advocates. Pvt. practice, Washington, 1961-79; prin. Jack H. Olender & Assocs., P.C., 1979—. Contbr. articles to profl. jours. Active World Peace through Law, Washington. Named to Hall of Fame Nat. Assn. Black Women Attys., 1987, D.C. Hall of Fame, 2000, Washington Bar Assn. Hall of Fame, 2000; recipient Presdl. award Nat. Bar Assn., 1996, 2000, 02, Advocate for Justice award Nat. Bar Assn., 2000, Internat. B'nai B'rith Pursuit of Justice award, 2001. Fellow Am. Coll. Trial Lawyers, Internat. Acad. Trial Lawyers and Inner Cir. Advs.; mem. ATLA, Nat. Bar Assn. (adv. for justice 2000), Am. Bd. Profl. Liability Attys. (bd. dirs.), Trial Lawyers Pub. Justice (bd. dirs.), Internat. Assn. Jewish Lawyers and Jurists (bd. dirs.), Bar Assn. of D.C. (pres. 1999-2000). Office: Jack H Olender & Assocs PC 888 17th St NW Fl 4 Washington DC 20006-3939

OLENDORF, DONNA, editor; b. Chgo., Sept. 11, 1949; d. Camille Frank Vozar and Lea Bertani Vozar Newman; m. Donald Olendorf, June 29, 1969; children: Patrice LeeAnn Boettcher, Sara Elizabeth Ortolan, Donald Patrick. BA with distinction, U. Mich., 1969; MA in Edn., Ea. Mich. U., Ypsilanti, 1973; MA in English cum laude, Wayne State U., Detroit, 1982. From asst. editor to sr. editor, project mgr. Gale Group, Farmington Hills, Mich., 1982—; editor in chief St. Luke's Epistle, Utica, 1998—2001; review panel manuscript Jour. Coll. Sci. Reading Nat. Sci. Tchrs. Assn., Arlington, Va., 1998-2000; with editl. bd. The Record, Detroit, 2000—; with Gale Group, Farmington Hills; series project mgr., editor select vols, Grzimek's Animal Life Ency., 2d edit., 2002—. Prodn. editor: Notable Twentieth Century Scientists, 1995 (RASD Outstanding Reference Books citation, 1995, Best Reference Libr. Jour., 1995); editor: Gale Encyclopedia of Medicine, 1999 (RUSA award Outstanding Ref., 2000, Editor's Choice award RRB/Booklist, 2000), Something about the Author, 1990-92, Contemporary Authors, 1992-94. Active Eisenhower Dance Ensemble, Rochester Hills, Mich., 1997—; clerk of vestry St. Luke's Episcopal Ch., Utica, Mich., 1998-2000. Recipient Blue Ribbon award for gen. excellence, Diocese of Mich., 2000, Red Ribbon award for gen. excellence, 2001. Mem.: Project Mgmt. Inst. Avocations: ballet, gardening. Office: Gale Group 27500 Drake Rd Farmington Hills MI 48331 E-mail: donna.olendorf@gale.com.

OLENDORF, WILLIAM CARR, JR. small business owner; b. Albany, N.Y., Oct. 3, 1945; s. William Carr Sr. and Mary Zilpha (Gillies) O.; m. Barbara Kay Cowan, Aug. 14, 1966; children: Mark, Julie, Jennifer. Student, Columbia Coll., 1964-65, So. Ill. U., 1965-66. Prodn. asst. Sta. WTTW-TV, Chgo., 1962-64; radio announcer Sta. WERX, Wyoming, Mich., 1967-68; sales rep. Sta. WCFL, Chgo., 1968-70, Sta. WJJD-AM & FM, Chgo., 1970-72; v.p. Promotion Network, 1972-74; account exec. AVCO-TV, 1974-76, Peters, Griffin & Woodward, Chgo., 1976-82, Petry TV, Chgo., 1982-83; owner, pres. Point South KOA Resort, Yemassee, S.C., 1983—. Commr. Point South Pub. Svc. Dist., 1987-88, Lowcountry & Resort Island Tourism Commn., 1994—; mem. tourism tax adv. bd. Jasper County, S.C., 1985--; chmn. Jasper County Hist. Preservation Commn., S.C., 1994-99; trustee S.C. Battleground Preservation Trust, Inc., 1994-98; mem. Low Country REvolutionary War Trail Commn. Recipient S.C. Honor award for Historic Preservation, Palmetto Trust for Historic Preservation, S.C. Dept. Archives and History, 1997. Mem. Nat. Campground Owners Assn. (campground nat. adv. bd. 1989-93, Take Pride in Am. award 1992), Kampground Owners Assn. (S.C. regiona pres. 1994-97, Award of Merit 1990), S.C. Campground Assn. (pres. 1987-88), Point South Mchts. Assn. (pres. 1990—), Jasper County Hist. Soc., Jasper County C. of C. (bd. dirs. 2001-2003). Republican. Episcopalian. Avocation: amateur radio operator. Home and Office: PO Box 1760 Yemassee SC 29945-1760 E-mail: pskoa@mykoa.com.

OLENGINSKI, JAN ANTHONY, surgeon; b. West Point, N.Y., May 29, 1964; s. Jan Anthony and Patricia Ann (Grabowski) O. BS, U. Scranton, 1986; DO, U. Health Scis., 1990. Intern Suburban Gen. Hosp., Norristown, Pa., 1990-91; resident in gen. surgery Phila. Coll. Osteo. Medicine, 1991-95, chief resident, 1994-95, fellow in vascular surgery, 1995-96; attending surgeon gen. and vascular surgery Tenet Hosps., Med. Coll. Pa., Frankford Hosp., Roxborough Hosp., Albert Einstein Med. Ctr., Phila., 1996—. Chmn. gen. surgery Pa. Osteopathic Med. Assn. (POMA); clin./assoc. prof. gen. and vascular surgery Phila. Coll. of Osteopathic Medicine. Mem. Am. Osteo. Assn., Am. Coll. Osteo. Surgeons, Am. Assn. Osteo. Postgrad. Physicians, Pa. Osteo. Med. Assn. (chmn. subcom. on gen. surgery), Pa. Med. Soc., Phila. County Med. Soc., Phila. County Osteo. Med. Soc. Republican. Roman Catholic. Avocations: golf, sports, running, art. Home: 7 Stevens Ct Lafayette Hill PA 19444 Office: 1331 E Wyoming Ave Ste 2110 Philadelphia PA 19124-3808

OLER, WESLEY M., IV, executive; b. Washington, Apr. 13, 1955; s. Wesley Marion III and Virginia (Craemer) O.; m. Debra Brown, Apr. 16, 1993; children: Wesley V, Phoebe. BA, Yale U., 1978. CFA. Deputy mgr. instl. sales Brown Bros. Harriman & Co., Zurich, 1982-88, mgr. internat. bankers N.Y.C., 1988-95, sr. mgr. equity trading, 1995-99; sr. portfolio mgr., pvt. client group, 1999—. Mem. ITS/CAES subcom. Nasdag Stock Market, N.Y.C., 1996—; mem. N.Y. Stock Exch., N.Y.C., 1998. Mem. Endowment Commn. Christ Ch., Greenwich, Conn. Mem. SAR (treas. 1995-96), Soc. Colonial Wars (coun. mem. 1993-94), Soc. Mayflower Descs., Securities Industry Assn. (mem. instnl. brokerage com. 1997—), N.Y. Soc. Security Analysts (mem. High Net Worth Investors Com.). Office: Brown Bros Harriman & Co 59 Wall St New York NY 10005-2808 E-mail: wesley.oler@bbh.com.

OLERTA, LESLIE ANNE, nuclear medicine technologist; b. Pa., July 9, 1968; d. Thomas Joseph and Elaine Louise (Pace) O. AS in Social Sci. magna cum laude, Luzerne County Cmty. Coll., 1996; BS Radiology Mgmt. with honors, Natl. Dean's List, Coll. Misercordia, Dallas, PA, 1999. Cert. nuclear Positron Emission Tomography technologist, radiologic technologist. Nuclear medicine technologist (part-time) Wyo. Valley Health Care Systems, Wilkes Barre, Pa.; radiologic technologist Pittston (Pa.) Med. and Emergency Complex; nuclear positron emission tomography technician Wyoming Valley P.E.T. Assocs., Forty-Fort, Pa., clin. operating mgr. Mem. Am. Soc. of Radiologic Technologists, Am. Soc. Nuclear Cardiology, Pa. Soc. of Radiologic Technologists, Soc. of Nuclear Medicine, Natl. Hon. Soc., Alpha Sigma Lambda (Beta Chi Chapter). Avocations: swimming, diving, biking, running, skiing. Home: 43 Memorial St Exeter PA 18643-2611 Office: Wyo Valley PET Assocs 190 Welles St Forty Fort PA 18704

OLERUD, JOHN GARRETT, professional baseball player; b. Seattle, Aug. 5, 1968; s. John E. Olerud. Student, Washington State U. Infielder Toronto Blue Jays, 1989-96, NY Mets, 1997-99, Seattle Mariners, 2000—. Mem. Am. League All-Star Team, 1993. winner A.L batting title, 1993. Office: Seattle Mariners 1st Ave S & Atlantic Seattle WA 98104*

OLES, PAUL STEVENSON (STEVE OLES), architect, perspectivist, educator; b. San Antonio, Sept. 26, 1936; s. Paul Stevenson Sr. and Suda (Willis) O.; m. Carole Simmons, Oct. 11, 1963 (div. 1991); children: Brian Thomas, Julia Oles Carr; m. Susan Thompson, Sept. 26, 1992. BArch, Tex. Tech U., 1960; MArch, Yale U., 1963. Registered architect, Mass. Draftsman The Architects Collaborative, Cambridge, Mass., 1963-65, Cambridge Seven Assocs., Cambridge, 1965-67; architect MIT, 1968-70; prin. architect Interface Architects, Newton, Mass., 1971—. Vis. faculty RISD, Providence, 1974-79; lectr. architecture Harvard Grad. Sch. Design, Cambridge, 1984-88, vis. scholar, 1989-91. Author: Architectural Illustration, 1979, Drawing the Future, 1988. Mem. vestry Episcopalian Ch., 1995-98. Named Loeb fellow Harvard Grad. Sch. Design, 1982. Fellow AIA (inst. honor 1983, fellow 1989), Boston Soc. Architects, Am. Soc. Archtl. Perspectivists (founder, pres. 1986-90, bd. dirs. 1993-97, Hugh Ferriss Meml. prize 1996). Democrat. Avocations: music, painting, photography. Office: Interface Architects 1 Gateway Ctr Ste 501A Newton MA 02458-2882 E-mail: steve@psoles.com.

OLES, STUART GREGORY, lawyer; b. Seattle, Dec. 15, 1924; s. Floyd and Helen Louise (La Violette) O.; m. Ilse Hanewald, Feb. 12, 1954; children: Douglas, Karl, Stephen. BS magna cum laude, U. Wash., 1947, JD, 1948. Bar: Wash., 1949, U.S. Supreme Ct. 1960. Dep. pros. atty. King County, Wash., 1949, chief civil dept., 1949-50; gen. practice law Seattle, 1950-95; sr. ptnr. firm Oles, Morrison & Rinker and predecessor, 1955-90, of counsel, 1991-95. Author: A View From the Rock, 1994, On Behalf of My Clients -- A Lawyer's Life, 1998. Chmn. Seattle Cmty. Concert Assn., 1955; pres. Friends Seattle Pub. Libr., 1956; mem. Wash. pub. Disclosure Commn., 1973-075; trustee Ch. Divinity Sch. of Pacific, Berkeley, Calif., 1974-75; mem. bd. curators Wash. State Hist. Soc., 1983; former mem. Seattle Symphony Bd.; pres. King County Ct. House Rep. Club, 1950, U. Wash. Young Rep. Club, 1947; Wash. conv. floor leader Taft, 1952, Goldwater, 1964; Wash. chmn. Citizens for Goldwater, 1964; chmn. King County Rep. convs., 1966, 68, 76, 84, 88, 90, 92, 96, Wash. State Rep. Conv., 1980. Served with USMCR, 1943-45. Mem. ABA (past regional vice-chmn. pub. contract law sect.), Wash. Bar Assn., Order of Coif, Scabbard and Blade, Am. Legion, Kapoho Bay Club (pres.), Am. Highland Cattle Assn. (v.p. and dir.), Phi Beta Kappa, Phi Alpha Delta. Home: 22715 SE 43rd Ct Issaquah WA 98029-5200 also: RR 2 Pahoa HI 96778-9802

OLESEN, CAROLYN MCDONALD, dance educator, choreographer; b. Blytheville, Ark., Aug. 27, 1963; d. Travis Eugene and Barbara Jean (Myers) McDonald; m. Donald John Olesen Jr., Nov. 3, 2001. BA in Dance, U. Calif., Irvine, 1987; MA in Edn., U. Iowa, 1998; choreographer, Coe Coll., 1998. Instr. dance Kirkwood C.C., Cedar Rapids, Iowa, 1987-90, choreographer, 1987—2001, artistic dir., 1990—2001; owner, pres. McDonald Arts Ctr., Marion, 1988—2001; instr. dance Coe Coll., Cedar Rapids, 1989—2001; choreographer show choir All Saints Mid. Sch., Marion, 1998-2000; choreographer color guard dance ensemble Washington H.S., Cedar Rapids, 1996-97; instr. fitness, gourmet cooking S.E. C.C., Lincoln, Nebr., 2002—; choreographer The Lofte Theatre, Manley, 2002; instr. S.E. C.C., Lincoln. Cons. Jane Boyd Cmty. House, Cedar Rapids, 1993—94. Singer/songwriter Rockit Science, 2000-01, Split Decision, 2001, Dark Horse, 2001--. Avocations: wine tasting, gourmet cooking, flying, gardening, song writing.

OLESEN, DONALD LOUIS, safety engineer, industrial hygienist, author; b. Chgo., Sept. 26, 1952; s. Burton Walter and Louise Elizabeth (Hersheway) O.; m. Regina Marie Clausen, Sept. 4, 1971; children: Angela Marie, Amy Michelle, Andrea Melissa. BS, Ill. State U., 1983; MBA, N.H. Coll., 1987. Registered profl. engr.; cert. safety profl. Assoc. safety adminstr. Wang Labs., Lowell, Mass., 1983-84, safety adminstr. Lawrence, 1984-85; safety and environ. mgr. Avco Rsch. Lab., Everett, 1985-86; corp. safety engr. Apollo Computer, Inc., Chelmsford, 1986-90; sr. v.p., mng. cons. Marsh Risk Consulting, Boston, 1990—. Instr. CSP rev. course Harvard U. Sch. Pub. Health. Contbr. articles to profl. jours. Mem. Am. Soc. Safety Engrs. (pub. rels. dir. 1988, treas. 1989-90, 2d v.p. 1990-91, 1st v.p. 1992-93, pres. 1993-94, chair profl. devel. conf. 1995, rep. regional operating com. 1995-96, area dir. 1997-2000, region XI spy 1998, Pres.'s award 1989, Safety Profl. of Yr. Boston Chpt. 1997), Am. Indsl. Hygiene Assn. Roman Catholic. Avocations: accomplished musician, power lifting. Office: 200 Clarendon St Boston MA 02116-5021 E-mail: donald.l.olesen@marshmc.com.

OLESEN, DOUGLAS EUGENE, research institute executive; b. Tonasket, Wash., Jan. 12, 1939; s. Magnus and Esther Rae (Myers) Olesen; m. Michaele Ann Engdahl, Nov. 18, 1964; children: Douglas Eugene, Stephen Christian. BS, U. Wash., 1962, MS, 1963, postgrad., 1965—67, PhD, 1972. Rsch. engr. space research divsn. Boeing Aircraft Co., Seattle, 1963—64; with Battelle Meml. Inst., Pacific NW Labs., Richland, 1967—84, mgr. water resources systems sect., water and land resources dept., 1970—71, mgr. dept., 1971—75, dep. dir. rsch. labs., 1975, dir. rsch., 1975—79, v.p. inst., dir. NW divsn., 1979—84; exec. v.p., COO Battelle Meml. Inst., Columbus, Ohio, 1984—87, pres., CEO, 1987—2001; ret., 2001. Bd. dirs. Goodrich Co., BattellePharma, Inc., Battelle for Kids. Mem. pres.'s coun. Columbus Mus. of Art; bd. dirs. Ohio State U. Found., Coun. on Competitiveness. Achievements include patents for on process and system for treating wastewater. Office: Battelle Meml Inst 505 King Ave Columbus OH 43201-2681

OLESKER, SARA LOIS, interior designer, merchandising firm executive; b. Chgo., Oct. 3, 1942; d. Irving and Libby (Rubenstein) Schwartz; m. Thomas Olesker, Jr., July 19, 1964; children— Elizabeth, Peter. B.F.A., Ind. U., 1964; postgrad. Ill. Inst. Tech., 1965-67, Chgo. Art Inst., 1967. Tchr. art pub. schs., Chgo., 1964-68; v.p. Childs-Dreyfus Group, Chgo., 1975-84; pres. Sara Olesker, Ltd., Chgo., 1983— , OSA, Inc., Chgo., 1984— ; mem. faculty Inst. Residential Mktg., Roosevelt U., Chgo., 1984— ; speaker, instr. at meetings. Contbr. articles to trade publs. Treas. Mother's Aid, Chgo. Lying In Hosp., 1981-82; bd. dirs. Chgo. Chamber Music Soc., 1982-83, pres., 1983-84. Mem. Greater Chgo. Home Builders Assn., Nat. Assn. Home Builders, Urban Land Inst., Inst. Residential Mktg. Office: Apt 3405 57 E Delaware Pl Chicago IL 60611-1632

OLESKIEWICZ, FRANCIS STANLEY, retired insurance executive; b. Chicopee, Mass., Jan. 2, 1928; s. Francis and Agata (Gniady) O.; m. Ruth M. Ventrice, June 16, 1951; children— Francis H., Laurie BS, Am. Internat. Coll., Springfield, Mass., 1953; LL.B, Western New Eng. Coll., 1961. Bar: Mass. 1962. With Ins. Co. N.Am., Boston, 1953-67; property mgr. Employers-Comml. Union, 1967-69; pres., chmn. Lexington Ins. Co., 1969-86; v.p. Am. Internat. Group, N.Y.C., 1979-86; retired, 1986; limited sole practice law Framingham, Mass., 1986—; ins. arbitrator. Chmn. bd. Risk Specialists Cos., Inc., Boston; vice chmn. Starr Assocs., N.Y.C., C.V. Starr & Co., Inc., Calif.; bd. dirs. Audubon Ins. Co., Baton Rouge, Union Atlantique d'Assurances S.A., Brussels; bd. trustees, mem. trustee com. We. New England Coll., Springfield, Mass., 1987—. Served as pfc. USMC, 1946-47, PTO Mem. Mass. Bar Assn. (vol. law speaker, 1988—), Marine Corps League, Am. Legion, Alpha Chi Home: 19 Hickory Hill Ln Framingham MA 01702-6113

OLESKOWICZ, JEANETTE, physician; b. N.Y.C., Oct. 10, 1956; d. John Francis and Helen (Zielinski) O. BA, NYU, 1977; D Chiropractic, N.Y. Chiropractic Coll., 1982; MS, U. Bridgeport, 1984; MD, U. Medicine and Dentistry N.J., 1990. Diplomate Am. Bd. Psychiatry and Neurology (cert. in addiction psychiatry). U.S. immigration officer U.S. Dept. Justice, N.Y.C., 1977; commd. med. officer USAR, 1983, advanced through grades to maj., 1990; resident and intern Eisenhower Army Med. Ctr., Ft. Gordon, Ga., 1990-94; chief psychiatry U.S. Army Hosp., Vicenza, Italy, 1994-95; cons.-liaison psychiatrist Brooke Army Med. Ctr., Tex., 1995-98; staff psychiatrist Value Options, Phoenix, 1998—2001, VA Med. Ctr., Roseburg, Oreg., 2001—. Am. sponsor for a crippled child's health care in Mid. East; active Cath. prison ministry. Decorated Army Commendation medal, Meritorious Svc. medal. Mem. AMA, Am. Psychiat. Assn. Home: 2515 NW Edenbower 20 Roseburg OR 97470 Office: Dept VA Affairs 913 Garden Valley Blvd Roseburg OR 97470

OLEVSKY, EUGENE A. research scientist, educator; b. Kiev, Ukraine, Mar. 6, 1962; came to U.S., 1995. s. Alex Isaak and Levina Jacob Olevsky; m. Renata Arn Kleiner, Apr. 12, 1987; children: Marina, Anna. MSME with honors, Kiev Poly. Inst., 1985; MS in Math. with honors, Kiev State U., 1986; PhD Powder Metallurgy/Composite Material, Ukraine Nat. Acad. Scis., Kiev, 1990. Rsch. assoc. Inst. for Problems of Materials Sci. NAS of Ukraine, Kiev, 1985-92; Alexander von Humboldt fellow Max Planck Inst., Stuttgart, Germany, 1992-94; rsch. fellow Cath. U. Leuven, Belgium, 1994-95; prof. San Diego State U., 1998—. Vis. scholar NSF Inst. for Mechanics and Materials, San Diego, 1995-98; invited prof. U. Metz, France, 1999. Contbr. numerous articles to sci. publs. Recipient Young Investigator (Career) award NSF, 2000, award for excellence in tchg. TRW, 2000; Long-term rsch. grantee Soros Internat. Sci. Found., 1994; scholar Bd. Govs., NSF Inst. for Mechanics and Materials, 1995-98. Mem. ASME, Internat. Inst. for Sci. of Sintering, Am. Powder Metallurgy Inst., Am. Soc. Engring. Edn. Office: San Diego State U 5500 Campanile Dr San Diego CA 92182-0002 Fax: (619) 594-3599. E-mail: olevsky@kahuna.sdsu.edu.

OLEY, NANCY H. biologist, educator; b. Manhattan, NY, Jan. 21, 1946; d. Arthur and Elizabeth Franklin Hurwich; m. Jordan Richard Pola, July 5, 1986; children: Loren Pola; m. James Leonard Kirkland (div.); m. Robert Carter Oley (div.). Student, Brandeis U., Waltham, Mass., 1963—65; Bachelors, Barnard Coll., 1967; Doctorate, Columbia U., 1973. Postdoctoral staff psychobiology Fla. State U., Tallahassee, 1972—74; asst. prof. psychology Augustana Coll., Rock Island, Ill., 1974—76, Trinity Coll., Hartford, Conn., 1976—83; dir. neurodiagnostic lab. Zuckerman & Zuckerman, MD, Bklyn., 1983—87; postdoctoral staff neuropsychology Columbia U., N.Y.C., 1983—85; prof. psychology Medgar Evers Coll./CUNY, Bklyn., 1988—. Vis. asst. prof. Columbia U., N.Y.C., 1984, N.Y.C., 87; adj. asst. prof. psychology Touro Coll., NY, 1987; chair rev. panel for the undergrad. course and curriculum devel. grants program NSF, Washington, 1992—94; software cons. PSYCH SOFT, Inc. Pres. Barnard Club of Hartford County, Hartford, Conn.; cons. Bklyn. AIDS Task Force, 1989; com. mem. Nassau County Dem. Com. Recipient Presdl. Rsch. award, Medgar Evers Coll., 2000; fellow faculty fellow, Columbia U., 1967—71, Postdoctoral fellow, NIMH, 1972—74; grantee Rsch. grant, PSC/CUNY Faculty Rsch. Award, 1991—92, Instrumentation & Lab. Improvement grant, NSF, 1991—95, Rsch. grant, CUNY Office Acad. Affairs, 1994, Software Devel. grant, Title III, 1994, Faculty Devel. grant, Medgar Evers Coll., 1994, 1995. Mem.: Soc. for Neurosci., N.Y. Neuropsychology Group (bd. dirs., webmaster 1987), Coun. on Undergrad. Rsch. (psychology councilor 2000—), Ea. Psychol. Assn. (liaison from Medgar Evers Coll. 1992), Am. Psychol. Soc., Psi Chi. Avocations: organic gardening, weaving. Home: 10 Arlington Pl Sea Cliff NY 11579 Office: Medgar Evers Coll/CUNY 1650 Bedford Ave Brooklyn NY 11225 E-mail: oley@mec.cuny.edu.

OLGAARD, ANDERS, economics educator; b. Aabenraa, Denmark, Sept. 5, 1926; s. Axel O. and Anna Lebeck; m. Alice Christiansen, 1951; three children. Dr. Polit., Univ. Copenhagen, 1966. Civil servant Econ. Sec., 1953-60; prof. econs., Univ. Copenhagen, 1962-96 ; adviser in Malaysia, Harvard U. Devel. Adv. Service, 1968-69; mem. Econ. Council, 1966-68, chmn., 1970-76. Author: Growth, Productivity and Relative Prices, 1966; The Danish Economy, EEC Economic and Financial Series, 1980. Mem. Danish Econ. Assn. (pres. 1983-88). Home: 12 Lerbaekvej DK-2830 Virum Denmark Office: U Copenhagen Inst Econs Studiestraede 6 DK-1455 Copenhagen Denmark

OLGUIN, VICTOR HUGO, school counselor, educator; b. Mexico City, July 28, 1941; came to U.S., 1967; s. Arnulfo and Columba (Rodriguez) O.; m. Vivian Karen Hogue, Apr. 21, 1967; 1 child, Nikolas Alejandro. Student, North Seattle C.C., 1970-72; BA in Psychology, U. Wash., 1974; MEd in Guidance and Counseling, City U., Bellevue, Wash., 1994. Cert. sch. counselor, Wash. Lang. instr. Berlitz Sch. Langs., Seattle, 1974-75; instr., interpreter, tech. translator Boeing Aircraft Co., 1975; human rels. assoc., spl. edn./vocat. edn. tchr., advisor Seattle Sch. Dist., 1975—. Rep. evening students adv. bd. U. Wash., Seattle, 1978. Sgt. Mexican Army, 1960-61. Mem. ACA, APA, NEA, Wash. Edn. Assn., Seattle Edn. Assn., U. Wash. Alumni Assn., City U. Alumni Assn. Avocations: landscaping, athletic equipment design and construction, painting, reading. Office: Seattle Sch Dist 815 4th Ave Seattle WA 98104-1603

OLHEISER, MARY DAVID, lawyer, educator; b. Dickinson, N.D., Jan. 13, 1918; d. Rudolph and Magdalen (Goetz) O. BA, Holy Names Coll., Spokane, Wash., 1942; MA, St. Louis U., 1952; PhD, Boston Coll., 1962; M in Ch. Adminstrn., Cath. U., 1976, Licentiate in Canon Law, 1977. Joined Sisters of the Order of St. Benedict, 1932. Elem. sch. tchr. Holy Rosary Sch., Tacoma, 1936-50; instr. edn. Coll. of St. Benedict, St. Joseph, Minn., 1952-62, prof. edn., 1962-77, v.p. for acad. affairs, 1972-74; defender of the bond St. Cloud (Minn.) Diocesan Tribunal, 1974-83, judge, 1983-97. Jud. cons. St. Benedicts Monastery, St. Joseph Carmelite Hermits, Alexandria, 1944—. Fedn. St. Benedict, St. Joseph, 1976—; lectr. on rights of women and code of canon law. Author: From Autonomy to Federations: An Historical Survey of Constitutional Development in Benedictine Monasteries, 1977. Trustee Coll. St. Benedict, St. Joseph, 1980-93; bd. dirs. Cath. Charities of the Diocese of St. Cloud, 1992-94; bd. dirs. Carmelite Hermits of Adoration, Inc., 1998—; dir. Eremitie Life Diocese of St. Cloud, 2001—. Mem. Canon Law Soc. Am. (com. chair 1977—). Home: 104 Chapel Ln Saint Joseph MN 56374-2020 Office: St Benedicts Monastery Saint Joseph MN 56374 E-mail: molheiser@csbsju.edu.

OLIAN, ROBERT MARTIN, lawyer; b. Cleve., June 14, 1953; s. Robert Meade and Doris Isa (Hessing) O.; m. Terri Ellen Ruther, Aug. 10, 1980; children: Andrew Zachary, Alix Michelle, Joshua Brett. AB, Harvard U., 1973, JD, M in Pub. Policy, 1977. Bar: Ill. 1977, U.S. Dist. Ct. (no. dist.) Ill. 1977, U.S. Ct. Appeals (7th cir.) 1983, U.S. Dist. Ct. (no dist. trial bar) Ill. 1992, U.S. Dist. Ct. (we. dist.) Mich. 1994. Assoc. Sidley & Austin, Chgo., 1977-84; ptnr. Sidley Austin Brown & Wood, 1985—. Editor: Illinois Environmental Law Handbook, 1988, 97. Panel atty. Chgo. Vol. Legal Svcs., Chgo., 1983—; mem. regional strategic planning/mktg. com. Alexian Bros. Ill., Inc., Elk Grove, 1985-88; trustee North Shore Congregation Israel, 1990—, sec., 1995-96, v.p., 1996—. Mem. ABA, Chgo. Bar Assn., Std. Club, Harvard Club (Chgo.). Jewish. Home: 85 Oakmont Rd Highland Park IL 60035-4111 Office: Sidley Austin Brown & Wood Bank One Plaza 10 S Dearborn St #5200 Chicago IL 60603-2003 E-mail: rolian@sidley.com.

OLICK, PHILIP STEWART, lawyer; b. N.Y.C., Oct. 2, 1936; s. Jack and Anita (Babsky) O.; m. Alice D. Chait, Mar. 25, 1961; children: Jonathan A., Jeffrey K., Diana M. BA, Columbia U., 1957; LL.B., NYU, 1960. Bar: N.Y. 1961, Mo. 1966. Ptnr. Benjamin, Galton, Robbins & Flato, N.Y.C., 1961-65; gen. counsel, v.p., sec. Nat. Bellas Hess, Inc., Kansas City, Mo., 1965-69, dir., 1970-76; ptnr. Burke & Burke, N.Y.C., 1970-73, Townley & Updike, 1973-89, Moses & Singer, 1989—. Bd. arbitrators N.Y. Stock Exch. Bd. dirs. Univ. Glee Club N.Y.C.; bd. dirs. The Young Peoples Chorus of N.Y.C. With AUS, 1960-61. Mem. N.Y. Bar Assn., Assn. of Bar of City of N.Y., Univ. Club

(N.Y.C.), Columbia Club. Home: 860 5th Ave # 19J New York NY 10021-5856 Office: 1301 Avenue Of The Americas New York NY 10019-6022 also: 4 Rosebud Ln East Quogue NY 11942-3627 E-mail: philipstew@aol.com., polick@mosessinger.com.

OLIET, SEYMOUR, endodontics educator, dean, dentist; b. Perth Amboy, N.J., July 12, 1927; s. Asher Jacob and Sarah Oliet; m. Sherry Roseff, July 2, 1949; children: Eric Jay, Amy Ellen Oliet Heller. Student, Rutgers U., 1945-46, 47-49; DDS with distinction, U. Pa., 1953. Diplomate Am. Bd. Endodontics. Instr. oral medicine Sch. Dental Medicine U. Pa., 1953-56, assoc. oral medicine, 1956-61, asst. prof. oral medicine, 1961-65, assoc. prof. oral medicine, 1965-71, prof. oral medicine, dir. undergrad. endodontics, 1971-72, founding chmn. dept. endodontics, 1972-80, prof. endodontics, interim chmn. endodontics, 1990-91, prof. emeritus, 1994—; attending dentist Albert Einstein Med. Ctr., Phila., 1953-60, sr. attending, chmn. endodontics, 1960-84; prof. endodontics Coll. Dental Medicine Nova Southeastern U., Ft. Lauderdale, Fla., 1996—, chmn. task force to estab. Dental Sch., 1995-96, dean Coll. Dental Medicine, 1996—. Cons. endodontics U.S. Army, Ft. Dix, N.J., and Walter Reed Army Hosp., Washington, 1955-80, VA Hosp., Phila., 1965-80; chmn. internat. to estab. I.B. Bender Endowment Fund, Israeli Endodontic Soc., Hebrew U., 1990-91; reviewer Jour. Am. Dental Assn., 1970—. Author: (with others) Endodontics Practice, 11th edit., 1988, Diagnosis and Treatment of Endodontic Emergences, 1981, Current Therapy in Dentistry, 1977, Diagnosis and Treatment Planning in Management of Diseases of the Pulp, 1963, Programmed Text Endodontics; editor Alpha Omega, 1956, (newsletter) Am. Assn. Endodontics, 1966-69; contbr. articles to profl. jours. Named Hon. Citizen of New Orleans; inducted Perth Amboy H.S. Hall of Fame, 1998; recipient Mayor's Citation, Perth Amboy, 1998. Fellow AAAS, Royal Soc. Health (Brit.), Internat. Assn. Dental Rsch., Am. Assn. Endodontists, Am. Coll. Dentists (sec.-treas. Phila. chpt. 1965-76, pres.-elect 1976-77, pres. 1976-77), Internat. Coll. Dentists, Phila. Coll. Surgeons; mem. ADA (life), Pa. Acad. Endodontics (founder, pres. 1977-79, adv. to pres. 1979), Phila. County Dental Soc. (membership com. 1954, indsl. dentistry com. 1954, chmn. sci. program com. 1963, chmn. essay and clins. com. 1964-65, chmn. mediation com. 1965-66, bd. govs. 1985-87, chmn. ad hoc com. ins. 1985-96, com. peer rev. 1985-96, com. on continuing edn. 1989-96, dir. liberty dental conf. 1987-91, gen. chmn. 1991-92, chmn. awards and banquets 1988-89, dir. sci. exhibits and programs 1989-90, del. Pa. Dental Assn. 1985-96, long-range planning com. 1993-96, historian, bd. govs. 1994-96), Brazilian Dental Soc. (hon.), N.Y. Acad. Sci., Am. Assn. Endodontists (arrangements com. 1958-60, libr. com. 1960-61, membership com. 1961-67, publ. chmn., editor newsletter, sci. 1966-69, sci. prof. chmn. 1970-71, bd. govs., exec. com. 1972-78, awards and hons. com. 1992-95), Eastern Dental Soc. (chmn. membership 1956-57, program com. 1957-59, chmn. publicity, editor 1957-59, sec. 1960-62, bd. dirs. 1958X, pres.-elect chmn. bd. govs. 1968-69, pres. 1969-70), Acad. Stomatology, Am. Assn. Dental Editors, Alpha Omega (Phila. alumni chpt., editor 1956, treas. 1956-60, adv. to alumni chpt., regent 1960-61, nat. dept. marshall 1961-62, pres.-elect 1961-63, pres. 1963-64). Avocations: tennis, golf, horseback trail riding, fishing. Office: Nova Southeastern U Coll Dental Medicine 3200 S University Dr Fort Lauderdale FL 33328-2018

OLIGARIO, MAX, retired accountant; b. Port-Au-Prince, Haiti, Sept. 17, 1920; arrived in U.S., 1958; s. Felix and Guillermina (Gonzales) Oligario; m. Gnislaine Romulus; children: Natasha, Sagine, Max Oligario Jr.; m. Fernande St. Leger (div.); 1 child Carole. AS in Engring. Scis., Nassau C.C., 1965; BBA, Hofstra U., 1969; MS in Pub. Acctg., C.W. Post Coll., 1972. CPA N.Y.; ordained 1999. Mgr. Champs Ednl. Supplies, Mineola, NY, 1958—66; asst. supr. cost acctg. Gt. Lakes Carbon, 1966—69; supr., auditor Sperry/Unisys, Nassau County, 1969—88; pvt. practice Brentwood, 1988—89; ret., 1990. Mem. Rep. Presdl. Task Force Presdl. Commn., Washington, 1986; mem. Presdl. Round Table, 1993—; life mem. Rep. Presdl. Task Force, 1989. Named Donor of Yr., Hospitalized Vets., 2002; recipient Order of Merit, Rep. Presdl. Legion of Merit, 1994, Cert. of Appreciation, Nat. Pk. Trust, 1995, Nat. Children's Cancer Soc., 2001, Royal honor, Principality of Hutt River Province, 1996—97. Home: 8784 Middlebrook Dr Fort Myers FL 33908

OLIKER, VLADIMIR, mathematician, educator; b. Ulianovsk, Russia, Oct. 7, 1945; came to U.S. 1975, naturalized 1980; s. Yosef and Sonia (Bakelman) Oliker; m. Elena Matis, Mar. 20, 1969; children: Olga, Aviva, Yosef Matis. MS, Leningrad U., Russia, 1967; PhD, Leningrad U., 1971. Sr. researcher Hydrometeorological Inst., Leningrad, Russia, 1970-72; group leader Dept. Transportation, 1972-74; vis. prof. Temple U., Phila., 1975-77; assoc. prof. to prof. U. Iowa, Iowa City, 1977-80, 80-84; prof. math. Emory U., Atlanta, 1984—. Vis. mem. Math Scis. Research Inst., Berkeley, Calif., 1983; vis. prof. U. Florence, Italy, 1983, Technische U., Berlin, 1982, U. Heidelberg, Fed. Republic Germany, 1981 Contbr. articles to profl. jours. Jewish. Home: 1565 Adelia Pl NE Atlanta GA 30329-3805 Office: Emory U Dept Math And Computer Sci Atlanta GA 30322-0001 E-mail: oliker@mathcs.emory.edu.

OLIN, KENT OLIVER, banker; b. Chgo., July 27, 1930; s. Oliver Arthur and Beatrice Louise Olin; m. Marilyn Louise Wood, May 27, 1956. BS in Econs., Ripon Coll., 1955. Dist. sales rep. Speed Queen Corp., Ripon, Wis., 1955—57; v.p. United Bank, Denver, 1957—71; exec. v.p., pres. Bank One Boulder (formerly Affiliated First Nat. Bank), Boulder, 1971—74; pres., CEO Bank One Colorado Springs, 1971—86; CEO Bank One Colo. (formerly Affiliated Bankshares of Colo.), Denver, 1986—91, vice chmn. bd., 1992—94, also bd. dirs. Trustee Colo. Coll., Colorado Springs, 1983-89, Falcon Found., Colorado Springs, 1983—; trustee El Pomar Found., Colorado Springs, 1992—, chair exec. com.; trustee Colorado Springs Fine Arts Ctr., 1992-95; sec.-treas. Air Force Acad. Found., Colorado Springs, 1988; dir., chair exec. com. Garden City (Kans.) Co.; bd. dirs. Rocky Mountain Arthritis Found., Denver, 1989-94, Goodwill Industries, Colorado Springs, 1993-99. Staff sgt. USAF, 1950-54. Mem. Broadmoor Golf Club (dir. 1975-88, 93-98). Office: El Pomar Found 10 Lake Cir Colorado Springs CO 80906-4201

OLIN, WILLIAM HAROLD, orthodontist, educator; b. Menominee, Mich., Mar. 7, 1924; s. Harold H. and Lillian (Hallgren) Olin; m. Bertha Spitters, May 6, 1950; children: William Harold, Paul Scott, Jon Edwards. DDS, Marquette U., 1947; MS, U. Iowa, 1948. Asst. prof. orthodontics Univ. Hosps., U. Iowa, Iowa City, 1948, assoc. prof., 1963-70, prof., 1970-93, prof. emeritus, 1995—. Chmn. bd. dirs. Hills Bank. Author: (book) Cleft Lip and Palate Rehabilitation, 1960; contbr. articles to profl. jours. Fund raiser, participant Ops. Smile. Served to capt. U.S. Army, 1952—54. Mem.: Am. Acad. Sports Dentistry (bd. dirs., sec./treas. 1989—95), Am. Cleft Palate Assn. (pres. 1970), Iowa Orthodontic Soc. (pres. 1959), Midwest Orthodontic Soc. (pres. 1968—69), Angle Orthodontic Soc. Midwest (pres. 1982), Univ. Athletic Club (bd. dirs.), Rotary (pres. Iowa City). Republican. Methodist. Avocations: coins, antique music boxes, sports, travel, political memorabilia. Home: 426 Mahaska Dr Iowa City IA 52246-1610

OLINER, ARTHUR AARON, physicist, educator; b. Shanghai, China, Mar. 5, 1921; s. Saul and Sarah (Schulsohn) O.; m. Frieda Ginsberg, June 16, 1946; children: Marian A., Eric J. BA, Bklyn. Coll., 1941; PhD, Cornell U., 1945. Research assoc. Microwave Research Inst., Poly. Inst. Bklyn., 1946-53, mem. faculty, 1953—, prof. electrophysics, 1957—, head dept., 1966-71; dir. Microwave Research Inst., 1967-82, head dept. elec. engring. and electrophysics, 1971-74. Walker-Ames vis. prof. U. Wash., summer 1964; vis. prof. Cath. U. Rio de Janeiro, Brazil, summer 1973; vis. research scholar Tokyo Inst. Tech., spring 1978; vis. prof. Central China U. Sci. and Tech., Wuhan, spring 1980; vis. prof. U. Rome, fall 1982; tech. cons. to industry; dir. Merrimac Industries, West Caldwell, N.J.; chmn. adv. panel Nat. Bur. Standards, 1960-64. Contbg. author: Microwave Scanning Antennas, 1966; contbr. numerous articles to profl. jours.; mem. editorial bd.: Advances in Microwaves, 1966-73, Electronics Letters, 1969-75; co-editor: Phased Array Antennas, 1972; editor, contbg. author: Acoustic Surface Waves, 1978. Guggenheim fellow Ecole Normale Superieure, Paris, 1965-66; recipient Instn. premium Instn. Elec. Engrs., London, 1963; citation for disting. rsch. Sigma Xi, 1974; honoree Spl. Session at Internat. Microwave Symposium, 1988. Fellow IEEE (Microwave prize 1967, Microwave Career award 1982, Centennial medal 1984, Disting. Educator award 1993, Heinrich Hertz Gold medal 2000, Millennium medal 2000), AAAS, Brit. Instn. Elec. Engrs.; mem. NAE, IEEE Microwave Theory and Techniques Soc. (hon. life, pres. 1959-60, nat. lectr. 1967, mem. publs. bd. 1971-74), Internat. Union Radio Sci. (mem. commn. B 1955—, chmn. U.S. commn. A 1959-62, co-chmn. U.S. commn. D 1983-88, mem. U.S. nat. com. 1985—, Van der Pol Gold medal 1990), Am. Phys. Soc., Optical Soc. Am. Home and Office: 11 Dawes Rd Lexington MA 02421-5926 E-mail: aao@merrimacind.com.

OLINGER, CARLA D(RAGAN), medical advertising executive; b. Cin., Oct. 8, 1947; d. Carl Edward and Selene Ethel (Neal) Dragan; m. Chauncey Greene Olinger, Jr., May 30, 1981. BA, Douglass Coll., 1975. Mgr. info. retrieval services Frank J. Corbett, Inc., N.Y.C., 1976—77; editor, proofreader, prodn. asst. Rolf W. Rosenthal, Inc., 1977—78, copywriter, 1978—80, copy supr., 1980—82, v.p. copy dept., 1982—83; v.p., group copy supr., adminstrv. copy supr. Rolf W. Rosenthal, Inc., divsn. Ogilvy & Mather, 1984—89; v.p., assoc. creative dir. RWR Advt., 1989; v.p., copy supr. Barnum & Souza, N.Y.C., 1990—92, Botto, Roessner, Horne & Messinger, Ketchum Comm., N.Y.C., 1992—95, Lyons Lavey Nickel Swift, N.Y.C., 1995—. Editor: Antimicrobial Prescribing (Harold Neu), 1979. Mem.: St. George's Soc. N.Y., Ch. Club N.Y. Office: Lyons Lavey Nickel Swift 220 E 42nd St New York NY 10017-5806

OLINGER, CHAUNCEY GREENE, JR. investment executive, editorial consultant; b. Long Beach, Calif., Jan. 16, 1933; s. Chauncey Greene and Cora Blount (Urquhart) O.; m. Carla R. Dragan, May 30, 1981. BA in Philosophy with honors, U. Va., Charlottesville, 1955; MA, Columbia U., N.Y., 1971. CFP. Coadjutant in philosophy Rutgers U., New Brunswick, N.J., 1968-72; rep. N.Y. World Federalists, USA, N.Y.C., 1970; dir. subcom. U.S. sec. of state adv. com. Dept. of State, Washington, 1972; editl. cons. Columbia U., N.Y.C., 1973-82; editor, pres. Metropolitan Rsch. Co., 1982-91; investment exec. First Albany, 1991-92, Janney Montgomery Scott, N.Y.C., 1992—; emeritus prof. Columbia U., 2001—. Sec. sem. on human nature Columbia U., N.Y.C., 1968-72, mem. sem. on orgnl. mgmt., 1972-84, mem. com. to increase corp. philanthropic giving, 1980-83, founder, co-chmn. U. seminar Hist. of Columbia U., 1998. Editor: World Enough, (Margaret Mead and Ken Heyman), 1975, A Celebration of Thanksgiving For the Life of I.I. Rabi, 1991, Columbia and the City: The University's Commitment to New York City, 1993, Courtney C. Brown: In Memory, 1995; author: New York City: An Economic Resource Profile, 1989, The I.I. Rabi Memorial Room, 1996. Pres. Fellowship of Young Churchmen, Episcopal Diocese of So. Va., 1950-52; trustee Cathedral Ch. St. John the Divine, 1988; nat. chmn. Coalition to Stop SST Environmental Damage, N.Y., 1975-78; pub. mem. human rights in rsch. com. N.Y. Hosp.-Cornell Med. Ctr., 1975-80; pres. grad. faculty alumni Columbia U., N.Y., 1977-81; bd. dirs. Bar Harbor (Maine) Festival, 1969-74, Bloomingdale House of Music, N.Y.C., 1976-81. Recipient Conspicuous Alumni Svc. medal Columbia U., 1980, Svc., Loyalty and Dedication award Grad. Faculty Alumni of Columbia U., 1988. Mem. Am. Philos. Assn., Nat. Inst. Social Science (dir. 1988-92), Pilgrims of the U.S., Am. Soc. Most Venerable Order of Hosp. of St. John of Jerusalem, St. Andrew's Soc. of the State of N.Y. (sec. 1991-95), St. George's Soc. N.Y., 1977—, Century Assn., Emeritus Profs. in Columbia (assoc.), The Ch. Club of N.Y. (v.p. 1985-86, 88-89, 96-97, pres. 1997-2000, trustee 1983-89, 93-), Laymen's Club of the Cathedral of St. John the Divine (pres. 1988, gov. 1982-). Episcopalian. Avocations: reading, writing, walking, theatre, ballet. Office: Janney Montgomery Scott 575 Lexington Ave New York NY 10022-6102

OLINS, ROBERT ABBOT, communications research executive; b. Cambridge, Mass., Sept. 25, 1942; s. Harry and Janice Olins; m. Irma Westrich, June 16, 1967; 1 son, Matthew Abbot. Student, Hobart Coll., 1961-62, San Francisco Art Inst., 1962; BA, U. Mass., 1967; postgrad., U. Tampa, 1968; MA, U. Mo., 1969, PhD, 1972. With Marsteller, 1972, N.W. Ayer, 1972, Post, Keys & Gardner, Chgo., 1973, Young & Rubicam, Chgo., 1973-76, mng. dir. comm. rsch. divsn., 1976-77; pres., CEO, subs. Comm. Rsch. Inc., 1978—, owner, chmn., 1979—. Pres., chief exec. officer Insights, Chgo., 1976—. Contbr. articles to profl. jours. Recipient Chgo./4 award for creative excellence, 1974; overall winner Chgo. Mackinac race, 1981; Am. Assn. Advt. Agys. grantee, 1968-71 Mem.: Mid North Assn. (bd. dirs., chmn. planning), Am. Mktg. Assn., Chgo. Yacht Club, Lake Michigan Yachting Assn., U.S. Sailing Club, Skyline Club. Avocations: skiing, sailing, power boating. Office: Communications Rsch Inc 233 E Wacker Dr Apt 2105 Chicago IL 60601-5110 E-mail: cri77@aol.com.

OLIPHANT, BETTY, retired ballet school director; b. London, Eng., Aug. 5, 1918; Studied classical ballet under Tamara Karsavina and Laurent Novikoff; student, Queen's and St. Mary's Colls.; LLD (hon.), Queen's U., 1978, Brock U., 1978, U. Toronto., 1980; DLitt, York U., 1992. Prin. dancer and arranger Prince & Emile Littler Prodns., London, 1936-46; dance arranger Howard & Wyndham, 1936-46; tchr. ballet, 1936-40; dancer, dance arranger and ballet mistress Blue Pencils Concert Party, Eng., 1944-46; tchr. ballet Oliphant Sch., Toronto, Can., 1948-59; ballet mistress Nat. Ballet of Can., 1951-62; prin. and dir. Nat. Ballet Sch., 1959; asso. artistic dir. Nat. Ballet of Can., 1969-75, artistic dir., 1975-89; founder Nat. Ballet Sch., 1959, dir., prin., ret., 1989, tchr., artistic advisor, 1989-91. Reorganized Ballet Sch. of Royal Swedish Opera, 1967, Royal Danish Theatre, 1978; mem. jury Internat. Ballet Competition, Moscow, 1977-81, III Internat. Ballet Competition, Jackson, MIss., 1986. Author: Miss O: My Life in Dance, 1996; contbr. articles on dance and teaching to profl. publs. Decorated officer Order of Can., 1972, Companion Order of Can., 1985; recipient Centennial medal, 1967, Molson prize, 1978, Diplome d'Honneur Can. Conf. Arts, 1982, Lifetime Achievement award, Toronto Arts Awards Found., 1989, Order of Napoleon, France, 1990, Commemorative medal 125th Anniversary Can., 1992, Gov. Gen.'s Performing Arts award, 1997, Order of Ontario, 2000; named Disting. Educator, Ont. Inst. for Studies in Edn., 1985. Fellow Imperial Soc. Tchrs. of Dancing (examiner); mem. Can. Dance Tchrs. Assn. (founder, past pres.), Internat. Soc. Tchrs. Dancing, Can. Assn. Profl. Dance Orgns. (founding mem.). Address: Anchor Pointe 540 Ontario St Unit 309 Saint Catharines ON Canada L2N 7S2

OLIPHANT, CHARLES ROMIG, retired physician; b. Waukegan, Ill., Sept. 10, 1917; s. Charles L. and Mary (Goss) R.; m. Claire E. Canavan, Nov. 7, 1942; children: James R., Cathy Rose, Mary G., William D. Student, St. Louis U., 1936-40, MD, 1943; postgrad., Naval Med. Sch., 1946. Intern Nat. Naval Med. Ctr., Bethesda, Md., 1943; pvt. practice medicine and surgery San Diego, 1947-99; ret., 1999. Bd. dirs. Midway Med. Enterprises; former chief staff Balboa Hosp., Doctors Hosp., Cabrillo Med. Ctr.; chief staff emeritus Sharp Cabrillo Hosp.; mem. staff Mercy Hosp., Children's Hosp., Paradise Valley Hosp., Sharp Meml. Hosp.; sec. Sharp Sr. Health Care, S.D., 1985-98; mem. exec. bd., program chmn. San Diego Power Squadron, 1985-93, 95; charter mem. Am. Bd. Family Practice. Served with M.C., USN, 1943-47. Recipient Golden Staff award Sharp Cabrillo Hosp. Med. Staff, 1990. Fellow Am. Geriatric Soc. (emeritus), Am. Acad. Family Practice, Am. Assn. Abdominal Surgeons; mem. AMA, Calif. Med. Assn., Am. Acad. Family Physicians (past pres. San Diego chpt., del. Calif. chpt.), San Diego Med. Soc., Pub. Health League, Navy League, San Diego Power Squadron (past comdr.), SAR, San Diego Yacht Club, Douglas County Scottish Soc. Home: Riverview Terr Unit # 109 1970 W Harvard Ave Roseburg OR 97470-2746

OLIPHANT, MARTHA CARMICHAEL, civic worker; b. Providence, Sept. 17, 1935; d. Leonard and Pearl (Kidston) Carmichael; m. S. Parker Oliphant, June 2, 1962 (dec. Jan. 2001); children: Leonard Carmichael, Samuel Duncan. BA, Wellesley Coll., 1957. Lab. asst. NIMH, Bethesda, Md., 1957-63. Bd. govs. Washington Home and Hospice, 1976—. Bd. dirs., past pres. All Hallows Guild, Washington Cathedral, 1971-93; mem. bd. lady visitors Childrens Nat. Med. Ctr., 1971-93, Children's Hosp. Found., 1974-90; mem. Com. of 100 of Fed. City, 1977-86; bd. dirs. Washington Home and Hospice, 1976—, also past pres.; past bd. dirs., v.p. Jr. League Washington; mem. Smithsonian Women's Com., Washington, 1993—. Recipient voluntarism award Jr. League Washington, 1988. Mem. Sulgrave Club (bd. dirs. 1985-88), Evergreen Garden Club (pres. 1989-91). Republican. Episcopalian. Avocation: golf. Home: 4977 Glenbrook Rd NW Washington DC 20016-3222

OLIPHANT, NAOMI JOYCE, music educator, performer; b. Toronto, Ont., Can., Jan. 24, 1953; d. James Leroy and Joyce Grace Gwendolyn (Stephens) O. BMus, U. Toronto, 1975, MMus, 1976; D of Musical Arts, U. Mich., 1982. Cert. tchr. piano. Lectr. U. Toronto, 1978; coach accompanist Banff (Ala.) Summer Sch. of Fine Arts, 1979, 80; asst. prof. music Brock U., St. Catharines, Ont., Can., 1976-83; prof., chair keyboard-vocal performance dept. U. Louisville, 1983-98, assoc. dean, 1998—, dir. Kentuckiana summer music festival piano program, 1986—. Clinician Frederick Harris Music Co., Ont., 1997—; com. mem. Nat. Conf. on Piano Pedagogy, 1988-95; pianist The McHugh/Oliphant violin and piano duo, 1983—; Disting. tchg. prof. U. Louisville, 1994. Piano soloist orchs. including Louisville Orch., Toronto Symphony, Hamilton Philharm., Niagara Symphony, many solo and chamber concerts, U.S., Can., Japan. Grantee Ky. Bus. and Profl. Women's Found., 1989, 96, Ky. Arts Coun., 1991, 92, 95, So. REgional Edn. Bd., 1989, 95. Mem. Louisville Bach Soc., Music Tchrs. Nat. Assn., Greater Louisville Music Tchrs. Assn., Ky. Music Tchrs. Assn. Presbyterian. Avocations: reading, walking, puzzles, swimming, needlework, gardening. Office: U Louisville Sch Of Music Louisville KY 40292

OLIPHANT, PATRICK, cartoonist; b. Adelaide, Australia, July 24, 1935; came to U.S., 1964; s. Donald K. and Grace L. (Price) O.; children: Laura, Grant, Susan. L.H.D. (hon.), Dartmouth Coll., 1981. Copyboy, press artist Adelaide Advertiser, 1953-55, editorial cartoonist, 1955-64; world tour to study cartooning techniques, 1959; editorial cartoonist Denver Post, 1964-75, Washington Star, 1975-81, L.A. Times Syndicate, 1965-80, Universal Press Syndicate, 1980—; represented by Susan Conway Gallery, Washington. Author: The Oliphant Book, 1969, Four More Years, 1973, An Informal Gathering, 1978, Oliphant! A Cartoon Collection, 1980, The Jellybean Society, 1981, Ban this Book, 1982, But Seriously Folks, 1983, The Year of Living Perilously, 1984, Make My Day, 1985, Between a Rock and a Hard Place, 1986, Up to There in Alligators, 1987, Nothing Basically Wrong, 1988, What Those People Need Is a Puppy, 1989, Fashions for the New World Order, 1991, Just Say No, 1992, Why do I Feel Uneasy?, 1993, Waiting for the Other Shoe to Drop, 1994, Off to the Revolution, 1995, Maintain The Status Quo, 1996, So That Where They Come From, 1997, Oliphant's Anthem, 1998, Are We There Yet?, 1999, Now We'll Have to Spray for Politicians, 2000, When We Can't See the Forest for the Bushes, 2001. Recipient 2d Place award as funniest cartoonist Internat. Fedn. Free Journalists in Fleet St., London, 1958, Profl. Journalism award Sigma Delta Chi, 1966, Pulitzer prize for editl. cartooning, 1967, Cartoonist of Yr. award Nat. Cartoonist Soc., 1968, 72, Best in Bus. award Washington Journalism Rev., 1985, 87, Premio Satira Politica award Forte de Marmi, 1992, Thomas Nast award, 1992. Office: Universal Press Syndicate 4520 Main St Ste 700 Kansas City MO 64111-7701 also: care Susan Conway Gallery 1214 30th St NW Washington DC 20007-3401

OLIPHANT, RANDALL, financial executive; B.Comm., U. Toronto, 1984. Acct. Coopers & Lybrand; with Barrick Gold Corp., Toronto, Ont., Can., 1987—, v.p. corp. devel. Can., v.p., treas. Can., CFO Can., 1994-99, exec. v.p., CFO Can., 1999, pres., CEO Can., 1999—, dir. Can., 1997—. Office: Royal Bank Plz S Twr #2700 200 Bay St PO Box 119 Toronto ON Canada M5J 2J3

OLIPHANT, URETZ JOHN, physician, surgeon; b. Chgo., May 9, 1953; s. John and Letha (Fryson) O.; m. Mercidita DeJesus, Jan. 11, 1985; children: Michael, Jonathan, Kathryn. AB, Boston U., 1976; MD, U. Minn., 1983. Diplomate Am. Bd. Surgery. Fellow in trauma/critical care Ill. Masonic Hosp./U. Ill., Chgo., 1991-92; attending surgeon Carle Found. Hosp., Urbana, Ill., 1992—, head divsn. trauma, 1995—; clin. assoc. prof. dept. surgery U. Ill. Coll. Medicine, 1994—, head dept. surgery, 1996—. Chmn. bd. dirs. Frances Nelson Cmty. Health Ctr., urbana, 1994—; chmn. Region 6 Trauma Com., Urbana, 1995-97. Founding mem. Nat. Safe Kids, Champaign, Ill., 1995—. Recipient Golden Apple Tchg. award U. Ill. Coll. Medicine, 1994, 95, 97, 99. Fellow ACS, Internat. Coll. Surgeons. Avocations: chess, basketball. Office: Carle Found Hosp 602 W University Ave Urbana IL 61801-2530

OLITSKI, JULES, artist; b. Snovsk, USSR, Mar. 27, 1922; came to U.S., 1923, naturalized, 1943; s. Jevel and Anna (Zarnitsky) Demikovsky; m. Gladys Katz, 1944 (div. 1951); 1 dau., Eve; m. Andrea Hill Pearce, Jan. 21, 1956 (div. 1974); 1 dau., Lauren; m. Kristina Gorby, Feb. 29, 1980. Student, Academie de la Grande Chaumiere, Paris, 1949-50; BA, NYU, 1952, MA, 1954; postgrad., Beaux Arts Inst., N.Y.C., 1940-42, Nat. Acad. Design, 1939-42, Ednl. Alliance, 1947, Ossip Zadkine Sch. Sculpture, Paris, 1949; hon. Doctorate of the Arts, U. of Hartford, CT, 1997, U of New Hampshire, NH, 1998. Assoc. prof. art SUNY, New Paltz, N.Y., 1954-55; curator Art Edn. Gallery, NYU, 1955-56; chmn. fine arts div. C.W. Post Coll. L.I.U., Greenvale, N.Y., 1956-63; tchr. Bennington Coll., 1963-67. Exhibited in many one-man shows including Galerie Huit, Paris, 1951, Iolas Gallery, N.Y.C., 1958, French & Co., N.Y.C., 1959-61, Poindexter Gallery, N.Y.C., 1961-68, Bennington (Vt.) Coll., 1962, Kasmin, Ltd., London, 1964-75, 89, Galerie Lawrence, Paris, 1964, David Mirvish Gallery, Toronto, Ont., Can., 1964-78, Nicholas Wilder, L.A., 1966, Corcoran Gallery, Washington, 1967, 74, Am. Pavillion, Venice Biennale Art Exhbn., 1966, 88, Andre Emmerich Gallery, N.Y.C., 1966-96, Zurich, Switzerland, 1973-78, Met. Mus. Art, N.Y.C., 1969, Inst. Contemporary Art, U. Pa., 1968, 86, Lawrence Rubin Gallery, N.Y.C., 1969, 71, 72, 73, Knoedler Contemporary Art, 1973-77, 79, 81, 83, 85, 87, Dart Gallery, Chgo., 1975, FIAL, Paris, 1976, Berlinische Galerie, 1977, Downstairs Gallery, Edmonton, Can., 1980, 82, Janus Gallery, L.A., 1981, Gallery One, Toronto, 1980-90, Yares Gallery, Scottsdale, Ariz., 1986-89, Galerie Wentzel, Hamburg and Cologne, Fed. Republic Germany, 1975, 77, 81, 89, Mus. Fine Arts, Boston, 1973, 77, Whitney Mus. Am. Art, 1973, Galleria Dell'Ariete, Italy, 1974, Corcoran Gallery Art, 1974-76, Waddington Gallery, London, 1975, Galerie Templon, Paris, 1984-85, Hirshhorn Mus., Washington, 1977, Edmonton (Alta., Can.) Art Gallery, 1979, Martha White Gallery, Louisville, 1982, Harcus/Krakow Gallery, Boston, 1978, 81, 82, Harcus Gallery, Boston, 1984, 86, Meredith Long, Houston, 1981, 82, 87, 90, (retrospective) Fondation du Chateau de Jau, Perpignon, France, 1984, La Musee de Valence, France, 1985, Hokin Gallery, Palm Beach, Fla., 1988, Associated Am. Artists, N.Y.C., 1989, (retrospective) Buschlen/Mowatt Gallery, Vancouver, B.C., Can., 1990, Salander-O'Reilly Galleries, N.Y.C., 1990, 92, 94, Gallery Camino Real, Boca Raton, Fla., 1987, 88, 90, 92, 94, 95, 96, 97, Thorne-Sagendorph Art Gallery, Keene, N.H., 1993, 96, 99, Long Fine Arts, N.Y.C., 1994, 95, 97, 98, 99, U. Miami, Coral Gables, Fla., 1994, C.S. Schulte Gallery, Milburn, N.J., 1995, 97, Drabinsky Friedland Gallery, Naples, Fla., and Toronto, 1996, 97, 99, Dorthy Blau Gallery, Bay Harbor Island, Fla., 1996, 97, 2001, Hodecker Gallery, Waterville Valley, NH, 1997, Belknap Mills, Laconia, NH, 1997, Butler Institute, Youngstown , OH, 1997, 2000, Portland Museum, ME, 1998, Grimaldis Gallery, Baltimore, MD, 1998, Virginia Lynch Gallery, Tiverton, RI, 1998, 99, 2000, 2001, Gould Academy, Bethel, ME, 1998, Bernard Jacobsen Gallery, London (Paintings 1965-75), 1999, Marianne Friedland Gallery, Naples, FL, 1999, 2000, 02 Galeria Metta, Madrid, 1999, Mary McGowan Fine Art, Concord , NH, 1999, Philharmonic Center for the Arts, Naples, FL, 1999, Annandale Galleries, Sydney, Australia, 2000, 2002, Charles Nodrum Gallery, Melbourne, 2000, The Butler Institute of American Art, Youngstown, OH, 2000, Ameringer-Howard Gallery, N.Y.C., 2000, Bunnington Gallery Notthingham Trent U., UK, 2001, Ameringer-Howard Fine Art, Boca Raton, FL, 2001; exhibited in many group shows including Carnegie Internat., Pitts., 1961, 1965, Washington Gallery Modern Art, 1963, Los Angeles County Mus., 1964, Fogg Art Mus. Harvard, 1965, Pasadena Art Mus., 1965, Mus. Basel, Switzerland, 1965, 74, Whitney Mus. Am. Art, 1972, 73, Musée d'Art Contemporain, Montreal, 1973, Hirshhorn Mus., 1974, Corcoran Gallery Art, 1975, Everson Mus. Art, Syracuse, N.Y., 1976, Bass Mus., Miami, Am. Embassy, Madrid, 1984, Ft. Worth Art Mus., Mus. Art, Ft. Lauderdale, 1986, Joseloff Gallery, Hartford, Conn., 1994, Galerie Piltzer, Paris, 1994, N.Y. Studio Sch., N.Y., 1996, Andre Emmerich Gallery, N.Y.C., 1997, 1998, Suzanne Lemberg Usdan Gallery, Bennington College, VT, 1998, Yares Gallery, Scottsdale, Ariz., 1998, Mus. Fine Arts, Boston, 2000, Portland Mus., Oreg., 2001; represented in permanent collections including Mus. Modern Art, N.Y.C., Art Inst. Chgo., Whitney Mus., Corcoran Art Gallery, Nat. Gallery Can., Met. Mus. Art, N.Y.C., Bklyn. Mus., Hirshhorn Mus., Washington, Everson Mus. Art, Syracuse, N.Y., Mus. Fine Arts, Boston, Norman MacKensie Art Gallery, Regina, Can., Portland Mus., Oreg.;also pvt. collections; subject book Jules Olitski by Kenworth Moffett, 1981, Nat. Acad. Design, N.Y., 1993, illustrator of limited edition book, Small Mountains (with W.D. Wetherell), 2000. Recipient 2d prize Carnegie Internat. 1961, 1st prize Corcoran Biennial, Washington, 1967, Award for Distinction in the Arts Univ Union, U. S.C., 1975, The Milton and Sally Avery Disting. Professorship, Bard Coll., 1987; named Assoc. Nat. Academician Nat. Acad. of Design, 1993, named Distinguished Artist, Arkansas Celebration of the Arts, Hot Springs, Arkansas, 1996. Fellow AAAS, Nat. Acad. Arts and Scis. E-mail: jolitski@sover.net.

OLIVA, LAWRENCE JAY, former academic administrator, history educator; b. Walden, N.Y., Sept. 23, 1933; s. Lawrence Joseph and Catherine (Mooney) Oliva; m. Mary Ellen Nolan, June 3, 1961; children: Lawrence Jay, Edward Nolan. BA, Manhattan Coll., 1955; MA, Syracuse U., 1957, PhD, 1960; postgrad., U. Paris, 1959; DHL (hon.) , Manhattan Coll., 1987; LLD (hon.) , St. Thomas Aquinas Coll., 1988; DHL (hon.) , Hebrew Union Coll., 1992; DLitt, Univ. Coll., Dublin, 1993; PhD, Tel Aviv U., 1994. Prof. history NYU, 1969—, assoc. dean, 1969—70, vice dean, 1970—71, dean faculty, 1971—72, dep. vice chancellor, 1970—75, v.p. acad. planning and services, 1975—77, v.p. acad. affairs, 1977—80, provost, exec. v.p. acad. affairs, 1980—83, chancellor, exec. v.p., 1983—91, pres., 1991—2002. Author: Misalliance: A Study of French Policy in Russia during the Seven Years' War, 1964, Russia in the Era of Peter the Great, 1969; editor: Russia and the West from Peter to Kruschev, 1965, Peter the Great, 1970, Catherine the Great, 1971; contbr. articles to profl. jours. Trustee Inst. Internat. Edn.; active Onassis Found., UN Assn. of N.Y. Adv. Coun., N.Y.C. Partnership, Assn. for Better N.Y., Am. Mus. Immigration; adv. bd. U. Athletic Assn.; bd. dirs. Chatham House, Royal Inst. Internat. Affairs, Am. Bd. Dirs. Coun. for U.S. and Italy Nat. Collegiate Athletic Assn., Pres.'s Commn.; adv. bd. Pres.'s Coun.; bd. dirs. N.Y. State Commn. on Nat. and Cmty. Svc. Recipient Medal of Sorbonne, U. Paris, 1992, Man. in Edn. award, Italian Welfare League, medal of honor, Ellis Island; fellow Fribourg fellow, 1959. Mem.: Irish-Am. Cultural Inst., Assn. Colls. and Univs. of State of N.Y, Am. Coun. Edn., Soc. Fellows NYU, Phi Gamma Delta, Phi Beta Kappa. Home: 33 Washington Sq W New York NY 10011-9154 Office: c/o NYU 70 Washington Sq S New York NY 10012-1091*

OLIVA, RALPH ANGELO, marketing educator; b. Tarrytown, N.Y., July 1, 1946; s. I. Ralph and Raechel O.; m. Kathryn Kaye Stembridge; children: Matthew Ralph, Christopher Charles. BS in Physics, Fordham U., 1966; MS and PhD in Physics, Rensselaer Poly. Inst., 1973. Mem. tech. staff Tex. Instruments Inc., Dallas, 1973-76, merchandising mgr., 1976-77, dir. learning ctr., 1977-79, mgr. merchandising strategy, 1979-81, dir. external edn., 1981-83, mgr. edn. mktg., 1983-85, mgr. worldwide mktg. communications, 1985-89, v.p. market communications/design, 1989-95; prof. mktg., exec. dir. Inst. for Study of Bus. Markets Pa. State U., 1995—. Co-author: Sourcebook for Programmable Calculators, 1979, Math on Keys, 1980, Calculating Better Decisions, 1981, Laboratory Physics, 1987; contbr. column to Mktg. Mgmt. Mag., 1996—. Crisis intervention counselor; lector at Good Shepherd Ch., State College, Pa. Mem. Am. Assn. Physics Tchrs. Roman Catholic. Avocation: sports cars. E-mail: ra08@psu.edu.

OLIVA, STEPHEN EDWARD, resource conservationist, lawyer; b. San Rafael, Calif., Jan. 31, 1946; s. George Verdelli Jr. and Dorothy Margaret (Austin) O.; m. Susan Rebecca Ellis, May 5, 1984; children: Stephanie, Mary. BA, U. Calif., Santa Barbara, 1972; JD, U. The Pacific, 1992. Bar: Calif. 1993, U.S. Dist. Ct. (ea. dist.) Calif. 1993. Naturalist Calif. Dept. Transp., San Francisco, 1973-76; planner Calif. Energy Commn., Sacramento, 1976, Calif. Air Resources Bd., Sacramento, 1976-79; spl. asst. to sec. The Resources Agy., 1979-80; spl. asst. Calif. Dept. Conservation, 1980, mgr. land conservation unit, 1981-87; spl. asst. Calif. Dept. Forestry, 1980-81; chief Office Land Conservation Calif. Dept. Conservation, 1987-89, dep. chief Calif. div. of recycling, 1989-91, environ. coord., 1991-92, staff counsel, legal office, 1992-99, sr. staff counsel, 1999-2001, supervising sr. staff counsel, 2001—. Governing bd. Calif. Tahoe Regional Planning Agy., South Lake Tahoe, 1979-81; policy adv. com. Sacramento County Local Agy. Formation Commn., 1988-89. With U.S. Army, 1966-68, Vietnam. Mem. ABA, Calif. State Bar, Sacramento County Bar Assn. Democrat. Avocations: snorkeling, photography. Office: Calif Dept Conservation 801 K St MS 24-03 Sacramento CA 95814-3500 E-mail: soliva@consrv.ca.gov.

OLIVA, SUZANNE DAPRA, lawyer, accountant; b. Tokyo, Mar. 2, 1965; (parents Am. citizens); d. Lawrence Gilbert and Kathleen Ann Dapra; m. Javier Francis Oliva, June 20, 1987; children: Stephen Andrew, Ryan Patrick, Christopher Lawrence, Blake Austin. BBA in Acctg., St. Mary's U., San Antonio, 1987. CPA, Tex. Office asst. Staff Judge Adv.'s Office, Vicenza, Italy, 1979; claims clk. U.S.A.A. Ins. Co., San Antonio, 1983, acctg. clk., 1984, 85; adv. staff acct. Ernst & Whinney, 1987-88; acct., office mgr. Psychiat. Assocs. of San Antonio, 1988-91; pvt. practice, San Antonio, 1991-93; atty. St. Mary's U. Sch. Law, 1993-96; assoc. Oliva, Saks & Garcia, LLP, 1996—. Soc. of Mary scholar, 1983-87, Jesse and Mary Jones scholar, 1985, Arthur Andersen acctg. scholar, 1986. Mem. Delta Mu Delta, Phi Alpha Delta. Roman Catholic. Avocation: foreign travel. Home: 6 San Isidro San Antonio TX 78261-2303 Office: 85 NE Loop 410 Ste 200 San Antonio TX 78216-5844 E-mail: oliva@ev1.net.

OLIVA, TERENCE ANTHONY, marketing educator; b. Rochester, N.Y., Feb. 21, 1943; s. Anthony J. and Teresa (Savasta) O.; children: Mark, Andrea. BA in Math. and Art, St. Mary's Coll., Calif., 1964; MBA with distinction, Fresno State U., 1971; PhD, U. Ala., 1974. Assoc. prof. mgmt. La. State U., Baton Rouge, 1974-82; vis. assoc. mktg. Columbia U., N.Y.C., 1982-83; assoc. prof., mktg. Rutgers U., Newark, 1983-88; vis. assoc. prof. Wharton Sch., U. Pa., Phila., 1985-87, assoc. prof., 1989-90; prof., dep. dir. Ctr. for Electronic Mktg. Temple U., 1990—. Mem. editl. bd. Org. Sci., 1993—. Author, editor: Production Mgmt., 1981; assoc. editor Mgmt. Sci. Dept. Tech., 1989-91; editl. bd. mem. Org. Sci.; contbr. 32 articles to profl. jours. Capt. USAF, 1965-69, Vietnam. Decorated Bronze Star; recipient Andrisani/Frank Undergrad Tchg. award, Leadership in Rsch. award SBM, 1998, Lindback Found. Tchg. award, 2001. Mem. Am. Mktg. Assn., INFORMS, Sigma Kappa Phi (Prof. of Yr. award), Phi Delta Kappa, Omicron Delta Epsilon, Mu Kappa Tau. Home: 605 S 48th St Philadelphia PA 19143-2010 *Swimming upstream is often very productive. Just be prepared to jump obstacles and have a hard head.*

OLIVARDIA, ROBERTO, clinical psychologist; m. Sharon Olivardia. BA in Clin. Psychology cum laude, Tufts U., 1994; MA, U. Mass., 1998, PhD, 2000. Psychology intern McLean Hosp./Harvard U. Med. Sch., Belmont, Mass., 1999-2000; clin. rsch. fellow Harvard Med. Sch., Boston, 2000—02, instr. psychology, 2002—; pvt. practice psychology, 2002—. Author: The Adonis Complex: The Secret Crisis of Male Body Obsession, (in English, Portuguese and German) 2000; contbr. articles to profl. jours., including Psychosomatics, Am. Jour. Psychiatry, Internat. Jour. Eating Disorders, others. Mem.: APA. Avocations: songwriting, fiction writing, playing drums, movies. Office: McLean Hosp Oaks Bldg 115 Mill St Belmont MA 02478 Fax: (617) 855-3585. E-mail: roberto_olivardia@hms.harvard.edu.

OLIVAS, DANIEL ANTHONY, lawyer; b. L.A., Apr. 8, 1959; s. Michael A. and Elizabeth M. (Velasco) O.; m. Susan L. Formaker, Oct. 19, 1986; 1 child, Benjamin Formaker-Olivas. BA in English Lit., Stanford U., 1981; JD with honors, UCLA, 1984. Bar: Calif. 1987, U.S. Dist. Ct. (cen. dist.) Calif. 1988, U.S. Ct. Appeals (9th cir.) 1988, U.S. Supreme Ct. 1995. Law clk., atty. Hunt & Cochran-Bond, L.A., 1984-88; atty. Heller, Ehrman, White & McAuliffe, 1988-90; dep. atty. gen. dept. of justice antitrust div. State of Calif., 1990-91, dep. atty. gen. dept. of justice land law sect., 1991—. State apptd. bd. dirs. Western Ctr. Law and Poverty, L.A., 1988-94; mem. Hispanic employees adv. com. Calif. Dept. Justice, 1990—. Contbr. articles to L.A. Daily Jour., and others; writer fiction and poetry. Recipient Atty. Gen.'s award for outstanding achievement in litigation, 1994; named one of Outstanding Young Men of Am., 1984. Mem. Mex.-Am. Bar Assn., Mex.-Am. Bar Found. (bd. dirs. 1993-94), L.A. County Bar Assn. (Jud. Appointments Com 1993-97), Stanford Chicano/Latino Alumni Assn. (pres.-elect 1992-93, pres. 1993-94). Democrat. Jewish. Office: State of Calif 300 S Spring St Ste 5212 Los Angeles CA 90013-1230 E-mail: olivasdan@aol.com.

OLIVAS, JOHN D. astronaut; b. North Hollywood, Calif. married; 4 children. BSME, U. Tex., El Paso; MSME, U. Houston; PhDME and Materials Sci., Rice U. Mech., materials engr. Dow Chem. Co., Freeport, Tex.; mem. support team Kelly AFB; mem. support team crew and thermal sys. directorate NASA, Johnson Space Ctr., Houston; sr. rsch. engr. Jet Propulsion Lab., program mgr. advanced interconnect and mfg. assurance program; astronaut, mission specialist candidate NASA, Johnson Space Ctr., Houston, 1998—. Contbr. articles to profl. jours. tech. confs. Named Most Promising Engr., HENAAC; recipient McDonald's Hispanos Triunfadores award. Mem.: Tex. Registered Profl. Engrs., Am. Soc. Materials Internat. Achievements include principal developer of seven inventions. Avocations: running, weightlifting, hunting, fishing, surfing. Office: Astronaut Office/CB NASA Johnson Space Ctr Houston TX 77058*

OLIVAS, VALERIE SEGURA, legal assistant; b. Marfa, Tex., July 20, 1954; d. Joe D. and Vidala (Gonzalez) Segura; divorced; 1 child, Donny Rey Martinez. AAS, El Paso C.C., 1987. Cert. legal asst., trial ct. coord. 1997, trial ct. mgmt. 1998, trial ct. adminstrn. 1999. Grad. vocat. nurse Big Bend Meml. Hosp., Alpine, Tex., 1974-78; lic. cosmetologist styling salon J.C. Penney, Inc., El Paso, 1980-88; paralegal Donald L. Williams Law Office, 1987-95; family law ct. coord. Hon. Donald L. Williams, 1995—. Mem. Tex. Assn. Ct. Adminstrs., El Paso Assn. Ct. Coord., El Paso Assn. Legal Assts. (v.p. continuing edn. and programs 1992-93, v.p. membership 1993-94, pres.-elect 1994-95, pres. 1995-96), El Paso Bar Assn. (assoc.), Family Law Bar Assn. (assoc.). Democrat. Roman Catholic. Home: 1625 Charles Owens Dr El Paso TX 79936-5210 Office: Family Law Ct 500 E San Antonio Ave Ste 1102 El Paso TX 79901-2425

OLIVE, DAVID MICHAEL, magazine writer, magazine editor; b. Toronto, Ont., Canada, Nov. 9, 1957; s. Harold Leslie and Alison Linton (Black) O.; m. Margaret Anne O'Reilly, Feb. 13, 1982 (div. June 1992). B of Applied Arts in Journalism, Ryerson Polytech. U., 1979. Copy editor Toronto Life Mag., 1979-81; assoc. editor Can. Bus. Mag., Toronto, 1981-84; sr. writer Report on Bus. Mag., 1984-87, Toronto Life Mag., 1988-90; editorial writer The Globe and Mail, Toronto, 1990-91, current affairs columnist, 1991-92, bus. ethics columnist, 1996-98; editor Report on Bus. Mag., 1991-97, sr. writer, 1997-98, Fin. Post, 1998, Nat. Post, Toronto, 1998—2001; bus. columnist Toronto Star, 2001—. Dir. Can. Ctr. for Ethics and Corp. Policy, 1988-91, Jessie's Ctr. for Teenagers, 1994—; pres. Jessie's Ctr. Non-Profit Homes Corp., 1994—; pres. Nat. Mag. Awards Found., 1988-90. Author: Just Rewards: The Case for Ethical Reform in Business, 1987, White Knights and Poison Pills: A Cynic's Dictionary of Business Jargon, 1990, Political Babble: The 1,000 Dumbest Things Ever Said by Politicians, 1992, Gender Babble: The Dumbest Things Men Ever Said About Women, 1993, Canadian Political Babble: A Cynic's Dictionary of Political Jargon, 1993, More Political Babble: The Dumbest Things Ever Said by Politicians, 1996, Canada Inside Out: How We See Ourselves, How Others See Us, 1996, No Guts, No Glory: How Canada's Greatest CEOs Built Their Empires, 2000, A Devil's Dictionary of Business Jargon, 2001, The Quotable Tycoon: A Treasury of Business Quotations, 2002. Recipient Silver, Nat. Mag. awards, 1987, Gold, 1988, hon. mention, 1983, 1985, 1987, 1989, 1996, Nat. Bus. Book awards, 2001. Mem. Can. Soc. Mag. Editors, Ethics Practitioners Assn. Can.

OLIVEIRA, FRANK DAVID, publishing executive; b. Hanford, Calif., June 9, 1946; s. Frank James and Mary Alice Souza Oliveira; life ptnr. Vichheka Thong. BA, Calif.State U., Fresno, 1969; cert. in data processing, U. Calif., Santa Barbara, 1983. Cert. life secondary tchr. Calif. Pub. Mille Grazie Press, Santa Barbara, 1993—. Founding dir. Santa Barbara Poetry Series, 1998—2002. Editor: Solo: A Journal of Poetry, 1995—; contbr. chapters to books; author: (book) In the Presence of Snakes, 2000; editor: How Much Earth: The Fresno Poets, 2001; co-author: A Near Country: Poems of Loss, 1999. Bd. dirs. Gay and Lesbian Resource Ctr., Santa Barbara, 1989—92; founding mem. March On, L.A., 1988—90. Recipient Individual Artist award, Santa Barbara Arts Commn., 1993, Poet Laureate of Santa Barbara award, City of Santa Barbara, 1999. Avocations: theater , travel, painting, book collecting. Office: 967 Clover Ln Hanford CA 93230 E-mail: pobiz@mail.com.

OLIVEIRA ALDAMIZ, JOSE MARIA, scriptwriter; b. Huelua, Spain, Mar. 8, 1934; m. Patricia Wright; children: Jonathan, Christopher, Maria, Patrick, Lily Ann, Jasmine. JD, U. Madrid, Madrid, Spain, 1957. Dir. William Morris Agy., Madrid, Spain, 1962—64; freelance agt. Spain, 1964—72; film prodr., write, dir. Oliveira Films, Spain, 1972—80; dir. ITT World Comm., Spain, 1980—83; freelance screen writer Salt Lake City, 1983—. Writer, director (films) Beware of Darkness, The Dead, the Devil and the Flesh (Nat., 1974). Home: 560 East South Temple C-101 Salt Lake City UT 84102

OLIVELLA, BARRY JAMES, financial executive; b. Can., 1947; BA, York U., Toronto, Ont., Can., 1968. Chartered acct., Ont. Ptnr. Arthur Young Clarkson Gordon and Woods Gordon (name now Ernst & Young), Toronto, 1968-87; v.p. fin. Bombardier Inc., Montreal, 1987-89, v.p. planning and acquisitions, 1989-93, v.p. acquisitions and strategic alliances, 1993-99, v.p. spl. projects, 1999—2002. Bd. dirs. NovaBus Corp., 1994-98. Pres. Uxbridge (Ont.) C. of C., 1986-87. Mem. Inst. Chartered Accts. Ont. and Can., Nat. Club (Toronto). Office: Bombardier Inc Ste 2900 800 Rene-Levesque Blvd W Montreal QC Canada H3B 1Y8

OLIVER, ANN BREEDING, secondary education educator; b. Hollywood, Fla., Sept. 21, 1945; d. Harvey James and Ruth (Lige) Breeding; m. John Russell Kelso, July 22, 1972 (div. Feb. 1984); 1 child, Anna Liege; m. Ted J. Oliver, June 29, 1996. BA in Fgn. Lang., U. Ky., 1967; MA in History of Art, Ohio State U., 1971. Curatorial intern Lowe Art Mus., Coral Gables, Fla., 1972; adj. faculty Fla. Atlantic U., Boca Raton, 1972-73, 78; lectr. Miami (Fla.) Dade C.C., 1974, with art-music workshop, 1980-81, lectr.-cons., 1972—, adj. faculty music dept., 1991; curator of edn. Ctr. for the Fine Arts, Miami, 1987-92, High Mus. of Art, Atlanta, 1992-96; Spanish tchr. Sprayberry H.S., Cobb County Bd. Edn., Marietta, 1997—. Mem. Artists in Edn. Panel, Ga. Coun. for Arts, 1994; field reviewer Inst. Mus. Svcs., 1994; adj. faculty in art history Kennesaw State U., Marietta, Ga., 1996—; Spanish tchr. Cobb County Bd. Edn., Atlanta, Spray H.S., Marietta, Ga. Contbg. editor African Art: An Essay for Teachers, 1993; project mgr. and contbg. author: Rings: Five Passions in World Art: Multicultural Curriculum Handbook, 1996. Mem. Cobb County Com. for Fgn. Lang. Curriculum Alignment. Recipient Nat. award for graphics Mead Paper Co., 1989, Gold Medal of Honor publication design S.E. Mus. Educators Publ. Design, 1994. Mem. Am. Assn. of Mus., Inst. Mus. Svcs., Nat. Art Edn. Assn., Am. Coun. Tchrs. Fgn. Langs., Fla. Art Edn. Assn. (dir. mus. divsn.), Ga. Art Edn. Assn. (dir. mus. divsn., Mus. Educator of Yr. 1993), Fgn. Lang. Assn. of Ga. Home: 2420 Mitchell Rd NE Marietta GA 30062-5321

OLIVER, BRUCE LAWRENCE, information systems specialist, educator; b. Westfield, Mass., Nov. 20, 1951; s. Ernest Lawrence and Elizabeth (Welchek) O. AS, Greater Hartford C.C., 1972; BS, U. Mass., 1974; MBA, U. Hartford, 1989. Cert. tchr. sec. and vocat. edn., Mass., Conn. Comml. sales Gordon Realty, Enfield, Conn., 1972-75; forestry tech. rsch. Dept. Environ. Protection, State of Conn., Hartford, 1973-1974; res. sales Forsman Realty, Enfield, 1975-77; substitute sec. tchr. Enfield Sch. Systems, 1975-78; collections mgr. New Eng. Bank & Trust, Enfield, 1978-79; ops. CCEC/McCullahg Leasing, Inc., S. Windsor, Conn., 1979-81; pres. Ollie & Ike's, Inc., Enfield, 1985-86; MBA Adj. U. Hartford, West Hartford, Conn., 1988-89; workstation engr. Travelers, Hartford, 1982-89. V.p. 1st Class Expert Sys., Inc., Wayland, Mass., 1989-90, Microsoft Corp., Boston, 1991-94; cons., pres. Profl. Office Solutions, Enfield, 1981—; pres. New Venture Inc., Enfield, 1994—; owner, nvi: Ednl. Multimedia Group, nvi: Webmaster Internet Devel.; del. leader Comparative Studies Assn.; Internat. Cultural Exch. with China, Washington; pub. spkr. Spkrs. Bur., U. Hartford; vis. mem. faculty mgmt. info. sci. U. Hartford, 1989-91. Author: A Novice's Guide to Personal Computer Buying, New Ventures to Egypt, New Ventures to China, Faith, Hope and Love: Coping With Life and Death. Gubernatorial appointee Conn. bd. trustees Reg. C.C.s, 1985-89; vice chmn. Student Affairs and Acad. Policies Com. Hartford, 1987; chmn., trustee Conn. Data Processing Curriculum Com., Hartford, 1989; elected com. mem. Enfield Dem. Com., 1975; chmn. regional adv. coun. Asnuntuck C.C.; notary pub. Conn., 1972—; gubernatorial appointee Conn. bd. trustees Community Tech. Colls., 1990-93. Recipient CTM degree Toastmaster Internat., Hartford, 1987, State Farmer degree Conn. Future Farmers Am., DeKalb Agrl. Accomplishment award, cert. of recognition Bicentennial (USA) Commn., Enfield, 1976, Vigil Hon. BSA Order of the Arrow, Hartford, 1972, Merit award State of Conn. Community-Tech. Colls. Bd. of Trustees, 1994. Mem. World Affairs Coun. of Hartford, Computer Soc. of IEEE, Am. Assn. for Artificial Intelligence, Assn. C.C. Trustees, Am. Assn. Cmty. and Tech. Colls., Microsoft AlumNet Assn., Internat. Platform Assn., Oldefield Farms Homeowners' Assn. (residence com. sec. 1990-91), Hartford County Soil and Water Conservation Dist., Nat. Press Club Found., Robert Schueller's Eagles Club, Masons. Democrat. Roman Catholic. Avocations: travel, refinishing antiques, tennis, hiking, real estate investment, photography. Home: 71 Oldefield Farms Enfield CT 06082-4565

OLIVER, CHARLES MONTGOMERY, retired English educator; b. Champaign, Ill., July 8, 1932; s. William Albert and Mary Maud (Thompson) O.; m. Helen Marie Vanover, Sept. 4, 1954; children: Mark Lee, Kent Thompson, Karl Henderson. BS, Western Ky. Coll., 1954; MA, U. Mo., Columbia, 1958; PhD, Bowling Green U., 1970. Sports writer Springfield (Mo.) News-Leader, 1958-60, South Bend (Ind.) Tribune, 1960-62; English tchr. Mt. Vernon (Ill.) H.S., 1962-65; prof. English Ohio No. U., Ada, 1965-92; ret., 1992. Author: Hemingway A to Z, 1999; editor: A Moving Picture Feast: The Filmgoer's Hemingway, 1989; editor The Hemingway Rev., 1979-92, The Hemingway Newsletter, 1979—. With U.S. Army, 1954-56. NEH grantee, 1975. Avocations: reading, writing. Home: 1417 Ricky Rd Charlottesville VA 22901-2609 E-mail: cmo7790@earthlink.net.

OLIVER, DALE HUGH, lawyer; b. Lansing, Mich., June 26, 1947; s. Alvin Earl and Jean Elizabeth (Stanton) Oliver; children: Nathan Corey, John Franklin; m. Sarah Elyse Sanders, Mar. 18, 2001. BA, Mich. State U., 1969; JD cum laude, Harvard U., 1972. Bar: D.C. 1973, U.S. Dist. Ct. (D.C. dist.) 1973, U.S. Ct. Appeals (D.C. cir.) 1976, U.S. Supreme Ct. 1980, U.S. Ct. Appeals (fed. cir.) 1983, U.S. Ct. Claims 1983, Calif. 1991. Assoc., ptnr. Jones, Day, Reavis & Pogue, Washington, 1975—79; ptnr. Crowell & Moring, 1979—84, Gibson, Dunn & Crutcher, Washington, 1984—87, Jones, Day, Reavis & Pogue, Washington, 1987—92, Quinn Emanuel Urquhart & Oliver, L.A., 1992—. Editor: (jour.) Pub. Contracts Law, 1980—86; contbr. articles to profl. jours. Spl. counsel 1980 Presdl. Inaugural Com., Washington, 1980; bd. dirs. L.A. coun. Boy Scouts Am., 1991—. Capt. USAF, 1973—75. Mem.: ABA (com. chmn. pub. contract sect. 1979—), Nat. Security Indsl. Assn., Nat. Contract Mgmt. Assn., Harvard Law Sch. Assn., Mich. State U. Alumni Club of Washington (pres., dir. 1984—88). Office: Quinn Emanuel Urquhart & Oliver & Hedges 865 S Figueroa St Fl 10 Los Angeles CA 90017-2543 E-mail: dho@qevo.com.

OLIVER, DAN DAVID, banker; b. Walla Walla, Wash., Mar. 11, 1952; s. Harold Allen and Nydia Jane (Munns) O.; children: Ana Mary, Whitney Leigh. Student, Univ. Coll., Cardiff, Wales, 1972-73; BA in Pre-Law with honors, Wash. State U., 1974; MBA in Taxation, Golden Gate U., 1979; JD, Western State U., 1978; grad. with trust specialization, Pacific Coast Banking Sch., U. Wash., Seattle, 1987; grad. Banking Law Sch., George Mason U., Washington, 1993; grad. Nat. Compliance Sch., U. Okla., 1994, nat. grad. Sch. Compliance Mgmt., 1997. Tax acct. John F. Forbes & Co., San Francisco, 1979-81; cat skinner James Francis Munns Farms, Inc., Prescott, Wash., 1981-82; law clk. Sherwood, Tugman, Gose & Reser, Walla Walla, 1975-79; trust adminstrv. asst. Baker-Boyer Nat. Bank, 1982-83, asst. trust officer, 1984, trust officer, 1985, asst. v.p., legal counsel, 1986, asst. v.p., legal/complaince officer, 1987, v.p. and legal/compliance officer, 1988—, v.p., legal counsel, compliance mgr., 1996—2002, v.p., legal dept. mgr., 2002—. Vice chmn. bd. dirs. Elite Turf Farm, Inc., West Richland, Wash., sr. v.p., sec., legal counsel, 1988-92; mem. Baker Boyer Bancorp Year 2000 Taskforce, 1998-2000; trip organizer/group leader diving expedition to Cozumel, Mexico, 1998; vet. of 18 internat. SCUBA diving trips to remote locations in Belize, Honduras, Saba, St. Kitts, Mexico, Bahamas, Cayman Islands, The Turks and Caicos Islands, humpback whale excursion to the Silver Banks of the Southern Atlantic Ocean, Great Barrier Reef, Coral Sea, Socorro Islands, Mex., The Bay Islands, Honduras, Martinique, Antigua, Saint Maarten, Tortola Brit. Virgin Islands, Puerto Rico, 1993—; participant, instr. Earth Day clean up dives Columbia River, 1995--; bd. mem. Blue Mountain Action coun., 2000—, treas., 2001—, Blue Mountain Se. Housing Group, Whitman St. Housing Group; exec. com., find. com. chmn., housing and energy com. chmn., planning and evaluation com., Blue Sr. Housing Group, 2000—. Commr. Walla Walla City Housing Authority, 1992—, vice chmn., 1997-98, chair housing and energy com., 2000—; mem. Homeless Coalition, 1994-99; bd. dirs. Prescott Sch. Dist., 1983-87, vice chmn., 1985, chmn., 1986; vol. spirits religious program St. Patrick's Cath. Ch., 1990-94; mem. Walla Walla Park and Recreation Adv. Bd., 1991-92, vice chmn., 1992; chmn. Park Improvement Com. for Irrigation, 1992; chmn. Walla Walla Area Com. for Housing, 1991-94; linesman Youth Soccer League; sch. vol. Prospect Point Elem. Sch.; organizer, co-chmn. DeSales H.S. Class of 1970 Reunion, 1995, chmn., treas. 2000 Reunion; mem. panel govt. and politics seminar Leadership Walla Walla, 1994; vice-chmn. Walla Walla City-County Regional Housing Com., 1997-98, chmn. 1998—; bd. dirs. Blue Mountain Action Coun., 2000—, chmn. sub-com. on housing and energy assistance, mem. fin. sub-com., mem. planning sub.com; participant Earth Day Columbia River, 1995-. Mem. Am. Bankers Assn., Nat. Assn. Housing and Redevel. Ofcls., Wash. Bankers Assn. (symposium panelist 1996, compliance com. 1990—, vice chmn. 1994-95, cmty. reinvestment act panel 1994, compliance symposium panelist of local experts), Walla Walla Valley Estate Planning Coun. (bd. dirs. 1986-87, treas. 1987-88, sec. 1988-89, v.p. 1989-90, pres. 1990-91), Nat. Arbor Day Found., Columbia Rural Elec. Assn., Nat. Assn. Underwater Instrs. (life, master diver, rescue diver, high altitude diving cert. 2000, open water I and II, advanced certs., cert. CPR, first aid, and oxygen provider, advanced cert. 1993—, ref. environ. edn. found. 1994—, instr. certification 1997, photography cert. 1996, Nitrox cert. 1999), treas. Atomic Ducks Dive Club, 1999-2000, Bergevin Family Reunion and Edn. Assn. (treas. 1993-96), Frenchtown Found. (charter), Walla Walla Men's Group (treas.), Walla Walla Exch. Club, Atomic Ducks Dive Club (bd. dirs., treas. 1999-2000), Beta Sigma Phi. Avocations: scuba diving, swimming, underwater photography, SCUBA kayaking, travel. Office: Baker Boyer Nat Bank Main and 2d Sts Walla Walla WA 99362 E-mail: oliverd@bakerboyer.com. *Personal philosophy: I believe we need to try to be all that we can be, with compassion for those who can not.*

OLIVER, DIANE FRANCES, publisher, writer; b. N.Y.C., Feb. 7, 1935; m. Ben Martin Oliver, Sept. 3, 1960 (div. 1973). BA, Syracuse U., 1955. Reporter Millinery Rsch. mag., N.Y.C., 1956-58; with N.Y.C. Bur., London Daily Mail and London Daily Sketch, 1964-69; editor The Celebrity Bull., Celebrity Svc. Inc., N.Y.C., 1971-78; pub. The Celebrity Bull., pres., owner Celebrity Svc. Ltd., London, 1978—. Former publicist Lake Lucerne (N.Y.) Playhouse, Bklyn. Acad. Music, Statler Hilton Hotel, N.Y.C. Author: Older Woman/Younger Man, 1975; columnist Palm Beach Social Pictorial mag., 1981-85. Avocations: music, ballet, films, theater, travel. Home: 44 Lennox Gardens London SW1X 0DJ England Office: Celebrity Svc Ltd 93/97 Regent St London W1B 4ES England E-mail: celebritylondon@aol.com.

OLIVER, DOMINICK MICHAEL, business educator; b. Niagara Falls, N.Y., Apr. 12, 1962; s. Dominick Jr. and Priscilla (Prenatt) O.; m. Vicki Anne Sellig, May 18, 1991. AAS, Niagara County C.C., Sanborn, N.Y., 1982; BS in Bus., Niagara U., N.Y., 1984, MS in Edn., 1986. Lic. tchr. bus. and distributive edn., N.Y.; bus. sch. lic. bus., mgmt., acctg., gen. academics, N.Y. Temporary instr. Niagara County C.C., Sanborn, 1986-87; tchr. on spl. assignment LaSalle Sr. H.S., Niagara Falls, N.Y., 1986-87; instr. St. Joseph Parochial Elem. Sch., 1987-88; instr., acad. dean Kelley Bus. Inst., 1988-91; instr. Cheryl Fell's Sch. Bus., 1991-92; instr., advisor Bryant and Stratton Bus. Inst., Buffalo, 1992—, sr. mentor, portfolio textbook curriculum com., 1996—. Bus. mgr. Dove Artworks, Buffalo, 1996—; instr. Adopt-A-H.S., Seneca Vocat. H.S., Kensington H.S., Lafayette H.S., Riverside H.S., Buffalo, 1996—. Life mem. Buffalo and Erie County Naval and Servicemen's Park, Buffalo, 1991—. Mem. Nat. Bus. Edn. Assn., Nat. Coun. Tchrs. English, Assembly for Tchg. English Grammar, Nat. Soc. Pub. Accts., Collegiate Press, N.Y. State Assn. Two Yr. Colls., N.Y. State Ind. Accts., Phi Delta Kappa. Republican. Roman Catholic. Avocations: sports (baseball, football, hockey), political history of United States, reading classical literature. Home: 119 Wendover Ave Buffalo NY 14223-2731 Office: The Huntington Learning Ctr 3086 Delaware Ave Kenmore NY 14217-2056

OLIVER, EDWARD CARL, state legislator, retired investment executive; b. St. Paul, May 31, 1930; s. Charles Edmund and Esther Marie (Bjugstad) O.; m. Charlotte Severson, Sept. 15, 1956; children: Charles E., Andrew T., Peter A. BA, U. Minn., 1955. Sales rep. Armstrong Cork Co., N.Y.C., 1955; registered rep. Piper, Jaffray & Hopwood, Mpls., 1958; mgr. Mut. Funds Inc., subs. Dayton's, 1964. NWNL Mgmt. Corp. subs. Northwestern Nat. Life Ins. Co., Mpls., 1968-72, v.p., 1972-81, pres., dir., 1981-90; mem. Minn. State Senate, 1992—, asst. minority leader, 1998—. Arbitrator/mediator, Nat. Assn.

Securities Dealers, 1988—; bd. dirs. 1st Minn. Bank, N.A. Commr. Gt. Lakes commn., 1993—; ch. elder, Presbyn. ch., Deephaven, Mpls. Mem. Internat. Assn. Fin. Planners (past pres. Twin City chpt., nat. governing com.), Psi Upsilon, Mpls. Club. Home: 20230 Cottagewood Rd Excelsior MN 55331-9300 Office: Washington Sq Securities Inc 100 Washington Ave S Ste 1600 Minneapolis MN 55401-2154 E-mail: sen.edward.oliver@senate.leg.state.mn.us.

OLIVER, ELIZABETH KIMBALL, writer, historian; b. Saginaw, Mich., May 21, 1918; d. Chester Benjamin and Margaret Eva (Allison) Kimball; m. James Arthur Oliver, May 3, 1941 (div. July 1967); children: Patricia Allison (dec.), Dexter Kimball. BA, U. Mich., 1940. Tchr. Dexter (Mich.) High Sch., 1940-41; libr. Sherman (Conn.) Libr. Assn., 1966-75; pres. Sherman (Conn.) Libr. Assn., 1983-84; writer, historian, 1976—. Reporter Sherman Sentinel, 1965-70; editor newsletter Sherman Hist. Soc., 1977-78; columnist Citizen News, Fairfield County, Conn.; 1981-83. Author: History of Staff Wives-AMNH, 1961, Background and History of the Palisades Nature Association, 1964, History and Architecture of Grace United Methodist Church, 1990, Legacy to St. Augustine, 1993, Franklin W. Smith and His Casa Monica Hotel, 2000; guest columnist Mandarin News, 1995-97; columnist St. Augustine Record, 1998—. Vol. N.Y. Hist. Soc., N.Y.C., 1961-65; treas. Coburn Cemetery Assn., Sherman, 1976-82; historian Greenbrook-Palisades Nature Assn., Tenafly, N.J., 1962-64; mem. St. Augustine Hist. Soc., Naromi Land Trust (life), Cedar Key Hist. Soc.; adv. bd. IBC (Eng.). Mem. AAUW, Friends of Libr. (life), Inst. Am. Indian Studies, Marjorie Kinnan Rawlings Soc. (charter), St. Augustine Woman's Club (archivist, cert. of appreciation 1990), Sherman Hist. Soc., Mandarin Hist. Soc. Republican. Congregationalist. Avocations: sacred choral music, research, reading, piano and dulcimer playing, botany. Home: 2292 Commodores Club Blvd Saint Augustine FL 32080-9161 *There are four words which I endeavor to live up to in my work, my personal contacts and every day life. They are the guideposts which I use in all I do: love, courage, integrity and steadfastness.*

OLIVER, GARY JACKSON, psychologist, educator; b. Great Falls, Mont., Sept. 20, 1947; m. Carrie Elizabeth Oliver, Dec. 27, 1980; children: Nathan, Matthew, Andrew. ThM, Fuller Sem., 1977; MA, U. Nebr., 1980, PhD, 1984. Cert. clin. psychology, Nebr., Colo., Ark. Sr. staff psychologist Lincoln (Nebr.) Family Med. Group, 1984-86; clin. dir. S.W. Counseling Assocs., Littleton, Colo., 1986-98; exec. dir., prof. The Ctr. for Marriage and Family Studies, John Brown U., Siloam Springs, Ark., 1998—. Program dir., prof. Denver Sem., 1988—; bd. mem. Today's Family, Branson. Author: Real Men Have Feelings Too, 1993, Made Perfect in Weakness: The Amazing Things God Can Do With Failure, 1998, (with H. Norman Wright) Hip Hop and His Famous Face, 1995, Bruce Moose and the What-Ifs, 1996, Fears, Doubts, Blues and Pouts, 1999, (with Gary J. Oliver) Raising Kids to Love Jesus, 1999, (with Carrie Oliver) Raising Sons...And Loving It!, 2000; contbg. editor New Man Mag., Marriage Partnership, Marriage & Family: A Christian Jour.; contbr. over 100 articles to profl. jours. and mags. Mem. APA, ACA, Am. Assn. Christian Counselors (bd. mem.), Am. Assn. for Marriage and Family Therapy, Assn. for Psychol. Type, Nat. Coun. on Family Rels., Christian Assn. for Psychol. Studies. Office: John Brown U Ctr for Marriage and Family Studies 2000 W University St Siloam Springs AR 72761-2112 E-mail: cmfs@jbu.edu.

OLIVER, G(EORGE) BENJAMIN, educational administrator, philosophy educator; b. Mpls., Sept. 17, 1938; s. Clarence P. and Cecile (Worley) O.; m. Paula Rae Foust, Sept. 15, 1963; children: Paul Benjamin, Rebecca Lee. BA with honors, U. Tex., 1960; MDiv, Union Theol. Sem., N.Y.C., 1963; MA, Northwestern U., 1966, PhD, 1967. Lectr. Northwestern U., Evanston, Ill., 1966-67; asst. prof. Hobart & William Smith Coll., Geneva, 1967-71, chmn. dept. philosophy, 1969-77, assoc. prof., 1971-77, prof., 1977; dean Southwestern U., Georgetown, Tex., 1977-89, provost, 1986-89; pres. Hiram (Ohio) Coll., 1989-2000, pres. emeritus, 2000—. Chmn. Coun. Acad. Deans and V.P.s of Tex., 1987-88. Contbr. articles to profl. jours. Trustee John Cabot U., Rome, 1989-2000, Grand River Acad., Austinburg, Ohio, 1991-2000, N.E. Ohio Coun. Higher Edn., 1991-2000, Ohio Found. Ind. Coll., 1989-2000, vice-chair, 1999-2000, exec. com., 1994-2000, co-chair strategic planning com., 1997-98; trustee Assn. Ind. Colls. and Univs. Ohio, 1993-2000, Nat. Assn. Ind. Colls. and Univs. Pol. Com. on Student Aid, 1999-2000, Am. Coun. Edn. Commn. Govtl. Rels., 1994-97, Cleve. Coun. on World Affairs, 1996-2000; chmn. bd. trustees East Ctrl. Coll. Consortium, 1993-95. Rockefeller Found. fellow, 1960-61, Internat. fellow Columbia U., 1962-63; rsch. grantee NEH, 1973-74. Mem. AAUP, Am. Coun. Edn. (commn. on govtl. rels.), Soc. for Values in Higher Edn., Assn. Ind. Coll. and Univs. Ohio (treas. 1993-94), East Ctrl. Colls. Consortium (chair, bd. trustees 1993-95), Ohio Found. Ind. Colls. (exec. com. 1994-2000, vice chair elect 1999-2000), Am. Assn. Higher Edn., Cleve. Coun. on Fgn. Rels. Episcopalian. Office: Hiram Coll Office of Pres Hiram OH 44234 E-mail: olivergben@msn.com.

OLIVER, HARRY MAYNARD, JR. retired brokerage house executive; b. Kansas City, Mo., Jan. 21, 1921; s. Harry Maynard and Marie (Curtin) O. BA, Williams Coll., 1943. Pres. M.A. Gesner & Co., Marsh & McLennan Co., Chgo., 1947-88. Chmn. Chgo. Commn. for Sr. Citizens, 1960-69; mem. Chgo. Bd. Edn., 1966-69; pres. Vol. Agys. Chgo., 1956-86; mem. vis. com. Sch. Edn. and div. of social scis., U. Chgo.; pres., bd. dirs. Benton House Settlement, 1953-58; bd. dirs. Adult Edn. Council Greater Chgo., Nat. Fedn. Settlements and Community Centers, 1961-67; trustee Old Peoples Home Chgo., Pub. Sch. Tchrs. Pension and Retirement Fund Chgo., 1966-69, George M. Pullman Ednl. Found., Field Mus. Natural History, 1971-75. Served to lt. (j.g.) USNR, World War II. Mem. Chgo. Club, Racquet Club, Commonwealth Club, Tavern Club, Onwentsia Club (Lake Forest, Ill.), Chi Psi. Home: 1948 N Lincoln Ave Chicago IL 60614-5476 also: PO Box 1319 Big Pine Key FL 33043 also: New Richmond PO Box 100 Fennville MI 49408-0100

OLIVER, JACK ERTLE, geophysicist, educator; b. Massillon, Ohio, Sept. 26, 1923; s. Chester L. and Marie (Ertle) O.; m. Gertrude van der Hoeven, Apr. 16, 1964; children: Cornelia Oliver, Amy Oliver. AB, Columbia U., 1947, MA, 1950, PhD, 1953; DSci (hon.), Hamilton Coll., 1988. Rsch. asst., then rsch. assoc. Columbia, 1947-55, mem. faculty, 1955-73, prof. geology, 1961-71, chmn. dept., 1969-71, adj. prof., 1971-73; Irving Porter Church prof. engring. dept. geol. scis. Cornell U., 1971-93, prof. emeritus, 1993—, chmn. dept., 1971-81; chmn. exec. com. COCORP. Terrestrial physicist USAF Cambridge (Mass.) Rsch. Labs., 1951; dir. Inst. for Study of the Continents, 1981-88; cons. AEC, 1969-72, ACDA, 1962-74, USAF Tech. Applications Ctr., 1959-65; mem. Polar Rsch. Com., 1959-71, also nat. commn. uppermantle program, 1963-71; mem. panel solid earth problems NAS, 1962; mem. adv. com. U.S. Coast and Geodetic Survey, 1962-66, on seismology, 1960-72, chmn., 1966-70; mem. Geophysics Rsch. Bd., 1969-70; U.S. coord. 2d U.S.-Japan Earthquake Prediction Conf., Palisades, 1966; earth sci. panel NSF, 1962-65; mem. USAF Sci. Adv. Bd., 1960-63, 64-69; mem. geophysics adv. panel Office Sci. Rsch., USAF, 1961-74, chmn., 1966-68; U.S. del. Test Ban Conf., Geneva, Switzerland, 1958-59; intergovtl. meeting seismology and earthquake engring., mem. exec. com. IASPEI, 1968-71; mem. governing com. Internat. Seismol. Summary Comm., 1963-67, 75-76; mem. exec. com. UNESCO, Paris, France, 1964, U.S.-Japan Earthquake Prediction Conf., Tokyo, 1964; mem. UNESCO Joint Com. on Seismology and Earthquake Engring., 1965-71; chmn. exec. com. Office Earth Scis., NRC, 1976-79, Internat. Seismol. Centre, 1976-78; mem. U.S. Geodynamics Com., 1979-87, chmn., 1984-87; mem. Geol. Scis. Bd., Assembly of Math. and Phys. Scis., NRC, 1981-84; Cabot Disting. vis. scholar U. Houston, 1985-86; commn. on phys. scis., math. and resources NRC, 1987-90, commn. on geoscis., environ. and resources, 1990—. Served with USNR, 1943-46. Recipient Hedberg award Inst. for Study of Earth and Man, So. Meth. U., 1990. Fellow Am. Geophys. Union (pres. seismology sect. 1964-68, Walter H. Bucher medal 1981), Geol. Soc. Am. (coun. 1970-73, v.p. 1986, pres. 1987, Woollard medal 1990, Penrose medal 1998), Geol. Soc. London (hon.); mem. AAAS (chmn. geol. geog. sect. 1993), NAS, Seismol. Soc. Am. (pres. 1964-65, bd. dirs. 1961-70, 72-76, Eighth medal 1984), Soc. Exploration Geophysicists (Virgil Kauffman Gold medal 1983), European Union Geoscis. (hon. fgn. fellow), Sigma Xi. Home: 125 Cayuga Park Rd Ithaca NY 14850-1405 E-mail: oliver@geology.cornell.edu.

OLIVER, JOHN EDWARD, bank strategic management and training consultant; b. Bedford, Eng., Apr. 14, 1951; came to U.S., 1978; s. Fred K. and Marjorie F. (Brown) O.; m. Jacqueline L. Alcock, Oct. 7, 1972; 1 child, Sophie Rose. Student, Mander Coll., Bedford, 1968-71. Mgr.'s asst. Nat. Westminster Bank, Bedford, 1971-73; credit analyst Kleinwort Benson Ltd., London, 1973-76; mktg. coord. Amex Bank Ltd., 1976-78; v.p. Continental Ill. Energy Devel. Corp., Houston, 1978-85; pres. Laurel Mgmt. Systems Inc., San Francisco, 1986—. Cons. various U.S. and internat. banks including Merita Bank, London, 1985—; bank edn. cons. Bank Am., San Francisco, 1986—; advisor Am. Inst. Banking, San Francisco, 1994—; pres. Global Bank Tng. Com., 1999—; lead faculty Cues Mgmt. Inst.; mem. faculty Bank Adminstrn. Inst. Author: What Really is Expected of Me?-The Role of the Community Bank Director, 1995, Strategic Bank Management in a Risk Environment, 1995, Strategic Management of Financial Institutions, 1998. Mem. ASTD, Assn. Bank Trainers and Cons. Office: Laurel Mgmt Systems Inc 3933 20th St San Francisco CA 94114-2906 E-mail: oliver@globalbanktraining.com.

OLIVER, JOHN PRESTON, chemistry educator, academic administrator; b. Klamath Falls, Oreg., Aug. 7, 1934; s. Robert Preston and Agnes May (McCornack) O.; m. Elizabeth Ann Shaw, Aug. 12, 1956; children: Karen Sue Oliver Vernon, Roy John, Gordon Preston. BA, U. Oreg., 1956; PhD, U. Wash., 1959. Asst. prof. chemistry Wayne State U., Detroit, 1959-64, assoc. prof., 1964-67, prof., 1967—, assoc. dean R&D, Coll. Liberal Arts, 1987-91, acting dean, 1991-92, interim dean Coll. Sci., 1992-93, dep. provost, 1996—. Chmn. organizing com. XIV Internat. Conf. on Organometallic Chemistry. Mem. Ferndale (Mich.) Bd. Edn., 1984-88. Mem. Am. Chem. Soc., Detroit sect. Am. Chem. Soc., Sigma Xi. Office: Wayne State Univ Rm 4101 FAB Detroit MI 48202-3489 E-mail: jpo@wayne.edu.

OLIVER, JOHN WILLIAM POSEGATE, minister; b. Vincennes, Ind., Apr. 9, 1935; s. Dwight L and Elizabeth (Posegate) Oliver; m. Cristina Shepard Hope, Oct. 19, 1968; children: John William Posegate Jr, Sloan Christian Shepard. BA, Wheaton Coll., 1956; BD, Fuller Theol. Sem., 1959; ThM, So. Bapt. Theol. Sem., 1963; DD, Western Conservative Bapt. Sem, 1996. Ordained to ministry Presby Ch, 1962. Asst. pastor Covenant Presbyn. Ch., Hammond, Ind., 1964-66, Trinity Presbyn. Ch., Montgomery, Ala., 1966-69; pastor 1st Presbyn. Ch., Augusta, Ga., 1969-97, Trinity Presbyn. Ch., Montgomery, Ala., 1997-99; prof. preaching and practical theology Reformed Theol. Sem., Charlotte, N.C., 1999—. Bd dirs Equip, Inc; moderator Cent Ga Presby, Presby Ch Am, 1976. Founder, trustee Westminster Schs, Augusta, 1972—97; bd comnrs Augusta Housing Authority, vice chmn, 1976—93; trustee, chmn bd Columbia Int Univ, 1978—; dir Bailey Manor Retirement Ctr, Clinton, SC, 1992—97; chmn clergy Augusta United Way Campaign, 1974; exec bd clergy staff Univ Hosp, Augusta, 1975—76; ministerial adv bd Reformed Theological Sem, Charlotte, 1996—99; bd dirs Mission to the World, Presby Am, 1984—89, 1992—96; ministerial adv. bd. Reformed Theol. Sem., Jackson, Miss., 1978—85, 1989—93. Mem.: Evang Theological Soc, Wynlakes Country Club, Nassau Club Princeton, Kappa Sigma. Home: 731 Stanhope Ln Matthews NC 28105-1516 Office: 2101 Carmel Rd Charlotte NC 28226-6318

OLIVER, JOYCE ANNE, journalist, editorial & film consultant, columnist; b. Coral Gables, Fla., Sept. 19, 1958; d. John Joseph and Rosalie Cecile (Mack) O. BA in Communications, Calif. State U., Fullerton, 1980, MBA, 1990. Corp. editor Norris Industries Inc., Huntington Beach, Calif., 1979-82; pres. J.A. Oliver Assocs., La Habra Heights, 1982—. Corp. editorial cons. Norris Industries, 1982, Better Methods Cons., Huntington Harbour, Calif., 1982-83, Summit Group, Orange, Calif., 1982-83, UDS, Encinitas, Calif., 1983-84, MacroMarketing, Costa Mesa, Calif., 1985-86, PM Software, Huntington Beach, Calif., 1985-86, CompuQuote, Canoga Park, Calif., 1985-86, Nat. Semicondr. Can. Ltd., Mississauga, Ont., Can., 1986, Maclean Hunter Ltd., Toronto, Ont., 1986-90; Frame Inc., Fullerton, Calif., 1987-88, The Johnson-Layton Co., L.A., 1988-89, Corp. Rsch. Inc., Chgo., 1988, Axon Group, Horsham, Pa., 1990-91, Am. Mktg. Assn., Chgo., 1990-92, Kenzaikai Co., Ltd., Tokyo, 1991, Penton Pub., Cleve., 1991, Bus. Computer Pub., Inc., Peterborough, N.H., 1991-92, Helmers Pub., Inc., Peterborough, 1992, Schnell Pub., Co., Inc., N.Y.C., 1992-93, Diversified Pub. Group, Carol Stream, Ill., 1993; mem. Rsch. Coun. of Scripps Clinic and Rsch. Found., 1987-92; pres. Oliver Vingtaine, 1999—. Contbg. editor Computer Merchandising/ Resell, 1982-85, Computer Reselling, 1985, Reseller Mgmt., 1987-89; contbg. editor Can. Electronics Engring., 1986-90, west coast editor, 1990, Chem. Bus. mag., 1992-93; spl. feature editor Cleve. Inst. Electronics publ. The Electron, 1986-89; bus. columnist Mktg. News, 1990-92; contbr. articles to profl. jours. and mags. Bd. dirs. Action Comms., 1993—. Mem. IEEE, AAUW, Internat. Platform Assn., Soc. Photo-optical Instrumentation Engrs., Inst. Mgmt. Scis., Nat. Writers Club (profl.), Internat. Mktg. Assn., Soc. Profl. Journalists, L.A. World Affairs Coun., Internat. Order of Merit, Nat. Trust for Hist. Preservation. Republican. Roman Catholic. Avocations: sailing, water skiing. Office: PO Box 2607 La Habra CA 90632-2607

OLIVER, KELLY, philosophy educator; d. Glen William and Virginia (Fay) O. BA in Comm./Philosphy summa cum laude, Gonzaga U., 1979; MA in Philosophy, Northwestern U., Evanston, Ill., 1980, PhD in Philosophy, 1987. Instr., tchr.'s asst. Northwestern U., Evanston, 1980-85; vis. asst. prof. Philosophy W.Va. U., 1986-88; vis. asst. prof. Philosophy and Women's Studies Miami U., 1988-90; asst. prof. Philosophy George Washington U., 1990-91; assoc. prof. Philosophy U. Tex., Austin, 1991—98; assoc. prof. Women's Studies & Philosophy Stony Brook U., 1998—99, prof. Women's Studies & Philosophy, 2000—, chair Philosophy Dept., 2001—. Dir. Popular Culture Conf., 1991-94. Author: Womanizing Nietzsche: Philosophy's Relation to "the feminine", 1994, Reading Kristeva: Unraveling the Double-bind, 1993; editor: (book) Ethics Politics and Difference in Julia Kristeva's Writing, 1993; reviewer SUNY Press, 1991—, U. Minn. Press, 1991—, Routledge Press, 1992—, Ind. U. Press, 1992—; contbr. articles to profl. jours. The Sch. of Lit. Criticism and Theory fellow, 1982, Summer Rsch. grantee Miami U., 1989, Small Rsch. grantee, 1989, Dilthey Faculty fellow, 1991, U. Tex. Spl. Rsch. grantee, 1991, U. Tex. Small Rsch. grantee, 1992. Mem. Am. Philos. Assn., Soc. for Women in Philosophy, N.Am. Nietzsche Soc., Soc. for Phenomenology & Existentialism, Internat. Assn. for Philosophy & Lit., Popular Culture Assn. Office: SUNY Womens Studies Old Chemistry 105 Stony Brook NY 11794-3456 also: SUNY Philosophy Dept Harriman Hall Rm 213 Stony Brook NY 11794-3750 Fax: 631-632-5729 , 631-632-7522. E-mail: koliver@sunysb.edu.

OLIVER, LEANN MICHELLE, government official; b. Eureka, Calif., Nov. 15, 1955; d. George L. and Laura Maxine (Jennings) O. BS, Willamette U., 1977; MPA, SUNY, Albany, 1980; cert., Nat. Comml. Lending Sch. of Am. Bankers Assn., Norman, Okla., 1982. Mgmt. trainee U.S. GAO, Albany, 1979-80; presdl. mgmt. intern U.S. SBA, Washington, 1980-83, fin. analyst, policy and program devel., 1983-89; dep. dir. for program devel. Office Econ. Devel., 1989-92; dep. dir. Office of Rural Affairs and Econ. Devel., 1992-94; acting dir. One Stop Office, Capital Shop Project, 1994; acting dir. Office Rural Affairs and Econ. Devel. SBA, Washington, 1995, dir. divsn. Program Devel., 1995-2000, dep. assoc. adminstr. for fin. assistance, 2000—. Bd. dirs. Lafayette Fed. Credit Union, Washington, 1986—, treas., 1997-2000, asst. treas., 2000—. Mem. Internat. Platform Assn. Roman Catholic. Office: SBA 409 3rd St SW Ste 8300 Washington DC 20416

OLIVER, MADISON E. retired mechanical engineer; b. Hermosa Beach, Calif., Apr. 14, 1925; s. Eldon Seymour and Gertrude Helen Oliver; m. Virginia E. Kellis. BS Applied Sci., Chico State U., 1951; BS Mech. Engring., Wash. State U., 1953. Registered profl. engr. N.Mex., 1956. Staff mem. Sandia Corp., Albuquerque, 1953—56, sect. supr. Livermore, Calif., 1957—60; design engr. Aerojet Gen. Corp., Sacramento, 1960—63; dir. of pub. works Govt. of Am. Samoa, Pago Pago, 1967—69, dep. dir. pub. works Antigua and Barbuda, 1963—67; project mgr. Parsons Hawaii, Honolulu, 1970—74, sr. project mgr., mgr. engring., 1974—82; v.p., gen. mgr. Parsons Hawaii (A unit of The Ralph M. Parsons Co.), 1982—91. Bd. dirs. KD2 Water & Energy Resources, Inc., Honolulu, 1983—85; territorial bldg. ofcl. Govt. of Am. Samoa, Pago Pago, U. S. Territory of American Samoa, 1967—69; sec. bd. of dirs. Marine Dry Dock, Pago Pago, 1968—69; project mgr. New Guam Internat. Air Terminal Parsons Hawaii, Honolulu, 1976—82, program director TRUK capital improvements, 1975—77, project mgr., trust ter. of the Pacific Islands airport sys. plan, 1975—76, prin. project mgr., engring. design of New Palau Hosp., 1988—91, spkr., west region conf. of Constrn. Specifications Inst.ific rim, 1982—82. Mem. Pacific & Asian Affairs Coun., Honolulu, 1982—90; mem., transp. com. Chamber of Commerce, 1982—90; bd. dirs. Marina Towers Condominium, 1980—83, pres. bd. dirs., 1983—86. Motor machinist's mate first class USN, 1943—46, PTO. Recipient Airport Beautification Award, Saipan Internat. Airport, FAA, Saipan, No. Mariana Islands, 1976. Mem.: Soc. Am. Mil. Engineers, ASME, Toastmasters Internat. (gov., area VI, dist. 39 1963—63), Toastmasters Internat., Raconteur Club, Folsom, Calif. (pres. 1962—63), Masonic Lodge (Golden Veterans Award 2000). Avocation: golf, writing, and fishing. Home: 1821 Jansen Way Woodburn OR 97071

OLIVER, MALCOLM BRUCE, physician; b. Anchorage, Mar. 28, 1963; s. James Harold Jr. and Arloeen Ann (Williams) O.; m. Mary Rose Williams, June 1, 1985; children: Benjamin Harold, Nathaniel Bruce, Esther Rose. BS, Southwestern Coll., 1985; MD, Ind. U., 1989. Diplomate Am. Bd. Family Practice. Intern St. Joseph Med. Ctr., South Bend, Ind., 1989-90, resident, 1990-92; physician St. Johns Physicians & Clinics, Republic, Mo., 1995—. Tchr. Sunday Sch. Maj. USAF, 1992-95. Fellow Am. Acad. Family Practice; mem. Mo. State Med. Soc., Kiwanis. Methodist. Avocations: fishing, golfing, reading. Office: Republic Family Medicine 332 S Main Ave Republic MO 65738-1861

OLIVER, MARGUERITE BERTONI, food service executive; b. Ann Arbor, Mich., June 5, 1929; d. Ralph Angelo and Margaret Amelia (Rovegno) Bertoni; m. William John Oliver, May 28, 1949; children: R. Scott, Catherine Oliver Allen, Susan M. Mgr. complaint dept. Sears Roebuck Co., Ann Arbor, 1949-50; dir. meals-on-wheels program U. Mich. Hosp., 1974-76; fund raiser U. Mich. Art Sch., 1976-80; founder Pastabilities (named outstanding pasta shop in U.S. by CNN TV), 1980—. Participant, speaker Midwest Assn. State Depts. Agr., 1987; mem. adv. com. Gov.'s Conf. on Future of Mich. Agr., 1988; co-chmn. Gov.'s Conf. on Agr., 1989. Bd. dirs. Washtenaw County Commn. Aging, 1970-74, Hands-On-Mus., Ann Arbor, 1980-82; mem. market commn. Ann Arbor, 1982—; founded Internat. Neighbors; mem., adv. com. Mich. Future 2020 Team; trustee Washtenaw Community Coll., 1989—; mem. Mich. Dept. Agr. Industry Task Force, 1990; invited del. Moscow Bus. Conf., 1991; fundraiser Mott Children's Hosp. U. Mich., 1979-80; fundraiser U. Mich. Musical Soc., 1997. Recipient Washtenaw Community Service award Washtenaw Community Coll., 1985. Roman Catholic. Home: 2892 Bay Ridge Dr Ann Arbor MI 48103-1704 Office: Pastabilities 708 State Cir Ann Arbor MI 48108-1648

OLIVER, MARLYS MAE, retired editor, writer; b. St. Paul, Mar. 23, 1930; d. Earle R. and Margaret A. (Parrott) Benner; m. Alfred Leo Oliver, Apr. 28, 1951; children— Stephanie Margaret, David Earle. AA, Lakewood C.C., 1970; student Metro State U., 1976-77. Graphic artist Lakewood C.C., White Bear Lake, Minn., 1968-70; corr. Women Sports mag., N.Y.C., 1973-77; editor Press Publs., White Bear Lake, 1972-76; mng. editor Frogtown Forum, St. Paul, 1976-77; mayor City of Birchwood, Minn., 1977-83; exec. editor Press Publs., White Bear Lake, 1982-92; owner Dolls by Marlys, 1992—; host weekly cable tel. talk show Come for Coffee, 1988-90; pres., dir. Cable Access Corp., 1985-87. Mem. White Bear Lake Arts Council, dir., 1975; bd. dirs. Lakeshore Players, 1984-85, White Bear Lake Area Hist. Soc.; chmn Ramsey Washington Counties Cable TV Commn. Recipient numerous awards in journalism. Mem. Minn. Press Women (past treas.), Midwest Writers Conf (com.) Mem. Democratic Farm Labor Party. Lodge: Job's Daus. (Queen 1949). Contbr. numerous articles and poems to popular mags. Home: 139 Birchwood Ave Saint Paul MN 55110-1611

OLIVER, MARY, poet; b. Maple Heights, Ohio, Sept. 10, 1935; d. Edward William and Helen Mary (Vlasak) O. Student, Ohio State U., 1955-56, Vassar Coll., 1956-57. Chmn. writing dept. Fine Arts Work Ctr., Provincetown, 1972-73, mem. writing com., 1984; Banister poet in residence Sweet Briar Coll., 1991-95. William Blackburn vis. prof. creative writing Duke U., 1995; Catharine Osgood Foster prof. Bennington Coll., 1996-2001. Author: No Voyage and Other Poems, 1963, enlarged edit., 1965, The River Styx, Ohio, 1972, The Night Traveler, 1978, Twelve Moons, 1979, American Primitive, 1983, Dream Work, 1986, House of Light, 1990, New and Selected Poems, 1992, A Poetry Handbook, 1994, White Pine, 1994, Blue Pastures, 1995, West Wind, 1997, Rules for the Dance, 1998, Winter Hours, 1999, The Leaf and the Cloud, 2000, What Do We Know, 2002; contbr. to Yale U. Rev., Kenyon Rev., Poetry, Atlantic, Harvard mag., others. Recipient Shelley Meml. award, 1970, Alice Fay di Castagnola award, 1973, Cleve. Arts prize for lits., 1979, Achievement award Am. Acad. and Inst. Arts and Letters, 1983, Pulitzer prize for poetry, 1984, Christopher award, 1991, L.L. Winship award, 1991, Nat. Book award, 1992, Lannan award, 1998; Nat. Endowment fellow, 1972-73; Guggenheim fellow, 1980-81. Mem. PEN. Home: care Molly Malone Cook Lit Agy PO Box 619 Provincetown MA 02657-0619

OLIVER, NANCY LEBKICHER, artist, retired elementary education educator; b. Stockton, Calif., 1939; d. John B. and Marjorie Lebkicher; m. Douglas C. Oliver, 1963; children: Charles, Elaine. BA with honors, San Jose State U., 1961. Summer playground dir. Recreation Dept., Redwood City, Calif., 1956-61; 1st grade tchr. Redwood City (Calif.) Elem. Sch. Dist., 1961-63; kindergarten tchr. Ukiah (Calif.) Unified Sch. Dist., 1963-67; assoc. tchr. kindergarten San Carlos (Calif.) Elem. Sch. Dist., 1976-81. Shopper for dept. store Macy's, San Francisco, 1975-82; asst. in hist. rsch., 2000—. Sunday sch. dir. St. Peter's Episcopal Ch., Redwood City, 1973-78; active White Oaks PTA, San Carlos, 1973-81, newsletter editor, 1978-81; leader Girl Scouts U.S.A., San Carlos, 1978-81; bd. mem. Sequoia H.S. Ednl. Found., co-chmn., 2000-2002, chmn. 2002—; bd. mem. San Mateo County Hist. Resources Adv. Bd. Mem. AAUW (San Carlos br. newsletter editor 1972-74, editor historic tour booklet 1981, editor historic resources booklet 1989, chmn. historic preservation sect. 1979—, pres. Willits br. 1966-67, co-res. San Carlos br. 2002—, Named Gift honoree 1976, pres. San Carlos br. 2002—), San Carlos Heritage Assn. (founder, dir. 1995—), Sequoia H.S. Alumni Assn. (founding sec., membership chmn. 1985—, centennial coord. 1992-95, pres. 1996-98, Unsung Hero award 1998), Internat. Order Rainbow Girls (grand officer Calif. 1957-58, mother advisor Redwood City 1987-89), SeriPrinters (serigrapher 1986—). Democrat. Episcopalian. Avocations: needlework, historic preservation activities, walking, calligraphy, classical music. Home: 147 Belvedere Ave San Carlos CA 94070-4818

OLIVER, ROBERT BRUCE, retired investment company executive; b. Brockton, Mass., Aug. 1, 1931; s. Stanley Thomas and Helen (Sabine) O.; m. Sylvia E. Bell, Feb. 17, 1954; children: Susan Pamela, Robert Bruce. AB, Harvard U., 1953; postgrad., Bus. Sch., 1971, Boston U. Law Sch., 1955-57; MA, Mich. State U., 1958. Ret. chmn., pres., chief exec. officer John Hancock Income Securities Trust, Boston, 1989. Ret. chmn., pres. chief exec. officer John Hancock Investors Trust, John Hancock Bond Trust, John Hancock Growth Trust, John Hancock Tax Exempt Cash Mgmt. Trust, John Hancock Govt. Securities Trust, John Hancock Tax Exempt Income Trust, John Hancock Cash Mgmt. Trust, John Hancock Spl. Equities Trust, John Hancock Global Trust, John Hancock World Trust, John Hancock High Income Trust, John Hancock Tax Exempt Series Trust; chmn., dir. John Hancock Distbrs.; vice chmn., chief exec. officer John Hancock Advisers, Inc.; chmn., mng. dir. John Hancock Advisers Internat. Ltd. 1st lt. USMCR, 1953-55. Mem. Marine Corps League Home: 6619 Trident Way Naples FL 34108-8243

OLIVER, RON, state official; Chmn. State Dem. Party, 2002—; owner First Ark. Bail Bonds. Democrat. Office: 1300 W Capitol Ave Little Rock AR 72201*

OLIVER, RONALD, retired medical technologist; b. New Orleans, July 16, 1949; s. Wilbert and Everlina (Theard) O.; m. Ora Grant, July 12, 1995; children: Nannette Marie, Joseph Byron. Diploma in bus. adminstrn., Meadows-Draughon Coll., New Orleans, 1972; AS in Environ. Health Tech., Delgado C.C., New Orleans, 1976; BS in Biology Edn., So. U., 1980, BS in Chemistry Edn., 1983; MA in Hosp. Adminstrn., Southwest U., La., 1986; PhD in Hosp. Adminstrn., Southwest U., 1987; cert., Charity Hosp. Sch. Nuclear Med, 1986; PhD in Pub. Health, Columbia State U., La., 1992; PhD in Health Adminstrn., Kennedy-Western U., 1993; PhD in Environ. Engring., Kensington U., Glendale, Calif., 1994; PhD in Electrophysiology, Summit U., New Orleans, 1995. Med. technologist, med. technologist supr. Charity Hosp., New Orleans, 1969-95, retired, 1995; mem. faculty Pacific Western U., 1993—, Kensington U.; rsch. scientist La. State U. Med. Ctr., New Orleans, 1999. Mem. faculty Tulane U. Pub. Health and Tropical Med. Sch., 1975-81, Kensington Univ., Glendale, Calif., 1996—; rsch. scientist Tech. La. State U.

Med. Sch., New Oreleans. Author 7 books, including A Primer in Electrocardiography with Technical and Some Evaluative Values, 1991, 2d edit., 1995, Electrocardiography, Theories, Applications and Practice, 1997; also articles. V.p. Friends of Amistad Rsch., Tulane U.; mem. U.S. Trade Adv. Bd., 1996. Recipient Outstanding Svc. award Charity Hosp., 1972, acknowledgement letter Nobel Found., 1992, cert. of acknowledgement Coll. Am. Pathologists, 1981, Am. Ex-mem. Assn. Profl. Cons.; candidate Pulitzer Prize, 1995. Mem. Am. Med. Technologists, Am. Coll. Healthcare Execs. (cert. of acknowledgment) , La. Environ. Health Assn. Methodist. Achievements include over 30 copyrights in the field of electrophysiology in Library of Congress; discovered the sigma wave in electracardiography, the electrical alternan theory, the intracerebral-intracranial theories; patentee in field, 1 registered U.S. Dept. Commerce. Home: 5131 Bundy Rd PO Box 8536 New Orleans LA 70182-8536

OLIVER, SAMUEL WILLIAM, JR. lawyer; b. Birmingham, Ala., Apr. 18, 1935; s. Samuel William and Sarah C. Oliver; m. Anne Holman Marshall, Aug. 26, 1961; children: Sarah Bradley Oliver Crow, Samuel William III, Margaret Nelson Oliver Little. BS, U. Ala., 1959, JD, 1962. Bar: Ala. 1962, U.S. Dist. Ct. (no. dist.) Ala. 1963. Law clk. Supreme Ct. Ala., Montgomery, 1962-63, U.S. Dist. Ct. (no. dist.) Ala., Birmingham, 1963; assoc. Burr & Forman, 1964-65, ptnr., 1966—, also chmn. bus./corp. law sect., 1990-93. Dir. Metalplate Galvanizing Inc., Birmingham; mem. panel arbitrators commercial Am. Arbitration Assn., Atlanta, 1981-99. Chmn. bd. govs. The Relay House, Birmingham, 1985-89; mem. Leadership Birmingham, 1990; bd. dirs. Jr. Achievement Greater Birmingham, Inc., 1975—; mem. diocese coun. Episcopal Diocese Ala., Birmingham, 1981-85; chmn. bd. trustees Highlands Day Sch. Found., Inc., Birmingham, 1980-81; bd. dirs. Ala. Kidney Found., Birmingham, 1990-94, hon. mem., 1995—. With U.S. Army, 1956-58. Mem. ABA (bus. law sect. 1965—, negotiated acquisitions com. 1990—, task force on joint venture and asset purchase agreements 1994—, corp. counsel com.), Internat. Bar Assn. (corp. law sect.), Southeastern Corp. Law Inst. (planning com. 1996—), Birmingham Bar Assn., Ala. Bar Assn., Summit Club (bd. govs., founding mem.), Monday Morning Quarterback Club, Rotary Club, Venture Club, Newcomen Soc. U.S. Episcopalian.

OLIVER, SANDRA, art dealer, painter; b. Bronxville, N.Y., Apr. 2, 1941; d. Clarence Charles and Mary Bell E. (McTeique) Simoni; m. Paul Alan Williams, May 2, 1982; children: John Mortimer Wilson, Melissa Anne Wilson, PHilip Keith Wilson. BA, BFA, Marymount Coll., 1963. Art and art history tchr. N.Y.C. Sch. System, 1963-65; art tchr. Diocese Cath. Sch., Westchester, N.Y., 1963-65; comml. artist rep. Weston, Conn., 1979-84; pres. Sandi Oliver, 1984—. Author catalog: American Impressionist Paul Williams: His Garden and His Oil Paintings, 1994. Recipient 1st prize Christmas Show, Pelham (N.Y.) C. of C., 1960, Bravo award, Revlon Corp., 1980, 1st prize, Braswell Galleries, 1998, honors, Westport Art Show, 2001, award, The Westport Downtown Merchants Assn., 2002, auction record (paintings), 1988—2001. Mem. New Eng. Appraisers Assn., Allied Arts Am. Inc., Am. Fedn. Artists, Nat. Mus. Women in Arts (charter mem.). Avocations: oil painting, antique collecting, gardening, walking, raising dogs. Home: 11 Tubbs Spring Dr PO Box 1203 Weston CT 06883-0203 Office: Sandi Oliver PO Box 1203 Weston CT 06883-0203 E-mail: sandioliver@aol.com.

OLIVER, SHEILA Y. county official; b. Newark, July 14, 1952; d. Charles Clay Sr. and Jennie Belle Oliver. BA cum laude, Lincoln U., Pa., 1974; MS, Columbia U., 1976. Dir. coop. edn. Lincoln U., 1976-78; dir. Office of Youth Svcs. City of Newark, 1978-80; exec. dir. The Leaguers, Inc., 1980-87; devel. dir. Newark Literacy Campaign, 1987-89; coord. career guidance Caldwell (N.J.) Coll., 1987-88; dir. Essex County Divsn. Cmty. Action, Newark, 1987-91; pres., CEO The Urban Ctr. for Pub./Pvt. Partnerships, East Orange, 1991—2000; asst. county adminstr., county freeholder Essex County, 2000—. Spl. asst. to the exec. dir. Tri-City Peoples Corp., Newark, 1991-2000. Mem. State Dem. Com., N.J., 1994-96; mem. East Orange Women's Commn., 1990-98; pres. East Orange Bd. Edn., 1994-2000; candidate for mayor City of East Orange, 1996. Named Minority Achiever, Blue Cross/Blue Shield and YM-YWCA N.J., 1990; named to Outstanding Young Women in Am., 1983. Avocations: the arts, politics, crafts, writing. Home: Crescent Park # 9M 320 S Harrison St East Orange NJ 07018-1309 Office: Essex County Hall of Records 465 MLK Blvd Rm 510 Newark NJ 07102

OLIVER, SOLOMON, JR. judge; b. Bessemer, Ala., July 20, 1947; s. Solomon Sr. and Willie Lee (Davis) O.; married; 2 children. BA, Coll. of Wooster, 1969; JD, NYU, 1972; MA, Case Western Res. U., 1974. Bar: Ohio 1973, U.S. Dist. Ct. (no. dist.) Ohio 1977, U.S. Ct. Appeals (6th cir.) 1977, U.S. Supreme Ct. 1980. Asst. prof. dept. polit. sci. Coll. of Wooster, Ohio, 1972-75; sr. law clk. to Hon. William H. Hastie U.S. Ct. Appeals (3d cir.), Phila., 1975-76; asst. U.S. atty. U.S. Atty.'s Office, Cleve., 1976-82, chief civil divsn., 1978-82; spl. asst. U.S. atty., chief appellate divsn. Dept. Justice, 1982, spl. asst. U.S. atty., 1982-85; prof. law Cleve. State U., 1982-94, assoc. dean faculty and adminstrn., 1991-94. Lectr. in law, trial practice Case Western Res. U., Cleve., 1979-82; vis. scholar Stanford U. Coll. Law, 1987; vis. prof. Comenius U., Bratislava, Czechoslovakia, 1991, Charles U., Prague, Czechoslovakia, 1991. Chair O.K. Hoover Scholarship com. Bapt. Ch., 1987-89; trustee Coll. of Wooster, Ohio, 1991-97, 2000—. Mem. ABA, Nat. Bar Assn. Office: 801 W Superior Ave Cleveland OH 44113-1838 Fax: 216-357-7176.

OLIVER, THORNAL GOODLOE, health care executive; b. Memphis, Aug. 26, 1934; s. John Oliver and Evelyn Doris (Goodloe) Mitchell; m. Pauline Reid, Oct. 1, 1959. B.S., Tenn. State U., Nashville, 1956; M.H.A., Washington U., St. Louis, 1973. Cert. nursing home adminstr., Mo. Asst. dir., King Meml. Hosp., Kansas City, Mo., 1973-75; evening mgr. Truman Med. Ctr., Kansas City, Mo., 1975-77; asst. adminstr. Mid-Am. Radiation Ctr. U. Kans. Coll. Health Sci., Kansas City, Kans., 1977-81; dir. CHS, Inc., Leawood, Kans., 1981-82; adminstr. Poplar Bluff Hosp., Mo., 1982-83; adminstr. The Benjamin F. Lee Health Ctr., Wilberforce, Ohio, 1983-86; asst. clin. prof. Dept. Community Medicine, Wright State U., Dayton, 1986-89; asst. patent adminstr. Munson Army Hosp., Ft. Leavenworth, Kans., 1987—; cons. Urban Health Assocs., Nashville, 1986-87, others. Contbr. articles to profl. jours. Served with U.S. Army, 1957-59, USAR, 1959-63. Fellow Am. Coll. Hosp. Adminstrs.; mem. Am. Hosp. Assn., Nat. Assn. Health Services Execs., Am. Med. Record Assn., Mo. League of Nursing Home Adminstrs. Home: 10641 N Grand Ave Kansas City MO 64155-1655 Office: Munson Army Hosp Fort Leavenworth KS 66027

OLIVER, WILLIAM ALBERT, JR. paleontologist, researcher; b. Columbus, Ohio, June 26, 1926; s. William Albert and Mary-Maud (Thompson) O.; m. Johanna L. Kramer, Sept. 1, 1948 (dec.); children: Robert A., James A. BS, U. Ill., 1948; MA, Cornell U., 1950, PhD, 1952. From instr. to asst. prof. geology Brown U., Providence, 1952-57; research geologist-paleontology U.S. Geol. Survey, Washington, 1957-93, emeritus scientist, 1993—; rsch. assoc. dept. paleobiology U.S. Nat. Mus. Natural History-Smithsonian Instn., 1967—; mem. U.S. Nat. Com. on Geology, 1975-79, chmn., 1978-79; U.S. rep. Internat. Subcommn. on Devonian Stratigraphy, 1973-92; chmn., 1984-89. Contbr. articles to profl. jours. Recipient Meritorious Svc. award Interior Dept., 1993. Fellow AAAS (coun. 1971-73), Geol. Soc. Am.; mem. Paleontol. Soc. (councilor 1964-69, 73-76, editor Jour. 1964-69, pres. 1974-75), Palaeontol. Assn. (London), Palaeontol. Rsch. Inst. (trustee 1976-89, pres. 1984-86, Harris award, 1994), Am. Geol. Inst. (dir. 1974-77, v.p. 1975-76, pres. 1976-77), Internat. Assn. for Study of Fossil Cnidaria (coun. 1971-88, pres. 1983-88), Internat. Palaeontological Assn. (sec. gen. 1984-89). Home: 4203 McCain Ct Kensington MD 20895-1321 Office: Smithsonian Instn MRC 137 Natural History Bldg #E-305 Washington DC 20560-0001

OLIVER, WILLIAM DONALD, orthodontist; b. Montreal, Dec. 14, 1945; s. Austen William and Margaret Kay (Donald) O. BS in Physics, Mt. Allison U., 1964; DDS, McGill U., 1968; MSD in Orthodontics, U. Pa., 1970. Pres. Orthodontic Enterprises Internat., Geneva, 1973-78; orthodontist Barrington, RI, 1979—94; pvt. practice Everett, Wash., 1993—. Instr. Frankfurt Carolinium, 1972-74; witness Senate Armed Services Com., 1975. Inventor Piezo Electric Bone Healing; contbr. articles to profl. jours. Mem. Olympic Ski Team, Squaw Valley, 1960. Served with USAF, 1970-73. Recipient Carter Meml. award, 1964, M.T. Dohan prize, 1966. Mem. ADA, Can. Assn. Orthodontists, Am. Assn. Orthodontists, European Orthodontic Soc., Can. Dental Assn., Fedn. Internat. d'Automobile (qualified and registered mem.), Royal Ocean Racing Club. Republican. Office: 10812 19th Ave SE Everett WA 98208-5153 E-mail: braces@seanet.com.

OLIVER, WILLIAM JOHN, pediatrician, educator; b. Blackshear, Ga., Mar. 30, 1925; s. John Wesley and Katherine (Schalwig) O.; m. Marguerite Bertoni, May 28, 1949; children: Ralph Scott, Catherine, Susan. Student, Ga. Southwestern Coll., 1942-43, Mercer U., 1943-44; MD cum laude, U. Mich., 1948. Diplomate Am. Bd. Pediatrics (examiner), Subsplty. Bd. Pediatric Nephrology. Intern, resident U. Mich. Med. Center, 1948-53, dir. pediatric labs., 1959-67; pvt. practice medicine specializing in pediatrics Ann Arbor, Mich., 1953—; instr. dept. pediatrics U. Mich., 1953-56, asst. prof., 1956-61, assoc. prof., 1961-65, prof., 1965, chmn. dept. pediatrics, 1967-79; chief pediatric service Wayne County Hosp., 1958-61. Co-chmn. task force on recent advances of coordinating com. on continuing edn. and recertification Am. Bd. Pediats. and Am. Acad. Pediats., 1977-80; mem. task force for pediatric rev. edn. program, 1980-88; mem. com. program for renewal certification in pediat. Am. Bd. Pediat., 1989-91, mem. exam writing com. for cert. pediatric nephrology, 1989-93, PRCP pilot test com., 1993-96; mem. rev. and question writing com. for Pediat. in Rev. Am. Acad. Pediat., 1991-97; cons. U. Riyadh, Saudi Arabia, 1980, Rsch. Rev. Com. on Pediat., 1989; ednl. cons. dept. pediat. Stanford U. Hosps., 1991-98; mem. self-assessment program for Pediat. in Rev., 1990-98; investigator adaptation primitive So. Ams. Indians, 1976—, African Pygmies, 1987—, worldwide primitive socs., 1997. Author: Primitive Peoples Without Salt, 1998; mem. editl. bd. IRCS Jour. Med. Sci., 1975-90. Pres. Mich. Kidney Disease Found., 1969, Washtenaw County br. Mich. Childrens Aid Soc., 1964; trustee Ann Arbor Hands-On Mus., 1983-88; pres. bd. trustees Perry Nursery Sch., Ann Arbor, 1989-90. With USNR, 1950-52. Fellow Am. Acad. Pediatrics (chmn. com. med. edn. 1974-80, chmn. council on pediatric edn. 1975-80, chmn. task force oversight of pediatric rev. and edn. program 1984-88, Clifford G. Grulee award 1979); mem. Soc. Pediatric Research, Midwest Soc. Pediatric Research (pres. 1968), Am. Soc. Nephrology, Assn. Med. Sch. Pediatric Dept. Chairmen (mem. council 1977-79), Soc. for Exptl. Biology and Medicine, Am. Pediatric Soc., Alpha Omega Alpha, Gamma Sigma Epsilon. Home: 2892 Bay Ridge Dr Ann Arbor MI 48103-1704

OLIVER, WILLIAM LANGDON, brokerage office executive; b. Savannah, Ga., June 9, 1954; s. Robert Lee and Martha (Farr) O.; m. Mary Claudette McCord, Oct. 10, 1987. BS, Vanderbilt U., 1976; MBA, Emory U., 1978. CFA. Officer Ga. R.R. Bank & Trust Co., Augusta, 1978-82; asst. v.p. Barnett Bank of Jacksonville (Fla.) N.A., 1982-83; valuation cons. Valuation Counselors, Inc., Atlanta, 1983-87; v.p. Equitable Securities Corp., Nashville, 1987-95; pres. Gulfstream Advisors LLC, 1995—; dir. rsch. Edgar M. Norris & Co., Inc., Greenville, S.C., 1995—. Mem. Nashville Soc. Fin. Analysts (sec.), Hillwood Country Club. Avocations: sports, reading, golf, soccer, travel. Home: 59 Stonehaven Dr Greenville SC 29607-3017

OLIVERI, EUGENE ALFRED, gastroenterologist; b. N.Y.C., Apr. 30, 1937; children: Gregory, Lisa, Michelle. Student, Bklyn. Coll., 1954-56, 58-60; DO summa cum laude, Kansas City Coll., 1964; LHD, U. Health Scis., 2000. Diplomate Am. Bd. Internal Medicine, Am. Bd. Gastroenterology. Intern Detroit Osteo. Hosp., 1964-65; resident in internal medicine Botsford/Ziegler Hosps., 1965-67; fellowship in gastroenterology VA Hosp., East Orange, N.J., 1967-68. Sr. mem. dept. internal medicine sect. of gastroenterology Botsford Gen. Hosp., assoc. program dir. gastroenterology residency emeritus; mem., courtesy staff emeritus dept. of internal medicine Huron Valley Hosp. With U.S. Army, 1956-58. Recipient Highest Acad. Achievement award Mead-Johnson, 1964, Outstanding Alumni Achievement award U. for Health Scis., Coll. Osteo. Medicine, 1991, Dr. J.O. Watson Disting. Lecr. Ohio Osteo. Assn., 1991, Walter Patenge medal for humanitarian svc. MSU, 1999; named Physician of Yr. Mich. chpt. Ileitis and Colitis Found., 1985, Botsford Profl. Staff, 1994. Fellow Am. Coll. Gastroenterology; mem. Am. Osteo. Assn. (pres. 1999-2000, trustee mem. bd., chair dept. of governmental affairs), Mich. Assn. Osteo. Physician and Surgeons (pres. 1991-92), Oakland County Osteo. Assn., Am. Coll. Osteo. Internists (pres. 1982-83, Disting. Svc. award 1982, Disting. Lectr. award 1983), Am. Coll. Gastroenterology, Am. Soc. Gastrointestinal Endoscopy, Am. Soc. Addiction Medicine, Am. Osteo. Found. (bd. dirs., chair bd. dirs., chair com. on awards), Am. Soc. Parenteral and Enteral Nutrition, Mich. Osteo. Coll. Found. (trustee, bd. dirs.), Crohn's and Colitis Found. Am. (Physician of Yr. 1991), Psi Sigma Alpha, Sigma Sigma Phi. Avocations: chef, health policy wonk. Home: 844 Old Milford Farms Milford MI 48381-3363 E-mail: docoli@aol.com.

OLIVERI, ROBERT PETER, retired social worker; b. Oct. 1, 1942; s. Ben and Lena (La Valle) O.; m. Anne Dullberg, June 23, 1973; children: Christopher Robert, Kenneth Mathew. BA, Adelphi U., 1965; MSW, SUNY, Albany, 1970; EdD, Nova Southeastern U., 1999. Cert. social worker, N.Y. Comty. orgn. specialist Suffolk County Dept. Social Svc., Hauppage, N.Y., 1966-97. Adj. asst. prof. sociology Dowling Coll., Oakdale, N.Y., 1999; dir. Dataflo Computer Services, Inc., Enfield, N.H., 1987, 88, also bd. dirs.; div. dir. Fgn. Lang. Ednl. Software Div., 1986-92; mem. adv. bd. on Decentralization of Social Services in Suffolk County, 1973-74; co-designer award winning programs for Nat. Assn. Counties, 1984, 89; co-author research study on social service delivery. Co-founder Foster Parents Adv. Coun. of Suffolk, 1972, Ind. Study Group, 1972. With U.S. Army, 1965. Recipient Ednl. Leave award Suffolk County Dept. Social Svcs., 1969, 70. Mem. NASW (v.p., bd. dirs. Suffolk County chpt. 1972-74, field rep.), Acad. Cert. Social Workers. Home: PO Box 642 Eastport NY 11941-0642 E-mail: bobo325@aol.com.

OLIVER-SIMON, GLORIA CRAIG, human resources advisor, consultant, lawyer; b. Chester, Pa., Sept. 19, 1947; d. Jesse Harper and Lavinia Craig Cuff; m. James Russell Norwood, Sept. 1970 (div.); 1 child, James Russell Jr.; m. Joseph M. Simon, Jan. 1993. BS, U. Md., 1987; JD, Am. U., 1990, MS, 1992. Bar: Pa. 1991, U.S. Ct. Appeals (fed. cir.) 1994, D.C. 1997. Pers. specialist VA Med. Ctr., Phila., 1974-80; pers./human resources specialist VA Ctrl. Office, Washington, 1980-90, human resources mgr., 1990-97; atty./adviser human resource mgmt./sr. human resources cons. VACO. Mem. VA Work Group on Minority Initiatives, 1990, 93—; VA coord., rep. Coun. for Excellence in Govts. Spkrs. Bur. Project, 1991-92, Pub. Employees Roundtable for Pub. Svc. Recognition Week, 1991-92; subcom. chair Student Employee Programs, Office of Pers. Mgmt. Work Group, 1993; coord. VA Caring and Courtesy Campaign Focus Group, 1993; mem. VA Veterans Health Adminstrn. Nursing Shortage Task Group, 1987, 93, VA Work Group on the Nat. and Cmty. Svc. Program, 1993-94, 95-96, Veterans Health Adminstrn. Healthcare Reform Work Group on Customer Svc., 1993-94; VA's Nat. Com. on Employment of Disabled Vets. and People with Disabilities, 1992-93; VA Office Human Resources Mgmt. coord. Pres.'s Com. on Employment of Persons with Disabilities/Dept. of Def. Student Employment Initiative, 1994-95; VA Office of Human Resources Mgmt. steering com. 1994-96; mem. Dept. of Energy Student Employment Task Group, 1994-96; VACO coord. Welfare to Work Initiative, 1997—; VACO coun. mem. VA Early Mediation Program, 1999—; mem. VACO Workgroup on Position Sensitivity and Suitability Adjudication, 1999—; mentor VA VACO Fed. Women's Program, 1999—. Bd. dirs. So. PG County Cmty. Charities, Inc., 1999—, pres., CEO, 2000. Mem. ABA, Fed. Bar Assn., Nat. Bar Assn., Fed. Cir. Bar Assn., D.C. Bar Assn., Bar Assn. of D.C., Phi Delta Phi, U. Md. Alumni Assn. (mentor program), Am. U. Alumni Assn. (admissions com., mentor program for grad. and law students), Leadership VA Alumni Assn. (chair promotions com. 1997-2000), AKA Sorority Inc., DAV Aux. (fed. unit 1), Zonta Internat., Am. Legion Aux. Avocations: reading, traveling. Home: 809 Braeburn Dr Fort Washington MD 20744-6022 Office: Dept Vets Affairs 810 Vermont Ave NW Washington DC 20420-0001

OLIVER-WARREN, MARY ELIZABETH, retired library science educator; b. Hamlet, N.C., Feb. 23, 1924; d. Washington and Carolyn Belle (Middlebrooks) Terry; m. David Oliver, 1947 (div. 1971); children: Donald D., Carolyn L.; m. Arthur Warren, Sept. 14, 1990 (dec. Feb. 1995). BS, Bluefield State U., 1948; MS, South Conn. State U., 1958; student, U. Conn., 1977. Cert. tchr., adminstr. and supr., Conn.; cert. pub. sch. substitute tchr., K-12, N.J. Media specialist Hartford (Conn.) Pub. Schs., 1952-86; with So. Conn. State U., New Haven, 1972—, asst. prof. Sch. Libr. Sci. and Instructional Tech., 1987-95, ret., 1995; substitute tchr. K-12 Windsor, 1999—. Mem. dept. curriculum com. So. Conn. State U., 1987-95, adj. prof., 1995—; cert. substitute tchr. Somerset County Pub. Schs., 1997—; cert. substitute tchr. Windser, Conn. Sch. Sys., 1999-. Author: My Golden Moments, 1988, The Elementary School Media Center, 1990, Text Book Elementary School Media Center, 1991, I Must Fight Alone, 1991, (textbook) I Must Fight Alone, 1994. Mem. ALA, Conn. Ednl. Media Assn., Black Librs. Network N.J. Inc., Assn. Ret. Tchrs. Conn., Black and Hispanic Consortium, So. Conn. State U. Women's Assn., Cicuso Club (v.p.), Friends Club (v.p.), Delta Kappa Gamma, Alpha Kappa Alpha. Avocations: reading, music, piano, walking. Home: 224 High Path Rd Windsor CT 06095-4103 Office: So Conn State U 501 Crescent St New Haven CT 06515-1330

OLIVET, JOSEPH FRANCIS, retired elementary school educator; b. N.Y.C., Oct. 8, 1945; s. Emil Bernard and Elizabeth Maria (Vivona) Olivet; m. Mildred Cruz LoBello, Dec. 31, 1985; children: Joseph, Yvette. BS, Marist Coll., Poughkeepsie, N.Y., 1968; MS, Herbert H. Lehman Coll., Bronx, 1975; CAS, SUNY, New Paltz, 1993. Cert. in phys. edn. and edn1. adminstrn. N.Y. Tchr. phys. edn., tchr. sci. N.Y.C. Bd. Edn., 1970—2001; ret., 2001. With Shortline Bus. Co., Mahwah, NJ, 1988—.

OLIVET, LINDA WALDROP, nursing educator, consultant, retired; b. Birmingham, Ala., June 1, 1942; d. Jesse Winfield Waldrop and Ruth (Poe) Waldrop Cummings; m. Ronald T. Olivet, June 19, 1965; children: David Wayne, Jeffrey Scott. BSN, U. Ala., Tuscaloosa, 1964, MSN, 1967; DSc in Nursing, U. Ala., Birmingham, 1985. RN, Ala. Instr. U. Hawaii, Honolulu, 1972, Coll. of St. Teresa, Rochester, Minn., 1973-78; head nurse pediat. unit Rochester Meth. Hosp., 1976-78; instr. nursing U. Ala., Birmingham, 1967-69; asst. prof. U. Ala. Capstone Coll. Nursing, Tuscaloosa, 1980-82, 84-86, assoc. prof., 1986-96, prof., 1996-2001, ret., 2001. Part-time staff nurse Univ. Hosp., Birmingham, 1965-69; part-time staff nurse Hospice of West Ala., Tuscaloosa, 1988-91, bd. dirs., sec., 1987-93; cons. Nigerian Christian Hosp., Oncha Ngwa, Nigeria, 1985, Dept. Human Resources, Tuscaloosa, 1996—. Co-author: Fitting It All Together, 1990; contbr. articles to nursing jours., chpts. to book. Tchr., coord. children's edn. Univ. Ch. of Christ, Tuscaloosa, 1980-90; bd. dirs., officer West Ala. chpt. ARC, 1992—. Recipient Outstanding Commitment to Tchg. award U. Ala.-Tuscaloosa Alumni Assn., 1987; named Coun. for Advancement and Support Edn. and Carnegie Ala. Prof. of Yr., 1995. Mem. Assn. for Death Edn. and Counseling (cert. death educator), Ala. Nurses Assn., Ala. League for Nursing, Sigma Theta Tau. Avocations: writing, tennis, travel. E-mail: lolivet@aol.com.

OLIVIER, JASON (JASON THOMAS OLIVIER), lawyer; b. New Orleans; s. Gerald L. and Beverly Olivier; m. Chellie Olivier, 1991. BS in Elec. Engring. Tech., Nicholls State U., Thibodaux, La., 1985; JD, Loyola U., New Orleans, 1990. Bar: La. 1990, U.S. Dist. Ct. (ea., we., and mid. dists.) La. Dir. music Sta. KNSU-FM, Thibodaux, 1984-85; prodn. dir. Sta. WTIX, New Orleans, 1987, 89; owner, pres. Jason T. Olivier, A P.L.C., Metairie, La., 1990-96; ptnr. Deas and Olivier, 1992—. CEO, pres., gen. counsel Interstate Collection Bur., New Orleans, 1993-99; host Hidden Talent Theatre TV Variety Show, Sta. WCOX, 1987; instr. Loyola Law Sch. Computer Ctr., 1988; extern U.S. Ct. Appeals (4th cir.) La. Author poetry; composer songs; vocal arranger, performer album Menagerie; mus. rev. columnist Rockaraound Mag., 1987-88. Pres., chair bd. Northlake Performing Arts Soc. Mem. Am. Collectors Assn., MAP Program (media rels. spokesperson, chmn. La. 1999), La. Bar Assn., Comm. Law Soc. (past v.p.), Federalist Soc., Comml. Law League Am., Tau Kappa Epsilon. Republican. Roman Catholic. Avocations: computers, web site programming, audio engineering, music. Office: PO Box 714 Mandeville LA 70470-0714

OLIVIER, MICHAEL JOSEPH, economic development executive; b. Franklin, La., Oct. 14, 1950; s. Thomas C. Sr. and Dorothy M. (Fournier) O.; m. Penelope Guest, May 20, 1977; children: Mallory E., Emily A. BS, U. Southwestern La., 1972, MS, 1974. Cert. econ. developer. Adminstr. U. Southwestern La., Lafayette, 1974-82; exec. Lafayette (La.) Econ. Devel. Authority, 1982—87; CEO HARCO Devel., Gulfport, Miss., 1987—. Bd. dirs. Pine Burr coun. Boy Scouts Am., 1995—; bd. dirs. Miss. Econ. Devel. Coun., 1991-95. Named one of Top Ten Most Outstanding ED Practitioners in the South, So. Bus. and Devel. Fellow Am. Econ. Devel. Coun. (bd. dirs. 1991-2000); mem. So. Indsl. Devel. Coun. (pres. 1995), Miss. Bus. Fin. Corp. (bd. dirs.), Miss. Enterprise for Tech. (bd. dirs. 1994-95), Gulfport Rotary Club (Paul Harris fellow 1996). Office: HARCO Development 1 Hancock Plz Ste 1105 Gulfport MS 39501-1947 E-mail: molivier@mscoast.org.

OLIVIERI, DONÉY GERARDO, director, educator; b. St. Jago De La Vega, Camaguey, Cuba, Sept. 2, 1956; s. Thomas Groves Bent and Luna Maude Anderson; 1 child Omar Enrique Sánchez. BA, U. D.C., 1978; MA, Am. U., 1980; ednl. specialist, Grambling State and U. D.C., 1997; PhD, Columbus U., 2000. Flight attendant Pan Am. World Airways, N.Y.C., 1979—80; tchr. Anne Arundel Pub. Sch., Annapolis, Md., 1980—81; content specialist D.C. Pub. Schs., Washington, 1985—. Adj. assoc. prof. U. D.C., Washington, 1986—98; spanish tchr. Fairfax County Pub. Schs., Falls Church, 1988—90; adj. lectr. II Howard U., Washington, 1998—2002; director-world language dept. D.C. Pub. Schs., Washington, 2000—02. Recipient Cert. of Completion, Office of Exec. Devel., 1997, cert., Middle States Assn. Colls. and Schs., 1999; fellow, Cafritz Found., 1995, NEH, Dept. Edn., 1997—98. Mem.: Am. Assn. Secondary Prins., Am. Assn. Tchrs. Spanish and Portuguese (recruiter 1997—2002). R-Consevative. Roman Catholic. Avocations: sailing, travel. Home: 1313 28th St SE Washington DC 20020-3602 Office: Howard University 2400 6th St NW Washington DC 20059 Home Fax: 202-581-6626. Personal E-mail: doney@olg.com.

OLIVIERI, JOSÉ ALBERTO, lawyer; b. San Juan, P.R., Aug. 28, 1957; s. José Juan Olivieri and Carmen Rivera; m. Jeanne Nikolai Olivieri, Aug. 12, 1978; children: Elisa, Lucas, Elena. BA in Polit. Sci. cum laude, Carroll Coll., 1978; JD, Marquette U., 1981. Bar: Wis. 1981. Lawyer Michael, Best & Friedrich, Milw., 1981. Asst. prof. law Marquette U., Milw., 1986-88, adj. prof., 1988—; bd. dirs. Firstar Bank, Milw. Articles editor Marquette Law Rev. Chmn. bd. dirs. Milw. Found., 1998; bd. dirs., pres. United Cmty. Ctr., Milw., 1987-92; mem. U. Wis. Bd. Regents, 1998—. Recipient Pro bono award Posner Found., Milw., 1985, Cmty. Svc. award Future Milw., 1987, Vol. Fundraiser award Nat. Assn. Fundraising Execs., 1993, Leadership award Milw. Civic Alliance, 1995; named Hispanic Man of Yr., United Migrant Opportunity Svcs., Milw., 1998. Mem. ABA, Wis. Hispanic Lawyers Assn. (pres. 1984), Wis. State Bar Assn. (chair labor and employment law sect. 1996), Milw. Bar Assn. Avocations: reading, sports. Office: Michael Best & Friedrich 100 E Wisconsin Ave Ste 3300 Milwaukee WI 53202-4108

OLK, FREDERICK JAMES, county official, paralegal; b. Clintonville, Wis., Apr. 30, 1952; s. James Howard and Bernice Helen (Durben) O. Student, Inst. Comp. Polit.& Econ. Sys., 1973; BS in Liberal Arts, U. Wis. River Falls, 1976; cert., Wis. Sch. Real Estate, Milw., 1980. Notary pub., Ill. Libr. asst. U. Wis., Stevens Point and Oshkosh, 1977-80; contract libr. U.S. Dept. Justice, Oxford, Wis., 1980; editl. libr. The Chgo. Cath. newspaper Archdiocese of Chgo., 1980-89; tax. examiner Cook County, Chgo., 1990—. Congl. intern U.S. Ho. of Rep., Washington, 1973; sales rep. Waupaca (Wis.) Pub. Co., 1978-79; freelance paralegal, Chgo., 1988—; security guard, account mgr. Glenbrook Security Svcs., Glenview, Ill., 1988—; asst. reference libr. Cicero (Ill.) Pub. Libr., 1989; genealogy rschr. Lineage Search Assocs., Mechanicsville, Va., 1980-99; v.p. New World Credit Union, Chgo., 1981-86. Columnist Looking back Chgo. Cath., 1985-89. Tutor Mercy Home for Boys, Chgo., 1987—88; coord. Friends of Vatican Libr., 1995—; mem. exec. bd. customer adv. coun. U.S. Postal Svc., Cicero, 1997—; Cicero rep. for Ill. 43d dist. Anti-Crime Adv. Bd., 1999—; precinct capt. Wis. and Ill. Rep. coms., 1973—; Rep. judge of election Cook County, 1980—; mem. Rome tour St. John Cantius Parish Resurrection Choir, 2001, sang at St. Peter's Basilica, 2001. Named adm. Nebr. Navy, State of Nebr., 1982, col. State of Ala., 1988, Internat. Citizen of Yr., Hutt River Province, Australia, 1995; recipient Legion of Merit Rep. Nat. Com., 1997, Order of the Arrow, Boy Scouts Am., 1971. Mem. Am. Soc. Notaries (life, chmn. govt. rels. 1984-85), Nat. Assn. Investigative Specialists, Am. Legion (life), Amtrak Hist. Soc. (asst. archivist 1996—), Chgo. Geneal. Soc. (life, bd. dirs. 1988-90), 20th Century R.R. Club (sec. 1994-98, Century Club 1996, dir. 1998-2000), KC (del. archdiocesan pastoral coun. 1996—). Avocations: rail travel, genealogy, reading, music, stamp collecting. Home: 5550 W 22nd Pl Apt 306 Cicero IL 60804-2769 Office: Cook County Clk 118 N Clark St Ste 434 Chicago IL 60602-1382

OLKINETZKY, SAM, artist, retired museum director and educator; b. N.Y.C., Nov. 22, 1919; s. Isidor and Jennie O.; m. Sammie Lee Sturdevant, Dec. 20, 1959; children: Jov Shan, Tova Shana. BA, Bklyn. Coll., 1942; postgrad., Inst. Fine Arts, N.Y. U., 1946-47. Asst. prof. art and humanities Okla. A&M U., Stillwater, 1947-57; vis. asst. prof. art U. Okla., Norman, 1957-58; assoc. prof. art Mus. of Art, 1959—; dir. Mus. Art U. Okla., Norman, 1959-83. Vis. prof. art and humanities U. Ark., Fayetteville, 1962-63, 67-68, Langston (Okla.) U., 1969-70; art cons. Kerr-McGee Industries, Inc.; advisor State of Okla. Visual Arts; mem. State Art Collection Com.; Mem. Norman Arts and Humanities Council One-man exhbns. include Arts Place II, Okla. Art Ctr., Firehouse Art Ctr., Norman, 1989; other exhbns. include Mus. Non-Objective Art, N.Y.C., Mus. Modern Art, N.Y.C.; 50-yr. Retrospective Exhbn., 1942-92, Norick Art Ctr., Oklahoma City, 1992; represented in permanent collections Philbrook Art Ctr., Tulsa, Okla. Art Ctr., Mus. Art. U. Okla., Philbrook Art Mus., Tulsa, Oklahoma City Mus. of Art. Served with USAAF, 1942-45. Recipient Gov.'s Art award, 1981. Mem. Okla. Museums Assn. (pres. 1978-79), Internat. Council Museums, Mountain-Plains Museums Assn., Am. Assn. Museums, Art Mus. Assn.

OLLAYOS, CLARE M. chiropractor; b. Elgin, Ill., Nov. 18, 1954; d. Robert W. and Margaret Irene (Knight) O.; m. Scott R. Fladland, Feb. 15, 1992. Student, Smith Coll., 1972-74; BS summa cum laude, Boston U., 1977; BS in Human Biology, Nat. Coll. Chiropractic, 1985, D of Chiropractic, 1987. Cert. acupuncturist Nat. Coll. Chiropractic; advanced cert. spine treatment of CAD injuries Rsch. Inst. San Diego; lic. chiropractic physician Ill., Mass. Instr. ballet Lisa Boehm Sch. of the Ballet, Elgin, 1975, 79-84; motor coordination remediation therapist Landmark Sch., Pride's Crossing, Mass., 1979, Summit Sch., Dundee, Ill., 1979-82; pvt. practice Elgin, 1988—. Lectr. in field. Soloist Lisa Boehm Ballet Theatre Nutcracker Ballet, 1970-76. Trustee Elgin C.C., 1995—, vice chmn., 1998—, chmn. bd. trustees, 2001—, cmty. chmn. Art a la Carte for grand opening of Visual and Performing Arts Ctr., 1993—94, mem. 50th Anniversary Task Force, chmn. opening event, 1999; mem., co-chair capital campaign Elgin C.C. Found., 1994—95; mem. Elgin Cultural Arts Commn., 1991—98, chmn., 1993—95, founder, chmn. Recognition Night, 1995—98; chmn. Smithsonian Midwest Region Sculpture Restoration and Preservation Conf., 1997; presenter Midwest Mus. Conf., Chgo., 1993; bd. dirs. Elgin Pub. Mus., 1993—. Named Outstanding Young Woman of Elgin, Elgin Jr. Woman's Club, 1986, Star Vol. of Yr., YWCA, 2001; recipient Margaret Hillis award for the arts, 1989, Elgin Image award, Elgin Image Adv. Commn., 1994, Spl. Recognition award, Elgin Cultural Arts Commn., 1998, Mayor's award for preservation, City of Elgin, 2000. Mem.: Ill. C.C. Coll. Trustees Assn. (govt. rels. com. 1996—, regional vice chmn. 1997—98, awards com. 1998—99, chmn. elect 1999—2000, state awards chmn. 2000, 2001), Assn. Cmty. Coll. Trustees (voting del. 1996—97, presenter), Fox Valley Chiropractic Coun., Ill. Chiropractic Soc., Am. Chiropractic Assn., Altrusa Internat. Avocations: ballet, reading, Egyptology. Home and Office: 1161 Florimond Dr Elgin IL 60123 E-mail: claremollayos@juno.com.

OLLENBURG, GUENTER WILHELM, retired economics educator, tax consultant; b. Berlin, Aug. 29, 1928; s. Wilhelm Friedrich and Wally Charlotte (Copernus) O.; m. Ingrid Leonore Hackel, Mar. 14, 1958; children: Heidrun, Kerstin, Karin, Stefanie. Diploma in econs., Free U. Berlin, 1952, Dr. Rer. Pol., 1960, Habilitation in econs., 1968. Theoretical cons. Enquete Econ. Concentration Dept. for Indsl. Econs., Frankfurt am Main, Germany, 1961-63; tchg. asst. Free U. Berlin, 1953-61, rsch. asst., 1963-68, prof. econs., 1970-84, prof. emeritus, 1984—; tax cons.,self employed Berlin, 1984—. Prin. editor: Economic Growth, Equilibrium and Dynamics, 1979. Mem. Assn. for Econs. and Social Scis. (sec. 1964-66), Royal Econ. Soc., List Assn., Numismatic Assn. Berlin (sec. 1990-93, designer medal for 150th anniversary 1993), Am. Numismatic Soc. Evangelical. Avocations: literature, stamps, medals. Home and Office: Teltower Damm 210 D-14167 Berlin Germany

OLLER, WILLIAM MAXWELL, retired energy company executive, retired naval officer; b. Lancaster, Pa., Apr. 7, 1924; s. John Secrist and Mabel Margaret (Coffman) O.; m. Doris Seitz Greenleaf, June 15, 1946; children: Arthur G., J. Richard. BS, U.S. Naval Acad., 1946; MBA, George Washington U., 1960. Commd. ensign USN, 1946, advanced through grades to rear adm., 1972; svc. in Samoa, Philippines and Italy; exec. officer Naval Supply Ctr., Newport, R.I., 1966-67, Ships Parts Control Ctr., Mechanicsberg, Pa., 1970-72; comdr. Def. Fuel Supply Ctr., Alexandria, Va., 1972-76; comdg. officer Naval Supply Ctr., Norfolk, 1976-77; gen. mgr. corp. supply and distbn. Champlin Petroleum Co., Houston, 1977-79, Ft. Worth, 1979-81; sr. v.p. Petroleum Ops. and Support Svcs., Inc., New Orleans, 1981-82, pres., 1982-84; spl. asst. to pres., CEO Kaneb Svcs., Inc., Houston, 1984-85; exec. v.p. Tex. Ea. Products Pipeline Co., 1986-90. Pres. Am. Leadership Forum, Houston, 1986. Decorated Legion of Merit with gold star, Meritorious Svc. medal with gold star, Joint Svc. Commendation medal. Mem. River Creek Club. Home: 46847 Grissom St Sterling VA 20165-3592

OLLEY, ROBERT EDWARD, economist, educator; b. Vendun, Que., Can., Apr. 16, 1933; s. Edwin Henry and Elizabeth (Reed) O.; m. Shirley Ann Dahl, Jan. 19, 1957; children— Elizabeth Anne, George Steven, Susan Catherine, Maureen Carolyn BA, Carleton U., Can., 1960; MA, Queen's U., Can., 1961, PhD in Econs., 1969. Vis. asst. prof. Queen's U., Kingston, Ont., Can., 1967-68; asst. prof. econs. U. Sask., Saskatoon, Can., 1963-67, 68-69, assoc. prof. Can., 1969-71, 73-75, prof. Can., 1975-93, prof. emeritus Can., 1993—; pres. Gen. Econs. Ltd., 1993—. Dir. rsch. Royal Commn. on Consumer Problems and Inflation, 1967-68; econ. advisor Bell Can., Montreal, Que., 1971-73, 78-79, Can. Telecom. Carriers Assn., 1978-85, Sask. Power Corp., 1980-83; econ. advisor AT&T, 1980-90, Waste Mgmt., Inc., 1990-92, SaskTel, 1989-93; chmn. adv. com. on consumer stds. Stds. Coun. Can., 1992-93; Can. rep. to ISO/COPOLCO, Geneva, 1992-93; bd. dirs. Niagra Hosp. Found., v.p., 1999—; v.p. Niagara-on-the-Lake Hosp. Found., 1999—. Author, editor: Consumer Product Testing, 1979; Consumer Product Testing II, 1981; Consumer Credit in Canada, 1966; Economics of the Public Firm: Regulation, Rates, Costs, Productivity Analysis, 1983, Total Factor Productivity of Canadian Telecommunications, 1984; Consumer Reps. Conf. Procs., 1st-4th, 1982-91. Bd. dirs. Can. Found. for Econ. Edn., 1974-82, Can. Gen. Standards Bd., 1977-81 Recipient Her Magesty The Queen silver Jubilee medal, 1977, Can.'s Jean P Carriere Exptl. Contbr. Vol. Standardization award, 1995. Mem. Royal Econ. History Soc., Royal Econs. Assn., Econ. History Assn., Am. Econ. Assn., Can. Econ. Assn., Consumers Assn. Can. (v.p. 1967-75, chmn. 1975-77), Can. Stds. Assn. (dir., mem. exec. com. 1971-93, vice chmn. 1985-87, chmn. 1987-89, Award of Merit 1995), Consumer's Assn. Found. Can. (v.p. 1989-95), Can. Comms. Rsch. Ctr. (dir. 1992-97), Internat. Telecom. Soc. (bd. dirs. 1986—), Shaw Guild, Niagara Hist. Soc. (bd. dirs. 1997-99). Home and Office: PO Box 1040 374 Queen St Niagara-on-the-Lake ON Canada L0S 1J0 E-mail: olley@niagara.com.

OLLIE, PEARL LYNN, artist, singer, songwriter; b. Highland Park, Mich., Oct. 15, 1953; d. Sam and Estelle Theresa Ollie; m. Christopher John Keyes, Nov. 29, 1975 (div. Nov. 1978); 1 child Shane Michael Fiondella. *Pearl Ollie's son, Shane M. Fiondella, of John Glen High School, graduate 2002, designed a vehicle for "Build Your Dream Vehicle" sponsored by Daimler Chrysler and was chief CEO for the project in a regional competition. His car took first place in design and concept and is now featured at Daimler Chrysler headquarters in Michigan. He has won a scholarship to Laurence Tech College in Michigan and is also interested in designing and engineering in Aeronautics.* Student, Henry Ford C.C., Dearborn, Mich., 1988-89, Soc. Arts and Crafts Coll., 1971-74, Ctr. for Creative Study, 1980-81. Tchr. ceramics Detroit Head Start, Mt. Zion, Mich., 1973; logo designer, platemaker, printer and painter Island Art Ctr., St. Simons Island, Ga., 1976-79; sec., receptionist High Performance Tube Inc., 1976-79; personal legal sec. State Senator Bill Littlefield, 1979; art coord., booking agt. Club Savoy Tivoli, San Francisco, 1979; tchr. art Redmond Hall, Skamokawa, Wash., 1980; artist Hollywood Costumes, Dearborn, 1960-90; account mgr. ins. Dr. Sheryl A. Ollie, Lynn, Mass., 1990; staff artist, acting, costumes Creative Currents, Ferndale, Mich., 1990—; art tchr. Art in Nahant, Mass., 1991-97. Make-up artist Paramount Costumes (was Hollywood Costumes), Dearborn; art tchr. music St. Lukes Montessori Sch., Detroit; artist Mich. Art and Design, Detroit, Dearborn Awnings, Lincoln Park, Mich.; instr. Aups, Provence, France, 1997. Make-up artist TV commls. and shows, movies; commd. portrait artist, illustrator; guest TV program All Star Kids. Co-pres. Nahant PTO, Johnson Sch., 1991-92; tchr. 8th grade religious edn.; vocalist area ch. chorus; choir dir. St. Anselms; vocal instr. Axis Music Musicians Inst.; instr. art, music and drama Hope of Detroit Acad. Roman Catholic. Avocations: paint, sculpting, singing, writing, piano. Office: POP Prodns 16886 Elwell Belleville MI 48111 E-mail: PEARLOLLIE2K@aol.com.

OLLINGER, GEORGE EDWARD, III, lawyer, commodities trader; b. Shuri City, Okinawa, Sept. 5, 1951; came to U.S., 1968; s. George Edward and Yoshiko Marie (Tonaki) O.; m. Bonnie Lee Noblet, Aug. 21, 1977; children: Joseph Bryan, Caitlin Marie. BA cum laude, UCLA, 1973; JD, U. Detroit, 1977. Bar: Fla. 1977, U.S. Dist. Ct. (mid. dist.) Fla. 1985, U.S. dist. Ct. (so. dist.) Fla. 1980, U.S. Ct. Appeals (5th and 11th cirs.), U.S. Tax. Ct. 1981, U.S. Supreme Ct. Clk. Dickinson, Wright et al, West Bloomfield, Mich., 1976-77; assoc. English, McCaughn & O'Bryan, Ft. Lauderdale, Fla., 1977-78; ptnr. Olds & Titone, P.A., 1978; owner Ollinger Law Firm, Melbourne, Ft. Lauderdale, 1978—. Legal rschr. Pima County Legal Aid, Tucson, 1995. Author: Ted Peck, 1989. Recipient Pro bono awrd Brevard County Legal Aid, 1996, others; Regents scholar UCLA, 1971-73. Mem. Fla. Bar. Christian. Avocations: golf, reading, information technology, cultural anthropology, horse breeding. Office: Ollinger Law Firm 100 Rialto Pl Ste 700 Melbourne FL 32901-3072

OLLINGER, W. JAMES, lawyer, director; b. Kittanning, Pa., Apr. 5, 1943; s. William James and Margaret Elizabeth (Reid) Ollinger; m. Susan Louise Gerspacher, Oct. 20, 1979; children: Mary Rebecca, David James. BA, Capital U., Columbus, Ohio, 1966; JD, Case Western Res. U., 1968. Bar: Ohio 1968, US Dist Ct (no dist) Ohio 1971. Ptnr. Baker & Hostetler, Cleve., 1968—. Bd dirs Parts Assocs Inc, Cleveland, Ohio. Mem Bentleyville Village Coun, Ohio, 1990—93; mayor Bentleyville, 1997—99. Mem.: Order of Coif, Phi Delta Phi. Office: Baker & Hostetler 3200 Nat City Ctr 1900 E 9th St Ste 3200 Cleveland OH 44114-3475 E-mail: jollinger@bakerlaw.com.

OLLMAN, BEVTELL, social sciences educator; b. Milw., Apr. 30, 1935; s. Cy and Marion Ollman; m. Paule Yvonne Ollman, Sept. 20, 1959; 1 son, Raoul. BA, U. Wis., 1956, MA, 1957; AB, Oxford (Eng.) U., 1959, MA, 1963, PhD, 1967. Asst. prof. U. W. Indies, Jamaica, 1963-66; prof. NYU, 1967—; pres. Class Struggle, Inc., N.Y.C., 1978-83. Author: Alienation, 1971, Dialectical Investigations, 1993, How to Take an Exam & Remake the World, 2001. Recipient Charles McCoy Life Achievement award New Polit. Sci. sect. Am. Polit. Sci. Assn., 2001; Fulbright fellow, 1994. Office: NYU Dept Polit Sci Washington Sq New York NY 10003 E-mail: obertell@netscape.net.

OLLWERTHER, WILLIAM RAYMOND, newspaper editor; b. Neptune, N.J., Jan. 1, 1950; S. William Frederick and Daphne Marie (Hawkins) O.; m. Arlene Judith Newman; children: Geoffrey Vaughan, Alyssa Irene. BA, Princeton U., 1971; MS, Northwestern U., 1972. Reporter Asbury Park (N.J.) Press, 1972-76, bur. chief, 1977-78, night suburban editor, 1979-82, from asst. to editor to asst. mng. editor, 1982-87; exec. editor Asbury Park (N. J.) Press, Neptune, 1988—, v.p. news, 1994-99, exec. v.p. news, 1999—. Adj. prof. Rutgers U., New Brunswick, N.J., 1988; bd. trustees Daily Princeton Pub. Co., 1996—. Editor: The Shore Catch, 1987. Commr. Ocean County Cultural & Heritage Commn., Toms River, N.J., 1977-78. Mem. Am. Soc. Newspaper Editors. Unitarian Universalist. Office: Asbury Park Press PO Box 1550 3601 Highway 66 Neptune NJ 07754-1551*

OLMAN, MARYELLEN, human resources administrator; b. Grand Rapids, Mich., Dec. 24, 1946; d. Norman Adolph and Mary Irene (McCarthy) O.; m. Richard Isaac Fine, Nov. 25, 1982; 1 child, Victoria Elizabeth. BA in Cmty. Svc., Mich. State U., 1968. Legis. rschr. to Hon. Gerald R. Ford, U.S. Ho. of Reps., 1969-71, spl. asst. to Hon. Jack F. Kemp, 1971-74; personnel analyst L.A. City Housing Authority, 1975-78; profl. placement rep. Gen. Telephone of Calif., Santa Monica, 1978-81, mgmt. staffing adminstr., 1981-84; human resource adminstr. Law Offices Richard I. Fine & Assocs., 1985—. Mem. Founders Cir., L.A. Music Ctr., L.A. World Affairs Coun., Chmn.'s Cir., L.A. Art Mus., Mus. Contemporary Art. Republican. Home: 12097 Summit Cir Beverly Hills CA 90210-1376

OLMSTEAD, CECIL JAY, lawyer; b. Jacksonville, Fla., Oct. 15, 1920; s. Cecil Jay Sr. and Bessie (Irby) O.; m. Frances Hughes; children: Cecil Jay III, Frank Hughes, Jane Olmstead Murphy, Amy Olmstead Vanecek. BA, U. Ga., 1950, LLB, 1951; Sterling Grad. fellow, Yale Law Sch., 1951-52; LLD (hon.), U. Hull, Eng., 1978. Bar: Ga. 1950, U.S. Supreme Ct 1964, D.C. 1978. Asst. to legal adviser Dept. State, counsel Mut. Security Agy., counsel Hoover Commn. on Orgn. Exec. Br. of Govt., 1952-55; prof. N.Y. U. Sch. Law, 1953-61; dir. Inter-Am. Law Inst., 1958-61, adj. prof. law, 1961-69; atty. Texaco, Inc., N.Y.C., 1961-62, asst. to chmn. bd., 1962-70, v.p., asst. to chmn. bd., 1970, v.p., asst. to pres., 1970-71, v.p., asst. to chief exec. officer, 1971-73, exec. dept., v.p., 1973-80; mem. firm Steptoe & Johnson, Washington, 1980—. Wang Disting. vis. prof. St. Johns U., 1987-90; mem. adv. panel on internat. law to sec. state; adv. com. law of sea State Dept.; also adv. com. transnat. enterprise; U.S. del. UN Com. on Law of Sea, 1972-73; U.S. del. UN Conf. on Law of Sea, 1974-76; Eisenhower lectr. Nat. War Coll., 1973; mem. U.S. del. UN Conf. on Code of Conduct for Transnat. Corps., ann. 1984-90; mem. World Bank's panel of conciliators of the Internat. Ctr. for Settlement of Investment Disputes, 1988-95; vis. fellow All Souls Coll., Oxford U., 1988; vis. scholar Yale Law Sch., 1990-91. With USAF, 1943-46, 8th and 20th Air Forces. ETO, PTO. Recipient Gold medal City of Brussels (Belgium, 1973, Gold medal City of Paris (France), 1984; named Commdr. Brit. Empire (hon.), 1990. Mem. Internat. Law Assn. (pres. Am. br. 1966-73, pres. 1972-75, vice chmn. exec. coun. 1975-86, chmn. exec. coun. 1986-88, patron 1989—), Am. Law Inst. (assoc. reporter Restatement of the Fgn. Rels. Law of the U.S., 1st edit. 1964, advisor 3d edit.), Coun. on Fgn. Rels., Washington Inst. Fgn. Affairs, Nat. Fgn. Trade Coun. (dir.), Am. Coun. on Germany (hon. dir.), Coun. on Ocean Law (dir.), Knickerbocker Club, Yale Club, Fairfield County Hunt Club (Westport), Cosmos Club (Washington), Order of Coif, Phi Beta Kappa. Home: 4 Sprucewood Ln Westport CT 06880-4021 Office: 1330 Connecticut Ave NW Washington DC 20036-1704

OLMSTEAD, WILLIAM EDWARD, mathematics educator; b. San Antonio, June 2, 1936; s. William Harold and Gwendolyn (Littlefield) Olmstead; m. Adele Cross, Aug. 14, 1957 (div. 1967); children: William Harold, Randell Edward. BS, Rice U., 1959; MS, Northwestern U., 1962, PhD, 1963. Mem. rsch. staff S.W. Rsch. Inst., San Antonio, 1959—60; Sloan Found. postdoctoral fellow Johns Hopkins, 1963—64; prof. applied math. Northwestern U., Evanston, Ill., 1964—, chmn. dept. engring. scis. and applied math., 1991—93. Vis. mem. Courant Inst. Math. Scis. NYU, 1967—68; faculty visitor U. Coll. London, England, 1973, Calif. Inst. Tech., 1987, 90. Contbr. articles to profl. jours. Named Technol. Inst. Tchr. of Yr., 1980, Charles Deering McCormick prof., 1994—97; recipient Award for Tchg. Excellence, Northwestern Alumni Assn., 1993. Mem.: Am. Contract Bridge League (silver life master), Soc. Indsl. and Applied Math. (editl. bd. jour. 1998—), Am. Phys. Soc., Am. Math. Soc., Am. Acad. Mechanics, Soc. Engring. Sci. (bd. dirs. 1998—2000), John Evans Club, Sigma Tau, Tau Beta Pi, Sigma Xi. Episcopalian. Home: 153 E Laurel Ave #203 Lake Forest IL 60045 Office: Northwestern U Dept Engring Scis And Applie Evanston IL 60208-0001

OLMSTED, AUDREY JUNE, communications educator, department chairman; b. Sioux Falls, S.D., June 5, 1940; d. Leslie Thomas and Dorothy Lucille (Else) Perryman; m. Richard Raymond Olmsted; 1 child, Quenby Anne. BA, U. No. Iowa, 1961, MA, 1963; PhD, Ind. U., 1971. Comm. instr. Boston U., 1964-71, acting chair comm., 1972-73, asst. prof. comm., 1971-74; debate coach R.I. Coll., Providence, 1978-92, asst. prof. comm., 1987—, chmn. dept. of comm., 1999—, internat. student advisor, 1980—. Text editor Prentice-Hall Pub., 1986-88. Recipient Faculty award R.I. Coll. Alumni Assn., 1987. Mem. Nat. Assn. Fgn. Student Advisors, Eastern Comm. Assn., Nat. Comm. Assn. Democrat. Office: RI Coll Dept Comm 600 Mount Pleasant Ave Providence RI 02908-1924

OLMSTED, DAVID JOHN, capital management company executive; b. Kearney, N.J., Aug. 18, 1939; s. Lawrence Joseph and Jane Veronica (Carberry) O.; m. Carole Colacurcio, June 29, 1962 (div. May 1974); children: David John, Kimberly Carole; m. Carol Ann Sunderlin, Oct. 12, 1974; children: Lauren Caryl, Kristy Lynne. BS in Mgmt., Fairleigh Dickinson U., 1968, postgrad., 1968-70. V.p. Midlantic Nat. Bank/Citizens, Englewood, N.J., 1968-77; exec. v.p. Trident Investment Mgmt. Co., Paramus, 1977-82; v.p. Donaldson, Lufkin & Jenrette, N.Y.C., 1982-84; pres. Centurion Capital Mgmt. Co., Nutley, N.J., 1984—. Sec. GT USA, Nutley, 1985—; pres. CCM Comm., Nutley, 1997—, Digital Creek Publ., Inc., 1999—. Chmn. Vincent Meth. Ch. Commn., Nutley, 1982-90; v.p. Nutley Recreation Soccer League, 1980-90, Nutley Recreation Basketball League, 1986-90; head coach Nutley Twp. Girls Softball Team, 1988-90; chmn. Essex coun. Boy Scouts Am., 1989-90. With USMC, 1958-61. Fellow Fin. Analysts Fedn., N.Y.C., 1976; named to United Way Hall of Fame, Newark, 1973, benefactor Boy Scouts Am., Newark, 1990. Mem. Assn. for Investment Mgmt., Paramus C. of C., Nutley Lions Club. Republican. Methodist. Avocations: coin-stamp-baseball card collecting, softball, volleyball, basketball. Home: 1 11th St Jamesburg NJ 08831

OLMSTED, JERAULD LOCKWOOD, telephone company executive; b. Des Moines, Aug. 26, 1938; s. George Hamden and Virginia (Camp) O.; m. Mary Karen Autenrieth, June 20, 1962 (div. Dec. 1986); children: Scott H., Victoria L., Jerauld; m. Gisele A. Child, June 17, 1988. BS, Iowa State U., 1961; MBA, George Washington U., 1979; Cert. mgmt. accountant. Vice-pres. First Nat. Bank of Washington, 1969; v.p., dir. Intermediate Credit Corp., 1969-73, Internat. Gen. Industries, Inc., 1974-79, pres., dir., 1980-82, IB Credit Corp., 1982-85, N.Am. Communications, Inc., Bethesda, Md., 1985—. Sr. v.p., dir. Internat. Bank, 1978-85. Bd. govs. Iowa State U. Found., 1980—; chmn. corporate adv. bd. div. arts and humanities U. Md., 1982—; sec.-treas. George Olmsted Found., 1970— . Served with U.S. Army, 1961-63. Decorated Knight of Malta, Order of St. John Mem. Fin. Execs. Inst., Mensa, Soc. Cincinnati, Beta Alpha Psi., Beta Gamma Sigma Clubs: Metropolitan, City, Georgetown (Washington). Republican. Episcopalian. Home and Office: 7735 Arrowood Ct Bethesda MD 20817-2821

OLMSTED, ROBERT AMSON, civil engineer; b. N.Y.C., Nov. 7, 1924; s. Harold McLain and Sophia (Amson) O.; m. Pauline Weiner, June 25, 1949; children: Elizabeth, Alan, Lawrence. BCE, Cornell U., 1946; MCE, Poly. Inst., Bklyn., 1953. Registered profl. engr., N.Y. Jr. civil engr. Triborough Bridge and Tunnel Authority, N.Y.C., 1946-49; civil engr. Port Authority of N.Y. and N.J., 1949-51; engr. TAMS Engrs., 1951-62; assoc. transp. engr. Office of Transp. State of N.Y., 1962-67; asst. dir. planning Met. Transp. Authority, 1967-89; transp. cons., 1989—. Adj. prof. Poly. Inst. Bklyn., 1966-70, Manhattan Coll., 1975-78, John Jay Coll., 1994. Contbr. articles to profl. jours. Sgt. U.S. Army, 1943-46, PTO. Mem. ASCE (bd. dirs. N.Y. sect. 1974-76, chmn. History and Heritage com. N.Y. sect. 1992—, Thomas Kavanaugh award N.Y. Met. sect. 1985), Inst. Transp. Engrs. (disting.), Am. Planning Assn., Regional Plan Assn., City Club, Transp. Rsch. Bd. (affiliate). Address: 33-04 91st St Jackson Heights NY 11372-1752 E-mail: rbtolmsted@aol.com.

OLMSTED, RUTH MARTIN, educator; b. Albany, N.Y., Oct. 26, 1950; d. Sterling Pitkin and Barbara (Starr) O.; m. Lawrence Daniel Syzdek, Oct. 27, 1990. Student, Oberlin Coll., 1968-69; AB in Lit. and Lang./History and Govt., Wilmington Coll., 1972; MA in Comparative Lit., U. Wis., 1973, PhD in Comparative Lit., 1976. Cert. tchr., Iowa, N.Y. Adj. faculty mem. in sociology Chatfield Coll., St. Martin, Ohio, 1974-75; adj. faculty mem. in writing and phys. edn. Wilmington (Ohio) Coll., 1975-77; adj. faculty mem. in writing, speech and adult basic edn. So. State Coll., Wilmington, 1975-77; asst. prof. English, drama and speech William Penn Coll., Oskaloosa, Iowa, 1977-82; substitute tchr. 10 sch. dists., So. Iowa, 1982-83; instr. in English and humanities Emma Willard Sch., Troy, N.Y., 1983-89; asst. prof. speech Sage Jr. Coll. of Albany, 1989-93; mng. editor assessment Regents Coll./Excelsior Coll., Albany, 1993—, asst. dean for test development, 1999—. Mem. workshops in medieval music-drama NEH, 1979, 81. Editor, desktop music pub. Theatre Wagon, 1994—; editor, translator: (plays) Crown Light Editions: Ordo Prophetarum, 1982, Iconia Sancti Nicolai, 1986. Life mem. Girl Scouts U.S., 1959—; mem. policy, pers. com., ann. meeting and gen. coms. Friends Com. on Nat. Legislation, Washington, 1979—. Ind. Study in Humanities fellow NEH, 1988. Mem. MLA, Nat. Coun. Tchrs. English, Tchrs. and Writers Collaborative, Country Dance and Song Soc. Am., Internat. Boethius Soc., Pokingbrook Morris Dancers (squire, foreman, treas. 1984—). Avocations: music, dance, raising sheep, camping, hiking, swimming. Office: Excelsior Coll Assessment 7 Columbia Cir Albany NY 12203-5159

OLNESS, KAREN NORMA, pediatrics and international health educator; b. Rushford, Minn., Aug. 28, 1936; d. Norman Theodore and Karen Agnes (Gunderson) O.; m. Hakon Daniel Torjesen, 1962. BA, U. Minn., 1958, BS, MD, 1961. Diplomate Am. Bd. Pediatrics, Am. Bd. Med. Hypnosis. Intern Harbor Gen. Hosp., Torrance, Calif.; resident Nat. Children's Hosp. Med. Ctr., Washington; asst. prof. George Washington U., 1970-74; assoc. prof. U. Minn., Mpls., 1974-87; prof. pediat., family medicine and internat. health Case Western Res. U., Cleve., 1987—. Named Outstanding Woman Physician, Minn. Assn. Women Physicians, 1987; recipient Christopherson award Am. Acad. Pediat., 1998, Aldrich award, Am. Acad. Pediat., 1999; named to Cleve. Med. Hall of Fame, 2000. Fellow Am. Acad. Pediat. (chair internat. health sect. 2001), Am. Acad. Family Physicians, Am. Soc. Clin. Hypnosis (pres. 1984-86), Soc. Clin. and Exptl. Hypnosis (pres. 1991-93); mem. Soc. for Behavioral Pediatrics (pres. 1991-92), Northwestern Pediat. Soc. (pres. 1977), Internat. Hypnosis Soc. (pres.-elect 2000). Office: Case Western Res U 11100 Euclid Ave Cleveland OH 44106-1736 E-mail: kno@po.cwru.edu.

OLNEY, JAMES, English language educator; b. Marathon, Iowa, July 12, 1933; s. Norris G. and Doris B. (Hawk) L.; children: Nathan, Marina Gobnait. BA, U. Iowa, 1955; MA, Columbia U., 1958, PhD, 1963. Asst. prof. Drake U., Des Moines, 1963-67; Fulbright lectr. Cuttington Coll., Liberia, 1967-69; prof. English N.C. Central U., Durham, 1970-83; Voorhies prof. English La. State U., Baton Rouge, 1983—. Vis. prof. Northwestern U., 1974, Amherst Coll., 1978-79 Author: Metaphors of Self, 1972, Tell Me Africa, 1973, the Rhizome & the Flower, 1980, The Language(s) of Poetry, 1993, Memory and Narrative, 1998 (Christian Gauss award 1999); editor: Autobiography, 1988; editor So. Rev., 1983—. Fellow NEH, 1975-76, Guggenheim Found., 1980-81, Nat. Humanities Ctr., Research Triangle Park, N.C., 1980-81 Mem. MLA (exec. coun. 1983-87), Am. Acad. Arts & Scis. Office: La State U Southern Review 43 Allen Hall Baton Rouge LA 70803-0001 Home: Apt D 2007 Los Trancos Dr Irvine CA 92612-4009

OLNEY, ROBERT C. diversified products manufacturing executive; b. Bklyn., Aug. 19, 1926; s. Herbert Mason and Martha L. (Otten) O.; m. Wanda G. Olney, July 17, 1948 (dec. 1988); children: Robert C. Jr., Thomas J., Douglas P.; m. Ann Waters Bell, Mar. 14, 1992. BA in Econs., Cornell U., 1946. With Chem. Bank, N.Y.C., 1946-48; various mgmt. positions 3M Co., from 1948; v.p., gen. mgr. 3M-Nat. Adv. Co., Bedford Pk., Ill., 1976-80; chmn., mng. dir. 3M UK plc, Bracknell, Eng., 1980-86; dir. Yale-Valor plc, Chiswick, London, Eng., 1986-91; chmn. Nutone Inc., Cin., 1987-91. Cons. Outdoor Consulting Inc., N.Y.C.; bd. dirs. Honeytree Inc., Mich. Mem. Greenville Country Club, Worshipful Co. of Upholders (London), Royal Automobile Club (London). Avocation: skiing. Home: PO Box 223 Montchanin DE 19710-0223 also: Oatlands Park 32 Lakeside Grange Weybridge Surrey England KT139ZE also: PO Box 1764 Avon CO 81620-1764

OLOFSON, TOM WILLIAM, computer executive; b. Oak Park, Ill., Oct. 10, 1941; s. Ragnar V. and Ingrid E. Olofson; m. Jeanne Hamilton, Aug. 20, 1960; children: Christopher, Scott. Various mgmt. positions Bell Telephone Co. of Pa., Pitts., 1963-67; sales mgr. Xerox Corp., Detroit, 1967-68, nat. account mgr. Rochester, N.Y., 1968, mgr. govt. planning, 1969, mgr. Kansas City (Mo.) br., 1969-74; corp. v.p. health products group Marion Labs., Inc., Kansas City, 1974-78, sr. v.p., mem. Office Pres., 1978-80; exec. v.p., dir. Electronic Realty Assocs., Inc., 1980-83; chmn. bd., CEO Emblem Graphic Sys., Inc., 1983-88, EPIQ Sys., Inc., 1988—. Dir. DemoGraFX, Elinco Internat., Access Industries, Inc., Saztec Internat., Capital Ptnrs. Bd. visitors U. Pitts., Joseph M. Katz Grad. Sch. Bus.; past trustee Barstow Sch.; past chmn. bd. trustees Village United Presbyn. Ch. Mem. Carlton Club (Chgo.), Kansas City Club, Omicron Delta Kappa, Sigma Chi. Republican. Presbyterian. Home: 400 W 49th Ter Kansas City MO 64112-2407 Office: EPIQ Sys Inc 501 Kansas Ave Kansas City KS 66105-1309

OLOGBENLA, ADESOJI OLAPOSI, financial advisor; b. Ile-Ife, Nigeria, Mar. 25, 1958; came to U.S., 1984; s. Adetunji Michael and Victoria (Adunni) O.; m. Olanike Adebimpe, Nov. 1, 1989; children: Adedeji Adedapo, Adedoyin. BS in Acctg., Brescia Coll., Owensboro, Ky., 1986; MBA in Fin., Delta State U., Cleveland, Miss., 1996. Acct. Walters Assocs., Miami, Fla., 1986-88; officer Devcom Mcht. Bank, Lagos, Nigeria, 1989-90; mgr. Chartered Bank, 1990-94; pres. S&N Assocs., Durham, N.C., 1996—. Vol. Bapt. Ch., Miami, 1986-88; mentor N.C. Ctrl. U., Durham, 1996—. Named to Outstanding Young Men of Am., 1987.

O'LOONEY, PATRICIA ANNE, medical program administrator; b. Bridgeport, Conn., Dec. 2, 1954; d. John Joseph and Marjorie Ellen (Curran) O'L. BA in Molecular Biology, Regis Coll., 1976; MS in Biochemistry, George Washington U., 1978, PhD in Biochemistry, 1982. Rsch. asst. biochemistry dept. George Washington Med. Sch., Washington, 1976-82, teaching asst., 1978-81, rsch. assoc., 1982-84, sr. rsch. scientist, 1984-86, asst. prof. medicine and biochemistry, 1986-88; asst. dir. The Nat. Multiple Sclerosis Soc., N.Y.C., 1988-90, assoc. dir. rsch. and med. programs, 1990-91, dir. rsch. and med. programs, 1991—. Vis. lectr. George Washington Med. Sch., 1988—. Author: Lipoprotein Lipase, 1987; contbr. articles to profl. jours. Recipient New Investigator Rsch. award NIH, 1985. Mem. Am. Soc. for Biochemistry and Molecular Biology, N.Y. Acad. Scis., Assn. for Women in Sci., The Mid-Atlantic Lipid Soc., Sigma Xi, Beta Beta Beta. Republican. Roman Catholic. Avocations: tennis, golf. Office: Nat Multiple Sclerosis Soc 733 3rd Ave New York NY 10017-3204 E-mail: patricia.olooney@nmss.org.

O'LOUGHLIN, JOHN KIRBY, retired insurance executive; b. Bklyn., Mar. 31, 1929; s. John Francis and Anne (Kirby) O'L.; m. Janet R. Tag, July 5, 1952; children: Robert K., Steven M., Patricia A., John A. BA in Econs., St. Lawrence U., Canton, N.Y., 1951. State agt. Royal Globe Ins. Group, 1953-58; with Allstate Ins. Co., 1958—, mktg. v.p., group v.p., then exec. v.p., 1972—; pres. Allstate Life Ins. Co., 1977—; chmn. bd. Allstate Ins. Co. and Life Co. Can., 1976—, sr. exec. v.p., chief planning officer, 1980-90; ret. Bd. dirs. all cos. in Allstate Ins. Group and Allstate Enterprises, Inc.; former pres. Allstate Enterprises, Inc.; pres., CEO Royal Link Ventures, Ltd., Pinehurst, N.C. Trustee St. Lawrence U.; bd. trustees, pres. U.S. Marine Corps U. Found., Inc.; bd. dirs. Marine Corps Assn., Am. Ireland Fund, USMC Scholarship Found. Inc., Coun. on Ind. Colls.; past chmn. No. Suburban Chgo. United Way; elder 1st United Presbyn. Ch. Capt. USMCR, 1951-53. Mem. Sales and Mktg. Execs. Internat. (bd. dirs., past chmn., pres.), Whispering Woods Golf Club, Pinehurst Country Club, Lahinch Club, Country Club of N.C., Army-Navy Club, Washington. Office: Royal Links Ventures Ltd PO Box 3579 Pinehurst NC 28374-3579

O'LOUGHLIN, SANDRA S. lawyer; b. Buffalo, Jan. 15, 1942; BA summa cum laude, Rosary Hill Coll., 1973; JD cum laude, U. Buffalo, 1978. Bar: N.Y. 1979. Atty. Hiscock & Barclay, LLP, Buffalo, 1978-79, ptnr., 1990—. Chmn. character and fitness com. appellate divsn. 4th dept. 8th jud. dist. N.Y. Supreme Ct., 1986—; adj. prof. SUNY Law Sch., Buffalo. Note editor Buffalo Law Rev., 1977-78. Mem. Erie County Legis. Task Force Mental Health, 1979-81; mem. adv. bd. Congregation of Sisters of St. Joseph, 1987—. Mem. ABA (bus. law com. on securities), Nat. Assn. Bond Lawyers, Am. Arbitration Assn., N.Y. State Bar Assn. (ethics com. 1984-94, 2000—, vice chmn. 1987-92, unauthorized practice of law com. 1998—), Erie County Bar Assn. (ethics com. 1984-87, chmn. 1987-89, corp. law com. 1984, grievance com. 1993—). Office: Hiscock & Barclay LLP 1100 M&T Ctr 3 Fountain Plaza Buffalo NY 14203-1486

OLSAK, IVAN KAREL, civil engineer; b. Nitra, Czechoslovakia, Apr. 30, 1933; came to the U.S., 1970; s. Innocenc and Jolana (Rutkovska) O.; m. Renata Gabriela Franclova, Sept. 26, 1959; children: Ruth E., Patricia L. Degree in civil and sanitary engring., Slovak Tech. U., 1958. Registered profl. engr., Pa., Fla. Chief engr. Keramoproject, Bratislava, Czechoslovakia, 1961-63; chief of commune hygien Slovak Dept. Health, 1963-68; draftsman Crippen Acres Ltd., Winnipeg, Canada, 1969-71; design engr. Bouguard & Assocs., Harrisburg, Pa., 1971-72; chief dept. engring. Adair & Brady, Inc., West Palm Beach, Fla., 1972-74; profl., engr., ptnr. Weimer & Co., Inc., 1974-75; pvt. practice Olsak & Assocs., 1975—. Rep. Presdl. Task Force, Washington, 1986-96, Nat. Com., Washington, 1989-97, Citizens Against Govt. Waste, Washington, 1988-96; hon. mem. Fla. Sherrif's Assn., 1992—. Recipient Cert. of Appreciation Palm Beach County Bar Assn., 1990, Fla. Assn. State Troopers, 1987. Mem. NSPE, Fla. Engring. Soc., Profl. Engrs. in Pvt. Practice. Roman Catholic. Achievements include research in oil refinery complex, influence of oil on ground water system. Home: 308 Greymon Dr West Palm Beach FL 33405-1922 Office: PO Box 6727 West Palm Beach FL 33405-6727

OLSCHWANG, ALAN PAUL, lawyer; b. Chgo., Jan. 30, 1942; s. Morton James and Ida (Ginsberg) O.; m. Barbara Claire Miller, Aug. 22, 1965; children: Elliot, Deborah, Jeffrey. BS, U. Ill., 1963, JD, 1966. Bar: Ill. 1966, N.Y. 1984, Calif. 1992. Law clk. Ill. Supreme Ct., Bloomington, 1966-67; assoc. Sidley & Austin and predecessor firms, Chgo., 1967-73; with Montgomery Ward & Co. Inc., 1973-81, assoc. gen. counsel, asst. sec., 1979-81; ptnr. Seki, Jarvis & Lynch, 1981-84, dir., mem. exec. com.; dir. Mitsubishi Electric & Electronics USA, Inc. and predecessors, N.Y.C., 1983-91, Cypress, Calif., 1991—. Mem. ABA, Am. Corp. Counsel Assn., Calif. Bar Assn., Ill. Bar Assn., Chgo. Bar Assn., N.Y. State Bar Assn., Bar Assn. of City of N.Y., Am. Arbitration Assn. (panel arbitrators). Office: Mitsubishi Elec & Electronics USA Inc PO Box 6007 5665 Plaza Dr Cypress CA 90630-0007

OLSEN, ALFRED JON, lawyer; b. Phoenix, Oct. 5, 1940; s. William Hans and Vera (Bearden) O.; m. Susan K. Smith, Apr. 15, 1979. BA in History, U. Ariz., 1962; MS in Acctg., Ariz. State U., 1964; JD, Northwestern U., 1966. Bar: Ariz. 1966, Ill. 1966, U.S. Tax Ct. 1970, U.S. Supreme Ct. 1970; C.P.A., Ariz., Ill. cert. tax specialist. Acct. Arthur Young & Co., C.P.A.s, Chgo., 1966-68; dir. firm Ehmann, Olsen & Lane (P.C.), Phoenix, 1969-76; dir. Streich, Lang, Weeks & Cardon (P.C.), 1977-78; v.p. Olsen-Smith, Ltd., 1978—. Chmn. tax adv. commn. Bd. Legal Specialization, 1990-92. Bd. editors: Jour. Agrl. Law and Taxation, 1978-82, Practical Real Estate Lawyer, 1983-95. Mem. Phoenix adv. bd. Salvation Army., 1973-81. Fellow: Am. Coll. Tax Counsel, Am. Coll. Trust and Estate Counsel (state chair); mem.: ABA (chmn. com. on agr., sect. taxation 1976—78, chmn. CLE com. sect. taxation 1982—84), AICPA, Internat. Acad. Estate and Trust Law (exec. coun. 1994—99), Nat. Cattlemen's Assn. (tax com. 1979—88), Am. Law Inst. (life; chmn. tax planning for agr. 1971—82), Ctrl. Ariz. Estate Planning Coun. (pres. 1972—73), State Bar Ariz., Ariz. Soc. CPAs, Phi Beta Kappa, Phi Kappa Phi, Beta Gamma Sigma, Sigma Nu Internat. (pres. 1986—88). Office: 3300 Virginia Fin Pla 301 E Virginia Ave Phoenix AZ 85004-1218

OLSEN, ARTHUR MARTIN, physician, educator; b. Chgo., Aug. 29, 1909; s. Martin I. and Aagot (Rovelstad) O.; m. Yelena Pavlinova, Sept. 16, 1936; children: Margaret Ann (Mrs. Frank A. Jost), David Martin, Karen Yelena (Mrs. Dori Kanellos), Mary Elizabeth. AB, Dartmouth Coll., 1930; MD, U. Chgo., 1935; MS, U. Minn., 1938. Diplomate Am. Bd. Internal Medicine. Intern Cook County Hosp., Chgo., 1935-36; fellow in medicine, resident Mayo Found., U. Minn., 1936-40, from instr. to prof. medicine, 1950-57, prof., 1957—. Cons. medicine Mayo Clinic, Rochester, Minn., 1940-76, chmn. divsn. thoracic diseases, 1968-71. Author numerous publs. on diseases of the lungs and esophagus. Mem. nat. heart and lung adv. coun. NIH, 1970-71; trustee Mayo Found., 1961-68, mem. subsplty. bd. pulmonary diseases, 1958—, chmn., 1961-63. Recipient Alexander B. Vishnevski medal Inst. Surgery, Moscow, 1966, Andres Bello medal Govt. of Venezuela, 1987, Disting. Alumnus award Rush Med. Coll., U. Chgo., 1989. Fellow ACP, Am. Coll. Chest Physicians (master, regent 1955—, chmn. 1959-66, pres. 1970, Disting. Fellow award 1978, dir. internat. activities 1976-83, cons. internat. activities 1983-85); mem. AMA (Billings gold meadl for exhibit on esophagitis 1955), Am. Soc. Gastrointestinal Endoscopy (pres. 1962-63), Minn. Respiratory Health Assn. (pres. 1964-68), Minn. Med. Assn., Am. Assn. Thoracic Surgery, Am. Thoracic Soc., Minn. Thoracic Soc. (pres. 1952), Am. Bronchoesophagol. Assn. (pres. 1969-70, Chevalier Jackson award 1973), Internat. Bronchoesophagol. Soc. (pres. 1979-81), Minn. Soc. Internal Medicine, Brit. Thoracic Soc. (hon.), Nat. Acad. Medicine of Buenos Aires (hon.), Portuguese Soc. Respiratory Pathology (corr.), Sigma Xi., Alpha Omega Alpha. Episcopalian. Home: 211 2nd St NW ALC #3-304 Rochester MN 55901

OLSEN, CLIFFORD WAYNE, retired physical chemist, consultant; b. Placerville, Calif., Jan. 15, 1936; s. Christian William and Elsie May (Bishop) O.; m. Margaret Clara Gobel, June 16, 1962 (div. 1986), remarried, Mar. 4, 2000; children: Anne K. Olsen Cordes Bothe, Charlotte Marie; m. Nancy Mayhew Kruger, July 21, 1990 (div. 1993). AA, Grant Tech. Coll., Sacramento, 1955; BA, U. Calif.-Davis, 1957, PhD, 1962. Physicist, project leader, program leader, task leader Lawrence Livermore Nat. Lab., Calif., 1962-93; ret., 1993; lab. assoc., 1993-95, 96—; cons. Holmes & Narver, 1995, Keystone Internat., 1996—, Am. Techs. Inc., 1997, Profl. Analysis, Inc., 1997-99. Mem. Containment Evaluation Panel, U.S. Dept. Energy, 1984—, mem. Cadre for Joint Nuclear Verification Tests, 1988; organizer, editor procs. for 2nd through 7th Symposiums on Containment of Underground Nuclear Detonations, 1983-93. Contbr. articles to profl. jours. Mem. bd. convocators Calif. Luth. U., 1976-78. Recipient Chevalier Degree, Order of DeMolay, 1953, Eagle Scout, 1952. Mem. AAAS, Am. Radio Relay League, Seismol. Soc. Am., Livermore Amateur Radio Klub (pres. 1994-96), Sigma Xi, Alpha Gamma Sigma (life), Gamma Alpha (U. Calif.-Davis chpt. pres. 1960-61). Democrat. Lutheran. Avocations: photography, amateur radio, music, cooking.

OLSEN, DAVID ALEXANDER, insurance executive; b. Bklyn., Nov. 29, 1937; s. Alexander and Meile (Anderson) O.; m. Roberta Ruth Garverick, May 11, 1963; children: Bradford, Amy. BA, Bowdoin Coll., 1959. With marine dept. Gt. Am. Ins. Co., N.Y.C. and Chgo., 1959-62; acct. exec. Johnson & Higgins, San Francisco, 1966-71, v.p., mgr. marine dept. Chgo., 1971-78, exec. v.p. Ill. br., 1978-79, br. mgr., exec. v.p. Houston, 1979-80, chmn., bd. dirs. Tex. br., 1980-85, exec. v.p. N.Y.C., 1985-87, pres., COO, 1987-93, CEO, 1990-97, chmn., 1991-98; dir. Marsh & McLennan, 1998—. Bd. dirs. U.S. Trust Corp. Bd. trustees Bowdoin Coll., Brunswick, Maine; trustee S. Street Seaport Mus., Salisburg (Conn.) Congrl. Ch., Salisbury Vol. Ambulence Svc.; vice chmn. Sharon (Conn.) Hosp . 1st lt. U.S. Army, 1960-62. Mem. India House (bd. dirs.), River Club, Sharon Country Club, Psi Upsilan. Republican. Avocations: art, photography, antiques, scuba diving, tennis, skiing. Office: J&H Marsh & McLennan 1166 Avenue Of The Americas New York NY 10036-2708

OLSEN, DAVID K. engineer, chemist, consultant; b. Leadville, Colo., Oct. 9, 1949; s. Kenneth R. and Catherine J. Olsen; m. Lois J. Bungo. BS in Chemistry, Colo. State U., 1971; MS, Idaho State U., 1973; DA in Chemistry, U. No. Colo., 1981. Registered environ. assessor, Calif. Prof. Colo. Northwestern C.C., Rangely, 1976-80; rsch. assoc. Getty Oil Rsch., Houston, 1980-84; sr. rsch. chemist, project leader Ill. Inst. Tech. Rsch. Inst., Bartlesville, Okla., 1984-94; sr. rsch. chemist Nat. Inst. for Petroleum and Energy Rsch., 1984-94; prin. engr. contract mgmt. BDM-Okla./Nat. Inst. for Petroleum and Energy Rsch., 1994-97; dir. UN Inst. for Tng. and Rsch. Centre for Heavy Crude and Tar Sands, Tulsa, 1996-98; dir. Internat. Centre for Heavy Hydrocarbons, 1999—; sci. advisor to U.S. Dept. Energy RMC Cons., Inc., 2000—. Author 3 books. Boetcher grad. fellow, 1973-75. Mem. Soc. Petroleum Engrs., Am. Chem. Soc. (petroleum divsn.), Am. Assn. Petroleum Geologists, Can. Inst. for Mining, Metalurgy and Petroleum, Sigma Xi. Achievements include patents in field. Office: Internat Ctr for Heavy Hydrocarbons 1 West 3d St Ste 1400 Tulsa OK 74103-3519

OLSEN, DAVID LESLIE, author, consultant; b. Berkeley, Calif., Dec. 13, 1943; s. Herbert Leroy and Eugenia Petrovna (Mjedloff) O.; m. Barbara Gail Schonborn, Mar. 17, 1985; children: Gregory Todd, Jeanine Lynne. BA in Chemistry, U. Calif., Berkeley, 1965; MBA in Mgmt., Golden Gate U., 1983; MA in English, Creative Writing, San Francisco State U., 1987. Cert. instr. cmty. coll. in bus., indsl. mgmt., mktg. and distbn., lang. arts and lit. With Shell Oil Co., various locations, 1965-76; mgr. energy mkts. SRI Internat., Menlo Park, Calif., 1976-83; project mgr., cons. Pacific Gas & Electric Co., San Francisco, 1983-86; sr. staff tech. writer/editor LSI Logic Corp., Milpitas, 1987-89; cons. dir. Schonborn Assocs., Westford, Mass., 1989—; editl. page columnist, drama critic Cmty. Newspaper Co., 1998—; On-line econ. analyst StockHouse, RagingBull, Yahoo, Arborwood, 1998—. Lectr. mktg. Golden Gate U., Mountain View, Calif., 1986-87; instr. English DeAnza Coll., Cupertino, Calif., 1987; book reviewer Title Pages, Palo Alto, 1985-86. Author: (stage plays) Captives, 1987, Shall We Begin Again, 1987, Two Roses, 1990, Third Person Singular, 1990, (poetry collection) Greatest Hits, 2001; contbr. to anthologies: Homeless Not Helpless, 1991, The Gulf War: Many Perspectives, 1992, The Literature of Poverty, World Bank Website, 1998; author stories, poems, essays, various lit. mags., websites, tech. and econ. reports; editl. page columnist Community Newspaper Co., 1998—; analyst econ. and fin. Stockhouse, Raging Bull, Yahoo, Arborwood websites. Recipient Trophy for Excellence in Poetry, Daly City Arts Commn., 1990, Westford Acad. Theater Arts Svc. award, 2001, about 30 lit. and fine arts prizes for individual works; Regents scholar U. Calif.-Berkeley, 1961, various scholarships from U. Calif., State of Calif., Hertz Meml. Found. Mem. ACLU, Dramatists Guild, Acad. Am. Poets, Poetry Ctr. San Francisco State U., Save the Redwoods League (life). Anglican Ch. Avocation: fine art photography. Home: 14 Vine Brook Rd Westford MA 01886-4212 E-mail: davidolsen65@alum.calberkeley.org.

OLSEN, DAVID MAGNOR, chemistry and astronomy educator; b. Deadwood, S.D., July 23, 1941; s. Russell Alvin and Dorothy M. Olsen; m. Muriel Jean Bigler, Aug. 24, 1963; children: Merritt, Chad. BS, Luther Coll., 1963; MS in Nat. Sci., U. S.D., 1967. Instr. sci., math. Augustana Acad., Canton, S.D., 1963-66; instr. chemistry Iowa Lakes Community Coll., Estherville, Iowa, 1967-69, Merced (Calif.) Coll., 1969—, instr. astronomy, 1975—, div. chmn., 1978-88, coord. environ. hazardous materials tech., 1989—. Trustee Merced Union High Sch. Dist., 1983—, pres., 1986-87, 97. Mem. NEA, Am. Chem. Soc., Astron. Soc. of the Pacific, Calif. Tchrs. Assn., Planetary Soc., Calif. State Mining and Mineral Mus. Assn. (bd. dirs., sec. 1990-93), Nat. Space Soc., Merced Coll. Faculty Assn. (pres. 1975, 93, 94, treas. 1980-90, 96, 97, bd. dirs., sec. 1990-91), Castle Challenger Learning Ctr. Found. (bd. dirs.), Merced Track Club (exec. bd. 1981), M Star Lodge, Sons of Norway (v.p. 1983), Rotary Internat. (pres. Merced Sunrise 2000-01). Democrat. Lutheran. Home: 973 Idaho Dr Merced CA 95340-2513 Office: Merced Coll 3600 M St Merced CA 95348-2806 E-mail: dmolsen@elite.net.

OLSEN, DONALD EMMANUEL, architect, educator; b. Mpls., July 23, 1919; s. Clarence Edward and Thea (Scharnell) O.; m. Helen Karen Ohlson, Apr. 2, 1944; 1 child, Alan Edward. B.Arch., U. Minn., 1942; M. Arch., Harvard U., 1946; postgrad. in civic design, U. Liverpool, Eng., 1953; postgrad. in philosophy of sci., London Sch. Econs., 1962-63, 68. Registered architect, Calif. Archtl. designer Saarinen, Swanson & Saarinen, Bloomfield Hills, Mich., 1946; project mgr. Skidmore, Owings & Merrill, San Francisco, 1948; designer, draughtsman Wurster, Bernardi & Emmons, 1949-51; pvt. practice architecture Berkeley, Calif., 1954—; prof. architecture U. Calif.-Berkeley, 1954-90, prof. emeritus, 1990—. Guest prof. various univs., lectr. in field, U.S., Eng., Germany, Denmark; lectr., tchr. Ecoles D'Art Améicaines de Fontainebleau, France; nominator Carnegie Grant Personality Assessment and Research Creativity Study Architects, 1959; profl. adviser City of San Francisco, 1961-62; juror, critic, evaluator, various programs, projects Contbr. articles, chpts. to profl. publs.; subject of numerous profl. publs. Numerous exhibits throughout U.S., Europe; prin. works include numerous design commns. Recipient awards, including nat. awards of Excellence Archtl. Record, Houses of 1966; scholar Harvard U., Cambridge, Mass., 1945-46; A. W. Wheelwright fellow Harvard U., 1953 Fellow AIA (2 nat. honor awards 1970, 8 various regional, local Honor, Excellence and Merit awards 1967-89); mem. Brit. Soc. for Philosophy of Sci., Soc. for Philosophy and Tech., Open Soc. and Its Friends Avocations: study of philosophy; travel and travel photography; opera. Office: Donald E Olsen & Assocs Architects 771 San Diego Rd Berkeley CA 94707-2025

OLSEN, EDGAR OLIVER, economics educator; b. New Orleans, Mar. 13, 1942; s. Edgar Oliver and Georgie Walker (Thompson) O.; m. Barbara Elliott Beasley, June 4, 1966; children— Robert Buckner, Melanie Guerry. B.A., Tulane U., 1963; Ph.D., Rice U., 1968. Postdoctoral fellow Ind. U.-Bloomington, 1967-68; vis. assoc. prof. econs. U. Wis., Madison, 1975-76, vis. prof., 1982-84; prof., U. Va., Charlottesville, 1970— ; economist Rand Corp., Santa Monica, Calif., 1968-70; vis. scholar HUD, Washington, 1978-79; cons., 1973-81; dir. Thomas Jefferson Ctr. for Polit. Economy, Charlottesville, 1984-87; bd. editors Am. Econ. Review, Princeton, N.J., 1985— . Contbr. articles to profl. publs. Ford Found. fellow, 1967; NIH fellow, 1983; Sesquicentennial assoc. Ctr. for Advanced Studies, 1975-76, 83-84; recipient Cert. Spl. Achievement, HUD, 1979. Mem. Econometric Soc., Am. Econ. Assn., Pub. Choice Soc., Assn. Pub. Policy Analysis and Mgmt., So. Econ. Assn. Home: 1606 Jamestown Dr Charlottesville VA 22901-3016 Office: Dept Econs U Va Charlottesville VA 22903

OLSEN, EDWARD JOHN, geologist, educator, curator; b. Chgo., Nov. 23, 1927; s. Edward John and Elizabeth (Bornemann) O.; children— Andrea, Ericka. AB, U. Chgo., 1951, MS, 1955, PhD, 1959. Geologist Geol. Survey Can., 1953, U.S. Geol. Survey, 1954—, Canadian Johns-Manville Co., Ltd., 1956, 57, 59; asst. prof. Case Inst. Tech., also Western Res. U., 1959-60; curator mineralogy Field Mus. Natural History, 1960-91, chmn. dept. geology, 1974-78; research assoc. prof. dept. geophys. scis. U. Chgo., 1977—. Adj. prof. U. Ill., Chgo. Circle, 1970-91. Assoc. editor Geochim. et Cosmochim. Acta., 1985-91. Fellow Mineral. Soc. Am.; mem. Mineral. Assn. Can., Geochem. Soc., Meteoritical Soc. Achievements include spl. research stability relations of minerals in earth's mantle and meteorites. Office: U Chgo Dept Geophys Sci Chicago IL 60637

OLSEN, EDWIN CARL, III, engineering educator, consultant; b. Salt Lake City, Dec. 20, 1932; s. Edwin Carl, Jr. Olsen and Ina G. Komes; m. Rebeca Villalobos Villalobos, Apr. 3, 1981; 1 child Ina Teresa 1 child Rebeca ;1 child Christopher Richard. PhD, Utah State U., Logan, 1963. Assoc. prof. Utah State U., Logan, 1968—99, prof. emeritus, 1999—. With USAF, 1951—54. Office: Dept Biol and Irrigation Engring Utah State U Logan UT 84322-4105 Home Fax: 435-797-1248; Office Fax: 435-797-1248. Personal E-mail: ted@cc.usu.edu. Business E-Mail: ted@cc.usu.edu.

OLSEN, ELAINE MERTZ, school administrator; b. Des Peres, Mo., Dec. 1, 1946; d. Pete and Aurel Mertz. BA in German and Psychology, Lindenwood Coll., St. Charles, Mo., 1968; MA in German, U. Wash., 1970; postgrad., Inst. European Studies, Vienna, Austria, 1966-67, U. Vienna, 1966-67. Cert. tchr., Wash., cert. counselor. Tchg. asst. dept. German U. Wash., Seattle, 1968-69; tchr. English and German Granite Falls (Wash.) H.S., 1970-71; instr. Olympic Coll., Bremerton, 1971-72; tchr., counselor Quinault Lake Sch. Dist., Amanda Park, Wash., 1972-73; guidance counselor Aberdeen (Wash.) Sch. Dist., 1973-98, dir. Harbor Homelink Program, 1998—. Coord.: Higher Education Book, 1989, 91, 93. Pubs. chmn. Wash. Coun. for H.S. Coll. Rels., 1988-93, mem. exec. com., 1983-94; adv. coun. for Wash., Am. Coll. Testing, Iowa City, 1987-90; lectr. on rape trauma Grays Harbor Sheriff's Dept., Montesano, Wash., 1980-82; crisis worker Grays Harbor Rape Crisis, 1981-86; treas. Our Savior's Luth. Ch., Aberdeen, 1988-89; mem. bd. and edn. com. Grays Harobr AIDS Task Force, Aberdeen, 1989-90. Recipient Wash. Award for Excellence in Edn., Office of Supt. of Pub. Instrn. and State Bd. Edn., 2000. Mem. NEA, Pacific N.W. Assn. Coll. Admissions Counselors (Outstanding Svc. to Youth award 1990-91), Wash. Edn. Assn., Olympians Hiking Club, Kiwanis (chpt. bd. dirs. 1999-2000, scholarship chair 1998-2000). Avocations: travel, hiking, psychology, world cultures, German language and literature.

OLSEN, FRANCES ELISABETH, law educator, theorist; b. Chgo., Feb. 4, 1945; d. Holger and Ruth Mathilda (Pfeifer) O.; m. Harold Irving Porter, June 8, 1984. Cert., Roskilde (Denmark) Højskole, 1967; BA, Goddard Coll., 1968; JD, U. Colo., 1971; SJD, Harvard U., 1984. Bar: Colo. 1972, U.S. Dist. Ct. Colo. 1972. Law clk. hon. Arraj U.S. Dist. Ct. Colo., Denver, 1972; lawyer Am. Indian Movement, Wounded Knee, S.D., 1973; pvt. practice Denver, 1973-74; law prof. U. Puget Sound, Tacoma, 1975-79, St. John's U., Jamaica, N.Y., 1982-83, UCLA, 1984—. Vis. fellow New Coll., Oxford (Eng.) U., 1987; vis. prof. U. Mich., Ann Arbor, 1988, Harvard U., Cambridge, Mass., 1990-91, Ochanomizu U., Tokyo, 1997, U. Tokyo, 1997, Cornell U., 1997, French UN Reunion, 2000; sr. Fulbright prof. U. Frankfurt, Germany, 1991-92; overseas fellow Churchill Coll., Cambridge, Eng., 1997-99; mem. faculty law Cambridge U., 1997-99; del. UN 4th World Conf. on Women, Beijing, China, 1995, NGO Forum, Huairou, China, 1995. Co-author: Cases and Materials on Family Law: Legal Concepts and Changing Human Relationships, 1994; editor: Feminist Legal Theory I: Foundations and Outlooks, 1995, Feminist Legal Theory II: Positioning Feminist Theory Within the Law, 1995; contbr. articles to law revs. Named Outstanding Alumnus U. Colo., 1989. Mem. Assn. Am. Law Schs. (chair jurisprudence sect. 1987-88, chair women in law tchg. sect. 1995-96), Conf. on Critical Legal Studies, European Conf. Critical Legal Studies. Avocations: windsurfing, bicycling, mountain climbing, hiking. Office: UCLA Sch Law 405 Hilgard Ave Los Angeles CA 90095-9000

OLSEN, GLENN WARREN, historian, educator; b. Mpls., Nov. 27, 1938; s. Warren Spandet and Alice Elvira (Lionstone) O.; m. Suzanne Miltner, Aug. 27, 1966; children: Teresa, Catherine, Gregory, John. BA, North Park Coll., Chgo., 1960; MA, U. Wis., 1962, PhD, 1965. Asst. prof. Seattle U., 1965-66, assoc. prof., 1969-72; asst. prof. Fordham U., Bronx, N.Y., 1966-69; prof. U. Utah, Salt Lake City, 1972—. Vis. prof. U. Notre Dame, Ind., 1990; v.p. Kairos Found., Erie, Pa., 1970—. Adv. editor: Cath. Hist. Rev., 1971—; cons. editor: Communio: Internat. Cath. Rev., 1988—; contbr. articles to profl. jours. Lectr. internat. sci. bd., confs. on European culture, U. Navarre, Pamplona, 1992—; regent St. Mary's Coll., Notre Dame, 1973-79. Fulbright grantee, 1963-65, travel grantee Am. Coun. Learned Socs., 1979, NEH grantee, 1990; David Piermont Gardner fellow U. Utah, 1977, fellow Inst. for Ecumenical and Cultural Rsch., 1978-79. Mem. Medieval Acad. Am., Am. Hist. Assn., Am. Cath. Hist. Assn., Soc. for Italian Hist. Studies, Medieval Assn. Pacific (councillor 1976-79, 92-95), Rocky Mountain Medieval & Renaissance Assn. (pres., councillor 1984-85), Am. Soc. Ch. History (councillor 1981-84). Roman Catholic. Avocations: travel, music, reading. Home: 2233 Bryan Cir Salt Lake City UT 84108-2711 Office: U Utah Dept History 208 Carlson Hall Salt Lake City UT 84112-1127

OLSEN, HANS PETER, lawyer; b. Detroit, May 21, 1940; s. Hans Peter and Paula M. (Olsen) O.; m. Elizabeth Ann Gayton, Sept. 14, 1968; children: Hans Peter, Heidi Susanne, Stephanie Elizabeth BA, Mich. State U., 1962; JD, Georgetown U., 1965; LLM, NYU, 1966. Bar: Mich. 1967, Pa. 1969, R.I. 1974. Law clk. Monaghan, McCrone, Campbell & Crawmer, Detroit, 1964; law clk. U.S. Ct. of Claims, Fed. Appellate Ct., Washington, 1966—68; assoc. Pepper, Hamilton & Scheetz, Phila., 1968—72; ptnr. Hinckley, Allen, & Snyder, Providence, 1972—. Adv. planning com. U. R.I. Fed. Taxation Inst.; continuing legal edn. adv. bd., tax symposium adv. bd. Bryant Coll.; mem. Gov.'s State Task Force, R.I. Pub. Expenditure Coun.; cons. Bur. Nat. Affairs; liaison Bar Assn. and North Atlantic region IRS; tax adminstrs. adv. com. R.I.; lectr. tax insts. and other profl. groups N.Y., L.A., Phila., Boston, R.I.; advisor R.I. Econ. Policy com. Contbr. numerous articles on taxation to legal jours. Fellow Am. Bar Found.; mem. ABA (sect. taxation, exempt orgns. com., subcom. healthcare, corp.-shareholders rels. com., partnerships com.), R.I. Bar Assn. (sect. taxation, sec.-treas. 1977-80, liaison with CPAs, specialization com., mem. various coms.), Providence C. of C., R.I. C. of C. (chmn. com. on bus. taxes and public spending, mem., past chmn. legis. action council), Mich. State Bar, Pa. State Bar. Home: 274 Olney St Providence RI 02906-2305 Office: 1500 Fleet Ctr Providence RI 02903 E-mail: holsen@haslaw.com., hpeterolsen@home.com.

OLSEN, HAROLD FREMONT, lawyer; b. Davenport, Wash., Oct. 17, 1920; s. Oscar E. and Dorothy (Sprowls) O.; m. Jeanne L. Rounds, Aug. 30, 1942; children: Eric O., Ronald R., Margaret Ruth. BA, Wash. State U., 1942; LL.B., Harvard U., 1948. Bar: Wash. 1948, U.S. Ct. Claims 1970, U.S. Supreme Ct. 1982; C.P.A., Wash. Instr. Oxford Bus. Sch., Cambridge, Mass., 1946-47; examiner Wash. State Dept. Pub. Utilities, 1948; with firm Perkins Coie (and predecessors), Seattle, 1949—, ptnr., 1954-88, of counsel, 1989—. Trustee Exec. Svcs. Corp. Wash., 1990-96. Bd. dirs. Northwest Hosp. Found., Northwest Hosp., 1980-90; trustee Wash. State U. Found., chmn. 1986-88; mem. adv. coun. Wash. State U. Sch. Bus. and Econs., 1978-90; trustee, mem. exec. com., pres. Mus. of Flight, 1991-92, chmn., 1993; trustee Horizon House, 1994-97. Maj. USAAF, 1942-45, NATOUSA, Mid. East, ETO. Decorated Silver Star. Mem. ABA, Wash. Bar Assn., Seattle Bar Assn., Aircraft Industry Assn. (chmn. legal com. 1957), Phi Beta Kappa, Phi Kappa Phi, Tau Kappa Epsilon, Rainier Club, Queenstown (New Zealand) Golf Club, Seattle Golf Club (pres. 1986-87), Sr. N.W. Golf Assn. Congregationalist. Home: 8875 Overlake Dr W Medina WA 98039-5347 Office: 1201 3rd Ave Ste 4500 Seattle WA 98101-3029 E-mail: olseh@perkinscoie.com., olseh@seanet.com.

OLSEN, HARRIS LELAND, writer, educator, retired real estate and international business executive, diplomat; b. Rochester, N.H., Dec. 8, 1947; s. Harries Edwin and Eva Alma (Turmelle) O.; m. Mimi Kwi Sun Yi, Mar. 15, 1953; children: Garin Lee, Gavin Yi, Sook Ja. AS, SUNY, Albany, 1983, BS, 1988; MA in Polit. Sci., U. Hawaii, 1990; PhD in Internat. Bus. Adminstrn.,

Kennedy Western U., Idaho, 1993. Enlisted USN, 1967, advanced through grades to, served in various nuclear power capacities Conn., 1971-76, Hawaii, 1976-87, ret., 1987; v.p. Waiono Land Corp., Honolulu, 1981-92, dir., 1993-95; v.p. Asian Pacific Electricity, 1988-89, Kapano Land Assocs., Honolulu, 1988-92, 94-95, MLY Networks, Inc., Honolulu, 1989-99, THO Consultants Corp., 1991—2002, Clarix Internat. Corp., 1994; consulate gen. Papua New Guinea, 1996—2002. Staff cons. Mariner-Icemakers, Honolulu, 1982-84, Transpacific Energy Corp., Honolulu, 1982-84; dir. Asian Pacific Devel. Bank, 1983; sr. cons. Western Rsch. Assocs., Honolulu, 1984-87, 94-95; quality assurance cons. Asian Pacific, Inc., Honolulu, 1987-88; instr., lectr. Asian history and culture U. Chaminade in Honolulu, 1991; nuclear reactor plant specialist Pearl Harbor Emergency Recall Team, 1991-95; instr. nuclear reactor theory Pearl Harbor, Hawaii, 1992-95; v.p. Schwartz, Inc., 1992-98, dir. Schwartz Jewelry Sch., 1996-98; cons. Waiono/Kapano Devel. Co., 1993; bd. dirs., sec. Pacific Internat. Engring. Corp., 1994-95; Keiretsu sec. Global Ocean Cons., Inc. and Assocs., 1994-95; joint venture Premier Fisheries Pty. Ltd., Papua New Guinea, 1995-98; cons. BFD Devel. Group, 1995-96; co-drafter Nat. Tuna Industry Devel. Plan for Papua New Guinea, 1995; quality analyst, Pearl Harbor, 1995; rep. for Min. for Fisheries, Papua New Guinea, Bi-lateral Fisheries Access Rights Japan and Papua New Guinea, 1996-97, drafter Bi-Lateral Fishing Treaty Japan and Papua New Guinea, 1996; U.S. del. to 4th World Tuna Conf., Manila, 1995, U.S. del. to 5th Aquatic Coninent Conf., Maui, Hawaii, 1995, 6th, 1996; apptd. rep. Abau Electorate, Papua New Guinea Timber Sales, 1995-98; apptd. hon. consul gen. and trade rep., dep. trade min. for Govt. of Papua New Guinea in Honolulu, 1996-2001; bd. dirs. Island Art; cons. Pew Global Devel. Corp., 1998-99, Niugini Enterprises LLC, 1999-2001, Niugini Millenium Co., Ltd., 1999-2001. Inventor, alternate power supply system; contbr. articles to profl. publs. Head coach USN Men's Softball, Honolulu, 1978-79; pres. Pearl Harbor (Hawaii) Welfare and Recreation Com., 1983-84; mem. Bishop Mus, Rep. Senatorial Inner Cir.; commd. hon. consul gen. Ind. State Papua New Guinea, 1996; mem. Consular Corps of Hawaii, 1997-2001. Named Alumnus of Yr., Kennedy Western U., 1993; recipient Citation of Leadership, Rep. Nat. Com., 1996, Letter of Commendation for Svc. During Aitape Tidal Wave Disaster in Papua New Guinea, 1998; selected to represent Hawaii at Presdl. Inauguration, Rep. Leadership U.S. Senate, 2001. Mem.: Plaza Club, Navy League, Fleet Res. Assn., USCG Aux., Internat. Fedn. Profl. and Tech. Engrs., Delta Epsilon Sigma. Republican. Roman Catholic and Buddhist. Avocations: chess, philosophy, Japanese haiku poetry, native American cultures. Home and Office: 94 1025 Anania Cir Apt 56 Mililani HI 96789-2045 E-mail: HarryTho@aol.com.

OLSEN, INGER ANNA, psychologist, educator; b. Copper Mountain, B.C., Can., Dec. 25, 1926; BS, Wash. State U., 1954, MS, 1956, PhD, 1962. Psychiat. nurse Provincial Mental Health Svcs. B.C., 1947-51, psychologist, 1956-58, Vancouver (B.C.) City Met. Health Svcs., 1958-60; psychologist Student Counseling Ctr., Wash. State U., Pullman, 1960-62; sr. psychologist Met. Health Svcs., Vancouver, 1962-66; instr. psychology Vancouver C.C., 1966-87. Contbr. articles to profl. jours. Docent Vancouver Aquarium Assn.; bd. dirs. Second Mile Soc., 1975—89. Mem. APA, Gerontol. Soc. Am., Can. Assn. Gerontology, Phi Beta Kappa, Sigma Xi, Alpha Kappa Delta. Home: 1255 Bidwell St Apt 1910 Vancouver BC Canada V6G 2K8

OLSEN, JAMES ARTHUR, college development officer; b. Boston, Aug. 27, 1959; s. Arthur Lloyd and Ruth Ann Olsen; m. Toshie Onai, Feb. 7, 1998. BA, Augustana Coll., Sioux Falls, S.D., 1983; MusM, Ind. U., 1990; MBA, U. Wis., Milw., 1998. Instr. All Sts. Elem. Sch., Sioux Falls, 1983-86; assoc. instr. Ind. U., Bloomington, 1988-90; adminstrv. coord. String Acad. Wis., Milw., 1990-93, asst. dir., 1993-97, mng. dir., 1997-2000; assoc. dir. devel. Med. Coll. Wis., 2000—. Vol. Habitat for Humanity, Milw., 1991-96; ptnr. Results, Milw., 1994-97, group leader, 1995-97; sec. Village Ch., Milw., 1996-98. Mem. Assn. Fundraising Profls. (cert.), Am. String Tchrs. Assn. Democrat. Lutheran. Avocations: chamber music, foreign languages. Office: Med Coll Wis Office of Devel 8701 Watertown Plank Rd Milwaukee WI 53226 E-mail: jolsen@mcw.edu.

OLSEN, JOHN WILLIAM, political organization worker; b. Greenwich, Conn., Mar. 27, 1950; s. William and Helen (Coombs) O.; m. Rose Smeriglio, Apr. 18, 1971; children: Amy, Elizabeth, Christopher. Student, Wright Tech. Sch., 1973. Apprentice Greenwich Plumbing and Heating, 1969-79; journeyman Stockenboyjer Plumbing and Heating, Greenwich, 1979-81; bus. mgr. U.A. Local 133, 1981-87, pres., 1978-79; sec., treas. Conn. State AFL-CIO, West Hartford, 1987-88, pres., 1988—. Truste Fairfield-New Haven Apprenticeship Sch., Bridgeport, 1983—, Conn. Plumbers and Pipefitters Pension Fund, Wallingford, 1979—; mem., subchair Conn. Employment and Tng. Com., Wethersfield, 1989—; mem. Conn. Innovations, Inc., Rocky Hill, 1989—. Mem. Dem. State Cen. Com., Hartford, 1986—, Greenwich Dem. Town Exec. Com., 1980—, Gov.'s Bldg. and Constrn. Adv. Com., Hartford, 1987-90, Gov.'s Mgmt. Study Commn., Hartford, 1989-91, State Democratic Chmn., Conn., 1995. Mem. Greenwich Bldg. and Constrn. Trades (pres. 1983-87), Kiwanis (2d v.p. Greenwich chpt. 1987-88). Democrat. Roman Catholic. Office: Conn State AFL-CIO 56 Town Line Rocky Hill CT 06067 also: Conn. Democratic Party 380 Franklin Ave. Hartford CT 06114*

OLSEN, JONATHAN ROBERT, political scientist; b. Topeka, Sept. 22, 1959; s. Robert Arthur and Marilyn Barr O.; m. Molly Elizabeth Hall, May 21, 1997; 1 child, Ian Kent. BA, U. Tex., 1983; MA, U. Kans., 1988; PhD, U. Md., 1997. Asst. prof. Schiller Internat. U., Heidelberg, Germany, 1989-90, U. Wis.-Parkside, Kenosha, 1997—. Author: Nature and Nationalism, 1999; contbr. articles to profl. jours. Fulbright fellow Fulbright Commn., 1988-89, 2000—, Wis. Tchg. fellow U. Tchg. Improvement Coun., 1999-2000, Wilson fellow Woodrow Wilson Ctr., 1997. Mem. Am. Polit. Sci. Assn., German Studies Assn., Western Polit. Sci. Assn., Conf. Group on German Politics. Democrat. Avocations: playing the flute, guitar, piano, singing, tennis. Office: 900 Wood Rd Kenosha WI 53144-1133 E-mail: jonathan.olsen@uwp.edu.

OLSEN, JOSEPHINE, federal agency administrator; B, U. Utah; MSW, PhD, U. Md. Vol. Peace Corps, Tunisia, 1966—68, various positions incuding chief of staff, regional dir. North Africa, Near East, Asia and the Pscific, country dir. Togo, 1979—84, 1989—92; exed. dirs. Coun. Internat. Exch. of Scholars, 1992—97; sr. v.p., dir. Peace Corps, 1997—2002, deputy dir., 2002—. Office: Peace Corps 1111 20th St NW Washington DC 20526-0001*

OLSEN, JUDITH JOHNSON, reference librarian; b. Manitowoc, Wis., May 13, 1948; d. Gordon Frank Johnson and Ellen Jeanette Knutson; m. Axel K. Olsen (div. 1999); children: Maren, Kristina. BA, Luther Coll., 1970; ML, U. S.C., 1976; MA, Villanova (Pa.) U., 1996. Reader's svcs. libr. Cabrini Coll., Radnor, Pa., 1977-88; ref. and publs. libr. Villanova (Pa.) U., 1988—. Mem. MLA, ALA, Assn. of Colls. and Rsch. Librs. Democrat. Office: Villanova U 800 Lancaster Ave Villanova PA 19085 E-mail: judith.olsen@villanova.edu.

OLSEN, KATHIE LYNN, federal agency administrator; b. Portland, Oreg., Aug. 3, 1952; d. Roland Berg and Gladys Elizabeth (Eldreth) O. BS, Chatham Coll., 1974; PhD, U. Calif., Irvine, 1979. Postdoct. fellow Harvard Med. Sch., Boston, 1979-80; rsch. scientist Long Island Rsch. Inst., Stony Brook, N.Y., 1980-83; rsch. asst. prof. SUNY, 1982-85, asst. prof., 1985-89; assoc. program dir. NSF, Washington, 1984-86, program dir., 1988, leader neurosci., 1991; assoc. director, tech. Off. Science and Tech. Policy, 1999—. Adj. assoc. prof. George Washington U., Washington, 1989—; cons. editor Hormones and Behavior, 1988—. Contbr. articles to profl. jours, chapters to books. Mem. Soc. Neurosci., Endocrine Soc., Women in Neurosci., Sod. Study of Reproduction, Internat. Acad. Sex Rsch. Office: Exec Off of the Pres Off Science and Tech Policy EEOB, 17th & Pennsylvania Ave NW Washington DC 20502*

OLSEN, KENNETH ALLEN, lawyer; b. Jersey City, June 6, 1953; s. George Anton and Dorothy (Mitschell) O.; m. Andrea M. Olsen. BA in Polit. Sci. and Pre-Law magna cum laude, Rutgers U., 1975; JD, Temple U., 1978. Bar: N.J. 1978, Pa. 1979; U.S. Dist. Ct. N.J. 1978, U.S. Dist. Ct. (mid. dist.) Pa. 1980, U.S. Dist. Ct. (ea. dist.) Pa. 1988; U.S. Ct. Appeals (3d cir.) 1979, U.S. Ct. Appeals (11th cir.) 1981, U.S. Ct. Appeals (D.C. cir.) 1982, U.S. Supreme Ct. 1983. Sole practice. Atty. Chgo. Title Ins. Co., Chelsea Title and Guaranty Co., Commonwealth Land Title Co., N.J. Realty Title Ins. Co. Named to Presdl. Classroom Young Ams. Mem. ABA (various sects. and coms.), N.J. State Bar Assn., Pa. Bar Assn., Morris County Bar Assn., Am. Acad. Polit. Sci., Am. Acad. Polit. and Social Sci., Assn. Transp. Practitioners, Temple U. Alumni Assn., Rutgers U. Alumni Assn., Newark Coll. Alumni Assn., Traffic Club Newark Inc., Transp. Lawyers Assn., Phi Beta Kappa, Pi Sigma Alpha. Lutheran. Avocations: tennis, golf, bowling.

OLSEN, M. KENT, lawyer, educator; b. Denver, Mar. 10, 1948; s. Marvin and F. Winona (Wilker) O.; m. Shauna L. Casement; children: Kristofor Anders, Alexander Lee, Nikolaus Alrik, Amanda Elizabeth. BS, Colo. State U., 1970; JD, U. Denver, 1975. Bar: Colo., U.S. Dist. Ct. Colo. 1982, U.S. Tax Ct. Law clk. Denver Probate Ct., 1973-75; assoc. ptnr. Johnson & McLachlan, Lamar, Colo., 1975-80; assoc. Buchanan, Thomas and Johnson, Lakewood, 1981-82, William E. Myrick, P.C., Denver, 1982-83; referee Denver Probate Ct., 1983-89; ptnr. Haines & Olsen, P.C., 1989-95; pvt. practice, 1995—2001; ptnr. Olsen & Traeger, LLP, 2001—. Adv. bd. Denver Paralegal Inst., 1993—, Elder Law Inst., 1994—. Mem. Gov.'s Commn. on Life and the Law, Denver, 1991-2000; bd. dirs. Adult Care Mgmt., Inc., Denver, 1985-95; bd. dirs. Arc of Denver, Inc., 1990—, pres., 1995-97; bd. dirs. Colo. Guardianship Alliance, Denver, 1990-91; bd. dirs. Colo. Fund for People with Disabilities, 1994—, pres., 1994-2000. Recipient Outstanding Vol. Svc. award Adult Care Mgmt., 1990, Outstanding Svc. award The Arc of Denver, 1991, Vol. Svc. award Colo. Gerontol. Soc., 1997, Pres.'s award Arc of Denver, 1998. Mem. ABA, Colo. Bar Assn. (past chair probate sect.), Am. Assn. Home for Aging, Nat. Acad. Elder Law Attys., Denver Bar Assn. Episcopalian. Avocations: running, skiing, racquetball, art, hiking. Home: 3030 S Roslyn St Denver CO 80231-4153 Office: 650 S Cherry St Ste 850 Denver CO 80246-1805 E-mail: mkolsen@earthlink.net.

OLSEN, MARTIN E. obstetrician, medical educator; b. Morgantown, W.Va., 1959; m. Natalie Ann Muschmann, June 25, 1985; 1 child, Karen Rebeca. MD, Med. Coll. Ohio, 1985. Diplomate Am. Bd. Ob-Gyn., Am. Bd. Family Practice. Resident in family practice Akron (Ohio) Gen. Med. Ctr., 1985-88; resident in ob-gyn. U. Tenn., Chattanooga, 1989-91; dir. residency program Johnson City (Tenn.) Med. Ctr., 1994—; mem. faculty East Tenn. State U., Johnson City, 1992—, chmn. dept. og-byn., 1999—. Contbr. Office: PO Box 70569 Johnson City TN 37614-1707 E-mail: olsen@etsu.edu.

OLSEN, MARY ANN, lawyer; b. Hoboken, N.J., Aug. 5, 1948; d. Charles Joseph and Margaret Nora (Power) O.; 1 child, Matthew Ellisen. AAS, Purdue U., 1973; BS, St. Peter's Coll., Jersey City, 1973; JD, Rutgers U., 1989. Bar: N.J. 1990, N.Y. 1991. Pvt. practice, Bayonne, N.J., 1991—. Cons. atty. Hudson County Protective Svc., West New York, N.J., 1993-96. Chmn. money mgmt. com. Bayonne Office on Aging, 1996-97; trustee Jersey City Cmty. Charter Sch.; bd. dirs. St. Joseph's Home for the Blind, Guardianship Assn. N.J., Inc. Mem. N.J. Bar Assn., Hudson County Bar Assn., Hudson Inn of Ct. Office: 8 E 35th St Bayonne NJ 07002-3925

OLSEN, RALPH A. science educator, researcher; b. Moroni, Utah, Jan. 30, 1925; s. John L. and Ethel E. Olsen; m. Vanona Fisher Olsen, Aug. 26, 1949; children: Ravona, Beverly, Karen, Loren, Paulette, Miriam, Amy. BS, Brigham Young U., Provo, UT, 1945—49; MS, Cornell U., Ithaca, NY, 1949—51; Ph. D, Cornell Universiy, Ithaca, NY, 1951—53; MS, Cornell U., Ithaca, NY, 1949—51; Ph. D, Cornell Universiy, Ithaca, NY, 1951—53. Soil chemist U.S. Dept. Agr., Beltsville, Md., 1953—56; chemistry educator Mont. State U., Bozeman, Mont., 1956—91. Post doctoral fellowship U. of Copenhagen, Copenhagen, 1965—66; mineral nutrition pioneering rsch. lab. Agrl. Rsch. Ctr., Beltsville, Md., 1961—62. Contbr. articles to profl. jour. Tec 5 Inf., 1944—46, California. Latter Day Saints. Achievements include research in Potentiometric measurements in colloidal suspensions; Validity Of The Soil Solution Hypothesis; Ion Transport Through Membranes Of Living Cells; Chemical Modification Of Their Environments By Plant Roots. Avocation: writing. Home: 1605 West Kagy Boulevard Bozeman MT 59715 Personal E-mail: ralphandvanona@juno.com.

OLSEN, REX NORMAN, trade association executive; b. Hazeltown, Idaho, Apr. 9, 1925; s. Adolph Lars and Pearl (Robbins) O. B.J., BA in English, U. Mo., 1950. Editor Clissold Pub. Co., Chgo., 1950-54; copy editor Am. Peoples Ency., 1955; asst. editor Am. Hosp. Assn., 1956-59, mng. editor, 1959-64, dir. jours. div., 1964-69, dir. publs. bur., 1969-75, exec. editor, asso. pub., 1975-79; v.p., treas. Am. Hosp. Pub., Inc., 1980-85; pres. Words Ltd., 1985—. Dir. publs. ETNA Comms., Chgo., 1997—. Served with USNR, 1943-46. Mem. Soc. Nat. Assn. Pubs. (sec. 1975-76, 2d v.p. 1976-77, 1st v.p. 1977-78, pres. 1978-79), Chgo. Bus. Publs. Assn. (dir. 1974-78, 4th v.p. 1978-79), Sigma Delta Chi. Home and Office: 3845 N Alta Vista Ter Chicago IL 60613-2907 E-mail: rexorudy@aol.com.

OLSEN, RICHARD GALEN, biomedical engineer, consultant; b. Colorado Springs, Colo., Aug. 10, 1945; s. Floyd Edwin and Ruth Elizabeth (Robinson) O.; m. Karen Fidler Brubaker, June 17, 1973; children: Kathryn Elizabeth, Nickolas Robert. BSEE, U. Mo., Rolla, 1968; MS, U. Utah, 1970, PhD, 1975. Registered profl. engr., Fla. Engr. Bendix Corp., Kansas City, Mo., 1968-69; elec. engr. Naval Aerospace Med. Rsch. Lab., Pensacola, Fla., 1975-79, chief engring. systems divsn., 1979-82, head bioengring. divsn., 1982-94; head bioengring. dept. Naval Health Rsch. Ctr. Detachment, Brooks AFB, Tex., 1994-2000; cons. in bioelectromagnetics Pensacola, 2001—. Tech. cons. Armstrong Lab., USAF, 1991-99, German Ministry of Def., Munster, 1994, Naval Surface Warfare Ctr., Dahlgren, Va., 1989-95, Naval Sea Sys. Command, Arlington, Va., 1989-91, Naval Command, Control and Ocean Surveillance Command, San Diego, 1996-97, Selicor Inc., 2001-. Contbr. articles to profl. jours. and books. With U.S. Army, 1970-72. Recipient NDEA fellowship U. Utah, 1969, Fred A. Hitchcock award Aerospace Physiologist Aerospace Med. Assn., 1987; named Engr. of the Yr., N.W. Fla. Engrs. Coun., 1991. Mem. IEEE (sr., chmn. Pensacola sect. 1982-83, SCC-28 and SCC-34 coms. 1982-2000, cert. of appreciation 1983), Bioelectromagnetics Soc. (charter, editl. bd. 1990-96), Sigma Xi, Eta Kappa Nu, Tau Beta Pi, Phi Kappa Phi. Achievements include conducting the first shipboard measurements of specific absorption rate (SAR) and of electromagnetic pulse (EMP) induced body current; patents in RF medical device to treat vascular insufficiency, RF coil for hypothermia resuscitation, RF dosimetry system, personal microwave and RF detector, and RF warming of submerged extremities. Home and Office: 1503 N Baylen St Pensacola FL 32501-2101 E-mail: olsen@pcola.gulf.net. *Live an ordinary life except in attainment.*

OLSEN, RICHARD JAMES, artist, art educator; b. Milw., Nov. 15, 1935; s. Edward Marinus and Ann Frances (Keymar) Olsen; m. Nina Marsh Civilette-Olsen, July 25, 1969; children: Dayna Kim, Dawn Beth(dec.) , Josh Keymar. BS, U. Wis., 1958, MFA in Painting and Printmaking, 1966. Tchg. asst. U. Wis., 1965-66; art tchr. grade 8 Winnequah Grade Sch., Monona, Wis., 1966-67; instr. printmaking Oper. Area Arts, Green Bay, 1967-69; instr. painting and drawing U. Ga., Athens, 1969-73, asst. prof., 1974-78, assoc. prof., 1978-94, prof., 1994-2000, Sandy Beaver prof., 1998-2000; emeritus prof. NOVUS, Inc., Atlanta, 2001—; represented by Berman Gallery, 1986-97, Novus Inc., Atlanta, 1990—, Maurine Littleton Gallery, Washington, 1990, Miriam Perlman Gallery, Chgo., 1991, EDL & Assocs., Atlanta, 1994, Elements of Art, Columbus, 1995, Ellen Wallace-Paushter, Art Cons., Chgo., 1999, Mercury Art Works, Athens, Ga., 2001—. Wrestling coach Monona Grove (Wis.) H.S., 1966-67; panelist Steinham Arts Festival St. Lawrence U., N.Y., 1987, Crossroads in Cultural Studies, Tampere, Finland, 1996; head praparator Reflexes and Reflections Russell Rotunda Capitol Hill, Washington, 1983, Lincoln Ctr., N.Y.C., 1984. One-man shows include , Claywork Gallery, Atlanta, 1986, H. Smith Gallery U. S.C., Spartanburg, 1991, Nat. Vietnam Vets. Art Mus., Chgo., 1999, exhibited in group shows at Brit. Internat. Print Biennale, Bradford, Yorkshire, Eng., 1971, U. Wis., Madison, 1975, SECAC, Winston-Salem, N.C., 1981, Chattahoochee Valley Arts Assn., LaGrange, Ga., 1982, N.A.M.E. Gallery, Chgo., 1982, Washington Project for the Arts, 1983, Cannon Rotunda, 1983, Russell Rotunda, 1983, Lincoln Ctr., N.Y.C., 1984, LBJ Libr., 1984, Claywork Gallery, Atlanta, 1986, Savannah Coll. Art and Design, 1989, R.H. Love, Contemporary, Chgo., 1992, Mus. Fine Arts, Ho Chi Ming City, Vietnam, 1994, Nat. Mus. Fine Arts, Hanoi, Vietnam, 1994, Berman Gallery, Atlanta, 1994, Am. Visionary Mus., Balt., 2001—, Peace Mus., Chgo., 2002—; featured Vietnam Reflexes and Reflections, N.Y. Times, New Art Examiner, Chgo. Tribune, "Q" A Jour. of Art, Panorama, AP, VFW mag., Stars and Stripes, Gravitas mag., War Lit. in the Arts, Bloomsbury Rev., Ninety Six Inc., (documentary) Reflexes/Reflections PBS, 1984; Represented in permanent collections Nat. Vietnam Vets. Art Mus., Chgo., Nat. Mus. Fine Art, Hanoi, Vietnam., one-man shows include Peace Mus., Chgo., 2002. With U.S. Army, 1959-63, Vietnam. Decorated Purple heart, 1963; Visual Arts fellow So. Arts Fdn./NEA, 1988; Sr. Faculty grantee U. Ga. Rsch. Found., Inc., 1991-93, 96-98, Individual Artist grantee Ga. Coun. Arts, 1993-94; recipient Purchase award 8th Annual Maine/Maritime Internat. Flatworks Exhibn., 1990. Mem. VFW, Mil. Order of the Purple Heart (comdr. 1999-2000), Vietnam Helicopter Pilots Assn. Home: 165 Springdale St Athens GA 30605-1237 E-mail: richard.j.olsen@att.net.

OLSEN, ROBERT C., JR. academic administrator, military officer; b. Bklyn. m. Maureen Olsen; 2 children. BS, USCG Acad., 1969; MS in Adminstrn., U.S. Naval Postgrad. Sch., Monterey, Calif.; MA in nat. Security and Strategic Studies, Naval War Coll. Commd. USCG, advanced through grades to rear admiral; exec. officer USCGC Madrona; commdg. officer various cutters USCG; commandant of cadets USCG Acad., asst. supt., maritime law enforcement and intelligence br. chief for 3d Coast Guard Dist. NY; mgr. surface forces Coast Guard Atlantic Area; detailer for officer assignments USCG Hdqrs., mem. tng. and edn. staff, dir. pers. mgmr.; supt. USCG Acad., New London, Conn. Decorated Legion of Merit (3), Meritorious Svc. medal, Coast Guard ommendation medal (4), Humanitarian Svc. medal (2). Office: US Coast Guard Academy 15 Mohegan Ave New London CT 06320-8100

OLSEN, ROBERT ERIC, lawyer, public interest litigator; b. Easton, Pa., July 10, 1944; s. Robert Thorvald and Frances (Wallburg) O.; m. Barbara Edith Mackay, July 25, 1992; 1 child, Alexander. AB, Harvard Coll., 1966; MA, U. Pa., 1967; JD, U. Denver, 1975. Bar: Md., Colo. Corp. planner Indsl. Valley Bank, Phila., 1968-73; sr. v.p. First Am. Indsl. Bank and First Am. Leasing Co., Denver, 1973-75; assoc. Calkins, Kramer, Grimshaw & Harring, 1975-79, Brenman, Epstein, Zerobnick, Raskin & Friedlob, Denver, 1979-80; ptnr. Olsen & Guardi, 1980-90; fgn. svc. officer U.S. Dept. of State, Washington, 1992-94; of counsel Goldstein & Baron, College Park, Md., 1995-97; atty. Olsen Law Firm, McLean, Va., 1997—99, 2001—; counsel to Greenberg Traurig, 1999—2001. On-air announcer, prodr., critic Sta. KVOD-FM, Denver, 1989-91. Democrat. Avocations: opera, photography, political policy development. Home: 922 Ridge Dr Mc Lean VA 22101-1632 E-mail: rolsen@cox.rr.com.

OLSEN, STEVEN KENT, dentist; b. Spanish Fork, Utah, Nov. 20, 1944; s. Earl Clarence and Adela (Faux) O.; children: Christopher, Sara Kate, Vanessa. *Steven Olsen's grandfather, F. Jabez Faux, won a national contest in the 1950's sponsored by General Motors by creating the "jingle:" "See the USA in your Chevrolet." He composed many original operas and published a well-known song for and about his wife entitled "Adoration." His grandmother, Florence Faux ("Flossy"), was famous for her philanthropic endeavors. In her later years, she would walk to the "old folk's home" and play the piano for the "old folks," who were generally much younger than herself. His mother, Adela F. Olsen, in her angelic way, wrote letters to various U.S. Presidents, and always received a personal reply.* BS, Brigham Young U., 1969; DDS, U. Pacific, 1974. Ptrn. practice dentistry in surg. and endodontics Brooks & Olsen, Salt Lake City, 1974—; gen. practice dentistry Steven K. Olsen, D.D.S., San Francisco, 1974-75; pres. S.K. Olsen, P.C., 1975—; ptnr. Olsen, H. & P., 1977-83; instr. U. Pacific, 1978—. Chmn. bd. Am. Dentists Ins. Corp., Grand Cayman, W.I., 1978-81; instr. Stanford (Calif.) Inst., Chabot Coll. Inst., 1979-82; med. staff Latter-day Saints Hosp.; cons. Calif. Inst., San Francisco, 1981—; ptnr. J.B. Devel. Co.; ptnr. Russell Harris Restorations, Ryan Bott Restorations, Jason Herget Restorations, D.W. Mmgt. Co., Bob Steck Mgmt. Co., Dave Olsen & Co.; bd. dirs. Wilks & Topper, Inc., San Francisco, Curt Facchino Ltd., Woodside. *Since 1975, Dr. Olsen has owned and operated Steven K. Olsen D.D.S., P.C., a highly successful professional practice in San Francisco. Staff members include an oral surgeon, orthodontist, periodontist, and ten other highly skilled doctors. His practice has developed numerous prototype systems, including the first dental office computer system (ROR) and the first board approved postdoctoral correspondence course with over 8000 member doctors. The American Dental Insurance Corporation (ADIC) was also established by Dr. Olsen's practice. Advanced techniques and state of the art equipment continues to be developed and practiced therein. His son, Christopher S. Olsen, plans on continuing to develop his practice upon completing his dental education.* Author: Accolade, 1963, (play) Lancer Ballade, 1963, (acad. course) World Religions, 1979; editor corr. course Calif. Inst., 1981. Recipient Good Citizenship medal SAR, 1963. Mem. Assn. Coll. of Physicians and Surgeons, ADA, Calif. Dental Assn., Utah Dental Assn., Physicians and Surgeons Club (San Francisco), Alpha Epsilon Delta. Home: 385 Old La Honda Rd Woodside CA 94062-2617 Office: 2 Embarcadero Ctr Promenade San Francisco CA 94111

OLSEN, TAVA MARYANNE LENNON, industrial and operations engineering educator; b. Aarhus, Denmark, Dec. 20, 1969; came to U.S., 1990; d. Michael James and Jennifer Anne Lennon; m. Timothy Robert Olsen, Dec. 30, 1995. BSc in Math. with honors, U. Auckland, New Zealand, 1989; MS in Stats., Stanford (Calif.) U., 1992, PhD in Ops. Rsch., 1994. Asst. prof. indsl. and ops. engring. U. Mich., Ann Arbor, 1994—2001; assoc. prof. Olin Sch. Bus., U. Washington in St. Louis, 2001—. Mem. Inst. Ops. Rsch. and Mgmt. Sci., Sigma Xi. Office: Campus Box 1133 PO Box 1133 Saint Louis MO 63188-1133

OLSEN, THOMAS RICHARD, SR. air force officer; b. Houston, June 28, 1934; s. Oscar Leonard and Catherine (Byers) O.; children: Thomas Richard Jr., Lisa Kendrick Olsen Wesolick; m. Jacquelyn Beasley Keels, June 28, 1998. BSME, Tex. A&M U., 1956; MS in Internat. Affairs, George Washington U., 1968. Mech. engr. Tex. Gas Corp., Houston, 1956; commd. 2d lt. USAF, 1957, advanced through grades to maj. gen., 1986; pilot trainee Greenville AFB, Miss., 1957-58; fighter pilot 326 FIS/526 FIS, U.S. and Fed. Republic Germany, 1958-65, 614 TFS/615 TFS, England AFB, La., 615 TFS, Phan Rang AB, Vietnam, 1966-67; instr. U.S. Naval Amphibious Sch., Coronado, Calif., 1968-71; fighter pilot 391 TFS, Mt. Home AFB, Idaho, 1971-72, squadron ops. officer, squadron comdr., 1972-74; chief rated officer Mgmt. Hdqrs. AFMPC, Randolph AFB, Tex., 1975-78; chief of staff Hdqrs. 9th Air Force, Shaw AFB, S.C., 1978-79; dep. comdr. Hdqrs. 314th Air Div., Seoul, Republic of Korea, 1979-81; dir. ops. Hdqrs. 5th Air Force, Yokota AFB, Japan, 1981-82; wing comdr. 51 TFW, Osan AB, Republic of Korea, 1982-83; dep. dir. ops. Hdqrs. Pacific Command, Camp Smith, Hawaii, 1983-85; asst. chief of staff ops. Hdqrs. AFCENT, NATO, Brunsuum, The Netherlands, 1985-87; dep. comdr., chief of staff Hdqrs. 4 ATAF, NATO, Heidelberg, Fed. Republic Germany, 1987-89; vice comdr. Hdqrs. 9th Air Force, Shaw AFB, S.C., 1989-91; dep. comdr. U.S. Cen. Command Air Forces (Desert Shield/Desert Storm), Riyadh, Saudi Arabia, 1990-91; ret., 1991. Exec. dir. Sumter Base Defense Com., 1994—. Mem. Optimist Club, Coronado, 1969-71. Mem. Air Force Assn., Ret. Officers Assn., Daedalians, Kiwanis, Rotary. Presbyterian. Home: 1008 Sparkleberry Ct Sumter SC 29150-2337 E-mail: tolsen@usc.net.

OLSEN-SPINA, TERESA ANN, health information specialist, consultant; b. Albany, N.Y., Nov. 6, 1961; d. James Edward and Mary Louise Olsen, Mary Louise Olsen; m. Thomas Spina, Jr.; children: Katherine Spina, Christopher Spina, Brian Spina. BS, Siena Coll., Loudonville, N.Y. Pub. Hawk Press, Albany, NY; pres., founder WellAssist KKC. Author: (book) "The Personal Health Diary", 2001, "HealthTrax - A Health Information Organizer", 1993. Mem.: N.Y. Inst. for Entrepreneurship, Women in Tech. Inst. Office: WellAssist LLC PO Box 729 Slingerlands NY 12159 Business E-Mail: tspina@wellassist.com.

OLSGAARD, JOHN NEWMAN, library science educator, university official; b. Jamestown, N.D., Dec. 29, 1953; s. Newman Benjamin and Doris Eileen (Olson) O.; m. Jane Lynell Kinch, Aug. 5, 1978; children: Sarah, Neal. BA, Jamestown Coll., 1974; MA, U. N.D., 1976; MLS, U. Iowa, 1977; PhD, U. Ill., 1984. Documents libr. U. S.D., Vermillion, 1977-81; asst. dean U. S.C., Columbia, 1984, 86-89, interim dean, 1985, assoc. prof. libr. sci., assoc. provost, 1989—. Author, editor: Principles and Practices of Information Science, 1989; contbr. articles to profl. jours. Founding mem. Thomas Cooper Soc., Columbia, 1991. Mem. ALA, Am. Assn. Higher Edn., Riverbanks Zoo Soc., Phi Kappa Phi, Phi Alpha Theta. Office: U SC Provost's Office Columbia SC 29208 E-mail: jo@gwm.sc.edu.

OLSHAKER, MARK BRUCE, author, film maker; b. Washington, Feb. 28, 1951; s. Bennett and Thelma A. (Abramson) O.; m. Carolyn M. Clemente, Aug. 28, 1977. BA, George Washington U., Washington, 1972. Spl. correspondent St. Louis Post Dispatch, Washington Bur., 1974-75; writer, author, film maker Washington Area, 1972—. V.p. Unicorn Projects, Inc., Washington, 1983—, Mindhunters, Inc. Vienna, Va., 1995—; bd. dirs. Shakespeare Guild, Washington. Author: (novels) Einstein's Brain, 1981, Unnatural Causes, 1986, Blood Race, 1989, The Edge, 1994, The Mindhunters: Broken Wings, 1999; (anthology) Unusual Suspects, 1996; (non-fiction) The Instant Image, 1978; co-author (with John Douglas), Mindhunter, 1995 (Anthony award nomination, Brit. Gold Dagger nomination, Edgar nomination, Mystery Writers of Am.), Unabomber: On the Trail of America's Most-Wanted Serial Killer, 1996, Journey into Darkness, 1997, Obsession, 1998, The Anatomy of Motive, 1999, The Cases That Haunt Us, 2000; (with C.J. Peters) Virus Hunter, 1997; (screen writing) Stormchasers, 1995, (CINE Golden Eagle), The Edge, 1996 (TV Writing and Prodn.) We All Came to America, 1974, A Moment in Time, 1975, Patent Pending, 1975 (silver medal Inst. Film & TV Festival N.Y.), Lewis Mumford: Toward Human Architecture, 1979, Castle, 1983 (Am. Film Festival Red Ribbon), Cathedral, 1985 (Am. Film Festival Blue Ribbon, Cine Golden Eagle) Pyramid, 1988 (CINE Golden Eagle, Nat. Ednl. Film and Video Festival Gold Apple), What's Killing the Children?, 1990, Discovering Hamlet, 1990 (Am. Film Festival Red Ribbon, Bronze medal Inst. Film & TV Festival N.Y.), Mind of a Serial Killer, 1992 (Emmy nomination news and documentary 1993), Roman City, 1994 (Emmy award), Bridge, 1998, Mill Times, 2001; contbr. articles to newspapers, mags., wrote exhibition films for Nat. Park Svc., and Nat. Bicentennial Grand Parade, 1976 Media advisor, NEH, Corp. Pub. Broadcasting, Washington, 1984, 89, 91, 98, D.C. Comm. Arts and Humanities; hearing com. D.C. Ct. of Appeal Bd. on Profl. Responsibility, 1988-91. Mem. Writers Guild of Am. East, The Authors Guild, The Cosmos Club, Nat. Press Club. Office: PO Box 1957 Vienna VA 22183-1957

OLSHEN, ABRAHAM CHARLES, actuarial consultant; b. Portland, Oreg., Apr. 20, 1913; m. Dorothy Olds, June 21, 1934; children: Richard Allen, Beverly Ann Jacobs. AB, Reed Coll., 1933; MS, U. Iowa, 1935, PhD, 1937. Chief statistician City Planning Commn., Portland, Oreg., 1933-34; rsch. asst. math. dept. U. Iowa, 1934-37; biometrics asst. Med. Ctr., 1936-37; actuary, chief examiner Oreg. Ins. Dept., 1937-42, 45-46; actuary West Coast Life Ins. Co., San Francisco, 1946—, chief actuary, 1953-63, v.p., 1947—, 1st v.p., 1963-67, senior v.p., 1967-68, bd. dirs., 1955-68. Cons. actuarial and ins. mgmt., pres. Olshen & Assocs., San Francisco, 1979—; bd. dirs. Home Federal Savs. & Loan Assn., San Francisco, 1972-85, vice-chmn. bd. 1979-85, bd. chmn. 1985-86; guest lectr. various univs. Contbg. writer Ency. Britannica, Underwriters' Report, The Nat. Underwriter, Life Underwriters Mag., Annals of Math. Stats., other publs. Mem. Calif. com. Health Ins. Coun., U. Calif. Med. Care Adminstrn. com., San Mateo County Retirement Bd. (1975-77). Rsch. assoc. Div. of War Rsch., 1942-44, Ops. Rsch. Gp., H/Q Comdr.-in-Chief, U.S. Fleet, 1944-45. Recipient U.S. Navy Ordnance Devel. award, 1945, Disting. Service award U.S. Office of Sci. Rsch. & Devel., 1945, Presdl. Cert. Merit, 1947. Fellow AAAS, Sigma Xi; mem. Health Ins. Assn. Am. (mem., past chmn. Blanks Com., actuarial & stat. com.), Actuarial Club of Pacific States (past pres.), Actuarial Club of San Francisco (past pres.), Am. Acad. of Actuaries (charter), Am. Math. Soc., Am. Risk and Ins. Assn., Calif. Math. Coun., Commonwealth Club (life), Fellow Conf. of Actuaries in Public Practice, Inst. Mgmt. Scis., Inst. Math. Stats., Internat. Actuarial Assn., Internat. Assn. Consulting Actuaries, Internat. Cong. Actuaries, Ops. Rsch. Soc. (charter), San Francisco Press Club (life). Office: Olshen & Assocs 760 Market St Ste 739 San Francisco CA 94102-2302

OLSHEN, RICHARD A. statistician, educator; b. Portland, Oreg., May 17, 1942; s. A.C. and Dorothy (Olds) O.; m. Susan Abroff, 1979. AB, U. Calif., Berkeley, 1963; PhD, Yale U., 1966. Rsch. staff statistician, lectr. Yale U., New Haven, 1966-67; asst. prof. stats. Stanford (Calif.) U., 1967-72; assoc. prof. stats. and math. U. Mich., Ann Arbor, 1972-75; assoc. prof. math. U. Calif., San Diego, 1975-77, prof. math., 1977-89, dir. lab. for math. and stats., 1982-89; prof. biostats. Sch. Medicine Stanford U., 1989—, prof. by courtesy dept. stats., 1990—, prof. by courtesy dept. elec. engring., 1995—, chief divsn. biostats., 1998—, assoc. chair dept. health rsch. and policy, 1999-2001. Office: Stanford U Sch Medicine Hrp Bldg Stanford CA 94305-5405 E-mail: olshen@stat.stanford.edu.

OLSINSKI, PETER KEVIN, international career continuation executive, coach; b. N.Y.C., Aug. 27, 1942; s. Peter Andrew and Mary Lucinda (O'Connor) O.; m. Joan Mary Mahon; children: Marybeth, Peter John. BA, Cathedral Coll., 1964; MS, St. John's U., Jamaica, N.Y., 1971; PhD, St. John's U., 1979. Dir. pers. Bklyn. Social Svcs., 1968-84; dir. Mainstream Access, N.Y.C., 1984-85; v.p. Fuchs Cuthrell & Co., 1985-88, from sr. v.p. to sr. exec. v.p., 1988-94, vice-chmn., 1994-96; also bd. dirs., 1991-96; sr. v.p. Goodrich & Sherwood Assoc., 1996—2001, Caliper Corp., 2001—02; pres. Olsenske Assocs., 2002—. Mem. Livingston Hist. Soc. Mem. Am. Psychol. Assn., Soc. for Indsl. & Orgnizational Psychology, Am. Soc. for Tng. and Devel., Soc. Human Resource Mgmt. Roman Catholic. Avocation: Civil War research.

OLSON, ANMARIE K. accountant; b. Teaneck, N.J., June 14, 1970; d. Henry Paul Olson and Maureen Frances Kennedy-Olson. BBA, Pace U., 1992. CPA, N.Y. Sr. auditor Marsh & McLennan Cos., Inc., N.Y.C., 1992-96; sr. acct. Ammirati & Puris Lintas, 1996, KPMG Peat Marwick, N.Y.C., 1996-98; sr. mgr. planning and forecasting Am. Express, 1998—. Roman Catholic. Avocations: tennis, swimming.

OLSON, BARBARA FORD, physician; b. Iowa City, June 15, 1935; d. Leonard A. and Anne (Swanson) Ford; m. Robert Eric Olson, 1959 (div. 1973); children: Katherine Gee, Eric Ford, Julie Marie. BA, Gustavus Adolphus Coll., 1956; MD, U. Minn., 1960. Diplomate Am. Bd. Family Practice, Am. Bd. Geriat. Medicine, added qualification geriat. medicine. Intern St. Paul-Ramsy Med. Ctr., 1960-61; resident in anesthesiology U. Hosp. Cleve., 1961-62, U. Minn. Hosp., Mpls., 1962-63; pvt. practice anesthesiology St. Johns Hosp. and Devine Redeemer Hosp., St. Paul, 1963-67, Mercy Hosp., Coon Rapids, 1967-74; staff physician Oak Terrace Nursing Home, Minnetonka, 1974-88; staff physician, med. dir. nursing home care unit VA Med. Ctr., St. Cloud, 1988—. Pres., bd. dirs. Alpha Epsilon Iota Med. Found., Mpls., 1980-86. Mem. Minn. Med. Assn., Minn. Women Physicians (pres. 1981-82), Minn. Nursing Home Med. Dirs. Home: PO Box 7306 Saint Cloud MN 56302-7306 Office: VA Med Ctr 4801 8th St N Saint Cloud MN 56303-2015 E-mail: Barbara.Olson@med.va.gov.

OLSON, BARRY GAY, advertising executive, creative director; b. Glendale, Calif., July 3, 1933; s. Gay Frank and Dorothy Barry (Guay) O. Student, U. So. Calif., 1952-54, UCLA, 1953, Coll. of San Mateo, Calif., 1954. In prodn. Neiman-Marcus, Dallas, 1956; prodn. mgr. Grant Advt., San Francisco, 1957-60; copywriter D'Arcy, MacManus, Masius, 1960-62, Norman, Craig & Kummel, N.Y.C., 1965-67, W. B. Doner, Balt., 1967-68, Ted Bates, L.A., 1969; creative dir., v.p. McCann-Erickson, Melbourne, Australia, 1963-65, J. Walter Thompson, Detroit, 1972-75, Vickers & Benson, Montreal, Can., 1976-77, Meldrum & Fewsmith, Cleve., 1971-72, 77-79, Stockton West Burkhart, Cin., 1981-82; creative dir. Hitchcock Fleming, Akron, Ohio, 1982-83, Muller Jordan Weiss, St. Louis, 1984-85; creative dir., v.p., shareholder Innis-Maggiore-Olson, Canton, Ohio, 1985-91; exec. v.p., creative dir., ptnr. Olson and Gibbons, Cleve., 1991-98, also bd. dirs.; exec. v.p., creative dir. Watt/Fleishman-Hillard Advt. Ltd., 1998—. Instr. creative advt. part-time Dynamic Graphics Edn. Found., Peoria, Ill., 1989. Contbr. to textbooks: American Corporate Identity 11 and 12, and to Contemporary Advertising. Trustee Big Bros., San Francisco, 1962, Palace Theater Assn., Canton, 1987, N.E. Ohio chpt. March of Dimes Birth Defects Found., 1991-93, Cleve. Signstage Theater, 1996—, Boy Scouts Am. Greater Cleve. Coun., 1999—; trustee, v.p. Cleve. Soc. Communicating Arts, 1971; mem. Mus. Modern Art, N.Y.C., 1980-95, Cleve. Mus. Art, 1996—. With USAF, 1954-55. Recipient Spl. Jury Gold award Atlanta Film Festival, 1975, Advertising Club of N.Y., Andy, 1975, Clio, 1976, One Show, Gold, 1976, Silver and Bronze Lions Cannes Film Festival, 1977, Ace award B/PAA of N.Y.C., 1989, Best of Show awards Columbus Advt. Club, 1981, Canton Advt. Club, 1988, 89, 90, Mktg. Mag. Silver award, Toronto, Can., 1976, Spl. Merit award Inst. Outdoor Advt., N.Y., 1986, Silver Microphone radio awards, Nat. Winners, 1987, 90, 96; 86 Gold Addy awards Akron Advt. Club, Canton Club, Cleve. Advt. Assn., Columbus Advt. Club, 1981, 85, 86, 87, 88, 90, 95, 5th Dist. Addy awards, 1995, 96, Gold Plaque award Chgo. Internat. Film Festival, 1992, Bronze Telly award, 1995, 96, Silver Telly award, 1996, 4 Gold Tower awards BMA Cleve., 1994, 96; voted one of top 100 creative people in Am. Ad Daily mag., 1971. Mem. Cleve. Advt. Assn., Cleve. Athletic Club, Hermit Club, Cleve. Play House Club. Home: 1742 W 29th Pl Cleveland OH 44113-3022 Office: Watt/Fleishman-Hillard Advt Ltd Key Tower 127 Pub Sq Ste #5200 Cleveland OH 44114 E-mail: barrycal@webtv.net., olsonb@fleishman.com.

OLSON, CAL WALLACE, editor; b. Vining, Minn., Nov. 13, 1924; s. Joseph Alvin and Ellen Jeanette Olson; m. Joanne Laverne, Apr. 16, 1950; children: Catherine, Charles. BA, U. Minn., 1948. City editor Daily News, Moorhead, Minn., 1948-50; mng. editor the Forum, Fargo, N.D., 1970-75; editor-in-residence Moorhead State U., 1975-76; producer, anchor KFME-TV, Fargo, 1977-78; editor Sioux City (Iowa) Jour., 1978-89, editor emeritus, 1989—. Author, editor 5 books. Nat. mktg. dir. Svc. Corps Ret. Execs., Washington, 1994-96. With Navy Air Corps, 1943-45. Recipient George Polk Meml. award L.I. U., 1966, Disting. Svc. award Iowa Newspaper Assn., Des Moines, 1987; co-recipient Pulitzer prize, 1957. Mem. Soc. Profl. Journalists, Shriners, Masons. Lutheran. Avocations: photography, fishing, clowning. Home: 2000 Outer Dr N #523 Sioux City IA 51104 E-mail: calolson@willinet.net.

OLSON, CANDY, school system administrator; b. Glen Ridge, N.J., Sept. 3, 1947; d. George Francis and Elizabeth Ehlers Sullivan; m. John Karl Olson, June 26, 1974; children: Elizabeth Ann, Katherine Louise. BA, Newton (Mass.) Coll., 1969; MBA, U. South Fla., Tampa, 1976. Staff Exec. Office Transp. and Constrn., Boston, 1972; registered rep. Josephthal & Co. and Estabrook & Co., 1972-73; analyst, adminstrv. asst. Endowment Mgmt. & Rsch., 1973-75; trust investment resource officer Exch. Bank, Tampa, 1976-77; dir. fin. and planning Drug Abuse Comprehensive Coord. Office, 1977-80; freelance writer, 1981-95. Mem. adv. bd. Child Abuse Coun., Tampa, 1990-99, Sch. Enrichment Resource Vols., T ampa, 1994—; mem. Hillsborough County Sch. Bd. 1994—, chair 1998-99; bd. dirs. United Way, Tampa, 1994-99, mem. fin. com., 1996—; bd. dirs. Lowry Pk. Zoo, Tampa, 1995—; bd. dirs., Fla. Edn. Leadership Found., Tallahassee, 1998—, Tampa Bay Performing Arts Ctr., 1998—, chair edn. com., 1999—; mem. parent bd. U. Del., 1998-2002, co-pres., 2000-2002. Mem. Jr. League Tampa, Athena Soc., Tiger Bay Club. Roman Catholic. Avocations: gardening, reading. Office: Hillsborough County Sch Bd 901 E Kennedy Blvd Tampa FL 33602-3507 E-mail: candy.olson@sdhc.k12.fl.us.

OLSON, CHARLES ERIC, economist; b. Wausau, Wis., June 2, 1942; s. Roland Anthony and Lois (Erickson) O.; m. Pamela Ann Templin, July 1, 1967 (div. Oct. 1973); children: Sonja Anne, Erika Christine; m. Carole Emily Collesian, Dec. 1, 1973 (div. Oct. 1990); children: Cora Elizabeth, Sarah Emily; m. Jeanne Esther Katz, Apr. 14, 1991. Student, U. Wis., Marathon County, 1960-62; BBA with honors, U. Wis., Madison, 1964; MS, U. Wis., 1966, PhD (Vilias fellow), 1968. Instr. U. Wis., Madison, 1966-68; asst. prof. U. Md., College Park, 1968-71, assoc. prof. bus. adminstrn., 1971-76; sr. economist H. Zinder & Assocs., Washington, 1976-77, v.p., 1977-79, sr. v.p., 1979-86, pres., 1986-2000, Olson & Co., Inc., 1980-86; vis. assoc. prof. R.H. Smith Sch. Bus., U. Md., College Park, 2000—. Cons. Devel. Adv. Service, atty. gens. N.C., Minn., Ky., Mass., Va. U.S. Postal Rate Commn., Dept. Def., numerous electric and gas utlities in U.S. and Can. Testified numerous pub. utility rate cases, before Senate Subcom. on Inter-govtl. Relations; mem. advisory com. research and devel. and energy conservation Fed. Power Commn., 1973-74, vice chmn. rate design task force, 1976—. Author: Cost Considerations for Efficient Electricity Supply, 1970; contbr. chpts. to books, articles to profl. jours. Mem. Prince Georges County (Md.) Citizens Airpark Advisory Com., 1970-71. Grantee Inst. Pub. Utilities, 1967-68; U. Md. 1970, 76. Mem. Transp. and Pub. Utilities Group, Beta Gamma Sigma. Home: 10822 Alloway Dr Rockville MD 20854-1503 Office: RH Smith Sch Bus Univ Md College Park MD 20742 E-mail: hzinder@aol.com.

OLSON, CLIFFORD LARRY, management consultant, entrepreneur; b. Karlstad, Minn., Oct. 11, 1946; s. Wallace B. and Lucille I (Pederson) O.; m. B.A. Blue Blodgett, March 18, 1967; children: Derek, Erin. BChemE, B in Physics, U. Minn., 1969; MBA, U. Chgo., 1972; Licence en Sci. Econ., U. Louvain, Brussels, 1972. CPA, Cert. mgmt. cons. Project engr. Procter & Gamble, Chgo., 1969-71; engagement mgr. McKinsey & Co., 1972-75; ptnr., midwest regional dir. mgmt. cons. Peat, Marwick, Mitchell, St. Louis, 1976-87; chmn. Casson Group, Inc., Mpls., 1987—; CEO AbelConn, 1997—. Mem. AICPA, Union League Club Chgo., Interlachen Country Club. Avocations: skiing, carpentry. Office: 9210 Science Center Dr New Hope MN 55428-3621

OLSON, DALE C. public relations executive; b. Fargo, N.D., Feb. 20, 1934; s. Arthur Edwin and Edith (Weight) Olson Neubauer. Sr. v.p., prin., pres. motion picture divsn. Rogers and Cowan, Inc., Beverly Hills, Calif., 1967-85; prin. Dale C. Olson & Assocs., 1985—. Cons. Filmex, L.A., 1972-83; U.S. del. Manila Film Festival, 1982-83. Editor L.A. edit. Theatre ann. Best Plays, 1963-67. V.p. Diamond Cir. City of Hope, Duarte, Calif., 1980-83; mem. adv. bd. Calif. Mus. Sci. and Industry, L.A., 1975-81; mem. bd. govs. Film Industry Workshops, Inc., 1965-80; pres. Hollywood Press Club, 1963-66; assoc. Los Angeles County Art Mus., 1981-83; bd. trustees Hollywood Arts Coun.; chair 1999 jury USA Film Festival, Dallas; cons. L.A. 2000. Recipient Golden Key, Pub. Rels. News, 1982, Les Mason and pub. svc. awards Publicists Guild, Golden Satellite award for lifetime achievement Internat. Press Acad., 1999, Prism award for pub. svc. Entertainment Industries Coun., 2000. Mem. NATAS, Acad. Motion Picture Arts and Scis. (chmn. pub. rels. coordinating com. 1982—), Actors Fund Am. (chmn. Western coun. 1991, trustee 1992, exec. com. 1998), Hollywood Arts Coun. (bd. dirs.), Pres.'s Club, Thalians. Lutheran. E-mail: dolson2000@earthlink.net.

OLSON, DAVID JOHN, political science educator; b. Brantford, N.D., May 18, 1941; s. Lloyd and Alice Ingrid (Black) O.; m. Sandra Jean Crabb, June 11, 1966; 1 dau., Maia Kari. BA, Concordia Coll., Moorhead, Minn., 1963; Rockefeller fellow Union Theol. Sem. N.Y.C., 1963-64; MA (Brooklings Instn. predoctoral research fellow 1968-69), U. Wis., Madison, 1966, PhD (univ. fellow 1967), 1971. Community planner Madison Redvel. Authority, 1965-66; lectr. U. Wis., 1966-67; from lectr. to asso. prof. polit. sci. Ind. U., Bloomington, 1969-76; prof. polit. sci. U. Wash., Seattle, 1976—, chmn. dept., 1983-88, Harry Bridges endowed chairlabor studies, 1992-94; bd. dirs. Harry Bridges Inst.; dir.Ctr. Labor Studies U. Wash., 1992-94; Disting. lectr. in labor studies San Francisco State U., 1994. Vis. prof. U. Bergen, 1987, Harvard U., 1988-89, U. Hawaii, 1989, U. Calif., Berkeley, 1996. Co-author: Governing the United States, 1978, Commission Politics, 1977, To Keep the Republic, 1975, Black Politics, 1971; co-editor: Theft of the City, 1974. Recipient Disting. Teaching award Ind. U., 1973, faculty fellow, 1973, Alumni Achievement award Concordia Coll., 1998. Mem. Am. Polit. Sci. Assn., Western Polit. Sci. Assn. (v.p. 1984, pres. 1985), Midwest Polit. Sci. Assn., So. Polit. Sci. Assn. Democrat. Lutheran. Home: 6512 E Green Lake Way N Seattle WA 98103-5418 Office: U Wash Dept Polit Sci Seattle WA 98195-0001

OLSON, DENNIS OLIVER, lawyer; b. Seminole, Tex., Oct. 19, 1947; s. Edwin and Beulah Matilda (Strang) O.; m. Leonee Lynn Claud, Jan. 30, 1971; children: James Edwin, Stacy Rae. BA in English, U. Tex., 1969; JD, Tex. Tech U., 1974. Bar: Tex. 1974, U.S. Ct. Mil. Appeals 1974, U.S. Dist. Ct. (no. dist.) Tex. 1978, U.S. Dist. Ct. (we. dist.) Tex. 1978, U.S. Ct. Appeals (5th cir.) 1984, U.S. Supreme Ct. 1985, U.S. Dist. Ct. (ea. dist.) Tex. 2002. Commd. USMC, 1969, advanced through grades to capt., 1973, infantry officer various locations including Vietnam, 1969-74, judge advocate, 1974-78, resigned, 1978; assoc. Carr, Evans, Fouts & Hunt, and predecessor, Lubbock, Tex., 1978-81, ptnr., 1981-85; pvt. practice Dallas, 1985-88; shareholder, co-chmn. bankruptcy sect. Godwin & Carlton, P.C., 1989-94; ptnr. Olson Nicoud Birne & Gueck, LLP & predecessor, 1994—. Bd. dirs. Presbyn. Ctr. Doctor's Clinic, Lubbock, 1983-85, United Campus Ministry, Tex. Tech U., Lubbock, 1984-85, Discovery Sch., Richardson, 1999-2002; elder Canyon Creek Presbyn. Ch., Richardson, Tex.; treas. bd. dirs. Lubbock chpt. ARC, 1975-77; vol. Lubbock United Way, 1978-80. Decorated Bronze Star; named Outstanding Young Man of Am., 1983. Fellow Tex. Bar Found. (sustaining life); mem. Dallas Bar Assn., Lubbock County Bar Assn. (bd. dirs. 1983-85), Tex. Young Lawyers Assn. (bd. dirs. 1981-83), Judge Advocates Assn. (bd. dirs. 1976-78), Lubbock C. of C. (grad. Leadership Lubbock program 1981), U. Tex. NROTC Alumni Found., (bd. dirs. 2001-), Phi Delta Phi. Home: 313 Forest Grove Dr Richardson TX 75080-1937 E-mail: denniso@dallas-law.com.

OLSON, DENNIS THORALD, religion educator; b. Luverne, Minn., Jan. 6, 1954; s. Toby and Esther (Heaak) O.; m. Carol Joyce Andersen, June 3, 1978; children: Eric Leif, Kristen Esther. BA, Augustana Coll., Sioux Falls, S.D., 1976; MDiv, Luther Theol. Sem., 1980; MA, Yale U., 1981, PhD, 1984. Tchg. fellow Yale Div. Sch., New Haven, 1981-84; parish pastor United Luth. Ch., Frost, Minn., 1984-87; instr. Luther Northwestern Theol. Sem., St. Paul, 1985-87; prof. of Old Testament Princeton (N.J.) Theol. Sem. Author: The Death of the Old and the Birth of the New: The Framework of the Book of Numbers and the Pentateuch, 1985, Deuteronomy and the Death of Moses, 1994, (interpretation commentary) Numbers, 1996, The Book of Judges (The New Interpreter's Bible), 1998; contbr. articles to profl. jours. N.Am. Ministerial fellowship Fund for Theol. Edn., 1976-80, Grad. Alumni fellowship Yale U., 1983-84; resident scholar Ctr. for Theol. Inquiry, Princeton, 1990—, Nat. Merit scholar, 1972-76. Mem. Soc. of Bibl. Lit. Office: Princeton Theol Sem CN821 Princeton NJ 08542 E-mail: dennis.olson@ptsem.edu. *There is no Paradise, no Garden of Eden, no ideal Promised Land in this life. But there are momentary glimpses of such places, glimpses which give hope and encouragement to carry on.*

OLSON, DIANA CRAFT, image and etiquette consultant; b. Langley, Va., May 5, 1941; d. Winfred O. and Joyce (Clark) Craft; m. Robert J. Olson, May 30, 1976; stepchildren: Stacey, Kirsten Lowry. BA, U. Tex., 1963; MA, San Francisco State U., 1970; cert. image cons., Fashion Acad., Costa Mesa, Calif., 1980; cert., Protocol Sch. Washington, 1988. Tchr. USAF, P.R., 1963-64, Long Beach (Calif.) Unified Sch. Dist., 1964-68, South San Francisco (Calif.) Unified Sch. Dist., 1968-79; founder Diana's Color Collage & Color Collage Inst., Pasadena, Calif., 1979—. Etiquette affiliates Dorthea Johnson and Marjabelle Stewart, Washington, 1988—; cons. Weight Watchers Internat., L.A., Ventura, Calif., 1987-90, Marriott Hotels, Long Beach, 1989, 1st Interstate Bank, L.A., 1990, Ritz Carlton Hotels, 1995. Designer: The Compassionate Friends nat. meml. pin, 1998; prodr. (book, CD and tape) The Secrets of Color and Style, 2001; contbr. articles to mags. Mem.: Assn. Image Consultants Internat. (sec. 1989—90, v.p. 1990—92, 2000—01, v.p. programs 2001—02, pres. So. Calif. chpt. 2002—). Republican. Presbyterian. Avocations: swimming, skiing. Studio: Diana's Color Collage 465 E Union St Ste 100 Pasadena CA 91101-1783 Fax: 626-584-1856. E-mail: olsonco465@aol.com.

OLSON, DONALD R. neurosurgeon, consultant; b. Edgerton, Wis., Dec. 13, 1936; m. Margie Olson; children: Jacy, Elisa, Kristina, Jon. BS, U. Wis., 1958, MD, 1961; MBA, George Fox U., Newberg, Oreg., 1996. Diplomate Am. Bd. Neurol. Surgery, Am. Bd. Pain Medicine. Resident in gen. surgery U. Wis. Med. Sch., Madison, 1965, resident in neurol. surgery, 1965-69; resident in neuropathology Neuropsychiat. Inst./U. Ill., Chgo., 1966; mem. faculty U. Nev. Med. Sch., Reno, 1971-81, clin. prof. surgery, 1980-81, clin. assoc. prof. neurosurgery, 1983-85; clin. instr. neurosurgery U. Calif. Med. Sch., San Francisco, 1974-81, clin. assoc. prof. neurosurgery San Diego, 1983-84; practice clin. neurosurgery/micro-neurosurgery, 1971-93; cons. neurosurgery in pvt. practice, 1993—; mem. staff Eisenhower Army Med. Ctr., Augusta, Ga., 1995-97; clin. prof. neurosurgery U. Oreg. Health Sci., 2001—. Fellow U. Paris, 1970-71; owner Olson Vineyard, Dundee, Oreg., 1985—; owner, pres. Torii Mor Winery, McMinnville, Oreg., 1993—; cons. med. devel. co. Pisxys, Boulder, Colo.; pres., CEO Pixsys NW/Pixsys Bohemia, 1994—; cons. minimally invasive neurosurgery N.W. Med. Teams, Portland; founder doctorii.com; mem. courtesy staff dept. neurosurgery Oreg. Health Sci. U. Contbr. articles to profl. jours.; presenter in field. Trustee Truckee Meadows C.C. Found., 1987-88, other civic activities; charter mem. Rep. Presdl. Task Force, 1983—; mem. Rep. Nat. Coun., 1984—, Rep. Senatorial Inner Circle, 1984—, Pres.'s Club of Rep. Nat. Com., 1984—; amb. to Czech Republic, Digneron d' Honneur Compagnons du Bordeaux. Capt. USAF, 1962-64, col. USAR, 1984—. Fellow ACS, Internat. Coll. Surgeons, Royal Soc. Medicine (London), Am. Soc. for Laser Medicine and Surgery, N.Am. Spine Soc., Am. Coll. Physician Execs.; mem. Am. Acad. Pain Medicine, Marion-Polk County Med. Assn., Laser Assn. Neurol. Surgeons Internat., Neurol. Soc. Nev. (founder), Western Neurol. Soc., Am. Assn. Neurosurgeons, Congress of Neurosurgery, Internat. Spinal Injection Soc., Capital Club (Washington), Porsche Club, Oreg. Wine Brotherhood. Office: 18325 NE Fairview Dr Dundee OR 97115-9112

OLSON, DONALD RICHARD, mechanical engineering educator; b. Sargent, Nebr., Dec. 26, 1917; s. Harry T. and Gyneth E. (Wittemyer) O.; m. Nancy Walker Benton, June 17, 1944; children: Walter H., Sally, Timothy W. BS, Oreg. State U., 1942; M.Engring., Yale U., 1944, D.Engring., 1951. Profl. engr., Conn. Asst. prof., asso. prof. mech. engring. Yale U., New Haven, 1951-62; prof. mech. engring. Pa. State U., University Park, 1962-83, prof. emeritus, 1983—; head underwater power plants Applied Research Lab., 1962-72, head dept. mech. engring., 1972-83; mem. engring. accreditation commn., 1979-82. Contbr. tech. papers in field to publs. Mem. ASME, Soc. Automotive Engrs. (dir. 1968-71), Sigma Xi. Home: 621 Glenn Rd State College PA 16803-3475 E-mail: dro@psu.edu.

OLSON, EDWARD CHARLES, entrepreneur, conservationist, writer, business consultant, foundation administrator; b. Jacksonville, Fla., July 6, 1956; s. Edward Charles and Marcine Era (Hall) O.; m. Krista Lynn Neuberger, Aug. 5, 1978; children: Laura Ellen, Edward Charles, Natalie Rose. BS, Miami U., Oxford, Ohio, 1978; MS, Wash. State U., 1980; PhD, Ohio State U., 1983. State dir. Nature Conservancy, Columbus, Ohio, 1983-86; pres., CEO Florida Keys Land & Sea Trust, 1986-93, Catalina Island Conservancy, Avalon, Calif., 1993-96; chmn., CEO E.C. Olson & Assocs., 1996—; ptnr. Oceanwatch Prodn. Group, 1996—. Cons. non-profit orgns., 1987—; chmn., CEO Man-O-War Clothing, Co., 1996—; pres., CEO St. Lucie Wetland Solutions, Inc., 1997—, Fla. Wetlands Stewardship Group, Inc., 1998—; dir. Reef Relief, 1997—; chmn., CEO Fregata Publ. Co., 1998—; pres., CEO MitBank-USA, 1999—. Editor: Guide to the Florida Keys, 1989; author: Winds of the Marquesas, 1996, Hardball, 1998, After Matthias, 1999. Bd. dirs. Catalina Cmty. Pub. Radio, 1993-96, Fla. Nat. Parks and Monuments Assn., Homestead, 1988-93, Fla. Keys Meml. Hosp., Key West, 1989-91, Fla. Keys Guidance Clinic, Marathon, 1990-92. Recipient Leadership Fla. Grad. award Fla. C. of C., 1990, Outstanding Young Floridian, Fla. Jaycees, 1991; named Man of Yr., Marathon Jaycees, 1990. Avocations: fishing, travel, reading, writing, Civil War study. Office: 205 Olive Ave Port Saint Lucie FL 34952-1347 E-mail: ecolson@inetw.net.

OLSON, ERNESTINE LEE, nurse; b. Gregory, S.D., Oct. 14, 1952; d. Ervin E. and Nila Lee (Ritterbush) Neiman; divorced; children: Nathan, Candice. BSN, U. Nebr., 1974; MSN, 2000. RN, Nebr. Family nurse practitioner Regional West Med. Ctr./Panhandle Health Svcs., Scottsbluff, Nebr. Mem. Gov.'s Rural Health Task Force; instr. CPR. Recipient Writing award Am. Jour. Nursing, 1984, Woman of Distinction award Girl Scouts Am., 1995. Mem.: VFW, ANA, Am. Heart Assn., Nebr. Nurses Assn. (dist. V pres., continuing edn. reviewer), S.W. Regional SIDS Coun., Am. Cancer Soc., Am. Legion Aux. Mennonite. Home: 2308 Avenue B Scottsbluff NE 69361-1637 Office: 4021 Avenue B Scottsbluff NE 69361-4602

OLSON, FERRON ALLRED, metallurgist, educator; b. Tooele, Utah, July 2, 1921; s. John Ernest and Harriet Cynthia (Allred) O.; m. Donna Lee Jefferies, Feb. 1, 1944; children: Kandace, Randall, Paul, Jeffery, Richard. BS, U. Utah, 1953, PhD, 1956. Ordained bishop LDS Ch., 1962. Research chemist Shell Devel. Co., Emeryville, Calif., 1956-61; assoc. research prof. U. Utah, Salt Lake City, 1961-63, assoc. prof., 1963-68, chmn. dept mining, metall. and fuels engring., 1966-74, prof. dept. metallurgy and metall. engring., 1968-96, prof. emeritus, 1996—. Cons. U.S. Bur. Mines, Salt Lake City, 1973-77, Ctr. for Investigation Mining and Metallurgy, Santiago, Chile, 1978; dir. U. Utah Minerals Inst., 1980-91. Author: Collection of Short Stories, 1985, (hist. book) Seymour Brunson: Defender of the Faith, 1998, (novel) Harriet Cynthia Allred Olson, 1995; contbr. articles to profl. jours. Del. State Rep. Conv., Salt Lake City, 1964; bishop, 1962-68, 76-82, missionary, 1988. With U.S. Army, 1943-46, PTO. Named Fulbright-Hayes lectr., Yugoslavia, 1974-75, Disting. prof. Fulbright-Hayes, Yugoslavia, 1980, Outstanding Metallurgy Instr., U. Utah, 1979-80, 88-89, Disting. Speaker U. Belgrade-Bor, Yugoslavia, 1974. Mem. Am. Inst. Mining, Metall. and Petroleum Engrs. (chmn. Utah chpt. 1978-79), Am. Soc. Engring. Edn. (chmn. Minerals div. 1972-73), Fulbright Alumni Assn., Am. Bd. Engring. and Tech. (bd. dirs. 1975-82). Republican. Achievements include research on explosives ignition and decomposition;

surface properties of thoria, silica gels, silicon monoxide in ultra high vacuum; kinetics of leaching of Chrysocolla, Malachite and Bornite; electrowinning of gold; nodulation of copper during electrodeposition. Home: 1862 Herbert Ave Salt Lake City UT 84108-1832 E-mail: oferron@aol.com.

OLSON, FLOYD PALMER, retired service company executive; b. Glencoe, Minn., May 12, 1932; s. Oscar Peter and Hazel Anna (Wolff) O.; m. Sandra Rae Larson, Feb. 5, 1955; children: Douglas, David, Clayton, Sarah. BS, U. Minn., 1954. Mgmt. trainee Wilson Meat Packing Co., Albert Lea, Minn., 1957-60, dept. mgr. Memphis, 1960-62, area mgr. Sao Paulo, Brazil, 1962-69, plant mgr. Oklahoma City, 1969-76; pres. Gol-Pak Corp., Oneida, N.Y., 1976-78; asst. West Coast mgr. Hygrade Food Products, Tacoma, 1978-79; owner, dir. Servpro, Gig Harbor, 1979-2000; ret., 2000. Bd. mem. Peninsula Light Co., Gig Harbor, 1992-95; state dir. Servpro Industries, Wash., 1982-2000. Organizer Jr. Achievement, Albert Lea, Minn., 1959; pres. couns. ch., 1975-74. With U.S. Army, 1955-57. Mem. Rotary Internat. (pres. Gig Harbor 1990-91, presdl. citation 1996, dist. gov. 1994-95, zone chmn. 1996-97, dir. elect, Paul Harris fellow 1993). Republican. Avocations: motorhoming, golf, travel.

OLSON, FRANK ALBERT, car rental company executive; b. San Francisco, July 19, 1932; s. Alfred and Edith Mary (Hazeldine) O.; m. Sarah Jean Blakely, Oct. 19, 1957; children: Kimberly, Blake, Christopher. AA, City Coll. San Francisco, 1961. V.p. and gen. mgr. Barrett Transp. Inc., San Francisco, 1950-64; v.p., gen. mgr. Valcar Co. subs. Hertz Corp., 1964-68; mgr. N.Y. zone Hertz Corp., N.Y.C., 1968-69, v.p., mgr. Ea. region, v.p., gen. mgr. rent-a-car divsn., exec. v.p. rent-a-car divsn. gen. mgr., also bd. dirs., 1973-77, pres., 1977-80; CEO, 1977-99; chmn. bd. dirs. Hertz Corp., N.Y.C., 1980, also dir., CEO, 1982—; chmn., CEO Allegis Corp., 1987; pres., CEO United Airlines, 1987; chmn., CEO Hertz Corp., Park Ridge, NJ, 1987-99, chmn.. bd. dirs., 1999—. Bd. dirs. Amerada Hess Corp., Becton Dickinson & Co., Fund Am. Enterprises Holdings, Inc. Bd. dirs., mem. exec. com. World Travel and Tourism Coun. Mem. Am. Assn. Sovereign Mil. Order of Malta, Pine Valley Golf Club (N.J.), Royal and Ancient St. Andrews (Scotland), Blind Brook Club, Met. Club (N.Y.C.), Seminole Golf Club (Fla.), Cypress Point Club (Calif.). Republican. Roman Catholic. Office: Hertz Corp Ste 100 One Maynard Dr Park Ridge NJ 07656-1888

OLSON, FREDERICK IRVING, retired history educator; b. Milw., May 30, 1916; s. Frank and Clara (Hansen) O.; m. Jane Marian Correll, June 8, 1946; children: David Frederick, Donald Frank, Roger Alan. BA magna cum laude, Harvard U., 1938, MA (George W. Dillaway fellow 1938-39), 1939, PhD in History, 1952. Mem. faculty U. Wis., Milw., 1946-85, prof. history, 1956-85, chmn. com. on univ. future, 1959-60, chmn. dept. history, 1960-62, 67-70, assoc. dean Coll. Letters and Sci., 1971-76, acting dean Sch. Library Sci., 1977-79; exec. dir. Milw. Humanities Program, 1979-84. Vis. prof. history U. Wis.-Madison, summer 1957; assoc. dean U. Wis. extension, Mil., 1960-68; dir. Ridge Stone Fin. Svcs., Brookfield, 1995-98. Author: (with Harry H. Anderson) Milwaukee: At the Gathering of the Waters, 1981, 2d edit., 1984, (with Frank Cassell and J. Martin Klotsche) The University of Wisconsin-Milwaukee: A Historical Profile, 1885-92, 1992, (with Jane Correll Olson) Dear Jane: A Soldier's Letters from Africa and the Middle East, 1942-45, 1994; contbr. articles and book revs. to profl. jours. Trustee Milw. Pub. Mus., 1951-52; bd. dirs. Milw. County Hist. Soc., 1947-85, 95—, pres., 1953-57, 72-75; bd. curators State Hist. Soc. Wis., 1961-91; mem. Milw. Landmarks Commn., 1964-71, Milw. County Landmarks Commn., 1976—, chmn., 1976-82; mem. rev. bd. Wis. Hist. Preservation, 1978-89; bd. dirs. Wis. Heritages, Inc., 1983-93, pres., 1989-90; bd. dirs. Wauwatosa Hist. Soc., 1984-96; mem. City of Wauwatosa Hist. Preservation Commn., 2001-. With AUS, 1942-45. Named Wauwatosa's Disting. Citizen of Yr., 2000. Mem. Orgn. Am. Historians, Wis. Acad. Scis., Arts and Letters, Lincoln Group (Boston), North Hills Country Club (Waukesha, Wis.), Phi Beta Kappa, Phi Alpha Theta, Phi Kappa Phi. Lutheran. Home: 2437 N 90th St Milwaukee WI 53226-1809

OLSON, GARY DUANE, history educator; b. Spring Grove, Minn., July 30, 1939; s. Raymond G. and Ethel N. (Storlie) O.; m. Rosaaen Marie Skifton, Sept. 4, 1960; children: Erik Lee, Timothy Karl, Lars Christian. BA, Luther Coll., 1961; MA, U. Nebr., 1965, PhD, 1968. Tchr. social studies Kerkhoven Pub. Schs., Minn., 1961-63; asst. prof. history Augustana Coll., Sioux Falls, S.D., 1968-73, assoc. prof., 1973-79, prof., 1979—, dean acad. svcs., 1981-87, v.p. acad. affairs, dean, 1987-95. Cons.-evaluator North Ctrl Assn., 1992—. Author: (with H. Krause) Prelude to Glory, 1974, (with E.L. Olson) Sioux Falls, South Dakota: A Pictorial History, 1985; contbr. articles to profl. jours. Mem. Orgn. Am. Historians, S.D. Hist. Soc., Vesterheim Mus. Assn., Norwegian-Am. Hist. Assn. Home: 2505 S Main Ave Sioux Falls SD 57105-4820 Office: Augustana Coll Sioux Falls SD 57197-0001 E-mail: olson@wise.augie.edu.

OLSON, GARY ROBERT, banker; b. Milw., May 9, 1946; s. Ward Louis and Mary Jane (Brown) O.; m. Mia Kristina Sohn, Feb. 26, 1972; children: Kristin Anne, Brian Ward. Student, Loyola U., Rome, 1966-67; AB, Marquette U., 1968; M Internat. Mgmt., Am. Grad. Sch. Internat. Mgmt., Glendale, Ariz., 1973. Instr. Sogang Jesuit U., Seoul, 1968-70, Hankuk U. Fgn. Studies, Seoul, 1971-72; grad. asst. Am. Grad. Sch. Internat. Mgmt., 1972; credit analyst Chase Manhattan Bank, N.A., N.Y.C. and Tokyo, 1973-75, asst. treas. N.Y.C., 1975-77, 2d v.p. Madrid, 1977, Paris, 1977-80, v.p., mgr. Regional Banking Office Chgo., 1980-83; v.p., regional mgr. Case Nat. Corp. Svcs., San Francisco, 1983-87; sr. v.p. Chase Bank Ariz., Phoenix, 1987-90; v.p. Bklyn. and S.I. commercial mgr. Chase Manhattan Bank, N.A., Bklyn., 1990-93, v.p., team leader Nassau mid. mkt. mgr. Melville, L.I., 1993-97; mgr. corp. banking L.I. Dime Savs. Bank, Huntington Station, N.Y., 1997-99; sr. v.p. comml. banking Dime Savings Bank, 2000—. Advisor English program USIS, Seoul, 1969; alumni domestic counselor Am. Grad. Sch. Internat. Mgmt., 1990—, Marquette U., 1990—; vol. Spl. Olympics, Phoenix, 1988-89; fund drive capt. Phoenix Econ. Growth Corp., 1988; trustee, bd. dirs. Variety Pre-schooler's workshop, 1994—; bd. dirs. L.I. chpt. Robert Morris Assocs., 1994—, chmn., 1995—; trustee, bd. dirs., mktg. com., chmn.'s coun. Hecksher Mus., Huntington, N.Y., 1995—. Mem. Robert Morris Assocs. (assoc.), Econ. Club Phoenix, World Trade Club. Republican. Roman Catholic. Avocations: reading, skiing, swimming, golf. Office: Washington Mutual Bank 1377 Motor Pkwy Farmingville NY 11749 E-mail: olsong@dime.com.

OLSON, GREGORY BRUCE, materials science and engineering educator, academic director; b. Bklyn., Apr. 10, 1947; s. Oscar Gustav Fritz and Elizabeth Rose (Dorner) Olson; m. Jane Ellen Black, May 10, 1980; 1 child Elise Marie. BS, MS in Materials Sci. and Engrng., MIT, 1970, ScD in Materials Sci. and Engrng., 1974. Rsch. assoc. dept. materials sci. and engrng. MIT, Cambridge, 1974-79, prin. rsch. assoc., 1979-85, sr. rsch. assoc., 1985-88; prof. materials sci. and engrng. Northwestern U., Evanston, Ill., 1988—, Wilson-Cook prof. engrng. design, 1999—. Cons. Army Materials Tech. Lab., Watertown, Mass., 1975-88, Lawrence Livermore (Calif.) Nat. Lab., 1983-89; Jacob Kurtz Exchange Scientist Technion-Israel Inst. Tech., 1979; SERC vis. prof. U. Cambridge, 1992; assoc. chmn. dept. materials sci. and engrng. Northwestern U., 1992-98, dir. materials tech. lab.-steel rsch.group, 1985—; founding mem. Questek Innovations LLC, 1997—. Editor: Innovative UHS Steel Technology, 1990, Martensite, 1992; contbr. numerous papers and articles to jours., encys., and symposia; inventor hydrogen-res. UHS steels, stainless bearing steel, ultrahard carburizing steels. Fellow AMAX Found., 1972-74; named N.Mex. Disting. lectr. in Materials, 1983; recipient Creativity Extension award NSF, 1983-85; Wallenberg grantee Jacob Wallenberg Found., Sweden, 1993, Technology Recognition award NASA, 1994, Tech. of Yr. award Industry Week mag. 1998. Fellow ASM (chmn. phase transformation com. 1987-90, Boston chpt. Saveur Meml. lectr. 1986, Phila. chpt. 1998, Alpha Sigma Mu lectr. 1996), ASM Internat., TMS-AIME (student affairs com.); mem. AAAS, Materials Rsch. Soc., Internat. Soc. Martensitic Transformation, ISS-AIME (M.R. Tenebaum award 1993), Assn. Univ. Related Rsch. Parks (Tech. Transfer award 1998). Lutheran. Avocations: sports cars, jazz trumpet. Office: Northwestern U Dept Materials Sci and Engring 2225 N Campus Dr Evanston IL 60208-3108

OLSON, HAROLD ROY, computer company executive; b. Escanaba, Mich., Apr. 8, 1928; s. Roy A. and Sara Calla Margarita (Carlson) O.; m. Angela Davis Hennessy, Sept. 26, 1959. BA in Journalism and Advt., Mich. State U., 1950. Mail clk. McCann Erickson Co., N.Y.C., 1950, 52-53; book promotion specialist, mgr. mag. promotion McGraw-Hill, 1953-56; mgr. mag. promotion Reinhold Pub. Co., 1956-58; space salesman McCall Corp., 1959-60; pres. Visual Identity, Inc., 1960-68; mktg. rep. Honeywell Info. Sys., Inc., 1969-86; pres. Hal Olson's EDGE-BUY Express, Inc., 1986—. With U.S. Army, 1950-52. Republican. Episcopalian. Avocation: sailing. Office: 26 Quirk Rd Milford CT 06460-3745

OLSON, HARRIETT JANE, corporate lawyer; b. Phila., May 5, 1958; d. Charles L. and G. Elizabeth O. BA, Houghton Coll., 1980; JD, Harvard Law Sch., 1983. Bar: N.J., Tenn. Ptnr. Pitney, Hardin, Kipp & Szuch, Morristown, N.J., 1990-96; sr. v.p. publ. United Meth. Publ. House, Nashville, 1996—. Methodist.

OLSON, HERBERT THEODORE, trade association executive; b. Bridgeport, Conn., Feb. 9, 1929; s. Herbert Theodore and Inez Evelyn (Lindahl) O.; children: Christina, Victoria; m. Kathleen A. Harrison, Dec. 27, 1988. Student, Heidelberg Coll., 1947-49; AB, Ohio U., 1951, postgrad., 1951-52. Asst. to dean of men Ohio U., Athens, 1951-52; with Union Carbide Corp., 1952-71, mgr. employee rels., coord. pub. affairs, 1969-71; exec. v.p. Am. Assn. for Aging, Washington, 1971-75; dir. spl. projects Am. Healthcare Assn., 1975-79; pres. Promotional Products Assn. Internat., Irving, Tex., 1979-96, pres. emeritus, 1996—. Event coord.-supplier Stars Showcase, 1998-2000; mem. adv. bd. Allied Bank. Mem. nat. exploring com., vice chmn. nat. events com., ann. meetings com., mem.-at-large nat. coun. Boy Scouts Am., 1980—; treas. U.S. Found. for Internat. Scouting, 1988—99, chmn. audit com., 1984—87, mem. internat. com., 1998—, mem. direct svc. coun. bd., 1997—2002; mem. long-term care for elderly rsch. rev. and adv. com. Dept. Health, 1972—77; mem. Longterm Care grant rev. com. HEW, 1972—77; mem. planning commn. City of Torrance, Calif., 1962—64, city councilman, 1964—67; chmn. Gov.'s Operation Leegit; mem. adv. bd. Irving Hosp.; chmn. bd. dirs. Irving Cancer Soc., 1997—; exec. bd. cir. 10 coun. Boy Scouts Am.; bd. dirs. Irving Conv. and Visitors Bur., 2001—, DFW Humane Soc., 2001—. Lord Baden Powell fellow, 1986; recipient Disting. Eagle award Boy Scouts Am., 1974, Silver Beaver award, 1968, Silver Buffalo award, 1998; named person of Yr. in Promotional Products in Counselor Mag., 1995, Hall of Fame Promotional Products Assn. Internat., 1997, Hall of Fame Can. Promo Prod. Assn., 1996. Mem. Meeting Planners Internat. (charter), Am. Soc. Assn., Execs., U.S. C. of C., Washington Soc. Assn. Execs., Nat. Assn. Exhibit Mgrs., Small Bus. Legis. Coun. (chmn. bd. 1993-95), Dallas Ft. Worth Soc. Assn. Execs. (v.p. 1985-87), Irving C. of C. (bd. dirs. 1999—), Am. Advt. Fedn., Tex. Sox. Assn. Execs., Las Colinas Country Club, Rotary (past bd. dirs.), Masons, Shriners, Kiwanis (lt. gov.)DFW Humane Soc. Irving (bd. dirs. 2000-). Baptist. Home: 2910 Pacific Ct Irving TX 75062-4624 Office: 807 W Pioneer Dr Irving TX 75061

OLSON, JAMES CLIFTON, historian, university president; b. Bradgate, Iowa, Jan. 23, 1917; s. Arthur Edwin and Abbie (Anderson) O.; m. Vera Blanche Farrington, June 6, 1941; children: Elizabeth, Sarah Margaret. AB, Morningside Coll., 1938, LLD, 1968; MA, U. Nebr., 1939, PhD, 1942, LittD, 1980, Chonnam Nat. U., Korea, 1978. Instr. Northwest Mo. State Tchrs. Coll., summers 1940-42; dir. Nebr. State Hist. Soc., 1946-56; lectr. U. Omaha, 1947-50, U. Nebr., 1946-54, part-time assoc. prof., 1954-56, prof., chmn. dept. history, 1956-65, Bennett S. and Dorothy Martin prof. history, 1962-65; dean Grad. Coll., univ. research adminstr., 1966-68, vice chancellor, 1968; chancellor U. Mo.-Kansas City, 1968-76; interim pres. U. Mo. System, 1976-77, pres., 1977-84, pres. emeritus, 1984—; OAS prof. Am. history El Colegio de Mexico, Mexico City, 1962. Vis. prof. U. Colo., summer 1965. Author: J. Sterling Morton, 1942, The Nebraska Story, 1951, History of Nebraska, 1955, 3d edit. (with Ronald C. Naugle), 1997, (with Vera Farrington Olson) Nebraska is My Home, 1956, This is Nebraska, 1960, Red Cloud and the Sioux Problem, 1965, paper edit., 1975, 79, (with Vera Farrington Olson) The University of Missouri: An Illustrated History, 1988, Serving the University of Missouri: A Memoir of Campus and System Administration, 1993; contbg. author: The Army Air Forces in World War II, 1951, 53; editor: Nebraska History, 1946-56; contbr. articles to profl. jours., encys. Bd. dirs. Mid-Am. Arts Alliance; trustee Midwest Rsch. Inst., Kansas City. Mem. Am. Assn. State and Local History, Coun. Basic Edn., Am. Hist. Assn., Orgn. Am. Historians, State Hist. Soc. Mo. (1st v.p.), Nebr. State Hist. Soc., We. Hist. Assn., Cosmos Club, Phi Beta Kappa, Omicron Delta Kappa, Phi Kappa Phi, Pi Gamma Mu. E-mail: olsonja@umkc.edu.

OLSON, JAMES RICHARD, retired transportation company executive; b. Alexandria, Minn., Mar. 11, 1941; s. Orie D. and Theresa Marie (Erickson) O.; m. Ronna Lee, Feb. 1, 1969 (dec.); 1 child, Trevor James. BS, N.D. State U., 1963; LLD, U. Minn., 1966; MBA, Harvard U., 1968. Asst. to v.p. finance Cargill Inc., Mpls., 1968-69; with Graco Inc., 1969-75, v.p. finance, 1972-75; exec. v.p. finance Ponderosa System, Inc., Dayton, Ohio, 1975-77; v.p. planning Pillsbury Co., Mpls., 1977-79, v.p. restaurant group, 1979-80; group v.p.-restaurants The Carlson Cos., Inc., Mpls., 1981-83; exec. v.p., chief fin. and adminstrv. officer Schneider Nat., Inc., 1983-87, pres. van group, 1987-92, pres. transp. sector, 1992-98. Mem. corp. bd. dirs. Curative Rehab. Ctr.; mem. bd. dirs The Ground Round, Inc., Meritex Enterprises, Inc. Mem. Financial Execs. Inst., Citizens League Mpls.-St. Paul, Harvard Bus. Sch. Club Minn. (past pres.) Lutheran. Home: Winslow House # 807 100 2d St NE Minneapolis MN 55414-2131 E-mail: jrolson1@att.net.

OLSON, JAMES WARREN, lawyer; b. Vermillion, S.D., July 20, 1949; s. Louis Burdette and Mary Cleola (Boden) O.; m. Shirley Mae Dappen, June 21, 1975; children: Neleigh Anne, Ethan Ellsworth. BA, U. S.D., 1971, JD, 1977. Bar: S.D. 1977, Nebr. 1983, U.S. Dist. Ct. S.D. 1977, U.S. Dist. Ct. Nebr. 1987, U.S. Ct. Appeals (8th cir.) 1984, U.S. Supreme Ct. 1984. Assoc. Kirby Law Office, Mitchell, S.D., 1977-78, Bubak Law Office, Tyndall, 1978; sole practice Armour, 1978-88; adminstrv law judge City of Salt Lake, 1988—, hearing office chief, 1990-92; adminstrv. law judge City of Spokane, Wash., 1992-2000, SSA/OHA. Spokane, 2000—. Adminstrv. law judge, Spokane, 1992-2000; states atty. Douglas County, S.D., 1981-84, city atty. Armour S.D., 1979-88; dep. states atty., Charles Mix County, S.D., 1980-84; gen. counsel, Yankton Sioux Tribe, Marty, S.D., 1985-86, various fin. insts., S.D., 1979-84. Active United Ch. of Christ Fin. Com., Armour. Capt. USAR. Mem. ABA (Nat. Conf. Adminstrv. Law Judges), S.D. State Bar Assn., Nebr. State Bar Assn., Assn. Trial Lawyers Am., S.D. Trial Lawyers Assn., S.D. Mcpl. Attys. Assn., Assn. Adminstrv. Law Judges, Armour C. of C., Jaycees, Lions. Republican. Avocations: skiing, racquetball, reading, horseback riding. Home: 17207 N Mount Spokane Park Dr Mead WA 99021-9768 Office: 316 W Boone Ave Spokane WA 99201-2354

OLSON, JAMES WILLIAM PARK, architect; b. St. Louis, Oct. 6, 1940; s. James William Park; s. Louis Garfield and Gladys Helen (Schuh) O.; m. Katherine Fovargue, June 11, 1971; children: Park, Reed. BArch, U. Wash., 1963. Registered architect, Wash., Oreg., Calif., Ill., Colo., Hawaii, Ga., Fla. Ptnr. Olson Sundberg Kundig Allen Architects, Seattle, 1985—. Assoc. architect New Seattle Art Mus., 1991. Prin. works include Pike and Virginia Bldg. (AIA Honor award 1980), Seattle's Best Coffee Retail Locations (AIA Honor award 1984), Hauberg Residence (AIA Honor award 1997), Mayer Lodo residence, Denver (AIA Honor award 1998, AIA N.W. and Pacific Regional Merit award 1999, AIA We. Internat. Design award 2000), St. Mark's Cathedral Renovation (AIA Commendation award), Seattle (IFFRA award 1998, AIA citation 1998, AIA and Pacific Regional Merit award 2000), numerous residences nationwide. Bd. dirs. Ctr. Contemporary Art, Seattle, 1982-86, Artist Trust, Seattle, 1986-90, U. Wash. Henry Art Gallery, Seattle, 1986-92, Seattle Art Mus., 1996—. Recipient Best Architect award Seattle Mag., 1985. Fellow AIA; mem. NEA (juror). Avocation: art. Work published in numerous mags, jours., including The AD 100 Architects, N.Y. Times, Archtl. Digest, Archtl. Record, Global Architecture and others. Office: Olson Sundberg Kundig Allen Architects 108 1st Ave S Ste 4 Seattle WA 98104-2557

OLSON, JEAN LOUNSBURY, social worker; b. Detroit, Feb. 19, 1942; d. James Breckinridge and Vivian Beatrice (Thomen) Lounsbury; children: James Gary Pittman, David Bern Pittman, Patrick Alan Pittman. BS, N.C. State U., Raleigh, 1975, BSW, 1976; MSW, U. N.C., Chapel Hill, 1985. Counselor Drug Action, Raleigh, NC, 1978-82; counselor, supr. Juvenile Restitution, 1978-82; clin. social worker Dorothea Dix Hosp., 1984-91; pvt. practice, 1991—. Liaison N.C. State Hosp., Raleigh, 1984-91; pvt. practice, Cary and Raleigh, N.C., 1991—. VISTA vol., Raleigh, 1977-78. Mem. NASW, AAUW, Am. Soc. Clin. Hypnosis, Am. Group Psychotherapy Assn., N.C. Soc. Clin. Hypnosis, N.C. Soc. Clin. Social Work (program com. 1984—). Democrat. Presbyterian. Avocations: swimming, tennis, oboe, trumpet, coaching basketball. Home: 2901 Day Lily Ln Apex NC 27539-

OLSON, JEANNE INNIS, technology and technical management executive; b. South Bend, Ind., May 10, 1960; d. Francis Bedford and Mary Ann Innis; m. Thomas Hilton Olson, Apr. 12, 1992; 1 child, Walter Samuel. Student, Purdue U., 1978-80; BS in Tech. & Mgmt. summa cum laude, U. Md., 1986; MS in Sys. Mgmt. with honors, U. So. Calif., 1991. Analyst Potomac Rsch., Inc., Alexandria, Va., 1980-82; staff specialist SWL, Inc., McLean, 1982-87; sr. staff Advanced Tech., Inc., El Segundo, Calif., 1987-89; prin. staff/section mgr. PRC, Inc., 1989-95, dep. dir. space sys. acquisition support, 1995-96, dir. space sys. acquisition support and LA operations, 1997-98; v.p., mgr. ANSWER program Litton PRC, 1998—2001; mgr. ANSWER program Northrop Grumman Info. Tech., 2002—. Mem. South Bay Friends Planned Parenthood, Calif., 1992—, v.p. fund raising, 1994. Recipient Vol. Recognition award Planned Parenthood L.A., 1994, 96. Mem. Innes Clan Soc. (v.p. 1984-91, pres. 1991-92), Innes Clan Ctr. Assn. (bd. dirs. 1993—), Nat. Def. Indsl. Assn. (bd. dirs. Greater L.A. chpt.), Phi Kappa Phi. Avocations: skiing, music, travel, Scottish heritage, family planning edn. Office: Northrop Grumman Info Tech Ste 1310 222 N Sepulveda Blvd El Segundo CA 90245-5648

OLSON, JOHN KARL, lawyer; b. Springfield, Mass., Aug. 14, 1949; s. Harold Gunnar and Louise Theodora (Shukis) O.; m. Ann Catherine Sullivan, June 16, 1973; children: Elizabeth Ann, Katherine Louise. AB, Harvard Coll., 1971; JD, Boston Coll., 1975. Bar: Fla. 1975, U.S. Dist. Ct. (mid. and so. dists.) Fla. 1976, U.S. Ct. Appeals (5th cir.) 1979, U.S. Supreme Ct. 1979; U.S. Ct. Appeals (11th cir.) 1981. From assoc. to ptnr. Carlton, Fields, Ward et al., Tampa, Fla., 1975-86; exec. v.p., gen. counsel, dir. Jet Fla., Inc., Miami, 1986-88; ptnr. Stearns Weaver Miller Weissler Alhadeff & Sitterson P.A., Tampa, 1988—. Author: Creditors and Debtors Rights in Florida, 1979, 89, Collier Bankruptcy Practice Guide, 1986. Trustee Tampa Mus. Art, 1992-98; mem. parent bd. U. Del., 1998-2002, co-pres., 2000-2002. Fellow U. Tampa, 1986—. Mem. ABA (vice-chmn. bankcruptcy com. 1984-86), Am. Bankruptcy Inst., Fla. Bar (chmn. bus. law sect. 1988-89), Harvard Club (pres. 1982-84), Turnaround Mgmt. Assn. (Ctrl. Fla. chpt. pres. 1995-96). Home: 2632 W Prospect Rd Tampa FL 33629-5358 Office: Sun Trust Fin Ctr 401 E Jackson St Tampa FL 33602-5233

OLSON, JOHN MICHAEL, communications executive; b. Eau Claire, Wis., May 1, 1970; s. Donald Lewis Olson and Mary Jane Weiland; m. Diana Lee Bitzer, Nov. 15, 1990; children: Amanda Jane, Alisha Lee. V.p. CSI, Chippewa Falls, Wis., 1992—. With USMC, 1988-92. Avocations: spending time with children, attending public functions. Home: E1997 Cedar Rd Eau Claire WI 54701-9630 Office: Comm Sys Internat 103 N Bridge St Chippewa Falls WI 54729-2478

OLSON, JOSEPHINE EVA, economics educator; b. Bronxville, N.Y., Aug. 25, 1942; d. Reinhold S. and Elizabeth S. (Deacon) O.; m. Jerome A. Spieckerman, May 24, 1980; 1 stepdaughter, Julia Louise Spieckerman. AB in Econs., Wellesley Coll., 1964; PhD in Econs., Brown U., 1970. Asst. prof. bus. adminstrn. CUNY, 1969-71, U. Pitts., 1971-75, assoc. prof. bus. adminstrn. and econs., 1975-91; prof. bus. adminstrn. and acctg., 1991—. Trustee Tchrs. Ins., N.Y.C., 1974-86; bd. advisors Health Am. of Pa., Pitts., 1977-91. Contbr. articles to profl. jours. and chpts. to books. NSF fellow, 1966-67, Fulbright fellow, Hungary, 1991. Mem. Transp. Rsch. Forum, Am. Econ. Assn., Acad. Mgmt. Democrat. Home: 5869 Beacon St Pittsburgh PA 15217-2003 Office: U Pitts Joseph M Katz Grad Sch Bus Pittsburgh PA 15260

OLSON, JUDITH MARY REEDY, retired public information officer, former state senator; b. Mitchell, S.D., June 24, 1939; d. John Marvin and Camille (Murphy) Reedy; m. Robert George Olson, Aug. 5, 1961; children: Jeffrey, Jennifer, Jon, Jaime, Jason, Jeremy. EdB, U. Tucson, 1961; MEd, S.D. State U., 1984; postgrad., U. S.D., 1985—. Cert. secondary tchr., edn. adminstrn. Tchr. jr. high sch. Mpls. Pub. Schs., 1961-63; mem. State Bd. Edn., S.D., 1972-83, pres., 1975-78; dir. S.D. Edn. Policy Seminar, 1975-79; substitute tchr. Rapid City (S.D.) Schs., 1979-81, tchr. adult basic edn., 1979-81, supr. community relations, 1981-88, supr. community edn., pub. info., 1988—95; senator S.D. Legis. (dist. 33), Pierre, SD, 1989—95; edn. dir. Career Learning Center of the Black Hills. Speaker, cons. sch. bds., adminstrs., tchrs., sch. dists., pub. relations, various states, 1972—. Bd. dirs. Black Hills Symphony, 1987—; chair, S.D. State Democratic Party, 1998—. Mem. AAUW (Women of Worth award), Rotary, PEO, Delta Kappa Gamma. Democrat. Roman Catholic. Avocations: reading, spectator sports. Home: 4603 Ridgewood St Rapid City SD 57702-2063 Office: South Dakota Democratic Party 207 East Capitol Pierre SD 57501-2724*

OLSON, KEITH WALDEMAR, history educator; b. Poughkeepsie, N.Y., Aug. 4, 1931; s. Ernest Waldemar and Elin Ingeborg (Rehnstrom) O.; m. Marilyn Joyce Wittschen, Sept. 10, 1955; children— Paula, Judy. BA, SUNY, Albany, 1957, MA, 1959; PhD, U. Wis., 1964; PhD (hon.), U. Tampere, Finland, 2000. Mem. history faculty Syracuse U., N.Y., 1963-66; mem. history faculty U. Md., College Park, 1966—, prof. history. Fulbright prof. U. Tampere, Finland, 1986-87, U. Oulu, Finland, 1993, U. Jyväskylä, Finland, 1994. Author: The G.I. Bill, the Veterans and the Colleges, 1974; Biography of a Progressive: Franklin K. Lane, 1979. Pres. Am. Scandinavian Found., Washington, 1977-79. Served with U.S. Army, 1952-54. U.S. Office Edn. grantee, 1965-66; U. Md. grantee, 1971, 76, 78. Mem. Am. Hist. Assn., Orgn. Am. Historians, Wis. Hist. Soc., Swedish Am. Hist. Soc., Finnish Hist. Soc., Soc. Historians of Am. Fgn. Rels., Cen. Study of Presidency, Am. Scandinavian Assn. (pres. 1998-99). Unitarian Universalist. Home: 10746 Kinloch Rd Silver Spring MD 20903-1226 Office: U Md Dept History College Park MD 20742-0001 E-mail: KO6@umail.umd.edu.

OLSON, KENNETH PAUL, vocational consultant; b. Providence, June 26, 1935; s. Gustave Frederick and Beatrice Evelyn (Backstrom) O.; m. Judith Luellan Hazard, Nov. 12, 1965; children: Glenn Edward Johnson. BA in Sociology, U. Denver, 1960; MA in Sociology, U. Colo., 1973. Cert. rehab. counselor, vocat. specialist; lic. profl. counselor, Colo. Exec. dir. Goodwill Industries, Colorado Springs, Co., 1960-65, San Francisco, 1965, Ft. Worth, 1966-70; counselor II Colo. Div. Rehab., Colorado Springs, 1972-83; pres. Olson Vocat. Svcs., 1983-97; pvt. practice vocat. cons., 1997—. Vocational expert Social Security Adminstn., Denver, 1984—; rehab counselor U.S. Dept. Labor, Denver, 1984-89. V.p. Bus. Arts Ctr., Manitou Springs, 1988—89; councilman, 1975—78; mem. Commn. for Rehab. Counselor Cert., 1979—85, Bd. for Rehab. Cert., 1984—86; pres. Manitou Art Project, 1994—95; mem. socioecon. adv. com. Pikes Peak Area Coun. of Govts., 1999—2002; bd. dirs. Econ. Devel. Com., Manitou Springs, 1998—. With USN, 1954—56. Fellow Nat. Rehab. Counseling Assn.; mem. Colo. Rehab. Counseling Assn. (pres. 1979, named Counselor of Yr. 1976), Great Plains Rehab. Assn. (pres. 1982-83), Colo. Rehab. Assn., Colo. Career Devel. Assn., El Paso County Assn. Lic. Profl. Counselors (treas. 1994-96), Colorado Springs C. of C. (Small Bus. Person of Yr. award 1991), Manitou Springs C. of C. (pres. 1986). Home: PO Box 226 Manitou Springs CO 80829-0226 Office: Kenneth P Olson MA CRC LPC Ste A 620 S Cascade Colorado Springs CO 80903-1814 E-mail: ken@kenolson.org.

OLSON, KENNETH RAY, soil scientist, educator; b. Stanley, N.D., July 16, 1947; s. Ray Lenard and Ethel Lydia Olson; m. Pamela Gail Reiss, Aug. 30, 1975; children: Susan Michelle, Kristina Reiss. BS with distinction, Ohio State U., 1969, MS in Agronomy, 1976; PhD in Soils, Cornell U., 1983. Cert. soil scientist Am. Soc. Agronomy. Lab. tech. Ohio State U., Columbus, Ohio, 1967—69; soil survey mapper Ohio Dept. Natural Resources, 1971—78; rsch. assoc. Cornell U., Ithaca, NY, 1978—83; prof. U. Ill., Urbana, 1983—. Mem. farmland assessment adv. bd. Ill. Dept. Revenue, Springfield, 1988—; mem. tech. adv. bd. USDA Natural Resource Conservation Svc., Champaign, Ill., 1990—. Contbr. chapters to books, articles to profl. jours. With U.S. Army, 1969—71. Recipient Erosion Rsch. award, Soil and Water Conservation, rbana, Ill., 1985. Mem.: Soil Sci. Soc. Am. (membership chair), Internat. Soil and Water Conservation Soc., Internat. Union Soil Sci., Phi Kappa Phi. Avocation: golf. Office: U Ill Dept Natural Resources 1102 S Goodwin Ave Urbana IL 61801

OLSON, KEVIN LORY, lawyer; b. Berkeley, Calif., Dec. 2, 1956; s. Lorimer Reuben and Norma Carolyn Olson; m. Linda Sue Gladish, June 16, 1978; children: Lisa Marie, Kimberly Ann, Karen Amanda. BS in Math., Ariz. State U., 1977; JD, Yale U., 1980. Bar: Ariz. 1980. Assoc. Lewis and Roca, Phoenix, 1980-85, ptnr., 1985-97, Steptoe & Johnson LLP, Phoenix, 1997—. Bd. dirs. East Valley Partnership, Mesa, Ariz., 1990—, pres.-elect, 2000-01, pres., 2001-02. Mem. ABA, State Bar of Ariz., Maricopa County Bar Assn., Tempe C. of C. (pres. 1995-96), Greater Phoenix C. of C. (v.p. transp. 2000-02). Office: 201 E Washington St Ste 1600 Phoenix AZ 85004 E-mail: kolson@steptoe.com.

OLSON, LEROY CALVIN, retired educational administration educator; b. Kane, Pa., Mar. 7, 1926; s. Vernon Reinhold and Gertrude Viola Olson; m. Miriam Marie Vogler, June 19, 1954; children— David Lee, Thomas Edward, Steven Andrew. BS, Clarion State Coll., 1949; M.Ed., Pa. State Coll., 1950; Ed.D., Pa. State U., 1962; postgrad., U. Del., 1964-65. Tchr.-counselor Boiling Springs (Pa.) High Sch., 1950-52, Gordon Jr. High Sch., Coatesville, Pa., 1952-54; guidance dir. Cen. Dauphin Sch. Dist., Harrisburg, 1954-57; coordinator pupil personnel services, asst. supt. for instrn. and personnel, acting supt. Alfred I. duPont Sch. Dist., Wilmington, Del., 1957-65; prof. ednl. adminstrn. Temple U., Phila., 1965-92, prof. emeritus, 1992—. Cons. to schs. bds. and dists., also Nat., Wis., Pa. sch. bds. assns. Contbr. articles to profl. jours. Trustee Luth. Ch., 1963-66, chmn. bd., 1976-78, chmn. various coms., discussion groups. Served with USNR, 1944-46, PTO. Recipient Disting. Alumni award Clarion State Coll., 1972 Mem. Am. Personnel and Guidance Assn., AAUP, Am. Assn. Sch. Personnel Adminstrs., Assn. Supervision and Curriculum Devel., Council Profs. Instrn. Supervision, Nat. Staff Devel. Council, Am. Legion, Phi Delta Kappa, Phi Kappa Phi. Republican. Home: 231 Prospect Dr Wilmington DE 19803-5331 *God's gift of life is a marvelous thing. My attempt to make the best use of that gift is to try to live an integrated and balanced life. This means that active attention must be paid to the physical, social, spiritual, and recreational aspects as well as to the work or career dimension. It also means we must share that gift through loving and caring about others.*

OLSON, LYNN, sculptor, painter, writer; b. Chgo., Mar. 23, 1952; s. Ellen (Nelson) Olson. Instr. direct cement sculpture workshops Montoya Art Studios, West Palm Beach, Fla., 1988-89, Alta. Sculptors Assn., Edmonton, Can., 1990, Mendocino (Calif.) Art Ctr., 1992-93, Sierra Nev. Coll. at Lake Tahoe, Incline Village, 1993, Lighthouse Art Ctr., Crescent City, Calif., 1990-96, Elisabet Ney Sculpture Conservatory, Austin, Tex., 1995, Tarrant County Jr. Coll., Ft. Worth, 1995, Arts Students League of Denver, 2000, Indpls. Art Ctr., 2002. Prin. works include Good Shepherd, Ch. Good Shepherd, Albion, Ind., Kneeling Figure, Manta Ray. World of Concrete, Addison, Ill., Rose, Carter Meml., Chesterton, Ind., Redwood Tree, Lighthouse Art Ctr., Crescent City, Calif., George Bartholomew Meml., Bellefontaine, Ohio, Color Concerto, Purdue U., Hammond, Ind., Continuity III, Tower East, Shaker Heights, Ohio, Aluma Beam, Aluma Corp., Toronto, Amobius, St. Joseph Coll., Rensselaer, Ind., Lake Sara, Effingham, Ill.; one-man shows include U. of Ill., Chgo., 2001, No. Ind. Arts Assn., Munster, CCT Gallery, Evanston Hall, Northwestern U. Settlement, Chgo., 2000—, 18 Artists Gallery, Chesterton, Ind.; exhibited in group shows at Danada Sculpture Show, Cantigny Park, Wheaton, Ill., 1999-2001, Prairie Arts Coun., Rensselaer, Ind., 2000, Ind. U. N.W., 2001, Effingham's 3d Ann. Sculpture on the Ave. Exhbn., Ill., 2001, McHenry County Coll., Crystal Lake, Ill., 2002, 4th Ann. Sculpture on Aves. Exhibit, Effingham, 2002, 15th Ann. Outdoor Sculpture Exhibit, Lawrence, Kans., 2002, Art in Pub. Places, Cedar Rapids, Iowa, 2002; author, pub.: Sculpting with Cement, 1981-2001; artist-in-residence St. Joseph Coll., 2000; contbr. over 50 articles to mags. Mem. Am. Concrete Inst. (com. 124 concrete aesthetics). Home and Office: Steelstone 4607 Claussen Ln Valparaiso IN 46383-1526

OLSON, MARGARET SMITH, program director, hospitality professional; b. Niagara Falls, N.Y. d. Andrew Maule and Mary Elizabeth (Hurst) Smith; m. Low Fletcher Mathews (div.); m. Richard Carlson Stevens (div.); m. Richard C. Olson, July 19, 1985; children: Kimberly Ann Mathews, Christopher Scott Mathews, Andrea Carlson Stevens. BA cum laude, Niagara U., 1972, MA cum laude, 1977. Instr. Niagara U., Niagara Falls, 1972-79; supr. mfg. Harrison Radiator divsn. GM, Lockport, N.Y., 1979-85; owner, mgr. Town House Restaurant, Ligonier, Pa., 1985-91; dir. restaurant mgmt., dir. acad. affairs Pa. Inst. Culinary Art, Pitts., 1992-97; sr. mgr. Gen. Cinema, Bridgewater, N.J., 1997-2001; dir. Ctr. for Workforce Excellence in Info. Tech. Middlesex Coll., Edison, NJ, 2001—. Advisor: (videos) Food Service Security, 1992, Sexual Harassment, 1994. Bd. dirs., treas. Hist. Soc. Ligonier, 1987-90; com. mem. Ligonier Libr. Arts, 1988-90; bd. dirs. Christian Charities, Ligonier, 1997—; mem. adv. bd. Goodwill Industries, Pitts., 1984-97. Named Hospitality Profl. of Yr. Allegheny County C.C., 1991. Mem. Nat. Restaurant Assn. (cert. food svc. mgmt. profl., cert. ServSafe serving safe food instr., instr. in sanitation 1992-97), Pa. Restaurant Assn. (state bd. dirs. 1988-95, bd. dirs. Western chpt. 1988-95, treas. Western chpt. 1990, pres. 1991, chmn. bd. 1992-93, lectr. 1992-95), Coun. Hotel, Restaurant & Instnl. Edn. Avocations: reading, cross-stitch, crossword puzzles, theater, music. E-mail: it_excellence@middlesexcc.edu., margaret_olson@middlesexcc.edu.

OLSON, MARIAN EDNA, nursing consultant, social psychologist; b. Newman Grove, Nebr., July 20, 1923; d. Edward and Ethel Thelma (Hougland) O. Diploma, U. Nebr., 1944, BSN, 1953; MA, State U. Iowa, 1961, MA in Psychology, 1962; PhD in Psychology, UCLA, 1966. Staff nurse, supr. U. Tex. Med. Br., Galveston, 1944-49; with U. Iowa, Iowa City, 1949-53, from supr. to asst. dir., 1953-59; asst. prof. nursing UCLA, 1965-67; prof. nursing U. Hawaii, 1967-70, 78-82; DON Wilcox Hosp. and Health Ctr., Lihue, 1970-77; chmn. Hawaii Bd. Nursing, 1974-80; prof. nursing No. Mich. U., 1984-88; ret., 1988; cons. nursing svcs. adminstr. practice and curriculum, 1988-2000; ret., 1988. Bd. dirs. Bay de Noc C.C. Home and Office: 6223 County 513 T Rd Rapid River MI 49878-9595

OLSON, MARIAN KATHERINE, management executive, consultant, publisher; b. Tulsa, Oct. 15, 1933; d. Sherwood Joseph and Katherine M. (Miller) Lahman; m. Ronald Keith Olson, Oct. 27, 1956 (dec. May 1991). BA in Polit. Sci., U. Colo., 1954, MA in Elem. Edn., 1962; EdD in Ednl. Adminstrn., U. Tulsa, 1969. Tchr. pub. schs., Wyo., Colo., Mont., 1956-67; tchg. fellow, adj. instr. edn. U. Tulsa, 1968-69; asst. prof. edn. Eastern Mont. State Coll., 1970; program assoc. rsch. adminstrn. Mont. State U., 1970-75; on leave with Energy Policy Office of White House then with Fed. Energy Adminstrn., 1973-74; with Dept. Energy and predecessor, 1975—, program analyst, 1975-79, chief planning and environ. compliance br., 1979-83; regional dir. Region VIII Fed. Emergency Mgmt. Agy., 1987-93; exec. dir. Search and Rescue Dogs of the U.S., 1993—. Pres. Marian Olson Assocs., Bannack Pub. Co.; mem. Colo. Nat. Hazards Mitigation Coun. Contbr. articles in field. Bd. dirs. Disaster Preparedness and Emergency Response Assn. Internat. Grantee Okla. Consortium Higher Edn., 1969, NIMH, 1974. Mem. Internat. Assn. Emergency Mgrs., Am. Soc. for Info. Sci., Am. Assn. Budget and Program Analysis, Assn. of Contingency Planners, Nat. Inst. Urban Search and Rescue (bd. dirs.), Nat. Assn. for Search and Rescue, Colo. Search and Rescue, Search and Rescue Dogs of U.S., Colo. Emergency Mgmt. Assn., Front Range Rescue Dogs, Kappa Delta Pi, Phi Alpha Theta, Kappa Alpha Theta. Republican. Home: 203 Iowa Dr Golden CO 80403-1337 Office: Marian Olson Assocs 203 Iowa Dr Ste B Golden CO 80403-1337 E-mail: mlolson@ix.netcom.com.

OLSON, MARK WALTER, banker; b. Fergus Falls, Minn., Mar. 17, 1943; s. Walter Roland and Agnes Marie (Peterson) O.; m. Renee Irene Korda, July 5, 1980; children: Benjamin, Stephanie. BA, St. Olaf Coll., 1965. With First Bank, St. Paul, 1966-70; legis. dir. Congressman Bill Frenzel, Washington, 1971-72; with Andrews Allen Co., St. Paul, 1972-74; dist. dir. Congressman Bill Frenzel, 1974-76; pres. Security State Bank, Fergus Falls, Minn., 1976-88; ptnr. Arthur Young, 1988—. Bd. dirs. Pioneer Home, Fergus Falls, 1977-86 , Lake Region Hosp., Fergus Falls, 1978-88, Fergus Falls Area YMCA, 1977-83, Security State Bank, Fergus Falls, 1976-88, Arthur Young Co., 1988—. Mem. Am. Bankers Assn. (chmn. govt. relations council, dir. 1982-84, pres. 1986-87), C. of C. (dir. 1980-84). Republican. Lutheran. Office: Fed Reserve System Bd of Gov 20th & C Streets NW Washington DC 20551 Office Fax: 202-452-3819.*

OLSON, MAXINE LOUISE, artist, lecturer; b. Kingsburg, Calif., June 29, 1931; d. Alfred and Lena A. Marshall; divorced; children: Todd Olson, Terry Olson. BA, Calif. State U., Fresno, 1973, MA, 1975. Asst. prof. U. Ga., Athens, 1986-89; lectr. Coll. of Sequoias, Visalia, Calif., 1973-96. Lectr. Fresno City Coll., 1990, Calif. State U., Fresno, intermittently 1973-96; tchr. U. Ga., Contona, Italy, 1987, 93; 6th Annual MicroPubl. Graphics, San Francisco, 1998, The World's Women On-Line United Nations Conf., Beijing, China, 1995. Exhibited works at Oakland Mus., Palazzo Casali, Venice, Italy, Forum Gallery, N.Y.C., Soho 20, N.Y., The World's Women on-line/UN 4th World Conf. on Women, Beijing, China, William Sawyer Gallery, Palm Springs Mus., Calif., Silicon Gallery, Pa. Recipient Gold award Art of Calif. Mag., 1992, IDN Design award, 1997-98. Mem. Coll. Art Assn. Roman Catholic. Avocations: painting, drawing, digital art. Home: 1555 Lincoln St Kingsburg CA 93631-1804 E-mail: molson@mobynet.com.

OLSON, MICHAEL LYNN, music educator; b. Omaha, Jan. 26, 1957; s. Franklin Roosevelt and Beverley Jeanne Olson. B Music, Concordia Coll., 1979; M Music, Southern Methodist U., Dallas, 1981. Organist, choir accompanist Lutheran Ch. of the Master, Omaha, 1969—75, Lutheran Ch. of Christ the King, Moorhead, Minn., 1976—79, Rosemount Christian Ch., Dallas, 1980; dir. music, organist Oak Cliff Lutheran Ch., 1980—81; dir. music, youth asst. Trinity Lutheran Ch., Fort Atkinson, Wis., 1981—85; min. of music First Lutheran Ch., Fargo, ND, 1985—. Pianist Downtown Fargo Kiwanis Club, 1986—95. Mem.: Fargo-Moorhead Music Tchrs. Assn. (treas. 1986—88), Am. Guild English Handbell Ringers, Am. Guild Organists (Red River Valley chpt. bd. dirs. 1999—). Republican. Lutheran. Avocation: stamp collecting. Home: 3410 2nd St N Unit 27 Fargo ND 58102-1192 Office: First Lutheran Ch 619 Broadway Fargo ND 58102-4492 Fax: 701-235-3245. Personal E-mail: pipeorgan10@hotmail.com.

OLSON, NANCY ANN, artist, educator; b. Warren, Minn., July 20, 1934; d. Orrin Cornelius and Ruth Emma (Matthews) Kruger; m. James Burton Olson; children: Mark James, Ruth Lynn, Alan Matthew. Elem. providional cert., Moorhead State U., 1955; BS, U. Minn., Morris, 1967. Elem. tchr. Marshall County (Minn.) Rural Schs., 1952-54; tchr. Glenwood (Minn.) Pub. Schs., 1955-58, Villard (Minn.) Pub. Schs., 1967-68, Starbuck (Minn.) Pub. Schs., 1968-77; tchr., mentor Five Wings Art Coun., Staples, Minn., 1992, watercolor students, Glenwood, 1992—. Cmty. edn. tchr., Morris, Minn., 19965. Exhibited in group shows Minn. State Fair, 1994, Humanities Fine Arts U. Minn., Morris, 1996, Red River Watercolor Soc., 1997, 98, 99, 2000, Waage Ctr. for Arts, Fergus Falls, 1997 (merit award 1997), Hawley (Minn.) Art Show, 1997, Lake Agassiz Libr., 1997 (purchase award 1997), Dille Ctr. Arts, 1997, MacRostie Gallery, Grand Rapids, Minn., Plains Mus., Western Colo. Watercolor, The Art Ctr., Grand Junction, Colo., 1998, Bismark Art and Galleries Assn.; one-women shows include Ctrl. Sq. Gallery, Glenwood, 1999, Waage Ctr. for the Arts, Fergus Falls, 1999-2000, Victoria's, Wolverton, 2000; represented in permanent collections Lake Agassiz Libr. Sys., Moorhead, Minn., Viking Libr. Sys., Fergus Falls, Minn., Glenwood Hosp., Minn., Am. Bus. Forms, Glenwood, LRAC Office, Glenwood Pub. Libr., Viking Libr., Fergus Falls, Minn. Bd. dirs. Lake Region Arts Coun., Fergus Falls, Minn., 1978-81, 91-94; co-organizer art workshops, Glenwood, 19935; co-organizer programs Glenwood Pub. Libr., 1998-2000. Individual artist grantee McKnight Found., Lake Region Arts Coun., 1994, 00; recipient Merit award Mathison's/Grumbacher Red River Watercolor Soc. Nat. Show, 1997, Merit award High Water Red River Watercolor Soc. Nat. Show, 1998. Mem. Glacial Ridge Artists (pres. 1985-87), Ottertail County Hist. Soc., Pope County Hist. Soc. (co-organizer exhbn. on physics 1994), Red River Watercolor Soc., Art of Lakes (newspaper com. 1995-97), Terrace Mill Found., Gen. Fedn. Women's Club (historian Glenwood 1996-97), Glenwood Federated Women's Club (mem. program com. 19995), Red River Watercolor Soc. (signature). Avocations: genealogy, photography, antiques, travel, historical writing and research. Home: 19707 County Road 18 Glenwood MN 56334-2346

OLSON, OSCAR JULIUS, international economist; b. Corpus Christi, Tex., Mar. 31, 1933; s. Oscar Julius and Kate (Arnold) O.; m. Patricia Kay Whipple, Nov. 12, 1955; children: Michael Alan, Kirsten Anne Olson Pruski, Kathleen Kay. BA, U. Tex., 1954; MA, Yale U., 1957; postgrad., Fletcher Sch. Law & Diplomacy, Medford, Mass., 1966-67. Fgn. svc. officer Dept. of State, Washington, 1957-84; exec. dir. U.S. Man & the Biosphere Program, 1976-80; counselor of embassy Am. Embassy, Quito, Ecuador, 1982-84; dir. Latin Am. BERI S.A., 1985—. Cons. internat. office Smithsonian Instn., Washington, 1984-85, Dept. of State, Washington, 1985—. Bd. dirs. Civitan Club of Arlington, Va., 1991—. Mem. Am. Fgn. Svc. Assn., Diplomatic and Consular Officers, Retired, Soc. for Internat. Devel., World Affairs Coun. of Washington, D.C., Latin m. Studies Assn., Phi Beta Kappa. Methodist. Avocations: music, travel, photography. Home: 691 Southview Ct Apt G Culpeper VA 22701-3722 Office: Beri SA PO Box 513 Friday Harbor WA 98250-0513

OLSON, PAUL BUXTON, retired social studies, marketing, and business educator; b. Waterloo, Iowa, Feb. 5, 1937; s. Ethan Sidney and Esther May O.; m. Jean Elaine Rinehart, Aug. 18, 1962 (div. 1993); children: Brent Sidney, Kimberly Jean, Julie Elaine; m. Rosalie Vera Nelson, Sept. 12, 1998. BA cum laude, Tarkio Coll., 1958; MEd, U. Mo., 1966; EdS, U. No. Iowa, 1975. Tchr. bus. edn. Riverton/Farragut Cmty. Schs., 1962-68; bus. tchr. Mason City (Iowa) Cmty. Schs., 1968-69, mktg. and disbributive edn. tchr., 1969-89, social studies tchr., 1989-96; ret., 1996. Adj. instr. mktg. No. Iowa Area C.C., Mason City, 1969-89. Bd. dirs. Jr. Achievement, 1970-88; pres. United Meth. Men, 1997-99; lay spkr. Meth. Ch. Served with U.S. Army, 1960-62. Named Outstanding Distributive Edn. Tchr. Iowa Distributive Edn. Tchrs. Assn., 1978, 89, to Mktg. Edn. Hall of Fame, 1985; recipient Leadership award Jr. Achievement, 1977, Writer's award Interstate Distributive Edn. Curriculum Consortium, 1975. Mem.: NEA (life; del. rep. 1963, 1967, 1993, 1994), Iowa Bus. Edn. Assn. (rep.), Iowa State Edn. Assn., Nat. Bus. Edn. Assn., Mktg. Edn. Assn. (life), Am. Vocat. Assn. (life), Sons of Norway (historian 1994—2001), Distributive Edn. Clubs Am., Delta Pi Epsilon (past treas.), Phi Delta Kappa (life; charter, past historian, pres. 1995—96). Republican. Methodist. Home: 600 Briarstone Dr #8 Mason City IA 50401-4632

OLSON, PAUL RICHARD, Spanish literature educator, editor; b. Rockford, Ill., Nov. 2, 1925; s. Oscar Wilhelm and Jenny Ingeborg (Taube) O.; m. Phyllis Elizabeth Edwards, Jan. 10, 1953; children: Thomas Jeremy, John Stephen, Carl Philip, Paul Andrew. AB, U. Ill., 1948, A.M., 1950; PhD, Harvard U., 1959. Instr. Dartmouth Coll., Hanover, N.H., 1956-59, asst. prof., 1959-61; asst. prof. modern Spanish lit. Johns Hopkins U., Balt., 1961-63, assoc. prof., 1963-67, prof., 1967-91, prof. emeritus, 1991—. Author: Circle of Paradox, 1967, Unamuno: Niebla, 1984, Unamuno and the Primacy of Language, 1989; editor: Unamuno: Como se hace una novela, 1977; gen. editor: Modern Lang. Notes, 1983-86. Guggenheim Found. fellow, 1964; Fulbright grantee, 1964-65; Am. Council Learned Socs. grantee, 1969 Mem. MLA, Acad. Lit. Studies, Asociacion Internacional Hispanistas

OLSON, PHILLIP DAVID LEROY, agriculturist, chemist; b. Anchorage, Feb. 3, 1940; s. Marvin Willard and Bernadette (McName) O.; m. Deborah Andreé Butler, Apr. 10, 1982; children from a previous marriage: Jamie Kay, Samuel Phillip, Jill Andre. BS, U. Idaho, 1963; MS, Oreg. State U., 1972. Technician U. Calif., Riverside, 1963-65; rsch. staff Oreg. State U., Corvallis, 1965-75; mgr. R & D, Hoechst-Roussel Agri-Vet Co., Somerville, N.J., 1975-91; owner, pres. Profl. Agrl. Cons., Palm Desert, Calif., 1991—. R & D cons. and quality assurance rsch. contractor, ret., 2000. Mem. Am. Mus. Natural History. Mem. Nat. Space Soc., Soc. Quality Assurance, Pacific Regional Quality Assurance Soc., Oreg. State U. Found. (hon.), Smithsonian Instn., Archaeol. Soc. Am., Acad. Model Aeronautics, Elks, Am. Mus. of Natural History, Planetary Soc., Scale Ship Modelers Assn. Avocations: reading, fishing, RC model building, scale boat modeling, HO train modeling. Home and Office: 42908 Scirocco Rd Palm Desert CA 92211-7697 E-mail: pdolson100@cs.com.

OLSON, PHILLIP ROGER, naval officer; b. Elmhurst, Ill., June 23, 1939; s. Willard Clarence and Carol (Schulz) O.; m. Marsha Andrea Lippert, July 10, 1966; children: Christine Carole, Phillip Roger Jr. B in Naval Sci., U.S. Naval Acad., 1962; M in Physics, Naval Postgrad. Sch., 1968. Commd. ens. USN, 1962, advanced through grades to rear adm., 1987, instr. ship material readiness group, 1978-81, commdg. officer USS Pharris (FF 1094) Norfolk, Va., 1981-82, commdg. officer USS Mississippi (CGN 40), 1983-86, sr. instr. ship material readiness group Newport, R.I., 1986-87; dep. dir. ops. Joint Staff, Washington, 1987-88; dep. dir. strategy & policy Joint Staff USN, 1988-89, comdr. logistics group two Norfolk, 1989-90, comdr. cruiser-destroyer group one San Diego, 1990-92, pres. bd. inspection & survey Norfolk, 1992-96; retired, 1996. Cons. on navy logistics support and operational engring.; exec. v.p. The Sigmon Group. Decorated Disting. Svc. medal. Mem. Surface Navy Assn. Lutheran. Avocations: golf, tennis.

OLSON, RAY ALAN, librarian; b. Yankton, S.D., Mar. 26, 1946; s. Oliver Bernard Olson and Mabel Highland; m. Carol Ann Nygaard; children: Eric Robert, Peter Alan. BA in History and Philosophy, Augustana Coll., 1968; MDiv, Luther Theol. Sem., St. Paul, 1972; MA in Libr. Sci., U. Minn., 1974; ThM, Luther Northwestern Sem., St. Paul, 1985. Reference and pub. svcs. supr. Luther Theol. Sem., St. Paul, 1972-74; reference libr. Luther Northwestern Sem., 1974-89; acting libr. Luther Sem., 1975-76, 81-82, 88-89, pub. svcs. libr., 1989-96, interim libr., 1996; sr. libr. Trinity Luth. Sem., Columbus, Ohio, 1996—. Co-editor: (with others) Landings Across the Ocean, 1997. Publicity chair Luth. Brotherhood Br. Bd., St. Paul, 1994-96. Mem.: Totenlag, Valdres Samband, Landings Laget (editor newsletter 1984—94, chair publs. com. 1994—2001), Am. Theol. Libr. Assn., Vesterheim Norwegian Am. Mus. (life), Ohio Theol. Libr. Assn. (life; pres. 1999—2001), Scandinavian Club Columbus. Avocations: reading, walking, genealogy, local history. Office: Hamma Libr Trinity Luth Sem 2199 E Main St Columbus OH 43209-2334

OLSON, RICHARD DAVID, psychology educator; b. Reading, Pa., Oct. 10, 1944; s. Milton Stuart and Sarah Ellen (Moyer) O.; m. M. Gayle Augustine, Aug. 26, 1967. BA, U. Redlands, 1966; MS, St. Louis U., 1968, PhD, 1970. Lic. psychologist, La. Asst. prof. psychology U. New Orleans, 1970-74, assoc. prof., chmn. dept. psychology, 1974-79, prof., chmn. dept., 1979-81, assoc. dean Grad. Sch., 1981-82, dean, 1982-88, vice chancellor, 1984-88, rsch. prof., 1988—; chmn. dept. psychology, 1995—2000. Cons. psychologist, New Orleans, 1973— ; pres. Statis. Cons. of New Orleans, 1977-82 Editor: Learning in the Classroom, 1971, The Comma After Love, The Selected Poems of Raeburn Miller, 1994, The Collected Poems of Raeburn Miller, 1997; contbr. articles to profl. jours. Grantee HEW, 1976-81 Fellow APA, Am. Psychol. Soc.; mem. Soc. for Neuroscis., Am. Statis. Assn. Home: 103 Doubloon Dr Slidell LA 70461-2715 Office: U New Orleans Dept Psychology Lake Front New Orleans LA 70148 E-mail: olson32@attglobal.net.

OLSON, RICHARD EARL, lawyer, state legislator; b. Elmhurst, Ill., Apr. 24, 1953; s. Earl Leroy and Helen Ellen (Wanamaker) O.; m. Patricia Michelle McKinney, May 16, 1976; children: Shelley, Rachel, Eric. BA, U. Miss., Oxford, 1975; JD, So. Meth. U., 1978. Bar: N.Mex. 1978. Ptnr. Hinkle, Cox, Eaton, Coffield & Hensley, Roswell, N.Mex., 1978—; mem. N.Mex. Ho. of Reps., 1989-95, mem. various coms. Bd. trustees Eastern N.Mex. Med. Ctr., 1995-98. Mem. Roswell City Coun., 1986—88, chmn. sts. and alleys com., mem. various other coms.; past chmn. pastor parish rels. com. 1st United Meth. Ch., Roswell; bd. dirs. Roswell Econ. Forum, Roswell Mus. and Art Ctr. Found., city coun. liaison; bd. dirs. Assurance Home, 1980—98; pres. Assurance Home Found., 2000—; former bd. dirs. N.Mex. 1st; bd. dirs. N.Mex. Conf. Meth. Found., 2001—. Mem.: Def. Rsch. Inst., Phi Kappa Phi, Order of the Coif. Republican. Home: 5003 Thunderbird Ln Roswell NM 88203-9386 Office: Hinkle Cox Eaton Coffield & Hensley PO Box 10 Roswell NM 88202-0010

OLSON, RICHARD GOTTLIEB, nuclear engineer; b. Terre Haute, Ind., Dec. 17, 1922; s. Gottlieb William and Lucille Adella (Clifton) O.; m. Virginia Ann Abbinett, June 22, 1947; children: Stephen Philip, Mary Ann. BSEE, Rose-Hulman Inst., Terre Haute, 1947; MSE, U. Mich., 1955; postgrad., U. Mass., 1970. Control and kinetics mgr. Atomic Power Devel. Assn., Inc., Detroit, 1955-64; supr. computer facilities and tng. Power Reactor Devel. Co., 1959-67; tech. work leader Detroit Edison, 1965-83, sr. nuclear fuel engr., 1982-89, ret., 1989. Instr. electrical engring. and math Rose Hulman Inst., Terre Haute, 1946-49, Wayne State U., Detroit, 1949-76; instr. computer devel. Cass Tech. High Sch., Detroit, 1960-70. Author: Dynamics of Fast Breeder Reactor, 1956 (Nucleonics award 1957), Instrumentation and Control, 1962 (Am. Nuclear Soc. award 1962). Mem. citizen's adv. com. Dearborn Bd. Edn., 1956-70. Sgt. U.S. Army, 1942-46, ETO, PTO, Korea. U. Mich. fellow, 1954, NSF fellow, 1970. Mem. IEEE (Svc. award 1954), Am. Nuclear Soc. (Svc. award 1966), Assn. for Computing Machines (Svc. award 1968), Tau Beta Pi. Home: 15191 Ford Rd Apt Bg224 Dearborn MI 48126-4699

OLSON, ROBERT EUGENE, physician, biochemist, educator; b. Minn., Jan. 23, 1919; s. Ralph William and Minnie (Holtin) O.; m. Catherine Silvoso, Oct. 21, 1944; children: Barbara Lynn, Robert E., Mark Alan, Mary Ellen, Carol Louise. AB, Gustavus Adolphus Coll., 1938; PhD, St. Louis U., 1944; MD, Harvard, 1951; MD (hon.), Chiang Mai U., Thailand, 1983. Diplomate: Nat. Bd. Med. Examiners, Am. Bd. Nutrition (pres. 1962-63). Postgrad. research asst. biochemistry St. Louis U. Sch. Medicine, 1938-43, asst. biochemistry, 1943-44, Alice A. Doisy prof. biochemistry, chmn. dept. biochemistry, 1965-82, asso. prof. medicine, 1966-72, prof. medicine, 1972-82; vis. prof. (sabbatical) dept. biochemistry U. Freiburg, Breisgau, West Germany, 1970-71; also Hoffman-La Roche Co., Basel, Switzerland, 1970-71; instr. biochemistry and nutrition Harvard Sch. Pub. Health, 1946-47; research fellow Nutrition Found., 1947-49, Am. Heart Assn., 1949-51, established investigator, 1951-52; house officer Peter Bent Brigham Hosp., Boston, 1951-52; prof., head dept. biochemistry and nutrition Grad. Sch. Pub. Health U. Pitts.; lectr. medicine Sch. Medicine, 1952-65; mem. panel malnutrition Japan-U.S. Med. Scis. Program, 1965-69; dir. Nutrition Clinic, Falk Clinic, 1953-65; mem. sr. staff Presbyn. Hosp., dir. metabolic unit, 1960-65; mem. staff St. Louis U. Hosp., 1965-81; prof. biochemistry, prof. medicine, assoc. dean acad. affairs U. Pitts. Sch. Medicine, 1982-84; prof. medicine, prof. pharm. scis. SUNY-Stony Brook, 1984-90, prof. emeritus, 1990—; prof. pediatrics U. South Fla., Tampa, 1994—. Cons. Mercy Hosp., U. Pitts. Med. Center; assoc. in medicine St. Margaret's Meml. Hosp., Pitts., dir. metabolic unit, 1954-60; cons. div. research grants USPHS, 1954-69, 72-76; dir. Anemia and Malnutrition Center, Chiang Mai, Thailand, 1967-77; vis. scholar dept. biochemistry Oxford (Eng.) U., 1961-62; vis. prof. dept. biochemistry U. Freiburg, West Germany, 1970-71; mem. food and nutrition bd. NRC, 1977-83; mem. adv. council Nat. Inst. Arthritis, Diabetes, Digestive and Kidney Diseases, 1981-85; William A. Noyes lectr. U. Ill., Urbana, 1980. Assoc. editor Nutrition Revs., 1954-56, editor, 1978-88; assoc. editor Am. Jour. Medicine, 1956-65, Circulation Rsch., 1956-76, Am. Heart Jour., 1958-65, Am. Jour. Clin. Nutrition, 1960-66, Methods in Med. Rsch., 1963-70, Biochem. Medicine, 1967-90, Molecular and Cellular Cardiology, 1967-78; assoc. editor Ann. Rev. Nutrition, 1979-84, editor, 1984-94; co-editor: Vitamins and Hormones, 1975-81. Bd. dirs. Nat. Nutrition Consortium, 1977-81, Am. Council on Sci. and Health, 1984-91. Served as lt. (j.g.) USNR, 1944-46. Recipient Fulbright award, 1961-62, Guggenheim Found. award, 1961-62, 70-71, McCollum award, 1965, Joseph Goldberger award, 1974; named Atwater Meml. lectr., 1978; Geiger Meml. lectr., 1979, William A. Noyes lectr. U. Ill., 1980, H. Brooks James lectr. N.C. State U., 1981, Virginia Beal lectr. U. Mass., 1990. Fellow ACP, Am. Pub. Health Assn. (chmn. food and nutrition sect. 1960-61), Am. Inst. Nutrition (pres. 1981-82, Conrad Elvehjem award 1998), Assn. Am. Physicians; mem. AAAS (sec. med. scis. N. sect. 1965-67), Am. Assn. Cancer Research, Am. Heart Assn., AMA (mem. council food and nutrition 1959-67, vice chmn. 1962-67), Royal Soc. Health (London), N.Y. Acad. Scis., Am. Fedn. Clin. Research, Am. Soc. Clin. Investigation, Boyleston Med. Soc., Am. Chem. Soc. (pres. biochemistry group Pitts. sect. 1960-61), Am. Soc. Biol. Chemists, Soc. Exptl. Biology and Medicine, Am. Soc. Clin. Nutrition (pres. 1961-62, McCollum award 1965, Herman award 2002), Assn. Med. Sch. Depts. Biochemistry (pres. 1979-80), Pa., St. Louis, Allegheny County med. socs., Am. Soc. Study Liver Diseases, Phi Beta Kappa, Sigma Xi, Phi Lambda Upsilon, Alpha Omega Alpha, Alpha Sigma Nu. Clubs: Cosmos (Washington), Countryside County Club (Clearwater, Fla.). Home: 2673 Camille Dr Palm Harbor FL 34684-2217 Office: U South Fla Dept Pediatrics 17 Davis Blvd Ste 200 Tampa FL 33606-3438 E-mail: rolson@hsc.usf.edu., roberteolsonr@cs.com.

OLSON, ROBERT EDWARD, coal mining executive; b. Phila., Aug. 5, 1927; s. Oscar E. and Marie B. (Kilgallon) O.; m. Jean Emilie Wadsworth, Dec. 31, 1955 (dec. Aug. 1997); children: Grace Olson, Nancy Olson Ashcraft, Karen Olson Culbertson. Student, U. Richmond, 1945, Duke U., 1945-46, U. Pa., 1946; BS in Mining Engring., Pa. State U., 1952. Registered profl. engr.,

Pa., W.Va. Indsl. engr. Island Creek Coal Co., Holden, W.Va., 1952-55; dir., treas., sr. assoc. Coal Standards, Inc., mgmt. cons., Charleston, 1955-61; v.p. adminstrn. Rochester & Pitts. Coal Co., Indiana, Pa., 1961-81; pres., COO Valley Camp Coal Co., Oil City, 1981-86, vice chmn., dir., mem. exec. com., 1986-88, ret., 1988. Past pres., chmn., dir. Kanawha and Hocking Coal & Coke Co., Kelley's Creek and Northwestern R.R. Co., Valley Camp Coal Sales Co.; pres., chief exec. officer Gt. Lakes Coal & Dock Co.; chmn., dir. Donaldson Mine Co., Elm Grove Coal Co., Shrewsbury Coal Co., Helen Mining Co., Valley Camp of Utah Inc.; chmn., CEO Pa. and W.Va. Supply Co. Bd. dirs. United Way of Venango County, 1983-88; pres. bd. trustees Venango County Cmty. Area Found., 1988-94, former dir.; mem. Ind. County C. of C., 1973-81, pres., 1976-77; mem. vestry Christ Episc. Ch., Oil City, 1989-92, 98. With USN, 1945-47. Mem. Ind. Rotary (club pres. 1979-80), Theta Delta Chi, Sigma Phi Sigma. Home: The Quadrangle Ste 8259 3300 Darby Rd Haverford PA 19041-2104

OLSON, ROBERT GRANT, lawyer; b. Ft. Dodge, Iowa, Mar. 29, 1952; s. Grant L. and R. June (Pohlmann) O.; m. Cynthia Lynn Murray, Sept. 7, 1978; children: Brendon, Elisabeth, Jeffrey, Daniel. BS, Iowa State U., 1973; JD, U. Iowa, 1976. Bar: Mo., 1976, Ill. 1977. Ptnr. Thompson & Mitchell, St. Louis, 1976-92, Riezman & Blitz, P.C., St. Louis, 1992-2000, Stone, Leyton & Gershman, P.C., St. Louis, 2000—. Editor Jour. Corp. Law, 1975-76. Vol. Gephardt for Pres. Campaign, 1988, Carnahan for Lt. Gov. Campaign, 1988, Carnahan for Gov. Campaign, 1992., Habitat for Humanity; arbitrator Better Bus. Bur. Taxpayer assistance program. Mem. ABA, Mo. Bar Assn., Ill. Bar Assn., Met. St. Louis Bar Assn., Downtown St. Louis Lions Club (pres. 1990-91). Home: 424 E Jackson Rd Saint Louis MO 63119-4128 Office: Stone Leyton & Gershman 7733 Forsyth Blvd Ste 500 Saint Louis MO 63105-1817

OLSON, ROBERT HOWARD, lawyer; b. July 6, 1944; s. Robert Howard and Jacquiline (Wells) O.; m. Diane Carol Thorsen, Aug. 13, 1966; children: Jeffrey, Christopher. BA in Govt. summa cum laude, Ind. U., 1966; JD cum laude, Harvard U., 1969. Bar: Ohio 1969, Fla. 1980, Ariz. 1985, Calif. 2001, U.S. Supreme Ct. 1973. Assoc. Squire, Sanders & Dempsey, L.L.P., Cleve., 1969, 70-71, 76-81, ptnr., 1981—, Phoenix, 1985—2002; sr. law clk. U.S. Dist. Ct., No. Dist., Ind., 1969-70; chief civil rights divsn. Ohio Atty. Gen.'s Office, Columbus, 1971-73, chief consumer protection, 1973-75, chief counsel, 1975, 1st asst. (chief of staff), 1975-76; ptnr. Squire, Sanders & Dempsey, San Francisco, 2002—. Instr. Ohio State U. Law Sch., Columbus, 1974; Cen. Phoenix com. to advise city council and mayor City of Phoenix, 1987—89; bd. dirs. Orpheum Theater Found., sec., 1989—90, pres., 1990—97, exec. com., 1997—99, The Ariz. Ctr. for Law in the Pub. Interest, 1989—2001, treas., 1992—93, 1997—2001, v.p., 1993—94; mem. Ariz. Ctr. for Disability Law, 1994—96, treas., 1994—95; mem. Valley Leadership Class XIV; rsch. com. Ariz. Town Hall, 1998—2001. Contbr. articles to profl. jours. Bd. dirs. 1st Unitarian Ch. Phoenix, 1987-89, 98-2001, v.p., 1987-89, 2000-2001, pres. 1998-99; bd. dirs. 1st Unitarian Ch. Found., 1987-93, pres., 1990-93. Named Arts Advocate of Yr. Bus. Vols. Arts/Phoenix, 1997. Mem. Ariz. State Bar Assn., Calif. Bar Assn., Phi Beta Kappa. Democrat. Office: Squire Sanders & Dempsey LLP One Maritime Plaza Suite 300 San Francisco CA 94111-3492

OLSON, ROBERT LEONARD, retired insurance company executive; b. Auburn, Mass., Aug. 11, 1930; s. Henry Leroy and Marie Albertina (Holquist) O.; m. Muriel E. Storms, Mar. 22, 1958; children: Cynthia L., Mark W., Keith E. AAS, Becker Jr. Coll., 1956; BBA, Clark U., 1958; grad. exec. program, Dartmouth Coll., 1986. Supr. payroll and expense acctg. Allmerica Financial Life, Worcester, 1958-66, asst. mgr. budget fiscal planning, 1966-68, mgr. cost acctg. Mass., 1966-72, asst. contr., 1972-75, asst. v.p., 1975-82, 2d v.p. fin. planning and reporting, 1982-85, v.p. fin. planning and reporting, 1985-87, v.p., contr., 1987-90, also bd. dirs. Asst. treas. Mass. affiliate Am. Heart Assn., 1982-90, mem. budget, fin. and audit com., 1983-90; treas. Auburn Dist. Nursing Assn., 1972—. Mem. Inst. Mgmt. Accts., Fin. Execs. Inst., Bus. Planning Bd., Am. Mgmt. Assn. (cert. mgmt. course 1982). Avocations: antique and classic cars. Home: 7 Ridgewood Dr Auburn MA 01501-2316 Office: Allmerica Fin Corp 440 Lincoln St Worcester MA 01653-0001

OLSON, ROBERT WILLIAM, writer, retired counselor; b. Chgo., Feb. 5, 1930; s. Milton Olaf Olson and Leonore Stillman; m. Seiko Itoyama, Jan. 16, 1955; children: Troy Olson Blair, Dean Kazu Olson, Trina Olson Harris. BA, George Williams Coll., 1952; MA, U. Chgo., 1959; 7th yr. cert. counselor-cons., Oreg. State U., 1967. 6th grade tchr. Matteson (Ill.) Elem. Sch., 1956-59; sch. counselor, cons. elem. schs., jr. and sr. h.s., various cities, Ill.,Wash., 1959-91; counseling instr. U. Wash., Seattle, 1979-81; family counselor, 1980-091. Behavioral rschr., U. Wash., 1979-81. Author: Memories with a Christmas Attitude, 1994; editor FOKUS Newsletter, 1998—; contbr. numerous articles to profl. counseling jours. Vol., Love and Forgiveness Seminar, Monroe Penitentiary, 1996—; bd. mem. Children Around the World Resource Ctr.; pres., King County (Wash.) Guidance Assn., 1978-79. With U.S. Army, 1952-56, Korea. Mem. NEA (life), Wash. Edn. Assn., Internat. Assn. Near-Death Studies, Full Gospel Businessmen Internat. (vol. King County Jail 1998—), Eastside Writers Assn. (hospitality chmn. 1999—), Northwest Christian Writers Assn. Avocations: ceramics, storytelling, swimming. Home and Office: 252 168th Ave SE Bellevue WA 98008

OLSON, ROBERT WYRICK, lawyer; b. Madison, Wis., Dec. 19, 1945; s. John Arthur and Mary Katherine (Wyrick) O.; m. Carol Jean Duane, June 12, 1971; children: John Hagan, Mary Catherine Duane. BA, Williams Coll., 1967; JD, U. Va., 1970. Assoc. Cravath, Swaine & Moore, N.Y.C., 1970-79; asst. gen. counsel Penn Cen. Corp., Cin., 1979-80, assoc. gen. counsel, 1980-82, v.p., dep. gen. counsel, 1982-87; sr. v.p., gen. counsel, sec. Am. Premier Underwriters, Inc. (formerly Penn Cen. Corp.), 1987-95, Chiquita Brands Internat., Inc., Cin., 1995—. Mem. ABA. Office: Chiquita Brands Internat 250 E 5th St Ste 25 Cincinnati OH 45202-4119 E-mail: bolson@chiquita.com.

OLSON, ROBERTA JEANNE MARIE, art historian, author, educator, curator; b. Shawano, Wis., June 1, 1947; d. Robert Bernard Olson and Emma Pauline (Dallmann) Hoops; m. Alexander Buchanan Vance Johnson, June 15, 1980; 1 child, Allegra Alexandra Olson Johnson. BA, St. Olaf Coll., 1969; MA, U. Iowa, 1971; MFA, Princeton U., 1973, PhD, 1976. Preceptor Princeton U., 1972-74; contbg. editor Arts Mag., N.Y.C., 1973-75; art news editor The Soho Weekly News, 1976-78; from asst. prof. to assoc. prof. Wheaton Coll., Norton, Mass., 1975-88, prof., 1988-2000, chmn. art dept., 1987-89, 92-93, 97-98, A. Howard Meneely chair, 1990-92. Mary L. Heuser faculty chair in the arts Wheaton Coll., 1997—2000; assoc. curator of drawings The N.Y. Hist. Soc., N.Y.C., 1999—; cons. Smithsonian Instn., Washington, 1984—86; bd. dirs. The Drawing Soc., N.Y.C., 1989—94, The Friends of Art; bd. advisers Halley's Comet Soc., 1986—; mem. vis. com. drawing and print dept. Met. Mus. Art, 1993—; mem. vis. com. drawing dept. Fogg Art Mus., Harvard U., 1997—. Author: Italian Nineteenth Century Drawings and Watercolors: An Album, 1976, Italian Drawings 1780-1890, 1980 (N.Y. Times Best Art Book award, 1981, Whole Earth Book award), Fire and Ice: A History of Comets in Art, 1985, Italian Renaissance Sculpture, 1992, French edit., 1993, Ottocento: Romanticism and Revolution in 19th Century Italian Painting, 1993; editor: The Art of Drawing: Selections from the Wheaton College Collection, 1997, Fire in the Sky: Comets and Meteors, the Decisive Centuries, in British Art and Science, 1998, The Florentine Tondo, 2000, Seat of Empire, 2002; contbr. articles to profl. jours. including Burlington Mag., Art Bull , Apollo, Master Drawings, Jour. History of Astronomy , Artibus et Historiae, Sci. Am., Mitteilungen des Kunsthistorischen Insts. in Florenz , Arte Cristiana, Mag. Antiques, Gazette des Beaux-Arts , Antologia di Belle Arti, Astronomy and Astrophysics , Print Quarterly, Art Jour. , Quarterly Jour. Royal Astronomical Soc., Sky and Telescope , Art in Am., Studies in History of Art, The Scis., Drawing, Connoisseur, numerous others, art exhbn. catalogs Six Centuries Sculptors' Drawings, The Drawing Ctr., N.Y.C., 1981, Disegni di Tommaso Minardi, 2 vols., 1982, Galleria Nazionale d'Arte Moderna, Rome, Old Master Drawings from the Mus. Art RISD, 1983; guest curator Art Mus. Princeton U. , 1974, Nat. Gallery of Art , 1980, N.-Y. Hist. Soc., 1990. Fellow Samuel H. Kress Found., 1973—74, Whiting Found. for Humanities, 1974—75, NEH, 1982—83; grantee, 1987—88, Am. Philos. Soc., 1989, Am. Coun. Learned Socs., 1990—91, Getty sr. rsch. grantee, 1994—95, Samuel H. Kress Found., 1996, 1999—2000. Fellow: The Morgan Libr.; mem.: Coll. Art Assn., Italian Art Soc., Drawing Soc., Assn. Univ. Profs. Italian, Phi Beta Kappa (pres. Kappa chpt. 1980—82). Avocations: running, yoga, collecting, horseback riding. Home: 1220 Park Ave Apt 3-c New York NY 10128-1733 Office: N-Y Hist Soc Two West 77th St New York NY 10024 E-mail: robertao@nyhistory.org.

OLSON, ROGER NORMAN, retired health service administrator; b. Spokane, July 3, 1936; s. Harry Leonard and Evelyn Helen (Pearson) O.; m. Joyce Marlene Markert, June 28, 1959; children: Leonard Mark, Brent Norman. BA, Pacific Luth. U., 1958; MDiv, Augustana Theol. Sem., 1962; MSW, U. Wash., 1970. Pastor Christ Luth. Ch., Des Moines, 1962-64; asst. pastor First Immanuel Luth. Ch., Portland, Oreg., 1964-68; planner Tri-County Community Coun., 1970-71; project coord. City-County Commn. on Aging, 1971-73; evaluation coord. Portland Bur. of Human Resources, 1973-74; asst. dir. Multnomah County Project Health Div., 1974-83; interim pastor Augustana Luth. Ch., 1984-85; dir. family support svcs. Met. Family Svc., 1985-91; dir. planning and rsch. Met. Family Svcs., 1992-94; dir. info. exch. Luth. Family Svc., 1994-98; performance improvement mgr. Kerr Youth and Family Ctr., Portland, 1998-2001, ret., 2001. Rockefeller Bros. fellowship Rockefeller Fund for Theol. Edn., 1958-59, fellowship NIMH, 1968-69, Adminstn. on Aging, 1969-70. Democrat. Lutheran. Avocations: music, reading, theatre. Home: 3939 NE 21st Ave Portland OR 97212-1432

OLSON, RONALD CHARLES, aerospace executive; b. Sioux Falls, S.D., Jan. 23, 1937; s. Arthur Helmer and Myrtle Esther (Gustafson) O.; m. Barbara Jean Newcomb, Apr. 7, 1957; children: Bradley Charles, Jodi Lynn. AA, North Idaho Coll., 1956; BS in EE, U. Idaho, 1958; grad. sr. exec. mgmt. program, MIT, 1988. Design engr. Boeing Aerospace, Seattle, 1958-72, engring. mgr., 1973-83; postgrad. in mgmt. MIT, 1988; program mgr. Boeing Defense and Space Group, 1985-95; pres., gen. mgr. Sea Launch Co., LDC, Cayman Islands, 1995-97; v.p. Boeing Comml. Space Co., Cayman Islands, 1995-97, exec. v.p., 1997-99, ret., 1999. Mem. engring. adv. bd. U. Idaho Coll. Engring., Moscow, 1988-95, chmn. bd., 1991-95. Recipient Gen. Ira C. Eaker, Air Force Assn., Vandenburg AFB, 1985; inductee U. Idaho Alumni Hall of Fame, 1998. Mem. Boeing Mgmt. Assn. (sec. 1981-85), Big Band Dance Club (instr. 1980-85), Twin Lakes Golf & Country Club. Republican. Lutheran. Avocations: golf, travel. Home: 1206 184th Avenue Ct E Sumner WA 98390-6443 E-mail: oleolson-1@msn.com.

OLSON, ROY ARTHUR, government official; b. Dec. 8, 1938; s. Elof Herman and Beatrice Lorraine (Dolezal) O.; m. Elisabeth Rigge Behrens, June 24, 1967; children: Heather Elisabeth, Peter Roy. BS, Northwestern U., 1960. Lic. real estate salesman, Ill. Writer, editor Chgo. Am., 1956-68; pres. Roy Olson Pub. Rels. Co., Oak Park, Ill., 1968-70; asst. regional adminstr. SBA, Chgo., 1970-95; Chgo. spokesman Ill. Dept. Transp., 1995—. Dir. Am. Food Industries, Chgo., Covenant Village Retirement Ctr., Northbrook, Ill., 1975-81, Brandel Care Ctr., Northbrook, 1975-81, Swedish Covenant Hosp., Chgo., 1995—. Chmn. Northbrook Covenant Ch., 1980-81, 97-2000. Mem. Soc. Profl. Journalists, Art Inst. Chgo., City Club (media com.), Execs. Club, Chgo. Press Club, Chgo. Headline Club (past dir. 1964-66), Northwestern Club. Home: 2015 Prairie St Glenview IL 60025-2824 Office: 310 S Michigan Ave Chicago IL 60604-4207 E-mail: olsonrb@aol.com.

OLSON, SANDRA LEE, aerospace engineer, research scientist; m. Randy L. Torboli; 2 children. BSChemE, U. Pitts., 1983; MS in Mech. and Aerospace Engring., Case Western Res. U., 1987, PhD in Mech. Engring., 1997. Mem. staff aerothermodynamics and fuels divsn. NASA Glenn Rsch. Ct., Cleve., 1983-84, mem. microgravity combustion sci. br., 1984—. Presenter sems., conf., symposia; keynote spkr. Internta. Space U., Gordon Conf., Hokkaido U., Sapporo, Japan, Miss. State U., Nat. Inst. Stds. and Tech., Mich. State U., U. Ill., Chgo.; jour. reviewer Nature, Combustion and Flame, Combustion Sci. and Tech., Jour. Heat Transfer (ASME), Internat. Jour. Fire and Materials, Nat. Inst. Stds. and Tech. Contbr. numerous articles to profl. jours. including Combustion and Flame. Recipient numerous grants. Mem. AAAS, Combustion Inst. (program rev. subcom.). Office: NASA Glenn Rsch Ctr Mail Stop 77-5 Cleveland OH 44135

OLSON, STEPHEN M(ICHAEL), lawyer; b. Jamestown, N.Y., May 4, 1948; s. Charles R. and Marilyn (Dietzel) O.; m. Linda C. Hanson, Aug. 24, 1968; children: Kevin, Darren. AB cum laude, Princeton U., 1970; JD, U. Chgo., 1973. Bar: Pa. 1973, U.S. Dist. Ct. (we. dist.) Pa. 1973, U.S. Ct. Appeals (3d cir.) 1975, U.S. Ct. Appeals (1st and D.C. cirs.) 1986, U.S. Ct. Appeals (7th cir. and 8th cir. 1988), U.S. Supreme Ct. 1986. Assoc. Kirkpatrick & Lockhart, Pitts., 1973-81, ptnr., 1981—. Bd. dirs. Sweetwater Art Ctr. Mem.: ABA (rlwy./airline labor law com.), Allegheny County Bar Assn., Pa. Bar Assn., Princeton Alumni Assn. West Pa., Duquesne Club. Avocations: photography, bicycling. Office: Kirkpatrick & Lockhart Henry W Oliver Bldg 535 Swithfield St Pittsburgh PA 15222-2312

OLSON, STEVEN STANLEY, social service executive; b. Longview, Wash., Aug. 5, 1950; s. Robert Martin and Martha Virginia (Duffin) O.; 1 child, Derek Thomas Dailey. BA, Wash. State U., 1972; MEd, Auburn U., 1977; postgrad., Seattle U., 1981-83. Cert. rehabilitation mgmt. Agrl. extensionist Action/Peace Corps, Popayan, Colombia, 1972-73; supr. Stonebelt Ctr. for the Mentally Retarded, Bloomington, Ind., 1974; adjustment counselor Exceptional Industries, Bowling Green, Ky., 1974-75, vocat. evaluator, 1975-76; alcohol counselor E. Ala. Mental Health, Opelika, 1976; intern Auburn Univ./Ptnrs. of the Americas, Guatemala City, Guatemala, 1976; planner, rschr. Marion County Mental Health, Salem, Oreg., 1977-78; assoc. dir. Reliable Enterprises, Centralia, Wash., 1979-80, exec. dir., 1980-98, Olympia (Wash.) Child Care Ctr., 1999—. Cons. in field, 1998-99; v.p. govt. affairs Rehab. Enterprises Wash., Olympia, 1984-86, chmn. regional rep., 1986-89, pres., 1990-91; treas. Arc of Wash., Olympia, 1983-85, 99—, govt. affairs chmn., 1983-89, v.p., 1989-90, sec., 1996-97; adv. coun. Lewis/Mason/Thurston Area Agy. on Aging, 1993-99. Contbr. articles to Vocat. Evaluation and Work Adjustment Bull., 1976, Rehab. World, 1977. Treas. Communities United for Reponsible Energy, Lewis County, Wash., 1979—; vice chairperson Wash. Solar Coun., Olympia, Wash., 1980-83; co-chair Early Childhood Help Orgn., Olympia, 1988. Home: 4333 Maytown Rd SW Olympia WA 98512-9239 Office: Olympia Child Care Ctr PO Box 7305 Olympia WA 98507

OLSON, THEODORE BEVRY, Federal Agency Administrator, Lawyer; b. Chgo., Sept. 11, 1940; 2 children. BA, U. Pacific, 1962; LL.B., U. Calif.-Berkeley, 1965. Bar: Calif. 1965, D.C. 1982. Assoc., ptnr. Gibson, Dunn & Crutcher, Los Angeles, 1972-81, 84—; asst. atty. gen. Dept. Justice, Washington, 1981—84; ptnr. Gibson, Dunn & Crutcher, 1984—2001; U.S. solicitor gen. Dept. Justice, 2001—. Mem. Calif. Commn. on Uniform State Laws, 1972-74; del. Republican Nat. Conv., 1976, 80. Fellow Am. Acad. of Appellate Lawyers, Am. Coll. Trial Lawyers; mem. ABA, L.A. County Bar Assn. Office: Office Solicitor Gen 950 Pennsylvania Ave NW Washington DC 20530-0001*

OLSON, TIMOTHY ALLAN, state official; b. Portland, Oreg., July 1, 1952; s. Lloyd Gordon and Emily Pauline (Winchester) O. BA, U. Calif., Santa Barbara, 1977. Dir. internat. program Calif. Energy Commn., Sacramento, 1978—. Democrat. Avocation: family history. Home: 1712 42nd St Sacramento CA 95819-4023 Office: Calif Energy Commn 1516 9th St Sacramento CA 95814-5504 E-mail: tolson@energy.state.ca.us. *Personal philosophy: Government policy influence and partnerships with private enterprise can enhance a climate for market forces to operate and stimulate international exports for U.S. business.*

OLSON, WALTER GILBERT, lawyer; b. Stanton, Nebr., Feb. 2, 1924; s. O.E. Olson and Mabel A. Asplin; m. Gloria Helen Bennett, June 26, 1949; children: Clifford Warner, Karen Rae Olson. BS, U. Calif., Berkeley, 1947, JD, 1949. Bar: Calif. 1950, U.S. Dist. Ct. (no. dist.) Calif. 1950, U.S. Tax Ct. 1950, U.S. Ct. Appeals (9th cir.) 1950. Assoc. Orrick, Herrington and Sutcliffe (formerly Orrick, Dahlquist, Herrington and Sutcliffe), San Francisco, 1949-54, ptnr., 1954-88, of counsel, 1989—. Bd. dirs. Alltel Corp., Little Rock, 1988-94; mem. Commn. to Revise Calif. Corp. Securities Law, 1967-69, Securities Regulatory Reform Panel, 1978-80; mem. corp. security adv. com. Calif. Commr. of Corps, 1975-88. Editor-in-chief Calif. Law Review, 1948-49. Bd. dirs. Internat. Ho., Berkeley, 1981-86. With U.S. Army, 1943-46, ETO. Fellow Am. Bar Found.; mem. ABA (trust divsn. nat. conf. of lawyers and reps. of Am. Bankers Assn.), Calif. Bar Assn. (chmn. corps com. 1975-76, exec. com. bus. law sect. 1977-78), San Francisco Bar Assn., U. Calif. Alumni Assn., Boalt Hall Alumni Assn. (bd. dirs. 1982-90, sec. 1985, v.p. 1987, pres. 1988), Order of Coif, Menlo Country Club (Woodside, Calif.), Pacific-Union Club. Office: Orrick Herrington & Sutcliffe 400 Sansome St San Francisco CA 94111-3143

OLSON, WALTER JUSTUS, JR. management consultant; b. Paterson, N.J., July 27, 1941; s. Walter Justus and Viola Patricia (Trautvetter) O. BS, BA, Brown U., 1964; MBA, Columbia U., 1967. CPA, Va. Design engr. Rockwell Internat., Inc., Downey, Calif., 1964-65; mgmt. officer CIA, Washington, 1969-73; sr. cons. Booz, Allen and Hamilton, Inc., 1973-78; corp. planning coordinator Washington Gas Light Co., 1978-82; prin. Walter J. Olson & Assoc., McLean, Va., 1982-83; dep. asst. sec. for export adminstrn. U.S. Dept. Commerce, Washington, 1983-86; prin. Walter J. Olson & Assoc., 1986—; sr. rsch. analyst U.S. House Select Com. Technology Transfer to PRC, 1998-99. Vice-chmn. fin. com. Fairfax County (Va.) Reps., 1982-83. Served to 1st lt., USAF, 1967-69. Mem. AICPA, Greater Wash. Soc. CPAs, Strategic Leadership Forum (pres. Washington chpt. 1990-91). Republican. Episcopalian. Home: 7348 Dartford Dr Mc Lean VA 22102-7348 Office: 8180 Greensboro Dr Ste 1070 Mc Lean VA 22102-3860

OLSON, WARREN KINLEY, operations research analyst, engineer, physicist; b. Minot, N.D., Aug. 11, 1943; s. Arthur Conrad and Dorothy Elenor (Kinley) O.; m. Colleen Kay Ude, Dec. 18. 1965; children: Christine Kay, Cynthia Dorine. BA in Physics and Math., St. Olaf Coll., 1965; MS in Stats., U. Del., 1974; PhD in Sci. Tech. and Pub. Policy, George Mason U., 2000. Mathematician Ballistics Rsch. Lab., Aberdeen Proving Ground, Md., 1962-69; ops. rsch. analyst Army Material Systems Analysis Agy., 1969-76; br. chief USA TRADOC Systems Analysis Activity, White Sands Missile Range, N. Mex., 1976-85; dir. rsch. USA TRADOC Ops. Rsch. Activity, 1985-86; div. chief USA TRADOC Analysis Command, 1986, dir. rsch., 1986-87; sr. staff engr. Honeywell Defense Systems Group, Edina, Minn., 1987-90, Alliant Techsystems, Inc., Hopkins, 1990-93; rsch. mem. Inst. for Def. Analysis, Alexandria, Va., 1993—2002, cons./tchr., 2002—. Mem. sci. staff NATO Joint Field Trials, Munich, Germany, 1973-74; chmn. U.S. Army ABCA QWG/AOR Spl. Work Group, White Sands, 1979-87; mem. def. sci. bd. MOBA Study, 1994; tech. expert on computer simulation, virtual reality. Co-author: (with others) (text) Military Strategy and Tactics, 1975, (handbook) Military Operations Research, 1994; contbr. tech. reports to profl., military publs., 1965-97. Elder Peace Luth. Ch., El Paso, Tex., 1985-87; mem. St. Olaf choir, 1963-65. Recipient Citizenship award, DAR, 1956, Civilian Svc. Commander's award, U.S. Army, Washington, 1979. Mem. Soc. for Preservation and Encouragement of Barber Shop Quartet Singing (bd. dirs. El Paso 1977-79, Internat. medalist 1991, 92, 93, Gt. No. Union Chorus), Mil. Ops. Rsch. Soc., Am. Def. Preparedness Assn., Nat. Mil. Intelligence Assn., Sigma Pi Sigma. Avocations: music, skiing, scuba diving, photography, model railroading, chess. Home and Office: 1755 Columbine Village Dr Woodland Park CO 80863-8390

OLSON, WILLIAM CLINTON, anthologist, international affairs specialist; b. Denver, Aug. 19, 1920; s. Albert Merrill and Frances (Murray) O.; m. Mary Elizabeth Matthews, Aug. 16, 1943; children: Jon Eric, Peter Murray, Elizabeth Ann. AB, U. Denver, 1942; PhD, Yale U., 1953; DHL (hon.), U. Denver, 1992; hon. diploma, Inter-Am. Def. Coll., 2001. Chmn. com. on internat. rels. Pomona Coll., 1953-61; sr. mem. St. Antonys Coll. Oxford (Eng.) U., 1959-60; assoc. dean sch. internat. affairs Columbia U., N.Y.C., 1965-67; assoc. dir. for social scis. Rockefeller Found., 1967-79; dean Am. U. Sch. Internat. Svc., Washington, 1979-86; vis. rsch. fellow Royal Inst. Internat. Affairs, London, 1986-87; dir. Bellagio Study and Conf. Ctr. of Rockefeller Found., Villa Serbelloni, Italy, 1970-79. Life fellow Clare Hall, Cambridge; cons. to vice chancellor U. Colombo, Sri Lanka, 1983. Author, editor: The Theory and Practice of International Relations, 1960, 9th edit., 1994; co-author: Internat. Relations Then and Now: Origins and Trends in Interpretation, 1991; bd. editors: Cambridge Studies in Internat. Relations, 1983-91. Mem. Brady Leadership Coun., 1999—; trustee Social Sci. Found. U. Denver, 1967, v.p., 1988—. Recipient Disting. Alumnus award Grad. Sch. Internat. Studies, Denver, 1986; received medal and named Hon. Ancien, NATO Def. Coll., 1989. Mem. Coun. Fgn. Rels., Washington Inst. Fgn. Affairs, Internat. Studies Assn. (nat. pres. 1968-69), Cosmos Club (Washington), Phi Beta Kappa (pres. Gamma of Calif. 1957-58), Sigma Iota Rho (founder). E-mail: deanolson@aol.com.

OLSON, WILLIAM JEFFREY, lawyer; b. Paterson, N.J., Oct. 23, 1949; s. Walter Justus and Viola Patricia (Trautvetter) O.; m. Janet Elaine Bollen, May 22, 1976; children: Robert J., Joanne C. AB, Brown U., 1971; JD, U. Richmond, 1976. Bar: Va. 1976, D.C. 1976, U.S. Ct. Claims 1976, U.S. Ct. Appeals (4th, 6th, 10th, and D.C. cirs.) 1976, U.S. Supreme Ct. 1982. Assoc. Jackson & Campbell, Washington, 1976-79; ptnr. Gilman, Olson & Pangia, 1980-92; prin. William J. Olson PC, McLean, Va. and Washington, 1992—. Sec., treas. bd. dirs. Victims Assistance Legal Orgn., McLean, Va., 1979—; presdl. transition team leader Legal Svcs. Corp., Washington, 1980; chmn. and bd. dirs. nat. Legal Svcs. Corp., 1981-82; mem. Pres.'s Export Coun. Subcom. on Export Adminstrn., Washington, 1982-84; spl. counsel bd. govs. U.S. Postal Svc., Washington, 1984-86. Author: Tuition Tax Credits and Alternatives, 1978; co-author: Debating National Health Policy, 1977, Executive Orders and National Emergencies, 1999. Trustee Davis Meml. Goodwill Industries, Washington, 1980-86, 88-93; chmn. Fairfax County Rep. Com., Fairfax, Va., 1980-82; mem. Rep. State Ctrl. Com., Richmond, Va., 1982-86. Mem. Va. Bar Assn., Assn. Trial Lawyers Am., Va. Trial Lawyers Assn. Republican. Baptist. Avocation: gardening. Office: 8180 Greensboro Dr Ste 1070 Mc Lean VA 22102-3860 E-mail: wjo@mindspring.com.

OLSON-HAGAN, ARLENE, parochial school administrator; b. Bklyn., May 30, 1926; d. Carl Bernard and Helen Loretta (Segerdell) Olson; m. Raymond G. Hagan, Feb. 15, 1979; stepchildren: David, Clifford, Richard, Bruce (dec.). AB in English, Hofstra U., 1948; MS in Edn., SUNY, New Paltz, 1952; Cert. Adv. Study, Hofstra U., 1976. Tchr. Island Trees (N.Y.) Pub. Schs., 1950-55; tchr., dist. pubs. editor Garden City (N.Y.) Pub. Schs., 1955-82; pub. info. officer Amityville (N.Y.) Pub. Schs., 1982-84; dir. external affairs St. Edward's Sch., Vero Beach, Fla., 1986-93. Editor, layout and design newsletters, spl. brochures for schs. Mem. Nat. Sch. Pub. Rels. Assn., Fla. Pub. Rels. Assn., Ctr. for the Arts. Episcopalian.

OLSON-HELLERUD, LINDA KATHRYN, elementary school educator; b. Wisconsin Rapids, Wis., Aug. 26, 1947; d. Samuel Ellsworth and Lillian (Dvorak) Olson; m. H. A. Hellerud, 1979; 1 child Sarah Kathryn Hellerud. BS, U. Wis., Stevens Point, 1969, tchg. cert., 1970, MST, 1972; MS, U. Wis., Whitewater, 1975; EdS, U. Wis., Stout, 1978. Cert. K-12 reading tchr. and specialist. Clk. U. Counseling Ctr. U Wis., Stevens Point, 1965-69; elem. sch. tchr. Wisconsin Rapids, 1970-76; sch. counselor, 1976-79; dist. elem. guidance dir., 1979-82; elem. and reading tchr., K-1 early intervention team, 1982—; also cons. Advocate Literacy Tutoring Program; adv. Moravian Ch. Sunday Sch. Mem.: NEA, Internat. Reading Assn., Internat. Reading Assn., Wood County Lit. Coun. (cons.), Wood County Hist. Soc., Wis. State Hist. Soc., Ctrl. Wis. Reading Assn. (family lit. com.), Wis. Reading Assn. (early intervention com.). United Ch. Christ. Avocations: literacy activities, piano, Spanish, technology, aerobics. Home: 1011 16th St S Wisconsin Rapids WI 54494-5371 Office: Howe Elem Sch Wisconsin Rapids WI 54494

OLSSON, CARL ALFRED, urologist, department chairman; b. Boston, Nov. 29, 1938; s. Charles Rudolph and Ruth Marion (Bostrom) O.; m. Mary DeVore, Nov. 4, 1962; children: Ingrid, Leif Eric. Grad., Bowdoin Coll., 1959; MD, Boston U., 1963. Diplomate Am. Bd. Urology (trustee 1988-94, pres. 1993-94). Asst. prof. urology Boston U. Sch. Medicine, 1971-72, assoc. prof., 1972-74, prof., chmn. dept., 1974-80; dir. urology dept. Boston City Hosp., 1974-77; chief urology dept. Boston VA Med. Ctr., 1971-75; urologist-in-chief Univ. Hosp., Boston, 1971-80; John K. Lattimer prof., chmn. dept. urology Coll. Phys. and Surgs., Columbia U., N.Y.C., 1980—. Dir. Squier Urol. Clinic, urology service Presbyn. Hosp., N.Y.C.; lectr. surgery Tufts U. Sch. Medicine. Boston Interhosp. Organ Bank, 1976-79; mem. working cadre Nat. Prostate Cancer Project, Nat. Cancer Inst., 1979-84; mem. adv. coun. Nat. Inst. Diabetes, Digestive Disease and Kidney. Editl. bd. Jour. Prostate, World Jour. Urology, Jour. Urodynamics and Neurourology, Jour. Urology; asst. editor Jour. Urology, 1978-89; contbr. chpts. to books, articles to med. jours. Recipient Disting. Alumnus award Boston U., 1985. Fellow ACS; mem. Am.

Urol. Assn. (coord. continuing med. edn. New Eng. sect. 1977-80, del. rsch. com., sec. elect 2001, sec. 2002, Gold Cystoscope award 1979, Grayson-Carroll award 1971, 73, Hugh Hampton Young award 2001), Boston Surg. Soc. (exec. com. 1976-80), Am. Assn. Clin. Urologists, Am. Surg. Assn., Am. Assn. Genitourinary Surgeons, Clin. Soc. Genitourinary Surgeons, Transplantation Soc., Soc. Urologic Oncology (pres. 1993), Soc. Univ. Urologists (pres. 1990), N.Y. Sect. Am. Urol. Assn., Am. Fertility Soc. (pres. elect 2001), AMA, Assn. Acad. Surgery, Am. Soc. Artificial Internal Organs, Am. Soc. Transplant Surgeons, Assn. Med. Colls., Can. Urol. Assn., Societe Internationale d'Urologie, Internat. Urodynamics Soc., Mass. Med. Soc., Soc. Govt. Urologists, Australasian Urol. Soc. (hon.), New Eng. Handicapped Sportsmen's Assn. (exec. com. 1977-81), U.S. Yacht Racing Union, Yacht Racing Union L.I. Sound Club, N.Y. Yacht Club, Cottage Park Yacht Club, Larchmont Yacht Club, Storm Trysail Club, Alpha Omega Alpha. Episcopalian. Home: 18 Elm Ave Larchmont NY 10538-3649 Office: Columbia-Presbyn Hosp P&S Box 44 630 W 168th St New York NY 10032-3702

OLSSON, CARMEN, interior designer; b. Lynwood, Calif., May 3, 1952; d. Manuel and Dorthy Marie (Sharrett) Chavez; m. Norman Allan Olsson, Apr. 8, 1972 (div. Sept. 1993); children: Kristian Eric, Mario Matthew, Rachel Lynn. AA, Chaffey Coll., Alta Loma, Calif., 1980; BA, UCLA, 1983. With Creative Interiors, Upland, Calif., 1975-78, David Allan Interiors, Tustin, 1978-80; pvt. practice interior design, Irvine, 1980—; CEO TAMC Mktg. & Distbn., 1993-99. Participant, designer Orange County (Calif.) Philharm. House of Design, Tustin, 1992, Santa Ana, 1993, Anaheim, 1994. Active HomeAid Project Playhouse, 1998, Assistance League Design House, Hancock Park, 1999. Mem. Am. Soc. Interior Designers, cert., profl., v.p. 1993-95, chmn. programs 1993-94), Chaffey Coll. Alumnae Assn. (pres. Anaheim, Calif. 1993-95), Am. Soc. of Interior Designers (pres-elect 1995-96, pres. 1996-97). Republican. Avocations: step aerobics, cross-training, cross-country running, volleyball. Office: PO Box 50552 Irvine CA 92619-0552 Fax: 949-559-8076. E-mail: colsson@compuserve.com.

OLSSON, NILS WILLIAM, former association executive; b. Seattle, June 11, 1909; s. Nils A. and Mathilda (Lejkell) O.; m. Dagmar T. Gavert, June 15, 1940; children: Karna B., Nils G. and Pehr C. (twins). Student, North Park Coll., Chgo., Northwestern U., U. Minn., 1929-34; A.M., U. Chgo., 1938, PhD, 1949, U. Uppsala, Sweden, 1968; LHD, North Park Coll., Chgo., 1990. Admissions counselor, instr. Swedish North Park Coll., 1937-39; asst. Scandinavian U. Chgo., 1939-42, instr., 1945-50, asst. prof., 1950; mem. U.S. diplomatic service, 1950-67; 2d sec., pub. affairs officer Am. legation, Reykjavik, Iceland, 1950-52; attache, pub. affairs officer Am. embassy, Stockholm, Sweden, 1952-55, 1st. sec., consul, 1955-57; pub. affairs adviser Dept. State, 1957-59; chief Am. sponsored schs. abroad, 1959-62; 1st sec. Am. embassy, Oslo, Norway, 1962-64, counselor for polit. affairs, 1964-66; diplomat in residence Ind. U., 1966-67; dir. Am. Swedish Inst., Mpls., 1967-73; exec. dir. Swedish Council of Am., 1973-84. Author: Swedish Passenger Arrivals in New York 1820-1850, 1967, Swedish Passenger Arrivals in U.S. Ports (except New York) 1820-1850, 1979, Tracing Your Swedish Ancestry, 1974, (with Erik Wiken) Swedish Passenger Arrivals in the U.S. 1820-1850, 1995; editor: A Pioneer in Northwest America, 1841-1858, vol. I, 1950, vol. II, 1959, Veckobladet, 1934-35; editor, pub.: Swedish American Genealogist, 1981—; editor: A Swedish City Directory of Boston 1881, 1986; contbr. to hist. and ednl. jours. Mem. bd. Evang. Covenant Hist. Commn., Chgo., 1958; asst. naval attache Am. legation, Stockholm, 1943-45. Served from lt. (j.g.) to lt. comdr. USNR, 1942-45. Decorated knight Order Vasa 1st class, knight comdr. Order North Star, Sweden; recipient Swedish Pioneer Centennial medal, 1948; King Carl XVI Gustaf Bicentennial Gold medal, Carl Sandburg medal Swedish Pioneer Hist. Soc., 1982, Charlotta medal Emigrant Inst. Växjö, Sweden; named Swedish Am. of Yr. Stockholm, 1969; recipient Hans Mattsson Plaque, Önnestad, Sweden, 1992; Victor Örnberg prize, Sweden, 1994. Fellow Geneal. Soc. (Finland), Geneal. Soc. (Sweden), Am. Soc. Genealogists; mem. Wermländska Sällskapet Stockholm (hon.), Nat. Geneal Soc., Carl Johan Soc. Sweden, Swedish-Am. Hist. Soc. (exec. sec. 1949-50, 57-68, pres. 1986-88), Royal Acad. Belles Lettres, History and Antiquities (Sweden, fgn. corr.), Pro Fide et Christianismo (Sweden, hon.), Royal Soc. Pub. Manuscripts Dealing with Scandinavian History (Sweden, fgn.). Clubs: Skylight (Mpls.); Grolier (N.Y.C.); Cosmos (Washington); Explorers (Central Fla.); Univ. (Winter Park, Fla.). Lodges: Rotary. Address: PO Box 2186 Winter Park FL 32790-2186

OLSSON, RONALD ARTHUR, computer science educator; b. Huntington, N.Y., Nov. 16, 1955; s. Ronald Alfred and Dorothy Gertrude (Hofmann) O. BA and MA, SUNY, 1977; MS, Cornell U., 1979; PhD, U. Ariz., 1986. Teaching asst. Cornell U., Ithaca, N.Y., 1977-79, rsch. asst., 1979; lectr. SUNY, Brockport, 1979-81; rsch. assoc. U. Ariz., Tucson, 1981-86; prof., vice chair Computer Sci. Dept. U. Calif., Davis, 1986—. Author (book) The SR Programming Language: Concurrency in Practice, 1993; contbr. articles to profl. jours. Grantee MICRO U. Calif., 1987, 92, NSF, 1988, 96, Dept. Energy, 1988-92, Advanced Rsch. Projects Agy., 1993—. Mem. Assn. for Computing Machinery. Avocations: bicycling, hiking, cross-country skiing, movies. Home: 2741 Brandywine Pl Davis CA 95616-2904 Office: U Calif Dept Computer Sci Davis CA 95616-8562

OLSTAD, ROGER GALE, science educator; b. Mpls., Jan. 16, 1934; s. Arnold William and Myra (Stroschein) O.; m. Constance Elizabeth Jackson, Aug. 20, 1955; children: Karen Louise, Kenneth Bradley. BS, U. Minn., 1955, MA, 1959, PhD, 1963. Instr. U. Minn., Mpls., 1956-63; asst. prof. U. Ill., Urbana, 1963-64; mem. faculty U. Wash., Seattle, 1964—, asso. prof. sci. edn., 1967-71, prof., 1971-95, assoc. dean grad. studies Coll. Edn., 1971-85; prof. emeritus, 1995—. Chair environ. quality commn. City of Lake Forest Park, Wash., 1997-2000, city coun., 2000—. Fellow AAAS; mem. NSTA (bd. dirs.) Wash. Sci. Tchrs. Assn. (pres. 1973-74), Nat. Assn. Rsch. Sci. Teaching (pres. 1977-78, bd. dirs.), N.W. Sci. Assn. (chmn. 1966-68), Assn. Edn. Tchrs. in Sci. (regional pres. 1966-68, pres. 1991-92), Nat. Assn. Biology Tchrs., Biol. Scis. Curriculum Study (chmn., bd. dirs. 1989-94), U. Wash. Faculty Club, Phi Delta Kappa. Home: 20143 53rd Ave NE Seattle WA 98155-1801 Office: U Wash Coll Edn Seattle WA 98195-0001

OLSTEAD, CHRISTOPHER ERIC, consulting executive, talent manager; b. Gainesville, Fla., Feb. 10, 1956; s. George Elias Olstead and Myra (Mahlow) Hinman; m. Rebecca Lynn Jeffries, Feb. 14, 1978; 1 child, Reneé. BS, SUNY, Albany, 1991; MBA in Internat. Bus., U. St. Thomas, 1994. Control sys. specialist Soltex Polymer, Etc., Houston, 1975-82; sr. instrument inspector Sohio Constrn. Co., Prudhoe Bay, Alaska, 1983-84; instrument engr. Arco Alaska, Kuparuk, 1984-85, Standard Alaska Prodn. Co., Prudhoe Bay, 1985-87; control sys. supr. S & B Engring., Houston, 1987-88; sr. control sys. engr. Bechtel Corp., 1988-90, microcomputer ops. mgr., 1990-92, project quality mgr., 1992-95, supply chain mgr., 1995-97; sr. exec. Arthur Andersen Bus. Cons., 1997-99; COO U.S. Space & Rocket Ctr., Huntsville, Ala., 1999-2000; sr. exec. Arthur Andersen Bus. Cons., Houston, 2000—02, Deloitte Cons., Houston, 2002—. Spkr. ASME-IEEE Internat. Conf., Boston, 1990; panelist Constrn. Industry Inst., San Antonio, Tex., 1993, Constrn. Productivity Inst., Austin, Tex., 1993. Lead author: Advances in Applied Business Strategies, 1995; contbr. articles to profl. jours. Mem. Project Mgmt. Inst., Instrument Soc. Am. (bd. dirs. 1989-92). Avocations: entertainment and management collectibles. Office: Deloitte Consulting Ste 2600 333 Clay St Houston TX 77002 E-mail: chrisolstead@hotmail.com.

OLTHOF, RANDY JAMES, commissioner; b. Elmira, N.Y., Oct. 21, 1950; s. Duane Elwood and Carol Pearl (Kelly) O.; m. Patricia Mary Baker, July 21, 1980; children: Emily Lucille, Katrina Angelique. BA, Elmira Coll., 1973; MPA, Pa. State U., 1975. Sr. regional planner Middle Peninsula Planning Dist. Commn., Glenns, Va., 1977-79; sr. cons. SMC-Mgmt. Tech., Washington, 1979-81; com. fiscal analyst Md. Gen. Assembly, Annapolis, 1981-85; commr. planning Chemung County, Elmira, N.Y., 1985—. Profl. mentor Empire State Coll., Binghamton, N.Y., 1989; statutory mem. Elmira Econ. Devel. Zone Adminstrn. Bd., 1988—; mem. Urban Land Inst., Washington, 1987—. Pres., bd. dirs. Elmira-Corning Ballet Co., Inc., 1985-87; incorporator Chemung Valley Living History Ctr., Wellsburg, N.Y., 1990-92; chmn. adv. com. Elmira Downtown Devel., Inc., 1990-94. Mem. Nat. Emergency Number Assn., Am. Planning Assn. Avocations: gardening, performing arts. Office: Chmung County Planning Dept 400 E Church St Elmira NY 14901-2803 E-mail: rolthof1@stny.rr.com.

OLTION, JERRY, author science fiction; m. Kathy Oltion. Author: Fram of Reference, 1987, German edit., 1992, Alliance, 1990, French edit., 1992, Humanity, 1990, Love Songs of a Mad Scientist, 1993, The Darkness Before the Dawn, 1995, Tales From the Yuletide, 1994, Twilights End, 1996, Buried Treasures, 1996, Mudd in Your Eye, 1997, You Only Die Twice, 1997, Hard Crase and Prophet's Power, 1998, Where Sea Meets Sky, 1998, Singing in the Rain, 1998, The Flaming Arrow (with Kathy Oltion), 2000, Abandon in Place, 2000, The Getaway, 2001; author numerous short stories, novelettes, novellas. Winner 1997 Nebula award for novella, Abandon in Place. Office: Tor Books 175 Fifth Ave, 14th Fl. New York NY 10010*

OLTZ, DONALD FREDERICK, research mineral resources executive; b. Duluth, Minn., Aug. 20, 1940; s. Donald F. and Helen J. (Richardson) O.; m. Theresa Z. Brooks, Sept. 1, 1962; children: Kristin Kara, Kurt Erich. BS, Alma Coll., 1962; PhD, U. Minn., 1968. Asst. prof. Alma Coll., Alma, Mich., 1967-72; exploration geologist Texaco, Inc., L.A. and N.Y., 1972-85; rsch. mgr. oil and gas sect. Ill. State Geol. Survey, Champaign, Ill., 1985-93, head energy and mineral resources group, 1993-96, group head mineral econs., minerals, energy, engring. environ. site assesment, 1996; state geologist, oil and gas supr. Geol. Survey Ala. and State Oil and Gas Bd., 1996—. Chmn., rsch. com., Inst. Oil and Gas Compact Commn., Oklahoma City, 1995-97; adv. com., Am. Assn. Petroleum Geologists, Tulsa, 1995-96; ofcl. rep. for Ala., Interstate Oil and Gas Compact Commn., 1996—; mem., ofcl. rep. for Ala., U.S. Minerals Mgmt. Svc. Outer Continental Shelf Policy Com., 1996—, vice chmn., 1999-2000, chmn., 2000—; chmn. N.Am. Coastal Alliance, Interstate Oil and Gas Compact Commn., 1997-2001; mem. Energy Coun. CLEER U. Adv. Bd., 1997-2001; Ala. ptnr. U.S. Energy Assn. Caspian Environmental Regulatory Partnership Program, 1999—. Editor: Symposium in Geochemistry, 1979; co-editor: Interior Cratonic Basins, 1991. Recipient Disting. Svc. award State of Ill., 1990, 92; numerous rsch. grants, 1989-95. Mem. Assn. Am. State Geologists (chmn. continental margins com., liaison to Am. Assn. Petroleum Geologists 1999—, liaison com. 2000—), Am. Assn. Petroleum Geologists (pres., eastern section, 1993-94, councillor divsn. environ. geosci., 1995-96, Disting. Svc. award 1996), Soc. Petroleum Engrs., Geol. Soc. Am., Ala. Geol. Soc., Sigma Xi. Avocations: pres. Soc. Am. Magicians, 1995-96. Office: Geological Survey Ala State Oil & Gas Bd PO Box 869999 Tuscaloosa AL 35486-6999 E-mail: dfoltz@aol.com.

OLUBADEWO, JOSEPH OLANREWAJU, pharmacologist, educator; b. Oroago, Kwara, Nigeria, Apr. 16, 1945; came to U.S., 1980; s. Solomon Akanbi and Leah Ifanike (Omodara) O.; m. Victoria Ibidunni Balogun, Aug. 20, 1972; children: Oludele, Oluseyi, Olubunmi, Oluwole. BSc with honors, Ahmadu Bello U., Zaria, Nigeria, 1970; PhD, Vanderbilt U., 1976. Asst. lectr. Ahmadu Bello U., 1970-75, lectr. II to lectr. I, 1975-80, sr. lectr., 1980; rsch. scientist U. Tenn. Ctr. Health Scis., Memphis, 1980-84, asst. prof., 1984-85; assoc. prof. Xavier U., New Orleans, 1985-91, prof., 1991—. Spl. reviewer NIH, 1989-92. Mem. editorial bd. Jour. Nat. Pharm. Assn., 1989; reviewer Annals of Pharmacotherapy, Cellular and Molecular Biology; contbr. articles to profl. jours. Fellow African-American Inst. Grad. Program, 1971-75, Am. Heart Assn., 1983, 84, NIH, 1987, 88. Mem. AAUP, Am. Soc. for Pharmacology and Exptl. Therapeutics, Southeastern Pharmacology Soc. (life), Am. Assn. Colls. Pharmacy, N.Y. Acad. Scis., West African Soc. Pharmacology (life). Baptist. Avocations: basketball, volleyball, aerobics, chess, writing poetry. Home: 13510 Dwyer Blvd New Orleans LA 70129-1530 Office: Xavier U La 7325 Palmetto St New Orleans LA 70125-1056

OLUBODUN, JOEL OLADAPO, medical researcher, physician; b. Ipoti, Ekiti, Nigeria, July 12, 1950; came to U.S., 1996; s. Samson Folayan and Alice Olawande O.; m. Margaret Olufunke, Feb. 21, 1981; children: David Oluwaseun, Israel Oladluwa, Elizabeth Ifejesu. BS, MB, U. Ibadan, Nigeria, 1977. Houseman Adeoyo Specialist Hosp., Ibadan, Nigeria, 1977-78; resident in internal medicine U. Coll. Hosp., 1979-85; rsch. fellow cardiology Freeman Hosp., Newcastle Upon Tyne, U.K., 1985-86; physician, cardiologist, sr. lectr. Ogun State U. Tchg. Hosp., Shagamu, Nigeria, 1988-91; sr. rschr. fellow U. Newcastle & Freeman Hosp., Newcastel Upon Tyne, 1991-96; resident U. Pa. Health Sys., Presbyn. Med. Ctr., Phila., 1996-2000; rschr. drug devel. Tufts U. Pfizer Ctrl. Rsch., Boston, 2000—. Chmn. cardiovas. svcs. bd. Ogun State U. Tchg. Hosp., 1989-91, disciplinary bd., 1989-91, acting head medicine dept., 1989-91, dept. rep. U. senate, 1989-91; cons. in field. Contbr. numerous articles to profl. jours.; editl. bd. Jour Ethnicity & Disease, 1999—. Active vol. African Christian Fellowship, 1996—. Med. officer 22d. armoured bridage, Ilorin, Nigeria, 1978-79. Recipient Elizabeth Wherry award, 1995, Searle Dist. Rsch. award 1996, med. degree (MRCP), Royal Coll. Physicians of Ireland, 1995, award Am. Coll. Clin. Pharmacology, 2001, award Am. Soc. Clin. Pharmacology and Therapeutics, 2002, James Bain award, 2002; fellow Assn. Commonwealth Univs., London, 1991, Pfizer, 1991. Fellow Postgrad. Med. Coll. Physicians Nigeria; mem. Royal Coll. Physicians Ireland, Royal Coll. Physicians Nigeria, Am. Coll. Physicians (bd. cert.), Internat. Soc. Hypertension in Blacks (editl. bd. 1990—, manuscript reviewer). Avocations: chess, travelling, writing. Home: 214 Chestnut W Randolph MA 02368 Office: Tufts Univ Med Sch 136 Harrison Ave Boston MA 02111 E-mail: olubodun@yahoo.com.

OLUBOWALE, FOLARIN ADEGBOYEGA, physician; b. Ibadan, Nigeria, Jan. 10, 1960; s. Isaiah Obayomi and Eunice Wuraola (Obakin) O.; m. Folasade Solaja, Dec. 3, 1994; children: Olayemi, Adeleye, Omolade. MBBS, U. Lagos (Nigeria), 1983. Diplomate Am. Bd. Internal Medicine, Am. Bd. Infectious Diseases. Resident Englewood (N.J.) Hosp., 1991-94; fellow in infectious diseases U. Medicine and Dentistry N.J., Newark, 1994-96; attending physician St. Francis Hosp., Dr.'s Hosp., The Med. Ctr., Columbus, Ga., 1997—. Mem. ACP, AMA, Infectious Disease Soc. Am., Soc. for Healthcare Epidemiology of Am. E-mail: folubowale@pol.net.

OLUYITAN, EMMANUEL FUNSO, communications educator; b. Efon-Alaye, Nigeria, July 25, 1940; BA cum laude in Polit. Sci., Bowie (Md.) State U., 1972; MPA in Policy Analysis and Journalism, Ind. U., 1975, EdD in Instructional Tech., 1980. News reporter Nigerian Nat. Press, Lagos, 1964-65; music libr., news translator, news reporter Nigerian Broadcasting Corp., 1965-69; pub. info. coord. Aerospace Rsch. Ctr., Sch. Pub./Environ. Affairs, Ind. U., Bloomington, 1973-75; victim assistance officer Indpls. Police Dept., 1975-76; prin. lectr. Nigerian TV Authority, Lagos, 1978-81; assoc. prof. dept. edn. Ahmadu Bello U., Zaria, Nigeria, 1981-88, asst. dean postgrad. studies Nigeria, 1985-88, head instructional tech. divsn. Nigeria, 1983-88; program officer Nat. Assn. for Equal Opportunity in Higher Edn., Washington, 1988-93; dir. Office of Pub. Rels. and Pubs. Lincoln University, Pa., 1993-96; dir. integrated info. tech. Bennett Coll., Greensboro, N.C., 1996-97; asst. prof. of comm. Wilberforce (Ohio) U., 1997—. Staff writer Office of Pub. Info., Bowie State U., 1973; vice chmn. bd. Adventures in Health, Edn. and Agrl. Devel., Inc., Rockville, Md., 1993—; bd. dirs. Anthony J. Cebrun Journalism Ctr., Nashville; founder, pres. Global Linkage Enterprises; CEO, Ase Internat. Photographer, fgn. news editor Ebony Tree, 1970-72; editor: African Insight, 1973, Nigeria Audio-Visual Newsletter, 1982-86, Nigeria Audio-Visual Jour., 1982-86, Global Vision, 1988-93, Update, 1988-93; assoc. editor Black Excellence, 1988-93; editor-in-chief Weekly Calendar, 1993-96, LU Newsletter, 1993-96, The Lincoln Lion, 1993-96, The Lincoln-Jour., 1993-96; contbr. articles to profl. jours., newspapers; contbr. photographs to books, jours.; prodr. numerous ednl. materials (videos, slides, pictures) Recipient Dir. Gen.'s Commendation, Nigerian TV Authority, 1987, Fed. Govt. of Nigeria's Postgrad. award, 1977-80, Award of Accomplishment and Worthiness, Indpls. Police Dept., 1976, Contr.'s Citation, Nigerian Broadcasting Corp., 1967. Mem. Assn. of Nigerians Against Corruption (founder), Nigerian Assn. for Ednl. Media and Tech., Internat. Assn. Black Profls. in Internat. Affairs, Assn. of Ednl. Comm. and Tech., Oxford Rotary Club (v.p. 1995-96). Avocations: tennis, ping-pong, photography, travel. Office: Wilberforce U LRC 115 Comm Divsn Wilberforce OH 45384 E-mail: eoluyita@wilberforce.edu.

OLVER, FRANK WILLIAM JOHN, retired research educator; b. Croydon, Eng., Dec. 15, 1924; came to U.S., 1961; s. John Adlbert and Susan Mary (Barnes) O.; m. Grace E. Smith, Sept. 25, 1948 (dec. 1980); children: Peter J., Linda M. (dec.), Sally E. Sondergaard; m. Claire L. Kellogg, June 22, 1990. BSc, U. London, 1945, MSc, 1948, DSc, 1961. Sr. prin. sci. officer Nat. Physical Lab., Teddington, Eng., 1945-61; mathematician Nat. Bureau of Standards, Washington, 1961-86; rsch. prof. U. Md., Coll. Park, 1969-92, prof. emeritus, 1992—. Author: Asymptotics and Special Functions, 1974; mem. editorial bd. SIAM Jour. on Mathematical Analysis, 1969-94, Mathematics of Computation, 1984-95, Methods and Applications of Analysis, 1992-2000; math. editor NIST Digital Libr. Math. Functions, 1998—; contbr. numerous articles to profl. math. jours. and books. Recipient Silver medal U.S. Dept. of Commerce, Washington, 1969. Fellow Inst. Math. and Its Applications; mem. Am. Math. Soc., Soc. for Indsl. and Applied Maths., Math. Assn. Am., Royal Soc. Scis. Uppsala (fgn. mem.), Sigma Xi. Avocation: billiards. Office: U Md Inst Phys Sci And Tech College Park MD 20742-2431 E-mail: olver@ipst.umd.edu.

OLVER, JOHN WALTER, congressman; b. Honesdale, Pa., Sept. 3, 1936; s. Helen Fulleborn Olver; m. Rose Alice Richardson, Sept. 12, 1959; 1 child, Martha. BS, Rensselaer Poly. Inst., 1955; MS, Tufts U., 1956; PhD, MIT, 1961. Asst. prof. chemistry U. Mass., Amherst, 1962-67; mem. Mass. Ho. of Reps., Boston, 1969-72, Mass. Senate, 1973-91, U.S. Congress from 1st Mass. dist., 1991—, mem. com. on appropriations, mem. subcoms. on transp. and mil. constrn., mil. appropriations; whip-at-large Dem. Caucus. Congressman; b. Honesdale, Pa., Sept. 3, 1936; s. Helen Fulleborn Olver; m. Rose Alice Richardson, Sept. 12, 1959; children: Martha. BS, Rensselaer Poly. Inst., 1955; MS, Tufts U., 1956; PhD, MIT, 1961. Asst. prof. chemistry, U. Mass., Amherst, 1962-68; mem. Mass. Ho. of Reps., Boston, 1969-72, Mass. Senate, 1973-91; mem. 101st-105th Congresses from 1st Mass. dist., 1991—, mem. com. on appropriations, mem. subcoms. on transp. and mil. constrn. Contbr. articles to profl. jours. Democrat. Avocations: hiking; gardening; tennis. Contbr. articles to profl. jours. Democrat. Avocations: hiking, gardening, tennis. Office: US Ho of Reps 1027 Longworth Hob Washington DC 20515-0001*

OLVER, MICHAEL LYNN, lawyer; b. Seattle, June 22, 1950; s. Manley Deforest and Geraldine (Robinson) O.; m. Wendy Kay, July 6, 1974; children: Erin, Christina. BA, U. Wash., 1972; JD, Calif. Western Sch. of Law, 1976. Assoc. Robbins, Merrick & Kraft, Seattle, 1976-77; lawyer, sole practitioner Michael L. Olver, 1977-80; ptnr., pres. Merrick & Olver, P.S., 1980—. Bd. dirs. Found. for Handicapped, Seattle, 1988—; commr. pro tem Ex part Dept. King County Superior Ct., Seattle, 1992—. Author: Bascomb's Rogue, 1994; assoc. editor Calif. Western Internat. Law Jour., 1975-76, contbr. numerous articles to profl. jours. Mem. Nat. Acad. Elder Law Attys. (pres. Wash. chpt. 2002), Wash. State Trial Lawyers Assn. Office: Merrick & Olver PS 9222 Lake City Way NE Seattle WA 98115-3268

OLVER, PETER JOHN, mathematician, educator; b. Twickenham, Eng., Jan. 11, 1952; s. Frank William John and Grace Elizabeth Olver; m. Chehrzad Shakiban; children: Parizad, Sheehan, Noreen. PhD, Harvard U., 1976. Prof. U. Minn., Mpls., 1980—. Author: Application of Lie Groups to Differential Equations, 1986, Equivalence, Invariants and Symmetry, 1995, Classical Invariant Theory, 1999. Baha'I. Office: School Math U Minn 206 Church St SE Minneapolis MN 55455

OLVERA, CARLOS NELSON, mechanical engineer, executive; b. Antioch, Calif., Aug. 16, 1942; s. Manuel Olvera and Faye Ames; m. Pamela Lords, Oct. 20, 1966 (div. 1979); children: Jason, Jared, Jamie, Janel; m. Georgelean Suitter, Mar. 19, 1983. BSME, Brigham Young U., 1972. Registered profl. engr., Calif., Idaho. Mgr. Westinghouse, Idaho Falls, Idaho, 1972-83; sr. engr. So. Calif. Edison, San Clemente, Calif., 1983-97; v.p., bd. dirs. SAI Engrs., inc., Santa Clara, 1997—2001; v.p. constrn. SAI Geothermal, Inc., 1997—2001. Cons. in field, 2000-. Author: Los Olvera, Journey to America. Chmn. Dana Point (Calif.) Planning Commn., 1990; pres. Dana Point Hist. Soc., 1992-94. Served with USN, 1963-69, USNR, 1974-90, comdr. ret. Mem. ASME. Home: 24901 Danafir Dana Point CA 92629-3153

OLVERA, JOE ENRIQUE, alcohol/drug abuse services professional; b. El Paso, Tex., July 21, 1944; s. Dario Ceniceros Olvera, Francisca (Jimenez) Olvera; m. Julieta Talamantes, July 21, 1992; children: Nila Lober, Malintzin Nolan; children: Ricky, Carlos, Diane. Student, U.Tex. El Paso, 1968—71. Tv reporter KROD-TV, Channel 4, El Paso, 1971—72; freelance writer, 1972—77; dep. dir. Aliviane NO-AD, Inc., 2002—. Columnist Eastside Reporter, El Paso, 2001—02; reporter/columnist El Paso Herald-Post, El Paso, 1982—85, El Paso Times, El Paso, 1987—94, USA Today, Gannett News Svc., Roslyn, Va. Author (poetry and short stories): Voces de la gente, 1972; author: Chicanismo: A Culture Trip, 1994; author: (gang intervention/prevention) The Saga of Jefitas y Vatos Locos: The School that Saves Lives, 1998. Mayoral candidate City Govt., El Paso, 1985. E-4 USAF, 1963—67. Named Columnist of Yr., El Paso Press Club, 1989. Avocation: Avocations: creative writing, motivational speaker. Home: 12400 Rojas Sp. 49 El Paso TX 79928-5208 Office: Aliviane NO-AD Inc 7722 N Loop Rd El Paso TX 79915 Home Fax: (915) 782-4040; Office Fax: (915) 782-4040. E-mail: jolvera@aliviane.org.

OLYAN, SAUL MITCHELL, religious studies educator; b. Toronto, Ont., Can., Feb. 2, 1959; s. Sidney David and Eve (Eisenberg) O.; life ptnr. Frederik Schockaert. BA, York U., Toronto, Ont., 1981; AM, Harvard U., 1984, PhD, 1985. Asst. prof. U. Winnipeg, 1985-87, Yale U., New Haven, 1987-92, Brown U., Providence, 1992-94, assoc. prof., 1994-2000, prof., 2000—. Author: Asherah and the Cult of Yahweh in Israel, 1988, A Thousand Thousands Served Him: Exegesis and the Naming of Angels in Ancient Judaism, 1993, Rites and Rank: Hierarchy in Biblical Representations of Cult, 2000; dissertation series editor Soc. Bibl. Lit., 1999-2002; mem. editl. bd. Jour. Bibl. Lit., 1993-98, Jour. History Sexuality, 1996-2000; contbr. articles to profl. jours. Mem. Soc. Bibl. Lit. (coun. 1999—), Am. Hist. Assn. Democrat. Jewish. Avocations: coin collecting, music, travel. Office: Brown U 163 George St Providence RI 02906 E-mail: saul_olyan@brown.edu.

OLYNYK, PATRICIA, artist, educator; b. Regina, Sask., Can., Oct. 4, 1961; came to the U.S., 1985; d. Mike Louis and Lil Olynyk. BFA, Alta. Coll. Art and Design, Calgary, 1983; MFA with distinction, Calif. Coll. Arts and Crafts, 1988. Rsch., vis. scholar Kyoto (Japan) Seika U., 1990-93; project mgr. Inner City Schs. Pub. Art Performance, Oakland, Calif., 1994; internat. student mgr. Calif. Coll. Arts and Crafts, San Francisco, 1994-96; instr. Acad. Art, 1996-98; vis. asst. prof. U. Nebr., Lincoln, 1999; asst. prof. U. Mich., Ann Arbor, 1999—. Cons., instr. Osaka (Japan) U., 1990; cons. Nisshin Electric, Osaka, 1990-93; advisor, cons. Inst. for Unpopular Culture, San Francisco, 1995; part-time instr. Kyoto Seika U., 1992-93, New Coll. Calif., San Francisco, 1995-97; artist in residence Villa Montalvo, Saratoga, Calif., 1999. One-woman shows include Ufer! Gallery, Kyoto, 1992, Galleria Grafica, Tokyo, 1993, 2002, Michael Himovitz Gallery, Sacramento, 1999, exhibited in group shows at Gray Gallery, East Carolina U., Bklyn. Mus. Art, Am. Mus. Papermaking, Atlanta, Museo Del Corso, Rome, Santa Maria Della Scala, Sienna, Italy, Michelle Brouta Gallery, Paris, Triton Mus. Art, Santa Clara, Calif., 1998. Project mgr. nebr. State Maximum Security Prison, Lincoln, 1999. Fellow Kala Inst. Residency fellow, Berkeley, Calif., 1996, Helmut Stern fellow, Inst. for Humanities, U. Mich., Ann Arbor; grantee Alta. Culture grantee for visual arts, Provincial Govt. Alta., 1984, 1985, 1986, 1987, Life Scis. Inst. and Office of V.P. for Rsch., U. Mich., Ann Arbor; scholar Monbusho scholar, Ministry Edn., Kyoto, 1989—91, Tokyu scholar for rsch., Tokyu Found., Kyoto, 1991—93. Mem.: YLEM, Women's Caucus for the Arts, Mid-Am. Print Coun. (presenter), Coll. Art Assn., Internat. Kendo Fedn., Internat. Assn. Papermakers and Hand Paper Artists (presenter). Avocations: hiking, jogging, music performance, film. Office: Univ Mich Sch Art and Design 2000 Bonisteel Dr Ann Arbor MI 48109-2069 E-mail: polynyk@umich.edu.

OLYPHANT, DAVID, cultural, educational association executive; b. N.Y.C., Feb. 3, 1936; s. John Kensett Olyphant and Adele (Hammond) Emery; m. Pamela Moore, Apr. 27, 1962 (div. Aug. 1988); children: Hillary, Fanny, David K., Elgin, Flora; m. Tatyana Doughty, Oct. 22, 1988 (div.); m. Eloise S. Watt, May 26, 2000. BA, Harvard U., 1958. V.p. Citibank, N.Y.C., 1959-75; ptnr. Harold Denton Assocs., Princeton, N.J., 1975-76; owner/operator Cluaran Farm, Pittstown, 1976-87; exec. dir., sec. English Speaking Union US, N.Y.C., 1987-2000; ret. Treas.-sec. Am. Trust for Brit. Libr., 1992-99; mem. adv. bd. N.Y. Marble Cemetery, 2001—. Fellow Met. Mus. Art (life), NAD (life); mem. St. Andrew's Soc. (life), Harvard Club N.Y., Porcellan Club (Cambridge, Mass.), Pilgrims of U.S. Presbyterian.

O'MAHONY, TIMOTHY KIERAN, writer; b. Cork City, Cork, Ireland, Feb. 16, 1953; came to U.S., 1982; s. Michael John and Bridget (Horan) O'M.; m. Mary Bernadette O'Leary, June 11, 1975 (div. 1998); children: Darragh Shane, Ronan Daniel, Madelein Caoimhe Anne. BA, Nat. U. Ireland, 1973, HDE, 1974, MEd, 1981. Tchr. H.S., Cork, Ireland, 1973-82; writer, pub. Educare Press, Seattle, 1983—. Pub. Glen Abbey Books, Seattle, 1990-93. Author: (short stories) To the Woods and Waters Wild, 1992, (trilogy) Geography, Education, 1988-94, Annals of a Small Press, 2000; editor: Valiant Captains, 1992. Fellow Royal Geog. Soc.; mem. Pubs. Mktg. Assocs. (Pub. Weekly Assn.), PublishingOnline.com. (affiliate). Avocations: sailing, mountaineering, white water kayaking, music, dancing. Office: Educare Press PO Box 17222 Seattle WA 98107-0922

O'MALLEY, CARLON MARTIN, judge; b. Phila., Sept. 7, 1929; s. Carlon Martin and Lucy (Bol) O'M.; m. Mary Catherine Lyons, Aug. 17, 1957; children: Carlon Martin III, Kathleen B. O'Malley Aikman, Harry Tighe, John Todd, Cara M. O'Malley Colombo. BA, Pa. State U., 1951; LLB, Temple U., 1954. Bar: Pa. 1955, Fla. 1973, U.S. Supreme Ct. 1973. Practiced law, 1957-61; asst. U.S. atty. for Middle Dist. Pa., Dept. Justice, 1961-69, U.S. atty., 1979-82; ptnr. O'Malley & Teets, 1970-72, O'Malley, Jordan & Mullaney (and predecessor firms), 1976-79; pvt. practice Pa. and Fla., 1972-79, 82-87; judge Ct. Common Pleas of Lackawanna County (45th Judicial Dist.), 1987-97, sr. judge, 1998—. Dir. pub. safety City of Scranton, 1983-86; lectr. Lackawanna Jr. Coll., 1982-86. Editorial bd.: Temple Law Rev, 1952-53. Pres. Lackawanna County (Pa.) unit Am. Cancer Soc., 1966-67; bd. dirs. Pa. Cancer Soc., 1967-68, Lackawanna county chpt. ARC, 1967-69; mem. solicitation team, govtl. divsn. Lackawanna United Fund, 1963-68; chmn. profl. divsn. Greater Scranton (Pa.) YMCA Membership Drives; trustee Everhart Mus., Scranton, 1987—. Pilot USAF, 1955-57, Pa. N.G., 1957-59. Mem. Am. Judges Assn., Nat. Assn. Former U.S. Attys., Pa. Bar Assn., Lackawanna County Bar Assn., Fla. Bar Assn., Country Club of Scranton, Elks (pres. Pa. chpt. 1978-79, judiciary com. 1985-89, justice Grand Forum 1991, 1995-97, chief justice 1992-93. nat. pres. 1997-98), K.C., Phi Kappa (pres.), Delta Theta Phi (pres.). Democrat. Office: Judges Chambers Lackawanna County Courthouse Scranton PA 18503

O'MALLEY, EDWARD, psychiatrist, consultant; b. Hudson, N.Y., May 30, 1926; s. Thomas Patrick and Helen Mary (Cornell) O. BS, St. John's U., Bklyn., N.Y., 1949; MS, Loyola U., Chgo., 1952, PhD, 1954; MD, SUNY, Bklyn., 1958. Diplomate Am. Bd. Forensic Examiners, Am. Bd. Psychiatry and Neurology. Psychiat. cons. dept. of corrections N.Y.C., 1962-68; psychiatrist Cath. Charities, N.Y.C., 1963-68; dir. of mental health Suffolk County Govt., Hauppauge, N.Y., 1968-70; commr. of mental health Orange County, Goshen, 1970-72; dir. drug abuse services State of N.Y., Bronx, 1972-78; lic. sch. psychiatrist N.Y.C. Bd. of Edn., 1982-82; chief psychiatry services VA, Huntington, W.Va., 1982-86; med. cons. State of Calif., San Diego, 1986—, psychiat. cons. dept. of corrections, 1987—. Asst. prof. psychiatry N.J. Med. Sch., Newark, 1975—; examiner Am. Bd. of Psychiatry and Neurology, Los Angeles, 1980; assoc. prof. psychiatry U. Calif., San Diego, 1980—; prof. psychiatry Marshall U. Sch. of Medicine, Huntington, 1982-86; dir. com. on sea cadets Navy League, San Diego, 1987—; cons. HHS, Social Security Adminstrn., Office of Hearings and Appeals, 1989—. Contbr. articles to profl. jours. Bd. dirs. Suffolk Community Council, Hauppauge, 1968-70, United Fund of Long Island, Huntington, 1968-70. Capt. ret. USNR, 1960-86. Scholar N. Y. State Coll., 1946-49, SUNY Joseph Collins Med. Sch., 1955-58; Teaching and Research fellow Loyola U., 1952-54. Fellow Am. Psychiat. Assn.; mem. San Diego Psychiat. Soc., Soc. of Med. Cons. to the Armed Forces, Soc. of Mil. Surgeons of U.S.A., N.Y. Celtic Med. Soc., Union Am. Physicians and Dentists (steward 1990—), State Employed Physicians Assn. (bd. dirs. 1993—). Roman Catholic. Home: 3711 Alcott St San Diego CA 92106-1212 E-mail: omalleyedwr@aol.com.

O'MALLEY, EDWARD JOSEPH, JR. financial services administrator; b. Flushing, N.Y., Jan. 4, 1942; s. Edward Joseph and Elsie Anne (Ende) O'M.; m. Iris Theresa Hill, Aug. 10, 1975. BS, Widener Coll., 1963; MBA, St. John's U., Jamaica, N.Y., 1976. Ins. agt. Liberty Mut. Ins. Co., N.Y.C., 1966-67; supr. group home Children's Village, Bayside, N.Y., 1967-69; unit head N.Y. Narcotic Addiction Control Commn., N.Y.C., 1970-71; exec. dir. sch. dist. drug and alcohol abuse program Howard Beach, N.Y., 1971-81; spl. asst. to Kings County Dist. Atty., 1982-85, adminstrv. asst., spl. advisor, 1986-89; sr. asst. comptr. City of N.Y., 1990-91, dep. comptr., 1991-93; exec. v.p. Improved Funding Techniques, Lynbrook, N.Y., 1993—; COO Accts. Proprietary Fin. ServiceNet Inc., 2000—. Past chmn., sec. N.Y.C. Coalition Sch. Based Drug Prevention Programs; past vice chmn. Comprehensive Health Planning Agy., Queens, N.Y.; mem. Queens Cmty. Planning Bd.; past v.p. Flushing Boys Club; past chmn. bd. dirs. Regular Dem. Club, Rockaway, N.Y.; mem. N.Y. State Dem. Com.; mem. Parish Coun. St. Camillus Ch.; mem. Chancellor N.Y.C. Bd. Edn. Task Force on Drug Abuse; bd. dirs. Queens chpt. ARC, N.Y.C. Health Systems Agy., Rockaway Task Force on Arts, Far Rockaway chpt. NAACP; chmn. Anti-Redlining Com. of Rockaways; vice chmn. Com. for Casino Gambling in the Rockaways, Surfside Housing Assn. for Tenants; mem. N.Y. State Urban Coalition Task Force Drug Abuse. Mem. Emerald Assn. L.I., Beta Gamma Sigma, Kiwanis (past pres. Rockaway club). Home: 79-19 210 St Flushing NY 11364 Office: Improved Funding Techniques 211 Broadway Ste 300 Lynbrook NY 11563-3291 also: Accts Proprietary Fin ServiceNet 622 3d Ave New York NY 10016 E-mail: edo@impfti.com.

O'MALLEY, EILEEN (EILEEN ANN O'MALLEY), medical/surgical nurse; b. N.Y., Nov. 16, 1960; d. Edward Joseph and Nancy Anne (Bonner) McNulty; m. Martin O'Malley, Sept. 12, 1987. Diploma, St. Vincent's Sch. Nursing, 1981; BS, Coll. of Mt. St. Vincent, 1987. Pvt. duty nurse Foley Nurses Registry, N.Y.C.; sch. health nurse Coll. of Mt. St. Vincent, Bronx; staff and charge nurse Valley Hosp., Ridgewood, N.J.; pvt. duty nurse S&L Nurse's Registry, Paramus, United Health Care, Montclair. Office: United Health Care 50 Church St Montclair NJ 07042-2745

O'MALLEY, JAMES TERENCE, lawyer; b. Omaha, Nov. 24, 1950; s. John Austin and Mayme Bernice (Zentner) O'M.; m. Colleen L. Kizer, May 22, 1972; children: Erin C., Michael B., Patrick J. BA magna cum laude, U. Notre Dame, 1972; JD, Stanford U., 1975. Bar: Calif. 1975, Tex. 1998. Ptnr. Gray, Cary, Ames & Frye, San Diego, 1975-87, of counsel, 1987-91, ptnr., 1991—; vice chmn., exec. v.p., gen. counsel Noble Broadcast Group, Inc., 1987-91; chmn. CEO Gray Care Ware & Freidenrich LLP, 1996—. Bd. dirs. The Corky McMillin Cos. Adv. bd. Hildebrandt Internat., Inc., 2001—; bd. dirs. San Diego Regional Econ. Devel. Corp., 1997—2002. Mem. San Diego Taxpayers Assn. (pres. 1986-87), Order of Coif. Avocation: jogging, music. Office: Gray Cary Ware & Freidenrich LLP Ste 1100 4365 Executive Dr San Diego CA 92121-2133 E-mail: tomalley@graycary.com.

O'MALLEY, JOHN DANIEL, law educator, banker; b. Chgo., Dec. 18, 1926; s. William D. and Paula A. (Skaugh) O'M.; m. Caroline Tyler Taylor, July 12, 1958; children: John Daniel, Taylor John. Grad., St. Thomas Mil. Acad., 1945; BS, Loyola U., Chgo., 1950, MA, 1952, JD, 1953; grad., U.S. Army Intelligence Sch., 1962, Command & Gen. Staff Coll., 1965. Bar: Ill. 1953, Mich. 1954, U.S. Supreme Ct. 1962. Asst. prof. law Loyola U., 1953-59, asso. prof., 1959-65; formerly spl. counsel and bond claims mgr. Fed. Ins. Co.; prof. law Loyola U. Grad. Sch. Bus., 1965—, chmn. dept. law, 1968-86. Trust officer, v.p. First Nat. Bank Highland Park (Ill.), Marina City Bank, Chgo., Hyde Park Bank & Trust Co., 1970-75; exec. v.p. Harris Bank Winnetka, Ill., 1975-95. Author: Subrogation Against Banks on Forged Checks, 1967, Common Check Frauds and the Uniform Commercial Code, 1969; Contbr. articles to profl. jours. and law revs. Served to maj. AUS, 1945-47, 61-62. Decorated knight grand cross Papal Order of Holy Sepulchre, knight comdr. with star Constantinian Order of St. George (Italy), knight Order of St. Maurice and St. Lazarus (Italy), knight of Malta. Mem. ABA, Chgo., Ill., Mich. bar assns., Chgo. Crime Commn., French Nat. Hon. Soc., Am., Chgo. bus. law assns., Mil. Govt. Assn. Home: 1630 Sheridan Rd 6-L Wilmette IL 60091-1830 Office: Loyola U 820 N Michigan Ave Ste 1316 Chicago IL 60611-2147

O'MALLEY, JOHN PATRICK, retired dean; b. Hoosick Falls, N.Y., Nov. 27, 1928; s. Thomas Joseph and Mary Alice (Mulvihill) O.'M.; m. Margaret Parlin, June 24, 1989. BA, Villanova U., 1950; MA, PhD, Cath. U., 1969. Tchr. Archbishop Carroll High Sch., Washington, 1954-68, prin., 1987-89; asst. prof. Cath. U., 1968-69, Merrimack Coll., North Andover, Mass., 1969-74, dean humanities, 1976-78; chair edn. dept. Emmanuel Coll., Boston, 1974-76; dean coll. arts and scis. Villanova (Pa.) U., 1978-84; provost St. Thomas U., Miami, Fla., 1985-86; assoc. prof. Widener U., Chester, Pa., 1990-99, ret., 1999. Editor: Non-Fiction, Books I and II, 1968. Home: PO Box 586 Norfolk CT 06058-0586 E-mail: momalley@snet.net.

O'MALLEY, MARGARET PARLIN, marketing administrator; b. Cin., Jan. 20, 1940; d. John Andrew and Agnes Sophia (Tietig) Parlin; m. Daniel L. Hutchinson, Nov. 6, 1965 (div. 1986); children: Daniel L., Jr., Agnes Alexina; m. John Patrick O'Malley, June 24, 1989. BA, Bryn Mawr Coll., 1961, postgrad., 1963-65; MBA, Villanova U., 1989. Tchr. The Shipley Sch., Bryn Mawr, Pa., 1961-63; adminstrv. asst. Bryn Mawr Coll., 1963-67, Villanova (Pa.) U., 1989—90; v.p. Winsor Assocs., 1990-91; mgr. mktg. and support svcs. Normandeau Assocs., Inc., Norfolk, Conn., 1992—. Mem. women's commn. Univ. Mus., U. Pa., Phila., 1969—76; trustee The Old Eagle Sch., Wayne, 1997—99; v.p. Phoenixville Area C. of C., 1998—99, commerce bd., 1997—99; bd. trustees The Norfolk Libr., 2001—; bd. dirs. Normandeau Assocs., 2001—02, Phila. Child Guidance Clinic, 1970—76, The Agnes Irwin Sch., Rosemont, 1982—85, Strings for Schs., Villanova, 1982—89, The West Hill Sch., Rosemont, 1970—87, The Schuylkill River Greenway, Assn., 1993—96. Mem. The Weeders Club, Norfolk Libr. Assocs. Republican. Episcopalian. Office: Normandeau Assocs Inc PO Box 586 Norfolk CT 06058-0586

O'MALLEY, MARTIN JOSEPH, mayor, former councilman, lawyer; m. Katie Curran; children: Grace, Tara. BA, Cath. U., 1985; postgrad, U. Md. Sch of Law, 1988. Asst. state's atty., Balt., 1988-90; staff asst. U.S. Congress; city councilman Balt.; pvt. practice law; mayor Balt., 1999—. Former state field dir. Senator Barbara Mikulski Senate Campaign; former state coord. Senator Bob Kerrey Dem. Primary. chmn. Com. of Taxation and Finance, chmn. of Legislative Investment. Recipient Svc. to Humanity award Md. Jaycees, 1994. Mem. Friendly Sons of St. Patricks. Democrat. Office: City Hall Rm 250 100 Holliday St Baltimore MD 21202-3417 E-mail: mayor@baltimorecity.gov.*

O'MALLEY, MARY KAY, elementary education educator; b. East Cleveland, Ohio, Feb. 12, 1959; d. Patrick Joseph and Ruth Mary (Friedmann) O'M. BA, Notre Dame Coll., 1980; MEd, John Carroll U., 1988. Cert. elem. tchr., Ohio. Asst. prin., tchr. 4th grade St. Francis of Assisi Sch., Gates Mills, Ohio, 1980—. Instr. dept. edn. John Carroll U., University Heights, Ohio, 1990—; adj. instr. dept. edn. Notre Dame Coll., South Euclid, Ohio, 1990—; presenter in field. Recipient Cleve. Diocese award, 1992, Ea. Region Diocese award, 1988, Diocese Excellence in Edn. award, 2000. Mem. ASCD, Internat. Reading Assn., Nat. Cath. Edn. Assn. Avocations: gardening, photography, bicycling, walking. Office: St Francis of Assisi Sch 6850 Mayfield Rd Gates Mills OH 44040-9635

O'MALLEY, PATRICIA, critical care nurse; b. Boston, May 13, 1955; d. Peter and Catherine (Dwyer) O'M. BSN, Coll. Mt. St. Joseph, Cin., 1977; MS, Ohio State U., 1984, PhD, 2000. Cert. critical care nurse. Clin. nurse specialist cardiology svcs. Miami Valley Hosp., Dayton, Ohio, nurse educator, cons. Adj. faculty Wright State U., Dayton. Contbr. articles to profl. jours., textbooks. Recipient honors Dayton Area Heart Assn., Ohio Ho. of Reps., 1994, Ohio Dept. Health, 1996. Mem. AACN, Soc. Critical Care Medicine, Midwest Nursing Rsch. Soc., Sigma Theta Tau. Office: Miami Valley Hosp 1 Wyoming St Dayton OH 45409-2722 E-mail: paomalley@interaxs.net.

O'MALLEY, ROBERT EDMUND, JR. mathematics educator; b. Rochester, N.H., May 23, 1939; s. Robert E. and Jeanette A. (Dubois) O'M.; m. Candace G. Hinz, Aug. 31, 1968; children: Patrick, Timothy, Daniel. BS in Elec. Engring., U. N.H., 1960, MS, 1961; PhD, Stanford U., 1966. Mathematician Bell Labs., Gen. Electric Research Co., RCA, summers 1961-63; asst. prof. U. N.C., Chapel Hill, 1965-66; vis. mem. Courant Inst., NYU, 1966-67; research mem. Math. Research Ctr., Madison, Wis., 1967-68; asst. prof., assoc. prof. NYU, N.Y.C., 1968-73; prof. math. U. Ariz., Tucson, 1973-81, chmn. applied math. program, 1976-81; prof. math. Rensselaer Poly. Inst., Troy, N.Y., 1981-90, chmn. dept. math. scis., 1981-84, Ford Found. prof., 1989-90; prof., chair applied math. U. Wash., Seattle, 1990-93, prof., 1993—. Sr. vis. fellow U. Edinburgh, (Scotland), 1971-72; guest prof. Tech. U. Vienna, 1987-88; vis. Univ. Lyon 1 and Univ. of Cambridge, 1994-95. Author: Introduction to Singular Perturbations, 1974; editor: Asymptotic Methods and Singular Perturbations, 1976, Singular Perturbation Methods for Ordinary Differential Equations, 1991, Thinking About Ordinary Differential Equations, 1997; editor ICIAM 91 procs.; co-editor Multiscale Phenomena, 1999; contbr. numerous articles to profl. jours. Mem. Soc. for Indsl. and Applied Math. (pres. 1991-92), Am. Math. Soc. Roman Catholic. Home: 3415 W Laurelhurst Dr NE Seattle WA 98105-5345 Office: U Wash Dept Applied Math Box 352420 Seattle WA 98195-2420 E-mail: omalley@amath.washington.edu.

O'MALLEY, SUSAN MARIE, lawyer; b. Evergreen Park, Ill., Apr. 11, 1968; d. Arthur Stephen and Mary Catherine O'Malley. BS cum laude, U. N.C., Charlotte, 1990; JD, U. N.C., 1994. Bar: N.C. 1994, D.C. 1996, U.S. Dist. Ct. (ea. dist.) N.C. 1998. Atty. Keel Law Offices, Tarboro, NC, 1995-98; ptnr. Keel, Kessler & O'Malley, LLP, 1998-2000, Keel O'Malley LLP, Tarboro, 2001—. Mem.: ATLA (social security sect. chair-elect 2000—01, chair 2001—02), N.C. Acad. Trial Lawyers (disability adv. sect. edn. chair 1998—99, vice-chair 2000—02, chair 2002—), Jaycees (v.p. 1998—99). Office: PO Box 1158 Tarboro NC 27886-1158

O'MALLEY, THOMAS ANTHONY, gastroenterologist, internist; b. St. Helens, Lancashire, Eng., Jan. 21, 1932; s. Michael and Margaret (Melia) O'M.; m. Margaret Mary O'Kane, Apr. 7, 1958 (dec. Apr. 1985); m. Marianne Rapier, Jan. 23, 1988; children: Anne, Patricia, Katherine, Jane, Margaret. MBChB, U. Liverpool, Eng., 1956; Lic. Medicine, U. State N.Y., 1964. Diplomate Am. Bd. Internal Medicine, State Bd. Med. Examiners Fla. House physician Royal Infirmary, Liverpool, 1956-57; house surgeon Royal Liverpool Children's Hosp., 1957; resident in medicine C.S. Wilson Meml. Hosp., Johnson City, N.Y., 1957-58; fellow internal medicine Lahey Clinic, Boston, 1958-59; USPHS trainee in gastroenterology U. Rochester (N.Y.), Strong Meml. Hosp., 1959-60; chief resident medicine/Segal Watson fellow gastroenterology Genesee Hosp., Rochester, 1960-61; gastroenterologist Cancer Clinic, Regina, Sask., Can., 1963; asst. dir. med. edn. Genesee Hosp., U. Rochester, 1967-72; clin. assoc. prof. medicine U. South Fla., Tampa, 1973—. Chief medicine Sarasota (Fla.) Meml. Hosp., 1973, Doctors Hosp., Sarasota, 1985. With RAF, 1961-62. Recipient Physician of Yr. award Doctors Hosp. Sarasota, 1985; listed among Best Dr.'s of Am., 1998. Fellow ACP, Am. Coll. Gastroenterology, Chevalier du Tastevin (comdr. 1985—), Cavalieri del Vini Nobili (amb. 1989—, pres. 1997). Office: O'Malley & Hall MD PA 2650 Bahia Vista St Sarasota FL 34239-2635

O'MALLEY, THOMAS D. petroleum industry executive; b. N.Y.C., 1941; Grad., Manhattan Coll., 1963. Vice chmn., dir. Salomon, Inc. (formerly Phibro-Salomon, Inc.), N.Y.C.; former chmn., chief exec. officer, pres. Phibro Energy Inc., Greenwich, Conn.; chmn. Argus Investments (formerly Argus Resources), Stamford, from 1987; now chmn., CEO Tosco Corp., 1989—. Office: Tosco Corp Hdqrs 72 Cummings Point Rd Ste 1 Stamford CT 06902-7922*

O'MALLEY, TIMOTHY PATRICK, otolaryngologist; b. Washington, Oct. 19, 1958; MD, Georgetown U., Washington, 1985. Diplomate Am. Bd. Otolaryngology. Intern Naval Hosp., San Diego, 1985-86, resident otolaryngology Oakland, 1989-93, dept. head otolaryngology Rota, Spain, 1996-99, head dept. otolaryngology Pensacola, Fla., 2000—02. Master: Am. Acad. Otolaryngology, Head and Neck Surgery; fellow: Am. Coll. Surgeons. Office: Naval Med Ctr Charlotte Health Care Ctr Bldg 2 Dept Oto-Head and Neck Surgery 27 Effingham St Portsmouth VA 23708 E-mail: TPOMalley@pcola.med.navy.mil.

OMAN, HENRY, retired electrical engineer, engineering executive; b. Portland, Oreg., Aug. 29, 1918; s. Paul L. and Mary (Levonen) O.; m. Winifred Eleanor Potter, June 17, 1944 (dec. Nov. 1950); m. Earlene Mary Boot, Sept. 11, 1954; children: Mary Janet, Eleanor Eva, Eric Paul. BSEE, Oreg. State U., 1940, MSEE, 1951. Registered profl. engr., Wash. Application engr. Allis Chalmers Mfg. Co., Milw., 1940-48; rsch. engr. Boeing Co., Seattle, 1948-63, engring. mgr., 1963-91. Author: Energy Systems Engineering Handbook, 1986; contbr. numerous articles to profl. jours. Mem. team that restarted amateur radio communication to the world from the People's Republic of China, 1981. Recipient prize paper award Am. Inst. Elec. Engrs., 1964. Fellow IEEE (founder power electronics systems confs., 1970—, v.p. Aerospace and Electronics Systems Soc. 1984-88, Harry Mimno award 1989, Third Millenium medal 2000, editor-in-chief IEEE Aerospace and Electronic Sys. mag. 1995-99/rated in top two by Inst. for Scientific Info.), AIAA (assoc.); mem. AAAS (bd. dir. Pacific divsn. 1992—). Republican. Methodist. Achievements include development of concepts for solar power satellite which generates power in geo-synchronous orbit 24 hours per day and beams it to the Earth surface with a microwave beam; research in simple battery-powered electric bicycles for low-cost, pollution-free transportation in developing nations. Home: 19221 Normandy Park Dr SW Seattle WA 98166-4129

OMAN, RALPH, lawyer; b. Huntington, N.Y., July 1, 1940; s. Henry Ferdinand and Annamarie (Retelsdorf) O.; m. Anne K. Henehan, Oct. 21, 1967; children: Tabitha Russell, Caroline Adams, Charlotte Ericsson. Diploma, Sorbonne U., Paris, 1961; BA, Hamilton Coll., 1962; LLD, Georgetown U., 1973. Bar: D.C. 1973, U.S. Dist. Ct. Md. 1973, U.S. Ct. Appeals (4th cir.) 1974, U.S. Supreme Ct. 1977. Law clk. to U.S. Dist. Ct. judge U.S. Dist. Ct. Md., Balt., 1973-74; trial atty U.S. Dept. Justice, Washington, 1974-75; chief minority counsel patents, trademarks and copyrights subcom. U.S. Senate, 1975-77; legis. dir. Senator Charles Mathias, 1977-78; minority counsel judiciary com. U.S. Senate, 1978-81, chief counsel, staff dir. criminal law subcom., 1981-82, chief counsel patents, copyrights and trademarks subcom., 1982-85; register of copyrights U.S. Copyright Office, 1985-94; counsel Dechert Price and Rhoads, 1996—. Adj. prof. copyright law George Washington U.; speaker in field. Contbr. numerous articles to profl. jours. Served to lt. USN, 1965-70, Vietnam. Mem. ABA (chair authors com.), Fed. Bar Assn. (past pres. Capitol Hill chpt.). Episcopalian. Home: 1110 E Capitol St NE Washington DC 20002-6225 Office: Dechert Price and Rhoads 1775 Eye St NW Ste 1100 Washington DC 20006-2424 E-mail: ralph.oman@dechert.com.

OMAN, RICHARD HEER, lawyer; b. Columbus, Ohio, Jan. 4, 1926; s. B. R. Oman and Marguerite H. (Oman) Andrews; m. Jane Ellen Wert, Oct. 5, 1963; children: Sarah M., David W. BA, Ohio State U., 1948, JD, 1951. Bar: Ohio 1951. Atty. Ohio Nat. Bank, Columbus, 1951-55; ptnr. Isaac, Postlewaite, O'Brien & Oman, 1955-71; dir. Columbus Found., 1955-77, counsel, 1955—; ptnr. Porter, Wright, Morris and Arthur (and predecessor firm), Columbus, 1972-89; of counsel Vorys, Sater, Seymour and Pease, 1990, ptnr., 1991-96, of counsel, 1997—. Mem. Columbus Airport Commn., 1960-64; trustee Reinberger Found., Cleve., 1980—, Columbus Acad., 1981-87, Grant Hosp., 1978-86, Harding Hosp., 1978-86; sr. warden Trinity Epsic. Ch., 1985-88. Fellow Ohio State Bar Found.; mem. ABA, Am. Coll. Trust and Estate Counsel, Ohio State Bar Assn. (past mem. bd. govs. probate and trust law sect.), Columbus Bar Assn., Columbus Club, Rocky Fork Hunt and Country Club, Nantucket (Mass.) Yacht Club, Kit Kat Club. Republican. Episcopalian. Office: Vorys Sater Seymour & Pease PO Box 1008 52 E Gay St Columbus OH 43215-3161 Fax: 614.714.4731. E-mail: rhoman@ussp.com.

O'MARA, JOHN ALOYSIUS, retired bishop; b. Buffalo, Nov. 17, 1924; s. John Aloysius and Anna Theresa (Schenck) O'M. Student, St. Augustine's Sem., Toronto, Ont., Can., 1944-51; J.C.L., St. Thomas U., Rome, 1953. Ordained priest Roman Catholic Ch., 1951; mem. chancery Archdiocese of Toronto, 1953-69; pres., rector St. Augustine's Sem., Toronto, 1969-75; pastor St. Lawrence Parish, Scarboro, Ont., 1975-76; bishop Diocese of Thunder Bay, 1976-94, Diocese of St. Catharines, 1994—2002. Pres. Ont. Conf. Cath. Bishops, 1986-92. Bd. dirs. Ont. Hosp. Assn., 1961-65; mem. Ont. Hosp. Services Commn., 1964-69. Named hon. prelate of Papal Household with title monsignor, 1954, hon. fellow U. St. Michael's Coll., Toronto, 1997. Mem. Cath. Ch. Ext. Soc. (bd. dirs. 1992-96), Cath. Health Assn. Ont. (bd. dirs. 1982-86, 88-92, 96—). Home: Holy Rosary Rectory 21 Queen St S Tjprp;d PM Canada L2V 3M7 E-mail: chancery@vaxxine.com.

O'MARA, ROBERT EDMUND GEORGE, radiologist, educator; b. Flushing, N.Y., Dec. 8, 1933; s. George Harold and Leonora (Potter) O'M.; m. Brenda Mae Millard, Feb. 15, 1964; children— Robert, Susan, Bridget. BS, U. Rochester, 1955; MD, Albany Coll. Medicine, 1959. Diplomate: Am. Bd. Radiology, Am. Bd. Nuclear Medicine (sec. 1982— , chmn. 1983-84). Resident in radiology St. Vincent's Hosp., N.Y.C., 1963-66; fellow in nuclear medicine Upstate Med. Center SUNY, Syracuse, 1966-67, instr. radiology, 1967-68, asst. prof. radiology, 1968-71; asso. prof. radiology, dir. nuclear medicine U. Ariz., Tucson, 1971-74, prof., dir. nuclear medicine, 1974-75; prof. radiology, chief div. nuclear medicine U. Rochester Sch. Medicine and Dentistry, 1975—; acting chmn. dept. radiology U. of Rochester, 1987-88, chmn. dept. radiology, 1988-93; med. dir. nuclear medicine tech. program Rochester Inst. Tech., 1976-92. Contbr. articles to med. jours. Pres. Clover Hills Assn., Rochester, N.Y., 1978-79; pres. Fruchtendler Parent Tchr. Assn., Tucson, 1974-75. Served with M.C. USAF, 1960-62. Fellow Am. Coll. Radiology (councillor 1983-89), Am. Coll. Nuclear Physicians (pres. 1980, trustee 1972-80, Ralph Robinson fellow 1996-97), N.Y. State Radiol. Soc. (pres. 1989-90); mem. Soc. Nuclear Medicine (trustee 1978-82, v.p. 1985-86, Gold medal for sci. exhibit 1977), Radiol. Soc. N.Am., Assn. Univ. Radiologists. E-mail: robert_o'mara@urmc.rochester.edu. Office: 601 Elmwood Ave Rochester NY 14642-0001

O'MARA, THOMAS PATRICK, manufacturing company executive; b. St. Catharine's, Ont., Can., Jan. 17, 1937; s. Joseph Thomas and Rosanna Patricia (Riordan) O'M.; m. Nancy Irene Rosevear, Aug. 10, 1968; children: Patricia Catharine, Tracy Irene, Sara Megan. BS, Allegheny Coll., 1958; MS, Carnegie Inst. Tech., 1960. Mktg. analyst U.S. Steel Corp., Pitts., 1960-65; dir. info. systems AMPCO Pitts. (formerly Screw & Bolt Corp.), 1965-68; v.p., gen. mgr. Toy div. Samsonite Corp., Denver, 1968-73; regional mgr. Mountain Zone, Hertz Corp., 1973-75; asst. to chmn. Allen Group, Melville, N.Y., 1975-76; group exec. v.p. fin. and adminstrn. Bell & Howell Co., Chgo., 1976-77, corp. controller, 1977-78, corp. v.p., 1978-85, pres. visual communications, 1978-85; pres., chief operating officer, dir. Bridge Product Inc., Northbrook, Ill., 1985-87; chmn., chief exec. officer Micro Metl Corp., Indpls., 1987-91; chmn. Omara Ptnrs., 1992—. Bd. dirs. Loyola U. Press; trustee Barat Coll., 1994—. Mem. Lake Forest H.S. Bd., 1989-96, pres. 1993-96. With USAR, 1961-66. Mem. Econs. Club Chgo., Newcomen Soc. U.S., Sigma Alpha Epsilon, Knollwood Club. Home: 1350 Inverleith Rd Lake Forest IL 60045-1540

O'MEARA, JOHN CORBETT, federal judge; b. Hillsdale, Mich., Nov. 4, 1933; s. John Richard and Karolyn Louise (Corbett) O'M.; m. Penelope Reingier Appel, June 9, 1962 (div. Feb. 1975); children: Meghan Appel, John Richard, Corbett Edge, Patrick Fitzpatrick, Tighe Roberts; m. Julia Donovan Darlow, Sept. 20, 1975; 1 child, Gillian Darlow. AB, U. Notre Dame, 1955; LLB, Harvard U., 1962. Bar: Mich. 1962. Assoc. Dickinson, Wright, Moon, Van Dusen & Freeman, Detroit, 1962-70; mem. faculty U. Detroit, 1965-70; ptnr. Dickinson, Wright, Moon, Van Dusen & Freeman, Detroit, 1970-94, head of labor group, 1985-94; judge U.S. Dist. Ct., 1994—. Bd. dirs. Mich. Opera Theatre, Detroit. Contr. articles to profl. jours. Fin. chmn. Dem. Party Mich., 1968-70; chmn. U.S. Cts. Com. State Bar Mich., 1984-94. Lt. USN, 1955-59. Fellow Am. Coll. Trial Lawyers, Am. Bar Found.; mem. ABA, U.S. Supreme Court Bar, Am. Judicature Soc., Mich. State Bar Assn., 6th Cir. Court Appeals Bar (life mem., 6th Cir. Jud. Conf. 1986). E-mail: john_corbett_o'meara@ck6.uscourts.gov. Office: US Dist Ct 231 W Lafayette Blvd Detroit MI 48226-2700

O'MEARA, JOHN FRANCIS, lawyer; b. Chgo., Apr. 14, 1936; s. John J. and Mary (Joyce) O'M.; children: Marcia A. Hiehle, John A., Timothy D. BS, Loyola U., 1959; JD, Northwestern U., 1960. Bar: Ill. 1961, U.S. Dist. Ct. (no. dist.) Ill. 1964, U.S. Ct. Appeals (7th cir.) 1992. Assoc., ptnr. Lord, Bissell & Brook, Chgo., 1961-74; atty. pvt. practice, Chgo. and Park Ridge, Ill, 1975—. Instr. John Marshall Sch. Law, Chgo., 1966-71. Author: Tort Liability of Illinois Land Occupiers, 1968. Bd. dirs. St. Mary of Angels, 1987—; founder, officer Ind. Precinct Orgn., Chgo., 1969-71. With U.S. Army Res., 1960-66. Mem. Holy Name Soc. Roman Catholic. Office: 1737 N Wolcott Ave Chicago IL 60622-1350

O'MEARA, NOEL P. priest, religious organization administrator; b. Gort, Galway, Ireland, Dec. 22, 1937; arrived in U.S., 1983; s. Thomas Joseph O'Meara and Moyna Theresa Pathe. BA, Nat. U. Ireland, Dublin, 1960, Higher Diploma, 1966; MEd, Trinity Coll., Dublin, 1973; PhD, Fordham U., 1987. Sr. dean Templeogue H.S., Dublin, 1966—73; provincial adminstr. Irish Province, Holy Spirit Order, 1973—77; missionary priest Congreção do Espirito Santo, São Paulo, Brazil, 1977—83; fund raiser Brazil missions Brazil Spiritan Missions, N.Y.C., 1983—88; dir. Mission Agy. Svcs., 1985; coord. Belem sector Archdiocese São Paulo, 1988—90; gen. sec. Congregation of Holy Spirit, Rome, 1990—93, provincial bursar Irish Province, Holy Spirit Order, 1994—2000, gen. bursar-adjoint, 2001—. Contbr. Parish priest Cath. Ch., São Paulo, 1978—90; pres. Spiritan Found., Washington, 2001—; gen. bursar adjoint Congregation of Holy Spirit, 2001—; bd. dirs. Des Places Ednl. Trust, Dublin, 1997—2000; chmn. bd. dirs. Aidlink Ngo, 1996—2000. Mem.: Fraternity of Sant. Egidio. Roman Catholic. Avocations: music, travel to underdeveloped countries, golf. Office: Spiritan Found 11411 Amherst Ave Silver Spring MD 20902

O'MEARA, ONORATO TIMOTHY, academic administrator, mathematician; b. Cape Town, Republic of South Africa, Jan. 29, 1928; arrived in U.S., 1957; s. Daniel and Fiorina (Allorto) O'M.; m. Jean T. Fadden, Sept. 12, 1953; children: Maria, Timothy, Jean, Kathleen, Eileen. B.Sc., U. Cape Town, 1947, M.Sc., 1948; PhD, Princeton U., 1953; LLD (hon.), U. Notre Dame, 1987. Asst. lectr. U. Natal, Republic South Africa, 1949; lectr. U. Otago, New Zealand, 1954-56; mem. Inst. for Advanced Study, Princeton, N.J., 1957-58, 62; asst. prof. Princeton U., 1958-62; prof. math. U. Notre Dame, Ind., 1962-76, chmn. dept., 1965-66, 68-72, Kenna prof. math., 1976-98, provost, 1978-96, provost emeritus, 1996—, Kenna prof. emeritus, 1998—. Vis. prof. Calif. Inst. Tech., 1968; Gauss prof. Göttingen Acad. Sci., 1978; mem. adv. panel math. scis. NSF, 1974-77, cons., 1960—. Author: Introduction to Quadratic Forms, 1963, 71, 73, 2000, Lectures on Linear Groups, 1974, 2d edit., 1977, 3d edit., 1988, Russian translation, 1976, Symplectic Groups, 1978, 82, Russian translation, 1979, The Classical Groups and K-Theory (with A.J. Hahn), 1989; contbr. articles on arithmetic theory of quadratic forms and isomorphism theory of linear groups to Am. and European profl. jours. Mem. Cath. Commn. Intellectual and Cultural Affairs, 1962—, Commn. on Cath. Scholarship, 1997-99; life trustee U. of Notre Dame, 1996—. Recipient Marianist award U. Dayton, 1988; Alfred P. Sloan fellow, 1960-63. Mem. Am. Math. Soc., Am. Acad. Arts and Sci., Collegium (bd. dirs. 1992-96). Roman Catholic. Home: 1227 E Irvington Ave South Bend IN 46614-1417 Office: U Notre Dame Office of Provost Emeritus Notre Dame IN 46556

O'MEARA, SARA, nonprofit organization executive; b. Knoxville, Tenn., Sept. 09; m. Robert O'Meara (dec.); children: John Hopkins, Charles Hopkins (dec.); m. Robert Sigholtz, Nov. 1986; stepchildren: Taryn, Whitney. Attended, Briarcliff Jr. Coll.; BA, The Sorbonne, Paris; D (hon.), Endicott Coll. Co-founder, chmn. bd., CEO CHILDHELP USA (formerly Children's Village USA), Scottsdale, Ariz., 1960—. Bd. dirs. Nat. Soc. for Prevention of Child Abuse and Neglect of Gt. Britain, Children to Children, Inc.; hon. com. mem. Learning Disabilities Found., Inc.; mem. Mayor's adv. bd., Defense for Children Internat., Nat. Soc. Prevention Cruelty to Children, World Affairs Coun.; adv. bd. mem. Ednl. Film Co.; bd. dirs. Internat. Alliance on Child Abuse and Neglect; sustaining mem. Spastic Children's League, past pres.; mem., past recording sec. Assistance League So. Calif. Recipient Cross of Merit, Knightly Order of St. Brigitte, 1967, Victor M. Carter Diamond award Japan-Am. Soc., 1970, Dame Cross of Merit of Order of St. John of Denmark, 1980, Official Seal of 34th Gov. Calif., 1981, Woman of Achievement award Career Guild, 1982, Women Making History award Nat. Fedn. Bus. Profl. Women's Clubs, 1983, Disting. Am. award for svc., 1984, Humanitarian award Nat. Frat. Eagles, 1984, Nat. Recognition award outstanding leadership Am. Heritage Found., 1986, Notable Am. award svc. to Calif., 1986, Dove of Peace award Pacific Southwest and Ctrl. Pacific Regions B'nai B'rith, 1987, Paul Harris fellow award Rotary Found., 1989, Internat. Collaboration to Prevention Child Abuse award HRH Queen of Eng., 1989, Living Legacy award Women's Internat. Ctr., 1989, Love and Help the Children award, 1990, Presdl. award, 1990, Kiwanis World Svc. medal, 1991, Family Circle award Family Circle Mag., 1992, Outstanding Woman for Tenn. award Nat. Mus. Women in Arts, 1993, Nat. Caring award Nat. Caring Inst., 1993, Hubert Humphrey award Touchdown Club Washington, 1993, numerous others. Mem. SAG, AFTRA, Victory Awards (exec. com.), Am. Biographical Inst. (nat. bd. advisors), Alpha Delta Kappa (hon.). Office: Childhelp USA 15757 N 78th St Scottsdale AZ 85260-1629

O'MEARA, THOMAS FRANKLIN, priest, educator; b. Des Moines, May 15, 1935; s. Joseph Matthew and Frances Claire (Rock) O'M. MA, Aquinas Inst, Dubuque, Iowa, 1963; PhD, U. Munich, Germany, 1967. Ordained priest Roman Cath. Ch., 1962. Assoc. prof. Aquinas Inst. of Theology, Dubuque, Iowa, 1967-79; prof. U. Notre Dame, South Bend, Ind., 1981-84, William K. Warren prof. of theology, 1985—. Author 14 books, including: Romantic Idealism and Roman Catholicism, 1983, Theology of Ministry, 1985, revised edit., 1999, Church and Culture, 1991, Thomas Aquinas: Theologian, 1997, Erich Przywara, S.J., His Theology and His World, 2002. Mem. Catholic Theol. Soc. Am. (pres. 1980). Office: U Notre Dame Dept Of Theology Notre Dame IN 46556 E-mail: o'meara.1@nd.edu.

O'MEARA, VICKI A. lawyer; b. Mpls., May 13, 1957; d. James Michael and Joan Kathleen (Shepers) O'M.; children: Joseph O'Meara Masterman, Nicolas James Reisinger O'Meara. BA in Polit. Sci., Cornell U., 1979; JD, Northwestern U., Chgo., 1982; MA in Environment & Natural Resource, George Washington U., Washington, 1987. Bar: Minn. 1982, D.C. 1983, Ill. 1989. Asst. to Army gen. counsel U.S. Army-Pentagon, Washington, 1982-86; spl. asst. to White House Counsel The White House Fellows Program, 1986-87; dep. exec. sec., domestic policy counsel, cabinet affairs The White House, 1987; dep. gen. counsel litigation and regional ops. U.S. EPA, 1987; ptnr. Jones, Day, Reavis & Pogue, Chgo., 1988-92, 93—; asst. atty. gen. U.S. Dept. Justice, 1992; exec. vice-pres., gen. counsel Ryder Systems Inc., Miami, FL. Hon. mem. faculty U.S. Army Logistics Mgmt. Sch., Ft. Lee, Va., 1982-85; adj. prof. The Union Inst., Cin., 1989-92. Author rev. Nat. Wetlands Newsletter, 1990; contbr. articles to profl. jours. Bd. dirs. Northwestern U. Alumni Assn., Chgo., 1988-90; mem. com. Chgo. Coun. Fgn. Rels. Mem. Chgo. Econ. Club Chgo. (com. fgn. affairs). Office: Ryder Stystem Inc 3600 NW 82nd Ave Miami FL 33166-6623

O'MEARA-WYMAN, KATHLEEN CECILE, marketing, advertising, public relations executive; b. Portland, OR, Feb. 18, 1953; d. Edward Francis and Frances M. O.; m. Thomas Albert Wyman, August 18, 1979; children: Patrick Michael. BA in Eng., Gonzaga Univ., Spokane, WA, 1975. News dir. Sta. KVNI, Coeur D'Alene, Idaho, 1975-77; stringer AP, Spokane, Wash., 1975-77; mktg. adminstr. Providence Health Sys., Yakima, 1977-98; owner O'Meara-Wyman & Assocs. Mktg. and Strategic Comm., 1999—. Bd. dirs. Healthy Mothers, Healthy Babies Coalition Wash., Seattle, 1993—; mem. nat. bd. Camp Fire Boys and Girls , Kansas City, Mo., 1993—95; pres. Healthy Mothers, 2000—. Author, calendar, 1992, co-chair, editor, Fund-raising Cookbook, Northwest Fresh, 1990. Campaign cabinet, United Way, Yakima County, WA, 1999-00, Allied Arts Coun., Allied Arts Coun. Yakima Valley, Wash., 1999-00; mem. steering com. Wash. Millennium Project, 1999—. Mem. Jr. League (corr. sec. 1986—), Rotary. Office: O'Meara-Wyman & Assocs Mktg & Strategic Comm 5210 Glacier Way Yakima WA 98908-2350 Fax: 509-966-0160. E-mail: kathyomw@aol.com.

OMELIANOWICH, JANET ANNE, home health caregiver; b. Grand Rapids, Mich., Apr. 9, 1940; d. Maurice Jonathon and Irene Esther (Machan) Ryan; m. James M. Kelly, Sept. 2, 1958 (div. 1965); m. James Q. Williams, July 1967 (div. 1971); m. James Omelianowich, May 26, 1978 (div. 1982); children: Patricia, Andrew, Elizabeth, Carol. Grad. high sch. Bookkeeper Tribbetts, Sturgis, Mich., 1959-63, Kalamazoo (Mich.) Ice 7 Fuel, 1964-65; staff acct. Alexander Grant & Co., Inc. CPAs, Kalamazoo, 1965-73, Goodman, Demink & Cerutti, CPAs, Kalamazoo, 1973-78; pvt. practice as acct. Gobles, 1978-86; religious sister Sisters of Charity, Boulder City, Nev., 1986-94; home health caregiver Eldercare, 1994—2000; acct. RMI HOA Divsn., 2001—. Caregiver, home health aide Avon & Bristol (England) Health Dist., 1987. Vol. caregiver Lend-A-Hand, Boulder City, 1990-96; leader, founder cadet and sr. troops Girl Scouts U.S.A., Gobles, 1980-86; bd. dirs., pres. Kairos Prison Ministries, Las Vegas, 1986—; treas. St. Christopher's Episc. Ch., Boulder, City, 1993, 94, lic. lay preacher, 1991—, lic. lay eucharistic min., 1982—, lic. lay reader, 1986—, sr. warden, 1995, 96, lay dep., 1994, alt. dep., 1991, 97, postulant for holy orders, 2002; treas. St. Mark's Episc. Ch., Paw Paw, Mich., 1983-86; bd. dirs. Cmty. Health Bd., Boulder City, 1988, 89. Mem. Episc. Diocese Nev. Democrat. Avocations: reading, sewing, drawing, writing. Home: 1305 Marwood St Boulder City NV 89005-2029 Office: Eldercare 1305 Marwood Boulder City NV 89005-2029

OMENN, GILBERT STANLEY, academic administrator, physician; b. Chester, Pa., Aug. 30, 1941; s. Leonard and Leah (Miller) O.; m. Martha Darling; children: Rachel Andrea, Jason Montgomery, David Matthew. AB, Princeton U., 1961; MD, Harvard U., 1965; PhD in Genetics, U. Wash., 1972. Intern Mass. Gen. Hosp., Boston, 1965-66, asst. resident in medicine, 1966-67; rsch. assoc. NIH, Bethesda, Md., 1967-69; fellow U. Wash., 1969-71, from asst. prof. medicine to assoc. prof., 1971-79, investigator Howard Hughes Med. Inst., 1976-77, prof. medicine, 1979-97, prof. environ. health, 1981—, chmn. dept., 1981-83; dean U. Wash. Sch. Pub. Health and Cmty. Medicine, 1982-97; exec. v.p. med. affairs, CEO health sys. U. Mich. Health Sys., Ann Arbor, 1997—2002; prof. internal medicine, human genetics and pub. health U. MIch., 1997—. Bd. dirs. Amgen, Rohm & Haas Co., Population Svcs. Internat.; White House fellow/spl. asst. to chmn. AEC, 1973-74; assoc. dir. Office Sci. and Tech. Policy, The White House, 1977-80; assoc. dir. human resources Office Mgmt. and Budget, 1980-81; vis. sr. fellow Wilson Sch. Pub. and Internat. Affairs, Princeton U., 1981; sci. and pub. policy fellow Brookings Instn., Washington, 1981-82; cons. govt. agys., Lifetime Cable Network; mem. Nat. Commn. on the Environment, Rene Dubos Ctr. for Human Environments, AFL-CIO Workplace Health Fund., Electric Power Rsch. Inst., Carnegie Commn. Task Force on Sci. and Tech. in Jud. and Regulatory Decision Making, adv. com. to dir., Ctrs. Disease Control, 1992-95, adv. com. Critical Technologies Inst., RAND; mem. Pres.'s Coun., U. Calif., 1992-97; chair, Pres. Congrl. Commn. on Risk Assessment and Risk Mgmt.; mem. Nat. Enterprise for the Environment. Co-author: Clearing the Air, Reforming the Clean Air Act, 1981. Editor: (with others) Genetics, Environment and Behavior: Implications for Educational Policy, 1972; Genetic Control of Environmental Pollutants, 1984; Genetic Variability in Responses to Chemical Exposure, 1984, Environmental Biotechnology: Reducing Risks from Environmental Chemicals through Biotechnology, 1988, Biotechnology in Biodegradation, 1990, Biotechnology and Human Genetic Predisposition to Disease, 1990, Annual Review of Public Health, 1991-97, Clinics in Geriatric Medicine, 1992; assoc. editor Cancer Rsch., Cancer Epidemiology, Biomarkers and Prevention, Environ. Rsch., Am. Jour. Med. Genetics, Am. Jour. Preventive Medicine; contbr. articles on cancer prevention, human biochem. genetics, prenatal diagnosis of inherited disorders, susceptibility to environ. agts., clin. medicine and health policy to profl. publs. Mem. Pres.'s Coun. on Spinal Cord Injury; mem. Nat. Cancer Adv. Bd., Nat. Heart, Lung and Blood Adv. Coun., Wash. State Gov.'s Commn. on Social and Health Svcs., Ctr. for Excellence in Govt.; chmn. awards panel Gen. Motors Cancer Rsch. Found., 1985-86; chmn. bd. Environ. Studies and Toxicology, Nat. Rsch. Coun., 1988-91; mem. Bd. Health Promotion and Disease Prevention, Inst. Medicine; mem. adv. com. Woodrow Wilson Sch., Princeton U., 1978-84; trustee Pacific Sci. Ctr., Fred Hutchinson Cancer Rsch. Ctr., Seattle Symphony Orch., Seattle Youth Symphony Orch., Seattle Chamber Music Festival, Santa Fe Chamber Music Festival, Univ. Mus. Soc., Ann Arbor; chmn. rules com. Dem. Conv., King County, Wash., 1972. Served with USPHS, 1967-69. Recipient Research Career Devel. award USPHS, 1972; White House fellow, 1973-74 Fellow ACP, AAAS, Nat. Acad. Social Ins., Western Assn. Physicians, Hastings Ctr., Collegium Ramazzini; mem. Inst. Medicine of NAS, White House Fellows Assn., Am. Soc. Human Genetics, Western Soc. Clin. Rsch., Assn. Am. Physicians, Am. Acad. Arts and Scis. Jewish. Home: 3340 E Dobson Ann Arbor MI 48105-2583 Office: Univ Mich M7324 Medical Sci I Bldg 1301 Catherine St Ann Arbor MI 48109-0626 Fax: 734-647-9739. E-mail: gomenn@umich.edu.

OMER, GEORGE ELBERT, JR. orthopaedic surgeon, educator; b. Kansas City, Kans., Dec. 23, 1922; s. George Elbert and Edith May (Hines) O.; m. Wendie Vilven, Nov. 6, 1949; children: George Eric, Michael Lee. BA, Ft. Hays Kans. State U., 1944; MD, Kans. U., 1950; MSc in Orthopaedic Surgery, Baylor U., 1955. Diplomate Am. Bd. Orthopaedic Surgery, 1959, (bd. dirs. 1983-92, pres. 1987-88), re-cert. orthopaedics and hand surgery, 1983, cert. surgery of the hand, 1989. 2nd lt. U.S. Army, 1945; advanced through grades to col., 1967; ret. U.S. Army, 1970; rotating intern Bethany Hosp., Kansas City, 1950-51; resident in orthopaedic surgery Brooke Gen. Hosp., San Antonio, 1952-55, William Beaumont Gen. Hosp., El Paso, 1955-56; chief surgery Irwin Army Hosp., Ft. Riley, Kans., 1957-59; cons. in orthopaedic surgery 8th Army, chief orthop. surgery 121st Evacuation Hosp., 1959-60; asst. chief orthopaedic surgery, chief hand surgeon Fitzsimons Army Med. Center, Denver, 1960-63; dir. orthopaedic residency tng. Armed Forces Inst. Pathology and Walter Reed Army Med. Ctr., Washington, 1963-65; chief orthopaedic surgery and chief Army Hand Surg. Center, Brooke Army Med. Center, 1965-70; cons. in orthopaedic and hand surgery Surgeon Gen. Army, 1967-70; prof. orthopaedics, surgery, and anatomy, chmn. dept. orthopaedic surgery, chief div. hand surgery U. N.Mex., 1970-90, med. dir. phys. therapy, 1972-90, acting asst. dean grad. edn. Sch. Medicine, 1980-81. Mem. active staff U. N.Mex. Hosp., Albuquerque, 1970—, chief of med. staff, 1984-86; cons. staff other Albuquerque hosps.; cons. orthopaedic surgery USPHS, 1966-85, U.S. Army, 1970-92, USAF, 1970-78, VA, 1970-2000; cons. Carrie Tingley Hosp. for Crippled Children, 1970-99, interim med. dir., 1970-72, 86-87, mem. bd. advisor 1972-76, chair, 1994-96. Mem. bd. editors Clin. Orthopaedics, 1973-90, Jour. AMA, 1973-74, Jour. Hand Surgery, 1976-81; trustee Jour. Bone and Joint Surgery, 1993-99, sec., 1993-96, chmn., 1997-99; contbr. more than 300 articles to profl. jours., numerous chpts. to books. Decorated Legion of Merit, Army Commendation medal with 2 oak leaf clusters; recipient Alumni Achievement award Ft. Hays State U., 1973, Recognition plaque Am. Soc. Surgery Hand, 1989, Recognition plaque N.Mex. Orthopaedic Assn., 1991, Recognition award for hand surgery Am. Osteo. Acad. Orthopaedics, 1982, Pioneer award Internat. Socs. for Surgery Hand, 1995, Rodey award U. N.Mex. Alumni Assn., 1997, Cornerstone award U. N.Mex. Health Scis. Ctr., 1997; recognized with Endowed Professorship U. N.Mex. Sch. Medicine, 1995; recognized with named Annual Orthop. Seminar and Alumni Day Brooke Army Med. Ctr., 1999. Fellow ACS, Am. Orthopaedic Assn. (pres. 1988-89, exec. dir. 1989-93), Am. Acad. Orthopaedic Surgeons, Assn. Orthopaedic Chmn., N.Mex. Orthopaedic Assn. (pres. 1979-81, 1999-2000), La. Orthopaedic Assn. (hon.), Korean Orthopaedic Assn. (hon.), Peru Orthopaedic Soc. (hon.), Caribbean Hand Soc., Am. Soc. Surgery Hand (pres. 1978-79), Am. Assn. Surgery of Trauma, Assn. Bone and Joint Surgeons, Assn. Mil. Surgeons U.S., Riordan Hand Soc. (pres. 1967-68), Sunderland Soc. (pres. 1981-83), Soc. Mil. Orthopaedic Surgeons, Brazilian Hand Soc. (hon.), S.Am. Hand Soc. (hon.), Groupe D'Etude de la Main, Brit. Hand Soc. (hon.), Venezuela Hand Soc. (hon.), South African Hand Soc. (hon.), Western Orthopaedic Assn. (pres. 1981-82), AAAS, Russell A. Hibbs Soc. (pres. 1977-78), 38th Parallel Med. Soc. (Korea) (sec. 1959-60); mem. AMA, Phi Kappa Phi, Phi Sigma, Alpha Omega Alpha, Phi Beta Pi. Achievements include pioneer work in hand surgery. Home: 316 Big Horn Ridge Rd NE Sandia Heights Albuquerque NM 87122 Office: U N Mex Dept Orthopaedic Surgery 2211 Lomas Blvd NE Albuquerque NM 87106-2745

OMER, ROBERT WENDELL, hospital administrator; b. Salt Lake City, Feb. 10, 1948; s. Wayne Albert and Melva Bernice (Thunell) O.; m. Deborah Jackson, May 4, 1972;children: Melinda, Carmen, Creighton, Preston, Allison. BS in Biology, U. Utah, 1972; MHA, Washington U., St. Louis, 1975. V.p. St. Luke's Hosp., Cedar Rapids, Iowa, 1974-80; asst. adminstr. Franciscan Med. Ctr., Rock Island, Ill., 1980-82, Latter Day Saints Hosp., Salt Lake City, 1982-85, Clarkson Hosp., Omaha, 1985-93, v.p., COO, 1993-97; CEO Creighton St. Joseph's Clinics, 1998-99; pres., CEO MCH Health Sys., Blair, 1999—2001; CEO Cooper County Hosp., Boonville, Mo., 2002—. Bd. dirs. ARC, Heartland chpt. Omaha; bd. dirs. Nebr. Scanning Svcs. Lt. col. USAR, 1972. Fellow Am. Coll. Healthcare Execs. (regent); mem. Nebr. Hosp. Assn., Omaha C. of C. (Leadership Omaha award 1978), Omaha Healthcare Execs. Group (pres. 1989-90), Rotary (bd. dirs. 1990). Republican. Mem. Lds Ch. Avocations: jogging, history, cycling, backpacking, racquetball. Home: 1310 Grace Ln Boonville MO 65233

OMHOLT, BRUCE DONALD, b. Salem, Oreg., Mar. 27, 1943; s. Donald Carl and Violet Mae (Buck) O.; m. Mavis Aronow, Aug. 18, 1963 (div. July 1972); children: Madison, Natalie; m. Darla Kay Faber, Oct. 27, 1972; 1 child, Cassidy. BSME, Heald Coll. Engring., San Francisco, 1964. Real estate salesman R. Lea Ward and Assocs., San Francisco, 1962-64; sales engr. Repco Engring., Montebello, Calif., 1964; various mfg., engring. and mgmt. positions Ford Motor Co., Rawsonville, Saline, Owosso and Ypsilanti, Mich., 1964-75; chief engr. E.F. Hauserman Co., Cleve., 1975-77; dir. design and engring. Am. Seating Co., Grand Rapids, Mich., 1977-80; pres. Trinity Engring., 1980-81, Rohnert Park, Calif., 1981—. Cons. in mfg., carrier rack apparatus, motorcycle improvements. Patentee in vertical mitre machine, merchandise display unit.

OMIDVAR, BIJAN, structural engineer, researcher; b. Tehran, Iran, Sept. 3, 1959; came to U.S., 1991; s. Reza and Parvin (Fekrazad) O.; m. Nahid Razmara, June 8, 1994. BS, U. Tehran, 1984, MS, 1986; PhD, U. Wis., Milw., 1995. Registered prof. engr., Iran. Structural engr. Sano Consulting Co., Tehran, 1984-86; project mgr. Djahad Assocs., Hamadan, Iran, 1986-90; mem. faculty Bu-Ali-Sina U., 1986-91; lectr. U. Wis., 1991-95, rsch. assoc., 1996—; engr. lead combustion design GE Power Sys., Schenectady, NY, 2000—, finite element analysis methods leader, 2001—. Adj. asst. prof. U. Wis. Ctr. Continuing Edn., 1994—, adj. asst. prof., 1996—. Contbr. articles to profl. jours. Scholar Asian Inst. Tech., 1986; grad. sch. fellow U. Wis., 1993; recipient 3d pl. award Student Rsch. Contest Soc. Exptl. Mechanics, Milw., 1995, Winner Best Rsch. Paper award, 1998. Mem. ASCE (assoc.). Achievements include development of new approach in defining "shear coefficient" in beams under bending. Home: 17 Leatherton Way Greenville SC 29615 E-mail: bijan.omidvar@ps.ge.com.

OMINSKY, ALAN JAY, lawyer, medical educator; b. Phila., Apr. 7, 1938; s. Benjamin B. and Ida S. (Snydman) O.; m. Marlene Lachman, Nov. 1, 1992; 1 child, Sara. BA, U. Pa., Phila., 1958, MD, 1962, JD, 1988. Bar: Pa. 1989, U.S. Supreme Ct. 1994; cert. Am. Bd. Anesthesiology, Am. Bd. Psychiatry. Assoc. prof. anesthesiology U. Pa., Phila., 1972-88, assoc. prof. psychiatry, 1975-88; assoc. Bernstein Silver & Agins, 1089-96. Mem. ABA, Pa. Bar Assn., Phila. Bar Assn. (chiar medicolegal com. 1993-95, mem. sr. lawyers, state civil, and computer users coms.), Assn. Trial Lawyers Am., Pa. Trial Lawyers Assn., Phil. Trial Lawyers Assn., Am. Soc. Anesthesiologists, Am. Psychiat. Soc., Lawyers Club Phila., Phi Beta Kappa. Home: 233 S 6th St Apt 701 Philadelphia PA 19106-3751

OMINSKY, ANDREW MICHAEL, lawyer; b. Phila., Jan. 8, 1965; s. Albert and Elaine Ominsky; m. Emma G. Ominsky, June 5, 1994; children: Jared, Emily, Elizabeth. BA, Duke U., 1987; JD, U. Denver, 1990. Bar: Colo. 1990, U.S. Dist. Ct. Colo. 1991, Pa. 1996, U.S. Dist. Ct. (ea. dist.) Pa. 1996. Jud. clk. Colo. Dist. Ct., Englewood, 1989-91; lawyer Burg & Eldredge, PC, Denver, 1991-96, Ominsky & Ominsky PC, Phila., 1996—. Apptd. to appellate ct. procedural rules com. Pa. Supreme Ct., 1999—. Bd. dirs. Linda Creed Breast Cancer Found., Phila., 1997—, J/CHAI, Phila., 1996—; founder Elaine Ominsky Circle of Friends, Wistar Inst., Gladwyne, Pa., 1997—. Mem. Colo. Bar Assn., Pa. Bar Assn., Pa. Trial Lawyers Assn., Phila. Bar Assn. Office: Two Penn Ctr 1500 JFK Blvd Ste 1210 Philadelphia PA 19102 E-mail: ominskylaw@yahoo.com.

OMINSKY, HARRIS, lawyer; b. Phila., Sept. 14, 1932; s. Joseph and Lillian (Herman) O.; m. Rosalyn Rita Rutenberg, June 4, 1961; children— Michelle, David BS in Econs., U. Pa., 1953, LL.B., 1956. Bar: Pa. 1956. Ptnr. Ominsky & Ominsky, Phila., 1958-64; ptnr. Blank, Rome, Comisky & McCauley, 1964—, mem. mgmt. com., 1981-84, 88-92, co-chmn. real estate dept., 1988-93. Lectr. Law Sch., Temple U., Phila., 1969-71, lectr. Real Estate Inst., 1996—. Author: Real Estate Practice: New Perspectives, 1996, Real Estate Practice: Breaking New Ground, 2001; weekly columnist Ominsky's Terrain, Phila. Legal Intelligencer, 1999—; contbr. numerous articles to profl. jours. Pres. bd. Phila. Singing City Choir, 1984-88; chmn. zoning com. Merion Civic Assn., Pa., 1984-91. Fellow Am. Bar Found.; mem. ABA (Harrison Tweed spl. merit award 1988), Pa. Bar Assn. (ho. of dels. 1984—), Pa. Bar Inst. (bd. dirs. 1981—, exec. com. 1986-93, v.p. 1988-89, pres. 1989-90, lectr., planner 1969—), Phila. Bar Assn. (chmn. real estate taxes subcom. 1984-85, real property sect. 1991-92, Leon J. Obermayer Edn. award 1989, Good Deed award real property sect. 1999), Am. Coll. Real Estate Lawyers (chmn. publs. com. 1987-91, bd. govs. 1993-95), Order of Coif. Home: 526 Baird Rd Merion Station PA 19066-1302 Office: Blank Rome Comisky & McCauley LLP One Logan Sq Philadelphia PA 19103-6998

OMIROS, GEORGE JAMES, medical foundation executive; b. Uniontown, Pa., Oct. 26, 1956; s. Chris George and Alice (Zervoudi) O.; m. Sophia Florent, June 28, 1980; children: Christopher George, Alicia Helene. BS in Polit. and Philosophy, U. Pitts., 1978; M, Cen. Mich. U., 1982. Campaign coordinator, program assoc. SW Pa. chpt. Am. Heart Assn., Greensburg, 1979, fundraising dir., 1979-80, dir. devel., 1980-84, v.p. devel., ops. Western Pa. chpt. Pitts., 1984-85, dep. exec. v.p., 1985-87, exec. v.p., 1987-88; exec. dir. Leukemia Soc. Am., The Leukemia and Lymphoma Soc., 1988—, nat. mktg. rep., 1988—, asst. v.p. nat. office, 1991-93; sr. exec. dir., nat. dir. Don Devel., 1993-95, sr. exec. dir., group dir., nat. dir. comm. camp., 1995—. Mem. coun., rev. com. Health Sys. Agy. S.W. Pa., Pitts., 1983—87; mem. com. Fayette County Rep. Party; mem. Order St. Andrew-Ecumenical Patriarchate Istanbul, 2001—; cons. devel. Greek Orthodox Archdiocese, Pitts., 1982—, v.p., 1987—, fin. chmn., 1999—; chair Pitts. met. com. Pitts. Metro Com.Internat. Orthodox Christian Charities, Balt., 1993—; mem. parish coun. St. Spyridon Greek Orthodox Ch., Monessen, Pa., 1982—2000; met. chmn. Internat. Orthodox Christian Charities. Decorated Order of St. Andrew, 2001. Mem. Nat. Soc. Fundraising Execs. (cert., founder 1980, pres. 1985-87, Outstanding Fundraising Exec. 1990), Oncology Nursing Soc. (chmn. Camp Raising Spirits 2000—), Pitts. Planned Giving Coun. (founding com. 1983—), Friends of George C. Marshall (steering com. 1990-92), Uniontown Country Club, Uniontown Rotary (local treas. 1985, sec. 1986, v.p. 1987, pres. 1988), Chestnut Ridge Rotary, Pitts. Rotary, Masons, Order St. Andrew. Republican. Greek Orthodox. Avocations: stained glass work, art collections, gardening, antiques. Office: Leukemia and Lymphoma Soc 13 North 2 Gateway Ctr Pittsburgh PA 15222-1425

OMLAND, JACQUELINE LEIGH-KNUTE, secondary school educator, small business owner; b. Grand Forks, N.D., Nov. 19, 1955; d. Denora Muriel and Jerry John Knute; m. Thomas Jay Omland, May 17, 1985; children: Brian. BS in Natural Scis., U. N.D., 1978; MS in Edn., No. State U., 1985. Sci. tchr. Thief River Falls (Minn.) Pub. Schs., 1978—79, Alvarado (Minn.) Pub. Schs., 1979—83; sci. instr. Aberdeen (S.D.) Pub. Schs., 1984—2002; adj. physics instr. Presentation Coll., 1995—; Matster E-Learning physics tchr. No. State U. Statewide E-learning Ctr., 2002—. Adj. physics instr. No. State U., Aberdeen, 1994. Police and fire commr. City of Aberdeen, 2001—. Named S.D. Tchr. of Yr. award, Coun. of Chief Sch. Officers, 1996; recipient Presdl. award for Excellence in Sci. and Math. Tchg., NSF, 1995, Walt Disney Am. Tchr. award, The Disney Corp., 1998. Mem.: Nat. Sci. Tchrs. Assn., Aberdeen Edn. Assn. (sec. 1984—85), NEA, Phi Delta Kappa, Am. Legion Auxiliary (pres. 1995—99, 2002—, Legionette of Yr. 2001, Legionette of Yr. 2002), Zonta (pres. 1997—99, Silver Plate), Delta Kappa Gamma (pres. 1996—98). Lutheran. Avocation: travel. Home: Box 1177 Aberdeen SD 57402-1177

OMMAYA, AYUB KHAN, neurosurgeon, educator; b. Pakistan, Apr. 14, 1930; came to U.S., 1961, naturalized, 1968; s. Sultan Nadir and Ida (Counil) Khan; m. Ghuzala Nangiana, 1984; children: David, Alexander, Shana, Aisha, Iman, Sinan. MD, U. Punjab, Pakistan, 1953; MA, Oxford U., Eng., 1956. Diplomate Am. Bd. Neurological Surgery. Intern Mayo Hosp., Lahore, Pakistan, 1953-54; resident in neurosurgery Radcliffe Infirmary, Oxford, Eng., 1954-61; vis. scientist NIH, Bethesda, Md., 1961-63, assoc. neurosurgeon, 1963-68, head sect. applied rsch., 1968-74, chief neurosurgery, 1974-79; clin. prof. George Washington U. Med. Sch., 1970—. Cons. VA, Armed Forces Radiobiology Rsch. Inst.; chmn. Inter-Agy. Com. for Protection Human Rsch. Subjects of Fed. Coordinating Coun. for Sci., Engring. and Tech., NAS; chmn. biomechanics adv. com. com. Nat. Hwy. Traffic Safety Adminstrn.; mem. adv. com. Nat. Ctr. Injury Control & Prevention, Atlanta; inaugural Lewin Meml. lectr. U. Cambridge, Eng., 1983; mem. adv. coun. CDC; Snively lectr. Am. Assn. Auto. Medicine, 1988; Ibn-Sina lectr. Islamic Med. Assn. N.Am. Contbr. articles to profl. jours.; inventor, patentee spinal fluid flow driven artificial organs for diabetes and degenerative diseases of the nervous system. Pres. Ctr. Integrative Neurosci., Bethesda; v.p., dir. rsch. Cyborgan, Inc., Bethesda. Recipient J. W. Kirkdaldy prize Oxford U., 1956, Lifetime Achievement award Internat. Coll. Surgeons, 1996; recipient Sitara-i-Imtiaz for Achievements in Neurosurgery Govt. Pakistan, 1981; Hunterian prof. Royal Coll. Surgeons, 1968; Rhodes scholar, 1954-60 Fellow ACS, Third World Acad. Scis. (assoc., med. scis. com.), Royal Coll. Surgeons Eng.; mem. ASME (exec. affiliate), Soc. for Neurosci., Am. Assn. Neurol. Surgeons, Rsch. Soc. Neurosurgeons, Brit. Soc. Neurol. Surgeons, Am. Assn. Pakistani Physicians (pres.), Internat. Brain Rsch. Orgn. (life), Pan-Am. Med. Assn. Home: 8901 Burning Tree Rd Bethesda MD 20817-3007 Office: 8006 Glenbrook Rd Bethesda MD 20814-2608

OMOHUNDRO, WILLIAM ADDISON, research marketing executive; b. Richmond, Va. s. Floyd Alvin and Mary Elizabeth (Gilliam) O.; m. Delight V. Dixon; children: William A., Jeffrey F., Robert L. BA, U. Va.; M Indsl. Engring., Ga. Tech. U.; MS, Columbia U. Mgr. new product devel. Gen. Electric, Bridgeport, Conn., mgr. new product engring.; mgr. product strategy Sperry Rand; dir. mktg. research Carrier Corp., Syracuse, N.Y., 1979—. Bd. dirs. Megafax, Inc., Syracuse. Patentee home hair dryer, negative ion generator, others. Pres. Stony Point Assn., Westport, Conn., 1978. Mem.: Am. Mktg. Assn. Republican. Home: 21 Camping Ridge Ct Stoney Creek Wintergreen VA 22958

OMOIKE, ISAAC IRABOR, chemist, publishing executive, writer; b. Iruekpen, Nigeria, Apr. 29, 1957; s. Matthew Ighodalo and Rosaline Alice (Amiolemen) Omoike; m. Brenda Gail Roberts, Sept. 20, 1980 (div. Dec. 1993); children: Ann, Angel, Jeremy. BS in Biology and Chemistry, U. La., 1980; PhD in Biochemistry and Food Sci., U. Palmersgreen, London, 1987; Cert. Law Enforcement/Pvt. Investigation, La. State U., 1995. Teaching asst. chemistry dept. La. State U., Baton Rouge, 1984, rsch. asst. food sci. dept., 1985-86; lab. analyst Fina Oil and Chem. Co., Caraville, 1987-88; chemist, supr. Bio-Now Lab. Inc., Amelia, 1989; lab. analyst Cibageigy corp., St. Gabriel, 1989-90; chemist West Paine Lab., Baton Rouge, 1991. Dir. Isaac Omoike Books, Baton Rouge, 1990—; owner Family Pizza Lover Restaurant, Baton Rouge; pres. rsch. and investigations, Baton Rouge, 1990—. Author: (book) Genocide: The Ultimate Threat of the Next Milleniums, 1991, Insider America, 1993, Euthanasia Right or Wrong (Tell-Tale Signs of Murder), 1995, The Murder of a Princess (An Investigational Analysis of the Death of Princess Diana), 1998, A Tribute to John F. Kennedy Jr., 2000, The Columbine High School Massacre: An Investigatory Analysis, 2000, Terror on America: Causes and Consequences, 2002. Mem.: ACLU, ALA, Pub. Mktg. Assn., U.S. Soccer Referees, Am. Chem. Soc. Avocations: soccer, volleyball, ping pong, bowling, athletics. Office: PO Box 44801 Fort Washington MD 20749-4801

OMOLE, GABRIEL GBOLABO, international venture capitalist; b. Akungba-Akoko, Nigeria, Mar. 15, 1940; came to U.S., 1975; s. Amos Akindele and Victoria Ola (Olutu) O.; children: Juliana Olufunke, Esther Oluremi, Christiana Oluseun, George Abayomi. PhD, D MSc. Chmn. Gay Omole & Co., Ltd., Lagos, Nigeria, 1968—, Akoko Indsl. Devel. Ltd., 1973—, Akoko Mktg. & Investment Ltd., 1973—, Johngay Enterprises, Ltd., Accra, Ghana, 1977—, Gayom Travel & Tours, Ltd., 1977—, Unifood Industries Nigeria Ltd., 1979—, Unity Village Complex, 1979—, 1st Akoko Internat. Corp., N.Y.C., 1978—, UCM Services Corp., N.Y.C., 1979—, The Akoko Group, Ltd., London, 1983—, Gay Omole Internat. Ltd., London, 1983—, Gay Omole Investment Ltd., Brunei Internat. Investors (West Africa) Ltd.; pres., CEO Mastercard Internat. Svcs. Ltd., 1996—; mng. dir. Galleria Tourist Devel. Property Co. Ltd., Lagos, 1993—, Galleria Transp. Systems Ltd., Lagos, 1993, Combined Billionaires Network Svcs. Ltd., 1996—, Direct Resources Internat. Ltd., 1996—, Galleria City Devel. Ltd., 1996—. Co-founder Brunei Resources (West Africa) Ltd., 1990—; pres., co-founder African Continental Corp., Miami, Fla.; dir.-gen. IBB World Leaders Gallery, Gay Omole Petroleum. Chmn. bd. dirs. Akoko Specialist Hosp., N.Y.C.; trustee, chmn., Gay Omole Found., Lagos, 1979—; founder Unity Ch. Mission, 1976, chmn. devel. fund, 1979—. Mem. Am. Mgmt. Assn., Akungba Devel. Union, Am. Mgmt. Internat., Assn. Venture Founders, Akure C. of C., N.Y.C. C. of C., Nigerian-Am. C. of C., Nigerian-ASEAN C. of C., Nigerian-South Africa C. of C., N.Y. Acad. Scis., Nat. Geo. Soc., London Inst. Dirs., U.S. C. of C. Home: PO Box 74147 Victoria Island Lagos Nigeria also: PO Box 4447 Garki Abuja Nigeria

O'MORCHOE, CHARLES CHRISTOPHER CREAGH, anatomical sciences educator, science administrator; b. Quetta, India, May 7, 1931; came to U.S., 1968; s. Nial Francis C. and Jessie Elizabeth (Joly) O'M.; m. Patricia Jean Richardson, Sept. 15, 1955; children: Charles Eric Creagh, David James Creagh. BA, Trinity Coll., Dublin (Ireland) U., 1953, MB, BCh, BAO, 1955, MA, 1959, MD, 1961, PhD, 1969, DSc, 1981. Resident Halifax Gen. Hosp., U.K., 1955-57; lectr. in anatomy Sch. Medicine Trinity Coll., Dublin (Ireland) U., 1957-61, 63-65, lectr. in physiology, 1966-67, assoc. prof. in physiology, 1967-68; instr. in anatomy Harvard Med. Sch., Boston, 1962-63; vis. prof. physiology U. Md. Sch. Medicine, Balt., 1961-62, assoc. prof. anatomy, 1968-71, prof. anatomy, 1971-74; chmn. anatomy bd. State of Md., 1971-73; prof., chmn. dept. anatomy Stritch Sch. Medicine Loyola U., Maywood, Ill., 1974-84; dean Coll. Medicine, U. Ill., Urbana-Champaign, 1984-98, prof. anat. scis. and surgery, 1984-98, emeritus dean and prof., 1998—. WHO cons., vis. prof. physiology Jaipur, India, 1967, S.M.S. Med. Coll., U. Rajasthan, vis. prof. anatomy, 1971. Assoc. editor: Anatomical Record, 1978-98, Am. Jour. Anatomy, 1987-91; contbr. articles to profl. jours. Elected fellow Trinity Coll., Dublin U., 1966; named faculty mem. of yr. Loyola U., Chgo., 1982. Mem. AMA, Am. Soc. Nephrology, N.Am. Soc. Lymphology (v.p. 1982-84, pres. 1984-86, sec. 1993-98, Cecil K. Drinker award 1992), Am. Assn. Anatomy Chairmen (emeritus), Am. Assn. Anatomists (dir. placement svc. 1981-91), Internat. Soc. Lymphology (exec. com. 1987-97, pres. 1993-95, Presdl. award 2001), Ill. State Med. Soc., Champaign County Med. Soc., Alpha Omega Alpha. Mem. Church of Ireland. Home: 5645 NE Lincoln Rd East Poulsbo WA 98370-7756 Office: U Ill Coll Medicine 190 Med Sci Bldg 506 S Mathews Ave Urbana IL 61801-3618 E-mail: cccom@uiuc.edu.

O'MORCHOE, PATRICIA JEAN, pathologist, educator; b. Halifax, Eng., Sept. 15, 1930; came to U.S., 1968; d. Alfred Eric and Florence Patricia (Pearson) Richardson; m. Charles Christopher Creagh O'Morchoe, Sept. 15, 1955; children: Charles E.C., David J.C. BA, Dublin U., Ireland, 1953, MB, Bch., BAO, 1955, MA, 1966, MD. Intern Halifax (Yorkshire) Gen. Hosp., Eng., 1955-57; instr., lectr. physiology Dublin U., 1957-61, 63-68; instr. pathology Johns Hopkins U., Balt., 1961-62, 68-72, asst. prof. pathology, 1972-74; rsch. assoc. surgery, pathology Harvard U., Boston, 1962-63; asst. prof. anatomy U. Md., 1970-74; assoc.prof., prof. pathology, anatomy Loyola U. Chgo., 1974-84; prof. pathology, cell and structural biology U. Ill., Urbana, 1984—, assoc. head dept. pathology, 1991-94, head dept. pathology coll. medicine, 1994-98; staff pathologist VA Hosp., Danville, Ill., 1989-98. Courtesy staff pathologist Covenant Hosp., Urbana, 1984-98, Carle Clinic, Urbana, 1990-98. Contbr. numerous articles to profl. jours. Recipient Excellence in Teaching award U. Ill., 1996, Spl. Recognition award U. Ill. Coll. Medicine at Urbana-Champaign, 1998. Mem. Internat. Acad. Cytology, Internat. Soc. Lymphology (auditor 1989-91, exec. com. 1991-93), N.Am. Soc. Lymphology (sec. 1988-90, treas. 1990-92, v.p. 1992-94, pres. 1994-98), Am. Soc. Cytology, Am. Assn. Anatomists, Ill. Soc. Cytology. Avocations: boating, needlework. Home: 5645 NE Lincoln Rd Poulsbo WA 98370-7756 Office: U Ill Coll Med 506 S Mathews Ave Urbana IL 61801-3618 E-mail: cccom@uiuc.edu.

OMOSHEYIN, ROTIMI, electronics engineer, real estate company executive; b. Yaba, Labos, Nov. 4, 1960; arrived in U.S., 1982; s. Matthew and Eunice Olamita Omusheyin; m. Rochelle Smith, Oct. 27, 1990; children: Rotimi, Dionte. BSC, Aero Space Inst., 1985; advanced cert., Harry S. Truman Coll., 1988. Lic. ins. agt. Ill.; real estate agt. Ill. Fgn. exch. specialist 1st Bank of Nigeria, Marina Lagos, 1979—82; sales cons. Century 21 Home Finder, Chgo., 1985—87; regional mgr. Al Williams and Assocs., 1988—92; electronics specialist Marshall Field and Co., 1986—; pres., CEO Binom Mgmt., 1995—. Author: Monster Zunga, 1997. Ambassador Bapt. Conv., Lagos, 1978. Mem.: Binom Club (pres. 1996—2000). Methodist. Achievements include invention of toddler cycle. Avocations: fishing, music, soccer, reading, travel. Home: 1455 W 115th St Chicago IL 60643 E-mail: Timiomo@yahoo.com.

OMURA, EMILY FOWLER, dermatologist, educator; b. Oklahoma City, Oct. 19, 1938; d. Richard William and Emma (Fraiser) Fowler; m. George A. Omura, Dec. 27, 1962; children: June, Susan, Ann, George F. BA cum laude, Barnard Coll., 1960; MD, Cornell U., 1964. Cert. Am. Bd. Dermatology, Am. Bd. Dermatopathology. Intern in mixed-medicine Roosevelt Hosp., N.Y.C., 1965-66; resident in dermatology Cornell/N.Y. Hosp., 1966-69, clin. instr. dermatology, 1969-70; asst. prof. dermatology U. Ala., Birmingham, 1970-75; assoc. prof. U. Ala. Med. Ctr., 1975-83, prof. dermatology, dir. dermatopathology, 1983-99, emeritus prof. dermatology, 1999—; with dermatopathology Skin Path Assocs., 1999—. Dir. dermatopathology fellowship training program U. Ala., Birmingham, 1983-99. Med Stud. Awd. for Outstanding Performance in Dermatology established by U. Ala. Birmingham, named for Emily F. Omura, 1999—. Fellow Am. Acad. Dermatology, Am. Soc. Dermatopathology (pres. 2000-01). Methodist. Avocations: dance, reading, museum docent. Office: Skin Pathology Assocs 3550 Independence Dr Birmingham AL 35209-5710 E-mail: mefomura@aol.com.

OMURA, GEORGE ADOLF, medical oncologist; b. N.Y.C., Apr. 30, 1938; s. Bunji K. and Martha (Pilger) O.; m. Emily Fowler, Dec. 27, 1962; children: June Ellen, Susan, Ann, George Fowler. BA magna cum laude, Columbia U., 1958; MD, Cornell U., 1962. Intern Bellevue Hosp., N.Y.C., resident, 1965-67; fellow Meml. Sloan Kettering Cancer Ctr., 1967-70; asst. prof. medicine U. Ala., Birmingham, 1970-73, assoc. prof. medicine, 1973-78, prof. medicine, 1978-95, prof. emeritus, medicine, 1995—, prof. ob-gyn., 1991-95; v.p. clin. devel. BioCryst Pharms., Inc., 1995-99, med. dir., 1996-99; prof. emeritus, ob-gyn U. Ala., 1996—. Cons. Nat. Cancer Inst., 1975-97; chmn. Southeastern Cancer Study Group, 1983-87; cons. to FDA, 1994-95; prin. investigator cancer and leukemia Group B for Ala., 1986-95. Contbr. articles to profl. jours. Served with USNR, 1963-65. Am. Cancer Soc. jr. faculty clin. fellow, 1971-74. Fellow A.C.P.; mem. Gynecol. Oncology Group (co-prin. investigator for Ala. 1988—), Am. Soc. Clin. Oncology, Am. Soc. Hematology, Am. Assn. Cancer Research, Phi Beta Kappa, Alpha Omega Alpha Home: 3621 Crestside Rd Birmingham AL 35223-1514 Office: University Sta Birmingham AL 35294-0001 E-mail: geoaomura@aol.com.

OMURA, YOSHIAKI, physician, educator; b. Tomari, Toyama-ken, Japan, Mar. 28, 1934; arrived in U.S., 1959, naturalized, 1979; s. Tsunejiro and Minako (Uozu) Omura; m. Rose Ninon Alexander, Sept. 8, 1962; children: Alexander Kenji, Vivienne Midori, Richard Itsuma. Assoc. degree, Nihon U., 1952—54; BSc in Applied Physics, Waseda U., 1957; MD, Yokohama City U., 1958; postgrad. exptl. physics, Columbia U., 1960—63; ScD (Med.), Coll. Physicians and Surgeons, Columbia U., 1965. Diplomate Internat. Coll. Acupuncture and Electro-Therapeutics, Am. Acad. Pain Mgmt., Am. Bd. Forensic Medicine, Am. Acad. Experts in Traumatic Stress. Rotating intern Tokyo U. Hosp., 1958, Norwalk (Conn.) Hosp., 1959; rsch. fellow cardiovasc. surgery Columbia U., N.Y.C., 1960; resident physician in surgery Francis Delafield Hosp., Cancer Inst., Columbia U., 1961—65; asst. prof. pharmacology and instr. surgery N.Y. Med. Coll., 1966—72; vis. prof. (summers) U. Paris, 1973—77; Maitre de recherche, Disting. Fgn. Scientist program of INSERM Govt. of France, 1977. Rsch. cons. orthop. surgery Columbia U., 1965—66; part-time emergency rm. physician Englewood Hosp., 1965—66; rsch. cons. pharmacology dept. N.Y. Downstate Med. Ctr., SUNY, 1966; co-founder, cons. Lincoln Hosp. Acupuncture Drug Detoxification Program, 1974—75; chmn. Columbia U. Affiliation and Cmty. Medicine com., Cmty. Bd. Francis Delafield Hosp., 1974—75; vis. rsch. prof. dept. elec. engring. Manhattan Coll., 1960—99; chmn. Sci. Divsn. Children's Art & Sci. Workshops, N.Y.C., 1971—92; dir. med. rsch. Heart Disease Rsch. Found., Bklyn., 1972—; adj. prof. dept. pharmacology Chgo. Med. Sch., 1982—93; adj. prof. physiology Sch. Med. Showa U., Tokyo, 1988—96; adj. prof. preventive medicine N.Y. Med. Coll., 1997—; vis. prof. Inst. Anesthesiology and Reanimation (summer) U. Padua, Italy, 1999; prof. dept. non-orthodox medicine Ukrainian Nat. Med. U., Kiev, 1993—; attending physician dept. neurosci. L.I. Coll. Hosp., 1980—88; cons. NY Pain Ctr., 1988—92, NIH Rsch. Grant Evaluation, 1994—96; v.p. Internat. Kirlian Rsch. Assn., 1981—; mem. N.Y. State Bd. Medicine, 1984—94; mem. alumni coun. Coll. Phys. and Surg. Columbia U., 1986—. Author: 6 books; contbr. chapters to books, over 190 articles to profl. jours.; mem. editl. bd. Alternative Medicine, 1985—93, Scandinavian Jour. Acupuncture and Electrotherapy, 1987—, Functional Neurology, 1988—2002, editl. cons. Jour. Electrocardiology, 1980—86; founder, editor-in-chief: Acupuncture & Electro-Therapeutics Rsch. Internat. Jour., 1974—. Recipient Acupuncture Scientist of Yr. award, Internat. Congress of Chinese Medicine, 1989, World 1st Qi Gong Scientist of Yr. award, Internat. Congress of Chinese Medicine & Qi Gong, 1990; fellow, Columbia U., 1960; grantee, Am. Cancer Soc. Inst., 1961—63, John Polacek Found., 1966—72, NIH, 1967—72, Heart Disease Rsch. Found., 1972—. Fellow: Internat. Coll. Angiology, N.Y. Cardiol. Soc., Am. Coll. Angiology, Am. Assn. Integrative Medicine (life), Am. Coll. Forensic Examiners (life), Royal Soc. Medicine (life), Internat. Coll. Acupuncture and Electro-Therapeutics (pres. 1980—), Am. Coll. Acupunture (life); mem.: N.Y. Japanese Med. Soc. (pres. 1963—73), Am. Soc. Artificial Internal Organs, Japan Bi-Digital O-Ring Test Med. Soc. (pres. 1990—), Japan Bi-Digital O-Ring Test Assn. (pres. 1986—), N.Y. Acad. Sci., Internat. Assn. for Study of Pain (founding mem. 1975—). Achievements include 5 U.S. patents and 5 Japanese patents. Home and Office: 800 Riverside Dr Ste 8I New York NY 10032-7400 Fax: 212-923-2279. Personal E-mail: dromura@aol.com. Business E-Mail: icaet@yahoo.com.

ONDETTI, MIGUEL ANGEL, chemist, consultant; b. Buenos Aires, Argentina, May 14, 1930; came to U.S., 1960, naturalized, 1971; s. Emilio Pablo and Sara Cecilia (Cerutti) O.; m. Josephine Elizabeth Garcia, June 6, 1958; children: Giselle Christine, Gabriel Alexander. Licensiate in Chemistry, U. Buenos Aires, 1955, D.Sc., 1957. Prof. chemistry Inst. Tchrs., Buenos Aires, 1957-60; instr. organic chemistry U. Buenos Aires, 1957-60; rsch. scientist Squibb Inst. Med. Rsch., Buenos Aires, 1957-60, rsch. investigator Princeton, N.J., 1960-66, rsch. supr., 1966-73, sect. head, 1973-76, dir. biol. chemistry, 1976-79; assoc. dir. Squibb Inst., 1980-82, v.p. rsch. cardiopulmonary disease, 1982-86, sr. v.p. cardiovascular rsch., 1987-91; pharm. cons., 1991—. Ad-hoc cons NIH; mem. adv. com. dept. chemistry Princeton U., 1982-86 Patentee in field (115); contbr. articles to sci. jours. Served with Argentine Army, 1950-51 Recipient Thomas Alva Edison Patent award R&D Coun. N.J., 1983, Ciba award for hypertension rsch. Am. Heart Assn., 1983, Perkins medal Soc. Chemistry Industry, 1991, Warren Alpert Found. award, 1991, Lasker award, 1999; scholar Brit. Coun., 1960, Squibb, 1956. Mem. AAAS, Am. Chem. Soc. (Alfred Burger award 1981, Creative Invention award 1992, Perkin medal 1992), Am. Soc. Biol. Chemists. Home: 79 Hemlock Cir Princeton NJ 08540-5405

ONDISH, ANDREA, museum educator; b. Scranton, Pa., Apr. 29, 1960; d. Andrew and Josephine (Mantione) O. AAS, Luzerne County C.C., 1980; BFA, Marywood Coll., 1985; MA, Ea. Ill. U., 1986; MFA, Ind. State U., 1992. Grad. asst. instr. art appreciation Ea. Ill. U., Charleston, 1985-86, art slide libr., 1986; art instr. Tarble Art Ctr., 1986; past up artist United Graphics, Mattoon, Ill., 1987-89; calligraphy instr. Lakeland Coll., 1989; tchg. asst. art appreciation Ind. State U., Terre Haute, 1991-92; silkscreen instr. Indpls. Art Ctr., 1995-98; instr. art. Swope Art Mus., Terre Haute, 1996-97, program and exhbns. coord., 1997-2001; curator edn. Marshall Fredericks Sculpture Mus., University Center, Mich., 2001—. Mem. panel adv. com. Ind. Arts Commn., Indpls., 1996-97, mem. individual artist com., 1997-98. Exhibited in one-person and group exhbns., including Sinclair C.C., Dayton, Ohio, 1994, Woman Made Gallery, Chgo., 1994, 95, 97, 99, ARC Gallery, Chgo., 1995, Sheldon Swope Art Mus., 1996, Indpls. Art Ctr., 1997, Sch. Profl. Psychology, Chgo., 1998, Lankershim Arts Ctr., North Hollywood, Calif., 1999, Olin Hall Galleries, Roanoke Coll., Salem, Va., 1999. Vol. grant reader Ind. Arts Commn., Indpls., 1996-98. Mem. Am. Print Alliance, Chgo. Artist Coalition, Mid Am. Print Coun., INprint. Home: PO Box 5146 Saginaw MI 48603 E-mail: ondish@svsu.edu.

ONDREY GRUBER, WILLIAM MICHAEL, lawyer; b. Cleve., Oct. 17, 1955; s. Roman Frederick and Mary Margaret (Moriarty) Gruber; m. Lynn Frances Ondrey Gruber, June 16, 1984; children: John Gruber, Elisabeth Gruber. BA, Georgetown U., 1977; JD, Case Western Res. U., 1982. Bar: Ohio 1982, U.S. Dist. Ct. (no. dist.) Ohio 1982. Asst. dir. law City of Cleve., 1982-89, chief asst. dir. law, 1989-98; pvt. practice Shaker Heights, Ohio, 1998—. Chmn. Mi Pueblo Latin Am. Culture Camp; chmn., trustee Concern for Children, Cleve., 1993—. Mem. ABA, Ohio Bar Assn., Cleve. Bar Assn., Cuyahoga County Law Dirs. Assn. Home and Office: 2714 Leighton Rd Shaker Heights OH 44120-1325 E-mail: gruberwl@aol.com.

ONDRUSEK, DAVID FRANCIS, discount store chain executive; b. Johnson City, N.Y., Aug. 8, 1955; s. Frank Joseph and Juanita Elizabeth (Seeley) O.; m. Tina G. Papapavlos, July 11, 1981; children: Stephanie Ann Albina, Michael David. BA, St. Michael's Coll., Winooski, Vt., 1977; BS, Idaho State U., Pocatello, 1980. Asst. mgr. Osco Drugs, Wenatachee, Wash., 1980, Richland, 1981-83, Thrift Drug, Williamsport, Pa., 1983; mgr. Revco Drug, 1983-88, dist. mgr. Morgantown, W.Va., 1988-92; pharmacy mgr. Wal-Mart, Salisbury, Md., 1992-94, dist. mgr. Lewisburg, Pa., 1994-99, regional mgr. Bentonville, Ark., 1999—. Head coach Lycoming Coll. Lacrosse Team, Williamsport, 1983-88. Mem. Am. Pharm. Assn., Nat. Assn. Retail Druggists, Wash. State Pharm. Assn., Pa. Assn. Chain Drug Stores (bd. dirs. 1996-99). Avocation: golf. Home: 313 NW LaSalle Dr Bentonville AR 72712 Office: Wal-Mart 702 SW 8th St Bentonville AR 72716-6299

O'NEAL, BARRON JOHNS, surgeon; b. Shreveport, La., June 12, 1952; s. Benjamin Franklin O'Neal and Nancy Johns; m. Mary Elizabeth Markaverich, Oct. 18, 1986; children: Barron Johns Jr., Benjamin Pearce, Cole Evan, Elizabeth K. BS, La. State U., 1974; MD, La. State U., Shreveport, 1978. Bd. cert. plastic and reconstructive surgery. Intern La. State U. Med. Ctr., Shreveport, 1978-79, resident in gen. surgery, 1979-82; resident in plastic surgery U. Louisville, 1982-84; fellow in hand surgery Hand Surgery Assocs., Louisville, 1984; asst. prof. surgery La. State U. Med. Sch., Shreveport, 1984—; ptnr. Brown's & O'Neal Med. Corp., 1986—. Chief of staff Physicians and Surgeons Hosp., Shreveport, 1990-94, Lagniappe Hosp., Shreveport, 1995-2000, dir. wound care, 1994—, chief of staff, 1997-2000; med. adv. bd. Pro Med Assets, Miami, Fla., 1998-99, Radiation Ctrs. Am., Ft. Lauderdale, Fla., 1998-2000. Contbr. articles to profl. jours. Bd. mem. St. Marks Cathedral Sch. Bd., 1998-2000; pres.-elect alumni affairs La. State U. Med. Ctr., Shreveport, 1998-2000, pres., 2001—. Mem. La. State Med. Soc. (del. 1986-99), Shreveport Med. Soc., Med. Sch. Faculty Assn. Republican. Episcopalian. Avocation: tennis. Office: Brown and ONeal Med Corp 2210 Line Ave Ste 204 Shreveport LA 71104-2134 E-mail: barononeal@aol.com., brownoneal@aol.com.

O'NEAL, DALE, JR. lawyer; b. Ft. Worth, Nov. 6, 1957; s. Dale O. and Delora (Neal) O'N.; m. Teresa Thompson, June 28, 1986. BBA, U. Tex., 1980; JD, South Tex. Coll., 1983. Bar: Tex. 1983, U.S. Dist. Ct. (no. dist.) Tex. 1988. Pvt. practice, Ft. Worth, 1983—. Adj. prof. family law U. Tex.; mem. State Bar Tex. Com. for Family Law Revisions, 1994-95. Author: Divorce: Understanding and Preparing for Trial, 1987, Security Agreements for Divorce Collateralization, 1989; asst. editor Tex. Young Lawyers Assn., mem. editl. bd., 1985-86; contbr. articles to profl. jours., convs., and seminars. Mem. Am. Acad. Matrimonial Lawyers, Tex. Young Lawyers Assn. (coun. mem. 1985-86, mem. family law com. 1989), Masons. Avocation: hunting. Office: PO Box 225 Fort Worth TX 76101-0225

O'NEAL, EDGAR CARL, psychology educator; b. St. Louis, Apr. 30, 1939; s. Clarence Edgar O'Neal and Alyce (Mullins) Redwine; m. Ellen Rose Luther, Aug. 31, 1963; children— Colleen Ruth, Patrick Blaine BA, Duke U., 1961; M.Div., Drew U., 1964; MA, U. Mo., 1968, PhD, 1969. Ordained to ministry United Meth. Ch., 1964. Minister Community Meth. Ch., Cold Spring Harbor, 1962-65; NIMH fellow U. Mo., Columbia, 1966-69; asst. prof., assoc. prof. psychology Tulane U., New Orleans, 1969-76, chmn. dept. psychology, 1978-84, prof. psychology, 1977—99, John Madison Fletcher prof. psychology, 1999—. Editor: Perspectives on Aggression, 1976; mem. editl. bd. Jour. Personality and Social Psychology, 1991-97, Jour. Non-verbal Behaviour, 1991-94, Aggressive Behavior, 1995—; contbr. articles to profl. jours. Fellow APA (coun. 1982-85); mem. Sigma Xi, Sigma Chi. Democrat. Methodist. Home: 7219 O'Neil Dr Harahan LA 70123-4844 Office: Tulane U Dept Psychology 2007 Stern Hall New Orleans LA 70118-5698 E-mail: edgar.oneal@att.net., edgar.oneal@tulane.edu.

O'NEAL, HANK, entertainment producer, business owner; b. Kilgore, Tex., June 5, 1940; s. Harold Lee and Sarah (Christian) O'N.; m. Shelley M. Shier, May 14, 1985. BA, Syracuse U., 1962. With CIA, Washington and N.Y.C., 1963-76; exec. v.p. Hammond Music Enterprises, N.Y.C., 1980-83; pres., owner Chiaroscuro Records Co./Downtown Sound recording studio, 1970-80, 85—; exec. v.p. HOSS, Inc., 1983—, Broadway Bound, Inc., 1998—. Instr., dept. head New Sch. for Social Rsch., N.Y.C., 1970-92; bd. dirs. Composer's and Choreographer's Theater, N.Y.C., The Jazz Found. Am., N.Y.C., The Gazz Gallery, N.Y.C.; pres. SOS Prodns., Wilkes Barre, Pa., 1987—. Author: Eddie Condon Scrapbook of Jazz, 1973, A Vision Shared, 1976, Berenice Abbott-American Photographer, 1982, Djuna Barnes 1978-81, 1990, Charlie Parker/The Funky Blues Date, 1995; author/photographer: The Floating Jazz Festival, 1985, The Ghosts of Harlem, 1997, Hank O'Neal, 2000; photographer: (books) Allegra Kent's Water Beauty Book, 1976, All the King's Men, 1990; producer, cover photographer/designer numerous record albums, 1967—. Capt. U.S. Army, 1963-67. Recipient various awards and prizes for books. Mem. Phi Gamma Delta. Home: Glenside PO Box 101 Thornhurst PA 18424-0101 Office: Chiaroscuro Records 830 Broadway New York NY 10003-4827 E-mail: chiarohank@aol.com.

O'NEAL, HARRIET ROBERTS, psychologist, psycholegal consultant; b. Covington, Ky., Dec. 28, 1952; d. Nelson E. and Georgia H. (Roberts) O'N. Student, U. Paris Sorbonne, 1972; BA in Psychology, Hollins Coll., 1974; JD, U. Nebr., 1978, MA in Psychology, 1980, PhD in Psychology, 1982. Therapist Richmond Maxi Ctr., San Francisco, 1979-81; clin. coord., therapist Pacifica (Calif.) Youth Svc. Bur., 1981-83; staff psychologist Kaiser Permanente Med. Ctr., Walnut Creek, Calif., 1983-91; pvt. practice psychotherapy Pleasant Hill, 1985-97; pvt. practice psychotherapy, psycholegal cons. San Francisco, 1995—. Cons. Employee Assistance Program, Pacific Bell, San Francisco, 1996—; psycholegal cons., Nebr., 1975-79, Calif. Bd. Behavioral Sci. Examiners, Sacramento, 1982—; psycholegal cons., presenter San Francisco State U., 1980, U. Calif., San Francisco, 1980, VA Med. Ctr., San Francisco, 1983. Cons. Nebr. Gov.'s Commn. on Status of Women, 1975, 78; vol. Make-A-Wish Found., 1992—. NIMH fellow, 1974-79. Mem. APA, Employee Assistance Profls. Assn., Phi Beta Kappa, Psi Chi. Avocations: dancing, swimming, hiking, travel, cycling.

O'NEAL, KATHLEEN LEN, communications executive, writer; b. Ft. Riley, Kans., May 24, 1953; d. Leonard Arthur and Mary (Modlin) O'Neal. BS with honors, U. Mo., 1975; MBA, Calif. Coast U., Santa Ana, 1991. Cert. secondary teacher. Tchr. math. Killian Sr. H.S., Miami, Fla., 1975-78; mfg. supr. Western Electric Co., Lee's Summit, Mo., 1978-79, prodn. control supr., 1979-81; dept. mgr. Lee Wards Co., Independence, Mo., 1981-83; materials mgmt. specialist Northrup-Wilcox Electric, Kansas City, 1983-84; bus. resource planning mgr. AT&T, Lee's Summit, 1984-85, product mgr. Berkeley Heights, N.J., 1985-87, fin. mgr. Bedminster, 1987-89, info. sys. devel. mgr. Piscataway, 1989-90, sr. fin. mgr. Jacksonville, Fla., 1990-91, asst. treas., 1992-95, sr. procurement mgr., 1995-96, procurement system design dist. mgr., 1997-98, payroll dist. mgr., 1998—2001; pres Kathy O'Neal Speaks, Inc, 2001—. Recipient Spec Recognition Award, United Way, 1980. Mem.: NOW, Am Production and Inventory Control Soc (vpres membership 1987—88, regional del 1988—89, instr inventory mgt 1987—88). Avocations: aerobics, reading. Office: PO Box 770655 Orlando FL 32877-0655 Personal E-mail: kathleen.oneal@celebration.fl.us. E-mail: kathy@accelerated-manager.com.

O'NEAL, MICHAEL RALPH, state legislator, lawyer; b. Kansas City, Mo., Jan. 16, 1951; s. Ralph D. and Margaret E. (McEuen) O'N.; children from a previous marriage: children: Haley Anne, Austin Michael; m. Cindy Wulfkuhle, Apr. 9, 1999. BA in English, U. Kans., 1973, JD, 1976. Bar: Kans. 1976, U.S. Dist. Ct. Kans. 1976, U.S. Ct. Appeals (10th cir.) 1979. Intern Legis. Counsel State of Kans., Topeka, 1975-76; assoc. Hodge, Reynolds, Smith, Peirce & Forker, Hutchinson, Kans., 1976-77; ptnr. Reynolds, Peirce, Forker, Suter, O'Neal & Myers, 1980-88; shareholder Gilliland & Hayes, P.A., 1988—, mng. ptnr., 2000—; mem. Kans. Ho. of Reps., 1984, chmn. jud. com., 1989-90, 93-94, 97—; pres. Gilliland & Hayes, P.C., 1999-2000; minority whip Kans. Ho. of Reps., 1991-92, majority whip, 1995-96, chmn. edn. com., 1995-96, mem. fiscal oversight com., 1997—, chair redistricting com., 2001—, mem. bus., commerce, labor com. Chmn. Ho. Reappointment Com.,

2001, instr. Hutchinson C.C., 1977-88. Vice chmn. Rep. Ctrl. Com., Reno County, Kans., 1982-86; bd. dirs. Reno County Mental Health Assn., Hutchinson, 1984-89, YMCA, 1984-86, Crime Stoppers (ex-officio), Hutchinson; chmn. adv. bd. dirs. Wesley Towers Retirement Cmty., 1984-96; mem. Kans. Travel and Tourism Commn., 1990-94; mem. bd. govs. U. Kans. Law Sch., 1991—; mem. Kans. Sentencing Commn., 1997—. Recipient Leadership award Kans. C. of C. and Industry, 1985; named one of Outstanding Young Men Am., 1986. Mem. ABA, Nat. Conf. State Legislatures (criminal justice com.), Kans. Assn. Def. Counsel, Def. Rsch. Inst., Kans. Bar Assn. (prospective legis. com., Outstanding Svc. award), Hutchinson C. of C. (ex-officio bd. dirs., Leadership award 1984), Am. Coun. Young Polit. Leaders (del. to Atlantic conf. biennial assembly), Kans. Jud. Coun., Commn. on Uniform State Laws. Avocations: basketball, tennis, golf. Home: 8 Windemere Ct Hutchinson KS 67502-2020 Office: Gilliland & Hayes PA 2d Flr Box 2977 20 W 2nd Ave Hutchinson KS 67504-2977 E-mail: mroneal@southwind.net.

O'NEAL, MICHAEL SCOTT, SR. lawyer; b. Jacksonville, Fla., Dec. 22, 1948; s. Jack Edwin and Lucille (Colvin) O'N.; m. Barbara Louise Hardie, Jan. 30, 1971 (div. Sept. 1974); 1 child, Jennifer Erin; m. Helen Margaret Joost, Mar. 18, 1985; children: Mary Helen, Angela Marie, Michael Scott O'Neal Jr. AA, Fla. Jr. Coll., 1975; BA in Econs. summa cum laude, U. No. Fla., 1977; JD cum laude, U. Fla., 1979. Bar: Fla. 1980, U.S. Dist. Ct. (mid. dist.) Fla. 1980, U.S. Dist. Ct. (no. dist.) Fla. 1981, U.S. Ct. Appeals (5th and 11th cirs.) 1981, U.S. Supreme Ct. 1986. Assoc. Howell, Liles, Braddock & Milton, Jacksonville, Fla., 1980-83; ptnr. Commander, Legler, Werber, Dawes, Sadler & Howell, 1983-91, Foley & Lardner, Jacksonville, 1991-93, Howell O'Neal & Johnson, Jacksonville, 1993-96, Howell & O'Neal, Jacksonville, 1996—. Pro bono atty. Legal Aid Soc., Jacksonville, 1980—; practicing atty. Lawyers Reference, Jacksonville, 1980—. Pres. Julington Landing Homeowners Assn., Jacksonville, 1980-83. Served to staff sgt. USAF, 1968-74. Mem. ABA, Jacksonville Bar Assn., Fed. Bar Assn., Assn. Trial Lawyers Am., Fla. Def. Lawyers Assn., Northeast Fla. Med. Malpractice Claims Coun. (pres. 1996), Jacksonville Assn. Def. Counsel (pres. 1999), Internat. Assn. Def. Counsel, Def. Rsch. Inst. Clubs: University, San Jose Country (Jacksonville). Republican. Methodist. Avocations: golf, music. Home: 1299 Norwich Rd Jacksonville FL 32207-7525 Office: Howell O'Neal 200 N Laura St Ste 1100 Jacksonville FL 32202-3500 E-mail: msoneal@hotmail.com.

O'NEAL, MOYA FRANCES, management consultant; b. Boston, Apr. 17, 1943; d. John Joseph and Frances Marie (Monagle) Moran; m. Donald Patrick O'Neal, Apr. 25, 1970; children: Patrick John, Sinead Kathleen, Dela Siobhan. BSBA, Western Carolina U., 1994. Mgr. St. Paul Hosp. Tumor Clinic, Dallas, 1965-70; artisan Moya's Stained Glass and Lapidary, Sylva, N.C., 1984—; pres. O'Neal Mgmt. Consulting Inc., 1995—. Mem. Phi Kappa Phi, Pi Gamma Mu. Office: O'Neal Mgmt Consulting Inc 52 Dixie Ln Sylva NC 28779-7385

O'NEAL, NELL SELF, retired principal; b. Glenwood, Ark., Feb. 19, 1925; d. Jewell Calvin and Nannie May (Bankston) Self; m. Billie Kenneth O'Neal, Apr. 1, 1943 (div. Jan. 1976); children: Kenneth Dan O'Neal, Rikki Devin O'Neal, Teresa Lynn Severson Gordon. BA, Little Rock U., 1964; MS in Edn., Ark. State Tchrs. Coll., 1965. Cert. tchr. mentally retarded, blind; cert. elem. sch. prin. Spl. edn. tchr. Little Rock Pub. Schs., 1961-65; prin. exceptional unit Ark. Sch. for the Blind, Little Rock, 1965-95; retired, 1995. Mem. LWV, AARP, NOW, NEA, AAUW, Assn. for the Edn., and Rehab. of Blind and Visually Impaired (J. Max Woolly Superior Svc. award 1990), Ark. Edn. Assn., Ark. Retired Tchrs. Assn., Sierra Club, Alpha Delta Kappa. Democrat. Methodist. Avocations: dancing, swimming, gardening, reading, writing. Home: 6513 Cantrell Rd Little Rock AR 72207-4218

O'NEAL, PATRICIA JANE, human resources specialist; b. Bayard, Nebr., Sept. 8, 1937; d. William B. and Freda (Ebel) Barrett; m. Ralph L. O'Neal, Feb. 4, 1955 (div. Dec. 1978); children: Michael, Douglas (dec. Dec. 1995), Steven, Darla, Kerry O'Neal. AA, Golden West Coll., 1975; BA in Mgmt., U. Phoenix, 1987. Cert. adminstrn. mgr.; cert. profl. sec. Pers. adminstr. Elec. Equipment Co., Phoenix, 1976-81; exec. asst. ITT Courier, 1980-81; pers. adminstr. Valley Seed Co., 1981-82; mgr. pers. and adminstrn. Kurta Corp., 1982-92; sole proprietor All Ink, 1992-96; pres. All Ink Corp., 1992-96; adminstrv. svcs. mgr. Superior Cos, 1995-97; dir. human resources Soc. St. Vincent de Paul, 1998—. Instr. Rio Salado C.C., Phoenix, 1988—, Phoenix Coll., 1984-87. Mem. Adminstrv. Mgmt. Soc. (pres. 1984-86, Mem. of Yr. 1986), Cert. Profl. Sec. Soc. Ariz. (bd. dirs. 1980-90, founding chmn.), Metro Phoenix Human Resources Assn. (dir. 1992). Republican. Avocations: motivational speaking to organizations, mentoring, travel, volunteerism.

O'NEAL, ROBERT STEVEN, criminologist, consultant, judge; b. Fayetteville, N.C., July 17, 1962; s. Bobby Gene and Brenda Faye (Coombs) O'N.; m. Theresa Angeline Michalak, Jan. 7, 1983. AAS in Police Sci., Wake Tech. Coll., Raleigh, N.C., 1982; BS in Criminal Justice summa cum laude, Western Carolina U., 1987; MS in Adminstrn. of Justice, Va. Commonwealth U., 1991. Pub. safety officer Durham N.C. Pub. Safety, 1982-84; dep. sheriff Wake County Sheriff's Dept., Raleigh, 1984-86; personnel mgr. Burns Internat. Security, Richmond, Va., 1987; investigations adminstr. Va. Dept. Health Professions, 1987-88; criminal justice program analyst Va. Dept. Criminal Justice Svcs., 1988-90, coord. drug enforcement, 1990-92; program mgr. ct. svcs. Va. Dept. Motor Vehicles, 1992-93, sr. policy analyst, 1993-98, asst. dir. investigations divsn., 1998—2001; dir. hearings and appeals office Va. Dept. ABC, 2001—. Pres. Legal Policy Cons., Richmond, 1987—; sr. staff cons. Va. Juvenile Adv. Com., Richmond, 1988-90; cons. pub. policy FBI Pub. Corruption Squad, Washington, 19932001; chief facilitator Va. Strategic Transp. Plan 1994-2000, Richmond, 1994-95. Author: Analysis of the Southern Subculture of Violence, 1991; contbr. articles to profl. publs. Pres. Cross Keys Civic Assn., 1998—2000; coord. Far West End. Va. Zoning Coalition, Tuchahoe, 1997; campaign mem. Kilgore for Atty. Gen., State of Va., 1997; mem. Henrico Rep. Com., Henrico County, Va., 1997—2001. Recipient Cmty. Crime Prevention award U.S. Dept. Justice, Washington, 1992, Commr's. Cup, State of Va., Richmond, 1997, Achievement award Nat. Coun. Family and Juvenile Ct. Judges, Seattle, 1993. Mem. Nat. Assn. Adminstrv. Law Judges, Va. Crime Prevention Assn., Ctrl. Va. Crime Clin., Phi Kappa Phi, Alpha Phi Sigma, Phi Alpha Delta, Pi Gamma Mu. Roman Catholic. Avocations: boating, navigation, orienteering, computer technology, game fishing. Home: 1844 Greenbriar Branch Dr Maidens VA 23102 Office: Va Dept ABC 2901 Hermitage Rd Richmond VA 23261 E-mail: rsoneal@aol.com., rsoneal@abc.state.va.us.

O'NEAL, SHAQUILLE RASHAUN, professional basketball player; b. Newark, Mar. 6, 1972; s. Philip A. Harrison and Lucille O'Neal. Student, La. State U. Center Orlando Magic, 1992-96, L.A. Lakers, 1996—. Appeared in movie Blue Chips, 1994, Kazaam, 1996. Named to Sporting News All-American first team, 1990-91; recipient Rookie of the Yr. award NBA, 1993; mem. NBA All-Star team, 1993, 94, Dream Team II, 1994; first pick overall, 1992 draft. Office: 555 N Nash St El Segundo CA 90245-2818

O'NEAL, STEVEN G. chemist, educator; b. Peru, Ind., Oct. 28, 1947; s. George Buckley and Myra Joan (Alger) O.; m. Cheryl Anne Poore, Jan. 24, 1970; 1 child, Kristina Marie. BA in Chemistry, Wabash Coll., Crawfordsville, Ind., 1970; PhD in Chemistry, U. S.C., 1977. Cert. tchr. secondary sci., Ariz., Okla. Instr. biology Wabash Coll., Crawfordsville, 1970-72; asst. prof. chemistry Okla. U., Norman, 1980-85; tchr. chemistry Norman (Okla.) H.S., 1989-97, Chandler (Ariz.) H.S., 1997-98, Hamilton H.S., Chandler, 1998-99; adj. prof. chemistry Chandler Gilbert C.C., 1999—; tchr. honors chemistry Desert Vista H.S., Tempe, 1999—. Advanced placement chemistry reader Coll. Bd., Princeton, N.J., 1999, 2000, chemistry cons., 2000—. Fellow AAAS; mem. Am. Chem. Soc., Nat. Sci. Tchrs. Assn., Sigma Xi (Okla. chpt. v.p., sec. 1995-97). Avocations: science fiction, walking, basketball, classical music. Home: 1435 W Remington Dr Chandler AZ 85248-1396 Office: Desert Vista High Sch 16440 S 32d St Phoenix AZ 85048

O'NEAL, VICKI LYNN, elementary education educator; b. Joplin, Mo., Feb. 20, 1950; d. Alven Rush Hall and Betty June (Cochran) Berry; m. Larry Dean O'Neal, June 17, 1977; children: Valerie Renee, Natalie Michelle. BS in Elem. Edn., Mo. So. Coll., 1972; MS in Edn., Pittsburg State U., 1979. Tchr. elem. Lincoln Elem. Sch., Baxter Springs, Kans., 1972—. Elder First Presbyn. Ch., Baxter Springs, 1989-91, 92-94. Grantee Southeast Kans. Ednl. Found., 1993-94, 94-95, 98-99, 2001—; named Educator of Yr. Baxter Springs C. of C., 1994; Peruvian Rainforest scholar, 1996, Fulbright Meml. Fund. Tchr. scholar, 1998, NASA Edn. Workshop scholar, 2000, Kans. Geography summer scholar, 2001. Mem. BT-PEO (corr. sec. 1994-96), Girl Scouts U.S.A. (leader/co-leader 1986-94, Green Angel 1992), Kans. Chpt. PEO Sisterhood, Beta Sigma Phi (scholarship co-chair 1993-95), Delta Kappa Gamma. Avocations: travel, walking, reading. Home: 3032 Edgewood Ave Baxter Springs KS 66713-2281 Office: Lincoln Elem Sch 801 Lincoln Ave Baxter Springs KS 66713-2429

O'NEIL, D. JAMES, lawyer; b. Hudson, N.Y., July 24, 1951; s. Daniel J. and Carolyn J. (Schug) O'N.; m. May 24, 1981; 1 child, Kimberley A. BS, Marist Coll., Poughkeepsie, N.Y., 1973; JD, U. vt., 1977. Bar: N.Y. 1977, U.S. Dist. Ct. (fed., so. and ea. dist.) N.Y. 1978. Asst. dist. atty. Dutchess County Dist. Atty.'s Office, Poughkeepsie, 1977—89; ptnr. Whalen Whalen O'Neil, 1989—91; pvt. practice, 1991—93; ptnr. Viglotti & O'Neil, Wappingers Falls, NY, 1993—2001, O'Neil and Burke, Poughkeepsie, 2001—. Mem. Arson Task Force, Dutchess County, 1984-86; atty. CJA (Fed. Criminal Panel Def.), 1990-93. Mem. N.Y. State Bar, Dutchess County bar Assn. Home: 5 Taconic View Ct Lagrangeville NY 12540-5517 Office: O'Neil and Burke 301 Manchester Mill Rt 55 Poughkeepsie NY 12601

O'NEIL, J(AMES) PETER, computer software designer, educator; b. Rockville Center, N.Y., Apr. 2, 1946; s. Clement Lee and Frances Rita (Theis) O'N.; m. Carol Ann Sypniewski, June 8, 1968; children: Kelly Ann, Thomas Joseph. BA in Psychology, Loyola U., Chgo., 1968; MA in Sci. Edn., Webster Coll., St. Louis, 1972. Cert. elem. tchr. K-8, Mo., elem. tchr. K-8, Wis., dir. instruction, Wis. Tchr., student tchr. Sacred Heart Sch., Florissant, Mo., 1968-73; tchr. sci. Waunakee (Wis.) Mid. Sch., 1973-96, chmn. K-8 sci. dept., chmn. K-12 dept., 1984-92; learning coord. Deforest (Wis.) Area Sch. Dist., 1992—. Dir. Waunakee Summer Sci. Program, 1975-91; dir. instrn./tech. Brodhead Wis., 1996-99; designer sci. curriculum computer CD-ROM programs Sci. Curriculum Assistance Program and Elem. Sci. Curriculum Assistance Program, 1990—; dir. instrn. DeForest (Wis.) Area Sch. Dist., 2000--. Feature editor: Science Scope, 1989-96; contbr. over 30 activities and articles to profl. jours. Group worker settlement houses Chgo., St. Louis; mem. Parish Coun.; dir. Waunakee Area Edn. Found. Named Master Tchr. NSF, Waunakee, 1986-96; recipient Tchr. of Yr. award Waunakee, 1984, 90, 92, Kohl Found. award, 1992, Mid. Sch. Tchr. of Yr. award Wis., 1992-93. Mem. Nat. Sci. Tchrs. Assn., Wis. Soc. Sci. Tchrs., Wis. Elementary Sci. Tchrs., NEA, Wis. Ednl. Assn. Roman Catholic. Avocations: computers, sports, writing, jogging. Home: 119 Simon Crestway Waunakee WI 53597-1721 Office: Deforest Area Sch Dist 520 E Holum St De Forest WI 53532-1316 E-mail: jponeil@deforest.k12.wi.us.

O'NEIL, JOHN, artist; b. Kansas City, Mo., June 16, 1915; s. Michael and Emma (Harms) O'N. BFA, U. Okla., 1936, MFA, 1939; student, Taos Sch. Art, 1942, U. Florence, Italy, 1951. Dir. U. Okla. Sch. Art, 1951-65; chmn. dept. fine arts Rice U., Houston, 1965-70; dir. Sewall Art Gallery, 1972-77, Joseph and Joanna Mullen prof. art and art history, 1979-81. Vis. lectr. NYU, U. Mich., U. Mass., l'Accademia di Belle Arti, Rome, Moana Olu Coll., Hawaii. One-man show, Mus. Art, U. Okla., Sask. (Can.) Art Centers, Seattle Art Mus., M-59 Galleries, Copenhagen, Denmark, Los Robles Galleries, Calif., La. Gallery, Houston, Philbrook Art Ctr., Tulsa, Firehouse Art Ctr., Norman, Okla.; works exhibited, Carnegie Inst., Artists West of Mississippi at Colorado Springs, Denver Art Mus., San Francisco Mus., Art Inst. of Chgo., U. Ill., Dallas Mus., Cin. Mus., Sadeer Gallery, Kuwait, Kauffman Galleries, Houston, Graham Gallery, Houston, Wierzbowski Gallery, Houston, N.Y. World's Fair, Pickard Gallery, Oklahoma City, U.S. Art Expo, San Francisco, McCormick Gallery, Chgo.; rep. collections, Philbrook Art Center, U. Mich., Denver Art Mus., Dallas Mus., Am. Arts., Kansas City, Chgo., Rice U., others. Recipient 30 painting and graphics awards. Painting fellow Huntington Hartford Found., MacDowell Colony, Montalvo Assn. Mem. Coll. Art Assn., Southwestern, Mid-Am. art confs., Delta Phi Delta. Home: 4718 Hallmark Dr Houston TX 77056

O'NEIL, JOHN JOSEPH, lawyer; b. Detroit, July 20, 1943; s. John J. and Dora J. (Collins) O'N.; children: Meghan, Kathryn. BA, Trinity Coll., 1965; LLB, U. Va., 1968. Bar: N.Y. 1969, U.S. Ct. Appeals (2d cir.) 1969, Fla. 1979, D.C. 1982. Assoc. Jackson & Nash, N.Y.C., 1968-71, Paul, Weiss, Rifkind, Wharton & Garrison, N.Y.C., 1971-77, ptnr., 1977—. Fellow Am. Coll. Trusts and Estates Counsel; mem. ABA (com. on spl. problems of aged), N.Y. State Bar Assn. (com. on taxation, trusts and estates sect.), Assn. Bar City N.Y. (com. on trusts and estates), Pi Gamma Mu. Office: Paul Weiss Rifkind Wharton & Garrison Ste 1225 1285 Avenue Of The Americas Fl 21 New York NY 10019-6028

O'NEIL, MICHAEL JOSEPH, engineer; b. Ottawa, Canada, Dec. 16, 1960; came to U.S., 1964; s. Robert A. and Mary A. (Duarte) O'N.; m. Elizabeth A. O'Neil, June 25, 1983; children: Michael J. Jr., Brian M., Conor Q. BS in Plastics Engring., U. Lowell, 1982, MS in Plastics Engring., 1983. Sr. engr. Travenol Labs., Inc., Round Lake, Ill., 1983-84; plastics molding engr. Critikon Divsn. of Johnson & Johnson, Southington, Conn., 1984-85, product/process scientist, 1985-87, sr. plastics engr., 1987-88, sr. devel. engr. Tampa, 1988-90, project devel. engr., 1990-91; project engr. Johnson & Johnson Profl., Raynham, Mass., 1991-94, sr. project engr., 1994-97, staff engr., 1997-99, DePuy AcroMed, Raynham, 1999—. Patentee in field; contbr. articles to profl. jours. Mem. Soc. Plastics Engrs. Avocations: windsurfing, golfing, skiing. Home: 121 Lombard Ave West Barnstable MA 02668-1415 Office: Johnson & Johnson DePuy AcroMed 325 Paramount Dr Raynham MA 02767-5110

O'NEIL, PATRICK MICHAEL, political scientist, educator; b. Norwich, N.Y., Dec. 3, 1947; s. Thomas Doyle and Edith (Byrne) O.'N. MA in English Lit., SUNY, Binghamton, 1973, MA in Philosophy, 1979, MA in History, 1981, PhD in History, 1993, MA in Social Sci., 2001. Adj. instr. SUNY-Morrisville, Norwich, N.Y., 1985-90; prof. in humanities and social scis. Broome C.C., Binghamton, 1985—. Adj. instr., tutor Empire State Coll., Binghamton, 1985-91; tour leader, guide Travelearn, Lakeville, Pa., 1993. Editor: Aristoi-An Interdisciplinary Journal of Philosophy; contbr. articles to profl. jours.; reporter, critic, reviewer: Sun Bulletin, 1971-72; editorial asst. ethics and religion sect. Evening Press, 1981-84. Congrl. candidate, Binghamton, 1972; chmn. Broome County Conservative Ctrl. Com., 1976-80, Chenango County Conservative Ctrl. Com., Norwich, 1980-90, Historians Caucus/Soc. Cath. Social Scientists. Mem. Am. Hist. Assn. (life), Am. Philos. Assn. (life), Am. Acad. Polit. Sci. (life), Soc. Cath. Social Scientists (chair historian's caucus), Nat. Assn. Scholars (life), Soc. Christian Philosophers. Republican. Roman Catholic. Avocations: hunting, fishing, chess. Home: 66 Riverside Dr Binghamton NY 13905-2106 Office: Broome CC Upper Front St Binghamton NY 13901-4713 E-mail: oneil_p@sunybroome.edu.

O'NEIL, THOMAS FRANCIS, III, lawyer, business executive; b. Fairfield, Conn., Apr. 8, 1957; s. Thomas F. Jr. and Carmen A. (Therrien) O'N.; m. Nancy D., Aug. 14, 1982; children: Caley Elizabeth, Patrick McGee. AB magna cum laude, Dartmouth Coll., 1975-79; JD, Georgetown U., 1979-82. Bar: Md. 1982, U.S. Dist. Ct. Md. 1983, U.S. Ct. Appeals (4th cir.) 1983, D.C. 1992. Legis. asst. Congressman Stewart B. McKinney, Washington, 1980-82; law clk. Hon. Alexander Harvey II U.S. Dist. Ct. Md.; assoc. Venable, Baetjer & Howard, Balt., 1984-86; asst. U.S. atty. U.S. Dept. Justice, 1986-89; assoc. Hogan & Hartson, 1990-91, ptnr., 1992-95; chief litigation counsel MCI Comms. Corp., Washington, 1995-98; chief legal counsel, sr. v.p. MCI Worldcom, Inc., 1998—; sr. v.p., gen. counsel MCI, 2001—. Bd. govs. Ged. Bar Assn., Balt., 1992; Walters Art Museum, ex officio trustee, 1995-96, trustee, 1999—; chairperson William T. Walters Assocs., Georgetown U. Law Ctr. mem., bd. visitors, 1999—; mem. adv. bd. Marbury Inst., 2000—; trustee The Contemporary Mus., 2001—. Recipient Chief Postal Insps. Spl. award U.S. Postal Svc., Washington, 1988, Letter of Commendation award Bur. of Investigation, Washington, 1989, Spl. Achievement award U.S. Dept. Justice, 1989. Mem. Serjeants Inn Law Club. Republican. Roman Catholic. Office: MCI Worldcom Inc 1133 19th St NW Washington DC 20036-3604

O'NEIL, THOMAS MICHAEL, physicist, educator; b. Hibbing, Minn., Sept. 2, 1940; married; 1 child. BS, Calif. State U., Long Beach, 1962; MS, U. Calif., San Diego, 1964, PhD in Physics, 1965. Rsch. physicist Gen. Atomic, 1965-67; prof. physics U. Calif., San Diego, 1967—. Mem. adv. bd. Inst. Fusion Studies, 1980-83, Inst. Theoretical Physics, 1983-86. Assoc. editor Physics Review Letters, 1979-83; correspondent Comments Plasma Physics & Controlled Fusion, 1980-84. Alfred P. Sloan fellow, 1971; recipient Disting. Alumnus award Sch. Natural Sci. CSULB, 1985, Alumni Disting. Tchg. award UCSD, 1996. Fellow Am. Phys. Soc. (award for excellence in plasma physics 1991, James Clerk Maxwell prize 1996). Achievements include research in theoretical plasma physics with emphasis on nonlinear effects in plasmas and on non-neutral plasmas. Office: Dept Physics 9500 Gilman Dr La Jolla CA 92093-5003 E-mail: toneil@ucsd.edu.

O'NEIL, WAYNE, linguist, educator; b. Kenosha, Wis., Dec. 22, 1931; s. L.J. and Kathryn (Obermeyer) O'N.; married; children: Scott Leslie, Patrick Sean, Elizabeth Erla. AB, U. Wis., 1955, AM, 1956, PhD, 1960; AM (hon.), Harvard U., 1965. Asst. prof. linguistics and lit. U. Oreg., 1961-65; prof. linguistics and edn. Harvard U., 1965-68, lectr. edn., 1968-72, vis. prof. edn., 1978-86; prof. linguistics MIT, 1968—, chmn. lit. faculty, 1969-75, chmn. linguistics program, 1986-97, head dept. linguistics and philosophy, 1989-97. Lectr. bilingualism Wheelock Coll., Boston, 1991—; lectr. Beijing Normal U., 1980, Beijing and Shanghai Fgn. Lang. Insts., 1981; lectr. linguistics Shandong (China) U., 1982-83, prof., 1984—; vis. prof. Kanazawa (Japan) Inst. Tech., 2001--; prof. Summer Inst. on Lang. Change, NEH, 1978; vis. prof. Tsuda Coll., Tokyo, 1983, Kanda U. Internat. Studies, Makuhari, Japan, 1997, Am. Indian Lang. Devel. Inst., 2000—, Kanazawa Inst. of Tech., Japan, 2001—; co-dir. MIT-Japan Sci. and Tech. mind articulation project, 1996—. Mem. editorial group Radical Teacher, 1975— ; author: (in Chinese) English Transformational Grammar, 1981, Linguistics and Applied Linguistics, 1983, (with S.J. Keyser) Rule Generalization and Optionality in Language Change, 1985, (with S. Flynn) Linguistic Theory in Second Language Acquisition, 1988, (with S. Flynn and G. Martohardjono) The Generative Study of Second Language Acquisition, 1998, (with A. Marantz and Y. Miyashita) Image, Language, Brain, 2000. Mem. steering com. Resist, 1967—, Peoples Coalition for Peace and Justice, 1970-72; co-founder, mem. Linguistics for Nicaragua, 1985—. With U.S. Army, 1952-54. Fulbright fellow in Iceland, 1961; Am. Council Learned Socs. study fellow M.I.T., 1964-65; George Watson fellow U. Queensland, Brisbana, Australia, 1998. Mem. AAAS, Linguistic Soc. Am., Nat. Coun. Tchrs. English, Am. Assn. Applied Linguistics. Office: MIT Dept Linguistics and Philosophy Cambridge MA 02139-4307 E-mail: waoneil@mit.edu.

O'NEIL, WILLIAM FRANCIS, academic administrator; b. Worcester, Mass., Mar. 26, 1936; s. John J. and Mary A. (Trahant) O'N.; m. Mary Elizabeth Dillon, Aug. 22, 1959; children: Kathleen, Mary Elizabeth. BS, Boston U., 1960; MEd, Worcester State Coll., 1963; diploma, U. Conn., 1970; EdD, Wayne State U., 1972; PhD in Pub. Edn. (hon.) , Bridgewater State Coll., 2002. Tchr. Worcester Pub. Schs., 1960-68, community sch. dir., 1968-73; assoc. prof., dir. community edn. devel. ctr. Worcester State Coll., 1973-75, dir. community svc., 1975-77, dean grad. and continuing edn., 1977-83, exec. v.p., 1983-85, Mass. Coll. Art, Boston, 1985-86, acting pres., 1986-87, pres., 1987-96; exec. officer Mass. State Coll. Coun. Pres., 1996—. Contbr. articles to profl. jours. Mem. Worcester Dem. City Com., Ward I Dem. Com., 1980—; pres., trustee Worcester Pub. Libr., 1977-82; mem. Mass. Bd. Libr. Commrs., 1984-89; bd. dirs. Worcester State Coll. Found., 2001—. Recipient Outstanding Alumni award field of edn. Worcester State Coll., 1996, citation Mass. Ho. of Reps., 1977, key City of Worcester, 1982; Mott fellow Charles Stewart Mott Found., 1971; Godine Cmty. Svc. medal, Mass. Coll. Art, 2002. Mem. Mass. Pub. Colls. and Univs. Pres. and Chancellors Assn. (chair 1991-92), Assn. Ind. Colls. Art and Design (bd. dirs. 1988-96), Mass. Cmty. Edn. Assn. (life; bd. dirs. 1972-77), Mass. State Colls. Pres. Assn. (chair 1992-93), Profl. Arts Consortium (v.p. Boston 1986-96, pres. 1993-94). Roman Catholic. Office: Worcester State Coll 486 Chandler St Worcester MA 01602-2832 E-mail: woneil@worcester.edu.

O'NEIL BIDWELL, KATHARINE THOMAS, fine arts association executive, performing arts executive; b. Dayton, Ohio, Mar. 23, 1937; d. Charles Allen and Margaret Stoddard (Talbott) Thomas; children: Margaret, Stephen, Thomas; m. J. Truman Bidwell. BA, Sarah Lawrence Coll., Bronxville, N.Y., 1959. Mng. dir. Met. Opera Assn., 1977-86, v.p., 1979-86; first v.p. Met. Opera Guild, N.Y.C., 1978-79, pres., chief exec. officer, 1979-86; dir. spl. projects Lincoln Ctr., 1986-96. Bd. dirs. Norlin Corp.; exec. cons. N.Y.C. Opera, 1997—. Bd. dirs. Lincoln Ctr. for Performing Arts, N.Y.C., Assn. of Mentally Ill Children, 1975-76, Valerie Bettis Sch. of Theater/Dance, 1976-79, Salisbury Sch., Conn., 1982-84; trustee Sarah Lawrence Coll., 1977-86; Westminster Choir Coll., 1986-91, Greenwall Found., 1986, Vol. Cons. Group, 1986; chmn. hon. mems. of chmn. coun. N.Y.C. Opera-Lincoln Ctr. Mem. Assn. Sarah Lawrence Coll. (pres. 1975-77), Chamber Music Soc. Lincoln Ctr. (bd. dirs. 1996—). Republican. Episcopalian. Home: 455 E 57th St New York NY 10022-3065

O'NEILL, ALBERT CLARENCE, JR. lawyer; b. Gainesville, Fla., Nov. 25, 1939; s. Albert Clarence and Sue Virginia (Henry) O'N.; m. Vanda Marie Nigels, Apr. 26, 1969; 1 child, Heather Marie. BA with high honors, U. Fla., 1962; LL.B. magna cum laude, Harvard U., 1965. Bar: Fla. bar 1965. Law clk. to judge U.S. Dist. Ct. (mid. dist.) Fla., Jacksonville, 1965-66; assoc. Fowler, White, Collins, Gillen, Humkey & Trenam, Tampa, Fla., 1966-69; ptnr. Trenam, Simmons, Kemker, Scharf & Barkin, 1970-77; mem. firm Trenam, Kemker, Scharf, Barkin, Frye, O'Neill & Mullis (P.A.), 1977—, also bd. dirs. Vis. lectr. law Stetson Law Sch., 1970-73; mem. adv. coun. IRS, 2001—. Exec. editor Harvard Law Rev., 1964-65; contbr. articles to profl. jours. Bd. dirs. Fla. Gulf Coast Symphony, Inc., 1975-86, U. Fla. Found., Inc., 1976-84, 97-2001, Fla. Orch., 1988—; adv. coun. IRS, 2001--. Mem. ABA (chmn. tax sect. 1992-93), Am. Law Inst., Am. Coll. Tax Counsel, Fla. Bar (chmn. tax sect. 1975-76), Am. Bar Retirement Assn. (pres. 2000-01, bd. dirs.), Phi Beta Kappa. Office: Trenam Kemker Scharf Barkin Frye O'Neill & Mullis 101 E Kennedy Blvd Ste 2700 Tampa FL 33602-5150 E-mail: aconeill@trenam.com.

O'NEILL, BEVERLY LEWIS, mayor, former college president; b. Long Beach, Calif., Sept. 8, 1930; d. Clarence John and Flossie Rachel (Nicholson) Lewis; m. William F. O'Neill, Dec. 21, 1952 AA, Long Beach City Coll., 1950; BA, Calif. State U., Long Beach, 1952, MA, 1956; EdD, U. So. Calif., 1977. Elem. tchr. Long Beach Unified Sch. Dist., 1952-57; instr., counsellor Compton (Calif.) Coll., 1957-60; curriculum supr. Little Lake Sch. Dist., Santa Fe Springs, Calif., 1960-62; women's advisor, campus dean Long Beach City Coll., 1962-71, dir. Continuing Edn. Ctr. for Women, 1969-75, dean student affairs, 1971-77, v.p. student svcs., 1977-88, supt.-pres., 1988—, exec. dir. LBCC, 1983—; mayor City of Long Beach, Calif., 1994—. Advisor Jr. League, Long Beach, 1976—, Nat. Coun. on Alcoholism, Long Beach, 1979—, Assistance League, Long Beach, 1982—; bd. dirs. NCCJ, Long Beach, 1976—, Meml. Hosp. Found., Long Beach, 1984-92, Met. YMCA, Long Beach, 1986-92, United Way, Long Beach, 1986-92. Named Woman of Yr., Long Beach Human Rels. Commn., 1976, to Hall of Fame, Long Beach City Coll., 1977, Disting. Alumni of Yr., Calif. State U., Long Beach, 1985, Long Beach Woman of Yr. Rick Rackers, 1987, Assistance League Aux., 1987, Woman of Yr., Calif. Legislature 54th Dist., 1995; recipient Hannah Solomon award Nat. Coun. Jewish Women, 1984, Outstanding Colleague award Long Beach City Coll., 1985, NCCJ Humanitarian award, 1991, Woman of Excellence award YWCA, 1990, Community Svc. award Community Svcs. Devel. Corp., 1991, Citizen of Yr. award Exch. Club, 1992, Pacific Regional CEO award Assn. Community Coll. Trustees, 1992, EDDY award, 1999, Long Beach Excellence in Leadership, 1999. Mem. Assn. Calif. Community Coll. Adminstrs. (pres. 1988-90, Harry Buttimer award 1991), Calif. Community Colls. Chief Exec. Officers Assn., Rotary, Soroptimists (Women Helping Women award 1981, Hall of Fame award 1984), U.S. Conf. Mayors (trustee, 2001-), League Calif. Cities (pres. 2002-). Democrat. Office: Office Mayor Civic Ctr Plz 333 W Ocean Blvd Fl 14 Long Beach CA 90802-4604*

O'NEILL, BRIAN, research organization administrator; b. Bristol, Eng., Sept. 20, 1940; s. Raymond and Phyllis Mary (Marshall) O'N.; m. Alayne O'Neill, Aug. 31, 1969 (div. Sept. 1987); children: Allison Sarah, Stuart Douglas, Leslie Alexandra; m. Karen O'Neill, Feb. 20, 1988. BSc in Math. and Stats., Bath. U. Tech., 1965. Cons. in stats. and ops. research Unilever Ltd., London, 1965-66; research assoc. Tech. Ops. Inc., Ft. Belvoir, Va., 1966-67; mgr. applied math. dept. Wolf Research & Devel. Corp., Riverdale, Md., 1967-69; v.p., sr. v.p., exec. v.p. Ins. Inst. for Hwy. Safety, Washington, 1969-85, pres., 1985—; v.p., sr. v.p., exec. v.p Hwy. Loss Data Inst., 1969-85, pres., 1985—. Witness at numerous fed. and state hearings on hwy. safety and transp. Contbr. numerous articles to profl. jours.; also presentations at profl. confs. Mem. Am. Pub. Health Internat. Com. on Alcohol Drugs and Traffic Safety, Royal Statis. Soc., Soc. Automotive Engrs. Office: Ins Inst for Hwy Safety 1005 N Glebe Rd Ste 800 Arlington VA 22201-5759

O'NEILL, BRIAN BORU, lawyer; b. Hancock, Mich., June 7, 1947; s. Brian Boru and Jean Anette (Rimpela) O'N.; m. Ruth Bohan, Sept. 18, 1991; children: Dru Groves, Brian Boru, Maggie Byrne, Phelan Boru, Ariel Margaret. BS, U.S. Mil. Acad., 1969; JD magna cum laude, U. Mich., 1974; D in Pub. Svc. (hon.), Northland Coll., 1999. Bar: Mich. 1974, U.S. Dist. Ct. Minn. 1977, U.S. Ct. Mil. Appeals 1975, U.S. Ct. Appeals (6th cir.) 1975, U.S. Ct. Appeals (8th cir.) 1977, U.S. Ct. Appeals (Fed. cir.) 1983, U.S. Ct. Appeals (7th cir.) 1985, U.S. Ct. Appeals (10th cir.) 1986, U.S. Ct. Appeals (9th cir.) 1990, U. S. Ct. Claims 1981, U.S. Supreme Ct. 1981. Asst. to gen. counsel Dept. Army, Washington, 1974-77; assoc., ptnr. Faegre & Benson, Mpls., 1977—. Mem. com. vis. Mich. Law Sch., 1994—; counsel Defenders of Wildlife, Washington, 1977—, also bd. dirs; counsel Sierra Club, Audubon Soc. Mng. editor: Mich. Law Rev., 1973—74. Served to capt. U.S. Army, 1969-77. Named Environmentalist of Yr. Sierra Club North Star, 1982, 96, 97, 98; recipient William Douglas award Sierra Club, 1985, Trial Lawyer of Yr. award Trial Lawyers for Pub. Justice, 1995. Fellow Am. Coll. Trial Lawyers, Order of the Coif; mem. Mpls. Golf, Mpls. Athletic. Office: Faegre & Benson 2200 Wells Fargo Tower 90 S 7th St Ste 2200 Minneapolis MN 55402-3901 E-mail: boneill@faegre.com.

O'NEILL, CHARLES KELLY, marketing executive, former advertising agency executive; b. Springfield, Mo., Apr. 2, 1933; s. Charles Chester and Frances (Kelly) O'N.; m. Kyoko Hirano, June 2, 1981. B.J., U. Mo., 1955. With Galvin-Farris-Alvine, Kansas City, Mo., 1957-58, copy chief, 1958; with Potts-Woodbury, Inc., Kansas City, 1958-61, chief time buyer, 1960-61; with Gardner Advt. Co., St. Louis, 1962-88, assoc. media dir., 1964-65, media dir., 1965-69, v.p., 1966-76, corp. media dir., dir. co., 1969-88, sr. v.p., 1976-78, pres., 1978-88; gen. mgr. Advanswers div., 1971-72; pres. Advanswers Media/Programming, Inc., 1973-78, chmn., 1978-88; v.p. Wells, Rich, Greene, N.Y.C., 1974-88, exec. v.p., 1979-88, dir., 1978-88; vice chmn. WRG-USA, 1981-88; chmn. O'Neill Mktg., Honolulu, 1988—; exec. v.p. Kyoko O'Neill, Inc., 1993—; dir. Colony Surf Ltd., Honolulu, 1990-94, chmn., bd. dirs., 1994. Bd. dirs. Waialae Iki Ridge Cmty. Assn., Honolulu, 1991—, 1st v.p., 1993-94. Lt. (j.g.) USN, 1955-57. Mem. St. Louis Advt. Club (gov. 1981-83), Outrigger Canoe Club (Honolulu), N.Y. Athletic Club, St. Louis Club, St. Louis Racquet Club, The Bridge (Navy League of the U.S.-Honolulu), Labrador Retriever Club of Hawaii, Sigma Chi, Alpha Delta Sigma. Episcopalian. Home: 1594 Hoaaina St Honolulu HI 96821-1345

O'NEILL, ELIZABETH STERLING, trade association administrator; b. N.Y.C., May 30, 1938; d. Theodore and Pauline (Green) Sterling; m. W.B. Smith, June 18, 1968 (div. Aug., 1978); 1 child, Elizabeth S. Kroese; m. Francis James O'Neill, May 19, 1984. BA, Cornell U., 1958; postgrad. studies, Northwestern U., 1959-60. Social sec. Perle Mesta Ambassador Luxembourg, N.Y.C.; spl. asst. Vivian Beaumont Allen, philanthropist; rep. Prentice-Hall Pub. Co., Eastern Europe; exec. dir. New Caanan (Conn.) C. of C., 1985-97. Speaker various orgns. including Lions Club, Exchange Club, Kiwanis, Rotary, Poinsettia Club; apptd. Commn. Small Bus. State of Conn., 1996. Pres. Newcomers, New Caanan, Conn.; pub. rels. rep. Girl Scouts of U.S., Fairfield County; bd. dirs. Young Women's Rep. Club; mem. Gov. Weicker's Com. for Curriculum Reform; mem. community bd. Waveny Care Ctr., New Caanan; apptd. mem. Gov. John Roland's Commn. on Small Bus., Conn., 1996—; bd. dirs., trustee Clinton (N.J.) Mus. Art; bd. trustees, Hunterdon Mus. Art, 2000, Tewksbury Women's Club (program chair). Recipient Service awards New Caanan YMCA, N.Y. ASPCA, certs. of appreciation New Caanan Lions Club, President Bush. Mem. AAUW (bd. dirs. New Canaan chpt.), Kiwanis, Woman's Club of Tweksbury Twp. (pres. 2002-03). Christian Scientist. Avocations: tennis, horses, travel. Home: 17 Lance Rd Lebanon NJ 08833-5007

O'NEILL, EUGENE FRANCIS, retired communications engineer; b. N.Y.C., July 2, 1918; s. John J. and Agnes (Willmeyer) O'N.; m. Kathryn M. Walls, Oct. 24, 1942; children— Kathryn Anne, Kevin, Jane A., Andrew Thomas. BS in Elec. Engring, Columbia U., 1940, MS, 1941; D.Sc. (hon.), Bates Coll.; D.Engring. (hon.), Politecnico di Milano; D.Sc. (hon.), St. John's U., N.Y.C. With Bell Telephone Labs., Holmdel, N.J., until 1983, engaged in radar devel., 1941-45, coaxial and submarine cable and microwave radio relay, 1945-56, headed devel. of speech interpolation terminals which doubled capacity submarine telephone cables, 1956-60, dir. Telstar satellite projects, 1960-66, exec. dir. network projects, 1966-83. Pulitzer prize; scholar Columbia, 1936-40 Fellow IEEE; mem. Nat. Acad. Engring., Sigma Xi, Tau Beta Pi. Home: 17 Dellwood Ct Middletown NJ 07748-3010

O'NEILL, EUGENE MILTON, mergers and acquisitions consultant; b. Richmond, Calif., Nov. 4, 1925; s. John Milton and Vivian Elda (Vogel) O'N.; m. Jane Prigmore; children: Karen, Kay, Mary. BS in Bus. and Pub. Adminstrn., Washington U., St. Louis, 1949. CPA, Mo. Acct., Jeff K. Stone & Co., St. Louis, 1948-52; controller Campbell Holton & Co. (div. Gen. Grocer Co.), Bloomington, Ill., 1953-54, pres., 1955-57; v.p. Gen. Grocer Co., St. Louis, 1957-60, pres., 1960-74, chmn. bd., pres., 1974-83. Founding trustee Food Industry Crusade Against Hunger. With USAAC, 1943-45. Mem. Food Distbrs. Internat. (past chmn.) Home: 8 Deacon Dr Saint Louis MO 63131-4803

O'NEILL, GEORGE DORR, business executive; b. N.Y.C., Dec. 27, 1926; s. Grover and Catharine (Porter) O'N.; m. Abby Milton, June 22, 1949; children: George D. Jr., Abby Caulkins, David M., Catharine Broderick, Wendy Wang, Peter M. BA, Harvard Coll., 1950. Registered rep. Harris Upham & Co., N.Y.C., 1949-53; with Chase Manhattan Bank, 1953-58; chmn. exec. com. Equity Corp., 1959-63, Train Cabot & Assocs., N.Y.C., 1963-76; chmn. Meriwether Capital Corp., 1977—; chmn., bd. dirs. Capewell Components Co LLC, South Windsor, Conn., 1981—, Chemstone Corp., Strasburg, Va., 1984-94, Victoreen Inc., Cleve., 1990-98, C&W Fabricators, Inc., Gardner, Mass., 1996—2001, Bulls Eye Environ., Inc., Bristol, Pa., 1999—, Redox Brands, Inc., West Chester, Ohio, 2000—, BPU Reynolds, Inc., Gregory, Tex., 2000—. Trustee Colonial Williamsburg (Va.) Found., 1966-94, Inc. Village of Oyster Bay (N.Y.) Cove, 1989-99, Ednl. Broadcasting Corp., N.Y.C., 1991—; commr. The Port Authority of N.Y. and N.J., N.Y.C., 1991-99. With U.S. Mcht. Marine Cadet Corps, 1945-46. Office: Meriwether Capital Corp 30 Rockefeller Plz Ste 5432 New York NY 10112-0245

O'NEILL, HARRIET, state supreme court justice; Undergrad. degree with honors, Converse Coll.; JD, JD, U. S.C., 1982. Practice law, Houston; with Porter & Clements, Morris & Campbell; pvt. practice, 1982-92; judge 152d Dist. Ct., Houston, 1992; justice 14th Ct. Appeals, 1995, Tex. Supreme Ct., 1998—. Lectr. continuing edn. courses; adv. bd. CLE Inst., 1996; panelist Tex. Ctr. Advanced Jud. Studies., Austin, 1993. Contbr. articles to profl. publs. Mem. U. S.C. academic honors soc.; law sch. rep. ABA. Office: Supreme Ct PO Box 12248 Austin TX 78711-2248*

O'NEILL, HARRY WILLIAM, survey research company executive; b. Atlantic City, Jan. 30, 1929; s. Harry William and Marian Elizabeth (Kuhl) O'N.; m. Carmel Gullo, Sept. 21, 1952; children: Sharon Ruth, Randal Bruce. BA, Colgate U., 1950; MS, Pa. State U., 1951. Lic. practicing psychologist, N.J. Research analyst Prudential Ins. Co., Newark, 1957-62; with Opinion Research Corp., Princeton, N.J., 1962-87, sr. v.p., 1970-73, exec. v.p., 1973-80, pres., 1980-85, vice chmn., 1985-87, Roper ASW, Princeton, NJ, 1988—. Mem. co-adj. faculty Rutgers U., 1959-64; vis. lectr. Woodrow Wilson Sch., Princeton U., 1980-82; mem. part-time faculty Rutgers U., 1999—. Editor Marketing Research: A Magazine of Management & Applications, 1988-93. Pres. Nat. Coun. Pub. Polls, 1984-94, trustee, 1994—; bd. dirs. Roper Ctr. for Pub. Opinion Rsch., 1984-94, chmn., 1994—; bd. dirs. Coun. Am. Survey Rsch. Orgns., 1981-83, chmn., 1982-83; vice chmn. Rsch. Industry Coalition, 1993-94, chmn., 1994-95; bd. dirs. Market Rsch. Inst. Internat., 1999—; mem. Highland Park (N.J.) Human Rights Commn., 1973-77; bd. dirs. Del-Raritan Lung Assn., 1974-88, v.p., 1977-82, chmn., 1982-84; fin. chmn. Highland Park Rep. Orgn., 1977-89. With USAF, 1951-54. Recipient Maroon citation, Colgate U., 1975, induction into Market Rsch. Coun. Hall of Fame, 1997, Lifetime Achievement award, Coun. Am. Survey Rsch. Orgns., 2001. Mem. Am. Psychol. Assn., Ea. Psychol. Assn., Am. Assn. Pub. Opinion Rsch. (Outstanding Achievement award N.Y. chpt. 1997), Assn. Consumer Rsch., Am. Mktg. Assn., Market Rsch. Coun., Highland Park Rep. Club, Masons, Elks. Presbyterian. Office: Roper ASW 1060 State Rd Princeton NJ 08540-1423 E-mail: honeill536@aol.com.

O'NEILL, JAMES ANTHONY, JR. pediatric surgeon, educator; b. N.Y.C., Dec. 7, 1933; m. Susan Pokorny; childen: James Anthony III, Elizabeth, Kathryn S. BS, Georgetown U., 1955; MD, Yale U., 1959. Diplomate Am. Bd. Surgery (bd. dirs. 1981-87, sr. 1988—), Am. Bd. Thoracic Surgery; lic. surgeon, Ohio, La., Tenn., Pa.; cert. instr. advanced trauma life support. Intern Vanderbilt U. Hosp., 1959-60, asst. resident, 1960-64, resident, instr. surgery, 1964-65; chief burn study divsn. U.S.A. Surgl Rsch. Unit Brooke Army Med. Ctr., 1965-67; resident, USPHS fellow in pediatric oncology Columbus Children's Hosp., 1967-69; instr. pediatric surgery Coll. Medicine Ohio State U., 1967-69; asst. prof. surgery and pediatrics, chief pediatric surg. svc. Sch. Medicine La. State U., 1969-70, assoc. prof. surgery, chief sect. pediatric surgery, 1970-71; prof. surgery, chmn. dept. pediatric surgery Sch. Medicine Vanderbilt U., 1971-81, chief med. staff Med. Ctr., 1976-77; prof. pediatric surgery Sch. Medicine U. Pa., Phila., 1981-95, C.E. Koop prof. pediatric surgery, 1988-95; surgeon-in-chief Children's Hosp. Phila., 1981-95; chmn. of surgery, J.C. Foshee Disting. prof. surgery Vanderbilt U. Med. Ctr., Nashville, 1995—. Site visitor residency rev. com. for surgery AMA; mem. trauma care subcom. med. adv. com. Phila. Emergency Med. Svcs. Coun.; surg. cons. U.S. Army Inst. Surg. Rsch., Ft. Sam Houston, Tex. Mem. editorial bd. Jour. Burn Care and Rehab., Jour. Enteral and Parenteral Nutrition, Jour. Surg. Rsch., Pediatrics, 1984—, Pediatric Emergency Care, 1984—, Pediatric Surgery, Pediatric Surgery Internat., 1988; mem. assoc. editorial bd. Jour. Pediatric Surgery; sect. editor Jour. Trauma, 1983—, Jour Vascular Surgery, 1992; contbr. 350 articles to med. jours. Mem. med. adv. bd. Hope Found.; mem. adv. bd. James Whitcomb Riley Rsch. Found., 1986-89; mem. standards com. State Pa. Found. for Trauma Care. Fellow Am. Acad. Pediatrics (surg., pediatric trauma care coord. Pa. chpt., sect. on oncology-hematology chmn. surg. sect. program com. 1975-77, adv. com. postgrad. edn. 1979-81, exec. com. surg. sect. 1977-80, chmn. 1980-81); mem. ACS (founding, cancer liason physician, Met. Phila. chpt., exec. com. trauma com. 1975-77, adv. coun. pediatric surgery 1977-83, 86-88, 90—, postgrad. edn. com. 1979-82, continuing edn. com. 1981-88, nominating com. 1986, regental ad hoc com. on legis issues in trauma in emergency med. svcs. 1987—, bd. govs. 1990—, com. to study fiscal affairs coll. 1992-93, subcom. on burns, spl. soc. gov. from. AM. Pediatric Surg. Assn. 1992—, coun. on acad. surgery 1993—, v.p. Phila chpt. 1993-94), Am. Assn. for Surgery Trauma, Am. Trauma Soc. (bd. dirs. 1974-78), Am. Burn Assn., Am. Pediatric Surg. Assn. (sec. 1976-79, chmn. edn. com. 1984-87, pres.-elect 1987-88, pres. 1988-89, manpower, trauma and issues and ethics coms.), Am. Surg. Assn. (1st v.p. 1997-98), Assn. for Acad. Surgery (membership com. 1973-74), Soc. for Surgery Alimentary Tract, Soc. Univ. Surgeons (edn. com. 1974-75), Assn. Program Dirs. in Surgery (steering com. 1990-94), Internat. Soc. for Burn Injuries, Internat. Soc. Parenatal Nutrition, Brit. Assn. Pediatric Surgeons, S.E. Surg. Congress (program com. 1979-82, 1st v.p. 1998-99, pres. 1999-2000), So. Gut Club, So. Soc. for Pediatric Rsch., So. Surg. Assn., Tenn. Med. Assn. (del. 1976, 77), Tenn. Pediatric Soc., New Orleans Surg. Soc., Phila. Acad. Surgery, Phila Pediatric Soc., Coll. Physicians Phila. (coun. 1988-91), Portland Surg. Soc. (hon.), Nashville Surg. Soc., Davidson County Med. Assn., James D. Rives Surg. Soc., Halsted Soc. (bd. govs. 1986-89), Alpha Omega Alpha. Office: Vanderbilt Univ Med Ctr Dept of Surgery 1001 Oxford House Nashville TN 37232-0001

O'NEILL, JAMES PAUL, psychiatrist; b. Elizabeth, N.J., Sept. 3, 1958; s. Paul James and Dorothy (Semansky) O'N.; m. Patricia Anne Scott, Aug. 1989. BS in Biology, Niagara U., 1980; MD, U. N.E., Mexico, 1984; MD Fifth Pathway, U Medicine & Dentistry, N.J., 1985. Diplomate Am. Bd. Psychiatry and Neurology (added qualification in addictions). Intern Jersey Shore Med. Ctr., Neptune, N.J., 1985-86; resident in psychiatry U. Medicine & Dentistry, Robert Wood Johnson Med. Sch., Piscataway, 1986-89, chief resident in psychiatry, 1988-89; pvt. practice, Avon By The Sea, 1989—. Attending psychiatrist Monmouth Med. Ctr., Long Branch, N.J.; clin. asst. prof. psychiatry U. Medicine and Dentistry of N.J., Robert Wood Johnson Med. Sch., U. Pa./Hahnemann Sch. Medicine. Contbr. articles to profl. jours. Mem. com. Gov.'s Coun. on Addictions Managed Care Round Table, 1992-93; mem. adv. bd. Cath. Charities, Monmouth County, N.J. NIMH fellow, 1988. Fellow Am. Psychiat. Assn.; mem. AMA (N.J. del. to resident physician sect. 1987-89, Physician Recognition award 1991, 94, 97, 2000), N.J. Psychiat. Assn. (founding pres. resident physician sect. 1987-88, chmn. addictive disorders treatment com., counselor/officer governing coun., treas. 2000-01, sr. v.p. 2001-02, pres.-elect 2002--), Monmouth Ocean County Psychiat. Assn. (pres-elect 1998-99, pres. 1999-2000), Am. Acad. Addiction Psychiatry (N.J. chmn.), Am. Soc. Addiction Medicine (cert., officer of N.J. chpt.), U.S. Life Saving Assn., Med. Soc. N.J. (del. Monmouth County 1990—), Med. Soc. N.J. Residents Assn. (chmn. 1987-89). Republican. Avocations: sports, travel. Office: 813 Main St Avon By The Sea NJ 07717-1023

O'NEILL, JEFF, professional hockey player; b. Richmond Hill, Ont., Can., Feb. 23, 1976; Ctr. Carolina Hurricanes, Morrisville, N.C., 1997—. Office: Carolina Hurricanes 1400 Edward Mills Rd Raleigh NC 27607-3624*

O'NEILL, JOHN, controller, accountant; b. Rochester, N.Y., July 10, 1948; s. Richard and Betty O'Neill; m. Janice O'Neill, Dec. 21, 1974 (div.); children: Sean, Brooke; m. Sandy O'Neill, May 12, 2001; children: Kelly, Cary, Chris, Matthew. BBA, Pa. State U., 1976. Mem. staff Patton Hunter & Co., Asheville, N.C., 1976-78; sr. staff CPA Hirsch Babush Neiman, Atlanta, 1978-80, Smith & Raab CPAs, Decatur, Ga., 1980-84; contr. Blackstone Group, Atlanta, 1984-90, Employee Benefit Trust Fund, Harrisburg, Pa., 1990-96, YAP, Harrisburg, 1996-97, Pa. Food Mchts. Assn., Wormleysburg, Pa., 1997—. With USMC, 1969-73. Mem. AICPAs, Pa. Inst. CPAs, Am. Soc. Assn. Execs. Office: Pa Food Mchts Assn 1029 Mumma Rd Wormleysburg PA 17043-1118

O'NEILL, JOHN H., JR. lawyer; b. Bainbridge, Md., Oct. 20, 1946; s. John Hardin and Lois May (Schnepfe) O'N.; m. Vivian Lidwina Gemelli, Nov. 29, 1969; children: Eric Michael, David Christopher, Sean Timothy, Daniel Ryan. BS with distinction in Naval Engring., U.S. Naval Acad., 1968; JD, Yale U., 1976. Bar: Md. 1976, D.C. 1977, U.S. Supreme Ct., U.S. Dist. Ct. D.C.; lic. to supervise operation, maintenance naval nuclear propulsion power plants AEC. Commd. ensign USN, 1968; advanced through grades to lt. comdr., 1975; officer on nuclear submarines USN, 1968-73; resigned, 1973; ptnr., chmn. energy practice group Shaw Pittman, Washington, 1976—, bd. dirs. Counsel various nuclear industry cos.; cons. in field to fgn. govs. Mem. ABA, Internat. Bar Assn. (coun. sect. on energy and natural resources), Internat. Nuclear Law Assn. Republican. Roman Catholic. Avocations: squash, tennis, skiing. E-mail: John.O'Neill@shawpittman.com. Office: Shaw Pittman 2300 N St NW Washington DC 20037-1172

O'NEILL, JOHN JOSEPH, speech educator; b. De Pere, Wis., Dec. 6, 1920; s. John Joseph and Elizabeth (Murray) O'N.; m. Dorothy Jane Arnold, Dec. 28, 1943; children— Katherine, Thomas, John, Philip. BS, Ohio State U., 1947, PhD, 1951. From instr. to assoc. prof. speech Ohio State U., 1949-59; prof. speech U. Ill. at Champaign, 1959-91, prof. emeritus, 1991—; prof. audiology U. Ill. Coll. Medicine, Chgo., 1965-79, head speech and hearing sci. dept., 1973-79. Research assoc. U.S. Naval Sch. Aviation Medicine, summers 1953, 54; cons. in field. Co-author: Visual Communication, 1961, 81;, Hard of Hearing, 1964, Applied Audiometry, 1966. Pres. Columbus Hearing Soc., 1956-58; Bd. dirs. Champaign County Assn. Crippled-United Cerebral Palsy, 1961-63. Served with inf. AUS, 1942-46. Decorated Purple Heart, Bronze Star with oak leaf cluster, Jubilee of Liberty medal, France, 2000; recipient Disting. Alumnus award dept. speech Ohio State U., 1969, recipient honors, 1979. Fellow Am. Speech and Hearing Assn. (pres. 1969), Ohio Psychol. Assn.; mem. Am. Bd. Examiners Speech Pathology and Audiology (pres. 1967-68), Acad. Rehabilitative Audiology (pres. 1969) Home: 1203 W University Ave Champaign IL 61821-3224 E-mail: j-oneill@uiuc.edu.

O'NEILL, JOHN JOSEPH, JR. business consultant, former chemical company executive; b. N.Y.C., Sept. 13, 1919; s. John Joseph and Margaret (Patterson) O'N.; m. Irene Ray, Apr. 18, 1940; children— Anne, Mary (Mrs. George Schuler). BS in Chem. Engring, Mo. Sch. Mines, 1940, Chem. Engr., 1951. Research engr. Western Cartridge Co., 1940-49; with Olin Industries, Inc., 1949-60, dir. prodn. explosives operations, energy div., 1959-60; with Olin Mathieson Chem. Corp., 1960-71, asst. to pres., 1963-64, staff v.p. planning, 1964-65, v.p. comml. devel., chems. group, 1965-67, corporate v.p. plastics, 1967-70, corporate v.p. product diverification, 1970-71; cons., 1971-72; exec. v.p., chief operating officer Kleer-Vu Inc., N.Y.C., 1972-76; v.p. planning and devel. Vertac Consol., 1976-77; pres., chief exec. officer Vertac, Inc., 1977-78, cons., 1979-80, vice chmn. bd., chief oper. officer, 1980-81; cons., 1981—; pres. Jonco, Inc., 1986-89. Mem. bd. advisors Am. Express Sr. Card, 2001. Contbr. articles to profl. jours.; patentee explosives, chemicals, ordnance items. Emeritus trustee St. Mary-of-Woods Coll., Terre Haute, Ind. Fellow Am. Inst. Chemists; mem. Am. Inst. Chem. Engring., Chemists Club (N.Y.C.). Clubs: Chemists (N.Y.C.). Home and Office: 7 Castlewood Ln PO Box 429 Pinehurst NC 28370-0429

O'NEILL, JOHN ROBERT, airline executive, retired; b. Bronxville, N.Y., Feb. 13, 1937; s. John R. and Hazel (Edwards) O'N.; m. Laura M. Bellmer, May 25, 1962; children: Amy, Wendy. BA, Hamilton Coll., 1958. Various positions in scheduling Eastern Airlines, Miami, Fla., 1961-71, dir. schedule planning, 1971-74, systems dir. schedule planning, 1974-75, dir. current schedules, 1975-80, dir. schedules, 1980-81, v.p. schedules, 1981-87; v.p. scheduling TWA Airlines, 1987-99, ret. Mem. Phi Beta Kappa Presbyterian.

O'NEILL, JOHN T. retired toy company executive; b. N.Y.C., Oct. 25, 1944; s. John and Rhoda (Dillon) O'N; m. Lois E. McGarry, Oct. 8, 1966; children: John, Margaret, Gregory, Brian. BS in Acctg., Providence Coll., 1962-66. Acct. Arthur Andersen & Co., Providence, 1966-67; ptnr. Peat Marwick, KPMG, 1970-84; mng. ptnr. Peat Marwick KPMG, 1984-87; sr. v.p. fin. Hasbro, Inc., Pawtucket, R.I., 1987-88, sr. v.p., CFO, 1988-89, exec. v.p., CFO, 1990—; ret., 1999. Mem. pres. coun. Providence Coll.; bd. dirs., past pres. Jr. Achievement R.I.; pres., bd. dirs. Galaxy Funds. Trustee Women and Infants Hosp. R.I., Providence; treas., bd. dirs. R.I. Philharmonic Orch., Providence, C. of C.; chmn. Catholic Charity Fund, Providence. Capt. Med. Svc. Corps, U.S. Army, 1967-70. Decorated Bronze Star. Mem. AICPA, R.I. CPA Soc., Inst. Mgmt. Accts., Fin. Execs. Inst., Warwick Country Club, Hope Club, Dunes Club, Bonita Bay Club, Univ. Club. Avocations: golf, outdoors, art. Office: Hasbro Inc 1011 Newport Ave Pawtucket RI 02861-2538

O'NEILL, JOSEPH DEAN, lawyer; b. Bayonne, N.J. s. Austin Joseph and Ann (Lynch) O'N. AB, Allegheny Coll.; JD, N.Y. Law Sch. Bar: N.J. 1968; cert. civil and criminal trial atty. Nat. Bd. Trial Advocacy. Pvt. practice, Vineland, N.J. Pres. Cumberland County Legal Aid Soc., Vineland, 1974-87. Contbr. articles to profl. publs. Assoc. counsel N.J. Jaycees. Recipient Outstanding Contbn. and Leadership award Nat. Assn. Criminal Def. Lawyers, 1978-79. Mem. Assn. Trial Lawyers Am. (pres. N.J. chpt. 1988-89, N.J. Legal PAC chmn. 1991-95), Cert. Trial Attys. (bd. dirs. 1988-90), Am. Bd. Trial Advocates (diplomate). Office: PO Box 847 30 W Chestnut Ave Vineland NJ 08360-5401

O'NEILL, JOSEPH F. health science association administrator; Grad., U. Calif., San Francisco, U. Calif., Berkeley. Diplomate Am. Bd. Internal Medicine. Former med. staff Chase Brexton Clin., Baltimore; former assoc. adminstr. for AIDS Health Resources and Svcs. Adminstrn., 1997—2001; with faculty Johns Hopkins U. Sch. Medicine; dir. Office of Nat. AIDS Policy, Wash., DC, 2002—. Vol. physician Hopkins AIDS Clin. Office: Office of Nat AIDS Policy 736 Jackson Pl NW Washington DC 20503*

O'NEILL, JOSEPH J. futures market executive; b. N.Y., Sept. 13, 1943; s. Vincent B. and Catharine (Carroll) O'N.; m. Margaret M. Lyons, June 20, 1964; children: Peggy Anne, Maureen, Patricia, Brian, Erin. BA, Manhattan Coll., 1967; MBA, Adelphi U., 1980. V.p., sec. N.Y. Cotton Exchg., N.Y., 1970-83, exec. v.p., 1983-84, pres., 1984—; exec. v.p. N.Y. Bd. Trade, N.Y.C., 1998—, sr. exec. v.p. Mem. bd. dirs. Nat. Futures Assn., N.Y., Nat. Assn. Futures Trading Adv., N.Y., Commodities Exchg. Ctr., N.Y. Contbr. articles to jours. in field.

O'NEILL, JUNE ELLENOFF, economist; b. N.Y.C., June 14, 1934; d. Louis and Matilda (Liebstein) Ellenoff; m. Sam Cohn, 1955 (div. 1961); 1 child, Peter; m. David Michael O'Neill, Dec. 24, 1964; 1 child, Amy. BA, Sarah Lawrence Coll., Bronxville, N.Y., 1955; PhD, Columbia U., 1970. Econs. instr. Temple U., Phila., 1965-68; rsch. assoc. Brookings Instn., Washington, 1968-71; sr. economist Pres.'s Coun. Econ. Advisors, 1971-76; chief human resources budget Congl. Budget Office, 1976-79; sr. rsch. assoc. The Urban Inst., 1979-86; dir. Office Policy and Rsch. U.S. Commn. Civil Rights, 1986-87; prof. econs. and fin., dir. Ctr. for Study Bus. and Govt. Baruch Coll., CUNY, 1987—; Morton Wollman Prof. Econs. Zicklin Sch. Bus. Baruch Coll., 1999—; dir. Congl. Budget Office U.S. Congress, Washington, 1995-99. Adj. scholar Am. Enterprise Inst., 1994-95, 99—; mem. Nat. Adv. Com., The Poverty Inst., U. Wis., 1988-95. Contbr. articles to profl. jours. Mem. Am. Econs. Assn. (v.p. 1998-99), Nat. Acad. Social Ins. Republican. Jewish. Home: 420 Riverside Dr New York NY 10025-7773 Office: CUNY Baruch Coll Ctr Study of Bus and Govt 17 Lexington Ave New York NY 10010-5518 E-mail: june_oneill@baruch.cuny.edu.

O'NEILL, KATHERINE TEMPLETON, journalist, museum administrator, former nursing educator; b. Moline, Ill., Jan. 13, 1949; d. Morris John and Patricia (Collins) Templeton; 1 child by previous marriage, Carolyn Patricia Coquillette; m. William James O'Neill Jr., July 18, 1987; stepchildren: Alec, Sara, Jessie, Laura O'Neill. BSN, U. Mich., 1971; postgrad., St. Clare's Hall, Oxford, Eng., 1971-72; MSN, Boston U., 1974. RN, Ohio, Mass. Instr. Mass. Gen. Hosp., Boston, 1974-76; assoc. prof. Ursuline Coll., Cleve., 1976-81; dir. devel. and pub. rels. Ohio Coll. Podiatric Medicine, 1985-87; dir. Chisholm Halle Costume Wing We. Res. Hist. Soc., 1988-90; fashion editor Chagrin Valley Times, 1989-2000. Vice-chair bd. dirs. Cleve. Health Edn. Mus., 1983-2000, Cleve. Music Sch. Settlement, 1983-97. Corp. bd. dirs. Hathaway Brown Sch., 1981—, pres. alumnae bd. dirs., 1984—86; bd. dirs. Cleve. Ballet, 1987—95, Cleve. Inst. Music, 1994—, Cleve. Scholarship Programs, 1995—, Mus. Arts Assn. The Cleve. Orch., 1995—; mem. adv. bd. Francis Paine Bolton Sch. Nursing and Mandel Sch. Applied Social Scis., Case Western Res. U., Cleve., 1990—, GAMUT, Cleve. State U., 1992—93; bd. dirs. Dress for Success, Cleve., 1998—2000, Cleve. Publs. Yearbook, 1993—95, Vis. Nurse Assn., 1995—, Cleve. Cmty. Bldg. Initiative, 2001—; founding trustee, vice chair Generation Found., Cleve., 1998—; mem. disbursements com. WMJ and Dorothy K. O'Neill Found., 1993—; trustee Cleve. C.C. Found., 2001—; bd. dirs. Great Lakes Sc. Ctr., 1999—, Ursuline Coll., 1996—; bd. dirs., chair Ursuline Coll. Outreach. Avocations: singing, gourmet cooking, orchidology. Office: Clanco Mgmt Pepper Pike OH 44124

O'NEILL, LAWRENCE, artist, poet; b. Bronx, Apr. 30, 1947; m. Christine S. O'Neill. BS, Mercy Coll., Dobbs Ferry, N.Y., 1973. Painter U. R.I., Kingston, RI, 1978—. Author: With Fire and Smoke, 1976, Daguerreotypes, 1991. Cpl. U.S. Army, 1967—68. Avocation: travel. Mailing: PO Box 9 Carolina RI 02812-0009

O'NEILL, MALCOLM R. aerospace transportation executive; b. Chgo. m. Judy O'Neill. BS in Physics, DePaul U.; MA in Physics, PhD in Physics, Rice U. Commd. U.S. Army, advanced through grades, ret., 1996, dir. Ballistic Missile Def. Orgn., dep. dir. Strategic Def. Initiative Orgn., dir. Army Acquisition Corps, comdr. Army Lab. Command; dep. for program assessment and internat. coop. Office of the Asst. Sec. of the Army; project mgr. multiple launched rocket system U.S. Army, dep. project mgr. NATO patriot systems; program mgr. strategic fire control systems Def. Advanced Rsch. Projects Agy.; v.p. mission success, ops. and best practices in space systems Lockheed Martin, Bethesda, Md., 1996—99, v.p., chief tech. officer, 1999—. Mem. Aero. and Space Engring. Bd., NAS. Office: Lockheed Martin Corp 6801 Rockledge Dr Bethesda MD 20817*

O'NEILL, MARGARET E. psychological counselor; b. Youngstown, Ohio, Jan. 23, 1935; d. Julius and Anna (Zakel) Huegel; children: Paul McCann, Kathleen McCann, Kevin McCann; m. Thomas B. O'Neill, Oct. 21, 1971 (div. 1979). BSN, UCLA, 1961, MSN, 1963; MA in Counseling, Calif. Luth. Coll., Thousand Oaks, 1974; PhD in Psychology, U.S. Internat. U., San Diego, 1986. Cert. hypnotherapist Calif., critical incident stress mgmt., trauma specialist. Instr. Ventura (Calif.) Coll., 1965-69, dept. chair, 1969-74, coord. Women's

Ctr., 1974-79, counselor, 1979-91; marriage, family and child psychologist Ventura, 1981-92, Morro Bay/San Luis Obispo, 1992—. Trainer; cons. County of Ventura, 1984—90, County of San Luis Obispo, 1991—98. Mem. commn. on the status of women San Luis Obispo County Bd. Suprs. Mem.: Coast Psychol. Assn., Rotary Morro Bay, Morro Bay C.of C. Democrat. Avocations: reading, dancing, hiking, walking, traveling. Office: 1203 Main St Morro Bay CA 93442-1945

O'NEILL, MARY JANE, not-for-profit developer; b. Detroit, Feb. 24, 1923; d. Frank Roger and Kathryn (Rice) Kilcoyne; m. Michael James O'Neill, May 31, 1948; children: Michael, Maureen, Kevin, John(dec.) , Kathryn. PhB summa cum laude, U. Detroit, 1944; postgrad., U. Wis., 1949—50. Editor East Side Shopper, Detroit, 1939—45; club editor Detroit Free Press, 1945—48; reporter UP, Milw. and Madison, Wis., 1949; dir. pub. rels. Fairfax-Falls Church (Va.) Cmty. Chest, 1955—60; copy editor Falls Church Sun-Echo, 1958—60; freelance writer Washington, 1960, 1963; assoc. editor Med. World News, 1963—66; dir. publ. rels. Westchester Lighthouse, N.Y. Assn. for Blind, 1967—71; dir. pub. edn. The Lighthouse, N.Y.C., 1971—73, dir. pub. rels., 1973—80; exec. dir., CEO Eye-Bank for Sight Restoration, Inc., 1980—2000, ret., 2000. Mem. N.Y. State Transplant Coun., 1991—; bd. dirs. N.Y. Organ Donor Network, Pro Mujer, 1997—, Found. of Women Execs. in Pub. Rels., 2000—. Named to Top 100 Irish Ams., Irish Am. Mag., 1999. Mem.: Pan Am. Eye Bank Assn. (bd. dirs. 1997—), Women Execs. in Pub. Rels. (dir. 1982—88, pres. 1986—87), Pub. Rels. Soc. Am., Eye Bank Assn. Am. (lay adv. bd. 1981—83, dir. 1983—86, pres. N.E. Region 1993—96, exec. com. 1994—96, EBAA Heise award 1997), N.Y. Acad. Scis., Women in Comm. (pres. N.Y. chpt. 1980—81), Cosmopolitan Club.

O'NEILL, MICHAEL, management educator; b. Washington, Sept. 2, 1938; s. John Patrick and Mary Lou (Maginnis) O'N.; m. Elfrieda Langemann, Apr. 10, 1993; 1 child, Susan Ewens. BA, St. Thomas Coll., 1960; MA, Cath. U., 1964; EdD, Harvard U., 1967. Supt. Cath. Diocese of Spokane (Wash.), 1967-76; assoc. prof., dir. pvt. sch. adminstrn. U. San Francisco, Sch. Edn., 1976-78, dean, prof., 1978-81, 1981-82; dir. fundraising No. Calif. Nuclear Weapons Freeze, 1982; prof., dir. inst. non-profit orgn. mgmt. U. San Francisco, Coll. Profl. Studies, 1983—2000. Tchr. Boston Coll., 1984, Ft. Wright Coll., 1970, 75, U. Notre Dame, 1968, 69. Author: How Good are Catholic Schools?, 1967, New Schools in a New Church, 1971, The Third America: Emergence of the Nonprofit Sector in the United States, 1989, Ethics in Nonprofit Management: A Collection of Cases, 1990, Nonprofit Nation: A New Look at the Third America, 2002; co-author: (with Dennis R. Young) Educating Managers of Nonprofit Organizations, 1988, (with Herman Gallegos) Hispanics and the Nonprofit Sector, 1991, (with Teresa Odendahl) Women and Power in the Nonprofit Sector, 1994, (with Kathleen Fletcher) Nonprofit Management Education: U.S. and World Perspectives, 1998, (with William L. Roberts) Giving and Volunteering in California, 2000; assoc. editor Nonprofit Mgmt. and Leadership, 1989-2000; mem. editl. bd. Harvard Ednl. Review, 1965-67; contbr. articles to profl. jours. Mem. membership com. Ind. Sector, 1993-98, rsch.com., 1989-92; bd. dirs. Nat. Acad. Ctrs. Coun., 1989-00. Teaching fellow Harvard U., 1965-67. Mem. Assn. for Rsch. Non-profit Orgns. and Vol. Action (bd. dirs. 1993-99, pres. 1996-98). Roman Catholic. Office: U San Francisco Coll Profl Studies 2130 Fulton St San Francisco CA 94117-1047

O'NEILL, MICHAEL JAMES, editor, author; b. Detroit, Nov. 19, 1922; s. Michael J. and Ellen Mary (Dacey) O'N.; B.A., U. Detroit, 1946, L.H.D. (hon.), 1977; postgrad. Fordham U., 1946-47; m. Mary Jane Kilcoyne, May 31, 1948; children: Michael, Maureen, Kevin, Kathryn. Writer Standard News Assn., N.Y.C., 1946-47; with UPI, 1947-56; Washington corr. N.Y. Daily News, 1956-66, asst. mng. editor, 1966-68, mng. editor, 1968-74, exec. editor, 1974-75, editor, 1975-82, v.p., 1971-79, exec. v.p., 1979-82, also dir.; freelance writer, lectr., 1983—. Mem. Nat. Adv. Coun. Health Professions Edn., 1967-71. Served with U.S. Army, 1943-45; ETO. Decorated Bronze Star. Recipient Nat. Affairs Reporting award Nat. Headliner's, 1956. Mem. Overseas Writers (pres. 1965), Am. Soc. Newspaper Editors (pres. 1981-82), Council Fgn. Relations. Club: Century (N.Y.C.). Author: (with L. Tanzer) The Kennedy Circle, 1961; China Today, 1976, Terrorist Spectaculars: Should TV Coverage Be Curbed, 1986, The Roar of the Crowd, How TV and People Power are Changing the World, 1993, (with K.M. Cahill) Preventive Diplomacy, 1996. Address: 23 Cayuga Rd Scarsdale NY 10583-6941

O'NEILL, MICHAEL WAYNE, civil engineer, educator; b. San Antonio, Feb. 17, 1940; s. Wayne Jackson and Delores Hazel (Shaw) O'N.; m. Jerilyne Arleen Busse, Jan. 22, 1972; 1 child, Ronald Christopher. PhD, U. Tex., 1970. Registered profl. engr., Tex. Rsch. assoc. U. Tex., Austin, 1970-71; div. mgr. Southwestern Labs., Inc., Houston, 1971-74; prof. U. Houston, 1974—, chmn. engrng. dept., 1989-93; rsch. assoc. U. Tex., Austin, 1970-71. Author: Design of Structures and Foundations for Machines, 1979, (with others) Construction and Design of Drilled Shafts, 1988, 1999 (2nd edition); contbr. articles to profl. jours. Capt. U.S. Army, 1965-67. Fellow ASCE (chmn. deep founds. com. 1982-86, John B. Hawley award 1975, 81, 90, Walter L. Huber Rsch. prize, 1986, Karl Terzaghi lecturship 1998); mem. Transp. Rsch. Bd., NSPE, Internat. Soc. for Soil, Mechanics and Geotech. Engrng. (chmn. exec. com. 1994-95). Lutheran. Achievements include research in reliability of load transfer on drilled shafts, interaction among piles in a group. E-mail: oneill@uh.edu.

O'NEILL, PAUL HENRY, secretary of the United States Treasury; b. St. Louis, Dec. 4, 1935; s. John Paul and Gaynald Elsie (Irvin) O'N.; m. Nancy Jo Wolfe, Sept. 4, 1955; children: Patricia, Margaret, Julie, Paul Henry. BA, Fresno State Coll., 1960; Haynes Found. fellow, Claremont Grad. Sch., 1960-61; postgrad., George Washington U., 1962-65; MPA, Ind. U., 1966; hon. degree, Clarkson U., 1993, Edinboro U., 1997, California U. Pa., 1998, Duquesne U., 1999, Calif. State U., Fresno, 1999. Site engr. Morrison-Knudsen, Inc., Anchorage, 1955-57; systems analyst VA, Washington, 1961-66; budget examiner Bur. of Budget, 1967-69; chief human resources program div. U.S. Govt. Office of Mgmt. and Budget, 1969-70, asst. dir., 1971-72, assoc. dir., 1973-74, dep. dir., 1974-77; v.p. Internat. Paper Co., N.Y.C., 1977-81, sr. v.p., 1981-85, pres., dir., 1985-87; CEO Alcoa Inc., Pitts., 1987-99, chmn., 1987-2000; sec. of the treas U.S. Dept. of the Treas, Wash., 2001—. Chmn. Pres.'s Edn. Policy Adv. Com., 1989—92. Bd. dirs. Gerald R. Ford Found., 1981—, Recipient Nat. Inst. Pub. Affairs Career Edn. award, 1965, William A. Jump Meritorious award, 1971; Fellow Nat. Inst. Pub. Affairs, 1966 Mem. Bus. Coun., Nat. Acad. Social Ins. (founding mem.), Inst. Internat. Econs., Mgmt. Exec. Soc. Methodist. Office: US Dept Treasury 1500 Pennsylvania Ave NW Washington DC 20220*

O'NEILL, PAUL JOHN, retired psychology educator; b. Taunton, Mass., Apr. 12, 1936; s. Clarence Bernard and Edna Mary (Burke) O'N.; 1 child, Maureen Kelly O'Neill. *Paul O'Neill's great grandfather, John James O'Neill (born 1829, Antrim, Ireland), immigrated to Taunton, Massachusetts where, in 1853, he married Agnes McGuiness (born 1829, County Down, Ireland). They both died in 1903. His grandfather, Daniel Augustus O'Neill (born 1857, Taunton), where, in 1880, he married Sarah Jane Farley (born 1860, Roxbury, Massachusetts). They resided in Taunton until they both died in 1929. His grandfather, Robert Michael Burke (born 1868, Londonderry, Ireland), immigrated to New Bedford, Massachusetts and married Annie Philamena Whalen (born 1872, Warren, Rhode Island). Annie died in 1934, and Robert died in 1950.* BA, St. Bonaventure (N.Y.) U., 1960; MA, Boston U., 1961; EdD, U. Ga., 1973. Lic. psychologist. Prof. psychology Jackson (Miss.) State U., 1972-93, dir. critical thinking and outcome measures program, 1987-93. Contbr. articles to profl. jours. With U.S. Army, 1954-56, Germany. Home: 7005 Copper Cv Ridgeland MS 39157-1044 E-mail: pj31957@yahoo.com.

O'NEILL, PHILIP DANIEL, JR. lawyer, educator; b. Boston, Sept. 19, 1951; s. Philip Daniel Sr. and Alice Maureen (Driscoll) O'N.; m. Lisa G. Arrowood, June 25, 1983; children: Alexander Edwin, Sean Matthew, Madeleine Clarice. BA, Hamilton Coll., 1973; JD cum laude, Boston Coll., 1977. Bar: Mass. 1977, N.Y. 1985, R.I. 1988. Assoc. Hale and Dorr, Boston, 1977-83, ptnr., 1983-87, Edwards & Angell, Boston, 1987—. Adj. rsch. fellow John F. Kennedy Sch. Govt., Ctr. for Sci. and Internat. Affairs Harvard U., 1983—86; adj. prof. law Boston U., 1992, 2001—, Boston Coll., 1988—; cons. Arms Control and Disarmament Agy. U.S. Dept. Def., 1983—84; guest lectr., commentator Boston Coll. Law Sch., Kennedy Sch. Govt., 1985, Boston U. Law Sch., 1990—91, Harvard Law Sch., 1994—95, 1998; current or past internat. and domestic comml. arbitrator Am. Arbiration Assn., Hong Kong Ctr. for Internat. Arbitration, N.Am. Free Trade Agreement, Internat. C. of C., London Ct. Internat. Arbitration, Stockholm and Milan Arb. Ctrs., Euro-Arab C. of C, World Intellectual Property Orgn.; panelist in internat. and domestic legal programs. Contbr. chpts. to books and articles to profl. jours. Fellow Chartered Inst. Arbitrators (Eng.); mem. ABA, Internat. Law Assn. (chmn. am. br. arbitration com. 1985-89, rep. internat. arbitration com. 1989—), Boston Bar Assn. (chmn. internat. law sect. 1994-96, past chmn. internat. litigation and arbitration com.), Am. Soc. Internat. Law. Home: 11 Blackburnian Rd Lincoln MA 01773-4317 Office: Edwards & Angell 101 Federal St Fl 23 Boston MA 02110-1800

O'NEILL, RALPH JAMES, lawyer; b. Berkeley, Calif., Apr. 12, 1958; s. Ralph James and Samantha Ann O'Neill; m. Andrea Lea Yuen, aug. 13, 1989; 1 child, Alyssa. AB, U. Calif., Berkeley, 1982; JD, U. Calif., 1987. Bar: Hawaii 1988, Calif. 1998. Ptnr. Reid Richards & Miyagi, Honolulu, 1993-98, MacDonald Rudy & Byrns, Honolulu, 1998—. Mem. ABA, Hawaii State Bar Assn., Rotary Internat. Avocations: reading, computers, kayaking, running. Office: MacDonald Rudy & Byrns 1001 Bishop St Honolulu HI 96813-3429

O'NEILL, ROBERT CHARLES, inventor, consultant; b. Buffalo, Dec. 3, 1923; s. Albert T. and Helen (Lynch) O'N.; m. Agnes Balischak; 1 dau., Eileen Anne. BS in Chemistry, Rensselaer Poly. Inst., 1945; PhD in Organic Chemistry, Mass. Inst. Tech., 1950. Sr. chemist Merck & Co., Inc., Rahway, N.J., 1950-56, marketing devel. specialist, 1956-58; v.p. Stauffer Pharms. div. Stauffer Chem. Co., N.Y.C., 1958-61; v.p., dir. R & D Cooper Labs., Inc., 1961-70, exec. v.p., 1970-76, gen. mgr., 1975-76, pres., 1976-77, also dir. Cons., inventor, 1977— Contbr. articles to profl. jours.; patentee in field. Served with USNR, 1943-46. Mem. Am. Chem. Soc., Chemists Club N.Y. Home: 10 Whitlaw Close Chappaqua NY 10514-1008

O'NEILL, ROBERT EDWARD, business journal editor; b. N.Y.C., Aug. 30, 1925; s. Joseph Michael and Ethel Agnes (Seymour) O'N.; m. Phyllis Ann Schreck, Apr. 19, 1952; children: Keith, Kathy, Kim, Karen. BA in Journalism, Syracuse (N.Y.) U., 1950. Reporter Southeasterner, Long Island, N.Y., 1950-51; rep. Bklyn. Daily, 1952; asso. editor Progressive Grocer, N.Y.C., 1952-62, sr. editor, 1962-69, exec. editor, 1970-86; editor in chief Monitor mag., Stamford, Conn., 1986-92; editorial dir. Progressive Grocer. Dir. Sopro Foods, Inc. Contbg. author/editor: Foodtown Study, 1954, Super Valu Study, 1957, Dillon Study, 1959, Colonial Study, 1961, Outstanding New Super Markets, 1961, Consumer Dynamics, 1963, A & P Study, 1970, Merchandising in Action, 1972, Consumer Behavior Study, 1976, Brand Power Study, 1977. Served with USN, 1944-47. Mem. Am. Bus. Press (editorial com. 1974-75, co-winner, Jesse H. Neal award 1961, 66, 74, 89, 90, Points of Light award 1991), Glacier Hills Assn. (pres. 1964-66), Sigma Delta Chi. Clubs: Overseas Press. Home: 67 Moraine Rd Morris Plains NJ 07950-2752 Office: O'Neill Assocs 67 Moraine Rd Morris Plains NJ 07950-2752 E-mail: lefcadio@optonline.net.

O'NEILL, RUSSELL RICHARD, engineering educator; b. Chgo., June 6, 1916; s. Dennis Alysious and Florence Agnes (Mathurin) O'N.; m. Margaret Bock, Dec. 15, 1939; children: Richard A., John R.; m. Sallie Boyd, June 30, 1967. BSME, U. Calif., Berkeley, MSME, 1940; PhD, UCLA, 1956. Registered profl. engr., Calif. Design engr. Dowell, Inc., Midland, Mich., 1940-41; design engr. Dow Chem. Co., 1941-44, Airesearch Mfg. Co., Los Angeles, 1944-46; lectr. engrng. UCLA, 1946-56, prof. engrng., 1956, asst. dean engrng., 1956-61, assoc. dean, 1961-73, acting dean, 1965-66, dean, 1974-83, dean emeritus, 1983—; staff engr. NAS-NRC, 1954; dir. Data Design Labs., 1977-86, dir. emeritus, 1986—. Mem. engrng. task force Space Era Edn. Study Fla. Bd. Control, 1963; mem. regional Export Expansion Coun. Dept. Commerce, 1960-66, Los Angeles Mayor's Space Adv. Com., 1964-69; mem. Maritime Transp. Rsch. Bd., 1974-81; bd. advisers Naval Postgrad. Sch., 1976-84; mem. Nat. Nuclear Accreditation Bd., 1983-88; mem. accrediting bd. Dept. Energy, 1992—. Trustee West Coast U., 1981-90; bd. dirs. Western region United Way, 1982-90. Mem. NAE, Am. Soc. Engrng. Edn., Sigma Xi, Tau Beta Pi. Home: 15430 Longbow Dr Sherman Oaks CA 91403-4910 Office: UCLA HSSEAS Box 951600 Los Angeles CA 90095-1600 E-mail: russ@ea.ucla.edu.

O'NEILL, SALLIE BOYD, educational consultant, business owner, sculptor; b. Ft. Lauderdale, Fla., Feb. 17, 1926; d. Howard Prindle and Sarah Frances (Clark) Boyd; AA, Stephens Coll., 1945; m. Roger H. Noden, July 8, 1945; children: Stephanie Ann Ballard, Ross Hopkins Noden; m. Russell R. O'Neill, June 30, 1967. Course coord. UCLA Extension, 1960-72, specialist continuing edn. dept. human devel., acad. appointment, 1972-83; pres. Learning Adventures, Inc., 1985-86; v.p., CFO The Learning Network, Inc., 1985-86; ednl. cons., 1986—; sculptor, 1987—. Bd. dirs. Everywoman's Village, Sherman Oaks, Calif., 1988-98, v.p. 1993-95. Mem. Women in Bus. (founding mem., v.p., bd. dirs. 1976-77, 86-87), Golden State Sculpture Assn., UCLA Assn. Acad. Women. Democrat. Home: 15430 Longbow Dr Sherman Oaks CA 91403-4910

O'NEILL, SHEILA, principal; Prin. Cor Jesu Acad., St. Louis. Recipient Blue Ribbon award U.S. Dept. Edn., 1990-91. Office: Cor Jesu Acad 10230 Gravois Rd Saint Louis MO 63123-4099

O'NEILL, THOMAS NEWMAN, JR. federal judge; b. Hanover, Pa., July 6, 1928; s. Thomas Newman and Emma (Cornpropst) O'N.; m. Jeanne M. Corr., Feb. 4, 1961; children: Caroline Jeanne, Thomas Newman, III, Ellen Gitt. AB magna cum laude, Catholic U. Am., 1950; LL.B. magna cum laude, U. Pa., 1953; postgrad. (Fulbright grantee), London Sch. Econs., 1955-56. Bar: Pa. 1954, U.S. Supreme Ct. 1959. Law clk. to Judge Herbert F. Goodrich U.S. Ct. Appeals (3d cir.), 1953-54; to Justice Harold H. Burton U.S. Supreme Ct., 1954-55; assoc. Montgomery, McCracken, Walker & Rhoads, Phila., 1956-63, ptnr., 1963-83; judge U.S. Dist. Ct. (ea. dist.) Pa., 1983—; counsel 1st and 2d Pa. Legis. Reapportionment Commns., 1971, 81. Lectr. U. Pa. Law Sch., 1973 Articles editor: U. Pa. Law Rev, 1952-53. Former trustee Lawyers Com. for Civil Rights Under Law; former mem. Gov.'s Trial Ct. Nominating Commn. for Phila. County; former mem. bd. overseers U. Pa. Mus. Fellow Am. Coll. Trial Lawyers; mem. Am. Law Inst. (life), Phila. Bar Assn. (chancellor 1976), Pa. Bar Assn. (gov. 1978-81), U. Pa. Law Alumni Soc. (pres. 1976-77), Pa. Conf. County Bar Officers (pres. 1981-82), Am. Inn of Ct. (founding chmn. U. Pa.), Order of Coif (pres. U. Pa. chpt. 1971-73), Merion Cricket Club, Edgemere Club, Broadacres Trouting Assn., Phi Beta Kappa, Phi Eta Sigma. Office: US Dist Ct 4007 US Courthouse 601 Market St Philadelphia PA 19106-1713

O'NEILL, THOMAS TYRONE, lawyer; b. Wichita, Kans., June 9, 1956; s. John Joseph and Dorothy Marie O'Neill; 1 child, Allison Rutherford Jones. BS in Geology, U. Kans., 1983, JD, 1986. Bar: Kans. 1986, U.S. Dist. Ct. Kans. 1986, U.S. Ct. Appeals (10th cir.) 1990. Assoc. Carson & Fields, Kansas City, Kans., 1987-91, ptnr., 1991-96, Carson & O'Neill, Kansas City, 1997—. Republican. Avocations: snow skiing, travel. Office: Carson & O'Neill 753 State Ave #460 Kansas City KS 66101

O'NEILL, TIMOTHY P. lawyer; b. Shotts, Scotland, Sept. 23, 1940; came to U.S., 1953; s. Thomas P. and Catherine (O'Connor) O'N.; m. Maria E. Karagianis, May 19, 1982; children: Katherine, Elizabeth. STB, Gregorian U., Rome, 1965; MA, Brandeis U., 1970; JD, Boston U., 1971. Bar: Mass. 1972, U.S. Dist. Ct. Mass. 1982, U.S. Ct. Appeals (1st cir.) 1982. Asst. dist. atty. Suffolk County, Mass., 1972-81; assoc. Driscoll and Gillespie, Lynn, 1981-83; ptnr. Murphy, DeMarco & O'Neill, Boston, 1983-93, Hanify & King, P.C., Boston, 1993—. Clin. supr. Sch. Law Harvard U., Cambridge, Mass., 1976-81; lectr. Mass. Continuing Legal Edn., 1988—. Chmn. fin. com. City of Boston, 1984-86. Recipient Disting. Prosecutor award Citizens for Decency Through Law, Phoenix, 1981. Mem. ABA, Internat. Assn. Defense Coun., Mass. Bar Assn., Inns Ct. Avocations: skiing, reading, classical music. Home: 145 Dudley Ln Milton MA 02186-4019 Office: Hanify & King PC One Federal St Boston MA 02110

O'NEILL, WILLIAM LAWRENCE, history educator; b. Big Rapids, Mich., Apr. 18, 1935; s. John Patrick and Helen Elizabeth (Marsh) O'N.; m. Elizabeth Carol Knollmueller, Aug. 20, 1960; children: Cassandra Leigh, Catherine Lorraine. AB, U. Mich., 1957; MA, U. Calif., Berkeley, 1958, PhD, 1963. Asst. prof. history U. Colo., 1964-66; asst. prof. U. Wis., 1966-69, asso. prof., 1969-71; prof. Rutgers U., New Brunswick, N.J., 1971—. Vis. asst. prof. U. Pitts., 1963-64; vis. asso. prof. U. Pa., 1969-70 Author: Divorce in the Progressive Era, 1967, Everyone Was Brave: The Rise and Fall of Feminism in America, 1969, rev. and repub. as: Feminism in America: A History, 1989, Coming Apart: An Informal History of America in the 1960's, 1971, The Last Romantic: A Life of Max Eastman, 1978, 2d edit., 1991, A Better World: The Great Schism: Stalinism and the American Intellectuals, 1982, repub. as: A Better World: Stalinism and the American Intellectuals, 1989, American High: The Years of Confidence, 1945-60, 1986, A Democracy at War: America's Fight at Home and Abroad in World War II, 1993. Nat. Endowment Humanities fellow, 1979-80 Mem. Am. Hist. Assn., Hist. Soc. Office: Rutgers U Dept History New Brunswick NJ 08903 E-mail: wlohp@aol.com.

O'NEILL, WILLIAM ROBERT, lawyer; b. Rahway, N.J., Aug. 8, 1950; s. Philip Thomas and Mary Ellen O.; m. Kathleen Kenney, Feb. 17, 1973; children: William, Garrett, Elizabeth. BA, Boston Coll., 1972; MA, U. Va., 1974, JD, 1977; LLM, NYU, 1983. Bar: Conn. 1977, Fla. 1978, U.S. Tax. Ct. 1980. Assoc. Cummings & Lockwood, Stamford, Conn., 1977-85, ptnr., 1985-89, ptnr. Naples, Fla., 1989-95; prin. Buckingham, Doolittle & Burroughs, 1995—2001; ptnr. Roetzel & Andress, 2001—. Contbr. articles Conn. Bar Jour., 1980, Bus. Lawyer, 1987. Bd. dirs. St. Joseph Med. Ctr. Found., Stamford, 1980-89, Bus. Press Ednl. Found., N.Y.C., 1984-89, S. Fla. chpt. Multiple Sclerosis Soc., 1991-95, Big Cypress Wilderness Inst., 1996-2002; dir. Econ. Devel. Coun. Collier County, 1993-96; mem. Attys. for Family-Held Enterprises, 1996—. Mem. ABA (subcom. exec. compensation, corps. sect. 1986-88), Conn. Bar Assn. (exec. com., taxation sect. 1983-85), Fla. Bar Assn., Collier County Bar Assn., Rotary (bd. dirs. 1988-89). Presbyterian. Avocations: gardening, choral singing, boating. Home: 263 Ridge Dr Naples FL 34108-2902 Office: Roetzel & Andress 850 Park Shore Dr Naples FL 34103 E-mail: woneill@ralaw.com.

O'NEILL, WILLIAM WALTER, physician, educator; b. Nov. 24, 1951; m. Carol; children: Brian, Katie, Julie, Molly. BS, U. Mich., 1972; MD, Wayne State U., 1977. Diplomate Am. Bd. Internal Medicine, Am. Bd. Cardiology. Intern in internal medicine U. Wis., Madison, 1977-78; resident in internal medicine Wayne State U., Detroit, 1978-80; fellow U. Mich., Ann Arbor, 1980-82, instr. internal medicine, 1982-83, asst. prof., 1983-86, assoc. prof., 1986-87; dir. cardiac catheterization lab. U. Mich. Hosp., 1984-87; dir. divsn. cardiology William Beaumont Hosp., Royal Oak, Mich., 1987—. Attending cardiologist VA Hosp., Ann Arbor, 1982-90; chmn. govt. rels. subcom. Nat. Cardiovasc. Network; rsch. peer rev. com. Am. Heart Assn. Mich., 1988-89; chmn. publs. com. Mansfield Scientific Balloon Valvuloplasty Registry; bd. govs. William Beaumont Hosp. Rsch. Inst.; presenter in field. Author: Myocardial Revascularization by Coronary Angioplasty or Bypass Surgery During MI in Acute Myocardial Infarction: New Approaches to Evaluation and Therapy, 1986, (chpt.) Acute Coronary Intervention, 1987, Current Perspective in Coronary Care, 1987, Interventional Cardiovascular Medicine, 1994, Acute Coronary Care, 2d edit., 1995; co-author: (chpts.) Cardiovascular Review, 6th edit., 1985, 8th edit., 1987, Tissue Plasminogen Activator in Thrombolytic Therapy, 1987, Techniques and Applications in Interventional Cardiology, 1991, Atherectomy, 1992, Emergency Medicine: A Comprehensive Study Guide, 3d edit., 1992, Adjunctive Therapy for Acute Myocardial Infarction, 1992, Manual of Interventional CArdiology, 1992, Cura Intensiva Cardiologica, Primary Coronary Angioplasty in Acute Myocardial Infarction; author, co-author: (chpt.) Interventional Cardiovascular Medicine, 1994; editl. cons. Jour. Intervention Cardiology; mem. editl. bd. Catheterization Cardiovasc. Diagnosis; contbr. over 400 articles to profl. publs. Grantee Smith/Kline Beecham, 1989-90, 90—, Advanced Cardiovasc. Sys., Inc., 1988-90, 90—, Midwest Heart Rsch. Found., Abbott Labs., 1990—, Duke U., 1990—, William Beaumont Hosp. Rsch. Inst., 1990—. Fellow Am. Coll. Cardiology (chpt. sec.-treas. 1993-94, reimbursement com.), Am. Coll. Chest Physicians, Coun. Clin. Cardiology; mem. AMA, ACP, Internat. Andreas Gruentzig Soc. Office: William Beaumont Hosp. 3601 W 13 Mile Rd Royal Oak MI 48073-6712

ONESTI, SILVIO JOSEPH, psychiatrist; b. San Francisco, Jan. 3, 1926; s. Silvio Joseph and Johanna (Kristoffy) O.; m. Jean Thomas, May 12, 1956; children: Sally Joanna, Stephen Thomas. BS, Stanford U., 1947; MD, McGill U., 1951. Diplomate Am. Bd. Psychiatry and Neurology. Instr. pediatrics Yale Med. Sch., New Haven, 1956-58; career tchr. psychiatry NIMH, Harvard Med. Sch., Beth Israel Hosp., Boston, 1963-65; head child psychiatry unit Beth Israel Hosp., 1965-73; dir. child and adolescent psychiatry McLean Hosp., Belmont, Mass., 1973-91, dir. Hall-Mercer Ctr. for children and adolescents, 1973-91; dir. child and adolescent psychiat. tng., 1973-92; dir. clin. svcs. McLean Hosp., Belmont, 1981-83; asst. prof. psychiatry Harvard Med. Sch., Boston, 1969—. Faculty Boston Psychoanalytic Soc. and Inst. Inc., Boston, 1971-81. Contbr. articles to profl. jours. With USN, 1944-46. Fellow Am. Psychiat. Assn., Am. Acad. Child and Adolescent Psychiatry, Am. Coll. Psychiatrists; mem. Group for Advancement of Psychiatry (fellow 1959-61, bd. dirs. 1987-89), Boston Psychoanalytic Soc. and Inst. Inc., Mass. Med. Soc., Alpha Omega Alpha. Home: 4 Gray Gdns W Cambridge MA 02138-2312 Office: McLean Hosp 115 Mill St Belmont MA 02478-1048

ONET, VIRGINIA C(ONSTANTINESCU), research scientist, educator, writer; b. Sarmasag, Salaj, Romania, Mar. 17, 1939; came to U.S., 1986; naturalized, 1991. d. Virgil and Eugenia (Marinescu) Constantinescu; m. Gheorghe Emil Onet, Sept. 3, 1981. DVM, U. Agriculture Scis., Cluj-Napoca, Romania, 1966; PhD, Coll. Vet. Med., Bucharest, Romania, 1974. Asst. prof., then assoc. prof. Coll. Vet. Medicine, Cluj-Napoca, 1966-81, lectr., 1981-85; pvt. rschr. Germany, 1985-86; ind. cons. Detroit, 1986-88; rsch. group leader Grand Labs., Inc., Larchwood, Iowa, 1988-92, mgr. R&D dept. parasitology, 1992-95, mgr. R & D dept. spl. rsch. projects, 1995—. Mem. profl. bd. Coll. Vet. Medicine, Cluj-Napoca, 1970-72, mem. faculty com., 1980-81; mem. Exam. Bd. for Screening Vet. Medicine Candidates, Cluj-Napoca, 1974-85. Author: Diagnosis Guide for Parasitic Disease, 1983; co-author: Laboratory Diagnosis in Veterinary Medicine, 1978; author 7 textbooks; contbr. over 45 articles to profl. jours. Merit scholar Coll. Vet. Medicine, Bucharest, 1964. Mem. AAAS, Am. Soc. Parasitologists, Am. Vet. Med. Assn., Am. Assn. Vet. Parasitologists, World Vet. Poultry Assn., World Assn. for Advancement Vet. Parasitology, Romanian Vet. Medicine Soc., Romanian Soc. Biologists, World Assn. Buiatrics, N.Y. Acad. Scis. Avocations: music, poetry, travel, crocheting, reading. Home: 4509 Mountain Ash Dr Sioux Falls SD 57103-4959 Office: Grand Labs Inc PO Box 193 Larchwood IA 51241-0193

ONG, CHEE-MUN, engineering educator; b. Ipoh, Perak, Malaysia, Nov. 23, 1944; came to U.S., 1978; s. Chin-Kok Ong and Say-Choo Yeoh; m. Penelope Li-Lok, July 17, 1971; children: Yi-Ping, Yi-Ching, Chiew-Jen. BE with honors, U. Malaya, 1967; MS, Purdue U., 1968, PhD, 1974. Registered profl. engr. Ind., Eng. Plant engr. Guinness Brewery, Malaysia, 1967; asst. lectr. U. Malaysia, 1968-73, lectr., 1976-78; rsch. asst. Purdue U., West Lafayette, Ind., 1973-74, vis. asst. prof., 1975-76, asst. prof., 1978-81, assoc. prof., 1981-85, prof., 1985—. Cons. SIMTECH, West Lafayette, 1978-85, L.A. Water and Power Co., 1986-88, Caterpillar, 1993-94, Franklin Electric, 1997-98, P Plus Corp., 1999-, PPlus, 1999-, Unibus, 2002. Author: Dynamic Simulation of Electric Machinery, 1998; contbr. articles to jours. in field. Fulbright-Hayes scholar, 1967-68; UNESCO fellow, 1969-70. Fellow Inst. Elec. Engrs. (U.K.); mem. IEEE (sr.). Avocations: gardening, fishing, reading. Office: Purdue U Dept Elec/Computer Engring West Lafayette IN 47907-1285

ONG, HIAP L. research, engineering, and manufacturing executive; s. Eng Seng and Ah Pang (Tan) O.; m. I-An Jennifer Tu, Jan. 25, 1990; children: Christina, Eric. BSc, Nanyang U., Singapore, 1978, BSc with honors, 1979; PhD, Brandeis U., 1984. Rsch. staff mem. IBM Thomas J. Watson Rsch. Ctr., Yorktown Heights, N.Y., 1984-93; dir. tech. transfer divsn., bd. mem. IBM Singapore Inst. Std. and Indsl. Rsch., 1992-93; v.p. LCD Rsch. Lab. Prime View Internat. Co., Ltd., Taiwan, 1993-95; v.p., gen. mgr., chief LCD technologist, Asia Divsn. Kopin Corp., 1995—. Tech. coun. mem. U.S. Display Consortium, 1996-97; display tech. cons. to U.S. and Taiwan Govts., display mfrs. and labs.; chmn. tech. project on liquid crystal tech., 1996-97; adv., mem. internat. confs. on displays; lectr. in field. Editor-in-chief World Sci. Pub. Co.'s Liquid Crystal Series and Info. Display Series, 1992—; editor Internat. Jour. Modern Physics, 1988—, Modern Physics Letters, 1988—; contbr. articles to profl. jours. Recipient 1st Glenn Brown award for Outstanding PhD Thesis in Field of Liquid Crystals, 11th Internat. Liquid Crystal Conf., Berkeley, Calif., 1986; Three Invention and Tech. Achievement award IBM, 1986-1992. Achievements include more than 10 U.S. patents and invention disclosures, more than 90 publications in major international journals, books, and publications, more than 30 invited presentations and 50 presentations at major international conferences. Office: Kopin Corp 125 North Dr Westborough MA 01581-3341 Fax: 508-870-0660. E-mail: hiap_ong@kopin.com.

ONG, JOHN DOYLE, ambassador, retired lawyer; b. Uhrichsville, Ohio, Sept. 29, 1933; s. Louis Brosee and Mary Ellen (Liggett) O.; m. Mary Lee Schupp, July 20, 1957; children: John Francis Harlan, Richard Penn Blackburn, Mary Katherine Caine. BA, MA, Ohio State U., 1954; LLB, Harvard, 1957; LHD, Kent State U., 1982; D Humanities (hon., Ohio State U., 1996; LHD (hon.), U. Akron, 1996. Bar: Ohio 1958. Asst. counsel B.F. Goodrich Co., Akron, 1961-66, group v.p., 1972-73, exec. v.p., 1973-74, vice chmn., 1974-75, pres., dir., 1975-77, pres., chief operating officer, dir., 1978-79, chmn. bd., pres., chief exec. officer, 1979-84, chmn. bd., chief exec. officer, 1984-96, chmn. bd., 1996-97, chmn. emeritus, 1997—; U.S. amb. to The Kingdom of Norway, 2002—. V.p. exploring Great Trail coun. Boy Scouts Am., 1974-77; bd. dirs. Nat. Alliance of Bus., 1981-84; trustee Mus. Arts Assn., Cleve., Bexley Hall Sem., 1974-81, Case Western Res. U., 1980-92, Kenyon Coll., 1983-85, Hudson (Ohio) Libr. and Hist. Soc., pres., 1971-72, Western Res. Acad., Hudson, 1975-95, pres. bd. trustees, 1977-95; nat. trustee Nat. Symphony Orch., 1975-83, John S. and James L. Knight Found., 1995-2002; mem. bus. adv. com. Transp. Ctr. Northwestern U., 1975-78, Carnegie-Mellon U. Grad. Sch. Indsl. Adminstrn., 1978-83; life trustee U. Chgo., 1991—; chmn. Ohio Bus. Roundtable, 1994-97; trustee Ohio Hist. Soc., 1998-2002; dir. New Am. Schs., 1991, chmn., 1998-2002. Mem. Ohio Bar Assn. (bd. govs. corp. counsel sect. 1962-74, chmn. 1970), Rubber Mfrs. Assn. (bd. dirs. 1974-84), Chem. Mfrs. Assn. (bd. dirs. 1988-91, 94-97), Conf. Bd., Bus. Roundtable (chmn. 1992-94), Bus. Coun., Portage Country Club, Union Club, Links, Union League, Ottawa Shooting Club, Met. Club, Rolling Rock Club, Castalia Trout Club, Phi Beta Kappa, Phi Alpha Theta. Episcopalian. Home: 230 Aurora St Hudson OH 44236-2941 Office: United States Embassy Norway Drammensveien 18 0244 Oslo Norway

ONG, MICHAEL KING, mathematician, educator, banker; b. Manila, Philippines, Dec. 16, 1955; s. Sanchez and Remedios (King) O. BS in Physics cum laude, U. Philippines, 1978; MA in Physics, SUNY, Stony Brook, 1979, MS in Applied Math., 1981, PhD in Applied Math., 1984. Asst. prof. Bowdoin Coll., Brunswick, Maine, 1984-91; sr. mathematician, fin. analyst Chgo. Rsch. & Trading Group Ltd., 1990-92; v.p., sr. rsch. analyst First Chgo. NBD, 1993-94; head market risk analysis unit First Chgo. Corp., 1994—, 1st v.p., head corp. rsch. unit, 1996-97; sr. v.p., head treasury bus. rsch. ABN-AMRO Bank, Chgo., 1997—, head of enterprise risk mgmt., 1999-2000; exec. v.p., chief risk officer Credit Agricole Indosuez, 2000—. Adj. prof. fin. markets and trading program Stuart Sch. Bus. Ill. Inst. Tech., 1990—, bd. dirs. Carr Global Advs., 2000—. Author: Internal Credit Risk Models--Performance Measurement and Capital Allocation, 1999; mem. editl. bd. Jour. Fin. Regulation & Compliance, Jour. of RISK; contbr. articles to profl. jours. Mem. Am. Fin. Assn., Am. Math. Soc., Math. Assn. Am., Soc. Indsl. and Applied Math., Consortium for Math. and Its Applications, Am. Phys. Soc., Phi Kappa Phi. Avocations: writing, singing, traveling, painting. Home: 2650 N Lakeview Ave Apt 4106 Chicago IL 60614-1833 Office: Credit Agricole Indosuez 666 Third Ave New York NY 10017 E-mail: michaelong123@aol.com.

ONGAN, NILGÜN ERDAL, decorator, architect, artist; b. Istanbul, Turkey, July 5, 1935; d. Galip and Fatma Zehra (Aliye) Erdal; m. Onay Ongan, July 18, 1981. Degree in interior arch., Fine Arts Acad., Istanbul, Turkey, 1957; Master degree (hon.), Rome Fine Arts Acad., 1963. Decorator TRT Ankara, 1968-80; asst. dir. TRT Istanbul, 1980-92; head decor and fgn. svcs. Interstar, Istanbul, 1992-95; dir. Kanal D, 1995-96; lectr. faculty comm., radio and TV dept. Istanbul U.; dir. HBB TV, Istanbul, 1996. Dir. decor, graphics chief Istanbul Turkish Radio TV, 1974. Decorator for theatrical and operatic prodns., including Hamlet, Rome, 1963, Falstaff, Rome, 1963, Gehrden Castle, Dortmund, Germany, 1963, (film) Bible, Rome, 1966; one-woman shows at Ankara Am. Culture Ctr., 1974, Istanbul Marmara Etap Hotel, 1979, Istanbul Italian Culture Ctr., 1990, Mandir Della Pace Congress, Assisi, Italy, 2000; group exhbns. include Club Internat. de Feminin, Paris, Vichy, Frankfurt, 1966, anniversary Fine Arts Acad. Soc., 2002, Galery Temore, 2002, Internat. Film Festival Antalya, 2002; represented in permanent collections in N.Am., Peru, Italy, Switzerland; designer oldstyle Turkish coffeehouse. Recipient Hon. Plaquette of High Merit, Turkish Radio TV, 1986. Mem. Fine Arts Soc., Fine Arts Acad. (mem. grads. assembly), Interior Architects Soc. Avocations: ceramics, drawing and sketching, decorating. Home: Kucuk Bebek Cad Nurhan Apt No 51/7 80810 Kucuk Bebek Istanbul Turkey

ONGGOSANUSI, EKO NUGROHO, electrical engineer, researcher; b. Indonesia, 1975; s. Gatot Wibowo and Christine Onggosanusi; m. Yenny Onggosanusi. PhD, U.of Wis., 2000. Rsch. asst. U. of Wis., Madison, 1997—2000; intern Tex. Instruments Inc., Dallas, 1999—2000, Mem. tech. staff, 2001—. Contbr. scientific papers to tech. confs. and seminars. Fellow Vilas Grad. Fellowship, U. of Wis., 1997. Mem.: IEEE. Avocation: running. Office Fax: 972-761-6966. Business E-Mail: eko@ti.com.

ONGMAN, JOHN WILL, lawyer; b. Chgo., July 19, 1951; s. John Warner and Helen Will (Dunbar) O.; m. Joanne Patricia Sawicki, Oct. 17, 1981; children: Peter Erik, Matthew Kristoffer. BS, Purdue U., 1972; MS, U. Ill., 1973; JD, Northwestern U., 1976. Bar: Ill. 1976, D.C. 1984, N.Y. 1990. Law clk. to Hon. Walter J. Cummings U.S. Ct. Appeals 7th cir., Chgo., 1976-77; assoc. Sidley & Austin, Chgo. and Washington, 1977-83; ptnr. Pepper Hamilton LLP, Washington, 1983—. Contbr. numerous articles to law jours. Mem. University Club of Chgo., Metropolitan Club of Washington. Office: Pepper Hamilton LLP 600 14th St NW Washington DC 20005-2008

ONISHI, KOSUKE, trading company executive; b. Ashiya, Japan, July 28, 1963; s. Hideo and Setsuko (Takano) O.; m. Masami Wake, Sept. 17, 1993. BA, MA, U. Chgo., 1987. Assistance mgr. Mitsubishi Corp., Tokyo, 1987-98; dir. Azabu Sogo Jimsho, 1998—. Author: Preppy Life, 1991. Avocation: driving.

ONISHI, YASUO, environmental researcher; b. Osaka, Japan, Jan. 25, 1943; came to U.S., 1969; s. Osamu and Tokiko (Domukai) O.; m. Esther Anna Stronczek, Jan 22, 1972; children: Anna Tokiko and Lisa Michiyo. BS, U. Osaka Prefecture, 1967, MS, 1969; PhD, U. Iowa, 1972. Rsch. engr. U. Iowa, Iowa City, 1972-74; sr. rsch. engr. Battelle Meml. Inst., Richland, Wash., 1974-77, staff engr., 1977-2001, mgr. rsch. program office, 1984-92, chief scientist, 2001—. Adj. grad. faculty Wash. State U., Tri-Cities, 1993—. Co-author: Principles of Health Risk Assessment, 1985, others; contbr. articles to profl. jours.; featured on TV program NOVA. Recipient Best Platform Presentation award ASTM, 1979. Mem. ASCE (chmn. task com. 1986-96), IAEA (advisor on environ. issues), U.S. coord. water and soil assessment bilateral joint work on Chernobyl nuclear accident, Nat. Coun. Radiation Protection and Measurements (adj., task com. 1983-96), Sigma Xi. Lutheran. Achievements include rsch. in bilateral USA/former USSR joint soil and environmental assessment of Chernobyl accident. Home: 144 Spengler Rd Richland WA 99352-1971 Office: Pacific NW Nat Labs Batelle Blvd Richland WA 99352

ONKEN, GEORGE MARCELLUS, retired lawyer; b. Bklyn., Aug. 15, 1914; s. William Henry and Lillian Charlotte (Dawe) O.; m. Mildred Ann Tausch, Dec. 13, 1958; children: Jane Elizabeth, Nancy Catherine. AB, Princeton U., 1936; LLB, Columbia U., 1948; LLM, NYU, 1952. Bar: N.Y. 1949. Asst. to pres. Welsbach Engring. and Mgmt. Corp., Phila., 1939-43; mem. legal staff L.I. R.R., 1949-78, gen. counsel, 1963-78, v.p., 1966-78, sec., 1968-78. Bd. dirs. Orphan Asylum Soc., Bklyn., 1958—, YMCA Greater N.Y., 1963-80, Pop Warner Little League, 1976-78; bd. mgrs. Pa. R.R. br. YMCA, N.Y.C., 1957-80, chmn., 1967-80; trustee Bklyn. YWCA, 1976-92. Lt. (j.g.) USNR, 1943-46. Recipient Man of Year award YMCA, 1977; Outstanding Svc. award Bklyn. Chpt. ARC Greater N.Y., 1994, Lifetime Commitment award Brookwood Child Care, 1998. Republican. Episcopalian (vestry 1958-64, 76-85). Clubs: Union League (N.Y.C.), Univ. (N.Y.C.), Church (N.Y.C.); Rembrandt (Bklyn.), Heights Casino (Bklyn.), Ihpetonga (Bklyn.). Home: 215 Adams St Brooklyn NY 11201-2856

ONKEN, HENRY DRALLE, plastic surgeon; b. St.Louis, Feb. 22, 1932; s. John Werner and Clara Ruth (Dralle) O.; m. Deborah Dorsett Smith, June 3, 1961; children: John D., Michael D., Katherine Minna. AB, Princeton U., 1953; MD, Harvard U., 1957. Diplomate Am. Bd. Plastic Surgery. Resident in gen. and plastic surgery Barnes Hosp., St. Louis, 1957-66; practice medicine specializing in plastic surgery, 1966—. Pres. staff Deaconess Hosp., St. Louis, 1986-89. Bd. dirs. St. Louis Christmas Carolers, 1981—; co-chmn. Theater Factory of St. Louis, Webster Groves, Mo., 1984-88. Capt. USMC, 1962-64. Mem. AFTRA, Am. Soc. Plastic and Reconstructive Surgeons, Mo. State Med. Assn., Midwestern Assn. Plastic Surgeons (pres. 1996-97), St. Louis Area Soc. Plastic Surgeons, St. Louis Med. Soc. (councilor 1996-99), Univ. Club, Princeton Club, Aesculapian Club (Boston). Democrat. Avocations: acting, clarinet, singing, collecting old maps. Office: 141 N Meramec Ave Ste 2 Clayton MO 63105-3750 E-mail: donken@artsci.wustl.edu.

ONO, KEN, mathematician, educator; b. Phila., Mar. 20, 1968; s. Sachiko Ono; m. Erika Dawn Anderson; children: Aspen, Sage. PhD, UCLA, 1993. Mem. Sch. Math., Inst. for Advanced Study, Princeton, NJ; prof. math. Pa. State U., University Park; prof. dept. math. U. Wis., Madison, 1997—. Recipient Young Investigator award, Nat. Security Agy., 1997, Career award, NSF, 1998, Presdl. Early Career award, Pre Clinton, 2000; fellow David and Lucile Packard fellow, David and Lucile Packard Found., 1999, Alfred P. Sloan Rsch. fellow, Alfred P. Sloan Found., 1999, H. I. Romnes fellow, U. Wis., 2002. Office: U Wis Dept Math 480 Lincoln Madison WI 53706

ONO, YOKO, conceptual artist, singer, recording artist; b. Tokyo, Feb. 18, 1933; U.S. citizen; m. John Ono Lennon, Mar. 20, 1969 (dec. 1980); children: Kyoko, Sean. Student, Peers' Sch., Gakushuin U., Tokyo, Sarah Lawrence Coll., Harvard U. One-woman shows include Alchemical Wedding, Albert Hall, London, 1967, Evening with Yoko Ono, Birmingham, 1968, Event, U. Wales, 1969, Everson Mus., Syracuse, N.Y., 1971, others; exhibited Fluxshoe, Sch. Art, Falmouth, Cornwall, Eng., 1972, Mus. Modern Art, Oxford, 1997; recorded albums: (with John Ono Lennon) Two Virgins, 1968, Life With Lions, 1969, Wedding Album, 1970, Live Peace in Toronto (1969), 1970, Some Time in New York City, 1972, Double Fantasy, 1980 (Grammy award Album of Yr. 1981), Milk and Honey, 1984; solo albums include Yoko Ono/Plastic Ono Band Two Vigins, 1968, Fly, 1971, Approximately Infinite Universe, 1972, Feeling the Space, 1973, Double Fantasy, 1980, Season of Glass, 1981, Starpeace, 1985, Ono Box, 1992, Rising, 1997; composer numerous songs including Don't Worry Kyoko, Mummy's Only Looking for her Hand in the Snow, Walking on Thin Ice (Grammy award nomination Best Female Rock Performance on Single 1981), Don't Be Sad; author: Grapefruit, 1964, Acorns, 1996; author 6 film scripts, Tokyo, 1964, 13 film scores, London, 1967, John & Yoko Calendar, 1970, (book) Grapefruit, 1964, London, 1970, A Hole to See the Sky Through, N.Y., 1971. Office: c/o John Hendricks 488 Greenwich St New York NY 10013-1313

ONOFRIO, JOE FREDERICK, III, piano company executive; b. Denver, Nov. 26, 1955; s. Joe Frederick, Jr. and Vivien C. (Pigossi) O.; m. Paula Marie Vann, Dec. 23, 1963; children: Stephania, Olivia, Angelica, Sylvana Rosa. BS in Acctg., Bus. Adminstrn., Regis U., 1981. Outfitter, horse wrangler, Colo., Ariz., Mont. , 1969-77; piano tech. Onofrio Piano Co., Denver, 1977-81; mfrs. rep. J&B Importers, 1981-91; pres. Onofrio Piano Co., 1991—. Sponsor Opera Colo., Denver, Colo. Ballet, Denver, 1993—, Ctrl. City (Colo.) Opera, 1993—. Recipient Joseph A. Ryan Excellence in Bus. Adminstrn. award Regis U., 1981. Mem. Alpha Sigma Nu. Republican. Roman Catholic. Avocations: sailing, horses, cycling. Office: Joe Onofrio Piano Co 1332 S Broadway Denver CO 80210-2205 E-mail: onofrio@onofriopiano.com.

ONORATO, NICHOLAS LOUIS, retired program director, economist; b. South Barre, Mass., Feb. 24, 1925; s. Charles and Amalia (Tartaglia) O.; m. Elizabeth Louise Settergren, July 19, 1947; children: Gary, Deborah, Nicholas, Jeffrey, Glenn, Charles, Lisa. BS in Pub. Relations, Boston U., 1951; MA in Econs, Clark U., 1952, PhD, 1959. Mem. faculty Becker Jr. Coll., Worcester, Mass., 1952-54; prof. econs. Worcester Poly. Inst., 1955-68, chmn. dept. econs., govt., bus., 1968-74, dir. Sch. Indsl. Mgmt., 1972-99; prof. emeritus Worcester (Mass.) Poly Inst., 1994. Vis. prof. Clark U., Worcester, 1964-66; fin. cons. Coz Chem. Co., Northbridge, Mass., 1959-95. Contbr. to newspapers and mags. Trustee Bay State Savs. Bank, Worcester. Served with USNR, 1943-46. Mem. Am. Finance Assn., Am. Econ. Assn., Am. Accounting Assn., Phi Kappa Theta. Clubs: Torch (pres. Worcester 1967, 87, 95). Home: 39 Knollwood Dr Shrewsbury MA 01545-3329

ONOVE, DANIEL JAMES, elementary educator; b. Newark, June 13, 1960; s. Salvatore William and Gretta (Knott) O.,; m. Donna Marie LaRiccia, Nov. 14, 1987; children: Daniel James II, Nicholas Matthew, Ryan Michael, Tyler Andrew. BA, Seton Hall U., 1983, postgrad., EdS, 1997; MA, Rutgers U., 1987. Cert. elem. and social studies tchr., prin., N.J. 6th grade tchr. Glen Ridge (N.J.) Bd. Edn., 1990-91, North Haledon (N.J.) Bd. Edn., 1991—. Faculty rep. Small Schs. Com., North Haledon, 1991—, Unity 2000, Passaic County, N.J., 1994; faculty coord. United Generations, North Haledon, 1991, mem. bd. continuing tchr. edn. Editor: Biographical Sketches, 1992; prodr., dir. TV documentary A Video History of North Haledon. NEH fellow, 1992; recipient Gov.'s Tchr. Recognition award State of N.J., 1993; grantee Coun. for Basic Edn., 1994. Fellow Coun. for Basic Edn.; mem. Kappa Delta Pi, Pi Sigma Alpha, Pi Lambda Theta. Republican. Presbyterian. Avocations: reading, writing, ice hockey, softball, philosophical research. Home: 220 W Passaic Ave Bloomfield NJ 07003-5541 Office: North Haledon Bd Edn 515 High Mountain Rd North Haledon NJ 07508-2603 E-mail: onove@northhaledon.k12.nj.us.

ONSAGER, DAVID RALPH, cardiothoracic surgeon, educator; b. Phoenix, Feb. 15, 1962; s. Ralph William and Margaret Carol (Engel) O. BA in Biochem., History & Sociology Sci., U. Pa., 1984; MD, Rush Med. Coll., 1988. Diplomate Nat. Bd. Med. Examiners, Am. Bd. Surgery, Am. Bd. Thoracic Surgery. Resident in gen. surgery Med. Coll. Wis. affiliated hosps., Milw., 1988-94; fellow in cardiopulmonary transplantation U. Wis. Hosp. and Clinics, Madison, 1994-95, fellow in cardiothoracic surgery, 1995-97, lectr. in cardiothoracic surgery, 1997-2000; attending surgeon Meth. Hosp., Omaha, 2000—. Contbr. articles to profl. jours. Recipient House Staff Excellence in Tchg. award Med. Coll. Wis., 1991, Cmty. Health Svc. award Rush Med. Coll., Chgo., 1988; Cancer Ctr. grantee Med. Coll. Wis., 1991. Fellow ACS (assoc.); mem. AMA, State Med. Soc. Nebr., Internat. Soc. Heart and Lung Transplantation, Soc. Thoracic Surgeons (candidate), Coun. Healthcare and Biomed. Advisors. Dem. Avocations: tennis, basketball, skiing, sailing, flying. Office: Cardiothoracic and Vascular Surgery 8111 Dodge St Ste 220 Omaha NE 68114-4117 Home: Apt 204 511 Aurora Ave Naperville IL 60540-6289 E-mail: donsager@earthlink.net.

ONTJES, DAVID AINSWORTH, medicine and pharmacology educator; b. Lyons, Kans., July 19, 1937; s. Max S. and Elizabeth (Ainsworth) O.; m. Sherri James, Aug. 27, 1960; children: Linden F., Sarah E., Ethan A., Jason A. BA, U. Kans., 1959; MA, Oxford U., 1961; MD, Harvard U., 1964. Am. Bd. Internal Medicine, sub-board endocrinology. Intern, resident Boston City Hosp., 1964-66; research assoc. NIH, Besthesda, Md., 1966-69; asst. prof. dept. medicine and pharmacology U. N.C., Chapel Hill, 1969-72, assoc. prof., 1972-76, prof., 1976—, Eunice Bernhardt Disting. prof., 1982—. Contbr. articles in field to profl. jours. Served with USPHS, 1966-69. Rhodes scholar Oxford U., 1959-61; USPHS grantee Nat. Ints. Arthritis and Metabolic Diseases, NIH, 1969-82; recipient Basic Sci. Teaching award U. N.C., 1978. Fellow ACP; mem. Endocrine Soc., Am. Soc. Clin. Investigation, Am. Soc. Pharmacology and Exptl. Therapeutics, Assn. Profs. Medicine Republican. Presbyterian. Office: U NC Sch Medicine Dept Medicine Chapel Hill NC 27599-0001

ONTON, ANN LOUISE REUTHER, chemist; b. Bridgeport, Conn., Sept. 29, 1943; m. Aare Onton, 1965; children: Alan David, Daryl John, Julie Ann. BS in Chemistry, Purdue U., 1965. Lab. chemist Great Lakes Chem. Corp., 1965-67; rsch. asst. Geigy Chem. Corp., 1967-70; abstractor Chem. Abstracts Svc., 1970-72; rschr. Cancer Prevention II Study, 1980-90; chemist Prototek Enzyme Sys. Products, 1992-93; rsch. assoc. Applied Biotech Concepts, Inc., 1995-98, Genaissance Pharms., 1999-2000; mgr. rsch. devel. and prodn. AllExcel, Inc., 2000—. NIH grantee, 1996, 97. Mem. NAFE, AAUW, Am. Chem. Soc., Assn. for Women in Sci. Achievements include development of novel materials and methods for improved electrophoresis and DNA sequencing technologies, development of methodologies for purification and testing of enzymes, U.S.A. Nat. and world medalist in Masters and Senior Olympic Swimming. Avocations: running, cycling, triathlon, competitive swimming. Office: AllExcel Inc 135 Wood St West Haven CT 06516-3700 E-mail: ontonalr69@yahoo.com.

ONUFROCK, RICHARD SHADE, pharmacist, researcher; b. Colorado Springs, Colo., July 5, 1934; s. Frank and Mildred Joy (Overstreet) O.; m. Karen Faye Larson, June 15, 1958 (div. 1980); children: Richard Alan (dec.), Amy Mildred. BS in Pharmacy, U. Colo., 1961; diploma, Famous Artists Schs., 1963. Registered pharmacist, Colo., Ariz., South Africa. Pharmacist Aley Drug Co., Colorado Springs, 1961-75, St. Joseph Hosp., Denver, 1976-77, Navajo Nation Health Found., Ganado, Ariz., 1977-81, Kearny (Ariz.) Kennecott-Samaritan Hosp., 1984-85, NIH, Warren G. Magnuson Clin. Ctr., Bethesda, Md., 1988—; dir. pharmacy, chief pharmacist Tintswalo Hosp., South Africa, 1981-84; pharmacist, chief pharmacist Miami (Ariz.)-Inspiration Hosp., 1985-88. Instr. Coll. of Ganado, 1979-80; asst. in textbook revision and illustration U. Colo., 1961; cons. Heritage Health Care Ctr., Globe, Ariz., 1988. Illustrator Pharmacy for Nurses, 1961, Colo. Jour. of Pharmacy, 1962-64; illustrations exhibited Colo. Springs Fine Art Ctr., 1964-66, Gilpin County Art Assn., Central City, Colo., 1968-74, 1st Nat. Space Art Show, Denver, 1969. Dem. precinct committeeman, 1974-76; den leader Boy Scouts Am., com. mem., 1975-76; fireman, Ft. Ganado Vol. Fire Dept., 1977-81; compassionate med. missionary Nazarene Ch., Tintswalo Hosp. Gazankulu, South Africa, 1981-84;bd. dirs. Friends of Libr., Kearny, 1985-87; active Grace Episcopal Ch. Mem.: Pharm. Soc. of S. Africa, Washington Met. Soc. Hosp. Pharmacists, Am. Soc. Health Sys. Pharmacists, Am. Pharm. Assn., Delta Sigma Phi, Phi Delta Chi. Avocations: traveling, bicycling, hiking, skiing, computers. Home: 12 Tygart Ct Gaithersburg MD 20879-4523 Office: NIH Clin Ctr Pharmacy 10 Center Dr 9000 Rockville Pike Bethesda MD 20892-0003 E-mail: pasquache@aol.com.

ONUIGBO, MACAULAY AMECHI, physician, nephrologist; b. Enugu, Nigeria, Mar. 17, 1958; came to U.S., 1994; MB BS, U. Nigeria, 1981, MSc, 1988. Renal registrar Queen Elizabeth Hosp., Birmingham, Eng., 1988; asst. prof. medicine/nephrology U. Nigeria, Enugu, 1990-94; ISN nephrology rsch. fellow U. Tex. Health Sci. Ctr., Houston, 1994-96; resident Greater Balt. Med. Ctr., 1997-99; fellow in nephrology U. Md., Balt., 2000—. Co-author: Handbook of Physiology, 1999; contbr. over 50 articles to profl. publs. Co-founder Cream Circle League, Enugu, 1990. E-mail: monui001@umaryland.edu., monuigbo27@hotmail.com.

ONUKWULI, FRANCIS OSITA, computer scientist, secondary education educator; b. Warri, Nigeria, Aug. 5, 1955; came to U.S., 1977; s. Chief Mathias Nwafor (deceased) and Mercy (Okonkwo) O.; m. Sandra Anthonia Mgbemena, Oct. 12, 1986; children: Francis Osita, Victor Chinedu, Anthony Tochukwu, Precious Chinenye. BS in Math. and Physics, Philander Smith Coll., Little Rock, 1981; MS in Computer Sci., Atlanta U., 1983; EdD in Ednl. Leadership Higher Edn., Clark Atlanta U., 1990. Billing and credit supr. Standard Bank Nigeria Ltd., Benin, 1975-77; tutor, counselor Philander Smith Coll., 1978-81; math. rsch. asst. Atlanta U., 1982-83; instr. computer sci. Spelman Coll., Atlanta, 1983-86; asst. prof. computer sci., mgr. computer and info. sci. lab. Morris Brown Coll., 1986-96, assoc. prof, chmn. computer sci. dept., 1991-92; tchr. math. Lovejoy (Ga.) H.S., 1998—. Cons. PBT Engring. Co., Atlanta, 1985-86; judge Ga. Sci. Fair, 1989, 90, 93, 94, 95, 99, 2001. Co-author: Computer Applications for the Twenty-First Century; author microcomputer materials for calculus students. Mem. NSF (co-chair proposal review panelist 1989-90), Math. Assn. Am., Assn. Computing Machinery, Am. Math. Soc., Internat. Devel. Edn. Coun. (sec. 1987), Igbo Union (pres. Atlanta chpt. 1986-91), Umuoji Improvement Union (nat. v.p. U.S. and Can. 2000—). Democrat. Roman Catholic. Home: 7544 Sedona Dr Jonesboro GA 30236-2740 Office: Lovejoy HS 1587 McDonough Rd Lovejoy GA 30250 E-mail: DrOnukwuli@aol.com.

ONUNKWO, EMMANUEL NWAFOR, economics educator; b. Ogbunike, Anambra, Nigeria, July 21, 1933; came to U.S., 1966; s. Justin Binyelum and Susannah (Anoma) O.; m. Hazel Herbalene Johnson, June 7, 1969. BA in Econs., U. Durham, Eng., 1960; M Pub. and Internat. Affairs, U. Pitts., 1968; MA in Econs., Georgetown U., 1970, PhD in Econs., 1973. Sr. asst. sec. Ministry of Econ. Planning, Enugu, Nigeria, 1971-73, prin. asst. sec. Nigeria, 1973-74, chief planning officer Nigeria, 1974, acting asst. contr. of planning Nigeria, 1974-75; asst. prof. econs. Fort Valley (Ga.) State Coll., 1975-78, S.C. State U., Orangeburg, S.C., 1978-82, prof. econs., 1987—, dept. chmn., 1988-92. Mem. Nigerian delegation World Bank, 1971; bd. dirs. Ctr. for Econ. Edn., S.C. State Coun. on Econ. Edn., DEEP adv. com., 1988-90. Mem. AAUP, Internat. Agribus. Mgmt. Assn., Nat. Econ. Assn., Ea. Econ. Assn., Nigerian Econ. Soc., Southeastern Econs. Assn., So. Agrl. Econs. Assn. Anglican/Methodist. Avocations: photography, bicycling, reading, music. Office: SC State U PO Box 7354 Orangeburg SC 29117-0001

ONYEJEKWE, CHIKE ONYEKACHI, physician, medical director; b. Ubaha-Okigwe, Nigeria, June 8, 1960; came to U.S., 1978; s. Eleweke and Agbara Caroline (Eloagu) O; 1 child, Chike I. BS in biology, BS in chem., Western Ky. U., 1981; MD, Howard U., 1986. Diplomate Nat. Bd. Medical Examiners. Medical officer D.C. Gen. Hosp., Washington, 1989-95; chief resident Howard Medical Svc. D.C. Gen. Hosp., 1989-90; medical officer Malcom Grow Hosp., 1989-90, Andrews Airforce Base, Washington, 1990; emergency room physician Oakland (Md.) Gen. Hosp., 1991; medical dir. Prime Medical Corp., Landover, Md., 1992-95; pres. Chykod Internat. Corp., 1993—. Mem. Am. Soc. Internal Medicine, Nat. Medical Assn., Southern Medical Assn., Grand Lodge. Avocations: soccer, photography, reading, running. Office: Chykod Internat Corp PO Box 7236 Pueblo CO 81007-0236

ONYEUKU, ALFRED EME, small business owner, consultant; b. Aba, Nigeria, Apr. 30, 1948; arrived in U.S.A., 1974; s. Jeremiah and Violet Onyeuku; m. Felicia Nkpola Onyeuku, Dec. 12, 1987; children: Nasarachi, Chisom, Ngwanna, Udobi. BS, BA, U. Nebr., 1976; MBA, Sam Houston State U., 1978. Mgr. finance U.S. West Comms., Denver, 1980—95; self employed Buffalo Grove, Ill., 1995—97; sr. cons. Internat. Profit Assoc., Chgo., 1997—98; acct. adv. Parks Coll. South, Aurora, Colo., 1998—; mng. ptnr. Interglobe Svcs. Internat., Denver, 2001—. Chmn. fin. com. 100 Black Men of Denver, Denver, 1996—97; chmn. fin. Headstart, Omaha, 1987—91. Mem.: Acad. Mgmt. Avocations: tennis, reading business journals, public speaking. Home: 1513 S Dearborn St Aurora CO 80012 Office: Parks College 14280 E Jewell Ave Aurora CO 80012 Fax: 303-632-7471. E-mail: onyeuku@aol.com.

OOLIE, SAM, manufacturing and investment company executive; b. N.Y.C., Aug. 11, 1936; s. Bernadt S. and Rose (Moyel) O.; m. Marjorie R. Oolie, Dec. 3, 1961; children: Janis Feldman, Caroline Gross, Tara. BS in Metallurgy, MIT, 1958; MBA, Harvard U., 1961. Chmn. Food Concepts, Inc., Rutherford, N.J., 1962-85; pres. CFC Venture Capital Corp., Fairfield, 1984-90; chmn. Oolie Enterprises, Upper Saddle River, 1985—; vice chmn. Am. Mobile, Inc., Secaucus, 1986-89; chmn. The Nostalgia Network, N.Y.C., 1987-90, New Thermal Corp., Keasbey, N.J., 1991-95, NoFire Tech., Inc., Upper Saddle River, 1995—. Bd. dirs. Comverse Tech., N.Y.C., NCT Group (formerly Noise Cancellation Tech.), Stamford, Conn. Mem. exec. com. State of N.J.-Israel Commn., 1989-93; commr. Essex County Improvement Authority, 1987-88; trustee Coun. Jewish Fedns., 1986—; bd. govs. Haifa U., 1986-90, 93-95; trustee Garden State Cancer Ctr., 1989-96, Beth Israel Med. Ctr., 1990-96, Assn. Reform Zionists Am., 1990-97, Am. Joint Distbn. Com., 1990-98; pres. United Jewish Fedn. Met. West N.J., 1988-90; vice chmn. United Jewish Appeal, 1986-96; chmn. Beth Israel Health Care Found., 1993-96. Recipient Gates of Jerusalem award Boys Town of Jerusalem, 1990, Israel 40th Ann. medal State of Israel Bonds, 1988. Mem. Harvard Club. Avocations: golf, numismatics. Office: 21 Industrial Ave Upper Saddle River NJ 07458 E-mail: SamOolie@cs.com.

OOMMEN, GEORGE, architect, painter; b. Munnar, India, Feb. 27, 1942; arrived in U.S., 1968; s. George and Achy (Abraham) O.; children: Mia, Christie, Sarah. BArch, Delhi U., 1964; MArch in Urban Design, Harvard U., 1970. Registered arch., planner. Prin. Khanna, Oommen, Jain, New Delhi, 1964-65, George Oommen & Assocs., Mepral, Kerala, India, 1964-67; archtl. designer Ewing Miller Assocs., Terre Haute, Ind., 1967-68; project planner Harvard U., Cambridge, Mass., 1970-72, planning officer, 1972-79, spl. asst. to v.p. adminstrn., 1979-84, critic Grad. Sch. Design, 1973-74, faculty Grad.

Sch. Design and Continuing Edn., 1983—, sr. property devel. officer Planning Group, 1984-95, sr. project mgr. Harvard Planning & Real Estate, 1995—. Faculty Boston Archtl. Ctr., 1970-73, Babson Exec. Edn. Program, 1985-86; cons. in field. Author: Program for Athletic Facilities, 1975; urban designer various jours., Eng., Greece, Italy, India, Japan, U.S.A.; creator first outdoor fine tuned track McCurdy Track, Harvard U., 1984; exhbns. include Wellbridge Ctr., Boston, 1994, Harvard Club Boston, 1994, Dru Arstark, N.Y.C., 1994, Kresge Gallery, Boston, 1994, Rocco's Charles St. South, Boston, 1994; guest artist Ellison Ctr. Arts, Duxbury, Mass. Art Heritage, New Delhi, Mingo Gallery, Beverly, Mass., Open Studio at 8 Elm St., Woodstock, Vt., Holyoke Ctr., Cambridge, Arlington, Mass. Exec. coun. Harvard/Radcliffe Child Care Coun., Cambridge, 1974; mem. Gov.'s Task Force Commonwealth of Mass., 1975; athletic cons. L.I. U., Franklin & Marshall Coll., Drew U., Babson Coll., Western Mont. Sports Medicine & Fitness Ctr., DePaul U., Assumption Coll., St. Marks Sch., McDonough (Md.) Sch., Mansfield U., The Nutrasweet Co., Hamline U., Adelphi U., St. Xavier U., SUNY New Paltz, Brooks Sch., North Andover, Mass., Brewster Acad., Wolfboro, N.H., Blair Acad., Blairstown, N.J. Recipient award of distinctioln for exhibit Internat. Conf. Archs., India, 1964, Cert. of Merit, Winthrop Housing Design Competition, Boston, 1975, Athletic Bus. Facility of Merit award, 1987, 88, 89, 90, Preservation Honor award Nat. Trust Hist. Preservation, 1987; John D. Rockefeller III Found. grantee, 1969. Mem. AIA (assoc.), Am. Inst. Cert. Planners, Am. Planning Assn., Am. Inst. Planners, Boston Soc. Archs., Mass. State Assn. Archs., Indian Inst. Archs. (assoc.), Harvard Club (Boston), Harvard Varsity Club (hon.). Office: Harvard Planning & Real Estate 912 Holyoke Ctr 1350 Massachusetts Ave Cambridge MA 02138-3846

OOMS, VAN DOORN, economist; b. Chgo., Oct. 29, 1934; s. Casper William and Ruth P. (Miller) O.; m. Theodora J. Parfit, June 17, 1961; children: Katrina, Alex, Tamara. BA summa cum laude, Amherst Coll., 1956, LHD (hon.), 1981; BA with 1st class honors, Oxford (Eng.) U., 1958, MA, 1962, Yale U., 1960, PhD, 1965. Lectr. Yale U., 1962, asst. prof. econs., to 1968; assoc. prof. Swarthmore Coll., 1968, prof., to, 1978; chief economist U.S. Senate Budget Com., Washington, 1977-78; asst. dir. for econ. policy U.S. Office Mgmt. and Budget, 1978-81; chief economist U.S. House Budget Com., 1981-91, exec. dir. for policy, 1989-91; sr. v.p., dir. rsch. Com. for Econ. Devel., 1991—2002, sr. fellow, 2002—. Rhodes scholar, Oxford U., 1958; Ford Found. Dissertation fellow Yale U., 1965. Office: 2000 L St NW Ste 700 Washington DC 20036-4915 E-mail: ooms@ced.org.

OORT, ABRAHAM HANS, meteorologist, researcher, educator; b. Leiden, The Netherlands, Sept. 2, 1934; came to U.S., 1961; s. Jan Hendrik and Johanna Maria (Graadt Van Roggen) O.; m. Bineke Pel, May 20, 1961; children: Pieter Jan, Michiel, Sonya. MS, MIT, 1963; PhD in Meteorology, U. Utrecht, The Netherlands, 1964. Rsch. meteorologist Koninklyk Nederlands Meteorologisch Instituut, De Bilt, The Netherlands, 1964-66, Geophys. Fluid Dynamics Lab/NOAA, Washington, 1966-68, Princeton, N.J., 1968-77, sr. rsch. meteorologist, 1977-96, ret., 1996. Prof. dept. geol. and geophys. scis. Princeton U., 1971-96; Shiatsu tchr. Kushi Inst. for Macrobiotic Studies, Becket, Mass., 1999--. Author: Physics of Climate, 1992; contbr. monographs in field. 2nd lt. Netherlands Air Force, 1959-61. NATO sci. fellow MIT, Cambridge, 1961-63; 10th Victor P. Starr Meml. lectr. MIT, 1988; recipient Gold medal U.S. Dept. Commerce, Washington, 1979. Fellow N.Y. Acad. Scis., Am. Meteorol. Soc. (Jule G. Charney award 1993), Royal Meteorol. Soc.; mem. Am. Geophys. Union. Democrat. Avocations: sculpture, shiatsu, meditation.

OOSTDYK, ARLENE ROSA, natural health educator, nurse; b. Oxford, N.J., Oct. 28, 1926; d. Ray William and Helen Anna (Renner) Frey; m. Marinus Joseph Oostdyk, Mar. 20, 1948; children: Darlene B. Oostdyk Haberer, Ray Marinus, James Marinus. Grad., Jersey City Hosp. Sch. Nursing, 1947; Nutritionist, Naturapathic Doctor, Bernadeen U., 1983. Cert. iridologist, nutritionist. Sch. nurse Bur. Maternal and Child Health, Alpha and Harmony, N.J., 1947-48, Hawthorne, N.J., 1948-49; nurse Hunterdon Med. Ctr., Flemington, 1953-60, Phillipsburg, 1953-60; sch. nurse Hampton Sch. Bd., 1960, Glen Gardner Sch. Bd., 1960; counselor in nutrition Asbury, N.J., 1981—; regional mgr. Natures Sunshine, Spanish Fork, Utah, 1986, divisional mgr., 1989—, nat. mgr., 1991—. Speaker in field. Clk., judge Election Bd., Asbury, N.J., 1967-87. Recipient Dedication of Classroom award India Internat. Gospel League, 1984. Mem. Am. Inst. Preventive Medicine (cert.), Sch. Natural Healing (cert.), Nat. Health Fedn. (life, million dollar club), Nat. Inst. Nutritional Edn., Jersey City Med. Ctr. Alumni Assn, Soc. Cert. Nutritionists. Republican. Baptist. Avocations: gardening, herbs, flowers, fishing, Bible studies. Home and Office: 292 Mountain View Rd W Asbury NJ 08802-1026 Fax: 908-689-5521. E-mail: ArleneO@usol.com.

OOSTEN, ROGER LESTER, medical manufacturing executive; b. Rock Valley, Iowa, Sept. 21, 1937; s. Henry and Martha (Kersbergen) O.; m. Patricia Nan Hanlon, Oct. 21, 1961; children: Kimberly Kay, Kurtis James, Jan Hendrik. BSEE, U. Iowa, 1967. Engr. Ball Bros. Research Corp., Boulder, Colo., 1967-73; pres. Mgmt. Bus. Machines, Inc., Denver, 1973-76; dir. research and devel. Neomed, Inc., Boulder, 1976-78; v.p. research and devel. Concept, Inc., Clearwater, Fla., 1978-81; v.p. surg. div. Birtcher Corp., El Monte, Calif., 1982-85; founder, pres. Bergen Mfg., Fla., 1985—. Patentee in field. Served with USN, 1956-60. Named Man of Yr., NASA, 1974. Home: 9345 Rookery Rd New Port Richey FL 34654-5546

OOSTWOUDER, PETER HENRY, family physician; b. Sioux City, Iowa, June 27, 1956; s. Cornelius and Alice Theresa (Roghair) O.; m. Joanna Ruth Field, June 7, 1997; children: Christina Elaine, Cornelius Wayne, Emily Theresa. BA cum laude, Washington U., St. Louis, 1978; MD, St. Louis U., 1982. Diplomate in family practice and geriatrics Am. Bd. Family Practice. Resident in family practice United Hosp., Clarksburg, W.Va., 1982-85; family physician Jasper Med. Svcs., Heidelberg, Miss., 1985-88, Ormond Family Physicians, Ormond Beach, Fla., 1989, Ctrl. Fla. Cmty. Clinic, Sanford, 1990—. Clin. assoc. prof. Nova Southeastern Sch. Osteo. Medicine, Ft. Lauderdale, Fla., 1997—. Contbr. articles to profl. jours. Mem. Am. Acad. Family Physicians, Sigma Xi. Republican. Mem. Christian Reformed Ch. Avocations: photography, travel, scuba diving, stamp collection. Home: 198 Poinciana Ln Enterprise FL 32738-9371 Office: Ctrl Fla Family Health Ctr 2400 State Rd 41S Sanford FL 32771-6012 E-mail: oostwouder@pol.net.

OPACICH, MILAN, protective services official, musician; b. Gary, Ind., Apr. 12, 1928; s. Mile and Roza (Perpic) O.; m. Rosalyn Helen Nicolich, Oct. 20, 1951; 1 child, Karin Joann. Grad. h.s., Gary, Ind. Tool and die maker Gary Screw and Bolt Co., 1947-58; lt. Gary Fire Dept., 1958-78; instr. Purdue U. NW, Hammond, Ind., 1978-80; luthier Schererville, 1950—. Lectr. in field; guest on numerous radio and TV shows. Writer Serb World, USA, 1984—; exhbns. include Mall, Washington, 1976, Remwick Gallery, Washington, 1978, 79-80, Smithsonian Inst., Washington, 1981, Bailey Ctr., 1982, Balzekas Lithuanian Culture Mus., Chgo., 1988, Arie Crown Theater, Chgo., 1990, Old Town Sch. Music, 1998; represented in permanent collection Roy Acuff Mus., Nashville; recordings include Bleda Djeva, Kreni Kreni, Jamin with Julius, Drina and Mel Dokich, Vintage 59 and Patriotic Songs of the Serbs; featured in books, magazines and newspaper articles. Founder, co-dir. Tamburitza Orch. St. Sava Orthodox Ch., 1964-70; founder First Tamburitza Extravaganza, 1971—. Recipient Pres.'s award for 50 yrs. of beautiful Tamburitza music, 1999; Am. Slavic Assn. honoree, 2000; Ind. Arts Commn. grant, 2000, Master Artist grant Traditional Arts Ind., 2002; inductee Tamburitza Assn. Am. Hall of Fame. Mem. Assn. Stringed Instrument Artisans. Ea. Orthodox. Avocations: collecting 78-RPM records, rare vintage instruments, documenting historical data, photographs, memorabilia tamburitza orchs. Home and Office: 2255 Robinhood Blvd Schererville IN 46375-1847

OPALA, MARIAN P(ETER), state supreme court justice; b. Lódz, Poland, Jan. 20, 1921; BSB in Econs., Oklahoma City U., 1957, JD, 1953, LLD (hon.), 1981; LLM, NYU, 1968; HHD, Okla. Christian U. Sci. & Arts, 1981. Bar: Okla. 1953, U.S. Supreme Ct. 1970. Asst. county atty., Oklahoma County, 1953-56; practiced law Oklahoma City, 1956-60, 65-67; referee Okla. Supreme Ct., 1960-65; prof. law Oklahoma City U. Sch. Law, 1965-69; asst. to presiding justice Supreme Ct. Okla., 1967-68; administrv. dir. Cts. Okla., 1968-77; presiding judge Okla. State Indsl. Ct., 1977-78; judge Workers Compensation Ct., 1978; justice Okla. Supreme Ct., 1978—, chief justice, 1991-92. Adj. prof. law Okla. City U., 1962—, U. Okla. Coll. Law, 1969—; prof. law U. Tulsa Law Sch., 1982—; mem. permanent faculty Am. Acad. Jud. Edn., 1970—; mem. NYU Inst. Jud. Adminstrn.; mem. faculty Nat. Jud. Coll., U. Nev., 1975—; chmn. Nat. Conf. State Ct. Adminstrs., 1976-77; mem. Nat. Conf. Commrs. on Uniform State Laws, 1982—. Co-author: Oklahoma Court Rules for Perfecting a Civil Appeal, 1969 Mem. Adminstrn. Conf. U.S., 1993-95. Recipient Herbert Harley award Am. Judicature Soc., 1977, Disting. Alumni award Oklahoma City U., 1979, Americanism medal Nat. Soc. DAR, 1984, ABA/Am. Law Inst. Harrison Tweed Spl. Merit award, 1987, Humanitarian award NCCJ, 1991, Jour. Record award, 1995, Constn. award Rogers State U., 1996, Jud. Excellence award Okla. Bar Assn., 1997, Leo H. Whinery Disting. Svc. award, 1999, Lifetime Achievement award Oklahoma City Univ. Sch. Law, 2000; inductee Okla. Hall of Fame, 2000. Mem. AbA (edn. com. appellate judges conf. 1984-93), Okla. Bar Assn. (Earl Sneed Continuing Legal Edn. award 1988, Jud. Excellence award 1997), Okla. County Bar Assn., Am. Soc. Legal History, Oklahoma City Title Lawyers Assn., Am. Judicature Soc. (bd. dirs. 1988-92), Am. Law Inst. (elected), Order of Coif, Phi Delta Phi (Oklahoma City Alumni award). Office: Okla Supreme Ct State Capitol Rm 238 Oklahoma City OK 73105

OPARA, EMMANUEL CHUKWUEMEKA, biochemistry educator; b. Lagos, Nigeria, July 4, 1951; came to U.S., 1984; s. Eugene Uba and Caroline (Adanma) O.; m. Clarice Adaku Njemanze, Mar. 28, 1980; children: Ogechi, Chiedu, Chukwuka, Ikenna. BS with honors, U. Nigeria, 1976; MS, U. Surrey, Eng., 1980; PhD, U. London, 1983. Assoc. Royal Coll. of Pathologists. Inspecting officer Food and Drug Adminstrn., Lagos, 1977-78; clin. biochemist Epsom (Eng.) Hosp. Labs., 1978-81; teaching asst. Chelsea Coll., London, 1981-83; rsch. fellow Mayo Clinic, Rochester, Minn., 1984-86; vis. fellow NIH, Bethesda, Md., 1986-88; rsch. assoc. Duke U. Med. Ctr., Durham, N.C., 1988-89, asst. prof. exptl. surgery, 1989-99, assoc. prof., 2000—. Mem. editl. bd. Pancreas, 1998—; contbr. articles to numerous scientific and med. jours. Com. chairperson Holy Cross Ch., Durham, 1992. WHO fellow, Geneva, 1984; Fogarty Internat. fellow, Bethesda, 1986; recipient Cystic Fibrosis Found. grant, 1990, Am. Diabetes Assn. grant, 1993. Mem. Am. Fedn. for Clin. Rsch., Am. Diabetes Assn., Am. Pancreatic Assn., Assn. Clin. Biochemists (U.K.), Biochemistry Soc., Am. Gastroenterological Assn. Democrat. Roman Catholic. Avocations: tennis, walking, current affairs, reading, television. Home: 2 Scarsdale Pl Durham NC 27707-5526 Office: Duke U Med Ctr Dept of Surgery PO Box 3065 Durham NC 27715-3065 E-mail: opara@mc.duke.edu.

OPARIL, SUZANNE, cardiologist, educator, cardiologist, researcher; b. Elmira, N.Y., Apr. 10, 1941; d. Stanley and Anna (Penkova) Oparil. AB, Cornell U., 1961; MD, Columbia U., 1965. Diplomate Am. Bd. Internal Medicine. Intern in medicine Presbyn. Hosp., N.Y.C., 1965—66; sr. asst. resident in medicine Mass. Gen. Hosp., Boston, 1967—68, clin. and rsch. fellow in medicine, cardiac unit, 1968—71; asst. prof. medicine Med. Sch., U. Chgo., 1971—75, assoc. prof., 1975—77; assoc. prof. dept. medicine U. Ala., Birmingham, 1977—81, asst. prof. physiology and biophysics, 1980—81, assoc. prof., 1981—, prof. medicine, 1981—, dir. vascular biology and hypertension program, 1985—, prof. med. physiology and biophysics, 1993—. Mem. vis. faculty Nat. High Blood Pressure Edn. Program, 1974—, Joint Nat. Com. on Detection, Evaluation and Treatment High Blood Pressure, 1991; mem. bd. sci. advisors Sterling Drug, Inc., 1988—91; lectr. in field; Selkurt lectr. Ind. U. Sch. Medicine, 1994; hon. prof. Peking Union Med. Coll., 1994; Louis Gross-Harold Segall lectr. Jewish Gen. Hosp., Montreal, Que., 1995; Joy Goodwin Disting. lectr. Auburn U., 1996; A Ross McIntyre award U. Nebr., 1996. Author books on hypertension; editor: Am. Jour. Med. Scis., 1984—94; assoc. editor: Hpertension, 1979—83, mem. editl. bd.: , 1984—, assoc. editor: Am. Jour. Physiology-Renal, 1989—91, mem. editl. bd.: Jour. Hypertension, 1989—98; contbr. over 450 articles to profl. jours., chapters to books. Recipient Young Investigator award, Internat. Soc. Hypertension, 1979, ann. award, Med. Coll. Pa., 1984; fellow, Am. Coll. Cardiology, 1992. Fellow: Am. Coll. Cardiology; mem.: AAAS, Am. Fedn. for Clin. Rsch. (midwest councillor 1974—75, nat. councillor 1975—78, sec.-treas. 1978—80, pres. 1981—82), Assn. Am. Physicians, So. Soc. for Clin. Investigation (Founder's award 1995), Soc. Exptl. Biology and Medicine (councillor 1993—), Am. Soc. for Clin. Investigation (sec.-treas. 1983—86), Am. Physiol. Soc. (clin. physiology advd. com. 1992—, Carl Ludwig disting. lectr. 2002), Am. Heart Assn. (coun. for high blood pressure rsch. 1973—, coun. on basic scis. 1978—, mem.-at-large, exec. com. 1979—81, chmn. Louis B. Katz Prize com. 1984—86, exec. com. 1985—90, vice chmn. 1986, v.p. Ala. affiliate 1986—87, pres.-elect Ala. affiliate 1987—88, pres. Ala. affiliate 1988—89, chmn. 1988—90, chmn. budget com. 1990—91, mem.-at-large bd. dirs. 1992, Lewis K. Dahl Meml. lectr. 1993, pres.-elect Ala. affiliate 1993—94, nat. pres.-elect 1993—94, nat. pres. 1994—, Arthur C. Corcoran Meml. lectr. 1998, Irving Page-Alva Bradley Lifetime Achievement award 2002), Assn. for Women in Sci., Am. Soc. Hypertension (sci. program com. 1990—92, pub. policy com. 1990—), Inter-Am. Soc. Hypertension, Endocrine Soc., Inst. Medicine of NAS (corr. com. on human rights 1992, chmn. com. adviser Dept. Def. 1993 Breast Cancer Rsch. Program), Phi Kappa Phi, Alpha Omega Alpha (mem. nat. bd. dirs., dir.-at-large 1991, treas. 1993), Sigma Xi, Phi Beta Kappa. Avocations: horseback riding, tennis, hiking, travel. Office: U Ala 703 S 19th St ZRB 1034 Birmingham AL 35294-0007 E-mail: soparil@uab.edu.

OPDAHL, CLARK DONALD, lawyer; b. St. Paul, June 22, 1956; s. Donald Arthur and Elizabeth Claire O.; m. Cynthia Ann Slipka, Sept. 2, 1977; children: Kyle, Shannon, Kelsey. BA, U. Minn., 1978; JD magna cum laude, William Mitchell Coll. of Law, St. Paul, 1986. Bar: Minn. 1987, U.S. Dist. Ct. Minn. Account exec., v.p. D.A. Opdahl & Assocs., Inc., Roseville, Minn., 1978-86; law clk. David G. Johnson, P.A., North St. Paul, 1984-86; atty. Henson & Efron, P.A., Mpls., 1986—. Baseball coach Blaine/Spring Lake Park Athletic Assn., Blaine, 1987-92, softball coach Spring Lake Park Athletic Assn., 1996-97. Mem. Minn. State Bar Assn., Hennepin County Bar Assn. (co-chmn. cmty. rels. 1989-93, 97-2000, co-chmn. publs. com. 1994-97). Avocations: golf, fishing. Office: Henson & Efron PA 220 S 6th St Ste 1800 Minneapolis MN 55402 E-mail: copdahl@hensonfron.com.

OPDAHL, VIOLA ELIZABETH, secondary education educator; b. Watervliet, N.Y., Jan. 6, 1925; d. Leslie Rouse and Violetta Frances (O'Bryon) Woodruff; m. Robert Clarence Opdahl, Aug. 4, 1956. BA, Skidmore Coll., 1945; MS in Edn., Cornell U., 1951; postgrad., SUNY, Albany, 1959-61. Cert. tchr. social studies, guidance. Tchr. social studies New Lebanon Ctrl. Sch., Lebanon Springs, N.Y., 1945-50, Patchogue H.S., 1951-55, Selkirk (N.Y.) Sch. Dist., 1955-56, Kingston (N.Y.) City Schs., 1956-58, secondary guidance, 1958-62, tchr. social studies, 1962-86; ret., 1986; coll. student tch. supr. SUNY, New Paltz, 1989-94; ret., 1994. Ad hoc syllabi and testing coms. N.Y. State Edn. Dept., Albany, 1967-82; adj. instr. psychology Marist Coll., 1972-86. Contbr. articles to profl. jours. Spl. activities organizer Town of Hurley Spl. Events Com., 1988—. Recipient Pres. award Marist Coll., 1986, Dean's award SUNY at New Paltz, 1989; named Outstanding Social Studies Tchr. Mid Hudson Soc. State Coun. of N.Y. State Coun., 1986. Mem. AAUW, LWV, Friends of the Senate House, Hurley Heritage soc. Avocations: reading, writing. Home: PO Box 218 431 Wynkoop Rd Hurley NY 12443-5108

OPDYCKE, LEONARD EMERSON, retired elementary, secondary and college-level educator, publisher; b. Boston, May 22, 1929; s. Leonard and Frances (Prescott) O.; m. Susan Wolcott, 1951 (div.); children: Susan, Deborah, Margot; m. Jeanne Bernhard, 1963 (div.); children: Sarah, Frances; m. Sandra S. Auchincloss, 1976. BA, Harvard U., 1951; MA, U. Rochester, 1965. Tchr. Southfield Sch., Shreveport, La., 1952-53, Dedham (Mass.) Country Day, Harley Sch., Rochester, N.Y., 1956-64; dir. Poughkeepsie (N.Y.) Day Sch., 1965-72; chair English dept. Rhinebeck (N.Y.) High Sch., 1974-77; adj. prof. Marist Coll., Poughkeepsie, 1977-84, 93-95. Author: French Aeroplanes before the Great War, 1999; editor, pub. WWI Aero, 1961—; pub. Skyways, 1987—. Mem. Phi Beta Kappa. Avocations: aviation history, linguistics, education. Home and Office: 15 Crescent Rd Poughkeepsie NY 12601-4405

OPEL, WILLIAM, medical research administrator; BA, Pepperdine U., 1968; MBA, U. So. Calif., 1993; PhD, Claremont Grad. U., 1998. Mem. staff Pasadena (Calif.) Found. Med. Rsch., Pasadena, Calif., 1961-63, rsch. assoc., 1964-70, asst. to dir., 1970-72, adminstr., 1972-76, exec. dir., 1976-82; acting exec. dir. Huntington Inst. Applied Med. Rsch., 1978-82; exec. dir. Huntington Med. Rsch. Inst., Pasadena, Calif., 1982—. Lectr. in technology, mgmt., Pepperdine U.; adj. prof. tech. mgmt. Claremont Grad. U. Mem. Beta Gamma Sigma, Phi Kappa Phi. Office: Huntington Med Rsch Insts 734 Fairmount Ave Pasadena CA 91105-3104

OPELT, RILLA ANNE, management consultant; b. Duluth, Minn., Aug. 7, 1939; d. Frank Louis and Mabel Hester (Chapman) DeBot; m. Alexander Lambi Stolis, May 6, 1961 (div. 1969); children: Alexander Jr., Roxanne Kathryn, Pauline Madeline, Rilla Marie; m. Bud T. Opelt, Nov. 8, 1969; children: Buddy Jr., Theanne Lenore. BA in Social Work, St. Scholastica, 1961, BA in Elem. Edn., 1969, MA in Psychology, 1988. Owner, operator Mother's Helper's Inc., Duluth, 1965-79; elem. tchr. Duluth Sch. Dist., 1969-75; sec. Minn. Power, Duluth, 1978; community rels. specialist Personalized Cons., 1990-95. Dir. Prolife Info. Network, Duluth, 1983—; dist. chmn. 7th Senate Dist. Reps., 1983-94; cand. for Minn. Ho. of Reps., 1988, 92, 94; exec. co-chmn. Citizens Coalition Gary-New Duluth, 1992-95; mem. Duluth Commn. on Aging, 1992-97; mem. Minn. State Sr. Olympics Bd., 1993-95; chair publicity com. Crime Stoppers Inc., 1993-95; superior program mgr. U. Wis., 1995—. Recipient Golden Poet award, 1990, Award for Outstanding Svc. to the Nat. Def., Nat. Guard and Reserves, 1991. Mem. Rep. Women. Clubs: Community. Roman Catholic. Avocations: dolls, miniatures, antiques collecting.

OPENSHAW, HELENA MARIE, investment company executive, portfolio manager; b. Beirut, July 30, 1953; d. Hubert J. and Lucile Openshaw. BA, U. South Fla., 1975, MA, 1977; PhD, SUNY, Buffalo, 1986. Tchg. asst. instr. SUNY, 1977-83; analyst specialist ValueLine, Inc., N.Y.C., 1986-88, sr. analyst, mem. portfolio mgmt. team, 1988-93; equity portfolio mgr. Ganz Capital Mgmt., Miami, Fla., 1993-94; v.p., sr. portfolio mgr. Comerica FSB, Ft. Lauderdale, 1994-95, Comerica Inc., Detroit, 1995-98; dir. Mackay Shields, N.Y.C., 1998—. Mem. Assn. for Investment Mgmt. and Rsch., Fin. Analysts Soc. N.Y. Office: Mackay Shields 9 W 57th St Ste 3410 New York NY 10019-2779

OPFER, GEORGE J. federal agency executive; b. N.Y.C., May 12, 1947; m. Elizabeth Opfer; 3 children. BS in Mgmt., St. John's U., 1969. With U.S. Secret Svc., spl. agt., treasury agt., asst. dir. Office of Investigations; nspector gen. FEMA, 1994—. Recipient Presdl. Rank of Meritorious Exec. award Sr. Exec. Svc., 1992. Office: Fed Emergency Mgmt Agy OIG 500 C St SW Rm 505 College Park MD 20742-0001*

OPFER, NEIL DAVID, construction educator, consultant; b. Spokane, Wash., June 1, 1954; s. Gus Chris and Alice Anna (Nibbe) Opfer. BS in Bldg. Theory cum laude, Wash. State U., 1976, BA in Econs. cum laude, BA in Bus. cum laude, Wash. State U., 1977; MS in Mgmt., Purdue U., 1982. Cert. cost engr., project mgr., profl. constructor; lic. gen. contractor. Estimator Standard Oil (Chevron), Richmond, Calif., 1975; gen. carpenter forman Opfer Constrn. Corp., Spokane, 1976; assoc. engr. Inland Steel Corp., East Chgo., Ind., 1977-78, millwright supr., 1978-79, field engr., 1979-82, project engr., 1982-84, sr. engr., 1984-87; asst. prof. construction and construction mgmt. Western Mich. U., Kalamazoo, 1987-89, U. Nev., Las Vegas, 1989-95, assoc. prof. construction and construction mgmt., 1995—. Contbr. articles to profl. jours. Bd. dirs. Christmas in April, 1993-98, Habitat for Humanity, 1991—. Mem. Am. Welding Soc. (bd. dirs. 1982-87), Am. Inst. Constructors, Am. Assn. Cost Engrs. (nat. bd. dirs. 1995-97, Order of Engr. award 1989), Project Mgmt. Inst., Constrn. Mgmt. Assn., Tau Beta Pi (life), Phi Kappa Phi (life). Methodist. Avocations: biking, running, marathons, triathlons. Home: 1920 Placid Ravine St Las Vegas NV 89117-5961 Office: Univ Nev Civil Engring 4505 S Maryland Pkwy Las Vegas NV 89154-4015 E-mail: opfern@ce.unlv.edu.

OPLINGER, CARL SPADT, biology educator; b. Walnutport, Pa., Oct. 6, 1936; s. Barton James and Erma Agnes (Spadt) O.; m. Marilee Ann Heckman, June 17, 1961; children: Anne Arlington, Amy Allison. BS, Mulhenberg Coll., 1958; MS, Lehigh U., 1960; PhD, Cornell U., 1963. Asst. prof. to prof. Muhlenberg Coll., Allentown, Pa., 1963—. Author: Natural History of the Poconos, 1988. Recipient Pa. Conservation Communicator of Yr., Pa. Wildlife Fedn., Harrisburg, 1989. Mem. Am. Inst. Biol. Sci., Ecol. Soc. Am., Soc. Conservation Biology, Herpetologists League. Lutheran. Home: 5071 Gary Dr Emmaus PA 18049-5051 Office: Muhlenberg Coll 2400 W Chew St Allentown PA 18104-5564 E-mail: oplinger@muhlenberg.edu.

OPOTOWSKY, ANNE A. scriptwriter, film producer; b. N.Y.C., July 19, 1959; d. Stanford Lester Opotowsky, Martha Coble Opotowsky. BA, Boston U., 1979; MFA, Am. Film Inst., 1993. Author: (documentary) The Poisoning of America, 1988 (Emmy award, 1988); prodr.: (documentary) The Poisoning of America, 1988. Mem.: PEN, Writers Guild Am.

OPPEDAHL, JOHN FREDRICK, newspaper publisher, publishing executive; b. Duluth, Minn., Nov. 9, 1944; s. Walter H. and Lucille (Hole) O.; m. Alison Owen, 1975 (div. 1983); m. Gillian Coyro, Feb. 14, 1987; 1 child, Max. BA, U. Calif., Berkeley, 1967; MS, Columbia U., 1968. Reporter San Francisco Examiner, 1967; reporter, asst. city editor Detroit Free Press, 1968-75, city editor, 1975-80, exec. city editor, 1981, exec. news editor, 1981-82, asst. mng. editor, 1983; nat. and fgn. editor Dallas Times Herald, 1983-85, asst. mng. editor, 1985-87; mng. editor/news L.A. Herald Examiner, 1987-89; mng. editor Ariz. Republic, Phoenix, 1989-93; exec. editor Phoenix Newspapers, Inc., 1993-95, pub., CEO, 1996—; pub. The Republic , 1996; chmn., pub., CEO San Francisco Chronicle, 2000—. Chmn. bd. The Daily Californian. Trustee Walter Cronkite Sch. Journalism and Telecomm., Ariz. State U.; bd. dirs. Found. for Am. Comms., Downtown Phoenix Partnership, Phoenix Cmty. Alliance; trustee Phoenix Art Mus.; bd. advisors Morrison Inst.; campaign chmn. Valley of the Sun United Way, 1999; mem. Greater Phoenix Leadership; past chmn. COMPAS; bd. visitors Columbia U. Journalism Sch. Mem. Am. Soc. Newspaper Editors, AP Mng. Editors, Newspaper Assn. of Am. Office: San Francisco Chronicle 901 Mission St San Francisco CA 94103*

OPPEDAHL, PHILLIP EDWARD, computer company executive; b. Renwick, Iowa, Sept. 17, 1935; s. Edward and Isadore Hannah (Gangstead) O.; m. Sharon Elaine Ree, Aug. 3, 1957 (dec. Aug. 1989); children: Gary Lynn, Tamra Sue, Sue Ann, Lisa Kay. BS in Naval Sci., Navy Postgrad. Sch., 1963, MS in Nuclear Physics, 1971; MS in Sys. Mgmt., U. S.C., 1978. Commd. ensign U.S. Navy, 1956, advanced through grades to capt., 1977; with Airborne Early Warning Squadron, 1957-59, Anti-Submarine Squadron, 1959-65; asst. navigator USS Coral Sea, 1965-67; basig jet flight instr., 1967-69; test group dir. Def. Nuclear Agy., 1972-74; weapons officer USS Oriskany, 1974-76; program mgt. for armament Naval Air Sys. Command, Washington, 1977-79; test dir. Def. Nuclear Agy., Kirtland AFB, N.Mex., 1979-82, dep. comdr., 1982-83; pres., CEO Am. Systems, Albuquerque, 1983—. Bd. dirs. BASIS Internat., 1991—. Author: Energy Loss of High Energy Electrons in Beryllium, 1971, Understanding Contractor Motivation and Incentive Contracts. Decorated DSM. Mem. Nava. Inst., Am. Nuclear Soc., Aircraft Owners and Pilots Assn., Assn. Naval Aviation, Navy League. Lutheran. Home and Office: 13504 Desert Zinnia Ct Albuquerque NM 87111-7156

OPPEGAARD, BRETT, journalist; b. Vancouver, Wash., Nov. 27, 1970; s. Eric Rae and Nancy Merle Oppegaard; m. Michelle Irma Wilfong, Jan. 15, 1995; 1 child Addy. BA in Comm., Wash. State U., 1993; MA in Comm., U. Portland, Oreg., 1999. Staff writer The Columbian, Vancouver, Wash., 1994—. Adj. prof. U. Portland, 2002—; journalism advisor Wash. State U., Vancouver, 2002—. Recipient award, Soc. Profl. Journalists, 1992, 1995, 1996, 2001. Mailing: The Columbian 701 W 8th St Vancouver WA 98660

OPPEL, ANDREW JOHN, computer systems consultant; b. Kerrville, Tex., Dec. 22, 1952; s. Wallace Churchill and Anne Kathryn (Smith) O.; m. Laura Lee Partridge, Aug. 26, 1972; children: Keith Andrew, Luke Andrew. BA in Computer Sci., Transylvania U., 1974. Computer programmer Johns Hopkins U., Balt., 1974-77; data base programmer Equitable Trust Co., 1977-78; sr. programmer, analyst Md. Casualty Co., 1978-79, Levi Strauss & Co., San Francisco, 1979-82, sr. requirements mgr., 1982-84, tech. cons., 1984-91, tech. advisor, 1991-93, mgr. database mgmt. sys., 1994-96, sr. sys. architect, 1996-97; sr. cons. Triadigm Internat., 1997-98; mng. prin. cons. Oracle Corp., Redwood Shores, 1998-99; database arch. Geoworks, Alameda, 1999-2000;

database group mgr. MBH Solutions, Inc., 2000—01; database designer ifb.net inc., 2001—. Instr. U. Calif. Extension, Berkeley, 1983—. Ops. officer Alameda County Radio Amateur Civil Emergency Svc., San Leandro, Calif., 1980-92; cub master Boy Scouts Am., Alameda, Calif., 1991-92; referee U.S. Soccer Fedn., Alameda, 1988—, referee instr., 1996—; sect. mgr. Am. Radio Relay League, 2000—. Democrat. Episcopalian. Avocation: amateur radio. Home: 1308 Burbank St Alameda CA 94501-3946 Office: 1fb.net, Inc 1000 Sansome St Ste 350 San Francisco CA 94111 E-mail: andy@andyoppel.com.

OPPEL, RICHARD ALFRED, newspaper executive; b. Newark, Jan. 30, 1943; s. Alfred William and Jane Genevieve (Owen) O.; m. Carol Freeman Van Aken, Apr. 1, 1967; children: Richard Alfred, Shelby Reid BA in Polit. Sci., U. South Fla. Reporter Tampa Tribune, Fla., 1963-65; newsman, corr., chief bur. AP, Tallahassee, Tampa, Miami and Detroit, 1965-76; assoc. editor Detroit Free Press, 1976-77; exec. editor, v.p. Tallahassee Democrat, 1977-78; v.p. Charlotte (N.C.) Observer, 1978-93; editor Charlotte News, 1985-87; chief Washington bur. Knight-Ridder Newspapers, Washington, 1993-95; editor Austin (Tex.) American Statesman, Austin, TX, 1998—. Pres. N.C. First Amendment Found. Served with USMCR, 1960-65 Recipient Disting. Alumni award U. South Fla.; named Editor of Yr. Nat. Press Found., 1987, Ralph McGill Lectr. U. Ga., 1992. Mem. N.C. Press Assn. (pres. 1992-93), Am. Soc. Newspaper Editors. Episcopalian. Avocations: long distance running, hunting, fishing. Office: Austin Am Statesman PO Box 670 Austin TX 78767-0670*

OPPENHEIM, ANTONI KAZIMIERZ, mechanical engineer; b. Warsaw, Poland, Aug. 11, 1915; came to U.S., 1948, naturalized, 1954; s. Tadeusz and Zuzanna (Zuckerwar) O.; m. Lavinia Stephens, July 18, 1945; 1 dau., Terry Ann. Diploma in Engring., Warsaw Inst. Tech., London, 1943; PhD in Engring., U. London, 1945; Diploma of Imperial Coll., 1945; DSc, U. London, 1976; Dr. Honoris Causa, U. Poitiers, France, 1981, Tech. U., Warsaw, 1989, Imperial Coll., 1995. Registered profl. engr., Calif. Research asst. City and Guilds Coll., 1942-48, lectr., 1946-48; asst. prof. mech. engring. Stanford U., 1948-50; faculty U. Calif. at Berkeley, 1950—, prof. mech. engring., 1958-86, Miller prof., 1961-62, prof. emeritus, 1986—; fellow Imperial Coll., 1995. Vis. prof. Sorbonne, Paris, 1960-61, U. Poitiers, France, 1973, 80; staff cons. Shell Devel. Co., 1952-60. Editor-in-chief: Acta Astronautica, 1974-79; contbr. articles to profl. jours., also monographs. Chmn. Heat Transfer and Fluid Mechanics Inst., 1958; IAA Com. on Gasdynamics of Explosions, 1968—; organizer Internat. Colloquia on Gas Dynamics of Explosions and Reactive Systems, 1967, 69, 71, 73, 75, 77, 79, 81, 83; mem. NASA, adv. com. fluid mechanics, 1963-69. Recipient Water Arbitration prize Inst. Mech. Engrs., 1948, Numa Manson medal Inst. for Dynamics of Explosions and Reactive Sys., 1981, Dionizy Smolenski medal Polish Acad. Scis., 1987, Alfred C. Egerton medal The Combustion Inst., 1988, citation U. Calif., Berkeley, 1988. Fellow Imperial Coll.; mem. U.S. Nat. Acad. Engring, Polish Acad. Scis. Achievements include research in research compressible fluid flow, gas turbines and internal combustion engines, heat transfer, combustion, detonation and blast waves. Home: 54 Norwood Ave Kensington CA 94707-1119

OPPENHEIM, DAVID JEROME, musician, retired university dean; b. Detroit, Apr. 13, 1922; s. Louis and Julia (Nurko) O.; m. Judy Holliday, 1948; 1 child, Jonathan; m. Ellen Adler, Apr. 14, 1957; children: Sara, Thomas; m. Pat Jaffe, June 13, 1987. Student, Julliard Sch. Music, 1939-40; MusB, U. Rochester, 1943. Dir. Masterworkd div. Columbia Records, N.Y.C., 1950-59; producer, dir., writer network news CBS-TV, 1962-68; exec. producer Pub. Broadcasting Lab., 1968-69; dean Tisch Sch. of Arts, NYU, 1969-92, dean emeritus, 1992—. Adv. com. Sta. WNCN; mem. Tony awards com., 1983-88. Clarinet soloist Casals Festival, Prades, France, 1955, San Juan, P.R., 1959, recs. include Budapest Quartet, Brahms Clarinet Quintet, Opus 115 and Mozart Clarinet Quintet in A Maj., (Stravinsky conducting) L'Histoire du Soldat, Octet, Septet, Bernstein Sonata, Leonard Bernstein, piano (dedicated to David Oppenheim), (with Julliard Quartet) Copland Sextet, (with New Music Quartet) Douglas Moore Quintet; co-producer (play) Saul Bellow's Last Analysis on Broadway, 1962; producer documentary films on Stravinsky and Casals, CBS News. Bd. dirs. emeritus Film Soc. Lincoln Center, Inc., Town Hall Found.; bd. dirs. Am. Stefan Wolpe Soc.; bd. advisors New Sch. Concerts. With AUS, World War II, ETO. Recipient Prix Italia Radiotelevisione Italiana, 1964. Mem. Nat. Soc. Lit. and Arts, Internat. Council Fine Arts Deans, N.Y. State Arts Deans, Town Hall Found., NYU Soc. of Fellows (charter), Am. Fedn. Arts (film program) Avocations: camping, reading, gardening, hiking.

OPPENHEIM, IRWIN, chemical physicist, educator; b. Boston, June 30, 1929; s. James L. and Rose (Rosenberg) O.; m. Bernice Buresh, May 18, 1974; 1 child, Joshua Buresh. AB summa cum laude, Harvard U., 1949; postgrad., Calif. Inst. Tech., 1949-51; PhD, Yale, 1956. Physicist Nat. Bur. Standards, Washington, 1953-60; chief theoretical physics Gen. Dynamics/Convair, San Diego, 1960-61; assoc. prof. chemistry MIT, Cambridge, 1961-65, prof., 1965—. Lectr. physics U. Md., 1953-60; vis. assoc. prof. physics U. Leiden, 1955-56, Lorentz prof., 1983; vis. prof. Weizmann Inst. Sci., 1958-59, U. Calif., San Diego, 1966-67; Van der Waals prof. U. Amsterdam, 1966-67. Author: (with J.G. Kirkwood) Chemical Thermodynamics, 1961; editor: Phys. Rev. E, 1992—. Recipient Hildebrand award 1998. Fellow Am. Phys. Soc., Am. Acad. Arts and Scis., Washington Acad. Sci.; mem. Phi Beta Kappa, Sigma Xi. Achievements include research in quantum statis. mechanics, statis. mechanics of transport processes, thermodynamics. Home: 140 Upland Rd Cambridge MA 02140-3623 Office: MIT 77 Massachusetts Ave #6-223 Cambridge MA 02139-4307 E-mail: irwin@mit.edu.

OPPENHEIM, JEFFREY SABLE, neurosurgeon; b. Queens, N.Y., Jan. 31, 1962; m. Ann Oppenheim; m. Samuel, Gabrielle, Julius. ABsumma cum laude, Princeton (N.J.) U., 1984; MD, Cornell U., 1988. Diplomate Am. Bd. Neurol. Surgeons. Resident in neurosurgery Mt. Sinai Hosp., N.Y.C., 1989-93, chief resident in neurosurgery, 1993-94; instr. Columbia U. Coll. of Physicians and Surgeons, 1994—; attending physician Nyack (N.Y.) Hosp., 1994—, Good Samaritan Hosp., Suffern, N.Y., 1994—, Arden Hill Hosp., Goshen, 1996—, Horton Hosp., Middletown, 1997—, Mercy Cmty. Hosp., Port Jervis, 1997—. Mem. bd. health Rockland County, 2001—. Mem. Am. Jewish Hist. Soc. (trustee 1995—), Rockland County Med. Soc. (pres. 1998-99), Med. Soc. State N.Y. (councillor 1999—). Office: 222 Route 59 Ste 205 Suffern NY 10901-5206 also: 30 Mathews St Ste 302 Goshen NY 10924-1963

OPPENHEIM, MARTHA KUNKEL, pianist, educator; b. Port Arthur, Tex., June 25, 1935; d. Samuel Adam and Grace (Moncure) Kunkel; m. Russell Edward Oppenheim, June 18, 1960; children: Lauren Susan, Kristin Lee Oppenheim Mortenson. MusB with honors, U. Tex., 1957, MusM, 1959; diploma in piano, Juilliard Sch. Music, 1960; student, Am. Conservatory, Fontainebleau, France, 1956, student, 1958. Soloist Amarillo (Tex.) Symphony, Austin (Tex.) Symphony, U. Tex. Orch., San Antonio Symphony, Dallas Symphony, Heilbronner Kammer Orch., Heilbron, Germany. Solo and chamber music recitals in Tex., N.Y., France; mem. Halcyon Trio, 1974—77; tchg. asst. U. Tex., 1957—59, 1968—69; pvt. piano tchr., San Antonio, 1962—; pianist in duo with cellist Dan Zollars, 1991—. Recipient 1st place award, Internat. Piano Rec. Festival, Nat. Guild Piano Tchrs., 1956, 1956, Tuesday Mus. Club Young Artist Competition, 1956, 1st place award Young Artist Competition, Amarillo Symphony, 1959, 1st place award G.B. Dealey competition, Dallas Symphony and Dallas Morning News, 1959; scholar, U. Tex., Juilliard Sch. Music. Mem.: San Antonio Music Tchrs. Assn., Tex. Music Tchrs. Assn., Music Tchrs. Nat. Assn., Tuesday Musical Club (San Antonio, bd. dirs.), Pi Kappa Lambda, Sigma Alpha Iota. Presbyterian. Home and Office: 9118 E Valley View Ln San Antonio TX 78217-5160 E-mail: moppenheim@satx.rr.com.

OPPENHEIM, ROBERT, beauty industry executive; b. N.Y.C., May 21, 1925; s. Hyman and Hannah (Lieberman) O.; m. Ruth Wigler, Feb. 7, 1954; children: Nancy Ellen, David Paul, Howard P. BS cum laude, Syracuse U., 1950. Product sales specialist McKesson & Robbins, Yonkers, N.Y., 1950-55; asst. sales mgr. Clairol, Inc., N.Y.C., 1955-60, pres. Salon div., 1976-83, chmn. Profl. Products div., 1983-87; dir. mktg. Haircolor div. Revlon, Inc., 1960-68, dir. mktg. and sales Salon div., 1968-70; exec. v.p. Milton R. Barrie Co., Inc., 1970-71; pres. Oppenheim Communications, N.Y.C., 1987—. Pub. Beauty Salon Newsletter, N.Y.C., 1971-83, Salon Update, 1988-95, The Oppenheim Letter, 1988-95; mgmt. cons., 1988—; contbg. commentator Beauty Store Bus., 1998—, Profl. Beauty Mfr., 1998-99; bd. dirs. Cosmetology Advancement Found., 1995-98, Internat. Haircolog Exch., 1995-96. Author: 101 Salon Promotions, 1999. With AUS, 1942-44, ETO. Decorated Purple Heart; recipient Spirit of Life award City of Hope, 1989, Showman Wall of Fame award Internat. Beauty Show, 1994; inducted into Nat. Cosmetology Assn. Hall of Fame, 1994, Barber & Beauty Supply Inst. Hall of Leaders, 1998. Mem. Nat. Beauty and Barber Mfrs. Assn. (pres. 1984-85), Am. Beauty Assn. (pres. 1985-86), Masons. Home: 241 Sickletown Rd West Nyack NY 10994-2905 Office: Oppenheim Communications PO Box 700 West Nyack NY 10994-0700

OPPENHEIMER, BEN R. research scientist; BA in Physics, Columbia U., 1994; PhD in Astronomy, Calif. Inst. Tech., 1999. Rsch. asst. NASA Goddard Inst. for Space Studies, 1988—91, Columbia Astrophysics Lab., 1991—94; Hubble rsch. fellow Am. Mus. Natural History, N.Y.C., 1994—2002, Kalbfleisch rsch. fellow, 2002—. Instr. Columbia U., 1993—95; instr. physics dept. Barnard Coll., 1993—94. Fellow Grad. Rsch. fellow, NSF, 1994—97, Miller Inst. for Basic Rsch. in Sci., 1999, Harvard-Smithsonian Ctr. for Astrophysics, 1999; scholar I.I. Rabi Sci. scholar, Columbia U., 1990—94, Douglass scholar, U. Ariz. Steward Obs., 2000. Mem.: AAAS, Astron. Soc. Pacific, Internat. Soc. Optical Engring., Am. Astron. Soc. Office: Am Mus Natural History Dept Astrophysics Central Park West at 97th St New York NY 10024*

OPPENHEIMER, FRANZ MARTIN, lawyer; b. Mainz, Germany, Sept. 7, 1919; s. Arnold and Johanna (Mayer) O.; m. Margaret Spencer Foote, June 17, 1944; children: Martin Foote, Roxana Foote, Edward Arnold. BS, U. Chgo., 1942; student, U. Grenoble, France, 1938-39; LL.B. cum laude (note editor Law Jour. 1945), Yale U., 1945. Bar: N.Y. 1946, D.C. 1955. Rsch. asst. com. human devel. U. Chgo., 1942-43; law clk. to Judge Swan, U.S. Circuit Ct. of Appeals, N.Y., 1945-46; assoc. atty. Chadbourne, Wallace, Parke & Whiteside, N.Y.C., 1946-47; atty. IBRD, Washington, 1947-57; individual practice law, 1958-59; ptnr. firm Leva, Hawes, Symington, Martin & Oppenheimer, 1959-83, Fort & Schlefer, Washington, 1984-94; pvt. practice, 1995-96; sr. of counsel Swidler Berlin Shereff Friedman (formerly Swidler & Berlin), 1996—2001; individual consulting and law practice, 2001—. Contbr. articles to profl. and other jours, chpts. to books. Bd. dirs. Internat. Student House; founding mem. Company of Christian Jews. Decorated officer's cross Order of Merit (Fed. Republic Germany), chevalier Nat. Order of Merit (France). Mem. ABA, Am. Soc. Internat. Law (hon. v.p., treas. 1964-76), Coun. Fgn. Rels., Yale Club, Century Assn. (N.Y.), City Tavern, Met. Club (Washington). Anglican. Home: 3248 O St NW Washington DC 20007-2847 E-mail: franzmfmo@aol.com.

OPPENHEIMER, JOHN JACOB, allergist, immunologist; b. Boston, June 22, 1960; BA, Lafayette Coll.; MD, Temple U., 1986. Diplomate Am. Bd. Allergy and Immunology, Am. Bd. Internal Medicine. Intern Robert Wood Johnson U. Hosp., New Brunswick, N.J., 1986-87, resident in internal medicine, 1987-89; fellow in allergy and immunology Nat. Jewish Ctr., Denver, 1989-91, staff, 1991-92; mem. staff Morristown (N.J.) Meml. Hosp., 1992—; pvt. practice, 1992-98. Asst. dir. U. Medicine and Dentistry N.J.-N.J. Med. Sch. Bd. dirs. clin. rsch. Pulmonary and Allergy Assn. Mem. Pulmonary and Allergy Assn. (dir. clin. rsch.). Home: 12 N Ridge Rd Denville NJ 07834-9629 Office: 101 Madison Ave Morristown NJ 07960-7305 E-mail: nallopp@pol.net.

OPPENHEIMER, MARTIN J. lawyer; b. Apr. 11, 1933; s. Julius and Sylvia (Haas) O.; m. Suzanne Rosenhirsch, July 3, 1958; children: Marcy, Evan, Joshua, Alexandra. BS with honors, U. Pa., 1953; LLB, Yale U., 1956. Assoc. Hays, Sklar & Hertzberg. Mendes & Mount; ptnr. Proskauer Rose Goetz & Mendelsohn, N.Y.C., 1958—. Contbr. articles to profl. jours. Chmn. City Ctr. of Music and Drama, Lincoln Ctr., N.Y., 1984—; vice chmn. N.Y.C. Opera, 1985—; bd. dir. 92nd St. YWCA, N.Y., 1985—, Lincoln Ctr. for Performing Arts, 1987—; bd. advs. Mailman Sch. of Pub. Health, Columbia U., 1991; chmn. Lincoln Ctr. Constituent Devel. Corp., 2001—. Fulbright scholar Goethe U., Frankfurt, Fed. Republic Germany, 1956-57. Home: 400 Claflin Ave Mamaroneck NY 10543-3906 Office: Proskauer Rose et al 1585 Broadway Fl 27 New York NY 10036-8299

OPPENHEIMER, MAX, JR. foreign language educator, consultant; b. N.Y.C., July 27, 1917; s. Max and Louise (Pourfuerst) O.; m. Christine Backus, Oct. 14, 1942; children: Edmund Max, Carolyn Christine Oppenheimer Burns. Bachelier ès Lettres, U. Paris, 1935; BA cum laude, NYU, 1941; MA, UCLA, 1942; PhD, U. So. Calif., 1947. Instr. fgn. langs. San Diego State Coll., 1947-49; asst. prof. Romance langs. Washington U., St. Louis, 1949-51; assoc. prof. modern langs. Fla. State U., Tallahassee, 1958-61; prof., chmn. dept. Russian U. Iowa, Iowa City, 1961-67; prof. SUNY, Fredonia, 1967-76, prof. emeritus, 1976—, chmn. dept. fgn. langs., 1967-74; prof. English Yunnan Normal U., Kunming, Peoples Republic of China, 1985-86. Intelligence officer CIA, 1956-58. Author: Outline of Russian Grammar, 1962; translator: Theory of Molecular Excitons (Davydov), 1962, Theory of Ship Waves and Wave Resistance (Kostyukov), 1968, The Fake Astrologer (Calderón de la Barca), 1976, 94, The Lady Simpleton (Lope de Vega), 1976, Don Juan (Tirso de Molina), 1976, Swim First and Last, 1981, An Innocent Yank at Home Abroad, 2000; contbr. articles to scholarly and profl. jours. Active YMCA, 1936—. Served to lt. col., MI, AUS, 1942-46, 52-56, lt. col. Res., ret. Decorated Bronze Star; Fla. State U. grantee, 1961, Office Naval Rsch. grantee, 1965, SUNY grantee, 1973. Mem.: MLA, Am. Soc. Geolinguistics (pres. 1975—76), Mil. Officers Assn. Am., Am. Soc. Dowsers, Dobro Slovo, Am. Mensa Ltd., Elks, Phi Beta Kappa, Alpha Mu Gamma, Pi Delta Phi (nat. pres. 1946—51), Sigma Delta Pi. Avocation: swimming. Home: 10963 W Coggins Dr Sun City AZ 85351-3346 E-mail: maxojr@earthlink.net. *When you speak, always say what you think, not what you think you should say for the sake of expediency. Steadfastly, stubbornly, cling to your ideals, principles and beliefs, but be flexible enough to change whenever changing them reflects wisdom, not weakness or compromise. Avoid ego trips or being awed by your own alleged accomplishments.*

OPPENHEIMER, MICHAEL, physicist; b. Bklyn., Feb. 28, 1946; s. Harry and Shirley Oppenheimer; m. Leonie Haimson, Dec. 31, 1986; children: Chloe, Nathaniel. S.B., MIT, 1966; PhD, U. Chgo., 1970. Research fellow Harvard Coll., 1971-73; lectr. astronomy Harvard U., 1973-81; physicist Harvard-Smithsonian Center for Astrophysics, Harvard U., 1973-81, Environ. Def., N.Y.C., 1981—2001, chief scientist, 1996-2001; Albert G. Milbank prof. geoscis. and internat. affairs Princeton U., 2002—. Mem. global change steering com. H. John Heinz III Ctr., 1998—; mem. panel on atmospheric effects of aviation NRC, 1995—99. Author: Dead Heat: The Race Against the Greenhouse Effect, 1990; contbr. Fellow, Union Carbide, 1969—70, A.F. Morrison, 1979, Guggenheim, 1978—79. Mem.: AAAS, Am. Meteorol. Soc., Am. Geophys. Union, Am. Phys. Soc. Office: Environ Def 257 Park Ave S New York NY 10010-7304 E-mail: moopenheimer@environmentaldefense.org.

OPPENHEIMER, NANCY BEA, artist; b. Morgantown, W.Va. d. Benjamin Rolland Oppenheimer and Betty Sylvia Bernson; m. Thomas Allen Smolen, Apr. 1, 1962. BFA in Studio Art cum laude, U. Hartford, 1972. Exhibited in one-woman shows at Blue Ridge Arts Ctr., Seneca, N.C., 1997, Opal Art Gallery, Pendleton, S.C., 1999, group show at Anderson (S.C.) Arts Ctr., 1997; represented in collections at Appalachian U., Prudential of Boston, Foster and Saad, Columbia, S.C., Litchfield (Conn.) Bank. Recipient Best New Eng. Newspaper Illustration of Yr., New Eng. Press., 1984. Home: 2016 Hampton Shores Dr Seneca SC 29672 Fax: (864) 888-0160. E-mail: oppenheimerart@mindspring.com.

OPPENHEIMER, PAUL, English comparative literature educator, poet, author; b. N.Y.C., May 1, 1939; s. Fred R. Oppenheimer and Gertrude Samuels; children: Julie Sarah, Ben. BA, Princeton U., 1961; MA, Columbia U., 1963, PhD, 1970. Lectr. Hunter Coll. CUNY, N.Y.C., 1964-67, lectr., poet-in-residence City Coll., 1967-70, from asst. prof. to assoc. prof. City Coll., 1970-84, prof. City Coll., 1984—; prof. comparative lit. The Grad. Ctr./CUNY, 2001—. Exch. prof., dir. CUNY student exch. program Sorbonne nouvelle, Paris, 1984-85; exch. prof. U. North London, Eng., 1989-90, Univ. Coll. London German Dept., 1993, 95, 97, 99; Fulbright prof. U. Osnabrück, Germany, 1993-94. Author: Before a Battle and Other Poems, 1967; translator: Till Eulenspiegel: His Adventures, 1972; author: Beyond the Furies, New Poems, 1985, The Birth of the Modern Mind: Self, Consciousness, and the Invention of the Sonnet, 1989; translator: Till Eulenspiegel: His Adventures, 1991, 1995; author: Evil and the Demonic: A New Theory of Monstrous Behavior, 1996, An Intelligent Person's Guide to Modern Guilt, 1997, Rubens: A Portrait, 1999, Blood Memoir, or the First Three Days of Creation, 1999, Infinite Desire: A Guide to Modern Guilt, 2000; translator: Till Eulenspiegel: His Adventures, 2001; author: The Flame Charts, New Poems, 2002. Woodrow Wilson fellow, 1961-62, Alfred Hodder fellow, 1969-70, Fulbright sr. fellow, Germany, 1993-94; recipient Eisner Scholars award Rifkind Ctr. for the Humanities, 1998. Mem. Dante Soc. Am. Home: 50 W 67th St New York NY 10023-6227 Office: CCNY Dept English and Comparative Lit NAC 138 St and Convent Ave New York NY 10031 Also: The Graduate Ctr CUNY Dept Comparative Lit 365 Fifth Ave New York NY 10016 E-mail: pauloppenheimer@hotmail.com.

OPPENHEIMER, PETER H. lawyer; b. N.Y.C., NY, 1964; m. Stephanie J. Oppenheimer, 1996. BA, Yale U., 1986, JD, 1992; MA in Law and Diplomacy, Tufts U., 1992. Staff asst. Coun. on Fgn. Rels., N.Y.C., 1987-88; atty. Bryan Cave LLP, Washington, 1992-99; atty. environ. and natural resources divsn. U.S. Dept. Justice, 1999—. Hon. sec. Am. br. Internat. Law Assn., N.Y.C., 1998-99. Contbr. articles to legal jours. Mem. Natural Resources and Environ. Law Com. Planning Bd., 1997-99. Recipient Hajo Holborn prize Yale U., 1985; German Acd. Exch. Svc. fellow, 1986-87. Mem. ABA, Phi Beta Kappa. Office: US Dept Justice 601 D St NW Washington DC 20004-2904 also: PO Box 4390 Ben Franklin Sta Washington DC 20044-4390 E-mail: peter.Oppenheimer@USDOJ.gov.

OPPENHEIMER, RANDOLPH CARL, lawyer; b. N.Y.C., Feb. 5, 1954; s. Bennett and Sandra (Haber) O.; m. Cynthia Ellen Shatkin, June 19, 1976; children: Benjamin David, Adam Jeremy, Jacob Aaron, Jordan Michael, Daniel Corey. BA, U. Vt., 1976; JD, Case Western Res. U., 1979. Bar: N.Y. 1980, U.S. Dist. Ct. (we. dist.) N.Y. 1980, U.S. Dist. Ct. (no. dist.) N.y. 1995, U.S. Bankruptcy Ct. 1980, U.S. Ct. Appeals (2d cir.) 1981. Assoc. Kavinoky & Cook, Buffalo, 1979-84, ptnr., 1984—. Instr. legal research, writing and adv., Case Western Res. U., 1978-79. Assoc. editor Case Western Reserve Law Rev., 1977-79. Mem. ABA, N.Y. Bar Assn., Erie County Bar Assn. E-mail (office). Home: 195 Greenaway Rd Buffalo NY 14226-4165 Office: Kavinoky & Cook 120 Delaware Ave Rm 600 Buffalo NY 14202-2793 E-mail: roppenheimer@kavinokycook.com.

OPPENHEIMER, STEPHEN MICHAEL, neurologist, administrator; b. London, Mar. 13, 1954; came to the U.S., 1991; BA, U. Oxford, Eng., 1975, MA, 1980, MD, 1995; MB, B of Surgery, U. London, 1980. Sr. house officer to registrar in medicine, cardiology and neurology U. London, 1980-85; resident in neurology U. Western Ont., London, Can., 1985-88; Can. Heart Found. Rsch. fellow Robarts Rsch. Inst., Can., 1988-91; asst. prof. clin. neurol. scis. U. Western Ont., 1990-91; dir. cerebrovascular program Johns Hopkins U. Sch. Medicine, Balt., 1991—, dir. neurocardiology program, 1995—; physician Johns Hopkins Hosp., 1991—; assoc. prof. neurology, assoc. prof. medicine Johns Hopkins U., 1996—; dir. neurosci. Pharmanet, Inc., Princeton, N.J.; prof. Neurosci. N.J. Neurosci. Inst., Seton Hall U., 2000—. Mem. sci. peer review com. NIH, Bethesda, Md., 1998—; chmn. Am. Heart Assn. Study Sect. 3, Mid Atlantic Region, Balt., 1998. Contbr. over 100 articles to profl. jours. Sec. clin. sect. Royal Soc. Medicine, London, 1995. Recipient Nat. prize Can. Stroke Soc., 1991. Fellow Royal Coll. Physicians Can., Royal Coll. Physicians London, Am. Coll. Physicians, Am. Coll. Cardiology (assoc.); mem. Royal Coll. Physicians (UK), United Univ. Club, Royal Overseas League. Avocations: antique bookcollecting, opera, walking. Office: Pharmanet Inc 504 Carnegie Ctr Princeton NJ 08540-6242 Fax: 609-951-6800. E-mail: soppenh@hotmail.com.

OPPENHEIMER, SUZI, state legislator; b. N.Y.C., Dec. 13, 1934; d. Alfred Elihu Rosenhirsch and Blanche (Schoen) O.; m. Martin J. Oppenheimer, July 3, 1960; children: Marcy, Evan, Josh, Alexandra. BA in Econs., Conn. Coll. for Women, 1956; MBA, Columbia U., 1958. Security analyst McDonnell & Co., N.Y.C., 1958-60, L.F. Rothschild Co., N.Y.C., 1960-63; mayor Village of Mamaroneck, N.Y., 1977-85; mem. N.Y. State Senate, Albany, 1985—. Ranking mem. edn., mem. fin., transp., water resources, health, ethics, environ. conservation and banking com., chmn. N.Y. State Women Legislators' Lobby, chmn. Senate Dem. Task Force on Women's Issues, treas. Legis. Women's Caucus, pres. Senate Club. Former pres. Mamaroneck LWV, Westchester County Mcpl. Ofcls. Assn., Westchester Mcpl. Planning Fedn. Recipient Humanitarian Svc. award Am. Jewish Com., 1988, Legis. Leadership award Young Adult Inst., 1988, Legis. award Westchester Irish Com., 1988, Hon. Svc. award Vis. Nurses Svcs., 1989, Humanitarian Svc. award Project Family, 1990, Meritorious Svc. award N.Y. State Assn. Counties, 1990, Friend of Edn. award N.Y. State United Tchrs., 1991, Assn. Health Care Providers award, 1993, Govtl. award Cmty. Opportunity Program, 1994, Spl. Recognition award Open Door Family Med. Group, 1995, Appreciation award, Careers for People with Disabilities, 1996, Dominican Sisters Family Health Svcs., 1996, Vets. Svc. award JWV, 1997; honoree Windward Sch. Ann. Dinner, 1992, others; named Legislator of Yr., N.Y. State Women's Press Club, Woman of Yr., Westchester ORT, 1990, Woman of Yr., Hope Cmty. Svcs. Club, Fedn. of Women's Clubs. Democrat. Jewish. Office: 222 Grace Church St Port Chester NY 10573-5168

OPPER, BARBARA NEGRI, financial economist; b. Torrington, Conn., Sept. 8, 1939; d. Albert Frederick and Anna (LaRocco) Negri; m. Franz Frederick Opper, Dec. 2, 1967 (dec. Mar. 1991); children: Gretchen Elizabeth, Stephen Frederick. BA, Conn. Coll., 1961; MA in Econs., U. Mich., 1965. Analyst Conn. Gen. Ins., Hartford, 1961-63; econ. rsch. assoc. Life Ins. Assn. Am., N.Y.C., 1965-66; corp. sec., dir. Krambo Corp., 1966-67; economist Fed. Res. Bd., Washington, 1967-72, sr. economist, 1976-83; fin. economist Travelers Ins. Cos., Hartford, 1972-76; lectr. Mt. Holyoke Coll., South Hadley, Mass., 1975-76; sr. advisor The World Bank, Washington, 1983-98; pres. ConFirm, Chevy Chase, Md., 1998—. Sec., bd. dirs. Bank Fund Staff Fed. Credit Union, Washington, 1997—; advisor sovereign debt mgmt. U.S. Treasury, Washington, 2000—. Contbr. articles to Fed. Res. Bull. Bd. dirs. Washington Bach Consort, 1998—. Mem.: Soc. Actuaries (com. on banks and fin. instns. 1993—2001), Cosmos Club, Phi Beta Kappa. Home: 7004 Meadow Ln Chevy Chase MD 20815

OPPERWALL, STEPHEN GABRIEL, lawyer; b. Racine, Wis., Aug. 14, 1953; s. Raymond and Helen Bertha Opperwall; m. Kathleen O'Neill, Oct. 27, 1990; children: Christopher Stephen, Scott O'Neill. BA, Calvin Coll., 1975; JD, U. Santa Clara, 1981. Bar: Calif. 1981, U.S. Dist. Ct. (no., ea., ctrl. and so. dists.) Calif. 1981, U.S. Tax Ct. 1994, U.S. Ct. Appeals (9th cir.) 1984; cert. specialist in creditor's rights. Tchg. asst. U. Santa Clara (Calif.) Sch. Law, 1979; judge's law clk. U.S. Ct. Appeals, 9th Cir., San Francisco, 1980; assoc. Pitto & Ubhaus, San Jose, Calif., 1980-82, Germino, Layne & Brodie, Palo Alto, 1982-87, Tarkington, O'Connor & O'Neill, San Jose, 1988-90, Smith & Smith, San Jose, 1990-92; pvt. practice Law Offices of Stephen G. Opperwall, Pleasanton, Calif., 1992—. Judge pro tem Santa Clara County Cts., 1986—, Alameda County (Calif.) Cts., 1992—; mem. adv. bd. Fremont (Calif.) Bank, 1996. Editor Santa Clara Law Review, 1980. Mem. bd. dirs. Fremont Symphony, 1994. Mem. Coml. Law League Am., Pleasanton C. of C. Avocations: golf, tennis, computers. Office: 4900 Hopyard Rd Ste 100 Pleasanton CA 94588-3149 E-mail: lawofcsgo@aol.com.

OPPEWALL, JEANNINE CLAUDIA, motion picture production designer; b. Whitinsville, Mass., Nov. 28, 1946; d. Garret Oppewall and Eva Edith Boutilier; m. Paul Schrader (div.). BA, Calvin Coll.; MA, Bryn Mawr Coll. Lectr. Harvard U., Am. Film. Inst., Otis Inst. of Art, Am. Inst. of Graphic Arts, others. Film prodn. designer L.A. Confidential, 1997 (Oscar nomination), Pleasantville, 1998 (Oscar nomination, L.A. Film Critics Assn. award for best prodn. design 1998), Wonder Boys, 1999, The Sum of All Fears, 2001, Catch Me if You Can, 2002, Maria's Lovers, Ironweed, The Music Box, White Palace, Love Letters, The Big Easy, Rooftops, Sibling Rivalry, The Bridges of Madison County, Snow Falling on Cedars, Tender Mercies Mem.: Art Dirs. Guild, United Scenic Artists.

OPPLER, RALPH LEO, retired publishing executive, advertising executive; b. N.Y.C., June 22, 1935; s. Charles Kurt and Jetta (Samuels) O.; m. Ruth Theresa Schoen, Sept. 22, 1957; children: Charles, Robin, Stephen. Student, Bryant Coll., 1951-52. Various sales positions, 1959-71; mem. sales staff Jour. Commerce Newspaper, N.Y.C., 1972-77; regional dir. B'nai B'rith Internat., Washington, 1978-88; fundraising mgr. Juvenile Diabetes Found., Essex

County, N.J., 1990-91; founder, pres. Bus. Builders Pub. Co., Inc., Fair Lawn, 1991-99; counselor Svc. Corps of Retired Execs., 2000—. Fundraising cons. Williams Ctr. Performing Arts, Rutherford, N.J., 1986, March of Dimes, Bergen County, N.J., 1980, Nat. Assn. Disabled Athletes, Ft. Lee, N.J., 1985; exec. analyst George B. May Co., Chgo., 1988. Pres., mem. Ridgefield (N.J.) H.S. Booster Club, 1970-80; v.p., coach, mgr. Ridgefield Boys Athletic Orgn., 1964-80; sponsor, coach basketball team Nat. Amateur Athletic Union, N.J., 1975-76; commr. Ridgefield Pks. and Recreation Commn., 1976-80; coach, Ridgefield 7/8 Grade Basketball, 1968-80; bd. dirs. Coun. Compulsive Gambling of N.J., 1997-99; mem. Svc. Corps of Ret. Execs., U.S. SBA. With USN, 1954-59. Mem. Commerce and Industry Assn. N.J., Fair Lawn C. of C., B'nai B'rith (Young Leadership award 1978; v.p. Paterson, N.J. lodge 1977; pres. Englewood lodge 1977-78), Jaycees (pres. Jacksonville, N.C. chpt. 1961). Democrat. Jewish. Avocations: basketball, jazz, ballroom dancing. Home: 10933 Royal Caribbean Cir Boynton Beach FL 33437-4222

OPPMAN, JOHN CHRISTOPHER, small business owner; b. Gary, Ind., Feb. 16, 1954; s. Ernest and Mary Oppman; divorced; children: Jennifer Kolosci, Elizabeth, Christine. BS in Criminal Justice, Ind. U., Gary, 1992; MPA, Western Mich. U., 1995. Asst. pers. dir. Sts. and Sanitation City of Gary, Ind., 1973; coke plant laborer U.S. Steel Corp., Gary, 1976-84; computer cons., 1985-88; drill instr. Camp Summit Juvenile Boot Camp State of Ind. Dept. Corrections, La Porte, 1995-97; owner, operator Specialty Logistics, Sawyer, Mich., 1998—. Asst. to pres. U.S.W.A. Local 1014, Gary, 1982-84. Polit. organizer Mayor Richard G. Hatcher campaign, Gary, 1970-73; campaign advisor, organizer Local 1014 presdl. campaign, Gary, 1978-84. Truman scholar, 1990. Mem. Gold Key, Sons of Italy. Episcopalian. Avocations: historical animation, interpretation.

OPPMANN, ANDREW JAMES, newspaper editor; b. Hopkinsville, Ky., Apr. 3, 1963; s. Patrick George Oppmann and Elizabeth Anne (Freeman) Peace; m. Emily Elise Wey, Oct. 8, 1988; children: Emily Katherine, Sarah Elizabeth. BA in Journalism, U. Ky., 1985. Staff writer The Orange County Register, Santa Ana, Calif., 1985-86; copy editor, staff writer Lexington (Ky.) Herald-Leader, 1986-87, bur. chief, asst. metro editor, 1988-91; urban affairs writer The Knoxville (Tenn.) News-Sentinel, 1987-88; asst. city editor The Houston Post, 1991-92, dep. met. editor, 1992, asst. to mng. editor, 1992, met. editor, 1992-94; Ky. editor The Cin. (Ohio) Enquirer, 1994-97; supervising editor The Ky. Enquirer, Ft. Mitchell, 1994-97; mng. editor Montgomery (Ala.) Advertiser, 1998-2001; exec. editor The Post-Crescent, Appleton, Wis., 2001—. Bd. vis. U. Ky. Sch. Journalism, 1994-97. Fellow U. Ky., 1984; recipient Gannett Newsroom Supr. Recognition award, 1995, 2000. Mem. U. Ky. Journalism Alumni Assn. (v.p. 1997-2000, pres. 2001—), Soc. Profl. Journalists (bd. dirs. Queen City chpt. 1995-97), Ala. AP Mng. Editors (bd. dirs. 1998—), U. Ky. Nat. Alumni Assn. (bd. dirs. 1998-2001) Office: The Post-Crescent PO Box 59 Appleton WI 54912 E-mail: oppedit@aol.com.

OPRE, THOMAS EDWARD, magazine editor, film company executive, corporate travel company executive; b. Evansville, Ind., Nov. 6, 1943; s. William Jennings and Ruth (Strouss) O.; children: Thomas Andrew, William Hartley. AB in Journalism, Ind. U., 1965. Writer sports and outdoors Decatur (Ill.) Herald and Rev., 1965-66; outdoor editor Detroit Free Press, 1966—91; field editor Midwest div. Field and Stream mag., 1971-81; editorial dir. Gt. Lakes Sportsman mag., 1972-75; editor-at-large and sports vehicles editor Outdoor Life mag., 1981-93; pres. Tom Opre Prodns., 1967—. Pres. TOP Safaris, Inc., 1986—. Author numerous articles in outdoor and travel fields. Recipient James Henshall award Am. Fish Tackle Mfrs. Assn., 1969, Teddy award Internat. Outdoor Travel Film Festival, 1973, Environ. award EPA, 1977, Nat. Writer's award Safari Club Internat., 1977, Deep Woods Writing award OWAA, 1977, Conservation Service award Ducks Unltd., 1977; World Wildlife Found. award, 1981; named to Internat. Fishing Hall of Fame, 1968, Conservation Communicator of Yr., 1985. Mem. Outdoor Writers Assn. Am. (past dir., pres., v.p., chmn. bd.), Assn. Gt. Lakes Outdoor Writers (past dir., chmn. bd., pres., v.p.), Mich. Outdoor Writers Assn. (v.p., pres., chmn. bd. dirs.), Alpha Tau Omega. Home and Office: 255 Powers Cv NE Marietta GA 30067-1503 E-mail: topsafaris@aol.com.

OPSAHL, ERHARD PETER, secondary education educator; b. Port Washington, Wis., Sept. 3, 1943; s. Peter Joseph and Caroline Hannah (Bruch) O.; m. Marta Mary Reeves, Dc. 7, 1968 (div. Aug. 1990); m. Carla Mae Beebe, Nov. 3, 1990; stepchildren: Kellie Brooke Endicott, Kaitlyn Carlene Endicott. BA, Northwestern Coll., Watertown, Wis., 1965; MA, U. Wis., Milw., 1972, PhD, 1994. Enlisted officer U.S. Army, 1965—91, advanced through grades to col., 1987; exec. asst. to adjutant gen. Wis. Dept. Mil. Affairs, Madison, 1992-96; tchg. Latin, journalism, Spanish, ancient medieval history Luther Prep. Sch., Watertown, 1995—. Adj. prof. history Wis. Luth. Coll., Milw., 1997. Co-editor: (online reference book) Military Orders , 1998—. Sec. Wis. Evang. Luth. Synod Hist. Inst., Milw., 1995-98; bd. dirs. Risen Savior Luth. Ch., McFarland, Wis., 1999—. Decorated Soldier's medal with Silver Star, U.S. Army, 1967-68, Bronze Star for Valour, Combat Infantryman's badge; recipient Order of St. George Silver medal U.S. Armor Assn., 1994. Mem. Medieval Acad. of Am., Soc. for Study of the Crusades and Latin East, N.G. Assn. of U.S. (life). Home: 5303 Dennis Dr Mc Farland WI 53558 Office: Luther Prep Sch 1300 Western Ave Watertown WI 53094 E-mail: eopsahlw@aol.com.

O'QUINN, NANCY DIANE, nurse, educator, consultant; b. Walton County, Ga., Nov. 22, 1944; d. L.C. Jr. and Eula (Hegwood) Kennedy; m. Charles Frank O'Quinn, Sept. 12, 1965; children: Robert, Spencer, Alan. Diploma, Ga. Bapt. Hosp., 1965; BSN, Valdosta State Coll., 1979, MEd, 1983; MSN, Valdosta State U., 1986; PhD in Social Work Adminstrn. & Policy, Fla. State U., 1999. Sr. nurse Tift County Health Dept., Tifton, Ga., 1979-80; instr. Abraham Baldwin Coll., 1980-85, assoc. prof., 1992-94; asst. prof. Valdosta (Ga.) State Coll., 1985-94; asst. prof. nursing Albany (Ga.) State U., 1990-92, 94-97; rsch. assoc. Fla. State U., 1998-99, Health Occupations Cook County, Ga., 1999; asst. dir. regional econ. devel. U. Ga., 2000—02; cons. O'Quinn Cons. Svcs., 2002—. Lt USNR, 1989—. Mem.: Alpha Chi, Sigma Theta Tau. E-mail: noquinn@planttel.net.

ORAL, BURC, geophysicist, consultant; b. Zonguldak, Turkey, Dec. 4, 1962; came to U.S., 1987; s. Firket and Suna Oral; m. Nancy Elizabeth Crandall; 1 child, Lily Demet Crandall-Oral. BS, Istanbul (Turkey) Tech. U., 1985, MS, 1987; PhD, MIT, 1994. Rsch. asst. Istanbul Tech. U., 1985-87; grad. rsch. asst., postdoctoral fellow MIT, Cambridge, 1987-94; programmer, analyst Scripps Insn. Oceanography, La Jolla, Calif., 1994-95; systems cons. Teradyne, Boston, 1995-96; software cons. Epsilon, 1996-97, Fidelity Investments, Boston, 1996-97; developer Miller Systems, Brookline, 1997-98; quality assurance cons. Delphi Info. Systems, Billerica, 1997-98; sr. quality assurance cons. Parametric Tech. Corp., Waltham, 1998-99; prin. software engr. Iona Tech., 2000—01; cons. Oracle/Amadeus E-travel, 2001—; pres. Dev Atma Techs. Inc., Melrose, 2001—. Cons. Eliassen/Masterworks, Wakefield, Mass., 1999—2000; sr. devel. engring. cons. Watershed Tech., Waltham, Mass., 1999—2000. Mem. Am. Geophys. Union. Avocations: yoga, philosophy, meditation. Home: 580 Lynn Fells Pkwy Melrose MA 02176-2327

ORAM, ROBERT W. library administrator; b. Warsaw, June 11, 1922; s. George Harry and Lottie Mae (Gresso) O.; m. Virginia White, June 16, 1949; 1 child, Richard W. BA, U. Toledo, 1949; MS in Library Adminstrn., U. Ill., 1950. Asst. to librarian U. Mo.-Columbia, 1950-56; circulation librarian U. Ill.-Urbana, 1956-67, dir. pub. service, 1968-71, assoc. univ. librarian, 1971-79, acting univ. librarian, 1975-76; dir. Central Univ. Libraries So. Meth. U., Dallas, 1979-89, dir. emeritus, 1989. Mem. adv. com. Ill. State Library, Springfield, 1975-79 Contbr. articles to profl. jours. Exec. sec. Friends of So. Meth. U. Librs., 1980-89; former mem. bd. dirs. Urbana Free Libr., Lincoln Trails Libr. Sys., Champaign, Ill.; trustee Friends Austin (Tex.) Pub. Libr., 1994-99. Mem. ALA (life, pub. com. 1975-79), Friends of Libraries U.S.A. (exec. bd. 1980-86), Ill. Library Assn. (treas. 1972-73), Democrat. Avocations: reading, music. Home: The Heritage 4409 Gaines Ranch Loop # 252 Austin TX 78735

ORAN, ELAINE SURICK, physicist, engineer; b. Rome, Apr. 16, 1946; d. Herman E. and Bessye R. (Kolker) Surick; m. Daniel Hirsh Oran, Feb. 1, 1969. AB, Bryn Mawr Coll., 1966; MPh, Yale U., 1968, PhD, 1972. Rsch. physicist Naval Rsch. Lab., Washington, 1972-76, supervisory rsch. physicist, 1976-88, sr. scientist reactive flow physics, 1988—. Head Ctr. for Reactive Flow and Dynamical Systems, 1985-87; mem. adv. bd. NSF; cons. to U.S. govt., agys., NATO.; mem. Aero. Adv. Coun. NASA, 1995-97. Author: Numerical Simulation of Reactive Flow, 1987, 2d edit., 2001, Numerical Approaches to Combustion Modeling, 1991; assoc. editor Jour. Computational Physics; mem. editl. bd. Prog. Ener. Comb. Sci.; mng. editor Shock Waves; contbr. numerous articles to profl. jours., chpts. to books. Named hon. prof., U. Wales, 2001—; recipient Arthur S. Flemming award, 1979, Women in Sci. and Engring. award, 1988, Oppenheim prize, 1999, Zeldovich Gold medal, 2000; grantee, USN, NASA, USAF, Def. Advanced Rsch. Projects Agy. Fellow AIAA (publs. com. 1986—, v.p. publs. 1993-97, Dryden Disting. lectr. 2002), Am. Phys. Soc. (exec. com. fluid dynamics divsn. 1986, 96, exec. com. computational physics 1989—, chair 1991-92); mem. Am. Geophys. Union, Combustion Inst. (bd. dirs. 1990—), Inst. Dynamics of Energetic Sys. (bd. dirs. 1989—, v.p.), Soc. Indsl. and Applied Math., Sigma Xi. Office: Naval Rsch Lab Code 6404 # 6004 Washington DC 20011 E-mail: oran@lcp.nrl.navy.mil.

ORANGE, CAROLYN, education educator; b. St. Louis, July 11, 1948; d. William, Sr. and Alma M.; m. John H. Orange, Nov. 22, 1970; children: Traci, Timothy, Tisha. BA, Harris-Stowe Coll., 1970; MS, Washington U., St. Louis, 1977, PhD, 1991. Cert. tchr., Mo. Tchr. St. Louis Pub. Schs., 1970-77; asst. staff mgr. Southwestern Bell, St. Louis, 1977-80; program dir. Maritz Motivation, 1983-85; instr. Maryville U., 1986-88; tchg. asst. Washington U., 1990, motivation cons., 1987-91; asst. prof. St. Louis U., 1991-93; assoc. prof. U. Tex., San Antonio, 1993—. Cons. St. Louis Pub. Schs., 1992, San Antonio Ind. Sch. Dist., Tex., 1995-97, Region 13, San Antonio, 1995, 97-98; book reviewer Merrill Edn. Prentice Hall, San Antonio, 1997; presenter confs. in field. Author: 25 Biggest Mistakes Teachers Make and How to Avoid Them, 2000, The Quick Reference Guide to Educational Innovations, 2002; author/prodr.: (video) Using Peer Models to Teach Self-Regulation, 1996; contbr. articles to profl. jours. Publicity chair Ebony Fashion Fair, Chgo., 1996, 97, 99; mem. human rels. com. City of University City, St. Louis, 1992. Recipient four-year scholarship Harris Stowe State, St. Louis Pub. Schs., 1966-70, univ. fellow Washington U., St. Louis, 1975-77, 88-89, Spencer fellowship Woodrow Wilson Found., Chgo., 1990-91, others; grantee in field. Mem. Am. Ednl. Rsch. Assn., Am. Psychol. Soc., Serious About Money Investment Club (pres. 1995--), Phi Theta Kappa. Avocations: collecting costume jewelry, writing, painting, mentoring. Office: Univ Tex 6900 N Loop 1604 W San Antonio TX 78249-1130 E-mail: jorange@swbell.net.

ORAZEM, PETER FRANCIS, economics educator; b. Ames, Iowa, Nov. 26, 1955; s. Frank and Slava (Furlan) O.; m. Patricia Mary Cotter; children: Matthew, Katherine. BA, Kans. U., 1977; M. Phil., Yale U., 1980, PhD, 1983. Asst. prof. dept. econ. Iowa State U., Ames, 1982-88, assoc. prof., 1988-94, prof., 1994—; interim assoc. dean Coll. Liberal Arts & Scis., 1998-2000, dir. Indsl. Rels. Ctr., 2000—. Vis. scholar World Bank, 1993-94. Contbr. articles to profl. jours. Grantee Inst. Rsch. on Poverty, U. Wis., 1985, Nat. Rsch. Coun., 1986-87, NSF, 1990, Carlson Sch. Mgmt., U. Minn., 1990, USDA, 1992, 93, World Bank, 1994—. Mem. Am. Econs. Assn., Am. Agrl. Econs. Assn., Midwest Econs. Assn., Soc. Labor Economists, Phi Beta Kappa. Roman Catholic. Avocations: fishing, camping, playing with his children, scouting. Home: 4941 Utah Dr Ames IA 50014-3004 Office: Iowa State U Dept Econs Ames IA 50011-0001

ORAZIO, PAUL VINCENT, financial planner; b. Flushing, N.Y., July 9, 1957; s. Louis D. and Joan (Politi) O.; m. PattiAnn DeMarzo, May 1, 1982; children: Louis D. II, Christina M. BS in Bus., Fordham U., 1979; cert. fin. planning, Coll. for Fin. Planning, 1987. Cert. fin. planner. Acct. exec. Levi Strauss & Co., Inc., San Francisco, 1979-83; v.p., sr. fin. planner Gary Goldberg & Co., Inc., Suffern, N.Y., 1983-91; v.p. Orazio Fin. Svcs., 1991—. Past pres., bd. dirs. Vol. Counseling Svc., New City, N.Y., 1985—; mem. Rockland Conservatory of Music, 2000--. Mem. adv. bd. Rockand Orange unit Arthritis Found., Haverstraw, N.Y., 1991—. Mem. Fin. Planning Assn., Internat. Bd. Standards and Practices for Cert. Fin. Planners, Inst. of Cert. Fin. Planners. Roman Catholic. Avocation: golf. Home: 43 Lorna Ln Suffern NY 10901-7110 Office: Orazio Fin Svcs 400 Rella Blvd Suffern NY 10901-4241 E-mail: porazio@nlfs.com.

ORBACH, RAYMOND LEE, physicist, educator; b. Los Angeles, July 12, 1934; s. Morris Albert and Mary Ruth (Miller) O.; m. Eva Hannah Spiegler, Aug. 26, 1956; children: David Miller, Deborah Hedwig, Thomas Randolph. BS, Calif. Inst. Tech., 1956; PhD, U. Calif., Berkeley, 1960. NSF postdoctoral fellow Oxford U., 1960-61; asst. prof. applied physics Harvard U., 1961-63; prof. physics UCLA, 1963-92, asst. vice chancellor acad. change and curriculum devel., 1970-72, chmn. acad. senate L.A. divsn., 1976-77, provost Coll. Letters and Sci., 1982-92; chancellor U. Calif., Riverside, 1992—2002, chancellor emeritus, 2002—; dir. office sci. U.S. Dept. Energy, Washington, 2002—. Mem. physics adv. panel NSF, 1970-73; mem. vis. com. Brookhaven Nat. Lab., 1970-74; mem. materials rsch. lab. adv. panel NSF, 1974-77; mem. Nat. Commn. on Rsch., 1978-80; chmn. 16th Internat. Conf. on Low Temperature Physics, 1981; Joliot Curie prof. Ecole Superieure de la Physique et Chimie Industrielle de la Ville de Paris, 1982, chmn. Gordon Rsch. Conf. on Fractals, 1986; Lorentz prof. U. Leiden, Netherlands, 1987; Raymond and Beverly Sackler lectr. Tel Aviv U., 1989; faculty rsch. lectr. UCLA, 1990; Andrew Lawson lectr. U. Calif., Riverside, 1992; mem. external rev. com. Nat. High Magnetic Fields Lab., 1994—. Author: (with A.A. Manenkov) SpinLattice Relaxation in Ionic Solids, 1966; divsn. assoc. editor Phys. Rev. Letters, 1980-83, Jour. Low Temperature Physics, 1980-90, Phys. Rev., 1983—; contbr. articles to profl. jours. Recipient Whitney M. Young Humanitarian award Urban League of Riverside and San Bernardino, 1998, El Sol Azteca award La Prensa Hispana, 2000; Alfred P. Sloan Found. fellow, 1963-67; NSF sr. postdoctoral fellow Imperial Coll., 1967-68; Guggenheim fellow Tel Aviv U., 1973-74. Fellow Am. Phys. Soc. (chmn. nominations com. 1981-82, counselor-at-large 1987-91, chmn. divsn. condensed matter 1990-91); mem. AAAS (chairperson steering group physics sect.), NSF (mem. rsch. adv. com. divsn. materials 1992-93), Phys. Soc. (London), Univ. Rsch. Assn. (chair coun. pres. 1993), Sigma Xi, Phi Beta Kappa, Tau Beta Pi. Home: 2950 Van Ness St NW Apt 212 Washington DC 20008 Office: Office of Sci Dept Energy 1000 Independence Ave SW Washington DC 20585*

ORBAN, CLARA ELIZABETH, foreign language educator; b. Teaneck, N.J., Jan. 3, 1960; f. Denes Mihail and Giuliana Zamboni O.; m. Elliot Stephen Weisenberg, June 16, 1985. BA in Italian & French with honors, U. Chgo., 1981; MA in French, U. Geneva, 1984, MA in Italian, 1985; PhD in Italian & French, U. Chgo., 1990. Lector U. Chgo., 1985; instr. Roosevelt U., Chgo., 1987; lectr. U. Chgo., 1985-90; asst. prof. DePaul U., Chgo., 1990-96, assoc. prof., 1996—. Vis. lectr. U. Ill., Chgo., 1990; dir. liberal arts & scis. honors program DePaul U., 1997—, exec. coun. humanities ctr., 1998—; peer rev. Literature and Medicine, Chgo., 1998. Author: Au Travail!, 1995, The Culture Fragments, 1997, Surrealist Case Studies, 2001; co-author: (chpt.) Mothers of Invention, 1995; translator: Cytomegalovirus, 1996; contbr. articles to profl. jours. Grantee Quality Instrn. Coun., DePaul U., 1991, U. Rsch. Coun., DePaul U., 1993, ill. Humanities Coun., 1993, Liberal Arts & Scis., De Paul U., 1993, 99, U. Rsch. Coun., DePaul U., 1997, Svcs. Culturels France, Montpellier, 1997; Nat. Italian Am. Found. fellow, 1988; U. Chgo. scholar, 1985. Mem. Am. Assn. Tchrs. French, Am. Assn. Tchrs. Italian, Am. Assn. Italian Studies, Internat. Assn. Word & Image Studies, Modern Lang. Assn., Golden Key Soc. (hon.). Office: DePaul U Modern Langs 802 W Belden Chicago IL 60614 E-mail: corban@depaul.edu.

ORBAN, EDMOND HENRY, political science educator; b. Heron, Liege, Belgium, Apr. 25, 1925; emigrated to Can., 1961; s. Edmond and Maria (Jamar) O.; m. Anne Marie Anciaux, May 10, 1955; children: Margaret, Christine, Yvon, Francois, Benoit. PhD in Polit. Sci., U. Louvain, Belgium, 1967. Asst. adminstr. Province of Kasaï Govt. of Belgium, 1951-59, adminstr. Province of Kasaï, 1961; prof. polit. sci. U. Montreal, Que., Can., 1961—. Vis. prof. Peoples Republic China, 1996-2000. Author: La Presidence moderne, 1974, Le Conseil legislatif, 1967, Le Conseil nordique, 1978; author-editor: Mecanismes constitutionnels, 1982, Dynamique de la Centralisation dans l'Etat Fédéral, 1984, Le Systeme politique des Etats-Unis, 1987, Federalism and Supreme Courts, 1991, Federalism, 1992, Systéme Politique Américain, 2001. Served as info.-commando Belgium Army, 1950-51. Decorated Medal of the Resistance, 1945, chevalier de l'Ordre de la Couronne (Belgium), 3 other decorations. Roman Catholic. Home: 337 Lac des chats Saint-Sauveur QC Canada J0R 1R1 Office: U Montreal Dept Sci Politique 2900 Boul Edouard Montpetit Montreal QC Canada H3C 3J7 E-mail: orbane@hotmail.com.

ORBAN, KURT, foreign trade company executive; b. S.I., N.Y., Aug. 6, 1916; s. Kurt and Gertrude (Astfalck) Orbanowski; children: Robert Arnold, Robyn Ann, Kurt-Matthew, Jonathan; m. Catherine Cheng, 2002. Grad. steel fgn. trade course, Stahlunion-Export GmbH, Duesseldorf, Germany, 1938. Fgn. trade corr. Stahlunion, Dusseldorf, 1938, rep. Bulgaria, 1939-40; steel export trader Steel Union Sheet Piling Co., N.Y.C., 1941; v.p. North River Steel Co., 1941; chmn., pres. Kurt Orban Co., Inc., Wayne, N.J., from 1946; now sr. ptnr., chmn./CEO Kurt Orban Ptnrs. LLC. Mem. field hockey games com. U.S. Olympic Com., 1948-61; playing mgr., team capt. U.S. Field Hockey Team., London, Eng., 1948, playing coach, Melbourne, Australia, 1956; U.S. rep. Bur. Internat. Hockey Fedn., Brussels, 1954-62. Served to 1st lt., pilot USAAF, 1943-45. Field Hockey Assn. Am. named its cup for each yrs. men's team competition for him. Mem. Am. Inst. for Internat. Steel (charter; pres. 1966-68, 78-80, bd. dirs. N.Y.C.), Am. Exporters and Importers Assn. (pres. 1972-73, bd. dirs.), West Coast Metal Importers Assn. (bd. dirs.), Wire Assn. Internat., Am. Wire Prodrs. Assn. (charter). Achievements include climbing Mt. Shasta, Calif. (14, 203') and Mt. Kilimanjaro (20, 103'), 1987, at age 71; national singles ranking 16th in USTA 80 years and over 2000, 1st in singles and doubles, No. Calif., 1997, 2nd in Nat. doubles 85 & over, 12th in singles, 2001, 1st in both singles and doubles in No. Calif., 2001. Avocations: sr. tennis, skiing, photography, languages. Address: PO Box 2010 Brisbane CA 94005-2010 E-mail: kurt@kurtorbanpartners.com.

ORBEN, JACK RICHARD, investment company executive, director; b. Bklyn., June 16, 1938; s. Stanley Souza and Helena Emily (Hall) O.; m. Patricia Wells, Dec. 17, 1960; children: Stacey Souza, Stephanie Anne, Bradford Richard. AA, Valley Forge, 1956; BA, Tufts U., 1960. Sales mgr. nat. accts. N.Y. Tel. Co., 1960-66; founder, exec. v.p. Facts, Inc., 1966-69; with Fiduciary Alliance, Inc., N.Y.C., 1970—, chmn., CEO, 1979—. Chmn., CEO Fiduciary Counsel, Inc., White Plains Charter Revision Commn.; mem. Fin. Com. City of White Plains; past pres. White Plains Child Day Care Assn., Thomas Slater Ctr.; past chmn., bd. dirs. YMCA Ctrl. and No. Westchester. With USNG, 1960-66. Mem. Larchmont Yacht Club, N.Y. Yacht Club, Union League Club, Windemere Island Club, Univ. Club, Down Town Assn., The Econ. Club of N.Y., The Pilgrims. Home: 177 Soundview Ave White Plains NY 10606-3825 Office: Fiduciary Counsel Inc 36 W 44th St New York NY 10036-8102 E-mail: jorben@fcounsel.com.

ORBEN, ROBERT, editor, writer; b. N.Y.C., Mar. 4, 1927; s. Walter August and Marie (Neweceral) O.; m. Jean Louise Connelly, July 25, 1945. Humor and speech writer for entertainment personalities, bus. execs., politicians, 1946—; writer Jack Paar Show, N.Y.C., 1962-63, Red Skelton Hour, Hollywood, Calif., 1964-70; editor Orben's Current Comedy, Wilmington, Del., 1971-89; cons. to Vice Pres. Gerald R. Ford, Washington, 1974; speechwriter Pres. Gerald R. Ford, 1974-75; spl. asst. to pres., dir. White House speechwriting dept., 1976-77; speaker on uses of humor in communication, 1977—. Author: 2500 Jokes to Start 'Em Laughing, 1979, 2100 Laughs for All Occasions, 1983, 2400 Jokes to Brighten Your Speeches, 1984, 2000 Sure-Fire Jokes for Speakers, 1986, Speaker's Handbook of Humor, 2000; numerous other books of humor for performers and pub. spkrs. Recipient World Humor award Workshop Libr. on World Humor, 1992; Literary fellow Acad. Magical Arts, 1996. Mem. Writers Guild Am. Clubs: Nat. Press (Washington). Unitarian Universalist. Avocations: travel, theater. Home: 3709 S George Mason Dr Apt 205E Falls Church VA 22041-3700 *I have spent most of my lifetime creating laughter and consider it a lifetime well spent. Laughter is one of the glories of the human experience. It warms, amuses, instructs, and opens emotional doors. For me, laughter has been a living and a loving as well.*

ORBISON, JAMES GRAHAM, civil engineer, educator; b. Cleve., Oct. 27, 1953; s. James Lowell and Olga Andrea (Dianich) O.; m. Nancy Anne Miller, June 11, 1977; children: Ryan Brantly, Eric James. BSCE, Bucknell U., 1975; MEC, Cornell U., 1976, PhD, 1982. Project engr. English Engring. Corp., Williamsport, Pa., 1976-77; lectr. Bucknell U., Lewisburg, 1977-78, asst. prof. civil engring., 1982-87, assoc. prof., 1987-93, prof., 1993-96, Presdl. prof., 1996-99, interim dean Coll. Engring., 2000—02, dean of engring., 2002—. Reviewer ASME, ASTM, Am. Inst. Steel Constrn., Prestressed Concrete Inst, Pa. Dept. Commerce, Harper & Row Pubs. Contbr. articles to profl. jours. Mem. ASCE (Lindback award for disting. tchg. 1988), Am. Acad. Mechanics, Am. Inst. Steel Constrn., Am. Soc. for Engring. Edn. (Excellence in Instrn. Engring. Students award AT&T Found. 1990), Pa. Soc. Profl. Engrs. (Engr. of Yr. award 1985). Office: Bucknell U Coll Engring Lewisburg PA 17837 E-mail: jorbison@bucknell.edu.

ORCHARD, HENRY JOHN, electrical engineer; b. Oldbury, Eng., May 7, 1922; came to U.S., 1961, naturalized, 1973; s. Richard John and Lucy Matilda O.; m. Irene Dorothy Wise, Sept. 13, 1947; 1 child, Richard John; m. Marietta Eugenie Gayet, Aug. 2, 1971. B.Sc., U. London, 1946, M.Sc., 1951. Prin. sci. officer Brit. Post Office, London, 1947-61; sr. staff GTE Lenkurt Inc., San Carlos, Calif., 1961-70; mem. faculty UCLA, 1970—, prof. elec. engring., 1970-91, prof. emeritus, 1991—, vice chmn. dept., 1982-91. Author over 50 pub. papers; patentee in field. Fellow IEEE (Best Paper award group circuit theory 1968), Cirs. and Systems Soc. (Golden Jubilee medal 1999). Democrat. Home: 828 19th St Unit E Santa Monica CA 90403-6705 Office: UCLA Elec Engring Dept Los Angeles CA 90095-1594

ORCHARD, ROBERT JOHN, theater producer, educator; b. Maplewood, N.J., Dec. 3, 1946; s. Robert Orchard and Beatrice (Gould) Todd; m. Pamela Marcy Pritchard, Sept. 6, 1969; children: Christopher, Katherine. Student, The Lawrence Acad., 1965; BA, Middlebury Coll., 1969; MFA, Yale U., 1972. Gen. mgr. Peterborough (N.H.) Players, 1967-70; asst. mng. dir. Yale Repertory Theatre, 1971-72, artistic admistr., 1972-73; instr. Yale Sch. Drama, 1972-73; mng. dir. Yale Repertory Theatre and Sch. Drama, 1973-79, Am. Repertory Theatre, Cambridge, Mass., 1979—2002, exec. dir., 2002—. Assoc. prof., co-chmn. theatre adminstrn. tng. program Yale Sch. Drama, 1975-79; mng. dir. Loeb Drama Ctr., Harvard U., 1979-2000, dir., 2000—, mng. dir. Inst. for Advanced Theatre Tng., 1979-2002, exec. dir., 2002—; orgn. ptnr. Inst. Arts and Civic Dialogue at Harvard U. Former mem. bd. dirs. Theatre Comms. Group; pres. bd. Mass. Cultural Edn. Collaborative, Am. Arts Alliance, Peterborough Players, Cambridge Multi-Cultural Arts Ctrs.; former exec. com. League of Residents Theatres; chmn. NEA, Profl. Theatre Cos., Opera/Mus. Theatre Panels. Office: Am Repertory Theatre 64 Brattle St Cambridge MA 02138-3443

ORCUTT, BEN AVIS, retired social work educator; b. Falco, Ala., Oct. 17, 1914; d. Benjamin A. and Emily Olive Adams; m. Harry P. Orcutt, 1946 (dec.). AB, U. Ala., 1936; MA, Tulane U., 1939, MSW, 1942; DSW, Columbia U., 1962. Social worker ARC, Lagarde Gen. Hosp., New Orleans; social worker, acting field dir. Fort Benning (Ga.) Regional Hosp., 1942-46; chief social work svc. VA Regional Office, Phoenix, 1946—51; chief work svc. unit outpatient office VA, Birmingham, Ala., 1954-57, 58; rsch. asst. Rsch. Ctr. Sch. Social Work, Columbia U., N.Y.C., 1960-62, field advisor social work, 1962, assoc. prof. social work, 1965-76, La. State U., Baton Rouge, 1962-65; prof. social work, dir. doctoral program U. Ala., University, 1976-84; ret. Rsch. cons. Tavistock Centre, London, 1972; cons. sch. social work U. Houston, 1990, Troy State System, 1992. Author: Science and Inquiry in Social Work Practice, 1990, (with Harry P. Orcutt) America's Riding Horses, 1958, (with Elizabeth R. Prichard, Jean Collard, Austin H. Kutscher, Irene Seeland, Nathan Lefkowitz) Social Work with the Dying Patient and the Family, 1977, (with others) Social Work and Thanatology, 1980; editor: Poverty and Social Casework Services, 1974; mem. editl. bd. Jour. Social Work, 1982-84; contbr. articles to profl. books and jours. Mem. alumni bd. Sch. Social Work, Columbia U., 1985-88, 91-94. Recipient Centennial award for edn. Columbia U. Sch. Social Work, 1998; named to Ala. Social Work Hall of Fame, 1999; NIMH fellow, 1957-60. Mem. NASW, Ala. Conf. Social Welfare, Group for Advancement Doctoral Edn. (steering com., editor newsletter 1980-83), Zonta, others. Episcopalian. Home: 222 Fox Run Tuscaloosa AL 35406 Office: PO Box 870314 Tuscaloosa AL 35487-0314

ORCUTT, JAMES CRAIG, ophthalmologist; b. Holyoke, Colo., July 22, 1946; s. John Potter and Irene M. (Falk) O.; m. Barbara McCallum, Feb. 9, 1974; children: John, Gale. BPh in Pharmacy, U. Colo., Boulder, 1969; PhD in Pharmacology, U. Colo., Denver, 1976, MD, 1977. Diplomate Am. Bd. Ophthalmology. Intern U. Wash., Seattle, 1977-78, resident, 1978-81; fellow in orbital disease Moorfields Eye Hosp., London, 1981-82; fellow in neuro-ophthalmology Hosp. for Nervous Diseases and Great Ormond St. Hosp., 1982; asst. prof. ophthalmology U. Wash., Seattle, 1983-88, adj. prof. otolaryngology, 1987-88, assoc. prof. ophthalmology/adj. assoc. prof. otolargyngology, 1988-95, prof. ophthalmology, adj. prof. otolaryngology, 1995—. Chief ophthalmology Seattle Vets. Affairs Ctr., 1983—95; chief ophthalmology and eye care VA Puget Sound Health Care System, 1995—, exec. dir. surg. and perioperative care, 2000—; ophthalmology cons. Vets. Affairs Hdqrs, Washington, 1993—. Pres. bd. trustees Northwest Sch., Seattle, 1996-99. Avocations: Northwest history, postal history, antique restoration. Office: U Wash Dept Ophthalmology PO Box 356485 Seattle WA 98195-6485 E-mail: jorcutt@u.washington.edu.

ORD, JOHN KEITH, statistics educator, researcher; b. Grimsby, Eng., Nov. 28, 1942; came to U.S., 1980; s. Kenneth and Edith (Snowball) O.; m. Janice Ann Derr, May 20, 1980; children— Jane Althea, Lawrence Neil. B.S. in Econs., London Sch. Econs., London U., 1963, Ph.D., 1967. Lectr. ops. research Bristol U., Eng., 1966-74; vis. assoc. prof. stats. Pa. State U., University Park, 1972, prof. mgmt. scis. and stats., 1980—; McKinley prof. bus. adminstrn., 1987—; sr. lectr. U. Warwick, Eng., 1974-78, reader, 1978-80, chmn. dept. stats., 1977-80. Author: Families of Frequency Distributions, 1972; (with others) Spatial Processes: Models and Applications, 1981, Spatial Diffusion: An Icelandic Example, 1981, The Advanced Theory of Statistics, vol. 3, 1983, vol. 1, 1987; Spatial Aspects of Influenza Epidemics, 1987. Contbr. articles to profl. jours. Recipient Disting. Faculty Scholars medal Pa. State U., 1985. Fellow Royal Statis. Soc. (local sec. 1967-70, research com. 1975-78); mem. Internat. Statis. Inst., Am. Statis. Assn., Decision Scis. Inst. Methodist. Club: Nittany Valley Track. Avocations: running. Home: 7838 Oracle Pl Potomac MD 20854-4029 Office: Dept Mgmt Sci Pa State U 303 Beam Bus Adminstrn Bldg University Park PA 16802

ORD, LINDA BANKS, artist; b. Provo, Utah, May 24, 1947; d. Willis Merrill and Phyllis (Clark) Banks; m. Kenneth Stephen Ord, Sept. 3, 1971; children: Jason, Justin, Kristin. BS, Brigham Young U., 1970; BFA, U. Mich., 1987; MA, Wayne State U., 1990. Asst. prof. Sch. Art U. Mich., Ann Arbor, 1994—. Juror Southeastern Mich. Scholastic Art Award Competition, Pontiac, 1992, Scarab Club Watercolor Exhbn., Detroit, 1991, Women in Art Nat. Exhbn., Farmington Hills, Mich., 1991, U. Mich. Alumni Exhbn., 1989-90; mem. dean's adv. coun. U. Mich. Sch. Art and Design, 2001-02. One-woman shows Atrium Gallery, Mich., 1990, 91; group shows include Am. Coll., Bryn Mawr, Pa., Riverside (Calif.) Art Mus., Kirkpatrick Mus., Oklahoma City, Montgomery (Ala.) Mus. Fine Arts, Columbus (Ga.) Mus., Brigham Young U., Provo, Utah, Kresge Art Mus., Lansing, Mich., U. Mich., Ann Arbor, Detroit Inst. Arts, Kirkpatrick Ctr. Mus. Complex, Oklahoma City, 1994, Riverside (Calif.) Art Mus., 1995, San Bernadino County Mus., Redlands, Calif., 1996, Neville Mus., Green Bya, Wis., 1996, Downey Mus. Art, Calif., 1996, Detroit Inst. Arts, 1996, Gallery Contemporary Art, U. Colo., Colorado Springs, 1996, Saginaw (Mich.) Art Mus., 1998, Springfield (Mo.) Art Mus., 1998, Art Inst. So. Calif., Laguna Beach, 1998, San Diego Art Inst., 1998, U. Mich., Dearborn, 1998, Hillsdale (Mich.) Coll., 1998, Ferris State U., Big Rapids, Mich., 1998, Sangre de Cristo Arts Ctr., Pueblo, Colo., 1999; works in many pvt. and pub. collections including Kelly Svcs., Troy, Mich., FHP Internat., Fountain Valley, Calif., Swords Into Plowshares Gallery, Detroit; work included in: (books) The Artistic Touch, 1995, Artistic Touch 2, 1996, Best of Watercolor-Painting Color, 1997, Best of Watercolor-Painting Light; Shadow, 1997, Artistic Touch 3, 1999; (mag.) Watercolor, An Am. Artist, 1996; subject of articles. Chairperson nat. giving fund Sch. Art U. Mich., 1993, Sch. art rep. Coun. Alumni Svcs., 1992—, mem. dean's adv. coun. Sch. Art and Design, 2001—02. Recipient 1st Pl. award Swords Into Plowshares Internat. Exhbn., Detroit, 1989, Silver award Ga. Watercolor Soc. Internat. Exhbn., 1991, Pres.'s award Watercolor Okla. Nat. Exhbn., Oklahoma City, 1992, Flint Jour. award Buckham Gallery Nat. Exhbn., 1993, Ochs Meml. award N.E. Watercolor Soc. Nat. Exhbn., Goshen, N.Y., 1993, Color Q award Ga. Watercolor Soc., 1994, St. Cuthberts award Tex. Watercolor Soc., 1996, Daler-Rowney award San Diego Watercolor Soc. Internat. Exhbn., 1998, Hon. Mention award Nat. Watercolor Okla. Exhbn., 1998, Winsor:Newton award N.e. Watercolor Soc., 22d Annual Nat. Exhbn., 1998; many state and nat. painting awards. Mem. U. Mich. Alumni Assn. (bd. dirs. 1992—, Sch. Art rep.), U. Mich. Sch. Art Alumni Soc. (bd. dirs. 1989-91, pres.), Mich. Watercolor Soc. (chairperson 1992-93, bd. dirs. adv. 1993-94). Avocations: music, theatre, tennis, golf, reading. E-mail: lbanksord@cox.net.

ORDAL, CASPAR REUBEN, business executive; b. Martell, Wis., May 5, 1922; s. Zakarias John and Sina Carlovna (Wulfsberg) O.; m. Ann Elizabeth Brady, June 7, 1947; Christopher Rolf, Peter Stuart. BS, Harvard Coll., 1946; M.P.A., Harvard U., 1947. Supr. central indsl. relations staff Ford Motor Co., Dearborn, Mich., 1947-53; dir. orgn. planning and mgmt. devel. Colgate-Palmolive Co., N.Y.C., 1953-65; v.p., gen. mgr. New Holland div. Sperry Rand Corp., (Pa.), 1965-76; corp. v.p. personnel Norton Simon Inc., N.Y.C., 1976-78; sr. v.p. adminstrn. Max Factor & Co., Hollywood, Calif., 1978-85. Served to 1st lt. USAAF, 1943-46. Mem. Personnel Round Table (chmn. 1983-84), Am. Mgmt. Assn. (Adv. council 1977-82), Phi Beta Kappa Clubs: Lancaster (Pa.) Country. Republican. Lutheran.

ORDAL, ERIK AKSEL, management consultant; b. Palo Alto, Calif., May 4, 1970; s. George Winford and Carol Christensen O.; m. Yumiko Yokochi, May 13, 2000. BEE, U. Minn., 1992; MBA, Columbia U., 2000. Mfg. engr. Seagate Tech., Bloomington, Minn., 1993-98; assoc. McKinsey & Co., Florham Park, N.J., 2000—. Home: 34 Norwood Terr Millburn NJ 07041 Office: McKinsey & Co 600 Campus Dr Florham Park NJ 07932 E-mail: EOrdal100@alumni.gsb.columbia.edu., erik_ordal@mckinsey.com.

ORDEN, ALEX, management science educator emeritus; b. Rochester, N.Y., Aug. 9, 1916; s. Abraham and Esther (Katz) O.; m. Susan Rabinowitz, Dec. 8, 1946; children: Ruth Diane, David Robert, Jeanne Hannah. BS in Optics, U. Rochester, 1937; MS in Physics, U. Mich., 1939; PhD in Math, Mass. Inst. Tech., 1950. Physicist Nat. Bur. Standards, 1942-47; instr. MIT, 1947-50; mathematician Hdqrs. USAF, 1950-52; mgr. applied math. sect. Burroughs Corp., 1952-58; dir. operations analysis lab. U. Chgo., 1958-62, prof. mgmt. sci., 1958-86, prof. emeritus, 1987—. Adj. prof. U. Ill., Chgo.; vis. prof. London (Eng.) Sch. Econs., 1964, 86; vis. Vasser Woolley prof. Ga. Inst. Tech., 1966, 67, 70; program chmn. Nat. Computer Conf., 1981 Contbr. articles to profl. jours. Mem. Ill. Sci. Adv. Council, 1965-67. Mem. Inst. Mgmt. Scis. (sec. 1953, chmn. nat. meeting 1969), Assn. Computing Machinery (nat. lectr. 1965, chmn. spl. interest group in math. programming 1969-71), Math Programming Soc. (chmn. organizing com. 1970-72, vice chmn. council 1982-83, chmn. council 1983-86), Phi Beta Kappa, Sigma Xi. Home: 5715 S Kenwood Ave Chicago IL 60637-1742

ORDIN, ANDREA SHERIDAN, lawyer; m. Robert Ordin; 1 child, M. Victoria; stepchildren: Allison, Richard. AB, UCLA, 1962, LLB, 1965. Bar: Calif. 1966. Dep. atty. gen. Calif., 1965-72; So. Calif. legal counsel Fair Employment Practices Commn., 1972-73; asst. dist. atty. L.A. County, 1975-77; U.S. atty. Central Dist. Calif. L.A., 1977-81; adj. prof. UCLA Law Sch., 1982; chief asst. atty. gen. Calif. L.A., 1983-90; ptnr. Morgan, Lewis & Bockius, 1993—. Mem. L.A. County Bar Assn. (past pres., past exec. dir.). Office: Morgan Lewis & Bockius 300 S Grand Ave Ste 22 Los Angeles CA 90071-3109 E-mail: aordin@morganlewis.com.

ORDONEZ, MAGGLIO, professional baseball player; b. Caracas, Venezuela, Jan. 28, 1974; Baseball player Chgo. White Sox, 1997—. Named to Am. League All Star Game, 1999. Office: Chgo White Sox 333 W 35th St Chicago IL 60616*

ORDORICA, STEVEN ANTHONY, obstetrician, gynecologist, educator; b. N.Y.C., Jan. 4, 1957; s. Vincent and Rose (Goiricelaya) O. BA magna cum laude, NYU, 1979; MD, Stony Brook U., 1983. Diplomate Am. Coll. Obstetrics and Gynecology, speciality cert. maternal-fetal medicine; lic. Nat. Bd. Med. Examiners. Resident obstetrics and gynecology NYU-Bellevue Hosp. Ctr., 1983-87, fellow maternal-fetal medicine, 1987-89, instr. obstetrics-gynecology, 1989-91; clin. instr. obstetrics-gynecology NYU, 1986-89, asst. prof. ob/gyn., 1989—2001, clin. assoc. prof. ob/gyn., 2001—; dir. perinatal clinics and prenatal diagnostic unit Gouverneur Hosp., N.Y.C., 1989-94. Perinatal cons. Bellevue Hosp. Ctr., N.Y.C., 1989—; faculty mem. perinatal div. NYU Med. Ctr., 1989—; presenter in field. Contbr. articles to Surgery, Am. Jour. Obstetrics and Gynecology, Am. Jour. Perinatal, Surgery, Obstetrics and Gynecology, Jour. Reproductive Medicine, Acta Geneticae Medicae et Gemellologiae, Jour. Rheumatology. Named NYU scholar; recipient Founder's Day award, NYU, Wash. Sq. Alumni award. Mem. Am. Coll. Obstetrics and Gynecology, Soc. Perinatal Obstetricians, N.Y. Acad. Scis., N.Y. State Perinatal Soc., AMA, Phi Beta Kappa, Beta Lambda Sigma. Achievements include research in investigating aspects of maternal-fetal physiology. Office: NYU Med Ctr 530 1st Ave Ste 10Q New York NY 10016-6402

ORDOVER, ABRAHAM PHILIP, lawyer, mediator; b. Far Rockaway, N.Y., Jan. 18, 1937; s. Joseph and Bertha (Fromberg) O.; m. Carol M. Ordover, Mar. 23, 1961 (dec. 1999); children: Andrew Charles, Thomas Edward; m. Eleanor Musick, Feb. 24, 2001. BA magna cum laude, Syracuse U., 1958; JD, Yale U., 1961. Bar: N.Y. 1961, U.S. Dist. Ct. (so. and ea. dists.) N.Y., U.S. Ct. Appeals (2d cir.), U.S. Supreme Ct. Assoc. Cahill, Gordon & Reindel, N.Y.C., 1961-71; prof. law Hofstra U., Hempstead, N.Y., 1971-81; L.Q.C. Lamar prof. law Emory U., Atlanta, 1981-91; CEO Resolution Resources Corp., 1991—; mediator and arbitrator. Vis. prof. Cornell U., Ithaca, N.Y., 1977; vis. lectr. Tel Aviv U., 1989, Am. Law Inst.; team leader nat. program Nat. Inst. Trial Advocacy, Boulder, Colo., 1980, 82, 84, 86, 89, tchr. program Cambridge, Mass., 1979-84, 88, adv. program Gainesville, Fla., 1978-79, northeast regional dir., 1977-81; team leader SE regional program, 1983; team leader Atlanta Bar Trial Tech. Program, 1981-91; lectr. in field; sr. v.p. Resolute Sys. Inc., bd. dirs. Author: Argument to the Jury, 1982, Problems and Cases in Trial Advocacy, 1983, Advanced Materials in Trial Advocacy, 1988, Alternatives to Litigation, 1993, Cases and Materials in Evidence, 1993, Art of Negotiation, 1994; prodr. ednl. films; contbr. articles to profl. jours. Bd. dirs. Atlanta Legal Aid Soc., 1984-91, 7 Stages Theatre, 1991-96. Recipient Gumpert award Am. Coll. Trial Lawyers, 1984, 85, Jacobsen award Roscoe Pound Am. Trial Lawyer Found., 1986. Fellow Am. Coll. Civil Trial Mediators; mem. ABA, N.Y. State Bar Assn., Assn. Am. Law Schs. (chair litigation sect.), Atlanta Lawyers Club, Am. Law Inst., Am. Acad. of Civil Trial Mediators. Avocation: photography. Office: Resolution Resources Corp 303 Peachtree St Atlanta GA 30308-3201 E-mail: ordover@rrcatlanta.com.

ORDOVEZA, JUANITO LINO, real estate company executive; b. Manila, Jan. 15, 1930; s. Fernando Carmelo and Virginia Baltazar (Lino) O.; m. Lourdes Javallena Montinola, Jan. 25, 1958; children: Juan M. Jr., Leah O. Pantaleon, Cristina O. Quimson, Fernando M. BA, Ateneo de Manila U., 1950; MA, Kans. State U., 1954; BS in Civil Engring., U. Philippines, 1953; PhD, Cornell U., 1956. Registered civil engr., Philippines; registered agrl. engr., Philippines, U.S. Pres., chmn. Ormon Devel. Corp., Manila, 1960—; chmn., CEO F.C. Ordoveza & Sons, 1960—; vice chmn., dir. Monja Estate & Securities Corp., 1980—; vice chmn., treas. Fil Hispano Ceraminics Inc., 1980—; pres., chmn. Rural Bank of Mulanay, Inc., Quezon, Philippines, 1960—, Bay Devel. Corp., Manila, 1970—. Chmn., dir. Activated CArbon Manila Pest Control, 1990—; agrl. engr. Kenram Palm Oil, Philippines, 1950-65; mem. Presdl. Econ. Staff, Philippines, 1964-66; cons. Rice Integrated Complex, Philippines, 1970-80. Inventor Mech. Grain Drying. Pres. Magallanes Parish Pastoral Coun., 1995—. Lt. Philippine Res. Officers Tng. Corp, 1946-50. Recipient Fulbright scholarship grant Fulbright Edn. Found., Philippines, 1954-56, Scholarship and Ednl. award Cornell U., N.Y.C., 1954-56; named one of Ten Outstanding Young Men Philippine Jaycees, Inc., 1965. Mem. Civil Engring. Philippines, Agrl. Engring. Philippines, Mgmt. Assn. Philippines, Manila Polo Club. Roman Catholic. Avocations: basketball, swimming, boating, hunting, agricultural activities. Home: Magallanes Village # 54 Lapu-Lapu Ave Makati Philippines Office: Bay Devel Corp Bay Laguna Philippines

ORDUNO, ROBERT DANIEL, artist, painter, sculptor; b. Ventura, Calif., Sept. 5, 1933; s. Octavio and Mary G.; children: Patrice Schulman, Nicole Franco. Pvt. and group tchr., Santa Fe, 1990—, Australia, 1993; guest lectr. Australian Coun. on Adult Edn., 1993; interviewed on local radio stas., 1996. One man show include Koshore Indian Mus. Le Junta, Colo., 1998; exhibited in Great Falls Tribune, J.M. Swanson, 1985, Gazette, Cody Bur, Wyo., Tom Howard, 1987, Aurora, Great Falls, Mont., Shirley Edam Diaz, 1988, S.W. Art Mag., J.M. Swanson, 1990; featured artist Shaman's Drum, 1992, The Advocate, Tasmania, Australia, 1993, The New Mexican, Santa Fe, 1994, Wheelright Mus. Am. Indian, Santa Fe, 1995, The World Times, 1995, Seasons Quarterly, 1996; featured artist and cover image Internat. Fine Art Collector, 1992, cover and featured artist Informart Mag., 1994, Counseling and Psychotherapy, 1998, Mathbook, 1998, Ken Burns PBS Documentary film, 1998. Recipient Best Oil, Denver Indian Mkt., Pine Ridge S.D., 1985, 86, 87, 1st and 2d graphics Red Cloud Indian Sch., Best Painting artists choice Great Falls Native Am. Exhibit, James Bama Purchase award, Best of Show, Best Contemporary Painting Buffalo Bill Hist. Ctr., Cody, Wyo., 1987, Best Painting Artists Choice award Great Falls Native Am. Exhibit, 1989, Best Show award, 1993, Okla. Indian Art competition, 1998. Avocations: skiing, surfing. Home: 153 Calle Don Jose Santa Fe NM 87501-2391

ORDWAY, FREDERICK IRA, III, educator, consultant, researcher, writer; b. N.Y.C., Apr. 4, 1927; s. Frederick Ira and Frances Antoinette (Wright) O.; m. Maria Victoria Arenas, Apr. 13, 1950; children: Frederick Ira IV, Albert James, Aliette Marisol. SB, Harvard, 1949; postgrad., U. Alger, 1950, U. Paris, France, 1950-51, 53-54, U. Barcelona, Spain, 1953, U. Innsbruck, Austria, 1954, Air U., 1952-63, Alexander Hamilton Bus. Inst., 1952-58, Indsl. Coll. Armed Forces, 1953, 63; DSc (hon.), U. Ala., 1992. Various geol., engring. positions Mene Grande Oil Co., San Tome, Venezuela, 1949-50, Orinoco Mining Co., Cerro Bolivar, Venezuela, 1950, Reaction Motors, Inc., Lake Denmark, NJ, 1951-53; with guided missiles divsn. Republic Aviation Corp., 1954-55; pres. Gen. Astronautics Research Corp., Huntsville, Ala., 1955-59, 65-66; v.p. Nat. R & D Corp., Atlanta, 1957-59; asst. to dir. Saturn Systems Office, Army Ballistic Missile Agy., Huntsville, 1959-60; chief space information systems br. George C. Marshall Space Flight Center NASA, 1960-64; prof. sci. and tech. applications Sch. Grad. Studies and Rsch., U. Ala. Rsch. Inst., 1967-73; cons. Sci. and Tech. Policy Office, NSF, 1974-75; cons. ops. analysis divsn. Gen. Rsch. Corp., 1974-75; asst. to adminstr. ERDA, 1975-77; Dept. Energy, 1977-94, policy/internat. affairs dir. spl. projects office, cons., 1994—; also participant internat. energy devel. program Office of Asst. Sec. Internat. Affairs, Dept. Energy, 1978-79. Cons. to industry, Ency. Britannica, Am. Coll. Dictionary of English Lang., M.G.M. film 2001: A Space Odyssey, 1965-66, Paramount Picture Corp., The Adventurers , 1968-69; internat. lectr. space flight and energy programs. Author: (with C.C. Adams) Space Flight, 1958, (with Ronald C. Wakeford) International Missile and Spacecraft Guide, 1960, Annotated Bibliography of Space Science and Technology, 1962, (with J.P. Gardner, M.R. Sharpe, Jr.) Basic Astronautics: An Introduction to Space Science, Engineering and Medicine, 1962, (with Adams, Wernher von Braun) Careers in Astronautics and Rocketry, 1962, (with Gardner, Sharpe, R.C. Wakeford) Applied Astronautics: An Introduction to Space Flight, 1963, (with Wakeford) Conquering the Sun's Empire, 1963, Life in Other Solar Systems, 1965, (with Roger A. MacGowan) Intelligence in the Universe, 1966, (with W. von Braun) History of Rocketry and Space Travel, 1966, 1969, 75, L'Histoire Mondiale de l'Astronautique, 1968, 70, Rockets Red Glare, 1976, (with C.C. Adams, M.R. Sharpe) Dividends from Space, 1972, Pictorial Guide to Planet Earth, 1975, (with W. von Braun) New Worlds, 1979, (with M.R. Sharpe) The Rocket Team, 1979, (with F.C. Durant and R.C. Seamans) Between Sputnik and the Shuttle, 1981, (with E.M. Emme) Science Fiction and Space Futures, 1982, (with von Braun, Dave Dooling) Space Travel: A History, 1985, (with Ernst Stuhlinger) Wernher von Braun: Aufbrach in den Weltraum, 1992, Wernher von Braun: Crusader for Space (2 vols.), 1994, revised 1996, also single vol. edition, 1996, (with Randy Liebermann) Blueprint for Space, 1992, Visions of Spaceflight, 2001; editor: Advances in Space Science and Technology, vols. I-XII, 2 supplements, 1959-72, (with R.M.L. Baker, N.W. Makemson) Introduction to Astrodynamics, 1960, (with others) From Peenemünde to Outer Space, 1962, Astronautical Engineering and Science, 1963; mem. editorial bd.: (with others) IX Internat. Astronautical Congress procs., 2 vols, 1959, Xth Congress procs., 2 vols, 1960; guest editor: Acta Astronautica, 1985, 94, History of Rocketry and Astronautics, Vol. IX, 1989, Digital book Mars: Target for Tomorrow Microsoft Network & Internet, 1996; Co-creation of biographical Film " He Conquered Space", Discovery channel, 1996, History of Astronautics Video, 1996, inter-active CD Rom, 1997, revised, 2001, interactive CD ROM and video versions) Mars: Past, Present, Future, 1998; contbr. (with others) numerous articles to profl. jours., U.S. and fgn. encys., chpts. to books, sects. to others; organizer Blueprint for Space exhbn., 1991-95, U.S. Space and Rocket Ctr., IBM Gallery of Sci. and Art, NASA Vis. Ctr., Houston, Spaceport USA, Cape Canaveral, Fla., Nat. Air and Space Mus., Washington, Va. Air and Space Ctr., exhibit Shaping The Vision contributions Art Inst. Chgo., 2001, Bruce Mus. Art and Scis., 2001, Hampton and numerous others. Served with USNR, 1945. Recipient (with W. von Braun) diplôme d'honneur French Commn. d'Histoire, Arts et Letters, Paris, 1969; commended for contbns. to U.S. Space and Rocket Ctr., Ala. Space Sci. Exhibit. Fellow: AIAA (history com. 1975—, internat. activities com. 1980—89, 2003 Centennial of Flight Ctr. 1998—, sel. com. hons. and awards 1996—, HErmann Oberth award 1977, K.E. Tsiolkowski award 1988), AAAS, Brit. Interplanetary Soc. (guest editor Jour. Brit. Interplanetary Soc. 1992—96); mem.: Eurasian Acad. Scis., Nat. Space Soc. (bd. dirs. 1986—95, mem. publs. com. 1987—88, nominating com. 1990—92, bd. govs. 1997—, Ctr. for Lunar Rsch. com. 1998—), Am. Astron. Soc. (Emme award 1994, Nat. Space Club award 1997), Internat. Acad. Astronautics (history if astronautics com. 1983—, chmn. 1989—95, space activities and soc. com. 1986—, peer rev. com. 1995—, Luigi Napolitano Lit. award 1992), Arthur C. Clarke Found. U.S. (bd. dirs. 2000—), Huntsville Racquet Club, Washington Golf and Country Club, Harvard Club N.Y., Cosmos Club (bd. mgmt. 1986—91, v.p. 1988—90, award 2001). Home and Office: 2401 N Taylor St Arlington VA 22207-4021 also: 3423 Lookout Dr SE Huntsville AL 35801 Fax: 703-524-5856. E-mail: ordmars@aol.com.

ORDWAY, JOHN DANTON, retired pension administrator, lawyer, accountant; b. Mpls., Mar. 19, 1928; s. John Dunreath Ordway and Inez Adelaide (Stahl) Larson; m. Mary E. Bateman, June 16, 1951 (div. 1978); 1 child, David; m. Patricia A. Nagle, Dec. 27, 1996. BBA, Am. U., 1963, JD, 1965. Bar: U.S. Dist. Ct. D.C. 1966; CPA, Minn. Dir. ins. Nat. Automobile Dealers Assn., Washington, 1957-69; v.p. Edward H. Friend and Co., Washington, 1969-74; exec. v.p. and CEO Pension Bds. United Ch. of Christ, N.Y.C., 1974-96. Alt. mem. Planning Bd., Stamford, Conn., 1982-86. With U.S. Army, 1946-47. Mem. AICPAs. Republican. Mem. United Ch. of Christ. Club: Westwood Country (Vienna, Va.); Quail Run Golf Club (Naples, Fla.). Lodge: Kena Temple. Home: 7520 Citrus Hill Ln. Naples FL 34109

O'REAR, EDGAR ALLEN, III, chemical engineering educator; b. Jasper, Ala., Feb. 24, 1953; s. Edgar Allen O'Rear Jr. and Edith Idzorek. BSChemE, Rice U., 1975; SM in Organic Chemistry, MIT, 1977; PhD, Rice U., 1981. Rsch. engr. Exxon Rsch. and Engring., Baytown, Tex., summer 1975; asst. prof. to assoc. prof. U. Okla., Norman, 1981-91, Conoco disting. lectr., 1987-92, prof., 1991—, dir. Bioengring. Ctr., 1999—, assoc. dean rsch. Coll. Engring., 1995-99. Vis. sr. rschr. Hitachi Cen. Rsch. Lab., Kokubunji, Japan, summer 1988; vis. scientist RIKEN-Inst. for Phys. and Chem. Rsch., Wako-Shi, Japan, summer 1992; vis. prof. Chulalongkorn U., Bangkok, Thailand; cons. Boehringer-Mannheim, Indpls., Baxter-Travenol, Deerfield, Ill., Associated Metallurgists, Norman; co-founder Inst. for Applied Surfactant Rsch.; organizer symposia; reviewer for funding agys. and profl. jours. Co-author: Fluid Mechanics Exam File, 1985; contbr. tech. articles to profl. jours. Usher, mem. parish coun. St. Thomas More U. Parish, Norman, GlenMary Home Missioners; People to People Phys. Scientist Del. to China; mentor Big Bros.,Big Sisters, Norman, 1984-86. Recipient Faculty Rsch. award Sigma Xi, 1986; rsch. grantee NSF, NIH, Whitaker Found., NASA, AHA, OCAST, Dept. of Def. Fellow Am. Inst. for Med. and Biol. Engring.; mem. AIChE, AAAS, Internat. Soc. Biorheology (sec. gen. 1992-99, v.p. 1999—), Am. Chem. Soc., Tau Beta Pi. Roman Catholic. Achievements include patent for production of polymeric films from a surfactant template; method and composition for treatment of thrombosis in a mammal. Avocations: reading, hiking, stamp collecting. Office: U Okla Dept Chem Engring SEC T335 100 E Boyd St Norman OK 73019-1000

OREFICE, GARY JAMES, state legislator; b. Hartford, Conn. BA, U. Conn., 1964; MBA, U. Hartford, 1978. Mem. East Lyme (Conn.) Bd. Selectmen, 1981-85, East Lyme Bd. Fin., 1985-92, Conn. Ho. of Reps., Hartford, 1993—. Democrat. Address: 47 Columbus Ave Niantic CT 06357-3138 Office: Conn Ho of Reps State Capitol Hartford CT 06106

O'REILLY, DAVID J. oil company executive; b. Dublin, Ireland, Jan. 1947; BS ChemE, University Coll., Dublin, 1968, Doctor (hon.) of Sci., 2002. Various positions Chevron Corp., 1968—91, v.p., 1991—94; pres. Chevron Products Co., San Francisco, 1994-98; dir., vice-chmn. Chevron Corp., 1998-2000, chmn. bd. dirs., CEO, 2000—01; CEO, chmn. ChevronTexaco Corp., 2000—. Bd. govs. San Francisco Symphony, Bay Area Coun. Mem.: Am. Soc. Corp. Execs., Bus. Coun., Nat. Petroleum Coun., Am. Petroleum Inst. (treas., bd. dirs.). Office: Chevron Corp 575 Market St San Francisco CA 94105*

O'REILLY, KENNETH WILLIAM, military officer; b. N.Y.C., July 17, 1953; s. Thomas Michael and Dorothy Marie (Garvin) O'R.; m. Ginger Lee Jacobs, Apr. 22, 1978; children: Ryan, Erin. AAS, SUNY, Farmingdale, 1973; BS, Dowling Coll., 1975; MA, Webster U., 1982. Sales rep. N.W. Airlines, N.Y.C., 1976-78; commd. 2d lt. USAF, 1978—, advanced through grades to lt. col.; student navigator 452 Flight Tng. Squadron, Mather AFB, Calif., 1979-80; KC135 unit navigator 11th Air Refueling Squadron, Altus AFB, Okla., 1980-83, instr. navigator, 1984-85; wing exec. officer 340 Air Refueling Wing, 1984-85; chief of navigation 34 Strategic Squadron, Zaragoza AB, Spain, 1985-88; strategic plans advisor 2 Airborne Command and Control Squadron, Offutt AFB, Nebr., 1988-91; action officer Hdqrs. SAC/Directorate of Strategic Plans, 1991-92; chief of tanker plans Hdqrs. Air Mobility Command/Dir. Ops. and Transp., 1992-93, chief personnel mgmt. br., 1993-96; chief opers. watch divsn., headqrs., dir. ops. and plans The Pentagon, Washington, 1996-97, chief command control and comms. divsn., dir. ops. and tng., 1997-2000, chief global command and ctrl. sys. br., dep. dir. cur. ops., 2000—. Committeeman Levittown South-North Wantagh, Rep. Club, N.Y.C., 1971-78. Decorated 3 Meritorious Svc. medal, 2 Commendation medals, others. Mem. Air Force Assn., Inst. of Navigation, Airlift Tanker Assn. Roman Catholic. Home: 6361 Regal Oak Dr Springfield VA 22152-2861 Office: The Joint Staff 20318-3000 Pentagon Washington DC 20330-0001 E-mail: oreillkw@js.pentagon.mil.

O'REILLY, PATRICK JAMES, public relations executive; b. Riverside, Calif., Oct. 4, 1965; s. Patrick Gerard and Anne Mary (Caslin) O'R. BA in Internat. Rels., U. So. Calif., 1989. Account exec. Geogeson & Co., N.Y.C., L.A., 1987-89; rsch. analyst Rep. Nat. Com., Washington, 1989; campaign mgr. Riverside (Calif.) County Supr. Norton Younglove Election, 1989-90; sr. account exec. Stoorza, Ziegaus & Metzger, Riverside, 1990—2001; pres. O'Reilly Pub. Rels., 2001—. Guest speaker in field. Republican. Roman Catholic. Office: O'Reilly Pub.Rels. 3403 10th St #110 Riverside CA 92501*

O'REILLY, RICHARD BROOKS, journalist; b. Kansas City, Mo., Feb. 19, 1941; s. Charles Alfred and Wilma Faye (Brooks) O'R.; m. Anne Pustmeuller, June 27, 1964 (div. 1978); children— Kathleen Marie, Randall Charles; m. Joan Marlene Sweeney, Jan. 1, 1981 (div. 1996). BA, U. Denver, 1966. Reporter Washington Park Times, Denver, 1963-64; mng. editor Aurora Advocate, Colo., 1964; police reporter Rocky Mountain News, Denver, 1964-66, night rewrite reporter, 1966, city hall reporter, 1966-67, statehouse reporter, 1967-68, investigative reporter, 1971-74; minority affairs reporter Denver Post, 1968-70; freelance writer St. Georges, Grenada, 1970; investigative reporter Orange County edition Los Angeles Times, 1974-78, chief county bur., 1978, asst. met. editor, 1978-80, environ. reporter, 1980-84, computer columnist, syndicated columnist, 1983-96, coord. tech. resources, 1984-89, dir. editorial computer analysis, 1989—. Adj. prof. journalism U. So. Calif., 1990-92; mem. electronic filing adv. com. Calif. Sec. of State, 1995. Named Colo. Journalist of Yr., Sigma Delta Chi, 1972; recipient Pub. Svc. award U.S. Justice Dept., 1973, McWilliams award Denver Press Club, 1974, Investigative Reporting award Orange Country Press Club, 1977, 95, Los Angeles Times, 1977, 97, Nat. Journalism award Soc. Profl. Engrs., 1983, Clean Air award Am. Lung Assn., 1985, award for non-deadline reporting

Sigma Delta Chi, 1996, medal for investigative reporting Investigative Reporters and Editors, 1996. Democrat. Avocations: flying; sailing; camping. Office: Los Angeles Times 202 W 1st St Los Angeles CA 90012

O'REILLY, RICHARD JOHN, pediatrician; b. Bklyn., Apr. 29, 1943; s. John Russell and Margaret (Cronin) O'R.; m. E. Jean Capitano, Nov. 1984; children from previous marriage: John, Steven. BS, Coll. Holy Cross, 1964; MD, U. Rochester, 1968. Diplomate Am. Bd. Pediatrics. Intern U. Minn. Hosp., Mpls., 1968-69; resident in pediatrics Children's Hosp. Med. Ctr. and Beth Israel Hosp., Boston, 1971-72; with dept. pediatrics Meml. Sloan Kettering Cancer Ctr., N.Y.C., 1973—; attending pediatrician, chmn. dept. pediatrics Meml. Hosp., 1986—; mem. dept. immunology Sloan-Kettering Inst. Cancer Research; prof. pediatrics Cornell U. Med. Coll., 1980, Lila Acheson Wallace prof. pediatric research, 1980, Vincent Astor prof. clin. research, 1984; chief marrow transplantation svc. Meml. Sloan-Kettering Cancer Ctr., 1981—; vice pres. elect Am. Soc. of Blood and Marrow Transplantation. Councillor Internat. Bone Marrow Transplant Registry; pres. Damon Runyon-Walter Winchell Cancer Fund, 1991-96. Editor-in-chief BBMT; assoc. editor Cancer Rsch., Clin. Cancer Rsch., Bone marrow Transplantation, NCI Study Sect. D. Served with USPHS, 1969-71. Recipient Louise and Allston Boyer-Young Investigator award for clin. research, 1980 Mem. AAAS, Am. Pediatric Soc., Am. Assn. Immunologists, Am. Acad. Pediatrics, Am. Assn. Pathologists, Soc. Pediatric Rsch., N.Y. Transplantation Soc., N.Y. Acad. Scis., Am. Assn. Clin. Radiology, Am. Soc. Hematology, Am. Soc. Blood and Marrow Transplantation (sec. 1993-95, v.p.-elect 1999). Democrat. Roman Catholic. Achievements include performing first application of marrow transplantation from unrelated donors and from genetically mismatched donors, 1973. Office: Meml Sloan-Kettering Cancer Ctr 1275 York Ave New York NY 10021-6094

O'REILLY, ROSANN TAGLIAFERRO, computer educator; b. Bronx, N.Y., July 4, 1948; d. Neil F. and Antoinette C. (Odierno) Tagliaferro; children: Jean Marie, Ann Maureen. BA in French, Fordham U., 1970. Cert. tchr., N.Y., Ohio. Asst. supr. EDP audit Deloitte Haskins and Sells, N.Y.C., 1968-72; payroll clk. U. Va., Charlottesville, 1972-74, Great Am. Ins., Cin., 1974-76; computer coord. St. Mary Sch., 1986-96; instnl. technologist Cin. Pub. Schs., 1996-98; computer coord. St. Ignatius Sch., 1998—. Pres. Hyde Park Neighborhood Coun., Cin., 1985; founder, pres. Sitters Anonymous, 1978. Mem. Mensa. Roman Catholic. Avocations: Broadway musicals, movies. Office: St Ignatius Sch 5222 North Bend Rd Cincinnati OH 45247-8026

O'REILLY, SALLY, musician, educator; b. Dallas, Oct. 23, 1940; Student, Curtis Inst. Music; MusB, Tex. Women's U., 1963; MusM, Ind. U., 1965. Ind. concert violinist, pianist, 1965—; faculty Manhattan Sch. Music, N.Y.C., 1972-81, La. State U., Baton Rouge, 1981-93, U. Minn., Mpls., 1993—. Sr. Fulbright lectr., Uruguay, 1982-83. Debut Dallas Symphony Orch., 1957; concert tours thru U.S., Can., S.Am., China, Mex., Europe; composer String Power Series, String Rhythms, Fiddle Magic, Quartet Sampler; rec. artist with Caecilian Trio. Recipient Hendl award, 1957, Van Katwijk Conducting prize, 1958, Dealey award, 1958; grantee Paul Found., 1979; Fulbright scholar, Belgium, 1970-72.

O'REILLY, SUSAN WHITE, health facility administrator; b. Kosciusko, Miss., Apr. 7, 1947; d. John L. and Corinne Wilson White; children: Eric White, Leigh Ann. BS, Miss. U. for Women, 1969; cert. med. tech., Mercy Hosp., 1971. Cert. med. tech. ASCP; BLM; lic. supr. Tenn. Med. tech. Vanderbilt Hosp., Nashville, 1973-75, Ctr. for Clin. Sci., Nashville, 1987-89; supr. spl. chemistry Nat. Ref. Lab./LABGORP, 1989-95; adminstrv. lab. dir. So. Hills Med. Ctr., 1995-99; lab. mgr. Centennial Med. Ctr., 1999—. Named to Outstanding Young Women of Am., 1997. Mem. Am. Soc. Clin. Pathologists, Clin. Lab. Mgmt. Assn., Am. Bd. Bioanalysis. Avocations: golf, walking, reading. Office: Centennial Med Ctr 2300 Patterson St Nashville TN 37203-1528 Home: 30103 N Course View Franklin TN 37067

O'REILLY, THOMAS EUGENE, human resources consultant, retired; b. Wichita, Kans., Sept. 7, 1932; s. Eugene William and Florence Irene (Gustner) O'R.; m. Lorraine Bryant, Feb. 9, 1957; children: Thomas Jr., Patricia, Susan, Gregory, Pamela. BA, Iona Coll., 1954; MBA, NYU, 1958. Mem. human resources staff Chase Manhattan Bank, N.Y.C., 1957-69, dir. employee rels., 1969-71, mgr. internat. personnel, 1971-75, dir. internal staffing, 1976-77, dir. mgmt. resources, 1978-80, dir. exec. resources, 1980-87; v.p., sr. cons. Lee Hecht Harrison, Inc., 1988-93; ret. Spl. agt. counter-intelligence corps, U.S. Army, 1954-57. Mem. Nat. Fgn. Trade Coun., Exec. Issues Forum. Republican. Roman Catholic. Home: 6200 E Cielo Run N Cave Creek AZ 85331-7645

O'REILLY, TIMOTHY PATRICK, lawyer; b. San Lorenzo, Calif., Sept. 12, 1945; s. Thomas Marvin and Florence Ann (Ohlman) O'R.; m. Susan Ann Marshall, July 18, 1969; children: T. Patrick Jr., Sean M., Colleen K. BS, Ohio State U., 1967; JD, NYU, 1971. Bar: Pa. 1971, U.S. Dist. Ct. (ea. dist.) Pa. 1971, U.S. Dist. Ct. (mid. dist.) Pa. 1972, U.S. Ct. Appeals (3d cir.) 1977, U.S. Supreme Ct. 1988. Ptnr. Morgan, Lewis & Bockius, Phila., 1978—. Editor: Developing Labor Law, 1989; contbr. articles to profl. jours. Bd. dirs. Notre Dame Acad. and Devon Preparatory Sch., bd. govs. Aronimink Golf Club. Elected to Coll. of Labor and Employment Lawyers. Mem. ABA (chmn. com. on devel. of the law under the Nat. Labor Rels. Act., editor-in-chief The Developing Labor Law jour., elected mem. coun. labor and employment sect.), Pa. Bar Assn., Phila. Bar Assn., Ohio State U. Alumni Assn., Aronimink Golf Club (bd. govs.). Avocation: golf. Home: 1127 Cymry Dr Berwyn PA 19312-2056 Office: Morgan Lewis & Bockius 1701 Market St Philadelphia PA 19103-2903 E-mail: toreilly@morganlewis.com

O'REILLY, WENDA BREWSTER, writer, researcher; b. Frankfurt, Fed. Republic of Germany, Mar. 29, 1948; d. William Russell Brewster and Harriet Stimson Bullitt; m. James Patrick Brewster O'Reilly, July 18, 1981; children: Andrea Mariele, Noelle Christine, Mariele Angelica. BA in Psychology, U. Wash., 1975; MEd, Harvard U., 1977; MA, Stanford U., 1977, PhD in Edn., 1983. Gen. asst. King Broadcasting Co., Seattle, 1965-66; media buyer Benton & Bowles Advt. Agy., N.Y.C, 1967-68; acct. exec. Young & Rubicam Advt. Agy., Milan, 1969-70; advt. producer McCann-Erickson Advt. Agy., 1971-73; rschr., scholar Inst. for Rsch. on Women and Gender Stanford (Calif.) U., 1983-91, statis. analyst, rsch. asst., 1978-81; exec. dir. The Birth Place, Menlo Park, Calif., 1985-87. Guest lectr., seminar leader in women in mgmt., communications and childbirth issues, 1979-93; speaker on homeopathic medicine, healthcare issues, 1995—; CFO Travelers' Tales, Inc., 1998—; v.p. Birdcage Books, 1998—. Author: (Book) The Beautiful Body Book, 1984; editor: (organon) An Organon of the Medical Art, 1998; creator (edu.games for children) The Renaissance Art Game, 2000, The Impressionest Art Game, 2001, Van Gogh and Friends Art Game, 2002; contbr. articles to profl.jours. Mem. adv. coun. Pacific Design Forum, 1991-93; v.p., bd. dirs. Calif. Assn. Free-standing Birth Ctrs., 1986-88; mem. bd. dirs. Leavenworth Summer Theater, 1995-98, Icicle Creek Music Ctr., 1996—. Grantee William H. Donner Found. Mem. Mid-peninsula Access Corp. (founding bd. dirs. Calif. chpt., v.p., founding bd. dirs. 1986-87). Democrat. Episcopalian.

OREL, HAROLD, literary critic, educator; b. Boston, Mar. 31, 1926; s. Saul and Sarah (Wicker) O.; m. Charlyn Hawkins, May 25, 1951; children: Sara Elinor, Timothy Ralston. BA cum laude, U. N.H., 1948; MA, U. Mich., 1949, PhD, 1952; postgrad., Harvard U., 1949. Teaching fellow U. Mich., 1948-52; instr. dept. English, U. Md., 1952-54, 55-56, overseas program Germany, Austria, Eng., 1954-55; tech. editor Applied Physics Lab., Johns Hopkins U., Balt., 1953-56; flight propulsion lab. dept. Gen. Electric Co., Cin., 1957; asso. prof. U. Kans., Lawrence, 1957-63, prof., 1963-74, Disting. prof. English, 1974-97, Disting. prof. emeritus, 1997—, asst. dean faculties and research adminstrn., 1964-67. Cons. to various univ. presses, scholarly jours., Can. Coun. Arts, Nat. Endowment Humanities, Midwest Rsch. Inst., 1958—93; lectr., Japan, 1974, Japan, 88, India, 85. Author: Thomas Hardy's Epic-Drama: A Study of The Dynasts, 1963, The Development of William Butler Yeats, 1885-1900, 1968, English Romantic Poets and the Enlightenment: Nine Essays on a Literary Relationship in Studies in Voltaire and the Eighteenth Century, vol. CIII, 1973, The Final Years of Thomas Hardy, 1912-1928, 1976, Victorian Literary Critics, 1984, The Literary Achievement of Rebecca West, 1985, The Victorian Short Story: Development and Triumph of a Literary Genre, 1986, The Unknown Thomas Hardy: Lesser-Known Aspects of Hardy's Life and Career, 1987, A Kipling Chronology, 1990, Popular Fiction in England, 1914-1918, 1992, The Historical Novel from Scott to Sabatini, 1995; contbg. author: Thomas Hardy and the Modern World, 1974, The Genius of Thomas Hardy, 1976, Budmouth Essays on Thomas Hardy, 1976, Twilight of Dawn: Studies in English Literature in Transition, 1987; contbr. numerous articles on English lit. history and criticism to various mags.; editor: The World of Victorian Humor, 1961, Six Essays in Nineteenth-Century English Literature and Thought, 1962, Thomas Hardy's Personal Writings: Prefaces, Literary Opinions, Reminiscences, 1966, British Poetry 1880-1920: Edwardian Voices, 1969, The Nineteenth-Century Writer and his Audience, 1969, Irish History and Culture, 1976, The Dynasts (Thomas Hardy), 1978, The Scottish World, 1981, Rudyard Kipling: Interviews and Recollections, 2 vols., 1983, Victorian Short Stories: An Anthology, 1987, Critical Essays on Rudyard Kipling, 1989, Victorian Short Stories 2: The Trials of Love, 1990, Sir Arthur Conan Doyle: Interviews and Recollections, 1991, Critical Essays on Sir Arthur Conan Doyle, 1992, Gilbert and Sullivan: Interviews and Recollections, 1994, Critical Essays on Thomas Hardy's Poetry, 1995, The Brontës: Interviews and Recollections, 1997, Charles Darwin: Interviews and Recollections, 2000; delivered orations Thomas Hardy ceremonies, Westminster Abbey, 1978, 90. With USN, 1944-46. Recipient Higuchi Endowment Rsch. Achievement award, 1990; grantee Am. Coun. Learned Socs., 1966, NEH, 1975, Am. Philos. Soc., 1964, 80. Fellow Royal Soc. Literature; mem. Thomas Hardy Soc. (v.p. 1968—), Am. Com. on Irish Studies (v.p. 1967-70, pres. 1970-72). Unitarian Universalist. Home: 713 Schwarz Rd Lawrence KS 66049-4507 Office: U Kans Dept English Lawrence KS 66045

OREL, VLADIMIR, linguist, educator; b. Moscow, Feb. 9, 1952; arrived in Israel, 1990; s. Emmanuil and Leah (Potiagailo) O.; m. Maria Osipov, July 1, 1981 (div. 1986); 1 child, Artiom; m. Natalia Zakharov, Mar. 25, 1989; children: Miriam, Elizabeth. BA, Moscow U., 1970, MA, 1973; PhD, Russian Acad. Scis., 1981. Rschr. Russian Acad. Scis., Moscow, 1981-87, sr. rschr., 1988-90; sr. lectr. Hebrew U., Jerusalem, 1991, Tel Aviv U., 1991-97; lectr., acad. dir. Coll. Pluralistic Judaism, Jerusalem, 1996—; sr. lectr. Bar-Ilan U., Ramat Gan, Israel, 1997-98, assoc. prof. Israel, 1998-2000; dir. linguistics ZI Corp., Calgary, Alta., Can., 2000-01; prin. rschr. ETS, Princeton, N.J., 2001—. Vis. scholar Wolfson Coll., Oxford, Eng., 1995-96. Author: Hamito-Semitic Etymological Dictionary, 1995, The Language of Phrygians, 1997, Albanian Etymological Dictionary, 1998, A Historical Grammar of Albanian, 2000; translator: Alice in Wonderland, Through the Looking Glass, 1980-85; contbr. articles to profl. jours. Guastalla Found. prize, 1991. Mem. Philol. Soc., Writers' Union Russia, World Union Jewish Studies. Jewish. Home: 352-B 8th Ave NE Calgary AB Canada T2E Opg E-mail: vladorel@hotmail.com.

OREM, CASSANDRA ELIZABETH, health corporation president and founder, educator, holistic health consultant and practicioner; b. Balt., Sept. 26, 1940; d. Ira Julius and Mabel Ruth (Peeples) O. Diploma, Ch. Home and Hosp. Sch. Nursing, 1962; BSN with honors, Johns Hopkins U., 1968; MSN, U. Md., 1972; cert., Balt. Sch. Massage, 1988; MA in Applied Psychology, U. Santa Monica, 1991, cert. in advanced applied psychology, 1992; cert., Waitley Masters Coaching Prog., 1996; postgrad., U. of the South, 2000—. Staff, charge nurse Ch. Home and Hosp., Balt., 1962-63; asst. instr. Ch. Home and Hosp. Sch. Nursing, 1963-64, instr., 1964-70; student rschr., clin.-primary investigator U. Md. Sch. Nursing, 1971-72; clin. nurse specialist Johns Hopkins Hosp., 1972-77, rsch., clin. co-investigator, 1975, asst. dir. nursing, 1977-79, asst. adminstr., DON, 1979-87; clin. assoc. faculty Johns Hopkins U. Sch. Nursing, 1984-87; program dir., instr. intermediate massage course Balt. Sch. Massage, 1988-98, instr., 1988—, instr. advanced massage course, 1991-98, program dir. advanced massage course, 1995-98, curriculum devel. coord., 1996-98, network mktg. cons., 1991—; ptnr., educator UBP Assocs., 1990-91. Pres. Nursing Edn. and Cons. Svc., Inc., Balt., 1976-78, Oasis Health Systems, Inc., Balt., 1987—; spkr. workshop facilitator, cons. profl. topics, Health and Wellness, Personal Growth, Time Mgmt., 1973—; adv. bd. integrative medicine nursing consult Integrative Medicine Comm., 1999-2000. Author: (profl. booklet, audio publs.) Patient Education Book and Related Materials, 1977, Time Management/Organizing Sys., 1995; contbr. chpts. and articles to profl. jours. Vol. Office on Aging, Balt., 1982-83, Boy Scouts Am., Balt., 1984-85, Cathedral of the Incarnation, Children's Peace Ctr., Balt., 2000-01, Help Increase the Peace Program for/with Children, 2000—. Mem. Am. Holistic Nurses' Assn., Ch. Home and Hosp. Sch. Nursing Alumni Assn. (treas. 1970-72, pres.-elect 1975-76), Am. Massage Therapy Assn., Md. Massage Therapy Assn., U. Md. Alumnae Assn., Sigma Theta Tau (Pi chpt.). Democrat. Episcopalian. Avocations: camping, photography, pets, birding, music.

OREN, BRUCE CLIFFORD, newspaper editor, artist; b. Mineola, N.Y., Aug. 31, 1952; s. Ralph and Bernice (Lands) O.; 1 child, Adam Nathaniel; m. Angela Malone Williams, Mar. 4, 1990. Student, U. Md., College Park, 1970-74. Archtl. sculptor Universal Restoration Inc., Washington, 1974-76; tech. illustrator Tex. Instruments, Stafford, Tex., 1976-77; graphic artist Houston Chronicle, 1977-79, photo editor, 1979-86, artist, 1986—, L.A. Times Syndicate, 1987-91. Named Best Art/Graphic, Hearst Newspapers, 1998, 2000; recipient Bronze medal, Soc. Newspaper Design, 1992. Jewish. Office: 801 Texas St Houston TX 77002-2904 E-mail: bruce.oren@chron.com.

OREN, JOHN BIRDSELL, retired coast guard officer; b. Madison, Wis., Dec. 27, 1909; s. Arthur Baker and Lucile Grace (Comfort) O.; m. Harriet Virginia Prentis, Feb. 9, 1934; children— Virginia Joan (Mrs. Luther Warren Strickler II), John Edward. BS, USCG Acad., 1933; MS in Marine Engring, MIT, 1942. Commd. ensign USCG, 1933, advanced through grades to rear adm., 1964; chief engring. div. (11th Coast Guard Dist.), 1957-59, (12th Coast Guard Dist.), 1960-61; dep. chief (Office Engring.), Washington, 1962-63, chief Office of Engring., 1964-68; now ret. Mem. Mcht. Marine Council, 1964— ; chmn. ship structures com. Transp. Dept., 1964— ; exec. dir. Maritime Transp. Research Bd., Nat. Acad. Scis., 1968— ; mem. nat. adv. bd. Am. Security Council Recipient Legion of Merit. Mem. Soc. Am. Mil. Engrs. (pres. 1966, Acad. of Fellows), Am. Soc. Naval Engrs. (pres. 1965), Internat. Inst. Welding (vice chmn. Am. coun. 1964), Ret. Officers Assn. (bd. dirs. 1978), Pan Am. Inst. Naval Engring., Vinson Hall Residents Assn. (v.p. 1998), Masons. Republican. Episcopalian. Home: Apt 221 6251 Old Dominion Dr Mc Lean VA 22101-4806

ORENSTEIN, MICHAEL (IAN ORENSTEIN), philatelic dealer, columnist; b. Bklyn., Jan. 6, 1939; s. Harry and Myra (Klein) O.; m. Linda Turer, June 28, 1964; 1 child, Paul David. BS, Clemson U., 1960; postgrad., U. Calif., Berkeley, 1960-61. Career regional mgr. Minkus Stamp & Pub. Co., Calif., 1964-70; mgr. stamp div. Superior Stamp & Coin Co., Inc., Beverly Hills, 1970-90; dir. stamp divsn. Superior Galleries, 1991-94; dir. space memorabelia Superior Stamp and Coin. Co., Inc., 1992-94; dir. stamp and space divsn. Superior Stamp & Coin an A-Mark Co., 1994-97; sr. buyer, appraiser Superior Stamp & Coin, 1997-2000; v.p., COO Superior Galleries, 2001; co-founder, ptnr., prin. AuroraGalleries Internat., 2002—. Stamp columnist L.A. Times, 1965-93; writer The Brookman Times, Scott Stamp Monthly; bd. Adelphi U. N.Y. Inst. Philatelic and Numismatic Studies, 1978-81. Author: Stamp Collecting Is Fun, 1990; philatelic advisor/creator The Video Guide To Stamp Collecting, 1988. With AUS, 1962-64. Recipient Medal of Yuri Gagarin, Fedn. Supporting Russian Cosmonauts. Mem. AAIA, Am. Stamp Dealers Assn., C.Z. Study Group, German Philatelic Soc., Confederate Stamp Alliance, Am. Philatelic Soc. (writers unit 1975-80, 89-93), Internat. Fedn. Stamp Dealers, Internat. Soc. Appraisers: Stamps, Space Memorabilia. Republican. Avocation: fishing. Address: 19546 Minnehaha Northridge CA 91326

ORENSTEIN, WALTER ALBERT, health facility administrator; b. N.Y.C., Mar. 5, 1948; m. Diane Rauzin; children: Eleza Tema, Evan William. BS, CCNY, 1968; MD, Albert Einstein Coll. Medicine, 1972. Intern U. Calif., San Francisco, 1972—73, resident in pediat., 1973—74; EIS officer divsn. immunization CDC, Atlanta, 1974—76; med. epidemiologist divsn. immunization Ctr. for Disease Control, 1976—77; resident pediat. Childrens Hosp. L.A., 1977—78; fellow infectious diseases U. So. Calif. Med. Sch., 1978—80; resident preventive medicine CDC, Atlanta, 1980—82, chief surveillance and investigations sect., 1982—88, dir. divsn. immunization, 1988—93; dir. nat. immunization program Ctrs. for Disease Control and Prevention, 1993—. Cons. smallpox eradication program WHO, Uttar Pradesh, India, 1974—75; med. adv. bd. CDC, Atlanta, 1981—84, nat. vaccine adv. com., 1988—; clin. assoc. prof. dept. cmty. health Emory U. Sch. Medicine, 1985; adj. prof. The Rollins Sch. Pub. Health, 1992—; cons. and presenter in field. Mem. editl. bd. Pediat. Infectious Disease Jour., 1987—2000; co-editor: Vaccines, 1999; contbr. articles. Asst. surgeon gen. USPHS, 1995. Fellow: Pediat. Infectious Diseases Soc. (past chmn. publs. com., past mem. coun.), Infectious Diseases Soc. Am., Am. Acad. Pediats. (com. on infectious diseases 1989—, liaison mem., nat. vaccine adv. com.); mem.: APHA, Soc. for Epidemiologic Rsch., Am. Epidemiol. Soc. Office: Nat Immunization Program MSC-EO5 1600 Clifton Rd Atlanta GA 30333

ORESKES, IRWIN, biochemistry educator; b. Chgo., June 30, 1926; s. Herman and Clara (Rubenstein) O.; m. Susan E. Nagin, June 18, 1949; children: Michael, Daniel, Naomi, Rebecca. BS in Chemistry, CCNY, 1949; MA in Phys. Chemistry, Bklyn. Coll., 1956; PhD in Biochemistry, CUNY, 1969. Cert. clin. lab. dir. N.Y.C., N.Y. State. Chemist Tech. Tape Co., Bronx, N.Y., 1949; technician NYU Sch. Medicine, 1950-51; phys. chemist Kingsbrook Jewish Med. Ctr., 1951-56; research fellow Poly. Inst., N.Y., 1957-58; research assoc. Mt. Sinai Hosp., 1959-68, dir. arthritis lab., 1961-90; rsch. asst. prof. Mt. Sinai Sch. Medicine, 1969-74, rsch. assoc. prof., 1974-91; assoc. prof. Hunter Coll. Sch. Health Scis., CUNY, 1970-74, prof., 1974—, dean, 1977-80; mem. doctoral faculty in biochemistry Grad. Center, CUNY, 1970—. Vis. prof. Johns Hopkins U. Sch. Health Services, 1976-77; cons. to diagnostic reagent and instrument mfrs., 1953— ; mem. Internat. Sci. Council, Albert Einstein Research Inst., Buenos Aires, Argentina, 1969-79; mem. bd. examiners for clin. labs. N.Y.C. Dept. Health, 1973-75; sr. cons. Biotech. Rev. Assocs., 1983-92. Co-editor: Rheumatology for the Health Care Professional, 1991; contbr. numerous articles to profl. jours. Served with U.S. Army, 1944-46. Nat. Inst. Arthritis and Metabolic Diseases grantee, 1961-69; Arthritis Found. grantee, 1961-65, 69, 72; Lupus Found. grantee, 1975-76; CUNY Found. grantee, 1982-83 Mem. Am. Chem. Soc., Am. Coll. Rheumatology, AAAS, N.Y. Acad. Scis., Am. Assn. Immunologists, Am. Assn. Clin. Chemistry, Harvey Soc., Nat. Acad. Clin. Biochemistry, Acad. Clin. Lab. Physicians and Scientists, Clin. Immunology Soc., Sigma Xi, Phi Lambda Upsilon. Home: 670 W End Ave New York NY 10025-7313 Office: Hunter Coll Sch Health Sci 425 E 25th St New York NY 10010-2547 *I have always tried to live and work by the idea that strength is not harshness, caring is not sentimentality, and honesty is not vulnerability.*

ORESKES, NAOMI, science historian; b. N.Y.C., Nov. 25, 1958; d. Irwin Oreskes and Susan Eileen Nagin Oreskes; m. Kenneth Belitz, Sept. 28, 1986; children: Hannah Oreskes Belitz, Clara Oreskes Belitz. BSc with honors, Imperial Coll., London, 1981; PhD, Stanford U., 1990. Geologist Western Mining Corp., Adelaide, Australia, 1981-84; rsch. and tng. asst. Stanford (Calif.) U., 1984-89; vis. asst. prof. Dartmouth Coll., Hanover, N.H., 1990-91, asst. prof., 1991-96; assoc. prof. Gallatin Sch. NYU, 1996-98, U. Calif., San Diego, 1998—. Consulting geologist Western Mining Corp., 1984-90; consulting historian Am. Inst. Physics, N.Y.C., 1990-96. Author: The Rejection of Continental Drift, 1999, Theory and Method in American Earth Science, 1999; editor: Plate Tectonics: An Insider's History of the Modern Theory of the Earth, 2001; contbr. articles to profl. jours. Recipient Lindgren prize Soc. Econ. Geologists, 1993, Young Investigator award NSF, 1994-99; fellow NEH, 1993. Mem. Geol. Soc. Am., History Sci. Soc. Jewish. Home: 14174 Bahama Cv Del Mar CA 92014-2901 Office: U Calif San Diego 9500 Gilman Dr La Jolla CA 92093-0104 E-mail: noreskes@ucsd.edu.

ORESKES, SUSAN, private school educator; b. N.Y.C., May 24, 1930; d. Morris and Sarah (Rudner) Nagin; m. Irwin Oreskes, June 19, 1949; children: Michael, Daniel, Naomi, Rebecca. BA, Queens Coll., 1952; dance student, Eddie Torres Sch., Manhattan, N.Y., 1984-90. Organizer Strycker's Bay Neighborhood Coun., N.Y.C., 1961-75; dir. weekly column cmty. newspaper Enlightenment Press, 1975-85; assoc. tchr. Riverside Ch. Weekday Sch., 1985-95. Organizer, v.p. F.D.R.-Woodrow Wilson Polit. Club, Manhattan, 1961-71; organizer Hey Brother Coffee House, 1968. Democrat. Jewish. Avocations: music, dance, travel. Home: 670 W End Ave New York NY 10025-7313

ORFIELD, GARY ALLAN, political scientist, educator; b. Mpls., Sept. 5, 1941; s. Myron Willard and Melba Berniece (Lindseth) O.; m. Antonia Marie Stoll, May 24, 1963; children: Amy, Sonia, Rosanna. BA, U. Minn., 1963; MA, U. Chgo., 1965, PhD, 1968. Asst. prof. politics and pub. affairs U. Va., Charlottesville, 1967-69, Princeton U., 1969-73; scholar-in-residence U.S. Civil Rights Commn., Washington, 1972-73; research assoc. Brookings Inst., 1973-77; asso. prof. U. Ill., Urbana, 1977-80, prof., 1980-81; prof. polit. sci., public policy, and edn. U. Chgo., 1982-91; prof. edn. and social policy Harvard U., 1991—; co-dir. Harvard Civil Rights Project, 1996—. Ct.-apptd. expert St. Louis, Los Angeles and San Francisco sch. desegregation cases; chmn. study group on desegregation research Nat. Inst. Edn., 1978-81; bd. dirs. Fund for an Open Society; cons. HUD, Dept. Edn., Dept. Justice, Ford Found.; founder Movement for a New Congress, 1970; mem. commn. on women's employment and related social issues NRC, 1981-85; adj. fellow Joint Ctr. for Polit. Studies, 1982— Author: Reconstruction of Southern Education: The Schools and the 1964 Civil Rights Act, 1969, Congressional Power: Congress and Social Change, 1975, Must We Bus? Segregated Schools and National Policy, 1978, Toward a Strategy of Urban Integration, 1982, Public School Desegregation in the United States, 1968-80, 1983, (with W. Ricardo Tostado) Latinos in Metropolitan Chicago, 1983, Chicago Study of Access and Choice in Higher Education, 1984, Job Training under the New Federalism: JPTA in the Industrial Heartland, 1985, (with Carole Ashkinaze) The Closing Door: Conservative Policy and Black Opportunity, 1991, (with Susan Eaton) Dismantling Desegregation, 1996, (with Mark Bachmeier) Deepening Segregation in American Public Schools, 1997; assoc. editor: Am. Jour. Edn., 1983-87. Danforth fellow; Woodrow Wilson fellow; Falk fellow; Brookings Inst. fellow; Spencer Found. sr. scholar; grantee Carnegie Found., Ford Found., Twentieth Century Fund, Joyce Found., Spencer Found., MacArthur Found., Woods Trust. Mem. Am. Polit. Sci. Assn., Soc. for Values in Higher Edn. Democrat. Roman Catholic. Office: Harvard U Gutman 442 6 Appian Way Cambridge MA 02138-3704

ORFORD, ROBERT RAYMOND, consulting physician; b. Winnipeg, Manitoba, Can., Apr. 18, 1948; came to U.S., 1988; s. Robert Raymond and Sarah Gloria L. (Gullden) O.; m. Dale Laura Stuart, June 2, 1972; children: Carolyn Tiffany, Andrew Craig, Loren Brent. BS, McGill U., 1969, MD, 1971; MS, U. Minn., 1975; MPH, U. Wash., 1976. Assoc. prof. cmty. medicine U. Alberta, Edmonton, Can., 1978-88; dir. med. svcs. Govt. of Alberta, Can., 1979-81, exec. dir. occupational health svcs. Can., 1981-85, deputy min. cmty. occupational health Can., 1985-88; med. dir. employee health U. Alberta Hosp., Can., 1988; sr. assoc. cons. Mayo Clinic, Rochester, Minn., 1988-91, cons. preventive medicine, 1991-96, Scottsdale, Ariz., 1996—. Asst. prof. Mayo Med. Sch., Rochester, 1988—; mem. Alberta Energy Resource Conservation Bd., 1988-89; chmn. divsn. preventive and occupl. medicine, dir. exec. health program, Mayo Clinic, Scottsdale, 1999—. Contbr. articles to profl. jours. Mem. Olmsted County Environ. Commn., Rochester, 1991-96, chair, 1994. Govt. of Can. Nat. Health fellow, 1975-76. Fellow Royal Coll. Physicians & Surgeons Can., Am. Coll. Occupational and Environ. Medicine, Am. Coll. Preventive Medicine, Aerospace Med. Assn.; mem. Internat. Commn. Occupational Health Medicine (nat. sec. 2001—). Presbyterian. Avocations: Spanish, skiing, travel. Home: 15516 E Acacia Way Fountain Hills AZ 85268-3158 Office: Mayo Clinic Scottsdale Divsn Preventive Medicine 13400 E Shea Blvd Scottsdale AZ 85259-5499 E-mail: rorford@mayo.edu.

ORGEBIN-CRIST, MARIE-CLAIRE, biology educator; b. Vannes, France, Mar. 20, 1936; License Natural Scis., License Biology, Sorbonne, U. Paris, 1957; D. Scis., Lyons U., France, 1961. Stagiaire dept. biochemistry faculty medicine, Paris, France, 1957-58; stagiaire Centre Nat. de la Recherche Scientifique, 1958-60, attachee de recherche, 1960-62; research assoc. Population Council (Med. Div.), N.Y.C., 1962-63; research assoc. dept. ob/gyn Vanderbilt Sch. Medicine, 1963-64, research instr., 1964-66, asst. prof., 1966-70, assoc. prof., 1970-73, Lucius E. Burch prof. reproductive biology, 1973—, prof. dept. anatomy, 1975—; dir. Vanderbilt Sch. Medicine (Center Reproductive Biology Research.), 1973—. Editor-in-Chief Jour. Andrology, 1983-89. Recipient Career Devel. award NIH, 1968-73, NIH Merit award, 1986,; Fogarty Internat. sr. fellow, 1977; Disting. Scientist award Am. Soc. Reproductive Medicine, 1996. Mem. Am. Assn. Anatomists, Am. Soc. Cell Biology, Am. Soc. Andrology (v.p. 1994-95, pres. 1995-96, Disting. Svc. award 1997, Disting. Andrologist award 1990), Internat. Com. on Andrology,

Endocrine Soc., Soc. for Study Fertility (Eng.), Soc. for Study Reprodn., N.Y. Acad . Scis. E-mial. Office: Vanderbilt U Sch Med Ctr Reproductive Biology Rsch Rm C-3306 MCN Nashville TN 37232-0001 E-mail: m-c.orgebin-crist@mcmail.vanderbilt.edu.

ORGEL, VIVIAN AUGUST, beauty expert; BA in Music and Psychology, C.W. Post, 1977. Educator, cons., rschr. for health, beauty, and well-being, stress re-educator and behavioral sci. for beauty trade pubs., Dermascope, the aesthetics and spa therapy mags., among others.; cited for the advancement and focus on the underlying causal roots to physical and psychological ailments. devel. pioneering strategies and philosophies to combat their effects.; former dir. electrolysis svcs. Bloomingdale's, N.Y.C. Consumer safety lectr. better health through edn.; interviews and books reviews by nat. and beauty trade mags. including N.Y. Times, GQ, Vogue, Glamour, Self, Seventeen, New Woman, Essence, others; appearances on numerous TV and radio programs. Author: Vanishing Hair: Treatment and Options, Anti-Aging Mastery: Wrinkle Prevention, Reduction and Elimination; Cosmetic Procedures: Treatments and Solutions; The Hair Removal and Skin Safety Resource Guide-Facts You Should Know; Hair's The Truth; Stress Control: Maintaining Beauty Under Pressure; Beauty Rituals That Work; Action Steps: De-stress and Grow Forward, Control Your Skin's Destiny; The Physical Ramification and Remedies; For Emotional, Psychological and Spiritual Growth; Perception, Reflection, Satisfaction; Weigh of Life: Emotional and Physiological Weight Loss; Gaining and Maintaining Energy: Making the Most of Your Age; Taming Tension and Coping With It's Effects; Defending Yourself From Health Reducing Ailments. (seminars) The Mind, Body, and Beauty Connection and Ageless Beauty. Vol. fundraiser Muscular Dystrophy. Mem. Author's Guild, Internat. Assn. Counseling and Therapists. Address: 628 Redgate Ave Unit A Norfolk VA 23507

ORI, JERRY ALLEN, management consultant; b. Highland Park, Ill., Aug. 20, 1944; s. Ralph and Edith Louise (Contratto) O. BS in Bus. Adminstrn., Roosevelt U., 1973, MPA, 1976; student, Pacific Western U., 1990-93. Assoc., prin. A.T. Kearney & Co., Chgo., 1970-75; pres. Belden Health Care Co., 1975-80; CEO Ancillia Health Care, 1980-89; mgmt. cons. Universal Life Associates, L.A., 1989—. Bd. dirs. Cuneo Fin. Svcs., 1995—. Contbr. polit. cartoons, various publs., 1998-99. Chmn. Citizens Action Com., Norwalk, Calif., 1994—. Grantee State of Ill., Chgo., 1970, Roosevelt U., Chgo., 1976. Mem. Internat. City Mgrs. Assn. (pres. 1976), Am. Mgmt. Assn. (v. chair 1981-88), Am. Hosp. Assn. (treas. 1978-79), YMCA. Independent. Avocations: golf, reading, investments, cycling, teaching. Home: PO Box 2138 Norwalk CA 90651-2138

ORIANI, RICHARD ANTHONY, metallurgical engineering educator; b. El Salvador, July 19, 1920; came to U.S., 1929, naturalized, 1943; s. Americo and Berta (Siguenza) O.; m. Constance Amelia Gordon, June 26, 1949; children—Margaret, Steven, Julia, Amelia. B. Chem.Engring, CCNY, 1943; MS, Stevens Inst. Tech., 1946; MA, Princeton U., 1948, PhD, 1949. Lab. asst. CCNY, 1943; chemist Bakelite Corp., Bloomfield, N.J., 1943-46; instr. physics Miss Fine's Finishing Sch., Princeton, 1946-47; research asso. Gen. Electric Corp. Research Lab., Schenectady, 1949-59; asst. dir. U.S. Steel Corp. Research Lab., Monroeville, Pa., 1959-80; prof. U. Minn., Mpls., 1980-89, dir. Corrosion Rsch. Ctr., 1980-87, prof. and dir. emeritus, 1989—. Cons. in field. Contbr. chpts. to books, articles to profl. jours. Founder, mem. Foxwood Civic Assn., Monroeville, 1959-80; founder, v.p. Monroeville Public Library, 1960-80. Recipient Alexander von Humboldt Sr. Scientist award, 1984, W.R. Whitney award, 1987. Fellow Am. Soc. for Metals, Am. Inst. Chemists, N.Y. Acad. Scis., Nat. Assn. Corrosion Engrs., Electrochem. Soc.; mem. AAAS, Am. Phys. Soc., Am. Inst. Metall. Engrs. Republican. Home: 4623 Humboldt Ave S Minneapolis MN 55409-2264 Office: U Minn 112 Amundson Hall 221 Church St SE Minneapolis MN 55455-0113 E-mail: orian001@tc.umn.edu.

ORIANS, GORDON HOWELL, biology educator; b. Eau Claire, Wis., July 10, 1932; s. Howard Lester and Marion Meta (Senty) O.; m. Elizabeth Ann Newton, June 25, 1955; children: Carlyn Elizabeth, Kristin Jean, Colin Mark. BS, U. Wis., 1954; PhD, U. Calif., Berkeley, 1960. Asst. prof. zoology U. Wash., Seattle, 1960-64, assoc. prof., 1964-68, prof., 1968-95, prof. emeritus, 1995—. Active Wash. State Ecol. Commn., Olympia, 1970-75, ecology adv. com. EPA, Washington, 1974-79; assembly life scis. NAS/NRC, Washington, 1977-83, environ. studies and toxicology bd., 1991—. Author: Some Adaptations of Marsh Nesting Blackbirds, 1980, Blackbirds of the Americas, 1985, Life: The Science of Biology, 2000; editor: Biodiversity and Ecosystem Processes in Tropical Forests, 1996. 1st lt. U.S. Army, 1955-56. Mem. AAAS, NAS, Am. Inst. Biol. Scis. (Disting. Svc. award 1994), Am. Ornithologists Union (Brewster award 1976), Am. Soc. Naturalists, Animal Behavior Soc., Royal Netherlands Acad. Arts and Scis., Orgn. for Tropical Studies (pres. 1988-94), Ecol. Soc. Am. (v.p. 1975-76, pres. 1995-96, Eminent Ecologist award 1998). Avocations: hiking, opera. Office: U Wash Dept Zoology PO Box 351800 Seattle WA 98195-1800 E-mail: blackbrd@serv.net.

ORIE, JANE CLARE, state senator; d. John R. Orie. BA, Franklin Marshall U.; JD, Duquesne U. Law Sch. Asst. dist. atty. Allegheny County Dist. Atty.'s Office, Pitts., 1989-93; dep. atty. gen. Pa. Office of Atty. Gen., 1993-96; state rep. 28th legis. dist. Pa. Ho. of Reps., Harrisburg, 1996—2001; state senator 40th senatorial dist. Pa. Senate, 2001—. Republican. Office: 9400 Mcknight Rd Ste 105 Pittsburgh PA 15237-6007 E-mail: jorie@pasen.gov.

ORIN, STUART I. lawyer; Exec. v.p. corp. affairs, gen. counsel UAL Corp., Elk Grove Village, Ill., 1996—. Office: UAL Corp PO Box 66100 Chicago IL 60666-0100

ORING, STUART AUGUST, visual information specialist, publisher, writer, photographer, researcher; b. Bronx, N.Y., Aug. 28, 1932; s. Irving and Helen Flora (Greenhut) O.; m. Mary Carolyn Barth, Aug. 22, 1957; children: Carlene Marie Oring, Sheri Alyce Oring. AAS, Rochester Inst. Tech., 1957; BFA, R.I. Tech., 1959; MA, Am. U., 1970. Photo lab asst. Nat. Geographic, Washington, summer 1957; photography asst. IJBeckerNepo-Nuss Advt Photo Studio Assocs. & Art Green Inc., N.Y.C., 1959-61; freelance photographer pvt. practice, Washington, 1961; indsl. photographer Vitro Corp., Rockville, Md., 1962-64; health photographer Nat. Ctr. Radiol. Health, 1964-67; visual info. specialist ARS Info. div. USDA, Washington, 1967-69; audio visual specialist Nat. AV Ctr., 1969-71; photojournalist Office of Econ. Opportunity, 1971-74; visual info. specialist ASCS, U.S. Dept. Agr., 1974-94; ret., 1994. Mgr., owner ISIS Visual Comms.; photography tchr. Prince George's C.C., Largo, Md., 1975-96; guest lectr. U. Md. Balt. County, Catonsville, Corcoran Gallery of Art, Washington; spkr. in field. Author, editor and pub.: (textbook/gallery text) Understanding Pictures-A Teacher's Planning Guide, 1994, Understanding Pictures-Theories, Exercises and Procedures, 1990, rev. 1992, rev. 1995, A Beginner's Guide to Looking at Pictures, 1997; contbr. numerous articles to profl. jours.; photos published in books, mags., brochures, pamphlets. Photographer with U.S. Army, 1952-55. Recipient Cert. Recognition award Eastman Kodak Co., 1973, Nat. Ctr. Radiol. Health, Rockville, Md., 1965. Mem.: APA (divsn. 10 psychology and the arts, program spkr. 105th ann. conf., 108th ann. conf.), Inst. for Psychol. Study of Arts (program spkr.), Am. Soc. Psychopathology of Expression (bd. dirs.). Achievements include research and development of new approaches for analyzing and interpreting art and photographs. Avocations: chess, swimming, classical music, oriental philosophy, art. Home and Office: 2570 Redbud Ln Owings MD 20736-4308 E-mail: stuartoring@comcast.net.

ORISEK, IVAN, financial executive; b. Prague, Czechoslovakia, May 29, 1945; came to U.S., 1976, naturalized, 1981; s. Frantisek and Bozena O.; m. Olga Dedina, Sept. 28, 1977; children: Philip, Vena. MSc, Czech Tech. U., Prague, 1967. Sr. rsch. analyst Rsch. Inst. Fuel and Energy Econs., Prague, 1970-75; head ops. rsch. sect. Am. Electric Power Svc. Corp., N.Y.C., 1976-81; prin. engr. Ebasco Svcs., Inc., 1981-86; pres. I&O Assocs. Mortgage Corp., Forestburgh, NY, 1986—. Mem. Inst. Ops. Rsch. and Mgmt. Scis., Sports Car Club Am. Avocations: race car driving. Home: Evergreens 2488 Rte 42 Forestburgh NY 12777 E-mail: iomortgage@aol.com., eurorally@aol.com.

ORITSKY, MIMI, artist, educator; b. Reading, Pa., Aug. 14, 1950; d. Herbert and Marcia (Sarna) O. Student, Phila. Coll. Art, 1968-70; BFA, Md. Inst. Coll. Art, 1975; MFA, U. Pa., 1979. Artist, supr. subway mural projects Crisis Intervention Network, Phila., 1978-83; instr. painting U. Arts, 1984, 89-93, Abington Art Ctr., Jenkintown, Pa., 1989—, Main Line Art Ctr., Haverford, 1993—. One-woman shows include Gross McCleaf Gallery, 1980-82, Callowhill Art Gallery, Reading, Pa., Amos Eno Gallery, N.Y.C., 1986, 89, 91, 94, 98, 01, Hahnemann U. Gallery, Phila., 1988, Kauffman Gallery, Shippensburg, Pa., 1989, 97, Kimberton (Pa.) Gallery, 1990, Rittenhouse Galleries, Phila., 1992-94; exhibited in group shows at Current Representational Painting in Phila., 1980, Gross McCleaf Gallery, 1980-82, Yearsley Spring Gallery, Phila., 1998, Phila. Art Alliance, 1998, Coll. Art Gallery, Coll. N.J., Trenton, 1996, 98, 2000,Brattleboro Mus., TW Wood Mus., Montshire Mus., Florence Griswold Mus., 2002-; pub. in NewAmerican Paintings, 2000. Recipient Purchase award Pa. Coun. Arts/Beaver Coll., 1983, award Pa. Coun. Arts Arcadia Coll., 1983, Reading Pub. Mus., 1984, Best of Show award Abington Art Ctr. Juried Annual, 1998; fellow Environment Found., 1980, Millay Colony for Arts, 1983. Mem. Coll. Art Assn. E-mail: gill1313@aol.com.

ORKAND, DONALD SAUL, management consultant; b. N.Y.C., Mar. 2, 1936; s. Harold and Sylvia (Wagner) O.; children: Dara Sue, Katarina Day. BS summa cum laude, NYU, 1956, MBA, 1957, PhD, 1963. Statistician Western Electric Co., N.Y.C., 1956-58; group v.p. Ops. Rsch., Inc., Silver Spring, Md., 1960-69; pres. Ops. Rsch. Industries, Ltd., Ottawa, Ont., Can., 1968-69; pres., CEO The Orkand Corp., Tysons Corner, Va., 1970—. Bd. dirs. U. Md. Found., Inc., College Park, 1993—. Contbr. articles to profl. jours. Bd. visitors coll. of bus. and mgmt. U. Md., College Park, 1985—; trustee Suburban Hosp., 1994-2000. 1st lt. Ordnance Corps, USAR, 1958-60. Mem. Am. Econs. Assn., Am. Statis. Assn., Ops. Rsch. Soc. Am. Republican. Jewish. Avocations: reading, theater, travel, exercise. Office: The Orkand Corp 7799 Leesburg Pike Ste 700N Falls Church VA 22043-2499

ORKIN, JENNA, writer; b. New York, Ny; d. Harvey Orkin; children: One. BA, Hunter Coll., Ny; JD, NY Law Sch., Ny; BA/MA, Oxford U., England. Chairperson Environ. Action, New York, NY, 2002—02; interviewer Exploring Post One, 1984—86; educator Juilliard, 1978—83.

ORKIN, LOUIS RICHARD, physician, educator; b. N.Y.C., Dec. 23, 1915; s. Samuel David and Rebecca (Rish) O.; m. Florence Fine, Mar. 5, 1938; 1 dau., Rita. BA, U. Wis., 1937; MD, N.Y. U., 1941; AAS in Marine Tech., Kingsborough Coll., 1992. Intern Bellevue Hosp., N.Y.C., 1942, resident anesthesiology, 1946-48; practice medicine specializing in anesthesiology Bronx, N.Y., 1946—; dir. anesthesiology Backus Hosp., Norwich, Conn., 1948-50; asst. prof. anesthesiology N.Y. U. Coll. Medicine, 1950-55; prof., chmn. dept. anesthesiology Albert Einstein Coll. Medicine, 1955-82, Disting. univ. prof., 1982-86, dist. univ. prof. emeritus, 1986—. Vis. prof. depts. bioengring., anesthesiology U. Calif., San Diego, 1971; Cons. VA, USPHS, USN; mem. com. anesthesiology Nat. Acad. Scis., 1964-69; mem. com. anesthetic drugs FDA, Dept. Health, Edn. and Welfare, 1970— Author: Patient in Shock, 1965, Physiology of Obstetrical Anesthesia, 1969; Contbr. articles to profl. jours. Vice pres., trustee Wood Library Mus. Served to capt. M.C. AUS, 1942-45. Decorated Bronze Star. Fellow Am. Coll. Chest Physicians, N.Y. Acad. Sci., N.Y. Acad. Medicine, Am. Coll. Anesthesiology (past chmn. bd. govs.); mem. N.Y. State Soc. Anesthesiologists (past pres.; Disting. Svc. award 2000). Home: 11 Stuyvesant Oval New York NY 10009-2001

ORKIN, NEIL S. management consultant, speaker; b. Plainfield, N.J., June 14, 1960; s. Saul and Maria Lydia Orkin. BA, U. Mich., 1982; MA, Columbia U., 1988; EdD, Rutgers U., 1998. Mktg. rep. Xerox Corp., Morris Plains, N.J., 1982-83; instr. Time T.I. Comms., Tokyo, 1985-87; instr., program coord. Rutgers U., New Brunswick, N.J., 1988-95; prin. Global Tng. Systems, Somerville, 1996—. Mem. ASTD, Inst. of Mgmt. Cons., Liberty Bell Spkrs. Assn., Nat. Spkrs. Assn., Soc. for Human Resource Mgmt. of Ctrl. N.J., v.p. Avocations: world travel, languages. Office: Global Tng Systems 12 Wolfe Dr Hillsborough NJ 08844

ORLANS, F(LORA) BARBARA, bioethics researcher; b. Birmingham, Eng., Jan. 14, 1928; came to U.S., 1956; d. Christopher and Flora Christine (Brookes) Hughes; m. Herbert C. Morton, June 19, 1982; children: Andrew Brookes Orlans, Nicholas Motcomb Orlans. BSc in Physiology/Anatomy, Birmingham (Eng.) U., 1949; MS in Physiology, London U., 1954, PhD in Physiology, 1956. Physiology instr. dept. medicine Johns Hopkins Hosp., Balt., 1956; rsch. pharmacologist Nat. Heart Inst., NIH, Bethesda, Md., 1956-60; freelance writer, 1967-73; sr. staff scientist Med. Ctr. George Washington U., Washington, 1973-74; health sci. adminstr. Nat. Heart, Lung & Blood Inst. NIH, Bethesda, 1974-77; exec. sec. Adv. Coun., Heart Inst. NIH, 1977-79; staff scientist cardiac diseases NIH, 1979-84; dir. Scientists Ctr. Animal Welfare, 1984-88; sr. rsch. fellow Kennedy Inst. Ethics Georgetown U., Washington, 1989—. Founding pres. Scientists Ctr. Animal Welfare, Bethesda, 1978-84; mem. Parks Found. for Animal Welfare, Richmond, Va., mem. grants com., 1981—, chair, 1987-90, 96-99. Author: Animal Care: From Protozoa to Small Mammals, 1977, In The Name of Science: Issues in Responsible Animal Experimentation, 1993; sr. author: The Human Use of Animals: Case Studies in Ethical Choice, 1998; editor: Scientific Perspectives on Animal Welfare, 1982, Effective Animal Care & Use Committees, 1987, Applied Ethics in Animal Research, 2002; contbr. articles to refereed jours. Grantee Geraldine R. Dodge Found., Morristown, N.J., 1980-90, ethics and values program NSF, 1987-88, 92-95, Kinnoull Found., 1989—; Rockefeller Found. scholar Bellagio, Italy, 1989. Mem. Am. Soc. Pharmacology, Nat. Assn. Biology Tchrs. Avocations: gardening, music, swimming. Office: Georgetown U Kennedy Inst Ethics Healy Hall 442 Washington DC 20057-0001 Fax: 202-687-8089. E-mail: orlansfb@.georgetown.edu.

ORLEBEKE, WILLIAM RONALD, retired lawyer, writer; b. El Paso, Tex., Jan. 5, 1934; s. William Ronald and Frances Claire (Cook) O.; m. Barbara Raye Pike, 1955 (div. 1981); children: Michelle, Julene, David; m. Susan K. Nash, 2000. BA, Willamette U., 1956; MA, Kans. U., 1957; JD, Willamette U., 1966. Bar: Calif. 1966, U.S. Dist. Ct. (no. dist.) Calif. 1967, U.S. Ct. Appeals (9th cir.) 1967, U.S. Ct. Appeals (7th cir.) 1989, U.S. Dist. Ct. (no. dist.) Ill. 1989, U.S. Dist. Ct. (cen. dist.) Calif. 1989. Mem. staff Travelers Ins. Co., Sacramento, 1957-61; branch claim mgr. N.Y. Life Ins. Co., 1961-62, Transamerica Ins. Co., San Francisco, 1962-63; assoc. Eliassen & Postel, 1966-69; ptnr. Coll, Levy & Orlebeke, Concord, 1969-77, Orlebeke & Hutchings, 1977-89; prin. Law Offices W. Ronald Orlebeke, 1989-98; hearing officer Contra Costa County, Calif., 1981-98; arbitrator Contra Costa County Superior Ct., 1977-98, U.S. Dist. Ct. No. Calif., 1978-98, Mt. Diablo Mcpl. Ct., 1987-89; ret., 1998. Judge pro tem Mt. Diablo Mcpl. Ct., 1973-77; adj. prof. Willamette U. Coll. of Law, 2001—. Author: Orlebeke Family in Europe and America, 1570-1990, 1988. Alumni bd. dirs. Willamette U., 1978-81, trustee, 1980-81 scholar chmn. Concord Elks, 1977-79; del. Joint U.S./China Internat. Trade Law Conf., Beijing, 1987. With USMCR, 1952-59. Sr. scholar Willamette U., 1955-56; Woodrow Wilson fellow Kans. U., 1956-57, U.S. Bur. Nat. Affairs fellow, 1966, others. Mem. SAR, Sons of Confederate Vets. (award of Merit 1989), Sons of Union Vets. Civil War, First Marine Divsn. Assn., Order Ea. Star (worthy patron 1980), Masons, Shriners, Elks, Rotary (charter pres. Clayton Valley/Concord Sunrise club 1987-88, chmn. dist. 5160 Calif. membership devel. 1989-90, dist. govs. liaison dist. 5160 1990-92, dist. Rotarian of Yr. 1989-90, Paul Harris fellow 1988, 1992 dist. conf. chmn. benefactor 1990, award of Merit 1990). Republican.

ORLIK, CHRISTINA BEAR, music educator; b. Detroit, Nov. 10, 1945; d. Robert William and Olive Marie (Evans) Bear; m. Peter Blythe Orlik, Aug. 18, 1967; children: Darcy Anne, Blaine Truen. BS in Edn., Wayne State U., 1967, MS in Edn., 1969. Tchr. clarinet pvt. practice, Detroit, 1961-69; elem. band dir. City Recreation Dept., Troy, Mich, 1964-67; dir. bands Crary Jr. High Sch., Waterford, 1967-69; instr. woodwind pvt. practice, Mt. Pleasant, 1970-84; dir. bands Montabella Jr. High Sch., Blanchard, 1974-76; substitute tchr. Mt. Pleasant Schs., 1976-84, libr. media profl., 1984-85, tchr. gen. music, 1985—, orch. dir., 1987—. Part-time instr. Cen. Mich. U. Tchr. Edn., 1989-91; organizing mem., mgr. Cen. Mich. Cmty. Band, Mt. Pleasant, 1973-75; clarinetist/bassoonist Alma (Mich.) Symphony Orch., 1973-86, Eddy Concert Band, Saginaw, Mich., 1973-2000. Tchr. Sunday sch. St. Andrew's Episcopal Ch., Clawson, Mich., 1966-67; treas., mem. chair LWV, Mt. Pleasant, 1972-73; chair Child Care Adv. Com., Mt. Pleasant, 1973-74. Mem. Am. String Tchrs. Assn. (program review grantee 1990), Mich. Edn. Assn., ch. Sch. Band and Orch. Assn. (Dist. 5 Orch. Tchr. of Yr. 2000), Music Educators Nat. Conf. Avocation: dancing. Home: 613 Kane St Mount Pleasant MI 48858-1949 Office: West Intermediate Sch 440 S Bradley St Mount Pleasant MI 48858-3052

ORLIN, JAMES BERGER, mathematician, management scientist, educator; b. Buffalo, Apr. 19, 1953; s. Albert Norman and Roslyn Louise (Berger) Orlin; m. Donna Lynn Hogan, Jan. 3, 1982 (dec. Oct. 2000); children: Jennifer Robin, Benjamin Aaron, Caroline Anne. BA, U. Pa., 1974; MS, Caltech, 1976; MMath, U. Waterloo, Ont., Can., 1976; PhD, Stanford U., 1981. Asst. prof. MIT, Cambridge, Mass., 1979-83, assoc. prof., 1983-87, prof., 1987—, co-dir. ops. rsch. ctr., 1998—. Vis. prof. Erasmus U., Rotterdam, The Netherlands, 1984-85; vis. sci. Collaborative Rsch. Inc., Waltham, Mass., 1992-93, Whitehead Inst., 1993-96. Co-author: Network Flows: Theory, Algorithms and Applications, 1993; assoc. editor: Networks, 1992—; contbr. over 70 articles to profl. jours. Fulbright Rsch. grantee, 1984-85, UPS fellow, 1991-94, 95-96; recipient Presdl. Young Investigator award NSF, 1985-90. Mem. Informs (co-recipient Lanchester prize 1993), Assn. Computing Machinery, Math. Programming Soc., Soc. Indsl. and Applied Math. Home: 10 Taft Dr Winchester MA 01890-3748 Office: MIT #E40-147 77 Massachusetts Ave Cambridge MA 02139-4307

ORLIN, LOUIS LAWRENCE, literature and history educator; b. Bayonne, N.J., Nov. 7, 1925; s. Bernard and Ruth Orlin; m. Jenny Lee Gray, June 24, 1988; children: Lesley, David, Hugh, Celia. BA, U. Mich., 1949, MA, 1950, PhD, 1960. Lectr. English lang. and lit. U. Mich., Ann Arbor, 1955-58, lectr. ancient near eastern lit. and history, 1956-61, asst. prof., 1961-65, assoc. prof., 1965, prof., 1970-89, dir. residential coll., 1973, prof. emeritus, 1989—. Vis. scholar Cambridge (Eng.) U., 1967-68; vis. prof. U. Queensland, Brisbane, Australia, 1982; regional cons. Nat. Humanities series NEH, 1973-75. Author: Ancient Near Eastern Literature, 1969, Assyrian Colonies in Cappadoua, 1970; editor: Janus: Essays in Ancient and Modern Studies, 1974, Michigan Oriental Studies in Honor of George G. Cameron, 1974. Violist Ann Arbor Symphony orch., 1960-85, VA Med. Musical Group, 1990s. With U.S. Army, 1943-45, ETO. Decorated Bronze Star, Purple Heart; recipient E. Harris Harbison award for disting. tchg. Danforth Found., 1967; Danforth Found. assoc., 1967—. Mem. Am. Oriental Soc., Am. Hist. Assn., Assn. Ancient Historians, Archaeol. Inst. Am., Phi Kappa Phi. Avocations: viola, lecturing, tennis, sailing, creative writing. Home: 4734 Northgate Dr Ann Arbor MI 48103 Office: U Mich Dept Near Eastern Studies Frieze Bldg Ann Arbor MI 48109

ORLITZKY, ROBERT, engineer; b. Nadrag, Romania, Dec. 5, 1960; came to U.S., 1965; s. Josef and Anna (Steingasser) O.; m. Barbara Ann Piazza, July 12, 1989; 1 child, Michael J. Student prof. aero., Embry Riddle Aero U., 1985-89. Master technician, USAF. Engr. product support Bendix Aerospace, Teterboro, N.J., 1983-85; engr. level V Test Tech., Inc., Hauppauge, N.Y., 1985-89; v.p. Bus. Svcs. Network, Balt., 1989-90; mgr. computer group Kohler & Co., Greenbelt, Md., 1990-91; mgr. systems group Sacks, McGibney & Trotta, P.A., Balt., 1992—. Conf. speaker Kohler Healthcare Cons., Balt., 1992—. Co-author, editor: Computerization in the Physicians Office, 1992; author: (software and documents) Nursing Employee Tracking System, 1990, MDCASH Cash Flow Projection, 1992. Community svc. Balt. (Md.) Bd. Edn., 1988-90; fundraiser Am. Heart Assn., Balt., 1991—, Am. Cancer Soc., Balt., 1991—. Sgt. USAF, 1978-82. Recipient Commendation, Gen. Dynamics Corp., 1981, Tech. Excellence award Strategic Air Command, 1981, Merit/Maintenance Support award Strategic Air Command, 1981. Mem. AIAA, IEEE , Air Force Assn. (life), Microcomputer Mgrs. Assn. Republican. Home: 1933 Kelly Ave Baltimore MD 21209-3656

ORLOFF, CHET, historian; b. Bellingham, Wash., Feb. 22, 1949; s. Monford A. and Janice (Diamond) O.; m. Wendy Lynn Lee, Sept. 20, 1970; children: Callman Labe, Hannah Katya, Michele Alison. BA, Boston U., 1971, U. Oreg., 1971; MA, Portland State U., 1978. Tchr. Peace Corps, Afghanistan, 1972-75; asst. dir. Oreg. Hist. Soc., Portland, 1975-86, exec. dir., 1991-2000, Ninth Cir. Hist. Soc., Pasadena, Calif., 1987-91. Adj. prof. Portland State U. Editor: Western Legal History, 1987-91, Law for the Elephant, 1992; sr. editor: Oreg. Hist. Quar.; contbr. articles to profl. jours. Commr. Met. Arts Commn., Portland, 1981-84, Portland Planning Commn., 1989-92; pres. Nat. Lewis and Clark Bicentennial Coun., 1996—. Mem. Phi Alpha Theta. Avocations: reading, tennis. Office: Oreg Hist Works 3332 NW Savier St Portland OR 97210

ORLOFF, GORDON MATTHEW, lawyer; b. Portland, Oreg., Aug. 23, 1958; s. Ronald L. and June L. (Yudenfreund) O. BA, Colgate U., 1980; JD, Duke U., 1984. Bar: Mass. 1985, U.S. Dist. Ct. Mass. 1985, U.S. Ct. Appeals 1988. Assoc. Palmer & Dodge, Boston, 1985-87, Rackemann, Sawyer & Brewster, Boston, 1987—. Chmn. bd. dirs. Dance Umbrella, Cambridge, Mass., 1988-92. Mem. ABA, Boston Bar Assn., Order of Coif. Office: Rackemann Sawyer & Brewster One Financial Ctr Boston MA 02111

ORLOFF, NEIL, lawyer, artist; b. Chgo., May 9, 1943; s. Benjamin R. and Annette (Grabow) O.; m. Jan Krigbaum, Oct. 9, 1971 (div. 1979); m. Gudrun Mirin, Oct. 2, 1992. BS, MIT, 1964; MBA, Harvard U., 1966; JD, Columbia U., 1969. Bar: D.C. 1969, N.Y. 1975, Calif. 1989, Utah 1993. Ops. officer World Bank, Washington, 1969-71; dir. regional liaison staff EPA, 1971-73; legal counsel Pres.'s Council on Environ. Quality, 1973-75; prof. dept. environ. engring. Cornell U., Ithaca, N.Y., 1975-88; sch. law UCLA, 1992; dir. Ctr. for Environ. Rsch., 1984-87, Am. Ecology Corp., 1986-88; of counsel Morgan, Lewis & Bockius, N.Y.C., 1986-87; ptnr. Irell & Manella, L.A., 1986-92, Parsons, Behle & Latimer, Salt Lake City, 1992—2001. Vice chmn. bd. dirs. S.W. Research and Info. Ctr., Albuquerque, 1975-84; vice chmn. air quality commn. ABA, Chgo., 1983-92, co-chmn. intensive course in environ. law ABA, 1994-96, co-chmn. roundtable sr. environ. lawyers ABA, 1996-97, membership officer sect. on natural resources, energy and environ. law, 1997-98; coun. mem. sect. on environ., energy and natural resources, 1998-2001; adviser Internat. Joint Com. Can., 1979-81; governing bd. N.Y. Sea Grant Inst., 1984-87; vice chmn. City of Ithaca Environ. Commn., 1976-77; adviser N.Y. Dept. Environ. Conservation, 1984-87; artist-in-residence MacDowell Colony, 2000, Yaddo, 2001; vis. prof. art Cornell U., 2001. Author: The Environmental Impact Statement Process, 1978, The National Environmental Policy Act, 1980, Air Pollution-Cases and Materials, 1980, Community Right-to-Know Handbook, 1988, Under the Fifth Street Overpass, 2000; mem. editl. bd. Natural Resources and Environ., 1984-87. E-mail: norloff@alum.mit.edu.

ORLOSKI, SHARON, secondary education educator; b. Taylor, Pa., Aug. 15, 1943; d. Leo Paul and Sophie Ann O. BS, Ctrl. Conn. State U., New Britain, 1965; MS, U. Conn., Storrs, 1970; CAS, Wesleyan U., Middletown, Conn., 1972. Cert. tchr. biology, chemistry and gen. sci., Conn. Gen. sci. tchr. Bridgeport (Conn.) Adult Edn., 1966-68; homebound tchr. Bridgeport Bd. Edn., 1966-67; tchr. biology Ctrl. H.S., Bridgeport Bd. Edn., 1965-82, Ctrl. Magnet H.S., Bridgeport Bd. Edn., 1982—. Master tchr. Bridgeport Bd. Edn., 1974, 2002; leader citywide workshops. Bd. dirs., pres., sec. Madison Gardens Condominium Assn. NSF grantee, 1967-71. Mem. NEA, Nat. Assn. Biology Tchrs., U. Conn. Alumni Assn. (life), Ctrl. Conn. State Alumni Assn. (life), Conn. Edn. Assn., Bridgeport Edn. Assn., Lladro Soc., U.S. Humane Soc. Avocations: New Haven Ravens, N.Y. Yankees, stocks, gardening. Office: Ctrl Magnet HS One Lincoln Blvd Bridgeport CT 06606

ORLOV, DARLENE, management consultant, educator; b. Elizabeth, N.J., July 13, 1949; d. Sol and Evelyn (Perlman) O.; m. Geoffrey M. Skolnik, Jan. 19, 1986. BA in English, Secondary Edn., Fairleigh Dickinson U., 1971, MA in English Lit., 1982; MBA in Mgmt. with distinction, N.Y. Inst. of Tech., 1981. Pers. dir. Kayser-Roth Corp., N.Y.C., 1975-76; pers. mgr. Corometrics Med. Systems, Wallingford, Conn., 1976-78; mgr. EEO and communications Internat. Playtex, N.Y.C., 1978-79; pres. Orlov Resources for Bus., Inc., 1979—. Adj. asst. prof. NYU, 1980-88; adj. prof. Marymount Manhattan Coll., N.Y.C., 1981-90. Author: Employee Termination: How to Reduce Your Risk, 1986; co-author: What Every Manager Needs to Know About Sexual Harassment, 1999. Trustee Fairleigh Dickinson U., Madison, N.J., 1989-94; bd. dirs., v.p. The Assoc. Blind, Inc., 1991-94; pres. WING, 1998. Recipient Pinnacle award Fairleigh Dickinson U., 1989. Mem.: Human Resources Assn. N.Y., Women's Econ. Roundtable. Home and Office: 25 Sutton Pl S New York NY 10022-2441 E-mail: Dorlov@OrlovResources.com.

ORLOVSKY, DONALD ALBERT, lawyer; b. East Orange, N.J., May 15, 1951; s. Manuel Martin and Eleanor Marie Orlovsky. AB, Cornell U., 1973; JD, Rutgers U., 1976. Bar: Fla. 1976, U.S. Ct. Appeals (5th cir.) 1976, N.J. 1977, U.S. Dist. Ct. (so. dist.) Fla. 1977, U.S. Dist. Ct. N.J. 1977, U.S. Supreme Ct. 1980, U.S. Ct. Appeals (11th cir.) 1981. Assoc. Smathers & Thompson, Miami, 1976-77; ptnr. McCune, Hiaasen, Crum, Ferris & Gardner, P.A., Ft. Lauderdale, Fla., 1978-86, Kamen & Orlovsky PA, West Palm Beach, 1988—. Sec. bd. dirs. Comprehensive Alcoholism Treatment Program, Inc.; bd. dirs. Fla. Lawyers Assistance, Inc., supervising monitor and counselor, 1991—. Author: Nova U. Law Review, 1977, U. Miami Law Review, 1978. Alumni bd. St. Andrew's Sch., Boca Raton, Fla., 1996—. Recipient All-Am. recognition in springboard diving, 1966-69; inducted Hall of Fame Newark Acad., Livingston, N.J., 1997. Mem. ABA, Fla. Bar (civil procedure rules com. 1981), Acad. Fla. Trial Lawyers, Assn. Trial Lawyers Am. Episcopalian. Office: 1601 Belvedere Rd Ste 402 West Palm Beach FL 33406-1541 E-mail: dao4law@aol.com.

ORLOW, DANIEL JOHN, photographer; b. Chgo., Jan. 29, 1952; s. Lewis Lucian and Margaret Isabel (Balke) O.; m. Patricia Sue Sortal, Sept. 8, 1979; 1 child, Kathryn Michelle. BS in Polit. Sci. & Sociology, Illinois State Univ., Normal, 1974; MSW, U. Ill., 1976. Faculty mem. Sch. Dist. 26, Mt. Prospect, Ill., 1979-80, Notre Dame High Sch., Niles, 1981-82; free-lance photographer. U. Ill. fellow, 1975. Democrat. Avocation: reading. Home: 1943 Burton Ln Park Ridge IL 60068-1571 E-mail: daniels31@juno.com.

ORLOW, DAWN M. mobile salon owner; b. Anaheim, Calif., Mar. 4, 1970; d. Patrick Rolf and Mary Ann (Dwyer) O. Cert., Colleen O'Hara's Beauty Sch., Anaheim Hills, Calif., 1989; AA in Mktg., FIDM, 1989-91; BS in Bus. Adminstrn. magna cum laude, ULV, 1994. Registered cosmetologist. Stylist Christopher's Salon, Fullerton, Calif., 1989-90; ind. contractor Hair Unique, Anaheim Hills, 1990; owner mobile salon Hair On Wheels, 1990—. Cons. Mary Kay Cosmetics, Tex., 1993—; distbr., educator Hi Products, Anaheim Hills, 1994—; distbr. Amway Products, Brea, Calif., 1996—; so. regional dir. Look Good Feel Better-Am. Cancer Soc., Santa Ana, Calif., 1995-97. Pub. (hair book) Inspire Quarterly vol. 21, 1997, (hair style book) Inspire Quarterly vol. 22, 1997. Mem. Crystal Cathedral Ch., Garden Grove, Calif., 1993. Recipient Best Publ. of Newsletter award Calif. Cosmetology Assn., Visalia, 1997, Membership Retention award calif. Cosmetology Assn., Visalia, 1997. Mem. Nat. Cosmetology Assn., Orange County Cosmetology Assn. (pres. 1994-97). Avocations: cruises, theater, boating. Home and Office: 903 S Cottontail Ln Anaheim CA 92808-1411 Address: 903 S Cottontail Ln Anaheim CA 92808-1411

ORLOWSKA-WARREN, LENORE ALEXANDRIA, art educator, fiber artist; b. Detroit, May 22, 1951; d. William Leonard and Aloisa Clara (Hrapkiewicz) Orlowski; m. Donald Edward Warren, May 11, 1990. AA, Henry Ford C.C., 1972; BS in Art Edn., Wayne State U., 1974, M in Spl. Edn., 1978; BFA, Ctr. for Creative Studies, 2000. Tchr. arts and crafts Detroit Pub. Schs., 1974—2002; fiber artist Detroit Inst. Arts. Cons. Arts Detroit Cmty. Plan, TRIACO Arts & Crafts, 1996—; instr., demonstrator weaving Detroit Inst. Arts. One-woman show at Dearborn C. of C., Ctr. for Creative Studies, 2000; exhibited in group shows, including alumni exhibit Henry Ford C.C., 1989, Detroit Artist Market, 1995-2000, Scarab Club, 1996, Lansing Art Gallery, 1997, Ctr. for Creative Studies, 1997, Yr. of the Woman Exhibit, 1998, Tom Thompson Meml. Art Gallery Juried Ontario Artists Exhibit, 1998, 2001, One Focus, Two Worlds Exhibit, 1999, Fashion Exhibit and Felt the Feeling of Fiber, U.245 Gallery, 1999, Ctr. Creative Studies, 2000, Ann Arbor Art Ctr., 2001, Downriver Coun. for the Arts, 2001, Alumni Fiber Artist exhibit Coll. Creative Studies, 2002, Outside The Lines Gallery, 2001, 2002; contbr. to Sch. Arts Mag. Mem. exec. bd. Springwells Pk. Assn., 1989-99, pres., 1994-96, chairperson youth act workshops; com. mem. Dearborn cmty. art coun. Art on the Ave., 1993-99, Gallery Crawl chairperson, 1998; chair Nat. Woman's History Month workshop, 1995. Mem. Nat. Art Edn. Assn. (electronic gallery coord. 1992-99), Mich. Art Edn. Assn. (presenter art advocacy workshop), Card Weaving Workshop presenter, 1999, Am. Craft Coun., Detroit Inst. Arts-Founders Soc., Birmingham Bloomfield Art Assn., Met. Mus. Art, The Nat. Mus. Women in Art Williamsburg Burgessess, The Textile Mus., Surface Design Assn., Downriver Coun. for Arts, Art Inst. of Chgo., Am. Tapestry Alliance, Cranbrook Acad. Art. Avocations: fiber art, travel, colonial gardening, reading colonial history and biographies. Home: 10 Berwick Ln Dearborn MI 48120-1102

ORLOWSKI, D. FAITH, lawyer; b. Cape Girardeau, Mo., July 28, 1954; d. Frank J. and Vera Don Orlowski; m. William George McMahan, Nov. 21, 1981. BA with highest honors, U. Tex., 1975, JD, 1978. Bar: Okla. 1978. Atty., shareholder, dir., mgr. Sneed Lang, P.C., Tulsa, 1978—. Editor newspaper The Tulsa Lawyer, 1999-2000; contbr. articles to profl. jours. Pres. Emergency Infant Svcs., Inc., Tulsa, 1996-98; bd. dirs. Arthritis Found. Ea. Okla., Tulsa, 1995-2000, Friends of Felines, Tulsa, 1996-2000; bd. dirs. Leadership Tulsa, 1992-93. Recipient Paragon award Leadership Tulsa, 1999. Mem.: Tulsa County Bar Assn. Mineral Lawyers (corp. sec. 2001—02, sec., treas., v.p., pres. 1996—99), Okla. Bar Assn. (chair, seminar organizer women in law com. 1998—2000, continuing edn. dir., budget officer, chmn.-elect, chair 2001, bd. dirs. real property law sect. 1996—, mem. title exam stds. com. 1996—2001). Office: Sneed Lang PC 2 W 2d St # 2300 Tulsa OK 74103 Fax: (918) 582-0410. E-mail: forlowski@sneedlang.com.

ORLOWSKI, KAREL ANN, elementary school educator; b. Fremont, Ohio, Dec. 22, 1949; d. Karl and Angeline Marie (Oudersluys) Kooistra; m. Paul Joseph Orlowski, Apr. 28, 1973; 1 child, Jennifer Frann. BA in Music Edn., U. Mich., 1971; MS in Elem. Edn., Dowling Coll., Oakdale, N.Y., 1978. Cert. tchr., N.Y. Tchr. vocal music Patchogue (N.Y.)-Medford Schs., 1971—, lead tchr. music dept., 1986-88, 91-94; dir. of musicals Eagle Elem. Sch., 1990-94. Dir. drama dept. River Elem. Sch., Patchogue, 1974-90, Chosen Few show choir South Ocean Mid. Sch., Patchogue, 1984-90, Notation! show choir Eagle Elem. Sch., 1990-94, 95—, A Chords show choir Barton Elem. Sch., 1994-95. Mem. N.Y. State Sch. Music Assn., Suffolk County Music Educators Assn. (co-chmn. so. divsn. I chorus 1993-95, divsn. II S.W. chorus 1996-97; asst. v.p. divsn. I festivals 1997-98, exec. v.p. for festivals 1998-2000, mem. standing coms. 1999-2000). Republican. Episcopalian. Avocations: reading, Renaissance music, vocal jazz, NASCAR SK class and figure-eight racing. Home: 37 Detmer Rd East Setauket NY 11733-1912 Office: Patchogue-Medford Schs 241 S Ocean Ave Patchogue NY 11772-3787

ORLOWSKI, RYSZARD, economist, educator; b. Brzozow, Poland, Dec. 21, 1927; s. Stanislaw and Wanda (Tietze) O.; m. Franciszka Wojtowicz, June 24, 1957; children: Magdalena, Wojciech. MA, Jagiellonian U., Krakow, Poland, 1951; PhD, U. Marii-Curie Sklodowskiej, Lublin, Poland, 1960. Asst. dept. econs. U. Marii-Curie Sklodowskiej, 1950-66, asst. prof., 1966-73, prof., 1973-92, full prof., 1992—, dean dept. econs., 1967-72, dep. rector, 1974-89. Prof. Coll. Computer Scis. and Mgmt., Rzeszow, 1996; rector Coll. Mgmt. and Pub. Adminstrn., Zamosc, 1998—. Author: Life Conditions and Struggle of Peasants in Zamoyski's Estate in the Second Half of XVIIIc, 1963, Social and Economic Activity of Andrzej Zamoyski, 1965; editor econ. group Annales Universitatis Mariae Curie-Skłodowska, 1977-2000. Recipient award Ministry of Edn., 1966, 71, 75, 77, 83, award Pres. Lublin, 1969. Mem. Polish Econ. Assn. (pres. 1970-79). Avocations: reading, travel, gardening, grandchildren. Home: 8/6 Sowinskiego 20-040 Lublin Poland Office: U Marii-Curie Sklodowskiej Plac M Curie Sklodowskiej 5 20031 Lublin Poland E-mail: rorlowski@wszia.edu.pl.

ORLOWSKY, PELAHIA DZVINIA, poet, publisher, educator; b. Cambridge, Ohio, May 13, 1953; d. Miroslaus and Tamara Orlowsky. BA, Oberlin Coll., 1975; MFA in Poetry, Warren Wilson Coll., 1991. Instr. Univ. Southern Maine, 2002; instr. creative writing workshops Mt. Holyoke Writers Conf., South Hadley, Mass., 1994, Boston Ctr. for Adult Edn., 1996-99, Stonecoast Writer's Conf., U. So. Maine, Gorham, 2000, 2001, Emerson Coll., Boston, 2000; guest lectr., poet Boston U., Emerson Coll., Harvard U., Putterham Br. Pub. Libr., Mt. Holyoke Writers Conf.; participant in numerous confs., workshops, sems. Author: Burying Dolls, 1992, A Handful of Bees, 1994, Edge of House, 1999; contbr. to anthologies including From Three Worlds: New Writing from the Ukraine, A Map of Hope: Women Writers and Human Rights in the World, A Hundred Years of Youth: A Bilingual Anthology of 20th Century Ukrainian Poetry; poetry contbr. to numerous jours. including Am. Poetry Rev., AGNI, Columbia: A Mag. of Poetry and Prose, Field, Jacaranda Rev., Ploughshares, Puerto del Sol, Sycamore Rev., The Jour., Pa. Rev., The Mass. Rev., among others; founding editor Four Way Books, 1992—. Mass. Cultural Coun. grantee, 1998, 99.

ORMAI-BUZA, ILDIKO, soprano, composer, organist, music educator; b. Budapest, Hungary, Dec. 21, 1927; came to U.S., 1949, naturalized, 1955; d. Janos and Margit Ormai; m. George Buza, Oct. 28, 1950; children: George F., Paul L. Student in piano and theory, Hannig Conservatory, Budapest, 1938-44; student, Ecole D'Arts Coll., Freiburg, Germany, 1947-49; studied voice with Carmela Cafarelli; studied composition and orchestration, Janos Kiss. Cert. pvt. voice, piano and organ tchr., Ohio. Organist, soloist St. Raphael Cath. Ch., Bay Village, Ohio, 1957-72; concert soprano Cafarelli Opera Co., Cleve., 1957-67; organist, soloist Holy Spirit Ch., Avon Lake, Ohio, 1972-97, Our Lady of Angels Ch., Cleve., 1998-99; frequent guest, organist, soloist St. Emeric Ch. Choir dir. Midnszenty Chamber Choir, Cleve., 1981-84; guest soloist Fatima World Congress, Germany, 1985, Portugal, 1992; guest concert soloist, U.S. and Can., 1960—. Composer: (organ and chorus) Mass of Adoration (Silver medal 1975), (choir and organ) Berzsenyi Poem: Supplication (Gold medal 1986), Piano Solos, 1996; performed solo concert Perpetual Adoration Ch., Budapest, 1989; soprano guest soloist West Suburban Philharm. Orch., Ann. Opera Concert, Cleve., 1980, 82, in concert record, 1981; commd. composer Hymn of Worldwide St. Ladislaus Order, 1989; prodr., announcer NBN weekly classical Hungarian Concert Hall Radio Hour, 1977-85; performer voice and piano Hungarian Assn., 1955—. Recipient Papal Blessing for composition Ave Maria, Pope John Paul II, 1987. Mem. Music Tchrs. Nat. Assn., Am. Guild Organists, Ohio Music Tchrs. Assn. (winner composition contest 1989, publicity com. 1981-97), St. Ladislaus Order (knighted Dame 1983, Cross of Honor 1987), Arpad Acad., Cleve. Piano Tchrs. Club. Avocations: painting, portrait drawing, sewing, dancing, poetry.

ORMAN, JOHN LEO, software engineer, writer; b. San Antonio, Mar. 19, 1949; s. Alton Woodlee and Isabel Joan (Paproski) O. BS in Physics, N.Mex. Inst. Mining & Tech., 1971, BS Math., MS Physics, 1974. Rsch. asst. N.Mex. Inst. Mining & Tech., Socorro, 1967-74; computer programmer State of N.Mex., Santa Fe, 1974-76; computer analyst Dikewood Corp., Albuquerque, 1976-83; nuclear engr. Sandia Nat. Labs., 1983-88, software engr., 1988—. Author numerous poems. NSF fellow, 1971-74; recipient 2d place award N.Mex. State Postry Soc., 1987. Mem. IEEE Computer Soc., Am. Assn. Physics Tchrs., Assn. for Computing Machinery, Nat. Writer's Club (poetry award 1987), Southwest Writers Workshop (3d place award non-fiction 1987), N.Mex. Mountain Club. Avocations: photography, travel, skiing, hiking, tennis. Home: 719 Vista Abajo Dr NE Albuquerque NM 87123-2246 Office: Sandia Nat Labs MS 0974 PO Box 5800 Albuquerque NM 87185-0100 E-mail: john.orman@att.net.

ORMAN, LEONARD ARNOLD, lawyer; b. Balt., June 15, 1930; s. Samuel and Bertie (Adler) O.; m. Barbara Gold, June 9, 1978; children: Richard Harold, Robert Barton. AB summa cum laude, U. Md., 1952, JD, 1955. Bar: Md. 1955, U.S. Ct. Appeals (4th cir.) 1956, U.S. Dist. Ct. Md. 1955, Ct. Appeals Md. 1955, U.S. Supreme Ct. 1977, U.S. Ct. Claims 1990, D.C. Ct. Appeals 1987; cert. civil trial advocate by Nat. Bd. Trial Advocacy. Law clk. Hon. Frederick W. Brune, Chief Judge Md. Ct. of Appeals, 1955-56; mem. dept. legis. reference Md. Legislature, 1957-58; mem. Gov.'s Commn. to Revise Criminal Code, 1958-59; pvt. practice law Balt., 1956—. Lectr. trial tactics. Mem. editorial bd.: Md. Law Rev, 1953-55; Contbr. articles to profl. jours. Pres. Young Dems. 2d Dist., Balt., 1960-63. With AUS, 1948-49; lt. col. USAF Res. ret. Rosco Pound Inst. fellow, trustee. Mem. Md. State Bar Assn. (various coms.), Balt. City Bar Assn. (various coms.), Nat. Coll. Trial Advocacy (trustee), Assn. Trial Lawyers Am. (numerous coms./offices, including nat. committeeman 1976-80, bd. govs. 1985—, exec. com. 1988-90, chmn. orgn. rev. com., home office and budget com., orgn. and home office com., election com., key man com., past mem. steering com., past mem. publ. com., past mem. ednl. adv. group 1989-90, chmn. Hall of Fame com., Stalwarts com., past vice-chair ABA-ATLA liaison com., M Club, co-chair conv. site planning com., co-chairpolit. insight com., long-range planning com., authhwy. adv. com., toy safety conf., med. malpractice adv. com., product liability adv. com., co-chair home office capital improvements adv. com., co-chmn. conv. planning com. Washington, Wiedmann/Wysocki award), Md. Trial Lawyers Assn. (bd. govs., pres. 1984-85), Order of Coif, Masons. Home: 2 Celadon Rd Owings Mills MD 21117-3010 Office: 26 South St Baltimore MD 21202-3215 Fax: (410) 962-0402. E-mail: lorman@triallaw.com.

ORMAN, NANETTE HECTOR, psychiatrist; b. Highland Park, Ill., Feb. 1, 1943; d. William Joseph and Agnes (Daly) Hector; m. John Christopher Orman, July 2, 1964; children: Laurel Anne, Nathaniel William. BA in Journalism, U. Calif., Berkeley, 1964; postgrad., Stanford U., 1978-81; MPH in Epidemiology, U. Calif., Berkeley, 1984, MS in Health and Med. Scis., 1985; MD, U. Calif., San Francisco, 1987. Diplomate Am. Bd. Psychiatry and Neurology; lic. physician, Calif. Psychiatrist San Jose (Calif.) State U., 1989-93; pvt. practice Los Altos, Calif., 1991—; staff El Camino Hosp., 1991-94, assoc. staff, 1994—; staff Stanford (Calif.) U. Hosp. and Med. Ctr., 1998—. Asst. clin. prof. Stanford (Calif.) U. Sch. Medicine, 1995—; oral bd. examiner Am. Bd. Psychiatry & Neurology, Deerfield, Ill., 1995—, chief resident in psychiatry, 1991; spkr. and cons. in field. Editor San Mateo County Planned Parenthood Assn. Newsletter, 1968-69. Bd. dirs. Mid-Peninsula Task Force for Integrated Edn., 1972-82; consumer mem. San Mateo County Mental Health Adv. Bd., 1987. Mem. Am. Psychiat. Assn. (pub. info. com. 1989—), No. Calif. Psychiat. Soc. (chair membership com. 1996-98, pub. info. com., media spokesperson, moderator ann. meetings 1993-94), Nat. Alliance for the Mentally Ill, San Francisco Depressive and Manic Depressive Assn. Office: 851 Fremont Ave Ste 98 Los Altos CA 94024-5602

ORMASA, JOHN, retired utility executive, lawyer; b. Richmond, Calif., May 30, 1925; s. Juan Hormaza and Maria Inocencia Olondo; m. Dorothy Helen Trumble, Feb. 17, 1952; children: Newton Lee, John Trumble, Nancy Jean Davies. BA, U. Calif.-Berkeley, 1948; JD, Harvard U., 1951. Bar: Calif. 1952, U.S. Supreme Ct. 1959. Assoc. Clifford C. Anglim, 1951-52; assoc. Richmond, Carlson, Collins, Gordon & Bold, 1952-56, ptnr., 1956-59; with So. Calif. Gas Co., L.A., 1959-66, gen. atty., 1963-65, v.p., gen. counsel, 1965-66; v.p., sys. gen. counsel Pacific Lighting Service Co., Los Angeles, 1966-72; v.p., gen. counsel Pacific Lighting Corp., Los Angeles, 1973-75, v.p., sec., gen. counsel, 1975. Acting city atty., El Cerrito, Calif., 1952. Served with U.S. Navy, 1943-46. Mem. ABA, Calif. State Bar Assn., Richmond (Calif.) Bar Assn. (pres. 1959), Kiwanis (v.p. 1959). Republican. Roman Catholic.

ORME, MELISSA EMILY, mechanical engineering educator; b. Glendale, Calif., Mar. 12, 1961; d. Myrl Eugene and Geraldine Irene (Schmuck) O.; m. Vasilis Zissis Marmarelis, Mar. 12, 1989; children: Zissis Eugene and Myrl Galinos (twins). BS, U. So. Calif., L.A., 1984, MS, 1985, PhD, 1989. Rsch. asst. prof. U. So. Calif., 1990-93; asst. prof. U. Calif., Irvine, 1993-96, assoc. prof., 1996—. Panel reviewer NSF, Arlington, Va., 1993—; cons. MPM Corp., Boston, 1993-97. Contbr. articles to profl. jours. Recipient Young Investigator award NSF, 1994, Arch T. Colwell Merit award SAE, 1994. Mem. AAUW, AIAA, ASME, Am. Phys. Soc., Minerals, Metals and Materials Soc. Achievements include 11 U.S. patents. Office: U Calif Dept Mech Engring Irvine CA 92697-0001

ORMES, JONATHAN FAIRFIELD, astrophysicist, science administrator, researcher; b. Colorado Springs, Colo., July 18, 1939; s. Robert Manly and Suzanne (Viertel) O.; m. Karen Lee Minnick, Dec. 26, 1960 (div.); 1 child, Laurie Kylee; m. Janet Carolyn Dahl, Sept. 12, 1964; children: Marina, Nicholas. BS, Stanford U., 1961; PhD, U. Minn., 1967. NRC assoc. Goddard Space Flight Ctr., NASA, Greenbelt, Md., 1967-69, astrophysicist, 1969, head cosmic radiations br., 1981-82, head nuclear astrophysics br., 1983-87, assoc. chief lab. for high energy astrophysics, 1987-90, chief lab. for high energy astrophysics, 1990-2000, project scientist for gamma ray astronomy obs., 1998—, dir. space scis., 2000—. Acting head high energy physics NASA hdqrs., Washington, 1982-83, mem. high energy astrophysics mgmt. ops. working group, 1975-83, mem. cosmic ray program working group, 1984-91; mem. com. on space and solar physics, com. on cosmic ray physics Nat. Acad. Sci., Washington, 1991-94. Editor: Essays in Space Science, 1987; assoc. editor astrophysics Phys. Rev. Letters, 1991-93; contbr. Astrophysics Jour., Phys. Rev. Letters, Astronomy and Astrophysics. Trustee Paint Br. Unitarian Universalist Ch., Adelphi, Md., 1987-88, chair bd. trustees, 1989, numerous positions, 1972—. Fellow: Am. Phys. Soc. (various divsn. offices); mem.: Am. Geophys. Union, Am. Astron. Soc. (sec.-treas. High Energy Astrophysics divsn. 1985—87), Internat. Astron. Union. Achievements include discovery of unusual isotopic abundance of Ne in galactic cosmic rays; research on composition and energy spectra of cosmic rays, antiprotons and gamma rays from the Milky Way galaxy. Office: NASA Code 600 Goddard Space Flight Ctr Greenbelt MD 20771-0001 E-mail: Jonathan.F.Ormes.1@gsfc.nasa.gov.

ORMOND, PAUL A. health facility executive; b. Aurora, Ill. B in Econs. with honors, Stanford U., 1971; MBA, 1973. Mem. corp. staff, positions with Glass Container divsn. Owens-Ill., Inc. (O-I), 1973-77; nat. mktg. mgr. soft drinks Glass Container divsn., 1977-78; mgr. Atlanta sales dist., 1978-80; asst. gen. mgr. Gerresheimer Glas internat. affil. O-I, Germany, 1980-82; v.p. Glass Container group, 1982-84; v.p. packaging ops., dir. market strategy and devel. O-I, 1984-91; corp. v.p., 1986-91; pres., CEO Health Care and Retirement Corp. (HCR) subs. O-I, Toledo, 1986-91; chmn., pres., CEO HCR now independent co., 1991-96; pres., CEO Manor Care, Inc., 1996—, chmn., 2001—; mem. board of dir. Nat. City Corp., Cleveland, Ohio. Bd. dirs. TRINOVA Corp., Nat. City Bank N.W. Office: Manor Care 333 N Summit St Toledo OH 43604-2617*

ORMSBY, ADAM JOHN, social worker; b. Urbana, N.Y., Feb. 5, 1965; s. John Carter and Katherine Ann Ormsby; m. Julie Loucks Ormsby, Oct. 8, 1994; children: Robin Marion, Evan Charles, Seth Carter. AAS in Criminal Justice, C.C. of Finger Lakes, 1989; BA in Psychology, Roberts Wesleyan Coll., 1992; MSW in Social Work, Syracuse U., 1994. Social worker Syracuse VA, 1994—. Spinal cord coord. VA Med. Ctr., Syracuse, 1997—. Staff sgt. USAF, 1983—87. Mem.: NASW, Psychologists and Social Workers, Am. Assn. Spinal Cord Injury. Republican. Methodist. Avocations: golf, bridge, music, computers. Home: 4485 Brickyard Falls Rd Manlius NY 13104 Office: VA Med Ctr Syracuse 800 Irving Ave Syracuse NY 13210

ORMSBY, ERIC LINN, educator, researcher, writer; b. Atlanta, Oct. 16, 1941; s. Robert and Virginia (Haire) O.; m. Dorothy Louise Hoffmann, July 22, 1967; children: Daniel Paul, Charles Martin. BA summa cum laude, U. Pa., 1971; MA, Princeton U., 1973, PhD, 1981; MLS, Rutgers U., 1978. Near East bibliographer libr. Princeton U., N.J., 1975-77, Near East curator libr., 1977-83; libr. dir. Cath. U. Am., Washington, 1983-86, McGill U., Montreal, Can., 1986-96, assoc. prof. Inst. Islamic Studies Can., 1986-96, prof. Can., 1996—. Cons. NYU, 1981-82; mem. libr. com. Mid. East Inst., Washington, 1985-87, Al Akhawayn U., Morocco, 1994-95, Saudi Arabian Monetary Agy., Riyadh, 1995-96; chmn. continuing edn. com. Washington Consortium, 1983-86; mem. bd. Ctr. Rsch. Librs., 1989-95. Author: Theodicy in Islamic Thought, 1984 (Choice Mag. award 1984), Bavarian Shrine and Other Poems, 1990 (QSPELL award for poetry 1991), (poems) Coastlines, 1992, (with others) Handlist of Arabic Manuscripts, 1986, For a Modest God: New and Selected Poems, 1997, (poems) Araby, 2001, (essays) Facsimiles of Time, 2001; editor: Moses Maimonides and His Time, 1989; contbr. articles and book revs. to profl. jours., poetry and essays to various mags., including New Republic, New Yorker, Grand St., Shenandoah, The New Criterion, The Yale Rev., So. Rev. and Chelsea. Instr. Princeton Adult Sch., 1978-80. DAAD fellow German Acad. Exch., 1973-74; recipient Ingram Merrill award, 1993. Mem. Middle East Librs. Assn. (v.p. 1981-82, pres. 1982-83), Hoelderlin Gesellschaft, Societe des Amis de Jean de la Fontaine, Can. Assn. Rsch. Librs. (v.p. 1988-89), Can. Libr. Assn., Assn. pour l'Avancement des Scis. et des Techniques de la Documentation, Conseil des recteurs et des principaux des univs. du Québec, Sous-Comité des Bibliotheques (pres. 1989-91). Roman Catholic. Avocations: natural history, writing, cooking, photography. E-mail: eormsb@po box.mcgill.ca. Office: McGill U Inst Islamic Studies 3458 McTavish St Montreal QC Canada H3A 1Y1

ORNAUER, RICHARD LEWIS, retired educational association administrator; b. Bklyn., Oct. 19, 1922; s. Edwin L. and Emma (Handler) O.; m. Jane Robb, May 15, 1955 (div. Jan. 7, 1976); children: David S., Michael J., SaraJo; m. J. Rexene Ashford, Nov. 24, 1985. BJ, U. Mo., 1947. Wire editor Coastal Georgian, Brunswick, Ga., 1947-48; reporter copyreader, night editor, city editor Nassau Daily Rev.-Star, Rockville Centre, N.Y., 1948-53; city editor L.I. Press, Jamaica, 1953-71; asst. commr. Nassau County Dept. Social Services, Mineola, 1971-74; pub. health info. program officer Nassau County Dept. Health, 1974-87; adminstr. Bur. Epidemiology, 1979-84; dir. communications N.Y. State Sch. Bds. Assn., Albany, 1987-89. Instr. Queens Coll., Flushing, N.Y., 1955-59; instr., mentor 55/Alive mature driving program AARP, Dover, Del., 1993—; asst. state coord. Kent County, Del., 1996—, mem. AARP Del. State Leadership Coun., 1996, 1999-2001, exec. bd. Hofstra U. Sch. Bd. Forum, 1969-87; chmn. Merrick Planning Com., 1959-61; mem. publs. com. N.Y. State Sch. Bds. Assn., 1961-64, cons. to com., 1980-81, mem. BOCES com., 1971-74; vice chmn. State Sch. Bd. Leaders Com., 1975-79, cons. to com., 1980, bd. dirs., 1979-87, v.p., 1981, 84, 85, 86, 87, mem. exec. com., 1981-87, cons. to disting. service com., 1984, 85; cons. cities com., 1986, cons. grants com., 1987; del. L.I. Ednl. Conf. Bd., 1967-86; trustee Merrick Bd. Edn., 1962-87, pres., 1966-71; trustee Bd. Coop. Ednl. Services Nassau County, 1967-87, v.p., 1967-71, pres., 1971-87; mem. exec. com. Nassau-Suffolk Sch. Bds. Assn., 1962-87, v.p., 1974-77, pres., 1977-79; mem. exec. com. Merrick Citizens Com. for Pub. Schs., 1959-87; mem. fed. relations network 4th Congl. dist. Nat. Sch. Bds. Assn., 1973-87, study com. on career edn., 1976-78, sub-chmn. for N.E. region presdl. task force on edn. of handicapped children, 1977-78, presdl. task force on critical viewing of TV by children, 1979-80; del. Northeast Region, Nat. Sch. Bds. Assn., 1980-87, vice chmn., 1985-87, chmn., 1987; adv. com. N.Y. State Senate Standing Com. on Civil Service and Pensions, 1978-79; mem. Instructional Service Television Com. WLIW-TV/Channel 21, pres., 1973-82; mem. Com. for Better Schs. of Merrick, 1975-87, Hist. Soc. Merricks, 1976-88; bd. dirs. L.I. Coalition Fair Broadcasting, 1979-82; mem. commr.'s adv. council N.Y. State Edn. Dept., 1980-87; mem. City of Dover Pub. Safety Issues Implementation Studies Commn., 1993—; advisory comm. on signage City of Dover, 1999-2000; comms. officer Dover AFB Mus., 1995-96. Mem. citizens adv. com. Dover/Kent County Met. Planning Orgn., 1993—, chmn. 1995—2001 del. Planned Parenthood, United Way; ptnr. Spl. Olympics, Medic Alert Internat.; active Sta. WHYY, Wilmington-Phila., Del. Hospice, Nat. Wildflower Rsch. Ctr., Am. Farmland Trust, Southern Poverty Law Ctr.; Kent County rep. to the prioritization sys. steering com. Del. Dept. Transp., 1996-98, mem. pub. adv. com. on calming devices, 1999-2000; founding mem. FDR Meml.; mem. Dover Transp. Com., 2001—. With AUS, 1942-45, PTO. Recipient citations N.Y. State Police Conf., 1949, citations Rockville Centre Police Benevolent Assn., 1953, citations Nassau Div. Am. Cancer Soc., 1961, citations Nassau Am. Legion, 1963, citations Nassau Library System, 1964, citations Firemen's Assn. of Nassau County, 1964, citations Nassau County Scholastic Press Assn., 1965, citations United Fund of L.I., 1970, citations Kiwanis Clubs Internat., 1971, citations Jewish War Vets., 1972, citations WLIW-TV, 1982; Educator of Yr. award Hofstra U. chpt. Phi Delta Kappa, 1973; Educator of Yr. award Assn. for the Help of Retarded Children, Nassau County chpt., 1977; Disting. Service award Nassau-Suffolk Sch. Bds. Assn., 1979, 87, Spl. Merit award Nassau-Suffolk Sch. Bds. Assn., 1987; named Educator of Yr. U.S. Congress, 1987, County of Nassau, 1987, Town of Hempstead (N.Y.), 1987, Merrick Bd. Edn., 1987, various depts. Nassau County Bd. Coop. Ednl. Services, 1987, Merrick Sch. Dist. Faculty Assn., 1987; named Man of Yr. L.I. Spl. Edn. Adminstrs. Assn., 1979, Man of Yr. Merrick C. of C., 1980, Man of Yr. N.Y. State Legislature, 1980, 87, Man of Yr. Nassau-L.I. dist. N.Y. State Congress Parents and Tchrs., 1980 Mem. Nat. Sch. Pub. Rels. Assn. (exec. com. N.Y. State chpt., Capital Dist. chpt.), Edn. Writers Assn., Am. Newspaper Guild, Nat. Congress Parents and Tchrs. (life), N.Y. State Congress Parents and Tchrs. (life), N.Y. State Pub. Health Assn., Assn. Emotionally Handicapped Children, Assn. to Help Retarded Children, Assn. Children With Learning Abilities, N.Am. Assn. Environ. Edn., N.Y. Citizens Com. Pub. Schs., Nat. Soc. Autistic Children, Am. Assn. Career Edn., Ad Hoc Planning Com. Mobilized Community Resources, L.I. Sch.-Community Relations Assn., N.Y. Civil Svc. Employees Assn., N.Y. State Outdoor Edn. Assn., Nat. Parks and Conservation Assn., Nat. Arbor Day Found., ARC, Nat. Audubon Soc., Consumers Union, Statue of Liberty-Ellis Island Found. (charter), Habitat for Humanity, U.S. Com. of UNICEF, LWV, World War II Meml. Com. (charter) Nature Conservancy, NatConf. Sch. Bds. Assn. Communicators, Am. Assn. Retired Persons (Greater Dover area chpt., bd. dirs. 1995-2001), Ednl. Press Assn. Am., U. Mo. Alumni Assn., Boise State U. Alumni Assn., Albany Inst. History and Art (charter mem.), N.Y. State Mus. Assocs., Smithsonian Inst. Assocs., Libr. Congress Assocs. (charter), U.S. Holocaust Meml. Mus. Assocs. (charter), Ret. Pub. Employees Assn. N.Y. State, Nat. Geographic Soc., Nat. Wildlife Fedn., Newtonville Neighborhood Assn., Mifflin Rd. Neighborhood Assn. (gov. rels. chmn., exec. com.), Deerfield Civ. Assn., Consumer Union Assocs., Common Cause, Nat. Com. to Preserve Social Security and Medicare, Soc. Profl. Journalists, Sigma Delta Chi (life, Empire State chpt.), Alpha Epsilon Pi (life). Jewish. Home: 17 Mifflin Rd Dover DE 19904-3316 E-mail: richrex@doverde.net.

ORNDOFF, ELIZABETH CARLSON, retired junior college librarian, educator; b. Spearville, Kans., Mar. 28, 1918; d. Carl Edward and Laura Rebecca (Pine) Carlson; m. John Delbert Orndoff, Dec. 26, 1942; children: Barbara Kay Orndoff Fazal, David Keith, Richard Lee. BA in Sociology, BEd, U. Colo., 1940; postgrad., U. So. Calif., 1941. Lic. pvt. pilot, 1941; cert. tchr. sociology. Physics dept. libr., sec. U. Colo., Boulder, 1937-40; head coll. librarian Trinidad (Colo.) State Jr. Coll., 1940-42, tchr. sociology, 1941-42; reference librarian Los Alamos (N.Mex.) Pub. Libr., 1963-73. Editor: (non-fiction book) All of These Things, 1974. Tchr. Sunday sch. Meth. Ch., Trinidad, 1940-41; den mother Boy Scouts Am., Los Alamos, 1953-55; leader Girl Scouts U.S.A., Los Alamos, 1955-56; charter mem. United Ch. Los Alamos, 1947—, historian, 1994, 95; mem. Friends Los Alamos Pub. Libr., 1989-90, 94—, Habitat for Humanity, 1994—; active Los Alamos Retirement Ctr., Inc., Blood Mobile, Svcs. and Aid for the Relief of the Poor, Inc., India, 1993—, Meals on Wheels, 1993-99. Mem. AAUW (life), United Ostomy Assn., U. Colo. Alumni Assn., Sr. Citizens, Los Alamos Ski Club, Am. Assn. Ret. Tchrs. Democrat. Avocations: playing piano, writing, skiing, dancing, teaching English grammar to foreigners upon request. Home: 997 B 48th St Los Alamos NM 87544-1886

ORNE, EMILY CAROTA, research psychologist; b. Boston, Sept. 7, 1938; d. Emil and Ruth (Farrell) Carota; m. Martin T. Orne, Feb. 3, 1962; children: Franklin Theodore, Tracy Meredith. BA, Bennington Coll., 1959. Rsch. assoc. Mass. Mental Health Ctr., Boston, 1963-64; rsch. psychologist Unit. for Exptl. Psychiatry, Phila., 1964-79, sr. rsch. psychologist, 1979-83, co-dir., 1982—; rsch. assoc. psychology U. Pa. Sch. Medicine, 1983—. Trustee Inst. Exptl. Psychiatry Rsch. Found., Mass., 1964—, assoc. co-dir., 1987-97, exec. dir., 1998—; bd. dirs. False Memory Syndrome Found., 1995—. Contbr. articles to profl. jours.; assoc. editor Internat. Jour. Clin. and Exptl. Hypnosis, 1977—. Recipient Benjamin Franklin Gold medal Internat. Soc. Hypnosis, 1982, Roy M. Dorcus award Soc. Clin. and Exptl. Hypnosis, 1985, Bernard B. Raginsky award, 1993, Morton Prince award Soc. Clin. and Exptl. Hypnosis and APA, 1994. Avocations: fishing, swimming, reading. Office: U Pa Sch Medicine 1013 Blockley Hall 423 Guardian Dr Philadelphia PA 19104-4209 Fax: 215-573-6410.

ORNISH, DEAN, medical educator, administrator; MD, Baylor Coll. Medicine. Resident in internal medicine Mass. Gen. Hosp., Boston, 1981-84; clin. fellow in medicine Harvard Med. Sch., 1981-84; clin. prof. medicine U. Calif., San Francisco, 1984—, co-founder Osher Ctr. Integrative Medicine, 1998; founder, pres. Preventive Medicine Rsch. Inst., Sausalito, Calif., 1984—; also bd. dirs. Physician cons. to Pres. Bill Clinton, U.S. Congress, others; U.S. bd. dirs. UN High Commn. on Refugees. Author: 5 books including Dr. Dean Ornish's Program for Reversing Heart Disease, 1990, Eat More, Weigh Less, 1993, Love & Survival: The Scientific Basis for the Healing Power of Intimacy, 1998; contbr. numerous articles to profl. jours. Recipient Outstanding Young Alumnus award U. Tex., 1994, U.S. Army Surgeon Gen. medal, Beckmann medal German Soc. Prevention and Rehab. Cardiovascular Diseases, 1996. Mem. Calif. Acad. Medicine. Office: Preventive Med Rsch Inst 900 Bridgeway Sausalito CA 94965-2100 Fax: 415-332-5730. E-mail: deanornish@aol.com.

ORNSTEIN, ALEXANDER THOMAS, lawyer; b. Detroit, Oct. 11, 1944; s. Charles and Martha (Lichter) O.; m. Harriet Rozenblum, July 5, 1970; children: Charles Allen, Deborah Rena. BS, Washburn U., 1969; postgrad., Detroit Coll. Law, 1970-72; JD, Wayne State U., 1974. Bar: Mich. 1972, U.S. Dist. Ct. (ea. dist.) Mich. 1972, U.S. Ct. Appeals (6th cir.) 1972, U.S. Supreme Ct. 1978. Counselor New Horizons of Oakland County, Pontiac, Mich., 1969-70; staff atty. Mich. Mut. Ins. Co., Detroit, 1973-74; assoc. Chambers, Steiner, Mazur, Ornstein & Amlin P.C., 1974-96; pvt. practice Southfield, Mich., 1996—. Hearing referee Mich. Dept. Civil Rights, Detroit and Flint, Mich., 1980—. Editor Metro Memo Newspaper, 1984, 86-88; editor-in-chief State Bar of Mich.'s Workers Compensation Law Rev., 1991-93. Internat. v.p. B'nai B'rith, 1996—99; bd. dirs. Great Lakes Region B'nai B'rith Youth Orgn., 1984—; mem. exec. com. B'nai B'rith Internat. Youth Commn., 1994—2000; past mem. mng. bd. Bais Chabad, Farmington Hills, Mich.; pres. Hillel Found. Met. Detroit, 1988—90, chmn. bd.; pres. Centennial Lodge, 1985, Dist. 6 B'nai B'rith; mem. men's club bd. Congregation Shaarey Zedek. Bancroft-Whitney scholar, 1971. Mem.: ATLA, ABA, Anti Defamation League (co-chair campus com. 1984—86), Am. Judicature Soc., Mich. Trial Lawyers Assn., Fed. Bar Assn., Detroit Bar Assn., Mich. State Bar Assn. (workers compensation coun., chmn. workers compensation sect. 2001—). Avocations: computers, vol. service, flute. Home: 32614 Olde Franklin Dr Farmington Hills MI 48334-1744 Office: 24445 Northwestern Hwy Ste 209 Southfield MI 48075

ORNSTEIN, DONALD SAMUEL, mathematician, educator; b. N.Y.C., July 30, 1934; s. Harry and Rose (Wisner) O.; m. Shari Richman, Dec. 20, 1964; children— David, Kara, Ethan. Student, Swarthmore Coll., 1950-52; PhD, U. Chgo., 1957. Fellow Inst. for Advanced Study, Princeton, N.J., 1955-57; faculty U. Wis., Madison, 1958-60, Stanford (Calif.) U., 1959—, prof. math., 1966—. Faculty Hebrew U., Jerusalem, 1975-76 Author: Ergodic Theory Randomness and Dynamical Systems, 1974. Recipient Bocher prize Am. Math. Soc., 1974 Mem. NAS, Am. Acad. Arts and Sci. Jewish. Office: Stanford U Dept Math Stanford CA 94305

ORNT, DANIEL B. physician, department chairman; b. Jan. 21, 1951; m. Jeanine Arden-Ornt. BA, Colgate U., 1973; MD, U. Rochester, 1976. Diplomate Am. Bd. Internal Medicine, subspecialty bds. nephrology, lic. physician N.Y. Sr. instr. medicine U. Rochester (N.Y.) Sch. Medicine and Dentistry, 1981—82, asst. prof. medicine, 1982—88, asst. prof. pediat., 1984—88, assoc. prof. medicine and pediat., 1988—97, acting chief divsn. nephrology, 1988—89, dir. clin. nephrology, 1991—99, prof. medicine and pediat., 1997—, assoc. chair clin. svcs. dept. medicine, 1998—2000, assoc. prof. GCRC, 1999—, vice-chair dept. medicine, 2000—, acting chief divsn. gastroenterology, 2000. Contbr. articles to profl. jours. Recipient Disting. Svc. award, Nat. Kidney Found., Inc., 1998. Fellow: ACP; mem.: Soc. for Clin. Trials, Am. Physiol. Soc., Am. Soc. Nephrology. Office: Univ Rochester Med Ctr Box MED 601 Elmwood Ave Rochester NY 14642 Office Fax: 585-756-5154. Business E-Mail: Daniel_Ornt@URMC.Rochester.edu.

ORO, DEBRA ANN, dentist; b. Mascoutah, Ill., May 12, 1953; d. Cyril John and Elizabeth Louise (Billhartz) Haas; m. Robert John Oro, June 17, 1979; children: Philip, Anna. BS in Biology with honors, U. Ill., 1975; postgrad., Harvard U., Boston, 1975-76; DMD, U. Pa., 1979. Lic. dentist, Pa., N.J., Ariz., N.Y. Dentist/rschr. NIH Dental Rsch., Bethesda, Md., 1977; dentist USPHS, Kotzebue, Alaska, 1978; resident Luth. Med. Ctr., Bklyn., 1979-80; attending/lectr. Brookdale Hosp. and Med. Ctr., 1980-81, Hudson Valley Hosp. Ctr., Cortlandt Manor, N.Y., 1982-96; pres., dentist Hudson Valley Dental Medicine, 1985-96; pres., co-founder Oro-Dontics, Inc., Oro Valley, Ariz., 1993—. Founder Dentistry as Children's Advocates, 1998; organizer, participant Great Debate Traditional vs. Managed Care Dentistry, 1999; nat. lectr. in field. Founder Dentistry As Children's Advocates. Cited as one of Top Clinicians, Acad. Gen. Dentistry, 1997, Mrs. Tucson-USA, 1997, Mrs. Congeniality, 3rd runner up Mrs. Ariz.-USA, 1997; James scholar U. Ill., 1972, Robert Woods Johnson scholar, 1975. Mem. Acad. Cosmetic Dentistry, N.Y. State Dental Soc., No. Westchester Dist. Dental Soc., So. Ariz. Dental Soc., Peekskill-Yorktown Dental Soc. (pres. 1987-88), Kappa Delta (v.p. 1973), Alpha Lambda Delta. Avocations: parenting, hiking, weight lifting, gardening, softball. Home: 991 W Wheatgrass Pl Tucson AZ 85737-8654

ORO, JOHN JAMES, neurosurgeon; b. Sept. 28, 1950; BS in Psychology, U. Houston, 1973; MD, U. Tex., Galveston, 1978. Diplomate Am. Bd. Neurol. Surgeons. Surgery intern U. Tex. Galveston, Columbia, 1979; neurosurgery resident U. Mo., 1984; assoc. prof. U. Mo. Health Scis. Ctr., 1987-99, prof., 1999—, chief divsn. neurosurgery, 1991—2002, dir. neurosurg. ICU, 1001—2002, program dir. neurol. surgery residence tng. program, 2002—. Mem.: Am. Assn. Neurol. Surgery (bd. dirs.). Office: Rm N521 One Hospital Dr Columbia MO 65212 E-mail: oroj@health.missouri.edu.

ORO, ROBERT JOHN, dentist, consultant, writer; b. Bklyn., Apr. 22, 1952; s. Philip Edward and Marie Catherine (Bruno) O.; m. Debra Ann Haas, June 17, 1979; children: Philip, Anna. BS in Econs. with honors, SUNY, Queens, 1974; DMD, U. Pa., 1979; Fellow, Acad. Gen. Dentistry, 1985, Master, 1988. Lic. dentist, N.Y., Ariz. Founder, dentist Free Dental Clinic, Guadalajara, Mex., 1976; jr. resident Brookdale Hosp. and Med. Ctr., Bklyn., 1979-80, sr. resident, 1980-81; pres., CEO Hudson Valley Dental Medicine, Cortlandt Manor, N.Y., 1981-96, Penn Dental Consultanta, Cortlandt Manor, 1996; v.p. Oro-Dontics, Inc., Oro Valley, Ariz., 1996—; CEO On Valley Denta Medicine, 1998—. Clin. instr. Brookdale Hosp. Med. Ctr., 1981-84; attending Hudson Valley Hosp. Ctr., 1981-96; officer Peekskill (N.Y.)-Yorktown Dental Soc., 1984-87, pres., 1988; co-founder, v.p. Dentistry as Children's Advocates; lectr. on patient advocacy and dental health. Author: How to Choose Your Dentist: Confessions of an Adrenaline Addict, 1997. Active health fairs/fundraisers Hudson Valley Hosp., 1981—96; fundraiser Casa del los Ninos, Tucson, 1996, 1997, St. Elizabeth's of Hungary, Tucson, 1996, 1997, Las Familias, 2000, spokesperson; active health fairs Tucson Pks. and Recreation, 1997—. Named Mr. Congeniality, Mrs. Ariz./USA Pagent, 1997; cited as one of four top clinicians Acad. Gen. Dentistry Ann. Meeting, 1997. Mem. ADA, Ariz. Dental Assn., N.Y. State Dental Soc., Pima County Dental Study Club, Peekskill Yorktown Dental Soc. (pres. 1981-96), Delta Omicron. Avocations: writing, sports, hiking. Office: Oro-Dontics Inc 991 W Wheatgrass Pl Tucson AZ 85737-8654

OROPESA, RALPH SALVADOR, sociologist; b. Detroit, Jan. 5, 1956; s. Ralph Manuel and Marcella Ruth Oropesa; m. Nancy Susan Landale; children: Sara, Alexandra. PhD, U. Wash., 1987. Strategic planning and rsch. assoc. DDB Needham Worldwide, Chgo., 1987—89, strategic planning and rsch. supr., 1989—90; asst. prof. sociology Pa. State U., University Park, 1990—96, assoc. prof. sociology and demography University Park , 1996—2002. Contbr. ; Mem. editl. bd.: Am. Sociol. Rev., 1998—2001. Recipient Runner-up for Outstanding Article award, Assn. for Rsch. on Non-Profit Orgns. and Vol. Action, 1995; grantee, Nat. Inst. Child and Human Devel., 1993—99. Mem.: Population Assn. Am., Am. Sociol. Assn. Office: Pa State U 201 Oswald Tower State College PA 16802 Office Fax: 814-863-8342. Personal E-mail: oropesa@pop.psu.edu. Business E-Mail: oropesa@pop.psu.edu.

O'RORKE, JAMES FRANCIS , JR. lawyer; b. N.Y.C., Dec. 4, 1936; s. James Francis and Helen (Weber) O'R.; m. Carla Phelps, Aug. 6, 1964. AB, Princeton U., 1958; JD, Yale U., 1961. Bar: N.Y. 1962. Assoc. Davies, Hardy & Schenck, 1962-69; ptnr. Davies, Hardy, Ives & Lawther, 1969-72, Skadden, Arps, Slate, Meagher & Flom, N.Y.C., 1972—. Dir. Clinipad Corp.; mem. adv. bd. Chgo. Title Ins. Co. N.Y. Trustee Mus. Am. Indian-Heye Found., 1977-80; dir. James Lenox House Assn., Inc., 1998-02. Mem. ABA, N.Y. State Bar Assn., Assn. Bar City N.Y., Am. Coll. Real Estate Lawyers, Princeton Club N.Y.C. Office: Skadden Arps Slate Meagher & Flom 4 Times Sq Fl 24 New York NY 10036-6595 Address: C/O Skadden Apts 4 Times Sq Rm 44200 New York NY 10036-6522

OROSEL, GERHARD OSKAR, economics educator; b. Vienna, Austria, July 31, 1946; s. Egon Walter and Auguste (Studnicka) O.; m. Renate Taubenbeck, July 30, 1971 (div. 1979); children: Christian, Stefan. JD, U. Vienna, 1970, Habilitation in Econ. Theory, 1974. Asst. Inst. Advanced Studies, Vienna, 1971; asst. dept. econs. U. Vienna, 1971-74, prof. econs., 1977—. Wissenschaftlicher rat and prof. econs. U. Bonn, Fed. Republic Germany, 1974-77; vis. scholar NYU, 1984, U. Calif., San Diego, 1987-88, dean of the sch. of social and econ. scis., 1989-91; acad. vis. London Sch. Econs., 1993; vis. scholar U. Boston, 1996-97, Harvard U., 1999-2000; vis. prof. Ctr. Econ. Studies, Munich, 1995. Mem. Amnesty Internat., 1975—. Mem. Am. Econ. Assn., Theoretischer Ausschuss des Vereins für Socialpolitik, Nationalökonomische Gesellschaft, European Econ. Assn., Econ. Soc. Home: Neubauguertel 4/17 A-1070 Vienna Austria Office: U Vienna Dept Econs Hohenstaufeng 9 A-1010 Vienna Austria E-mail: gerhard.orosel@univie.ac.at.

OROST, JOSEPH MARTIN, computer scientist; b. Jersey City, 1956; s. Joseph and Jean Orost; m. June Deli, Oct. 4, 1980 (div.); 1 stepchild, Jeffrey Liscik. BS in Computer Sci., Thomas A. Edison State Coll., 1991; MS in Computer Sci., Rutgers U., 1995. Programmer Interdata, Oceanport, N.J., 1974-78; sr. cons. tech. staff Concurrent Computer Corp., Tinton Falls, 1978-91, project leader, 1985-91; tech. staff AT&T Echo Logic, Holmdel, 1991-93; tech. mgr. AT&T Labs., Lincroft, 1994—. Author: UNIX compress, 1985, BENCH++, 1995. Past advancement chmn. Troop 82 Boy Scouts Am., Jackson, N.J. Mem. Assn. Computing Machinery, Internat. Platform Assn. Avocations: music, electronics. Office: AT&T Labs 200 Laurel Ave Middletown NJ 08755 Home: 1556 Church Rd Toms River NJ 08755-2116 E-mail: orost@att.com.

O'ROURKE, C. LARRY, lawyer; b. Colusa, Calif., Dec. 10, 1937; s. James Harold and Elizabeth Janice (Jenkins) O'R.; m. Joy Marie Phillips, May 22, 1965; children: Ryan, Paula. BSEE, Stanford U., 1959, MBA, 1961; JD, George Washington U., 1972. Bar: Va. 1971, D.C. 1974, U.S. Ct. Appeals (fed. cir.) 1973, U.S. Patent and Trademark Office 1971, U.S. Supreme Ct. Patent atty. Westinghouse Elec., Washington, 1969-70, Pitts., 1970-73; assoc. Finnegan, Henderson, Farabow, Garrett & Dunner, Washington, 1974-79, ptnr., 1979—, mng. ptnr. Palo Alto, Calif. Dir. Zest Inc., Md., 1988, chmn. bd. dirs., 1990-95; mem. George Washington Law Sch. I.P. adv. coun., mem. bd. dirs. Stanford Bus. Sch. Alumni and mem. devel. coun. Stanford GSB. Mem. ABA, Am. Intellectual Property Law Assn., Inter-Pacific Bar Assn. Democrat. Presbyterian. Office: Finnegan Henderson Farabow Garrett & Dunner 700 Hansen Way Palo Alto CA 94304-1016

O'ROURKE, JAMES LOUIS, lawyer; b. Bridgeport, Conn., July 5, 1958; s. James G. and Margaret Elizabeth (Fesco) O'R.; m. Margaret C. DiCicco, Sept. 18, 1994. BS, U. Bridgeport, 1984, JD, 1987. Bar: Conn. 1988, U.S. Dist. Ct. Conn. 1989, Mashantucket Pequot Tribal Bar 1995, Supreme Ct. of U.S., 1998. Pvt. practice, Stratford, Conn., 1987—. With USN, 1976-79. Mem. ABA, ATLA, Conn. Trial Lawyers Assn., Conn. Bar Assn., Greater Bridgeport Bar Assn. Roman Catholic. Avocations: boating, gardening, fishing, cycling, swimming. Office: The Barnum Profl Bldg 1825 Barnum Ave Ste 201 Stratford CT 06614-5333

O'ROURKE, JOAN B. DOTY WERTHMAN, retired educational administrator; b. N.Y.C., June 7, 1933; d. George E. Doty and Lillian G. Bergen; 10 children, 8 stepchildren. BA summa cum laude, Marymount Manhattan Coll., 1953; MA, Columbia U., 1958; PhD, St. John's U., 1971. Tchr. history Marymount H.S., N.Y.C., 1953-55; instr. history Marymount Manhattan Coll., 1957-59; acting chmn. history dept. Nassau C.C., Mineola, N.Y., 1959-60; prof. history Westchester C.C., Valhalla, 1963-74; prin. Pius X Sch., Scarsdale, 1974-77; assoc. dir. alumni rels. Fordham U., N.Y.C., 1980-84; co-founder, dir. Assn. for Profl. Psychol. and Ednl. Counseling, Wilmette, Ill., 1987-91; ptnr., pres. O'Rourke and Assocs., 1993-97; ret., 1997. Dir., writer Sta. WFAS, White Plains, 1963-64; adj. prof. social sci. Fordham U., 1974-76. Mem. resident bd. Del Webb, Sun City, Calif., 2001—; bd. mem. Catholic Christian , San Bernardino; mem. fin. com. St. Francis of Assisi Ch., LaQuinta, 2001—; bd. dirs. Cath. Charities Diocese of San Bernardino, 2001—. Recipient alumni award Marymount Coll., 1988; tchg. fellow St. John's U., Jamaica, N.Y., 1968. Mem. Soc. Mayflowers Descs. Ill., Michigan Shores Club, Order of Holy Sepulchre (lady). Democrat. Roman Catholic. E-mail: doctorjoan@web.tv.net.

O'ROURKE, THOMAS DENIS, civil engineer, educator; b. Pitts., July 31, 1948; s. Lawrence Robert and Adel Mildred (Moloski) O'R.; m. Patricia Ann Lane, Aug. 12, 1978; 1 child, Adele Christina. BSCE, Cornell U., 1970; MSCE, U. Ill., 1973, PhD, 1975. Soils engr. Dames & Moore, N.Y.C., 1970; rsch. asst. U. Ill., Urbana, 1970-75, asst. prof., 1975-78, Cornell U., Ithaca, N.Y., 1978-80, assoc. prof., 1981-87, prof., 1987-98, Thomas R. Briggs prof. engring., 1999—. Fellow: AAAS; mem.: ASTM (C.A. Hogentogler award 1976), ASME, NAE, ASCE (pres. Ithaca sect. 1981—82, chair exec. com. tech. coun. lifeline earthquake engr. 1998—99, Collingwood prize 1983, Huber prize 1988, C. Martin Duke award 1995, Stephen D. Bechtel pipeline engring. award 1997), U.S. Com. on Tunnelling Tech. (chmn. 1987—88), Internat. Soc. Rock Mechanics, Internat. Soc. Engring. Geology, Earthquake Engring. Rsch. Inst. (bd. dirs. 1998—2000, v.p. 2000, pres.-elect 2002, Outstanding Paper award 1996). Home: 10 Twin Glens Rd Ithaca NY 14850-1041 Office: Cornell U Sch Civil Environ Engring 273 Hollister Hall Ithaca NY 14853-3501 E-mail: tdo1@cornell.edu.

O'ROURKE, TIMOTHY JOHN, physician; b. Mpls., Aug. 1, 1950; s. Edward Clarence and Rita Margaret (Brosnan) O'R.; m. Debra Dee Dickerson, May 19, 1979; children: Michael J., Jacob J. BS, Mich. State U., 1971; MS, U. Mich., 1975, MD, 1976. Commd. 2d lt. U.S. Army, 1976, advanced through grades to col., retired, 1996. Fellow Am. Coll. Physicians; mem. AMA, Am. Soc. Hematology, Am. Soc. Clin. Oncology, Am. Assn. Cancer Rsch. Roman Catholic. Office: Cancer & Hematology Ctrs Western Mich 710 Kenmoor Ave SE Grand Rapids MI 49546-2379 E-mail: timothyorourke@sprintmail.com.

OROZCO, LUZMARIA, language educator, educator; b. Mexico City, Nov. 3, 1933; came to U.S., 1953; BA in French and English, Marycrest Coll., Davenport, Iowa, 1956; MA in English, Marquette U., 1958; PhD in Comparative Lit., U. Minn., 1973. Chair humanities divsn. Marycrest Internat. U., Davenport, Iowa, 1975-78, prof. English and Spanish. Humanities rep. human rights commn. Palmer Sch. Chiropracters, 1979—; official translator Latin Am. affairs Diocese of Davenport, 1978; vis. prof. St. Agnes Coll., Md., 1978, St. Jerome Coll., Waterloo, Ontario, Canada, 1976, Yale U., New Haven, Conn., 1986-87; cons., participant Iowa Program in Humanities, 1975-79; translator, cons. testing program on bilingual edn. U. Iowa, 1978. Editor of publs. Sister of Humility of Mary, 1960-85; contbr. numerous poems to competitions. Danforth Instn. grantee, 1967-69, Fulbright grantee, 1970-72; recipient award for teaching excellence and campus leadership Sears-Roebuck and Found. for Ind. Higher Edn., 1990. Mem. MLA, Popular Culture Assn., Spanish-Speaking Commn., Chaparral Poetry Assn. Roman Catholic. Avocations: tennis, swimming, fighting illiteracy. Home: 1607 W 12th St Davenport IA 52804-4034 Office: Marycrest Internat U Dept English Davenport IA 52804

ORPHANIDES, GUS GEORGE, research chemist; b. N.Y.C., Jan. 27, 1947; s. Gus G. and Savesta (Agapetus) O.; m. Jeanne Wood, Feb. 3, 1968; children: Alyson, Paul, Lindsay. BS with honors, Hobart Coll., 1967; PhD, Ohio State U., 1972. Chemist E.I. Du Pont de Nemours & Co., Wilmington, Del., 1974-79, Beaumont, Tex., 1979-81, Air Products, Allentown, Pa., 1981-84, applications mgr., 1984-85, comml. mgr., 1985-88, rsch. mgr., 1988-91, sr. comml. devel. mgr., 1991-94, comml. devel. mgr., 1995-96, R&D mgr., 1996-98, global tech. svc. mgr., 1998—2000, dir. applications devel., tech. svc., chem. tech., 2000—02, dir. intellectual asset mgmt. and licensing, 2002—. Contbr. articles to profl. publs.; patentee in field; developed new polymers for adhesives, non-wovens, paper coatings, polyurethane elastomers, rubber cross-linking. Phys. rehab. hosp. vol. in occupl. therapy. 1st lt. U.S. Army, 1972-74. Decorated Army Commendation medal; recipient Army Cert. of Achievment, Raker Meml. award Good Shepherd Hosp.; N.Y. State Regents scholar, 1963-67. Mem. Am. Chem. Soc., Licensing Exec. Soc. Republican. Presbyterian. Achievements include development of novel emulsion polymers and polymer intermediates, international technology transfer, technology licensing, lab-to-plant technology transfer, plant start-up, commercialized new products. Avocations: traveling, classical music, crossword puzzles, reading. Home: 4046 Providence Ct Schnecksville PA 18078-3524 Office: Air Products 7201 Hamilton Blvd Allentown PA 18195-1526

ORPHANIDES, NORA CHARLOTTE, ballet educator; b. N.Y.C., June 4, 1951; d. M.T. and Mary Elsie (Tilly) Feffer; m. James Mark Orphanides, July 1, 1972; children: Mark, Elaine, Jennine. BA, CUNY, 1973; student, Joffrey Ballet Sch., N.Y.C., 1970-75; postgrad., Princeton Ballet Sch., 1976-86. Cert. speech and hearing handicapped tchr. With membership dept. M.M.A., N.Y.C., 1987—2002; mem. faculty Princeton (N.J.) Ballet Sch., 1983—, trustee emeritus, 1992—. Mem. cast Princeton Ballet ann. Nutcracker, 1985-90, now Am. Repertory Ballet Co., 1993—; appeared in Romeo & Juliet, 1995-96, 2000. Fundraising gala chmn. Princeton Ballet, 1985, 86, 91-92, chmn. spl. events, 1987—, trustee, 1986—, chmn. Nutcracker benefit, 1990—, Dracula benefit, 1991, honoree, 1999; dept. chmn. June Fete to benefit Princeton Hosp., 1988, 90-91, 92, 96, 2000, trustee, 1995-99; vol. Nat. Hdqrs. Recording for the Blind, 1991-93; dinner chmn. Nassau Ch. Music Festival, 1992, Handel Festival, Nassau Ch., 1993, Princeton Chamber Symphony, 1993; hon. chmn. Princeton Ballet Gala, 1993; chmn. Christmas Boutique, Princeton Med. Ctr., 1993; trustee, Princeton Med. Ctr. Aux. Bd., 1992—, trustee 1995—, pres., 1997-99, past pres., 2000—; choreographer Stuart Country Day Sch., Princeton, 1996-99; chmn. benefit dinner Eden Inst., 2000. Named honoree Princeton Ballet, 1999. Democrat. Avocations: piano, skiing, tennis. Office: 301 N Harrison St Princeton NJ 08540-3512

ORR, ANITA CHRISTINE, government relations representative; b. Texarkana, Tex., Mar. 11, 1960; d. David Guss and Prudie Luther O.; children: Steven, Chloe. BA, U. Ark., 1982; MPA, U. Ark., Little Rock, 1986. Legis. asst. Congressman Tommy Robinson, Washington, 1985-88; sr. legis. asst. Congresswoman Jolene Unsoeld, 1989-90; regulatory specialist Am. Nat. Red Cross, 1991-96; govt. rels. rep. San Francisco Bay Area Rapid Transit Dist., Oakland, Calif., 1996—. Office: Bay Area Rapid Transit Dist 800 Madison St Oakland CA 94607-4730 Home: 4952 Cache Peak Dr Antioch CA 94531-8319

ORR, BOBETTE KAY, diplomat; b. Oak Park, Ill., Oct. 28, 1941; d. Robert Jay and Neta (Hoobler) Potle; m. William Rucker Orr, Oct. 11, 1974; step children: Bridgette, Brietta, Alyson, William Jr. BA in Econs., Conn. Coll. for Women, 1963; student auditor Internat. Econs., London Sch. of Econs., 1964; postgrad. studies in Internat. Econs., George Washington U., 1964-65. Rsch. asst. C. of C. USA, Washington, 1965-66; country desk officer for Scandanavia U.S. Dept. Commerce, 1966-69, country desk officer for France, 1970-72, 79-81, country desk officer for Belgium, Netherlands, Luxembourg, 1974-77, country desk officer for Japan, 1981-82; mkt. rsch. officer United States Trade Ctr., Stockholm, 1973, trade promotion officer London, 1977-78; asst. comml. attache Am. Embassy, Paris, 1982-87; comml. attache Am. Consulate Gen., Auckland, New Zealand, 1988-92, consul gen. Edinburgh, Scotland, 1992-95; comml. counselor Am. Embassy, London, 1995-99, Cairo, 1999—2002; regional dir. Africa, Near East and South Aisa U.S. Dept. Commerce, Washington, 2002—. Mem. bd. dirs. U.S. Dept. Commerce Fed. Credit Union, Washington, D.C., 1972-77, pres., 1976-77, mem. supervisory com., 1979-81; equal employment opportunity counselor for Greater Washington Met. Area, 1972-75; mission dir. for USDOC's Concrete Constrn. Techniques Seminar Mission to Hong Kong, Singapore, Malaysia, 1980; detailed to Office of Dir. Fgn. Comml. Svc. as evaluator of candidates for Fgn. Comml. Svc., 1981. Author: (with others) 10 pamphlet series, on free enterprise, The Power of Choice, 1966; contbr. to Bus. Am., 1966-81, Overseas Bus. Reports 1966-76 (Dept. Commerce publs.). Mem. Am. Women's Club of Edinburgh, (hon. pres.), The English Speaking Union. Avocations: skiing, bicycle riding. Home: PO Box 63 Great Falls VA 22066-0063 Office: ANESA/USFCS/ITA Dept Commerce 14th & constitution NW Rm 1223 Washington DC 20230

ORR, CAROL WALLACE, book publishing executive; b. Newton, Mass., Dec. 17, 1933; d. Barton Stuart Wallace and Mary (Blanthorne) Stigler; children: Brett Amanda, Ross Wallace. Student, Boston U., 1951-53; BA, Douglass Coll., 1966. Successively permissions mgr., paperback editor, reprint editor, asst. to assoc. dir. Princeton (N.J.) U. Press, 1966-75, exec. asst. to dir. then asst. dir., 1975-78; dir. U. Tenn. Press., Knoxville, 1978-91. Aerobics instr., freelance editor, 1992—. Mem. editorial bd. Book Rsch. Quar., 1988-92; contbr. articles to Scholarly Pub. jour., 1974-86. Recipient Book Woman award Women's Nat. Book Assn., 1987, Disting. Career award Needham (Mass.) H.S., 1995. Mem. Assn. Am. Univ. Presses (pres. 1987-88), Internat. Assn. Scholarly Pubs. (sec.-gen. 1980-83), Women in Scholarly Pub. (first pres. 1980-81), AAUP Lang. Task Force (chair 1989-91), AAUP Golden Fluke Award Com. (chair 1984-91), Phi Beta Kappa, Phi Kappa Phi. Avocations: jogging, tennis, gardening, travel, music.

ORR, CAROLE, artist; b. Alexandria, Ind., June 10, 1933; d. Carl Victor and Marian Martha (Long) Coonse; m. Larry D. Ribble (dec. July 1953); m. Thomas LeRoy Orr, Nov. 10, 1950 (div. Oct. 1979); children: Karen Sue, Terri Ribble, David Thomas; m. Lev C. Hamblet Jr., Feb. 5, 1982 (div. Oct. 1998); stepchildren: James, Jean, Laura, Anne. Cert., Famous Artist Sch., Westport, Conn., 1956, Art Instrn. Schs., Mpls., 1962. Asst. art dir. La Gallerie du Mall, Houston, 1975-78; freelance fine artist Lantern Ln. Gallery, 1968-81, asst. mgr., design cons., 1979-81; artist Artist Showroom, 1982—. Participating artist Assistance Guild, Houston, 1968, Beaux Arts, Houston, 1968-70, Houston Gamma Phi Gallery, 1971-72, Houston Delta Gamma Found., 1978-81, Glassell Sch. of Art Houston, 1983; art instr. children's art Houston Park and Recreational Programs, 1964-68. One-woman shows include Nobler Gallery, Houston, 1967, Art Gallery, Pasadena, Tex., 1968, Gallarie La Rue, Austin, Tex., 1971, Gallery 12, Houston, 1972, Main St., Houston, 1974, La Galerie de Mall, Houston, 1976-78, Triumvirate Gallery, Santa Fe, N.Mex., 1980, Houshang's Gallery, Dallas, 1980-82, Battle Horn Galleries Ltd., Santa Fe, 1984, New Trends Inc., Santa Fe, 1985-88, Horizons Galleries, Houston, 1990-93, Houston C.C., 1992, Heinen Theatre, 1992, Windsor Gallery, Ft. Lauderdale, Fla., 1994; exhibited in group shows at Motorola Invitational, Houston, 1964, Assistance Guild Houston, 1968, Am. Gen. Bldg., Houston, 1968, Beaux Arts, Houston, 1968-70, Gamma Phi Gallery, Houston, 1971-72, Lantern Ln. Gallery, Houston, 1971-72, Delta Gamma Found., Houston, 1978-81, Glassell Sch. Art, Houston, 1983, New Trends Gallery Inc., Santa Fe, N.mex., 1985-88, Pasadena (Tex.) Art Invitational, 1988, Double Tree Hotel, Houston, 1990, Horizons Gallery, Houston, 1990-93, Windsors Gallery, Dania, fla., 1993. Art instr. adults Ch. of the Advent, Houston, 1968-70; adult edn. instr. arts Ch. Sch. Conf., Dept. Christian Edn., Trinity Ch., Diocese of Tex., Houston, 1969. Recipient Profl. Best Ann. Competition Art Instrn. Schs., Mpls., 1965; named Best-Selling Artists of Yr., 2001. Avocations: self-study in psychology, music, dance. Home and Office: Artist Showroom DBA 880 Tully Rd Apt 29 Houston TX 77079-5418

ORR, CYNTHIA HUJAR, lawyer; b. Panama City, Fla., Oct. 4, 1957; d. Thomas Stanley and Joan Theresa (Sigler) Hujar; m. John David Orr, Aug. 1, 1981. BBA, U. Tex., 1979; JD, St. Mary's U., 1988. Assoc. Goldstein, Goldstein & Hilley, San Antonio, 1986—; law clk. Fed. Dist. Judge Emilio Garza, 1988. Mem. Nat. Assn. Criminal Def. Lawyers (bd. dirs.), San Antonio Criminal Def. Lawyers Assn. (past pres.), Tex/ Criminal Def. Lawyers Assn. (1st v.p.). Assn. Cert. Specialists Criminal Law (past pres.). Home: 231 Pinewood Ln San Antonio TX 78216-6722 Office: Goldstein Goldstein & Hilley 29th Fl Tower Life Bldg San Antonio TX 78205

ORR, DENNIS PATRICK, lawyer; b. N.Y.C., Dec. 29, 1952; s. Gerard Samuel and Mary Ellen (Dowd) O.; m. Laurie Louise Lawless, Jan. 15, 1977; children: Kathryn, Kristen, Megan, Matthew. BA, Boston Coll., 1975; JD, St. John's U., 1978. Bar: N.Y. 1979, U.S. Dist. Ct. (so. and ea. dists.) N.Y. 1979, U.S. Ct. Appeals (2d cir.) 1986. Assoc. Shearman & Sterling, N.Y.C., 1978-86, ptnr., 1987-97, Mayer, Brown & Platt, N.Y.C., 1997—. St. Thomas More scholar St. John's Law Sch., Jamaica, N.Y., 1975. Mem. ABA, N.Y. State Bar Assn. Roman Catholic. Office: Mayer Brown Rowe & Maw 1675 Broadway Fl 19 New York NY 10019-5820

ORR, ELAINE LOUISE, public policy writer; b. Washington, Aug. 14, 1951; d. Miles D. and H. Rita (Rooney) O. BA, U. Dayton, 1972; MA, Am. U., 1974. Evaluator GAO, Washington, 1974-78, spl. asst. to asst. comptr. gen., 1979-80, dir. internat. liaison, 1979-86; sr. cons. Nat. Acad. Pub. Adminstr., 1987—. Editor Internat. Jour. Govt. Auditing, 1983-86, Nat. Young Profls. Forum News, 1982-83; assoc. editor The Public Manager, 1987-89. Mem. ASPA (life, pres. Nat. Capital Area chpt. 1991-92), AAUW (pres. Ottumwa area br. 2001-03), Writers Ctr. Bethesda, DAR (gov. DC. Girls State 1968). Democrat. Avocations: gardening, reading, theatre, family history research. E-mail: elaineorr55@yahoo.com.

ORR, EMMA JANE, pharmacist, educator; b. Pennington, Va., Sept. 30, 1956; d. Clyde Wilson and Monnie Lee (Daugherty) O.; m. Allen Emerson Clark, Oct. 24, 1981; 1 child, Katherine Wilson. BS in Pharmacy, Med. Coll. Va., 1979; D of Pharmacy with highest hons., U. Ky., 1981. Registered pharmacist, Va., Ky., Tenn. Asst. dir. pharmacy St. Mary's Hosp., Norton, Va., 1980-84, Norton Community Hosp., 1984-90; clin. coord. Hoston Valley Hosp., Kingsport, Tenn., 1990—. Adj. faculty Mountain Empire C.C., Big Stone Gap, Va., 1981—; asst. clin. prof. dept. pharmacy and pharmaceutics Med. Coll. Va., Richmond, 1982—; clin. prof. So. Sch. Pharmacy Mercer U. Tchr., children's spkr. Ch. United Meth. Ch., Duffield, Va., Mountain Empire Older Citizens, Wise, Va., 1983-85; leader Girl Scouts, Duffield, Va. Named Young Career Woman of Yr. Bus. and Profl. Women's Club, 1983. Mem.: Va. Soc. Hosp. Pharmacists, Am. Soc. Hosp. Pharmacists. Methodist. Avocations: reading, needlework, skiing, swimming. Home: 100 Quillen Dr Duffield VA 24244 E-mail: e_jane_orr@wellmont.org.

ORR, FRANK HOWARD, III, architect; b. Jasper, Ala., Sept. 4, 1932; s. Frank Howard Jr. and Lola Ruth (Lynch) O.; m. Nancy Gayle Gentry, Apr. 13, 1957; children: Mark Daniel, Steven Gentry, Karen Diann, Amy Ruth. B in Applied Art, Auburn U., 1961. Registered Ala., Fla., Ga., Ky., N.C., Tenn., Va., Miss. Assoc. architect Edwin A. Keeble Assocs., Nashville, 1962-70, Bianculli & Tyler, Inc., Chattanooga, 1970; prin. Frank Orr Architects, Nashville, 1970-76; pres., prin. Orr/Houk & Assocs. Architects, Inc., 1976-2001; v.p. Hart Freeland Roberts, Inc. (merged with Orr/Houk), Brentwood, 2001—. V.p. Hart Freeland Roberts, Inc., Brentwood, Tenn.; adj. faculty O'More Sch. Design, Franklin, Tenn., 1972—77, Nashville State Tech. Inst., 1978—79; guest lectr. Sch. Arch., Victoria U., Wellington, New Zealand, 1987; exam grader Nat. Coun. Archtl. Registration Bds., Ft. Lauderdale, Fla., 1985; guest lectr. Coll. Arch., Auburn U., 2001. Author: Professional Practice in Architecture, 1982, Scale in Architecture, 1985; author (column) Urban Life, Nashville Bus. Jour., 1995; editor: Notable Nashville Architecture 1930-1980; contbr. articles to profl. jours.; prin. works include Woodmont Bapt. Ch. (design commendation 1979, Design award of Merit 1990), Appalachian Ctr. for Crafts, Two Rivers Bapt. Ch. (design commendation 1979), 1st Bapt. Ch., Hendersonville, Tenn. (design award of merit 1992), First Bapt. Ch., Athens, Ala., First Bapt. Ch., Pasadena, Tex., Tenn. Bapt. Camps, Carson and Linden, First Baptist Ch., Joelten, Ind., Lake Providence Missionary Baptist Ch., Nashville. Active Citizens com. Met. Nashville Gen. Plan, 1994; missionary trips including Guatemala, 1977, 82, Mexico, 1980, Sierra Leone, 1985, 88, Poland, 1998, Brazil, 2000. Recipient Scarab Archtl. hon. award, Auburn U., 1961. Mem. AIA (dir. Mid. Tenn. chpt. 1971-78, chmn. chpat. com. design awards 1985, com. environ. edn. 1972-76), Tenn. Soc. Architects (sec.-treas. 1977), Nashville C. of C. (regional transp. com. 1993-94), Scarab. Baptist. Avocations: sketching, writing. Office: 7101 Executive Center Dr Ste 300 Brentwood TN 37027-3207

ORR, FRANKLIN MATTES, JR. petroleum engineering educator; b. Baytown, Tex., Dec. 27, 1946; s. Franklin Mattes and Selwyn Sage (Huddleston) O.; m. Susan Packard, Aug. 30, 1970; children: David, Katherine. BSChemE, Stanford U., 1969; PhDChemE, U. Minn., 1976. Asst. to dir. Office Fed. Activities EPA, Washington, 1970-72; research engr. Shell Devel. Co., Houston, 1976-78; sr. engr. N.Mex. Petroleum Recovery Research Ctr., Socorro, 1978-84; assoc. prof. petroleum engring. Stanford (Calif.) U., 1985-87, prof., 1987—, interim dean Sch. Earth Scis., 1994-95, dean Sch. Earth Scis., 1995—. Contbr. articles to profl. jours. Bd. dirs. Wolf Trap Found. for the Performing Arts, 1988-94, Monterey Bay Aquarium Rsch. Inst., 1987—, Am. Geol. Inst. Found., 1997—, David and Lucile Packard Found., 1999—; chair sci. adv. com. David and Lucile Packard Found. Fellowships for Sci. and Engring. With USPHS, 1970-72. Recipient AIME Robert Earll McConnell award, 2001. Mem. NAE, AIChE, AAAS, Soc. Petroleum Engrs. (Disting. Lectr. award 1988-89, Disting. Achievement award for petroleum engring. faculty 1993), Soc. Indsl. and Applied Math. Office: Stanford U Sch Earth Scis Mitchell Bldg Rm 101 Stanford CA 94305-2210

ORR, JIM (JAMES D. ORR), editor, writer; b. Buffalo, Feb. 7, 1960; s. David James and Doris Kathleen (Wolos) O.; m. JoEllen Black, June 4, 1994. B in Journalism, Ind. U. of Pa., 1982, M in Comm., 1987. Station mgr. Sta. WIUP-TV, Ind., Pa., 1983-84; sports writer, news writer Ind. (Pa.) Gazette, 1984-88; reporter Stuart (Fla.) News, 1988-89; staff writer, columnist Gannett Rochester (N.Y.) Newspapers, 1989-96; staff writer The Bus. Jour., Fresno, Calif., 1997; sr. writer The Fresno Bee, 1998-99; spl. projects/weekend editor, page designer The Westerly (R.I.) Sun, 2000—. Columnist Orrdinary People, 1994-95; freelance writer, publicist, 1996—. Moderator polit. debate Edu-Cable Corp., Greece, N.Y., 1993. Recipient Agrl. Writing 1st Place award Penn-Ag Industries, 1985, 2d place Keystone State Press award Pa. Newspaper Pub. Assn., 1987, 2 Scripps Howard writing awards, 1989, Award Gannett Enterprise Project, 1994, Cmty. Svc. award N.Y. Newspaper Pubs. Assn., 1994-95, Spl. Series 2d pl. award R.I. Press Assn., 2000. Home: 42 Rosewood Dr Vernon Rockville CT 06066-6229

ORR, JOHN TRAYLOR, JR. lawyer; b. Birmingham, Ala., July 9, 1946; s. John Traylor and Robena (Evins) O.; m. Anita Jean Black, Jan. 27, 1979; 1 child, Lauren Elizabeth; stepchildren: Angela Marie Adams, Michelle Swan. BS, Emory U., 1967, JD, 1975. Bar: Ga. 1975, U.S. Dist. Ct. (no. dist.) Ga. 1979. Chem. engr. Turco Products div. Purex Corp., Atlanta, 1971-72; trial atty. antitrust div. U.S. Dept. Justice, 1975-86, chief Atlanta regional office antitrust div., 1986—97, 1998—2002, dir. criminal enforcement antitrust div. Washington, 1997-98; pvt. practice Marietta, Ga., 2002—; owner Mountain River Cabins, L.L.C., 2002—. Mem. faculty law trial techniques program Emory U., Atlanta, 1982-2002. Lt. (j.g.) USN, 1968-71, Vietnam. Mem. State Bar Ga. (past pres. sect. antitrust law), Oak Creek Estates Swim and Tennis Club (Marietta, Ga.). Avocations: tennis, golf, travel. Home and Office: 1530 Wood Valley Dr Marietta GA 30066-4146

ORR, JOSEPH ALEXANDER, educational administrator; b. West Palm Beach, Fla., Nov. 20, 1929; s. Joseph Alexander and Eula (Terry) O.; m. Ardis W. Orr (div.); children: Eric, Pamela, Tracey; m. Linda F. Orr. BS, Fla. A&M U., 1951; MS, Mich. State U., 1953; MEd, Fla. Atlantic U., 1965; PhD, Fla. State U., 1972. Sci. tchr. Roosevelt Sr. H.S., West Palm Beach, Fla., 1953-68; counselor, coord. Adult Edn. Dept. Sch. Sys., Palm Beach County, 1960-72; dean of students Palm Beach H.S., West Palm Beach, 1968-70; asst. dean Fla. A&M U., Tallahassee, 1970-72; adj. prof. Ind. U., Bloomington, 1972-73; prin. Ctrl. Sr. H.S., Louisville, 1972-74, Jupiter (Fla.) H.S., 1974-78; adj. prof. Fla. Atlantic U., Boca Raton, 1978—; asst. supt. Palm Beach County (Fla.) Sch. Bd., 1978-84, assoc. supt., 1984-92, dep. supt., chief acad. officer, 2001—; exec. dir. Palm Beach County Sch. Adminstrs. Assn., 1992-2001. Chair State Adv. Bd. for Severely Emotionally Disturbed. Contbr. articles to profl. jours. Bd. dirs. Children's Home Soc. Fla., Palm Beach County Coun. Arts; past chair Health and Human Svcs. Bd., Palm Beach County, Inst. New Dimensions, Palm Beach C.C., Assn. Retarded Citizens, Inc., West Palm Beach; past pres. Scholastic Achievement Found. Palm Beach County, Edn. Found. Palm Beach County. Recipient Disting. Svc. award NEA, Pioneer award for excellence in pub. svc. Nat. Forum of Pub. Adminstrn., Outstanding Achievement award Fla. Assn. Cmty. Educators, Four Seasons award Nat. Assn. for Year Round Edn. Mem. ASCD, Fla. Assn. Sch. Adminstrs., Am. Assn. Sch. Adminstrs., Nat. Assn. Secondary Sch. Prins., Nat. Cmty. Edn. Assn. (Sch. Leadership award), Kiwanis Internat. Democrat. Episcopalian. Avocation: boating. Office: Palm Beach County Sch Adminstrs Assn PO Box 31511 Palm Beach Gardens FL 33420

ORR, JOSEPH NEWTON, recreational guide, outdoor educator; b. San Francisco, Oct. 25, 1954; s. James Neewah and Verna Louise (Butler) O. BA in Spanish, Sul Ross State U., 1981. Cert. swiftwater rescue technician, wilderness first responder, open water scuba diver, Grand Canyon river guide, Tex. master naturalist. Instr. astronomy lab. Sul Ross State U., Alpine, Tex., 1972-75; svc. sta. attendent, store clerk Nat. Park Concessions, Big Bend Nat. Park, 1975-78; surveyor's aide Gila Nat. Forest U.S. Dept. Agriculture, N. Mex., 1979; instr. ESL Centro Universitario de Idiomas, Mexico City, 1981; English and Spanish tutor Ctr. Student Devel. Sul Ross State U., 1980-83, instr. ESL, Intensive Summer Lang. Tng. Inst. Tex., 1980-83; ednl. cons. Chihuahuan Desert Rsch. Inst., 1983; editor The Skyline (student newspaper) Sul Ross State U., 1984; interpreter, translator, guide Dr. John M. Miller, Mexico, 1980-85; guide in U.S., Mex., Belize, Guatemala and Honduras for Far Flung Adventures, Terlingua, Tex., 1986-94, Remarkable Journeys, Houston, 1994-98; with Ceiba Adventures, Flagstaff, 1998—. Active Grand Canyon River Guides, Pre-Columbian Art Rsch. Inst., Chihuahuan Desert Rsch. Inst., Friends of Big Bend Nat. Park. Mem. Internat. Dark Sky Assn., Grand Canyon Assn., Nature Conservancy, Am. Rock Art Rsch. Assn., Aubudon Soc., Am. Birding Assn., Tex. Ornithol. Soc., Big Bend Natural History Assn., Alamo Pre-Columbian Soc., San Antonio Astron. Assn., Beta Beta Beta. Democrat. Avocations: astronomy, archaeology, birding. Home and Office: Apt 932 1835 Lickhill Slema Rd San Antonio TX 78213-1564 E-mail: josephorr@aol.com.

ORR, KENNETH BRADLEY, academic administrator; b. Charlotte, N.C., Mar. 15, 1933; s. Frank Wylie and Kate Harriett O.; m. Ruth Douglas Currie; children: Kevin, Jeffrey, Jonathan. BA, Duke U., 1954; MDiv, Union Theol. Sem., 1960, ThM, 1961; PhD, U. Mich., 1978; LittD, Carroll Coll., 1990; DD, Presbyn. Coll., 1997. Ordained to ministry, Presbyn. Ch., 1961. Minister West End Presbyn. Ch., Roanoke, Va., 1961-64; asst. to pres. Union Theol. Sem., Richmond, 1964-68, v.p., 1968-74; pres. Presbyn. Sch. Christian Edn., Richmond, 1974-79, Presbyn. Coll., Clinton, S.C., 1979-97, pres. emeritus, 1997—; sr. v.p. John McRoe & Assocs., Atlanta, 1997—. Past mem. coun. presidents Nat. Assn. Intercollegiate Athletics, Kansas City, Mo., chmn. S. Atlantic Conf., 1989—91; mem. nat. adv. com. on instnl. quality and integrity U.S. Dept. Edn., 1995—2001. Contbr. to religious and ednl. publs. Mem. Assn. Presbyn. Colls. and Univs. (pres. 1994, exec. com.), Coun. Ind. Colls. (bd. dirs. 1993-96), Laurens County C. of C. (past pres.), Kiwanis. Democrat. Avocations: reading, travel, tennis, classical music.

ORR, MARCIA, child development researcher, child care consultant; b. Anamosa, Iowa, Mar. 2, 1949; d. Harold Edward Eiben and Clara Elizabeth (Hubbard) E.; m. Robert J. Orr, Sept. 6, 1969; 1 child, Jennifer. Student, U. Iowa, 1977; BS, St. Xavier U., Chgo., 1981; MEd in Early Childhood Leadership, Nat. Louis U., 1996. Bookkeeper Monticello State Bank, 1967-69; exec. sec. Davenport Bank and Trust, 1969-73; asst. educator Elisabeth Ludeman Devel. Ctr., Park Forest, Ill., 1979; tchr. Flossmoor Hills (Ill.) Elem. Sch., 1980-1984; exec. dir. Co-Care, Inc., Park Forest, 1984-89; child devel. rschr., Flossmoor, Ill., 1989—; tchr. Nazarene Nursery Sch. and Kindergarten, Chicago Heights, 1991; child care ctr. cons. Matteson Sch. Dist. 162, Park Forest, 1991—; founder, exec. dir. Before and After Sch. Enrichment, 1991—; adv. mem. project early start Matteson Sch. Dist. 162, 1991—, home-sch. coord., 1992—. Grant writer Matteson Sch. Dist. 162 and Before and After Sch. Enrichment, Inc.; officer Boleo Childcare Ctr., Iowa City, 1975-77; mentor to dirs. child care programs early childhood edn. dept. Nat.-Louis U., Ill, 1994—; co-founder Reaching New Horizons, Inc., 1996—. Tchr. religion Infant Jesus of Prague Ch., Flossmoor, Ill., 1982—; mem. Flossmoor PTO, 1987-89; music chmn. Dist. 161 PTO, 1980-90; exec. dir. Before and After Sch. Enrichment, Inc.; parent resource coord. Matteson Sch. Dist. 162. McCormick fellow, 1995—; recipient Golden Achievement award Nat. Sch. Pub. Rels. Assn., 2001; named Best Practices and Rsch. honoree Louis U., Evanston, Ill., 2001. Mem. NAFE, Nat. Assn. for Edn. Young Children (validator), Women Employed Orgn., Internat. Platform Assn., Parent Inst., South Suburban Small Bus. Assn. (charter). Democrat. Roman Catholic. Avocations: piano, classical music, travel. Home: 9411 Fox Run Ct Frankfort IL 60423-1380 Office: Before and After Sch Enrichment 210 Illinois St Park Forest IL 60466-1100

ORR, RICHARD CLAYTON, financial modeler, futures trader; b. Oakland, CA, Mar. 28, 1941; s. James Clayton Orr, Helen Kittle Orr; m. Marilyn Ellard. PhD Mathematics, Syracuse University, Syracuse, New York, 1966—69, MA Mathematics, 1964—66; AB Mathematics, Humboldt State College, Arcata, California, 1962—64. Managing Director Calibar, LLC, West Hartford, CT, 2000—02; General Partner ROME Partners, Marblehead, MA, 1995—2002; President Chronos Corp., Lexington, 1990—95; Vice President for Research John Gutman Investments Corp., New Britain, CT, 1984—90; President Contratrend, Inc., Lexington, MA, 1981—84; Chairman, Department of Mathematics State University of New York, Oswego, NY, Assistant and Associate Professor, 1969—81. Referee Market Technicians Association, New York, NY, 1989—2002, Associate Editor, NY, 1985—89. Author: (9 articles over 13 years) Market Technicians Association, 1992, (article) Journal of Number Theory, 1971, Journal of the London Mathematical Society, 1969. Mem.: Market Technicians Association. Avocation: Meteorology, Sailing, Hiking. Office: Calibar, LLC 30 Gloucester Lane West Hartford CT 06107 Office Fax: 860-561-4910. Business E-Mail: orrbars@aol.com.

ORR, RITA HOPE, artist; b. Calif., Mo., Nov. 2, 1953; d. Rulo Ira and Helen Roberta (Helton) Mathews; m., Joseph Charles Orr, June 14, 1974. Grad. h.s., Tipton, Mo. Artist pvt. practice, Osage Beach, Mo., 1975—. Artist: exhbns. include Two Views, Dunnegan Mus., Bolivar, Mo., 1991, Two Views, Rozier Gallery, Jefferson City, Mo., 1992, Where We Live, Norfolk (Nebr.) Art Ctr., 1996, The Song Within Us, Ashby-Hodge Gallery, Fayette, Mo., 1997, M. Harwell Mus., Poplar Bluff, Mo., 1999. Home: 1405 Highway Kk Osage Beach MO 65065-9805 Office: Orr's Studio & Gallery State Rte KK Osage Beach MO 65065 Fax: 573-348-2232. E-mail: orrstudios@onemain.com.

ORR, ROBERT ANDREW, management consultant; b. Atlantic City, Sept. 1, 1952; s. Robert Andrew and Frances Rita Orr; m. Kathleen Theresa Kovach, June 1, 1975; children: Sarah Christine, Caolan Andrew and Samuel Patrick Kovach-Orr. BA in Psychology, Seton Hall U., 1974; MA in Psychology, Fairleigh Dickinson U., 1982. Cert. sr. profl. in human resources, Human Resources Cert. Inst. Asst. mgr., quality assurance Guyon Alloys, Inc., Harrison, N.J., 1975-82; edn. coord. J.F.K. Med. Ctr., Edison, N.Y., 1982-84; sr. human resource devel. cons. Port Authority N.Y. and N.J., N.Y.C., 1984-88; dir. human resources GRE Ins. Group, 1988-91; sr. human resources cons. Ins. Svcs. Office, Inc., 1991—; faculty Nat. Transit Inst. (Rutgers), New Brunswick, N.J., 1993—; ptnr. Combined Resources, Metuchen, 1993—. Mem. faculty Rutgers Ctr. for Mgmt. Devel., 1996—. Vestry mem. St. Luke's Episcopal Ch., Metuchen, 1983-84, chair self-study commn., 1999-2000. Mem. ASTD, ASME (affiliate mem.), Soc. for Human Resource Mgmt., U.S. Rowing. Avocations: rowing, woodworking, music. Home: 28 Homer Pl Metuchen NJ 08840-2007

ORR, ROBERT F. state supreme court justice; b. Norfolk, Va., Oct. 11, 1946; AB, U. N.C., 1971, JD, 1975. Bar: N.C. 1975. Pvt. practice, Asheville, NC, 1975—86; assoc. judge N.C. Ct. Appeals, 1986—94; assoc. justice N.C. Supreme Ct., Raleigh, 1994—. Mem. N.C. Beverage Control Commn., 1985—86; adj. prof. appellate advocacy N.C. Ctrl. U. Sch. Law, 1989—, adj. prof. N.C. State constl. law, 1998. Mem. Asheville-Revitalization Commn., 1977—81, Asheville-Buncombe Hist. Resources Commn., 1980—81; bd. trustees Hist. Preservation Found. N.C., 1982—85; mem. Nat. Park Sys. Adv. Bd., 1990—95, chmn., 1992—93; bd. visitors U. N.C.-Chapel Hill, 1996—; mem. NCBAs Appellate Rules Study com., 1999—, Gov.'s Crime Commn. With U.S. Army, 1968—71. Mem.: N.C. Bar Assn., 28th Jud. Dist., N.C. State Bar. Republican. Office: PO Box 1841 Raleigh NC 27602-1841 also: 302 Justice Bldg 2 E Morgan St Raleigh NC 27601-1428

ORR, SAN WATTERSON, JR. lawyer; b. Madison, Wis., Sept. 22, 1941; s. San Watterson and Eleanor Augusta (Schalk) O.; m. Joanne Marie Ruby, June 26, 1965; children: San Watterson III, Nancy Chapman. BBA, U. Wis., 1963, JD, 1966. Bar: Wis. 1966; CPA, Wis. Sec., tres., bd. dirs. Yawkey Lumber Co., Wausau, Wis., 1971—; pres. Forewood, Inc., 1979—, also bd. dirs.; dir. Marshall & Ilsley Bank, 1988—, vice chmn., 1997—; dir. Marshall & Ilsley Corp., 1994—; chmn. bd., chmn. exec. com. Wausau-Mosinee Paper Corp., 1997—. Dir. Wausau Ins. Cos., 1982-98, M&I Marshall & Ilsley Bank, Milw., , 1983-2001, MDU Resources Group, Inc., Bismarck, N.D., 1978-2000; chmn. Marathon Electric Mfg. Corp., Wausau, 1982-97, Mosinee (Wis.) Paper Corp., 1987-97; chmn. bd. Wausau Paper Mills Co., 1989-97. Editor: U. Wis. Law Rev., 1962-63. Bd. dirs. The Aytchmonde Woodson Found., Inc., Wausau, 1966—, The Leigh Yawkey Woodson Art Mus., Inc., Wausau, 1981—, Wis. Taxpayers Alliance, Madison, 1983—, Competitive Wis., Inc., Milw., 1989—, Wis. Mfrs. and Commerce, 2001—, U. Wis. Found., Madison, 1991—; dir. Wis. Policy Rsch. Inst., Milw., 1995—; mem. bd. regents U. Wis. Sys., Madison, 1993-2000, pres., 1998-2000; v.p., bd. dirs. Wausau YMCA Found., 1979—; dir. Wausau Health Found., Inc., 1981—, pres., 1998—. Mem. Wis. Bar Assn., Am. Law Inst., Wausau Club, Minocqua Country Club, Country Club of Fla., Ocean Club of Fla. Office: Yawkey Lumber Co 500 3rd St Ste 602 Wausau WI 54403-4857

ORR, SANDRA JANE, civic worker, pharmacist; b. Marion, Ohio, June 27, 1930; d. Lawrence Edward and Wanita Izell (Noyes) Schneider; m. Ross Moore Orr, Jr., Aug. 12, 1951; children: Sandra K. Orr Whiston, Sara L. Orr Cochrane. BS in Pharmacy, Med. Coll. Va., 1952. Pharmacist Atkison & Howard, Richmond, Va., 1952-54, Schneider's Walgreen Agy., Kenton, Ohio, 1954-73. Part-time pharmacist Drug Svc., Bethlehem, Pa., 1954-57, Fastchnacts' Drug, Bethlehem, 1954-57. One-woman shows in oils, pastels and watercolors. Chmn. ball St. Luke's Hosp., Bethlehem, 1985, 87; bd. dirs. Hist. Bethlehem, 1988—; dir. liturgical dance 1st Presbyn. Ch., 1968, 78; instr. needlework YMCA, 1980-81; instr. movement Orff tchrs.; instr. ballet Lehigh U. football team, 1966; docent Allentown Art Mus., 1956-68, Art Goes to Sch., 1960-62. Mem. Jr. League Lehigh Valley. Republican. Presbyterian. Avocations: flying, boating, motor home travel, golf, gourmet cooking. Home: 405 High St Bethlehem PA 18018-6103

ORR, STANLEY CHI-HUNG, financial executive; b. Shanghai, China, May 19, 1946; s. Chiu-Lai and Chiu-Chun (Ma) O.; children: Simon K., Edmund K., Norman K. Grad., Hong Kong Bapt. U., 1966; M in Econs., Chu Hoi Coll., Hong Kong, 1973; post grad., East Anglia U., Eng., 1975; MBA, Bradford U., Eng., 1977, West Coast U., L.A., 1980. CPA, Calif.; CMA, Eng.; notary pub. Chief acct. Cordial Knitting Factory Ltd., Hong Kong, 1966-69, mgr., 1969-71; chief acct. for Asia Mark Holding Co. Ltd., 1971-74; chief fin. officer Knits-Cord Ltd., Montebello, Calif., 1977—. Broker Dept. of Real Estate, 1992—. Treas., sec. World Univs. Svc., Hong Kong, 1965-66. Mem. AICPA, Chinese-Am. CPA Soc. (chmn., pres. 1991), Calif. Soc. CPAs. Republican. Office: Knits-Cord Ltd 1600 Date St Montebello CA 90640-6371

ORR, STEVEN DEREK, international development consultant; b. Joplin, Mo., Feb. 11, 1940; s. Charles Thomas and Janice Laura (MacKinnon) O.; m. Maureen Jane Dumm, May 25, 1968; children: Sean Christopher, Brendan Huan. BA, U. Ariz., 1972. Cert. Accounting (22 CFR 226); USAID Audit (A-133). Vol. Peace Corps, Panama, 1964-66; fgn. svc. officer Dept. State, Vietnam, 1966-68; mgr. Am. Express, N.Y.C., 1969-70; dir. edn. Planned Parenthood, Tucson, 1972-76; adminstr. Ariz. Med. Assn., Ft. Apache Indian Reservation, 1976-78; cons. Ariz. Dept. Pub. Health, 1975—78; regional dir. Family Planning Internat. Assistance, Bogotá, Colombia, 1978-84; cons. USAID/El Salvador, 1989—92; med. data analyst HMO, 1994—98; field programs del. ARC/Internat. Relief and Devel., 1999—2000; warehouse mgr. ARC-Disaster Svcs. of World Trade Ctr. 9-11-01 Disaster, 2001; fin. adminstrn. mgr. AirServ Internat., Dem. Republic of Congo , Uganda and Kigali, Rwanda, 2001—02. Internat. devel. cons. Mgmt. Scis. for Health, Inc., The Futures Group, Inc., MD Resources, Inc., Juarez & Assocs., Inc., Devel. Assocs., Inc., Acad. for Ednl. Devel., Inc., U.S. Ctrs. for Disease Control, USAID; observer/testifier with U.S. Ho. of Reps. on World Trade Ctr. Disaster, 2001. Pres. Ariz. Pub. Health Assn., Phoenix, 1978, Miami-Killian H.S. Band Patrons Assn., 1988-89. With USAF, 1957-60. Mem. Nat. Coun. Internat. Health, Med. Group Mgmt. Assn., Fla. Spkrs. Assn., Am. Mgmt. Assn., Nat. Coun. Returned Peace Corps Vols., Returned Peace Corps Vols. South Fla. (co-founder, treas. 1987-88, dir. 1995—, v.p. 1996-98, pres. 1998-99), Toastmasters.

ORRILL, ROBERT THOMAS, foundation executive, former history educator; b. Madison, Ind., Jan. 20, 1939; s. Edward Morris and Katherine (Erny) O.; m. Linda Berg, June 22, 1963 (div. Jan. 1994); children: Andrea, Jeannie; m. Dorothy Schneirla Downie, Sept. 8, 1999. BS in English, Purdue U., 1961; BA, MA in Modern History, Oxford (Eng.) U., 1864; MA in Am. Social-Intellectual History, U. Wis., 1968. Tchg. fellow dept. history U. Wis., Madison, 1967-68; prof. dept. Am. studies Skidmore Coll., Saratoga Springs, N.Y., 1969-75; coord. for humanities, sr. acad. assoc. SUNY Empire State Coll., 1976-78, asst. v.p. for acad. devel., 1978-82, chmn. grad. coun., chief adminstr. grad. program, 1982-85; exec. dir. Office ACad. Affairs, Coll. Bd., N.Y.C., 1985-99; prof. edn. reform Princeton U. Woodrow Wilson Sch. Pub. and Internat Affairs, NJ, 2001—02; exec. dir. Nat. Coun. on Edn. and the Disciplines, Princeton, 1999—; sr. advisor Found. Woodrow Wilson Nat. Fellowship Found., 1999—. Advisor Alliance for Curriculum Reform, Am. Assn. Colls. and Univs., Am. Coun. on Tchg. Fgn. Langs., Am. Coun. Learned Socs., Assn. New Am. Colls., CUNY, Coun. on Basic Edn., U.S. Mil. Acad., to SUNY Faculty Task Force on Core Curriculum; co-chmn. policy task force Arts Edn. Partnership; organizer, facilitator summer insts. Coalition Essential Schs.; mem. adv. bd. Coun. Chief State Sch. Officers, EXTEND, Learning Productivity Network, NEH, Nat. Fgn. Lang. Ctr.; dir. funded project Nat.

Assessment Governing Bd.; external reviwer Fund for Improvement Postsecondary Edn.; cons. to English chairs dept. Nat. Coun. Tchrs. English; evaluator Nat. Coun. Tchrs. Math., New Press, NSF. Exec. editor: Reading Reconsidered, 1988, Languages of Thought, 1989, Thinking Historically, 1990, Thinking Through Mathematics, 1990, Taking Full Measure, 1991, The Future of Educaton, 1994, The Condition of American Liberal Education, 1995, Inquiry and Learning, 1996, Literacy Redefined, 1996, Quantitatite Literacy, 1996, Education and Democracy, 1997, Why Numbers Count, 1997, Mathematics and Democracy, 2001. Rhodes scholar, 1963-64; fellow U. Wis., Yale U.; granted Fund for Improvement Postsecondary Edn., MacArthur Found., Mellon Found., Getty Ctr. for Edn. in Arts, Pew Charitable Trusts, 1999, 2000, Carnegie Corp. N.Y., 2000. Writer Neighbors for Bucks County Preservation, Inc., Solebury, Pa. Avocation: writing. Home: PO Box 442 2733 Creamery Rd Solebury PA 18963 Office: 5 Vaughn Dr Princeton NJ 08540-6313

ORRINGER, MARK BURTON, surgeon, educator; b. Pitts., Apr. 19, 1943; s. Harry B. and Alta (Moses) O.; m. Susan Michaels, June 20, 1964; children: Jeffrey Scott, Lisa Jill. BA, U. Pitts., 1963, MD, 1967. Diplomate Am. Bd. Surgery, Am. Bd. Thoracic Surgery. Resident Johns Hopkins Hosp., Balt., 1967-73; from asst. prof. to prof. surgery U. Mich. Med. Sch., Ann Arbor, 1973-80, prof. surgery, 1980—, John Alexander disting. prof. thoracic surgery, 1996. Head sect. thoracic surgery U. Mich. Med. Sch., Ann Arbor, 1985-98, head sect. gen. thoracic surgery, 1998—; dir. Am. Bd. Thoracic Surgery, 1988-95. Co-editor: (with Waldhausen) Complications in Cardiothoracic Surgery, Mosby Year Book, 1991, (with Zuidema) Shackelford's Surgery of the Alimentary Tract, vol. 1 - The Esophagus, 3d edit., 1991, 5th edit. 2002; contbr. over 175 articles to profl. jours., over 100 chpts. to books. Capt. USAR, 1974-76. Named among the Best Med. Specialists in the U.S., Town and Country mag., 1984, 89, among the 400 Best Drs. in Am., Good Housekeeping mag., 1991, One of Best Drs. in Am., 1993-94, 96-97, 99, The 318 Top Cancer Specialists, Good Housekeeping mag., 1999; recipient Bicentennial Medal of Distinction, U. Pitts., 1987. Fellow ACP; mem. Thoracic Surgery Dirs. Assn. (sec., treas. 1991-95, pres. elect 1995-97, pres. 1997-99), Soc. Thoracic Surgeons (pres. elect 2000, pres. 2001), Am. Coll. Chest Physicians, Am. Assn. Thoracic Surgery, Soc. Univ. Surgeons, Internat. Soc. Surgery, Am. Surg. Assn., Internat. Soc. Diseases Esophagus, Halsted Soc., Phi Beta Kappa, Alpha Omega Alpha. Avocations: swimming, scuba diving, hiking. Office: U Mich Med Ctr 1500 E Med Ctr Dr Ann Arbor MI 48109 E-mail: morrin@umich.edu.

ORRIS-MODUGNO, MICHELE MARIE, public relations, marketing and advertising consultant; b. Norwalk, Conn., Feb. 23, 1958; d. Stephen Joseph and Arcenia (Rodriguez) O. Student, U. N.Mex., 1976-78; BA with honors, U. Bridgeport, 1980, postgrad., 1981-83. Tchr. Norwalk Pub. Schs., 1981-83; head tchr. presch. Norwalk YMCA, 1983-84; exec. dir. Norwalk Seaport Assn., 1984-86; cons., 1986-87, Barnum Festival, Bridgeport, Conn., 1987-88, P.T. Barnum Found., Bridgeport, 1987; mgr. communications Human Resources Inc., Stamford, Conn., 1987; owner, mgr. Michele Orris, Norwalk, 1988—. Dir. pub. rels. YWCA of Stamford (Conn.), 1989-90. Past sec., pres. Marvin Beach Assn., East Norwalk; asst. dir. pub. rels. Conn. Women's Celebration, 1986; chmn. subcom. auditorium com. New City Hall, Norwalk; active numerous other civic orgns.; bd. dirs. Southwestern Conn. coun. Girl Scouts U.S., 1987-88, Cmtys. In Schs. of Norwalk, Inc., 2000-01; gdn. dirs. Levitt Pavilion Performing Arts, Westport, Conn., 1991-93; mgr. Orch. New Eng., 1993-95; mem. Unquowa parents Assn., 2000—. Recipient award City of Norwalk, 1987. Mem. Greens Farms Acad. Alumni Assn. (pres., class sec.), Phi Sigma Iota (life). Democrat. Roman Catholic. Avocations: reading, tennis, bicycling, golf, art museums. Home and Office: 455 Primrose Ln Fairfield CT 06432-2343 E-mail: ENTMOM@aol.com.

ORRJE, OLLE, civil engineer, jazz musician, poet; b. Kristianstad, Skåne, Sweden, Apr. 7, 1937; s. Alfred and Svea (Holmberg) O.; m. Stina Jacobsson, Dec. 1, 1962; children: Henrik, Carl Fredrik, Peter, Jacob. Degree in Civil Engring., Royal Inst. Tech., Stockholm, 1965, D in Tech., 1968. Research engr. Swedish Geotech. Inst., Stockholm, 1965-69; research asst. Royal Inst. Tech., 1965-69; head dept. geotech. engring. Alfred Orrje AB, 1969-96, dir., 1977-96. Recipient Swedish Louis Armstrong award, 1981, Albert Bonniers poetry award, 1993, Swedish Acad. poetry award, 1999. Mem. Swedish Geotech. Soc., Soc. Swedish Engring. Geology, Swedish Union of Writers. Home: Brötvägen 39 S-16766 Bromma Sweden E-mail: olle.orrje@swipnet.se.

ORRMONT, ARTHUR, writer, editor; b. Albany, N.Y., July 3, 1922; m. Lora Orenstein, Oct. 6, 1956 (div. 1965); m. Leonie Rosenstiel, Aug. 22, 1995. Student, U. Ala., 1941, U. Mich., 1942-45, Cornell U., 1945; BA, U. Mich., 1945. Editl. dept. head Farrar, Straus & Co., N.Y.C., 1945-51; sr. editor Popular Libr., 1951-55; exec. editor Fawcett Books, 1955-57; pres., editl. dir. Author Aid Assocs., 1967-97; v.p. Rsch. Assocs. Internat., 1980-97; pres. Literary Cons., Albuquerque, 1997—. Lectr. creative writing CCNY, 1966, Columbia U., 1967; judge Hopwood Awards, U. Mich., 1999. Author: Love Cults and Faith-Healers, 1961, (with Capt. Marion Aten RAF) Last Train Over Rostov Bridge, 1962, Brit. edit., 1962, Indestructible Commodore Matthew Perry, 1962, Japanese edit., 1963, Amazing Alexander Hamilton, 1964, Portuguese edit., 1965, Master Detective: Allan Pinkerton, 1965 (Jr. Literary Guild selection), Chinese Gordon: Hero of Khartoum, 1966, Fighter Against Slavery: Jehudi Ashmun, 1966, Mr. Lincoln's Master Spy: Lafayette Baker, 1966, Diplomat in Warpaint: Chief Alexander McGillivray of the Creeks, 1967, Richard Burton, 1969, Brit. edit., 1969, James Buchanan Eads: The Man Who Mastered the Mississippi, 1970, (with Fr. Joseph Lauro) Action Priest, 1970, French edit., 1970, Requiem for War: The Life of Wilfred Owen, 1972; editor: (with Leonie Rosenstiel) Literary Agents of North America, 1984, 5th edit., 1995; editor Nat. Hall of Fame Biography series, 1970-72. With U.S. Army, 1942. Recipient Avery Hopwood award for short story U. Mich., 1943, 44, 45. Mem. Assn. Lit. Critics Scholars. E-mail: rosensti@concentric.net.

ORSAK, CHARLES GEORGE, college district official; b. Wichita Falls, Tex., May 18, 1945; s. Charlie George Sr. and Virginia Lorene (King) O.; m. Lana Beth Lawson; children: Clessa Ann, Erik Lawson, Charles Aaron. BA in English, Speech, Midwestern State U., 1968, MA in English, 1970; MEd in Adult and Continuing Edn., East Tex. State U., 1984; PhD in Secondary and Higher Edn., Tex. A&M U., 1987. Instr. U. Md., Heidelberg, Germany, 1972-73; curriculum devel. specialist project transition U.S. Army Europe Gen. Edn. Div., Worms, Germany, 1972-74; dir. community coll. programs Cen. Tex. Coll., Wiesbaden, Germany, 1974-76, dir. Far East programs Seoul, Republic of Korea, 1976; instr., dir. institutional devel. and effectiveness Navarro Coll., Corsicana, Tex., 1976-84, dean off-campus ctrs. Ellis County, 1985-86; fgn. expert Hefei (China) U. Tech., 1986-87; acting dir. learning resource ctr. Navarro Coll., Corsicana, 1987-90; exec. dir. Superconducting Super Collider Tng. Project Navarro Coll./Dallas County C.C. Dist., Waxahachie, Tex., 1990-92, ESL instr., 1992-93; dir. instnl. rsch., dir. R & D, Houston C.C. Sys., 1997-99; v.p. for rsch. and instnl. effectiveness San Jacinto Coll. Dist., Pasadena, Tex., 1999—. Dir. Dept. of Energy Nat. Solar Manpower Needs Assessment and Task Analysis, Corsicana, 1976-77; curriculum devel. specialist Tex. Edn. Agy. Energy Conservation Curriculum Project, Corsicana, 1977-78; prin. investigator NSF Solar Tech. Curriculum Project, Corsicana, 1978-82; cons. alcohol fuels curriculum Navarro Coll., Corsicana, 1982; cons. Title III Carl Perkins NSF, 1983-91; cons. grantsmanship, Cairo, Egypt, 1988; cons. Roboz-Katona Assoc., Budapest, Hungary, 1991; cons. in field. Contbr. articles to profl. jours. Mem. Navarro County Hist. Soc., Corsicana, 1980-91; mem. Navarro County Drug and Alcohol Abuse Com., Corsicana, 1987-91. 1st lt. U.S. Army, 1970-72. Mem. ASCD, Nat. Coun. Resource Devel., Am. Assn. Community Jr. Colls., Tex. Jr. Coll. Tchrs. Assn., C.C. Coll. Adminstrs. Assn. (pres.), Phi Delta Kappa (founding pres. Bluebonnet chpt. 1988-90). Avocations: travel, historical preservation and restoration, grants research. Home: 212 N 30th St Corsicana TX 75110-4219 E-mail: corsak@sjcd.cc.tx.us.

ORSAK, JOSEPH CYRIL, retired civil engineer; b. Port Arthur, Tex., Aug. 28, 1928; s. Adolph and Marie Veronica (Repka) O.; m. Patricia Ann Viau, May 30, 1951; children: Joseph Cyril Jr., David, Darlene, Karen, James, Patricia Elaine. BSCE, Syracuse U., 1957. Project engr. Firestone Tire & Rubber Co., Akron, Ohio, 1957-69; project mgr. Firestone Brema, Bari, Italy, 1969-76, Firestone Australia Pty., Sydney, 1976-78, Firestone Can. Ltd., Hamilton, Ont., 1978-80, Firestone Fire & Rubber Co., Memphis, 1980-81; prin. Orsak Project & Constrn. Mgmt., Bartlett, 1981-83; constrn. adminstr. Askew Nixon Ferguson Wolfe Architects, Memphis, 1983-90; project mgr. Memphis-Shelby County Airport Authority, 1990—2001. Sgt. U.S. Army, 1950-51, Japan. Mem. ASCE (life), Assn. Profl. Engrs. Ont. Roman Catholic. Home: 5932 Spruce Hollow Cv Bartlett TN 38134-5541

ORSATTI, ALFRED KENDALL, organization executive; b. Los Angeles, Jan. 31, 1932; s. Alfredo and Margaret (Hayes) O.; m. Patricia Decker, Sept. 11, 1960; children: Scott, Christopher, Sean. BS, U. So. Calif., 1956. Assoc. prodr., v.p. Sabre Prodns., L.A., 1957-58; assoc. prodr. Ror Vic Prodns., 1958-59; bus. rep. AFTRA, 1960-61; Hollywood exec., sec. SAG, 1961-81, nat. exec. dir., 1981—, trustee Pension Welfare Plan, 1971—. Del. Los Angeles County Fedn. Labor, Los Angeles, Hollywood Film Council, Los Angeles; v.p., mem. exec. Calif. Fedn. Labor; pres. Calif. Theatrical Fedn.; chmn. arts, entertainment and media com. dept. profl. employees AFL-CIO Mem. Mayor's Film Devel. Com., Los Angeles. Mem. Actors and Artists Am. Assn. (1st v.p.) Office: SAG 5757 Wilshire Blvd Los Angeles CA 90036-3635

ORSATTI, ERNEST BENJAMIN, lawyer; b. Pitts., Nov. 14, 1949; s. Ernest Ubaldo and Dorothy Minerva (Pfeiffer) O.; m. Ingrid Zalman, May 3, 1975; 1 child, Benjamin E. BA, Marquette U., 1971; JD, Duquesne U., 1974; postgrad., Army Command and Gen. Staff Coll., 1984. Bar: Pa. 1974, U.S. Dist. Ct. (we. dist.) Pa. 1974, U.S. Ct. Appeals (3d cir.) 1977, U.S. Supreme Ct. 1978, U.S. Ct. Appeals (6th cir.) 1992. Assoc. Jubelirer, Pass & Intrieri, Pitts., 1974-81, ptnr., 1981—. Contbg. editor: The Developing Labor Law, 4th edit., 1992—. Bd. dirs. Am. Italian Cultural Inst., Pitts. Served to capt. U.S. Army, 1975, lt. col., USAR, ret. Mem. ABA, ACLU (legal com. 1996—), Am. Arbitration Assn., Pa. Bar Assn., Allegheny County Bar Assn. (profl. ethics com. 2000—), Am. Legion. Democrat. Roman Catholic. Home: 9343 N Florence Rd Pittsburgh PA 15237-4815 Office: Jubelirer Pass & Intrieri 219 Fort Pitt Blvd Pittsburgh PA 15222-1576 E-mail: ebo@jpilaw.com., eborsatti@aol.com.

ORSBON, BENJAMIN THOMAS, transportation planner; b. North Wilkesboro, N.C., Nov. 28, 1951; s. Richard Chapman and Ruby (Wyatt) O. BA, U. N.C., 1973, MRP, 1975. Regional planner Region D Coun. Govt., Pierre, S.D., 1976-77; policy aide State Planning Bur., 1977-79, dep. commr., 1979-84; transp. planner S.D. Dept Transp., 1985-99, mgr. Office of Planning and Programs, 1998—. Bd. dirs. Western Planning Resources, Helena, Mont., pres., 1989, chair WASHTO standing com. on planning, 1998—. Contbr. articles to profl. jours. Backpacking instr. Boy Scouts Am. Mem. Am. Planning Assn. (pres. western ctrl. chpt. 1996), Am. Inst. Cert. Planners, Kiwanis. Lutheran. Avocations: knife-making, skiing, backpacking, basketball, shooting.

ORSILLO, JAMES EDWARD, computer systems engineer, company executive; b. Elmira, N.Y., Oct. 30, 1939; s. Giacomo and Irene (Heppy) O.; 1 child, June Lynne. BEE, RCA Insts., 1962; BS in Elec. Engring. and Math., Ind. Inst. Tech., 1964; MS, Rensselear Poly., 1968; BS in Nuclear Engring., Capital Radio Electronic Inst., 1974. Communications engr. Bell Telephone Labs., Holmdel, N.J., 1962-63; video engr. Westinghouse, Elmira, N.Y., 1965-66; computer engr. GE, Pittsfield, Mass., 1966-67; systems specialist Control Data Corp., Mpls., 1968-70; software specialist Computer Sci. Corp., Morristown, N.Y., 1970-72; prin. cons. Computer Cons. Assocs., Elmira, 1972-78; CEO ORTHSTAR, Inc., 1974—; acquired Hughes Tng., Inc. Rail Simulation Bus., 1996—. Owner, pres. Shadowstand Properties, Inc. (FKA O-K Properties), Elmira, 1984—, Thundering Hooves Stables, Elmira, 1985—. Mem. IEEE, Am. Nuclear Soc., Soc. Indsl. and Applied Math., Am. Helicopter Soc., Army Aviation Assn. Am., Internat. Flying Engrs., USAF Assn., U.S. Naval League, U.S. Polo Assn. Republican. Achievements include invention of Integrated Data Acquisition System (IDAS), of Thread Algebra used in simulation development, of Extended Sentient Non-linear Ensemble (ESNE). Office: ORTHSTAR Inc Airport Corp Park PO Box 459 Big Flats NY 14814-0459 E-mail: orsillo@orthstar.com.

ORSINI, ERIC ANDREW, army official; b. Lodi, N.J., Jan. 7, 1918; s. Serafino and Valentina Lena (Dinino) O.; m. Mildred Jean Andre, Feb. 8, 1947; children: Donna Jean, Debra Jane. BS, GED, Fort Knox, Ky., 1948; student, Def. Sys. Mgmt. Coll., Ft. Belvoir, Va., 1978, Harvard U., 1982, George Washington U., 1986. Registered mech. engr. Commd. capt. armor U.S. Army, 1943, advanced through grades to col., 1965, transfer to Ordinance Corps., 1958, ret., 1971, appt. dep. asst. sec. for logistics, 1975—. Developer policy guidance mil. identification symbology technologies LOGMARS, 1982; policy developer mil. ordnance/maintenance policies and procedures. Decorated Purple Heart, Silver Star, Bronze Star, Legion of Merit; named to Ordnance Hall of Fame, 1991; recipient Presdl. Meritorious Exec. award, 1991, 94, Logistics Emeritus award Nat. Security Indsl. Assn., 1999. Avocations: golf, fishing. Home: 11204 Gray Fox Pt Spotsylvania VA 22553-4660

ORSINI, PAUL VINCENT, music educator; b. Albany, N.Y., Oct. 4, 1955; s. Paul Vincent and Lucia (Rutolo) O. MusB in Music Edn., SUNY, Potsdam, 1977; MusM in Performance, Syracuse U., 1979. Cert. K-12 music tchr., N.Y. Musician Mirage, 1978-79; entertainer The Carmen Canavo Show, Tampa, Fla., 1979-83; freelance entertainer Albany, 1983-86; substitute tchr. Suburban Coun. Schs., 1983-86; tchr. Corinth (N.Y.) Sch. Dist., 1986-87, Shenendehowa Sch. Dist., Clifton Park, N.Y., 1987—. Owner, leader High Society Big Band, Clifton Park, 1988-91. Premiered trumpet compositions of Dr. Brian Israel Syracuse Univ., 1977-79. Advisor Shenendehowa Crisis Intervention Team, Clifton Park, 1988-93; faculty rep., exec. bd. Friends of Music of Shenendehowa, Clifton Park, 1993; active Shenendehowa Partnership Team, 1995-97; lead trumpet Greg Nazarian Big Band, 1998—; prin. trumpet Meml. Concert Band of Colonie, 2000—; rep. Unified Arts, Shenendehowa, 1999; prin. trumpet South Colonie Meml. Wind Ensemble, 2000—. Mem. Albany Musicians Assn., Internat. Trumpet Guild, N.Y. State Congress of Parents and Tchrs. (hon. life mem.). Avocations: fishing, sports, travel, reading, jazz. Home: 54 Via Da Vinci Clifton Park NY 12065-2906

ORSKI, C. KENNETH, consulting company executive, lawyer, publisher; b. Warsaw, Poland, Mar. 7, 1932; came to U.S., 1946, naturalized, 1953; s. Thaddeus and Irene Orski; m. Jocelyne Schule, Aug. 27, 1968; children: Karine N., Monica J.; m. Barbara K. Klema, Apr. 28, 1978; 1 child, Christopher P. AB, Harvard U., 1953, LLB, JD, 1956. Atty. AEC, 1956-61; asst. to pres. Gen. Dynamics Corp., Washington, 1961-66; dir. OECD Paris; fgn. svc. officer U.S. Dept. State, 1966-73; assoc. adminstr. U.S. Dept. Transp., Washington, 1974-78; pres. Urban Mobility Corp., 1982—. Contbg. author books in field, 1982, 85; editor, pub. Innovation Briefs, 1991—; Washington corr. Traffic Tech. Internat.; contbr. articles to profl. jours. Recipient Outstanding Pub. Svc. award U.S. Dept. Transp., 1985, Disting. Svc. award, 1977, Meritorious Svc. award, 1975. Republican. Home: 10200 Riverwood Dr Potomac MD 20854-1536 E-mail: korski@erols.com.

ORSOMARSO, DON FRANK, school system administrator; b. Queens, N.Y., Oct. 23, 1925; s. Frank and Angela (Aliano) O.; m. Marguerite Angela Rocco, July 2, 1955; children: Donald Frank, Gail Marie. BA, NYU, 1949, MA, 1953, 55, MBA, 1959; EdD, Nova U., 1975. Tchr. Shaw Ave Sch. Dist. 30, Valley Stream, N.Y., 1955-61; asst. supt. Maple Shade (N.J.) Pub. Schs., 1961-64, Valley Cen. Schs., Montgomery, N.Y., 1964-65, Union Free Sch. Dist. 17, Franklin Sq., 1965-70, Newington (Conn.) Sch. System, 1970-78, East Islip Schs., Islip Terr., N.Y., 1978-92; ret., 1992. Mem. Am. Assn. Sch. Bus. Officials, Conn. Assn. for Advancement Sch. Adminstrs. (v.p. 1976-77, pres. 1977-78), Am. Assn. Sch. Adminstrs., East Islip C. of C., Lions, Phi Delta Kappa. Lodges: Lions. Avocation: golf. Home: 32 Adelhaide Ln East Islip NY 11730-2202

ORSON, BARBARA TUSCHNER, actress; b. N.Y.C., May 19, 1929; d. Jonah Tuschner and Rebecca Traceman; m. Jay M. Orson, June 24, 1956; children: Beth-Diane, Theodore. Student, Dramatic Workshop, N.Y.C., 1948-50. Singer Am. Savoyards, N.Y.C., 1950-51, 53-55; actress Trinity Repertory, Providence, 1964—. Founding mem. Trinity Sq. Repertory Co., Providence, 1964—. Actress Edinburgh Festival, Scotland, 1968, Am. Repertory Theatre, Cambridge, Mass., 1981-85, Williamstown (Mass.) Theatre, 1985-89, Dallas Theatre Ctr., 1985, Yale Repertory Co., New Haven, Conn., 1991; appeared in: (film) Mission Hill (Adrian Hall award 2002), Code of Ethics, My One and Only, Swimming Upstream, (TV) Theatre in America, Feasting with Panthers, Life Among the Lowly, House of Mirth, Camera Three, RI Demon Murder, Miller's Court, (Am. premiere) The Suicide, 1980, (world premiere) Grown Ups, 1981, God's Heart, 1995; founding mem., appeared in over 100 prodns. Trinity Sq. Repertory Co., Providence, 1964—; (radio) House of Mirth, Masterpiece Radio Theatre with Jane Alexander; guest artist (Lady Macbeth), Brown U. Recipient Adrian Hall award, 2002. Mem. Am. Fedn. Radio and TV Artists, Screen Actors Guild, Actor's Equity Assn., Trinity Rep. Co. (founder). Home: 281 Hillside Ave Pawtucket RI 02860-6119

ORSZAG, JONATHAN MARC, economic consultant; b. Boston, Apr. 15, 1973; s. Steven Alan and Reba Karp O.; m. Rica Rodman, June 17, 2000. AB, Princeton (N.J.) U., 1995; MS, Oxford (Eng.) U., 1997. Econ. policy advisor The White House Nat. Econ. Coun., Washington, 1996-99; dir. policy and stratetic planning U.S. Dept. Commerce, 1999-2000; mng. dir. Sebago Associates, Marina del Rey, Calif., 2000—. Mem. Calif. Workforce Investment Bd., Sacramento, 2000—; mem. Calif. Tech. Adv. Group, Sacramento, 2000—; adj. lectr. U. So. Calif., 2002—. Recipient Leadership award, Corp. Enterprise Devel., 1999; scholar Marshall scholarship, 1996. Mem. Pacific Coun. on Internat. Policy, L.A. World Affairs Coun., Asis Soc., Am. Econ. Assn., Am. Polit. Sci. Assn. Avocation: golf. Home: 1 Northstar St Apt 301 Marina Del Rey CA 90292 Office: Sebago Assocs Inc 13428 Maxella Ave #451 Marina Del Rey CA 90292 E-mail: jorszag@sbgo.com., jorszag@yahoo.com.

ORSZAG, PETER RICHARD, economist; b. Boston, Dec. 16, 1968; s. Steven Alan and Reba (Karp) O.; m. Cameron Rachel Hamill; children: Leila Madeleine, Joshua Nathaniel. AB summa cum laude, Princeton U., 1991; MS, London Sch. Econs., 1992, PhD, 1997. Econ. advisor Ministry of Fin., Moscow, 1992-93; staff economist Coun. Econ. Advisers, Washington, 1993-94; prof. rsch. staff London Sch. Econs., 1994-95; sr. economist Coun. Econ. Advisers, Washington, 1995-96, sr. adviser, 1996; sr. econ. advisor Nat. Econ. Coun., 1997, spl. asst. to pres for econ. policy, 1998; pres. Sebago Assocs., 1998—. Lectr. in econs. U. Calif., Berkeley, 1999—2000; rsch. assoc. Ctr. Retirement Rsch., Boston Coll., 2000—; Joseph A. Pechman sr. fellow in tax and fiscal policy The Brookings Instn., 2001—. Marshall scholar, 1991-92. Mem. Nat. Acad. Social Ins., Phi Beta Kappa. Office: The Brookings Instn 1775 Massachusetts Ave NW Washington DC 20036-2188 E-mail: porszag@brookings.edu.

ORT, PAUL JOSEPH, orthopedic surgeon, educator; b. Prague, Czechoslovakia, Apr. 15, 1936; s. Miloslav Ort; m. Vicky Harnik, Oct. 23, 1982. MD, Charles U., 1961. Diplomate Am. Bd. Orthop. Surgery. Intern Bronx-Lebanon Hosp., N.Y.C., 1964-65; resident in gen. surgery Bellevue Hosp.-Cornell U., 1965-67; resident in orthop. surgery Bellevue Hosp.-NYU, 1967-70; attending physician Cabrini Med. Ctr., N.Y.C., 1971-88; from instr. to assoc. prof. clin. orthop. surgery NYU Med. Ctr., 1975-96, prof. clin. orthop. surgery, 1996—. Fellow ACS, Am. Acad. Orthopaedic Surgery; mem. AMA, NYU Alumni Assn. (pres. 1989-91)m Bellevue Soc. (pres. 1994). Office: 530 1st Ave New York NY 10016-6402 E-mail: orthopjo@aol.com.

ORTBALS, GERALD RAY, lawyer; b. St. Louis, Jan. 20, 1941; s. Ray W. and Ruth M. (Krost) O.; m. Mary L. Colligan, Aug. 13, 1966; children: Stephanie, Andrea, Joanna. BS, St. Louis U., 1963, JD, 1966; postgrad. in pub. comm., Boston U., 1968-69. Atty. Fordyce & Mayne Law Firm, St. Louis, 1971-74; ptnr. Ziercher & Hocker Law Firm, 1975-82, Greensfelder, Hemker & Gale, P.C. Law Firm, St. Louis, civ, 1982—. Chair ctr. justice campaigen Legal Svcs. Eastern Mo., St. Louis, 1995—. Contbr. articles to newspapers. Pres. St. Patrick Ctr. Cath. Charities, St. Louis, 1996—, White House Retreat, Inc., St. Louis, 1986-87; bd. dirs. Mid-Am. Transplant Assn., Mo. and Ill., 1991—, exec. com.; dem. candidate U.S. Senate, Mo., 1994; chief staff Office Gov., Mo., 1977-78; pres. Young Dem., 1962. Capt. USAF, 1966-72. Recipient Pro Bono Publico award Mo. Bar, 1989, Alumni Leadership award St. Louis Univ. Law Sch., 1990, Vol. award United Way, 1991, Found. award St. Louis Bar Found., 1995. Mem. Mo. Lawyers Trust Found. (bd. dirs. 1992-97), Bar Assn. Met. St. Louis (pres. 1990-91), Lawyers Assn. St. Louis (pres. 1986-87). Roman Catholic. Avocations: fitness, golf, reading, jazz. Address: 100 S 4th St Ste 700 Saint Louis MO 63102-1823

ORTEGA, ALEXANDER N. medical educator, researcher; b. Clovis, N.Mex. s. Alexander C. and Marie Annette Ortega. MPH, Boston U., 1994; PhD, U. Mich., 1998. Sr. rsch. assoc. U. Pa., Phila., 1995—98; asst. prof. Yale U. Sch. Medicine, New Haven, 1998—. Mem.: APHA, Acad. of Health Svcs. Rsch. and Health Policy, Internat. Soc. for Advancement of Respiratory Psychopathology, Am. Coll. Epidemiology. Office: Yale U Sch Mediicine PO Box 208034 60 College St New Haven CT 06520 Personal E-mail: alexander.ortega@yale.edu. Business E-mail: alexander.ortega@yale.edu.

ORTENZI, REGINA (GINA RAE ORTENZI), home fashion products designer, educator; b. Cin., Oct. 23, 1949; d. Anthony Henry and Esther (Ciener) O.; m. Robert George Button, May 28, 1978. Student fashion design, U. Cin., 1967-69; B Design, U. Fla., 1972; MFA, U. Ga., 1975. Design dir. Tempo Advt. Agy., Winter Park, Fla., 1972-73, Gloria Vanderbilt, Gloria Concepts, Inc., N.Y.C., 1975-82; pres., co-owner Ortenzi/Button Designs, Jersey City, 1983-94; dir. design Beacon Looms, Inc., Teaneck, N.J., 1990-96; co-owner Ortenzi/Button Designs, Jersey City, 1996—99; ptnr. RPC Imports, Bellevue, Wash., 1998-2000. Instr. U. Ga., Athens, 1974-75, Rollins Coll., Winter Park, 1975, Parsons Sch. Design, N.Y.C., 1982-93; vis. instr. Pratt-Phoenix Sch. Art and Design, N.Y.C., 1980-83. Recipient 1st place award S.E. div. Ford Motor Co. Pinto Competition, 1972, 2d place award Cen. Fla. ADDY Competition, 1973. Mem. Graphic Artists Guild (nat. prse. 1985-87), Internat. Furnishings and Design Assn., Fashion Group, Surface Design Assn., Color Mktg. Group (chairholder 2000—). Jewish. Avocations: reading, travel, swimming. Office: Ortenzi/Button Designs 3348 Kennedy Blvd Jersey City NJ 07307-4233 E-mail: ginarae111@aol.com.

ORTH, PAUL WILLIAM, retired lawyer; b. Balt., May 7, 1930; s. Paul W. and Naomi (Howard Bevard) O.; m. Isle Haertle, June 15, 1956; children: Ingrid, Ilse Christine. AB, Dartmouth Coll., 1951; JD, Harvard U., 1954. Bar: Mass. 1954, Conn. 1957, U.S. Dist. Ct. Conn. 1958, U.S. Ct. Appeals (2d cir.) 1960, U.S. Ct. Appeals (1st cir.) 1983, U.S. Supreme Ct. 1960. Assoc. Hoppin, Carey & Powell, Hartford, Conn., 1957-62, ptnr., 1962-86, Shipman & Goodwin, Hartford, 1987-2000, MacDermid, Reynods & Glissman P.C., Hartford, 2000—. Instr. Sch. Law U. Conn., 1959-81. Editor: Every Employee's Guide to the Law, 1993, 96. Chmn. Farmington Conservation Commn., 1982-83; mem. town com. Town of Farmington, 1973-81; dir. Conn. Opera Assn., 2000—. With AUS, 1954-56. Fellow Am. Bar Found., Conn. Bar Found.; mem. ABA, Hartford County Bar Assn. (pres. 1983-84), Conn. Bar Assn. (chmn. coms.). Democrat. Office: MacDermid Reynold & Glissman PC 86 Farmington Ave Hartford CT 06105 E-mail: porth@mrglaw.com.

ORTHMANN, ROSEMARY ANN, editor; b. Ridgewood, N.J., Oct. 10, 1952; BA, Washington Coll., 1974; MA, U. Minn., 1977; PhD, Ind. U., 1987. Editl. asst. Am. Historical Review, Bloomington, Ind., 1977-80; asst. book editor 21st Century Books, Frederick, Md., 1987-88; mng. editor U. Publ. of Am., 1987-88, editor, 1988-2000; mng. editor LexisNexis Acad. and Libr. Solutions, Bethesda, 2000—. Author: Out of Necessity, 1991; contbr. articles to profl. jours. Mem. steering com. Commn. for Women, Frederick, 1991-92; mem. Frederick County Commn. for Women, 1992-97; mem. Walters Art Gallery, Planned Parenthood, U.S. Holocaust Meml. Mus. Internat. Rsch. and Exch. Bd. fellow, 1980-81, Social Sci. Rsch. Coun. fellow, 1981-82; Fulbright-Hays scholar, 1981-82, German Acad. Exch. Svc. scholar, 1974-75. Mem. AAUW, ACLU, Nat. Mus. Women in Arts, Nat. Abortion Rights Action League, LWV, Planned Parenthood, U.S. Holocaust Meml. Mus., Folger Shakespeare Libr., Walters Art Gallery, Whitman Walker Clinic, Vietnam Vets. Meml. Funds. Democrat. Avocations: reading, soccer, basketball, listening to music, science fiction. Office: LexisNexis Acad and Libr Solutions 4520 E West Hwy Bethesda MD 20814-3389

ORTHWEIN, WILLIAM COE, mechanical engineer; b. Toledo, Jan. 27, 1924; s. William Edward and Millie Minerva (Coe) O.; m. Helen Virginia Poindexter, Feb. 1, 1948; children— Karla Frances, Adele Diana, Maria Theresa. BS, M.I.T., 1946; MS, U. Mich., 1951, PhD, 1959. Registered profl. engr., Ill., Ind., Ky. Aerophysicist Gen. Dynamics Co., Ft. Worth, 1951-52; research asso. U. Mich., 1952-59; adv. engr. IBM Corp., Owego, N.Y., 1959-61; dir. computer centers U. Okla., Norman, 1961-63; research scientist Ames Lab., NASA, Moffett Field, Calif., 1963-65; mem. faculty So. Ill. U., Carbondale, 1965—, prof. engring., 1967—. Cons. in field. Author: Clutches and Brakes, 1986, Machine Component Design, 1990; papers, revs., books in field. Pres. Jackson County (Ill.) Taxpayers Assn., 1976. Served with AUS, 1943-46. Mem. ASME (Outstanding Svc. award 1972), Am. Gear Mfrs. Assn., Am. Acad. Mechanis, Soc. Automotive Engrs., Ill. Acad. Sci., Ill. Soc. Profl. Engrs. (chmn. salary and employment com. 1974, chmn. ad hoc com. continuing edn. 1975), NRA, Aircraft Owners and Pilots Assn., Sigma Xi. Mem. Lds Ch. Home: 22 Meffert Ct Highland IL 62249-2699 *Success in engineering is, I believe, contingent upon one's ability to see the world as it really is, to quickly gain insight enough to detect fundamental parameters that determine behavior of the system in question, to conduct a straightforward check of one's analysis, and to simply synthesize a means of modifying and/or controlling the parameters to obtain the desired results. These ingredients apply to both physical mechanisms and to human organizations— only the means of implementation differ.*

ORTIGUEIRA, SALVADOR, economist, educator, researcher; b. Pontevedra, Spain, July 22, 1966; came to U.S., 1998; s. Manuel Ortigueira and Maria Victoria Silva. BA in Econs., Santiago de Compostela, Galicia, Spain, 1990; MA in Econs., Carlos III, Madrid, 1992, PhD in Econs., 1995. Asst. prof. ITAM, Mexico City, 1995-98; asst. prof. econs. Cornell U., Ithaca, N.Y., 1998—. Vis. scholar U. Chgo., 1995. Contbr. articles to profl. jours. Mem. Am. Econ. Assn., Econometric Soc. Office: Cornell U Uris Hall Ithaca NY 14850

ORTINAU, DAVID JOSEPH, marketing specialist, educator; b. Harvey, Ill., Dec. 14, 1948; s. Harold Raymond and Lois Agnice (Reich) O.; m. Shirley Keating, Aug. 15, 1975 (div. Nov. 1979); m. Renee Susan Hess, Apr. 30, 1983 (div. Aug. 1993). BS in Mgmt., So. Ill. U., 1970; MS in Bus. Adminstrn., Ill. State U., 1971; PhD in Mktg., La. State U., 1979. Sr. research analyst, dir. projects Rabin Research Co., Chgo., 1971-73; adminstrv. asst., instr. mktg. Coll. Bus., Ill. State U., Normal, 1973-76; grad. teaching assoc., instr. mktg. Coll. Bus., La. State U., Baton Rouge, 1976-79; from asst. prof. mktg. to assoc. prof. Coll. Bus., U. South Fla., Tampa, 1979-84, assoc. prof., 1984-95, prof., 1995—, coord. PhD program dept. mktg., 1989-91; dir. mktg. and rsch. Market Research Group, 1980-83. V.p. mktg. Neaves, Neaves and Ortinau, Normal, 1974-77. Author: Marketing Research: Withing a Changing Information Environment, 2002; co-author: Marketing Research: A Practical Approach in the New Millennium, 2000 Marketing Research: Within a Changing Information Environment, 2002; mem. editl. rev. bd. Jour. Acad. Mktg. Sci., 1989— (Disting. Merit award for Outstanding Reviewer 1992-93, Outstanding JAMS Rev. 1997-2000), Jour. Bus. Rsch., 2000—; contbr. articles to Jour. Health Care Mktg., Jour. Mktg. Edn., Jour. Bus. Rsch., Jour. Svcs. Mktg., Jour. Acctg. Horizons, Jour. Retailing, others. Recipient Disting. Merit award Advt. Fedn. S.W. Fla., 1983, Coba Outstanding Rsch. award U. South Fla., 1987, Outstanding Tchg. award, 1980, 81, 82, 86, 90, 95. Mem. Am. Mktg. Assn. (doctoral consortium fellow 1978, reviewer 1982—), Assn. Consumer Rsch., So. Mktg. Assn. (reviewer 1975—, chmn. 1976—, sec. 1990-91, treas. 1992-95, pres. elect 1995-96, pres. 1996-97, chmn. Svcs. Mktg. Customer Satisfaction Track Program 1990-92, co-chair doctoral consortium 1998, 99, Outstanding Articles award 1981, 86, 87, 90, 92), Acad. Mktg. Sci. (reviewer 1988—, chmn. 1989, 92, Reviewer of Yr. 1992, session chair new tech. and retail store images at 1999 conf.), Acad. Bus. Adminstrn. (track program chmn. 1993), Soc. for Mktg. Advances (bd. dirs. 1998—, co-chair doctoral consortium 1998-99, fellow award 2001), Beta Gamma Sigma (pres. Fla. chpt. 1990-91). Avocations: all sports, reading, gardening, the arts. Research and consulting specializations focus on attitudinal, motivational, multivariate measurement and data analysis methods in areas of services marketing and quality, customer satisfaction and evaluation models, advertising, marketing education topics/issues, diffusion and evaluative diagnostic performance processes of product innovations, consumer services and interactive marketing technologies. Home: 2305 Windsor Oaks Ave Lutz FL 33549-5880 Office: U South Fla Mktg Dept Tampa FL 33620 E-mail: dortinau@cdoa.usf.edu.

ORTIQUE, REVIUS OLIVER, JR. city official, retired state supreme court justice; b. New Orleans, June 14, 1924; s. Revius Oliver and Lillie Edith (Long) O.; m. Miriam Marie Victorianne, Dec. 29, 1947; 1 child: Rhesa Marie (Mrs. Alden J. McDonald). AB, Dillard U., 1947; MA, Ind. U., 1949; JD, So. U., 1956; LLD (hon.), Campbell Coll., 1960; LHD (hon.), Ithaca Coll., 1971; LLD (hon.), Ind. U., 1983, Morris Brown Coll., 1992, Loyola U. South, 1993, Dillard U., 1996. Bar: La. 1956, U.S. Dist. Ct 1956, Eastern Dist. La 1956, U.S. Fifth Circuit Ct. of Appeals 1956, U.S. Supreme Ct 1964. Practiced in, New Orleans, 1956-78; judge Civil Dist. Ct. for Orleans Parish, 1978-92; assoc. justice La. Supreme Ct., 1993-94; chmn. New Orleans Aviation Bd., 1994—2002. Lectr. labor law Dillard U., 1950-52, U. West Indies, 1986; formerly assoc. gen. counsel Cmty. Improvement Agy.; former gen. counsel 8th Dist. A.M.E. Ch.; former mem. Fed. Hosp. Coun., 1966, Pres.'s Commn. on Campus Unrest, 1970, Bd. Legal Svcs. Corp., 1975-83; chief judge civil cts. Orleans Parish, 1986-87; spkr. in field; U.S. alt. rep. to 54th Gen. Assembly UN, 1999-2000. Contbr. articles to profl. jours. Former pres. Met. Area Com.; former mem. Bd. City Trusts, New Orleans, New Orleans Legal Assistance Corp. Bd., Ad Hoc Com. for Devel. of Ctrl. Bus. Dist. City of New Orleans; bd. dirs. Cmty. Rels. Coun., Am. Lung Assn.; trustee Antioch Coll. Law, New Orleans chpt. Operation PUSH, 1981-84; pres. Louis A. Martinet Soc., 1959; active World's Fair, New Orleans, 1984, Civil Rights Movement, 1960-79; bd. dirs., mem. exec. com. Nat. Sr. Citizens Law Ctr., L.A., 1970-76, Criminal Justice Coordinating Com., UN Assn. New Orleans, 1980—; former mem. exec. bd. Nat. Bar Found.; mem. exec. com. Econ. Devel. Coun. Greater New Orleans; past chmn. Health Edn. Authority of La.; trustee, mem. exec. com. Dillard U.; former mem. bd. mgmt. Flint Goodridge Hosp.; former mem. adv. bd. League Women Voters Greater New Orleans; former mem. men's adv. bd. YWCA; trustee AME Ch., former connectional trustee; former chancellor New Orleans Fedn. Chs.; bd. dirs. Nat. Legal Aid and Defender Assn.; trustee Civil Justice Found.; served on over 50 bds., commns. 1st lt. AUS, 1943-47, PTO. Recipient Arthur von Briesen medal Disting. Svcs. Disadvantaged Ams. NLADA, 1971, Weiss award NCCJ, 1975, Brotherhood award NCCJ, 1976, Nat. Black Achievement award, 1979, Poor People's Banner award, 1979, William H. Hastie award, 1983, Outstanding Citizen award Kiwanis of Pontchartrain, 1986, Civil Justice award, 1989, Daniel E. Byrd award NAACP, 1991, A.P. Tureaud Meml. medal La. State NAACP, 1993; Revius O. Ortique Jr. Law Libr. named in his honor, Lafayette, La., 1988; named Outstanding Young Man Nat. Urban League, 1958, Outstanding Person in La. Inst. Human Understanding, 1976, Citizen of Yr. Shreveport, 1993. Mem. ABA (del., Legal Svcs. program, Nat. adv. coun., 1964-71, jud. divsn., Thurgood Marshal award 2000), Nat. Bar Assn. (pres. 1965-66, exec. bd., Raymond Pace Alexander award, jud. coun. 1987, William Hastie award 1982, Gertrude E. Rush award 1991, Thurgood Marshall award 2000), La. State Bar Assn. (former mem. ho. of dels., Lifetime Achievement award 1986, WTC award for Exceptional Internat. Distinction, 2001), Nat. Legal Aid and Defender Assn. (past pres., mem. exec. bd.), La. District Judges Assn., Am. Judicature Soc. (bd. dirs. 1975-79), Civil Justice Found. (trustee 1989-93), Louis A. Martinet Legal Soc., World Peace Through Law (charter mem.), Blue Key Honor Soc., Phi Delta Kappa, Alpha Kappa Delta. Home: 10 Park Island Dr New Orleans LA 70122-1229 Office: New Orleans Aviation Bd PO Box 20007 New Orleans LA 70141-0007 *In 1989 the National Black Law Journal in cooperation with the UCLA Law Center published: Struggle: A Power Reserved to the People, which was distributed nationwide in commemoration of Black History month, the State of Louisiana thru the office of the Secretary of State has installed a life size portrait of Justice Ortique in the gallery of the State Archives, 1986-1994, 99. Appointed U.S. Alternate Representative to the 54th General Assembly of the United Nations, 2000. Delivered U.S. position on Taliban and terrorism before General Assembly. "With little or no effort on our part, life unfolds with opportunities and rewards, except that we permit our frailties to enslave our ambitions. I am grateful that there are only horizons.".*

ORTIZ, ANA ALICIA, physician; b. Rio Piedras, Puerto Rico, Mar. 16, 1947; d. Carlos Gilberto and Maria (Rivas) Silva; m. Julio Enrique Ortiz, June 14, 1969; children: Ana, Julio, Annette. BS in Biology, U. Puerto Rico, 1969, MD, 1973. Diplomate Am. Bd. Pediatrics, Am. Bd. Allergy Immunology. Commd. 2d lt. U.S. Army, 1973, advanced through grades to col.; intern in pediats. Brooke Army Med. Ctr., 1973, resident in pediats., 1974-76, staff pediatrician, 1976-78, Ft. Bliss, 1978-79; fellow in allergy and immunology Walter Reed Army Med. Ctr., 1979-81; chief allergy clinic Tripler Army Med. Ctr., 1981-84; chief allergy and immunology Brooke Army Med. Ctr., San Antonio, 1984-98; ret. U.S. Army, 1998; pvt. practice asthma, allergy and immunology, San Antonio, 1998—. Roman Catholic. Office: 7950 Floyd Curl Dr Ste 102 San Antonio TX 78229-3916

ORTIZ, ANDREW FLORES, management consultant; b. Tempe, Ariz., June 7, 1969; s. Joe Angel and Celia (Flores) O.; m. Deborah René Ortiz. BA in Polit. Sci., Ariz. State U., 1992, JD, 1998, MPA, 1999. V.p. Hispanic Bus. Assn., Tempe, 1988-89; customer svc. staff Drug Emporium of Ariz., 1989-90; dir. bus. enrichment and acad. preparation program Coll. Bus., Ariz. State U., 1990-91; legis. aide Ariz. State Capitol, Phoenix, 1992—; pres., CEO Ortiz Leadership Cons., Tempe, 1990—. Bd. dirs. AIT/Am. Express Travel, Tempe, 1989-90; dir. League Corp. Advisors, Hispanic Bus. Students Assn., 1989. Contbg. author: Dear Mr. Gorbachev, 1991. Bd. dirs. Ariz. State U. Career Svc., Tempe, 1985-87, Parham Youth Ctr., Mesa, 1985-87, Sen. John McCain's Adv., Phoenix, 1989-91; chmn. Army Canned Food Dr., 1986; vol. United Way, 1986-87, Chicanos Por La Causa, 1991-92, De Colores Battered Women's Shelter, 1992; co-chmn. Tempe Mayor's Adv. Com., 1986; tutor, mentor Tempe Scales Devel. Sch., 1992; v.p. Ariz. State U. Liberal Arts Coun., Tempe, 1992; pres. Young Dems. of Ariz., Phoenix, 1993. Recipient City of Tempe Leadership award, 1986, Presdl. Points of Light award Pres. George Bush, 1991, Leadership award New Times Newspaper, GM Vol. Spirit award, 1991, Gold Congl. award U.S. Congress, 1993, Marin Luther King Cmty. Svc. award, 1994; Ctr. for Study of Pres. nat. fellow, 1992-93. Mem. NAACP (Ariz. State U. chpt. founder, Image award 1990), Am. Mgmt. Assn. (pres.'s coun. 1988), Am. Polit. Sci. Assn., Ariz. State U. Alumni Assn., Assoc. Students Ariz. State U. (v.p. grad. student affairs 1996—, pres. 1997-98), Beta Sigma Phi, Omega Delta Phi (v.p. 1991), Internat. Platform Assn., ABA, Alpha Epsilon Lambda. Roman Catholic. Avocations: sports, travel, painting, foreign languages. Home: 1203 W 9th St Tempe AZ 85281-5305 Office: Ortiz Leadership Cons 1230 W 9th St Tempe AZ 85281-5306

ORTIZ, ANGEL VICENTE, church administrator; b. L.A., Nov. 9, 1956; s. Benjamin and Petra (Santiago) O.; m. Michele Annette Gaunt, May 5, 1979; children: Angela Nicole, Michael David. BS in Bibl. Studies, Ft. Wayne (Ind.) Bible Coll., 1982. Ordained to ministry Christian and Missionary Alliance, 1987. Pastor, ch. planter Christian and Missionary Alliance, Chula Vista, Calif., 1983-90, supt. Spanish western dist. Escondido, 1991-96, also nat. conf. spkr., evangelist; asst. to the pres. for program devel. Nyack (N.Y.) Coll., 1996-97, v.p. student devel., dean students, 1997—2002; sr. pastor First Ch. Christian and Missionary Alliance, N.Y.C., 2002—. Republican. Avocations: camping, woodworking, refinishing, travel, teaching. E-mail: angelortiz@firstchurchnyc.org.

ORTIZ, ANTONIO IGNACIO, public relations executive; b. Mexico City, Feb. 22, 1961; came to U.S., 1988; s. Antonio and Sylvia (Vega) O.; m. Socorro Chinolla, June 12, 1982. B Bus., Autonoma U. Baja Calif., Tijuana, 1984. With acctg. dept. Bank of Atlantic, Tijuana, 1979-83; mgr. Aldaco, 1983-84; dir. pub. rels. Oh! Laser Club, 1984-88, Iguanas, Tijuana, 1988-90, Euebe, S.A., Tijuana, 1990-2000, R. Noble Enterprises, La Jolla, Calif., AAP, Inc., Chula Vista, SPD Transport Inc., Chula Vista. Cons. R.P. Noble Enterprises, La Jolla, Ca.; dir. pub. rels. R. Noble Enterprises, AAP, Inc., Chula Vista, Calif., 2000-; gen. ptnr. SPD Transport, Inc., Chula Vista, Calif., 2001-. Avocations: swimming, watching TV. Home: PO Box 431859 San Diego CA 92143-1859 Office: 482 W San Yaidro Blvd #642 San Ysidro CA 92173

ORTIZ, FERNANDO, JR. commissioner; b. Havana, Cuba, Dec. 2, 1951; came to the U.S., 1961; m. Frances K. Ortiz; children: William, Fernando III. Attended, Miami-Dade C.C., 1972-74, U. Miami, Coral Gables, Fla., 1974-75, Fla. Internat. U., Miami, 1975-76; MD, U. Centro Estudios Technicos, Santo Domingo, Dominican Republic, 1981; postgrad, Syracuse U., postgrad., 1998—. Mgr. Ortiz Transp., Miami, 1981-84; ptnr. Astrum, Syracuse, N.Y., 1984-91; bus. developer Rebuild Syracuse, Inc., 1991-92; coord. Urban Bus. Opportunity Ctr. City of Syracuse, 1992-96, sr. econ. devel. officer, 1996-2000, budget dir., 2000-01, commr. cmty. devel., 2001—. Mem. adv. bd. Greater Syracuse Small Bus. Loan Program, 1993-99; bd. dirs. Consol. Industries, Inc., Child Care coun. of Onondago County; mem. educare com. Success By Six, 2000. Sec. bd. dirs. Onondaga Spanish Action League, Syracuse, 1994-95, pres., 1996-2000; Cultural Resources Coun., 1997-2000; active Onondaga Citizens League, Syracuse, 1995; bd. dirs. Syracuse Neighborhood Housing Svcs., 1997-2000, Met. Water Bd., 1998—, Leadership Greater Syracuse, 2000—; corp. mem. United Way Ctrl. N.Y.; mem. bus. and industry adv. bd. Onondaga C.C.; mem. Leadership Greater Syracuse Class of '93, alumni bd. dirs., bd. mem., 2001—; active F.O.C.U.S. Greater Syracuse, 1997—. Named Min. Small Bus. Adv. of Yr., U.S. SBA, Syracuse, 1995. Mem. U.S. Assn. Small Bus. and Entrepreneurship, Thursday Morning Roundtable. Avocations: reading, gardening, music. E-mail: bus. Home: 1412 Lemoyne Ave Syracuse NY 13208-1339 Office: City of Syracuse Dept Cmty Devel 201 E Washington St Rm 412 Syracuse NY 13202 E-mail: fortiz@ci.syracuse.ny.us., fortizsyr@yahoo.com., fortiz@twcny.yr.com.

ORTIZ, FERNANDO, JR. scriptwriter, film researcher, stage manager; b. N.Y.C., Mar. 28, 1965; s. Fernando and Helen Ortiz. BA in Comm., St. Francis Coll., Bklyn., 1988; MA in Liberal Studies, NYU, 1996. Asst. photo rschr./filer The Bettmann Archive, N.Y.C., 1985-88; rsch. asst. Fleishman-Hillard, Inc., 1988-90; rsch. coord. NYU, 1990-95; patron rschr. Carnegie Hall, N.Y.C., 1996-98; asst. bldg. mgr. Columbia U., 1998-99; stage mgr. various prodns., 1998—; film rschr. Archive Films, 1999-2000; adminstrv. officer Columbia U. Health Scis. Adminstrn., 2000—02. Casting asst. Casting Solutions, 2000-2001. Asst. stage mgr. Mutt Repp Prodns., N.Y.C., 1998, property master, mem. crew, 1998; asst. stage mgr. Infinite Prodns., N.Y.C., 1999; stage mgr. The Shakespeare Project, N.Y.C., 1999. Vol. Lower East Side Tenement Mus., N.Y.C., 1998-2000, Hartley Ho., N.Y.C., 1983-85. Mem. Actor's Equity Assn., Film Soc. of Lincoln Ctr., Ford Falcon Club of Am. Democrat. Roman Catholic. Avocations: writing, running, music, dance, photography.

ORTIZ, FRANCIS VINCENT, JR. retired ambassador; b. Santa Fe, Mar. 14, 1926; s. Francis Vincent and Margaret Mary (Delgado) O.; m. Dolores Duke, May 2, 1953; children: Christina, Francis, Stephen, James. BS, Georgetown U., 1950, postgrad., 1951-53, U. Madrid, Spain, 1950, Am. U. Beirut, Lebanon, 1952; MS, George Washington U., 1967; LLD (hon.), U. N.Mex., 1986. Joined U.S. Fgn. Service, 1951; asst. officer charge Egyptian affairs State Dept., 1951-53; 3d sec. embassy Addis Ababa, Ethiopia, 1953-55; 2d sec. Am. embassy, Mexico City, 1955-57; spl. asst. to ops. coordinator Office Undersec. State, 1957-60, staff asst. to asst. sec. interam. affairs, 1960-61; spl. asst. Am. ambassador to Mexico, 1961-63; officer charge Spanish affairs State Dept., 1963-66; assigned Nat. War Coll., 1966; chief polit. sect. Am. embassy, Lima, Peru, 1967-70, dep. chief of mission Montevideo, Uruguay, 1970-72, charge' d'affairs, 1973; country dir. for Argentina, Uruguay and Paraguay, 1973-75; dep. exec. sec. Dept. State, 1975-77; ambassador to Barbados and Grenada, spl. rep. to Antigua, Dominica, St. Christopher-Nevis-Anguilla, St. Lucia & St. Vin, 1977-79; U.S. ambassador to Guatemala, 1979-80; spl. advisor for polit. affairs U.S. So. Command, Panama, 1980-81; U.S. ambassador to Peru, 1981-83; to Argentina, 1983-86; diplomat-in-residence U. N.Mex., Santa Fe, 1986-88; spl. asst. to under sec. of state for mgmt., 1988-90; ret., 1990. Regent Mus. of N. Mex., 1999. With USAAF, 1944-46. Decorated Air medal; Knight of Malta; recipient Honor award Dept. State, 1952, Superior Service award, 1964, Unit Superior Service award, 1973, Meritorious Civilian Svc. award U.S. Sec. of Def. 1981; Orden del Quetzal (Guatemala), 1980; Gran Cruz Merito Civil award (Spain), 1980; Gran Cruz Orden de Mayo (Argentina), 1991; U.S., Mexican Presdl. Chamizal Commemorative medals, 1964. Mem. Am. Fgn. Service Assn., Sigma Chi. Roman Catholic. E-mail: fvo14@aol.com.

ORTIZ, GERMAINE LAURA DE FEO, secondary education educator, counselor; b. Astoria, N.Y., Aug. 6, 1947; d. Andrew and Germaine Laura (Fournier) De Feo; m. Dennis Manfredo, June 6, 1970 (annulled July 1975); m. Angel Manuel Ortiz, July 11, 1975; 1 child, Germaine Angela. AA, Suffolk County C.C., Selden, N.Y., 1969; BA magma cum laude, SUNY, Stony Brook, 1971, MALS, 1974; MS in Edn. with distinction, Hofstra U., 1989. Cert. N-6, 7-12 social studies tchr., sch. counselor, N.Y.; cert. rank II social studies, jr. coll. tchr., sch. counselor, Fla. Tchr. social studies, guidance counselor Connetquot Cen. Sch. Dist. Islip, Bohemia, N.Y., 1971—. Guidance counselor Connetquot Ctrl. Sch. Mem. ASCD, NEA, N.Y. State Unified Tchrs., Connetquot Tchrs. Assn., Nat. Coun. for Social Studies, N.Y. Coun. for Social Studies, L.I. Coun. for Social Studies, Hofstra U. Alumni Assn., Suffolk County C.C. Alumni Assn., DAV Aux., Vietnam Vets. Am. Aux. Roman Catholic. Avocations: swimming, exercise, meteorology. Home: 5 Honey Ln W Miller Place NY 11764-1719 Office: Connetquot Cen Sch Dist Islip 780 Ocean Ave Bohemia NY 11716-3631

ORTIZ, GUILLERMO, banker; BA, Universidad Nacional Autonoma de Mexico; PhD Economics, Stanford U. Economist Ministry of the Presidency of Mex., 1971—72; mgr. & deputy mgr. Econ. Rsch. Bureau of Bank of Mex., 1977—84; exec. dir. IMF, 1984—88; undersecretary of finance and public credit, 1988—94; sec. telecommunications and transportation Zedillo Adminstrn.; sec. finance and public credit Mexican Fed. Govt., 1994—97; gov. Bank of Mex., 1998—. Instr. Univ. in Mex. and U.S. Author: books and papers on econ. and finance in specialized jour. and mag. Office: Governor Banco de Mexico Avda 5 de Mayo 2 Centro 06059 Mexico City Mexico E-mail: gortiz@banxico.org.mx.

ORTIZ, JAIME, business educator; b. Santiago, Chile, Jan. 20, 1958; s. Sergio Ortiz and Pilar Arizabalo; m. Pamela Caballero, June 20, 1987; children: Maria Pamela, Maria Alejandra. BSc, U. Chile, Santiago, 1980, Diploma, 1981; MA, Inst. Social Studies, The Hague, The Netherlands, 1988; PhD, Va. Poly. Inst. and State U., 1993. Freelance bus. and econ. cons., Santiago, 1980-82; econ. analyst Inter-Am. Inst. Cooperation on Agriculture, Ecuador, 1983-85; mgmt. advisor Ecumenical Ch. Loan Fund, Quito, 1985-87; rsch. asst. dept. applied econ. Va. Tech. U., 1989-93; team leader Euroconsult B.V., Quito, Ecuador, 1994-95; sr. advisor COASER, 1995-96; internat. coord. Pre-investment Orgn. OPALC, 1996-97; gen. coord. Intern Am. Devel. Bank, 1997; mem. faculty, asst. dir. internat. programs Fla. Atlantic U. Coll. Bus., Boca Raton, 1998—. Sr. mgmt. cons. Abastefrut S.A., Santiago, 1994, World Bank, Quito, 1995, GTZ gmbH, Quito, 1995, Inter Am. Devel. Bank, Caracas, Venezuela, 1996 Author: Small-scale Agriculture: Its Evolution in Ecuador, 1988, Small and Medium Enterprises as an Alternative to Macroeconomic Adjustments, 1997; contbr. articles to profl. jours., including Jour. Internat. Devel., Econ. Devel., Microfin., Am. Acad. Bus., Food Policy. Roman Catholic. Office: Fla Atlantic U Coll Bus 777 Glades Rd Boca Raton FL 33431-0991

ORTIZ, JAMES GEORGE, educator; b. Boston, June 6, 1961; BA suma cum laude, Monterey Inst. Internat. Studies, 1989, MA, 1990. Instr. lang. Blue Mountain C.C., Pendleton, Oreg., 1990-2000; pres., CEO, Data Info. Svc., Inc., Toppenish, Wash., 1991-93; safety dir. Marlette Homes, Inc., Hermiston, Oreg., 1993-97; COO Michael James LLC, Toppenish, Wash., 1999—; dep. exec. dir. ADRA Nicaragua, 2000; case mgr. CAPECO, 2000—02, State of Oreg., 2002—. Founder JGO Internat., 1990—. Regional dir. CASA of Oreg., Hermiston, 1990. Scholar Chevron Co., 1988-89. Mem. Am. Soc. Safety Engrs. Republican. Adventist. Avocations: marathon running, scuba diving, piloting small engine aircraft. Home: 1025 W Madrona Ave Hermiston OR 97838-1511

ORTIZ, JAY RICHARD GENTRY, lawyer; b. Washington, Mar. 21, 1945; s. Charles and Catherine Gentry (Candlin) Ortiz; m. Lois Wright Hatcher Greer, June 12, 1982. BA, Yale U., 1967; postgrad., Stanford U., 1967—68; JD, U. N.Mex., 1972. Bar: N.Mex. 1973, Mo. 1978, Tenn. 1982, Ga. 1991, U.S. Dist. Ct. N.Mex. 1973, U.S. Ct. Appeals (10th cir.) 1973, U.S. Supreme Ct. 1977, U.S. Dist. t. (we. dist.) Mo. 1978, U.S. Dist. t. (no. dist.) Ga. 1991, U.S. Ct. Appeals (8th cir.) 1978, U.S. Ct. Appeals (11th cir.) 1991. Assoc. Rodey, Dickason, Sloan, Akin & Robb, Albuquerque, 1972—75; ptnr. Knight, Sullivan, Villella, Skarsgard & Michael, 1975—77; litigation atty. Monsanto Co., St. Louis, 1977—81; environ. atty. Eastman Kodak Co., Kingsport, Tenn., 1981—84; sr. atty. AT&T, Atlanta, 1984—91; gen. counsel AMS Group, Inc., 1991—96, 1998—, ConsultaAmerica Internat., 1994—97, Vision Net, Inc., 1994—, Cross Constrn. Internat., Inc., 1996—97, Ophthalmic Solutions LLC, 1996—97, Univest Ltd., 1996—97; pres. VMS, Inc., 1994—. Precinct vice chmn. Dem. Party, Albuquerque, 1971—77. Lt. (j.g.) USN, 1969—70. Mem.: ABA, English Speaking Union, Tenn. Bar Assn., Mo. Bar Assn., N.Mex. Bar Assn., Ga. Bar Assn., Yale Club of Ga., Order of the Coif, Delta Theta Phi (tribune 1972—77). Episcopalian. Home: 1000 Buckingham Cir NW Atlanta GA 30327-2704

ORTIZ, KATHLEEN LUCILLE, travel consultant; b. Las Vegas, N.Mex., Feb. 8, 1942; d. Arthur L. and Anna (Lopez) O. BA, Loretto Hghts. Coll., 1963; MA, Georgetown U., 1966; cert. in tchg., Highlands U., 1980; cert. in travel, ABQ Travel Sch., 1984. Mgr. Montezuma Sq., Las Vegas, 1966-70; office mgr. Arts Food Market, 1971-75; tchr. Robertson HS, 1976-80; registered rep. IDS Fin. Svcs., 1980-84; travel cons. VIP Travel & Tours, Albuquerque, 1985-86, New Horizons Travel, Albuquerque, 1986-87, All World Travel, Albuquerque, 1987-90, Premium Travel Svcs., Albuquerque, 1990-91; travel cons., group tours Going Places Travel, 1991—. Contbr. 100 articles to newspapers. Founding mem. Citizens Com. for Hist. Preservation, Las Vegas, 1977-79; fund raiser St. Anthony's Hosp., Las Vegas, 1969-75; mem. Hispanic Geneol. Rsch. Ctr., N.Mex., 1996—. Mem. LWV (numerous positions), Internat. Airlines Travel Agent Network, Airlines Reporting Corp. Agent, Georgetown Club of N.Mex. (bd. dirs. at large 1991-94). Avocations: tennis, langs., photography, writing. Home: 7600 Adele Pl NE Albuquerque NM 87109-5362 Office: Going Places Travel 6400 Uptown Blvd NE Ste 429E Albuquerque NM 87110-4290

ORTIZ, LOIDA A. communications executive; b. Vega Baja, P.R. d. Luis and Alicia Ortiz. AA in Computer Scis., U. P.R., 1979; BA in Comm., U. Sacred Heart, 1985; M in Mass. Comm., Fla. Internat. U., 1998. From field prodr. to news dir. Sta. WSJN-TV, Hato Rey, P.R., 1987-90; news editor Stas. WIPR-Radio and WKAQ-Radio, 1989-90; announcer Sta. WMDO Radio Mundo, Tampa, Fla., 1990-91; media cons. Am. Region United Bible Socs., Miami, 1991—. Office: United Bible Socs 1989 NW 88th Ct Miami FL 33172-2641

ORTIZ, MARY THERESA, biomedical engineer, educator; b. N.Y.C., Mar. 25, 1957; d. Henry and Viola (Rega) O. BS, Wagner Coll., 1979; MS, Rutgers U., 1981, PhD, 1987. Emergency med. technician, N.Y. Adj. lectr. N.Y.C. Tech. Coll., Bklyn., 1981-89; teaching/rsch. asst. Rutgers U., New Brunswick, N.J., 1982-86; rsch. scientist N.Y. State Inst. for Basic Rsch., S.I., 1988-93; assoc. prof. Kingsborough C. C., Bklyn., 1993—. Adj. asst. prof. Coll. S.I., 1989-94, NASA SLSTP faculty counselor, 1994, NASA/ASEE summer faculty fellow, 1995. Contbr. articles to sci. jours. Mem. youth adv. coun. N.Y.C. Youth Bd. Beame Adminstrn., 1970's; participant N.Y.C. Tech. Coll. Access for Women, Bklyn., 1980's, Rutgers U. Coll. Engrs. Open House, Piscataway, 1985-86. Grad. Prof. Opportunities Program fellow Rutgers U., 1979-82, Grad. Student Dissertation and Research Support grantee, 1986; Women's Rsch. and Devel. Fund grantee CUNY, 1988. Mem. IEEE, N.Y. Acad. Scis. (judge city and boro sci. fairs), Nat. Engrs. Honor Soc., IEEE, ASEE, NSPE, Kappa Mu Epsilon, Beta Beta Beta. Democrat. Roman Catholic. Home: 31 Ruth Pl Staten Island NY 10305-2430 Office: Kingsborough C C 2001 Oriental Blvd Brooklyn NY 11235-2333 E-mail: MOrtiz@kbcc.cuny.edu.

ORTIZ, PAUL ANDREW, history educator; b. Norfolk, Va., Mar. 12, 1964; s. Paul Pedro O. and Johnine Ivonne Powell; m. Sheila A. Payne, June 11, 1995; children: Joshua Redmond-Payne. BA, Evergreen State Coll., Olympia, Wash., 2000; PhD, Duke U., Durham, N.C., 2000. Rsch. asst. (privately employed), Olympia, 1989—91; living skills instr. South Sound Options Unltd., 1990—93; rsch. asst. Duke U., Durham, NC, 1993—96, rsch. coord. Ctr. Documentary Studies, 1996—2001; prof. U. of Calif., Santa Cruz, Calif., 2001—. Hist. cons. Sunflower County Civil Rights Reunion Com., Indianola, Miss., 2000—, Reality Works Radio Documentary, Tampa, Fla., 2000—; vis. asst. prof. history Duke U., Durham, 2000—01. Editor: Remembering Jim Crow: African Americans Tell About Life in the Segregated South, 2001; contbr. . Bd. dirs. Inst. So. Studies, Durham, 1999—2001; steering com. mem. Resource Ctr. for Nonviolence, Santa Cruz, Calif., 2002; bd. dirs. N.C. Farm Workers Project, Benson, NC, 1993—2001, Student Action with Farm Workers, Durham, 1999—2001. Sgt. U.S. Army, 1982—86. Decorated Army Achievement Medal with oak leaf cluster U.S. Army; fellow Minority Scholar-in-Residence fellow, Grinnell Coll., 1996; grantee Faculty Rsch. Grant, U. Calif., 2001. Mem.: Santa Cruz Faculty Assn. (mem. exec.com. 2002), Orgn. Am. Historians, Oral Hisotry Assn. (Outstanding Oral History

Project 1996), Am. Hist. Assn. Labor. Avocation: basketball. Home: 125 Hagar Ct Santa Cruz CA 95064 Office: U Calif 1156 High St Santa Cruz CA 95064-1077 Home Fax: 831-459-3518; Office Fax: 831-459-5583. Personal E-mail: portiz@cats.ucsc.edu. E-mail: portiz@cats.ucsc.edu.

ORTIZ, SOLOMON P. congressman; b. Robstown, Tex., June 3, 1937; children: Yvette, Solomon P. Student, Del Mar Coll., Corpus Christi, Tex., 1965—67; cert., Inst. Applied Sci., Chgo., 1962; student, Nat. Sheriff's Tng. Inst., Los Angeles, 1977. Constable Nueces County, Tex., 1965—68, commr., 1969-76, sheriff, 1977—83; mem. 98th-106th Congresses from 27th Tex. dist., Washington, 1983—; ranking mem. ho. armed svcs. readiness 98th-105th Congresses from 27th Tex. dist. Mem. subcoms. for resources com.: fisheries, wildlife & oceans, energy & mineral resources; mem. Congrl. Hispanic Caucus; co-chair Congrl. Border Caucus. Served with U.S. Army, 1960-62. Named Man of Yr., Internat. Order Foresters, 1981, one of Hispanic Bus. 100 Most Influential Hispanics in U.S., Hispanic Bus. Mag., 1999. Mem. Nat. Sheriff's Assn., Sheriff's Assn. Tex. Office: US Ho Reps 2136 Rayburn Bldg Washington DC 20515-4327*

ORTIZ, WILLIAM, composer, music educator; b. Salinas, P.R., Mar. 30, 1947; s. William and Guillermina (Alvarado) O.; m. Candida, Mar. 26, 1988; children: Aleyda Enid, Nicole Samara, Amaya E. MusB, P.R. Conservatory of Music, 1976; MA in Composition, SUNY, Stony Brook, 1978; PhD in Composition, SUNY, Buffalo, 1983; B in Music Edn., P.R. Conservatory Music, 1999. Cons./auditor N.Y. State Arts Coun., N.Y.C., 1976-86; asst. dir. Black Mountain Coll. II, Buffalo, 1982-86; music advisor P.R. Symphony Orch., San Juan, 1988-90; prof. music U. P.R. , Bayamon, 1986—; dir. humanities dept. U. P.R., 1997—. Dir./conductor, U. P.R. Band, Bayamon, 1986—, Grammy award nomination, 2001; music critic San Juan Star, 1993-94; composer-in-residence for Music-in-Motion program Atlantic Ctr. for the arts, 1996-97; artist-in-residence René Marquez Mid. Sch., 1999-2000. Composer: (music) 124 E. 107th St., 1979 (Felipe Gutierrez Internat. Composition prize 1980), Llego la Banda, 1984 (Composers Guild Internat. Composition prize 1985), Dos Gritos y una Cancion, 1986 (Composition award Ateneo Puertorriqueno 1989); composer more than 100 works for orchestra, chamber groups, opera, others. Assoc. mem. Hispanic Womens League, Buffalo, 1982-86. Recipient commns. P.R. Symphony, San Juan, 1990, Camerata Caribe, San Juan, 1990, grants Inst. of Puerto Rican Culture, San Juan, 1990, P.R. Community Found., San Juan, 1990, Casals Festival, 1995, Orquesta Baja California, Mex., 1999, 2001; guest composer Festival Musica Nova, Sao Paulo, Brazil, 1988, Festival Latinoamericano de Musica, Caracas, Venezuela, 1991, 92, 94, 98, Am. Composers Orch. "Sonidos de las Americas," 1997, VIII Tribuna Musical para América Latina, Mex., 1997. Mem. Am. Composers Alliance, Am. Music Ctr., Coll. Music Soc., Composers Alliance of Buffalo (pres. 1984), Assn. de Compositores Puertorriquenos. Home: Plaza de La Fuente 1275 Calle España Toa Alta PR 00953 Office: U PR Bayamon Gardens Sta Bayamon PR 00959 E-mail: w_ortiz@upr.edu.

ORTIZ-BUTTON, OLGA, social worker; b. Chgo., July 12, 1953; d. Luis Antonio and Pura (Acevedo) Ortiz; m. Dennis Vesley, Aug. 11, 1973 (div. 1976); m. Randall Russell Button, Nov. 3, 1984 (div. Oct. 1993); children: Joshua, Jordan, Elijah. BA, U. Ill., 1975; MSW, Western Mich. U., 1981. Cert. social worker, sch. social worker. Social svcs. dir. Champaign County Nursing Home, Urbana, Ill., 1976; social svcs. and activity dir. Lawton (Mich.) Nursing Home, 1977; job developer Southwestern Mich. Indian Ctr., Watervliet, 1977-78; staff asst. New Directions Alcohol Treatment Ctr., Kalamazoo, 1978; counselor, instr. Alcohol Hwy. Safety, 1978-79; clin. social worker Mecosta County Community Mental Health, Big Rapids, Mich., 1981-84; program dir. substance abuse Sr. Svcs., Inc., Kalamazoo, 1984-85; sch. social worker Martin (Mich.) Pub. Schs., 1985-96, J.C. Huizenga Charter Schs., Grand Rapids, Mich., 1996—; owner, therapist Plainwell (Mich.) Counseling Ctr., 1989-98; co-dir. Everlasting Covenant Ministry, Kalamazoo, 1997—. S.W. cons. Med. Pers. Pool, 1993-94. Vol. social worker Hospice-Wings of Hope, Plainwell, 1984-85; mem. Hospice Quality Rev. Bd., 1993-96; supporter Students Against Aparteid South Africa, Kalamazoo, 1979-81; mem. World Vision and Countertop Ptnr., 1984—, Christian Life Ctr., Kalamazoo, 1996; sponsor, vol. People for Ethical Treatment of Animals, 1986-91; vol. helper Sparkies for Awana Club Ch., 1989-95; consortium mem. Mich. Post Adoption Svc. System, 1994-97; co-founder Everlasting Covenant Ministry, Kalamazoo, 1997; sch. social worker Nat. Heritage Acads., 1997—. NIMH Rural Mental Health grantee, 1979-81. Mem.: NASW, Nat. Assn. Christian Social Workers, Am. Assn. Christian Counselors, Mich. Assn. Sch. Social Workers. Avocations: jogging, plants, cross country skiing. Home: 1339 Cadet Ln Kalamazoo MI 49009-1838 E-mail: obutton@ureach.com.

ORTIZIO, DEBRA LOUISE, elementary education educator; b. Hoboken, N.J., Mar. 2, 1955; d. Louis Mario and Mary Evelyn (Borra) O. BA in Elem. Edn., Jersey City State Coll., 1977, MA in Reading, Reading Specialist, Jersey City State Coll., 1985, postgrad., 1986. Lic. elem. edn. tchr., reading specialist, N.J. Remedial reading tchr. St. Joseph Man Power Program, Union City, N.J., 1977-78; basic skills tchr. Gilmore Sch.-Union City (N.J.) Bd. Edn., 1978-86, 6th grade tchr., 1986-97, 4th grade tchr., 1997—2002, 5th grade tchr., 2002—. Coach advisor rifles and flag twirlers Emerson H.S., Union City, 1981-83; Students Awareness of Substance Abuse advisor Gilmore Sch., Union City, 1991-92, 93-98, Earth Day coord., 1990, 91; fund raiser advisor Christmas Gifts for Christ Hosps., Gilmore Sch., Union City, 1989-98, student coun. advisor, 1993-94. Ednl. task force Sch. Mgmt. Team, 1999—. Recipient Tchr. Recognition award Hudson County, 1993, Tchr. Recognition award State of N.J., 1993. Roman Catholic. Home: 308 Passaic Ave Hasbrouck Heights NJ 07604-1704 Office: Gilmore Sch Union City NJ 07087

ORTLIP, PAUL DANIEL, artist; b. Englewood, N.J., May 21, 1926; s. Henry Willard and Aimee (Eschner) O.; m. Mary Louise Krueger, June 1981 (dec. May 2001); children from previous marriage: Carol, Kathleen, Sharon (dec.), Danielle (dec.), Michelle. *Generations of artists beginning with Grandfather William Henry Ortlip of Norristown, Pennsylvania, who befriended American painter Thomas Eakins. Great Uncle Henry McCarter of Philadelphia, an artist and an art teacher from the 1890's to 1920's. Father Henry Willard Ortlip and Mother Aimee Eschner met as art students in William Merritt Chase's class in 1903 at the Pennsylvania Academy of Fine Arts Philadelphia. They raised a family of seven children. They excelled as artists and teachers. They painted portraits murals and illustrations that graced the covers of such magazines as Colliers, Christian Herald and Literary Digest during the 1920's and 1930's.* Diploma, Houghton Acad., 1944; student, Art Students League, 1947-49; diploma, Acad. la Grande Chaumiere, Paris, 1950; DFA (hon.), Houghton Coll., 1988. Tchr. Fairleigh Dickinson U., Teaneck, N.J., 1956-68, artist in residence, curator Rutherford, 1968-72. Official USN artist on assignment, Cuban missile crisis, Fla., 1963, Gemini 5 Recovery, Atlantic Ocean, 1965, Vietnam, 1967, Apollo 12 recovery, Pacific Ocean, 1969, Apollo 17 recovery, Pacific Ocean, 1972, Internat. Naval Rev., N.Y. harbor, 1976, USCG Sta., Key West, Fla., 1985; mem. USN Art Coop. and Liason Com. *While in the U.S. Army in Italy during World War II, then Korea and China, Paul had a sketchbook with him. From the 1940's through the 1980's, he painted portrait commissions and murals, and taught art clases. He filled sketchbooks while his five, little daughters were underfoot. As an official U.S. Navy artist on assignment, he sketched Apollo astronauts on recovery from lunar landings, and sketched on the spot Viet Cong rocket attacks in Danang Vietnam in 1967. His artist Wife Mary is often portrayed in these moments to be remembered.* Exhbns. include Salonde L'Art Libre, Paris, 1950, Nat. Acad. Design, 1952, Allied Artists of Am., N.Y.C., Acad. Sci., Rundell Gallery, Rochester, N.Y., Monclair Art Mus., Hist. Mus., Lima, Ohio, Butler Art Inst., Youngstown, Ohio, Fine Arts Gallery, San Diego, State Capitol Bldg., Sacramento, Calif., Capitol Mus., Olympia, Wash., Mus. Gt. Plains, Lawton, Okla., Witte Meml. Mus., San Antonio, Nimitz Meml. Mus., Fredericksberg, Tex., Pentagon Collection of Fine Arts, James Hunt Barker Galleries, Palm Beach, Fla., Nantucket, Mass, N.Y.C., Smithsonian Inst., Gallerie Vollem Breuse, Biarritz, France, Galerie Mouffe, Paris, Guggenheim Gallery, London, Wickersham Gallery, N.Y.C., Soc. Illustrators, N.Y.C.; retrospective exhbn. Bergen Community Mus., Paramus, N.J. 1970, The Curzon Gallery, 1987, 88, 89, 93, Ardennes et de l'Eifel, Charleville Mézières, France, June-Sept. 1990; represented permanent collections including Salmagundi Club N.Y.C., Houghton (N.Y.) Coll., Portrait Meml. J.F. Kennedy Library, Fairleigh-Dickinson U., Nat. Air and Space Mus., Smithsonian Inst., Intrepid Sea-Air Space Mus., N.Y.C., Hist. Mural Visitors Ctr., Palisades Interstate Pk., Ft. Lee, N.J., Vets. Med. Ctr., East Orange, N.J., USN Exhbn. Ctr., Washington Navy Yard, Am. Coll. Clin. Pharmacology, N.Y.C., N.J. U. Dentistry & Medicine, Newark, Bergen County Ct. House, Hackensack, N.J., Dickinson Coll., Carlisle, Pa., George Washingtogn Meml Pk., Paramus, N.J., Marietta (Ohio) Coll., Mcpl. Bldg., Ft. Lee, N.J., Navy League U.S., Arlington, Va., Nat. Archives and Records Adminstrn., Washington, (mural) Pub. Libr., Fort Lee, N.J., Bush Presdl. Libr., College Station, Tex., Underwater Demoltion Team Seal Mus., Fort Pierce, Fla. Served to sgt. U.S. Army, 1944-47, ETO, PTO, 1946-47. Recipient 1st prize Am. Artists Profl. League State Exhibit N.J. chpt., Paramus, 1960, 1st prize U.S. Armed Forces Exhibit Far East, Seoul, Korea, Tokyo, 1946, Franklin Williams award, Salmagundi Club, N.Y., 1967, Outstanding Achievement award for oil painting, USN, 1968, Artist of Yr. award, Hudson Artists, Jersey City (N.J.) Mus., 1970, Statue of Victory World Culture prize, Academia Italia, Parma, 1982, Men of Achievement medal Cambridge, Eng., 1990, Connaissance de Notre Europe Gold medal Charleville-Mézières, France, 1990. Mem. Allied Artists Am. (art coop. and liaison com. with USN), Nat. Soc. Mural Painters, Nat. Soc. Arts and Letters, Bergen County Artists Guild (pres. 1960-62), Portrait Soc. Am., Inc., Artists Fellowship, Inc., U.S. Coast Guard Art Program, Art Students League N.Y. (life), Navy League U.S., VFW (life), Am. Legion. Clubs: Salmagundi (N.Y.C.) (art chmn. 1979-81); Gov.'s of the Palm Beaches (Fla.). Home: 2917 S Ocean Blvd Apt 703 Highland Beach FL 33487-1836 Office: c/o The Curzon Gallery 501 E Camino Real Boca Raton FL 33432-6127

ORTLOFF, GEORGE CHRISTIAN, SR. (CHRIS ORTLOFF), journalist, state legislator; b. Lake Placid, N.Y., Sept. 20, 1947; s. Carl Jacob and Lillian Grace (Travis) O.; m. Ruth Mary Hart, Jan. 28, 1978; children: George Christian Jr., Jonathan Hart. BS, Rensselaer Poly. Inst., 1969; MA, U. Mich., 1975. Reporter, producer Sta. WUOM-FM, Ann Arbor, Mich., 1973-75; reporter Nat. Pub. Radio, 1973-75, Adirondack Daily Enterprise, Saranac Lake, N.Y., 1976-77, Sta. WNBZ-Am, Saranac Lake, 1975-77; pub. rels. dir. Ctr. for Music, Drama and Art, Lake Placid, 1975-76; pres. Macromedia, Inc., 1976-82; anchor, mng. editor Sta. WPTZ-TV, Plattsburgh, N.Y., 1981-85; mem. N.Y. State Assembly, Albany, 1986—, ranking minority mem. Legis. Commn. on Sci. and Tech., 1987-97, chmn. Rep. program com., 1993-98, vice-chair Rep. conf., 1999—2002, ranking minority mem. legis. task force redistricting, 1998—, mem. higher edn. budget com., 1998—, dep. minority whip, 2002, asst. minority whip, 2002—. Mem. health and human svcs. task force Am. Legis. Exch. Coun., 1994-97; N.Y. state chmn., 1997. Author: Lake Placid, The Olympic Years: 1932-80, 1976, A Lady in the Lake, 1985; reporter, producer (TV news series) "Special Segment", 1981-85 (N.Y. State Broadcasters Best Series award 1982, 83, 84, 85), (TV documentary) "A Time to Choose", 1985 (N.Y. State Broadcasters Best award 1986). Chief ceremonies 1980 Olympic Winter Games, Lake Placid, 1978-80; field asst. to congressman David O'B. Martin, Plattsburgh, 1981; chmn. Clinton County Rep. Com., 1995—; committeeman Essex County Rep. Com., 1980-81; trustee Lake Placid Village, 1977-81, Olympic & Winter Sports Mus., 1980-84, Battle of Plattsburgh Assn., 1998-2001, St. Lawrence Aquarium and Ecol. Ctr., 1997-2001, Adirondack Mus., 2001—; lay reader Episcopal Ch., Lake Placid and Plattsburgh, 1976-92. Mem. VFW, AMVETS, Am. Legion, North Country Vietnam Vets. Assn., Elks, Kiwanis (pres. Lake Placid 1980-81). Avocations: skiing, piano, trumpet, painting, woodworking. Home: 23 Morrison Ave Plattsburgh NY 12901-1417 Office: NY State Assembly 450 Legislative Office Bldg Albany NY 12248-0001

ORTMAN, GEORGE EARL, artist; b. Oakland, Calif., Oct. 17, 1926; s. William Thomas and Anna Katherine (Noll) O.; m. Conni Whidden, Aug. 5, 1960 (dec.); 1 stepson, Roger Graham Whidden. Student, Calif. Coll. Arts and Crafts, 1947-49, Atelier Stanley William Hayter, 1949, Acad. Andre L'Hote, Paris, 1949-50, Hans Hoffman Sch. Art, 1949-50. Co-founder Tempo Playhouse, N.Y.C., 1954; Instr. painting and drawing NYU, 1962-65; co-chmn. fine arts Sch. Visual Arts N.Y.C., 1963-65; artist-in-residence Princeton U., 1966-69, Honolulu Acad. Art, 1969; head painting dept. Cranbrook Acad. Art, Bloomfield Hills, Mich., 1970-92. One-man exhbns. include Tanager Gallery, 1954, Wittenborn Gallery, 1955, Stable Gallery, 1957, 60, Howard Wise Gallery, 1962, 63, 64, 66, 69, Gimpel-Weitzenhoffer Gallery, 1972 (all N.Y.C.), Swetzoff Gallery, Boston, 1961-62, Fairleigh Dickinson U., 1962, Mirvish Gallery, Toronto, Can., 1964, Walker Art Center, Mpls., 1965, Milw. Art Center, 1966, Dallas Mus. Art, 1966, Portland Mus. Art, 1966, Akron Inst. Art, 1966, U. Chgo., 1967, Princeton U. Art Mus., 1967, Honolulu Acad. Art, 1969, Reed Coll., 1970, Cranbrook Acad. Art, 1970, 92, Indpls. Mus. Art, 1971, J.L. Hudson Gallery, Detroit, 1971, Gimpel-Weitzenhoffer, N.Y.C., 1972, 73, Gertrude Kasle Gallery, Detroit, 1976, Lee Hoffman Gallery, Detroit, 1977, Flint (Mich.) Mus. Art, 1977; other one-man exhbns. include Cranbrook Mus. Art, 1982; exhibited numerous group shows including Whitney Mus. Am. Art Annual, 1962, 63, 64, 65, 67, 73, Carnegie Internat., Pitts., 1964, 67, 70, Jewish Mus., N.Y.C., 1964, Corcoran Mus., Washington, 1964, others; represented permanent collections, Walker Art Center, Mpls., Mus. Modern Art, Whitney Mus. Am. Art, (both N.Y.C.), Guggenheim Mus., N.Y.C., Albright-Knox Mus., Buffalo, NYU, Christian Theol. Sem., Indpls., Indpls. Mus. Art, Cleve. Mus. Art, Mus. Am. Art, Washington, Honolulu Acad. Art, Newark Mus. Art, Container Corp. Am., Chgo. Ind. U. Music Bldg., Wausau (Wis.) Hosp. Center, Unitarian Ch., Princeton, Mfr. Hanover Trust Bldg., Albert Kahn & Assos., Detroit, Renaissance Center, Detroit, Mich. State Univ. Performing Arts Ctr., East Lansing, Detroit Inst. Arts. Guggenheim fellow, 1965-66; Ford Found. grantee, 1966; One of five Am. artists selected for 1965 Japanese Bi-ann.; recipient Gov. N.J.'s Purchase award 2d ann. exhbn. art, 1967; Best of Show Religion in Art Exhbn., Birmingham, Ala., 1966 Mem. Nat. Acad. of Design. also: Tim Hill Gallery 1527E 72d St Apt 12H New York NY 10021

ORTMAN, HAROLD RODEBAUGH, retired prosthodontist; b. Buffalo, Dec. 19, 1917; s. Harold Taylor and Marguerite (Rodebaugh) O.; m. Betty Hellriegel (div.); children: Jeffrey, Lance, Jay, Paul; m. Virginia Love Ortman, June 30, 1960; step-children: William, Bruce Barton. DDS, U. Buffalo, 1941. Diplomate Am. Bd. Prosthodontists. (fellow). Instr. in removable prosthodontics U. Buffalo Dental Sch., 1942-46, asst. prof., 1947-51, assoc. prof., 1952-62, prof., 1962-88, chmn., head. dept. prosthodontics, 1962-88, prof. emeritus, 1988—. Mem. exec. com. Sch. Dental Medicine U. Buffalo, 1970-88. Author: (with others) Complete Denture Prothodontics, 1979, 2d rev. edit., 1988; lectr: over 52 lectrs. on complete dentures in U.S. and 7 fgn. countries.; contbr. articles to profl. jours. Named Alumni Man of Yr., U. Buffalo; SUNY dental med. clinic named in his honor, 1980. Fellow Am. Coll. Dentists; mem. Am. Prosth. Soc. (all offices including v.p. and pres., exec. com.), Am. Dental Assn., Rocky Mt. Dental Study Club, Erie County Dental Assn., Am. Coll. Prosthodontists (life), Pres. Assocs. SUNY, Greater N.Y. Acad. Prosthodontists (life). Avocations: hunting, fishing, hiking, skiing. Home and Office: 3800 Main St Buffalo NY 14226-3238 E-mail: hrortman@acsu.buffalo.edu.

ORTMEYER, CARL EDWARD, retired demographer; b. Charles City, Iowa, Mar. 12, 1915; s. Arthur Herman and Sarah Emilie (Stoeber) O.; m. Anne Babuska O'Brien, Aug. 3, 1947 (dec. Dec. 15, 1995); 1 child, Kerry Michael; m. Ruth Forberg, Oct. 5, 1996. BA, U. Iowa, 1939; MS, Iowa State U., 1948, PhD in Rural Sociology, Demography, 1954. Rsch. assoc. bur. pub. health econs. Sch. Pub. Health U. Mich., Ann Arbor, 1954—56; sociologist Legis. Reference Svc., Libr. Congress, Washington, 1956—57; rsch. assoc. Social Security Adminstrn. U.S. Dept. HEW, 1957—58; rsch. assoc. Sch. Medicine Howard U., 1958—59; demographer Nat. Ctr. Health, Statistics Pub. Health Svc. U.S. Dept. HEW, 1959—68, demographer Nat. Inst. Occpl. Safety and Health CDC, 1968—80. Vol. caregiver Benedictine Nursing Ctr., Mt. Angel, Oreg., 1990-96, Wesley Homes Health Ctr., Des Moines, Wash., 1996—; mem. Wesley Found., Ams. for Democratic Action. Sgt. U.S. Army, 1941-45. Travel grantee London Sch. Econs. Rockefeller Found., 1969. Fellow APHA AAAS; mem. N.Y. Acad. Sci. Democrat. Mem. United Meth. Ch. Avocation: dancing. Home: 816 S 216th St Apt 211 Des Moines WA 98198-6332 E-mail: rortmeyer@aol.com.

ORTNER, DONALD J. biological anthropologist, educator; b. Stoneham, Mass., Aug. 23, 1938; s. A.W. and Marie B. (Schweizer) O.; m. Joyce E. Walker, April 9, 1960; children: Donald J. Ortner Jr., Allison A. May, Karen L. Ortner. BA, Columbia Union Coll., 1960; MA, Syracuse U., 1967; PhD, U. Kans., 1970; DSc (hon.), U. Bradford, England, 1995. Asst. curator Smithsonian Instn., Washington, 1969-71, assoc. curator, 1971-76, curator, 1976—, chmn. anthropology, 1988-92; acting dir. Nat. Mus. Natural History, 1994-96. Vis. prof. U. Bradford, 1988—; pres. Paleopathology Assn. , 1999—2001. Author: (book) Identification of Pathological Conditions in Human Skeletal Remain, 1981; editor: How Humans Adapt, 1983; co-editor: Human Paleopathology, 1991. Mem. Am. Assn. Phys. Anthropology (mem. exec. com. 1987-90), Internat. Skeletal Soc., Paleopathology Assn. Office: Smithsonian Inst Nat Mus Natural History 10th & Constitution Ave NW Washington DC 20560-0001 E-mail: ortner.don@nmnh.si.edu.

ORTNER, EVELYN MAVIS JACOBS, organization executive; b. N.J. d. Samuel Jacobs and Bronislawa Wilson; m. Robert Ortner, May 21, 1947; children: Peter Colby, Nicole Jane. BA, Montclair State U., 1972; MA, Drew U., 1973. Lectr. contemporary lit. Brandeis U. Studies Group, N.J., 1970's; sr. advisor, speechwriter Sec. Health and Human Svcs., U.S. Govt., Washington, 1980's; founder, exec. dir. The Unity Group, Inc., Millburn, N.J., 1990—. Bd. visitors Drew U., Madison, N.J.; spkr. in field; appeared on numerous TV and radio programs. Author: By Nature a Sociable Fellow. Biography of the Amrican Poet; contbr.: (chpt.) Domestic Violence: A Loss of Selfhood; contrb. articles to profl. publs., mags., newspapers. Founder Inter-Group Com., Essex County, N.J., 1950's; officer LWV, Short Hills, N.J., 1960's; commr. Essex County (N.J.) Commn. on Status of Women, 1990's. Recipient Cert. of Appreciation, U.S. Dept. Justice, Washington, 1998, Commending Resolution, N.J. Senate and Gen. Assembly, Trenton, 1999, Annual Vol. award Gov. N.J., 1999. Avocations: theater, writing, reading, dancing. Office: The Unity Group Inc PO Box 333 Short Hills NJ 07078

ORTNER, EVERETT HOWARD, magazine editor, writer; b. Lowell, Mass., Aug. 25, 1919; s. Herman and Anne (Ehrenhaus) O.; m. Evelyn Frances Gelbman, Jan. 1, 1953. BA, U. Ark., 1939. Editor Popular Publs., N.Y.C., 1946-52; assoc. editor Popular Sci., 1953-56, copy chief, 1956-70, group editor, 1970-76, mng. editor, 1976-80, editor, 1980-85. Pres. Brownstone Revival Coalition N.Y., 1968-76, chmn., 1986—; founder, pres. Back to the City, Inc., N.Y.C., 1974-83, chmn. bd., 1983—; v.p. L.I. Hist. Soc., Bklyn., 1979-83; chmn. bd Preservation Vols. Inc., 2000—. Lt. U.S. Army, 1942-46, ETO. Recipient Cinderella award Bklyn. Union Gas Co., 1978, Honor citation Borough Pres. Bklyn., 1983, Disting. Citizen award City Louisville, 1979, Quality of Life award Kings County Hosp. Ctr., Bklyn., 1976, Spirit of Life award N.Y. Congl. Home, 1994, Excellence in Hist. Preservation award Preservation League NY State, 2002, Grassroots Preservation award Hist. Dists. Coun., 2002. Mem. Overseas Press Club, Montauk Club, Ft. Hamilton Officers Club. Home: 272 Berkeley Pl Brooklyn NY 11217-3904

ORTOLANO, LEONARD, civil engineering educator, water resources planner; b. Bklyn., Sept. 26, 1941; s. Salvatore Thomas and Anna Ortolano. BSCE, Poly. Inst. Bklyn., 1963; MS in Engring., Harvard U., 1966, PhD, 1969. Sanitary engr. USPHS, Denver, 1963-65; rsch. scientist Ctr. for the Environment and Man, Hartford, Conn., 1969-70; prof. civil enging. Stanford (Calif.) U., 1970—, dir. program on urban studies, 1980—. Vis. prof. Inst. Ricerca sulle Acqua, Rome, 1979, South China Environ. Inst. Sci., Guanzhou, 1987, Ecole Nat. des Ponts et Chaussées, Paris, 1987-88, Inst. Universitario Architecture Venice, Italy, 1996, 98, Nat. Poly. Inst. of Toulouse, France, 2000; vis. scholar Kyoto (Japan) U., 1992; vis. lectr. Nat. Sci. Coun. China, 1991. Author: Environmental Planning and Decision Making, 1984 (Chinese edit. 1989), Environmental Regulation and Impact Assessment, 1997, Ecologia dell'Impatto Ambientale, 2000; co-author: Implementing Environmental Policy in China, 1995, Environmental Regulation in China, 2000, Ecologia dell' Impatto Ambientale, 2000. Resources for the Future Natural Resources fellow, 1968-69; Fulbright-Hays grantee, 1979, 87. Mem. Internat. Water Resources Assn., Internat. Assn. for Impact Assessment. Office: Stanford U Dept Civil Engring Stanford CA 94305

ORTON, COLIN GEORGE, medical physicist; b. London, England, June 4, 1938; came to U.S., 1966; s. Frederick G. and Audrey V. (Sewell) O.; m. Barbara G. Scholes, July 25, 1964; children: Nigel, Susanne, Philip. BS in Physics with honors, Bristol U., 1959; MS in Radiation Physics, London U., 1961, PhD in Radiation Physics, 1965; MA (hon.), Brown U., 1976. ABR, ABMP. Instr. London U. St. Barts' Hosp., 1961-66; assoc. prof. NYU Med. Ctr., 1966-75, Brown U., R.I., 1975-81; prof., chief physicist Wayne State U., Harper Hosp., Detroit, 1981—. Dir., grad program, Wayne State U., 1981—. Author: Radiation Physics Review Books I, 1971, II, 1978; editor: Electron Treatment Planning, 1978, Progress in Medical Physics I, 1982, II, 1985, Radiation Dosimetry, 1986; editor Med. Physics, 1997—. Marie Curie Gold Medal, Health Physics Soc., 1987. Fellow Am. Assn. Physicists in Am. (pres. 1981, William D. Coolidge award 1993), Am. Coll. Med. Physics (chmn. 1985, Marvin M. D. Williams Award, 1997), Inst. Physics London, Am. Coll. Radiology; mem. Internat. Orgn. for Med. Physics (sec. gen. 1988-94, pres. 1997-2000), Am. Brechytherapy Soc. (pres. 2001—). Avocations: golf, badminton, tennis, running, squash. Home: 15810 Lakeview Ct Grosse Pointe Park MI 48230-1806 Office: Harper Hosp 3990 John R St Detroit MI 48201-2097 E-mail: ortonc@kci.wayne.edu.

ORTON, GEORGE FREDERICK, aerospace engineer; b. Flushing, N.Y., Aug. 8, 1941; s. Harry and Evelyn (Brostrom) O.; m. Susan K., Dec. 21, 1962; children: Karen, Kevin, Kristen. BS in Aeron. Engring., U. Md., 1964; MS in Engring. Mechanics, St. Louis U., 1971. Engr. propulsion McDonnell Douglas Co. (now The Boeing Co.), St. Louis, 1964-73, sr. engr. propulsion, 1973-77, unit chief propulsion, 1977-81, sect. chief propulsion, 1981-86, br. chief nat. aerospace plane, 1986-90, staff dir. nat. aerospace plane, 1990-92, dir. space programs, 1992-93, program mgr. Hypersonics Ctr. Excellence, 1993—, mem. air force sci. adv. bd., 2000—. Mem. adv. bd. Ga. Inst. Tech., 1998—. Contbr. articles to profl. jours. Advisor Explorer Post 9005, St. Louis, 1980-87; sci. advisor University City (Mo.) Schs. Fellow AIAA (assoc., mem. liquid propulsion tech. com. 1980-84, 91-96, mem. hypersonics program com. 1994—, Best Paper award 1986), St. Louis Head Injury Assn. Methodist. Achievements include patent for propellant acquisition device for zero-g engine starts, patent for propellant resupply system, NASA technology cash award for work on shuttle auxiliary propulsion. Office: The Boeing Co PO Box 516 Mailcode S1067250 Saint Louis MO 63166-0516 E-mail: george.f.orton@boeing.com.

ORTON, JOHN STEWART, lawyer; b. Cin., Nov. 25, 1949; s. Stewart and Hanni (S.) O.; m. Katharine Fleming Wilson, Aug. 8, 1975; children: Elizabeth Fleming, Virginia Stewart. BA in Polit. Sci., Trinity Coll., 1972; JD, Washington and Lee U., 1975. Bar: Tex. 1975, U.S. Dist. Ct. (so. dist.) Tex. 1976, Colo. 1990. Assoc. Rowland & Keim, Houston, 1976-77, Greenwood & Koby, Houston, 1977-80; assoc., ptnr. Barrow, Bland & Rehmet, 1980-85; ptnr. Thompson & Knight, LLP, 1985—. Bd. dirs. Planned Parenthood Houston and S.E. Tex., 1987-96, St. John's Sch. Alumni Assn., Houston, 1991-94, Glassell Sch. Art, Houston, 1988—, Career and Recovery Resources, Inc., Houston, 1999—, Houston Symphony, 1999—. Mem. State Bar Tex. Assn., State Bar Colo., Houston Bar Assn., Briar Club, Houston Club, Galveston Country Club. Avocations: tennis, golf, skiing, hiking. Office: Thompson & Knight LLP 1200 Smith St Ste 3600 Houston TX 77002-4313

ORTON, MARION ROGERS, civic volunteer, former mayor; b. Rochester, Minn., June 22, 1928; d. James Creighton Thomas and Fanny Little (Armstrong) Rogers; m. William R. Orton, Sept. 6, 1950 (dec. May 1990); children: Lori Ann Orton Vu, William R. III, Lisa Marion, Benjamin Rogers. Student, Carlton Coll., 1946-48; BA, U. Ill., 1950. City dir. City of Fayetteville, Ark., 1969-77, 83-86, mayor, 1975-77, dir., organizer cmty. recycling ctr., pollution control com., 1970-74, mem. bd. of adjustment and sign appeals, 1994—; vol. dept. local svcs. State of Ark., Little Rock, 1974-77; vol. Ozark Guidance Ctr., 1976-82; bd. dirs., pres. Pub. Access TV, Fayetteville, 1979-85, 89-95; bd. dirs., pres., various offices LWV, 1956—, pres., 1970-72, 1st v.p., 1994-99; pres. Habitat for Humanity, 1996-98; bd. dirs. Butterfield Trail Village, 1996—. Cited for Outstanding Svc. to Cmty., Lions, Fayetteville, 1980; named First Lady of Fayetteville, Beta Epsilon Omega, Fayetteville, 1975. Democrat. Presbyterian. Avocations: horseback riding, watercolor painting, environmental issues, travel, video photography. Home: 1641 W Halsell Rd Fayetteville AR 72701-3904

ORTON, PATRICIA OSBORN, marina owner, real estate investor; b. Memphis, Jan. 25, 1940; d. John Marion Lee Osborn and Lillie Ann (Bass) Osborn; m. Ed Orton. Degree in bus. ins. and pension planning, Newkirk Rsch. and Rev., 1976. Sales and mgmt. exec. Occidental Life of Calif.,

Memphis and Nashville, 1972-80; owner Anchor High Marina, Hendersonville, Tenn., 1976-80, Pirates Chest Yacht Club, Quinton, Ala., 1986—; mem. mgmt. Provident Life, Chattanooga, 1981-86; real estate investor. Contbr. poetry to lit. publs. Recipient Women's Leader Roundtable award Nat. Assn. Life Underwriters, 1975, 76, 77, Nat. Sales Achievement award, 1975, 76, 77, Nat. Quality award, 1975, 76, 77, Editors Choice award Nat. Libr. Poetry, 1996. Mem. Internat. Soc. Poets. Avocations: yachting, genealogy.

ORTON, WILLIAM H. (BILL ORTON), former congressman, retired lawyer; b. North Ogden, Utah, Sept. 22, 1948; BS, Brigham Young U., 1973, JD, 1979. Adj. prof. Portland (Oreg.) State U./Portland C.C., 1974-76, Brigham Young. U., Provo, Utah, 1984-85; tax auditor IRS, 1966-77; owner/lectr. Tax Tng. Inst., Inc., 1978-90; lectr. continuing edn. seminars Real Estate Tax Inst., N.W. Ctr. Profl. Edn., and Tax Tng. Inst., various locations in U.S., 1978-90; corp. counsel WI Forest Products, Inc., Portland, Oreg., 1980-81; of counsel Merritt & Tenney, Atlanta, 1986-90; tax atty. pvt. practice, Utah, 1980-90, Washington, 1986-90; atty., 1980-90; mem. 102d-104th Congresses from 3f Utah dist., 1990-97, fgn. affairs com., small bus. com., budget, banking and fin. svcs. coms.; ptnr. Jones, Waldo, Holbrook & McDonough, Washington, 1997-99. Democrat. Mem. Lds Ch. Office: Jones Waldo Holbrook & McDonough 1500 Wells Fargo Plz 170 S Main St Salt Lake City UT 84101-1605 also: 550 E 2100 N Ogden UT 84414-3130

ORTTUNG, WILLIAM HERBERT, chemistry educator; b. Phila., June 16, 1934; s. Elmer Herbert and Rosalind Orttung; married; children: Robert W., Mark. H. SB, MIT, 1956; PhD, U. Calif., Berkeley, 1961. Asst. prof. chemistry Stanford (Calif.) U., 1960-63, U. Calif., Riverside, 1963-69, assoc. prof., 1969-79, prof., 1979-94; emeritus prof., 1994—. Mem. AAAS, Am. Chem. Soc., Am. Phys. Soc. E-mail: worttung@worldnet.att.net.

ORULLIAN, B. LARAE, bank executive; b. Salt Lake City, May 15, 1933; d. Alma and Bessie (Bacon) O. Cert., Am. Inst. Banking, 1961, 63, 67; grad. Nat. Mortgage Sch., Ohio State U., 1969-71. With Tracy Collins Trust Co., Salt Lake City, 1951-54, Union Nat. Bank, Denver, 1954-57; exec. sec. Guaranty Bank, 1957-64, asst. cashier, 1964-67, asst. v.p., 1967-70, v.p., 1970-75, exec. v.p., 1975-77, also bd. dirs.; chair, CEO, pres. The Women's Bank N.A., 1977-97, Colo. Bus. Bankshares, Inc., 1980-97; vice chmn. Guaranty Bank and Trust Co., Denver, 1998—. Bd. dirs. Guaranty Corp., Anthem Ins. Co., Indpls., Lange Golf Co., Holladay (Utah) Bank; vice-chmn. bd. dirs. Frontier Airlines. Treas. Girl Scouts U.S., 1981-87, 1st nat. v.p., chair exec. com., 1987-90, nat. pres., 1990-96; 1st vice chair world bd. World Assn. Girl Guides Girl Scouts, London. Recipient Woman Who Made a Difference award Internat. Women's Forum, 1994; named to Colo. Women Hall of Fame, 1988; named Colo. Entrepreneur of Yr., Inc. Mag. and Arthyr Young and Co., 1989, Woman of Yr., YWCA, 1989, Citizen of Yr., EMC Lions Club, 1995, laureate Colo. Bus. Hall of Fame, 1999. Mem. Bus. and Profl. Women Colo. (3d Century award 1977), Internat. Women's Forum, Am. Bankers Assn. (adv. bd. edn. found.), Com. of 200. Republican. Mem. Lds Ch. Home: 6650 W 10th Pl Denver CO 80214

ORVANANOS, MARCELA DE ROVZAR, philanthropist; b. Mexico City, Oct. 20, 1950; d. Eduardo Zuniga and Teresa (Hernández) O.; m. Alexis E. Rovzar, Dec. 1, 1972; 4 children. Degree in architecture, Iberoamericana U., Mex., 1972; cert. in mgmt. non-profit/fundraising, Indiana Ctr. Philanthropy, 1993. Vol. Mex. Found. Rural Devel., Mex., 1989-90, dir. of devel. Mex., 1990-92, v.p. Mex., 1992-94; founder Procura A.C., Mex., 1994-2000, mem. hon. bd. Mex., 2000—. Mem. cmty. bd. Jr. League, Mex., 1997—; bd. dirs. UNICEF, Save the Children, 1999—; trustee Ctr. Mex. Filantropia, Mex., 2000—. Roman Catholic. Avocations: painting, sculpture, ceramics. Home: Au Desierto de Los Leones 6153-2 Mexico City Mexico Office: Av Contreras 517-A 10200 Mexico City Mexico E-mail: procura_ac@yahoo.com.

ORVICK, GEORGE MYRON, church denomination executive, minister; b. Hanlontown, Iowa, Jan. 9, 1929; s. George and Mabel Olina (Mandsager) O.; m. Ruth Elaine Hoel, Aug. 25, 1951; children: Daniel, Emily, Mark, Kirsten. AA, Bethany Luth. Coll., Mankato, Minn., 1948, candidate of theology, 1953; BA, Northwestern Coll., Watertown, Wis., 1950. Ordained to ministry Evang. Luth. Synod, 1953. Pastor Our Saviour Luth. Ch., Amherst Junction, Wis., 1953-54, Holy Cross Luth. Ch., Madison, 1954-86; cir. visitor Evang. Luth. Synod, Mankato, 1964-69, pres., 1970—76, 1980—2002, dir. dept. archives and history, 2002—. Author: Our Great Heritage, 1966; columnist: The Luth. Sentinel, 1982-2002. Home: 1117 Lori Ln Mankato MN 56001-4728 Office: Evang Luth Synod 6 Browns Ct Mankato MN 56001-6121 E-mail: gorvick@blc.edu.

ORVIN, GEORGE HENRY, psychiatrist; b. Columbia, S.C., Aug. 6, 1922; s. Jesse Wright and Ruth Veril (Walton) O.; m. Rosalie Greer Salvo, Sept. 16, 1944; children: Candace, Jay Scott, Debra Anne, Nancy Lee. BS, The Citadel, 1943; MD, Med. U. S.C., Charleston, 1946; MD (hon.), The Citadel, 1996. Diplomate Am. Bd. Psychiatry. Pvt. practice, Charleston, S.C., 1948-57; resident psychiatry Med. U. S.C., 1957-60; clin. asst. U. London, 1960-61; instr. Med. U.S.C., 1961; with Maudsley Hosp. Inst. of Psychiatry/U. London, 1960-61; chief adolescent psychiatry Med. U. S.C., 1967-89, pres. faculty senate, 1977-79, prof. psychiatry, 1977-89, emeritus prof. psychiatry, 1993; founder, chmn. New Hope Treatment Ctrs., Inc., Charleston, 1984—. Author: Understanding the Adolescent, 1995; sr. editor Annals Adolescent Psychiatry, 1985-98; contbr. chpts. to books, articles to profl. jours. Vice-chmn. S.C. Com. Alcohol/Drug Abuse, 1973-89; mem. Gov.'s Cabinet for Children, 1984, Gov.'s Task Force Adolescent Pregnancies, 1985. Fellow Am. Psychiat. Assn. (life), Am. Soc. Adolescent Psychiatry (life), Royal Soc. Medicine, St. Andrews Soc., Citadel Brigadier Club (founder, pres. 1948-53). Episcopalian. Achievements include development of new treatment modalities for adolescents. Home: 84 S Battery St Charleston SC 29401-2301 Office: New Hope Inc 225 Midland Pky Summerville SC 29485-8104

ORVIS, ANDREA LEIGH, fine technology scientist, researcher; b. Titusville, Fla., Mar. 3, 1964; d. Orel Dighton Orvis III and Marjorie Dale (Cheyney) Weil; 1 child, Cheyney Renae. BS in Physics, LeMoyne Coll., 1995; postgrad., U. Tex., 1997—. Tchg. asst. Seminole C.C., Sanford, Fla., 1988-90, U. Tex., San Antonio, 1992-93, LeMoyne Coll., Syracuse, N.Y., 1993-95; scientist in fine tech. S.W. Rsch. Inst., San Antonio, 1996—. Editor: Laboratory Manual for Digital Electronics, 1994, Laboratory Manual for Analog Electronics, 1994; contbr. articles to profl. jours. Mem. Soc. for Physics Students (sec. 1994-96), Alpha Sigma Nu, Phi Theta Kappa. Republican. Office: SW Rsch Inst PO Box 28510 San Antonio TX 78228-0510

ORWOLL, GREGG S. K. lawyer; b. Austin, Minn., Mar. 23, 1926; s. Gilbert M. and Kleonora (Kleven) O.; m. Laverne M. Flentie, Sept. 15, 1951; children: Kimball G., Kent A., Vikki A., Tristen A., Erik G. BS, Northwestern U., 1950; JD, U. Minn., 1953. Bar: Minn. 1953, U.S. Supreme Ct. 1973. Assoc. Dorsey & Whitney, Mpls., 1953-59, ptnr., 1959-60; assoc. counsel Mayo Clinic, Rochester, Minn., 1960-63, gen. counsel, 1963-87, sr. legal counsel, 1987-91, sr. counsel, 1991-92. Gen. counsel, dir. Rochester Airport Co., 1962-84, v.p., 1981-84; gen. counsel Mayo Med. Svcs., Ltd., 1972-90; bd. dirs., sec. and gen. counsel Mayo Found. for Med. Edn. and Rsch., 1984-90; gen. counsel Mid-Am. Orthop. Assn., 1984—, Minn. Orthop. Soc., 1985-95; counsel Norwegian Am. Orthopaedic Soc., 1999—; asst. sec./sec. Mayo Found., Rochester, 1972-91; sec. Mayo Emeritus Staff, 1998-99, vice chair, 1999-2000, chair, 2000-2001; bd. dirs. Charter House, 1986-90; dir., officer Travelure Motel Corp., 1968-86; dir., v.p. Echo Too Ent., Inc.; dir., v.p. Oberhamer Inc., 1989-99; bd. dirs. Am. Decal and Mfg. Co., 1989-93, sec., 1992-93; adj. prof. William Mitchell Coll. Law, 1978-84. Contbr. articles and chpts. to legal and medico-legal publs.; mem. bd. editors HealthSpan, 1984-93; mem. editl. bd. Minn. Law Rev., 1952-53. Trustee Minn. Coun. on Founds., 1977-82, Mayo Found., 1982-86; trustee William Mitchell Coll. Law, 1982-88, 89-98, mem. exec. com. 1990-98; bd. visitors U. Minn. Law Sch., 1974-76, 85-91; mem. U. Minn. Regent Candidate Adv. Coun., 1988-99, Minn. State Compensation Coun., 1991-97. With USAF, 1944-45. Recipient Outstanding Svc. medal U.S. Govt., 1991. Mem. ABA, AMA (affiliate), Am. Corp. Counsel Assn., Minn. Soc. Hosp. Attys. (bd. dirs. 1981-86), Minn. State Bar Assn. (chmn. legal/med. com. 1977-81), Olmsted County Bar Assn. (v.p., pres. 1977-79), Rochester C. of C., U. Minn. Law Alumni Assn. (bd. dirs. 1973-76, 85-91), Rochester U. Club (pres. 1977), The Doctors Mayo Soc., Mid Am. Orthop. Assn. (hon.), Mayo Alumni Assn. (hon.), Phi Delta Phi, Phi Delta Theta. Republican. Home: 2233 5th Ave NE Rochester MN 55906-4017 Office: Mayo Clinic 200 1st St SW Rochester MN 55905-0002

ORWOLL, MARK PETER, magazine editor; b. Lynwood, Calif., Dec. 3, 1953; s. Sylfest Peter Jr. and Frances Patricia (Giffin) O.; m. Kathleen F. Fox, Aug. 6, 1983; children: Caitlin, Gillian, Rory. BA in Journalism, San Diego State U., 1978, MA in English, 1985. Reporter Star-News, Chula Vista, Calif., 1978-79; staff writer The Reader, San Diego, 1979-81; features editor Woman's World, Englewood, N.J., 1981; bus. editor American Salon, N.Y.C., 1981-83; editor Transfer, San Francisco, 1983-84; sr. editor USAir Mag., N.Y.C., 1985-87; mng. editor Travel & Leisure, 1987—. Lectr. Rice U. Pub. Program, Houston, 1994, Seabourn Cruise Line, India-Singapore, 1994, S.W. Writers Workshop, Albuquerque, 1998; spkr. Am. Soc. Journalists and Authors, N.Y.C., 1991, New Sch. Social Rsch., N.Y.C., 1992, Hospitality Sales and Mktg. Assn. Internat., Anaheim, 1998, others. Author: Teach Yourself e-Travel Today, 2000; media appearances on CBS, CNN, ABC, MSNBC, Fox News Channel, NBC, others. Ky. col. Hon. Order Ky. Cols., Frankfort, 1995. Mem. Am. Soc. Mag. Editors, 1990—. Office: Travel & Leisure 1120 Avenue Of The Americas New York NY 10036-6700

ORY, STEVEN JAY, physician, educator; b. Houston, Aug. 4, 1950; s. Edwin Marvin and Norma Gertrude O.; m. Kathleen Higgins, Jan. 10, 1981; children: Eleanor Claire, Edward Michael. BA, Washington and Lee U., 1972; MD, Baylor Coll., 1976. Diplomate Am. Bd. Obstetrics and Gynecology, subsplty. cert. in Reproductive Endocrinology and Infertility. Asst. prof. Duke U., Durham, N.C., 1981-82, Northwestern U., Chgo., 1982-85; assoc. prof., cons. Mayo Clinic, Rochester, Minn., 1985-95, chmn. sect. reproductive endocrinology and infertility, 1985-95; pvt. practice reproductive endocrinology and infertility; mem. ob-gyn. staff N.W. Ctr. for Infertility and Reproductive Endocrinology, Margate, Fla., 1995—; assoc. clin. prof. obstets. and gyn. U. Miami, 1999—. Assoc. dir. Am. Fertility Soc., Birmingham, Ala., 1986-87. Asst. editor: Fertility and Sterility, 1988-96; contbr. articles to profl. jours. Mem. Internat. Soc. for Advancement of Humanistic Studies in Medicine (bd. dirs. 1999—), Am. Soc. Reproductive Medicine (chmn. practice com. 1998—, bd. dirs., 1999—), Soc. Reproductive Endocrinologists (sec.-treas., pres. 2001—), Ft. Lauderdale Ob-Gyn. Soc. (pres. 1998-2000). Address: 2825 N State Road 7 Ste 302 Margate FL 33063-5737

ORZECHOWSKI, ALICE LOUISE, accountant; b. Washington, Jan. 14, 1952; d. Casimir T. and Frances (Zemaites) O.; m. Scott Mitchell Hoyman Jr. BS in Econs., U. Md., 1973, BS in Acctg., 1976; MS in Adminstrn. and Mgmt., Hood Coll., 1983. CPA, Md.; cert. mgmt. acct. Mgr. Gen. Bus. Svcs., Rockville, Md., 1972-78, Ross Assocs., Alexandria, Va., 1978-87; owner Alice L. Orzechowski, CPA, Cert. Mgmt. Acct., Frederick, Md., 1987-97, OAO CPAs LLC, Frederick, 1998—. Adj. faculty Frederick (Md.) C.C., 1990-92, Montgomery Coll., Rockville, Md., 1992-98; spkr. in field. Named Outstanding Young Marylander, Md. Jaycees, 1991. Mem. Nat. Spkrs. Assn., AICPA, Am. Women's Soc. CPAs, Md. Assn. CPAs, Nat. Assn. Accts., Nat. Assn. Tax Profls., Downtowne Frederick Toastmasters (pres. 1991, Toastmaster of Yr. 1990), Frederick C. of C. (chair small bus. coun. 1990-91, dir. 1992-96, Entrepreneur of Yr. 1992). Office: 25 E Patrick St Frederick MD 21701-5671 E-mail: AliceO@oaocpa.com.

OSAKA, MICHI, artist, printmaking educator; b. Brooks, Oreg., May 15, 1927; d. Otoichi and Fumiyo (Masukawa) Umemoto; m. Tom S. Osaka, May 30, 1945; children: Janice Vinnedge, Gordon, Kurt. BA magna cum laude, U. Puget Sound, 1978; BFA, U. Wash., 1981, MFA, 1984. Artist, Tacoma, 1978—. Exhbn. chair Nat. Am. Pen Women Wash., Tacoma, 1983. Author, artist: Peace and Harmony, 1991 (Artist Trust 1991), Michi Osaka's Path, 1997, Best of Show 1997); 23 solo exhns., regionally and nationally, exhibited in group shows at Puget Sound Artists, Tacoma, 1981, 82, 83, Regional South Profl. Puyallup, Olympia, 1985, Pacific Gallery Artists, Tacoma, 1985, Puget Sound Sumie Artists, Tacoma and Seattle, 1975, 93 and others; exhibited in traveling exhibit N.W. Print Coun., Portland, 1982. Artist Ford Found. Grant, U. Wash., 1982; artist-chmn. Sister City of Kitakyushu, Tacoma, 1987. Nine Best of Show awards nationally and regionally N.W. Watercolor Soc.; cert. excellence Internat. Art Competition, N.Y., 1988; fine arts recognition Pierce County Arts Commn., Tacoma, 1992. Mem. Sumie Soc. Am. (pres. 1985-86), Women's Painter Wash. (1st v.p. 1995-96), N.W. Print Coun. (Best of Show), Nat. Northcoast Collage Soc. (Merit award), N.W. Watercolor Soc. (1st place award), Phi Kappa Phi. Avocations: Bonsai, calligraphy, Saga floral arrangements. Home: 1115 62d Ave E Tacoma WA 98424

OSAKI, MARK STEPHEN, writer, development administrator; b. Sacramento, Oct. 7, 1952; s. Tadashi Melvin and Haruye (Murata) O. BA, U. Calif., Berkeley, 1974; PhD, Georgetown U., 1984. Assoc. dir. RAND Corp., Santa Monica, Calif., 1992-97, cons., 1997-2001; dir. devel. Disabled Sports USA Far West, Citrus Heights, 2000—. Comm. dir. U. Calif., 1984-90; dir. devel. Coro Found., San Francisco, 1996-97, Second Harvest Food Bank, San Jose, Calif., 1997-2000, Toigo Found., Sacramento, 1997-98. Author: Poetry of the Vietnam War, 1989, Men of Our Time: An Anthology of Male Poetry in Contemporary America, 1992. Nat. Endowment for Arts fellow, 1981. Home: 6615 Fordham Way Sacramento CA 95831 Office: Disabled Sports USA Far West Ste 2540 6060 Sunrise Vista Dr Citrus Heights CA 95610 E-mail: markosaki@msn.com., mark@dsusafw.org.

OSANDER, JOHN, secondary school educator; AB in English cum laude, Princeton U.; postgrad., U. Minn., Rider U., St. Thomas U., Macalester Coll., Yale U.; MEd in English Tchg. and Adminstrn., Harvard U. Cert. secondary sch. English and social studies tchr., cert. elem. and presch. tchr., prin. and sch. adminstr. Tchr. Blake Sch., Mpls., 1957—60, Lincoln-Sudbury Regional H.S., Mass., 1961—63; dir. admissions Princeton U., 1963—71; tchr. Exptl. Work on Writing with Children, NJ, 1974—77, NY, 1974—77; sr. dep. to the pres. Carnegie Found., 1980—97; writing and theater vol. Washburn H.S., Mpls., 2000—. Cons. in field; founding dir. tchr. recruitment and placement office N.J. State Dept. Edn., 1984—91. Author: (novels) Country Matters, 2000. Mem.: Loft Literary Ctr., Playwrights' Ctr., Authors League Am., Dramatists Guild. Home: 4831 Portland Ave S Minneapolis MN 55417

OSANI, STEVEN LEO, physician assistant, medical educator; b. Oct. 8, 1964; BS, Touro Coll., 1994; MPAS, Nebr. State U., 2000. Asst. prof. medicine Touro Coll., Dix Hills, N.Y., 1994—; physician asst. Office of Dr. Neil J. Dash, Massapequa, 1999. Ind. cons. Merck Pharm., Park Davis Pharm., 1999. Mem. N.Y. State Soc. Physician Assts. (chmn. scholarship com. 1999), Fed. Order of Police (physician asst. rep. 1999). Address: 159 Hunter Ave North Babylon NY 11703-4719

OSAWA, PAULA MARIANI, trading company executive; b. St. Petersburg, Fla., Jan. 31, 1951; d. Alfred and Velma Mariani; m. Yuichi Osawa, 1999. BS, U. Fla., 1972, MS, 1973. Pres. Orientations Japan, Hawaii and Tokyo, 1979-87; protocol advisor Mitsui & Co., Ltd., Tokyo, 1987—, Japan External Trade Orgn., Tokyo, 1992—. TV commentator Japan Ednl. TV, 1991—; radio commentator Japan Ednl. Radio, 1985-90. Contbr. articles to profl. jours.; profiled on CNN TV as successful Am. woman working in Japan, on CBS TV as success in Japan market. Mem. Am. C. of C. in Japan. Avocations: Kung Fu (Black Belt), marathon running. Office: Mitsui & Co Ltd 1-2-1 Otemachi, Chiyoda-ku Tokyo 100-0004 Japan

OSBALDESTON, GORDON FRANCIS, business educator, former government official; b. Hamilton, Ont., Can., Apr. 29, 1930; s. John Edward and Margaret (Hanley) O.; m. Geraldine Keller, Oct. 3, 1953; children— Stephen, David, Robert, Catherine B.Commerce, U. Toronto, Ont., Can., 1952; MBA, U. Western Ont., London, 1953, LL.D., 1984, York U., Toronto, 1984, Dalhousie U., Halifax, N.S., 1985, Carleton U., Ottawa, Ont., Can., 1987. Fgn. service officer Dept. Trade and Commerce, Ottawa, 1953-54, vice consul, asst. trade commr. Sao Paula, Brazil, 1954-57, Chgo., 1957-60, consul, trade commr. Los Angeles, 1960-64, asst. dir., personnel trade commr. service Ottawa, 1964-66, asst. dir. ops. trade commr. service, 1966-67, exec. dir. trade commr. service, 1967-68; asst. dep. minister Dept. Consumer and Corp. Affairs, 1968-70, dep. minister, 1972-73; dep. sec. Treasury Bd. Secretariat, 1970-72, sec., 1973-76; dep. minister Dept. Industry, Trade and Commerce, 1976-78; sec. Ministry of State for Econ. Devel., 1978-82; undersec. of state Dept. External Affairs, 1982; clk. privy council, sec. to cabinet Privy Council Office, 1982-86; mem. Queen's Privy Coun. for Can., 1986; prof. emeritus Western Bus. Sch. U. Western Ont., 1986—. Bd. dirs. DuPont of Can. Inc., Great West Lifeco Inc., Great West Life Assurance Co., London Group Ins. Inc., London Life Co. Author: Keeping Deputy Ministers Accountable, 1989, Organizing to Govern, 1990. Decorated officer Order of Can., companion, 1997; recipient Outstanding Achievment award Can. Govt., 1981, Vanier medal Inst. Pub. Adminstrn., 1990. Mem. London Hunt and Country Club, Psi Upsilon Roman Catholic. Avocations: philately, golf. Home: 1353 Corley Dr N London ON Canada N6G 4L4 E-mail: gordon5304@aol.com.

OSBERG, TIMOTHY MICHAEL, psychologist, educator, researcher; b. Buffalo, Aug. 11, 1955; s. John Carlton and Adeline Rose (Weichsel) O.; m. Debra A. Morreale, July 14, 1990; children: John Peter, Erika Evelyn. BA, SUNY, Buffalo, 1977, MA, 1980, PhD, 1982. Lic. psychologist NY. Intern VA Med. Ctr., Buffalo, 1981-82; asst. prof. Niagara U., N.Y., 1982-86; assoc. prof., 1986-90; prof., 1990—; pvt. practice Niagara U., Niagara Falls, N.Y., 1985—, 1985—. Psychologist Optifast Weight Loss Program, Niagara Falls, 1989-92; editorial bd. Jour. Personality and Social Psychology, 1988-92, Teaching of Psychology, 1991-99, Jour. Correctional Edn., 1993-97, Jour. Clin. Psychology, 1999-2001; instr. Attica Correctional Facility, 1980-93; presenter in field. Contbr. articles to profl. jours. Vol. group leader pre-release program Attica (N.Y.) Correctional Facility, 1984-90, exec. com. Psychol. Assn. Western N.Y., Buffalo, 1982-87. Recipient Feldman-Cohen Meml. award SUNY, Buffalo, 1977, Disting. Faculty award Consortium of Niagara Frontier, 1993. Fellow APA; mem. Am. Psychol. Soc., Eastern Psychol. Assn., Soc. for Personality Assessment, Assn. Advancement Behavior Therapy, Phi Beta Kappa. Democrat. Roman Catholic. Avocations: spectator sports, running, golf, tennis, hockey. Home: 109 Hidden Oaks Ct Grand Island NY 14072-2575 Office: Niagara U Dept Psychology Niagara University NY 14109 E-mail: tosberg@niagara.edu.

OSBORN, ANN GEORGE, retired chemist; b. Nowata, Okla., Aug. 1, 1933; d. David Thomas and Alice Audrey (Giles) George; m. Charles Wesley Osborn, Nov. 8, 1958 (dec. Dec. 1977); 1 child, Charles David. BA in Chemistry, Okla. Coll. Women, 1955. Rsch. chemist thermodynamics rsch. lab. Bartlesville (Okla.) Energy Rsch. Ctr., U.S. Dept. Energy, 1957—; ret., 1983. Contbr. articles to profl. jours. Mem. AAAS (emeritus), Am. Chem. Soc. Republican. Mem. Christian Ch. (Disciples Of Christ). Home: 647 S Pecan St Nowata OK 74048-4015

OSBORN, DEVERLE ROSS, insurance company executive; b. Leesburg, Ind., Sept. 29, 1925; s. Leland John and Beth (Bunnell) O.; m. Edith Helaine Germann, June 27, 1948 (dec. Mar. 1990); children: Bradford, Pamela, Andrea, Randall; m. Lillian C. Fellwock, Aug. 1990. Student, U. Notre Dame, 1944; BS in Air Transp. Engring., Purdue U., 1947. CLU. Spl. agt. FBI, Louisville, 1948, N.Y.C., 1948-53; life ins. agt. Conn. Mut. Life, 1953-56; life ins. exec. Conn. Mutual Life, Hartford, 1956-65, Allentown, Penn., 1965-70, Aid Assn. Luths., Appleton, Wis., 1970-78, Evansville, Ind., 1978-91; ret. Chmn. adv. coun. Law Enforcement of Bergen County, N.J., 1955-56. Liaison State Legislators Justice Fellowship, Washington, 1982-85, chmn., 1989-92; fin. dir. Prescott, Ariz. Spl. Olympics, 1996-98; bd. dirs. Atlantic dist. Luth. Ch.-Missouri Synod, 1961-65, Habitat for Humanity, Evansville, Ind., 1991-92, Meals on Wheels, Prescott, 1997-2000, Prayer Family Internat., 1999-2002. Naval Aviation cadet, 1943-45, lt. (j.g.) res., 1950-60. Named Nat. Vol. Yr. Justice Fellowship, 1989. Mem. Soc. CLUs (v.p., pres. local chpts. 1968,70), Gen. Agt. Mgr. Assn. (treas., v.p., pres. local chpts. 1966-68), Nat. Assn. Life Underwriters. Republican. Lutheran. Avocation: flying. Home: 394 Sunny Cove Cir Prescott AZ 86303-5734 E-mail: nrobso@interwrx.com.

OSBORN, DONALD ROBERT, lawyer; b. N.Y.C., Oct. 9, 1929; s. Robert W. and Ruth C. (Compton) O.; m. Marcia Lontz, June 4, 1955; children: David, Judith, Robert; m. Marie A. Johnson, Sept. 11, 1986. BA, Cornell U., 1951; LLB, Columbia U., 1957. Bar: N.Y. 1957, U.S. Tax Ct. 1958, U.S. Ct. Claims 1961, U.S. Ct. Appeals (2d cir.) 1974, U.S. Ct. Appeals (8th cir.) 1974, U.S. Dist. Ct. (so. and ea. dists.) N.Y. 1975, U.S. Supreme Ct. 1975. Assoc. Sullivan & Cromwell, N.Y.C., 1957-64, ptnr., 1964-96, sr. counsel, 1997—. Trustee Hamilton Coll., 1978-88, Mus. of Broadcasting, 1975-80; trustee, treas. Kirkland Coll., 1969-78; mem. coun. White Burkett Miller Ctr. Pub. Affairs, 1976-82; bd. dirs., pres. Stevens Kingsley Found., 1967—; sec., treas. Dunlevy Milbank Found., 1974—; bd. dirs. Spanel Found., 1978-88, CBS, Inc., 1975-80. Served with USN, 1951-54. Mem. ABA, N.Y. State Bar Assn., Assn. of Bar of City of N.Y., Am. Bar Found., Scarsdale Golf Club, India House, Regency Whist Club, Country Club of the Rockies. Presbyterian. Home: 1049 Park Ave New York NY 10028-1061 Office: Sullivan & Cromwell 125 Broad St Fl 32 New York NY 10004-2498

OSBORN, FREDERICK HENRY, III, foundation executive; b. Phila., Dec. 31, 1946; s. Frederick Henry Osborn Jr. and Anne de Witt (Pell) O.; m. Anne Hampton de Peyster Todd, July 10, 1971; children: Frederick Henry IV, Elisabeth Van Cortlandt, Graham Livingston. Student in Econs., Princeton U., 1964-66; BA in Bus. Adminstrn., Colby Coll., 1971; postgrad., Nat. Planned Giving Inst., 1987, Philanthropy Tax Inst., 1988. Registered investment advisor. Pres. Call-Us, Inc., Edgartown, Mass., 1969-72; exec. v.p. Hall Labs., Boston, 1972-74; fin. officer Episcopal Diocese Mass., 1972-76; diocesan adminstr. Episcopal Diocese Maine, Portland, 1976-80; dir. adminstrn. Episcopal Diocese Conn., Hartford, 1980-86; dir. of devel. and planned giving Nat. Episcopal Ch., N.Y.C., 1987-94; dir. of devel. programs Episcopal Ch. Found., 1995-97; dir. devel. The Nature Conservancy of N.Y., 1997-99; dir. philanthropic svcs. Episcopal Ch. Found., 1999—. Bd. dirs. Living Music, Inc., Ulysses Co., William O. Benson Co., FAN Trusts, Oslands, Inc., Boscobel Restoration, Inc., Garrison Sta. Plz., Inc., Garrison Landing Assn., Covenant Svcs., Inc.; prin. Cat Rock Counsel, Garrison, N.Y., 1990—. Co-author: Planned Giving for the Episcopal Parish, 1989, Funding Future Ministry, 2000. Bd. dirs. The Giraffe Project, chmn. 1989-93, Alice Desmond & Hamilton Fish Libr.; chmn. bd. dirs. Hudson Highlands Land Trust; v.-chair., bd. dirs. Scenic Hudson, Berkeley Divinity Sch. Yale U., Nature Conservancy (lower Hudson chpt. chair 1994-97); trustee Tabor Acad., 1993-99, Cathedral Ch. St. John the Divine, chair Hudson Highlands Music Festival, 1994-96, 99-2001, St. Francis Found., The Constn. Island Assn. With U.S. Army, 1966-68, Vietnam. Mem. Nat. Soc. Fund Raising Execs., Nat. Planned Giving Assn., Nat. Environ. Le adership Coun., Planned Giving Group Greater N.Y., Social Investment Forum, Coun. Econ. Priorities, Social Venture Network, Century Assn., Constitution Is. Assn., St. Andrews Soc. of N.Y., Highlands Country Club, N.Y. Yacht Club, Portland Yacht Club, Dauntless Club, Garrison Yacht Club, Princeton Club (N.Y.), Internat. Platform Assn., Yale club (N.Y.). Avocations: sailing, music, photography. Home: PO Box 347 Garrison NY 10524-0347 Office: The Episcopal Ch Found 815 2nd Ave New York NY 10017-4563

OSBORN, GERALD GUY, psychiatrist, educator, consultant; b. Cin., Nov. 6, 1947; s. Guy Henry and Doris Irene (Taylor) O.; m. Sue Ellen Granger, July 9, 1983; children— Erica Tyrell, Eric Gerald, Ellen Stephanie. B.A., Wilmington Coll., 1969; student Schiller U., Klein-Ingersheim, Germany, 1968-69; D.O., Kirksville Coll. Osteo. Medicine, 1973; postgrad. in psychiatry U. Sheffield (Eng.), 1973; M in Philosphy Cambridge U., 1986. Diplomate Am. Osteo. Bd. Neurology and Psychiatry (bd. examiners 1982), Am. Bd. Psychiatry and Neurology. Rotating intern Lansing (Mich.) Gen. Hosp., 1973-74; resident, postdoctoral fellow dept. psychiatry Mich. State U., East Lansing, 1974-77, chief resident in psychiatry, 1976-77, instr. in psychiatry, 1974-77, asst. prof., 1977-82, assoc. prof., 1982— , dir. residency tng. osteo. div., 1979-81, assoc. dean for acad. affairs Coll. Osteo. Medicine, 1981-83; chmn. dept. psychiatry St. Lawrence Hosp., Lansing, 1986—; assoc. adj. prof. dept. history Mich. State U., 1986—; cons. in field; psychiat. reviewer Mich. Dept. Social Services; chmn. Lansing Area Psychiatry Council, 1983. Med. dir. Catholic Social Services and Family and Child Services of Lansing; active Physicians for Social Responsibility, East Lansing. Recipient Med. Writing award Mich. Osteo. Coll. Found., 1976; teaching awards Mich. State U., 1979, 80, 82, Prof. of Yr. award, 1981; Kettering scholar, 1968. Mem. Am. Osteo. Assn. Mich. Assn. Osteo. Physicians and Surgeons, Ingham County Osteo. Soc., Am. Psychiat. Assn., Mich. Psychiat. Soc., Am. Coll. Neuropsychiatrists (sr.; bd. govs. 1982—, pres.-elect 1986—), Mich. Osteo. Neuropsychiat. Soc., Osteo. Physicians and Surgeons Calif. (assoc.), Am. Assn. Dirs. Psychiat.

Residency Tng., Aircraft Owners and Pilots Assn., U.S. Internat. Sailing Assn., Sigma Sigma Phi. Democrat. Quaker. Contbr. articles to profl. publs. Office: Kirksville Coll of Osteopathic Med Office of Dean 800 West Jefferson St. Kirksville MO 63501*

OSBORN, JAMES HENSHAW, operations research analyst; b. Carbondale, Pa., May 22, 1941; s. Daniel Cargill Jr. and Marguerite Isabel (Henshaw) O.; m. Mary Inez Tompkins, Nov. 26, 1966; children: Kevin Daniel, James Clifton. BA, Northeastern U., 1964; MA, U. Rochester, 1966; PhD, U. Wis., 1972. Computer programmer Sylvania Applied Rsch. Lab., Waltham, Mass., 1962-64, sr. engr., 1966-67; vis. asst. prof. Wright State U., Dayton, Ohio, 1972-73; systems analyst Computer Scis. Corp., Moorestown, N.J., 1973-75; ops. rsch. analyst Hdqs. Tactical Air Command, Langley AFB, Va., 1975-90, dir. ops. analysis, 1990-91; chief scientific analyst Air Combat Command, Joint Studies Group, 1991-92, analyst ops. rsch., 1992—. Lectr. George Washington U., Hampton, Va., 1977-79, Golden Gate U., Langley AFB, Va., 1982-87; mem. Air Force Chief Scientists Group, Washington, 1990-92. Treas. York River Community Orch., Yorktown, Va., 1989-90. Mem. Math. Assn. of Am., Ops. Rsch. Soc. of Am. Episcopalian. Home: 404 Old Dominion Rd Yorktown VA 23692-4733 Office: Studies and Analyses Squadron HQ ACC/XP-SAS Langley AFB VA 23665-2778

OSBORN, JOHN DAVID, credit union executive; b. Indpls., Feb. 29, 1948; s. John Isaac and Belva M. (Grubb) O.; m. Wanda Sue Hall, June 22, 1974; children: John David II, Heather Marie, James Michael. BBA, U. Ga., 1971. Office mgr. United Empire Life Ins. Co., Indpls., 1971-73, adminstrv. v.p., 1973-76; mgr. data and devel. Ind. Telco Fed. Credit Union, 1976-82; pres. Fin. Ctr. Fed. Credit Union, 1982-92, Anheuser-Busch Employees Credit Union, St. Louis, 1992—. Treas., past chmn. Mo. Corp. Credit Union, St. Louis; past bd. dirs., past vice chmn. Ind. Corp. Credit Union, Indpls., Fin. Ctr. Svc. Corp., Indpls.; past chmn. Def. Credit Union Coun., Washington; past bd. dirs. Teeter Found., Noblesville, Ind.; bd. dirs. Co-op Network. Pres. Wellington North Civic Assn., Noblesville, Ind., 1985-86. Mem. Credit Union Execs. Soc., Nat. Exch. Club (pres. Lawrence 1985). Republican. Methodist. Avocations: basketball, golf. Office: Anheuser Busch Employees Credit Union 1001 Lynch St Saint Louis MO 63118-1818

OSBORN, JOHN EDWARD, lawyer, pharmaceutical and biotechnology industry executive, former government official, writer; b. Davenport, Iowa, Sept. 4, 1957; s. Edward Richard and Patricia Anne (O'Donovan) O.; m. Deborah Lynn Powell, Aug. 11, 1984; children: Delaney Powell, Keeley Rush. Student, Coll. William and Mary, 1975-76; BA, U. Iowa, 1979; cert., Georgetown U., 1980; JD, U. Va., 1983; cert., Wadham Coll., Oxford U., 1987; M Internat. Pub. Policy, Johns Hopkins U., 1992; cert., Wharton Sch., U. Pa., 1994-95; postgrad., Princeton U., 1997-99. Bar: Mass. 1985, U.S. Supreme Ct. 2001. Law clk. to Hon. Albert V. Bryan U.S. Ct. Appeals (4th cir.), Alexandria, Va., 1983-84; assoc. Hale and Dorr, Boston, 1984-88, Dechert Price & Rhoads, Phila., 1988-89; spl. asst. to legal adviser U.S. Dept. State, Washington, 1989-92; sr. counsel DuPont Merck Pharm. Co., Wilmington, Del., 1992-94, assoc. gen. counsel, 1994-96, v.p., assoc. gen. counsel, asst. sec., 1996—97; v.p. legal affairs Cephalon, Inc., West Chester, Pa., 1997—98, sr. v.p., gen. counsel, sec., 1998—. Vis. lectr. U. Mich. Bus. Sch., 1997—; vis. scholar East European studies Woodrow Wilson Internat. Ctr. for Scholars, Washington, 1991; vis. fellow dept. politics Bobst Ctr. Princeton U., 2002—. Contbr. articles to profl. jours. and newspapers; articles editor Va. Jour. Internat. Law, 1982—83. Bd. advisors U. Pa. Inst. Law and Econs., Phila., 1999—; mem. Friends of Child Devel. Ctr., Georgetown U. Med. Ctr., Washington, 1999—, Johns Hopkins U. Alumni Coun., Balt., 1997—, U. Va. Law Sch. Bus. Adv. Coun., Charlottesville, 1996—, U. Iowa Liberal Arts Dean's Adv. Bd., Iowa City, 1999—; trustee Tower Hill Sch., Wilmington, Del., 1997—, Del. Art Mus., 1999—, asst. sec., 2001—; mem. Del. Rep. State Com., 1995—99; del. Rep. Nat. Conv., 1996; rsch. aide, speechwriter George Bush for Pres. Com., 1979—80, 1987—88; bd. dirs. Del. Ctr. for the Contemporary Arts, 1994—, v.p., 1997—99; bd. dirs. Am. Civil Liberties Found. Del., 1995—98, adv. bd., 1998—; bd. dirs. World Affairs Coun. of Wilmington, 2001—. Recipient study grant, Andrew W. Mellon Found., 1999; fellow Eisenhower fellow, Ireland, 1998. Mem. Atlantic Coun. of the U.S., Coun. Fgn. Rels., Greenville Country Club, Capitol Hill Club, Princeton Club N.Y., Fieldstone Golf Club, Met. Club Washington, Mortar Bd., Phi Beta Kappa, Phi Delta Phi, Omicron Delta Kappa, Omicron Delta Epsilon. Republican. Roman Catholic. Home: 5 Doe's Lane Way Ridge Wilmington DE 19807-1548 Office: 145 Brandywine Pkwy West Chester PA 19380-4245 E-mail: josborn@cephalon.com.

OSBORN, JOHN SIMCOE, JR. lawyer; b. Louisville, Jan. 14, 1926; s. John S. and Ruby (Pinnell) O.; m. Mary Jo Fishback, Sept. 6, 1947; children—Robert, John, Donna LLB, U. Louisville, 1949. Bar: Ky. 1949, U.S. Dist. Ut. (ea. and we. dists.) Ky. 1952. Exec. v.p., gen. counsel Louisville Title Ins. Co., 1954-72; ptnr. Tarrant Combs & Bullitt (name changed to Wyatt Tarrant & Combs 1980), Louisville, 1972—. Chmn. bd. Beargrass Corp. Capt. JAGC, U.S. Army, 1952-54. Fellow Am. Bar Found.; mem. Ky. Bar Assn., Louisville Bar Assn., ABA, Am. Land Title Assn., Am. Coll. Real Estate Lawyers, Rotary. Democrat. Lutheran. Office: Wyatt Tarrant & Combs 2800 Citizens Plz Louisville KY 40202

OSBORN, JUNE ELAINE, pediatrician, microbiologist, educator, foundation administrator; b. Endicott, N.Y., May 28, 1937; d. Leslie A. and Dora W. (Wright) Osborn; children: Philip I. Levy, Ellen D. Levy, Laura A. Jana. BA, Oberlin (Ohio) Coll., 1957; MD, Western Res. U., 1961; DSc (hon.) , U. Med. Dental Sch. N.J., 1990; DMS (hon.) , Yale U., 1992; DSc (hon.) , Emory U., 1993, Oberlin Coll., 1993; LHD (hon.) , Med. Coll. Pa., 1994; DSc (hon.) , Rutgers U., 1994, Case Western Res. U., 1997, SUNY, Stony Brook, 1999. Intern, resident in pediatrics Harvard U. Hosp., 1961—64; fellow Johns Hopkins, 1964—65, U. Pitts., 1965—66; prof. med. microbiology and pediat. U. Wis. Med. Sch., Madison, Wis., 1966—84, prof. pediat. and microbiology, 1974—84, assoc. dean Grad. Sch., 1975—84; dean Sch. Pub. Health U. Mich. Sch. Pub. Health, 1984—93; prof. epidemiology, pediat. and communicable diseases U. Mich. Sch. Pub. Health and Med. Sch., 1984—96, prof. emeritus, 1997—. Pres. Josiah Macy, Jr. Found., 1997—; mem. rev. panel viral vaccine efficacy FDA, 1973—79, mem. vaccines and related biol. products adv. com., 1981—85; mem. exptl. virology study sect. Divsn. Rsch. Grants, NIH, 1975—79; mem. med. affairs com. Yale U. Coun., 1981—86; chmn. life scis. associateships rev. panel NRC, 1981—84; mem. U.S. Army Med. R&D Adv. Com., 1983—85; chmn. working group on AIDS and the Nation's Blood Supply NHLBI, 1984—89; chmn. WHO Planning Group on AIDS and the Internat. Blood Supply, 1985—86. Contbr. articles to profl. jours. Active task force in AIDS, Inst. of Medicine, 1986; mem. adv. com. Robert Wood Johnson Found. AIDS Health Svcs. Program, 1986—91; mem. nat. adv. com. on health of pub. program Pew and Rockefeller Founds.; mem. health promotion and disease prevention bd. Inst. Medicine, 1987—90; mem. Global Commn. on AIDS, WHO, 1988—92; chmn. Nat. Commn. on AIDS, 1989—93; trustee Kaiser Found., 1990—98, Case Western Reserve U., Cleve., 1993—97; mem. coun. Inst. Medicine, 1995—2000; mem. Nat. Vaccine Adv. Cte., HHS, 1995—98; mem. adv. coun. Nat. Inst. on Drug Abuse, 1995—98; Legal Action Ctr., 1994—2001; Ctr. for Health Care Strategies, 1998—. Recipient NIG Pub. Svc. award, 2000, Scientific Freedom and Responsibility award, AAAS, 1994; grantee NIH, 1969, 1972, 1974—75, Nat. Multiple Sclerosis Soc., 1971. Fellow: Infectious Diseases Soc. Am., Am. Acad. Microbiology, Am. Acad. Arts and Scis., Am. Acad. Pediat.; mem.: Inst. Medicine, Soc. Pediat. Rsch., Am. Assn. Immunologists. Office: Josiah Macy Jr Found 44 E 64th St New York NY 10021-7306

OSBORN, KENNETH LOUIS, financial executive; b. Belleville, Ill., Jan. 9, 1946; s. William Arthur and Louise Mary (Brueggemann) O.; BBA, U. N.Mex., 1968; m. Roberta Marie Vodicka, Oct. 23, 1971; 1 son, David Anthony. Auditor, Ernst & Ernst, Albuquerque, 1968; budge mgr. Rockwell Internat., Chgo., 1970-74; mgr. internat. acctg. Allied Van Lines, Chgo., 1974-76; fin. mgr. Sealy, Inc., Chgo., 1976-79; sr. fin. analyst Newark Electronics, Chgo., 1979-80, internat. dir. credit, 1980-82; bus. mgr. Prime Computer, 1982-90; acctg. mgr., CFO Flexonics, Inc., Chgo., 1990-96; contr. and chief fin. ofcr. Jackson Industries, Chgo., 1996—; fin. cons. Am. European Expres. Mem. Rep. Nat. Com., presdl. task force. With AUS, 1968-70. Decorated Air medal. Mem. Mensa, Soc. Am. Baseball Rsch., Inst. Mgmt. Accts.

OSBORN, LA DONNA CAROL, clergywoman; b. Portland, Oreg., Mar. 13, 1947; d. T.L. and Daisy (Washburn) O.; m. Cory A. Nickerson, Dec. 11, 1981; children: Tommy O'Dell, LaVona Thomas, Daneesa Dolan, Donald O'Dell. Student, Assemblies of God Coll., 1963; BA, Okla. City U., 1994; DD, Bethel Coll., 1995; Doctor of Humane Letters (hon.), Wesley Synod, 1998; MA, Oral Roberts U., 2000; D in Ministry, Am. Christian Coll. and Sem., 2001; DD, Zoe Univ., 2001. Fgn. mission corr., purchaser, personnel agt. Osborn Found., Tulsa, 1969-75, exec. asst., 1975-76, internat. gen. mgr., 1976-81, internat. editor-in-chief, 1981-86, corp. pres., 1986-93; assoc. pastor Internat. Gospel Ctr., 1986-89, sr. pastor, 1989-94, sr. pastor, overseer, 1994-97; bishop Internat. Gospel Ctr. (IGC) Chs., Okla., 1997—; mem. Coll. of Bishops Internat. Communion of Charismatic Chs., 1998—; v.p., CEO OSFO Internat., 1998—. Internat. minister, religious tchr., and motivational spkr. Nigeria, Kenya, Uganda, Colombia, Papua New Guinea, France, Russia, Belarus, Kazakhstan, Kyrgyzstan, Ukraine, Russia, Sweden, Eng., Holland, Can., India, Zambia, Guatemala, Ecuador, China, U.S.; internat. spiritual advisor Christian Women's Fellowship Internat. Nigeria; founder Internat. Gospel Ctr. Ch. and Ministries, Believers' Network Internat., Internat. Gospel Ctr. Fellowship of Chs. and Ministries, Women's Internat. Network. Author: (book) Jesus & Women, 2000, God's Big Picture, 2001; author, editor Bible tng. courses. Republican. Avocations: Jewish Biblical history, interracial issues, Biblical equality, women's issues. Home: 3111 E 89th St Tulsa OK 74137-3362 E-mail: revldo@aol.com.

OSBORN, MALCOLM EVERETT, lawyer; b. Bangor, Maine, Apr. 29, 1928; s. Lester Everett and Helen (Clark) O.; m. Claire Anne Franks, Aug. 30, 1953; children: Beverly, Lester, Malcolm, Ernest. BA, U. Maine, 1952; postgrad., Harvard U., 1952-54; JD, Boston U., 1956, LLM, 1961. Bar: Maine 1956, Mass. 1956, U.S. Dist. Ct. Mass. 1961, U.S. Tax Ct. 1961, U.S. Claims Ct. 1961, N.C. 1965, U.S. Supreme Ct. 1979, U.S. Ct. Appeals (4th cir.) 1980, Va. 1991. Tax counsel State Mut. Life Assurance Co., Worcester, Mass., 1956-64; v.p., gen. tax counsel Integon Corp. and other group cos., Winston-Salem, N.C., 1964-81; ptnr. House, Blanco & Osborn, P.A., 1981-88; v.p., gen. counsel, dir. Settlers Life Ins. Co., Bristol, Va., 1984-89; prin. Malcolm E. Osborn, P.A., Winston-Salem, 1988—. Lectr. The Booke Seminars, Life Ins. Co., 1985-87; adj. prof. Wake Forest U. Sch. Law, Winston-Salem, 1974-82; Disting. guest lectr. Ga. State U., 1965; guest lectr. NYU Ann. Inst. Fed. Taxation, 1966, 68, 75, 80. Com. editor The Tax Lawyer, ABA, 1974-76; author numerous articles in field. Trustee N.C. Coun. Econ. Edn., 1968-76; bd. dirs. Christian Fellowship Home, 1972-80; co-founder Bereaved Parents Group Winston-Salem, 1978—. Mem. ABA (chmn. com. ins. cos. of taxation sect. 1980-82, chmn. subcom. on continuing legal edn. and publs. 1982-88), Am. Bus. Law Assn. (mem. com. fed. taxation 1968—, chmn. 1972-75), Assn. Life Ins. Counsel (com. on co. tax, tax sect. 1965—), N.C. Bar Assn. (com. taxation 1973—), Fed. Bar Assn. (taxation com. 1973—), Maine State Bar Assn., Va. State Bar Assn., Internat. Bar Assn. (com. on taxes of bus. law sect. 1973—), AAUP, Southeastern Acad. Legal Studies in Bus., Masons (Lincoln, Maine). Office: PO Box 5192 Winston Salem NC 27113-5192

OSBORN, MARK ELIOT, dentist; b. Buffalo, Apr. 22, 1950; s. Thomas Earl and Ruth Frances (Martin) O. BA, U. Mo., Columbia, 1972; DDS, U. Mo., Kansas City, 1977. Dir. Westport Free Health Clinic, Kansas City, Mo., 1974-76; clinician St. Louis Dept. Health, 1977-82; gen. practice dentistry Troy, Mo., 1978-92; pvt. practice St. Louis, 1993-94; mem. gen. practice staff Gravois-Gustine Dental Group, 1994-96; pvt. practice gen. dentistry, 1996-97; pvt. practice Chestnut Park Dental, 1997—. Mem. ADA, Greater St. Louis Dental Soc. (bd. dirs. 1999—), Am. Soc. Dentistry for Children, St. Louis Dental Rsch. Group, Delta Sigma Delta, Troy C. of C., Rotary (Troy chpt., dir. dental program 1985—, sec. 1988, pres. 1989, bd. dirs. 1989-91). Home: 360 W Point Ct Saint Louis MO 63130-4028 Office: Chestnut Park Dental 4583 Chestnut Park Plz Ste 201 Saint Louis MO 63129-3163 E-mail: meosborn@swbell.net.

OSBORN, MARVIN GRIFFING, JR. educational consultant; b. Baton Rouge, Sept. 7, 1922; s. Marvin Griffing and Mamie (Hester) O.; m. Sarah Fleming, Aug. 3, 1945; children: Jane Fleming, Charles Porter. BA, La. State U., 1942, MA, 1946; LLD, St. Xavier U., 1971; DHum, Phillips U., 1977. Pub. relations counsel La. State U., 1945-47, acting dir. bur. pub. service, 1947; assoc. prof., chmn. dept. journalism and dir. pub. relations Howard Coll. (now Frank Samford U.), 1947-49; dir. pub. relations, lectr. journalism Miss. State Coll. (now Miss. State U.), 1949-53; dir. information Washington U., 1953-58, pub. relations adviser, 1955-58, dir. Devel. Funds, 1958-61; cons. coll. and univ. adminstrn., 1961—, including Drake, Duke, Phillips, Tampa, Tex. Christian univs., Atlantic Christian Coll. (now Barton Coll.), Bethany (W.Va.), Eckerd, Loretto Heights, St. Xavier U., Tenn. Wesleyan, Webster U., Hendrix, Mercy (Detroit), Bethel (Tenn.), McMurry U., St. Scholastica, Coker Coll., Christian Ch. Found., Nat. Meth. Found. Christian Higher Edn., Lexington Theol. Sem., Memphis Theol. Sem., Nat. Benevolent Assn. Christian Ch., Sisters of Loretto. Interim pres. St. Xavier Coll., now St. Xavier U., 1968-69; mem. planning com. Conf. for Advancement Understanding and Support Higher Edn., White Sulphur Springs, W.Va., 1958; mem. exec. com. program and arrangements com. Gen. Assembly Christian Ch., 1977, 87-89. Bd. dirs. St. Louis Heart Assn., 1969-75, Fla. Christian Ctr., 1986-88; trustee Nat. City Christian Ch. Corp., 1981-85; mem. Christian Ch., bd. dirs., exec. com., sec. divsn. of higher edn., 1973-77, mem. panel to study fin. procedures of Christian Ch. (Disciples of Christ), 1987-89, Cypress Village Devel. Coun., Jacksonville, Fla., 1992-98, co-chair, 1992-98. Served from lt. to capt. 28th Inf. Divsn. AUS, 1942-45, ETO. Recipient Harry T. Ice disting. svc. award Christian Ch. Found., 1991. Mem. Am. Coll. Pub. Rels. Assn. (v.p. dists. 1951-52, v.p. membership 1952-53, sec.-treas. 1953-55, pres. 1959-60), Nat. Benevolent Assn. (amb. 1992—), Soc. Profl. Journalists, Omicron Delta Kappa, Sigma Chi. Home: 13655 Myrica Ct Jacksonville FL 32224-6626

OSBORN, MARY JANE MERTEN, biochemist, educator; b. Colorado Springs, Colo., Sept. 24, 1927; d. Arthur John and Vivien Naomi (Morgan) Merten; m. Ralph Kenneth Osborn, Oct. 26, 1950. BA, U. Calif., Berkeley, 1948; PhD, U. Wash., 1958. Postdoctoral fellow, dept. microbiology NYU Sch. Medicine, N.Y.C., 1959-61, instr., 1961-62, asst. prof., 1962-63; asst. prof. dept. molecular biology Albert Einstein Coll. Medicine, Bronx, N.Y., 1963-66, asso. prof., 1966-68; prof. dept. microbiology U. Conn. Health Ctr., Farmington, 1968—, dept. head, 1980—2002. Mem. bd. sci. counselors Nat. Heart, Lung and Blood Inst., 1975-79; mem. Nat. Sci. Bd., 1980-86; adv. coun. Nat. Inst. Gen. Med. Sci., 1983-86, divsn. rsch. grants NIH, 1989-94, chair, 1992-94; trustee Biosci. Info. Systems, 1986-91, chair, 1990-91; mem. German Am. Acad. Coun., 1994-97; mem. space scis. bd. NRC, 1994-2000, chair com. space biology and medicine, 1994-2000. Assoc. editor Jour. Biol. Chemistry, 1978-80; contbr. articles in field of biochemistry and molecular biology to profl. jours. Mem. rsch. com. Am. Heart Assn., 1972-77, chair, 1976-77. NIH fellow, 1959-61; NIH grantee, 1962-95 ; NSF grantee, 1965-68; Am. Heart Assn. grantee, 1968-71 Fellow Am. Acad. Arts and Scis. (coun. 1988-91), NAS (coun. 1990-93, com. sci. engring. and pub. policy 1993-96); mem. Am. Acad. Microbiology (bd. govs. 1994-2000), Am. Fedn. Soc. Exptl. Biology (pres. 1982-83), Am. Soc. Biol. Chemists (pres. 1981-82), Am. Soc. Microbiology. Democrat. Office: U Conn Health Ctr Dept Microbiology Ctr Farmington CT 06030-0001

OSBORN, PATRICIA ANN, writer, teacher; b. Dayton, Ohio, Jan. 15, 1931; d. Harold Joseph and Vera (Houck) O. BA in Ednl. Journalism, Bowling Green State U., 1952. Newspaper reporter Marion (Ohio) Star, 1952-54; advt. copywriter Lasalle's (Macy's) Dept. Stores, Toledo, 1954-62; tchr. English, journalism advisor, chmn. English City of Toledo Bd. Edn., 1962-92. Author: How Grammar Works, 1989, 2d edit., 1999, Finding America, 1995, Reading Smarter, 1995, Poetry by Doing, 1992, School Newspaper Advisers Survival Guide, 1998. Organizer, dir. TJS Claude Black Nature of Jazz Project, Toledo, 1999—. Mem. Nat. Coun. Tchrs. English, Toledo Jazz Soc. (newsletter editor, bd. dirs.), English Speaking Union (publicity chmn.) Glass Club of Toledo (publicity chmn. 1999—). Avocations: visiting and exploring Mexico City graphic design, trvel, photography, jazz. E-mail: elpatoo@aol.com.

OSBORN, RALPH J. retired electrical engineer; b. Pawhuska, Okla., Oct. 26, 1923; s. Ray J. and Lena (Tebo) O.; m. Ruth Rains, Nov. 6, 1943; children: Marsha Hayes, Ronald J. BSEE, Kans. State U., 1948. Registered profl. engr., Kans. Engr. Arco Pipeline, Independence, Kans., 1948-73, supervisor elec. engring. divsn., 1973-74, project mgr. Bayport/Olefins Houston, 1974-85, mid-continent regional mgr. Independence, 1976-85. Bd. dirs. Independence Pub. Schs., 1956-60, 62-64, Independence C.C., 1972-74, 94-98, Independence Pub. Libr., 1988-98. Ensign USN, 1943-46. Mem. IEEE (pipeline subcom. 1954-75), Am. Petroleum Inst. (pipeline automation com. 1960-76). Disciples of christ. Avocations: photography, computers, travel. Home: 419 S 4th St Independence KS 67301-3938

OSBORN, SUSAN CHANEY, educator, writer; b. Ft. Campbell, Ky., Jan. 7, 1953; d. Lawrence Elvie and Wilma Barbara (Powell) Howard; m. Nicholas Lourick, Aug. 1, 1976 (div. Oct. 1981); m. Steve Osborn, Mar. 20, 1993; 1 child. BS, Ga. State U., 1989; MS, U. Colo., 1997. Lic. tchr., Colo, pvt. occupational tchr., Colo. Owner, photographer Creative Assistance, Atlanta, 1979-89; educator St. Mary's Acad., Cherry Hills Village, Colo., 1989-90, Denver Pub. Schs., 1990-92; internet resource coord. Nat. Renewable Energy Lab., Golden, Colo., 1993-95; writer Diners Club Internat., Englewood, 1995-96; owner, writer, coord. Publs. Resolution, Denver, 1996—. Website advisor Colo. Dept. Pub. Health and Environment, Denver, 1998-99; advisor Houghton-Mifflin Co., Boston, 1992; mem. math. text seclection com. Denver Pub. Schs., 1991; cons. Hauser Chem. Co., Boulder, Colo., 1994. Author: Public Service Company Classroom Connection, 1992, photography manual. Art/photography dir. Boy's Club, Marietta, GA., 1987; art show sect. organizer Girl's Club, Atlanta, 1988; implementor Bear Creek Blvd. Civic Assn., Lakewood, Colo., 1995; pub. rels. coord. Resolve Rocky Mountain Assn., Denver, 1996. Fellow Colo. Writing Project; mem. NEA, Golden Key. Avocations: creative writing, creative photography, theatre, hiking, mountain biking. Office: Publs Resolution PO Box 37263 Denver CO 80237

OSBORN, SUSAN RAMEY, piano teacher, pianist; b. Plainfield, N.J., Nov. 6, 1960; d. Douglas Marion and Elizabeth Ann (Bowden) O. BA in Music, Smith Coll., 1982; MusM in Piano Performance, U. N.C., 1986; cert. tchg., New Sch. for Music Study, Princeton, N.J., 1987; MusD in Performance and Pedagogy, Northwestern U., 1995. Instr. Northwestern Music Acad., Evanston, Ill., 1987—; lectr. class piano DePaul U., 1991—2002; class and ensemble piano instr. Interlochen (Mich.) Arts Camp, 1996—; lectr. keyboard skills Northwestern U., Evanston, Ill., 2002—. Harriet Hale Woodley scholar Fondation des Etats Unis, Paris, 1982. Mem. Music Tchrs. Nat. Assn. Avocations: photography, drawing. Office: Northwestern U MAB Rm 401 711 Elgin St Evanston IL 60208

OSBORN, SUSAN TITUS, editor; b. Fresno, Calif., July 11, 1944; d. Clifford Leland Feldt and Jane (Taylor) Cousins; m. Richard G. Titus, Aug. 28, 1965 (div. Dec. 1990); children: Richard David, Michael Craig; m. Richard A. Osborn, Aug. 22, 1992. BA in Religious Studies, Calif. State U., Fullerton, 1988, MA in Comm., 1993. Svc. rep. Mountain Bell Tel., Colorado Springs, Colo., 1965-67; freelance writer Fullerton, Calif., 1978—; assoc. dir. Biola U. Writers Inst., La Mirada, 1986-92; co-dir. Christian Communicators Conf. The Master's Coll., Santa Clarita, 1993-95, adj. prof., 1993-96, Pacific Christian Coll., 1996—. Mem. adv. bd. Christian Writers Fellowship, Huntington Beach, Calif., 1987-93; mem. adv. bd. Christian Communicator, San Juan Capistrano, Calif., 1989-94, mng. editor, 1991-92, editor, 1992-98, contbg. editor, 1998—; pub. cons. Ednl. Ministries, Brea, Calif., 1989- 91; conf. spkr. numerous cities, 1987—; tchr. India Comm. Inst., Bombay; bd. dirs. Moscow Christian Sch. Psychology, 1992-95; mem. adv. bd. Am. Christian Writers, 1996—. Author: Parables for Young Teens, 1986, You Start With One, 1990, Meeting Jesus, 1990, Eyes Beyond the Horizon, 1991, Children Around the World Celebrate Christmas, 1993, The Complete Guide to Christian Writing and Speaking, 1994, Rest Stops for Single Mothers, 1995, Potpourri of Praise, 1997, The Complete Guide to Writing for Publication, 1999, Beanie Baby Stories, 1999, Parables in Action series, 2000, Just Write!, 2000, Heartlifters for Sisters, 2001, Ten Friends Together, 2002. Bd. dirs. Jr. Ebell Club, Fullerton, 1969-75, Youth Sci. Ctr., Fullerton, 1970-75, YMCA Swim Club, Fullerton, 1976-82; pres. Troy Swim Boosters, Fullerton, 1982-88, Moscow Christian Sch. Psychology, 1992-95. Recipient Spl. Recognition award Troy Swim Boosters, 1986. Mem. Presbyn. Writers Guild., Spiritual Overseers Svc. Republican. Evangelical. Avocations: writing, reading, gardening, theatre, beach.

OSBORN, WILLIAM GEORGE, savings and loan executive; b. Alton, Ill., Dec. 9, 1925; s. Ralph A. and Pauline J. (Horn) O.; m. Hilda M. Alexander, Aug. 12, 1950; children: Barbara K., David A., Robert W., James A. BS in Math., Shurtleff Coll., 1947; certificate, Grad. Sch. Savs. and Loan, Ind. U., 1946-48; A.M. in Econs., St. Louis U., 1962. With Germania Fed. Savs. and Loan Assn., Alton, 1946-90, exec. officer, 1955-86, pres., 1964-86, chmn., 1981-86, chmn. trust com., 1982-86; pres. Fin. Service Assocs., Ft. Lauderdale, Fla., 1986—. Pres. Germania Fin. Corp., 1970-86; owner Fin. Guidance, Alton, 1951—; mem. Opportunities Unltd., 1954-58; instr. Am. Savs. and Loan Inst.; bd. dirs. Nat. Coun. Savs. Instns., Washington, 1984-86. Author: Savings and Loan Operating Policies Manual, 1960, Economic Factors Influencing Savings and Loan Interest Rates, 1962. Pres. Alton Wood River Community Chest, 1959; bd. dirs. Piasa Bird coun. Boy Scouts Am., 1961-88, Mississippi Valley Jr. Achievement, Alton Area United Fund, 1961-63; founder, bd. dirs., treas. New Piasa Chautauqua Ch. Assembly, 1982-86; treas. Lewis and Clark Community Coll. Found., 1976-86; bd. dirs., sec. Riverbend Civic Progress, 1984-86. Served to lt. (j.g.) USNR, 1943-46, 50-52. Mem. Nat. Assn. Bus. Economists, Nat. Economists Club, St. Louis Economists Club, Am. Inst. Mgmt. Presbyterian (elder). Clubs: Masons (Alton); Shriners; Lockhaven Country (Alton); Chautauqua (Ill.) Yacht.

OSBORN, WILLIAM PALMER, writer, English language educator; b. Hastings, Mich., Oct. 6, 1946; s. Palmer Osborn and Elizabeth Grose Dubuque; m. Sylvia Ayano Watanabe, Mar. 26, 1991. BA, U. Calif., San Diego, 1981; MFA, Bowling Green State U., 1983; PhD, SUNY, Binghamton, 1986. Prof. English Grand Valley State U., Allendale, Mich., 1988—. Contbr. short fiction to jours. including Carolina Quar., So. Humanities Rev., Miss. Rev., nonfiction to publs. including Chgo. Rev., Manoa, San Francisco Rev. Books. Home: 145 Crestwood NW Grand Rapids MI 49504 Office: Grand Valley State U Allendale MI 49401

OSBORNE, BARTLEY PORTER, JR. aeronautical engineer; b. Akron, Ohio, Sept. 1, 1934; s. Bartley P. and Cordelia Inez (Sims) O.; m. Carol Ann Eubanks, Jan. 15, 1966; children: Roxane Elizabeth, Ashley Hamilton. BSME, Carnegie Mellon U., Pitts., 1956; MS in Aerospace Engring., U. So. Calif., 1962. Sr. stress analyst N. Am. Aviation, Columbus, Ohio, 1956-66; sr. design engr. Lockheed Aircraft, Burbank, Calif., 1966-70, project engr., 1970-74; staff specialist aeronautics and ocean vehicles Office Sec. of Def., Washington, 1974-78; engring. prog. mgr. Lockheed Aircraft, 1978-82, chief adv. design engr., 1982-85, chief engr. ATF, 1985-87, dep. chief adv. design engr., 1987-89; prog. mgr. Lockheed Aero. Sys. Co., Burbank, 1989-90; v.p., engr. Lockheed Aero. Systems Co., Marietta, Ga., 1990-96, v.p. advanced concepts, 1996-97; retired; cons. Aerotec Solutions, 1998—. Chmn. NASA Aeronautics Adv. Com., 1994-97; chmn. Aerospace Coun. SAE, 1997-2001, Quiet Supersonic prgm. planning com., 2001-02; bd. dirs. Aerofon Corp., San Diego; guest lectr. Carnegie Mellon U., 2001. Pres. Chesterfield Mews Homeowners Assn., Fairfax, Va., 1977-78. 1st lt. U.S. Army, 1956-58. Pa. State scholar, 1952; recipient Disting. Pub. Svc. medal U.S. Govt., 1997. Fellow Royal Aero. Soc., AIAA (assoc.); mem. L.A. Violin Cello Soc. Democrat. Avocation: cellist. Home: 405 White Horse Trl Palm Desert CA 92211-8947 Fax: 760-772-6842. E-mail: spdfrk@aol.com.

OSBORNE, BURL, newspaper publisher, editor; b. Jenkins, Ky., June 25, 1937; s. Oliver and Juanita (Smallwood) O.; m. Betty S. Wilder, Feb. 14, 1974; 1 son, Burl Jonathan. Student, U. Ky., 1955-57; BA in Journalism, Marshall U., 1960; MBA, L.I. U. Sch. Bus., 1984; A.M.P., Harvard Bus. Sch., 1984. Reporter Ashland (Ky.) Daily Ind., 1957-58; reporter, editor Sta. WHTN-TV, Huntington, W.Va., 1958-60; corr. AP, Bluefield, 1960-62, statehouse corr. Charleston, 1963-64, corr. Spokane, Wash., 1964-67, news editor Denver, 1967-70, chief of bur. Ky., 1970-72, Ohio, 1972-74, asst. chief of bur. Washington, 1974-76, mng. editor, 1977-80; exec. editor Dallas Morning News, 1980-83, v.p., 1981, sr. v.p., editor, 1983-84, pres., editor, 1985-90, pub., editor, 1991—2001, pub. emeritus, 2001—. Bd. dirs., pres. publ. divsn. Belo Corp.; bd. dirs. AP, chmn. elect, 2001; bd. mem. adv. com. Nieman Found., Harvard U.; mem. journalism adv. com. Knight Found., 1991—97; bd. dirs. Nat. Kidney Found., S.W. Transplant Alliance. Named Newspaper Exec. of Yr., Nat. Press Found., 1992; inducted to Ky. Journalism Hall of Fame, 1994; recipient Disting. Alumnus award Marshall U., 1997, Freedoms Found.

Next Millinium award, 1999. Mem.: Newspaper Assn. Am. (bd. dirs. 1996—), World Assn. Newspapers (bd. dirs., mem. exec. com. 1998—2001), So. Newspaper Pub. Assn. (bd. dirs. 1995—, pres. 2000—01), Tex. Daily Newspaper Assn. (bd. dirs. 1982—92, pres. 1993), Am. Press Inst. (chmn. 1988—93), Am. Soc. Newspaper Editors (bd. dirs. 1982—91, pres. 1990—91), Orgn. Profl. Journalists. Home: 4030 Centenary Dallas TX 75225-7727 Office: Dallas Morning News PO Box 655237 Dallas TX 75265-5237 E-mail: bosborne@belo.com.

OSBORNE, CHRISTINE MEGAN, musician, educator; b. Kingsport, Tenn., May 16, 1960; d. Charles Edward and Columbine (Amici) Osborne; m. Kenneth Allen Engstrom, Aug. 30, 1997; children: Alexander Erik Anders Engstrom, Nicholas Brennan Tristan Engstrom. MusB, performer's cert., Eastman Sch. Music, 1982; MusM, U. So. Calif., L.A., 1985; postgrad., U. Utah, 1993-96. Bassoonist Utah Symphony, Salt Lake City, 1985—. Pvt. music tchr., Salt Lake City, 1985—; chamber music performer NOVA chamber music series, 1987—; prin. bassoon Utah Chamber Artists, 1994-99, Sun Valley Summer Symphony, 1987-89, 92-98; adj. asst. prof. bassoon U. Utah, Salt Lake City, 1992-99. Author (op-ed pieces) Salt Lake Tribune, 1989, Deseret News; contbr. articles to profl. jours. Pub. lands chair, pub lands activist Utah Chpt. Sierra Club, Salt Lake City, 1988—; voting dist. chair, del. Dem. Party Utah, Salt Lake City, 1992-96; mem. Salt Lake County Dem. Ctrl. Com., 1992-96. Recipient Concerto Competition winner, Music Acad. of the West, Santa Barbara, Calif., 1980, chamber music competition winner, Coleman Nat. Chamber Music Competition, Pasadena, Calif., 1983, hon. mention Dalmas Nelson Best MPA Paper award, 1994. Mem. Am. Fedn. Musicians (shop steward 1993-98, bd. dirs. local 104 1994, media spokesperson 1994—), Utah Symphony Musicians (negotiating com. 1999, 2000, chmn. musicians ad hoc com. 2002, chmn. musicians transition team 2002), Am. Soc. for Pub. Adminstrn., Utah Progressive Network (trustee 1995-98), Utah Wilderness Coalition (bd. dirs. 1995-98), Sierra Club (Utah chpt. exec. com. 1992-93). Office: Utah Symphony 123 W South Temple Salt Lake City UT 84101-1496

OSBORNE, CLAUDINA ROSETTA, financial analyst; b. Montserrat, Mar. 19, 1965; d. Joseph William and Mary Edith Osborne; 1 child, Bryan A. M. BS, Herbert H. Lehman Coll., 1994; M in Pub. Adminstrn. and Fin., L.I. U., 2000. Fin. analyst AIG, N.Y.C., 1998—2001; sr. fin. analyst Primerica Fin. Svcs., 1999-2000; ops. analyst Morgan Stanley Dean Witter, 2000—. Mem. MPA task force L.I. U., 1998-2000. Mem. Caribbean Women Orgn., Bronx, 1995-97; leader Boy Scouts of Am., 1995-97. Recipient Hiroshima Japanese scholarhip award Herbert Lehman Coll., 1993. Mem. NAFE, Am. Soc. for Pub. Adminstrn., N.Y. Women Agenda, Sigma Beta Delta. Episcopalian. Avocations: traveling, reading, meeting people, tennis. Home: 2435 Boston Rd Bronx NY 10467 E-mail: dinaosborne@aol.com.

OSBORNE, DUNCAN ELLIOTT, lawyer; b. Orange, N.J., May 24, 1944; s. Walter Dodd Osborne and Anne (Boaz) Treanor; m. Elizabeth May Bachman, Dec. 29, 1965; children: Ellen Osborne Ray, Mark Elliott, Michael Cleveland. BA, Stanford U., 1966; MA, U. Tex., 1968, JD with honors, 1971. Bar: Tex. (cert. estate planning and probate law) 1971, U.S. Supreme Ct. 1975, U.S. Tax Ct. 1975, U.S. Fed. Ct. Claims 1997. Atty. Graves Dougherty, Austin, Tex., 1971-93, Osborne, Lowe, Helman & Smith L.L.P., Austin, 1993-2000, Osborne & Helman L.L.P., Austin, 2001—. Bd. dirs. Boatmen's Nat. Bank Austin, 1995-97, Hill Country Bank, Austin, 1998. Author, editor: Asset Protection: Domestic and International Law and Tactics; contbr. articles to profl. jours.; mem. Tex. Law Rev. Trustee Susan Vaughan Found., Houston, Still Water Found., Austin; chair bd. trustees St. Stephens Episcopal Sch., Austin, 1985-91, St. Andrews Episcopal Sch., Austin, 1978. Fellow Am. Coll. Trust and Estate Counsel, Coll. of State Bar of Tex.; mem. ABA, Internat. Tax Planning Assn., Offshore Inst., Internat. Acad. Estate and Trust Law (exec. com.), Asset Protection Planning Commn. (chair 1996-98)), Order of Coif. Avocation: scuba diving. Office: Osborne & Helman LLP 301 Congress Ave Ste 1910 Austin TX 78701-2959 E-mail: deosborne@osbornehelman.com.

OSBORNE, FRANK R. lawyer, educator, lecturer; b. Cleve., Dec. 7, 1946; s. Thomas L. and Doris E. O.; m. Charlotte A. Caston, July 8, 1972; children: James, Thomas, Patricia, Janet, Karen, Kathleen, Linda, Jennifer. AB in Polit. Sci., John Carroll U., 1969; JD, Cleve. State U., 1973. Bar: Ohio 1973, U.S. Dist. Ct. (no. dist.) 1975, U.S. Supreme Ct. 1979, U.S. Ct. Appeals (6th cir.) 1979, U.S. Tax Ct. 1980, U.S. Ct. Appeals (7th cir.) 1982. Law clk. to Hon. John V. Corrigan Ohio Ct. Appeals (8th appellate dist.), Cleve., 1973-76; atty. Roudebush, Brown & Ulrich, LPA, 1976-86, Arter & Hadden, LLP, Cleve., 1986—. Adj. prof. law Ohio civil procedure Cleve. Marshall Coll. Law, Cleve. State U., 1994—; alternative dispute resolution neutral U.S. Dist. Ct. (no. dist.), Cleve., 1990—. Co-author: Civil Discovery Practice in Ohio, 1995. Mem. Ohio State Bar Assn., Cleve. Bar Assn. Home: 1278 Croyden Rd Lyndhurst OH 44124-1413 Office: Arter & Hadden LLP 1100 Huntington Bldg Cleveland OH 44115 Fax: 216-696-2645. E-mail: fosborne@arterhadden.com.

OSBORNE, FREDERICK SPRING, JR. academic administrator, artist; b. Phila., Sept. 10, 1940; s. Frederick Spring and Katherine (Mitchell) O.; m. Deborah H. Cooper, June 30, 1964 (div. June 1979); children: Thomas, Sophia, Jessica; m. Judith K. M. Barbour, Feb. 15, 1986. BFA in Sculpture, Temple U., 1963; MFA in Sculpture, Yale U., 1965. From instr. to asst. prof. Grad. Sch. Fine Arts U. Pa., Phila., 1966-77; dir. continuing edn. Phila. Coll. Art, 1977-85; co-founder, dir., trustee Vt. Studio Ctr., Johnson, 1983—; dean, dir. Pa. Acad. Fine Arts, Phila., 1985-99, v.p. for external and alumni affairs, 1999—; dir. Violette deMazia Trust edn. program Barnes Found., 1998—. Lectr. Smith Coll., 1966, Phila. Coll. Art, 1976-85, U. Maine, 1980; cons. Inst. Internat. Edn., N.Y.C., 1984, Jury for Korean War Vet. Meml., Washington, 1989. Exhibited in group shows, including Cheltenham Art Ctr., Woodmere Gallery, 1962, Pa. Acad. Fine Arts, Mackler Gallery, 1963, Smith Coll., 1966, Haverford Coll., 1970, Mus. Phila. Convention Ctr., 1974, Gallery 1st Fed. Bank, 1982. Trustee Mantua-Powelton Edn. Fund, 1978-81, Assn. Ind. Coll. Art & Design, 1991-95, Grass Roots Art and Comm. Effort, 1990—, Choral Arts Soc. Phila., 1997-98; mem. Phila. Redevel. Authority Fine Arts Com., 93-99; co-chmn. Internat. Sculpture Conf., Phila., 1991. Mem. Nat. Assn. Sch. Art and Design (bd. dirs. 1989-96), Coll. Art. Assn., Nat. Art Edn. Assn. Home: 3621 Hamilton St Philadelphia PA 19104-2327 Office: Pa Acad Fine Arts 118 N Broad St Philadelphia PA 19102-1598 E-mail: fojo@bellatlantic.net.

OSBORNE, GAYLA MARLENE, sales executive; b. Owenton, Ky., Aug. 9, 1956; d. Frederick Clay and Helen Beatrice (Mason) O. AAS, No. Ky. U., 1982, BS, 1986; cert. in Chinese Mandarin, Def. Lang. Inst., 1975. Pers. clk. Dept. Edn. State Ky., Frankfort, 1974; sec. Dept. Health, Edn., Welfare Nat. Inst. Occupational Safety Health, Cin., 1977-79; specialist sales promotion U.S. Postal Svc., 1980, coord. customer liaison, task force pub. image, account rep., 1986-87, with stamp distbn. task force, 1993—; reservation sale agt. Delta Airlines, 1987-89. Councilmember Florence City Coun., Ky. 1984-87; vol. Children's Home, Covington, 1982, 87. With USAF, 1974-76. Named to Hon. Order Ky. Cols. Mem. Disabled Am. Veterans, No. Ky. U. Alumni Assn., Nat. Assn. Postmasters U.S., Boone County Fraternal Order Police, Ky. Assn. Realtors, Nat. Bd. Realtors, Women in Mil. Svc. for Am. (charter). Clubs: Fraternal Order Police. Democrat. Baptist. Avocations: horseback riding, travel, organizing seminars. Home: 8395 Juniper Ln Florence KY 41042-9279

OSBORNE, GLENNA JEAN, social and health services administrator; b. East Rainelle, W.Va., Jan. 5, 1945; d. B.J. and Jean Ann (Haranac) Osborne; m. Thomas Joseph Ferrante Jr., June 11, 1966 (div. Nov. 1987); 1 child, Thomas Joseph Osborne; m. Brian Mark Popp, Aug. 13, 1988 (div. Oct. 1999). BA cum laude, U. Tampa, 1966; MA, Fairleigh Dickinson U., 1982; cert., Kean Coll., 1983. Cert. English, speech, dramatic arts tchr., prin./supr.; cert. nursing child assessment feeding scale and nursing child assessment tchg. scale, DENVER II cert., HOME cert. Tchr. Raritan H.S., Hazlet, N.J., 1966, Keyport (N.J.) Pub. Schs., 1968-86, coord. elem. reading and lang. arts, 1980-84, supr. curriculum and instrn., 1984-86; prin. Weston Sch., Manville, N.J., 1986-88, The Bartle Sch., Highland Park, 1988-91, Orange Ave. Sch., Cranford, 1991-92; dir. The Open Door Youth Shelter, Binghamton, N.Y., 1992-94; child protective investigator supr. Dept. Health and Rehab. Svcs., Orlando, Fla., 1994-95; program supr. Children's Home Soc., Sanford, 1995; clin. supr. Healthy Families-Orange, Orlando, 1995-98; dir. program ops. Children's Home Soc., Tavares, 1998—. Regional trainer Individualized Lang. Arts, Weehawken, N.J., 1976-86; cons. McDougal/Littel Pubs., Evanston, Ill., 1982-83; chair adv. bd. women's residential program Ctr. for Drug Free Living, Orlando, 1996. Contbr. chpt.: A Resource Guide of Differentiated Learning Experiences for Gifted Elementary Students, 1981. V.p. Sch. Readiness Coalition for Lake County, 1999; mem. adv. coun. Lake Cmty. Action Agy., Head Start, 1999; bd. mem. Mount Dora Cmty. Trust, 2002; vice chair Lake County Sch. Readiness Coalition, 2000—02; mem. Ctrl. Healthy Start Coalition, 1999—2002; Sunday sch. tchr. Reformed Ch., Keyport, 1975—80, supt. Sunday sch., 1982—84; bd. dirs. Ctrl. Health Start Coalition, 1999. Mem.: Elks, Order Ea. Star, Kiwanis (Mt. Dora bd. dirs. 2000, pres. 2002—), Phi Delta Kappa. Republican. Methodist. Avocation: writing. Office: Children's Home Soc 1300 S Duncan Dr Bldg D Tavares FL 32778-4223

OSBORNE, HAROLD WAYNE, sociology educator, consultant; b. Eldorado, Ark., Sept. 5, 1930; s. Carl Clinton and Mary Eunice (Peace) O.; m. Alice June Williams, Feb. 15, 1953; children— Michael, Van, Samuel BA in History, Ouachita Bapt. Coll., 1952; MA in Sociology, La. State U., 1956, PhD in Sociology, 1959. Research assoc. dept. rural sociology La. State U., 1954-56; social sci. analyst USDA, Baton Rouge, 1956-58; asst. prof. sociology Baylor U., Waco, 1958-60, assoc. prof., 1960-63, prof., 1963—, dir. grad. studies dept. sociology, 1963-87, chair dept. sociology, anthropology, social work and gerontology, 1988-2000. Cons. in field; dir. workshops on crime and delinquency Co-editor: Research Methods: Issues and Insights, 1971; co-author: Sociology: A Pragmatic Approach, 1981, 86; assoc. editor for sociology Social Sci. Quar., 1965-75. Bd. dirs. Mclennan County Mental Health Assn., Tex., 1970-80. Served with inf. U.S. Army, 1952-54 Named Outstanding Baylor Prof., Baylor U., 1976, Master Tchr., 1993. Mem. Am. Sociol. Assn., Southwestern Sociol. Assn. (v.p. 1985-87, pres. 1987-88), Southwestern Social Sci. Assn., Population Assn. Am., Population Reference Bur., Am. Social Health Assn. (bd. dirs. Southwestern region) Democrat. Baptist. Home: 2717 Braemar St Waco TX 76710-2118 Office: Baylor U Dept Sociology Waco TX 76798 E-mail: harold_osborne@baylor.edu.

OSBORNE, HARRY ALAN, orthodontist; b. Youngstown, Ohio, Mar. 9, 1934; s. Kenneth L. and Marguerite (Filmer) O.; m. Carol June Williams, June 30, 1956 (dec. 1989); children: Elizabeth Ann, J. Scott, Linda J., Robert K.; m. Linda Sue Leister Simmons, May 9, 1993; stepchildren: William A. Simmons, John S. Simmons, Susan Jane Simmons. Student, Westminster Coll., New Wilmington, Pa., 1952-55; DDS, U. Pitts., 1959; MS, Northwestern U., 1962. Diplomate Am. Bd. Orthodontics. Intern Youngstown Hosp. Assn., 1959; practice dentistry specializing in orthodontics Canton, Ohio, 1964—. Supt. adv. com. North Canton Sch. Dist., 1960-87; mem. adv. com. Soc. Bank, Canton, 1962-89; chmn. bldg. com. Faith United Meth. Ch., 1975-80; chmn. cmty bd. YMCA, North Canton, 1986-96, charter mem. Heritage Club (Canton YMCA); v.p. Hills and Dales Homeowners Assn., 1993-96; trustee Christ Presbyn. Ch., Canton, Ohio, elder. Recipient Disting. Service award, Jaycees, 1968. Mem. ADA, Pierre Fauchard Acad., Am. Assn. Orthodontists, Coll. of Diplomates of Am. Bd. Orthodontists (charter), Gt. Lakes Orthodontic Assn., Ohio Dental Assn., Cleve. Orthodontic Soc. (pres. 1983), Stark County Dental Soc. (pres. 1975-76, inductee Disting. Dental Svc. Acad. 2001), World Fedn. Orthodontists, Internat. Coll. Dentists, Shady Hollow Country Club (Massillion, Ohio) (bd. dirs. 1984-85, 87—), Brookside Country Club. Republican. Avocation: golf. Home: 2410 Strathmore Dr NW Canton OH 44708-1364 Office: 1021 Schneider St SE Canton OH 44720-3857

OSBORNE, JAMES ALFRED, religious organization administrator; b. Toledo, July 3, 1927; s. Alfred James and Gladys Irene (Gaugh) O.; m. Ruth Glenrose Campbell, Nov. 26, 1945; 1 child, Constance Jean (Mrs. Donald William Canning). Grad., Salvation Army Coll., 1947; student, U. Chattanooga, 1954-55; D of Pub. Svc. (hon.), Gordon Coll., 1991. Corps officer Salvation Army, Magness, Nashville, 1947, Southside, Memphis, 1948, Owensboro, Ky., 1949-54, comdg. officer Chattanooga, 1954-61, city comdr. Miami, Fla., 1961-65, divisional sec. Ky.-Tenn. Div., 1965-68, gen. sec. N.C. and S.C. Div., 1968-70, pub. rels. sec. 15 so. states, D.C. and Mex., 1970-71, divisional comdr. Md. and No. W.Va. Div., 1971-73, divisional comdr. Nat. Capital and Virginias Div., 1973-78, divisional comdr. Fla. Div., 1978-80, chief sec. Western Ter., 1980-84, nat. chief sec. N.J., 1984-86, territorial comdr. so. states Atlanta, 1986-89; nat. comdr., Republic of Marshall Islands, Guam, P.R., Virgin Islands Salvation Army USA, 1989-93. Chmn. Salvation Army Nat. Planning and Devel. Commn., 1974-76, 84-86; exec. bd. Vision Interfaith Satellite Network, Nat. Assn. Evangelicals, Christian Children's Fund Inc.; chmn. bd. Christian Mgmt. Assn., 1993-94; exec. com. religious alliance Against Pornography; rep. Salvation Army to numerous orgns. Bd. dirs. Nat. Law Ctr. for Children and Families; sec. Tenn. Conf. on Social Welfare, 1959, v.p., 1960; pres. Fla. Conf. on Social Welfare, 1965; pres. Ky. Welfare Assn., 1970. Mem. Chattanooga Pastors Assn. (pres. 1958), Va. and W. Va. Welfare Confs., Rotary. E-mail: josborne@attglobal.net.

OSBORNE, JOHN WALTER, historian, educator, author; b. Bklyn., Aug. 19, 1927; s. Douglas Walter and Gertrude Ann (Purcell) O.; m. Frances Patricia Hannon, Aug. 2, 1958; 1 son, David. BA, Rutgers U., 1957, MA (Louis Bevier fellow), 1959, PhD, 1961. Asst. prof. history Kean Coll. of N.J., 1961-63, N.J. Inst. Tech., 1963-64; asst. prof. Rutgers U., New Brunswick, N.J., 1964-66, assoc. prof., 1966-69, prof., 1969-93, prof. emeritus, 1993—. Author: William Cobbett-His Thought and His Times, 1966, The Silent Revolution: The Industrial Revolution in England as a Source of Cultural Change, 1970, John Cartwright, 1972; co-author: Cobbett in His Times, 1990; editor: Jour. of Rutgers U. Libraries, 1975-80; co-editor: A Grammar of the English Language, 1983; contbr. articles to profl. jours. Recipient Henry Browne award for disting. teaching Rutgers U., 1988; Am. Philos. Soc. grantee, 1966, 75 Home: PO Box 426 Ivoryton CT 06442-0426

OSBORNE, JUDITH BARBOUR, artist, art educator; b. Winnipeg, Man., Can., Oct. 14, 1950; came to U.S., 1952; d. John Anderson and Laura May (Jones) Barbour; m. Frederick Spring Osborne Jr., Feb. 15, 1986; 1 child, Sheila. BFA, Univ. of Arts, Phila., 1974; student, Vt. Studio Ctr., 1984-89; MFA, Pa. Acad. Fine Arts, Phila., 1997. Prin. Barbour CalliGraphics, Phila., 1976—; dir. publs. and publicity Phila. Conf. on Calligraphic Arts, 1982; mem. faculty Phila. Coll. Art (now Univ. of Arts), 1982-85, 92, 00, Drexel U., Phila., 1991—; faculty Innovations Internat. Calligraphy Conf., N.Y., 1987; exhbns. coord. Calleidoscope Internat. Calligraphy Conf., Trenton, N.J., 1993. Guest curator Kamin Gallery, U. Pa., Phila., 1993, 95; exhbn. juror Phila. Calligraphers' Soc., 1989, 91, 94-95, 98, Phila. Sketch Club, 2002. One-woman shows include Rourke Art Gallery, Moorhead, Minn., 1999, Phila. Art Alliance, 1999, Artists' House, 1998, 2000, 02, Living Arts, Tulsa, Okla., 2000, Shipley Sch., Bryn Mawr, Pa., 2000; exhibited in group shows at Nat. Arts Club, N.Y.C., 1990, Pa. State Mus., Harrisburg, 1994, 2000-01, Am. Coll., Bryn Mawr, Pa., 1996, Nexus Found. for Today's Art, Phila., 1997, Del. Ctr. for Contemporary Art, 2002; represented in permanent collections at Fed. Res. Bank Phila., Blue Cross, Rourke Art Gallery Mus., Moorhead, Barbour/Ladouceur Archs., Mpls.; also pvt. collections; collaborator Sophia Osborne Dance Assocs., 1999—; contbr. articles to mags. and newspapers. Recipient Best of Show Abington (Pa.) Art Ctr., 1990; Pa. Acad. Fine Arts fellow, Phila., 1997, Independence Found. fellow, 2001. Mem. Coll. Art Assn., Phila. Calligraphers' Soc. (bd. mem., publs. editor 1980-85), Inst. Noetic Scis. Avocation: metaphysics. Home: 3621 Hamilton St Philadelphia PA 19104-2327 Studio: Studio 5 314 Brown St Philadelphia PA 19123-2202 E-mail: fojo@bellatlantic.net.

OSBORNE, KERMIT CHARLES, JR. contractor, consultant; b. Kingsport, Tenn., Dec. 21, 1942; s. Kermit Charles Osborne, Sr. and Loretta June Osborne. BSEE, Trinity Coll. and Univ., Sioux Falls, S.D., 2001. Cert. electricity II Scott County Vocat. Ctr., 1980, electricity I Scott County Vocat. Ctr., 1981, HVACR VA Highlands C.C., 1995, refrigerant recovery type I AHAM-NARDA, 1994, computer tech. 2000, computer fundaments 2001, computer electronics specialist 2000, motor vehicle refrigerant recovery IMACA, 1998, profl. locksmithing Foley-Belsau, 1995, advanced locksmithing Foley-Belsau, 1995, amp fiber optic and LAN cabling NJATC, 2001, type I and II refrigerant recovery 1994, flexible gas piping Track Pipe, 1999, registered safe tech. Nat. Safemanis Orgn., 2001. Journeyman wireman IBEW 934, Blountville, Tenn., 1992—; owner Millenium Security Svcs., Nickelsville, Va., 1995—. Scott County area vol. rep. Citizen Corps. Mem.: Internat. High IQ Soc., Nat. Safeman's Orgn., Nat. Locksmiths Assn., Masonic Lodge. Avocations: collectibles, amateur inventor, astronomy, nature, computers. Home: Rte 2 Box 533 Nickelsville VA 24271-9546 Personal E-mail: charles_osborne@hotmail.com.

OSBORNE, LINDA BARRETT, writer, editor; b. N.Y.C., Feb. 1, 1949; d. James and Josephine (Valeri) Barrett; m. Robert John Osborne, Sept. 23, 1972; children: Catherine, Nicholas. BA, Swarthmore Coll., 1971. Freelance writer, editor, Washington, 1977—2000; writer, editor Libr. of Congress, 2000—. Author: Song of the Harp, 1977, (with Casey King) Oh, Freedom!, 1997 (Flora Stieglitz Straus award for non-fiction Children's Book Com.), also short stories, over 100 book revs. in Washington Post, N.Y. Times. Grantee D.C. Commn. on Arts and Humanities, 1990; recipient Pen Syndicated Fiction award 1988-89. Mem. Nat. Book Critics Cir.

OSBORNE, LISETTE KIRSTIE, neonatal nurse practitioner, nursing administrator; b. Austin, Tex., Feb. 15, 1956; d. Calvin Herbert and Kathleen Ada Ohl; children: Stephanie, Nathaniel, Zachary, Roger, Wesley; m. Earney Osborne, Jan. 1997. BSN, U. Tex., San Antonio, 1986, MSN, 1991. RN, Tex., Md. Neonatal nurse Brackenridge Hosp., Austin, Tex., 1980-91; neonatal nurse practitioner Ochsner Med. Found., New Orleans, 1992; supr. spl. edn. sch. health Balt. City Health Dept., 1993-98, dir. sch. health nursing, 1998—2002, supr. hearing and vision program, 1996—2002, adminstrv. dir. Sch. Health Programs, 2002—. Mary Gibbs Jones scholar. Mem. APHA, Nat. Assn. Sch. Nurses, Assn. Women's Health, Obstet. and Neonatal Nurses, Nat. Assn. Neonatal Nurses, Am. Acad. Nurse Practitioners, Greater Balt. Asthma Alliance (chair 2001—), Md. Assn. Sch. Health Nurses (pres. 2001-02). Home: 1406 Beetree Ct Bel Air MD 21014-2494 E-mail: ohlosborne@aol.com.

OSBORNE, MARGERY DIANE, education educator; b. New Milford, Conn., Sept. 9, 1955; d. John Frost and Mary Simons Osborne; 1 child Larkin Kennedy 1 child Cornelia. AB, Wellesley Coll., 1977; PhD, U. Western Ont., London, Ont., Can., 1983, Mich. State U., 1993. Assoc. prof. U. Ill., Champaign, 1993—. Author: (book) Constructing Knowledge in the Elementary School Classroom, 1999, Teaching science in diverse settings: Marginalized discourses and classroom practice, 2001, The Love We Call Science: Constructing A Womanist Science from Observations of Practice , 2002. Office: U Ill 1310 S 6th St Champaign IL 61820

OSBORNE, MARY POPE, writer; b. Ft. Sill, Okla., May 20, 1949; d. William Perkins and Barnette (Dickens) Pope; m. William R. Osborne, May 16, 1976. BA in Religion, U. N.C., 1971. Author: Run, Run, As Fast As You Can, 1982, Love Always, Blue, 1983, Best Wishes, Joe Brady, 1984, Mo to the Rescue, 1985, Last One Home, 1986, Beauty and the Beast, 1987, Favorite Greek Myths, 1988, American Tall Tales, 1990, The Many Lives of Benjamin Franklin, 1990, Moon Horse, 1991, George Washington, Leader of a New Nation, 1991, Spider Kane Mystery Series, 1992, 93, Magic Tree House Series, 1992-02, Haunted Waters, 1994, Molly and the Prince, 1994, Favorite Norse Myths, 1996, One World, Many Religions, 1996, Rocking Horse Christmas, 1997, Favorite Medieval Tales, 1998, Standing in the Light, 1998, The Life of Jesus, 1998, Adaline Falling Star, 2000, My Brothers Keeper, 2000, My Secret War, 2000, Kate and the Beanstalk, 2000, The Brave Little Seamstress, 2002, After the Rain, 2002, The One-Eyed Giant, 2002, The Land of the Dead, 2002, New York's Bravest, 2002, Tales from the Odyssey, 2002. Recipient Disting. Alumna award U. N.C., Chapel Hill, 1994, Distinctive Contbn. to Arts, N.Y. Carolina Club. Mem. PEN, Authors Guild (pres. 1993-97), Authors League Fund (bd. dirs.). Office: Brandt & Brandt Lit Agy 1501 Broadway Ste 2310 New York NY 10036-5689

OSBORNE, MICHAEL PIERS, surgeon, researcher, health facility administrator; b. Sutton, Surrey, Eng., Jan. 6, 1946; came to U.S., 1980; s. Arthur Frederick and Leonora Kate Hope (Miller) O.; m. Carolyn Patricia Malkinson, June 22, 1974; children: James, Simon, Andrew, Emma. MB, BS, London U., 1970, MS in Surgery, 1980. Diplomate Royal Coll. Surgeons of Eng., Am. Coll. Surgeons. Intern Charing Cross Group of Hosp., England, 1970-71; resident Brompton Hosp., London, St. James Hosp., London, West Herts Hosp., Eng.; hon. lectr. surgery Royal Marsden Hosp., London, 1977-81; fellow in surg. oncology Meml. Sloan-Kettering Cancer Ctr., N.Y.C., 1980-81, attending surgeon, 1981-91, head breast cancer rsch. lab., 1984-91; chief breast surgery N.Y. Hosp.-Cornell Med. Ctr., 1991—; prof. surgery Cornell U. Med. Coll., 1991—; dir., CEO Strang Cancer Prevention Ctr., 1991-95, pres., CEO, 1995—; dir. Strang- Cornell Breast Ctr., 1991—. Mem. adj. faculty Rockefeller U. Hosp., N.Y.C., 1981-89, vis. physician, 1983—; mem. sci. adv. com. Am.-Italian Found., N.Y.C., 1991—; bd. trustees Nat. Consortium Breast Ctrs., 1992-95; pres. N.Y. Met. Breast Cancer Group, 1995-97. Contbr. 12 chpts. to textbooks; contbr. over 150 articles to profl. jours. Recipient Gov.'s Clin. Gold medal Charing Cross Hosp. Med. Sch., 1970, Prize in Surgery, Charing Cross Hosp. Med. Sch., 1970, Raven prize British Assn. Surg. Oncology, 1978; Wellcome Trust fellow, 1975. Mem. Am. Surg. Assn., N.Y. Acad. Scis., N.Y. Surg. Soc., Brit. Assn. Surg. Oncology, Soc. Surg. Oncology, Royal Soc. Medicine, Am. Soc. Breast Disease (trustee 1993-95), Am. Assn. Cancer Rsch., Am. Soc. Clin. Oncology, Internat. Soc. for Cancer Chemoprevention (sec.-gen.). Office: Strang Cancer Prevention Ctr 428 E 72d St Ste 600 New York NY 10021-4635 E-mail: osborne@strang.org.

OSBORNE, QUINTON ALBERT, psychiatric social worker, inspector of institutional services; b. Hopkinsville, Ky., May 14, 1951; s. Willie Lee and Elizabeth (Talley) O.; m. Gwendolyn G. Flowers, Oct. 19, 1991; 1 adopted child, Quinton A. Jr.; children: Ashley Elain, Shelbie Elizabeth. BS in Sociology, Austin Peay State U., 1978; MS in Health Adminstrn., Calif. Coll. Health Sci., 1996. Lic. social worker, Ohio, Ky., D.C. Fin. specialist U.S. Army, Karlsruhe, Fed. Republic Germany, 1972-75; resident advisor Breckinridge Job Corps, Morganfield, Ky., 1978; clk., typist Govt. D.C., Washington, 1979; asst. worker's compensation Dept. Labor, Mt. Sterling, Ky., 1979-80; social svc. asst. U.S. Forest Svc., Mariba, 1980-85; mil. pay clk. Ky. N.G., Frankfort, 1985-86; social worker Cin. VA Med. Ctr., 1986-88; equal opportunity specialist US Dept. HUD, Columbus, Ohio, 1988-90; family tchr. Maryville Acad., 1991-93; inspector of instnl. svcs. Lebanon Correctional Instn., 1999; social worker Warren Correctional Instn., 1999—. Mem. Victorian Eva Vet. Group, Cin., 1975—, task force for homeless U.S. Dept. HUD, Columbus, 1988-89; chair ptnrs. in edn. VA Med. Ctr., Cin., 1986-88, Op. Feed, Columbus, 1988-89; social worker Vets. Homeless Program, Cin., 1988—; sect. and employees asst. coord., chairperson Adopt-A-Sch. Program, 1991—. Mem. Ptnrs. in Edn. (chairperson 1986-88), Alpha Phi Alpha (pres. Clarksville, Tenn. chpt. 1977-78), Alpha Phi Alpha (Clarksville chpt.). Republican. Baptist. Avocations: tennis, bowling, biking, reading, traveling. Home: 509 14th Ave Middletown OH 45044-5601 Office: Warren Correctional Instn Lebanon OH 45036

OSBORNE, RICHARD DE JONGH, mining and metals company executive; b. Bronxville, N.Y., Mar. 19, 1934; s. Stanley de Jongh and M. Elizabeth (Ide) O.; m. Cheryl Anne Archibald, Dec. 14, 1957; children: Leslie Coleman, Lindsay Vogel, Nicholas de J., Stanley de J. AB in Econs., Princeton U., 1956. With Cuno Engring. Corp., Meriden, Conn., 1956-60; fin., planning and mktg. exec. IBM Corp., Armonk, N.Y., 1960-69; investment adviser Sherman M. Fairchild, N.Y.C., 1969-70; exec. v.p. fin. and bus. devel., dir. Fairchild Camera & Instrument Corp., Mountain View, Calif., 1970-74; v.p. fin. ASARCO Inc. (formerly Am. Smelting & Refining Co.), N.Y.C., 1975-77, exec. v.p., 1977-82, pres., 1982-85, chmn., pres., chief exec. officer, 1985-99. Bd. dirs. Schering-Plough Corp., Goodrich Corp., NACCO Industries, Inc., The Tinker Found.; non-exec. chmn., bd. dirs. Datawatch Corp.; treas. Ams. soc. Mem. Nat. Mining Assn. (hon. dir.), Coun. Fgn. Rels., Econs. Club NY, River Club, Brook Club, Sakonnet Golf Club. Home: 40 E 94th St Apt 32B New York NY 10128-0759 Office: Asarco Inc Ste 1902 156 W 56th St New York NY 10019 Office Fax: 212-307-5376.

OSBORNE, RICHARD ERNEST, mechanical engineer, writer; b. Indpls., May 2, 1931; s. Gilbert Thomas and Frances Anne (Riebel) Osborne; m. Josephine Roque-Novo Osborne, Feb. 7, 1957; children: Gary Thomas, Audrey, Anna Marie. BSME, U. Ill., 1954. Seaman USN, Calif., 1957; ptnr. Calrk & Osborne, Indpls., 1957—88; pub. Riebel-Roque Publ., 1988—. Rschr. in field. Author: Tour Book for Antique Car Buffs, 1990, World War II Sites

In The United States, 1996, 2d edit., 1998, Casablanca Companion, The Movie and Its Place in History, 1997, World War II in Colonial Africa, 2001; contbr. articles to profl. jours. Avocations: research on WWII, antique automobiles.

OSBORNE, RICHARD HAZELET, anthropology and medical genetics educator; b. Kennecott, Alaska, June 18, 1920; s. Clarence Edward and Margaret Jerenne (Hazelet) O.; m. Barbara White, Oct. 14, 1944; children: Susan, Richard, David; m. Barbara Teachman, Sept. 1, 1970. Student, U. Alaska, 1939-41; BS, BA, U. Wash., 1949; postgrad., Harvard U., 1949-50; PhD (Viking Fund Pre-doctoral fellow, Spl. fellow Inst. for Study Human Variation), Columbia, 1956; hon. doctor odontology, U. Oulu, Finland, 1994; DSc (hon.), U. Alaska, Fairbanks, 2001. Research asso. Columbia U., 1953-58; asst. Sloan-Kettering Inst., N.Y.C., 1958-60, asso., 1960-62, asso. mem., head sect. human genetics, 1962-64; prof. anthropology and med. genetics U. Wis., Madison, 1964-86, prof. emeritus, 1986—; rsch. assoc. Quatenary Ctr. U. Alaska, Fairbanks, 1993—. Asso. prof. preventive medicine Cornell Med. Coll., 1962-64; clin. geneticist Meml. Hosp. for Cancer, N.Y.C., 1963-65; vis. scientist Forsyth Dental Center, Boston, 1969-71; cons. human genetics Newington (Conn.) Childrens Hosp., 1971-73; Mem. com. on epidemiology and vets. follow-up studies NRC, 1969-73; mem. perinatal research com. Nat. Inst. Neurol. Diseases and Stroke, NIH, 1970-72; mem. cultural anthropology fellowship and rev. NIMH, 1969-73 Author: Genetic Basis of Morphological Variation, 1959, Biological and Social Meaning of Race, 1971; Editor: Social Biology, 1961-77, 81—99 ; contbr. articles to profl. jours. Served to maj. USAAF, 1942-46. Decorated D.F.C., Air medal with 3 oak leaf clusters.; Named Health Research Council Career Scientist City N.Y., 1962-64 Fellow Explorers Club; Mem. Am. Assn. Phys. Anthropology (exec. com. 1965-67, v.p. 1968-70), Am. Soc. for Human Genetics (dir. 1960-61, 67-69), Behavior Genetics Assn. (pres. pro-tem 1970-71), Soc. for Study Social Biology (editor Social Biology 1961-99, dir. 1981-83, 86-99), Pioneers of Alaska (life), Sigma Xi. Office: 1129 E 8th St Port Angeles WA 98362-6628 E-mail: rho66@columbiau.edu.

OSBORNE, RICHARD JAY, electric utility company executive; b. N.Y.C., Feb. 16, 1951; s. Victor and Evelyn Celia (Sweetbaum) O. BA, Tufts U., 1973; MBA, U. N.C., 1975. Fin. analyst Duke Power Co., Charlotte, N.C., 1975-78, sr. fin. analyst, 1978-80, mgr. fin. rels., 1980-81, mgr. treasury activities, 1981, treas., 1981-88, v.p. fin., CFO, 1988-94, sr. v.p., CFO, 1994-97; exec. v.p., CFO Duke Energy Corp., 1997-2000, PRO, 2000—, exec. v.p., chief risk officer, 2001—. Bd. dirs. Charlotte Jewish Fedn., New South Healthcare, Echo Found., Sch. of Pub. Health, U. N.C., Chapel Hill, Mus. New South, Charlotte Symphony Orch., Johnson Smith U., Nuc. Elec. Ins. Ltd. Mem. Fin. Execs. Inst. Democrat. Jewish. Office: Duke Energy Corp 526 S Church St Charlotte NC 28202-1802

OSBORNE, SEWARD RUSSELL, writer; b. Catskill, N.Y., June 28, 1946; s. Seward Russell and Doris Virginia (Tompkins) O.; m. Jean Marie Shaver, June 22, 1968; children: Dean, Sarah. Historic site technician Senate House State Historic Site, Kingston, N.Y., 1976-77; contbg. editor Mil. Images, 1980—; contbg. author Mil. Collector & Historian, 1984—; historian Ulster County Civil War Round Table, 1994—; photographic cons. Arts and Entertainment Network, 1996. Cons. in field. Author: Holding the Left, The 20th New York State Militia at Gettysburg, July 1, 1863, 1990, The Saga of the Mountain Legion (156th N.Y. Vols.) in the Civil War and the Modest Hero Who Saved Our Flag, 1994, The Ninety Days Service of the 20th New York State Militia, 1998; editor: The Civil War Diaries of Col. Theodore B. Gates, 20th New York State Militia, 1991; contbr. articles to North South Trader's Civil War, 1970s, 1980s, Ulster County Gazette, 1970s, 1980s; photographic cons. Legacy TV Prodn. Three Days at Gettysburg, 1994. Active Friends of the Ulysses S. Grant Cottage; founder, dir. 120th Monument Restoration Fund, 1996-97. Cited for erection of monument to 20th N.Y. State Militia on the Gettysburg Battlefield, 1981, 20th N.Y. State Militia on the Battlefield of 2nd Bull Run (Manassas), 1986; selected for inclusion in the Book of Buffs, Masters, Mavens and Uncommon Experts, 1980. Fellow The Co. of Mil. Historians; mem. DAV (life), NRA, Ulster County Com. to Save the Grant Cottage (founder, chmn. 1990), N.Y. State Mil. Heritage Inst., 1997, Ulster County Geneal. Soc. (Civil War history cons.), Zadock Pratt Mus (hon. life), Kingston Area Libr. (Civil War history cons.), Friends of Nat. Parks at Gettysburg, Inc., Surratt Soc. (life), Gettysburg Battlefield Preservation Assn., Lexington Historical Soc. (hon. life), Friends of Albany Rural Cemetery, NRA. Avocations: historical sites, collecting Civil War artifacts. Home: 1329 County Road 2 Olivebridge NY 12461-5417

OSBORNE, SOLOMON CURTIS, lawyer, consultant; b. Miss., May 26, 1948; s. Cassie and Doris (McCool) O.; m. Deborah Osborne; children: Solomon, Kai, Shadwich, Alyah. BA in Polit. Sci., Tougalou Coll., 1970; JD, U. Ill., Champaign, 1973. Bar: Miss. 1975, U.S. Dist. Ct. (no. and so. dists.) Miss., U.S. Ct. Appeals (5th and 11th cirs.). Staff atty. No. Miss. Rural Legal Svcs., West Point, 1973-74, mng. atty. West Point and Greenwood, 1974-78, sr. atty., 1982—; exec. dir. S.W. Miss. Legal Svcs., McComb, 1978-82; CEO, Osborne Lawe Office and Legal Clinic, Greenwood, 1990—. Adj. prof. Tougaloo Coll., 1982; Mississippi Valley State U., Itta Bena, 2000; cons. in field. Recipient Cmty. Svcs. award Greenwood Voters League, 1978; named Atty. of Yr., No. Miss. Rural Legal Svcs., 1978. Mem. ABA, Nat. Conf. Black Lawyers (bd. dirs.) Magnolia Bar Assn., Alpha Phi Alpha. Baptist. Address: 216 Star St Greenwood MS 38930-7527

OSBORNE, STEPHEN J. philatelist; b. Hove, Sussex, Eng., Mar. 22, 1953; s. Stephen J. and Pauline (Compton) O.; m. Vanessa Mack, 1973 (div. 1976); 1 child, Stephen; m. Nicola Edwards, Aug. 19, 1978 (div. 1990); children: Francesca, James; m. Lorraine Gaetan, Dec. 31, 1994; children: Sean, Callum. Attended, Lancing Coll., Eng. Prin. Osborne Ltd., 1974—. Contbr. articles to profl. jours. Parliamentary candidate for Brighton, Eng., 1974, 79; trustee Cardinal Spellman Mus., Weston, Mass., 1994-98; mem. Smithsonian Mus., Washington, 1995. Mem. Odd Fellows (hon.). Democrat. Avocation: philosophy of Ludwig Wittgenstein. Address: PO Box 378 Jeffersonville VT 05464 Fax: 802 644 6512.

OSBORNE, THOMAS EUGENE, oral and maxillofacial surgeon; b. Santa Barbara, Calif., Nov. 25, 1954; s. Thomas and Inez (Terres) O.; m. Joan Boubek; children: Elisabeth, Tommy. BA, U. Calif., Santa Barbara; DDS, Loyola U., Chgo., 1982; cert. in oral and maxillofacial surgery, Johns Hopkins U., 1983-87. Diplomate Am. Bd. Oral and Maxillofacial Surgery. Asst. chief of svcs. Johns Hopkins Hosp., Balt., 1986-87; asst. prof. Sch. Dentistry Emory U., Atlanta, 1987-91; asst. chief oral and maxillofacial surgery Grady Meml. Hosp., 1987-91; pvt. practice oral surgery Tucker, Ga., 1991—; pres. exec. coun., COO, bd. dirs. Benchmarq Healthcare Sys., Atlanta, 1995-97, CEO, 1999—. Chmn. continuing edn. com. No. Dist. Dental Soc., Atlanta, 1993-94. Author: Hospital Dentistry, 1992; contbr. articles to profl. jours., chpt. to book. Cub scout leader Boy Scouts Am., Tucker, 1994—; vol. World Relief. Fellow Am. Bd. Oral and Maxillofacial Surgery, Hinman Dental Soc.; mem. ADA, Am. Assn. Oral and Maxillofacial Surgery, Ga. Soc. Oral and Maxillofacial Surgery, Ga. Dental Assn., Johns Hopkins Med. and Surg. Soc., Xi Psi Phi. Avocations: skiing, writing, running, rollerblading, weightlifting. Office: 2163 Northlake Pkwy Tucker GA 30084-4102 E-mail: yanker2@aol.com.

OSBORNE, TOM, congressman, former college football coach; b. Feb. 23, 1937; m. Nancy Tederman; children: Mike, Ann, Susie. BA, Hastings Coll., 1959; MA, U. Nebr., 1963, PhD in Ednl. Psychology, 1965. Flankerback Washington Redskins, NFL, 1959-61, San Francisco 49ers, NFL, 1961-62; asst. football coach U. Nebr., 1962-73, head football coach, 1973-97; coach team U. Nebr. (Cotton Bowl), 1974, U. Nebr. (Sugar Bowl), 1971, U. Nebr. (Astro-Bluebonnet Bowl), 1976, U. Nebr. (Liberty Bowl), 1977, U. Nebr. (Sun Bowl), 1980, U. Nebr. (Orange Bowl), 1979, 83, 84, 89, 92-95; prof. emeritus U. Nebr., 1998-2000; mem. U.S. Congress from Nebr. 3rd Dist., 2001—; mem. agr. com., edn. and the workforce com., resources com. Served in U.S. Army. Named Big Eight Coach of Yr., 1975, 78, 80; named Bobby Dodds Nat. Coach of Yr., 1978 Coached team to NCAA Divsn. IA Nat. Championship, 1994-95. Office: US Ho of Reps 507 Cannon HOB Washington DC 20515-2703*

OSBORNE, WILLIE CARROLL, geologist, consultant; b. McGehee, Ark., Aug. 16, 1923; s. John Carroll Osborne and Lola Almedia Mangum; m. Dixie Beth Tarver, Nov. 24, 1944; children: Janet Lee, John Carroll II. BS, Centenary Coll. La., 1943. Area geologist Tide Water Assoc. Oil, Midland, Tex., 1946—50, dist. geologist, 1950—51, Union Oil & Gas Corp., Midland, 1951—57; exploration mgr. Am. Trading and Prodn., 1957—69, gen. mgr., 1969—70; pvt. practice cons. geologist, 1970—. Pres. Apex Oil and Gas Corp., Midland, 1985—90. Author: Looking Back, 1992, Running High/Looking Good, 1996, Freemasonry & America, 2000. Trustee Scottish Rite Hosp., Dallas, 2000. Lt. USN, 1943—46, PTO. Mem.: West Tex. Geol. Soc., Green Tree Country Club (developer 1980—, pres. 1981). Republican. Baptist. Avocations: reading, traveling. Home: 2110 N I St Midland TX 79705-7523 Office: Ste 405 401 W Texas Midland TX 79701

O'SCANNLAIN, DIARMUID FIONNTAIN, federal judge; b. N.Y.C., Mar. 28, 1937; s. Sean Leo and Moira (Hegarty) Diarmuid; m. Maura Nolan, Sept. 7, 1963; children: Sean Diarmuid, Jane Diarmuid, Brendan Diarmuid, Kevin Diarmuid, Megan Diarmuid, Christopher Diarmuid, Anne Diarmuid, Kate Diarmuid. BA, St. John's U., 1957; JD, Harvard U., 1963; LLM, U. Va., 1992. Bar: Oreg. 1965, N.Y. 1964. Tax atty. Standard Oil Co. (N.J.), N.Y.C., 1963—65; oassoc. Davies, Biggs, Strayer, Sotel & Boley, Portland, Oreg., 1965—69; dep. atty. gen. State of Oreg., 1969—71, pub. utility commr., 1971—73; dir. Oreg. Dept. Environ. Quality, 1973—74; sr. ptnr. Ragen, Roberts, O'Scannlain, Robertson & Neill, Portland, 1978—86; judge U.S. Ct. Appeals (9th cir.), San Francisco, 1986—, mem. exec. com., 1988—89, 1993—94; mem. Jud. Coun. 9th Cir., 1991—93. Mem. U.S. Jud. Conf. Com. on Automation and Tech. , 1990—; cons. Office of Pres.-elect and mem. Dept. Energy Transition Team (Reagan Transition), Washington, 1980—81; chmn. com. adminstrv. law Oreg. State Bar, 1980—81. Mem. coun. of legal advisors Rep. Nat. Com., 1981—83, mem., 1983—86; chmn. Oreg. Rep. Party, 1983—86; del. Rep. Nat. convs., 1976, 1980, chmn. Oreg. del., 1984; nominee U.S. Ho. of Reps., 1st Congl. Dist., 1974; team leader energy task force Pres.'s Pvt. Sector Survey on Cost Control, 1982—83; trustee Jesuit H.S.; bd. visitors U. Oreg. Law Sch., 1988—; mem. citizens adv. bd. Providence Hosp., 1986—92. Maj. USAR, 1955—78. Mem.: ABA (sec. Appellate Judges Conf. 1989—90, exec. com. 1990—, chmn. elect 1994—), Fed. Bar Assn., Multnomah Club, Arlington Club. Roman Catholic. Office: US Ct Appeals 313 Pioneer Courthouse 555 SW Yamhill St Ste 104 Portland OR 97204-1321*

OSCARSON, KATHLEEN DALE, retired writing assessment coordinator, educator; b. Hollywood, Calif., Sept. 16, 1928; d. Chauncey Dale and Hermine Marie Rulison; m. David Knowles Leslie, June 16, 1957 (div. Aug. 1970); m. William Randolph Oscarson, Apr. 27, 1974. AB, UCLA, 1950, MA, 1952; Cert. Advanced Study, Harvard U., 1965; Diplomé Elementaire, Le Cordon Bleu U. Paris, 1972. Gen. secondary life credential, Calif. Cons. Advanced Placement English Calif. Dept. Edn., Sacramento, 1968-70; reader Calif. Assessment Program, 1989-2000; instr. individual study U. Calif. Extension, Berkeley, 1979-92; reader, leader Ednl. Testing Svc., Princeton, N.J., 1967—, Oakland, Calif., 1967—; reader San Jose (Calif.) State U., 1991-2000; tchr. English, counselor Palo Alto (Calif.) Unified Sch. Dist., 1954-90, H.S. writing assessment coord., 1987-2000, ret., 2000. Adj. lectr. English Santa Clara (Calif.) U., 1990-91; commr. Curriculum Study Commn., San Francisco Bay Area, 1978—; chair tchrs. English Spring Asilomar Conf., Pacific Grove, Calif., 1992, Asilomar 44, Pacific Grove, 1994; advanced placement faculty cons. in English Collegeboard N.J., 1967-73, 91—. Mem. lang. arts assessment adv. com. Calif. State Dept. Edn., Sacramento, 1975-90; mem.-at-large exec. bd. Ctrl. Calif. Coun. Tchrs. English, Bay Area, 1969-71; mem. Medallion Soc. San Francisco Opera, 1984—; mem. ann. summer event com., membership com. Internat. Diplomacy Coun. Mem. MLA, Nat. Coun. Tchrs. English (group leader, presenter conf. San Francisco), Calif. Assn. Tchrs. English (presenter), Internat. Diplomacy Coun. San Francisco (membership and events coms. 1996), Harvard Club San Francisco, Christopher Marlowe Soc. Avocations: cuisine, voice, writing. Home: 840 Carrousel Ct Lincoln CA 95648-8650

OSE, DOUGLAS, congressman; b. Sacramento, 1955; m. Lynnda ose; children: Erika, Emily. BS, U. Calif., Berkeley, 1977. Project mgr. Ose Properties, Sacramento, 1977-85; owner real estate devel. and investment co., 1986—; mem. U.S. Congress from 3d Calif. dist., 1999—; mem. agr., fin. svcs., and govt. reform coms. Former bd. dirs. Citrus Heights C. of C., Sacramento Housing and Redevel. Commn.; mem. Citrus Heights Incorporation Project. Republican. Office: 215 Cannon Ho Office Bldg Washington DC 20515-0001*

OSEAS, NANNETTE N. industrial hygienist, toxicologist, educator; b. Inglewood, Calif., Feb. 14, 1964; d. Elliot S. and Irene Harriet (Pollinger) O. BS in Indsl. Hygiene, Calif. State U., Northridge, 1986, MS in Environ. Sci., 1989. Cert. indsl. hygienist. Indsl. hygienist Lockheed, Burbank, Calif., 1987-89, Dept. Indsl. Rels., Van Nuys, 1989-94; chief indsl. hygiene and field safety Dept. Toxic Substances Control, Sacramento, 1994—2002. Mem. com. Am. Conf. of Govtl. Indsl. Hygienist Threshold Values, 1999-2002. Contbr. articles on occupl. health and safety to profl. pubs. Mem. Am. Indsl. Hygiene Assn., Am. Bd. Govtl. Indsl. Hygienists, Internat. Occup. Hygiene Assn. Avocations: hiking, biking, the environment, tennis, child advocacy. Office: Calif EPA PO Box Hq-26 Sacramento CA 95812-0806

OSEGUERA, PALMA MARIE, retired career officer; b. Kansas City, Mo., Dec. 29, 1946; d. Joseph Edmund and Palma Louise (Utke) O'Donnell; m. Alfonso Oseguera, Jan. 1, 1977; stepchildren: Kristie M. Daniels, Michelle L. Nielson, Lori A. Kelley. BA in Phys. Edn., Marycrest Coll., 1969. Commd. 2d lt. USMC, 1969, advanced through grades to col., 1991; asst. Marine Corps exch. officer Hdqs. and Hdqs. Squadron, Marine Corps Air Sta., Beaufort, S.C., 1969-71; classified material control officer Hdqs. and Svcs. Battalion, Camp S.D. Butler, Okinawa, 1971-73; adminstrv. officer, asst. Marine Corps exch. officer Marine Corps Air Sta., El, Toro, Santa Ana, Calif., 1973-76, Marine Corps exch. officer Yuma, Ariz., 1976-77; asst. Marine Corps exch. officer Hdqrs. and Support Bn., Marine Corps Devel. and Edn. Command, Quantico, Va., 1977-79; Marine Corps exch. officer Hqrs. Marine Corps, Washington, 1979-80; adminstrv. officer Marine Air Base Squadon 46, Marine Air Group 46, Marine Corps Air Sta., El Toro, Santa Ana, 1981-83, Hdqs. and Maintanence Squadron 46, Marine Air Group 46, Marine Corps Air Sta., El Toro, Santa Ana, 1983-85, Mobilization Tng. Unit Calif. 53, Landing Force Tng. Command, Pacific, San Diego, 1985-89, 3d Civil Affairs Group, L.A., 1989; dep. asst. chief of staff G-1 I Marine Expeditionary Force, Individual Mobilization Augumentee Detachment, Camp Pendleton, Calif., 1990-91; assoc. mem. Mobilization Tng. Unit Del. 01, Del., 1992-94; adminstrn. officer Mobilization Tng. Unit, CA-53, EWTG Pac, NAB, Coronado, San Diego, 1994-96; exch. officer MWRSPT ACT IMA Det MCB, Camp Pendleton, Calif., 1996-99; ret. from 30 yrs. commissioned svc. USMCR, 1999. Mem. choir St. Elizabeth Seaton, Woodbridge, Va., 1978-80, St. Patricks, Arroyo Grande, Calif., 1990-94; vol. Hospice, San Luis Obispo, 1995—; mem. Los Osos (Calif.) veteran's events com. Mem. AAUW (past libr.), Marine Corps Assn., Marine Corps Res. Officer Assn., Marine Corps Aviation Assn. (12 dist. dir. 1987), Women in Mil. Svc. for Am., Woman Marine Assn., Marine Corps League. Republican. Roman Catholic. Avocations: skiing, gardening, reading, pet care/sitting, horseback riding. Home: 728 Scenic Cir Arroyo Grande CA 93420-1617

OSEN, GREGORY ALAN, water conditioning company executive; b. Beloit, Wis., Mar. 14, 1951; s. Vincent Darryl and Mavis Lucille (Lasher) O.; m. Deborah Ann Churchill Bladorn, Jan. 29, 1972 (div. Jan. 1987); m. Christine Adel Dauenbaugh Pulliam, Oct. 8, 1987; children: Leah Michelle, Felicia Ann. BA in Music Edn. with honors, Milton (Wis.) Coll., 1973; postgrad., Cardinal Stritch Coll., 1985. Machinist, assembler Nat. Detroit, Rockford, Ill., 1973-78; sales tech. Ill. Water Treatment, 1978-79, sales engr., 1979-80, dist. sales engr., 1980-85; sales mgr. Glegg Water Technologies, Guelph, Ont., Can., 1985-2000; v.p. mktg. & sales Process Equipment Unltd., Londonderry, N.H., 2000—. Pres. Seekers, Strawbridge Meth. Ch., 1995-96, mem. adminstrv. bd., 1996, mem. choir, 1995-96; trumpeter Harris County Big Band, 1993-95. Mem. Am. Water Works Assn., AIChe Avocation: video prodn., sports cars, auto racing. Home: 6012 Canyon Rd Sanger TX 76266-7451 Office: Process Equipment Unltd 46 Nashua Rd Bldg B Ste 9A Londonderry NH 03053 also: Glegg Water Conditioning 29 Royal Rd Guelph ON Canada N1H 1G2 E-mail: peunh@aol.com.

OSGOOD, CHRISTOPHER MYKEL, radio sales executive; b. Northampton, Mass., Nov. 8, 1963; s. Robert Mansfield and Susanne (Mykel) O.; m. Angela Baxter; 1 child, Robert Marley. BS, Cornell U., 1989. Media rsch. mktg. analyst Vitt Media Internat., N.Y.C., 1988-89; acct. exec. KAOI AM/FM Radio, Maui, Hawaii, 1989-91, KTXH-TV, Houston, 1991-92; dir. advt. Oilers News, Browns News Illustrated, 49ers Report, Cleve., 1992-93; acct. exec. KRBE-FM, Houston, 1993-96, KLOL-FM, Houston, 1996-99; local sales mgr. KUCD-FM, Honolulu, 1999-2001, KLOL-FM, Houston, 2001—, gen. sales mgr., 2002—. Coach Bear Creek Basketball League, Houston, 1993-94. Mem. Cornell Alumni Assn. of Greater Houston, Cornell Soc. Hotelmen. Office: KLOL 3050 Post Oak Blvd Ste 1200 Houston TX 77056 E-mail: chrisosgood@clearchannel.com.

OSGOOD, FRANK WILLIAM, urban and economic planner, writer; b. Williamston, Mich., Sept. 3, 1931; s. Earle Victor and Blanche Mae (Eberley) O.; children: Ann Marie, Frank William Jr. BS, Mich. State U., 1953; M in City Planning, Ga. Inst. Tech., 1960. Prin. planner Tulsa Met. Area Plnning Commn., 1958-60; sr. assoc. Hammer & Co. Assocs., Washington, 1960-64; econ. cons. Marvin Springer & Assocs., Dallas, 1964-65; sr. assoc. Gladstone Assocs., Washington, 1965-67; prof. urban planning Iowa State U., Ames, 1967-73; pres. Frank Osgood Assoc./Osgood Urban Rsch., Dallas, 1973-84; dir. mktg. studies MPSI Americas Inc., Tulsa, 1984-85, Comarc Systems/Roulac & Co., San Francisco, 1985-86; pres. Osgood Urban Rsch., Millbrae, Calif., 1986-95; freelance writer Millbrae and L.A., 1994—; VISTA vol. coord. Chrysalis, Santa Monica, 1995-96; pres. Osgood Urban Rsch., L.A., 1996—. Adj. prof. U. Tulsa, 1974-76; lectr. U. Tex., Dallas, 1979, U. Tex., Arlington, 1983. Author: Control Land Uses Near Airports, 1960, Planning Small Business, 1967, Continuous Renewal Cities, 1970, (novel) Region Aroused, 2001; contbr. articles to profl. jours. Chmn. awards Cub Scouts Am., Ames, 1971-73; deacon Calvary Presbyn. Ch., San Francisco, 1987-90. 1st lt. USAF, 1954-56. Recipient Community Leaders and Noteworthy Americans award 1976. Mem. Am. Inst. Cert. Planners (peninsula liaison 1987-89, dir. pro-tem 1990 No. Calif. sect., edn. coord. 1991-92, Calif., dir. N. Cen. Tex. sect., Tex. chpt. 1983), Am. Planning Assn., Am. Inst. Planners (v.p. Okla. chpt. 1975-77), Okla. Soc. Planning Cons. (sec., treas. 1976-79), Urban Land Inst., Nat. Assn. Regional Couns., So. Calif. Assn. Govts. (regional adv. coun. 1998—, vice-chmn. 1999-2000, chair 2000-01), Writer's Bloc & Novel Group, Cypress. Home: 5605 Nelson St Cypress CA 90630-3148 E-mail: fwosgood@worldnet.att.net.

OSGOOD, RICHARD MAGEE, JR. applied physics educator, electrical engineering educator, research administrator, educator; b. Kansas City, Mo., Dec. 28, 1943; s. Richard Magee and Mary Neff (Russell) O.; m. Alice Rose Dyson, June 25, 1966; children— Richard Magee, III, Nathaniel David, Jennifer Anne BS in Engring., U.S. Mil. Acad., 1965; MS in Physics, Ohio State U., 1968; PhD, MIT, 1973. Rsch. assoc. dept. physics MIT, Cambridge, 1969-72, rsch. staff Lincoln Lab., 1973-80, project leader Lincoln Lab., 1980-81; assoc. prof. applied physics and elec. engring. Columbia U., N.Y.C., 1981-82, prof., 1982-91, Higgins prof., 1989—. Assoc. dir. Brookhaven Nat. Lab., Upton, NY, 2000—; dir. Microelectronics Sci. Labs., 1984—90; mem. Army Sci. and Tech. Basic Energy Scis. Adv. Com., Def. Scis.-Advanced Rsch. Projects Agy.; cons. Los Alamos Nat. Lab.; mem. ad hoc com. Air Force Sci. Adv. Bd. Editor: Laser Diagnostics and Photochemical Processing of Semiconductor Devices, 1983; contbr. articles to profl. jours.; patentee in field Served to capt. USAF, 1965-69 Recipient Samuel Burka award USAF Avionics Lab., 1968, Leos Travelling Lectr. award, 1986-87, Disting. Travelling Lectr. APS, R.W. Wood Prize, 1991, Optical Soc. Am.; John Simon Guggenheim fellowship, 1989. Fellow IEEE, Am. Phys. Soc., Optical Soc. Am. (R.W. Wood award, 1991); mem. Am. Chem. Soc., Materials Rsch. Soc. (councillor 1983-86), Optical Device Assn. (Japanese hon. lectr. 1990), Am. Phys. Soc. (travelling lectureship 1992). Home: 345 Quaker Rd Chappaqua NY 10514-2615 Office: Columbia U Radiation Laboratory New York NY 10027

OSGOOD, RUSSELL KING, academic administrator; b. Fairborn, Ohio, Oct. 25, 1947; s. Richard M. and Mary Russell Osgood; m. Paula Haley, June 6, 1970; children: Mary, Josiah, Micah, Iain. BA, Yale U., 1969, JD, 1974. Bar: Mass. 1974, U.S. Dist. Ct. Mass. (admitted to) 1976. Assoc. Hill & Barlow, Boston, 1974—78; assoc. prof. Boston U., 1978—80; prof. Cornell U., Ithaca, NY, 1980—88, dean law sch., 1988—98; pres. Grinnell (Iowa) Coll., 1998—. Lt. USNR, 1969—71. Mem.: Selden Soc., Stair Soc., Mass. Hist. Soc. Office: Grinnell Coll 1121 Park St Grinnell IA 50112-1640 E-mail: osgood@grinnell.com.

OSGUTHORPE, JOHN DAVID, otolaryngologist, educator; b. Fairbanks, Alaska, 1948; MD, U. Utah, 1973. Intern UCLA, 1973-74, resident surgery, 1974-75, resident otolaryngology, 1975-78; prof. Med. U. S.C., Charleston, 1979—; otolaryngologist Med. U. Hosp. Skull Base fellowship U. Zurich. Mem.: HNS, AMA (del.), Sinus Allergy Health Partnership (bd. dirs. 1998—), Am. Rhinologic Soc. (bd. dirs. 1998—2001, editor 1998—2001), Am. Laryngological Assn., Am. Acad. Otolaryngic Allergy (pres. 1995), Am. Acad. Otolaryngology, Head and Neck Surgery (bd. dirs. 1997—, coord. continuing edn. 2000—, Disting. Svc. award 1995), Am. Acad. Facial Plastic and Reconstructive Surgery. Office: Med Univ SC Dept Otolaryngology 150 Ashley Ave Charleston SC 29401-5803 E-mail: osguthjd@worldnet.att.net.

O'SHANICK, GREGORY JOHN, physician, medical association administrator; b. Akron, Ohio, Nov. 22, 1953; s. Peter and Mary (Popadics) O'S; m. Alison Moon, Oct. 8, 1991; children: Beth, Peter, Van, Alexis, Drew. Student, Ohio State U., 1971-73; MD, U. Tex., 1977. Diplomate Am. Bd. Disability Analysts. Intern to chief resident, fellow Duke U. Med. Ctr., Durham, N.C., 1977-81; asst. staff psychiatrist Meml. Southwest Hosp., Houston, 1981-84; assoc. The Hauser Clinic and Assoc., P.A., 1981-82; clin. asst. prof. psychiatry, clin. instr. family practice U. Tex. Health Scis. Ctr., 1981-82, asst. prof. psychiatry, assoc. dir. cons.-liason svc., 1982-84; asst. prof. psychiatry, dir. med./psychiatry svc. Med. Coll. Va., Richmond, 1984-89, asst. prof. rehab. medicine, 1985-89, dir. inpatient psychiatry svcs., 1987-90, co-dir. rehab. rsch. and tng. ctr. in brain injury, 1989-90, chmn. divsn. inpatient psychiatry, 1989-90, assoc. prof. psychiatry and rehab. medicine, 1989-91; attending physician VA Med. Ctr., Richmond, 1987-91; dir. Ctr. Neurorehab. Svcs., 1991—; assoc. med. dir. neurorehab. program HealthSouth Med. Ctr., 1993-96. Cons. neuropsychiatric PATE Rehab. Endeavors, Inc., Dallas, 1990-91; spl. cons. traumatic brain injury initiative Nat. Inst. Handicapped Rsch., 1986-87; assoc. prof. neurosurgery U. Va. Health Sci. Ctr.; mem. neuromed. adv. bd. N.E. Ctr. for Spl. Care, 1998-2000. Author: Head Trauma Psychiatric Medicine, 1989; (with others) MMPI 168 Codebook, 1984, Psychiatric Aspects of Trauma, 1986; contbg. author: (with others) Neuropsychological Treatment of Head Injury, 1989, Principles of Medical Psychiatry, 1987, Community Reentry for Person with Traumatic Brain Injury, 1989, Psychiatric Aspects of Traumatic Brain Injury, 1994; editl. bd. Neurorehabilitation: An Interdisciplinary Jour.; numerous nat. presentations; contbr. articles, papers, letters and editls. to numerous profl. jours. Mgr., coach Huguenot Little League, Chesterfield, Va., 1991—; mem. selection com. Keep our Streets Safe and Sober, 1996; bd. dirs. Nat. Head Injury Found., 1989, chair psychiatry adv. com., 1988-90, mem. legis. com. profl. divsn., 1986-87, com. revise DSM-IV listings TBI, 1985, spl. cons., 1984; mem. task force dually diagnosed Southern Regional Edn Bd., 1986; mem. Va. Brain Injury Coun., 1987-2000, vice-chair, 1997-2000, chair, 1998-99; mem. adv. bd. Va. Head Injury Found., Inc., 1988-91; mem. task force cognitive retraining Gen. Assembly Commonwealth Va., 1992; mem. task force evaluate and modify traumatic brain injury program Woodrow Wilson Rehab. Ctr., Va., 1993; bd. dirs. Transitional Learning Cmty., Galveston, Tex., 1983-85, adv. bd. 1985-91; mem. com. psychol. edn. Am. Diabetes Assn., Houston chpt., 1983-84. Named Bus. Assoc. Yr. award Am. Bus. Women's Assn., Shockoe Valley chpt., 1989; Hamilton Ford award for Excellence, 1977; grantee Roering Pharm., 1983-85, UTHSCH, 1983; Va. Commonwealth Univ. Grants-In-Aid Program, 1985-86, DMHMR, 1988, 1988-89, 1989-90, 1990-91, NIDRR, 1988-89, 1986-89, 1989-93, 1989-90, 1992-93, Dept. Edn., 1991-92, N.Y. State Dept. Edn., 1993, US DOE RSA, 1995-96. Fellow Am. Psychiat. Assn. (com. mem. life, accident and health ins. 1981-89, subcom. ins. code system 1983-84, task force traumatic brain injury 1990, assoc. editor Brian Injury: Jour. Internat. Brain Injury Assn. 1985-91); mem. AMA, Am. Neuropsychiat. Assn., Am. Soc. Neurorehab., Brain Injury Assn. (med. dir. 1996—, bd. dirs. Rubin Rsch. Fund 1997), Assn. Medicine and Psychiatry, Am. Acad. for Cert. of Brain Injury Specialists (bd. dirs.), Psychiat. Soc. Va., Am. Acad. Neurology, Sigma Xi. Republican. Avocations: golf, skiing, travel, reading. Office: Ctr Neurorehab Svc 11315 Polo Pl Midlothian VA 23113-1434 E-mail: gjocns@aol.com.

O'SHAUGHNESSY, ERIN JEANNE, government official, consultant; b. Cambridge, Mass., Feb. 6, 1970; d. Daniel William and Janice Edna (Mathews) O'S. BA, U. N.H., 1992; MA, Yale U., 1996. Tchg. fellow Yale U., New Haven, 1995-96; intelligence officer CIA, Washington, 1997-99, chmn. mgmt. adv. group Office Transnat. Issues, 1998-99; bus. intelligence cons. KPMG Cons., 1999-2000; knowledge and bus. mgr. GAO, 2000—. Developer, instr. bus. process improvement course Bus. Process Improvement Overview, 2000 (award Nat. Reconnaissance Office 2000). Lyndon B. Johnson Congl. scholar, 1991. Mem. Phi Alpha Theta (life), Pi Gamma Mu (life). Avocations: rock climbing, reading, cooking, computers. Office: GAO 441 G St NW Washington DC 20548 Fax: 202-512-8786. E-mail: oshaughnessye@gao.gov.

O'SHAUGHNESSY, JAMES PATRICK, lawyer; b. Rochester, N.Y., Mar. 3, 1947; s. John Andrew and Margaret May (Yaxley) O'S.; m. Terry Lee Wood. BS cum laude, Rensselaer Poly. Inst., 1972; JD, Georgetown U., 1977. Bar: Va. 1977, Ohio 1979, Wis. 1987. Assoc. Squire, Sanders & Dempsey, Cleve., 1978-81; ptnr. Hughes & Cassidy, Sumas, Wash., 1981-84; patent counsel Kimberly-Clark Corp., Neenah, Wis., 1984-85; ptnr. Foley & Lardner, Milw., 1986-96; v.p., chief intellectual property counsel Rockwell Internat. Corp., 1996—, corp. officer. Founder Innovatech Co., 1996—; mem. tech. adv. coun. Ideation Internat., Inc., 1999—; mem. adv. bd. Licensing Econs. Rev.; mem. bd. visitors Georgetown U. Sch. Nursing, 1996-2000; mem., bd. dir. Intellectual Property Owners; frequent lectr., chmn. seminars to legal and bus. groups. Contbg. author: Technology Licensing: Corporate Strategies for Maximizing Value, 1996, Profiting From Intellectual Capital: Extracting Value From Innovation, 1998; contbr. articles to profl. jours. Bd. dirs. Skylight Opera Theatre, 1991-92, Milw. Florentine Opera Co., 1999—. With USN, 1964-68. Mem. CPR Inst. for Dispute Resolution (mediation/arbitration panel), Lic. Execs. Soc., Am. Intellectual Property Law Assn., Assn. Chief Patent Coun.; Disabled Am. Vets., Tau Beta Pi, Alpha Sigma Mu. Home: 3207 W Donges Bay Rd Mequon WI 53092-5119 Office: Rockwell Automation Inc. 777 E Wisconsin Ave Ste 1400 Milwaukee WI 53202-5302

O'SHEA, CATHERINE LARGE, marketing and public relations consultant; b. Asheville, N.C., Feb. 27, 1944; d. Edwin Kirk Jr. and Mary Mitchell (Westall) Large; m. Roger Dean Lower, Dec. 19, 1970 (dec. Sept. 1977); children: Thaddeus Kirk Lower and David Alexander Lower (twins, dec.); m. Michael Joseph O'Shea, Dec. 29, 1980. BA in History magna cum laude, Emory U., 1966. Mktg. staff mem. Time Inc., N.Y.C., 1966-69; mktg. adminstr. Collier-Macmillan Internat., 1970-71; circulation mgr. Coll. Entrance Exam. Bd., 1971-73; spl. asst. to pres. Wayne Dressel Assocs. Exec. Search, 1973-75; freelance writer, editor, pub. rels. Princeton, N.J., 1975-78; dir. constituency rels. Emory U., Atlanta, 1978-80; devel. assoc. U. Del., Newark, 1981-83; asst. to pres. Elizabethtown (Pa.) Coll., 1983-85; assoc. v.p. Beaver Coll., Glenside, Pa., 1985; cons. mktg. and pub. rels. Phila., S.C., Ga., 1985—. Co-author: 50 Secrets of Highly Successful Cats, 1994 (trans. German edit. Schnurrende Tyrannen by Manfred Sommer, 1996); editor Elizabethtown mag., 1983-85; contbr. articles to nat. mags. and profl. jours. Founder Helping Hands Internat.; trustee Large Found.; founding trustee Newberry Opera House Found.; promotions coord. St. Joseph Fan. Mem. Pub. Rels. Soc. Am. (accredited), Mortar Bd., Phi Beta Kappa, Phi Mu.

O'SHEA, LYNNE EDEEN, management consultant, educator; b. Chgo., Oct. 18, 1950; d. Edward Fisk and Mildred (Lessner) O'S. BA, BJ in Polit. Sci. and Advt., U. Mo., MA in Comms. and Mktg. Rsch., 1971; PhD in Consumer Cultures, Northwestern U., 1977; postgrad., Sch. Mgmt. and Strategic Studies, U. Calif., 1988. Congl. asst., Washington, 1969-70; brand mgr. Procter & Gamble Co., Cin., 1971-73; v.p. Foote, Cone & Belding, Inc., Chgo., 1973-79; v.p. corp. communications Internat. Harvester Co., 1979-82; dir. communications Arthur Andersen & Co., 1983-86; v.p. bus. devel. Gannett Co., Inc., 1987-94; pres., chief oper. officer Shalit Place L.L.C., 1995—; exec. v.p. Mus. Broadcast Comm., Chgo., 1996-97; cons. A.T. Kearney, Chgo., 1998—. Prof. mktg. U. Chgo. Grad. Sch. Bus., 1979—80, Kellogg Grad. Sch. mgmt., 1983—84, 1994—95, 2000—; exec.-in-residence DePaul U., 2000—; dir. AskRex.com, 1999—, Clark/Bardes Inc., 1999—. Bd. dirs. Off-the-Street Club, Chgo., 1977-86; mem. adv. bd. U. Ill. Coll. Commerce, 1980-95, Chgo. Crime Commn., 1987—; bus. adv. bd., DePaul U., 1989—, Roosevelt U., 1994—; dir., Merle Ruskin Theatre bd., 2001—. Recipient numerous Eagle Fin. Advt. awards, Silver medalist Am. Advt. Fedn., 1989; named Advt. Woman of Yr. Chgo. Advt. Club, 1989; named Glass Ceiling Commn., 1991-95, Com. 21st Century, 1992—. Fellow Internat. Leadership Forum; mem. Internat. Women's Forum (v.p. devel., v.p. communications, exec. com., bd. dir.), Chgo. Network, Women's Forum Chgo., Women's Forum Mich., Tarrytown Group, Social Venture Network, Execs. Club Chgo., Mid-Am. Club (bd. govs. 1990—), Women's Athletic Club Chgo., Cleve. Yachting Club. Office: AT Kearney Inc 222 W Adams St Fl 25 Chicago IL 60606-5227 E-mail: lynne.o'shea@atkearney.com., loshea@depaul.edu.

O'SHEA, PATRICK MICHAEL, conductor, music educator; b. Worcester, Mass., Feb. 15, 1967; s. Martin William and Crystal Alice (Bilodeau) O'Shea; m. Amy Meyer, July 31, 1993. MusB summa cum laude, Shenandoah Conservatory, 1989; MusM, U. Ill., 1990; D of Musical Arts, Ariz. State U., 1995. Vis. asst. prof. Stephen F. Austin State U., Nacogdoches, Tex., 1995-97; asst. prof. music St. Mary's U., Winona, Minn., 1997—. Chmn. Winona Fine Arts Commn. Composer (choral music) Three Marian Motets, 1996, (choral/orchestral) Te Deum, 1997, (choral cycle) Freedom River, 1999; author (essayist). Capt. spl. ops.., adv. group S.C. Mil. Dept. Mem. ASCAP, Internat. Fedn. Choral Music, Am. Choral Dirs. Assn., Mensa, Internat. Soc. for Philos. Enquiry, Gaelic Heritage Soc. (pres.), Am. Coll. Heraldry (fellow, bd. govs.), O'Shea Clan Soc. (pres.), Imperial Order of the Star of Honor of Ethiopia (grand officer). Democrat. Roman Catholic. Avocations: Irish history, genealogy. Home: 850-A Highway 14 Winona MN 55987-7602 Office: St Marys Univ 700 Terrace Hts # 1447 Winona MN 55987-1321 Fax: 507-457-1439. E-mail: poshea@smumn.edu.

O'SHEA, PATRICK JOSEPH, lawyer, electrical engineer; b. Chgo., Apr. 10, 1950; s. John Raymond and Alta M. (Bauert) O'S.; m. Patricia Ann Dalaker, Aug. 11, 1980; children: Erin, Tarah, Brian, Maghan. BSEE, U. Ill., 1972; JD, John Marshall Law Sch., 1979. Bar: Ill. 1979, U.S. Dist. Ct. (no. dist.) Ill. 1979, U.S. Patent Office 1982. Elec. engr. elec. div. City of Chgo. Police Dept., 1976-79; elec. engr. Commonwealth Edison, Chgo., 1972-76; atty. Patricik Mazza & Assocs., 1979-80, Richard E. Alexander & Assocs., Chgo., 1980-81; sole pratice Chgo. and Lombard, Ill., 1981—; spl. asst. states atty. Du. Page County, 1988. Spl. appellate prosecutor, 1989. Elected Rep. committeeman, York Twp., Ill., 1982, chmn. rep. committeeman's orgn., 1996; mem. exec. com. York Twp. Rep. Committeeman's Orgn., vice-chmn., 1992, chmn., 1996; mem. exec. com. DuPage County Bd., 1989—, chmn. landfill com., 1989, 94, vice chmn. legis. com., 1994; commr. Forest Preserve, 1992; gen. counsel Ill. Rep. Party; gen. counsel Ill. Rep. Party. Mem. Ill. Bar Assn., DuPage Bar Assn., Chgo. Bar Assn., Lombard C. of C., Lombard Rotary. Roman Catholic. Avocations: politics, golf, chess. Home: 1051 S Fairview Ave Lombard IL 60148-4035 Office: 156 S Main St Lombard IL 60148-2628

OSHEROFF, DOUGLAS DEAN, educator, physicist, researcher; b. Aberdeen, Wash., Aug. 1, 1945; s. William and Bessie Anne (Ondov) Osheroff; m. Phyllis S.K. Liu, Aug. 14, 1970. BS in Physics, Calif. Inst. Tech., 1967; MS, Cornell U., 1969, PhD in Physics, 1973. Mem. tech. staff Bell Labs., Murray Hill, NJ, 1972—82, head solid state and low temperature physics research dept., 1982—87; prof. Stanford (Calif.) U., 1987—, J.G. Jackson and C.J. Wood prof. physics, 1992—; chair physics, 1993—96; assoc. chair physics, 2001—. Rschr. on properties of matter near absolute zero of temperature, co-discoverer of superfluidity in liquid 3He, 1971, nuclear antiferromagnetic resonance in solid 3He, 1980. Co-recipient Simon Meml. prize, Brit. Inst. Physics, 1976; recipient Oliver E. Buckley Solid State Physics prize, 1981, Nobel prize in Physics, 1996, Walter J. Gores award, 1991; fellow John D. and Catherine T. MacArthur prize, 1981. Fellow: Am. Acad. Arts and Scis., Am. Phys. Soc.; mem.: NAS. Office: Stanford U Rm 150 Varian Physics Bldg 382 Via Pueblo Mall Stanford CA 94305-4060*

OSHIDA, YOSHIKI, materials scientist, researcher; b. Tokyo, Dec. 17, 1941; s. Yoshiteru and Michiko Koizumi Oshida; m. Michiko Koizumi, Nov. 29, 1969; 1 child Yoshiko Neugebauer 1 child Kenichi. PhD, Waseda U., Tokyo, 1970. Assoc. prof. Syracuse U., Syracuse, NY, 1980—90; prof. Ind. U. Sch. Dentistry, Indpls., 1990—. Sr. rschr. Mitsubishi Heavy Industries, Yokohama, Japan, 1970—80; presenter in field. Mem. editl. adv. bd.: Jour. Biomed. Materials and Engring., 1994—; contbr. numerous peer-reviewed articles to profl. jours. Fellow rsch. fellow, Nat. Inst. for Std. and Tech., 1995. Mem.: Internat. Assn. for Dental Rsch., Japanese Soc. for Dental Materials and Devices, Japan Soc. Oral Implantology, Am. Assn. for Dental Rsch., Internat. Acad. Shape Memory Metals for Medical Use, Am. Inst. for Mining, Metallurgical, and Petroleum Engrs., Am. Soc. of Metals. Home: 310 Haddonfield Dr Syracuse NY 13214 Office: Ind U Sch Dentistry 1121 W Michigan St Indianapolis IN 46202-5186 Home Fax: 315-446-1036; Office Fax: 317-274-2419. Personal E-mail: yoshida@iupui.edu. Business E-Mail: yoshida@iupui.edu.

O'SHIELDS, RICHARD LEE, retired natural gas company executive; b. Ozark, Ark., Aug. 12, 1926; s. Fay and Anna (Johnson) O'S.; m. Shirley Isabelle Washington, Nov. 8, 1947; children: Sharon Isabelle O'Shields Boles, Carolyn Jean, Richard Lee Jr. BS in Mech. Engring. U. Okla., 1949; MS in Petroleum Engring, La. State U., 1951. Registered profl. engr., Kans., Tex. Instr. petroleum engring. La. State U., 1949-51; prodn. engr. Pure Oil Co., 1951-53; sales engr., chief engr., v.p. Salt Water Control, Inc., Ft. Worth, 1953-59; cons. engr. Ralph H. Cummins Co., 1959-60; with Anadarko Prodn. Co. and parent co. Panhandle Eastern Pipe Line Co., 1960-88; pres. Anadarko Prodn. Co., 1966-68; exec. v.p. Panhandle Eastern Pipe Line Co., 1968-70, pres., chief exec. officer, 1970-79, chmn., chief exec. officer, 1979-83, chmn., 1983-88, also bd. dirs., 1969-93. Pres., CEO Trunkline Gas Co., 1970-79, chmn., CEO, 1979-83, chmn., 1983-88. With USAAF, 1945. Mem. Am. Petroleum Inst., Soc. Petroleum Engrs., Ind. Natural Gas Assn. Am., Gas Research Inst., Ind. Petroleum Assn. Am., So. Gas Assn., Tau Beta Pi. Republican. Methodist. Home: 511 Oakland Hills Ln Kerrville TX 78028-6427 E-mail: richloshields@aol.com.

OSHIMA, MICHAEL W. lawyer; b. Big Rapids, Mich., Apr. 4, 1957; s. Walter W. and Mitsue Oshima. AB, Brown U., 1979; MA, Harvard U., 1984; JD, NYU, 1987. Bar: N.Y. 1988, D.C. 1989. Sr. rsch. asst. Harvard U. John F. Kennedy Sch. Govt., Cambridge, Mass., 1981-84; assoc. Davis Polk & Wardwell, N.Y.C., 1987-90, Arnold & Porter, N.Y.C., 1990-96, ptnr., 1997—. Contbr. articles, reports to profl. publs. Mem. Am. Sociol. Assn., Law and Soc. Assn., N.Y. State Bar Assn., Assn. Bar City N.Y. Office: Arnold & Porter 399 Park Ave Fl 35 New York NY 10022-4690 E-mail: michael_oshima@aporter.com.

OSHIN, DIANE, publisher; married; two children. BA in Polit. Sci. and French, Tufts U.; MBA in Mktg. and Fin., Columbia U. Formerly with Woman's Day, Conde Nast Traveler, Ogilvy & Mather, others; former advt. dir. Vogue; v.p., group pub. The Parenting Group AOL Time Warner, N.Y.C., 1994—. Office: Time Inc The Parenting Grp Time Inc The Parenting Grp 530 Fifth Ave New York NY 10036

OSHYPKO, JOHN, artist, set designer; b. Phila., Sept. 7, 1928; s. Nicholas and Olga Oshchypko. BFA, BS Edn., postgrad., Temple U. Cert. Computer Aided Drafting/Design 1994. Prodn. designer Cape May (N.J.) Playhouse, 1966; set designer Valley Forge (Pa.) Music Fairs, 1955—58; prodn. designer, art dir. Phila. Co-Opera Co., 1953—58. Art cons. Cardion Electronics, Woodbury, NY, 1989—99. One-man shows include , Brentwood, N.Y., 1990, Smithtown, N.Y., 1992, Westhampton Beach, N.Y., 1995, exhibited in group shows at Internat. Art Competition, 1988 (cert. of excellence, 1988), Artitudes 7th Internat. Exhbn., 1989 (cert. of excellence, 1989), Manhattan Arts Internat., 1998 (cert. of excellence, 1998), Brentwood Libr., Westhampton Beach Gallery, Smith Haven Mall Bank, Bellport Libr. Avocation: gardening. Home and Office: 13 S 5th Ave Brentwood NY 11717-5420 E-mail: oshypko@optonline.net.

OSIAS, RICHARD ALLEN, international financier, investor, real estate investment executive, corporate investor; b. N.Y.C., Nov. 13, 1940; s. Harry L. and Leah (Schenk) O.; children: A. Kimberly, Alexandra Elizabeth. Student, Columbia U., 1963; postgrad. theolog. works, David Lipscomb U., 1988-92; PhD in Bus. Adminstrn., Shaftesbury U., 2000, DD, 1984. Owner Osias Enterprises, Inc., numerous locations, 1953—98. Mem. bus. cabinet David Lipscomb U.; bd. dirs. Am. 21. Prin. works include city devel., residential and apt. units, founder City North Lauderdale, Fla., founder City of Lauderhill, Fla., complete residential housing communities, shopping centers, country clubs, golf courses, hotel chains, comprehensive housing communities; contributed Greystone Raquet and Tennis Club to Nolensville, Tenn.; owner, operator Coolsprings Exec. Plz., landmark office bldg., Internat. Common Market Shopping Complex and other office bldgs., shopping ctrs. in mid-southern region; co-author: South Florida Uniform Building Code. Mem. North Lauderdale City Coun., 1967—, mayor, 1968, police and fire commr., 1967—; mem. Gold Cir., Atlanta Ballet; benefactor Atlanta Symphony Soc.; founder Boys Clubs Broward County, Tower coun. Pine Crest Prep. Sch. (founder), v.p., bd. dirs. LaCiel Park Tower Condominium Assn.; bd. dirs. Tenn. Children's Home, MASS, Tenn. chpt. MADD, MADD Tenn. Children's Home. Recipient Best Am. House award Am. Home mag., 1962, Westinghouse award, 1968, Cert. of Merit for outstanding achievement and contbn. to City of Atlanta by Mayor Andrew Young, 1982; named Builder of Yr., Sunshine State Info. Bur., Fla. and Sunshine State Sr. Citizen, Fla., 1967-73, Builder of Month, Builder/Arch. Mag., 1992, Hon. Police Chief, Nashville, Tenn., 1995, N.Y.C., 1980; profiles on nat. and internat. media, including Dateline/CBS TV, NBC TV, CBS TV and Fuji Network (Japan). Mem. Fla. Sheriff's Assn., Ft. Lauderdale BBB, N.Y. BBB, Nashville BBB, Offshore Power Boat Racing Assn., Fraternal Order Police Assn. (pres.), U.S. C. of C., Fla. C. of C., Margate C. of C., Ft. Lauderdale C. of C., Smithsonian Instn., Soc. Founders U. Miami, Tower Coun., Columns Soc., Pinecrest Prep. Sch. (founder), Nat. Assn. Home Builders, Bankers Club (Miami, Fla.), Bankers Top of First Club, Quarter Deck Club (Galveston, Tex.), Boca Raton (Fla.) Yacht and Country Club, Maunalua Bay Club (Honolulu), Tryall Golf and Country Club (Jamaica), Top of the Home Club, Svc. Plus Club (France), Ensworth Red Gables Soc., Hawaii Loa Ridge Assn., Cannes Island Yacht Club, Canary Islands Yacht Club, Collier's Reserve Country Club (Naples, Fla.), Grey Oaks Country Club (Naples), Le Ciel Club (Naples; v.p. bd. dirs.), Hawaii Loa Ridge Assn. Home: 482 Maono Loop Honolulu HI 96821 Fax: 808-373-8885. E-mail: osias1@aol.com.

OSINSKI, MARTIN HENRY, healthcare consultant; b. N.Y.C., Apr. 23, 1954; s. Stanley and Shirley (Bobick) O.; children: Ashley, Brett. BBA in Acctg., U. Miami, 1975, MBA, 1977. Grad. asst. U. Miami, Fla., 1975-77; staff acct. Ernst & Ernst, CPA, Miami, 1977-78; asst. buyer, dept. mgr. Burdines Dept. Stores, 1978-80; buyer menswear Jefferson Ward Dept. Stores, 1980-82, Richway Dept. Stores, Atlanta, 1982-84; pres. Nat. Health Search, Inc., Miami, 1984-95; chief oper. officer MD Resources, Inc., 1989-95; prin. Am. Med. Consultants, Inc., 1996—. Bd. dirs. Congregation Bet Breira, 1994-98. Mem.: Am. Mktg. Assn., Nat. Assn. Physician Recruiters (bd. dirs. 1989—96, v.p. 1990—91, prs. 1991—, ethics com. 2001—, Presdl. award 1991), Iron Arrow Soc. U. Miami, Mens Club (pres. 1992—94). Office: Am Med Consultants Inc 11625 SW 110th Rd Miami FL 33176-3152

OSIPOW, SAMUEL HERMAN, psychology educator; b. Allentown, Pa., Apr. 18, 1934; s. Louis Morris and Tillie Osipow; m. Sondra Beverly Feinstein, Aug. 26, 1956; children: Randall A., Jay I., Reva S., David S. BA, Lafayette Coll., Easton, Pa., 1954; MA, Columbia U., 1955; PhD, Syracuse U., 1959. Lectr. U. Wis., Madison, 1961; psychologist, asst. prof. Pa. State U., 1961-67; mem. faculty Ohio State U., Columbus, 1967-98, prof. psychology, 1969-98, chmn. dept., 1973-86, prof. emeritus, 1998—. Vis. prof. Tel Aviv U., 1972, U. Md., 1980—81; vis. rsch. assoc. Harvard U., 1965; cons. to govt. Author: Strategies in Counseling for Behavior Change, 1970, Theories of Career Development, 1968, 4th edit. 1996, Handbook of Vocational Psychology, 2 vols., 1983, 2d edit. 1995, A Survey of Counseling Methods, 1984; editor: Jour. Vocat. Behavior, 1970-75, Jour. Counseling Psychology, 1975-81, Applied and Preventive Psychology, 1993-99. Served to 1st lt. U.S. Army, 1959-61. Erskine fellow U. Canterbury, New Zealand, 1997. Mem. APA (bd. dirs. 1985-88), Nat. Register Health Svc. Providers in Psychology (bd. dirs. 1982-89, chmn. 1986-89). Home: 330 Eastmoor Blvd Columbus OH 43209-2022 E-mail: sosipow@aol.com.

OSIS, DAIGA GUNTRA, lawyer; b. Riga, Latvia, July 24, 1943; d. Voldemars and Sandra (Seja) Amatnieks; m. Aivars Osis, Dec. 2, 1967; 1 child, Andre. BA cum laude, CUNY, Bklyn., 1971; JD, U. (Bridgeport) Conn., 1980. Bar: Conn. 1980, U.S. Dist. Ct. Conn. 1981, U.S Ct. Appeals (2d cir.) 1982, U.S. Supreme Ct. 1984. Assoc. DePiano & Palmesi, Bridgeport, 1980-85; ptnr. Gans, Leo & Osis, 1985-88, Gans, Osis, Reynolds & Riccio, Bridgeport, 1989-90, Gans, Osis & Reynolds, Bridgeport, 1990-94; pvt. practice law, 1994—. Asst. prof. law U. Bridgeport, 1982-83. Research editor U. Bridgeport Law Review, 1979-80. Mem. Bd. Edn., Trumbull, Conn., 1982-84; bd. dirs. Conn. Inst. of Vocal Arts, Southport, Conn., 1984-87. Mem.: Conn. Bar Assn. Democrat. Lutheran. Home: 175 Middlebrooks Ave Trumbull CT 06611-3016 Office: 325 Reef Rd Ste 212 Fairfield CT 06430-6537 E-mail: osisatty@aol.com.

OSIYOYE, ADEKUNLE, obstetrician, attorney medical and legal consultant, gynecologist, educator; b. Lagos, Nigeria, Jan. 5, 1951; came to U.S., 1972; s. Alfred and Grace (Apena) Oshiyoye; m. Toyin Osinowo Oshiyoye, Dec. 28, 1991; children: Adekunle Jr., Adedayo Justice. Student, Howard U., 1972-73; BS, U. State of N.Y., 1974; postgrad., Columbia U., 1974-78; MD, Am. U., Montserrat, West Indies, 1979; JD, Thomas Cooley Law Sch., Lansing, Mich., 1997. Bar: Mich. 1998. Intern South Chgo. Community Hosp., 1980-81; intern dept. obstetrics-gynecology Cook County Hosp., Chgo., 1981-82, resident physician, 1982-84, chief resident physician dept. obstetrics-gynecology, 1984-85; assoc. prof. dept. obstetrics-gynecology Chgo. Osteo. Coll. Medicine, 1986—; health physician, cons. physician City of Chgo. Dept. Health, 1989—. Attending physician St. Bernard Hosp., Chgo., 1985—, Hyde Park Hosp., Chgo., 1986—, Mercy Hosp., Chgo., 1987—, Roseland Hosp., Chgo., 1985—, Columbus Hosp., Chgo., 1985—, Jackson Park Hosp., Chgo., 1985—; coord. emergency rm. Cook County Hosp., 1983-85, cons. medical, legal residential care, CEO, pres., atty. Law Offices Dr. Emmanuel Oshiyo M.D., J.D., P.C., 1998—. Med. editor African Connections, 1990—; med. columnist Newsbreed Mag., 1990—; founding mem. Ob-Gyn Video Jour. Am. Organizer Harold Washington Coalition, Chgo., 1983-87; operation mem. Operation P.U.S.H., Chgo., 1987—; active Chgo. Urban League, 1989—, Cook County Dem. Party, 1988—; mem. Mayor's Commn. on Human Rels., Chgo., 1990—, State of Ill. Inaugural Com., 1991. Shell scholar, 1965-69; recipient Fed. Govt. scholarship award, 1972, Howard Univ. scholarship award, 1973, Fed. Govt. Nigeria grad. med. scholarship award, 1975-79, Cerebral Palsy rsch. award, 1977, Ob-gyn. Video Jour. award, 1989, Role Model award Chgo. Police Dept., 1991, 92, Chgo. Bd. Edn., 1991, Chgo. 100 Black Men, 1991, Gov.'s Recognition award, 1992; named one of Best Dressed Men in Chgo., Chgo. Defender, 1990, 91. Fellow Am. Coll. Internat. Physicians, Am. Coll. Obstetricians & Gynecologists; mem. AMA (physician recognition award 1986), Am. Coll. Glegal Medicine (edn. com.), Am. Soc. Law Medicine, Am. Pub. Heart Assn., Nat. Med. Assn., Ill. Med. Soc., Chgo. Med. Assn., Chgo. Gynecol. Soc., Cook County Physician Assn., Nigerian Am. Forum (chmn. health com., chmn. election com.), Cook County Hosp. Surg. Alumni Assn., Howard U. Alumni Assn. (regent, chmn. scholarship com. Chgo. chpt.), Eureka Lodge (investigating com.), Masons, Shriners, Order of Eastern Star, Alpha Phi Alpha (life mem., mem. Labor Day com., dir. ednl. programs Xi Lambda chpt. 1990—, co-chmn. courtesy Black & Gold com. 1989, 90, Recognition award 1991), Pan Hellenic Action Coun. (chmn. pub. rels. com.), Ill. Maternal and Child Health Coalition, Beta Kappa Chi, ABA, State Bar Mich., Oakland County Bar, Mich. Trial Lawyers Assn., Am. Immigration Lawyers Assn., Wayne County Med. Soc. (Legislative Com.), Mich. State Med. Soc. Apostolic. Avocations: ping pong, fishing, golf, basketball, swimming. Home: PO Box 2940 Southfield MI 48037-2940 Office: Dept Health 37 W 47th St Chicago IL 60609-4657

OSKOUIE, ALI KIANI, chemical and environmental engineer; b. Tabriz, Iran, Aug. 9, 1960; came to U.S., 1988; s. Mohammad Kiani Oskouie and Azam Heidari; m. Mojgan Rassouli, June 14, 1989; children: Suzanne, Melissa. BS, U. Tabriz, 1986; MS of Civil Engring., U. Mich., 1990; PhD, Ill. Inst. Tech., 1996. Tchg. asst. Ill. Inst. Tech., Chgo., 1990-95, rsch. asst., 1996, postdoctoral faculty rsch. assoc., 1996-97; adj. prof. dept. chem. and environ. engring. dept. civil adn archtl. engring. Stuart Sch. Bus., Environ. Mgmt. program, 1997; coord. water treatment program jt. project with City Chgo. Ill. Inst. Tech. Cons. Amherst (Mass.) Process Instruments, 1992—; supr. grad. students, particle lab. establishment Ill. Inst. Tech., Chgo., 1996—; coord. pharmaceutical rsch. with Gen. Hosp. and U. of Ottawa, Can.; rsch. scientist Met. Water Reclamation Dist. Greater Chgo., 2001. Mem. grad. and undergrad. housing focus group Ill. Inst. Tech., Chgo., 1996. Rsch. grantee Am. Air Liquide, 1996. Mem.: ASCE, Water Environment Fedn., Am. Water Works Assn., Am. Assn. Aerosol Rsch. Achievements include devel. of technique to determine particle size, density and shape factor using time-of-flight sizers in supersonic flow field, technique for surfactant characterization, technique for BOD characterization; invented a multi-beam system in time-of-flight sizers; patentee apparatus for generating aroma upon electronic signal for Tele-Aroma Drive. Office: Ill Inst Tech 10 W 33rd St Chicago IL 60616-3730 E-mail: oskouie@iit.edu.

OSLER, GORDON PETER, retired utility company executive; b. Winnipeg, Man., Can., June 19, 1922; s. Hugh Farquarson and Kathleen (Harty) O.; m. Nancy A. Riley, Aug. 20, 1948; children: Sanford L., Susan Osler Matthews, Gillian Osler Fortier. Student, Queen's U., Kingston, Ont., Can., 1940-41. Pres. Osler, Hammond & Nanton Ltd., Winnipeg, 1952-64, UNAS Investments Ltd., Toronto, Ont., Can., 1964-72; chmn. Slater Steel Industries, Hamilton, Can., 1972-86, N.Am. Life Assurance Co., Toronto, 1986-95, TransCan. Pipelines, Toronto, 1983-89, ret., 1993. Lt. Can. Army, 1942-45, ETO. Mem. Toronto Club, York Club (Toronto), Everglades Club (Palm Beach, Fla.). Avocation: golf. Home: 17 Lamport Ave Toronto ON Canada M4W 1S7

OSLER, HOWARD LLOYD, retired controller; b. Camden, N.J., Nov. 24, 1927; s. Howard B. and Miriam Osler; m. Barbara C. Skufca, 1987; children by previous marriage: Carol, Peter, Andrew, Bruce. BA, Antioch Coll., 1951. CPA, D.C. Pub. acct. Peat, Marwick Mitchell & Co., Boston, 1949-55; staff asst. to corp. contr. Gillette Co., 1957-59, gen. mgr. Panamanian subs., 1959-61; asst. to pres. Gillette Co. Argentine subs., 1961-63; asst. to corp. contr. Gillette Co., Boston, 1963-65, contr. mil. Far East div., 1965-67; contr. U.S. div. Foxboro Co., Mass., 1967-68, corp. contr., 1968-87, sec., clk., 1976-86, v.p., contr., 1981-87, ret., 1987. Trustee Gilmanton Cemeteries, 1988—, Trust Funds, 1990—91, 1994—2001; commr. Gilmanton Corner Precinct, 1989—; mem. Gilmanton Budget Com., 1990—2000, Sch. Bldg. Com., 1988, 1990, Zoning Bd. Adjustment, 1990—91, 1998—2001; mem. Gilmanton Bd. Selectmen, 1991—94. Home: PO Box 190 Gilmanton NH 03237-0190 E-mail: posler@worldpath.net.

OSMAN, EDITH GABRIELLA, lawyer; b. N.Y.C., Mar. 18, 1949; d. Arthur Abraham and Judith (Goldman) Udem; children: Jacqueline, Daniel. BA in Spanish, SUNY, Stony Brook, 1970; JD cum laude, U. Miami, 1983. Bar: Fla. 1983, U.S. Dist. Ct. (so. dist.) Fla. 1984, U.S. Dist. Ct. (mid. dist.) Fla. 1988, U.S. Ct. Appeals (11th cir.) 1985, U.S. Supreme Ct. 1987, U.S. Ct. Mil. Appeals 1990. Assoc. Kimbrell & Hamann, PA, Miami, 1984-90, Dunn & Lodish, PA, Miami, 1990-93; pvt. practice, 1993-98; shareholder Carlton Fields, 1998—. Spkr. in field. Adv. com. for Implementation of the Victor Posner Judgement to Aid the Homeless, 1986-89. Recipient Breaking the Glass Ceiling award Ziff Mus., 2000, In the Company of Women award Dade County, 2000, Judge Mattie Belle Davis award, 2000; selected for photographic exhibit Florida Women of Achievement, 2000. Fellow Am. Bar Found.; mem. ABA (family law, Ho. of Dels. 1998—, standing com. on independence of judiciary 2000—), Fla. Bar Assn. (budget com. 1989-92, 97-98, voluntary bar liaison com. 1989-90, spl. com. on formation of All-Bar Conf. 1988-89, chair mid-yr. conv. 1989, long range planning com. 1988-90, bd. govs. 1991-98, spl. commn. on delivery of legal svcs. to the indigent 1990-92, bus. law cert. com. 1995-96, practice law mgmt. com. 1995-96, chair program evaluation com., 1993-94, exec. com. 1992-93, 96—, rules and bylaws com., 1993-94, vice-chair disciplinary rev. com. 1994-95, investment com. 1994-95, vice-chair rules com. 1994-95, All-Bar Conf. chair 1997, chair grievance mediation com. 1997-99, pres.-elect 1998-99, pres. 1999-2000, exec. coun. family law sect., vice-chair legis. 2001—), Dade County Bar Assn. (fed. ct. rules com. 1985-86, chmn. program com. 1988-91, 96-97, exec. com. 1987-88), Fla. Assn. Women Lawyers Assn. (Dade County chpt. bd. dirs. 1984-85, treas. 1985-86, v.p. 1986-87, pres. 1987-88), Fla. Assn. Women

Lawyers (v.p. 1988-89, pres. 1989-90), Fla. Bar Found. (dir. 1998—), Nat. Conf. Women's Bar Assn. (dir. nat. conf. 1990-91), Fla. Acad. Trial Lawyers, Dade County Trial Lawyers Assn., Nat. Conf. Bar Pres., So. Conf. Bar Pres. Office: Carlton Fields PA 100 SE 2nd St Ste 4000 Miami FL 33131-2148 E-mail: eosma@carltonfields.com.

OSMAN, STEPHEN EUGENE, historic site administrator; b. Berkeley, Calif., Aug. 8, 1949; s. Eugene Lee and June Elizabeth (Claus) O.; m. Wendy Kay Holmberg, June 21, 1975; children: Rachel Ann, Austin Thomas, Laurel Suzanne. BA in History and Edn. cum laude, St. Olaf Coll., 1971. Program mgr. Historic Ft. Snelling, St. Paul, 1971-85, dir., 1985—. Program mgr. Legis. Commn. on Minn. Resources, 1985; mem. Coun. on Am.'s Mil. Past, Midwest Open Air Mus. Coord. Coun.; lectr. in field. Author: The Soldiers Handbook, 1825, 1972; contbr. articles to profl. jours. Fellow Co. Mil. Historians; mem. Assn. Living History Farms and Agrl. Mus., Living History Soc. Minn. Republican. Lutheran. Avocations: 19th Century military uniforms and equipment, historic crafts. Office: Minn Hist Soc Ft Snelling History Ctr Saint Paul MN 55111 E-mail: stephen.osman@mnhs.org.

OSMENT, LAMAR SUTTON, retired dermatologist, educator; b. Pascagoula, Miss., Apr. 9, 1924; s. Eugene Algernon and Julia Ann Maria (Lowry) O.; m. Nelda Dutton; 1 child, Rachael Osment Pippen. BS, Birmingham-So. Coll., 1945; MD, U. Ala., 1951. Instr. dermatology Sch. Medicine U. Ala., Birmingham, 1955-57, asst. prof., 1957-60, assoc. prof., 1960-70, prof., 1970-89, prof. emeritus, 1989—. Author: The Yellow Fever Epidemic of 1878, 1990, History of the University of Alabama Birmingham Department of Dermatology, 1996; contbr. chpts. to books. Bd. dirs. Arlington Antebellum Home, Birmingham, 1990—. Mem. Ala. Dermatol. Soc. (Lifetime Achievement award 1997), So. Med. Assn. (pres. 1980). Republican. Avocations: geneaology, history of medicine, tennis.

OSMER-MCQUADE, MARGARET, business executive, broadcast journalist; b. N.Y.C. d. Herbert Bernard and Margaret Normann (Brunjes) O.; m. Lawrence Carroll McQuade, Mar. 15, 1980; 1 son, Andrew. BA, Cornell U., 1960. Assoc. producer UN Bur., CBS News, N.Y.C., 1962-69; producer 60 Minutes, 1969-72; reporter, producer Bill Moyer's Jour., Pub. Broadcasting Service, 1972-73, Reasoner Report, ABC News, N.Y.C., 1973-75; corr., anchor person Good Morning Am., ABC Morning News, Washington, 1975-77; corr. ABC TV News, 1977-79; v.p., dir. programs Council on Fgn. Relations, 1979-93; pres., CEO Qualitas Internat., N.Y.C., 1994—. Dir. Dime Savs. Bank, 1980—; cons. pub. broadcasting; mem. program com. Ditchley Found. Producer, reporter: TV news shows Come Fly A Kite (Nat. Press Photographer's award 1974), Kissinger, 1970, No Tears for Rachel, 1972, Calder: Master of Mobiles, 1975; moderator, producer World in Focus, publ. TV series for Coun. Fgn. Relations/Sta. WNYC, PBS, Worldnet, 1988-93. Mem. U.S. delegation World Conf. on Cambodian Refugees, Geneva, 1980; mem. Def. Adv. Com. on Women in the Service, 1978-82; trustee Cornell U.; mem. bd. overseers Cornell U. Med. Coll., pres.'s coun. Cornell Women; mem. program com. The Ritchley Found., 1994—, task force N.Y. Sch. Vols., 1994—; vol. Nat. Svc. Learning, 1994—. Recipient Peabody award Staff of 60 Minutes, 1970 Mem. NATAS, Coun. Fgn. Relations, program comm. The Mitching Found., Task Force N.Y. Sch. Vol., Nat. Press Club, Mid. Atlantic Club., vol. Nat. Svc. Learning. Clubs: Cosmopolitan, Century.

OSMOND, DENNIS GORDON, medical educator, researcher; b. N.Y.C., Jan. 31, 1930; s. Ernest Gordon and Marjorie Bertha (Milton) O.; m. Anne Welsh, July 30, 1955; children: Roger Gordon, Martin Henry, David Richard. BSc with first class honors, U. Bristol, Eng., 1951, MB, ChB, 1954, DSc, 1975. House surgeon Royal Gwent Hosp., Newport, Eng., 1954-55; house physician Bristol Royal Infirmary, 1955; demonstrator, lectr. anatomy U. Bristol, 1957-60, 61-64; instr. anatomy U. Wash., Seattle, 1960-61; assoc. prof. anatomy McGill U., Montreal, Que., Can., 1965-67, prof., 1967-74, Robert Reford prof. anatomy, 1974-00, chmn. dept. anatomy and cell biology, 1985-95, Robert Reford emeritus prof. anatomy, 2000—. Vis. scientist Walter and Eliza Hall Inst. Med. Research, Melbourne, Australia, 1972-73; hon. sr. research fellow U. Birmingham, Eng., 1979; vis. scientist Basel Inst. Immunology, Switzerland, 1980, 96; Gaylord scholar Okla. Med. Rsch. Found., 1995. Contbr. numerous articles to profl. jours. Served with Royal Army Med. Corps, 1955-57. Fellow Royal Soc. Can.; mem. Am. Assn. Anatomists, Can. Assn. Anatomists, Anat. Soc. Gt. Britain and Ireland, Am., Can. assns. for immunology, Am. Assn. Immunology, Internat. Soc. for Exptl. Hematology. Home: 1380 Revell Dr Manotick ON Canada K4M 1K8 E-mail: osmond@med.mcgill.ca.

OSMONT, GHYSLAIN LOUIS, accountant; b. Paris, Mar. 17, 1961; came to U.S., 1983; s. Lucien Henri and Marie-Therese Osmont; m. Macaire Henderson, Aug. 12, 1989; children: Leslie, Clara, Simon. BBA in Internat. Bus. and Acctg., U. Tex., 1987. CPA, N.Y. Acct. Mazars LLP, N.Y.C. Mem. AICPA, N.Y. Soc. CPA, N.J. State Soc. CPA, French-am. C. of C., Conseillers du Commerce Exterior, Paris-Am. Club. Home: 22 Maple Dr Colts Neck NY 07722 Office: Mazars LLP 135 W 50th St New York NY 10020 E-mail: losmont@mrweiser.com.

OSMUNDSEN, BARBARA ANN, sculptor; b. Jacksonville, N.C., Apr. 21, 1945; d. Robert Nygaärd and Catherine Ann (Wilent) Osmundsen; m. Baxter Smith Rains III, Sept. 20, 1986; 1 child, Holly Christine Delaney. Student, Vanderbilt U., 1963-64; BS, U. Tenn., Chattanooga, 1967; postgrad., U. Tenn., Knoxville, 1969-70, Va. Mus. of Fine Arts, Richmond, 1988-89. Fashion, accessory designer, Atlanta, 1972—85; ptnr. Bara Designs, Richmond, 1987—88; art instr. Mus. Art and Sci., Melbourne, Fla., 1998—, Vero Beach Ctr. for the Arts, 2000—; artist in residence Brevard Cultural Alliance, Viera, Fla., 1999—. V.p., cons. artist Hope Dragon Found., Indian Harbour Beach, Fla., 1996. Exhibitions include Arlington Arts Ctr., 1991, Raleigh Gallery, Boca Raton, 1992—97, Gaier Contemporary Gallery, Orlando, 1994—96, Renee Foosaner Ctr., Mus. Art and Sci., Melbourne, 1998—, Marine Resources Coun. East Fla., Rockledge, 1999, Ctr. for the Arts, Vero Beach, Fla., 2000—, Mus. of Arts and Sci., Melbourne, 2001, one-woman shows include Melbourne Internat. Airport, 2001, Represented in permanent collections Freedom 7 Cmty. Ctr., Wuesthoff Health Sys. Found., Caron Wills Collection, Killaloe/Bullina, Ireland, Mort Harris Collection, Detroit, Sch. Dist. Brevard County, Viera, Fla., pvt. collections;one-woman shows include Brevard County Govt. Complex, Viera, Fla., 2001—02; co-editor, author: Studio Link newsletter, 1994. Adv. bd. Women's Shelter, Valdosta, Ga., 1987; co-founder bd. govs. Vector Arts Endowment, 1997-2000. Mem.: Internat. Sculpture Assn., Internat. Platform Assn., Nat. League Am. Pen Women (pres. Cape Canaveral Br., Fla. 2000—02). Avocations: organic gardening, gourmet cooking. Office: PO Box 372628 Indian Harbor Beach FL 32937-0628

OSNES, PAMELA GRACE, special education educator; b. Burke, S.D., Sept. 10, 1955; d. John Ruben and Dortha Grace (Wilson) O.; children: Jocelyn Fern, Logan John. BS in Spl. Edn., BS in Elem. Edn., U. S.D., 1977; MA in Clin. Psychology, W.Va. U., 1981; PhD in Spl. Edn., 1998. Spl. edn. tchr. Sioux Falls (S.D.) Sch. Dist., 1977-79; instr. psychology dept. W.Va. U., Morgantown, 1982-85; dir. Carousel Preschool Program, 1982-85; assoc. prof. U. South Fla., Tampa, 1986-93, adminstrv. coord. advanced grad. programs dept. spl. edn., 1994-97, instr. dept. spl. edn., 1997-98, assoc. prof., 1999—, coord. Master's Program in Applied Behavior Analysis, 2000—. Mem. Assn. for Behavior Analysis, Coun. for Exceptional Children (div. early childhood, div. rsch., tchr. edn. div.), Coun. Adminstrs. Spl. Edn., Coun. for Children with Behavior Disorders.

OSNOS, DAVID MARVIN, lawyer, director; b. Detroit, Jan. 10, 1932; s. Max and Florence (Pollock) O.; m. Glenna DeWitt, Aug. 10, 1956; children: Matthew, Alison AB summa cum laude, Harvard U., 1953, JD cum laude, 1956. Bar: D.C. 1956. Assoc. Arent, Fox, Kintner, Plotkin & Kahn, Washington, 1956-61, ptnr., 1962—, chmn. exec. com., 1978-97. Bd. dirs. EastGroup Properties, Jackson, Miss., VSE Corp., Alexandria, Va., Washington Real Estate Investment Trust, Rockville, Md., Washington Wizards Basketball Club, Washington. Trustee Mt. St. Mary's Coll., Emmitsburg, Md., 1981-90; bd. dirs. Greater Washington Jewish Cmty. Found., Rockville, Md., Jewish Cmty. Ctr. Greater Washington, 1964-75. Avocations: tennis, music, enology. Office: Arent Fox Kintner 1050 Connecticut Ave NW Ste 600 Washington DC 20036-5339 E-mail: osnosd@arentfox.com.

OSNOS, GILBERT CHARLES, management consultant; b. Detroit, Nov. 23, 1929; s. Herman Sol and Helen (Yudkoff) O.; m. Margaret N. Paysner, Aug. 18, 1957; children: Steven, Elisabeth. BA, U. Mich., 1951; MBA, Harvard U., 1953. Dept. mgr. Sams, Inc., Detroit, 1956-57, asst. buyer, 1957-58, dir. store ops., 1958, buyer, 1958-59, mdse. buyer, 1959-62; buyer Topps Divsn. Interstate Dept. Stores, N.Y.C., 1962-65; mdse. mgr. Arlans Dept. Stores, 1965-68; pres. Nazareth Mills divsn. Kayser Roth, 1968-73, Rosenau Bros., Phila., 1973-75, Warnaco Men's Sportswear, 1975-78; with Grisanti and Galef, 1979-81, ptnr., 1981—; pres. Grisanti, Galef & Osnos, N.Y.C., 1983—. Chmn. Osnos & Co., Inc., 1986—; bd. dirs. ehomecare.com Ltd., Strauss Auto Stores, Mrs. Fields Original Cookie Co., Turnaround Mgmt. Assn., chmn., 1990-91. Lt. j.g. USNR, 1953-56. Mem. Am. Apparel Assn. (consumer affairs com.), Am. Bankruptcy Inst., Bus. Execs. for Nat. Security, Harvard Club, Halloween Yacht Club, Harvard Bus. Sch. Club of N.Y.C. Avocations: sailing, opera, classical music, photography, reading. Office: Osnos & Company Inc 230 Park Ave Ste 1546A New York NY 10169-0005 E-mail: osnos@msn.com.

OSNOS, PETER LIONEL WINSTON, publishing executive; b. Bombay, India, Oct. 13, 1943; s. Joseph Lionel and Marta (Bychowski) O.; m. Susan R. Sherer, Aug. 18, 1973; children: Katherine Mason, Evan L.R. BA, Brandeis U., Waltham, Mass., 1964; MS in Journalism with honors, Columbia U., 1965. Editorial asst. I.F. Stone's Weekly, Washington, 1964-65; corr., editor Washington Post, 1966-84; v.p, assoc. pub. Random House Trade Books and pub. Times Books, Random House, Inc., N.Y.C., 1984-96; cons. 20th Century Fund, 1996-97; pub., chief exec. Public Affairs, 1997—. Contbr. articles to profl. publs. Bd. dirs. Human Rights Watch, chmn. Europe and Ctrl. Asia divns.; bd. dirs. Baltic-Am. Partnership, U. Mich. Fellowship Journalists, 2000. Fellow NEH, 1973-74. Mem. Assn. Am. Pubs. (vice chmn. gen. pub. divsn. 1993-96), Coun. on Fgn. Rels., Century Club. Office: Pub Affairs 250 W 57th St New York NY 10107 E-mail: peter.osnos@persevsbooks.com.

OSOFSKY, BARBARA LANGER, mathematician, educator; b. Beacon, N.Y., Aug. 4, 1937; d. Theodore William and Shirley Alpert Langer; m. Abraham Joseph Osofsky, Aug. 31, 1958; children: Deena Shapiro, Laura Rabinowitz, Samuel. BA, Cornell U., 1959, MA, 1960; PhD in Math., Rutgers U., 1964. Assoc. mem. tech. staff Bell Lab., Whippany, NJ, 1960; instr. math. Douglass Coll., New Brunswick, 1961—63; asst. prof. math. Rutgers U., 1964—67, assoc. prof. math., 1967—71, prof. math., 1971—. Mem. of editl. bd. Procs. of the Am. Math. Soc., Providence, RI, 1973—77, mng. editor, Providence, 1975—77; mem. of editl. bd. Jour. of Algebra, Academic Press, 1980—90; mem. of bd. of governors Math. Assn. of Am., Washington, 1993—96, first v.p. Contbr. articles; mem. editl. bd.: Jour. Algebra., 1980—90. Fellow, NSF, 1967—68. Mem.: Assn. Women Math., Am. Math. Soc. (mem. editl. bd. proceedings 1973—77, mng. editor proceedings 1975—77), Math. Assn. Am. (life; first v.p. 2000—02, bd. govs. 1993—96). Avocations: amateur radio, swimming. Office: Dept Math Rutgers Univ 110 Frelinghuysen Rd Piscataway NJ 08854-8019 Business E-Mail: osofsky@math.rutgers.edu.

OSOWIEC, DARLENE ANN, clinical psychologist, educator, consultant; b. Chgo., Feb. 16, 1951; d. Stephen Raymond and Estelle Marie Osowiec; m. Barry A. Leska. BS, Loyola U., Chgo., 1973; MA with honors, Roosevelt U., l980; postgrad. in psychology, Saybrook Inst., San Francisco, 1985-88; PhD in Clin. Psychology, Calif. Inst. Integral Studies, 1992. Lic. clin. psychologist, Mo., Ill., Calif. Mental health therapist Ridgeway Hosp., Chgo., l978; mem. faculty psychology dept. Coll. Lake County, Grayslake, l98l; counselor, supr. MA-level interns, chmn. pub. rels. com. Integral Counseling Ctr., San Francisco, l983-84; clin. psychology intern Chgo.-Read Mental Health Ctr. Ill. Dept. Mental Health, 1985-86; mem. faculty dept. psychology Moraine Valley C.C., Palos Hills, Ill., 1988-89; lectr. psychology Daley Coll., Chgo., 1988-90; cons. Gordon & Assocs., Oak Lawn, 1989; adolescent, child and family therapist Orland Twp. Youth Svcs., Orland Park, 1993; psychology fellow Sch. Medicine, St. Louis U., 1994-95; pvt. practice Geneva, 1996—; founder Maximum Potential, Chgo., 1996—. Contbr., author: Transpersonal Hypnosis, 1999. Ill. State scholar, 1969-73; Calif. Inst. Integral Studies scholar, 1983. Mem. APA (chair edn. and tng. com. divsn. 30 1998-2000, chair mem. svcs. 2001—), Am. Psychol. Soc., Am. Women in Psychology, Ill. Psychol. Assn., Calif. Psychol. Assn., Mo. Psychol. Assn., Fla. Psychol. Assn., Am. Soc. Clin. Hypnosis, Internat. Platform Assn., Chgo. Soc. Clin. Hypnosis, NOW (chair legal adv. corps, Chgo. 1974-76). Avocations: playing piano, gardening, reading, backpacking, writing. E-mail: d.osowiec@worldnet.att.net.

OSSERMAN, ROBERT, mathematician, educator, writer; b. N.Y.C., Dec. 19, 1926; s. Herman Aaron and Charlotte (Adler) O.; m. Maria Anderson, June 15, 1952; 1 son, Paul; m. Janet Adelman, July 21, 1976; children— Brian, Stephen. BA, NYU, 1946; postgrad., U. Zurich, U. Paris; MA, Harvard U., 1948, PhD, 1955. Tchg. fellow Harvard U., 1949-52, vis. lectr., rsch. assoc., 1961-62; instr. U. Colo., 1952-53; mem. faculty Stanford U., 1955-94, prof. emeritus, 1994—, prof. math., 1966—, chmn. dept. math., 1973-79, Mellon Prof. Interdisciplinary Studies, 1987-90; dep. dir. Math. Scis. Rsch. Inst., Berkeley, Calif., 1990-95, dir. spl. projects, 1995—. Mem. NYU Inst. Math. Scis., 1957-58, Math. Scis. Rsch. Inst., Berkeley,, 1983-84, head math. br. Office Naval Rsch., 1960-61; researcher and author publs. on differential geometry, complex variables, differential equations, astronomy, cosmology, especially minimal surfaces, isoperimetric inequalities. Author: Two-Dimensional Calculus, 1968, A Survey of Minimal Surfaces, 1969, 2d edit., 1986, Poetry of the Universe, 1995; author videos: Fermat's Last Theorem, 1994, Mathematics in Arcadia, 1999, Galileo: A Dialog, 2000. Fulbright lectr. U. Paris, 1965-66; Guggenheim fellow, 1976-77; vis. fellow U. Warwick, Imperial Coll., U. London. Fellow AAAS; mem. Am. Math. Soc., Math. Assn. Am., Astrom. Soc. Pacific. Office: Math Sci Rsch Inst 1000 Centennial Dr Berkeley CA 94720-5070

OSSEWAARDE, ANNE WINKLER, real estate developer; b. Dallas, June 2, 1957; d. Lowell Graves and Ruth Lenore (Lind) Winkler; m. Kirk L Ossewaarde, Apr. 27, 1991. BBA in Fin. with honors, Emory U., 1979; MBA in Acctg. and Fin. with honors, U. Tex., 1983; MS in Real Estate Devel., MIT, 1988. Cert. comml. investment mem., Comml. Investment Real Estate Inst. Mgmt. trainee Citizens & So. Nat. Bank, Atlanta, 1979-81; banking assoc. Continental Ill. Nat. Bank, Chgo. and Dallas, 1983-85; asst. v.p., devel. assoc. Trammell Crow Residential, Dallas, 1985-87, Seattle, 1988-91; devel. mgr. Blackhawk Port Blakeley Cmtys., 1991-93; v.p., real estate portfolio mgr. Aegon U.S.A. Realty, Atlanta, 1994-98. Dir. UBS Brinson Realty Investors (formerly Allegis Realty Investors), Dallas, 1998-2000; regional v.p. Lend Lease Real Estate Investments, Inc. Atlanta, 2000—. Charles Harritt Jr. Presdl. scholar U. Tex., 1982, Alexander Grant scholar, 1982. Mem. Jr. League of Dallas, Comml. Real Estate Women, MIT Ctr. for Real Estate Alumni Assn., Alpha Epsilon Upsilon. Methodist. Avocations: singing, photography, bicycling, reading. Home: 3170 Windsor Lake Dr Atlanta GA 30319

OSSI, JAMES MATTHEW, artist; b. Wyckoff, N.J., Jan. 7, 1947; s. Peter and (Hildegarde) O.; m. Diana Louise Wege (divorced); children: Sara, Peter; m. Marie Decarie, Aug. 18, 1997. Grad. in Indsl. Rsch., Parsons Sch. of Design, 1970. Sculptures located in The Mus. of Modern Art, N.Y.C., 1969, MIT Mus. Cambridge, Mass., 1983, Saibu Gas Mus., Fukuoka, 1989, math. dept. Princeton U., 1998, physics lobby MIT, 2000. Home: 21 Baywater Dr Darien CT 06820 E-mail: james.ossi@GTE.net.

OSSIAN, CLAIR RUSSELL, geologist, paleontologist; b. Red Oak, Iowa, Jan. 4, 1941; s. Almond Frances Claire and Elizabeth Fanny (Dilts) O.; m. Eleanor Lorraine Smith, Sept. 5, 1964; children: Merit Laural, Robert Henry. BS in Geology, U. Nebr., Lincoln, 1966; MS in Geology, Mich. State U., 1970; PhD in Geology, U. Tex., Austin, 1974. Prof. St. Edwards U., Austin, 1970-74; prin. rsch. geologist Arco Oil & Gas Co., Plano, Tex., 1974-91; prof. geology Tarrant County Coll., Hurst, 1993—. Pres. Am. Rsch. Ctr. in Egypt, Dallas, 1997-2000. Author: Insights in Earth Science, 1999, 2d edit., 2001; contbr. articles to profl. jours. Mem. AAAS, Am. Assn. Petroleum Geologist (cert.), Am. Orchid Soc. (rsch. com. 1979—), Sigma Xi. Avocations: Egyptology, photography, koi, orchids.

OSSIKOVSKI, RAZVIGOR BOJIDAROV, research and development engineer, physicist; b. Russe, Bulgaria, June 8, 1967; arrived in France, 1991; s. Bojidar Tzvetanov and Vania Danova (Mileva) O.; m. Marie Madeleine Gallardo, Dec. 23, 1995; 1 child, Anne. BSc, High Tech. Sch., Russe, Bulgaria; MSc, Ecole Poly., Palaiseau, France, 1992, PhD, 1995. R & D engr. Instruments SA, Longjumeau, France, 1996-99; R & D engr., optical designer Corning SA, Fontainebleau, France, 1999-01; project mgr. Highwave Optical Techs., Lannion, France, 2001—. Part-time prof. quantum mechanics Ecole Poly., France, 2001—. Contbr. articles to profl. jours.; inventor in field. Mem. European Commn. Scientific Expert, Bulgarian Amateur Radio Assn. Avocations: amateur radio, rowing, bridge. Home: 13 Ave du Gen de Gaulle 91140 Villebon sur Yvette France Office: Highvave Opt Techs 9 ave Laponie 91951 Les Ulis France E-mail: ossikovski@aol.com.

OSSIP, MICHAEL J. lawyer; b. N.Y.C., Nov. 9, 1954; s. William L. and Jeannette (Linial) O.; m. Karen Silverstein, May 28, 1978; 1 child, Brian. BS in Inds. and Labor Rels., Cornell U., 1976; JD, U. Pa., 1979. Bar: Pa. 1979, U.S. Dist. Ct. (ea. dist.) Pa. 1980, U.S. Dist. Ct. (mid. dist.) Pa. 1994, U.S. Ct. Appeals (3d cir.) 1981, U.S. Ct. Appeals (4th cir.) 1982, U.S. Ct. Appeals (9th cir.) 1985, U.S. Ct. Appeals (D.C. cir.) 1986, U.S. Ct. Appeals (7ht cir.) 2002, U.S. Ct. Appeals (5th cir.) 2002, U.S. Supreme Ct. 1989. Law clk. to judge U.S. Dist. Ct., Wilmington, Del., 1979-80; assoc. Morgan, Lewis & Bockius LLP, Phila., 1980-88, ptnr., 1988—. Mem. faculty Cornell U., N.Y.C., 1987—; lectr. Pa. Bar Inst., Phila., Harrisburg and Pitts., 1987—. Pres., bd. dirs. Nat. Tay-Sachs and Allied Diseases Assn. Delaware Valley, Jenkintown, Pa., 1993-98; bd. dirs. Nat. Tay-Sachs and Allied Diseases Assn., Delaware Valley, Jenkintown, Pa. Mem. ABA (com. chair sect. labor law), Pa. Bar Assn., Phila. Bar Assn. Office: Morgan Lewis & Bockius LLP 1701 Market St Philadelphia PA 19103-2903 E-mail: mossip@morganlewis.com.

OSSMAN, SUSAN MARIE, educator; b. Chgo., May 19, 1959; arrived in France, 1980; d. Edward Thomas Ossman and Camille Joan Radzicki; m. Jean-Philippe André Dorent, Dec. 12, 1981 (div. 1990); 1 child Nathanael Philippe ; life ptnr. Mamoun Fandy. AB, U. Calif., Berkeley, 1980, MA, 1986, PhD, 1991; Diplôme d'etudes approfondies, U. Paris VII, 1983. Documentalist San Francisco Chronicle, 1984-85; rschr. U. Calif., Berkeley, 1991-92; dir., rschr. Inst. de Rsch. sur le Maghreb Contemporain, Rabat, Morocco, 1993-96; assoc. prof. Am. U. Paris, 1996—. Dir. rsch. program on comm. IRMC, Rabat, 1993—96; rsch. assoc. Lab. Comm. et Politique, Paris, 1996—99; vis. prof. U. Liege, Belgium, 1996—97, Georgetown U., Washington; lectr. Celsa U. Paris IV, Levallois-Perret, France, 1996—98. Author: Picturing Casablanca: Portraits of Power in a Modern City, 1994; editor: Miroirs Maghrébins Itinéraires de Soi et Paysages de Rencontre, 1998; editor Mimesis: Imiter, représenter, circular, 1998; mem. editl. bd. Jour. North African Studies, 2000—. Recipient Bourse Chateaubriand, French Govt., 1986; grantee Fulbright, Morocco, 1988, 89. Mem. Internat. Comm. Assn., Am. Anthropol. Assn., Am. Inst. Maghrebi Studies. Avocations: painting, piano, poetry. E-mail: S.Ossman@net-up.com.

OSSOFF, ROBERT HENRY, otolaryngological surgeon; b. Beverly, Mass., Mar. 25, 1947; s. Michael Max and Eve Joan (Kladky) G.; m. Lynn Spilman, 1984; 1 child, Leslin; 1 child by previous marriage, Jacob. BA, Bowdoin Coll., 1969; DMD, Tufts U., 1973, MD, 1975; MS in Otolaryngology, Northwestern U., 1981. Intern Northwestern Meml. Hosp., Chgo., 1975-76; resident in otolaryngology Northwestern Med. Sch., 1976-80, NIH rsch. fellow dept. otolaryngology, 1977-78, Am. Cancer Soc. clin. fellow, 1980-81, jr. faculty clin. fellow, 1981-84; pvt. practice surgery, laryngology and care of profl. voice, 1975-86, Nashville, 1986—; chmn. dept. otolaryngology Vanderbilt U. Hosp., 1986—; exec. med. dir. Vanderbilt Voice Ctr., 1991—. Staff Children's Meml. Hosp., Chgo., 1980—81, Nashville VA Hosp., 1986—; chief divsn. otolaryngology Evanston (Ill.) Hosp., 1983—86; chief otolaryngology VA Lakeside Hosp., Chgo., 1982—86; mem. staff Northwestern Meml. Hosp., 1981—86, Children's Meml. Hosp., 1981—84; asst. prof. Northwestern U. Dental Sch., 1980—86; assoc. prof. Northwestern U. Med. Sch., 1985—86; Guy M. Maness prof., chmn. dept. otolaryngology Vanderbilt U. Sch. Medicine, 1986—; assoc. dir. Vanderbilt Free-Electron Laser Ctr. Med. and Materials Rsch., 1992—95; assoc. vice chancellor for health affairs and chief of staff Vanderbilt U. Hosp., 1995—97, assoc. vice chancellor for health affairs, 1995—. : mem. editl. bd. Otolaryngology-Head and Neck Surgery, 1988—, : sr. editor Lasers in Suegery and Medicine, 1987—94, : editor-in-chief, 1995—; co-editor: Complications in Head and Neck Surgery W.B. Saunders Co., 1993—; : mem. editl. bd. Clin. Laser Monthly, 1984—, : mem. editl. bd. Jour. of Voice, 1987—, : mem. editl. bd. The Laryngoscope, 1988—, : mem. editl. bd. Operative Techniques in Otolaryngology-Head and Neck Surgery, 1989—, : mem. editl. bd. Head and Neck Surgery, 1989—, : mem. editl. bd. Jour. of Laser Applications, 1989—, : with editl. adv. bd. Gen. Surgery News, 1990—99, : assoc. editor Diagnostic and Therapeutic Endoscopy, 1992—; contbr. articles to profl. jours., chpts. to books. Bd. dirs. Laser Inst. Am., 1984—90; dir. Am. Bd. Otolaryngology, 1995—; trustee Midwest Biolaser Inst., Chgo., 1981—86. Recipient Lederer-Pierce award Chgo. Laryngol. and Otol. Soc., 1978. Fellow: ACS (bd. govs.); mem.: AMA, Cartesian Soc., Am. Laryngol. Assn. (coun. 1996—, sec. 1998—), The Triological Soc. (coun. 1996—99, v.p. so. sect. 2002—), Am. Broncho-Esophagological Assn. (treas. 1980—84, pres.-elect 1994—95, pres. 1995—96), Am. Soc. Head and Neck Surgery (coun. 1991—94), Soc. Head and Neck Surgeons, Am. Soc. Laser Medicine and Surgery (bd. dirs. 1985—88, pres.-elect 1988—89, pres. 1989—90, William B. Mark award 1992), Am. Acad. Otolaryngology-Head and Neck Surgery (chmn. laser surgery com. 1983—89, chmn. self instl. package com. 1990—96, bd. dirs. 1992—95, coord. for devel. 2001—, Cert. of Honor 1984, Disting. Svc. award 1995, Presdl. citation 1999), Am. Acad. Oral Pathology, Am. Acad. Oral Medicine. Office: Vanderbilt U Med Ctr Dept Otolaryngology S-2100 Med Ctr N Nashville TN 37232-0001

OSSONT, DAVID ROBIN, science educator; b. Amsterdam, N.Y., May 19, 1955; s. Willard Earle and Lorraine H. (Hoobler) O.; m. Pamela Joan Stone, Sept. 6, 1986; children: Kyle, Hayley. BS, SUNY, Utica, 1977; MS, SUNY, Cortland, 1990. Cert. tchr., N.Y. Wildlife technician N.Y. State Dept. Environ. Conservation, Utica, 1977-85; tchr. sci. Oneida (N.Y.) City Schs., 1986—. Mem. Nat. Sci. Tchrs. Assn. (nat. cert.), Sci. Tchrs. Assn. N.Y. State, Soc. of Children's Book Writers and Illustrators. Avocations: bicycling, hiking. Office: Otto Shortell Mid Sch Markell Dr Wampsville NY 13163

OSTAPENKO, ALEXIS, civil engineer, educator; b. Ukraine, Oct. 1, 1923; came to U.S. 1951; s. Peter and Natalia O.; married; 3 children. Dipl.Ing., Tech. U. Munich, Germany, 1951; ScD, MIT, 1957. Structural engr. Fay, Spofford & Thorndike, Boston, 1952, Thomas Worcester, Boston, 1952-54, various firms, 1955-57; from asst. prof. to prof. civil engring. Lehigh U., Bethlehem, Pa., 1957—. Rsch. grantee USN, PennDOT, USCG, U.S. Dept. of Transp., U.S. Dept Interior, U.K. Dept. Energy, Exxon, Mobil, many others, 1958—. Mem. ASCE, Sigma Xi. Office: Lehigh Univ Fritz Engring Lab 13 E Packer Ave Bethlehem PA 18015-3176

OSTAR, ALLAN WILLIAM, academic administrator, higher education consultant; b. East Orange, N.J., Sept. 4, 1924; s. William and Rose O.; m. Roberta Hutchison, Sept. 10, 1949; children. Cert. engring., U. Denver, 1943; BA, Pa. State U., 1948; postgrad., U. Wis., 1949-55; LL.D., U. No. Colo., 1968, Eastern Ky. U., 1972, Whittier Coll., 1973; L.H.D., U. Maine, 1975; D.Letters, Central Mich. U., 1975; D.P.S., Bowling Green State U., 1975, R.I. Coll., 1983; D.Higher Edn., Morehead State U., 1977; L.H.D., Appalachian State U., 1977, No. Mich. U., 1978, Dickinson State Coll., N.D., 1979, Towson State U., 1980, Salem State Coll., 1980, Mont. Coll. Mineral Sci. and Tech., 1983, Ball State U., 1984; LL.D., U. Alaska, 1978, Ill. State U., 1983, Western Mich. U., 1984; D. Polit. Sci., Kyung Hee U., Korea, 1984; L.H.D., Fitchburg State Coll., 1986, Bridgwater State Coll., 1988, No. State Coll., 1988, Harris-Stowe State Coll., 1986; LLD, Edinboro U. Pa., 1987, Loch Haven U., Pa., 1989; LHD, No. Ariz. U., 1990, Shepherd (W.Va.) Coll., 1992, SUNY, 1993, Lincoln U., Mo., 1995. Dir. nat. pub. relations U.S. Nat. Student Assn., 1948-49; exec. asst. Commonwealth Fund, N.Y.C., 1952-53; asst. to dean extension div. U. Wis., 1949-52, dir. office communications services, 1954-58; dir. Joint Office Instnl. Research, Nat. Assn. State Univs. and Land Grant Colls., Washington, 1958-65; pres. Am. Assn. State Colls. and Univs., 1965-91, pres. emeritus, 1991—; sr. cons. Acad. Search Consultation Svc., 1991—. Adj. prof. edn. Pa. State U., 1990—. Co-author: Colleges and Universities for Change, 1987; contbr. chpts. in books. Mem. 42d (Rainbow) div. U.S. Army, 1943-46. Decorated 2 Bronze Stars; recipient Centennial award for disting. svcs. to edn. U. Akron, 1970, Fogelsanger award Shippensburg (Pa.) State Coll., 1974, World Peace Through Edn. medal Internat. Assn. U. Pres., 1975, Disting. Achievement award, U. So. Colo., 1979, Chancellor's award U. Wis., 1985, Chancellor's medal CUNY, 1986, Disting. Alumnus award Pa. State U., 1989, svc. award Coun. on Internat. Ednl. Exch., 1990, Chancellor's medal Internat. Svc. U. Ark., Little Rock, 1990, Disting. Pub. Svc. medal Dept. of Def., 1991; Alumni fellow Pa. State U., 1975. Unitarian-Universalist. Home: 5500 Friendship Blvd Chevy Chase MD 20815-7219

OSTASHEV, VLADIMIR E. physicist, researcher; b. Moscow, Russia, Feb. 12, 1953; s. Evgeni I. Ostashev and Klara M. Ostasheva; m. Alla M. Zaharova, June 27, 1981; children: Evgeni. Master Diploma(hon.) , Moscow Inst. of Physics and Tech., 1976, PhD in Physics, 1979; D of Phys. and Math. Scis., Acoustics Inst., Moscow, 1992. Rsch. scientist Russian Acad. of Scis./Inst. of Atmospheric Physics, Moscow; sr. rsch. scientist Acoustics Inst., 1989—93; sr. vis. scientist Phys. Sci. Lab., N.Mex State U., Las Cruces, 1994; vis. sr. scientist The Open U., Milton Keynes, England, 1995—96; sr. rsch. assoc. Nat. Rsch. Coun./NOAA, Environ. Tech. Lab., Boulder, 1999—2000; rsch. assoc. U. of Colo., CIRES/NOAA, Environ. Tech. Lab., 2000—02; prof. physics N.Mex State U., Las Cruces, 1996—. Vis. prof. physics U. Miss., Oxford, 1992, Ecole Centale de Lyon, France, 1994—95, 1999; guest prof. physics U. Oldenburg, Germany, 1993—95; sr. vis. scientist N.Mex. State U., 1994, 1999—2000, The Open Univ., Eng., No. Ireland, 1995—96; head Russian del. Internat. Meeting for Wave Propagation in Random Media, Seattle, 1992; chair of session: "acoustics" Internat. Workshop "Tomography and Acoustics: Recent Developments and Methods", Leipzig, Germany, 2001; dir. of the army rsch. office N.Mex State U., Las Cruces, 2000—. Author: Sound Propagation in Moving Media, 1992, Acoustics in Moving Inhomogeneous Media, 1997; contbr. over 140 articles to sci. and tech. jours., chapters to books. Recipient Associateship award, NRC, 1999; fellow, Royal Soc. of London, 1995, Royal Soc. Exquota, 1995, French Ministry of Edn. and Rsch., 1999; grantee, Internat. Sci. Found., 1993, German Sci. Found., 1993. Mem.: Russian Acoustical Soc., German Acoustical Soc., European Acoustical Assn., Acoustical Soc. Am. Office: NOAA/Environ Tech Lab 325 Broadway Boulder CO 80305

OSTASZEWSKI, ALYCE VITELLA, religion educator; b. Chgo., Apr. 24, 1936; d. Peter Anthony and Cleta Earline (Chastain) Indelli; m. Gerald Earl Nelson (div. 1967); children: Peter J., Maryalice C., William P., Paula A.; m. Stanley Joseph Ostaszewski; children: Vinson Shaw, Stacean V. Grad. high sch. Immaculata, Chgo., 1954. Tchr. religious edn. St. John the Evangelist Ch., Streamwood, Ill., 1962-68; tchr. religious edn., facilitator Rite of Christian Initiation of Adults, St. Thomas More Ch., Elgin, 1980-86; tchr. religious edn., young adult min. St. Julie Billiart Ch., Newbury Park, Calif., 1987-89, confirmation coord., 1990-91; confirmation asst. coord. St. Paschal Baylon Ch., Thousand Oaks, 1991-92; master chatechist basic faith formation program L.A. Diocese, Santa Barbara Region, 1990-93. Com. mem. Santa Barbara Regional Conf., 1988-93; workshop spkr. Santa Barbara Regional Conf., 1992; confirmation tchr. Holy Cross Parish, Batavia, Ill., 1993-94; 3rd grade religion edn. tchr., 1994-96, Saturday ch. staff asst. 1997—, U. Dayton catechist formation program, 1997-98, 99, 00. Sec. Village of Streamwood Homeowners Assn., 1957-58; bd. dirs. Oak Ridge Estates Homeowners Assn., Newbury Park, Calif., 1986-88; lifetime mem. Streamwood Hist. Soc., 1993—; woman's team 7 C.R.H.P. Witness'er, 1994; mem. choir St. Thomas More, St. Julie Billiart, Holy Cross; vol. picture person program for McWayne Sch., Batavia, Ill., 1998-99. Recipient Bishop O'Neill award, 1999.

OSTBERG, HENRY DEAN, corporate executive; b. Bocholt, Germany, July 21, 1928; came to U.S., 1939, naturalized, 1945. s. Fred and Lotte (Hertz) O.; m. Sydelle Burns, Dec. 13, 1987; 1 child, Neal; stepchildren: Elysa Bari, Brent Adam, Ross Jay. LLB, N.Y. Law Sch., 1950; MBA, Ohio State U., 1953, PhD, 1957. Pres. H.D. Ostberg Assocs., N.Y.C., 1950—; assoc. prof. mktg. NYU, 1954—63. Chmn. bd. Admar Group,Inc., 1960; dir. Self-Instructional Devel. Corp., Amherst Group, Porter Industries, Inc.; pres. Eastman Enterprises, Inc. Contbr. articles to profl. jours. Trustee Ostberg Found.; chmn. Givat Haviva Edn. Found. Capt. USAF, 1950—53. Jewish. Office: Admar Group Inc 278 Fountain Rd Englewood NJ 07631-4403 E-mail: hdousa@earthlink.net.

OSTBY, FREDERICK PAUL, JR. meteorologist, retired government official , science administrator; b. New Haven, Jan. 20, 1930; s. Frederick Paul and Edna Maria (Kruckenberg) O.; m. Joanne Bernice Sorvig, Jan. 1, 1955 (div. 1989); children: Paul, Neil, Karen, Lynn; m. Barbara Richards, Mar. 17, 1989. BS in Meteorology, NYU, 1951, MS, 1960. Cert. Consulting Meteorologist. Meteorologist TWA, N.Y.C., 1953-54, Kansas City, Mo., 1955-56, N.E. Weather Service, Lexington, Mass., 1955, Travelers Weather Service, Hartford, Conn., 1956-60; research scientist Travelers Research Center, 1960-70; meteorologist Nat. Weather Service, Silver Spring, Md., 1970-72; dep. dir. Nat. Severe Storms Forecast Center, Dept. Commerce, Kansas City, Mo., 1972-80; dir. Nat. Severe Storms Forecast Center, 1980-96; assoc. Climatological Cons. Corp., 1997—. Severe weather cons. The Weather Channel, 1997—. Contbr. papers to profl. lit. Served with USAF, 1951-53. Fellow Am. Meteorol. Soc. (council 1977-80, 84-87). Home: 12537 Broadmoor St Overland Park KS 66209-3234 E-mail: fostby@attglobal.net.

OSTDAHL, ROGER HAROLD, neurological surgeon; b. Richland, Wash., May 1, 1946; s. Harold Everett and Lorraine (DeWall) O.; m. Maureen Callahan, May 8, 1976; children: Maggie, Shannon. BA in Chemistry magna cum laude, Duke U., 1969, MD, 1973. Bd. cert. Nat. Bd. Med. Examiners, Am. Bd. Neurol. Surgery. Neurol. surgeon Neurol. Surgery Ltd., Harrisburg, Pa., Pinnacle Health Sys., Harrisburg, Holy Spirit Hosp., Camp Hill, 1979—. Contbg. author: (book chpts.) Neurosurgery, 1985, The Drez Operation, 1996; contbr. articles to profl. jours. Neurol. coord. Think First Program, Harrisburg, 1988-94. Fellow ACS; mem. AMA, Am. Assn. Neurol. Surgeons, Congress Neurol. Surgeons, Am. Trauma Soc. (bd. dirs. Pa. divsn. 1989—), Pa. Med. Soc., Pa. Neurol. Soc., Alpha Omega Alpha. Avocations: tennis, skiing, reading, travel, scuba diving. Office: Neurol Surgery Ltd 920 Century Dr Mechanicsburg PA 17055-4351

OSTDICK, WAYNE WILLIAM, orthodontist; b. Elgin, Ill., Apr. 28, 1961; s. William Theodore Ostdick and Mary Jane Bush; m. Laurie Ann Pautz, Sept. 20, 1986. BA, Augustana Coll., Rock Island, Ill., 1983; DDS, U. Iowa, 1992; MS, Northwestern U., Chgo., 1994. Lic. dentist, Wis., Ill. Assoc. orthodontist Norman Garn, DDS, MS, Chgo., 1994, Assoc. Orthodontists, Waukesha, Wis., 1994-95, Stan Biel, DDS, MS, Hoffman Estates, Ill., 1994-97; clinic instr. Waukesha County Tech. Coll., Pewaukee, Wis., 1996-2001; orthodontist Marion Dental, Milw., 1996-2000; orthodontist/owner Advanced Orthodontics, Sussex, Wis., 1996—. Vol. dentist St. Joseph's Med. and Dental Clinic, Waukesha, 1996—. Mentor sch.-to-work program Waukesha County, Sussex, 1999—2000; vol. dentist St. Joseph's Med. and Dental Clinic, Waukesha, 1996—99; vol. emergency med. tech. Sussex Fire Dept., 1999—2001. Recipient Dean's Leadership award U. Iowa, 1990, Pre-doctoral Orthodontic Lab. tchg. award, 1991, Am. Acad. Oral Pathology award, 1992. Mem. ADA, Am. Assn. Orthodontists, Midwestern Soc. Orthodontists, Wis. Soc. Orthodontists, Wis. Dental Assn., Waukesha County Dental Soc., Sussex Area C. of C., Omicron Kappa Upsilon. Avocations: swimming, hiking, cooking, foreign films. Office: Advanced Orthodontics N64w24050 Main St Sussex WI 53089-3000

OSTEEN, LOUIS, chef; b. Anderson, S.C. m. Marlene Osteen. Chef, owner Pawleys Island Inn, SC, 1980; chef Charleston Grill, 1989—. Former mem. food bd. New Eng. Culinary Inst. Appearances Gourmet, Bon Appetit, Southern Living, GQ, Esquire, Saveur, Food & Wine, Town & Country , Great Chefs of the South. Bd. dirs. DiRoNa; founding co-organizer Charleston's Share Our Strength State of the Nation event. Nominee James Beard Found., 1996; named to Fine Dining Hall of Fame, Nation's Restaurant News A, 1994; recipient Great Am. Express Chef S.E. award, Ivy award, Restaurants & Institutions mag., Golden Dish award, Alan Richman, GQ's Mag.'s food and wine writer, 1994. Office: Louis's 200 Meeting St Charleston SC 29401*

O'STEEN, RANDY A. nursing administrator; b. Oklahoma City, Sept. 14, 1954; s. Jim D. and June A. (Davis) O'S. AS, Oklahoma City Community Coll., 1981; BA in Mgmt., So. Nazarene U., Bethany, Okla., 1990. Charge nurse, post anesthesia care unit Bapt. Med. Ctr. of Okla., Oklahoma City, 1983-88, head nurse, post critical care unit, 1988-89, head nurse, nursing resource unit, 1989-91; dir. Nursing Systems, 1991-93; dir. systems and devel. Integris Health, Oklahoma City, 1993-97, dir. care continuum, info. sys., 1997-2001; dir. R&D Christus Health, Houston, 2001—. Editor newsletter Vital Signs, 1984-87. Mem. ANA, Am. Soc. Post Anesthesia Nurses, Okla. Nurses Assn., Okla. Soc. Post Anesthesia Nurses (pres. Oklahoma City chpt. 1983-86, chmn. publs. com. 1985-86), Okla. Orgn. Nurse Execs., Am. Med. Informatics Assn., Health Level Seven, Health Info. Mgmt. Sys. Soc., Am. Telemedicine Assn. Home: 229 NW 33rd St Oklahoma City OK 73118-8613 E-mail: okcrolk@swbell.net.

O'STEEN, VAN, lawyer; b. Sweetwater, Tenn., Jan. 10, 1946; s. Bernard Van and Laura Emelyne (Robinson) O.; m. Deborah Ann Elias, May 18, 1974; children— Jonathan Van, Laura Ann. B.A., Calif. Western U., 1968; J.D. cum laude, Ariz. State U., 1972. Bar: Ariz. 1972, U.S. Dist. Ct. Ariz. 1972, U.S. Ct. Appeals (9th cir.) 1973, U.S. Supreme Ct. 1975. Staff atty. Maricopa Legal Aid Soc., Phoenix, 1972-74; atty. Bates & O'Steen, Legal Clinic, Phoenix, 1974-77; atty. O'Steen Legal Clinic, Phoenix, 1977-80; mng. ptnr. Van O'Steen and Ptnrs., Phoenix and Tucson, 1980—; pres. Van O'Steen Mktg. Group, Inc., Phoenix, 1985—. Author numerous self-help legal books. Founding dir. Ariz. Ctr. for Law in the Pub. Interest, 1974-80. Served with USNR, 1963-69. Mem. ABA (chmn. spl. com. delivery legal services 1982-85), Am. Legal Clinic Assn. (pres. 1979), Assn. Trial Lawyers Am. Democrat. Address: 3605 N 7th Ave Phoenix AZ 85013-3638

O'STEEN, WENDALL KEITH, neurobiology and anatomy educator; b. Meigs, Ga., July 3, 1928; s. Wellna Hubert and Lillian (Powell) O'S.; m. Sandra Lynn Kraeer, July 30, 1983; children: Lisa Diane, Kerry Keith, Buckley Powell. BA, Emory U., 1948, MS, 1950; PhD, Duke U., 1958. Asst. prof. Emory U. Jr. Coll., Valdosta, Ga., 1948-49; instr. Emory U., Atlanta, 1950-51; prof. Emory U. Sch. Medicine, 1968-77; from asst. prof. to prof. med. br. U. Tex., 1958-67; asst. prof. Wofford Coll., Spartanburg, S.C., 1951-53; prof., chmn. dept. neurobiology and anatomy, Bowman Gray Sch. Med. Wake Forest U., Winston-Salem, N.C., 1977-93, prof. emeritus, 1993—. Mem. anatomy com. Nat. Bd. Med. Examiners, Phila., 1982-87. Contbr. over 150 articles to books, nat. and internat. jours. Served to lt. col. USAR. Recipient Golden Apple teaching award Med. Br. U. Tex., Galveston, 1967, Outstanding Tchr. award Emory U., 1973, Williams Disting. Teaching award Emory U., 1974, award for teaching excellence Bowman Gray Sch. Medicine, Wake Forest U. Mem. Am. Assn. Anatomists (exec. com. 1980-84, v.p. 1990-92), Assn. Anatomy Chairmen (exec. com. 1982-84, pres. 1990-91), So. Soc. Anatomists (pres. 1975-76), Soc. for Neurosci., N.C. Soc. Neurosci. (pres. 1980-81), Western N.C. Soc. Neurosci. (pres. 1987-88), Assn. Rsch. in Vision and Ophthalmology, Alpha Omega Alpha. Republican. Methodist. Avocations: gardening, music. Office: Wake Forest U Bowman Gray Sch Medicine Dept Of Neurobiology & Anatomy Winston Salem NC 27157-0001

OSTENDORF, LANCE STEPHEN, lawyer, investor, financial consultant and planner; b. New Orleans, Aug. 16, 1958; 1 child, Christine Marie Ostendorf. BBA summa cum laude, Loyola U., 1976, JD, 1980. Bar: La. 1980, U.S. Dist. Ct. (ea. dist.) La. 1981, U.S. Dist. Ct. La., U.S. Supreme Ct. 1980, U.S. Dist. Ct. (we. and mid. dists.) La. 1983. Founder Law Firm of Ostendorf, Tate, Barnett & Wells PLC, New Orleans, Calif. and Tex.; owner RCO Internat. Inc. Treas., CFO La. State U. Med. Ctr. Found., New Orleans, 1992—; lectr. Lorman Ednl. Seminars; bd. dirs. La. State U. Med. Ctr. Found., New Orleans, tech. transfer com.; speaker and tchr. Lorman Ednl. Svcs., Inc. Author: Insurance Law; contbr. articles to profl. jours. Mem. ABA, Fed. Bar Assn., Internat. Bar Assn., La. Bar Assn., Metairie Bar Assn., Maritime Law Assn., Comite Maritime Internat., Assn. for Transp. Law, Trucking Industry Def. Assn., Logistics and Policy, Assn. Average Adjusters of U.S., Jefferson Bar Assn., New Orleans Bar Assn., La. Restaurant Assn., Am. Trial Lawyers Assn., La. Bar Assn., Jefferson Bar Assn., Fifth Cir. Bar Assn., Def. Rsch. Inst., La. Trial Lawyers Assn., Law Def. Lawyers Assn., Houston Mariners Club, Southeastern Adm. Law Inst., St. Thomas Moore Club, La. Notary Soc., Blue Key Honor Soc. Office: The Poydras Ctr Ste 1460 650 Poydras St New Orleans LA 70130 Fax: 504-527-5111. E-mail: lanceostendorf@otbw-law.com.

OSTER, LEWIS HENRY, manufacturing executive, engineering consultant; b. Mitchell, S.D., Jan. 18, 1923; s. Peter W. and Lucy (Goetsch) O.; m. Mary Mills, Aug. 17, 1948; children— David, Lewis, Nancy, Susan. B.S. in Engring., Iowa State U., 1948; M.B.A., Syracuse U., 1968. Registered profl. engr., Iowa. Mgr., Maytag Co., Newton, Iowa, 1953-59; sr. staff engr., mgr. Philco-Ford Corp., Phila., 1959-62; mgr. mech. and indsl. engring. Carrier Corp., Syracuse, N.Y., 1962-75; v.p. Superior Industries Internat., Van Nuys, Calif., 1981— ; v.p., gen. mgr. Superior/Ideal, Inc., Oskaloosa, Iowa, 1975— ; engring. cons., Louisville, 1951-53. Author: MTM Application Manual, 1957. Leader, Boy Scouts Am., Syracuse, 1965-73; fund chmn. United Fund, Syracuse, 1965-73. Served to lt. col. USAFR, 1942— ; ETO. Decorated Purple Heart, Disting. Flying Cross, air medal with four oak leaf clusters. Mem. Am. Inst. Indsl. Engrs. (pres. 1951-53), Oskaloosa Country Club, Retired Officers Assn., Elks, Am. Legion.

OSTER, MARTIN WILLIAM, oncologist, educator; b. Apr. 9, 1947; s. Joseph A. and Bella Oster; m. Karen A. Strauss, May 18, 1975; children: Bonnie Felice, Michelle Rae, Nancy Meredith. BA summa cum laude, Columbia U., 1967, MD, 1971. Diplomate Am. Bd. Internal Medicine and subsplty. med. oncology. Intern, resident in medicine Mass. Gen. Hosp., Boston, 1971-73; clin. assoc. divsn. of cancer treatment Nat. Cancer Inst., Bethesda, Md., 1973-76; asst. prof. medicine Columbia Coll. Physicians and Surgeons, 1976-86, assoc. prof. clin. medicine, 1986—. Asst. attending physician Columbia-Presbyn. Med. Center, N.Y.C., 1976-86, assoc. attending physician, 1986—; vice chair protocol com. Columbia U. Cancer Ctr., 1998, chmn., 1999. With USPHS, 1973-76. Am. Cancer Soc. jr. faculty clin. fellow, 1976-79. Fellow ACP; mem. AMA (Physician Recognition awards 1976-78, 79-81, 82-84), Am. Assn. Cancer Rsch., N.Y. Cancer Soc., Am. Soc. Clin. Oncology, N.Y. Met. Breast Cancer Group, Phi Beta Kappa, Alpha Omega Alpha. Home: 6 Arrowhead Ln Armonk NY 10504-1301 Office: 161 Fort Washington Ave New York NY 10032-3713

OSTER, PATRICK RALPH, journalist; b. Harvey, Ill., Oct. 9, 1944; m. Sally Anne Jacobsen. BS with honors, Loyola U., Chgo., 1966; postgrad., Glasgow (Scotland) U. Soviet Inst., 1968-69; JD, Cornell U., 1970. Assoc. firm Price, Cushman, Keck, Mahin and Cate, Chgo., 1970-72; atty., investigator Better Govt. Assn., 1972-73; reporter Chgo. Sun-Times, 1973-74, Washington corr., 1977-78, chief Washington bur., 1978-84; assoc. editor U.S. News & World Report, Washington, 1974-77; chief Mexico City Bur. Knight-Ridder Newspapers, 1984-88; corr. Business Week, Brussels, 1990-94; asst. mng. editor The Bakersfield Californian, 1994-96; mng. ediitor Nat. Law Jour., N.Y.C., 1996-97, editor-in-chief, 1997—2001; legal editor Bloomberg News, 2001—. Author: The Mexicans: Personal Portrait of a People, 1989. Recipient Silver Gavel award (3) ABA; InterAm. Press Club award, 1984; Worth Bingham award, 1982, citation Overseas Press Club, 1986; others.

OSTER, ROSE MARIE GUNHILD, foreign language professional, educator; b. Stockholm, Feb. 26, 1934; came to U.S., 1958; d. Herbert Jonas and Emma Wilhelmina (Johnson) Hagetorn; m. Ludwig F. Oster, May 17, 1956; children: Ulrika, Mattias. Fil. mag., U. Stockholm, 1956; PhD, Kiel (Germany) U., 1958. Postdoctoral rsch. fellow linguistics Yale U., 1958-60, rsch. fellow Germanic langs., 1960-64, lectr. Swedish, 1964-66; mem. faculty U. Colo., Boulder, 1966-80, assoc. prof. Germanic langs. and lits., 1970-77, prof., 1977-80, chmn. dept., 1972-75, assoc. dean Grad. Sch., 1975-79, assoc. vice chancellor for grad. affairs Grad. Sch., 1979-80; dean for grad. studies and rsch. U. Md., College Park, 1980-83, prof. Germanic langs. and lits., 1980—, acting chair dept., 1997—2001. Mem. Fulbright Nat. Screening Com., Scandinavia, 1973, 83-87, chair, 1986-87; mem. selection com. Scandinavia Internat. Exch. of Scholars, 1982-86; cons. panelist Nat. Endowment for Humanities, 1975—, mem. bd. cons., 1980—; state coord. Am. Coun. on Edn., Colo., 1978-80, Md., 1981-83, dir. dept. leadership program, 1986-91; mem. exec. com. Assn. Grad. Schs., 1980-83; mem. dean's exec. com. African-Am. Inst., 1981-85; interim dir. Washington Sch. Psychiatry, 1994-95; cons. in field. Contbr. articles and revs. to profl. publs. Bd. dirs. Washington Sch. Psychiatry, Am.-Swedish Hist. Mus., Phila., Open Theatre, Washington; mem. nat. fellowship com. Am.-Scandinavian Found., 1997—, bd. trustees, 2001—. Carnegie fellow, 1974; grantee Swedish Govt., Am. Scandinavian Found., German Acad. Exch. Svc.; recipient Translation prize Am.-Scandinavian Found., 1997. Mem. NOW, MLA (mem. Del. Assembly 1995—), AAUP, Soc. Advancement Scandinavian Studies (pres. 1979-80), Am. Scandinavian Assn. of Nat. Capital Area (pres. 1983-86, 96—), Am.-Scandinavian Found., Am. Assn. Higher Edn., Modern Lang. Assn. (mem. del. assembly). Home: 4977 Battery Ln Bethesda MD 20814-4931 Office: U Md Dept Germanic Studies College Park MD 20742-0001 E-mail: ro8@umail.umd.edu.

OSTERBERG, JORJ O. retired civil engineer; Prof. Northwestern U., Chgo., prof. emeritus Evanston, Ill. Recipient Nova award for constrn. innovations, 1994. Mem. ASCE (Karl Terzaghi award 1993), Nat. Acad. Engring. Achievements include patents for Holder 11 patents. Home: 16416 E Powers Pl Aurora CO 80015-4059

OSTERBERG, SUSAN SNIDER, communications educator, farmer; b. Balt. d. Ray and Helen (Taubkins) Snider; m. Edward C. Osterberg Jr., Aug. 26, 1967; 1 child, E. Charles III. BS in Speech, Northwestern U., 1966; MS in Speech, So. Ill. U., 1967; EdD in Reading, U. Houston, 1980. Adj. prof. dept. arts and humanities U. Houston, 1967-72, 84—, field supr. Coll. Edn., 1975-76; farmer Citrus Grove, Ft. Pierce, Fla., 1995—. Dir. drama Longfellow Elem. Sch. for Creative and Performing Arts, 1976-78, cons. to gen. supt. of schs., 1982-83; tchr. Merry-Go-Round Theatre Sch., Nina Vance Alley Theatre, Houston, 1970-85; arts edn. rep. to China, 1977; mem. African/Am. educators program AAUW, Internat. Comm. Agy and Sierra Leone Assn. Univ. Women, Washington, 1981; artist-in-residence Hambidge Ctr. for the Arts, 1981. Editor Opera Cues mag., 1972-74; author of plays. Fellow program for arts mgr. Nat. Endowment for the Arts, Washington, 1979. Mem. ASCD, Internat. Assn. Theatre for Children and Young People, Internat. Reading Assn., Internat. Theatre Inst., Am. Alliance for Theatre and Edn., Am. Assn. for Theatre in Secondary Edn. (bd. dirs.), Am. Assn. of Theatre for Youth (adminstrv. com.), Am. Coun. for the Arts, Assn. Performing Arts (presenter), Assn. for Theatre in Higher Edn., Children's Theatre Assn. Am. (regional critic), Nat. Assn. for Cmty. Leadership, Nat. Soc. for Internships and Exptl. Edn. (cons. peer assistance network in exptl. learning), So. States Comm. Assn., S.W. Theatre Conf., Theatre for Young Audiences, Delta Kappa Gamma (chair Beta Omicron), Kappa Delta Pi. Methodist. Office: U Houston 11222 Wilding Ln Houston TX 77024-5308 E-mail: eosterberg@aol.com.

OSTERBERG, THOMAS KARL, construction company executive; b. Worthington, Minn., Sept. 20, 1953; s. Milton A. and Lucille I. (Pawek) O.; m. Pamela L. Adams, June 14, 1980; children: Emily L., Tucker S. AA, Worthington C.C., 1975; BA, Minn. State U., 1978. Football coach Worthington C.C., 1973-75, Mankato (Minn.) State U., 1975-78; carpenter Pepper Constrn., Mankato, 1976-78; prin. Osterberg Constrn., 1978-82; project mgr. Constrn. 70, Inc., Roseville, Minn., 1982-83; gen. mgr., exec. v.p. Carlson-LaVine, Inc., Mpls., 1983-94; ptnr., exec. v.p. Benson-Orth Assocs., Inc., Minnetonka, 1994—. Mem. Young Execs. Mpls., 1985; exec. Mgmt. Com., Mpls., 1988-91. Mem. Am. Swedish Inst., The Swedish Soc. Lutheran. Avocations: winter camping, hunting, fishing, cross country, skiing. Home: 17500 64th St SW Cokato MN 55321-4700 Office: 14300 Ridgedale Dr Ste 320 Minnetonka MN 55343

OSTERBROCK, DONALD E(DWARD), astronomy educator; s. William Carl and Elsie (Wettlin) O.; m. Irene L. Hansen, Sept. 19. 1952; children: Carol Ann, William Carl, Laura Jane. PhB, SB, U. Chgo., 1948, SM, 1949, PhD, 1952; DSc (hon.), Ohio State U., 1986, U. Chgo., 1992, U. Wis., Madison, 1997. Postdoctoral fellow, mem. faculty Princeton, 1952-53; mem. faculty Calif. Inst. Tech., 1953-58; faculty U. Wis.-Madison, 1958-73, prof. astronomy, 1961-73, chmn. dept. astronomy, 1966-67, 69-72; prof. astronomy and astrophysics U. Calif., Santa Cruz, 1972-92, prof. emeritus, 1993—. Dir. Lick Obs., 1972-81; mem. staff Mt. Wilson Obs., Palomar Obs., 1953-58; vis. prof. U. Chgo., 1963-64, Ohio State U., 1980, 86; Hill Family vis. prof. U. Minn., 1977-78. Author: Astrophysics of Gaseous Nebulae, 1974, James E. Keeler, Pioneer American Astrophysicist and the Early Development of American Astrophysics, 1984, Astrophysics of Gaseous Nebulae and Active Galactic Nuclie, 1989, Pauper and Prince: Ritchey, Hale and Big American Telescopes, 1993, Yerkes Observatory, 1892-1950: The Birth, Near Death and Resurrection of a Scientific Research Institution, 1997, Walter Baade: A Life in Astrophysics, 2001; co-author: (with John R. Gustafson and W.J. Shiloh Unruh) Eye on the Sky: Lick Observatory's First Century, 1988; editor: (with C.R. O'Dell) Planetary Nebulae, 1968, (with Peter H. Raven) Origins and Extinctions, 1988, (with J.S. Miller) Active Galactic Nuclei, 1989; Stars and Galaxies: Citizens of the Universe, 1990; letters editor Astrophys. Jour., 1971-73. With USAAF, 1943-46. Recipient Profl. Achievement award U. Chgo. Alumni Assn., 1982, Antoinette de Vaucouleurs Meml. lecture and medal U. Tex., Austin, 1994, Hans Lippershey medal Antique Telescope Soc., 1999, Alumni medal U. Chgo. Alumni Assn., 2000, LeRoy Doggett prize and lecture AAS Hist. Astronomy Divsn., 2002; Guggenheim fellow Inst. Advanced Studies, Princeton, N.J., 1960-61, 82-83, Ambrose Monnell Found. fellow, 1989-90, NSF sr. postdoctoral rsch. fellow U. Coll., London, 1968-69. Mem. NAS (chmn. astronomy sect. 1971-74, sec. class math. and phys. sci. 1980-83, chmn. class math and phys. sci. 1983-85, councilor 1985-88), Am. Acad. Arts and Scis., Internat. Astron. Union (pres. commn. 34 1967-70), Royal Astron. Soc. (assoc., Gold medal 1997), Am. Astron. Soc. (councilor 1970-73, v.p. 1975-77, pres. 1988-90, vice chmn. hist. astronomy div. 1985-87, chmn. 1987-89, Henry Norris Russell lectr. 1991), Astron. Soc. Pacific (chmn. history com. 1982-86, Catherine Wolfe Bruce medal 1991, bd. dirs. 1992-95), Wis. Acad. Scis. Arts and Letters, Am. Philos. Soc., State Hist. Soc. Wis. Congregationalist. Home: 120 Woodside Ave Santa Cruz CA 95060-3422 E-mail: don@ucolick.org.

OSTERGARD, PAUL MICHAEL, not for profit executive; b. Akron, Ohio, Apr. 1, 1939; s. Paul and Janette Beryl (Laube) O.; m. Elizabeth K. McCombs, Jan. 1965 (div. Nov. 1971). AB magna cum laude, Case-Western Res. U., 1961; JD, U. Mich., 1964; MPA, Harvard U., 1969; diploma in hispanic studies, U. Madrid, Spain, 1960. Bar: Ohio 1964. Atty. U.S. Steel Corp., Pitts., 1967-69; gen. atty. TWA Inc., N.Y.C., 1969-71; v.p. adminstrn., sec., counsel Pa. Co. (now Penn Ctrl. Corp.), 1971-74, and subs. Buckeye Pipe Line Co., N.Y.C., 1972-74; pub. affairs exec. GE, Fairfield, Conn., 1974-84; pres. GE Found., 1984-90; chmn., CEO, bd. dirs. Citigroup Found., N.Y.C., 1990-99; pres. Com. to Encourate Corp. Philanthropy, 1999-2001; pres., CEO Jr. Achievement Internat., 2001—. Bd. dirs. Bond Market Found., Found. for Tchg. Econs., Jr. Achievement Internat., Jr. Achievement Inc. Decorated Bronze Star, Legion of Merit (Vietnam); Univ. scholar, 1957-61; Littauer fellow, 1968-69 Mem. Harvard Club, Wexford Plantation Club, Phi Beta Kappa, Omicron Delta Kappa. Episcopalian. Office: JA Internat 460 Abernathy Rd NE Atlanta GA 30328 Home: 54 Wexford on Green Hilton Head Island SC 29928 E-mail: paul@jaintl.org.

OSTERGREN BAITS, MARCIA, elementary education educator; b. Sao Paulo, Brazil, Oct. 24, 1944; came to U.S., 1965; d. Eduardo and Oraide G. Ostergren; m. David F. Baits, July 31, 1971; children: Mark David, Anelise Christine. MusB, Birmingham So. Coll., 1969; M of Music Edn., Wright State U., 1997. Cert. elem. tchr., Ohio. Music tchr. Sao Paulo Grad Sch., 1970-73, St. John Internat. Sch., Waterloo, Belgium, 1977-81; kindergarten tchr. ECLC, Columbus, Ohio, 1986-87; French immersion tchr. Columbus Pub. Sch., 1987-88, elem. tchr., 1988-89; music tchr. Wilmington (Ohio) City Sch., 1997-98, Dayton (Ohio) Pub. Schs., 1998—. Asst. Montessori Acad., Dallas, 1969. Playwright: O Cedarville; contbr. National Anthology, Poetic Voices of America, 1994. Co-founder Cedarville Opera House Soc., 1994; founder Cedarville News, 1995; active Food for the Hungry, Crisis Pregnancy Ctr., Foster Care. Invited to Presdl. Prayer Breakfast The White House, Washington, 1969.; Outstanding Freshman scholar, Andrew Coll., 1965; Birmingham So. Coll. jr. scholar, 1967. Mem. Cedarville Opera House Soc. (co-founder 1994), Mortar Bd., Kappa Delta Pi, Phi Theta Kappa. Avocations: volleyball, tennis, guitar, piano, translator. Home: 179 Detroit Blvd Xenia OH 45385-2241 Office: Dayton City Scsh Edison Elem 228 N Broadway Dayton OH 45407 E-mail: mbaits@dps.k12.oh.us.

OSTERHAUS, GREG S. artist, graphic designer; b. Hinsdale, Ill., Apr. 28, 1963; s. Gordon Frederick and Leona Osterhaus; m. Janie D. Osterhaus, May 9, 1987; children: Taylor W., Madeline Q., Kyle J. BFA, Va. Poly. Inst. and State U., 1985. Artist oil paintings, also acrylics, watercolors, pastels. One-mans shows include Roanoke County Pub. Libr., 1987, Studios on the Square, Roanoke, 1994, 96, 99, YMCA Rotating Gallery, Roanoke, 1996, The Little Gallery, Smith Mt. Lake, Va., 1996, 99, Shenandoah Club, Roanoke, 1997, Frame Scapes, Roanoke, 1998, Allehany Highlands Ctr., Clifton Forge, Va., 1998, Artworks Gallery, Norfolk, Va., 1999; exhibited in group shows

Depot Gallery, Roanoke, Studios on the Square, 1994, Gallery at Shanaz!, Lynchburg, Va., 1995, The Little Gallery, 1996, 97, Gallery at Szent Györgyi, Falmouth, Mass., 1998. Avocations: music, reading, guitar. Home and Office: 2351 Denniston Ave SW Roanoke VA 24015-1904

OSTERHAUS, WILLIAM ERIC, television executive; b. N.Y.C., July 31, 1935; s. Eric Hugo and Helen (McAuliff) O.; m. Nancy Jean Heinemann, June 19, 1960 (dec.); children: Eric Frank, Marc Andrew; m. Annemarie Clark, Dec. 28, 1985 Student, Fordham U., 1953-54, Harvard U. Bus. Sch., summer 1970. Staff producer news and spl. events dept. Sta. WNBC-AM-TV, N.Y.C., 1956-61; exec. producer Sta. KYW-TV, Cleve., 1961-64, Sta. KPIX, San Francisco, 1964-67, gen. mgr., 1969-73; program mgr. Sta. KYW-TV, Phila., 1967-69; pres., gen. mgr. Sta. KQED Inc., San Francisco, 1973-78; pres. SiteLine Comms., Inc., 1979—; chmn. bd. VariCom Inc., 1982-86. Chmn. TV adv. com. Calif. Pub. Broadcasting Commn., 1977-78; mem. joint com. on film and broadcasting Indo-U.S. Subcommn. on Edn. and Culture., 1975-85; chmn. TV com. San Rafael Redevel. Agy., Calif., 1977-78; mem. citizens adv. com. CATV, San Rafael, 1976-77, Dominican Coll., San Rafael, 1972-80; bd. dirs. Downtown Parking Corp. Bd. dirs. The Ctr. for the Arts, San Francisco, 1985—; bd. dirs. Zeum, 1995—. 1st lt. U.S. Army, 1958-60. Recipient Peabody award and Hillman award for One Nation Indivisible documentary, 1968. Office: 703 Market St Ste 1108 San Francisco CA 94103-2121

OSTERHELD, R(OBERT) KEITH, chemistry educator; b. Bklyn., Apr. 19, 1925; s. Albert Henry and Hilda Pearl (Heatlie) O.; m. Jean Drake Evans, June 28, 1952; children: Robert Keith, Albert Laighton, James Evans, Thomas Heatlie. BS in Chemistry, Poly. Inst. Bklyn., 1945; PhD in Inorganic Chemistry, U. Ill., 1950. Instr. Cornell U., Ithaca, N.Y., 1950-54; asst. prof. chemistry U. Mont., Missoula, 1954-58, assoc. prof., 1958-65, prof., 1965-90, prof. emeritus, 1990—, chmn. dept., 1973-90. Contbr. articles to profl. jours. Mem. Florence (Mont.) Sch. Bd., 1969-75, chmn., 1972-73, 74-75; bd. dirs. Mont. Sch. Bd. Assn., Helena, 1973-75; council mem. Florence-Carlton Community Ch., 1965-90, treas., 1965-90. Served to sgt. USAAF, 1945-47. Mem. Am. Chem. Soc., N.Am. Thermal Analysis Soc., Sigma Xi. Home: 524 Larry Creek Loop Florence MT 59833-6705 Office: U Montana Dept Chemistry Missoula MT 59812-0001

OSTERHOFF, JAMES MARVIN, retired telecommunications company executive; b. Lafayette, Ind., May 18, 1936; s. Abel Lyman and Mildred Paulene (Post) O.; m. Marilyn Ann Morrison, Aug. 24, 1958; children: Anne Michelle Bitsie, Amy Louise Olmsted, Susan Marie BSME, Purdue U., 1958; MBA, Stanford U., 1963. Staff asst. FMC Corp., San Jose, Calif., 1963-64; with Ford Motor Co., Dearborn, Mich., 1964-84; v.p. fin. Ford Motor Credit Co., 1973-75; controller car ops. N. Am. Automotive Ops., Ford Motor Co., 1975-76, asst. controller, 1976-79; controller tractor ops. Ford Motor Co., Troy, Mich., 1979-84; v.p. fin., CFO Digital Equipment Corp., Maynard, Mass., 1985-91; exec. v.p., CFO U.S.West Inc., Englewood, Colo., 1991-95. Bd. dirs. Arkwright Mutual Ins. Co., FSA Ltd., GenCorp, Inc., Pvt. Sector Coun., Colo. Neurol. Inst., Goodwill Industries of Denver. Served to lt. (j.g.) USN, 1958-61. Recipient Disting. Engring. Alumnus award Purdue U.; named Outstanding Mech. Engring. Alumnus, Purdue U.

OSTERHOLM, J(OHN) ROGER, humanities educator; b. Worcester, Mass., Nov. 24, 1936; s. Walfred Anders and Ellen Olivia (Hendrickson) O.; m. Jo-Ann M. Doiron, Dec. 22, 1962 (div. 1981); children: Doreen, Jon R., Don J.; m. Diane Jane Ungerer, May 1, 1982 (div. 2002). BA, Upsala Coll., 1959; MA, CCNY, 1966; PhD, U. Mass., 1978; postgrad., Tex. Tech U., 1961-62, Worcester (Mass.) State Coll., 1965-66, Clark U., 1972. Announcer, disk jockey Sta. WFMU, East Orange, N.J., 1957-59; instr. Worcester Jr. Coll., 1962; supr. Aetna Life Ins. Co., N.Y.C., 1963-65; tchr. Wachusett Regional H.S., Holden, Mass., 1965-66; assoc. prof. Ctrl. N.E. Coll., Worcester, 1966-79, chmn. humanities, 1977-79; prof. Embry-Riddle Aero. U., Daytona Beach, Fla., 1979—. Cons. Am. Mil. U., 1998—; spkr. on journalism, aviation films and Bing Crosby; advisor to coll. student publs., 1969-94, 97—; designer on-line comm. and humanities courses Integrated Curriculum in Engring, Embry-Riddle Aero. U., 1998—. Author: Literary Career of Isaiah Thomas, 1978, Bing Crosby: A Bio-bibliography, 1994; editor: The Riddle Reader, 1988; co-author: MiG-15 to Freedom, 1996; contbr. articles to profl. jours. and Guide to U.S. Popular Culture (Encyclopedia). Dirs. Daytona Playhouse, Daytona Beach, 1980-83; lector Grace Luth. Ch., Ormond Beach, Fla., 1989—; pres. Civility at Large, 1998—. With USAF, 1960-62. Recipient Best Supporting Actor award Daytona Playhouse, 1981. Mem. Popular Culture Assn., Air Force Assn., Soc. Collegiate Journalists, Internat. Crosby Circle, Alpha Phi Omega, Rho Tau Sigma. Republican. Avocations: acting, airplane models, computer simulations. Office: Embry-Riddle Aero U Humanities Dept Daytona Beach FL 32114 E-mail: DocJollyR@aol.com.

OSTERHOUT, SUYDAM, physician, educator; b. Bklyn., Nov. 25, 1925; s. Howard and Edna Cornell (Davison) O.; m. Shirley Elizabeth Kirkman, Sept. 17, 1960; children— Mark, Martin, Ann. BA, Princeton, 1945; MD (Hanes fellow), Duke, 1949; PhD, Rockefeller U., 1959. Diplomate: Am. Bd. Internal Medicine. Intern pathology Cleve. City Hosp., 1950; intern internal medicine Mass. Meml. Hosp., Boston, 1950-51; resident Duke Hosp., 1953-56; faculty Duke Med. Sch., Durham, N.C., 1959—, now prof. medicine, prof. microbiology, asso. dean. Contbr. articles to profl. jours. Served with M.C. USAF, 1951-53. Recipient NIH Career Devel. award, 1960-65; Markle scholar in medicine, 1959-64 Fellow A.C.P.; mem. Am. Soc. Micro-Biology, Am. Fedn. Clin. Research, Sigma Xi, Alpha Omega Alpha. Home: 5133 N Willowhaven Dr Durham NC 27712-1956 Office: PO Box 3007 Durham NC 27715-3007

OSTERLOH, ELIJAH RAEL, elementary school educator; b. Baltimore, Md., Oct. 21, 1976; s. Steven Bradley and Nina Marie Osterloh. BS in Music Edn., U. Md., 1999. Cert. tchr. Md., 1999. Dir. bands Martin Luther King, Jr. Mid. Sch., Beltsville, Md., 1999—. Marching band drill design Long Reach H.S., Columbia, Md., 1999—2001, U. Md. Marching Band, College Park, 1997—99; pvt. studio clarinet instr., Ellicott City, Md., 1997—; adjudicator Md. All State Band, 1999—, Prince George's County Solo and Ensemble Festival, Md., 1999—, Fairfax County Solo and Ensemble Festival, Fairfax, Va., 2001—. Dir.: Prince George's County Band Festival, 2002 (highest score in festival, 2002), Fiesta-Val Music Festival, 2001; musician: Waterford Music Festival, 2002, Garrett Lakes Art Festival, 1998. Assoc. prin. clarinet Capital Wind Symphony, Fairfax, Va., 1999; bass clarinetist Prince George's Philharm. Orch., Beltsville, Md., 2000; prin. clarinet Free State Winds, Aberdeen, 1996—99, U. Md. Symphonic Wind Ensemble, College Park, 1998—99. Recipient Otto Sebeneichen Leadership award, U. Md. Bands, 1999. Mem.: Music Educators Nat. Conf. (pres. College Park collegiate chpt. 1996—98), Golden Key, Kappa Kappa Psi (joint sec./treas. Gamma Xi chpt. 1997, joint chair 1998). Democrat. Avocations: camping, hiking, bicycling, science fiction, reading. Personal E-mail: erosterloh@aol.com.

OSTERMAN, EURYDICE V. music educator; b. Atlanta, Apr. 5, 1950; d. Francis Alexander and Ella Louise (Lockett) O. BMus, Andrews U., Berrien Springs, Mich., 1972, MMus, 1975; DMA, U. Ala., Tuscaloosa, 1988. Cert. tchr., Ala. Tchr. Mt. Vernon (Ohio) Acad., 1972-76, Southwest Region Conf. 7th Day Adventists, Dallas, 1976-78; prof. Oakwood Coll., Huntsville, Ala., 1978—. Composer: numerous organ compositions. Recipient award for arrangement of Amazing Grace, Am. Guild Organists, 1994. Mem. Am. Guild Organists, Soc. Composers, Internat. Adventists Musicians Assn., So. Conf. Afro-Am. Studies, Phi Kappa Lambda. Avocations: walking, crocheting. Office: Oakwood Coll Huntsville AL 35896 E-mail: eosterman@oakwood.edu.

OSTERMEYER, MARYANN, secondary school educator, writer; b. Indpls., Dec. 9, 1950; d. Kenneth Dale and Mary Ida Ostermeyer. AB in English, San Diego State U., 1972, M of History, 1981. Cert. secondary tchg.credential/Clad credential. Tchr. Cajon Valley Union Sch. Dist., El Cajon, Calif., 1975—; freelance writer San Diego County Office of Edn., 1983; curriculum writer Heritage Pub. Co., El Cajon, 1985—86; writer I Love a Clean San Diego, 1995—96; tchr. refugee students/ESL Internat. Rescue Com., San Diego, 1996—. Bd. dirs. Friends of Classics, San Diego; AVID dist. coord. Cajon Valley Union Sch. Dist., El Cajon, 1997—98; developer of dist. AVID programs Hillsdale Mid. Sch. and Cajon Valley Mid. Sch.; collaborator with Survivors of Torture Internat. Cajon Valley Mid. Sch., San Diego, 2001—02. Contbr. ednl. curriculum; author: (book) El Cajon: A Pictorial History, 1986; contbr. curriculum text; author: (biographical sketch) In My Heart and On My Mind, 2003. Mem. El Cajon Hist. Soc.; tchr. rep. Cmtys. Against Substance Abuse, El Cajon, 1990—92; Bd. dirs. City of El Cajon Fire Dept., 2001—02; Community Panel Representative - Vision 2000 City of EL Cajon Mayor's Recommendation Committee, El Cajon, CA, 1990—92. Recipient World of Difference Inst. OutstandingTchr. Recognition award, Anti-Defamation League, 1998, NEH Tchr. Summer Inst. Program, 1993, Outstanding Tchr. Yr. Emerald Mid. Sch./Cajon Valley Mid. Sch., PTA, 1985, 1991. Mem.: Cajon VAlley Ednl. Assn. Avocations: gardening, needlepoint, writing, dog walking, community philanthropic services. Home: 1114 Evilo St El Cajon CA 92021 Office: Cajon Valley Union Sch Dist 189 Roanoke Rd El Cajon CA 92021 Personal E-mail: magistrao@aol.com.

OSTERN, WILHELM CURT, retired holding company executive; b. Geisenheim am Rhein, Germany, Sept. 29, 1923; came to U.S., 1956, naturalized, 1970; s. Wilhelm A. and Margarete R. (Seul) Ostern; m. Olga Atterbury, Nov. 24, 2001; children from previous marriage: Karen, Ellen, Wilhelm. Grad., Staatliches Realgymnasium, Geisenheim, 1941. With Bayer AG, and predecessor, 1941-88, officer and/or dir. subsidiaries and affiliates, 1956-89; vice chmn., chief fin. officer Mobay Corp., Pitts., 1974-86. Vice chmn. Bayer USA, Inc., Pitts., 1986—88, chmn., 1988—91; bd. dirs., chmn. fin. com. ACE Ltd., 1987—91; bd. dirs. Schott Corp., Inc., Carl Zeiss, Inc. Mem. Carnegie Mus. Sustaining Fund. With German Army, 1942-45. Hon. Consul Fed. Republic of Germany. Mem. Soc. Contemporary Crafts, Pitts. (bd. dirs.). Clubs: Brook (N.Y.C.); Duquesne (Pitts.). Home: Rhinebrook Farms Hartle Rd Sewickley PA 15143

OSTERTAG, ROBERT LOUIS, lawyer; b. N.Y.C., June 21, 1931; s. Frederick C. and Lillian (Bishop) O.; m. Ann Mary Flynn, Aug. 28, 1954; children— Thomas J., Daniel V., Debra A. BA, Fordham U., 1953; LL.B., St. John's U., Bklyn., 1956; LL.M., Georgetown U., 1960. Bar: N.Y. 1957, U.S. Dist. Ct. (so. dist.) N.Y. 1969, U.S. Tax Ct. 1965, U.S. Ct. Mil. Appeals 1959, U.S. Supreme Ct. 1960. Atty. office chief counsel IRS, Washington, 1958-60; ptnr. Guernsey, Butts & Walsh, Poughkeepsie, N.Y., 1963-90, Guernsey, Butts, Ostertag & O'Leary, Poughkeepsie, 1991-95, Ostertag, O'Leary & Barrett, Poughkeepsie, 1995—; adj. prof. paralegal studies Marist Coll., 1975-91; adj. prof. Fordham U. Sch. of Law, N.Y.C., 1993—. Counsel Agr. Com., N.Y. State Assembly, 1967-68; mem. Gov.'s Jud. Screening Com., 1987-93; counsel to cons. and draftsman of proposed county charters and adminstrv. codes for Sullivan, Fulton, Orange and Onondaga Counties, N.Y., City of Poughkeepsie, N.Y.; mem. 9th Jud. Dist. Grievance Com., 1975-79, 9th Jud. Dist. Med. Malpractice Panel, 1975-91, mem. 9th Jud. Dist. Arbitration Panel, 1980—; mem. Chief Judges Com. on Pro Bono Legal Svc., 1992-93. Trustee Joseph F. Barnard Meml. Law Libr., Poughkeepsie, 1979—; dir. Hudson Valley Philharm. Soc., 1973—76; v.p., dir. High Tor Opera Co., 1967—70; dir. United Fund of Dutchess County, 1973—78; dir. Dutchess County chpt. Am. Heart Assn., 1975—81, 1984—89; trustee Sports Mus. Dutchess County, 1989—93, chmn., 1989—90; dir. Hudson Valley Stadium Corp., 1995—, chair, 1998—; mem. Dutchess County (N.Y.) Charter Commn., 1966—67, Dutchess County Bd. Health, 1964—70, pres., 1966—70; chmn. Dutchess County Charter Revision Task Force, 1979—88; dep. supr. Town of Poughkeepsie, 1976; bd. dirs. Com. for Modern Cts., 1975—99; dir. Std. Gage Co., 1972—88; mem. adv. coun. Pace U. Sch. Law, 1975—84; paralegal adv. coun. Marist Coll., 1975—. Served to capt. JAGC USAF, 1956—58. Recipient Recognition award Cen. Poughkeepsie Exch. Club, 1967, Marist Coll. Pres.'s award, 1991. Mem.: ABA (chmn. conf. of state bar gen. practice leaders of gen. practice sect. 1980—87, mem. coun. 1982—86, ho. of dels. 1985—98, Gavel awards com. 1989—, standing com. on solo and small firm practitioners 1992—95), Dutchess County Bar Assn. (sec. 1969—79, pres. 1984—85), N.Y. State Bar Assn. (exec. com. 1983—85, 1986—93, ho. of dels. 1973—79, 1980—, pres. 1991—92, chmn. unlawful practice of law com. 1977—81, chmn. com. on law office econs. and mgmt. 1982, chmn. sect. on gen. practice of law 1980—82, com. profl. ethics 1986—90, 1996—99, 2000—, chmn. comm. on future of profession 1998, spl. com. on law governing firm structure and operation 1999—), N.Y. Bar Found., Am. Bar Found., Hudson Valley Estate Planning Coun. (pres. 1965—66, dir. 1969—74), Delta Theta Phi. Home: 5 Pat Dr Poughkeepsie NY 12603-5626 Office: 17 Collegeview Ave Poughkeepsie NY 12603-2406 E-mail: rlodmo@vh.net.

OSTERUD, HAROLD TRUMAN, public health and preventive medicine physician, researcher; b. Richmond, Va., May 1, 1923; s. Hjalmer Lauritz Osterud and Zella Surfus; m. Jessie Harrison Binford, Mar. 3, 1949; children: Bruce Harrison, Lauritz Binford, Erin Lee. BS, Randolph-Macon, Ashland, VA, 1940—43; MD, Med. Coll. Va., Richmond,VA, 1943—47; Master-Public Health, U. NC, Chapal Hill, NC, 1950—51. Lic. American Board Preventive Medcine Va. & Oreg. Internship Good Samaritan Hosp., Portland, Oreg., 1947—48; health officer Wasco-Sherman Health Dept., The Dalles, 1948—50, Coos County Health Dept., Coqville, 1953—55, Ln. County Health Dept., Eugene, 1956—61; assoc. prof. Oreg. Health Sciences U., Portland, 1961—66; prof. & chmn. pub. health Oreg. Health Sci. U., 1967—89; prof. emeritus Oreg. Health Sciences U., 1990—. Cons. Gov., State Legislature, Salem, Oreg., 1958—93; physician YMCA, Adv. Bd., Portland, Oreg.; mem. Oreg. State Senate, Salem, Oreg., 1976—78. Author: (book) Parasitic Protocols. Testimoney on bills Oreg. State Legislature, Salem, Oreg.; enviornmental activities Bull Run Heritage Found., Portland, 1972—2002. Capt. US Army, 1951—53, Japan & Korea. Recipient Alpha Omega Alpha, AOA Honor Med. Soc., 1947, John N. Sippy Award, APHA, 1969, Outstanding Leadership, Oreg. Pub. Health Assn., 1969 & 1988. Mem.: Oreg. Med. Assn. (chmn., pn & safety 1981—91, Presdl. Citation 1991), Oreg. Pub. Health Assn. (life; pres. 1948—2002), Portland Art Mus. Presbyterian. Achievements include PPreventive Medcine & Dentistry Review Committee, National Institutes of Health; United States Army, Bronze Star, Third Infantry Division, Korea, 4/9/1953; Oregon's first local medical examiner, Lane County Oregon, 1958-1961. Avocations: music, photography, hiking, building doll houses. Home: 64 Wheatherstone Court Lake Oswego OR 97035 Office: Oregon Health Science University 3181 SW Sam Jackson Park Rd Portland OR 97201-3011 Home Fax: 503-494-4981. E-mail: austind@ohsu.edu..

OSTLING, RICHARD NEIL, journalist, author; b. Endicott, N.Y., July 14, 1940; s. Acton Eric Sr. and Christine Cathryn (Cumins) O.; m. Joan Elaine Kerns, July 8, 1967; children: Margaret Anne, Elizabeth Anne. BA, U. Mich., 1962; MS in Journalism, Northwestern U., 1963; MA in Religion, George Washington U., 1970; LittD (hon.), Gordon (Mass.) Coll., 1989. Reporter, copyreader Morning News and Evening Jour., Wilmington, Del., 1963-64; asst. news editor Christianity Today mag., Washington, 1965-67, news editor, 1967-69; staff corr. Time mag., N.Y.C., 1969-74, religion writer, 1975-94, sr. corr., 1994-98; broadcaster Report on Religion, CBS Radio, 1979-98; religion corr. Newshour with Jim Lehrer formerly MacNeil/Lehrer Newshour, 1991-98; religion writer Associated Press, N.Y.C., 1998—. Adv. bd. Ctr. for Religion and the News Media, Northwestern U., 1994—. Author: Secrecy in the Church, 1974; co-author: Aborting America, 1979, Mormon America, 1999. Served with USNG, 1964-70. McCormick Found. fellow, 1962-63; recipient Supple, Templeton, Am. Acad. Religion and Wilbur awards for religion writing. Mem. Religion Newswriters Assn. (pres. 1974-76), Northwestern U. Alumni Hall of Achievement (charter), Phi Beta Kappa. Mem. Christian Reformed Ch. Home: 280 Hillcrest Rd Ridgewood NJ 07450-2400 Office: Associated Press 50 Rockefeller Plz New York NY 10020-1666 E-mail: rostling@ap.org.

OSTLUND, H. GOTE, atmospheric and marine scientist, educator; b. Stockholm, June 26, 1923; came to U.S., 1963; s. Sven and Ruth (Lundin) O.; m. Doris Beck, Sept. 30, 1950; children: Stellan, Goran. Fil Kand., U. Stockholm, 1949, Fil Lic., 1958; hon. doctorate, U. Gothenburg, 1984. Research asst. U. Stockholm, 1944-46; tchr. Technol. Night Coll., Stockholm, 1946-51; research asst. Royal Inst. Tech., 1947, asst. instr., 1948-52; head of lab. Swedish Nitrogen Fertilizer Works, Ltd., 1952-54, Radioactive Dating Lab., Stockholm, 1954-63; asst. instr. Royal Inst. Tech., 1956-57; vis. research asso. prof. Inst. Marine Scis., U. Miami (Fla.), 1960-61, asso. prof. geochemistry, 1963-67, prof. marine and atmospheric chemistry Rosenstiel Sch. Marine and Atmospheric Sci., 1967-97, chmn. div. chem. oceanography, 1970-72, coordinator Geochem. Oceans Sects., 1976-86, mem. exec. com. Geochem. Oceans Sects., 1973-86, coordinator Transient Tracers in Ocean, 1977-85, prof. emeritus, 1997—. Assoc. editor: Revs. of Geophysics and Space Physics, 1974-76; mem. editorial bd.: Marine Chemistry, 1974-93; mem. adv. bd.: Tellus B; contbr. articles to profl. jours. Served in Royal Swedish Air Force, 1943-44, 46. Mem. Am. Geophys. Union, Am. Meteorol. Soc., AAAS, Swedish Chem. Soc., Swedish Geophys. Soc., Fla. Acad. Scis. Office: U Miami 4600 Rickenbacker Cswy Miami FL 33149-1031 E-mail: gostlund@rsmas.miami.edu.

OSTRAGER, BARRY ROBERT, lawyer; b. N.Y.C., July 14, 1947; m. Pamela Goodman, Apr. 8, 1972; children: Anne Elizabeth, Katie, Jane. BA, CCNY, 1968, MA, 1973; JD, NYU, 1972. Bar: N.Y. 1973, Calif. 1996. Sr. ptnr., trial lawyer Simpson Thacher & Bartlett, N.Y.C., 1973—. Co-author: Handbook on Insurance Coverage Disputes, 11th edit. , 2002, Modern Reinsurance Law and Practice, 2d edit., 2000. Mem. Am. Law Inst., Assn. of Bar of City of N.Y. Office: Simpson Thacher & Bartlett 26th Fl 425 Lexington Ave Fl 26 New York NY 10017-3903 E-mail: b_ostrager@stblaw.com.

OSTRANDER, ROBERT EDWIN, retired United Nations interregional advisor, petroleum company executive; b. Pitts., June 30, 1931; s. Robert Jesse and Elizabeth Raymond (Comstock) O.; m. Margaret Valentina Servello, Dec. 21, 1958; children: Robert Glen, Roseanne. BA, Cornell U., 1953. Cert. petroleum geologist; registered geol. scientist. Area reservoir engr. Mene Grande Oil Co., San Tome, Venezuela, 1956-61; dist. engr. Oasis Oil Co. of Libya, Tripoli, 1962-67; reservoir/petroleum chief engr. Occidental Oil of Libya, 1967-71; divsn. head Iranian Oil Consortium, Ahwaz, Iran, 1972-75; mgr. ops. Ultramar Co. Ltd., Mt. Kisco, N.Y., 1975-81; v.p. engring. Weeks Petroleum Ltd., Westport, Conn., 1982-85; mng. dir. Reomag Inc., South Salem, N.Y., 1980—. Cons. World Bank, Washington, 1981—; cons. UN Secretariat, 1994—; advisor to govts. of China, India, others in Asia, Africa, Middle East; guest lectr. Asian univs., internat. seminars. Contbr. articles to profl. jours. Sec. Rep. Com., Town of Lewisboro; chair conservation adv. coun. Town of Lewisboro; pres. Ostrander Family Assn.; mem. Rep. Com. Westchester County; past. bd. dirs. Oakridge Condominium Assn., Vista, N.Y.; fellow Herbert F. Johnson Mus. Art, Cornell U., 1999—. Served to 1st lt. U.S. Army, 1953-55. Mem. Am. Assn. Petroleum Geologists, Soc. Petroleum Engrs. Home: 5715 State Route 89 Romulus NY 14541-9546 Address: 5715 State Route 89 Romulus NY 14541-9546 E-mail: reomag@flitg.net.

OSTRANDER, THOMAS WILLIAM, investment banker; b. Detroit, July 20, 1950; s. Roland J. and Sybil (Swartout) O.; children: John Charles, Elizabeth Ann, Brian Thomas. AB, U. Mich., 1972; MBA, Harvard U., 1976. CPA, Mich. Staff acct. Ernst & Whinney, Detroit, 1972-74, sr. acct., 1974, Cleve., 1975; assoc. Kidder, Peabody & Co., N.Y.C., 1976-78, asst. v.p., 1978-80, v.p., 1980-86, mng. dir., 1986-89, Salomon Bros., Inc., N.Y.C., 1989-97, Salomon Smith Barney, N.Y.C., 1997—. Bd. dirs. Westmoreland Coal Co.; mem. adv. bd. Paton Sch. Accountancy U. Mich., 1984-87, mem. vis. com. Lit., Sci. and Arts Sch., 1988-90, 95—. Pres. Ballet Hispanico, 1996—. Mem. AICPA, Met. Club, Harvard Club, Hasty Pudding Club, The Creek, Bond Club, Beaver Dam Winter Sports Club, Theta Delta Chi. Office: Salomon Smith Barney 388 Greenwich St New York NY 10013-2339 Home: 240 E 39th St Apt 46G New York NY 10016

OSTREM, WALTER MARTIN, librarian, educator, consultant; b. Mpls., May 27, 1930; s. Oscar Martin and Helen Therese (Marcio) O.; m. Gertrud Franciska Tunkel, Aug. 6, 1956; children: Thomas, Paul, Francine. BA, U. Minn., 1953, MA, 1958; BS, Mankato State U., 1962, MS, 1964; postgrad., U. Mich., U. Iowa. Serials libr. Agr. Libr. U. Minn., 1958-59; acquisitions libr. Mankato State U., Minn., 1959-66, Eastern Mich. U., 1966-67; dir. media Iowa City Sch., 1967-69; libr. John F. Kennedy Sch., Berlin, 1969-73; disting. profl. libr. St. Paul Schs., 1973-90; libr. Open Sch. St. Pauls Schs., 1990-93; cons. in field. Librarian, educator, consultant; b. Mpls., May 27, 1930; s. Oscar Martin and Helen Therese (Marcio) O.; m. Gertrud Franciska Tunkel, Aug. 6, 1956; children— Thomas, Paul, Francine. B.A., U. Minn., 1953, M.A., 1958; B.S., Mankato State U., 1962, M.S., 1964; postgrad. U. Mich., U. Iowa. Serials librarian Agr. Library U. Minn., 1958-59; acquisitions librarian Mankato State U., Minn., 1959-66, Eastern Mich. U., 1966-67; dir. media Iowa City Sch., 1967-69; librarian John F. Kennedy Sch., Berlin, W.Ger., 1969-73; dist. profl. librarian St. Paul Schs., 1973-90; librarian Open Sch. St. Pauls Schs., 1990-93; cons. in field. Served to 1st lt. U.S. Army, 1954-55. Recipient Ency. Brit. 1st place Sch. Library Media System award, 1969. Mem. Minn. Ednl. Media Orgn., Am. Fedn. Tchrs., M Club, Phi Delta Kappa. Contbr. articles in field. Contbr. articles to profl. jours. Served to 1st lt. U.S. Army, 1954-55. Recipient Ency. Brit. 1st place Sch. Libr. Media System award, 1969. Mem. Minn. Ednl. Media Orgn., Am. Fedn. Tchrs., M Club, Phi Delta Kappa. Home: 5536 Harriet Ave Minneapolis MN 55419-1830 *Personal philosophy: I believe school libraries and school librarians are essential for increasing children's understanding of themselves and their society.*

OSTRIKER, ALICIA SUSKIN, poet; b. N.Y.C., Nov. 11, 1937; d. David and Beatrice (Linnick) Suskin; m. Jeremiah P. Ostriker, 1958; children: Rebecca, Eve, Gabriel. BA, Brandeis U., 1959; MA, U. Wis., 1961, PhD, 1964. Asst. prof. Rutgers U., New Brunswick, N.J., 1965-68, assoc. prof., 1968-72, prof. English, 1972—. Author: Vision and Verse in William Blake, 1965, Songs, 1969, Once More Out of Darkness, and Other Poems, 1974, A Dream of Springtime, 1979, The Mother/Child Papers, 1980, A Woman Under the Surface: Poems and Prose Poems, 1982, Writing Like a Woman, 1983, The Imaginary Lover, 1986 (William Carlos Williams prize Poetry Soc. Am. 1986), Stealing the Language: The Emergence of Women's Poetry in America, 1986, Green Age, 1989, Feminist Revision and the Bible, 1993, The Nakedness of the Fathers: Biblical Vision and Revisions, 1994, The Crack in Everything, 1996 (Nat. Book award finalist 1996, Paterson Poetry prize 1996, San Francisco State Poetry Ctr. award 1997), The Little Space: Selected and New Poems, 1998 (Nat. Book award finalist 1998), Dancing at the Devil's Party: Essays on Poetry, Politics, and the Erotic, 2000, The Volcano Sequence, 2002; editor: William Blake: Complete Poems, 1977. Nat. Coun. on Humanities grantee, 1968; NEA fellow, 1976-77, N.J. Arts Coun. fellow, 1982, Guggenheim Found. fellow, 1984-85, faculty fellow Rutgers Ctr. for Hist. Analysis, 1995-96, Rockefeller Found. fellow, 1982; recipient Strousse Poetry prize Prairie Schooner, 1986, Edward Stanley award Prairie Schooner, 1994, Anna David Rosenberg Poetry award, 1994, Best American Poetry award, 1996, Paterson prize, 1997, San Francisco State Poetry Ctr. award, 1997, Pushcart prize, 1999, Larry Levis prize 2001. Office: Rutgers Univ Dept of English New Brunswick NJ 08903 E-mail: ostriker@rci.rutgers.edu.

OSTRIKER, JEREMIAH PAUL, astrophysicist; b. N.Y.C., Apr. 13, 1937; s. Martin and Jeanne (Sumpf) Ostriker; m. Alicia Suskin, Dec. 1, 1958; children: Rebecca, Eve;1 child Gabriel. AB, Harvard, 1959; PhD (NSF fellow), U. Chgo., 1964; postgrad., U. Cambridge, Eng., 1964—65; degree (hon.) , U. Chgo., 1992. Rsch. assoc., lectr. astrophysics Princeton (N.J.) U., 1965—66, asst. prof., 1966—68, assoc. prof., 1968—71, prof., 1971—, chmn. dept. astronomy, dir. obs., 1979—95, Charles A. Young prof. astronomy, 1982—; provost Princeton (N.J.) U. Obs., 1995—2001; Plumian prof. astronomy and exptl. philosophy U. Cambridge, England, 2001—. Author: Development of Large-Scale Structure in the Universe, 1991; editl.bd., trustee Princeton U. Press; contbr. articles to profl. jours. Recipient Vainu Bappu Meml. award, Indian Nat. Sci. Acad., 1993, Karl Schwarzschild medal, Astronomische Gesellschaft, 1999, U.S. Nat. medal of Sci., 2000; fellow Alfred P. Sloan, 1970—72. Fellow: AAAS; mem.: NAS (counselor 1992—95, bd. govs. 1993—95), Royal Netherlands Acad. Arts and Scis. (fgn.), Am. Acad. Arts and Scis., Am. Philos. Soc., Internat. Astron. Union, Am. Astron. Soc. (councilor 1978—80, Warner prize 1972, Russel prize 1980), Royal Astron. Soc. (assoc.), Am. Mus. Natural History (trustee 1997—). Home: 33 Philip Dr Princeton NJ 08540-5409 Office: Princeton U Dept Astrophys Scis Peyton Hall Princeton NJ 08544 E-mail: jpo@astro.princeton.edu.

OSTROFSKY, ANNA, music educator, violinist; b. N.Y.C., June 27, 1953; d. Joseph and Lena (Cipollone) Simeone; m. Frederick Ostrofsky, May 26, 1975; 1 child, Jacqueline. BMus, Manhattan Sch. Music, 1974, MMus, 1975; profl. diploma, Fordham U., 1990. Orch. dir., tchr. Harlem Sch. Arts, N.Y.C., 1975-76; first violinist N.J. Symphony Orch., Newark, 1975-76; string instr. Hoff-Barthelson Sch. Music, Scarsdale, N.Y., 1976-79; concertmaster Chappaqua (N.Y.) Chamber Orch., 1976-89; orch. dir./string instr. City Sch. Dist. New Rochelle (N.Y.), 1978-83; first violinist Hudson Valley Philharmonic Orch., Poughkeepsie, N.Y., 1981-89; 1st violinist Ea. Philharm. Orch., Greensboro, N.C., 1982-83; orch. dir. Briarcliff Union Free Sch. Dist., Briarcliff Manor, N.Y., 1983—; 1st violinist Concert Soc. Putnam and Northern Westchester, 1982—; first violinist New Rochelle (N.Y.) Opera,

1997, 98; adj. prof. violin/viola King's Coll., Briarcliff Manor, 1989-94. Coord. employment opportunities Westchester County (N.Y.) Sch. Music Assn. Debut Carnegie Recital Hall, 1976; conductor Westchester Elem. All-County Orch., 1997. Recipient First prize Artists' Internat. Mgmt., 1975, Excellence in Chamber Music Teaching award Chamber Music Am., 1991. Mem. N.Y. State Acad. Teaching and Learning. Democrat. Roman Catholic. Avocations: writing music composition and orchestration, reading, swimming, walking, cooking. Home: PO Box 396 Somers NY 10589-0396 Office: 444 Pleasantville Rd Briarcliff Manor NY 10510-1922 Fax: 914-769-2509.

OSTROM, DON, political science educator; b. Chgo., Mar. 9, 1939; s. Irving and Margaret (Hedberg) O.; m. Florence Horan, Jan. 13, 1972; children: Erik, Rebecca, Katherine. BA, St. Olaf Coll., Northfield, Minn., 1960; MA, Washington U., 1970, PhD, 1972. Prof. polit. sci. Gustavus Adolphus Coll., St. Peter, Minn., 1972—; state rep. Minn. Ho. of Reps., St. Paul, 1988-96. Co-editor: Perspectives on Minnesota Government and Politics, 1998. Democrat. Home: 405 N 4th St Saint Peter MN 56082-1921 E-mail: dostrom@gac.edu.

OSTROM, KATHERINE ELMA, retired educator; b. L.A., Dec. 30, 1928; d. Charles W. and Mabel M. (Christensen) Shults; m. Carl R. Ostrom, Jan. 29, 1949 (dec.); children: Margaret K. Larson, Carl R. Jr. BA cum laude, U. Wash., 1966, MA in Tchg. English, 1973, EdD, 1994. Std. tchg. cert. grades K-12, Wash.; continuing prins. cert.-secondary, Wash. Substitute tchr. Renton, Kent & South Ctrl. Sch. Dists., 1966; tchr. Foster H.S., Tukwila, Wash., 1966-67, 75-76, Showalter Middle Sch., Tukwila, 1967-79, dept. chair, 1968-87, vice prin., 1979-87; tchr., supr. student tchrs. U. Wash., Seattle, 1989-91; subs. tchr. Tukwila Sch. Dist., 1999—. Tchr. Western Wash. State Coll., Bellingham, 1967-68; liaison, supr. Jr. Achievement, Seattle, 1988-89; cons., trainer Nat. Assn. Elem. Sch. Prins., 1992-98; vol. tchr. Immigrant & Refugee Resources Ctr., Seattle, 1996—; dir. Forum on Edn., PDK, Seattle, 1997; mem. Citizen Adv. Com. in Curriculum, Renton, S.D., 2001—, chair, 2002--. Host del. Tukwila-Ikawa (Japan) Sister Cities, 1980—, chair, 1999—2002, block watch organizer King Co. (Wash.), 1994—, key cummunicator Renton (Wash.) Sch. Dist., 1996—, tutor Skyway Meth. Ch., Seattle, 1997—2001, staff Parish Com., 1996—. Named Vol. of Yr., BPW, Tukwila, Wash., 1990; Coll. scholar U. Puget Sound, Tacoma, Wash., 1946. Mem. Assn. Wash. Sch. Prins. (chair state vice prins.' conf. 1986, regional dir. 1986-88), Wash. Physicians for Social Responsibility (del. to Mid. East 1994), Key Players, Prosser Piano and Organ Club, Phi Delta Kappa (pres. chpt. 1991-95, newsletter editor 1988-90, 95—, area coord. 1995-2001), Phi Beta Kappa (bd. dirs., trustee Puget Sound chpt. 2000—, Pathfinder award 1997). Democrat. Home: 12817 80th Ave S Seattle WA 98178-4911 E-mail: kateostrom@aol.com.

OSTROM, VINCENT A(LFRED), political science educator; b. Nooksack, Wash., Sept. 25, 1919; s. Alfred and Alma (Knudson) O.; m. Isabell Bender, May 20, 1942 (div. 1963); m. Elinor Awan, Nov. 23, 1963. BA in Polit. Sci., UCLA, 1942, MA in Polit. Sci., 1945, PhD in Polit. Sci., 1950. Tchr. Chaffey Union H.S., Ontario, Calif., 1943-45; asst. prof. polit. sci. U. Wyo., Laramie, 1945-48, U. Oreg., Eugene, 1949-54, assoc. prof. polit. sci., 1954-58, UCLA, 1958-64; prof. polit. sci. Ind. U., Bloomington, 1964-90, Arthur F. Bentley prof emeritus polit. sci., 1990—. Hooker disting. vis. scholar McMaster U., 1984-85; rsch. assoc. Bur. Mcpl. Rsch., 1950, Resources for Future, Inc., 1962-64; assoc. dir. Pacific NW Coop. Program in Ednl. Adminstrn., 1951-58; co-dir. Workshop in Polit. Theory and Policy Analysis, Ind. U., Bloomington, 1973—; cons. and lectr. in field. Author: Water and Politics, 1953, The Political Theory of a Compound Republic, 1971, 2nd rev. edit., 1987, The Intellectual Crisis in American Public Administration, 1974, 2nd edit., 1989, The Meaning of American Federalism, 1991, The Meaning of Democracy and the Vulnerability of Democracies, 1997; co-author: Understanding Urban Government, 1973, Local Government in the United States, 1988; co-editor: Comparing Urban Service Delivery Systems, 1977, Guidance, Control and Evaluation in the Public Sector, 1986, Rethinking Institutional Analysis and Development, 1988, 2d. edit. 1993; mem. bd. editors Publius, 1972—; mem. editl. bd. Constnl. Polit. Economy, 1989—, Nigerian Jour. Fin. and Human Resources Mgmt., 1996—, Internat. Jour. Orgn. Theory and Behavior, 1997—; contbr. articles to profl. jours. Program coord. Wyo. Assessors' Sch., 1946-48, Budget Officer's Sch., 1947-48; exec. sec. Wyo. League of Municipalities, 1947-48; cons. Wyo. Legis. Interim Com., 1947-48, Nat. Resources, Alaska Constitutional Convention, 1955-56, Tenn. Water Policy Commn., 1956; mem. founding bd. Com. on Polit. Economy of the Good Soc., 1990—. Grantee and fellowships Social Sci. Research Council, 1954-55, Ctr. Advanced Study in Behavioral Scis., 1955-56, Ctr. Interdisciplinary Rsch., 1981-82. Mem. AAAS, Am. Polit. Sci. Assn. (Spl. Achievement award for Significant Contbns. to Study of Federalism, 1991, Best Book on Federalism and Intergovtl. Rels. award 1999), Am. Econ. Assn., Am. Soc. Pub. Adminstrn., Pub. Choice Soc., Internat. Polit. Sci. Assn. Home: 5883 E Lampkins Ridge Rd Bloomington IN 47401-9726 Office: Ind U Workshop in Polit Theory 513 N Park Ave Bloomington IN 47408-3895 E-mail: workshop@indiana.edu., ghiggins@indiana.edu.

OSTROV, JEROME, lawyer; b. Boston, Dec. 2, 1942; s. Harold S. and Etta (Resnick) O.; m. Roberta S. Baruch, Sept. 3, 1978; children: Rebecca Ann, Max Abraham, Julia Grace. BSBA cum laude, Boston U., 1964; JD, Union U., 1967; LLM in Taxation, NYU, 1968; MPA, Harvard U., 1980. Bar: N.Y. 1968, D.C. 1971, Md. 1991. Mem. Friedlander, Misler, Sloan, Kletzkin & Ochsman PLLC, 1985—; ptnr. N.Y.C., 1968-69; law clk. to presiding judge U.S. Tax Ct., Washington, 1969-71; pvt. practice, 1971-73; dep. assoc. gen. counsel U.S. EPA, 1973-79; fellow John F. Kennedy Sch. Govt., Harvard U., 1979-80; staff counsel U.S. Ho. of Reps., Washington, 1982-83; pvt. practice, 1983—. Bd. dirs. Am. Assocs. Ben Gurion U. of Negev, N.Y.C. Author: (law treatise) Tax Planning with Real Estate, 2001; contbr. articles. Bd. dirs. Jewish Social Svcs. Agy. Mem. ABA. Democrat. Jewish. Avocations: family, jogging, hiking, skiing, classical music, ballet. Office: Friedlander Misler Sloan Kletzkin Ochman PLLC 1101 17th St NW Ste 700 Washington DC 20036-4711 E-mail: jostrov@dclawfirm.com.

OSTROVSKII, MIKHAIL IOSIFOVICH, mathematician; b. Kharkov, Ukraine, USSR, Dec. 26, 1960; s. Iosif Vladimirovich and Larisa Semyenovna (Kudina) O.; m. Marina Anatol'evna Likhosherst, Apr. 20, 1991; 1 child, Stanislav Mikhailovich. MSc, Kharkov (USSR) State U., 1982; PhD, Kharkov Inst. Mcpl. Engrs., 1985. Rsch. fellow Inst. for Low Temperature Physics and Engrng. Ukrainian Acad. Scis., Kharkov, 1985-89; sr. scientist Inst. for Low Temp. Physics and Engrng. Ukrainian Acad. Sci. Contbr. articles to profl. jours. Mem. Kharkov Math. Soc. Office: Ukrainian Acad Scis Inst Physics 47 Lenin Ave 310164 Kharkov Ukraine

OSTROVSKY, LEV ARONOVICH, physicist, oceanographer, educator; b. Vologda, USSR, Dec. 10, 1934; s. Ahron L. Ostrovsky and Lidiya A. (Warshawskaya) Khvilivitskaya; children: Svetlana, Alexander. Cert. rsch. physicist in radiophysics, U. Gorky, USSR, 1957; PhD, U. Gorky, 1964; Dr Sci, Acoust. Inst., Moscow, 1973. Lead engr. Design Bureau, Gorky, 1957-59; asst. prof., then assoc. prof. physics Poly. Inst., 1962-65; sr. researcher Radiophys. Rsch. Inst., 1965-77; chief scientist and head lab. Inst. Applied Physics Russian Acad. Sci., Nizhni Novgorod (formerly Gorky), 1977—; assoc. prof to prof U. Nizhni Novgorod, 1966-94; prof. sr. rsch. scientist U. Colo./NOAA Environ. Tech. Lab., Boulder, 1994-2001; Orson Andersen fellow Inst. Geophys. and Planet. Physics Los Alamos Nat. Lab., 1998-99; sr. scientist Zel Tech./NOAA Environ. Tech. Lab., 2001—. Co-author: Nonlinear Wave Processes in Acoustics, 1990, English edit., 1998, Modulated Waves, 1999; author or co-author 3 lectr. notes, numerous articles in profl. jours., patented various inventions; editor 3 book translations from English to Russian, 3 paper collection books, a topical dictionary; mem. editorial and adv. bds. Chaos, Ultrasonics, various Russian sci. jours. Recipient State Prize of USSR, 1985, USSR State Discovery Cert., 1982. Fellow Acoustical Soc. Am.; mem. Acoustical Soc. Russia, European Geophys. Soc., Am. Geophys. Union. Office: Zel Tech/NDAA ETL R/ETL-O Boulder CO 80305 E-mail: lev.a.ostrovsky@noaa.gov.

OSTROW, JOSEPH W. advertising executive; b. N.Y.C., Feb. 22, 1933; s. Meyer H. and Helen (Small) O.; m. Francine Lee Goldberg, Sept. 4, 1955; children: Elizabeth Sara, Peter Mathew, William Nathan. BS in Mktg., NYU, 1955. Researcher W.R. Simmons, N.Y.C., 1954-55; with Young & Rubicam, 1955-87, sr. v.p., dir. communication planning, 1972-73, exec. v.p., dir., dir. communications services, 1973-87, mem. N.Y. exec. com., U.S.A. bd. dirs.; pres., chief operating officer worldwide Direct Mktg. Group of Cos., 1983-84; exec. v.p., dir. media worldwide Foote, Cone & Belding Co., N.Y.C., 1987-94; pres., CEO Cabletelevision Advt. Bur., 1994—. Bd. dirs. Cabletelevision Advt. Bur., Multichannel Advt. Bur. Internat.; hon. chair bd. dirs. Cable Positive; past chmn. Traffic Audit Bur.; dir. Audit Bur. Circulations; bd. dirs., past mem. exec. com. Advt. Info. Svcs., Advt. Rsch. Found.; lectr. in field. Mem. nat. coun. Boy Scouts Am. Mem. Media Dirs. Coun. (past pres.), Am. Assn. Advt. Agys. (past vice chmn. media policy com.), Internat. Radio and TV Found. (bd. dirs.), Advt. Coun. (bd. dirs.), John Reisenbach Found. (bd. dirs.). Office: Cable TV Advt Bur 830 3rd Ave New York NY 10022-7523 E-mail: joeo@cabletvadbureau.com. *It is important that one continue to set goals that seem unachievable and at the same time live by standards that remain consistently high. The maintenance of integrity and adherence to principles which support it, are especially critical when dealing with consumer commercial persuasion. Anything less would be detrimental to the proper pursuit of both personal and business achievements.*

OSTROW, MICHAEL JAY, lawyer; b. Baldwin, N.Y., Apr. 25, 1934; s. Oscar I. and Ethel M. (Morganstern) O.; m. Judith L. Loewenthal, Aug. 25, 1957; children: Thomas L., Kenneth A., Nancy M. BA, Alfred U., 1955; JD, Cornell U., 1958. Bar: N.Y. 1958, U.S. Supreme Ct. 1964, U.S. Dist. Ct. (so. and ea. dists.) N.Y. 1970; diplomate Am. Coll. Family Trial Lawyers. Ptnr. Taylor & Ostrow, Mineola, N.Y., 1961-69, Taylor Atkins & Ostrow, Garden City, 1969-96, Ostrow and Taub, Garden City, 1996-2000. Bd. dirs., lectr Advanced Practice Inst. Hofstra Law Sch., Hempstead; lectr. Practicing Law Inst., N.Y.C. Mem. ABA, Acad. Matrimonial Lawyers (pres. N.Y. chpt. 1980-81, sec. nat. acad. 1988-90, nat. v.p. 1990-94, pres.-elect 1995-96, pres. 1996-97), Internat. Acad. Matrimonial Lawyers (bd. govs. 1990-92), Am. Coll. Family Trial Lawyers (diplomate), N.Y. State Bar Assn. (chmn. family law sect. 1976-78), Nassau County Bar Assn. (pres. 1984-85, chmn. judiciary com. 1992-93), Order of Coif, Zeta Beta Tau, Phi Delta Phi. Home: 8 Randolph Dr Dix Hills NY 11746-8308 Office: Schlissel Ostrow Karabatos Poepplein Cender & Fisher PLLC 200 Garden City Plz Garden City NY 11530 E-mail: MJODIX@aol.com.

OSTROW, ROBERT, publishing executive; Account mgr. PC World, Framingham, Mass., 1986—87, senior account mgr., 1988—90, adv. dir., 1991—99, pub., 2000—. Office: PC World 492 Old Connecticut Path Framingham MA 01701*

OSTROW, RONA LYNN, librarian, educator; b. N.Y.C., Oct. 21, 1948; d. Morty and Jeane Goldberg; m. Steven A. Ostrow, June 25, 1972; 1 child, Ciné Justine. BA, CCNY, 1969; MS in LS, Columbia U., 1970; MA, Hunter Coll., 1975; PhD., Rutgers U., 1998. Cert. libr., N.Y. Br. adult and reference libr. N.Y. Pub. Libr., N.Y.C., 1970-73, rsch. libr., 1973-78; asst. libr. Fashion Inst. Tech., 1978-80; assoc. dir. Grad. Bus. Resource Ctr., Baruch Coll., CUNY, 1980-90, assoc. prof., 1980-90; assoc. dean of librs. for pub. svcs. Adelphi U., Garden City, N.Y., 1990-94; chief libr. Marymount Manhattan Coll., N.Y.C., 1994-98; asst. provost Fairleigh Dickinson U., Teaneck, N.J., 1998-2000; chief libr. Lehman Coll. CUNY, Bronx, 2000—. Author: Dictionary of Retailing, 1984, Dictionary of Marketing, 1987; co-author: Cross Reference Index, 1989. Mem.: ALA, Assn. Coll. and Rsch. Librs. Office: CUNY Lehman Coll Libr 250 Bedford Park Blvd W Bronx NY 10468-1589 E-mail: rostrow@lehman.cuny.edu.

OSTROW, STUART, theatrical producer, educator, writer; b. N.Y.C. m. Ann Elizabeth Gilbert; children: Julie Elizabeth, Katherine Ann, John Stuart. Disting. univ. prof. theater U. Houston. Pres. Stuart Ostrow Found., Inc., Musical Theatre Lab.; former mem. opera-musical theatre panel NEA; mem. bd. overseers com. to visit Loeb Drama Ctr., Harvard U. Prodr.: We Take the Town, 1961, The Apple Tree, 1966, 1776, 1969, Scratch, 1971, Pippin, 1972, The Moony Shapiro Songbook, 1981, American Passion, 1983, M. Butterly, 1988, La Bête, 1991, Face Value, 1993, Doll, 1995, Coyote Goes Salmon Fishing, 1996; prodr., dir.: Here's Love, 1963, Swing, 1980; author, producer: Stages, 1978; assoc. dir.; Chicago, 1975; author: A Producer's Broadway Journey, 1999, Thank You Very Much, 2002. Mem. Pulitzer Prize Drama Jury; chmn. bd. trustees Inst. for Advanced Study in Musical Theatre, 2002. Served with USAF, 1952—55. Office: 10 S Briar Hollow Ln Unit 87 Houston TX 77027-2891 E-mail: sostrow@uh.edu.

OSTROWSKI, THOMAS JOHN, accountant; b. Scranton, Pa., Dec. 23, 1956; s. Bernard H. and Marilyn J. (Blackledge) O.; m. Dianne C. Anderson, July 9, 1988; children: Brittany, Courtney, Brandon, Brian. BS in acctg., U. Scranton, 1978. CPA, Pa. Acct.-spl. studies Texaco Inc., White Plains, N.Y., 1978; staff acct. Eckersley and Eckersley PC, Scranton, 1980-87; ptnr. Eckersley and Ostrowski LLP, 1987—. Adv. bd. Scranton State Sch. for the Deaf, 1987—; treas. Bob Casey for Auditor Gen., 1996—; asst. treas. Casey for Gov. com., 1987-94. Mem. AICPA, Pa. Inst. CPAs, Estate Planning Coun. of N.E. Pa., Internat. Soc. CPAs (founding). Democrat. Avocations: golf, tennis. Office: Eckersley and Ostrowski LLP 434 Lackawanna Ave Scranton PA 18503-2051

OSTRY, SYLVIA, academic administrator, economist; b. Winnipeg, Man., Can. d. Morris J. and B. (Stoller) Knelman; m. Bernard Ostry; children: Adam, Jonathan. BA in Econs., McGill U., 1948, MA, 1950; PhD in Econs., Cambridge U. and McGill U., 1954; also 18 hon. degrees. Lectr., asst. prof. econs. McGill U.; rsch. officer Inst. Stats., U. Oxford, Eng.; assoc. prof. U. Montreal, Can.; with dept. stats. Econ. Coun. Can., Ottawa, 1964-72, chmn., 1978-79; chief statistician Stats. Can., 1972-75; dep. minister consumer and corp. affairs Govt. Can., 1975-78, dep. minister internat. trade, coordinator internat. econ. relations, 1984-85, ambassador for multilateral trade negotiations, personal rep. of Prime Minister for Econ. Summit, 1985-88; chancellor U. Waterloo, 1991-96; head dept. econs. and stats. OECD, Paris, 1979-83; chmn. Ctr. for Internat. Studies U. Toronto, Ont., Can., 1990-97, disting. rsch. fellow Munk Ctr. for Internat. Studies Can., 1997—. Lectr. Per Jacobssen Found., 1987; chmn. nat. coun. Can. Inst. Internat. Affairs, 1990-95; western co-chmn. Blue Ribbon Commn. for Hungary's Econ. Recovery, 1990-94; mem. adv. bd. Inst. Internat. Econs., Washington; founding mem. Pacific Coun. on Internat. Policy; Volvo Disting. vis. fellow Coun. on Fgn. Rels., N.Y.C., 1989. Author: Governments and Corporations in a Shrinking World: The Search for Stability, 1990, The Threat of Managed Trade to Transforming Economies, 1993; co-author: (with Richard Nelson) Technonationalism and Technoglobalism: Conflict and Cooperation, 1995; co-editor: (with Karen Knop, Richard Simeon, Katherine Swinton) Rethinking Federalism: Citizens, Markets and Governments in a Changing World, 1995; New Dimensions of Market Access, 1995, (with Gilbert R. Winham) The Halifax G-7 Summit: Issues on the Table, 1995, Who's on First: The Post-Cold War Trading System, 1997, APEC and Regime Creation in the Asia-Pacific: The OECD Model?, 1998, Technology, Productivity and Multinational Enterprise, 1998, Intellectual Property Protection in the World Trade Organization: Major Issues in the Millennium Round, 1999, Globalization Implications for Industrial Relations, 1999, The Future of the World Trading System, 1999, Convergence and Sovereignty: Policy Scope for Compromise?, 2000, Regional Versus Multilateral Trade Strategies, 2000, Making Sense of it All: A Post Mortem on the Meaning of Seattle, 2000; The Uruguay Round North-South Grand Bargain: Implications for Future Negotiations, 2000, Regional Dominos and the WTO: Building Blocks or Boomerang?, 2000, Business, Trade and the Environment, 2000, The Changing Scenario in International Governance, 2000, Looking Back to Look Forward: The Multilateral Trading System after 50 Years, 2000, The WTO: Post Seattle and Chinese Accession, 2001, The WTO and International Governance, 2001, The WTO After Seattle: Something's Happening Here, What It Is Ain't Exactly Clear, 2001, WTO Membership for China: To Be & Not To Be. Is That The Answer?, 2001, The Question of the Q's: What Cue Should Quebec Send to Qatar?, 2001, The WTO and Internat. Governance, 2001, WTO Membership for China: To Be & Not To Be, Is That the Answer?, 2001, The Question of The Q's: What Cue Should Quebec Send to Qatar?, 2001, Global Integration: Currents and Counter-Currents, 2002; contbr. articles on empirical and policy-analytic subjects to more than 90 profl. publs. Decorated companion Order of Can., 1990; recipient Outstanding Achievement award Govt. of Can., 1987, Hon. Assoc. award Conf. Bd. of Can., 1992; Disting. vis. fellow Volvo, 1989-90. Fellow Royal Soc. Can., Am. Statis. Assn.; mem. Am. Econ. Assn., Can. Econ. Assn., Royal Econ. Soc. (founding), Ctr. for European Policy Studies (internat. adv. coun.), Group of Thirty, Inst. for Internat. Econs. (adv. bd.). Avocations: films, theatre, contemporary reading. Office: Munk Ctr Internat Studies U Toronto 1 Devonshire Pl Toronto ON Canada M5S 3K7 E-mail: sylvia.ostry@utoronto.ca.

OSTWALD, MARTIN, classics educator emeritus; b. Dortmund, Germany, Jan. 15, 1922; came to U.S., 1946, naturalized, 1956; s. Max and Hedwig (Strauss) O.; m. Lore Ursula Weinberg, Dec. 27, 1948; children: Mark F., David H. BA, U. Toronto, 1946; AM, U. Chgo., 1948; PhD, Columbia U., 1952; D (hon.) , Fribourg (Switzerland) U., 1995, Dortmund (Germany) U., 2001. Instr. classics and humanities Wesleyan U., Middletown, Conn., 1950-51; from lectr. to asst. prof. Greek and Latin, Columbia U., 1951-58; mem. faculty Swarthmore Coll., 1958—, prof. classics, 1966-92; prof. classical studies U. Pa., 1968-92, prof. emeritus, 1992—. Vis. assoc. prof. Princeton, spring 1964; vis. prof. U. Calif. at Berkeley, summer 1969, Tel-Aviv U., 1996—; vis. fellow Balliol Coll., Oxford (Eng.) U., 1970-71, Wolfson Coll., Oxford, 1987, 91; dir. fellowships-in-residence in classics NEH, 1976-77, dir. d'etudes, EHESS, Paris, 1991. Author: Autonomia, Its Genesis and Early History, 1982, From Popular Sovereignty to the Sovereignty of Law, 1987, Ananke in Thucydides, 1988, Oligarchia, 2000, (with T.G. Rosenmeyer and J.W. Halporn) The Meters of Greek and Latin Poetry, 2d edit., 1980, Nomos and the Beginnings of the Athenian Democracy, 1969; translator with intro., notes and glossary Nicomachean Ethics (Aristotle), 1962; mem. editl. bd. Cambridge Ancient History, 1976-94; contbr. articles to profl. jours. Fulbright research fellow Greece, 1961-62; fellow Am. Council Learned Socs., 1965-66; fellow Nat. Endowment Humanities, 1970-71, 90-91; mem. Inst. for Advanced Study Princeton, 1974-75, 81-82, 90-91, Inst. Advanced Studies, Tel Aviv, 1994; Guggenheim fellow, 1977-78; Lang. fellow Swarthmore Coll., 1986-87. Fellow AAAS; mem. Am. Philos. Soc., Am. Philol. Assn. (pres. 1986-87), Classical Assn. Can., Soc. Promotion Hellenic Studies (hon.), Classical Assn. Atlantic States, Soc. Ancient Philosophy. Home: 408 Walnut Ln Swarthmore PA 19081-1137 E-mail: mostwal1@swarthmore.edu.

OSTWALD, RAY E. conductor, music educator; b. Appleton, Wis., June 15, 1967; s. Sam R. and Jean P. Ostwald. BA Math, BA Music, Lawrence Univ., Appleton, WI, 1990; MA Music Ed. Orch. dir. Elgin H.S., Elgin, Ill., 1990—96, York Cmty. H.S., Elmhurst, 1996. Violinist Solisti Di Camera, Elgin, Ill., 1998—, Various Orchestras, Chicago, Ill., 1990—; condr. Various Orchestras And Festivals, Chicago, Ill., 1991—. Editor: (musical work) Mozart: Fugue in D, k.173; arranger (musical work) Brahms: Symphony No. 3, Andante, contbg. author (book) Teaching Music Through Performance in Orchestra, Vol. 1, Teaching Music Through Performance in Orchestra, Vol. 2. Recipient Educator of the Yr., Elgin Youth Symphony, IL, 1991, 2002. Mem.: Am. String Teachers Assn., Music Educators Nat. Conf. (dist. orch. chmn. 1989), Pi Kappa Lambda, Phi Beta Kappa. Achievements include guest conductor, Ecuador National Symphony, Quito, Ecuador, 1996. Avocation: long distance motorcycle touring. Home: 330 Woodridge Circle Apt G South Elgin IL 60177 Office: York Community High School 355 W Saint Charles Road Elmhurst IL 60126

O'SULLIVAN, CHRISTINE, retired executive director social service agency, consultant; b. Washington, July 5, 1947; d. George Albert and Mary Ruth (Stalcup) Markward; m. Donald Phillip O'Sullivan, June 27, 1985; 1 child: Kimberly Molly. Sec. Gas Distributors Info. Svc., Washington, 1966-70; adminstr. asst. Nat. Airlines, 1970-71; office mgr. Tire Industry Safety Coun., 1971-75; pres. Type-Right Exec. Sec. Svc., Washington, Pitts., 1976-91; exec. dir. Eastside Cmty. Ministry, Zanesville, Ohio, 1991—2001. Chair FEMA Emergency Bd., Muskingum, Morgan and Perry Counties, Ohio, 1994-97, 99-2000; chair United Way Exec. Dirs. Coun., 1994-97; v.p. Muskingum County Hunger Network, Zanesville, 1993-99. Author: Write a Good Resume, 1976. Mem. task force Literacy Coun., 1993—2000; mem. steering com. Muskingum County Operation Feed, 1992—99; trustee Disability Network of Ohio-Solidarity, 2001; mem Zanesville City Sch. Bldg. Adv. Coun., Ohio, 2001—02; v.p. Muskingum County Women's Rep. Club, 1994, sec., 1995; mem. Downtown Clergy Assn., 1992—, pres., 1995—96; bd. dirs. Human Care Ministry, Ohio dist. Luth. Ch., Mo. Synod, PRO-Muskingum, 1995—2000; commr. Mo. Synod Luths. to Commn. on Religion in Appalachia, 1996—98; bd. dirs. Muskingum County Women's Coalition, 1994—97, Families and Children First Coun., 1995—2000, Interfaith Response to Ohio Disaster, 1988—91, Luth. Social Svcs. Emergency Assistance Com., 1998—99, Muskingum County Family Adv. Team, 2000—01. Recipient Cert. of Achievement for Mil. Family Support, U.S. Army, 1991, Excellence in Cmty. Svc. award Aid Assn. Luths., 1993, Excellence in Cmty. Svc. award Muskingum County DAR, 1994, Positive Action award, NOW, 1997, YWCA Woman of Achievement award, 1997, Americanism award VFW, 1992, Cmty. Involvement award Richvale Grange, 1997, Cmty. Citizen award State of Ohio Grange, 2000; named Outstanding Cmty. Vol. Zanesville Daybreak Rotary Club, 1997. Mem.: Bus. and Profl. Women's Club Zanesville, Nat. Multiple Sclerosis Soc. (program com. Buckeye chpt. 2001—02), Muskingum County Respiratory Assn. (bd. dirs. 2001—02), Disability Network Ohio Solidarity (trustee 2001—02), Richvale Grange, Kiwanis (Zanesville chpt. bd. dirs. 1997—99, spiritual aims com. chair Dist. 18 of Ohio 1998—99). Avocations: creative writing, music. Home: 509 Van Horn Ave Zanesville OH 43701-2562 Office: Eastside Cmty Ministry 221 Stillwell St PO Box 965 Zanesville OH 43702-0965 E-mail: eastsidecommunityministry@juno.com.

O'SULLIVAN, EUGENE HENRY, retired advertising executive; b. Plainfield, N.J., June 8, 1942; s. Patrick J. and Helen (Callahan) O'S.; 1 child, Meredith. BBA, U. Notre Dame, 1964. Media buyer Foote Cone Belding, N.Y.C., 1967-68; account exec., mgmt. supr. Group Dtr; exec. v.p., dir. client svcs. Young & Rubicam, 1968-84; sr. v.p., group dir. Ogilvy & Mather, 1984-86, 87; exec. v.p. Hill, Holliday, Boston, 1986-87; exec. v.p., gen. mgr. McCann Erickson, N.Y.C., 1988-90; ret., 1990. Served to lt. (j.g.) USN, 1964-66. Mem. Lotos Club. Democrat. Home: 21 E 10th St New York NY 10003-5923 E-mail: eugeneo@earthlink.net.

O'SULLIVAN, GERALD JOSEPH, association executive; b. Chgo., Dec. 9, 1941; s. Gerald Thomas and Norine Rita (Herbert) O'S.; m. Joan Griffin, June 14, 1992; children from previous marriage: Stacey Marie, Lauren Ann; 1 stepchild, Kelly. Student, Chgo. Tchrs. Coll., Roosevelt U., MPA, 1974. Cert. tchr., Ill.; cert. law enforcement officer, Ill. Pub. health adminstr. Chgo. Dept. Health, 1968-76, dir. fiscal svcs., 1976-78, dir. mgmt. and ops., 1978-81, adminstrv. dir., 1981-83; dir. personnel Ill. Atty. Gen. Office, Chgo., 1983-86, dir. ops., 1986-91; dir. program devel. Genesis Schs., Inc., 1991-93; sr. v.p. ops. World Trade Ctr. Chgo. Assn., 1993-94; sr. ops. mgr. Chgo. Mfg. Tech. Ctr., 1994-95; supt. Impact Incarceration Cook County Sheriff's Office, 1995-96; exec. dir. Cook County Sherrif's Tng. Acads., 1997—. Community prof. Gov. State U., Chgo., 1986-88; prof. grad. program Roosevelt U., Chgo., 1974-81; cons E.W. Lynch Vocat. Sch., Chgo. Mem. steering com. Ill. Juvenile Justice Inst., 1992-93; bd. dirs. Apple Canyon Lake Property Owners' Assn., Apple River, Ill., 1988-90; mem. City of Chgo. Task Force Brownnfields Land Redevel., 1995. Staff sgt. U.S. Army, 1964-66. Mem. Soc. Human Resource Mgmt., Nat. Sheriff's Assn., Law Enforment Tng. Mgrs. Assn., Ill. Chiefs Police Assn., Ill. Juvenile Justice Inst. (steering com. 1992-93), Chgo. Bar Assn. (justice for youth com. 1992-93), Ill. C. of C., Sierra Club, City of Chgo. Exec. Alumni (past v.p.), Thunderbird Internat. Sch. Mgmt. Alumni. Roman Catholic. Office: Cook County Sheriffs Tng Inst 2000 N 5th Ave River Grove IL 60171-1907

O'SULLIVAN, JAMES MICHAEL, lawyer; b. Boston, Jan. 21, 1958; s. James M. and Edith I. (Fielding) O'S.; m. Mary Ann Hayes, Mar. 28, 1992; children: Mary Elizabeth, Sheila Joanne, Bridget Eileen. BA, U. Mass.; JD, Northeastern U., Boston, 1983. Bar: Mass. 1983, U.S. Ct. Appeals (1st cir.) 1984, U.S. Dist. Ct. Mass. 1984, U.S. Supreme Ct. 1988. Mem. Thayer, Cannon & O'Sullivan, P.C., Quincy, Mass., 1986-90; prin. O'Sullivan & Gizzarelli, P.C., Norwell, 1990-92, O'Sullivan & Assocs., P.C., Norwell, 1992—. Adj. instr. Ea. Nazarene Coll., Quincy, 1992—, New Eng. Banking Ins., Boston, 1989—; examiner Mass. Land Ct. Co-author: Bank Operations, 1990, 2d edit. 1994. Pres., bd. dirs. Cath. Alumni Sodality, Boston, 1984—, South Boston Cmty. Health Ctr., 1982-94; mem. Vols. Lawyers Project. Mem.

Mass. Bar Assn., Mass. Conveyancers Assn., KC. Democrat. Roman Catholic. Avocations: running, woodwork, reading. Office: O'Sullivan & Assocs PC 17 Accord Park Dr Norwell MA 02061-1629

O'SULLIVAN, JUDITH ROBERTA, lawyer, author, artist; b. Pitts., Jan. 6, 1942; d. Robert Howard and Mary Olive (O'Donnell) Gallick; m. James Paul O'Sullivan, Feb. 1, 1964; children: Kathryn, James. BA, Carlow Coll., 1963; MA, U. Md., 1969, PhD, 1976; JD, Georgetown U., 1996. Editor Am. Film Inst., Washington, 1974-77; assoc. program coord. Smithsonian Resident Assocs., 1977-78; dir. instl. devel. Nat. Archives, 1978-79; exec. dir. Md. State Humanities Coun., Balt., 1979-81, 82-84, Ctr. for the Book, Libr. of Congress, Washington, 1981-82; dep. asst. dir. Nat. Mus. Am. Art, 1984-87, acting asst. dir., 1987-89; pres., CEO The Mus. at Stony Brook, N.Y., 1989-92; exec. dir. Nat. Assn. Women Judges, Washington, 1993; clk. Office Legal Adviser U.S. Dept. State, 1994-96; trial atty. Atty. Gen.'s honors program U.S. Dept. Justice, 1996—; spl. asst. U.S. atty. U.S. Dist. Ct. (ea. dist.) Va., 1998—; asst. U.S. atty. U.S. Dist. Ct. Ariz., Tucson, 1999—2000. Assoc. Piper & Marbury, Balt., summer 1995; chair Smithsonian Women's Coun., Washington, 1988-89. Author: The Art of the Comic Strip, 1971 (Gen. Excellence award Printing Industry Am.); Workers and Allies, 1975; (with Alan Fern) The Complete Prints of Leonard Baskin, 1984, The Great American Comic Strip, 1991; editor Am. Film Inst. Catalogue: Feature Films, 1961-70, 1974-77; mem. editl. bd. Am. Film Inst., 1979—. Trustee Child Life Ctr., U. Md., College Pk., 1971-74; chair Smithsonian Women's Coun., 1988-89. Univ. fellow U. Md., 1967-70, Mus. fellow, 1970-71, Smithsonian fellow Nat. Collection Fine Arts, Washington, 1972-73. Mem.: AAUW, D.C. Bar Assn., Md. Bar Assn., Mid-Atlantic Mus. Conf., Am. Assn. Mus., Assn. Art Mus. Dirs. Avocations: landscape painting, mystery writing. Home: # 606 7111 Woodmont Ave Chevy Chase MD 20815 Office: US Dept Justice Northern Alien Smuggling Task Force Criminal Divsn Washington DC 20530 E-mail: Judith.R.O'Sullivan@usdoj.gov.

O'SULLIVAN, KEVIN PATRICK, foundation administrator; b. N.Y.C., Apr. 13, 1928; s. Patrick Joseph and Christina Nora (O'Sullivan) O'S.; m. Carole Evelyn Christensen, Apr. 19, 1958; 1 child, Erin Anne. BA in Polit. Sci., CUNY, 1950. Profl. singer and actor TV, theatre, night clubs, N.Y.C., 1951-55; mem. radio-TV promotion staff Ronson Corp., Newark, 1955-57; gen. sales mgr. Ind. TV Corp., N.Y.C., 1958-61; dir. program svcs. Harrington, Righter & Parsons, Inc., 1961-67; v.p., gen. sales mgr. domestic sales div. ABC Films, Inc., 1967-68, v.p., gen. mgr., 1969, pres., 1969-73, ABC Internat. TV, N.Y.C., 1970-73; pres., CEO, Worldvision Enterprises, Inc., 1973-80, chmn., CEO, 1981-87; pres. The O'Sullivan Children Found., Inc., Westbury, N.Y., 1981—. Pres., CEO entertainment group Gt. Am. Broadcasting Co., N.Y.C., 1987-88. Bd. dirs. St. Francis Hosp., Roslyn, N.Y., Telicare, Uniondale, N.Y., Nat. Ethnic Coalition Orgns.; nat. bd. dirs. Boys Hope, St. Louis; former chmn. bd. trustees Old Westbury (N.Y.) Sch. of Holy Child. Recipient Ellis Island medal of hon., 1990. Fellow NATAS (life, founding bd. dirs., past chmn. bd. trustees found. of internat. coun., past treas., vice chmn.); mem. Internat. Radio and TV Soc., Am. Film Inst., Motion Picture Acad. Arts and Scis., 7th Rgt. Club (N.Y.C.), Brookville Country Club (L.I., N.Y.), Atlantis Golf Club (Palm Beach, Fla.). Avocations: golf, tennis, reading history. Home: 4 Bridle Path Dr Old Westbury NY 11568-1608 Office: O'Sullivan Children Found 355 Post Ave Westbury NY 11590-2265

O'SULLIVAN, LYNDA TROUTMAN, lawyer; b. Oil City, Pa., Aug. 30, 1952; d. Perry John and Vivian Dorothy (Schreffler) Troutman; m. P. Kevin O'Sullivan, Dec. 15, 1979; children: John Perry, Michael Patrick. BA, Am. U., 1974; JD, Georgetown U., 1978, postgrad., 1982-83. Bar: D.C. 1978. Ptnr. Perkins Coie, Washington, 1985-92, Fried, Frank, Harris, Shriver & Jacobson, Washington, 1993-97, Miller & Chevalier, Washington, 1997—. Former mem. adv. bd. Govt. Contract Costs, Pricing & Acctg. Report, 1997-99; mem. faculty govt. contracts program George Washington U., 1990-99; lectr. Contbr. articles to profl. jours. Fellow Am. Bar Found.; mem. ABA (chair truth in negotiations com. 1991-94, chair acctg., cost and pricing com. 1996-2000, coun. sect. pub. contract law 1993-95). Office: Miller & Chevalier 655 15th St NW Ste 900 Washington DC 20005-5799 E-mail: losullivan@milchev.com.

O'SULLIVAN, PAUL KEVIN, business executive, management and instructional systems consultant; b. Syracuse, N.Y., May 10, 1938; s. John Hugh and Helen Troy (Smith) O'S.; m. Lynda Troutman; children: Mary Kathleen and Karin Jennifer (twins), John Perry, Michael Patrick. A.B., Dartmouth Coll., 1960. Communications specialist Gen. Electric Co., Schenectady, N.Y., 1963-66; nat. inst. dir. Gen. Learning Corp., Washington, 1966-67; sr. con. ednl. systems. Aries Corp., McLean, Va., 1967-69; dir. profl. devel. Nat. Audio-Visual Assn., Fairfax, Va., 1969-74; exec. dir. Am. Soc. Tng. and Devel., Madison, Wis., 1974-80; sr. v.p. Sterling Inst., Washington, 1980-87, nat. account mgr. Orgnl. Dynamics, Inc., 1987-94; account exec. Zenger Miller, 1995-96, pres. The O'Sullivan Group, Inc., 1996—; staff dir. Nat. Audio-Visual Inst. for Effective Communications Ind. U., 1969-74; chief adminstr. Internat. Fedn. Tng. and Devel. Orgns., 1974-80; dir. Internat. Symposia for Tng. Communications in Switzerland, Australia and Middle East. Producer and dir. films and multi-media presentations; author communications and tng. courses, textbooks; contbr. articles to profl. jours. Served to lt. (j.g.), USNR, 1956-63. Recipient Honor medal for Literature Freedoms Found., 1963; Writers Gold Cup award Gen. Electric, 1966; Resolution for Outstanding Achievement Nat. Audio-Visual Assn., 1974, Pres.'s award for bus. achievement, 1989, 90, 91, 92, 93. Mem. Nat. Soc. for Performance and Instrn. (Presdl. citation 1977), Am. Soc. Assn. Execs. (Grand award for mgmt. achievement 1978), Am. Soc. Tng. and Devel. (hon. life).

O'SULLIVAN, THOMAS J. lawyer; b. New Haven, Apr. 7, 1940; s. Thomas J. and Marjorie (Hession) O'S.; m. Anita Brady, Aug. 10, 1968; children: Kathleen, Margaret, Mary Tess, Anne Elizabeth. BA in History, Yale U., 1961; LLB, Harvard U., 1966. Bar: Conn. 1966, U.S. Dist. Ct. Conn. 1967, N.Y. 1967, U.S. Dist. Ct. (so. and ea. dists.) N.Y. 1967, U.S. Ct. Appeals (2d cir.) 1971, U.S. Supreme Ct. 1971, U.S. Dist. Ct. (no. dist.) N.Y. 1976. Assoc. White & Case, N.Y.C., 1966-74, ptnr., 1974—. 1st lt. U.S. Army, 1961-63. Mem. ABA, N.Y. State Bar Assn., Assn. of Bar of City of N.Y., Internat. Bar Assn. Clubs: Milbrook (Greenwich, Conn.); Yale (N.Y.C.). Home: 56 Hillside Rd Greenwich CT 06830-4835 Office: White & Case Bldg Ll 1155 Avenue of The Americas New York NY 10036-2787

OSVATH, LUDOVIC LAJOS, minister; b. Lupoaia, Romania, July 22, 1938; came to U.S., 1980; s. Lajos and Anna (Feher) O.; m. Jolan Pacso, May 4, 1963; 1 child, Judith. Grad., Inst. Tech., Romania, 1954, Inst. Bus., 1957, Ady Endre Coll., 1978; student, Heritage Bapt. Inst., Cleve., 1986. Ordained to ministry Bapt.Ch., 1955. Preacher Bapt. Ch., Romania, 1955—, mem. coms. Romania, 1955-65, treas., mem. com. Zalau, Romania, 1965-73; pres. Hungarian Missionary Soc. Inc., Cleve., 1989—. Del. Romanian Bapt. Congress, Bucharest, Romania, 1978; maintenance exec. Sponge, Inc., Cleve., 1985—. Underground rep. Amnesty Internat., Romania, 1977-80; founding mem. Defenders of Religious Freedom and Ideas, Romania, 1978, persecuted and excluded from the country; mem. Internat. Christian Solidarity, Zurich, Switzerland. Mem. Christian Mgmt. Assn., Bocskai Cultural Soc. (sec. 1988—). Office: Hungarian Missionary Soc PO Box 6327 Cleveland OH 44101-1327

OSVER, ARTHUR, artist; b. Chgo., July 26, 1912; s. Harry and Yetta (Woodrov) O.; m. Ernestine Betsberg, Aug. 12, 1940. Student, Northwestern U., 1930-31, Art Inst. Chgo., 1931-36, Dartmouth U., 1997. Instr. art Washington U., St. Louis, 1960-83. Works exhbtd., Art Inst. Chgo., Pa. Acad. Art, Carnegie Inst., Whitney Mus., St. Louis Art Mus., Nelson Gallery, Atkins Mus., Corcoran Art Gallery, U. Ill. Ann., Mus. Modern Art, Met. Mus., others, works in permanent collections, Whitney Mus., Toledo Mus., Isaac Delgado Mus., Peabody Mus., Rio de Janeiro Mus.; artist in residence, U. Fla., 1954-55; trustee emeritus Am. Acad Rome, 1993, artist in residence, 1957-58, one man shows, Wilson Gallery, Chgo., 1940, Grand Central Moderns, N.Y.C., 1947, 49, 51, 56, U. Tenn., 1948, Syracuse U., 1949, Hamline U., 1950, U. Fla., 1951, 55, Fairweather-Hardin Gallery, Chgo., 1953, 55, 69, Dartmouth U., Hanover, N.H., 1997, St. Louis Art Mus., 2000, others. Recipient John Barton Paine medal Va. Mus., 1944, purchase prize U. Ill., 1949, Temple gold medal and purchase prize Pa. Acad., Prix de Rome, 1952, 53, J. Henry Schiedt prize Pa. Acad. Fine Arts, award Am. Acad. and Inst. Arts and Letters, 1991, Arts & Edn. Excellence in Painting award, Arts and Edn. Coun. Greater St. Louis, 1994; James Nelson Raymond traveling fellow, 1936-38; Guggenheim fellow, 1950-51; sabbatical leave grantee Nat. Endowment Arts. Mem. Audubon Artists, Artists Equity. Address: 465 Foote Ave Webster Groves MO 63119-1502

OSWALD, EVA SUE ADEN, insurance executive; b. Ft. Dodge, Iowa, Feb. 2, 1949; d. Warren Dale Aden and Alice Rae (Gingerich) Aspeslet; m. Bruce Elliott Oswald, Nov. 27, 1976. BBS, U. Iowa, 1972. With Great Am. Ins. Co., 1975—, v.p. mktg. div. Calif., 1987, v.p. profit ctr., 1988-90; pres. Garden of Eva, Inc., 1990—. Mem. Snelling-Selby Bus. Coun. Mem. Nat. Assn. Ins. Women, State Guarantee Fund (bd. dirs. 1986-87), Exec. Women St. Paul, Midway C. of C. Methodist. Office: 1585 Marshall Ave Saint Paul MN 55104-6222

OSWALD, HAROLD NICHOLAS, JR. lay worker; b. Joliet, Ill., Nov. 29, 1961; s. Harold N. and Judith D. (Taylor) O. Diploma, Waldron (Mich.) Area Schs., 1980. Asst. song leader Prattville (Mich.) Community Ch., 1987-91; mem. Christian Family Centre, Adrian, Mich., 1991—. Mgr. Centre Lanes, Christian Family Ctr., 1992—; info. exch. mgr.. Christian Family Ctr., 1997—. Author: TOP Devotional Guide, 1991. Pres. Young Am. Bowling Alliance for Lenawee County, 1996-2000. Recipient Bowler of Yr. award Lenawee County Am. Bowling Congress, 1999. Mem. Sons Am. Legion (West Unity, Ohio)., Lenawee County Men's Bowling Assn. (bd. dirs. 2001—). Republican. Evangl. Free Ch. Office: Christian Family Ctr 1800 W Us Highway 223 Adrian MI 49221-8479 E-mail: noswald@core.com.

OSWALD, JAMES MARLIN, education educator; b. Plainview, Tex., Aug. 17, 1935; s. James Buchanan and Eula Bea (Marlin) O.; m. Dorothy Anne Veigel, Dec. 27, 1956; children: Richard, Ramona, Roberta. BS, West Tex. State Coll., 1957, MA, 1958; EdD, Stanford U., 1970. Tchr., supr. Salt Lake City Pub. Schs., 1958-66; curriculum specialist Am. Insts. Rsch., 1966-68; staff assoc. Nat. Coun. Social Studies, 1968-69; asst. prof. social studies and social sci. edn. Syracuse (N.Y.) U., 1969-72; rschr.-writer, dir. global cultural studies edn. projects Am. Univs. Field Staff, 1972-75; asst. supt. instrn. East Penn Sch. Dist., Emmaus, Pa., 1975-78; field coord. Pa., Del. and N.J. citizen edn. Rsch. for Better Schs., Phila., 1978-80; instrnl. devel. specialist C.C. Phila., 1980-96; energy conservation cons., 1959—; edn. cons., 1963—. Propr. Energy Cons. and Main Line Stoves, 1972—; pres. N.Y. State Coun. Social Studies, 1971-72; co-founder, pres. Inst. Plant Based Nutrition, 1996—; pres. PlantKingdom.com, VeganFund.com, VeganQuality.com, 2000—. Author: The Monroe Doctrine: Does It Survive?, 1969; Research in Social Studies and Social Science Education, 1972; co-author: Earthship, 1974, Planet Earth, 1976, Our Home, the Earth, 1980, Marco Polo Vegan Cuisine, 1998, Christopher Columbus Vegan Cuisine, 1999, Criteria for Nutritional Guidelines for Century 21, 1999, Ferdinand Magellan Vegan Cuisine, 2000; introduced concepts of global cultural studies, 1972, humanself, 1972, veganomics, 1998, veganocracy, 1998, veganagro, 1998; editor quar. newsletter Plant Based Nutrition; contbr. articles to profl. jours.; cons. on energy efficiency, ecol. conservation, plant based econ. devel., vegan nutrition, veganic-organic gardening, fin., life, career and retirement planning. With U.S. Army, 1957-58, USAR, 1958-68. Recipient Sertoma Svc. to Mankind award, Salt Lake City, 1966; grantee Stanford U., NSF, U.S. Office Edn., Inst. Internat. Studies; Henry Newell fellow Stanford U., 1966-68; Fulbright-Hays SEAsia U. Singapore Study Program fellow, 1967. Mem. Am. Vegan Soc., Vegan Soc. (U.K.), Vegetarian Union N.Am., Vegan Organic Network Horticulture-Agr. (U.K.), Hastings-Halliburton Vegetarian Assn. (Can.), Inst. Nutrition Edn. and Rsch. (bd. advisors), Internat. Vegetarian Union, Inst. Plant Based Nutrition, N.Am. Vegetarian Soc., Physicians Com. for Responsible Medicine, People for Ethical Treatment Animals, Farm Sanctuary, Vegetarians of Phila. (bd. dirs., editor Veggie News quar.), Vegetarian Resource Group, Toronto Vegetarian Assn., Main Line Vegetarian Soc. (founding pres.), Am. Youth Hostels (past pres. Delaware Valley coun.), Hindu Temple Soc. Am., Internat. Soc. Kirsna Consciousness, Food for Life Internat., Internat. Oak Soc., Internat. Platform Assn., Social Sci. Edn. Consortium, Tex. Panhandle-Plains Hist. Soc., Utah Hist. Soc., Nat. Trust Hist. Preservation, Desc. Founders of Ancient Windsor, Windsor Hist. Soc., Pa. Assn. for Sustainable Agr., Farm Animal Reform Mvmt., Pa. Hort. Soc., Pa. Forestry Assn., State Hort. Assn. (Pa.), Pa. Fruit Grower Assn., Pa. Vegetable Growers Assn., Vegetable Growers Assn. N.J., Lower Merion Hist. Soc., Pa. Hist. Soc., Stanford Club Phila., Phi Delta Kappa, Keystone Trails Assn. Home and Office: 333 Bryn Mawr Ave Bala Cynwyd PA 19004-2606 E-mail: jmoswald@bellatlantic.net.

OSWALD, ROBERT BERNARD, science administrator, nuclear engineer; b. Detroit, May 25, 1932; s. Robert Bernard and Leona Virginia (LeFave) O.; m. Judith Ann Dick, Feb. 3, 1964; children: Robert Vernon, Susan Marie. BSME, BS in Math., U. Mich., 1957, MSME, 1958, PhD in Nuclear Engring., 1964. Rsch. physicist Harry Diamond Labs., U.S. Army, Washington, 1964-69, chief radiation, phys. br., 1970-72, chief rsch. lab., 1972-76, assoc. tech. dir. Adelphi, Md., 1976-79; asst. to dep. dir. sci. and tech. Def. Nuclear Agy., Alexandria, Va., 1979-81; tech. dir. Electronic R&D Command, U.S. Army, Adelphi, 1981-85; corp. v.p. Sci. Application Internat. Corp., McLean, Va., 1985-87; dir. R&D C.E. Washington, 1987-96; exec. dir. strategic environ. R&D program, 1992-94; ret., 1996. Vis. prof. dept. nuclear engring. U. Mich., Ann Arbor, 1969-70. Contbr. articles to profl. jours. With USAF, 1950-53. Recipient Louis J. Hamilton award U. Mich., 1973, Disting. Exec. award Pres. of U.S., 1983, Meritorious Exec. Pres. award, 1991; Meritorious Exec. Pres. award, 1996; Boeing fellow, 1957-58, Atomic Energy Spl. fellow, 1961-63. Fellow IEEE; mem. Am. Phys. Soc., Soc. Mil. Engrs., Cath. Acad. Scis., Cosmos Club. Republican. Roman Catholic. Avocations: sailing, woodworking, gardening, golf.

OSWALD, RUDOLPH A. economist; b. Milw., Aug. 4, 1932; s. Carl J. and Anne O.; m. Mary Louise Hurney BA, Holy Cross Coll., 1954; postgrad. (Fulbright scholar), U. Munich, W. Ger., 1954-55; MS, U. Wis., Madison, 1958; PhD in Econs., Georgetown U., 1965. Research and edn. dir. Internat. Assn. Fire Fighters, Washington, 1959-63; economist research dept. AFL-CIO, 1963-72, asst. dir. edn. dept., 1975-76, dir. research dept., 1976-96, economist-in-residence George Meany Ctr for Labor Studies, 1996—. Vis. prof. Cornell U., 1997, 99, 2000; rsch. dir. Svc. Employees Internat. Union, Washington, 1972-75; adj. prof. econs. George Washington U., 1966-75; mem. Fed. Employees Pay Coun., 1970-72, Sec. Navy's Adv. Bd. Edn. and Tng., 1975-78, Nat. Commn. Employment and Unemployment Stats., Fgn. Investment Adv. Com.; mem. adv. coun. Indsl. Labor Rels. Sch., Cornell U., 1981-85, 95-99, Sch. Bus. U. S.C. 1992-98; mem. Consumer Adv. Com. Securities and Exchange Com., 1994-98, Labor Rsch. Adv. Coun. to Bur. Labor Stats., mem. adv. com. on trade, 1984-98; mem adv. com. Ex-Im Bank, 1989-92. Bd. dirs. Nat. Industries for the Blind, 1965-71. Served with U.S. Army, 1956-57. Mem. Am. Econ. Assn., Am. Statis. Assn., Indsl. Rels. Rsch. Assn. (past pres.), Nat. Bur. Econ. Rsch. (dir.), Nat. Policy Assn. (dir.), Nat. Coun. on Econ. Edn. (dir.). Home: 11804 Devilwood Dr Rockville MD 20854-3407 Office: George Meany Labor Studies Ctr 10000 New Hampshire Ave Silver Spring MD 20903-1706

OSWALD, STANTON S. lawyer; b. Phila., Oct. 15, 1927; s. Sylvan J. and Myra O.; m. Bernice Boorstein, June 17, 1951; children: Jane Easley, Eve Robbins, David Oswald, Beth Oswald. BA, U. Pa., 1949; LLB magna cum laude, Harvard U., 1952. Bar: Pa., 1953. Law clk. to Judge William L. Hastie U.S. Ct. Appeals Third Circuit, Phila., 1952-53; assoc. Wolf, Block, Schorr & Solis-Cohen, 1953-63, ptnr., 1963-95, of counsel, 1995—. Trustee, hon. dir. Congregation Adath Jeshurun, Melrose Park; past chmn. bd. dirs. Pa. affiliate Am. Diabetes Assn., past chmn. bd. dirs. Phila. chpt. With USAAF, 1946-47. Mem. ABA, Pa. Bar Assn., Phila. Bar Assn. Democrat. Jewish. Office: Wolf Block Schorr & Solis-Cohen LLP 1650 Arch St 22d Fl Philadelphia PA 19103-2029 E-mail: soswald@wolfblock.com.

OSWALT, ARIA LUCINDA, real estate broker; b. Marion, Ind., July 11, 1953; d. Chester Von and Georgia Shoaff (Waltz) O. AB in French, Ind. U., 1975. Cert. residential specialist; accredited buyer rep. Real estate broker Owens Bryan & Reed, Bloomington, Ind., 1977-89, F.C. Tucker Co., Bloomington, 1989—2001, v.p. residential divsn., 1994—; real estate broker F.C. Tucker/OBR Realtors, 2001—. Bd. dirs. Bloomington YMCA, 1994-2000. Mem. Realtors Nat. Mktg. Inst. (coun. residential specialists), Real Estate Buyer Agy. Coun., Ind. Assn. Realtors (bd. dirs. 1990-94, chmn. bd. leadership forum 1992-93), Bloomington Bd. Realtors (bd. dirs. 1990-94, pres. 1991-92, chmn. strategic planning com., 1993, v.p. multiple listing svc. 1994-95, pres. multiple listing svc., 1995-96, Realtor of Yr. 1995), Realtors Honor Soc., Greater Bloomington C. of C., Friends of Art Ind. U., Friends of Music Ind. U., Ind. U. Alumni Assn., Pres. Club (life), Phi Beta Kappa. Avocations: gardening, travel, mystery novels, cooking. Office: F C Tucker/OBR Realtors 487 S Clarizz Blvd Bloomington IN 47401-5517

OSWALT, ROY E. baseball player; b. Kosciusko, Miss., Aug. 29, 1977; m. Nichol Oswalt. Baseball player Houston Astros, 2001—. Named Rookie of Yr., Baseball Writers Assn. Am. (BBWAA) Houston chpt.; named to TOPPS All-Rookie team; recipient Sporting News NL Rookie Pitcher of Yr. honors. Office: Houston Astros Po Box 288 Houston TX 77001-0288*

OTANI, MIKE, optical company executive; b. Atsumi, Aichi, Japan, July 25, 1945; s. Yuichi and Miyako (Suzuki) O.; m. Jane Ashley Campbell, Aug. 25, 1976; 1 child, Michael Taro. Degree in Internat. Fin. and Econs., Shiga U., Japan, 1967. Office mgr. Kumagai-Gumi Ltd, Osaka, Japan, 1968-73; dude rancher Tumbling River Ranch, Grant, Colo., 1974-77; merchandiser Nobel, Inc., Denver, 1978-82; v.p. Charmant Eyewear, Inc., Morris Plains, N.J., 1983-88, pres., CEO, 1988—; chmn., CEO, bd. dirs. Aristar, Inc., 1994—. Bd. dirs. Charmant Optical Co., Ltd., Fukui, Japan, Charmant Optical GmbH Europe, Munich, Charmant Eyewear, Inc., Charmant Eyewear, Inc., London and Paris; pres. Charmant Internat. de Mexico, 1997—. Donor Project Literacy U.S., Pitts., 1990, Pa. Coll. Optometry, Phila., 1990; organizer N.J.-Fukui Sister State Activity, 1990; active Big Bros. and Big Sisters of Morris County, 1993—. Recipient Vendor of Yr. award Walmart, Inc., 1991, Cole Nat. & Pearl Vision, 1997. Mem. Optical Mfrs. Assn. (bd. dirs. 1988-92, Star of Vision award 2002), Fukui-N.Y. Club (chmn. 1996-). Avocations: golf, horseback riding, reading, traveling, fishing. Office: Charmant Eyewear Inc 400 American Rd Morris Plains NJ 07950-2461

OTELSBERG, JONAH, business educator; b. Warsaw, Poland, Aug. 6, 1932; came to U.S., 1962; d. Abraham and Esther (Goldwag) O.; m. Nissim Capuano, Aug. 16, 1951 (div. 1956); m. Peter David Goodwin, Dec. 22, 1976. B in Econs., History, Math., Hebrew U. Jerusalem; MBA, CUNY, 1967, PhD in Bus., 1976. Surveyor Govt. Israel, 1951-56, dir. standards Cen. Bur. Stats., 1960-62; editorial asst. Internat. Media Guide, 1962-63; mgr. rsch. Nat. Knitted Outerwear Assn., 1963-64; staff asst. product devel. and evaluation Mut. N.Y., 1965-66; project dir. Schwerin Rsch., 1966-67; mgr. statis. design and methods McGraw-Hill Info. Systems Co., 1967-76; project dir. Ctr. Social Rsch. CUNY, 1976-79, adj. prof. Grad. Sch. and Univ. Ctr., 1978-79, assoc. prof. bus., 1979—, dir. Data Svc., 1982-86. Adj. prof. grad. sch. bus. L.I. U., 1978-79; organizer, leader various confs. and workshops, 1977-86. Contbr. articles to profl. jours. Mem. Acad. mktg. Sci., Am. Mktg. Assn., Am. Statis. Assn. (past chair com. small area stats.), Internat. Assn. Survey Statisticians; Fulbright lectr., USSR, 1990-91. Jewish. Avocation: bird watching, hiking, music, ballet, theatre. Home: 45 W 54th St New York NY 10019-5404 Office: York Coll Cuny Jamaica NY 11451-0001

OTEY, RHEBA L. librarian, educator; b. Xenia, Ohio; d. E. Byron and Lottie (Myers-Jenkins) Washington; m. Robert C. Otey (dec.); 1 child, James Edward. AB cum laude, Wilberforce U., 1942; Libr. Cert., Ohio Dominican Coll., 1964; MA in English, Ohio State U., 1969, PhD in English Edn., 1978. Cert. tchr. English, libr. sci., earth sci., Ohio. Lectr., coord. job devel. Ohio Bur. Employment, Columbus, 1956-62; columnist Ohio Sentinel, 1960-64; head libr. Columbus Pub. Schs., 1964—, mem. prin.'s adv. coun., 1965-71, chmn., 1972, 77-80, coord. gifted and talented program, 1980-96, advisor libr. stds., 1998—; ret. Pub. rels. cons., 1960—; former ptnr. Assocs. Resource Inst., Inc., cons. in human devel. svcs.; columnist Columbus Post; dir. Black Studies program Monroe Jr. H.S., Columbus, 1969-73, Medina Mid., 1974—; moderator Edn. Devel. Model Cities Workshops, 1970-73; presenter Phi Delta Kappa Workshop; del. Ohio White House Conf. on Libr. and Info. Svc.; chair tech. plan Medina Mid., 1997; mem. Medina Mid. Sch. Continuous Improvement Plan, 1998—. Author: Mercury Identifies: A Study of The Nature of Man, (collection short stories) That's the Way Life Is; contbr. articles, papers to profl. jours.; author poems. Vol. United Negro Coll. Fund, Columbus Cmty. House, numerous others; nat. pub. rels. officer Continental Socs., Inc.; founder Columbus chpt. Chums, Inc., past local pres., nat. officer; pub. spkr. Holistic Approach to Successful Goal Setting. Recipient Ohio gov.'s proclamation for outstanding cmty. svc., award for outstanding cmty svc. Columbus sect. Nat. Coun. Negro Women, also numerous certs. of merit from Ohio and U.S. govt. agys.; named Famous Poet, Famous Poet Soc., 1996. Mem. NEA, Ohio Edn. Assn., Columbus Edn. Assn., Phi Delta Kappa, Zeta Sigma Pi, Sen Mer Rekh. Roman Catholic.

OTHERSEN, HENRY BIEMANN, JR. pediatric surgeon, physician, educator; b. Charleston, S.C., Aug. 26, 1930; s. Henry and Lydia Albertine (Smith) O.; m. Janelle Lester, Apr. 4, 1959; children: Megan, Mandy, Margaret, Henry Biemann III. BS, Coll. Charleston, 1950; MD, Med. Coll. S.C., 1953. Diplomate: Am. Bd. Surgery, Am. Bd. Thoracic Surgery, Am. Bd. Pediatric Surgery. Intern Phila. Gen. Hosp., 1953-54; postgrad. U. Pa., 1956-57; resident in gen. surgery Med. Coll. S.C., Charleston, 1957-62; resident in pediatric surgery Ohio State U. and Columbus Children's Hosp., 1962-64; research fellow Harvard U., Mass. Gen. Hosp., Boston, 1964-65; asst. prof. pediatric surgery Med. U. S.C., Charleston, 1965-68, assoc. prof., 1968-72, prof., 1972—, chief pediatric surgery, 1972-98; med. dir. Med. U. S.C. Hosp., 1981-85, Children's Hosp., 1985—2001, med. dir. profl. staff, 1996—2001, physician liaison for documentation, 2002—; acting chief surgery VA Hosp., 2002—. Editor The Pediatric Airway; mem. editorial bd. Jour. Pediatric Surgery, Jour. Parenteral and Enteral Nutrition; contbr. articles on pediatric oncology, esophageal, tracheal strictures to profl. jours. Bd. dirs., pres. S.C. div. Am. Cancer Soc., 1977-79. Served with USN, 1954-56, Korea. Fellow ACS, Am. Acad. Pediatrics; mem. Am. Pediatric Surg. Assn. (bd. govs. 1986-89, pres.-elect 1996, pres. 1997), Brit. Assn. Pediatric Surgeons (overseas coun.), Am. Surg. Assn., So. Surg. Assn., Am. Trauma Soc., Charleston County Med. Soc. (pres. 1980), Alpha Omega Alpha (councilor 1978-94). Office: 246 North Tower PO Box 250332 169 Ashley Ave Charleston SC 29425-0001 Fax: (843) 792-5114. E-mail: othershb@musc.edu. *A man ought to do what he thinks is right.*

OTHERSEN-KHALIFA, CHERYL LEE, insurance agent, realtor; b. Bay City, Mich., Aug. 17, 1948; d. Andrew Julius and Ruth Emma (Jacoby) Houthoofd; m. Wayne Korte Othersen, Sept. 5, 1964 (div.); 1 child Angela Othersen ; m. Imed M. B. Salah Khalifa, Sept. 27, 1997 (div.). Lic. ins., Mich. State U., 1980, lic. realtor, 1981. Owner, operator Glad Rags Boutique, Unionville, Mich., 1976-79; dept. mgr. Gantos, Saginaw, 1979-80; agt., bookkeeper Othersen Ins. Agy., Inc., Unionville, 1979-81, v.p., 1981—; realtor Osentoski Realty Corp., 1981—; benefits specialist AFLAC Ins. Co., 1995—. Active Mich. chpt. Nat. head Injury Found., Mich. chpt. Crohn's and Colitis Found. Am., Inc., Nat. Mus. in Arts, Nat. Trust Hist. Preservation; assoc. mem. Am. Mus. Natural History; charter supporter U.S. Holocaust Meml. Mus.; vol. local Rep. campaigns, 1982, 1984, 1986. Fellow: John F. Kennedy Libr. Found. (hon.); mem.: Saginaw County Homebuilders Assn., Nat. Mus. Women in the Arts, Profl. Ins. Agts., Saginaw Christian Women's Assn., Saginaw County C. of C., Saginaw Twp. Bus. Assn. (bd. dirs. 2002), Unionville Bus. Assn. Avocations: sports, painting, travel, gardening, reading. Home: 2575 Ranier St Saginaw MI 48603-3325 Office: Othersen Ins Agy Inc 6639 Center St Unionville MI 48767-9482 also: Cheri Othersen Agy 2575 Ranier St Saginaw MI 48603

OTHMAN, TALAT MOHAMAD, financial consultant, investment banker; b. Betunia, Palestine, Apr. 27, 1936; came to U.S., 1947, naturalized, 1954; s. Mohamad Racheed and Damelize (Ahmed) O.; children— Joseph, Suad, Jamil, Rashid; m. Haleema Othman. Student Northwestern U. With Harris Bank, Chgo., 1956-78, v.p., div. head, 1974-78; gen. mgr., chief exec. officer Saudi Arab Fin. Corp., S.A., Paris, 1978-83; pres. Dearborn Financial, Inc., Arlington Hts., Ill., 1983-95; chmn. Grove Fin. Inc., 1995—; bd. dirs. Bank One Wis. Corp., Milw., Harken Oil and Gas Co., Dallas, Pathogenesis Corp., Seattle; chmn. Dansk Internat. Designs, Inc., Mt. Kisko, N.Y., 1985-91, Goodson Polymer, Inc., Troy, Ohio, 1987-88. Contbr. chpts. to Technique of Foreign Exchange Trading, 1975; also articles and booklets. Bd. dirs. Inst. World Affairs, Milw., 1986-89, Khail Gibran Meml. com., Washington, D.C., 1987-89; pres. Islamic Cultural Ctr.; mem. adv. bd. Kennedy Sch. Govt.,

Harvard U.; mem. hon. bd. Mid. East Studies Ctr., U. Chgo. Recipient Outstanding Pres. award proclaiming Talat M. Othman Day in Ill., Nov. 1, 1997. Mem. Arab Bankers Assn. (pres. 1985-87, bd. dirs. 1984-89, recipient plaque of Appreciation), Forex Assn. of N.Am. (chmn., founding pres. Chgo. chpt. 1976, recipient plaque of Appreciation), Mid Am. Arab C. of C. (bd. dirs. 1974-78, 84-91, founding pres. 1977, recipient plaque of Appreciation), Chgo. Club. Moslem. Avocations: tennis, racquetball, reading. Office: 3432 Rfd Long Grove IL 60047-8106 E-mail: grovefinancial@worldnet.att.net.

OTHMER, DAVID ARTMAN, television and radio consultant; b. West Medford, Mass., Mar. 18, 1941; s. Murray Eade and Mary (Artman) O.; m. Nancy Trumbull, Sept. 12, 1965 (div. Dec. 1982); 1 child, Rachel; m. Maureen Barden, June 4, 1983; 1 child, Matthew. BA, Harvard Coll., 1963; MBA, Harvard U., 1966. Asst. to pres. Sta. WNET, N.Y.C., 1974-75, dir. broadcasting, 1975-82, dir. telecommunications, 1982-83; v.p., sta. mgr. Sta. WHYY, Phila., 1983-2000; cons., 2000—. Exec. producer (TV show) Science Spots, 1985 (Ohio State award 1985); producer (TV show) Who is Red Grooms?, 1986 (Emmy 1986), various other TV shows, 1980— (Emmy nominations). Avocations: growing grapes and making wine. Home and Office: 4220 Spruce St Philadelphia PA 19104-4040 E-mail: davidothmer@aol.com.

OTHS, JOSEPH ANTHONY, lawyer; b. Valhalla, N.Y., Dec. 6, 1934; s. Joseph William and Martha Mary (Walker) O.; m. Jane Matthews, Aug. 7, 1982; children (previous marriage): Michael, Kathryn, Christine Masson, Jennifer Martindill, Amy Montgomery; stepchildren: Debora Roth, Catherine Gravois, Laurie Gaston, Stacey Nicchio. BA, U. Dayton, 1956; LLB/JD, No. Ky. U., 1961. Bar: Ohio 1961, U.S. Dist. Ct. (so. dist.) Ohio 1963, U.S. Supreme Ct. 1971, Fla. 1986, La. 1987, U.S. Ct. Appeals (6th cir.) 1993. Lawyer various ptnrs. and solo practice, Wellston, Ohio, 1961—; sr. ptnr. Oths, Heiser & Miller, 1995—. Bd. dirs. First Nat. Bank of Wellston, 1980—. City solicitor City of Wellston, 1965-72; trustee (mem. exec. com.) Rio Grande (Ohio) Coll., 1975-79; mem. Ohio Lottery Commn., 1980-82; chmn. Revolving Loan Fund City of Wellston, 1988-2001. Fellow Am. Bar Found.; mem. ABA (coun. dels. 1980-84), Ohio State Bar Assn. (pres. 1979-80). Democrat. Avocations: travel, reading, computers. Office: Oths Heiser & Miller 16 E Broadway Wellston OH 45692-0309 E-mail: joths@ohlaw.com.

OTIS, DENISE MARIE, editor, writer; b. Detroit, July 25, 1927; d. J. Hawley and Florence Ruth O. AB cum laude, Radcliffe Coll., Cambridge, Mass., 1949. English tchr. Cambridge Sch., Weston, Mass., 1949-50; asst. to feature editor House and Garden, N.Y.C., 1952-53, assoc. decorating editor, 1953-56, editor, entertaining dept., 1956-66, assoc. editor, 1966-80, deputy editor, 1980-87; sr. editor and cons. Conde Nast Publs., 1987-93. Consulting editor Vogue Decoration, Paris, 1989-91. Author: Decorating with Flowers, 1978, Grounds for Pleasure: Four Centuries of the American Garden, 2002; contbg. editor Garden Design, 1997—; contbr. articles to profl. jours. Fulbright scholar Inst. Internat. Edn., France, 1950-51. Mem. Internat. Dendrology Soc., Decorators Club, Phi Beta Kappa. Episcopalian. Avocations: cooking, photography, gardening.

OTIS, JACK, social work educator; b. N.Y.C., Feb. 13, 1923; s. Abraham and Esther (Goldberg) O.; children: Elisabeth H., Erich R., Greta M., Marcus H., Alicia. AB, Bklyn. Coll., 1946; MS in Social Work, U. Ill., 1948, M.Ed., 1955, PhD, 1957. Social worker Jewish Social Svc. Bur. Dade County, 1948-49; Psychiat. social worker Free Synagogue Social Service, N.Y. U., 1949-50; asso. prof. U. Ill., 1950-61; dep. dir. Office Juvenile Delinquency and Youth Devel., Dept. Health, Edn. and Welfare, 1961-65; dean Grad. Sch. Social Work U. Tex., 1965-77, prof. emeritus, 1993—. Cons. to govt., 1961—; presenter Internat. Coun. on Social Welfare, Inter-Univ. Consortium for Internat. Social Devel., Internat. Assn. Schs. Social Work, 1994; mem. President's Com. Juvenile Delinquency and Youth Crime, 1961-65; spl. cons. for Am. social work edn. and rsch. European Ctr. for Social Welfare Tng. and Rsch., Vienna, Austria, 1976—; Dean Dan Sanders Meml. lectr. U. Ill., 1999. Author: (with George Barnett) Corporate Society and Education, 1961; contbr. article on child labor to Ency. Social Work, 1995. Bd. overseers Ctr. for Study Violence, Brandeis U., 1966-70; commencement spkr. U. Tex. Sch. Social Work, 2001. With AUS, 1943-46, PTO. Fulbright-Hays research fellow Austria, 1977-78 Mem. AAUP, Coun. on Social Work Edn. (commn. on accreditation), Philosophy of Edn. Soc., Nat. Assn. Social Workers (chair Calif. Task Force on Child Labor 2001--), Am. Acad. Polit. and Social Sci., N.Y. Acad. Sci., Johannesburg Child Welfare Soc. (rsch. cons. South Africa chpt. 1990-91), Phi Kappa Phi (pres.). *The meaning of my life is whether I have added to the meaning of another's.*

OTIS, JAMES, JR. architect; b. Chgo., July 8, 1931; s. James and Edwina (Love) O.; m. Diane Cleveland, Apr. 9, 1955; children: James III, Julie C., David C. BArch cum laude, Princeton U., 1953; postgrad., U. Chgo., 1955-57. Registered architect, Ill., Ariz., Colo., Ind., Iowa, Wis., N.Mex., Mo. Designer Irvin A. Blietz Co., Wilmette, Ill., 1955-57; pres. Homefinders Constrn. Corp., 1957-59, O & F Constrn. Co., Northbrook, Ill., 1959-61; chmn. bd., chief exec. officer Otis Assocs., Inc., 1960-89; pres. Otis Co., 1981—. Bd. dirs. Banco Popular, Chgo. Prin. works include GBC Corp. Hdqrs., Zurich Towers Office Complex, Schaumburg, Ill., AON Ins. Co. Corp. Hdqrs., Performing Arts Ctr., Northbrook, Ill., All State Regional Hdqrs., Skokie, Ill., Zurich Nat. Hdqrs.-Zurich Towers Schaumburg. Trustee Evanston (Ill.) Hosp., 1971-93, Better Govt. Assn., Chgo., Graham Found., 1984-86; chmn. bd. trustees North Suburban YMCA, Northbrook, 1990-97; governing mem. Shedd Aquarium; bd. govs. Chgo. Zool. Soc.; mem. adv. bd. Cook County Forest Preserve Dist.; mem. founder's coun. Field Mus., Chgo.; bd. dirs. Ill. Nature Conservancy. Lt. USNR, 1953-55. Mem. AIA, Nat. Coun. Archtl. Registration Bds., Urban Land Inst., Northwestern U. Assocs., Princeton Club (pres. 1971-72), Econ. Club, Commonwealth Club, Chgo. Club, Comml. Club, Glen View Golf Club, Old Elm Club, Coleman Lake Club, Angler's Club. Republican. Episcopalian. Office: Otisco 1450 American Ln Ste 1250 Schaumburg IL 60173-6010 E-mail: jotisjr@otiscompany.com.

OTIS, JAMES A.D. physician, educator; b. N.Y.C., Aug. 8, 1959; AB, Harvard Coll., Cambridge, Mass., 1980; AM, Harvard U., Cambridge, Mass., 1981; MD, N.Y. Med. Coll., Valhalla, 1985. Diplomate Am. Bd. Psychiatry, Am. Bd. Neurology. Resident in medicine Lenox Hill Hosp., N.Y.C., 1985-86; resident in neurology Boston U. Med. Ctr., 1986-88, chief resident, 1988-89, fellow in EEG and epilepsy, 1989-90; fellow in pain and neuro-oncology Meml.-Sloan-Kettering Cancer Ctr., N.Y.C., 1990-91; asst. prof. neurology Sch. Medicine Boston U., 1991-99, asst. dir. neurology residency program, 1991, assoc. prof., 1999—. Dir. Pain Mgmt. Ctr. Boston Med. Ctr., 1991. Contbr. articles to profl. jours. Office: Boston U Sch Medicine Pain Ctr DOB 707 720 Harrison Ave Boston MA 02118-2334

OTIS, JOHN JAMES, civil engineer; b. Syracuse, N.Y., Aug. 5, 1922; s. John Joseph and Anna (Doy) O.; m. Dorothy Fuller Otis, June 21, 1958; children: Mary Eileen Dawn, John Leon. BChemE, Syracuse U., 1943, MBA, 1950, postgrad., 1951-55. Registered profl. engr., Ala., Tex. Jr. process engr. GM, Syracuse, 1951-53, prodn. engr., 1954-58, process control engr., 1958-59, process engr., 1960-61; engr., writer GE, 1961-63, configuration control engr. Phila., 1969; assoc. rsch. engr. Boeing Co., Huntsville, Ala., 1963-65; assoc. Planning Rsch. Corp., 1965-67; prin. engr. Brown Engring. Co. subs. Teledyne Co., 1967-69; mech. designer Drever Co., Beth Ayres, Pa., 1970-71; civil engr. U.S. Army Corps Engrs., Mobile, Ala., 1971-74, Galveston, Tex., 1974—. Lector, lay minister Roman Cath. Ch. Served with USNR, 1944-50. Mem. Am. Inst. Indsl. Engrs. (past v.p. Syracuse and Huntsville chpts.), Tex. Soc. Profl. Engrs. (dir. Galveston County chpt. 1976-79, sec.-treas. 1979-80, v.p. 1980-81, pres. 1982-83), Am. Legion, Tau Beta Pi, Phi Kappa Tau, Alpha Chi Sigma, Chi Eta Sigma. Home: 2114 Yorktown Ct N League City TX 77573-5056 Office: US Army Corps Engrs Jadwin Bldg 2000 Fort Point Rd Galveston TX 77550-3038

OTIS, LEE LIBERMAN, lawyer, educator; b. N.Y.C., Aug. 19, 1956; d. James Benjamin and Deen (Freed) L.; m. William Graham Otis, Oct. 24, 1993. BA, Yale U., 1979; JD, U. Chgo., 1983. Bar: N.Y. 1985, D.C. 1994. Law clk. U.S. Ct. Appeals (D.C. cir.), Washington, 1983-84; spl. asst. to asst. atty. gen., civil div. U.S. Dept. Justice, 1984-86, dep. assoc. atty. gen., 1986, assoc. dep. atty. gen., 1986; law clk. to Justice Antonin Scalia U.S. Supreme Ct., Washington, 1986-87; asst. prof. law George Mason U., Arlington, Va., 1987-89; assoc. counsel to the Pres. Exec. Office of the Pres., Washington, 1989-92; assoc. Jones, Day, Reavis & Pogue, 1993-94; chief judiciary coun. U.S. Sen. Spence Abraham, 1995-96; chief counsel subcom. on immigration Com. on the Judiciary, U.S. Senate, 1997-2000; chief counsel U.S. Dept. Energy, 2001—. Adj. prof. law Georgetown Law Sch., 1995, 96. Mem. Federalist Soc. for Law and Pub. Policy (founder). Republican. Jewish. Avocations: sailing, computers.*

OTIS, RICHARD DICKINSON, pathologist; b. Meriden, Conn., Dec. 26, 1924; s. Fessendon Newport and Anna (Gerstenmaier) O.; m. Mary Tourtellot Hamlen, June 10, 1949; children: James H., Richard D. Jr., Christopher N., John B. Student premed. tng. program, Trinity Coll., 1945; MD, Yale U., 1949. Diplomate Am. Bd. Pathology, Internat. Bd. Cytopathology. Pathologist Sch. Medicine Yale U., New Haven, 1952-55; sr. pathologist, dir. anatomic pathology Hartford (Conn.) Hosp., Md., 1955-86, cons. pathologist, 1986—. Contbr. articles to profl. jours. Lt. USN, 1950-52. T. Stewart Hamilton grantee TSH Found.; Harvard U. fellow, 1979. Mem. AMA, Internat. Acad. Pathologists, Internat. Acad. Cytology, New Eng. Cancer Soc., Coll. Am. Pathologists. Republican. Avocations: antique cars, sailing, photography, wood working. Home and Office: 181 Meadow Neck Rd East Falmouth MA 02536-7712

OTIS, ROY JAMES, lawyer; BA, Stanford (Calif.) U., 1968; JD, Golden Gate U., 1980. Bar: Calif. 1980, U.S. Dist. Ct. (no. dist.) Calif. 1980; cert. specialist in workman's compensation. Ptnr. Gearheart & Otis, Pleasant Hill, 1996—. Mem. Calif. Applications Atty. Assn. (pres. no. Calif. chpt., 1994-96, bd. govs. 1997—), Assn. of Trial Lawyers of Am. (workplace injury litigation group sect. 1996—). Democrat. Office: Gearheart & Otis 367 Civic Dr Ste 17 Pleasant Hill CA 94523-1935

O'TOOLE, AUSTIN MARTIN, lawyer; b. New Bedford, Mass., Oct. 5, 1935; s. John Brian, Jr. and Helen Veronica O'T.; children: Erin Ann, Austin Martin Jr. BBA, Coll. Holy Cross, 1957; JD, Georgetown U., 1963. Bar: N.Y. 1965, D.C. 1963, Tex. 1975. Law clk. to judge U.S. Ct. Appeals, Washington, 1962-63; assoc. White & Case, N.Y.C., 1963-74; sr. v.p., sr. counsel, sec. Coastal Corp., Houston, 1974—2001. Bd. editors Georgetown Law Jour., 1962-63. Bd. dirs. Nat. Coun. on Alcoholism and Drug Dependency, Inc., 2001—; charter mem., certificated mediator Inst. for Responsible Dispute Resolution, Houston, 2000—; bd. dirs. Houston Marathon Com., 1973—2002. Officer USMC, 1957—60. Mem. ABA, Am. Soc. Corp. Secs. (bd. dirs. 1982-85), State Bar of Tex., Houston Bar Assn. (past chmn. corp. counsel sect. 1979-80), Am. Arbitration Assn. (comml. com.). Home: 1400 Hermann Dr Unit 14-c Houston TX 77004-7137 Office: 509 Nineteenth St Galveston TX 77550 E-mail: otoole@msn.com.

O'TOOLE, DENNIS P. music educator, musician; b. Louisville, Feb. 21, 1972; s. Donald P. and Barbara A. O'Toole; m. Lauraine D. Thomson, Aug. 2, 1998; 1 stepchild Albanie Knight. Grad. in surg. tech., Madisonville Tech Coll., 1992. Surgeon's asst. Trover Clinic, Madisonville, Ky., 1992—93; owner, instr. Dennis O'Toole Guitar Instrn., Denison, Tex., 1995—. Author: (instrnl. book) Dennis O'Toole Presents Basic Theory For The Beginning Guitarist, 2000; musician, co-prodr., co-writer, co-arranger (CD) Einabla, 2000. Avocations: exercising, swimming. Home: 1901 S Crockett Ave Denison TX 75021-6743 Office: Dennis O'Toole Guitar Instrn 1901 S Crockett Ave Ste 101 Denison TX 75021-6743 Personal E-mail: tko.dla@att.net. Business E-Mail: dennisotoole@netscape.net.

O'TOOLE, FRANCIS J. lawyer; b. Dublin, Ireland, Feb. 10, 1944; came to U.S., 1960; s. Francis Herbert and Josephine (McCarthy) O'T.; m. Carole Ann Leland, Apr. 11, 1977; children: Kathleen, Kirra. AB, Harvard U., 1967; JD, U. Maine, 1970. Bar: Maine 1970, U.S. Supreme Ct. 1977, U.S. Dist. Ct. D.C., U.S. Dist. Ct. (ea. dist.) Va., U.S. Ct. Appeals (1st, 2d, 4th, 5th, 7th, 8th, 9th and 10th cirs.). Assoc. Fried, Frank, Harris, Shriver & Jacobsen, Washington, 1971-78, ptnr., 1978-92, Sidley & Austin, Washington, 1992—. Editor-in-chief U. Maine Law Rev., 1969-70; contbr. articles to profl. jours. Reginald Heber Smith fellow Calif. Indian Legal Services, 1970-71. Mem. ABA. Avocations: horse breeding and racing. Home: 7700 Burford Dr Mc Lean VA 22102-2105 Office: Sidley & Austin 1722 I St NW Fl 7 Washington DC 20006-3705

O'TOOLE, JAMES JOSEPH, business educator; b. San Francisco, Apr. 15, 1945; s. James Joseph and Irene (Nagy) O'T.; m. Marilyn Louise Burrill, June 17, 1967; children: Erin Kathleen, Kerry Louise. BA, U. So. Calif., L.A., 1966; DPhil, Oxford (Eng.) U., (Eng.), 1970. Corr. Time-Life News Service, L.A., 1967-68, Nairobi, Kenya, 1967-68; mgmt. cons. McKinsey & Co., San Francisco, 1969-70; coordinator field investigations Pres.'s Comm. on Campus Unrest, Washington, 1970; spl. asst. to sec. HEW, 1970-73; prof. mgmt. U. So. Calif., L.A., 1973-93, Univ. Assocs. Chair of Bus., 1982-93; v.p. Aspen Inst., 1994-97; mng. dir. Booz-Allen & Hamilton Leadership Ctr., San Francisco, 1997—; rsch. prof. Ctr. for Effective Orgn., U. So. Calif., 1999—. Chmn. sec.'s com. work in Am. HEW, Washington, 1971-72; exec. dir. The Leadership Inst., 1990-93; bd. dirs. Radica Games. Prin. author: Work in America, 1973, Energy and Social Change, 1976; author: Work, Learning and the American Future, 1977, Making America Work, 1982 (Phi Kappa Phi prize 1982), Vanguard Management, 1985, The Executive's Compass, 1993, Leading Change, 1995, Leadership A to Z, 1999; bd. editors: Ency. Britannica, 1981-87; editor: New Management, 1983-89, The American Oxonian, 1996-98. Active Project Paideia, Chgo., 1981-83. Rhodes scholar, 1966; recipient Mitchell prize Woodlands Conf., 1979. Mem. Phi Beta Kappa. Home: 23852 Pacific Coast Hwy Ste 364 Malibu CA 90265-4879 Office: U So Calif Ctr Effective Orgns Los Angeles CA 90089-0806 E-mail: otoole_jim@bah.com.

O'TOOLE, JOHN MUNSTER, humanities educator; b. Clinton, Mass., July 19, 1937; s. Henry Aloysius and Mary Ellen (Munster) O'T.; m. Joan P. Curé, Aug. 22, 1964; children: John J., Marie, Philip E. BA in History, Worcester State Coll., 1968; MA in History, Northeastern U., Boston, 1971. Cert. secondary sch. tchr., Mass. Tchr. history Worcester (Mass.) Pub. Schs., 1969-99. Vis. instr. Holocaust and mil. history Worcester State Coll., 1993—; spkr., lectr. in ctrl. Mass., 1992—. Author (book) Tornado; 84 Minutes, 94 Lives, 1993; co-author: Clinton (Mass.) World War II Tribute Volume, 2000; contbr. photos and taped interviews to documentary Tornadoes: The Wrath of God, 1998. Horace Mann Tchr. grantee Mass. Dept. Edn., 1987, NEH grantee, 1992, 95, Coun. for Basic Edn. grantee, 1993. Mem. Am. Hist. Assn., New Eng. Hist. Assn., Ret. Officers Assn. Republican. Avocations: trout fishing, gourmet dining, book research. Home: 84 Clark St Worcester MA 01606-1758

O'TOOLE, LAURENCE JOSEPH, political science educator, researcher; b. Syracuse, N.Y., Dec. 7, 1948; s. Laurence Joseph and Marjorie Rose (Weinheimer) O.; m. Mary Irene Gilroy, June 26, 1971; children: Conor Gilroy O'Toole, Kathleen Easton O'Toole. BS with high honors, Clarkson U., 1970; MPA, Syracuse U., 1972, PhD, 1975. Asst. prof. polit. sci. U. Va., Charlottesville, 1975-79; assoc. prof. polit. sci. Auburn (Ala.) U., 1979-85, prof. polit. sci., 1985-92, U. Ga., Athens, 1992—, M. Hughes and Robert T. Golembiewski prof. pub. adminstrn., 2000—. Vis. rschr. Internat. Inst. Mgmt. Sci. Ctr., Berlin, 1978; rsch. advisor Ctr. for Clean Tech. and Environ. Policy, Twente U., The Netherlands, 1994—; sr. rsch. assoc. Carl Vinson Inst. of Govt., U. Ga., Athens, 1994—; mem., bd. editors Adminstrn. and Society, Blacksburg, Va., 1995—, Adminstrv. Theory and Praxis, San Francisco, 1995—, Beleidswetenschap Groningen, The Netherlands, 1997—, Evaluation and Program Planning, 2000—, Jour. Pub. Affairs Edn., 2001—. Co-author: American Government: Origins, Institutions and Public Policy, 1984, Regulatory Decision Making: The Virginia State Corporation Commission, 1984, Implementation Theory and Practice, 1990; editor: American Intergovernmental Relations, 1985, American Intergovernmental Relations, 2d rev. edit., 1993, American Intergovernmental Relations, 3d edit., 2000; co-editor: International Comparative Policy Research, 1992, Networks for Water Policy, 1995, Participation and the Quality of Environmental Decision Making, 1998, Advancing Public Management, 2000, Johns Hopkins Studies in Governance and Public Management, 2001—; author: Institutions, Processes and Outputs for Acidification, 1998—; contbr. articles to profl. jours. Recipient outstanding prof. award Ga. Students for Pub. Adminstrn., Athens, 1994, 95; vis. scholar Erasmus U., Rotterdam, The Netherlands, 1989, 94. Mem. ASPA (Burchfield award 1979, Mosher award 1987, Stone award 1999, Levine award 2002), Am. Polit. Sci. Assn. (chair pub. admin. sect. 1985), So. Polit. Sci. Assn. Home: 190 Avalon Dr Athens GA 30606-3235 Office: Univ Ga Sch Pub and Internat Affairs Baldwin Hall Athens GA 30602 E-mail: cmsotool@arches.uga.edu.

O'TOOLE, ROBERT JOHN, II, telemarketing consultant; b. Binghamton, N.Y., Mar. 24, 1951; s. Robert John and Joan Ceclia (Martin) O'T.; m. Donna Sue Stevenson, Jan. 28, 1978 (div. 1984); 1 child, Irene Grace; m. Karen Irene Cady, Dec. 21, 1994. Student, Corning (N.Y.) C.C., 1969-71, SUNY, Brockport, 1970-71; BA, Wake Forest U., 1973; MBA, Southwestern Coll., 1986. Asst. dir. devel. Duvall Home for Children, DeLand, Fla., 1978-81; gen. mgr. Royale Art Advt., Odessa, Tex., 1981-82; v.p. Barnes Assocs. Advt., 1982-84, Tex. Assn. for Blind Athletes, Austin, 1985-86; sales mgr. Los Amables Pub., Albuquerque, 1987-88; dir. devel. Albuquerque (N.Mex.) Help for the Homeless, 1988-91; chmn., CEO Advantage Ventures, Inc. (formerly Advantage Mktg., Inc.), Albuquerque, 1991—; CEO LaCourt, Medina & Sterling, 1993-96. Cons. Nat. Child Safety Coun., Austin, 1985, Assn. Profl. Fire Fighters, Austin, 1985, Reynolds Aluminum, Austin, 1986, N.Mex. State Legis., 1990, Children's Charity Fund, 1996, N.Am. Found. for AIDS Rsch., 1992-93, N.Am. Pediatric AIDS Found., 1995. Author: Telemarketing Tickets, 1988, Fishing Secrets of the Florida Poachers, 1993; founder, editor: (newspaper) Albuquerque Street News, 1990; publisher: (newspaper) The New Mexican, 1991; contbr. articles to jours. Founder Permian Basin Rehab. Ctr., Odessa, 1983, Albuquerque (N.Mex.) Help for the Homeless, Inc., 1988. Recipient Cert. of Merit, Small Bus. Adminstrn., Odessa, 1984. Mem. Direct Mktg. Assn., Amnesty Internat. Avocations: restoration of historic bldgs., archeo-geomantics, travel. Office: Advantage Ventures Inc 1019 2nd St SW # B Albuquerque NM 87102-4124

O'TOOLE, WILLIAM GEORGE, lawyer; b. Chgo., Oct. 25, 1934; s. George P. and Margaret (Battenhouse) O'T.; m. Gail M. McGregor, Aug. 13, 1960; children: Joyce M. Masterton, Paul G., Katherine A. Gorski. BS, U. Detroit, 1956; JD, DePaul U., 1961. Bar: Ill. 1961, U.S. Dist. Ct. (no. dist.) Ill. 1962. Assoc. Jaros, Tittle & O'Toole (and predecessor firm), Chgo., 1961-74, ptnr., 1974-90, pres., 1990—. Mem. ABA, Ill. Bar Assn., Ill. Mortgage Bankers Assn. (bd. dirs.), Chgo. Bar Assn., Southwest Bar Assn. (past pres.), Chgo. Athletic Assn., Abbey Springs Country Club, Ridge Country Club, Elks, K.C., Beta Alpha Psi. Roman Catholic. Home: 10736 S Kolmar Ave Oak Lawn IL 60453-5349 Office: Jaros Tittle & O'Toole 20 N Clark St Ste 510 Chicago IL 60602-4188

OTOROWSKI, CHRISTOPHER LEE, lawyer; b. Teaneck, N.J., Nov. 20, 1953; s. Wladyslaw Jerzy and Betty Lee (Robbins) O.; m. Shawn Elizabeth McGovern, Aug. 4, 1978; children: Kirsten, Hilary. BSBA cum laude, U. Denver, 1974, MBA, JD, U. Denver, 1977. Bar: Wash. 1977, Colo. 1977, U.S. Dist Ct. (we. dist.) D.C. 1977, U.S. Dist. Ct. (we. dist.) Wash. 1978. Asst. atty. gen. Wash. State Atty. Gen., Spokane, 1978-79; atty. Bassett, Gemson & Morrison, Seattle, 1979-81; pvt. practice, 1981-88; atty. Sullivan, Golden & Otorowski, 1988-91, Morrow & Otorowski, Bainbridge Island, 1996—; pvt. practice Morrow and Otorowski, Wash., 1991-96. Contbr. articles to profl. jours. Bd. dirs. Bainbridge Edn. Support Team, Bainbridge Island, 1991-97. Mem. Fed. Bar Assn. We. Dist. Wash. (sec. 1979-82, trustee 1990-93), Wash. State Trial Lawyers Assn. (bd. govs. 1991-93), Assn. Trial Lawyers Am., Seattle Tennis Club, Seattle Yacht Club. Avocations: photography, sailing. Office: 298 Winslow Way W Bainbridge Island WA 98110 E-mail: clo@medilaw.com.

OTOSHI, TOM YASUO, electrical engineer, consultant; b. Seattle, Sept. 4, 1931; s. Jitsuo and Shina O.; m. Haruko Shirley Yumiba, Oct. 13, 1963; children: John, Kathryn. BSEE, U. Wash., 1954, MSEE, 1957. Tech. staff Hughes Aircraft Co., Culver City, Calif., 1956-61; tech. sr. staff Jet Propulsion Lab. Calif. Inst. Tech., Pasadena, 1961—. Cons. in field. Contbr. articles to profl. jours.; patentee in field. Treas. West L.A. United Meth. Ch., 1958-60; active Towne Singers, La Canada, Calif. Recipient New Tech. NASA award, Exceptional Svc. medal, 1994. Fellow IEEE (life); mem. Sigma Xi, Tau Beta Pi. Home: 3551 Henrietta Ave La Crescenta CA 91214-1136 Office: Jet Propulsion Lab 4800 Oak Grove Dr Pasadena CA 91109-8001

OTSTOTT, CHARLES PADDOCK, company executive, retired army officer; b. Ft. Worth, June 2, 1937; s. Daniel Dushane and Sarah May (Paddock) O.; m. Candice Lee Curley, Nov. 6, 1982; 1 child, Kelley Ann; 1 child from previous marriage, James Boyd. BS, U.S. Mil. Acad., West Point, N.Y., 1960; MS, Purdue U., 1967. Commd. 2d lt. U.S. Army, 1960, advanced through grades to lt. gen., 1990; bn. advisor Republic of Vietnam, 1964-65; co. cmdr., S-3, 2d bn. 502 Inf. (Airborne) 101st Airborne Div., 1967-68; comdr. 1st bn. 46 Inf., 1st Armored Div., Erlangen, Fed. Republic Germany, 1976-78; student Nat. War Coll., Ft. McNair, D.C., 1978-79; comdr. 2d brigade 9th High Tech. Light Div., Ft. Lewis, Wash., 1979-82, chief of staff, 1982-83; exec. to SACEUR Supreme Hdqrs. Allied Powers Europe, Belgium, 1983-85; asst. div. comdr. 1st Armored Div., Bamberg, Fed. Republic Germany, 1985-86; comdg. gen. Combined Arms Combat Devel. Activity, Ft. Leavenworth, Kans., 1986-88, 25th Inf. Div. (Light), Schofield Barracks, Hawaii, 1988-90; dep. chmn. NATO Mil. Com., Brussels, 1990-92; ret., 1992; pvt. cons. strategic planning, 1992-94; with Innovative Logistics Techniques (Innolog, Inc.), 1994-96; v.p. advanced program devel. Bolt, Beranek, and Newman (BBN), 1996-99; v.p. command and control sys. Global InfoTek, 1999—2001; pvt. cons., 2001—. Instr then asst, prof. dept. physics U.S. Mil. Acad., West Point, 1968—71. Chmn. adv. com. Brussels Am. Sch., 1990-92. Decorated Def. D.S.M., Army D.S.M., Def. Superior Svc. medal, Silver Star, Legion of Merit. Avocations: handball, jogging, picture framing, woodworking. E-mail: cotstott@aol.com.

OTT, ANDREW EDUARD, lawyer; b. Vancouver, B.C., Can., Sept. 23, 1962; s. Eduard Karl and Elfriede Marie (Petryc) O. BA in English, Seattle U., 1986, JD, 1989; D (hon.), U. Graz, Austria, 1986. Bar: Wash. 1990, U.S. Dist. Ct. (we. dist.) Wash. 1992. Contract atty. Keller Rohrback, Seattle, Lieff Cabraser Heimann & Bernstein, San Francisco, Jamin, Ebell, Schmitt & Mason, Kodiak, Alaska, 1989—. Cons. OMNI Tech. Engring., Bothell, Wash., 1986-2000. Actor musicals and theater, 1992, 93, 95, 96, 98, 99, 2000; musician Cmty. Orch. and Jazz, 1990-2000. Trustee Kodiak Arts Coun. Mem. ABA, ATLA, Nat. Assn. Self-Employed. Avocations: snow skiing, soccer, bike riding, running, acting. Office: Jamin Ebell Schmitt & Mason 323 Carolyn Ave Kodiak AK 99615-6348 E-mail: Andrew@JESMKOD.com.

OTT, C(LARENCE) H(ENRY), citizen ambassador, accounting educator; b. Richmond, Mich., Jan. 20, 1918; s. Ferdinand and Wilhelmina (Radkte) O.; m. Helen Louis McKay, Oct. 29, 1942 (dec. Apr. 1994); children: James Richard, Dennis McKay, Richard Darrel, Delene Michelle. BA, Valparaiso U., 1940; MBA, Northwestern U., 1970; PhD, Southeastern U., 1980. CPA, N.Y.; cert. mgmt. acct., N.Y. Chief acct. G.E. X-Ray Corp., Chgo., 1940-41; pub. auditor Arthur Andersen & Co., 1941-43; renegotiator contracts U.S. Army Air Corps, 1943-45; internal auditor David Bradley Mfg. (Sears), Bradley, Ill., 1945-48; contr., treas. Manco Mfg. Co., 1948-59; owner, operator Yellow-Checker Cab Co., Kankakee, Ill., 1959-70; chmn. acctg., prof. Rochester (N.Y.) Inst. Tech., 1970-73, Southwestern Mich. Coll., Dowagiac, Mich., 1973—; citizen amb. People to People Internat., Kansas City, Mo., 1992—. Curriculum advisor Southwestern Mich. Coll., Dowagiac, 1992—. Del. to Russia to faciliate their transition to Dem. form of govt.; del. leader Wharton Sch. Fin., U. Pa., Phila., 1992, Citizen Ambassador to many countries including Tahita, Bora Bora, Moorea, Cuba, Quebec, Can., Ecuador, Galapagos Islands, Israel, Egypt, Hong Kong, Mainland China, Greece, Greek Islands, Turkey, Singapore, India, Japan, France, Morocco, Portugal, Spain, Russia, British Isles, Italy, Iceland, Greenland. Mem. Nat. Assn. Accts., Inst. Cert. Mgmt. Accts., Planning Execs. Inst. (spkr., chmn.), Alpha Kappa Psi, Pi Kappa Alpha, Pi Gamma Mu. Republican. Avocations: travel, golf, bowling, reading, exercise. Home: 30992 Middle Crossing Rd Dowagiac MI 49047-9268

OTT, CLARICE JEAN, social worker; b. Delhi, N.Y., June 18, 1944; d. Luther Ernest and Clara Grace (Helman) O. BA in English, Elizabethtown Coll., 1966; MSW, U. Pitts., 1973. Cert. social worker; lic. social worker, Pa. Tchr. secondary English World Ministries, Ch. of the Brethren, Nigeria, West Africa, 1966-69; caseworker Westmoreland County Bd. Assistance, Greensburg, Pa., 1970-73, social worker, 1973-75; social worker, counselor Dundalk Youth Svc. Ctr., Balt., 1975-83, supr. counseling svcs., 1976-83; family counselor New Day, Inc., Johnstown, Pa., 1983-84; social worker Conemaugh Meml. Med. Ctr., 1984—. Mem. NASW. Mem. Ch. of the Brethren. Home: 1100 Grove Ave Windber PA 15963-1562

OTT, DAVID JAMES, diagnostic radiologist; b. Toledo, Apr. 19, 1946; s. Jack Melvin and Betty June (Miller) O.; m. Susan Emily Becker, July 12, 1970; 1 child, Stephen Louis. BS, U. Mich., 1967, MD, 1971. Intern Bowman Gray Sch. Medicine, Winston-Salem, N.C., 1971-72, resident in radiology, 1972-75, from instr. to assoc. prof. radiology, 1977-86, prof., 1986. Author: (with Meschan) Introduction to Diagnostic Imaging, 1984, (with Fayez) Hystero-Salpingography, 1991, 2d edit., 1998, (with Chen, Zagoria, Gelfand) Radiology of the Small Bowel, 1992, (with Gelfand, Chen) Manual of Gastrointestinal Fluoroscopy, 1996; editor: (with Castell) Gastroesophageal Reflux Disease, 1985, Polypoid Disease of the Colon, 1986, (with Chen, Pope) Basic Radiology, 1996; contbr. articles to profl. jours. Served to maj. Med. Service Corps, U.S. Army, 1975-77. Recipient Quinn Teaching award Bowman Gray Sch. Medicine 1984, 96. Fellow Am. Coll. Gastroenterology, Am. Coll. Radiology; mem. Radiol. Soc. N.Am., Am. Roentgen Ray Soc., Am. Gastroent. Assn., Soc. Gastrointestinal Radiologists. Unitarian Universalist. Avocations: wine, music, woodworking. Office: Wake Forest U Sch Medicine Radiology Dept Winston Salem NC 27157-0001 E-mail: dott@wfubmc.edu.

OTT, DAVID MICHAEL, engineering company executive; b. Glendale, Calif., Feb. 24, 1952; s. Frank Michael and Roberta (Michie) O.; m. Cynthia Dianne Bunce. BSEE, U. Calif., Berkeley, 1974. Electronic engr. Teknekron Inc., Berkeley, 1974-79; chief engr. TCI, 1979-83; div. mgr. Integrated Automation Inc., Alameda, Calif., 1983-87, Litton Indsl. Automation, Alameda, 1987-92; founder, chmn. Picture Elements Inc., Berkeley, 1992—. Inventor method for verifying denomination of currency, method for processing digited images, automatic document image revision. Mem. IEEE, AAAS, Assn. Computing Machinery, Union of Concerned Scientists. Office: Picture Elements Inc 777 Panoramic Way Berkeley CA 94704-2538

OTT, DORIS ANN, librarian; b. Elgin, N.D., Sept. 24, 1942; d. Oscar Edward Hirning and Lorraine Wilhelmina Greubele; m. Richard Donald Ott, Nov. 21, 1998; m. Bernnett Gordon Reinke, Sept. 1961 (div.); 1 child, Scott Bernnett Reinke; m. James Lee Daugherty, June 1974 (div.). BS, Dickinson State U., 1964; MLS, George Peabody Coll., 1965. Lic. Ind. life tchr. Elem. tchr. Mott (N.D.) Pub. Schs., 1963-64; asst. prof. Dickinson (N.D.) State U., 1965-73; media specialist Minot (N.D.) Pub. Schs., 1973-74; head tech. svcs. Bartholomew County Libr., Columbus, Ind., 1974-75; media specialist Rushville (Ind.) Pub. Schs., 1975-86; head interlibr. loan N.D. State Libr., Bismarck, 1986-87, asst. state libr., 1987—2001, state libr., 2001—. Image cons. Beauty For All Seasons, 1984—. Mem. Humane Soc. Mem. ALA, N.D. Libr. Assn., Mountain Plains Libr. Assn. Avocation: image consulting. Office: ND State Libr 604 E Boulevard Ave Dept 250 Bismarck ND 58505-0800 E-mail: dott@state.nd.us.

OTT, GILBERT RUSSELL, JR. lawyer; b. Bklyn., Apr. 15, 1943; s. Gilbert Russell Sr. and Bettina Rose (Ferrel) O.; m. Lisa S. Weatherford, Apr. 12, 1986; children: Gilbert R. III, Laura Elisabeth. BA, Yale U., 1965; JD, MBA, Columbia U., 1969. Bar: N.Y. 1970. Assoc. Chadbourne, Parke, Whiteside & Wolff, N.Y.C., 1969-72, LeBoeuf, Lamb, Leiby & MacRae, N.Y.C., 1972-78; assoc. gen. counsel Kidder, Peabody & Co., Inc., 1978-96, asst. sec., 1978-91, asst. v.p., 1978-79, v.p., 1979-86, mng. dir., 1986-91, sr. v.p., sec., 1992-96; v.p. Kidder, Peabody Group Inc., 1989-96, asst. sec., 1986-96; exec. v.p., gen. counsel, sec. Rodman & Renshaw Capital Group, Inc., Chgo. and N.Y.C., 1996-98; counsel Cadwalader, Wickersham & Taft, N.Y.C., 1998-99; dep. gen. counsel Datek Online Holdings Corp., Jersey City, 1999—, N.Y.C. Mem. Assn. of Bar of City of N.Y., Cold Spring Harbor Lab. Assn. (dir.), Piping Rock Club, Univ. Club. Home: 260 Highwood Cir Oyster Bay NY 11771-3205 E-mail: gott@datek.com.

OTT, JAMES DANIEL, journalist, educator; b. Dayton, Ky., Mar. 24, 1938; s. Arthur Daniel and Grace Mary (Bennett) O.; m. Charlotte Elizabeth Freihofer, Aug. 1, 1964; children: Alec, Stephen, Anthony, James, Michael. AB in English Lit., Thomas More Coll., 1961; MEd in Comms. Arts, Xavier U., 1973. Reporter Cin. Enquirer, 1959-65, Ky. editor, 1965-69; pub. rels. dir. Thomas More Coll., Crestview Hills, Ky., 1969-74, Cath. U. Am., Washington, 1974-78; transport editor Aviation Week and Space Tech., 1978-84, sr. transport editor, 1984-94, contbg. editor Ft. Mitchell, Ky., 1994—. Freelance writer, McGraw-Hill, Inc., Ft. Mitchell; online editor Aviation Week Group, Ft. Mitchell. Author: Jets, Airliners of the Golden Age, 1993, Airline Odyssey, 1995. Mem. adv. bd. The Messenger, 1999—. With USAR, 1956-63. Mem. Soc. Aerospace Communicators, Cathedral Found. (bd. dirs. 1997—). Republican. Roman Catholic. Avocations: swimming, hiking, reading. E-mail: jim. Office: Aviation Week and Space Tech 825 Rosewood Dr Crescent Springs KY 41017 E-mail: ott@aviationnow.com.

OTT, JOHN HARLOW, museum administrator; b. Ottawa, Ont., Can., Jan. 29, 1944; s. Thomas Gordon and Lois Elizabeth (Wright) O.; m. Lili Reineck, May 20, 1972; children— Jennie Elizabeth, Michael James Hutchins BA, Eastern Bapt. Coll., St. David's, Pa., 1966; MA, SUNY-Oneonta, 1975; postgrad. Mus. Mgmt. Inst., U. Calif., Berkeley, 1987. Curator Hancock Shaker Village, Inc., Pittsfield, Mass., 1970-72, dir., 1972-83; exec. dir. Atlanta Hist. Soc., 1983-91, B&O R.R. Mus., Inc., Balt., 1991-99, The Nat. Heritage Mus., Lexington, Mass., 1999—. Curator Ga. Hist. Soc., Savannah, 1983-87; mem. adv. bd. Concord (Mass.) Mus. Author: Hancock Shaker Village, 1976 Bd. dirs. Devens Hist. Mus., 2001—. Decorated Bronze Star; named mus. profl. of yr. in Ga., 1991, profl. of yr. Acad. for Travel, Hospitality and Tourism, 1996. Mem. Am. Assn. Mus. (accrediting officer 1982—), Am. Assn. for State and Local History, Mid-Atlantic Mus. Assn., Ga. Soc. Assn. Execs., Nat. Hist. Communal Socs. Assn. (pres. 1983-84), Nat. Soc. Fund Raising Execs. (bd. dirs. Ga. chpt. 1985-91, bd. dirs. Md. chpt. 1993), Balt. City C. of C. (bd. dirs., past chmn.), Md.Assn. History Mus. (bd. dirs. 1996), Freedom's Way Heritage Assn. (bd. dirs. 2000—), Lexington C. of C. (chmn. 2002-); bd. dirs. Merrimack Valley Convention & Vis. Bureau. Republican. Episcopalian. Office: The Nat Heritage Mus 33 Marrett Rd Lexington MA 02421-5703 E-mail: jott@monh.org.

OTT, JOSEPH JOHN, computer specialist, writer; b. Williamsport, Pa., Feb. 22, 1931; s. Chester Leroy and Agnes Julia (Lyaski) O.; divorced; children: Susan, John, Carol. BA, Lycoming Coll., 1961. Computer specialist Dept. Commerce, Washington, 1961-64, Dept. HHS, Washington, 1964-81; freelance writer, 1984; contbg. editor Gulf Coast Fisherman, Port Lavaca, Tex., 1992. Sgt. USMC, 1950-54, Korea. Mem. Am. Legion (reporter 1954-56, 86-92), NRA, 1st Marine Divsn. Assn., A/1/7 Marine Assn. Democrat. Roman Catholic. Avocations: hunting, fishing, marksmanship.

OTT, KARL OTTO, nuclear engineering educator, consultant; b. Hanau, Germany, Dec. 24, 1925; came to U.S., 1967, naturalized, 1987; s. Johann Josef and Eva (Bergmann) O.; m. Gunhild G. Göring, Sept. 18, 1958 (div. 1986); children: Martina, Monika; m. Birgit Fehse, May 1, 1995. BS, J. W. von Goethe U., Frankfurt, Germany, 1948; MS, G. August U., Göttingen, Fed. Republic Germany, 1953, PhD, 1958. Physicist Nuclear Rsch. Ctr., Karlsruhe, Fed. Republic Germany, 1958-67, sect. head Fed. Republic Germany, 1962-67; prof. Sch. Nuclear Engring. Purdue U., West Lafayette, Ind., 1967-2001, prof. emeritus, 2001—. Cons. Argonne (Ill.) Nat. Lab., 1967—; prof. emeritus, 2001—. Author: Nuclear Reactor Statics, 1983, 2nd edit., 1989, Nuclear Reactor Dynamics, 1985, Chinese edit., 1991. Fellow Am. Nuclear Soc. (Arthur Holly Compton award 1993). Office: Sch Nuclear Engring Purdue U Lafayette IN 47907-1290 E-mail: ott@ecn.purdue.edu.

OTT, WALTER RICHARD, academic administrator; b. Bklyn., Jan. 20, 1943; s. Harold Vincent and Mary Elizabeth (Butler) Ott; m. Carla M. Narret, May 27, 2001; children: Regina Winter Burrell, Christina W. Chiappetta, Walter R. Jr. BS in Ceramic Engring., Va. Poly. Inst. and State U., 1965; MS in Ceramic Engring., U. Ill., 1967; PhD in Ceramic Engring., Rutgers U., 1969. Registered profl. engr., Pa. Process engr. Corning Inc., Buckhannon, W.Va., 1965-66; staff research engr. Champion Spark Plug Co., Detroit, 1969-70; prof. engring. Rutgers U., New Brunswick, N.J., 1970-80; dean, assoc. provost N.Y. State Coll. Ceramics, Alfred, 1980-88; provost, chief acad. officer Alfred U., 1988-2000; pres. Predictive Edge, Inc., West Orange, NJ, 2000—. Rsch. assoc. Atomic Energy Commn.-E.I. duPont de Nemours, Aiken, S.C., 1971; cons. Haight & Hofeldt Inc., Chgo., 1984-88, Pillsbury, Mpls., 1977-79, Ctr. for Profl. Advancement, New Brunswick, 1971-79, Hammond (Ind.) Lead Products, 1970-80; bd. dirs. Victor (N.Y.) Insulator Inc., UNIPEG, 1987-88; treas., Alfred Tech. Resources N.Y.; bd. dirs. Grads Found., N.Y.C. Contbr. articles to profl. jours.; patentee in field. Recipient Ralph Teetor award Soc. Automotive Engrs., 1973, PACE award Nat. Inst. Ceramic Engrs., 1975, Ann. award Ceramic Assn. N.J., 1980; named to Greaves Walker Roll, Keramos, 1991. Fellow Am. Ceramic Soc. (trustee 1980-83, v.p. 1988-89); mem. Ceramic Ednl. Coun. (pres. 1976-77), Ceramic Assn. N.Y. (treas. 1980-88, bd. dirs.), Ceramic Assn. N.J. (bd. dirs. 1974-80), Keramos (pres. 1982-84, Greaves-Walker Roll of Honor 1991), Tau Beta Pi. Avocations: tennis, reading. Home: 165 Clarken Dr West Orange NJ 07052-3429 Office: PO Box 144 West Orange NJ 07052-0144

OTT, WAYNE ROBERT, environmental engineer; b. San Mateo, Calif., Feb. 2, 1940; s. Florian Funstan and Evelyn Virginia (Smith) O.; m. Patricia Faustina Bertuzzi, June 28, 1967 (div. 1983). BA in Econs., Claremont McKenna Coll., 1962; BSEE, Stanford U., 1963, MS in Engring, 1965, MA in Comm., 1966, PhD in Environ. Engring., 1971. Commd. lt. USPHS, 1966, advanced to capt., 1986; chief lab. ops. br. U.S. EPA, Washington, 1971-73, sr. systems analyst, 1973-79, sr. rsch. engr., 1981-84, chief air toxics and radiation monitoring rsch. staff, 1984-90; vis. scientist dept. stats. Stanford (Calif.) U., 1979-81, 90—; vis. scholar Ctr. for Risk Analysis and dept. stats., civil engring., 1990-93; sr. environ. engr., EPA Atmospheric Rsch. and Exposure Assessment Lab, 1993-95; consulting prof. of civil engring. Stanford (Calif.) U., 1995—; dir. field studies Calif. Environ. Tobacco Smoke Study, 1993-95. Author: Environmental Indices: Theory and Practice, 1976, Environmental Statistics and Data Analysis, 1995; contbr. articles on indoor air pollution, total human exposure to chems., stochastic models of indoor exposure, motor vehicle exposures, personal monitoring instruments, and environ. tobacco smoke to profl. jours. Decorated Commendation medal USPHS, 1977; recipient Nat. Statistician award for outstanding contribution to environ. statistics EPA, 1995, Commendable Svc. Bronze medal for assessing human exposure from motor vehicle pollution, 1996. Mem. Internat. Soc. Exposure Analysis (v.p. 1989-90, Jerome J. Weselowski Internat. award for career achievement in exposure assessmemt 1995), Am. Statis. Assn., Am. Soc. for Quality Control, Air and Waste Mgmt. Assn., Internat. Soc. Indoor Air Quality and Climate, Phi Beta Kappa, Sigma Xi, Tau Beta Pi, Kappa Mu Epsilon. Democrat. Clubs: Theater, Jazz, Sierra. Avocations: hiking, photography, model trains, jazz recording. Developer nationally uniform air pollution index, first total human exposure activity pattern models. Home: 1008 Cardiff Ln Redwood City CA 94061-3678 Office: Stanford U Dept Stats Sequoia Hall Stanford CA 94305

OTTAWAY, DAVID BLACKBURNE, journalist; b. Endicott, N.Y., Oct. 27, 1939; s. James Haller Sr. and Ruth Blackburne (Hart) O.; m. Marina Seassaro, July 18, 1963; children: Eric, Robin. BA, Harvard U., 1962; MA, Columbia U., 1964, PhD, 1972. Dep. fgn. editor Washington Post, 1971-73, Africa corr., 1974-79, Mid. East corr., 1981-85, nat. security corr., 1985-90, South Africa corr., 1990-92, Ea., So. and Ctrl. South Europe corr., 1992-94, investigative reporter, 1994—. Chmn., pres. Buck Hill Falls Co., Buck Hills, Pa., 1995-98, bd. dirs., 1999—. Co-author: (with Marina Ottaway) Algeria - The Politics of a Socialist Revolution, 1965, Ethiopia - Empire in Revolution, 1978, Afrocommunism, 1983; author: Chained Together - Mandela, De Klerk and the Struggle to Remake South Africa, 1993. Pres. NBO Found., 1995-98, trustee, 1998—; trustee Lawrenceville Sch., 1998—. Mem. Harvard Club of Washington. Avocations: skiing, hiking, jogging, tennis. Office: Washington Post 1150 15th St NW Washington DC 20071-0002

OTTAWAY, JAMES HALLER, JR. newspaper publisher; b. Binghamton, N.Y., Mar. 24, 1938; s. James Haller and Ruth Blackburne (Hart) O.; m. Mary Warren Hyde, June 16, 1959; children— Alexandra, Christopher, Jay. Grad., Phillips Exeter Acad., 1955; BA, Yale U., 1960; DJournalism (hon.), Suffolk U., Boston, 1970; DBA (hon.), Southeastern Mass. U., 1984. 1962reporter, mgmt. trainee New-Times, Danbury, Conn., 1960; reporter, mgmt. trainee Times Herald-Record, Middletown, NY, 1962—63; editor Pocono Record, Stroudsburg, Pa., 1963—65; publisher New Bedford (Mass.) Standard-Times, 1965—70; pres. Ottaway Newspapers, Inc., Campbell Hall, NY, 1970—85, CEO, 1976—88, chmn. bd., 1979—, CEO, 1998—. V.p. Dow Jones & Co., 1980-86, sr. v.p., 1986—, also bd. dirs.; dir., vice-chmn. Associated Press, 1982-91. Past. v.p. bd. trustees Phillips Exeter Acad.; trustee Am. Sch. Classical Studies at Athens, chmn., 1996-99; trustee, vice-chmn. Storm King Art Ctr., Mountainville, N.Y., World Wildlife Fund USA, 1993-96; trustee Bard Coll., 1996—; chmn. World Press Freedom Com., 1996—; past pres., bd. dirs. Arden Hill Hosp. Found., Goshen, N.Y. Mem. Am. Newspaper Pubs. Assn., Am. Soc. Newspaper Editors. Episcopalian. Office: PO Box 401 Campbell Hall NY 10916-0401 also: Dow Jones & Co Inc 200 Liberty St Fl 11 New York NY 10281-1003 E-mail: jottaway@ottaway.com.

OTTE, LYNDA ELLEN, neonatal nurse; b. Washington, Apr. 14, 1946; d. Robert Grover and Esther Ellen (Watson) O. BSN, U. Md., 1968. RNC; cert. Nat. Cert. Corp. for the Ob-Gyn. and Neonatal Nursing Specialties. Staff nurse Children's Hosp., Washington, 1968-73, 76-78, nursery instr., 1973-74, primary nurse II, 1978-85, clin. mgr. I, 1985-88, 91-93, clin. nurse III, 1988-91; clin. nurse II, 1993-94; staff nurse George Washington U. Hosp., Washington, 1975-76, Anne Arundel Med. Ctr., Annapolis, Md., 1994—. Treas. bd. dirs. Prince George's Oak Pond Homeowners Assn., Bowie, Md., 1987—2000, v.p., 2000—; vol. for ann. fund drive Am. Cancer Soc. Residential Campaign, 1989, 1991—93; vol. Mothers March of Dimes, 1993—96, 1999—2001, Am. Diabetes Assn. fund drive, 1994—96, Nat. Kidney Found. Ask Your Neighbor campaign, 1997, Am. Lung Assn. of Md., 1997—2001, Leukemia and Lymphoma Soc. Am. Friends and Neighbors Campaign, 1997, 1999—2001. Mem. Nat. Assn. Neonatal Nurses (charter), Washington Met. Assn. Neonatal Nurses (charter, co-chair strategic planning com. 1990-92, pres.-elect 1992-94, pres. 1994-96, co-chmn. mem. com. 1996—). Baptist. Avocations: reading, knitting, gardening, travel. Home: 3060 New Oak Ln Bowie MD 20716-1350 Office: Anne Arundel Med Ctr Rebecca Clatanoff Pavilion 2001 Medical Pkwy Annapolis MD 21401-3030 E-mail: lo99@erols.com.

OTTE, PAUL JOHN, academic administrator, consultant, trainer; b. Detroit, July 10, 1943; s. Melvin John Otte and Anne Marie (Meyers) Hirsch; children: Deanna Kropf, John. BS, Wayne State U., 1968, MBA, 1969; EdD, Western Mich. U., 1983. With Detroit Bank and Trust Co., 1965-68; teaching fellow Wayne State U., Detroit, 1968-69; auditor, mgr. Arthur Young & Co., 1969-75; contr., dir. Macomb Community Coll., Warren, Mich., 1975-79, v.p. bus., 1979-86; pres. Franklin U., Columbus, Ohio, 1986—, prof. undergrad. and grad. programs, 1986—. Author various tng. manuals, 1982. Cpl. USMC, 1961-65. Teaching fellow Wayne State U., 1968-69. Mem. AICPA, Mich. Assn. CPAs (chmn. continuing profl. edn. com. 1980-82, leadership com. 1981-83), Nat. Assn. Coll. and Univ. Bus. Officers (acctg. prins. com. 1986), Assn. Ind. Colls. and Univs. Ohio (bd. dirs.), Greater Detroit C. of C. (leadership award 1983), Columbus C. of C. (info. svc. com.). Roman Catholic. Avocations: travel, speaking engagements. Office: Franklin U 201 S Grant Ave Columbus OH 43215-5399

OTTEN, ARTHUR EDWARD, JR. lawyer, corporate executive; b. Buffalo, Oct. 11, 1930; s. Arthur Edward Sr. and Margaret (Ambrusko) O.; m. Mary Therese Torri, Oct. 1, 1960; children: Margaret, Michael, Maureen Staley, Suzanne Hoodecheck, Jennifer Shankle. BA, Hamilton Coll., 1952; JD, Yale U., 1955. Bar: N.Y. 1955, Colo. 1959. Assoc. Hodges, Silverstein, Hodges & Harrington, Denver, 1959-64; ptnr. Hodges, Kerwin, Otten & Weeks (predecessor firms), 1964-73, Davis, Graham & Stubbs, Denver, 1973-86; gen. counsel Colo. Nat. Bankshares, Inc., 1973-93; mem. Otten, Johnson, Robinson, Neff & Ragonetti, P.C., Denver, 1986—. Rec. sec. Colo. Nat. Bankshares, Inc., Denver, 1983-93; gen. counsel Regis U., Denver, 1994-99; mediator Denver Dist. Ct., 1997-99; com. bd. Centura Health, Denver, St. Anthony Hosps., Denver. Bd. dirs. Cath. Charities Archdiocese of Denver, 1998—. Lt. USN, 1955-59. Mem. ABA, Colo. Bar Assn., Denver Bar Assn., Am. Arbitration Assn. (panel arbitrators, large complex case panel, mediator panel), Nat. Assn. Securities Dealers (bd. arbitrators), Law club, Univ. Club, Denver Mile High Rotary (pres. 1992-93), Phi Delta Phi. Republican. Roman Catholic. Avocations: hiking, biking, church activities. Home: 3774 S Niagara Way Denver CO 80237-1248 Office: Otten Johnson Robinson Neff & Ragonetti PC 950 17th St Ste 1600 Denver CO 80202-2828 E-mail: aeotten@ojrnr.com.

OTTEN, JEFFREY, former hospital administrator; Pres. and CEO Brigham and Women's Hosp., Boston, 1994—2002; pres. JRO Ventures, 2002—. Chmn. Ardais Corp.; bd. mem. Fossa. Recipient Outstanding Leadership in Healthcare, Linkage, Inc., 2002. Office: Ardais Corp 128 Spring St Lexington MA 02421*

OTTEN, RICHARD HEUSE, physician; b. Indpls., Aug. 22, 1944; s. Claude Frederick and Lois Jean (Heuse) O.; m. Paulette Ballrd, June 8, 1968 (dec. Oct. 1990); children: David, Dennis; m. Maribeth Deguzman, Nov. 11, 1995; children: Richard Jr., Kristen Lois. BS, Wabash Coll., 1966; MD, Ind. U., 1970. Diplomate Am. Bd. Family Practice. Commnd. 2d lt. USN, 1975, advanced through grades to capt., 1995, ret., 1995; physician Metro Health, Indpls., 1995-96; locum tenens physician, 1996-98; physician Sharp Med. Group, San Diego, 1998—. Fellow Am. Acad. Family Practice. Republican. Methodist. Avocations: traveling, snowskiing, running. Home and Office: 1256 Santa Lucia Rd Chula Vista CA 91913-1502

OTTEN, WESLEY PAUL, lawyer; b. Duluth, Minn., July 29, 1959; s. Wesley Leo and Mary Ellen Otten; m. Deborah Smoger, Dec. 31, 1987; children: James, Elizabeth. BA, U. Minn., Duluth, 1982; JD, William Mitchell Coll. Law, St. Paul, 1986. Bar: Minn. 1988, U.S. Dist. Ct. Minn. 1990. Pvt. practice Otten Law Offices, Burnsville, Minn., 1988-96; mng. ptnr. Otten & Knutson, P.L.L.P., 1996-98; pres. Otten & Assocs., P.A., 1999—. Chmn. bd. Cmty. Action Coun., Inc., Lakeville, Minn., 1998-2000. Mem. ATLA, Minn. Bar Assn., Minn. Trial Lawyers Assn. (bd. govs.), Dakota County Bar Assn. Republican. Lutheran. Avocations: sports, travel. Fax: 952736340070. E-mail: wpotten@aol.com.

OTTENSMEYER, DAVID JOSEPH, retired neurosurgeon, retired healthcare executive; b. Nashville, Jan. 29, 1930; s. Raymond Stanley and Glenda Jessie Ottensmeyer; m. Mary Jean Langley, June 30, 1954; children: Kathryn Joan, Martha Langley BA, Wis. State U., Superior, 1951; MD, U. Wis., Madison, 1959; MS in Health Svcs. Adminstrn., Coll. St. Francis, 1985. Diplomate Am. Bd. Neurological Surgery. Intern then resident in gen. surgery Univ. Hosps., Madison, Wis., 1959-61, resident in neurol. surgery, 1962—65; staff neurosurgeon Marshfield Clinic, Wis., 1965-76; from instr. of neurol. surgery to clin. asst. prof. U. Wis. Med. Sch., Madison, 1964-77; CEO Lovelace Med. Ctr., Albuquerque, 1976-86, chmn., 1986-91; clin. prof. community medicine U. N.Mex., 1977-79, clin. prof. neurol. surgery, 1979-92; exec. v.p., chief med. officer Equicor, 1986-90; part-time cons. pvt. practice, 1996. Bd. dirs. AABC; v.p. Marshfield Clinic, 1970-71, pres., CEO, 1972-75; pres., CEO The Lovelace Insts., 1991-96; sr. v.p., chief med. officer Travelers Ins. Co., 1990-91; served on numerous adv. and com. posts. Contbr. articles to profl. jours. Col. USAR, 1960-90. Fellow ACS, Am. Coll. Physician Execs. (pres. 1985-86); mem. Am. Group Practice Assn. (pres. 1983-84), Am. Bd. Med. Mgmt. (bd. dirs. 1989-95, chmn. 1995). Republican. Episcopalian. Avocations: flying, golf, travel. Address: 102 Crofton Ct Fairhope AL 36532-6306 E-mail: ottensmeyer@msn.com.

OTTENSTEIN, DONALD, psychiatrist; b. N.Y.C., Feb. 2, 1922; s. Morris Zachary and Sadelle (Fertig) O.; m. Leah May Helpern, Dec. 24, 1944; children: Paul, John, Beth, Daniel. BS, Harvard U., 1942; MD, Columbia U. Intern Boston City Hosp., 1948-49; resident Mass. Mental Health Ctr., Boston, 1950-53; fellow D.O. Thom Clinic, 1955-56; cons. Met. State Hosp., Waltham, Mass., 1955-58; dir. South Shore Mental Health Ctr., Quincy, 1959-67; asst. psychiatrist Beth Israel Hosp., Boston, 1959—. Attending psychiatrist McLean Hosp., Belmont, Mass., 1970-85, Newton Wellesley Hosp., 1979-85; asst. clin. prof. Harvard U. Med. Sch., Boston, 1974-89. Contbr. articles to profl. jours. Served to capt. U.S. Army, 1953-55. Fellow Mass. Med. Soc., Am. Psychiat. Assn., Am. Orthopsychiat. Assn., Am. Acad. Child Psychiatry. Avocations: art collecting, tennis. Home and Office: 65 Gale Rd Belmont MA 02478-3945

OTTER, CLEMENT LEROY (BUTCH OTTER), congressman; b. Caldwell, Idaho, May 3, 1942; s. Joseph Bernard and Regina Mary (Buser) O.; m. Gay Corinne Simplot, Dec. 28, 1964; children: John Simplot, Carolyn Lee, Kimberly Dawn, Corinne Marie. BA in Polit. Sci., Coll. Idaho, 1967; PhD, Mindanao State U., 1980. Mgr. J.R. Simplot Co., Caldwell, Idaho, 1971-76, asst. to v.p. adminstrn., 1976-78, v.p. adminstrn., 1978-82, internat. pres., from 1982, now v.p.; lt. gov. State of Idaho, Boise, 1987-2000; mem. U.S. Congress from Idaho 1st Dist., 2001—; mem. transp. and infrastructure, resources and govt. reform coms. Mem. Presdl. Task Force-AID, Washington, 1982-84; com. mem. invest tech. devel. State Adv. Council, Washington, 1983-84; mem. exec. council Bretton Woods Com., 1984—; mem. U.S. C. of C., Washington, 1983-84. Mem. Young Pres.' Orgn., Sales and Mktg. Execs., Idaho Assn. Commerce and Industry, Idaho Agrl. Leadership Council, Idaho Ctr. for Arts, Idaho Internat. Trade Council, Pacific N.W. Waterways Assn., N.W. Food Producers, Ducks Unltd. Clubs: Arid, Hillcrest Country. Lodges: Moose, Elks. Republican. Roman Catholic. Avocations: jogging, music, art collecting, horse training, fishing. Office: US Ho of Reps 1711 Longworth HOB Washington DC 20515*

OTTER, JOHN MARTIN, III, television advertising consultant, retired; b. Pottsville, Pa., Nov. 26, 1930; s. John Martin and Ruth A. (Knipe) O.; m. Susan Morgan Eaves, May 21, 1960; children— John Martin, IV, Robert Marshal. BA, Cornell U., 1953. Comml. producer Arlene Frances Home Show, 1953-55; producer Dave Garroway Today Show, 1956-59; dir. spl. programs sales NBC-TV, 1959-61, v.p. nat. sales, 1962-64, v.p. charge sales, 1965-73; cons. sta. WNET-TV, Practising Law Inst., also Dragonwk Prodns., 1973-75; v.p., dir. network programming SSC&B Inc., 1975-78; sr. v.p., dir. network programming SSC&B Lintas Worldwide, N.Y.C., 1978-84; sr. v.p. dir. nat. broadcast McCann-Erickson U.S.A., 1984-88; sr. v.p. spl. projects McCann-Erickson Worldwide, 1988; pres. RETTO Internat. Inc., 1989-94; retired, 1994. Mem. The Landings Club, The Landings Yacht Club. Republican. Episcopalian. Home: Four Seafarer's Cir Savannah GA 31411

OTTERBOURG, ROBERT KENNETH, public relations consultant, writer; b. N.Y.C., Jan. 26, 1930; s. Albert Marcus and Frances (Roset) O.; m. Susan Delman, Apr. 14, 1957; children— Laura Ann, Kenneth Douglas. BA, Colgate U., 1951; MS, Columbia U., 1954. Reporter, editor Fairchild Publs., N.Y.C., 1953-57; editor McGraw-Hill Pub. Co., 1957-59; v.p. pub. rels. Charles Mathieu & Co., 1959-61; pres. pub. rels. Otterbourg & Co., N.Y.C., 1962-69, 71—. Sr. v.p. Daniel J. Edelman, 1970. Author: It's Never Too Late, 1993, Retire and Thrive, 1995, 2d edit., 1999, Switching Careers, 2001; contbr. articles to profl. and consumer jours. Legis. asst. N.Y. State Senate, 1962-64; mem. exec. com. Columbia U. Sch. Journalism, N.Y.C., 1980-93, pres. exec. com., 1985-87; trustee Flat Rock Nature Ctr., pres., 1991-92; trustee Planned Parenthood Bergen County, 1985-88, v.p., 1986-88; trustee Urban League for Bergen County, 1988-93; chmn. Durham County Libr. Exec. Svc. Corps of the Greater Triangle; bd. dirs. Colgate U. Alumni Corp., 1969-93. 1st lt. USAF, 1951-53. Mem. Pub. Rels. Soc. Am., Columbia U. Grad. Sch. Journalism Alumni Assn. (pres. 1985-87). Democrat. Jewish. Home and Office: 68 Beverly Dr Durham NC 27707-2224

OTTERNESS, TOM, artist; b. Wichita, Kans., June 21, 1952; s. Garnet Otterness; m. Coleen Fitzgibbon; 1 child, Kelly. Student, Art Students League, 1970, Whittney Mus of Am. Art, 1973. One man shows include James Corcoran Gallery, Santa Monica, Brooke Alexander, N.Y., 1990, IVAM Centre Julio Gonzalez, Valencia, Spain, Portikus/Senckenbergmuseum, Frankfurt, Germany, Haags Gemeentemuseum, The Hague, The Netherlands, 1991, The Mus. Modern Art, 1987, Nancy Drysdale Gallery, Washington, 1991, Brooke Alexander, N.Y., 1992, Galerie Weber, Muenster, Westfalen, Germany, 1993, John Berggruen Gallery, San Francisco, 1993, 99, The Carnegie Mus. of Art, Pitts., 1993, Gallery of Contemporary Art, Krannert Art Mus., Champaign, Ill., 1994, MetroTech Ctr., Bklyn., 1995, Wichita Art Mus., 1995, Doris Freedman Plaza, 1995, Marlborough Gallery, N.Y., 1997, Marlborough Gallery, Madrid, Spain, 1999; exhibited in numerous group exhibitions including Whitney Mus. Am. Art, N.Y.C., 1985, Marlborough gallery, N.Y., 1995-96, Ubu Gallery, N.Y., 1995-96, Mus. of Modern Art, N.Y., 1996, The White House, Washington, 1996, Detroit Inst. of Arts, Mus. of Fine Arts, Boston, Mpls. Inst. of Arts, San Diego Mus. of Art, Ctr. for the Fine Arts, Miami, 1996-97, John Berggruen Gallery, 1997, San Jose Mus. of Art, Calif., 1997-98; pub. commns. include Edward R. Roybal Fed. Bldg., L.A., 1991, Gov. Nelson A. Rockefeller Park, N.Y.C., 1992, State Libr., Munster, Germany, 1993, Roosevelt Island, N.Y., 1996, Mark O. Hatfield U.S. Courthouse, Portland, 1997, Cleve. Pub.

Libr., 1998, Fed. Courthouse, Sacramento, 1999, Western Wash. U., Bellingham, 1999, Fed. Courthouse, Mpls., 1999, Hilton Times Sq., N.Y.C., 2000, MTA Arts for Transit, N.Y.C., 2000; represented in man pvt. and permanent collections including Bklyn. Mus., Carnegie Mus. Art, Guggenheim Mus., N.Y.C., Israel Mus., Jerusalem, IVAM Ctr. Julio Gonzalez, Valencia, Spain, Mus. Modern Art, N.Y.C., Whitney Mus. Am. Art, Miyagi Mus. Art, Sendai, Japan, Mus. Tamayo, Mexico City, Carl Sagan Discovery Ctr. Children's Hosp. Montefiore Med. Ctr., Bronx, N.Y., 2000. Founding mem. Collaborative Project, Inc., N.Y., 1977-82. Fellowship Nat. Endowment for the Arts, 1994. Studio: 202 Plymouth St Brooklyn NY 11201-1124 E-mail: ottrness@rcn.com.

OTTESON, HOLLY CAROL HARVICK-WARD, poet, artist, educator; b. Bismarck, N.D., Dec. 20, 1941; d. Bennie Arthur and Mary Laura (Bawden) Harvick; m. Denis Martin Ward, June 7, 1963 (dec. Dec. 1986); children: Scott John Ward Harvick, Lauren Heather Ward; m. Lyle William Otteson, Feb. 3, 1996 (dec. July 2001); stepchildren: Tracy, Kip, Joelle. BS, U. N.D., 1963; MA, U. Mo., Kansas City, 1982. Life cert. tchr. Mo., cert. counselor, tchr. N.D. Pvt. art tutor, Bismarck, ND, 1962—69, Bismarck, 2001—02, Oswego, NY, 1974. Author: (poetry) The Desert Sun, Anthology of N.Am. Poetry, A View from the Edge, New American Poetry Anthology, Great Poems of Our Time, Selected Works of Our World's Best Poets, Our Worlds Favorite Poems, Whispers in the Wind; poetry pub. various jours. Active Jr. Women's Symphony Alliance, Symphony Women's League; vol. Bismarck Pub. Schs., 2001. With USMC, 1980-88, U.S. Army, 1963. Recipient Silver and Bronze medals for working with disabled vets. Mem. AAUW, Internat. Soc. Poets, Nat. Geog. Soc., Nat. Hist. Trust, Smithsonian Instn., N.D. State Hist. Soc. (hon. mem.), Comdrs. Club of DAV, U. Mo. Womens Club, Kappa Alpha Theta. Republican. Lutheran. Avocations: dancing, diving, music, animals, plants. Home and Office: 1017 Mandan St Bismarck ND 58501

OTTINGER, MARY LOUISE, podiatrist; b. Valley City, N.D., July 8, 1956; d. Roy A. and Harriet A. Ottinger. BS, N.D. State U., 1978; D of Podiatric Medicine, Scholl. Coll. Podiatric Med., Chgo., 1983. Diplomate Am. Bd. Podiatric Surgery. Resident in podiatric medicine J.A. Haley VA Hosp., Tampa, Fla., 1983-84; podiatrist Med. Ctr. Podiatry Group, Augusta, Ga., 1984—. Author: (with others) Podiatric Dermatology, 1986. Fellow Am. Coll. Foot Surgeons; mem. Am. Podiatric Med. Assn., Ga. Podiatric Med. Assn., Am. Diabetes Assn. Methodist. Avocation: photography. Office: Foot and Ankle Group 811 13th St Ste 11 Augusta GA 30901

OTTINGER, MAURICE ARMAND, software engineer, educator; b. Knoxville, Tenn., July 10, 1962; s. Charles Love and Nana Marie (Matthews) O.; m. Lorie Lee Spin, July 20, 1985; children: Emily Marie, Maurice Allan. BMus magna cum laude, Carson-Newman Coll., 1984; MS in Adminstrn., Ctrl. Mich. U., Mt. Pleasant, 1986; postgrad., U. Tenn., 1993—. Course mgr. Jolly Frog Golf Course, Powell, Tenn., 1981-84; chief enlisted mgmt. U.S. Army Missile Sch., Redstone Arsenal, Ala., 1984-85; exec. officer/assoc. bandmaster 214th Army Band, Ft. McPherson, Ga., 1985-86; chief pers. svc. Hdqs. U.S. Army Garrison, 1986-87; chief adminstrn. and logistics U.S. Army Recruiting, Marietta, Ga., 1988-89; chief planning and ops. Hdqs. 8th Pers. Command, Seoul, Korea, 1990-91, hdqs. co. comdr., 1991-92; adminstrv. officer 3292d USAR Forces Sch., Knoxville, 1993-96; software engr. U.S. Army Info. Support Activity, St. Louis, 1996—. Lectr. bus. and fin. St. Leo Coll., Ft. McPherson, 1987-88; instr. data processing Ga. Mil. Coll., Ft. McPherson, 1987-89. Treas. HSW Orphanage Coun., Seoul, 1991-92; active Boy Scouts Am., 1986-92; choir dir. Post Chapel, Ft. McPherson, 1987-88; acting music dir., deacon Cumberland Bapt. Ch., Knoxville, 1993-96; deacon, asst. music dir. Geyer Rd. Bapt. Ch., Kirkwood, Mo., 1997—. Maj. U.S. Army, 1984—. Recipient Meritorious Svc. medal U.S. Army, 1992, 96, Commendation medal, 1988, 89, Achievement medal, 1985. Mem. Assn. of U.S. Army, Adjutant Gen.'s Corps Regimental Assn., Officers' Christian Fellowship of the U.S.A., Nat. Eagle Scout Assn., Rev. Officers Assn. of U.S., Interallied Confedn. of Res. Officers and Med. Res. Officers. Baptist. Avocations: study of comparative religion and Biblical prophecy. Office: US Army Info Support Activity 9700 Page Ave Saint Louis MO 63132-1547 Home: Apt Y204 450 S Peachtree Pkwy Peachtree Cty GA 30269-6839

OTTINO, JULIO MARIO, chemical engineering educator, scientist; b. La Plata, Buenos Aires, Argentina, May 22, 1951; came to U.S., 1976; naturalized, 1990; s. Julio Francisco and Nydia Judit (Zufriategui) O.; m. Alicia I. Löffler, Aug. 20, 1976; children: Jules Alessandro, Bertrand Julien. Diploma in Chem. Engring., U. La Plata, 1974; PhD in Chem. Engring., U. Minn., 1979; exec. program Kellogg Sch. Mgmt., Northwestern U., 1995. Instr. in chem. engring. U. Minn., Mpls., 1978-79; asst. prof. U. Mass., Amherst, 1979-83, adj. prof. polymer sci., 1979-91, assoc. prof. chem. engring., 1983-86, prof., 1986-91; Chevron vis. prof. chem. engring. Calif. Inst. Tech., Pasadena, 1985-86; sr. rsch. fellow Ctr. for Turbulence Rsch. Stanford (Calif.) U., 1989-90; Walter P.Murphy prof. chem. engring. Northwestern U., Evanston, Ill., 1991-2000, chmn. dept. chem. engring., 1992-2000; McCormick Inst. prof., 2000—; George T. Piercy Disting. prof. U. Minn., 1998, prof. mech. engring., 2001—. Cons. to U.S. and European corps.; Allan P. Colburn Meml. lectr. U. Del., 1987; Merck Sharp & Dohme lectr. U. P.R., 1989, Stanley Corrsin lectr. Johns Hopkins U., 1991; Centennial lectr. U. Md., 1994, William N. Lacey lectr. Calif. Inst. Tech., 1994, P. V. Danckwerts Meml. lectr. Inst. Chem. Engring., Eng., 1999; Robb lectr. Pa. State U., 2002; mem. tech. adv. bd. Dow Chem.; mem. bd. dirs. Coun. Chem. Rsch. Author: The Kinematics of Mixing: Stretching, Chaos and Transport, 1989; contbr. articles to profl. jours.; assoc. editor Physics Fluids A, 1991—; mem. editl. bd. Internat. Jour. Bifurc. Chaos, 1991—; assoc. editor Am. Inst. Chem. Engring. Jour., 1991-95, assoc. editor., 1995—; one man art exhibit, La Plata, 1974. Recipient Presdl. Young Investigator award NSF, 1984, Alpha Chi Sigma award AIChE, 1994, W.H. Walker award AIChE, 2001, E.W. Thiele award AIChE, Chgo., 2002; Univ. fellow U. Mass., 1988, J.S. Guggenheim fellow, 2001; Lacey lectureship, Calif. Inst. Tech., 1994, Danckwerts lectureship Royal Instn., 1999, Robb lectr. Pa. State U. Fellow Am. Phys. Soc., AAAS; mem. Am. Chem. Soc., Am. Phys. Soc., Soc. Rheology, Am. Soc. Engring. Edn., NAE, Sigma Xi (disting. lectr. 1997-99), Coun. for Chem. Rsch.(gov. bd. coun. 1999-2001). Achievements include research in fluid dynamics, chaos, complex systems, mixing and granular flows. Avocations: visual arts, painting. Home: 1092 Crescent Ln Winnetka IL 60093-1501 Office: Northwestern U Dept Chem Engring 2145 Sheridan Rd Evanston IL 60208-0834 E-mail: jm_ottino@northwestern.edu.

OTTLEY, JOHN K., JR. entrepreneur; b. Atlanta, Oct. 8, 1931; s. John King and Mary Hinton (Harvey) O.; widowed; four children. AB, Davidson Coll., 1953; MS, Columbia U., 1954; grad., U.S. Army Command/Staff Coll., Ft. Leavenworth, Kans., 1975, Army War Coll., Carlisle Barracks, Pa., 1977. Infantry unit comdr., aviator U.S. Army, 1953-58; from editl. trainee to staff reporter Charlotte (N.C.) Observer, 1958-63; from staff reporter to mng. editor Marietta (Ga.) Daily Jour., 1960-63; pub. rels. mgr. So. Svcs., Inc., Atlanta, 1963-68; v.p. Manning, Selvage & Lee, 1968-78; exec. dir. So. Assn. Orthodontists, 1978-96, Coll. Diplomates Am. Bd. Orthodontics, Atlanta, 1996-98; owner J.O. Svcs., 1998—. Pubs., editor Midwest Poetry Rev., 1995-2000; assoc. editor The Village Writer, 1991-93. Past dir. Families First, Atlanta; dir. Howell Pl. Condominium, 1997-98. Recipient Army Legion of Merit award, Master Army Aviator badge, Expert Infantryman badge, Three times 1st place winner Byron Herbert Reece Internat. Poetry award, Disting. Svc. award So. Assn. Orthodontists. Mem. So. Assn. Orthodontists, S.C. Assn. Orthodontists, Am. Assn. Execs., Ga. Soc. Assn. Execs., Ga. State Poetry Soc. (dir., pres. 2001—), Atlanta Writers Club, Village Writers Group, Inquiry Club (pres. 2000—), Capital City Club. Office: JO Svcs PO Box 20236 Atlanta GA 30325-0236

OTTLEY, WILLIAM HENRY, professional association director, consultant; b. N.Y.C., Mar. 7, 1929; s. James Henry and Margaret (Deeble) O. BA, Yale U., 1950; spl. cert., Georgetown U., 1953; D of Aero. Sci. (hon.), Embry Riddle Aero. U., 1979. Dir. pub. rels. Thomas A. Edison Co., West Orange, N.J., 1953-56; exec. v.p. Career Publs., Inc., N.Y.C., 1956-60; dir. spl. exhibits N.Y. World's Fair, 1960-65; exec. dir. Nat. Pilots Assn., Washington, 1965-77, U.S. Parachute Assn., Washington, 1978-92, Nat. Aero. Assn., Washington, 1992-93; pres. Internat. Gen. Aviation Commn., Paris, 1994-99. V.p. Fedn. Aero. Internat., Paris, 1994-99. 1st lt. USAF, 1951-53. Recipient Skydiving Lifetime Achievement award, 1994. Mem. Am. Mus. Sport Parachuting (pres.), Met. Club Washington, Soc. of Cin. Republican. Episcopalian. Avocations: skydiving (world record holder 1982), flying (world record holder 1985), scuba diving, waterskiing, snow skiing. Home and Office: 2627 Woodley Pl NW Washington DC 20008-1525 E-mail: whottley@erols.com.

OTTO, CATHERINE NAN, clinical laboratory scientist; b. Stockton, Calif., Dec. 17, 1953; d. Edward Joseph Otto and Arlene Maude (Holmes) Naylor. BS in Microbiology, Oreg. State U., 1976; BS in Med. Tech., Oreg. Health Scis. U., 1981; BA in French, Portland (Oreg.) State U., 1986, MBA, 1990; PhD in Law, Policy and Soc., Northeastern U., 1998. Cert. clin. lab. scientist, clin. lab. dir., clin. lab. supr., clin. lab. specialist in hematology, med. technologist. Med. technologist night shift Ore. Health Scis. U., Portland, 1981-85, Bess Kaiser Med. Ctr., Portland, 1985, med. technologist hematology, 1985-86; lab. supr. div. med. office Kaiser Permanente, 1986-87, lab. supr. Vancouver Med. Office, 1987-94; instr. U. N.C., Chapel Hill, 1997-98, asst. prof., 1999—. Adj. asst. prof. Mass. Coll. Pharmacy, 1995-96. Bd. dirs. Friends of Ore. Pub. Broadcasting, Portland, 1985-88; mem. allied health subcom. Am. Cancer Soc., Portland, 1985-87. Mem. AAUW, APHA, Assn. for Oreg. Med. Tech. (pres. 1986-87, bd. dirs. 1984-85, Mem. of Yr. 1989, 91, pres. Portland Dist. 1983-84), Am. Soc. Clin. Lab. Sci. (chair region IX immunology/immunohematology sci. assembly 1984-87, vice chair 1987-88, chair polit. action com. 1990-91, trustee polit. action com. 1987-91, commr. profl. and econ. affairs 1989-91, dir. at large 1991-92, sec.-treas. 1992-95, mem. govt. affairs com. 1995-98, com. on profl. affairs 1998-2001, chair 1999-2000, vice chair 2000-2001), Clin. Lab. Mgmt. Assn., Beaverton Internat. Tng. in Comms. (sec. 1985-86). Avocations: golf, skiing, bicycling, oil painting. Office: Univ NC Chapel Hill Med Sch Wing E CB # 7145 Chapel Hill NC 27599-7145 E-mail: cotto@med.unc.edu.

OTTO, FRED DOUGLAS, chemical engineering educator; b. Hardisty, Alta., Can., Jan. 12, 1935; BSc, U. Alta., 1957, MSc, 1959; PhD in Chem. Engring., U. Mich., Ann Arbor, 1963. From asst. prof. to assoc. prof. U. Alta., Edmonton, 1962-70, chmn., 1975-84, prof. chem. engring., 1970-96, dean engring., 1985-94, prof. emeritus, 1996—; pres., CEO DB Robinson & Assocs. Ltd., 1998—. Mem. governing coun. NRC, 1991-94. Recipient donald L. Katz award Gas Processors Assn., 1998. Fellow Can. Acad. Engring.; mem. AIChE, Can. Soc. Chem. Engrs. (pres. 1986-87), Assn. Profl. Engrs., Geologists and Geophysicsts of Alta. (1st v.p. 1995-96, pres. 1996-97, Centennial award 1993), Can. Coun. Profl. Engrs. (bd. dirs. 1997—). Office: 9419 20th Ave Edmonton AB Canada T6N 1E5

OTTO, HARRY CLAUDE, manufacturing executive; b. Chgo., Feb. 7, 1957; s. Edward and Carol (Greengard) Urbanski; m. Linda Jean Schneller, Sept. 13, 1980. Diagnostic ctr. mgr. Panafax Corp., Chgo., 1979-83, spl. project mgr. Melville, N.Y., 1983-86; product mgr. Brother Internat. Corp., Piscataway, N.J., 1986—; dir. mktg. Toshiba Am. Info. Systems, Irvine, Calif., 1990-92; exec. v.p. Danka Omnifax, L.A., 1992—; gen. mgr. Samsung Electronics Am., 1997—. Contbr. articles to profl. jours. Mem. Facsimile Systems Equipment Engring., Electronic Industries Assn., Telecommunications Industry Assn., Am. Mgmt. Assn. Republican. Methodist. Avocations: skiing, weightlifting, running. Office: Samsung Electronics Am Ste 250 3351 Michelson Dr Irvine CA 92612

OTTO, INGOLF HELGI ELFRIED, banking institute fellow; b. Duesseldorf, Germany, May 7, 1920; s. Frederick C. and Josephine (Zisenis) O.; m. Carlyle Miller, 1943 (div. 1960); children: George Vincent Edward, Richard Arthur Frederick. A.B., U. Cin., 1941; M.A., George Washington U., 1950, Ph.D., 1959. CPCU. Assoc. prof. fin. NYU, N.Y.C., 1960-62; prof. fin. U. Nuevo Leon, Monterrey, Mexico, 1962-65, U. So. Miss., Hattiesburg, 1965-67, U. So. Ala., Mobile, 1967-81; sr. fellow Inst. Banking and Fin., Mexico City, 1981—. Contbr. articles on fin. to profl. jours. Served to col. U.S. Army, 1941-46. Decorated Legion of Merit, Meritorious Service medal, Purple Heart. Mem. Am. Econ. Assn., N.Am. Econ. and Fin. Assn.

OTTO, JEAN HAMMOND, journalist; b. Kenosha, Wis., Aug. 27, 1925; d. Laurence Cyril and Beatrice Jane (Slater) Hammond; m. John A. Otto, Aug. 22, 1946; children: Jane L. Rahman, Mary Ellen Takayama, Peter J. Otto; m. Lee W. Baker, Nov. 23, 1973. Student, Ripon Coll., 1944-46. Women's editor Appleton (Wis.) Post-Crescent, 1960-68; reporter Milw. Jour., 1968-72, editorial writer, 1972-77, editor Op Ed page, 1977-83; editorial page editor Rocky Mountain News, Denver, 1983-89, assoc. editor, 1989-92, reader rep., 1992-99; endowed chair U. Denver, 1992-97. Founder, chmn. bd. trustees First Amendment Congress, 1979-85, chmn. exec. com., 1985-88, 89-91, pres. 1991-96, mem. bd. trustees, 1979-96; founding mem. Wis. Freedom of Info. Council. Recipient Headliner award Wis. Women in Communications, 1974; Outstanding Woman in Journalism award YWCA, Milw., 1977; Knight of Golden Quill Milw. Press Club, 1979; spl. citation in Journalism Ball State U., 1980; James Madison award Nat. Broadcast Editorial Assn., 1981; spl. citation for contbn. to journalism Nat. Press Photographers Assn., 1981; Ralph D. Casey award U. Minn., 1984; U. Colo. Regents award, 1985; John Peter Zenger award U. Ariz., 1988; Paul Miller Medallion award Okla. State U., 1990; Colo. SPJ Lowell Thomas award, 1990, Disting. Alumna award Ripon Coll., 1992, Hugh M. Hefner First Amendment Lifetime Achievement award Playboy Found., 1994; named to Milw. Press Club Hall of Fame, 1993, Freedom of Info. Hall of Fame, 1996. Mem. Colo. Press Assn. (chmn. freedom of info. com. 1983-89), Assn. Edn. in Journalism and Mass Communications (Disting. Svc. award 1984), Am. Soc. Newspaper Editors (bd. dirs. 1987-92), Soc. Profl. Journalists (nat. treas. 1975, nat. sec. 1977, pres.-elect 1978, pres. 1979-80, First Amendment award 1981, Wells Key 1984, pres. Sigma Delta Chi Found. 1989-92, chair Found. 1992-94), Milw. Press Club (mem. Hall of Fame 1993). E-mail: jottofirst@aol.com.

OTTO, JEFFREY BRUCE, industrial research and development executive; b. Lowell, Mass., Dec. 23, 1943; s. Harry Frederick Otto and Winifred Evelyn (Pike) Otto Nutting; m. Carolyn Elaine Heimall, July 7, 1973; children: Jared Harris, Jacob Edward, Jedidiah Corbin. BA in Math. and Stats., U. Conn., 1966. From sr. devel. engr. to dir. product devel. Rogers (Conn.) Corp., 1965-93; exec. dir. Tech. for Conn., New London, 1994-96; v.p. R&D The Butcher Co., Marlborough, Mass., 1996—. Divsn. dir. Chem. Splty. Mfgrs. Assn., Washington, 1996—. Inventor, patentee in field; presenter in field. Chief Mortlake Fire Co., Brooklyn, Conn., 1971-97; treas. Windham-Tolland Firemen's Assn., 1984—; pres. Quinebaug Valley Emergency Comms., Danielson, Conn., 1974—; chair Bd. Fin., Brooklyn, Conn., 2000—. Mem. Am. Chem. Soc., Materials Rsch. Soc., Manchester Pipe Band (pres. 1998—), South Cemetery Assn. (pres. 1989—). Avocation: public safety. Home: PO Box 153 Brooklyn CT 06234-0153 Office: The Butcher Co 67 Forest St Marlborough MA 01752-3075 E-mail: jotto@butchers.com.

OTTO, LUDWIG, publisher, educator, consultant, evangelist; b. N.Y.C., Mar. 15, 1934; s. Ludwig and Anna V. (Messina) O.; m. Sara S. Sheffield, Apr. 18, 1966 (div. 1987); children: Molly, Ryan, Matthew, Katherine; m. Maxine Z. Knight, Sept. 1, 1991; children: David, Jeffrey. LLB, Blackstone Sch., Chgo., 1958; BA, CUNY, 1975; MDiv, Southwestern Bapt. Sem., Ft. Worth, 1978, D of Ministry, 1980; PhD, Am. U., 1996; postgrad., U. Dallas, 2001; MLA, So. Meth. U. Ordained minister, Baptist Ch., 1975. Mgr. computer div. NCR, various locations, 1957-64, Honeywell, Houston, 1964-66; pres. U. Computer Scis., 1966-74; pastor, evangelist So. Bapt. Ch., Tex., 1974—; publ. Franklin Publ. Co., Arlington, 1987—; dir. Fed. and Found. Grants Adminstrn. Paul Quinn Coll.; pres. Prometheus Internat. Inc.; evangelist, 1971—. Exec. dir. Nat. Ethics Inst., 1992—; mem. adj. faculty El Centro Coll., Collin County C.C., Northlake Coll., Irvine, Tex., U. Tex., Arlington; assoc. prof., chair divsn. arts and scis. Paul Quinn Coll., Dallas, 1994—, dir. fedn. and found. rels. and grant adminstrn; v.p. Paul Quinn Cmty. Devel. Corp.; pres., CEO Franklin Devel. Corp., 1966—; prof. lit. DeVry Inst. Tech., Tarrant County Coll, Columbia Coll.; CEO Franklin Global Svcs., 2001; sr. ptnr. Franklin Ednl. Travel. Author: Introduction to Computer Math, 1967, 69, Training Church Members, 1980, How to Protect Your Children, 1982, Critical Thinking Strategies, 1993, Reading for Speed and Comprehension, 1993, Plato in New York, Born Poor in the USA; pub. monthly newspaper Your Opinion Counts, 1997; host radio program Your Opinion Counts, 1997. 2d lt. U.S. Army, 1950-53. Mem. North Tex. Alumni Assn. of CCNY (pres. 1993—), Prometheus Internat. (pres.), Sigma Tau Delta. Home and Office: Franklin Global Svcs 2723 Steamboat Cir Arlington TX 76006-3705 E-mail: ludotto@aol.com.

OTTO, MARIE (BERTHA OTTO), educational administrator, educational consulting company executive; b. Houston, July 11, 1930; d. Robert Lillard and Bertha Irene (Allen) Davis; m. Robert Lee Otto, Jan. 7, 1950; children: Lois Ann Otto Buschmann, Barbara Jeane Otto Hunt, Robert Lee Jr. Student, Tex. Christian U., 1947-49, Hardin-Simmons U., summers 1947, 49, 54; BA in Speech, Drama and Edn., Sul-Ross State U., 1954; postgrad., U. Wyo., 1961, U. Calif., Santa Barbara, 1962, Calif. State U., Northridge, 1964; MA, Calif. State U., Long Beach, 1969, postgrad., 1980-82. Lic. tchr., Tex., secondary tchr., Wyo., Calif.; lic. psychologist; lic. marriage and family counselor. Tchr. high schs., Tex., Wyo. and Calif., 1956-64; tchr., counselor Excelsior High Sch., Norwalk, Calif., 1964-66; counselor Neff High Sch., La Mirada, 1966-69; psychologist Huntington Beach (Calif.) Union High Sch. Dist., 1969-74, project mgr., dir. pupil pers., 1974-80, asst. supt., 1980-84, supt., 1984-88, supt. emeritus, 1988—. V.p. Poole-Young-Koehler Assocs., Inc., Long Beach, 1964-79; pvt. practice marriage and family counselor, Fountain Valley, Calif., 1970—; pres. Marie Otto Assocs., Fountain Valley, 1979—; supr. student tchrs. Chapman Univ. Orange, Calif., 1988—; sec.-treas., Ctr. for Teaching Thinking, Huntington Beach, 1991—. Mem. Fountain Valley Human Svcs. Com., Huntington Beach Human Resources Commn., state planning com. Girl Scouts U.S., Worland, Wyo., 1959-61; pres. Spl. Edn. Local Plan Orgn., 1983-84; bd. dirs. Humana Hosp. Huntington Beach, Golden West Coll. Found., Huntington Beach, Huntington Beach Community Clinic, Orange County chpt. ARC, Santa Ana, Calif, No on Drugs, 1988—; sec., treas. Ctr. for Teaching of Thinking, Huntington Beach, 1992—. Recipient numerous plaques, 1985—, including Fountain Valley Human Svcs. Com., 1979, City of Fountain Valley, 1975, 79, 88, City of Huntington Beach, 1988, Fountain Valley C. of C., 1988, City of Westminster, 1988, Orange Coast Coll., 1988, Golden West Coll., 1988, Ocean View Sch. Dist., 1988, Spl. Edn. Local Plan Orgn., 1984; named Woman of Yr., Soroptimist Club, Westminster, 1984, Disting. Alumnus, Grad. Sch. Edn. Calif. State U.-Long Beach, 1988. Home and Office: 16689 Mount Hoffman Cir Fountain Valley CA 92708-2435

OTTO, RANDAL ALLEN, otolaryngologist, educator; b. Sheboygan, Wis., June 17, 1954; MD, U. Mo., 1981. Cert. in otolaryngology. Resident in pathology Queens Med. Ctr., Honolulu, 1981-82; resident in otolaryngology U. Mo., Columbia, 1982-87; prof. dept. otolaryngology U. Tex. Health Sci. Ctr., San Antonio, 1987—, interim chmn., 1999-2001, chmn., 2001—. Fellow ACS, Am. Acad. Otolaryngology-Head and Neck Surgery, Triologic Soc.; mem. AMA, Am. Soc. for Head and Neck Surgeons, Tex. Med. Assn. E-mail: otto@uthscsa.edu.

OTTO, TERRE A. artist, writer; b. N.Y.C., Aug. 8, 1941; d. Sigfried S. and Ethyl (Goldstein) Alper; children: Regan Alexis, Tiffany Ariana, Dylan Richard. BA, Bennington Coll., 1963; postgrad., Columbia U., 1964, U. Geneva, 1960. Pres. Primiterre Assocs., Port Washington. Dir. Nassau County Family Ct. Nursery. Office: Primiterre Assocs PO Box 1030 Port Washington NY 11050-0204

OTTO-DINIZ, SARA JEAN, art education administrator, consultant; b. Wilkes-Barre, Pa., Feb. 9, 1948; d. Henry Habel and Mildred Jean (Gordon) Otto; m. Elvidio Vidalito Olavo Bernadino Diniz, Sept. 6, 1975; children: Cecilia Giana Diniz, Gabriel Bernard Diniz. BA with honors, Wilson Coll., 1970; MA, U. Tex., 1983; postgrad., U. N.Mex., 1998—. Dir., founder Art in Sch., Inc., Albuquerque, 1985—; instr. Coll. Santa Fe, 1989-00. Grantee McCune Charitable Found., 1999-2000, Albuquerque Cmty. Found., 1989-2002, Urban Enhancement Trust Fund, Albuquerque, 1994-96, 99-2001, Honeywell Def., Albuquerque, 1993-95, N.Mex. Arts, 1998-2002. Mem. Nat. Art Edn. Assn., N.Mex. Art Edn. Assn., N.Mex. Alliance for Art Edn., Albuquerque Arts Alliance. Democrat. Roman Catholic. Avocation: travel. Home: 8720 La Sala Del Centro NE Albuquerque NM 87111-4522 Office: Art in Sch Inc PO Box 3416 Albuquerque NM 87190-3416

OTTOO, RICHARD EBIL, business educator; b. Paimol, Uganda, Dec. 28, 1958; came to U.S., 1990; s. Jevenino and Sabina (Lamoji) O.; 1 child, Emily Alimo. B of Stats., Makerere U., Kampala, Uganda, 1985; MBF, Finafrica Found., Milan, 1989; MBA, Baruch Coll., 1997; PhD, Baruch, CUNY, 1998. Spl. asst. to min. Ministry of Health, Govt. of Uganda, Entebbe, 1985-86; project mgr. Action Internationale, Kampala and Kotido, Uganda, 1986-88; lectr. Baruch Coll., N.Y.C., 1992-97; asst. prof. Pace U., 1998—. Accounts trainee Nat. Water Corp., Entebbe, 1981-83; bd. dirs. Global Edn. Assocs., N.Y.C. Contbr. articles to profl. jours. Italian Ministry Fgn. Affairs scholar, 1988; Rockefeller Bros. Fund fellow, 1990; John C. Whitehead Found. fellow, 1991. Mem. Am. Fin. Assn., Fin. Mgmt. Assn., Eastern Fin. Assn., N.Y. Soc. Security Analysts. Home: 1425 Amsterdam Ave New York NY 10027-7454 Office: Pace U Lubin Sch Bus One Pace Plz New York NY 10038

OTTOSON, HOWARD WARREN, agricultural economist, former university administrator; b. Detroit Lakes, Minn., Sept. 18, 1920; s. John Henry and Hilma Marie (Johnson) O.; m. Margaret Jane Featherstone, Oct. 22, 1944; children— Keith Richard, John Howard, David Thomas BS, U. Minn., 1942, MS, 1950; PhD, Iowa State U., 1952. Chmn. dept. agrl. econs. U. Nebr., Lincoln, 1956-66, Bert Rodgers prof., 1965, dir., dean, 1966-79, asst. vice chancellor, 1979-81, vice chancellor, 1981-82, exec. v.p., provost, 1982-85, prof. agrl. econs. emeritus, 1985—. Cons. USDA, Washington, 1961, 64, AID, Buenos Aires, Argentina, 1962, Colombian Inst. Agr., Bogota, 1970; mem. USDA Policy Adv. Com. on Feed Grains, Washington, 1966-68; chmn. Gt. Plains Agrl. Council, Lincoln, Nebr., 1971, 79; bd. dirs. Farm Found. Bd., Chgo., 1977-85. Sr. author: Land and People in the Northern Plains Tranition Area, 1966; sr. author Agrl. Land Tenure Research bull., 1962; editor: Land Use Problems and Policies in the U.S., 1963; co-editor: Transportation Problems and Policies in the Trans Missouri West, 1967. Pres. Lincoln Coun. Chs., Nebr., 1958-59, Nebr. divsn. UN Assn.-U.S.A., Lincoln, 1977-78; chmn. Mayor's Adv. Com. on Taxation, Lincoln, 1991; mem. Nebr. Commn. on Local Govt. Innovation and Restructuring, 1996-2000; pres. Pelican Lakes Property Owners Assn., 2000—. Served to lt. USNR, 1944-46, PTO. Mem.: LWV (bd. dir. Nebr. 1993—99), Internat. Assn. Agrl. Economists (travel fellow 1958, 1964), Am. Agrl. Econs. Assn., Open Forum (pres. 1991—92), Norden Club (pres. 1985—87), Pelican Lake Property Assn. (pres. 2000—01), Farm House, Fifty-Fifty Club, Phi Delta Kappa, Gamma Sigma Delta, Phi Kappa Phi, Sigma Xi, Alpha Zeta. Democrat. Presbyterian. Avocations: golf; skiing; woodwork; Civil War history; gardening. Home: 3001 S 51 # 2205 Lincoln NE 68506

OTTUM, BRIAN DOUGLAS, research and marketing consulting executive; b. Madison, Wis., Mar. 28, 1961; s. Robert Warren and Margaret Gertrude (Richards) O.; m. Mona Schultz Ottum, Aug. 20, 1988; children: Paul Robert, Sarah Elizabeth. BSChemE, U. Wis., 1983; MBA, Xavier U., Cin., 1989; PhD, U. Utah, 1994. Product devel. mgr. Procter & Gamble, Cin., 1983-88; internat. market rsch. mgr. Procter & Gamble Internat., 1988-90; tchg. fellow U. Utah, Salt Lake City, 1990—94; ptnr. Axion Group, Mpls., 1994-96; pres. Ottum Rsch. & Cons., Ann Arbor, Mich., 1995—. Adj. prof. U. Mich. Bus. Sch., Ann Arbor, 1996—. Contbg. author: Handbook of New Product Development, 1997; contbr. articles to profl. jours. Rsch. dir. Com. for Quality Cmty., Saline, Mich., 1995—. Doctoral fellow Am. Assn. Collegiate Schs. Bus., 1993. Mem. Product Devel. and Mgmt. Assn. (founder, past pres., now v.p. Mich. chpt. 1994—, Meritorious Svc. award 1996). Republican. Lutheran. Avocations: astronomy (owns largest observatory in Midwest). Office: Ottum Rsch & Cons 398 Green Hills Dr Saline MI 48176-8718 Fax: 734-429-8329. E-mail: ottum@comcast.net.

OTTWEIN, MERRILL WILLIAM GEORGE, real estate company executive, veterinarian; b. Troy, Ill., Apr. 24, 1929; s. Oscar J. and Hilda (Bardelmeier) O.; m. Grace Marie Schmidt, Jan. 22, 1932; children: Ann Marie, Amy Sue, Paul John, Emily Carol. BS with highest honors, U. Ill., 1951, MS in Agrl. Econs., 1952, BS in Vet. Medicine, 1954, DVM with honors, 1956. Lic. veterinarian, Ill., real estate broker, Ill. Pvt. practice, Edwardsville, Ill., 1956-66; dir. Diakonia, Ch. World Svc., Honduras, 1967; mem. Ill. Senate, Springfield, 1968-70; real estate developer Cottonwood Sta. Corp., 1970-81; real estate broker Coldwell Banker, Edwardsville, 1981-91; exclusive buyer broker relocation svcs., 1991—, O'Fallon, Ill., 1992—. Mem. vet. med. adv. com. U. Ill., Urbana, 1960-64. Pres. Cahokia Mounds coun. Boy Scouts Am., 1969-71; mem. bd. for world ministries United Ch. of Christ, N.Y.C., 1970-74; active local Rep. politics. Mem. Nat. Assn. Exclusive Buyer Agts. (treas. 1995, 96, pres. 1998), Ill. Assn. Realtors, Edwardsville-Glen Carbon C. of C.,

Edwardsville-Collinsville Bd. Realtors, Land of Goshen C. of C. (pres. 1974-75), U. Ill. Vet. Medicine Alumni Assn. (pres. 1960-61), Rotary (pres. Edwardsville 1976), Phi Kappa Phi, Alpha Zeta. Avocations: vocal and instrumental music, photography. Address: 515 W Highway 50 O'Fallon IL 62269-2012 E-mail: Buyerside@aol.com.

OTWELL, RALPH MAURICE, retired newspaper editor; b. Hot Springs, Ark., June 17, 1926; s. Walter Clement and Pearl Oda (Tisdale) O.; m. Janet Barbara Smith, July 18, 1953; children— Brian Thornton, Douglas Keith, David Smith. Student, U. Ark., 1947-48; BS, Northwestern U., 1951; postgrad. (Nieman fellow), Harvard, 1959-60. Reporter, telegraph editor So. Newspapers, Inc., Hot Springs, 1943-44, 47; asst. city editor Chgo. Sun-Times, 1953-59, news editor, 1959-63, asst. mng. editor, 1963-65, asst. to editor, 1965-68, mng. editor, 1968-76, editor, 1976-80, exec. v.p., editor, 1980-84. Mgmt. bd. newspaper div. Field Enterprises, Inc., 1967-84; lectr. Medill Sch. Journalism, Northwestern U., 1955— ; charter mem. Nat. News Council, 1973-80 Trustee Garrett-Evang. Theol. Sem., 1965-79; Mem. nat. bd. Christian Social Concerns, United Meth. Ch., 1968-72; mem. bd. Community Renewal Soc., 1987-90, Chgo. Reporter, 1987-90, student publs. Northwestern U., 1968-72. Served to 1st lt. AUS, 1944-47, 51-53. Recipient Page One award Chgo. Newspaper Guild, 1964; named Ill. Journalist of Year No. Ill. U., 1974 Mem. Am. Soc. Newspaper Editors (chmn. ethics com. 1976-77), AP Mng. Editors Assn., Soc. Profl. Journalists (dir. 1966-71, sec. 1971-72, v.p. 1972-73, pres. 1973-74), Northwestern U. Alumni Assn. (dir. 1965-68, 91-93, sec. 1993-94, Merit award 1969, Svc. award 1995, chair seminar day com. 2001-2002), Sigma Delta Chi (pres. 1987-89), Kappa Tau Alpha, Econ. Club, Headline Club (pres. Chgo. chpt. 1965-66), Harvard Club Chgo., Chgo. Press Club (dir. 1968-77), Northwestern Club. Home: 2750 Hurd Ave Evanston IL 60201-1268 E-mail: ralph@otwell.com., r-otwell@northwestern.edu.

OU, FONG-LIEH, civil engineer; b. Chung-Hua, Taiwan, Sept. 8, 1940; came to U.S., 1967, naturalized, 1978; s. Ja and Mee (Wu) O.; m. Julie Chen, Sept. 5, 1967; children— King, Harris. B.S., Chung-Yang U., Taiwan, 1964; M.S., Pa. State U., 1970; Ph.D., U. Utah, 1980. Registered profl. engr., D.C. Lectr., U. Chinese Culture, Taipei, Taiwan, 1966-67; transp. planner Pa. Dept. Transp., Harrisburg, 1968; planning analyst Pa. State Planning Bd., Harrisburg, 1969-75; research asst. Pa. Transp. Inst., State College, 1975-77; civil engr. Salt Lake Internat. Airport, 1978-80, U.S. Dept. Agr., Washington, 1980— ; cons. Govt. Taiwan, Trans Systems, Vienna, Va., Allstar Engring., Washington. Contbr. articles to profl. jours. Mem. ASCE, Western Regional Sci. Assn., Sigma Xi. Home: 3333 Happy Heart Ln Annandale VA 22003-1176 Office: US Dept Agr PO Box 96090 Washington DC 20090-6090

OU, LO-CHANG, physiology educator; b. Shanghai, Oct. 16, 1930; came to U.S., 1964; m. Cynthia Chin Ou, June 10, 1960; children; Winnie, Edward, Emily, Joseph. BS, Peking U., Beijing, 1954; PhD, Dartmouth Coll., 1971. Tchg. asst., dept. biochemistry Peking U., Beijing, 1954-60, lectr., dept. biochemistry, 1960-62; demonstrator, dept. physiology Hong Kong U., 1962-64; asst. prof. dept. physiology Dartmouth Med. Sch., Hanover, N.H., 1977-80, assoc. prof., 1980-85, rsch. prof., 1985—, prof. emeritus (active), 1998—. NIH rsch. grantee, 1977-94. Mem. Am. Physiol. Soc. Achievements include research on pathophysiology of high altitude. Office: Dartmouth Med Sch Dept Physiology Lebanon NH 03756 E-mail: Lo.Chang.Ou@Dartmouth.edu.

OU, YEN-CHUAN, urologist; b. Taichung, Taiwan, Jan. 31, 1961; s. Wen-Guey and Haw (Jeng) Ou; m. Hui-Min Chen, Nov. 23, 1987; children: Hsien-Kuei, Hsien-Che, Hsien-Chi. B, Nat. Def. Med. Coll., Taipei, Taiwan, 1986. Resident Taichung Vets. Gen. Hosp., 1986—90, chief resident, 1990—91, urology specialist, 1991-92, 94—; chief urology Puli Vets. Hosp., Nan-Tou, Taiwan, 1993-94; rsch. assoc. U. Va., 1997—99, Inst. Medicine, Chung Shan Med. U., 2001—. Contbr. articles to profl. jours. Capt. Chinese Air Force, 1992-93. Nat. Sci. Coun. grantee, 1992. Mem. Urol. Assn. China, Assn. Andrology China, Surg. Assn. China. Mem. Nationalist Party. Avocations: table tennis, basketball, traveling, mountain climbing, music. Office: Taichung Vets Gen Hosp 160 SEc 3 Taichung-Kong Rd Taichung 407 Taiwan

OUDENS, GERALD FRANCIS, architect, architectural firm executive; b. Manchester, N.H., May 18, 1934; s. John and Louise Esther (Wagner) Oudens; m. Monica Elizabeth Wohlfert, June 16, 1962; children: Elizabeth Marian, Matthew Thomas, Katherine Frances. BA in Architecture cum laude, Yale U., 1956, MArch, 1958. Registered arch., D.C., Va., Md., Ind., Nat. Coun. Archtl. Registration Bds. Intern arch. Koehler & Isaak, Manchester, 1955-58; staff architect Office Surgeon Gen. USAF, Washington, 1958-61; assoc. Metcalf & Assocs., 1961-69; prin. Oudens & Knoop Architects, PC, Chevy Chase, Md., 1970—. Vis. critic, thesis advisor dept. architecture Cath. U. Am., 1968—88; mem. adv. com. Acad. Med. Ctr. Study Sch. Architecture Rice U., 1975; mem. abulatory care adv. panel U.S. VA, 1974—75; mem. adv. panel No. Ind. Health Sys. Agy., 1977—81, AIA Rsch. Corp., 1978, Nat. Inst. Bldg. Scis., 1982—88; mem. design award juries Modern Healthcare Ann. Design Awards, 1992, Soc. Critical Care Medicine/AACN/AIA ICU Design Awards, 1992—97, 1999—2001, AIA Health Facilities Rev. Jury, 1995; presenter in field. Prin. works include NIH Master Plan, Bethesda, Md., Sibley Meml. Hosp., Washington, Washington Hosp. Ctr. Master Plan, Washington Adventist Hosp., Takoma Park, Md., Martha Jefferson Hosp., Charlottesville, Va., Marion (Ind.) Gen. Hosp., Humana Lucerne Hosp., Orlando, Fla., Hosp. de Pedregal, Mexico City, Fairfax Hosp., Falls Church, Va., Humana Audubon Hosp. and Heart Inst., Louisville, Humana Greensboro (N.C.) Hosp., Centre Universitaire des Scis. de la Sante, Younde, Cameroon, Washington Home and Hospice, Cuttington U. Coll., Suakoko, Liberia, Escuela Agricola Panaericana, El Zamorano, FM, Honduras, others; contbr. articles to profl. jours. Recipient Nat. Capital Architecture award, D.C. Coun. Engring. and Archtl. Socs./Washington Acad. Scis., 1961, ICU Design citation, Soc. Critical Care Medicine, 1998. Fellow: AIA (acad. architecture for health 1971—, past pres. and dir., nat. healthcare policy task force 1993—, mem. adv. com. Am. Collegiate Schs. Architecture coun. archtl. rsch. 1994—, Am. Hosp. Assn. Grad. Fellowship Rev. Panel, Henry Adams award 1958, Honor award Ky. chpt. 1980, Outstanding Leadership and Commitment to Healthcare Design award 1987, Merit award Washington Met. chpt. 1989, Citations for Design Excellence 1988, 1990), Am. Coll. Healthcare Archs. (bd. regents); mem.: Forum Health Care Planning, Internat. Hosp. Fedn., Am. Hosp. Assn. (mem. faculty continuing edn. insts. 1972—76, adv. panel 1978), Lambda Alpha Internat. Office: Oudens & Knoop Architects PC 2 Wisconsin Cir Chevy Chase MD 20815-7003 E-mail: goudens@okarch.com.

OUDERKIRK, MASON JAMES, lawyer; b. Des Moines, Feb. 1, 1953; s. Mason George and Florence Astor (Lowe) O.; m. Kari Aune Hormel, May 28, 1983; 1 child, Mason Christopher. BA, Drake U., 1975, JD, 1978. Bar: Iowa 1978, U.S. Dist. Ct. (so. dist.) Iowa 1978, U.S. Ct. Appeals (8th cir.); lic. real estate broker. Assoc. M.G. Ouderkirk Law Office, Indianola, Iowa, 1978-79; ptnr. Ouderkirk Law Firm, 1979-96; sr. mem. Ouderkirk, Ouderkirk & Dougherty, P.L.C., 1996-98; proprietor Ouderkirk Law Firm, Iowa, 1998—; pres. Avanti Realty Co. (formerly Landmark Real Estate, Ltd.), 1978—, Avanti Builders Co., Indianola, 1991—. Mem. Vol. Lawyers Project of Iowa, 1987-93. Mem. Indianola Police Retirement Bd., 1983-88; instr. Eric Heintz Black Belt Acad., 1988-93, Indianola Parks and Recreation Dept., 1988-93; mem. Nominating Commn., Warren County Assoc. Dist. Ct., 1999—; mem. Jud. Nominating Commn. for 5A Jud. Dist. of Iowa, 2002--. Mem. ABA, Iowa Bar Assn. (pub. rels. com. 1989-94, family law com. 1989-90), Warren County Bar Assn. (sec., treas. 1985-89, v.p. 1989-90, pres. 1990-92), 5th Jud. Dist. Bar Assn. (sec., treas. 1995), Assn. Trial Lawyers Am., Iowa Trial Lawyers Assn. Episcopalian. Avocations: fishing, hunting, gardening. Office: Ouderkirk Law Firm 108 S Howard St PO Box 156 Indianola IA 50125-0156 Home: PO Box 156 Indianola IA 50125-0156 Fax: 515-961-0304. E-mail: ouderkirklaw@earthlink.net.

OUE, EIJI, conductor, music director; b. Hiroshima, Japan; Student, Toho Sch. Music, Tanglewood Music Ctr.; artist diploma in conducting, New England Conservatory Music. Assoc. condr. Buffalo (N.Y.) Philharmonic, 1987-91; music dir. Erie (Pa.) Philharmonic, 1991-95, Minn. Orch., 1995—2002; chief condr. Hannover Radio Orch., Germany; prof. Hochschule Für Musik und Theater. Co-creator, resident condr. Pacific Music Festival, Sopporo, Japan, 1990-92; music dir., condr. Grand Teton Music Festival, Wyo.., 1997; guest condr. London Symphony Orch., Shinsei Symphony, N.Y. Philharmonic, Phila. Orch., Nat. Symphony, others. Recipient Koussevitzky prize Tanglewood, 1980, First prize Salzburg Mozarteum, 1981, Hans Haring Gold medal, 1981. Office: Minn Orch Orch Hall 1111 Nicollet Ave Minneapolis MN 55403-2406*

OUELLET, ANDRÉ, business executive; b. St. Pascal, Can., Apr. 6, 1939; s. Albert and Rita (Turgeon) O.; m. Edith Pagé, July 17, 1965; children: Sonia, Jean, Olga, Pierre. BA, U. Ottawa, Ont., Can., 1960, D (hon.), 1995; LLL, U. Sherbrooke, Can., 1963. Mem. Can. Parliament, Ottawa, 1967-93, min. consumer and corp. affairs, 1974-76, 80-83, min. state urban affairs, 1976-78, min. public works, 1978-79, min. labor, 1983-84; postmaster gen. Can., 1972-74, 80-81; min. fgn. affairs Can. Parliament, 1993-96; chmn. bd. Can. Post Corp., 1996-99, pres., CEO, 1999—. Office: Canada Post Corp 2701 Riverside Dr Ste N1250 Ottawa ON Canada K1A 0B1 E-mail: andre.ouellet@canadapost.ca.

OUELLETTE, DEBRA LEE, association administrator, consultant; b. Butte, Mont., Aug. 1, 1962; d. Eugene George and Avonne Gail (Smeltzer) O.; m. Anthony Lee Jaeger, Aug. 27, 1994 (div.). BA in Soc. and Tech., Mont. Coll. Mineral Sci. and Tech., 1985. Photographer, trainer Mountain States Energy, Butte, 1984-85; lab. asst. Western Energy, 1985-86, receptionist, 1986; acctg. data entry clk. N.Am. Resources, 1986, lease and oil data entry clk., 1986-87; data entry clk. Spl. Resource Mgmt., 1987-89; adminstrv. asst. N.Am. Indian Alliance, 1989-97, asst. dir., 1998-99; dir. Butte Parent-Aide Program, 1999; adminstrv. asst. Human Resources Coun. Dist. XII, 2000—01; site coord. Continental Gardens Housing Corp., 1999—. Designer chem. dependency forms. Mem.-at-large Vol. Ctr., Butte, 1995-96; vol. CPR first aid instr. ARC, 1999. Outstanding Pub. Svc. award Soc. Security Adminstrn., Proctective Payee Program.Personnal Invitation to Pres. Inaugration. Mem. VFW Ladies Aux. (sr. v.p. 1994-96, jr. vice trustee 1998—, 3 yr. trustee dist. 4 State of Mont. 1999—, pres. dist. 4 2001-02). Avocations: reading, assisting urban Indian programs with policy and procedures, traveling. Office: Continental Gardens 100 Gardens Way Butte MT 59701-2840

OUELLETTE, JENNIFER JOHN, newscaster, writer; b. Wareham, Mass., May 5, 1976; d. Wilfred Noel, Sr. Ouellette and Joan Elizabeth (Howland) Ouellette. BA in English, U. Mass., Dartmouth, 1998. Cert. broadcasting. Tour guide Fearing Tavern Mus., Wareham, 1994—98; writer, reporter Wanderer Comm., Mattapoisett, 1996—97, Chronicle, Dartmouth, 2000—01; freelance writer Publs. Internat., Ltd., Lincolnwood, Ill., 2000—, Marian Heath Greeting Cards, Wareham, 2000—; radio news anchor, reporter Sta. WQRC Radio, Hyannis, 2000—; writer Inside Cape Cod Mag., Sandwich, 2002—. Roman Catholic. Avocations: rollerblading, shopping. Office: WQRC Radio 737 W Main St Hyannis MA 02601 Personal E-mail: Jeno4745@cs.com. Business E-Mail: wqrcnews@cape.com.

OUGHTON, THOMAS VICTOR, engineer; b. Denver, Oct. 12, 1951; s. Victor William and JoAnne (Speicher) O.; m. Kelly Ann Gomer, June 14, 1980; children: Kevin Thomas, Theodore Powell, Elizabeth Ann. BS in Engring. Physics, U. Colo., 1975. Researcher U. Colo. Health Scis. Ctr., Denver, 1976-81; engring. programmer UNISYS, Thorton, Colo., 1981-94; programmer Auto-trol Tech., Denver, 1994-98; tech. svc. engr. Sun Microsystems, Broomfield, Colo., 1998—. Asst. scoutmaster Boy Scouts Am., Broomfield, Colo., 1992-2000. Mem. Star Fleet Club (sec. 1988-95). Clubs: Star Fleet (Arvada, Colo.) (sec. 1988—). Republican. Avocations: camping, volleyball, swimming. E-mail: thomas.oughton@sun.com., tomoug@hotmail.com.

OUJO, JACK DOMINIC, accountant; b. Irvington, N.J., Aug. 12, 1958; s. Dominic and May Audrey (Rone) O.; m. Eileen Prout, Sept. 27, 1986; children: Kaitlin, Christopher. AAS in Acctg., Middlesex C.C., Edison, N.J., 1978; BSBA, Seton Hall U., 1980; MS in Taxation, Fairleigh Dickinson U., 1993. CPA, N.J.; CFP. Profl. umpire Baseball Umpire Devel. Program, St. Petersburg, Fla., 1981-88; tax cons. Ernst & Young, CPA's, N.Y.C., 1988-89; sr. Gentile, Wiener, Penta & Co., CPA's, Neptune, N.J., 1989-90; ptnr. Pierson & Co., CPA's, Sea Girt, 1990—. Fellow Internat. Bd. Cert. Fin. Planners. Fellow AICPA, N.J. Soc. CPA's (chmn. legis. com. 1992-93), Spring Lake C. of C. (bd. dirs. 1993). Republican. Roman Catholic. Avocations: golf, over 30 baseball. Home: 797 Holly Berry Ln Brick NJ 08724-5122 Office: Pierson & Co CPA's 2100 Route 35 Ste E Sea Girt NJ 08750-1001

OULTON, RICHARD JAMES, lawyer, entrepreneur; b. Peekskill, N.Y., Jan. 8, 1945; s. John and Martha (Smith) Outhouse; m. Ava Liu, July 4, 1986; children: John Lawrence, Alexis Xaioying, Jamie Richard. BA, SUNY, Buffalo, 1970, JD, 1973; MBA, CUNY, N.Y.C., 1976. Bar: N.Y. 1974, Va. 1989, D.C. 1990; U.S. Ct. Appeals (4th cir.) 1989. Asst. adminstr., atty. Roosevelt Hosp., N.Y.C., 1973-77, N.Y. Med. Coll., N.Y.C., 1977-78; 2d v.p. Va. Ins. Reciprocal, Richmond, 1978-87, v.p., 1987-88; pres. Oulton Assocs. Inc., Glen Allen, Va., 1988—, Affiliated Attys., Inc., Richmond, 1989—, Attys. Ins. Agy., Inc., Richmond, 1989—, Affiliated Accts., Inc., Richmond, 2000—, Affiliated Agts. Inc., Richmond, 2000—, Am. Flag Alliance, Inc., 2001—. Mem. Adv. Bd. on Edn. and Pubs., 1984-88, Adv. Bd. Joint Commn. on Accreditation of Hosps., Chgo.; asst. prof. dept. health care adminstrn. Va. Commonwealth U., Richmond, 1982-87, assoc. prof., 1987—; liaison, legis. officer Order of Purple Heart VA, 1991-92, 2001; spkr. numerous seminars; founding dir. 1st Battalion, 9th Marines Network Inc., The Walking Dead, 1997—. Editor: quality assurance risk mgmt. newsletter; mem. editl. adv. com. Quality Rev. Bull., 1984-89; contbr. articles to profl. jours. With USN/USMC, 1964-67, Vietnam. Decorated Purple Heart, USMC Combat Action Ribbon, Vietnam Cross of Gallantry. Mem. ABA, Va. Bar Assn., Am. Coll. Health Care Execs., Am. Acad. Hosp. Attys., Nat. Health Lawyers Assn., Outhouse Family Hist. Soc., Inc. Home: 11900 Alor Ct Glen Allen VA 23059-7068 Office: Affiliated Attys Inc 8515 Mayland Dr Richmond VA 23294-4701 E-mail: oulton@affiliatedattorneys.com.

OUNJIAN, MARILYN J. employment and training company executive; Student, U. Md, Founder, pres. Today's People, Phila., 1973-81; chmn., founder, chief exec. officer Careers USA, 1981—; pres., chief exec. officer The Career Inst., 1981—. Mem. Rep. Senatorial Inner Circle; bd. dirs. Phila. Econ. Devel. Coalition. Named Entrepreneur of Yr. Venture Mag, 1988, Woman Bus. Owner of Yr. Arthur Young and Assoc., 1989; Inc. 500 Corp. Careers USA, 1988. Mem. NAFE, Nat. Assn. Women Bus. Owners, Inst. Am. Entrepreneurs, Greater Phila. C. of C., Pa. C. of C. Avocations: swimming, horseback riding, gardening. Office: Careers USA 1825 John F Kennedy Blvd Philadelphia PA 19103-1701

OURSLER, FULTON, JR. editor, writer; b. West Falmouth, Mass., June 27, 1932; s. Fulton and Grace (Perkins) O.; m. Anne Noel Nevill, Nov. 29, 1954; children: Theresa Noel, Fulton III, Mark Nevill, James Randall, Carroll Grace. BA, Georgetown U., 1954. With Reader's Digest, Pleasantville, N.Y., 1956-87, book editor, 1968-70, sr. staff editor, 1970-72, asst. mng. editor, 1973, mng. editor, 1974-82, exec. editor, 1982-85, dep. editor-in-chief, 1986-87; editor-in-chief Guideposts mag., 1992-98; editor-in-chief, founding editor Angels on Earth mag., 1995-98, editl. dir., 1998-99; roving editor Guideposts mag., 2001—. Established: Fulton Oursler Meml. Collection, Georgetown U. Library.; editor: (commentary) Behold This Dreamer, 1964. Bd. dirs. Georgetown U. Library Assocs. Mem.: Friends of the Nyacks, Univ. Club. Home: 2 Laveta Pl Nyack NY 10960-1604 *Man makes two journeys in life: one in matter, the other in spirit. The first journey is outward and manifest; it leads to family, society, and career. The second journey is inward and invisible; it leads to the kingdom of God. The first journey is limited by logic, flesh, and time. The second is infinite, and its pathway is paradox. Self-preservation is the strongest instinct on the first journey; freedom, maturity, self-knowledge, power, and abundance seem to be important goals. But on the second journey, one learns that to find our truest selves, we must lose the sense of self; that to grow we must become as a child; that freedom is won by surrender, that the one counts for more than the many, that the meek are powerful, and the poor are rich. On both journeys, to gain life one must lose it, and be reborn.*

OUSELEY, WILLIAM NORMAN, security services consultant; b. N.Y.C., May 26, 1935; s. Norman J. Ouseley and Helen (Accurso) Loffredo; m. Josephine B. Ouseley, Mar. 3, 1962; children: John W., Elizabeth A. BA, Coll. of William & Mary, 1957; LLB, Fordham U., 1960. Spl. agt., supervisory spl. agt. organized crime FBI, nationwide, 1960-85; security rep. NFL, Kansas City, Mo., 1985-2000. Adv. bd. YMCA, Kansas City, 1987-88. Mem. Soc. Former FBI Spl. Agents (chmn. Kansas City chpt. 1992-93). Avocations: sports, outdoor activities.

OUSSANI, JAMES JOHN, stapling company executive; b. Bklyn., Jan. 3, 1920; s. John Thomas and Clara (Tager) O.; m. Lorraine G. Tutundgy, Apr. 25, 1954; children: James J., Gregory P., Rita C. B.M.E., Pratt Inst., 1938-42; J.D. (hon.), Coll. Boca Raton, Lynn U.; LLD. Dir. research, mfg. Supertronic Co., N.Y.C., 1943-46; sr. partner Perl-Oussani Machine Mfg. Co., N.Y.C., 1946-49; founder The Staplex Co., Bklyn., 1949, pres., 1949—; exec. dir. Lourdes Realty Corp.; dir. Junios Corp.; producer air sampling equipment for radioactive fallout AEC, 1951—. Mem. Bur. Research Air Pollution Control, Pres.'s Council on Youth Opportunity, Cardinal's Com. for Edn.; trustee Ch. of Virgin Mary; bd. dirs. St. Joan Arc Found., Boca Raton; founding mem. Lumen Christi-Palm Beach Diocese; founder, bd. dirs. Oussani Found.; founder James J. & Lorraine G. Oussani Scholarship Fund, Coll. Boca Raton; mem. cardinal's com. of laity, bishop's com. of laity; mem. Lumen Christi Found.; bd. overseers Lynn U., Boca Raton. Recipient Blue Ribbon Mining award, Sch. Mgmt. award, Aerospace Pride Achievement award; installed Knight of Jerusalem. Mem. Adminstrv. Mgmt. Soc., Office Adminstrn. Assn., Nat. Stationery and Office Equipment AssOffice Equipment Assn., Office Execs. Assn., Nat. Office Machine Mfg. Assn., Nat. Office Machine Dealers Assn., Nat. Office Products Assn., Bus. Equipment Mfrs. Assn., Our Lady Perpetual Help Holy Name Soc., Knights of Holy Sepulchre, Knights of St. Gregory, Knights of Malta, Rotary, Salaam Club, Mahopac Golf Club (Lake Mahopac, N.Y.), Internat. Club of Boca Raton, Boca Raton Hotel and Resort Club. Inventor automatic electric stapling machine. Patentee in field. Office: 777 5th Ave Brooklyn NY 11232-1626

OUTCALT, DAVID LEWIS, academic administrator, mathematician, educator, consultant; b. Los Angeles, Jan. 30, 1935; s. Earl Kinyon and Alberta Estes Ferguson O.; m. Marcia Lee Beach, July 1, 1956; children— Jeffrey David, Kevin Douglas, Gregory Mark, Eric Matthew. BA in Math., Pomona Coll., 1956; MA in Math., Claremont Grad. Sch., 1958; PhD in Math., Ohio State U., 1963; D.Pub. Adminstrn. (hon.), Kyung Hee U., Korea, 1984. Asst. prof. math. Claremont McKenna Coll., 1962-64; asst. prof. to prof. math. U. Calif.-Santa Barbara, 1964-80, chmn. dept. math., 1969-72, dean instrnl. devel., 1977-80; vice chancellor acad. affairs U. Alaska, Anchorage, 1980-81, prof. math., 1980-86, chancellor, 1981-86; prof. natural and applied sci. U. Wis., Green Bay, 1986-93, chancellor, 1986-98, chancellor emeritus, 1998—, Hendrickson prof. econ. devel., 1994-98. Pres. Mid-Continent athletic conf., 1990-91. Author math. textbooks; contbr. articles on math. and higher edn. to profl. jours. Moderator bd. trustees Humana Hosp. Anchorage, 1982-83; mem. exec. bd. Western Alaska coun. Boy Scouts Am., 1982-86, Bay-Lakes coun., 1987-97, v.p. exploring, 1988-92, v.p. ops., 1992-93, pres., 1993-94; mem. Anchorage Symphony bd., 1986, Green Bay Symphony Bd., 1988-97, mem. Weidner Ctr. Presents Bd., 1994-98; peer reviewer NCAA, 1994-99; trustee, v.p., treas. Kauai Internat. Theatre, 1998-2000; trustee Kauai C.C. Fund, 2000—. Grantee USAF Office Sci. Research, 1964-71, U. Calif., 1975-78, NSF, 1976-79. Mem. Math. Assn. Am., Internat. Assn. Univ. Pres.'s (exec. com. 1988-96, internat. com. on tech. in higher edn. 1996—, N.Am. coun. exec. com. 1988—, vice chair, 1988-94, newsletter editor 1994-95), Greater Green Bay C. of C. (advance bd. 1987-97, bd. dirs. 1991-94, 95-97), Brown County Indsl. Devel. (pres. bd. dirs. 1994-97), Rotary (exec. com. Kapaa club 1999—), Sigma Xi. Mem. Congregational Ch. Home: 6414A Puupilo Rd Kapaa HI 96746-9463 E-mail: outcalt@aloha.net.

OUTIN, MARY LOUISE, business, multi-cultural history and geneology educator; b. Peak, S.C., July 18, 1948; d. Ralph T. Williams and Mary Frances Wicker-Outin, Theopolis Outin (Stepfather). BA in Bus. Adminstrn., Columbia Coll., Columbia, South Carolina, 1987; MEd, Lesley U., 1999; grad., S.C. Sch. Real Estate, 1986. Owner MO Businesses, Inc., Columbia, 2000—. N/A. Mem.: S.C. Afro-Am. Hist. and Geneal. Soc., Inc. (co-pub. rels. dir. 1998—2000), Am. Legion Aux. (Unit 219 2000). Avocations: family history research, genealogy, cooking, reading. Office: MO Businesses Inc P O Box 3393 Columbia SC 29230 Office Fax: 803-736-9566.

OUTLAW, KITTI KIATTIKUNVIVAT, plastic surgeon; b. Bangkok, Aug. 24, 1964; came to U.S., 1974; s. Bert G. and Vilai (Chittachot) O. BS, U. South Ala., 1987, MD, 1992. Diplomate Am. Bd. Surgery. Resident in surgery La. State U. Affliated Hosps., New Orleans, 1992-96; chief resident La. State U. Dept. Surgery, 1996-97; assoc. River Parishes Surg. Assocs., La Place, La., 1997-98; fellow divsn. plastic and reconstructive surgery Med. Coll. Ga., 1998-2000; with Plastic & Reconstructive Surgery, Mobile, Ala., 2000—. Contbr. articles to profl. jours. Physician Boy Scouts of Am., Pensacola, Fla., 1982-90. Recipient Excellence in Tchg. award, Med. Coll. Ga., 2000. Avocations: outdoors, running, biking. Home: 5965 Shimmering Pines St Pace FL 32571-7332 Office: 3290 Dauphin St Ste 204 Mobile AL 36606-4014 E-mail: kkoutlaw@hotmail.com.

OUTMAN, WILLIAM DELL, II, lawyer; b. St. Petersburg, Fla., Nov. 10, 1940; s. Boyd Johnson and Marion Lucetta (Banks) O.; m. Sally Rockwell June 29, 1963 (dec. Sept. 1998); children: William Dell III, Stephanie O. Kiker, Sarah O. Brophy. BS in Bus. Adminstrn., Wash. & Lee U., 1962; JD, Georgetown U., 1965, LLM in Taxation, 1968. Bar: DC 1966, NY 1999. Assoc. atty. Baker & McKenzie, Wash., 1965-70, ptnr., 1970-97, mng. ptnr. N.Y.C., 1997-2000, ptnr. Washington, 2000—. Staff sgt. U.S. Army, 1965—71. Mem. Customs and Internat. Trade Bar Assn. (pres., bd. dirs. 1992—), Ct. Internat. Trade Adv. Com. (current chmn. 1990—), Congl. Country Club, Met. Club, Omicron Delta Kappa. Office: Baker & McKenzie 815 Connecticut Ave NW Ste 900 Washington DC 20006-4004 E-mail: william.d.outman@bakernet.com.

OUTTEN, KRISTINA MARIE, secondary education educator; b. Ogden, Utah, Dec. 6, 1973; d. Burrett William and June J. Clay; m. Todd Edgar Outten, Nov. 16, 1996. BA in English Edn., U. Ariz., 1996, MA in Ednl. Psychology, 2000. Lead trainer Macayo's Mexican Food, Tucson, 1991-95; bar mgr. Bushwacker, 1995-96; student tchr. Tucson H.S. Tucson Unified Sch. Dist., 1996, tchr. Alice Vail Mid. Sch., 1996—; bartender Applebee's Thomas & King, Tucson, 1996—. Com. mem. 504 rev. team, awards and site-based decision making team Vail Mid. Sch., 1998—. Author: And So It Begins..., 1999; contbr. poetry to Nat. Libr. of Poetry-Libr. of Congress, A View from Afar, The Peace We Knew, A Muse to Follow, Blossom in the Dawning, The Colors of Thought, Serenity at Daybreak; author poems (Editor's Choice awards 1996, 97, 98). Regents scholar U. Ariz., 1991; Vocal Talent scholar Am. Legend, 1991. Mem. Tucson Edn. Assn., Internat. Soc. Poets. Avocation: writing, singing, reading, travel.

OUTTEN, OUTTEN, JR. metal products executive; b. St. Louis, July 2, 1920; s. Burnet Outten; children: John A., Janet A. Gaines, David B., Doris A. Southern, Carol A. Hinkle. Student, Cornell U., 1938—39. Founder, ptnr. Western Metal Products Co, St. Louis, 1941—. 1st lt. USAAF, 1942—45. Mem.: Am. Astron. Soc. (assoc.). Republican. Achievements include invention of metallurgical processes; discovery of nucleosynthesis process. Home and Office: 1300 Weber St Orlando FL 32803-3336

OUTWATER, JOHN OGDEN, mechanical engineering educator; b. London, Eng., Jan. 2, 1923; came to U.S., 1924; s. John Ogden and Nenny (Boe) O.; m. Alice Hooker Davidson, Dec. 13, 1952; children— Anne Hooker (Mrs. Dale Sarver), Catherine Boe (Mrs. Carl B. Colby), Alice Brookfield (Mrs. Robert B. Lang), John Ogden III. BA, Cambridge (Eng.) U., 1943, MA, 1948, PhD, 1976; Sc.D. (Timken fellow), Mass. Inst. Tech., 1950. Registered profl. engr. Research engr. DuPont Co., 1950-52; project engr. Universal Moulded Products, 1952-53; indsl. liaison officer Mass. Inst. Tech., 1954-55; prof. mech. engring. U. Vt., Burlington, 1955—, chmn., 1955-93, prof. emeritus, 1993—. Leader archaeol. expdns. Wenner-Gren Found., Central Mexico, 1954, Yucatan, 1955, Peru-Bolivia, 1957, Haiti, 1959; cons. non-metallic materials Naval Ordnance Lab., Nat. Acad. Scis., Monsanto Research Corp., Smithsonian Instn. Author: (with others) Engineering Materials, 1959, Esplendor del Mexico Antigua; papers on metal cutting, plastics, archaeology, bones, ski safety. Chmn. Vt. Instrument Co., Inc.; Mem. Vt. Conf. Econ. Growth; vestryman St. Paul's Cathedral, Burlington. Served as officer Brit. Army, 1943-47. Named Vt. Engr. of Year, 1970 Fellow ASME; mem. Am. Soc.

Testing Materials, Holland Soc., Vt. Soc. Engrs., Delta Psi, Tau Beta Pi. Patentee in field. Home: 62 Overlake Park Burlington VT 05401-4012 Office: 321 S Union St Burlington VT 05401-4595

OUYANG, ANN, physician, researcher, educator; b. Kaoshiung, Taiwan, Feb. 20, 1950; came to U.S., 1970; d. Mid and Ching Chao Liu O.; m. Michael Rusli; children: Andrew Ouyang Rusli, Robert Ouyang Rusli. BSc, U. London, 1971, MB BS, 1974. Diplomate Am. Bd. Medicine and sub-bd. Gastroenterology. House surgeon Guy's Hosp., London, 1974; house physician St. Olave's Hosp., 1974-75; intern and resident in medicine Pa. Hosp., Phila., 1975-78; fellow in gastroenterology U. Pa., 1978-80, rsch. assoc. in medicine, 1980-81, asst. prof. in medicine, 1981-90, assoc. prof. medicine, 1990-92; prof. medicine Pa. State U., Hershey, 1992—, chief divsn. gastroenterology and hepatology, 1992—. Mem. study sect. NIDDKD/NIH, Bethesda, Md., 1991-95, ad hoc mem. 1989, 90; mem. Am. Found. Aging Rsch. Nat. Screening Adv. Coun., 1995, NIH Health Reviewers Res., 1995—; mem. subsplty. bd. on gastroenterology Am. Bd. Internal Medicine, 1993—, med. sec., 1984-89. Mem. editl. bd. Annals Internal Medicine, 2000; contbr. articles to profl. jours. and chpts. to books. Recipient Career Devel. award NIH, 1986, Rsch. award, 1989. Fellow ACP (mem. publ. com. 2000, 01); mem. AAAS, Am. Gastroenterological Assn. (rsch. com. 1986-89, admissions com. 1993-96, nominating com. 1993-95, chmn. 1995, abstract rev. com. Hormones and Receptors sect. 1994, tng. and edn. com. 1997-98, manpower and tng. com. chair 2000—, Elsevier rsch. initiative award 1993), Am. Motility Soc. (steering com. 1991-94), Am. Physiol. Soc., Am. Fedn. for Clin. Rsch., Soc. for Neurosci., Women in Gastroenterology, Phila. Gastrointestinal Rsch. Group (pres. 1986-87), Sigma Delta Epsilon. Avocations: violin, art. Office: The Milton S Hershey Med Ctr Rm C5800 PO Box 850 Hershey PA 17033-0850

OUYANG, JINSONG, computer science researcher; b. Chengdu, Sichuan, China, Oct. 27, 1966; came to U.S., 1997; s. Shen-Zhang Ou and Shu-Qun Lan; m. Lan Yan, Feb. 6, 1991. PhD, U. NSW, Australia, 1997. Computer arch. Sichuan Sky Software Co., Chengdu, 1991-94; rschr. HP Labs and HP Open View, Palo Alto, Calif., 1997—. Mem. IEEE Computer Soc., Assn. Computing Machinery. Office: Ms5726 8000 Foothills Blvd Roseville CA 95747-6553 Fax: 916-785-9893. E-mail: jinsong_ouyang@hp.com.

OUYANG, LIANGBIAO, petroleum engineer, researcher, petroleum engineer, educator; b. Nanan, Fujian Province, China, Sept. 16, 1964; s. Teng Ouyang, Zhangjia Ouyang; m. Bin Cao; children: Yafei, Amy. BSc, U.Sci.& Tech.of China, Hefei, Anhui, China, M in Engring., 1988; MSc, Stanford U., 1995, PhD, 1998. Lectr. U. Sci. & Tech. of China, Hefei, China, 1988—93; lead rsch. scientist Chevron Petroleum Tech. Co., Hosuton, Tex., 1998—2001; sr. rsch. scientist ChevronTexaco Exploration & Prodn. Tech. Co., Houston, 2001—. Contbr. articles to profl. jours. Student adv. U. Sci.& Tech. of China, 1988—93. Fellow The Shell Found. fellow, Stanford U., 1995, The Rsch. fellow, 1994—98. Mem.: Soc. Profl. Well Log Analysts, So.of Petroleum Engr., Internat. (tech. editor SPE Reservoir Evaluation & Engring. Jour. 2001—, tech. editor SPE Prodn. & Facilities Jour. 2001—, mem. editl. review com. 2000—). Avocations: Classical Music, bridge, badminton, tennis. Office: ChevronTexaco Corporation 2202 Oil Center Court Houston TX 77073

OUYANG, YING, environmental scientist, educator; b. Wan Ning, Hainan, China; s. Jia Xing and Nan C. Ouyang; m. Min Li; children: Yu, Bo. PhD, Oreg. State U., 1990. Post doctoral rsch. assoc. U. of Calif., Riverside, 1990—91, U. of Fla., Gainesville, 1991—94; project scientist ManTech Environ. Tech. Inc., U.S.-EPA Nat. Risk Mgmt. Rsch. Lab., Ada, Okla., 1995—97; rsch. scientist U. of Ala., Tuscaloosa, 1997—99; environ. scientist St. Johns River Water Mgmt. Dist., Palatka, Fla., 1999—. Contbr. articles to profl. jours. Mem.: Soil Sci. Soc. Am., Am. Geophys. Union. Office: St Johns River Water MgmtDist PO Box 1429 Palatka FL 32178 Business E-Mail: youyang@sjrwmd.com.

OUZTS, EUGENE THOMAS, minister, secondary education educator; b. Thomasville, Ga., June 7, 1930; s. John Travis and Livie Mae (Strickland) O.; m. Mary Olive Vineyard, May 31, 1956. BA, Harding U., Searcy, AR, 1956, MA, 1957; postgrad., Murray State U., KY, U. Ark., U. Ariz., Ariz. State U., No. Ariz. U. Cert. secondary tchr., Ark., Mo., Ariz.; cert. c.c. tchr., Ariz.; ordained minister Church of Christ, 1956. Min. various chs., Ark., Mo., Tex., 1957-65; tchr. various pub. schs., Ark., Mo., Ariz., 1959-92; min. Ch. of Christ, Clifton and Morenci, Ariz., 1965—; 1st lt. CAP/USAF, 1980, advanced through grades to lt. col., 1989, chaplain Ariz., 1982—, asst. wing chaplain, 1985—. Adviser student activities Clifton (Ariz.) Pub. Schs., 1965-92; bd. dirs. Ariz. Ch. of Christ Bible Camp, Tucson, 1966—. Mem. airport adv. bd. Greenlee County, Clifton, Ariz., 1992—. Recipient Meritorious Svc. award, 1994, Exceptional Svc. award, 1997, Civil Air Patrol; named Ariz. Wing Chaplain of Yr, 1984, Thomas C. Casaday Unit Chaplain of Yr., 1985, Ariz. Wing Safety Officer of Yr., 1989, Ariz. Wing Sr. Mem. of Yr., 1994, Southwest Region Sr. Mem. of Yr., 1995, Civil Air Patrol. Mem. Mil. Chaplains Assn., Disabled Am. Vets., Am. Legion, Elks. Democrat. Avocations: flying, building and flying model aircraft, reading. Home and Office: HC 1 Box 557 Duncan AZ 85534-9720

OVADIAH, JANICE, cultural institute executive; m. Isaac Ovadiah; children: Meir Benjamin, Simha Victoria Miriam. BA, Washington U., St. Louis, 1965; MA, Columbia U., 1967, PhD, 1978. Dir. profl. study tours Am. Odysseys, Inc., 1973-84; escort, interpreter in French U.S. Dept. State, 1978-84; asst. to exec. dir. Meml. Found. for Jewish Culture, 1984-87; exec. dir. Congregation Shearith Israel/The Spanish & Portuguese Syn., N.Y.C., 1987—, Sephardic House, N.Y.C., 1987—. Instr. French Rutgers U., New Brunswick, N.J., 1978-79; asst. to dir. of The Maison Franclase, Columbia U., 1970-72; instr. French Columbia U., 1968-70; lectr. in field. Author: (books) Toward a Concept of Cinematic Literature: An Analysis of Hiroshima, Mon Amour, 1983, The Far Away Island of the Grey Lady, 1979, others; contbr. articles to profl. jours. Office: Sephardic House 15 W 16th St New York NY 10011-6301 Fax: 212-294-6149. E-mail: sephardichouse@cjh.org.

OVARY, ZOLTAN, pathology educator; b. Kolozsvar, Hungary, Apr. 13, 1907; came to U.S., 1954; s. Elemer and Olga (Purjesz) O. Degree, Reformed Coll. at Kolozsvar, 1924; MD, U. Paris, 1932. Scientist Med. Sch., Johns Hopkins U., Balt., 1954-59; assoc. prof. Sch. Pathology, NYU, N.Y.C., 1959-62, prof., 1962—. Author: Souvenirs: Around the World in Ninety Years; contbr. over 300 articles to sci. jours. Achievements include first to demonstrate passive cutaneous anaphylaxis, diversity of antibody functions related to isotype bridging or crosslinking as first step of cellular activation. Home: 343 E 30th St Apt 14A New York NY 10016-6438 Office: NYU Med Sch Dept Pathology 550 1st Ave New York NY 10016-6402

OVERBECK, GENE EDWARD, retired airline executive, lawyer; b. St. Louis, June 16, 1929; s. Harry C. and Edna (Kessler) O.; m. Patricia June Bay, Oct. 5, 1957; children: Richard, Thomas, Elizabeth, Katherine. BA, U. Mich., 1951, JD, 1953. Bar: Mich. 1953, Mo. 1954, N.Y. 1958, Tex. 1980. Asso. firm Sullivan & Cromwell, N.Y.C., 1957-59; gen. atty. Am. Airlines, 1959-67, v.p., gen. counsel, 1967-72, sr. v.p., 1972-90. Served with AUS, 1954-57. Home: 13606 Rex Terrace Rd Rapid City MI 49676-9628 E-mail: GEOverbeck@aol.com.

OVERBECK, THOMAS JEROME, university liturgist, consultant; b. Cin., Nov. 21, 1946; s. Thomas Jerome and Virginia Glen (Scully) Overbeck. AB in Classics, Loyola U., Chgo., 1970; MEd in Counseling, Xavier U., 1972; MDiv, Jesuit Sch. Theology, 1974, ThM, 1975, STL, 1982; PhD, Grad. Theol. Union, 1983. Mem. univ. ministry Xavier U., Cin., 1970-72; mem. faculty and univ. ministry Santa Clara (Calif.) U., 1974-76, Loyola U., Chgo., 1976-79, univ. liturgist, 1983—. Liturg. cons. Loyola U., Chgo., 1983—, Archdiocese of Chgo., 1983—; cons. to Jesuit superior Loyola U. Jesuit Cmty., Chgo., 1996—; co-dir. summer counseling program Xavier U., 1970—72. Author: (book) Ancient Fonts, Modern Lessons, 1998, Preparing Your Catholic Wedding, 2002; contbr. Counselor Berkeley Free Clinic, 1973, Cin. Free Clinic, 1971. Mem.: The Liturg. Conf., Am. Sch. Counselors Assn., Societas Liturgica, Am. Counseling Assn., Assn. Jesuit Liturgists, N.Am. Acad. Liturgy, Golden Key Honor Soc., Alpha Sigma Nu. Roman Catholic. Avocation: Avocations: racquetball, bike riding, ice skating. Office: Loyola U 6525 N Sheridan Rd Chicago IL 60626

OVERBY, OSMUND RUDOLF, art historian, educator; b. Mpls., Nov. 8, 1931; s. Oscar Rudolph and Gertrude Christine (Boe) O.; m. Barbara Ruth Spande, Mar. 20, 1954; children: Paul, Katherine, Charlotte. BA, St. Olaf Coll., 1953; B.Arch., U. Wash., 1958; MA, Yale U., 1960, PhD, 1963. Asst. in instruction dept. of history of art Yale U., 1959-60, 61-62; architect Hist. Am. Bldgs. Survey, U.S. Nat. Park Service, 1960-61, summers 1959, 62, 63, 65, 68, 69, 70, 73, 85; lectr. dept. fine arts U. Toronto, Ont., Can., 1963-64; faculty dept. art history and archaeology U. Mo., Columbia, 1964—, dept. chmn., 1967-70, 75-77, prof. art history, 1979-98, prof. emeritus, 1998—, dir. Mus. of Art and Archaeology, 1977-83. Vis. prof. dept. architecture U. Calif., Berkeley, 1980; Morgan prof. U. Louisville, 1989; vis. prof. dept. art history and archaeology Washington U., St. Louis, 1996; bd. advisors Nat. Trust for Hist. Preservation, 1974-83; cons., panelist Nat. Endowment for Humanities, 1974— ; bd. Mo. Mansion Preservation Commn., 1974-87; advisor Heritage/St. Louis Survey, 1974-76; counsellor to St. Louis Landmarks Assn., 1977— ; chmn. Task Force on Hist. Preservation City of Columbia, 1977-78; cons. on hist. preservation; active Mo. Adv. Council on Hist. Preservation, 1967-82; lectr., exhibitor profl. confs. in field Author: Historic American Buildings Survey, Rhode Island Catalog, 1972, William Adair Bernoudy, Architect, Bringing the Legacy of Frank Lloyd Wright to St. Louis, 1999; co-author: Laclede's Landing, a History and Architectural Guide, 1977, The Saint Louis Old Post Office, A History and Architectural Guide to the Building and Its Neighborhood, 1979; co-author, editor: Illustrated Museum Handbook, A Guide to the Collections in the Museum of Art and Archaeology, University of Missouri-Columbia, 1982; editor in chief Buildings of the United States series, 1990-96; contbr. sects. to books, articles to profl. publs. in field. Served with U.S. Army, 1953-55. Recipient various fellowships and grants in field. Mem. Soc. Archtl. Historians (bd. dirs. 1968-73, 78-81, Jour. editor 1968-73, dir. Mo. Valley chpt., session chmn. ann. meeting 1976, v.p. 1982-86, pres. 1986-88, chmn. coms.), Mid-Continent Am. Studies Assn. (editorial bd. American Studies 1965-70), Midwest Art History Soc. (bd. 1975-78, gen. chmn. annual meeting 1977), Mid-Am. Coll. Art Assn. (session chmn. annual meeting 1975), Mo. Heritage Trust (pres. 1976-79, 81-83, bd. dirs. 1979—), Coll. Art Assn., Landmarks Assn. St. Louis. Lutheran. Home: 1118 W Rollins Rd Columbia MO 65203-2221 Office: U Mo Dept Art History & Archaeolo Columbia MO 65211-0001 E-mail: overbyo@missouri.edu.

OVERFELT, CLARENCE LAHUGH, lawyer; b. Big Timber, Mont., Apr. 15, 1935; s. Leo and Clara (Drivdahl) O.; m. Joyce Overfelt, Feb. 15, 1959 (div. 1977); children: Kent Leo, Reed Allen; m. Allyce Overfelt, Nov. 21, 1977. BA, U. Mont., 1958, JD, 1968. Bar: Mont. 1968, U.S. Dist. Ct. Mont. 1968. Ptnr. Randono Overfelt & Gianotti, Great Falls, Mont., 1968-73; pvt. practice Overfelt Law Firm, 1973-91, pres., sr. mem., 1980—. Tchr. Cut Bank (Mont.) Pub. Schs., 1959-60, Helena (Mont.) Pub. Schs., 1960-65. Mem. Assn. Trial Lawyers Am., Mont. Trial Lawyers Assn., Civil Justice Found., Meadowlark Country Club, Elks, Kiwanis. Democrat. Episcopalian. Avocations: golf, skiing, music, woodworking, gardening. Home: 128 Lower River Rd Great Falls MT 59405-8203 Office: Overfelt Law Firm PC 121 4th St N Ste 2E Great Falls MT 59401-2570

OVERGAARD, MITCHELL JERSILD, lawyer; b. Chgo., Jan. 9, 1931; s. Kristen Mikkelsen and Rose Eunice (Jersild) O.; m. Joan Marquardt, Aug. 2, 1958; children: Wade, Kristin Bond, Neil. BA, U. Chgo., 1950, JD, 1953. Bar: Ill. 1957, U.S. Supreme Ct. 1975. Assoc. Dale, Haffner & Grow, Chgo., 1957-63; ptnr. Overgaard & Davis, 1963-2000, of counsel, 2001—. Dir. Cmty. Bank of Homewood-Flossmoor, Homewood, Ill., 1973—83. Trustee Village of Homewood, 1965-69, 85-95; commr. Homewood-Flossmoor Park Dist., 1969-77; past pres., bd. dirs. Family Svcs. and Mental Health Ctr. of South Cook County, Homewood Youth Coun.; bd. dirs. Ill. Philharm. Orch., 1992-95, South Star Svcs., 1998—. With U.S. Army, 1953-56. Mem.: Rotary. Mem. Reformed Ch. in America (elder) Home: 19137 Loomis Ave Homewood IL 60430-4431 Office: Overgaard & Davis 134 N La Salle St Chicago IL 60602-1086

OVERGAARD, ROBERT MILTON, retired religious organization administrator; b. Ashby, Minn., Nov. 6, 1929; s. Gust and Ella (Johnson) O.; m. Sally Lee Stephenson, Dec. 29, 1949; children: Catherine Jean Overgaard Thuleen, Robert Milton, Elizabeth Dianne Overgaard Almendinger, Barbara, Craig, David (dec.), Lori Overgaard Noack. Cert., Luth. Brethren Sem., 1954; BS, Mayville (N.D.) State U., 1959; MS, U. Oreg., 1970. Ordained to ministry Ch. Luth. Brethren Am., 1954. Pastor Elim Luth. Ch., Frontier, Sask., Can., 1954-57, Ebenezer Luth. Ch., Mayville, 1957-60, Immanuel Luth. Ch., Eugene, Oreg., 1960-63, 59th Street Luth. Ch., Bklyn., 1963-68, Immanuel Luth. Ch., Pasadena, Calif., 1969-73; exec. dir. world missions Ch. Luth. Brethren Am., Fergus Falls, Minn., 1973-86, pres., 1986—2001, ret., 2001. Editor Faith and Fellowship, 1967-75. Home: 806 W Channing Ave Fergus Falls MN 56537-3221 Office: Ch Luth Brethren Am PO Box 655 Fergus Falls MN 56538-0655 E-mail: rmo@clba.org.

OVERGAARD, WILLARD MICHELE, retired political scientist, jurisprudent; b. Montpelier, Idaho, Oct. 16, 1925; s. Elias Nielsen and Myrtle LaVerne (Humphrey) O.; m. Lucia Clare Cochrane, June 14, 1946; children: Eric Willard, Mark Fredrik, Alisa Claire. BA, U. Oreg., 1949; Fulbright scholar, U. Oslo, 1949-50; MA (non-resident scholar 1954-55), U. Wis., Madison, 1955; PhD in Polit. Sci. (adminstrv. fellow 1955-56, research fellow 1962-64), U. Minn., 1969. Instr., Soviet and internat. affairs Intelligence Sch., U.S. Army, Europe, 1956-62, dir. intelligence rsch. tng. program, 1958-61; asst. prof. internat. affairs George Washington U., 1964-67; sr. staff polit. scientist Ops. Research Inst., U.S. Army Inst. Advanced Studies, Carlisle, Pa., 1967-70; assoc. prof. polit. sci., chmn. dept., dir. Internat. Studies Inst., Westminster Coll., New Wilmington, 1970-72; prof. polit. sci. and pub. law Boise (Idaho) State U., 1972-94, chmn. dept., 1972-87, acad. dir. M.P.A. degree program, personnel adminstr., mem. humanities council interdisciplinary studies in humanities, 1976-87, prof. of pub. law emeritus, 1994—, dir. Taft Inst. Seminars for Pub. Sch. Tchrs., 1985-87, coord. Legal Asst. Program, 1990-95. Mem. comml. panel Am. Arbitration Assn., 1974—; mem. Consortium for Idaho's Future, 1974-75; adv. com. Idaho Statewide Tng. Program Local Govt. Ofcls., 1974-78; adv. group Gov. Idaho Task Force Local Govt., 1977; co-dir. Idaho State Exec. Inst., Office of Gov., 1979-83; grievance hearing officer City of Boise, 1981-85; arbitrator U.S. Postal Svc., 1988-90; cons. in field. Author: The Schematic System of Soviet Totalitarianism, 3 vols, 1961, Legal Norms and Normative Bases for the Progressive Development of International Law as Defined in Soviet Treaty Relations, 1945-64, 1969; co-author: The Communist Bloc in Europe, 1959; editor: Continuity and Change in International Politics, 1972; chief editor: Idaho Jour. Politics, 1974-76. Served with USAAF, 1943-45; with AUS, 1951-54; ret. maj. USAR. Named Disting. Citizen of Idaho, Idaho Statesman, 1979. Mem. ABA (assoc.), Res. Officers Assn. (life), Am. Legion. Home: 2023 S Five Mile Rd Boise ID 83709-2316 E-mail: wgaard@velocitus.net.

OVERHAUSER, ALBERT WARNER, physicist; b. San Diego, Aug. 17, 1925; s. Clarence Albert and Gertrude Irene (Pehrson) Overhauser; m. Margaret Mary Casey, Aug. 25, 1951; children: Teresa, Catherine, Joan, Paul, John, David, Susan, Steven. AB, U. Calif., Berkeley, 1948, PhD, 1951; DSc (hon.) , U. Chgo., 1979; LLD (hon.) , Simon Fraser U., 1998. Research assoc. U. Ill., 1951—53; asst. prof. physics Cornell U., 1953—56, assoc. prof., 1956—58; supr. solid state physics Ford Motor Co., Dearborn, Mich., 1958—62, mgr. theoret. scis., 1962—69, asst. dir. phys. scis., 1969—72, dir. phys. scis., 1972—73; prof. physics Purdue U., West Lafayette, Ind., 1973—74, Stuart disting. prof. physics, 1974—. With USNR, 1944—46. Recipient Alexander von Humboldt sr. U.S. scientist award, 1979, Nat. medal of Sci., Pres. of U.S., 1994. Fellow: Am. Acad. Arts and Scis., Am. Phys. Soc. (Oliver E. Buckley Solid State Physics prize 1975); mem.: NAS. Home: 236 Pawnee Dr West Lafayette IN 47906-2115 Office: Purdue U Dept Of Physics West Lafayette IN 47907 E-mail: awo@physics.purdue.edu.

OVERHOLT, HUGH ROBERT, lawyer, retired army officer; b. Beebe, Ark., Oct. 29, 1933; s. Harold R. and Cuma E. (Hall) O.; m. Laura Annell Arnold, May 5, 1961; children: Sharon, Scott. Student, Coll. of Ozarks, 1951-53; BA, U. Ark., 1955, LL.B., 1957. Bar: Ark. 1957. Commd. 1st lt. U.S. Army, 1957, advanced through grades to maj. gen., 1981; chief Criminal Law Div., JAG Sch., Charlottesville, Va., 1971-73; chief personnel, plans and tng. Office of JAG, U.S. Army, Washington, 1973-75; staff judge adv. XVIII Airborne Corps, Ft. Bragg, N.C., 1976-78; spl. asst. for legal and selected policy matters Office of Dep. Asst., 1978-79; asst. judge adv. gen. for mil. law Office of JAG, Washington, 1979-81, asst. judge adv. gen., 1981-85, judge adv. gen, 1985-89; atty. Ward & Smith, New Bern, N.C., 1989—. Notes and comment editor Ark. Law Rev, 1956-57. Decorated Army Meritorious Service medal with oak leaf cluster, Army Commendation medal with 2 oak leaf clusters., Legion of Merit, Def. Meritorious Service medal, D.S.M. Mem. ABA, N.C. Bar Assn., Ark. Bar Assn., Assn. U.S. Army, Delta Theta Phi, Omicron Delta Kappa, Sigma Pi. Presbyterian. Office: Ward and Smith 1001 College Ct New Bern NC 28562-4972

OVERHOLT, MILES HARVARD, cable television consultant; b. Glendale, Calif., Sept. 30, 1921; s. Miles Harvard and Alma Overholt; A.B., Harvard Coll., 1943; m. Jessie Foster, Sept. 18, 1947; children: Miles Harvard, Keith Foster. Mktg. analyst Dun & Bradstreet, Phila., 1947-48; collection mgr. Standard Oil of Calif., L.A., 1948-53; br. mgr. RCA Svc. Co., Phila., 1953-63, ops. mgr. Classified Aerospace project RCA, Riverton, N.J., 1963; pres. CPS, Inc., Paoli, Pa., 1964-67; v.p. Gen. Time Corp.; mem. pres.'s exec. com. Gen. Time Corp., Mesa, Ariz., 1970-78; gen. mgr., dir. svc. Talley Industries, Mesa, 1967-78; v.p., gen. mgr. Northwest Entertainment Network, Inc., Seattle, 1979-81; v.p., dir. Cable Communication Cons., 1982—; mcpl. cable cons., 1981—; pub. The Mcpl. Cable Regulator. Served with USMCR, 1943-46. Decorated Bronze Star, Purple Heart (two). Mem. Nat. Assn. TV Officers and Advisors. Home: 8320 Frederick Pl Edmonds WA 98026-5033 Office: Cable Communication Cons 502 E Main St Auburn WA 98002-5502

OVERKAMP, SUNSHINE JANDA, marketing professional; b. Norfolk, Va., Dec. 16, 1943; d. Vojt Allen and Willa Martha (Hall) Janda; m. Richard Thomas Overkamp, Sept. 1, 1964; children: Cherie Maranda, Mari Elizabeth, Richard Thomas, Jr. BA in Comms., Mich. State U., 1968; MBA, Pepperdine U., 1980; postgrad., Harvard U. Grad. Sch. Bus., 1982—. Exec. v.p. United Way of Tri-State, N.Y.C.; sr. v.p. Tri-State Market for United Way of Am., 1983-85, United Way of the Tex. Gulf Coast, Houston, 1979-83, 85-87, United Way of Am., 1987-93; v.p. mem., mktg. and comms. Coun. on Founds., Washington, 1993—. Contbg. author: A Communicator's Guide to Marketing. Recipient numerous nat., state and local awards for comms. programs, advt., promotion and publs., including an Emmy, Nat. Acad. TV Arts and Scis. Mem. Pub. Rels. Soc. Am. (nat. bd. dirs., cert., chmn. ethics promotion com., chair of honors and awards com., recipient Bronze Anvil), Internat. Assn. Bus. Communicator's Mktg. Coun. (past chmn., Gold Quill award), Corp. Rels. Roundtable, Women Execs. in Pub. Rels. Home: 6331 Alderman Dr Kingstowne VA 22315-3731 Office: Coun on Foundations 1828 L St NW Ste 300 Washington DC 20036-5104

OVERLUND, ERVIN KENNETH, pastor; b. Silverton, Oreg., May 6, 1928; s. Oscar Reinhart and Emma Charlotte (Johnson) O.; m. Sylvia Adrene Moe, Nov. 25, 1954; children: Ruth Gorham, Mary C. Sluke, Timothy E., Joel K., Rachel Waggoner. BA, Augsburg Coll., 1956; B of Divinity, Luther Sem., 1961. Specialized ministry (chaplaincy), 1978. Pastor Coulee (N.D.) Luth. Parish, 1961-65, Benedict (N.D.) Parish, 1965-68, Fordville (N.D.) Parish, 1969-78; chaplain Lake Region Luth. Home, Devil's Lake, N.D., 1978-90, Good Samaritan Ctr., Devil's Lake, 1981-96; pastor Argyle Luth. Parish, Glenboro, Man., Can., 1991-95, St. Matthew Luth. Ch., Beaverton, Oreg., 1997—. Dean Grafton Conf., East N.D. Dist., Am. Luth. Ch., 1973; treas. Devil's Lake Ministerial Assn., 1979-96. V.p. United Way of Devil's Lake, 1982. Mem. ACPE, Assn. Luths. Specializing in Pastoral Care Ministries, Am. Soc. on Aging, Rotary Club Devil's Lake (sec. 1979-95, Paul Harris fellow 1995), Sunrise Rotary (treas. N.W. Rotary Prostate Awareness Project 2000-01, sec. 2001—). Avocations: personal computer, walking, traveling. Office: St Matthew Luth Ch 10390 SW Canyon Rd Beaverton OR 97005-1996 E-mail: ekosao@aol.com.

OVERMAN, LARRY EUGENE, chemistry educator; b. Chgo., Mar. 9, 1943; s. Lemoine Emerson and Dorothy Jane Overman; m. Joanne Louise Dewey, June 5, 1966; children: Michael, Jackie. BA in Chemistry, Earlham Coll., 1965; PhD in Organic Chemistry, U. Wis., 1969. Asst. prof. chemistry U. Calif., Irvine, 1971-76, assoc. prof. chemistry, 1976-79, prof. chemistry, 1979-94, chair dept. chemistry, 1990-93, disting. prof. chemistry, 1994—. Mem. sci. adv. bd. Pharmacopeia, Inc., 1993—; co-chair bd. chem. scis. and tech. NRC, 1997-2000. Editor-in-chief Organic Reactions, 1999—; bd. editors Organic Reactions, 1984-97, Organic Syntheses, 1986-94; hon. mem. editl. adv. bd. Ann. Reports in Hetero Chem., 1989-95, Synlett, 1989—, Jour. Am. Chem. Soc., 1996-, Chem. Revs., 1996-2000, Accounts Chem. Rsch., 1996-99; mem. cons. editors Tetrahedron Publs., 1995—; mem. editl. bd. Procs. NAS, 1998-2000. Recipient Sr. Scientist award Alexander von Humboldt Found., 1985-87, Jacob Javits award Nat. Inst. Neurol. Sci., 1985-92, 92-99, Disting. Faculty award Earlham Coll., 1999, S.T. Li prize for achievements in sci. and tech., 1999, Yamada prize, 2002; fellowship Japan Soc. for Promotion of Sci., 2000; predoctoral fellow NIH, 1966-69, postdoctoral fellow, 1969-71; fellow A.P. Sloan Found., 1975-77, Guggenheim fellow, 1993-94, Japan Soc. Promotion Sci. fellow, 2000; Arthur C. Cope scholar, 1989. Fellow NAS, AAAS, Am. Acad. Arts and Scis.; mem. Am. Chem. Soc. (exec. com. organic divsn., Cope Scholar award 1989, Creative Work in Synthetic Organic Chemistry award 1995), Royal Soc. Chemistry (Centenary medal 1997). Achievements include research in new methods for organic synthesis, natural products synthesis, medicinal chemistry. Office: U Calif Irvine Dept Chemistry 516 Rowland Hl Irvine CA 92697-2025 E-mail: leoverma@uci.edu.

OVERMYER, DANIEL LEE, Asian studies educator; b. Columbus, Ohio, Aug. 20, 1935; s. Elmer Earl and Bernice Alma (Hesselbart) O.; m. Estella Velazquez, June 19, 1965; children: Rebecca Lynn, Mark Edward. BA, Westmar Coll., LeMars, Iowa, 1957; BD, Evang. Theol. Sem., Naperville, Ill., 1960; MA, U. Chgo., 1966, PhD, 1971. Pastor Evangel. United Brethren Ch., Chgo., 1960-64; asst. prof. dept. religion Oberlin (Ohio) Coll., 1970-73; prof. Asian studies U. B.C., Vancouver, Can., 1973—, acting head religious studies Can., 1984-85, head Asian studies Can., 1986-91. Vis. prof. Princeton U., 1983, U. Heidelberg, 1993, Nat. Chengchi Univ., Taiwan, 2002; prof. Chinese U. Hong Kong, 1996-98; hon. prof. Shanghai Normal U., 1997—. Author: Folk Buddhist Religion, 1976, Religions of China, 1986; (with David Jordan) The Flying Phoenix, 1986, Precious Volumes: An Introduction to Chinese Sectarian Scriptures From the Sixteenth and Seventeenth Centuries, 1999; edit. Ethnography in China Today:A Critical Assessment of Methods and Results, 2002; contbr. articles to encys. and profl. jours. Chmn. Sch. Consultative Com., Vancouver, 1976-77; coord. Vancouver Boys Soccer League, 1979-81; adult edn. coord. United Ch. Can., Vancouver, 1981-84; co-chmn. Endowment Lands Regional Park Com., 1987-90; co-chair China and Inner Asia Coun., Assn. Asian Studies, 1992—. With USNR, 1953-61. Recipient Killam faculty rsch. prize U. B.C., 1986, Killiam faculty tchg. prize, 2000; NEH fellow, 1978, 79, China Rsch. fellow, 1981, sr. fellow coun. humanities Princeton U., 1983, Wang Inst. Grad. Studies fellow, 1985-86. Fellow Royal Soc. Can.; mem. Am. Soc. Study Religion, Soc. Study Chinese Religions (pres. 1985-88), Assn. Asian Studies. Democrat. Methodist. Avocations: photography, swimming, hiking, gardening. Home: 3393 W 26th Ave V Vancouver BC Canada V6S 1N4 Office: U BC Dept Asian Studies Vancouver BC Canada V6T 1Z2 E-mail: dano@interchange.ubc.ca.

OVERTON, EDWIN DEAN, campus minister, educator; b. Dec. 2, 1939; s. William Edward and Georgia Beryl (Fronk) O. BTh, Midwest Christian Coll., 1963; MA in Religion, Ea. N.Mex. U., 1969, EdS, 1978; postgrad., Fuller Theol. Sem., 1980. Ordained to ministry Christian Ch., 1978. Min. Christian Ch., Englewood, Kans., 1962-63; youth min. 1st Christian Ch., Beaver, Okla., 1963-67; campus min. Cen. Christian Ch., Portales, N.Mex., 1967-68, Christian Campus House, Portales, 1968—; tchr. religion, philosophy, counseling Ea. N.Mex. U., 1970—, acting chmn. religion dept., 2000. Dir. Campus Christian House, 1980—; farm and ranch partner, Beaver, Okla., 1963—. State dir. Beaver Jr. C. of C., 1964-65; pres. Beaver H.S. Alumni Assn., 1964-65; elder Cen. Christian Ch., Portales, 1985-88, 90-93; chmn. Beaver County March of Dimes, 1966; neighborhood chmn. Portales March of Dimes, 1997; pres. Portales Tennis Assn., 1977-78. Mem. U.S. Tennis Assn., Am. Assn. Christian Counselors, Ea. N.Mex. U. Faith in Life Com., Lions Club. Republican. Home: 1129 Libra Dr Portales NM 88130-6123 Office: Christian Campus House 223 S Avenue K Portales NM 88130-6643 E-mail: campusmin@juno.com.

OVERTON, ELIZABETH NICOLE, elementary school educator, aerobics instructor; b. Fayetteville, N.C., Dec. 22, 1966; d. Hilton Rudolph and Pearl Elizabeth (Jackson) Barefoot; m. Stephen Mark Overton, Mar. 29, 1997; children: Jessup Colton, Caden Jackson. BA in English, Campbell U., 1989, MEd in English Edn., 1996, MEd in Elem. Edn., 1999. Lic. tchr., N.C.; cert. fitness instructor, Nat. Dance Exercis Instr.'s Tng. Assn. Tutor gifted students Campbell U., Buies Creek, N.C., 1987-88; tchr. secondary English and journalism Sampson County Schs., Clinton, 1989-97; tchr. 2d grade reading Harnett County Schs., Lillington, 1997-2000; instr. aerobics Hardbodies, Erwin, 1997—; tchr. 3d grade Harnett County Schs., Dunn, NC, 2000—. Advisor yearbook Raider, Sampson County Schs., 1990-97, asst. editor lit. mag. Lyricist, 1987-88; editor, pub. newsletter Tiger Times, 1997—; entertainer as Belkie Bear, Easter Bunny, Chelsie the Clown, Dunn, N.C., 1983-89. Judge Miss Erwin Denim (Little Miss), 1996; mem., soloist adult choir Stoney Run Ch., Dunn, 1981—, tchr. vacation Bible sch., 1988—, tchr. Sunday sch., 1990-91, 1999-2001. Mem. Nat. Coun. Tchrs. of English, N.C. Assn. Educators (bldg. rep. 1991-92), Woodmen of the World, Omicron Delta Kappa, Kappa Delta Pi, Phi Kappa Phi. Republican. Baptist. Avocations: fitness training, hiking, reading, travel. Home: 13339 Harnett-Dunn Hwy Dunn NC 28334 Office: Harnett Primary Sch 800 W Harnett St Dunn NC 28334

OVERTON, GEORGE WASHINGTON, lawyer; b. Hinsdale, Ill., Jan. 25, 1918; s. George Washington and Florence Mary (Darlington) O.; m. Jane Vincent Harper, Sept. 1, 1941; children— Samuel Harper, Peter Darlington, Ann Vincent AB, Harvard U., 1940; JD, U. Chgo., 1946. Bar: Ill. 1947, U.S. Dist. Ct. (no. dist.) Ill. 1947, U.S. Supreme Ct. 1951. Assoc. Pope & Ballard, Chgo., 1946-48; ptnr. Overton & Babcock, 1948-51, Taylor, Miller, Busch & Magner, Chgo., 1951-60; pvt. practice, 1960; sr. prin. Overton, Schwartz & Fritts and predecessor cos., 1961-81; of counsel Wildman Harrold Allen & Dixon, 1981—. Bd. dirs. Ill. Inst. Continuing Legal Edn., 1974-81, chmn. 1980-81; mem. com. on profl. responsibility of Ill. Supreme Ct., 1986-97, chmn., 1990-93. Contbr. articles to profl. jours. Ill. reporter Cornell U. Nat. Legal Ethics Project, 1981—; bd. dirs. Open Lands Project, 1961—, pres., 1978—81; bd. dirs. Canal Corridor Assn., 1981—, chmn., 1981—84. 1st lt. U.S. Army, 1942—45. Mem. ABA (mem. com. on counsel responsibility 1985—, com. on nonprofit corps., adv. coun. ethics 2000), Ill. Bar Assn., Chgo. Bar Assn. (bd. mgrs. 1981-83), Assn. of Bar of City of N.Y., Am. Law Inst., Univ. Club. Office: Wildman Harrold Allen & Dixon 225 W Wacker Dr Chicago IL 60606-1224 E-mail: overton@wildmanharold.com.

OVERTON, MARCUS LEE, performing arts administrator, actor, writer; b. Calhoun, Ga., Aug. 13, 1943; s. Marcus Burl Jr. and Eva Mae (Greene) O. BS in Speech and Theatre, Northwestern U., 1965. Actor, tchr. Southeastern Shakespeare Festival, Atlanta, summer 1965; actor, co. mgr. Eagles Mere Assocs. Repertory Co., Chgo., 1966; prodn. stage mgr. Lyric Opera of Chgo., 1966-72; mgr. Ravinia Festival, Highland Park, Ill., 1973-77; performing arts program mgr. Smithsonian Instn., Washington, 1983-92; exec. dir., prod. dir. Spoleto Festival U.S.A., Charleston, S.C., 1992-94; program prodr., host Who Do You Know S.C. Pub. Radio, 1994-97; instr. in theatre and arts mgmt. Coll. Charleston, 1995-97. Narrator talking books Libr. Congress, Washington, 1982-83; adv. panelist Nat. Endowment for Arts, 1977-79, D.C. Commn. on Arts and Humanities, 1989, 90, 92; bd. dirs. Nat. Cultural Resources, 1989-90, Performing Arts Assistance Corp., 1992-97; cons. in field. Prodr. Falstaff (L.A. Philharm.), 1981-82; prodr., host Spoleto Today, S.C. Pub. Radio, 1996—, Supertitles, San Diego Opera, 1999—. Northwestern U. scholar, 1961-65. Avocations: travel, prehistoric cave art, motorcycle touring, linguistics, French culture. Address: Columbia Terr # 14 2959 Columbia St San Diego CA 92103-6073 E-mail: marcoverton@k-online.com.

OVERTON, NICOLE YOLANDA, program analyst; b. Buffalo, Feb. 24, 1973; d. Dewitt David and Mary Lee Overton. BS, Buffalo State Coll., 1996. EDI programmer Ingram Micro, Buffalo, 1996—; cashier supr. Quality Markets, 1991-96. Tchg. asst., tutor for computers Buffalo State Coll., application designer, career dept. Troop leader Girl Scouts Buffalo and Erie County, 1996—, trip dir., treas., axcct., 1999—. Democrat. Baptist. Avocations: drawing, dancing, reading novels, music, movies. Office: Ingram Micro 1740 Wehrle Dr Buffalo NY 14221-7032

OVERTON, ROSILYN GAY HOFFMAN, financial services executive; b. Corsicana, Tex., July 10, 1942; d. Billy Clarence and Ima Elise (Gay) Hoffman; m. Aaron Lewis Overton, Jr., July 2, 1960 (div. Mar. 1975); children: Aaron Lewis III, Adam Jerome; m. Mardiros Hatsakorzian, 1991. BS in Math., Wright State U., Dayton, Ohio, 1972, MS in Applied Econs. (fellow), 1973; postgrad. N.Y. U. Grad. Sch. Bus., 1974-76; Cert. Coll. Fin. Planning, 1987. CFP. Research analyst Nat. Security Agy., Dept. Def., 1962-67; bus. reporter Dayton Jour.-Herald, 1973-74; economist First Nat. City Bank, N.Y.C., 1974, A.T. & T. Co., 1974-75; broker Merrill Lynch, N.Y.C., 1975-80; asst. v.p. E.F. Hutton & Co., N.Y.C., 1980-84; v.p., nat. mktg. dir. investment products Manhattan Nat. Corp., 1984-86; pres. R.H. Overton Co., N.Y.C., 1986—; ptnr. Brown & Overton Fin. Svcs., 1987—. Named Businesswoman of Yr., N.Y.C., 1976. Mem. Inst. Cert. Planners, Internat. Assn. Fin. Planning (pres. N.Y. chpt.), Gotham Bus. and Profl. Womens Club, Rotary Internat., Wright State U. Alumni Assn., Mensa, Zonta. Methodist. Office: 25418 Northern Blvd Ste 5 Little Neck NY 11362-1451

OVERWEG, NORBERT IDO ALBERT, physician; b. Enschede, The Netherlands; s. Ido and Bella Theresa (Lievenboom) Overweg; m. Angelique de Gorter; children: Eleanore, Elizabeth, Harold. MD, U. Amsterdam, 1957. Intern Univ. Amsterdam Hosp., 1958-60; resident Rochester (N.Y.) Gen. Hosp., 1961-62; postdoctoral fellow dept. pharmacology Columbia U. Coll. Physicians and Surgeons, 1962-65; instr. dept. public health Columbia U., 1965-66; rsch. assoc. dept. surgery Columbia U., Coll. Physicians and Surgeons, 1967-71; rsch. collaborator, asst. attending physician Brookhaven Nat. Lab., 1966-67; asst. prof. dept. physiology and pharmacology N.Y. U., 1971-78; cons. Lung Rsch. Ctr. Yale U. Sch. Medicine, New Haven, 1972-73; pvt. practice medicine specializing in internal medicine N.Y.C., 1967—. Attending staff St. Clare's Hosp. and Health Center, Cabrini Med. Ctr.; clin. investigator antihypertension, anti-depressant, anti-anxiety, Alzheimer's Disease, migraine headache, panick attack, and gastro-intestinal drugs. Contbr. articles to profl. jours. NIH fellow, 1964-65. Mem. Am. Soc. Pharmacology and Exptl. Therapeutics, Am. Physiol. Soc., Am. Soc. Hypertension, Am. Coll. Clin. Pharmacology, NY. Acad. Scis., AAAS, AAUP, Royal Dutch Soc. Advancement of medicine, Harvey Soc., Eastern Hypertension Soc., N.Y. County Med. Soc., Med. Soc. of N.Y., Sigma Xi. Clubs: Netherlands of N.Y., Inc. E-mial. Office: 133 E 73rd St New York NY 10021-3556 E-mail: norbertoverweg@msn.com.

OVIATT, LARRY ANDREW, retired secondary school educator; b. Boone, Iowa, Mar. 13, 1939; s. Eli Charles and T. Mae (Lathrop) O.; children: Julia, Vanessa, Dana. BA, Drake U., Des Moines, 1962; MS, San Diego State U., 1975. Tchr. art San Diego City Schs., 1969-96, mentor tchr., 1992-96; owner Perfect Travel of La Jolla, 1989-97; prof. art edn. Calif. State U., Northridge, 1998—. Prof. art edn. Calif. State U., Northridge. San Diego dir. Anderson for Pres., 1976; dist. coord. Hedgecock for Mayor, San Diego, 1984; dir. elder Help Corp., San Diego, 1988; v.p. Afrian Am. Mus., 1989-92; pres. Sushi Gallery, 1980-82; bd. dirs. Mingei Internat. Mus., 1983-87; pres. Cmty. Svc. Assn., 1984-88; past pres. Diversionary Theatre, African Am. Mus.; dir. AIDS Walk for Life, 1988, 89; bd. dirs. AIDS Art Alive. Named 1986 Tchr. of Yr. Urban League, 1986, Sec. Art Tchr. of Yr. Calif. Art Tchrs. Assn., 1988, Art Tchr. of Yr. Calif. Art Tchrs. Assn., 1992, Vol. of Yr. San Diego City Schs., 1993. Mem. So. Calif. Art Tchrs. Assn. (pres. 1984-89), Calif. Art Edn. Assn. (dir. 1984-89, conf. adminstr., Art Edn. Tchr. of Yr. award 1992), Nat. Art Edn. Assn. (dir. 1987-93). Avocations: reading, basketball, art. Home: 1500 E Ocean Blvd # 519 Long Beach CA 90802 E-mail: rsmith4720@aol.com.

OVISSI, NASSER, artist; b. Tehran, Iran, Aug. 13, 1934; s. Shaban and Batool O.; m. Ruby; 1 child, maryam. LLB, Tehran U., 1959; BA, U. Rome, 1965. Diplomat fgn. ministry, 1960-79; art cons., 1979-85. Artworks exhibited in Italy, France, Eng., Greece, Germany, Switzerland, Sweden, Spain, India, Can., U.S., Turkey, Brazil, Yugoslavia, Monaco, China, and Iran; permanent collections in mus. in Athens, Barcelona, Belgrade, Brussels, Campione, Italy, N.C., Kerman, Iran, Madrid, N.Y., Ottawa, Paris, Pasadena, Calif., Rome, Tehran, Washington, in palaces in His Royal Majesty Juan Carlos of Spain and Her Imperial Majesty Farah Pahlevi of Iran. Recipient numerous awards including gold medal Internat. Salon of Campione (Italy), 1968, grand prize Internat. Art Exhbn. in Monaco, 1974, gold medal, Madrid, 1979. Home: 1381 Park Lake Dr Reston VA 20190-3936

OVITSKY, STEVEN ALAN, musician, symphony orchestra executive; b. Chgo., Oct. 12, 1947; s. Martin N. and Ruth (Katz) O.; m. Camille Levy; 1 child, David Isaac. MusB, U. Mich., 1968; MusM, No. Ill. U., 1975. Fine arts dir. Sta. WNIU-FM Pub. Radio, Dekalb, Ill., 1972-76; program mgr. Sta. WMHT-FM Pub. Radio, Schenectady, N.Y., 1976-79; gen. mgr., artistic dir. Grant Park Concerts, Chgo., 1979-90; v.p., gen. mgr. Minn. Orch., Mpls., 1990-95; v.p., exec. dir. Milw. Symphony Orch., 1995-99, pres., exec. dir., 1999—. Panelist Ill. Arts Coun., 1986, 87, 88, Chgo. Artists Abroad, 1987-91, Nat. Endowment for the Arts, 1987-89, 98-99; bd. dirs. Ill. Arts Alliance, Chamber Music Chgo.; hon. dir. Chgo. Sinfonietta. With U.S. Army, 1968-71, Korea. Mem. NARAS, Am. Symphony Orch. League. Jewish. Avocations: audio, record collecting, softball. Office: Milw Symphony Orch 700 N Water St Ste 700 Milwaukee WI 53202-4278 Business E-Mail: ovitskys@milwaukeesymphonyorchestra.org.*

OVITT, GARY C. mayor; b. May 3, 1947; BA, U. Redlands, 1969. Tchr. Chaffey H.S., Ontario, Calif.; mayor City of Ontario, 1998—. Chmn. dept. edn. Chaffey Joint Unified Sch. Dist., 1970—. Mem. Ontario (Calif.) City Coun., 1992-99. Office: City Hall 303 E B St Ontario CA 91764-4105*

OVITZ, MICHAEL S. communications executive; b. 1946; m. Judy Reich, 1969; 3 children. Grad., UCLA, 1968. With William Morris Agy., 1968-75; co-founder, chmn. Creative Artists Agy., L.A., 1975-95; pres. Walt Disney Co., Burbank, Calif., 1995-97; owner CKE Cos., Beverly Hills, 1998—. Chmn. exec. bd. dirs. UCLA Hosp. and Med. Ctr.; bd. advisors Sch. Theater, Film and TV UCLA; bd. dirs. Livent, Inc., Gulfstream Aero. Corp., J. Crew Group, Inc. Trustee Mus. Modern Art, N.Y.C.; bd. govs. Cedars-Sinai Hosp., L.A.; mem. exec. adv. bd. Pediatric AIDS Found. Mem. Coun. Fgn. Rels., Zeta Beta Tau. Avocations: contemporary art, African antiques, Chinese furniture. Office: Artists Management Group 9465 Wilshire Blvd Ste 212 Beverly Hills CA 90212-2610

OVREBO, JUDITH, retired physical education educator; b. Wausau, Wis., Mar. 28, 1950; d. Donald Irving and Rozella Eileen (Boggs) O.; m. Harold Marvin Oberg, July 5, 1975 (div.); children: Jessica Kristine, Deborah Elisabeth. BS, U. Conn., 1972; MS in Phys. Edn., U. R.I., 1978; grad., So. Conn. State U., 1986, postgrad., 1992. Tchr. phys. edn. Fitch Jr. High Sch., Groton, Conn., 1972-79, Fitch Sr. High Sch., Groton, 1979-97. Mentor co-op. tchr. State of Conn., Groton, 1988—; evaluator New Eng. Assn. Schs. and Colls., 1993. Chairperson phys. edn. sub-com. New Eng. Assn. of Schs. and Colls., Groton, Conn., 1988-90; bd. dirs. Ledyard (Conn.) Girls Softball League, 1989—, mgr., coach, 1989—; coach Ledyard Youth Basketball League, 1991—; mentor Take Stock in Children, Ocala, Fla.; organizer Connections, 2000—; vol. Hospice Merion County, 2002. Mem. AAHPERD, NEA, Am. Softball Assn., Conn. Assn. Health, Phys. Edn., Recreation and Dance, Conn. Edn. Assn., Groton Edn. Assn., Nat. Assn. Sports and Phys. Edn., Nat. Assn. Girls and Women Sports, Phi Kappa Phi. Avocations: swimming, organ. church involvement, reading. Home: 7598 SW 81st Pl Ocala FL 34476-6924 E-mail: jovrebo@cs.com.

OVSHINSKY, STANFORD ROBERT, physicist, inventor, energy executive, information company executive; b. Akron, Ohio, Nov. 24, 1922; s. Benjamin and Bertha T. (Munitz) O.; m. Iris L. Miroy, Nov. 24, 1959; children— Benjamin, Harvey, Dale, Robin Dibner, Steven Dibner. Student public schs., Akron; DSc (hon.), Lawrence Inst. Tech., 1980; DEng (hon.), Bowling Green State U., 1981; DSc (hon.), Jordan Coll., Cedar Springs, Mich., 1989. Pres. Stanford Roberts Mfg. Co., Akron, 1946-50; mgr. centre drive dept. New Britain Machine Co., Conn., 1950-52; dir. research Hupp Corp., Detroit, 1952-55; pres. Gen. Automation, Inc., 1955-58, Ovitron Corp., Detroit, 1958-2000; pres., CEO, chief scientist Energy Conversion Devices, Inc., Troy, Mich., 1978—. Adj. prof. engring. scis. Coll. Engring., Wayne State U.; hon. advisor for sci. and tech. Beijing (China) Inst. Aeronautics and Astronautics (name changed to Beijing U. Aeros. and Astronautics); chmn. Inst. for Amorphous Studies. Contbr. articles on physics of amorphous materials, neurophysiology and neuropsychiatry to profl. jours. Recipient Diesel Gold medal German Inventors Assn., 1968, Coors Am. Ingenuity award, 1988, Karl W. Böer solar energy medal of merit U. Del. and Interna. Solar Energy Soc., 1999; named to Mich. Chem. Engring. Hall of Fame, 1983, Mich. Scientist of Yr., Impression 5 Sci. Mus., 1987, Hero for the Planet, Time mag., 1999, Hero of Chemistry, Am. Chem. Soc., 2000, Sir William Grove award IAHE, 2000. Fellow AAAS, Am. Phys. Soc.; mem. IEEE (sr.), Soc. Automotive Engrs., N.Y. Acad. Scis., Electrochem. Soc., Engring. Soc. Detroit, Cranbrook Inst. Sci. (bd. govs. 1981). Office: Energy Conversion Devices Inc 2956 Waterview Dr Rochester MI 48309

OWADA, HISASHI, government official; b. Shibata, Nigata, Japan, Sept. 18, 1932; s. Takeo and Shizuka (Tamura) O.; m. Yumiko Egashira, Oct. 7, 1962; children: Masako, Reiko, Setsuko. BA, U. Tokyo, 1955; LLB, Cambridge U., Eng., 1956. Dir. legal affairs Ministry Fgn. Affairs, New York, 1959, pvt. sec. to min. Tokyo, 1971, dir. UN polit. affairs div., 1972-74, dir. treaties div., 1974-76; pvt. sec. to prime min. Govt. of Japan, 1976-78; min. Japanese Embassy, Washington, 1979-81, Moscow, 1981-84; dir. gen. treaties bur. and for law of sea Ministry Fgn. Affairs, 1984-87, dep. vice minister, 1987-88; amb. extraordinary and plenipotentiary Permanent Mission of Japan to OECD, Paris, 1988-89; dep. min. fgn. affairs Min. Fgn. Affairs, Tokyo, 1989-91, vice min., 1991-93, advisor to mins. fgn. affairs, 1993-94; perm. rep. of Japan UN, N.Y.C., 1994-98; assoc. Inst. Internat. Law. Adj. lectr. U. Tokyo, 1963-88; vis. prof. Harvard U., Cambridge, Mass., 1979-81, 87, 89; adj. prof. Internat. Law Columbia U., 1994-2000; Inge Rennert disting. vis. prof. N.Y.U., 1994—; sr. advisor to Pres. of World Bank, advisor to Min. Fgn. Affairs of Japan, Pres. Japan Inst. Internat. Affairs, 1999—. Author: Japanese Practice in the Field of International Law, 1984, From Involvement to Engagement, 1994, Diplomacy, 1996. Bd. dirs. Aspen Inst., Ditchley Found., Salzburg Sem. Mem. Japanese Assn. Internat. Law (exec. coun.). Avocations: skiing, mountain walking, music. Fax: 83-3-3503-7411. E-mail: owada@jiia.or.jp.

OWEISS, IBRAHIM MOHAMED, economist, educator; b. Egypt, Sept. 25, 1931; came to U.S., 1960; s. Mohamed Zaki and Warda (Zeiden) O.; m. Celine M. J. Lesuisse, July 19, 1975; children: Yasmeen, Kareem. B.Com., Alexandria U., Egypt, 1952; MA, U. Minn., 1961, PhD, 1969. Tchr., 1953-55; econ. dir. indsl. projects Cairo, 1958-60; mem. faculty U. Minn., Mpls., 1961-67, Georgetown U., Washington, 1967—2002, prof. econs., 1973-75; mem. faculty Johns Hopkins U., 1971-74; first undersec. state econ. affairs Govt. Egypt, Cairo, 1977; ambassador, 1977-79; chief Egyptian Econ. Mission to U.S., 1977-79; prof. econs. Harvard U., 1997-98. Cons. econs., 1971—; mem. Pres. Coun. on Egyptian-Am. Rels., 1999—. Author: Pricing of Oil in World Trade, 1974, The Israeli Economy, 1974; editor: The Dynamics of U.S.-Arab Economic Relations, 1980, Economic Development of Egypt, 1982, Arab Civilization, Challenges and Responses, 1988, Political Economy of Contemporary Egypt, 1990, The Arab Gulf Economies: Challenges and Prospects, 2000. Pres. Assn. Egyptian-Am. Scholars, 1984-88; chmn. bd. dirs. Arab-Am. Bus. and Profl. Assn., Howard and Georgeanna Jones Inst. for Reproductive Medicine, 1984-90, Egyptian Am. Cultural Assn., 1975-77, Faith and Hope Project, 1975-77. Officer Egyptian Army, 1955-58. Decorated Egyptian Merit decoration 1st Order, Order of St. John, knight Order of Queen of Sheba, grand cordon Order Mohammed Ali Pasha; Ford Found. fellow, 1979-80. Mem. Am. Econ. Assn. Clubs: University (N.Y.C.). Moslem. Home: 4017 Glenridge St Kensington MD 20895-3708 Office: Georgetown University Dept Econs Washington DC 20057-0001 E-mail: oweissi@att.net.

OWEN, AMY, library director; b. Brigham City, Utah, June 26, 1944; d. John Wallace and Bertha (Jensen) O. BA, Brigham Young U., 1966, MLS, 1968. Systems libr. Utah State Libr., Salt Lake City, 1968-72, dir. reference svcs., 1972-74, dir. tech. svcs., 1974-81, dep. dir., 1981-87; dir., 1987—; serials com. chmn. Utah Coll. Libr. Coun., Salt Lake City, 1975-77, exec. sec., 1978-84, coun. mem. 1987—; mem. staff Gov.'s Utah Systems Planning Task Force, Salt Lake City, 1982; staff liaison Utah Gov.'s Conf. on Libr. and Info. Svcs., 1977-79, chair exec. planning com., 1990-91; mem. pres.'s adv. panel Baker & Taylor Co., Somerville, N.J., 1977-78; panelist U.S. Dept. Edn., 1992; mem. rsch. project adv. com. U. Wis. Sch. Libr. and Info., Madison, 1992-94; mem. adv. panel Nat. Commn. Libr. and Info. Svcs., 1985; Alumni Honor lectr. Coll. Humanities, Brigham Young U., 1990. Contbr. chpts. to books, also contbg. author various manuals; cons. and trainer in field. Coun. mem. Utah Endowment for Humanities, 1986-91, vice chmn., 1987-88, chair, 1988-90; trustee Bibliographic Ctr. for Rsch., 1987—, pers. com., 1988-89, chmn. pers. com., 1989-90, nominating com., 1984, v.p. bd. trustees, 1989-91, pres, 1991-93; active Chief Officers of State Libr. Agys., 1987—, stats. com., 1988-93, mem. network com., 1993—, state info. policy workshop com., 1988, bd. dirs., 1992—; mem. conf. program com. Fedn. of State Humanities Couns., 1988; mem. coop. pub. libr. data system task force Nat. Commn. on Libr. and Info. Svcs., 1988-90; grant rev. panelist NEH, 1988, 92, panel mem. reading and discussion groups, 1988; regional project mgmt. bd. mem. Intermountain Community Learning and Info. Ctr. Project, 1987-90; mem. midcontinental regional adv. com. Nat. Libr. Medicine 1991-94; mem. adv. com. Brigham Young U. Sch. Libr. and Info. Svcs. Named Libr. of Yr., Libr. Jour., 1990. Mem. Utah Libr. Assn. (pres. 1978-79, exec. bd. 1976-80, Spl. Svc. award 1989), Mountain Plains Libr. Assn. (rec. sec. 1979-80, fin. com. 1982-84, Disting. Svc. award 1989), ALA (bd. dirs. ASCLA divsn. 1984-86, 93-96, pres. ASCLA divsn. 1994-95, fin. com. 1984-86, 89-92, 93-96, planning, orgn. and bylaws com. 1981-85, SLAS program com. 1984-86, pres. program com. 1986, exec. bd. mem., 1988-90, 93-94; clene roundtable mem. com. 1984-86, nominations com. 1986-87, nat. adv. bd. office communications svcs., voices and visions project 1988-89; LITA div. Satellite Conf. Task Force mem. 1982; PLA div. editor column. 1987-89, PLA div. goals, guidelines and standards com. 1987-90, chair, 1990-91, PLA pub. libr. data svc. adv. com. 1988-91, PLA Kellogg Phase III EIC project adv. com. chair 1990-92, PLA strategic issues and directions com., 1991-92, PLA non MLS involvement com., 1990-91, ALA Office for Rsch. coop. pub. libr. data system adv. com. 1985-89), Dynix Snowbird Leadership Inst. (nat. adv. bd. 1990—), Utah Edn. Network (steering com. 1996—), Utah Partnership Edn. and Econ. Devel. (rsch. com. 1995—), Phi Kappa Phi, Alpha Lambda Delta. Home: 4786 Naniloa Dr Salt Lake City UT 84117-5547 Office: Utah State Libr 250 N 1950 W Ste A Salt Lake City UT 84116-7901*

OWEN, BRADLEY SCOTT, lieutenant governor; b. Tacoma, May 23, 1950; s. Laural Willis; m. Linda Knoll, Jan. 20, 1983; children: Shanie, Dana, Mark, Sherrie, Adam, Royce. Student pub. sch., Germany. State rep. Wash. Ho. Rep., Olympia, 1976-82; state senator Wash. State Senate, 1983-96; lt. gov. State of Wash., 1997—. Mem. Wash. State substance abuse coun., 1997—. Mem. Elks. Democrat. Office: Wash State Lt Gov PO Box 40400 Olympia WA 98504-0400*

OWEN, CAROL THOMPSON, artist, educator, writer; b. Pasadena, Calif., May 10, 1944; d. Sumner Comer and Cordelia (Whittemore) Thompson; m. James Eugene Owen, July 19, 1975; children: Kevin Christopher, Christine Celese. Student, Pasadena City Coll., 1963; BA with distinction, U. Redlands, 1966; MA, Calif. State U., L.A., 1967; MFA, Claremont Grad. Sch., 1969. Cert. community coll. instr., Calif. Head resident Pitzer Coll., Claremont, Calif., 1967-70; instr. art Mt. San Antonio Coll., Walnut, 1968-96, prof. art, 1996—, 1996-97, prof. emeritus, 1997, dir. coll. art gallery, 1972-73. Group shows include Covina Pub. Libr., 1971, U. Redlands, 1964, 65, 66, 70, 78, 88, 92, Am. Ceramic Soc., 1969, 97, 99, 2000, Mt. San Antonio Coll., 1991, The Aesthetic Process, 1993, Separate Realities, 1995, Sequence 1, 2001, San Bernardino County Mus., 1996, 97, 98, 99, Tampa Fla. Black, White & Gray, Artists Unltd., 1998, Current Clay VII, La Jolla, Calif., 1998, Westmoreland Art Nats., 1998, 99, Riverside Art Mus., 1998, Fine Art Inst. Juried Show, San Bernardino, 1998, 99, 2000, Parham Gallery, L.A., 1998, Angels Gate Cultural Ctr., San Pedro, Calif., 1998, Los Angeles County Fair, Pomona, Calif., 1998, Monrovia Arts Festival, 1998, Art for Heavens Sake Festival, 1998, 99, Riverside Art Mus., 1998, 99, 2000, Birger Sandzen Meml. Gallery, McPherson, Kans., 1998, 2000, Earthen Art Works Gallery, L.A., 1999, State Polytechnic U., Pomona, 1999, 2001, Mo. State U., Warrensburg, 1999, City of Brea Gallery, 1999, 2000, All Media Exhibit, Chico, Calif., 1999, Period Gallery, Omaha, Nebr., 1999, 2000, 2001, 2002, Mixed Media, Period Gallery, 2002, Franklin Square Gallery, Southport, N.C., 1999, 2000, Judson Gallery, L.A., 1999, Parham Gallery, L.A., 1999, San Angelo (Tex.) Mus. Fine Arts, 2000, So. Calif. Juried Art Exhbn., San Bernardino, Calif., 2000, Gallery 212, Ann Arbor, Mich., 2000, Judson Gallery, L.A., 2000, Artists Unlimited, Inc., Tampa, Fla., 2000, Urban Inst. Contemporary Arts, Grand Rapids, Mich., 2000, Tri-Lakes Ctr. for Arts, Palmer Lake, Colo., 2000, Santa Cruz Art League, Calif., 2000, Fine Arts Inst., San Bernardino County Mus., Redlands Calif. 2000, Vermont Artisan Designs, Brattleboro, 2000, USA Craft '99, New Caanan, Conn., 1999, Keith Gallery, Dexter, Mich., 1999, Claremont Forum Gallery, 1999, Parham Gallery, Santa Monica, Calif., 1999 (Grand prize 1999), City of Brea Galleries, Calif., 2000, 2001, Chiarosouro Galleries, Chgo., 2000, TLD Design Ctr. and Gallery, Westmont, Ill., 2000, 2001, North Tahoe Art Ctr., Calif., 2000, Palos Verdes Art Ctr., Rancho Palos Verdes, Calif., 2000, Peck Gallery, Providence, 2000, Alder Gallery, Oreg., 2001, Rocky Mt. Arts Ctr., N.C., 2001, Esmay Fine Art Gallery, Rochester NY, 2001, Hillcrest Festival, 2001, Dysfunctional Business of Art Center, Manitou Springs, Colorado, 2001, National Juried Exhbn. Gallery 214, Montclair, New Jersey, 2002, Period Gallery, Omaha, 2001, 2002, Mt. San Antonio Coll., Walnut, Calif., 2001, Nat. Juried Exhbn., Gallery 214, Montclair, N.J., 2002, Gallery Mia Tyson, Wilmington, N.C., 2002, numerous others; ceramic mural commd. and installed U. Redlands, 1991; represented in permanent collections Redlands Art Assn. Gallery, Redlands, Calif.. Recipient award San Bernardino County Mus., 1996, Hon. Mention, 1998, 99; Past Pres.'s Monetary award, 1997, Jack L. Conte Design Cons. Purchase award Westmoreland Art Nats., 1998, 3rd Pl. Monetary award All Calif. City of Brea Galleries, 2000, Honorarium for teapots Urban Inst. Contemporary Arts, Grand Rapids, Mich., 2000. Mem. Am. Ceramic Soc. (design divsn., Design chpt. monetary award 1999), Calif. Scholarship Fedn., Coll. Art Assn. Am., Friends of Huntington Library, L.A. County Mus. Art, Redlands Art Assn., Heard Mus. Assn., Riverside Art Mus., Fine Arts Inst., Sigma Tau Delta. Republican. Presbyterian.

OWEN, CHARLES THEODORE, journalist, publisher; b. Beech Grove, Ind., June 14, 1941; s. James Robert and Helen Maurine (Sayre) O.; m. Kathleen Rose Dellaria, Apr. 29, 1967. AS in Journalism, Vincennes U., 1972; BA in Social Sci., Chapman U., 1976; MBA, Nat. U. San Diego, 1984. Enlisted U.S. Marine Corps, 1959-72, commd. 2d lt., 1973, advanced through grades to capt., 1979; combat journalist/photographer, Vietnam, 1967-68; dep. dir. Joint Pub. Affairs Office, Camp Pendleton, 1976-79; dir. Pub. Affairs Office, Marine Corps Recruit Depot, San Diego, 1980-81; dir. comm. and mil. affairs div. Greater San Diego C. of C., 1981-82, v.p. 1987—, bd. dirs., 1982-87; now pres., pub. San Diego Bus. Jour., 1987—; host TV program Focus on San Diego Bus. Bd. dirs. San Diego Conv. and Visitors Bur., San Diego Econ. Devel. Corp.; econ. devel. advisor to Mayor of San Diego; presenter in field. Decorated Cross of Gallantry, Joint Svc. Commendation medal with Combat V (3 awards), medal of Honor 2d class (Vietnam); recipient Thomas Jefferson award, 1981. Republican. Pub. Newswriting Program Instruction, 1972. Office: 4909 Murphy Canyon Rd Ste 200 San Diego CA 92123-5381

OWEN, CYNTHIA CAROL, sales executive; b. Ft. Worth, Oct. 16, 1943; d. Charlie Bounds and Bernice Vera (Nunley) Rhoads; m. Franklin Earl Owen, Oct. 20, 1961 (div. Jan. 1987); children: Jeffrey Wayne, Valeria Ann, Carol Darlena, Pamela Kay; m. John Edward White, Jan. 1, 1988 (div. Sept. 1991). Cert. Keypuncher, Comml. Coll., 1963; student, Tarrant County Jr. Coll., 1974-77; BBA in Mgmt., U. Tex., Arlington, 1981. Keypunch operator Can-Tex. Industries, Mineral-Wells, 1966-67; sec. Electro-Midland Corp., 1967-68; exec. sec. to v.p. sales Pangburn Co., Inc., Ft. Worth, 1972-78; bookkeeper, sec. CB Svc., 1978-82; project mgr. Square D Co., 1982—. Mem. NAFE, NOW, AAUW. Baptist. Avocations: miniature golf, volleyball. Home: 1221 Pine Ridge Rd Roanoke TX 76262 Office: Square D Co 204 Airline Dr Ste 300 Coppell TX 75019-4663 E-mail: owenc@squared.com.

OWEN, DANIEL HUGH, writer; b. Vincennes, Ind., May 26, 1922; s. William Allen and Zenith Euclid (Wilkes) O.; divorced; children: Susan, Patrick William. BS in Photography and Pub. Rels., Art Ctr. Sch., L.A., 1947; M in Edn., Ind. U., 1958; D in Comms., Syracuse U., 1963. Photographer in motion picture industry, 1947; reporter, photographer Indpls. Star, AP; instr. Ind. U. Sch. Fine Arts and Sch. Edn., Syracuse U. Sch. Fine Arts, Syracuse U. Sch. Journalism, Syracuse U. Sch. Edn.; owner photography bus.; v.p.

Conklin, Labs & Bebee; founder Pizza-Porter, Inc., Dan-Lee Aviation Corp., Imagination Unlimited; v.p. Manlius Mil. Acad.; v.p. pub. rels., fundraising, advt. and student recruitment Alaska Methodist U.; pres., chmn. bd. dirs. Action Resources, Inc., Wilmington, N.C., Pitts., L.A., Detroit. Instr. Purdue U. Extension, Indpls.; spkr. in field; mem. UN coms.; bd. dirs., co-chmn. Russian Firm. Author: Circumvention of Article VI 1786, 1936, 1001 Lovers, 1968; editor The Local Paper; contbr. articles to profl. jours.; columnist La Prensa Libre. Dir. Nixon Campaign, N.Y., co-chmn.; chmn. County Republicans, Syracuse, N.Y., 1963-68; bd. dirs. Rescue Mission Syracuse, 1961-73; chmn. bus. betterment Republican Better Bus., Syracuse, 1964-67; mem. Russian Humanitarian Coms. Capt. USAF, 1941-45. Decorated Air Medal, Silver Star, Purple Heart, Presdl. Citation, French Croix de Guerre. Mem. Internat. Under Water Explorers Soc., Navy League (life), Lions, Rotary, Masonic Order, Kiwanis. Avocations: scuba diving, hot air balloon, bungee jumping, flying, archeology. Home and Office: Action Resources Inc 993C S Santa Fe Ave Ste 215 Vista CA 92083-6910 also: 5A Ave A 13-16 Zona 9 Guatemala City Guatemala

OWEN, DANIEL THOMAS, entrepreneur, venture capitalist; b. Dec. 6, 1947; s. Jesse Taylor and Loretta (Kirchner) O.; m. Margaret Wynne Chilton, Jan. 12, 1980; stepchildren: Margaret Ann Worsham Oden, Joseph Irion Worsham II. BA, U. Dayton, 1969. Dir. fundraising KERA-TV, Dallas, 1972-75; founder KERA-FM, 1973; v.p. mktg. and programming Spectradyne, Inc., 1975-87, exec. v.p., COO, 1987-89, internat. pres., 1989-90; founder, chmn. Focus Networks, 1991-95; gen. ptnr. HO2 Ptnrs., 1997—. Bd. dirs. Daisytek Internat. Inc. (DZTK). North Tex. Pub. Broadcasting, Inc., 1994—. Mem. World Pres.'s Orgn. Episcopalian. Home: 3925 Potomac Ave Dallas TX 75205-2116 Office: HO2 Ptnrs Galleria Tower Two 13455 Noel Rd Ste 1670 Dallas TX 75240 E-mail: dan@ho2.com.

OWEN, DUNCAN SHAW, JR. physician, medical educator; b. Fayetteville, N.C., Oct. 24, 1935; s. Duncan S. and Mary Gwyn (Hickerson) O.; m. Irene Lacy Rose, Oct. 22, 1966; children: Duncan Shaw III, Robert Burwell, Frances Gwyn. BS, U. N.C., 1957, MD, 1960. Diplomate Am. Bd. Internal Medicine (proctor 1977-97). Intern Med. Coll. Va., Richmond, 1960-61; jr. asst. resident in medicine N.C. Meml. Hosp., Chapel Hill, 1961-62; asst. resident in medicine Med. Coll. Va., Richmond, 1964-65, fellow in rheumatic diseases, 1965-66; internal medicine and rheumatology physician Va., 1966—; from instr. in medicine to assoc. prof. Med. Coll. Va., 1966-78, prof. dept. internal medicine, 1978—; Taliaferro/Scott Disting. prof. internal medicine Med. Coll. Va., Va. Commonwealth U., 1989-2000, emeritus prof., 2000—; dir. residency tng. Med. Coll. Va. Hosp.; dir. rheumatology clinics. Dir. clin. tng. divsn. rheumatology, allergy, immunology, 1975-98, chmn. clin. activities comm., dept. internal medicine, 1970-90; chmn. med. adv. com. Richmond br. Arthritis Found., 1966-75, nat. patient edn. com., 1979-80; med. advisor Social Security Adminstrn., HHS, 1967—; co-chmn. arthritis project Va. Regional Med. Program, 1975-76; prodr. Your Health TV series Va. Ednl. TV, 1978-79; prodr. Update in Medicine, Good Morning Virginia TV show, 1980; cons. McGuire VA. Contbr. articles to profl. jours.; assoc. editor: Va. Med., 1978-98; editl. reviewer Jour. AMA, 1979—, Arthritis Rheumatism, 1981—, Jour. Rheumatology, 1984—. Mem. usher's guild First Presbyn. Ch., Richmond, Va., 1966-70, deacon, 1974-77, chmn. of diaconate, 1976-77, elder, 1978—, chmn. witness com., 1978-80; co-chmn. physicians statewide capital funds campaign Va. Commn. U., 1986-87; bd. dirs. Mooreland Farms Assn., 1971-73, 77-81, Va. chpt. Arthritis Found., 1970-85; mem. Va. Mus., Richmond Symphony; bd. dirs. Richmond Area Health Care Coalition, 1980-84. Capt. MC, 1962-64. Nat. Inst. Arthritis and Metabolic Diseases fellow, 1965-66; recipient Gerard B. Lambert award, 1974-75, Disting. Service award Arthritis Found., 1971, U. N.C., Chapel Hill, 1999. Fellow ACP (Laureate award 1997), Am. Coll. Rheumatology; mem. AMA (expert on diagnostic and therapeutic tech. assessment program 1990-99), Am. Rheumatism Assn. (exec. com. 1979-80), Richmond Acad. Medicine (pres. 1982, chmn. bd. 1983, parliamentarian 1988-99), Med. Soc. Va. (com. on aging 1980-89, v.p. 1973, 75, del. 1972-99, scholarship com. 1980-89), Richmond Soc. Internal Medicine (bd. dirs. 1971-73), Met. Richmond C. of C. (bd. dirs. 1981-84), Jr. Clin. Club (emeritus), Country Club Va., Custis Hunting and Fishing Club, Alpha Omega Alpha. Avocations: hunting, fishing, photography, amateur radio. Home: 8910 Brieryle Rd Richmond VA 23229-7704 E-mail: dowen75089@aol.com.

OWEN, ELLYNN BARBARA, medical/surgical nurse; b. Balt., May 24, 1961; d. Homer and Florence Elaine (Harding) Works; m. Douglas Owen, May 2, 1987; children: Matthew Heath, Jennifer Kristen. BSN, Salisbury State Coll., 1983. Staff coord. Med. Temps, Inc., Marietta, Ga., 1985-86, staff RN cardiac surg., 1986-87; clin. mgr. cardiac surg. floor St. Joseph's Hosp., Atlanta, 1987-89, staff intensive care unit cardiac surg., 1989-92; nursing supr. South Eastern Health Svcs., 1992—. Home: 400 S Maryland Ave Delmar MD 21875-1521 Office: Southeastern Health Svcs 3200 Downwood Cir NW Atlanta GA 30327-1610

OWEN, H. MARTYN, lawyer; b. Decatur, Ill., Oct. 23, 1929; s. Honore Martyn and Virginia (Hunt) O.; m. Candace Catlin Benjamin, June 21, 1952; children: Leslie W., Peter H., Douglas P. AB, Princeton U., 1951; LLB, Harvard U., 1954. Bar: Conn. 1954, U.S. Ct. Appeals (2d cir.) 1961, U.S. Dist. Ct. Conn. 1962, U.S. Supreme Ct. 1963, U.S. Dist. Ct. Vt. 1965. Assoc. Shipman & Goodwin, Hartford, Conn., 1958-61, ptnr., 1961-94, of counsel, 1995-96. Mem. Simsbury (Conn.) Zoning Bd. Appeals, 1961-67, Simsbury Zoning Commn., 1967-79; sec. Capitol Region Planning Agy., 1965-66; bd. dirs. Symphony Soc. Greater Hartford, 1967-73; trustee Renbrook Sch., West Hartford, Conn., 1963-72, treas. 1964-68, pres., 1968-72, hon. life trustee, 1972—; trustee Simsbury Free Libr., 1970-84; pres. Hartford Grammar Sch., 1987-98, trustee; corporator Hartford Hosp., 1984-96; vestry St. Alban's Ch., Simsbury, 1988-94; warden, vestry St. Paul's Ch., Brunswick, Maine, 1999-2001. Lt. USNR, 1954-57. Mem. ABA, Conn. Bar Assn., Hartford County Bar Assn., Am. Law Inst., Princeton (N.Y.C.) Club, Ivy Club (Princeton, N.J.). Democrat. Episcopalian. Home: 80 Matthew Dr Brunswick ME 04011-3275

OWEN, HARRISON HOLLINGSWORTH, management consultant; b. Evanston, Ill., Dec. 2, 1935; s. Raymond Smith and Mary Crawford (Siter) Owen; m. Ethelyn Abbot, July 9, 1967; children: Cameron, Amy, Barry, Mary, Harrison Jr. BA, Williams, 1957; BD, Va. Sem., 1960; MA, Vanderbilt U., 1965. Pres. H.H. Owen & Co., Potomac, Md., 1979—. Author: (book) Riding the Tiger, 1992, Millennium Orgn., 1994, Tales from Open Space, 1995, (users guide) Open Space Technology, 2d edit., 1997, Expanding Our Now, 1997, Growing Our Now, 1997, The Spirit of Leadership, 1999, The Power of Spirit: How Organizations Transform, 2000. Home and Office: 7808 River Falls Dr Potomac MD 20854-3878 E-mail: owenhh@mindspring.com.

OWEN, HENRY, former ambassador, consultant; b. N.Y.C., Aug. 26, 1920; AB, Harvard U., 1941. Economist Dept. State, Washington, 1946-55, mem. policy planning staff, 1955-62, dep. counselor, vice chmn. policy planning coun., 1962-66, chmn. coun., 1966-69; dir. fgn. policy studies Brookings Instn., 1969-77; personal rep. of Pres. U.S. with rank of ambassador to participate in preparations for summit meetings, 1977-81; sr. adviser Salomon Bros., 1981—. Editor: Next Phase of U.S. Foreign Policy, 1971, (with Charles Schultze) Setting National Priorities, 1976. Served to lt. USN, 1942-46. Office: 1616 H St NW Washington DC 20006-4903 Fax: 202-393-4655.

OWEN, JACK EDWARD, JR. lawyer; b. Port Arthur, Tex., June 14, 1951; s. Jack Edward and Hessie (Williams) O.; m. Lucy Ross; children: Sean Rhys, MarrGwen Rhys. BS, U.S. Naval Acad., 1973; JD, Harvard U., 1979; MA, U. Tex., 1995. Bar: Tex. 1979, U.S. Ct. Mil. Appeals 1979, U.S. Supreme Ct. 1982. Judge advocate USMC, 1979-83; assoc. prof. U. Tex., Austin, 1983-86; shareholder Graves, Dougherty, Hearon & Moody, 1986-93; mng. ptnr. Osborne, Lowe, Helman & Smith, LLP, 1993—. Contbr. articles to profl. jours. Mem. U.S. Naval Acad. Alumni Assn. (trustee 1987-90). Avocation: American military history. Home: 5813 Trailridge Dr Austin TX 78731-4245 Office: Osborne Lowe Helman & Smith 301 Congress Ave Ste 1900 Austin TX 78701-2959

OWEN, JOHN, retired newspaper editor; b. Helena, Mont., June 10, 1929; s. John Earl and Ella Jean (McMillian) O.; m. Alice Winnifred Kesler, June 9, 1951; children— David Scott, Kathy Lynn. BA in Journalism, U. Mont., 1951. Sports editor Bismarck (N.D.) Tribune, 1953-55; wire editor Yakima (Wash.) Herald, 1956; with Seattle Post-Intelligencer, 1956-94, sports editor, 1968-80, assoc. editor, 1980-94, columnist, 1968-94. Author: Intermediate Eater Cookbook, 1974, Gourmand Gutbusters Cookbook, 1980, Seattle Cookbook, 1983, Great Grub Hunt Cookbook, 1989, Press Pass, 1994, Gluttony Without Guilt, 1997, Seattle Walks, 2000; also short stories. Served with AUS, 1951-52. Named Top Sports Writer in Wash. Nat. Sportswriters Orgn., 1966, 68, 69, 71, 74, 85, 88. Home: 611 Bell St Apt 4 Edmonds WA 98020-3065

OWEN, JOHN ATKINSON, JR. physician, educator; b. South Boston, Va., Sept. 24, 1924; s. John Atkinson and Mary Helen (Carrington) O.; m. Wanda Earle Reamy, Nov. 29, 1952; children— John Atkinson III, Ryland R. BS, Hampden-Sydney Coll., 1944; MD, U. Va., 1948. Intern Cin. Gen. Hosp., 1948-49; resident, fellow U. Va. Hosp., 1950-52; rsch. fellow Duke Med. Center, 1954-56; asst. prof. medicine Med. Coll. Ga., 1956-58, George Washington U. Med. Sch., 1958-60; mem. faculty U. Va. Sch. Medicine, 1960-96, prof., 1970-96, vice chmn. dept. internal medicine, 1972-74, James M. Moss prof. diabetes, sr. assoc. dean, 1995-96, prof. emeritus, 1997—. Mem. Va. Vol. Formulary Bd.; Mem. exec. com. U.S. Pharmacopeia, 1970-75, pres., 1975-80, trustee, 1975-85 Mem. editorial bd.: Jour. Clin. Pharmacology, 1971-84; editor-in-chief: Hosp. Formulary, 1974-83. Served with USNR, 1942-45, 48-50, 52-53; capt. M.C. Res. Recipient Raven award U. Va., 1948; co-recipient Horsley Research prize, 1962, Walter Reed Disting. Achievement award, 1998; laureate ACP, 1998. Mem. AMA, ACP, Am. Fedn. Clin. Rsch., So. Soc. Clin. Investigation, Med. Soc. Va. (pres. 1990-91), Am. Diabetes Assn., Endocrine Soc. Presbyterian. (elder 1965—). Home: 106 Tally Ho Dr Charlottesville VA 22901-2034

OWEN, JUNE LOIS, artist; b. Berlin, June 10, 1930; d. Raymond and Maude (O'Bryan) Legru; m. Frank Swain Owen, June 21, 1952; children: Jody Ann, Polly Swain. BFA, R.I. Sch. Design, 1952. Solo exhbns. include New Britain (Conn.) Mus. Am. Art, 1973, Munson Gallery, New Haven, Chatham, Mass., 1979, Pindar Gallery, N.Y.C., 1986-88, Slater Meml. Mus., Norwich, Conn., 1994, Main St. Gallery, Nantucket, Mass., 1975-97, Kerygma Gallery, Ridgewood, N.J., 2000; group exhbns. include Mattatuck Mus., Waterbury, Conn., 1977, DeCordova Mus., Lincoln, Mass., 1972. Avocation: cooking.

OWEN, KENNETH EMERSON, retired librarian; b. Oklahoma City, July 27, 1940; s. Emerson Copeland and Thelma Dawson Owen. BA, Okla. U., 1961; MS in Libr. Sci., La. State U., 1968. Libr., La. colonial archivist La. State Mus., New Orleans, 1964—67; libr. U. New Orleans, 1968-96; dir. Am. Italian Renaissance Found. Mus. and Libr., New Orleans, 1997-99; ret., 1999. Archivist La. Hist. Soc., New Orleans, 1973-79; cons., founding libr. New Orleans City Park Botanical Gardens, 1996. Editor Publications of the Louisiana Historical Society, Series II, 1974, Louisiana Renaissance, 1977; compiler, editor Cumulative Index to the Louisiana Historical Quarterly, vols. 34-55, 1974, Complete Cumulative Index to the Publications of the Louisiana Historical Society, 1895-1917, 1984. Advisor New Orleans City Coun., 1983-85. Avocations: horticulture, aviculture, local history. Home: 3128 Annunciation St New Orleans LA 70115-1102

OWEN, KENNETH DALE, orthodontist, real estate broker; b. Charlotte, N.C., May 9, 1938; s. Olin Watson and Ruth (Watlington) O.; m. Lura Aven Carnes, Feb. 14, 1958; children: Kenneth Dale, Aven Anna. BS, Davidson Coll., 1959; DDS, U. N.C., 1963, MSc in Orthodontics, 1967. Diplomate Am. Bd. Orthodontics. Pvt. practice dentistry specializing in orthodontia, Charlotte, 1966—. Asst. clin. prof. U. N.C. Shc. Dentistry, 1969-72; bd. dirs. N.C. Dental Found., 1973-81, 89-90, exec. com., 1974-80, v.p., 1976-77, pres., 1978-79; bd. dirs. Holiday Dental Conf. Found., 1989—, v.p., 1990—, exec. dir., 1995—. Adminstrv. bd. Myers Park United Meth. Ch., 1976-79, 93-95, 99-2001. Served with Dental Corps., AUS, 1963-65. Fellow Internat. Coll. Dentists (dep. regent N.C. 1986, 87), Am. Coll. Dentists; mem. ADA (ho. of dels. 1981-92, 95, 16 trustee dist. caucus vice chmn. 1986-89, chmn. 1989-92, ADPAC bd. 1994-99, exec. com. 1997-99), Am. Assn. Orthodontists (ho. of dels. 1980-88, 90-93), So. Assn. Orthodontists (trustee 1983-85, dir. 1987-93, pres. 1991-92, Oren A. Oliver Disting. Svc. award 2001), N.C. Assn. Orthodontists (bd. dirs. 1976-80, sec. treas. 1976-78, pres. elect 1978-79, pres. 1979-80), N.C. Dental Soc. (ho. of dels. 1969-77, 81-94, parlmentarian 1994—, trustee 1980-91, sec. treas. 1987-88, pres. elect 1988-89, pres. 1989-90, N.C. Dental Polit. Action Com. chmn. 1996—, Disting. Svc. Scroll 2000), 2d Dist. Dental Soc. (editor 1967-69, sec.-treas. 1971-74, pres. 1975-76, exec.. coun. 1971-77, 80-87), Charlotte Dental Soc. (chmn. various coms., dir. 1978-79, v.p. 1980-81), Stanly County Dental Soc. (program chair 1997—), Coll. Diplomates Am. Bd. Orthodontics, U. N.C. Orthodontic Alumni Assn. (sec.-treas. 1971, v.p. 1972-73, pres. 1974-75, exec. com. 1971-76), U. N.C. Gen. Alumni Assn. (life), U. N.C. Dental Alumni Assn., Orthovista Orthodontic Study Group, Delta Sigma Delta (life; pres. N.C. grad. chpt. 1970-71), Omicron Kappa Upsilon, Kappa Sigma, Alpha Epsilon Delta. Home: 3724 Pomfret Ln Charlotte NC 28211-3726 Office: 497 N Wendover Rd Charlotte NC 28211-1064 also: 325 N 2d St Albemarle NC 28001

OWEN, LARRY GENE, academic administrator, educator, electronic and computer integrated manufacturing consultant; b. Pine Bluff, Ark., Oct. 2, 1932; s. Cecil Earl and Helen Marie (Jacks) O.; m. Ruth MyrNewton, Sept. 3, 1953; children: Deborah, Patricia, Larry Gene, Shea. BS in Physics and Math., U. So. Miss., 1967; postgrad., Inst. Tech., 1974-75; MS n Ops. Mgmt., U. Ark., 1987. Enlisted USAF, 1951, advanced through ranks to master sgt., 1968, electronic technician, 1951-61, comms. supt., 1961-71, ret., 1971; tchr. math. and Physics Southwestern Tech. Inst., Camden, Ark., 1971-72, tchr. electronics, 1972-75; dean tech. engring.omputer Integrated Mfg. Ctr. So. Ark. U. Tech., 1988-89, dean, dir. divsn. Computer Integrated Mfg. Ctr., 1989-91, dean, prof., 1991-97, assoc. vice chancellor, 1996-98, dean emeritus, 1996—. Adj. asst. prof. So. Ark. U.; project dir. Ark. Consortium for Mfg. Competitiveness So. Growth Policies Bd., 1988-98; vice chair South Ark. Fiber Optics Coun., 1997. Contbr. articles to profl. jours. Mem. Rep. Task Force; chair Atea Coll. Cons., 1991—. Mem. Instrumentation Soc. Am. (sr.), Am. Assn. Physics Tchrs. Am. Tech. Edn. Assn. (rep. Ark. 1989-91, 95-96, pres. so. region 1992-93, chair Coll. of Cons.), Soc. Mfg. Engrs. (sr., chmn. South Ark. chpt. 1991-92, mem. govs. mfg. network adv. com.), Am. Legion (fin. dir. post 45). Baptist. Home: 306 Lakeside Ave Camden AR 71701-3237

OWEN, LARRY LESLI, management educator, retired military officer, small business owner; b. Dothan, Ala., Sept. 21, 1945; s. Lesley Homer and Doris (Teuten) O.; m. Betty Aldredge, Aug. 4, 1966; children: Kimberley, Larry Allen, Jonathan. BA in Human Resources, Pepperdine U., 1979; MS in Personnel Mgmt., Troy State U., Ala., 1986. Enlisted U.S. Army, 1963, advanced through grades to maj., battlefield commn., commd. 2d lt. Socialist Republican of South Vietnam, 1970, inf. officer, 1970-85, ret., 1985. Instr. mgmt. Chattahoochee Valley State Coll., Phenix City, Ala., 1987-90, Patrick Henry Jr. Coll., 1990-92; instr. tng. for bus. and industry program Ala. So. Coll. Sys., 1992-94, Wallace C.C.-Selma, 1994-2000; tng. mgr., Riverdale Mill, 1994-2000; cons. Mil. Profl. Resources, Inc.; mem. Boise Cascade Tng. Task Force, 1992, chmn. Mgr.'s Roundtable, 1992. Designer, developer interactive video disc Combat Decision-Making, 1986 (Designer of Yr. award 1986), Mortar Tactical Tng., 1987. Chmn. Ft. Mitchell Nat. Cemetery, Phenix City, 1986-87, trustee, 1988-90; chmn. Vietnam Wall Com., Columbus, Ga., 1986-87; trainer Econ. Improvement Project, Phenix City, 1987-90; chmn. Nat. Am. Flag Run Com., 1989; chmn. tourism com. Phenix City C. of C., 1989; mem. scholarship and recruitment com. Auburn U. Paper/Pulp Found.; tech. adv. com. State of Ala., Dept. Edn. Named Instr. of Yr. U.S. Army, 1982. Mem. TAPPI (career devel. com. 1991—), ASTD, Soc. Human Resource Mgrs., Soc. Applied Learning Tech., Internat. Paper Maintenance Selection/Testing Com., Ala. State Dept. of Edn. Technology/Tech. Adv. com., Ala. State Workforce Devel Com., Jackson C. of C. (pride com.), Phenix City/Russell County C. of C. (chmn. tourism com., bd. dirs.), 1st Cav. Assn. (Follow Me chpt., pres. 1985-87, 88-90), Chattahoochee Valley Vets. Coun. (co-chmn. 1986-90). Baptist. Avocations: fishing, hunting. Home: 1634 Northpointe Dr Deatsville AL 36022-2557

OWEN, MAUREEN A. poet; b. Graceville, Minn., July 6, 1943; d. Vincent Robertson and DeLoris Phalen; divorced; children: Ulysses, Patrick, Kyran Owen-Mankovich. Grad. h.s., 1961. Publ. tel. books, N.Y.C., Guilford, Conn., 1970-84; adminstrv. asst., arts adminstr. St. Mark's Poetry Project, N.Y.C., 1973-76, co-dir. arts adminstrn., 1976-80, tchr. book prodn., 1984-85; mng. editor The Inland Book Co., East Haven, Conn., 1982-96; sr. editor Morton Pub. Co., Guilford, Denver, 1996-99; prof. Edinboro (Pa.) U., 1999-2000; mng. editor LPC Group, Milford, Conn., 2000—. Tchr. creative writing St. Joseph Coll., Hartford, Conn., 1980—; program coord. The Poetry Project, N.Y.C., 2001—. Author (book of poetry) Hearts in Space, 1980, Amelia Earhart, 1984, Zombie Notes, 1985, American Rush: Selected, 1999. Poetry writing fellow Nat. Endowment for Arts, 1980-81; grantee Found. for Contemporary Performance Arts, 1998-99. Avocations: Tai Chi, biking, horseback riding. Home: 109 Dunk Rock Rd Guilford CT 06437 E-mail: pomowen@ix.netcom.com.

OWEN, MICHAEL, entertainer; b. Nashville, Dec. 6, 1948; s. Grace Puckett and Syroun Albert Owen. Ptnr. All Access, Nashville, 1998. Named Supplier of Yr., Tenn. chpt. Meeting Profls. Internat., 1999—2000; recipient Pres.'s award, Meeting Profls. Internat., 2000—01, Pres.'s Disting. Svc. award, Tenn. chpt. Meeting Profls. Internat., 2000—01. Mem.: Profl. Conv. Mgmt. Assn., Internat. Entertainment Buyers Assn., Country Music Assn., Tenn. Soc. Assn. Execs. Office: All Access PO Box 111949 Nashville TN 37222-1949 Business E-Mail: m.owen@allaccess.cc.

OWEN, MICHAEL LEE, lawyer; b. L.A., Aug. 17, 1942; s. Richard M. Owen and Betty Hamilton; m. Espy Bolivar-Owen. AB in Econ. with distinction, Stanford U., 1964; LLB, Harvard U., 1967. Bar: Calif., 1968, N.Y. 1968. Assoc. Reid & Priest, N.Y.C., 1967-69; mem. legal dept. Bank of Am. NT&SA, San Francisco, 1969-81; corp. sec. BRE Properties, 1970-75; v.p., assoc. gen. counsel Bank of Am. NT&SA, L.A., 1979-81; ptnr. and chair L.Am. practice group Paul, Hastings, Janofsky & Walker, LLP, 1981—. Vice chair adv. bd. Inst. for Internat. Law and Commerce Ctr. for Am. and Internat. Law (formerly Southwestern Legal Found.). Contbr. articles to profl. jours. regarding legal issues affecting financing and investment in Latin Amer. Bd. dirs. Constnl. Rights Found. Mem. Am. Arbitration Assn. (internat. panel of arbitrators), U.S.-Mex. Law Inst. (bd. dirs.), U.S.-Mex. C. of C. (bd. dirs. Pacific chpt.). Office: Paul Hastings Janofsky & Walker LLP 515 S Flower St 25th Fl Los Angeles CA 90071-2229 E-mail: michaelowen@paulhastings.com.

OWEN, PRISCILLA RICHMAN, state supreme court justice; BA, Baylor U., JD, 1977. Bar: Tex. 1978, U.S. Ct. Appeals (4th, 5th, 8th and 11th cirs.). Former ptnr. Andrews & Kurth, L.L.P., Houston; justice Supreme Ct. Tex., Austin, 1995—. Liaison to Tex. Legal Svcs. for Poor Spl. Supreme Ct. Tex., Supreme Ct. Adv. Com. on Ct.-Annexed Mediations. Named Young Lawyer of Yr., Baylor U., Outstanding Young Alumna. Office: Supreme Ct Tex PO Box 12248 Austin TX 78711-2248*

OWEN, RAY DAVID, biology educator; b. Genesee, Wis., Oct. 30, 1915; s. Dave and Ida (Hoeft) O.; m. June J. Weissenberg, June 24, 1939; 1 son, David G. BS, Carroll Coll., Wis., 1937, ScD, 1962; PhD, U. Wis., 1941, ScD, 1979, U. of Pacific, 1965. Asst. prof. genetics, zoology U. Wis., 1944-47; Gosney fellow Calif. Inst. Tech., Pasadena, 1946-47, assoc. prof. div. biology, 1947-53, prof. biology, 1953-83, also chmn., v.p. for student affairs, dean of students, prof. emeritus, 1983—. Research participant Oak Ridge Nat. Lab., 1957-58; Cons. Oak Ridge Inst. Nuclear Studies; mem. Pres.'s Cancer Panel. Author: (with A.M. Srb) General Genetics, 1952, 2d edit. (with A.M. Srb, R. Edgar), 1965; Contbr. articles to sci. jours. Recipient Gregor Mendel medal Czech Acad. Scis., 1965, Medawar prize The Transplantation Soc., 2000. Fellow AAAS; mem. Genetics Soc. Am. (pres., Thomas Hunt Morgan medal 1993), Am. Assn. Immunologists (Excellence in Mentoring award 1999), Am. Soc. Human Genetics, Western Soc. Naturalists, Am. Soc. Zoologists, Am. Genetics Assn., Nat. Acad. Scis., Am. Acad. Arts and Scis., Am. Philos. Soc., Am. Acad. Allergy and Immunology (hon.), Internat. Soc. Animal Genetics (hon.), Sigma Xi. Home: 1583 Rose Villa St Pasadena CA 91106-3524 Office: Calif Inst Tech # 156-29 Pasadena CA 91125-0001

OWEN, RICHARD, federal judge; b. N.Y.C., Dec. 11, 1922; s. Carl Maynard and Shirley (Barnes) O.; m. Lynn Rasmussen, June 6, 1960; children: Carl R., David R., Richard. AB, Dartmouth Coll., 1947; LLB, Harvard U., 1950; MusD (hon.), Manhattan Sch. Music, 1989. Bar: N.Y. 1950. Practiced in, N.Y.C., 1950-74; assoc. Willkie Owen Farr Gallagher & Walton, 1950-53, Willkie Farr Gallagher Walton & Fitzgibbon, 1958-60; pvt. practice, 1960-65; ptnr. Owen & Aarons, 1965-66, Owen & Turchin, 1966-74; asst. U.S. atty. So. Dist. N.Y., 1953-55; trial atty. antitrust div. U.S. Dept. Justice, 1955-58; U.S. dist. judge So. Dist. N.Y., 1974-89, sr. judge, 1989—. Asst. prof. N.Y. Law Sch., 1951-53; adj. prof. law Fordham U. Sch. Law, 1996—. Composer, librettist operas Dismissed with Prejudice, 1956, A Moment of War, 1958, A Fisherman Called Peter, 1965, Mary Dyer, 1976, The Death of the Virgin, 1980, Abigail Adams, 1987, Tom Sawyer, 1989, Sadie Thompson, 1997. Trustee Manhattan Sch. Music, N.Y.C.; founder, bd. dirs. Maine Opera Assn., 1975-85; pres., bd. dirs. N.Y. Lyric Opera Co. 1st lt. USAAC, 1942-45. Decorated D.F.C. with oak leaf cluster, Air medal with 3 oak leaf clusters. Mem. ASCAP, Century Assn., Chelsea Yacht Club. Republican. Mem. Soc. Of Friends. Office: US Dist Ct US Courthouse Foley Sq New York NY 10007-1501

OWEN, ROBERT FREDERICK, internist, rheumatologist; b. Poplar Bluff, Mo., Oct. 19, 1927; s. John Clarence and Lydia Anna (Laverty) O.; m. Edith Suzanna Trugly, June 11, 1960; 1 child, Suzanne Marie. AB summa cum laude, Princeton U., 1948; MD, Yale U., 1952. Diplomate Am. Bd. Internal Medicine, Nat. Bd. Med. Examiners. Med. intern Barnes Hosp. (Washington U.), St. Louis, 1952-53; asst. resident in internal medicine St. Louis City Hosp. (Washington U. Med. Svc.), 1953-54, 56-57, med. resident, 1957-58; pvt. practice in internal medicine and rheumatology St. Louis, 1958—98. Instr. clin. medicine Washington U. Sch. Medicine, St. Louis, 1958-98, emeritus, 1998—; cons. Arthritis Clinic Washington U. Clinics, St. Louis, 1958-78; attending physician inpatient and outpatient tchg. svcs. at Washington U. and Mo. Baptist, St. Luke's, and Deaconess Hosps., St. Louis, 1958-79. Chmn. Instnl. Rev. Bd. Mo. Baptist Hosp. (monitoring biomed. and behavioral rsch.), 1977-96; mem. St. Louis Cmty. Clin. Oncology Program Human Subjects Rsch. Instnl. Rev. Bd., 1983-96. Capt. U.S. Army Med. Corps, 1954-56, Korea. Commendation by surgeon, Eighth U.S. Army, Far East, 1955. Fellow ACP; mem. AMA (Physician's Recognition award annually 1977—), Sigma Xi, Phi Beta Kappa. Avocations: piano, organ, photography. Office: St Francois Med Ctr 1224 Graham Rd Ste 3008 Florissant MO 63031-8028

OWEN, ROBERT HUBERT, lawyer, former real estate broker; b. Birmingham, Ala., Aug. 3, 1928; s. Robert Clay and Mattie Lou (Hubert) O.; m. Mary Dane Hicks, Mar. 14, 1954; children: Mary Kathryn, Robert Hubert. BS, U. Ala., 1950; JD, Birmingham Sch. Law, 1956. Bar: Ala. 1957, Ga. 1965. Methods and procedures analyst, supr. Ala. Power Co., Birmingham, 1952-58; assoc. Martin, Vogtle, Balch & Bingham, 1958-63; asst. sec. So. Services, Atlanta, 1963-69; sec. Southern Co., 1969-71, sec., asst. treas., 1971-77; exec. v.p., sec., gen. counsel, dir. Proverbs 31 Corp., Atlanta, 1978-81, 90-97; broker Bob Owen Realty, 1990-97; pvt. practice law Marietta, 1978-85; v.p., gen. counsel Hubert Properties, 1985-86. Atlanta area rep. Inst. Basic Life Principles, 1970-80; elder Calvary Bapt. Ch., 1997-. Served to maj. USAF, 1951-52, 61-62. Mem. Jasons, Delta Chi, Omicron Delta Kappa, Beta Gamma Sigma, Delta Sigma Pi, Phi Eta Sigma. Home and Office: 6590 Bridgewood Valley Rd NW Atlanta GA 30328-2906 Fax: 404-255-9479. E-mail: rowen2000@attbi.com.

OWEN, ROBERTS BISHOP, lawyer, arbitrator; b. Boston, Feb. 11, 1926; s. Roberts Bishop and Monica Benedict (Burrell) O.; m. Kathleen Comstock von Schrader, Aug. 27, 1966; children— David Roberts, Lucy Leffingwell, William Atreus. Student, Dartmouth Coll., 1943-44; AB cum laude, Harvard U., 1948, LL.B. cum laude, 1951; Dip.C.L.S., Cambridge U., Eng., 1952. Bar: D.C. 1952, U.S. Ct. Appeals (D.C. cir.) 1953, U.S. Supreme Ct. 1958. Assoc. Covington & Burling, Washington, 1952-60, ptnr., 1960-79, 81—; the legal advisor U.S. Dept. State, Washington, 1979-81. Sr. advisor Sec. of State former Yugoslavia, 1995; arbitrator Fedn. Bosnia and Herzegovina, 1995; mem. Permanent Ct. Arbitration, The Hague, The Netherlands, 1980—86, 1993—98; mem. arbitration panel Internat. Ctr. for Settlement of Investment Disputes, 1995—; chair bd. dirs. Internat. Human Rights Law Group, 1996—99; mem. Claims Resolution Tribunal , 1998—; sr. U.S. negotiator U.S.-Can. Pacific Salmon Treaty dispute, 1998; vice chair, sr. claims judge Claims Resolution Tribunal , 2001—02. Served to ensign USN, 1943-46. Fulbright scholar, 1951-52; recipient Disting Honor award Dept. of State, 1981, Sec. of State Disting. Svc. award, 1996, Sec. of Defense's medal for outstanding pub. svc., 1996. Fellow Am. Coll. Trial Lawyers; mem. ABA,

Council Fgn. Relations, Am. Soc. Internat. Law (exec. council 1981-85). Clubs: Royal Ocean Racing (London); Metropolitan (Washington). Office: Covington & Burling PO Box 7566 1201 Pennsylvania Ave NW Washington DC 20004

OWEN, STEVEN KEITH, utility executive; b. Enterprise, Ala., Aug. 16, 1959; s. Charlie Glenn Owen and O. Beatrice Gibson; m. Kim Cruce, July 15, 1984 (div. July 1995). BSCE, Auburn U., 1981. Asst. engr. So. Co. Svcs., Birmingham, Ala., 1981—83, AP600 project mgr., 1990—92, field engr. Augusta, Ga., 1983—84, startup test supr., 1984—87, project staff engr., 1987—89, project engring. mgr., 1989—90, So. Energy/So. Co., Atlanta, 1993—96, project dir., 1996—98, bus. unit mgr. Chgo., 1998—2000, dir. Midwest bus. units, 2000—01; v.p. Mirant Corp., Atlanta, 2001—. Coach basketball and baseball youth teams, Birmingham, 1991-93; membership chmn. So. Co. Svcs. PAC, Birmingham, 1991-93; bd. dirs. United Way, Lake County, Ind., 1998—. Mem. ASME (com. mem.), Ind. State C. of C. (environ. bd., congrl. affairs bd. 2000—), Beta Theta Pi Alumni Assn. (Auburn chpt. pres., treas. 1981-85). Avocations: golf, running, reading. Office: Mirant Corp 1155 Perimeter Center W Atlanta GA 30338

OWEN, THOMAS LLEWELLYN, investment executive; b. Patchogue, N.Y., June 24, 1928; s. Griffith Robert and Jeanette Roberts (Hatfield) O. AB in Econs., Coll. William and Mary, 1951; postgrad., Columbia U., 1952, N.Y. Inst. Fin., 1960-62; MBA, NYU, 1966. Exec. trainee Shell Oil Co., N.Y.C. and Indpls., 1951-59, supr., 1958-59; petroleum and chem. investment analyst Paine, Webber, Jackson & Curtis, N.Y.C., 1959-62; sr. oil investment analyst DuPont Investment Interests, Wilmington, Del., N.Y.C., 1962-66, dir. rsch., 1964-66; v.p., sr. investment officer, mem. policy, investment coms. Nat. Securities and Rsch. Corp., N.Y.C., 1966-75; sr. investment exec., v.p., portfolio mgr. F. Eberstadt & Co. and Eberstadt Asset Mgmt., Inc., 1975-85, mem. policy com., 1979-85, also dir. portfolio rev. com.; sr. investment exec., portfolio mgr. Brown Brothers Harriman, 1985-89; pres., CEO Owen Capital Mgmt., 1989—. Contbr. chpt. "Oil and Gas Industries" to Financial Analysts Handbook, 1975. Chmn. bd. trustees Congl. Ch. Patchogue, N.Y. Mem. N.Y. Soc. Security Analysts, Assn. of Investment Mgmt. and Rsch., Oil Analysts Group N.Y., Am. Econ. Assn., Investment Assn. N.Y., Am. Petroleum Inst., Nat. Assn. Petroleum Investment Analysts, Internat. Assn. Energy Economists. Home and Office: 251 E 32nd St New York NY 10016-6304

OWEN, THOMAS BARRON, retired naval officer, space company executive; b. Seattle, Mar. 19, 1920; s. Thomas Barron and Ruth (Deane) O.; m. Rosemary Stolz, Dec. 24, 1944; children— Catherine Adams, Thomas Barron, James Rowell, Nancy Deane. BS cum laude, U. Wash., 1940; postgrad., U.S. Naval Postgrad. Sch., 1946-47; PhD in Chemistry, Cornell U., 1950; postgrad., U. Amsterdam, 1950-51, Indsl. Coll. Armed Forces, 1961-62, Harvard Grad. Sch. Bus. Adminstrn., 1964. Commd. ensign U.S. Navy, 1940, advanced through grades to rear adm., 1967, combat duty with Pacific Fleet, 1940-45; officer distbn. div. Bur. Naval Personnel, 1945-46; with armaments br. and mil. operations br. Office Naval Research, 1951-53; asst. repair supt. (hull) and prodn. analysis supt. Long Beach (Calif.) Naval Shipyard, 1953-57; dir. applied scis. div., dir. research and devel. planning div. Navy Bur. Ships, 1957-61; mil. asst. to dep. dir. def. research and engring. engring. and chemistry, 1962-63; assigned Office Asst. Sec. Navy Research and Devel., 1963; dir. support services Naval Research Lab., 1963-65, dir., 1965-67; chief naval research, 1967-70; ret., 1970; asst. dir. nat. and internat. programs NSF, 1970-74; assoc. dean grad. affairs and rsch. Am. U., Washington, 1974-76, asst. provost, 1976-79; asst. adminstr. NOAA, Dept. Commerce, Rockville, Md., 1979-81; mgr. program planning Fairchild Space & Electronics Co., Germantown, 1981-83; sr. dir. systems effectiveness Fairchild Space Co., 1983-84, v.p. procurement, 1984-86. Author profl. papers. Decorated D.S.M., Silver Star, Bronze Star. Fellow AAAS; mem. Am. Chem. Soc., U.S. Naval Inst., Philos. Soc. Washington, Sigma Xi, Phi Kappa Phi, Phi Lambda Upsilon, Tau Beta Pi, Chi Psi. Clubs: Cosmos (Washington). Home: 8409 Magruder Mill Ct Bethesda MD 20817-2746 E-mail: wonkpop@aol.com. *Demand high standards of excellence for self and others. Achieve respect of others through own performance. Be direct; avoid circumspection. Develop empathy; listen; consider feelings and rights of others. Maintain philosophy of "Onward and Upward!".*

OWEN, THOMAS JAMES, artist, educator; b. Coca-Rockledge, Fla., Aug. 20, 1945; s. Irwin Arthor and Esther Ethel (Sensinig) O.; m. Judith Lea Pasternak, June 21, 1969 (div. Feb. 1983); m. Koreen Clay, June 26, 1986; 1 child, Gillian Clay. BS in Edn., N.W. Mo. State U., 1968. Cert. tchr., Mo., Nebr. Secondary educator Avon-Grove Sch. Dist., West Grove, Pa., 1968-69, Dist. # 60 Schs., Pueblo, Colo., 1969-72, Wymore (Nebr.) Unified Dist., 1972-73; art educator Sangre De Cristo F.A.C., Pueblo, 1981-86, Colorado Springs (Colo.) F.A.C. Bemis Art Sch., 1982-96, Cottonwood Art Acad., Colo. Springs, 1997—; pvt. practice Black Forest, Colo., 1996—. Art dir. Columbine Cellers, Denver and Palisade, Colo., 1989-96; guest instr. Adams State Coll., Alamosa, Colo., 1990-95. Exhibited Kans. Watercolor Soc. (Purchase selection), Wichita Ctr. for Arts. Recipient Juror's Choice award San Diego Nat. Watermedia, 1981, Adirondack's Wilderness award, The Rouse Gold medallion, Adirondack's Nat. Exhbn. Am. Watercolors, 1995, Florene and H. Samuel Slater meml. award, 1999, Gold Medal New World Internat. Wine Label Competition, 1994, Dr. Martin's award Soc. Watercolor Artists, 1997, Silver Brush award 1999, New West award Watermedia IX, 1998, Meyer award Rocky Mt. Nat. Water Media Exhbn. Signature, 1998, 2000, Best Transparent Watercolor Watermedia X, 1999, Omni Trax award, 1999, Mid Continent Engring. award Kans. 7 state exhbn., 1999, 2000, Atlantic Papers award Western Colo. Nat. Watercolor Exhbn., 1999, Best of Show award Soc. Watercolor Artists, 2000, Carillion Gallery award, Best of Show award, 2000, Honorarium award Kans. Watercolor Soc., 2000, Connoisseur Art award, 2000, 4th Pl. medallion Pa. Watercolor Soc., 2000. Mem. Nat. Watercolor Soc. (signature mem., Rocky Mtn. br. bd. dirs., Hariett Wexler Bartsch Meml. award 1994), Colo. Artists Assn. (v.p. 1982-86), Nickerbocker Artists (assoc.), Pikes Peak Watercolor Soc. (v.p. 1990—), Watercolor West (juried mem. 1999), Acad. Sertoma Club. Avocations: trout fishing, skiing, model railroading. Home and Office: 11935 Vollmer Rd Colorado Springs CO 80908-4086 E-mail: tomowen@hotbot.com.

OWEN, THOMAS WALKER, banker, broker; b. Everett, Wash., June 7, 1925; s. Thomas Walker and Frances (Yantis) O.; m. Barbara May Neils, Oct. 20, 1951; children: Thomas W., Gerhard, Caroline, Jeffrey; m. Ingrid Lundgren, June 7, 1975. BA, U. Wash., 1949, MA in Finance, 1953; postgrad., Pacific Coast Banking Sch., 1956. Adminstrv. trainee Seattle Trust & Savs. Bank, 1949-54, asst. br. mgr., 1954-56, trust investment officer, 1956-57, mgr. investment dept., chmn. investment com., 1957-59; v.p., mgr. investment dept. Nat. Bank Wash., Tacoma, 1959-66, vice chmn., 1967-71; exec. v.p. bank adminstrn. Pacific Nat. Bank Wash., 1971-73; v.p. Reeder, Owen & Co., Inc., 1975-92; pres., chmn. Owen, Reeder, Inc., Merrill Lynch, 1991-92; bd. dirs. West One Bank Wash., Tacoma, 1981-93. Served with AUS, 1943-45. Decorated Bronze Star, Purple Heart. Mem. N.W. Forum, Wash. Athletic Club, Tacoma Club (past pres.), Tacoma Country and Golf Club, Phi Gamma Delta. Home: 11204 Tower Rd SW Lakewood WA 98498

OWEN, TIMOTHY ANDREW, minister; b. La Grange, Ky., May 16, 1959; s. James Andrew and Donnie Ashley Owen; m. Janet Rebecca Anderson; children: Ashlee, Jared. BA, Southeastern Coll. of the Assemblies of God, Lakeland, Fla., 1981; M.Religion, Heritage Bible Coll., Huntsville, Ala., 1987; DMin, So. Bapt. Sch. for Bibl. Studies, Jacksonville, Fla., 1999. Ordained Bishop Ch. of God (Cleveland, Tenn.), 1986. Evangelist Assemblies of God, New Castle, Ky., 1976—81; pastor Waynesboro Ch. of God, Waynesboro, Tenn., 1995—; adminstrv. dean Hardin County Sch. of Ministry, Savannah, 2001—. Dist. overseer Waynesboro Dist. Ch. of God, Waynesboro, Tenn., 1995—; bd. dirs. So. Bapt. Sch. for Bibl. Studies, Jacksonville, 2000—; adminstr. Estill Springs Christian Acad., Estill Springs. Com. mem. Wayne County Families First Adv. Com., Waynesboro. Mem.: Wayne County Min. Assn. (pres. 1999—2001), Soc. for Pentecostal Studies, Sons of Confederate Vets., Hon. Order of Ky. Cols. Pentecostal. Avocation: baseball. Mailing: 522 Hwy 64 W Waynesboro TN 38485

OWEN, WADSWORTH, oceanographer, consultant; b. N.Y.C., Sept. 4, 1932; S. George Wadsworth and Helen Owen; m. Elaine M. Brewster, Oct. 26, 1955 (div. 1973); children: Leslie Shore, Victoria Rand, Samantha; m. Margaret W. Emslie, May 31, 1975 (div. July 22, 1992); 1 child, Joanna W. BS in Physics and Math., U. Mass., 1961; MA in Phys. Oceanography, Johns Hopkins U., 1969. Asst. scientist Avco R&D, Wilmington, Mass., 1956-61; rsch. asst. Johns Hopkins U., Balt., 1961-64; engr. sonar devices Westinghouse-Undersea, 1964-66; sr. engr. Sikorski Aircraft, Stratford, Conn., 1966-67; mgr. marine tech. Raytheon Subsig, New London, 1967-69; divsn. mgr. marine sci. and v.p. underwater vehicles VAST, Inc., Waterford, 1969-73; divsn. dir. phys. sci. divsn. Normandeau Assocs., Bedford, N.H., 1973-77; dir. marine ops. Coll. Marine Studies, U. Del., Lewes, 1977-94. Contbr. articles to profl. jours.; patentee in field. Adv. bd. New Eng. Marine Rsch. Info. Program, R.I., 1970-73. Sgt. USMC, 1952-55, PTO. U. Mass. scholar, 1958-61; NDEA fellow, 1961-64. Mem. So. N.E. Marine Scis. Assn. (chmn. exec. bd. 1970-73), Am. Inst. Physics (pres. student sect. 1960-61), Lewes C. of C. (treas. 1990-91), Univ. Nat. Oceanography Lab. Sys. Assn., Rsch. Vessel Ops. Coun., Marine Tech. Soc., Acad. Model Aeronautics, Nat. Free Flight Soc. Avocations: model aircraft design and construction, art, history, boats, diving. Home: PO Box 268 Friendship ME 04547-0268

OWEN, WALTER SHEPHERD, materials science and engineering educator; b. Liverpool, Eng., Mar. 13, 1920; s. Walter L. and Dorothea (Lunt) O. B.Engring., U. Liverpool, 1940, M.Engring., 1942, PhD, 1950, D.Eng., 1972. Metallurgist English Electric Co., 1940-46; mem. research staff MIT, 1951-57; prof. metallurgy U. Liverpool, 1957-66; prof., dir. materials sci. and engring. Cornell U., 1966-70; dean Tech. Inst., 1970-71; v.p. sci. and research Northwestern U., Evanston, Ill., 1971-73; prof. and head materials sci. and engring. MIT, 1973-82, prof. phys. metallurgy, 1982-85, prof. emeritus materials sci. and engring., 1985—. Cons. to industry. Author research papers. Commonwealth Fund fellow, 1951 Fellow ASM; mem. NAE, AIME, Instn. Metallurgists, N.Y. Acad. Scis., Inst. Metals, Materials Rsch. Soc., Japan Inst. Metals (hon.). Home: 1 Marine Ter Porthmadog LL49 9BL Wales E-mail: wsowen@aol.com.

OWEN, WILLIAM MICHAEL, real estate developer; b. Houston, Sept. 27, 1950; s. W. Frank and Lois Marie (Nelson) O.; m. Debra Ann Phillips, Jan. 9, 1971 (div.); 1 child, Heather Ann; m. Pamela C. Birkhead, Feb. 18, 1983; children: Sean Michael, Blane William. BA in Econs., U. North Tex., 1992, MBA in Fin., 1996. Pres. Owen Resource & Devel., Inc., Denton, Tex., 1992—; pub., editor The Profit Connection Fin. Newsletter, 1994—. V.p. Ivey & Owen Investments, Inc., Las Vegas, 1992—; pres. Owen Fin. Group, Denton, 1978—. Home: PO Box 50832 Denton TX 76206-0832

OWENS, ARNE WESLEY, mental health commissioner; b. Burbank, Calif., Feb. 15, 1954; s. Ralph Hayes and Margaret Caroline O.; m. Arlene Austra, Sept. 11, 1982; 1 child, Wesley Paul. BS, U.S. Mil. Acad., 1977; MS, U. So. Calif., 1983. Commd. 2d lt. U.S. Army, 1977, advanced through grades to lt. col., 1994, retired, 1997; exec. asst. to asst. sec. def., pub. affairs Dept. Def., Washington, 1992-93; pub. affairs plans exec. U.S. Dept. Def., 1993-95, press spokesperson, 1995-97; dir. comm. Christian Coalition, Chesapeake, Va., 1997-98; pub. rels. cons. Virginia Beach, 1998-99; dep. commr. mental retardation and substance abuse Va. Dept. Mental Health. Mem. World Affairs Coun., Hampton Rds., Va., 1998-99. Mem. Pub. Rels. Soc. Am., Assn. U.S. Army, Army & Navy Club, Assn. Grads. U.S. Mil. Acad., The Econs. Club Hampton Rds. Republican. Baptist. Avocations: music, mountaineering, bicycling, running, reading. Home: 12820 Pennmardel Ln Richmond VA 23233-7684

OWENS, BARBARA ANN, English educator; b. Muskogee, Okla., Jan. 11, 1947; d. Carl Howard Fullbright and Iris Oleta (Staffan) Evans; children: Shelia DeLynn, Katherine Elizabeth, David Warren III. BS, Northeastern Okla. State U., 1976; MEd, U. Okla., 1990. Cert. reading specialist. Tchr. Muldrow (Okla.) Pub. Schs., 1976-77, Stafford (Mo.) Pub. Schs., 1977-79, Oklahoma City C.C., 1991—, Moore (Okla.) Pub. Schs., 1979—. Sponsor, state pres. Moore West Nat. Jr. Honor Soc.; global classroom dir., chair reading dept. Moore West Sch. Bd. dirs. Moore Parks & Recreation, 1988-89. Mem. NEA, Oklahoma Edn. Assn., Okla. Reading Coun., Okla. Romance Writers Am.)v.p.), Romance Writers Am., Moore Assn. Classroom Tchrs. Avocations: travel, writing, reading, painting, golf. Office: Moore Pub Schs 9400 S Pennsylvania Ave Oklahoma City OK 73159-6903

OWENS, BETSY KINGSOLVER, writer; b. Abingdon, Va., June 19, 1932; d. James Clarence and Elizabeth Kathleen (Carr) O. BS in Home Econs., Madison Coll., 1953; MS in Home Econs., U. Tenn., 1953, MA in English, 1964. Lab. technician Tenn. Eastman Co., Kingsport, 1954-57; writer Abingdon, 1964—. Author: Summer Bonding, 1988, Mango Valentine, 1993, Justin's Quest, 1995; (poems) Guided Voices, 1998, Cherished Poems of the Western World, 1998, A Gift of Love (winner Bristol Herald Courier Christmas Story contest 1999). Campaign worker Rep. Party, Washington County, Va.; singer Joyful Singers of Abingdon Sr. Ctr., 1991—; musician St. Columba's Anglican Cath. Ch., 2000. Anglican Catholic. Avocations: singing, playing recorder, reading, knitting, crocheting.

OWENS, BILL, governor; b. Ft. Worth, Oct. 22, 1950; m. Frances Owens; children: Monica, Mark, Brett. BA, Stephen F. Austin State U.; MPA, U. Tex. With Touche Ross & Co., Gates Corp.; state repr. Colo. Ho. Reps., 1983-89; state sen. Colo. State Sen., 1989-94; state treas. State of Colo., 1994-98, gov., 1999—. Guest host Mike Rosen, Ken Hamblin and Chuck Baker talk shows; lectr. Russia. Contbr. more than 50 articles to profl. jours. Named One of Country's Ten Up-and-Coming leaders Robert Novak. Office: Office Gov 136 State Capitol Bldg Denver CO 80203-1792 E-mail: governorowens@state.co.us.*

OWENS, CATHERINE, writer; b. Charlotte, N.C., Oct. 21, 1965; d. Charles Eugene and Barbara Joan (Maletta) W. Diploma, N.C. Sch. Sci. and Math., Durham, 1984; BA, U. N.C., 1990. Editl. asst., rsch. intern Smithsonian Instn., Washington, 1991-93; tech. writer Nuclear Regulatory Commn., 1993-96, Ga. Pacific Corp., Atlanta, 1996-98, The Coca-Cola Co., Atlanta, 1996-98, IBM, Olympics Sports Tech., Atlanta, 1998, Info. Am., Atlanta, 1998-2000, Clarify/Nortel, Raleigh, N.C., 2000. Author: (poetry in anthologies) Whispers in the Wind, 1990, Promises to Keep, 1998, Am. Poetry Ann., 1998, Moments, 1998; prodr.-dir., founder Pretend Prodns., 2001; exec. prodr. Four Chicks Prodns.; writer, dir., prodr. N.C. Lore Documentary Movies, The Devil's Tramping Grounds, 2001; prodr., dir., filmmaker (TV series) BackBone, 2001. Recipient Presdl. Lit. awards Am. Acad. Poets, 1998, 99, Most Notable Poet Duke U. Med Ctr., 2000, Poet's award Lit. Illiad Press, 1999, 2000. Mem. Soc. Tech. Communicators, 4-H Nat. Hon. Club (life). Avocations: ballet, travel. Home: 1501 NC Hwy 86 N Hillsborough NC 27278 E-mail: catherineowens@msn.com.

OWENS, CHARLES A. cardiovascular and interventional radiologist; b. Champaign, Ill., Nov. 8, 1956; s. Albert and Sue Ella (Baumgartner) O.; m. Susan Louis Ballin, Sept. 7, 1988; children: David Christian, Michael Charles, Katherine Louise. BS in Psychology, U. Ill., 1980, BS in Biology, 1981; MD, U. Ill., Chgo., 1985. Diplomate in radiology, diagnostic radiology, vascular and interventional radiology Am. Bd. Radiology; diplomate Nat. Bd. Med. Examiners. Resident in diagnostic radiology U. Ill. Med. Ctr., Chgo., 1987-91; fellow in interventional radiology Mass. Gen. Hosp., Boston, 1991-92; asst. prof. U. Ill. Med. Ctr., Chgo., 1992-98, assoc. prof., 1998—, physician and surgeon, 1992—. Co-dir. sect. cardiovascular and interventional radiology, dir. peripheral vascular animal lab, dir. continuing med. edn. dept. radiology U. Ill. Med. Ctr., Chgo. Contbr. articles to profl. jours. Grantee Johnson & Johnson, 1994, Dow Corning Wright, 1994, Abbott Labs., 1995, 97, Nycomed, 1995. Mem. Am. Soc. Cardiovascular and Interventional Radiology, Am. Roentgen Ray Soc., Radiol. Soc. N.Am., Cardiovascular and Interventional Soc. Europe, Assn. Univ. Radiologists, Am. Gastroenterol. Assn. Avocations: skiing, swimming, golf, basketball. Home: 331 Fuller Rd Hinsdale IL 60521-3626 Office: U Ill Med Ctr 1740 W Taylor St Chicago IL 60612-7232

OWENS, CHARLES VINCENT, JR. diagnostic company executive and consultant; b. Kansas City, Mo., May 15, 1927; s. Charles Vincent and Helen (Barrett) O.; m. Cheryl Kreighbaum, Feb. 12, 1955; children: Melody, Kevin, Michael, John, Barbara. BS, U. Notre Dame, 1948; MS (Univ. fellow), U. N.C., 1949. Public health educator Richmond County (N.C.) Health Dept., 1949-51; with Miles Labs., Inc., Elkhart, Ind., 1951-82, pres. Ames Co. div., 1967-71, group v.p. profl. products group, 1971-77, exec. v.p. internat. ops., 1977-82; chmn., CEO Kyoto Diagnostics, Inc., 1982—. Bd. dirs. Chronimed Inc.; CEO Genesis Inc., 1982—91. Bd. dirs. St. Jude Med Ctr., Elkhart YWCA, 1972-76; vice chmn. Elkhart County Bd. Health, 1973-77; chmn. Child Abuse Task Force, Elkhart County, Ind., 1977-78. Served with M.C., USAAF, 1945-47. Mem. Am. Public Health Assn., Health Industry Mfg. Assn. (dir.), Pharm. Mfrs. Assn., Nat. Pharm. Council (pres. 1970-71, dir. 1965-73), Am. Mgmt. Assn., Am. Diabetes Assn., Am. Assn. Diabetes Educators, Internat. Diabetes Fedn., Am. Soc. Med. Tech., Elcona Country Club (bd. dirs.), Nat. Notre Dame Monogram Club (bd. dirs.). Republican. Roman Catholic.

OWENS, DEBRA ANN, chiropractor; b. Poplar Bluff, Mo., Dec. 21, 1953; d. James Alva and Veleta Frances (Pierce) Stutts; 1 child from previous marriage, Jacqueline. BS in Edn., S.E. Mo. State U., 1975; DC, Logan Coll. Chiropractic, 1991; fellow, Internat. Acad. Clin. Acupunct, 1996. Chiropractor Albers Chiropractic, Washington, 1991-92, Owens Chiropractic Ctr., P.C., Dexter, 1992—. Mem. Chiropractors Restoring Energy Worldwide Humanitarian Chiropractic Mission, Costa Rica, 2000. Mem. Humanitarian Chiropractic Mission to Panama City, Panama, 1997, Humanitarian Chiropractic Mission to South Africa, 1999. Mem. Am. Chiropractic Assn., Internat. Chiropractors Assn., Mo. Chiropractors Assn., World Congress of Women Chiropractors, Logan Coll. Alumni Assn. (Alumni Rsch. award 1991), Dexter C. of C. (2nd v.p. 1993, 1st v.p. 1994, pres. 1995, sec. devel. corp. 1996, v.p. devel. corp. 1997, pres. devel. corp. 1998, 99, econ. devel. com. 1996), Kiwanis (bd. dirs. 1994-98, 2nd v.p. 1997-98. Avocations: swimming, boating, patchwork quilting, flying. Office: Owens Chiropractic Ctr PC 907 N Harris Dr Ste B PO Box 678 Dexter MO 63841-0678

OWENS, DONALD STANLEY, judge; b. Ann Arbor, Mich., Dec. 25, 1943; s. James Samuel and Marion (Borgerding) O.; m. Carolyn Hickok, Aug. 20, 1966 (div. June 1990); children: Michael, Daniel, Stephen, Elizabeth; m. Jeanie Leyden, Nov. 2, 1991. Student, Oberlin Coll., 1962-64; BA, U. Mich., 1966, MBA, 1967, JD, 1969. Bar: Mich. 1969, U.S. Dist. Ct. (we. dist.) Mich. 1969. Atty. MacLean, Seaman, Laing & Guilford, Lansing, Mich., 1969-74; judge Ingham County Probate Ct., 1974-99, Mich. Ct. Appeals, Lansing, 1999—. Assoc. editor jour. Inter-Com, 1980s. Hon. dir. Lansing Area Safety Coun.; merit badge counselor Boy Scouts Am., Mason, Mich., 1980s; mem. adv. bd. Big Bros.-Big Sisters, Lansing, 1990s; deacon First Presbyn. Ch., 1992. Recipient Amb. award Peckham Vocat. Industries, 1989; named Mich. Judge of Yr., Mich. Assn. Ct. Apptd. Spl. Advocates, 1999. Mem. State Bar Mich. (chair jud. conf. 1990-91), Mich. Probate Judges Assn. (pres. 1990-91, Mich. guardianship ombudsman 2000-01), Mich. Judges Assn., Beta Gamma Sigma. Avocations: sailing, golf, running, gardening. Office: Mich Ct Appeals PO Box 30022 Lansing MI 48909-7522

OWENS, GARLAND CHESTER, accounting educator; b. Wilson, N.C., Dec. 12, 1922; s. James F. and Leona (Owens) O.; m. Mary Elizabeth Wade, June 19, 1948; 1 dau., Lynn Carol. BS, U. Richmond, 1947; MS, Columbia U., 1948, PhD, 1956. C.P.A., N.Y. State. Acct. Arthur Young & Co. (C.P.A.s), N.Y.C., 1950-53; mem. faculty Columbia Grad. Sch. Bus., 1956-86, prof., 1964-86; prof. emeritus Columbia U., 1986; assoc. dean Columbia Grad. Sch. Bus., 1962-70; prof. Mercer U. Sch. Bus., 1986-93; prof. emeritus Mercer U., 1993; program dir. Mgmt. Devel. Center, Belo Horizonte Minas Gerais, Brazil, 1973-75. Controller Arctic Inst. N.Am., 1957-77 Author: Cost Basis in Business Combinations, 1956, (with James A. Cashin) Auditing, 1963; former reading editor: Jour. Accountancy. Mem. bd. edn. Union Free Sch. Dist. 5, Greenburgh, N.Y., 1964-69, v.p., 1965-68, pres., 1968-69; mem. N.E. Regional Postmaster Selection Bd., U.S. Postal Service, 1969-75. Served to capt. USAAF, 1942-45. Decorated D.F.C., Air medal Mem. Am. Inst. C.P.A.s, N.Y. State Soc. C.P.A.s, Ga. State Soc. C.P.A.'s, Am. Acctg. Assn., Beta Gamma Sigma. Methodist. Home: 12 Cole Pl Palm Coast FL 32137

OWENS, GARY, broadcast personality, entrepreneur, author; b. Mitchell, S.D., May 10; s. Bernard and Vennetta O.; m. Arleta Lee Markell, June 26; children: Scott, Christopher. Student (speech and psychology scholar), Dakota Wesleyan U., Mitchell; student, Mpls. Art Inst. With Sta. KMPC, L.A., 1962-82; with Sta. KPRZ, 1982—, Sta KFI, L.A., 1986-90; pres. Foonman & Sons, Inc., 1987—; v.p., creative dir. GoldenWest Broadcasters, 1981-82. V.p., nat. creative dir. Gannett Broadcasting, 1984; TV performer, 1963—. Writer Jay Ward Prodns., 1961-62; syndicated radio show The G.O. Spl. Report, from 1969; host: world-wide syndicated show Soundtrack of the 60's, 1981—, Biff Owens Sports Exclusive, 1981—; USA Today, Mut. Broadcasting System, 1982-83; radio host Gary Owens Music Weekend, Lorimar Telepictures, 1987—; performer, writer: world-wide syndicated show Sesame St, 1969—, Electric Co, 1969—, Dirkniblick (Mathnet) CTW, 1988; performer over 3000 animated cartoons including Dyno-Mutt, ABC-TV, 1975, Roger Ramjet, 1965, Space Ghost, 1966—, Perils of Penelope Pitstop, 1970, Square One, 1987, Godzilla's Power Hour, 1979, Space Heroes, 1981, Mighty Orbots, 1984, World's Greatest Adventures, 1986, Garfield, Cops, Bobby's World, 1990, 96, The 3 Musketeers, Return of Roger Ramjet, Alice in Wonderland, The Count of Monte Cristo, 20,000 Leagues Under the Sea, Godzilla, Mickey Mouse, Donald Duck, Goofy Chip N'Dale, Bill & Ted's Great Adventure, Tom & Jerry Jr., Eek the Cat, Swat Kats, Two Stupid Dogs, Ren & Stimpy, Bonkers, Dirk Niblick, Felix the Cat, numerous others, 1990; appeared: in films The Love Bug, 1968, Prisoner of Second Ave., 1975, Hysterical, 1982, Nat. Lampoon's European Vacation, 1985, I'm Gonna Get You Sucka, 1988, Kill Crazy, 1988, How I Got Into College, 1988, Say Bye Bye, 1989, Green Hornet, 1966 Regular on series; performer on camera more than 1000 nat. TV shows; regular The Rosie O'Donnell Show, 1996; performer: Rowan and Martin's Laugh-in, 1968-73; TV host: Gong Show, ABC-TV, 1976, Monty Pythons Flying Circus, 1975; regular performer: TV Games People Play, 1980-81, Breakaway, 1983; TV spls. include Bob Hope Spls., Like Hep, The Muppets Go Hollywood, Perry Como Visits Hollywood, The Gary Owens All-Nonsense News Network, Jonathan Winters & Friends, NBC's 50 Years, CBS's 50 Years, Battle of Beverly Hills, America's Choice, The American Comedy Awards, 1986—, Flip Wilson's Spls., Saturday Night at the Superbowl, Mickey Mouse's 50th Birthday, Mad About You, The Jeff Foxworthy Show, Night Court, Funniest Comedy Duos; author: Elephants, Grapes and Pickles, 1963; 12 printings The Gary Owens What To Do While Your're Holding the Phone Book, revised edit., 1973, A Gary Owens Chrestomathy, 1980; host Encore Pay TV, 1992; author: (screenplay) Three Caraway Seeds and an Agent's Heart, 1979; columnist: Radio and Records newspaper, 1978—, Hollywood Citizen-News, 1965-67, Hollywood mag., 1983—, The Daily News, 1981—; rec. artist MGM, ABC, Epic, Warner Bros., RCA, Reprise, Decca; TV announcer NBC, 1968-80, ABC, 1980—; host many top video's in U.S. including Dinosaurs, More Dinosaurs, Son of Dinosaurs, TV's Greatest Bits; host: How to Collect Comic Books, Aliens, Dragons, Monsters and Me, Gone Fishing, 1993, The Gary Owens All-Nonsense News Network. Chmn. Multiple Sclerosis dr. L.A., 1972; chmn., grand marshall So. Calif. Diabetes Dr., 1974—; mayor City of Encino, Calif., 1972-74; bd. govs. Grammy Awards, 1968—, Emmy Awards, 1972; mem. adv. bd. Pasadena (Calif.) City Coll., 1969—, Sugar Ray Robinson Youth Found., 1971—; mem. nat. miracle com. Juvenile Diabetes Found., 1981—, nat. com. for Carousel Ball Children's Diabetes Found. Denver; radio adv. bd. U. So. Calif., 1980—; hon. chmn. Goodwill Industries Sporting Goods Dr., 1986, chmn., 1986; active telethons Cerebral Palsy, 1980, DARE program, 1985—, S.A.N.E. program, 1985—, comic relief to help U.S. Homeless, 1986. Named outstanding radio personality in U.S., 1965-79, top Radio Personality in World, Internat. Radio Forum, Toronto, 1977, Man of Yr. All-Cities Employees Assn., City of Los Angeles, 1968, Top Radio Broadcaster, Nat. Assn. Broadcasters, 1986, Radio Man of Yr. Nat. Assn. Broadcasters, 1986; recipient Distinguished Service award Hollywood Jaycees, 1966, David award, 1978, Hollywood Hall of Fame award, 1980, Am. award Cypress Coll., 1981, Carbon Mike award Pacific Broadcasters, 1987, 5 Grammy nominations, Emmy award for More Dinosaurs, 1986; Star on Hollywood Walk of Fame, 1981; honored by U.S. Dept. Treasury, 1985, Am. Diabetes Assn., 1990, Variety Clubs Internat., 1990; inducted into Nat. Broadcasters Hall of Fame, 1994, Radio Hall of Fame, 1994, Nat. Assn. Broadcasters Hall of Fame, 1995. Mem. Nat. Cartoonists Soc., So. Calif. Cartoonists Assn., Cartoonists and Artists Profl. Soc. Office: 2444 Wilshire Blvd Ste 506 Santa Monica CA 90403-5813 *Without sounding like a coffee break Voltaire, the apothegm that "Everyman is his own Pygmalion" may be correct. I have tried to enrich my life by performing, reading, writing, creating, and helping others whenever* *possible. I try to stand up for what I believe, for it is better to give ulcers than to receive! Humor has helped protect me from the bruises of life, in addition to a daily supply of fantasy and illusion.*

OWENS, GARY MITCHELL, family physician; b. Salisbury, Md., July 31, 1949; s. Avery Donovan and Elizabeth (Mitchell) O.; m. Loretta Andrews; children: Aaron David, Scott Christopher, Stefanie Erin, Avery Tyler, Thomas Edward, Danielle Caroline. BA, U. Pa., 1971; MD, Thomas Jefferson U., 1975. Diplomate Am. Bd. Family Practice, 78. Resident in family medicine Wilmington (Del.) Med. Ctr., 1975-78, chief resident, 1978, tchg. assoc. dept. family medicine, 1978-91; practice medicine specializing in family practice, Wilmington, 1978-91; tchg. assoc. dept. family medicine St. Francis Hosp., 1978-91; med. dir. Phoenix Steel Co., 1980-87, Delaware Valley HMO, Delaware Plan, 1985-91; assoc. med. dir. quality assurance, chmn. credentials com. Delaware Valley HMO, 1987-91; vice chmn. dept. family practice Med. Ctr. of Del., Wilmington, 1990—91; med. dir. Keystone Health Plan East, Phila., 1991-94, sr. med. dir., 1994-95; chmn. pharmacy and therapeutic com. Independence Blue Cross, 1994—; sr. med. dir., 1995-96; v.p. patient care mgmt., 1996—. Bd. dirs. Phila. Health Mgmt. Corp., 2000—; mem. interdisciplinary coun. on lifestyle and obesity mgmt., 1997; staff, coun. mem., chmn. reappointment com. Med. Ctr. Del., vice chmn. dept. family practice, 1990-91; cons. NorAm. Chem. Co., 1984-91; mem. Ladership Phila. Core Class, 2001-02. Fellow: Am. Acad. Family Physicians; mem.: Biotech Med. Mgmt. Assn. (bd. dirs. 1997—2002), Am. Coll. Physician Execs., Alpha Epsilon Delta, Alpha Omega Alpha. Roman Catholic. Home: S Palmer Dr Glen Mills PA 19342 Office: PO Box 7516 1901 Market St Philadelphia PA 19101-7516 E-mail: gary.owens@ibx.com.

OWENS, GUY, neurosurgeon; b. Amarillo, Tex., Jan. 25, 1926; s. Guy Fitzhugh Owens and Mary Helen Virgin; m. Lillian Janet Parkinson, June 20, 1949; children: Victoria Ann, Guy Parkinson. BS, Tufts U., 1946; MD, Harvard U., 1950. Diplomate Am. Bd. Neurol. Surgery. Asst. prof. Vanderbilt U., Nashville, 1958—62; assoc. prof. SUNY, Buffalo, 1963—68; prof. surgery, head dept. U. Conn. Med. Sch., Farmington, Conn., 1968—75; pvt. prractice neurol. surgery New Britain, 1975—. Author: Neurologic and Neurosurgical Nursing, 1975; contbr. over 130 articles to profl. jours. Office: 40 Hart St New Britain CT 06052

OWENS, HELEN DAWN, elementary school educator, reading consultant; b. Eastman, Ga., Oct. 9, 1949; d. Eli B. and Irene (Harrell) Branch; m. Bobby Lee Owens, Dec. 9, 1967; children: Leslie Owens-McDonald, Monica Dawn. AA, Miami (Fla.) Dade Jr. Coll., 1969; BS, Fla. Internat. U., 1978; MEd, Mercer U., 1986, EdS, 1991. Cert. presch.-12th grade, reading specialist, early childhood edn. specialist, Ga. Youth ctr. dir. Dept. Def., Clark AFB, Philippines, 1969-70; English lang. instr. Chinese Mil. Acad., Feng Shan, Taiwan, 1973-75; tchr., music instr. ABC Presch., Miami, 1976-78; kindergarten and music tchr. Berkshire Sch., Homestead, Fla., 1978-79; tchr., reading specialist Perdue Elem. Sch. Houston County Bd. Edn., Warner Robins, Ga., 1979—. Mem. nominating com. mem. Ga. picture book of yr. U. Ga., Athens, 1990-91; reading cons. for schs., county edn. bds., regional reading ctrs., Ctrl. Ga., 1990—. Author: With Loving Hands and Tender Hearts, 1975. Exec. bd. dirs. Ladies Ministries, Ch. of God., Warner Robins, 1990-94; dir. Internat. City Girls' Club, Warner Robins, 1990-96. Recipient 25-Yr. Bible Tchr. Svc. award Internat. City Ch. of God., 1991; named Fla. State Family Tng. Dir. of Yr., Fla. Ch. of God, 1979, Ga. Girls' Club Coord. of the Year, 1995. Mem. Internat. Reading Assn. (Ga. coun. 1979-96, dir. mem. devel. 1993-96, v.p. 1996-97, pres. elect 1997-98, pres. 1998-99, past pres. HOPE coun. 1990-92, Annette Hopson Svc. award 1998), Profl. Assn. Ga. Edn., Internat. Platform Assn. Republican. Avocations: reading, sewing, touring foreign countries, swimming, storytelling. Home: 111 Crestwood Rd Warner Robins GA 31093-6803 Office: Perdue Elem Sch 856 Highway 96 Warner Robins GA 31088-2222

OWENS, JANA JAE, entertainer; b. Great Falls, Mont., Aug. 30, 1943; d. Jacob G. Meyer and Bette P. (Sprague) Hopper; m. Sidney Greif (div.); children: Matthew N., Sydni C.; m. Buck Owens. Student, Interlochen Music Camp, 1959, Internat. String Congress, 1960, Vienna (Austria) Acad. Music, 1963-64; BA magna cum laude, MusB magna cum laude, Colo. Womens Coll., 1965. Tchr. music Ontario (Oreg.) Pub. Schs., 1965-67, Redding (Calif.) Pub. Schs., 1969-74; entertainer Buck Owens Enterprises, Bakersfield, Calif., 1974-78, Tulsa, 1979—. Concertmistress Boise (Idaho) Philharm., 1965-67, Shasta Symphony, Redding, 1969-74. Rec. artist (violinist, vocalist) Lark Records, 1978—. Avocations: skiing, tennis, swimming. Office: Jana Jae Enterprises Lake Record Prodns Inc PO Box 35726 Tulsa OK 74153-0726

OWENS, JOHN FRANKLIN, health care administrator, consultant, nurse; b. Slatington, Pa., May 19, 1935; s. William and Goldie Irene (Zerfass) O.; m. Shirley Ann Spade, June 15, 1957; children: Terri Ann Owens Albright, Rick Todd. Student, Orange County Community Coll., 1954-55; grad. Sch. of Nursing, student, SUNY, 1954-57, Pa. State U., 1964, U. Pa., 1967. Pvt. practice, 1960-72; pvt. cons., 1961-72; nursing supr., instr. Easton (Pa.) Hosp., 1961-65, dir. in-svc. edn., 1963-65; dir. svcs. Northampton County Homemaker Svc., Bethlehem, Pa., 1965-67; exec. dir. Bucks County Homemaker-Home Health Aide Svc., Doylestown, 1967-72; zone mgr. UpJohn Healthcare Svcs., N.J., 1972-73, govt. adminstr., 1973-79, zone mgr. Fla., 1979-82, bus. mgr., 1982-84, asst. to pres., 1984-85, regional mgr., 1985-88, govt. contracts nat. program mgr., 1989-90, dir. Nat. Govt. Affairs, 1990-91; pvt. cons. New Port Richey, Fla., 1991—; long term territory mgr. Kinetic Concepts, Inc., New Port richey, 1992-94, acct. exec. Hudson, 1994-96; ret., 1996. Author: PA Training Guide for Homemaker Home Health Aides, 1972, Government Contracting, 1990. Chmn. Bucks County Reps., Doylestown, 1972; founding pres. Pa. Homemaker-Home Health Aide Coun., 1970. With U.S. Army, 1953-54. Mem. Am. Pub. Health Assn., Am. Mgmt. Assn., Jr. Chamber Internat., Nat. Conf. on Aging, Jaycees (1st v.p. 1969-70, pres. 1970-71, chmn. bd. 1971-72). Republican. Avocation: sports.

OWENS, LARRY BRENT, nurse, anesthetist; b. Paintsville, Ky., July 13, 1948; s. James Woodrow and Anna Yvonne (Stamper) O.; m. Julie Lynn Wilson, May 19, 1979 (div. Nov. 1986); m. Mary Drane Whaley, Oct. 28, 1989; children: Miller W., Magaret V. A in Nursing, Ea. Ky. U., 1973; cert. in nurse anesthesia, Charleston (W.Va.) Area Med. Ctr.; BS in Nursing, U. Ky., 1983. Supr. operating rooms Louisa (Ky.) Community Hosp., 1975; nurse anesthetist Cave Run Clinic, Morehead, Ky., 1977-79; sr. nurse anesthetist Anesthesia Assocs., Lexington, 1979—; freelance anesthetist, 1990—. With USN, 1969-73, comdr. Nurse Corps, USNR, 1987—, specialty advisor for nurse anesthetist-oper. rm. nurses, 1999—. Mem. Am. Assn. Nurse Anesthetists (asst. chmn. coun. on practice 1985-91, coun. on pub. interest in anesthesia 1985-91, mem. com. on practice 1986-92, acting chmn. com. on practice 1990), Ky. Assn. Nurse Anesthetists (past pres., v.p., sec., treas., bd. dirs., mem. adv. bd. coun. on practice Ky. Bd. Nursing 1985-93, editor, pub. Pacemaker). Avocations: sailing, running, amateur radio, volleyball, tennis. Home: 4816 Firebrook Blvd Lexington KY 40513-1404 E-mail: LarryOwensCRNA@aol.com.

OWENS, LUVIE MOORE, association consultant; b. Cleve., July 26, 1933; d. Dan Tyler and Elizabeth (Oakes) Moore; m. Lloyd Owens, Jan. 1, 1955; children: Luvie Owens Myers, Elizabeth, Lloyd H. Student, Smith Coll., Northampton, Mass., 1956. Tchr. Howard Jr. High Sch., Wilmette, Ill., 1971-75; U.S. ops. mgr. Frank T. Ross & Co., Evanston, 1976-86; chief exec. officer Internat. Platform Assn., Winnetka, 1986-98, dir., 1972—99; ret., 1999. Mem. jr. league Cleve. Mus. Art, 1954—98, treas., mem. jr. coun., 1964—65; commr. Police and Fire Commn., Winnetka, 1986—87; mem. alumnae bd. Madeira Sch., Greenway, Va., 1984—88; chmn. bd. Lake Shore Unitarian Ch., Winnetka, 1986—87. Mem.: Rotary.

OWENS, MAJOR ROBERT ODELL, congressman; b. Memphis, June 28, 1936; m. Marie Cuprill; children: Christopher, Geoffrey, Millard, Carlos, Cecilia. Grad. with high honors, Morehouse Coll., 1956; MS, Atlanta U., 1957. Mem. Internat. Commn. on Ways of Implementing Social Policy to Ensure Maximum Pub. Participation and Social Justice for Minorities, The Hague, Netherlands, 1972, U.S. Congress from 11th N.Y. dist., 1983—; chmn. select edn. & civil rights subcom., edn. and workforce com.; ranking minority mem. subcom. on workforce protections; mem. govt. reform and oversight com. Featured speaker White House Conf. on Librs., 1979. Pub. author and lectr. on library sci. Chmn. Bklyn. Congress Racial Equality; v.p. Met. Coun. on Housing, 1964; community coord. Bklyn. Pub. Library, 1964-66; exec. dir. Brownsville Community Coun., 1966-68; commr. N.Y.C. Community Devel. Agy., 1968-73; bd. dirs. community media program Columbia U., N.Y.C., 1973-75; mem. N.Y. State Senate, 1975-82, chmn. Dem. Ops. Com. Major R. Owens Day, named in his honor, City Bklyn., 1971. Office: US Ho of Reps 2309 Rayburn Ho Office Bldg Washington DC 20515 : 289 Utica Avenue Brooklyn NY 11213*

OWENS, MARILYN MAE, elementary school educator, secondary school educator; b. Poland, Ohio, Nov. 17, 1932; d. S. Reed and Vernice Mae (Flickinger) Johnson; m. J. Edward Owens, July 23, 1953; children: Charlene, Preston, Lorraine. BS in Art Edn., Millersville State U., 1970, elem. cert., 1983; MEd in Art, Towson U., 1975; elem. prin. cert., Western Md. U., 1984. Cert. elem. and secondary tchr. art, elem. tchr., Pa.: art supr. elem. and secondry, prin. elem., Md. Tchr art. k-12 Northeastern Sch. Dist., Manchester, Pa., 1970-99; ret., 1999. Adj. instr. humanities, art appreciation York Coll. of Pa., 1977-81; mem. long range planning com., Northeastern Sch. Dist., Manchester, 1988-90, supt.'s adv. bd., 1990-91, elem. adv. bd. Orendorf Sch., 1990-92, 97-98, dist. budget com., 1991-92, elem. budget com. Conewago Elem. Sch., 1993-98, computer tech. elem. com., 1993-95, instrnl. and profl. devel. com., 1994-98, calligraphy tchr. Northeastern Adult Cmty. Edn., 1988-90. Leader Girl Scouts of U.S., Penn Laurel, York, Pa., 1963-67; mem. Northeastern Art Out-Reach program, Northeastern Edn. Assn. Cmty. Rels. Com., Northeastern Sch. Dist.'s Portfolio Com.; vol. Susan B. Byrnes Health Ctr., Conewago Elem. Sch., Northeastern Sch. Dist., Spl. Olympics, York. Recipient scholarship Ind. (Pa.) State Coll., 1950; grantee Northeastern Sch. Dist., Manchester, 1989-90. Mem. AAUW, Nat. Art Edn. Assn., Northeastern Edn. Assn. (v.p. 1987-88, pres. 1988-89, cmty. rels. program 1998-99), Pa. Art Edn. Assn. (ret., Ret. Art Educator of Yr. 1999), Pa. Guild of Craftsmen (Yorktowne chpt., mailing com. 2001—), Pa. Inst. CPA (Women's Aux. S. Ctrl. chpt.), York Quilters Guild, York County Heritage Trust, Clearfield Hist. Soc. (life), York Art Assn., Kiwanis Club York, Phi Delta Kappa (scholarship com. 1990-94, scholarship chair 1998-99, 2000-02, Disting. Svc. award 1999). Avocations: painting, crafts, hiking, camping, sewing. Home: 2505 Schoolhouse Ln York PA 17402-3918

OWENS, MARK ERNEST, lawyer, legal administrator; b. Columbus, Ohio, Sept. 1, 1956; s. Charles Ernest and Rebecca Jean (Graham) O.; m. Debra L. Kellereskie, May 19, 1979; children: Matthew, Emily. BA in Polit. Sci., Wright State U., 1978; JD, U. Dayton, 1981. Bar: Ohio 1981, U.S. Dist. Ct. (so. dist.) Ohio. Atty. Reid & Assocs., Beavercreek, Ohio, 1981-84, Bates, Riley, Sorrell, Tell & Owens, Dayton, 1985-89; asst. prosecutor Montgomery County Prosecutor, 1986-89; referee Dayton Mcpl. Ct., 1989-91, clk. of ct., 1991—. Legal counsel Montgomery County Dem. Party, Dayton, 1988—, vice-chmn., 1994—. Mem. ABA, Ohio State Bar Assn., Dayton Bar Assn., Ohio Assn. Mcpl. Ct. Clks. (2d v.p. 1995-96), Optimists. Roman Catholic. Office: Clk of Cts 301 W 3rd St Dayton OH 45402-1446

OWENS, MARSHA, library director; b. Birmingham, Ala., Apr. 5, 1956; d. Clarence Austin and Virginia (Hamilton) O.; m. James Alfred Smith, May 19, 1984 (div. Dec. 1990); m. William Kelly Key, Jan. 7, 1995. BS in Journalism, U. Ala., 1982, MLS, 1992. Staff photographer, reporter Daily Mountain Eagle, Jasper, Ala., 1983-84; paraprofl. librarian Birmingham Pub. Libr., 1988-90; dir. Orange Beach Pub. Libr., 1992—. Bd. dirs. South Baldwin Literacy Coun., Foley, Ala., 1993-97; mem. Ala. Electronic Access Com., 1997-98. Mem. ALA, Ala. Libr. Assn. (convention com. 1994-97, 98), Beta Phi Mu. Avocations: hiking, camping, reading, sports cars, gardening. Home: 26759 Magnolia Ave Orange Beach AL 36561-4915 Office: Orange Beach Pub Libr 26267 Canal Rd PO Box 1649 Orange Beach AL 36561-1649 E-mail: owensmar@hotmail.com.

OWENS, MARVIN FRANKLIN, JR. oil company executive; b. Oklahoma City, Feb. 20, 1916; s. Marvin Franklin and Levis (Coley) O.; m. Jessie Ruth Hay, June 15, 1941; children: Marvin Franklin III, William Earl, Jack Hay. BS, U. Okla., 1937; postgrad., Stonier Grad. Sch. Banking Rutgers U., 1960-62. Petroleum engr. Brit. Am. Oil Producing Co., Oklahoma City, 1937-41; chief petroleum engr. Bay Petroleum Corp., Denver, 1946-54; sr. v.p. Cen. Bank of Denver, 1954-81. Elder Presbyn. Ch., Denver. With U.S. Army, 1941-46; col. Res. ret. Mem. Cherry Hills Country Club. Home: 3899 S Glencoe St Denver CO 80237-1024

OWENS, MERLE WAYNE, executive search consultant; b. Barnsdall, Okla., Mar. 30, 1933; s. Jesse Raymond and Beulah Juanita (Thompson) O.; m. Nettie Natalie Norris, June 6, 1953; children: Jesse Wayne, Jennifer Lee. BBA, U. Okla., 1955. Sales engr. Nat. Supply Co., Tulsa, 1956-60; underwriter Allstate Ins., Dallas, 1960-63; regional mgr. Blue Cross Blue Shield, 1963-78; sr. v.p. Paul R. Ray & Co., Ft. Worth, 1978-93; owner Merle Owens & Assocs., 1993—. 1st lt. U.S. Army, 1955-56. Republican. Baptist. Avocations: hunting, fishing, woodworking. Home: 420 Blue Jay Ct Bedford TX 76021-3201 Office: Merle W Owens & Assocs 401 Harwood Rd Ste B Bedford TX 76021-4151

OWENS, ROBERT GEORGE, psychologist, researcher; b. Devils Lake, N.D., Oct. 10, 1932; s. Clarence George and Anne Marie (Ebner) O.; m. Ruth Ann Johnson, Aug. 21, 1955 (dec. Sept. 1993); children: Scott George, Bruce Robert, Laura Marie. PhB, U. N.D., 1954, MA, 1955. Lic. psychologist, Wis. Lectr. U. Wis., Madison, 1964-66; cons. psychologist various mental health facilities and cts., Wis., 1966-86; profl. spkr. in field of psychology Wis., N.Y., 1962—. Founder, pub., editor The Internat. Jour. of Clin. Neuropsychology, 1979-84; contbr. articles to profl. publs. Mem. APA, Am. Psychol. Soc., Nat. Register Health Svc. Providers in Psychology, Nat. Acad. Neuropsychologists (life). Republican. Episcopalian. Avocation: book collecting. Home and Office: 6666 Odana Rd Madison WI 53719-1012

OWENS, ROBERT PATRICK, lawyer; b. Spokane, Wash., Feb. 17, 1954; s. Walter Patrick and Cecile (Phillippay) O.; m. Robin Miller, Aug. 12, 1978; children: Ryan Barry, Meghan Jane. BA, Wash. State U., 1976; JD, Gonzaga U., 1981; LLM in Admiralty Law, Tulane U., 1983. Bar: Wash. 1982, Alaska 1984, U.S. Dist. Ct. (ea. dist.) Wash. 1982, U.S. Dist. Ct. Alaska 1984, U.S. Ct. Appeals (5th cir.) 1983. Assoc. Groh, Eggers & Price, Anchorage, 1983-88; mng. atty. Taylor & Hintze, 1988-90; Anchorage office mgr. Copeland, Landye, Bennett and Wolf, 1990-99; prin. Law Offices of Robert P. Owens, PC, 2000—. V.p. bd. dirs. Hope Cmty. Resources, Inc., 1999-2001, pres., 2001—. Coord. supplies Insight Seminars, Anchorage, 1985-86. Mem. ABA (dist. 27 rep. young lawyers div. 1988-90), Alaska Bar Assn., Wash. State Bar Assn., Anchorage Bar Assn. (pres. 1991-92, v.p. 1990-91, pres. young lawyers sect. 1986-88), Alaska Fly Fishers, Phi Alpha Delta. Roman Catholic. Avocations: fishing, photography, skiing, softball. Office: Law Offices Robert P Owens PC 310 K St Ste 200 Anchorage AK 99501 E-mail: rpowens@alaska.com.

OWENS, ROCHELLE, poet, playwright; b. Bklyn., Apr. 2, 1936; d. Max and Molly (Adler) Bass; m. George Economou, June 17, 1962. Fellow, Yale Sch. Drama, 1968. Writer-in-residence, Brown U., 1989; tchr. U. Calif. 1982, U. Okla., 1985, 87, 88, U. Southwestern La., 1998, Tex. A and M Univ. Author: (plays) The String Game, 1965, Istanboul, 1965, Futz, 1967, Homo, 1966, Beclch, 1966, Futz and What Came After, 1968, He Wants Shih, 1969, Farmers Almanac, 1969, The Queen of Greece, 1969, Kontraption, 1970, The Karl Marx Play, 1971, O.K. Certaldo, 1975, Emma Instigated Me, 1976, The Widow and the Colonel, 1977, Mountain Rites, 1977, Who Do You Want, Peire Vidal, 1978, Chucky's Hunch, 1981, Who Do You Want, Peire Vidal, 1982, Plays by Rochelle Owens, 2000, (poetry) Not be Essence That Cannot Be, 1961, Salt and Core, 1968, I am the Babe of Joseph Stalin's Daughter, Poems from Joe's Garage, The Joe 82 Creation Poems, The Karl Marx Play & Others, The Joe Chronicles, Part 2, Four Young Lady Poets, 1962, Shemuel, 1979, French Light, 1984, Constructs, 1985, Anthropologists at a Dinner Party, 1985, Who Do You Want Peire Vidal, 1986, W.C. Fields in French Light, 1986, How Much Paint Does the Painting Need, 1988, New and Selected Poems: 1961-1996, Black Chalk, 1992, Rubbed Stones: Poems from 1960-1992, 1994, Luca: Discourse on Life and Death, 2001, (radio play) Sweet Potatoes, 1979 (Obie award 1982); (feature film) Futz, 1969; editor: (plays) Spontaneous Combustion (Obie award 1967); recs. include: From a Shaman's Notebook, 1968, The Karl Marx Play, 1974, Totally Corrupt, 1976, Black Box 17, 1979, (play) Three Front, 1990, (radio play) Guerre a'Trois, 1991; reading performances at St. Mark's Poetry Project, Mus. Modern Art, Guggenheim, Whitney Mus., Oxford U., Am. Coll., Paris; host of The Writer's Mind; prodr. radio show, U. Okla.; (video) Oklahoma Too, 1987, How Much Paint Does the Painting Need; reading performance: Am. Coll. Athens, Greece. Founding mem. N.Y. Theatre Strategy, Women's Theatre Council. Ford Found. grantee, 1965, Creative Arts Pub. Svc. grantee, 1973, Nat. Endowment for Arts grantee, 1974, Rockfeller Found. grantee, 1974; Guggenheim fellow, 1971; honors N.Y. Drama Critics Cir.; Rockefeller Found. Bellagio resident, 1993; recipient Nomination in poetry Okla. Ctr. for the Book, 1995. Mem. Dramatists Guild, ASCAP. Achievements include being in anthologies. Address: 226 W Rittenhouse Sq Apt 1001 Philadelphia PA 19103 *Creativity and idealism have enabled me to pursue the world of ideas, transforming itself always into art.*

OWENS, RODNEY JOE, lawyer; b. Dallas, Mar. 7, 1950; s. Hubert L. and Billie Jo (Foust) O.; m. Sherry Lyn Bailey, June 10, 1972; 1 child, Jonathan Rockwell. BBA, So. Meth. U., 1972, JD, 1975. Bar: Tex. 1975, U.S. Dist. Ct. (no. dist.) Tex. 1975, U.S. Tax Ct. 1975, U.S. Ct. Appeals (5th cir.) 1975. Assoc. Durant & Mankoff, Dallas, 1975-78, ptnr., 1978-83, Meadows, Owens, Collier, Reed, Cousins & Blau, Dallas, 1983—. Contbr. articles to profl. jours. Baptist. Home: 6919 N Jan Mar Dr Dallas TX 75230-3111 Office: Meadows Owens Collier Reed 901 Main St Ste 3700 Dallas TX 75202-3725 E-mail: rowens@meadowsowens.com.

OWENS, RUTH WILMA, principal; b. Birmingham, Ala. d. G. T. Townsel, Inez (Harrison) Townsel; m. Blanton B. Owens, Dec. 28, 1960; children: Blanton B. Owens Jr., Phil, Marc. BS, Ala. State U., 1956, MEd, 1965; postgrad., U. Wis., 1975, Marquette U., 1979. Christian counselor HR Ednl. Complex, Milw., 1997—. Pres. Help One Another Club, Milw., 1970—. Grantee Mex. Travel grant, U. Wis., Counseling Grant, GE. Mem.: Christian Bus. and Profl. Alliance, Ala. State U. Alumni Assn. Milw. chpt. Avocation: Avocations: reading, chess, exercising. Office: HR Ednl Complex 3500 W Mother Daniels Way Milwaukee WI 53209

OWENS, SANDRA NELL, nurse; b. Birmingham, Ala., Aug. 6, 1948; d. Willie Toney Jr. and Eleanor Johnson; children: Zondra Newson, Cassondra Bess, Kendra Owens, Marlon Riley II. BS in Chemistry and Math., Paine Coll., 1969; A in Bus. IBM/Clerical, So. Jr. Coll., Birmingham, 1971; AS in Nursing, Grayson County Jr. Coll., Denison, Tex., 1977; PhD in Healthcare Svc. Mgmt., LaSalle U., 1996. RN, Ala.; ordained to ministry Bapt. Ch., 1992, World Christian Ch., 1995. Tchr. Boggs Acad., Keysville, Ga., 1971-72; packaging engr. Johnson and Johnson, Sherman, Tex., 1972-74; teletype operator, train mover SLSF R.R., 1974-75; tchr. Sch. of Open Learning, 1975-76; insp. Oscar Mayer Corp., 1976-77; nurse St. Vincent's Hosp., Birmingham, 1990—. Worship team singer Internat. Nurses Conv., Birmingham, 1994; del. conf. on cancer prevention and detection in Black Ams., Oncology Nursing, Atlanta, 1991. Author (pamphlet) Let's Talk PMS, 1993, Talking PMS from Philosophical and Theological Point of View, 1997; contbr. poems to lit. publs. (Internat. Soc. Poets awards 1994, 95). Mem. care of the poor com. St. Vincent's Hosp., 1992-93; instr. ARC, 1993—, Birmingham AIDS Outreach, 1994. Recipient Ala. Quality award Examiner, 1999—. Mem. Birmingham City C. of C. (active corp. leadership 1995—). Avocations: singing, cooking, writing, painting, sewing. Home: 528 Avenue T Birmingham AL 35214-5568 Office: Saint Vincent's Hosp 833 Saint Vincents Dr Birmingham AL 35205-1606

OWENS, TERRELL, football player; b. Dec. 7, 1973; Postgrad in merchandising, Univ. Tenn., Chattanooga. Wide receiver San Francisco 49ers, 1996—. Achievements include making NFL history for most receptions in one game in 2000. Office: San Francisco 49ers Ltd 4949 Centennial Blvd Santa Clara CA 95054*

OWENS, TYLER BENJAMIN, chemist; b. Norfolk, Va., Aug. 28, 1944; s. Arthur Samuel and Julia Tyler (Downs) O.; m. Brenda Anne Coates, Sept. 5, 1980; children: Brooks Downs, Elizabeth Tyler. BA in Chemistry, Campbell U., Buies Creek, N.C., 1967; postgrad., N.C. State U., 1967-69. Sanitarian State of Va. Health Dept., Manassas, Va., 1971-72; chief chemist Goodmark Foods, Raleigh, N.C., 1972-75; real estate broker Nadine Hodge Realty, 1976-77; sales engr. Hewlett Packard Co., Palo Alto, Calif., 1977-80; sales rep. Sperry Univac Corp., Blue Bell, Pa., 1980-81; sales engr. Spectra Physics Corp., San Jose, 1981-83; pres. Batchelor & Owens, Inc., Raleigh, 1983-88; territory mgr. Extrel Corp., Pitts., 1988-90; sales mgr. Delsi Nermag Instruments, Paris, 1990-91, Viking Instruments Corp., Reston, Va., 1989-93; account exec. Dean Witter, Raleigh, 1993-95, Bodman Industries, Raleigh, 1995—; organic sales engr. Leco Corp., 1998—. Active YMCA, Raleigh, 1989—; bd. dirs. Stonebridge Homeowners Assn., Raleigh, 1990-93, pres., 1993; bd. govs. Friends of the Children, Wake Meml. Hosp., Raleigh, 1990-93; precinct del. Wake County Rep. Party, Raleigh, 1985; vestry Episcopal Ch. of the Nativity, Raleigh, 1988-90, sr. warden, 1988-89. Mem. Am. Soc. Mass Spectrometry, N.C. Real Estate Commn., Triangle Mass Spectrometer Discussion Group, Wake County Rep. Men's Club. Episcopalian. Avocations: running, flying, ham radio, bridge. Home and Office: 1009 Carrington Dr Raleigh NC 27615-1212

OWENS, VIVIAN ANN, plant science educator, researcher; b. Conway, S.C., Sept. 2, 1948; d. Zack Jr. and Frances (Mishoe) O. BS, Howard U., 1971, MS, 1974; PhD, Cornell U., 1984; MLS, U. Md., 1998. Assoc. prof. plant sci. Hampton (Va.) U., 1988-95. Faculty fellow EPA, Washington, summer 1990. Contbr. articles to profl. jours. Vol. Friends of Kennedy Ctr., 1996. E-mail: owens600@aol.com.

OWENS, WARNER BARRY, physical therapist; b. Detroit, Apr. 29, 1939; s. Wendell Lee and Flora Lucille (Maddox) O.; m. Frances Hutton, June 11, 1960 (div. May 1973); children— Jeffrey, Karen; m. Sandra Irene Olstyn, Nov. 16, 1974. B.S., UCLA, 1962. Staff phys. therapist Valley Phys. Therapy Ctr., Van Nuys, Calif., 1962-63; chief phys. therapist St. Joseph Med. Ctr., Burbank, Calif., 1963-70, dir. rehab., 1970— , bd. dirs. Credit Union, 1974-76, 83-91, pres., 1986-91; pres. Therapeutic Assocs. Inc., Sherman Oaks, 1992—; dir. Tetrad and Assocs., Sherman Oaks, 1972— ; chmn. bd. dirs. Nat. Physical Rehab. Network, Inc.; mem. admissions com. phys. therapy option Calif. State U.-Northridge, 1976— . Childrens Hosp. Sch. Phys. Therapy Kate Crutcher scholar, 1961; recipient Outstanding Contbn. to Profession award Calif. State U.-Northridge, 1983. Mem. Am. Phys. Therapy Assn. (chmn. jud. com. 1981-82), Am. Coll. Sports Medicine, Phys. Therapy Dirs. Forum, Internat. Wine and Food Soc. (bd. dirs. San Fernando Valley 1979— , pres. 1980). Republican. Home: 780 Rockbridge Rd Montecito CA 93108-1127 Office: Therapeutic Assocs Inc 7100 Fort Dent Way Seattle WA 98188-7500

OWENS, WILBUR DAWSON, JR. federal judge; b. Albany, Ga., Feb. 1, 1930; s. Wilbur Dawson and Estelle (McKenzie) O.; m. Mary Elizabeth Glenn, June 21, 1958; children: Lindsey, Wilbur Dawson III, Estelle, John. Student, Emory U., 1947-48; JD, U. Ga., 1952. Bar: Ga. 1952. Mem. firm Smith, Gardner & Owens, Albany, 1954-55; v.p., trust officer Bank of Albany, 1955-59; sec.-treas. Southeastern Mortgage Co., Albany, 1959-65; asst. U.S. atty. Middle Dist. Ga., Macon, 1962-65; assoc., then ptnr. Bloch, Hall, Hawkins & Owens, 1965-72; judge U.S. Dist. Ct. for Mid. Dist. Ga., 1972—, now sr. U.S. dist. judge. Served to 1st lt., JAG USAF, 1952-54. Mem. State Bar Ga., Macon Bar Assn., Am. Judicature Soc., Phi Delta Theta, Phi Delta Phi. Clubs: Rotarian, Idle Hour Golf and Country. Republican. Presbyterian. Office: US Dist Ct PO Box 65 Macon GA 31202-0065

OWENS, WILLIAM DEAN, lawyer; b. Topeka, July 3, 1931; s. Claude and Melvina Owens; m. Doris McConnell, June 10, 1953; children: Steven D., Susan Bloom, Sarah Steele. BS in Bus., U. Kans., Lawrence, 1953, JD, 1968. Bar: Kans. 1968. Mgr. McConnell Lumber Co., Lawrence, 1955-65; ptnr. Hampton & Royce, L.C., Salina, Kans., 1968—. Trustee, chmn. Kansas Wesleyan U., Salina, 1990-99, Salina Regional Health Found., 1986—; trustee Eisenhower Found., 1999—. Capt. USMC, 1953-55, Japan. Fellow Kans. Bar Found.; mem. ABA, Kans. Bar Assn. Republican. Presbyterian. Avocations: golf, travel, woodworking. Home: 2126 Melrose Ln Salina KS 67401-3543 Office: Hampton & Royce LC 119 W Iron Ave Salina KS 67401-2600 E-mail: wdowens@hamptonlaw.com.

OWENS, WILLIAM DON, anesthesiology educator; b. St. Louis, Dec. 12, 1939; s. Don and Caroline Wilhemena (Raaf) Owens; m. Patricia Gail Brown, Dec. 12, 1964; children: Pamela, David, Susan. AB, Westminster Coll., 1961; MD, U. Mich., 1965. Diplomate Am. Bd. Anesthesiology. Resident and fellow Mass. Gen. Hosp. and Harvard Med. Sch., Boston, 1969—72; instr. Harvard

Med. Sch., 1972—73; asst. prof. anesthesiology Washington U. Sch. Medicine, St. Louis, 1973—76, assoc. prof., 1976—82, prof., 1982—, chmn. dept., 1982—92. Bd. trustees Barnes Hosp., St. Louis, 1987—89; bd. dir. Anesthesia Found., 1994—, pres., 1999—; sec.-treas. An. Bd. Anesthesiology, 1991—94, pres., 1995—96, bd. dirs., 1984—96. Contbr. Served to lt. comdr. USN, 1966—69. Fellow: Am. Coll. Anesthesiology; mem.: Assn. Univ. Anesthesiologists, Acad. Anesthesiology, Internat. Anesthesia Rsch. Soc., Am. Soc. Anesthesiologists (bd. dirs. 1989—99, 1st v.p. 1995—96, pres. 1997—98). Office: Washington U Sch Med Dept Anesthesiology 660 S Euclid Ave Saint Louis MO 63110-1010

OWINGS, ALISON JUNE, writer, journalist; b. Pasadena, Calif., June 17, 1944; d. Kenneth Brown and Alice Case (Roberts) O.; m. Jonathan Brittain Perdue, May 1, 1993. Student, Freiburg (Germany) U., 1964-65; BA, Am. U., 1966. Writer, rschr. Congl. Quar., Washington, 1966; rschr. Dem. Nat. Com., 1966-67; news asst. ABC, 1967-69; assoc. prodr. documentary series WRC, 1969-71; assoc. prodr. WNBC TV, N.Y.C., 1971-73; TV newswriter CBS TV, 1973-77, 80-85; freelance TV newswriter, 1982-99; freelance editor, 1999—. Author: Wander Women's Phrasebook, 1987, Frauen: German Women Recall the Third Reich, 1993 (NY Times Notable Books of Yr., 94), Hey, Waitress! The USA from the Other Side of the Tray, 2002. Founder Don't Tear It Down (now D.C. Preservation League), Washington, 1971. Resident writer Edna St. Vincent Millay Colony for Arts, 1977; travel/rsch. grantee West German Press Office, 1985, German Dem. Republic, 1985; John J. McCloy fellow Am. Coun. on Germany, 1987; recipient award for newswriting Writers Guild Am., 1977. Democrat. Avocations: theater, American antiques, gardening, pondering. Home and Office: 145 Richardson Dr Mill Valley CA 94941-2413 E-mail: AlysounO@aol.com.

OWINGS, DONALD HENRY, psychology educator; b. Atlanta, Dec. 7, 1943; s. Markley James and Loyce Erin (White) O.; m. Sharon Elizabeth Calhoun, Jan. 29, 1966; children: Ragon Matthew, Anna Rebekah. BA in Psychology, U. Tex., 1965; PhD, U. Wash., 1972. Asst. prof. psychology U. Calif., Davis, 1971-78, assoc. prof., 1978-83, prof., 1983—, chair dept., 1989-93. Editor: (with M.D. Beecher & N.S. Thompson) Perspectives in Ethology, Vol. 12: Communication, 1997, (with R.G. Coss & K.R. Henry) Introduction to Psychobiol., 1998, 99 (2nd edit.); author: (with E.P. Morton) Animal Vocal Communication: A New Approach, 1998; contbr. articles to profl. jours., book chpts. NSF rsch. grantee, 1978-80, 82-84. Fellow Animal Behavior Soc.; mem. Internat. Soc. for Ecol. Psychology, Internat. Soc. for Behavioral Ecology, Internat. Soc. for Comparative Psychology. Democrat. Avocations: hiking, wildlife, travel, reading. Home: 815 Oeste Dr Davis CA 95616-1856 Office: U Calif Dept Psychology 1 Shields Ave Davis CA 95616-8686 E-mail: dhowings@ucdavis.edu.

OWINGS, MALCOLM WILLIAM, retired management consultant; b. Cin., Feb. 5, 1925; s. William Malcolm and Margaret (Benvie) O.; m. Margie M. Gehiker, Sept. 4, 1948 (dec. June 2000); children: Lynn A., Sandra S., Wendy K., Cheryl M; m. Doris Marie Gorman, Aug. 23, 2002. BS in Bus. Adminstrn., Miami U., Oxford, Ohio, 1950, LL.D., 1976; A.M.P., Harvard U., 1975. With Continental Can Co., 1950-83, corp. v.p., from 1971; v.p., gen. mgr. pub. affairs Continental Packaging Co (Continental Group, Inc.), 1982-83; owner, pres. Owings Assocs., Inc., Pinehurst, N.C., 1983-92. Dir. First Bank, Pinehurst, N.C.; adviser to Am. del. Internat. Tin Council, 1978-82 Columnist The Pilot, Southern Pines, N.C., 1997—. Dean's assoc. exec. in residence Sch. Bus., Miami U., 1973, mem. alumni coun., 1958-65, meem. pres.'s devel. coun., 1965-69, meem. resource devel. bd., 1982; trustee Village of Thiensville, Wis., 1956-59; mem. N.C. Clean, 1985-94, chmn., 1986-93; bd. dirs. Barrington Area Devel. Coun., 1974-79, Sales Mgmt. Execs. Grad. Sch., Am. Soc. Environment, 1976, Keep Am. Beautiful, 1980-81, also chmn., 1990; chmn. Keep N.C. Beautiful Coun., Raleigh, 1988-92, Moore Meml. Hosp. Found., Pinehurse, N.C., 1986-89; mem. Moore Regional Hosp. Scroll Soc., 1991—, chmn., 1992-93; chmn. Moore County (N.C.) Rep. Party, 1986-88; co-founder Rep. Presdl. Task Force; mem. U.S. Senate Bus. Adv. Bd., 1981-91; commr. Moore County, 1988-96, Youth Svcs., 1993-95; apptd. to N.C. Watershed Protection Adv. Com. by N.C. Environ. Mgmt. Commn., 1990-92; bd. dirs. Pub. Edn. Found., 1994-99, Ptnrs. for Children and Family, 1994-97, Drug-Free Moore County Inc., 1995-98, Dispute Settlement Ctr. of Moore County, 1995-97, Keep Moore County Beautiful, 1997—; mem. Moore County Bd. of Health, 1994-97; pres. Belle Meade Residents Assn., 2000. Recipient Cert. of Meritorious Svc. Miami U., 1967, Meritorious Svc. award Keep Moore County Beautiful, Inc., 1993-94; named Alumnus of Yr. Miami U., 1970; 1st Am. recipient Order of Apteryx Earth Awareness Found., 1971, Order of Long Leaf Pine. Mem. Ill. C. of C. (bd. dirs. 1976-78), Miami U. Alumni Assn. (nat. pres. 1964-65), Omicron Delta Kappa, Sigma Chi, Delta Sigma Pi Clubs: Pinehurst Country, Country of N.C. (Pinehurst). Home and Office: Belle Mead Retirement Resort 107 Caritas Ct Southern Pines NC 28387-2242 E-mail: mwowings@ac.net. *The Golden Rule - "treating others as thyself" is not only a cornerstone for success, it is the foundation of personal happiness. However, it is well to remember that none of this is possible without political freedom and the contingent responsibilities that freedom requires.*

OWINGS, SUZANN M. consultant, educator; b. L.A., Jan. 26, 1947; d. Theodore Raymond and Elizabeth Marie O'Malley. BA, Calif. State Coll., L.A., 1969; MAT, Ind. U., 1971; PhD, U. N.Mex., 1978. Adminstr. Ind. U., Bloomington, 1970-71; tchr. Compton (Calif.) Sr. High Sch., 1971-75; cons. Owings, Albuquerque, 1975-78; assoc. dir. Energy Consumers of N.Mex., 1978-79; statewide comprehensive planner CES, N.Mex. State U., 1979; strategic planner Bechtel Inc., San Francisco, 1979-83; dean Golden Gate U., 1983-84; cons. Bitn Assocs., Corrales, N.Mex. and L.A., 1984—; coord. Albuquerque Pub. Schs., 1992—. Instr. mgmt. Troy State U., U. Phoenix, Chapman U.. Co-author, co-editor: Southwest Images and Trends: Factors in Community Development, 1979, numerous others. Co-organizer Rio Rancho 2000, 1992-93; mem., chmn. Sandoval County Intergovtl./Bus. Adv. Coun., Bernalillo, N.Mex., 1993—; mem. Sandoval County Econ. Devel. Com., 1991—. Mem. ASTD (pres.- elect, v.p., bd. dirs.), Am. Soc. for Pub. Adminstrn. (pres.-elect, chairperson Pub. Policy Inst.), Optimist (bd. dirs., pres. N.W. Albuquerque club). Avocations: walking, cycling, gardening. Home: PO Box 872 Placitas NM 87043-0872

OWINGS, VICKIE ANN, librarian; b. Caldwell, Idaho, Apr. 29, 1953; d. A. Henry and Mary Elizabeth (Bellaire) Kinsey; m. Keith A. Owings; children: Nicholas, Christopher, Holly. BS in Elem. Edn., U. Idaho, 1974. Elem. tchr. Hagerman (Idaho) Sch. Dist., 1975-77; 3d grade tchr. Kimberly (Idaho) Sch. Dist., 1978-81, elem. sch. libr., 1981—, tech. mentor, 1995—. Ch. libr. Presbyn. Ch., 1995-97. Mem. Delta Kappa Gamma. Home: 3081 E 3500 N Twin Falls ID 83301-0310 Office: Kimberly Elem Sch 311 Main St S Kimberly ID 83341-2081

OWNBEY, LENORE F. DALY, motivational speaker; b. Fremont, Nebr., Feb. 24; d. Joseph E. and Anna R. (Godel) Daly; m. Amos B. Ownbey, June 18, 1948; children: Kenton, Stephen. BBA, U. Nebr. Cert. comml. investment mem. Former real estate and comml. investment specialist, 1976—; motivational spkr. Recipient Ptnrs. in Excellence Achievement award Colo. chpt. Nat. Speakers Assn., 1988, Cert. of Proclamation Internat. Women of Yr., 1992-93, 96. Mem. Nat. Assn. Realtors, Denver Bd. Realtors (life mem.), Comml. Investment Real Estate Inst. (life mem., cert. comml. investment mem.). E-mail: lfdownbey@worldnet.att.net.

OWNBY, DENNIS RANDALL, pediatrician, educator, allergist, researcher; b. Athens, Ohio, July 14, 1948; s. Dillard Ralph and Miriam (Lee) Ownby; m. Helen Louise Engelbrecht, May 24, 1970; children: David Randall, Kathryn Louise. BS, Ohio U., 1969; MD, Med. Coll. Ohio, 1972. Diplomate Am. Bd. Allergy and Immunology (bd. dirs. 1993-98, chair 1998, residency rev. com. 1995-2000), Am. Bd. Pediat., Nat. Bd. Med. Examiners. Intern and resident Duke U. Sch. Medicine, Durham, NC, 1972—74, asst. prof., 1977—80; staff physician Henry Ford Hosp., Detroit, 1980—97, dir. Allergy Rsch. Lab., 1986—97; prof. pediat. Case Western Res. U., Cleve., 1997; prof. pediat. and medicine Med. Coll. Ga., Augusta, 1998—. Clin. asst. prof. pediat. U. Mich., Ann Arbor, 1980—86, clin. assoc. prof. pediat., 1986—95. Contbr. articles to med. jours., chpts. to books. Fellow: Am. Acad. Allergy, Am. Acad. Pediat. Office: Med Coll Ga Sect Allergy & Immunology BG-1019 Augusta GA 30912-3790 E-mail: downby@mail.mcg.edu.

OWNBY, JERRY STEVE, landscape architect, educator; b. Shawnee, Okla., Jan. 25, 1939; s. Hugh H. and N. Lorraine (Hopkins) O.; children by previous marriage: Gregory Steve, Mitchell Hugh; m. Arnola Colson, Dec. 19, 1971; 1 child, Steven Cory BS, Okla. State U., 1961; MS in Landscape Architecture, Kans. State U., 1964, M in Landscape Architecture, 1970. Coun. Landscape Archtl. Registration Bds. cert. and registered landscape architect, Ariz., Kans., Okla., Mo., Tex. Extension landscape architect Kans. State U., Manhattan, 1963-64, instr., 1969-70; landscape architect Beardsley & Talley, Seattle, 1964-65; extension specialist Okla. State U., Stillwater, 1965-69, from asst. prof. to prof. landscape architecture and coordinator landscape architecture, 1970-85; pvt. practice, 1985—. Chmn. Okla. Landscape Architect Registration Bd., 1980-85; mem. 1985 Expert Panel for Uniform Nat. Exam., 1984-85; gov.'s appointee Mo. Coun. Landscape Architects, 1991-97 Designs include Las Laderas residence, 1978 (Merit award 1981), Student Union courtyard Okla. State U., 1981 (Honor award 1983). Chmn. Oklahomans for Landscape Architecture, 1979-80; chmn., vice chmn. Stillwater Park and Recreation Adv. Bd., Okla., 1971-79. Recipient Outstanding Prof. award Okla. State U. chpt. Alpha Zeta, 1975, svc. award Stillwater City Commn., 1980, design awards Springfield Planning and Zoning Commn.., 1988, 89, 90, 99, design award Springfield Environ. Adv. Bd., 1990, Gov.'s landscape design award for Andy Williams' Moon River Theatre, Branson, Mo., 1992, for Charley Pride Theater, Branson, 1995, design award Watershed Com., 1993; alumni fellow Kans. State U., 1995. Fellow Am. Soc. Landscape Architects (v.p. 1983-85, Okla. chpt. Svc. award 1980); mem. Nat. Coun. State Garden Clubs (accredited instr. 1964—), Nat. Coun. of Educators in Landscape Architecture, Mo. Assn. of Landscape Architects, Coun. Landscape Archtl. Registration Bds. (cert.), Phi Kappa Phi, Sigma Lambda Alpha. Republican. Baptist. Avocations: travel; photography; fishing. Home: 234 Sunset Cove # 109 Branson MO 65616-3604 Office: Ownby Assocs 654 S Hickory Ave Springfield MO 65809-1335 E-mail: jsownby@aol.com.

OWSLEY, JOHN QUINCY, III, plastic surgeon; b. Manila, Philipines, Oct. 2, 1928; came to U.S., 1930; s. John Quincy Owsley Jr. and Sara Christine Maxwell; m. Mary Leslie Marriott, Apr. 27, 1957 (div. 1969); children: John Quincy IV, Sara Elizabeth; m. Sharon Theresa Anton, Jan. 2, 1971. BA, Vanderbilt U., 1950, MD, 1953. Intern U. Calif. Med. Ctr., San Francisco, asst. resident in surgery, asst. resident, chief resident plastic surgery, 1956-60, clin. instr. to asst. prof. to assoc. prof., clin. prof. surgery, 1960-80; pvt. practice, 1960—. Dir. Aesthetic Surgery Fellowship, 1989—; vis. prof. Columbia U. Coll. of Physicians and Surgeons, 1989, Divsn. of Plastic Surgery U. Pa., 1993; Donald P. Hause Meml. lectr. U. Calif., Davis Med. Ctr., 1993; guest reviewer Jour. of Plastic and Reconstructive Surgery. Author: Aesthetic Facial Surgery, 1994; contbr. chpts. to books and articles to profl. publs. Fellow ACS; mem. Am. Soc. of Plastic Surgeons (chmn. ethics com. 1973-76), Am. Soc. for Aesthetic Plastic Surgery (sec. 1975-77), Am. Assn. of Plastic Surgeons, Am. Cleft Palate Assn. (pres. 1977-78), Bohemian Club. Avocations: sailing, bird hunting, traveling. Office: 45 Castro St Ste 111 San Francisco CA 94114 E-mail: Owsley@DrjohnOwsley.com.

OWUSU, AKUA, psychiatrist; b. Mar. 2, 1960; MB ChB, U. Ghana, 1986. Diplomate in psychiatry Am. Bd. Psychiatry and Neurology. Outpatient psychiatrist Associated Rehab. Clinic, Jacksonville, Fla., 1996—. Office: Associated Rehab Clinic 2032-4 Southside Blvd Jacksonville FL 32216

OXELL, LOIE GWENDOLYN, fashion and beauty educator, consultant, columnist; b. Sioux City, Iowa, Nov. 17, 1917; d. Lyman Stanley and Loie Erma (Crill) Barton; m. Eugene Edwin Eschenbrenner, Aug. 8, 1936 (dec. 1954); children: Patricia Gene, Eugene Edward (dec. Feb. 1994); m. Henry J. Oxell, Nov. 3, 1956 (dec. July 1994). AS in Fashion Merchandising, Broward C.C., Davie, Fla., 1978. Fashion rep. Crestmoor Suit & Coat Co., St. Louis, 1951-56; appeared on "To the Ladies" weekly TV show KSD-TV, 1950s; cons./instr. Miami-Herald Newspaper Glamor Clinic, Miami, Fla., 1957-71; pres./owner Loie's (Loy's) Inc., 1958-71; pres., owner West Coast East Talent Agy.; instr./lectr. Charron-Williams Coll., Miami, 1973-77; instr. Fashion Inst. Ft. Lauderdale, Fla., 1977-86; pres./owner Image Power Unltd., Plantation, 1992—. Lectr. in field; columnist Sr. Life and Boomer Times, Fla., 1993-97, Sr. Life, 1997-98, The Entertainer, 1997-98 Author: I'd Like You to Meet My Wife, 1964, Executive Wives, A.C. Sparkplug Co., So! We're in Our 60's, 70's, 80's Plus; regularly appeared in comedy skits, fashion segments, commentary, and TV comml̃s. Del Russo Beauty Show, 1960s; actress Red Skelton TV show, Miami, Fla., also fashion show prodns., TV commls. Vol. Insight for the Blind, The Work Force, lectr., instr. The AARP Sr. Cmty. Svc. Employment Program, Ft. Lauderdale and Hollywood, Fla., 1987—, keynote spkr. nat. conv., Charlestown, S.C., 1986; life mem. women's com. Miami Children's Hosp. Aux.; faculty advisor Nu Tau Sigma sorority Charron Williams Coll., 1973-77; pres. Venice of Am. chpt. Am. Bus. Women's Assn., 1975-76. Recipient Cert. of Appreciation Dade County Welfare Dept. Youth Hall, Miami, 1966, Community TV Found., Miami, 1966, 71, Woman of the Yr. award Am. Bus. Women's Assn. (Venice of Am. chpt.), 1976-77, Award for Svc. AARP Sr. Community Svc. Program, 1993. Mem. The Fashion Group Internat. Avocations: bridge, golf. Office: Image Power Unltd 1859 N Pine Island Rd MB339 Plantation FL 33322-5224

OXENDINE, BESS HOLLAND, language educator; b. Hazelton, Pa., July 12, 1933; d. Raleigh Leroy and Pearl Allie (Shook) Holland; m. Denford Harold Oxendine, Jan. 12, 1956; children: Denny, Laura. AA, Mars Hill Coll., 1953; BA, Berea Coll., 1956; MA in English, U. NC, Chapel Hill, 1970; Cert. of Advanced Study, U. NC, Charlotte, 1981. English tchr. St. Andrews and North Charleston H.S., Charleston, SC, 1956—60; English and social studies tchr. JW Cannon Jr. H.S., Kannapolis, NC, 1961—70; English and journalism tchr. Al Brown H.S., 1971—90; tchr. summer program for gifted students Gov.'s Sch. of NC, Laurinburg, 1979—80; instr. English dept. Rowan-Cabarrus C.C., Salisbury, 1989—. Author: (children's book) Miriam, 1995, Samuel, 2001, (novel) Grace Beyond Measure, 2000, (poetry) Running Over, 2001. NC del. NEA, Dallas, 1978—80; v.p., pres. NC Assn. Educators, Kannapolis, 1977—78. Democrat. Baptist. Avocations: writing, reading, photography, RV travel, public speaking. Home: 1193 Daybrook Dr Kannapolis NC 28081

OXENHANDLER, NEAL, language educator, writer; b. St. Louis, Feb. 3, 1926; s. Joseph and Billie (Lutsky) O.; m. Jean Romano (div. May 1976); children: Noelle, Daniel, Alicia; m. Judith I. Josel, Dec. 12, 1979; stepchildren: Rebecca, Marjorie Menza. AB, U. Chgo., 1948; MA, Columbia U., 1951; PhD, Yale U., 1955; MA (hon.), Dartmouth Coll., 1973. Lectr. French St. Louis U., 1951-52; asst. instr. Yale U., New Haven, 1952-54, instr., 1954-57; asst. prof. UCLA, 1957-60, assoc. prof., 1960-65, U. Calif., Santa Cruz, 1965-66, prof., 1966-69, Dartmouth Coll., Hanover, N.H., 1969—, Edward Tuck prof., 1987—, chmn. dept. French and Italian, 1987-91. Dir. NEH Summer Seminar in Comparative Lit., 1981. Author: Scandal and Parade: Theater of Jean Cocteau, 1957, Aspects of French Literature, 1961, French Literary Criticism: The Basis of Judgment, 1966, Max Jacob and Les Feux de Paris, 1964, (novel) A Change of Gods, 1962, Looking for Heroes in Post-War France, 1995; adv. editor Film Quar., Berkeley, 1958-91; mem. editl. com. U. Calif. Press, Berkeley, 1966-69; asst. editor French Rev., 1969-73; contbr. articles, revs., poetry and translations to profl. jours. With U.S. Army, 1941-43, ETO, PTO. Fulbright scholar, Italy, 1953; Cross-Disciplinary fellow Soc. for Values in Higher Edn., France, 1966, Guggenheim fellow, France, 1962, Inst. for Shipboard Edn., 1995. Mem. MLA (adv. editor proc. 1977-80), Internat. Assn. Philosophy and Lit., Internat. Comparative Lit. Assn. Democrat. Roman Catholic. Avocation: writing poetry. Home: # 502 97 Sunset Dr Sarasota FL 34236 Office: Dartmouth Coll Dept French Hanover NH 03755 E-mail: nealoxen@aol.com.

OXFORD, HUBERT, III, lawyer; b. Beaumont, Tex., Sept. 25, 1938; s. Hubert Burton and Virginia Mary (Cunningham) O.; m. Cynthia Lynn Culp, Apr. 25, 1987; children: Mary Francelia, Hubert IV, Mary Cunningham, Virginia Barrett, Alaina Danielle, Adriana Victoria, Gabriella Elizabeth. BSME, Tex. A&M U., 1960; JD, U. Tex., 1963. Bar: Tex., 1963, U.S. Ct. Appeals (5th cir.), 1967, (11th cir.), Tex., U.S. Dist. Ct. (ea., so., no., we. dists.) Tex., U.S. Supreme Ct., 1975, U.S. Dist. Ct. (we. dist.) Okla., Mont., 1996, Wyo., 1996, Okla., 1996, DC 1998, Colo. 1998. Briefing atty. to U.S. dist. judge Eastern Dist. Tex., Beaumont, 1966; asst. dist. atty. Jefferson County, Tex., 1967; mng. ptnr. firm Beckenstein & Oxford, L.L.P., Beaumont, 1966; gen. counsel Jefferson County Nav. Dist., Lower Neches Valley Authority. Mem. Gov. Reorganization Commn. Tex. 70th Legislature, 1987-88, Tex. Oil Spill Commn.; U.S. Commr. Ea. Dist. Tex., 1968-70; mem. Tex. Bd. Registration for Profl. Engrs., 1994-2000. Assoc. editor Tex. Law Rev., 1962-63. Bd. dirs. Ducks Unltd., 1978-86, Gulf Coast Conservation Assn., 1978-86; sec. bd. regents Lamar U., 1978-84, gen. counsel, 1986; mem. Tex. Air Control Bd., 1984-90; chmn. Tex. Clean Air Study Com., 1989. Capt. JAGC, USAF, 1963-66. Fellow Tex. Bar Assn., Internat. Soc. Barristers, Am. Bar. Assn.; mem. ABA, ATLA, Southeastern Admiralty Law Inst., Internat. Assn. Def. Counsel, Tex. Assn. Def. Lawyers, Nat. Bd. Trial Advocacy, State Bar Tex. (chmn. CLE com. 1979-81, course dir. admiralty and maritime seminar 1991, 96, grievance com. Dist. 3A, dir. Dist. 3 1997-2000), Maritime Law Assn., Jefferson County Bar Assn. (pres. 1987-88, Outstanding Young Lawyer 1972), Def. Rsch. Inst., Beaumont C. of C. (dir. 1978-84), Phi Delta Theta, Tau Beta Pi, Phi Kappa Phi, Phi Delta Phi. Democrat. Roman Catholic. Home: 490 Yount Beaumont TX 77706-5328 Office: Benckenstein & Oxford LLP 3535 Calder Ave Ste 300 Beaumont TX 77706-5087 E-mail: hubertoxford@benoxford.com.

OXLEY, ANN, television executive; b. Canton, Ohio, Aug. 3, 1924; d. Edward and Dorothy (Duffy) Adang; m. Jack Raymond Oxley, Aug. 10, 1946 (dec.); children: Kathleen Oxley Wiggins, Maureen Oxley Gaff, Joseph, Jeffrey, Christeen Oxley Rhodes, Daniel (dec.), Sister Julie Marie Oxley, Jamie, Kevin, Valerie Oxley Fouch, Amy. BA with distinction, Ind. U., 1974, MPA, 1982. Advt. account salesperson Ft. Wayne (Ind.) Jour. Gazette, 1945-47; office mgr. Ind. Equestrian Assn., Ft. Wayne, 1971-73; rsch. dir. Taxpayers Rsch. Assn., 1974-76; exec. dir. Ft. Wayne Pub. TV Inc., 1976-86. Active Bicentennial Com., 1976; adviser Media Arts Panel Ind. Arts Commn.; pres. Allen County Coun. on Aging. Found., 1995-98. Mem. AAUW, Svc. Corps Ret. Execs. (publicity chair 1986, nat. mktg. dir. 1989-90), Mensa Internat. (nat. coord. Project Inkslinger Mensa Ednl. Rsch. Found. 1998-2000), C. of C. (cultural com.), Phi Alpha Alpha. Roman Catholic. Home: 4305 Arlington Ave Fort Wayne IN 46807-2635 Office: SCORE 1300 S Harrison Federal Bldg Fort Wayne IN 46807

OXLEY, JAMES GRIEVE, mathematics educator; b. Sale, Victoria, Australia, Feb. 4, 1953; s. William A. and Dilys C. (Grieve) O.; m. Judith Danute Surkevicius; children: Margaret Catherine, David Grieve (dec.). BSc, U. Tasmania, 1974; MSc, Australian Nat. U., 1975; PhD, U. Oxford, 1978. Lectr., rsch. fellow Australian Nat. U., 1978-82; asst. prof. La. State U., Baton Rouge, 1982-85, assoc. prof., 1985-90, prof., 1990-99, alumni prof., 1999—. Vis. instr. U. N.C., Chapel Hill, 1978. Author: Matroid Theory, 1992.; mem. editorial bd. Combinatorics, Probability and Computing; reviewer Mathematical Reviews, Zentralblatt für Mathematik; contbr. chpts. to books, articles to profl. jours. Grantee NSF, 1985-87, 89-91, La. Edn. Quality Support Fund, 1987-94, Nat. Security Agy., 1994—, others; Fulbright postdoctoral fellow U. N.C., 1980; named Disting. Rsch. Master of Engring, Sci. and Tech., La. State U., 1999. Mem. Am. Math. Soc., London Math. Soc. Office: La State U Math Dept Baton Rouge LA 70803-4918

OXLEY, MARGARET CAROLYN STEWART, elementary education educator; b. Petaluma, Calif., Apr. 1, 1930; d. James Calhoun Stewart and Clara Thornton (Whiting) Bomboy; m. Joseph Hubbard Oxley, Aug. 25, 1951; children: Linda Margaret, Carolyn Blair Oxley Greiner, Joan Claire Oxley Willis, Joseph Stewart, James Harmon, Laura Marie Oxley Brechbill. Student, U. Calif., Berkeley, 1949-51; BS summa cum laude, Ohio State U., 1973, MA, 1984, postgrad., 1985, 88, 92. Cert. tchr., Ohio. 2d grade tchr. St. Paul Sch., Westerville, Ohio, 1973—. Presenter in field. Mem. editl. bd. Reading Tchr., vol. 47-48, 1993-94, Jour. Children's Lit., 1996—; co-author: Reading and Writing, Where it All Begins, 1991, Teaching with Children's Books: Path to Literature-Based Instruction, 1995, Adventuring With Books, 2000. Active Akita Child Conservation League, Columbus, Ohio, 1968-70. Named Columbus Diocesan Tchr. of Yr., 1988; Phoebe A. Hearst scholar, 1951, Rose Sterheim Meml. scholar, 1951; recipient Mary Karrer award Ohio State U., 1994. Mem. Nat. Coun. Tchrs. English (Notable Children's Books in the Lang. Arts com. 1993-94, chair 1995-96, treas. Children's Literature Assembly bd. dirs. 1996-99, co-chair fall breakfast children's lit. assembly, 2000—, excellence in poetry for children com. 2001-), Internat. Reading Ass (Exemplary Svc. in Promotion of Literacy award 1991), Literacy Connection (pres.), Children's Lit. Assembly, Ohio Coun. Tchrs. English Lang. Arts (Outstanding Educator 1990), Phi Kappa Phi, Pi Lambda Theta (hon.). Democrat. Roman Catholic. Avocations: reading, writing, travel, gardening, working with children. Home: 298 Brevoort Rd Columbus OH 43214-3826

OXLEY, MICHAEL GARVER, congressman; b. Findlay, Ohio, Feb. 11, 1944; s. George Garver and Marilyn Maxine (Wolfe) O.; m. Patricia Ann Pluguez, Nov. 27, 1971; 1 child, Michael Chadd. BA, Miami U., Oxford, Ohio, 1966; JD, Ohio State U., 1969. Bar: Ohio 1969, U.S. Supreme Ct. 1985. Agt. FBI, 1969-71; mem. Ohio Ho. of Reps., 1973-81, U.S. Congress from 4th Ohio dist., Washington, 1981—; chmn. fin. svcs. com. Mem. ABA, Ohio Bar Assn., Findlay Bar Assn., Soc. Former Spl. Agts. FBI, Ohio Farm Bur., Sigma Chi. Lodges: Rotary, Elks. Office: US Ho Reps 2233 Rayburn Ho Office Bldg Washington DC 20515-3504*

OXMAN, DAVID CRAIG, lawyer; b. Summit, N.J., Mar. 10, 1941; s. Jacob H. and Kathryn (Grear) O.; m. Phyllis Statter; children— Elena, Lee AB, Princeton U., 1962; LL.B., Yale U., 1969. Bar: N.Y. 1970, N.J. 1974, U.S. Dist. Ct. (so. and ea. dists.) N.Y. 1974, U.S. Ct. Appeals (2d cir.) 1974, U.S. Tax Ct. 1977, U.S. Supreme Ct. 1974. Assoc. Davis Polk & Wardwell, N.Y.C., 1970-76, ptnr., 1977-95, sr. counsel, 1995—. Served with USN, 1962-66 Fellow Am. Coll. Trust and Estate Counsel; mem. ABA, N.Y. State Bar Assn., Assn. of Bar of City of N.Y. Office: Davis Polk & Wardwell 450 Lexington Ave Fl 31 New York NY 10017-3982

OXMAN, MARK, sculptor, educator; b. N.Y.C., 1940; Student, Adelphi U., 1958-61, Pa. Acad. Fine Arts, 1961-65, City and Guilds of London Art Sch., 1965-67. Lectr., artist-in-residence Haverford Coll., 1967-70; asst. prof. Amherst Coll., 1970-76; assoc. prof. Am. U., Washington, 1975-94; prof., 1994—. One-man shows include Harmony Hall Gallery, Ft. Washington, Md., 2001, Hobart and William Smith Colls., Geneva, N.Y., 2000, Washington and Jefferson Coll., Pa., 2000, Maryland Arts Place, 2000, Elizabethtown Coll., 1993, West Chester (Pa.) U., 1994, Washington Coll., Md., 1994, Arts Alive Montgomery County, 1993, Salisbury State U., 1993, Mary Baldwin Coll., 1992, Western Md. Coll., 1992, Watkins Gallery, 1990, 2001, Bond Gallery, Sch. Architecture, U. Notre Dame, 2002, others; exhibited in group shows at Emerson Gallery, McLean, Va., 2000, Watkins Gallery, 1992, Art Spring, Loudon, Va., 1992, Johnson' Garden Ctr., 1990, Washington Flower Show, 1990, 16 Sculptors, 1995 Washington Fig. Sculptors Md. Coll. of Art and Design, 1995, Sculpture On and Off the Wall A Salon ltd., 1995, Artist to Artist The Art Barn, 1995 and others. Mem. Washington Figurative Sculptors (founder and dir. 1991—), N.Y. Acad. Art (grad. accredidation com. 1988), Alexandria Commn. on Arts (subcom. on acquisition policy 1985), Phila. Coll. Art (external rev. com. sculpture program 1985). Home: 620 Gist Ave Silver Spring MD 20910-5232 Office: American Univ Art Dept Washington DC 20016

OXNARD, CHARLES ERNEST, anatomist, anthropologist, human biologist, educator; b. Durham, Eng., Sept. 9, 1933; arrived in Australia, 1987; s. Charles and Frances Ann (Golightly) O.; m. Eleanor Mary Arthur, Feb. 2, 1959; children: Hugh, David. BSc. with 1st class honors, U. Birmingham, Eng., 1955, MB, BChir in Medicine, 1958, PhD, 1962, D.Sc., 1975. Med. intern Queen Elizabeth Hosp., Birmingham, 1958-59; rsch. fellow U. Birmingham, 1959-62, lectr., 1962-65, sr. lectr., 1965-66, court govs., 1958-66; assoc. prof. anatomy, anthropology and evolutionary biology U. Chgo., 1966-70, prof., 1970-78, gov. biology collegiate div., 1970-78, dean coll., 1973-77; dean grad. sch. U. So. Calif., Los Angeles, 1978-83, univ. rsch. prof. biology and anatomy, 1978-83, univ. prof., prof. anatomy and cell biology, prof. biol. scis., 1983-87; prof. anatomy and human biology U. Western Australia, 1987-98, dir. ctr. for human biology, 1989-99, head div. agr. and sci., 1990-92, prof. emeritus, 1998—, sr. rsch. fellow, 1998—; Leverhulme prof. U. Liverpool (U.K.), Univ. Coll., London, 2000—. Rsch. assoc. Field Mus. Natural History, Chgo., 1967; overseas assoc. U. Birmingham, 1968—; Lo Yuk Tong lectr. U. Hong Kong, 1973, 94, 97, hon. prof., 1978, Chan Shu Tzu lectr., 1980, Octagon lectr. U. Western Australia, 1987, Latta lectr. U. Nebr., Omaha, 1987; Stanley Wilkinson orator, 1991, Lo Yuk Tong Found. lectr., U.

Hong Kong, 1994; rsch. assoc. L.A. County Natural History Mus., 1984—, George C. Page Mus., L.A., 1986; vis. scholar U. Hong Kong, 1995, Shaw Coll. Chinese U. of Hong Kong, 1995, U. of Hong Kong, 1996; bd. dirs. U. Western Australia Press, 1993-95; adv. on human biology World Sci. Pub. Co., 1993—; vis. prof. Northwestern U., Xian, China, 1999. Author: Form and Pattern in Human Evolution, 1973, Uniqueness and Diversity in Human Evolution, 1973, Human Fossils: The New Revolution, 1977, The Order of Man, 1983, Humans, Apes, and Chinese Fossils, 1985, Fossils, Teeth and Sex, 1987, Anatomies and Lifestyles, 1990; series editor Recent Advances in Human Biology Series World Sci. Pub., Vol. I, The Origin and Past of Modern Humans, 1995, Vol. 2, Bone Structure and Remodeling, 1995, Vol. 3 The Origins and Past of Modern Humans: Towards Reconciliation, 1998, Vol. 4 The Natural History of the Doucs and Snub-nosed Langurs, 1998, Vol. 7 Morphometrics for the Life Sciences, 2000, Perspectives in Human Biology, Vol. 1 Genes, Ethnicity and Aging, 1995, Vol. 2 Humans in the Australasian Region, 1996, Vol. 3 Human Adaptability: Future Trends and Lessons from Past, 1998, Vol. 4, Is Human Evolution a Closed Chaptr, 1999, Vol. 4, Child Growth, Secular Trends and Continuing Human Evolution, Vol. 4, Dento-Facial Variation in Perspective, 1999, Vol. 5 Towards Consilience, 2000; mem. editl. bd. Annals of Human Biology; cons. editor: Am. Jour. Primatology, Jour. Human Biology, Jour. Human Evolution: Australia com. mem. Ency. Britannica, 1991-99; bibliographic referee Britannica On-Line, 1994, 99; contbr articles to anat. and anthrop. jours. Mem. Pasteur Found., 1988; bd. dirs. West Australian Inst. for Child Health, 1991-98; mem. electoral bd. Freemantle Hosp., 1991-94. Recipient Book award Hong Kong Coun., 1984, S.T. Chan Silver medal U. Hong Kong, 1980; grantee USPHS, 1960-71, NIH, 1974-87, NSF, 1971-87, Raine Found., 1988-91, Viertel Found., 1993-94, Australian Acad. Sci., 1995, Charles Darwin Lifetime Achievement award Am. Assn. Phys. Anthropology, 2001. Fellow N.Y. Acad. Sci., AAAS, So. Calif. Acad. Sci. (bd. dirs. 1985); mem. Chgo. Acad. Soc. (hon. life), Australasian Soc. for Human Biology (pres. 1987-90), Australia and New Zealand Anat. Soc. (pres. 1989-90), Anat. Soc. Gt. Britain and Ireland (councillor 1992-94), Nat. Health and Med. Rsch. Coun. (grantee 1994-97, 2001—), Australian Rsch. Coun. (grantee 1988-2004), Soc. for Study Human Biology (treas. 1962-66), Sigma Xi (pres., nat. lectr. 1990), Phi Beta Kappa (pres. chpt.), Phi Kappa Phi (pres., Book award 1984). Office: U Western Australia Nedlands WA 6009 Australia Fax: 618-08-9380-1051. E-mail: coxnard@cyllene.uwa.edu.au.

OXNER, GLENN RUCKMAN, financial executive; b. Greenville, S.C., July 10, 1938; s. G. Dewey and Frances O.; m. Kathleen Gallagher, 1992. Student, Duke U., 1956-57; BS, U.S.C., 1961. Trainee stock bd. broker Alester G. Furman Co., Greenville, S.C., 1961, v.p., 1964-67, exec. v.p., 1967-75; pres. S.C. Securities Co., 1975-77; sr. v.p. Interstate Securities, Charlotte, N.C., 1977-82, exec. v.p., 1982-85; chmn. First Tryon Securities, 1986-89; mng. dir. Nations Bank Investment Banking Co., 1989-92; chmn. Edgar M. Norris & Co., 1992-2001; exec. v.p. Scott & Stringfellow, Greenville, SC, 2001—. Served with U.S. Army, 1957. Mem. Nat. Assn. Security Dealers (com. chmn. dist. 7 1974, gov. 1981-84), Security Industry Assn. (gov. 1974), Security Dealers Carolinas (pres. 1977). Home: 18 Woodland Way Cir Greenville SC 29601-3824 Office: Scott & Stringfellow PO Box 247 Greenville SC 29602-0247

OXTOBY, DAVID WILLIAM, chemistry educator; b. Bryn Mawr, Pa., Oct. 17, 1951; s. John Corning and Jean (Shaffer) O., m. Claire Bennett, Dec. 17, 1977; children: Mary-Christina, John, Laura. BA, Harvard, 1972; PhD, U. Calif., Berkeley, 1975. Asst. prof. U. Chgo., 1977-82, assoc. prof., 1982-86, prof., 1986—, Mellon prof., 1987-92, dir. James Franck Inst., 1992-95, dean physical scis. divsn., 1995—, William Rainey Harper prof., 1996—. Co-author: Principles of Modern Chemistry, 1986, Chemistry: Science of Change, 1990. Trustee Bryn Mawr Coll., 1989—, Tchrs. Acad. Math. and Sci., 1999—; mem. bd. govs. Argonne Nat. Lab., 1996—, Astrophys. Rsch. Consortium, 1998—. Recipient Quantrell award U. Chgo., 1986; Alfred P. Sloan Found. fellow, 1979, John Simon Guggenheim Found. fellow, 1987; Camille and Henry Dreyfus Found. tchr.-scholar, 1980. Fellow Am. Phys. Soc.; mem. Am. Chem. Soc., Royal Soc. Chemistry (Marlow medal 1983), Phi Beta Kappa. Office: James Franck Inst U Chgo 5640 S Ellis Ave Chicago IL 60637-1433

OXYER, MINA JANE STEVENS, nurse; b. Esmond, N.D., July 18, 1932; d. Carl Marshall and Olive Rose (Walter) Stevens; m. Edward Wayne Oxyer, Aug. 7, 1955 (div. June 1979); children: James, Lenders, David. RN, Bismarck Hosp. Sch. Nursing, 1953; student, N.W. Nazarene Coll., 1953-54. Cert. in advanced obstetrics and fetal monitoring. Staff nurse Samaritan Hosp., Nampa, Idaho, 1953-54; night charge nurse NB nursery Meml. Hosp. Laramie County, Cheyenne, Wyo, 1954-55; staff nurse Loring AFB Hosp., Limestone, Maine, 1955, Ramey AFB Hosp., Aquadilla, P.R., 1957-59, Mt. View Gen. Hosp., Tacoma, 1960, Beale AFB (Calif.) Hosp., 1968-69; night charge nurse OB Dept. United Gen. Hosp., Sedro-Woolley, Wash., 1971-83; night charge nurse MiraVista Care Ctr., Mt. Vernon, 1983—.

OYESIKU, NELSON MOBOLANLE, neurosurgeon, neuroscientist; s. Nelson M. and Margaret M. Oyesiku; m. Lola M. Afolabi, Nov. 20, 1982; children: Angela, Linda, Nelson III. MD, U. Ibadan, Nigeria, 1979; MSc, U. London, 1982; PhD, Emory U., 1995. Cert. neurol. surgery. Asst. prof. neurol. surgery Emory U., Atlanta, 1993—2000, assoc. prof. neurol. surgery, 2000—. Author: (book) Patient Care in Neurosurgery, 1990; contbr. chapters to books, articles to profl. jours. Bd. dirs. Brain Injury Assn. Ga., Atlanta, 1997—99, Med. Assn. Atlanta, 1997; trustee Emory U. Alumni Exec. Bd., 1997—2000; bd. dirs. Druid Hills Civic Assn., 1994—96. Recipient Augustus McCravey award, So. Neurosurg. Soc., 1992, Young Investigator award, Brain Trauma Found./AANS/CNS, 1994, Minority Med. Faculty Devel. award, Robert Wood Johnson Found., 1994, Clinician Investigator Devel. award, NIH, 1994; fellow Young Investigator Travel fellow, Internat. Stroke Congress, 1989; scholar Commonwealth scholar, Brit. Govt., 1981. Fellow: ACS; mem.: AMA, Ga. State Med. Assn., Pituitary Soc., Nat. Med. Assn., So. Neurosurg. Soc., Med. Assn. Atlanta (bd. dirs. 1997), Ga. Neurosurg. Soc. (sec.-treas. 2001—), Am. Assn. Neurol. Surgeons, Congress Neurol. Surgeons (exec. com. 1998), Atlanta Soc. Episcopalian. Avocation: golf. Home: 1917 Durand Mill Dr NE Atlanta GA 30307 Office: Emory University 1365B Clifton Rd NE Atlanta GA 30322 Home Fax: 404-778-4472; Office Fax: 404-778-4472.

OYLER, GREGORY KENNETH, lawyer; b. Moses Lake, Wash., Sept. 16, 1953; s. Eugene Milton and Annetta Diane (Williams) O.; m. Evelyn Hartwell Wright, Oct. 18, 1986; 1 child, Elizabeth Atwood. AB, Princeton U., 1975; JD, Georgetown U., 1978; LLM, NYU, 1981. Bar: Pa. 1978, U.S. Tax Ct. 1978, U.S. Ct. Appeals (D.C. cir.) 1979, D.C. 1981, U.S. Supreme Ct. 1982, U.S. Ct. Fed. Claims 1983, U.S. Ct. Appeals (fed. cir.) 1987. Law clk. to judges U.S. Tax Ct., Washington, 1978-80; assoc. Hamel & Park, Washington, 1981-85; ptnr. Hopkins & Sutter, 1985-95, Scribner, Hall & Thompson, Washington, 1995—. Mem. adv. com. IRS Info. Reporting Program, 1993-94. Mem. ABA (tax sect., ins. and govt. submissions coms.), D.C. Bar Assn. (tax sect.), Fed. Bar Assn., Soc. Preservation Md. Antiquities (bd. dirs. 1991-97), Clark-Winchcole Found. (trustee 1999—). Office: Scribner, Hall & Thompson 1875 Eye St NW Ste 1050 Washington DC 20006-5441

OZ, EFFY, management and information science educator; b. Ramat-Gan, Israel, Mar. 22, 1950; s. Aharon and Haya (Silberberg) O.; m. Narda Green, Dec. 8, 1974; children: Sahar, Adi, Noam, Ron. BA in Econs. and Stats., Hebrew U., Jerusalem, Israel, 1974, MBA, 1978; DBA, Boston U., 1990. Dep. dir. fin. Israel Aircraft Industries, Lod, 1974-85; lectr. Boston U., 1986-89, Boston Coll., 1988-90; asst. prof. mgmt. info. sys., coord. MIS program Wayne State U., Detroit, 1980-96; assoc.prof. mgmt. sci. and info. sys. Pa. State U., Malvern, 1996—. Author: Management Information Systems, 1998, 2000, 2002, The Manager's Bible, 1998, Foundations of E-Commerce, 2002; mem. editl. bd. Ency. of Info. Sys., 1999—, Jour. Global Info. Tech. Mgmt., 1997—; contbr. articles to profl. jours. Mem. Chester County Internat. Trade Coun., West Chester, Pa., 1998—. Mem. Beta Gamma Sigma. Avocation: numismatics. Office: Pa State U 30 E Swedesford Rd Malvern PA 19355-1488 E-mail: effyoz@psu.edu.

OZ, MEHMET CENGIZ, physician, writer; b. Cleve., June 11, 1960; s. Mustafa and Suna (Atabay) O. BA, Harvard U., 1982; MD, U. Pa., 1986; MBA, Wharton Bus. Sch., Phila., 1986. Resident Columbia-Presbyn. Med. Ctr., N.Y.C., 1986—93, physician, assoc. prof., 1993—, dir. Cardiovascular Inst. Bd. dirs. Siga Corp. Author: Healing from the Heart, 1998 (Best Book award Books Better Am.). Mem.: Found. Advancement of Cardiac Therapies (bd. dirs.), Am. Thoracic Soc. (bd. dirs.), Global Leader Tomorrow, World Econ. Froums, Am. Soc. Artificial Internal Organs, Am. Coll. Cardiology, Am. Heart Assn., Turkish-Am. Physicians Assn., Assn. Acad. Surgery, Internat. Soc. for Heart and Lung Transplantation, Am. Bd. Surgery, Am. Bd. Thoracic Surgery, Am. Assn. Thoracic Surgeons. Office: Columbia Presbyterian Med Ctr 177 Fort Washington Ave New York NY 10032-3713 E-mail: mco2@columbia.edu.

OZAG, DAVID, finance educator; b. Connellsville, Pa., Apr. 16, 1962; s. Joseph and Barbara Lee (Brady) O. BS, U. Md., 1984, postgrad., 1985; MBA, Mt. St. Mary's Coll., Md., 1987; EdD, George Washington U., 2001. CPA. Acct. Aronson Greene Fisher and Co., Bethesda, Md., 1984-86, Keller, Zanger and Co., Frederick, 1986-87; controller Grove Hill Enterprises Inc., Md., 1985-88; v.p. Standard Fed. Savs. Bank, Gaithersburg, 1988-95; owner DJ Liquors, Frederick, 1991-95; project mgr. First Nationwide Mortgage Co., 1995-98; prof. Gettysburg Coll., 1998—; owner Hope Again, Inc., 1998—. Basketball coach Gov. Thomas Johnson HS, Frederic, Md., 1987—95; instr. Frederic C.C., 1986—88, Carroll C.C., 1990—93, U. Md., 1997—. Mem. AICPA, Md. Assn. CPA, U. Md. Alumni Assn. Roman Catholic. Home: 402 Birmingham Dr Frederick MD 21701-6361 Office: Gettysburg Coll Gettysburg PA 17325

OZAKI, NANCY JUNKO, performance artist, performing arts educator; b. Denver, Feb. 14, 1951; d. Joe Motoichi and Tamiye (Saki) O.; m. Gary Steven Tsujimoto, Nov. 12, 1989. BS in Edn., U. Colo., 1973; postgrad., U. Colo., Denver, 1977, Metro State Coll., 1982, Red Rocks C.C., 1982-83, U. No. Colo., 1982, U. N.Mex., 1985, U. No. Colo., 1988. Elem. tchr. Bur. Indian Affairs, Bloomfield, N.Mex., 1973-75, Aurora (Colo.) Pub. Schs., 1977-83, Albuquerque Pub. Schs., 1983-84, Denver Pub. Schs., 1984-87, Oak Grove Sch. Dist., San Jose, Calif., 1988-89, San Mateo (Calif.) City Elem. Dist., 1990-92; performing artist Japanese drums Young Audiences, San Francisco, 1992-93, Denver, 1994-97, Walt Disney World, Epcot Ctr., Orlando, Fla., 1993-97; co-dir., mgr., performer One World Taiko, Japanese Drum Troupe, Denver, 1997—2001, Seattle, 2001—, 2001—. Vol. worker with young Navajo children; co-sponsor girl's sewing and camping groups. Mem. Kappa Delta Pi (Theta chpt.). Avocations: reading, sewing, skiing, hiking, snorkeling. Office: PO Box 80158 Seattle WA 98108 E-mail: oneworldtaiko@earthlink.net.

OZANICH, CHARLES GEORGE, real estate broker; b. Aug. 11, 1933; s. Paul Anthony and Alma Bertha (Sablotna) O.; m. Betty Sue Carman, Feb. 20, 1955; children: Viki Lynn, Terri Sue, Charles Anthony, Nicole Lee. Student, Am. River Coll.; degree, Sierra Coll. Owner, broker Terrace Realty, Basic Realty, Grass Valley, Calif., 1971—. Compliance inspector Dept. Vets. Affairs. Mem. Grass Valley Vol. Fire Dept., 1965-93. Served with USAF, 1951-55, Korea. Decorated Bronze Star with three oak leaf clusters, Korean Presdl. citation, UN citation. Mem. Nevada County Bd. Realtors (dir. 1973-74). Lodges: Am. Legion, Masons, Shriners, Moose (charter mem.). Achievements include receiving the Nat. Champion award Truck Drivers Rodeo class 5 semi-trailer 18 wheeler divsn., 1954. Home and Office: 15053 Chinook Ln Grass Valley CA 95945-8846 E-mail: cozanich@hotmail.com.

OZAWA, MARTHA NAOKO, social work educator; b. Ashikaga, Tochigi, Japan, Sept. 30, 1933; came to U.S., 1963; d. Tokuichi and Fumi (Kawashima) O.; m. May 1959 (div. May 1966). BA in Econs., Aoyama Gakuin U., 1956; MS in Social Work, U. Wis., 1966, PhD in Social Welfare, 1969. Asst. prof. social work Portland (Oreg.) State U., 1969-70, assoc. prof. social work, 1970-72; assoc. rsch. prof. social work NYU, 1972-75; assoc. prof. social work Portland State U., 1975-76; prof. social work Washington U., St. Louis, 1976-85, Bettie Bofinger Brown prof. social policy, 1985—. Author: Income Maintenance and Work Incentives, 1982; editor: Women's Life Cycle: Japan-U.S. Comparison in Income Maintenance, 1989, Women's Life Cycle and Economic Insecurity: Problems and Proposals, 1989; editl. bd. Social Work, Silver Spring, Md., 1972-75, 85-88, New Eng. Jour. Human Svcs., Boston, 1987—, Ency. of Social Work, Silver Spring, 1974-77, 91-95, 99—, Jour. Social Svc. Rsch., 1977-97, Children and Youth Svcs. Rev., 1991—, Social Work Rsch., 1994-97, Jour. Poverty, 1997—. Grantee Adminstrn. on Aging, Washington, 1979, 84, NIMH, 1990-93. Mem. Nat. Assn. Social Workers (presdl. award 1999), Nat. Acad. Social Ins., Nat. Conf. on Social Welfare (bd. dirs. 1981-87), The Gerontol. Soc. Am., Coun. Social Work Edn., Soc. for Social Work and Rsch., Washington U. Faculty Club (bd. dirs. 1986-91). Avocations: photography, tennis, swimming, gardening. Home: 13018 Tiger Lily Ct Saint Louis MO 63146-4339 Office: PO Box 1196 Saint Louis MO 63188-1196 E-mail: awazo@gwbmail.wustl.edu.

OZAWA, TERUTOMO, economics educator, consultant; b. Yokohama, Japan, Jan. 17, 1935; came to U.S., 1959, naturalized, 1973; s. Hanjiro and Tsuru (Teramura) O.; m. Hiroko Aoyama, Nov. 4, 1967; children: Edwin, Clare. BA, Tokyo U. of Fgn. Studies, 1958; MBA, Columbia U., 1962, PhD, 1966. Prof. econs. Colo. State U., Ft. Collins, 1974—; vis. rsch. assoc. Ctr. for Policy Alternatives, MIT, Cambridge, Mass., 1975-76; vis. scholar Cambridge (Eng.) U., 1982-83; vis. prof. U. Paris, Sorbonne, 1993, 96, U. Tokyo, 1996; cons. to UN agys. and OECD. Author: Multinationalism, Japanese Style, 1979, Japan's General Trading Companies: Merchants of Economic Development, 1984, Recycling Japan's Surpluses for Developing Countries, 1989, Business Restructuring in Asia, 2001; also other books and articles. Mem. Am. Econ. Assn. Home: 648 Heather Ct Fort Collins CO 80525-2209 Office: Colo State U Dept Econs Fort Collins CO 80523-0001

OZBOLT, JUDY G. nursing educator; b. Dothan, Ala., Nov. 16, 1944; d. Bernard R. and Cleo Grace (Whiddon) O.; m. Samuel R. Kaplan, July 14, 1981; children: Jay Y. Kaplan, Rebecca J. Kaplan, Ira D. Kaplan. BSN, Duke U., 1967; MS, U. Mich., 1974, PhD, 1976. Visiting prof. Institut Internat. de Formation des Cadres de Santé, Lyon, France; assoc. prof. U. Pitts., U. Mich., Ann Arbor; prof./dir. doctoral program U. Va., Charlottesville; prof. nursing and biomed. informatics Vanderbilt U., Nashville. Chmn. priority expert panel nursing inf. systems, Nat. Ctr. Nursing Rsch. Author: (with Vandewal and Hannah) Decision Support Systems in Nursing, 1990; contbr. articles to profl. jours. Am. Acad. Nursing fellow, Am. Coll. Med. Info. fellow. Founding fellow Am. Inst. for Med. and Biol. Engring.; mem. Am. Med. Informatics Assn. (bd. dirs., sec., co-chmn. profl. specialty group).

OZDEMIR, PHILLIP, inventor, entrepreneur, consultant; b. N.Y.C., June 28, 1959; s. Talat and Elin (Hamilton) O. BS, Columbia U., 1981; MS, 1986. Cons. Caithness Corp., N.Y.C., 1983-87; founder, CEO The Skybone Group, Smyrna, N.Y., 1987—. Patentee in laser radar and detection of atmospheric trace gases. Chmn. (hon.) Clean Air Initiatives, Williamstown, Mass., 1999—. Mem. The Explorer's Club. Avocations: skiing, chess, hiking, sculpture, music. Home: 476 Hopkins Crandall Rd Smyrna NY 13464

OZDENER, MEHMET HAKAN, physician, biochemist; b. Corum, Sungurlu, Turkey, Mar. 27, 1963; MD, Med. Sch., Samsun, Turkey, 1987; PhD, ICGEB/Ondokuz Mayis U., Turkey, 1996. Intern Ondokuz Mayis U. Hosp., 1986—87; instr. Ondokuz Mayis U., 1996-98, asst. prof., 1998; postdoctoral fellow U. Pa., Phila., 2000—, Thomas Jefferson U., Phila., 1998-2000. Author: Hepatitis E, Virus, HIV. Fellowship UN Devel. Programs, 1998, NATO, 1993, 96. Mem.: Soc. Exptl. Biology and Medicine, AAAS, N.Y. Acad. Scis. Home: 375-B Beverly Blvd Upper Darby PA 19082 Office: U Pa 415 Curie Blvd 280 CRB Philadelphia PA 19104

OZEL, TUGRUL, engineering educator; b. Izmir, Turkey, Jan. 4, 1967; s. Rafet and Kaya Sadriye Ozel; m. Muge Ozel; children: Pelin. PhD, Ohio State U., 1998. Asst. prof. Cleve. State U., 1998—2001, Rutgers U., Piscataway, NJ, 2002—. Fellow Summer Faculty fellow, NASA, 1999. Mem.: ASME, AAUP, N.Am. Mfg. Rsch. Inst., Soc. Mfg. Engrs. Office: Rutgers U 96 Frelinghuysen Rd Piscataway NJ 08854

OZELLI, TUNCH, economics educator, consultant; b. Ankara, Turkey, May 18, 1938; came to U.S., 1962; s. Sufyan and Saziye (Ozmorali) O.; m. Lale A. Baymur, Dec. 30, 1960 (div. Mar. 1972); children: Selva, Kerem; m. Nancy Ann Goldschlager, Feb. 3, 1974 (div. Dec. 1984); m. Meral Ozdemir, May 9, 1992. MBA, Fla. State U., 1963; PhD, Columbia U., 1968. Rsch. fellow Harvard U., Cambridge, Mass., 1969-70; econ. advisor Office Prime Minister, Ankara, 1970-72; prof. mgmt. N.Y. Inst. Tech., N.Y.C., 1972—. Spl. advisor State Planning Orgn., Ankara, 1989-92. Contbr. articles to profl. jour. Ford Found. scholar, 1963-64, Found. for Econ. Edn. fellow, 1968. Mem. Am. Econ. Assn., Middle East Studies Assn., Turkish Mgmt. Assn., Delta Mu Delta. Avocation: equestrian activities. Office: Dept of Economics NY Inst Tech Old Westbury NY 11568

OZER, MARTHA ROSS, school psychologist, counselor; b. Richmond, Ky., Sept. 4, 1932; d. Robert Lee and Virginia Eudelle (Hurst) Ross; m. John Dudley Redden, Dec. 27, 1953 (dec. June 1969); children: Mary, Patricia, Robert, Mark; m. Mark N. Ozer, Aug. 12, 1979. BA in Elem. Edn., Georgetown Coll., 1954; MA in Counseling, Murray State U., 1966, MS in Psychology, 1968; EdD in Edn. Adminstrn., U. Ky., 1976; LLD (hon.), Georgetown Coll., 1995; postdoctoral cert. in infant and young child mental health program, Wash. Sch. Psychiatry, 1995-96. Cert. sch. psychologist with autonomous functioning, Ky. Bd. Psychology; lic. sch. psychologist, Va. Dept. Edn., D.C. Pub. Schs., lic. profl. counselor, D.C.; nat. cert. sch. psychologist Nat. Assn. Sch. Psychologists. Elem. tchr. Jefferson County Pub. Schs., Louisville, 1954-58, Hickman County Pub. Schs., Campbellsburg, 1960-62; tchr. emotional disturbed, dir. psychol. svcs. Paducah (Ky.) Pub. Schs., 1965-70; psychologist, program dir. Louisville Pub. Schs., 1970-74; doctoral intern Bur. Edn. for Handicapped U.S. Dept. Edn., Washington, 1974-75; program dir. project sci. tech. and disability AAAS, 1975-86; postdoctoral intern NYU Brain Trauma Program NYU Med. Ctr., N.Y.C., 1986-87; program dir., adminstr., asst. prof. dept. rehab. medicine Med. Coll. Va., Richmond, 1987-89; psychologist MCV Pediatric Devel. Ctr., 1989; sch. psychologist Fairfax (Va.) County Pub. Schs., 1989-98; pvt. practice, 1998—; dir. Project Link, William Wendt Ctr. for Loss and Healing, Washington, 2000—; dir. Ednl. Diagnostics Inst., Inc., 1998—. Cons. Am. Coun. on Edn., Washington, 1976-97; project coord. Higher Edn. and the Handicapped Am. Coun. on Edn., 1976-86; cons. rehab. and spl. edn., Brazil, Saudi Arabia, Qatar, Turkey; numerous other profl. and disability orgns. Authored more than 20 books and contbr. articles to profl. jours. on access for persons with disabilities to sci. edn. and careers, contbn. of sci./tech. to persons with disabilities. Advisor Disability Rights, 1975—. Recipient U.S. Presdl. Pvt. Sector award, award Am. Coalition Citizens with Disabilities, 1980, Alumni award Georgetown Coll., 1985, Disting. Alumni award Murray St. U., 1996; grantee U.S. Dept. Edn., 1975-86, U.S. Dept. Civil Rights, 1975-82, Grant Found., 1975-77, Exxon Found., 1976, IBM, 1976, NSF, 1977-86, Nat. Inst. for Rehab. Rsch., 1978-84. Mem. NSTA (award), APA (bd. dirs. rehab. sect.), NASP (nat. cert.), Va. Psychol. Assn., Assn. Handicapped Student Svc. Programs in Post-Secondary Edn. (editor jour. 1988-91). Avocations: photography, pottery, travel. Home: 3420 38th St NW Apt A-415 Washington DC 20016-3032 E-mail: mr2oz@aol.com.

OZEREKO-DECOEN, MARY T. therapeutic recreation specialist and therapist; b. Salem, Mass., Oct. 4, 1961; d. Domenic S. and Monica M. (Gesek) Ozereko; m. Jeffrey G. deCoen, Nov. 21, 1987. BS, U. Mass., 1982; MEd, Springfield Coll., 1987. Cert. therapeutic recreation specialist, Pa.; cert. golf club maker. Dir. promotions and ops. Wheat Thins mayors cup race Nabisco, Salem, 1984-86; conf. planner Pioneer Valley Conv. and Visitors Bur., Springfield, Mass., 1986-87; dir. tennis and recreation Village of Smugglers Notch, Vt., 1987-88; mental health profl., therapeutic recreation specialist Hoffman Homes for Youth, Gettysburg, Pa., 1988-89; therapeutic recreation aide Chambersburg (Pa.) Hosp., 1990; caseworker, therapeutic recreation specialist Tressler Wilderness Sch., Boiling Springs, Pa., 1989-92, Harrisburg, 1993-98; behavior specialist cons., 1998-99; health edn. specialist Automated Health Sys., 2000—. Owner GolfAugusta Pro Shops, Hershey, Pa., 1995—; cons. clin. seminars on recreational therapy for mental health profls.; adj. instr. prof. York (Pa.) Coll., 1997—; health edn. specialist Automated Health Sys., Pitts., 1999—. Mem. Hershey Partnership, 1995—, Pa. Children's Panel, Harrisburg, 1992—. Mem. NAFE, Nat. Recreation and Parks Assn., Pa. Mental Health Providers Assn., Pa. Parks and Recreation Assn., Ctrl. Pa. C. of C. (golf planner ea. amputee spl. olympics 1996—), U.S. Golf Assn., Cert. Golfmakers Assn., Nat. Coun. for Therapeutic Recreation Cert., U. Mass.-Keystone Alumni Assn. (pres. 1994—), Harrisburg Exec. Womens Com. Democrat. Roman Catholic. Avocations: sports, soccer, golf, collecting old toys and antiques, clubmaking. Office: 744 E Chocolate Ave Hershey PA 17033-1211 E-mail: gaps@prodigy.net.

OZERO, BRIAN JOHN, chemical engineer; b. Winnipeg, Manitoba, Can., Dec. 14, 1932; came to U.S., 1963; s. Daniel and Mary Ozero; m. Ila Atlas, Dec. 14, 1985. BS in Chem. Engring., Queens U., Kingston, Ontario, Can., 1954; MS in Chem. Engring., NYU, 1968. Technologist Shell Oil Co., Montreal, Quebec, Can., 1954-60; design engr. Chem. Constrn. Co., London, 1960-63; sr. process engr. Sci. Design Co., N.Y.C., 1963-65, process mgr., 1965-75; tech. dir. Halcon SD Group Inc., 1976-85; sr. process mgr. Tech. Evaluation and Devel. Assocs., Hoboken, N.J., 1986; pres., prin. cons. Scientech Assocs. Inc., N.Y.C., 1986—. Recognized expert in ethylene oxide/ethylene glycol, VCM, propylene oxide; contbr. articles and chpts. to tech. jours. and encyclopedias in field; patentee in field. Pres. Barrier Beach Preservation Assn., Westhampton, N.Y., 1985-88. Mem. Am. Inst. Chem. Engrs., Rotary. Republican. Roman Catholic. Avocations: reading, tennis, skiing. Home: PO Box 1524 Westhampton Beach NY 11978-7524 Office: Scientech Assoc Inc PO Box 768 Westhampton Beach NY 11978-0768

OZGOKMEN, TAMAY MEHMET, oceanography educator; b. Istanbul, Turkey, Apr. 29, 1965; s. Tarhan Hanefi and Sevgi O. BSME, Bosphorus U., Istanbul, Turkey, 1988; MSME, U. Miami, 1991; PhD in Engring., Dartmouth Coll., 1995. Rsch. asst. prof. U. Miami (Fla.), 1995—. Mem. Am. Geophys. Union. Office: RSMAS/MPO 4600 Rickenbacker Causeway Miami FL 33149-1098 E-mail: tozgokmen@rsmas.miami.edu.

OZICK, CYNTHIA, author; b. N.Y.C., Apr. 17, 1928; d. William and Celia (Regelson) O.; m. Bernard Hallote, Sept. 7, 1952; 1 dau., Rachel Sarah. BA cum laude with honors in English, NYU, 1949; MA, Ohio State U., 1950; LHD (hon.), Yeshiva U., 1984, Hebrew Union Coll., 1984, Williams Coll., 1986, Hunter Coll., 1987, Jewish Theol. Sem. Am., 1988, Adelphi U., 1988, SUNY, 1989, Brandeis U., 1990, Bard Coll., 1991, Spertus Coll., 1991, Skidmore Coll., 1992, Seton Hall U., 1999, Rutgers U., 1999, U. N.C., Asheville, 2000, NYU, 2001, Bar-Ilan U., Israel, 2002. Author: Trust, 1966, The Pagan Rabbi and Other Stories, 1971, Bloodshed and Three Novellas, 1976, Levitation: Five Fictions, 1982, Art and Ardor: Essays, 1983, The Cannibal Galaxy, 1983, The Messiah of Stockholm, 1987, Metaphor and Memory: Essays, 1989, The Shawl, 1989, Epodes: First Poems, 1992, What Henry James Knew, and Other Essays on Writers, 1994, Portrait of the Artist as a Bad Character, 1996, The Cynthia Ozick Reader, 1996, Fame and Folly, 1996, The Puttermesser Papers, 1997; (plays) Blue Light, 1994, The Shawl, 1996; guest editor Best Am. Essays, 1998, Quarrel & Quandary: Essays, 2000; also poetry, criticism, revs., translations, essays and fictions in numerous periodicals and anthologies. Phi Beta Kappa orator, Harvard U., 1985. Recipient Mildred and Harold Strauss Living award Am. Acad. Arts and Letters, 1983, Rea award for short story, 1986, PEN/Spiegel-Diamonstein award for the Art of the Essay, 1997, Harold Washington Literary award City of Chgo., 1997, John Cheever award, 1999, Lannan Found. award for fiction, 2000, Koret Found. award for lit. studies, 2001, Nat. Book Critics Circle award for nonfiction, 2001; Lucy Martin Donnelly fellow, Bryn Mawr Coll., 1992, Guggenheim fellow, 1982. Mem. PEN, Authors League, Am. Acad. of Arts and Scis., Am. Acad. of Arts and Letters, Dramatists Guild, Académie Universelle des Cultures (Paris), Phi Beta Kappa. Office: care Alfred A Knopf Co 299 Park Ave New York NY 10171

OZIER, IRVING, physicist, educator; b. Montreal, Que., Can., Sept. 7, 1938; s. Harry and Peppi (Schwartzwald) O.; m. Joyce Ruth Weinstein, July 4, 1963; children: Elizabeth, David, Douglas. BA, U. Toronto, 1960; AM, Harvard U., 1961, PhD, 1965. Rsch. fellow Harvard U., Cambridge, Mass., 1965-67, MIT, Cambridge, 1966-67; tech. staff Rockwell Internat. Sci. Ctr., Thousand Oaks, Calif., 1966-70; assoc. prof. physics U. B.C., Vancouver, B.C., Can., 1970-77, prof. Can., 1977—. Vis. rsch. fellow Cath. U., Nijmegen, The Netherlands, 1976-77, U. Nijmegen, 1997; vis. rsch. officer Nat. Rsch. Coun. Can., Ottawa, 1982-83; vis. prof. Eidgenossische Technische Hochschule, Zurich, Switzerland, 1988-89, 98. Author research articles in molecular spectroscopy. Alfred P. Sloan research fellow, 1972-74; Izaak Walton Killiam Meml. Sr. fellow U. B.C., 1982-83 Mem. Am. Phys. Soc., Can. Assn. Physicists Office: U BC Dept Physics & Astron 5224 Agricultural Rd Vancouver BC Canada V6T 1Z1

OZKAN, UMIT SIVRIOGLU, chemical engineering educator; b. Manisa, Turkey, Apr. 11, 1954; came to U.S., 1980; d. Alim and Emine (Ilgaz) Sivrioglu; m. H. Erdal Ozkan, Aug. 13, 1983. BS, Mid. East Tech. U., Ankara, Turkey, 1978, MS, 1980; PhD, Iowa State U., 1984. Registered profl. engr., Ohio. Grad. rsch. assoc. Ames Lab. U.S. Dept. Energy, 1980-84; asst. prof. Ohio State U., Columbus, 1985-90, assoc. prof. chem. engring., 1990-94, prof., 1994—, assoc. dean for rsch. Coll. Engring., 2000—. Contbr. articles to profl. jours. French Ctr. NAt. Rsch. Sci. fellow, 1994-95; recipient Women of Achievement award YWCA, Columbus, 1991, Outstanding Engring. Educator Ohio award Soc. Profl. Engrs., 1991, Union Carbide Innovation Recognition award, 1991-92, NSF Woman Faculty award in sci. and engring., 1991, Engring. Tchg. Excellence award Keck Found., 1994, Ctrl. Ohio Outstanding Woman in Sci. & Tech., 1996, Pitts.-Cleve. Catalysis Soc. Outstanding Rsch. award, 1998, Achievement award SWE, 2002, Columbus Outstanding Rsch. award ACS, 2002. Fellow Am. Inst. Chemists; mem. NSPE, N.Am. Catalysis Soc., Am. Inst. Chem. Engring., Am. Soc. Engring. Edn., Am. Chem. Soc., Combustion Inst., Sigma Xi. Achievements include research in selective oxidation, hydrogenation, NO reduction, hydrodesulfurization, hydrodeoxygenation, hydrodenitrogenation, fuel reformulation, in-situ spectroscopy. Office: Ohio State U Chem Engring 140 W 19th Ave Columbus OH 43210-1110

OZMENT, STEVEN, historian, educator; b. McComb, Miss., Feb. 21, 1939; s. Lowell V. and Shirley M. (Edgar) O.; children by previous marriage: Joel, Matthew, Katherine, Amanda, Emma. BA, Hendrix Coll., 1960; BD, Drew Theol. Sch., 1964; PhD, Harvard U., 1967; MA (hon.), Yale U., 1975. Asst. prof. Inst. Late Medieval and Reformation Studies, U. Tübingen, Fed. Republic Germany, 1966-68; asst. prof. history and religious studies Yale U., New Haven, 1968-72, assoc. prof., 1972-75, prof., 1975-79; prof. history Harvard U., 1979—, McLean prof. ancient and modern history, 1991—, assoc. dean undergrad. edn., 1984-87. Bonsall vis. prof. Stanford U., 1991. Author: Homo Spiritualis, 1969, The Reformation in Medieval Perspective, 1971, Mysticism and Dissent, 1973, The Reformation in the Cities, 1975; author: (with others) The Western Heritage, 1979, The Western Heritage, 7th edit., 2000, The Age of Reform, 1980, Reformation Europe: A Guide to Research, 1982, When Fathers Ruled: Family Life in Reformation Europe, 1983, The Heritage of World Civilizations, 1985, The Heritage of World Civilizations, 6th edit., 2002; author: Magdalena and Balthasar: An Intimate Portrait of Life in 16th Century Europe, 1986, Three Behaim Boys: Growing Up in Early Modern Germany, 1999, Protestants: The Birth of a Revolution , 1992, The Burgermeister's Daughter: Scandal in a 16th Century German Town, 1996, Flesh and Spirit: Private Life in Early Modern Germany, 1999, Ancestors: The Loving Family in Old Europe, 2001; mem. editl. bd.: Archive for Reformation History, 1976—93, mem. editl. bd.: Sixteenth Century Jour., 1976—, mem. editl. bd.: Jour. Am. Acad. Religion, 1972—77, mem. editl. bd.: Jour. Hist. Ideas, 1986—, mem. editl. bd.: Netherlands Archive for Ch. History, 1987—. Recipient Disting. Alumnus award Hendrix Coll., 1997; Morse fellow, 1970-71, Guggenheim fellow, 1978, Cabot fellow, 1992. Mem. Am. Soc. Reformation Rsch. (dir. 1979-83). Home: 69 High Rd Newbury MA 01951-1725 Office: Harvard Univ Robinson Hall Cambridge MA 02138 E-mail: steven0z@juno.com.

OZMON, KENNETH LAWRENCE, retired university president, educator; b. Portsmouth, Va., Sept. 4, 1931; emigrated to Can., 1968; s. Howard Augustine and Anna Josephine (Lynch) O.; m. Elizabeth Ann Morrison, July 6, 1968; children: Angela Francene, Kendi Elizabeth. BA in Philosophy and History magna cum laude, St. Bernard Coll., Ala., 1955; MA in Psychology, Cath. U., 1963; PhD in Psychology, U. Maine, 1968. Lic. psychologist, N.S. Instr. U. Maine, Orono, 1966-68; vis. lectr. St. Dunstan's U., P.E.I., Can., 1967; asst. prof. Calif. State U., Chico, 1968-69; chmn. dept. psychology U. P.E.I., Charlottetown, 1969-72, dean of arts, 1972-79; pres. St. Mary's U., Halifax, N.S., 1979-2000, pres. emeritus, 2000—. Chmn. pres.' coun. N.S. U., 1982—85; chmn. Met. Halifax U. Pres.' Com., 1982—84, 1986—87, 1992—; co-chmn. coordinating com. Nat. Univ. Week, 1983, 1986—87; hon. prof. U. Internat. Bus. and Econs., Beijing, 1986. Contbr. numerous articles to psychol. jours. Bd. dirs. United Way Halifax-Dartmouth, 1980-82, Friends N.S. Mus. Industry Soc., 1993-95, Greater Halifax Partnership, 1995-2000; bd. dirs. Interuniv. Svcs., Inc., 1987-94, chmn., 1992-94; provincial bd. dirs. Can. Assn. Mentally Retarded, 1980-82; co-chmn. Found. for Irish and Can. Studies, 1993; mem. nat. coun. Can. Human Rights Found., 1976; mem. selection com. J.H. Moore Awards for Excellence, Toronto, 1983-92; hon. chmn. ann. campaign N.S. div. Can. Paraplegic Assn., 1985-86; mem. fundraising com. Phoenix House, 1986-88, Charitable Irish Soc. Halifax; chmn. Human Rights Commn., 1990-96; mem. adv. coun. Order of Can., 1991-95; area chair for N.S. Internat. Coun. Psychologists, 1992-93. Decorated Order of Can.; named one of 100 Nova Scotians of Century, Daily News, 2000, Can.'s Top 50 CEO's, Atlantic Bus. Mag., 2000; recipient Gov. Gen. of Can. medal for 125th Anniversary of Can. Confedn., 1993, Jerusalem award, Atlantic Jewish Congress, 1994, Disting. Cmty. Svc. award, St. Mary's U., 2000, Can.'s Top 50 CEO's, Atlantic Bus. Mag., 2001. Mem. Assn. Atlantic Univs. (vice chmn. l983-85, chmn. l985-87), Assn. Commonwealth Univs (governing coun. l988-91), Assn. Univs. and Colls. Can. (exec. coun. 1985-89, vice chmn. 1990-91, chmn., 1991-93, mem. audit com. 1991—, chmn. exec. com. 1991—, vice-chmn. nominating com. 1990-91), Can. Psychol. Assn. (Nat. Univ. Week coordinating com. l983, co-chmn. l986-87, audit com. 1985—, co-chmn. steering com. Halifax Met. Econ. Summit II 1994), Halifax Bd. Trade (internat. trade com. 1985-91, bd. dirs. 1989-91), Halifax Club, Ashburn Golf Club. Roman Catholic. Avocations: fishing, golf, running. Home: 139 Kingswood Dr Hammonds Plains NS Canada B4B 1K4 Office: St Mary's U President Emeritus Halifax NS Canada B3H 3C3 E-mail: kenneth.ozmon@stmarys.ca.

OZOLINSH, SANDIS, hockey player; b. Aug. 13, 1972; Defense Fla. Panthers, 2001—, Carolina Hurricanes, 2000—01, Colo. Avalanche, 1995—2000, San Jose Sharks, 1992—96. Office: Nat Car Rental Ctr 2555 Panther Pky Sunrise FL 33323*

OZSVATH, DAVID L. geologist, educator; b. Summit, N.J., June 19, 1954; s. Daniel R. and Janet C. Ozsvath; m. Janet S. Ogden, Oct. 27, 1956; children: Daniel, David. BA, U. Vt., 1976; MS, Pa.State U., 1978; PhD, SUNY, Binghamton, 1985. Cert. profl. geologist. Prof. geology U. Wis., Stevens Point, 1987—; sr. hydrogeologist Ctrl. Wis. Engrs. and Archs., Weston, 1987—. Vis. prof. geology Lafayette Coll., Easton, Pa., 1986—87. Mem.: AWRA (pres. Wis. sect. 2001—), Nat. Ground Water Assn. Office: Dept Geography/Geology Univ Wisconsin-Stevens Point Stevens Point WI 54481 Office Fax: 715-346-3372. E-mail: dozsvath@uwsp.edu.

PAALZ, ANTHONY L. beverage company executive; b. Louisville, Apr. 18, 1924; s. Leon A. and Rose M. (Westendick) P.; m. Elaine Wolf, Feb. 11, 1956 (dec. Dec. 1981); children: Teresa Dawson, Eileen Baldwin, Anthony L. Jr.; m. Alison Kerr, May 3, 1986. BS, U. Ind., 1949. Chief acct. J.E. Seagram & Sons Inc., N.Y.C., 1959-69, asst. controller, 1969-72, dir. of taxes, 1972-84, v.p. taxes, 1984—. Served with USN, 1943-45, PTO. Decorated numerous battle stars. Mem. Tax Execs. Inst. Avocation: golf. Home: 29 Treeview Dr Melville NY 11747-2413 Office: Joseph E Seagram & Sons Inc 800 3rd Ave New York NY 10022-7604 E-mail: apaalz@msn.com.

PAANANEN, VICTOR NILES, English educator; b. Ashtabula, Ohio, Jan. 31, 1938; s. Niles Henry and Anni Margaret (Iloranta) P.; m. Donna Mae Jones, Aug. 15, 1964; children: Karl, Neil. AB magna cum laude, Harvard U., 1960; MA, U. Wis., 1964, PhD, 1967. Instr. English Wofford Coll., Spartanburg, S.C., 1962-63; asst. prof. Williams Coll., Williamstown, Mass., 1966-68, Mich. State U., East Lansing, 1968-73, assoc. prof., 1973-82, prof., 1982—, asst. dean Grad. Sch., 1977-82, chmn. dept. English, 1986-94. Vis. prof. Roehampton Inst., London, 1982, 96, hon. fellow, 1992. Author: William Blake, 1977, 2d edit., 1996, British Marxist Criticism, 2000; contbr. articles to profl. and scholarly jours. Univ. fellow U. Wis., 1962, 63-64, Roehampton Inst. hon. fellow, London, 1992—; Harvard Nat. scholar, 1956-60. Home: 350 Revere Beach Blvd 5-5W Revere MA 02151-4851 E-mail: paananen@msu.edu.

PAARLBERG, ROBERT L. political science educator; b. Hall, N.Y., Aug. 25, 1945; s. Don and Eva P.; m. Marianne Perlak, Aug. 21, 1971. BA, Carleton Coll., 1967; PhD, Harvard U., 1975. Prof. polit. sci. Wellesley (Mass.) Coll., 1976—; assoc. Weatherhead Ctr. for Internat. Affairs Harvard U., Cambridge, Mass., 1976—. Vis. prof. govt. Harvard U., Cambridge, 1988-89; cons. Internat. Food Policy Rsch. Inst., Washington, 1996—; mem. adv. com. on emerging markets U.S. Dept. Agr., 1997—, cons. Nat. Intelligence Coun. Author: (books) Food Trade and Foreign Policy, 1985, Fixing Farm Trade, 1988, Leadership Abroad Begins at Home, 1995; co-author: Policy Reform in American Agriculture, 1999, Politics of Precaution, 2001. Advisor to candidates, Dukakis, Tsongas, Mass., 1988, 92; congressional witness, Washington, 1991-95; chmn. of working group Nat. Commn. on Internat. Trade Devel. and Cooperation, Washington, 1996-97. Recipient Pinanski prize Wellesley (Mass.) Coll., 1998. Mem. Am. Agrl. Econs. Assn., Am. Polit. Sci. Assn., Phi Beta Kappa. Office: Wellesley Coll Polit Sci Dept Wellesley MA 02481 E-mail: rpaarlberg@wellesley.edu.

PAASWELL, ROBERT EMIL, civil engineer, educator; b. Red Wing, Minn., Jan. 15, 1937; s. George and Evelyn (Cohen) P.; m. Rosalind Snyder, May 31, 1958; children: Judith Marjorie, George Harold. BA (Ford Found. fellow), Columbia U., 1956, BS, 1957, MS, 1961; PhD, Rutgers U., 1965. Field engring. asst. Spencer White & Prentis, Washington, 1954-56, engr. N.Y.C., 1957-59; rsch. scientist Davidson Lab., N.J., 1964; rsch. fellow Greater London Council, 1971-72; rsch. and teaching asst. Columbia U., 1959-62; asst. prof. civil engring. SUNY, Buffalo, 1964-68; chmn. bd. govs. Urban Studies Coll., 1973-76, assoc. prof., 1968-76, prof. civil engring., 1976-82; dir. Center for Transp. Studies and Research, 1979-82, chmn. dept. environ. design and planning, 1980-82; prof. transp. engring. U. Ill., Chgo., 1982-86, 89-90, dir. Urban Transp. Ctr., 1982-86; exec. dir. Chgo. Transit Authority, 1986-89; dir. transp. rsch. consortium, prof. civil engring. CCNY, 1990—, disting. prof., 1991—; dir. CUNY Inst. Urban Systems, 2000—. Faculty-on-leave Dept. Transp., 1976-77, cons., 1981—; v.p. Faculty Tech. Cons., Inc., Midwest Sys. Scis., Inc., 1982-86; dir. Urban Mass Transp. Adminstrn. Summer Faculty Workshop, 1980, 81; cons. transp. planning, energy and soil mechanics; spl. cons. to Congressman T. Dulski, 1973; vis. expert lectr. Jilin U. Tech., Changchun, Peoples Republic of China, 1985, hon. prof. transp., 1986—; bd. dirs. E'Escuto Archs. and Engrs., Chig, Hickling Co., Ottawa, Can., Transic Devel. Corp.; chmn. transp. steering adv. bd. Office of Tech. Assessment for Infrastructure and the Urban Core Project, 1994—; faculty Lincoln Inst. of Land Policy, 1994-95; vis. scholar Tel Aviv U., Israel, 1995—; arbitrator in productivity Met. Transp. Authority, N.Y.C., 1996—; mem. exec. com. Coun. on Transp., 1996—, NSF Ctr. for Infrastructure Sys.; cons. Coun. of North East Govs., 1997—; faculty "Conflict Resolution," NYU, 1998—; mem. exec. com. Inst. for Civil Infrastructure Sys. (NSF), 1998—; chair panel new paradigms in transit Transp. Rsch. Bd.; bd. dirs. Transit Stds. Consortium, chmn., 2000—. Author: Problems of the Carless, 1977; contbg. author: Transport and Urban Development, 1995, Panels for Transportation Planning, 1997, Studies in Israel Planning, 1996, Dynamic Networks and Spatial Change, 1999, After the World Trade Center, 2002; editor: Site Traffic Impact Assessment, 1992; contbg. author: Decisions for the Great Lakes, 1982, World Book Encyclopedia, 1992, 93, 94, Transport and Urban Development, 1995, Israel Planning Studies, 1996, 97, Panels for Transportation Planning, 1997, New Contributions to Transportation Analysis in Europe, 1999; mem. bd. editors Jour. Environ. Systems, 1974—, Transp., 1978—, Jour. Urban Tech., 1992—; contbr. articles to profl. jours. Mem. Buffalo Environ. Mgmt. Commn., 1972-74; mem. Area Com. for Transit, Mayor's Energy Adv. Bd., 1974, Block Grant Rev. Com., City of Buffalo; chmn. com. on transp., mem. rev. adv. bd. Rsch. and Planning Coun. Western N.Y.; mem. transp. com. Chgo. 1992 Worlds Fair; mem. citizens' adv. bd. Chgo. Transit Authority, 1985—; mem. strategic planning com. Regional Transp. Authority, 1985; mem. steering com. Nat. Transit Coop. Rsch. Program, 1991—, Borough pres. (Manhattan) Trans. Adv. Bd., Bronx Ctr. Devel. Project; bd. dirs. Transit Devel. Corp., 1992—; exec. bd. Transp. Council, 1996—; mem. exec. com. Colin Powell Ctr. Recipient Dept. Transp. award, 1977; SUNY faculty fellow, 1965-66 Fellow ASCE (past pres. Buffalo sect., chmn. steering com. 1992 specialty conf. traffic impact analysis); mem. AAAS, Transp. Rsch. Bd. (chmn. com. on transp. disadvantaged, mem. exec. com., peer rev. com. nat. transp. ctrs. 1988—), Inst. Transp. Engrs. (transit coun., exec. com., chmn. legis. policy com., rsch. com. surface transp. policy project 1995—), Coun. on Transp. (bd. dirs. 1996—), N.Y. Acad. Scis., Sigma Xi. Office: CCNY Inst Transp Systems Rm 220-Y 135th St and Convent Ave New York NY 10031

PAAVO, JARVI, conductor; b. Tallinn, Estonia; Studied under Leonard Bernstein; student in percussion and conducting, Tallinn Sch. Music; student under Otto-Werner, Max Rudolf, Curtis Inst. Music; student under Leonard Bernstein , L.A. Philharmonic Inst. Music dir. Cin. Symphony Orch., 2001—. Prin. guest conductor Royal Stockholm Philharmonic , City of Birmingham (Eng.) Symphony Orch., guest conductor N.Y. Philharmonic , Berlin Philharmonic, Munich Philharmonic, London Philharmonic , San Francisco Symphony , Phila. Orch. (Carnegie Hall debut) , NHK Symphony, Tokyo Symphony , Israel Philharmonic, St. Petersburg Philharmonic , Orch. Filarmonica della Scala, L.A. Philharmonic, Philharmonic orch. and many others, (works by Bernstein) City of Birmingham Symphony Orch., (recorded performances Stenhammar pieces) Royal Stockholm Philharmonic Orch., (recordings with Estonian composers Part, Tuur, and Tubin) Searching for Roots, Sibelius' Kullervo, Lemminkainen Suite , (concerts with cellist Turls Mork). Office: Cin Symphony Orch 1241 Elm St Cincinnati OH 45210*

PABARCIUS, ALGIS, investment executive; b. Telsiai, Lithuania, May 1, 1932; came to U.S., 1950, naturalized, 1956; s. Vacius and Brone (Ziuryte) P.; m. Eleanor A. Rakovic, Aug. 18, 1956; children: Nina, Lisa, Algis. BS, U. Ill., 1955; MS, Ill. Inst. Tech., 1958, PhD, 1964; postgrad., Technische Hochschule Muenchen, Germany, 1962. Registered prof. engr. Ill., D.C., structural engr. Ill. Engr. Esso Rsch. & Engring. Co., Linden, N.J., 1955-56; instr. U. Ill., Chgo., 1956-59, asst. prof., 1959-64; ptnr. Zubkus, Semaitis & Assocs., Architects and Engrs., Chgo., Washington, 1959-67; v.p. Garden Hotels Investment Co. and Whitecliffe Corp., Lanham, Md., 1967-75; pres. Aras Investment Corp., 1975-79, Colony Funding Corp., Washington, 1979-92, Amtrust Corp., Alexandria, Va., 1992—. Danforth Found. grantee, 1960-61; NSF Faculty fellow, 1961-62. Mem. ASCE, Sigma Xi, Tau Beta Pi, Sigma Tau, Chi Epsilon, Phi Kappa Phi. Home: 7620 Old Georgetown Rd Bethesda MD 20814-6150 Office: Amtrust Corp 218 N Lee St Alexandria VA 22314-2631 E-mail: pabarcius@erols.com.

PACALA, LEON, retired association executive; b. Indpls., May 3, 1926; s. John and Anna (Ferician) P.; m. Janet Lefforge, Dec. 28, 1947 (dec. July 1987); children: Mark, Stephen, James; m. Virginia Strasenburgh, Mar. 10, 1990. AB, Franklin (Ind.) Coll., 1949; BD, Colgate Rochester Div. Sch., 1952; PhD, Yale U., 1960; LLD (hon.), Nazareth Coll., 1980; LHD (hon.), Franklin Coll., 1987. Ordained to ministry Baptist Ch., 1952. Asst. prof. philosophy and religion DePauw U., 1956-61; participant study religion undergrad. coll. Lilly Found., 1957-59; assoc. prof. religion Bucknell U., 1961-68, prof., 1968-73, chmn. dept., 1961-64, dean, 1962-73; pres. Colgate Rochester (N.Y.) Div. Sch.; also Bexley Hall, Crozer Theol. Sem., 1973-80; exec. dir. Assn. Theol. Schs. in U.S. and Can., 1980-91. Cons. acad. adminstrn. Beirut Coll. Women, 1972. Author: The Role of ATS in Theological Education, 1980-90, 1998; contbr. articles to profl. jours. Exec. com. Christian Faith in Higher Edn. Projects, 1965-68; trustee Franklin Coll., 1967-73, 98—; bd. dirs. Rohesters Jobs, Inc., 1973-80, Union Theol. Sem., N.Y.C., 1999—; trustee Rochester Area Colls., 1973-80; dir. Nat. Housing Ministries, Am. Bapt. Chs., 1976-80; mem. adv. bd. Colgate Rochester Div. Sch., 1997—. With USAAF, 1944-45. Internat. Rotary scholar, Louvain U., Belgium, 1952-53. Mem. Am. Conf. Acad. Deans (exec. com., treas., chmn., presiding officer 1973-74), Am. Assn. Higher Edn., Assn. Am. Colls. (commn. religion higher edn.), Assn. Theol. Schs. (com. accreditation), World Conf. Assns. Theol. Instns. (v.p. 1988-93), Am. Bapt. Assn. Sem. Adminstrs. (chmn 1975-80). Home: 3515 Elmwood Ave Rochester NY 14610-3464

PACALO, PATRICK JOHN, writer; b. Pensacola, Fla., Sept. 4, 1963; s. Nicholas and Rose Barbera Pacalo. B of Polit. Sci., Indiana U. of Pa., 1988; M in History, Youngstown State U., 1995. Author: (www.coldwar.net) Cold Warfare: A Compact History, 2001; contbr. editls. and articles to newspapers and profl. publs. Chairperson of bd. trustees Pride Ctr. of Greater Youngstown, Youngstown, 2000—02. Capt. U.S. Army, 1980—94. Mem.: Pi Sigma Alpha, Pi Gamma Mu, Phi Alpha Theta. Roman Catholic. Avocations: fitness walking, Internet, music. Office: Hist Rsch Enterprises Youngstown OH Personal E-mail: info@coldwar.net. Business E-Mail: info@coldwar.net.

PACCONE, DAVID E. management consultant; b. N.Y.C., July 31, 1963; BA, Hofstra U., 1985. Adj. undergrad. tchg. program Maxwell Sch., Syracuse U., NY, 1990—93; dir. govt. affairs STF Svc., East Syracuse, 1993—98. Mem. Pacc. Bros. Consulting, Albany, NY, 1992—2002. Home: 34-H N St Marcellus NY 13108 Personal E-mail: brodleus@aol.com.

PACE, CAROLINA JOLLIFF, communications executive, commercial real estate investor; b. Dallas, Apr. 12, 1938; d. Lindsay Gafford and Carolina (Juden) Jolliff; student Holton-Arms Jr. Coll., 1956-57; BA in Comparative Lit., So. Meth. U., 1960; m. John McIver Pace, Oct. 7, 1961. Promotional advisor, dir. season ticket sales Dallas Theatre Ctr., 1960-61; exec. sec. Dallas Book and Author Luncheon, 1959-63; promotional and instl. cons. Henry Regnery-Reilly & Lee Pub. Co., Chgo., 1962-65; pub. trade rep. various cos., instl. rep. Don R. Phillips Co., Southeastern area, 1965-67; Southwestern rep. Ednl. Reading Svc., Inc.-Troll Assocs., Mahwah, N.J., 1967-72; v.p., dir. multimedia div. Melton Book Co., Dallas, 1972-79; v.p. mktg. Webster's Internat., Inc., Nashville, 1980-82; pres. Carolina Pace, Inc., 1982—; mem. adv. bd. Nat. Info. Ctr. of Spl. Edn. Materials; mem. materials rev. panel Nat. Media Ctr. for Materials of Severely-Profoundly Handicapped, 1981; mem. mktg. product rev. bd. LINC Resources, 1982, 83, 84, mktg. task force, 1983, adv. bd., 1987; reviewer spl. edn. U.S. Dept. Edn., 1975-79, 85; rev. cons. Health and Humas Svcs., 1982, 83, 84, 86; product rev. task force CEC, 1984, 85, 86; cons. Ednl. Cable Consortium, Summit, N.J., 1982-87. Mem. adv. coun. Grad. System Sch. Libr. and Info. Sci. Found., U. Tex., 1987—; co-vice chair Friends Highland Park Libr., 1989; mem. focus group City Dallas Growth Policy Plan; mem. art and design com. Downtown Ctrs.; active Dallas City Wide Parking Task Force, Ctrl. Transp. Forum Ctrl. Bus. Dist., Union Sta. Art & Design Com., Downtown Transfer Ctrs., Art and Design Com., West End Task Force, Ctrl. Bus. Dist. Task Force, Tex. Parking Assn.; co-founder Operation TexRec, 1990-91; bd. dirs. Transp. Mgmt. Assn., 1995—; chair Vanpool Use Study, 1995; budget chmn. Dallas County Sesquicentennial com., 1996; adv. bd. mem. Friends of Old Red Courthouse, 1997—, Trinity River Econ. Devel. Bd., 1998—. Mem. Ctrl. Dallas Assn. (transportation com. 1996—, planning and greenspace com. 1998—), Dallas Plan (focus com.), Nat. Audio Visual Assn. (conf. panelist 1979), Internat. Comm. Industries Assn., Assn. Ednl. and Comm. Tech., Assn. Spl. Edn. Tech. (nat. dir., v.p. publicity 1980-82), Women's Nat. Book Assn, Women in Comm., Dallas Founders, Friends of the West End (pres. 1988—), West End Assn. Dallas (chmn. subcom. on traffic and parking 1986-87, com. demographic study 1987-88), Pub. Rels. Soc. Am., Coun. Exceptional Children (dir. exhibitors com., chmn. publ. com. 1979 conf., conf. speaker 1981), Downtown Transp. Mgmt. Assn. (adv. bd., chmn. vanpools subcom., 1995—), adv. bd., Friends of Old Red Courthouse, 1997—, Planning a Greenspace com., Central Dallas Assn., 1998—, Transportation com., Central Dallas Assn., 1996—. Econ. Adv. bd., Trinity River Devel., 1998—, DAR (Jane Douglas chpt.), Dallas Zool. Soc., Dallas West End Hist. Dist. Assn., Dallas Mus. of Art, Dallas Southern Meml. Tex. Parking Assn., Kimball Art Mus., Alpha Delta Pi. Presbyterian. Producer ednl. videos; contbr. articles to profl. jours. Home: 4524 Lorraine Ave Dallas TX 75205-3613

PACE, CHARLES ROBERT, psychologist, educator; b. St. Paul, Sept. 7, 1912; s. Charles N. and Lenore (Lee) P.; m. Rosella Gaarder, Dec. 18, 1937; children: Rosalind, Jenifer. BA, De Pauw U., 1933; MA, U. Minn., 1935, PhD, 1937. Instr. in gen. coll. U. Minn., 1937-40; research asso. Am. Council Edn., 1941-42; research psychologist Bur. Naval Personnel, Navy Dept., 1943-47; mem. faculty Syracuse U., 1947-61, asso. dir., then dir. evaluation service center, 1947-52, asst. to chancellor, 1948-52, prof. psychology, chmn. dept., dir. psychol. research center, 1952-61; prof. higher edn. UCLA, 1961-82, prof. emeritus, 1982—. Mem. adv. coms. Am. Council Edn., Coll. Entrance Exam. Bd., Social Sci. Research Council. Author: They Went to College, 1941, (with M. E. Troyer) Evaluation in Teacher Education, 1944, The Junior Year in France, 1959, (with F.H. Bowles and J.C. Stone) How to Get Into College, 1968, College and University Environment Scales, 2d edit, 1969, Education and Evangelism, 1972, The Demise of Diversity?, 1974, Measuring Outcomes of College, 1979, Measuring the Quality of College Student Experiences, 1984, CSEQ: Test Manual and Norms, 1987, The Undergraduates, 1990. Post-doctoral fellow Rockefeller Found., 1940-41; fellow Center Advanced Study Behavioral Scis., 1959-60; recipient citation for meritorious civilian service Navy Dept., 1946, E.F. Lindquist award Am. Ednl. Research Assn. and Am. Coll. Testing Program, 1984, Suslow award for outstanding svc. Assn. for Instl. Rsch., 1989. Mem. APA, Am. Ednl. Rsch. Assn. (Disting. Rsch. award divsn. postsecondary edn. 1992), Assn. for Study Higher Edn. (Disting. Career award 1989), Am. Assn. Pub. Opinion Rsch. E-mail: crp7001@axe.humboldt.edu.

PACE, ERIC DWIGHT, journalist, writer; b. N.Y.C., Oct. 13, 1936; s. Eric and Eleanor Robertson (Jones) Paepcke; m. Suzanne Monique Wiedel, June 12, 1976 (div. Jan. 1987); children: Christine, Lydia. Grad., Phillips Exeter Acad., 1953; student, U. Heidelberg, Germany, 1955-56; BA magna cum laude, Yale, 1957; MA, Johns Hopkins, 1959. Reporter San Angelo (Tex.) Standard Times and Evening Standard, 1957-58; mem. staff Life mag., N.Y.C., 1959-61, assigned to Bonn, 1961, Paris, 1961-62; corr. Time mag., Bonn., 1962-63, Hong Kong, 1963-65; mem. staff New York Times, N.Y.C., 1965-66, assigned to Saigon, 1966, Cairo, 1966-69, Paris, 1969-70, Beirut, 1970-71, N.Y.C., 1971-74, Teheran, 1974-77, N.Y.C., 1977—. Author: novels Saberlegs, 1970, Any War Will Do, 1973, Nightingale, 1979; contbr. articles to Fgn. Affairs, also others. Served with AUS, 1957. Recipient George Polk Meml. award Overseas Press Club, 1968, Page One award N.Y.C. Newspaper Guild, 1968 Mem. Mystery Writers Am., Crime Writers Assn. (Gt. Britain), Am. P.E.N. Clubs: Century (N.Y.C.), Squadron A (N.Y.C.). Unitarian Universalist. Office: New York Times 229 W 43rd St New York NY 10036-3959

PACE, ESTON A. systems administrator; b. Richmond, Va., Feb. 7, 1960; s. James Eston and Thelma Marie Winston P.; m. Vivian J. Cox, Mar. 31, 1985 (div. Aug. 1988); m. Wendy Jane Unison, Apr. 4, 1999. Diploma, Huguenot Acad., 1978; student, J. Sargent Reynolds. Microsoft Cert. network essentials, NT4.0 workstation, windows 2000, Windows 2000 destop adminstrn. Sr. officer, field tng. officer Va. Dept. of Corrections, Starkfarm, Va., 1995-2000; owner We Try Harder Computer Co., Richmond, 1998—; network adminstr. Philip Morris, Va., 1999-2000; customer svc. analyst, network adminstr. Chaparral Steel/TXI, Petersburg, 2000—. Lt. Fine Creek Vol. Fire Dept., Powhatan, Va., 1983-85, 86-90, capt. 1985-86, chief, 1982-83, in-charge emergency med. tech. Powhatan Vol. Rescue Squad, 1974-84. Recipient Svc. award Fine Creek Vol. Fire Dept., 1986, Cert. of Appreciation, 1991; Svc. award Va. Dept. Corrections, 2000. Mem. Comp TIA-IT Profl., Internat. Internet Assn., Internat. Footprints Assn. Avocations: literature, creative cooking, amature chef, genealogy. Office: WTHCC 7005 Fernwood #411 Richmond VA 23228 E-mail: wthcc@erols.com.

PACE, FRANK ANTHONY, television producer; b. White Plains, N.Y., Feb. 14, 1950; s. Dominick Edward and Rose T. (Papillo) P.; m. Karen Lynn Huggins, Nov. 5, 1983; 1 child, Erin Lynn. BS in Bus., Jacksonville U., 1972. Co-producer Winner Never Quits ABC, Los Angeles, 1985; producer Head of the Class, 1986-90, supervising producer, 1991; producer Murphy Brown CBS, 1988; producer Ferris Bueller NBC, 1990, Babe Ruth NBC, 1991, Billy ABC, 1991; producer pilot & series Daddy Dearest FOX, 1993-94, Something Wilder NBC, 1994-95, Bless This House CBS, 1995-96, Suddenly Susan NBC, 1996—; producer For Your Love Warner Bros. Network, 1997-2000, Nikki, 2000—. 1st Am. producer in Moscow, 1988. Author: Rod Carew's Art and Science of Hitting, 1986. Named EMMY nominee Murphy Brown CBS, 1988. Mem. Dirs. Guild Am., Am. Acad. TV Arts and Scis. Office: Warner Bros 4000 Warner Blvd Burbank CA 91522-0002

PACE, JOHN EDWARD, III, chemical engineer; b. Ridgeway, Va., Apr. 6, 1948; s. John Edward Jr. and Retta Jean Stanley Sheppard; m. Carolyn Ann Gray, Aug. 31, 1969; children: Brian Edward, Kimberly Carol. BSChemE, Va. Poly. Inst. and State U., 1971, MS in Chem. Engring., 1972. Registered profl. engr., W.Va. Summer engr. Exxon, Baytown, Tex., 1971; devel. engr. Dow Badische, Anderson, S.C., 1972-76; process devel. engr. Borg Warner, Parkersburg, W.Va., 1976-88, GE Plastics, Parkersburg, 1988-97, process engring. leader, 1997-99; prin. engr. Global Process Engring. Group, 1999—. Contbr. articles to profl. jours. Recipient Charles F. Reed award for process innovation, GE Global Tech., 2000. Mem. AIChE, Elfuns. Republican.

Baptist. Achievements include 3 patents on ABS processes; development of bulk SAN and bulk ABS processes. Home: 51 Bethel Pl Washington WV 26181-9579 Office: General Electric Plastics PO Box 68 Washington WV 26181-0068

PACE, KAREN YVONNE, mathematics and computer science educator; b. Jefferson City, Mo., Dec. 29, 1957; d. William John and Georgia (Loesch) Sippel; m. Charles Edward Pace, Dec. 27, 1982. EdB, Mo. State U., 1980; EdM, Drury U., 1985. Cert. secondary tchr. Tchr. Salem (Mo.) Sch. Dist., 1980—, Southwest Bapt. U., Boliver, Mo., 1985—. Dist. chair Career Ladder Com., Salem, 1991-92; treas. Cmty. Tchrs. Orgn., Salem, 1992-93; assessment expert Salem Sch. Dist., 1993-94; sr. leader Mo. Assessment Project 2000, 1994. Pres. Community Cause Club, Salem, 1994. Mem. Salem Tchrs. Assn. (budget com. chair 1992-94). Democrat. Avocation: music. Home: PO Box 795 Salem MO 65560-0795 Office: Salem Sch Dist 1400 W 3rd St Salem MO 65560-1769

PACE, LEONARD, retired management consultant; b. Torrington, Conn., Oct. 24, 1924; s. Anthony and Maria G. P.; m. Maureen Therese Murphy, Sept. 15, 1956; children: Leonard Anthony, Susan Maria, Daniel Graham, Thomas William, Mary Macaire, Cathleen Anne. Student, Syracuse U., 1943; BSM.E., U. Conn., 1949; postgrad., N.Y. U., 1951-52, Wayne U., 1955. Cert. mgmt. cons. With GAF, 1949-57, asst. to div. controller, 1954-57; with Deloitte Haskins and Sells, N.Y.C., 1957—, head N.Y. mgmt. adv. services, 1965-67, head Eastern region, 1967-76, nat. dir. mgmt. adv. services, 1976-85, chmn. internat. mgmt. adv. svcs. com. Served as officer, pilot USAAF, 1943-45. Mem. Am. Mgmt. Assn., Inst. Mgmt. Cons. (dir., chmn. profl. standards com.) Clubs: Baltusrol Golf, Union League, Circumnavigators. Home: 35 Little Wolf Rd Summit NJ 07901-3112

PACE, ORLANDO LAMAR, football player; b. Sandusky, Ohio, Nov. 4, 1975; Attended , Ohio State Univ. Lineman St. Louis Rams, 1997—; winner Super Bowl 34, 2000; 1st overall pick NFL Draft, 1997; earned 2nd consecutive Pro Bowl Invitations; no sacks allowed St. Louis vs. Minn. , 1999. Donater Disadvantaged Kids; participant Spearheads Annual Offensive Line Thanksgiving Project, Chesterfield, Mo. Achievements include first to make history by becoming the first player to win two consecutive Lombardi awards in 1996. Office: 1 Rams Way Saint Louis MO 63045*

PACE, ROSA WHITE, lawyer; b. Borger, Tex., Nov. 5, 1932; d. John Herron and Anna Mae (Caldwell) White; m. Carroll Pace, Jan. 3, 1968; children: Ann Catherine, Virginia Gale, Mary Jane. BA, William Jewell Coll., 1953; JD, U. Tex., 1956. Bar: Tex. 1956. Ptnr. White & White Attys., Borger, 1956-62, White, White & White Attys., Borger, 1962-65; pvt. practice, 1966—. Co-author: Borger, a History, Hutchinson County History, 1983. Chmn. Hutchinson County Hist. Commn., 1985-94. Recipient Professionalism award Coll. of State Bar of Tex., 1996. Mem. ABA, State Bar Assn. Tex., Borger Bar Assn., DAR (local regent 1975-76), Beta Sigma Phi (women of yr. 1978). Office: 431 Deahl St Borger TX 79007-4113

PACE, STANLEY CARTER, retired aeronautical engineer; b. Waterview, Ky., Sept. 14, 1921; s. Stanley Dan and Pearl Eagle (Carter) P.; m. Elaine Marilyn Cutchall, Aug. 21, 1945; children: Stanley Dan, Lawrence Timothy, Richard Yost. Student, U. Ky., 1939-40; BS, U.S. Mil. Acad., 1943; MS in Aero. Engring., Calif. Inst. Tech., 1949; LLD (hon.), Maryville Coll., 1987; LHD (hon.), U. Mo., 1990. Commd. 2d lt. USAAF, 1943, advanced through grades to col., 1953; pilot, flight leader B-24 Group, 15th Air Force, 1943-44; chief power plant br., procurement div. Hdqrs. Air Materiel Command Wright-Patterson AFB, Ohio, 1945-48; assignments, procurement div. Hdqrs. Air Materiel Command, 1949-53; dep. chief prodn. Hdqrs. Air Materiel Command, 1952-53; resigned, 1954; with TRW, Inc., Cleve., 1954-85, successively sales mgr., asst. mgr., mgr. West Coast plant; mgr. jet div. Tapco plant; asst. mgr. Tapco group, 1954-58, v.p., gen. mgr., 1958-65, exec. v.p. co., 1965-77, pres., 1977-85, vice chmn., 1985, dir., 1965-85; vice chmn., dir. Gen. Dynamics Corp., St. Louis, 1985, chmn., chief exec. officer, 1985-90, also bd. dirs. Head United Way drive, Cleve., 1984; former council commr., pres. Great Cleve. Council Boy Scouts Am.; former trustee Nat. Jr. Achievement, Denison U., Washington U., Judson Park; former chmn. Greater Cleve. Roundtable, Cleve. Found., Nat. Assn. Mfrs., Aerospace Ind. Assn. Decorated Air medal with oak leaf clusters, Purple Heart; recipient James Forrestal award Nat. Security Indsl. Assn.; named d'Officier de lóorder de Leopold Belgium Govt. Mem. AIAA, Soc. Automotive Engrs., Union Club, Country Club, Chagrin Valley Hunt Club, Pepper Pike Club, Eldorado Country Club, Rolling Rock Club, St. Louis Country Club, Delta Tau Delta. Home: 1709 Berkshire Rd Gates Mills OH 44040-9747

PACE, STANLEY DAN, lawyer; b. Dayton, Ohio, Dec. 10, 1947; s. Stanley Carter and Elaine (Cutchall) P.; m. Judy Roehm, Sept. 8, 1973; children: Stanley Carter, Barbara Roehm. BA, Denison U., Granville, Ohio, 1970; JD, U. Toledo (Ohio), 1975. Bar: U.S. Dist. Ct. (so. dist.) Ohio 1975, U.S. Dist. Ct. (no. dist.) Ohio 1977, U.S. Ct. Appeals (6th cir.) 1975. Atty. ARMCO Steel Corp., Middletown, Ohio, 1975-77; assoc. Spieth, Bell, McCurdy & Newell, Cleve., 1977-82, dir., 1982—, co-mng. dir., 1987—. Bd. mem. Indsl. Rels. Rsch. Assn., Cleve., 1985. Bd. pres. Judson Retirement Community, Cleve., 1985; bd. mem. Arthritis Found. N.E. Ohio, Cleve., 1984, Western Res. Hist. Soc., 1998. Mem. ABA, Ohio Bar Assn., Greater Cleve. Bar Assn., The Country Club, Pepper Pike Club, Tavern Club, Rolling Rock Club. Office: Spieth Bell McCurdy & Newell 2000 Huntington Bldg Cleveland OH 44115

PACE, STEPHEN SHELL, artist, educator; b. Charleston, Mo., Dec. 12, 1918; s. John C. and Ora K. (Reeves) P.; m. Palmina Natalini, Feb. 26, 1949. Student, Inst. Fine Arts, San Miguel, 1945-46, Art Students League, N.Y.C., 1948-49, Grande Chaumiere, Paris, 1950, Inst. D'Arte Statale, Florence, Italy, 1951, Hans Hofmann Sch., N.Y.C., 1951-52; ArtsD (hon.) , U. So. Ind., 2002. Artist in residence Washington U., 1959; instr. painting Pratt Inst., N.Y.C., 1961-69; artist in residence Des Moines Art Ctr., 1970; vis. artist U. Calif., 1968; asso. prof. Bard Coll., 1969-71, Am. U., 1975-83. One-man shows include Hendler Gallery, 1953, Artists Gallery, 1954, Poindexter Gallery, 1956, 57, Washington U., St. Louis, 1959, Holland-Goldowsky Gallery, Chgo., 1960, Howard Wise Gallery, Cleve., 1960, N.Y., 1960, 61, 63, 64, Dilexi Gallery, San Francisco, 1960, HCE Gallery, 1956-59, 61-63, 66, Dwan Gallery, Los Angeles, 1961, Hayden Gallery, Cambridge, Mass., 1961, Ridley Gallery, Evansville, Ind., 1966, U. Calif. at Berkeley, 1968, Graham Gallery, N.Y.C., 1969, Des Moines Art Center, 1970, U. Tex., Austin, 1970, Kansas City Art Inst., 1973, A.M. Sachs Gallery, N.Y.C., 1974, 76, 77, 78, 79, 81, 83, 85, Drew U., 1975, Bard Coll., 1975, Am. U., 1976, Roberto Polo Gallery, Washington, 1976, New Harmony (Ind.) Gallery, 1977, Farm Gallery, Far Hill, N.J., 1978, Barbara Fiedler Gallery, Washington, 1980, Chastenet Gallery, Washington, 1981, Katherina Rich Perlow Gallery, N.Y.C., 1987, 89, 91, 94, 97, 98. 2000, 2002, Vanderwoude-Tananbaum Gallery, N.Y.C., 1991, U. N.C., Greensboro, 1991, Evansville Mus., 1992, Maine Coast Artists, Rockport, 1994, Bates Coll. Mus., Lewiston, Maine, 1994, Union Coll., Schenectady, NY, 1999; exhibited in group shows in U.S., Europe, Japan, Middle East, India, Burma, Australia, N.Z., Hawaii, Central and S.Am.; represented in permanent collections, Whitney Mus., Chrysler Mus., Norfolk, Va., Provincetown (Mass.) Mus., Evansville (Ind.) Mus., U. So. Ill., Carbondale, Michener Found., Walker Art Center, U. Calif., CIBA-Geigy Collection, Hallmark Collection, Bundy Art Gallery, U. N.C., Greensboro, Chase Manhattan Bank, Munson-Williams-Procter Inst., Utica, N.Y., Des Moines Art Center, Boston Mus. Fine Arts, Met. Mus., N.Y.C., Phillips Collection, Washington, Am. U., Washington, Corcoran Gallery, Washington, Curie Inst., Paris, Hirshhorn Mus., Washington, Bristol Myers Collection, Indpls. Mus., Portland (Maine) Mus., Bowdoin Coll. Mus., Brown U., Providence, Oberlin (Ohio) Coll. Mus, Farmsworth Art Mus., Rockland, Maine, Bates Coll. Mus., Lewiston, Maine, Nat. Mus. Am. Art, Washington, Columbus Mus. Art, Yale U., New Haven, U. of S. Indiana, Evansville, Union Coll., Schenectady, Newark Art Mus., N.J., U. No. Iowa, Cedar Falls, Colby Coll. Mus., Waterville, Maine, Rutgers U. Mus., NB, NJ, New Orleans Mus. Art. Served with AUS, 1941-45, ETO. Recipient Dolian Lorian award for promising Am. painters, 1954; Hallmark award, 1961; Guggenheim fellow, 1980; Creative Artists Pub. Service Program grantee, 1973. Mem.: Nat. Acad. Design (Benjamin Altman prize 1993, Edwin Palmer Marine prize 2001). Address: 345 W 29th St New York NY 10001-4780

PACE, THOMAS M. lawyer; b. Mesa, Ariz., Feb. 5, 1952; s. Lemuel Max and Ann (Green) P.; m. Vi Garrett Pace, Jan. 24, 1981; children: Melanie, Brittany. BA, Stanford U., 1973; JD, U. Ariz., 1976. Bar: Ariz.; cert. real estate specialist. Assoc. Martin, Feldhacker & Freidl, Phoenix, 1976-77, Trew & Woodford, Phoenix, 1977-78; ptnr. Hecker, Phillips & Hooker, Tucson, 1978-88; sr. ptnr. O'Connor Cavanagh, 1988-95; pvt. practice Law Office of Thomas M. Pace, 1995—. Mem. Mayor's Housing Task Force, Tucson, 1993; bd. dirs. Tucson Urban League, 1986-96; chmn. So. Ariz. Homebuilders Polit. Action Com., 1995, 96. Mem. So. Ariz. Homebuilders (tech. com), Stanford Club So. Ariz. Democrat. Office: 2525 E Broadway Blvd Ste 102 Tucson AZ 85716-5398 E-mail: tpace2@mindspring.com.

PACELLA, BERNARD LEONARDO, psychiatrist; b. Toronto, Ont., Can., July 25, 1912; m. Theresa Rita Domalakes; children: Karen Pacella Oldham, Richard B., Madelyn Joyce Nichols, Bernard Leonard Jr. BS, U. Colo., 1931, MD, 1935; postgrad., N.Y. Psychoanalytic Inst., 1946-51. Cert. child, adolescent, and adult psychoanalyst; Diplomate Am. Bd. Psychiatry and Neurology. Intern Kings County Hosp., Bklyn., 1935-37, resident in pediat., 1937-38; resident in psychiatry Columbia U. and N.Y. State Psychiat. Inst., N.Y.C., 1938-40; rsch. fellow in psychiatry Columbia Presbyn. Med. Ctr., 1940-41, instr. mil. psychiatry, 1943-46; lectr. clin. psychiatry Columbia U. Coll. Physicians and Surgeons, 1942-44; from assoc. clin. psychiatry to clin. prof. emeritus Columbia U., 1944-84; lectr., faculty Columbia U. Ctr. Pshychoanalytic Tng. and Rsch., 1984—; clin. prof. emeritus Columbia U., 1990—. Faculty Ctr. for Psychoanalytic Tng. and Rsch., Columbia U. Contbr. articles to profl. jours.; reviewer Psychoanalytic Quar. Pres. Margaret S. Mahler Psychiat. Rsch. Found., 1970-88, bd. dirs.; sec.-treas., bd. dirs. Sigmund Freud Archives; pres. Psychoanalytic Assistance Fund, 1974-89, bd. dirs.; bd. dirs. Freud London Mus.; co-trustee Mary S. Sigourney award, 1990. With Colo. N.G., 1930-35, M.C. USAR, 1935-40. Decorated Cavaliere Officiale dell Ordine al Merito (Italy), 1958. Fellow Am. Coll. Psychoanalysis, Am. Acad. Child and Adolescent Psychiatry, N.Y. Acad. Medicine, Am. Psychiat. Assn.; mem. AMA, Am. Soc. Adolescent Psychiatr, Am. Psychoanalytic Assn. (reviewer jour., pres.-elect 1990, pres. 1992—, treas. 1983—), Assn. Child Psychoanalysis, Group Advancement Psychiatry, Assn. Psychoanalytic Medicine, N.Y. Psychoanalytic Soc. and Inst. (bd. dirs.), Internat. Psychoanalytic Assn., N.Y. Psychiat. Soc., N.Y. Coun. Child and Adolescent Psychiatry, Alpha Omega Alpha. Home and Office: 115 E 61st St New York NY 10021-8183

PACH, PETER BARNARD, newspaper columnist and editor; b. Bklyn., Aug. 3, 1951; s. Stewart Warner and Constance (Barnard) P.; m. Kathleen Ann Megan, Sept. 7, 1985; children: Nell, Samuel. BA in English, Union Coll., 1973. Reporter Record Jour., Meriden, Conn., 1974-78, Wallingford bur. chief, 1978-83; Middletown bur. chief Hartford Courant, 1983-84, columnist, 1984-95; mem. editorial bd. Hartford (Conn.) Courant, 1992—. Vis. instr. Wesleyan U., Middletown, Conn., 1985—. Recipient First Bus. and Econ. Reporting award New England Press Ass., 1977. Mem. Dedham County and Polo Club. Avocations: running, skiing, golf, gardening, reading. Home: PO Box 46 Middle Haddam CT 06456-0046 Office: Hartford Courant 285 Broad St Hartford CT 06115-2510

PACHAN, MARY JUDE KATHRYN DOROTHY, guidance counselor; b. East Otto, N.Y., Jan. 29, 1933; d. Nicholas and Mary (Podolinsky) P. BS in Edn., Medaille Coll., 1964; MS in Edn., St. Bonaventure U., 1972. Cert. guidance counseling, N.Y., elem. edn. tchr., N.Y. 3d grade tchr. Holy Cross Sch., Buffalo, 1955-56; 3d and 4th grade tchr. Immaculata Heart of Mary Sch., 1956-60; 8th grade tchr. Our Lady of Loretta Sch., 1960-64; tchr. English DeSales High Sch., Lockport, N.Y., 1964-68; counselor campus ministry SUNY, Buffalo, 1968-72; counselor St. Joseph's Collegiate Inst., 1973—. Dir. guidance svcs. St. Joseph's Collegiate Inst., Buffalo, 1989-96. Grantee in English, Nazareth Coll., Rochester, N.Y., 1965, journalism grantee Wall St., Boston U., 1966. Mem. N.Y. State Pers. and Guidance Assn., Counseling and Devel. Hospice Tng., AACD. Avocations: cross country skiing, horseback riding, concerts. Home: 557 Burroughs Dr Amherst NY 14226-3900 Office: St Josephs Collegiate Inst 845 Kenmore Ave Buffalo NY 14223-3195

PACHECO, FELIPE RAMON, lawyer; b. Sagua la Grande, Las Villas, Cuba, Aug. 22, 1924; came to U.S., 1962; s. Felipe and Eugenia America (Rodriguez) P.; m. Maria Infiesta, Apr. 5, 1945; children: Carmen Pacheco Weber, Lilian C. Porter. D in philosophy and art, U. Havana, Cuba, 1947, D of laws, 1953; MS, Syracuse U., 1967; JD, U. Fla., 1975. Bar: Fla. 1975, U.S. Dist. Ct. (mid. dist.) Fla. 1976. Dir. librs. Ctrl. U. Las Villas, Santa Clara, Cuba, 1953-61; asst., assoc. catalog libr. Cornell U., Ithaca, N.Y., 1962-68, asst. law libr., 1969-70; law libr. Carlton, Fields, Tampa, Fla., 1971-75; pvt. practice, 1976—. Roman Catholic. Office: 4509 N Armenia Ave Tampa FL 33603-2703

PACHECO, MANUEL TRINIDAD, academic administrator; b. Rocky Ford, Colo., May 30, 1941; s. Manuel J. and Elizabeth (Lopez) P.; m. Karen M. King, Aug. 27, 1966; children: Daniel Mark, Andrew Charles, Sylvia Lois Elizabeth. BA, N.Mex. Highlands U., 1962; MA, Ohio State U., 1966, PhD, 1969. Prof. edn., univ. dean Tex. A&I U., Laredo, 1972-77, exec. dir. Bilingual Edn. Ctr., Kingsville, 1980-82; prof. multicultural edn., chmn. dept. San Diego State U., 1977-78; prof. Spanish and edn. Laredo State U., 1978-80, pres., 1984-88; assoc. dean Coll. Edn. U. Tex., El Paso, 1982-84, exec. dir. for planning, 1984; chief policy aide for edn. to gov. N.Mex., 1984; pres. U. Houston-Downtown, 1988-91, U. Ariz., Tucson, 1991-97, U. Mo. Sys., Columbia, 1997—. Cons. lang. divsn. Ency. Britannica, 1965-72; bd. dirs. Valley Nat. Bank Corp., Nat. Security Edn. Program, ASARCO; mem. exec. com. Bus.-Higher Edn. Forum. Co-editor: Handbook for Planning and Managing Instruction in Basic Skills for Limited English Proficient Students, 1983; producer: (videotapes) Teacher Training, 1976. Treas. adv. com. U.S. Commn. on Civil Rights, L.A., 1987-91; trustee United Way of Houston, 1988-91; chmn. pub. rels. Buffalo Bayou Partnership, Houston, 1988-91; bd. dirs. Ctr. for Addiction and Substance Abuse, Greater Tucson Econ. Coun., Ariz. Econ. Coun., Ariz. Town Hall. Recipient Disting. Alumnus award Ohio State U., Columbus, 1984; named Most Prominent Am.-Hispanics Spanish Today mag., 1984, one of 100 Outstanding Hispanics Hispanic bus., 1988, Man of Yr. Hispanic Profl. Action Com., 1991; Fulbright fellow U. de Montepellier, France, 1962. Mem. Am. Assn. State Colls. and Univs., Nat. Acad. of Pub. Adminstrn., Hispanic Assn. Colls. and Univs., Tex. Assn. of Chicanos in Higher Edn., Rotary, Phi Delta Kappa. Office: U Mo Sys Office of Pres 321 University Hall Columbia MO 65211-3020 Business E-Mail: pachecom@umsystem.edu.

PACHECO-RANSANZ, ARSENIO, Hispanic and Italian studies educator; b. Barcelona, Spain, Feb. 8, 1932; s. Arsenio Pacheco and Jacoba Ransanz-Alvarez; m. Mercedes Olivella-Sole, Sept. 1, 1956; children: Arsenio-Andrew, David-George. MA, U. Barcelona, 1954, PhD, 1958. Tutor Colegio Mayor Hispanoamericano Fray Junipero Serra, Barcelona, 1954-56; lectr. Hochschule für Wirtschaft und Sozialwissenschaften, Nurnberg, 1956; asst. lectr. U. Glasgow, Scotland, 1957-59; lectr. U. St. Andrews, Scotland, 1960-70; vis. prof. U. Pitts., 1966; prof. Hispanic and Italian studies U. B.C., Vancouver, Can., 1970-97, prof. emeritus, 1997—. Editor: Historia de Xacob Xalabin, 1964, Testament de Bernat Serradell, 1971, Varia fortuna del soldado Pindaro, 1975, Obres de Francesc de la Via, 1997; contbr. articles to profl. jours. Bd. dirs. Can. Fedn. Humanities, 1981-84. Fellow Royal Soc. Can.; mem. Can. Assn. Hispanists (pres. 1978-81), Asociacion Internacional de Hispanists, MLA, Assn. Hispanists Gt. Britain and Ireland, N.Am. Catalan Soc. (v.p. 1984-87, pres. 1987-90), Anglo Catalan Soc., Associacio Internacional de Llengua i Literatura Catalana. Roman Catholic. Office: U BC Dept Frnch Hispanic Ital Vancouver BC Canada V6T 1Z1 E-mail: arp@interchange.ubc.ca.

PACHMAN, DANIEL J. physician, educator; b. N.Y.C., Dec. 20, 1911; s. Louis and Ann (Kleinman) P.; m. Vivian Allison Futter, Nov. 8, 1935; children— Lauren Merle, Grace Allison. AB, U. N.C., 1931; MD, Duke U., 1934. Diplomate Nat. Bd. Med. Examiners, Am. Bd. Pediatrics. Intern pediatrics U. Chgo., 1934-35, instr. pediatrics, 1937-40; intern pediatrics N.Y. Hosp., 1935-36; resident pediatrics, attending pediatrician Duke Hosp., Durham, N.C., 1936-37; instr. Duke U., 1936-37, Northwestern U., 1940-42; practice medicine specializing in pediatrics Chgo., 1940-96; ret., 1996; clin. asst. prof. pediatrics U. Ill., 1950-59, clin. assoc. prof., 1960-67, clin. prof., 1967-81, emeritus prof., 1981—. Attending pediatrician Ill. Research and Edn. Hosp., 1950-81; cons. Presbyn.-St. Luke's Hosp., Chgo., 1971-81, South Shore Hosp., 1955-60, Ill. Central Hosp., 1970-72, chmn. dept. pediatrics, 1962-70; attending pediatrician Trinity Hosp., 1971— ; prof. pediatrics Rush Med. Coll., 1971-81, emeritus prof., 1981— ; staff Children's Meml. Hosp.; courtesy staff Chgo. Lying-in Hosp; Med. cons. Bd. Edn., S. Shore High Sch., 1954-56; mem. advisory com. on sch. health Chgo. Bd. Health, 1962— , Chgo. Bd. Edn., 1962-66; pediatric cons. Ill. Council for Mentally Retarded Children, 1960-66; chmn. subcom. on sch. health Chgo. Med. Sch., 1961-67; chmn. Ill. Pediatric Coordinating Council, 1969-76 Contbr. numerous articles to profl. jours. Mem. com. on rights of minors Ill. Commn. on Children, 1975-77; mem. Mayor's Com. on Sch. Bd. Nominations, 1965-68; mem., co-chmn. Ill. Bd. for Opinions on Profl. Nursing, 1980— . Served to lt. col. M.C. U.S. Army, 1942-46. Recipient Archibald L. Hoyne award Chgo. Pediatric Soc., 1977 Fellow Am. Acad. Pediatrics (mem. exec. com. Ill. 1961-69, rep. to adv. council on child health Nat. Congress Parents and Tchrs., chmn. sci. exhibits com. 1964-72), Am. Cancer Soc. (pub. edn. com. 1967-69), Chgo. Inst. Medicine (mem.-at-large jt. com. on sch. services 1961-64), Chgo. Med. Soc. (past chmn. child health com.), Chgo. Pediatric Soc., AMA (med./edn. com. on sch. and coll. health), Phi Beta Kappa, Sigma Xi. Clubs: Quadrangle (bd. dirs. 1969-72), Carlton. Home: 1212 N Lake Shore Dr Chicago IL 60610-2371 *Knowledge, perception and an outlook of acceptance and encouragement make the life of a pediatrician an interesting and disciplined adventure.*

PACHMAN, FREDERIC CHARLES, library director; b. Paterson, N.J., Apr. 16, 1952; s. Morris J. and Barbara M. (Haagen) P.; m. Donna Kearns, May 2, 1982; children: Rick, Kristina. BA, Syracuse U., 1973; MLS, Columbia U., 1976; cert., Rutgers U., New Brunswick, N.J., 1996. Libr. dir. Hamilton Twp. (N.J.) Pub. Libr., 1981-83, Middletown Twp. (N.J.) Pub. Libr., 1983-85, Monmouth Med. Ctr., Long Branch, N.J., 1985—. Mem. exec. bd. Hist. Soc. Ocean Grove, N.J., 1985—. Interagy. Coun. on Info. Resources for Nursing, N.Y.C., 1985—; cons. Caucus Archival Program Evaluation Svc., N.J., 1990—; mem. adv. com. on preservation and access N.J. State Libr., 1992-95. Contbr. articles to profl. jours. Asst. scoutmaster troop 32 Boy Scouts Am., River Plaza, N.J., 1993—. Mem. ALA, N.J. Libr. Assn., Med. Libr. Assn., League Hist. Socs. N.J., Mid Atlantic Regional Archives Conf., Acad. Health Info. Profls. (disting.), Monmouth Librs. Assn. (pres. 1985-86, 1999-2000), Order of the Arrow (brotherhood mem.). Avocations: backpacking, reading, historic preservation, archives, kayaking. Office: Monmouth Med Ctr 300 2d Ave Long Branch NJ 07740-6300 E-mail: fpachman@sbhcs.com.

PACHNER, JOAN HELEN, art historian, curator; b. N.Y.C., Oct. 14, 1956; d. Charles W. and Janice F. (Frenkel) P.; m. Richard A. Newman, Sept. 24, 1989; children: David, Joshua. BA in Art History cum laude, Conn. Coll., New London, 1978; MA, NYU, 1982, PhD, 1993. Guest curator Cooper-Hewitt Mus., N.Y.C., 1982; organizer, cataloger Estate of Theodore Roszak, 1983-84; cataloger Hans Namuth, 1984; rsch. asst. NYU Inst. Fine Arts, 1983-85, Stuart Davis Catalogue Raisonné, N.Y.C., 1985-86; guest co-curator Westfälisches Landesmuseum, Münster, Germany, 1988; photo rschr., editl. prodr. Mus. Modern Art, N.Y.C., 1990, curatorial asst., 1995; curator Storm King Art Ctr., Mountainville, N.Y., 1993—; cons. archivist, curator Estate of David Smith, N.Y.C., 1994—. Lect. various galleries, colls. and art ctrs.; cons. Mus. Modern Art, N.Y.C. 1998 exhibit; vis. assoc. prof. dept. fine arts NYU, summer 2001. Contbr. articles to profl. jours. Mem. Coll. Art Assn., Am. Assn. Museums, Art Table. Democrat. Jewish. Avocations: bicycle riding, movies, reading, swimming, museums. Home: 56 Midvale Rd Hartsdale NY 10530 Office: Storm King Art Ctr PO Box 280 Old Pleasant Hill Rd Mountainville NY 10953-0280 E-mail: jpachner@aol.com.

PACHOLSKI, RICHARD FRANCIS, retired securities company executive, financial advisor, consultant; b. Seattle, June 18, 1947; s. Theodore Francis and Nellie (Tarabochia) P.; m. Dorothy Irene Nelson, May 25, 1974; children: Nicolas, Tara. BA cum laude, U. Wash., 1969, MBA summa cum laude, 1970. CPA, Wash. Mgr. Arthur Andersen & Co., Seattle, 1970-76; v.p., contr. SNW Enterprises, 1976-82; sr. v.p., treas., sec., dir. Seattle N.W. Securities, 1982-93; cons. Carl & Co., Portland, Oreg., 1984-88, Ellis & Carl Inc., Portland, 1979-83; pres. R. Pacholski, P.C., Redmond, Wash., 1979—. Adj. prof. U. Wash., Seattle, 1976-80. Mem. AICPA, Nat. Assn. Securities Dealers (past bd. dirs. local dist.), Wash. Athletic Club, PacWest Club (Redmond, Wash.). Roman Catholic. Home and Office: 5060 164th Ct NE Redmond WA 98052-5294 E-mail: pacholski@prodigy.net.

PACHT, ERIC REED, pulmonary and critical care physician; b. Madison, Wis., Mar. 24, 1954; s. Asher Roger and Perle (Landau) P.; m. Karen Sue Dalpiaz, Aug. 7, 1982; children: Ben, Lora. BA summa cum laude, Lawrence U., 1976; MD cum laude, U. Wis., Madison, 1980. Diplomate Nat. Bd. Med. Examiners, Am. Bd. Internal Medicine. Intern, resident Ohio State U. Hosps., 1980-83, fellow in pulmonary and critical care medicine, 1983-86; asst. prof. Ohio State U., 1986-91, assoc. prof., 1991-99; staff phys. Mt. Carmel Med. Ctr. and St. Annis Hosp., Columbus, Ohio, 1999-01, Licking Meml. Heatlh Profls., Columbus, 2001—. Asst. dir. pulmonary and critical care Ohio State U., 1988-96, dir. pulmonary and critical care fellowship tng. program, 1988-99, med. sch. rep. to Am. Fedn. for Clin. Rsch., 1990-94, med. dir. lung transplantation program, 1992-95, dir. clin. rsch., 1993-99. Contbr. articles to profl. jours. Vol. Am. Lung Assn., Columbus, Ohio, Columbus Cancer Clinic. Recipient numerous rsch. awards. Fellow Am. Coll. Chest Physicians; mem. Am. Thoracic Soc., Ohio Thoracic Soc., Am. Fedn. Clin. Rsch., Phi Beta Kappa. Achievements include description of new form of respiratory failure and emphysema in patients with HIV. Home: 1224 Leicester Pl Columbus OH 43235-2181 Office: Bldg 6 1272 W Main St Newark OH 43055 E-mail: EPacht@aol.com.

PACHTER, IRWIN JACOB, pharmaceutical consultant; b. N.Y.C., July 15, 1925; s. Nathan and Ethel Lillian (Thomases) P.; m. Elaine Anna White, Aug. 23, 1953; children: Wendy, Jonathan. BS, UCLA, 1947; MS, U. N.Mex., 1949; PhD, U. So. Calif., 1951; postgrad., U. Ill., 1951-52, Harvard U., 1952-53. Research chemist Ethyl Corp., 1953-55; asso. research chemist Smith Kline & French, 1955-62, asst. sec. head, 1962; dir. medicinal chemistry Endo Labs., 1962-66; dir. research Endo div. du Pont Co., 1967-70; v.p. research and devel. Bristol Labs. div. Bristol-Myers Co., 1970-82; lectr. Adelphi U., 1963-69. Contbr. articles to profl. jours.; patentee in field Trustee Gordon Research Conf., 1972-75; chmn. medicinal chemistry study group Walter Reed Inst. Research, 1975-77. Served with USN, 1944-46. Mem. Am. Chem. Soc. (chmn. div. medicinal chemistry 1974-76), Pharm. Mfrs. Assn. (chmn. research and devel. sect. 1975-76) Home: 101 Woodberry Ln Fayetteville NY 13066-1745

PACHTER, LEE M. pediatrician; b. Bklyn., Mar. 12, 1957; s. Harvey Leonard and Rosalind Blau Pachter. BA, Franklin & Marshall Coll., 1979; DO, Phila. Coll. Osteopathic Med., 1983. Diplomate Am. Bd. Osteopathic Physicians. Intern Metro. Hosp., Springfield, Pa., 1983-84; resident in pediatrics St. Christopher's Hosp. Children, Phila., 1984-87; fellow in pediatrics Children's Hosp. Phila., 1987-89; from asst. prof. to assoc. prof. pediats. and anthropology U. Conn. Sch. Medicine, Farmington, 1989—, head divsn. gen. pediat., 1998—. Trustee The Artists Collective, Hartford, Conn., 1989—. Fellow Am. Acad. Pediatrics, Soc. Applied Anthropology; mem. Am. Anthropol. Assn., Ambulatory Pediat. Assn., Soc. Rsch. & Child Devel., Soc. Applied Anthropology. Office: St Francis Hosp & Med Ctr 114 Woodland St Hartford CT 06105-1208 E-mail: lpachter@stfranciscare.org.

PACI, PIERELLA, economist; b. Rome, Italy, Aug. 18, 1957; d. Orazio and Rosa (Galassetti) P.; m. Adam Wagstaff, July 15, 1989; children: Benedict, Lilli Ruth. Grad., U. Rome, 1980; diploma, U. York, Eng., 1981; PhD, U. Manchester, Eng., 1986. Lectr. U. Sussex, Brighton, Eng., 1985-89; from lectr. to sr. lectr. City U., London, 1989-99; hon. rsch. fellow Inst. Edn., 1994—; sr. economist World Bank, Washington, 1998—; regional gender coord. Europe and Ctrl. Asia. Author: Wage Differentials between Men and Women: Evidence from Cohort Studies, 1996, Unequal Pay for Women and Men, 1998 (Noteworthy Books in Indsl. Rels. and Labor Econs. award 1999); contbr. articles to profl. jours. including Jour. Health Econs., Social Sci. and Medicine, Jour. Human Resources, Cambridge Jour. Econs., others. Office: The World Bank 1818 H St NW Washington DC 20433-0002

PACIFIC, JOSEPH NICHOLAS, JR. educator; b. Honolulu, Oct. 27, 1950; s. Joseph Nicholas Sr. and Christine Mary (Mondelli) P.; m. Paulette Kay Miller, July 7, 1975. BA in Math., BS in Biology, BSEE, Gonzaga U., 1974; MMSc in Clin. Microbiology, Emory U., 1978. Cert. tchr., Hawaii, Wash. Rsch. specialist Ctr. Disease Control, Atlanta, 1978-82; supr. Joe Pacific Shoe Repair, Honolulu, 1983; lab. technician Mont. State U., Bozeman, 1984; sci. tchr. Hawaii Preparatory Acad., Kamuela, 1985-87; unit mgr. Hawaii Med. Service Assn., Honolulu, 1987-88; tchr. biology St. Andrew's Priory Sch., 1988—. Mem. Nat. Registry Microbiologists, Sigma Xi, Pi Mu Epsilon, Phi Sigma, Kappa Delta Pi, Alpha sigma Nu. Avocations: microscopy, bicycling. Office: St Andrews Priory Sch 224 Queen Emma Sq Honolulu HI 96813-2388

PACIFICO, ALBERT DOMINICK, cardiovascular surgeon; b. Bklyn., Sept. 24, 1940; s. Dominick Vincent and Amelia Catherine (Jannelli) P.; m. Vicki Lynne Overton, May 16, 1980; children: Albert D., Nicole M., Paul V. BS, St. Johns U., 1960; MD, N.J. Coll. Medicine, 1964. Diplomate Am. Bd. Surgery, Am. Bd. Thoracic Surgery. Med. intern Jersey City Med. Ctr., Seton Gall Coll. Medicine, 1964-65; asst. resident in surgery Mayo Clinic, Rochester, Minn., 1965-67; research fellow in surgery U. Ala., Birmingham, 1967-69, sr. resident, then chief resident surgery, resident in thoracic and cardiovascular surgery, 1968-72, mem. faculty dept. surgery, 1970—, prof. surgery, 1978-83, John W. Kirklin prof. cardiovascular surgery, 1983—, vice chmn. dept. surgery, 1990, dir. div. cardiothoracic surgery, 1984—, dir. Congenital Heart Disease Diagnosis and Treatment Ctr., 1985—. Mem. staff gen., thoracic and cardiovascular surgery Univ. Hosp., Birmingham, 1972—, VA Hosp., Birmingham, 1972—; mem. staff Children's Hosp., Birmingham, 1971—, chief gen., thoracic and cardiovascular surgery, 1984—. Author: (with others) Pediatric Cardiac Surgery, 1985, Cardiology, 1985, Textbook of Surgery, 13th edit., 1986, The Treatment of Congenital Cardiac Anomalies, 1986, Perspectives in Pediatric Cardiology, 1988, Current Therapy in Cardiothoracic Surgery, 1989, Decision Making in Surgery of the Chest, 1989, Cardiac Surgery: Cyanotic Congenital Heart Disease, 1989, Reoperation in Cardiac Surgery, 1989, others; mem. editorial bd. Am. Jour. Cardiology, 1983—, Heart and Vessel, 1985—, Jour. Cardiac Surgery, 1985—; cons. editorial referee Ala. Jour. Med. Scis., 1974-75; contbr. articles to med. jours. Fellow ACS, Am. Coll. Cardiology, Am. Surg. Assn.; mem. AMA, Ala. State Med. Soc., Jefferson County Med. Soc., Am. Heart Assn. (Paul Dudley White Internat. Svc. Citation 1977), Am. Assn. Thoracic Surgery, Soc. Thoracic Surgeons, Am. Surg. Soc., Internat. Coll. Pediatrics, John Kirklin Soc., Congenital Heart Surgeons Soc., Assn. Acad. Surgery, Ala. chpt. Mayo Clinic Alumni Assn., Panamanian Soc. Cardiology (hon.), Peruvian Soc. Thoracic and Cardiovascular Surgery (hon.), Soc. Nat. Inst. Cardiology Mex. (hon.), Cardiac Soc. Australia and New Zealand (corr.), Peruvian Soc. Cardiology (corr.), Alpha Omega Alpha. Republican. Roman Catholic. Office: Univ Ala UAB Sta Dept Surgery Birmingham AL 35294-0001

PACIN, MICHAEL P. internist, allergist; b. Chgo., Jan. 9, 1944; AB magna cum laude, Washington U., St. Louis, 1965, MD, 1969. Diplomate Am. Bd. Internal Medicine, Am. Bd. Allergy and Immunology. Intern Jewish Hosp., St. Louis, 1969-70, resident in internal medicine, 1970-71, Jackson Meml. Hosp., Miami, Fla., 1971-72; fellow in allergy and immunology Long Beach (Calif.) VA Hosp., 1972-74; asst. prof. family medicine U. Miami (Fla.), 1974-84; pvt. practice Miami, 1974—. Mem. Am. Acad. Allergy, Asthma and Immunology, Am. Coll. Allergy, Asthma and Immunology, Fla. Med. Assn., Dade County Med. Assn., Fla. Allergy and Immunology Soc., Joint Coun. Allergy and Immunology, Phi Beta Kappa. Office: Fla Ctr for Allergy and Asthma 8970 SW 87th Ct Ste 100 Miami FL 33176-2207 also: 4302 Alton Rd Ste 840 Miami Beach FL 33140-2899

PACINO, AL (ALFREDO JAMES PACINO), actor; b. N.Y.C., Apr. 25, 1940; s. Salvatore and Rose P. Student, High Sch. of Performing Arts, N.Y.C., Actors Studio, from 1966. Formerly mail deliverer editorial offices Commentary Mag.; formerly messenger, movie theatre usher, bldg. supt.; co-artistic dir. The Actors Studio, Inc., N.Y.C., 1982-84. Served apprenticeship as actor, dir. and comedy writer in Off-Off Broadway theatres, Elaine Stewart's Cafe La Mama, Julian Beck & Judith Malina's Living Theatre; appeared in New Theatre Workshop prodn. of The Peace Creeps, Dec., 1966; joined Charles Playhouse, Boston, fall, 1967, and performed in New Theatre Workshop prodn. of America Hurrah and Awake and Sing; appeared in a one-act play Off Broadway The Indian Wants the Bronx, opened Astor Pl. Theater on Jan. 17, 1968 (Obie as best actor in Off-Broadway prodn. 1967-68); made Broadway debut in Does A Tiger Wear A Necktie?, 1969 (Tony award as best dramatic actor in a supporting role, named most promising new Broadway actor in a Variety poll of metropolitan drama critics); appeared in The Local Stigmatic at Actors Playhouse, N.Y.C., opening 1969; joined Repertory Theater of Lincoln Center, N.Y.C.; other plays include The Basic Training of Pavlo Hummel, Boston Repertory Theater, 1972, Camino Real, Richard III, 1973, 79, Jungle of Cities, 1979, The Connection, Hello Out There, Tiger at the Gates, American Buffalo, Julius Caesar, 1988, Salome, Chinese Coffee, Circle in the Square, 1992, Dir. and Performer, Hughie, 1996; (films) debut in Me, Natalie, 1969, Panic in Needle Park, 1971, The Godfather, 1972 (Best Actor award Nat. Soc. Film Critics, Acad. award nominee), Scarecrow, 1973, Serpico, 1973 (Acad. award nominee), The Godfather, Part II, 1974 (Acad. award nominee), Dog Day Afternoon (Acad. award nominee), 1975, Bobby Deerfield, 1977, And Justice for All, 1979 (Acad. Award nomination), Cruising, 1980, Author! Author!, 1982, Scarface, 1983, Revolution, 1985, Sea of Love, 1990, Dick Tracy, 1990 (Acad. award nominee), The Godfather Part III, 1990, Frankie and Johnny, 1991, Glengarry Glen Ross, 1992 (Acad. award nominee), Scent of a Woman, 1992 (Acad. award for Best Actor), Carlito's Way, 1993, Two Bits, 1994, Heat, 1995, City Hall, 1996, Donny Brasco, 1996, Devil's Advocate, 1997, Chinese Coffee, 1999, Man of the People, 1999, Any Given Sunday, 1999; actor, prodr., dir., writer Looking for Richard, 1996. Recipient Am. Comedy award film Dick Tracy, 1991. Office: CAA care Rick Nicita 9830 Wilshire Blvd Beverly Hills CA 90212-1804

PACIS, JOANN FIDES, pediatrics nurse; b. Lakewood, Nj, June 7, 1974; d. Romeo and Carmencita Villena Pacis. BS, Rutgers U., Newark, NJ, 1993—96, MS, 1996—2000. Cert. Emergency Nurse, Emergency Nurses Assn., Registered Nurse, ANCC, Clinical Nurse Specialist, ANCC, registered Advanced Nurse Practitioner, ANCC. Rn Kimball Med. Ctr., Lakewood, NJ, 1996—2001; lectr. Rutgers U., Newark, 1999—2001; pnp Pvt. Practice, Toms River, 2000—01; rn practitioner/clin. nurse specialist Lee Meml. Health Sys., Fort Myers, Fla., 2001—. Mem.: Am. Assn. of Nurse Practitioners, AAUP, Emergency Nurses Assn. Avocations: piano, cello, spanish and italian languages. Office: Lee Memorial Health System 2776 Cleveland Ave Fort Myers FL 33901 Office Fax: 239-336-6899. E-mail: joann.pacis@leememorial.org.

PACK, ALLEN S. retired coal company executive; b. Bramwell, W.Va., Dec. 11, 1930; s. Paul Meador and Mable Blanche (Hale) P.; m. Glenna Rae Christian, June 21, 1952; children: Allen Scott Jr., David Christian, Mark Frederick, Andrew Ray. BS, W.Va. U., 1952. Gen. mgr. Island Coal Co., Holden, W.Va., 1969-70, pres., 1970-73, v.p. adminstrn. Lexington, Ky., 1973-75; exec. v.p. Cannelton Holding Co., Charleston, W.Va., 1975-77, pres., chief ops. officer, 1977-80, pres., chief exec. officer, 1980-91; chmn., 1991-93; ret., 1993. Bd. dirs. Bucksin coun. Boy Scouts Am., Charleston, 1976—, pres., 1980, chmn., 1994, 95, 96; bd. dirs. W.Va. Univ. Found., Morgantown, 1978-96; trustee Davis and Elkins Coll., 1981. Capt. USMC, 1952-54. Recipient Silver Beaver award Boy Scouts Am., 1981; inductee W.Va. Coal Hall of Fame, 1998. Presbyterian. E-mail: pack747@webtv.net.

PACK, BOBIGENE, minister; b. Sumter, S.C., Mar. 3, 1949; d. Altomount Pack and Maybelle Farmer Thompson; m. Albert Alonzo Turner (div.); children: Kwind, Emory Harrison Turner; m. Jesse Miller (div.). Student, U. S.C., 1974; cert., Forsyth Tech., 1983; diploma, Rhema Bible Tng. Ctr., 2000. Owner, adminstr. New Beginnings Assisted Living, Winston-Salem, NC, 1983—97; founder, pres. Love in Action Outreach, Ellenwood, Ga., 1998—; founder, radio personality Your Dreams Can Come True, Tulsa, Okla., 2000—01. Active The Salvation Army Child Devel. Ctrs., Tulsa, 1998—99. Office: Love in Action Outreach PO Box 766 Ellenwood GA 30294

PACK, LEONARD BRECHER, lawyer; b. Seattle, Feb. 7, 1944; s. Howard David and Vivian (Brecher) P.; m. Barbara-Jane Lunin (div. Sept. 1978); children: Jesse, Justin; m. Adele Susan Weisman, Jan. 7, 1979; 1 child, Anna Rae. BA, Columbia U., 1966, JD, MIA, Columbia U., 1970. Bar: N.Y. 1971. Law clk. to judge U.S. Ct. Appeals D.C. Circuit, 1970-71; assoc. Fried, Frank, Harris, Shriver & Jacobson, N.Y.C., 1971-78; sec., assoc. gen. counsel Metromedia, Inc., Secaucus, N.J., 1979-86; sr. v.p., gen. counsel Orion Pictures Corp., N.Y.C., 1986-90; ptnr. Berger Steingut & Stern, 1990-93; pvt. practice, 1993—. Bd. dirs., v.p. Dance Theatre Workshop. Mem. ABA. Democrat. Jewish. Avocation: music. Office: 116 John St Fl 33 New York NY 10038 Fax: 212-847-7955.

PACK, NANCY J. special education educator, speech therapist; b. Santa Monica, Calif., May 28, 1952; d. James Neil and Muriel Elaine (Stone) Hess; m. Albert Richard Pack, Mar. 22, 1986; children: Ember, Andrea, Galen. BA in Speech/Drama, Chico State U., 1975, MA in Speech Pathology, 1977. Cert. in early childhood spl. edn., Wash. Lang. disorders specialist Shasta County Office of Edn., Redding, Calif., 1977-80; tchr. hearing impaired Tehama County Dept. Edn., Red Bluff, 1983-89, speech and lang. pathologist, 1983-89, spl. edn. tchr., 1989-94, North Kitsap Sch. Dist., Poulsbo, Wash., 1994—. Mem. adv. bd. Spl. Edn. Steering Com., Poulsbo, 1996-97, Spl. Edn. Tech. Com., Poulsbo, 1997-98; presenter in field. Tchr. adult edn. Tehama County Dept. Edn., Red Bluff, 1980-82. Recipient Tchr. of Yr. award Tehama County Edn. Found., 1992-93, Exemplary Educator award Calif. Coun. for Edn. Exceptional Children, 1993-94."Who" award Redd ing Svc. Ctr. Coun. of Calif. Tchrs. Assn., 1993. Mem. Am. Speech and Lang. Assn. (cert. clin. competence), Tehama County Cert. Employees Assn. (pres. 1988-94), Coun. for Exceptional Children, Nat. Assn. Edn. of Young Children, Wash. Educators Assn. Avocations: backpacking, mountain climbing, cross country skiing, windsurfing, camping. Home: 2255 Dalarna Ct NE Poulsbo WA 98370-7590

PACK, RUSSELL T. theoretical chemist; b. Grace, Idaho, Nov. 20, 1937; s. John Terrell and Mardean (Izatt) P.; m. Marion Myrth Hassell, Aug. 21, 1962; children: John R., Nathan H., Allen H., Miriam, Elizabeth, Quinn R., Howard H. BS, Brigham Young U., 1962; PhD, U. Wis., 1967. Postdoctoral fellow U. Minn., Mpls., 1966-67; asst. prof. Brigham Young U., Provo, 1967-71, assoc. prof., 1971-75, adj. prof., 1975-88; staff scientist Los Alamos (N.Mex.) Nat. Lab., 1975-83, fellow, 1983—, assoc. grp. leader, 1979-81. Vis. prof. Max Planck Institut, Gottingen, 1981; chmn. Gordon Rsch. Conf., 1982; lectr. in field. Contbr. articles to profl. jours. Named Sr. U.S. Scientist, Alexander Vol Humboldt Found., 1981. Fellow Am. Phys. Soc. (sec.-treas. div. Chem. Physics 1990-93); mem. Am. Chem. Soc., Sigma Xi. Mem. Ch. of Jesus Christ of Latter Day Saints. Home: 240 Kimberly Ln Los Alamos NM 87544-3526 Office: Los Alamos Nat Lab T 12 Ms # B268 Los Alamos NM 87545-0001 E-mail: pack@lanl.gov.

PACK, SANDRA L. federal agency administrator; Bus. degree, Notre Dame Coll. CPA. Dir. of treasury Bush for Pres., Inc., Bush-Cheney 2000, Inc.; dep. dir. treasury Bob Dole for Pres., Inc., Washington; dir. treasury Phil Gramm for Pres., Inc.; dir. planning and ops. MicroProse divsn. Spectrum Holobyte, Inc., Hunt Valley, Md.; dir. small bus. cons. and acctg. svcs. Ernst & Young, Balt., dir. microcomputer consulting and acctg. svcs. Atlanta; asst. sec. Army for fin. mgmt., contr. Dept. Def., Washington, 2001—. Office: Dept Def 109 Army Pentagon Washington DC 20310-0109

PACK, SUSAN JOAN, art consultant; b. N.Y.C., June 15, 1951; d. Howard Meade and Nancy (Buckley) P. BA summa cum laude, Princeton U., 1973. Copywriter Laurence Charles & Free, N.Y.C., 1978-83, Warwick Advt., N.Y.C., 1983-85; sr. copywriter Saatchi & Saatchi Compton, 1985-88; pres. The Pack Collection, 1989—. Author: Film Posters of the Russian Avant-Garde, 1995. Mem. Princeton (N.J.) U. Libr. Coun., 1985-93; trustee Pack Found. for Med. Rsch., N.Y., 1983—; bd. dirs. The Poster Soc., N.Y., 1985-87. Recipient 4 Clio awards, 1981, 1 Clio award, 1982; named one of top art collectors under 40 Art and Antiques Mag., 1985, one of top 100 collectors in U.S., 1996. Mem. Phi Beta Kappa. E-mail: spdesign@pacbell.net.

PACKARD, JOHN MALLORY, physician; b. Saranac Lake, N.Y., Sept. 25, 1920; s. Edward Newman and Mary Bissell (Betts) P.; m. Ann Maurine Schoonover, June 15, 1944; children: Michael David, John Mallory, Ann Maurine, Mary Betts, Charles Edward, Kris Asvananda, Frank Schoonover, Charlotte Mellen. BA, Yale U., 1942; MD, Harvard U., 1945. Diplomate Am. Bd. Internal Medicine. Intern Presbyn. Hosp., N.Y.C., 1945-46; resident in internal medicine Peter Bent Brigham Hosp., Boston, 1948-49; practice medicine specializing in internal medicine and cardiology Pensacola, Fla., 1954-68; prof. medicine, asso. dean Med. Sch. U. Ala., Birmingham, 1968-76; exec. dir. Ala. Regional Med. Program, 1968-73; corp. v.p. med. edn. Bapt. Med. Centers, 1976-92; ret. Contbr. articles to med. jours. Served with USN, 1946-54. Fellow ACP, Am. Coll. Cardiology, AHA; mem. Jefferson County Med. Soc., Med. Assn. Ala., AMA, Am. Soc. Internal Medicine, Ala. Soc. Internal Medicine (pres. 1981-82), Alpha Omega Alpha. Republican. Episcopalian.

PACKARD, MILDRED RUTH, middle school educator; b. Boulder, Colo., Sept. 8, 1947; d. Peter L.M. and Jane G. Packard. BA, Lynchburg Coll., 1969; MS, Va. Poly. Inst. and State U., 1973. Cert. phys. edn. tchr., Va. Tchr., basketball, gymnastics and track coach Osbourn High Sch., Manassas, Va., 1969-73; tchr., coach girls softball, basketball and volleyball Rippon Mid. Sch., Woodbridge, 1973-89, athletic dir., 1982-89; tchr., athletic dir., volleyball coach Lake Ridge Mid. Sch., 1989—. Mem. NEA, AAHPERD, Va. Edn. Assn., Prince William Edn. Assn., Va. Assn. Health, Phys. Edn., and Recreation. Avocations: volleyball, golf, reading. Office: Lake Ridge Mid Sch 12350 Mohican Rd Woodbridge VA 22192-1757

PACKARD, PETER, medical educator, retired internist; b. Evanston, Ill., Mar. 14, 1927; s. George and Marianna (Dickinson) P.; m. Jenifer Carr, Aug. 28, 1951 (div. 1969); m. Mary Jane P., Nov. 8, 1969; children: Patricia Ann Langlais, Charles Barklay Langlais, Georgia Packard, Caroline L. Gregger, Louise Moskowitz-Packard, Victoria P. Aase, Adam L. Packard. BA, U. Calif., Berkeley, 1945; MD, U. Calif., San Francisco, 1948. Diplomate Am. Bd. Internal Medicine. Intern San Francisco Gen. Hosp., 1948-49; vol. arzt fellow infectious diseases Children's Hosp., Zurich, 1949-50; asst. res. in medicine Franklin Hosp., U. Calif., San Francisco, 1950-51; capt., med. corps USAF, Riverside, Calif., 1951-53; asst. res. medicine Ft. Miley VA Hosp., San Francisco, 1953-54, U. Calif. Hosp., San Francisco, 1954-55; pvt. practice Mills Hosp., Peninsula Med. Lab., San Mateo, Burlingame, Calif., 1955-91. Med. dir., vice chmn. bd. dirs., Peninsula Med. Lab., Menlo Park, Calif., 1980-94; chief of medicine, chief of staff Mills Hosp., San Mateo, 1967-74; assoc. clin. prof. medicine, U. Calif. San Francisco, 1955—. Founding trustee, v.p. Mills-Peninsula Found., 1974-90, trustee emeritus, 1990—; pres., mem. bd. San Mateo County Heart Assn., 1964-74. Capt. M.C., USAFR, 1951-53, Korea. Mem. AMA, Calif. Med. Assn., San Mateo County Med. Assn. (various coms., bd. dirs., 1959-91), Am. Soc. Internal Medicine, Calif. Soc. Internal Medicine (del. off and on 1960-93), Calif. Soc. Medicine, U. Calif. San Francisco Assn. Clin. Faculty. Avocations: tennis, golf, teaching, history, politics. Home and Office: 720 Seabury Rd Hillsborough CA 94010-6532

PACKARD, ROCHELLE SYBIL, elementary school educator; b. June 25, 1951; d. Dave Wallace and Jeanette (Goddy) P. BA in Early Childhood Edn., Point Park Coll., 1973; MEd in Elem. Edn., U. Pitts., 1975. Instrnl. II permanent tchg. cert., Pa. Substitute tchr. Pitts. Pub. Bd. Edn., 1973-77, tchr. kindergarted, 1st grade, 2d grade, 1977—. Chair Israel Day Parade, Pitts., 1981; mem. Hadassah, Pitts., 1983—, Pioneer Women, Pitts., 1982—, ORT, Pitts., 1975—. Mem. Pitts. Fedn. Tchrs., Pitts. State Edn. Agy. Democrat. Jewish. Home: 4100 Lydia St Pittsburgh PA 15207-1135

PACKARD, RONALD C. former congressman; b. Meridian, Idaho, Jan. 19, 1931; m. Jean Sorenson, 1952; children: Chris, Debbie, Jeff, Vicki, Scott, Lisa, Theresa. Student, Brigham Young U., 1948-50, Portland State U., 1952-53; D.MD, U. Oreg., Portland, 1953-57. Gen. practice dentistry, Carlsbad, Calif., 1959-82; mem. 98th-106th Congresses from 48th (formerly 43d) Calif. dist., 1983-2001; chmn. appropriations legis. com.; former mem. pub. works and transp. com., sci., space, tech.; also chmn. appropriations fgn. ops. and transp. subcoms. Mem. Carlsbad Sch. Dist. Bd., 1962-74; bd. dirs. Carlsbad C. of C., 1972-76; mem. Carlsbad Planning Commn., 1974-76, Carlsbad City Coun., 1976-78; Carlsbad chmn. Boy Scouts Am., 1977-79; mayor City of Carlsbad, 1978-82; mem. North County Armed Svcs. YMCA, North County Transit Dist., San Diego Assn. Govts., Coastal Policy Com., Transp. Policy Com.; pres. San Diego div. Calif. League of Cities. Served with Dental Corps USN, 1957-59. Republican. Mem. Ch. LDS.*

PACKARD, SANDRA PODOLIN, education educator, consultant; b. Buffalo, Sept. 13, 1942; d. Mathew and Ethel (Zolte) P.; m. Martin Packard, Aug. 2, 1964; children: Dawn Esther, Shana Fanny BFA, Syracuse U., 1964; MSEd, Ind. U., 1966, EdD, 1973. Cert. tchr. art K-12, N.Y. Asst. prof. art SUNY-Buffalo, 1972-74; assoc. prof. art Miami U., Oxford, Ohio, 1974-81, spl. asst. to provost, 1979-80, assoc. provost, spl. programs, 1980-81; dean Coll. Edn. Bowling Green State U., 1981-85; provost and vice chancellor for acad. affairs U. Tenn., Chattanooga, 1985-92; pres. Oakland U., Rochester, Mich., 1992-95, prof. edn., 1995—; sr. fellow, dir. tech. in edn. Am. Assn. State Colls. and Univs., 1995; coord. Nat. Coun. for Accreditation of Tchr. Edn., Washington, 1995—2001. Cons. Butler County Health Ctr., Hamilton, Ohio, 1976-78; vis. prof. art therapy Simmons Coll., 1979, Mary Mount Coll., Milw., 1981; bd. dirs. SE Ctr. for Arts in Edn., 1994-96; mem. corp. adv. com. Corp. Detroit Mag., 1994-95; cons. Univ. of the North, South Africa Project of the Am. Coun. on Edn., 1995; bd. mem. Fellows Coun. Am. Coun. on Edn., 1994-96. Sr. editor Studies in Art Edn. jour., 1979-81; editorial adv. bd. Jour. Aesthetic Edn., 1984-90; editor: The Leading Edge, 1986; contbr. articles to profl. jours., chpts. to conf. papers Chmn. com. Commn. on Edn. Excellence, Ohio, 1982-83, Tenn. State Peformance Funding Task Force, 1988, Tenn. State Task Force on Minority Tchrs., 1988; reviewer art curriculum N.Y. Bd. Edn., 1985; mem. supt. search com. Chattanooga Pub. Schs., 1987-88; mem. Chattanooga Met. Coun., 1987-88, Chattanooga Ballet Bd., 1986-88, Fund for Excellence in Pub. Edn., 1986-90, Tenn. Aquarium Bd. Advisors, 1989-92, Team Evaluation Ctr. Bd., 1988-90; mem. Strategic Planning Action Team, Chattanooga City Schs., 1987-88, Siskin Hosp. Bd., 1989-92, Blue Ribbon Task Force Pontiac 2010: A New Reality, City of Pontiac Planning Divsn., 1992—; steering com., cultural action bd. Chattanooga, planning com United Way, 1987; Jewish Fedn. Bd., 1986-91; mem. coun. for policy studies Art Edn. Adv. Bd., 1982-91; ex-officio mem. Meadow Brook Theatre Guild, 1992-95; bd. chair Meadow Brook Performing Arts Co., 1992-95; chair World Cup Soccer Edn. Com./Mich. Host Com. 1993-95; bd. dirs. Ptnrs. for Preferred Future, Rochester Cmty. Schs., 1992-95, Traffic Improvement Assn. Oakland County, 1992-95, Oakland County Bus. Roundtable, 1993-95; Rochester C. of C. host com. chair on edn. World Cup, 1992-95; mem. fin. adv. com. Jewish Fedn. Detroit, 1995-97; bd. dirs. United Way Southeastern Mich., 1992-95: bd. dirs. United Way Oakland County, 1992-95, Pontiac 2010: A New Reality, mayor's transition team city/sch. rels. task force: team evaluation leader Dept. of State Am. Univ. Bulgaria, 1995; bd. trustees Cohn's & Colitis Found., 1996-97. Am. Coun. on Edn. and Mellon fellow Miami U., 1978-79; recipient Cracking the Glass Ceiling award Pontiac Area Urban League, 1992. Fellow Nat. Art Edn. Assn. (disting.); mem. Am. Assn. Colls. for Tchr. Edn. (com. chair 1982-85), Am. Art Therapy Assn. (registered), Nat. Art Edn. Assn. Women's Caucus (founder, pres. 1976-78, McFee award 1986), Am. Assn. State Colls. and Univs. (com. profl. devel. 1993-95, state rep. 1994-95), Econ. Club Detroit (bd. dirs. 1992-95), Rotary Club, Great Lakes Yacht Club (social chmn. 1996-97, ground chmn., bd. dirs. 1997-98), Phi Delta Kappa (Leadership award 1985). Avocation: sailing. Home: Apt 204 6127 Orchard Lake Rd West Bloomfield MI 48322 Office: Oakland U 316 Odowd Hall Rochester MI 48309-4423 E-mail: packard@oakland.edu.

PACKARD, STEPHEN MICHAEL, lawyer; b. Hartford, Conn., Nov. 26, 1953; s. Charles David and Anne (Moriarty) P.; m. Eileen Mary Joyce, May 23, 1981; children: Stephen Michael Jr., Sheila Marie, James Charles, Brian Joseph. BS, Fairfield U., 1975; JD magna cum laude, N.Y. Law Sch., 1981. Bar: N.Y. 1981, U.S. Dist. Ct. (ea. and so. dists.) N.Y. 1981, U.S. Dist. Ct. Conn. 1983, Conn. 1984. Assoc. Mudge, Rose, Guthrie, Alexander & Ferdon, N.Y.C., 1981-83, Wiggin & Dana, New Haven, 1983-87; atty. Aetna Life & Casualty, Hartford, 1987-96; ptnr. Accenture, N.Y.C., 1996—. Adj. prof. law U. Bridgeport Law Sch., Conn., 1987. Bd. dirs. New Haven Literacy vols., 1985-87. Mem. Conn. Bar Assn., N.Y.C. Bar Assn., Fed. Bar Coun., Conn. Def. Lawyers Assn. Roman Catholic. Office: Accenture One Financial Plz Hartford CT 06103

PACKENHAM, RICHARD DANIEL, lawyer; b. Newton, Pa., June 23, 1953; s. John Richard and Mary Margaret (Maroney) P.; m. Susan Patricia Smillie, Aug. 20, 1983. BA, Harvard U., 1975; JD, Boston Coll., 1978; LLM in Taxation, Boston U., 1985. Bar: Mass. 1978, Conn. 1979, U.S. Dist. Ct. Mass. 1979, U.S. Dist. Ct. Conn. 1979, U.S. Ct. Appeals (1st cir.) 1981, U.S. Supreme Ct. 1985. Staff atty. Conn. Superior Ct., 1978-79; ptnr. McGrath & Kane, Boston, 1979-94, Packenham, Schmidt & Federico, Boston, 1994—. Mem. ABA, Mass. Bar Assn., Conn. Bar Assn., Boston Bar Assn., Mass CLE (faculty). Clubs: Harvard (Boston). Democrat. Roman Catholic. Home: 1062 North St Walpole MA 02081-2307 Office: Packenham Schmidt & Federico 10st James Ave Boston MA 02116

PACKER, CORINNE ANGÉLINE AGNES, human rights law consultant; b. Winnipeg, Man., Can., Apr. 7, 1967; d. Aimé Urbain and Aline Marie-Thérèse (Soetaert) Vandewaeter; m. Frederick John Packer, Aug. 26, 1988; children: Sébastien Alexandre, Nicholas Aimé. BA in French with 1st class honors, U. Man., Winnipeg, Can., 1989; MA Applied Popul. Rsch. with distinction, Exeter (Eng.) U., 1993; MPhil in Internat. Rels., Cambridge (Eng.) U., 1995; PhD in Internat. Human Rights Law, Utrecht U., 2002. Cons. info. officer ILO, Geneva, 1993—2000; lectr., rschr. Utrecht (Netherlands) U., 2000—. Pres. The Themis Found., Inc., Can., 1996—; cons. Netherlands Ministry Social Welfare, The Hague, 1999, Netherlands Ministry Fgn. Affairs, The Hague, 1997, UN High Commr. for Refugees, Geneva, 1995. Author: The Right to Reproductive Choice, 1996; contbr. chpts. to books, articles to profl. jours. Mem. World Assn. for Med. Law, Can. Rsch. Inst. for Advancement of Women. Home: Neuhuyskade 76 2596 XM The Hague Netherlands Office: Netherlands Inst Human Rts Janskerkhof 3 3512 BK Utrecht Netherlands Fax: 31.30 253 71.68. E-mail: packer10@zonnet.nl .

PACKER, DIANA, retired reference librarian; b. Cleve., Sept. 04; d. Herman and Sabina (Hochman) Reich; m. Herbert Packer, June 21, 1964 (dec.); children: Cynthia, Jeremy, Todd. BA, Case Western Res. U., 1951, MLS, 1952. Libr. Horizons Rsch. Inc., Cleve., 1952-64, Cleveland Heights (Ohio) University Heights Pub. Libr., 1969-98, ret., 1998. Officer Cleveland Heights PTA, 1971-84; bd. dirs. LWV, Cleveland Heights, 1974—; officer Spl. Librs. Assn., 1952-64. Mem. Ohio Libr. Assn. Avocations: travel, theater, art, music, reading. Home: 2201 Acacia Park Dr Apt 522 Lyndhurst OH 44124-3841

PACKER, KAREN GILLILAND, cancer patient educator, researcher; b. Washington, Apr. 27, 1940; d. Theodore Redmond and Evelyn Alice (Johnson) Gilliland; m. Allan Richard Packer, Sept. 27, 1962; 1 child, Charles Allan. Student, Duke U., 1957-59, U. Ky., 1959-60, 61-62, U. P.R. Sch. Medicine, 1960-61. Genetics researcher U. Ky., Lexington, 1959-60, 61-62; biologist Melpar Inc., Nat. Cancer Inst., Springfield, Va., 1964-66; rsch. assoc., epidemiology rsch. ctr. U. Iowa Coll. Medicine, Iowa City, 1981-85; founder, dir. Marshalltown (Iowa) Cancer Support Group, 1987—. Mem. County Health Planning Comm., Marshalltown, 1989-96; mem. adv. bd. Cmty. Nursing Svc., Marshalltown, 1990—; v.p. Cmty. Svcs. Coun., Marshalltown, 1992-96, pres. 1996-97; mem. Marshall County Bd. of Health, 1996—. Editor The Group Gazette, 1988—. Bd. dirs. 1st United Ch. Christ, Hampton, Va., 1973-75; corr. sec. DAR, Marshalltown, 1988-92; chmn. cancer and rsch. aux. VFW, Marshalltown, 1990—; chmn. Marshall County Commn. Aging, 1999—, sec., 2000—. Recipient Leadership award Marshalltown Area C. of C., 1988, Spl. recognition Nat. Coalition for Cancer Survivorship, 1990, Iowa Senate 1995, 1st place in state award Cmty. Cancer Edn. VFW Aux., 1990-98, Nat. Vol. Hero of Yr. award Coping Mag., 1995; Genetics Rsch. grantee NSF, 1959-60, NIH, 1961-62. Mem. AAAS, Nat. Guard Bur. Officers Wives Club (publ. editor 1965-68), Nat. Alliance Breast Cancer Orgns., Nat. Cancer Registrars Assn., Iowa Cancer Registrars Assn., N.Y. Acad. Scis. Mem. Congregational Ch. Achievements include establishment of regional orgn. for cancer info. and edn. Home and Office: 1401 Fairway Dr Marshalltown IA 50158-3825

PACKER, KATHERINE HELEN, retired library educator; b. Toronto, Ont., Can., Mar. 20, 1918; d. Cleve Alexander and Rosa Ruel (Dibblee) Smith; m. William A. Packer, Sept. 27, 1941; 1 dau., Marianne Katherine. BA, U. Toronto, 1941; A.M.L.S., U. Mich., 1953; PhD, U. Md., 1975. Cataloguer William L Clements Library, U. Mich., 1953-55, U. Man. (Can.) Library, Winnipeg, 1956-59; cataloguer U. Toronto Library, 1959-63; asst. prof. Faculty Library Sci., 1967-75, asso. prof., 1975-78, prof., dean, 1979-84, prof. emeritus, 1984—. Head cataloguer York U. Library, Toronto, 1963-64; chief librarian Ont. Coll. Edn., Toronto, 1964-67. Author: Early American School Books, 1954. Mem. property tax working group Ont. Fair Tax Commn., 1991-92; mem. assessment reform working group City of Toronto, 1992-97. Recipient Disting. Alumnus award U. Mich., 1981. Mem.: Ex Libris Assn. (Howard Phalin award 1972), Phi Kappa Phi. Home: 53 Gormley Ave Toronto ON Canada M4V 1Y9 Office: U Toronto Fac Info Studies 140 Saint George St Toronto ON Canada M5S 3G6 E-mail: packer@interlog.com.

PACKER, MARK BARRY, lawyer, financial consultant, foundation official; b. Phila., Sept. 18, 1944; s. Samuel and Eve (Devine) P.; m. Donna Elizabeth Ferguson (div. 1994); children: Daniel Joshua, Benjamin Dov, David Johannes; m. Helen Margaret (Jones) Klinedinst, July, 1995. AB magna cum laude, Harvard U., 1965, LLB, 1968. Bar: Wash. 1969, Mass. 1971. Assoc. Ziontz, Pirtle & Fulle, Seattle, 1968-70; pvt. practice Bellingham, Wash., 1972—. Bd. dirs., corp. sec. BMJ Holdings (formerly No. Sales Co., Inc.), 1977—; trustee No. Sales Profit Sharing Plan, 1977—; bd. dirs. Whatcom State Bank, 1995-98. Mem. Bellingham Planning and Devel. Commn., 1975-84, chmn., 1977-81, mem. shoreline subcom., 1976-82, capital improvements adv. com., 1999-01; mem. Bellingham Mcpl. Arts Commn., 1986-91, landmark rev. bd., 1987-91; chmn. Bellingham campaign United Jewish Appeal, 1979-90; bd. dirs. Whatcom Cmty. Coll. Found., 1989-92; trustee, chmn. program com. Bellingham Pub. Sch. Found., 1991-98, Heavy Culture classic lit. group, 1991—, Jewish studies group, 1993—; trustee Kenneth L. Kellar Found., 1995—; mng. trustee Bernard M. & Audrey Jaffe Found.; Torah reader; pres. Congregation Eytz Chaim, Bellingham, 1998-2000. Recipient Blood Donor award ARC, 1979, 8-Gallon Pin, 1988, Mayor's Arts award City of Bellingham, 1993. Mem. Wash. State Bar Assn. (sec. environ. and land use law, sec. bus. law, sec. real property, probate and trust, com. law examiners 1992-94). Office: PO Box 1151 Bellingham WA 98227-1151 E-mail: Packer@nas.com.

PACKER, REKHA DESAI, lawyer; b. N.Y.C., Apr. 20, 1955; d. Rajanikant C. and Santosh (Nagpaul) Desai; m. Michael Benjamin Packer, Aug. 11, 1979. AB magna cum laude, Harvard U., 1976, JD, 1979. Bar: Mass. 1979, U.S. Dist. Ct. Mass. 1979, U.S. Tax. Ct. 1980. Assoc. Gaston & Snow, Boston, 1979-87, ptnr., 1987-91; sr. ptnr. Hale and Dorr, 1991-96; tax dir. Pricewaterhouse Coopers LLP, 1997-99; ptnr. Stradley, Ronon, Stevens & Young, LLP, Phila., 1999—. Speaker Fed. Tax Inst., 1987—, World Trade Inst., 1986—. Mem. Internat. Bar Assn. (mem. com. on investment cos., funds and trusts 1989—), ABA (mem. com. on regulated investment cos., labor law sect. 1986—, com. on U.S. activities of foreigners 1988—), Boston Bar Assn. (labor law sect. 1987—, co-chmn. internat. tax. com. 1987-89), Phi Beta Kappa. Office: Stradley Ronon Stevens & Young LLP 2600 1 Commerce Sq Philadelphia PA 19103-7098

PACKER, SAMUEL, ophthalmologist; b. N.Y.C., Jan. 26, 1941; s. Frank and Thelma (Miller) P.; m. Donna Ann Samborsky, May 24, 1957; children: Heidi, Adam, Marisa, Andrew. BA, NYU, 1962; MD, SUNY, Bklyn., 1966. Diplomate Am. Bd. Ophthalmology. Intern Kings County Hosp., Bklyn., 1966-67; resident in internal medicine Yale-New Haven Hosp., 1967-71; instnl. rev. bd. North Shore U. Cornell U. Med. Coll., Manhasset, N.Y., 1975—, med. ethics com., 1986—, chmn., 1986-92; chmn. dept. ophthalmology North Shore U. Hosp./NYU Sch. Medicine, 1989—. Dir. North Shore U. Hosp. Eye Surgery Ctr., Syosset, N.Y., 1996—. Contbr. numerous articles to profl. jours. Lt. comdr. USN, 1971-73. Fellow N.Y. Acad. Medicine; mem. Am. Acad. Ophthalmology (ethics com. 1990—, vice chair 1996-2000, chair 2001—), N.Y. State Ophthal. Soc. (pres. 1998—), L.I. Ophthal. Soc. (pres . 1991), Nassau Acad. Medicine (chmn. sect. ophthalmology 1987-88, bd. dirs. 1994—, pres. 1996-97), Nassau County Med. Soc. (comm. and media com., bylaws com. 1991—, sec. 1992-93), Med. Soc. State N.Y. (sci. adv. 1985-92, bioethics. com. 1993—, rules com. 1994, chmn. rules com. 1995), N.Y. State Ophthal. Soc. (bd. dirs. 1988—, pres.-elect 1996-97, pres. 1998-99), The Lions Eye Bank for L.I. (exec. dir. 1986—). Office: 600 Northern Blvd Great Neck NY 11021-5200

PACKER, STEPHEN BARRY, economist; b. Bklyn., Dec. 8, 1928; s. Morris Emanuel and Paule (Ginsberg) P.; m. Alice Barbara Sandberg, Aug. 12, 1956; children: Robert, Richard. B.A., Columbia U., 1948; M.A. in Econs., U. Chgo., 1950. Economist various cos., 1953-58; bond market analyst Standard & Poors Corp., N.Y.C., 1958-63; mgr. econ. and sales analysis Continental Can Co., N.Y.C., 1963-67; planning mgr. Mobil Corp., N.Y.C., 1967-74, chief economist, 1974-88; prof. of econs. St. Peter's Coll., Jersey City, 1988—. Contbr. articles to profl. jours. Served with USN, 1951-53. Fellow Nat. Assn. Bus. Economists (mem. coun. 1968-73); mem. N.Y. Soc. Security Analysts, Beach Point Club (Mamaroneck, N.Y.). Home: 4 Ellen Ct Rye NY 10580-2610 Office: St Peters Coll 2641 John F Kennedy Blvd Jersey City NJ 07306-5943

PACKERT, G(AYLA) BETH, lawyer; b. Corpus Christi, Tex., Sept. 25, 1953; d. Gilbert Norris and Virginia Elizabeth (Pearce) P.; m. James Michael Hall, Jan. 1, 1974 (div. 1985); m. Richard Christopher Burke, July 18, 1987; children: Christopher Geoffrey Makepeace Burke Packert, Jeremy Eliot Marvell Packert Burke. BA, La. Tech. U., 1973; MA, U. Ark., 1976; postgrad., U. Ill., 1975-81, JD, 1985. Bar: Ill. 1985, U.S. Dist. Ct. (no. dist.) Ill. 1985, U.S. Ct. Appeals (7th cir.) 1987, Va. 1988, U.S. Dist. Ct. (we. dist.) Va. 1989. Assoc. Jenner & Block, Chgo., 1985-88; law clk. U.S. Dist. Ct. Va. (we. dist.), Danville, 1988-89; asst. commonwealth atty. Commonwealth of Va., Lynchburg, Va., 1989-95; pvt. practice, 1995—. Notes and comments editor U. Ill. Law Rev., 1984-85. Mem. Phi Beta Kappa. Home: 3900 Faculty Dr Lynchburg VA 24501-3110 Office: PO Box 529 Lynchburg VA 24505-0529

PACKHAM, MARIAN AITCHISON, biochemistry educator; b. Toronto, Ont., Can., Dec. 13, 1927; d. James and Clara Louise (Campbell) A.; m. James Lennox Packham, June 25, 1949; children: Neil Lennox, Janet Melissa. BA, U. Toronto, 1949, PhD, 1954; DSc honoris causa, Ryerson Poly. U., 1997. Sr. fellow dept. biochemistry U. Toronto, 1954-58, lectr. dept. biochemistry, 1958-63, 66-67; rsch. assoc. dept. physiol. scis. Ont. Vet. Coll., U. Guelph, 1963-65; rsch. assoc. blood and cardiovascular disease rsch. unit U. Toronto, 1965-66; asst. prof. U. Toronto dept. biochemistry, 1967-72, assoc. prof., 1972-75, prof., 1975-89, acting chmn. dept. biochemistry, 1983, univ. prof., 1989—2002; ret., 2002. Contbr. articles to profl. jours. Royal Soc. Can. fellow, 1991; recipient Lt. Govs. Silver medal Victoria Coll., 1949; co-recipient J. Allyn Taylor Internat. prize in Medicine, 1988. Mem.: Can. Atherosclerosis, Internat. Soc. Thrombosis and Haemostasis, Can. Soc. Clin. investigation, Can. Soc. Hematology, Am. Soc. Hematology, Molecular and Cellular Biology, Can. Soc. Biochem. Office: U Toronto Dept Biochemistry Toronto ON Canada M5S 1A8

PACTER, PAUL ALLAN, accounting standards researcher; b. N.Y.C., Jan. 26, 1943; s. Bernard David and Hilda Libby (Margolies) P. BS, Syracuse U., 1964; PhD, Mich. State U., 1967. C.P.A., N.Y. Asst. prof. N.Y.U., 1967-69; rsch. mgr. Peat Marwick, N.Y.C., 1969-73; exec. dir. Fin. Acctg. Standards Bd., Stamford, Conn., 1973-84; commr. fin. City of Stamford, 1984-90; prof. acctg., MBA program U. Conn., Stamford, 1990-96, adj. prof., 1982-84. Adj. prof. NYU, 1982-84; project cons. Fin. Acctg. Standards Bd., 1990-96, fellow Internat. Acctg. Standards Com., London, 1993-2000, dir. Deloitte Touche Tohmatsu, Hong Kong, 2000—. Consulting editor The Jour. of Accountancy, 1968-73 Chmn. Stamford Commn. on Human Rights, 1977-84, Stamford Film Commn., 1984-90; mem. Charter Revision Commn., Stamford, 1979-80, Gov.'s Tourism Coun., Conn., 1984-90, acctg. adv. coun. U. Conn., 1984-90; pres. N. Stamford Dem. Club, 1983-84, treas., 1987-95; dir. Stamford Coliseum Authority, 1984-90; vice chmn. govtl. acctg. stds. adv. coun., 1984-91; vice chmn. China Beijing Ctr. for Asia-Pacific Fin. and Acctg. Rsch., 2000—; treas. Conn. Tourism Assn., 1987-90, North Stamford Assn., 1993-94; bd. dirs. Stamford Ctr. for the Arts, United Way Stamford, Stamford Theatre Works, Stamford Cmty. Fund, Housing Devel. Fund of Fairfield County. Earhart Found. fellow Mich. State U., 1966-67; U.S. Office of Edn. grantee, 1967 Mem. AICPA, Am. Acctg. Assn. (coun.), N.Y. State Soc. CPA's, Beta Gamma Sigma, Beta Alpha Psi. Jewish. Office: Deloitte Touche Tohmatsu 111 Connaught Rd Central Hong Kong Hong Kong E-mail: pau.pacter@deloitte.com.hk.

PADBERG, DANIEL IVAN, agricultural economics educator, researcher; b. Summersville, Mo., Nov. 9, 1931; s. Christopher Edward and Ruth (Badgley) P.; m. Mildred Frances True, Aug. 5, 1956 (dec. Dec. 15, 1997); children: Susan Elizabeth, Jean Ellen, Carol Natalie; m. Sarah O'Brien, Dec. 30, 1998. BS, U. Mo., 1953, MS, 1955; PhD, U. Calif.-Berkeley, 1961. Asst. prof. Ohio State U., Columbus, 1961-65; project leader Nat. Commn. on Food Mktg., Washington, 1965-66; prof. Cornell U., Ithaca, N.Y., 1966-75; head dept. agrl. econs. U. Ill., Urbana, 1975-81; dean U. Mass., Amherst, 1981-83, prof. agrl. econs., 1983; cons. Farm Credit System, 1983-84; head dept. agrl. econs. Tex. A&M U., College Station, 1984-90, prof., 1990-95, ret., 1995; Fulbright chair internat. econs. U. Tuscia, Viterbo, Italy, 1997. Mem. White House Task Force on Farmer Bargaining, Washington, 1968; mem. food and nutrition bd. Nat. Acad. Sci., Washington, 1974-77; cons. Office Tech. Assessment, Washington, 1975-82; pres. Am. Agrl. Econs. Assn., 1987-88; exec. dir. Food and Agrl. Mktg. Consortium, 1993-98; chmn. Nat. Adv. Com. on Concentration in Agr l., 1996. Author: Economics of Food Retailing, 1968, Todays Food Broker, 1971; editorial council: Am. Jour. Agrl. Econs., 1970-73, Jour. Consumer Affairs, 1974-76. Pres. council First Congregational Ch., Ithaca, 1971-72. Served to lt. (j.g.) USN, 1955-58, PTO. Consumer Research Inst. grantee, 1970; FDA grantee, 1971; USDA/NRI grantee, 1992; Simon research fellow U. Manchester, Eng., 1972-73 Mem. Am. Agrl. Econs. Assn. (Quality of Discovery award 1975, Quality of Communication in Research award 1977, chmn. awards 1979-80) Home: 90 S Highland Ave Apt 216 Tarpon Springs FL 34689-5344 E-mail: danpad7@hotmail.com. *Not always right, but never in doubt.*

PADBERG, FRANK THOMAS, JR. surgeon, educator; b. 1947; BA, Vanderbilt U., 1969; MD, U. Ark., 1973. Resident in surgery Harvard Surg. Svcs., Boston, 1973-76, resident and chief resident, 1977-79; registrar in surgery Aberdeen (Scotland) Royal Infirmary, 1976-77; fellow in vascular surgery, 1979-81; asst. prof. surgery, 1981-88; assoc. prof. surgery, 1988-94; prof. surgery N.J. Med. Sch. U. Medicine and Dentistry of N.J., Newark, 1994—. Assoc. dir. clin. surgery Univ. Hosp., Newark, 1985-88; assoc. chief surgery, chief sect. vascular surgery VA Med. Ctr., East Orange, N.J., 1988—; rsch. peer rev. com. Am. Heart Assn., N.J., 1991-97; prin. investigator VA Coop. Studies, 1986—. Mem. editl. bd. Jour. Vascular Surgery, 1998—; contbr. articles to profl. jours. U. Medicine and Dentistry of N.J. Found. grantee, 1984-85, Merit Rev. grantee Dept. VA, 1999—. Fellow: ACS (bd. govs. 1995—98); mem.: Ea. Vascular Soc., Am. Assn. Vascular Surgery, Am. Assn. Surgery of Trauma, Am. Venous Forum (program chair 1995—98, treas. 1998—2001, pres. elect 2002—03), Internat. Soc. Cardiovasc. Surgery (N.Am. chpt.), Soc. Vascular Surgery, Vascular Soc. N.J. (pres. 1989—90), Peripheral Vascular Surgery Soc. (pres. 1992—93). Avocations: history, antiquarian cartography.

PADBERG, HARRIET ANN, mathematics educator; b. St. Louis, Nov. 13, 1922; d. Harry J. and Marie L. (Kilgen) P. AB with honors, Maryville Coll., St. Louis, 1943; MMus, U. Cin., 1949; MA, St. Louis U., 1956, PhD, 1964. Registered music therapist; cert. tchr. math. and music, La., Mo. Tchr. elem. math. and music Kenwood Acad., Albany, N.Y., 1944-46; tchr. secondary math. Acad. of Sacred Heart, Cin., 1946-47; instr. math. and music Acad. and Coll. of Sacred Heart, Grand Coteau, La., 1947-48; secondary tchr. music Acad. Sacred Heart, St. Charles, Mo., 1948-50; instr. math. and music Acad. and Coll. Sacred Heart, Grand Coteau, 1950-55, Maryville Coll., St. Louis, 1955-56; tchr. elem. and secondary math. and music Acad. Sacred Heart, 1956-57; asst. prof. Maryville Coll., 1957-64, assoc. prof., 1964-68, prof. math., 1968-92, prof. emeritus, 1992—; music therapist Emmaus Homes, Marthasville, Mo., 1992—. Recipient Alumni Centennial award Maryville Coll., St. Louis, 1986; grantee Danforth Found., Colorado Springs, 1970, Tallahassee, 1970, Edn. Devel. Ctr., Mass., 1975, U. Kans., 1980. Mem. Assn. Women in Math., Am. Math. Soc., Math. Assn. Am., Nat. Coun. Tchr. Math., Mo. Acad. Sci., Delta Epsilon Sigma (sec. local chpt. 1962), Pi Mu Epsilon (sec. local chpt. 1958), Sigma Xi. Avocations: computer music, organist, knitting. E-mail: hpadberg@rscj.org.

PADBERG, HELEN SWAN, violinist; b. Shawnee, Okla. d. Frank P. and Birdie B. (Rudell) Swan; m. Frank Padberg, Feb. 6, 1943; children: Frank, Kristen. AA, Stephens Coll., 1938; MusB, U. Okla., 1940; MusM, Northwestern U., 1941; student, Jacques Gordon. Solo performances and concerts, 1932—; mem. faculty string quartet and symphony soloist Stephens Coll., 1937-38; violinist Oklahoma City Symphony Summer Concerts, 1940; soloist Northwestern U. Symphony, 1941; violinist USO Tours World War II, 1941-43; mem. Nat. Orchestral Assn. and Am. Youth Orch., N.Y.C., 1944-46; tchr. strings Maywood (Ill.), 1946-47; asst. concertmaster West Suburban Symphony, Chgo., 1947-48; mem. Chgo. Women's Symphony, Chgo. Civic Orch. and chamber music groups, 1947-51; violinist Ark. Piano Trio, 1952-58; concertmaster Ark. Symphony and Little Rock Philharm., 1953-57, Marjorie Lawrence TV Series, Ark., 1953-54; pvt. tchr. violin Little Rock, 1953-66; accompanist and performer on piano, harp. Pres. Ark. Med. Soc. Alliance, 1962-63, historian, 1963-94. Co-founder Little Rock Chamber Music Soc., 1954; pres. bd. dirs. Vis. Nurse Assn. of Pulaski County, Ark., 1967-69; bd. dirs. Internat. Visitors Ctr., Chgo., 1988—, Stephens Coll. Alumna Assn. Bd.; elder, trustee Presbyn. ch. Mem.: Mu Phi Epsilon, Internat. Women Assocs. (pres. 1988—91), Am. Opera Soc. Chgo. (v.p. and program chmn. 1981—82, pres. 1984—87), Am. Opera Soc. (historian 1987—), Am. Fedn. Musicians, Chgo. Harp Soc. (sec. 1979—84), Am. Harp Soc., English Spkg. Union (Chgo. br., bd. govs. 1997—), Musicians' Club of Women (Chgo., bd. dirs.), Women's Athletic of Chgo. Club, Aesthetic Club (pres. Little Rock), Pi Beta Phi (pres. Little Rock Alumnae Club), Pi Kappa Lambda. Home: 175 E Delaware Pl Chicago IL 60611-1756

PADDER, TANVEER A, cardiologist, researcher; s. Ghulam Mohammad Padder and Sajida Begum; m. Tasleem Kousar, June 27, 2001. MD (hons.), UTESA Sch. of Medicine, Santo Domingo, 1999. Rsch. assoc. cardiology Hahnemann U. Hosp., Phila., 2000. Author: (Scientfic Paper) Safe and effective management of infected Pacemaker and ICD devices - our experience of 400 patients from Jan.1991 to Dec.2000. Seventh International Workshop on Cardiac Arrhythmias, Venice, Italy, October 2001 , 2001 (Best oral communication on sudden death- certificate and cash award, 2001); contbr. articles to profl. jours. Mem.: AMA (assoc.), Womens Heart, Internat. Soc.Heart Rsch. (Europe and U.S.A.), Cardiac Electrophysiology Assn.USA, Physicians for Nat. Health Program USA, American Soc. Nuclear Cardiology (assoc.), World Med. Assn. (assoc.), Nat. Assn. Physicians for Homeless USA. Moslem. Avocations: music, reading, travel. Home: 317 N. Broad St. Apt. 711 Philadelphia PA 19107 Office: Divsn Cardiac Electrophys MS. 470 Broad and Vine Philadelphia PA 19102 Home Fax: 215-762-3028; Office Fax: 215-762-3028. Personal E-mail: tanveer3333@yahoo.com. Business E-Mail: tanveer3333@yahoo.com.

PADDISON, DAVID ROBERT, lawyer; b. Savannah, Ga., May 15, 1949; s. Richard Milton and Josephine Butler (Bowles) P.; m. Frances M. Phares (div. Mar. 1995); children: Hunt, Brian, Margery; m. Jane Ingrid Caddell, Mar. 30, 1996; 1 child, Ethan David. BSBA, La. State U., 1971; JD, Tulane U., 1976. Bar: La. 1976; U.S. Dist. Ct. (ea. dist.) 1976; U.S. Ct. Appeals (5th cir.) 1976; bd. cert. specialist in family law La. State Bar Assn., 1995; U.S. Tax. Ct. 2001. Asst. dist. atty. Dist. Atty.'s Office, Covington, La., 1983-86, New Orleans, 1978-83; pvt. practice Covington, 1986—. Advisor Contemporary Arts Ctr., New Orleans, 1978-79; clin. advisor Tulane U. Sch. Law, New Orleans, 1980-81; spl. cons. Dist. Atty.'s Office, New Orleans, 1981. Legal advisor Christ Episcopal Church (sch. planning com., lector, usher). Mem. Covington Bar Assn., La. Trial Lawyers Assn., ATLA. Republican. Episcopalian. Avocations: golf, sailing, snow skiing. Office: PO Box 1830 Covington LA 70434-1830

PADDOCK, ANTHONY CONAWAY, financial consultant; b. Paris, July 9, 1935; came to U.S., 1940; s. H. Watson and Mildred V. (Decker) P.; m. Wendy E. Brewer, Apr. 24, 1971. AB, Harvard U., 1957, JD, 1960; MBA, Columbia U., 1961. Bar: N.Y. 1961. Assoc. investment bank Merrill Lynch & Co., N.Y.C., 1961-69; v.p. Chase Manhattan Bank, 1970-78, Standard Rsch. Cons., N.Y.C., 1978-84; mng. dir. Benchmark Valuation Cons., 1978-84; prin. KPMG Peat Marwick, 1984-96; mng. dir. Empire Valuation Cons., 1997—. Adj. prof. NYU, 1979-90. Trustee Sun Capital Advisors Trust, 1998—. Mem. Assoc. for Corp. Growth, Inst. Mgmt. Cons. (cert.). Episcopalian. Home: 14 N Chatsworth Ave Larchmont NY 10538-2142 Office: Empire Valuation Cons 350 5th Ave Ste 5513 New York NY 10118-5513 E-mail: acpaddock@empireval.com.

PADDOCK, AUSTIN JOSEPH, retired engineering executive; b. Washington Court House, Ohio, July 18, 1908; s. Leon A. and Nellie (Hare) P.; m. Janet Nevin, Aug. 3, 1934 (dec. Aug. 1964); children: Larry C. and Linda M. (twins), Jane M.; m. JoAnn Rourke, May 1966; 1 child, Jennifer Jo. BSCE, U. Mich., 1929. With Am. Bridge divsn. U.S. Steel Corp., 1929-61; from timekeeper constrn. dept., through ops. and sales to pres.; corp. adminstrv. v.p. fabrication and mfg. U.S. Steel Corp., 1961-69; chmn. bd., pres., CEO Blount, Inc., 1969-75; exec. v.p., COO Pa. Engring. Corp., Pitts., 1975-78, vice-chmn. bd., dir., 1978-87. Dir., exec. com. Pitts.-Des Moines Corp.; past dir. bldg. research adv. bd. Nat. Acad. Sci.; past dir. Am. Standards Inst., Steel Structures Paint Council; past dir. constrn. affairs com. U.S. C. of C.; past chmn. research tech. com. Am. Iron and Steel Inst. Past bd. dirs. Allegheny council Boy Scouts Am. Mem. NAM (past dir.), Duquesne Club (Pitts.), Montgomery Country Club. Home: 3875 Taylor Rd Montgomery AL 36116

PADDOCK, PAULA J. geriatrics nurse; b. Rochester, N.Y., Oct. 26, 1956; d. Eugene J. and Marguerite R. (Bailey) O'Brien; m. Wayne W. Paddock, Jan. 3, 1981; children: Keith Allen, Eric William. AAS in Nursing, C.C. Finger Lakes, 1977. RN, N.Mex., N.Y. Float nurse, charge nurse emergency Lovelace Bataan Med. Ctr., Albuquerque, 1978-79; asst. head nurse pediat., charge surg. specialist St. Joseph Hosp., 1979-83; head nurse Ontario County Health Facility, Canadaigua, N.Y., 1983-86; head nurse, relief supr. Hurlbut Nursing Home, Rochester, 1986-88; nurse mgr. Episcopal Ch. Home, 1988-90; asst. v.p. nursing, nurse mgr., svc. leader post acute Thompson Continuing Car Ctr., Canandaigua, 1990—. Nurse trainer pediatrics in field. Mem. CNA (program coord., program instr., clin. evaulator), Nat. Nurses Assn. Home: 2115 Elton Rd Ionia NY 14475-9701

PADEN, HARRY, municipal official; children: Shahara, Angela. Student, Am. U., 1971-73, Essex County (N.J.) Coll., 1981-83. Dir. social svcs. Unity Freedom Bapt. Ch., Newark, 1989-92; aide to freeholder pres. Essex County, 1992-96; code enforcement officer Township of Irvington, N.J., 1992-94, chief field rep. Office Neighorhood Preservation, 1994-98. Host, prodr. (cable T.V. program) Parent to Parent; contbg. writer Jersey Girl mag.; columnist Irvington Herald. Chmn. Irvington juvenile conf. com. Superior Ct.; v.p., former pres. PTA Irvington H.S.; program coord. Neighborhood Preservation, 1998—; parent coord. Essex County PTA; ednl. liaison mayor of Irvington; aide Irvington West Ward Council; celebrity reader Essex and Hudson County chpts. United Way; deacon, adminstrv. asst. to pastor Unity Freedom Bapt. Ch., Newark; mem. Irving Bd. Edn. Named Irvington African Am. Male of Yr., 1994, One of 100 Most Influential in State, City News, 1997; recipient Pinnacle award Being Single mag., 1995, Spl. Civil award Irvington C. of C. Home: 31 Civic Sq W Apt 14 Irvington NJ 07111-2425

PADEN, JOHN BRUCE, community resource executive; b. St. Louis, Aug. 19, 1944; s. John Milton Paden and Erma Maye Wheeler; m. Kristin Alexander, Nov. 17, 1983; 1 child, Rebecca Margaret. BSBA, U. Mo., 1971, MBA, 1973; cert. networks and telecom., Johnson County C.C., Overland Pk., Kans., 1994. Sr. sales exec. Xerox Corp., St. Louis, 1973-78; v.p. investments Drexel Burnham Lambert Merrill Lynch, Overland Pk., 1978-87; regional sales dir. Mark Twain Bankshares, Kansas City, Mo., 1987-88; pres., owner 1st Capital Source, Overland Pk., 1988-93; instr. Johnson County C.C., 1993-96; dir. info. mgmt. St. Mary Coll., Leavenworth, Kans., 1996-2001; CEO Cmty. Resource Network, Kansas City, 2001—. Mem. adv. bd. info. tech. Johnson County C.C., Overland Pk., 1998-00. Avocations: flying, skiing. Home: 12437 S Ellsworth St Olathe KS 66062-4970 Office: Cmty Resource Network 106 W Eleventh St Ste 110 Kansas City MO 64105 E-mail: jpaden@crn.org.

PADEN, LARRY J. consulting electronics engineer, lawyer; b. Tulsa, Mar. 21, 1957; s. Jackson Taylor Jr. and Mary Lois (Dilday) P.; m. Carol Denise McAlister, July 28, 1979 (div. 2000); children: John Lawrence, Zachary Taylor, Katherine Elizabeth, Robert Nathaniel. BSEE, Okla. State U., 1979, MEE, 1980, PhD in Elec. Engring., 1991; JD, Oklahoma City U., 1995. Cert. electromagnetic compliance engr.; registered profl. engr., Okla.; bar: Okla. 1996. NSF rsch. asst. dept. physics U. Tex., Arlington, 1977; engring. intern Amoco Prodn. Rsch. Ctr., Tulsa, 1978-79; tchg. asst. Sch. Elec. and computer Engring. Okla. State U., Stillwater, 1979, grad. rsch. asst., 1979-80, rsch. asst. Consortium for Enhancement Well Log Data, 1983-85; devel. engr. AT&T Western Elec., Oklahoma City, 1980-83, 85-90; patent law clk. McCarthy & Assocs., 1993-95; electronics, computer engring.-software cons. profl. engr. Aaden Engring., LLC, Broken Arrow, Okla., 1996—. Vis. instr. computer arch. U. Okla. Sch. Elec. Engring. and Computer Sci., Norman, 1989, 91; cons. profl. engr. in electronics U.S. Post Office Maintenance Tech. Support Ctr., Norman, 1996-2000, Uptown Thrift Store, 1997—; ILS electronics engr. flight safety Internat. Simulation Sys. Divsn., Broken Arrow, Okla. Contbr. articles to profl. jours.; newsletter editor Royal Oaks Neighborhood assn., 1988-92. Quality control sec., pres. Jr. Achievement, Tulsa, 1972-75; pres. Vocat. Indsl. Clubs of Am., Sand Springs, Okla., 1973-75; mem. Cherokee Nation, Tahlequah, Okla., 1986—; bd. dirs. Royal Oaks Neighborhood Assn., Oklahoma City, 1988-92; mem. Civic Music Assn., Oklahoma City, 1995—, bd. dirs., 1998—. Okla. State U. Regents Disting. scholar, 1975, Sigma Xi scholar, 1976, Albrecht Naeter scholar, 1977. Mem. ABA, IEEE (Oklahoma City sect. vice chmn. 1994-95, chmn. 1995-98, newsletter editor 1994-97), Okla. Soc. Profl. Engrs. (pres. Okla. City chpt. 1999-2000), Am. Assn. Individual Investors (life), Internat. Soc. for Philos. Enquiry, Citizens Police Acad. Alumni Assn., Intertel, Masons (master of ceremonies in 19th deg.), Civic Music Assn. (bd. dirs. 1998—), Eta Kappa Nu. Democrat. Baptist. Avocations: swimming, hiking, ham radio, tennis, Aikedo. Office: Aaden Engineering LLC 2612 S Dogwood Ave Broken Arrow OK 74012-7347 Home: 2612 S Dogwood Ave Broken Arrow OK 74012-7347 E-mail: Aaden@aol.com.

PADEREWSKI, SIR CLARENCE JOSEPH, architect; b. Cleve., July 23, 1908; BArch, U. Calif., 1932. Chief draftsman Sam W. Hamill, 1939-44; with Heitschmidt-Matcham-Blanchard-Gill & Hamill, 1943; prin. C.J. Paderewski, 1944-48; pres. Paderewski, Mitchell, Dean & Assoc., Inc. (and predecessor), San Diego, 1948-78. Instr. adult edn. San Diego city schs., 1939-44, U. Calif. extension div., 1945, 56; lectr. in field. Prin. works include Charactron Labs, Gen. Dynamics Corp., Convair, S.D., 1954, South Bay Elem. Schs., S.D., 1948-74; additions to El Cortez Hotel; including first exterior passenger glass elevator in the world and New Travolator Motor Hotel, S.D., 1959, Palomar Coll., San Marcos, 1951-80, San Diego County U. Gen. Hosp., San Diego Internat. Airport Terminal Bldgs., Fallbrook Elem. Schs., 1948-74, Silver Strand Elem. Sch., Coronado, Tourmaline Terrace Apt. Bldg., San Diego Salvation Army Office Bldg. Mem. adv. bd. Bayside Social Service Center, 1953-75, San Diego Polonia Newspaper, 1994—; mem. San Diego Urban Design Com.; adv. bd. Camp Oliver, 1963—, pres., 1975-76; bd. dirs. San Diego Symphony Orch. Assn., 1954-62, San Diego chpt. ARC, 1971-74; bd. dirs., chmn. coms., pres. San Diego Downtown Assn., 1963—; bd. dirs. Nat. Council Archtl. Registration Bds., 1958-66, bd. dirs. other offices, 1961-64, pres., 1965-66, chmn. internat. relations com., 1967-68, Salvation Army, vice-chmn., 1989, life mem. adv. bd., 1993—, Copernicus Found., 1994—; mem. Calif. Bd. Archtl. Examiners, 1949-61, past pres., commr., 1961—; mem. Nat. Panel Arbitrators, 1953—, Nat. Council on Schoolhouse Constrn.; hon. chmn. Ignacy Jan Paderewski Meml. Com., 1991; adv. bd. S.D. Balboa Park Cmty. Endowment Fund, 1995—. Decorated Knight Order Polonia Restituta, Polish govt. in exile, 1982, recipient Commodore cross, 2002; recipient Award of Merit for San Diego County Gen. Hosp., San Diego chpt., AIA, 1961, Honor award for San Diego Internat. Airport Terminal, Honor award Portland Cement Co., Golden Trowel award Plastering Inst., 1958-60, 4 awards Masonry Inst., 1961, award Prestressed Concrete Inst., 1976, Outstanding Community Leadership award San Diego Downtown Assn., 1963-65, 80, Polish Engring. award for outstanding arch. and achievement, 2000, Gold award Engring. Soc., 2000, Outstanding INdividual Polish Am. award Polish Ctr. of L.A., 2001. Fellow AIA (pres. San Diego chpt. 1948, 49, bd. dirs. 1947-53, chmn. several coms., spl. award 1977, Calif. Coun. Spl. award 1979, Calif. Coun. Disting. Svc. award 1982, Lifetime Achievement award 2000); mem. San Diego C. of C. (bd. dirs. 1959-62, 64-67), Am. Arbitration Assn. (San Diego adv. coun. 1969—), Sister City Soc. (bd. dirs.), Lions (past pres. Hillcrest Club, Lion of Yr. 1990, fellow internat. found. 1991), Father Serra Club (charter, past pres.), Outboard Boating Club San Diego, Chi Alpha Kappa, Delta Sigma Chi. Home: 2837 Kalmia Pl San Diego CA 92104-5418

PADGET, JOHN E. management professional; b. L.A., Aug. 26, 1948; s. LeRoy and Gladys (Black) P. BA, U. Kans., 1969, postgrad., 1970. Instr. bridge Am. Contract Bridge League, 1971-77; owner Hectors, Kirkland, Wash., 1978-84; producer TV show Sta. 2, Oakland, 1985-88; regional mgr. Keithwood Agy.-Am. Health Care Adv., Pleasanton, Calif., 1991-92; exec. v.p. J. & J. Warren Co., Walnut Creek, 1991-97; pres. BBH Ltd., 1997—. Pres. BBH Ltd. Author: Winning Style, 1977. Mem. AAAS, Mensa, Internat. Platfrom Soc. Jewish. Avocations: hiking, reading, travel, internet publishing.

PADGETT, FRANK DAVID, former associate state supreme court justice; b. Vincennes, Ind., Mar. 9, 1923; LLB, Harvard U., 1948. Bar: Hawaii 1949, U.S. Supreme Ct. 1967. Assoc., then ptnr. Robertson, Castle & Anthony, Honolulu, 1949-66; ptnr. Padgett & Greeley, 1966-67, Padgett, Greeley & Marumoto (and predecessor firms), Honolulu, 1968-74; assoc. judge Intermediate Ct. Appeals State Hawaii, 1980-82; assoc. justice Hawaii Supreme Ct., Honolulu, 1982-92. Mem.: ABA, Hawaii Bar Assn. Office: PO Box 61 Kula HI 96790-2560 Business E-Mail: padgettf@aol.com .

PADGETT, GREGORY LEE, lawyer; b. Greenfield, Ind., May 9, 1959; s. William Joseph and Anna Katherine (Hyre) Padgett; m. Ruth Anne Dorworth, June 5, 1982; children: Joshua David, William Joel, Emily Xiao Lei. BA summa cum laude, DePauw U., 1981; JD, Northwestern U., 1984. Bar: Ill., U.S. Dist. Ct. (no. dist.) Ill. 1984, U.S. Ct. Appeals (7th cir.) 1986, Ind. 1988, U.S. Dist. Ct. (no. & so. dists.) Ind. 1988. Assoc. Kirkland & Ellis, Chgo., 1984-88, Baker & Daniels, Indpls., 1988-92; ptnr. Johnson, Lawhead, Buth & Pope, P.C., 1992-2000; of counsel Barnes & Thornburg, 2000—. Adj. prof. Butler U., 1989-90. Mem. Marion County Prosecutor's Rev. Task Force, Indpls., 1991; pres., bd. dirs. Theatre on the Square, Indpls., 1994-95; mem. coun. Hope Evang. Covenant Ch., 1992-96; bd. dirs. Meridian St. Found., 1994-96. Mem. Ind. State Bar Assn., Indpls. Bar Assn. (exec. com. alternative dispute resolution sect.), Christian Legal Soc., Phi Beta Kappa. Avocations: theatre arts, vocal music, hiking, writing. Office: Barnes & Thornburg 11 S Meridian St Indianapolis IN 46204 E-mail: gpadgett@btlaw.com.

PADGETT, NANCY WEEKS, law librarian, consultant, lawyer; b. Newberry, S.C., June 3, 1932; d. Price John and Caroline (Weeks) P.; m. David Lazar, Aug. 6, 1953 (div. Feb. 1994). BS, Northwestern U., 1953; MLS, U. Md., 1972; JD, Georgetown U., 1977. Bar: D.C. 1977. Asst. law libr. U.S. Ct. Appeals for D.C., Washington, 1972-74; supervisory law libr. U.S. Ct. Appeals for D.C. Dist., 1974-84, circuit libr., 1984—. Mem. ALA, D.C. Bar Assn., Am. Assn. Law Librs. Home: 5301 Duvall Dr Bethesda MD 20816-1873 Office: US Ct Appeals for DC Cir Judges' Libr 5518 US Court House Washington DC 20001-5618

PADILLA, DAVID JOSEPH, lawyer, diplomat; b. Detroit, Feb. 9, 1944; s. David J. and Irene C. (Clos) P.; m. Kathryn E. Grant, Apr. 19, 1970; children: Sarah, Elizabeth, Rebecca. AB cum laude, U. Detroit, 1966, JD, 1969; MA, U. Pa., 1974; LLM with highest distinction, George Washington U., 1979; MPA, Harvard U., 1982. Bar: Mich. 1970, D.C. 1975. Tchr. St. Mary's H.S., Detroit, 1969-70; vol. Peace Corps, Venezuela, 1970-72; asst. prosecutor Wayne County Prosecutor's Office, Detroit, 1973; dir. legal svcs. OAS, Washington, 1975-80, asst. exec. sec. Inter-Am. Commn. Human Rights, 1980—2001, dir. human resources, 1985-86. Adj. prof. Am. U., Washington, 1987-96. Co-author: Municipal Development Institutions in Latin America, 1976; book reviewer Revista Interam. Bibliografía, 1982; contbr. numerous articles to profl. jours., chpts. to books. Pres. Ayuda, Inc., Washington, 1982—. Recipient Best Paper award Inter-Am. Bar Assn., 1979; named Outstanding Vol. Ayuda, Inc., 1993. Mem. Mich. Bar Assn., DC Bar Assn., U.S. Supreme Ct. Bar Assn., Theta Xi. Avocations: pilot, marathons, juggling. Home: 6838 Woodland Dr Falls Church VA 22046-2324 E-mail: dpadilla44@aol.com.

PADILLA, DEREK SHANE, director, secondary school educator; b. Redwood City, Calif., Nov. 22, 1973; s. Napoleon and Marlene Padilla. BA in English and Creative Writing, San Francisco State U., 1997. Single subject tchg. credential in English 1997. Dir. activities El Camino H.S., South San Francisco, Calif., 1997—. Editor, contbr.: comic book anthology Spasm, 1993, author, editor: poetry anthology Eloquent Graffiti, 2001. Named Hero of the Bay, San Francisco Chronicle and KNBR, 2000. Mem.: Calif. Assn. Dirs. of Activities (Dir. of Yr. Area B 2001). Avocations: poetry, coaching. Home: PO Box 2427 Daly City CA 94017-2427 Office: El Camino HS 1320 Mission Rd South San Francisco CA 94080 Business E-Mail: dpadillaechs@hotmail.com.

PADILLA, ELSA NORMA, retired school system administrator; b. Guines, Havana, Cuba, Feb. 25, 1947; came to U.S., 1962; d. Regulo and Esther (Beato) Cuesta; m. Pedro Manuel Padilla, June 10, 1967; children: Jorge Alberto, Alejandro Manuel. BA, U. Ariz., 1970, MEd, 1972, cert. administration, 1982. Cert. elem. tchr. bilingual endorsement, spl. edn., adminstrn., Ariz. Spl. edn. tchr. Tucson Unified Sch. Dist., 1970, 1972-76, spl. edn. program specialist, 1976-78, spl. edn. tchr., 1978-81, bilingual diagnostician, 1981-84, asst dir. spl. edn., 1984-89; principal Ochoa Elem. Sch. Tucson Unified Sch. Dist., 1989-96, compliance coord., 1996-99; ednl. cons. Tuscon Unified Sch. Dist., 1999—. Part time instr. Ariz. Dept. Edn., 1980-87, No. Ariz. U., 1983-89, U. Ariz., Tucson, 1983-88; mem. bilingual diagnostic team Tucson Sch. Dist., 1978, author Bilingual Spl. Edn. Program, 1980; prin. in restructuring of sch. project funded by Charles Stewart Mott Found.; grant reader Office Bilingual Edn. and Minority Lang. Affairs, U.S. Dept. Edn., 1995—; cons. in field. Co-author: Courage to Change. Bd. dirs. TETRA Corp., Tucson, 1988-94, Vista Adv. Coun., Tucson, 1990-93; mem. City of South Tucson Econ. Devel. Adv. Bd., 1993-96. Grantee: U.S. Dept. Edn., Tucson, 1984; recipient NEA Excellence award, 1994. Democrat. Avocations: cooking, swimming. E-mail: enpadilla@cs.com.

PADILLA, JAMES EARL, lawyer; b. Miami, Fla., Dec. 28, 1953; s. Earl George and Patricia (Bauer) P. BA, Northwestern U., 1975; JD, Duke U., 1978. Bar: Ill. 1978, U.S. Ct. Appeals (5th and 7th cir.) 1978, U.S. Supreme Ct. 1981, Colo. 1982, U.S. Ct. Appeals (10th cir.) 1982, D.C. 1985, N.Y. 1989. Assoc. Mayer, Brown & Platt, Chgo. and Denver, 1978-84, ptnr. Denver, 1985-87, N.Y.C., 1988-96; private investor, 1996—. Contbg. author: Mineral Financing, 1982, Illinois Continuing Legal Education, 1993. Mem. ABA, Ill. Bar Assn., D.C. Bar Assn., Colo. Bar Assn., N.Y. State Bar Assn. Avocation: golf.

PADILLA, MARIO RENÉ, literature educator, writer, actor; b. Detroit, Oct. 4, 1949; s. Marcelino Ramos and Nina Consolata (Macioce) P.; children: Francesca, Miguel, Marcello, Gabriella; m. Christine Jasiorkowski; stepchildren: Trevor, Laura. BS, Ohio State U., 1971; MA, Loyola Marymount U., 1987; PhD, U. So. Calif., 1993. Prodn. supr. CBS TV, L.A., 1972-78; actor, 1980—; prof. English lit. and creative writing, Latin Am. lit. Santa Monica (Calif.) Coll., 1994—. Author: Reaching Back for the Neverendings, 1993, Borges, Faulkner, Hemingway: Young Poets of Prose, 1993 (Fulbright award 1993); composer (ballet) The Harbinger of Evolution, 1980 (ASCAP award 1981), (song) I Found Love, and numerous other songs and ballets; actor including Mario on Falcon Crest, 1981-83, Jimmy Rivera on Hunter, 1991-92, officer Lopez in General Hosp., 1993-2000. Capt. U.S. Army, 1971-72. Mem. ASCAP, MLA, Screen Actors Guild, Am. Fedn. TV Radio Artists, Actor's Equity. Avocations: Karate, soccer, basketball, coaching children's sports, Yoga. Home: 1211 Vienna Way Venice CA 90291-4026 E-mail: Padilla_mario@smc.edu.

PADMANABHAN, CAPE S. geriatrician; b. Trivandrum, Kerala, India, Sept. 2, 1943; s. Shankar and Jeyalakshmi Iyer; m. Lalitha Padmanabhan, Jan. 20, 1973; 2 children. MB BS, JIPMER, Pondicherry, India, 1967. Diplomate Am. Bd. Internal Medicine, Am. Bd. Geriatric Medicine. Intern Booth Meml. Hosp., Flushing, N.Y., 1970-71; resident Met. Hosp. Ctr.-N.Y. Med. Ctr., N.Y.C., 1971-73; chief geriat. medicine VA Med. Ctr., Castle Point, N.Y., 1983-96; assoc. med. dir. Masonic Home, Utica, 1996-97, Shorefront Jewish Geriatric Ctr., Bklyn., 1998; med. dir. VA Primary Care Clinic, Glens Falls, N.Y., 1999-2000; fellow Norwalk (Conn.) Hosp., 1973-74; geriatrician VA, Bedford, Mass., 2000—. Cons. Geriat. Svcs., P.C., Yonkers, N.Y., 1999—, Hudson Valley Health Care System, Castle Point, N.Y. Mem. ACP. Avocations: classical music, tennis. Home: PO Box 807 Bedford MA 01730 also: 280 Bishops Forest Dr Waltham MA 02452

PADMANABHAN, SIVAKUMAR, physician; b. Thanjavur, Tamil Nadu, India, Jan. 20, 1967; came to U.S., 1995; s. Sundararajulu and Vasantha (Parthasarathy) P.; m. sridevi Jeyasekar, Feb. 10, 1995; children: Aparna Pushkara, Gokul Pushkaran. M.B.BS, Thanjavur Med. Coll., 1990. Diplomate Am. Bd. Internal Medicine, Am. Bd. Pulmonary Diseases, Am. Bd. Critical Care Medicine. Med. officer AKC Nursing Home, Thanjavur, 1990-93; sr. house officer Royal Hull and East Yorkshire Hosps., Eng., 1994-95; resident Brookdale U. Hosp. and Med. Ctr., Bklyn., 1995-98, fellow pulmonary medicine, 1998-2000; fellow in critical care medicine U. Tex. Med. Br., Galveston, 2000-01; inpatient mgr., hospitalist Spohn Shoreline Hosp., Corpus Christi, 2001—. Mem. AMA, ACP, ACCP, Am. Thoracic Soc., Soc. Critical Care Medicine, Tex. Med. Assn. Hindu. Office: Inpatient Med Svcs Ste 1020 1225 North Loop West Houston TX 77008 Home: 5622 Les Parre Corpus Christi TX 78414-6074 E-mail: sivapadman@hotmail.com.

PADNOS, MARK, library administrator, literary translator; b. N.Y.C., Sept. 24, 1944; s. Morton and Edna (Nass) P.; m. Alla Lipina, July 8, 1997 (div. 2000). BA, U. Iowa, 1966; MLS, L.I. U., 1978; cert. in advanced librarianship, Columbia U., 1992; MA in Liberal Studies-Translation, CUNY, 1993. Asst. libr. YIVO Inst. for Jewish Rsch., N.Y.C., 1978-80; libr. dir. Anthology Film Archives, 1980-82; libr. aviation week & space technology McGraw-Hill, 1982-84; ref. libr. Bronx (N.Y.) C.C., 1986-89; asst. dir. multimedia ctr. Pratt Inst., Bklyn., 1989-90; reference libr. Fordham U., Bronx, 1991-93; humanities reference libr. grad. sch. CUNY, N.Y.C., 1993-98; coord. pub. svcs. Bronx (N.Y.) C.C. Libr., 1998—, acting chief libr., 2000—. Rsch. cons. and book reviewer in field. Translator: (German poetry) Contemporary Literature in Translation, 1971, Modern Poetry in Translation, 1973, Romanian Library Bulletin, 1973, Dimension: Contemporary German Arts and Letters, 1994. Con Edison grantee, 1985. Mem. Am. Libr. Assn., Am. Literary Translators Assn., Poetry Soc. Am., Spl. Libr. Assn. (sec. info. tech. group), Assn. Jewish Libr. Jewish. Avocations: poetry, short fiction, genealogy, weight training. Office: CUNY Bronx CC W 181st St and Univ Ave Bronx NY 10453

PADOS, FRANK JOHN, JR. investment company executive; b. Easton, Pa., Feb. 9, 1944; s. Frank John and Mary Helen (Pokrifscak) P.; m. Barbara Janselwitz, July 6, 1968; children— Frank John (dec.), Kelly Ann, Kristin, Matthew John, Kaitlyn. BA cum laude in Econs. Boston Coll., 1966; MBA, U. Pa., 1968. Securities analyst Tchrs. Ins. and Annuity Assn., N.Y.C., 1971-74, investment officer, 1975-77, v.p., 1977-78, sr. v.p., mgr. securities div., 1978-83; mng. dir. Trust Co. of the West, 1983-95; exec. v.p. Desai Capital Mgmt., N.Y.C., 1995—. Dir. Candlewood Hotels, Inc. Served with U.S. Army, 1969-70. Decorated Bronze Star. Mem. Wharton Club, Sky Club. Roman Catholic. Home: 57 Thornley Dr Chatham NJ 07928-1360 Office: 540 Madison Ave New York NY 10022-3213 E-mail: fjp@desaicapital.com.

PADOVANO, ANTHONY THOMAS, theologian, educator; b. Harrison, N.J., Sept. 18, 1934; s. Thomas Henry and Mary Rose (Cierzo) P.; m. Theresa Lackamp, 1974; children— Mark, Andrew, Paul, Rosemarie BA magna cum laude, Seton Hall U., 1956; S.T.B. magna cum laude, Pontifical Gregorian U., Rome, Italy, 1958, S.T.L. magna cum laude, 1960, S.T.D. magna cum laude, 1962; Ph.L. magna cum laude, St. Thomas Pontifical Internat. U., Rome, 1962; MA, NYU, 1971; PhD, Fordham U., 1980. Ordained priest Roman Cath. Ch., 1959. Asst. chaplain Med. Center, Jersey City, 1960; asst. St. Paul of the Cross Ch., 1962, St. Catharine Ch., Glen Rock, N.J., 1963; prof. systematic theology Darlington Sem., Mahwah, 1962-74; prof. Am. lit. Ramapo Coll., 1971—; founding faculty mem., adj. prof. theology/religious studies Fordham U., 1973-93. Mem. Archdiocesan Commn. Ecumenical and Interreligious Affairs, 1965, Commn. Instrn. Clergy in Documents Vatican II, 1966; del. dialogue group Luth.-Roman Cath. Theol. Conversations, 1969; del.-at-large senate of priests Archdiocese of Newark; Danforth assoc., 1975—; Cath. pastor Inclusive Cmty. World Coun. Chs., 1986—; lectr. in field, also appearances on radio and TV; parish min. St. Margaret of Scotland, Morristown, N.J. Author: The Cross of Christ, the Measure of the World, 1962, The Estranged God, 1966, Who is Christ, 1967, Belief in Human Life, 1969, American Culture and the Quest for Christ, 1970, Dawn Without Darkness, 1971, Free to be Faithful, 1972, Eden and Easter, 1974, A Case for Worship, 1975, America: Its People, Its Promise, 1975, Presence and Structure, 1975, The Human Journey, 1982, Trilogy, 1982, Contemplation and Compassion, 1984, Winter Rain: A Play, 1985, His Name is John: A Play, 1986, Christmas to Calvary, 1987, Love and Destiny, 1987, Summer Lightening: A Play, 1988, Conscience and Conflict, 1989, Reform and Renewal, 1990, A Celebration of Life, 1990, The Church Today: Belonging and Believing, 1990, Scripture in the Streets, 1992, A Retreat with Thomas Merton, 1996, Hope is a Dialogue, 1998; editor: Centenary Issue Roman Echoes, 1959; editl. bd. The Advocate, 1966-73; contbr. articles to mags., Padovano Collection, personal and profl. papers, Archives, U. Notre Dame. Active Diocese Paterson Ecumenical Commn.; founding pres. Justice and Peace Commn., Diocese of Paterson, active Resigned Priests Com. Mem. Cath. Theol. Soc. Am., Mariological Soc. Am., Nat. Fedn. Priests Councils (ofcl. rep. to Constl. Conv., Chgo. 1968), Corpus (pres.), Fedn. Christian Ministries, Internat. Fedn. of Married Cath. Priests (v.p. for N.Am.). Home: 9 Millstone Dr Morris Plains NJ 07950-1536 Office: Dept of American Lit Ramapo Coll New Jersey Mahwah NJ 07430 E-mail: anthonypadovano@mail.com. *People rather than ideas have been most formative in my life. More accurately, people, as they embodied certain ideas have proved most decisive. There is nothing more persuasive than an idea which becomes so vital that it transforms the person who proclaims it.*

PADULA, FRED DAVID, filmmaker; b. Santa Barbara, Calif., Oct. 25, 1937; s. Fred and Mary (Adams) P.; married; 1 child. BA in Music, San Francisco State U., MA in Art, 1965. Adj. faculty U. Calif., San Francisco Art Inst., San Francisco State U.; artist-in-residence U. Minn., Mpls. Filmmaker: Ephesus, 1965 (1st pl. award San Francisco Internat. Film Festival, awards N.Y. Film Festival, Chgo. Internat. Film Festival, others), The Artist Speaks, Two Photographers: Wynn Bullock and Imogen Cunningham, Little Jesus (Hippy Hill), Anthology of Boats, David and My Porch, Salmon River Run, El Capitan (awards: Grand Prize Festival Internat. de Film D'Aventure Uecue, La Plagne, France, Grand Prize Film Festival Internat. Montagna Esplorazione, Trento, Italy, Grand Prize Banff Festival of Mountain Films, Can., Grand Prize Mountain Film, Telluride, Colo., Gold medal Festival Internat. du Film Alpine, Les Diablerets, Switzerland; electronic music compositions include: Barking Dogs, Charnet Loops, others; one-man shows (photography) include aerial photographic survey of Mayan Indian Ruins, Yucatan, Mex., 1989, San Francisco Internat. Airport, San Francisco Mus. Modern Art, Kalamazoo Inst. Arts, DeYoung Mus., San Francisco, San Fernando Valley State Coll., Bakersfield Coll., Wash. State U., West Chester Coll., Valhalla,N.Y., George Eastman House, represented in permanent collections, Kalamazoo Inst. Arts, State of Calif., George Eastman House, San Francisco Internat. Airport, Crocker Art Mus., Oakland Mus. Art, 1004 Gallery, Port Townsend, Wash., New Horizons Nat. Bank Hdqs., San Rafael, Calif., SUNY/Westchester C.C., Valhalla, N.Y., Grace Mus., Abilene, Tex. Address: 47 Shell Rd Mill Valley CA 94941-1551

PADVE, MARTHA BERTONNEAU, urban planning and arts consultant, fundraiser; b. Scobey, Mont., Feb. 22; d. Henry Francis and Marie (Vaccaro) Bertonneau; m. Jacob Padve, May 9, 1954 (div. 1980). Student, Pasadena Jr. Coll., 1938-40; cert., S.W. U. Bus. Coll., L.A., 1940-41, Pasadena Inst. for Radio, 1946-47; student, Claremont Colls., 1972-74, U. So. Calif., 1983-84, Community Coll., Pasadena, 1987-88. Juvenile roles Pasadena (Calif.) Cmty. Playhouse, 1935-37; ptnr., bus. mgr. restaurant devel. ventures, Pasadena, 1940-50; club dir. Red Cross, Nfld., Can., 1944-45; leading roles Penthouse Theatre, Altadena, Calif., 1946-48; club dir. armed forces spl. svcs. Red Cross, Austria, 1949-52; head dept. publs. Henry E. Huntington Libr., San Marino, Calif., 1953-57; cons. art planning Model Cities program, Omaha, 1975; founding instr. contemporary art collecting class, 1979-80; dir. devel. Bella Lewitzky Dance Found., L.A., 1980-81; instr. Art. Ctr. Coll. Design, Pasadena, 1981-82, assoc. dir. devel., 1981-83; instr. U. So. Calif. Coll. Continuing Edn., L.A., 1983-84; urban planning and arts cons. The Arroyo Group, Pasadena, 1979-94; freelance writer, journalist, playwright, 1994—. Developer edn. program Mus. Contemporary Art, L.A., 1984-86; author arts segment Pasadena Gen. Plan, 1980-83. Contbr. articles to newspapers. Trustee, v.p. Pasadena Art Mus., 1967-74; co-chair bldg. fund Norton Simon Mus. Art, Pasadena 1968-70; chair Pasadena Planning Commn., 1973-81, Pasadena Street Tree Plan, 1975-76, Pasadena High Rise Task Force, 1979, San Gabriel Valley Planning Coun., 1977-78; mem. Pasadena Downtown Urban Design Plan, 1980-83; founding mem. Arts, Pks. & Recreation Task Force, 1978-80; vice-chair Pasadena Design Review Commn., 1974-78; founding chair So. Calif. Fellows of Contemporary Art, 1976-78; adv. com. U. So. Calif. Art Galleries, 1976-82, UCLA oral history program contemporary art, 1983-94; chair audit com. L.A. County Grand Jury, 1986-87; founder Pasadena Robinson Meml., Inc., 1990-92, bd. dirs. 1992-93; curator Vroman's Art on the Stairwell, 1992-2002; exec. com. St. Andrew's Sch. Bd., 1993-94; co-chair restoration adv. com. St. Andrew's Ch., 1994; judge Pasadena Tournament of Roses, 1994; bd. dirs. San Juan Cmty. Theatre, 1997-2001, exec. com., 1999-2001, mem. acting exec. dir. team, 1999-2000; monologue produced Playwrights Festival, 2001. Named Woman of the Yr., Pasadena Women's Civic League, 1980; recipient Gold Crown award Tenth Muse, Pasadena Arts Coun., 1983, Commendation awards Pasadena City Dirs., 1975, 80, 82-83, Commendation award L.A. County Bd. Suprs., 1987, Graphic Arts award Southern Calif. Fellows Contemporary Art, 1978. Republican. Roman Catholic. Avocations: theater, music, wine, food. Home and Office: 57 Olympic View Dr Friday Harbor WA 98250-8933 E-mail: mbp10@outerisland.net. *Personal philosophy: I have come to believe that nothing is a coincidence; that our lives are a series of interconnections with people and events; that our destiny is largely controlled by exterior forces. A lesson to remember is that we never know where or when a chance acquaintance (or subordinate) may become a major player in our lives.*

PAEZ, RICHARD A. federal judge; b. 1947; BA, Brigham Young U., 1969; JD, U. Calif., Berkeley, 1972. Staff atty. Calif. Rural Legal Assistance, Delano, Calif., 1972—74, Western Ctr. on Law and Poverty, 1974—76; sr. counsel, dir. litig., acting exec. dir. Legal Aid Found. of LA, 1976—81; judge LA Mcpl. Ct., 1981—94, U.S. Dist. Ct. (ctrl. dist.) Calif., LA, 1994—2000, U.S. Dist. Ct. (9th cir.), Pasadena, 2000—. Active Hollywood-Los Feliz Jewish Cmty. Ctr. Mem.: Calif. Jud. Coun., Mex.-Am. Bar Assn. LA County, LA County Bar Assn., Calif. State Bar Assn. Office: US Ct Appeals Edward R Roybal Ctr & Fed Bldg 125 S Grand AveRm 204 Pasadena CA 91105-1652*

PAGÁN, GILBERTO, JR. clinical psychologist; b. San Juan , P.R., Dec. 30, 1950; s. Gilberto Sr. and Juanita (Quiñones) P.; m. Grissele Camacho, Aug. 6, 1972; children: Mariel, Lauren. Exch. student, SUNY, Albany, 1969-70; BA in Psychology magna cum laude, U. P.R., 1972; MS in Devel. Psychology, Rutgers U., 1974, PhD in Clin. Psychology, 1984. Lic. psychologist, N.J.; cert. sch. psychology. Psychometrician Well Baby Clinic of New Brunswick, N.J., 1972-73; staff psychologist Community Orgn. for Mental Health and Retardation, Inc., Phila., 1976-77; intern in clin. psychology Multimodal Therapy Inst., Kingston, N.J., 1979-80; sch. psychologist New Brunswick Pub. Sch. System, 1980-83; mental health clinician Community Mental Health Ctr. U. Medicine and Dentistry N.J., Piscataway, 1983-93; sch. psychologist Perth Amboy Pub. Sch. Sys., 1993-95; pvt. practice clin. psychology Newark, 1988—; sch. psychologist Jersey City Pub. Sch. Sys., 1995-98, Elizabeth (N.J.) Pub. Sch. Sys., 1998—. Assoc. in psychiatry Univ. of Medicine and Dentistry of N.J., Piscataway, 1988-98; field supr. Rutgers U., New Brunswick, N.J., 1988—; cons. in field to clients including Bloomfield Pub. Sch. System, Div. of Youth and Family Svcs. of State of N.J., Project Head Start, Plainfield, N.J. Columnist San Juan Star, 1990-93, 97-98, El Hispano, Phila., 1977-78; contbr. profl. publs.; presenter in field. Pres. N.J. chpt. Nat. Com. for Puerto Rican Statehood, 1990-95. NIMH fellow, 1978-79; predoctoral rsch. fellow Inst. for Rsch. in Human Devel., Divsn. Psychol. Studies of Ednl. Testing Svc., Princeton, N.J., 1974-75; recipient P.R. Psychol. Assn. award, 1972, Puerto Rican Action Bds. Parents Assn. award 1985; inducted into Nat. Honor Soc. in Psychology, 1973. Mem. APA, NEA, N.J. Edn. Assn., N.J. Psychol. Assn., Elizabeth Edn. Assn. Democrat. Roman Catholic. Home: 422 Johnstone St Perth Amboy NJ 08861-3330 Office: 467 Mount Prospect Ave Newark NJ 07104-2907

PAGAN, KEITH AREATUS, music educator, academic administrator; b. Beggs, Okla., June 7, 1931; s. Areatus and Opal Gail (Facker) P.; m. Betty Lois Wallace; children: Melva Joy, Lisa Lynne, Beryl Kay. B in Music Edn., Bethany Nazarene Coll., 1952; M in Music Edn., Okla. U., 1953; D in Music Edn. with honors, Ind. U., 1970. Asst. prof. music Bethany (Okla.) Nazarene Coll., 1952-53, 55-58; prof. music Pasadena (Calif.) Coll., 1961-76; acad. dean, v.p. acad. affairs Point Loma Nazarene Coll., San Diego, 1976-88, prof. music, chair dept. music., 1989—98. Dir. S.W. Music Symposium, San Diego, 1991—; cons. Sch. for Creative and Performing Arts, San Diego, 1990—, Chula Vista, Calif., 1992—; mem. vis. team Western Coll. Assn., Calif., 1977-82. Arranger (choral) To God be the Glory, (brass) Keith A. Pagan Brass Quintet Series, The King Shall Come; mem. editorial bd. Christian Scholars Rev., 1986—, EverGreen Morning Music Press. Trustee Christian Scholars Rev., 1994—. With U.S. Army, 1953-55. Recipient WHO award Calif. Higher Edn. Assn., 1971, Lawrence Vredevoe Disting. Leadership award 1986, Spl. Svc. to Music award Calif. Music Educators Assn., 1991; winner 4th ann. anthem contest Choral Condrs. Guild; grantee Danforth Found., 1960. Mem. Calif. Coll. and Univ. Faculty Assn. (pres. 1969-70), Music Tchrs. Assn. Calif. (parliamentarian 1971-73), Western Assn. Schs. and Coll. (accreditation liaison 1976-88). Avocations: travel, photography. Home: 7450 Margerum Ave San Diego CA 92120-2025

PAGANELLI, CHARLES VICTOR, physiologist, educator; b. N.Y.C., Feb. 13, 1929; s. Charles Victor and Mary Paganelli; m. Barbara Harriet Slauson, Sept. 18, 1954; children: William, Kathryn, Peter, Robert, John. AB, Hamilton Coll., Clinton, N.Y., 1950; MA, Harvard U., 1952, PhD, 1957. Instr. physiology U. Buffalo, 1958-60, asst. prof., 1960-63; assoc. prof. SUNY, Buffalo, 1963-71, prof. physiology, 1971-97, disting. svc. prof., 1997—. Interim chair SUNY, Buffalo, 1991-98, emeritus, 1998. Editor: Physiological Function in Special Environments, 1990; contbr. articles to profl. jours. Recipient Elliott Coues award Am. Ornithologists Union, 1981, Newman award 1998. Mem.: Phi Beta Kappa, Am. Physiol. Soc., Sigma Xi, Alpha Omega Alpha.

PAGANI, ALBERT LOUIS, aerospace system engineer; b. Jersey City, Feb. 19, 1936; s. Alexander C. and Anne (Salvati) P.; m. Beverly Cameron, Feb. 23, 1971; children: Penelope, Deborah, Michael. BSEE, U.S. Naval Acad., 1957; MBA, So. Ill. U., 1971. Commd. 2d lt. USAF, 1957, advanced through grades to col., 1978, navigator La., 1957-63, pilot McGuire AFB, N.J., 1963-65, command pilot Anchorage, 1965-68, mgr. airlift Saigon, Socialist Repubublic of Vietnam, 1968-69, chief spl. missions Scott AFB, Ill., 1969-74; commd. tactical airlift group USAF Europe, Mildenhall, Eng., 1974-76, dep. comdr. Rhein Main Air Base Frankfurt, Fed. Republic Germany, 1976-78; chief airlift mgmt. USAF Mil. Airlift Command, Scott AFB, Ill., 1978-81, dir. tech. plans and concepts, 1981, dir. command and control, 1982-85; ret., 1985; program mgr. Lockheed Missile and Space Co., Sunnyvale, Calif., 1985-94; dir. data applications, dir. adv. programs PAR Govt. Sys. Corp., New Hartford, NY, 1994-97; pres. Computer Solutions Group, N.Y., 1997—; prin. Beval Assocs., Inc., 1997—; CEO CSG, Canada, 1999—; dir. B-Net, N.Y., 1999—; prin., dir. Asset Trax, Inc., 2000—. V.p. Cath. Ch. Coun., Mildenhall, 1974, pres., 1975. Decorated Legion of Merit, Bronze Star, Air medal, Vietnam Cross of Gallantry. Mem. Nat. Def. Transp. Assn. (sr.), Soc. Logistics Engrs., Air Force Assn., Armed Forces Comm. and Electronics Assn., Air Lift Assn., Inst. Noetic Scis., Daedalions, Mensa. Avocations: woodworking, neurolinguistics, volunteer senior executive consulting. Home: 8592 Red Hill Rd Clinton NY 13323-4210 E-mail: csq@bevalinc.com.

PAGANO, ALICIA I. education educator; b. Sidney, N.Y., June 29, 1929; d. Neil Gadsby Leonard and Norma (Carr) Collins; m. Thomas McNutt, Feb. 20, 1954 (div. Nov. 1962); m. LeRoy Pagano, Feb. 26, 1963 (div. Oct. 1985); children: Janice, Daniel, Jack, Pier. BA in Music, Barrington Coll., 1952; MAT in Music, Rollins Coll., 1964; EdD in Edn. Adminstrn., Am. U., 1972. Tchr. music Prince Georges County Pub. Schs., Beltsville, Md., 1966-69; asst. prof. Medgar Evers Coll., Bklyn., 1973-78; nat. program dir. Girl Scouts USA, N.Y.C., 1978-83; nat. dir. vol. development U.S. Com. UNICEF, 1983-84; pres. Pagano Consulting Internat., Jersey City, 1984—; asst. prof. mgmt. Coll. Staten Island, CUNY, 1985-89; adj. prof. museum studies NYU, N.Y.C., 1986-91; assoc. exec. dir. Louis August Jonas Found., Red Hook, N.Y., 1988-89; assoc. prof. edn. N.J. City U., 1990—. Chair Wingspread Nat. Conf./Nat. Collaboration for Youth, Washington, 1982; adv. bd. dirs. Early Childhood Ctr.; rschr., cons. in early childhood edn. in West Africa, 1988—. Author, editor: Social Studies in Early Childhood, 1979; author: The Future of American Business, 1985, (with others) Learning Opportunities Beyond

School, 1987; co-editor: International Early Childhood Teacher Education, 1999; contbr. articles to profl. jours. Judge annual awards Girls, Inc., N.Y.C., 1985-90; reader Jersey City Spelling Bee, 1991; vol. Girl Scouts USA, Essex/Hudson Counties, N.J., 1995—, Boys & Girls Clubs, Hudson County, N.J., 1995—. Mem. ASCD, AAUW, Am. Ednl. Rsch. Assn., Nat. Assn. Early Childhood Tchr. Edn. (bd. dirs. 1995—), N.J. Assn. Early Childhood Tchr. Educators (v.p. 1994-97, pres. 1997-99), Orgn. Mondiale pour l'Edn. Prescolaire (N.J. regional dir. 1996-98). Avocations: hiking, swimming, international travel. Home: PO Box 413 Mastic Beach NY 11951-0413 E-mail: apagano@njcu.edu.

PAGANO, CELESTE ANN, social services administrator; b. Bridgeport, Conn., Apr. 12, 1950; d. Peter Angelo and Carmella Marie (Carrafiello) P. AAS in Broadcast Journalism, Grahm Jr. Coll., Boston, 1970; BA magna cum laude, Fairfield U., 1997; MPA, NYU, 2000. Self employed real estate investor, property mgr. Pagano-Albert, 1981-97; cmty. rels. coord., vol., bd. mem. Vol. Ctr. Greater Bridgeport, 1997-99; program and vol. coord. Interfaith Vol. Caregivers, 1999-2000; program coord. Bridgeport Supportive Housing Program, 2000—02; domestic violence coord. Ctr. for Women and Families, 2002—. Guest spkr. on discrimination Conn. Realtors Conv., Hartford, 1987. Mem. adv. bd. Coordinated Assessment and Referral for the Elderly Program, Bridgeport Hosp., 1999; steering com. mem. Caring Connections Program, Cath. Family Svcs., 2000-02. Recipient Outstanding Fair Housing Action award Bridgeport Fair Housing, 1986. Democrat. Avocations: writing, music, kayaking, cross-country skiing. Home and Office: 56 Livingston St Bridgeport CT 06605-3303

PAGANO, EUGENE SALVATORE ROONEY, lawyer; b. N.Y.C., Apr. 29, 1951; s. Vito Venero and Virginia Marie (Rooney) P. BA summa cum laude, Spring Hill Coll., Mobile, Ala., 1973; JD, U. Va., 1976; LLM, Harvard U., 1983. Bar: N.Y. 1977, D.C. 1977, U.S. Dist. Ct. (so. dist.) N.Y. 1978, U.S. Dist. Ct. (ea. dist.) N.Y. 1979, U.S. Ct. Appeals (D.C. cir.) 1981, U.S. Ct. Appeals (2d cir.) 1985, U.S. Supreme Ct. 1987. Law clk. to Hon. Stanley S. Harris D.C. Ct. Appeals, Washington, 1976-77; self-employed. Contbr. articles to profl. jours. Mem. Nassau County Bar Assn. (vice chair appellate practice com. 2000—, Pres.'s award 1991). Roman Catholic. Avocation: history. E-mail: jurisconsultus@earthlink.net.

PAGANO, FILIPPO FRANK, financial broker, commercial loan consultant; b. East Paterson, N.J., Feb. 4, 1939; s. Frank and Katherine (Tavano) P.; m. Rose Ann Melisi, June 10, 1960 (div. Dec. 1972); children: Paul, Cynthia Pagano Grube, Stefanie; m. Darlene Ann Coryea, Mar. 1987 (div. June, 1998). BS in Pharmacy, Rutgers U., 1960. Registered pharmacist, profl. ski instr.; lic. capt. master USCG. System analyst Parke-Davis & Co., Detroit, 1964-72; sr. mktg. analyst internat. Schering-Plough Pharm. Co., Kenilworth, N.J., 1972-73; v.p. Robert S. First, N.Y.C., 1973-74; pres. M-P Consultations Inc., 1974-75; chief exec. officer Nordic Inn, Landgrove, Vt., 1975-83; sea capt. Bahamas, 1983-85; food and beverage dir. Meredith Guest House, Durham, 1985-86, gen. mgr., 1986-88; pres. Flagship Yachts, Beaufort, N.C., 1988—; gen. mgr. Inter-Global Capital, Raleigh, 1989—. Co-author: Nordic Inn Book of Soups, 1979; contbr. articles on skiing to newspapers and mags. Mem. Vt. Ski Touring Operators Assn. (pres. 1979-81), Beaufort Off-Shore Sailing Soc., Boss Club (Beaufort), Kappa Psi. Republican. Roman Catholic. Avocations: sailing, snow skiing, culinary interests. Home and Office: PO Box 145 Beaufort NC 28516-0145

PAGANO, JOSEPH STEPHEN, physician, researcher, educator; b. Rochester, N.Y., Dec. 29, 1931; s. Angelo Pagano and Marian (Vinci) Signorino; m. Anna Louise Reynolds, June 8, 1957; children: Stephen Reynolds, Christopher Joseph. AB with honors, U. Rochester, 1953; MD, Yale U., 1957. Resident Peter Bent Brigham Hosp. Harvard U., Boston, 1960-61; fellow Karolinska Inst., Stockholm, 1961-62; mem. Wistar Inst., Phila., 1962-65; from asst. to assoc. prof. medicine & microbiology U. N.C., Chapel Hill, 1965-73, prof., 1974—, dir. divsn. infectious diseases, 1972-75; founder, dir. U. N.C. Lineberger Comprehensive Cancer Ctr., 1974-97, dir. emeritus, 1997—. Attending physician U. Hosps., Chapel Hill; vis. prof. Swiss Inst. Cancer Rsch., Lausanne, 1970-71, Lineberger prof. cancer rsch., 1986—; mem. virology study sect. NIH, Bethesda, Md., 1973-79; recombinant DNA adv. com. USPHS, 1986-90; bd. dirs. Burroughs Wellcome Fund, 1993-2001; chmn., adv. com. N.C. Cancer Coord. and Control, 1993—; Mclaughlin vis. prof. U. Tex. Med. Br., 1996; Norma Berryhill Disting. lectr. U. N.C., 1997; Harry Eagle lectr. Albert Einstein Coll. Medicine, 1997; Harry F. Dowling lectr. U. Ill. Sch. Med., 1991; Gertrude & Werner Henle lectr. in viral oncology, 1990. Mem. editorial bd. Jour. Virology, Jour. Immunology, Cancer Rsch., Jour. Gen. Virology, Antimicrobial Agts. and Chemotherapy, 1974-93; contbr. articles to profl. jours., chpts. to books. Awards assembly GM Cancer Rsch. Found., 1997-2001. Recipient Sinsheimer award, 1966-68, USPHS Research Career award NIH, 1968-73, N.C. award in sci., 1996. Mem. AAAS (Newcomb Anderson prize selection com. 1984-88), Inst. Med. (sr. mem.), Am. Assn. Cancer Rsch., Am. Assn. Cancer Insts. (bd. dirs. 1992-99, pres., chmn.), Internat. Assn. for Rsch. in Epstein-Barr Virus (pres. 1990-94), Chapel Hill Tennis Club (pres. 1980-82), Carolina Club, Baldhead Island Club. Episcopalian. Avocations: tennis, squash. Home: 114 Laurel Hill Rd Chapel Hill NC 27514-4323 Office: U NC CB7295 Lineberger Comp Cancer Ctr Chapel Hill NC 27599-0001

PAGANO, MICHAEL PRO, advertising executive; b. Tulsa, Dec. 25, 1946; s. Michael Anthony and Irene Lucille (Burns) P.; m. Laura Iris Silverman, Oct. 12, 1969 (div. May 1981); children: Brian Paul, Anthony Michael. BA, Okla. U., 1974, BS Physician Assoc., 1977, MA in English, 1984, PhD in Health Comm., 1990. Cert. physician asst. Lectr. U. Okla., Norman, 1984-86; physician asst. Atoka (Okla.) Meml. Hosp., 1986-88, Vinita (Okla.) Med. Assocs., 1988-92, St. Mary's Hosp., Racine, Wis., 1992-94; prof., chmn. dept. Physician Asst. U. Health Scis./Chgo. Med. Sch., 1992-94; physician asst. Stamford (Conn.) Hosp., 1995—; adj. faculty Sch. Labor rels. Cornell U., N.Y.C., 1995—2000; sr. v.p. Lyons Lavey Nickel Swift, 1994—2002, assoc. creative dir., dir. internet devel.; pres., chief creative officer DrCreative, Inc., 2002—. Author: Communicating Effectively in Medical Records, 1992, Communication Skills for Professional Nurses, 1992; contbr. articles to profl. jours. With U.S. Army, 1965-68. Recipient Rx Club Award of Excellence, 1997, 98, 2000; Western Speech Comm. Assn. scholar, 1987, AD/RX award New Eng. Jour. Medicine, 1998, Readex award, Med Ad News, 1998. Fellow Am. Acad. Physician Assts., Am. Med. Writers Assn., Conn. Acad. Physician Assts.; mem. Healthcare Mktg. and Comm. Coun. Avocations: golf, writing fiction, reading. bus. Home: 3 Shorefront Park Norwalk CT 06854-3752 Office: DrCreative Inc 3 Shorefront Park Norwalk CT 06854-3752 E-mail: drmpp@optonline.net., drmpp@drcreative.biz.

PAGANO, RICHARD DONALD, physical education educator, researcher; b. Phila., Jan. 17, 1951; s. Joe Thomas and Mary Irene Pagano; m. Ann Theresa Pagano, June 17, 1977; children: Lauren Ann, Ryan Richard. BS, East Stroudsburg U., 1973; MEd, West Chester U., 1981. Cert. tchr., Pa. Health and phys. edn. tchr. Upper Darby (Pa.) Sch. Dist., 1974—. Columnist Town Talk Newspaper, 1987— (Sportsman of Yr. 1999); author: Life of Fred Luehring, 1981, History of Delco Hall of Fame, 1988. Trustee Stuzebecker Found., 1998—; bd. dirs. Crozer-Keystone Healthplex Sports Mus., 1998—, Pa. Sports Hall of Fame, 1995—, Delaware County Athletes Hall of Fam Com., 1988—, sport historian, 1988—. Named to Delaware County Athletes Hall of Fame, 1991, Pa. Sports Hall of Fame, 1997, Ridley Twp. Old Timers Hall of Fame, 1991. Mem. AAPHERD. Avocations: sports research, writing, collecting sports books. Home: 1311 Donna Ave Woodlyn PA 19094-1126 Office: Westbrook Park Sch Westbrook Dr Clifton Heights PA 19018

PAGAN ORTIZ, ALEX OMAR, computer systems analyst, educator; b. Ponce, P.R., Dec. 8, 1967; s. Javier E. Pagan and Brunilda Ortiz Collazo. BS in Computer Sci., Sacred Heart U., 1993; MS in Computer Sci., Temple U., 1997. Computer scientist U.S. Dept. Def., Fort Meade, Md., 1998-99; sr. cons. Oracle Corp., Columbia, 1999-2000; internal sys. engr. Digital Courier Techs., Clearwater, Fla., 2000-2001; data analyst Eli Lilly Export S.A., Hato Rey, PR, 2001—02. Faculty assoc. Johns Hopkins U., Washington, 1998-2000. Avocations: tennis, swimming. Home: 1628 W Holden Ave # 172 Orlando FL 32839 E-mail: aopagan@yahoo.com.

PAGE, ALBERT LEE, soil science educator, researcher; b. New Lenox, Ill., Mar. 19, 1927; s. Thomas E. and Hattie O. (Pease) Pugh; m. Shirley L. Jessmore, Sept. 14, 1952; children— Nancy, Thomas BA in Chemistry, U. Calif.-Riverside, 1956; PhD in Soil Sci., U. Calif.-Davis, 1960. Prof. soil sci. U. Calif.-Riverside, 1960—. Dir. Kearney Found., Univ. Calif.-Riverside, program of excellence in energy research Editor: Methods of Soil Analysis, 1983, Utilization of Municipal Wastewater and Sludge on Land, 1983, Heavy Metals in the Environment, 1977 Served as QMQ1 USN, 1945-52 Recipient Environ. Quality Research award Am. Soc. Agronomy, 1984, Disting. Teaching award U. Calif., Riverside, 1976, Disting. Svc. award USDA, 1991; Fullbright scholar, 1966-67; Guggenheim Meml. Found. fellow, 1966-67 Fellow AAAS, Am. Soc. Agronomy, Soil Sci. Soc. Am.; mem. Internat. Soil Sci. Soc., Western Soil Sci. Soc., Soc. Environ. Geochemistry and Health, Sigma Xi. Home: 5555 Canyon Crest Dr Apt 1F Riverside CA 92507-6443 Office: U Calif Dept Soil & Environ Sci Riverside CA 92521-0001 E-mail: albert.page@ucr.edu.

PAGE, ALICE CECILIA, artist, educator; b. Greenwich, Conn., Nov. 29, 1965; d. Donald Rothwood Gregory and Alice Cecilia (Duffy) Page; children: John Gregory, Kathleen Alice. BFA, Parsons Sch. Design, 1988; MA, Columbia U., 1991. Textile designer The Echo Design Group, N.Y.C., 1988; tchr. art New Milford (Conn.) Pub. Schs., 1997—. Editor newsletter Family Focus, 1995-97. Vol. Vis. Nurse Assn., Washington, Conn., 1992-97; chmn. Inland Wetlands and Conservation Commn., Washington, 1993-99; mem. profl. adv. com. Vis. Nurse and Homecare N.W., Litchfield, Conn., 1995-97; mem. conservation plan com. Town of Washington, 1996—; sec. and elected mem. Zoning Commn., Washington, Conn., 1999—; mem. Head Start Policy Coun. of N.W. Conn., 2000-2001. Mem. NEA, Conn. Edn. Assn. Republican. Roman Catholic. Office: Hill and Plain Elem Sch Old Town Park Rd New Milford CT 06777

PAGE, ANN, stock brokerage executive; b. Carbondale, Ill., Apr. 12, 1958; d. Richard Frank and Marilyn Kay (Bays) P. BFA in Theatre, S.W. Mo. State U., 1990. V.p. individual retirement products Paine Webber, N.Y.C., 1984-86, v.p. bank trust products, 1986-88, v.p. equity sales, 1988-91; asst. br. mgr. Paine Webber, Inc., Chesterfield, Mo., 1991-92, sales mgr. Houston, 1992—. Sponsor March of Dimes, N.Y.C., 1982-88, Symphony Space, N.Y.C., 1988; bd. dirs. Greater Greenspoint Mgmt. Dist., 1993—. Mem. NAFE, Soc. for Parapsychol. Rsch., Internat. Found. Employee Benefit Plans, Internat. Assn. Fin. Planners., North Greenspoint C. of C. (bus. and econ. devel. coms. 1992—). Avocations: parapsychology, French, skiing, singing jazz/blues. Office: Paine Webber Inc 5 Post Oak Park Houston TX 77027-3409

PAGE, ANNE RUTH, gifted education educator, education specialist; b. Norfolk, Va., Apr. 13, 1949; d. Amos Purnell and Ruth Martin (Hill) Bailey; m. Peter Smith Page, Apr. 24, 1971; children: Edgar Bailey, Emmett McBrannon. BA, N.C. Wesleyan Coll.; student, Fgn. Lang. League; postgrad., N.C. State U.; student, Overseas Linguistic Studies, France, Spain, Eng., 1978, 85, 86. Cert. tchr., N.C. Tchr. Cary (N.C.) Sr. High Sch., 1971-72; tchr., head dept. Daniels Mid. Sch., Raleigh, N.C., 1978-83; chmn. fgn. lang. dept. Martin Mid. Gifted and Talented, 1983—. Leadership team Senate Bill 2 Core co-chair; dir. student group Overseas Studies, Am. Coun. for Internat. Studies, France, Spain, Eng., 1982, 84, 86, 88; bd. dirs. N.T.H., Inc., Washington; cert. mentor tchr. Wake County Pub. Schs., 1989; dir. student exchs. between Martin Mid. Sch. and Sevigné Inst. of Compiegne, France. Sunday sch. tchr. Fairmont United Meth. Ch., Raleigh, 1983-85. Mem. Alpha Delta Kappa. Democrat. Home: 349 Wilmot Dr Raleigh NC 27606-1232 Office: Martin Mid Sch GT 1701 Ridge Rd Raleigh NC 27607-6737

PAGE, CURTIS MATTHEWSON, minister; b. Columbus, Ohio, Oct. 24, 1946; s. Charles N. and Alice Matthewson P.; m. Martha Poitevin, Feb. 12, 1977; children: Allison, Charles, Abigail. BS, Ariz. State U., 1968; MDiv, San Francisco Theol. Sem., 1971, D Ministry, 1985. Ordained Presbyn. Ch., 1971. Pastor Ketchum (Idaho) Presbyn. Ch., 1972-80, Kirk O'The Valley Presbyn. Ch., Reseda, Calif., 1980-90; campaign dir. Kids 1st Edn. Reform Partnership, L.A., 1990-91; sr. pastor Orangewood Presbyn. Ch., Phoenix, 1991-93, First Meridian Heights Presbyn. Ch., Indpls., 1993—. Mem. com. Ch. Devel., Ind., 1995—; bd. dirs. Express Pub., Ketchum. Chmn. com. on preparation for the ministry, San Fernando, Calif., 1988-90; chmn. Ketchum City Zoning Commn., 1979-80; L.A. Mayor's Citizen's Adv. Task Force on Ethics, 1990; co-chmn. Voice Cmty. Orgn. L.A., 1988-90; chair Family CARES, Indpls., 1995—; founding pastor AliveTime, 1995; leading innovator in mainline Protestant worship and urban ministry. Avocations: tennis, snow skiing, coaching softball. Office: First Meridian Heights Pres 4701 Central Ave Indianapolis IN 46205-1828 E-mail: FMHPC@aol.com.

PAGE, EARL MICHAEL, management specialist; b. Providence, Sept. 5, 1950; s. Earl Gee and Joan V. (Moran) P.; m. Marilyn Martin Wagner, Nov. 30, 1984; children: Michael Page, Keri Wagner, Michael Wagner. BA, Boston Coll., 1972; MEd., Northea. U., 1977; MBA, Fla. Atlantic U., 1986. Program coord. Mass. Gen. Hosp., Boston, 1972-76; unit dir. Chandler St. Ctr., Worcester, Mass., 1977-80; pres. Page Three, Inc., North Palm Beach, Fla., 1981-83, Palm Beach Mgmt. Cons., Pompano Beach, 1983—; mgr. tng. and devel. AAA East Fla., Miami, 1986-87; v.p. adminstrn. and human resources City Furniture, Waterbed City, 1987—. Prof. Coll. Bus. and Pub. Adminstrn. Fla. Atlantic U., Boca Raton, Fla. Mem. ASTD, Soc. Human Resource Mgmt., Phi Kappa Phi. Republican. Roman Catholic. Avocations: tennis, guitar, investments. Home: 6701 N Hiatus Rd Tamarac FL 33321-4021 Office: 6701 N Hiatiss Rd Tamarac FL 33321

PAGE, ELLIS BATTEN, psychologist, educator; b. San Diego; s. Frank Homer and Dorothy (Batten) P.; m. Elizabeth Latimer Thaxton, June 21, 1952 (dec. 2000); children: Ellis Batten (Tim), Elizabeth Page Sigman, Richard Leighton. AB, Pomona Coll.; MA, San Diego State U.; EdD, UCLA, 1958. Tchr. secondary schs., Calif.; dean Coll. Edn., prof. edn. and psychology Tex. Woman's U., 1960-62; prof. ednl. psychology U. Conn., 1962-79; prof. ednl. psychology and research Duke U., 1979—. Vis. prof. U. Wis., 1960, 62, Stanford U., 1965, Harvard U., 1968-69, U. Javeriana, Bogotá, 1975; leader Ford Found. rsch. adv. team Venezuelan Ministry Edn., Caracas, 1969-70; vis. prof. Spanish Ministry Edn., 1972, 80, 82-85; rsch. cons. U.S. Office Edn., USN, Nat. Inst. Edn., Bur. Edn. Handicapped; chmn. nat. planning com. Nat. Ctr. Edn. Stats.; adviser Brazilian Ministry Edn., 1973, 80; chief Ministerial Commn. Edn., Bermuda, 1983-85; mem. Adv. Coun. for Edn. Stats., U.S. Dept. Edn., 1987-90; pres. TruJudge, Inc., 1993—. Author, editor in field. Capt. USMCR. Recipient Disting. Alumnus award San Diego State U., 1980; NSF fellow, 1959, IBM fellow, 1966-67. Fellow AAAS (life), APA (pres. ednl. psychology 1976-77), Am. Psychol. Soc., John Dewey Soc., Am. Assn. Applied and Preventive Psychology, Nat. Conf. Rsch. English, Philosophy Edn. Soc.; mem. Am. Coun. Assn., Am. Ednl. Rsch. Assn. (pres. 1979-80), Am. Statis. Assn. (officer N.C. chpt.), Assn. Computational Linguistics, Nat. Assn. Scholars, N.C. Assn. Rsch. Edn. (Disting. Rsch. award 1981, 91, pres. 1984-85), Rhetoric Soc. Am. (dir.), Psychometric Soc., Sociedad Española de Pedagogia (hon.), Sigma Xi, Phi Kappa Phi, Phi Gamma Delta, Psi Chi, Kappa Delta Pi, Phi Delta Kappa (life, svc. key). Episcopalian. Home: 110 Oakstone Dr Chapel Hill NC 27514-9585 E-mail: EBPage@Duke.edu.

PAGE, ERNEST, medical educator; b. Cologne, Germany, May 30, 1927; came to U.S., 1936, naturalized, 1942; s. Max Ernest and Eleanor (Kohn) P.; m. Eva Veronica Gross, June 5, 1967; 1 son, Thomas J. AB, Calif., Berkeley, 1949; MD, Calif., San Francisco, 1952. Intern Peter Bent Brigham Hosp., Boston, 1952-53, resident, 1953-54, 57-58; research assoc. Harvard Med. Sch., 1957-65; assoc. prof. medicine and Physiology U. Chgo. Med. Sch., 1965-69, prof., 1969-98, prof. emeritus, 1998—. Editor: (jour.) Am. Jour. Physiology: Heart and Circulatory Physiology, 1981—86; editor: (sections) (handbook) Handbook of Physiology Vol. I The Heart, 2002. Served with AUS, 1945-46. Established investigator Am. Heart Assn., 1959-65 Mem. Am. Physiol. Soc., Biophys. Soc., Am. Soc. Cell Biology, Soc. Gen. Physiologists, Assn. Am. Physicians. Home: 5606 S Harper Ave Chicago IL 60637-1832 Office: U Chgo Med Sch 5841 S Maryland Ave Chicago IL 60637-1463 E-mail: epage@medicine.bsd.uchicago.edu.

PAGE, FREDERICK WEST, business consultant; b. East Orange, N.J., Oct. 19, 1932; s. Frederick West and Dorothy (Donham) P.; m. Miriam Lowell Jones, Feb. 14, 1959; children: William, Janet, Thomas, James. AB, Dartmouth Coll., 1954; postgrad., Wharton Grad. Sch. Bus., U. Pa., 1956-57; MBA, NYU, 1960. With Schering Corp. (now Schering-Plough), 1957-91, various mktg. positions, 1957-73, gen. mgr. animal health products, 1973-80, pres. U.S. Animal Health Products Div., 1980-83, v.p. pharm. ops., 1983-91; pres. Bus. Cons. Svcs., 1991—; dir. Immune Tech. Inc., 1996-98. Served with U.S. Army, 1954-56. Mem. Animal Health Inst. (exec. com. 1978-81, chmn. 1979-80) Clubs: Phi Kappa Psi. Republican. Home and Office: 22 Martin Rd West Caldwell NJ 07006-7419

PAGE, GEORGE ALFRED, JR. lawyer; b. Evanston, Ill., June 30, 1932; AB, Princeton U., 1954; JD, Harvard U., 1959; LLM in Taxation, Boston U., 1964. Bar: Mass 1959. From assoc. to ptnr. Peabody & Arnold, Boston, 1959-79; sr. ptnr. Csaplar & Bok, 1979-90; pvt. practice, 1990—. Lectr grad tax program Boston Univ Sch Law, 1974—77; gen counsel to bd dirs and sr mgmt Woodside Mgmt Sys Inc, Boston, 1978—87. 1st lt USAR, 1954—56. Mem.: ABA (mem real property, probate and trust law sect), Boston and Essex County Estate Planning Couns, Boston Probate Forum, Boston Bar Asn (chmn state tax comt 1971—74, sect taxation 1974—75, fed tax comt 1980—82, sr sect 1994—96, mem trusts and estates law sect, mem estate planning comt). Home: 1 Risley Rd Marblehead MA 01945-3720 Office: 50 Congress St Ste 350 Boston MA 02109-4008

PAGE, HARRY ROBERT, business administration educator; b. Milw., Mar. 22, 1915; s. Harry Allen and Lydia (Rosendahl) P.; m. Jeanne Tompkins, Apr. 1, 1945; children: Patricia Jeanne, Margaret Berenice. AB, Mich. State U., 1941; postgrad., U.S. Army Command and Staff Coll., 1945-46, Indsl. Coll. Armed Forces, 1958-59; MBA, Harvard, 1950; PhD, Am. U., 1966. Served from 2d lt. to lt. col. U.S. Army, 1941-46; from lt. col. to col. USAF, 1947-61; exec. officer logistics directorate U.S. Joint Chiefs of Staff, Washington, 1959-61; asst. prof. bus. adminstrn. George Washington U., 1961-65, assoc. prof., chmn. dept., 1965-69, prof., chmn. dept. bus. adminstrn., 1970-74, assoc. dean, 1975-80, prof. emeritus, 1981—. Cons. Advanced Study program Brookings Instn., Washington, 1966-70, Ednl. Svcs. Inst., U.S. Postal Svc., 1985-92. Author: Church Budget Development, 1964, An Analysis of the Defense Procurement Program Decision-Making Process, 1966, Public Purchasing and Materials Management, 1980, rev. edit., 1989; co-author: Federal Contributions to Management, 1972. Chmn. task force edn. and tng. Commn. Govt. Procurement, 1972-73; bd. dirs., treas. Coun. Chs., Greater Washington, 1963-68; bd. dirs. Hunter Assocs. Lab., Inc.; deacon Rock Spring Congregational Ch., 1994-97. Decorated Air medal, Purple Heart, Legion of Merit. Fellow Nat. Contract Mgmt. Assn.; mem. Acad. mgmt., Nat. Assn. Purchasing Mgmt., Internat. Fedn. Purchasing and Materials Mgmt., Harvard Bus. Sch. Assn., Air Force Assn., Nat. Parks and Conservation Assn. (trustee), Air Force Sgts. Assn. (trustee, chmn. scholarship bd. 1971—), Harvard Bus. Club, Sch. of Wash. Club (dir., pres. 1980-81), Alpha Phi Omega, Lambda Chi Alpha Alpha Kappa Psi, Pi Sigma Alpha, Beta Gamma Sigma. Home: 3612 N Glebe Rd Arlington VA 22207-4317

PAGE, JACK RANDALL, lawyer; b. Waco, Tex., Aug. 1, 1956; s. Jack Bennett and Mary Elizabeth (Cobbs) P.; m. Shirley Jean Hull, Aug. 5, 1978; children: Anna Christine, Sara Elaine. BBA magna cum laude, Baylor U., 1977, JD, 1980. Bar: Tex. 1980, U.S. Tax Ct. 1985, U.S. Dist. Ct. (we. dist.) Tex. 1987, U.S. Ct. Appeals (5th cir.) 1989; cert. in tax law Tex. Bd. Legal Specialization; CPA, Tex. Acct. Allie B. Gates Jr., CPA, Waco, 1975-78; assoc. Pakis, Giotes, Page & Burleson, P.C., 1980-86, ptnr., 1986—. Chmn. exploring sales team Heart O' Tex. coun. Boy Scouts Am., 1983, dist. chmn., 1984-85, v.p., 1986-88, coun. commr., 1989-91, coun. pres., 1991-94, asst. coun. commr., 1994-95, v.p., 1995-96, mem. adv. coun. Longhorn Coun., 2000—; mem. adv. coun. dept. acctg. Baylor U., 1993—; co-chmn. Food for Families, 1995—. Recipient Dist. Award of Merit Heart O' Tex. coun. Boy Scouts Am., 1985, Silver Beaver award 1993, Commrs. Key, 1994. Fellow Tex. Bar Found.; mem. AICPA, Tex. Bar Assn., Coll. of State Bar of Tex., Waco-McLennan County Bar Assn., Tex. Soc. CPAs, Waco Estate Planning Coun. (pres. 1983), Rotary (Paul Harris fellow), Order of Demolay (chevalier 1975). Roman Catholic. Avocations: hiking, fly fishing, outdoor activities. Office: Pakis Giotes Page & Burleson PC 801 Washington Ave Ste 800 Waco TX 76701-1266

PAGE, JOHN GARDNER, research administrator, scientist; b. Milw., Sept. 14, 1940; s. Raymond G. and Leone B. (Churchill) P.; m. Joyce Ann Krueger, July 7, 1962; children: Teresa Ann, Kimberly Christine. BS, U. Wis.-Madison, 1963, MS, 1966, PhD, 1967. Diplomate Am. Bd. Toxicology. Sr. scientist NIH, Bethesda, Md., 1967-69, Eli Lilly Co., Indpls., 1969-77; dir. toxicology and pathology Rhone Poulenc, Inc., Ashland, Ohio, 1977-79; dir. toxicology Toxigenics, Inc., Decatur, Ill., 1979-83; sr. rsch. advisor Battelle Meml. Inst., Columbus, Ohio, 1983-87; head preclin. toxicology divsn. So. Rsch. Inst., Birmingham, Ala., 1987—; dir. NGVL-Nat. Toxicology Ctr., 2001—. Adj. prof. U. Ill., 1981-83, ctr. for AIDS rsch., U. Ala., Birmingham, 1987—, sch. pub. health, 1988—, sch. medicine, 1997—. Contbr. articles to profl. jours. Bd. dirs. Am. Cancer Soc., Greenfield, Ind., 1973-77. Recipient Rennebohm Outstanding Tchr.'s award U. Wis., 1964. Mem. AAAS, Fedn. Am. Socs. Exptl. Biology, Am. Soc. Pharm. Exptl. Therapeutics, Soc. Toxicology, Am. Coll. Toxicology, Internat. Soc. for Study Xenobiotics, Sigma Xi, Rho Chi. Avocations: photography, hiking, fishing. Home: 3700 Rockhill Rd Birmingham AL 35223-1562 Office: So Research Inst 2000 9th Ave S Birmingham AL 35205-5305 E-mail: page@sri.org., toxman1@worldnet.att.net.

PAGE, JOHN HENRY, JR. artist, educator; b. Ann Arbor, Mich., Jan. 18, 1923; s. John Henry and Lucille (Bennett) P.; m. Mary Lou Franks, July 22, 1945; children: Jonathan, Marilyn, Jeremy. Student, Mpls. Sch. Art, 1940-42; B.Design, U. Mich., 1948; M.F.A., U. Iowa, 1950. Instr. Mankato (Minn.) State Coll., 1950-54; asst. prof. art U. No. Iowa, Cedar Falls, 1954-55, asst. prof., 1955-59, assoc. prof., 1959-64, prof., 1964-87, acting head dept. art, 1984-85. Head art dept. U. Omaha, 1959-60 One-man exhbns. include Luther Coll., Decorah, Iowa, 1981, Laura Musser Mus., Muscatine, Iowa, 1978, Coe Coll., Cedar Rapids, Iowa, 1975, Sheldon Gallery, Lincoln, Nebr., 1974, Creighton U., Omaha, 1969, Augustana Coll., Rock Island, Ill., 1964, Muskegon (Mich.) Mus. Art, 1983, retrospective (in three parts) Gallery of Art U. No. Iowa, Hearst Ctr. for the Arts, Cedar Falls, Iowa, Waterloo (Iowa) Mus. of Art, 1992; group exhbns. include 10th Nat. Print Show Bklyn. Mus., 1956, 9 Iowa Artists Gov. Exhbn., 1971-72, Walker Art Ctr., Mpls., 1973, Regional Invitational Exhbn., U. Omaha, 1978, Fragile Giants, Brunner Gallery, 1994-96; represented in permanent collections, Library of Congress, Walker Art Center, Des Moines Art Center, Joslyn Art Mus., Omaha, Carnegie Inst., Pitts. Served with U.S. Army, 1943-45. Nat. Endowment Arts grantee, 1975 Unitarian Universalist. Home: 114 E Los Arcos Green Valley AZ 85614-2429 E-mail: jmlpage@earthlink.net.

PAGE, JONATHAN ROY, investment analyst; b. Harrisburg, Pa., Sept. 10, 1946; s. John and Ellen (Smith) P.; m. Patrice Marie Margerm, May 17, 1975; children: Elizabeth, Gregory, Richard, Brian. BA, Dartmouth Coll., 1968; MBA, Tuck Sch. Dartmouth, 1969. Chartered fin. analyst. Investment officer Irving Trust Co., N.Y.C., 1970-75; portfolio mgr. to mng. dir. Morgan Stanley Investment Mgmt., 1975—. Vestry person St. John's Ch., Ramsey, N.J., 1984-88. Mem. N.Y. Soc. Security Analysts, Fin. Analysts Fedn. Republican. Episcopalian. Avocations: tennis, golf, skiing, landscaping. Fax: 201-209-8568. E-mail: jonathan.page@morganstanley.com.

PAGE, LARRY KEITH, neurosurgeon, educator; b. Rayville, La., July 7, 1933; s. Ardie Lee and Edris Estelle (Chaney) P.; m. Joan Marie Doherty, Aug. 27, 1960; children: Matthew, Elizabeth, Jennifer. BS, La. State U., 1955, MD, 1958. Diplomate: Am. Bd. Neurol. Surgery. Intern Grad. Hosp., U. Pa., Phila., 1958-59; resident Children's Hosp. and Peter Bent Brigham Hosp., Boston, 1962-66; assoc. neurosurgeon Children's Hosp., assoc. surgeon Peter Bent Brigham Hosp., 1966-71; cons. Beverly Hosp., Mass., Robert Breck Brigham Hosp., Boston, Pondville Hosp., Boston, West Roxbury VA Hosp., Boston VA Hosp.; clin. instr. neurosurgery Harvard U., Boston, 1966-71; prof., vice chmn. dept. neurosurgery U. Miami, Fla., 1971-95, prof. emeritus, 1995—, chief div. pediatric neurosurgery, 1971-95; neurosurgeon VA Hosp., Miami, 1971-88, Jackson Meml. Hosp., Miami, 1971-95, dir. neurosurgery, 1994-95; chief neurosurgery Mt. Sinai Hosp., 1990-94. Neurosurg. cons. FDA; neurosurg. cons. NASA Mem. editorial bds., contbr. articles to profl. jours. Served to lt. USN, 1959-62. Mem. ACS, Am. Acad. Pediatrics, Am. Assn. Neurol. Surgeons, Internat. Soc. Pediatric Neurosurgery, Am. Soc. Pediatric Neurosurgery, Congress Neurol. Surgeons, Fellowship of Acad. Neurosurgeons,

Internat. Neurosurg. Forum, Royal Soc. Medicine, Soc. for Rsch. in Hydrocephalus and Spina Bifida, New Eng. Neurosurg. Soc., Fla. Neurosurg. Soc. (pres. 1989-90), Mass. Med. Soc., Dade County Med. Assn., Internat. Palm Soc., Alpha Omega Alpha. Roman Catholic. Home and Office: 13845 SW 73rd Ct Miami FL 33158-1213

PAGE, LESLIE ANDREW, disinfectant manufacturing company executive; b. Mpls., June 5, 1924; s. Henry R. and Amelia Kathryn (Steinmetz) P.; m. DeEtte Abernethy Griswold, July 6, 1952 (div. Sept. 1975); children: Randolph, Michael, Kathryn, Caroline; m. Mary Ellen Decker, Nov. 26, 1976. BA, U. Minn., 1949; MA, U. Calif., Berkeley, 1953, PhD, 1956. Asst. microbiologist, lectr. U. Calif., Davis, 1956-61; cons. San Diego Zoological Soc. Zoo Hosp., 1957-60; microbiologist, research leader Nat. Animal Disease Ctr., USDA, Ames, Iowa, 1961-79; ret., 1979; specialist in Chlamydial nomenclature and disease; med. text cons. Bay St. Louis, Miss., 1979-85; founder, pres., chmn. bd. Steri-Derm Corp., San Marcos, Calif., 1987—. Cons. McCormick Distilling Co., Weston, Mo., 1994-95. Editor: Jour. Wildlife Diseases, 1965-68, Wildlife Diseases, 1976; contbr. chpts. to med. texts, over 70 articles to profl. jours.; patentee Liquid Antiseptic Composition, 1989. Pres. Garden Island Cmty. Assn., Bay St. Louis, Miss., 1980—81; chief commr. East Hancock Fire Protection Dist., 1982—83; treas. Woodridge Escondido Property Owners Assn., 1986—88; pres. Westminster Men's Group, Westminster Presbyn. Ch., Escondido, Calif., 2002. Fellow Am. Acad. Microbiology (emeritus); mem. Wildlife Disease Assn. (pres. 1972-73, Disting. Svc. award 1980, Emeritus award 1984), Am. Soc. for Microbiology, Zool. Soc. San Diego, Sigma Xi, Phi Zeta (hon.). Home and Office: 1784 Deavers Dr San Marcos CA 92069-3359 E-mail: steriderm@hotmail.com., steriderm@home.com.

PAGE, LEWIS WENDELL, JR. lawyer; b. Scottsboro, Ala., Nov. 6, 1947; s. Lewis Wendell and Maymie Elizabeth (Parks) P.; m. Dollie Lucretia Roberts, Dec. 24, 1977; children— Margaret Amelia, Katherine Elizabeth. B.A., Auburn U., 1970; J.D., U. Ala., 1973; LL.M., George Washington U., 1975. Bar: Ala. 1973, U.S. Dist. Ct. (no. dist.) Ala. 1974, U.S. Ct. Appeals (5th cir.) 1973, U.S. Ct. Appeals (11th cir.) 1978, U.S. Supreme Ct. 1982. Assoc. firm Sadler, Sadler, Sullivan & Sharp, Birmingham, Ala., 1973-74; assoc. firm Lange, Simpson, Robinson & Somerville, Birmingham, 1975-80, ptnr. 1980-93, Page Law Firm, 1993—; pres., CEO Controllex, L.L.C., 1997—. Served to 2d lt. U.S. Army, 1973. Mem. Ala. State Bar Assn. (chmn. antitrust sect. 1983-84, co-chmn. permanent code commn. 1986-88), Birmingham Bar Assn. (panel chmn. grievance com. 1983-84, chmn. fee arbitration com. 1984-85, exec. com. 1998—), ABA (antitrust sect., litigation sect., patent, copyright and trademark sect.), Auburn U. Bar Assn. (pres. 1993-94).

PAGE, LINDA KAY, banking executive; b. Wadsworth, Ohio, Oct. 4, 1943; d. Frederick Meredith and Martha Irene (Vance P. Studnet, Ohio U., 1976-77; grad. banking program, U. Wis., 1982-84; BA, Capital U. cert. in pers. Am. Bankers Assn. Asst. v.p., gen. mgr. Bancohio Corp., Columbus, 1975-78, v.p., dist. mgr., 1979-80, v.p., mgr. employee rels., 1980-81, v.p., divsn. mgr., 1982-83; commr. of banks State of Ohio, 1983-87, dir. Dept. Commerce, 1988-90; pres., CEO Star Bank Ctrl. Ohio, 1990-92; state dir. Rural Devel/USDA, 1993-2000; pub. svc. dir. City of Columbus, 2000. Bd. dirs. Clark County Mental Health Bd., Springfield, Ohio, 1982-83, Springfield Met. Housing, 1982-83, Pvt. Industry Coun. Franklin County, 1990-2000—, Ohio Highe Edn. Facilities Commn., 1990-93, Ohio Devel. Corp., 1995—; bd. advisers Orgn. Indsl. Standards, Springfield, 1982-83; trustee League Against Child Abuse, 1986-90; treas. Ohio Housing Fin. Agy., 1980-90; vice chair Fed. Res. Bd. Consumer Adv. Coun., 1989-91; trustee, treas. Columbus State C.C. Found., 1990-2000, pres., 1997-99; bd. dirs. Columbus Urban league, 1992-98; mem. CompDrug Bd., 1998-2000. Recipient Leadership Columbus award Sta. WTVN and Columbus Leadership Program, 1975, 82, Outstanding Svc. award Clark County Mental Health Bd., 1983, Giles Mitchell Housing award, 1996. Mem.: LWV (treas. edn. fund 1992—2000), Women in Transp., Robert Morris Assocs., Women in Transp. (bd. trustees Ohio chpt. 2000, bd. dirs. 2002), Internat. Womens Forum, Am. Pub. Works Assn. (treas. Ohio chpt. 2000, treas. 2002), Ohio Mortgage Bankers Assn. (legis. commn. 1998), Ohio Devel. Assn., Ohio Bankers Assn. (bd. dirs. 1982—83, 1991—92), Conf. State Bank Suprs. (dist. chmn. 1984—85, sec.-treas. 1985—90, bd. dirs.), Women Execs. in State Govt., Am. Bankers Assn. (govt. rels. coun. 1990—92), Nat. Assn. Bank Women (pres. 1980—81). Democrat. Avocations: animal protection, reading, cultural arts, travel. Home: 641 Mirandy Pl Reynoldsburg OH 43068-1602 Office: 90 W Broad St Columbus OH 43215-9000 E-mail: lkpage@cmhmetro.net., lpage@ix.netcom.com.

PAGE, LORNE ALBERT, physicist, educator; b. Buffalo, July 28, 1921; s. John Otway and Laura (Stewart) P.; m. Muriel Emily Jamieson, Sept. 7, 1946; children: J. Douglas (dec. Nov. 2001), Kenneth L., James F., Donald S., David K. BSc, Queen's U., Can., 1944; PhD, Cornell U., 1950. Mem. faculty U. Pitts., 1950—, prof. physics, 1958-86, prof. emeritus, 1987—. Vis. physicist Stanford U., Palo Alto, Calif., 1962, Lawrence Livermore Lab., Calif., 1970. Contbr. articles to Phys. Rev., Rev. Modern Physics, Ann. Rev. Nuc. and Particle Sci. Lt. Royal Can. Navy, 1944-45. Guggenheim fellow Upsala U., Sweden, 1957-58; Alfred P. Sloan research fellow, 1961-63 Fellow Am. Phys. Soc.; mem. Sigma Xi. Episcopalian. Achievements include definitive measurement of electron-electron (Moller) scattering, measurement of the positron's mass, identification of positronium in condensed matter; development of method for analyzing circular polarization of high energy x-rays, first measurement of inherent polarization of positive beta particles. Home: 157 Lloyd Ave Pittsburgh PA 15218-1645 E-mail: page@sgi.net.

PAGE, MICHEL, biochemist, researcher; b. Quebec, Que., Can., Feb. 18, 1940; s. Hector and Alma (Dussault) P.; m. Marthe Boudreau, Dec. 17, 1966; children: Brigitte, Marie, Charles, Madeleine. BA, Laval U., 1960; B.Sc., Ottawa U., 1965, PhD, 1969. Nat. Cancer Inst. postdoctoral fellow U. Colo., Boulder, 1968-70; research fellow Mt. Sinai Sch. Medicine, N.Y.C., 1970-71; clin. biochemist Hotel Dieu Hosp., Quebec, 1971-81; research scholar Nat. Cancer Inst. Can., 1975-81; prof. biochemistry U. Laval, Quebec City, 1982—; pres., founder BCM Biotech, Inc., 1988, BCM Développement Inc., 1993; founder BCM Oncologia Inc., 1995. Mem. grant panels Med. Rsch. Coun., Nat. Cancer Inst.; pres. BCH Biotech Inc., BCH Devel. Inc.; sci. advisor Bioxel Pharma Inc. Author: La cuisine sans cholesterol, 1975, Cancer, 1983, Cancérologie expérimentale, 1993; contbr. over 140 articles to sci. publs; patentee in field. Mem. Ordre des Chimistes du Que., AAAS, Canadian Biochem. Soc., Canadian Immunol. Soc., Am. Soc. Cell Biology., Am. Assn. Clin. Research Roman Catholic. Home: 125 Dalhousie #217 Quebec QC Canada G1K 4C5 Office: Faculty of Medicine U Laval Quebec QC Canada G1K 7P4

PAGE, OSCAR C. academic administrator; b. Bowling Green, Ky., Dec. 22, 1939; s. Elizabeth Page; m. Anna Laura Hood, June 12, 1965; children: Kristen, Matt. BA in Social Sci., Western Ky. U., 1962; MA in History, U. Ky., 1963, PhD in Early Modern European History, 1967. Instr. history Western Ky. U., Bowling Green, 1964; asst. prof., asst. chair history dept. U. Ga., Athens, 1967-71; dean Wesleyan Coll., Macon, Ga., 1971-78; v.p. acad. affairs Lander Coll., Greenwood, S.C., 1978-86, acting pres., 1985, provost, v.p. acad. affairs, 1986-88; pres. Austin Peay State U., Clarksville, Tenn., 1988-94, Austin Coll., Sherman, Tex., 1994—. Mem. adv. com. Master of Mil. Art & Sci. Program, Leavenworth, Kans., 1994—96. Bd. dirs. United Way, Sherman; mem. pres.'s commn. NCAA, 1990—94, mem. mgmt. coun., 1998—; Bd. dirs. Meml. Hosp., Clarksville, Nations Bank, Clarksville; pres. Assn. Tex. Colls. and Univs., 1998—99. Mem.: Sherman C. of C., Rotary Club. Office: Austin Coll 900 N Grand Ave Sherman TX 75090-4440

PAGE, PHYLLIS ELEANOR, physician; b. Newton, Mass., Aug. 28, 1930; d. Joseph Westley and Alice Florence (Wainwright) P.; m. Joseph Tabrisky, Apr. 23, 1955; children: Joseph Page, William Page, Elizabeth Ann Tabrisky Richardson. BS, Rutgers U., 1952; MD, Tufts U., 1956; postgrad., U. Colo., 1958-60. Diplomate Am. Bd. Phys. Medicine and Rehab. Staff physician Coco Solo Hosp., Crestobal, Canal Zone, 1961-62, Ft. Hood Army Hosp., Killeen, Tex., 1963; instr. rehab. medicine Boston U., 1964-66; asst. prof. phys. medicine and rehab. U. Colo., Denver, 1966-68; staff physician phys. medicine and rehab. VA Med. Ctr., Long Beach, Calif., 1968-91, chief phys. medicine and rehab., 1991—. Asst. prof. phys. medicine and rehab. U. Calif., Irvine, 1972-75, assoc. prof., 1975-82, clin. prof., 1982—, vice chair phys. medicine and rehab., 1982—. Mem. AMA, Am. Acad. Physical Medicine and Rehab., Am. Congress Rehab. Medicine, Assn. of Acad. Therapists (bd. trustees 1995-97). Republican. Episcopalian. Avocation: U.S. history. Home: 2748 Coral Ridge Rd Rolling Hills Estates CA 90275

PAGE, REX L, computer scientist, educator, software consultant; b. Wichita, OK, Feb. 4, 1944; s. Warren Rector Page, Mildred Irene Page; m. Lucy Garcia Garcia Lopez; m. Beverly Jane Brown (div. Mar. 15, 1991); children: Peter Nicholas, Kathleen Alanna, Cammie Jane. AB, Stanford University, Stanford, CA, 1962—66; PhD, University of California at San Diego, La Jolla, CA, 1966—70. Professor of Computer Science University of Oklahoma, Norman, OK, 1993—2002; Senior Member of Technical Staff Eclipse International, Mountain View, CA. Software Architect Amoco, Houston, 1982—93; Professor of Computer Science Colorado State University, Fort Collins, CO, 1970—82. Author: (book) Fortran for Humans, 1974, Using Basic, 1980, Symbolic Computing with Lisp and Prolog, 1986. Office: University of Oklahoma 200 Felgar Street - EL120 Norman OK 73019

PAGE, RICHARD LEIGHTON, cardiologist, medical educator, researcher; b. San Diego, Mar. 8, 1958; s. Ellis Batten and Elizabeth Latimer (Thaxton) P.; m. Jean Reynolds, Oct. 12, 1985; children: Franklin Reynolds, Gillian Grace, Edward Batten. BS in Zoology magna cum laude, Duke U., 1980, MD, 1984. Diplomate Nat. Bd. Med. Examiners, Am. Bd. Internal Medicine, subspecialties cardiovascular disease and clin. cardiac electrophysiology; lic. physician, Tex. Rsch. fellow in pharmacology Columbia Presbyn. Med. Ctr., 1982-83; intern dept. medicine Mass. Gen. Hosp., Boston, 1984-85, resident dept. medicine, 1985-87; cardiology fellow clin. electrophysiology Duke U. Med. Ctr., Durham, N.C., 1987-89, clin. cardiology fellow, 1989, lectr. medicine divsn. cardiology, 1989-90, assoc. in medicine, 1990, asst. prof., dir. clin. electrophysiology lab., 1990-92; asst. prof. medicine U. Tex. Southwestern Med. Ctr., Dallas, 1992-95, assoc. prof., 1995-2001, prof., 2001—. Dir. sect. clin. electrophysiology U. Tex. Southwestern Med. Ctr., Dallas, 1992—; dir. clin. electrophysiology lab., arrhythmia and pacemaker svc., Parkland Meml. Hosp., Dallas, 1992—; holder Dallas Heart Ball Chair in Cardiac Arrhythmia Rsch., 1997—; dir. Stanley J. Sarnoff Endowment for Rsch. in Cardiovasc. Sci., Inc., Bethesda, Md., 1990—, co-chmn., 1992; Dallas Heart Ball chair in Cardiac Arrhythmia Rsch., 1997—. Mem. editl. bd. Cardiac Chronicle, 1993, Am. Heart Jour., 1998—, Am. Jour. Cardiology, 1999—; author: (with others) Manual of Clinical Problems in Cardiology, 5th edit., 1995; contbr. articles to profl. jours., chpt. to book. Sarnoff Endowment fellow, 1982, Sarnoff scholar, 1987. Fellow Stanley J. Sarnoff Soc., Am. Heart Assn., Am. Coll. Cardiology; mem. N.Am. Soc. Pacing and Electrophysiology, Tex. Med. Assn., Dallas County Med. Soc., North Tex. Electrophysiology Soc. (trustee), Sigma Xi, Alpha Omega Alpha. Episcopalian. Avocations: tennis, sailing, gardening. Home: 1500 Ramsgate Cir Plano TX 75093-5044 Office: U Tex Southwestern Med Ctr 5323 Harry Hines Blvd Dallas TX 75390-7208

PAGE, ROBERT HENRY, engineer, educator, researcher; b. Phila., Nov. 5, 1927; s. Ernest Fraser and Marguerite (MacFarl) P.; m. Lola Marie Griffin, Nov. 12, 1948; children: Lola Linda, Patricia Jean, William Ernest, Nancy Lee, Martin Fraser. BS in Mech. Engring, Ohio U., 1949; MS, U. Ill., 1951, PhD, 1955. Instr., research assoc. U. Ill., 1949-55; research engr. fluid dynamics Esso Research & Engring. Co., 1955-57; vis. lectr. Stevens Inst. Tech., 1956-57, dir. fluid dynamics lab., prof. mech. engring., 1957-61; prof. mech. engring., chmn. dept. mech., indsl. and aerospace engring. Rutgers-The State U., 1961-76, prof., research cons., 1976-79; dean engring. Tex. A&M U., 1979-83, Forsyth prof., 1983-93, prof. emeritus mech. engring., 1994—. Spl. research base pressure and heat transfer, wake flow and flow separation. Contbr. over 200 articles to profl. publs.; inventor impingement nozzles. Served with AUS, 1945-47, Pacific Theatre of Operations. Recipient Western Electric Fund award for excellence in engring. edn. Am. Soc. Engring Edn., 1968; Lindback Found. award for disting. tchg., 1969; Disting. Alumnus award U. Ill., 1971; Disting. Service award, 1973; Life Quality Engring. award, 1974, James Harry Potter Gold medal, 1983, Ohio U. medal, 1983; named hon. prof. Ruhr U., Buchum, Fed. Republic Germany, 1984; named to Acad. Disting. Grads., Ohio U., 2001, Halle of Fame, Ctrl. H.S., Phila., 2002. Fellow AAAS, AIAA, ABET, Am. Astron. Soc. (chmn. nat. space engring. com. 1969-70, 72-76), Am. Soc. Engring. Edn. (Centennial medal 1993); mem. ASME (hon. mem. award 1988), Am. Phys. Soc. Home: 1905 Comal Cir College Station TX 77840-4818 E-mail: rpage@mengr.tamu.edu.

PAGE, ROBERT WESLEY, engineering and construction company executive, federal official; b. Dallas, Jan. 22, 1927; s. Arch Cleo and Zelma (Tyler) P.; m. Nancy Ann Eaton, Sept. 17, 1952; children: Robert W. Jr., David, Mark, Margaret. BS in Archtl. Engring., Tex. A&M U., 1950. Asst. prof. Am. Univ., Beirut, 1952-54; project mgr. Aramco, The Hague and Saudi Arabia, 1954-56; dir. constrn. and devel. Internat. Coll., Beirut, N.Y.C., 1956-58; internat. mgr. Bechtel Co., N.Y.C., 1958-64; v.p. Rockresorts Co., 1964-71; pres., chief exec. officer George A. Fuller Co., from 1971; corp. v.p. Northrop Corp., from 1971; pres., chief exec. officer Rust Engring. Co., Birmingham, Ala., 1976-81, Kellogg Rust Inc., Houston, 1981-85, chmn., chief exec. officer, dir., 1985-86; pres., chief exec. officer PM Co., 1986; asst. sec. U.S. Dept. of Army, Washington, 1987-90; chmn. Panama Canal Commn., 1989-90; exec. v.p. McDermott Internat., Washington, 1990—; sr. lectr. MIT, 1993; chmn. Pegasus Cons., Inc., Cambridge, Mass., 1996—; vice-chmn. Indevo Group, 2001—. Adj. prof. Georgetown U.; bd. dirs. I.C.F./Kaiser Internat.; bd. dirs. Thormatrix, Inc., San Jose, Calif. Trustee Internat. Coll. Beirut; mem. Pres.'s Coun., U. Ala.; bd. dirs. Coll. Football Hall of Fame. With USNR, 1944-46, PTO. Trustee Am. U. in Cairo; trustee Wortham Theatre Ctr., Houston, Internat. Coll. Beirut; mem. Pres.'s Council, U. Ala.; mem. adv. bd. John E. Gray Inst., Lamar U.; bd. dirs. Coll. Football Hall of Fame. Served with USNR, 1944-46, PTO. Mem. ASME, ASCE, Rolling Rock Club (Ligoner, Pa.), Internat. Club (Washington), Army-Navy Club (Washington), Georgetown Club (Washington), Sakonnet Country Club (Little Compton, R.I.), Tau Beta Pi. Home: 3025 P St NW Washington DC 20007-3054 Office: 1850 K St NW Ste 950 Washington DC 20006-2213

PAGE, ROY CHRISTOPHER, periodontist, scientist, educator; b. Campobello, S.C., Feb. 7, 1932; s. Milton and Anny Mae (Eubanks) P. BA, Berea Coll., 1953; DDS, U. Md., 1957; PhD, U. Wash., 1967; ScD (hon.), Loyola U., Chgo., 1983. Cert. in periodontics. Pvt. practice periodontics, Seattle, 1963-98; asst. prof. U. Wash. Schs. Medicine and Dentistry, 1967-70, prof., 1974—, Disting. prof. dentistry, 1996-98, dir. Ctr. Research in Oral Biology, 1976-96; dir. grad. edn. U. Wash. Sch. Dentistry, 1976-80, dir. rsch., 1976-94, dir. Regional Clin. Dental Rsch. Ctr., 1990—, assoc. dean rsch., 1994-2000. Vis. scientist MRC Labs., London, 1971-72; cons., lectr. in field; fellow Pierre Fauchard Acad. Author: Periodontal Disease, 1977, 2d edit., 1990, Periodontitis in Man and Other Animals, 1982. Recipient Gold Medal award U. Md., 1957; recipient Career Devel. award NIH, 1967-72, Disting. Alumnus award U. Wash. Sch. Dentistry, 2000. Fellow Internat. Coll. Dentists, Am. Coll. Dentists, Am. Acad. Periodontology (Gies award 1982, fellowship award 1989, spl. citation 1998); mem. ADA (Norton Rose award for clin. rsch. 1998), Am. Assn. Dental Rsch. (pres. 1982-83, disting. scientist award 2001), Am. Soc. Exptl. Pathology, Internat. Assn. Dental Rsch. (pres. 1987, basic periodontal rsch. award 1977). Home: 5583 171st Ave SE Bellevue WA 98006-5503 E-mail: roypage@u.washington.edu.

PAGE, SALLY JACQUELYN, university official; b. Saginaw, Mich., 1943; d. William Henry and Doris Effie (Knippel) P. BA, U. Iowa, 1965; MBA, So. Ill. U., 1973. Copy editor C.V. Mosby Co., St. Louis, 1965-69; editl. cons. Editl. Assocs., Edwardsville, Ill., 1969-70; rsch. adminstr. So. Ill. U., 1970-74, asst. to pres., affirmative action officer, 1974-77; officer of instn. U. N.D., Grand Forks, 1977—, lectr. mgmt., 1978—. Polit. comentator Sta. KFJM, Nat. Public Radio affiliate, 1981-90; mem. mayor's com. Employment of People With Disabilities, 1980-97. Contbr. articles to profl. jours. Chmn. N.D. Equal Opportunity Affirmative Action Officers, 1987-2002; pres. Pine to Prairie coun. Girl Scouts U.S., 1980-85; mem. employment com. Ill. Commn. on Status of Women, 1976-77; mem. Bicentennial Com., Edwardsville, 1976, Bikeway Task Force, Edwardsville, 1975-77, Bus. Leadership Network, ARC Upper Valley; bd. dirs. Grand Forks Homes, 1985—, pres., 1996-2001; mem. Civil Svc. Rev. Task Force, Grand Forks, 1982, civil svc. commr., 1983-98, chmn., 1984, 86, 88, 92, 96; ruling elder 1st Presbyn.; mem. Grand Forks Mayor's Adv. Cabinet, 1998-2000. Mem. AAUW (dir. Ill. 1975-77), PEO, Coll. and Univ. Pers. Assn. (rsch. and publs. bd. 1982-84), Soc. Human Resource Mgmt., Am. Assn. Affirmative Action. Democrat. Presbyterian. Home: 3121 Cherry St Grand Forks ND 58201-7461 Office: U ND Grand Forks ND 58202 E-mail: Sally-Page@mail.und.nodak.edu.

PAGE, STEPHEN JEFFREY LAWRENCE, management consulting company executive; b. London, Apr. 29, 1955; came to U.S., 1979; s. Allan and Joan Vera (Wheatcroft) P. Diploma in Math. and Telecomms., Merton Coll., Surrey, Eng., 1974. With exec. mgmt. program Brit. Telecom, 1971-74; product mgr. Sperry Univac Fed. Systems Divsn., Europe, 1974-78, Itel Internat., Frankfurg, Germany, 1978-80; cons. Ctrl. Bank, San Francisco, 1980-81; CEO Page-Wheatcroft & Co., Ltd., Dallas, 1981—. Cons. Republic Bank, Dallas; bd. dirs. Union Bank of Dallas, Micronyx Inc., eJobs, Inc., eresume, Inc. Bd. dirs. Trutle Creek Centre for Arts, 1981—, Shakespeare Festival of Dallas, United Cerebral Palsy, 1990—. Named to Outstanding Young Men of Am., 1982. Mem. Brit. Am. Commerce Assn. (bd. dirs.), Dallas C. of C. (lasso club 1981—), G-Tree (bd. dirs.). Republican. Home: 5852 Glendora Ave Dallas TX 75230-5050 Office: 14131 Midway Rd Ste 680 Addison TX 75001-3655

PAGE, TIM, music critic, writer, producer; b. San Diego, Oct. 11, 1954; s. Ellis Batten and Elizabeth Latimer (Thaxton) P.; m. Vanessa Weeks, Mar. 3, 1984 (divorced); children: William Dean, Robert Leonard, John Sherman. Student, Tanglewood Music Ctr., 1970, 74, 75, Mannes Coll. Music, 1975-77; BA, Columbia U., 1979. Music critic Soho News, N.Y.C., 1979-82; music writer N.Y. Times, 1982-87; music critic Newsday, 1987-95; writer Washington Post, 1995—. Artistic advisor St. Louis Symphony, 1999-2000; lectr. in field. Author: Music From the Road, 1992, William Kapell, 1992, Dawn Powell: A Biography, 1998, Tim Page on Music, 2001; editor: The Glenn Gould Reader, 1984, Selected Letters of Virgil Thomson (with Vanessa Weeks Page), 1988, Dawn Powell at Her Best, 1994, The Diaries of Dawn Powell, 1995, Selected Letters of Dawn Powell, 1999, The Unknown Sigrid Undset, 2001; radio host WNYC-FM, N.Y.C., 1981-92. Recipient Pulitizer prize for criticism, N.Y., 1997. Mem. The Century Assn. Office: Washington Post 1150 15th St NW Washington DC 20071-0002

PAGE, WILLIAM MARION, lawyer; b. Columbus, Ga., July 31, 1917; s. Roger McKeene and Louise Olivia (Seals) P.; m. Lucy Quillian Page, Feb. 8, 1941 (dec. 1982); children: John Roger, Jane Quillian Page McCamy, William Franklin (dec.); m. Barbara Brown Waddell, May 10, 1985. LLB, U. Ga., 1939, JD. Bar: Ga. 1938, U.S. Supreme Ct. 1955. Ptnr. Page Scrantom Sprouse Tucker & Ford P.C., Columbus, Ga., 1939—. Bd. visitors U. Ga. Law Sch., 1969-74. With U.S. Army, 1941-46. Fellow: Am. Coll. Trial Lawyers; mem.: ABA, Columbus Bar Assn. (bd. govs. 1946—47), Chattahoochee Circuit Bar Assn. (pres. 1948—49), State Bar Ga. (bd. govs. 1964—71), Chattahoochee River Club, Big Eddy Club, Kiwanis. Home: 916 Overlook Dr Columbus GA 31906-3029 Office: PO Box 1199 Columbus GA 31902-1199

PAGE, WILLIS, conductor; b. Rochester, N.Y., Sept. 18, 1918; Grad. with distinction, Eastman Sch. Music, Rochester., 1939. Mem. Rochester Philharm., 1937-40, Rochester Civic, 1939-40; prof. conducting Eastman Sch. Music, 1967-69; prof. conducting, dir. orchestral activities Drake U., Des Moines, 1969-71. Guest condr. Sony concerts, Chiba, Japan, 1992. Mem. Boston Symphony Orch., 1940-55; prin. bass Boston Pops, 1947-55; condr. Cecilia Soc. Boston, 1952-54, New Orchestral Soc. Boston; assoc. condr. Buffalo Philharm., 1955-59; music dir./condr. Nashville Symphony Orch., 1959-67; music dir. Linwood Music Sch., 1955-59; 1st condr. Yomiuri Nippon Symphony, Tokyo, 1962-63; condr. Des Moines Symphony, 1969-71, Jacksonville (Fla.) Symphony Orch., 1971-83; founder, condr. St. John's River City Band, 1985-86; guest condr. Boston Pops, Toronto, Rochester Civic, Eastman-Rochester, Denver, Muncie, Jerusalem, St. Louis, Colorado Springs, Memphis, Hartford orchs., Yomiuri Nippon Symphony, 1988, 92; founding condr., exec. dir. First Coast Pops Orch., 1989; condr. all-state orchs. of N.Y., Iowa, Ky., Tenn., Fla., also regional festivals; condr. 13 L.P. recordings including Symphony of the Air (Roger Williams soloist), Boston Festival Orch., Cook Labs., Nashville Symphony. Sgt. 95th inf. divsn. U.S. Army, 1943-45. Decorated Bronze Star; recipient Ford Found. European travel award, 1967. E-mail: wpage17@bellsouth.net.

PAGELS, CARRIE FANCETT, psychologist; b. Newberry, Mich., Jan. 5, 1958; d. William Henry and Ruby Evelyn (Skidmore) F.; m. Jeffrey D. Pagels; 1 child, Cassandra Rose. BA in Psychology, Lake Superior State Coll., 1978; MA in Sch. Psychology, U. S.C., 1981, PhD in Sch. Psychology, 1984. Lic. psychologist; cert. sch. psychologist. Rsch. asst. U. S.C., Columbia, 1979-80, 81-83, instr., 1983, Lake Superior State Coll., Sault Ste. Marie, Mich., summer 1981; mental health cons. Head Start Program, Columbia, 1983-86, Charleston, S.C., 1987-95; child psychotherapist Counseling and Readjustment Svcs., Columbia, 1985-86; psychologist Richland Meml. Children's Hosp., 1983-86; clin. asst. prof. U. S.C. Sch. Medicine, 1984-87; sch. psychologist Berkeley County Schs., 1986-87; pvt. sch. psychologist North Charleston, 1987-94; sch. psychologist Erie 1 Boces Presch., Depew, N.Y., 1995-96; asst. prof. Valdosta (Ga.) State U., 1996-98; sch. psychologist Williamsburg James City County Schs., Va., 1998—2001; clin. psychologist Christian Psychotherapy Svcs., Newport News, 1999-2001, Beacon Counseling and Cons., Williamsburg, 2001—. Learning disability diagnostician spl. svcs. program, 1996-98; pvt. practice Midtown Psychol. Assocs., Valdosta, 1996-98; cons. Richland Meml. Hosp., Columbia, 1983, Divorce Mediation Project, Columbia, 1982, Life Satisfaction Grant, Columbia, 1979-81. Book reviewer Contemporary Psychology, 1998; contbr. chpt. to book. Campaign aide Dem. Party, U.S. Senate race, Sault Ste. Marie, Mich., 1978. Stephenson scholar, 1978, NIMH fellow, 1980-81. Mem. Am. Psychol. Assn., Nat. Assn. of Sch. Psychologists, Children and Adults with Attention Deficit Disorder. Baptist. Avocations: computers, crafts, walking. Home: 200 Grafton District Rd Yorktown VA 23692-4045 E-mail: cfpagels@aol.com.

PAGELS, JÜRGEN HEINRICH, balletmaster, dance educator, dancer, choreographer, writer; b. Lübeck, Germany, Apr. 16, 1925; came to U.S., 1955; s. Heinrich and Margret (Haas) P. Artists diploma, Hamburg (Fed. Republic Germany) State Exam Bd., 1947; advanced soloist exam. with honors, Assn. Russian Ballet, London, 1952, advanced tchrs. exam. with honors, 1961, sr. tchrs. exam. with honors, 1969; DFA, Pacific Western U., 1988. Ballet soloist Atlantic Theater, Lübeck, 1945-46, Stadt-Theater, Lübeck, 1946-47; prin. dancer Dortmund, Fed. Republic Germany, 1947-48, Operette and Stattl. Schauspielhaus Theater, Hamburg, 1949-50; ballet soloist Ballet Theater Co., 1950-51; prin. dancer Ballet Legat, London, 1951-52, Ballet Legat and Yugoslav Nat. Ballet, touring throughout Europe, 1952-53; guest ballet soloist Ballet Etoile, Paris Opera, Paris, 1954; dir., owner Pagels Legat Sch. Ballet, Dallas, 1955-62; guest tchr. ballet numerous dance acads. and ballet cos., worldwide, 1962-70; prof. dance Ind. Univ., Bloomington, 1970-90; prof. emeritus Ind. U., 1990—. Guest tchr. ballet numerous orgns. including Vaganova Choreography Inst., Leningrad, USSR, Ballet do Rio de Janeiro, Egypt Nat. Ballet of Cairo, Ballet Intezet, Hungary, Nat. Ballet, Istanbul, Turkey, Royal Danish Ballet, Tex. Christian Univ., Ft. Worth, Legat Sch., Eng., Nat. Ballet, Nicaragua; condr. master classes for Ballet Guatemala, Escuela Nacional de Danza, San Salvador, Academia de Danza Classica, Costa Rica, Nat. Ballet Venezuela, T.W. Univ., Dallas Ballet Co., Columbia Nat. Ballet, Nat. U. Costa Rica, Bellas Artes, Honduras, Ballet Nacional Nicaragua; co-founder, dir. Dallas Civic Ballet; art dir. Ballet Guatemala, 1978-79, Nat. Ballet Salvador; guest tchr. Ulm Theatre, Germany, Ballet Co., 1995, Ballet Nat.-Mcpl., Lima, 1999, Artemis, Amsterdam, Holland, State Ballet Ecuador, Quito; Internat. Ballet competition Managua, Nicaragua, 1995; examiner Russian Ballet Soc., Eng., 1969—; guest tchr., lectr. Cuba State Ballet Co. Author of character dance books and ballet dance books in English, German and Spanish, 1991; collaborator and coach to Dame Margot Fonteyn. U.S. judge Internat. Ballet Competition, Trujillo, Peru, 1989-91, 99, Internat. Competition, Camaguey, Cuba, 1999. Served as sgt. German Army, 1942-45. Research grantee Ind. Univ., 1977. Avocations: exhibited sculptor, tennis, deep-sea fishing. Home: Curtius Str 6 23568 Luebeck Germany

PAGET, JOHN ARTHUR, mechanical engineer; b. Ft. Frances, Ont., Can., Sept. 15, 1922; s. John and Ethel (Bishop) P.; B. in Applied Sci., Toronto, 1946; m. Vicenta Herrera Nunez, Dec. 16, 1963; children: Cynthia Ellen, Kevin Arthur, Keith William. Chief draftsman Gutta Percha & Rubber, Ltd., Toronto, Ont., 1946-49; chief draftsman Viceroy Mfg. Co., Toronto, 1949-52; supr., design engr. C.D. Howe Co. Ltd., Montreal, Que., Can., 1952-58, sr.

design engr. Combustion Engring., Montreal, 1958-59; sr. staff engr. Gen. Atomic, Inc., La Jolla, 1959-81. Mem. ASME, Soc. for History Tech., Inst. Mech. Engrs., Brit. Nuclear Energy Soc. Patentee in field. Home: 3183 Magellan St San Diego CA 92154-1515

PAGILLO, CARL ROBERT, elementary school educator; b. Bklyn., Apr. 11, 1950; s. Nicholas and Rachel (Rhyne) P.; m. Joanne Ferro, Aug. 1, 1992. BA, Queens Coll., 1973, MS in Elem. Edn., 1975; advanced in edn. adminstrn., Bklyn. Coll., 1993. Tchr. grade 3, 5, and 6 Pub. Sch. 207 Queens, Howard Beach, N.Y., 1983-93; tchr. multimedia PS 20 YQ, 1983-93; tchr. lang. arts PS 56 Q, Richmond Hill, 1993—. Pres., founder Catherine St. Block Assn., Lynbrook, 1987-91; baseball coach, mgr. Little League, Pony League and Baby Ruth League, Nassau County, 1974-92; capt. Lynbrook 4.0. tennis team, 1984-93. Recipient Ely Trachtenberg award United Fedn. of Tchrs., 1986. Mem. Phi Delta Kappa. Avocation: tennis. Home: 17 Catherine St Lynbrook NY 11563-1207

PAGLIA, CAMILLE, writer, humanities educator; b. Endicott, N.Y., 1947; d. Pasquale John and Lydia (Colapietro) P. BA in English summa cum laude with highest honors, SUNY, Binghamton, 1968; MPhil, Yale U., 1971, PhD in English, 1974. Mem. faculty Bennington (Vt.) Coll., 1972-80; vis. lectr. Wesleyan U., 1980, Yale U., New Haven, 1980-84; prof. humanities U. Arts, Phila., 1984-2000, univ. prof. and prof. humanities and media studies, 2000—. Author: Sexual Personae: Art and Decadence from Nefertiti to Emily Dickinson, 1990, Sex, Art, and American Culture, 1992, Vamps and Tramps: New Essays, 1994, Alfred Hitchcock's "The Birds", 1998; columnist: Salon-.com, 1995—2001; contbg. editor: Interview Magazine, 2001—. Office: Univ Arts 320 S Broad St Philadelphia PA 19102-4994

PAGLIARI, RICHARD M. lawyer, estate planner; b. L.A., Jan. 5, 1964; BA, U. So. Calif.; JD, U. West Los Angeles, Culver City, Calif. Bar: Calif. 1994. Pvt. practice, L.A., 1994—. Office: 6535 Wilshire Blvd Ste 200 Los Angeles CA 90048-4905

PAGLIARINI, JOHN RAYMOND, public affairs executive; b. Providence, Oct. 2, 1961; s. John Vincent and Florence Marie (Piacitelli) P. BA, Fairfield U., 1983; MA, George Washington U., 1986. Planning intern City of Cranston, R.I., 1979-83; legis. intern Senator John Chafee, Washington, 1984, Congresswoman Claudine Schneider, Washington, 1984; mgr., exec. aide, policy assoc. Gov.'s Office, Providence, 1986-90; account exec. Strategy Corp., Cranston, 1991-92; dir. comms. Mayor's Office, Warwick, R.I., 1993-96; mgr. cmty. devel. program City of Warwick, 1997-98; dir. govt. rels. United Healthcare of New England, 1998—. Mem. R.I. Statewide Planning Tech. Com., 1987-90, Gov's Ins. Commn., 1987-90, Multi-Purpose Arts Ctr. Study Com., 1988, Commn. on Vets. Registration Plates, 1989, Commn. on Local Cmty. Econ. Devel., 1989, Coalition N.E. Govs.' Source Reduction Task Force, 1989, chmn. subcom. on consumer softgoods 1989; chmn. R.I. Take Pride in Am. Com., 1988-89, Warwick Hazard Mitigation Strategy Com., 1998; coord. R.I. Statewide Bond Referenda, 1989, Greenwich Bay Bond Referendum, 1994; mem. Ctrl. R.I. Econ. Devel. Corp. Organizing Com., 1995-96, Providence Jour. Tourism Roundtable Panel, 1997, Nat. Cmty. Devel. Assn., 1997-98, Commn. to Study the Utilization Rev. Act, 1999. Walk Am. com. mem. March of Dimes, Warwick, 1993-99; chmn. Ward 5 Rep. Com., Warwick, 1993-99; bd. dirs. Willow Glen Condominiums, Warwick; bd. dirs., sec., R.I. chpt. Amyotrophic Lateral Sclerosis Assn., 1999—; alt. state ctrl. com. R.I. Rep. Com., 2001—, mem. exec. bd., chmn. nominating com, state ctrl. com. Mem. Amyotrophic Lateral Sclerosis Assn. (R.I. chpt.). Roman Catholic. Avocations: running, skiing, photography, travel. Office: United Healthcare New England 475 Kilvert St Warwick RI 02886-1392 E-mail: jpagliar@uhc.com.

PAGLIARO, FRANK CARL, JR. collection agency executive, city official; b. Derby, Conn., Apr. 5, 1929; s. Frank Carl and Mary (Nacrella) P.; m. Elizabeth Malec; children: John, Frank Carl III (dec.), Robert; stepchildren: Susan, Fred. AS, U. New Haven, 1950. Cert. mgr. patient accounts. Contr. Park City Hosp., Bridgeport, Conn., 1959-65; comptr. Griffin Hosp., Shelton, 1966-74, v.p. fin., 1974-81; mng. ptnr. Universal Adjustment, 1982-88; owner, mgr. Collect Assocs., 1989—91; welfare commr. City of Shelton, 1991-95, treas., 1995—. Chmn. Shelton Rep. Com., 1991—. Recipieent John Davis Lodge award Shelton Rep. Com., 1994. Fellow Hosp. Fin. Mgmt. Assn.; mem. Conn. Assn. Collection Agys., Rotary. Roman Catholic. Home: Vaccaro Heights Shelton CT 06484 Office: Collect Assocs 392 River Rd Shelton CT 06484-4426

PAGLIARO, JAMES DOMENIC, lawyer; b. Phila., Aug. 18, 1951; s. Domenic A. and Nancy I. (D'Amore) P.; m. Susan B. Boag, Aug. 25, 1973; children: Jamie C., Justin A. BA cum laude, LaSalle U., 1973; JD, Dickinson Law Sch., 1976. Bar: Pa. 1976, U.S. Dist. Ct. (ea. dist.) Pa. 1977, U.S. Ct. Appeals (3d, 4th, 8th, 9th and 10th cirs.) 1989, U.S. Supreme Ct. 1989. Regional atty. Gov. of Pa., Phila., 1976-79; sr. trial atty. office regional solicitor U.S. Dept. Labor, 1979-85; assoc. Morgan, Lewis & Bockius, LLP, 1985-88, ptnr. litigation, 1988—, mng. ptnr. litigation sect., 1999—. Chmn. Home & Sch. Bd. Norwood Acad., Chestnut Hill, Pa., 1983-87; vestry Hist. St. Paul's Ch., Elkins Park, Pa., 1993-94. Fellow Am. Coll. Trial Lawyers; mem. ABA, Pa. Bar Assn. (speaker continuing legal edn. 1987—), Phila. Bar Assn., Woolsach Honors Soc. Home: 1120 Timbergate Dr Rydal PA 19046-2509 Office: Morgan Lewis & Bockius LLP 1701 Market St Philadelphia PA 19103-2903 E-mail: jpagliaro@morganlewis.com.

PAGLIARULO, MICHAEL ANTHONY, physical therapy educator; b. Amityville, N.Y., May 15, 1947; s. Anthony and Louise (Cipriani) P.; m. Patricia Marilyn Salm, Mar. 22, 1975; children: Michael, David, Elisa. BA in Biology, SUNY, Buffalo, 1969, BS in Phys. Therapy, 1970; MA in Phys. Therapy, U. So. Calif., 1974; EdD in Postsecondary Edn. Adminstrn., Syracuse U., 1988. Lic. phys. therapist, N.Y., Calif. Staff phys. therapist Brunswick Hosp. Ctr., Amityville, 1970; lectr. U. So. Calif., L.A., 1974-75, U. Calif., San Francisco, 1975-80; curriculum coord. Ithaca (N.Y.) Coll., 1980-82, asst. prof., 1982-89, acting dir., 1986-89, assoc. prof., dir., 1989-94, assoc. prof. phys. therapy, 1994—, chair, 1989-94, 97-98. Author: Introduction to Physical Therapy, 1996, 2d edit., 2001. Bd. dirs. Marin/Roundtree Homeowners Assn., San Rafael, Calif., 1978-80; cubmaster Boy Scouts Am., Ithaca, 1989-91. Capt. U.S. Army, 1970-72. Named to Copiague H.S. Hall of Achievement, 1998. Mem.: Am. Phys. Therapy Assn. (bd. dirs. Calif. chpt. 1979—80, treas. N.Y. chpt. 1989—91, speaker del. assembly 2001, Merit award 1988, 1995, 1997, Norma Chadwick award 1993, Outstanding Svc. award 1997, Dr. Marilyn Moffat Disting. Svc. award 1998, Ithaca Coll. Excellence in Svc. award 2001). Congregationalist. Avocations: scuba diving, water and snow skiing, model trains. Office: Ithaca Coll Dept Phys Therapy Danby Rd Ithaca NY 14850

PAGNI, PATRICK JOHN, mechanical and fire safety engineering science educator; b. Chgo., Nov. 28, 1942; s. Frank and Helen P.; m. Carol DeSantis, Dec. 26, 1970 (div. Jan. 2000); children: Christina Marie, Catherine Ann, Patrick John Jr. B in Aeronautical Engring. magna cum laude, U. Detroit, 1965; SM, MIT, 1967, ME, 1969, PhD, 1970. Registered profl. mechanical engr., Calif., fire protection engr., Calif. Research asst. MIT, Cambridge, 1965-70; asst. prof. Mech. Engring. Dept. U. Calif., Berkeley, 1970-76, assoc. prof., 1976-81, prof., 1981—, vice chmn. grad. study, 1986-89; acting assoc. dean Coll. Engring. U. Calif., 1990; assoc. faculty scientist Lawrence Berkeley Lab., 1976—. Vis. scientist Factory Mut. Research Corp., Norwood, Mass., 1980; cons. on fire safety sci. various orgns., 1972—; affiliate prof. fire protection engring. dept. Worcester Poly. Inst., 2000—; vis. rsch. scholar U. Ulster, No. Ireland, 2000—. Editor: Fire Science for Fire Safety, 1984, Fire Safety Science--Procs. of the First Internat. Symposium, 1986, Procs. of the Second Internat. Symposium, 1989; contbr. articles to profl. jours. Grantee NSF, NASA, Nat. Bur. Standards, Nat. Inst. Standards and Tech., 1971—; Applied Mechanics fellow Harvard U., 1974, 77; Pullman Found. scholar, 1960. Mem. ASME, Am. Phys. Soc. (life), Combustion Inst., Soc. Fire Protection Engrs. (Bono award for best paper 1999), Internat. Assn. Fire Safety Sci. (life mem., vice chmn., exec. com., chmn. program com.), Tau Beta Pi, Pi Tau Sigma, Alpha Sigma Nu. Democrat. Roman Catholic. Home: 1901 Ascot Dr Moraga CA 94556-1412 Office: U Calif Coll Engring Mech Engring Dept Berkeley CA 94720-1740 E-mail: pjpagni@me.berkeley.edu.

PAGON, ROBERTA ANDERSON, pediatrics educator; b. Boston, Oct. 4, 1945; d. Donald Grigg and Erna Louise (Goettsch) Anderson; m. Garrett Dunn Pagon Jr., July 1, 1967; children: Katharine Blye, Garrett Dunn III, Alyssa Grigg, Alexander Goettsch. BA, Stanford U., 1967; MD, Harvard U., 1972. Diplomate Am. Bd. Pediatrics, Am. Bd. Med. Genetics. Pediatric intern U. Wash. Affiliated Hosp., Seattle, 1972-73, resident in pediatrics, 1973-75; fellow in med. genetics U. Wash. Sch. Medicine, 1976-79, asst. prof. pediatrics, 1979-84, assoc. prof., 1984-92, prof., 1992—. Supr. Helix: A Directory of Medical Genetics Labs., Seattle, 1992—. Sponsor N.W. region U.S. Pony Club, 1985-94. Mem. Am. Soc. Human Genetics, Phi Beta Kappa. Avocations: hiking, backpacking, horseback riding. Office: Children's Hosp Med Ctr Divsn Med Genetics CH 25 4800 Sand Point Way NE Seattle WA 98105-3901*

PAGONIS, WILLIAM GUS, retired army general; b. Charleroi, Pa., Apr. 30, 1941; s. Constantinos V. and Jennie (Kontos) P.; m. Cheryl Elaine Miller, June 14, 1964; children: Gust, Robert. BS, Pa. State U., 1964, MBA in Bus. Logistics, 1970; D in Pub. Svc. (hon.), Washington Jefferson Coll., 1997. Commd. 2d lt. U.S. Army, 1964, advanced through grades to lt. gen., 1991; comdr. 1097th Transp. Co., Vietnam, 1968; div. transp. officer, then exec. officer 2d bn., 501st inf., 101st Airborne Div., Vietnam, 1970-71; pers. staff officer U.S. Army Mil. Pers. Ctr., Alexandria, Va., 1973-75; staff officer Office Chief of Legis. Liaison, Washington, 1975-76; comdr. 10th transp. bn. 7th Transp. Group, Ft. Eustis, Va., 1977-78; chief of staff 193d Inf. Brigade, Panama, 1980-81, comdr. Logistics Support Command Panama, 1981-82; comdr. Div. Support Command, 4th Inf. Div., Ft. Carson, Colo., 1982-85; dir. transp., energy and troop support Office Dep. Chief of Staff for Logistics, Washington, 1989-90; comdg. gen. 22d Support Command, Dhahran, Saudi Arabia, 1990-91, Saudi Arabia, 1990-92, 21st Support Command Europe, Germany, 1992-93; lt. gen., ret. U.S. Army, 1993; exec. v.p. logistics Sears & Roebuck Co., Hoffman Estates, Ill., 1993—. Author: Moving Mountains (Logistics Leadership and Management of the Gulf War), (one of top 30 best bus. books of 1992, top leadership book 1992 Soundview Exec. Book Summaries, 1992), 1992. Decorated D.S.M., Silver Star, Legion of Merit with oak leaf cluster, Bronze Star with 3 oak leaf clusters, Air medal with 2 oak leaf clusters, Meritorious Svc. medal with 4 oak leaf clusters, King Abdul Aziz 2d Class award Chief of Staff, Saudi Arabian Army, 1991, Kuwait Liberation medal Chief of Staff, Kuwait Army, 1992; recipient Merit and Honor award Govt. of Greece, 1991, Joseph C. Scheleen award Am. Soc. Transp. and Logistics, 1991, Man of Yr. award Modern Materials Handling, 1991, Grad. Man of Yr. award Alpha Chi Rho, 1991, AHEPA Man of Yr., 1992, Disting. Alumni award Pa. State U., 1994; named Hellenic Man of Yr., 1992; Pa. State U. fellow, 1992. Home: 25190 N Pawnee Rd Barrington IL 60010-1354 Office: Sears Roebuck & Co 3333 Beverly Rd Hoffman Estates IL 60192-3322

PAGTER, CARL RICHARD, lawyer; b. Balt., Feb. 13, 1934; s. Charles Ralph and Mina (Amelung) P.; m. Judith Elaine Cox, May 6, 1978; 1 child by previous marriage: Corbin Christopher. AA, Diablo Valley Coll., 1953; BA, San Jose State U., 1955; LLB, U. Calif., Berkeley, 1964. Bar:Calif. 1965, D.C. 1977, U.S. Supreme Ct. 1976. Law clk. Kaiser Industries Corp., Oakland, Calif., 1963-64, counsel, 1964-70, assoc. counsel Washington, 1970-73, counsel Oakland, Calif., 1973-75, dir. govt. affairs Washington, 1975-76; v.p., sec., gen. counsel Kaiser Cement Corp., Oakland, Calif., 1976-88, cons., gen. counsel San Ramon, 1988-98, cons., 1998—. Author: (with A. Dundes) Urban Folklore from the Paperwork Empire, 1975, More Urban Folklore from the Paperwork Empire, 1987, Never Try to Teach a Pig to Sing, 1991, Sometimes the Dragon Wins, 1996, Why Don't Sheep Shrink When It Rains, 2000. With USNR, 1957-61, to comdr., 1978. Mem. Calif. Bar, Am. Folklore Soc., Calif. Folklore Soc., Calif. Bluegrass Assn. (founder), Mariners Square Athletic Club, Univ. Club. Republican. Home and Office: 17 Julianne Ct Walnut Creek CA 94595-2610

PAHIRA, JOHN JOSEPH, urology educator; b. Abington, Pa., Aug. 18, 1948; s. Joseph Charles and Jean (Shaller) P. BS in Biology, St. Joseph's Coll., 1970; MD, Pa. State U., 1974. Intern in surgery Abington (Pa.) Meml. Hosp., 1974-75, resident in surgery, 1975-76; resident in urology Hosp. of the U. of Pa., 1976-79; prof. urology Georgetown U. Med. Ctr., Washington, 1979—. Contbr. chpt. to book, articles to profl. jours. Mem. Am. Urologic Assn. (mid-atlantic sect. 1997—), Washington Urologic Soc (pres. 1995-96). Office: Georgetown U Med Ctr 3800 Reservoir Rd NW Washington DC 20007-2113

PAHK, SANG KEE, gastroenterologist; b. Korea, Oct. 5, 1930; s. Chang Won and Soon Nam (Kim) P.; m. Hong Ja Lee, Mar. 3, 1973; children: Albert, Patricia. MD, Seoul (Korea) Nat. U., 1956, MS, 1958, PhD, 1963. Diplomate Am. Bd. Internal Medicine and Gastroenterology. Dir. medicine Korean Air Force Hosp., Seoul, 1961-62; assoc. dir. medicine Seoul Red Cross Hosp., 1964-69; asst. clin. prof. medicine Seoul Nat. U. Coll. Medicine, 1967; dir. medicine Maryknoll Hosp., Pusan, Korea, 1969-71; assoc. clin. prof. medicine Cath. Med. Coll., Seoul, 1969-71; gastroenterologist St. John's Queens Hosp., Elmhurst, N.Y., 1981—. Fellow: ACP, Am. Coll. Gastroenterology; mem.: Am. Soc. Gastrointestinal Endoscopy, Korean Assn. Gastroenterology (councillor), Am. Gastroenterol. Assn. Avocations: photography, golf. Office: 13630 Maple Ave Apt 1D Flushing NY 11355-3866

PAHL, RANDALL, principal, parochial school educator; b. Green Bay, Wis., Nov. 15, 1958; s. Roger Pahl, Margaret Pahl; m. Judith Wangerin; children: Jason, Eric, Karen. AA, Wis. Luth. Coll., 1978; BS, Dr. Martin Luther Coll., 1981. Head math depart. East Fork Luth. H.S., Whiteriver, Ariz., 1981—90; prin., jr. high instr. St. Paul's Luth. Sch., Wisconsin Rapids, Wis., 1990—. Conservative. Lutheran. Avocations: fishing, golf. Office: St Paul's Luth Sch 311 14th Ave S Wisconsin Rapids WI 54495

PAHMAN, DAVID A. principal; b. Greenville, Miss., Oct. 29, 1971; s. Larry Pahman Jr., Anita Pahman; m. Sarah A. Allen; children: Hannah, Leah. BS in Secondary Math. Edn., Faulkner U., 1993; MS in Secondary Math. Edn., Troy State U., 1997, MS in Ednl. Leadership, 1998. Cert. profl.educator Fla., 2000. Math. tchr. & coach Goshen H.S., Goshen, Ala., 1993—98; asst. prin. Ala. Christian Acad., Montgomery, 1998—2000; secondary prin. Christian Home & Bible Sch., Mount Dora, Fla., 2000—. Recipient Outstanding Tchr. award, Tandy Tech. Scholars, 1996. Mem.: Assn. for Supervision & Curriculum Devel., Nat. Assn. Secondary Sch. Prin. Ch. Of Christ. Office: Christian Home & Bible School 301 West 13th Avenue Mount Dora FL 32757 Office Fax: 352-383-1942. Personal E-mail: dpahman@chbs.org. Business E-Mail: dpahman@chbs.org.

PAHNKE, GREG RANDOLPH, surgeon; b. Wilmington, Del., Sept. 30, 1951; MD, U. Pa., 1977. Diplomate Am. Bd. Surgery. Intern U. Tex. Health Scis. Ctr., Houston, 1977-78, resident, 1978-82; fellow in surg. oncology MD Anderson Hosp., 1982-83; staff Med. Ctr. Del., Wilmington; pvt. practice, 1983—; med. dir. Christiana Care Breast Ctr., 1999—. Fellow Am. Coll. Surgeons; mem. AMA, Stanley J. Dudrick MD Soc. Office: Lombardy Med Ctr 410 Foulk Rd Ste 200A Wilmington DE 19803-3802 Fax: 302-764-3501. E-mail: gpahnke@dca.net.

PAHNKE, LYLE DOUGLAS, JR. surgeon; b. Chgo., Nov. 5, 1944; MD, Washington U., St. Louis, 1970. Diplomate Am. Bd. Surgery. Intern Bellevue Hosp. Ctr.-NYU Med. Ctr., N.Y.C., 1970-71, resident in surgery, 1971-75, chief resident, 1975; fellow in transplantation Sloan Kettering Cancer Ctr., 1975-76; dept. chief surgeon San Bernardino (Calif.) Cmty. Hosp., 1991-93; dept. chief surgery St. Bernardines Hosp., Calif., 1991-93, courtesy staff, 1995-99; active staff surgery St. Marys Hosp., Centralia, Ill., 1994—; courtesy staff Good Samaritan Hosp., Mt. Vernon, 1997; chief surgery St. Mary's Hosp., 2002—; staff Crossroads Cmty. Hosp., Mt. Vernon, 2000—. Fellow ACS; mem. AMA, ACSurgEons, Ill. State Med. Soc., So. Ill. Med. Assn. Office: Ste 106 1050 Martin Luther King Dr Centralia IL 62801

PAHWA, RAJESH, physician; b. Apr. 9, 1960; MD, U. Bombay, 1983. Diplomate Am. Bd. Psychiatry and Neurology. Resident in medicine KEM Hosp., Bombay, India, 1984-85; intern Baylor Coll. Medicine, Houston, 1987-88, resident in neurology, 1988-91; fellow in movement disorders U. Kans. Med. Ctr., Kansas City, 1991-92, from instr. to assoc. prof. neurology, 1992—, dir. Parkinson's Disease and Movement Disorder Ctr. Office: Kans U Med Ctr Dept Neurology 3901 Rainbow Blvd Kansas City KS 66160-0001

PAI, DEVDAS MIZAR, educator; b. Burnpur, India, Oct. 5, 1960; came to U.S., 1982; s. Mizar Shrinivasa P. BTech, Indian Inst. Tech., Madras, 1982; MS, Ariz. State U., 1984, PhD, 1987. Registered profl. engr., N.C. Faculty assoc. Ariz. State U., Tempe, 1987-88; asst. prof. N.C. A&T State U., Greensboro, 1988-93, assoc. prof., 1993—. Contbr. articles to numerous jours. Vol. ARC, Tempe, Ariz., 1983-87. Recipient Ralph Teetor Ednl. award Soc. Automotive Engrs., 1996; Herman B. Demund scholar Ariz. State U., 1985. Mem. ASME (vice chmn. local chpt. 1992, chmn. 1993, faculty advisor student sect. 1993—), NSPE (faculty advisor student chpt. 1989-93), Soc. Mfg. Engrs., Hindu Soc. N.C. (treas. North Ctrl. region 1988-90, sec. 1996), Indian Assn. Greensboro (sec. 1988-90, treas. 1992-93), Sigma Xi. Avocation: reading. Office: NC A&T State U Dept Mech Engring Greensboro NC 27411-0001

PAI, RAVINDRA, naval architect; b. Coondapoor, India, July 21, 1967; s. Wandan and Mukta (Bhandarkar) P.; m. Seema Sharma, Dec. 6, 1994. BTech. with honors, Indian Inst. Tech., Kharagpur, 1989; MSc, Va. Poly. Inst. and State U., 1991; MBA, U. Chgo., 2000. Engr. Aker Engring., Houston, 1992, Bechtel/PMB, Houston, 1992; project engr. Offshore Pipelines Internat., 1992-94; engr., project mgr. Aker Omega, 1995—98; assoc. Deutsche Bank, 2000—02, Prudential Securities, 2002—. Named Best All Rounder, Am. Bur. Shipping, Kharagpur, 1989. Mem. Soc. Naval Archs. Marine Engrs. (chmn. tech. paper com. 1996-97, publicity chair 1995-96). Home: 201 E 86th St Apt 17F New York NY 10028-3043

PAICOPOLOS, ERNEST MICHAEL, public opinion research company executive; b. Boston, July 11, 1951; s. Michael Frank and Irene Anne (Bosia) P.; m. Gail Miriam Bloom, Feb. 15, 1976; 1 child, Adam Nathaniel. BS, Northeastern U., 1974, postgrad., 1974-75, U. Mass., 1976-77. Field researcher Nat. Opinion Rsch. Ctr., Chgo., 1976-77; rsch. asst. Mass. Dept. Mental Health, Boston, 1977-78; v.p. Cambridge (Mass.) Reports, Inc., 1978-88; prin. Opinion Dynamics Corp., Cambridge, 1988—; pres. Am. Insight, 1989—. Author, editor Dextra, polit. newsletter, 1971. Researcher Carter-Mondale Reelection Com., Dem. Nat. Conv., 1980; mem. fin. com. Paleologos for Lt. Gov., Boston, 1990. Mem. Am. Assn. for Pub. Opinion Rsch., Am. Assn. Polit. Cons., Cable TV Pub. Affairs Assn. Avocations: reading, photography. Home: 27 Somerset Dr Andover MA 01810-1249 Office: Opinion Dynamics Corp 1030 Massachusetts Ave Ste 3 Cambridge MA 02138-5335 E-mail: epaicopolos@opiniondynamics.com.

PAIDOUSSIS, MICHAEL PANDELI, mechanical engineering educator; b. Nicosia, Cyprus, Aug. 20, 1935; emigrated to Can., 1953, naturalized, 1976; s. Pandelis Aristeidis and Parthenope (Leptou) P. B in Engring., McGill U., 1958; PhD in Engring., U. Cambridge, 1963. Overseas fellow Gen. Electric Co., Erith, Kent, Eng., 1958-60; rsch. officer Atomic Energy of Can., Chalk River, Ont., 1963-67; with McGill U., Montreal, 1967—, prof., dept. mech. engring., 1976—, chmn., 1977-86, Thomas Workman prof., 1986—2000, 2000—. Cons. and rschr. in field. Editor Jour. Fluids and Structures; contbr. articles in field. Pres. Hellenic-Can. Solidarity Com. for Cyprus, 1974-80, Com. Pan-Can. de Solidarite pour Chypre, 1978-83; hon. consul gen. Republic of Cyprus, Montreal, 1983—. Recipient Brit. Assn. medal for high distinction in mech. engring., 1958, George Stephenson prize Inst. Mech. Engrs., 1976, commemorative medal for 125th ann. of Confederation of Can., 1993, medal Can. Congress Applied Mechs., 1995. Fellow Instn. of Mech. Engrs., ASME (Fluids Engring. award 1999), Can. Soc. Mech. Engring., Royal Soc. Can., Am. Acad. Mechanics, Can. Acad. Engring.; mem. Internat. Assn. Hydraulic Rsch., Internat. Assn. Structural Mechanics in Reactor Tech., Order Engrs. Que. Home: 2930 Edouard Montpetit #PH2 Montreal QC Canada H3T 1J7 Office: 817 Ouest Rue Sherbrooke Montreal QC Canada H3A 2K6 E-mail: maryf@mecheng.mcgill.ca.

PAIER, ADOLF ARTHUR, computer software and services company executive; b. Branford, Conn., Oct. 27, 1938; s. Adolf Arthur and Margaret Mary (Almond) P.; m. Geraldine Shnakis, Sept. 17, 1966; children: Nathaniel Jason, Andrew Joseph, Alena Catherine. AA, Quinnipiac Coll., 1958; BS in Econs., U. Pa., 1960. Audit mgr. Touche Ross & Co., Phila., 1960-67; pres., dir. Safeguard Scientifics, Inc., Wayne, Pa., 1967-92; chmn., CEO, pres. Healthworks Alliance, Inc., King of Prussia, 1992—; pres., CEO Novus Corp., Radnor, 1992—. Bd. dirs. Deltapaper, Croydon, Pa., Analytical Graphics, Malvern, Pa. Bd. dirs. Univ. of Arts, Phila., Lincoln Ctr. Family and Youth, Bridgeport, Pa.; bd. overseers U. Pa. Mus. Archaeology and Anthropology. Mem. Chief Execs. Orgn., Phila. Pres. Orgn., Phila. Country Club (bd. govs.). Office: Novus Corp 5 Radnor Corp Ctr 100 Matsonford Rd Ste 520 Radnor PA 19087-4526

PAIGE, GLENN DURLAND, political scientist, educator; b. Brockton, Mass., June 28, 1929; s. Lester Norman and Rita Irene (Marshall) P.; m. Betty Gail Grenier, Jan. 2, 1949 (div.); children: Gail, Jan, Donn, Sean, Sharon, Van; m. Glenda Hatsuko Naito, Sept. 1, 1973. Grad., Phillips Exeter Acad., 1947; AB, Princeton U., 1955; MA, Harvard U., 1957; Ph. D., Northwestern U., 1959; PhD (hon.), Soka U., 1992. Asst. prof. pub. adminstrn. Seoul Nat. U., 1959-61; asst. to assoc. prof. politics Princeton U., 1961-67; prof. polit. sci. U. Hawaii, Honolulu, 1967-92, prof. emeritus, 1992—. Cons. Fla. Martin Luther King, Jr., Inst. for Nonviolence, 1997. Author: The Korean Decision, 1968, The Scientific Study of Political Leadership, 1977, To Nonviolent Political Science, 1993, Nonkilling Global Political Science, 2002; editor: Political Leadership, 1972, (with George Chaplin) Hawaii 2000, 1973, (with Sarah Gilliatt) Nonviolence in Hawaii's Spiritual Traditions, 1991, Buddhism and Nonviolent Global Problem-Solving, 1991, (of Petra K. Kelly) Nonviolence Speaks to Power, 1993, (with Chaiwat Satha-Anand) Islam and Nonviolence, 1993; social sci. editor: Biography, 1977-2000. Program chmn. Hawaii Gov.'s Conf. on Yr. 2000, 1970; faculty UN Univ. Internat. Leadership Acad., 1997; pres. Non-profit Ctr. for Global Nonviolence, 1994—. With U.S. Army, 1948-52. Decorated Commendation medal; recipient Seikyo Culture prize, 1982, Dr. G. Ramachandran award for internat. understanding, 1986, Anuvrat award for internat. peace, 1987, Jai Tulsi Anuvrat award, 1995; named Woodrow Wilson nat. fellow, 1955-56, Princeton U. Class of 1955 award, 1987, 3rd Gandhi Meml. lectr., New Delhi, 1990. Mem. Internat. Peace Rsch. Assn., Internat. Polit. Sci. Assn., World Future Studies Fedn., Am. Polit. Sci. Assn, Phi Beta Kappa. Home: 3653 Tantalus Dr Honolulu HI 96822-5033 E-mail: cgnv@hawaii.rr.com. *Political science is a science that can help liberate humankind from violence. To do so, it must first liberate itself. This will require five related transformations: normative, empirical, theoretical, institutional, and educational. Political scientists in the 21st century must carry these transformations forward, consolidate them, and extend their influence throughout global society. A nonkilling world is possible.*

PAIGE, HILLIARD WEGNER, corporate director, consultant; b. Hartford, Conn., Oct. 2, 1919; s. Joseph Wegner and Ruth (Hill) P.; m. Dorothea Magner, Dec. 8, 1945; children: Elizabeth, Deborah, Hilliard, Jr. BSME, Worcester Poly. Inst., 1941, D of Engring. (hon), 1971. Sr. v.p. for aerospace and computer ops. Gen. Electric, N.Y.C., 1941-71; pres. Gen. Dynamics, St. Louis, 1971-73; chmn., CEO Satellite Bus. Systems, Inc., Washington, 1973-76; vice-chmn. bd. Internat. Energy Assocs., Ltd., 1976-85; chmn. bd. H.A. Knott, Ltd., Silver Spring, Md., 1984-89. Vice-chmn. The Atlantic Coun. of U.S., 1987—, Gallager Marine Systems, Inc., 1993—. Patentee in field; contbr. articles to profl. jours. Mem. Def. Sci. Bd. U.S. Dept. Def., Washington, 1973-78; trustee Worcester Poly. Inst., Mass., 1974—. Recipient Pub. Service award NASA, 1969, Order of Merit Italy, 1970, Engr. of Year award Greater Phila. Engring Council, 1960 Fellow AIAA, Explorers Club (nat.); mem. NAE. Clubs: Metropolitan, Chevy Chase (Washington); Conquistadores del Cielo. Republican. Congregationalist. Avocations: skiing, tennis, scuba diving, golf. Home: 905 E Boca Raton Rd Boca Raton FL 33432-4119 Office: 5163 Tilden St NW Washington DC 20016-1961

PAIGE, RODERICK R. federal agency administrator; b. Monticello, Miss., 1943; Bachelor's, Jackson State U.; master's, doctorate, Ind. U. Coach coll. level athletics; dean Coll. Edn. Tex. So. U., developer Ctr. Excellence in Urban Edn.; supt. Houston Ind. Sch. Dist.; sec. edn. Dept. Edn., Washington, 2001—. Est. Ctr. for Excellence in Urban Edn., Tex. Southern U.; created Peer Exam., Evaluation, Redesign (PEER) program. Co-author: A Declaration of Beliefs and Visions. Mem. NAACP; mem. adv. bd. Tex. Commerce Bank, Am. Leadership Forum. Recipient Harold W. McGraw, Jr. Prize in Edn., 2000; named Supt. Yr. award, Nat. Assn. Black Sch. Educators', 2000, Nat. Supt.

Yr., Am. Assn. Sch. Adminstr., 2001. Mem. review coms. Tex. Edn. Agy., State Bd. Edn. Task Force H.S. Edn.; chair, Youth Employment Issues Nat. Com. Employment Policy U.S. Dept. Labor subcom.; mem. Nat. Assn. Advancement Colored People, Edn. Com. States, Coun. Great City Schs.(recipient Richard R. Green award for Outstanding Urban Educator, 1999). Office: Dept Edn Office of Sec 400 Maryland Ave SW Washington DC 20202-0100*

PAIGEN, KENNETH, geneticist, director; b. N.Y.C., Nov. 14, 1927; s. Alexander and Ida (Kantor) P.; m. Beverly Vandermolen, June 14, 1970; children: Susan, Gina, Mark, David, Jennifer AB, Johns Hopkins U., Balt., 1946; PhD, Calif. Inst. Tech., Pasadena, 1950. Staff mem. Roswell Park Meml. Inst., Buffalo, 1955-72, dept. head, 1972-82; prof. dept. genetics U. Calif., Berkeley, 1982-89; dir., sr. staff scientist Jackson Lab., Bar Harbor, Maine, 1989—. Mem. AAAS, Am. Assn. for Cancer Rsch., Internat. Mammalian Genome Soc., Human Genome Orgn., Genetics Soc. Am., Am. Soc. for Biochemistry and Molecular Biology, Sigma Xi, Phi Beta Kappa. Democrat. Jewish. Avocation: sailing. Home: Old Farm Rd Bar Harbor ME 04609 Office: Jackson Lab 600 Main St Bar Harbor ME 04609-1500 E-mail: nrv@jax.org.

PAIK, JOHN KEE, structural engineer; b. Seoul; came to U.S., 1955; s. Nam Suk and Kyong Ock (Yun) P.; m. Aine Fenoula Ievers, Feb. 20, 1970; 1 child, Brian Ievers Paik. BSCE, So. Meth. U., 1961; PhD, NYU, 1975. Lic. profl. engr. N.Y., N.J., Conn., Pa., Md., Mass., Vt., Ga., Fla., N.C. Chief engr. T.Y. Lin and Assocs., N.Y.C., 1960-67; chief structural engr. Soros Assocs., 1967-68; sr. project engr. Stauffer Chem. Co., Dobbs Ferry, N.Y., 1975-77; prin., founder Paik and Assocs., Westchester County, 1977—; chmn., founder The Future Home Tech. Inc., Port Jervis, 1986—; chmn., pres. J.K.P. Constrn. Co. Inc., Mohegan Lake, 1989—. Adj. assoc. prof. Grad. Sch. Engring. Manhattan Coll., Bronx, 1985; lectr. Grad. Sch. Engring. Polytech. U., Bklyn., 1973-85, Cooper Union, N.Y.C., 1972. Mem. ASCE, NSPE, Am. Inst. Steel Constrn., Prestressed Concrete Inst., N.Y Acad. Scis., Am. Concrete Inst., Post Tensioning Inst., Constrn. Specifications Inst., Am. Arbitration Assn. (dispute arbitrator, constrn.), So. Meth. U. Alumni Club (pres. 1964), Chi Epsilon. Republican. Methodist. Achievements include the design of over 100 million sq. feet of comml., residential, indsl. and instnl. structures including several highrise bldgs. over 40 stories in N.Y.C. and White Plains, N.Y. Home: Dyckman Dr Mohegan Lake NY 10547 Office: Paik and Assocs 115 Stevens Ave Valhalla NY 10595-1252 E-mail: jkpaid@earthlink.net.

PAIKEDAY, THOMAS M. lexicographer and language consultant; came to U.S., 1962, Can. 1964; s. Manuel Thomas and Anna (Poovelickal) P.; m. Mary Kurien Kizhakethottam, Jan. 4, 1967; children: Anthony, Anne-Marie. L.Ph., Coll. of the Jesuits, Shembaganur, India, 1955; BA with 1st class honors, Madras Christian Coll., Tambaram, India, 1958; MA, U. Madras, India, 1960; postgrad, Boston Coll., 1962-63, U. Mich., 1963-64. Lectr. English St. Joseph's Coll., Tiruchy, Madras, 1958-59, Ramjas Coll., Delhi, India, 1960-61; copy editor The Statesman, New Delhi, India, 1961-62; asst. lexicographer W.J. Gage Ltd., Toronto, Ont., Can., 1964-66; editor Ont. Min. Edn., 1966-67; head lexicography div. Holt, Rinehart & Winston, 1967-73; chief lexicographer Lexicography, Inc., Brampton, Ont., 1973—. Cons. Collier-Macmillan Can., Toronto, 1980-81, Can. advisor Collins Publishers, Glasgow, Scotland, 1981-82, User's Webster. Author: The Native Speaker is Dead!, 1985; contbr. articles. Mem. Dictionary Soc. N.Am., MLA, Am. Dialect Soc., Am. Name Soc. Roman Catholic. Avocations: computer applications in lexicography, tennis, swimming. Office: Lexicography Inc 83 Sunny Meadow Blvd Brampton ON Canada L6R 1Z3 E-mail: t.paikeday@sympatico.ca.

PAILES, WILLIAM, astronaut; b. Hackensack, N.J., June 26, 1952; married. BS in Computer Sci., USAF Acad., 1974; MS in Computer Sci., Tex. A&M U., 1981. Commd. 2d lt. USAF, 1974, advanced through grades to maj.; pilot McClellan AFB, Calif., 1975—80, Royal AFB, Woodbridge, England, 1975—80; mgr. mini-computer operating systems software devel. Hqrs. Mil. Airlift Command, Scott AFB, Ill., 1982; manned spaceflight engr. Manned Spaceflight Engring. Program, L.A. Air Force Sta., 1983—; astronaut NASA, Houston. Achievements include logged over 97 hours in space; payload specialist STS-51J Atlantis (1985). Office: Astronaut Office/CB NASA Johnson Space Ctr Houston TX 77058*

PAIN, BETSY M. lawyer; b. Albertville, Ala., Aug. 29, 1950; d. Charles Riley and Jean Faye (Rains) Stone; m. William F. Pain, Nov. 18, 1977; children: Taylor Holland, Emily Anne Pain. AA, Northeastern Okla. A&M, Miami, Okla., 1970; BA, U. Okla., 1974, JD, 1976. Bar: Okla. 1977; U.S. Dist. Ct. (we. dist.) 1979. Staff atty. Okla. Dept. Corrections, Oklahoma City, 1978-79; gen. counsel Okla. Pardon and Parole Bd., 1979-84, exec. dir., 1983—88; corp. counsel Roberts, Schornick & Assocs., Inc., Norman, 1990-2000, Atkins Benham, Inc., 2002; chief legal officer Atkins Americas, Inc., 2002—. Editor: (newsletter) RSA Environmental Report, 1991—. With extended family program Juvenile Svcs., Inc. Cleveland County, Okla., 1983-91. Mem. NAFE, Okla. Bar Assn. Democrat. Methodist. Avocations: reading, needlework, church activities. Office: Atkins Americas Inc 9400 N Broadway Oklahoma City OK 73114 E-mail: betsy.pain@atkinsamericas.com.

PAINCHAUD, PHILLIP ANDRE, metrologist; b. Somerville, Mass., Apr. 24, 1919; s. Phillip Andre Painchaud and Gertrude Marie Shanley; m. Josephine Daisy Wandschneider, Dec. 18, 1943 (dec. Feb. 1988); children: Phillip A. III, Denise Michele, Valerie Yvonne; m. Arlene Roberts Painchaud, July 12, 1992 (dec. Dec. 1999). Student, MIT and U. Ill., 1943, R.I. State Coll., 1938-41; BS in Engring., Pacific States U., 1947. Lic. profl. engr., Calif. Gen. supr. metrology Northrop Corp., Anaheim, Calif., 1948-65; dir. corp. stds. E-H Rsch. Labs., Oakland, 1965-70; sr. scientist Alcon Labs., Ft. Worth, 1970-71; dir. mktg. Metron Corp., Upland, Calif., 1971-72, 78-79; cons. Painchaud Cons., Brea, 1970—. Vice-chair Calif. Profl. Metrology Com., Sacramento, 1965-74; chair Gov.'s Commn. Metrology, Sacramento, 1967-68; mem. metrology adv. bd. Calif. State Poly. U., San Luis Obispo, 1970-76. Columnist The Std., 1993— Mem. curriculum bd. Calif. State U.-Dominguez Hills, Carson, 1998—. With U.S. Signal Corps, 1942-45. Recipient Woodington Laureate award Meas. Sci. Conf. Inc., 1996; disting. vis. scholar Butler County C.C., 1996. Fellow Precision Measurements Assn. (life, pres. 1963-64), IEEE (life, sr. mem.); mem. Internat. Soc. Weighing and Measurements (life, sr. mem., gov. precision measurement divsn. 1997-99), Instrument Soc. Am. (life, sr. mem., dir. met. divsn. 1966-70), Am. Soc. for Quality (sr. mem.), ENG Club San Francisco. Avocations: computer operations, photography. Home and Office: 1110 W Dorothy Dr Brea CA 92821-2017 E-mail: painchaud4@cs.com.

PAINE, DAVID M. public relations executive; b. N.Y.C., Sept. 25, 1956; BA in Polit. Sci., Union Coll., 1979. Press advanceman The White House, Washington, 1980; with N.Y. State Assembly Judiciary Com.; acct. exec. Burson-Marsteller, N.Y.C.; founder, pres. Paine & Assocs., Costa Mesa, Calif., 1986—. Mem. Pub. Rels. Soc. Am. Office: Paine PR 1900 MacArthur Blvd Irvine CA 92612*

PAINE, SUSAN MARY, pharmacist; b. Superior, Wis., Dec. 8, 1966; d. Thomas Michael and Delores Agnes Sitek; m. Terry Richard Paine, May 15, 1993; 1 child, Paxton. BS in Pharmacy, U. Wis., Madison, 1990. Registered pharmacist, Wis. Pharmacist North Star Drug, Superior, 1990—.

PAINO, JAVIER E. physician; b. Lima, Peru, Mar. 5, 1965; arrived in U.S., 1989; s. Aldo L. Paino and Maria M. Scarpati; m. Nelida C. Heredia, Jan. 4, 1982; 1 child Isabella M. MD, Fed. Parana (Brazil) U., 1990; PhD, George Washington U., 1994; postgrad., NYU, 1999—. Cert. Peruvian Coll. Medicine and Surgery. Rescue diver Marine Corps, Lima, Peru, 1982—83; asst. prof. Stanley Kaplan, Washington, 1992—96, Balt., 1992—96. New product devel. Peikard Labs., Lima, PR, Peru, 1989—95. V.p. biochemistry students body George Washington U., Washington, 1995. Scholar, Brazilian Govt., 1983—89. Mem.: N.Y. Acad. Sci., Soc. for Neurosci., Am. Assn. Neurol. Surgery, N.Am. Skull Base Soc.

PAINTER, DIANA JEAN, urban designer, artist, architectural historian; b. Seattle, Dec. 29, 1953; d. Robert Cook and Nancy Marie (Chivers) P.; m. John Hazen McKean, Aug. 10, 1973 (div. Feb. 1975). BA, Western Wash. U., 1977; MUP, U. Wash., 1984; postgrad., U. Pa., 1987; PhD, U. Sheffield, England, 1990. Cert. planner. Designer Cope Linder Assn., Phila., 1987-88, Dagit-Saylor Architects, Phila., 1988; urban designer WRT, 1989; designer Edwin Schlossberg Inc., N.Y.C., 1989-90; urban designer The SWA Group, Laguna Beach, Calif., 1990-91; assoc. planner City of Tukwila, Wash., 1993-97; project mgr. Sound Transit, Seattle, 1997—2000. Cons. Diana J. Painter Archtl. & Cmty. History, Seattle, 1982—; instr. U. Wash., Seattle, 1986, 2000; printmaking instr. Sev Shoon Arts Ctr.; presenter in field. Exhibited prints throughout West Coast; contbr. articles to profl. jours. Active Allied Arts of Seattle Downtown Com., 1984-85; bd. dirs. Greystone Found., Pullman, Wash., 1992-93. Fellow Northwest Inst. Architecture & Urban Studies in Italy; mem. Am. Inst. Cert. Planners, Am. Assn. Planning (head mentoring program 1995—, vice-chmn. urban design divsn.), Am. Inst. Architects L.A. (urban design com. 1990-91). Avocations: painting, rowing.

PAINTER, JACK TIMBERLAKE, civil engineer; b. Kincaid, W.Va., July 23, 1930; s. Troy Earl and Nannie Bell (Proffit) P. BSCE, W.Va. U., 1950, MSCE, 1955. Instr. civil engring. W.Va. U., 1950-51, 53-55; mem. faculty La. Tech U., Ruston, 1955—; prof. civil engring. La. Tech. U., 1962-92, prof. emeritus, 1992—; Alumni Found. prof. La. Tech U., 1977-78. Vis. lectr. Manhattan Coll., Coll. Forestry, SUNY, Syracuse, Cornell U., U. Wis., summers 1954-60 Nat. pres. Circus Fans Assn. Am., 1967; lic. layreader Episcopal Ch. Served with USNR, 1951-52. Faculty fellow NSF, 1958-59; named Man of Year Omicron Delta Kappa, 1972 Fellow ASCE (life, 11 Outstanding Prof. award 1969-90); mem. Am. Congress Surveying and Mapping, La. Engring. Soc. (Charles M. Kerr Pub. Rels. award 1990), Am. Soc. Engring. Edn., Tau Beta Pi (Outstanding Prof. award 1963, 68, 74, 78), Chi Epsilon (Nat. Excellent Tchg. award 1985). Address: 1303 Hodges Ave Ruston LA 71270-5507

PAINTER, JOHN HOYT, electrical engineer; b. Winfield, Kans., Mar. 27, 1934; s. John Paul and Marjorie Marietta (Slack) P.; m. Joy Lou Vaughan, June 7, 1955; children— John Mark, Paul Burton, William Vaughan, Joy Lynn. BS, U. Ill., Urbana, 1961; Gen. Electric Found. fellow, MS, 1962; PhD, So. Meth. U., 1972; postgrad., Coll. William and Mary, 1967-69. Apollo comm. engr., tchr. astronauts NASA Manned Spacecraft Ctr., Houston, 1962-65; sr. engr. Motorola Govt. Electronics divsn., Scottsdale, Ariz., 1965-67; rsch. engr. NASA Langley Rsch. Ctr., Hampton, Va., 1967-74; assoc. prof. elec. engring. Tex. A&M U., College Station, 1974-79, prof. elec. engring., 1979—, prof. computer sci., 1989—, prof. aerospace engring., 1999—. Pres. ALTAIR Corp. cons., College Station, 1980—; tchr. Christian eschatology seminars. Author: The Church Visited, 2002; patentee digital signal processing and fuzzy logic. Served with USAF, 1953-58. Recipient Recognition cert. NASA, 1975 Mem. IEEE (sr.), AIAA. Home: 1119 Merry Oaks Dr College Station TX 77840-2606 Office: Tex A&M U Dept Aero Engring College Station TX 77843-3141 E-mail: painter@aero.tamu.edu.

PAINTER, MARK PHILIP, judge; b. Cin., Apr. 6, 1947; s. John Philip and Marjorie (West) P.; m. Sue Ann Painter. BA, U. Cin., 1970, JD, 1973. Bar: Ohio 1973, U.S. Dist. Ct. (so. dist.) Ohio 1973, U.S. Supreme Ct. 1980. Assoc. Smith & Schnacke (now part of Thompson Hine), 1973-78; pvt. practice Cin., 1978-82; judge Hamilton County Mcpl. Ct., 1982-95, Ohio 1st Dist. Ct. Appeals, Cin., 1995—. Adj. prof. law U. Cin., 1990—; lectr. in field. Author: The Legal Writer: 30 Rules for the Art of Legal Writing, 2002; co-author: Ohio DUI Law, 1988, 11th edit., 2002; mem. editl. bd.: Criminal Law Jour. Ohio, 1989—92; contbr. articles to profl. jours. Mem. bd. commrs. on grievances and discipline Ohio Supreme Ct., 1993—95; mem. Rep. Ctrl. Com., Cin., 1972—82; bd. dirs. Citizens Sch. Com., 1974—76; trustee Freestore Foodbank, 1984—90, Friends of William Howard Taft Birthplace, 2002—, Mary Jo Brueggeman Meml. Found., Cin., 1981—92. Recipient Superior Jud. Svc. award Ohio Supreme Ct., 1982, 84, 85. Mem. ABA, Ohio State Bar Assn., Cin. Bar Assn. (trustee 1988-90), Am. Judges Assn., Am. Judicature Soc., Am. Soc. Writers on Legal Subjects, Potter Stewart Inn of Ct. (master of bench emeritus), Bankers Club. Home: 2449 Fairview Ave Cincinnati OH 45219-1170 Office: Ct of Appeals William Howard Taft Law Ctr 230 E 9th St Cincinnati OH 45202-2174 E-mail: JuqPainter@aol.com.

PAINTER, PAUL WAIN, JR. lawyer; b. Cleveland, Tenn., Aug. 10, 1945; s. Paul Wain and Juanita (Davis) P.; m. Judith Ann Babine, Aug. 28, 1971; 1 child, Paul Wain III. BS, Ga. Tech., 1968; JD, U. Ga., 1974. Bar: Ga. 1974, U.S. Dist. Ct. (so. dist.) Ga., U.S. Ct. Appeals (11th cir.). Assoc. Bouhan, Williams & Levy, Savannah, Ga., 1974-79; ptnr. Karsman, Brooks, Painter & Callaway, 1979-88, Ellis, Painter, Ratterree & Bart, Savannah, 1988—. Faculty mem. Nat. Inst. Trial Advocacy, Emory U. Sch. Law, 1982-90; mem. com. on lawyer qualifications and conduct U.S. Ct. Appeals for 11th Cir., 1995—; mem. ct. adv. com. U.S. Dist. Ct. (so. dist.) Ga., 1992-2000; mem. Gov.'s Adv. Com. on Tort Reform, Atlanta, 1986; mem. Ga. Bd. Bar Examiners, 1998—. Trustee Ga. Inst. Continuing Legal Edn., Athens, 1992-95; pres. Savannah Arthritis Found., 1982-83; bd. dirs. Ga. Arthritis Found., Atlanta, 1983; grad. Leadership Savannah, 1986-88. Lt. (j.g.) USN, 1968-71. Fellow Am. Coll. Trial Lawyers; mem. ABA, State Bar Ga. (chair trial sect. 1992-93), Def. Rsch. Inst. (Ga. state chmn. 1988-91), Savannah Bar Assn. (pres. 93), Ga. Def. Lawyers Assn. (pres. 1986-87), U. Ga. Law Sch. Alumni Assn. (dir. 1997-2000, pres. 2002-2003). Avocations: golf, reading history and fiction, hunting, fishing. Office: Ellis Painter Ratterree Bart PO Box 9946 Savannah GA 31412-0146 E-mail: ppainter@eprb-law.com.

PAINTER, ROBERT LOWELL, surgeon, educator; b. Winchester, Ind., Jan. 13, 1934; s. Lowell Walter and Lillian Genevieve (Pierson) P.; m. Esther Lillian Reece, Sept. 21, 1957 (div. Sept. 1977); children: Elizabeth Haines, Bradley, Robert R., Andrew, Jane Macy-Painter; m. Nancy Sue Macy, Feb. 10, 1980. BA, Earham Coll., Richmond, Ind., 1955; MD, Ind. U., 1959. Intern and resident Hartford (Conn.) Hosp., 1959-65; resident Baylor U. Sch. Medicine, Houston, 1967-68; attending surgeon Day Kimball Hosp., Putnam, Conn., 1962-91; chmn., dir. surgery St. Francis Hosp., Hartford, 1991-98; med. practice, cons., 1999—2001. Cons. Hartford Hosp., 1969-99; assoc. prof. surgery U. Conn., 1991-99, anatomy instr., 2000—. Councilman Ct. Common Coun., Hartford, Conn., 2001—. Capt. USAF, 1965—67. Fellow ACS, Am. Coll. Physician Execs.; mem. New Eng. Surg. Soc., New Eng. Vasc. Soc., Soc. Thoracic Surgery. Republican. Avocations: hiking, gardening, saxaphone, birdwatching.

PAINTER, RUTH ROBBINS, retired environmental biochemist; b. Bethel, Conn., July 21, 1910; d. Bradford Hilton and Clara Mae (Davis) Robbins; m. Edgar Page Painter, July 4, 1940; children: Jane Painter Clapp, Page Robbins Painter. BS, U. Hawaii, 1931, MS, 1934. Cert. nutrition specialist. Nutrition investigator U. Hawaii, Honolulu, 1931-36; assoc. chemist USDA Bur. Home Econs., Washington, 1937; nutrition chemist Wash. State U., Pullman, 1937-40; asst. chemist agrl. toxicology pesticide residue rsch. U. Calif., Davis, 1960-66; assoc. specialist Environ. Toxicology, U. Calif., 1967-73, specialist, 1973-76. Cons. Nutrition and Food Toxicology, Davis, 1940-60. Contbr. articles to profl. jours. and books. Pres. PTA Coun., Davis, 1959-60; chmn. UN Assn. Davis, 1963-65, chmn. Yolo County, Calif. chpt. ARC, 1988. Recipient Clara Barton medal Yolo County, Calif. ARC, U. Hawaii Gold medal, 1931. Mem. Am. Chem. Soc. (emeritus), Inst. Food Technologists (profl.), Entomological Soc. Am. (emeritus, chmn. Yr. publs. 1973-75), Sigma Xi, Phi Kappa Phi. Home: 815 Miller Dr Davis CA 95616-3622

PAINTER, THEOPHILUS SHICKEL, JR. internist, allergist; b. Austin, Tex., Apr. 29, 1924; s. Theophilus Shickel and Anna Mary (Thomas) P.; m. Dorothy Bulkley, July 11, 1957; children: Dana Parkey, Amy Hur, Theophilus III. BA, U. Tex., 1944, MD, 1947. Diplomate Am. Bd. Internal Medicine, Am. Bd. Allergy and Immunology. Rotating intern Univ. Hosp., U. Mich., Ann Arbor, 1947-48, resident in internal medicine, 1948-51, fellow, jr. clin. instr., 1956-58; pvt. practice, Austin, Tex., 1958—. Capt. USAF, 1951-53. Fellow ACP, Am. Coll. Allergy and Immunology, Am. Acad. Allergy and Immunology. Avocations: fishing, carving, hunting, painting. Home: 3222 Tarryhollow Dr Austin TX 78703-1639 Office: 800 W 34th St Ste 201 Austin TX 78705-1146 E-mail: tspainterjr@cs.com.

PAINTER, WILLIAM HALL, law educator; b. Pitts., May 2, 1927; s. John Littleton Dawson and Eleanor Cramer (Hall); m. Marion Symmes Homer, July 9, 1955; children: Richard William, Edward Homer. AB, Princeton U., 1950; JD, Harvard U., 1954. Bar: N.Y. 1955. Assoc. Debevoise, Plimpton & McLean, N.Y.C., 1954-58; teaching fellow Harvard U.Law Sch., Cambridge, Mass., 1958-59; prof. Villanova U. Law Sch., Phila., 1959-65; vis. prof. U. Mich. Law Sch., Ann Arbor, 1965; prof. U. Mo., Kansas City, 1965-71; spl. counsel, dir. study securities industry U.S. Ho. Reps., Washington, 1971-72; prof. U. Ill. Coll. Law, Champaign, 1972-81, Albert E. Jenner Jr. prof., 1981-87; Theodore Rinehart prof. law George Washington U., Washington, 1987—. Author: Federal Regulation of Insider Trading, 1968, Corporate and Tax Aspects of Closely Held Corporations, 1971, 2d edit., 1981, Problems and Materials in Business Planning, 1975, 3d edit., 1994, The Federal Securities Code and Corporate Disclosure, 1979, Painter on Close Corporations, 1991; contbr. articles to legal publs. Mem. Ill. Bus. Corp. Act Revision Com., 1981-83. Mem. ABA (fed. securities commn. sect. corp., banking and bus. law, chmn. subcom. on legis. 1974-81), Assn. Am. Law Schs. (chmn. sect. bus. assn. 1976), Am. Law Inst., Phi Beta Kappa. Home: 6652 32d St NW Washington DC 20015 Office: George Washington U Nat Law Ctr 720 20th St NW Washington DC 20006-4306 E-mail: wpainter@main.nlc.gwu.edu.

PAINTON, RUSSELL ELLIOTT, lawyer, mechanical engineer; b. Port Arthur, Tex., Dec. 5, 1940; s. Clifford Elliott and Edith Virginia (McCutcheon) P.; m. Elizabeth Ann Mullins, July 2, 1965 (div. Dec. 1977); 1 child, Todd Elliott; m. Mary Lynn Weber, May 9, 1981. BS in Mech. Engring., U. Tex.-Austin, 1963, JD, 1972. Bar: Tex. 1972; registered profl. engr., Tex. Engr. Gulf States Utilities, Beaumont, Tex., 1963-66, Tracor, Inc., Austin, 1966-70, corp. counsel, 1973-83, v.p., gen. counsel, 1983-98, corp. sec., 1991-98; atty. Brown, Maroney, Rose, Baker & Barber, 1972-73, Childs, Fortenbach, Beck & Guyton, Houston, 1973; corp. sec. Westmark Systems, Inc., Austin, 1990-91; sole practitioner, 1998—. Gen. counsel Paramount Theatre for Performing Arts, 1977-83, 2d vice chmn., 1978-80, 1st vice chmn., 1980-82, chmn. bd., 1982-84, retiring chmn., 1984-85; mem. Centex chpt. ARC; mem. adv. bd. Austin Sci. Acad., 1985-88, 93-95; mem. adv. coun. Austin Transp., 1985-88; bd. dirs. Tex. Industries for the Blind and Handicapped, 1988-95, vice chmn., 1990-91. Named Boss of Yr. Austin Legal Secs. Assn., 1981. Mem.: Rockport Yacht Club, Am. Electronics Assn. (chmn. Austin coun. 1985—86), Better Bus. Bur., Nat. Chamber Litigation Ctr. (arbitrator 1983—), Travis County Bar Assn., Tex. Bar Assn. (treas. corp. counsel sect. 1982—83), ABA, Houston Yacht Club, Order Blue Gavel, Austin Yacht Club (race comdr. 1968—69, treas. 1970—71, sec. 1972, 1975, vice commodore 1980, commodore 1981, fleet comdr. 1986), Delta Theta Phi. Republican. Episcopalian. E-mail: sailor44@swbell.net.

PAIRO, PRESTON ABERCROMBIE, JR. lawyer; b. June 5, 1927; s. Preston Abercrombie and Blossom Winona (Pritchett) P.; m. Carol May Rupprecht, Aug. 12, 1950; 1 child, Preston Abercrombie III. AA, U. Balt., 1948; JD, 1951. Bar: Md. 1951. Legal investigator Office of City Solicitor, Balt., 1947-50; mem. Md. Ho. Dels., 1950-54; asst. states atty. State of Md., Balt., 1954-58; atty. Liquor Bd. City of Balt., 1958-60; savs. and loan atty., 1960—90. Mem. Md. Criminal Def. Bar (bd. dirs., past pres.), Assn. Trial Lawyers Am., Md. Bar Assn., Howard County Bar Assn. Democrat. Episcopalian. Club: Ellicott City Optimists (pres. 1968). Lodges: Ben Franklin, Masons, Shriners, Jesters. Home: 9032 Overhill Rd Ellicott City MD 21042-5221 Office: Pairo & Pairo 9050 Frederick Dr # A Ellicott City MD 21042-4014 E-mail: pairojr@aol.com., pairo@pairo.com.

PAIROLERO, PETER CHARLES, surgeon; b. Bessemer, Mich., 1938; MD, U. Mich., 1963. Diplomate Am. Bd. Surgeons, Am. Bd. Thoracic Surgeons, Am. Bd. Gen. Vascular Surgeons. Intern St. Mary's Hosp., Duluth, Minn., 1963-64; resident gen. surgery Mayo Grad. Sch. Medicine, Rochester, 1966-71, fellow cerebral vascular resch., 1968-69, resident thoracic-cardio surgery, 1971-73; chmn. American Board of Thorasic Surgery, 2001—. Mem. AMA. Office: 200 1st St SW Rochester MN 55905-0001*

PAISE, MICHELE PAYNTER, music educator; b. Westminster, Md., Jan. 20, 1970; d. John Reese and Kathleen Adele Paynter; m. John Robert Paise, Oct. 9, 1999. BA in Secondary Edn., Shepherd Coll., 1993; M in Music, Johns Hopkins U., 1997. Cert. tchr. Tenn., Orff-Schulwerk level I and II. Choral dir., music tchr. N. Frederick (Md.)Elem. Sch., 1993—97, Cedar Grove Elem. Sch., LaVergne, Tenn., 1997—2000; music prof. Mid. Tenn. State U., Murfreesboro, 1999—2001; choral dir. Centennial H.S., Franklin, 2000—. Sponsor Tri-M Music Honor Soc. Centennial H.S., Franklin, 2001—02, vocal musical dir. various sch. prodns.; mem. Balt. Symphony Chorus, 1993—95; mem. chorus Aida by Verdia Nashville Opera, 1997, mem. chorus Turandot by Puccini, 2001, mem. chorus The Pearl Fishers by Bizet, 02. Vocal coach St. Ignatius Orthodox Ch., Franklin, 2001—02, mem. choir, chair ann. ch. yard sale; chair children's activities s.e. region Parish Life Conf. Orthodox Chs., 2002. Recipient Sword of Honor, Sigma Alpha Iota, 1993. Mem.: Am. Choral Dirs. Assn., Mid. Tenn. Vocal Assn., Music Educators Nat. Conf., Kappa Delta Pi. Avocations: theater , reading, antiques, walking, attending performances. Home: 813 Del Rio Pike #B6 Franklin TN 37064

PAISLEY, KEITH WATKINS, former state senator, retired small business owner; b. Mpls., Dec. 29, 1928; s. Manley G. and Maxine Alice (Watkins) P.; m. Jean Clare Robson, Sept. 23, 1950; children: Mark, Susan, Julie, Jeanne. BA, Hamline U., 1950. Owner Robson Hardware, Sioux Falls, S.D., 1972-93; mem. S.D. Ho. of Reps., Pierre, 1981-84, S.D. Senate, Pierre, 1985-2000. Lutheran. Home: 2409 S Elmwood Ave Sioux Falls SD 57105-3315

PAITICH, OLIVIA, project coordinator, office manager; b. Bucharest, Romania, May 29, 1965; came to U.S., 1987; d. Lucian and Floarea (Dragan) Dragulinescu; m. Srgian Paitich, June 20, 1992; children: Ashley Gordana, Justin Eric. AA, Northeastern U., Chgo., 1990. Legal sec. Casualty Ins. Co., Chgo., 1990-91, legal asst., 1991-95; exec. asst. Fremont Compensation, 1995-2001; tech. exec. asst. ABN AMRO, 2001—. Mem. NAFE, Chgo. Coun. Fgn. Affairs. Eastern Orthodox. Avocations: reading, jogging, travel. Home: 4844 N Nordica Ave Chicago IL 60656-3821 Office: ABN AMRO 181 W Madison Ave # 2900 Chicago IL 60602 E-mail: olivia.paitich@abnamro.com.

PAIVA, CLIFFORD ANTHONY, physicist, consultant; b. Honolulu, Jan. 9, 1947; s. John Albert and Dorothy (Martin) P.; m. Jerrine Dunn, Oct. 13, 1972; children: Antonette, Alexander, Allison, Martin. BS in Geophysics, Christian Heritage Coll., El Cajon, Calif., 1978; MS in Astrogeophysics, Inst. Creation Rsch., El Cajon, Calif., 1988. Physicist Naval Warfare Assessment Ctr. Naval Weapons Sys., Seal Beach, Corona, Calif., 1979-83; physicist USAF Rsch. Lab. Rocket Propulsion Directorate Edwards AFB, 1986-91; physicist Naval Surface Warfare Ctr. Dahlgren (Va.) Divsn., 1991-2000; founder, pres. Battle Sci. Mgmt., California City, 2001—; engring. physicist EDO-AIL Techs. Inc., Lancaster, Calif., 2002—. Mem. East Asia Working Group, Ctr. for Strategic and Internat. Studies, Washington, automatic target recognition working group Def. Advanced Rsch. Agy., Theater Missile Def. Asia Pacific sector, Washington; sr. councilor Atlantic Coun. U.S., Washington. Contbr. articles to profl. jours. Tenor Masterworks Chorus, King George, Va., 1996-98, Fredericksburg (Va.) Master Chorale, 1996-98, Antelope Valley Master Chorale, 2000—. With USAF, 1965-69. Mem.: BSM Assn. (pres., founder), Am. Optical Soc., U.S. Naval Inst. Engrs., Creation Rsch. Soc., Optical Soc. Am., Internat. Soc. Optical Engrs., Am. Geophys. Union, APS, U.S. Naval Intelligence Profl. (life). Republican. Assemblies Of God Ch. Achievements include implementation of advanced morphological target segmentation and extraction techniques, leading to accurate predictive computer simulations of threat target sets for ballistic missile defense; research in Air Force airborne high energy laser program. Avocations: piano, guitar. Home and Office: Edwards AFB 159 Camp Fire Drive California City CA 93505 E-mail: aanthony@as.net.

PAJAK, DAVID JOSEPH, lawyer, consultant; b. Buffalo, June 19, 1956; s. William H. and Theresa A. (Granato) P.; m. Peggy J. Fisher, Aug. 1, 1981; children: Andrew J., Karl W. BA, State Coll. Buffalo, 1978; JD, U. Buffalo, 1982. Bar: N.Y. 1983, U.S. Dist. Ct. (we. dist.) N.Y., 1991. Social svcs. counsel Genesee County Dept. Social Svcs., Batavia, N.Y., 1984-93; pvt. practice Corfu, 1983—, Buffalo, N.Y., 1993—; town justice Town of Pembroke, N.Y., 1994—; with Genesee County Attys. Office, 2001—. Mem. legis. com. N.Y. Fed. on Child Abuse and Neglect, Albany, 1986—99, bd. dirs., 1987—89; cons. N.Y. Pub. Welfare Assn., Albany, 1987—92; pres. Social Svcs. Attys. Assn. N.Y. State, 1990—91; instr. Bill Adam's Martial Arts & Fitness Ctr., Buffalo, 1988—2000. Contbr. articles to profl. jours. Mem.: Western Genesee County Bus. Assn., Corfu Area Bus. Assn., Genesee County Magistrate's Assn., Genesee County Bar Assn., Erie County Bar Assn., N.Y. State Magistrate's Assn., N.Y. State Bar Assn. Republican. Avocations: karate, martial arts. Home: 17 E Main St Corfu NY 14036-9665 Office: 170 Franklin St Ste 701 Buffalo NY 14202-2412 E-mail: dave@djpajak.com.

PAJAK, ROGER F. federal official, writer; s. Frank F. and Martha D. Pajak; m. Lillian M. Murawski; children: Melinda, Lisa, Jeffrey. BA, Mich. State U., 1958; MA, Harvard U., 1960; PhD, Am. U., 1966; graduate, Nat. War Coll., 1980. Sr. foreign affairs adv. U.S. Arms Control Agy., Washington, 1971—80; nat. security adv. Dept. Treasury, 1981—97; dir. nat. security Orion Sci. Sys., McLean, Va., 1997—2001; coord. tng. Dept. Energy, Washington, 2001—. Prof. strategy U.S. Naval War Coll., Newport, RI, 1987—88; lectr. in field. Contbr. articles to profl. jours. Col. USAR, 1963—89. Mem.: Phi Kappa Phi. Avocation: playing piano. Home: 43252 Golf View Dr Fairfax VA 20152

PAJAMA, HELEN, advocate; b. Sanford, Maine, May 21; d. Cyrille Joseph Parent and Georgieanna M. Suominen; m. John Pajanen, July 21, 1962 (div. Mar. 1967); children: Candence Joleen, Martin John, Carlene Ida, Jason Howard; m. Bradley A. Bouton, Oct. 21, 1989. Dormitory counselor Gallaudet Sch. for Deaf Students, Washington, 1974; paralegal, legal asst. Nat. Acad. for Paralegal Studies, Atlanta, 1993. Abolitionist Murder Victims Families for Reconciliation, Portage, Ind., 1993-97; abolitionist, activist for ending the death penalty in the U.S., 1990-2000. Author: A Door Will Open, 1971; poet: (chapbook) Pajama Lady and Death Row Friends, 1995. Prison ministry St. Mary's Ch., County Jail, Bangor, Maine, 1990-94; with Bangor Clowns, 1996-97; soup kitchen vol. St. John's Ch., Bangor, 1987-89; vol. pastoral care ministry Fla. Hosp., 2001. Mem. NAACP (exec. bd. dirs. 1996-97). Roman Catholic. Avocations: photography, music, art, reading, swimming (5 Gold medals Sr. Olympics 1997). Home: PO Box 530095 Debary FL 32753-0095

PAJUNEN, GRAZYNA ANNA, electrical engineer, educator; b. Warsaw, Poland, Dec. 15, 1951; d. Romuald and Danuta (Trzaskowska) Pyffel; m. Veikko J. Pajunen (div. 1990); children: Tony, Thomas, Sebastian. MSc, Warsaw Tech. U., 1975; PhD in Elec. Engring., Helsinki (Finland) U., 1984. Grad. engr. Oy Stromberg Ab, Helsinki, 1974, design engr., 1975-79; teaching/rsch. asst. Helsinki U. Tech., 1979-85; vis. asst. prof. dept. elec. and computer engring. Fla. Atlantic U., 1985-86, asst. prof. elec. and computer engring., 1986-90, assoc. prof. elec. engring., 1990—; vis. asst. prof. dept elec. engring. UCLA, 1988-89. Cons. Motorola; lectr. in field. Author: Adaptive Systems - Identification and Control, 1986; contbr. articles to profl. jours.; holder 14 patents in field. Grantee Found. Tech. in Finland, Ahlstrom Found., 1982, Wihuri Found., 1982, Foun.d Tech. in Finland, 1983, Acad. Finland, 1984, EIES Seed grantee, 1986, Finnish Ministry Edn., 1985, NSF, 1988-89, 93-94, State of Fla. High Tech. and Industry Coun., 1989. Mem. IEEE, Control Sys. Soci., N.Y. Acad. Sci., AAUW, SIAM, Control and Sys. Theory Group. Roman Catholic. Avocations: jazz, ballet, piano, jogging, skiing. Office: Fla Atlantic U Dept Elec Engring Boca Raton FL 33431

PAK, BO HI, foundation executive; b. Ah-San, Chung Nam, South Korea, Aug. 18, 1930; s. Dong Hyun and Pyung Chun (Han) P.; m. Ki Sook Yoon, Nov. 29, 1953; children: Na Kyung, Jun Sun, Jin Sung, Hoon Sook, Yun Sook, Jin Kyung. Student, Georgetown U., 1962-64; HHD, La Plata Cath. U. of Argentina, 1984. Pres. The Washington Times Corp., Washington, 1982-92, CAUSA Internat., N.Y.C., 1981—; chmn., pres. Korean Cultural Found., Seoul and Washington, 1969—; pres. Universal Ballet Found., Washington, 1986—; chmn. bd. Panda Motors Corp., Hong Kong, 1990—; chmn. Kumgangsan Internat. Group, Seoul, 1998—. Pres. The Summit Coun. for World Peace, Washington, 1987-97; pres., pub. News World Comm., Inc., N.Y., 1976-90; asst. mil. attache Embassy of Korea, Washington, 1961-64; spl. asst. to vice min. of def. Govt. of Republic of Korea, 1958-68. Author: The Truth is My Sword, 1999, Messiah: My Testimony to Reverend Sun Myung Moon, 2000. Lt. col. Republic of Korean Army, 1950-64. Decorated Medal of Gold Star Hwa-Rang Republic of Korea Govt., 1953, Nat. medal Dong Baek, 1971; recipient Investiture of Acad. Mexican Acad. of Internat. Law, 1990, Order of Liberty and Unity Assn. for the Unity of Latin Am., 1992. Office: Summit Coun for World Peace 3rd Fl 3600 New York Ave NE Fl 3 Washington DC 20002-1947 E-mail: bohipak@aol.com.

PAK, HYUNG WOONG, community developer; b. Ham-Hoong, Korea, Nov. 6, 1932; came to U.S., 1955, naturalized, 1968; s. Kyung-Koo and Myung-Sook (Lee) P.; m. Diana Lee Stenen Woodruff, 1975; children: Jonathan Tong-Hee, Michelle Hyun-Mi Lee. AB, U. Chgo., 1958. Editor and publisher Chgo. Rev., 1958-63, cons., 1963-65; assoc. editor Ency. Britannica Press, Chgo., 1963-64, sr. editor social scis. and humanities, 1964-66; ednl. dir. Bantam Books, Inc., N.Y.C., 1966-69; gen. mgr. sch. dept. Appleton-Century-Crofts/New Century, 1970-72; v.p., editorial dir. D. Van Nostrand Co., 1972-74, pres., 1974-76, Chatham Sq. Press, N.Y.C., 1976-83; pub. Urizen Books, Inc., 1978-81; exec. v.p. Bus. Software Mag., Palo Alto, Calif., 1983-84; pub., editor Asian High-Tech. Report, 1984-90; exec. dir. The Philip Jaisohn Meml. Found., Inc., Phila., 1990-99; pres. Asian Cmty. Devel. Corp., 2000—. Fellow Hoover Instn., Stanford, Calif., 1984-85. Author: The Pacific Rim, 1990; columnist The Phila. Bus. Rev., 1993-99. Mem. Bd. Sch. Dist. Cheltenham Twp., Pa., 1987-94; mem. Asian task force Phila. Sch. Dist., 1988-95; co-chmn. bus. adv. com. Montgomery County, Pa., 1991-93; del. Citizens' Assembly for a Greater Phila., 1991-95; chmn. Pan Asian Assn. Greater Phila., 1992-96, mem. bd. fellowship commn., 1992-95; bd. dirs. Brandywine Art Ctr., 1995-99, vice chair, 1998-99; Pa. del. The White Ho. Conf. on Aging, 1995; trustee Abington Meml. Hosp. Found., 1995-2000; mem. cmty. adv. com. Keystone Mercy Health Plan, 1998-2002; bd. dirs. Nat. Conf. Cmty. and Justice, 2000-02. Mem. ACLU (life), AHA (mem. comms. com. 1998-2000, mem. Phila. All-Am. city host com. 1998-99), Phila. Mus. Art. Home: 1015 Sharpless Rd Elkins Park PA 19027-3040 Office: PO Box 7167 Elkins Park PA 19027-0167 E-mail: hwpak@aol.com.

PAKALUK, DEBRA LORRAINE BEHM, science educator, community service coordinator; b. North Chicago, Ill., Dec. 25, 1959; d. Thomas Gerald and Bonnie Lorraine Behm. BS, Cornell U., 1982; MA, Kans. U., 1984; tchg. cert., Washburn U., 1990. Cert. tchr. secondary biology, secondary sci., Kans. Sci. camp dir., instr. Topeka Collegiate Sch., 1984-90, sci. tchr., dept. head, 1984-91, Yeshiva Greater Washington, Silver Spring, Md., 1991-92, Norwood Sch., Bethesda, 1992—. Sci. camp dir., instr. Kans. State Dept. Edn., Kansas City, 1989; workshop presenter. Contbr. articles to profl. mags. Sci-Math. fellow Coun. for Basic Edn., 1992; Fulbright Tchr. Exch. fellow, 1997; Fulbright Meml. Fund scholar, 2000. Mem. Nat. Sci. Tchrs. Assn. Avocations: travel, reading, piano, photography. Office: Norwood Sch 8821 River Rd Bethesda MD 20817-2600 E-mail: dpakaluk@norwoodschool.org.

PAKENHAM, ROSALIE MULLER WRIGHT, magazine and newspaper editor; b. Newark, June 20, 1942; d. Charles and Angela (Fortunata) Muller; m. Lynn Wright, Jan. 13, 1962; children: James Anthony Meador, Geoffrey Shepard; m. E. Michael Pakenham, Sept. 29, 2001. BA in English, Temple U., 1965. Mng. editor Suburban Life mag., Orange, N.J., 1960-62; assoc. editor Phila. mag., 1962-64, mng. editor, 1969-73; founding editor Womensports mag., San Mateo, Calif., 1973-75; editor scene sect. San Francisco Examiner, 1975-77; exec. editor New West mag., San Francisco and Beverly Hills, Calif., 1977-81; features and Sunday editor San Francisco Chronicle, 1981-87, asst. mng. editor features, 1987-96; v.p. and editor-in-chief Sunset Mag, Menlo Park, Calif., 1996—2001. Tchr. mag. writing U. Calif., Berkeley, 1975-76; participant pub. procedures course Stanford U., 1977-79; chmn. mag. judges at conf. Coun. Advancement and Support of Edn., 1980, judge, 1984. *During Rosalie Muller Wright Pakenham's five-year editorship of Sunset Magazine (1996-2001), circulation grew from 1.3 to 1.5 million (readership, 5 million) : profits from $14 to $25 million, renewal rates to 70%. She won for the magazine a record 12 Maggies, a Folio Gold Award and a Henry Luce Award for editorial excellence. She managed a $5 million budget and was involved in circulation, advertising, and production strategies while managing 65 editors/writers/artists. As executive editor of New West, she broke the Jim Jones and Peoples Temple story in 1977 and the Firestone 500 expose in 1978, for which New West won a National Magazine Award.* Contbr. numerous mag. articles, critiques, revs., Compton's Ency. Mem. Am. Assn. Sunday and Feature Editors (treas. 1984, sec. 1985, 1st v.p. 1986, pres. 1987, Hall of Fame 1999), Am. Newspaper Pubs. Assn. (pub. task force on minorities in newspaper bus. 1988-89, Chronicle minority recruiter 1987-94), Internat. Women's Forum, Women's Forum West (bd. dirs. 1993—, sec. 1994), Am. Soc. Mag. Editors. E-mail: rzzzw@aol.com. *Keep a sharp eye out for talent, recognize it and reward it, and everyone profits.*

PAKES, ARIEL S. economist, educator; b. Edmonton, Alta., Can., Nov. 15, 1949; s. Saul and Lillian Pakes; m. Juliana Rojas; children: Michael Joey, Sol Matthew. BA, Hebrew U. Jerusalem, 1971, MA, 1973, Harvard U., 1976, PhD, 1979. Lectr. econs. Hebrew U. Jerusalem, 1980—84, sr. lectr. econs., 1984—86; assoc. prof. U. Wis., Madison, 1986—88; prof. econs. Yale U., New Haven, 1988—97, Charles and Dorthea Dilley prof. econs., 1997—99; prof. Harvard U., Cambridge, Mass., 1999—. Invited plenary lectr. Econometric Soc., Berlin, 1998; invited lectr. The Richard T. Ely Lectures, John Hopkins U., Balt., 2001, Jour. Applied Econs. Invited Lectures, 2002; lectr. in field. Editor: The RAND Jour. Econs., 1999—; contbr. articles to profl. jours. Fellow: Econometric Soc. (Frisch medal 1986); mem.: Am. Econ. Assn. Home: 215 Brattle St Cambridge MA 02138 Office: Harvard Univ Dept Econs Littauer Rm 117 Cambridge MA 02138

PAKHOMOV, ANDREW VALERIEVICH, physicist, educator; b. Moscow, Jan. 22, 1961; came to U.S., 1992; s. Valeriy P. and Eleonora M. Pakhomov; m. Yelena N. Zakin, Nov. 2, 1995. BS, MS in Semiconductor Materials Sci., Moscow Technol. U., 1983; PhD in Physics, Mich. Tech. U., 1996. Rsch. assoc. Inst. of Rare Metals, Moscow, 1983-92; vis. prof. physics N.Mex. Highlands U., Las Vegas, 1996-98; asst. prof. U. Ala., Huntsville, 1998—. Adj. prof. Ctr. for Applied Optics, U. Ala. Huntsville, 1999—. Propulsion Rsch. Ctr., U. Ala., 1999—. Contbr. over 50 articles to profl. jours.; patentee in field. Fellow fellow, Mich. Tech. U., 1993—96; grantee N.Mex. Space Grant Consortium grantee, 1997, 1998, minigrant, U. Ala., 2000, 2001, NASA, 2000—01, 2002—. Mem. AIAA, Am. Phys. Soc. Avocations: backcounty tourism. Office: U Ala Huntsville Dept Physics Huntsville AL 35899-0001

PAKOLA, RICHARD STEPHEN, psychiatrist; b. Hazleton, Pa., Nov. 12, 1943; s. Stephen Joseph and Lottie Carol (Valagene) P.; m. Casimira Susan Saladigo, Dec. 10, 1966; children: Richard, Stephen, Jennifer, Rebecca, James. BA in Biology, LaSalle Coll., 1966; MD, Temple U., 1970. Diplomate Am. Bd. Psychiatry & Neurology. Internat Ch. Home and Hosp., Balt., 1970-71; resident in psychiatry Naval Regional Med. Ctr., Phila., 1971-74, psychiatrist Portsmouth, Va., 1974-76; physician, chief Philhaven Hosp., Mt. Gretna, Pa., 1976—. Fellow Am. Psychiat. Assn.; mem. Psychiat. Physicians of Pa., Ctrl. Pa. Psychiat. Assn. (pres.), Mental Health Assn. (pres. Lebanon County 1977-2000). Avocations: golf, gardening. Office: Philhaven PO Box 550 Mount Gretna PA 17064-0550

PAKTER, JEAN, maternal and child health consultant; b. N.Y.C. d. David and Lillian (Kunitz) P.; m. Arnold L. Bachman, MD, Sept. 17, 1939 (dec. Dec. 1992); children: Ellen Bachman Mendelson, MD, Donald M. Bachman, MD. BS, NYU, 1931, MD, 1934; MPH, Columbia U., 1955. Diplomate Am. Bd. Pediat. Intern Mt. Sinai Hosp., N.Y.C., 1934-36, resident in pediat., 1937-39; pvt. practice, 1939-43; dir. Bur. Dept. Health, Maternity, Newborn and Family Planning, 1950-82; cons., lectr. maternity, child health Columbia U. Sch. Pub. Health, 1984—, dep. dir. maternal and child health program, 1984-94, lectr. maternity, child health, 1970—. Contbr. numerous articles to profl. med. jours. Advisor March of Dimes, N.Y.C., 1975—. Recipient Fund for City of N.Y. Pub. Svc. award, 1974, Jacobi medal Mt. Sinai Hosp., 1975. Fellow APHA (Martha May Eliot award 1990), Am. Acad. Pediatrics, N.Y. Acad. Medicine (trustee 1979-83), N.Y. Obstet. Soc. (assoc.); mem. Pub. Health Assn. N.Y.C. (bd. dirs. 1992-96), Women's City Club, Alpha Omega Alpha. Avocations: concerts, opera, theatre, reading. Home: 1175 Park Ave New York NY 10128-1211

PAKULA, DENNIS PAUL, writer, photographer; b. Detroit, Oct. 26, 1954; s. John Maximilian Pakula, Jr. and Helen Frances (Kacakowsky) Pakula. BS in Physics/Math., Oakland U., Rochester Hills, Mich., 1976; MS in Physics, U. Mich., 1977; MA in Religious Studies, U. Colo., 1995. Process engr. Ford Motor Co., Utica, Mich., 1978—80; staff engr. to engr. Martin Marietta, Denver, 1980—88; tchg. asst./tutor U. Colo., Boulder, 1990—95. Author: (book) New Story, New God, 1999, God: An Autobiography, 2002; contbr. photography. Grantee, Iliff Sch. Theology, Denver, 1995—97, U. Colo. Grad. Sch., 1991—94. Avocations: canoeing, hiking, backpacking, rock climbing, mountaineering.

PAKULA, HANNAH, writer; b. Omaha, July 23, 1933; d. Mayer Louis and Gertrude (Marks) Cohn; m. Robert L. Boorstin, Dec. 31, 1953 (dec. May 1969); children: Anna, Robert O., Louis C.; m. Alan J. Pakula, Feb. 17, 1973 (dec. Nov. 1998). Student, Wellesley Coll., 1951-53, Sorbonne, 1953-54; BA, So. Meth. U., 1956. Author: Historic Biography of Queen Marie of Romania, The Last Romantic, 1985, Historic Biography of Empress Frederick of Germany, An Uncommon Women, 1995. Bd. dirs. Princess Margarita of Romania Found. Recipient Eleanor Roosevelt Val-Kill medal for human rights, 1999. Mem. PEN (co-chmn. Freedom to Write com.), Coun. Fgn. Rels. Democrat. Jewish.

PAL, PRABIR KUMAR (SUNNY PAL), retired aluminium company executive; b. Chittagong, Bengal, India, Feb. 17, 1936; arrived in Can., 1969; s. Niranjan and Renuka (Mitter) P.; m. Nandinee Majumdar, Dec. 13, 1960; 1 child, Nobina. BA in Law with honors, Cambridge U., 1958, MA, 1972; diploma in indsl. mgmt., Geneva U., Geneva, 1964. From legal asst. to v.p., chief legal officer, sec. Indian Aluminium Co. Ltd. (subs. Alcan), various, 1959—88, v.p., chief legal officer, sec., 1988—99. Bd. dirs. Transparency Internat. Can. Inc. Bd. dirs. Lester B. Pearson Coll. of the Pacific, Opera Lyra Ottawa. Fellow Inst. Chartered Secs. and Adminstrs.; mem. Internat. Bar Assn., Univ. Club Montreal, Rideau Club. Avocations: photography, rowing. E-mail: sunny@flavellkubrick.com.

PAL, PRATAPADITYA, curator; b. Bangladesh, Sept. 1, 1935; came to U.S., 1967; s. Gopesh Chandra and Bidyut Kana (Dam) P.; m. Chitralekha Bose, Apr. 20, 1968; children— Shalmali, Lopamudra. MA, U. Calcutta, 1958, D.Phil., 1962; PhD (U. K. Commonwealth Scholar), U. Cambridge, Eng., 1965. Research assoc. Am. Acad. of Benares, India, 1966-67; keeper Indian collections Mus. Fine Arts, Boston, 1967-69; sr. curator Indian and Southeast Asian art Los Angeles County Mus. Art, L.A., 1970-95, acting dir., 1979; vis. curator Indian and S.E. Asian art Art Inst. Chgo., 1995—; cons. curator Norton Simon Mus., Pasadena, Calif., 1995—. Adj. prof. fine arts U. So. Calif., 1971-89; vis. prof. U. Calif., Santa Barbara, 1980, Irvine, 1994-95; William Cohn lectr. Oxford U., 1983; Catherine Mead meml. lectr. Pierpont Morgan Libr., N.Y.C., 1986; Ananda K. Coomaraswamy meml. lectr. Prince of Wales Mus., Bombay, 1987; D.J. Sibley prehistoric art lectr. U. Tex., Austin, 1989; Anthony Gardner meml. lectr. Victoria and Albert Mus., London, 1993, keynote spkr. 1st Internat. Conf. on Tibetan Art, 1994; mem. commr.'s art adv. panel IRS, Washington, 1986-96. Author: The Arts of Nepal, vol. 1, 1974, vol. 2, 1979, The Sensuous Immortals, 1977, The Ideal Image: Gupta Sculptures and its Influence, 1978, The Classical Tradition in Rajput Painting, 1978, Elephants and Ivories, 1981, A Buddhist Paradise: Murals of Alchi, 1982, Art of Tibet, 1983, Tibetan Painting, 1984, Art of Nepal, 1985, From Merchants to Emperors, 1986, Indian Sculpture, vol. 1, 1986, Icons of Piety, Images of Whimsey, 1987, Indian Sculpture, vol. 2, 1988, Buddhist Book Illuminations, 1988, Romance of the Taj Mahal, 1989, Art of the Himalayas, 1991, Pleasure Gardens of the Mind, 1993; Indian Painting, vol. 1, 1993, The Peaceful Liberators: Jain Art from India, 1994, On the Path to Void, 1996, A Collecting Odyssey, 1997, Divine Images, Human Visions, 1997, Tibet Change and Tradition, 1997, Desire and Devotion, 2001; gen. editor: Marg mag., 1993—. Bd. dirs. Music Circle, Pasadena, Calif. John D. Rockefeller III Fund fellow, 1964, 69, fellow NEA, 1974; Getty scholar, 1995-96. Fellow Asia Soc. (Bombay, hon.); mem. Asiatic Soc. (Calcutta, B.C. Law gold medal 1993).

PALACIO, JUNE ROSE PAYNE, nutritional science educator; b. Hove, Sussex, Eng., June 14, 1940; came to U.S., 1949; d. Alfred and Doris Winifred (Payne) P.; m. Moki Moses Palacio, Nov. 30, 1968. AA, Orange Coast Coll., Costa Mesa, Calif., 1960; BS, U. Calif., Berkeley, 1963; PhD, Kans. State U., 1984. Registered dietitian. Asst. dir. food svc. and res. halls Mills Coll., Oakland, Calif., 1964-66; staff dietitian Servomation Bay Cities, 1966-67; commissary mgr. Host Internat., Inc., Honolulu, 1967-73; dir. dietetics Straub Clinic and Hosp., 1973-80; instr. Kans. State U., Manhattan, 1980-84; prof. and program dir. Calif. State U., L.A., 1984-85; prof., asst. dean Pepperdine U., Malibu, Calif., 1985—. Instr. Kapiolani Community Coll., Honolulu, 1973-79, U. Hawaii, Honolulu, 1975-80, Ctr. for Dietetic Edn., Woodland Hills, Calif., 1986—; cons. Clevenger Nutritional Svcs., Calabasas, Calif., 1985—, Calif. Mus. Sci. and Industry, L.A., 1989—, Calif. State Dept. Edn., Sacramento, Calif., 1985—. Author: Foodservice in Institutions, 1988, Introduction to Foodservice, 1992, 97, 2001, The Profession of Dietetics, 1996, 2000. Mem. Am. Dietetic Assn. (del. 1977-80, 86-89, commr. Commn. for Accreditation of Dietic Edn. 1997—), Calif. Dietetic Assn. (pres. 1992-93), L.A. Dist. Dietetic Assn., Foodsvc. Systems Mgmt. Edn. Coun., Dietetic Educators of Practitioners, Gamma Sigma Delta, Omicron Nu, Phi Upsilon Omicron. Republican. Episcopalian. Avocations: tennis, running, reading, traveling. Home: 24319 Baxter Dr Malibu CA 90265-4728 Office: Pepperdine U 24255 Pacific Coast Hwy Malibu CA 90263-0002 E-mail: june.palacio@pepperdine.edu.

PALACIOS, ALANA SUE, computer programmer; b. Taylor, Tex., June 21, 1950; d. Alphonse T. and Doris Marie (Speegle) Hanzelka; m. Roberto C. Palacios, Mar. 10, 1956. BBA with honors, U. Tex., 1978; MPA, Calif. State U., 1993. Asst. staff mgr. Southwestern Bell Telephone, St. Louis, 1978-80; sr. analyst Mountain Bell Telephone, Denver, 1980-81; asst. staff mgr. Southwestern Bell Telephone, 1981-84; project leader Hughes Aircraft, Long Beach, Calif., 1984-86; programmer, analyst City of Long Beach, 1986—. Civil svc. commr. Signal Hill, Calif., 1994-99. Mem. NAFE, Phi Kappa Phi, Pi Alpha Alpha. Democrat. Episcopalian. Avocation: the Internet. Office: City of Long Beach 333 W Ocean Blvd Fl 12 Long Beach CA 90802-4664

PALACIOS, LUIS E. lawyer; b. San Jose, Costa Rica, June 25, 1975; arrived in Peru, 1980; s. Enrique C. Palacios and Teresa Cisneros. LLB, Cath. U., Lima, Peru, 1998; LLM, Duke U., 2000. Bar: Peru. Assoc. Estudio Aurelio Garcia Sayan Abogados, Lima, 1998-99; internat. assoc. Milbank, Tweed, Hadley & McCloy, LLP, N.Y.C., 2000—01, assoc. L.A., 2001—. Mem. Ius et Veritas Law Jour., 1996-97. Home: 4750 Lincoln Ave Apt 349 Marina Del Rey CA 90292 Office: Milbank Tweed Hadley Et Al 601 S Figueroa St Fl 30 Los Angeles CA 90017 E-mail: lpalacios@milbank.com.

PALACKAL, JOSEPH JOSEPH, researcher, musician; s. Joseph Kurian Palackal, Rosamma Mathai Kochery. MA(Ethnomusicology), Hunter College, New York, 1990—95; MA (Psychology), Maharaja Sayajirao University, Baroda, India, 1982—84, BPA (Indian classical music), 1982—85; BTh (Theology), Dharmaram Pontifical Institute, Bangalore, India, 1975—80. Dean of Studies Kalabhavan Academy, Cochin, India, 1986—89; pres. Indus Society Inc, New York, NY, 1999—2002. Prodr.: (Compact Disc) Syriac (Aramaic) Chants From South India, 2002; contbr. articles; author: (master's thesis) Puthen Pana: A Musical Study, 1995; contbr. articles; singer: (LP Record) Christian Bhajans, 1979; composer: (pre-recorded cassette) Karunamrutham (Christian devotional songs), 1987; singer: Christu sahasra namam (Thousand names of Christ), 1985. Mem.: Society for Ethnomusicology, Christian Musicological Society of India (life; President 2000—02), Indus Society Inc (life). Home: 57-15 61st Street Maspeth NY 11378-2713 Office: Graduate Center, City Univ. of New York 365 Fifth Avenue New York NY Personal E-mail: palackal@erols.com.

PALADE, GEORGE EMIL, biologist, educator; b. Jassy, Romania, Nov. 19, 1912; arrived in U.S., 1946, naturalized, 1952; s. Emil and Constanta Cantemir Palade; m. Irina Malaxa, June 12, 1941 (dec. 1969); children: Georgia Teodora, Philip Theodor; m. Marilyn G. Farquhar, 1970. Bachelor, Hasdeu Lyceum, Buzau, Romania; MD, U. Bucharest, Romania. Instr., asst. prof., then assoc. prof. anatomy Sch. Medicine, U. Bucharest, 1935—45; vis. investigator, asst. assoc., prof. cell biology Rockefeller U., 1946—73; prof. cell biology Yale U., New Haven, 1973—83, sr. research scientist, 1983—89; prof.-in-residence Med. Sch., U. Calif., San Diego, 1990—2001, dean sci. affairs emeritus, 1990—2001. Contbr. articles to sci. jours. Recipient Albert Lasker Basic Rsch. award, 1966, Gairdner Spl. award, 1967, Horwitz prize, 1970, Nobel prize in Physiology or Medicine, 1974, Nat. Medal Sci., 1986. Fellow: Am. Acad. Arts Scis.; mem.: NAS, Royal Belgian Acad. Medicine, Romanian Acad., Leopoldina Acad. (Halle), Royal Soc. (London), Pontifical Acad. Sci. Achievements include correlated morphological and biochemical studies by electronmicroscopy and cell fractionation of subcellular components; discovery of ribosomes; discovery and elucidation of the secretory, exocytic pathway and studies on membrane biogenesis; discovery of and regulation of proteins and membrane traffic in animal eukaryotic cells.

PALADINO, ALBERT EDWARD, venture capitalist; b. N.Y.C., Aug. 4, 1932; s. Albert E. and Jennie (Fiato) P.; m. Dorothy M. Hayes (div. June 1979); children: Thomas A., Robert E., Catherine J., Paul F.; m. Susan Flynn, June 11, 1983. BS in Ceramic Engring., Alfred U., 1954, MS in Ceramic Engring., 1956; ScD in Materials Sci., MIT, 1962. Registered profl. engr., Mass. Staff mem. Raytheon Co. Rsch. Div., Waltham, Mass., 1955-59, mgr. materials and crystal growth lab., 1962-69; mgr. materials and techniques group Raytheon Co. Microwave & Power Tube Div., 1969-72, mgr. electronics materials group, 1972-75; program mgr. materials Office of Tech. Assessment U.S. Congress, Washington, 1975-78; asst. dir. telephone ops. tech. ctr. GTE Labs., Waltham, 1978-79; dep. dir. Office Energy Programs U.S. Dept. Commerce, Nat. Inst. Standards and Tech., Washington, 1979-81; mng. ptnr. Advanced Tech. Ventures, Boston, 1981-98. Chmn. Telaxis Comm. Corp., South Deerfield, Mass., 1988—, Electro-Scan Corp., Billerica, Mass., 1990-95, Onex Comm. Corp., 1999-2001; bd. dirs. TranSwitch Corp., Shelton, Conn., 1988—, Microwave Networks, Houston, 1990-95, Thunderbird Techs., Morrisville, N.C., 1992-98; chmn. Micro Devices, Greensboro, N.C., 1992—; telecomm. bd. advisors Prism Ventures, 1997—, Early Stage Enterprises, 1997—. Contbr. articles to profl. jours.; patentee in field. Pres. West Needham (Mass.) Civic Assn., 1967-69; bd. trustees Alfred U., 1991—; mem. Needham Town Meeting, 1973-74. Recipient Disting. Svc. resolution Office of Tech. Assessment U.S. Congress, 1978. Fellow Am. Ceramic Soc. (chmn. basic sci. div. 1968-69, chmn. New Eng. sect. 1969-70, Disting. New Eng. Ceramic award), Nat. Venture Capital Assn. Avocations: painting, music, physical fitness, hiking, tennis, reading.

PALADINO, BERNARD, physician, psychiatrist; b. Mt. Pleasant, Pa., Mar. 7, 1943; s. Benjamin and Donna P.; m. Rose Mary Zoracki (div.); 1 child, Elysia; m. Mary Beth Plunkett Paladino, June 25, 1977; children: Elizabeth, Elana, Bernadette, Michael. AB, Cornell U., 1965, MD, 1969; JD, Jefferson Law Sch., San Diego, 1992. Bar: Calif.; diplomate Am. Bd. Psychiatry. Intern St. Francis Gen. Hosp., Pitts., 1970; resident Inst. of Living, Hartford, Conn., 1970—72; fellow No. Va. Mental Health Inst., 1973; attending psychiatrist Fairfax Hosp., Falls Church, Va., 1972-76, Alvarado Hosp., San Diego, 1983-87; staff psychiatrist Ky. River Cmty. Care, Hazard, 1994; attending psychiatrist Charlotte Hungerford Hosp., Torrington, Conn., 1995-96; staff psychiatrist Stanislaus County Mental Health, Modesto, Calif., 1995; attending psychiatrist Contra Costa (Calif.) County Hosp., 1995; staff psychiatrist Lahey Hitchcock Clinic, Nashua, N.H., 1995; chief intake psychiatrist Ctrl. Calif. Women's Prison, Chowchilla, 1997; chief psychiatrist Desert Regional Med. Hosp., Palm Springs, Calif., 1998; attending psychiatrist Kern County Med. Ctr., Bakersfield, 1999; chief psychiatrist Humboldt County Mental Health Ctr., Eureka, 2000—. Outpatient staff psychiatrist Long Beach Mental Health Clinic, Long Beach, Calif., 2002—. Avocation: collecting Presidential memorabilia. Home: 4410 Narragansett Ave San Diego CA 92107 E-mail: brenrad2000@go.com.

PALAHNUK, DONALD WALTER, JR. chemical engineer; b. Elmont, N.Y., June 8, 1965; s. Donald W. Palahnuk Sr. and Lucy (Solecito) Gugliotta. BS in Chemistry, SUNY, Stony Brook, 1988; postgrad., Clemson U., 1988-90; MS in Chemical Engring., Lehigh U., 1998. Process engr. Takeda Chem. Products, Wilmington, N.C., 1990-92; assoc. engr. Hoffman-La Roche Inc., Belvidere, N.J., 1992-96; sr. engr. Heico Chemical, Del. Water Gap, Pa., 1996-98; sr. devel. engr. Procter & Gamble, Norwich, N.Y., 1998—. Mem. AICHE, Math Assn. Am., Mensa. Roman Catholic. Avocations: guitar, chess, gardening, woodworking, computers, math. Office: Procter and Gamble Pharm Rte 320 Woods Corners Norwich NY 13815 E-mail: palahnuk.d@pg.com.

PALANCA, TERILYN, software industry analyst; b. Chicago Heights, Ill., Aug. 15, 1957; d. Raymond Anthony and Barbara Jean (Schweizer) P. BA, Coll. William and Mary, 1979; MBA, Rutgers U., 1983. Chief auditor, mgr. Williamsburg (Va.) Hilton, 1979-81; corp. auditor RCA, Princeton, N.J., 1982-83; EDP cons. Price Waterhouse & Co., N.Y.C., 1983-84; data base adminstr. Chubb & Son, Inc., Warren, N.J., 1984-85; cons., tech. mgr. Applied Data Rsch., Inc., Princeton, 1985-88; mgr. bus. devel. and product Oracle Corp., Belmont, Calif., 1988-91; mgr. market analysis Sybase, Inc., Emeryville, 1991-92, dir. product mgmt., 1993-95, sr. dir. corp. mtkg., 1996-99; rsch. dir. Giga Info. Group, Cambridge, Mass., 1999—. Mem. NAFE, Assn. of

Inst. for Cert. Computer Profls. (cert. in data processing), Savannah Symphony Chorus. Avocations: music, literature, outdoor activities, animal and environmental aid, conservation. Office: Giga Info Group 526 E Taylor St Savannah GA 31401 E-mail: tpalanca@gigaweb.com.

PALANS, LLOYD ALEX, lawyer; b. St. Louis, Aug. 6, 1946; s. Hyman Robert and Mae (Sherman) P.; m. Deborah Regn, Aug. 5, 1972; children: Emily Rebecca, Samantha Jane. BS, Tulane U., 1968; JD, U. Mo., 1972. Bar: Mo. 1972, U.S. Dist. Ct. (ea. and we. dists.) Mo. 1972, U.S. Ct. Appeals (8th cir.) 1972, U.S. Ct. Appeals (5th cir.) 1974, U.S. Supreme Ct. 1975, U.S. Ct. Appeals (9th cir.) 1992. Ptnr. Kramer, Chused, Kramer, Shostak & Kohn, St. Louis, 1972-77, Blumenfeld, Marx & Tureen, P.C., St. Louis, 1978-8l, Gallop, Johnson & Neuman, St. Louis, 1981-90, Bryan Cave, LLP, St. Louis, 1990—. Adj. prof. Washington U. Sch. Law, St. Louis, 1989—. Bd. dirs. St. Louis Chpt. ARC, 1987—, St. Louis Chpt. Leukemia Soc., 1988—, Combined Health Appeal Greater St. Louis, 1988—, Combined Health Appeal of Am., 1990. Fellow Am. Coll. Bankruptcy; mem. ABA, Mo. Bar, St. Louis Met. Bar Assn. Office: Bryan Cave LLP 1 Metro Sq 211 N Broadway Saint Louis MO 63102-2733

PALAUSI, NICOLE (NICOLE GALINAT), artist; b. Paris, Feb. 8, 1922; came to U.S. 1956; d. Henry and Marguerite (Pinel) P.; m. Edmund Galinat (dec.); children: Danuta, Beatrice. Student, Ecole des Beaux Arts, Paris; studies with Othon Friesz. One-woman shows include Salon Pernod, Paris, 1955, Galerie du Front de Mer, Royan, France, 1955, Galerie Mouffe, Paris, 1975, Big Ben Gallery, Rouen, 1975, Casino de Cannes, France, 1976, 77, Alliance Francaise, Washington, 1976, Retrospective at Springfield (Ohio) Mus., 1976, Galerie Ban Lao, Paris, 1977-78, Galerie La Mandragore Internationale, Paris, 1981, Paris Health Club, N.Y.C., 1996, 1st Unitarian Soc., Plainfield, N.J., 1997; exhibited in over 60 group exhbns., France, U.K., Luxemburg, Germany, Italy, Spain, Tunisia, Brazil, Argentina, U.S., 1952—; represented in permanent collections Springfield (Ohio) Art Mus. Decorated Knight Internat. Order of Arts and Letters, France, 1976; recipient 1st prize Internat. Festival, Lyon France, People's Choice, Michelangelo Found., France, 1977, Grand prize, Deauville, France, 1979, Targa D'Aurea, Oscar d'Oro, Napoli, Italy, 1980 (gold oscar to fgn. artist), Dio Pan Firenze, Italy, 1981 (art critics' award).

PALAY, SANFORD LOUIS, retired scientist, educator; b. Cleve., Sept. 23, 1918; s. Harry and Lena (Sugarman) P.; m. Victoria Chan Curtis, 1970 (div. Nov. 1990); children: Victoria Li-Mei, Rebecca Li-Ming. AB, Oberlin Coll., 1940; MD (Hoover prize scholar 1943), Western Res. U., 1943. Teaching fellow medicine, rsch. assoc. anatomy Western Res. U., Cleve., 1945-46; NRC fellow med. scis. Rockefeller Inst., 1948, vis. investigator, 1953; from instr. anatomy to assoc. prof. anatomy Yale U., 1949-56; chief sect. neurocytology, lab. neuroanatomical scis. Nat. Inst. Neurol. Diseases and Blindness, NIH, Washington, 1956-61, chief lab. neuroanatomical scis., 1960-61; Bullard prof. neuroanatomy Harvard, Boston, 1961-89, prof. emeritus, 1989—. Linnean Soc. lectr., London, 1959; vs. investigator Middlesex Hosp. (Bland-Sutton Inst.), London, Eng., 1961; Phillips lectr. Haverford Coll., 1959; Ramsay Henderson Trust lectr. U. Edinburgh, Scotland, 1962; George H. Bishop lectr.. Washington U., St. Louis, 1990; Disting. Scientist lectr. Tulane U. Sch. Medicine, 1969, 75; vis. prof. U. Wash., 1969; Rogowski Meml. lectr. Yale, 1973; Disting. lectr. biol. structure U. Miami, 1974; Disting. Scientist lectr. U. Ark., 1977; Disting. scholar-in-residence dept. biology Boston Coll., Chestnut Hill, Mass., 1994—; other Disting. lectureships; vis. prof. U. Osaka, Japan, 1978, Nat. U. Singapore, 1983; spl. vis. prof. U. Osaka, 1988; chmn. study sect. on behavioral and neural scis. NIH, 1984-86; mem. fellowship bd. NIH, 1958-61, cell biology study sect., 1959-65, adv. com. high voltage electron microscope resources, 1973-80, mem. rev. com. behavioral and neurol. scis. fellowships, 1979-86; chmn. Gordon Research Conf. Cell Structure and Metabolism, 1960; asso. Neuroscis. Research Program, 1962-67, cons. assoc., 1975—; mem. anat. scis. tng. com. Nat. Inst. Gen. Med. Scis., 1968-72; mem. sci. adv. com. Oreg. Regional Primate Research Center, 1971-76 Author: The Fine Structure of the Nervous System, 1970, 3d edit., 1991, Cerebellar Cortex, Cytology and Organization, 1974; editor: Frontiers of Cytology, 1958, The Cerebellum, New Vistas, 1982; mem. sci. coun. Progress in Neuropharmacology and Jour. Neuropharmacology, 1961-66; mem. editorial bd. Exptl. Neurology, 1959-76, Jour. Cell Biology, 1962-67, Brain Research, 1965-71, Jour. Comparative Neurology, 1966—, Jour. Ultrastructure Research, 1966-86, Jour. of Neurocytology, 1972-87, Exptl. Brain Research, 1965-76, Neurosci, 1975-95, Anatomy and Embryology, 1968; co-mng. editor, 1978-88; editor in chief Jour. Comparative Neurology, 1981-93, editor emeritus, 1994—; mem. adv. bd. editors Jour. Neuropathology and Exptl. Neurology, 1963-82, Internat. Jour. Neurosci, 1969-74, Tissue and Cell, 1969-86; contbr. articles to profl. jours. Served to capt. M.C. AUS, 1946-47. Recipient 50 Best Books of 1974 award Internat. Book Fair, Frankfurt, Fed. Republic Germany, Best Book in Profl. Readership award Am. Med. Writers Assn., 1975, Biomed. Rsch. award Assn. Am. Med. Colls., 1989, Lashley award Am. Philos. Soc., 1991, Camillo Golgi award Fidia Rsch. Found., 1992; Guggenheim fellow, 1971-72; Fogarty scholar-in-residence NIH, Bethesda, 1980-81. Fellow Am. Acad. Arts and Scis.; mem. NAS, Am. Assn. Anatomists (chmn. nominating com. 1964, mem. exec. com. 1970-74, anat. nomenclature com. 1975-78, pres. 1980-81, Henry Gray award 1990), Histochem. Soc., Electron Microscope Soc. Am., AAAS, Am. Soc. Cell Biology (program com. 1975), Internat. Soc. Cell Biology, Soc. for Neurosci. (Gerard award 1990), Washington Soc. Electron Microscopy (organizing com., sec.-treas. 1956-58), Soc. Francaise de Microscopie Electronique (hon.), Royal Microscopical Soc. (hon.), Golgi Soc. (hon.), Anat. Soc. Gr. Britain and Ireland (hon.), Cajal Club (pres. 1973-74), Am. Philos. Soc., Phi Beta Kappa, Sigma Xi, Alpha Omega Alpha. Home: 78 Temple Rd Concord MA 01742-1520

PALAZZO, ROBERT PAUL, lawyer, accountant; b. L.A., Apr. 14, 1952; s. Joseph Francis and Mickey Palazzo. BA in Econs., UCLA, 1973; MBA, JD, U. So. Calif., 1976; postgrad., U. Oxford, 1979. CPA Calif., Nev., Colo.; Bar: Calif. 1976, U.S. Dist. Ct. (so. dist.) Calif. 1977, U.S. Tax Ct. 1977, U.S. Ct. Appeals (9th cir.) 1978, U.S. Supreme Ct. 1980. Assoc. Graham & James, L.A., 1976-78; ptnr. Rader, Cornwall, Kessler & Palazzo CPAs, 1978-81, Palazzo & Kessler, L.A., 1978-81; pvt. practice L.A., Darwin, Calif., 1981—. Judge pro tem L.A. Mcpl. Ct., 1982—; bd. dirs. Cons. Am. Oil Co., Fin. Systems Internat. Inc.; alumni advisor UCLA, 1977-81, mem. adv. and scholarship com., 1978-81; mem. profl. adv. com. West L.A. Coll., 1993-96; lectr. U. Oxford, 1979, U. So. Calif., 1986, Calif. Poly. Inst., Pomona, 1997; hist. cons. A&E Civil War Jour., Death Valley Memories (motion picture), A&E Biography, (history channel) Guns of Infamy; spkr. Calif. State U., Northridge, 1996, Death Valley 49ers Encampment, 1996, 6th Death Valley History Conf., 1999; hist. cons. A&E Biography, Medieval Conf. Plymouth State Coll. U. N.H., 1999, 2000; session chair Medieval and Renaissance Conf., Aris. State U., 2000, 2001; spkr. in field; archival cons. Haunted History, History Channel, hist. cons. Author: Darwin, California, 1996; contbg. editor: The Gun Report; prodr. (motion picture) L.A. Bounty, the 20 Mule Team of Death Valley, (History channel) Magnificent Failures, Haunted History, 20th Century Infamous Guns; contbr. articles to profl. jours.; featured Tales of the Gun, History Channel, 1998, 99, 2000. Founder Ohio History Flight Mus.; bd. dirs. Calif. Cancer Found., L.A., 1978-85, pres., 1979-80; bd. dirs. Friends of William S. Hart Park and Mus., 1990-93, v.p. Mus. Relations; chmn. dist. bd. dirs. Darwin Community Svcs., 1990-92. Mem. L.A. County Bar Assn. (arbitration com., fee dispute resolution program), Italian Am. Lawyers Assn. (bd. govs. 1980—, 1st v.p. 1984-88), Nat. Acad. Rec. Arts and Scis., Western Writers Assn., Century City Bar Assn. (vice-chmn. estate planning, trust and probate com. 1979-80), English Westerners' Soc., Nat. Italian Am. Bar Assn., Am. Numismatic Assn. (dist. rep. Carson City 1981-82, L.A. 1982-83), Medieval Acad. Am., English Westerners Soc., S.E. Ohio Oil and Gas Assn., Death Valley History Assn. (life, conf. spkr. 1992, 95, 99), Medieval Acad. Am. (conf. session chair 2001), Mensa, Wig and Pen Club (London), So. Calif. Autograph Soc. (v.p.), Omicron Delta Epsilon, Beta Alpha Psi (pres. 1972), Pi Gamma Mu, Phi Alpha Delta, Zeta Phi Eta. Office: 3002 Midvale Ave Ste 209 Los Angeles CA 90034-3418 also: 230 S Main St Darwin CA 93522

PALDUS, JOSEF, mathematics educator; b. Bzi, Czechoslovakia, Nov. 25, 1935; emigrated to Can., 1968; s. Josef and Ludmila (Danicek) P.; m. Eva Zdena Bajer, Jan. 26, 1961; 1 dau., Barbara Alice. MSc, Charles U., Prague, 1958, DrSc, 1995; PhD, Czechoslovak Acad. Sci., Prague, 1961. Research scientist Czechoslovak Acad. Scis., Prague, 1961-62, 64-68; postdoctoral fellow NRC, Ottawa, Can., 1962-64; assoc. prof. applied math. U. Waterloo, Ont., Can., 1968-75, prof. Can., 1975-2001, disting. prof. emeritus Can., 2001—; assoc. dir. Fields Inst., 1992-95. Vis. prof. U. Rheims, 1973, U. Louis Pasteur, Strasbourg, France, 1975-76, 82-83, Cath. U., Nijmegen, Holland, 1981, Technion, Haifa, Israel, 1983, Max Planck Inst. for Astrophysics, Munich, Germany, 1997, 98, 99; vis. scientist NRC, Ottawa, 1966-68, Free U. Berlin, 1981; adj. prof. chemistry U. Fla., Gainesville, 1984—; fellow Inst. for Advanced Study, Berlin, 1986-87. Mem. editl. bd. Comtex Sci., 1981-83, Advances in Quantum Chemistry, 1986, Jour. Chem. Physics, 1987-89, Can. Jour. Chemistry, 1994-96, Internat. Jour. Quantum Chemistry, 1996; mem. adv. editl. bd. Internat. Jour. Quantum Chemistry, 1977-88, Theoretica Chimica Acta, 1988-94, Jour. Math. Chemistry, Switzerland, 1989; contbr. numerous articles to profl. jours., chpts. to books. Killam Rsch. fellow, 1987-89; recipient prize Chemistry divsn. Czechoslovak Acad. Scis., 1962, 67, J. Heyrovsky Gold medal Czechoslovak Acad. Sci., 1992, Gold medal Faculty of Math and Physics, Comenius U., Slovakia, 1994, Alexander von Humboldt Sr. Scientist award, 1996. Fellow Royal Soc. Can.; mem. Internat. Acad. Quantum Molecular Sci., Internat. Soc. Theoretical Chem. Physics (bd. dirs.), European Acad. Scis., Czech Learned Soc. (hon. mem.), Arts and Letters (corr.), Am. Inst. Physics, N.Y. Acad. Scis., Applied Math. Soc. Can., Can. Soc. for Chemistry, Chem. Inst. Can. Roman Catholic. Office: U Waterloo Dept Applied Math University Ave Waterloo ON Canada N2L 3G1 E-mail: paldus@theochem.uwaterloo.ca

PALEN, J(OSEPH) JOHN, sociology educator; b. Dubuque, Iowa, Feb. 24, 1939; s. Joseph John Palen and Mary (Rowan) Toner; m. Karen Ann Doody, June 9, 1962; children: Joseph John, Elizabeth Ann, Ellen Marye. BA, U. Notre Dame, 1961; MS, U. Wis., Madison, 1963, PhD, 1967. Demographer UN, Addis Ababa, Ethiopia, 1971-72; assoc. prof. U. Wis., Milw., 1972-77, prof., 1977-80; vis. prof. Nat. U. Singapore, 1983-84; prof. sociology, chmn. dept. Va. Commonwealth U., Richmond, 1983—. Author: Gentrification, Displacement and Revitalization, 1984; Urban World, 6th edit., 2002; City Scenes, 2nd edit., 1981, The Suburbs, 1995; Social Problems for the Twenty-first Century, 2001. Leader Boy Scouts Am., Wis., 1973-80, Torch Club 1980-. Rockefeller found. grantee, 1985; NIH grantee, 1980-82; Ford Found. grantee, 1979; NIMH grantee, 1976; NSF grantee, 1985; Sr. Fulbright scholar, Taiwan, 1992, Fulbright Disting. Lectr. and Chair in N.Am. Studies, U. Calgary, 1997; Disting. scholar Va. Commonwealth U., 1995. Mem. Fellow Am. Sociol. Assn., So. Sociol. Soc.; mem. Urban Affairs Assn. Avocations: hiking, canoeing, civil war. Home: 500 Gardiner Rd Richmond VA 23229-6919 Office: Va Commonwealth U Dept Sociology And Anthropo Richmond VA 23284

PALEN, JOSEPH WILLIAM, chemical process research company executive; b. Springfield, Mo., June 4, 1935; s. John Carlyle and Jean Allen (Gravely) P.; m. Louise Kibler, Sept. 13, 1956 (div. 1977); children: Patti, Joni, James; m. Kasdina Kasdan, June 4, 1977; children: Indradini, Indrasto, Indrastati. BS in Chem. Engring., U. Mo., 1957; MS in Chem. Engring., U. Ill., 1965; PhD in Chem. Engring., Lehigh U., 1988. Process design engr. Phillips Petroleum Co., Bartlesville, Okla., 1957-63; rsch. engr. Heat Transfer Rsch., Inc., Alhambra, Calif., 1965-68, asst., then assoc. tech. dir., 1968-86, prin. staff cons., 1988-90; prin. rsch. engr. Heat Transfer Rsch. Inc., College Station, Tex., 1992—; adj. prof. Bandung Inst. Tech., Indonesia, 1990-92. Patentee in field; editor: Heat Exchanger Sourcebook, 1986; contbr. to tech. publs. Lectr., UNESCO, Yugoslavia, 1981. Fellow AIChE (lectr. internat. heat transfer conf. 1986, D.Q. Kern award 1995); mem. Tau Beta Pi. Democrat. Baptist. Avocations: reading, fitness, music, personal computers. Home: 1514 Wayfarer Ln College Station TX 77845-9378 Office: Heat Transfer Rsch Inc 1500 Rsch Pky College Station TX 77840

PALEOLOGOS, EVANGELOS, hydrologist, educator; b. Athens, Greece, June 26, 1958; came to U.S., 1983; s. Constantine E. and Kathy A. (Michos) P.; m. Cleo L. Kalemkeris, Apr. 30, 1989; children: Katrina, Demi. BSCE, MSCE, Poly. U., 1986; PhD in Hydrology, U. Ariz., 1994. Tchg. asst. Poly. U., N.Y.C., 1984-85, adj. lectr., 1985-86; grad. rsch. asst. U. Ariz., Tucson, 1986-92; sr. staff cons. Intera Inc., Las Vegas, Nev., 1992-95; asst. prof. U. S.C., Columbia, 1995-2001, assoc. prof., 2001—. Editl. bd. Jour. Stochastic Hydrology and Hydraulics, Stochastic Environ. Rsch. and Risk Assessment, 1998—, over 20 publs; author 2 books on environmental risk analysis. Organizing com. Champman Conf., 1998; faculty senator U. S.C., 1997—. Dept. Energy Nat. Water Rsch. Ctr. and Environ. Mgmt. grantee, 1997; U. S.C. Rschr. scholar, 1995-96; recipient Initializers award S.C. Rsch. Inst., 1998. Mem. Am. Geophys. Union, European Geophys. Soc. Greek Orthodox. Avocations: art collecting, gardening. Office: Dept Geol Scis U Sc Columbia SC 29208-0001 E-mail: epal@geol.sc.edu.

PALERMO, ANTHONY ROBERT, lawyer; b. Rochester, N.Y., Sept. 30, 1929; s. Anthony C. and Mary (Palvino) P.; m. Mary Ann Coyne, Jan. 2, 1960; children: Mark Henry, Christopher Coyne, Peter Stuart, Elisabeth Megan McCarthy, Julie Coyne Lawther, Gregg Anthony. BA, U. Mich., 1951; JD, Georgetown U., 1956. Bar: D.C. 1956, N.Y. 1957, U.S. Supreme Ct. 1961. Trial atty. U.S. Dept. Justice, Washington, 1956-58, asst. U.S. atty. N.Y.C., 1958-60, asst. U.S. atty. in charge Rochester, N.Y., 1960-61; ptnr. Brennan, Centner, Palermo & Blauvelt, 1962-81, Harter, Secrest & Emery, Rochester, 1981-94, Hodgson, Russ, Andrews, Woods & Goodyear, LLP, Rochester, 1994-97, of counsel, 1998, Woods Oviatt Gilman LLP, Rochester, 1999—. Note editor Georgetown Law Jour., 1956. Bd. dirs. McQuaid Jesuit H.S., Rochester, 1978-84, St. Ann's Home for Aged, Rochester, 1974-2001; bd. dirs., sec. St. Ann's Found., Rochester, 1989-2001; trustee, charter chmn. Clients' Security Fund N.Y. (now Lawyer's Fund for Client Protection), 1981-90; chmn. Govs. Jud. Screening Com. 4th Jud. Dept., mem. statewide com., 1987-89; chair magistrate selection com. U.S. Dist. Ct. (we. dist.) N.Y., 1995, 98; mem. N.Y. Chief Judge's Commn. on Jud. Salaries, 1997—; mem. N.Y. Office Ct. Adminstrn. Commn. on Fiduciary Appointments, 2000—. Fellow Am. Bar Found., N.Y. State Bar Found. (bd. dirs. 1978-91), Am. Coll. Trial Lawyers; mem. ABA (ho. dels. 1980-98, state del. 1982-85, bd. govs. 1985-88, 1989-93, sec. 1990-93), N.Y. State Bar Assn. (pres. 1979-80, ho. dels. 1973-75, 77—), Monroe County Bar Assn. (pres. 1973), Oak Hill Country Club. Roman Catholic. Avocation: golf. Home: 38 Huntington Meadow Rochester NY 14625-1813

PALERMO, JAMES W. artistic director; b. Cleve. BMus, MMus, Ind. U. Gen. mgr. Evansville (Ind.) Philharmonic Orch., 1989-92; orch. mgr. Louisville Orch., 1992-95; artistic and gen. dir. Grant Park Orch., Chgo., 1995—. Musician Spoleo Festival Orch., Orquesta Sinfonica Del Valle, Cali, Columbia; intern Chgo. Office Fine Arts. Active Grant Park Cultural and Ednl. Cmty., program planning com. Sherwood Conservatory, search com. Chgo. Youth Symphony Orch., 25th anniversary com. Chgo. Opera Theater. Orch. Mgmt. fellow Am. Symphony Orch. League. Office: Grant Park Orch 425 E Mcfetridge Dr Chicago IL 60605-2791*

PALERMO, NORMAN ANTHONY, lawyer; b. Whittier, Calif., Mar. 14, 1937; s. Anthony and Alice Lucille (Ingram) P.; m. Wynne Harrison Kieffer, Apr. 12, 1989; children by previous marriage: David I., Pamela B. BS in Geology, Tulane U., 1958; LLB, Georgetown U., 1966. Bar: Colo. 1966, U.S Dist. Ct. Colo. 1966, U.S. Ct. Appeals (10th cir.) 1966, U.S. Supreme Ct. 1971. Assoc., ptnr. Quigley Wilder & Palermo, Colorado Springs, Colo., 1966-75; v.p. Quigley & Palermo, P.C., 1975-85; pres. Norman A. Palermo, P.C., 1985—. Chmn. El Paso County Rep. Cen. Com., Colorado Springs, 1985-87; bd. dirs. Goodwill Industries, Colorado Springs, 1973—; mem. State Commn. on Jud. Performance, 1993-97; bd. dirs. Colorado Springs Symphony, 1981-87; bd. dirs. Centura Health Penrose-St. Francis Health Svcs. Cmty. Bd., 2000—, chmn., 2001—; co-chmn. SPRINGS 2000; mem. Colo. Commn. on Taxation, 2000—. Comdr. USNR, 1958-66. Mem. ABA, Colo. Bar Assn. (bd. govs. 1999-2001), El Paso County Bar Assn., Colorado Springs C. of C. (bd. dirs. 1980-83, 93-97, chmn. bd. dirs. 1993-95, chmn. Chamber Found. 1996-97). Republican. Avocations: golf, travel. Home: 1835 Cantwell Grv Colorado Springs CO 80906-6911 Office: 102 E Pikes Peak Ave 5th Fl Colorado Springs CO 80903-1823 also: PO Box 1718 Colorado Springs CO 80901-1718 E-mail: norm@palermolaw.com.

PALERMO, ROBERT JAMES, architect, consultant, inventor; b. N.Y.C., Mar. 25, 1949; s. Vitorio and Simone (DiFlorio) P.; m. Lore Bernadette Bilbao, July 22, 1972 (dec. Feb. 1977); m. Patricia Dolores Ward, June 14, 1981; children: Jaime, Justin, Kristen Leigh. BS, CCNY, 1971, BArch, 1972; MBA, Baruch Grad. Ctr., 1974; postgrad., Nat. Asbestos Tng. Inst., 1987. Lic. asbestos investigator; registered architect, N.Y., NJ. Architect Rongved, Wilcox, Erickson, N.Y.C., 1972-73, Welton Becket Assocs., N.Y.C., 1973-75; architect, prin. Jaime Lore Design, Bklyn., 1976—. Bd. dir. Nat. Meddlex Med. Constrn. Corp., Hicksville, N.Y., 1981-85; pres. Corp. Design of Am., P.C., 1989—. Mem. Am. Inst. Archs., Soc. Am. Registered Archs., Cert. Interior Decorators Assn., Phi Sigma Kappa. Republican. Roman Catholic. Avocations: rare coin collecting, philatelics, Beaux Art prints. Home: 160 Pelican Rd Middletown NJ 07748-3042 Office: Corp Design of Am PC 461 Park Ave S New York NY 10016-6822 E-mail: rpale52235@aol.com.

PALESKY, CAROL EAST, tax accountant; b. Orange, N.J., May 13, 1940; d. Neil Norell and Marie R. Reiss; m. Jacob Palesky; children: Donna, Lewis. AB, Am. Inst., Pleasantville, N.J., 1973; postgrad., Am. Inst., Portland, Maine, 1980; student, Atlantic C.C., Mays Landing, N.J., 1971-73. With mgmt. First Nat. Bank of South Jersey (now First Fidelity), Pleasantville, N.J., 1967-74; loan officer Maine Savs. Bank, Portland, 1980-81; acct., owner East Acctg. Assocs., Topsham, Maine, 1985—. Pres. Sensible Tax Limits Coalition, 1995—. Treas., bd. dirs. Congl. Term Limits Coalition, Topsham, 1993—; bd. dirs. Maine Citizens Rev. Bd., Portland, 1993—. Scholar Nat. Taxpayer Union, 1992, 94; recipient United to Serve Am. award, 1992. Mem. Nat. Assn. Small Business Owners, Maine Taxpayers Action Network (pres. 1990—), Topsham Taxpayer Assn. (pres. 1991—). Roman Catholic. Home and Office: 24 Sokokis Cir Topsham ME 04086-1615 E-mail: cep@mtan.org.

PALEVEDA, CARL AUGUST, accountant; b. Tampa, Fla., Dec. 31, 1955; s. Nicholas Luke Paleveda, Jr. and Florence Cecelia Paleveda. BA in Acctg., U. South Fla., 1978. Lic. real estate salesperson Fla. Acct. Nick Paleveda Press, Tampa, 1973—86; tax acct. Montgomery-Jackson Tax Svc., 1979—85, Edith A. Fernandez Acctg., Tampa, 1987; pvt. practice tax acctg., 1988—. Author: (book) Is the U.S. Constitution Unconstitutional?, 1990. Achievements include copyrighted formula for factoring numbers into their aciquot parts. Avocations: chess, military wargames.

PALEVSKY, MAX, industrialist; b. Chgo., July 24, 1924; s. Isadore and Sarah (Greenblatt) P.; children: Nicholas, Madeleine, Alexander, Jonathan, Matthew. Ph.B., BS, U. Chgo., 1948; postgrad., U. Calif.-Berkeley, U. Chgo., UCLA, 1951-52. Mathematician Computer div. Bendix Corp., Los Angeles, 1952-56; v.p., gen. mgr., dir. Packard Bell Electronics, 1957-61; pres., chmn. bd. Sci. Data Systems; chmn. bd. Xerox Data Systems, Inc., El Segundo, Calif., 1961-72; dir. Xerox Corp., 1969-72, chmn. exec. com. of bd., 1969-72. Bd. dirs. Intel Corp., Santa Clara, Calif., Komag, Inc., Milpitas, Calif. Organized George McGovern's campaign for Pres. of U.S., 1972; organized and ran Tom Bradley's campaign for Mayor of L.A., 1973; mem. Folger com. Folger Shakespeare Libr., Washington, 1977—; mem. Dem. Adv. Com., 1968—; bd. dirs. ACLU, Constl. Rights Found.; trustee The Inst. for Advanced Study, Princeton U., 1988—. With USAAF, 1943-46. Office: 924 Westwood Blvd Ste 700 Los Angeles CA 90024-2928

PALEY, GERALD LARRY, lawyer; b. Albany, N.Y., Sept. 11, 1939; s. Arthur and Mary (Peckner) P.; m. Joyce R., June 25, 1961 (div. June 1985); children: Jonathan, Eric, Suzanne; m. Sheryl Gae, Aug. 14, 1985. BA, Union Coll., 1961; JD with distinction, Cornell U., 1964. Bar: N.Y. 1964. Assoc. Nixon, Hargrave, Devans & Doyle, Rochester, N.Y., 1964-69; assoc. solicitor Dept. Labor, Washington, 1969-71; ptnr. Nixon, Hargrave, Devans & Doyle, Rochester, 1971-87, Phillips, Lytle, Hitchcock, Blaine & Huber, Rochester, 1987—. Author: Handbook of Federal Labor Relations Laws, 1981, Understand Employee Regulations, 1984. Mem. ABA. Republican. Jewish. Office: Phillips Lytle Hitchcock et al 1400 First Federal Plz Rochester NY 14614-1981

PALEY, GRACE, author, educator; b. N.Y.C., Dec. 11, 1922; d. Isaac and Mary (Ridnyik) Goodside; m. Jess Paley, June 20, 1942; children: Nora, Dan.; m. Robert Nichols, 1972. Ed., Hunter Coll., NYU. Formerly tchr. Columbia, Syracuse U.; ret. mem. lit. faculty Sarah Lawrence Coll., Stanford, Johns Hopkins, Dartmouth, CUNY. Author: The Little Disturbances of Man, 1959, Enormous Changes at the Last Minute, 1974, Learning Forward, 1985, Later the Same Day, 1985, Long Walks and Intimate Talks, 1991, New and Collected Poems, 1992, The Collected Stories, 1994 (Nat. Book award nomination, 1994), Just As I Thought , 1998, Begin Again Collected Poems, 2000; contbr. stories to Atlantic, New Yorker, Ikon, Genesis West, others. Sec. N.Y. Greenwich Village Peace Center. Recipient Literary award for short story writing Nat. Inst. Arts and Letters, 1970, Edith Wharton award N.Y. State, 1988, 89, Rea award for short story, 1993, Vt. Gov.'s award for Excellence in the Arts, 1993, award for contbn. to Jewish culture Nat. Found. Jewish Culture; Guggenheim fellow. Mem. Am. Acad. and Inst. Arts and Letters. Office: PO Box 620 Thetford VT 05074-0620

PALFFY, ZIGMUND (ZIGGY PALFFY), professional hockey player; b. Skalica, Skovakia, May 5, 1972; Hockey player N.Y. Islanders, 1993—99, L.A. Kings, 1999—. Mem. Czechoslovakia Nat. Jr. Team, World Jr. Championships, Saskatoon, 1991, Czechoslovakian team Can. Cup, 1991, Slovakia team Lillehammer Olympics, 1994, World Championships, 1996 Office: LA Kings The Staples Center 1111 S. Figueroa St. Los Angeles CA 90015*

PALGON, SHELDON, physician; b. Bklyn. BA magna cum laude, YEshiva U., 1975; MD, Albert Einstein Coll. Medicine, 1979. Intern in surgery Montefiore Med. Ctr., 1979-80; resident in otolaryngology Albert Einstein Coll. Medicine, 1980-83; attending physician Brookdale Hosp., Bklyn., 1984-96, L.I. Coll. Hosp., Bklyn., 1992—, Manhattan Eye, Ear & Throat Hosp., N.Y.C., 1996—, Lenox Hill Hosp., N.Y.C., 2002—. Fellow Am. Acad. Otolaryngology. Office: 127 E 61 St New York NY 10021-9006

PALIA, ASPY PHIROZE, marketing educator, researcher, consultant; b. Bombay, Nov. 27, 1944; came to U.S., 1973; s. Phiroze E. and Homai P. (Irani) P. BE in Mech. Engring., U. Bangalore, 1966; MBA, U. Hawaii at Manoa, 1976; DBA, Kent State U., 1985. Sales engr. Larsen & Toubro Ltd., 1966-72, export sales engr., 1972-73; teaching fellow Coll. Bus. Adminstrn. Kent State U., 1977-80, instr. Coll. Bus. Adminstrn., 1982-84; asst. prof. Coll. Bus. Adminstrn. U. Hawaii, Manoa, 1984-89, assoc. prof., 1990-95, prof., 1996—, pres. faculty coun., 1995-96; senator U. Hawaii Manoa Faculty Congress, 1996-98; sr. fellow dept. mktg. Nat. U. Singapore, 1998-99, vis. sr. fellow dept. mktg., 2000—02. Vis. prof. Coll. Mgmt. Nat. Sun Yat-sen U., Kaohsiung, Taiwan, 1992, Chulalongkorn U., Bangkok, 1992, 93, 97, U. Otago, New Zealand, 1995, Adminstrv. Staff Coll. India, Hyderabad, 1992, Indian Inst. Mgmt., Ahmedabad, 2000, Asian Inst. Tech., Bangkok, 2001; mem. U. Hawaii Manoa Ctr. for Teaching Excellence Faculty Adv. Group, 1991; mem. mktg. plan adv. com. U. Hawaii, Manoa, 1994, mem. honors and awards com., 1990—91, pres. faculty coun., 1995—96, mem. faculty adv. com. on acad. freedom, 1997; vis. scholar faculty bus. adminstrn. Nat. U. Singapore, 1991, Mktg. Inst. Singapore Exec. Devel. Seminars, 1991, 1994—95, 1997, Hong Kong Inst. Mktg. Exec. Devel. Seminar, 1996, Kathmandu Coll. Mgmt. Exec. Devel. Workshop, 2000, others; sr. fellow dept. mktg. faculty of bus. adminstrn. Nat. U. Singapore, 1998—99; affiliate faculty Japan Am. Inst. Mgmt. Sci., Honolulu, 1989—; vis. prof. Grad. Sch. Internat. Mgmt., Internat. U. Japan, Uhrasa, Yamato-machi, 1991, U. Internat. Bus. and Econs., Beijing, 1991, U. Kebangsaan Malaysia, Bangi-Selangor, Kuala Lumpur, Malaysia, 1991, 92, Mt. Carmel Inst. Mgmt., Bangalore, India, 1997, Vietnam Nat. U., Hanoi Sch Bus., 2002; lectr., cons., presenter in field. Editor: (with Dennis A. Rondinelli) Project Planning and Implementation in Developing Countries, 1976; assoc. editor e-Services Quar., 1999—; contbr. conf. procs. and articles to profl. jours. and books, including Indsl. Mktg. Mgmt., Internat. Bus. Jour., Asia-Pacific Jour. Mgmt., Internat. Mktg. Rev., European Jour. Mktg., Fgn. Trade Rev., Internat. Rev. Econs. & Bus., others; contbr. to numerous confs. and symposia in field; developer various mktg. decision support systems and decision-making tools for use in strategic market planning and in marketing simulations. Mem. various program rev. coms. Pacific and Asian Mgmt. Inst., Acad. Internat. Bus., Assn. Bus. Simulation and Exptl. Learning, others; bd. examiners Nat. U. Singapore Sch. Postgrad. Mgmt. Studies, 1991; external examiner Bd. Grad. Studies, Nat. U. Singapore, 2001; mem. adv. bd. Soc. Coll. of Bus. Adminstrn. Alumni and Friends Exec. Com., 1991-93; adv. bd.

Salvation Army Residential Treatment Facilities for Children and Youth Adv. Coun., 1989-96, vice chair, 1987-89; chair Salvation Army Family Treatment Svcs. Adv. Coun., 1997-98; mem. Salvation Army Honolulu Adv. Bd., 1997-98; treas., bd. dirs. Kings Gate Homeowners Assn., 1994-96; bd. advisors Ctr. for Nat. Competitiveness Inst. Indsl. Policy Studies, Korea, 1998—. Univ. fellow Kent State U., 1983; East-West Ctr. scholar East-West Ctr., 1973-75; Ednl. Improvement Fund grantee, 1989, Instrl. Travel and Devel. Fund grantee Office Faculty Devel. and Acad. Support, 1991, 95, joint rsch. grants U. Kebangsaan Malaysia, Nat. U. Singapore, U. So. Queensland, Australia, U. Otago, New Zealand, Lingnan Coll., Hong Kong; recipient Internat. Agreements Fund award Office Internat. Programs and Svcs., 1990-91, 91-92, ORA travel award U. Rsch. Coun., 1986, 88, 89, 91, 92, 94-98. Mem. Am. Mktg. Assn. (academia editor Honolulu chpt. 1986-87), Acad. Internat. Bus. (chair Pacific Basin Region 1995, chair Pacific Basin chpt. 1996—, co-chair Asia Pacific Conf. 1997), Pacific Asian Consortium for Internat. Bus. Edn. and Rsch., Assn. for Bus. Simulation and Exptl. Learning, Pan-Pacific Bus. Assn. (charter), Mortar Bd. (Outstanding Educator award 1993, Mentor award 1995), East-West Ctr. Alumni Assn. U.S. (v.p. Hawaii chpt. 1987-89, ad campaign com. 1987-88), Beta Gamma Sigma (faculty advisor, sec.-treas. Alpha of Hawaii chpt. 1990—, Outstanding Svc. award 1992-93, Bd. Govs. Commitment to Excellence award 1997), Mu Kappa Tau, Pi Sigma Epsilon. Avocations: music, photography, swimming, reading, hiking. Home: 2724 Kahoaloha Ln # 1605 Honolulu HI 96826-3337 Office: U Hawaii Manoa Dept Mktg 2404 Maile Way Honolulu HI 96822-2223

PALIHNICH, NICHOLAS JOSEPH, JR. retail executive; b. Montclair, N.J., Nov. 9, 1939; s. Nicholas Joseph and Lucille (Pflugh) P.; m. Diane Lorraine Parise, Nov. 12, 1966; children: Nicholas, Kristin, Danielle. BBA, U. Notre Dame, 1961. Retail buyer R.H. Macy, N.Y.C., 1961-66, Korvettes, Inc., N.Y.C., 1966-69; retail v.p., gen. mdse. mgr. Mangurians Inc., Ft. Lauderdale, Fla., 1970-72; sr. v.p. retail mgmt. Korvettes Inc., N.Y.C., 1973-79, pres., 1979-81; sr. v.p. retail mgmt. Lane Bryant, 1981-83; pres. retail mgmt. Dan Inc., 1984-86; exec. v.p. retail Bally U.S.A. 1987-93; gen. mgr. retail, dir. The Rockport Co., Canton, Mass., 1994—. Served with U.S. Army, 1962. Republican. Roman Catholic. Office: 1895 JW Foster Blvd Canton MA 02021

PALILEO, HAZEL VALENCIA, videographer; b. Pila, Laguna, Philippines, May 22, 1951; came to U.S., 1971, naturalized citizen, 1979; d. Lauro Gomez and Edna (Valencia) P. BFA in Photography and Media, Wright State U., 1976; student, DeVry Inst. Tech., 1995-97; diploma, Applied Multimedia Tng. Ctrs., 1998; cert. web designer, U. Calgary, 2002. Lab. tech. Valdhere Films, Inc., Dayton, Ohio, 1973-76; news photographer Sta. WDTN-TV, 1977-79; videographer Sta. WKEF-TV News, 1979-86, chief videographer, 1983-86; videographer, still photographer Wycliffe Bible Translators, Calgary, Alta., Can., 1986-92, co-mgr. media prodns. dept. Can., 1990-92; video mgr., media coord. Cornerstone Comms., 1992-94; photographer, videographer and multi media specialist freelance, 1994—; media technician U. Calgary, 1998—. Videographer (TV news) Haviland Ave. Fire, 1984 (Emmy 1984). Recipient Best Video award Nat. Cath. Stewardship Conf., 1993. Mem. Anglican Ch. of Canada. Avocations: reading, photography, travelling, walking. E-mail: palileo@ucalgary.ca.

PALIN, MICHAEL EDWARD, actor, screenwriter, writer; b. May 5, 1943; s. Edward and Mary P.; m. Helen M. Gibbins, 1966; 3 children. BA, U. Oxford, Eng., 1965. Writer, performer BBC Corp., 1965-69. Presenter in field. Actor, writer: (TV shows) Monty Python's Flying Circus, 1969-74, Ripping Yarns, 1976-80; (films) And Now for Something Completely Different, 1970, Monty Python and the Holy Grail, 1974, Monty Python's Life of Brian, 1978, Time Bandits, 1980, Monty Python's The Meaning of Life, 1982, American Friends, 1991; TV presenter, writer Great Railway Journeys of the World, 1980, Around the World in 80 Days, 1989, Pole to Pole, 1993, Palin's Column, 1994, Great Railway Journeys of the World, 1994, Full Circle, 1997, Michael Palin's Hemingway Adventure, 1999, Sahara with Michael Palin, 2002; television presenter: Palin on Redpath, 1997, The Bright Side of Life, 2000, Michael Palin and the Ladies Who Loved Matisse, 2002; actor: (TV shows) Three Men in a Boat, 1975, GBH, 1991; (films) Jabberwocky, 1976, A Private Function, 1984, Brazil, 1985, A Fish Called Wanda (Best Supporting Actor Brit. Acad. Film and TV Arts, 1989), Fierce Creatures, 1998; actor, writer and co-prodr.: The Missionary, 1982; writer (stage play) The Weekend, 1994; author: Monty Python's Brand New Bok, 1973, Dr. Fegg's Encyclopeadia of All World Knowledge, 1984, Limericks, 1985, Around the World in 80 Days, 1989, Pole to Pole, 1993, Pole to Pole: The Photographs, 1994, Hemingway's Chair 1995, Full Circle, 1997, Full Circle: The Photographs, 1997; (children's books) Small Harry and the Toothache Pills, 1981, The Mirrorstone, 1986, The Cyril Stories, 1986. Co-recipient (with Monty Python) Michael Balcon award for outstanding contbn. to cinema Brit. Acad. of Film and TV Arts, 1987; named to CBE New Year's Honours List for Svc. to TV, Drama & Travel, 2000. Avocations: reading, running, railways. Office: 34 Tavistock St London WC2E 7PB England

PALION, PETER THADDEUS, financial planner; b. Warsaw, Poland, Jan. 14, 1966; came to U.S., 1982; s. Karol and Zofia (Biernacka) P.; m. Monica Witak, Jan. 18, 1992. Student, CUNY, 1984-85; CFP, Coll. Fin. Planning, Denver, 1993. CFP. Fin. cons. Shearson Lehman Bros., N.Y.C., 1987-88; fin. planner IDS Fin. Svcs., Inc., 1988-94; pres., chmn. bd. dirs. Master Plan Advisory, Inc., 1994—; registered rep. FSC Securities Corp., 1994-96; registered prin. Securities Am., Inc., 1996-98; registered rep. Long Grove Trading Co., 1998-99, Cambridge Investment Rsch., Inc., 1999—. Stock market cons. Polish Govt., Warsaw, 1990; guest speaker on East European markets Voice of Am., Washington, 1990-93, on investments N.Y.C. Channel 31 Polish TV, 1991, CNNfn, 1997, 98, Neighborhood News 13; featured spkr. Times/Ledger Newspapers-IAFP Person Finance Day, 1998, 99, 2000; tchr. investment planning courses Hofstra U., 1999—. Author article series Kariera, 1990. Mem. Fin. Planning Assn. (practitioner divsn.). Avocations: tennis, skiing, reading, motorsports. Office: Master Plan Advisory Inc 60 E 42nd St Fl 46 New York NY 10165-4699

PALIOTTA, ARMAND, lawyer; b. N.Y.C., Mar. 17, 1967; s. Armand R. and Margaret R. Paliotta; m. Amanda M. Dry, Aug. 29, 1992; 1 child, Joshua Armand. BBA, U. Okla., 1989, JD, 1992. Bar: Okla. 1992. Ptnr. Hartzog Conger Cason & Neville, Oklahoma City, 1992—. Office: Hartzog Conger Cason & Neville 1600 Bank of Oklahoma Plz Oklahoma City OK 73102 E-mail: apaliotta@hartzoglaw.com.

PALISI, ANTHONY THOMAS, psychologist, educator; b. Rahway, N.J., Mar. 8, 1930; s. Anthony Francis and Marianne Catherine (Picone) P.; m. Dyane Cassidy, Apr. 19, 1954; children: Jane, Anthony Francis II, Phyllis, Damian-Marie. BS, Seton Hall U., 1951, MA, 1958; EdD, Temple U., 1973. Cert. secondary tchr., elem. prin., psychologist, rehab. counselor, N.J.; mem. Nat. Register Health Care Profls. in Psychology. Tchr., coach pub. schs., Rahway, 1953-60; sports editor Rahway News-Record, 1950-60; prin. elem. pub. sch. Franklin Twp., N.J., 1960-65; asst. prof. edn. Seton Hall U., 1965-73, assoc. prof., 1974-77, prof., 1977-82, acting grad. dean, 1976-77, dir., 1969-80, indsl. cons. group dynamics, 1967-97; dir. cons. divsn. FormTech Graphics, Inc., 1997—. Contbr. articles and short stories to profl. jours. and popular periodicals. Mem. Rahway Bd. Edn. 1961-62; trustee Rahway Libr., 1961-68, pres. 1967-68. Recipient award N.J. Sportswriters' Assn., 1953. Mem. APA, ACA, Am. Mgmt. Assn. (co-author video tng. program), N.J. Psychol. Assn., Assn. for Specialists in Group Work (mem. rsch. com. 1980-82), N.Y. Acad. Scis., Nat. Acad. Counselors and Family Therapists (chmn., exec. dir. 1988-93, co-editor Family Letter 1985-93), Nat. Register of Health Svc. Providers in Psychology, Am. Coll. Counselors. Roman Catholic. Fax: (732) 223-5379. E-mail: atpalisi@wallnet.com.

PALITZ, ANKA A. KRISER, manufacturing and distributing company executive; b. Sofia, Bulgaria, Aug. 19, 1934; came to U.S., 1951; d. Angel Georgieff, Rayna Tomoff Georgiewa; m. David B. Kriser (div. 1978); m. Clarence Y. Palitz Jr., 1989 (dec. Nov. 2000). BA, Art Acad., Munich, 1950. Cert. interior designer. V.p. Revlon, N.Y.C., 1955-61; pres. Decart Design, N.Y.C., Lancaster, Pa., 1978-83, also chair, 1983-89; pres. The Baroness Collection, N.Y.C., 1983—; art dealer, 1989—. Adv. bd. Mus. Am. Illustrator Art, Newport, R.I. Contbr. articles to profl. jours. Bd. dirs. N.Y.C. Opera Guild, 1965—78, Beth Israel Hosp. Guild, N.Y.C., N.Y. Hosp. Nursing Com., 1975—78, 910 Fifth Ave. Bldg., N.Y.C., 1984—, Am. Ballet Theater, Career Transition for Dancers, Met. Opera, Golden Horseshoe; mem. adv. bd. Nat. Mus. Am. Illustration; contbg. mem. Met. Mus., N.Y. Philharm. Mem. Benefactor Coun. Soc. of the Four Arts (Palm Beach, Fla.). Avocations: the arts, travel, skiing. Home and Office: 880 Fifth Ave New York NY 10021-4951

PALIWAL, DINESH KUMAR, diplomat, educational administrator; b. Muzaffar Nagar, India, June 5, 1957; s. Rajendra Prasad and Kaushal P.; m. Neeta Paliwal, Dec. 8, 1982; children: Abhishek, Ankit. BS, Meerut U., India, 1976; MS, Agra U., India, 1979; PhD, Indian Inst. Tech., Delhi, India, 1996. Lectr. Kishan Lal Pub. Coll., Rewari, India, 1981-88; tchr. fellow Indian Inst. Tech., New Delhi, India, 1988-92; asst. ednl. adv. dept. edn. Govt. of India, 1992-97; consul edn. Consulate Gen. India, New York, 1997—. Contbr. articles to profl. jours. Mem. Indian Soc. Tech. Edn. Fax: 212-879-7914. E-mail: dinesh_paliwal@hotmail.com.

PALL, ELLEN JANE, writer; b. N.Y.C., Mar. 28, 1952; d. David B. and Josephine H. (Blatt) P.; m. Richard Holmes Dicker, July 12, 1986; 1 child, Benjamin. BA, U. Calif., Santa Barbara, 1973. Freelance writer for several jours., 1987—. Staff assoc. Bread Loaf Writers Conf., Middlebury, Vt., 1986; instr. UCLA-Ext., 1980-83; adj. asst. prof. Fordham U./Coll. at Lincoln Ctr., N.Y.C., 1990-93. Author: (under pen name Fiona Hill) The Trellised Lane, The Wedding Portrait, The Practical Heart, Love in a Major Key, Sweet's Folly, The Autumn Rose, The Love Child, The Stanbroke Girls, 1981, The Country Gentleman, 1987, (as Ellen Pall) Back East, 1983, Among the Ginzburgs, 1996, Corpse de Ballet, 2001; contbr. articles to N.Y. Times Mag., N.Y. Times Arts & Leisure, New Yorker Mag., Chgo. Tribune, Washington Post; book reviewer. Shane Stevens fellow Bread Loaf Writer's Conf., Vt., 1983. Mem. Am. PEN (freedom to write com.). Office: care Mary Evans Inc 242 E 5th St New York NY 10003-8501

PALLADINO-CRAIG, ALLYS, museum director, educator; b. Pontiac, Mich., Mar. 23, 1947; d. Stephan Vincent and Mary (Anderson) Palladino; m. Malcolm Arnold Craig, Aug. 20, 1967; children— Ansel, Reed, Nicholas. BA in English, Fla. State U., 1967; grad., U. Toronto, Ont., Can., 1969; MFA, Fla. State U., 1978, PhD in Humanities, 1996. Editorial asst. project U. Va. Press, Charlottesville, 1970-76; instr. English Inst. Franco Americain, Rennes, France, 1974; adj. instr. Fla. State U., Tallahassee, 1978-79, dir. Four Arts Ctr., 1979-82, dir. U. Mus. of Fine Arts, 1982—, prof. mus. studies. Mem. grad faculty Mus. Studies Cert. Program Fla. State U. Curator, contbg. editor: articles and exhbn. catalogues Nocturnes and Nightmares, curator, contbg. editor: articles and exhbn. catalogues Monochrome/Polychrome, curator, contbg. editor: articles and exhbn. catalogues Chroma, contbg. editor: articles and exhbn. catalogues Body Language, curator, contbg. editor: articles and exhbn. catalogues others, guest curator, author: Mark Messersmith: New Mythologies, author: Jack Nichelson: Micro-Theatres, author: Alexa Kleinbard: Talking Leaves, curator, author: The Abridged Walmsley--Selections from the Career of William Aubrey Walmsley, curator, author: Albert Paley--Sculpture, Drawings, Graphics and Decorative Arts; author: Jake Fernandez--Ethereal Journeyman, Jim Roche-Sense of Place; gen. editor: Athanor I-XXI, 1980—; Represented in permanent collections Fla. Ho. of Reps., Barnett Bank, IBM; author: Jim Roche--Wayfaring Stranger. Individual artist fellow Fla. Arts Coun., 1979 Mem. Am. Assn. Mus., Fla. Art Mus. Dirs. Assn. (sec. 1989-91), Phi Beta Kappa. Democrat. Avocation: antique American fountain pen collecting. Home: 1410 Grape St Tallahassee FL 32303-5636 Office: Fla State U Mus of Fine Arts 250 Fine Arts Bldg Tallahassee FL 32306-1140 E-mail: apcraig@mailer.fsu.edu.

PALLAI, DAVID FRANCIS, publishing executive; b. N.Y.C., Nov. 7, 1950; s. Alfiero and Clara Aurora (Dignani) P.; m. Jean Therese Leary, June 25, 1977; children: Matthew Gian, Jeremy Michael. BA, Boston Coll., 1972, MA, 1974, Yale U., 1981. Sales rep. Prentice Hall, Inc., Englewood Cliffs, N.J., 1976-77, field editor, 1977-78; acquisitions editor Allyn & Bacon, Inc., Boston, 1978-80; sr. editor PWS Pubs., 1980-87, Addison-Wesley Pub. Co., Reading, Mass., 1987-88, exec. editor, 1988-90; v.p., pub. Acad. Press, Cambridge, 1990-94; pres., founder Charles River Media, Inc., Rockland, 1995—. Com. mem. Duxbury (Mass.) Hist. Commn., 1984-87. With USNG, 1972-78. Mem. Math. Assn. Am., Mensa, KC, Harvard Club, Yale Club of Boston. Republican. Roman Catholic. Avocations: softball, model shipbldg. Home: 65 Bayview Rd Duxbury MA 02332-5043 Office: Charles River Media Inc Ste 3 20 Downer Ave Hingham MA 02043-1132

PALLAM, JOHN JAMES, lawyer; b. Cleve., May 19, 1940; s. James John and Coralia (Gatsos) P.; m. Evanthia Venizelos, Nov. 29, 1969; 1 child, Alethea. BA, Case Western Res. U., 1962; JD, Ohio State U., 1965. Bar: Ohio 1965, U.S. Ct. Claims 1969, U.S. Ct. Mil. Appeals 1969, U.S. Supreme Ct. 1970. Law clk. to presiding justice Cuyahoga County Ct., Cleve., 1965-66; assoc. Burke, Habor & Berick, 1970-73; corp. atty. Midland Ross Corp., 1973-80, corp. counsel, 1980-87; v.p., gen. counsel Brush Wellman Corp., 1987—. Guest lectr. Nat. Foundry Assn., Chgo., 1986—. Contbr. articles on labor and environ. matters to jours. Legal advisor Am. Hellenic and Prog. Assn., Cleve., 1966—. Served to capt. JAGC U.S. Army, 1966-70, Vietnam. Decorated Bronze Star with oak leaf cluster. Mem. Ohio Bar Assn. (committeeman 1984—), Cleve. Bar Assn. (merit svc. award 1972), Hellenic Bar Assn., Hellenic Univ. Club, Rowfant. Greek Orthodox. Avocations: history, antiques, golfing, rare books, railroading. Office: 17876 Saint Clair Ave Cleveland OH 44110-2602

PALLASCH, B. MICHAEL, lawyer, director; b. Chgo., Mar. 30, 1933; s. Bernhard Michael and Magdalena Helena (Fixari) P.; m. Josephine Catherine O'Leary, Aug. 15, 1981; children: Bernhard Michael III and Madeleine Josephine (twins). BSS, Georgetown U., 1954; JD, Harvard U., 1957; postgrad., John Marshall Law Sch., 1974. Bar: Ill. 1957, U.S. Dist. Ct. (no. dist.) Ill. 1958, U.S. Tax Ct. 1961, U.S. Ct. Claims 1961, U.S. Ct. Appeals (7th cir.) 1962. Assoc. Winston & Strawn, Chgo., 1958-66, resident mgr. br. office Paris, 1963-65, ptnr. Chgo., 1966-70, sr. capital ptnr., 1971-91; sr. ptnr. B. Michael Pallasch & Assocs., 1991—. Corp. sec. Tanis, Inc., Calumet, Mich., 1972-2000, Greenbank Engring. Corp., Dover, Del., 1976-91, C.B.P. Engring. Corp., Chgo., 1976-91, Arthur Andersen Assocs., Inc., Chgo., 1976-98, Chgo. Cutting Svcs. Corp., 1977-88, L'hotel de France of Ill., Inc., Chgo., 1980-85, Water & Effluent Screening Co., Chgo., 1988-91. Bd. dirs. Martin D'Arcy Mus. Medieval and Renaissance Art, Chgo., 1975— ; bd. dirs. Katherine M. Bosch Found., 1978— ; asst. sec. Hundred Club of Cook County, Chgo., 1966-73, bd. dirs., sec., 1974— . Served with USAFR, 1957-63. Knight of Merit Sacred Mil. Constantinian Order of St. George of Royal House of Bourbon of Two Sicilies, knight comdr. with star Sovereign Mil. Order of Temple of Jerusalem; named youth mayor City of Chgo., 1950; recipient Outstanding Woodland Mgmt. Forestry award Monroe County (Wis.) Soil and Water Conservation Dist., 1975. Mem. Ill. Bar Assn. (tax lectr. 1961), Advs. Soc., Field Mus. Natural History (life), Max McGraw Wildlife Found., English Speaking Union. Clubs: Travellers (Paris); Saddle and Cycle (Chgo.). Roman Catholic. Home: 737 W Hutchinson St Chicago IL 60613-1519 Office: 35 W Wacker Dr Ste 4700 Chicago IL 60601-1614 *Personal philosophy: We define and measure success in various ways: achievement, position, wealth: and attribute it to the application of various attributes but is there any degree of success that we can achieve that is worthier than the knowledge that we have faithfully served those who depend upon and trust in us?.*

PALLASCH, MAGDALENA HELENA (MRS. BERNHARD MICHAEL PALLASCH), artist; b. Chgo., Sept. 6, 1908; d. Frank and Anna (Meier) Fixari; m. Bernhard Pallasch, Nov. 26, 1931 (dec. Nov. 1977); children: Bernhard Michael, Diana Pallasch Miller Student, Chgo. Acad. Fine Arts, 1922-26, Am. Acad. Fine Arts, 1926-30, U. Chgo., 1960, Art Inst. Chgo.; pvt. study with Joseph Allworthy, 1935-38, hon. doctorate, 1985. Contbr. two murals and ten life size figures for Woman's World Fair, Chgo., 1928, Century of Progress Exhbn., Chgo., 1933-34; portrait artist, subjects include Cardinal Cody, Chgo., 1980—, Cardinal Francis George, Chgo., 1998, Carlotta Ames, Boston, Mrs. Timothy Kingston, Arlington Heights, Ill., Dr. Neal Coleman, Hinsdale, Ill., Catherine Eardley Murphy, Lake Forest, Ill., Anita Mangels, Sao Paulo, Brazil; mural St. Mary of the Lake Ch., Chgo., 1987; exhbn. at Montifiori Estate, 1992, 93, 94, Hinsdale Art Ctr., 1995, 96, 97; represented in pvt. and pub. collections Loyola U., Chgo., Barat Coll., Lake Forest, Ill., Internat. Coll. Surgeons, Chgo., Med. Library, Columbus Hosp. Recipient first award for still life Arts Club, N.Y.C., 1960; First award Nat. League Am. Pen Women, 1972; 1st place and best of show State Exhibit, Springfield, Ill., 1973; 1st award Chgo. Woman's Club, 1978; hon. mention for portrait Italian Cultural Ctr.; hon. alumna award Loyola U., Chgo., 1983; award of excellence for portrait of author Gail Brook Burket, Wheaton Hist. Mus., 1987; Gold Medal of Honor for disting. lifelong achievements, 1987; award of honor for portrait of sculptor Lisa Gengler, 1989; named Dame Commandeur with Starbust, 1997, Sovereign Mil. Order Temple of Jerusalem, 1995. Mem. Presentation Ball Aux.; mem. President's Club, Loyola U., also mem. women's bd. Nat. League Am. Pen Women (v.p. Chgo. br. 1966-68, art chmn. 1978-80, Margaret Dingle Meml. award 1979), Mcpl. Art League Chgo., Nat. Soc. Arts and Letters (art chmn. chgo. chpt. 1982—, apptd. nat. chmn. 1997—), Friends of Austria, Friends of D'Arcy Gallery of Medieval and Renaissance Art, Ill. Cath. Women Club (gov. 1979—), Cuneo Mus. (Vernon Hills, Ill.). Home: 723 W Junior Ter Chicago IL 60613-1512

PALLEY, HOWARD A. social work educator; b. N.Y.C., Mar. 22, 1936; s. Abraham and Henrietta (Sher) P.; m. Marian Judith Lief, April 21, 1961; children: Stephen D., Elizabeth S. BA cum laude, Bklyn. Coll., 1957; MS, Yeshiva U., 1959; PhD, Syracuse U., 1963. Asst. prof. William Paterson Coll., Wayne, NJ, 1962—65, U. Wis.- Milw., 1965—66; assoc. prof. Adelphi U., Garden City, NY, 1966—70, U. Md., Balt., 1970—77, prof., Sch. Social Work, 1977—, prof. dept. epidemiology and preventive medicine, 1991—. Vis. prof. Chung-Ang U., Seoul, Korea, 1990, Hebrew U., Israel, 1978, 85, Brookdale Inst. of Gerontology, 1985, Otago U., New Zealand, 2000; conf. presenter in field. Author: Implementing The Canadian National Health Insurance Program, 1985; co-author: The Chronically Limited Elderly, 1983; mem. editl. bd. Soc. Devel. Issues, 1983—, Jour. Health and Soc. Policy, 1992—; contbr. articles to profl. jours. Co-dir. NASW Policy Rsch. Project Nat. Assn. Social Workers, Washington, 1980-82; mem. inter-univ. consortium for international social devel. Recipient Fulbright Rsch. award, Ukraine, Coun. Internat. Exch. of Scholars, Washington, 1990. Mem. Nat. Assn. of Social Workers, Am. Political Sci. Assn., Am. Assn. of U. Profs., Council on Soc. Worl Edn., Inter Univ. Consortium for Internat. Social Devel. (instnl. rep. to bd. dirs.). Democrat. Jewish. Avocations: hiking, travel, chess. Home: 11 N Townview Ln Newark DE 19711-7416 Office: U Md Sch of Social Work 525 W Redwood St Baltimore MD 21201-1705 E-mail: hpalley@ssw.umaryland.edu.

PALLEY, MARIAN LIEF, political science educator, author; b. N.Y.C., June 28, 1939; d. Samuel and Frances Rose (Levy) Lief; m. Howard A. Palley, Apr. 21, 1961; children: Stephen, Elizabeth. BA, Syracuse U., 1961, MA, 1963; PhD, NYU, 1966. Acting instr. U. Wis., Milw., 1966; asst. prof. Rutgers U., Newark, 1967-70; asst. prof., assoc. prof., prof. polit. sci. U. Del., 1970—, chairperson polit. sci. dept., 1979-84, dir. women's studies dept., 1989-90, 99—. Vis. prof. polit. sci. Hebrew U., 1985, U. Adelaide, Australia, 1985; vis. scholar women's studies Ewha U., Korea, 1988, 90, 93; cons. Agy. for Instrnl. Tech., Bloomington, Ind., 1985-87; William Evans fellow Otago U., New Zealand, 2000. Co-author: Women and Public Policies, 1982, 87, 96, Urban America and Public Policies, 1977, 81, Politics of Federal Grants, 1981, Tradition and Change in American Party Politics, 1975, Women of Japan and Korea, 1994; contbr. articles to profl. jours. Am. Coun. Edn. fellow, 1974-75, Fulbright Found. fellow, 1988; grantee Korea Rsch. Found., 1993, Women's Rsch. and Edn. Inst., 1986. Mem. Am. Polit. Sci. Assn. (sec. 1980-81), Am. Soc. Pub. Adminstrn. (nat. coun. mem. 1990-93), Women's Caucus for Polit. Sci. (pres. 1983-84), So. Polit. Sci. Assn. (pres. 1996). Democrat. Avocations: swimming, hiking, cooking. Office: U Del Dept Polit Sci Newark DE 19716 E-mail: mpalley@udel.edu.

PALLINI, ROBERT ANTHONY, engineering executive; b. Phila., Feb. 13, 1953; s. Massimini C. and Carmela R. (De Carolis) P.; m. Margaret M. Pfizenmaier, May 13, 1978; children: Christine, Robert C. BSME, Drexel U., 1976; MS in Engring., Pa. State U., 1981. Product design engr. Messinger Bearings Inc., Phila., 1976-77; sr. rsch. engr. Franklin Rsch. Ctr., 1977-83; sr. engring. scientist SKF Industries, Inc., King of Prussia, Pa., 1983-88; cons. engr. J. V. Poplawski & Assocs., Bethlehem, 1988; mgr. sales and engring. Nice Ball Bearings Inc. div. RBC Bearings, Kulpsville, 1989—. Lectr. in field. Contbr. articles to profl. jours. Chmn. bearings tech. com. Am. Soc. Lubrication Engrs., 1982. Recipient Walter D. Hodson award Am. Soc. Lubrication Engrs., 1985. Mem. ASME. Office: Nice Ball Bearings Inc 2060 Detwiler Rd Kulpsville PA 19443 also: PO Box 307 Kulpsville PA 19443 E-mail: BPALLINI@aol.com.

PALLMEYER, REBECCA RUTH, judge; b. Tokyo, Sept. 13, 1954; arrived in U.S., 1957; d. Paul Henry and Ruth (Schrieber) Pallmeyer; m. Dan P. McAdams, Aug. 20, 1977; children: Ruth McAdams, Amanda McAdams. BA, Valparaiso (Ind.) U., 1976; JD, U. Chgo., 1979. Bar: Ill. 1980, U.S. Ct. Appeals (7th cir.) 1980, U.S. Ct. Appeals (11th and 5th cirs.) 1982. Jud. clk. Minn. Supreme Ct., St. Paul, 1979-80; assoc. Hopkins & Sutter, Chgo., 1980-85; judge administrv. law Ill. Human Rights Commn., 1985-91; magistrate judge U.S. Dist. Ct. No. Dist. Ill., 1991-98, dist. judge, 1998—. Mem. jud. resources com. Jud. Conf. U.S., 1994—2000. Nat. adv. coun. Christ Coll., Valparaiso U., 2002—; bd. dirs. Augustana Ctr., 1990—91. Mem.: FBA (bd. mgrs. Chgo. chpt. 1995—99), Chgo. Bar Assn. (chair devel. law com. 1992—93, David C. Hilliard award 1990—91), Fed. Magistrate Judges Assn. (bd. dirs. 1994—97), Nat. Assn. Women Judges, Womens Bar Assn. Ill. (bd. mgrs. 1995—98), Valparaiso U. Alumni Assn. (bd. dirs. 1992—94). Lutheran. Avocations: choral music, sewing, running. Office: US Dist Ct 219 S Dearborn St Ste 2178 Chicago IL 60604-1877

PALLONE, ADRIAN JOSEPH, research scientist; b. Lille, France, Apr. 8, 1928; came to U.S., 1946; s. Giovanni and Laurina (Caccia) P.; m. Teresa Maria Violino, June 12, 1954; children— John M., Anne Marie, Janet M., Joan L. BS in Aero. Engring., Poly Inst. Bklyn., 1952, MS in Aero. Engring., 1953, PhD in Applied Mechanics, 1959; cert., Sloan Sch. Mgmt., MIT, 1984. Research assoc. Poly. Inst. Bklyn., 1955-59; mgr. Avco Systems Div., Wilmington, Mass., 1959-63; mem. faculty NYU, N.Y.C., 1963-67; dir. Avco Systems Div., Wilmington, 1967-78, chief scientist, 1978-87; aerospace cons. Textron Def. Systems, Wilmington, 1987-91; pres. Aerophysics Systems & Tech., Inc., Silver Lake, N.H., 1992—. Patentee in field. Contbr. articles to sci. jours. Fellow AIAA; mem. N.Y. Acad. Scis., Sigma Xi, Sigma Gamma Tau. Roman Catholic. Avocations: skiing; sailing; hiking. Office: Aerophysics Systems & Tech Inc PO Box 189 Silver Lake NH 03875-0189

PALLONE, FRANK, JR. congressman; b. Long Branch, N.J., Oct. 30, 1951; Grad. cum. laude, Middlebury Coll., 1973; MA, Tufts U., 1974; JD, Rutgers U., 1978. Councilman City of Long Branch, 1982-88; mem. N.J. Senate, 1984-88, U.S. Congress from 6th N.J. dist., 1988—; mem. commerce com., resource com. Democrat. Roman Catholic. Office: US Ho of Reps 420 Cannon Hob Washington DC 20515-0001 Address: 504 Broadway Ste 118 Long Branch NJ 07740-5951*

PALLONE, NATHANIEL JOHN, psychologist, educator; b. Chgo., Oct. 30, 1935; s. Louis T. and Adeline (Tenkach) P.; m. Letitia Clarke, Sept. 19, 1983; children: Andrea, Angela. AB, Cath. U. Am., 1957, MA, 1960; PhD, NYU, 1963. Lic. psychologist, N.J. Psychologist St. Francis Coll., Bklyn., 1960-63; asst. prof. U. Notre Dame, South Bend, Ind., 1963-66; dept. chair NYU, N.Y.C., 1966-72; assoc. dean U. Hartford, Conn., 1972-73; dean Rutgers U., New Brunswick, N.J., 1973-79, acad. v.p., 1979-87, univ. disting. prof. psychology, 1987—. Vis. prof. Harvard U., Cambridge, Mass., 1987-88; case cons. Office of Pub. Defender, New Brunswic, 1987-91; cons. social svc. agys., criminal justice agys., 1963—; chair classification rev. bd. for sex offenders N.J. Dept. Corrections, 1975—. Editor: Jour. Offender Rehab., 1989—; exec. editor Current Psychology, 1989—; sr. editor Society, 1992-98; author 24 books; contbr. numerous articles to profl. publs. Fellow Am. Psychol. Assn., Am. Coll. Forensic Psychology, Am. Psychol. Soc.; mem. Am. Bd. Profl. Psychology (diplomate), Phi Beta Kappa. Office: Rutgers Univ 213 Smithers Hall New Brunswick NJ 08903

PALLOT, JOSEPH WEDELES, lawyer; b. Coral Gables, Fla., Dec. 23, 1959; s. Richard Allen Pallot and Rosalind Brown (Wedeles) Spak; m. Linda Fried, Oct. 12, 1956; children: Richard Allen, Maxwell Ross. BS, Jacksonville U., 1981; JD cum laude, U. Miami, Coral Gables, Fla., 1986. Bar: Fla. 1986. Comml. lending officer S.E. Bank, N.A., Miami, 1981-83; ptnr. Steel Hector & Davis, 1986-2000, Devine Goodman Pallot & Wells, P.A., Miami, 2000—. Bd. dirs. MOSAIC: Jewish Mus. Fla., Miami Beach, 1993—; dir. Fla. Grand Opera, 1996—, The Beacon Coun., 1997—, exec. com., 2001-. Avocations: golf, tennis. E-mail: jpallot@devinegoodman.com.

PALLOTTA, JOHANNA ANTONIA (JOHANNA STEPHEN), physician, educator, researcher; b. Boston, May 7, 1937; d. John and Antonia (Lanni) P.; m. Michael John Stephen, Aug. 13, 1966; children: Jacqueline, Antonia, Michael, Andrew. *Parents John and Antonia Pallotta emigrated from Italy in 1920. Her husband Michael J. Stephen is a physics professor. Het children Jacqueline, Antonia and Michael are physicians. Her son Andrew is a third year medical student. She considers her family to be her greatest accomplishment.* BS in Chemistry magna cum laude, Boston Coll., 1958; MD, N.Y. Med. Coll., 1962. Diplomate Am. Bds. Internal Medicine, Endocrinolgoy and Metabolism; lic. N.Y., Mass., Calif. Intern St. Elizabeth's Hosp., Boston, 1962-63; resident in medicine N.Y. Med. Coll. Metro. Hosp., N.Y.C., 1963-64; resident in medicine, fellow radioisotope svc. VA Hosp., Bronx, 1964-66; fellow metabolism and endocrinology Yale U. Sch. Medicine, 1966-67; instr. medicine Harvard Med. Sch., 1967-69, Beth Israel Deaconess Hosp. Harvard Med. Sch., Boston, 1969-70; asst. prof. medicine Harvard Med. Sch., 1970—. Tutor med. scis. Harvard Med. Sch., 1972-73; dir. endocrinology clinic Beth Israel Deaconess Hosp., Boston, 1967—, dir. radioimmunoassay lab., 1972-83, clin. cons., 1984—, asst. in medicine, 1967-69, assoc. in medicine, 1969-70, asst. physician, 1970-79, assoc. physician, 1979-87, sr. physician, 1987—, dir. clin. rsch. ctr. core radioimmunoassay lab., 1984-93; cons. staff Mount Auburn Hosp., Cambridge, 1974-90; mem. numerous other coms., 1969—. Researcher in field; contbr. articles to profl. jours. Recipient S. Robert Stone Harvard Med. Sch.-BIDMC tchg. award, 1998; scholar Carl Shapiro, BIDMC-Harvard Med. Sch., 2000—. Fellow: ACP; mem.: Am. Fedn. Clin. Rsch., Am. Thyroid Assn., Am. Assn. Clin. Endocrinology, Endocrine Soc., Harvard Aesculapian Club, Alpha Omega Alpha Honor Soc. Roman Catholic. Home: 16 Fresh Pond Ln Cambridge MA 02138-4616 Office: Beth Israel Hosp Harvard Med Sch 330 Brookline Ave Boston MA 02215-5491 E-mail: jpallott@caregroup.harvard.edu.

PALLOZOLA, CHRISTINE, non-profit historic site administrator; b. St. Louis, Mar. 28, 1952; BS, U. Mo., 1974. Purchasing and sales mgmt. computer industry, Mo., 1984-92; exec. dir. Cahokia Mounds Mus. Soc., Collinsville, Ill., 1993—. Mem. Nat. Soc. Fundraising Execs. Office: St Louis Arts & Edn Coun 3526 Washington Ave Saint Louis MO 63103-1019

PALM, CHARLES GILMAN, university official; b. Havre, Mont., Apr. 25, 1944; s. Victor F. and Laura (McKinnie) P.; m. Miriam Willits, Sept. 15, 1968. AB, Stanford U., 1966; MA, U. Wyo., 1967; MLS, U. Oreg., 1970. Asst. archivist Stanford (Calif.) U., 1971—74, dep. archivist, 1974-84, archivist, 1984-87, head libr., 1986-87, assoc. dir., 1987-90; dep. dir. Stanford U., Palo Alto, Calif., 1990—2001, dep. dir. emeritus, 2002—. Co-author: Guide to Hoover Institution Archives, 1980, Herbert Hoover, Register of His Papers in the Hoover Institution Archives, 1983; mem. editl. bd. Internat. Democracy Found., Moscow. Mem. Calif. Heritage Preservation Commn., Sacramento, 1988—, vice chmn., 1993-97, chmn., 1997—; mem. Nat. Hist. Records and Publs. Commn., Washington, 1990-96; mem. history & edn. ctr. adv. bd. ARC, 1994—; trustee Golden State Mus. Corp., 1997—. Fellow Soc. Am. Archivists; mem. Soc. Calif. Archivists (pres. 1983-84), Bohemian Club. Republican. Office: Hoover Instn Stanford CA 94305

PALM, MARION, educator; b. Aug. 6, 1940; children: Peter, Mari, Noah. BA, U. Minn., 1978; MS, Bank Street, 1995. Founder, dir. Poets Under Glass, Bklyn., 1987—. Dir. Proclamation for literacy programs, Borough Pres. Bklyn., N.Y.C., 1998; featured reader, various instns. and orgns., N.Y.C.; adj. prof. Bklyn. Coll. Author books of poetry. Fundraiser Cornell U., N.Y.C.; liasion dir. Cmty. Coun. Police Precinct #72, Bklyn. Recipient Cmty. Svc. awards Chase Bank, N.Y.C., 1991-93; Bklyn. Arts Coun. grantee, 1986, 88, 90. Mem. Poetry Soc. Am., Acad. Am. Poets, U.M. Alumni Assn. Home: 705-41 St Brooklyn NY 11232 E-mail: marionpalm@aol.com.

PALMA, NICHOLAS JAMES, lawyer; b. Newark, Oct. 28, 1953; s. James Thomas and Venice Maria (Dibenedetto) P.; m. Mary Jo Cugliari, Sept. 1, 1973; children: Nicholas J., Valerie Michele, James Michael. BS cum laude, William Paterson U., 1975; JD, Seton Hall U., 1979. Bar: N.J. 1979, U.S. Dist. Ct. N.J. 1979, U.S. Ct. Appeals (3d cir.) 1985, N.Y. 1986; cert. firearms expert, Hudson County, N.J. Investigator N.J. Pub. Defender's Office, Essex Region, Newark, 1974-75; investigator Hudson County Prosecutor's Office, Jersey City, 1975-79, asst. prosecutor, 1979-81; ptnr. A.J. Fusco, Jr., P.A., Passaic, N.J., 1981-90; sole practice, Clifton, N.J., 1990—. Recipient Commendation, Dade County Sheriff, Fla., 1976. Mem. Passaic County Bar Assn., N.J. State Bar Assn. Roman Catholic. Home: 221 Cedar St Cedar Grove NJ 07009-1615 Office: 1425 Broad St Clifton NJ 07013-4201

PALMATIER, MALCOLM ARTHUR, editor, consultant; b. Kalamazoo, Nov. 11, 1922; s. Karl Ernest and Cecile Caroline (Chase) P.; m. Mary Elizabeth Summerfield, June 16, 1948 (dec. Oct. 1982); children: Barnabus, Timothy K., Duncan M.; m. Marie-Anne Suzanne van Werveke, Jan. 12, 1985. BS in Math., Western Mich. U., 1945; MA in English, UCLA, 1947; MA in Econs., U. So. Calif., 1971. Instr. English Pomona Coll., Claremont, Calif., 1949-51; editor Naval Ordnance Test Sta., Pasadena, 1951-54; head editl. unit Rocketdyne, L.A., 1954-55; editor The RAND Corp., Santa Monica, Calif., 1955-87, cons. editor, 1987—. Instr. English UCLA, L.A., summer 1950. Mng. editor, cons. editor Jour.: Studies in Comparative Communism, L.A., 1968-80; co-editor Perspectives in Economics, 1971; contbr. chpts. to book, book revs. and articles to profl. jours. Chmn. bd. New Start, West L.A., 1982-84. With USNR, 1943-45. Mem. Jonathan Club. Avocations: music, travel. Home: 516 Avondale Ave Los Angeles CA 90049-4804 Office: 1700 Main St Santa Monica CA 90401-3208 E-mail: Malcolm_Palmatier@rand.org.

PALMEDO, PHILIP FRANKLIN, management consulting company executive; b. N.Y.C., Mar. 11, 1934; s. Roland and Elizabeth (Franklin) P.; m. Elisabeth Sheerin, May 27, 1961; children: P. Christopher, Lawrence. BA, Williams Coll., Williamstown, Mass., 1956; MS, MIT, 1958, PhD, 1961. Physicist Brookhaven Nat. Lab., Upton, N.Y., 1964-79; pres. Internat. Resources Group, Washington, 1979-80, chmn., 1980—; pres. Kepler Fin. Mgmt., Setauket, N.Y., 1988-91, L.I. Rsch. Inst., Setauket, 1992-97, Palmedo Assocs., Setauket, 1998—. Dir. EHR Investments, Point Vedra Beach, Fla., Grodyne Corp. Am., St. James, N.Y. Co-author: Wines of Long Island, 1994, Voices in Bronze, 1999. Mem. bd. L.I. Mus. Sci. and Tech., Melville, N.Y., 1996—; trustee Gallery North, Setauket, 1987—; dir. Stony Brook (N.Y.) Found., 1987—. Avocations: writing, sports, art. Home: 4 Piper Ln Saint James NY 11780-1122 Office: Palmedo Assocs 100 N Country Rd Setauket NY 11733-1300 E-mail: ppalmedo@cs.com.

PALMEIRO, RAFAEL CORRALES, professional baseball player; b. Havana, Cuba, Sept. 24, 1964; Degree in Comml. Art, Miss. State U. With Chgo. Cubs, 1986-88, Tex. Rangers, 1988-93, 98—; first baseman Balt. Orioles, 1994-98. Named to Coll. All-Am. Team, 1985, to Nat. League All-Star Team, 1988, 95, 98, to Am. League All-Star Team, 1991; named Eastern League Most Valuable Player, 1986; recipient Gold Glove award, 1997, 98. Office: Texas Rangers Oriole Park at Camden Yards 1000 Ballpark Way Arlington TX 76011-5168*

PALMER, ADA MARGARET, systems analyst, consultant; b. Feb. 8, 1940; d. Mark Lloyd Palmer and Eunice Elizabeth (Thompson) Palmer Schnitzer. AA, Colo. Woman's Coll., 1960; BA, George Washington U., 1962. Programmer, analyst U.S. Navy Dept., Washington, 1962-66, Schroder Trust, N.Y.C., 1967-68; v.p. EDP Learning Systems, 1968-69; cons. JWI Assoc. Tech. Group, 1969; adv. sr. programmer Merrill Lynch, 1969-72; sys. analyst Tchrs. Ins. & Annuity, 1972-77; sys. specialist N.Y. Times, 1977-81; computer cons. Applied Sys. Resources, Inc., 1981-82; asst. sec. Chase Bank, 1982-94; computer cons. A.Z. Software Shop Inc., Garden City, N.Y., 1994-95; sys. acct. UN, N.Y.C., 1995-99; computer cons. AMP Consulting, Inc., 1999—. Mem. Women's Assn. of the Wichita Symphony, Allegro Movement Soc. of the Wichita Symphony. Recipient George Washington U. Alumni Svc. award, 1992. Mem. AAUW, Archeol. Inst. Am., Colo. Woman's Coll. Alumni Club, George Washington U. Alumni Club of N.Y.C. (past pres.). Republican. Presbyterian. Home and Office: Apt 1707 550 W Central Wichita KS 67203-4238

PALMER, ANN THERESE DARIN, lawyer; b. Detroit, Apr. 25, 1951; d. Americo and Theresa (Del Favero) Darin; m. Robert Towne Palmer, Nov. 9, 1974; children: Justin Darin, Christian Darin. BA, U. Notre Dame, 1973, MBA, 1975; JD, Loyola U., Chgo., 1978. Bar: Ill. 1978, U.S. Supreme Ct. 1981. Reporter Wall Street Jour., Detroit, 1974; freelancer Time Inc. Fin. Publs., Chgo., 1975-77; extern, Midwest regional solicitor U.S. Dept. Labor, 1976-78; tax atty. Esmark Inc., 1978; counsel Chgo. United, 1978-81; ind. contractor Legal Tax Rsch., 1981-89; fin. and legal news contbr. The Chgo. Tribune, 1991—, Bus. Week Chgo. Bur., 1991—, Automotive News, 1993-97, Crain's Chgo. Bus., 1994-2000. Mem. Woman's Athletic Club Chgo. Home: 873 Forest Hill Rd Lake Forest IL 60045-3905

PALMER, ARNOLD DANIEL, professional golfer; b. Youngstown, Pa., Sept. 10, 1929; s. Milfred Jerome and Doris M. Palmer; m. Winnie Walzer, Dec. 20, 1954 (dec. Nov. 1999); children: Peggy Palmer Wears, Amy Palmer Saunders. Student, Wake Forest Coll., LLD, 1970. Profl. golfer, 1954—; businessman, entrepreneur, 1960—. Nat. spokesman Pennzoil Petroleum Products, Sears Can., Rolex, Cadillac Motor Car, Verizon, Golf mag., Rayovac, Textron, Lexington Furniture, Office Depot, Cooper Tires, Callaway Golf, PNC Bank Corp., Home Depot, Microsoft, Sanford, Capital Mercury, KRB Seed, Encore Bank; nat. spokesman Invacare, GlaxoSmithKline; designer numerous golf courses. Author: Arnold Palmer's Golf Book, 1961, Portrait of a Professional Golfer, 1964, My Game and Yours, 1965, rev. edit., 1983, Situation Golf, 1970, Go for Broke, 1973, Arnold Palmer's Best 54 Holes of Golf, 1977, Arnold Palmer's Complete Book of Putting, 1986, Play Great Golf, 1987, (with Thomas Hauser) A Personal Journey, 1994, (with James Dodson) Arnold Palmer, A Golfer's Life, 1999, Playing by the Rules, 2002. With USCG, 1951-54. Winner over 90 major golf tournaments, 1955—, including Masters Championship, 1958, 60, 62, 64, U.S. Open, 1960, U.S. Amateur, 1954, Brit. Open, 1961, 62; recipient numerous golf awards including Bob Jones award U.S. Golf Assn., William D. Richardson award Golf Writers Assn. Am., Herb Graffis award Nat. Golf Found.; named AP Athlete of Decade, 1969, Sportsman of Yr. Sports Illustrated mag., 1960, Player of Yr. Profl. Golfers Assn., 1960, 62; Profl. Golfers Assn. Tour Money Leader, 1958, 60, 62, 63; elected to World Golf Hall of Fame, Profl. Golfers Assn. Hall of Fame. Mem. Latrobe (Pa.) Country Club, Laurel Valley Golf Club, Rolling Rock Club (Ligonier, Pa.), Bay Hill Club, Duquesne Club (Pitts.). Avocation: aviation. Home and Office: PO Box 52 Youngstown PA 15696-0052

PALMER, ARTHUR EUGENE, retired nursing home administrator; b. Newark, Nov. 23, 1923; s. Frederick A. and Grace (Miller) P.; m. Rosemary Louise Pierce, June 11, 1949; children: Christine, David. BA in Econs., Coll. Wooster, 1947; MBA, NYU, 1955. Traffic engr. N.J. Bell Tel., Newark, 1947-57; bus. mgr. Coll. of Wooster, Ohio, 1958-78, dir. gen. svcs., 1978-79; adminstr. Lima (Ohio) Convalscent Home, 1979-87, Allen County Health Care Ctr., Lima, 1988; nursing home cons., West Central, Ohio, 1988-98; ret. Nursing Home Cons., West Ctrl., 1998. Pres. Ohio Assn. Coll. Univ. Bus. Officers, 1971, Ohio Assn. Ednl. Buyers, 1973-74; com. chmn. Planning Sabbatical Leaves, 1975-78, Ea. Assn. Coll. and Univ. Bus. Officers. Health facility coord. United Way, Lima, 1975-78; fundraiser Lima Symphony Orch., 1974-85; elder Presbyn. Ch., 1949—, Sunday sch. tchr. and dept. supt., 1953-59, head usher, 1982-87; bd. dirs. Marimor Industries for MRDD, 1985-93; mem. advisi ng bd. Wooster Outdoor Ctr., 1970-79. With U.S. Army, 1943-45, ETO. Decorated Bronze Star. Mem. Allen County Diabetes League (pres. 1985-88), Kiwanis (sec. 1980-2000, Disting. sec. 1989, 92, 93, Kiwanian of Yr. 1995, tablet of honor 1998), Lima Men's Garden Club (Disting. Svc. award 1998). Republican. Avocations: gardening, travel, music, reading. Home: 2815 Lowell Ave Lima OH 45805-3032

PALMER, BEVERLY BLAZEY, psychologist, educator; b. Cleve., Nov. 22, 1945; d. Lawrence E. and Mildred M. Blazey; m. Richard C. Palmer, June 24, 1967; 1 child, Ryan Richard. PhD in Counseling Psychology, Ohio State U., 1972. Lic. clinical psychologist, Calif. Adminstrv. assoc. Ohio State U., Columbus, 1969-70; rsch. psychologist Health Svcs. Rsch. Ctr. UCLA, 1971-77; commr. pub. health L.A. County, 1978-81; pvt. practice clin. psychology Torrance, Calif., 1985—; prof. psychology Calif. State U., Dominguez Hills, 1973—. Reviewer manuscripts for numerous textbook pubs; contbr. numerous articles to profl. jours. Recipient Proclamation, County of LA, 1972, 1981, Fulbright scholarship, Malaysia, 2001, Fulbright Sr. Specialist award, 2002. Mem. Am. Psychol. Assn. Office: Calif State U Dominguez Hills Dept Psychology Carson CA 90747-0001

PALMER, BONITA ANN, physician, marriage and family therapist; b. Mineola, N.Y., Mar. 25, 1949; d. Donald Rich and Regina Batchelder Palmer. AB cum laude, Vassar Coll., 1971; MD, U. Vt., 1976; MA in Integral Counseling Psychology, Calif. Inst. Integral Studies, 1992; MDiv, Ch. Div. Sch. of the Pacific, 2002; diploma in Art Spiritual Direction, San Francisco Theological Seminary, 2001. Cert. in clin. interactive guided imagery, Reiki level II practitioner, cert. spiritual emergence syndromes. Counselor, advocate Vt. Women's Health Ctr., Burlington, 1973-74; resident physician San Francisco Gen. Hosp., 1976-78; staff physician Berkeley (Calif.) Women's Health Collective, 1978-80, 88-90; tng. in advanced clairvoyang counseling and psychic healing Psychic Horizons, San Francisco, 1985-87; pvt. practice MinAn Health Ctr., 1987-89, Holistic Gen. Medicine, San Francisco, 1989-97; staff physician St. Luke's Neighborhood Clinic, 1992-96; clin. facilty mem. family and cmty. medicine U. Calif., 1991—. Co-chmn, founder Commn. on Health and Healing Ministries, Episcopal Diocese Calif., 1998—; founding bd. dirs. Integrative Ctr. for Culture and Healing, St. Luke's Hosp., 1997—99, Lilly Endowment seminarian intern, 2001—02. Contbr. to book: Wolf Girls at Vassar: Lesbian and Gay Experience, 1993; contbr. articles to profl. publs. Bd. dirs. Bay Area Physicians for Human Rights, San Francisco, 1978-79; mem. Com. on the Status of Women, Nat. Episcopal Ch., 1991-97; bd. dirs., co-chair The Parsonage, Diocesian Gay/Lesbian Ministry Episcopal Diocese of Calif., San Francisco, 1989-91; alt. dep. to gen. conv. Episcopal Ch., 1997, 2000; facilitator, Formation for Healing Ministry, Diocese of Calif., 2002-. Fellow Am. Acad. Family Physicians; mem. Am. Assn. Pastoral Counselors, Assn. for Transpersonal Psychology, Internat. Assn. for Guided Imagery, Spiritual Dirs. Internat., Calif. Assn. Lesbian Physicians (founding mem.), Am. Holistic Med. Assn. (charter mem.). Democrat. Avocations: spiritual healing. Home and Office: 3667 A 20th St San Francisco CA 94110 E-mail: bonita.ann.palmer@ecunet.com.

PALMER, BRADLEY BERAN, sportscaster; b. Madison, Wis., July 21, 1940; s. Robert and Cerise (Beran) P.; m. Patricia Carey, Oct. 19, 1974; two children. BS in Comms., U. Ill., 1963. Officer USN, U.S.S. Shangri-La, 1963-65; news anchor, reporter KGLO-AM/TV, Mason City, Iowa, 1965; news reporter WTVO-TV, Rockford, Ill., 1965-66; news writer, prodr. WGN-AM/TV, Chgo., 1966-68; sports dir. WBBM-AM, 1968-85; sports anchor, reporter WLS-TV, 1985—. Named Ill. Sportscaster of Yr., Nat. Sportscaster & Sportwriters Assn., 1980, 82, 86, 87, 88, 93, 95, 98.

PALMER, BRIAN EUGENE, lawyer; b. Mpls., May 16, 1948; s. Eugene Philip and Virginia Breeze (Rolfshus) P.; m. Julia Washburn Morrison, Dec. 29, 1972; 1 child, Julia Hunter. AB, Brown U., 1970; JD, William Mitchell Coll. of Law, 1974. Bar: Minn. 1974, U.S. Dist. Ct. Minn. 1975, U.S. Dist. Ct. (ea. dist.) Wis. 2001, U.S. Ct. Appeals (8th cir.) 1980, U.S. Ct. Fed. Claims 1984, U.S. Supreme Ct. 1980. Asst. pub. defender Hennepin County Pub. Defender, Mpls., 1974-78; assoc. Dorsey & Whitney LLP, 1978-82, ptnr., 1983—. Home: 1190 Lyman Ave Wayzata MN 55391-9671 Office: Dorsey & Whitney LLP 50 South Sixth St Ste 1500 Minneapolis MN 55402-1498 E-mail: palmer.brian@dorseylaw.com.

PALMER, CHRIS, professional football coach; b. Brewster, N.Y., Sept. 23, 1949; m. Donna Palmer; children: Mark, Kristin. BS, MS, So. Conn. State U. Asst. coach U. Conn., 1972-75; wide receivers coach Lehigh U., 1975-76; offensive coord. Colgate U., 1976-82; offensive line coach Montreal Concords, 1983-84; coach receivers, quarterback coach, offensive coord. N.J. Generals, 1984-86; head coach U. New Haven, 1986-87, Boston U., 1988-89; coach wide receivers Houston Oilers, 1990-92; with New Eng. Patriots, 1994-97, quarterback coach, 1996-97; offensive coord. Jacksonville Jaguars, 1997-99; head coach Cleveland Browns, 1999—2001; offensive coord. Houston Texans, 2002—. Office: The Houston Texans Two Reliant Park Houston TX 77054*

PALMER, CRUISE, newspaper editor; b. Kansas City, Kans., Apr. 9, 1917; s. Thomas Potter and Margaret Scroggs (McFadden) P.; m. Dorraine Humphreys, Sept. 7, 1946; children: Thomas Cruise, Martha D. Sprague. BS in Journalism, Kans. State U., 1938. With Kansas City (Mo.) Star, 1938—, news editor, 1963-64, mng. editor, 1965-66; exec. editor and bd. Star and Times, 1967—78, cons., 1978—. Dir. Purtec Systems, Inc. Mem. bd. govs. Am. Royal Live Stock and Horse Show Assn., 1967-91; bd. dirs. ARC, 1978-91, Kansas City Mayor's Corps Progress, 1978-91; found. trustee Kans. State U.; trustee Kansas City Sister Cities Commn., 1978-91. Served to lt. (j.g.) USNR, 1943-46. Recipient Distinguished Service award Kans. State U., 1967; First Place award Pro-Am. Southgate Open Golf Tournament, 1973; Second Place award Pro-Am. Hawaiian Open, 1973, 85; Third Place, 1981; First Place award Jim Colbert Celebrity Tournament, 1981, First Place Team award Kansas City area Am. Cancer Soc. Golf Tournament, 1986. Mem. Am. Soc. Newspaper Editors, Soc. Profl. Journalists, Kansas City Sr. Golf Assn., Kansas City Press Club (pres. 1953-54, 64-65, permanent trustee, pres. scholarship found. 1989), Kansas City Club, Chiefs Red Coat Club, Milburn Golf and Country Club, Beta Theta Pi (Greater Kansas City Beta of Yr. 1980). Episcopalian (former vestryman and lay reader). Home: Lakeview Retirement Village 14100 W 90th Ter Apt 504 Lenexa KS 66215-5430 Office: 1729 Grand Ave Kansas City MO 64108-1413

PALMER, CURTIS DWAYNE, cardiopulmonary practitioner, microbiologist, researcher, builder; b. Leesville, La., Aug. 5, 1947; s. Curtis and Freda Elaine (Franklin) P.; children: Derrick Mitchell, Elizabeth Merritt. BSc, Northwestern U., Natchitoches, La., 1971; MSC, Northwestern U., 1972; cardiopulmonary diploma, U. Chgo., 1975. Registered respiratory therapist. From dir. pulmonary rsch. to rsch. assoc. La. State U., Shreveport, 1972-75, 79-81; pres., chmn. Pulmonary Care Assocs., 1975-79; med. student St. Lucia U., El Paso, Tex., 1981-83; supr. pulmonary svcs. Glenwood Reg. Med. Ctr., West Monroe, La., 1987-93; v.p. DeBlieux-Palmer Ltd., Natchitoches, 1994—. Contract adminstr. Therapeutic Svcs., Shreveport, 1986-90; regional mgr. TriTek Industries, Inc., 1987-93; pres., chmn. Dwayne Palmer Realty Inc., Shreveport, 1974-80; faculty Inst. Microbiology and Pulmonary Rsch., La. Sch. Medicine, Shreveport, Northwestern U. Contbr. articles to profl. jours. Bd. dirs. March of Dimes, Shreveport, 1977; realtor Bd. Realtors, Shreveport, 1975-82, Natchitoches, 1995—; contractor La. Bd. Licensing Contractors, 1976—, Palmer Constrn. Co., Inc., 1993—. Mem. Nat. Bd. Respiratory Care, Am. Assn. Respiratory Care, Nat. Assn. Home Builders, La. Soc. Respiratory Care (chmn. judiciary bd. 1976), Soc. Critical Care Medicine, Nat. Bd. Realtors, Shreveport-Bossier Bd. Realtors, Kappa Sigma (Epsilon chpt.). Republican. Methodist. Avocations: scuba diving, tennis, pilot. Home: 14150 Azalea Park Ave Ste B Baton Rouge LA 70816-1106

PALMER, DAVE RICHARD, retired military officer, academic administrator; b. Ada, Okla., May 31, 1934; s. David Furman and Lorena Marie (Clardy) P.; m. LuDelia Clemmer, Apr. 13, 1957; children: Allison, J. Kersten. BS, U.S. Military Acad., 1956; MA in History, Duke U., 1966; postgrad., Army War Coll., 1972-73; PhD (hon.), Duke U., 1990. Commd. U.S. Army, 1956, advanced through grades to lt. gen.; mem. faculty dept. history U.S. Mil. Acad., 1966-69; mem. staff (Pentagon), 1973-76, Joint Chiefs of Staff, 1979-81; comdr. Baumholder Mil. Community, W. Ger., 1981-83; dep. comdt. Command and Gen. Staff Coll., Ft. Leavenworth, Kans., 1983-85; comdg. gen. 1st Armored Div., W.Ger., 1985-86; supt. U.S. Mil. Acad., 1986-91, ret., 1991; pres. Walden U., 1995-99; CEO Walden Corp., 1999-2000. Author: The River and the Rock, 1969, The Way of the Fox, 1975, Summons of the Trumpet, 1978, 1794-America, Its Army, and The Birth of the Nation, 1994, First in War, 2000, Provide for the Common Defense, 2001. Bd. dirs. Walden U., 1992-2001. Decorated Legion of Merit (3); Bronze Star (2), D.S.M.(2). Mem. Assn. U.S. Army, Armor Assn., Mil. History, Soc. Cin. E-mail: lucpalmer4@cs.com.

PALMER, DAVID GILBERT, lawyer; b. Lakewood, N.J., Jan. 10, 1945; s. Robert Dayton and Lois (Gilbert) P.; m. Susan Edmundson Walsh, Aug. 17, 1968; children: Jonathan, Megan. AB, Johns Hopkins U., 1967; JD, U. Colo., 1970. Bar: Colo. 1970, U.S. Dist. Ct. Colo. 1970, U.S. Ct. Appeals (9th and 10th cirs.) 1970, U.S. Supreme Ct. 1970. Ptnr., chmn. litigation dept. Holland & Hart, Denver, 1970-87, Gibson, Dunn & Crutcher, Denver, 1987-97; ptnr. Zevnik, Horton, Palmer, 1997-2001, Greenberg Taurig LLP, Denver, 2001—. Chmn. N.W. region Am. Heart Assn., Dallas, 1986—, bd. dirs., 1986—, sec., 1990—, nat. chmn., 1992-93; pres., bd. dirs. Colo. Heart Assn., Denver, 1974; bd. dirs. C.H. Kempe Nat. Ctr. for Prevention of Child Abuse, Denver, 1984-90, pres., 1989-90; bd. dirs. Goodwill Industries, Denver, 1981-84. Mem. ABA, Colo. Bar Assn., Denver Law Club, Univ. Club, Mile High Club. Home: 3120 Ramshorn Dr Castle Rock CO 80104-9073 Office: Greenberg Taurig 1200 17th St Ste 2400 Denver CO 80202 E-mail: palmerdg@gtlaw.com.

PALMER, DAVID SCOTT, political scientist, educator; b. Boston, July 16, 1937; s. Walter S. and Jean (Stuart) P.; m. Sarah Crawford, 1966 (dec. Nov. 1985); children: Walter Scott, Henry Crawford, Asa MacAdam; m. Diane Nagel, 1998. BA in Internat. Rels. cum laude, Dartmouth Coll., 1959; MA in Hispanic Am. Studies, Stanford U., 1962; PhD in Comparative Govt., Cornell U., 1973. Vol. leader Peace Corps, Peru, 1962-64; asst. dean freshmen, asst. to dir. admissions Dartmouth Coll., Hanover, N.H., 1964-68; from instr. to asst. prof. dept. govt. Bowdoin Coll., 1972-76; professorial lectr. Sch. Advanced Internat. Studies Johns Hopkins U., Washington, 1977-88; assoc. dean for programs Fgn. Svc. Inst., Dept. State, 1984-88, chair Latin Am. and Caribbean studies, 1976-88; prof. polit. sci. Boston U., 1988—, prof. internat. rels., 1990—, assoc. chair undergrad. studies internat. rels. dept., 1997-99, chair dept. polit. sci., 1998-2001. Vis. lectr. Princeton U., 1978—79, Georgetown U., 1985; vis. scholar Inter-Am. Dialogue, 2001—02. Author: Peru: The Authoritarian Tradition, 1980, (with Kevin Middlebrook) Military Government and Political Development: Lessons from Peru, 1975 (with Robert Wesson and others) The Latin American Military Institution, 1985; editor, contbr.: Shining Path of Peru, 1992, 2d edit., 1994; contbr. chpts. to books, articles and revs. to profl. jours. Recipient Meritorious Honor award U.S. Dept. of State, 1981; Daniel Webster nat. scholar, 1955-59; Edward John Noble Found. leadership grantee 1959-62; Fulbright fellow, 1998. Mem. Latin Am. Studies Assn. (exec. com. 1983-86), New Eng. Coun. Latin Am. Studies (exec. com. 1989-98, 2000—, pres. 1993-94), Interam. Coun. of Washington (pres. 1978-79), Phi Beta Delta, Phi Kappa Phi, Sigma Delta Pi. Home: 69 Waverley St Belmont MA 02478-1958 Office: Boston U 152 Bay State Rd Boston MA 02215-1501 E-mail: dspalmer@bu.edu.

PALMER, DEBORAH JEAN, lawyer; b. Williston, N.D., Oct. 25, 1947; d. Everett Edwin and Doris Irene (Harberg) P.; m. Kenneth L. Rich, Mar. 29, 1980; children: Andrew, Stephanie. BA, Carleton Coll., 1969; JD cum laude, Northwestern U., 1973. Bar: Minn. 1973, U.S. Dist. Ct. Minn. 1973, U.S. Ct. Appeals (8th cir.) 1975, U.S. Supreme Ct. 1978, U.S. Ct. Appeals (11th cir.) 1999. Econ. analyst Harris Trust & Savs. Bank, Chgo., 1969-70; assoc. Robins, Kaplan, Miller & Ciresi LLP, Mpls., 1973-79, ptnr., 1979—. Trustee Carleton Coll., 1984-88; mem. bd. religious edn. Plymouth Congl. Ch., 1992-95; bd. dirs. Mpls. YWCA, 1996-99; mem. Dist. Minn. Civil Justice Reform Act Adv. Group, 1990-93; bd. dirs. RKM&C Found. Edn., Pub. Health & Social Justice, 1999—. Mem. ABA, Minn. Bar Assn., Minn. Women Lawyers Assn. (sec. 1976-78), Minn. Fed. Bar Assn. (chpt. bd. dirs. 1996-98), Hennepin County Bar Assn., Hennepin County Bar Found. (bd. dirs. 1978-81), Carleton Coll. Alumni Assn. (bd. dirs. 1978-82, sec. 1980-82), Women's Assn. of Minn. Orch. (bd. dirs. 1980-85, treas. 1981-83). Home: 1787 Colfax Ave S Minneapolis MN 55403-3008 Office: Robins Kaplan Miller & Ciresi LLP 800 Lasalle Ave Ste 2800 Minneapolis MN 55402-2015 E-mail: djpalmer@rkmc.com.

PALMER, DENISE, publishing executive; V.p. strategy and fin. Chgo. Tribune; now pres., CEO CLTV, Oakbrook, Ill. Office: Baltimore Sun PO BOX 1377 501 N Calvert St Baltimore MD 21278-0001*

PALMER, DENNIS DALE, lawyer; b. Alliance, Nebr., Apr. 30, 1945; s. Vernon D. Palmer and Marie E. (Nelson) Fellers; m. Rebecca Ann Turner, Mar. 23, 1979; children: Lisa Marie, Jonathan Paul. BA, U. Mo., 1967, JD, 1970. Bar: Mo. 1970, U.S. Dist. Ct. (we. dist.) Mo. 1970, U.S. Ct. Appeals (8th and 10th cirs.) 1973, U.S. Supreme Ct. 1980. Staff atty. Legal Aid Soc. Western Mo., Kansas City, 1970-73; assoc. Shughart, Thomson & Kilroy, P.C., 1973-76, ptnr., bd. dirs., 1976—. Contbr. articles on franchise and employment law to legal jours. Bd. dirs., chmn. legal assts. adv. bd. Avila Coll., Kansas City, 1984-87. 2d lt. U.S. Army, 1970. Mem. ABA (litigation com. 1980, forum com. on franchising 1987), Mo. Bar Assn. (antitrust com. 1975—, civil practice com. 1975—), Kansas City Bar Assn. (chmn. franchise law com. 1987—), Univ. Club. Avocations: jogging, golf, tennis, outdoor activities, reading. Home: 13100 Canterbury Rd Leawood KS 66209-1700 Office: Shughart Thomson & Kilroy 12 Wyandotte Plz 120 W 12th St Fl 17 Kansas City MO 64105-1902

PALMER, DONALD CURTIS, interdenominational missionary society executive; b. Nelson, Minn., Oct. 8, 1934; s. Roy August Adn Cora (Bergner) P.; m. Dorothy Mae Nordquist, Mar. 16, 1962; children: Jean Marie, John Eric. Student, U. Minn., 1952-55; BS in Bible, Briercrest Bible Coll., Caronport, Can., 1958; MA in Missions, Trinity Divinity Sch., Deerfield, Ill., 1967; D in Ministry, Trinity Divinity Sch., 1989. Missionary Colombia GMU Internat., Kansas City, Mo., 1959-71, dir. evangelism, 1969-71, field sec. Latin Am., 1971-73, v.p. field ministries for Latin Am., 1973-85, v.p. research and strategy, 1985-92; gen. dir. Am. Missionary Fellowship, Villanova, Pa., 1992—2002. Vis. prof. Grace Coll. of the Bible, Omaha, 1982—92; mem. Frontier People's Com., 1985—92, Evang. Missiological Soc., 1991—. Author: Explosion of People Evangelism, 1974; (with others) Dynamic Religious Movements, 1978, Managing Conflict Creatively, 1990. Republican. Baptist. Avocations: golf, tennis, hiking. Home: 200 Cohasset Ln West Chester PA 19380-6504 Office: Am Missionary Fellowship 672 Conestoga Rd Villanova PA 19085-1499 E-mail: amfpalmer@aol.com. *The greatest inner quality that a person can possess is a thankful, grateful spirit.*

PALMER, DOUGLAS S., JR. lawyer; b. Peoria, Ill., Mar. 15, 1945; AB cum laude, Yale U., 1966; JD cum laude, Harvard U., 1969. Bar: Wash. 1969. Mem. Foster Pepper & Shefelman PLLC, Seattle, 1975—2002, Hillis Clark Martin & Peterson, P.S., Seattle, 2002—. Office: Hillis Clark Martin & Peterson PS 500 Galland Bldg 1221 Second Ave Seattle WA 98101-2925

PALMER, EARL A. ophthalmologist, educator; b. Winchester, Ohio, July 2, 1940; m. Carolyn Mary Clark; children: Andrea, Aaron, Genevieve. BA, Ohio State U., 1962; MD, Duke U., 1966. Diplomate Am. Bd. Pediatrics, Am. Bd. Ophthalmology. Resident in pediatrics U. Colo. Med. Ctr., Denver, 1966-68; resident in ophthalmology Oreg. Health Scis. U., Portland, 1971-74; fellow Baylor Coll. Medicine, Houston, 1974-75; asst. prof. Pa. State U., Hershey, 1975-79; prof. Oreg. Health Scis. U., 1979—. Chmn. Multicenter Outcome Study of Retinopathy of Prematurity; eye alignment specialist. Contbr. articles to profl. jours. Fellow: Am. Acad. Ophthalmology (Honor award); mem.: Am. Assn. Pediatric Ophthalmology and Strabismus (pres. 1996—97). Avocation: golf. Office: Casey Eye Inst 3375 SW Terwilliger Blvd Portland OR 97201-4197

PALMER, EDWARD LEWIS, banker; b. N.Y.C., Aug. 12, 1917; s. William and Cecelia (Tierney) P.; m. Margaret Preston, Jan. 5, 1940; children: Edward Preston, Jane Lewis. AB, Brown U., 1938. With N.Y. Trust Co., 1941-59, v.p., 1952-59; with Citibank, N.A., N.Y.C., 1959-82, sr. v.p., 1962-65, exec. v.p., 1965-70, dir., chmn. exec. com., 1970-82; pres. Mill Neck Group, Inc., 1982. Bd. dirs.SunResorts Ltd., FondElec Group Inc.; dir. emeritus Corning Inc.; trustee emeritus Mut. N.Y. Trustee emeritus Met. Mus. Art, Brown U. Served to lt. comdr. USNR, 1942-46. Mem. Phi Gamma Delta. Home: Horseshoe Rd Mill Neck NY 11765 Office: 425 Park Ave New York NY 10022-3506

PALMER, FLOYD HUGH, retired secondary school educator; b. Houston, Feb. 17, 1932; s. Walter Leslie Palmer and Leona Lucile McGowen; m. Mildred Elsie Sudds (div.); children: Floyd Steven, Keith David, Toni Lynn. Student, San Jacinto Coll.; degree in criminal justice, Cleve. CC. Tchr. Rockvale (Tex.) Ind. Sch. Dist.; policeman City of Everett, Wash.; with Exec. Security Sys., Austin, Tex. Author: Guam Hold Out, 1953. Coach Little League, Everett; com. chmn. Boy Scouts Am., Houston; first aid instr. USNR, Everett; police officer's assoc.; counselor elem. sch. and youth orgns., Houston. Staff sgt. USAF, 1950—55, PTO. Recipient Order of the Arrow, Boy Scouts Am., Houston. Mem.: VFW (sgt. at arms), Elks. Home: 350 W Bell Ave Rockdale TX 76567

PALMER, GARY ANDREW, portfolio manager; b. Stamford, Conn., Dec. 30, 1953; s. Andrew and Edna Balz (Brogan) P.; m. Suzanne Branyon, Oct. 10, 1981; children: Gregory Allen, Kimberly Lynn. BS in Bus. Adminstrn., U. Vt., 1977; MBA, U. N.C., 1979. Sr. fin. analyst Carolina Power and Light Co., Raleigh, NC, 1979—80; dir. fin. planning and analysis Fed. Home Loan Mortgage Corp., Washington, 1980—85; sr. v.p. capital markets Imperial Corp. of Am., San Diego, 1985—90; sr. v.p., treas. Pacific 1st Fin. Corp., Seattle, 1990—92, Gentral Capital Corp., Seattle, 1993—95; CFO So. Pacific Funding Corp., Lake Oswego, Oreg., 1995—97; pvt. practice, 1998—99; CFO FiNet.com, Inc., San Ramon, Calif., 1999—2000; exec. v.p. Capital Mkts., LoanCity.com, San Jose, 2001; dir. fin. engring. Fannie Mae, Washington, 2002—.

PALMER, GARY STEPHEN, health services administrator; b. Murphy, N.C., Jan. 19, 1949; s. Bruce and Mary Frances (Patterson) P.; m. Kathleen Hart Middleton, June 12, 1976; children: Eric S., Brian S. BS in Bus. Adminstrn., U. N.C., 1971; MHA, Baylor U., 1982. Commd. U.S. Army, 1972, advanced through grades to lt. col., 1990; dir. program budget Letterman Army Med. Ctr., San Francisco, 1979-80; adminstrv. resident Womack Community Hosp., Fayetteville, N.C., 1981-82, ambulatory healthcare adminstr., 1982-83, asst. adminstr. profl. svcs., 1983-85; ambulatory healthcare adminstr. USA Health Svcs., San Antonio, 1985-88; COO U.S. Army Den Activity, Killeen, Tex., 1988-91; dir. managed care Tripler Army Med. Ctr., Honolulu, 1991-93; inspector gen. Womack Army Med. Ctr., Ft. Bragg, N.C., 1993-94; assoc. dir. exec. master's program Sch. Pub. Health U. N.C., Chapel Hill, 1994—, dir. network devel. and external affairs, 1996-99. Mem. Eastern N.C. Regent's Adv. Coun., 1997-2000. Fellow Am. Coll. Healthcare Execs. (army regent's adv. coun. 1988-92); mem. Med. Group Mgmt. Assn., Career Activities Network, Sch. Pub. Health , Ret. Officers Assn., Pi Kappa Phi. Home: 103 William White Ct Carrboro NC 27510-4120 Office: U NC Sch Pub Health CB 7411 Dept Health Policy Adminstn Chapel Hill NC 27599-7411 E-mail: emp@unc.edu.

PALMER, GEORGE THOMAS, artist; b. Buffalo, Mar. 23, 1925; s. George Joseph and Margaret Alice P.; m. Gloria Theresa Palmer, Oct. 17, 1953; children: Lisa Haug, Maria Buscemi, Beth Palmer, Mark Palmer, Eric Palmer. Cert. art, Albright Art Sch., 1949; studied with Robert Brachman, Art Students League, 1949-52; BFA, SUNY, Buffalo, 1969. Portrait painter Little Studio, N.Y.C., 1953-56; operator George Palmer Gallery, Buffalo, 1958-65; instr. art D'Youville Coll., 1962-72, Genesee C.C., Batavia, N.Y., 1965-70; operator George Palmer Studio, Buffalo, 1965—. Mem. faculty Erie County C.C., D'Youville Coll., Genesee C.C.; lectr. in field; hon. exhibiting mem. Buffalo Soc. Artists. One-man shows include Art Ctr. Williamsville, N.Y., 1977, Kenan Ctr., Lockport, N.Y., 1980, Patterson Gallery, Westfield, N.Y., 1981, Washington Arts Club, 1995; exhibited in groups shows at Art Dialogue Gallery, 1996, 97, others; featured in article Artists Mag., We. N.Y. C. of C. Mag. Active Williamsville Art Soc. and Fine Arts League; founder Kenmore Art Soc.; mem. Carnegie Cultural Ctr., We. N.Y. Artists Group; mem. arts com. City Hall, Buffalo. With USN, 1943-46. Recipient Best of Show award Art 1961 Exhbn., The Promising Young Realist award Art 1961 Exhbn., Gold medal Annual Fine Arts League Show, Jr. League Buffalo Soc. Artists Annual, The Promising Young Artists award Jr. League Buffalo Soc. Artists Annual.

PALMER, HARVEY JOHN, dean; b. N.Y.C., Apr. 3, 1946; s. Harvey Anthony and Pearl Edna (Weber) P.; m. Donna Mary Partigan, July 11, 1966; children— Harvey D., Angeline, Thomas BSC.E., U. Rochester, 1967; PhD in Chem. Engring., U. Wash., 1971. Lic. profl. engr., N.Y. Asst. prof. chem. engring. U. Rochester, N.Y., 1971-77, assoc. prof., 1977-84, prof., 1984-00, assoc. dean for grad. studies, 1983-89, chair dept. chem. engring., 1990-00; dean Kate Gleason Coll. Engring. Rochester Inst. Tech., 2000—. Cons. Pfaudler Co., Rochester, 1978-79, Eastman Kodak Co., Rochester, 1982-92, Helios Corp., Mumford, N.Y., 1983-91, Boehringer Mannheim Corp., Indpls., 1993; bd. dirs. Transmation Inc., Rochester. Contbr. articles to profl. jours. Mem. sch. bd. Honeoye Falls-Lima Central Schs., N.Y., 1983-92, pres., 1988-90. Recipient Undergrad. Teaching award Coll. Engring., U. Rochester, 1979, 82 Mem. Am. Inst. Chem. Engrs. (sec. Rochester sect. 1976-77, chair 1998-00), Am. Chemical Soc., Tau Beta Pi, Sigma Xi. Office: Rochester Inst Tech Coll Engring Rochester NY 14623-5603 E-mail: hjpeen@rit.edu.

PALMER, HUBERT BERNARD, dentist, retired military officer; b. San Antonio, Sept. 6, 1912; s. Hubert Victor and Rosemary (Garvey) P.; student St. Mary's U., 1931-34; D.D.S., Baylor U., 1938; postgrad. George Washington U., 1946-47, U. Md., 1950-53; m. Elizabeth Harriet McAlary, Aug. 16, 1945; children— Hubert Bernard II, Robert Leldon. Commd. 1st lt. USAAF, 1938, advanced through grades to col. USAF, 1971; chief dept. dental research U.S. Army, 1946-50; chief dept. exptl. dentistry, USAF, 1953-54, chief research dentistry div. 1954-56; command dental surgeon, 1958-59, 63-65, 65-68; dental staff officer, 1959-62, dir. dental services, 1968-71; dir. Eastside Dental Clinic San Antonio Met. Health Dist., 1972-81; dir. Mirasol Dental Clinic, 1982-83; clin. asst. prof. U. Tex. Dental Sch., San Antonio, 1973-76. Decorated Legion of Merit, Commendation medal First Oak Leaf Cluster, Meritorious Service medal. Fellow AAAS; mem. Am. Dental Assn., Internat. Assn. Dental Research, Soc. Gen. Microbiology, Am. Soc. Microbiology, Omicron Kappa Upsilon. Contbr. articles to profl. jours. Research reduction decalcification tooth enamel. Home: 6115 Forest Timber St San Antonio TX 78240-3357

PALMER, IRENE SABELBERG, university dean and educator emeritus, nurse, researcher, historian; b. Franklin, N.J., May 28, 1923; d. John Joseph and May (Heiser) Sabelberg. BS, N.J. State Tchrs. Coll., 1945; diploma, Jersey City Med. Center Sch. Nursing, 1945; MA, NYU, 1951, PhD, 1963. Edn. dir. Diploma Schs. Nursing, N.J., Mass., 1948-52; edn. dir. Glenn Dale (Md.) Hosp., D.C. Dept. Pub. Health, 1956, dir. nursing svc. and edn., 1956-61; assoc. clin. prof. nursing Georgetown U., 1960-61; USPHS trainee, 1961-62; assoc. chief nursing svc. for rsch. VA Hosp., San Francisco, 1963-64; rsch. nurse cons. HEW, USPHS, Div. Nursing, Nursing Rsch. Field Center, 1964-66; asst. dean, assoc. prof. nursing U. Colo. Sch. Nursing, Denver, 1966-68; dean, prof. nursing Boston U. Sch. Nursing, 1968-74; prof. Hahn Sch. Nursing, U. San Diego, 1974-91, prof. emeritus, 1991—, dean, 1974-87, dean emeritus, 1988—. Lectr. Clasical Alliance of the western States, Uskudar, Turkey, 1994, Italy, 1995. Editor: Nursing Clinics of North America, 1970; Contbr. articles to profl. jours. Served to capt. Nurse Corps U.S. Army, 1953-56. Internat. Nightingale scholar; Nat. Health Svc. fellow; recipient Excellence in Nursing Scholarship award Orgn. Nurse Execs., 1993. Fellow Nat. League Nursing (bd. visitors 1977-87), Am Acad. Nursing; mem. ANA, Am. Assn. History Nursing, Am. Assn. Colls. Nursing (hon.), Boston U. Nursing Archives, German Rsch. Assn. (pres. 1995), Sigma Theta Tau (Leadership award Zeta Mu chpt. 1986, Excellence in Nursing award 1991).

PALMER, JAMES DANIEL, information technology educator; b. Washington, Mar. 8, 1930; s. Martin Lyle and Sarah Elizabeth (Hall) P.; m. Margret Kupka, June 21, 1952; children: Stephen Robert, Daniel Lee, John Keith. AA, Fullerton Jr. Coll., 1953; BS (Alumni scholar), U. Calif., Berkeley, 1955, MS, 1957; PhD, U. Okla., 1963; DPS (hon.), Regis Coll., Denver, 1977. Chief engr. Motor vehicle and Illumination Lab. U. Calif., Berkeley, 1955-57; assoc. prof. U. Okla., Norman, 1957-63, prof., 1963-66, asst. to dir. Rsch. Inst., 1960-63, cons. Rsch. Inst., 1966-69, dir. Sch. Elec. Engring., 1963-66, dir. Systems Rsch. Center, 1964-66; dean sci. and engring., prof. elec. engring. Union Coll., Schenectady, 1966-71; pres. Met. State Coll., Denver, 1971-78; rsch. and spl. programs adminstr. Dept. Transp., Washington, 1978-79; v.p., gen. mgr. rsch. and devel. div. Mech. Tech., Inc., Latham, N.Y., 1979-82; exec. v.p. J.J. Henry Co., Inc., Moorestown, N.J., 1982-85; BDM internat. prof. info. tech. George Mason U., Fairfax, Va., 1985-95, prof. emeritus, 1995—; software cons., 1995—. Bd. dirs. J.J. Henry Co., Inc.; cons. Sym Mgmt. Co., Boston, Higher Edn. Exec. Assocs., Denver, PERI, Princeton; adj. prof. U. Colo. Co-author: (with A.P. Sage) Software Systems Engineering, (with Aseltine, Beam and Sage) Introduction to Computer Systems, Analysis, Design and Application. Bd. dirs., exec. v.p. adv. com. U.S.A. Vols. for Internat. Tech. Assistance, 1967-83, exec. v.p., 1970-71, chmn. exec. com.; trustee, vice chmn. Nat. Commn. on Coop. Edn.; mem. exec. policy bd. Alaska Natural Gas Pipeline, 1978-79; trustee Auraria Higher Edn. Program, Denver; mem. Fulbright fellow Selection Com., Colo.; bd. mgrs., mem. exec. com. Hudson-Mohawk Assn. Colls. and Univs., trustee, chmn. bd., 1970-71; adv. com. USCG Acad., 1972-82, chmn. adv. com., 1979-82; mem. Colo. Gov.'s Sci. and Tech. Adv. Council; pres. Denver Cath. Community Services Bd.; mem. Archdiocesan Catholic Charities and Community Services; mem. bd. U. Okla. Rsch. Inst.; mem. adv. com. Mile-Hi Red Cross. With USMC, 1950-51. Case-Western Res. Centennial scholar, 1981; recipient U.S. Coast Guard award and medal for meritorious pub. service, 1983 Fellow IEEE (exec. and adminstrv. coms., v.p. long-range planning and finance, chmn. com. on large scale systems, Joseph E. Wahl Outstanding Career Achievement award 1993, Millennium medal 2000); mem. Systems, Man and Cybernetics Soc. (pres., Outstanding Contbns. award 1981), alumni assns. U. Calif. and U. Okla., Inst. Internat. Edn. (bd. dir. Rocky Mt. sect.), Soc. Naval Architects and Marine Engrs., Am. Soc. Engring. Edn., Am. Mil. Engrs., N.Y. Acad. Sci., Navy League, Sigma Xi, Eta Kappa Nu, Pi Mu Epsilon, Alpha Gamma Sigma. Home: 860 Cashew Way Fremont CA 94536-2646 Office: George Mason U Sch of Info Tech & Engring Fairfax VA 22030 E-mail: jdpalmer@ix.netcom.com.

PALMER, JAMES DANIEL, protective services official; b. Oklahoma City, Aug. 11, 1936; s. Athol Ford and Marjorie Lorraine (Ward) P.; m. Gail Dorothy Myers, June 1954 (div. Sept. 1956); 1 child, James Douglas; m. Gloria Jean West, Dec. 14, 1963; children: Diana Lorraine, Elana Louise, Sheri Francis. BA in Police Sci., San Jose (Calif.) State U., 1963, BA in Psychology, 1964; MPA, Golden Gate U., 1972. Cert. Calif. police officers standards and tng. Asst. foreman Hunts Foods, Inc., Hayward, Calif., 1959-64; spl. investigator Dept. A.B.C. State of Calif., Oakland, 1964-67; criminal inspector Contra Costa County Dist. Atty., Martinez, Calif., 1967-72, lt. of inspectors, 1972-92; ret., 1992. Pres. Contra Costa County Peace Officers, Richmond, 1974-75; past v.p. Contra Costa County Dist. Atty's Inv. Assn., Martinez, 1971, tng. officer, 1990-92. Contbr. articles to profl. jours. Past pres. South Hayward (Calif.) Dem. Club, 1976, 77, San Leandro (Calif.) Dems., 1975; mem. Gov's Law Enforcement Adv. Commn., Sacramento, Calif., 1972-76, Calif. Dem. Coun., 1972-73; rev. Am. Fellowship Protestant Ch., 1990—, min., 1990—. With USAF, 1955-58. Avocations: stocks, bonds, real estate, family, church. Home: 2788 Sydney Way Castro Valley CA 94546-2738

PALMER, JAMES EDWARD, public relations executive; b. Evansville, Ind., July 30, 1935; s. James Edward and Verble (Hearin) P. BA in English, N.Y.U., 1955. Reporter Evansville Courier, 1955-59; non-fiction editor Cosmopolitan mag., N.Y.C., 1959-61, exec. editor, 1961-65; editor Mag. Mgmt. Co., Inc., 1971-72; editor-in-chief Liberty mag., N.Y.C., 1972-73; dir. mag. and book dept. Carl Byoir & Assos., 1973-76; corp. public relations dir. Macmillan, Inc., 1977-80; pres. James Palmer Assos., 1980-88, The Palmer Group, Houston, 1988—. Mem. Sigma Chi. Office: PO Box 90422 Houston TX 77290-0422

PALMER, JANICE MAUDE, lawyer; b. Greeley, Colo., Sept. 7, 1951; d. William L. and Cleo E. (White) P.; children: Emilie Halladay, Eileen Halladay, Michael W. Halladay III. BS, Ariz. State U., 1979, JD, 1982. Bar: Ariz. 1983, U.S. Dist. Ct. Ariz. 1983, U.S. Ct. Appeals (9th cir.) 1985. Assoc. Law Office of Guy Buckley, Mesa, Ariz., 1983-86, Slater & Santiquida, Mesa, 1986-89; pvt. practice Phoenix, 1989-92, Mesa, 1992—. Democrat. Office: 2111 E Baseline Rd Ste F-8 Tempe AZ 85283-1519

PALMER, JEFFERY DEAN, systems engineer, consultant; b. Monroe, La., Apr. 11, 1960; s. Kenneth Dean and Martha Jean Palmer; m. Sharman Ann Taylor. BSEE, La. State U., Baton Rouge, 1979—83. Registered profl. engr., Tex., 1989, EIT La., 1983, cert. reliability engr., Am. Soc. for Quality, 1998. Engr. General Dynamics, Fort Worth, Tex., 1983—90, Japan, 1991—92; sys. engr. sr. staff Lockheed Martin, Fort Worth, Tex., 1993—. Mem.: Am. Soc. for Quality. Avocation: guitar playing. Home: 228 Valley Ranch Rd Weatherford TX 76087 Office: Lockheed Martin 1000 Lockheed Blvd Fort Worth TX 76108 Personal E-mail: plmrjd@aol.com. Business E-Mail: jeff.d.palmer@lmco.com.

PALMER, JEFFRESS GARY, hematologist, educator; b. Bklyn., Oct. 7, 1921; s. William Ware and Margaret Lee (Boswell) P.; m. Jane Ann Cartwright, Feb. 2, 1951; children: Kristin Cartwright, Julie Mitchell. BS, Emory U., 1942, MD, 1944. Intern N.C. Bapt. Hosp., 1944-45; resident in medicine Emory U., Atlanta, 1947-49; fellow hematology U. Utah, Salt Lake City, 1949-52; from asst. prof. to prof. medicine U. N.C., Chapel Hill, 1952—. Capt. M.C. AUS, 1945-47. Mem. AAAS, AAUP, AMA, Am. Fedn. for Clin. Rsch., So. Soc. for Clin. Investigation, N.Y. Acad. Scis., Am. Soc. Hematology. Home: Morgan Creek Rd Chapel Hill NC 27514 E-mail: jgpal@med.unc.edu.

PALMER, JOCELYN BETH, civic worker; b. Salina, Kans., Dec. 19, 1927; d. Paul Franklin and Josie Murtle (Schultz) Swartz; m. Gerald Keith Palmer, Dec. 28, 1952; children: David, Paula, Brian, April. AA, Christian Coll., Columbia, Mo., 1947; BS, Kans. State U., 1949; MA, U. Iowa, 1951. Grad. asst. presch. U. Iowa, Iowa City, 1949-51; instr. U. Ill., Urbana, 1951-52; co-dir. child devel. ctr. Long Beach (Calif.) City Coll., 1954-56. Mem. task force Early Childhood Edu., 2000-2001. Tchr. trainer, presch. tchr., cons., chmn. nursery com., elder, deacon Presbyn. Ch.; mem. Com. to Develop Stds. for Presch. Handicapped, Salina, 1981-83; pres., bd. dirs. # 305 Salina Sch. Dist., 1975-87; com. chair, bd. dirs. St. Francis Boyd Home, Salina, Ellsworth, 1984-87; bd. dirs. YWCA, 1993-97; bd. dirs. Asburg Hosp. Aux., 1993-96, sec. 1994-96; mem. com. planning early childhood edn. USD 305. Mem. Clippership Mariners (chaplain 1991-93, logkeeper 1994-95, 2000—, skipper 1997), Saline County Med. Alliance (bd. dirs. 1992-96, 98-2000), Twentieth Century Forum (courtesy chmn. 1989-93, 2000—), PEO (pres. 1989-91, 94-95, treas. 1993-95), Salina Downtown Lioness (bd. dirs. 1988-89, 91-93, program chair 1997, pres. 2000—), Priority Action Team of Future of USD. Republican. Avocations: sewing, reading, music, swimming.

PALMER, JOHN ANTHONY, III, secondary education educator; b. Worcester, Mass., May 18, 1955; s. John Jr. and Barbara (Dufresne) P. BA in Spanish, Worcester State Coll., 1977, MEd in Ednl. Adminstrn., 1988. Cert. Spanish, French, German and music tchr., Mass. Tchr., head dept. fgn. langs. Mahar Regional Sch., Orange, Mass., 1979-88; tchr. French, Spanish and German, Doherty Meml. H.S., Worcester, 1993-99, Burncoat Sr. High, 1999—. Adj. prof. Spanish, Worcester State Coll., 1988-90, Fla. Atlantic U., 1991-93, Quinsigamond Cmty. Coll., 1997—; instr. voice Worcester Poly. Inst., 1979-81; cantor Ch. of St. Peter, 1977-81, Worcester Eglise Notre Dame des Canadiens, Worcester, 1981-83; adjudicator vocal auditions All-State Music Educators Conf., 1988. Tenor soloist Regis Coll., Boston, Worcester Poly. Inst., Worcester Chorus, Salisbury Singers, Simmons Coll., Boston, Ft. Lauderdale Opera Co., Opera Worcester, Smith Coll., North Hampton, Wells Coll., Aurove, N.Y. Mem. ASCD, Am. Coun. Tchrs. Fgn. Langs., Nat. Assn. Secondary Sch. Prins., Mass. Assn. Sch. Supts., Mass. Fgn. Lang. Assn., Sigma Delta Pi. Democrat. Roman Catholic. Home: 14 Waterford Dr Botany Bay Worcester MA 01602 E-mail: jpalmerIII@aol.com.

PALMER, JOHN BERNARD, III, lawyer; b. Ft. Wayne, Ind., May 18, 1952; s. John Bernard and Dorothy Alma (Lauer) P. BA, Mich. State U., 1974; JD, U. Mich., 1977. Bar: Ill. 1977, U.S. Dist. Ct. (no. dist.) Ill. 1977, U.S. Tax Ct. 1979. Assoc. Mayer Brown & Platt, Chgo., 1977-80, Hopkins & Sutter, Chgo., 1980-83, ptnr., 1983-2001, Foley & Lardner, Chgo., 2001—. Adj. prof. Ill. Inst. Tech.- Kent Coll. of Law, Chgo., 1984—. Mem. ABA. Office: Foley & Lardner Three First Nat Plaza Chicago IL 60602

PALMER, JOHN DERRY, physiology educator; b. Chgo., May 26, 1932; s. John and Florence (Eley) P.; m. Carla Bianchi, Sept. 15, 1960; 1 child, John Charles. BA, Lake Forest Coll., 1957; MS, Northwestern U., 1959, PhD, 1962. Asst. prof. U. Ill., Chgo., 1961-63; fellow NSF, U. Bristol, Eng., 1963-64; prof., dept. chmn. NYU, 1964-74; prof. U. Mass., Amherst, 1974—, dept. chmn., 1974-80. Edit. bd. Marine Behavior and Physiology, 1988—, Chronobiology Internat., 1986—; author: Textbook of Modern Biology, 1968, The Biological Clock: Two Views, 1970, Biological Clocks in Marine Organisms: The Control of Physiological and Behavioral Tidal Rhythms, 1974, An Introduction to Biological Rhythms, 1976, (with others) Biological Rhythms and Living Clocks, 1977, Human Biological Rhythms, 1983, The Biological Rhythms and Clocks of Intertidal Animals, 1995, The Living Clock, 2000; contbr. articles to profl. jours. With U.S. Army, 1953-55. Fellow AAAS, Explorers Club; mem. Internat. Soc. of Chronobiology, Nat. Assn. of Scholars, Marine Biol. Lab., Phi Beta Kappa, Sigma Xi (pres., v.p., treas. N.Y. chpt., Disting. Rschr. award 1968). Avocations: trout and saltwater fishing. Office: U Mass Dept of Biology Amherst MA 01003 E-mail: ftodd@bio.umass.edu.

PALMER, LARRY GEORGE, chemist; b. Edwards, Calif., June 8, 1959; s. Richard and Marilyn Joan (Wynn) P. BS in Chemistry summa cum laude, U. Okla., 1982. Rsch. assoc. U. Okla., Norman, 1982-84; developer Digital Equipment Corp., Maynard, 1984-94, cons. engr., 1995-98; pvt. practice Norman, 1998—. Patentee in field; contbr. articles to profl. jours. including Digital Tech. Jour. Mem. Phi Beta Kappa. Avocations: puzzles, reading, gardening, golf, cooking. E-mail: palmers@sprintmail.com.

PALMER, LARRY ISAAC, lawyer, educator; b. 1944; AB, Harvard U., 1966; LLB, Yale U., 1969. Bar: Calif. 1970. Asst. prof. Rutgers U., Camden, N.J., 1970-73, assoc. prof., 1973-75, Cornell U., Ithaca, N.Y., 1975-79, prof. law, 1979—, vice provost, 1979-84, v.p. acad. programs, 1987-91, v.p. acad. program and campus affairs, 1991-94. Vis. fellow Cambridge U., 1984-85. Author: Law, Medicine, and Social Justice, 1989, Endings and Beginnings: Law, Medicine and Society in Assisted Life and Death, 2000. Mem. Am. Law Inst. Office: Cornell U Law Sch 120 Myron Taylor Hall Ithaca NY 14853-4901 E-mail: lip1@cornell.edu.

PALMER, LOUIS THOMAS, pathologist; b. Omaha, Dec. 12, 1937; s. Harry Calvin and Helen Irene (Hansen) P.; m. Rosario Garcia, Dec. 28, 1977; children: Ria Charrise, Ryan Christopher. BS, Wash. State U., 1960; MS, Kans. State U., 1965; PhD, U. Minn., 1968. Cert. profl. plant pathologist. Plant pathologist Rockefeller Found., Mex. and India, 1968-71; extension plant pathologist U. Nebr., Lincoln, 1971-75; plant pathologist Internat. Rice Rsch. Inst., Sukamandi, Indonesia, 1975-79; dir. United Fruit Co., La Lima, Honduras, 1979-81; field devel. biologist E.I. duPont de Nemours, Campinas, Brazil, 1982-85, mgr. Madera, Calif., 1985-88; cons. Checchi & Co., Dhaka, Bangladesh, 1988-91; field rsch. mgr. Calif. Agriculture Rsch., Kerman, Calif., 1992; plant pathologist Harris Moran Seed Co., Ruskin, Fla., 1992—. Contbr. articles to profl. jours. Advisor Boy Scouts Am., Campinas, 1983-85, councilor, Madera, 1985-88, leader Tiger Club, Dhaka, 1988-90, cubmaster, 1990-91, den. leader, Madera, 1991-92, asst. den leader Brandon, 1993. Recipient Eagle Scout award Boy Scouts Am., 1955; Carl Raymond Grey scholar Union Pacific R.R., 1955, Carl J. Erickson scholar Benton County, Washington, 1956. Mem. Am. Phytopathol. Soc. Roman Catholic. Avocations: photography, swimming, tennis. Home: 1343 Monte Lake Dr Valrico FL 33594-8109 Office: Harris Moran Seed Co 4331 Cockroach Bay Rd Ruskin FL 33570-2636

PALMER, LYNNE, writer, astrologer; b. El Centro, Calif., Dec. 14, 1932; d. Clarence Lee and Paquita Mae (Hartley) Hafer; m. Bruno Cazzaniga, Mar. 13, 1964 (div. 1965); m. Sidney Latter, Nov. 29, 1997. Student, Ch. of Light, 1957-62, Calif. Sch. Escrows, L.A., 1960; theatre mgmt. degree, Mus. Arenas Theatres Assn., N.Y.C., 1963. Asst. teller Western Mortgage, L.A., 1957-58; head teller Sutro Mortgage Svc., 1958-61; freelance astrologer N.Y.C., 1961-92, Las Vegas, Nev., 1962—; owner, operator, tchr. astrology sch. N.Y.C., 1970-72; owner Star Bright Pubs., Las Vegas, 1996—. Spkr. in field; interviewed in N.Y. Post and other major newspapers and mags. including Life and Oggi (Italy), Veja (Brazil), Wall St. Jour., People Mag., Globe, Die Welt am Sonntag (West Germany), New Woman Mag., Forbes. Author: Prosperity, Nixon's Horoscope, Astrological Almanac, Astrological Compatibility (Profl. Astrologers award 1976), Horoscope of Billy Rose, ABC Basic Chart Reading, ABC Major Progressions, ABC Chart Erection, Pluto Ephemeris (1900-2000), Daily Positions, Is Your Name Lucky For You?, Do-It-Yourself Publicity Directory, Your Lucky Days and Numbers, Money Magic, Astro-Guide to Nutrition and Vitamins, Gambling to Win, The Astrological Treasure Map, Dear Sun Signs, Are You Compatible With Your Boss, Partner, Coworkers, Employee, Client?, Bet to Win; columnist: Self, House Beautiful, Gold; record album: Cast and Read Your Horoscope; TV appearances include The Johnny Carson Tonight Show, What's My Line, 60 Minutes, CBS News Night Watch, Cosmos (BBC), Sci. Series (Italian TV), Fantastico (Brazilian TV), Japan TV, News (Nippon), Do We Really Need It? (ASAHI), The World is Calling (Uranai); contbr. articles to mags. and newspapers. Mem. AFTRA, Am. Fedn. Astrologers (cert.). Avocation: travel. Home: 850 E Desert Inn Rd Apt 912 Las Vegas NV 89109-2100 Office: Star Bright Pubs 2235 E Flamingo Rd Las Vegas NV 89119-5129 E-mail: lynnepalmer@lynnepalmer.com.

PALMER, MARILYN JOAN, English composition educator; b. Mahoning County, Ohio, Mar. 3, 1933; d. Rudolph George and Marian Eleanor Wynn; m. Richard Palmer, Nov. 10, 1956 (dec. 1987); children: Ricky, Larry, Kevin. Phys. therapy cert., UCLA, 1954, BS, 1955; MA in Philosophy, Ohio State U., 1969; PhD, U. Okla., 1996. Phys. therapist Neil Ave. Sch. for Handicapped, Columbus, Ohio, 1968-69; instr. philosophy Ohio State U., 1969; instr. English Youngstown (Ohio) State U., 1970-71; writer, editor The Economy Co., ednl. publs., Oklahoma City, 1977-81; grad. asst. in English U. Okla., Norman, 1981-87, lectr. in English, 1988-90, tech. writing instr. ind. studies, 1988-97. Free-lance editing and cons.; cons. for on-line CD-ROM to accompany a textbook, 2002. Author: Technical Writing for Science, Business and Industry, 1988, An Enthymeme as a Platform for Understanding Audience Values, 1997; editor: Kindergarten Keys Teacher's Guidebook, 1982, author parochial supplement, 1982. Fund-raiser Easter Seal Soc., 1965-68; den mother coord. Boy Scouts Am., 1966, 67. Dept. Energy grantee, 1976. Mem. AAUP, Am. Phys. Therapy Assn., Soc. for Women in Philosophy, Alpha Xi Delta (nat. editor Quill 1984-86). E-mail: doclynn@cox.net.

PALMER, MICHAEL PAUL, lawyer, mediator, educator; b. San Francisco, Mar. 7, 1944; s. Coy Cornelius and Fay Janetta (Conley) P.; m. Gisela Schultz, Jan. 8, 1969; children: Eva Rebecca, Esther Marie. BA, McMurry Coll., Abilene, Tex., 1967; MA, Freie U., Berlin, 1971, PhD, 1976; JD, Georgetown U., 1980. Bar: Ill. 1980, Vt. 1987. Asst. prof. Freie U., Berlin, 1971-76; assoc. Jenner & Block, Chgo., 1980-87; pres. Palmer Legal Svcs., Middlebury, 1987—. Adj. prof. Kent U., Ill. Inst. Tech., Chgo., 1983, Middlebury Coll., 1995; pres. The Negotiation Ctr., Palmer Legal Svcs.; mem. Rule of Law Project, Karelia, Russia. Author: Das Problem der Technik, 1976, Problem Solving Negotiation: The Art of a Just Peace, 1999, The Respectful Workplace, 2001; contbr. articles to profl. jours. Active Amnesty Internat.; bd. dirs. Middlebury Union H.S. Hon. mention Ammy award Am. Lawyer, 1982. Mem. ACLU, Vt. Bar Assn., Soc. of Profls. in Dispute Resolution. Office: Palmer Legal Svcs PO Box 528 Middlebury VT 05753-0528

PALMER, PATRICIA EILEEN, retired nurse anesthetist; b. Jersey City, Mar. 23, 1934; d. John Martin and Lillian Bigelow Enright; m. Ralph V. Palmer, Nov. 22, 1956; children: Kathleen Cheryl, Michele Diane. Diploma, Mercer Hosp., 1954; postgrad., Harris Hosp., 1956. Nurse anesthetist Haris Hosp., Ft. Worth, 1956, Meth. Hosp., Omaha, 1968-79, Midlands Community Hosp., Papillion, Nebr., 1979-81; relief nurse anesthetist Grape Cmty. Hosp., Hamburg, Iowa, 1976-81, Myrtue Meml. Hosp., Harlen, 1978-79. Pres. PEP Svcs. Inc., Plattsmouth, Nebr., 1981—; owner Chasemore Farms, Plattsmouth, 1976—, Teeny Tiny Tack Shop, 1998— Pres. Boston MAC Syndicate, Plattsmouth, 1980, Windchester Syndicate, Plattsmouth, 1980. Mem. Am. Assn. Nurse Anesthetists (cert. 1956, 95), Am. Quarter Horse Assn., Nebr. Assn. Nurse Anesthetists, Quarter Horse Assn. Nebr. Republican. Roman Catholic. Home and Office: 219 Hwy 66 Plattsmouth NE 68048-9089

PALMER, PATRICK ASA, former banker, lecturer; b. Amherst, N.S., Can., Mar. 29, 1943; s. James Asa and Evelyn Elizabeth (Hatt) P.; m. Margaret Ann Teixeira, Feb. 8, 1964; children: Mark, Ingrid, Petrina, Kara-Lynn. B in Commerce with honors, U. Windsor, Ont., Can., 1970; FICB, U. Toronto, 1972. Mgr. mktg. program Royal Bank of Can., Toronto, Ont., 1976-78, mgr. nat. bus. met., 1978-79, mgr. comml. markets, 1979-81, v.p. comml. mktg. and svcs. Ont., 1981-82, v.p. comml. mktg. Can., 1982-83, v.p. planning, comml. banking and nat. accounts, 1983-86, v.p. sales and svcs. Can., 1986-88, v.p. corp. mktg. and sales Can., 1988-89, v.p. retail banking Can., 1989-94; sr. v.p. channel mgmt. RBFG, 1994-97; pres. Where Eagles Soar, Inc., 1997—. Lectr. Sheridan Coll., Oakville, Ont., 1979-81, George Brown Coll., Toronto, 1979; bd. dirs. Janes Family Foods Ltd., Kinfolk Mgmt. Inc., Penetangore Ridge, Inc; mem. adv. bd. Mphasis. founder Cappy Ride, Motorcycle Charity Ride; past bd. dirs. Ont. Export, Inc., C. of C., Ont., C. of C., CDN C. of C., Gov. Gen.'s Can. study conf., U. Windsor, CDN Tourism Assn.. Econ. Devel. Assn. Can., CDN Tourism Mgmt. Ctr., other non-profit orgns.; mem. devel. bd. Windsor/Essex Hosp. Found. Contbr. articles to profl. jours. Double Gold medalist, U. Windsor, 1970. Mem. Alliance for Ont. Univs. (hon.). Home: 8078 8th Line RR # 4 Kenilworth ON Canada NOG 2E0 Office: Where Eagles Soar Inc 5720 Timberlea Blvd Ste 201 Mississauga ON Canada L4W 4W2 E-mail: pat@whereeaglessoar.com.

PALMER, PATRICK EDWARD, radio astronomer, educator; b. St. Johns, Mich., Dec. 6, 1940; s. Don Edward and Nina Louise (Kyes) P.; m. Joan Claire Merlin, June 9, 1963; children: Laura Katherine, Aidan Edward, David Elijah. SB, U. Chgo., 1963; MA, Harvard U., 1965, PhD, 1968. Radio astronomer Harvard U., Cambridge, Mass., 1968; asst. prof. astronomy and astrophysics U. Chgo., 1968-70, assoc. prof., 1970-75, prof., 1975—. Vis. assoc. prof. astronomy Calif. Inst. Tech., Pasadena, 1972; vis. radio astronomer Cambridge (Eng.) U., 1973; vis. rsch. astronomer U. Calif., Berkeley, 1977, 86; vis. scientist Nat. Radio Astronomer Obs., 1980-2002. Contbr. articles on radio astron. investigations of comets and interstellar medium to tech. jours. Recipient Bart J. Bok prize for contbns. to galactic astronomy, 1969, Alfred P. Sloan Found. fellow, 1970-72, Helen B. Warner prize, 1975. Fellow AAAS (chmn. sect. D astronomy 1984); mem. AAUP, Am. Astron. Soc. (chmn. nominating com. 1981, mem. publs. bd. 1985-86, mem. Warner Prize selection com. 1977-78), Royal Astron. Soc., Internat. Astron. Union, U. Chgo. Track Club. Home: 5549 S Dorchester Ave Chicago IL 60637-1720 Office: Univ Chgo Astronomy & Astrophysics Ctr 5640 S Ellis Ave Chicago IL 60637-1433 E-mail: ppalmer@oskar.uchicago.edu.

PALMER, PAUL RICHARD, librarian, archivist; b. Cin., Jan. 21, 1917; s. Gardiner O. and Sarah Ellen (Christy) P. BA, U. Cin., 1949; MS, Columbia U., 1950, MA, 1955. Asst. br. libr. Bklyn. Pub. Libr., 1950-51; libr. Columbia U., N.Y.C., 1951-67, libr. sch. libr. svc., 1968, libr. and curator Brander Matthews Dramatic Mus., 1969-73, bibliographer Avery Archtl. Libr., 1974, curator Columbiana Collection, 1974—. Cons. Am. Libr. Assn., Chgo. and N.Y.C., 1954-59. Contbr. articles to profl. jurs. Founder fund for collection and preservation of film stills and formats, Mus. Modern Art. Fellow The Pierpont Morgan Libr.; mem. Theatre Libr. Assn. (exec. coun. 1970-74), Mus. Modern Art, Metro. Mus. Art, Am. Film Inst., Am. Mus. Britain, French Inst., Soc. Hist. Preservation, Lincoln Ctr. Film Soc., Manuscript Soc., Grolier Club, Church Club N.Y., St. George Soc. N.Y., VFW, Order St. John of Jerusalem, Phi Beta Kappa. Episcopalian. Home: 560 Riverside Dr Apt 21-b New York NY 10027-3236

PALMER, PHILIP EDWARD STEPHEN, radiologist; b. London, Apr. 26, 1921; Ed., Kelly Coll., Tavistock, Eng., 1938; MB BS, U. London, 1944, DMR, 1946, DMRT, 1947. Intern, then resident Westminster Hosp.; cons. radiologist West Cornwall (Eng.) Hosp. Group, 1947-54; sr. govt. radiologist Matabeleland, Rhodesia-Zimbabwe, 1954-64; prof. radiology U. Cape Town, South Africa, 1964-68; prof. U. Pa., 1968-70; prof. diagnostic radiology and vet. radiology U. Calif., Davis, 1970—. WHO cons. in field. Author: The Imaging of Tropical Diseases, 1980 and 2nd edit.: 2000; contbr. 200plus articles to profl. publs. Recipient German Röentgen award, 1993, 1st Béclère medal Internat. Soc. Radiology, 1996, 1st Antoine Béclère lectr. Internat. Soc. Radiology, 1996, Presdl. award Radiol. Soc. N.Am., 2000. Fellow Calif. Radiol. Assn., Royal Coll. Physicians (Edinburgh), Royal Coll. Radiologists (Eng.), Romanian Soc. Radiol. and Nuclear Med.; mem. Brit. Inst. Radiology, Brit. Med. Assn., Calif. Med. Assn., Internat. Skeletal Soc., Assn. Univ. Radiologists, Radiol. Soc. N.Am. (Spl. Pres.'s award 2000), Kenya Radiol. Soc., South African Coll. Medicine, Egyptian Soc. Radiology and Nuclear Medicine, Yugoslav Assn. for Ultrasound, West African Assn. Radiologists. Address: 821 Miller Dr Davis CA 95616-3622

PALMER, RAYETTA J. technology coordinator, educator; b. Tribune, Kans., Dec. 9, 1949; d. Raymond H. and Helen Jean (Whittle) Helm; children: Carol Lynn, Eric Lee. BA in Bus. Edn., U. No. Colo., 1970; MA in Computer Edn., Lesley Coll., 1990. Cert. vocat. educator, Colo. Bus./computer tchr. Dept. Def. Schs., Mannheim, Germany, 1983-87; computer tchr./coord. Cheyenne County Sch. Dist., Cheyenne Wells, Colo., 1987—. Part-time instr. Lamar C.C., 1987—; instr. Colo. Online Consortium Schs., 1999—; part-time bookkeeper Scherler Sales, Inc., 2000—. Treas. Cheyenne County Rep. Ctrl. Com., Colo., 1989—; elected mem. Cheyenne Wells City Coun., 2000. Mem. Internat. Soc. for Tech. in Edn., Pi Omega Pi. Republican. Avocations: reading, bridge, travel, church organist. Home: PO Box 771 Cheyenne Wells CO 80810-0771 Office: Cheyenne County Sch Dist PO Box 577 Cheyenne Wells CO 80810-0577

PALMER, RAYMOND ALFRED, administrator, librarian, consultant; b. Louisville, May 8, 1939; BA in Biology, U. Louisville, 1961; MLS, U. Ky., 1966. Adminstrv. asst. Johns Hopkins Med. Libr., Balt., 1966-69; asst. librarian Harvard Med. Libr., Boston, 1969-74; health scis. librarian Wright State U., Dayton, Ohio, 1974-82, assoc. prof. library adminstrn., 1974-82; exec. dir. Med. Libr. Assn., Chgo., 1982-92, Am. Assn. Immunologists, Bethesda, Md., 1992-95; dir. info.-edn. svcs. Nat. Ctr. Edn. Maternal-Child Health Georgetown U., Arlington, Va., 1995-97—. Cons. Acad. Mil. Med. Scis. Libr., Beijing, 1990, Alzheimer's Assn., Chgo., 1991. Author: Management of Library Associations; mng. editor: Jour. Immunology, 1992-95; contbr. articles to profl. jours. Mem. ALA, Am. Soc. Assn. Execs., Greater Washington Soc. Assn. Execs., Spl. Librs. Assn., Biomed. Communication Network (chmn. 1980-82), Am. Mgmt. Assn. (strategic planning adv. coun. 1987-91), Coun. Biology Editors, Friends of Nat. Libr. Medicine (bd. dirs. 1989-92, 94-97), Internat. Fedn. Libr. Assns. and Instns. (exec. com. Round Table for Mgmt. of Libr. Orgns. 1989-92), Med. Libr. Assn. E-mail: rap539@aol.com.

PALMER, RICHARD ALAN, chemistry educator; b. Austin, Tex., Nov. 13, 1935; s. Ernest Austin and Eugenia Rosalie (Robey) P.; m. Janice Leah Boyce, June 30, 1961; children: William D., Leah D., Sarah L., Benjamin C. BS, U. Tex., 1957; MS, U. Ill., 1962, PhD, 1965. Asst. prof. chemistry Duke U., 1966-71, assoc. prof., 1971-78, prof., 1978—, dir. grad. studies dept. chemistry, 1979-82, dir. Chemistry for Executives Program, 1992—. Author: Problems in Structural Inorganic Chemistry, 1971; mem. editorial bd. Applied Spectroscopy, 1990—. Served with USN, 1957-60. NIH fellow, 1965-66; NSF Internat. Study grantee, 1980-81. Mem. Am. Chem. Soc. (nat. coun. 1993—), Soc. Applied Spectroscopy, Coblentz Soc. (bd. mgrs. 1992—), Phi Beta Kappa, Sigma Xi, Phi Lambda Upsilon. Home: 126 Pinecrest Rd Durham NC 27705-5813 Office: Duke U Chemistry Dept Durham NC 27706

PALMER, RICHARD JOSEPH, communications director; b. Mpls., June 23, 1929; s. Charles Henry and Josephine (Shimek) P.; m. Bernice Arvilla Schumacher, Sept. 18, 1954; children: Howard, Penny Rae, Pamela, Randall, Roger. Diploma in Journalism, U. Minn., 1957. Reporter/photographer Fairmont Daily Sentinel, Minn., 1953-54, 57-59; newsman, capitol corrs. AP, Mpls., Fargo and Bismarck, N.D., 1959-67; comms. dir. N.D. Education Assn., Bismarck, 1967-93; comms. cons. NEA, Washington, 1993—. Pres., State Edn. Editors of NEA, 1974, sec./treas. Pub. Rels. Coun., 1977-79, chmn. Sml. States Printing Consortium, 1977-88. Editor/photographer: (video) Come In, Please, To My World, 1990 (Best of Show in NEA Pub. Rels. Coun. 1991); contbr. publs. in field. Coun. mem. Trinity Luth. Ch., Bismarck, 1994-96. Ssgt. U.S. Army, 1950-52, Korea. Named Outstanding Male Grad. in Journalism, Sigma Delta Chi, 1957; recipient Friend of Edn. award N.D. Edn. Assn., Bismarck, 1993. Mem. N.D. Wildlife Fedn. (Conservation Comms. award 1971), Soc. for Profl. Journalists, Lions (3d to 1st v.p. Bismarck club 1994-96). Avocations: photography, hunting, fishing, travel, woodcarving. Home: 1801 Marian Dr Bismarck ND 58501-1552 Office: Palmer Comms 1801 Marian Dr Bismarck ND 58501-1552

PALMER, RICHARD WARE, lawyer; b. Boston, Oct. 20, 1919; s. George Ware and Ruth French (Judkins) P.; m. Nancy Fernald Shaw, July 8, 1950; children: Richard Ware Jr., John Wentworth, Anne Fernald. AB, Harvard U., 1942, JD, 1948. Bar: N.Y. 1950, Pa. 1959. Sec., dir. N.Am. Mfg. Co., Natick, Mass., 1946-48; assoc. Burlingham, Veeder, Clark & Hupper, Burlingham, Hupper & Kennedy, N.Y.C., 1949-57; ptnr. Rawle & Henderson, Phila., 1958-79, Palmer, Biezup & Henderson, Phila., 1979-95, of counsel, 1996—. Sec., bd. dirs. Underwater Technics, Inc., Camden, N.J., 1967-85; adv. on admiralty law to U.S. del. Inter-Govtl. Maritime Consultative Orgn., London, 1967, U.S. del. 30th-34th internat. confs.; mem. U.S. Shipping Coordinating Com., mem. Washington legal sub com., 1967—; Titular mem. Comité Maritime Internat.; v.p., sec., bd. dirs. Phila. Belt Line R.R.; bd. dirs. Mather (Bermuda) Ltd. Editor: Maritime Law Reporter. Mem., permanent adv. bd. Tulane Admiralty Law Inst., Tulane U. Law Sch., New Orleans, 1975—; trustee Seamen's Ch. Inst., Phila., 1967—2001, pres., 1972—84; mem. exec. com. Harvard Law Sch. Assn., 1986—; bd. dirs. Havrford (Pa.) Civic Assn., 1972—85, pres., 1976—79; consul for Denmark State of Pa., 1980—91, consul emeritus, 1992—; bd. dirs. Woodlands Cemetary Co. of Phila., Woodlands Trust for Historic Preservation. Lt.comdr. USNR, 1942—46. Fellow World Acad. Art and Sci. (treas. 1988-2002); mem. ABA (former chmn. stdg. com. on admiralty and maritime law 1978-79), N.Y.C. Bar Assn., Phila. Bar Assn., Am. Judicature Soc., Maritime Law Assn. (chmn. limitation liability com. 1977-83, 2d v.p. 1984-86, 1st v.p. 1986-88, pres. 1988-90, immediate past pres. 1990-92), Internat. Bar Assn., Assn. Average Adjusters USA and Gt. Britain, Port of Phila. Maritime Soc., Harvard Law Sch. Assn. of Phila. (exec. com. 1986—), Fgn. Consul assn. of Phila., Danish Order of Dannebrog, Merion Cricket Club, Phila. Club, Rittenhouse Club, India House, Geneal. Soc. Pa. (bd. dirs. 1997—), Harvard Club of N.Y.C. and Phila. (exec. com. 1983-86, 94-97). Republican. Episcopalian. Home: 432 Montgomery Ave Haverford PA 19041-1527 Office: Palmer Biezup & Henderson Pub Ledger Bldg 620 Chestnut St Philadelphia PA 19106-3409

PALMER, RICKY SAMUEL, physicist; b. Waco, Tex., Aug. 24, 1957; s. Richard and Marilyn Joan (Wynn) P. BS in Physics magna cum laude, BS in Math., U. Okla., 1980, MS in Physics, 1982. Rsch. assoc. U. Okla., Norman, 1982-84; developer Digital Equipment Corp., Maynard, Mass., 1984-94, cons. engr., 1995-98; pvt. practice Norman, 1998—. Patentee in field; contbr. articles to profl. jours. including Digital Tech. Jour. Mem. Mu Alpha Theta. Avocations: reading, gardening, music, collecting, travel. E-mail: palmers@sprintmail.com.

PALMER, ROBERT ALAN, lawyer, educator; b. Somerville, N.J., June 29, 1948; BA, U. Pitts., 1970; JD, George Washington U., 1976. Bar: Va. 1977. Dir. labor relations Nat. Assn. Mfrs., Washington, 1976-79; assoc. gen. counsel Nat. Restaurant Assn., 1979-85, gen. counsel, 1985-87; assoc. prof. Pa. State U., State College, 1987-88, Calif. State Poly. U., 1988-92, prof., 1992—. Mem. ABA, Va. State Bar Assn. Home: 557 Fairview Ave Arcadia CA 91007-6736 Office: 3801 W Temple Ave Pomona CA 91768-2557

PALMER, ROBERT ARTHUR, private investigator; b. St. Augustine, Fla., May 20, 1948; m. Christine Lynn Creger, May 14, 1974. AA, Glendale C.C., 1975; BS, U. Phoenix, 1981; MA, Prescott Coll., 1993; PhD, Union Inst., 1999. Lic. pvt. investigator, Ariz.; bd. cert. forensic examiner. Dep. sheriff Maricopa County Sheriff's Office, Phoenix, 1971-79; owner Palmer Investigative Svcs., Prescott, Ariz., 1980-90; pres. The Magnum Corp., 1990—. V.p. Mountain Club Homeowners, Prescott, 1986—. Mem. Internat. Assn. Chem. Testing, World Assn. Detectives, Nat. Assn. Legal Investigators, Nat. Assn. Profl. Process Servers, Am. Coll. Forensic Examiners, Ariz. Assn. Lic. Pvt. Investigators (pres. 1984), Ariz. Process Servers Assn. (pres. 1985-86), Prescott C. of C. (v.p. 1987-90). Avocations: photography, collecting western art. Office: Palmer Investigative Svcs PO Box 10760 Prescott AZ 86304-0760

PALMER, ROBERT BAYLIS, librarian; b. Rockville Centre, N.Y., Apr. 5, 1938; s. John Frederick and Marion (Baylis) P.; divorced; 1 child, Michele Palmer Fracasso. AB, Kenyon Coll., Gambier, Ohio, 1960; MS in L.S, Simmons Coll., Boston, 1965; MA in English, Middlebury (Vt.) Coll., 1965. Tchr. Brooks Sch., North Andover, Mass., 1960-65, librarian, 1961-65; acting librarian Columbia Coll., 1965-66; asst. to dir. libraries Columbia U., 1965-67; dir. Barnard Coll. Library, 1967-81. Fulbright lectr. Tribhuvan U. Library, Kathmandu, Nepal, 1972-73, Kathmandu, 1980; vol. lectr. USIS, library cons., Asia, 1976; Fulbright lectr. Wuhan, Peoples Republic China, 1984-85; library cons., advisor, Peoples Republic China, 1986-87, Zanzibar, Tanzania, 1988; lectr., cons. Kenya, Ethiopia, Zimbabwe, 1988; English lang. escort officer U.S. Dept. State, 1989—. Mem. ALA. Address: 190 Riverside Dr New York NY 10024-1008 *From my many world travels, I have learned that much curiosity, low maintenance and no quick movements, left or right, make for pleasant survival.*

PALMER, ROBERT CHRISTOPHER, music educator, musician; b. St. Joseph, Mo., Mar. 11, 1954; s. Michael Gordon and Margaret Ann Palmer; m. Kathleen Mary Berg, May 12, 1979; children: Jon Michael, Nicole Kathleen, Matthew Gene. BA in Piano, St. John's U., 1976; MM in Piano Performance, Peabody Conservatory of Music, 1978; DMA in Piano Performance, U. Minn., 1988. Vis. lectr. music St. John's U., Collegeville, Minn., 1978—81; asst. prof. music Southwestern Coll., Winfield, Kans., 1983—86; disting. prof. music Ball State U., Muncie, Ind., 1986—, Mauzy-Porter disting. prof. music, 2001. Piano master class clinician various univs. and colls., 1978—. Pianist (solo recital) Carnegie Hall debut, 1979, (performances) Carnegie Hall, 1980, 1994, Libr. of Congress, 1984. Named Music Tchr. of Yr., Ind. Music Tchrs. Assn., 1998. Mem.: Music Tchrs. Nat. Assn. Avocations: reading, golf, tennis, travel, exercise. Office: Ball State U Sch Music Muncie IN 47306 Office Fax: 765-285-5401. Business E-Mail: rpalmer@bsu.edu.

PALMER, ROBERT ERWIN, association executive; b. Texarkana, Ark., Feb. 6, 1934; s. Burgess Prince and Ruth (Erwin) P. BJ, U. Tex., 1961. Reporter Texarkana Gazette, 1961; editor Southwestern Bell Telephone, Houston, 1961, info. specialist St. Louis, 1961-63; editor Shell Oil Co., Houston and Chgo., head office pub. relations N.Y.C.; dir. pub. relations Nat. PTA, Chgo., 1969-74; program dir. Nat. Assn. Realtors, 1974-76; corp. communications mgr. The Milw. Rd., 1976-78; staff v.p. Soc. Real Estate Appraisers, 1978-83, exec. v.p., 1983-90; sr. v.p. communications, 1991—; co. exec., v.p. Appraisal Inst., Chgo., 1992-93, v.p. mem. svcs., 1993-98. Bd. dirs. Tower Advt., Chgo., Costumes Unltd. ltd., Chgo. Founding mem. Chgo. Crime Commn., 1967. Served to staff sgt. USAF, 1953-57. Recipient Award of Merit, Chgo. Internat. Film Festival, 1970, 71, Spl. Corrs. Pring Feature award, 1971, 72, Golden Trumpet award Realtor Week promotion, 1975, Golden Trumpet award Pvt. Property Week promotion, 1977, Golden Trumpet award Realtor bicentennial program, 1977, Gold Circle award Chpt.-by-Chpt. program, 1982. Mem. Pub. Relations Soc. Am., Am. Soc. Assn. Execs., Sigma Delta Chi. Clubs: Chgo. Headline. Methodist.

PALMER, ROBERT LESLIE, lawyer; b. Porterville, Calif., Apr. 10, 1957; s. Harrison Rowe and Margaret Elizabeth (Witty) P.; m. Huisuk Kim, Feb. 1, 1986; 1 child, Aaron Rowe. BA, Tulane U., 1979; JD, Georgetown U., 1982. Bar: D.C. 1982, U.S. Ct. Mil. Appeals 1985, Tex. 1987, Ala. 1987, U.S. Dist. Ct. (no. dist.) Ala. 1987, U.S. Ct. Appeals (11th cir.) 1987. Assoc. Lewis Martin Burnett & Dunkle, P.C., Birmingham, Ala., 1987-89, Lewis and Martin, Birmingham, 1989-90, Martin, Drummond and Woosley, Birmingham, 1990-91, bd. dirs., 1991-92, Martin, Drummond, Woosley and Palmer, Birmingham, 1992-95; atty. Environ. Litig. Group, P.C., Ala., 1995—. Ala. del. 6th Joint Conf. between Korea and S.E. U.S., Kyongju, Republic of Korea, 1991, 7th Joint Conf., Atlanta, 1992. Capt. JAGC, U.S. Army, 1983-87, USAR, 1987-91. Recipient commendation Republic of Korea Ministry of Justice, 1984. Mem. ATLA, Christian Legal Soc., Phi Beta Kappa, Omicron Delta Kappa. Independent. Baptist. Home: 1408 E Whirlaway Helena AL 35080-4102 Office: Environ Litig Group PC 3529 7th Ave S Birmingham AL 35222-3210

PALMER, ROBERT P. professional association executive; b. Indpls., Dec. 29, 1967; s. Frederick Grant and Phyllis Anne Palmer; m. Kimberly Ann Palmer, July 20, 1996. BA in Polit. Sci., The Citadel, 1990; MPA, Ind. U., 1998. Exec. dir. Sheet Metal Contractors Assn. Ctrl. Ind., Indpls., 1991-93; spl. asst. Office of U.S. Rep. Steve Buyer, Kokomo, Ind., 1994; assoc. mgr. Ctrl. Ind. chpt. Nat. Elec. Contractors Assn., Indpls., 1995-97; exec. v.p. Associated Gen. Contractors Ind., 1997—. Dean's industry adv. com. Sch. Engring. and Tech. Ind. U.-Purdue U., Indpls., 1999—; bd. dirs. Jameson Inc., Indpls. Columnist Indiana Constructor, 1997—. Bd. dirs. Christamore House, Indpls., 1999—. Mem. Am. Soc. Assn. Execs. Republican. Avocations: military history, international affairs, golf, canoeing. Office: AGC Ind 1050 Market Tower 10 W Market St Indianapolis IN 46204-2954

PALMER, ROBERT ROSWELL, historian, educator; b. Chgo., Jan. 11, 1909; s. Roswell Roy and Blanche (Steere) P.; m. Esther Howard, Dec. 19, 1942; children: Stanley, Richard, Emily. Ph.B., U. Chgo., 1931, LL.D., 1963; PhD, Cornell U., 1934; Litt.D., Washington U., St. Louis, 1962; L.H.D., Kenyon Coll., 1963, U. New Haven, 1980; Dr. honoris causa, U. Toulouse, France, 1965, U. Uppsala, Sweden, 1977. Mem. faculty Princeton U., 1936-63, 66-69, prof. history, 1946-63, Dodge prof. history, 1952-63; dean faculty arts and sci., prof. history Washington U., St. Louis, 1963-66; prof. history Yale U., 1969-77, emeritus, 1977. Adj. prof. U. Mich., 1977-80; vis. prof. U. Chgo., summer 1947, U. Colo., summer 1951, U. Calif. at Berkeley, summer 1962, U. Mich., 1969, 75 Author: Catholics and Unbelievers in 18th Century France, 1939, Twelve Who Ruled, 1941, A History of the Modern World, 1950, (with Joel Colton) A History of the Modern World, 2d edit., 1955, 8th edit. 1994, also in Swedish, Italian, Finnish, Spanish and Chinese, The Age of the Democratic Revolution, 1959, vol. II, 1964, also German, Italian edits., World of the French Revolution, 1971, also in French, School of the French Revolution, 1975, The Improvement of Humanity: Education and the French Revolution, 1985, From Jacobin to Liberal, Marc-Antoine Jullien 1775-1848, 1993, J.b. Say Economist in Troubled Times, 1997; editor, translator: The Two Tocquevilles, Father and Son on the Coming of the French Revolution, 1987; co-author: Organization of Ground Combat Troops, 1947, Procurement and Training of Ground Combat Troops, 1948; editor: Rand McNally Atlas of World History, 1957. Served hist. div. U.S. Army, 1943-45. Recipient of ACLS Spl. prize, 1960, Bancroft prize, 1960, Antonio Feltrinelli Internat. prize, Rome, 1990. Mem. Am. Acad. Arts and Scis., Mass. Hist. Soc., Am. Philos. Soc., Am. Hist. Assn. (pres. 1970), Soc. French Hist. Studies (pres. 1961), Acad. Naz. dei Lincei. Home: Pennswood Village # K205 Newtown PA 18940-2401

PALMER, ROBERT TOWNE, lawyer, banker; b. Chgo., May 25, 1947; s. Adrian Bernhardt and Gladys (Towne) P.; m. Ann Therese Darin, Nov. 9, 1974; children: Justin Darin, Christian Darin. BA, Colgate U., 1969; JD, U. Notre Dame, 1974. Bar: Ill. 1974, D.C. 1978, U.S. Supreme Ct. 1978. Law clk. to Hon. Walter V. Schaefer Ill. Supreme Ct., 1974-75; assoc. McDermott, Will & Emery, Chgo., 1975-81, ptnr., 1982-86, Chadwell & Kayser, Ltd., Chgo., 1987-88, Connelly, Mustes, Palmer & Schroeder, Chgo., 1988-89; of counsel Garfield & Merel Ltd., 1990-2000. Mem. adj. faculty Chgo. Kent Law Sch., 1975—77, Loyola U., 1976—78; mem. adv. com. Fed. Home Loan Mortgage Corp., 1988—89; dir. Ctrl. Fed. Savs. & Loan Assn. of Chgo., 1988—, chmn., 2000—, Chgo. Assn. Fin. Insts., 2001—, sec., 2002—; mem. Chgo. Ctr. Adv. Bd. Voyageur Outward Bound Sch., 1988—91; chmn. Lake Forest Cemetery Commn., 2001—. Contbr. articles to legal jours. and textbooks. Mem. Chgo. Crime Commn., 2001-, dir., 2002—. Mem. ABA, Ill. State Bar Assn. (Lincoln award 1983), Chgo. Bar Assn., Chgo. Club, Dairymen's Country Club, Lambda Alpha. Office: Central Fed Savs 1601 W Belmont Ave Chicago IL 60657-3044

PALMER, R(OBIE) MARK (ROBIE MARCUS HOOKER PALMER), banker; b. Ann Arbor, Mich., July 14, 1941; s. Robie Ellis and Katherine (Hooker) P.; m. Sushma Palmer. BA, Yale U., 1963. Copy asst. N.Y. Times, N.Y.C., 1963; asst. to producer WNDT-TV, 1963-64; entered U.S. Fgn. Service, 1964; third sec. U.S. Embassy, New Delhi, India, 1964-66; internat. relations officer NATO affairs, Dept State, Washington, 1966-68; second sec. U.S. Embassy, Moscow, 1968-71; prin. speechwriter Sec. of State Rogers, Kissinger, Washington, 1971-75; counselor for polit. affairs U.S. Embassy, Belgrade, Yugoslavia, 1975-78; dir. office disarmament and control of arms Bur. of Polit.-Mil. Affairs Dept. State, Washington, 1978-81, dep. to undersec. for polit. affairs, 1981-82, dep. asst. sec. state for European affairs, 1982-86; amb. U.S. Embassy, Budapest, Hungary, 1986-90; pres., CEO Cen. European Devel. Corp., Washington, 1990-97; CEO Capital Devel., 1997—. Pres., CEO Television Devel. Ptnrs., Inc., 1996-97. Author: speeches for five Secs. of State and three Presidents Recipient Superior Honor award Dept. State, 1980, Presdl. Meritorious Service award, 1984. Mem. Council Fgn. Relations, Am. Fgn. Service Assn., Phi Beta Kappa. Episcopalian. Avocation: tennis. Home and Office: 4437 Reservoir Rd NW Washington DC 20007-2021

PALMER, ROGER CAIN, information scientist; b. Corning, N.Y., Oct. 14, 1943; s. Wilbur Clarence and Eleanor Louise (Cain) P. AA, Corning (N.Y.) C.C., 1964; BA, Hartwick Coll., 1966; MLS, SUNY, Albany, 1972; PhD, U. Mich., 1978. Tchr. Penn Yan (N.Y.) Acad., 1966-68, 70-71; dep. head, grad. libr. SUNY, Buffalo, 1972-75; asst. prof. UCLA, 1978-83; sr. tech. writer

Quotron Sys., Culver City, 1984; sr. sys. analyst Getty Art History Info., Santa Monica, Calif., 1984-90, mgr. tech. devel., 1990-93; mgr. internal cons. group The J. Paul Getty Trust, 1993-96, mgr. ITS Infrastructure Ops. L.A., 1996-97; v.p. China and N.Am. Bus. Assocs., Inc., 1997-2000; CIO, v.p. ops. Webchoir, Inc., 2001—. Gen. ptnr. Liu-Palmer, L.A., 1989—2000. Author: Online Reference and Information Retrieval, 1987, dBase II and dBase III: An Introduction, 1984, Introduction to Computer Programming, 1983. With U.S. Army, 1968-70. Mem. IEEE Computer Soc., ALA, Am. Soc. for Info. Scis., Spl. Librs. Assn., Art Librs. Soc. of N.Am., Assn. for Computing Machinery, Pi Delta Epsilon, Beta Phi Mu. Home: 8205 Santa Monica Blvd # 1-295 Los Angeles CA 90046-5967 Office: Webchoir Inc Los Angeles CA 90046

PALMER, ROGER FARLEY, pharmacology educator; b. Albany, N.Y., Sept. 23, 1931; m. Nelida Santiago, Apr. 1994. BS in Chemistry, St. Louis U., 1953; postgrad., Fla. State U., 1955-56, Woods Hole Marine Biology Lab., 1956; MD, U. Fla., 1960. Intern Johns Hopkins Hosp., 1960-61, resident in medicine, 1961-62; asst. dept. biochemistry U. Fla., Gainesville, 1957; asst. medicine Osler Med. Service, 1960-62; instr. pharmacology and therapeutics U. Fla., 1962, asst. prof. pharmacology, therapeutics and medicine, 1964-67, assoc. prof. pharmacology and medicine, 1967-69, prof. medicine, chief div. clin. pharmacology, 1969-70, 71-82; prof., chmn. dept. pharmacology, prof. medicine U. Miami, Fla., 1970-81, clin. prof. medicine, 1982—. Chmn. pharmacology sect. Nat. Bd. Med Examiners, 1977-81; cons. Nat. Acad. Scis.; chmn. pharmacology sect. Nat. Bd. Med. Examiners, 1977-81. Editorial bd. Pharmacol. Revs.; assoc. editor Advances in Molecular Pharmacology; ad hoc editor Am. Heart Jour.; editor Horizons in Clinical Pharmacology, 1976; author abstracts; contbr. over 100 articles to profl. jours. Served with USAR. Mosby scholar, 1957-60; Markle scholar in acad. medicine, 1965-70; recipient Basic Sci. Teaching award U. Miami, 1975-76; Meritorious Service medal Am. Heart Assn., 1972; citation for meritorious Service So. Region Am. Heart Assn., 1979; Visitante Distinguido award, Costa Rica, 1979; Outstanding Tchr. award U. Miami, 1982. Mem. Am. Coll. Clin. Pharmacology, Am. Fedn. Clin. Rsch., Am. Therapeutic Soc. (prize essay award 1970), Am. Soc. Pharmacology and Exptl. Therapeutics (emeritus), N.Y. Acad. Scis., So. Soc. Clin. Investigation, U.S. Pharmacopeia Revision Com., Internat. Study Group Rsch. Cardiac Metabolism, Am. Soc. Internal Medicine, Royal Soc. Health, Key Biscayne Yacht Club (bd. govs. 1994-97, fleet surgeon 1999-2000), Sigma Xi. Office: 240 Crandon Blvd Ste 215 Key Biscayne FL 33149-2009

PALMER, ROGER RAYMOND, accounting educator; b. N.Y.C., Dec. 31, 1926; s. Archibald and Sophie (Jarnow) P.; m. Martha West Hopkins, June 7, 1986; children by previous marriage: Kathryn Sue, Daniel Stephen, Susan Jo. BS, U. Wis., 1949; MBA, Cornell U., 1951; postgrad., NYU, 1951-54. Auditor, Ernst and Ernst, CPA's, N.Y.C., 1953-54; auditor Gen. Dynamics Corp., 1956-60; mgr. corp. audits Tex. Instruments, 1960-64; auditor 1st Nat. Bank, St. Paul, 1964-68, v.p. planning, 1968-69, v.p., comptr., 1969-75, sr. v.p., contr., 1975-82; chmn. dept. fin. Coll. of St. Thomas (now U. St. Thomas), 1996—. Dir. First Met. Travel, Inc.; guest lectr. U. Minn., 1966; conf. leader, speaker, 1959— Contbr. articles to publs. Bd. dirs. Waterford (Conn.) Civic Assn., 1959-60, Friends of St. Paul Pub. Library, 1967, Mpls. Citizens League; chmn. bd. dirs. Film in the Cities, 1983-85; mem. acctg. adv. council U. Minn.; trustee, chmn. fin. com. Hazelton Found. With U.S. Maritime Svc., 1945-47; with U.S. Army, 1954-56. Mem. Inst. Internal Auditors (pres. So. New Eng chpt. 1957-60, edn. chmn. Dallas 1961, Twin City chpt. 1965-66), Nat. Assn. Accts. (dir. Norwich, Conn. chpt. 1958-60), Nat. Assn. Accountants (St. Paul chpt. 1967), Assn. Bank Audit, Control and Operation, Am. Inst. Banking, Fin. Execs. Inst., Planning Forum (pres. Twin Cities chpt. 1984-85), Univ. Club (St. Paul). Clubs: St. Paul Athletic. Home: 415 Oak Ridge Dr San Marcos TX 78666 E-mail: rrpalmer@stthomas.edu.

PALMER, ROSE, foundation director, nurse; b. Pitts., Oct. 14, 1943; d. William Woodrow and Marion (Kuhn) Robbins; m. Anthony Joseph Palmer, (div. 1977); children: Tony, Kim; m. Alvin Phelps, 1985; stepchildren: Todd, Craig, Dean, Ryan, Mindy. AS in Nursing, Community Coll. Allegheny County, 1979; student, Carlow Coll., 1989. RN, Pa. Dir. SUPPORT, Pitts., 1979—. Legis. chair Allegheny County Transit Council, Pitts., 1985-87; candidate 45th legis. dist. Pa. Ho., 1988, 90; mem. steering com. Pitts. Women's Commn. Recipient Take Charge award Clairol, 1988. Mem. ABA (adv. bd. Child Support Advocacy Project 1987—), Nat. Child Support Coalition (treas. 1986—), Am. Acad. Family Mediators (assoc. 1986—), Family Mediation Coun. of Western Pa. (legis. com., bd. dirs.), Joint Family Law Coun. Pa., NOW, Women's Agenda Pa. Avocations: painting, needlework, macrame, gardening. Office: SUPPORT 429 Forbes Ave Ste 429 Pittsburgh PA 15219-1604

PALMER, RUSSELL EUGENE, investment executive; b. Jackson, Mich., Aug. 13, 1934; s. Russell E. and Margarite M. (Briles) P.; m. Phyllis Anne Hartung, Sept. 8, 1956; children: Bradley Carl, Stephen Russell, Russell Eugene, III, Karen Jean. BA with honors, Mich. State U., 1956; D in Comml. Sci. (hon.), Drexel U., 1980; MA (hon.), U. Pa., 1984; PhD (hon.), Chulalongkorn U., 1988, Free U. Brussels, 1989, York Coll., 1989. With Touche Ross & Co., N.Y.C., 1956-83, mng. ptnr., CEO, 1972-82, also bd. dirs., exec. coms.; mng. dir., CEO Touche Ross Internat., 1974-83; dean, Reliance prof. mgmt. and pvt. enterprise Wharton Sch. U. Pa., 1983-90, CEO. Bd. dirs. Verizon Corp., The May Dept. Stores Co., Honeywell Internat., Inc.; corp. bd. Safeguard Scientifics, Inc., Fed. Home Loan Mortgage Corp. Mem. pub. bds. Dirs. & Bds., Mergers & Aquisitions, Directory Corp. Affiliations, Directory Leading Pvt. Cos. Chmn. bd. trustees U. Pa. Health Care Sys.; pres. Fin. Acctg. Found., 1979-82; trustee Acctg. Hall of Fame, U. Pa.; bd. dirs. Joint Coun. Econ. Edn., 1978-83, United Fund Greater N.Y., 1980-83, UN Assn. U.S.A.; mem. Bus. Com. Arts, 1977-83; mem. Pres.'s Mgmt. Improvement Coun., 1979-80; mem. N.Y. adv. bd. Salvation Army, past mem. nat. adv. bd.; former mem. adv. coun. Sch. Internat. and Pub. Affairs Columbia U., Grad. Sch. Bus. Stanford U., Womens Way; mem. assocs. coun. Bus. Sch. Oxford U.; mem. adv. panel Comptr. Gen. U.S.; mem. U.S. Sec. Labor's Commn. on Workforce Quality and Labor Market Efficiency; pub. mem. Hudson Inst., mem. adv. bd. Radnor Venture Ptnrs.; bd. dirs. SEI Ctr. for Advanced Studies in Mgmt. Recipient Gavin Meml. award Beta Theta Pi, 1956, Disting. Community Svc. award Brandeis U., 1974, Outstanding Alumnus award Mich. State U., 1978, Humanitarian award Fedn. Jewish Philanthropies, 1979, Disting. Aux. Svc. award Salvation Army, 1979, LEAD Bus. award, 1984, Good Scout award Phila. coun. Boy Scouts Am., 1987. Mem. Merion Cricket Club, Merion Golf Club, Lost Tree Country Club, Conf. Bd. (bd. dirs.), Beta Gamma Sigma (mem. bd. govs.). Presbyterian. Office: The Palmer Group 3600 Market St Ste 530 Philadelphia PA 19104-2649

PALMER, SAMUEL COPELAND, III, lawyer; b. Phila., June 9, 1934; s. Samuel Copeland Jr. and Vivian Gertrude (Plumb) P.; divorced; children: Samuel C. IV, Sarah Anne, Bryan Douglas. Grad., Harvard Sch., Los Angeles, 1952; student, Yale U., 1953; AB, Stanford U., 1955; JD, Loyola-Marymount U., Marymount, 1958. Bar: Calif. 1959, U.S. Dist. Ct. (cen., ea. and so. dists. Calif.) 1959, U.S. Ct. Appeals (9th cir.) 1970, U.S. Supreme Ct. 1971. Dep. city atty., Los Angeles, 1959-60; assoc. firm Pollock & Deutz, 1960-63; ptnr. firm Pollock & Palmer, 1963-70, Palmer & Bartenetti, Los Angeles, 1970-81, Samuel C. Palmer III, P.C., 1981-85; ptnr. Thomas, & Snell, 1985—. Adj. prof. Calif. State U., Fresno, 1993. Trustee Western Ctr. Law and Poverty; bd. dirs. Big Bros./Big Sisters, Fresno, Arte Ams., Lively Arts Found., Nat. Sleep Found., Vols. in Parole; pres., bd. dirs. Poverello House; founder, pres. Fresno Crime Stoppers. Mem. ABA, State Bar Calif. (disciplinary subcom., bar examiners subcom.), Fresno County Bar Assn. (pres., bd. dirs. 1988-93), Pickwick Soc., Am. Bd. Trial Advocates, Chancery Club, Downtown Club, Calif. Club, Fig Garden Tennis Club, Rotary, Delta Upsilon, Phi Delta Phi. Office: 2445 Capitol St Fresno CA 93721-2224 also: 820 Suffolk St Cambria CA 93428-2508 E-mail: spalmer@thomasnell.com.

PALMER, SHARON-JOY, agricultural research company executive; b. S.I., N.Y., Oct. 16, 1947; d. James Murdock Palmer and Lillian Elinore (Nelson) Daniels; 1 child, Cameron Nelson Polland. Student, Wayne U., Chgo., 1966-68; student in real estate, Dade Jr. Coll., 1969-73; BS in Edn./Ch. Ministries, Liberty U., 1989, ThM, MAR/Counseling, 1994. Dental asst. Francis J. Byron Jr., DDS, S.I., N.Y., 1966-69; flight attendant Delta Airlines, Miami, 1969-77; realtor D.W. Hyder and Assocs., Albuquerque, 1976-78; sales rep. Postique of Colo., Denver, 1976-78; dir. Combanc Internat., Inc., Albuquerque, 1976-80; mfr.'s rep. Innovative Mktg. Concepts, 1977-79, owner; developer, owner Angel Skye Investments, Ltd., Angel Fire, N.Mex., 1979-82; econ. adv. Am. S.S.T. Corp., Parkersburg, W.Va., 1982-85; chmn., pres. Sci. Econ. Environ. Devel. Internat., Inc., Albuquerque, 1980—. Ptnr. Angel Skye Investments, 1980—; bd. dirs. Asia Enterprise Ltd., Tokyo, Condoc-Paraguay Ltd., Asuncion, Victory Internat. Inc., Panama City, Republic of Panama, Sci Econ. Environ. Devel. Kenya Ltd., Nairobi, 1980—, Sci. Econ. Environ. Devel. Internat. Del., Mountains Herbs and Spices, Albuquerque, 1980—. Inventor agrl. energy efficient units, 1982; inventor, designer above ground and underground "mighty seed" units for food prodn., seed programmable environ. controller and modular housing. Active Embassy Kenya, Washington for Agrl. Devel., Nairobi, Kenya, East Africa, 1982; mem. various childrens' hosps., Miami, 1973, Westside Assn., Coralles, N.Mex., 1980. Mem. Am. Dental Assts. Assn., Better Bus. Bur., Bd. Realtors, NAFE (nat. dir.), Nat. Platform Assn., Entrepreneur's Assn. Clubs: Angel Fire Country, Rio Rancho (N.Mex.) Country. Republican. Baptist. Home: 3208 Sue Cir Albuquerque NM 87124

PALMER, STUART HUNTER, sociology educator; b. N.Y.C., Apr. 29, 1924; s. Herman G. and Beatrice (Hunter) P.; m. Anne Barbara Scarborough, June 22, 1946; 1 dau., Catherine. BA, Yale U., 1949, MA, 1951, PhD, 1955; LHD (hon.), Daniel Webster Coll., 1997. Asst. to dean Yale Coll., New Haven, 1949-51; instr. sociology New Haven Coll., 1949-51, 53-55; faculty U. N.H., Durham, 1955—, prof., 1964—, chmn. dept. sociology and anthropology, 1964-69, 79-82, dean Coll. Liberal Arts, 1982-95, dir. London program, 1995-96. Disting. vis. prof. SUNY, Albany, 1970-71; vis. behavioral scientist N.H. Div. Mental Health; vis. prof. U. Sussex, Eng., 1976, U. Ga., 1977; cons. U.S. Office Edn., USPHS, U.S. Office Delinquency and Youth Devel., Dept. Justice; mem. adv. com. for sociology Com. on Internat. Exchange of Persons; mem. exec. com. N.H. Gov.'s Commn. on Crime and Delinquency; co-chmn. Internat. Symposium on Univs. in Twenty-First Century; co-chmn. Internat. Confs. on Stress Rsch., Nat. Commn. Arts and Scis. Author: Understanding Other People, 1955, A Study of Murder, 1960, (with Brian R. Kay) The Challenge of Supervision, 1961, Deviance and Conformity, 1970, (with Arnold S. Linsky) Rebellion and Retreat, 1972, The Violent Society, 1972, The Prevention of Crime, 1973, (with John A. Humphrey) Deviant Behavior, 1980, Role Stress, 1981, Deviant Behavior: Patterns, Sources, and Controls, 1990, The Universities Today, 1998; contbr. articles to profl. jours. Chmn. bd. trustees Daniel Webster Coll., New Eng. Aero. Inst. Served to lt. AC AUS, 1942-45; Served to lt. AC USAF, 1951-53. Decorated Air medal with 3 oak leaf clusters; fellow Henry Page. Mem. Am. Sociol. Assn., Eastern Sociol. Soc., Internat. Sociol. Soc., Internat. Soc. Criminology, Internat. Soc. Forecasters, Am. Assn. Colls., Council for Liberal Learning, Am. Assn. Higher Edn., Council Colls. Arts and Scis., Nat. Assn. State Univs. and Land-Grant Colls., AAAS, Am. Acad. Polit. and Social Scis., N.Y. Acad. Scis., Am. Assn. Suicidology, Soc. Cross-Cultural Research, Am. Soc. Criminology, Assn. Gov. Bds. Univs. and Colls., Phi Beta Kappa (hon.), Sigma Xi, Alpha Kappa Delta. Home: PO Box 904 Durham NH 03824-0904 *Be honest with yourself.*

PALMER, TERESA ANNE, nurse practitioner; b. Somerville, N.J., July 15, 1954; BSN, Seton Hall U., 1976, MS in Nursing, 1985. Cert. adult nurse practitioner, acute case nurse practitioner. Nurse practitioner inpatient psychiat. svcs. Cmty. Mental Health Ctr.-U. Medicine/Dentistry N.J., Piscataway, 1985-91; nurse practitioner adult cardiac surgery unit Robert Wood Johnson U. Hosp., New Brunswick, N.J., 1991-94; asst. prof. nursing acute care nurse practitioner U. Medicine and Dentistry, Newark, 1994; nurse practitioner internal medicine Internal Medicine and Urgent Care, Edison, 1994—. Holistic health educator/cons. Rx for Optimal Wellness. Contbr. articles to profl. jours. Mem. ANA, Am. Acad. Nurse Practitioners, N.J. Forum for Nurses in Advanced Practice. Home: 2484 Allwood Rd Scotch Plains NJ 07076-4502

PALMER, TIMOTHY TROW, safety and health consultant; b. Evanston, Ill., Mar. 22, 1938; s. Clinton Foster and Josephine Margaret (Squires) P.; m. Eloise Ann Ellson, Jun 16, 1962; children: Timothy Foster, Jennifer Ann, Jonathan Blair. BA in Chemistry, Zoology, Carleton Coll., Northfield, Minn., 1960; MS in Zoology, U. Minn., 1964, PhD in Zoology, 1974; MS in Safety, U. So. Calif., L.A., 1981. Cert. safety profl.; registered profl. engr., Mass. Commd. U.S. Navy, 1964, advanced through grades to lt. comdr., ret. 1984; asst. to dir. Gorgas Meml. Lab., Panama, 1976-79; safety prog. mgr. NMRI, Bethesda, Md., 1979-84; pres. Tepee Ltd., Annapolis, 1984-90; dir. environ. assessments and tng. Profl. Safety Cons. Co., Seabrook, 1986—2000, ret., 2000. Contbr. articles to profl. jours. Merit badge counselor Boy Scouts Am., Bloomington, Minn., 1967-76; risk mgmt. cons. Episcopal Diocese of Washington, 1981-88. Mem. Am. Soc. Safety Engrs., Nat. Safety Mgmt. Soc. (bd. dirs. 1985-87, 89-91, pres. 1987-89), Am. Nat. Standards Inst., Am. Soc. Tropical Medicine and Hygiene, Am. Legion, Masons. Republican. Episcopalian. Avocations: fishing, hunting, gardening. Home: 3232 Chrisland Dr Annapolis MD 21403-4350

PALMER, TOM GORDON, political scientist; b. Moetsch, Germany, Nov. 12, 1956; s. Gordon Felix and Martha Alice Palmer; life ptnr. Matthew Coombes. BA, St. John's Coll., 1982; MA, Catholic U. Am., 1993; DPhil, Oxford U., 2000. Editor Dollars and Sense, Washington, 1984-86; dir. student affairs Inst. Humane Studies George Mason U., Fairfax, Va., 1986-93; H.B. Earhart fellow Hertford Coll., Oxford, England, 1993-95; dir. spl. projects Cato Inst., Washington, 1995-99; dir. Cato U., 1999—; sr. fellow Cato Inst., 2001—. Dir Eastern European programs Carl Menger Inst, Inst Humane Studies, Vienna, 1989—93; policy analyst Coun for competitive Econ, Washington, 1982—83. Editor: The Ency. of Libertarianism, Humane Studies Rev., 1986—94. Youth coord Libertarian Party, Washington, 1975; asst dir MacBride for Pres Campaign, 1975—76; asst communications dir Clark for Pres Campaign, 1979—81; newsletter ed Nat Taxpayers Legal Fund, 1981—82; nat secy Comt Against Registration and the Draft, 1979—81; trustee Found Econ Educ, NY, 1998—. Avocations: hiking, weightlifting, self-education, promotion of liberty and the rule of law. Office: Cato Inst 1000 Massachusetts Ave NW Washington DC 20001 E-mail: TomGPalmer@hotmail.com.

PALMER, TREVELYAN EDWARD, physician, thoracic and cardiovascular surgeon; b. Perth, Australia, Sept. 14, 1924; came to U.S., 1954; s. Robert Trevelyan and Florence Mabel (Taaffe) P.; m. Claudia Ann Shaiko, May 17, 1958; children: Diana Alison, Andrew Trevelyan, Geoffrey Grant. MB, BS, U. Melbourne, 1952; MD, U. State of N.Y., Albany, 1979. Diplomate Am. Bd. Surgery, Am. Bd. Thoracic Surgery. Fellow in surgery Lahey Clinic, Boston, 1958-59; resident in gen. surgery Presbyn. Hosp., Phila., 1956-58, resident in thoracic surgery, 1959-62; attending thoracic and cardiovascular surgeon St. Christopher's Hosp. for Children, 1964-67, Temple U. Hosp., Phila., 1964-67, St. Agnes and White Plains (N.Y.) Hosps., 1967-91, chief thoracic and cardiovascular surgeon; hon. thoracic and cardiovascular surgeon White Plains Hosp., 1991—. Asst. instr. in surgery U. Pa. Sch. Medicine, Phila., 1956-58, prosector in anatomy, 1957-58; asst. prof. surgery Temple U. Sch. Medicine, 1964-67; cons. cardiothoracic surgeon Royal Hobert Hosp., Australia, 1989, Royal Perth Hosp., 1990; overseas vis. surgeon All India Inst. Med. Sci., New Delhi, 1992. Contbr. articles to profl. jours. Served with Royal Australian Air Force, 1942-45, U.K. and Middle East. Fellow ACS, Am. Coll. Chest Physicians, Royal Coll. Surgeons Can., Royal Australasian Coll. Surgeons, Royal Coll. Surgeons Edinburgh; mem. N.Y. Soc. Cardiovascular Surgery, N.Y. Soc. Thoracic Surgery. Avocations: aviation, travel, locum surgery in foreign countries. Home: 15 Gorham Rd Scarsdale NY 10583-1117

PALMER, VENRICE ROMITO, lawyer, educator; b. Springfield, Mass., Jan. 11, 1952; s. Venrice Wellesley and Mildred Adlay (Foster) P. Higher diploma, U. Besançon, France, 1973; AB maxima cum laude, King's Coll., Wilkes-Barre, Pa., 1974; JD, Harvard U., 1977. Bar: N.Y. 1978, U.S. Dist. Ct. (so. and ea. dists.) N.Y. 1979, Ill. 1986, Calif. 1997. Spl. asst. atty. gen. Office N.Y. Atty. Gen., N.Y.C., 1977-79; staff atty. SEC, 1979-82, br. chief, 1982-83, spl. trial counsel, 1983-85, acting asst. regional adminstr., 1984-85; sr. counsel Sears, Roebuck and Co., Hoffman Estates, Ill., 1985-97, Bank of Am., San Francisco, 1997-99; counsel McCutchen, Doyle, Brown & Enersen, LLP, 1999—2002, Bingham McCutchen LLP, San Francisco, 2002—. Guest lectr. St. John's U. Bus. Sch., N.Y.C., 1984; lectr. Practicing Law Inst., N.Y.C., 1995—, Glasser LegalWorks, Little Falls, N.J., 1997—, Am. Soc. Corp. Secs., 1997-99, Nat. Bus. Inst., Eau Claire, Wis., 2000—. Contbr. articles to various law publs. Recipient cert. of appreciation N.Y. State Bar Assn., 1978. Mem. ABA, Calif. State Bar Assn. (mem. fin. instns. com. 2000—). Avocations: opera, ballet, reading. Home: 1200 Gough St Apt 7A San Francisco CA 94109-6616 Office: Bingham McCutchen LLP Three Embarcadero Ctr San Francisco CA 94111 E-mail: venricepalmer@bingham.com.

PALMER, VERNON VALENTINE, law educator; b. New Orleans, Sept. 9, 1940; s. George Joseph and Juliette Marie (Wehrmann) P. BA, Tulane U., 1962, LL.B., 1965; LL.M., Yale U., 1966; PhD, Pembroke Coll., Oxford U., 1985. Bar: La. 1965, U.S. Supreme Ct. 1981. Asst. prof. law Ind. Sch. Law, Indpls., 1966-70; lectr. law U. Botswana, Lesotho & Swaziland, Roma, Lesotho, 1967-69; prof. Tulane Law Sch., New Orleans, 1970—, Clarence Morrow research prof. law, 1980—, Thomas Pickles prof. law, 1989—; external examiner Nat. U. Lesotho, Roma, 1978-81. Dir. Tulane Paris Inst. European Legal Studies, European Legal Studies; reporter for revision of civil code La. Law Inst. 1979; vis. prof. Faculty Law, U. Strasbourg, 1988, The Sorbonne, U. Paris, 1986, 92, Universite des Antilles, Martinique, 1998, Universidad Ramon Llull, Barcelona, 1998, U. Trento, 1999—, U. Laussanne, 2000, U. Geneva, 2000. Author: The Roman-Dutch and Lesotho Law of Delict, 1970, The Legal System of Lesotho, 1971, The Paths to Privity, 1992, The Civil Law of Lease in Louisiana, 1997, Louisiana: Microcosm of a Mixed Jurisdiction, 1999, Mixed Jurisdictions Worldwide: The Third Legal Family, 2001; contbr. numerous articles to profl. jours. Pres. French Quarter Residents Assn., 1973-75, Alliance for Good Govt., 1974-75; del. Nat. Democratic Conv., N.Y.C., 1976; chmn. World Congress on Mixed Jurisdictions, 2002. Decorated chevalier L'ordre des Palmes Académiques. Mem. La. Law Inst. Democrat. Roman Catholic. Home: 3311 Coliseum St New Orleans LA 70115-2401 Office: 6329 Freret St New Orleans LA 70118-6231 E-mail: vpalmer@law.tulane.edu .

PALMER, WAYNE LEWIS, television director and producer; b. Camden, N.J., Jan. 24, 1949; s. Paul John and Edna L. (Mitten) P.; m. Nicola E. Williams; 1 child, Shawn Mireille. BS cum laude, Ithaca Coll., 1971. Engr. Sta. WFIL-TV, Phila., 1968-71, Sta. WHYY-TV, Phila., 1971-72, ABC-TV, N.Y.C., 1972-73, Sta. WNET-TV, N.Y.C., 1973-79, assoc. dir., 1979-90, Dick Cavett Show, Bill Moyers' Journal; assoc. dir. then dir. MacNeil/Lehrer Newshour, N.Y.C., 1983-95. Judge ACE Cable Awards, N.Y.C., 1986; dir. duPont-Columbia Journalism Awards, 1998—. Prodr., writer Cancer: A Family Matter, PBS, 1996 (Nat. Med. Info. award 1997); dir. Internet In Action, PBS, 1998, The World of Elie Wiesel, PBS, 1992 Rep. and Dem. Nat. Conv., PBS, 1996 Nat. Issues Conv., PBS, News Hour with Jim Lehrer, 1996, Op Sail 2000, PBS, 2000, That Money Show, PBS, 2000-2001; dir. Time to Choose-A PBS Voter's Guide, 2000, (PBS) Moyers In Conversation: America Responds, 2001, Wide Angle, PBS, 2002; photography exhbns. Trenton (N.J.) City Mus., 1989, Abington Art Ctr., Phila., 1989, The Armory, Phila., 1990, Oakland (Calif.) Mus., 1990; represented in permanent collection Mus. City of N.Y. Recipient Graphic and Design award Nat. Assn. Ednl. Broadcasters, 1980. Mem. Dirs. Guild Am. Avocation: photography. Home: 23 W 73d St New York NY 10023-3104

PALMER, WILLARD ALDRICH, III, magician, writer, actor; b. Houston, July 25, 1942; s. Willard Aldrich and Ruby Lenoir (Touchstone) P.; m. Carol Ann Houston. BA in Germanics, Rice U., 1964; MA in Leetrs, Music, Profl. Studies, World U. Advanced Studies of Hawaii, 1995, Phd in Germanics, 2000. Instr. Charlie Cash Music Studios, Houston, 1962-70; performer various venues, Houston, Montreal, Can., 1965—; writer Alfred Music Co., Los Angeles, 1968-86; official magician Todd Mission, Tex., 1984—; owner, operator Bill Palmer Magic Shows, Bellaire, 1984—. Dir. Tex. Renaissance Festival, Todd Mission, 1978-79; writer, dir. Ren Fair Prodns., Inc., Houston, 1979-81; writer, cons. Exclusive Magical Pubs., Houston, Mexico City, 1986— (mem. editoral bd. 1986). Author: (books) How To Play Folk and Bluegrass Banjo, 1965, A Guide For The Texas Renaissance Festival Performer, 1978, Early History of the Paddle Trick in Print, 1995, How to be a Professional Entertainer, 1996; translator: Magical Adventures and Fairy Tales (Punx) 1987, Punx's Fourth Dimensional Mysteries, 1990, Farewell Performance (Punx), 1990, Paramiracles, 1996, Shenerazade (Borodin), 2001. Dir., pres. Houston Soc. for Psychic Research, 1972—. Mem. Soc. Am. Magicians (pres. Houston chpt. 1985-86), Internat. Brotherhood Magicians (pres. Houston chpt. 1984-85), Tex. Assn. Magicians, Houston Assn. Magicians (pres. 1978-79), The Inner Magic Circle (assoc.), Phi Mu Alpha (warden 1966-67), Delta Phi Alpha. Lutheran. Avocation: psychic research. Home and Office: Bill Palmer Magic Shows 7902 Roos Rd Houston TX 77036-6440 E-mail: bill@billpalmer.com.

PALMER, WILLIAM D. judge; b. Adrian, Mich., 1952; BS in Mgmt. cum laude, Rensselaer Poly. Inst., 1973; JD cum laude, Boston Coll., 1976. Bar: Fla. 1976; cert. civil mediator, family mediator, arbitrator, Fla. Assoc. Carlton, Fields, Ward, Emmanuel, Smith & Cutler, Orlando, Fla., 1976-82, ptnr., 1982-97, Palmer & Palmer, PA, Orlando, 1997-2000; dist. judge 5th dist. Fla. Ct. Appeal, Daytona Beach, 2000—. Lectr. in field. Editor-in-chief Boston Coll. Environ. Affairs Law Rev., 1975-76. Past bd. dirs. Fla. Hosp. Found., Life for Kids Adoption Agy.; past chmn. bd. dirs. Ctrl. Fla. Helpline; bd. dirs. Boys and Girls Club of Ctrl. Fla. Mem.: Orange County Bar Assn. (chmn. various coms.), Fla. Bar (mem. litigation, appellate law and family law sects., chair Fla. Bar jour. com. 1993—95, vice chair amicus com. 1993—95, chair jud. nominating procedures com. 1992—94, mem. jud. adminstrn. selection and tenure com. 1995—98). Office: 5th Dist Ct Appeal 300 S Beach St Daytona Beach FL 32114-5097 E-mail: palmerw@flcourts.org.

PALMER, WILLIAM JOSEPH, accountant; b. Lansing, Mich., Sept. 3, 1934; s. Joseph Flammin Lacchia and Henrietta (Yagerman) P.; m. Judith Pollock, Aug. 20, 1960 (div. Nov. 1980); children: William W., Kathryn E., Leslie A., Emily J.; m. Kathleen Francis Booth, June 30, 1990; stepchildren: Blair T. Manwell, Lindsay H. Manwell. BS, U. Calif., Berkeley, 1963. CPA. With Coopers & Lybrand, 1963-80; mng. ptnr. Sacramento, 1976-80; ptnr. Arthur Young & Co., San Francisco, 1980-89, Ernst & Young, San Francisco, 1989-94; prof. U. Calif., Berkeley, 1994—. Bd. dirs. The Dutra Group; chair constrn. industry group Coopers & Lybrand, 1973-80, Arthur Young, 1980-89, Ernst & Young, 1989-94; guest lectr. Engring. Sch. Stanford U., 1976; lectr. Golden Gate Coll., 1975. Author: (books) Businessman's Guide to Constuction, 1981, Construction Management Book, 1984, Construction Accounting and Financial Management, 5th edit., 1994, Construction Litigation-Representing The Contractor, 1992, Construction Insurance, Bonding and Risk Management, 1996. Bd. dirs. Sacramento Met. YMCA, 1976-82, V.p., 1979-82; bd. dirs. Sacramento Symphony Found., 1977-80; asst. state fin. chmn. Calif. Reagan for Pres., 1980. Lt. USN, 1953-59. Mem. AICPA (vice chmn. com. constrn. industry 1975-81), Nat. Assn. Accts. (pres. Oakland/East Bay chpt. 1972, Man of Yr. 1968), Calif. Soc. CPA's, Assn. Gen. Contractors Calif. (bd. dirs. 1971-74), World Trade Club, Commonwealth Club (San Francisco), Del Paso Country Club, Sutter Club, Lambda Chi Alpha. Roman Catholic. Avocations: antique boats, sailing, tennis, book collecting, pipe collecting. Home: 6 Heather Ln Orinda CA 94563-3508 Office: Ernst & Young 1331 N California Blvd Walnut Creek CA 94596-4537 E-mail: sherry-swanson@ey.com.

PALMERI, MARLAINA, school executive; b. Rochester, N.Y., Feb. 20, 1950; d. Joseph Michael and Eleanor Louise (Polisseni) P. BA, SUNY, Plattsburgh, 1971; MA, SUNY, Brockport, 1984; EdD, U. Rochester, 1997; student, U. Matlock, England, U. Copenhagen, Denmark, U. Moscow, Russia. Cert. Sch. Dist. Adminstr., Sch. Administr. Supr., N-6, N.Y. Tchr. Rochester (N.Y.) City Schs., 1972-86, supr. elem. magnet schs., 1986-88, vice prin., 1988-92, prin., 1992-99; v.p. Edison Schs. Inc., N.Y.C., 1999—. Named Disting. Educator, N.Y. State, 1997. Mem. ASCD, Nat. Assn. Elem. Sch. Prins., Phi Delta Kappa. Avocations: tennis, golf. Home: 254 Mendon Ionia Rd Honeoye Falls NY 14472-9742 Office: The Edison Project 521 5th Ave New York NY 10175-1600

PALMERI, SHARON ELIZABETH, freelance writer, community educator; b. Gary, Ind., July 23, 1948; d. Theodore and Alberta (Bias) Wozniak; m. John James Palmeri, Apr. 9, 1969; 1 child, Renee Suzanne. BS in Edn. English/Journalism with honor, Ind. U. NW, 1991. Health columnist Lake County Star, Crown Point, Ind., 1989-92; corr. Post Tribune, Gary, 1992-93; feature corr. The Munster (Ind.) Times, 1993—95; educator creative and news writing Merrillville (Ind.) Adult Edn., 1989—95; educator writer's workshop continuing edn. dept. Purdue U. Calumet, Hammond, Ind., 1990—95, composition educator English dept., 2001—02; educator creative writing Purdue U. N. Ctrl., Westville, 1995—; educator of composition Purdue U., Calumet, 2001—02; corr. Post Tribune, 2002—. Dir. Write-On Hoosiers, Inc., Crown Point, 1989—; educator news and creative writing Bethlehem Steel Career Devel. Ctr., 1996—98; educator Forest Ridge Acad., 1996—; bood doctor, publicity agt., local book and mag. promoter The Creative Connection. Exec. editor: Hoosier Horizon, 1991-96; co-editor: Hoosier Horizon Children's Mag., 1993—; contbr. short stories and essays to Spirits Mag., 1990, 91. Bd. dirs. N.W. Ind. Arts and Humanities Consortium, Gary, 1994—2000. Recipient Best of Show award Southlake Camera Club, Crown Point, 1975, Focal Point Camera Club, Portage, 1982. Mem. Nat. Coun. Tchrs. English, Soc. Profl. Journalists, N.W. Ind. Arts Assn. (educator 1997—), Communicators N.W. Ind., Ind. U. Alumni Assn., Kappa Delta Pi (newsletter editor 1991-94). Avocations: sailing, photography. Home and Office: 3605 Kingsway Dr Crown Point IN 46307-8934

PALMERIO, ELVIRA CASTANO, art gallery director, art historian; b. Cin., July 23, 1929; d. John and Josephine Castano; m. Carlo Palmerio, June 1, 1958 (dec.); 1 child, Marina. B Lit. Interpretation, Emerson Coll., 1950; postgrad., Pius XII Inst., Florence, Italy, 1954-55; student opera with Cesare Sturani. Curator Castano Art Gallery, Boston, 1965-78, dir. Needham, Mass., 1978-98; rschr. for Archivies of Am. Art Smithsonian Instn., Boston, 1988-89; performed voiceover in Italian for Nova PBS TV Series, Nova, Italy, 1997; gov. adv. com., 1997. Vatican translator; interpreter Italian art specializing in Macchiaioli art; Italian interpreter Ritz Carlton Internat. Festival, (Italian) Mayor's Office Sister Cities Internat. Conv.; appointed sec. World Affairs Coun., Boston; tchr. Emmanuel Coll. Boston, 1953. Mem. Rep. Presdl. Task Force, Nat. Rep. Senatorial Com., Presdl. Inner Circle; active Boston chpt. UN; bd. dirs. Needham Hist. Soc., Boston U. Women's Coun.; vol. Sail Boston, 1992; del. Presdl. Trust, 1992; apptd. Gov.'s Com. on Women's Issues; del. to Nat. Fedn. of Rep. Womens Conv., 1999, 2002. Cardinal Spellman scholar; recipient Pirandello Lyceum award, I Migliori, 1997, Vol. award Nat. Fedn. Commns. Women, 1999, Nat. Assn. Commissions for Women, 1999. Mem. UN, Boston U. Women's Coun., Boston Browning Soc., Fogg Art Mus. of Harvard U., Friends of Needham Libr., Archives Am. Art Boston, Alliance Francaise Boston, World Affairs Coun. Boston (sec.), Nat. Mus. Women in Arts, Needham Hist. Soc. (bd. dirs.), Nat. Italian Am. Found., French Libr., World Boston. Avocations: current events, internat. affairs, writing, travel, music. Address: 50 Grove St Wellesley MA 02482-7713

PALMERLEE, APRIL WAHLESTEDT, government official; b. Cheverly, Md., Apr. 9, 1968; d. James Anthony Pazienza and Beth Lewisa Catherwood; m. Claes R. Wahlestedt, June 15, 1991 (div. July 1996); m. David Luke Palmerlee, May 28, 2000. BS in Fgn. Svc., Georgetown U., 1989; M Internat. Affairs, Columbia U., 1999. Program asst. Spanish Inst., N.Y.C., 1990-92; spl. asst. Oscar de la Renta, Ltd., 1992-94, 95-96; rschr. Bank Credit Analyst, Montreal, Que., Can., 1994-95; dir. comms. Coun. on Fgn. Rels., N.Y.C., 1996—2002; sr. coord. internat. women's issues U.S. Dept. State, Washington, 2002—. Republican. Episcopalian. E-mail: palmerleeAW@state.gov.

PALMGREN, NADINE R. lawyer; b. Geneseo, Ill., Sept. 9, 1954; d. Wayne A. and Helen L. (Lulich) Stohl; m. Charles F. Palmgren, May 17, 1975; children: Lynn M., Brad M. Student, Black Hawk Coll., 1972-74, No. Ill. U., 1974-76, Augustana Coll., 1975-76; BS, No. Ill. U., 1976; MBA, St. Ambrose U., 1990; JD with honors, Drake U., 1993. Bar: Ill. 1993, Iowa 1993, U.S. Dist. Ct. (cen. dist.) Ill. 1995. Jud. clk. 14th Jud. Cir. Ct., Rock Island, Ill., 1992; ptnr. Stone & Palmgren, Geneseo, 1993—. Adj. prof. Black Hawk Coll., Moline, Ill., 1993-97. Author: Understanding Iowa Law, 1993. V.p. Bus. and Profl. Women, Geneseo, 1994; chmn. N & W. Henry County unit Am. Cancer Soc., Geneseo, 1989-90; mem. cmty. devel. com. Jr. Women's Club, Geneseo, 1989-90. Mem. Ill. Bar Assn., Iowa Bar Assn, Henry County Bar Assn. Office: Stone & Palmgren 211 S State St Geneseo IL 61254-1454 Fax: (309) 944-4629.

PALMIERE, CATHERINE EMILIA, executive recruiter; b. Yonkers, N.Y., Apr. 4, 1959; d. Michael Anthony and Raffaela Theresa (Celentano) P. BS, Manhattan Coll., 1981, MBA, 1995. Cert. personnel cons., temporary staffing specialist, internat. personnel cons., search specialist. V.p. Adam Pers. Inc., N.Y.C., 1981-92; dir. Advice Pers. Inc., 1992-2000; prin. Adam Pers., 2000—. Mem. Internat. Confedn. Pers. Svcs. Assns., Nat. Assn. Pers. Svcs., Delta Mu Delta. Home: 500 E 77th St Apt 1417 New York NY 10162-0005 E-mail: cpalmiere@adampersonnel.com.

PALMIERI, RODNEY AUGUST, retired state agency administrator, pharmacist; b. Santa Rosa, Calif., July 12, 1944; s. August John and Olga G.; m. Phyllis Scott, Aug. 14, 1965; children: Christopher August, Joshua Scott. AA, Santa Rosa Jr. Coll., 1964; B of Pharmacy, U. Colo., 1968. Pvt. practice pharmacist, Santa Rosa, 1968—71; pharm. cons. State of Calif., San Jose, 1971-75, chief pharm. cons. Sacramento, 1975-80, sr. mgr., 1991-95; project dir. Vital Record Improvement Project, 1991-95; gen. ptnr. Cold Springs Office Devel., Placerville, Calif., 1984-98; chief Office Vital Records, 1995-2000; dep. state registrar State of Calif., 1995-2000; owner Palmieri Cons. Svcs., 2001—. Mem. El Dorado County Grand Jury, 1990; Webelos leader Boy Scouts Am., 1976-77, scoutmaster, 1977-82; referee, coach El Dorado (Calif.) Youth Soccer League, 1977-83; dir. El Dorado County Fair, 1991-99; chmn. City of Placerville Pers. Bd., 1995-98; cert. profl. guide and instr. for whitewater rafting. Mem. Rho Chi (pres. 1967-68), Phi Delta Chi. Avocations: gourmet cooking, collecting wine, martial arts, backpacking, golf.

PALMIERI, VICTOR HENRY, lawyer, business executive; b. Chgo., Feb. 16, 1930; s. Mario and Maria (Losacco) P.; children: Matthew B., John W.; m. Cathryn Connors, July 6, 1990. AB in History, Stanford U., 1951, JD, 1954. Bar: Calif. 1954. Assoc. O'Melveny & Myers, L.A., 1955-59; exec. v.p. Janss Investment Corp., 1959-63, pres., 1963-68; chmn. Pa. Co. and its subs. Great S.W. Corp., 1969-77; chmn. bd. Palmieri Co., N.Y.C., 1969—. Chmn. PHL Corp., Inc. (formerly Baldwin-Unitaed Inc.), Phila., 1983—87; trustee, CEO Colo.Ute Electric Assn., Inc., 1990—92; spl. dep. rehabilitator Confedn. Life Ins. Co., 1994—98; dep. rehabilitator, CEO Mut. Benefit Life Ins. Co., 1991—94; pres., CEO MBL Life Assurance Corp., 1994—95; chmn. Alix-Palmieri Assocs., 1997—99; dir. William Carter Corp., 1992—95, Outlet Comms., Inc., 1993—95, Broadcasting Ptnrs., Inc., 1994—95; bd. dirs. Mullin Cons., Inc., vice chmn., 2002—; bd. dirs. M Fin. Holdings Inc. Ambassador-at-large, U.S. coord. refugee affairs Dept. State, 1979—81; chmn. Am. Learning Corp., 1970—85; dep. exec. dir. Nat. Adv. Commn. on Civil Disorders, 1967—68; mem. Coun. on Fgn. Rels.; trustee Rockefeller Found., 1979—89; pres., bd. dirs. Lincoln Ctr. Theater, 1985—89; chmn. Overseas Devel. Coun., 1985—91; bd. trustees The Police Found., 1996—2002. Office: Mullin Cons Inc 644 S Figueroa St Los Angeles CA 90017 E-mail: Victor.Palmieri@mullinconsulting.com.

PALMINTIER, MICHAEL CARTER, lawyer; b. Linz, Austria, Feb. 6, 1949; arrived in U.S., 1949; s. Dominic John and Betty Brownsbeger Palmintier; m. Laura Vannoy Palmintier, June 11, 1970; children: Dominic, Joshua, Blake, Ellen. BS, La. State U., 1972, JD, 1975. Assoc. Due & Dodson, Baton Rouge, 1975—78; pvt. practice, 1978—87; founding ptnr. de Gravelle Palmintier Holthaus & Frugé, 1987—. Mem. Alliance for Jud. Excellence, Baton Rouge, 1995—; mem. govs. panel to establish uniform informed consent State of La., Baton Rouge, 1996—, vice chair , 1999—. Mem.: ATLA, ABA, Baton Rouge Bar Assn. (court liason 1998—99), La. Trial Laawyers Assn. (pres. 2000—01), La. State Bar Assn. Democrat. Roman Catholic. Avocations: music, literature, travel. Office: de Gravelles Palmintier Holthaus and Frugé 628 St Louis St Baton Rouge LA 70802

PALMISANO, ELSALYN, library director, consultant, archivist; b. Corvallis, Oreg., Mar. 20, 1943; d. Vincent S. and Charlotte (Harman) Palmisano; m. Harris Drucker, Aug. 6, 1966; children: David, Jason. BA, U. Del., 1965; MS in LS, Drexel U., 1968; student, Modern Archives Inst., Washington, 1989, Rutgers U., 1995. Cert. in archives, in preservation mgmt. Libr., archivist Monmouth County Hist. Assn., Freehold, N.J., 1974-78; media specialist Brookdale C.C., Lincroft, 1978-81; libr. dir. Ann May Sch. Nursing/Jersey Shore Med Ctr, Neptune, 1980-88; dir. West Long Branch (N.J.) Pub. Libr., 1990—. Cons. CAPES, N.J., 1988—. Mem.exec. bd. Hist. Soc. Ocean Grove, N.J., 1985—. Recipient award ofr recognition N.J. Hist. Commn., 1990, cert. of recognition Bd. of Freeholders, Monmouth County, N.J., 1993. Mem. ALA, Monmouth Librs. Assn. (pres. 1983, 97-99), Mid Atlantic Regional Archives Conf., N.J. Libr. Assn., Monmouth County Hist. Assn., Beta Phi Mu. Unitarian Universalist. Avocations: kayaking, walking, bicycling, reading. Office: West Long Branch Pub Libr 95 Poplar Ave West Long Branch NJ 07764-1653 Home: Marina Bay Club # 74 580 Patten Ave Long Branch NJ 07740-7853 E-mail: epalmisa@hawkmail.monmouth.edu.

PALMISANO, SAMUEL J. information technology executive; With IBM, Balt., 1973; sr. mng. dir. ops. IBM Japan; sr. v.p., group exec. IBM Personal Systems Group; pres., CEO Integrated Systems Solutions Corp., IBM subs.; sr. v.p., group exec. IBM Global Svcs., IBM Enterprise Systems Group; pres., COO IBM, White Plains, NY, pres., CEO, 2002—. Office: IBM 1133 Westchester Ave White Plains NY 10604*

PALMORE, CAROL M. state official; b. Owensboro, Ky., Jan. 13, 1949; d. P.J. and Carrie Alice (Leonard) Pate; m. John Stanley Palmore Jr., Jan. 1, 1982. BS in History and Polit. Sci., Murray State U., 1971; JD, U. Ky., 1977. Social worker Dept. Human Resources, Frankfort, Ky., 1971-74; assoc. Rummage, Kamuf, Yewell & Pace, Owensboro, 1977-81; hearing officer Ky. Bd. Claims, Frankfort, 1980-81; gen. counsel Ky. Labor Cabinet, 1982-83, dep. sec. labor, 1984, 1986-87, sec. labor, 1987-90, 91-94; ptnr. Palmore & Sheffer Attys., Henderson, Ky., 1984-86; dep. sec. Ky. Pers. Cabinet, Frankfort, 1996-98, acting sec., 1998, sec., 1998—. Bd. dirs. Ky. Employer's Mutual Ins., Ky. Retirement Sys., Ky. Pub. Employees Deferred Comp. Authority, Govtl. Svcs. Ctr. Authority, Gov.'s Collective Bargaining Task Force, Gov.'s Minority Mgmt. Trainee Program Task Force, State Parks Commn., Ky. Group Health Ins. Bd.; chmn. Ky. Safety & Health Stds. Bd., Frankfort, 1987-90, 91-94; co-chmn. Ky. Labor Mgmt. Adv. Coun., Frankfort, 1987-90, 91-94; bd. dirs. Ky. Workers' Comp Funding Commn., Frankfort, 1987-90, 91-94, Community Svc. Commn., Frankfort, 1993-94, Ky. Info. Resources Mgmt. Commn., Frankfort, 1994, Sch.-to-Work Partnership Coun., Frankfort, 1994; ex-officio bd. dirs. Pub. Employees Collective Bargaining Task Force, Frankfort, 1994, Ky. Workforce Partnership Coun., Frankfort, 1994. Labor liaison Jones for Gov., Lexington, 1990-91; del. Dem. Nat. Conv., N.Y.C., 1992; mem. inaugural class Ky. Women's Leadership Network, Frankfort, 1993; bd. dirs. Alliant Health Systems Adult Oper. Bd., Louisville, 1992-96, Ky. Commn. Homeless, Frankfort, 1993-94; candidate for Sec. State Commonwealth Ky., 1995; chair Dem. Women's Think Tank, 1995. Mem. Ky. Bar Assn. (del. ho. dels. 1985-86, chair law day/spkr. bur. 1985-86, mem. 1986-90), Ky. Bar Found. (bd. dirs. 1985-92, sec. 1986-89, pres. elect 1989-90, pres. 1990-91), Rotary (program chair Frankfort chpt. 1993-94). Episcopalian. Avocations: antiques, reading, vintage jewelry, walking. Home: 2310 Peaks Mill Rd Frankfort KY 40601-9437 Office: Personnel Cabinet 200 Fair Oaks Ln Frankfort KY 40601-1134

PALMORE, ERDMAN BALLAGH, education educator, researcher; b. Tokuyama, Japan, June 3, 1930; arrived in U.S., 1936; s. Peyton Lee Palmore, Jean McAlpine Palmore; m. Brydie S. Palmore; children: Karen Beckerman, Julia Shaida. PhD, Columbia U., 1959. Assoc. prof. Yale U., New Haven, 1959—63; social scientist Social Security Adminstrn., Balt., 1963—67; prof. Duke U., Durham, NC, 1967—. Author: Facts on Aging Quiz, 1998, Ageism: Negative & Positive, 1999. Sec. W. Triangle UN Assn., Chapel Hill, NC, 1998—2002. Named Disting. Acad. Gerontologist, So. Gerontol. Soc., 1989. Fellow: Gerontol. Soc. Am. Unitarian Universalist. Avocations: physical fitness, singing, hiking. Home: 3908 Stoneycreek Rd Chapel Hill NC 27514 Office: Duke Univ Box 3003 DUMC Durham NC 27710 Business E-Mail: ebp@geri.duke.edu.

PALMORE, JOHN STANLEY, JR. retired lawyer; b. Ancon, C.Z., Aug. 6, 1917; s. John Stanley and Antoinette Louise (Gonzalez) P.; m. Eleanor Anderson, July 31, 1938 (dec. 1980); 1 child, John Worsham (dec.); m. Carol Pate, Jan. 1, 1982. Student, Western Ky. State Coll., 1934-36; LL.B. cum laude, U. Louisville, 1939. Bar: Ky. 1938. Practice law, Henderson, 1939-42, 47-59; judge Ct. Appeals Ky. (name changed to Supreme Ct. Ky. 1975), 1959-82, chief justice, 1966, 73, 77-82; practice law Frankfort, Ky., 1983-84; ptnr. Palmore & Sheffer, Henderson, 1984-86; sr. counsel Jackson & Kelly, Lexington, Ky., 1986-92; ret., 1992. City pros. atty., Henderson, 1949-53, city atty., 1953-55; commonwealth's atty. 5th Circuit Ct. Dist. Ky., 1955-59 Served to lt. USNR, 1942-46, 51-52. Mem. VFW, Ky. Bar Assn., Am. Legion, Ky. Hist. Soc., Frankfort Country Club, Lexington Club, Frankfort Rotary Club (pres. 1993-94), Masons, Shriners, Elks, Phi Alpha Delta. Episcopalian (past vestryman, sr. warden). Home: 2310 Peaks Mill Rd Frankfort KY 40601-9437

PALMS, JOHN MICHAEL, academic administrator, physicist; b. Rijswijk, The Netherlands, June 6, 1935; naturalized, 1956; s. Peter Joannes and Mimi Adele (DeYong) P.; m. Norma Lee Cannon, June 2, 1958; children: John Michael, Danielle Maria, Lee Cannon. BS in Physics, The Citadel, 1958, DSc (hon.), 1980; MS in Physics, Emory U., 1959; PhD, U. N.Mex., 1966. Commd. 2d lt. USAF, 1958, retired capt. Res., 1970; lectr. physics dept. U. N.Mex., 1959-60; instr. physics dept. USAF Acad., 1961-62; staff mem. Western Electric Sandia Lab., 1961-62, U. Calif. Los Alamos Sci. Lab., 1962-66, Oak Ridge Nat. Lab., 1966; asst. prof. Emory U., Atlanta, 1966-69, assoc. prof., 1969-73, chmn., assoc. prof. dept. physics, asso. prof. radiology dept. Med. Sch., 1973-74, prof., chmn. dept. physics, 1969-74, dean Coll. Arts and Scis., 1974-80, acting chmn. dept. math. and computer sci., 1976-77, v.p. arts and scis., acting chmn. dept. anthropology, 1979-80, acting dean Emory Coll., 1979-80, acting dir. Emory U. Computing Ctr., 1980-82, v.p. acad. affairs, 1982-88, interim dean Grad. Sch., 1985-86, Charles Howard Candler prof. nuclear, radiation and environ. physics, 1988-90; pres., prof. physics Ga. State U., Atlanta, 1989-91, U. S.C., Columbia, 1991—. Bd. dirs. Fortis, Inc., N.Y.C., Exelon Corp., Chgo., NCAA, Simcom Internat. Holdings, Inc., Atlanta; adv. com. Oak Ridge Nat. Lab., 1985-89; mem. nat. nuclear accrediting bd. Inst. Nuclear Power Ops., 1985-91, mem. nat. adv. coun., 1997-2001; mem. panel for semicondr. detectors NAS/NRC, 1963-74; cons. Acad. Natural Scis., Phila., Hughes, Inc., Santa Barbara, Calif., Tennelec, Inc., Three Mile Island Environ. Study, TRW Space Sys. Divsn., L.A., Ga. Dept. Human Resources, Nat. Cancer Inst.; mem. high tech. task force Atlanta C. of C. Contbr. articles on nuclear, atomic, med. and environ. physics to profl. jours. Mem. adv. bd. The Citadel, Oak Ridge Nat. Lab.; mem. exec. bd. Atlanta Area Coun. Boy Scouts of Am., 1989-90; mem. cmty. rels. bd. U.S. Penitentiary, Atlanta; trustee, chmn. Inst. Def. Analyses, Wesleyan Coll., 1984-89, Pace Acad., 1984-89, St. Joseph's Hosp., Atlanta, 1987-89, Ga. Rsch. Alliance, 1988-89; mem. S.C. Univs. Edn. Found., Devel. Found. and Rsch. Found., S.C. Rsch. Inst. Bds.; bd. dirs. Civic-Atlanta Partnership Bus. and Edn., Inc., 1988-90, United Way; chair Rhodes scholar selection com., 1987, S.C., 1995-99; bd. dirs. Nat. Merit Scholarship Corp. Mem. AAAS, Am. Phys. Soc., Am. Assn. Physics Tchrs., IEEE (Nuclear Sci. Group), Am. Nuclear Soc., Am. Coun. Edn., Coun. Provosts and Acad. V.P.s, Am. Conf. Acad. Deans, Soc. Nuclear Medicine, Health Physics Soc., Greater Columbia C. of C. (bd. dirs.), Rotary, Columbia C. of C., Phi Beta Kappa, Sigma Xi, Phi Kappa Phi, Omicron Delta Kappa, Sigma Pi Sigma. Home and Office: Pres U SCO Osborne Bldg Columbia SC 29208-0001

PALMS, ROGER CURTIS, educator, editor, clergyman; b. Detroit, Sept. 13, 1936; s. Nelson Curtis and Winifred Jessie (Bennett) P.; m. Andrea Sisson, Aug. 22, 1959; children— Grant Curtis, Andrea Jane BA, Wayne State U., 1958; B.D., Eastern Baptist Sem., Phila, 1961, M.Div., 1971, D.D., 1977; MA, Mich. State U., 1971. Ordained to ministry Am. Bapt. Chs., 1961. Pastor Ronceverte Bapt. Ch., W.Va., 1961-64; pastor 1st Bapt. Ch., Highland Park, N.J., 1964-67; chaplain Am. Bapt. Student Found., Mich. State U., East Lansing, 1967-73; assoc. editor Decision mag. Billy Graham Evang. Assn., Mpls., 1973-76, editor, 1976-98. Guest lectr. at schs of evangelism writers' confs., colls. and seminaries. Author 15 books including Enjoying the Closeness of God, 1989, Let God Help You Choose, 1989, An Unexpected Hope, 1998, Effective Magazine Writing, 2000; newspaper columnist. Trustee No. Bapt. Theol. Sem., 1973— Mem. Evang. Press Assn. (pres. 1991-93). *Investing in people's spiritual lives, giving time and counsel, will bring multiplied results for generations. It is one of the most far-reaching ways I can put faith to work.*

PALÓCZ, ISTVÁN, electrical engineer, educator; b. Budapest, Hungary; s. Bodog and Stephanie Palócz; m. Suzane Zimmerman; children: Patricia, Spencer. Engring. diploma, U. Tech. Scis., Budapest, 1948, Docent, 1953; PhD in Electrophysics, Polytech. Inst. Bklyn., 1962; PhD (hon.) , U. Tech. Scis., Budapest. Rschr. Tungstram Co. , Budapest, 1945—48, head quality control, 1948—53; asst. prof., rschr., docent Tech. U., Budapest, 1950—56; mem. rsch. staff IBM, N.Y.C., 1957—65; prof. NYU, 1965—73, Polyech. Inst. , Bklyn., 1973—91, prof. emeritus, 1991—. Cons. Tungstrom, Budapest, 1950—56, INPE, San Jose of Candos, Brazil, 1992. Achievements include discovery of first self consistent calculation of Smith-Purcell effect. Presented the first measurement of precursors. Home: 1 N Main St Cranbury NJ 08512

PALOLA, HARRY JOEL, international affairs executive, consultant; b. Kaukola, Viipuri, Finland, May 13, 1943; came to U.S., 1961; s. Heikki and Mary Dagmar (Ahokas) P.; m. Rita Hannele Ahokas, Sept. 15, 1968 (div. July 1992); children: Christine, Kathy, Kimberly. AA, L.A. City Coll., 1966; BS in Mech. Engring., Calif. State U., Long Beach, 1971; MA in Internat. Affairs, Calif. State U., Sacramento, 1995. Registered engr.-in-tng., Calif. Design engr. Northrop Corp., Hawthorne, Calif., 1971-77, Ford Aerospace and Comm. Corp., Newport Beach, 1977-81, B&M Assocs., San Diego, 1982; mech. engr. Raytheon Corp., Goleta, Calif., 1982-84; electronic packaging engr. LPL Tech. Svc., Seattle, 1984-86; design/test engr. Boeing Co., Seattle and Vandenberg, Calif., 1986-92; CEO Internat. Consultancy Corp., Santa Ynez, 1993—. Cons. in basic and applied rsch. in human comm., 1993—. Author: International Finnish Studies: Language, History and Culture, 1995, The Karjala Question-Thoughts on Religious Directions, 1997. Econ. devel. student intern City of Sacramento, 1992-93. Sgt. USNG, 1966-72. Republican. Lutheran. Avocations: ocean sailing, private flying, Finno-Urgic and Ural-Altaic languages. Office: Internat Consultancy Corp 1041 N Refugio Rd Santa Ynez CA 93460-9316

PALOMBO, JOSEPH, clinical social worker; b. Cairo, July 18, 1928; came to U.S., 1949; s. Albert H. and Regina (Costi) P.; m. Dorothy D. Denton, Aug. 4, 1957. PhB, New Sch. Social Rsch., N.Y.C., 1954; MA in Philosophy, Yale U., 1958; MSW, U. Chgo., 1959; cert. in child therapy, Inst. Psychoanalysis, Chgo., 1964; DHL (hon.), Inst. for Clin. Social Work, Chgo., 1999. Cert. social worker, Ill. Pvt. practice, Chgo., 1970—; dean Inst. Clin. Social Work, 1981-92, founding dean, 1992—; assoc. dir. Rush Neurobehavioral Ctr. dept. pediats. Rush-Presbyn.-St. Luke's Med. Ctr., 1995-97; rsch. coord. Rush Neurobehavioral Ctr. Rush-Presbyn. St. Luke's Med. Ctr., 1997—. Adminstrv. dir. child therapy program Inst. Psychoanalysis, 1970-78, mem. faculty, 1970—; adminstrv. dir. Barr-Harris Ctr. Inst. Psychoanalysis, Chgo., 1976-78; mem. faculty advanced cert. program Smith Coll. Sch. Social Work, 1985-87. Contbr. articles to profl. jours. Mem. NASW, Acad. Cert. Social Workers, Assn. Child Psychotherapists (pres. 1976), Nat. Acads. Practice in Social Work (founding), Ill. Soc. Clin. Social Workers. Democrat.

PALOMBO, LISA, artist; b. Providence, Mar. 1, 1965; d. Joseph Christopher Palombo and Catherine Ann Walsh. BFA, R.I. Sch. Design, 1987. Featured artist: (books) The Best of Oil Painting, 1996, Exploring Color, 1998. Recipient honors recognition Artist's Mag., 2002. Mem.: Oil Painters of Am., N.J. Am. Artists Profl. League. Office: Palombo Studios 55 Mountain Ave Caldwell NJ 07006 E-mail: art@lisapalombo.com.

PALOMINO, KRISTI SUZANN, elementary school educator; b. Garden Grove, Calif., Mar. 19, 1970; d. Stephen James and Jeanne Frances (Prelesnik) T.; m. Jessie Palomino Jr.; 1 child, Sophia. BA in Liberal Studies, San Francisco State U., 1992, credentials in multiple subject edn., 1993. Cert. elem. tchr., Calif., crosscultural lang. acquisition devel. Tchg. asst. San Francisco State U., 1988-92; substitute tchr. Newark (Calif.) Unified Sch. Dist., 1992-93, New Haven Unified Sch. Dist., Union City, Calif., 1992-93; tchr. after-sch. program Milpitas (Calif.) Unified Sch. Dist., 1993, elem. substitute tchr., elem. tchr., 1994, elem. tchr., 1994-95, Newark (Calif.) Unified Sch. Dist., 1995-99, literacy coord., 1998-99, prin., 2001, kindergarten tchr., 2001—. After-sch. tutor Chpt. 1 program Milpitas Unified Sch. Dist., 1994-95. Mem. Calif. Tchrs. Assn. Democrat. Avocations: exercise, reading, gardening, theatre, scrapbooking. Home: 6324 Lafayette Ave Newark CA 94560-2435 E-mail: kpalomino@nusd.k12.ca.us.

PALOVCIK, REINHARD ANTON, research neurophysiologist; b. Dornheim, Hessen, Germany, June 30, 1950; came to U.S. 1956; s. Anton and Elfriede (Lankus) P. BS, U. Mich., 1973; MA, Wayne State U., Detroit, 1979, PhD, 1982. Rsch. asst. E.B. Ford Inst. Med. Rsch., Detroit, 1973-78; teaching asst. Dept. Psychology, Wayne State U., 1978-79, grad. trainee, 1979-81, grad. asst., 1981-82; postdoctoral assoc. dept. physiology U. Fla., Gainesville, 1982-86, postdoctoral assoc. dept. neurosci., 1986-89, postdoctoral assoc. dept. neurosurgery, 1989-90, postdoctoral assoc. neurology dept., 1991, rsch. cons.; rsch. health scientist rsch. svc. VA Med. Ctr., 1990-95, clin. rsch. cons., 1995—. U. Mich. Regents Alumni scholar, 1969; NIMH predoctoral tng. grantee, 1979; NIH Nat. Rsch. Svc. awardee, 1983; Epilepsy Rsch. Found. Fla. postdoctoral grantee, 1990. Mem. AAAS, IEEE, Soc. for Neurosci., Am. Statis. Assn., Internat. Neural Network Soc. Avocations: classical and modern music, Japanese culture, creative photography, poetry. Home: 2209 NE 15th Ter Gainesville FL 32609-8934

PALOYAN, EDWARD, physician, educator, researcher; b. Paris, Mar. 19, 1932; s. Michael and Renee (Palaian) P.; m. Geraldine Richveis, July 7, 1957 (dec. June 1996); children: Vivian, Regina, Edmund, Grace; m. Mary Marcella Driscoll, May 19, 2000. MD, U. Chgo., 1956. Intern U. Chgo. hosps. and clinics, 1956-57; resident in surgery, 1957-58, 1960-65; asst. prof. surgery, 1965-68; asso. prof. surgery U. Chgo. Hosps. and Clinics, Pirtzker Sch. Medicine, 1968-73; prof. surgery Loyola U. Stritch Sch. Medicine, Maywood, Ill., 1973-94; chief endocrine surgery Loyola and Hines, 1980-94; assoc. chief of staff for rsch. VA Hosp., Hines, 1973-94; assoc. staff Hinsdale (Ill.) Hosp., 1991—. Author: (with A.M. Lawrence) Endocrine Surgery, 1976, (with A.M. Lawrence, F.H. Straus) Hyperparathyroidism, 1973. Served with USN, 1958-60. Recipient McClintock award U. Chgo. Med. Sch., 1971 Mem. Am. Surg. Assn., Soc. Univ. Surgeons, Endocrine Soc., Central Surg. Assn., Am. Assn. Endocrine Surgeons (pres. 1987) Home: 827 Taft Rd Hinsdale IL 60521-4836 also: 40 S Clay St Ste 217W Hinsdale IL 60521-8806

PALSER, BARBARA F. botany researcher, retired educator; b. Worcester, Mass., June 2, 1916; d. G. Norman and Cora A. (Munson) P. AB, Mt. Holyoke Coll., 1938, A.M., 1940, D.Sc. (hon.), 1978; PhD, U. Chgo., 1942. From instr. to prof. botany U. Chgo., 1942-65; from assoc. prof. to prof. botany Rutgers U., New Brunswick, N.J., 1965-83, dir. grad. program in botany, 1973-80; adj. prof. botany U. Mass., Amherst, 1991—. Erskine fellow U. Canterbury, Christchurch, N.Z. 1969; vis. prof. Duke U., Durham, N.C., fall 1962; vis. research fellow U. Melbourne, Parkville, Victoria, Australia, fall 1984-85 Author lab. manual Principles of Botany, 1973, also numerous research papers in bot. jours.; bot. adviser Ency. Brit., Chgo., 1958-59; editor Bot. Gazette, Chgo., 1960-65 Named Outstanding Tchr., Rutgers Coll., 1977 Mem. Bot. Soc. Am. (sec. 1970-74, v.p. 1975, pres. 1976, Merit award 1985), Torrey Bot. Club (pres. 1968), Internat. Soc. Plant Morphologists, N.J. Acad. Scis. (pres. elect 1987-88, pres. 1988-89, Outstanding Svc. award 1985, 90). Avocations: hiking, stamp collecting, photography. Home: 330 Spencer Dr Amherst MA 01002-3367 Office: U Mass Dept Biology Morrill (South) PO Box 35810 Amherst MA 01003-5810

PALSER, BETH ANNE, painter; b. Chester, Pa., Nov. 26, 1964; d. John Frank Palser Jr. and Barbara Mower Urban; adopted d. John Frank and Anita (Dietrich) P.; m. William Joseph Quindlen III, Aug. 26, 1963. AD in Specialized Tech., Art Inst. Phila., 1984. Mech./paste-up artist, draftsman Southco, Inc., Concordville, Pa., 1985; artist, asst. David E. Gordon Studios, Phila., 1985-87; freelance artist Franklin Mint, Wawa, Pa., 1988; artist, owner Beth Palser Studios, Oxford, 1988—; represented by San Pebbles Gallery Ocean City, N.J. Bd. dirs. Rittenhouse Sq. Fine Arts Assn., Phila., 1991-94, 98—, treas., 1992-94; exhbn. chair Artist Guild of Delaware County, Springfield, Pa., 1996-98; bd. dirs. Rittenhouse Sq. Fine Arts Annual, 1998—. Exhibited in one-woman show at Darlington Fine Arts Ctr., Wawa, 1994, 95, 97; exhibited in group shows including Pavilion Galleries Nat. Art Exhbn., Mt. Holly, N.J., 1992, Camden County Cultural Heritage Regional Watercolor Exhbn., Camden, N.J., 1994 (2d place award 1994), Pearl S. Buck Found. Regional Show, Lehigh Valley, Pa., 1995, Lansdale (Pa.) Fine Art Show, 1994, 96 (Best of Show award 1994, Excellence in Watercolor award 1996), Cape May (N.J.) Promenade Art Show, 1996, Phila. Sketch Club Watercolor Exhbn., 1997, Bianco Gallery Ann. Regional Exhbn., Buckingham, Pa., 1997, Cape May (N.J.) Promenade Fine Art Show, 1997 (2d place award 1996, 1st pl. award 1997), Chestnut Hill Art Show, Pa., 1998 (hon. mention 1998, 1st pl. award 2000), Spirit of Art, Wilmington, Del., 1998 (hon. mention 1998),

Roxborough Fine Art Festival, Phila., 1999 (Award of Merit, watercolor 1999), Rittenhouse Sq. Fine Arts Festival (2d place award 2000), Cape May (N.J) Promenade Art Show (2d place award 2000), Chestnut Hill Art Show (1st place award 2000); exhibited in charity art shows at Children's Hosp. Phila., 1994-95, South Jersey Arthritis Found., 1995-98, Brandwine Sch. Nursing, 1998-99, United Cerebral Palsy Del., 1998-2001, Ronald McDonald House Art Fest, Del., 1999-2001; represented in Newman Galleries, Phila, Chadds Ford Art Gallery, Pa., Tyme Gallery, Haverton, Pa., Deck the Walls, Exton, Pa.; represented by The Total Picture Gallery, Hockessin, Del., Artworks Gallery, Kennett Square, Pa., Sand Pebbles Gallery; exhibited in two-person show Artworks Gallery, Kennett Square, Pa., 1999. Recipient numerous awards for art. Mem. Balt. Watercolor Soc. (signature mem.), Chester County Art Assn., Phila. Watercolor Club, Pa. Watercolor Soc. (signature mem.). Republican. Avocations: photography, travel, cooking, aerobics. Home: 107 Midland Dr Oxford PA 19363-1125 E-mail: billnbeth@brandywine.net.

PALTER, ROBERT MONROE, philosophy and history educator; b. N.Y.C., June 19, 1924; s. Meyer and Mildred (Gilder) P.; m. Ruth Rappeport, July 15, 1945; 1 child, Alixe Daphne Cielo; m. Toni Ann Inman, Apr. 5, 1955; children: Geoffrey Meyer, Jennifer Thorn Allan, Nicholas Trask, Adam Finch; m. Annette B. Weiner, May 21, 1979 (div. 1982). AB, Columbia U., 1943; PhD, U. Chgo., 1952. From instr. to asso. prof. phys. scis. and philosophy U. Chgo., 1949-64; prof. philosophy and history U. Tex., Austin, 1964-82; Dana prof. history of sci. Trinity Coll., Hartford, Conn., 1983-91, prof. emeritus, 1991—. Author: Whitehead's Philosophy of Science, 1960; editor: Toward Modern Science, 1961, The Annus Mirabilis of Sir Isaac Newton, 1971. Served with AUS, 1944-46. Mem. Phi Beta Kappa.

PALTROW, GWYNETH, actress; b. L.A., Sept. 28, 1973; Appeared in films Shout, 1991, Hook, 1991, Malice, 1993, Flesh and Bone, 1993, Mrs. Parker and the Vicous Circle, 1994, Jefferson in Paris, 1995, Moonlight and Valentino, 1995, Seven, 1995, The Pallbearer, 1996, Emma, 1996, Hard Eight, 1996, Sliding Doors, 1998, (voice) Out of the Past, 1998, Duet, 1998, Great Expectations, 1998, Hush, 1998, A Perfect Murder, 1998, Shakespeare in Love, 1998, The Talented Mr. Ripley, 1999, Duets, 1999, The Intern, 2000, Bounce, 2000, The Anniversary Party, 2001, The Royal Tenenbaums, 2001, Shallow Hal, 2001, Possession, 2002; TV films Cruel Doubt, 1992, Deadly Relations, 1993; theatre Picnic, The Adventures of Huck Finn, Sweet Bye and Bye, The Seagull, Proof. Won Golden Satellite Best Actress in a Motion Picture Emma, 1997, Best Actress Oscar, American Academy Awards, Shakespeare in Love, 1999; Golden Globe Awards, Best Actress, Shakespeare in Love, 1999, Best Actress FFCC, 1999. Mem. Screen Actors Guild (Outstanding Performance with others). Office: CAA c/o Rick Kurtzman 9830 Wilshire Blvd Beverly Hills CA 90212-1804 also: Screen Actors Guild 5757 Wilshire Blvd Los Angeles CA 90036-3635*

PALUMBO, BENJAMIN LEWIS, public affairs consulting company executive; b. Boston, Mar. 4, 1937; s. Guido Americo and Stella Marie (Lombardo) P.; m. Magdalene Julia Palinczar, Nov. 18, 1961; children: Matthew, Jason, Guy. BA, Rutgers U., 1959, MA, 1961. Adminstrv. asst. to Gov. Richard J. Hughes, N.J., 1963-65; dir. rsch. N.J. Dem. Com., Trenton, 1965-66; asst. to commr. N.J. Dept. Transp., 1966-70; asst. dean Woodrow Wilson Sch., Princeton (N.J.) U., 1970-71; adminstrv. asst. to Senator Harrison Williams, U.S. Senate, Washington, 1971-73, staff dir. U.S. Ho. Dem. caucus, 1975-77, Ho. subcom. on govt. activities and transp., 1977-78; nat. campaign dir. Bentsen for Pres., 1973-75; dir. fed. govt. rels. Phillip Morris, Inc., 1978-83; chmn., CEO Palumbo & Cerrell, Inc., 1983—. Bd. dirs. Washington Performing Arts Soc., Nyumbani Child of God Hospice and Orphage. Mem.: Phillips Collection Assn., N.J. State Soc., Am. League Lobbyists, Nat. Dem. Club, Rutgers Club Washington, Nat. Press Club. Democrat. Roman Catholic. Office: 1717 K St NW Ste 500 Washington DC 20036-5346 Fax: 202-466-9009. E-mail: pnc@clark.net.

PALUMBO, EDWARD PAUL, real estate appraiser, writer; b. Providence, Mar. 4, 1960; s. George J. and Corinne Palumbo. BA, U. of R.I., 1982. Cert. General Certified Appraiser 1991. Prin., owner CSA Valuation Svc., Warwick, RI, 1990—. Author: (poem) Shells, 1998 (First Prize award The Poet's Page 2nd Ann. Poetry Contest, 1998); contbr. poems to various pub. Mem.: SRA (mem. appraisal inst. 1990), The Acad. of Am. Poets (assoc.). Republican. Avocation: antiques. Home and Office: CSA Valuation Svc 115 Crane Street Warwick RI 02889 Fax: 401-736-0443., 401-736-0443.

PALUMBO, FRANCIS XAVIER BERNARD, pharmacy educator; b. Scranton, Pa., June 19, 1945; s. Frank Bernard and Marcia DeSales (Fidati) P.; m. Karen Ann Setterlund, June 26, 1971; 1 child, Janice Lynn. BS in Pharmacy, Med. U. S.C., 1968; MS, U. Miss., 1973, PhD in Health Care Adminstrn., 1974; JD, U. Balt., 1982. Bar: Md., D.C.; lic. pharmacist S.C., Md. Asst. prof. pharmacy U. Md., Balt., 1974-79, assoc. prof., 1979-91, assoc. dir. Ctr. on Drugs and Pub. Policy, 1988-98, dir., 1998—, prof., 1991—, chmn. dept. pharmacy practice and adminstrv. sci., 1991-93. Atty. Hyman, Phelps & McNamara, P.C., Washington, 1988-89; mem. study sect. NIH, Bethesda, Md., 1984-88; cons. in field. Co-author: Containing Costs in Third Party Drug Programs, 1979. Bd. govs. Rodgers Forge Cmty. Assn., Balt., 1987-95; bd. dirs. Luth. Health Care Corp., Balt., 1988-93, Edenwald Continuing Care Retirement Cmty., 1996—. With U.S. Army, 1969-71. Mem. Am. Pharm. Assn. (chair econ., social and adminstrn. sci. 1992-93), Acad. Pharm. Rsch. and Sci. (pres. 1994-95), Am. Assn. Coll. Pharmacy, Am. Soc. Pharmacy Law, Internat. Soc. for Pharmacoecons. and Outcomes Rsch. Home: 1209 Mapleleaf Ct Hunt Valley MD 21030-1982 Office: U Md Sch Pharmacy Ctr Drugs and Pub Policy 100 N Greene St Fl 6 Baltimore MD 21201-1563 E-mail: fpalumbo@rx.umaryland.edu.

PALUMBO, JAMES FREDRICK, financial services company executive; b. Everett, Mass., Nov. 30, 1950; s. Bruno James and Lillian Elizabeth (Picardi) P.; m. Nancy Laurie Richards, July 24, 1976; children: Elizabeth Richards, Andrew Reid, Alexander Thomas. BA, Lake Forest Coll., 1973; MBA, Washington U., 1975. Market surveillance analyst Nat. Assn. of Securities Dealers, Washington, 1975-76, asst. treas., 1976-78; regional rep. Student Loan Mktg. Assn., 1978-79, mgr., 1979-81, dir., 1981-82, asst. v.p., 1982-83, v.p., 1983-87; sr. v.p. Connie Lee Mgmt. Svcs. Corp., Coll. Constrn. Loan Ins. Assn., 1987-95; with N.Y. Life Ins. Co., N.Y.C., 1995-2001, N.Y. Life Securities Inc., N.Y.C., 1995-2001; prin. Treasury Investment Svcs., Reston, Va., 1999—; mng. dir. TransCapital Group, 1999—. Participant Govt.-Univ.-Industry Rsch. Roundtable, Washington, 1986; chmn. Palumbo Properties L.L.C.; chmn. Capital Holdings Ltd., Great Falls, Va. Actor popular and children's theater, 1973-76. Chmn. sports announcers com. D.C. Spl. Olympics, Washington, 1986, 87, D.C. Regional Counsel, Lake Forest Coll., Washington, 1976-80; mem. Elliott Soc. membership com. Washington U., 1986—, Great Falls (Va.) Hist. Soc., Great Falls Citizens Assn., 1996—; bd. govs. Lake Forest Coll., 1978-82, trustee, 1992-99; trustee Abruzzo and Molise Heritage Soc., 2002--. Mem.: Washington Soc. Investment Analysts, Nat. Assn. Ins. and Fin. Advisors, Assn. for Investment Mgmt. and Rsch., Great Falls Swim and Tennis Club (bd. dirs. 1988—91), Alpha Psi Omega. Avocations: polo, horseback riding, decoy painting. Office: Ste 500 11490 Commerce Pk Dr Reston VA 20191 E-mail: jpalumbo@transcapital.net.

PALUMBO, LORRAINE REIKO MINATOISHI, architectural historian; b. Honolulu, June 3, 1966; d. Merton Chikayuki and Eleanor Machiko (Suda) M.; m. Charles Haigler Palumbo, Feb. 16, 1995; children: Sara Minatoishi, Hana Machiko. BArch, U. Hawaii, 1989; MArch, U. Oreg., 1993; postgrad., Waseda U., Tokyo, 1994-95, PhD in Archtl. History, 1999. Designer, draftsperson DMJM Architects, Engrs. Planners, Honolulu, 1989-91; rsch. intern Mizusawa Constrn. Co., Tokyo, 1992-93; archtl. historian Mason Archs., Inc., 2000—. Seminar leader Waseda U., 1996-97. Editor Hawaii Buddhism Newsletter, 1999—. Grad. tchg. fellow U. Oreg., 1991, Patricia Roberts Harris fellow U.S. Govt., Oreg., 1991-92; recipient Japanese Mombusho scholarship Japanese Govt. Min. of Edn., 1994-98; grantee Toyota Corp. Fellowship, 1997-98. Mem. Archtl. Inst. Japan, Hist. Hawaii Found., U. Oreg. Alumni Assn. Avocations: travel, ocean activities, visiting architectural sites. Office: Mason Archs Inc 119 Merchant St Ste 501 Honolulu HI 96813 E-mail: imp@masonarch.com.

PALUMBO, MATTHEW ALOYSIUS, marketing executive; b. Queens, N.Y., Sept. 17, 1961; s. John Christopher and Seiko (Murakami) P. BS, Cornell U., 1986; MBA in Mktg. Mgmt., St. John's U., 1990. Mortgage clk. Salomon Bros., Inc., N.Y.C., 1986; mut. fund adminstr. Bank of N.Y. Co., Inc., 1986-88; copywriter Pierce Assocs., 1988-90; dir. mktg. cons. Palumbo Assocs., S.I., 1989-90; adj. prof. St. John's U., 1990; mktg. dir., copy dir. Flaghouse Inc., Mt. Vernon, N.Y., 1990-93; spl. projects mgr., group product mgr. Global Computer Supplies, Port Washington, 1993-97; dir. product mktg. Cyberian Outpost, Kent, Conn., 1997—2000; pres. Palumbo Consultants, 2000—. Guest lectr. Am. direct mktg. techniques Sheffield Halleron U. (Eng.), 1993; guest lectr. designed and acquired funding Cornell U., Ithaca, 1992—. N.Y. State Regents scholar, 1979, Annette Brodsky scholar, 1988. Mem. Am. Assn. MBA Execs., Cornell Asian Alumni Assn. (v.p. alumni affairs 1993-95), Cornell ILR Alumni, Direct Mktg. Club N.Y., Cornell Club N.Y., Cornell Club Fairfield County, Cornell U. Quadrangle Club, Beta Gamma Sigma. Avocations: reading, sports, music. E-mail: mpal999@aol.com.

PALVINO, JACK ANTHONY, broadcasting executive; b. Rochester, N.Y., May 28, 1934; s. John Charles and Mary Aurelia P.; m. Joyce Ann Vilkaitis, Oct. 8, 1960; children: John Charles, Jill Marie, Jason Allen. BS, St. John Fisher Coll., 1955. Broadcaster, program dir. Sta. WGVA, Geneva, 1958-60; radio personality Sta. WBBF, Rochester, 1958-78; pres. Sports and Spls. TV, 1970-73; co-owner, exec. v.p. Lincoln Group Ltd., 1978-98; gen. mgr. Stas. WHAM, WVOR, WHTK, WPXY, Rochester, 1978-98; ret., 1998. Chmn. bd. trustees St. John Fisher Coll. Served with U.S. Army, 1957-58. Mem. St. John Fisher Alumni Assn., Nat. Assn. Broadcaster, Rochester Radio Broadcasters Assn. (pres. 1987-97), N.Y. State Broadcasters Assn., Rochester C. of C. Clubs: University, Rochester Press Radio (pres. 1974), Rotary. Roman Catholic.

PALVINO, NANCY MANGIN, retired librarian; b. Rochester, N.Y., Nov. 22, 1937; d. John Bernard and Miriam Lucille (Fox) Mangin; m. Lawrence Robert Palvino, July 2, 1960; children: Mark, Laurie, Lisa, Katharine, Thomas. BS, SUNY, Geneseo, 1959; MLS, U. Buffalo, 1993. Cert. libr., N.Y. Libr. Spencerport (N.Y.) Elem. Sch., 1959-60; tchr. East Greenbush (N.Y.) Elem. Sch., 1960-63; libr. # 41 Sch., Rochester, 1993—2001; ret., 2001. Author: (bibliography) Autism, 1991. Fundraiser Rochester Philharm. Orgn., 1970; mem. women's bd. dirs. St. Mary's Hosp., Rochester, 1980—, giftshop chairperson, 1989-92, exec. coun., 1989-92, chmn. of ball, 1985, Imperial Ball Meml. Art Gallery, 1987, Holiday Open House, 1988; v.p. women's coun. Meml. Art Gallery, Rochester, 1989-91. Grantee DeWitt Wallace Reader's Digest Fund, 1994. Mem. ALA, N.Y. Libr. Assn. (scholarship 1992), Greater Rochester Areas Media Specialists (chmn. scholarship com. 1994-95, scholarship 1992), Phi Delta Kappa. Avocations: golf, reading, walking, knitting. Home: 345 Kilbourn Rd Rochester NY 14618-3632

PAM, ELEANOR, behavorial sciences educator; b. Bklyn., June 24, 1936; d. Simon and Berta (Field) Pam; m. Robert Emanuel Juceam, May 24, 1970; children: Daniel James, Jacquelyn Brooke, Gregory Andrew. BA, Brandeis U., 1958; MA, NYU, 1960, MA, 1963, PhD, 1969. Exec. asst. to pres. Queensboro C.C., CUNY, 1969-72, assoc. dean coll., 1969-72, dir. spl. programs, 1972-73, 1978-79; dept. chair, prof. behavioral scis. Hostos C.C., CUNY, 1981-96; prof. John Jay Coll. Criminal Justice, CUNY, 1996-2000, dir. John Jay Rsch. and Resource Ctr. Inmate Edn. Pres. coun. Brandeis U., Waltham, Mass., 1972—. Active Mayor's Commn. Combat Domestic Violence; vis. prof., dir. John Jay Rsch. and Resource Domestic Violence Ctr., 1997-2000 Recipient Founders Day award NYU, 1969, Appreciation award CUNY, 2000, Medal of Honor Vet. Feminists Am., 2001. Mem. NOW, Women and Soc., City U. Women's Coalition, Vet. Feminists of Am. (hon. bd. mem.). Jewish. Home: 106 Hemlock Rd Manhasset NY 11030-1214 E-mail: EleanorPam@aol.com.

PAMEL, GREGORY JAMES, ophthalmologist; b. Ann Arbor, Mich., June 21, 1961; BS in Biomed. Sci., U. Mich., 1983, MD, 1986. Diplomate Am. Bd. Ophthalmology. Intern Ill. Masonic Med. Ctr., Chgo., 1986-87; resident in opthalmology U. Calif. at San Diego, La Jolla, 1987-90; clin. fellow, instr. U. Conn. Health Ctr., Farmington, 1990-91; pvt. practice, N.J., 1991-94, N.Y.C., 1994—. Attending surgeon Manhattan Eye, Ear and Throat Hosp., N.Y.C., 1994—; clin. investigator for several FDA clin. trials for lens implants and laser surgery. Contbg. author: Corneal Surgery, 1994; contbr. articles to med. jours., including Am. Jour. Ophthalmology, Jour. Neurology, Archives Ophthalmology. Fellow Am. Acad. Ophthalmology; mem. Am. Soc. Cataract and Refractive Surgery, Internat. Soc. Refractive Surgery, Internat. Ocular Surface Soc. Avocations: golf, skiing, art collecting, music, reading. Office: Pamel Vision and Laser Group 115 E 61st St New York NY 10021 E-mail: gjpmd@aol.com.

PAMIN, DIANA DOLHANCYK (DIANA DOLHANCYK), poet; b. Cleve., Dec. 13; d. Peter and Diana (Dribes) Dolhancyk; m. Leonard Pamin, Aug. 28; children: Diana Anne, Louis Peter. Grad., Titus Coll. Cosmetology. Author: The Parting in Journey of the Mind, 1994 (Editor's Choice award), The Parting in East of the Sunrise, 1995 (Editor's Choice award), Stormy in Songs on the Wind, 1994 (Editor's Choice award), Stormy in Beyond the Stars, 1995 (Editor's Choice award), Shadow Side in At Water's Edge, 1995 (Editor's Choice award), Eclipse in A Delicate Balance, 1995 (Editor's Choice award), Burnt By Love in Windows of the Soul, 1995 (Editor's Choice award), Web of Guilt in Where Dawn Lingers, 1996 (Editor's Choice award), The View in A Muse to Follow, 1996 (Editor's Choice award), The View in Portraits of Life, 1996 (Editor's Choice award), Photographer in Fields of Gold, 1997 (Editor's Choice award), Photographer in Dappled Sunlight, 1997 (Editor's Choice award), Shadow Side II in Of Moonlight and Wishes, 1997 (Editor's Choice award), Love No More in Best Poems of 1996 (Editor's Choice award), The Happening in Best Poems of the '90s, 1997 (Editor's Choice award), Rain in Journey to Our Dreams, 1996 (Accomplishment of Merit award for Literary Achievement), CAT in Promises to Keep, 1996 (Editor's Preference award of Excellence for Lit. Achievement), CAT in Starburst Jour., Winter Wedding, in Of Sunlight and Shadows, 1997 (Editor's Preference award of Excellence for Lit. Achievement), Unrequited Love, Web of Guilt, Sighs of Love, Autumn Symphony, A Dream, Happiness, Swan Song, Lost Song, in Of Sunlight and Shadows, 1997, Red Satin Box, in The Golden Wings of Time, 1997 (Editor's Preference award of Excellence for Lit. Achievement), Snowscape, Rain, Letters, Love No More, Happiness, in Best New Poems, 1996, 10 Elite award winning poems for Lit. Excellence in The Fourth Dimension, 1998, The Swing, Seasons of Love, The Goodbye, Betrothal, Not Our Own, Association, Gypsy, Heady Lilacs, Our Enchantment, Love No More, Sea of Dreams, A Furtive Tear, The Treasure, When Lips Cared, others; Association (poem), artwork cover Starburst Jour., 1999, Sea of Dreams, Starburst Jour., 1999 (elite award lit. excellence), Winter Wedding, Winds of the Universe, You, Loves Deception, The Soothing, Caress, He in Starburst Jour., 1997, His Name is Peter, "But, Isn't The Flower Lovely?," PaPa, in the Sparrowgrass Family Poetry Album, 2000, others. Inducted Internat. Poetry Hall of Fame Mus. Mem. Internat. Soc. Poets (life), Poet's Guild, Internat. Soc. Authors and Artists, Nat. Authors Registry. Home: 6282 Akins Rd North Royalton OH 44133

PAMPLIN, ROBERT BOISSEAU, SR. retired textile manufacturing executive; b. Sutherland, Va., Nov. 25, 1911; s. John R. and Pauline (Beville) P.; m. Mary K. Reese, June 15, 1940; 1 child, Robert Boisseau Jr. BBA, Va. Poly. Inst. & State U., 1933; postgrad., Northwestern U., 1933-34; LLD (hon.), U. Portland (Oreg.), 1972; LHD (hon.), Warner Pacific Coll., 1976. With Ga.-Pacific Corp., Portland, 1934-76, sec., from 1936, adminstrv. v.p., 1952-55, exec. v.p., 1955-57, pres., 1957-67, chmn. bd., chief exec. officer, from 1967; ret., 1976; with R.B. Pamplin Corp., 1957—, chmn. bd., CEO, to 1996, Mt. Vernon Mills Inc., (subs. R.B. Pamplin Corp.), Greenville, S.C., retired, 1996. Office: R B Pamplin Corp Ste 2400 805 SW Broadway Portland OR 97205-3341

PAMPLIN, ROBERT BOISSEAU, JR. manufacturing company executive, minister, writer; b. Augusta, Ga., Aug. 3, 1941; s. Robert Boisseau and Mary Katherine (Reese) P.; m. Marilyn Joan Hooper; children: Amy Louise, Anne Boisseau. Student, Va. Poly. Inst., 1960-62, BS in Acctg., 1965, BS in Econs., 1966; BS (hon.), Va. Tech., 2001; LHD (hon.), Va. Poly. Inst., 1995, Pacific U., 2001; DHL (hon.), Va. Poly. Inst., 1995; MBA, U. Portland, 1968, LLD (hon.), 1972, MEd, 1975; MCL, Western Conservative Bapt. Sem. (name now Western Sem.), 1978, DMin, 1982, D of Sacred Letter (hon.), 1991, MA, 2000; PhD, Calif. Coast U.; DHL (hon.), Warner Pacific Coll., 1988; LLD (hon.); Western Baptist Coll., 1989; cert. in wholesale mgmt., Ohio State U., 1970; cert. labor mgmt., U. Portland, 1982; cert. in advanced mgmt., U. Hawaii, 1975; DD (hon.), Judson Baptist Coll., 1984; DBA (hon.), Marquis Giuseppe Scicluna Internat. U. Found., 1986; LittD (hon.), Va. Tech. Inst. and State U., 1987, LHD (hon.), Western Seminary, 1991; DD, Western Evang. Sem., 1994; DBA (hon.), U. S.C., 1996; D Pub. Svc. (hon.), DHL, U. Puget Sound, Pacific U., 1999, 2001; BS in Bus. Adminstrn. (hon.), Va. Inst. Tech., 2001. Pres., CEO R.B. pamplin Corp., Portland, Oreg., 1964—. Chmn. bd., CEO Columbia Empire Farms Inc., Lake Oswego, Oreg., 1976—, Pamplin Comms.; chmn. bd., CEO Mt. Vernon Mills Inc.,; pres., CEO Ross Island Sand & Gravel; lectr. bus. adminstrn. Lewis and Clark Coll., 1968-69; adj. asst. prof. bus. adminstrn., U. Portland, 1973-76; pastor Christ Cmty. Ch., Lake Oswego; lectr. in bus. adminstrn. and econs. U. Costa Rica, 1968, Va. Tech. Found., 1986; chmn. bd. dirs. Christian Supplly Ctrs. Inc.; prof. with tenure U. Portland, 1999. Author: Everything is Just great, 1985, The Gift, 1986, Another Virginian: A Study of the Life and Beliefs of Robert Boisseau Pamplin, 1986; author: (with others) A Portrait of Colorado, 1976, Three in One, 1974, The Storybook Primer on Managing, 1974, One Who Believed, Vol. I, 1988, vol. II, 1991, Climbing the Centuries, 1993, Heritage the Making of an American Family, 1994, American Heroes, 1995, Prelude to Surrender, 1995, Alaska Gold, 1998, Robert Reese, 1998; editor: Oreg. Mus. Sci. and Industry Press, 1973; trustee Oreg. Mus. Sci. and Industry Press, 1971, 1974—; editor: Portrait of Oregon, 1973; editor: (with others) Oregon Underfoot, 1975. Trustee Lewis and Clark Coll., 1989—, chmn. bd. trustees, 1991; hon. life pres. Western Conservative Bapt. Sem.; chmn. regents Western Sem., 1994; mem. nat. adv. coun. on vocat. Edn., 1975—; mem. Western Interstate Com. on Higher Edn., 1981-84; co-chmn. Va. Tech. $50 Million Campaign for Excellence, 1984-87, Va. Tech. Found., 1986—, Va.-Oreg. State Scholarship Commn., 1974—, chmn. 1976-78; mem. Portland dist. adv. coun. SBA, 1973-77; mem. rewards rev. com., City of Portland, 1973-78, chmn., 1973-78; bd. regents U. Portland, 1971-79, chmn. bd., 1975-79, regent emeritus, 1979—; trustee Oreg. Episc. Schs., 1979, Linfield Coll., U. Puget Sound, 1989—; dr. pub. svc., U. Puget Sound, 1999. Named Outstanding Philanthropist of Yr. award, Nat. Soc. Fund Raising Execs., 1997, Textile World's Top 10, 1999, Portland First Citizen, Portland Met. Assn. Realtors, 1999, Parents of Yr., Juvenile Diabetes Found., 2001, Entrepreneur of Yr., Oreg. Entrepreneur Forum, 2001, Va. Tech. Coll. Bus. Adminstrn. renamed R.B. Pamplin Coll. Bus. Adminstrn. in his honor, Western Conservative Bapt. Sem. Lay Inst. for Leadership, Edn. Devel. and Rsch. named for R.B. Pamplin Jr., 1988; recipient Disting. Alumnus award, Lewis and Clark Coll., 1974, ROTC Disting. Svc. award, USAF, 1974, bronze medal, Albert Einstein Acad., 1986, Disting. Leadership medal, Freedoms Found., Disting. Bus. Alumnus award, U. Portland, 1990, Nat. Caring award, Caring Inst., 1991, Pride of Portland award, Portland Lions Club, Hero Athlete award, 1994, Herman Lay Entrepreneurship award, 1995, Thomas Jefferson award, Oreg. Hist. Soc., 1998, Aubrey R. Watzek award, Lewis and Clark Coll., 1998, Leadership award, Portland Living Mag., 1998, Unique Contbns. to Comms. award, Portland Advt. Fedn., 2001, Oliver Wendell Holmes, Jr. award for Civil War Preservationalist of Yr., 2001, Govs. Arts award, 2001. Mem. Acad. Mgmt., Delta Epsilon Sigma, Beta Gamma Sigma, Sigma Phi Epsilon, Waverley Country Club, Arlington, Multnomah Athletic Club, Capitol Hill Club, Greenville Country Club, Poinsett Club, Eldorado Country Club, Thunderbird Country Club, Rotary. Republican. Episcopalian. Office: RB Pamplin Corp Inc Ste 2400 805 SW Broadway Portland OR 97205-3341

PAMPUSCH, ANITA MARIE, foundation administrator; b. St. Paul, Aug. 28, 1938; d. Robert William and Lucille Elizabeth (Whaley) P. BA, Coll. of St. Catherine, St. Paul, 1962; MA, U. Notre Dame, 1970, PhD, 1972. Tchr. St. Joseph's Acad., St. Paul, 1962-66; instr. philosophy Coll. of St. Catherine, 1970-76, assoc. acad. dean, 1979, acad. dean, 1979-84, pres., 1984-97; Am. Council Edn. fellow Goucher Coll., Balt., 1976-77; pres. Bush Found., St. Paul, 1997—. Bd. dirs. St. Paul Cos.; head Women's Coll. Coalition, 1988-91. Author: (book rev.) Philological Quarterly, 1976; contbr. articles to profl. jours. Mem. adv. com. Instl. Leadership project, Columbia U., 1986—; dist. chmn. Rhodes Scholarship Selection com., Mo., Neb., Minn., Kans., N.D., S.D., 1987—; exec. com. Women's Coll. Coalition, Washington, 1985—. Mem. Coun. for Ind. Colls. (bd. dirs. 1987—, chair 1991—), Am. Philos. Assn., St. Paul C. of C. (bd. dirs. 1986—), St. Paul's Athletic Club, Mpls. Club, Phi Beta Kappa. Roman Catholic. Avocations: swimming, camping, reading, music. Home: 161 Stonebridge Rd Saint Paul MN 55118

PAMUKCU, SIBEL, civil engineering educator; b. Istanbul, Turkey, Feb. 10, 1956; came to U.S., 1979, naturalized, 1994; d. Necmi an dMediha (Ardal) Taboglu; m. Derya Pamukcu, June 23, 1979; children: Deniz Ozan, Erin Melis. BS in Civil Engring., Bogazici U., Istanbul, 1978; MS in Civil Engring., La. State U., 1981, PhD in Civil Engring., 1986. Project engr. Dept. Hwys./Transp., Istanbul, 1978-79; teaching asst. La. State U., Baton Rouge, 1979-83, rsch. asst., 1983-86; asst. prof. Lehigh U., Bethlehem, Pa., 1986-92, assoc. prof., 1992—. Advisor Lehigh U. chpt. Soc. Women Engrs., 1994. Contbr. book chpts., articles to profl. jours. Mem. ASCE, Am. Soc. Testing and Materials, Am. Soc. Engring. Edn., Transp. Rsch. Bd. (sec. com. soil and rock 1988-95, chair com. soil and rock 1995—), Internat. Soc. for Soil Mechanics and Found. Engring., Sigma Xi, Phi Beta Kappa. Moslem. Avocations: biking, classical music, choral music. Office: Lehigh U Dept Civil and Environ Engring 13 E Packer Ave Bethlehem PA 18015-3101

PAN, CHAI-FU, engineering educator; b. Loshon, Szechwan, China, Sept. 8, 1936; arrived in U.S., 1960; s. I-Chen Pan, Shih-Liang Shih; m. Maria Chia-Yao Shih, Aug. 18, 1962; children: Lawrence, Mariette. BS in Chem. Engring., Nat. Taiwan U., 1956; PhD in Phys. Chemistry, U. Kans., 1966. Assoc. prof. Ala. State U., Montgomery, 1966—71, prof., 1971—91, prof. emeritus, 1881—. Contbr. Recipient Rsch. award, Ala. State U., 1985; grantee Misip grantee, NSF, 1985. Fellow: Am. Inst. Chemists; mem.: Am. Chem. Soc. (referee), Phi Lambda Upsilon. Achievements include derived Pan equations; proposed methods to study hydrophilic and hydrophobic phenomena in electrolyte solutions. Avocations: reading, writing, gardening, photography. Home: 2420 Wentworth Dr Montgomery AL 36106

PAN, CYNTHIA X. geriatrician, educator, researcher; b. Taipei, Taiwan, Aug. 17, 1965; d. James T.M. pan and Hsiang Yu; m. Darrell C. Sandel. BA, Harvard/Radcliffe U., 1987; MD, SUNY, Stony Brook, 1992. Diplomate Am. Bd. Internal Medicine. Asst. prof. in geriatrics, dir. edn. palliative care program Mt. Sinai Sch. Medicine, N.Y.C., 1997—. Mem. AMA, ACP, Am. Geriatrics Soc. (com. mem.), Am. Acad. Hospice and Palliative Medicine. Avocations: swing dancing, movies, travel. Office: Mount Sinai Sch Medicine PO Box 1070 New York NY 10029-0310 E-mail: cynthia.pan@mssm.edu.

PAN, HENRY YUE-MING, clinical pharmacologist; b. Shanghai, Dec. 27, 1946; came to U.S. 1969; s. Chia-Liu and Siu-Ging (Sung) P.; m. Mary Agnes Tse; children: Lincoln Jonathan, Gregory Kingsley. BSc (hon.), McGill U., Montreal, 1969; MS in Toxicology, U. Hawaii, 1973, PhD in Pharmacology, 1974; MD, U. Hong Kong, 1979. Rsch. asst. U. Hawaii, Honolulu, 1969-74, tchg. asst., 1970-74; med. officer Queen Mary Hosp., Hong Kong, 1979-81; asst. prof. medicine U. Hong Kong, 1981-85; vis. asst. prof. Stanford (Calif.) U., 1983-85; from asst. clin. pharmacology dir. to exec. dir. clin. rsch. Squibb Inst. Med. Rsch., Princeton, N.J., 1985-91; v.p. clin. rsch. Bristol-Myers Squibb Pharm. Rsch. Inst., 1991-92; v.p. clin. R & D DuPont Merck Pharm. Co., Wilmington, Del., 1992-93, sr. v.p. drug devel., 1993-96, exec. v.p. R & D, 1996-97; pres. MDS Pharm. Svcs., 1997-99; pres., CEO, mng. ptnr. Integrated Drug Devel. Svcs. and Pharmacologics, LLC, 1998-2000; mng. dir. VennWorks LLC, N.Y.C., 2000—01; CEO VennWorks RTP, 2000—01; exec. v.p., chief med. officer Neurocrine Bioscis., Inc., San Diego, 2001—. Bd. dirs. Predict, Inc., Proband, Inc.; chmn. EastWest Pharm. Internat. LLC. Contbr. articles to profl. jours. Stanford Asian Med. Fund grant, 1983-85. Fellow: Inst. Biol. and Clin. Investigation, Acad. Medicine N.J., Am. Coll. Cardiology, Am. Heart Assn. Coun., Am. Coll. Clin. Pharmacology; mem.: Am. Coll. Clin. Pharmacology, Drug Info. Assn., Am. Fedn. Med. Rsch., Am. Soc. Pharmacology and Exptl. Therapeutics, Am. Soc. Clin. Pharmacology and Therapeutics, Am. Assn. Pharm. Scientists, AMA, AAAS. Roman Catholic. Avocations:

tennis, golf, distance running, cycling, baseball. Office: Neurocrine Bioscis 10555 Science Center Dr San Diego CA 92121-1147 Home: PO box 675552 Rancho Santa Fe CA 92067 E-mail: henrypan@att.net., hpan@neurocrine.com.

PAN, HUO-HSI, mechanical engineer, educator; b. Fuzhou, Peoples Republic of China, Nov. 11, 1918; came to the U.S., 1948; s. Bai-ming and Won-ching (Chen) P.; m. Chao Pan, June 4, 1960; children: Lillian, Nina. BS in Mech. Engring., Nat. S.W. Associated U., Kunming, Peoples Republic of China, 1943; MS in Mech. Engring., Tex. A&M U., 1949; MS in Applied Mechanics, Kans. State Coll., 1950; PhD, U. Calif., Berkeley, 1954. Asst. engr. Yunnan Smelting Plant, Peoples Republic of China, 1942-43; from mem. tech. staff to head inspection dept. 21st Arsenal, Peoples Republic of China, 1943-47; from teaching asst. to assoc. mech. engring. U. Calif., Berkeley, 1950-53; rsch. engr. Portland Cement Assn., 1954; asst. prof. U. Toledo, 1954-55, U. Ill., Champaign, 1955-57; asst. prof. engring. mechanics NYU, 1957-59, from asst. prof. to prof. applied mechanics, 1957-73; prof. applied mechanics, mech. engring. Poly. U., 1973-90, prof. emeritus, 1990—. Cons. Frankford Arsenal, Picatinny Arsenal, Petro-Chem Devel. Co.; referee Jour. Applied Mechanics, AIAA Jour., Internat. Jour. Mech. Sci., Internat. Jour. Solid and Structures, NSF; reviewer Applied Mechanics Revs.; sect. chmn. Internat. Modal Analysis Confs.; lectr. Kunming Inst. Tech., Tsinghua U., Jilin U. Tech., Jilin U., 1984. Contbr. numerous articles to Jour. Applied Mechanics, AIAA Jour., Jour. Mecanique, Jour. Engring. Mechanics, Jour. Applied Math. and Physics, Quar. Jour. Mechanics and Applied Math., Quar. Applied Math., Internat. Jour. Mech. Sci., Bull. Acad. Polonaise des Scis., Jour. Sound and Vibration, many others. Grantee NSF, 1964-67, NASA, 1966-68. Mem. ASME, AIAA, Am. Acad. Mechanics, Soc. Engring. Sci., Soc. for Indsl. and Applied Math., U.S. Assn. for Computational Mechanics, Internat. Assn. for Computational Mechanics, Phi Kappa Phi, Sigma Xi, Tau Beta Pi, Pi Tau Sigma, Pi Mu Epsilon. Achievements include development of method for reduction of vibrational systems, general method of modal analysis, solution for ordinary differential equation containing symbolic functions, eigenfunction expansion method in vibration problems of viscoelestic bodies. Home: 76 Edgars Ln Hastings On Hudson NY 10706-1137 Office: Poly U Dept Mech Engring 6 Metrotech Ctr Brooklyn NY 11201-3840

PAN, JWO, engineering educator; b. Taipei, Taiwan, May 22, 1952; s. Hsiao-Tung and Mei-Chin Pan; m. Hsiao-Ching Lin; children: Selina. BS, Nat. Taiwan U., 1974; MSc, Brown U., 1978, PhD, 1981. Rsch. scientist Battelle Meml. Inst., Columbus, Ohio, 1981—84; asst. prof. U. Mich., Ann Arbor, 1984—90, assoc. prof., 1990—99, prof., 1999—. Dir. Ctr. Automotive Structural Durability Simulation, Ann Arbor, 1994—98, Ctr. Advanced Polymer Engring Rsch., Ann Arbor, 2001—. Assoc. editor : Jour. Pressure Vessel Tech., 1997—, mem. editl. bd.: Internat. Jour. Damage Mechanics, 1996—, mem. editl. bd.: Internat. Jour. Fatigue, —. Faculty advisor Taiwanese Student Assn., Ann Arbor, 1991—2002. Fellow: ASME (material and fabrication com. 1996—2002, Fellow 1997); mem.: Am. Ceramics Soc., Am. Acad. Mechanics, Soc. Engring. Sci., Soc. Automotive Engrs. (ferrous com. 1996—2002). Office: Dept Mech Engring Univ Mich Ann Arbor MI 48109-2125

PAN, MARY AGNES, banker; b. Hong Kong, Oct. 20, 1951; came to U.S., 1970; d. Andrew and Priscilla (Ho) Tse; m. Henry Y.M. Pan, June 14, 1974; children: Lincoln, Gregory. BBA with honors, U. Hawaii, 1974. Asst. v.p. Citibank, Hong Kong, 1974-79; v.p. Bankers Trust Co., 1979-84, Bank of Am., Palo Alto, Calif., 1984-86, Midlantic Nat. Bank, Metro Park, N.J., 1987-88; fin. cons. Merrill Lynch, Lawrenceville, 1988; v.p. Citibank, N.Y.C., 1988-94; 1st v.p. Republic Nat. Bank of N.Y., 1994-98; sr. v.p. Bank of Am., 1998-2000, HSBC Bank (U.S.), N.Y.C., 2000—. Home: PO Box 675552 Rancho Santa Fe CA 92067 E-mail: mary.pan@us.hsbc.com.

PAN, XIAOCHUAN, physicist, researcher; b. Chongqing, Sichuan, China, Nov. 15, 1960; came to U.S., 1986; s. Jiezeng and Yunxiang (Shi) P.; m. Marie Meiying Jiang, Mar. 1986; 1 child, Jennifer Megan. BS in Physics, Beijing U., 1982; MS in Physics, Academia Sinica, Beijing, 1985; PhD in Physics, U. Chgo., 1991. Asst. prof. Grad. Sch. Academia Sinica, 1985-86; assoc. prof. dept. radiology U. Chgo., 1994—. E-mail: xpan@uchicago.edu.

PAN, YI, computer science educator; b. Wujiang, Jiangsu, China, May 12, 1960; came to U.S., 1987; s. Jun and Xiuzhen (Fei) P.; m. Hong Miao, Aug. 4, 1986; children: Marissa, Anna. BEng, Tsinghua U., Beijing, 1982, MEng, 1984; MSc, U. Pitts., 1988, PhD, 1991. Rsch. asst. Tsinghua U., 1982-86; tchg. asst. U. Pitts., 1987-89, tchg. fellow, 1989-91; asst. prof. computer sci. U. Dayton, Ohio, 1991-96, assoc. prof., 1996-2000; assoc. prof. computer sci. Ga. State U., Atlanta, 2000—. Director of Graduate Studies in Computer Science University of Dayton, Dayton, 1998—2000. Contbr. articles to profl. jours. Recipient Rsch. Opportunity award NSF, 1995, Investment Competition Fund award Ohio Bd. Regents, 1996; Mellon Found. fellow 1990, Summer Rsch. fellow U. Dayton Rsch. Coun., 2000, Air Force Office for Sci. Rsch., JSPS fellow, 1998. Mem. IEEE Computer Soc. (sr.), Assn. for Computing Machinery. Home: 615 Summer Breeze Ter Alpharetta GA 30005-6431 Office: Ga State U Computer Sci Dept Atlanta GA 30303 E-mail: pan@cs.gsu.edu.

PAN, YI, neurologist; b. Beijing, China, Oct. 4, 1955; came to U.S., 1986; d. Yutang and Xiangchun (Zhang) P.; m. Randolph H. Bretton, Sept. 14, 1997. MD, Beijing Med U., 1982, MS, 1986; PhD, Howard U., 1992. Diplomate Am. Bd. Psychiatry and Neurology. Resident in neurology St. Louis U., 1993-97, fellow in neurophysiology, 1997-98; neurologist So. Ill. Neurologic Inst., Belleville, Ill., 1998-2000; asst. prof. dept. neurology St. Louis U., 2000—. Postdoctoral fellow Harvard Med. Sch., 1992-93. Mem. Am. Acad. of Neurology, Soc. for Neurosci., Am. Physiolog. Soc. Home: 2440 Pro Tour Dr Belleville IL 62220-4847 Office: St Louis U Dept Neurology 3635 Vista Ave Saint Louis MO 63110 E-mail: pany@slu.edu.

PAN, ZIGANG, engineering educator; s. Dejia Pan and Meilin Zhang; m. Ying Gu, Dec. 26, 1990; 1 child Tina. BS, Shanghai Jiao Tong U., 1990; MSc, U. Ill., 1992, PhD, 1996. Rsch. engr. dept. elect. and computer engring. U. Calif. , Santa Barbara, 1996; asst. prof. dept. elect. engring., Polytechnic U., Bklyn., 1996—98; assoc. prof. dept. automation Shanghai Jiao Tong U., Shanghai, 2000; asst. prof. dept. elect., computer engring. and compter sci. U. Cin., 2001—. Contbr. chapters to books, articles to profl. jours. Recipient Silver prize, 28th Internat. Math. Olympiad, 1987, First prize, Shanghai Assn. Sci. and Technology, 2000. Mem.: IEEE (George S. Axelby Outstanding Paper award 1995, cert. CDC Best Student Paper award competition 1992), Phi Kappa Phi. Office: U Cin Dept of Elec & Comp Eng & Comp Sci Cincinnati OH 45221-0030

PAN, ZUOHONG, economist, researcher; b. Guangzhou, Guangdong, China, Sept. 11, 1957; s. Zhigang Pan and Linxian Wu; m. Xiaomei Gong; 1 child Felicia. BA, Renmin U. China, Beijing, 1982, MA, 1985; Ph D, Wayne State U., 1995. Lectr. Renmin U. China, 1985—88; sr. rsch. analyst Automated Mktg. Sys., Inc., Detroit, 1994; assoc. prof. Western Conn. State U., Danbury, 1995—2002. Rsch. fellow Tech. and Economy Devel. Ctr., State Coun. ChinaState Council, Beijing, 1984; econ. cons. Internat.Credit & Investment Corp. China, Beijing, 1986; fin. cons. Real Investment & Mgmt. Inc., N.Y.C., 2000; strategic alliance cons. Millennium Capital Quest Corp., Wolcott, 1999—2000; referee Procs. of the Complex & Chaotic Sys. Track of the 30th Ann. Hawaii Internat. Conf. on Sys. Scis. (HICSS-30), 1997; guest prof. Renmin U., 1996—2002. Author: (book) The Methodology of Social Sciences, 1990; contbr. book, ; translator: (book) Economics by Paul A. Samuelson, 10th edit., 1991; editor: (22-book series) American Studies Series, 2000; author: (book) Investment Banking in the U.S., 2000; contbr. book, ; reviewer: Macroeconomics by Ralph T. Byrns and Gerald W. Stone, 7th edit., 1999, reviewer: Economics Today by Miller, 1999—2000. Fellow Thomas C. Rumble univ. grad. fellow, Wayne State U., 1993; grantee CSU/AAUP rsch. grantee, Connecticut State U., 1996, 1997, 1998; scholar CEERC scholar, NAS and Ford Found., 1988—89. Mem.: Assn. Chinese Social Scis. Profs., Am. Econ. Assn. Office: Western Conn State U 181 White St Danbury CT 06810 Business E-Mail: panz@wcsu.ctstateu.edu.

PANACCIONE, BRUCE ROY, systems analyst, geographer; b. Van Nuys, Calif., Dec. 22, 1958; s. Thomas Edward and Dorothy Louise (Bogert) P.; m. Kaori Tokushiku, July 11, 1987; 1 child, Thomas Morio. AA in Photojournalism, L.A. Pierce Coll., 1987, AS, 1979; BA in Geography magna cum laude, Calif. State U., Northridge, 1990, postgrad. studies, 1990-92. Accredited adviser in ins. Ins. Inst. Am. Exploration technician Unocal Corp., L.A., 1989-92; sr. market rsch. analyst, Geog. Info Sys. project leader Automobile Club of So. Calif., Costa Mesa, 1992—. Mem. Spkrs.' Bur. Orange County chpt. ARC, 1997-2000; mem. steering com. Orange County Disaster Preparedness Acad. Recipient Geography Scholarship, Nat. Coun. for Geog. Edn., 1989. Mem. Assn. Am. Geographers, Soc. Ins. Rsch. Office: Automobile Club So Calif 3333 Fairview Rd Costa Mesa CA 92626-1610 E-mail: panaccione.bruce@aaa-calif.com.

PANAGARIYA, ARVIND, economics educator; b. Jaipur, Rajasthan, India, Sept. 30, 1952; s. Baloo Lal and Mohan (Golecha) P.; m. Amita Somani, Jan. 17, 1981; children: Ananth, Ajay. BA, Rajasthan Coll., India, 1971; MA, U. Rajasthan, 1973; PhD, Princeton U., 1978. Asst. prof. econs. U. Md., College Park, 1978-83, assoc. prof. econs., 1983-89, prof. econs., 1989—; sr. economist World Bank, Washington, 1989-93. Editor: (with Jaime de Melo) New Dimensions in Regional Integration; contbr. articles to profl. jours. Mem. Am. Econ. Assn. Jain Religion. Home: 8402 Old Seven Locks Rd Bethesda MD 20817-2007 Office: U Md Dept Econs College Park MD 20742-0001

PANAGIDES, JOHN, pharmacologist; b. N.Y.C., Aug. 15, 1944; s. Chris and Sophie (Marmar) P.; m. Kathleen Ann Heimann, July 9, 1967; children: Christopher, Melissa, Adrienne. BS, CCNY, N.Y.C., 1966; MS, U. N.C., 1968; PhD, SUNY, Buffalo, 1972. Rsch. assoc. Rockefeller U., N.Y.C., 1972-73; sr. scientist Lederle Labs., Pearl River, N.Y., 1973-83; sr. clin. monitor Ayerst Labs., N.Y.C., 1983-87; dir. clin. projects, CNS Organon Inc., West Orange, N.J., 1987-99, sr. dir. clin. projects, CNS, 1999—. Contbr. articles to profl. jours. NDEA Title IV fellow, Chapel Hill, 1966-68. Mem. AAAS, Am. Soc. Pharmacology and Exptl. Therapeutics, Am. Coll. Neuropsychopharmacology, N.Y. Acad. Scis. Achievements include development of haemophilus influenza vaccine, 23-valent pneumococcal vaccine, fenbufen, lodine, cotazym, cotazym-S, zymase, remeron. Home: 7 Catawba Dr West Nyack NY 10994-2304 Office: Organon Inc 375 Mount Pleasant Ave West Orange NJ 07052-2798 E-mail: j.panagides@organoninc.com.

PANAGIOSOULIS, GABRIEL, cook; b. Kefalonia, Greece, Nov. 21, 1933; arrived in U.S., 1970; s. Costas Panagiosoulis and Panorea Parginou; m. Hortencia Argueta, June 28, 1962; children: Panorea, Cleopatra, Gabriela-Constantina. Chief steward Mcht. Marine; chief personal plastics factory, Guatemala; taxi driver Guatemala; cook NY; ret. Author: (book) Adventures at Sea, 1995, Fifty Years Back, 1996, Quest for a Dream, 1997. Mem.: Cephalonian Soc., Hellenic Lit. Soc. Avocations: reading, writing. Home: 2718 Gifford Ave Bronx NY 10465 Personal E-mail: gabrielkp@aol.com.

PANARESE, WILLIAM C. civil engineer; b. Framingham, Mass., Mar. 6, 1929; s. Angelo and Stephanie (Di Profio) P. BSCE, Purdue U., 1952. Structural research engr. Assn. Am. Railroads, Chgo., 1952-55; with Portland Cement Assn., Chgo. and Skokie, Ill., 1957-76, 80-94, mgr. concrete tech. sect., 1973-76, assoc. mgr. bldg. constrn. sect., 1980-83, mgr. bldg. tech. dept., 1983-86, mgr. constrn. info. services dept., 1987-94. Author, editor Design and Control of Concrete Mixtures, Concrete Masonry Handbook for Architects, Engineers, Builders, High Strength Concrete, Concrete Floors on Ground, Fiber Reinforced Concrete, Cement Mason's Guide, other bldg. guides and handbooks; editor Concrete Constrn. mag., 1976-80, Concrete Tech. Today newsletter, 1980-94. Served with C.E. U.S. Army, 1955-57. Fellow Am. Concrete Inst. (coms. 302 on constrn. of concrete floors, 332 on residential concrete work, chmn. 332 1984-88). Roman Catholic. Home: 1625 Glenview Rd Unit 304 Glenview IL 60025-2973 E-mail: wmpanarese@aol.com.

PANARETOS, JOHN, mathematics and statistics educator; b. Kythera, Lianianika, Greece, Feb. 23, 1948; s. Victor and Fotini (Kominu) P.; m. Evdokia Xekalaki; 1 child, Victor. First degree, U. Athens, 1972; MSc, U. Sheffield, Eng., 1974; PhD, U. Bradford, Eng., 1977. Lectr. U. Dublin, Ireland, 1979-80; asst. prof. U. Mo., Columbia, U.S, 1980-82; assoc. prof. U. Iowa, Iowa City, U.S., 1982-83, U. Crete, Iraklio, Greece, 1983-84; assoc. prof. div. applied math., Sch. Engring. U. Patras, Greece, 1984-87, prof. Greece, 1987-91, assoc. dean sch. engring., chmn. div. applied math. Greece, 1986-87, vice-rector Greece, 1988-91; prof. Athens U. Econs., 1991—, dir. grad. program, chair dept. stats., 1993-96; pres. Nat. Coun. Edn. of Greece, 1996—. Sec.-gen. Ministry Edn. and Religious Affairs, Greece, 1988-89, 95-96. Contbr. articles to profl. jours. Mem. Sci. Coun. of Greek Parliament, 1987—; mem. ednl. com. OECD, 1994-97; mem. governing bd. CERI of OECD, 1994-97; chmn. rsch. com., pers. com. U. Patras, 1988-91. Mem. N.Y. Acad. Sci., Am. Statis. Assn., Inst. Math. Stats., Bernoulli Soc. for Probability and Math. Stats., Greek Math. Soc., Greek Statis. Inst., Internat. Statis. Inst. Office: Athens U Econs 76 Patision St 10034 Athens Greece E-mail: jpan@aueb.gr.

PANARO, JOSEPH, financial services company executive; b. Stamford, Conn., May 15, 1950; s. Anthony and Ruth (Scharf) P.; m. Janet Lyn Lucas, June 17, 1972; children: Jennifer, Alyson. BS, N.H. Coll., 1972; MBA, U. Bridgeport, 1976; postgrad., U. Pa., 1987, 89. Asst. v.p. Western region Jos. E. Seagram and Sons, N.Y.C., 1976-81; region mktg. mgr. Coca-Cola Co., Atlanta, 1981-86; divsn. sales mgr. RJR Nabisco, East Hanover, N.J., 1986-92; region v.p. Western Union, Paramus, 1992-94; v.p. Info. Resources, Chgo., 1994-95, MasterCard Internat., Purchase, N.Y., 1995—. Team leader Emmaus, New Canaan, Conn., 1991-93. Mem. New Canaan Field Club (bd. dirs. 1993-95), K.C. (advocate 1994-95). Republican. Roman Catholic. Avocations: tennis, paddle tennis. Home: 76 Glen Dr New Canaan CT 06840-3636 Office: MasterCard Internat 2000 Purchase St Purchase NY 10577-2405

PANAYIOTIS, CHINAS, school psychologist, consultant; b. Cyprus, July 19, 1948; arrived in Greece, 1982; BA in Psychology, U. Lyon, France, 1974; degree in psychology, U. Paris V, 1979, Diplome Etudes Approfondies, 1980; Diplome Etudes Superieures Specialisees, Inst. Psychology, France, 1981. Asst. child and family welfare Social Svcs., Cyprus, 1975-76; rsch. exec. Middle East Rsch. Bur., 1976-78; counsellor office for adult edn. Ministry of Edn., Athens, 1983-84; dir. dept. spl. edn. svc. Mental Health Ctr., 1984-89; sch. psychologist Exptl. Spl. Sch. Maraslio Didaskalio Dimotikis Ekpedeusis-Tchrs. Coll., 1989—. Tchr. psychology and spl. edn. Sch. Social Work, IAKE, Athens, 1982-85; tchr. psychology and group work Sch. of Nurses, PIKPA, 1983-85; dir. specialization courses, social educator and spl. needs Ministry of Youth, CEE, 1986-89; coord. seminars and workshops on spl. needs Dist. Pieria, Greece, 1985; spl. edn. coord. Best Buddies U. Athens, 1993-96; v.p. coun. Nat. Welfare Orgn. for the Child and Mother, Athens, 1993-96; mem. commn. for reform of spl. edn. Ministry of Edn., 1994; mem. commn. for tng. needs and the devel. of social svcs. Ministry of Health and Social Svcs., 1997-99. Editor, translator; contbr. articles to profl. jours. Mem. Assn. Greek Psychologists, Internat. Sch. Psychology Assn., Am. Soc. for Quality Control, Greek Assn. Sch. Psychologists (founding mem., pres. 2000—). Home: Antifanous 3 15773 Athens Greece E-mail: chinas@iname.com.

PANAYIRCI, SHARON LORRAINE, textiles executive, design engineer; b. San Diego, Nov. 11, 1957; d. Robert Vernon and Edna Ruth (Bayless) Reed; m. Mehmet Vefki Panayirci, Mar. 1, 1985; 1 child, Ruth Naile. AAS cum laude, Sinclair Coll., 1981; B in Tech. cum laude, U. Dayton, 1984. Designer Dayton (Ohio) Progress Corp., 1981-85; design engr. Hartzell Propeller Inc., Piqua, Ohio, 1987-88; v.p. Patex Exim Inc., Dayton, 1986-93, Aegean Apparel, Dayton, 1993—. Cons. Cepateks A.S. Indsl. Engr., Denizli, Turkey, 1985-86; fin. cons. Aegean Apparel Inc., Dayton, 1991-93. Mem.: AAUW, NAFE, USA Equestrian. Democrat. Avocations: horseback riding, auto repair and restoration. Office: Aegean Apparel Inc 4365 Lisa Dr Tipp City OH 45371-9463

PANCERO, JACK BLOCHER, restaurant executive; b. Cin., Dec. 27, 1923; s. Howard and Hazel Mae (Blocher) P.; m. Loraine Fielman, Aug. 4, 1944; children: Gregg Edward, Vicki Lee. Student, Ohio State U., 1941-44. Ptnr. Howard Pancero & Co., Cin., 1948-66; stockbroker Gradison & Co., Cin., 1966-70; real estate assoc. Parchman & Oyler, Cin., 1972-87; v.p. Gregg Pancero, Inc., Kings Mills, Ohio, 1972—. Mem. Vineyards C. of C., Western Hills Country Club, Univ. Club (Cin.), Cin. Engrs. Table, Pelican Bay Club, Vineyard Country Club, Royal Poinciana Golf Club, Met. Club., Collier Athletic Club, Masons, Shriners. Methodist. Home and Office: 806 Rue De Vl Naples FL 34108-8531 Office: Kings Island Kenwood Ctr Bldg 7565 Kenwood Rd Cincinnati OH 45236-2800

PANCHAL, CHANDRAKANT B. chemical engineer, researcher; b. Naroli, India, June 14, 1948; came to U.S., 1977; s. Bhanabhai C. and Kamlaben (Mistry) P.; m. Padma C. Mistry, Feb. 10, 1978; children: Surbhi, Vishal. BS in Chem. Engring., U. Bombay, 1972, MS in Chem. Engring., 1974; PhD in Chem. Engring., U. Manchester (Eng.), 1977. Rsch. assoc. Okla. State U., Stillwater, 1977-79; asst. chem. engr. Argonne (Ill.) Nat. Lab., 1979-82, chem. engr., 1982—. Cons. devel. program UN, New Delhi, 1985-86, NASA, Cleve., 1987-88. Editor: Fouling Mitigation, 1997; contbr. chpt. to book. Recipient FLC Award Tech. Transfer Fed. Lab. Consortium, 1995. Mem. AIChE (divsn. chair 1998). Achievements include revitalization of research on fouling mitigation. Avocations: travel, camping, cycling, reading. Office: Argonne Nat Lab 9700 Cass Ave Bldg 362 Argonne IL 60439-4815 also: Energy Concepts Co 627 Ridgeley Ave Annapolis MD 21401

PANCHALAVARAPU, POORNACHANDRA RAO, industrial engineer, consultant; s. Purushotham and AdiLakshmi Panchalavarapu; m. SriPadmaja S Ogirala, June 12, 1969; children: Manoj, Niraj. PhD, Case Western Res. U., 2000. Logistics engr. Schneider Logistics Inc., Green Bay, Wis., 1998—2001, lead logistics engr., 2001—. Contbr. articles; mem. editl. bd.: Internat. Jour. Indsl. Engring., 2000—. Mem.: Inst. Ops. Rsch. and Mgmt. Sci. Hindu. Avocation: travel. Home: 2980 Conesta Dr Green Bay WI 54311 Office: Schneider Logistics Inc 3101 South Packerland Drive Green Bay WI 54313 Personal E-mail: ppc_rao@hotmail.com. E-mail: panchalavarapur@schneider.com.

PANCHERI, EUGENE JOSEPH, chemical engineer; b. South Bend, Ind., Jan. 23, 1947; s. Raymond Albert and Dora Lugenia (Martin) P.; m. Janice Edwina Sutton, Mar. 9, 1986; children: Brent Jason, Ayrie Ann, Joseph Sutton. BSChE, Purdue U., 1969. Staff mem. Procter & Gamble, Cin., 1969-74, group leader, 1974-92, prin. engr., 1993-95, rsch. fellow, 1995—. Author: Famiglia Pancheri, 1991, The Gospel, 2000. Mem. Brit. Zeolite Assn., Internat. Com. Natural Zeolites, Am. Oil Chemists Soc., Nat. Geneal. Soc., Trentini nel Mondo, Phi Eta Sigma, Alpha Tau Omega. Achievements include 23 U.S. patents and 24 foreign patents for dishwashing and laundry cleaning products. Office: Procter & Gamble ITC 5299 Spring Grove Ave Cincinnati OH 45217-1025 E-mail: ginopan@hotmail.com.

PANCOSKA, PETR, research and development company executive, educator; b. Zlin, Czech Republic, Oct. 1, 1952; s. Vojtech Pancoska and Ludmila Pancoskova; m. Eva Krejcova; 1 child Lenka Martinova 1 child Petra. PhD in Physics, Charles U., Prague, 1981, MA Chemistry, 1977. Sr. rsch. assoc.e Charles U., Prague, Czech Republic, 1977—; assoc. prof. U. Ill., Chgo., 1994—; exec. bd. dirs. DIMATIA Rsch. Ctr., Prague, 1995—; founder, dir. R&D Bioinformatics DNA Codes, Chgo., 1999—. Cons. Tm Biosci., Toronto, Canada. Contbr. sci. papers to profl. jours. Mem.: Biophys. Soc. Achievements include invention of methods and tools for nucleic acid sequence analysis, selection, and generation. Home: 901 Hinman Ave Evanston IL 60202 Office: Bioinformatics DNA Codes Ste 2W 316 South Halsted St Chicago IL Office Fax: 312-258-9687. Personal E-mail: pancoska@uic.edu. Business E-Mail: ppancoska@dnacodes.com.

PANDA, RAJESH KUMAR, ceramics and materials engineer; b. Berhampur, India, 1972; s. Jagannath and Jyoshna Panda; m. Smruti Rekha Panda, 1999. B Tech. in Metall. Engring., Indian Inst. Tech., Bombay, 1994; MS in Ceramics and Materials Engring., Rutgers U., 1996, PhD in Ceramics and Materials Engring., 1998. Undergrad. rsch. asst. Indian Inst. Tech., 1993-94; grad. rsch. asst. Rutgers U., Piscataway, N.J., 1994-98, tchg. asst., 1997-98; R&D design engr. Hewlett Packard Co./Agilent Tech., Andover, Mass., 1998—2001, Philips, 2001—. Cons. Ethicon (a J&J Co.), Somerville, N.J., 1997-98, Exogen Inc., Piscataway, 1996-97; presenter, spkr. in field. Contbr. articles to profl. jours.; patentee in field. Tchr. Nat. Social Svc. Orgn., Bombay, 1990-92. Recipient Best Paper award SAMPE, 1996, Rsch. Excellence award N.J. Ctr. for Biomaterials and Med. Devices, 1996, award for excellence Literati Club, 1999 Mem. IEEE. Avocations: current affairs, hiking, travel. Office: Agilent Techs 3000 Minuteman Rd # Ms0095 Andover MA 01810-1032 E-mail: rkpanda@yahoo.com.

PANDE, PRAKASH NARAIN, cardiologist, educator, consultant; b. Basti, U.P., India, Jan. 1, 1942; came to U.S., 1971; s. Bhawnath and Chandra (Misra) P.; m. Lora Joann Kargina, June 19, 1974; children: Jennifer, Robby. BSc, U. (India) Lucknow, 1958, MBBS, 1964, MD in Internal Medicine, 1968. Diplomate Am. Bd. Internal Medicine, Am. Bd. Cardiovascular Diseases. Rotating house officer Associated Hosps. Med. Coll. (India) Kanpur, 1964-66, resident med. officer, 1966-67; sr. house officer Bury and Rosendale Hosp., Eng., 1969-71; resident in medicine Rochester (N.Y.) Gen. Hosp., 1971-73; trainee in cardiology U. Rochester, 1973-75; cons. cardiology, attending physician Rochester (N.Y.) Gen. Hosp., 1975-98, dir. cardiac catheterization labs., 1982-90, head cardiology unit, 1990-97; from clin. asst. prof. medicine to clin. prof. U. Rochester, 1980-97, adj. prof., 1998—99; prof. clin. medicine, cardiology Ind. U. Sch. Medicine, Indpls., 1998—. Cardiologist Krannert Inst. Cardiology, Indpls.; dir. Johnson Meml. Homecare, 1998—, chair credentials com., 2001—. Editor Clarian Cardiology newsletter, 1998—. Fellow Sr. rsch. fellow, Coun. Scientific and Indsl. Rsch., 1968. Fellow ACP, Am. Heart Assn. (coun. clin. cardiology 1990), Am. Coll. Cardiology (Ind. councilor 1994, 1996), Soc. Cardiac Angiography and Interventions (sr.), Coun. Geriatric Cardiology; mem. Assn. Subspecialty Profs. Mem. Reformed Ch. Am. Office: Krannert Inst Cardiology 1800 Capitol Indianapolis IN 46202-4832 E-mail: ppande@iupui.edu.

PANDEY, RAMESH CHANDRA, chemist, executive; b. Naugaon, India, Nov. 5, 1938; came to U.S., 1967; s. Gauri Dutt and Jivanti Pandey. BSc, U. Allahabad, India, 1958; MSc, U. Gorakhpur, India, 1960; PhD, U. Poona, India, 1965. Jr. rsch. fellow CSIR Nat. Chem. Lab., Poona, 1960-64, rsch. officer, 1965-67, scientist organic divsn., 1970-72; rsch. assoc. dept. chemistry U. Ill., Urbana, 1967-70, vis. scientist, 1972-77; sr. scientist fermentation program Nat. Cancer Inst. Frederick (Md.) Cancer Rsch. Facility, 1977-82, head chem. sect., 1982-83; sr. scientist Abbott Labs., North Chicago, Ill., 1983-84; pres. Xechem, Inc., Melrose Park, 1984-90, pres., CEO, dir. tech. devel. New Brunswick, N.J., 1990—; chmn., CEO, pres. Xechem Internat. Inc., 1994—, Xetapharm Inc., 1996—. Cons. Washington U. Sch. Medicine, St. Louis, 1976-85, LyphoMed, Inc., Melrose Park, 1984-85; vis. prof. Waksman Inst. Rutgers U., Piscataway, N.J., 1984-86; mem. life sci. adv. bd. NJTC, 1999—. Mem. editl. bd. Internat. Jour. Antibiotics, 1986—; patentee graft thin layer chromatography; several U.S. and internat. patents for the isolation and purification of antibiotics and anticancer agents. Mem. Middlesex County (N.J.) Work Force Investment Bd., 1999—; mem. adv. com. for sci. transfer and sci. tech. program Middlesex County Coll., Edison, N.J., 1999-2001. Fellow Am. Inst. Chemists; mem. Am. Chem. Soc., Am. Soc. Microbiology, Am. Soc. Mass Spectrometry, Am. Assn. Cancer Rsch., Am. Soc. Hosp. Pharmacists, Am. Soc. Pharmacognosy, Soc. Indsl. Microbiology, N.Y. Acad. Scis., Indian Sci. Congress Assn., Rotary Club (Paul Harris fellow 1996—, pres. New Brunswick club 1999-2000). Office: Xechem Internat Inc New Brunswick Tech Ctr 100 Jersey Ave Bldg B Ste 310 New Brunswick NJ 08901-3200 E-mail: xechem@erols.com.

PANDEY, VIVEK K. finance educator, researcher; b. Chapra, Bihar, India, Feb. 4, 1965; came to U.S., 1987; s. Gopal K. and Shobha (Tiwary) P. BCom, Andhra U., India, 1986; MBA, Western Carolina U., Cullowhee, N.C., 1988; DBA, Miss. State U., 1994. Grad. rsch. asst. Western Carolina U., 1987-88, Miss. State U., 1988-93; instr. Miss. U. for Women, Columbus, 1993, asst. prof., 1994-98; asst. prof. dept. econs. and fin. Murray (Ky.) State U., 1998—; asst. prof. U. Tex., Tyler, 1999—. Contbr. articles to profl. jours. Recipient Outstanding Paper award Southwestern Fin. Assn., 1991, Anbar Highest Quality rsch. award, 1998, Distig. Rsch. award Allied Acads., 1999; named Faculty Mem. of Yr., Divsn. of Bus., Miss. U. for Women, 1995. Mem. Am. Fin. Assn., Fin. Mgmt. Assn., Eastern Fin. Assn., So. Fin. Assn. Avocations: philately, camping, biking, reading. Office: U Tex at Tyler 3900 University Blvd Tyler TX 75701-6622

PANDOLFI, FRANCES, health facility administrator; b. N.Y.C., Sept. 7, 1944; d. Frank Pandolfi and Rose McGinn; m. Edmund Lewiska Menelik Bobbitt, May 19, 1973. BA, Vassar Coll., 1965; MPA, NYU, 1990. Health planner N.Y.C. Dept. City Planning, 1965-74; planner West Midlands County Coun., Birmingham, Eng., 1974-81, dir. recreation and tourism planning Eng., 1981-85, dir. strategic planning, 1985-86; dep. dir. housing coord. N.Y.C.

Mayor's Office, 1987-89; dir. nurses housing N.Y.C. Health & Hosps. Corp., 1989-92, exec. asst. to v.p., 1992-94, asst. v.p., 1994-97; chief of staff N.Y.C. Health and Hosps. Corp., 1998-2001, chief info. officer, 2001—. Dir. Women in Housing and Fin., N.Y.C., 1990-96. Mem. Am. Soc. Pub. Adminstrn., Royal Town Planning Inst. Office: NYC Health & Hosps Corp 125 Worth St New York NY 10013-4006

PANDRES, DAVE, JR. science educator, researcher; b. Duncan, Okla., Jan. 10, 1928; s. Dave and Goldye (Hart) P.; m. Irene Shirley Pandres, July 21, 1953; children: Ronald Mark, Leo Philip, Keith Alan, Lisa Ann. BSEE, U. Tex., Austin, 1949, MA in Applied Math., 1956; PhD in Physics, U. Tex., 1958. Sr. engr. Chance-Vaught Aircraft Co., Dallas, 1951-52; advanced rsch. scientist Marathon Oil Co. Rsch. Ctr., Littleton, 1958-60; assoc. rsch. scientist Martin-Marietta Corp., Denver, 1960-62; sr. rsch. & devel. scientist Lockheed-California Co., Burbank, 1962-64; dir. Math. Scis. Divsn. Douglas Adv. Rsch. Labs., Huntington Beach, Calif., 1964-70; asst. prof. Dept. Math. N. Ga. Coll., Dahlonega, 1971-74, assoc. prof. Dept. Math., 1974-78, prof. Dept. Math., 1978—. Vis. lectr. U. Calif., 1965-66; vis. prof. Inst. Math. Scis., Madras, India, 1970. Contbr. articles to profl. jours. LTJG U.S. Navy, 1952-55. Grantee NSF, 1974, 76. Mem. APS. Democrat. Jewish. Avocations: boating, photography. Home: PO Box 1275 Dahlonega GA 30533-0022 Office: N Ga Coll Dept Math & Computer Science College Ave Dahlonega GA 30597-0001

PANE, MICHAEL ANTHONY, lawyer, consultant; b. New Brunswick, N.J., Nov. 1, 1942; s. Remigio Ugo Quirino and Philomena (Pascale) P.; m. Frances Eleanor Heckert, May 7, 1966; children: Michael Anthony Jr., Natalia Eugenia. AB, Princeton U., 1964; JD, Harvard U., 1967. Bar: N.J. 1967, U.s. Dist. Ct. N.J. 1967. Rsch. assoc., then rsch. dir. N.J. County and Mcpl. Govt. Study Commn., 1967-71; exec. v.p. Cmty. Program Assistance, Inc., Trenton, N.J., 1971-75; sr. rsch. analyst Synectics, 1971-75; assoc. firm Warren Goldberg and Berman, Trenton and Princeton, 1975-77; pvt. practice Hightstown, 1978—. Cons. and counsel various state and mcpl. govtl. bodies, orgns. and assns.; lectr. numerous legal and local govtl. profl. meetings; past pres. N.J. Inst. Mcpl. Attys., 1994-96, 96-97; dep. gen. counsel N.J. State League of Municipalities, 1989-90; counsel Mcpl. Clk.'s Assn. N.J., 1983—, N.J. Health Officer's Assn., 1983—, Govt. Fin. Officer's Assn. N.J., 1990—, Mcpl. Welfare Assn. N.J., 1994—; asst. counsel N.J. Fedn. Planning Ofcls., 1986—; adj. prof. local govt. Rutgers U., Camden, N.J., 1997-2000. Author: Functional Fragmentation and the Traditional Forms of Local Government in New Jersey, 1986, N.J. Local Governmental Law (Volumes 30, 34, 35 and 35A West's N.J. Practice Series), 1999, Code Enforcement in New Jersey, 1990; contbr. numerous articles to profl. publs.; editor N.J. Inst. Mcpl. Attys. Law Rev., 1986—. Campaign chmn. Mercer County unit Am. Cancer Soc., 1975-76, bd. mem. 1993-97; active local and county Dem. Coms., 1967-83. Recipient Disting. Svc. award N.J. State League Municipalities, 1985, 2000, Osborne Disting. Svc. to Pub. Health award, 1988, Fred Stickel award N.J. Inst. Mcpl. Attys., 2000, Achievement in Planning award N.J. Planning Ofcls., 2001. Mem. N.J. Bar Assn., Italy and Colonies Study Circle (U.S.A.)(treas., quar. nat. jour. editor 1981-84, 91—). Roman Catholic. Home: 1 Hidden Springs Ln Hightstown NJ 08520-6102 Office: 307 N Main St Hightstown NJ 08520-3101 E-mail: mapanepc@aol.com.

PANEC, WILLIAM JOSEPH, lawyer; b. Pawnee City, Nebr., June 22, 1937; s. Albert and Thelma I. (Sebring) P. BS, U. Nebr., 1962, JD, 1965. Bar: Nebr. 1965, Colo. 1999, U.S. Dist. Ct. Nebr. 1965, U.S. Supreme Ct. 1991, U.S. Ct. Appeals (8th cir.) 1991. Sole practice, Fairbury, Nebr., 1965—; county judge Jefferson County, 1965-70. Mem. Nebr. Jud. Qualifications Commn., 1968-70; chmn. Region XIV Crime Commn., 1968-71; cons., 1971-79; cons. for regions VIII, IX, XIV Regional Jail Study, 1972; profl. instr. Nebr. Law Enforcement Adv. Council, 1972; county atty. Jefferson County, 1973-75; village atty. Diller, Nebr., 1975-95; atty. Fairbury Airport Authority, 1981—, Greeley Airport Authority, 1990-2000; organizer Nebr. Jud. Reform, 1969. Author: Probate Procedures and the Uniform Probate Code, 1969. Bd. dirs. Housing Authority, Fairbury, 1979—90, chmn., 1983—90; bd. dirs. Legal Svcs. S.E. Nebr., 1984—2000, v.p., 1992—94, pres., 1994—98; chmn. Law Day, Jefferson County, 1972, 1973, Jefferson County Mental Health Bd., 2001—. U.S. Army, 1955—56, honorably discharged Sgt. U.S. Army. Mem. Nebr. Assn. Trial Attys., Assn. Trial Lawyers Am., Am. Judicature Soc., Nebr. County Judges Assn. (v.p., pres.), Jefferson County Bar Asssn., Internat. Footprinters Assn., U. Nebr. Alumni Assn., Masons, Delta Theta Phi. Address: 1140 Main Ave Crete NE 68333-2258

PANEK, EDWARD STANLEY, JR. lawyer; b. Phila., Jan. 10, 1945; s. Edward S. and Clara S. P.; m. Marlene Lazzaro, Sept. 26, 1981; 1 child, Marilyn O. Primiano. BA, St. Joseph's U., Phila., 1966; JD, Villanova U., 1969. Bar: Pa. 1971, U.S. Cir. Ct. (8th cir.) 1976, U.S. Cir. Ct. (3d cir.) 1982. Counsel Phila. Civil Svc. Commn., 1969; trial atty. antitrust divsn. U.S. Dept. Justice, Phila., 1971—. Mem. Logan Sq. Neighborhood Assn., Phila., 1990—. With U.S. Army, 1969-71. Mem. Union League Phila. Roman Catholic. Avocations: sports, investing, wines, real estate, dining. Home: 2137 Race St Philadelphia PA 19103-1009 Office: US Dept Justice Antitrust Divsn 650 Curtis Ctr 7th & Walnut Philadelphia PA 19106 E-mail: edward.panek@usdoj.gov.

PANES, JACK SAMUEL, publishing company executive; b. N.Y.C., Apr. 6, 1925; s. Max S. and Sophie (Levine) P.; m. Pearl Shaine, Dec. 25, 1949; children— Stephanie Jill, Michael Jonathan. BA, Bklyn. Coll., 1947; MS in Journalism, Northwestern U., 1949. Editor, pub. The Howe Service, Inc., N.Y.C., 1949-54; founder, pub. Publs. for Industry, 1955—, Panes Publs., Inc., N.Y.C., 1959—; owner Drug Products Display Service Advt. Co., 1955—, Supplies for Industry Co., N.Y.C., 1956—; pres. Senap Devel. Corp., Great Neck, N.Y., 1972—. Pres. Russsell Woods Civic Assn., Great Neck. Served with inf. AUS, 1942-45, ETO. Decorated Silver Star medal, Bronze Star medal. Mem. Deadline Club, Sigma Delta Chi. Home: 21 Russell Woods Rd Great Neck NY 11021-4644 Office: Panes Publications Inc Great Neck NY 11021

PANESCU, DORIN, biomedical scientist; b. Deva, Romania, Nov. 10, 1960; came to U.S., 1990; s. Petre and Sevastita Panescu; children: Julia, Tenzi. BSEE, Poly. Inst., Timisoara, Romania, 1985; MSEE, U. Wis., 1991, PhD, 1993. Rsch. engr. Elec. Instrumentation Enterprise, Timisoara, 1985-87, Inst. Automation, Cluj, Romania, 1987-90; rsch. asst. U. Wis., Madison, 1991-93; rsch. scientist EP Technologies, Sunnyvale, Calif., 1993—96; dir. R&D Boston Sci., San Jose, 1996—. Cons. U. Wis., 1993—. Co-author: Biomedical Digital Signal Processing, 1993; reviewer IEEE Transactions on Biomed. Engring., 1993—; contbr. over 80 articles and abstracts to profl. jours. Mem. IEEE (sr. mem., chair indsl. rels. 1997-98, mem. EMBS AdCom 1997-98). Achievements include 100 patents related to cardiac mapping and ablation. avocations: tennis, Internet. Office: Boston Scientific 2710 Orchard Pkwy San Jose CA 95134-2012

PANETH, DONALD JOSEPH, editor, writer; b. N.Y.C., Feb. 28, 1927; s. Irving and Maud (Kramer) P.; m. Elma Olans, Apr. 10, 1949 (dec. 1987); children: Thea, Ira. BBA, CCNY, 1948; postgrad., Columbia U., 1949-50. Reporter N.Y. Times, 1947-49; free-lance journalist N.Y.C., 1950-56, 73-75, 77-83, 94—; rewriteman Daily Mirror, 1956-63; copy editor The Morning Telegraph, 1964-65; staff writer Med. Tribune, 1966-72; copy editor L.I. Press, Queens, N.Y., 1975-77; editor-in-chief News Dictionary: People, Places and Events, 1977-80; editor, writer Yearbook of the UN, N.Y.C., 1986-93; documents editor UN Office Conf. Svcs., 1993-94; recruiting asst., crew leader U.S. Bur. Census, 2000. Adj. lectr. English York Coll., CUNY, 1983-86; cons. study of lit. of far right extremist groups in U.S. Anti-Defamation League, N.Y., 1995-96. Author: William Baziotes: A Literary Portrait, 1961, Current Affairs Atlas, 1979, The Ency. of American Journalism, 1983; contbr. articles to Commentary mag., The Nation, Village Voice, Current Biography, Peacework, WorldPaper, N.Y. Indypendent, others; work included in anthologies Commentary on the American Scene, 1953, New York City Folklore, 1956. Mem. Am.-Scandinavian Found., N.Y. Soc. Libr. Avocation: reading. Home and Office: 240 Cabrini Blvd Apt 1E New York NY 10033-1113

PANETH, NIGEL SEFTON, epidemiologist, pediatrician; b. London, Sept. 19, 1946; s. Philip and Rita Zena (Kremer) P.; m. Ellen Margaret Pollak, Dec. 16, 1973; children: Rachel Ilana Rose, Tessa Tatiana Tamar. AB, Columbia Coll., 1968; BMS, Dartmouth Med. Sch., 1970; MD, Harvard Med. Sch., 1972; MPH, Columbia U., 1978. Diplomate Am. Bd. Pediatrics, Nat. Bd. Med. Examiners. Intern, jr., sr. and chief resident in pediatrics Albert Einstein Coll. Medicine/Bronx Mcpl. Hosp. Ctr., N.Y.C., 1972-76; fellow human devel. biology Albert Einstein Coll. Medicine, 1976-77; asst. clin. prof. dept. pediatrics Albert Einstein Coll. Medicine/Yeshiva U., 1977-78; asst. prof. dept. pediatrics and epidemiology Columbia U., N.Y.C., 1978-85, assoc. prof. 1985-89; assoc. prof. dept. pediatrics and human devel. Mich. State U. and Program in Epidemiology, East Lansing, 1989-92, prof., 1992—, prof., chair dept. epidemiology, 1997—; assoc. dean for rsch. Coll. of Human Medicine Mich. State U., 2000—. Vis. lectr. dept. neurology Harvard Med. Sch., Boston, 1988-89; nat. sci. advisory com. mem. March of Dimes Found., White Plains, N.Y., 1993—; cons. Inst. of Medicine, NAS, Washington, 1980s; study sect. mem. NIH, Bethesda, Md.; nat. adv. com. All Kids Count Immunization Effort, Atlanta, 1993-98; mem. rsch. adv. coun. United Cerebral Palsy Rsch. and Ednl. Found., 1999—. Co-author: (book) Brain Damage in the Preterm Infant, 1994; mem. editl. bd. Pediatric & Perinatal Epidemiology, The Future of Children. Recipient Rose Seegal award Harvard Med. Sch., 1972, Kathleen Lyle Murray award Am. Acad. Cerebral Palsy, 1986. Jewish. Home: 839 Wildwood Dr East Lansing MI 48823-3048 Office: Mich State U Dept Epidemiology 4660 S Hagadorn Rd East Lansing MI 48823-5376 E-mail: paneth@msu.edu.

PANETTA, JOSEPH DANIEL, biotechnology executive; b. Syracuse, N.Y., Mar. 1, 1954; s. Salvatore and Josephine Mary (Sbardella) P.; m. Karin Ann Hoffman, Oct. 21, 1978; children: Lauren Marie, Christopher Daniel. BS, LeMoyne Coll., 1976; MPH, U. Pitts., 1979. Environ. protection specialist EPA, Washington, 1979-82, sr. policy analyst, 1982-84; project leader Schering Corp./NorAm Chem Co., Wilmington, Del., 1984-85; mgr. regulatory affairs agrchems. divsn. Pennwalt Corp., Phila., 1985-88; mgr. corp. regulatory affairs Mycogen Corp., San Diego, 1988-90, dir. corp. regulatory affairs and quality assurance, 1990-92, dir. corp. regulatory, environ. affairs, 1992-97, v.p. govt. and pub. affair, 1998-99; pres., CEO BIOCOM/san diego, 1999—. Chmn. agr. and environment subcom. Internat. Bioindustry Forum; chmn. maneb data task force Inter-industry, Washington, 1985-88; guest lectr. biotech. U. Calif., San Diego, and Calif. Western Law Sch.; advisor bd. on agr. NAS; mem. San Diego Pub. Utilities Adv. Commn., 2002—; mem. Calif. Food Biotech. Adv. Com., 2002—. Columnist San Diego Daily Transcript, 1999—; contbr. articles to profl. jours. Mem. Rep. State Com. Del., 1987; bd. dirs. San Diego Work Force Partnership; mem. exec. com. Calif. Cmty. Colls. Econ. Devel. Network; mem. adv. bd. UCSD-Connect. Mem. Am. Crop Protection Assn. (chmn. com. biotech.), Nat. Agrl. Chems. Assn. (mem. registrations com. 1986-89), Biotech. Industy Orgn. (mem. food and agr. steering com., chmn. bipesticides com., internat. affairs com.), Calif. Indsl. Biotech. Assn. (mem. agrl. affairs com.), Am. Chem. Soc. (mem. agrl. div.), Am. Seed Trade Assn. (chmn. steering com. biotech.), Gov.'s Biotech. Coun. (Calif.), San Diego C. of C. (mem. pub. policy com.), San Diego Workforce Partnership (mem. youth coun.). Roman Catholic. Avocations: yachting, skiing, classical piano. Home: 5459 Shannon Ridge Ln San Diego CA 92130-4808 Office: BIOCOM San Diego 4501 Executive Dr San Diego CA 92121-3025

PANETTA, LEON EDWARD, federal official, former congressman; b. Monterey, Calif., June 28, 1938; s. Carmelo and Carmelina Panetta; m. Sylvia Marie Varni, July 14, 1962; children: Christopher, Carmelo, James. BA magna cum laude, U. Santa Clara, Calif., 1960, LL.B., JD, 1963. Bar: Calif. bar 1965, U.S. Supreme Ct. 1965, U.S. Dist. Ct. (no. dist.) Calif. 1965, U.S. Ct. Appeals 1965. Legis. asst. to U.S. Sen. Thomas Kuchel, Washington, 1966-69; dir. U.S. Office Civil Rights, HEW, 1969-70; exec. asst. to Mayor of N.Y.C., 1970-71; ptnr. Panetta, Thompson & Panetta, Monterey, 1971-76; mem. 95th-103d Congresses from 17th Calif. dist., 1977-93, chmn. budget com., mem. agr. com., adminstrn. com., also com. dep. majority whip for budget issues, mem. select com. on hunger; dir. U.S. Office Mgmt. and Budget, Washington, 1993-94; chief of staff The White House, 1994-97; founder Panetta Inst., CA State U., Monterey, Monterey Bay, CA, 1998—. Author: Bring Us Together, 1971. Counsel Monterey Regional Park Dists.; counsel NAACP, 1971-76; bd. trustees U. Santa Clara Law Sch.; founder Monterey Coll. Law; mem. Monterey County Dem. Cen. Com., 1972-74; v.p. Carmel Valley Little League, 1974-75. Served with AUS, 1964-66. Recipient Lincoln award NEA, 1970, Disting. Svc. award NAACP, 1972, Bread for World award, 1978, Nat. Hospice Orgn. award, 1984, Golden Plow award Am. Farm Bur. Fedn., Pres.'s award Am. Coun. on Tchr. of Fgn. Langs., 1991, Coastal and Ocean Mgmt. award Coastal Zone Found., 1991, Food Rsch. and Action Ctr. award, 1991; named Lawyer of Yr., Law Sch. U. Santa Clara, 1970. Mem.: Calif. Bar Assn. Roman Catholic. Office: The Panetta Inst Calif State U Monterey 100 Campus Ctr Bldg 86E Seaside CA 93955-8000

PANETTA, MICHAEL JON, state agency administrator, educator, writer, researcher; b. Lansing, Mich., Sept. 9, 1949; s. Frank Anthony P. and Elizabeth Virginia Rocchetti; m. Susan Marie Cottrill, May 1, 1971; children: Mary Elizabeth Panetta-Lowe, Michelina Anne Panetta-Cantu, Joseph Andrew. AA, Lansing (Mich.) C.C., 1970; BA, Mich. State U., East Lansing, 1971, MS, 1972, MA equivalency, 1988, DPhil, 2000. Cert. paramedic Mich., lic. emergency med. technician Mich.; cert. pvt. detective Mich. Fed. Manpower adminstr. Manpower Area Planning Coun., Lansing, Mich., 1970—73; spl. agent med. fraud auditor State of Mich., 1973—78, supr. fed. food stamp program, 1977—78, emergency med. svcs. program specialist, 1978—89, program specialist Gov.'s Coun. Environ. Quality, 1989—90, departmental policy and procedure specialist, 1990—91, fin. specialist, contract adminstr. child and family health programs, 1991—; prof. Spring Arbor U., 2001—02. Dir. youth and vet. program Nat. Alliance of Businessmen, Lansing, 1970—73; suggestion award program adminstr. Mich. Dept. Pub. Health, Lansing, 1990—91. Author: Leader Behavior & Member Response in an Institutional Setting, 1972, Citizens Perceptions of Police & Community Policing, 2000, pamphlets, booklets, guides. Co-founder, pres., v.p. Citizen's to Save Lansing Mich., Lansing, 1992—99; founder Citizens to Save Vets. Civic Ctr., 1992—99; co-founder, v.p. Citizens Against the Rain Tax of Lansing, 1994—2000. Recipient award, Soc. Study Social Problems Columbia U., 1986; scholar grad. rsch. scholarship, Mich. State U. Bd. Trustees, 1971. Fellow: Am. Lit. Assn.; mem.: Nat. Assn. Welfare Adminstrs., NRA, Mich. State U. Alumni Assn. (life), KC (assoc.; grand knight Richard coun. 1988—90, assoc. mem. Msgr. John A. Gabriels coun., charter grand knight Msgr. John A. Gabriels coun. 1993—95, Knight of Yr. Richard Coun. 1989, Top Proposer of Yr. Richard Coun. 1990, Knight of Yr. Msgr. John A. Gabriels Coun. 1993—95, Papal medallion 1992, Star Coun. award, Columbian award, Founders award 1993—95), Alpha Kappa Delta (life). Republican. Roman Catholic. Avocations: teaching, writing, travel, bicycling, camping.

PANG, IOK-HOU, research scientist, science educator; b. Macao, China, June 27, 1956; arrived in US, 1980; d. Pui-Hong Pang and Choi-Kam Choi; m. Ophelia Chan; children: Priscilla, Garrick. BS, Nat. Def. Med. Ctr., Taipei, Taiwan, 1978; PhD, U. Tex., Dallas, 1985. Cert. cert. pharmacist Taiwan. High sch. sci. tchr. Colegio Estrela do Mar, Macao, China, 1978—79; sr. scientist Alcon Lab, Inc., Ft. Worth, 1990—97, prin. scientist, 1998—2000; asst. dir. Alcon Rsch., Ltd., 2001—. Adj. faculty U. North Tex. Health Sci. Ctre, Ft. Worth, 1993—, North Tex. Eye Rsch. Inst., Ft. Worth, 1993—. Contbr. articles. Mem.: Am. Soc. Pharmacol. Exptl. Therapy, Soc. Neurosci., Assn. Rsch. Vision and Ophthalmology. Avocations: painting, chess. Office: Alcon Rsch Ltd 6201 S Freeway R3-24 Fort Worth TX 76134

PANG, JOSHUA KEUN-UK, trade company executive; b. Chinnampo, Korea, Sept. 17, 1924; came to U.S. 1951, naturalized, 1968; s. Ne-Too and Soon-Hei (Kim) P.; m. He-Young Yoon, May 30, 1963; children: Ruth, Pauline, Grace. BS, Roosevelt U., 1959. Chemist Realemon Co., Chgo., 1957-61; chief-chemist chem. divsn. Bell & Gossett Co., 1961-63, Fatty Acid Inc., divsn. Ziegler Chem. & Mineral Corp., Chgo., 1963-64; sr. chemist-supr. Gen. Mills Chems. Inc., Kankakee, Ill., 1964-70; pres., owner UJU Industries Inc., Broadview, 1971—, also dir. Bd. dirs. Dist. 92, Lindop Sch., Broadview, 1976-87; chmn. Proviso Area Sch. Bd. Assn., Proviso Twp., Cook County, Ill. 1976-77; bd. dirs. Korean Am. Cmty. Svcs., Chgo., 1979-80; mem. governing bd. Proviso Area Exceptional Children, Spl. Edn. Joint Agreement, 1981-84, 85-87; alumni bd. govs Roosevelt U., 1983-89; pres. Korean Am. Sr. Ctr., 1991-92; pres. Korean Am. Srs. Assn., Chicagoland, 1992—. Mem. Am. Chem. Soc., Am. Assn. Arts and Sci., Am. Inst. Parliamentarians (region 2 treas. 1979-81, region 2 gov. 1981-82), Internat. Platform Assn., Ill. Sch. Bd. Assn., Nat. Assn. Sch. Bds., Chgo. Area Parliamentarians, Parliamentary Leaders in Action (pres. 1980-81), Nat. Spkrs. Assn. (dir. Ill. chpt. 1981-82, nat. parliamentarian 1982-84, 2d v.p. chpt. 1983-84), Toastmasters (dist. gov. 1969-70), DADS Assn. U. Ill. (chmn. Cook County 1985-98, bd. dirs. 1987-95, treas. 1990-91, v.p. 1991-92), Korean Am. Assn. Chgo. (exec. dir. 1990), World Future Soc. (Chgo. area chpt. coord. 1988-99, pres. Greater Chicagoland Futurists 1991-95, 97-98, chmn. 1998 ann. conf. World Future Soc. Chgo.), Chicagoland C. of C. (ednl., environ. and Pacific-Rim coms., internat. divsn.). Home: 2532 S 9th Ave Broadview IL 60155-4804 Office: UJU Industries Inc PO Box 6351 Broadview IL 60155-6351 E-mail: jokupang@worldnet.att.net., j.pang@att.net.

PANG, MAYBELINE MIUSZE (MAYBELINE CHAN), software testing and systems engineer, analyst; b. Shanghai, China, Sept. 9, 1945; came to U.S. from Hong Kong, 1964; d. Yee Sun and Margaret H. (Kong) Chan; m. Patrick Yewwah Pang, Aug. 4, 1968 (div. 1987); children: Elaine Weikay, Irene Weisum, George Siu-On. BS in Physics/Math, Lincoln U., 1967; postgrad, U. Mo., 1967-68, U. Ariz., 1984-86. Application programmer Ariz. Health Sci. Ctr., Physiology Lab., Tucson, 1984-85; software engr. System and Software Engring. Dalmo Victor, Singer, 1985-88, McDonnell Douglas Helicopter Co., Mesa, Ariz., 1988-90, Sperry Marine, Charlottesville, Va., 1990—. Cons., worked with Air Force (F111 Weather Simulation), Army (Advanced Apache Helicopter), Navy (Seawolf weapons, ship control, CNO-Automatic Depth Finder LPD17) projects; comml. (Integrated Software Analysis Sys.; Sperry's docking sys., Guardian Star, SRD-500 SpeedLog, Voyage Mgmt. Sys.) projects; familiar with sys. analysis and design; software devel. and testing; algorithms, pulse processing, sys. engr. and analyst for Marine Sensors; active in Sperry's New Tech. Group. Recipient Nat. Sci. Honor Soc. award, 1967, Teaching assistantship U. Mo., 1968. Avocations: Chinese healing and martial arts, spirit/mind/body medicine, religion, life philosophy metaphysics, reading and research. Home: 1517 Westfield Ct Charlottesville VA 22901-1602 Office: Litton Marine Sys Seminole Trail Charlottesville VA 22901

PANG, SAMUEL CHOW-ERN, reproductive endocrinologist, gynecologist-obstetrician; b. Singapore, Oct. 28, 1959; came to U.S., 1988; s. Teck Soon and Wendy Chew-Eng (Poh) P. Student, Vancouver (B.C., Can.) C.C., 1976-77; BSc, U. B.C., 1982, MD, 1983. Diplomate Am. Bd. Ob.-Gyn., Am. Bd. Reproductive Endocrinology. Adj. asst. prof. UCLA Sch. Medicine, 1988-90; asst. prof. Loma Linda (Calif.) U. Sch. Medicine, 1990-93; assoc. med. dir. Reproductive Sci. Ctr., Boston, 1993—; chief ob-gyn. Deaconess Waltham (Mass.) Hosp., 1995-00. Fellow ACOG, Royal Coll. Surgeons (Can.); mem. AMA, Am. Soc. Reproductive Medicine, Mass. Med. Soc., Soc. for Reproductive Endocrinology & Infertility, Boston Fertility Soc. (pres. 2001—), Obstet. Soc. Boston, Charles River Dist. Med. Soc. (sec. 2000—), Soc. Male Reproduction and Urology (charter). Avocations: masters swimming, tennis, piano, choral singing, stamp and coin collecting. Office: Deaconess Waltham Hosp Hope Ave Waltham MA 02453-2774

PANG, YUAN-PING, synthetic and computational chemist; b. Shanghai, China, Sept. 9, 1962; came to U.S., 1987, naturalized, 1999; s. Qi-Yang and Li-Kang (Wang) P.; m. Bee-Darn Chao, July 26, 1996. BS, Amoy U., Xiamen, China, 1984; PhD, U. Pitts., 1990. Rsch. assoc. Mayo Clinic, Jacksonville, Fla., 1991-92, assoc. cons., 1992-97, chief rational drug design lab., 1996-97, mem. rsch. exec. subcom., 1995-97, sr. assoc. cons. Rochester, Minn., 1997-2001, cons., 2001—; asst. prof. dept. pharmacology Mayo Med. Sch., 1998-2001, assoc. prof., 2001—. Inventor neuroprotectives, drugs for Alzheimer's, drugs for schizophrenia, and antidotes for organophosphate poisonings. Author: (with others) Excitatory Amino Acids, 1991, Trends in QSAR and Molecular Modeling '92, 1993, QSAR and Molecular Modelling: Concepts, Computational Tools and Biological Applications, 1995; contbr. more than 70 articles to profl. jours. including Nature, Nature Struct. Biol., Procs. NAS USA, Jour. Phys. Chemistry, Jour. Medicinal Chemistry, Jour. Biol. Chemistry, Molecular Pharmacology, Jour. Organic Chemistry, Jour. Am. Chem. Soc., Protein Sci., Protein, others. Grantee NIH, NIMH, Def. Advanced Rsch. Projects Agy. Achievements include inventions of the multiple template approach for developing nonpeptidic mimetics, the cationic dummy atom approach to molecular modeling of metalloproteins and the dimeric analog approach for prototype drug optimization; contbn. to conformational selection mechanism for bindings of biologically active proteins; and leadership in developing automated computer docking program, ligands of cholinesterase and neurotensin receptor, model of ligand binding site of transmembrane receptor for neurotension and in silico screening of chemical databases for drug leads. Avocations: playing the violin, computer programming. Office: Mayo Clinic Dept Pharmacology 200 1st St SW Rochester MN 55905-0002

PANG-WHITE, ANN A. philosophy educator, researcher; b. Taichung, Taiwan, China, June 23, 1964; came to U.S., 1989; d. Jee-Zen and Ai-Chu (Huang) Pang; m. David Alan White, July 22, 1995. BA, Tung-Hai U., Taichung, 1986; MA, U. S.C., 1991; PhD, Marquette U., 1997. Asst. prof. philosophy U. Scranton, Pa., 1997—, mem. instn. rev. bd. for protection human subjects, 1998—, parliamentarian faculty senate, 1998-2000, mem. honors com., 1999—, mem. commencement com., 2000—. Contbr. articles to profl. jours. Mem. adv. bd. St. Pius X Sem., Dalton, Pa., 1998—. Recipient James W. Oliver prize in logic U. S.C., 1991, Faculty Svc. and Tchg. award Dexter Hanley Coll. Student Govt., U. Scranton, 1999. Mem. Am. Philos. Assn., Soc. of Medieval and Renaissance Philosophy, N.Am. Patristic Soc., Am. Cath. Philos. Assn. Office: Univ of Scranton Dept Philosophny Scranton PA 18510

PANIAN, STEVEN PAUL, surgeon; b. Portland, Oreg., Sept. 21, 1958; MD, U. Oreg. Health Sci. U., 1985. Diplomate Am. Bd. Surgery. Intern St. Joseph Hosp., Denver, 1985-86, resident in gen. surgery, 1986-90; gen./vascular surgeon Kaiser Permenente, 1990—; attending surgeon St. Joseph Hosp., St. Luke's PSC, Denver, 1992—. Chmn. St. Joseph Hosp. Gen. Surgery Edn. com. Fellow: ACS; mem.: AMA, Western Surg. Soc., Denver Acad. Surgery, Colo. Thoracic Soc. Home: 99 Lupine Way Golden CO 80401-5023 Office: Kaiser Permanente 2045 Franklin Denver CO 80205

PANICCIA, MARIO DOMENIC, architect; b. Torrice, Italy, May 13, 1948; s. Sebastiano and Clara (Mancini) P.; m. Tatiana Petropavlovskaya, 1995. BArch, Cooper Union, 1972. Nat. Coun. Archtl. Registration Bds.; registered arch. Conn., N.Y., Tex., Minn., N.J., R.I., Idaho, S.C., Ala., W.Va., Ga., Ill., Tenn., Ind., Mich., Mo., Fla., La., Md., Ma., N.C., Ohio, Pa., Iowa, Va., Calif., Del., D.C., Tex. (interior), Conn. (interior). With William F. Griffin & Assocs., Milford, Conn., summers 1968-72; designer Raffone, Elovitz & Fischer, Archs. & Engrs., Bridgeport, 1972-75; prin. Paniccia Assocs., Archs. & Planners, 1975-86, Paniccia Archs. and Engr. Inc., Monroe, Conn., 1987—. Commr. Monroe Conservation & Water Resources and Inland Wetland Commn., 1986-90, reapptd., 1990—. Mem. AIA (nat. housing com. 1988-89, commr. conservation com. 1980—), Conn. Soc. Archs. (dir. 1979-80, commr. chpt. affairs 1979, commr. cmty. affairs 1980, commr. profl. practice 1985-86), Bridgeport Assn. Archs. (dir. 1979, v.p. 1980, 83, pres. 1981), Nat. Trust Hist. Preservation, Nat. Pks. Conservation Assn., Inst. Urban Design, Bridgeport C. of C., Elks (Fairfield, Conn.), KC (3d degree), Exch. Club (Monroe, Conn.), Pyramid Temple Shriners (Milford). Roman Catholic. Office: Paniccia Archs & Engrs Inc 25 Easton Rd Monroe CT 06468

PANICH, DANUTA BEMBENISTA, lawyer; b. East Chicago, Ind., Apr. 9, 1954; d. Fred and Ann Stephanie (Grabowski) B.; m. Nikola Panich, July 30, 1977; children: Jennifer Anne, Michael Alexei. AB, Ind. U., 1975, JD, 1978. Bar: Ill. 1978, U.S. Dist. Ct. (no. dist.) Ill. 1978, U.S. Dist. Ct. (ctrl. dist.) Ill. 1987, U.S. Ct. Appeals 1987, U.S. Dist. Ct. (no. dist.) Ind. 2001. Assoc. Mayer Brown & Platt, Chgo., 1978-86, ptnr., 1986—2001, Mayer Brown Rowe & Maw, Chgo., 2002—. Bd. dirs. Munster (Ind.) Med. Rsch. Found., 1990—. Mem. ABA, Ill. Bar Assn. Republican. Roman Catholic. Office: Mayer Brown Rowe & Maw 190 S La Salle St Ste 3100 Chicago IL 60603-3441 E-mail: dpanich@mayerbrownrowe.com.

PANICHI-EGBERTS, MICHELE A. healthcare facility manager; b. Phila., Dec. 12, 1959; d. Emil J. and Mary T. (Walsh) P. BS, Millersville U. Pa., 1981. Lic. nuclear medicine, N.J.; cert. nuc. medicine tech. Staff nuc. medicine technologist James C. Giuffré Med. Ctr., Phila., 1981-86; chief technologist nuclear medicine Rancocas Hosp., Willingboro, N.J., 1986-89; dir. nuclear medicine W. Jersey Health System, Marlton, 1989-99; radiation safety officer Syncor Internat., Sharon Hill, Pa., 1999—. Mem. adj. faculty Glouchester County C.C., 1992-98. Mem. adv. com. for nuclear medicine N.J. State Dept.

of Environ. Protection. Mem. Am. Soc. Nuc. Cardiology, Am. Soc. Radiol. Tech., Soc. Nuc. Medicine, Am. Registry Radiologic Tech. Home: 21B E Daisey Ln Mount Laurel NJ 08054-2579 E-mail: panichiegbertsm@syncor.com.

PANICKER, GIRISH KUMAR, agricultural scientist, consultant; b. Paravur, Kerala, India, Jan. 11, 1949; s. Sukumar and Pankajam Panicker; m. Rani Girish Kumar, Apr. 27, 1988; 1 child, Aja Girish. BS in Agr., U. Kerala, 1972; MS in Agronomy, Alcorn State U., 1992; PhD in Hort., Miss. State U., 1999. Rsch. asst., tech. officer Dept. Agr., Kerala, 1972-78, asst. dir., 1978-80; prin. inspector agr. Dept. Sci. and Tech., Sokoto, Nigeria, 1980-89; grad. rsch. asst. agr. Alcorn State U., Lorman, Miss., 1990-92, rsch. assoc. soil conservation rsch. project USDA, 1992-96; grad. rsch. asst. Miss. State U., Starkville, 1996-99; project coord. soil conservation rsch. project USDA Alcorn State U., Lorman, 1999—. Recruitment bd. cons. agr. Pub. Svc. Commn., Sokoto, Nigeria, 1986-89; cons. in agronomy for gen. pub., Miss., 1997—. Contbr. more than 25 articles to profl. jours. Coord. India Assn., Sokoto, 1986-89. Mem. Am. Soc. Agronomy, Soil and Water Conservation Soc. Am., World Assn. Soil and Water Conservation, Am. Soc. Hort. Sci., Internat. Union Soil Scis., Miss Acad. Scis. (elected chmn. divsn. agr. and plant scis. 2002-), Fruit and Vegetable Growers Assn. Avocations: ornamental and vegetable gardening, reading, writing scientific articles, watching the discovery channel and national geography channel. Office: Alcorn State U 1000 Asu Dr # 1434 Lorman MS 39096-7510

PANICO, ELAINE HARTMAN, nurse; b. Phila., July 13, 1924; d. Edward Earl and Eleanor Mayo (Adams) Hartman; children: Frederick, Robert, Eleanor, Lorne, Earl, John, William, Richard, Louise. BSN, BS in Edn., N.J. City U., 1946; postgrad., U. Pa., 1946-49. RN, N.J. Nurse Summer Boys Camp, Winaukee, N.H., 1948; instr. Rowan Univ., Glassboro, N.J., 1948, nurse, asst., 1946-48; dir. nurses Osteo. Hos., Phila., 1948-49; instr. pharm. math. Osteo. Hosp., 1948-49; eye surg. nurse Cornell-N.Y. Hosp., N.Y.C., 1949-50; surg. supr. Balt. City Hosps., 1950-52; nurse in charge Taj Mahal Med. Office, Atlantic City, 1990; surg. office nurse Ventnor, 1960—. Pub. health spkr. elem. schs., Boston, 1950; RN internat. confs., Stony Brook, N.Y., 1980-85, A.C. Med. Ctr. Eye Clinic, Atlantic City, 1987-90; creator earliest postoperative surg. ICU, Balt. City Hosps., 1950-52. Cert. classic ballet, 1932-42. Bd. dirs. PTA, Ventnor, 1960-83, Atlantic Performing Arts Ctr., Atlantic City, 1970-90; mem. Holy Spirit Mothers Assn., Absecon, N.J., 1966-83; sponsor South Jersey Regional Theatre, Atlantic Community Concerts, Stockton Coll. Performing Arts; fin. sec. Atlantic City Med. Ctr. Aux., 1963; chmn. spl. projects Miss. Am. Pageant Scholarship Found., Very Important Hostess, 1967—. Recipient Lifetime Recognition award Great Books Found., 1966-67, 15-yr. Gold award Miss Am. Pageant, 1982. Mem. AAUW, Atlantic County Med. Aux. (pres. 1984-90), U.S. Golf Assn., Internat. Platform Assn., RNs Cancer Heart Meml. Fund. (bd. dirs.), Hydrangea Club (chmn. 1964, Silver 15 Yr. award). Avocations: travel, oil painting, fishing, Chinese gourmet cooking, horseback riding. Home: 102 S Dudley Ave Ventnor City NJ 08406-2837 Office: 10 S Somerset Ave Ventnor City NJ 08406-2846

PANIK, MICHAEL JOSEPH, economics educator; b. McKees Rocks, Pa., May 20, 1940; s. Michael and Emily J. (Petrovich) P.; m. Paula Cusano, Sept. l0, l966; children: Michele, Marie. AB, St. Vincent Coll., Latrobe, Pa., l963; AM, Boston Coll., l965, PhD, l970. Lectr. econs. Boston Coll., Chestnut Hill, Mass., l966-68; prof. econs. U. Hartford, West Hartford, Conn., l968—, chmn. dept., 1980—86. Cons. Conn. Dept. Motor Vehicles, Wethersfield, 1970-73; cons. to mfg. cos., banks, health orgns., Hartford, Conn., l975—. Author: Classical Optimization, 1976, Fundamentals of Convex Analysis, 1993, Linnear Programming, 1996; contbr. articles on managerial econs. and quantitative methods to profl. jours. NASA fellow, l970-73; Exxon Oil Co. grantee, 1977, 80. Mem. Am. Econ. Assn., Econometric Soc., Math. Program Soc., Informs, Soc. Econ. Assn., Western Econ. Assn. Am. Math. Soc., Math. Assn. Am. Democrat. Roman Catholic. Avocations: tennis, weightlifting. Home: 21 Long Hill Rd Windsor CT 06095-2650 Office: U Hartford Dept Econs 200 Bloomfield Ave West Hartford CT 06117-1545

PANIKOV, NICOLAI SERGEYEVICH, microbiologist, researcher; b. N-Udinsk, Russia, Mar. 1, 1950; s. Sergey Dmitriyevich and Alexandra Fedorovna (Tichomirova) P.; m. Elena Livovna (Stepanova), Feb. 20, 1974, (div. Feb. 1994); children: Anna, Sergey; m. Maria Vyacheslavovna Sizova, Mar. 24, 1994; 1 child, Fedor. BSc, Moscow Univ., Russia, 1972; PhD, Moscow Univ., 1976, DSci, 1989. Jr. researcher Moscow Univ., 1975-83; postdoctoral Queen Elizabeth Coll., London, 1976-77; sr. researcher Moscow Univ., 1983-89; head of lab., Soil Microbiology Inst. of Microbiology, Moscow, 1989—2001; vice dir. Inst. of Microbiology Russian Acad. of Sci., 1991-96; prof. dept. chemistry and chem. biology Stevens Inst. Tech., 1999—. Vis. prof. Mich. State Univ., East Lansing, 1995-96, Univ. of Louisville, 1996-97. Author: Microbial Growth Kinetics, 1995, The Kinetics of Microbial Growth: General Principles and Ecological Applications, 1992, Individual Components of Soil Humus, 1984; contbr. articles to profl. jours. Recipient numerous rsch. grants, 1995, 1998—, 1992-94. Avocations: poetry, tourism, swimming. Home: 807 Castle Point Ter Hoboken NJ 07030 Office: Stevens Inst Tech Castle Point on Hudson Hoboken NJ 07030 Fax: 201-216-8240. E-mail: npanikov@steven-tech.edu.

PANISH, MORTON B. physical chemist, consultant; b. N.Y.C., Apr. 8, 1929; s. Isidore and Fanny (Glasser) P.; m. Evelyn Wally Chaim, Aug. 20, 1951; children: Steven, Paul, Deborah. Student, Bklyn. Coll., 1946-48; BS in Chemistry, Denver U., 1950; MS in Chemistry, Mich. State U., 1951, PhD in Phys. Chemistry, 1954. Chemist Oak Ridge (Tenn.) Nat. Lab., 1954-57; mem. tech. staff RAD div. AVCO Corp., Wilmington, Mass., 1957-61, sect. chief, 1961-64; mem. tech. staff Bell Telephone Labs. (now Bell Labs.), Murray Hill, N.J., 1964-69, dept. head, 1969-86, disting. mem. tech. staff, 1986-92; cons., 1992—. Mem. com. on microgravity rsch. NRC, 1991-96, mem. com. on future of space sci. rsch. priorities, 1994-95, space studies bd., 1996-98; mem. com. on human rights NAS, 1996—. Co-author: Heterostructure Lasers, 1978, Gas Source Molecular Beam Epitaxy, 1993; contbr. numerous articles to profl. jours.; patentee in field. Mem. dean's adv. bd. Coll. Natural Sci., Mich. State U., 1990-95. Recipient Electrochem Soc. Electronics Divsn. award, 1972, Solid state medal, 1979, C&C Found. prize, Japan, 1986, Internat. Crystal Growth award Am. Assn. Crystal Growth, 1990, John Bardeen award The Minerals, Metals and Materials Soc., 1994, The Kyoto prize, 2001. Fellow IEEE (Morris N. Liebmann Meml. award 1991), Am. Phys. Soc.; mem. Nat. Acad. Engring., Nat. Acad. Scis. Avocation: photography. Home and Office: 9 Persimmon Way Springfield NJ 07081-3605 E-mail: mort@worldnet.att.net.

PANITZ, LAWRENCE, physician; b. Apr. 30, 1928; s. Max and Gussie (Gorenstein) P.; m. Adrienne Ruth Luke, June 20, 1965; children: Jennifer, Michael. BA, NYU, 1962; MD, SUNY, Syracuse, 1966. Diplomate Am. Bd. Family Practice. Intern St. Joseph's Hosp., Syracuse, N.Y., 1966-67; practice gen. medicine Elmsford, 1967-90, Hawthorne, 1968—. Affiliated with Docs Physicians Beth Israel Med. Ctr., N.Y.C., Shrub Oak, N.Y., Hartsdale, N.Y., Larchmont, N.Y., Yonkers, N.Y., Thornwood, N.Y., Crestwood, N.Y., New City, N.Y., West Haverstraw, N.Y., and numerous other cities, 1992-97; mem. staff New Rochelle (N.Y.) Hosp., St. Agnes Hosp., White Plains, N.Y., Phelps Meml. Hosp., North Tarrytown, N.Y., Westchester County Med. Ctr., Valhalla, N.Y., Dobbs Ferry Hosp., Beth Israel Hosp. Med. Ctr., N.Y.C., New Rochelle Hosp. Med. Ctr., Sound Shore Med. Ctr.; dep. dir. dept. family practice Phelps Meml. Hosp.; dir. Elmsford Med. Ctr.; police surgeon Tarrytown and North Tarrytown, Sleepy Hollow, Elmsford, Town of Greenburgh; med. dir. Margaret Chapman Sch. for Exceptional Child, Hawthorne; med. dir., prin. rschr. Clin. Tech. Assoc., Elmsford, N.Y., CNS Biosvcs., Pleasantville, N.Y.; physician Westchester County Correctional Health Dept., Valhalla; sch. physician Elmsford, N.Y. With U.S. Army, 1946-48, 82-88; lt. col. M.C. USAR; ret. Fellow AMA, Am. Acad. Family Physicians, Med. Soc. State of N.Y., Westchester County Med. Soc., Westchester Acad. Medicine, Shriners, Masons. Jewish. Home and Office: Riveredge 3 David Ln Yonkers NY 10701-1122 Office: 5 Bradhurst Ave Hawthorne NY 10532-2154 E-mail: lp711md@aol.com.

PANKEN, PETER MICHAEL, lawyer; b. N.Y.C., Dec. 30, 1936; s. Harold Ira and Sylvia Rita (Haimes) P.; m. Beverly Muriel Goldner, June 19, 1960; children: Aaron, Melinda. BA cum laude, Haverford Coll., 1957; LLB magna cum laude, Harvard U., 1962. Bar: N.Y. 1962, U.S. Dist. Ct. N.Y. 1962, U.S. Ct. Appeals (2d cir.) 1969, 3d cir. 1988, (10th cir.) 1989, U.S. Supreme Ct. 1989. Assoc. Paul Weiss Rifkind Wharton Garrison, N.Y.C., 1962-66, Poletti Freiden Prashker Feldman & Gartner, N.Y.C., 1966-67, Parker Chapin Flattau & Klimpl, N.Y.C., 1967-72, ptnr., 1973-99, chair employment and labor law dept., 1986-99; mem. Epstein Becker & Green PC, 1999—. Editor: Harvard Law Rev., 1961-62; editor-in-chief: ALI-ABA Resource Materials on Labor and Employment Law (1st to 9th edits.), 1982—; Author: A State-by-State Survey of the Law of Religion in the Workplace, 2001; contbr. articles on law and bus. to profl. jours. Pres., bd. dirs. Fedn. of Handicapped, N.Y.C., 1984-92; bd. dirs. Fedcap Rehab. Svcs., 1993—; pres. metro N.Y. chpt. Soc. for Human Resource Mgmt., 1990-92, gen. counsel, 1993—. Mem. ABA (labor and employment sect., com. on NLRB law), N.Y. State Bar Assn. (labor and employment law sect., continuing legal edn. com.), Am. Law Inst.-ABA (chmn. employment and labor law programs), Am. Law Inst. (com. on restatement of agy.), SHRM (com. on employment practices). Office: Epstein Becker & Green PC 250 Park Ave Ste 1200 New York NY 10177-1211 E-mail: ppanken@ebglaw.com.

PANKEY, GEORGE ATKINSON, internist, educator, researcher; b. Shreveport, La., Aug. 11, 1933; s. George Edward and Annabel (Atkinson) P.; m. Patricia Ann Carreras, Sept. 22, 1972; children: Susan Margaret, Stephen Charles, Laura Atkinson, Edward Atkinson. Student, La. Poly. Inst., 1950-51; BS, Tulane U., 1954, MD, 1957; MS, U. Minn., 1961. Diplomate Am. Bd. Internal Medicine, Am. Bd. Infectious Disease. Intern U. Minn. Hosps., 1957-58, resident in internal medicine, 1958-60, Mpls. VA Hosp., Mpls. Gen. Hosp., 1960-61; practice medicine New Orleans, 1961—; partner Ochsner Clinic, 1968-99; asst. vis. physician Charity Hosp. La., 1961-62, vis. physician, 1962-75, sr. vis. physician, 1975-95; cons. infectious diseases Ochsner Clinic Found., 1963—, head sect. infectious diseases, 1972-94, dir. infectious disease training program, 1972—94, dir. infectious disease rsch., 1999—; instr. dept. medicine, div. infectious diseases Tulane U. Sch. Medicine, New Orleans, 1961-63, clin. instr., 1963-65, clin. asst. prof. medicine, 1965-68, clin. assoc. prof., 1968-73, clin. prof., 1973—; clin. prof. dept. medicine La. State U. Sch. Medicine, 1979—; clin. prof. oral diagnosis, medicine and radiology La. State U. Sch. Dentistry, 1983—. Cons. World Health Info. Services Inc., 1974; dir., founder Century Nat. Bank, New Orleans; mem. medicine test com. Nat. Bd. Med. Examiners, 1979-83; mem. infectious diseases adv. bd. Hoffman-LaRoche, 1982—; cons. Federal Air Surgeon, 1997—. Author: A Manual of Antimicrobial Therapy, 1969, (with Charles W. Gross and Michael G. Mendelsohn) Contemporary Diagnosis and Management of Sinusitis, 1997, 2d edit., 1998, 3d edit., 2000; editor: (with Geoffrey A. Kalish) Outpatient Antimicrobial Therapy - Recent Advances, 1989, Infectious Diseases Digest, 1983-95, So. Med. Assn. Program for Infectious Diseases Dial-Access, 1983-92, Ochsner Clinic Reports on Serious Hosp. Infections, 1985—, Ochsner Clinic Reports on Geriatric Infectious Diseases, 1990-93, Ochsner Clinic Reports on the Management of Sepsis, 1991-93, Infectious Disease Clinics of North America, 1994; bd. editors: Patient Care, 1969-75, Today in Medicine, 1990; mem. editl. bd. Nat. Infectious Disease Info. Network, 1983; mem. editl. adv. bd. Compendium Continuing Edn. in Dentistry, 1984—, Quinolones Bull., 1985-93, Ochsner Jour., 1999—, Infectious Disease News, 2001—; contbr. numerous articles to profl. jours. Dir. Camp Fire Inc.; Pres. New Orleans Young Republican Club, 1969-71; adv. bd. Angie Nall Sch. Hosp., Beaumont, Tex.; trustee Nall Found. for Children, Beaumont. Recipient cert. merit Am. Acad. Gen. Practice, 1969, 70 Fellow ACP-ASIM (laureate award La. chpt. 1997), Am. Coll. Preventive Medicine, Infectious Disease Soc. Am. (clinician award 1996), Am. Coll. Chest Physicians, Royal Soc. Medicine; mem. Am. Soc. of Transplantation, Assn. Contamination Control (chpt. pres. 1968-70), Am. Fedn. Med. Rsch., So. Med. Assn. (certificate of award 1970), Am. Soc. Internal Medicine (del. ann. meeting 1971-72), Am. Soc. Microbiology, Am. Thoracic Soc., New Orleans Acad. Internal Medicine (pres. 1977-78, 96-97), AMA, Aerospace Med. Assn., Am. Soc. Tropical Medicine and Hygiene, Am. Venereal Disease Assn., Am. Soc. Parasitologists, Internat. Travel Medicine Soc., La. Soc. Internal Medicine (pres. 1972-73), La. Med. Soc., La. Thoracic Soc. (chmn. program com. 1968, governing council 1976-80), Surg. Infection Soc., Immunocompromised Host Soc., Musser Burch Soc., Orleans Parish Med. Soc., N.Y. Acad. Scis., Pan Am. Med. Assn. (diplomate mem. sect. internal medicine 1971, sect. pres. infectious diseases and virology 1978-85), SAR, Huguenot Soc. Founders Manakin in Colony of Va., Aviation Med. Examiner. Clubs: Masons (32 deg), Shriners. Home: 5910 Prytania St New Orleans LA 70115-4348 Office: Ochsner Clinic & Hosp 1514 Jefferson Hwy New Orleans LA 70121-2483 E-mail: gpankey@ochsner.org.

PANKIN, JAYSON DARRYL, entrepreneur, biotechnologist, venture capitalist, e-mail system developer; b. Newark, June 2, 1957; s. Harvey A. and Edythe R. (Simons) P. BBA in Acctg., George Washington U., 1979, MBA in Internat. Bus., 1980. Chmn., pres. PolyCell, Inc., Detroit, 1983-95; v.p. Growth Funding Ltd., 1983-95; v.p., dir. Venture Funding Ltd., 1983-95; treas., v.p. U. Sci. Ptnrs., Inc., 1984-85; pres., sec., chmn. Quest Blood Substitute, 1986—, also bd. dirs.; co-founder, chmn. bd., pres. ACT Biomed., Inc., 1986-95; co-founder, v.p., dir. Acid Rain Control, Inc., 1992-94; CEO Pankin Internat., 1995—; v.p. alliances and fin. planning, sec.-treas. Originus, Inc., 2002—. Founder, v.p. VFS, Inc., 1992, Imperial Midwest Underwriting Svc. Inc., Imperial Midwest Ins. Co.; bd. dirs., v.p. Quest Biotech., Inc., Quest Am., Inc. Co-founder, v.p., treas., bd. dirs. Art Renaissance, Inc., 1992-94; CEO, co-founder The Pankin Found., 1995—. Achievements include pioneering the commercialization of artificial blood; bifunctional monoclonal antibodies for disease detection and therapy and adoptive immunotherapy utilizing effector cells; Broadcasting anti-totalitarianism documentaries over television in the former Soviet Union and developing western businesses in Russia. Home: 1033 Bedford Rd Grosse Pointe Park MI 48230-1408

PANKIW, JIM, member of parliament; Mem. 37th Parliament, House of Commons, Ottawa, Canada. Office: House of Commons Ottawa ON K1A 0A6 Canada also: Box 2061 8th St E Saskatoon SK 57H 5N9 Canada*

PANKOPF, ARTHUR, JR. lawyer; b. Malden, Mass., Feb. 1, 1931; BS in Marine Transp., Mass. Maritime Acad., 1951; BS in Fgn. Svc. and Internat. Transp., Georgetown U., 1957, JD, 1965. Bar: Md. 1965, D.C. 1966, U.S. Supreme Ct. 1977. Ea. area mgr. Trans Ocean Van Service of Consol. Freightway, 1958-61; with U.S. Maritime Adminstrn., 1961-65; assoc. firm Preston, Thorgrimson, Ellis & Holman, Washington, 1976-77; minority chief counsel Com. on Mcht. Marine & Fisheries U.S. Ho. of Reps., 1965-69; minority chief counsel, staff dir. Com. on Commerce, U.S. Senate, 1969-76; mng. dir. Fed. Maritime Commn., 1977-81; pvt. practice Washington, 1981-84; dir. legis. affairs Corp. Pub. Broadcasting, 1984-86, v.p., gen. counsel, sec., 1986-88; pvt. practice Washington, 1988-90, 96—; dir. fed. affairs Matson Navigation Co. Inc., 1990-95. Mem. Maritime Adminstrv. Bar Assn. (pres. 1995-96), Propeller Club Port of Washington (bd. govs. 1992—). Address: 7819 Hampden Ln Bethesda MD 20814-1108 E-mail: a.pankopf@worldnet.alt.net.

PANKOVE, JACQUES ISAAC, physicist, researcher; b. Chernigov, Russia, Nov. 23, 1922; came to U.S., 1942, naturalized, 1944; s. Evsey Leib and Miriam (Simkine) Pantchechnikoff; m. Ethel Wasserman, Nov. 24, 1950; children: Martin, Simon. BSEE, U. Calif., Berkeley, 1944, MSEE, 1948; PhD in Physics, U. Paris, 1960; DSc (hon.), Nat. Poly. Inst., Grenoble, France, 2000. Mem. tech. staff RCA Labs., Princeton, N.J., 1948-70, physicist, fellow, 1970-85; prof. U. Colo., Boulder, 1985-93, prof. emeritus, 1993—, Hudson Moore Jr. Univ. prof., 1989-93, program mgr. materials and devices Ctr. for Optoelectronic Computing Systems, 1986-89; Disting. Rsch. fellow Nat. Renewal Energy Lab. (formerly Solar Energy Rsch. Inst.), 1985-93; v.p. for rsch. and tech. Astralux, Inc., 1993—. Vis. McKay lectr. U. Calif., Berkeley, 1968-69; vis. prof. U. Campinas, Brazil, 1975; Disting. vis. prof. U. Mo., Rolla, 1984; participant NAS sci. exch. program with Romania, 1970, Hungary, 1972, Yugoslavia, 1976. Mem. hon. editl. bd. Solid State Electronics, 1970-94, Solar Energy Materials, 1984—, Optoelectronics, 1986-95; regional editor Crystal Lattice Defects and Amorphous Materials, 1984-90; author: Optical Processes in Semiconductors, 1971, 75, (ednl. film) Energy Gap and Recombination Radiation, 1962; editor: Electroluminescence, 1977, Display Devices, 1980, Hydrogenated Amorphous Silicon, 1984; co-editor: Hydrogen in Semiconductors, 1991, Wide Bandgap Semiconductors, 1992, III-Nitrides, 1997, Gallium Nitride Vol. I, 1998, Vol. II, 1999; designer: laser sculpture, Bklyn. Mus., 1968; contbr. articles to profl. jours.; patentee in field. Trustee Princeton Art Assn., 1970-82; mem. Experiment-in-Arts-and-Tech., Berkeley, 1968-69. Served with U.S. Army, 1944-46. Recipient RCA achievement awards, 1952, 53, 63, Faculty Rsch. award U. Colo. Coll. Engring. and Applied Sci., 1997, Rank Prize award Optcelectronics, 1998; David Sarnoff scholar, 1956, Disting. Alumnus award U. Calif., Berkeley, 2000. Fellow IEEE (J. J. Ebers award 1975, assoc. editor Jour. Quantum Electronics 1968-77, mem-at-large IEEE awards bd. 1992-95), Am. Phys. Soc.; mem. AAAS, NAE (hon.), Materials Rsch. Soc., Internat. Soc. for Optical Engring., Sigma Xi. Home: 809 10th St Boulder CO 80302-7551 also: Astralux Inc 2500 Central Ave Boulder CO 80301-2864 E-mail: pankove@astrraluxinc.com.

PANNAPACKER, WILLIAM ALBERT , III, humanities educator; b. Camden, N.J., Apr. 25, 1968; s. William Albert Jr. and Gertrude Cecelia (Rieck) P.; m. Teresa Jenkins, May 30, 1992; children: Rebecca, Jessica. BA in English, St. Joseph's U., Phila., 1990; MA in English, U. Miami, Coral Gables, Fla., 1993; AM in English and Am. lit., Harvard U., 1997, PhD History Am. Civilization, 1999. Lectr. English U. Miami, 1992-93, Miami-Dade C.C., 1993; lectr. Am. Studies Brandeis U., Waltham, Mass., 1996; project supr. W.E.B. DuBois Inst., Cambridge, 1995-97; tchg. fellow history and lit., English, fine arts, comparative literature Harvard U., 1995-98, lectr., 1999-2000; asst. prof. English Hope Coll., Holland, Mich., 2000—. Sr. cons. History Assocs., Inc., Washington, Rockville, Md., 2000. Contbr. articles to lit., hist., polit. and reference publs.; columnist Chronicle of Higher Edn., 1998—. Recipient Bowdoin prize, 1994, 99, Bell prize, 1995, 98, Hofer prize, 1996, Arnold prize, 1998; Whiting fellow, 1998-99; Mellon Faculty Devel. grantee, 2001-02; Mellon Found. Curriculum Devel. grantee, 2002--. Mem. AAUP, MLA (mem. del. assembly 2000—), Am. Studies Assn. (task force on employment in higher edn. 1999--), Am. Lit. Assn. Avocations: book collecting, travel, sports, photography. Office: Hope Coll Dept English 321 Lubbers Hall Holland MI 49422-9000

PANNEBAKER, JAMES BOYD, lawyer; b. Middletown, Pa., Mar. 9, 1936; s. Boyd Alton and Kathryn Kennedy (Brindle) P.; divorced; children: Jeffery B., Renee E. Pannebaker Bench, Traci Lee Pannebaker. BS, Elizabethtown Coll., 1958; JD, U. Mich., 1961. Bar: Pa. 1962, U.S. Dist. Ct. (mid. dist.) Pa., U.S. Ct. Appeals (3d cir.), U.S. Supreme Ct. 1969. Pvt. practice, Harrisburg, 1965-86; pres. Pannebaker & Jones, P.C., Middletown, 1986—. Mem. regional adv. bd. Mellon Bank, Harrisburg, 1980—. Bd. dirs. Cmty. Gen. Osteo. Hosp., harrisburg, 1970-98; trustee Elizabethtown (Pa.) Coll., 1972-78; mem. adv. bd. Villa Teresa Nursing Home, Harrisburg, 1985—; past chmn. Middletown chpt. ARC; pres. Keystone Area coun. Boy Scouts Am. Capt. U.S. Army, 1962-65. Mem. Am. Legion, Masons, Shriners, Elks. Republican. Methodist. Avocations: skiing, sailing, horseback riding, outdoor activities. Office: Pannebaker & Jones PC 4000 Vine St Middletown PA 17057-3565 E-mail: jim@pannebaker-jones.com.

PANNER, BERNARD J. pathologist, educator; b. Youngstown, Ohio, Oct. 9, 1928; s. Morris W. and Matilda (Giber) P.; m. Molly R. Seidenberg, Feb. 11, 1962; children— Morris J., Aaron M., Daniel Z. AB, Western Res. U., 1949, MD, 1953. Diplomate Am. Bd. Pathology. Intern in internal medicine Kings County Hosp., Bklyn., 1953-54; resident in pathology Boston City Hosp., 1954-55, Strong Meml. Hosp., Rochester, N.Y., 1958-60; asst. prof. pathology Sch. Medicine, U. Rochester, 1960-67, assoc. prof., 1967-72, prof., 1972-96, emeritus prof., 1996—; pathologist Strong Meml. Hosp., Rochester, 1972-96. Cons. Genesee Hosp., Rochester, 1974-96. Contbr. articles to profl. jours. Served with USNR, 1955-57 Recipient Mapstone Teaching prize Sch. Medicine, U. Rochester, 1981 Mem. Internat. Acad. Pathology, Am. Assn. Pathologists, Internat. Soc. Nephrology, Am. Soc. Nephrology, Sigma Xi Democrat. Jewish. Home: 330 Wilmot Rd Rochester NY 14618-2947 Office: U Rochester Sch Medicine Dept Pathology 601 Elmwood Ave Rochester NY 14642-0001 E-mail: Bernard_Panner@urmc.rochester.edu.

PANNER, JEANNIE HARRIGAN, retired electrical engineer; b. Malone, N.Y., Jan. 4, 1948; d. Martin Thomas and Marjorie (Boyea) Harrigan; m. John Charles Panner, Aug. 17, 1974. BS summa cum laude, SUNY, Plattsburgh, 1970; MA in Math., U. Vt., 1974, MSEE, 1993. Programmer Microelectronics Divsn. IBM, Burlington, Vt., 1970-71, assoc. programmer, 1971-74, sr. assoc. programmer, 1974-79, staff engr., 1979-85, adv. engr., 1985-90, sr. engr., 1990-97, sr. tech. staff, 1997-2000; ret., 2000. Contbr. articles to engring. jours.; patentee in field. Mem. IEEE. Avocations: golf, travel, gardening. Home: 55 Maple Leaf Farm Rd Underhill VT 05489-9361 E-mail: jeanpanner@aol.com.

PANNER, OWEN M. federal judge; b. 1924; Student, U. Okla., 1941-43, LL.B., 1949. Atty. Panner, Johnson, Marceau, Karnopp, Kennedy & Nash, 1950-80; judge, now sr. judge U.S. Dist. Ct. Oreg., Portland, 1980—, sr. judge, 1992—. Recipient Am. Bd. Trial Advocates Trial Lawyer of Yr., 1973. Mem. Am. Coll. Trial Lawyers, Am. Bd. Trial Advs., Order of Coif. Office: US Dist Ct 1000 SW 3rd Ave Ste 1207 Portland OR 97204-2942

PANNETON, JACQUES, librarian; b. Trois-Rivières, Que., Can., May 7, 1943; s. Marcel and Bernadette (Page) P.; children— Anne-Marie, Luce. B.L.S., U. Montréal, 1964. Cataloguer Bibliothèque de Trois-Rivières, 1964-65; dep. librarian, then head librarian Bibliothèque Centrale de Pret de la Mauricie, Trois-Rivières, 1965-74; head librarian Bibliothèque de la Ville de Montréal, 1974—; prof. pub. libraries U. Montréal Library Sch., 1974-75; mem. Com. Cons. du Livre, Govt. Que., 1976; mem. adv. bd. Nat. Library Can., 1978—. Mem. com. d'étude sur bibliothèques publiques Govt. Qué., 1987; invited guest German libraries, German Fed. Republic, summer 1976, Brit. libraries, spring 1978; mem. Planning Com. for a New Provincial Libr. in Que., 1997; bd. dirs. La Grande Bibliothiques du Que., 1998—. Contbr. articles to profl. jours. Mem. Canadian, Am., Que. library assns., Corp. Profl. Librarians Que. (past pres.), Assn. pour l'avancement des sci. et des techniques de la documentation, Council Adminstrs. Large Urban Pub. Libraries, Internat. Fedn. Library Assns., Internat. Assn. Met. City Libraries. Office: Bibliothèque de Montreal 5650 d'Iberville St Ste 400 Montreal QC Canada H2G 3E4

PANNKE, PEGGY, long term care insurance agency executive; b. Chgo., Oct. 26; d. Victor E. and Leona (O'Leary) Stich; m. Craig D. Smith, July 18, 1998; children from previous marriage: Thomas Scott, David Savonne, Heidi Mireille, Peter. V.p. long term care ins. Sales & Seminars, Des Plaines, 1986-90; pres., founder Nat. Consumer Oriented Agy., 1990—. Cons. on long-term care ins. The Travelers, Tchrs. Inc. & Annuity Assocs., others; spkr. Exec. Enterprises, N.Y.C., 1988—93. Columnist Sr. News, Vital Times, Daily Herald, Sr. Connection, Sr. Marketplace News, Pioneer Press, Boulder Daily Camera, Longmont Times-Call, Aurora Sun, Mature Lifestyles Mag. Sponsor Ill. Alliance for Aging, Chgo., 1990—, Ill. Assn. Homes for Aging, 1990-91; bd. govs. St. Matthew Luth. Home, Park Ridge, Ill., 1993-95. Recipient Speakers awards Health Ins. Assn. Am., Washington, 1990, Ret. Officers Assn., Glenview, Ill., 1991, 93, Nat. Assn. Sr. Living Industries, Denver, 1992, Exec. Enterprises, N.Y.C., 1993, Gov.'s Conf. on Aging, Chgo., 1996, Golden Harvest Long Term Care award Ret. Officers Assn., 2001, Nat. awards UNUM, 2001, AIG 2002, Conseco, 2000, Allianz, 2002. Mem.: Internat. Soc. for Retirement Planning, Am. Soc. on Aging, Mature Am., Nat. Coun. on Aging (ad hoc com.), Ctr. for Applied Gerontology, Nat. Assn. Sr. Living Idustries, Nat. Assn. Long Term Care Profl. (corr.), Friends of the Colo. Trail, Colo. Mountain Club, Boulder C. of C., Park Ridge C. of C., Kiwanis (bd. dir. Park Ridge 1992—98, pres. 1996—97), Am. Mensa (program dir. in Ill. 1983—85, Colo. chpt. 1999—). Avocations: showshoeing, travel, sketching wildflowers, hiking, trekking the Colorado Trail. Office: Nat Consumer Oriented Agy 2200 E Devon Ave Ste 359 Des Plaines IL 60018-4505 also: Cherry Creek 300 S Jackson St Denver CO 80209-3176 also: 4450 Arapahoe Ave Boulder CO 80303-9123 E-mail: NCOAmmp@AOL.com.

PANNO, SAMUEL VINCENT, geochemist; b. Streator, Ill., Aug. 24, 1949; s. Samuel Vincent and Edith Tabb (Sullivan) P.; m. Dorey Day, June 8, 1974; children: Scott Christopher, Brent Anthony, Daniel Charles. BS in Biology, Eureka Coll., 1972; BS in Geology, Oreg. State U., 1976; MS in Geology, So. Ill. U., 1978. Cert. ground water profl. Mining geologist Atlas Minerals Corp., Maob, Utah, 1978-79; assoc. geochemist Brookhaven Nat. Lab., Upton, N.Y., 1979-83; geochemist, hyrdogeologist Rogers and Assocs. Engring., Washington, 1983-88; sr. geochemist Ill. State Geol. Survey, Champaign, Ill., 1988—. Contbr. articles to profl. jours. Grantee Johns Hopkins U., 1994, U. Ill.,

Champaign, 1996, 99, 2000, State of Ill. Environ. Protection Trust Fund, Springfield, 1994-98, State of Ill. Conservation 2000 Fund, 1999. Avocations: drawing, caving, running. Office: Ill State Geol Survey 615 E Peabody Dr Champaign IL 61820-6918 Fax: 217-244-2785.

PANNU, SARDUL SINGH, science educator, researcher; b. Wadala Banger, Panjab, India, Nov. 1, 1935; s. Bhim Pannu Singh and Gurdip Kaur Pannu; m. Shindi Grewal Pannu, Aug. 16, 1966; children: Sandip, Yashdip, TejPaul. BS(hon.) , Panjab U., Panjab, India, 1956, MS (hon.) , 1958; PhD, George Wash. U., Washington, DC, 1965. Asst. chemistry educator Randolph-Macon Coll., Ashland, Va., 1966—69; assoc. educator Fed. City Coll., Washington, 1969—71; chemistry educator U. of Dist. of Colombia, 1971—2002. Contbr. Encyclopedia of Chemistry. Fellow The Kawecki Fellowship, The Kawecki Chem. Co., 1963. Home: 413 Grand Champion Drive Rockville MD 20850 Office: University of DC 4200 Connecticut Ave NW Washington DC 20008

PANOFF, STEPHEN EDWARD, music educator; b. Washington, May 24, 1961; s. Robert and Kathleen Dorothy Panoff. BS in Math. and Music, Coll. of William and Mary, Williamsburg, Virginia, 1984; MusM Edn., Shenandoah U., Winchester, Va., 1997. Cert. postgrad. profl. tchr, Va., 2001. Asst. dir. of bands Tabb (Va.) H.S., 1984—96; dir. of bands Tallwood H.S., Virginia Beach, 1996—. Adjudicator Fiesta-Val Music Festivals, Richmond, Va., 1985—86; dir. Brass Menagerie, Tabb, Va., 1990—96; asst. dir. Shenandoah U. Fine Arts Camp, Winchester, Va., 1997—2001. Contbr. world premiere musical composition; dir.(conductor): (musical performance) Heroes, Lost and Fallen, 2000, To Those Who Serve, 2001, (music performance to honor 9/11 victims) Band-aide, 2001, (conductor) (musical performance) Danzas Brillantes, 2002. Basketball rules interpreter Peninsula Bd. #125, Newport News, Va., 2000—02, basketball ofcl., 1985—2002. Nominee for Disney Am. Tchg. Award, 1998—2002. Mem.: Internat. Jazz Educators Assn., Va. Band and Orch. Dirs' Assn., Va. Music Educator Assn. Roman Catholic. Avocation: golf. Home: 1023 Marlbank Dr Yorktown VA 23692 Office: Tallwood HS 1668 Kempsville Rd Virginia Beach VA 23464 Home Fax: 757-479-5534. Personal E-mail: sepanoff@aol.com. E-mail: sepanoff@vbcps.k12.va.us.

PANOFSKY, WOLFGANG KURT HERMANN, physicist, educator; b. Berlin, Germany, Apr. 24, 1919; arrived in U.S., 1934, naturalized, 1942; s. Erwin and Dorothea (Mosse) Panofsky; m. Adele DuMond, July 21, 1942; children: Richard, Margaret, Edward, Carol, Steven. AB, Princeton U., 1938; PhD, Calif. Inst. Tech., 1942; DSc (hon.) , Case Inst. Tech., 1963, U. Sask., 1964, Columbia U., 1977, U. Hamburg, Germany, 1984, Princeton U., 1983, Yale U., 1985, U. Beijing, 1987, U. Rome, 1988; degree (hon.) , Uppsala U., Sweden, 1991. Mem. staff mem. radiation lab. U. Calif., 1945-51, asst. prof., 1946-48, asso. prof., 1948-51; prof. physics Stanford U., 1951-62, prof. Stanford Linear Accelerator Ctr., 1962-89, prof. emeritus, 1989—; dir. Stanford (High Energy Physics Lab., Stanford Linear Accelerator Center), 1962-84, dir. emeritus, 1984—. Am. del. Conf. Cessation Nuclear Tests, Geneva, 1959; mem. Pres.'s Sci. Adv. Com., 1960—64; cons. Office Sci. and Tech., Exec. Office Pres., , 1965—73, U.S. ACDA, 1968—81; mem. gen. adv. com. to White House, 1977—81; mem. panel Office Sci. and Techl. Policy, 1977; with nat. def. rsch. Calif. Inst. Tech. and Los Alamos, 1942—45; mem. JASON, 1965—; chmn. bd. overseers Superconducting Supercollider Univs. Rsch. Assn., 1984—93; mem. com. to provide interim oversight Dept. Energy nuclear weapons complex NAS, 1988—89; mem. panel on nuclear warhead dismantlement and special materials control Dept. Energy, 1991—92; mem. Commn. on Particles and Fields Internat. Union Pure and Applied Physics, 1985—93. Decorated officier Legion of Honor; named Calif. Scientist of Yr., 1966; recipient Lawrence prize, AEC, 1961, Nat. med. of Sci., 1969, Franklin medal, 1970, Ann. Pub. Svc. award, Fedn. Am. Scientists, 1973, Enrico Fermi award, U.S. Dept. Energy, 1979, Shoong Found. award for sci., 1983, Hilliard Roderick prize Sci., AAAS, 1991, Matteucei medal, 1997. Fellow: Am. Phys. Soc. (pres. 1974); mem.: AAAS, NAS (mem. com. on internat. security and arms control 1985—, chmn. com. 1985—93, mem. scis. com. on scholarly comm. with China 1987—92), Nat. Acad. Lincei (Italy), Russian Acad. Scis., French Acad. Scis. (fgn.), Am. Philos. Soc. (pres. 1974—75), Sigma Xi, Phi Beta Kappa. Home: 25671 Chapin Rd Los Altos CA 94022-3413 Office: Stanford Linear Accelerator Ctr PO Box 20450 Stanford CA 94309-0450 E-mail: pief@slac.stanford.edu.

PANSEGRAU, PHAEDRA RENÉE, lawyer; b. Rantoul, Ill., Jan. 19, 1967; d. Robert A. and Shonna Noles Leidecker; children: Lauren, Reed. BBA, Baylor U., 1989, JD, 1991. Bar: Tex. 1991, U.S. Dist. Ct. (so. dist.) Tex. Assoc. Wesley, Wilson & Herzog, Houston, 1991-95; corp. counsel Compass Group USA, Inc., Charlotte, N.C., 1996-99, sr. ops. counsel Columbia, S.C., 2000—. Office: Compass Group USA Inc 104 Hurlingham Dr Columbia SC 29223 E-mail: phaedra_pansegrau@exch.compass-usa.com.

PANSINI, MICHAEL SAMUEL, tax and financial consultant; b. Molfetta, Italy, July 12, 1928; came to U.S., 1935; s. Ralph and Isabel (Cirilli) P.; m. Anna D'Angelo, June 5, 1949 (div. 1970); children: Elizabeth, Valerie, Michael; m. Elizabeth Bischoff, Oct. 3, 1970 (div. Feb. 1992); 1 child, Elissa Michelle. BS, NYU, 1950, MBA, 1952, LL.M., 1960; LL.D., Fordham U., 1956. Bar: N.Y. 1956, U.S. Tax Ct. Tax mgr. Pfizer Corp., N.Y.C., 1951-64; asst. treas. Hooker Chem. Corp., 1964-69; treas., dir. United Indsl. Corp., 1969-72; sr. v.p., gen. counsel Beker Industries Corp., Greenwich, Conn., 1972-87; pres., dir. Panmer, Inc., 1987—; tax, fin. cons., 1988—; v.p., corp. counsel Champion Energy Corp. and affiliates, 1991-93, Champion Holdings Co. and affiliates, 1993-96. V.p., chmn. various coms. Tax Exec. Inst., N.Y.C., 1963-72; pres., dir. Fed. Tax Forum, Inc., N.Y.C., 1961-72; dir. Intelligent Bus. Communications Corp. Mem. Rep. Town Com. 19th Dist., Stamford, Conn., 1993—; commr., vice chmn. Econ. Devel. Commn., Stamford, 1994—; bd. dirs. Stamford Sr. Ctr., 2000—. Mem. North Stamford Assn. (bd. dirs. 1999—, v.p. 2000, pres. 2001). Republican. Home and Office: 76 Lawrence Hill Rd Stamford CT 06903-2120

PANSLER, KARL FREDERICK, lawyer; b. Canton, Ohio, Sept. 30, 1961; s. Clarence E. and Ruth E. Pansler; m. Heather Ann Craft, Sept. 9, 1985; children: Christopher, Karlene, Chase, Charles, Karen. BA, Southeastern Coll., 1982; JD, Oral Roberts U., 1985. Bar: Okla. 1985, Fla. 1987, U.S. Dist. Ct. (mid. dist.) Fla. 1988, U.S. Dist. Ct. (ea. and no. dists.) Okla., U.S. Ct. Appeals (11th cir.). Assoc. Melone & Shepard, Tulsa, Okla., 1985-87, Frost & Purcell, Bartow, Fla., 1987-91; ptnr. Pansler & Moody, 1991—. Pres. Intrepid Dolphin Investments, Bartow, 1994—. Contbg. author: Christian Ministries and the Law, 1990. Character edn. com. Polk County Pub. Schs., Bartow; pres., bd. chmn. Beacon Christian Sch., Lakeland, Fla., 1991-95; active Rep. Nat. Com., 2001—. Named Young Alumnus of Yr., Southeastern Coll., Lakeland, 1991, Fla. Businessman of Yr., Nat. Rep. Congressional Com., 2000, Medal of Distinction, 2001. Mem.: ATLA, Southeastern Coll. Alumni Assn. (pres. 1998—2000), Fla. Bar, Okla. Bar, Acad. Fla. Trial Lawyers. Republican. Avocations: Tae Kwon Do (black belt), running marathons, golf. Office: Pansler & Moody PA 575 N Broadway Ave Bartow FL 33830-3919

PANTAGES, LOUIS JAMES, lawyer; b. Plainfield, N.J., Apr. 29, 1916; s. Dimitrios Louis and Bessie (Massas) P.; m. Dorothea Carol Adams, Dec. 16, 1950; children: James, Peter, Elaine Marie. AB, Rutgers U., 1938, LLB, 1940. Bar: N.J. 1941, U.S. Dist. Ct. N.J. 1941, U.S. Dist. Ct. (so. dist.) N.Y. 1955, U.S. Supreme Ct. 1960, U.S. Ct. Appeals (3d cir.) 1967. Since practiced in, Newark; with firm Cox & Walburg, 1938-54; partner Mead, Gleeson, Hansen & Pantages, 1954-68, Gleeson, Hansen & Pantages, 1968-72, Hansen, Pantages, Sellar & Zavesky, 1972-77, Pantages Sellar Richardson & Stuart, 1977-82, Stein, Bliablias, McGuire, Pantages & Gigl, 1982—; trial lawyer in cts. of N.J., U.S. Dist. cts. of N.J., U.S. Dist. Ct., So. Dist. N.Y., U.S. Supreme Ct., others. Capt. C.W.S., AUS, 1942-46; Capt. M.I., U.S. Army, 1950-52. Fellow Am. Coll. Trial Lawyers, Internat. Acad. Law and Sci.; mem. ABA, N.J. Bar Assn., Essex County Bar Assn., Am. Judicature Soc., Trial Attys. N.J., N.J. Def. Assn., Internat. Assn. Def. Counsel, Fedn. Ins. and Corp. Counsel, Def. Rsch. Inst., Am. Arbitration Assn., Arbitration Forums, Inc., Rutgers Law Sch. Alumni Assn., Essex Fells Country Club, Hellenic Univ. Club N.Y. Republican. Greek Orthodox. Avocations: art, antiques, music. Home: Claridge II unit 5NE Claridge Dr Verona NJ 07044 Office: 354 Eisenhower Pkwy Livingston NJ 07039-1022

PANTALEO, JACK, writer, composer, social worker, harpist; b. Melrose Park, Ill., Nov. 30, 1954; s. Jack Sam Pantaleo and Sophia Mannozzi Pantaleo Cicero. Psychiat. Tech., C.C., San Francisco, 1981; BA in Humanities, New Coll. Calif., San Francisco, 1986; MA in Writing, U. San Francisco, 1988. Lic. psychiat. technician. Asst. to dean U. San Francisco Sch. Nursing, 1984-88; grammar sch. tchr. St. Michael's Cath. Sch., San Francisco, 1989-91; instr. English Vista C.C., Berkeley, Calif., 1990-93; social worker City and County of San Francisco, 1991—. Founder, dir. Evangelicals Concerned, San Francisco, 1978-85; co-founder, co-dir. AIDS InterFaith Network, San Francisco, 1983-88. Author: (novel) Mother Julian and the Gentle Vampire, 2000; Playwright/composer musical The Gospel According to the Angel Julius translated into German and performed in Hamburg, Germany, 1999; (one-act play): Uncle Fred's Ex-Staight Ministry in Wilma Loves Betty, 1999; contbg. author: (collection of meditations) The Road to Emmaus, 1990; author booklet and articles. Caregiver for babies with AIDS, The Bridge, San Francisco, 1989-93. Work included in Silver Quill, The David Ross Meml. Competition, Wichita, 1996. Mem. Social Workers Union, Nat. Writers Union. Democrat. Episcopalian. Avocations: harp, lecturing. E-mail: jackp100@onebox.com.

PANTANOWITZ, LIRON, pathologist, researcher; b. Klerksdorp, South Africa, Nov. 1, 1968; came to U.S., 1999; s. Philip and Phyllis Pantanowitz; m. Heidi Schwartz, Dec. 8, 1996; 1 child, Joshua. BSc, U. Witwatersrand, Johannesburg, South Africa, 1987, MB BChir, 1996. Med. officer U. Witersrand Hosps., Johannesburg, 1998-99; pathology registrar South African Inst. Med. Rsch., 1999; pathology resident Beth Israel Deaconess Med. Ctr., Boston, 1999—. Med. rschr. Harvard Med. Sch., Mass., 2000. Office: Beth Israel Deaconess Med Ctr 330 Brookline Ave Boston MA 02215 E-mail: Lpantanowitz@hotmail.com.

PANTEL, GLENN STEVEN, lawyer; b. Plainfield, N.J., Sept. 25, 1953; s. Donald and Sarah Libby (Pearlman) P.; m. Lisa Pamela Krop, June 28, 1981; 1 child, Adam Scott. AB, Johns Hopkins U., 1975; JD, U. Pa., 1978. Bar: N.J. 1978, U.S. Dist. Ct. N.J. 1978, Pa. 1978, Fla. 1980, U.S. Ct. Appeals (3d cir.) 1982. Law clk. to presiding judge U.S. Dist. Ct. (so. dist.), Miami, Fla., 1978-79; from assoc. to ptnr. Shanley & Fisher P.C., Morristown, N.J., 1979-99, also bd. dirs.; ptnr. Drinker Biddle and Shanley LLP, Florham Park, 1999—. Trustee Integrity, Inc., Drug and Alcohol Abuse Program, Newark; trustee, mem. scholarship com. 200 Club of Somerset County. Mem. ABA, Fla. Bar Assn., N.J. Bar Assn., Morris County Bar Assn., Phi Beta Kappa. Avocations: skiing, sailing. Home: 3 Cross Way Mendham NJ 07945-3120 Office: Drinker Biddle & Shanley LLP 500 Campus Dr Florham Park NJ 07932-1047

PANTEL-BAKST, SHARON S. social worker; b. Bklyn., Feb. 11, 1953; d. Meyer and Ayala (Wachsman) Pantel; m. Michael S. Bakst. BA summa cum laude, CUNY, 1973; MSW, NYU, 1977. Diplomate Am. Bd. Examiners in Clin. Social Work. Case aide Jewish Assn. for Svcs. for the Aged, Bklyn., 1973-75; social work asst. Jewish Hosp. Med. Ctr./Interfaith Med. Ctr., 1975-76; social work intern Brookdale Hosp.-Community Mental Health Ctr., 1976-77; caseworker family svcs. N.Y. Assn. for New Ams., N.Y.C., 1977-81; social worker neonatal ICU SUNY/Health Sci. Ctr., Bklyn., 1981-92, social work coord. neonatal bereavement program, 1983-92; dir., social worker Hadassah-WIZO Can. Rsch. Inst., Israel, 1993-96; rsch. and clin. data mgr. bone marrow transplantation dept. Hadassah U. Hosp., Israel, 1997—. Social work cons. Bklyn. Parent Ednl. Program, 1982—. Mem. Bklyn.-S.I. Perinatal Network, Bklyn. Inter-Hosp. Coalition on Child Abuse and Neglect, 1982-83. Recipient Excellence Award N.Y. State United Univ. Professions, 1990. Mem. NASW, Phi Beta Kappa. Home: 66 Hai Taieb St 93878 Jerusalem Israel Office: Hadassah Univ Hosp Ein Kerem Jerusalem Israel E-mail: bakst@netvision.net.il., sharon@hadassah.org.il.

PANTELOPOULOS, NICHOLAS EVAN, lawyer, ship's officer; b. Athens, Greece, Oct. 21, 1964; s. Evan and Helene Pantelopoulos; m. Lea Trataros, June 27, 1993; children: Eleni, Athena, Evan. BS, U.S. Merchant Marine Acad., 1986; JD, Union U., 1990; LLM, Fordham U., 1991. Bar: Conn. 1990, N.Y. 1991, D.C. 1991, U.S. Dist. Ct. (no. dist.) N.Y. 1991, U.S. Dist. Ct. (so. and ea. dists.) N.Y. 1995, U.S. Ct. Appeals (2d cir.) 1996, U.S. Supreme Ct. 2000, U.S. Ct. Internat. Trade 2000. Pvt. practice, NY, 1991—95; atty. DeOrchis & Ptnrs., N.Y.C., 1995—97; ptnr. Biedermann, Hoenig, Massamillo & Ruff, P.C., 1997—. Mem. Maritime Law Assn. of U.S., N.Y. State Bar Assn. Avocations: sailing, traveling, photography. Home: 1 Bradford Pl Harrison NY 10528-2703 Office: Biedermann Hoenig Massamillo & Ruff PC 90 Park Ave New York NY 10016-1301

PANTENBURG, MICHEL, hospital administrator, health educator, holistic health coordinator; b. Denver, Oct. 6, 1926; d. Arthur Robert and Alice (McKenna) P. Diploma, Providence Nursing Sch., Kansas City, Kans., 1951; BS in Nursing Edn., St. Mary Coll., Leavenworth, Kans., 1958; M. in Nursing, Cath. U. Am., 1960. Joined Sisters of Charity, Roman Catholic Ch., 1945; lic. amateur radio operator. Dir. nursing Providence Hosp., Kansas City, Kans., 1958-62; nursing coordinator Sisters of Charity, Leavenworth, 1962-67; hosp. adminstr. St. Mary Hosp., Grand Junction, Colo., 1967-73, St. Vincent Hosp., Billings, Mont., 1973-84; dir. focus on leadership program Gonzaga U., Spokane, Wash., 1985-92; chaplain pastoral care dept. St. Marys Hosp. and Med. Ctr., Grand Junction, Colo., 1994-99, integrative medicine, 1999—. Dir. Norwest Bank, Billings Co-author, editor: Management of Nursing (CHA award 1969), 1967 Bd. dirs. De Paul Hosp., Cheyenne, Wyo., 1980-85, Ronald McDonald House, Billings, 1982-85, St. Joseph Hosp., Denver, 1994-97. Named Woman of Yr., Bus. and Profl. Women, Billings, 1979 Mem. Cath. Hosp. Assn. (bd. dirs., sec.), Am. Hosp. Assn. (regional del. 1975-80), Am. Coll. Hosp. Adminstrn., Mont. Hosp. Assn. (pres.), Billings C. of C. (v.p. 1977-78). Avocations: hiking; skiing. Office: Pastoral Care Dept St Marys Hosp & Med Ctr Grand Junction CO 81502

PANTER, IRWIN, lawyer; b. Chgo., Apr. 16, 1914; s. Phillip and Mollie (Bender) P.; m. Ruth Schwartz, June 18, 1950; children— Michael Richard, Deborah, Janet. A.B., U. Chgo., 1935, J.D., 1937. Bar: Ill., U.S. Dist. Ct. (no. dist.) Ill., U.S. Supreme Ct. Sole practice, Chgo., 1937-47; ptnr. Panter, Nelson & Bernfield, 1947-82; counsel Deutsch, Levy & Engel, 1982-; dir. Wesley Jessen, Inc., Nat. Clothier Corp., Plastic Contact Lens Corp., Tiara Corp. Bd. dirs. Nat. Eye Research Found. Served to 2d lt. Signal Corps, USAAC, 1941-43. Mem. ABA, Ill. Bar Assn., Chgo. Bar Assn., Decalogue Soc. Contbr. articles to legal jours. Office: Deutsch Levy & Engel 33 N Dearborn St Chicago IL 60602-3102

PANTER, TERRY EVE, accountant; b. Copperhill, Tenn., Apr. 30, 1957; d. Wallace Lloyd Panter and Lelia Louise Burk. BBA, Kennesaw (Ga.) Coll., 1983. CPA, Ga. Owner Panter Acctg. Svcs., Marietta, Ga. Mem.: Kennesaw Coll. Alumni Assn. Avocations: physical fitness, music, art. Home: 727 Bonnie Dell Dr Marietta GA 30062-3430 Office: General Delivery Mineral Bluff GA 30559-9999 E-mail: epantercpa@netscape.net.

PANTOJAS-CONCEPCION, CARLOS A. rheumatologist; b. Santurce, P.R., Aug. 27, 1958; s. Hipolito and Carmen D. (Concepcion) Pantojas; m. Margarita S. Barbosa, Sept. 5, 1987; 1 child, Karla. MD, U. Ctrl. del Caribe, P.R., 1984. Cons. rheumatology Caguas (P.R.) Regional Hosp., 1990—, Ashford-Presbyn. Hosp., Santurce, 1992—, Pavia Hosp., Santurce, 1995—; asst. prof. San Juan Baptista Sch. Medicine, Caguas, 1995—. Pres. ethics com. Caguas Regional Hosp., 1991—. Recipient Dr.'s Choice award in Rheumatology, PR, 2000, 2001. Mem.: ACP, AMA (Physician Recognition award 1993, 1996, 1999), Women's Health Adv. Bd., Am. Acad. Pain Mgmt., PR Soc. for Pain Mgmt., Sociedad Reumatologos PR (chmn. sci. com. 2001—02, pres. 1999—2000), Am. Coll. Rheumatology.

PANTOS, WILLIAM PANTAZES, mechanical engineer, consultant; b. Ann Arbor, Mich., May 15, 1957; s. William Van and Lillian William (Skinner) P. BS in Mech. Engring., Northwestern U., Evanston, Ill., 1979; MS in Mech. Engring., San Diego State U., 1991. Registered profl. engr., Calif. Owner Signs & Symbols, Niles, Ill., 1975-80; engr. Hughes Aircraft, El Segundo, Calif., 1980-83, Gen. Dynamics, San Diego, 1983-85; staff engr. TRW, 1985-90; pres. Tekton Industries, Carlsbad, Calif., 1990—. Patentee animal lift and transport apparatus. NROTC scholar USN, 1975. Mem. Am. Soc. Mech. Engrs., Nat. Soc. Profl. Engrs., Alpha Delta Phi. (pres. 1978). Greek Orthodox. Home: 1571 San Elijo Ave Cardiff By The Sea CA 92007-2420 E-mail: w.pantos@worldnet.att.net.

PANTUSO, MICHAEL VINCENT, graphic design company executive; b. Morgantown, W.Va., Aug. 21, 1963; s. John Anthony and Bonnie Ruth (Fisher) P.; m. Shari Ann Urso, Oct. 6, 1990; 1 child: Elliott Anthony. BA, Flagler Coll., 1986. Art dir. Mktg. Comms. Firm, Chgo., 1986-90; prin. Michael Pantuso Design, 1990—. Works exhibited at AIDS Benefit, 1994, 95, Hotel d'Angleterre, 1995. Mem. Am. Inst. Graphic Arts. Avocations: painting, art collecting, traveling, interactive multimedia, writing. Home: 419F W Grand Ave Chicago IL 60610-4008

PANTUSO, VINCENT JOSEPH, food service consultant; b. Charleston, W.Va., Aug. 13, 1940; s. Fortunato F. Pantuso and Josephine Malcom (Ginestra) Pantuso Messer; m. Carol Barber, Dec. 10, 1964 (div. 1976); children: Lisa, Barbara, Tina; m. Nancy Josephine Chellman, Sept. 30, 1978 (div. 1995). Student, Drexel U.; BSBA, St. Joseph's U., 1968; postgrad., Rollins Coll., 1984-85. Asst. mgr. Marriott Hotels, Inc., Bethesda, Md., 1962-64; v.p. sales mktg. ARA Services, Inc., Phila., 1964-72; sr. v.p. Interstate United Corp., Chgo., 1972-84; pres. V.J. Pantuso Services, Inc., Orlando, Fla., 1984—, New Vista Services, Inc., 1988-97. Mem. Nat. Assn. Concessionaires (bd. dirs. 1982—, pres. 1989-91, chmn. 1991-94, Master Concessionaire, Chgo. 1985), Nat. Assn. Food Equipment Mfrs. (doctorate 1989). Republican. Episcopalian. Avocation: fishing. Home: Apt 5 120 Monarch Cir Casselberry FL 32730-2718

PANTZER, JOHN G. retired physician; b. Apr. 6, 1932; AB, Wabash Coll., 1954; MD, Ind. U. Diplomate Am. Bd. Plastic and Reconstructive Surgery. Retired from career as plastic and reconstructive surgeon. Fellow ACS (life); mem. Am. Soc. Aesthetic Surgery, Am. Soc. Plastic and Reconstructive Surgery.

PANUSKA, JOSEPH ALLAN, academic administrator; b. Balt., July 3, 1927; s. Joseph William and Barbara Agnes (Preller) P. BS, Loyola Coll., Balt., 1948; PhD, St. Louis U., 1958; STL, Woodstock Coll., 1961; LLD (hon.), U. Scranton, 1974; degree (hon.), Trnava (Slovakia) U., 1997; LHD (hon.), Marywood Coll., 1992. Joined S.J., 1948; ordained priest Roman Cath. Ch., 1960. Instr. dept. physiology Emory U. Sch. Medicine, 1962-63; asst. prof. biology Georgetown U., 1963-66, assoc. prof., 1966-72, prof., 1973; provincial, bd. dirs. Jesuit Conf. Md. Province (S.J.), 1973-79; acad. v.p., dean faculties, prof. biology Boston Coll., 1979-82; pres. U. Scranton, Pa., 1982-98, pres. emeritus, 1998—; rector Jesuit Ctr., 1998—. Mem. Pa. Commn. Ind. Colls. and Univs., 1982-98, mem. exec. com., treas., 1987-91, vice chmn., 1988-89, chmn., 1990-91; mem. President's Commn., NCAA, 1989-90. Mem. editl. bd. Crybiology, 1968-88, editor-in-chief, 1971-74; contbr. chpts. to books, articles to sci. rsch. jours. Mem. corp. Am. Found. Biol. Rsch., 1967-85, pres. bd. dirs., 1974-79, v.p., 1979-83; trustee Loyola Coll., 1979-85, St. Joseph's U., 1979-84, U. Scranton, 1970-73, St. Peter's Coll., 1971-72, Woodstock Coll., 1973-76, Fordham U., 1982-88, Cambridge Ctr. for Social Studies, 1973-79 (pres. 1973-79), Corp. Roman Cath. Clergymen, 1973-79 (pres. 1973-79); rector Jesuit Community at Georgetown U., 1970-73; bd. dirs. United Way Pa., 1985-87, Scranton Preparatory Sch., 1984-90, Scranton Area Found., 1997-98; chmn. Pa. Commn. for Ind. Colls. and Univs., 1990-91; bd. dirs. John Carroll U., 1992-98, Nat. Inst. Environ. Renewal, 1992-98, Woodstock Theol. Ctr., Washington, 1998-2001, St. Joseph's Prep. Sch., Phila., 1998-2001, Alvernia Coll., 2001—; bd. visitors Panuska Coll. Profl. Studies, U. Scranton, 1998-. NIH postdoctoral fellow, 1962-63; recipient Danforth Found. Harbison prize for disting. teaching, 1969, B'nai B'rith Americanism award, 1997, recipient from 2001, Michelini award Outstanding Svc. to Higher Edn. AICUP (Assoc. Indep. C and U. Pa.), 2001; vis. fellow St. Edmunds Coll., Cambridge U., 1969; college named J.A. Panuska College of Professional Studies, Univ. at Scranton. Mem. Am. Physiol. Soc., Soc. for Cryobiology, Soc. Exptl. Biology and Medicine, Assn. Jesuit Colls. and Univs. (bd. dirs. 1982-98, treas. 1993-96), Pa. Assn. Colls. and Univs. (exec. com., adv. com. to State Bd. Edn. 1990-91), Scranton C. of C. Home and Office: Jesuit Ctr PO Box 223 Wernersville PA 19565-0223 E-mail: jescntsec@talon.net. *In order to be happy in a leadership role and to succeed in it, I have to possess a sense of coherence with my life values. I also need to recognize that my own activity makes a real difference in the empowerment of others so that there is a multiplier effect which extends me beyond my own person and activity.*

PANY, KURT JOSEPH, accounting educator, consultant; b. St. Louis, Mar. 31, 1946; s. Joseph Francis and Ruth Elizabeth (Westerman) P.; m. Darlene Dee Zabish, June 3, 1971; children: Jeffrey, Michael. BSBA, U. Ariz., 1968; MBA in Mgmt., U. Minn., 1971; PhD in Accountancy, U. Ill., 1977. CPA, Ariz., cert. fraud examiner. Staff auditor Arthur Andersen & Co., Mpls., 1968-69, Touche Ross & Co., Phoenix, 1971-73; teaching asst. U. Minn., Mpls., 1969-71; teaching asst. auditing and acctg. U. Ill., Urbana, 1972-76; asst. prof. acctg. Ariz. State U., Tempe, 1977-81, assoc. prof., 1981-85, Arthur Andersen/Don Dupont prof. acctg., 1985-91. Mem. acctg. and auditing standards com. State of Ariz., Phoenix, 1989—; reviewer Jour. Acctg. and Pub. Policy, 1983—. Contbg. author: CPA Exam. Rev., 1983—; co-author: Principles of Auditing, 1988—, Auditing, 1993—; co-editor Auditing: A Jour. Practice and Theory, 1984-88; mem. editl. bd. Advances in Acctg., 1982—, Jour. Acctg. Edn., 1983—; reviewer Acctg. Rev., 1984—, ad hoc editor, 1989—; contbr. numerous articles to profl. jours. Active various child-related orgns. Peat, Marwick, Mitchell & Co. Found. grantee, 1985. Fellow AICPA (auditing stds. divsn. 1989-90, acctg. lit. selection com. 1989-90, acctg. lit. awards com. 1979-83, mem. auditing stds. bd. 1995—); mem. Am. Acctg. Assn. (tech. program com. 1980-81, chairperson Western region auditing sect. 1981-83, acctg. lit. nominating com. 1982-84, 88-89, acctg. lit. selection com. 1989-90, dir. auditing stds., chmn. auditing stds. com. 1989-90), Ariz. Soc. CPA's (auditing stds. com. 1978-81, ethics com. 1981-84). Avocation: baseball. Address: 7411 S Rita Ln Unit 116 Tempe AZ 85283-4792 Office: Ariz State U Sch Accountancy Tempe AZ 85287

PANZARELLA, PHILIP PATRICK, engineer; b. N.Y.C., Mar. 17, 1939; s. John Joseph and Josephine Catherine (Cassella) P.; m. Susan Kay Barga, Sept. 3, 1966; children: Michael Anthony, Gregory Stephan, David John. BS in Aero. Engring., St. Louis U., 1960; MS in Aerospace/Mech. Engring., Air Force Inst. Tech., 1965; MS in Indsl. Mgmt., MIT, 1979; PhD in Engring. Mgmt., Union Inst., Cin., 1992. Registered profl. engr., Calif. Commd. 2d lt. USAF, 1960, advanced through grades to capt., 1965; flight test engr. Armament Devel. Test Ctr., Eglin AFB, Fla., 1960-63; project/flight test engr. Aero. Sys. Divsn., Wright-Patterson AFB, Ohio, 1965-69, Dep. for Flight Test, Wright-Patterson AFB, 1969-73; chief modification engr. 4950th Test Wing, Aero. Sys. Divsn., 1973-79, dir. aircraft modification, 1979-86; chief scientist, chief engr. Air Force Logistics Command, 1986-91; chief engr. Air Force Sys. Command, Andrews AFB, Md., 1991-92, Air Force Material Command, Wright-Patterson AFB, 1992-94; exec. dir. Electronic Sys. Ctr., Hanscom AFB, Mass., 1994-96; v.p. EER Systems Inc., 1996—. Active Leadership Dayton, Ohio, 1990-94; mem. local fed. coordinating com. Greater Boston Fed. Exec. Bd., 1994—. Recipient Meritorious Rank award Pres. of the U.S., 1991, Disting. Rank award, 1994. Mem. Soc. Automotive Engrs. (mem. tech. stds. bd. 1993—), Air Force Comm. Electronics Assn., Sys. Safety Society (v.p.). Republican. Roman Catholic. Achievements include discovery of phenomenon of parallel secondary injection control of fluid jets. Office: EER Systems Inc 10289 Aerospace Rd Lanham Seabrook MD 20706-2280

PANZER, MARY CAROLINE, historian, museum curator; b. Flint, Mich., May 29, 1955; d. Milton and Caroline Alice (Weis) P. BA, Yale U.; MA, Columbia U., 1980; PhD, Boston U., 1990. Asst. prof. U. Kans., Lawrence, 1989-91; curator photographs Spencer Mus. Art, 1989-91; asst. dir. SMART Mus. Art U. Chgo., 1991; curator photographs Nat. Portrait Gallery Smithsonian Instn., Washington, 1992-2000; ind. historian N.Y.C., 2000—. Author: Philadelphia Naturalistic Photography, 1982, Rudolf Eickemeyer, Jr. and the Art of the Camera, 1986, Mathew Brady and the Image of History, 1997, Halsman: A Retrospective, 1998, Brady 55, 2001, Hine 55, 2002; contbg. editor Am. Photo, 2002; editor, Separate, But Equal. Mem. Am. Studies Assn., Coll. Art Assn., Oracle, Mid-Atlantic Radical Historians Orgn., Orgn. Am. Historians.

PAOLINI, CLAIRE JACQUELINE, dean, educator; b. Newton, Mass., May 19, 1934; d. Frank and Angelina Landro; m. Gilberto Paolini, June 18, 1960; children: Angela J., John F. BA, Boston U., 1956; MA, Middlebury (Vt.) Coll., 1958; PhD, Tulane U., 1982. Instr. Spanish U. Mass., Amherst, 1956-60,

U. New Orleans, 1970-75; from dir. internat. student affairs to assoc. dean Loyola U., New Orleans, 1975-83, assoc. dean arts and scis., 1983-97; dean coll. arts and scis., prof. spanish Sacred Heart U., Fairfield, Conn., 1997—. Author: The Narrative Art of Domingos Monteiro, 1979, Valle-Inclán's Modernism: Use and Abuse of Religious and Mystical Symbolism, 1986; editor: LA CHISPA '95: Selected Proceedings, 1995, LA CHISPA '97: Selected Proceedings, 1997; co-editor: La CHISPA '99: Selected Proceedings, 1999; assoc. editor: LA CHISPA '93: Selected Proceedings, 1993; mem. editl. bd. LA CHISPA, 1983, 85, 87, 89, NACADA Jour., 1995-97. V.p. Soc. Espanola, New Orleans, 1977-81, bd. mem. 1976-97. Mem. Nat. Assn. Academic Affairs Administrators (Administrator of Yr. award 1996-97), Modern Lang. Assn., Council Colls. Arts Scis., Am. Assn. Tchrs. Spanish and Portuguese, Coll. Consortium Internat. Studies (bd. mem. 1997—), Am. Assn. Higher Edn. Home: 3 Gregory Farm Rd Easton CT 06612-2049 Office: Sacred Heart Univ 5151 Park Ave Fairfield CT 06432-1000

PAOLINI, GILBERTO, literature and science educator; b. L'Aquila, Italy; naturalized citizen, 1954; s. John and Assunta Angela (Turavani) P.; m. Claire Jacqueline Landro; children: Angela Janet, John Frank. BA, U. Buffalo, 1957, MA, 1959; postgrad., Middlebury Coll., summer 1960, 61; PhD, U. Minn., 1965. Lectr. Spanish Rosary Hill Coll., Buffalo, 1957-58; instr. Italian and Latin lit. U. Mass., Amherst, 1958-60; instr. Spanish and Italian Syracuse U., 1962-65, asst. prof., 1965-67; assoc. prof. Spanish lit. Tulane U., New Orleans, 1967-76, prof., 1976—, dir. Tulane scholars and honors program, 1981-83, chmn. colloquia dept., 1981-83. Originator Spanish Culture Week, New Orleans, 1977, 79; chmn. adv. com. Jambalaya program Nat. Endowment Humanities, New Orleans, 1975-80; Spanish essay reader Ednl. Testing Svc., Princeton, 1979-85; founder, gen. chmn. La. Conf. on Hispanic Langs. and Lits., 1981, 83, 85, 87, 89, 93, 95, 97, 99. Author: Bartolome Soler: novelista: Procedimientos estilísticos, 1963; An Aspect of Spiritualistic Naturalism in the Novel of B.P. Galdos: Charity, 1969; mem. editorial bd.: Forum Italicum, 1967-71, Critica Hispanica, 1979—, Discurso Literario, 1985—, Letras Peninsulares, 1987—; assoc. editor: South Central MLA Bull, 1978-80; editor: La Chispa'81: Selected Procs., 1981, Papers on Romance Literary Relations, 1983, La Chispa '83: Selected Procs., 1983, La Chispa '85: Selected Procs., 1985, La Chispa '87: Selected Procs. 1987, La Chispa '89: Selected Prods., 1989, La Chispa '93: Selected Procs. 1993; cons. editor South Central Rec., 1988-92; gen. editor: La Chispa '95: Selected Proceedings, 1995, La Chispa '97: Selected Proceedings, 1997, La Chispa '99: Selected Proceedings, 1999; contbr. articles to profl. jours. With AUS, 1952-54, USAFRES, 1954-57. Recipient Disting. Service award Sociedad Espanola, 1979, Knight Cross of Order of Isabel the Catholic, 1984; subject of Festscrift Studies, Honor of Gilberto Paolini, 1996. Mem. MLA, AAUP, Am. Assn. Tchrs. Spanish and Portuguese (chmn. pub. rels. com. 1981-86, pres. La. chpt. 1979-81, 88-89), Am. Assn. Tchrs. Italian, Am. Assn. Advancement Humanities, Soc. for Lit. and Sci., Asociacion Internacional de Hispanistas, Southeastern Am. Soc. 18th Century Studies (exec. v.p.), Assn. Internat. Galdosistas, Soc. Literatura Española del Siglo XIX, Phi Sigma Iota, Sigma Delta Pi (v.p. for S.W. 1989-92). Office: Tulane Univ 304 Newcomb Hall New Orleans LA 70118 E-mail: gpaolini@tulane.edu.

PAOLINO, MICHAEL ANTHONY, engineering educator; b. Albany, N.Y., Mar. 8, 1939; s. Anthony and Bessie (Malatesta) P.; m. Carole Montgomery, Dec. 2, 1961; children: Patrick, Kevin, John. BS, Siena Coll., 1960; MS, U. Ariz., 1967, PhD, 1972. Registered profl. engr., Va. Commd. officer U.S. Army, 1960, advanced through grades to col., 1982; served as prof. U.S. Mil. Acad., West Point, N.Y., 1973-86; ret. U.S. Army, 1986; prof., dean engring. Lafayette Coll., Easton, Pa., 1986—2000, Dana prof. mech. engring., 2000—. Recipient Ralph R. Teetor award Soc. Automotive Engrs., Detroit, 1978. Mem. ASME, Am. Soc. Engring. Edn., Tau Beta Pi, Phi Kappa Phi, Pi Tau Sigma. Roman Catholic. Avocations: skiing, hiking, boating.

PAOLINO, RONALD MARIO, clinical psychologist, consultant, psychopharmacologist, pharmacist; b. Providence, Mar. 15, 1938; s. Lawrence and Mary Corinne (Guglielmi) P.; m. Eileen Frances Quimby, June 18, 1960; children: Lisa Katherine, David Lawrence. Student, Providence Coll., 1955-56; BS in Pharmacy, U. R.I., 1959, MS, 1961; PhD in Pharmacology/Toxicology, Purdue U., 1963; postdoctoral studies Exptl. Psychology, Yale U., 1963-65; doctoral studies in clin. psychology, Purdue U., 1972-74; postdoctoral studies in existential analytic psychotherapy, Okla. Inst. Existential Analysis and Psychotherapy, 1974-75; Hostage Negotiation, FBI, 1991, Advanced Hostage Negotiation, 1995; Crisis Negoitaition, FBI Acad., 1994; MA (hon.), Brown U., 1977. Lic. psychologist, R.I., pharmacist R.I.; nat. registered health svc. provider in psychology; cert. arbitrator; cert. nat. registered group psycho-therapists; cert. edn. provider N.Y.; diplomate Am. Bd. Forensic Examiners, Am. Bd. Forensic Medicine. Intern dept. psychiatry and behavioral scis. U. Okla. Health Scis. Ctr., 1974-75; David Ross predoctoral fellow dept. pharmacology/toxicology Purdue U., 1961-63; NIMH postdoctoral fellow in psychology dept. psychology Yale U., 1963-65; asst. prof. pharmacology U. Conn. Sch. Pharmacy, 1965-67; assoc. prof. psychopharmacology Purdue U., 1967-74; NIMH fellow in clin. psychology U. Okla. Health Scis. Ctr., 1974-75; coord. group psychotherapy tng. program Brown U. Program in Medicine, 1983-85, assoc. prof. psychiatry and human behavior, 1976-90; pvt. practice; chief drug dependency treatment program VA Med. Ctr., Providence, 1975-87, dir. biofeedback clinic, 1977-87, primary hostage negotiator, 1991—. Psychiatric cons. VA Police, alternative Dispute Resolution Mediator, New Eng. Veterans Integrated Svc. Network, 1996—, pain mgmt. bd., 1999—; mem. Pharmacology and Therapeutic Agts. Com., 1979-87, VA Med. Ctr., coord. VA Contracted Half-Way Project for Substance Dependent Vets., 1981-85, chmn. Pain Mgmt. Task Force, 1984-85, mem. Supervisory Level Pharmacy Profl. Standards Bd., 1990—, mem. Mgmt. Suicidal and Violent Patient Task Force, 1990-91, chmn. Com. Prevention & Mgmt. of Disturbed Behaviors, 1991—, chief crisis mgmt. program, 1993-96, advisor FBI Hostage Negotiations, 1991—, Instr. R.I. State Police Acad., 1994, Instr., Drug Recognition Experts Recert PRGM, R.I. Dept Health, 1995, Faculty, Law Enforcement Mgmt. Command Sch. U.R.I., 1991—, Va. Nat. Law Enforcement Tng. Ctr., 1997; chmn. Outpatient Psychiatry Svcs. Reorganization Task Force, 1991, mem. VA DOD Desert Storm Emergency Plan Com., 1991; advisor OSHA Dept. Labor for Violence in the Work Place, 1994-95; mem. E. Prov. Clergy & Mental Health Providers Alliance, 1995—; mem. substance abuse and prevention grant application rev. com. R.I. Adv. Coun. on Substance Abuse, 1982-92, prevention, edn. and tng. com. on substance abuse, 1981—, chmn. 1981-82; adj. assoc. prof. psychology, U. R.I., 1982—, clin. assoc. prof. pharmacy U. R.I., 1998—; mem. planning com. State Conf. on Substance Abuse in the Hispanic Community, 1986; mem. alcohol awareness commn. Episc. Diocese of R.I., 1983-85; gubernatorial appointee Gov.'s Permanent Coun. on Drug Abuse Control, 1978-82; mem. rev. com. for funding of state drug abuse programs R.I. Single State Agy. on Drug Abuse, R.I. Dept. Mental Health Retardation and Hosps., 1978-82; cons. Nurses Renewal Com., 1980-81, substance abuse prevention edn. for elem. sch. children R.I. chpt. ARC, 1977, mem. suicide prevention steering com., 1977; mem.Interagy. Drug Abuse Steering Com., Lafayette, Ind. 1969-72; bd. dirs. Providence VA Med. Ctr. Credit Union; mem. bd. cert. for alcoholism counselors R.I. Assn. Alcohol Counselors, 1979-81; mem. Gov.'s Task Force on Substance Abuse at Adult Correctional Instn., 1977-78, Gov.'s Task Force on Mental Health Svcs. at Adult Correctional Instn., 1977-78, chmn. reclassification of inmates com., 1977-78; chmn. com. on edn. and cert. biofeedback practioners Conn. Biofeedback Soc., 1977-78; summer faculty fellow U. Conn., 1967; vis. scientist lectr. Assn. Am. Colls. Pharmacy, 1972-73; cons. to bus., unions, law enforcement. Author: (2 chpts.) Drug Testing: Issues and Options, 1991; contbr. 37 articles to profl. jours. Bd. dirs. R.I. chpt. Samaritans Internat. Suicide Prevention Orgn., 1978-84; v.p. Experience Jesus Inc.; mem. com. adv. bd. Cpina Bifida Assn. R.I., 1980-83; mem. R.I. East Bay Interfaith Mental Health Alliance; congressman appointee (Patrick J. Kennedy); mem. veterans adv. commn., 1995—. Recipient Citation award for svc. and contbns. to formulation of state policy for treatment and prevention of drug abuse Gov. R.I., 1983, Letter of Commendation, Gov.'s R.I. Adv. Coun. on Substance Abuse, 1986, vc. Recognition award DAV, 1990, Spl. Contbn. award Providence VA Med Ctr., 1990, 98, 99, 2000, Outstanding Performance award, 1991, 92, 93, 94, 97, cert. appreciation for continued excellence in patient care, 1999; named to Cranston Hall of Fame, 2001. Fellow Am. Coll. Forensic Examiners; mem. AMA, Am. Psychotherapy Assn., Am. Soc. Pharmacology Exptl. Therapeutics, Internat. Brain Rsch. Orgn., Internat. Narcotic Enforcement Officers Assn., R.I. Group Psychotherapy Soc. (pres. 1991-93, continuing edn. dir. psychologists 1990-95, exec. bd. 1986—, tng. faculty 1985—, co-dir. tng. 1986-87, tng. adv. bd. 1985-86), R.I. Psychol. Assn. (chmn. substance abuse ins. subcom. 1986-87, rep. Gov.'s Coun. on Mental Health State Plan Com. 1982-84), Hostage Negotiators Am. Office: PO Box 159 Barrington RI 02806-0159 E-mail: rmpne50@aol.com.

PAOLUCCI, ANNE ATTURA, playwright, poet, English and comparative literature educator, educational consultant; b. Rome; d. Joseph and Lucy (Guidoni) Attura; m. Henry Paolucci(dec.). BA, Barnard Coll; MA, Columbia U., PhD, 1963; hon. degree, Lehman Coll., CUNY, 1995. Mem. faculty English dept. Brearley Sch., N.Y.C., 1957-59; asst. prof. English and comparative lit. CCNY, 1959-69; univ. research prof. St. John's U., Jamaica, N.Y., 1969-75, prof. English, 1975-77, acting head dept. English, 1973-74, chmn. dept. English, 1982-91, dir. doctor of arts degree program in English, 1982-97; ednl. cons.; editl. cons. Bagehot Coun. Fulbright lectr. in Am. drama U. Naples, Italy, 1965-67; spl. lectr. U. Urbino, summers 1966-67, U. Bari, 1967, univs. Bologna, Catania, Messina, Palermo, Milan, Pisa, 1965-67; disting. adj. vis. prof. Queens Coll., CUNY; bd. dirs. World Centre for Shakespeare Studies, 1972— ; spl. guest Yugoslavia Ministry of Culture, 1972; rep. U.S. at Internat. Poetry Festival, Yugoslavia, 1981; founder, exec. dir. Council on Nat. Lits., 1974— ; mem. exec. com. Conf. Editors Learned Jours.-MLA, 1975— ; del. to Fgn. Lang. Jours., 1977— ; mem. adv. bd. Commn. on Tech. and Cultural Transformation, UNESCO, 1978— ; vis. fellow Humanities Research Centre, Australian Nat. U., 1979; rep. U.S. woman playwright Inter-Am. Women Writers Congress, Ottawa, Ont., Can., 1978; organizer, chmn. profl. symposia, meetings; TV appearances; hostess Mags. in Focus, Channel 31, N.Y.C., 1971-72; mem. N.Am. Adv. Council Shakespeare Globe Theatre Center, 1981— ; mem. Nat. Grad. Fellows Program Fellowship Bd., 1985— ; mem. Nat. Garibaldi Centennial Com., 1981; mem. Nat. Grad. Fellows Program, 1985—; trustee Edn. Scholarship, Grants Com. of NIAF, 1990—; guest speaker with E. Albee Ohio No. State U., 1990. Author (with H. Paolucci) books, including: Hegel On Tragedy, 1962, new edition, 2001, From Tension to Tonic: The Plays of Edward Albee, 1972, new edit., 2000, Pirandello's Theater: The Recovery of the Modern Stage for Dramatic Art, 1974, Henry Paolucci: Selected Writings on Literature and the Arts; Sci. and Astronomy; Law, Govt., and Pol. Sci., 1999, Dante's Gallery of Rogues, 2001, Do Me a Favor (and other short stories), 2001, Poems Written for Sbek's Mummies, Marie Menken, and Other Important Persons, Places, and Things, 1977, Eight Short Stories, 1977, Sepia Tones, 1985, 2nd edit., 1986; plays include: Minions of the Race (Medieval and Renaissance Conf. of Western Mich. U. Drama award 1972), Cipango!, 1985, pub. as book, 1985, 86, videotape excerpts, 1986, revision, 1990; performed N.Y.C. and Washington, 1987-88, Winterthur Mus., U. Del., 1990; The Actor in Search of His Mask, 1987, Italian translation and prodn., Genoa, 1987, The Short Season, Naples, 1967, Cubiculo, N.Y., 1973, German translation, Vienna, 1996, mini-prodn. of Minions of the Race, The Players, 1999, In the Green Room (play), 1999, Three Short Plays, 1995; poems Riding the Mast Where It Swings, 1980, In the Green Room (orig. play), 1999; Gorbachev in Concert, 1991, Queensboro Bridge (and other Poems), 1995 (Pulitzer prize nominee 1995-96), Terminal Degrees, 1997; contbr. numerous articles, rev. to profl. jours.; editor, author introduction to: Dante's Influence on American Writers, 1977; gen. editor tape-cassette series China, 1977, 78; founder Coun. on Nat. Lit.; gen. editor series Rev. Nat. Lits., 1970-2000, CNL/Quar. World Report, 1974-76, semi-ann., 1977-84, ann., 1985-2000; full-length TV tape of play Cipango! for pub. TV and ednl. TV with original music by Henry Paolucci, 1990; featured in PBS psl. Italian-Americans II: A Beautiful Song, 1998. Pres. Reagan appointee Nat. Grad. Fellows Program Fellowship Bd., 1985—86, Nat. Coun. Humanities, 1986—, Ann. award FIERI, 1990; bd. dirs. Am. Soc. Italian Legions of Merit, chmn. cultural com., 1990—; bd. dirs. Italian Heritage and Culture City-wide com., 1986—; pres. Columbus: Countdown 1992 Fedn.; mem. Gov. Cuomo's Heritage Legacy Project for Schs., 1989—; trustee CUNY, 1996—, chairwoman bd. trustees, 1997—99; mem. adv. com. on edn. N.Y. State Senate, 1996—. Named one of 10 Outstanding Italian Ams. in Washington, awarded medal by Amb. Rinaldo Petrignani, 1986; named Cavaliere Italian Republic, 1986, "Commendatore" of the Italian Republic Order of Merit, 1992; recipient Notable Rating for Mags. in Focus series N.Y. Times, 1972, Woman of Yr. award Dr. Herman Henry Scholarship Found., 1973, Amita award, 1970, award Women's Press Club N.Y., 1974, Order Merit Cavaliere, Commendatore Italian Republic, 1986, Gold medal for Quincentenary Can. trustee NIAF, 1990, ann. awards Consortium of Italian-Am. Assns., 1991, Am.-Italian Hist. Assn., 1991, 1st Columbus award Cath. Charities, 1991, Leone di San Marco award Italian Heritage Coun. of Bronx and Westchester Counties, 1992, Children of Columbus award Order of Sons of Italy in Am., 1993, 1st Nat. Elena Cornaro award Order of Sons of Italy, 1993, Golden Lion award, 1997, Ann. award Am. Italian Cultural Roundtable, 1997, Am. Italian Tchrs. Lifetime Achievement award, 1997, Italian-Am. Legislator's award, Albany, 1997, N.Y. State Italian-Am. Legis. Lifetime Achievement award, 1997, Columbus Citizens Fedn. Ann. award, 1997, Italian Welfare League award, 1998, Queens Coun. on Arts award, 1998, N.Y. State Conservative Party Bronx com. award, 1998, Woman of Distinction award Kingsborough C.C./CUNY, 1999; Columbia U. Woodbridge hon. fellow, 1961-62; Am. Coun. Learned Socs. grantee Internat. Pirandello Congress, Agrigento, Italy, 1978; recipient Woman of Distinction award N.Y. State Senate, 2000. Mem. Internat. Shakespeare Assn., Shakespeare Assn. Am., Renaissance Soc. Am., Internat. Comparative Lit. Assn., Am. Comparative Lit. Assn., MLA, Am. PEN, Hegel Soc. Am., Dante Soc. Am. (v.p. 1976-77), Am. Found. Italian Arts and Letters (founder, pres.), Pirandello Soc. (pres. 1978-85), Am. Soc. Italian Legions of Merit (bd. dirs. 1990-93). *My own first practical premise has been to organize every task (even routine chores) so that there is always time and energy for whatever important projects come up. There is enough room in the day for doing a number of things— and for creating "space" every so often to do one's own special work (writing fiction or poetry or plays, in my case). Organization is all-important; but perhaps the basic premise in intellectual things is organic growth, letting "in" those things that are meaningful because they already suggest an intrinsic pattern. In my case, I discovered long after the projects and books themselves had taken shape and had been published, that I had been tending for a number of years more and more exclusively toward drama and dramatic criticism and theory. Well, that, obviously, was my own potential "law" organizing from within my various interests. One must continue to allow for new interests to revitalize those already familiar.*

PAOLUCCI, ROBERT D. translator; b. Quincy, Mass. s. Salvatore and Adelina (Romano) P. BA, Don Bosco Coll. Translator, N.Y.C. Author: Middle East Maelstrom; translator: The Tree of Knowledge, The Church: Icon of the Trinity, He Loved Them to the End, Italian, Spanish, French, Portuguese and Latin. Mem. Editl. Freelancers Assn. Roman Catholic. Avocations: acting, singing, theatrical production. Home: 433 W 45th St New York NY 10036-3586 E-mail: robertp@gis.net.

PAOLUCCI, UMBERTO, information technology executive; b. Ravenna, Italy; M in Elec. Engring., DHC in Info. Tech. and Bus. Stats., Bologna (Italy) U. Prof. High Tech. Sch., Italy; systems analyst Hewlett-Packard Co.; various mgmt. pos. Gen. Automation; gen. mgr. in charge of establishing and running Italian subs. Microsoft, Redmond, Wash., 1985, regional dir., So. European region, corp. v.p., Europe, Middle East and Asia (EMEA) region. Office: One Microsoft Way Redmond WA 98052-6399*

PAONE, PETER, artist; b. Phila., Oct. 2, 1936; s. George and Angelina (Vitrella) P.; m. Alma Alabilikian, 1976. BA, Phila. Mus. Coll. Art, 1958. Instr. Phila. Mus. Coll. Art, Pratt Inst., others; head graphics dept. Fleisher Art Meml., 1959-62; tchr. Pa. Acad. Fine Arts, 1978— , also chmn. graphics dept.; instr. Positano Art Sch., Italy, 1961 One man shows include Ft. Worth Mus., 1963, Grippi Gallery, 1959, 60, 61, Phila. Print Club, 1961-64, 83, Robinson Gallery, Houston, 1978-79, Pa. Acad. Fine Arts, 1983, Ryder Coll., Pa., 1991, Merlin Verlag, Hamburg, Germany, 1996; exhibited in group shows at Phila. Mus. Art, 1960, 61, 63, Contemporary Am., 1961, Lehigh (Pa.) U., Bklyn. Mus., 1962, Paris Biennial, 1963, Dallas Mus., Otis Art Inst., L.A., Syracuse U., 1964, La Escuela Nacional, Mexico City, Vanderbilt U., N.Y. World's Fair, Exhbn. Pakistan, 1967, Clydie Jessop Gallery, London, 1968, David Gallery, Houston, Kennedy Gallery, N.Y.C., 1970-72, Hooks-Epstein Gallery, 1978, 80, 81, 82, 83, 85, 87, 88, 90, Rider Coll. N.J., 1991, Merlin Verlag, 1996, Dresden, Germany, 1996, Pascal Robinson Gallery, Houston, 2000, 176 Ann. 2001 Nat. Acad. Design, N.Y.C.; represented in permanent collections of Libr. of Congress, Phila. Mus. Art, Sumner Found., N.Y. Mus. Modern Art, Princeton Libr., Phila. Libr., Gen. Mills, Phila. Print Club, Rosenwald Collection, Carl Sandburg Meml. Libr., Syracuse U., Ft. Worth Mus., Victoria and Albert Mus., Brit. Mus., Art Inst. Chgo., Yale U.; artist of the Commonwealth Realism in Pa. Painting, 1950-2000. Recipient award of merit Phila. Print Club, 1983, Painting prize Nat. Acad., 199y; Tiffany Found. grantee, 1962, 64; John Simon Guggenheim fellow, 1965-66; grantee Penn Council for the Arts, 1985. Mem. NAD (assoc.) Home: 1027 W Westview St Philadelphia PA 19119-3718 E-mail: ppaone@aol.com. *Somewhere between the world of realism and surrealism, there is a world that deals with the reality of relationships, favoring the substance of the imagination rather than the substance of everyday vision. Objects that seemingly have no real relationship to each other in their existence are juxtaposed in the life of the artist. They have touched each other and have become part of the vision, and in turn have become his iconography. There is no urgency in this vision. The private reality has always been there and always will be. The viewer is allowed to question his knowledge of it, and in doing so, he often is uneasy and bewildered before the assemblage. This, at first, implies fantasy; this is not true. Instead, this is a reconstruction of reality, not an escape from it.*

PAONESSA, M. SUZANNE, budget analyst; b. Albany, N.Y., May 1, 1974; d. Thomas and Mary Laura (Maresca) P. BS in Fin., Siena Coll., 1996. Fin. mgmt. specialist U.S. Dept. Energy, Schenectady (N.Y.) Naval Reactors Office, 1996-99; assoc. dir. fin. aid Siena Coll., 1999-2001; assoc. dir. budget and bus. svcs. U. Maine, Orono, 2001—. Treas. Schenectady Naval Reactors Office Employee Assn., 1997-98. Co-dir. Siena Coll. Friendly's Fanfest, 1997-98; mem. Siena Coll. Career Advisory Network; vol. instr. Maine Hello Program. Mem.: Nat. Youth Sports Coaches Assn., Sigma Beta Delta, Delta Epsilon Sigma, Alpha Kappa Alpha, Kensho-Do Karate Club (asst. instr. 1998—2000), DOE Women's Golf League (treas. 1998—, named Most Improved Player 1998), 21st Century Leaders Soc., Fin. Mgmt. Assn. Roman Catholic. Avocations: karate (brownbelt), golf, yoga, softball. E-mail: sqboo@yahoo.com.

PAPA, MICHAEL JOSEPH, real estate broker; b. Bklyn., Sept. 29, 1948; s. Joseph and Lena Helen (Bellofatto) P.; m. Lana Susan Turner, Oct. 30, 1967 (div. Dec. 1969); 1 child, Dawn Michelle; m. Barbara Moehringer-Papa, May 17, 1992 (div. Dec. 1997). Lic. Real Estate Broker, Fla. Real Estate Careers, Orlando, 1992; Lic. Mortgage Broker, Kambuck Inst., Inc., Orlando, 1994. Pres. Universal Trading Co., Huntington, N.Y., 1969-70; v.p. Interspec Trading, Inc., Lake Grove, 1970-72; pres. Quality World Ctrs., Inc., Deer Park, 1973-83, Jewels By Shalet, Inc., Deer Park, 1983-87; v.p. Quality Treasures, Inc., Patchogue, N.Y., 1980-81; pres. Select Acquisitions, Inc., Denver, 1987-91, Watches "R" Us, Inc., Smithtown, N.Y., 1988-91, Time for You, Inc., Smithtown, 1989-91, Progressive Realty Am., Inc., Cocoa, Fla., 1993—; owner Success Foundation.com., 1998—, Realty Executives Specialists, Sacramento, 2000—. Pres. Investors Home Realty, Inc., Cocoa, All Svc. Mortgage of Am., Universal Satellite, Success Found., 1998—; real estate and mortgage broker, owner realty-execs. specialists, Sacramento, 2000. Author: "Good Communication" A Lost Art, 1998. Cert. Housing and Urban Devel., Brevard County, Fla., 1994-95. Mem. Rosicrusian Order (guard 1980-89). Avocations: holography, lighting effects, weapons, coins and stamps, 1st Degree Black Belt/Moo Do Kwan Tang Soo Do-Tai Kwan Do. Home: 5740 Audrey Way Fair Oaks CA 95628-3004 Office: Realty Execs 165A Commerce Cir Sacramento CA 95815-4201 Fax: 916-966-1231. E-mail: michaelpapa@realtyexecutives.com.

PAPA, VINCENT T. insurance company executive; b. N.Y.C., Dec. 11, 1946; s. Frank R. and Carmela (Farruggia) P.; m. Karen Ann Conroy, July 4, 1969; children: Kimberly, Jennifer, Kristen. AA, Nassau C.C., 1967; BBA, Hofstra U., 1969. CPA, N.Y. Staff acct. Arthur Andersen & Co., N.Y.C., 1969-72; comptr. Finserv Corp., 1972-80; sr. v.p. Orion Capital Corp., 1980-99; chmn. bd. dirs. Wm. H. McGee & Co. Inc., 1995-99; CEO NYMAGIC Inc., 1999. Mem. AICPAs, Am. Mgmt. Assn. (mem. ins. and risk mgmt. coun.), N.Y. State Soc. CPAs.

PAPACHRISTOU, CHRISTOS A. engineering educator; b. Chalkis, Greece, Mar. 27, 1943; s. Apostole and Helen Papachristou; m. Patricia Washburn; children: Markos. PhD, Johns Hopkins U., 1974; MSEE, Philips Technol. Inst., Eidhoven, Holland, 1965; BSEE, Nat. Poly. U., Athens, 1964. Cert. profl. engr., 1965. Asst. prof. Drexel U., Phila., 1974—78; assoc. prof. U. of Cin., 1978—85, Case Western Res. U., Cleve., 1985—90, prof., 1990—2002. Cons. Ind. Cons. Svc., Cleve., 1990—2002. Grantee, NSF, 1999—2002, NASA, 1989—93, 2001—02, US Army Rsch. Office, 1981—85, Semiconductor Rsch. Corp. (SRC), 1989—93, 1994—98, Rsch. Indsl. Grant, Rockwell, 1996—2001. Mem.: Assn. for Computing Machinery (program committees 1987—95, SIGDA Faculty Awards 1988—89), IEEE (conf. program committees 1990—2002, Svc. Award in Microarchitecture Cmty. 1990). Office: Case Western Reserve University 10900 Euclid Ave Cleveland OH 44106 Business E-Mail: cap2@po.cwru.edu.

PAPACHRISTOU, PATRICIA TOWNE, economics educator; b. Hartford, Conn., Oct. 16, 1946; d. George Robert and Lois Katherine (Stretch) Towne; m. Gerald Christopher Papachristou, Aug. 23, 1969; children— Mark Andrew, Angela Marie. B.A. in Polit. Sci. cum laude, Trinity Coll., Washington, 1968; M.A. in Polit. Sci., Duke U., 1970; M.A. in Econs., Memphis State U., 1975, M.B.A., 1979; postgrad. U. Miss., 1979— . Tchr., chairperson social studies dept. Immaculate Conception High Sch., Memphis, 1971-78; instr. Christian Bros. Coll., Memphis, 1980-84, asst. prof. economics, 1984-87, assoc. prof. econ., 1988-95, prof. econs., 1995—; intern Kaiser-Permanente Health Services Research Ctr., Portland, Oreg., summer 1984. Contbr. articles to profl. jours. Non-service fellow U. Miss., 1979-80; Jane Cassels Record scholar Kaiser Health Research Ctr., 1983. Mem. Am. Econ. Assn., Atlantic Econ. Soc., MidSouth Economists, Missouri Valley Econ. Assn., Omicron Delta Epsilon, Pi Gamma Mu, Delta Sigma Pi. Roman Catholic. Avocations: bridge, camping. Home: 2858 Shelley Cv Memphis TN 38115-1814 E-mail: ppapachr@cbu.edua.

PAPADAKIS, CONSTANTINE N. university executive; b. Athens, Greece, Feb. 2, 1946; came to U.S., 1969; s. Nicholas and Rita (Masciotti) P.; m. Eliana Apostolides, Aug. 28, 1971; 1 child, Maria. Diploma in Civil Engring., Nat. Tech. U. Athens, 1969; MS in Civil Engring., U. Cin., 1970; PhD in Civil Engring., U. Mich., 1973. Registered profl. engr., Ohio, Greece. Engring. specialist, geotechnical group Bechtel, Inc., Gaithersburg, Md., 1974-76, supr. and asst. chief engr. geotechnical group Ann Arbor, Mich., 1976-81; v.p., bd. dirs. water resources div. STS Cons. Ltd., 1981-84; v.p. water and environ. resources dept. Tetra Tech-Honeywell, Pasadena, Calif., 1984; head dept. civil engring. Colo. State U., Ft. Collins, 1984-86; dean Coll. Engring. U. Cin., 1986-95, dir. Groundwater Rsch. Ctr., 1986-95; dir. Ctr. Hill Solid and Hazardous Waste Rsch. Ctr. EPA, Cin., 1986-93; pres. Drexel U., Phila., 1995—. Adj. prof. civil engring. U. Mich., 1976-83; cons. Gaines & Stern Co., Cleve., 1983-84, Honeywell Europe, Maintal, Fed. Republic of Germany, 1984-85, Arthur D. Little, Boston, 1984-85, Camargo Assocs., Ltd., Cin., 1986, King Fahd U. Rsch. Inst., Dhahran, Saudi Arabia, 1987, King Abdulaziz City for Sci. and Tech., Riyadh, Saudi Arabia, 1991, Henderson & Bodwell Cons. Engrs. Inc., 1991, Cin. Met. Sewer Dist., 1992, Ohio River Valley Water Sanitation Commn., 1994; acting pres. Ohio Aerospace Inst., 1989-90; interim pres. Inst. Advanced Mfg. Scis. Ohio Edison Tech. Ctr., 1989-90; bd. govs. Edison Materials Tech. Ctr., 1988-95; adv. bd., founding mem. Hamilton County Bus. Incubator, 1988-95; bd. dirs. Nat. Commn. for Coop. Edn., U. City Sci. Ctr., Ben Franklin Tech. Ctr., WHYY Inc., Fidelity Fed. Bank, Opera Co. of Phila., Corcell, Inc., Greater Phila. First, Hellenic Coll./Holy Cross Acad. Author: Problems on Strength of Materials, 1968, Sewer Systems Design, 1969; editor: Fluid Transients and Acoustics, 1978, Pump-Turbine Schemes, 1979, Small Hydro Power Fluid Machinery, 1982; Megatrends in Hydraulics, 1987; contbr. more than 65 articles to profl. jours. Mem. Greater Cin. C. of C. Blue Chip Campaign for Econ. Devel. Task Force, 1988-93, bd. dirs. Bus. Assistance Ctr., 1989-95; mem. Ohio Coun. on Rsch. and Econ. Devel., 1988, Ohio Sci. and Tech. Commn. Adv. Group, 1989-90, 92-95; coun. mem. St. Nicholas Ch. Parish, Ann Arbor, 1981-84; mem. City of Ft. Collins Drainage Bd., 1984-86; bd. dirs. Dan Beard coun. Boy Scouts Am., 1995, Intelligent Vehicle Hwy. Soc. Ohio, 1994-95; bd. dirs. Liberty Bell Coun. of the Boy Scouts of Am., 1996—. Recipient Horace W. King scholarship civil engring. dept. U. Mich., 1971-73, 6 Bechtel Merit awards, 1974-79, Young Engr. of Yr. award Mich. Soc. Profl. Engrs., Ann Arbor, Mich., 1982, Disting. Engr. award Engrs. and Scientists Cin. Tech. Socs. Coun., 1989, Acad. of Achievement in Edn. award Am. Hellenic Ednl. Progressive Assn., 1995, Hellenic Univ. Club of Phila. Achievement award, 1996, Krikos Disting. Hellene Leader award, 1996. Fellow ASCE (pres. Ann Arbor br. 1980-81, pres.-elect Mich. sect. 1983-84, hydraulics divsn. publ. com. 1980-83), ASME (chmn. fluid transients com. 1978-80, mem. fluids engring. divsn. awards com. 1981-84), Am. Soc. Engring. Edn.; mem. NSPE (legis. and govt. affairs com. 1994-95, chair profl. engrs. in edn. divsn. 1995), Order of the Engr., Internat. Assn. for Hydraulic Rsch., Ohio Engring. Dean's Coun. (chmn.-elect 1989-91), Rotary, Sigma Xi, Chi Epsilon, Tau Beta Pi. Greek Orthodox. Avocations: photography, classical music, travel, swimming, racquetball. Home: 75 Crestline Rd Wayne PA 19087-2611 Office: Drexel Univ Main Building 310 3141 Chestnut St Philadelphia PA 19104-2875*

PAPADAKIS, EMMANUEL PHILIPPOS, physicist, consultant; b. N.Y.C., Dec. 25, 1934; s. Philippos E. and Helen (Eastman) P.; m. Stella Christopher, Sept. 4, 1960; children: Susan H., Philip E., Christopher E., Nicholas E. S.B. in Physics, M.I.T., 1956, PhD in Physics, 1962; M.M. in Mgmt, U. Mich., 1979. Mem. tech. staff Bell Telephone Labs., Allentown, Pa., 1962-69; dept. head Panametrics, Inc., Waltham, Mass., 1969-73; prin. staff engr. Ford Motor Co., Detroit, 1973-75, supr., 1975-87; ptnr. E&S Antiques, 1978—; pres. Quality Sys. Concepts Inc., 1991—; assoc. dir. Ctr. for Nondestructive Evaluation, Iowa State U., Ames, 1988-95. Adj. prof. Northeastern U. ext., Waltham, 1970-73, elec. engring. and computer engring. Iowa State U., 1988-95; cons. quality, NDT, TQM, ISO-9000, acoustics and ultrasonic testing sys., 1969-73, 88—. Contbr. numerous articles on electronics, ultrasonics, acoustics, nondestructive testing and quality to profl. jours.; tech. editor Materials Evaluation, 1988—; reviewer various jours. in physics, testing materials and sci. instrumentation; guest editor for Academic Press, 1995-2000; reviewer proposals to various govtl. agencies; patentee in field. Fellow IEEE, Acoustical Soc. Am. (Biennial award 1968), Am. Soc. for Nondestructive Testing (Mehl honor lectr. 1979, tutorial award 1993); mem. ASTM, Am. Phys. Soc., Soc. Mfg. Engrs., Am. Soc. Metals, Am. Soc. Quality, Am. Foundrymen's Soc., Soc. Automotive Engrs., Soc. Engring. Mechanics, Sigma Xi. Achievements include developing method and instrument for measuring ultrasonic velocity, method for bonding thin slabs to substrates, instrument for sheet metal texture determination, method using DSSS in ultrasonic flaw detection, method to calculate effect of quality on profitability quantitatively, new economic field of nanoeconomics. Office: QSC Inc 379 Diem Woods Dr New Holland PA 17557-8800

PAPADAKIS, PANAGIOTIS AGAMEMNON, financier, international business executive; b. Athens, Greece, Mar. 29, 1935; s. Agamemnon Ioannou and Anna Karyatis (Kyriakopoulou) P.; m. Alexandra Argyropoulou, July 12, 1959. Student, U. Athens, 1953-57. Registered rep., Del., Athens, Greece, Zurich, Switzerland, Washington, 50 other countries. Pub., owner newspaper Peristeri, Athens, 1953-64; owner, gen. dir. printing house, advt. office, ins. agy., 1953-64; leader Nat. Radical Party Youth, 1958-59; founder, gen. dir. Servis Advt., 1963-78, Book-Servis, Athens, 1974-78; pres. Investments Promotions and Assocs. of Chgo., 1979-85; chmn. Internat. Investments World Co. Inc., Athens and Zurich, 1985—, Internat. Bus. Co. Inc., Internat. Comml. Co. Inc., Athens and Zurich, 1985—, Papadakis Internat. Fin. Co. Inc., Guarantor Co. Inc., Athens and Zurich, 1992—, Internat. Banker Fin. Co. Inc., Athens and Zurich, 1992—. Chmn. Internat. Pap Financing and Investment Group, Vaduz Liechtenstein, Konekt Financing Investment Group AG, Griscaviation AG, Graubunden, Switzerland. Author, editor: Historical Biography of President Karamanlis, 1974-77; author: Why the Revolution of 21 April 1967 Happened, 1968; author numerous articles in Recently Humanity '93, Human Rights. Mem. Internat. C. of C., Internat. Soc. Financiers, World Trade Ctr. of Basel, Acad. Scis. Zurich (hon.), Assn. de Soutier A L'Universite De Dalout (hon.). Mem. New Democracy Party. Christian Orthodox. also: 1329 Connecticut Ave NW Washington DC 20036-1846 Office: Internat Invest World Co Inc PO Box 140 88 115 10 Athens Greece also: Bahnhofstrasse 52 8001 Zurich Switzerland also: 24 Pontou St Ilisia 115 28 Athens Greece

PAPADAKOS, DOROTHY JEAN, composer, organist; b. Coral Gables, Fla., Oct. 22, 1960; d. Peter James Papadakos and Dorothy Mae Johnson. BA, Barnard Coll., 1982; MM, Juilliard Sch., 1986. Organist, choirmaster St. Mark's Ch., Islip, N.Y., 1980-85; asst. organist Cathedral of St. John the Divine, N.Y.C., 1987-89, cathedral organist, 1990—. Artistic dir. Vespers Improvisation Series, Cathedral St. John the Divine, N.Y.C., 1995; mem. Paul Winter Consort, Litchfield, Conn., 1984—; project dir. Gt. Organ Restoration Fund, Cathedral St. John the Divine, N.Y.C., 1990—. Composer: (orch. works for ballet) Triantafilia, 1992, Overture and Variation in E flat, 1991; improviser, performer: (CD rec.) Dorothy Over the Rainbow, 1996, (commd. mass) Missa Divinum Mysterium, 1996; incidental music for Mona 7, 1997. Mem. adv. bd. AIDS Action, Internat., N.Y.C., 1994—. Composition grantee Meet the Composer, 1991, 92. Mem. ASCAP, Am. Guild Organists (1st prize N.Y.C. chpt. 1983). Democrat. Episcopalian. Avocations: travel, astronomy, mythology, antique furniture. Home and Office: Cathedral St John Divine 1047 Amsterdam Ave New York NY 10025-1747

PAPADAKOS, NICHOLAS PETER, retired state supreme court justice; b. Hoboken, N.J., Jan. 24, 1925; s. Petros and Olga (Christopoulou) P.; m. Roula Sakellariou, 1950; children: Peter, James, Thomas BA, Dickinson Coll., 1949; LLB, Columbus Law Sch., Washington, 1952. Bar: D.C. 1952, Pa. 1957, U.S. Supreme Ct. 1975. Atty. Dept. Labor, Washington, 1950-55; office mgr. Pa. Dept. Labor, McKeesport, 1955-57; pvt. practice Pa., 1957-75; judge Ct. of Common Pleas, Pitts., 1976-84; justice Pa. Supreme Ct., 1984-95. Solicitor Versailles Sch. Dist., McKeesport, Pa., 1964-65, Port Vue Borough, Pa., 1969-75, City of McKeesport, 1974-75; instr. in bus. law Pa. State U.-McKeesport, 1960-75; mem. nat. panel arbitrators Am. Arbitration Assn., 1986. Trustee Hellenic Coll./Holy Cross Greek Orthodox Sch. of Theology; mem. charter rev. com. Greek Orthodox Archdiocese Am.; del. World Coun. Hellenes Abroad; Laic chmn. Greek Orthodox Diocese of Pitts.; past mem., past chmn. U.S. Selective Service Bd., McKeesport, Pa., early 1970s; bd. dirs. Mendelssohn Choir, Pitts. Sgt. A.C., U.S. Army, 1943-46; PTO Recipient Ellis Island Medal of Honor. Mem. Pa. State Trial Judges Conf., Greek-Am. Progressive Assn., Am. Hellenic Ednl. Progressive Assn., Tall Cedars Club, Optimists Club, Lions, Elks, Masons. Democrat.

PAPADAKOS, PETER JOHN, critical care physician, educator; b. Bklyn., Feb. 4, 1957; s. John and Irene (Vahaviolos) P.; m. Susan E. Dantoni; 1 child, Yanni. BA, NYU, 1979; MD, CUNY, 1983. Intern, then resident in surgery Roosevelt Hosp., N.Y.C., 1983-85; resident in anesthesiology Mt. Sinai Hosp., 1985-87, fellow in critical care medicine, 1987-88; assoc. prof. anesthesiology and surgery U. Rochester (N.Y.) Sch. Medicine, 1988—, also dir. divsn. critical care medicine, 2000—. Prof. respiratory care SUNY. Editor: (textbook) The Intensive Care Manual, 2001; editor-in-chief Controversies in Critical Care; sect. editor Intensive Care Medicine Jour. Applied Cardiopulmonary Pathophysiology, Internet Jour. Emergency and Intensive Care Medicine, Intensive Care & Shock; contbr. articles to profl. jours., numerous chpts. to books. Trustee Incurable Illness Found., N.Y.C., 1986-88. Recipient rsch. award USN, 1975, Pres.'s citation Soc. Critical Care Medicine, 1996. Fellow Coll. Critical Care Medicine, Am. Coll. Chest Physicians; mem. Shock Soc., Soc. Critical Care, Thoracic Soc. Achievements include research on effect of inverse ratio ventilation and pressure regulated volume control on acute respiratory distress syndrome, research on septic shock and oxygen delivery, basic science work on pulmonary pathophysiology of acute lung failure; research on nitric oxide in treatment of lung failure and acute respiratory distress syndrome. Office: U Rochester 601 Elmwood Ave Rochester NY 14642-0001 E-mail: peter_papadakos@urmc.rochester.edu.

PAPADIAS, CONSTANTINOS BASIL, electrical engineer; b. Athens, Jan. 16, 1969; s. Basil C. and Vassiliki B. Papadias. Diploma of elec. engring., Nat. Tech. U. Athens, 1991; PhD with highest honors, Ecole Nat. Supérieure des Télécomms., Paris, 1995. Cert. engr., Tech. Chamber of Greece. Mem. tech. staff Bell Labs. Wireless Rsch. Lab., Holmdel, NJ, 1997—2002, tech. mgr., 2002—. Author: (book chpt.) Multiple Antenna Transceivers for Wireless Communications, 2002, (stds. contbns.) Downlink improvement through Space-Time Spreading , 1999 (Inclusion in cdma-2000 std. for 3G wireless comms., 1999); contbr. articles to profl. jours. Mem. Hellenic Assn. at Stanford (HELL.A.S), Stanford, 1995—97. Recipient FITNESS project on smart antennas rsch., European Commn., 2001—03, award for grad. studies abroad, Eugenides Found., Greece, 1991, Award for top class undergrad. records, Nat. Bursaries Found. Greece, 1990. Mem.: IEEE, Tech. Chamber of Greece. Achievements include patents for detectors for CDMA systems. Avocations: guitar, swimming, tennis, reading. Office: Bell Labs Lucent Techs Rm R-133 791 Holmdel-Keyport Rd Holmdel NJ 07733-0400 Business E-Mail: papadias@lucent.com.

PAPADIMITRIOU, DIMITRI BASIL, economist, college administrator; b. Salonica, Greece, June 9, 1946; came to U.S., 1965, naturalized, 1974; s. Basil John and Ellen (Takas) P.; m. Rania Antonopoulos; children: Jennifer E., Elizabeth R. BA, Columbia U., 1970; PhD, New Sch. U., 1986. V.p., asst. sec. ITT Life Ins. Co. N.Y., N.Y.C., 1970-73; exec. v.p., sec., treas. William Penn Life Ins. Co. N.Y., 1973-78, also dir.; exec. v.p., provost Bard Coll., 1978—, Jerome Levy prof. econs., 1978—; exec. dir. Bard Ctr., 1980—; pres. Levy Econs. Inst., 1988—. Adj. lectr. econs. New Sch. U., 1975-76; fellow Ctr. for Advanced Econ. Studies, 1983; Wye fellow Aspen Inst.; bd. dirs. William Penn Life Ins. Co. N.Y.; mem. adv. com. Hudsonia, Inc.; bd. govs. Levy Econs. Inst., 1986—; mem. subcoun. capital allocation Competitiveness Policy Coun.; mem., vice-chmn. Congrl. Commn. to Rev. the Trade Deficit; mem. adv. com. Women's World Banking; radio econs. commentator Sta. WAMC, NPR, PRI, Money Radio. Author: Employment Policy Community Development and the Underlcass, 1997, Employment Policy: Theory and Practice, 1998; co-author: Community Development Banking, 1993, A Path to Community Development, 1993, An Alternative in Small Business Finance, 1994, Monetary Policy Uncovered: The Federal Reserve's Experiment with Unobservables, 1994, Targeting Inflation: The Effects of Monetary Policy on the CPI and Its Housing Component, 1996, The Fed Should Lower Interest Rates More, 1998, What to Do With the Surplus, 1998, How Can We Provide for the Baby Boomers in their Old Age?, 1999, Can Social Security Be Saved, 1999, Fiscal Policy for the Coming Recession, 2001; editor, contbr. Profits, Deficits and Instability, 1992, Aspects of Distribution of Wealth and Income, 1994, Stability in the Financial System, 1996, Modernizing Financial Systems, 1998, Employment Policies: Theories and Evidence, 1999; co-editor, contbr.: Poverty and Prosperity in the USA in the Late Twentieth Century, 1993, Financial Conditions and Macroeconomic Performance, 1992; bd. editors Ea. Econ.Jour., Rev. of Income and Wealth; book reviewer Econ. Jour., Ea. Econ. Jour. Bd. dirs. Catskill Ballet Theatre, William Penn Life Ins. Co.; trustee, treas. Am. Symphony Orch. Mem. Am. Econ. Assn., Am.-Hellenic Banker Assn., Royal Econ. Soc., Am. Fin. Assn., Econ. Club N.Y., European Econ. Assn., Eastern Econ. Assn., Econ. Sci. Chamber of Greece, Assn. for Evolutionary Econs., Econ. Club N.Y. Home and Office: Bard Coll Annandale On Hudson NY 12504

PAPADOPOULOS, PATRICIA MARIE, healthcare professional; AAS, No. Va. C.C., 1970; BS, George Mason U., 1988; MS in Edn., Va. Poly. Inst., 1992. RN, Va.; cert. nursing adminstr. Staff nurse ICU, PACU Jefferson Meml. Hosp., Alexandria, Va.; dept. dir. PACU Nat. Hosp. for Orthopedics and Rehab., Arlington, 1977-82, dir. med. surg. dept., 1982-85, house supr., 1985-89, dir. nursing ops. Va., 1989-92; asst. dir. emergency svcs. Potomac Hosp., Woodbridge, 1992-95; dir. ICU Nat. Hosp. Med. Ctr., Arlington, 1995, dir. nursing resources and ops., 1995-97; house adminstr. Pentagon City Hosp. (formerly Nat. Hosp. Med. Ctr.), 1997-99; hosp. analyst USAID, Cairo, 1999-2000; nursing supr. No. Va. Cmty. Hosp., Arlington, 2000—; clin. mgr., ATC, surg. holding Wash. Hosp. Ctr. , 2001—.

PAPAGEORGE, TOD, photographer, educator; b. Portsmouth, N.H., Aug. 1, 1940; s. Theodore and Eileen Elizabeth (Flanigan) P.; m. Pauline Whitcomb, Feb. 3, 1962 (div. 1970); m. Deborah Flomenhaft, June 21, 1987; 1 child, Theo. BA in English Lit., U. N.H., 1962; MA, Yale U., 1979. Lectr. in photography MIT, Cambridge, Mass., 1974-75; lectr. in visual studies Harvard U., 1975-76; Walker Evans prof. of photography Yale U., New Haven, 1978—. Vis. instr. in photography The Parsons Sch. Design, N.Y.C., 1969-72, The Pratt Inst. of Art, N.Y.C., 1971-74, The Cooper Union Sch. Art, N.Y.C., 1971-74; adj. lectr. in photography Queens Coll., N.Y.C., 1972-74. Guest dir. exhbn., Mus. Modern Art, N.Y.C., 1977, Yale Art Gallery, 1981; one-man shows include Light Gallery, N.Y.C., 1973, 79, Cronin Gallery, Houston, 1977, Art Inst. Chgo., 1978, Galerie Zabriskie, Paris, 1979, Stills Photography Group, Edinburgh, Scotland, 1980, Daniel Wolf Gallery, N.Y.C., 1981, 85, Akron (Ohio) Art Mus., 1981, Sheldon Meml. Art Gallery, Lincoln, Nebr., 1981, Franklin Parrasch Gallery, N.Y.C., 1991; group shows include Mus. Modern Art, N.Y.C., 1971, 73, 74, 76, 77, 78, 79, 91, 97, 99, 2002, Lowe Art Mus., Coral Gables, Fla., 1974, Balt. Mus. Art, 1975, Mus. Fine Arts, Boston, 1976, 91, Thomas Gibson Gallery, London, 1976, Galerie Zabriskie, Paris, 1977, 87, U. Colo., 1977, Houston Mus. Fine Arts, 1977, Art Inst. Chgo., 1979, Corcoran Gallery Art, Washington, 1980, Fraenkel Gallery, San Francisco, 1981, Daniel Wolf Gallery, N.Y.C., 1982, 83, 86, Albright-Knox Mus., Buffalo, 1983, The Whitney Mus. Art, N.Y.C., 1983, The Photographer's Gallery, London, 1983, Nat. Mus. Am. Art, Washington, 1984, The Dog Mus., N.Y.C., 1984, The Barbican Nat. Gallery, London, 1985, Light Gallery, N.Y.C., 1985, Centro Reina Sophia, Madrid, Spain, 1987, N.Y. State Mus., Albany, 1987, Worcester (Mass.) Art Mus., 1990, 94, Jewish Mus. Art, Wellesley, Mass., 1990, Musee De La Photographie, Mont-Sur-Marchienne, Belgium, 1991, Franklin Parrasch Gallery, N.Y.C., 1992, Yale Art Gallery, New Haven, 1999, Greenberg Van Doren Gallery, N.Y.C., 1999, others; represented in permanent collections Mus. Modern Art, Art Inst. Chgo., Boston Mus. Fine Arts, Yale U. Art Gallery, Bibliothéque Nationale, Paris, Mus. Fine Arts, Houston, Dallas Mus. Fine Arts, Nat. Mus. Am. Art, Washington, J.B. Speed Mus., Louisville, Seattle Art Mus., Kunsthaus, Zurich, Switzerland, others; commd. by Seagrams Corp., 1975, Mus. Modern Art, N.Y., 1977, AT&T, 1978, Yale U. Art Gallery, 1981, Warner Comm., 1983; author: Walker Evans and Robert Frank: An Essay on Influence, 1981; editor: Public Relations: The Photographs of Garry Winogrand, 1977. Guggenheim fellow, 1970, 77; Nat. Endowment Arts fellow, 1973, 76 Achievements include being subject of numerous articles and publs. Home: 122 Cottage St New Haven CT 06511-2406 Office: Yale U Sch Art PO Box 208339 New Haven CT 06520-8339 E-mail: tod.papageorge@yale.edu.

PAPAGEORGIS, JACK, business owner; b. Gaitani, Zakynthos, Greece, Feb. 19, 1933; came to U.S., 1951; s. Anastasios and Eftihia P.; m. Maria Papageorgis, Oct. 1, 1959 (div. Sept. 1993); 1 child, Marie D. BS, Seton Hall U., 1974, Cert. in Internat. Bus., 1983; MBA, Fairleigh Dickinson U., 1978, Seton Hall U., 1987. Gen. helper Libby's Lunch, Paterson, N.J., 1951-54, cook, 1954-56, counterman, 1956-58, mgr., 1958-63; co-owner, sec., treas. Libby's A Corp., 1963-83, co-owner, pres., 1983-85; officer Passaic County Sheriff's Dept., 1985-88; family svc. specialist III Divsn. Youth Family Svc., Newton-Pompton Lakes, 1990-92; food svc. assoc. Sodexho-Marriott William Paterson U., 1993—. Active St. Nicholas Greek Orthodox Ch., 1970—. Mem. Am Hellenic Progressive Assn. (25th anniversary award 1992), Panzakynthian Brotherhood (sec., v.p.). Home: 441 Preakness Ave Paterson NJ 07502-1100

PAPAI, BEVERLY DAFFERN, library director; b. Amarillo, Tex., Aug. 31, 1949; d. Clarence Wilbur and Dora Mae (Henderson) Daffern; m. Joseph Andrew Papai, Apr. 3, 1976. BS in Polit. Sci., West Tex. State U., Canyon, 1972; MSLS, Wayne State U., 1973. Head extension dept. and Oakland County Subregional Libr. The Farmington Cmty. Libr., Farmington Hills, Mich., 1973-79, coord. adult svcs., br. head, 1980-83, asst. dir., 1983-85, dir., 1985—. Cons. U.S. Office of Edn., 1978, Battelle Meml. Inst., Columbis, Ohio, 1980; presenter in field. Contbr. articles to profl. jours. Bd. dirs. Mich. Consortium, 1987-91, Oakland Literacy Coun., 1998—, vice chair, 2000-01, chair, 2001—; trustee Libr. of Mich., 1989-92, vice chair, 1991, 97-98, chair, 1992; del. White House Conf. on Librs. and Info. Svcs., 1991; founder, treas., fiscal agt. METRO NET Libr. Consortium, 1993—; mem. edn. com. Child Abuse and Neglect Coun. of Oakland County, 1998-2000; mem. Commn. on Children, Youth and Families, 1996—, Multiracial Cmty. Coun., 1995—; chair Edn. and Tng. Com., 2000—. Recipient Athena award Farmington/Farmington Hills C. of C. and Gen. Motors, 1994, Chairperson's Rainbow award, 2001; Amarillo Pub. Libr. Friends Group fellow, 1972, Wayne State U. Inst. of Gerontology fellow, 1972. Mem. ALA (officer), Mich. Libr. Assn. (chair specialized libr. svcs. roundtable 1975, chair conf. program 1982, chair pub. policy com. 1988-89, chair devel. com. 1994-95, chair ann. conf. and program coms. 1995-96, pres. 1996-97, Loleta D. Fyan award 1975), LWV of Mich., Farmington Exch. Club, Coun. on Resource Devel. Democrat. Roman Catholic. Home: 6805 Wing Lake Rd Bloomfield Hills MI 48301-2959 Office: The Farmington Cmty Libr 32737 W 12 Mile Rd Farmington Hills MI 48334-3302 E-mail: papaibev@farmlib.org.

PAPAI, SZILVIA, economist; b. Budapest, Hungary, Feb. 24, 1965; d. Janos Papai and Jolan Bakos; m. William Mitchell Kelly. PhD, Calif. Inst. Tech., 1995. Contbr. articles to profl. jours. Office: U Notre Dame Dept Fin and Bus Econs Notre Dame IN 46556

PAPAIOANNOU, EVANGELIA-LILLY, psychologist, researcher; b. Thessaloniki, Greece, Mar. 22, 1963; came to U.S. 1984; d. Nicholas and Ekaterini (Goulias) P. Bus. studies cert. with high honors, Anatolia Coll., Thessaloniki, 1983; BA in Psychology magna cum laude, Smith Coll., 1986; postgrad., Am. U., 1989; PhD in Philos. Psychology, Georgetown U., 2002. Guest researcher NIH, Bethesda, Md., 1986—. Author articles in press and profl. jours. Active in Hellenic Soc. for the Health Scis., Bethesda, 1987—. Recipient: scholarships Smith Coll. and Anatolia Coll. Mem. APA, Jean Piaget Soc., Internat. Platform Assn., Washington Soc. for Jungian Psychology, Washington Soc. for Jungian Psychology, Washington Accueil, Alliance Francaise, Friends of Goethe Internat., Smith Coll. Alumnae Assn., Japan-Am. Soc. Washington, Anatolia Coll. Alumni Assn., Nat. Mus. Women in the Arts, Brazilian-Am. Cultural Inst., Smith Coll. First Group Scholar, Phi Beta Kappa, Psi Chi. Greek Orthodox. Avocations: modern and jazz dance, classical ballet, horseback riding, travel, fencing. Home: 5225 Pooks Hill Rd Apt 1818N Bethesda MD 20814-6771

PAPAIOANOU, HELEN ANTOINETTE, retired allergist, pediatrician, educator; b. Springfield, Mass., July 21, 1928; d. John Xenophon and Assunta (Raverta) P.. BS, Bates Coll., 1949, DSc (hon.), 1997; MD, Boston U., 1953; MS, U. Mich., 1968. Diplomate Am. Bd. Allergy and Immunology, Am. Bd. Pediatrics. Intern Boston City Hosp., 1953-54, resident in pediatrics, 1954-55, fellow in child psychology, 1956-57; pvt. practice pediatrics Westfield, Mass., 1959-66; resident in pediatrics U. Mich. Hosp., Ann Arbor, 1955-56; fellow in allergy and immunology U. Mich. Med. Ctr., 1966-68; pvt. practice allergy/immunology Grosse Pointe, Mich., 1969-80; dir. allergy Children's Hosp. Mich., Detroit, 1980-91, dir. allergy/immunology tng. program, 1980-91; asst. prof. pediatrics Wayne State U., 1980-91; pvt. practice allergy/immunology Bloomfield Hills, 1991-94; ret., 1994. Chief pediatrics McDowell (Ky.) Meml. Hosp., 1957-59. Pres. Mich. Allergy Soc., Detroit, 1976-77. Fellow Am. Acad. Allergy and Immunology, Am. Acad. Pediatrics; mem. AMA. Home: 353 Neff Rd Grosse Pointe MI 48230-1644

PAPAKONSTANTINO, STACY, English language educator; b. San Francisco, Feb. 27, 1967; d. Demetrios and Eugenia (Yiallely) P. AA, City. Coll. of San Francisco, 1987; BA in English Lit., San Francisco State U., 1989, MA in English Lang. Studies, 1991. Cert. in tchg. composition and postsecondary reading. English, ESL tutor City Coll. of San Francisco, 1986-87, instr. of English, 1991—; Greek instr. Holy Trinity Sch., 1988-90. Chair student grade and file rev. com., City Coll. of San Francisco, 1996—, resource mem. student success com., 1997—, mem. student complaint com., 1997—, mem. composition/lit./reading com., 1996—. Mem. Nat. Coun. Tchrs. of English. Democrat. Orthodox. Avocations: reading, movies and plays, helping needy people, spiritual worship, fitness. Home: 48 Westpark Dr Daly City CA 94015-1055 Office: City Coll San Francisco 50 Phelan Ave San Francisco CA 94112-1821 E-mail: spapak@hotmail.com.

PAPAKOSTAS, ACHILLEAS, telecommunications engineer, researcher; b. Larissa, Greece, Sept. 23, 1967; came to U.S., 1990; s. Ioannis and Dimitra Papakostas; m. Sheila Ann Papakostas, Apr. 27, 1996; children: Maria Margarita, Demitra Eleni, Erini Gianna. MS, U. Mass., 1993; PhD, U. Tex., Dallas, 1996. Cert. engr., Greece. Telecom. engr. NEC Am., Irving, Tex., 1996—. Contbr. articles to profl. jours. Tchr. Greek Orthodox Ch., Dallas, 1994-97; pres. Hellenic Cultural Soc. Dalls, 1996-97. Mem. IEEE, Greek Tech. Chamber, Soc. Indsl. and Applied Math. Avocations: reading, teaching Greek, cycling. Office: NEC Am 6535 N State Hwy 161 Irving TX 75039-2402 E-mail: apapakostas@necam.com.

PAPALEO, ANTHONY See FRANCIOSA, ANTHONY

PAPALEO, LOUIS ANTHONY, accountant; b. N.Y.C., Sept. 15, 1953; s. Domenico Vincent and Antoinette (Pica) P.; children: Leigh, Domenic, Adriana. BS in Acctg., Iona Coll., 1975, MBA, 1986. Staff acct. Papaleo & Co., New Rochelle, N.Y., 1975-80, v.p., 1980-84, pres., 1984—. Enrolled to practice IRS, 1990. Chmn. Downtown Businessman's and Merchants Assn., New Rochelle, 1984. Fellow Nat. Tax Practice Inst. (accredited tax advisor 1996); mem. Nat. Acctg. Assn., N.Y. State Acct. Assn., Nat. Soc. Pub. Accts. Lodges: Masons. Republican. Roman Catholic. Office: Papaleo & Co 3010 Westchester Ave Purchase NY 10577-2535 E-mail: papaleo1@msn.com.

PAPALIA, DIANE ELLEN, human development educator; b. Englewood, N.J., Apr. 26, 1947; d. Edward Peter and Madeline (Borrin) P.; m. Jonathan Finlay, June 19, 1976 (div. 1999); 1 child, Anna Victoria Finlay. AB, Vassar Coll., 1968; MS, W.Va. U., 1970, PhD (NSF fellow), 1971. Asst. prof. child and family studies U. Wis., Madison, 1971-75, assoc. prof., 1975-78, prof., 1978-87, coordinator child and family studies, 1977-79. Adj. prof. psychology in pediatrics U. Pa. Sch. Medicine, 1987-89. Author (with Sally W. Olds and Ruth D. Feldman): A Child's World: Infancy Through Adolescence, 1975, 9th edit., 2002; author: (with others) Human Development, 1978, 8th edit., 2001, Psychology, 1985, 2d edit., 1988; author: (with Harvey Sterns, Cameron J. Camp and Ruth D. Feldman) Adult Development and Aging, 1996, 2d edit., 2002; contbr. articles to profl. jours. Am. Council on Edn. fellow, 1979-80; U. Wis. grantee. Fellow: Gerontol. Soc.; mem.: APA, Nat. Coun. Family Rels., Soc. Rsch. in Child Devel., Am. Psychol. Soc., Psi Chi. Home: 316 E 18th St New York NY 10003-2803 E-mail: depapalia@aol.com.

PAPAMITSAKIS, NIKOLAOS I.H. neurologist; b. Chania, Crete, Greece, Apr. 15, 1968; came to U.S., 1994; s. Ioannis N. and Henrietta E. (Ritsataki) P. MD, U. Crete, 1991. Resident in internal medicine Maimonides Med. Ctr., Bklyn., 1994-95; resident in neurology Mt. Sinai Med. Ctr., N.Y.C., 1995-98; fellow in stroke Oreg. Health Scis. U., 1998-99, Henry Ford Hosp., 1999-2000, sr. staff physician dept. neurology, 2000—. U. Crete scholar, 1996. Mem. AMA, Am. Acad. Neurology, Am. Heart Assn., European Fedn. Neurol. Soc Office: Henry Ford Hosp 2799 W Grand Blvd Detroit MI 48202-2689 E-mail: papa@neuro.hfh.edu.

PAPANEK, GUSTAV FRITZ, economist, educator; b. Vienna, Austria, July 12, 1926; s. Ernst and Helene P.; m. Hanna Kaiser, June 13, 1947; children: Thomas H., Joanne R. Papanek Orlando. BA in Agrl. Econs, Cornell U., 1947; MA in Econs, Harvard U., 1949, PhD, 1951. Economist, dep. dir. program planning for Asia, tech. coop. adminstrn. Dept. State, 1951-53; econ. adv., then dir. adv. group to planning commn. Harvard U., Pakistan, 1954-58, dep. dir., then dir. Devel. Adv. Svc., 1958-70, dir. adv. group to planning commn. Indonesia, 1971-73; prof. econs. Boston U., 1974-92, prof. emeritus, 1992—, chmn. dept., 1974-83, interim dir., 1977-80, dir. Ctr. for Asian Devel. Studies, 1983-90, dir. Asian program, 1991-92; dir., cons. team devel. studies to planning commn. Govt. of Indonesia, 1987-89; pres. Boston Inst. for Developing Econs., Ltd. (BIDE), 1987—; dir. policy adv. team to Federated States of Micronesia, 1995—2002. Cons. on econ. crisis Govt. of Indonesia, 1998—; cons. in field. Author: Pakistan's Development: Social Goals and Private Incentives, 1967, The Indonesian Economy, 1980, Development Strategy, Growth Equity and the Political process in Southern Asia, 1986; co-author: Decision Making for Economic Development, 1971, The Indian Economy, 1988; several other books; contbr. articles to profls. jours. With AUS, 1944-46. Grantee Ford Found., AID, World Bank, UN Devel. Program, UN Univ., HEW, Asian Devel. Bank. Mem. Am. Econs. Assn., Am. Agrl. Econs. Assn., Soc. Internat. Devel. (past mem. exec. com.), Assn. Comparative Econ. Studies (pres. 1982), Assn. Asian Studies (pres. New Eng. conf. 1975-77), Pakistan Econ. Assn. Home and Office: 2 Mason St Lexington MA 02421-6315 E-mail: papanek@bide.com.

PAPAS, GEORGE NICK, bakery company executive; b. Milw., Sept. 21, 1961; s. Nicholas Peter and Angeline (Petropoulos) P. B of Fin., U. Wis. Milw., 1986, MBA, 1988. Baker Nick Papas & Son Bakery, Milw., 1975-81, ptnr.,

1982-89; pres. Papas Bakery, Inc., 1989—. Owner, mgr. various investment properties, Milw., 1985—. Mem. Phi-Hellenic Profl. Soc., Beta Gamma Sigma. Office: Papas Bakery Inc 6055 S Howell Ave Milwaukee WI 53207-6233

PAPASTOITSIS, GRIGORIS, biochemist; b. Athens, Greece, Dec. 2, 1958; came to U.S., 1980; s. George and Mosxa (Zarbis) P.; m. Shaunna L. Harrington, June 18, 1990. BS, Suny Binghamton, Bingahmton, NY, 1985; MA, Suny Binghamton, Binghamton, NY, 1987, PhD, 1990. Scientist Repligen, Cambridge, Mass., 1993—94, Seragen, Hopkington, 1994—96; sr. scientist Serono, Randolph, 1996—98, Millennium Pharma, Boston, 1999—. Lectr. in chemistry Roxbury C.C., Boston, 1992-93. Contbr. articles to profl. publs.; author abstracts in field. Recipient Outstanding Contbr., Millennium Pharma, 2001. Mem. AAAS, N.Y. Acad. Scis. Avocations: snorkeling, racquetball, photography, films. Home: 34 Phillips Street Watertown MA 02472-3918 Office: Millennium Pharma 640 Memorial Drive Cambridge MA 02139 Home Fax: 617-926-3830. E-mail: gpapastoitsis@mac.com.

PAPATHOMAS, GEORGIA NIKOLAKOPOULOU, communications company executive, engineer; b. Kato Achaia, Greece, Sept. 11, 1950; d. Andreas and Corina (Fotopoulou) Nikolakopoulos; m. Thomas Vergil Papathomas, Aug. 15, 1976; children: Lia Natassa, Alexander Vergil. BS in Engrng. Sci., Columbia U., 1973, MS in Engrng. Sci., 1974, PhD in Engrng. Sci., 1978; cert. in bus. devel., U. Pa., 1994; cert. in strategic mktg., Harvard U., 1995. Mem. tech. staff Bell Labs., Murray Hill, N.J., 1978-84, supr. Whippany, 1984-90, program mgr., 1990-93; dir. strategy AT&T, Morristown, 1993-96, dir. ops. Bedminster, 1996-98; v.p. network solutions Lucent Tech., 1998—. Adj. asst. prof. engrng. Rutgers U., New Brunswick, NJ, 1979—82. Sloan Found. rsch. fellow, N.Y.C., 1974. Mem. ASCE, Soc. Women Engrs., Sigma Xi.

PAPAY, FRANCIS ANTHONY, plastic surgeon, researcher; b. Lorain, Ohio, Sept. 24, 1953; s. Frank Steven and Virginia Kay (Plato) P.; m. Patricia Lynn Lake, Dec. 27, 1991 (div. Aug. 1998); m. Michelle Lynn Balsamo, Oct. 28, 2000. BA in Chemistry, Zoology cum laude, Ohio U., 1975; MS in Biomed. Engrng., Case Western Res. U., 1984; MD, Northeastern Ohio U., Rootstown, 1984; profl. fellows program Weatherhead Sch. Mgmt., Case Western Reserve U., 2001. Diplomate Am. Bd. Plastic Surgery, Am. Bd. Otolaryngology, Nat. Bd. Med. Examiners, Am. Bd. Clin. Engrs. Clin. engr. Lake County Meml. Hosp., Willoughby, Ohio, 1976-77; biomed. engr. NASA, Cleve., 1978-79; intern Riverside Meth. Hosp., Columbus, 1983-84; intern in gen. surgery Cleve. Clinic Found., 1984-85, resident in otolaryngology, 1985-89, resident in plastic and reconstructive surgery, 1989-91, clin. staff, 1992—, co-dir. craniofacial-occuloplastic surgery, 1992—, head sect. pediat. plastic surgery, 1992—, head sect. craniofacial plastic surgery, 1995—, co-acad. chairperson dept. plastic surgery sch. medicine, 1995—, dir. cleft palate clinic; fellow craniofacial surgery Primary Childrens Med. Ctr., U. Utah, 1991-92. Preceptor facial plastic surgery New Orleans Facial Plastic Surg. Ctr., 1988; founder, pres. N.E. Ohio Tissue Engrng. Consortium , 1998—; mem. surg. staff Primary Children's Med. Ctr., Salt Lake City, 1991, Holy Cross Hosp., Salt Lake City, 1991; courtesy staff LDS Hosp., Salt Lake City, 1991; asst. prof. Ohio State U.; with dept. plastic reconstructive surgery Fairview Health Sys., Cleve.; dir. craniomaxillofacial clynic Elyria (Ohio) Health Dept., Lake and Ashtabula Counties, Painesville, Ohio; co-dir. Kaiser Permanente Craniomaxillofacial Clinic, Beachwood, Ohio; vis. prof. Hosp. Clinicas Jose San Martin, Buenos Aires, 1997, Hosp. Clinicias Dept. Pediat. Surgery, Puerto Montt, Chile, 1997; mem. Children's Oncology Svcs. Northeastern Ohio, Inc.; presenter in field. Co-author: (chpt.) The Otolaryngologic Clinics of North America: Advance Techniques for Management of Head and Neck Neoplasms, Vol. 24, 1991, Instructional Courses-Otolaryngology-Head and Neck Surgery, Vol. 4, 1991, Complications of Head and Neck Surgery, 1993, Duane's Clinical Ophthalmology, Vol. 2, 1993; mem. editl. bd. Pediat. Perspectives, 1994—; sect. editor Cleft Palate-Craniofacial Jour., 1994, 98, Jour. Craniofacial Surgery, 1998; contbr. articles to Jour. Craniofacial Surgery, Laryngoscope Jour., Annals Plastic Surgery, Otolaryngolgoy, Head and Neck Surgery, Am. Jour. Ophthalmology, Plastic Reconstructive Surgery Jour., Internat. Jour. Aesthetic Restorative Surgery, Archives Pediat. Adolescent Medicine, Jour. Am. Acad. Dermatology, Cleft Palate Craniofacial Jour., Surg. Forum, Facial Plastic Surgery, Jour. Burn Rehab., Operative Techniques Otolaryngology, Head Neck Surgery, Ear Nose Throat Jour., Otolaryngol. Clinic N.Am., Laryngoscope, Am. Jour. Rhinology, Cleve. Clinic Jour. medicine, Archives Otolaryngology, Ear Nose Throat Jour., Ohio State Med. Jour. Prin. Ambulatory Care. Founding mem. Interplast Ohio, surg. vol. mission, Puerto Viejo, Ecuador, 1990, Santiago, Chile, 1991, Temuco, Chile, 1992, Orsono, Chile, 1992, 94, 95, 96, Puerto Montt, 1995, 96; Nat. judge BF Goodrich Collegiate Inventors Program, Cleve., 1997, 98, 99, 2000, 2001; founding mem. Aboutface, Cleve.; trustee Ronald McDonald House, Cleve. Recipient Northeastern Ohio Otolaryngology and Maxillofacial Surgery Rsch. award, 1989, Outstanding Young Men In USA award Jaycees, 1992, Servico Salud Osorno, 1996; Melvin E. Jones Rsch. Found. Meml. scholar, 1981, Maxillofacial Surg. Internat. scholar A-O Synthes, 1990; George and Grace Crile Traveling Surg. fellow U. Basel Kantonspital, 1991, Craniomaxillofacial and Pediat. Plastic Surgery fellow Primary Children's Ctr., 1991-92; grantee Cleve. Clinic Found., 1987-88, 90-96, 98, U. Utah, 1992-93, Calif. Birth Defects Monitoring Program, 1995, NIH, Leibinger Surg., others. Fellow ACS, Am. Acad. Pediat., Am. Acad. Otolaryngology; mem. AAAS, Internat. Coll. Surgeons, Internat. Soc. Craniofacial Surgeons, Lipoplasty Soc. N.Am. (continguing med. edn. com.), Am. Cleft Palate-Craniofacial Assn. (internat. rels. com., publs. com.), Am. Soc. Plastic Reconstructive Surgeons (ednl. tech. com., internat. rels. com., managed care com., rep. young plastic surgeons com.), Am. Rhinologic Soc., Assn. Am. Med. Instrumentation, Am. Bd. Clin. Engrs., Am. Soc. Maxillofacial Surgeons., Utah State Med. Assn., Ohio State Med. Assn. (pres. med. student sect. 1983, coun. 1983, Student Leadership award 1983), Ohio Valley Soc. Plastic Reconstructive Surgeons (Resident Rsch. award 1990), Tissue Engrng. Soc., Bur. Children Med. Handicaps, Plastic Surgery Rsch. Coun., No. Ohio Pediat. Soc. (assoc.), Cleve. Med. Soc., Robin Anderson Soc. (founding), A-O Maxillofacial Fellowship Alumni. Republican. Roman Catholic. Achievements include patents for Subcutaneous Mandibular Bone Distractor, Pneumatic Cranial Molding Helmet, Osseous Integrated Bone Anchor, Anti Sids Sleep Cradle. Home: 30548 Royal Woods Pl Westlake OH 44145-3771 Office: Cleve Clinic Found 9500 Euclid Ave Cleveland OH 44195-0001 E-mail: papayf@ccf.org.

PAPAZIAN, DENNIS RICHARD, history educator, political commentator; b. Augusta, Ga., Dec. 15, 1931; s. Nahabed Charles and Armanouhe Marie (Pehlevanian) P.; m. Mary Arshagouni. BA, Wayne State U., 1954; MA, U. Mich., 1958; NDG, Moscow State U., 1962; PhD, U. Mich., 1966. Head dept. social and behavioral scis. U. Mich., Dearborn, 1966-69, head div. lit., sci. and the arts, 1969-73, assoc. dean acad. affairs, 1973-74; dir. Armenian Assembly Am., Washington, 1975-79; dir. grad. studies U. Mich., Dearborn, 1979-85, prof. history, dir. Armenian Rsch. Ctr., 1985—. Fellow Ctr. for Russian and East-European Studies, U. Mich., Ann Arbor, 1982-92; chmn. bd. dirs. Mich. Ethnic Heritage Studies Ctr., U. Mich., 1987-92. Author: St. John's Armenian Church, 1974; editor: The Armenian Church, 1983, Out of Turkey, 1994; editor Jour. of Soc. Armenian Studies, 1994—. Bd. dirs. Armenian Apostolic Soc., Southfield, Mich., 1968-78; chmn. bd. dirs. Alex Manoogian Found., Taylor, Mich., 1969-77; mem. evaluation team Ind. Schs. Assn. Ctrl. States, Chgo., 1985; polit. commentator WXYZ-TV, ABC, Detroit, Southfield, 1984—, WWJ-Radio, Detroit, 1984—; bd. dirs. Southeastern Mich. chpt. ARC, 1988-98, chmn. internat. svcs. com., 1988-98, disaster and mil. family svcs. com., 1988-98. Scholar/diplomat U.S. Dept. State, Washington, 1976; grantee NEH, Washington, 1977, AID, Washington, 1978. Mem. AAUP (chpt. pres. 1962-65), Nat. Assn. Armenian Studies and Rsch. (bd. dirs. 1961-91), Nat. Ethnic Studies Assn. (bd. dirs. 1976-85), Am. Hist. Assn., Soc. Armenian Studies (pres. exec. com. 1988-91, 97—, sec./treas. exec. com. 1991-97), Am. Assn. Advancement of Slavic Studies, Am. Acad. Polit. Sci., Armenian Students Assn. (Arthur S. Dadian Armenian Heritage award 1993), Knights of Vartan. Armenian Orthodox. Avocations: reading; travel. Home: 1935 Bluff Ct Troy MI 48098-6616 Office: U Mich 4901 Evergreen Rd Dearborn MI 48128-1491 E-mail: papazian@umich.edu.

PAPE, PATRICIA ANN, social worker, consultant; b. Aurora, Ill., Aug. 2, 1940; d. Robert Frank and Helen Louise (Hanks) Grover; children: Scott Allen, Debra Lynn. BA in Sociology, Northwestern U., 1962; MSW, George Williams Coll., 1979. Cert. addictions counselor, Ill.; lic. clin. social worker, sch. social worker, Ill. Pvt. practice family counseling, 1979—; coord. community resources DuPage Probation Dept., Wheaton, Ill., 1977-80; dir. The Abbey Alcoholism Treatment Ctr., Winfield, 1980-81; prin. Pape & Assocs., Wheaton, 1982—; dir. alcoholism counselor tng. program Coll. of DuPage, Glen Ellyn, Ill., 1982-87. Chgo. affiliate Employee Assistance Program, 1982—; cons. Luth. Soc. Services Ill., 1979-82. Contbr. articles to profl. jours. Mem. alcohol drug task force Ill. Synod Luth. Ch. Am., Chgo., 1985—. Named Woman of Yr., Entrepreneur Women in Mgmt., Oak Brook, Ill, 1986, Social Worker of Yr. Fox Valley Dist., 1998. Mem. Assn. Labor-Mgmt. Adminstrs. Cons. Alcoholism (women's issues com. 1984—), Acad. Cert. Social Workers, Am. Assn. Marriage Family Therapists, Nat. Assn. Soc. Workers, Women in Mgmt. Home: 26 W 360 Churchill Rd Winfield IL 60190-2104 Office: Pape & Assocs 618 S West St Wheaton IL 60187-5038

PAPE, SHERI, music director, educator, artist; b. Pekin, Ill., Dec. 27, 1961; d. Gerald Barter and Evelyn Lucille Poe; children: Trevor, Jared. BA, No. Ill. U., 1987, postgrad., 1988—; MA in Music Edn., St. Regis U., 2001; CAS in Musical Theater, History, Film, St. Lourdes U., 2002; EdD in Early Chilhood Devel., Blackstone U., 2002. Music dir., educator Pape Piano Conservatory, Rockford, Ill., 1984—. Composer piano solos. Mem. Music Tchrs. Nat. Assn., Ill. State Music Tchrs. Assn., Greater Rockford Music Tchrs. Assn. (scholarship chair 1996-99, historian 1999—), Sigma Alpha iota. Mem. Evang. Free Ch. Am. Avocations: music, art, classic movies. Home and Office: Pape Piano Conservatory 3646 Cavalier Ct Rockford IL 61114

PAPE, STUART M. lawyer; b. Paterson, N.J., Dec. 24, 1948; BA, U. Va., 1970, JD, 1973. Bar: Va. 1973, U.S. Ct. Appeals (6th cir.) 1975, U.S. Supreme Ct. 1976, D.C. 1980. Law clk. to Hon. Leonard Braman Superior Ct. D.C., 1973-74; exec. asst. to commr. FDA, 1979; mng. ptnr. Patton Boggs LLP and predecessors, Washington. Mem. ABA (com. food and drug law, sect. adminstrv. law 1973-2002), Va. State Bar, D.C. Bar. Address: 2950 Chain Bridge Rd NW Washington DC 20016-3408 E-mail: spape@pattonboggs.com.

PAPE, WILLIAM JAMES, II, newspaper publisher; b. Waterbury, Conn., Aug. 14, 1931; s. William B. and Helen (Cronan) P.; m. Patricia Moran, Oct. 15, 1959; children: William B. II, Andrew J. BS, U.S. Naval Acad., 1953; MBA, Harvard U., 1959; LHD (hon.), Teikyo Post U., 1991. Commd. ensign USN, 1953, advanced through grades to lt., 1955, resigned, 1957; asst. treas. Ea. Color Printing Co., Waterbury, 1959-63, pres., treas. Avon, Conn., 1977-87; v.p., asst. treas. Am.-Republican Inc., Waterbury, 1963-64, asst. publisher, comptroller, v.p., treas., 1964-72, pres., 1972—, treas., 1972-98; pub. Waterbury Republican-Am., 1972—, editor, 1988—; also bd. dirs.; v.p., asst. treas. & dir. Paper Delivery, Inc., 1972—. Bd. dirs. Platt Bros., Waterbury. Bd. dirs. Conn. Coun. Freedom of Info., 1968-88, Conn. Bus. and Industry Assn., 1980-83, Naugatuck Valley Devel. Corp., Regional Action Coun., Waterbury, 1991; bd. dirs. Conn. Citizens for Jud. Modernization, pres., 1973-75; bd. dirs. Waterbury YMCA, 1970-78, trustee, 1972-2001, chmn. trustees, 1976-85; trustee Northeast Utilities, 1974-2001, Greater Waterbury Health Network Inc., 1993-95; mem. Conn. Pub. Expenditure Coun. Inc., 1974-77, dir. Conn. policy and econ. coun., 1994—; trustee Teikyo Post U., 1976-96; grants com. Waterbury Found., 1980-87; pub. affairs com. Waterbury Hosp., 1984-90, past trustee; incorporator Conn. Found. for Open Govt. Inc.; active Conn. Legislature Commn. to Study Modernization and Unification of Cts., 1973-75, Citizens for Better Govt. Through Reorganization, 1977. Mem. Am. Judicature Soc. (assoc. dir. 1975-76), New England Newspaper Assn. (Conn. bd. govs. 1983-87), Conn. Bar Assn. (task force conflict of interest 1979), Conn. Daily Newspaper Assn. (pres. 1970, exec. com. 1971-91), Waterbury C. of C. (exec. com., v.p. 1975, chmn. 1977-79, dir. 1980-2001, vice-chmn. transp. 1981-2001), Navy League U.S. (comms. bd. 1982), Waterbury Club, Madison Beach Club, Highfield, Liverpool Nautical Rsch. Soc. Republican. Roman Catholic. Avocations: sailing, firearms, walking, carpentry. Home: Old Sherman Hill Rd Woodbury CT 06798 Office: Waterbury Rep-Am PO Box 2090 389 Meadow St Waterbury CT 06722-2090 E-mail: wjpape@rep-am.com.

PAPELL, HELEN GERTRUDE, poet, retired librarian; b. N.Y.C., Apr. 8, 1924; d. Henry and Anna (Gimpel) Sobel; m. Robert Papell, June 1, 1949; 1 child, David H. BA, U. Mo., 1949; MLS, Pratt Inst., 1969; cert. profl. pub. libr., SUNY, 1973. Libr. trainee Bklyn. Pub. Libr., 1967-69, libr., storyteller, puppeteer, sr. libr., supervising libr., 1969-84; libr., cataloger Jewish Women's Resource Ctr. Nat. Coun. Jewish Women, N.Y.C., 1984-98; ret., 1998. Puppeteer in librs., schls., chs., st. fairs, N.Y.C., Bklyn., 1969-84. Author: (poems) Talking with Eve, Leah, Hagar, Miriam, 1996; contbg. editor Jewish Women's Lit. Ann. Grantee Poets and Writers, 1991, 93. Mem. Nat. Coun. Jewish Women, Phi Beta Kappa. Avocations: reading Judaica, folklore and mysteries, visiting museums, attending plays. Home: 720 W End Ave New York NY 10025-6299

PAPELL, NATHAN, real estate broker, business broker, accountant; b. Bronx, N.Y., Apr. 5, 1931; married. BBA, CCNY, 1956. CPA, N.Y. Acct. various CPA firms, N.Y.C., 1956-68; pres. Federated Bus. Agencies, 1968—. With U.S. Army, 1952-54, Korea. Mem. N.Y. State Soc. CPAs. Office: Federated Business Agencies 15 Hunter Dr Eastchester NY 10709-5205 also: Radio City Sta PO Box 234 New York NY 10101-0234 E-mail: papell@msn.com.

PAPENFUSE, EDWARD CARL, JR. archivist, state official; b. Toledo, Oct. 15, 1943; m. Sallie Fisher; children: Eric, David. BA in Polit. Sci., Am. U., 1965; MA in History, U. Colo., 1967; PhD, Johns Hopkins U., 1973. Assoc. editor Am. Hist. Rev., Washington, 1970-73; asst. archivist Md. Hall of Records, Annapolis, 1973-75, archivist, 1975—, commr. land patents, 1975—. Archivist, state official; b. Toledo, Oct. 15, 1943; m. Sallie Fisher; children: Eric, David. BA in Polit. Sci., Am. U., 1965; MA in History, U. Colo., 1967; PhD, Johns Hopkins U., 1973. Assoc. editor Am. Hist. Rev., Washington, 1970-73; asst. archivist Md. Hall of Records, Annapolis, 1973-75, archivist, 1975—, commr. land patents, 1975—. Author: In Pursuit of Profit: The Annapolis Merchants in the Era of the American Revolution, 1975, (with others) Directory of Maryland Legislators, 1635-1789, 1974, (with others) Maryland: A New Guide to the Old Line State, 1976, The Hammond-Harwood House Atlas of Historical Maps of Maryland, 1608-1908, 1982, Doing Good to Posterity, 1995; also articles and revs. Mem. Johns Hopkins U. Med. Archives. NEH grantee; recipient Disting. Svc. award to State Govt. Nat. Gov.'s Assn., 1985, Marylander of Yr. award Md. Colonial Soc., 1985. Fellow Soc. Am. Archivists, Md. Hist. Soc., Am. Antiquarian Soc. Author: In Pursuit of Profit: The Annapolis Merchants in the Era of the American Revolution, 1975, (with others) Biographical Dictionary of Maryland Legislators, 1635-1789, 1974, (with others) Maryland: A New Guide to the Old Line State, 3d edit., 1999, The Hammond-Harwood House Atlas of Historical Maps of Maryland, 1608-1908, 1982, Doing Good to Posterity, 1995; contbr. articles and revs. to profl. jours. Mem. Johns Hopkins U. Med. Archives. NEH grantee; recipient Disting. Svc. award to State Govt. Nat. Gov.'s Assn., 1985, Marylander of Yr. award Md. Colonial Soc., 1985. Fellow Soc. Am. Archivist, Md. Hist. Soc., Am. Antiquarian Soc. Home: 206 Oakdale Rd Baltimore MD 21210-2520 Office: Md State Archives 350 Rowe Blvd Annapolis MD 21401-1686 E-mail: edp@mdarchives.state.md.us.

PAPENTHIEN, RUTH MARY, fiber artist, retired educator; b. Milw., Aug. 30, 1924; d. Roy Oliver and Hazel Mary (Heyer) P. BA, U. Wis., 1946; student, The Konstfackskolan, Stockholm, 1959-60; MFA, Cranbrook Acad. Art, Bloomfield Hills, Mich., 1965. Elem. sch. tchr. Milw. Pub. Schs., 1948-63; instr. fiber art Alverno Coll., Milw., 1966-67; vis. instr. fiber art Sch. Fine Arts Ohio State U., Columbus, 1967-72; fiber art instr. Arrowmont Sch. Arts and Crafts, Gatlinburg, Tenn., summer 1970; vis. artist fiber art Ball State U., Muncie, Ind., 1972; asst. prof. fiber art Tyler Sch. Art Temple U., Phila., summer 1973. Tchr. Cheley Colo. Camps, Estes Park, 1956-59, 64, 65. One-woman shows include Alverno Coll., Milw., 1967, Ohio State U. Union, Columbus, 1968, The Liturgical Arts, St. Luke's Meth. Ch., Oklahoma City, 1970, exhibited in group shows in Wis. Designer Craftsmen exhbns. at Milw. Arts Ctr. (Anonymous Donor award 1963, 64, Court of Honor 1965, 66, 70, 71), Miss. River Craft Exhbn., Brooks Meml. Art Gallery, Memphis, 1963, Detroit Art Inst., 1964, Rockford (Ill.) Art Assn. Burpee Gallery of Art, 1964, 65 (1st pl. and hon. mention 1966), Rochester (Minn.) Art Ctr., 1967, Capital U., Columbus, Ohio (Liturgical Art award 1967, 71, 73), Coll. of Wooster, Ohio, 1970, Midland (Mich.) Art Ctr., 1972, Ball State U., Muncie, Ind., 1972, S.C. Johnson Collection Contemporary Crafts, 1970-72, Ohio State U., 1972, Huntington Nat. Bank and Trust Co., Columbus, 1972, Ozaukee Art Ctr., Cedarburg, Wis., 1976, West Bend (Wis.) Gallery Fine Arts, 1978, Peninsula Mus. Art, Newport News, Va., 1995, Blue Skies Gallery, Hampton, Va., 1997, 98; represented in permanent collections Alverno Coll., Milw., Ohio Hist. Ctr., Columbus, Ohio Med. Indemnity Inc., Columbus, Karlsberger and Assoc. AIA, Columbus, U. Rochester (N.Y.) Meml. Gallery, IBM Bldg., Columbus, The Prairie Archives, Milw. Art Ctr.; represented in pvt. collections in Ohio, Wis., Fla., La., Calif., Va.; contbr. artwork to jours. Home: 208 Woodmere Dr Williamsburg VA 23185-3935

PAPER, LEWIS J. lawyer, educator; b. Newark, Oct. 13, 1946; s. Sidney and Dorothy (Nieman) P.; m. Jan Clachko, Sept. 4, 1972; children: Lindsay, Brett. BA, U. Mich., 1968; LLM, Harvard U., 1971; JD, Georgetown U., 1972. Bar: D.C. 1971, N.J. 1975, Md. 1984. Fellow Inst. Pub. Interest Representation Georgetown U. Law Sch., Washington, 1971-72; staff atty. Citizens Comms. Ctr., 1972-73; legis. counsel to Sen. Gaylord Nelson U.S. Senate, 1973-75; assoc. atty. Lowenstein, Sandler, Brochin, Kohl & Fisher, Newark, 1975-78; asst. gen. counsel FCC, Washington, 1978-79, assoc. gen. counsel, 1979-81; ptnr. Grove Engelberg & Gross, 1981-86, Keck, Mahin & Cate, 1986-95, Dickstein, Shapiro, Morin & Oshcinsky LLP, Washington, 1995—. Adj. prof. law Georgetown U. Law Sch., Washington, 1983-86. Author: John F. Kennedy: The Promise and the Performance, 1975, 79, Brandeis: An Intimate Biography, 1983, Empire: William S. Paley and the Making of CBS, 1987; contbr. articles to newspapers, mags., and profl. jours. Office: Dickstein Shapiro Morin & Oshinsky LLP 2101 L St NW Washington DC 20037-1526 E-mail: paperl@dsmo.com.

PAPERNIK, JOEL IRA, lawyer; b. N.Y.C., May 4, 1944; s. Herman and Ida (Titefsky) Papernik; m. Barbara Ann Barker, July 28, 1972; children: Deborah, Ilana. BA, Yale U., 1965; JD cum laude, Columbia U., 1968. Bar: NY 1969. Assoc. Shea & Gould, N.Y.C., 1968-76, ptnr., 1976-91; ptnr., chmn. corp. and securities dept., mem. mgmt. com. Squadron, Ellenoff, Plesent & Sheinfeld, 1991-2000; ptnr., chair mergers and acquisitions practice group, mem. bus. fin. dept. and opinion com. Mintz, Levin, Cohn, Ferris, Glovsky and Popeo PC, 2000—. Lectr various panels. With 11th Spl. Forces USAR, 1967—73. Mem.: ABA (sect. corp. law), Negotiated Acquisitions Com., NY Tri-Bar Opinion Com., Assn. Bar City NY (mem. securities regulation com. 1992—95, chmn., lectr., mem. corp. law com.), NY State Bar Assn. (lectr. various panels, mem. securities law com.), NY Biotech. Assn. (lectr. various panels), Yale Club. Office: Mintz Levin Cohn Ferris Glovsky and Popeo PC 666 3rd Ave New York NY 10017-4011 E-mail: jpapernik@mintz.com.

PAPI, LIZA RENIA, artist, writer, educator; b. Malacacheta, Minas Gerais, Brazil, Jan. 19, 1949; came to U.S., 1978; d. Rivadavia and Lair Bronzon P.; 1 child, Mourrice O. BA, Inst. Fine Arts Rio de Janeiro, 1974; MFA, CUNY, 1992. Art instr. CUNY, Henry St. Settlement, N.Y.C., Third St. Music; illustrator Studio T. Graphics. Artist in residence Mus. del Barrio, N.Y.C.; dir. publicity Art Sphere Cultural Ctr., N.Y.C., 1990-91; coord. Americanos, N.Y.C., 1990-94. Author: The Vanishing Beetles, 1991, Carnavalia, African Brazilian Folklore and Crafts, 1994. Residency planning grantee N.Y. Found. Arts, 1994, Anneberg Art-in-Edn. grantee, 1998—. Mem. Soka Gakkai Internat., Coll. Art Assn., The Fgn. Press. Buddhist. Avocations: contemprary dance, biking. Office: Apt 6P 400 Chambers St New York NY 10282-1006

PAPILA, MELIH, aeronautical engineer, researcher, aerospace engineer; b. Ankara, Turkey, Sept. 27, 1968; s. Gonul and Mithat Papila; m. Nilay Uzgoren; children: Ada. BS in Aero. Engrng., Mid. East Tech. U., Ankara, Turkey, 1990, MS in Aero. Engrng., 1995; PhD in Aero. Engrng., U. Fla., 2001. Rsch., tchg. asst. aero. engrng. Mid. East Tech. U., 1990—93; rsch. engr. Roketsan, 1993—97; rsch. asst. aero. engrng. U. Fla., Gainesville, 1997—2001, post-doctoral assoc., 2002—. Vis. engr. structural testing dept. CASA, Madrid, 1992—; cons. Roketsan, Ankara, 1993. Reviewer Jour. Composite Materials. Mem.: AIAA. Avocation: basketball. Office: Univ Fla. 231 Aerospace Bldg Gainesville FL 32611

PAPIRNO, ELISSA, journalist, newspaper editor; b. Bklyn., Aug. 9, 1949; d. Ralph and Cecile (Worby) P. AB, Brandeis U., 1971; MS in La, Yale U., 1978. Reporter Lowell (Mass.) Sun, 1971-72, Hartford (Conn.) Courant, 1972-77, editl. writer, 1978-81, dep. editor editl. page, 1982-94, assoc. editor, reader rep., 1995—. Ford Found. fellow Yale U. Law Sch., 1977-78; fellow Am. Leadership Forum, Hartford, 1994-95, sr. fellow, 1995—. Mem. Nat. Conf. Editl. Writers (exec. bd. 1987-88, 90-91), Orgn. News Ombudsmen (exec. bd. 1996—, v.p. 1999—, pres. 2000—). Office: Hartford Courant 285 Broad St Hartford CT 06115-2510 E-mail: papirno@courant.com.

PAPKE, WILLIAM C. carpenter; b. Rockford, Ill., Dec. 6, 1959; s. Frank Albert Papke and Leah Francis; m. Thayer Anna Marie, Sept. 30, 2000. Grad., Vocat. Ctr., Rockford, 1977. Janitor Humphey Cadillac and Olds, Rockford, 1975; stock boy United Banks, 1975—76; truck driver Rockton (Ill.) Lumber, 1975—76; woodworker Wood Trends Mfg., Rockford, 1985—86; carpenter Rock Valley Coll., 1986—. Foreman Project Playworks, Rockford. Contbr. ; puzzle game. Fellow: Forest City Woodcrafters. Lutheran. Achievements include patents for bookworm bookshelves; lightning bug powered flashlight. Avocations: fishing, arts and crafts, hiking, birdwatching. Home: 11560 Zahm Rd Rockton IL 61072 Office: Rock Valley Coll 3301 Mulford Rd Loves Park IL 61111

PAPKIN, ROBERT DAVID, lawyer; b. New Bedford, Mass., Feb. 26, 1933; s. Barney and Rose (Shuster) P.; m. Rachel Friedberg, Aug. 29, 1965; children: Steven C., Daniel M. AB, Harvard U., 1954, LLB, 1957. Bar: Mass. 1957, D.C. 1964. Legal asst. NRLB, Washington, 1958-61; assoc. Cox, Langford & Brown, 1963-66, ptnr., 1966-73, Squire, Sanders & Dempsey, Washington, 1973—. Trustee Art Svcs. Internat., 1990—. Served with U.S. Army, 1957-58, 61-62. Mem. ABA, D.C. Bar Assn., Fed. Bar Assn., Internat. Bar Assn., Met. Club Washington D.C., Cosmos Club. Democrat. Jewish. Home: 9702 Leeds Landing Cir Easton MD 21601-5564 Office: Squire Sanders & Dempsey PO Box 407 1201 Pennsylvania Ave NW Washington DC 20004-2491 E-mail: rpapkin@ssd.com.

PAPLAUSKAS, LEONARD PAUL, academic administrator, health science educator; b. Wiesbaden, Germany, June 22, 1949; came to U.S., 1950; s. Leonardas and Emilija (Sadauskas) P.; m. Lynn Ellen Verhoeven, Nov. 24, 1972 (div. Jan. 1988); 1 child, Grant Peter; m. Judith Ann Jones, June 30, 1990. BS, Loyola U., 1970; masters equivalent, So. Ill. U., 1972, postgrad. Asst. sec. U.S. adopted names coun. AMA, Chgo., 1974-75; rsch. adminstr. Health & Hosp. Governing Commn., 1975-76; asst. dir. Office Rsch. & Sponsored Programs Northwestern U., Evanston, Ill., 1976-84, dir. Office Rsch. & Sponsored Programs, Med. Sch. Chgo., 1977-84, instr. div. biol. sci. Evanston, 1983-84; instr. dept. natural sci. Loyola U., Chgo., 1982-84; asst. v.p. rsch. U. Conn. Health Ctr., Farmington, 1984-2000, assoc. v.p. rsch. adminstrn., 2000—. Cons. NIH, Bethesda, Md., 1977—. Contbr. articles to profl. jours. Bd. dirs./pres. Currier Woods Assoc./Currier Woods Tax Dist., Cheshire, Conn., 1991—; bd. dirs., exec. com., v.p., corp. sec. Conn. United for Rsch. Excellence, 1990-99. NIH grantee, 1987—. Mem. AAAS, Nat. Coun. Univ. Rsch. Adminstrs., Soc. Rsch. Adminstrs., Mus. of Natural History, Smithsonian Instn. Avocations: skiing, fishing, mountain biking. Office: U Conn Health Ctr 263 Farmington Ave Farmington CT 06030-0002 E-mail: paplauskas@adp.uchc.edu.

PAPP, DANIEL STEPHEN, international affairs educator; b. Cleve., July 11, 1947; s. Stephen Geza and Lucille Louise (Hammer) P.; m. Nancy Wilson, Jan. 14, 1978; children: William, Alexander. BA, Dartmouth Coll., 1969; PhD, U. Miami, 1973. Prof. internat. affairs Ga. Tech, Atlanta, 1973—, dir. Sch. Social Sci., 1980-90, dir. Sch. Internat. Affairs, 1990-94, exec. asst. to pres., 1994-97. Rsch. prof. Army War Coll., Carlisle, Pa., 1977-78, Air War U., Montgomery Ala, 1983-84; vis. prof. Fudan U., Shanghai, 1984; interim pres. So. Poly. State U., Marietta, Ga., 1997-98; cons. to various bus., 1973-98, So. Ctr. for Internat. Studies, Atlanta, 1980-98, U.S. Dept. Def., Washington, various times. Author: Soviet Polices in the Developing World, 1986, Contemporary International Relations, 1997; editor: As I Saw It, 1990; editor, author: The Information Age Anthology, 1997. Recipient Outstanding Civilian Svc. medal U.S. Army, 1979. Mem. Am. Polit. Sci. Assn. (bd. dirs. disarmament sect.),

Am. Assn. for Advancement Slavic Studies, Internat. Inst. for Strategic Studies, Internat. Studies Assn. (chmn. Am.-Soviet sect.), Soc. Internat. Bus. Fellows. Lutheran. Avocations: running, rugby, basketball, skiing, diving. Office: Board of Regents of U System of GA 270 Washington St SW Atlanta GA 30334-1450 Fax: 404-463-6682. Business E-Mail: Dan.Papp@usg.edu.

PAPP, LASZLO GEORGE, architect; b. Debrecen, Hungary, Apr. 28, 1929; came to U.S., 1956; m. Judith Liptak, Apr. 12, 1952; children: Andrea, Laszlo-Mark (dec. 1978). Archtl. Engr., Poly. U. Budapest, 1955; MArch, Pratt Inst., 1960; D of Liberal Arts, Tech. U. Budapest, 1998. Designer Harrison & Abramovitz, Architects, N.Y.C., 1958-63; ptnr. Whiteside & Papp, Architects, White Plains, N.Y., 1963-67; pres. Papp Architects, P.C., 1967-96, chmn., 1996—; exec. dir. Urban Redevel. Commn., Stamford, Conn., 2001—. Mem. Pres.'s Adv. Com. on Pvt. Sector Initiatives, 1980-85; mem. adv. com. Westchester C.C., 1971-75, Iona Coll., New Rochelle, N.Y., 1982-87, Norwalk State Tech. Coll., 1983-95; v.p. Clearview Sch., 1985-89, pres., 1990-91; mem. Town Coun. New Canaan, Conn., 1993-99. Fellow AIA (reg. dir. 1983-85); mem. Internat. Union Architects (rep. habitat com. 1986-90), N.Y. State Assn. Architects (v.p. 1977-80, pres. 1981), Am.-Hungarian Engrs. Assn. (bd. dirs. 1978-90), Am. Coun. World Fedn. Hungarians (pres. 1993-97, regional pres. 1996-2000), Hungarian Univ. Assn. (pres. 1958-60), Westchester County C. of C. (bd. dirs. 1968-71, vice chmn. bd. for area devel. 1983-89, chmn. bd. dirs. 1989-90), Am.-Hungarian C. of C. (charter 1989—). Home: 1197 Valley Rd New Canaan CT 06840-2428 Office: Urban Redevel Commn 888 Washington Blvd Stamford CT 06901 E-mail: papparch@aol.com.

PAPPAS, BARBARA ESTELLE, Biblical studies educator, author; b. Chgo., July 26, 1941; m. George G. Pappas, Sept. 20, 1964; children: Dheanna Pappas Fikaris, Michele Pappas Glavanovits, Laina Pappas Krabbe. Lay asst. Holy Apostles Ch., Westchester, Ill., 1976—. Sec., lectr. Diocese of Chgo. Religious Edn. Commn., 1982—; founder, dir. Holy Apostles Resource Ctr., Westchester, 1984—. Author: Are You Saved?, The Orthodox Christian Process of Salvation, 4th edit., 1997, The Christian Life in the Early Church and Today, Commentaries on Paul's Epistles to the Corinthians, Vol. I, 1989, Vol. II, 1998, God's Bubbly, Gurgly, Overwhelming, Overflowing Love, 2000. Mem. ASCD. mem. Archdiocese Am.Teenage Curriculum Com. Greek Orthodox. Home: 379 Arboretum Cir Wheaton IL 60187 E-mail: ayspappas@msn.com.

PAPPAS, CHARLES ENGELOS, plastic surgeon; b. Phila., May 20, 1946; s.Engelos George and Angelina (Biniaris) P.; children: Evan, Angela, Chrysten. BA, BS, U. Pa., 1968; MD, Temple U., 1972. Intern, then resident in gen. surgery Johns Hopkins Hosp., Balt., 1972-75; resident in gen. surgery Temple U. Hosp., Phila., 1975-76, resident in plastic surgery, 1976-78, clinical fellow cardiac surgery, 1972-73; clinical fellow transplant Harvard Med. Sch., 1973; chmn. dept. plastic surgery Temple U. Hosp., Phila., 1978-81, clin. assoc. prof. surgery, 1981—; chief dept. plastic surgery Meml. Hosp., 1986—; clin. assoc. plastic surgery Chestnut Hill Hosp., 1979—, chief/dir. dept. plastic surgery, 1994—; med. dir. Ft. Washington Surgery Ctr., 1994—. Dir. Inst. for Aesthetic Plastic Surgery, Ft. Washington, Pa., 1985—; chmn. bd. Am. Gaming Industries, 1984—; dir., ptnr. Tristate Quicklube Co., 1982-91, Medars; pres., dir. two carwash cos., Phila., 1989—; med. dir. Fort Washington Surgery Ctr., 1995—, dir., trustee, 1996—; med. dir. Aesthetica, Inc., 1996—; nat. med. dir. Aesthetics Med. Mgmt., Inc., 1996—, med. advisor, 1997—; dir., CEO Spa Aesthetika, 1998—; CEO, dir. Aesthetic Health Care Ctrs., 1999—, SPA Aesthetika, 1999—; founder, CEO Papco Ventures, Inc., 2000--. Contbr. articles to profl. jours. Trustee Germantown Acad., Ft. Washington, 1986—, Commonwealth Nat. Country Club, Horsham, 1988—, Patrons' Charity Found. Fellow ACS, Royal Coll. Surgeons; mem. Am. Soc. Plastic Reconstructive Surgeons (diplomate), Am. Soc. Aesthetic Plastic Surgeons (diplomate), Phila. Soc. Plastic Surgeons (pres. 1990-92). Greek Orthodox. Avocations: golf, tennis, development and investing, skiing. Office: The Aesthetic Health Care Ctr 467 Pennsylvania Ave Ste 202 Fort Washington PA 19034-3420 E-mail: cepmd@aol.com.

PAPPAS, DAVID CHRISTOPHER, lawyer; b. Kenosha, Wis., Mar. 18, 1936; s. theros and Marion Lucille (Piperas) P.; m. Laurie Jean LaCaskey, Nov. 26, 1956 (div. 1969); children: Christopher David, Andrea Lynn; m. Nancy Marie Pratt, June 11, 1983. BS, U. Wis., 1959, JD, 1961. Bar: Wis. 1961, U.S. Dist. Ct. (ea. and we. dists.) Wis. 1965, U.S. Supreme Ct. 1971; lic. master mariner. Asst. corp. counsel Racine County (Wis.), 1961; atty., advisor U.S. Dept. Labor, Washington, 1961-62; staff atty. U.S. Commn. Civil rights, 1962-63; asst. city atty. City of Madison (Wis.), 1963-65; atty. pvt. practice, Madison, 1965—. Chmn. Madison Mayor's Citizen Adv. Com., 1964-65; pres. Wis. Cup Assn., Madison, 1965; c0-chmn. 2d Congl. Dist. Humphrey for Pres., Madison, 1972. Recipient commendation for Supreme Ct. work Madison County Coun., 1965, commendation resolution City of Madison, 1965. Mem. Wis. Bar Assn., Dane County Bar Assn., Wis. Acad. Trial Lawyers, Am. Assn. Trial Lawyers, Lawyer-Pilot Bar Assn. (master mariner), Gt. Lakes Hist. Soc., Madison Club, South Shore Yacht Club (Milw.). Home and Office: 1787 Strawberry Rd Deerfield WI 53531-9779

PAPPAS, DAVID WAYNE, guidance counselor, consultant; b. Chgo., May 19, 1958; s. Danny and Roselle Pappas. BS in Adminstrn. Justice, So. Ill. U., 1981, M Bus. Edn., 1988; ednl. specialist degree in curriculum and instrn., No. Ill. U., 1993, MEd in Counseling, 1997, EdD in Curriculum Inst. and Supervision, 2001. Cert. tchr., in guidance, gen. supervisory cert., profl. counselor, Ill.; nat. cert. counselor; cert. in scuba diving. Tng. specialist Dawson Tech. Inst., Chgo., 1985-92; coord. coop. edn. Chgo. City-Wide Coll., 1987-89, ast. dir. curriculum and tng., 1989-90, dir. Life Skills Employment Awareness Program, 1990-92; dir. opportunities program Harold Washington Coll., Chgo., 1992-94; tchr. tech. Taft H.S., 1994-2001, lead tchr. summer sch., 1999; coord. Chgo. Police and Firefighters Tng. Acad., Chgo. Bd. Edn., 1999—, guidance counselor, 2001—. Cons. Strategies, Inc., Chgo. Mem. ACA, Am. Sch. Counseling Assn., Ill. Counseling Assn., Phi Delta Kappa, Chi Sigma Iota. Democrat. Roman Catholic. Avocations: international travel, scuba diving, running, swimming, skiing. Home: 700 W Bittersweet Pl Apt 1010 Chicago IL 60613-2385 Office: Chgo Bd Edn 6545 W Hurlbut Chicago IL 60631 Fax: 773-534-1027. E-mail: dwpappas@ix.netcom.com.

PAPPAS, DEAN, internist; b. Nafpactos, Greece, Apr. 10, 1947; came to U.S., 1956; s. Chris and Stavroula (Agnostopoulos) P.; m. Mary Pappous, May 31, 1981; children: Chris, George, Arlene. BS, Fla. So. Coll., 1969; MD, U. Athens, Greece, 1978. Diplomate Am. Bd. Internal Medicine. Intern then resident in internal medicine Mt. Sinai Svcs., Elmhurst, N.Y., 1979-82, fellow in gastroenterology, 1982-84; pvt. practice Gastrointestinal Assoc. Long Island, 1984—. Capt. U.S. Army, 1969-72. Fellow ACP; mem. Am. Hellenic Ednl. Progressive Assn. (v.p.). Office: 139 Plandome Rd Manhasset NY 11030-2331

PAPPAS, EDWARD HARVEY, lawyer; b. Midland, Mich., Nov. 24, 1947; s. Charles and Sydell (Sheinberg) P.; m. Laurie Weston, Aug. 6, 1972; children: Gregory Alan, Steven Michael. BBA, U. Mich., 1969, JD, 1973. Bar: Mich. 1973, U.S. Dist. Ct. (ea. dist.) Mich. 1973, U.S. Dist. Ct. (we. dist.) Mich. 1980, U.S. Ct. Appeals (6th cir.) 1983, U.S. Supreme Ct. 1983. Ptnr. firm Dickinson & Wright, P.L.L.C., Detroit and Bloomfield Hi, Mich., 1973—. Mediator Oakland County Cir. Ct., Pontiac, Mich., 1983—; hearing panelist Mich. Atty. Discipline Bd., Detroit, 1983—, chmn., 1987—; mem. bus. tort subcom. Mich. Supreme Ct. Com. Standard Jury Instructions, 1992-94; bd. commrs. State Bar Mich., 1999—. Trustee Oakland Community Coll., Mich., 1982-90, Oakland-Livingston Legal Aid, 1982-90, v.p., 1982-85, pres., 1985-87; trustee, adv. bd. Mich. Regional Anti-Defamation League of B'nai B'rith, Detroit, 1983-90; planning commr. Village of Franklin, Mich., 1987-91, chmn. 1989-91, councilman, 1991-92, chmn. charter com., 1993-94; chmn. State Bar Mich. Long Range Planning com.; pres.-elect Oakland County Bar Assn., 1996-97, pres., 1997-98, chmn. Jud. Selection Task Force, 1997; bd. dirs. Franklin Found., 1989-92; trustee The Oakland Medication Ctr., 1992-96. Master Oakland County Bar Assn. Inn of Ct.; fellow Mich. State Bar Found., Oakland Bar-Adams Pratt Found., ABA Found.; mem. ABA, Fed. Bar Assn., State Bar Mich. (co-chmn. nat. moot ct. competition com. 1974, 76, com. on legal aid, chmn. standing com. on atty. grievances 1989-92, comml. litigation com., civil procedure com. 1992-94, bd. commrs. 1999—), Oakland County Bar Assn. (vice-chmn. continuing legal edn. com., chmn. continuing legal edn. com. 1985-86, mediation com. 1989-90, chmn. mediation com. 1990-91, bd. dirs. 1990-98, chmn. select com. Oakland County cir. ct. settlement week 1991, chmn. strategic planning com. 1992-93, editor Laches monthly mag. 1986-88, co-chair task force to improve justice systems in Oakland County 1993—, pres.-elect, bd. dirs. 1996-97, pres. 1997-98), Am. Judicature Soc., Mich. Def. Trial Lawyers, Def. Rsch. and Trial Lawyers Assn. (com. practice and procedure), B'nai B'rith Barristers. Home: 32223 Scenic Ln Franklin MI 48025-1702 Office: Dickinson Wright Moon Van Dusen & Freeman 525 N Woodward Ave Bloomfield Hills MI 48304-2971

PAPPAS, EFFIE VAMIS, English and business educator, writer; b. Cleve., Dec. 26, 1924; d. James Jacob and Helen Joy (Nicholson) Vamis; m. Leonard G. Pappas, Nov. 3, 1945; children: Karen Pappas Morabito, Leonard J., Ellen Pappas Daniels, David James. BBA, Western Res. U., 1948; MA in Edn., Case Western Res. U., 1964, postgrad., 1964-68; MA in English Lit., Cleve. State U., 1986; postgrad., Indiana U. Pa., 1979-86. Cert. elem. and secondary tchr., Ohio. Tchr. elem. schs., Ohio, 1963-70; office mgr. Cleve. State U., 1970-72, adminstr. pub. relations, 1972-73; med. adminstr. Brecksville (Ohio) VA Hosp., 1974-78; lectr. English, econs./bus. mgmt., math., comm., composition Cuyahoga C.C., Cleve., 1978-92. Tchg. asst. Case Western Reserve U., 1979-80; lectr. bus. comms. Cleve. State U., 1980; participant in Sci. and Cultural Exch. dels. Am. Inst. Chemists, to Peoples Republic of China, 1984 and to Soviet Union, 1989. Feature writer The Voice, 1970-78; editor, writer Cleve. State U. newsletter and mag., 1970-73. Cub scout leader Boy Scouts Am., Brecksville, 1960; mem. local coun. PTA, 1965-70; sec. St. Paul's Coun., 1990-91; Sunday Sch. tchr., mem. choir Brecksville United Ch. of Christ, 1975-76, mem. bd. missions, 1966-67, membership com. 1993, St. Paul Ladies Philoptohos, 1990—; active Women's Equity Action League, 1995—; mem. planning com. for edn. Case Western Res. U., Cleve. Coll. 75th Anniversary steering com.; mem. Greater Cleve. Learning Project. Recipient Editor's Choice award for outstanding achievement in poetry Nat. Libr. of Poetry, 1995, 2000; grantee Cuyahoga C.C., 1982. Mem. NEA, NAFE, AAUW (legis. chair, del. Ohio meetings 1993-94, del. Ohio Coalition for Change, 1993-94, mem. Ohio and Cleve. br. del. Gt. Lakes regional meeting 1994, co-chair Cleve. br. 1994, 96-97, chair 1997-98, del. to S.W. regional meeting 1995, del. to Internat. Fedn. Univ. Women triennial meeting Stanford U. 1992), AARP, Ohio Edn. Assn. (rep. assembly Columbus 1994, 99-2001), Nat. Mus. Women in Arts (hon. roll mem.), Nat. Trust for Hist. Preservation, Smithsonian Instn. Avocations: travel, art, legal studies, theater, correspondence with national and international friends. Home: 8681 Brecksville Rd Brecksville OH 44141-1912

PAPPAS, GEORGE DEMETRIOS, anatomy and cell biology educator, scientist; b. Portland, Maine, Nov. 26, 1926; James and Anna (Dracopoulos) Pappatheodoros; m. Bernice Levine, Jan. 14, 1952; children: Zoe Alexandra, Clio Nicollette. BA, Bowdoin Coll., 1947; MS, Ohio State U., 1948, PhD, 1952; DSc (hon.), U. Athens, Greece, 1988. Vis. investigator Rockefeller Inst., N.Y.C., 1952-54; assoc. in anatomy Coll. Physicians and Surgeons, Columbia U., 1956-57, asst. prof. anatomy, 1957-63, assoc. prof., 1963-66; prof. anatomy Albert Einstein Coll. Medicine, Yeshiva U., 1967-77, prof. neurosci., 1974-77, vis. prof. neurosci., 1977-97; prof., head dept. anatomy and cell biology U. Ill. Coll. Medicine, Chgo., 1977-96, prof. cell biology and psychiatry, 1996—. Trustee Marine Biol. Lab., Woods Hole, Mass., 1975-81 Author: (with others) The Structure of the Eye, 1961, Growth and Maturation of the Brain, vol. IV, 1964, Nerve as a Tissue, 1966, The Thalmus, 1966, Pathology of the Nervous System, vol. 1, 1968, Structure and Function of Synapses, 1972, Methodological Approaches to the Study of Brain Maturation and Its Abnormalities, 1974, Advances in Neurology, vol.12, 1975, The Nervous System, vol. 1 The Basic Neurosciences, 1975, Cellular and Molecular Basis of Synaptic Transmission, 1988, also author many conf. procs.; contbr. over 200 articles to profl. jours.; former mem. editorial bd. Anatomical Record, Biol. Bull., Brain Rsch., Jour. Neurocytology, Microstructure, Neurol. Rsch.; patentee method inducing analgesia by implantation of cells releasing neuroactive substances. Arthritis and Rheumatism Found. fellow, 1954-56; recipient career devel. award Columbia U., 1964-66; rsch. grantee NIH Fellow AAAS, N.Y. Acad. Scis., Inst. Medicine Chgo.; mem. Am. Soc. Cell Biology (pres. 1974-75), Am. Assn. Anatomists (chmn. pub. policy com. 1981-82), Assn. Anatomy Chmn. (exec. com. 1978-80, pres. 1981-82), Electron Microscopy Soc. Am. (program chmn. 1984-85), N.Y. Soc. Electron Microscopy (pres. 1967-68), Soc. for Neurosci. (pres. Chgo. chpt. 1985-86), Harvey Soc., Internat. Brain Rsch. Orgn., Cajal Club, Sigma Xi. Home: Apt 512 S 680 N Lake Shore Dr Chicago IL 60611 Office: U Ill Psychiat Inst MC 912 1601 W Taylor St Chicago IL 60612-4310 E-mail: gdpappas@uic.edu.

PAPPAS, GEORGE FRANK, lawyer; b. Washington, Oct. 5, 1950; s. Frank George and lora Marie (Stauber) P.; m. Susan Elizabeth Bradshaw, Apr. 25, 1980; children: Christine Bradshaw, Alexandra Stauber. BA, U. Md., 1972, JD, 1975. Bar: Md. 1976, D.c. 1991, u.S. Dist. Ct. Md. 1976, U.S. Dist. Ct. (d.C. cir.) 1986, U.S. Dist. Ct. (we. dist.) Tex. 1993, U.S. Ct. Appeals (4th cir.) 1976, U.S. Ct. Appeals (d.c. cir.) 1984, U.S. Ct. Appeals 9fed. cir.) 1991, U.S. Ct. Appeals (2d cir.) 1993, U.S. Ct. Appeals (6th and 7th cirs.) 1994, U.S. Supreme Ct. 1984, U.S. Ct. of Fed. Claims, 1995. Assoc. H. russell Smouse, Balt., 1976-81, Melnicove, Kaufman, Wiener & Smouse, Balt., 1981-83, prin., 1983-88; ptnr. Venable, Baetjer and howard, 1986—. Lectr. Wash. Coll. Law, Am. U., Washington, 1980-84; mem. moot ct. bd., 1974-75; Master of the Bench , Inn XIII, Am. Inns of Ct., 1989; mem. U.S. Dist. Ct. of Delaware Judges' Intellectual property Adv. Com., 1998—; mem. Dist. Judge Edn. Adv. Com. for the Fed. Jud. Ctr., 2001—. Founding editor-in-chief Internat. Trade law Jour., 1974-75. Mem. bd. vis. U. Md. Sch. of Law, 2000—. 1st lt. USAF, 1972-76. Mem. ABA, Internat. Assn. Def. Counsel, Md. Bar Assn. (chmn. internat. coml. law sect., 1980-81), Am. Intellectual Property Law Assn., U.S. Trademark Assn., Omicron Delta kappa, Phi Kappa Phi, Phi Beta Kappa, L'Hirondelle Club. Republican. Greek Orthodox. Home: 9 Roland Ct Baltimore MD 21204-3550 Office: Venable Baetjer & Howard 2 Hopkins Plz Ste 2100 Baltimore MD 21201-2982 also: 1201 New York Ave NW Ste 1000 Washington DC 20005-6197

PAPPAS, GEORGE JAMES, educator; b. N.Y.C., May 13, 1969; s. James and Julia P.; m. Anna Papafragou, Oct. 31, 2000. BS in Computer & Systems Engring., Rensselaer Polytech. Inst., 1991, MS in Computer & Systems Engring., 1992; PhD in Elec. Engring. & Computer Scis., U. Calif., Berkeley, 1998. Rschr. U. Calif., Berkeley, 1999-2000; prof. U. Pa., Phila., 2000—. Cons. Honeywell Tech. Ctr., Mpls., 1997—. Contbr. articles to profl. jours. Mem. IEEE, Tau Beta Pi, Eta Kappa Nu. Avocations: travel, sports, music, opera. Office: U Pa Dept Elec Engring 200 S 33d St Philadelphia PA 19104 Fax: 215-573-2068. E-mail: pappasg@ee.upenn.edu.

PAPPAS, JAMES PETE, university administrator; b. Price, Utah, June 30, 1939; s. Pete S. and Dia P. (Metrakis) P.; m. Peggy Ann Kunz, Aug. 30, 1964; children: C. Jennifer, Peter T. AS in Psychology, Coll. Eastern Utah, 1959; BA in Psychology, U. Utah, 1961; MS in Counseling Psychology, Ohio U., 1964; PhD in Clin. Psychology, Purdue U., 1968; cert. in Mgmt., Stanford U., 1979; cert. in adminstrn., Harvard U., 1985. Asst. dir. counseling ctr. U. Utah, Salt Lake City, 1969-72, dir. ctr. for acad. advising, assoc. dean liberal edn., 1975-78, assoc. dean divsn. of continuing edn., 1978-87; prof. ednl. psychology and liberal studies U. Okla., Norman, 1987—, v.p. for univ. outreach; dean Coll. of Continuing Edn., 1994-00, Coll. of Liberal Studies, 2000—. Author: (book) Windows of Opportunity: Preparing University Based Residential Continuing Education for the Twenty-First Century, 1992, The University's Role in Economic Development: From Research to Outreach, 1997; co-author: (workbook) Promotional Techniques, 1987. Mem. Norman Econ. Devel. Coalition, 1996—; state chmn. Utah Endowment for Humanities, 1985-88; pres. Norman Arts and Humanities Coun., 1994-95. Recipient St. Paul award Greek Orthodox Ch. of N. Am., Denver, 1990, Christopher Outstanding Leadership and Bittner Svc. awards U. Continuing Edn. Assn.; inductee Internat. Adult and Continuing Edn. Hall of Fame, 1997. Mem. Am. Assn. Counseling and Devel. (nat. senator 1975-77), Assn. Acad. Affairs Adminstr. (bd. dirs. 1977-78), Adult Edn. Assn. Utah (bd. dirs. 1979-82), Univ. Continuing Edn. Assn. (pres. 1996-97), Nat. Assn. State Univs. and Land Grant Colls. (bd. dirs. 1994-97), Assn. Grad. Liberal Studies Programs (bd. dirs. 2002—). Avocations: reading, cmty. svc., writing, sports, travel. Office: Coll Continuing Edn 1700 Asp Ave Rm 111 Norman OK 73072-6407

PAPPAS, JIM D. federal bankruptcy judge; b. 1952; Chief bankruptcy judge U.S. Bankruptcy Ct., Boise, 1993—. Office: US Bankruptcy Ct 550 W Fort St Msc 042 Boise ID 83724-0001

PAPPAS, JOHN DOUGLAS, cardiologist; b. Galveston, Tex., June 23, 1955; s. Patrick Henry and Margaret Jean P.; m. Maricela, May 5, 1990; children: John, Melissa, Laura. BA, Tex. Tech. U., 1977; JD, U. Houston, 1980; MD, Tex. Tech. U., 1987. Diplomate Am. Bd. Internal Medicine. Atty. Carson, Boyd & Strother, Houston, 1980-83; resident Tex. Tech. HSC, Lubbock, Tex., 1987-90; cardiology fellow U. Tex., Houston, 1990-93; cardiologist Heart Assocs., Corpus Christi, Tex., 1993-96, Cardiology Assocs., Corpus Christi, 1996—. Prin. investigator clin. trials; chief cardiology Doctors Regional Med. Ctr., Corpus Christi, 1995-97, Spohn Meml. Hosp., Corpus Christi, 1997—. Fellow Am. Coll. Cardiology; mem. Am. Heart Assn. (bd. dirs. 1993—, pres. Corpus Christi chpt. 1995). Office: Cardiology Assocs 1521 S Staples St Ste 700 Corpus Christi TX 78404-3160 E-mail: dougmdjd@davlin.net.

PAPPAS, LEAH AGLAIA, civic worker, political consultant; b. Ogden, Utah, Mar. 23, 1936; d. George Thomas and Maria (Harames) P. BA, Coll. St. Mary of the Wasatch, 1959. Tchr. Bishop Gorman High Sch., Las Vegas, Nev., 1959-64; with Dist. Atty.'s staff, 1972-75; tchr. Weber State Coll., 1985. Civic worker various orgns., including Opera Guild, Heart Fund, City of Hope, March of Dimes, also groups for prevention of blindness, sr. citizens' groups, others, Ogden and Las Vegas, 1955—; cons. numerous polit. campaigns, Ogden, Las Vegas and Boston, L.A., John F. Kennedy campaign, 1959; alt. del. Chgo. Nat. Conv.; vol. Senator Robert Kennedy Campaign, 1968; supr. Senator Edward M. Kennedy Campaign, Boston, 1970, 76, Presdl. Campaign, 1980; campaign worker Gov. Jerry Brown, L.A., 1978, office mgr., Reagan-Bush campaign, 1984, Pres. Bill Clinton, 1996. Greek Orthodox. Home: 1323 Marilyn Dr Ogden UT 84403-0424

PAPPAS, MICHAEL, financial services company executive; b. N.Y.C., Sept. 10, 1940; s. Michael Papadopoulos and Despina (Vrioni) Kokindo; m. Eileen McGovern, Jan. 25, 1969. BBA in Acctg. and Data Processing, Pace U., N.Y.C., 1973. Mgr. acctg. E.F. Hutton, N.Y.C., 1972-75, bus. unit mgr., 1976-77; mgr. payroll and commn. acctg. Drexel Burnham Lambert, 1977-81, v.p., project mgr., 1981-83, v.p., mgr. gen. acctg., 1983-85, v.p., mgr. fin. info. systems, 1985-86, v.p., govt. reporting coord., 1986-89; dir. compensation Gruntal & Co., Inc., 1989-2000; v.p. Donaldson, Lufkin, Jenrette, 2000—. Sgt. U.S. Army, 1963-65. Mem. Am. Payroll Assn. (N.Y. Met. chpt. pres. 1998—), Securities Industry Assn. (tech. tax com. 1986-88), Hellenic Am. Bankers Assn. (bd. dirs. 1991-92, v.p. 1992-94, pres. 1995-98, treas. 1998—). Greek Orthodox. Avocations: golf, bowling, collecting award winning movies. Office: Gruntal & Co Inc 1 Liberty Plz Fl 18 New York NY 10006-1404

PAPPAS, MILTON J. venture capitalist; b. Cleve., Nov. 13, 1928; s. John Milton and Helen Stajos Pappas; m. Christine Kanillos, Nov. 7, 1953; children: Jeannine, William. BBA, Case Western Res. U., 1950; LLB, Cleveland Marshall Law Sch., 1956. Bar: Ohio 1956; cert. Inst. Chartered Analysts. Trust investment officer Cleve. Trust Co., 1954-60; fin. analyst Merrill Turben & Co., Cleve., 1960-62; sr. v.p. First of Mich., Detroit, 1962-66; v.p. Drexel, Harrman Ripley, N.Y.C., 1966-70, Euclid Ptnrs., N.Y.C., 1970—. Bd. dirs. IntraLinks, Inc., N.Y.C., Vision RX.com, Inc., Elmsford, NY, Xanoptix, Inc., Merrimack, NH. Lt. (j.g.) USCG, 1952-54. Mem. N.Y. Venture Capital Forum. Greek Orthodox. Avocations: opera, ballet, theater, travel, jogging. Office: Euclid Ptnrs Corp 45 Rockefeller Plz Ste 3240 New York NY 10111-0999

PAPPAS, PHILIP JAMES, real estate company executive; b. Chgo., Sept. 29, 1954; s. Nicholas James and Ann (Nicholson) P.; m. Ana Lucia Sant'Anna; children: Tiago, Marcelo, Amanda. BA, Shimer Coll., 1975. Mgr. Cook County Hosp., Chgo., 1975-77, purchasing agt., 1977-81; pres. L.G. Properties, 1980—, Tiamar Real Estate, 1990—. Docent Chgo. Architecture Found., 1976-78. Pres. Lincoln Park Builders Assn., 1997-99, Lake View Developers, 1988-89; trustee Shimer Coll., 1997—. Recipient 1st pl. award for best interior restoration Nat. Trust for Hist. Preservation, 1991, Good Neighbor award for exceptional property restoration Chgo. Assn. Realtors, 1992, 95, 96, 97, 98, 99, 2000, 01, 02. Mem. Nat. Assn. Realtors, Oxford Union Soc. (life), Chgo. Assn. Realtors, Owassippe Staff Assn. Boy Scouts Am. (life). Greek Orthodox. Office: LG Properties 3654 N Lincoln Ave Chicago IL 60613-3536

PAPPAS, WILLIAM JOHN, principal, educator; b. Detroit, Oct. 23, 1937; s. John Basil and Susan (Kurlas) P.; m. Susan Kay Payne, Aug. 18, 1962; 1 child Laurie Ann. BA, Western Mich. U., 1962; MA, Eastern Mich. U., 1966; cert. in edn. spl., Wayne State U., 1971. Tchr. Mt. Clemens (Mich.) High Sch., 1962-67, asst. prin., 1967-71; prin., co-dir. system-wide curriculum Northview High Sch., Grand Rapids, Mich., 1971—, co-dir. curriculum, 1989—. Adj. prof. grad. sch. Ctrl. Mich. U., Mt. Pleasant, 1974—; regional rep. North Ctrl. Assn. Mich., 1995-2001; spl. cons. Charter Schs. Ctrl. Mich. U., 1995-2001; ednl. cons. Detroit Charter Schs. Adminstrv. Svcs. Contbr. articles to profl. jours. Recipient Northview High Sch. Exemplary Sch. Recognition award U.S. Dept. Edn., 1985, 89, 93; I/D/E/A fellow, 1974-76, 78-84, 86-89, 90-92; named to Mich. Educators Hall of Fame, 1997. Mem. NASSP (Mich. state coord. 1990-93), Mich. Assn. Secondary Sch. Prins. (exec. bd. 1975-86, 91-94, pres. 1981-82, Outstanding Secondary Prin. Yr. 1985-86), Lions (pres. N.E. Grand Rapids chpt. 1976), Elks, Eagles, Moose, Am. Hellenic Ednl. Progressive Assn., Phi Delta Kappa. Greek Orthodox. Avocations: reading, athletics, politics. Home: 6234 Miramonte Dr NE Rockford MI 49341-8516 E-mail: wjpap@msn.com.

PAPPAS-SPEAIRS, NINA, financial planner, educator; b. Hazard, Ky., Oct. 8, 1928; d. Steve E. and Martha (Hicks) Kalfas; m. Harry J. Pappas, 1951 (div.); children: John J., Nicholas S., Vivian E. Pappas Unger, Mark A., Carol A. Pappas Siegel; m. Mitchell F. Speairs, 1992. BS, U. Cin., 1950; MA, Northwestern U., 1957; PhD, U. Ill., 1978. Faculty St. Mary's H.S., Chgo., Sch. Dist. 102, LaGrange, Ill., U. Ill., Chgo., 1969-79, U. Tex., Arlington, 1979-82, Tex. Wesleyan Coll., Ft. Worth, 1982-83; realtor Merrill Lynch Realty, 1983-84; fin. planner Cigna Corp., Irving, Tex., 1984-90; pvt. practice fin. planning and investments, Ft. Worth, 1990—. Organizer, condr. lst U.S. Olympic Acad., Chgo., 1977; collaborator Internat. Olympic Acad., Olympia, Greece, 1977, guest lectr., 1977, 78; chief of mission to Greece U.S. Olympic Com., 1977; guest lectr. Nat. Olympic Acad. Republic of China, 1982; mem. Sch. Bd. Lagrange, Ill. Dist. 107, 1971-74. Author: History and Development of the International Olympic Academy: 1927-1977, 1978; editor: Perspectives of the Olympic Games, 1979; also articles. Vice chair Edn. Coun. U.S. Olympic Com., 1977-85; pres. Opera Guild Ft. Worth, 1982. Recipient Silver Medal Internat. Olympic Acad., Olympia, Greece, 1981. Mem. Lecture Found. Ft. Worth, Ft. Worth Sister Cities Internat., Symphony League, Opera Guild, English Speaking Union, Woman's Club, River Crest Country Club, Ft. Worth Boat Club. Republican. Greek Orthodox. Avocations: golf, reading, sailing, dancing. Home: 7705 Lake Highlands Dr Fort Worth TX 76179-2809 E-mail: cordovacorporation@earthlink.net.

PAPPER, EMANUEL MARTIN, anesthesiologist; b. N.Y.C., July 12, 1915; s. Max and Lillian (Weitzner) P.; m. Patricia Meyer, Nov. 30, 1975; children: Richard Nelson Papper, Patrick Goldstein, Amy Goldstein. AB, Columbia U., 1935; MD, NYU, 1938; MD (hon.), Univ. Uppsala, Sweden, 1964, U. Turin, Italy, 1969, U. Vienna, Austria, 1977; DSc (hon.), Columbia U., 1988; PhD, U. Miami, 1990. Diplomate Am. Bd. Anesthesiology (dir. 1956-65, pres. 1964-65). Fellow medicine NYU, 1938-39, fellow physiology, 1940, asst. prof., 1946-49, assoc. prof., 1949; intern Bellevue Hosp., 1939-40, resident in anesthesiology, 1940-42; prof. anesthesiology, chmn. dept. Columbia U.; also dir. anesthesiology service Presbyn. Hosp., 1949- 69; dir. anesthesiology, vis. anesthesiologist Francis Delafield Hosp., 1951-69; v.p. med affairs, dean, prof. anesthesiology U. Miami, 1969-81, prof. pharmacology, 1972-81. Dir. Abbott Labs., No. Trust Bank of Fla., Miami; cons. div. med. scis. NRC, 1954-69, Huntington (N.Y.) Hosp., 1949-69; nat. cons. surgeon gen. USAF, 1963-70; mem. surgery study sect. NIH, 1958-62; civilian cons. First Army, USN; prin. cons. Nat. Inst. Gen. Med. Scis., 1965-66, chmn. project com. gen. med. research program, 1966-70; mem. nat. heart council NIH, 1962-66; hon. cons. Royal Prince Alfred Hosp., Sydney, Australia Author 350 sci. papers pub. in various med. jours., 3 textbooks, 2 non-fiction books. Bd. dirs. PBS-Channel 2, Miami, 1984—. Served from 1st lt. to maj. M.C. U.S. Army, 1942-46; chief anesthesiology sect. Torney, Dibble and Walter Reed hosps. Recipient Silver medal City of Paris, 1972, 1st prize History of Medicine, Am. Med. Writers

Assn., 1996, Davdi M. Little prize Am. Anesthesia Assn., 1998; established E.M. Papper chair in anesthesiology Columbia U. Coll. Physicians and Surgeons, 1984, E.M. Papper lectures in anesthesiology Columbia U. and UCLA, 1978 Hon. fellow Royal Coll. Anaesthetists (England), Royal Coll. Surgeons (Ireland, faculty anaesthetists), Royal Soc. Medicine (England), Australian and New Zealand Coll. Anesthesiologists ; mem. N.Y. Acad. Medicine (1st pres. sect. anesthesiology), Am. Surg. Assn., Am. Soc. Anesthesiologists (pres. 1967-68), N.Y. State Soc. Anesthesiologists (past pres.), NRC (chmn. com. anesthesia 1962-67), Am. Coll. Anesthesiologists, World Fedn. Soc. Anesthesiologists (v.p.), Am. Soc. Pharmacology and Exptl. Therapeutics, AMA, N.Y. Acad. Scis., N.Y. Co. Med. Soc., Am., N.Y. socs. anesthesiologists, AAAS, Am. Assn. Thoracic Surgery, Harvey Soc, Am. Soc. Clin. Investigation, Am. Thoracic Soc., Assn. Univ. Anesthetists (co-founder, 1st pres.), Pan Am. Med. Assn., Assn. Anaesthetists Gt. Britain and Ireland (hon.), Swedish Soc. Anesthesiologists (hon. mem.), Finnish Soc. Anesthesiologists (hon. mem.), Israeli Soc. Anesthesiologists (hon. mem.), Australian Soc. Anaesthesiologists (hon. mem.), N.Y. State Soc. Anesthesiologists (hon. mem.), D.C. Soc. Anesthesiologists (hon. mem.), Calif. Soc. Anesthesiologists (hon. mem.), German Soc. Anesthesiologists (hon. mem.), Halsted Soc., Japan Soc. Anesthesiologists (hon.), Am. Soc. Anesthesiologists (pres. 1969), European Acad. Anesthesiology (hon., Gold medal), Grolier Club (N.Y.C.), Phi Beta Kappa, Sigma Xi, Alpha Omega Alpha. Clubs: Cosmos (Washington); Century Assn. (N.Y.C.). Home: Apt 1501 1 Grove Isle Dr Miami FL 33133-4100 Office: PO Box 016370 Miami FL 33101-6370 E-mail: painpill@aol.com.

PAPPS, BRUCE WILLIAM, chartered financial analyst, investment company executive; b. Mt. Kisco, N.Y., Jan. 19, 1962; s. Ernest W. and Annette (Lazration) P. BS in Econs., U. Pa., 1985. CFA, 2000. Broker tng. program Shearson Lehman, N.Y.C., 1989-93, 94-96; pres., CEO Papps Capital Group, Inc., 1996—. Adj. prof. SUNY, Valhalla, 1996—98. Mentor P.R.I.D.E., Harlem, N.Y., 1996-98. Mem. N.Y. Soc. Securities Analysts (mem. com.), Wharton Club. Avocations: sky diving, scuba diving, boating, skiing. Office: Papps Capital Group Inc 67 Wall St Ste 2411 New York NY 10005-3101 E-mail: CEO@papps.com.

PAPYRIN, ANATOLII NIKIFOROVICH, biophysicist, researcher; b. Novosibirsk, Russia, Apr. 2, 1942; s. Nikitor Vasilievich Papyrin and Kaleria Sergeevna Chirkovskaya; m. Valentina Semenovna Papyrin, Oct. 3, 1962 (div. Mar. 19, 1980). PhD, State U., Tomsk, Russia, 1971; MS, Sate Tech. U., Novosibirsk, Russia, 1965. Sr. rschr. K Tech. Corp., Albuquerque, 2000—; sr. rschr. assoc. Penn State U., State Coll., Pa., 1997—2000; visiting prof. McGill U., Montreal, Canada, 1990—91; assoc. prof. State U. , Novosibirsk, Russia, 1972—85, prof. Russia, 1985—90; sr. scientist, head of lab. ITAM of RAS, Russia, 1971—97; rsch. asst. Inst. Nuclear Physics , Russia, 1965—71. Coord. Metallurgical Plant, Novosibirsk, Russia, 1986—89; cons. ASB Ind. Inc., Barberton, Ind., 1996—97, Round Table Group, Inc., Wash., DC, 2001—; mem. Cold Spray Consortium. Author: (book) Supersonic Two-Phase Flows, 1980 (SB of RAS award), Methods of Experimental Physics, 1981; contbr. articles. Mem. Social Coun. Edn., Novosibirsk, Russia, 1981—86. Mem.: ASM Internat. Achievements include invention of gas dynamic spraying method. Avocations: basketball, tennis, music. Office: K Tech Corp 2201 Buena Vista SE Ste 400 Albuquerque NM 87106-4265

PAQUE, JOAN MICHAELS, multimedia artist, author, educator; b. Menominee, Mich. d. Frank E. and Gertrude (Pfotenhauer) Michaels; m. Henry Paul Paque, July 13, 1957. Student, Layton Sch. Art, Milw., 1955-58, Marquette U., 1955-58. Owner JMP Atelier, Milw., 1969—. Bd. dirs. Artists Working in Edn.; vis. artist Internat. Forum for the Arts, Australia, 1989, 98, 2001; resident vis. artist Australian Nat. U. Sch. Art, Canberra, 2001. Multimedia artist, exhibiting in Japan, Australia, Europe, Mex., Can. and U.S.; commns. for law firm, archtl. firm, others; one-woman show Luth. Coll., Milw., 2000; contbr. to Fiberarts Mag., Fiber Forum Mag., others; works in pvt. collections. Cons., African Am. Children's Theatre, Milw, 1994-99, 00. Recipient numerous awards; grantee NEH, Cardinal Stritch U., Eli Lilly, Roundy's Corp., 2000. Mem.: Midwest Weavers, Handweavers Guild Inc., Am. Crafts Coun., Milw. Arts Mus. (artists adv. bd.), Fiber Forum. Avocations: research, experimenting, writing. Home: JMP Atelier 4455 N Frederick Ave Milwaukee WI 53211

PAQUET, GARY LEE, elementary school educator; b. Marquette, Mich., Feb. 28, 1963; s. Herbert Russell and Rena Ann McEachern. MusB, No. Mich. U., 1985; MA in Child Devel., Mich. State U., 1995. Music tchr. grades K-5 Algonac (Mich.) Cmty. Schs., 1985—93, tchr. 3d grade, 1993—. Conductor Rainbow Singers Cmty. Honor Choir, Port Huron, Mich., 1998—99; soloist Schubert Male Chorus, 1998—2001. Mem.: Algonac Edn. Assn. (bldg. rep. 1996—99, exec. bd. 1998—99, pres. 2001—). Avocation: art. Home: 362 4th St Marysville MI 48040 Office: Algonzac Cmty Schs 9541 Phelps Rd Algonac MI 48001

PAQUETTE, JACK KENNETH, management consultant, writer; b. Toledo, Aug. 14, 1925; s. Hector J. and Nellie (McCormick) P.; m. Jane Russell, Sept. 13, 1947; children: Jan Eriksen, Mark Russell, Mary Beth, John Eric. Student, Baldwin-Wallace Coll., 1943-44, Marquette U., 1944; BA, Ohio State U., 1949, MA, 1951; postgrad., Wayne State U., 1966. Editor monthly pub. Bur. Motor Vehicles, State of Ohio, 1947-49; asst. city editor, copy editor Ohio State Jour., 1949-51; copywriter Owens-Ill., Inc., Toledo, 1951-53, copy chief mktg. dept., 1953-55, asst. advt. mgr. mktg. dept., 1955-59; advt. mgr. Owens-Ill., Inc. (Libbey div.), 1959-61; mgr. advt. and sales promotion Owens-Ill., Inc. (Libbey products), 1961-64, mgr. customer mktg. services glass container div., 1964-67, dir. corporate orgn. planning, 1967-69, v.p. adminstrv. div., dir. corp. relations, 1969-70, corporate v.p., dir. corp. relations, 1970-80, corp. v.p., asst. to chmn. bd., 1980-84, cons., 1984-86; pres. Paquette Enterprises, 1984—; owner The Trumpeting Angel, antiques, 1985—. Mem. adv. bd. Cresset Chem. Co., 1987—. Author: A History of Owens-Illinois Inc., (1818-1984), 1985, The Glassmakers, Blowpipes, 2002. Bd. dirs. Toledo YMCA, 1970-74, Vis. Nurse Svc., 1970-73, Children's Svcs., Lucas County, 1973-80, Toledo coun. Boy Scouts Am., trustee, v.p. fin., 1978-84; trustee Owens Tech. Coll. Found, 1978-81; mem. Advt. Club Toledo, 1951-75, trustee, 1960-62; hon. bd. dirs. Greater Toledo area chpt. ARC, 1970—; mem. adv. bd. Mercy Hosp., Toledo, 1981-84, Mary's Adult Day Care Ctr., 1989-93, St. Anthony's Children's Ctr., 1993, Mid-Coast Hosp., Brunswick, Maine, 1998—; mem. pub. rels. com. Cath. U. Am., 1979-82; chmn. U.S. Savs. Bonds, Lucas County, 1977-79; trustee Bowling Green State U. Found., 1976-83, pres., 1980-82; mem. Nat. Commn. on a Free and Responsible Press, 1980-83; v.p. trustee, Toledo Repertoire Theatre, 1984-88; trustee Crosby Gardens, 1983-89, chmn. 1987-88; trustee Toledo Bot. Gardens, 1989-90, chmn. emeritus and hon. lifetime trustee, 1990—; mem. pres.'s coun. Toledo Mus. Art, Bowling Green State U.; trustee Riverside Hosp. Found., 1984-94, chmn. 1986-89; mem. Juvenile Justice Adv. Bd., 1986-87; advisor R.B. Hayes Presdl. Ctr., 1990-92. With USNR, 1943-46, PTO. Recipient Gold Key award Pub. Rel. News, 1970, Silver Anvil award Pub. Rel. Soc., 1971, 72; named to Toledo Clean Hall of Fame, 1983. Mem. Soc. Profl. Journalists (co-founder Columbus and Toledo chpts.), Ohio Mfrs. Assn. (v.p., trustee 1969-84), Keep Am. Beautiful, Inc. (nat. chmn., exec. com., 1978-84, chmn. emeritus, mem. nat. adv. coun. 1984—), Bus. Com. for the Arts (corp. liason 1980-84), U.S. C. of C. (cons. affairs com. 1980-84), Western Great Lakes Hist. Soc. (life, trustee 1998—), Lucas County/Maumee Valley Hist. Soc., Maine Maritime Mus., Toy Soldier Collectors of Am. Soc., Glass Club Toledo, USN Armed Guard Assn., Sampson WWII Navy Vets. Assn., OSU Alumni Assn. (life), Am. Legion (Toledo post), Pi Sigma Alpha. Clubs: Toledo Press (founding trustee), Toledo, Torch, Rotary (Paul Harris fellow). Home and Office: 2355 Parliament Sq Toledo OH 43617-1256

PAQUETTE, STEVEN A. lawyer; b. Westport, N.Y., Nov. 30, 1955; s. Ronald A. and Mildred Paquette; m. Cynthia J. Sardino, Sept. 18, 1982; children: Aimee, Sarah, Chelsea. BS in Journalism, Syracuse U., N.Y., 1977, JD, 1979. Bar: N.Y. 1979, U.S. Dist. Ct. (no. dist.) N.Y. 1980, U.S. Dist. Ct. (we. dist.) N.Y. 1986, U.S. Supreme Ct. 1986. Atty. Meggesto Paquette Badera, Syracuse, N.Y., 1979-86, Sardino Paquette, Syracuse, 1986—2001, N.Y. State Dept. Taxation, Syracuse, 1985-91, N.Y. State Assembly, Albany, 1995—2001; chair Dem. Party Onondaga Cty., Syracuse, 1993—2000. Mem. alumni bd. Delta Tau Delta Fraternity, Indpls., 1981—; mem. parish coun. St. Michael's Ch., Syracuse, N.Y., 1994—. Mem. N.Y. State Bar Assn., Onondaga Cty. Bar Assn. Democrat. Roman Catholic. Office: Green and Seifler PILC 900 One Lincoln Ctr Syracuse NY 13202

PAQUIN, EDWARD H., JR. state legislator, state agency administrator; b. Bennington, Vt., Feb. 2, 1953; s. Edward H. Sr. and Alice Marie (Tremblay) P.; m. Patricia LaRose, July 4, 1981; 1 child, Katherine Marie. BA, U. Vt., 1975. Various positions including silversmith and factory worker; builder; rep. Vt. Gen. Assembly, Montpelier, 1991—2002, mem. natural resources and energy com.; exec. dir. Vt. Protection and Advocacy, Inc. Dir. summer camp for low-income rural children CAMP!; bd. dirs. Vt. Ctr. Ind. Living. Recipient Victory award Nat. Rehab. Hosp., 1991. Democrat. Baptist. Home: PO Box 219 Fairfax VT 05454-0219 Office: Vt Gen Assembly 133 State St Montpelier VT 05633-0001

PAQUIN, JEFFREY DEAN, lawyer; b. Milw., Dec. 7, 1960; s. James DeWayne and Helen Ann (Walter) P. BA, U. Wis., 1983; JD, U. Ky., 1986. Bar: Ga. 1986, U.S. Dist. Ct. (no. dist.) Ga. 1986, U.S. Ct. Appeals (11th cir.) 1986, U.S. Dist. Ct. (mid. dist.) Ga. 1987, D.C. 1989, U.S. Ct. Appeals (D.C. cir.) 1989, U.S. Supreme Ct. 1990. Assoc. Powell, Goldstein, Frazer & Murphy, Atlanta, 1986-94; chief litigation counsel United Parcel Svc., 1994-98; nat. practice leader ADR and litig. mgmt. Price Waterhouse, 1998; global practice leader Legal Mgmt. Svcs. Ernst & Young, LLP, 1998-2000; practice leader ADR and conflict mgmt. svcs. Kritzer & Levick, 2000-01; ptnr. Paquin Victor LLP, 2001—. V.p. Prodn. Values, Inc., Atlanta, 1987-88. Exec. editor U. Ky. Law Rev., 1985-86. Bd. dirs. Children's Motility Disorder Found., 1995-2000, Ctr. Corp. Counsel Innovation, 2000-02. Mem. ABA, FBA, The Ombudsman Assn., Am. Corp. Counsel Assn. (bd. dirs. Ga. 1997-98), D.C. Bar Assn., Ga. Bar Assn., Atlanta Bar Assn. (v.p., dir. alternative dispute resolution sect.), Mortar Board, Phi Delta Phi, Sigma Epsilon Sigma, Psi Chi. Roman Catholic. Home: 3620 Woodshire Chase Marietta GA 30066-8719 Office: Paquin Victor LLP 4403 Northside Parkway Ste 1101 Atlanta GA 30327 E-mail: jeff.paquin@adrcms.com.

PAQUIN, THOMAS CHRISTOPHER, lawyer; b. Quincy, Mass., Feb. 12, 1947; s. Henry Frederick and Rita Marie (St. Louis) P.; m. Jean Jacqueline O'Neill, Aug. 5, 1972; children: Martha, Edward. BS in Acctg., Bentley Coll., 1969; JD, U. Notre Dame, 1974. Bar: Mass. 1974, U.S. Dist. Ct. Mass. 1976. Tax atty. Coopers and Lybrand, Boston, 1974-76; assoc. Cargill, Masterman & Cahill, 1976, Wilson, Curran & Malkasian, Wellesley, Mass., 1976-77; ptnr. Bianchi and Paquin, Hyannis, 1977-98; shareholder, dir. Quirk and Chamberlain, P.C., Yarmouthport, 1998—. Bd. dirs., chmn. nominating com. Elder Svcs. Cape Cod and Islands, Inc., Dennis, Mass., 1986-91; bd. dirs., corporator Vis. Nurse Assn. Cape Cod Found., Inc., Dennis, 1988-97; pres. Life Svcs. Inc., 1991-95; bd. dirs. Woodside Cemetery Corp., 1998—, pres., 1999—. Mem. Bass River Golf Commn., Yarmouth, Mass., 1980-83, chmn., 1982-83; chmn. Yarmouth Golf Course Bldg. Com., 1985-89; mem. hearing com. bd. Bar Overseers of the Supreme Jud. Ct., 1989-95; bd. dirs. Project Coach, Inc., 1990-97; conciliator Barnstable Superior Ct., 1992—; trustee Cape Symphony Orch., 1999—. Fellow Mass. Bar Found.; mem. ABA, Mass. Bar Assn. (del. 1986-87, mem. com. on bicentennial U.S. Constn. 1986-88, fee arbitration bd. 1985-86, chmn. spkrs. and writers subcom. 1986-88), Barnstable County Bar Assn. (chmn. seminar com. 1979-83, mem. exec. com. 1981-84, v.p. 1984-86, pres. 1986-87), Estate Planning Coun. Cape Cod (exec. com. 1985-98, sec. 1991-93, pres.-elect 1993-95, pres. 1995-97), Mass. Conveyancers Assn., Mid-Cape Men's Club (v.p. 1992, pres. 1993), Cummaquid Golf Club. Office: PO Box 38 Yarmouth Port MA 02675-0038

PÂQUIN, TRUDY, gerontological nurse; b. Wantagh, N.Y., May 23, 1954; d. William Carl and Gertrude Mary (Kryl) Bauer; m. Alfred Joseph Pâquin III, July 30, 1977. AAS, John Tyler C.C., Chester, Va., 1982; BA magna cum laude, So. Conn. State U., 1993; gerontol. nurse cert., U. Conn., 1994, nurse mgmt. cert., 1995. cert. psychiat. and mental health nurse. Animal trainer, 1972—; pet therapist, 1974—; Alzheimer's rschr., 1995; therapy dog tng. nurse, educator, 1983—; adj. faculty dept. sociology So. Conn. State U., 2001—. Mem. Antarctic Expdn., 1996; adj. faculty dept. sociology So. Conn. State U., 2001; qualitative rsch. on psychiat. patient interaction, 02. Author: Pet Therapy Handbook, 1998, One Man's Journey to America, 1996; composer numerous musical works. Mem. Harness Goat Soc. Avocations: songwriting, fiddling, training and showing dogs, swimming, packing with llamas. Office: Fowler Nursing Ctr 10 Boston Post Rd Guilford CT 06437 E-mail: Trudy@prodigy.net.

PARA, GERARD ALBERT, lawyer, real estate broker, consultant; b. Oak Park, Ill., June 27, 1953; s. Bruno Joseph and Bernice Agnes Para; m. Gayle Louise Keegan, Sept. 15, 1979; children: Eric, Teresa. BA with honor, De Paul U., 1973, JD, 1976. Bar: Ill. 1977, U.S. Dist. Ct. (no. dist.) Ill. 1977, U.S. Ct. Appeals (7th cir.) 1977, Fed. Trial Bar. 1984; lic. real estate broker, Ill., 1981. Jud. law clk. Ill Appellate Ct. (1st dist.), Chgo., 1977-78; divsnl. counsel Household Internat. Franchisor Divsns., Prospect Heights, 1978-85; v.p. Bannockburn (Ill.) Pk. Concepts, Inc., 1986-93; dir. real estate ops., asst. gen. counsel Ben Franklin Stores, Carol Stream, Ill., 1994-96; v.p., gen. counsel DiMucci Devel. Corp., Palatine, 1996-97; gen. counsel Urban Investment Trust Inc., Chgo., 1998-99; prin. Franchise ESQ.sm, Lincolnshire, 1999—; arbitrator 19th Jud. Cir., Lake County, 1999—, 18th Jud. Cir., DuPage County, 2000—, Cir. Ct. of Cook County, 2000—; candidate 19th Jud. Cir. Judge, Dem. Party, Lake and McHenry Counties, 2002. Real estate broker, Long Grove, Ill., 1987—; franchise cons. Elliotts' Off Broadway Deli, Oak Brook, Ill., 1993—. Editor: Medical Malpractice, 1975, Trial Technique, 1975. Asst. coach Little League Buffalo Grove (Ill.) Recreation Assn., 1988-2000; asst. scoutmaster Boy Scouts Am., Long Grove, 1995—. Mem. ABA, Internat. Coun. Shopping Ctrs., Internat. Corp. Real Estate Execs. (bd. dirs. Chgo. chpt.), Chgo. Bar Assn., Internat. Franchise Assn., Coun. Franchise Suppliers. Roman Catholic. Avocations: lap swimming, boating, scuba diving, weightlifting. Office: Franchise ESQ sm 125 Shelter Rd #450 Lincolnshire IL 60069 E-mail: franchiseesq@aol.com.

PARADA, LUIS FERNANDO, science educator; b. Santa Fe de Bogota, Colombia, July 18, 1954; came to the U.S., 1993; s. Alfonso and Clara Parada. BS, U. Wis., 1979; PhD, MIT, 1985. Postdoctoral fellow Pasteur Inst., Paris, 1985-87; group leader Nat. Cancer Inst., Frederick, Md., 1988-91, sect. chief ABL, 1991-94; prof., dir. Ctr. Devel. Biology U. Tex. Southwestern Med. Ctr., Dallas, 1994—, Dana and Richard C. Strauss disting. chmn. in devel. biology, 1994—, dir. Kent Waldrep Ctr. for Basic Rsch. on Nerve Growth, 1997—, Southwestern Bell disting. chair in basic neurosci. rsch., 1998—. Mem. sci. adv. bd. Rett Syndrome Found., N.Y., 1999—, Christopher Reeve paralysis Found., N.Y.C., 1996—; mem. sci. adv. coun. Damon Runyan-Walter Winchell Cancer Fund., N.Y.C., 1998—, Nat. Neurofibromatosis Found., N.Y.C., 1997—; chmn. bd. sci. counselors Nat. Inst. Neurol. Disorders and Stroke, Bethesda, Md., 1999—; mem. bd. sci. counselors Nat. Cancer Inst., Bethesda, 1995-99; rschr. in field. Patentee in field. Office: U Tex Southwestern Med Ctr 6000 Harry Hines Blvd Dallas TX 75390-9133

PARADIS, DONALD EDWARD, lawyer, arbitrator; b. West Harwick, R.I., Dec. 17, 1923; s. Charles Desire and Elizabeth Agnes (Murphy) P.; m. Elizabeth Evans Reid, Mar. 15, 1947 (dec. Mar. 1996); children: Nancy, Martha, Timothy. BA, Wesleyan U., Middletown, Conn., 1943; JD, Harvard Law Sch., 1950. Bar: Mass., N.Y. Assoc. gen. counsel Economic Coop. Adminstrn., Paris, France, 1950-52; dep. U.S. observer European Army, 1952-53; atty. Cahill, Gordon, Reindel & Ohl, N.Y.C., 1953-57; legal advisor Imperial Ethiopian Govt., Addis Ababa, 1957-68; pres., CEO Chappaqua Oil Corp., London, 1969-73, Excalibur Oil Co., London, 1971-73; ptnr. Casey, Lane & Mittendorf, 1974-79; internat. arbitrator pvt. practice, Washington, 1980—. Lt. JG, U.S. Navy, 1943-46. Recipient Grand Officer Star of Ethiopia, Imperial Ethiopian Govt., 1968. Mem. Metropolitan Club, University Club. Avocations: reading, music, travel. Home: 2737 Devonshire Pl NW Washington DC 20008-3479 E-mail: thebigdep@aol.com.

PARADISE, LOUIS VINCENT, educational psychology educator, university official; b. Scranton, Pa., Apr. 19, 1946; s. Louis Benjamin and Lucille (Bochicchio) P.; children: Christopher, Gabrielle,Victoria. BS, Pa. State U., 1968; MS, Bucknell U., 1974; PhD, U. Va., 1976. Lic. psychologist, profl. counselor; cert. sch. psychologist. Assoc. prof. Cath. U. Am., Washington, 1976-83; prof. edn., chmn. edn. leadership U. New Orleans, 1983-90, dean Coll. Edn., 1990-92, univ. vice chancellor and provost, 1992-94, exec. vice chancellor, provost, 1994—. Author: Ethics in Counseling and Psychotherapy, 1979, Questioning: Skills for the Helping Process, 1979, Counseling in Community College, 1982. 1st lt. U.S. Army, 1968-72. DuPont scholar U. Va., 1974. Mem. APA, ACA (ethics com. 1986-89), Am. Edn. Rsch. Assn., So. Assn. Counselor Edn. (chmn. ethics com. 1988-89), Acad. Counseling Psychology, Chi Sigma Iota (founding chpt. pres. 1985-87). Roman Catholic. Avocations: running, cycling. Office: U New Orleans Office Acad Affairs New Orleans LA 70148-0001 E-mail: louis.paradise@uno.edu.

PARADISE, PAUL RICHARD, writer, editor; b. N.Y.C., July 4, 1950; s. Paul L. and Ann (Ho) P. BA in Journalism, Wash. State U., 1975; MLS, Pratt Inst., Bklyn., 2002. Staff writer T.F.H. Publs., Neptune, N.J., 1977-79; legal indexer Matthew Bender, N.Y.C., 1980-86; free-lance writer, 1988—. Author: Raccoons, 1976, Amazon Parrots, 1978, African Gray Parrots, 1979, Cockatiels, 1987, Trademark Counterfeiting, Product Piracy and the Billion Dollar Threat to the U.S. Economy, 1999. Mayors Grad. scholar, 2001—. Mem. Soc. Profl. Journalists. Home: 722 Willow Ave Hoboken NJ 07030-4034 E-mail: prpirate@aol.com.

PARADYSZ, MARSHA L. academic administrator; b. Clinton, Ind., May 1, 1957; d. Claude Derrill and Bessie Faye (Brown) Wilson; children: Matthew Dustin Hickman, Jessica Faye Hickman; m. William David Paradysz; 1 child, Tara Star. BS in Mgmt. of Human Resources, Oakland City (Ind.) Coll., 1991; postgrad., Ind. U. S.E., New Albany. Asst. dist. mgr. Avon Products, Cin., 1978-87; asst. to English and math. profs. Oakland City U., Bedford, 1987-89; admissions counselor Bedford (Ind.) Coll. Ctr., 1994-96; adminstrv. asst. Orange County Child Care Cooperative, Paoli, Ind., 1988-90, dir. youth svcs., 1990-93; dir. Lawrence County First Steps and Step Ahead, 1996; exec. dir. Orange County Child Care Coop., Paoli, 1997-98; asst. dir. devel. Sarasota Ballet of Fla., 1998-99; instr. Ind. Bus. Coll., 1999—2002, dir. continuing edn., 2002—. Mem. svc.-learning adv. com. Middle Grades Improvement, Paoli, 1992-93; mem. gifted and talented adv. com. Paoli Schs., 1990-98; asst. property mgr. Meridian Mgmt., 1999—. Actor, singer, dancer Orange County Players, Paoli, 1985-98; bd. dirs. Internat. Network for Children and Families, 1998-99; elder Presbyn. Ch., 1998—. Named one of Outstanding Young Women Am., 1986; Youth as Resources grantee Nat. Crime Prevention Coun., 1992, 91, Cmty. Guidance for Youth grantee Lilly Endowment, 1993; recipient Gov.'s Voluntary Action award State of Ind., 1992, 93. Presbyterian. Avocations: music, canoeing, writing, reading, theater. Home: 5508 E Rawles Ter Indianapolis IN 46219-7121

PARAGAS, ROLANDO G. physician; b. Philippines, Apr. 15, 1935; came to U.S., 1959; s. Epifanio Y. and Ester (Guiang) P.; m. Liwayway Galvey, May 5, 1963; children: Suzanne, Richard, Esther, Dawn. AA, U. Philippines, 1953; MD, Far Eastern U., 1958. Physician pvt. practice, Burlington, Iowa, 1968—. Fellow Am. Acad. Pediatrics; mem. AMA, Assn. Philippine Physicians in Am., Iowa Med. Soc. Office: 828 N 7th St Burlington IA 52601-4921

PARAISO, JOHNNA KAYE, elementary education educator; b. Wyandotte, Mich., Nov. 17, 1961; d. John Calvin and Ruth (Hughes) Underwood; m. Normandy Paraiso, Oct. 6, 1984; children: Sophia Elisabeth, Abigail Mahalia, Genevieve Christine. BS, Bob Jones U., 1983. Cert. ACSI, educator K-8 (all subjects). Tchr. fifth grade Temple Christian Sch., Redford, Mich., 1983-86; music tchr. Fairlane Christian Sch., Dearborn Heights, 1986-90; tchr. 2d grade Internat. Christian Sch., San Francisco, 1992-93, dept. head primary childhood edn., 1992-93. Freelance musician children's concerts; leader Curriculum Selection Com.; initiator Elem. Music Program; dir. several dramatic prodns.; tchr. piano, guitar. Children's minister 1st Bapt. Ch., San Francisco, 1991-94. Mem. Pi Lambda Theta. Home: 2024 Stonebrook Dr Murfreesboro TN 37128-5334

PARALEZ, LINDA LEE, technology management consultant; b. Raton, N.Mex., Oct. 29, 1955; AS, Amarillo Coll., 1975; student, West Tex. State U., 1975-77; BBA, Century U., Beverly Hills, Calif., 1984, MBA, 1987, PhD in Bus. Mgmt. and Econ. Tchg. asst. Amarillo (Tex.) Coll., 1974-75; drafter natural gas divsn. Pioneer Corp., Amarillo, 1975-76; sr. drafter exploration divsn. Amarillo Oil Co., 1976-77; drafting supr., engring. svcs., supr., dir. spkrs. bur. Thunder Basin Coal Co., Atlantic Richfield Co., Wright, Wyo., 1977-86; pres. Rose Enterprises, Inc., 1986-99, Treefarm Ctr. Inc., 1999—; prof. tech. mgmt. U. Phoenix, Utah, 1995-96; owner, pres., CEO Treeform Ctr. Cons., Poulsbo, Wash.; CEO REZ Global, Doulsbo. Adj. prof. Weber State U., Ogden, Utah; tech. writer Eaton Corp., Riverton, Wyo., 1986-88; cons. State Wyo. Office on Family Violence and Sexual Assault, Cheyenne, 1986-89, Diamond L. Industries, Inc., Gillete, Wyo., 1986-88; tech. writer, pubs. cons. Thiokol Corp., Brigham City, Utah, 1987-89, design specialist space ops., 1989-90, mgr. total quality mgmt. ctr. space ops., 1990-98; cons. organizational effectiveness and quality mgmt. principles; cons. incident investigation team NASA Space Shuttle Solid Rocket Booster Program, Huntsville, Ala.; cons. process improvement Puget Power, Seattle, Wash., Pub. Svc. Co. of Colo., W.R. White; cons. process design Microsoft Corp., Seattle; mgmt. cons., consulting dir. Western Regional Water Utilities Benchmarking Group; process redesign cons. City of Seattle, 1995—; rsch. specialist Child Abuse Prevention Ctr., 1994-99; rsch. benchmarking specialist Western Regional Water Utilities Benchmarking Group, 1996-99. Author: (poetry) God was Here, But He Left Early, 1976, Gift of Wings, 1980, 89; contbg. author: The Changing Water Utility, 1999; columnist Wytech Digest; contbr. numerous articles to profl. jours. Vol. NASA Young Astronauts Program Adv. Com., 1991—; bd. dirs. Campbell County Drafting Adv. Coun., 1984-85; sec. bd. dirs. exec. com. Am. Inst. Design and Drafting, 1984-85, tech. publ. chairperson, 1984-85; vol. educator, data specialist child abuse prevention coun., Ogden. Named Most Outstanding Woman, Beta Sigma Phi, 1980, 81; recipient Woman in the Industry recognition Internat. Reprographics Assn., 1980; grand prize winner Wyo. Art Show with painting titled Energy, 1976. Mem. AAUW, NAFE, NOW, Am. Soc. Quality Control, Am. Productivity and Quality Coun., Am. Legion Aux, Ocean Rsch. Edn. Soc., Gloucester, Mass. (grant proposal writer, 1984), Soc. Tech. Communications, 4-H Club. Home: 22259 Treefarm Ln NE Poulsbo WA 98370-9064

PARAN, MARK LLOYD, lawyer; b. Cleve., Feb. 1, 1953; s. Edward Walter and Margaret Gertrude (Ebert) P. AB in Sociology cum laude, Harvard U., 1977, JD, 1980. Bar: Ill. 1980, Mass. 1986, Tex. 1993. Assoc. Wilson & McIlvaine, Chgo., 1980-83, Lurie Sklar & Simon, Ltd., Chgo., 1983-85, Sullivan & Worcester, Boston, 1985-92; pvt. practice, 1992, Euless, Tex., 1992—. Mem. ABA, State Bar Tex. Avocations: tornado hunting, severe thunderstorms, photography. Home and Office: 1050 W Ash Ln Apt 1015 Euless TX 76039-2171 E-mail: tornado@attbi.com.

PARASCOS, EDWARD THEMISTOCLES, engineering consultant; b. N.Y.C., Oct. 20, 1931; s. Christos and Nina (Demitrovich) P.; m. Jenny Morris, July 12, 1978; children: Jennifer Mellissa, Edward T., Jr. BSME, CCNY, 1956, MSME, 1958; postgrad. ops. rsch., NYU, 1964. Registered profl. engr., Calif. Design engr. Ford Instrument, 1957-61; reliability engring. supr. Kearfott divsn. Gen. Precision Inc., 1961-63; staff cons. Am. Power Jet, 1963-64; reliability mgr. Perkin Elmer Corp., 1964-66; dir. system effectiveness CBS Labs., Stamford, Conn., 1966-72; pres. Dipar Cons. Svcs. Ltd., East Elmhurst, N.Y., Lapa Trading Corp.; gen. mgr., prin. reliability engr. engring. Consol. Edison Co., N.Y.C., 1972-95, mgr. transp. and stores environ. affairs, 1995-98, ret., 1998; sr. reliability engring. cons. Morris Cons. Agy., 1998—. Pres., chmn. bd. RAM Cons. Assocs.; pres., 1978-80; chmn. 1st Reliability Engring. Conf. Electric Power Industry, 1974, also 4th and 18th confs.; chmn. bd. Inter-Ram Q Conf. for electric power industry; gen. chmn. 18th Inter-Ramq Conf. for electric power industry; lectr. in field. Fellow Am. Soc. Quality Control (vice chmn. Reliability divsn. 1968-70, sr. mem.); mem. ASME, Soc. Reliability Engrs., Edison Engring. Soc. Home: 30-02 83rd St Jackson Heights NY 11370-1919 Office: Morris Consulting Agy 82-18 30th Ave Jackson Heights NY 11370 E-mail: ETP1919@aol.com.

PARASURAMAN, T. V. pharmaceutical executive; b. Calcutta, India, June 5, 1965; s. Perambaur V. and Saradha Venkateswaran; m. Bhash M. Mukherjee; children: Kurran, Rajat. BPharm, Birla Inst. Tech., Mesra, India, 1988; PhD, U. La., Monroe, 1992. Prin. scientist GlaxoWellcome, Research Triangle Park, NC, 1992—97; dir. worldwide human health mktg. Merck & Co., Whitehouse Station, NJ, 1997—98; exec. dir. Hastings Health Care Group, Pennington, 1998—99; dir. global health outcomes assessment Wyeth-Ayerst Rsch.,

Radnor, Pa., 1999—2001; sr. dir. global health outcomes assessment Wyeth, St. Davids, 2001—. Sr. sci. cons. Hastings Health Care Group, Pennington, 1998—99; spkr. in field. Author: (theoretical social integration model) Development of a model of social integration, 2000, (continuing med. edn. credit) Estimating the economic impact of viral meningitis, 2000; contbr. sci. articles to profl. jours. Mem.: Indian Students Assn. (sec. 1989—92), Internat. Soc. for Pharmacoeconomics and Outcomes Rsch. Hindu. Avocation: travel. Office: Wyeth 555 E Lancaster Ave Wayne PA 19087 Office Fax: 610-995-3310. Business E-Mail: parasut@war.wyeth.com.

PARATJE, MERCEDES, bank executive; b. Barcelona, Spain; m. Sergio Verdu; 1 child, Ariana Verdu. Grad. telecommunications engring., Poly. U. Barcelona, 1981; MA in Labor Rels., U. Ill., 1983, MBA in Fin., 1985. Lic. stockbroker. Engr. N.V. Philips, Barcelona, 1978-81; fin. analyst Ctr. Internat. Fin. Analysis, Princeton, N.J., 1985-87, rsch. mgr., 1987-88; 2nd v.p., investment strategist internat. pvt. bank Chase Manhattan Bank, N.Y.C., 1988-90, 2d v.p., internat. equity analyst, 1990-91; v.p., portfolio mgr. pvt. banking internat. The Chase Manhattan Pvt. Bank, 1991-94; v.p., global product head equity adv. svcs. Citicorp Securities Pvt. Bank Divsn., 1994-98; chief investment officer Americas pvt. bank divsn. Barclays Bank, N.Y.C., 1998-2000; global head Investment Adv. Svcs., N.Y.C., London, 2000—. Co-editor: Worldscope, Industrial, 1988; contbg. researcher: Worldscope, Financial, 1988, International Accounting Trends, 1989; contbr. articles to profl. publs. Mem. European Register Tech. Professions, Nat. Assn. Tech. Engrs. (prize 1981), Sigma Iota Epsilon. Home: 6 Farrand Rd Princeton NJ 08540-6777 Office: Barclays Pvt Bank 34th Fl Tower 49 12 E 49th St New York NY 10017-1028

PARAZYNSKI, SCOTT E. astronaut; b. Little Rock, July 28, 1961; m. Gail Marie Vozzella; 2 children. BS in Biology, Stanford U., 1983, MD with honors, 1989. Intern Brigham and Women's Hosp., 1990; resident in emergency medicine Denver; astronaut NASA, Houston, 1992, crew rep. Astronaut Office Mission Devel. Br., crew rep. Astronaut Office Ops. Planning Br., dep. Astronaut Office ISS Br. Team coach for the Philippines Olympic Winter Games, Calgary, Canada, 1988. Recipient Predoctoral Tng. award in cancer biology, NIH, 1983. Mem.: Aircraft Owners and Pilots Assn., Exptl. Aircraft Assn., Assn. Space Explorers, Wilderness Med. Soc. (Rsch. award 1991), Am. Soc. Gravitational and Space Biology, Aerospace Med. Assn., Am. Alpine Club. Achievements include logged over 2,000 flight hourse in a variety of aircraft; logged over 1.019 hours in space; 20 hours EVA; crew STS-66 (1994), STS-86 Atlantis (1997), STS-95 Discovery (1998) and STS-100 Endeavour (2001). Avocations: mountaineering, rock climbing, flying, scuba diving, skiing. Office: Astronaut Office/CB NASA Johnson Space Ctr Houston TX 77058*

PARCELL, JOHN CLEO, music educator; b. Oskaloosa, Iowa, July 17, 1945; s. John Melvin and Verda Louella May Parcell; m. Cathy Kay Hardy, Sept. 30, 1990; m. Gretchen Paullette Van Gorp, Aug. 28, 1966 (div. Aug. 0, 1990); children: Kent Bradley, Khristina Lynn. BS, NE Mo. St U., Kirksville, MO, 1967; MA, Truman St U., Kirksville, MO, 1968; MS, Ctrl. Mo. St U., Warrensburg, MO, 2000; DMA, U. Mo., Kansas City, MO, 1990. DESE-Life Certification Mo., Orff Schulewerk Level J Mo., Elementary Administration-DESE Mo. Band dir. Rich Ctrl. H.S., Olympia Field, Ill., 1967—69, Tipton Cmty. Sch., Tipton, Iowa, 1969—72, Maynard (West Ctrl.), Maynard, 1972—73, Carl Junction R-I Schools, Carl Junction, Mo., 1973—73; choir dir. Meml. H.S., Joplin, 1980—82; music and instrumental music tchr. Joplin R-8, 1982—88; elem. music tchr. Kans. City Sch. Dist., Kansas City, 1990—; adj. prof. Longview CC, Lee's Summit, 1992—. Music critic Pk. Forest Star, Park Forest, Ill., 1967—69; trumpet player Chgo. Hgts Symphony, Chicago Heights, Ill., 1967—69; member-european tour Mid Am. Jazz & Concert Band-Coe Coll., Cedar Rapids, Iowa, 1972; member-mexican tour Kans. City Symphony Chorus, Kansas City, Mo., 1988; mem. Mid. Sch. Music Curriculum Committe, Joplin, Mo., 1984, Profl. Devel. Com., Kansas City, Mo., 1990—2000, Kans. City Sch. Dist. Core Curriculum and Textbook Com., Kansas City, Mo., 1999—2000. Camelot cast mem. Joplin Little Theater, Joplin, Mo., 1983—83; asst. condr. Carthage Cmty. Band, Carthage, 1985—87; mem. Blue Springs Summer Musical Orch., Blue Springs, 1990—95. Recipient Cowlgill & Blair Incentive Award, SW Mo. Teachers Assoc, 1986, Phi Kappa Phi, Ctrl. Mo. St U., 2000. Mem.: Mo. Music Educators Assn., Music Educators Nat. Conf. Southern Baptist. Avocations: music listening, music listening, landscaping, instrument and vocal music performance. Home: 5433 Appleton Ave Raytown MO 64133 Office: Kansas City School District 12th & McGee Kansas City MO 64109 Office Fax: 816-672-2078. Personal E-mail: john-cathy@sbcglobal.net.

PARCELLS, FREDERICK R. underwriter; b. Chgo., May 14, 1957; s. Charles Hubbard and Winifred Elaine (Summer) P. AA, Barton County C.C., Great Bend, Kans., 1977; BA in Fin., U. Ill., 1980; MBA, Ind. U., 1985. CFP, CPCU; assoc. in risk mgmt., assoc. in reinsurance/Ins. Inst. Am. Actuarial trainee CNA Ins., Chgo., 1980-81; actuarial technician Sentry Ins., Stevens Point, Wis., 1982-83; scouting intern The Buffalo Bills, Orchard Park, Fredonia, N.Y., 1984; underwriting trainee Kemper Group, Chgo., 1986-87, casualty underwriter Chgo. and St. Louis, 1987-88; acct. underwriter Northbrook P&C Ins. (subs. Allstate), Chgo., 1988-91; sr. account underwriter Northbrook Property and Casualty Ins., Chgo./Rolling Meadows, 1991; sr. underwriter Allstate Ins., South Barrington, Ill., 1991-95; product analyst CNA Ins. Cos., Chgo., 1995-97; sr. splty. exec. underwriter Interstate Ins. Group, 1997-2000; sr. underwriter Apex Ins. Mgrs., 2001—. Asst. chmn. civic affairs com., Cambridge Forest Assn., Lincolnshire, Ill., 1980-81; treas. Santa Claus Anonymous, Chgo., 1990-91, 91-92, pres., 1992-93; vol. duplex constrn. Habitat for Humanity, Chgo., 1988, 89. Mem. CPCU Soc. (sec. Chgo. chpt. 1994-95, bd. dirs./pub. rels. chmn. 1993-94, mem. nat. underwriting sect. com. 1994—, treas. Chgo. chpt. 1995-96, v.p. Chgo. chpt. 1996-97, pres. Chgo. chpt. 1997-98, past pres. 1998-2000com. chair 2001-). Presbyterian. Home: 1330 N Lasalle St Chicago IL 60610-1986 Office: Apex Ins Mgrs LLC 500 W Madison St Ste 450 Chicago IL 60661 E-mail: fparcells@apexamerican.com.

PARDAVI-HORVATH, MARTHA MARIA, physicist, educator; b. Budapest, Hungary, Feb. 3, 1940; came to U.S., 1985; d. Elek and Katalin (Sattelberger) H.; m. Ferenc Pardavi, July 7, 1967; 1 child, Martha. PhD in Physics, Hungarian Acad. Sci., Budapest, 1985, R. Eotvos U., 1988. Rsch. assoc. Hungarian Acad. Sci., Budapest, 1967-75, head lab., 1975-85; rsch. assoc. Ohio State U., Columbus, 1988; vis. prof. NRC, Rome, 1989; prof. George Washington U., Washington, 1989—. Author: Microelectronic Technology, Magnetic Multilayers, Nonlinear Microwave Signal Processing, Magnetic Systems; contbr. more than 140 articles to profl. jours. Mem. IEEE (chpt. chair 1989), AAAS, N.Y. Acad. Scis., Am. Phys. Soc., Internat. Soc. Interdisciplinary Study of Symmetry (sec.), Sigma Xi. Office: George Washington U Dept ECE 801 22nd St NW Washington DC 20052

PARDE, DUANE ARTHUR, association executive; BA in Polit. Sci., History, U. Kans. Legis. rsch. asst. Atty. Gen. Office, Topeka, 1986-87; dir. state legis. rsch. Am. Legis. Exchange Coun., Washington, 1989-92; dir. state affairs Coun. Affordable Health Ins., Alexandria, Va., 1992-95; chief of staff Am. Legis. Exchange Coun., 1995-96, exec. dir., 1996—. Bd. adv. Kans. Pub. Policy Inst. Mem. Am. Soc. Assn. Exec. Office: Am Legis Exchange Coun 910 17th St NW Fl 5 Washington DC 20006-2601

PARDEE, ARTHUR BECK, biochemist, educator; b. Chgo., July 13, 1921; s. Charles A. and Elizabeth B. (Beck) Pardee; m. Ruth Sager (dec.); m. Ann Goodman; children: Michael, Richard, Thomas. BS, U. Calif. at Berkeley, 1942; MS, Calif. Inst. Tech., 1943, PhD, 1947; D (hon.) (hon.) , U. Paris, 1993. Merck postdoctoral fellow U. Wis., 1947—49; mem. faculty U. Calif. at Berkeley, 1949—61, assoc. prof., 1957—61; NSF fellow Pasteur Inst., 1957—58; prof. biology, chmn. dept. biochem. scis. Princeton, 1961—67; prof. biochemistry Princeton U., 1961—75; Donner prof. sci. Princeton, 1966; prof. Dana Farber Cancer Inst. and biochem. pharmacology dept. Harvard Med. Sch., Boston, 1975—. Co-author: Experiments in Biochemical Research Techniques, 1957; editor: Biochemica et Biophysica Acta, 1962—68. Mem. rsch. adv. coun. Am. Cancer Soc., 1967—71; trustee Cold Spring Harbor Lab. Quantitative Biology, 1963—69. Named Princess Takamatu lectr., 1990, hon. faculty mem., Nanjing U., 1999; recipient Young Biochemists travel award, NSF, 1952, Krebs medal, Fedn. European Biochem. Socs., 1973, Rosenstiel award, Brandeis U., 1975, 3M award, Fedn. Am. Socs., Exptl. Biology, 1980, CIIT Prize, 1993, Disting. Alumnus awar, Calif. Inst. Tech., 1999; fellow fellow, Internat. Inst. for Advanced Studies, 1999. Fellow: AAAS; mem.: Chem. Industry Inst. Toxicology (Founders award, Boehringer-Mannheim award 1998), Ludwig Inst. Cancer Rsch. (sci. com. 1988—), Japanese Biochem. Soc., Am. Philos. Soc., Am. Soc. Microbiologists, Am. Assn. Cancer Rsch. (pres. 1985—86), Am. Soc. Biol. Chemists (treas. 1964—70, pres. 1980—81), Am. Chem. Soc. (Paul Lewis award 1960), NAS (editl. bd. proc. 1971—73, com. on scis. and pub. policy 1973—76). Office: 44 Binney St Boston MA 02115-6013 E-mail: pardee@mbcrr.harvard.edu.

PARDEE, JEFFREY CLARK, county government official; b. N.Y.C., May 14, 1944; s. Jack Howard II and Florence (Brennan) P.; m. Mary Anna Weil, Dec. 23, 1966; children: Brennan James, Kennedy Clark. BBA, Eastern Mich. U., 1968; MBA in Fin., U. Detroit, 1971; postgrad., Nova U., 1975-81. Cert. pub. fin. officer. Fin. analyst Sterling Axle Plant div. Ford Motor Co., Sterling Heights, Mich., 1968-73; budget dir. Genesee County, Flint, 1973-76, Oakland County, Pontiac, 1976-95, dep. dir. mgmt. and budget, 1996-99, dir. mgmt. and budget, 1999—. Treas. Flint-Genesee Corp. for Econ. Growth, 1978-81; pres. Genesee County Econ. Devel. Corp., Flint, 1982-84; bd. dirs. Forward Devel. Corp; chmn. bd. dirs. Communications Services Network, Inc.; adj. prof. pub. budgeting U. Mich., Flint, 1984-85. Editor Statewide News-Mich. Rental Housing Assn. Newsletter, 1985-95. Merit counselor Boy Scouts Am., Grand Blanc, Mich., 1982—, dist. com. chmn. Tall Pines Coun., 1998-2001; councilman City of Grand Blanc, 1985—; treas. Crime Watch Assn., Grand Blanc, 1985—, Genesee County Met. Alliance, Flint, 1986-91; bd. dirs. Flint-Genesee Revolving Loan Fund, 1980-90; treas. Partnership Saginaw Bay Watershed, 1987-2001, Grand Blanc Vision 2020, 1998—; pres. Mich. Mcpl. Fin. Officers Assn., 1995-96; mem. GFOA Mgmt. Budget Com., 1998—; mem. City Coun., Grand Blanc, Mich., 1985--. Recipient Fin. Officer award CFO Mag., 2000. Mem. Govt. Fin. Officers Assn. U.S. and Can. (review com. 1984—, Disting. Budget Presentation award, Excellence in Fin. Reporting award), Am. Soc. Pub. Adminstrs., G.M.I. Mgmt. and Engring. Inst. (adv. bd. 1984-87). Republican. Mem. Lds Ch. Avocations: racquetball, auto racing. Home: 11390 Grand Oak Dr Grand Blanc MI 48439-1219 Office: Oakland County Dept Mgmt & Budget 1200 N Telegraph Rd Pontiac MI 48341-0407 E-mail: pardeej@co.oakland.mi.us.

PARDEE, MARGARET ROSS, violinist, violist, educator; b. Valdosta, Ga., May 10, 1920; d. William Augustus and Frances Ross (Burton) P.; m. Daniel Rogers Butterly, July 4, 1944. Diploma, Juilliard Sch. Music, 1940, grad. diploma, 1942; diploma, Juilliard Grad. Sch., 1945. Instr. violin and viola Manhattanville Coll. Sacred Heart, N.Y.C., 1942-54, Juilliard Sch., N.Y.C., 1942, Meadowmount Sch. Music, Westport, N.Y., 1956-84, 88-92, Bowdoin Coll. Music Festival and Sch., Maine, summer 1987. Mem. faculty Estherwood Sch. and Summr Festival, 1984-86, Killington (Vt.) Music Festival, 1993—, Mannes Sch. Music, 1996—; concert master Gt. Neck (L.I., N.Y.) Symphony, 1954-85; adj. assoc. prof. Aaron Copeland Sch. Music, Queens Coll., CUNY, Flushing, 1978—, Adelphi U., Garden City, N.Y., 1979-83; adj. prof. SUNY, Purchase, 1980-93; vis. prof. Simon Bolivar Youth Orch. and Conservatory, Caracas and Barquisimeto, Venezuela, 1988, 89, Conservatorio Orch. Nat. Juvenil, Caracas, 1988, 89; mem. jury for internat. competitions; guest artist profl. 1st Internat. Festival for Young Violinists, Caracas, 1988; guest vis. prof. Orch. Filarmonica Nat. y Mcpl. Sinfonica Caracas, 1992, 97. Debut N.Y. Town Hall, 1952; toured U.S. as soloist and in chamber music groups; soloed with symphony orchs., Miss., N.J., D.C., N.Y. Bd. dirs. Meadowmount Sch. Music. Recipient Andres Bello award Venezuela Min. Edn., 1993. Mem. Soc. for Strings (dir. 1965-92), Assoc. Music Tchrs. League N.Y. (cert.), N.Y. State Music Tchrs. Assn. (cert., citation 1989), Music Tchrs. Nat. Assn., Am. String Tchrs. Assn. (citation for exceptional leadership 1990), Am. Fedn. Musicians, Viola Rsch. Soc. Office: care Juilliard Sch Lincoln Ctr Plz New York NY 10023

PARDEE, OTWAY O'MEARA, computer science educator; b. Seattle, June 26, 1920; s. Otway and Mary Gertrude (O'Meara) P.; m. Marilynn Lowrie, Aug. 9, 1946; children— Irene, Loraine, Suzanne BS in Elec. Engring., U. Wash., 1941; PhD in Elec. Engring., Stanford U., 1948. Instr. math. Syracuse U., N.Y., 1948-52, asst. to assoc. prof., 1952-69, dir. Computing Ctr., 1962-69, prof. computer sci., 1969-86, prof. emeritus, 1986—. Served with U.S. Navy (USNR) 1944-46. Mem. AAUP (pres. Syracuse U. chpt. 1960), Assn. Computing Machinery (chmn. Syracuse chpt. 1963), Am. Math. Soc., Math. Assn. Am., Am. Phys. Soc., IEEE, Sigma XI, Tau Beta Pi. Avocations: camping; photography. Home: 843 Maryland Ave Syracuse NY 13210-2502 Office: Syracuse U Ctr for Sci and Tech Ste 2-175 Syracuse NY 13244-0001 E-mail: oopardee@syr.edu.

PARDEE, SCOTT EDWARD, securities dealer; b. New Haven, Oct. 11, 1936; s. William Durley and Catherine (Eames) P.; m. Aida Milagros Fuentes Tavarez, Jan. 29, 1966; 1 child, Alan Alexander. BA, Dartmouth Coll., 1958; PhD, MIT, 1962. Research asst. Fed. Res. Bank, Boston, 1959-62; teaching asst. in econs. MIT, Cambridge, Mass., 1961-62; research economist Fed. Res. Bank N.Y., N.Y.C., 1962-66, mgr. fgn. dept., 1967-70, asst. v.p. fgn. dept., 1970-74, v.p. fgn. dept., 1974-79; tchr. banking and fin. NYU, 1965-67, Am. Inst. Banking, 1969-72; adj. prof. Grad. Sch. Bus. Columbia U., N.Y.C., 1972-75; dep. mgr. fgn. ops. Fed. Res. System Open Market Account, 1975-79, mgr. fgn. ops., 1979-81; exec. v.p., dir. Discount Corp. N.Y., N.Y.C., 1981-86; dir. Am. Internat. Group, 1982-86; vice chmn. Yamaichi Internat. Am. Inc., N.Y.C., 1986-88, chmn., 1988-95, sr. advisor, 1995-97; sr. lect., exec. dir. Fin. Rsch. Ctr., MIT Sloan Scool of Mgmt., 1997-99; adj. prof. Grad. Sch. of Business, U. Chicago, Chicago, IL, 1997-98; Alan R. Holmes prof. of monetary econs. Middlebury Coll., Vt., 2000—. Bd. dirs. Renaissance Holdings, Ltd. Author: A Study of Inter-City Wage Differentials, 1962. Trustee Woodrow Wilson Fellowship Found., 1994—; mem. Coun. on Fgn. Rels., 1995—. Woodrow Wilson fellow MIT, 1958-59; recipient Dr. Louis M. Spadaro award Fordham U., 1980 Mem. Phi Beta Kappa. Home: 250 South End Ave New York NY 10280-1074 Office: Middlebury Coll Econs Dept Middlebury VT 05753

PARDEN, ROBERT JAMES, engineering educator, management consultant; b. Mason City, Iowa, Apr. 17, 1922; s. James Ambrose and Mary Ellen (Fahey) P.; m. Elizabeth Jane Taylor, June 15, 1955; children— Patricia Gale, James A., John R., Nancy Ann. BS in Mech. Engring, State U. Iowa, 1947, MS, 1951, PhD, 1953. Reg. profl. engr. Iowa, Calif.; lic. gen. contractor Calif. Indsl. engr. LaCrosse Rubber Mills, 1947-50; asso. dir. Iowa Mgmt. Course, 1951-53; asso. prof. indsl. engring. Ill. Inst. Tech., 1953-54; prof. engring. mgmt. Santa Clara U., 1955—, dean Sch. Engring., 1955-82; prin. Saratoga Cons. Group (Calif.), 1982—. Mem. Sec. Navy's Survey Bd. Grad. Edn., 1964 Mem. Saratoga Planning Commn., 1959-61. Served to 1st lt., Q.M.C. AUS, 1943-46. Named to Silicon Valley Engring. Hall of Fame Silicon Valley Engring. Coun., 1993. Mem. ASME (chmn. Santa Clara Valley sect. 1958), Am. Soc. Engring. Edn. (chmn. Pacific N.W. sect. 1960), Am. Inst. Indsl. Engrs. (edn. chmn. 1958-63, dir. ASEE-ECPD affairs 1963-68), Nat. Soc. Profl. Engrs., Engrs. Council Profl. Devel. (dir. 1964-65, 66-69), Soc. Advancement Mgmt., ASEM, Sigma Xi, Tau Beta Pi. Roman Catholic. Home: 19832 Bonnie Ridge Way Saratoga CA 95070-5010 Office: Santa Clara U Sch Engring Santa Clara CA 95053-0001 E-mail: bobparden@attbi.com, rparden@scu.edu.

PARDES, HERBERT, psychiatrist, educator; b. Bronx, N.Y., July 7, 1934; s. Louis and Frances (Bergman) P.; m. Juidith Ellen Silber, June 9, 1957; children: Stephen, Lawrence, James. BS, Rutgers U., 1956; MD, SUNY, Bklyn., 1960; DSc (hon.), SUNY, 1990. Straight med. intern Kings County Hosp., 1960-61, resident in psychiatry, 1961-62, 64-66; asst. prof. psychiatry Downstate Med. Ctr., Bklyn., 1968-72, prof., chmn. dept., 1972-75; dir. psychiat. svcs. Kings County Hosp., 1972-75; prof., chmn. dept. psychiatry U. Colo. Med. Sch., 1975-78; dir. psychiat. svcs. Colo. Psychiat. Hosp., Denver, 1975-78; dir. NIMH, Rockville, Md., 1978-84; asst. surgeon gen. USPHS, 1978-84; prof. psychiatry Columbia U., N.Y.C., 1984—, chmn. dept., 1984—, dir. Psychiat. Inst., 1984-89, v.p. for health scis., dean faculty medicine, 1989—99; pres., CEO N.Y.-Presbyn. Hosp., 2000—. Contbr. articles to med. jours. Pres. sci. bd. Alliance for Rsch. on Schizophrenia and Depression. Capt. M.C., AUS, 1972-74. Named Ann. Hon. Lectr. Downstate Med. Ctr. Alumni Assn., 1972; recipient Alumni Achievement medal, 1980, William Menninger award ACP, 1992, Dorothy Dix award Mental Illness Fedn., 1992, Vester Mark award, 1994, Salmon award, 1996. Mem. Assn. Am. Med. Colls. (chair 1995-96), Am. Psychiat. Assn. (v.p. 1986-88, pres. 1989-90, Disting. Svc. award 1993), Inst. Medicine, Am. Psychoanalytic Assn., Coun. of Deans (adminstrv. bd., chair-elect 1993-94, chair 1994-95), Assoc. Med. Schs. N.Y. (pres. 1995-2000), Phi Beta Kappa, Alpha Omega Alpha. Office: NY Presbyn Hosp Pres and CEOs Office 161 Ft Washington Ave New York NY 10032 also: 525 E 68th St New York NY 10021

PARDIECK, ROGER LEE, lawyer; b. Seymour, Ind., Mar. 1, 1937; s. Martin W. and Lorna (Wente) P.; m. Mary Ann Pardieck; children: Amy, Andrew, Melissa, Duncan. AB, Ind. U., 1959, LLB, 1963; student, Internat. Grad. Sch., Stockholm, 1960. Bar: Ind. 1963, U.S. Dist. Ct. (so. dist.) Ind. 1964, U.S. Ct. Appeals (7th cir.) 1965; diplomate Am. Bd. Trial Advocates. Tchg. asst. Ind. U., Bloomington, 1963-64; spl. prosecutor Jackson County, Ind., 1964-65; ptnr. Montgomery, Elsner and Pardieck, 1965-84; prin. Pardieck & Gill, PC, Seymour, Ind., 1985—. Faculty Nat. Inst. Trial Advocacy, Ind.; lectr. in field. Contbr. articles to profl. jours. Bd. dirs. Seymour Girls Club, 1968-72, Seymour C. of C., 1971-75; bd. dirs. Luth. Comty. Home, 1964-82, pres., 1970; trustee Immanuel Luth. Ch., 1977-80, bd. Immanuel Luth. Sch., 1980-83; adv. bd. Ind. U., Purdue U.-Indpls., 1981-83. Fellow Am. Coll. Trial Lawyers, Ind. Trial Lawyers Assn. (bd. dirs. 1969—, pres. 1975), Ind. Coll. Trial Lawyers, Roscoe Pound Found., Ind. Bar Assn.; mem. FBA, ATLA (bd. govs. 1985-88), Ind. State Bar Assn. (bd. govs. 1980-82), Inst. for Injury Reduction (bd. dirs. 1992-95), Nat. Bd. Trial Advocacy, Safety Attys. Fedn. (bd. dirs. 1993-95), Internat. Soc. Primerus Law Firms (bd. dirs. 1995—), Am. Bd. Trial Advocates, Trial Lawyers Pub. Justice (IN coord. 1991-), Am. Judicature Soc., Inner Cir. Advocates. Office: 100 N Chestnut St PO Box 608 Seymour IN 47274-0608 E-mail: pgv@pgvlaw.com., rlp@pardieckgilllaw.com.

PARDO, GABRIEL, neuro-ophthalmologist, neurologist, researcher; b. Lincoln, Nebr., July 5, 1962; s. Jaime H. and Wilma E. (Tovar) P.; m. Diana E. Hampton. MD, U. Militar Nueva Granada, Bogota, Colombia, 1986. Resident ophthalmology U. Militar Nueva Granada, Bogota, 1986; fellow neuro-ophthalmology U. Tex., Galveston, 1995; resident neurology U. Okla., Oklahoma City, 1999; vice-dean Med. Sch. U. Militar Nueva Granada, Bogota, 1992-93, asst. prof. ophthalmology, 1992-95, basic scis. sect. chief Med. Sch., 1992; clin. asst. prof. ophthalmology U. Okla., Oklahoma City, 2000—, clin. asst. prof. neurology, 2000—; rschr. Okla. Med. Rsch. Found., 2000—01; med. dir. Multiple Sclerosis Ctr. Neurosci. Inst. Mercy Hosp., 2002—. Bd. mem. Nat. Med. Edn. Coun., Bogota, 1992; cons. Coll. Optometry, U. Houston, 1993-95. Contbr. articles to profl. jours. Mem.: Nat. Multiple Sclerosis Soc. (bd. mem. Okla. chpt.), Okla. State Med. Assn., N.Am. Neuro-ophthalmology Soc., Am. Acad. Neurology, Am. Acad. Ophthalmology, AMA. Office: Med Neurologists Inc Neurosci Inst at Mercy 4120 W Memorial Rd Ste 218 Oklahoma City OK 73120 E-mail: gabriel-pardo@ouhsc.edu.

PARDO, JOSEPH FRANK, JR. telecommunications industry executive; b. New Orleans, Feb. 2, 1952; s. Joseph Frank Sr. and Rita Marie (Eckert) P.; m. Deborah Ann Duggan, Apr. 26, 1975; children: Joseph Frank III, Rebecca Rose, Michael Jerome. BS, U. New Orleans, 1974, postgrad., 1976-78, Christian Bros. U., 1980—, Bellcore, 1980—. Docket clk. U.S. Dist. Ct., New Orleans, 1975-76; svc. rep. South Cen. Bell, 1976-77, comm. cons., 1977-78, customer svc. rep. data dept., 1978-80, account exec. industry cons. fin. dept., 1980-85, systems integrator, tech. cons. Birmingham, Ala., 1988-90, systems integrator, tech. support, 1990—; telecom. mgr. Hibernia Nat. Bank, New Orleans, 1985-88; sys. designer III tech. support Bell South Comm. Inc., Birmingham, 1990-93; sys. designer III emerging techs. Bell South Bus. Sys., 1993-94, sys. mgr., 1994-98, broadband ATM applications devel. mgr., 1998—. Cub master, asst. scout master Cub Scout & Boy Scouts Am., Metairie, La. and Birmingham, 1983—. Fellow U. New Orleans Alumni Assn., K.C., Optimists; mem. La. Telecommunications Assn. (1st v.p. New Orleans chpt. 1985-86, pres. 1986-87, bd. dirs. 1987-88), Archbishop Rummel High Sch. Alumni Assn. (class rep.). Republican. Roman Catholic. Avocations: reading, stamp collecting, fishing, hunting, coaching little league. Home: 5248 Valleybrook Trce Birmingham AL 35244-1986

PARDO, MARIAN URSULA, investment company executive; b. Rockville Centre, N.Y., Sept. 23, 1946; d. Francis V. and Dorothy E. (Bellidora) P.; m. Michael S. Toonkel. BA, Barnard Coll., 1968. With J.P. Morgan Cos., N.Y.C., 1968-98, v.p. investment group, 1980-95, mng. dir., 1995-98, J.P. Morgan Investment Mgmt., N.Y.C., 1998—. Former chmn. bd. dirs. Opportunity Resources for the Arts; mem. Columbus Citizens Found. Mem. Fin. Analysts Assn. Office: JP Morgan Investment Mgmt 522 5th Ave New York NY 10036-7601

PARDO-MAURER, ROGELIO, federal agency administrator; b. Danbury, Conn., June 10, 1963; s. Rogelio Pardo-Evans and Susan Clarke Maurer. BA, Yale U., 1984; postgrad., Cambridge U., 1986. Pres. Emerging Market Access, Washington, 1992—2001; dep. asst. sec. def. we. hemispher Dept. Def., 2001—. Author: The Contras: A Special Kind of Politics, 1990, Access Mexico, 1993. Sgt. 20th spl. forces group (airborne). Mem.: Elizabethan Club, Potomac Boat Club, Met. Club. Episcopalian. Avocations: classical piano, rowing, painting. Home: 1221 Connecticut Ave 3rd Fl Washington DC 20036 Office: 4C800 Defense Pentagon Washington DC 20301-2400

PARDUE, A. MICHAEL, retired plastic and reconstructive surgeon; b. Nashville, June 23, 1931; s. Andrew Peyton and Ruby (Fly) P. BS, U. of the South, 1953; MD, U. Tenn., 1957. Resident in gen. surgery Pittsfield (Mass.) Affiliated Hosps., 1966; resident in plastic surgery N.Y. Hosp./Cornell Med. Ctr., 1968; plastic surgeon A. Michael Pardue, M.D., Thousand Oaks, Calif., 1968-98. Lt. comdr. USN, 1956-62. Fellow ACS; mem. Am. Soc. Plastic Surgeons, Am. Soc. Aesthetic Plastic Surgery, Calif. Soc. Plastic Surgeons. Episcopalian. Avocations: fly fishing, skiing, golf, equestrian, African safaris.

PARDUE, DANA BAUGH, interior designer; b. Nashville, Dec. 24, 1959; d. John Thomas Jr. abd Nell (Apple) B. Student, Seminole Coll., 1983. Sr. designer Packer & Assocs., Brentwood, Tenn., 1984-86; co-owner, sr. interior designer Maddux-Pardue Design Cons., 1986—. Chmn. Heart Gala Heart Assn., Nashville, 1987. Named one of Outstanding Young of Am., 1985, Best Interior Designer, 1984, 85, Young Careerist, 1985. Mem. Nashville Home Builders Assn., Bus. Profl. Women Assn. Republican. Avocations: boating, skiing, entertaining, travel. Office: Maddux-Pardue Design Cons 5020 Harpeth Dr Brentwood TN 37027-7510

PARDUE, DWIGHT EDWARD, venture capitalist; b. North Wilkesboro, N.C., Aug. 3, 1928; s. Gilbert F. and Nina (Glass) P.; m. Annie Eller, Mar. 24, 1951; children: Richard S., Dwight E. Cert., Clevenger Bus. Coll., 1956. Dir. warehousing Lowe's Co., Inc., North Wilkesboro, 1956-57, store mgr. Sparta, N.C., 1957-59, Richmond, Va., 1959-70, regional v.p. North Wilkesboro, 1970-75, sr. v.p. store ops., 1975-78, exec. v.p. sales and store ops., 1978-86, sr. exec. v.p., 1986-90; pres., investor D. Pardue & Assocs., Wilkesboro, N.C., 1990—. Mem. steering com. Home Ctr. Leadership Coun., Nat. Home Ctr. Home Improvement Congress and Exposition, 1983-86; bd. dirs. Northwestern Nat. Bank, Inc., Wilkesboro, N.C.; chmn. bd. Community Bancshares, Inc., Wilkesboro, 1992—. Served with U.S. Army, 1950-52. Mem. Oakwoods Country Club, Jefferson Landing Golf Club, Masons. Office: D Pardue & Assocs PO Box 791 North Wilkesboro NC 28659-0791

PARDUE, KAREN REIKO, elementary education educator; b. Honolulu, June 13, 1947; d. Rex Shinzen and Ruth Fujiko (Arakawa) Ishiara; m. Jerry Thomas Pardue, Oct. 21, 1978 (dec. Sept. 1994); 1 child, Holly; m. Nicholas Lambiase, Mar. 17, 1998 (div. July 1999). BS, Western Ill. U., 1969; MA, U. No. Colo., 1971, 72. Tchr. home econs. Galesburg (Ill.) H.S., 1969-70; tchr. spl. edn. Jefferson County Pub. Schs., Golden, Colo., 1973-85, 87-94; tchr. 2d and 3d grade Englewood (Colo.) Christian Sch., 1985-86; tchr. 2d grade Jefferson County Pub. Schs., 1994—. Adj. instr. Colo. Christian U., Lakewood, 1989—; mem. recommended basic list com. Jefferson County Pub. Schs., 1993-95. Grantee Colo. Dept. Edn., 1976, Jefferson Found. Venture, 1988. Mem. ASCD, Colo. Coun. Learning Disabilities, Jefferson County Ednl. Assn., Jefferson County Internat. Reading Assn., Delta Kappa Gamma (rec. sec. 1988-89, pres. 1990-92, treas. 1994-96, Values award for exemplary performance 2001-2002). Avocations: reading, sewing. Home: 6827 S Webster St Unit D Littleton CO 80128-4469

PARDUE, MARY-LOU, biology educator; b. Lexington, Ky., Sept. 15, 1933; d. Louis Arthur and Mary Allie (Marshall) P. BS, William and Mary Coll., 1955; MS, U. Tenn., 1959; PhD, Yale U., 1970; D.Sc. (hon.), Bard Coll., 1985. Postdoctoral fellow Inst. Animal Genetics, Edinburgh, Scotland, 1970-72; assoc. prof. biology MIT, Cambridge, 1972-80, prof., 1980—, Boris Magasanik prof. biology, 1995—. Summer course organizer Cold Spring Harbor Lab., NY, 1971—80; mem. rev. com. NIH, 1974—78, 1980—84, nat. adv. gen. med. scis. coun., 1984—86; sci. adv. com. Wistar Inst., Phila., 1976—; mem. health and environ. rsch. adv. com. U.S. Dept. Energy, 1987—94; bd. trustees Associated Univs., Inc., 1995—97; mem. Burroughs Wellcome Adv. Com. on Career Awards in Biomed. Scis., 1996—2000, now bd. dirs.; chair Inst. of Medicine Com. on Biol. Basis of Sex and Gender Differences, 1999—2001. Mem. editorial bd. Chromsoma; contbr. articles to profl. jours. Mem. rev. com. Am. Cancer Soc., 1990-93, Howard Hughes Med. Inst. Adv. Bd., 1993-2000. Recipient Esther Langer award Langer Cancer Rsch. Found., 1977, Lucius Wilbur Cross medal Yale Grad. Sch., 1989; grantee NIH, NSF, Am. Cancer Soc. Fellow AAAS, NAS (chmn. genetics sect. 1991-94, coun. 1995-98), Am. Acad. Arts and Sci. (coun. mem. 1992-96); mem. NRC (bd. on biology 1989-95), Genetics Soc. Am. (pres. 1982-83), Am. Soc. Cell Biology (coun. 1977-80, pres. 1985-86), Phi Beta Kappa, Phi Kappa Phi, Sigma Xi. Office: MIT Dept Biology 68-670 77 Massachusetts Ave Dept 68-670 Cambridge MA 02139-4307

PARE', CRAIG THOMAS, musician, educator; b. Pawtucket, Ri, Sept. 5, 1955; s. Roland Conrad and Thelma Louise Pare'; m. Barbara Ann Fatzinger, Oct. 28, 1962; children: Alexander. Dr. of Musical Arts, U. of Cin., Cincinnati, Ohio, 1990—93; MusM, Fla. State U., Tallahassee, Florida, 1986—88; MusB, Barrington Coll., Barrington, Rhode Island, 1973—78. Assoc. prof. of music DePauw U., Greencastle, Ind., 1993—; prin. timpanist Terre Haute Symphony Orch., Terre Haute, 1999—; dir. of bands Western State Coll., Gunnison, Colo., 1988—90; percussionist Savannah Symphony Orch., Savannah, Ga., 1986—88; prin. timpanist and percussionist Spoleto Festival, U.S.A., Charleston, SC, 1980—83, Festival Dei Due Mondi, Italy; percussionist RI Philharm., Providence, 1979—83; timpanist and percussionist Philharmonia à vent, Terre Haute, Ind., 1999—2002. Contbr. chpts. to Teaching Music Through Performance In Band; , editor Inner Game of Music workbooks; conductor (compact disc recordings) DePauw University Band CD Recording Project. Recipient Joan Westmen Battey Disting. Tchg. Award, DePauw U., 1999-2001, DePauw U./United Meth. Ch. Exemplary Tchg. Award, DePauw U./United Meth. Ch., 1999, John Price Durban John Disting. Professorship, DePauw U., 2001. Mem.: Am. String Teachers Assn., Ind. Music Educators Assn., Coll. Band Directors Nat. Assn., Percussive Arts Soc., Music Educators Nat. Conf., Pi Kappa Lambda. Home: 617 E Walnut Street Greencastle IN 46135 Office: School of Music DePauw University 600 South Locust Street Greencastle IN 46135 Office Fax: 765-658-4042. E-mail: cpare@depauw.edu.

PAREDES, BERT (NORBERT PAREDES), computer systems engineer; b. Frankfurt, Germany, Dec. 27, 1947; s. George and Elfriede (Kleebach) P.; m. Linda L. Stubblefield, July 5, 1968 (div. 1986); m. Katherine Blacklock, Feb. 4, 1989. BS in Computer Sci., SUNY, Albany, 1970; postgrad., U. Colo., 1977-78. Enlisted U.S. Army, 1970, programmer/analyst, 1970-79, resigned, 1979; staff engr. Martin Marietta, Denver, 1979-81, sr. staff engr., 1984-92; regional analyst, mgr. Gould Computer Systems, 1981-84; mgr. tech. analysis and support Denelcor, Inc., Aurora, Colo., 1984; v.p. C-Quad Systems, Inc., Littleton, 1992-94, pres., 1994—. Pres., chief exec. officer A.C.T., Inc., Denver, 1982-84. Contbr. articles to profl. jours. Nat. Merit scholar, 1966. Mem. Assn. Computing Machinery, Armed Forces Communications and Electronics Assn., Am. Rose Soc., Mensa, Denver Bot. Gardens. Lutheran. Home: 6859 N Beaver Run Littleton CO 80125-9202 Office: C-Quad Systems Inc 26 W Dry Creek Cir Ste 600 Littleton CO 80120-8066

PAREDES, JAMES ANTHONY, anthropologist, educator; b. N.Y.C., Sept. 29, 1939; s. Antonio Paredes Piñeiro and Mildred Olene (Brown) P.; m. Anna Hamilton, Nov. 25, 1959 (div. 1984); children: J. Anthony Jr., Anna Teresa P. Lesinski, Sara Caroline P. Campbell; m. Elizabeth Dixon Purdum, Aug. 10, 1985 (div. 1994): 1 stepchild, David Joseph Plante. BA, Oglethorpe U., 1961; MA, U. N.Mex., 1964, PhD, 1969. Rsch. coord. Upper Miss. Mental Health Ctr., Bemidji, Minn., 1964-67; asst. prof., acting dir. Am. Ind. Studies Bemidji State Coll., 1967-68; community devel. specialist U. Minn. Agrl. Extension Svc., Bemidji, 1967-68; asst. prof. dept. anthropology Fla. State U., Tallahassee, 1969-74, assoc. prof., 1974-78, prof., 1979-99, emeritus prof., 1999—, chmn. dept., 1974-77, 84-90; chief ethnography and Indian affairs S.E. regional office Nat. Park Service, Atlanta, 1999—. Adj. prof. dept. anthropology U. Fla., Gainesville, 1979—; cons. Nat. Marine Fisheries Svc., Galveston, Tex., 1987-88, Bur. Indian Affairs, Washington, 1985, 92, Fed. Recognition Panel, Assn. on Am. Indian Affairs, N.Y.C., 1987-88. Author: Indios de los Estados Unidos Anglosajones, 1992; editor: Anishinabe: Six Studies of Modern Chippewa, 1980, Indians of the Southeastern United States in the Late 20th Century, 1992; co-editor: Classics of Practicing Anthropology: 1978-1998, 2000; co-editor: Anthropologists and Indians in the New South, 2001; author or co-author numerous articles, chpts. in books, revs. Mem. Sci. and Statis. Com., Gulf of Mex. Fishery Mgmt. Coun., Tampa, Fla., 1978-88. Recipient svc. award Poarch Creek Indians, 1990, Woodrow Wilson Found. fellow U. N.Mex., 1961-62; Nat. Inst. Mental Health predoctoral fellow U. N.Mex., 1968-69; Rockefeller Ctr. for Study of So. Culture and Religion fellow, Fla. State U., 1978. Fellow Am. Anthrop. Assn., Soc. for Applied Anthropology (assoc. editor 1983-88, pres. 1993-95); mem. So. Anthrop. Soc. (pres. 1988-89), Fla. Acad. Scis. (sect. chair 1984-85), Sigma Xi (Fla. State U. chpt. pres. 1977-78). Democrat. Avocation: walking. Office: Nat Park Svc SE Region 100 Alabama St SW Atlanta GA 30303-8701 E-mail: Tony_Paredes@nps.gov.

PARENT, DAVID HILL, investment company executive; b. Salem, Oreg., Apr. 13, 1940; s. Donald Allan and Pauline Louise (Lyons) P.; m. Christine Hedwige Marie Thérèse Wielezynski, Sept. 25, 1976; children: Marc Alexander Lair Thompson, Nathalie Jacqueline Marie Pauline. BS, U. Calif. Berkeley, 1963; MBA, Columbia U., 1965. Internat. fellow Columbia U., N.Y.C., 1963; dir. mktg. Europe Vendo Internat., Brussels, 1965-69; exec. v.p. T.S.I., Hempstead, N.Y., 1969-70; v.p. mktg. Gateway-Globus, Forest Hills, 1970-72; mgr. Ctrl. Africa, Leon Tempelsman & Son, N.Y.C., 1972-79; pres. The Parent Co., Plano, Tex., 1979—. Advisor to pres. of Gabon, Libreville, 1976-79. Charter rep. troop 285 Boy Scouts Am., Plano. Mem. Rockwall Citizen's Counc. (exec. com.), Rockwall C. of C., Plano C. of C. Republican. Roman Catholic. Avocations: travel, skiing, scuba diving. Home and Office: 4948 Stony Ford Dr Dallas TX 75287-7235

PARENT, RODOLPHE JEAN, Canadian air force officer, pilot; b. Thurso, Que., Can., June 16, 1937; s. Eugène Jean and Eliane Marie (Raby) P.; m. Michelle Marie Masse, Aug. 10, 1963; children— Stéphane, Nathalie, Cynthia Student, Coll. Militaire Royal de St-Jean, 1958-61; B.Sc., Royal Mil. Coll. Can., Kingston, Ont., 1963. Commd. Royal Can. Air Force, 1958; advanced through grades to brig.-gen., 1984; joined 425 Squadron for ops. on CF-101 aircraft Bagotville, Que., 1964-69; worked for Directorate of Recruiting and Selection at Nat. Def. Hdqrs., Ottawa, Ont., Can., 1969-71; chief of ops. 433 Tactical Fighter Squadron, Bagotville, 1972-75, Can. Forces Base Bagotville, 1975-76; comdg. officer 433 Tactical Fighter Squadron, 1976-80; asst. dir. personnel careers Nat. Def. Hdqrs., Ottawa, 1980-81; base comdr. Can. Forces Base Lahr, Federal Republic Germany, 1981-83; commandant Coll. Militaire Royal de Saint-Jean, Que., 1983-86; dir. gen. personnel careers other ranks Nat. Def. Hdqrs., Ottawa, 1986-89; def. attaché Paris, 1989-92; ret., 1992. Decorated Order of Mil. Merit, Order of St. John of Jerusalem Roman Catholic. Avocations: hockey; tennis; windsurfing. E-mail: rudy.michelle@sympatico.ca.

PARENTE, LOUISE, social worker; b. Bklyn., Apr. 11, 1945; d. Frank and Lucy (Coppola) Russo; m. John Parente, Sr., Dec. 23, 1967; children: John Jr., Donald, Steven. B in Social Work summa cum laude, Kean U., 1984; MSW, NYU, 1985, PhD, 1998. Cert. social worker N.Y., N.J., eating disorder specialist, bd. cert. diplomate. Pvt. practice, S.I., NY, 1989—; staff social worker Very Spl. Pl., Inc., 1985-86; staff social worker, psychotherapist Children's Cmty. Ctr., S.I. Mental Health Svc., 1986-88; clin. social worker, psychotherapist S.I. Hosp. Outpatient Psychiat. Clinic, 1988-95. Part-time lectr. NYU, N.Y.C., 1995—2000. Chmn. Boy Scouts Am. Mem.: NASW, Internat. Assn. Eating Disorder Profls., Am. Anorexia/Bulimia Assn., Acad. Eating Disorders, Acad. Cert. Social Workers, Soc. Clin. Social Work Psychotherapists (corr. sec.), Kappa Delta Phi, Phi Kappa Phi, Alpha Delta Mu. Home: 103 Augusta Ave Staten Island NY 10312-3232

PARENTE, WILLIAM JOSEPH, political science educator; b. Chgo., July 7, 1937; s. Salvatore S. and Genevieve (Rooney) P.; m. Diane Alpern, Nov. 30, 1963; children: Elizabeth, Margaret, William Joseph, Caroline, Rebecca, Catherine, Abigail, Christopher, Natalya. AB cum laude, Xavier U., Ohio, 1961; PhD (Woodrow Wilson fellow, Woodrow Wilson dissertation fellow), Georgetown U., 1970. Woodrow Wilson intern Wilberforce (Ohio) U., 1965-66; asst. prof., chmn. polit. sci. dept. Antioch Coll., 1966-69, assoc. dean faculty, 1969-70; dean Coll. Arts and Scis., U. Scranton, Pa., 1970-85, assoc. prof. polit. sci., 1970-73, prof., 1973—; Fulbright scholar Chulalongkorn U., Bangkok, Thailand, 1985-86, Inst. for Policy Studies, Washington, 1986-87. Mem. nat. Fulbright screening com. for East Asia, Southeast Asia; mem. adv. com. Inst. Internat. Edn.; cons. on world affairs to Peace Corps. Author articles in field. Fellow Inst. Acad. Deans, 1971, Inst. Ednl. Mgmt., Harvard Bus. Sch., 1972, Fulbright fellow, Korea, 1974, Indonesia, 1978, Germany, 1980, Thailand, 1985-86, fellow NEH Seminar, U. Va., 1976, Harvard U., 1985, Columbia U., 1988, George Mason U., Va., 1990, UCLA, 1991, U. Mich., 1992, William and Mary, 1993, U. Iowa, 1994, U. Accra, Ghana, 1996; scholar-diplomat program State Dept., 1970, 73; vis. scholar in humanities NYU, 1989. Fellow Union Experimenting Colls. and Univs., Inst. for Policy Studies, Soc. for Religion in Higher Edn.; mem. Am. Polit. Sci. Assn., Assn. Jesuit Colls. and Univs. (chmn. conf. on internat. edn. 1981-85), Alpha Sigma Nu (nat. sec.-treas. 1979-82, nat. pres. 1983-85), Pi Sigma Alpha, Eta Sigma Phi, Alpha Sigma Lambda, Tau Kappa Alpha, Phi Alpha Theta. Roman Catholic. Home: 1608 Summit Pointe Scranton PA 18508-1034 Office: U Scranton Coll Arts & Sciences Scranton PA 18510

PARENTI, KATHY ANN, sales professional; b. Gary, Ind., Sept. 24, 1957; d. Lee Everett Huddleston and Barbara Elizabeth (Daves) Tilley; m. Michael A. Parenti, Mar. 31, 1979 (div. Sept. 1990); m. S. Curtis McCoy, Sept. 6, 1996. Student, Ind. U., Gary, 1977; cert., U. Nev., Las Vegas, 1978; diploma, Interior Design Inst., Las Vegas, 1984. Supr. Circus Circus Hotel, Las Vegas, 1980-87; owner Interior Views, 1984-87; sales rep. Win-Glo Window Coverings, 1987-88; owner Dimension Design, 1988-90; sales rep. Sidney Goldberg & Assoc., Las Vegas, 1990-99; sales rep.. Parenti & Assocs., 1990—. Mem.: Rep Network, Construction Specification Inst., Network of Exec. Women in Hospitality, Am. Soc. Interior Designers. Avocations: exercise, reading, piano, guitar and singing.

PARESKY, DAVID S. travel company executive; b. Boston, Sept. 27, 1938; s. Paul and Ada (Rudnick) P.; m. Linda Kotzen, Aug. 18, 1963; children: Pamela, Laura, Mark. BA, Williams Coll., 1960; JD, Harvard U., 1963, MBA, 1965. Bar: Mass. Pres., chmn. bd. Crimson Travel Svc., Inc., Cambridge, Mass., 1965-89; pres., CEO, chmn. bd. Thomas Cook Travel, 1989-94. Mem. Bd. Higher Edn., Boston, 1980; trustee New Eng. Med. Ctr., 1982-83; mem. Bd. Regents of Higher Edn., Boston, 1980-86. Mem. Young Pres. Orgn. (chmn. New Eng. chpt. 1985), Chief Execs. Orgn., Phi Beta Kappa, Fisher Island Club (bd. dirs.).

PARESKY, LINDA K. travel company executive, educator; b. Cambridge, Mass., Mar. 18, 1943; d. Gilbert Milton and Marcia (Brown) Kotzen; m. David S. Paresky, Aug. 18, 1963; children: Pamela, Laura, Mark. BA, Simmons Coll., 1964; MA, Harvard U., 1965; PhD, Boston Coll., 1988; hon. degree, Simmons Coll., 1999, Bay Path. Coll., 2000. Chmn., CEO Travel Edn. Ctr., Cambridge, 1975-98; pvt. investor. V.p. Crimson Travel, Cambridge, 1965-89; co-chmn. Thomas Cook Travel, Cambridge, 1989-94; chair bd. trustees Simmons Coll., Boston, 1994-98; chair bd. dirs. Com. 200 Found., Chgo., 1997-98; bd. dirs. Thryoid Found. Am., Boston, 1994-97. Adv. com. Investment Svcs. and Policy Adv. Com., U.S. Trade Dept., Washington, 1995-2000. Recipient Bus. Leadership award New England Coun., 1994; named Outstanding Woman Entrepreneur, Pres. Reagan, 1986, Top 50 Women Bus. Owners, Nat. Found. Woman Bus. Owners and Working Woman Mag., 1994, Outstanding Bus. Leader award Northwood U., 2001. Mem. Internat. Women's Forum, (Mass. chpt., pres. 1994-96), Travel Bus. Roundtable (policy com.), Acad. Travel and Tourism (adv. bd.), Com. 200. Avocations: travel, sports. Home: 7212 Fisher Island Dr Miami FL 33109-0725 Office: 41212 Fisher Island Dr Miami FL 33109-1253

PARET, PETER, historian; b. Berlin, Apr. 13, 1924; s. Hans and Suzanne Aimée (Cassirer) P.; m. Isabel Harris, Sept. 23, 1961; children: Suzanne Aimée, Paul Louis Michel. BA, U. Calif., Berkeley, 1949; PhD, U. London 1960, DLitt, 1992; LittD, U. S.C., 1995; HHD, Coll. of Wooster, 1996. Resident tutor, delegacy of extramural studies Oxford U., 1959-60; research assoc. Center of Internat. Studies, Princeton U., 1960-62, 63; vis. asst. prof. U. Calif., Davis, 1962-63, assoc. prof., 1963-66, prof., 1966-69; prof. history Stanford U., 1969-77, Raymond A. Spruance prof. internat. history, 1977-86; Andrew W. Mellon Prof. in humanities Inst. Advanced Study, Princeton, N.J., 1986-97, Andrew W. Mellon Prof. in humanities emeritus, 1997—. Mem. Inst. for Advanced Study, Princeton, 1966-67; fellow Ctr. for Advanced Study in Behavioral Scis., Stanford, Calif., 1968-69; vis. fellow London Sch. Econs., 1972-73; NEH fellow, 1979-80; sr. fellow Hoover Instn., Stanford U., 1988-93. Author: (with John Shy) Guerrillas in the 1960's, 1962, French Revolutionary Warfare from Indochina to Algeria, 1964, Yorck and the Era of Prussian Reform, 1966, Clausewitz and the State, 1976, rev. edit., 1985; The Berlin Secession, 1980, Art as History, 1988, (with Beth Irwin Lewis and Paul Paret) Persuasive Images, 1992, Understanding War, 1992, Imagined Battles, 1997, German Encounters with Modernism, 1840-1945, 2000; editor, translator: (with Michael Howard) On War (C. v. Clausewitz), 1976, (with Daniel Moran) Historical and Political Writings (C. v. Clausewitz), 1992; editor: Frederick the Great, 1968, Frederick the Great: A Historical Profile, 1972, Sisyphus or the Limits of Education, 1973, The Age of German Liberation, 1977, Berliner Secession, 1981, Makers of Modern Strategy, 1986, (with Ekkehard Mai) Sammler, Stifter & Museen, 1993. Served with inf. U.S. Army, 1943-46. Decorated Officer's Cross, Order of Merit, Germany. Fellow AAAS, Royal Hist. Soc., Leo Baeck Inst., London Sch. Econs. (hon.); mem. Am. Philos. Soc. (Jefferson medal), Hist. Kom zu Berlin, Soc. for Mil. History (Samuel Eliot Morison medal), Clausewitz Gesellschaft (hon.). Office: Sch Hist Studies Inst Advanced Study Princeton NJ 08540

PARETTE, HOWARD P. college dean, special education educator; b. Pine Bluff, Ark., July 9, 1952; s. Howard Phillips Parette and Marjorie Edith Wright. BS, U. Ark., 1976, MSE, 1979; EdD, U. Ala., 1982. Asst. prof. La. Tech. U., Ruston, La., 1982-84; rsch. assoc. U. Ark. for Med. Scis., Little Rock, 1988-89; asst. prof. U. Ark., 1989-92; prof. Southeast Mo. State U., Cape Girardeau, Mo., 1993-2000, dean grad. sch., 2000—. Coord. Ark. Easter Seal Soc., Little Rock, 1992-93. Author, editor 4 books, 1997-2000; contbr. over 120 articles to profl. jours., chpts. to books. Mem. Am. Assn. Colls. of Tchr. Edn., Midwest Assn. Grad. Schs., Coun. of Grad. Schs., Coun. for Exceptional Children (newsletter editor 1993-99). Democrat. Methodist. Avocations: running, gardening, weightlifting, fine art. Home: 1428 Bessie Cape Girardeau MO 63701 Office: SE Mo State U Grad Sch One University Pla Cape Girardeau MO 63701 E-mail: pparette@semo.edu.

PARFENOV, ALEXANDER VSEVOLODOVITCH, physicist, researcher; b. Kazan, USSR, Apr. 3, 1954; s. Vsevolod A. Parfenov and Ludmila P. Jemeljanova; m. Zinaida P. Semenova, July 7, 1979; children: Stanislav, Anna. Diploma, Moscow Engring. Physics Inst., 1977; PhD (hon.), P.N. Lebedev Physics Inst., Moscow, 1981. Cert. in physics. Jr. rschr. P.N. Lebedev Physics Inst., 1980-86, sr. researcher, 1986—. Lectr. Moscow Elec. Engring. Inst, 1984-88. Author: Spatial Light Modulators, 1987; contbr. over 100 articles to prof. jours. Recipient USSR State Prize in Sci. and Engring., 1985. Achievements include 20 inventions including new electrooptical effect in liquid crystal. Office: Physical Optics Corp 20600 Gramercy Pl Bldg 100 Torrance CA 90501 E-mail: parfenov@softhome.net.

PARFET, A. JAMES, engineer; b. Haybro, Colo., Apr. 4, 1938; s. Aaron Lee and I. Lucelle (Woody) P.; m. Barbara Louise Geiser, May 2, 1956; children: John R., Janet L., Joan E., Joyce D. Intern in mfg. div. Woodward Govner Co., Ft. Collins, Colo., 1956-62, with machine design div., 1962-67, with engring. design and devel. div., 1968-78, wiht mktg. sales div., 1978-84, engr. project mgmt. div., 1984—. Instr., speaker indsl. scis. dept. Colo. State U., 1981—. Contbr. articles to profl. jours. Advisor Colo. Gov.'s Excellence in Edn. Com., Denver, 1987-90; co-chmn. Indsl. Tech. Coun., Southwestern Okla. State U., 1983-90. Mem. Nat. Assn. Inst. Tech. (pres. indsl. div. 1989-90), Soc. Mfg. Engrs. (chpt. chmn. 1981, regional chmn. 1988, internat. bd. dirs. 1990—). Achievements include patents in field. Office: Woodward Govner Co 1000 E Drake Rd Fort Collins CO 80525-1824

PARFET, JOHN RICHARD, business development specialist; b. Ft. Collins, Colo., Jan. 23, 1957; s. A. James and Barbara Parfet; m. Kristie Ann Rohde, Oct. 4, 1987; children: Erin Nicole, Alyson Rose. BS, Colo. State U., 1980; MS, Purdue U., 1984; MBA, William Woods U., 1995. Rsch. technician Colo. State U., Ft. Collins, 1977-81; lab. mgr. Purdue U., West Lafayette, Ind., 1981-84; tech. cons. Monsanto Co., St. Louis, 1985-87; rsch. assoc. U. Mo., Columbia, 1985-90; diagnostic sales rep. ICN Pharm., Costa Mesa, Calif., 1990; client svcs. rep. ABC Labs., Columbia, 1990-93, bus. devel. specialist, 1993—. Contbr. numerous articles to profl. publs. Mem. exec. com. Meml. Day Corp., Columbia, 1991—; coord. for sci. program Ptnrs.-in-Edn., Columbia, 1993. Named Vol. of Yr., Meml. Day Corp., 1993. Mem. Rotary (chmn. youth exch. 1996—, bd. dirs. 1996—). Avocations: fly fishing, reading, computers. Home: 1810 Garden Dr Columbia MO 65202-1251

PARGAMENT, FRANCES P. social worker, psychotherapist; b. N.Y.C., Mar. 17, 1944; d. Dave and Hilda Pargament; m. Paul Oliver, May 4, 1986. BA, CCNY, 1967; MSW, U. Mich., 1971. Cert. social worker. Social worker N.Y. State Edn. Dept., Albany, 1979—, sch. social worker, 1990—; sch. social worker specialist Nat. Assn. Social Workers, Washington, 1992—; psychotherapist in pvt. practice, Bklyn. and Poughkeepsie, N.Y., 1982—; pvt. supr. for social workers, 1980—. Mem. NASW. Avocations: swimming, showshoeing, hiking, reading, dancing.

PARGOFF, ROBERT MICHAEL, small business owner; b. Garden City, Mich., May 22, 1961; s. Andrew Stephen and Virginia (Dimanin) P.; m. Diane Elizabeth Bailey, Feb. 25, 1985; children: Andrew Stephen III, Patrick Robert, Mark James. BS in Indsl. Mgmt., Glen Cullen U., 1994. Beverage mgr. Hilton Hotels, Plymouth, Mich., 1980-82; food and beverage dir. Holiday Inn, Inc., Farmington Hills, 1982-83; v.p., sec. Mich. Info. Systems, Plymouth, 1983-84; group ops. John Hancock Ins., Farmington Hills, Mich., 1986-88; chmn., pres. B. Bear Industries, Inc., 1985—; sales mgr. Huston Tech., Inc., Southfield, Mich., 1995-2000; ops. mgr. Rosso Mgmt. Co., Birmington, 2001—. Assoc. Presdl. Re-election Campaign, Detroit, 1984; mem. Young Macedonian Polit. Orgn., past pres., 1979-80, 83-85, Rep. Nat. Com. Mem. Am. Mgmt. Assn., Ind. Mgmt. Soc., Highlander Club, Oakland Athletic Club. Eastern Orthodox. Avocations: racquet sports, photography, golf. E-mail: pargoff21@msn.com.

PARHAM, ANNETTE RELAFORD, librarian; b. Petersburg, Va., Dec. 13, 1954; d. William Rosley and Sarah Matthews (Pierce) Relaford; m. Keith Lionel Parham, June 14, 1975; children: Loretta Springfield, Alison Nicole. BSBA, Va. Union U., 1977; MS in Libr. and Info. Sci., Cath. U., Washington, 1998. File clk. Va. Farm Bur. Mut. Ins., Richmond, Va., 1981-82, ins. rater, 1982-83; file clk. tech. svcs. dept. of libr. Colonial Williamsburg (Va.) Found., 1987-89, acquisitions libr., 1989—. Named to Outstanding Young Women of Am., 1981. Democrat. Baptist. Avocations: singing, bowling, reading. Office: Colonial Williamsburg Found John D Rockefeller Jr Libr 313 1st St Williamsburg VA 23185-4306

PARHAM, BETTY ELY, credit bureau executive; b. Drumright, Okla., Aug. 14, 1928; d. Wayne Albert and Edith May (Ledgerwood) Bingamon; m. Richard D. Ely, Dec. 22, 1946 (dec. Jan. 1971); children: Richard Wayne, Stephen Wyatt; m. Billy S. Parham, Mar. 10, 1991. BS, East Cen. U., Ada, Okla., 1962, M Teaching, 1965. Office mgr. Louiis M. Long, Loans, Ada, 1946-78; owner Credit Bur. Ada, 1956—, mgr., 1978—. Mem. Soc. Cert. Credit Bur. Execs., Assoc. Credit Burs. Okla. (bd. dirs. 1980—, pres. 1990), AAUW (cert. of achievement 1989), Ada Bus. and Profl. Women (chmn. YC, Pres.'s award 1991), Toastmasters (pres. Ada 1984, Presdl. Excellence award 1984), Kiwanis (bd. dirs. Ada 1990-92). Democrat. Avocations: boating, travel, reading. Home: PO Box 506 Ada OK 74821-0506 Office: Credit Bur Ada 304 E 12th St Ada OK 74820-6510

PARHAM, DAVID MARION, pathologist; b. Somerville, Tenn., Feb. 26, 1951; s. David Norman and Mildred Myrtle (Weatherly) P.; m. Jane Jarvis, June 18, 1973 (div. Mar. 1977); m. Norma Jean Manning, Feb. 18, 1979; children: Andrew Mason, Zachary Allen. BS, U. Tenn., 1972; MD, U. Tenn., Memphis, 1976. Pathology resident U. Tenn., Memphis, 1976-80; pathology fellow Meml. Sloan-Kettering Hosp., N.Y.C., 1980-81; pathologist St. Jude Children's Rsch. Hosp., Memphis, 1981-95. Faculty pathologist U. Tenn., Memphis, 1981-95, Ark. Childrens Hosp., 1995—, U. Ark. Med. Sci., 1995—. Contbr. articles to Human Pathology, Cancer, Am. Jour. Pathology, Am. Jour. Clin. Pathology. Mem. Internat. Acad. Pathology, Soc. Pediatric Pathology, Arthur Purdy Stout Soc., Phi Beta Kappa. Methodist. Achievements include description of grading system for childhood sarcomas and work on the phenotype and morphology of rhabdoid tumors, rhabdomyosarcomas, and peripheral neuroepitheliomas. Office: Ark Children's Hosp. marshall St Little Rock AR 72202

PARHAM, DEBORAH, health facility administrator; BSN, U. Cin.; PhD Pub. Health, U. N.C.; MS Pub. Health, MS Pub. Health. RN. Capt. USPHS Commd. Corps.; dep. assoc. adminstr. HAB, 2000—, acting assoc. adminstr., 2002—; pub. health analyst, chief nurse., perinatal coord. HRSA HIV/AIDS Bur., HHS, 1983, assoc. adminstr., 2002—. Office: US Dept Health and Human Svcs Health Resources Svcs Adminstrn 5600 Fsihers Ln Rm 14-45 Rockville MD 20857 Office Fax: 301-443-1989.*

PARHAM, IRIS ANN, gerontology educator; b. Orange, Tex., Nov. 14, 1948; d. George Kevlin and Nina Mabel Parham; m. Edward Swarbrick, Aug. 9, 1975; 1 child, Erin Elsbeth. BA, U. Tex., 1970; MA, W.Va. U., 1973; PhD, U. So. Calif., 1976. Asst. prof. gerontology Va. Commonwealth U., Richmond, 1976-81, assoc. prof., 1981-91, prof., 1991—. Exec. dir. Va. Geriatric Edn. Ctr. Co-editor: Modular Gerontology Curriculum, 1982, vol. II, 1984, Access, 1990, Resource Guides--Geriatrics, 2990, Gerontological Social Work, 1992, Alcoholism and Aging, 1995, Jour. Social Issues, 1980; spl. editor Jour. Minority Aging. Grantee Adminstrn. on Aging, 1978-79, 79-82, 85-87, Adjusting to Widowhood Va., 2978-79, Temple U., 1983-84, Health Resources and Svcs. Adminstrn., 1985-90, 91-94, 97-01, 00—. Fellow Gerontol. Soc. Am., So. Gerontol. Soc. (treas. 1984-87); mem. APA, Aassn. Gerontology in Higher Edn. (charter fellow), Sigma Xi. Avocation: photography. Office: Va Commonwealth U Med Coll Va Campus Dept Gerontology PO Box 980228 Richmond VA 23298-0228

PARHAM, LINDA DIANE, occupational therapist, researcher, educator; b. Guantanamo, Cuba, Aug. 28, 1952; d. Gerald Dathel and Shirley (Melzer) Parham; m. Harry Edward Trigg III, June 1, 1985; 1 child Dorothy Helen Trigg. BS, U. Fla., 1974; MA, U. So. Calif., L.A., 1980; PhD, U. Calif., L.A., 1989. Asst. dir. occupl. therapy Bayberry Psychiat. Hosp., Hampton, Va., 1974-75; sr. occupl. therapist Maryview Cmty. Mental Health Ctr., Portsmouth, 1975-78; pvt. practice L.A., 1980-84; asst. prof. U. So. Calif., 1986-92, assoc. prof., 1992—. Adj. instr. Univ. So. Calif., 1979—80, 1985—86; dir. edn. Ayres Clinic, Torrance, Calif., 1985—96; dir. edn. and rsch. Pediatric Therapy Network, Torrance, Calif., 1996—. Editor: (book) Play in Occupl. Therapy for Children; mem. edtl. rev. bd.: Occupl. Therapy Jour. Rsch., 1988—90; contbr. articles to profl. jours. and textbooks. Recipient Jean Ayres Award, Am Occupl. Therapy Found, 1998, Leadership Commendation, 1999; fellow Am. Occupl. Therapy Found, 1988; scholar Ctr. Study Sensory Integrative Dysfunction, 1980. Fellow: Am. Occupl. Therapy Assn.; mem.: Assn. Study of Play (v.p. 2000—01, pres. 2001—02), Soc. Rsch. Child Devel., Sensory Integration Internat. (faculty emeritus, sec. 1986—87), World Fedn. Occupl. Therapists, Occupl. Therapy Assn. Calif. Office: U So Calif 1540 Alcazar St # 133 Los Angeles CA 90089 Personal E-mail: ldiane@pacificnet.net. Business E-Mail: lparham@hsc.usc.edu.

PARHAMI, BEHROOZ, engineering educator, consultant; b. Tehran, 1947; s. Salem and Kowkab Parhami; m. Vida Parhami; children: Sepehr, Sepand, Sepideh. PhD, UCLA, 1973. Chartered engr., Engring. Coun. U.K. Acting asst. prof. UCLA, 1973—74; prof. math. and computer sci. Sharif (formerly Arya-Mehr) U. Tech., Tehran, 1974—88; prof. elec. and computer engring. U. Calif., Santa Barbara, 1988—. Author: (book) Computer Appreciation, 1984, Introduction to Parallel Processing: Algorithms and Architectures, 1999,

Computer Arithmetic: Algorithms and Hardware Designs , 2000. Fellow: IEEE (chmn. Iran sect. 1977—85, Centennial medal 1984), Brit. Computer Soc.; mem.: Informatics Soc. Iran (pres., editor-in-chief 1979—84, disting. mem. 1985), Assn. for Computing Machinery. Office: U Calif Dept Elec and Computer Engring Santa Barbara CA 93106-9560 Business E-Mail: parhami@ece.ucsb.edu.

PARIENTE, BARBARA J. state supreme court justice; b. Dec. 24, 1948; m. Frederick A. Hazouri. Grad. with high honors, Boston U., 1970; JD with highest honors, George Washington U., 1973. Bar: Fla. 1973; cert. civil trial lawyer Fla. Bar; cert. Nat. Bd. Trial Advocacy. Law clk. to hon. Norman C. Roettger, Jr. U.S. Dist. Ct. (so. dist.) Fla., 1973-75; ptnr. Cone Wagner Nugent, 1975-83, Pariente & Silber, P.A., 1983; pvt. practice; judge U.S. Ct. of Appeals (4th dist.), 1993-97; justice Fla. Supreme Ct., Tallahassee, 1997—. Participant Twenty-First Century Justice Conf.; mem. Judicial Cir. Grievance Com., 1989-92, chair, 1990-92; mem. nominating com. U.S. Ct. Appeals (15th cir.), 1980-84. Contbr. articles to profl. jours. Bd. dirs. Fla. Bar Found.; mentor Take Stock in Children; active Palm Beach County Youth Ct. program, 1997, Cities in Schs. mentoring program, 1993, Temple Judea, Palm Beach County Sephardi Fedn., Jewish Cmty. Ctr., Ballet Fla., Palm Beach County Commn. on Status of Women. Recipient award for disting. svc. to the arts Palm Beach County Bar Assn., 1987, Civil Litigation Pro Bono award Legal Aid Soc., 1993. Mem. ABA, Nat. Assn. Women Judges, Am. Inns. of Ct. (founding mem. Palm Beach County chpt.), Acad. Fla. Trial Lawyers (bd. dirs., chair Spkr.'s Bur. program 1984-87, outreach com. 1991-92, co-chair Workhorse Seminar 1991-92), Assn. Trial Lawyers Am. (vice chair profl. rsch. and devel. dept. 1980-82, chair comml. litigation sect. 1984-85, women's trial lawyer caucus 1986-87; mem. ethics com. 1989-90, conv. planning com. 1992-93), Fla. Assn. Women Lawyers. Office: State Supreme Ct of Florida 500 S Duval St Tallahassee FL 32399-1925*

PARINS, ROBERT JAMES, professional football team executive, judge; b. Green Bay, Wis., Aug. 23, 1918; s. Frank and Nettie (Denissen) P.; m. Elizabeth L. Carroll, Feb. 8, 1941; children: Claire, Andrée, Richard, Teresa, Lu Ann. BA, U. Wis., 1940, LL.B., 1942. Bar: Wis. Supreme Ct. 1942. Pvt. practice, Green Bay, Wis., 1942-68; dist. atty. Brown County, 1949-50, cir. judge, 1968-82, res. judge, 1982—; pres. Green Bay Packers, Inc., 1982-90, chmn. bd., 1990-92; hon. chmn. bd., 1992-94. Mem.: Wis. State Bar Assn. Roman Catholic.

PARIS, STEVEN MARK, software engineer; b. Boston, May 26, 1956; s. Julius Louis and Frances (Keleishik) P. BS, Rensselaer Poly. Inst., 1978; MS, Boston U., 1980, postgrad., 1980-84. Sr. software engr. Prime Computer Inc., Framingham, Mass., 1978-82; sr. analyst Computervision Corp., Bedford, 1982-84; prin. engr. Lotus Devel., Inc., Cambridge, 1984-88; pres. Tri-Millennium Corp., 1988-91; sr. researcher Tech. Edn. Rsch. Ctr., Cambridge, Mass., 1990-93; prin. engr. Beyond, Inc., Burlington, 1993, Bus. Matters Inc., Waltham, 1994-96; v.p. engr. Ambit, Inc., Brighton, 1996—. Dep. chief Civil Def., Somerville, Mass. Recipient Boston Sci. Fair 1st prize, 1973, 74, State of Mass. Sci. Fair 3d prize, 1973, 2d prize, 1974. Mem. Assn. for Computing Machinery, IEEE, Boston Computer Soc., Planetary Soc. Jewish.

PARIS, WAYNE, social worker, researcher; b. Claremore, Okla., Nov. 8, 1949; s. Arch LaVerne and Aileen Rosella (McGraw) P.; m. Donna Marie Lindley, Mar. 20, 1982; 1 child, Joel Michael. BA, Northeastern State U., 1972; MSW, U. Okla., 1979; postgrad., U. Huddersfield, Eng., 2000—. Lic. clin. social worker, Okla. Med. social worker Bapt. Med. Ctr., Oklahoma City, 1979-84; clin. transplant social worker Nazih Zuhdi Transplantation Inst., 1985—. Pvt. practice, cons. Wayne Paris & Assocs., Edmond, Okla., 1993—; grant reviewer The Wellcome Trust, London, 1999. Author: Yearbook of Surgery, 1994; : mem. editl. bd. Jour. Transplant Coordination, 1996—; : Progress in Transplantation, 2000, : invited reviewer Jour. Heart and Lung Trandplantation, 1995—, : invited reviewer, 1999—, : invited reviewer, 2001—, : invited reviewer Rsch. on Social Work Practive, 1999—; contbr. articles to med. jours. Mem.: NASW, Internat. Soc. for Heart and Lung Transplantation (co-chair edn. com. nursing and social sci. com. 2001—02), Soc. for Social work and Rsch. (charter), Soc. for Transplant Social Work (charter, chmn. abstract rev. com. 2000, bd. dirs.). Avocations: coin collecting, sailing. Office: Nazih Zuhdi Transplantation Inst 3300 NW Expwy Oklahoma City OK 73112-4418

PARIS CAMMER, BARBARA ELAINE, geriatrician; b. N.Y.C., July 20, 1951; AB, Columbia U., 1973; MD, SUNY, Bklyn., 1977. Diplomate Am. Bd. Internal Medicine, Am. Bd. Geriatrics. Resident in medicine St. Vincent's Med. Ctr., N.Y.C., 1977-80; assoc. prof. medicine and geriatrics Mount Sinai Med. Ctr., 1996—, med. dir. geriatric inpatient svcs., 1998—, fellow in geriats., 1983-86. Bd. nat. com. for prevention of elder abuse, 1989-2001. Asst. editor Mount Sinai Jour. of Medicine, 1999—; author: (with others) A Guide to the Care of the Elderly, 1996; contbr. articles to profl. jours. Fellow ACP; mem. AMA (Physicians Recognition award 1998—), Am. Geriatric Soc. (Geriatrics Recognition award 1999—). Office: Mount Sinai Med Ctr Box 1070 New York NY 10029-0310

PARISE, MARC ROBERT, banker; b. Chgo., Feb. 19, 1953; s. Donald Louis and Dorothy Anne (Merva) P.; m. Margaret Mary Baldwin, June 21, 1975; children: Megan, Matthew. BS in Fin., No. Ill. U., 1975; MBA in Fin., DePaul U., Chgo., 1980; postgrad., St. Ambrose U., Davenport, Iowa, 1998—. Credit analyst, asst. v.p. Amalgamated Bank, Chgo., 1975-79; v.p. Met. Bank, 1979-82, First Nat. Bank, Mt. Prospect, Ill., 1982-84; sr. v.p. First Midwest Bank/Joliet, 1984-87; pres., chief exec. officer First Midwest Bank/Danville, 1987-91; pres., bd. dirs. First Midwest Bank, Moline, 1991—. Chmn. Danville Area Econ. Devel. Corp., 1989-91, Danville Polymed Found., 1989-91; Danville Area C.C. Found., 1987-91; mem. pres.'s coun. No. Ill. U., 1989-91; fin. com. Trinity Med. Ctr., 1992—; East Moline Citizens Adv. Com., 1992-93; Moline Ctr. on the Miss. Project Mgmt. Team Moline Ctr., 1992-94; bd. dirs. Quad City Devel. Group, 1992-94, Quad Cities Charitable Health Trust, 1992-97, Jr. Achievement, 1994-99, Trinity Physician Hosp. Orgn., 1994-2000, Quad Cities Contbrs. Coun., 1995—; bd. dirs. United Way, 1994-2000, chmn. gen. campaign, 1996; trustee Trinity Coll. Nursing, 1993-96, Robert Young Ctr., 1998-99; bd. trustees Trinity Regional Health System, 1999—; bd. mem. Trinity Vis. Nurses and Hmkrs. Assn., 1999—, bd. chair 2002—. Named Outstanding Young Alumni No. Ill. U. Coll. Bus., 1991. Mem. Moline Rotary. Roman Catholic. Avocations: shooting, hunting. Office: First Midwest Bank 506 15th St Moline IL 61265-7997 E-mail: marc.parise@firstmidwest.com.

PARISE, RONALD A. astronaut; b. Warren, Ohio, May 24, 1951; s. Henry and Mrs. Henry Parise; m. Cecelia M. Sokol; 2 children. BS in Physics, Youngstown State U., 1973; MS in Astronomy, U. Fla., 1977, PhD in Astronomy, 1979; DSc (hon.) , Youngstown U., 1996. With Ops. Rsch. Inc., 1979—80; data mgmt. scientist, Internat. Ultraviolet Explorer (IUE) ops. ctr. Computer Scis. Corp., 1980, sect. mgr. IUE hardcopy facility, 1981, developer Ultraviolet Imaging Telescope (UIT), Spacelab experiment, 1981; payload specialist NASA, 1984; astronaut NASA STS-35/Astro-1 Columbia, 1990, NASA STS-67/Astro-2 Endeavor, 1995; supporter Goddard Space Flight Ctr. Networks and Mission Svcs. Project. Recipient Quest for Excellence award, Allied Signal, 1997. Mem.: Internat. Astron. Union, Assn. Space Explorers, Astron. Soc. of the Pacific, Am. Astron. Soc., Phi Kappa Phi, Sigma Xi. Avocations: amateur radio, flying, scuba diving, sailing, hiking. Office: Astronaut Office/CB NASA Johnson Space Ctr Houston TX 77058*

PARISH, BARBARA SHIRK, writer, educator; b. Nov. 28, 1942; MA in English, U. Mo., 1968, MA in L.S., 1969. Writer, Memphis, 1970—; instr. Shelby State C.C., 1995-98, State Tech. Inst. Memphis, 1996—, U. Memphis, 1999, Christian Bros. U., Memphis, 1999—, Crichton Coll., Memphis, 2000—. Home: 4293 Beechcliff Ln Memphis TN 38128-3423 E-mail: nativestones@aol.com.

PARISH, DIEDRE LORNA, transportation executive; b. Chateauroux, France, Jan. 29, 1958; d. Paul Eugene and Jean Petronella Parish. BA, U. Balt., 1984, MPA, 2000. Pers. security asst. Def. Investigative Svcs., Balt., 1985-86; supr. group living Palmer Family, Inc., Crownsville, Md., 1986-88; fin. aid counselor U. Md., College Park, 1988-92, asst. registrar Balt., 1993-96; sr. assoc. records and registration Goucher Coll., 1996-98; program mgr. Md. Transp. Authority, 2000—. Grad. fellow Schaefer Ctr. for Pub. Policy, Balt. Mem. Am. Soc. for Pub. Adminstrn. (Md. chpt. coun. 2000-2001), Alpha Epsilon Lambda (hon.). Office: Md Transp Authority 303 Authority Dr Baltimore MD 21222-2201 Office Fax: (410) 288-8495. E-mail: dparish@mdtransportationauthority.com.

PARISH, J. MICHAEL, lawyer, writer; b. Decatur, Ill., Nov. 9, 1943; s. John Mitchell and Gladys Margaret (Daulton) P.; m. Susan Lee Sgarlat, July 24, 1976 (div.); m. Ellen R. Harnett, Dec. 3, 1991; children: Margaret Ruth, William Walter. AB cum laude, Princeton U., 1965; LLB, Yale U., 1968. Assoc. LeBoeuf Lamb et al, N.Y.C., 1968-73, ptnr., 1974-89, Winthrop Stimson Putnam & Roberts, N.Y.C., 1989-95, Thelen, Reid & Priest, N.Y.C., 1995—2002, Wolf, Block, Schorr & Solis-Cohen, N.Y.C., 2002—. Bd. dirs. Forum Funds, Portland, Maine, Core Trust. Contbr. stories and poetry to mags. Dir. PBS Am. Poetry Project, 1985-90; coord. Yale Law Sch. Clinton Election com.; class sec. Princeton Class of 1965. Univ. scholar Princeton U., 1965. Mem. Princeton Club N.Y. Avocation: creative writing. Home: 100 Riverside Dr New York NY 10024-4822 Office: Wolf Block 250 Park Ave New York NY 10177

PARISH, JAMES ROBERT, author, cinema historian; b. Cambridge, Mass., Apr. 21, 1944; s. Fred Arthur and Ann Lois (Magilevy) P. BA, U. Pa., 1964, LLB, 1967. Pres. Entertainment Copyright Rsch.Co. Inc., N.Y.C., 1967-68; film reporter, reviewer, interviewer Variety, Motion Picture Daily, 1968-69; entertainment publicist Harold Rand & Co., 1969-70; free-lance writer, publicist, film book cons., film reviewer, novelist, 1970—; acquisition editor Renaissance Books, 1996-99. Author: (with P. Michael) The Emmy Awards: A Pictorial History, 1970, The Fox Girls, 1971, The Great Movie Series, 1971 (with A.H. Marill) The Cinema of Edward G. Robinson, 1972, The Slapstick Queens, 1972, The Paramount Pretties, 1972, (with R. Bowers) The MGM Stock Company, 1973, Actors TV Credits, 1950-72, 73, Good Dames, 1973, (with M.R. Pitts) The Great Spy Pictures, 1973, The RKO Gals, 1973, (with S. Whitney), The George Raft File, 1973, (with M.R. Pitts) Film Directors: A Guide to Their American Pictures, 1974, Hollywood's Great Love Teams, 1974, (with S. Whitney) Vincent Price Unmasked, 1974, The Great Movie Heroes, 1975, (with D. Stanke), The Glamour Girls, 1975, The Debonairs, 1975, (with L. DeCarl) Hollywood Players: The Forties, 1975, (with J. Ano) Liza! (The Liza Minnelli Story), 1975, (with M.R. Pitts) The Great Gangster Pictures, 1975, The Elvis Presley Scrapbook, 1975, (with W. Leonard) Hollywood Players: The Thirties, 1976, (with D. Stanke) The All Americans, 1976, Film Directors: A Guide for Western Europe, 1976, Great Child Stars, 1976, The Jeanette McDonald Story, 1976, (with D. Stanke) The Leading Ladies, 1977, (with M.R. Pitts) The Great Science Fiction Pictures, 1977, Film Actors Guide: Western Europe, 1977, The Elvis Presley Scrapbook (update), 1977, (with M. Trost) Actors TV Credits: Supplement One, 1977, (with M.R. Pitts) Hollywood on Hollywood, 1978, (with R. Braff et al.) Hollywood Character Actors, 1978, (with G. Mank and D. Stanke) The Hollywood Beauties, 1978, (with W. Leonard) The Funsters, 1979, (with D. Stanke) The Forties Gals, 1980, (with G. Mank) The Hollywood Reliables, 1980, The Great American Movies Book, 1980, (with G. Mank) The Best of MGM, 1981, (with M.R. Pitts) The Great Spy Pictures II, 1986, (with M.R. Pitts) The Great Gangster Pictures II, 1987, (with M.R. Pitts) The Great Western Pictures II, 1988, Black Action Pictures from Hollywood, 1989, (with M.R. Pitts) The Great Science Fiction Pictures II, 1990, (with V. Terrace) Complete Actors TV Credits, 1990, (with M.R. Pitts) Hollywood Songsters, 1990, The Great Cop Pictures, 1990, Prison Pictures from Hollywood, 1991, (with M.R. Pitts) Hollywood's Great Musicals, 1992, (with D. Stanke) Hollywood Baby Boomers, 1992, Prostitution in Hollywood Film, 1992, The Hollywood Death Book, 1992; Let's Talk: America's Favorite Talk Show Hosts, 1993, Gays and Lesbians in Mainstream Cinema, 1993, Hollywood's Celebrity Death Book, updated and expanded, 1994, Ghosts and Angels on the Hollywood Screen, 1995, Today's Black Hollywood, 1995, Pirates and Seafaring Swashbucklers, 1995, The Great Child Stars, 1996, The Unofficial "Murder She Wrote" Casebook, 1997, Rosie: Rosie O'Donnell's Biography, 1997, updated edit., 1998, Whoopi Goldberg: From Poverty to Mega Stardom, 1997, updated edit., 1999, Jason Biggs, 2000, The Hollywood Book of Death, 2001, Gus Van Sant, 2001, Hollywood Bad Boys, 2002, Jet Li, 2002, The Encyclopeida of Ethnic Groups in Hollywood, 2002, Hollywood Divas, 2002, I Don't Hear Wedding Bells, 2003; assoc. editor: The American Movies Reference Book, 1969, TV Movies, 1969, The Great American Movie Book, 1980. Mem. Phi Beta Kappa. Avocations: docent, reading, writing. Address: 4338 Gentry Ave Unit 1 Studio City CA 91604-1764 *To succeed in one's ambitions requires an unyielding avoidance of other people's skepticisms.*

PARISH, RICHARD LEE, engineer, consultant; b. Kansas City, Mo., May 31, 1945; s. Charles Lee and Ruth (Duncan) P.; m. Patricia Ann Erickson, June 2, 1968; children: Christie Lynn White, Kerry Anne Parish-Philp. BS in Agrl. Engring., U. Mo., 1967, MS in Agrl. Engring., 1968, PhD, 1970. Registered profl. engr., Ohio. Asst., then assoc. prof. engring. Univ. Ark., Fayetteville, 1969-74; mgr. mech. research and devel. O.M. Scott & Sons Co., Marysville, Ohio, 1974-83; assoc. prof., then prof. La. State U., Baton Rouge, 1983-97; prof. Hammond Rsch. Sta., 1995—. Cons. in equipment patents, design and evaluation; expert witness testimony in agrl. and hort. equipment, patents, 1984—. Contbr. over 100 articles to profl. jours. and trade pubs.; patentee in field (3). Bd. dirs. Agrl. Devel. Found. Recipient Quality award, ITT, 1979, Doyle Chambers award for excellence in rsch., La. State U. Agrl. Ctr., 2001; fellow NSF, 1967—69; grantee rsch., Cotton Inc., 1970—74, 1991—93, 1995—96, La. Dept. Natural Resources, 1985—87, Italian Trade Commn., 1988—90. Mem. Am. Soc. Agrl. Engrs. (chmn. agrl. chem. application com. 1982-83, power and machinery div. program com. 1986-87, chmn. cultural practices equipment com. 1994-95, chmn. fruit and vegetable prodn. engring. com. 1999-2001), La. Vegetable Growers Assn., Am. Soc. Hort. Sci. Republican. Baptist. Avocations: gardening, woodwork, bicycling. Home: 21135 Highway 16 Amite LA 70422-4733 Office: Hammond Rsch Sta 21549 Old Covington Hwy Hammond LA 70403-0533 E-mail: dparish@agctr.lsu.edu.

PARISH, THOMAS SCANLAN, human development educator; b. Oak Park, Ill., Jan. 24, 1944; s. Robert S. and Florence Catherine (Fleming) P.; children: Robert V., Kimberly E., David G., Thomas P., Kathryn E., Lydia E.; m. Jocelyn G. Parish, Dec. 29, 2000. BA, No. Ill. U., 1968; MA, Ill. State U., 1969; PhD, U. Ill., 1972. Instr. psychology Parkland Coll., Champaign, Ill., 1971-72; asst. prof. Okla. State U., Stillwater, 1972-76; assoc. prof. Kans. State U., Manhattan, 1976-80, prof., 1980—, asst. to dean of edn., 1992-97; assoc. dir. ARIOS-Kan., 1994-96. Rsch. coord. for Midwest Desegration Asst. Ct., 1994-96; regional dir. Excel Comm., 1997—. Assoc. editor Jour. of Social Studies Rsch., 1994-98; cons. editor Jour. Genetic Psychology, 1984—, Internat. Jour. Reality Therapy, 1992—, The Genetic, Social and General Psychology Monographs, 1984—; contbr. articles to profl. jours. Bd. dirs. Friendship Tutoring Program, Manhattan, 1982-91, Stillwater Awareness Coun., 1973-74; co-founder, bd. dirs. Youth Alternatives, Inc., Champaign, 1971-72; pres. Mid-Western Edn. Rsch. Assn., 1998-99. Fellow Am. Psychol. Soc.; mem. Am. Ednl. Rsch. Assn., APA, Assn. Reality Therapists, Soc. for Rsch. in Child Devel., Phi Delta Kappa, Phi Kappa Phi. Office: Kans State U Coll of Edn Bluemont Hall Manhattan KS 66506 Home: PO Box 516 Fayette IA 52142-0516 E-mail: thomas_s_parish@hotmail.com., tparish@ksu.edu.

PARISI, CHERYL LYNN, elementary school educator; b. Hackensack, N.J., Aug. 26, 1955; d. Elza A. and Constance Leah (Sculley) Sockey; m. Albert J. Parisi, Apr. 18, 1981; 1 child, Christopher Thomas. BA, Fairleigh Dickinson U., 1977. Cert. tchr., N.J. Piano instr., Bergen County, N.J., 1972-79; art tchr. Meml. Sch., South Hackensack, 1979-80, Hackensack Mid. Sch., 1980-84, Nellie K. Parker Sch., Hackensack, 1984—. Exhibited in group shows at The Jacob Javits Conv. Ctr., N.Y.C., 1990, The Designer Craftsmen's Gallery, New Brunswick, N.J., 1993, Gloucester County Coll., Sewell, N.J., 1993, Johnson and Johnson Corp., Titusville, N.J., 1993, Arts Coun. Princeton, N.J., 1993, Montclair State U., Upper Montclair, N.J., 1992, 94, named to panel for selection of educators for the NEH seminar Amer. and Brit. Chldrns. Lit., Princeton, 1999. Author and co-dir. of chldrns. musical: Claude Monet: A Bridge to the Past, 1999. Recipient Art Educator Achievement award Fantasy Fund Inc. at the Cathedral of St. John the Divine, N.Y.C., 1992; grantee Hackensack Edn. Found., 1991; NEH fellow Princeton U., 1991. Mem. Art Educators N.J. (chairperson 1993 Yr. of the Am. Craft 1991-93, publicity 50th anniversary conf. 1990; pres. Bergen County chpt. 1984-86, Achievement award 1989), Nat. Art Edn. Assn. Avocations: playing the piano, reading. Home: 167 Godwin Ave Wyckoff NJ 07481-2004 Office: Nellie K Parker Sch 261 Maple Hill Dr Hackensack NJ 07601-1497

PARISI, JOSEPH (JOSEPH ANTHONY PARISI), magazine editor, writer-consultant, educator; b. Duluth, Minn., Nov. 18, 1944; s. Joseph Carl Parisi and Phyllis Susan (Quaranta) Schlecht BA with honors, Coll. St. Thomas, 1966; MA, U. Chgo., 1967, PhD with honors, 1973. Asst. prof. Roosevelt U., Chgo., 1969-78; assoc. editor POETRY Mag., 1976-83, acting editor, 1983-85, editor, 1985—. Vis. prof. U. Ill., Chgo., 1978-87; cons., writer ALA, Chgo., 1980—; cons. NEH, 1983—. Author: The Poetry Anthology, 1912-1977, 1978, Voices and Visions Reader's Guide, 1987, Marianne Moore: The Art of a Modernist, 1990, (listener's guide) Poets in Person, 1992, 97, A History of Poetry in Letters, 2002, The Poetry Anthology, 1912-2002, 2002; contbr. articles and reviews to profl. jours.; producer, dir. (audio series on NPR) Poets in Person, 1991. Recipient Alvin Bentley award, Duns Scotus Coll., 1963; fellow, U. Chgo., 1966—69, Guggenheim, 2000, Churchill Coll., Cambridge. Mem. Arts Club of Chgo., Cliff Dwellers Club, Delta Epsilon Sigma Avocations: piano, photography, book and record collecting. Office: Poetry Mag 60 W Walton St Chicago IL 60610-7324

PARISI, MARITA, artist, art gallery director; b. Bad Kreuznach, Germany, July 29, 1946; came to U.S., 1984; d. William and Irma Acker. BA, Wilfred Laurier U., Waterloo, Can., 1968; MEd, U. Toronto, Can., 1969. Tchr. Halton Bd. Edn., Oakville, Ont., Can., 1971-83; pres., owner Nature Art Gallery, Lake Katrine, N.Y., 1995—. Cons., workshop leader York U., Toronto, 1977-82, tchr., 1978-79. Artist cover N.E. Wildlife Exposition, Albany, N.Y., 1987-89, Smithsonian, 1989; represented in permanent collection N.Y. State Art Mus., Albany, Sundancer Gallery, Cocoa Village, Fla., Amrita Gallery, Poughkeepsie, N.Y., Long Ago and Far Away, Manchester Ctr., Vt.; exhibited in numerous one-woman and group shows. Mem. Ward Found., Md., 1991-92. Rotary Club Can. scholar, 1964, Ont. scholar, 1966; Ministry Edn. Hilroy fellow, Ont., 1983; recipient award in art Washington Project, 1993; named Best of Show, Bonita Springs, Fla., 1995, first in category Mandarin Art Festival, Fla., 1996, Higginbotham award, 1998, Best of Show, Stuart, Fla., 1998, Best of Show, Martin Coun. for Arts, 1999, Award of Excellence, Ft. Lauderdale, 2001. Mem. Ulster Arts Alliance, Empire States Crafts Alliance, Nat. Mus. Am. Indian, Kingston (N.Y.) C. of C., So. Vt. Art Ctr. Avocations: photography, wildlife, travel, writing, reading. Home and Office: PO Box 1028 Citra FL 32113

PARISIO, TAMARA LYNN, marketing professional; b. Appleton, Minn., July 4, 1960; d. Merlyn Eugene and Patricia Yvonne (Johnson) Munsterman; m. James Warren Burke, Jr., Mar. 26, 1983 (div. June 1993); 1 child, Madelyn Amanda; m. Douglas Eugene Parisio, Sept. 2, 2000; stepchildren: Chalynn, BriAnne Lea, Justine. BA, U. Minn., 1982; postgrad., Calif. Luth. U., 1999. Asst. acct. exec. Sheggeby Advt., Mpls., 1982-83, BBDO, Inc., L.A., 1983-84; program mgr. Cable Music Channel, Hollywood, Calif., 1984-85; acct. exec. Ogilvy & Mather, L.A., 1985-88; mktg. mgr. Teleflora, 1988-93; asst. mgr. mktg. & merchandising Jafra Cosmetics Internat. Inc. (A Gillette Co.), Westlake Village, Calif., 1993-97, mgr. product mktg., 1997-98; mgr. mktg. Jafra Cosmetics Internat. Inc., 1998-99; group mktg. mgr. Sebastian Internat., Inc., Woodland Hills, Calif., 1999—2001, dir. global mktg., 2001—. Mentor Pepperdine U. Recipient Silver Clio award, 1986, N.Y. Internat. Film and TV Festival bronze award, 1986, Ogilvy & Mather Creative Excellence award, 1986, Disting. Scholar award Calif. Luth. U., 1998, Am. Beauty Assn. award, 2000. Mem. L.A. Mus. Art, L.A. World Affairs Coun., L.A. Conservancy, Rho Lambda, Sigma Beta Delta. Office: Sebastian Internat Inc 6109 DeSoto Ave Woodland Hills CA 91367 E-mail: tparisio@sebastian-intl.com.

PARISO, JEAN BRUNNER, real estate agent; b. Reinholds, Pa., Dec. 26, 1925; d. Emory Lutz and Rachel Ebling (Keith) Brunner; m. Jesse Francis Pariso, Aug. 11, 1956; 1 child, Penelope Ann. BA, Cedar Crest Coll., Allentown, Pa., 1947; postgrad., Columbia U., 1948-50. Social caseworker Edwin Gould Found., Inc., N.Y.C., 1947-50; asst. dir. pub. rels. Toy Guidance Coun., 1950-51; sec. to pres. Charles Schlaifer & Co., 1951-52; legal sec., asst. prod. ABC, 1952-54; dir. pub. rels. Cushman & Wakefield, Inc., 1954-62; asst. dir. Coun. Community Svcs., Princeton, N.J., 1970-72; dir. pub. rels. The Princeton (N.J.) Ballet Soc., 1972-81; sales assoc. Richard A. Weidel Corp. Realtors, Hopewell, NJ, 1987—2002. Pub. info. cons. Community Guidance Ctr., Mercer County, 1988-89. Mem. Montgomery Twp. Bd. Edn., Skillman, N.J., 1962-65; mem. Somerset County Bd. Elections, Somerville, N.J., 1987—; co-chmn. Citizens Com. to elect Kennedy-Johnson, Montgomery Twp., 1960; active Aux. of Princeton Med. Ctr. Mem. Montgomery Cultural Ctr. (charter), Van Harlingen Hist. Soc. Democrat. Lutheran. Avocations: reading, swimming. Home: 404 Skillman Rd Skillman NJ 08558-1523

PARISOTTO, GLORIA, publishing executive, poet; b. São Paulo, Brazil, July 4, 1938; came to U.S., 1980; d. Luiz and Antonia (Guimarães) P.; m. Onofre Pereira Mendonca, Dec. 13, 1954 (div. 1980); children: Marco Antonio, Marco Tulio, Maria Emilia. Degree in tchg., Inst. Fernando Costa, Prudente, 1954; student, Brazilian Acad. Fine Arts, Rio de Janeiro, 1985. Cert. tchr., Brazil. Tchr. Sch.-Pres. Bernardes, São Paulo, Brazil, 1954-56, Maristas H.S., Parana, P.R., 1954-66; hosp. supr. Sanatory Maringa Ltd., P.R., 1955-90; pres. Sunrising Publ. Co., N.Y.C., 1991—. Author: Learning Portuguese Without a Teacher, 1991, The Extraterrestrial and the Blue Planet, 1992, My Poems (3 langs.), 1992; (poems) The Flower (Poet of Merit award Am. Poetry Assn. 1990), Mother (Poet of Merit award Internat. Poetry soc. 1991); contbr. poetry to numerous anthologies; one-woman art show at Cricket Club, Nfianii, U.S., 1981; exhibited art in group shows at Assn. de Criticos y Comentaristas de Arte, Miami, Fla., 1981, Hispanic Heritage Festival, Miami, 1981, Internat. Festival, Nhan-@, 1982, Nouvelle Gailerie, Geneva, Switzerland, 1983, UNESCO, Paris, 1984, Brazilian Artists Show, Rio de Janeiro, 1985, Internat. Expo, N.Y.C., 1986, Internat. Art Expo, Montreal, Que., Can., 1986, Pub. Libr., Gt. Neck, N.Y., 1987 (Excellence medal), Am. Embassy, Brasilia, Brazil, 1987, House of Spain, Rio de Janeiro, 1987, Lever House, N.Y.C., 1987, Mcpl. Gallery, São Paulo, 1989, Lincoln Ctr. Cork Gallery, N.Y.C., 1989, Icaro Gallery, N.Y.C., 1990, Epiphany Gallery, N.Y.C., 1990, Vanderbilt Mus., L.I., N.Y., 1992, Rio Design Ctr. Gallery, 1993 (hon. mention), Portal Gallery, São Paulo, 1993, Who's Who Artists, Edinburgh, Scotland, 1994, IPS's Conv. Art Show, Washington, 1995, Art Show, Capetown, South Africa, 1995, Am. & Internat. Bio Ctr., San Francisco, 1996, Oxford (Eng.) Gallery, 1997. Rep. abroad Brazilian Ecology Assn., Rio de Janeiro, 1988, Pan Am. Writers Assn., Brazilian Acad. Fine Arts, Rio de Janeiro, 1988. Recipient Bronze medal L'Amounier Gallery, Rio de Janeiro, 1981, Hebrew Cmty., Rio de Janeiro, 1981, Silver medal Brazilian Assn. Drawing and Visual Arts, Rio de Janeiro, 1982, Mil. Assn. Art Show, Rio de Janeiro, 1982, Gold medal Internat. Blenal, Rio de Janeiro, 1983, Ho. of Reps., Rio de Janeiro, 1983, Planetarium Gallery, Rio de Janeiro, 1984, Nat. Acad. Fine Arts, Rio de Janeiro, 1985, Palace "Espelho D'Agua", Belem, Portugal, 1986, Civil Police Acad., Rio de Janeiro, 1986, Gold Palette award Exhbn. Brazilian Artists, Salvador, Bahia, Brazil, 1987, Editor's award Nat. Libr. of Poetry, Washington, 1993, 94, Excellentia Order of Merit award, 1995, 1st prize award Famous Poetry Soc., Calif., 1996; semi-finalist nat. contest Internat. Poetry Soc.; named Poet of Merit, Internat. Poetry Assn., Washington, 1990, 91, 92. Mem. Nat. League Am. Pen Women, Inc., Internat. Platform Assn., Writers and Poets Soc., Acad. Am. Poets, Française-Italian Cultural Inst. Avocations: tennis, gym, traveling, reading, music. Home and Office: 150 W 56th St Apt 3407 New York NY 10019-3843

PARIZEK, ELDON JOSEPH, geologist, educator, dean; b. Iowa City, Apr. 30, 1920; s. William Joseph and Libbie S. P.; m. Mildred Marie Burger, Aug. 9, 1944; children— Richard, Marianne, Elizabeth, Amy. BS, U. Iowa, 1942, MS, 1946, PhD, 1949. Instr. U. Iowa, 1947-49; asst. prof. geology U. Ga., 1949-54, asso. prof., 1954-56, U. Kansas City, 1956-63; prof. U. Mo., Kansas City, 1963—, chmn. dept. geoscis., 1968-78; dean U. Mo. (Coll. Arts and Scis.), 1979-86. Served with USN, 1942-45. Fellow Geol. Soc. Am.; mem. AAUP, Assn. Mo. Geologists, AAAS, Sigma Xi. Roman Catholic. Achievements include research, numerous publs. on mass wasting, slope failure, underground space, geology of West Mo. Home: 6913 W 100th Shawnee Mission KS 66212 Office: 5100 Rockhill Rd Kansas City MO 64110-2481

PARIZO, MARY ANN, retired state legislator; b. Rochester, N.Y., Dec. 3, 1934; m. Bernard E. Parizo (dec.); two children. BS, U. Vt., 1958. Tchr., grades 6-8 (ret.); mem. Vt. Ho. of Reps., Montpelier, 1990—2000. Mem. spl. health care com., Vt. Ho. Reps., 1993-94. Bd. of justice of peace Woodside Juvenile Facility; bd. trustees U. Vt.; mem. Civil Bd. Authority, 1990-97; vice chair govt. ops. com.; mem. bd. Fanny Allen Sch. Nursing; mem. Commn. Sister State Karelia, Russia, Vt. Mem. NEA (life), Alpha Delta Kappa. Home: 10 Prospect St Essex Junction VT 05452-3613 E-mail: map1934@aol.com.

PARK, BEVERLY GOODMAN, lawyer; b. Boston, Nov. 10, 1937; d. Morris and Mary (Keller) Goodman; divorced; children: Glynis Forcht, Seth, Elyse. BS, Simmons Coll., 1959; MS, Ea. Conn. State U., 1968; JD, Western N.E. Coll. Law, 1998. Bar: Mass. 1998. Asst. dir. comty. svc. Hartford (Conn.) Courant, 1976-79; mayor Borough of Colchester, Conn., 1979-83; lifestyle editor Chronicle, Willimantic, 1980-82, suburban editor, 1982-84; officer mktg. & comm. U. Conn. Health Ctr., Farmington, 1984-97; assoc. Etheredge and Steuer, Northampton, Mass., 1998—. Selected team mem. radiation exposure info. study Belorussia, 1993; mem. adv. bd. Hosp. News; mem. women's affairs com. U. Conn. Health Ctr. Women's Networking Task Force; mem. Univ. Adminstrv. Staff Coun.; mem. minority awards com. U. Conn. Health Ctr., mem. John N. Dempsey hosp. disaster plan com. Designer: (libr. studies curriculum) Classroom Instruction on the Use of Books and Libraries, 1972; pub.: (edn1. booklets) Have You Made Plans for the Future?, 1977-78; editor of edn. holiday and bridal supplements The Chronicle, 1980-84; editor: U. Conn. Health Ctr. Anniversary Mag., 1986, U. Conn. Health Ctr. Med. Catalog, 1986, (ann. pub.) Salute, 1988, U. Conn. Health Ctr. 30th Anniversary Supplement, 1991. Bd. dirs. Ea. Conn. Found. for Pub. Giving, Norwich, 1990-96; women's club officer Dem. Town Com., Colchester, Conn., 1963-90; active Hadassah, Northampton/Amherst, 1996—, Women's League for Conservative Judaism. Recipient Lifestyle Page award New England Press Assn., 1980, Media Excellence in Covering Human Svcs. award Conn. chpt. NASW, 1982, Ragan Report Arnold's Admirables award for excellence in graphics and typography, 1985, Gold award Healthcare Mktg. Report, 1987, award for video ACS, 1990. Mem. NOW (membership com. Southea. chpt., mem. legis. task force, Meritorious Svc. award Southea. Conn. chpt. 1985), Am. Soc. for Hosp. Mktg. and Pub. Rels., Am. Mktg. Assn., Assn. Am. Med. Colls. (mem. group on pub. affairs), Conn. Hosp. Assn. (participant hosp. pub. rels. conf.), State of Conn. Pub. Info. Coun. (mem. steering com.), Mass. Bar Assn., Hampshire County and Franklin County Bar Assns., New England Hosp. Pub. Rels. and Mktg. Assn. (bd. dirs. 1987, 88). Avocations: swimming, hiking, spending time with grandchildren. Home: 116 N Main St Florence MA 01062-1220 Office: 64 Gothic St Northampton MA 01060-3042 E-mail: parklegal@aol.com.

PARK, BYIUNG JUN, textile engineer; b. Seoul, Republic of Korea, Feb. 28, 1934; came to U.S., 1954; s. Kyung Hak and Tansil (Kiu) P.; m. Chunghi Hong, June 28, 1958. BS, R.I. Sch. Design, 1958; MS, MIT, 1961, Mech. Engr., 1963; PHD, Leeds U., Eng., 1966. Rsch. asst. MIT, Cambridge, 1961-63; v.p. Consumer Testing Labs., Inc., Canton, Mass., 1966-84, sr. v.p., 1984-86; pres. Merchandise Testing Labs., Brockton, 1986—. Contbr. articles to profl. jours. Recipient Bronze medal No. Textile Assn., Boston, 1958; Rsch. fellow Internat. Wool Secretariat, Leeds, 1964-66. Mem. ASTM (Harold Dewitt Smith Meml. award 1997), Textile Inst., Am. Assn. Textile Chemists and Colorists, Am. Assn. Textile Technology, Am. Soc. for Quality Control, Indls. Fabrics Assn. Internat. Achievements include research in understanding mechanical behavior of textile assemblages. Office: Merchandise Testing Labs 244 Liberty St Brockton MA 02301-5554 E-mail: bj_park@mtlusa.com.

PARK, CHAN HYUNG, cell biologist, physician; b. Seoul, Korea, Aug. 16, 1936; s. Chung Suh and Yoon Sook Yuh; m. Mary Hyungrok Kim, Apr. 16, 1966; 1 child, Christopher Myungwoo. MD, Seoul Nat. U., 1962, MS, 1964; PhD, U. Toronto, 1972. Diplomate in internal medicine and med. oncology Am. Bd. Internal Medicine. Asst. prof. U. Kans. Med. Ctr., 1974-80, assoc. prof., 1980-86, prof., 1986-89; prof., chief divsn. oncology/hematology, dept. internal med. Tex. Tech U. Health Scis. Ctr., 1989—94; dir. Cancer Ctr., Samsung Med. Ctr., Seoul, 1994—2001, head divsn. hematology/oncology dept. medicine, 1994-99, cons. physician, 2001—; sr. rsch. scientist The Ctr. for the Improvement of Human Functioning Internat., Inc., Wichita, Kans., 2001—; cons. physician Aidan, Inc., Tempe, Ariz., 2001—. Transl. novel from German to Korean; mem. editl. bd. Jour. Nutrition, Growth and Cancer, 1986-87; mem. editl. bd. Internat. Jour. Hematology, 1999—; contbr. articles to biomed and sci. jours. Recipient Rsch. Career Devel. award USPHS, NIH, 1979-84. Fellow: ACP; mem.: Am. Soc. Hematology, Internat. Soc. Exptl. Hematology, Am. Soc. Clin. Oncology, Am. Assn. Cancer Rsch. Home: 8814 E Churchill Cir Wichita KS 67206 Office: The Ctr for the Improvement Human Functioning Internat Inc 3100 N Hillside Wichita KS 67219

PARK, CHERYL ANTOINETTE, women's health nurse, educator; b. Pitts., Mar. 4, 1945; d. Louis Joseph and Rose Gertrude (Rosenberger) Seethaler; m. Phocion Samuel Park Jr., Dec. 17, 1983; children: Louis Joseph, Phocion Samuel III. Diploma, St. Francis Med. Ctr., Pitts., 1974; BS in Edn., Carlow Coll., Pitts., 1971; MEd, U. Pitts., 1977; BSN magna cum laude, U. Tex., Houston, 1988. Cert. natural family planning practitioner, Am. Acad. Natural Family Planning. Primary therapist, staff nurse Western Psychiat. Inst. and Clinic/U. Pitts., 1975-76; dir., instr. psychiat. nursing edn. Ohio Valley Gen. Hosp. Sch. Nursing, McKees Rocks, Pa., 1976-78; charge nurse, clin. nurse St. Joseph Hosp., Houston, 1978-88; pres. N.W. Natural Family Planning Svcs. Contbr. articles to profl. jours. Charter mem. bd. dirs. Natural Family Planning Adv. Bd., Houston, 1982—. Mem. Assn. Christian Therapists, Med. Quality Found., Sigma Theta Tau. Home: 8114 Trail Side Dr Houston TX 77040-2655

PARK, CHRISTOPHER S. chairman civil service board; b. Bedford, N.Y., Mar. 27, 1950; BA, Stetson U., 1972, MBA, 1973. With Barnett Banks of Fla., 1973-77; investment banker, 1977-82; v.p., real estate The Haskell Co., 1982—; chmn. civil svc. bd. City of Jacksonville, Fla., 1995—; exec. v.p. Haskel Enterprise Group, Jacksonville, 1999—. Mem. Jacksonville Com. of 100, Fla., 1983—. Mem. Nat. Assn. Office Indsl. Parks, Fla. Chambers. Office: The Haskell Co 111 Riverside Ave Fl 1 Jacksonville FL 32202-4950 E-mail: cspark@thehaskellco.com.

PARK, CHUNG, painter, educator, computer software developer; b. Pusan, Korea, Oct. 27, 1941; s. Byung Ho Park and Jung Sun Im; m. Sue Bok Park, May 9, 1974; children: Paul, Janet Suejean Park. Diploma, Pusan Tchr.'s Coll., 1962; BFA, U. Mich., 1979; MFA, Pratt Inst., 1981. Cert. secondary edn. tchr., Korea. Art prof. Pusan Women's U., Korea, 1984-87, Pusan Nat. U., Korea, 1983-84; instr. painting & drawing Sch. of Visual Arts, N.Y.C., 1990-92, 94—; adj. prof. fine arts Nyack (N.Y.) Coll., 1992-93; asst. adminstr. Upsala Coll., Orange, N.J., 1993-94; exec. dir. Uran Tech., Inc., Palisades Park, 1994—. Trustee Bd. of Edn., Tenafly, 1997-2000; chmn. Korean-Am. Elected Sch. Bd. Mem. Assembly, 1998-2000; mem. adv. com. N.J. State Dept. Edn., Bilingual Edn., 1998-2000; founder Korean-Am. Youth Ctr. N.J., 1998—, Korean-Am. Parents Assn. N.J., 1998—; exec. dir. Asian Am. Youth and Cultural Ctr., 2000—' apptd. mem. com. human rels. Bergen County, N.J., 2001-. Mem. Coll. Art Assn., Korean-Am. Tchrs. Assn. N.J. (founder), Korean-Am. Contemporary Artists Assn. Greater N.Y. (founder). Home: 101 Prospect Ave Apt 8-D Hackensack NJ 07601-1995 Office: Uran Tech Inc 261 1st St Palisades Park NJ 07650 Office Fax: 201-489-0712. E-mail: chungpark@parkchung.com.

PARK, CHUNG IL, librarian; b. Chang-won, Korea, Aug. 25, 1938; s. Zung S. and Bong-y (Choo) P.; m. Jung Yoo, Aug. 30, 1969; children: Charlotte, Sue, Andrew. BA, Yonsei U., 1961; MLS, U. So. Calif., L.A., 1971; postgrad., U. Ill., 1975. Libr., mem. faculty Malcolm X Coll., Chgo., 1972—. Compiler, editor: (books) Best Sellers and Best Choices 1980-83, Best Books by Consensus 1984-88, Advertisement Digest: Library and Information Services, 1979; editor COINT, 1980-88; contbr. articles to profl. jours. Mem. ALA, Am. Fedn. Tchrs. Avocation: automobile travel. Office: Malcolm X Coll 1900 W Van Buren St Chicago IL 60612-3145 Home: Apt 1 8542 Georgiana Ave Morton Grove IL 60053-2996

PARK, DAVID ALLEN, physicist, educator; b. N.Y.C., Oct. 13, 1919; s. Edwin Avery and Frances (Paine) P.; m. Clara Justine Claiborne, Aug. 18, 1945; children: Katharine, Rachel, Paul, Jessica. AB, Harvard, 1941; PhD, U. Mich., 1950. Instr. Williams Coll., 1941-44; ops. research on radar countermeasures Harvard U. and Eng., 1944-45; instr. U. Mich., 1950; mem. Inst. Advanced Study, Princeton, 1950-51; mem. faculty Williams Coll., 1952-88, prof. physics, 1960-88, emeritus, 1988—; sr. vis. Cambridge (Eng.) U., 1962-63; vis. lectr. U. Ceylon, 1955-56, 72, Mass. Inst. Tech., 1966; vis. prof. U. N.C., 1964. Author: Quantum Theory, 1964, 3d edit., 1991, Contemporary Physics, 1964, Strong Interactions, 1966, Classical Dynamics and Its Quantum Analogues, 1979, 2d edit., 1990, The Image of Eternity, 1980, (with P.J. Davis) No Way, 1987, The How and the Why, 1988, The Fire Within the Eye, 1997. Fellow Am. Phys. Soc.; mem. Internat. Soc. for Study Time (pres. 1973-76). Office: Williams Coll Dept Physics Williamstown MA 01267 E-mail: dpark@williams.edu.

PARK, EDWARD CAHILL, JR. retired physicist; b. Wollaston, Mass., Nov. 26, 1923; s. Edward Cahill and Fentress (Kerlin) P.; m. Helen Therese O'Boyle, July 28, 1951. AB, Harvard U., 1947; postgrad., Amherst Coll., 1947-49; PhD, U. Birmingham, Eng., 1956. Instr. Amherst (Mass.) Coll., 1954-55; mem. staff Lincoln Lab., Lexington, Mass., 1955-57, Arthur D. Little, Inc., Cambridge, 1957-60, group leader electronic systems Santa Monica, Calif., 1960-64; sr. staff engr., head laser system sect. Hughes Aircraft Co., Culver City, 1964-68, sr. scientist El Segundo, 1986-88; mgr. electro optical systems sect. Litton Guidance and Control Systems, Woodland Hills, 1968-70; sr. phys. scientist The Rand Corp., Santa Monica, 1970-72; sr. scientist R&D Assocs., Marina Del Rey, Calif., 1972-1986, cons., 1986-89; sr. tech. specialist Rockwell Internat., N.Am. Aircraft, Seal Beach, 1988-94. Contbr. articles to profl. jours.; patentee in field. Served to 1st lt. USAAF, 1943-46. Grantee Dept. Indsl. and Sci. Research, 1953. Fellow Explorers Club (sec. So. Calif. chpt. 1978-79); mem. IEEE, Optical Soc. Am., Soc. Archtl. Historians, N.Y. Acad. Scis., Acad. Am. Poets, Sigma Xi. Clubs: 20-Ghost (Eng.), Harvard (So. Calif.). Democrat. Avocations: music, art, architecture, body surfing, gardening. Home: 932 Ocean Frnt Santa Monica CA 90403-2410

PARK, EUISU, research scientist; b. KwangJoo, JeonNam, Republic of Korea, Feb. 24, 1963; s. YoungJin Park, SeokOk Kim; m. JiYoung Lee; children: Yena, WonII. PhD, U. Mich., 1999. Rschr. Kia Motors Co., Seoul, Republic of Korea, 1988—91; asst. rsch. scientist U. Mich., Ann Arbor, 1999—. Contbr. articles to profl. jours. Mem.: ASEE, IEEE. Office: U Mich 4110 EECS 1301 Beal Ave Ann Arbor MI 48109-2122 Office Fax: 734-863-8041. Business E-Mail: euisu@umich.edu.

PARK, GLORIA, family physician, consultant; b. Spokane, Wash., Apr. 13, 1930; d. George Edmund and Nellie Edessa (Dorman) Knowles; m. Orlo Edward Park, Aug. 9, 1952; children: Kevin, Loren, Galen, Diane. BS in Zoology cum laude, Wash. State Coll., 1952; MD, U. Colo., 1955. Cert. Nat. Indian Health Bd. Intern St. Anthony Hosp., Denver, 1955-56; chief outpatient svc. Alaska Native Med. Ctr., Anchorage, 1956-61, acting chief profl. svc., 1961-63, dir. outpatient dept. and field health, 1963-71, asst. dir. svc. unit affairs, 1971-74, dir. ambulatory care, 1974-85, mem. cons. staff family medicine svc., 1985—. Cons. hepatitis program Alaska Native Health Bd., Anchorage, 1986-87; clin. instr. U. Wash., Anchorage, 1978-85. Med. reviewer Alaska Medicine, 1987—. Former mem. Alaska Gov.'s Com. on Edn.; mem. Anchorage Municipality Libr. Bd., 1981-86; life mem. Alaska Coun. on Smoking or Health, 1981—. Recipient recognition award Anchorage Bus. and Profl. Women, 1968, award Nat. Indian Health Bd., 1985, 88, Alumni Achievement award Wash. State U., 1994. Fellow Am. Acad. Family Physicians (com. minority health affairs 1980-85); mem. AMA, Am. Assn. Sr. Physicians, Alaska Acad. Family Physicians (pres. 1981-83), Alaska Med. Assn. (councilor 1984-88), Anchorage Med. Soc. (com. mem.), Alaska Pub. Health Assn. (life), Alaska Heart Assn. (life), Cook Inlet Hist. Soc. (life). Republican. Avocations: travel, fishing, reading, genealogy. Office: Alaska Native Med Ctr 4315 Diplomacy Dr # Mailrm Anchorage AK 99508-5926

PARK, GYOUNGWON, electrical engineer, research scientist; b. Seoul, Korea, Oct. 19, 1969; s. Taehyun and Kija Lee Park; m. Soyoun Kim, June 25, 1996. BS in Physics, Seoul Nat. U., 1992, MS in Physics, 1996; PhD, U. Tex., 2001. Rsch. asst. Seoul Nat. U., 1994-96; tchg. asst. U. Tex., Austin, 1996-97, rsch. asst., 1997—. Contbr. articles to profl. jours. Mem. IEEE. Office: Honeywell Internat VCSEL Products Div Honeywell Tech Div 12001 State Hwy 55 MN 14-3 B20 Plymouth MN 55441 E-mail: gyoungwon@yahoo.com.

PARK, JAMES WALLACE, economics educator; b. Forest, Miss., May 1, 1934; s. Ulric Z. and Estelle Park; m. Martha A. Mayes, June 5, 1958; children: Julia C., Mary J. BS, U. Miss., 1958, M in Bus. Edn., 1959; PhD, U. Ala., 1974. Asst. prof. bus. U. N.Mex., Albuquerque, 1959—68; asst. prof. econs. Miss. U. for Women, Columbus, 1968—70; prof. bus. Jackson (Miss.) State U., 1974—77; prof. econs. Belhaven Coll., 1977—2001, prof. emeritus, 2001—. Contbr. articles to profl. jours. Mem. Gov.'s Task Force on Miss. Economy, 1981; pres. Men of Ctrl. Miss. Presbytery, 1981—84. Recipient Tchg. Excellence and Campus Leadership award, Sears-Roebuck Found., 1991. Democrat. Avocation: writing. Home: 810 Fairview St Jackson MS 39202-1626 Office: Belhaven Coll 1500 Peachtree St Jackson MS 39202-1754 E-mail: jwmpark@aol.com.

PARK, JEFFREY JOHN, science educator; b. L.A., Feb. 10, 1958; s. Heath John and Pierina Park; m. Dorothy Marie Koch; children: Helen, Naomi. AB, Princeton U., 1979; PhD, U. Calif.-San Diego, La Jolla, 1985. Asst. prof. Yale U., New Haven, 1985—90, assoc. prof., 1990—2000, prof., 2000—, chmn. environ. studies maj., 2002—. Chmn., bd. dirs. Incorporated Rsch. Instns. for Seismology, Washington, 1992—94. Author: (scientific articles) about seismology, paleoclimate, historical clinmate change. Fellow: Royal Astron. Soc.; mem.: AAAS, Seismol. Soc. Am., Am. Geophys. Union (pres. seismology sect. 2000—02). Episcopalian. Home: 131 Old Coach Hwy New Haven CT 06518-2024 Office: Yale U Dept Geology and Geophysics PO Box 208109 New Haven CT 06520-8109 Personal E-mail: jeffrey.park@yale.edu. Business E-Mail: jeffrey.park@yale.edu.

PARK, JOHN, finance, investment consultant; b. Seoul, Korea, Nov. 29, 1925; came to U.S., 1949; s. Young-Kee and In-Oak P.; m. Nancy A. King, Dec. 21, 1961 (div. Nov. 1969); children: John K., Ben C.; m. Kwi Yong Lee, Aug. 14, 1990; 1 child, Angela L. AB, Coll. St. Thomas, 1953; MA, U. Nebr., 1955, PhD, 1959. Chmn., dept. econs., bus. Tarkio (Mo.) Coll., 1957-62; sr. prof. econs., bus. Clarkson Coll., Potsdam, N.Y., 1962-65, Northeast Mo. State U., 1965-67; prof. bus. econs Southwest Mo. State U., 1967-70; chmn., dept. econ., bus. adminstrn. Frostburg (Md.) State U., 1970—93, prof., econs., bus. adminstrn., 1970—78. Investment advisor, Met. Securities Corp., St. Louis, 1966-70. Mem. Am. Econs. Assn., Am. Fin. Assn., Nat. Assn. Securities Dealers, Am. Assn. Polit. Social Scis., Eastern Fin. Assn., Fin. Mgmt. Assn., Alpha Kappa Delta, Pi Gamma Mu. Republican. Methodist. Avocation: classical music. Home and Office: PO Box 3436 451 Beacon Knoll Ln Fort Mill SC 29708-7952

PARK, JOHN THORNTON, academic administrator; b. Phillipsburg, N.J., Jan. 3, 1935; s. Dawson J. and Margaret M. (Thornton) P.; m. Dorcas M Marshall; June 1, 1956; children: Janet Ernst, Karen Daily. BA in Physics with distinction, Nebr. Wesleyan U., 1956; PhD, U. Nebr., 1963. NSF postdoctoral fellow Univ. Coll., London, 1963-64; asst. prof. physics U. Mo., Rolla, 1964-68, assoc. prof. physics, 1968-71, prof., 1971-2000, prof. emeritus, 2000—, chmn. dept. physics, 1977-83, vice chancellor acad. affairs, 1983-85, 86-91, interim chancellor, 1985-86, 91-92, chancellor, 1992-2000, chancellor emeritus, 2000—. Vis. assoc. prof. NYU, 1970-71; pres. Talema Electronics, Inc., St. James, Mo., 1983-99, Tortran Corp., 1990—; prin. investigator NSF Rsch. Grants, 1966-92; bd. dirs. Mo. Tech. Corp., Jefferson City, Mo., 1994—, Mo. Enterprise, 1990—, Phelps County Bank, 1997—. Contbr. articles to profl. jours. Recipient Most Disting. Scientist award Mo. Acad. Sci., 1994. Fellow Am. Phys. Soc. (mem. divsn. elec. and atomic physics); mem. Am. Assn. Physics Tchrs., Rotary. Methodist.

PARK, JOHN WONSUH, internist, oncologist, educator; b. Carmel, Calif., Oct. 19, 1959; s. Seung P. and Sunzah E. Park. AB, Harvard U., 1982; MD, Stanford U., 1986. Diplomate Am. Bd. Internal Medicine, Am. Bd. Med. Oncology. Intern UCLA, 1986-87, resident in internal medicine, 1987-89; fellow in hematology and med. oncology U. Calif., San Francisco, 1989-92, adj. asst. prof., 1993—, mem. staff, 1992—. Contbr. numerous articles to med. jours., chpts. to books. Mem. Am. Soc. Clin. Oncology, Am. Assn. for Cancer Rsch.

PARK, JON KEITH, dentist, educator; b. Wichita, Kans., May 26, 1938; DDS, U. Mo., 1964; BA, Wichita State U., 1969; MS in Dental Hygiene Edn., U. Mo., 1971; MS in Oral Pathology, U. Md., 1982; cert. in dental radiology, U. Pa. Sch. Dental Medicine, 1982. Diplomate Am. Bd. Oral and Mixillofacial Radiology. Pvt. practice dentistry, Wichita, 1964-67; chmn. dept. dental hygiene Wichita State U., 1967-72; assoc. prof. oral diagnosis, dir. oral radiology Balt. Coll. Dental Surgery, U. Md., 1972—. Program dir. U. Md. dental externship, 1974-77; lectr. Essex C.C., Harford County C.C.; cons. in radiology VA Hosp., Medix Sch. Dental Assisting; mem. Md. StateRadiation Control Adv. Bd., 1981—; chmn. devel. com. Introduction to Basic Concepts in Dental Radiography, Dental Assisting Nat. Bd., Inc., Am. Dental Assts. Assn., 1991 Editor Am. Acad. Oral and Maxillofacial Radiology Newsletter; patentee pivotal design dental chair. Mem. Ute Pass Hist. Soc. Recipient U. Md. Media Achievement award, 1977, 78. Fellow Am. Coll. Dentists, Am. Acad. Dental Radiology; mem. ADA, Md. State Dental Assn., Balt. City Dental Soc. (ad hoc com. radiation safety, exec. coun.), Am. Acad. Oral Pathology, Am. Acad. Oral and Maxillofacial Radiology (ednl. standards com., editor newsletter), Orgn. Tchrs. oral Diagnosis, Am. Theater Organ Soc., Kans. Dental Hygienists Assn. (hon.), Balt. Music Club, Am. Assn. Dental Schs., Internat. Assn. Dental and Maxillofacial Radiology, Balt. Opera Guild, Engring. Soc. Balt., Met. Opera Guild, Balt. Symphony Orch. Assn., Ute Pass Cmty. Assn., Univ. Club, Omicron Kappa Upsilon, Psi Omega. Episcopalian. E-mail: jpark@umaryland.edu.

PARK, JOON BU, biomedical engineer, researcher, educator; b. Pusan, Korea, June 20, 1944; came to U.S., 1964; s. Sung Sub and Jung Ju (Kim) P.; m. Hyonsook Yoo, Apr. 15, 2000; children: Misun, Yoon Ho, Yoon Il, Lajong. Student, Seoul Nat. U., Korea, 1962-64; BS, Boston U., 1967; MS, MIT, 1969; PhD, U. Utah, 1972. NIH postdoctoral fellow U. Wash., Seattle, 1972-73; vis. asst. prof. U. Ill., Urbana, 1973-76; asst./assoc. prof. Clemson (S.C.), 1976-81; prof. Tulane U., New Orleans, 1981-83; prof. biomed. engrng. U. Iowa, Iowa City, 1983—. Advisor/cons. FDA, Rockville, Md., 1980—. Author: Biomaterials: An Introduction, 1979, 2nd edit., 1992, Biomaterials Science and Engineering, 1984, also more than 100 jour. articles, more than 100 abstracts. Recipient McQueen Quattlebaum award Clemson U., 1980. Fellow Am. Inst. Med. and Biol. Engring.; mem. Soc. for Biomaterials (founding mem.), Biomed. Engring. Soc., Orthop. Rsch. Soc., N.Y. Acad. Scis. Achievements include 7 patents. Home: 1810 Country Club Dr Coralville IA 52241-1183 Office: Univ of Iowa Dept Biomedical Engring Iowa City IA 52242

PARK, JOSEPH CHUL HUI, computer scientist; b. Seoul, Korea, Aug. 6, 1937; came to U.S., Nov., 1955; s. Don Gil and Eui Kyung (Shin) P.; m. Young Ja Yoon, Aug. 17, 1968; children: Esther Y.J., Maria Y.S., David Y.W., Jonathan Y.S. BA, Coll of Wooster, Ohio, 1959; BS, MIT, 1959; MS, U. Ill., 1961, PhD, 1967. Mem. rsch. staff Stanford Linear Accelerator Ctr Stanford U., 1969-72, 73-75; assoc. prof., then prof. computer sci. Korea Advanced Inst. of Sci., Seoul, 1975-82; head Computer Sci. Rsch. Ctr. Korea Advanced Inst. Sci., Korea, 1980-82; mem. tech. staff Braegen Corp., Milpitas, Calif., 1982-86, Hewlett-Packard Labs., Palo Alto, 1986-92; tech mgr. compiler Advanced Processor div. Intergraph Corp., 1992-93; sr. staff engr. Sun Microsystems, Inc., Calif., 1993—. Lectr. in computer engring. Santa Clara (Calif.) U., 1987-94. Mem. IEEE, Assn. Computing Machinery. Baptist. Home: 14800 Masson Ct Saratoga CA 95070-9715 E-mail: joseph.park@sun.com.

PARK, JULIA R. editor, poet; b. Fremont, Calif., Feb. 20, 1963; d. William Frederick and Elizabeth Bailey Park; m. Joseph Rodrigues, Oct. 8, 1989 (div. Mar. 1, 2002); children: Simone Petra Rodrigues, Anastasia Elizabeth Rodrigues;1 child from previous marriage Michaela Suzanna Romero. BA in Journalism, San Francisco State U., 1986; MA in English, Calif. State U., Hayward, 2000. Freelance writer, 1982—; publicist for local theatres Oakland, Calif., 1994—2001; newsletter editor, writer cmty. orgns. and bus. San Leandro, 1989—; features editor East Bay Pub., 2000—01; editor The Alameda (Calif.) Sun newspaper, 2001—. Vis. scholar, 1998—. Contbg. editor: Maxie mag., 2001—; contbr. chapters to books; , author poetry. Recipient Frederick C. Fallon award, Chabot Coll., Hayward, 1996. Mem.: Jane Austen Soc. N.Am. (reporter 1998—), Pen West/Pen USA, Soc. Profl. Journalists. Avocations: reading, traveling.

PARK, LEE (LEE PARKLEE), artist; b. Seoul, South Korea; s. Chung-Kun Park and Mil-Hwa Kim; m. Chai Kyung Lim, June 3, 1994. MA, Fla. State U., 1986. Group shows include Shinpara Gallery, L.A., Up-Stairs Gallery, L.A., Beverly Plz. Hotel, Pacific Mus., Pasadena, Calif., Barnsdall Art Gallery, Hollywood, Calif., Brand XXII The Assn. of Brand Art Ctr., Glendale, Calif., Asia Invitation Art Exhibn., Sejong Cultural Ctr., Seoul, la Peintre Moderne Coreend '93, Paris, Korea-Japan Interchange Exhbn., Tokyo, 1994, Downtown Lives '96 Art Exhbn., L.A., City Hall of Paris, 4, Biennale Internat. de Paris, 1994, Musee d'Art Moderne de la Commanderie d'Unet, Paris, 1994, Bridgeport U., N.Y., 1995, San Bernardino County Mus., 1995, Kong-Ja Culture Art Exhbn., China, 1995, His Majesty the King's 50th Anniversary Art Exhbn., Thailand, 1996, 1st Venice Annual Internat. Open Art Exbhn., Venice, 1998, 1st Internat. Biennial Contemporary Art, Perugia, Italy, 1998, Heukyong-gangsung Internat. Art Exhbn., China, 1998, Ting Shao-Kuang Fine Art Ctr., Beverly Hills, Articulture Gallery, Hermosa Beach, Calif., 1998, '99 World Peace Art Exhbn., Sejong Cultural Ctr., Seoul, 1999; 2 person shows include Cosmos Gallery, Honolulu, The City of L.A. Cultural Affairs Dept.; solo exhibits include Modern Art Gallery, L.A., Olympic Gallery, L.A., Sun Space Gallery, L.A., Gallery Nuevo, Pusan, Korea; publ. artwork in American References, Art of California mag., Artweek mag., The Biweekly Art Jour., Seoul, Artprint mag., Washington, Art Exposure mag., Calif., Encyclopedia of Living Artists mag., Calif., Art 2000, Seoul, Art Diary Internat. 98/99, Milan, Italy. Recipient Bronze award Art of Calif., 1993, Gold award Art Addiction, Stockholm, 1997. Avocations: collecting stamps and antiques, music, reading books, jogging, playing tennis. Home: 1935 S La Salle Ave Apt 31 Los Angeles CA 90018-1627

PARK, LEE CRANDALL, psychiatrist; b. Washington, July 15, 1926; s. Lee I. and Alice (Crandall) P.; m. Barbara Ann Merrick, July 1, 1953; children: Thomas Joseph, Jeffrey Rawson; m. Mary Woodfill Banerjee, Apr. 27, 1985; stepchildren: Stephen Kumar, Scott Kumar. Grad., Putney Prep. Sch., Vt.; BS in Zoology, Yale U., 1948; MD, Johns Hopkins U., 1952. Diplomate Nat. Bd. Med. Examiners, Am. Bd. Psychiatry and Neurology. Intern medicine Johns Hopkins Hosp., Osler Clinic, Balt., 1952-53; resident psychiatry USN Hosp., Oakland, Calif., 1953-54, Henry Phipps Psychiat. Clinic, Johns Hopkins Hosp., Balt., 1955-59, asst. psychiatrist, 1955-59, staff psychiatrist, 1959—, staff dept. medicine, 1970—, hon. staff dept. medicine, 1991—, dir. psychiat. outpatient svcs. and community psychiatry program, 1972-74, asst. dir. clin. svcs. dept. psychiatry, 1973-74, mem. departmental coun., 1974-76. Fellow psychiatry Johns Hopkins U., 1955-59, faculty in psychiatry, 1959—, assoc. prof., 1971—, physician charge psychiat. svcs. student health svc., 1961-73; vis. psychiatrist Balt. City Hosp., 1960-61; co-prin., prin. investigator NIMH Psychopharmacology Rsch. Br. Outpatient Study of Drug-Set Interaction, 1960-68, co-dir. (with Eugene Meyer) Time-Limited Psychotherapy Rsch. Grant, 1969-73; pvt. practice psychiatry, 1964—; cons. Met. Balt. Assn. Mental Health, 1961-63, Bur. Disability Ins., Social Security Adminstrn., 1964-81; attending staff Seton Psychiat. Inst., 1966-73, exec. bd., 1970-73; staff Sheppard and Enoch Pratt Hosp., 1974—; rsch. includes borderline and narcissistic conditions, long-term effects of childhood emotional abuse and neglect, psychotherapy, interrelationships of psychotherapy and pharmacotherapy, ethical considerations in clin. rsch. Co-author: A Primer on Mental Disorders: A Guide for Educators, Families and Students, 2001; contbr. articles and chpts. to profl. jours. and books. Served to lt. M.C., USNR, 1953-55, div. psychiatrist 1st Marine Div., Korea, staff psychiatrist USN Hosp., Camp Pendelton, Calif., 1954-55; mem. Md. Interdisciplinary Coun. for Children and Adolescents, 1978-98, treas., 1980-87. Fellow: AAAS, Am. Psychiat. Assn. (life; mem. assembly 1983—93, Psychiat. Rsch. Network 1994—, disting. fellow); mem.: SAR, AAUP, AMA, Johns Hopkins Med. and Surg. Assn., Balt. County Med. Assn., Balt. City Med. Soc., Med. and Chirurg. Faculty Md., Group Therapy Network, N.Y. Acad. Scis., Soc. Psychotherapy Rsch., Md. Psychiat. Soc. (pres. 1978—79), Md. Assn. Pvt. Practicing Psychiatrists, Am. Assn. Pvt. Practicing Psychiatrists, Am. Coll. Neuropsychopharmacology, Am. Soc. Adolescent Psychiatry, Internat. Soc. Study of Personality Disorders, Am. Psychosomatic Soc., Md. Found. for Psychiatry (bd. dirs. 1995—, pres. 2000—), Nat. Assn. Scholars, Sons of Union Vets. of Civil War, Avery Assn., Denison Soc., Crandall Assn., Van Kouwenhoven-Conover Assn., Van Voorhees Assn., Parke Soc., Nat. Soc. of the Sons and Daus. of the Pilgrims, Gen. Soc. of War of 1812 (bd. dirs. State of Md. 1997—99, officer, surgeon 2000—), Descendants of Mexican War Vets, Nat.

Huguenot Soc., Chevy Chase (Md.) Country Club, Met. Club (Washington), Johns Hopkins Club (Balt.), Farmington Country Club (Charlottesville, Va.), Phi Beta Pi. Episcopalian. Home: 308 Tunbridge Rd Baltimore MD 21212-3803 Office: 1205 York Rd Ste 35 Lutherville Timonium MD 21093 E-mail: lpark3@jhmi.edu.

PARK, LELAND MADISON, librarian; b. Alexandria, La., Oct. 21, 1941; s. Arthur Harris and Jane Rebecca (Leland) P. Student, McCallie Sch., 1957-59; AB, Davidson Coll., 1963; M.L.S., Emory U., 1964; postgrad., Simmons Coll., 1968; Adv.M. in L.S., Fla. State U., 1973, PhD, 1974. Reference librarian Pub. Library of Charlotte and Mecklenburg County, N.C., 1964-65; head reference and student personnel Davidson (N.C.) Coll. Library, 1967-70, asst. dir., 1970-75, dir., 1975—. Cons. coll. cons. network So. Assn. Colls and Schs.; vis. lectr. Emory U., summer 1972; temporary instr. Fla. State U., 1973; libr. cons.; conf. spkr.; chmn. state adv. com. Libr. Svcs. and Constrn. Act, 1975-79; mem. N.C. State Libr. Commn., 1983-85, 87-92, chmn., 1989-92; mem. Davidson (N.C.) Town Appearance Commn., 1986-93, 98—, Hist. Preservation Commn., 1994-96. Editor Southeastern Librarian, 1976-78; acad. sect. editor N.C. Libraries, 1972-77; contbr. articles to profl. jours. Mem. Wake County Citizens for Better Librs., N.C., 1965-67; sec. com. libr. affairs Piedmont U. Ctr., 1969-70, chmn., 1970-72; mem. nat. bd. cons. NEH, 1976—; clk. mission com. St. Alban's Episcopal Mission, Davidson, N.C., 1969-72, layreader, 1970-75, treas., 1975-86; bd. dirs. statewide computer libr. resource network NC-LIVE, 1997—. Recipient H.W. Wilson library periodical award, 1979, Alumni Achievement award The McCallie Sch., 1989, Order of Long Leaf Pine presented by N.C. Gov. James G. Martin, 1993. Mem. ALA, Southeastern Libr. Assn. (chmn. coll. and univ. sect. 1976-78, exec. bd. 1976-78), N.C. Libr. Assn. (2d v.p. 1975-77, 1st v.p. 1981-83, pres. 1983-85), Metrolina Libr. Assn. (pres. 1969-71), Mecklenburg County Libr. Assn. (treas. 1969-70), Soc. of Cin. (2d v.p. Ga. Soc. 1982-83), SAR, Mil. Order World Wars, Raleigh Jaycees (chmn. libr. com. 1965-67), Res. Officer Assn., SCV, Soc. Colonial Wars, S.C. Huguenot Soc., Beta Phi Mu, Sigma Nu, Omicron Delta Kappa. Lodges: Rotary. Home: PO Box 777 235 Ney Circle Davidson NC 28035-7200 Office: Davidson Coll E H Little Libr PO Box 7200 Davidson NC 28035-7200 E-mail: lepark@davidson.edu.

PARK, LESLIE DESMOND, health organization executive; b. Chgo., May 23, 1925; s. Andrew Gordon Park and Edith Emily Windsor; m. Jeannette Irene Park; children: Kathy Jean, Pamela Louise, Jane Ann. BA, Northwestern U., 1949, MA, 1950. Tchr. Ill. State Normal U., 1949-54; exec. dir. United Cerebral Palsy, Ill., Bloomington, 1954-58, United Cerebral Palsy of Pa., Harrisburg, 1959-67, United Cerebral Palsy of N.Y.C., 1967-88; chmn., founder Disabled and Alone/Life Svcs. for the Handicapped, Inc., N.Y.C., 1988—. Author: How to be a Friend to the Handicapped; contbr. articles to profl. jours. Founder, dir. The Open Congregation, 1984—; adult bible sch. tchr., 1951—; ordained elder Presbyn. Ch.; mem. Internat. Studies on Manoradde Needs, Camp Hill, Bloomington, Ill. Lt. (j.g.) USN, 1943-45. Recipient Founder's award The Open Congregation, 1986, Henry Kessler Human Dignity award Kessler Rehab. Inst., 1984, Hon. award Schuylkill County, 1968, Profl. award Outstanding Exec. in Cerebral Palsy Work, 1964, Svc. to Soc. award Northwestern U., 1997; named Hon. chief Coun. for Handicapped, Nigeria. Mem. Am. Acad. for Devel. Medicine, Internat. Cerebral Palsy Soc. Presbyterian. Achievements include research in needs of the handicapped in Bahrain, Greece, Nigeria, U.S. Avocations: gardening, hiking, Bible study. Office: Disabled and Alone Life Svcs for Handicapped Inc 352 Park Ave S Ste 703 New York NY 10010

PARK, LINDA SUE, writer; b. Ill. BS in English, Stanford U. Pub. rels. writer major oil co., 1981—83; writer, 1997—. Author: Seesaw Girl, 1999, The Kite Fighters, 2000, A Single Shard, 2001 (Newbery Medal, 2002), When My Name Was Keoko, 2002. Avocations: cooking, travel, movies, crossword puzzles. Office: Clarion Books 215 Park Ave S New York NY 10003*

PARK, MARY WOODFILL, information consultant; b. Nevada, Mo., Nov. 20, 1944; d. John Prossor and Elizabeth (Devine) Woodfill; m. Salil Kumar Banerjee, Dec. 29, 1967 (div. 1983); children: Stephen Kumar, Scott Kumar; m. Lee Crandall Park, Apr. 27, 1985; stepchildren: Thomas Joseph, Jeffrey Rawson. BA, Marywood Coll., 1966; postgrad., Johns Hopkins U., 1983, Goucher Coll., 1986. Asst. to dir. U. Pa. Librs., Phila., 1968-69; investment libr. Del. Funds, 1969-71; investment officer Investment Counselors Md., Balt., 1980-84, 1st Nat. Bank Md., Balt., 1984-85; founder Info. Consultancy, 1985—. Lectr. Loyola Coll., Balt., 1991-92, Cath. U., 1993. Author: InfoThink—Practical Strategies for Using Information in Business, 1998; editor, contbr. to profl. publs. Vol. Internat. Visitors' Ctr., Balt., 1979-80, 91; del. White House Conf. on Librs.; v.p. bd. dirs. Friends of Goucher Libr., 1988-90; mem. industry applications com. Info. Tech. Bd., State of Md., 1993-96; mem. info. tech. com. of the Tech. Coun., Greater Balt. Com., 1993-98. Named One of Md.'s Top 100 Women, Warfield's Bus. Publn., 1996. Mem.: DAR, Huguenot Soc. Md. (bd. mem. 2001—), Nat. Huguenot Soc., Md. Found. for Psychiatry (bd. mem. 1998—), Md. Libr. Assn., Assn. Ind. Info. Profls., Info. Futures Inst., Spl. Librs. Assn. (pres. Balt. chpt. 1991—92, mem. network coord. coun. Sailor project 1993—95, govt. rels. chair 1998—), Soc. of Daughters of Holland Dames, Friends of the Holland Soc. N.Y. (assoc.), Ryker-Riker Hist. Soc., Nat. Soc. Colonial Dames XVII Century, Nat. Soc. of the Sons and Daus. of the Pilgrims, Nat. Soc. Dames Ct. Honor, Nat. Soc. Daus. Am. Colonists, Friends of New Netherlands, Nat. Soc. of U.S. Daus. of 1812, The Soc. of Daughters of Holland Dames, Three Arts Club Homeland, Hamilton St. Club (bd. dirs. 1989—92). Episcopalian. Office: The Information Consultancy 308 Tunbridge Rd Baltimore MD 21212-3803 E-mail: mwpark@informationconsultancy.com.

PARK, MYUNG KUN, medical educator; b. Suhung, Hwanghae, Korea, Sept. 30, 1934; came to U.S., 1962; s. Jung-Jin and Sonnyu (Lee) P.; m. Issun Kim, Jan. 21, 1967; children: Douglas, Christopher, Warren. Diploma for premed. course, Seoul Nat. U., 1956, MD, 1960. Asst. prof. U. Kans. Coll. of Medicine, Kansas City, 1973-76; assoc. prof. U. Tex. Med. Sch., San Antonio, 1976-83, prof., 1983—; prof., chmn. pediatrics Arabian Gulf U. Med. Coll., Bahrain, 1995-98. Author: How to Read Pediatric ECG, 1982, 3rd rev. edit., 1992, Pediatric Cardiology for Practitioners, 1984, 3rd rev. edit., 1996, The Pediatric Cardiology Handbook, 1991, 2nd rev. edit., 1997; contbr. articles to profl. jours. Rsch. fellowship NIH, 1971-73, Postdoctoral fellowship NIH, 1965-68, fellowship Maternal and Child Health Bur., 1991-95; recipient Gold medal Seoul Nat. U., 1960. Fellow Am. Coll. Cardiology, Am. Acad. Pediatrics; mem. Soc. for Pediatric Rsch., Sigma Xi Rsch. Soc. Home: 3318 Buckhaven St San Antonio TX 78230-3956 Office: U Tex Med Sch 7703 Floyd Curl Dr San Antonio TX 78284-6200

PARK, NO-HEE, academic administrator; b. Jan. 30, 1944; m. Yu Bai Yuly, 1969; 1 child Jennifer. DDS, Seoul Nat. U., 1968, MSD, 1970; PhD, Med. Coll. Ga., 1978; DMD, Harvard U., 1982. Postdoctoral fellow in oral biology and pharmacology Med. Coll. Ga., 1975—78; rsch. assoc., Eye Rsch. Inst. Harvard Med. Sch., Boston, 1978—80, instr., dept. ophthalmology, 1978—82, asst. scientist, Eye Rsch. Inst., 1980—82, assoc. scientist, Eye Rsch. Inst., 1982—83; asst. prof., oral biology and pathophysiology Harvard U. Sch. Dental Medicine, 1982—83; assoc. prof., oral biology UCLA Sch. Dentistry, L.A., 1984—85, prof., 1985—, assoc. dean rsch., 1997—98, dean, 1998—; assoc. dir. UCLA Dental Rsch. Inst., 1986—90, dir., 1995—, UCLA Wound Healing Rsch. Ctr., L.A., 1997—. Contbr. articles to profl. jours.; editl. bd. Internat. Jour. Oncology, Electronic Jour. Biotechnology, editor-in-chief Internat. Jour. Oral Biology, ad-hoc reviewer for various publs. Mem.: Internat. Coll. Dentistry, Omicron Kappa Upsilon Dental Soc. Achievements include research in the role of telomerase in oral carcinogenesis, gene therapy for oral cancer, molecular mechanism of replicative senescence in normal human oral keratinocytes and viral and chemical oncogenesis; cellular proto-oncogenes and tumor suppressor genes, cell cycle and DNA repair, and antiviral chemotherapy. Office: UCLA 10833 Leconte Ave Rm 53-038 Los Angeles CA 90095*

PARK, PATRICIA WEILL, controller; b. N.Y.C., June 30, 1939; d. Harold and Lisbeth (Goldmann) W.; m. Richard Alan Rosenthal, June 10, 1962 (div. 1985); children: Pamela Gail Rosenthal, Mark Carroll Rosenthal; m. Richard Darrow Park, Jan. 9, 1992 (dec. July 1995); 1 child, Heather. BS in Publs., Simmons Coll., 1961; postgrad., Northeastern U., 1981-82; Cert. in Acctg., Bentley Coll., 1987. Assoc. editor various TV and fan mags., N.Y.C., 1961-62; free-lance writer N.Y.C., N.J. and Mass., 1962-78; asst. to mgr. credit/receivables Dodge Co., Cambridge, Mass., 1980-83; asst. controller Edward R. Marden Corp., Allston, 1983-86; controller Aarlan, Inc., Cambridge, 1986-87; asst. controller SDK Healthcare Info. Systems (now Eclipsys Solutions Corp.), Boston, 1987-99; A/R cons. Eclipsys Solutions Corp., 1999; tax specialist H&R Block, 2000—. Script writer Two Collection, WCBH-TV. Vol. tutor Adult Literacy Program, Brighton, Mass., 1988-90; pres. Class of 1961 Simmons Coll., 1991-96, v.p., 1996-2001; pres., bd. mgrs. condominium assn., 1987-89, v.p., 1991-92, pres. 1993-94; vol. tour guide WGBH-TV, 1998-99. Mem. Mensa. Avocations: concerts, theatre, Feng Shui, travel, computers.

PARK, PENNY SHERAN, elementary school educator, writer; b. Tulare, Calif., July 13, 1948; d. Sheridan Lee Roy Harris and Jeanne Avril Lightbody. AA, Coll. of the Sequoias, Visalia, CA, 1968; B in Music Edn., U. of Pacific, 1971; M in Music Edn., U. Calif., Fresno, 1980. Registered music therapist Nat. Assn. Music Therapy, 1971. Music therapist mental health wing Emmanual Hosp., Turlock, Calif., 1971; music therapist Brandel Manor Nursing Home, 1971, Kings County Mental Health Day Treatment Ctr., Hanford, 1971—77; self-employed, 1977—85; music therapist Lee Richmond Sch. -Spl. Edn., 1979—84; resource tchr.- music The Learning Ctr., 1984—85; tchr. Hanford Elem. Sch. Dist., 1985—. Consulting music therapist & music educator various, Hanford, 1977—79; program developer Kings County Supt. Schs.-Spl. Edn., 1979—84; chorale instr. Hanford Elem. Sch. Dist., 1985—90; trainer The Activities In Math & Sci. Found.- Fresno (Calif.) Pacific Coll., 1987—92. Author: Five Merry Santas, 1992; editor: Community Treasures, 2000. Mem.: Hanford Elem. Tchrs. Assn., Calif. Tchrs. Assn., Ea. Star (25 year pin 1997). Avocations: writing, reading, music, scrapbooks, computer games. Office: Hanford Elem Sch Dist 741 White St Hanford CA 93232 Business E-Mail: ppark@hesd.k12.ca.us.

PARK, ROY HAMPTON, JR. advertising executive; b. N.C., 1938; s. Roy Hampton and Dorothy Goodwin (Dent) P.; m. Elizabeth Tetlow Parham; children: Elizabeth P. Fowler, Roy H. III. BA in Journalism, U. N.C., 1961; MBA, Cornell U., 1963. Sr. acct. exec., rev. bd. exec., advt. planning dir., J. Walter Thompson Co., N.Y.C. and Miami, 1963-70; v.p. mktg. and account mgmt. Kincaid Advt. Agency divsn. First Union Nat. Bank Corp., Charlotte, N.C., 1970-71; v.p. Park Outdoor Advt., Ithaca, N.Y., 1971-75; v.p. advt. and promotion Park Broadcasting Inc., 1976-81; dir., 1993-95; mng. editor Park Comm. Newsletter, Ithaca, 1976-81; mng. dir. Agrl. Rsch. Advt. Agy., 1976-81; v.p., gen. mgr. Park Outdoor Adv., 1981-84; pres., CEO, dir. Park Outdoor Advt. of N.Y. Inc., 1984—; pres. Outdoor Advt. Coun. N.Y. Inc., 1986-91, chmn., dir., 1992-95; dir., sr. v.p. RHP Inc., 1994-96, RHP Properties Inc., 1994-96. Mem. region I planning bd. Inst. Outdoor Advt., 1984—86. Dir., vice chmn. Boyce Thompson Inst. for Plant Rsch. Inc., 1995—; trustee Park Found. Inc., 1995—, Cornell U., 1999—; mem. adv. coun. Cornell U. Johnson Grad. Sch. Mgmt., 1996—, founding mem. alumni exec. com., 1984-88; bd. vis. U. N.C. Sch. Journalism and Mass Comm., 1994—; chmn. Ithaca Assembly Cotillion, 1979-81; dir. pub. rels. Tompkins County Conf. and Tourist Coun., 1976; exec. com. Tompkins County Rep. Fin. Com., 1983-84; chmn. fin. com. MacNeil for Assembly, 1984-86, co-chmn. 1978-82; bd. dirs. Tompkins County Coun. Arts, 1976; chmn. pub. rels. com. United Way Tompkins County, 1973-74, loaned publicity exec., 1977; bd. chmn., publicity dr. Jr. Olympics, 1973-74; dir. pub. rels. United Fund Raleigh, N.C., 1971; fin. com. Spl. Childrn's Ctr., 1979. Mem. Tompkins County C. of C. (chmn. legis. action com. 1976, acting chmn. nominating com. 1976, chmn. sign ordinance com., 1975-76, pub. rels. coun. 1976, Project of Yr. award 1974, Recognition award 1975), Charlotte C. of C. (pub. rels. com. 1970-71), N.C. Soc. of N.Y., Beach Preservation Assn. Pine Knoll Shores (adv.), Ithaca Yacht Club, Ithaca Country Club, Boca Bay Pass Club. Office: Park Outdoor Advt PO Box 4680 Ithaca NY 14852-4680

PARK, SEOK-KYUN, civil engineer, educator; b. Seoul, Oct. 10, 1961; s. Keum-Churl and Chae-Bong (Kim) P.; m. Hyun-Joo Na, May 10, 1985; 1 child, Jeong-Min. BE, U. Hanyang, Seoul, Korea, 1984, M in Engring., 1986; PhD, U. Tokyo, 1996. Asst., tchr. U. Hanyang, Seoul, 1984-86; rschr. Ssangyong Rsch. Ctr., Taejon, 1986-94, sr. rschr., project mgr., 1995-96; postdoctoral fellow U. Tokyo, 1996-97; lectr. Korea Infrastructure Safety and Tech. Corp., Goyang, 1998—; asst. prof. U. Taejon, 1998—. Vis. prof. Ssangyong Rsch. Ctr., Taejon, 1998—; expert advisor Korea Inst. of Contrn. Tech., Seoul, 1998—; cons. prof. Korea Infrastructure Safety and Tech. Corp., Goyang, 1999—; design cons. Adv. Com. of Cheonju City Hall, 1999—; mem. internat. exchange com., U. Taejon, 1999—; hon. supr. Subway Constrn. Hdqs. Taejon City, 2000—; mem. Asian Model Code Com.; exec. sec. study com. smart concrete structures, study com. repair and reinforcement of concrete structures, tech. com. concrete structure instrumentation, 2000; mem. tech. coun. of Chungmam provincial govt., 2001—. Author: Evaluation and Repair of Concrete Structures, 1998, Design and Maintenance of Civil Structures, 2000, Reinforced Concrete Engineering, 2002, Construction Materials, 2002, Diagnosis and Maintenance of Concrete Structures, 2002; contbr. articles to profl. jours., including Jour. Japan Soc. Civil Engrs., INSIGHT (jour. Brit. Inst. Non-Destructive Testing), Concrete Libr. Internat., Jour. Korean Soc. Non-Destructive Testing, Jour. KCI, Jour. KSCE Recipient Best Acad. prize U. Hanyang, 1981, grand prize Ssangyong Cement Ind. Co. Ltd., 1993. Mem. Japan Soc. Civil Engrs. (Best Presentation award 1995, 96), Japan Concrete Inst., Korea Concrete Inst. (mem. editl. bd. 1999—, design cons.), Korean Soc. Civil Engrs. (design cons.), Korea Inst. for Structural Maintenance Inspection, Taeduk Sci. Forum. Achievements include patent for ultrasonic measurement system for concrete setting time; radar image processing system for non-destructive evaluation of concrete; composite material of high tenacity and non-retraction grouting material which includes powder of wasted tire and powder of plastic. Avocations: tennis, mountaineering, golf, listening to music, seeing movies, cycling. Home: 115-1401 Nurie APT Wolpyung-dong Seo-gu Taejon 302-280 Republic of Korea Office: U Taejon Dept Civil Engring 96-3 Yongwoon-dong Tong-gu Taejon 300-716 Republic of Korea E-mail: skpark@dju.ac.kr.

PARK, SOONG-KOOK, internist, researcher; b. Pyung-Yang, Korea, Aug. 9, 1938; s. Tae-Soo and Wha-Sil (Lee) P.; m. Sine-Ja, Oct. 9, 1965; children: Han-Kil, See-Nae, Han-Sol. BA, MD, Kyung-Pook Nat. U., Daegu, Korea, 1963. Med. diplomate. Surgeon gen. Republic of Korea, 1963-67; hosp. intern Bklyn. Jewish Hosp., 1968-69; resident in internal medicine Grassland Hosp., Valhalla, N.Y., 1969-72; fellow in gastroenterology Lahey Clinic, Boston, 1972-74; chief internal medicine Dongsan Presbyn. Hosp., Daegu, 1974-76; cons. in internal medicine, chief staff Mariana Med. Ctr., Guam, 1977-78; chief internal medicine Bak Hosp., Seoul, Korea, 1978, Dongsan Presbyn. Hosp., Daegu, 1978-90; prof. Keimyung U. Med. Sch., 1980—. Supt. Dongsan Med. Ctr., Daegu, 1990-94, Kyungju Dongsan Hosp., Kyungju, Korea, 1994-96; v.p. for med. affairs Keimyung U., 1996-98; dir. Dongsan Med. Ctr., 1996-98. Elder Sungji Presbyn. Ch., Daegu, 1976—; bd. dirs. YMCA, Daegu, 1980—, chmn., 1999-2001; dist. gov. Y's Men's Internat., Daegu, 1987-88; regional dir. Korea East region Y's Men's Internat., 2001-2002; internat. svc. dir. Internat. Bro. Club, Y's Men's Internat.; comdt. Med. Drs. Soccer Team, Daegu, 1990-94, 96—; pres. Korea Christian Hosp. Assn., 1997-98. Mem. Korean Assn. Internal Medicine (councilor 1980, v.p. 1999), Korean Assn. Gastroenterology (councilor 1980—), Korean Soc. Gastrointestinal Endoscopy (coun. 1988—, pres. 1996), Korean Soc. Gastrointestinal Motility Study (pres. 1993), Am. Coll. Gastroenterology (internat.) N.Y. Acad. Scis. Presbyterian. Avocations: tennis, soccer, choir. Home: Eunhatown 101-1708 Sangin-Dong 42 Dalseo-Ku Daegu 704-370 Republic of Korea Office: Dongsan Med Ctr 194 Dongsan-Dong Daegu 700-712 Republic of Korea E-mail: skpark@dsmc.or.kr.

PARK, STEVE, race car driver; b. Islip, N.Y., Aug. 23, 1967; s. Bob and Dorothy Park. Racecar driver Dale Earnhardt Inc., 1996—. Named Most Popular Driver, NASCAR Featherlite Modified Tour, 1995, one of Top 10 Drivers to Watch, Sports Illustrated, 1997, Rookie of Yr., Busch Series, 1997; recipient 2d pl., NASCAR Featherlite Modified Tour Championship, 1995, 5th pl., GoRacing.com 500, 2000, 4th pl., Cracker Barrel 500, 2000, Chevrolet Monte Carlo 400, 2000, Dover Downs Internat. Speedway, 2000, 3d pl., Checker Auto Parts 500, 2000, 1st pl., Winston Open, 2000, Dura Lube 400, 2001. Avocations: motorcycling, boating, golf. Office: Dale Earnhardt Inc 1675 Coddle Creek Hwy Mooresville NC 28115-8245*

PARK, THOMAS JOSEPH, biology researcher, educator; b. Balt., June 8, 1958; s. Lee Crandall and Barbara Ann (Merrick) P.; m. Stephanie Suzanne Reynolds, June 22, 1985; 1 child, Nicholas Timothy. BA, Johns Hopkins U., 1982; PhD, U. Md., 1988. Vis. scientist Coll. of France, Paris, 1988-89; rsch. fellow U. Tex., Austin, 1989-94; Alexander von Humboldt rsch. fellow U. Munich, 1994-95; with U. Ill. dept biol. scis., Chgo., 1995—. Contbr. chpt. to book, articles to Jour. Neurosci., Jour. Comparative Psychology, Hearing Rsch., Jour. Neurophysiol. Grantee NIMH, 1986, Nat. Ctr. Sci. Rsch., Paris, 1988, Alexander von Humboldt Found., 1994, NIH, 1996. Mem. AAAS, Soc. for Neurosci., Assn. for Rsch. in Otolaryngology. Office: U Ill at Chgo Dept Biol Scis Chicago IL 60607

PARK, WILLIAM ANTHONY (TONY PARK), lawyer; b. Blackfoot, Idaho, June 4, 1934; s. William Clair and Thelma Edelweiss (Shear) P.; m. Elizabeth Taylor, Aug. 26, 1961 (div.); children: Susan E., W. Adam, Patricia A.; m. Gail Chaloupka, Aug. 6, 1983. AA, Boise Jr. Coll., 1954; BA, U. Idaho, 1958; JD, U. Idaho, 1963. Bar: Idaho 1963. Sole practice, Boise, Idaho, 1963-70, 82-83; atty. gen. State of Idaho, 1971-75; ptnr. Park & Meuleman, Boise, 1975-81, Park & Burkett, Boise, 1983-84, Martin, Chapman, Park & Burkett, Boise, 1984-90, Park, Costello & Burkett, Boise, 1990-93, Park, Redford, Thomas & Burkett, Boise, 1994-97, Park, Thomas, Burkett & Williams, Boise, 1997-99; of counsel Huntley, Park, Thomas, Burkett, Olsen & Williams, 1999—. Chmn. Idaho Bicentennial Commn., 1971—77; bd. dirs. ACLU, Idaho, 1996—2000, pres., 1997—99; chmn. Idaho State Dem. Party, 1998—99; bd. dirs. Radio Free Europe/Radio Liberty, Inc., , 1977—82, Am. Lung Assn., 1978—90, Am. Lung Assn. of Idaho/Nev., 1976—96, 1999—, pres., 1991—95, 2002—. Served with U.S. Army, 1956—58. Recipient Disting. Svc. award. Home: 706 Warm Springs Ave Boise ID 83712-6420 Office: PO Box 2188 Boise ID 83701-2188 E-mail: gchaloupka@msn.com.

PARK, WILLIAM H(ERRON), financial executive; b. Monongahela, Pa., Sept. 19, 1947; s. William M. and Marjorie (Herron) P.; m. Mary Cornell, June 25, 1977; children: William H., Douglas C. BS in Indsl. Engring. with distinction, Cornell U., 1969, MBA, 1970. Engr. True Temper Corp., Geneva, 1970-72; with Price Waterhouse & Co., Boston, 1972-82; exec. v.p., CFO United Asset Mgmt. Corp., 1982—2001; v.p. The UAM Funds, 1982—2001; pres. and CEO Prizm Capital Mgmt., 2001—. Bd. dirs. No. Light Asset Mgmt., 1992—; bd. dirs. The Chautauqua Found., Inc., 1992—, v.p., treas., 1996—; bd. dirs. Nat. Com. to Preserve Social Security and Medicare, 1997—, chmn., 2000—. Treas., trustee Tower Sch. in Marblehead, 1982-92; trustee Proctor Acad., 1998—, Spry Found., 2000-01. Home: 3 Fort Sewall Ter Marblehead MA 01945-3505 Office: United Asset Mgmt Corp One Internat Pl Boston MA 02110

PARK, WILLIAM LAIRD, agricultural economics educator, consultant, college associate dean; b. Mar. 29, 1931; s. William D. and Ardella (Laird) Park; m. Ann Payne, Aug. 7, 1953; children: Leslie, David W., Wayne L., Andrea, John L. BS, Utah State U., 1957, MS, 1958; PhD, Cornell U., 1963. Dep. chief coop. rels. NY/NJ Milk Mktg. Adminstrn., N.Y.C., 1958—65; assoc. prof. agrl. econs. Rutgers U., New Brunswick, NJ, 1965—68, chmn. dept. agrl. econs. and mktg., 1970—77; sr. agrl. economist Devel. and Resources Corp., Sacramento, 1969—70; chmn. dept. agrl. econs. Brigham Young U., Provo, Utah, 1977—83, prof., 1983—, assoc. dean agr., 1988—98; now ret. Pres. Ag-Econ Rsch. Assocs., Orem, Utah, 1978—; bd. dirs. N.E. Agrl. Econs. Coun., 1972—77; cons. agr., agribus. Author: Estimating Demand and Price Structures by Residual Analysis, 1970; author: numerous bulls., reports on dairy econs., feasibility analysis, internat. econ. devel.; contbr. articles to profl. jours. Cpl. U.S. Army, 1953—55. Mem.: Am. Agrl. Econs. Assn., Western Agrl. Econs. Assn., Phi Kappa Phi, Sigma Xi. Republican. Mem. Lds Ch. Home: 7807 White Pine Way Sandy UT 84094-0256

PARK, WILLIAM WYNNEWOOD, law educator; b. Phila., July 2, 1947; s. Oliver William and Christine (Lindes) P. BA, Yale U., 1969; JD, Columbia U., 1972; MA, Cambridge U., 1975. Bar: Mass. 1972, DC 1980. Law practice, Paris, 1972-79; prof. law Boston U., 1979—. V.p. London Ct. Internat. Arbitration; dir. Boston U. Ctr. Banking Law Studies, 1990-93; vis. prof. U. Dijon, France, 1983-84, Inst. U. Hautes Etudes Internat., Geneva, 1983, U. Hong Kong, 1990; fellow Selwyn Coll., Cambridge, Eng., 1975-77; arbitrator Claims Resolution Tribunal for Dormant Accts., Switzerland, 1998-2002. Author: International Chamber of Commerce Arbitration, 3d edit., 2000, International Forum Selection, 1995, International Commercial Arbitration, 1997, Annotated Guide to the 1998 ICC Arbitration Rules, 1998, Arbitration in Banking and Finance, 1998; contbr. articles and book revs. to profl. jours. Trustee Mass. Bible Soc.; sr. warden King's Chapel, Boston. Fellow Chartered Inst. Arbitrators (Chartered Arbitrator U.K.), Coll. Comml. Arbitrators. Home: 36 King St Cohasset MA 02025-1304 Office: Boston U Law Sch 765 Commonwealth Ave Boston MA 02215-1401

PARK, WON KUK, foundation administrator; b. Bukchang Dong, Chung-Ku, Korea, Mar. 24, 1929; s. Jun Seop and Kum Sun (Song) P. BA in Economics, Sungkyunkwan U., Seoul, Korea, 1957; MA in Economics, Am. U., 1960; PhD in Economics, Kyunghee U., Seoul, Korea, 1975; PhD (hon.) , Caldwell Coll., 1997. Asst. prof. Duksung Women's Coll., Seoul, Korea, 1961-63, Kyunghee U., Seoul, Korea, 1963-65; assoc. prof. Duksung Women's Coll., Korea, 1965-67, v.p. Korea, 1965-70, prof. Korea, 1967-77, pres. Korea, 1970-77; v.p. Korean Pvt. Ednl. Found., Korea, 1987-90, Korean Assn. for Univ. Found., Seoul, Korea, 1987-92; chmn. bd. trustees Duksung Sch. Found., Republic of Korea, 1977—2001. Dir. Korean Pvt. Ednl. Found., Seoul, 1978—, Korean Assn. for Univ. Found., 1987—. Chmn. bd. trustees Jungam Found. of Culture in Korea, 2002—. Recipient Choon Kang award, Republic of Korea, 1995. Mem. Korean Sect. World Edn. Fellowship (v.p. 1987—); The Seoul Ctrl. Club of Good Will. Office: D-201 The Sungbookville Ho 330-21 Sungbuk 2-dong Sungbuk-ku Seoul 136-022 Republic of Korea

PARK, YOONDONG, research scientist; b. Seoul, Republic of Korea; s. Kwonsik Park and Bokie Eun; m. Heesook Yoon, Mar. 2, 1991; 1 child, Nicola. BS, Hanyang U., 1988; MS, U. So. Calif., 1997, PhD, 1999. With Nat. Indsl. Tech. Inst., Seoul, 1989-95, Small and Med. Bus. Adminstrn., Seoul, 1995-99; rsch. assoc. U. So. Calif., L.A., 1999-2000. Rschr. scholar Carnegie Mellon U., Pitts., 1993. Short-Term fellow Korean Govt., 1993, Long-Term fellow, 1995-99. Mem. IEEE (sr., mem. editl. bd. 1998-99, assoc. editor 1999-2000), Soc. Neuroscience. Home: 1200 Dale Ave Apt 101 Mountain View CA 94040-3331 Office: 2880 Scott Blvd Santa Clara CA 95050-2554 Fax: 408-588-5434.

PÁRKÁNYI, MARIE HŘEBIČEK, real estate broker; b. Prague, Nov. 18, 1939; d. František and Marie Schmittová Hrebícek. BS in Psychology with honors, U. Tex., El Paso, 1978-81, attended, 1982-85. Technical editor, technical artist Intra-Science Rsch. Found., L.A., 1968-70; tchr. & translator B.I. Lang. Svcs., El Paso, Tex., 1981, 83; psychol. evaluations testing asst. El Paso Guidance Ctr., 1983-84, Clinic U. Tex., El Paso, 1984-85; pvt. lang. tchr., 1985; lang. instr. U.S. Army, MI Unit, Fort Bliss, 1986-87; real estate broker, assoc. Gimelstob Realty, Inc., Boca Raton, 1989-98, Coldwell Banker Residential Real Estate, Boca Raton, 1998—. Patentee in semiconductors. Mem. Nat. Assn. Realtors, Fla. Assn. Realtors, Boca Raton Assn. Realtors. Roman Catholic. Avocations: music & arts, gardening, skiing, hiking, swimming. Home: 245 NW 69th St Boca Raton FL 33487-2390 E-mail: mparkanyi@earthlink.net.

PARKE, DAVID WILKIN, II, ophthalmologist, educator, healthcare executive; b. Columbus, Ohio, May 19, 1951; s. David William Parke and Eunice Joyce Erikson; m. Julie Diane Thorne, Sept. 15, 1975; children: David W. III, Laura Thorne, Lindsey Diane. AB, Stanford U., 1973; MD, Baylor Coll. Medicine, 1977. Diplomate Am. Bd. Ophthalmology. Resident in internal medicine Baylor Coll. Medicine, Houston, 1977-78, resident in ophthalmology, 1978-81, fellow in med. retina, 1981-82, asst. prof., 1983-90, assoc. prof., 1990-92; fellow diseases and surgery of the retina and vitreous Med. Coll. of Wis., 1982-83; prof., chair dept. ophthalmology U. Okla., Oklahoma City, 1992—; pres., CEO McGee Eye Inst., 1992—. Bd. dirs. Medem, Inc. Active Okla. Econ. Devel. Found., 1992, Okla. Health Ctr. Found., 1992—; trustee Presbyn. Health Found., 1995—, Casady Sch., 1997—, vice chair, 1999—; mng. dir. Stephenson Laser Ctr., 1996—; bd. mgrs. Okla. Health Alliance, 1995-97; dir. Oklahoma City C. of C. Fellow: Am. Acad. Ophthalmology (assoc. sec. 1983—92, trustee 2000—, sr. sec. for ophthalmic practice 2002—,

Honor award 1980, Sr. Honor award 1998); mem.: Vitreous Soc., Retina Soc., Assn. Univ. Profs. Ophthalmology (trustee 1997—, pres. 2001—02), Greater Oklahoma City C. of C. (bd. dirs. 1998—99), Alpha Omega Alpha. Office: Dean A McGee Eye Institute 608 Stanton L Young Blvd Oklahoma City OK 73104-5065 E-mail: david-parke@ouhsc.edu.

PARKE, JOHN SHEPARD, marketing consultant; b. N.Y.C., Nov. 11, 1933; s. John S. and Dorothy (Simpson) P.; m. Mary J. Lundy, Aug. 20, 1955; children: John Shepard III, Suzanne Lundy. AB, Dartmouth Coll., 1956; MBA, Amos Tuck Sch., 1957. Sales mgr. Procter & Gamble Co., Cin., 1960, advt. mgr., 1961-69; mktg. dir. Ralston Purina Co., St. Louis, 1969-74, v.p. mktg., 1974-79; v.p. mktg. and sales Bausch & Lomb, Rochester, N.Y., 1979-81; founder, pres. PPI Mktg. Group, 1982—. Chmn. Nathanial Rochester Soc.; chmn. bd. Episc. Sr. Life Com., Rochester; chmn. Coll. of Liberal Arts Adv. Coun., Rochester Inst. Tech.; bd. dirs. Meml. Art Gallery of U. Rochester. Capt. USAF, 1957—60. Mem. Genesse Valley Club (Rochester), U.S. Tennis Assn. (chair umpire). Republican. Episcopalian. Avocations: tennis, squash. Home and Office: 215 Ambassador Dr Rochester NY 14610-3404 E-mail: jsparke@rochester.rr.com.

PARKE, ROBERT LEON, retired communications executive; b. Jersey City, Aug. 28, 1940; s. Edwin Gager and Alice Elizabeth (Servis) P.; m. Geraldine R. Pavlick, Sept. 2, 1967; children: Cheryl Lynn, Tracy Ann, David Scott. Grad. high sch., Jersey City. Asst. bookkeeper Snow-Kist Frozen Foods, Jersey City, 1964-67; supr. accounts receivable Swift Line Transfer Co., Inc., North Bergen, N.J., 1967-69; contr. Imperial Cartage Co., Inc., Jersey City, 1969-79; mgr. logistic svcs. Vista United Telecommunications, Lake Buena Vista, Fla., 1980-2000. Corp. sec. Imperial Warehouse Co., Inc., Jersey City, 1968-79, Arbe Transfer Co. Inc., 1968-79; v.p. Cole Foods, Inc., Jersey City, 1968-79 Spl. min. of the eucharist Diocese Orlando, Fla., 1992; vol. Give Kids The World, Kissimmee, Fla., 1992-98; mem. Pemberton Twp. Zoning Bd., Browns Mills, N.J., 1977-79; trustee, bd. dirs. Browns Mills Improvement Assn., 1974-79; life trustee Rebecca Worf Meml. Fund Browns Mills, N.J., Parke Soc., S.E. Milw.; hon. trustee Am. Indian Relief Coun. Recipient Cert. Appreciation Am. Indian Relief Coun., 1996, 97, 98, 99, 2000, hon. trustee, 1999, 2000; recipient spl. recognition award masters degree program in Nat. Security Studies, Grad. Sch. of Georgetown U., 1996; Bob Parke day proclaimed by Twp. of Pemberton, 1979, Customer Appreciation Award GN Netcom/Unex, 1997, Partners in Excellence Award Walt Disney Co., 1997. Mem. Nat. Notary Assn., Fla. Notary Assn., Am. Soc. Notaries, Nat. Assn. Purchasing Mgmt. Ctrl. Fla. (named scholar), Nat. Assn. Purchasing Mgmt. (scholarship for continued edn., Ctrl. Fla. Most Supportive Mem. 1994, accrediated purchasing practitioner cert. 1998), Fla. Sheriffs Assn. (life, hon.), Soc. Descs. of the Colonial Clergy (life), Nat. Soc. Sons and Daus. of Pilgrims, Soc. Sons and Daus. Am.'s First Families (life), Winthrop Soc., KC (mem. coun.) E-mail: rlparke828@aol.com. *Everyone can have a dream, but only those that care and show perseverance will achieve success.*

PARKE, STEPHEN JOHN, theoretical physicist; b. Gisborne, New Zealand, Dec. 14, 1950; came to U.S., 1973; s. William and Muriel P.;m. Winifred Haun, Nov. 27, 1988; children: Athena, Iris. BSc, Auckland U., New Zealand, 1973; MA, PhD, Harvard U., 1980. Postdoctoral fellow Stanford Linear Accelerator Ctr., Stanford, Calif., 1980-83; assoc. scientist Fermi Nat. Accelerator Lab., Batavia, Ill., 1983-88, scientist, 1988-95, sr. scientist, 1995—. Contbr. numerous articles to various jours. including Phys. Rev. Letters, Phys. Rev., Physics Letters, Physics Reports, Nuclear Physics. Bd. dirs. Winifred Haun and Dancers, 1991—. Fellow Am. Phys. Soc. Achievements include contributions to research that advanced the understanding of top quark and Higgs physics, neutrino physics and quantum chromodynamics. Office: Fermi Nat Accelerator Lab PO Box 500 Batavia IL 60510-0500 E-mail: parke@fnal.gov.

PARKEL, JAMES G. health association administrator; BS in elec. engring., U. Denver; LLD (hon.) , Am. Grad. Sch. Internat. Mgmt. Exec. mgmt. IBM Internat. Found., 1961—93; pres.-elect AARP, 2000—02, pres., 2002—. Chair AARP Andrus Found.; mem. bd. councilors Andrus Gerontology Ctr., U. So. Calif. Mem. Madison Coun. Libr. of Congress; pres. and CEO Junior Achievement Internat.; chair Junior Achievement Westchester; nat. bd. mem. Junior Achievement; bd. dirs. Danbury Hosp., New Fairfield Cmty. Trust, Am. Grad. Sch. Internat. Mgmt. Mem.: Soc. Human Resource Mgmt. (past nat. chair). Office: Am Assn Retired Persons 601 E St NW Washington DC 20049*

PARKER, ALAN JOHN, veterinary neurologist, educator, researcher; b. Portsmouth, Eng., Oct. 28, 1944; arrived in U.S., 1969, naturalized, 2002; s. William Barton and Emily (Begley) P.; m. Heather Margaret Nicholson, Oct. 30, 1971; children: Alyxander John, Robert William. B.Sc. with honors, Bristol U., 1966, B.V.Sc. with honors, 1968; MS, U. Ill., 1973, PhD, 1976. Diplomate Am. Coll. Vet. Internal Medicine-Neurology, European Coll. Vet. Neurology. Intern Vet. Coll., U. Calif.-Davis, 1969-70; instr. vet. clin. medicine U. Ill., Urbana, 1970-71, 72-76, asst. prof., 1976-77, assoc. prof., 1977-82, prof., 1982-2000, prof. emeritus, 2001—. Cons. pharm. cos., seminar presenter; cons. in neurology Berwyn Vet. Hosp., Chgo., 1973— , Lake Shore Animal Hosp., Chgo., 1978— Contbr. numerous articles to sci. jours., chpts. to books. Active Boy Scouts Am., Champaign, Ill., 1982—; active Presbyn. Ch., Monticello, Ill., 1979—. Recipient Vigil Honor and Founder's award Order of the Arrow, Silver Beaver award Boy Scouts Am.; sci. grantee various orgns., 1972-2000. Mem. AVMA, Am. Animal Hosp. Assn., Brit. Vet. Assn., Ill. State Vet. Assn. Republican. Office: 2845 S Harlem Ave Berwyn IL 60402 E-mail: a-parker@staff.uiuc.edu.

PARKER, ALAN WILLIAM, film director, writer; b. London, Feb. 14, 1944; s. William Leslie and Elsie Ellen P.; m. Annie Inglis, July 30, 1966; children: Lucy Kate, Alexander James, Jake William, Nathan Charles. Student Brit. schs. Advt. copywriter, 1966-69; dir. TV commls. Author: screenplay Melody, 1968; novel Bugsy Malone, 1975, Puddles in the Lane, 1977; author, dir.: No Hard Feelings, 1972, Our Cissy, 1973, Footsteps, 1973, Bugsy Malone, 1975 (5 Brit. Acad. awards), Come See the Paradise, 1990; dir.: The Evacuees (Brit. Acad. award, Internat. Emmy award, Press Guild U.K. award), Midnight Express (6 Golden Globe awards, 3 Brit. Acad. awards, 2 Oscar awards), Fame, 1980 (Brit. Acad. award, Golden Globe award, 2 Oscar awards), Shoot the Moon, 1982, Pink Floyd-The Wall, 1982, Birdy, 1984 (Grand Prix Spl. du Jury, Cannes Film Festival), A Turnip Head's Guide to the British Cinema, 1986 (British Press Guild award), Angel Heart, 1987, Mississippi Burning, 1988 (Oscar award), The Commitments, 1991 (4 BAFTA awards), The Road to Wellville, 1994, Evita, 1996 (3 Golden Globe awards), Angela's Ashes, 1999, The Life of David Gale, 2002. Recipient 4 Brit. Acad. awards. Mem. Brit. Acad. Film and TV Arts, Brit. Film Inst. (chmn. 1997-99, chmn. film coun. 1999—), Dirs. Guild Am., Writers Guild G.B., Writers Guild Am., Dirs. Guild G.B., Acad. Motion Pictures Arts and Scis. Office: care Michael Wimer Creative Artists Agy 9830 Wilshire Blvd Beverly Hills CA 90212-1804

PARKER, ALICE, composer, conductor; b. Boston, Dec. 16, 1925; d. Gordon and Mary (Stuart) P.; widowed; children: David, Timothy, Katharine, Mary, Elizabeth. BA, Smith Coll., Northampton, Mass., 1947; MS, Juilliard Sch., N.Y.C., 1949; MusD (hon.), Hamilton U., 1979, Macalester Coll., St. Paul, 1989, Bluffton (Ohio) Coll., 1991, Westminster Choir Coll., Princeton, N.J., 1996. Arranger Robert Shaw Chorale, N.Y.C., 1948-66; artistic dir. Melodious Accord, 1985—. Tchr., workshop leader Westminster Choir Coll., Princeton, N.J., summers, 1972-98. Composer 4 operas, 35 cantatas, 8 song cycles and numerous anthems and suites. Recipient composer's award ASCAP, 1968—, AGO Disting. Composer of the Yr., 2000, Barlow Endowment, 1992, spl. award Nat. Endowment Arts, 1976. Fellow Hymn Soc., Hymn Soc. Am.; mem. Am. Choral Dirs. Assn., Am. Condrs. Guild, Chorus Am. (Founders award 1994), Am. Music ctr., Sigma Alpha Iota. Office: Melodious Accord Inc Park West Sta PO Box 20801 New York NY 10025-1523

PARKER, ALICE CLINE, computer engineering educator, consultant; b. Birmingham, Ala., Apr. 10, 1948; d. Joseph Kalman Cline and Elizabeth (Wenk) Jebeles; m. Donald Joseph Bebel, Aug. 9, 1980; 1 child, Joseph Cline Bebel. BEE, N.C. State U., 1970; MEE, Stanford U., 1971; PhD, N.C. State U., 1975. Asst. prof. Carnegie-Mellon U., Pitts., 1975-80, U. So. Calif., L.A., 1980-83, assoc. prof., 1983-91, prof., 1991—, computer engring. divsn. dir., 1991-93, acad. senate pres.-elect, 1993-94, vice provost for rsch., dean grad. studies, 1994-96, vice provost rsch. and grad. studies, 1996—97. Cons. Hughes Aircraft, El Segundo, Calif., 1983, Xerox, El Segundo, 1982-83, Aerospace Corp., El Segundo, 1981-91. Contbr. articles to profl. jours. Program chmn. 11th Microprogramming Workshop, Asilomar, Calif., 1978. IBM rsch. grantee, 1981-86, U.S. Army rsch. grantee, 1976-87; NSF fellow, 1970, grantee, 1984; recipient NSF award for women in sci. and engring., 1991. Fellow IEEE; mem. IEEE Computer Soc. (bd. govs. 1994), Assn. Computing Machinery (treas. spl. interest group 1979-83, 83-87, v.p. 1981-83), Stanford Profl. Women. Presbyterian. Office: U So Calif Eeb 348 Mc 2562 Los Angeles CA 90089-2562

PARKER, ALLAN LESLIE, marketing executive; b. Bronx, N.Y., Aug. 31, 1938; s. Henry S. and Sylvia G. (Gross) P.; m. Vicky Ann Williams, Aug. 25, 1965; 1 child, David Henry. BSBA, Syracuse U., 1960; MBA, Creighton U., 1966. Cert. data processor. Acct. Hertz Corp., N.Y.C., 1960-62; systems analyst J.C. Penney Co., 1966-67; mktg. mgr. Xerox Corp., Rochester, N.Y., 1967-78; nat. mktg. mgr. Cheshire div. Xerox Corp., Mundelein, Ill., 1978-82; v.p., chief oper. officer Internat. Software Enterprises, Arlington Heights, 1982-83; v.p. sales and mktg. First Computer Corp., Westmont, 1983-85; mktg. mgr. Wang Labs., Rosemont, 1985-87; mgr. ea. region Odesta Corp., Northbrook, 1987-88; gen. mgr. Zenith Electronics Corp., Glenview, 1988—94; dir. mktg. and sales Oryx Power Products, Mt. Prospect, 1994-97; v.p. N.Am. sales and channel programs EOS Corp., Camarillo, Calif., 1997-99; nat. channel mgr. Force Computers Inc., San Jose, 1999-2000; sales and mktg. cons. Pahrump, Nev., 2000—. Pres. A&V Assocs., Hoffman Estates, Ill., 1987-90; co-owner A&V Printing, Hoffman Estates, 1987-90; instr. bus. Rochester Inst. Tech., 1966-78, Keller Grad. Sch. Mgmt., Lincolnshire, Ill., 1986-99, West Hills, Calif., 2000-2001. 1st lt. USAF, 1962-66. Mem. Am. Philatelic Soc., Creighton U. Alumni Assn. (coll. recruiting coordinator 1987—), Beta Gamma Sigma. Republican. Jewish. Avocations: stamp collecting, computers, travel, reading, sports. Home and Office: Apt 4 1040 Indio Ct Pahrump NV 89048-2703

PARKER, ARNOLD JOHN, minister; b. Wis., Oct. 13, 1924; s. Edgar Martin and Grace May Parker; m. Esther-Jean Parker, Aug. 19, 1926; children: Jon, Winifred Parker Jeffers, Claudia Parker Kikuta. Diploma, Moody Bible Inst., Chgo., 1957. Ordained to ministry Conservative Baptist Ch., 1958. Seamen's pastor Chgo. Am. Bible Soc., Chgo., 1954-64, Seamen's Internat. Christian Assn., Wonder Lake, Ill., 1954-64; min. various Bapt. chs., Ill., INd., Wis., Ohio, 1964-90; adminstr., supt. Cmty. Christian Acad., Wisconsin Rapids, Wis., 1990-99. Chaplain Marine Hosp., Chgo. Active in jail visitation in Chgo. and Crown Point, Ind. Republican. Home: Apt 223 2521 10th St S Wisconsin Rapids WI 54494-6391

PARKER, BARBARA L. educator; b. Phila., Dec. 8, 1933; d. Benjamin and Nettie Vivian (Rademan) Parker. BA, UCLA, 1957; MA, CCNY, 1970; PhD, NYU, 1982. Prof. English William Paterson U., Wayne, N.J., 1989—. Editor: Ecology of Endemic Diseases in the Dez Irrigation Pilot Area: A Report to the Govt. of Iran, 1962; author: A Precious Seeing: Love and Reason in Shakespeare's Plays, 1987; contbr. articles to profl. jours. Active Friends of N.Y. Pub. Libr., 1983—, Friends of Bobst Libr., 1982—, Bklyn. Hts. Assn., 1975—. Mem. MLA, Renaissance Soc. Am., Shakespeare Assn. Am., Columbia U. Seminars, Assn. Lit. Scholars and Critics. Avocations: photography, portrait artist, poet. Home: 145 Hicks St Apt A64 Brooklyn NY 11201-2330 E-mail: ParkerB@wpunj.edu.

PARKER, BARRINGTON D., JR. federal judge, lawyer; b. Washington, Aug. 21, 1944; BA, Yale U., 1965, JD, 1969. Bar: N.Y. 1971. Law clk. to Hon. Aubrey E. Robinson, U.S. Dist. Ct. for D.C., Washington, 1969-70; assoc. Sullivan & Cromwell, N.Y.C., 1970-77; ptnr. Parker Auspitz Neesemann & Delehanty, P.C., 1977-87, Morrison & Foerster, N.Y.C., 1987-94; judge U.S. Dist. Ct. for so. dist. N.Y., White Plains, 1994—2001, U.S. Ct. Appeals (2nd Ct.), NY, 2001—. Bd. dirs., v.p. NAACP Legal Def. and Educational Fund, Inc., 1980—; com. on grievances, com. on civil discovery U.S. Dist. Ct. (so. dist.) N.Y., 1983—; com. on pre-trial phase civil cases U.S. Ct. Appeals (2nd cir.) 1983—. Trustee Governance Inst., Greenwich Acad., South Africa Legal Svcs. and Legal Edn. Project, Inc.; successor trustte an mem. Yale Corp. Mem. ABA, Fed. Bar Coun., Assn. Bar City N.Y. (com. on the judiciary 1978-82, exec. com. 1982-86, nominating com. 1987), Coun. on Fgn. Rels. Office: US Courthouse 300 Quarropas St Rm 633 White Plains NY 10601-4150 also: Thurogood Marshall US Courthouse 40 Foley Square New York NY 10007*

PARKER, BRENT MERSHON, retired medical educator, internist, cardiologist; b. St. Louis, July 3, 1927; s. William Bahlmann and Florence (Mershon) P.; m. Martha Shelton, Aug. 1, 1953; children: Martha Parker Burgess, Elizabeth, Margaret. MD cum laude, Wash. U., St. Louis, 1952. Diplomate Am. Bd. Internal Medicine. Intern and asst. resident N.Y. Hosp.-Cornell, N.Y.C., 1952-54; asst. resident, fellow Barnes Hosp., Wash. U., St. Louis, 1954-57; cardiology sect. chief VA Hosp., U. Oreg., Portland, 1957-59; asst. prof. to assoc. prof., co-dir. cardiovascular div., chief adult cardiac catherization Wash. U. Sch. Medicine, St. Louis, 1959-73; prof. medicine U. Mo., Columbia, 1973-89, prof. emeritus, 1989-94, chief of staff, assoc. dean, 1976-82, chief of cardiology, 1983-89. Mem. colloquium faculty Merck, Sharp and Dohme, West Point, Pa., 1980-86. Author or co-author 58 papers in referred jours., 6 book chpts., teaching papers, others. Bd. dirs. St. Louis Heart Assn., 1962-73, v.p. 1972-73; bd. dirs. Mo. Heart Assn., 1965-75, pres. 1970-71. Served with USN, 1945-46. Recipient Arthur Strauss award St. Louis Heart Assn., 1973, 3 teaching awards U. Mo. Sch. Medicine, 1974, 75, 86, Preventive Cardiology Acad. award, Nat. Heart Lung and Blood Inst., 1982-87, Alumni Achievement award Washington Univ. Sch. Medicine, 1992; Brent Mershon Parker professorship estab. in honor U. Mo., 1989. Fellow ACP, Am. Coll. Cardiology (Mo., Kans. council rep. 1973-77), Clin. Cardiology Soc. Am. Heart Assn.; mem. Am. Fedn. Clin. Research, Cen. Soc. for Clin. Research, Alpha Omega Alpha, Sigma Xi. Episcopalian. Avocations: choral singing, jogging, camping, back packing.

PARKER, BRET I. lawyer; b. N.Y.C., 1968; m. Katharine; children: Matthew, Benjamin. BA, U. Pa., 1990; JD, Fordham U., 1993. Bar: N.Y. 1994, U.S. Dist. Ct. (so. dist.) N.Y., U.S. Dist. Ct. (ea. dist.) N.Y. Law clk. to Hon. K. Michael Moore U.S. Dist. Ct. (so. dist.) Fla., Miami, 1993-94; assoc. Townley & Updike, N.Y.C., 1994-95, Dorsey & Whitney, N.Y.C., 1995-97; counsel trademark and copyright Colgate-Palmolive Co., 1997—. Mem. Internat. Trademark Assn. (bd. dirs.), N.Y.C. Bar Assn. (chair com. trademarks and unfair competition 1996—). Office: Colgate-Palmolive Co 300 Park Ave New York NY 10022-7499

PARKER, BRIAN PRESCOTT, forensic scientist; b. Norfolk, Va., Aug. 31, 1929; s. Milton Ellsworth and Louise Randall (Smith) P.; m. Sonia Garcia Rosario, Dec. 23, 1960; children: Robin Marie, Augustin Keith. BS in Quantitative Biology, MIT, 1953; JD, Northwestern U., 1957; M in Criminology, U. Calif., Berkeley, 1961, D in Criminology, 1967. Rsch. asst. U. P.R. Med. Sch., 1961; cons. P.R. Justice Dept., 1961-63; spl. asst. FDA, Washington, 1964; lectr., then asst. prof. criminology U. Calif., Berkeley, 1964-70; sr. criminalist, then sr. forensic sci. and criminal justice Calif. State U., Sacramento, 1973-92, prof. emeritus, 1988—. Project dir. phys. evidence Dept. Justice, 1969-70; vis. fellow Nat. Police Research Unit, Australia, 1985; vis. prof. Elton Mayo Sch. Mgmt., South Australia Inst. Tech., 1985. Co-author: Physical Evidence in the Adminstration of Criminal Justice, 1970, The Role of Criminalistics in the World of the Future, 1972; assoc. editor Law, Medicine, Science-and Justice, 1964; contbr. to Ency. Crime and Justice, 1983. Mem. Am. Chem. Soc. Home: 5117 Ridgegate Way Fair Oaks CA 95628-3603 E-mail: bparker@saclink.csus.edu.

PARKER, BRUCE D. business executive; BS in Bus. and Econs., MS in Bus. and Fin., U. Kans. Pres. Sabre devel. svcs. Am. Airlines; sr. v.p. mgmt. info. sys., chief info. officer Ryder Sys., Inc.; sr. v.p., chief info. officer United Airlines, 1997-99; exec. v.p. Sapient Corp., Cambridge, Mass., also bd. dirs. Leader info. sys. tech. nat. coun. Boy Scouts Am. Office: Sapient Corp 1 Memorial Dr Cambridge MA 02142-1313

PARKER, CATHERINE SUSANNE, psychotherapist; b. Norwood, Mass., Nov. 4, 1934; d. George Leonard and Hazel Olga (Remmer) P. BA, Bates Coll., 1956; MSW, U. Denver, 1961. Diplomate Acad. Cert. Social Workers; cert. social worker, Colo. Social worker Taunton (Mass.) State Hosp., 1956-59, Ft. Logan Mental Health Ctr., Denver, 1961-66, clin. team leader, 1966-72; dir. adult services Western Inst. Human Resources, 1973-74; pvt. practice psychotherapy, 1974—. Workshop facilitator Arapahoe C.C., 1986-90. Mem. NASW. Avocations: tennis, skiing, fishing, antiques, gardening. Home: 6453 S Downing St Littleton CO 80121-2517 Office: Denver Mental Health 165 Cook St Ste 100 Denver CO 80206-5308

PARKER, CHARLES WALTER, JR. consultant, retired equipment company executive; b. nr. Ahoskie, N.C., Nov. 22, 1922; s. Charles Walter and Minnie Louise (Williamson) P.; m. Sophie Nash Riddick, Nov. 26, 1949; children: Mary Parker Hutto, Caroline Parker Robertson, Charles Walter III, Thomas Williamson. BS in Elec. Engring, Va. Mil. Inst., 1947; Dr. Engring. (hon.), Milw. Sch. Engring., 1980. With Allis-Chalmers Corp., 1947-87, dist. mgr. Va., 1955-57, Phila., 1957-58, dir. sales promotion industries group Milw., 1958-61, gen. mktg. mgr. new products, 1961-62, mgr. mktg. services, 1962-66, v.p. mktg. and public relations services, 1966-70, v.p., dep. group exec., 1970-72, staff group exec. communications and public affairs, 1972-87, ret., 1987; prin. Charles Parker & Assocs., Ltd., Milw., 1987—. Founding mem. World Mktg. Contact Group, London; bd. dirs. Internat. Gen. Ins. Corp., Dinermite Corp. Gen. chmn. United Fund Greater Milw. Area, 1975; trustee Boy Scouts Am. Trust Fund, Milw.; bd. dirs., pres. Jr. Achievement; pres. bd. trustees Univ. Sch. Milw., 1978-80; trustee Carroll Coll., Waukesha, Wis.; bd. dirs. Milw. Children's Hosp.; bd. regents Milw. Sch. Engring.; mem. Greater Milw. Com.; chmn. bd. dirs. Milw. Found., 1987-89. Served to capt. AUS, 1943-46, ETO. Decorated Bronze Star. Mem. NAM (dir.), Wis. C. of C. (pres. 1974-76), Sales and Mktg. Execs. Internat. (pres., CEO 1974, 75, Eduardo Rihan Internat. Mktg. Exec. of Yr. award 1979), Wis. Mfrs. and Commerce Assn. (exec. com.), Pi Sigma Epsilon (pres. 1976-77, trustee and chmn. nat. edn. found. 1979-86), Kappa Alpha. Home: 4973 N Newhall St Milwaukee WI 53217-6049 Office: PO Box 92398 828 N Broadway Milwaukee WI 53202-3611

PARKER, CHERYL JEAN, small business owner; b. Kansas City, Kans., Feb. 3, 1948; d. Mildred Eileen (Mayer) Ross; m. Jack W. Parker, June 25, 1977; children: Brian Scott, Kimberly Michelle. BS, Kans. State U., 1970; MA, U. Mo., Kansas City, 1975; postgrad., Dept. Def. Info. Sch., 1984. Cert. tchr. Mo., Kans. Migrant tchr. Piper Unified Schs. 203, Kansas City, Kans., 1970-72; tchr. North Kansas City Pub. Schs., 1970-75; elem. guidance counselor Excelsior (Mo.) Springs Pub. Schs., 1975-77; rsch. asst. foster parent rsch. project Coll. Human Ecology, Manhattan, Kans., 1977-78; test examiner 1st Inf. Div., Fort Riley, 1980-82, pub. affairs specialist, 1983-85; pers. clerk 3rd ROTC Div. Hdqrs., 1982-83; tchr. Living Word Christian Sch., Manhattan, 1985-86; program mgr., career counselor Army Community Svcs., Army War Coll., Carlisle, Pa., 1987-90; elem. guidance counselor Shawnee Mission (Kans.) Pub. Schs., 1990-96; small bus. owner, 1996—. Recording sec. Career Edn. Com., Excelsior Springs, 1975-77; career counselor personal contacts and referrals, Carlisle, 1986-90; career counselor relocation/outplacement, U.S. Army, Carlisle, 1987-90; job fair coord. Army Community Svcs., Carlisle, 1989-90; guest speaker various clubs, confs., Carlisle, Excelsior Springs. Author: (with others, catalog) Foster Parent Resources, 1977-78; contbr. articles to profl. jours. Violinist Christ Community Ch. Orch., Camp Hill, Pa., 1986-89, Full Faith Ch. Psalm 150 Orch., 1993; mem. hospitality com. PTA, Carlisle, 1987-88; mem. Suggestion Awards Rev. Com., Fort Riley, 1983-85. Hollis Award scholar Kans. State U., 1968, Kansas City Star scholar Kansas City Star Newspaper, 1966-70. Mem. Kans. NEA, Kans. Assn. Counseling and Devel. (Spurs Acad. hon. mem.), Carlisle Area Pers. Assn., Federally Employed Women (nomination chmn. 1989—), Federal Women's Program (program mgr. 1988-89, certificate 1989), Alpha Lambda Delta. Mem. Christian Ch. Avocations: Christian and classical music, reading, needlework, travel, swimming. Home: 9824 W 132nd Ter Overland Park KS 66213-3319

PARKER, CHRISTINE WRIGHT, medical director; b. Redcar, Eng., Mar. 6, 1957; d. Henry Glyn and Patricia (Lynas) Wright; m. William Shelley Parker Jr., Dec. 29, 1981; children: William Shelley III, Jennifer Lynn. BS, U. Tenn., 1978, MD, 1982. Diplomate Am. Bd. Internal Medicine. Intern, then resident internal medicine Erlanger Med. Ctr., Chattanooga, 1982-85, chief resident internal medicine, 1985-86; asst. med. director Provident Life & Accident, 1986-90, assoc. med. dir., 1990-91, asst. v.p., med. dir., 1991-94, v.p. med. policy and assessment, 1994-97; med. dir. Meml. Health Svcs., 1997—. Chmn. IRB, Meml. Hosp., Chattanooga; mem. working group exploring implications of genetic testing in life, disability and health ins. Human Genome Project. Mem. ACP, AMA (past mem. current procedural terminology editorial panel), Health Ins. Assn. Am. (past chair health care tech. com.), Hamilton County Med. Soc. (bd. dirs. 2000), Internal Medicine Soc., Tenn. Med. Assn., Mortar Bd., Blue Key, Chattanooga Golf and Country Club, Tri Beta. Republican. Episcopalian. Avocations: piano, running, downhill skiing. Home: 1055 River Hills Cir Chattanooga TN 37415-5611 Office: Memorial Health Services 2525 De Sales Ave Chattanooga TN 37404

PARKER, CHRISTOPHER WILLIAM, lawyer; b. Evanston, Ill., Oct. 26, 1947; s. Robert H. and Dorothy Boynton P.; m. Mary Ann P., Dec. 28, 1984. BA, Tufts U., 1969; JD, Northeastern U., 1976. Bar: Mass. 1977, U.S. Dist. Ct. Mass. 1977, U.S. Dist. Ct. (we. dist.) Tex. 1986, U.S. Ct. Appeals (1st cir.) 1988, U.S. Supreme Ct. 1988. Law clk. to judge U.S. Bankruptcy Ct. Mass. dist., Boston, 1976-77; assoc. Fletcher, Tilton & Whipple, Worcester, Mass., 1977-79; counsel U.S. Trustee, Boston, 1979-81; assoc. Craig and Macauley P.C., 1982-84, ptnr., 1984-87; counsel Hinckley, Allen, Snyder & Comen, 1987-88, ptnr., 1989-91, McDermott, Will & Emery, Boston, 1991—. Mem. ABA, Mass. Bar Assn., Am. Bankruptcy Inst. Boston Bar Assn., Comml. Law League. Clubs: Union Boat (Boston). Home: 11 Tophet Rd Lynnfield MA 01940-1616 Office: McDermott Will & Emery 28 State St Boston MA 02109-1775 E-mail: cparker@mwe.com.

PARKER, CLEA EDWARD, retired university president; b. Talisheek, La., Apr. 2, 1927; s. William A. and Lutritia (Davis) P.; m. Peggy Ann Faciane, June 21, 1953; children— Brian, Stephen, Karen, Robin. BA, Southeastern La. U., 1948; M.Ed., La. State U., 1952, Ed.D., 1965. Coach, tchr. Rugby Acad., New Orleans, 1948-50; tchr., prin., supr. instr., dir. curriculum and instrn. St. Tammany Parish Sch. Bd., 1950-67; prof. edn., head dept. student teaching Nicholls State Coll., Thibodaux, La., 1967-68; acting pres. Southeastern La. U., Hammond, 1968, pres., 1968-80, pres. emeritus, 1980—. Liaison La. State Dept. Edn., Higher Edn. and Bds. for Edn. in La., 1986; vis. lectr. La. State U., 1965-69; Past pres. St. Tammany Parish Tchrs. Assn., La. Assn. Supervision and Curriculum Devel.; past pres. elementary dept. La. Tchrs. Assn.; chmn. Pres.'s Council La. Bd. Edn., 1972-73; v.p. Conf. La. Colls. and Univs., 1973-74, pres., 1974-75; pres. elect Gulf South Conf., 1974-75, pres., 1975-76; mem. Steering Com. on Curriculum Devel. and Revision for Career Edn. for State La., 1973; mem. adv. council for State Plan for Career Edn., 1973 Mem. planning com. Gov.'s Conf. on Aging, 1976; v.p. chpt. 15 La. Good Samaritans, 1987-88; bd. dirs. Assn. for Retarded Citizens, pres.-elect, 1981; mem. Zemurray Park Recreation Commn., Hammond, 1992-95; chmn. bd. dirs. Lallie Kemp Meml. Hosp., 1993-94; bd. dirs. Lallie Kemp Med. Ctr., 1994—, chmn., 1994-95. With USCGR, 1945, 93-94. Named Hon. State Farmer La., 1970, Disting. Alumnus of Yr., Southeastern La. U. Alumni Assn., 1977, 91, 92; inductee La. Spl. Olympics Hall of Fame, 1998. Mem. Am. Assn. State Colls. and Univs. (com. on nat. svc. 1972-73, task force on aging 1975-76, 78-79, nominating com. 1977—, state Rep. for La. 1979—, com. agr. renewable resources and rural devel. 1979-80, Svc. to Edn. award 1980), Hammond C. of C., La. Assn. for Sch. Execs., Ozone Ramblers Camping Club (pres. 1988), KC (lectr. 1982, 85, 90-91, chancellor 1983-84, 87—, dep. grand knight 1995-96), Rotary (bd. dirs. Hammond, internat. svc. dir. 1972), Phi Delta Kappa, Kappa Delta Pi. Home: 10 Golden Dr Hammond LA 70401-1010 E-mail: CEPARKER@I-55.com.

PARKER, DALTON AUSTIN, sales professional; b. Laneview, Va., Mar. 10, 1938; s. Oliver Robert Parker and Nora Mandy Lumpkin; m. Barbara Buddin; children: Mandy Elizabeth, Amy Layton. BS, U. Richmond, 1962. Comml. sales rep. Va. Electric & Power, Norfolk, 1967-73; chem. field sales rep. Metropolitan Refining Co., Long Island City, N.Y., 1973-78; mgr. sales Met. Life Ins. Co., Columbia, S.C., 1978-81; ednl. sales rep. Devry Inc., Evanston, Ill., 1984-87; chem. field sales rep. Garrett-Callahan Co., Burlingame, Calif., 1987-89; mgmt. rep. The Cardinal Cos., LP, Columbia, 1993-2001; quality mgr. global products BC Components, 2001—. Author: The Lumpkin Family of King and Queen Couty, Va., 1990; editor ISOGRAM tng. manual, 1993—. Coord. United Way of the Midlands, Columbia, 1993—; sponsor, advisor Jr.

Achievement, Norfolk, 1968-70; bd. dirs. Norfolk Jr. C. of C., 1968-70. comdr. USNR, 1962-83. Mem. Environ. Mgmt. System Netowrk, Midlands ISO Network, Midlands Camellia Soc. (sec. 1998-99), Midland Daylily Soc., Am. Soc. for Quality. Avocations: dogbreeding, daylilies, historical research and genealogy. Home: 531 Lockshire Rd Columbia SC 29212 Office: BC Components 3071 St Andrews Rd Columbia SC 29212

PARKER, DENNIS GENE, former sheriff, martial arts instructor; b. Kansas City, Kans., Jan. 5, 1956; s. Billy Gene and Lola Ruth (Martens) P.; children: Heatheryn Ruth, Jessica Elise. Student, U. Kans., 1984. Nat. accredited police firearms instr. and expert., police side handle baton instr. Martial arts instr. Northland Tai-Ryuku, Kansas City, Mo., 1974-84; anti-terrorist/hostage rescue specialist ITC CITRO, 1977-78; police cpl. Atchison (Kans.) Dept. Police, 1984-90; estate investigator Am. Rsch. Bur., L.A., 1990; sheriff Atchison County, Kans., 1990-94; instr. martial arts, including Shito-Ryu Okinawate, Tang Soo Do Mu Duk Kwon, Chinese Wu-Shu Chkn Na. Bd. dirs. Atchison County Community Corrections; team mem. Atchison County Multidisciplinary Child Protection Team, 1992—; bd. dirs. N.E. Kans. Drug Task Force, Oskaloosa, 1990-91. Bd. dirs. N.E. Kans. Community Action Program, Atchison, 1991—, Atchison Area Drug Task Force, 1993—. Recipient Silver Star for Bravery Am. Police Hall of Fame, 1992, Honor award, 1992, John Edgar Hoover Meml. award Nat. Assn. Chiefs of Police and Police Hall of Fame, 1993, State of Kans. medals of valor, 1992, 93, Pres.'s Nat. medal of patriotism, 1993, APD Life Saving award and commendation, 1987, knight chevalier medal Am. Police Hall of Fame, 1992, Medal of Valor Atchison County, 1992, U.S. Cold War Recognition award, 2000. Mem. World Black Belt Bur., Sandan-3d Level Black Shito-Ryu Okinawa Te. Baptist. Home and Office: 5125 NW Parkdale Rd Kansas City MO 64151-3205 E-mail: d.g.parker@worldnet.att.net.

PARKER, DIANA LYNNE, restaurant manager, special events director; b. Eureka, Calif., June 21, 1957; d. Carol Dean and Lynne Diane (Havemann) P. BA in English, Humboldt U., 1981, postgrad., 1982-84. Lic. real estate agent, Calif. Retail clk. Safeway, Inc., Eureka, 1977-84; caterer, owner TD Catering, 1982-84; asst. buyer Macy's Calif., San Francisco, 1984-85; realtor Mason-McDuffie, Alameda, Calif., 1985-87; host, rotunda Neiman Marcus, San Francisco, 1987-89, asst. mgr., rotunda, 1989—, dir. spl. events, 1989—. Mem.: San Francisco Visitor and Conv. Bur., Women Chefs and Restaurateurs, Mus. Modern Art, Commonwealth Club Calif. Republican. Avocations: gourmet chef, artist, antique collecting. Office: Rotunda at Neiman Marcus 150 Stockton St San Francisco CA 94108-5807

PARKER, DONALD EDWARD, aeronautics and aerospace educator; b. Chgo., Apr. 6, 1936; s. Kenneth Coldwell and Florence (Wilson) P.; m. Lynn Goodrich, Sept. 27, 1959 (dec. Apr. 1986); children: Katherine, Susan, Geoffrrey, Rebecca; m. Sharon Lynne Parker, Aug. 19, 1987. BA in Psychology and Econs., DePauw U., 1958; PhD in Exptl. Psychology, Princeton U., 1961. Postdoctoral fellow Auditory Rsch. Lab. Princeton (N.J.) U., NIMH, 1961-62; sr. postdoctoral fellow Max Planck Inst., NIMH, Germany, 1965-66; asst. prof. psychology Miami U., Oxford, Ohio, 1966-69, assoc. prof. psychology, 1969-72, prof. psychology, 1972-93, chair dept. psychology, 1977-80, prof. emeritus dept. psychology, 1993—; affiliate prof. otolaryngology U. Wash., Seattle, 1993—. Vis. scientist Space Biomed. Rsch. Inst. NASA, Houston, 1983, 85-87, project scientist pre-flight adaptation trainer project, 1987-89, co-investigator, 1989-94; clin. prof. cmty. medicine Wright State U., Dayton, Ohio, 1984—; assoc. investigator Spatial Orientation Rsch. Project Harry G. Armstrong Aerospace Med. Rsch. Lab. Wright-Patterson AFB, Dayton, 1988-93; faculty assoc. Human Interface Tech. Lab., 1994— Contbr. numerous articles to profl. jours. Capt. USAF, 1962-65. Numerous grants NIH, USAF, NASA, 1965—. Mem. Internat. Acad. Astronautics, Barany Soc. Avocation: hiking. Office: Dept Otolaryngology Box 357923 U Wash Seattle WA 98195-7923

PARKER, DONALD FRED, college dean, human resources management educator; b. Oilton, Okla., Nov. 7, 1934; s. Robert Fred Parker and Georgia Marie (Culley) Meek; m. Jo Ellen Dunfee, Apr. 6, 1963; children: Margaret Elizabeth, Emily Lyle. BA in Sociology, U. Okla., 1957; MS in Personnel Adminstrn., George Washington U., 1966; PhD in Human Resource Mgmt., Cornell U., 1975. Commd. ensign USN, 1957, advanced through grades to capt., 1977, staff officer with chief naval ops., 1969-71, comdg. officer, exec. officer, Patrol Squadron Ten Brunswick, Maine, 1974-76, prof. Naval War Coll. Newport, R.I., 1976-78, comdg. officer Navy Personnel Research & Devel. Ctr. San Diego, 1978-80, ret., 1980; asst. prof. Grad. Sch. Bus., U. Mich., Ann Arbor, 1980-84; prof. , dean Coll. Commerce and Industry U. Wyo., Laramie, 1984-91; Sara Hart Kimball dean bus., prof. human resources mgmt. Oreg. State U., Corvallis, 1991—2001. Advisor U.S. West Wyo. State Bd. Advisors, Cheyenne, 1986-91; ex-officio dir. Wyo. Indsl. Devel. Corp., Casper, 1987; vis. prof. Acad. Internat. Econ. Affairs, Hsinchu, Taiwan, 1986-91. Author numerous articles, book chpts., case studies. Mem. Acad. of Mgmt. (human resource mgmt. divsn. dir. 1983-85), Midwest Assn. Deans and Dept. Chairs in Bus. (pres.), Western Assn. Collegiate Schs. Bus. (bd. dirs., pres. 1999), Phi Kappa Phi, Beta Gamma Sigma (pres. 1998-2000, past pres. 2000—02). Avocations: jogging, hiking. Home: 4400 NW Honeysuckle Dr Corvallis OR 97330-3355 Office: Oreg State U Coll Bus 200 Bexell Hall Corvallis OR 97331-8527 E-mail: parker@bus.orst.edu.

PARKER, DOUGLAS MARTIN, retired lawyer, writer; b. Chgo., Mar. 6, 1935; s. Lewis Wallace and Elaine (Schulz) P.; m. Angela Macintosh, June 5, 1965; children: Heather Louise, Melissa Meredith. AB, Cornell U., 1956, LL.B., 1958. Bar: N.Y. 1959, U.S. Supreme Ct. 1966, D.C. 1969. Assoc. Mudge Rose Guthrie Alexander & Ferdon, N.Y.C., 1958-59, 62-69, ptnr., 1977-94, of counsel, 1995; ptnr, Lankler & Parker, Washington, 1969-73; with Office of Counsel to Pres., 1973; dep. gen. counsel HUD, 1974-77. Served to capt. U.S. Army, 1959-62. Republican. Congregationalist. Home: 7 Highwood Rd South Orleans MA 02662 E-mail: dmparker@capecod.net.

PARKER, ELLIS JACKSON, III, lawyer, broadcaster; b. Haleyville, Ala., Oct. 2, 1931; s. Ellis J. and Elizabeth (Funderburg) P.; m. Nancy Elizabeth Bealer; children: Francis Hill, Ellis Stuart. Student, U.S. Mil. Acad., West Point, N.Y., 1953-57; AB, U. Ala., 1958, LLB, 1960, JD, 1961; diploma, Droit Compare, Luxembourg, 1959; cert., Acad. Internat. Law, Hague, The Netherlands, 1960. Bar: Ala. 1960, U.S. Tax Ct. 1960, U.S. Supreme Ct. 1966, D.C. Ct. Appeals 1972, U.S. Ct. Appeals D.C. 1972, Md. Ct. Appeals 1973, U.S. Ct. Claims 1977. Legis. atty. IRS, Washington, 1961-62; chief of staff to U.S. Congressman Grant Ala., 1963-64; pvt. practice Birmingham, 1964-84; spl. advisor to Pres. Richard Nixon White House, Washington, 1968-69; v.p., counsel Birmingham Broadcasting Co., 1964-83; ptnr. Taylor, Smith & Parker Law Office, Upper Marlboro, Md., 1970-86; prin., owner Ellis J. Parker, Law Office, Washington, 1986—. V.p., sec. Constrn. Components Corp., Upper Marlboro, Md., 1968-72; pres. Washington-Ala. News Reports, Washington, 1980-01; pres. Sta. WNPT-AM-FM, Tuscaloosa, Ala.; v.p. Sta. WLPH, Birmingham, Parker Real Estate, Birmingham, N.B. Devel. Co., Washington; chmn. bd. Blackbelt Broadcasting Co., Selma, Ala.; founding mem. Women's Nat. Bank, Washington; CEO Birmingham Broadcasting Co.; ptnr. Linden Radio Joint Venture, Faunsdale, Ala., 1969-89; bd. dirs. 17th St L.L.C., Bealer-Parker, LLC, Washington. Mem. Presdl. Inaugural Com., inaugural protocol officer V.p. Agnew, 1968; mem. steering com. Rep. Party, Balt., 1972; chmn. bd. trustees Prince George's Hist. and Cultural Trust, Upper Marlboro, 1974; chmn. bd. advisors Prince George's Equestrian Ctr., Upper Marlboro, 1980; founder, pres. bd. dirs. Hospice of Prince George's County, Upper Marlboro, 1982; mem. Upper Marlboro Devel. Com. Mem. IEEE, ABA, FCC Bar Assn., Fed. Bar Assn., Inter-Am. Bar Assn., Ala. Bar Assn., Md. Bar Assn., Nat. Assn. Broadcasters, Ala. Broadcasters Assn., Balt. Coun. Fgn. Affairs, Assn. Grads. U.S. Mil. Acad., Chevy Chase Club, Md. Club, St. Andrews Soc., Met. Club, Ala. Alumni Assn., Scabbard and Blade (chmn. nat. alumni coun.), Pi Kappa Alpha, Sigma Delta Kappa. Home and Office: 9220 Cranford Dr Potomac MD 20854-2229 Home: Chateau Rambouillet 2165 Ibis Island Palm Beach FL 33480 E-mail: eparker124@aol.com.

PARKER, ELLIS D. retired career officer, aviation executive; b. Adams, Tenn., Nov. 1, 1932; s. Ellis A. and Lorene (Qualls) P.; m. Judy C. Matthews, Dec. 24, 1952; children: Donald S., Phillip R., David B. BS in Psychology, U. Nebr., 1972; MPA, Shippensburg U., 1979; LLD (hon.), Miles U., 1989. Rated aviator FAA. Commd. 2d lt. U.S. Army, Korea, 1957, advanced through ranks to lt. gen., 1992, aviation officer, comdr. 17th aviation brigade Korea, 1978-80, asst. divsn. comdr. 101st airborne divsn. Ky., 1983-84, comdg. gen. Army Aviation Ctr. Sch. Fort Rucker, Ala., 1984-89; dir. requirements army staff Pentagon, Washington, 1980-83, dir. army staff, 1989-92; bd. dirs. Canadian Aviation Electronics, 1993—. Bd. dirs. West Star Corp., St. Louis, Doss Aviation, Colorado Springs; chmn., bd. dirs. Hammer Constrn. Co., Samson, Ala. Contbr. articles to profl. jours. Chmn. Fort Rucker Mus. Found., 1995—; adv. bd. Troy State U., Dotham, 1992—;chair retiree coun. for chief of staff U.S. Army, 1993-99; co-chair Dept. of Def. Retiree Coun., 1994-99. Decorated D.S.M. with oak leaf cluster, D.F.C., Legion of Merit, Bronze Star with two oak leaf clusters, Meritorious Svc. medals, 23 Air medals; named to Hall of Honor Bd. by Gov. Ala., 1993—. Mem.: Enterprise (Ala.) C. of C. (chmn bd. 1995—), Assn. U.S. Army (mem. exec. com. Fort Rucker chpt. 1994, named to Army Aviation Hall of Fame 1994), Ret. Officers Assn. (1st vice-chmn.), Army Aviation Assn. Am. (pres., Order of St. Michel, Gold 1992), Enterprise Rotary Club (Paul Harris fellow). Republican. Avocations: flying, hunting, fishing, volunteering in community. Home and Office: 128 Deer Run Strut Enterprise AL 36330-7812

PARKER, EUGENE NEWMAN, retired physicist, educator; b. Houghton, Mich., June 10, 1927; s. Glenn H. and Helen (MacNair) Parker; m. Niesje Meuter, 1954; children: Joyce, Eric. BS, Mich. State U., 1948; PhD, Calif. Inst. Tech., 1951; DSc (hon.) , Mich. State U., 1975; DHC in Physics and Math. (hon.) , Univ. Utrecht, The Netherlands, 1986; DHC in Theoretical Physics (hon.) , U. Oslo, 1991. Instr. math. and astronomy U. Utah, 1951—53, asst. prof. physics, 1953—55; mem. faculty physics U. Chgo., 1955—95, prof. dept. physics, 1962—95, prof. dept. astronomy and astrophysics, 1967—95, prof. emeritus, 1995—. Author: Interplanetary Dynamical Processes, 1963, Cosmical Magnetic Fields, 1979, Spontaneous Current Sheets in Magnetic Fields, 1994. Recipient Space Sci. award, AIAA, 1964, Chapman medal, Royal Astron. Soc., 1979, Gold medal, 1992, Disting. Alumni award, Calif. Inst. Tech., 1980, Karl Schwarzschild award, Astronomische Gesselschaft, 1990, Bruce medal, Astron. Soc. Pacific, 1997, medal, Assn. Internat. Devel. Nice (France) Obs., 1997. Mem.: NAS (H. K. Arctowski award 1969, U.S. Nat. medal of Sci. 1989), Norwegian Acad. Sci. and Letters, Am. Geophys. Union (John Adam Fleming award 1968, William Bowie medal 1990), Am. Astron. Soc. (Henry Norris Russell lectr. 1969, George Ellery Hale award 1978). Achievements include development of theory of the origin of the dipole magnetic field of Earth; prediction and theory of the solar wind and heliosphere; theoretical basis for the X-ray emission from the Sun and stars. Home: 1323 Evergreen Rd Homewood IL 60430-3410 E-mail: parker@odysseus.uchicago.edu.

PARKER, EVERETT CARLTON, clergyman; b. Chgo., Jan. 17, 1913; s. Harry Everett and Lillian (Stern) P.; m. Geneva M. Jones, May 5, 1939; children: Ruth A. (Mrs. Peter Weiss), Eunice L. (Mrs. George Kolczun, Jr.), Truman E. AB, U. Chgo., 1935; BD magna cum laude, Chgo. Theol. Sem., 1943, Blatchford fellow, 1944-45, DD, 1964, Catawba Coll., Salisbury, N.C., 1958; L.H.D., Fordham U., 1978, Tougaloo Coll., 1987; LLD, Coll. St. Elizabeth, 2000. Pastor Waveland Ave. Congl. Christian Ch., 1943; asst. pub. service and war program mgr. NBC, 1943-45; founder-dir. Protestant Radio Commn., 1945-50; lectr. communication Yale Div. Sch., 1946-58, dir. communications research project, 1950-54; dir. Office Communication United Ch. Christ, 1954-83; sr. research assoc., adj. prof. Fordham U., 1983—; founder citizen movement to protect minority rights in media, 1963—. Chmn. broadcasting and film commn. Nat. Coun. Chs., 1969-72, mem. gen. bd., 1966-72; chair Study Commn. on Theology, Edn. and Electronic Media, 1985-87; founder Found. for Minority Interests in Media, 1985—, treas., 1985—, Hispanic Telecommunications Network, 1986—; mem. adv. com. on advanced TV svcs., Consumer Adv. Group FCC, 1988-92. Producer-dir.: nat. TV programs including series Off to Adventure, 1956, Tangled World, 1965; originator: series Six American Families, PBS-TV, 1977; Author: Religious Radio, 1948, Film Use in the Church, 1953, The Television-Radio Audience and Religion, 1955, Religious Television, 1961, (with others) Television, Radio, Film for Churchmen, 1969, Fiber Optics to the Home: The Changing Future of Cable, TV and The Telephone, 1989, Social Responsibility of Television in the United States, 1994. Recipient Human Relations award Am. Jewish Com., 1966, Faith and Freedom award Religious Heritage Found., 1966, 77, Alfred I. DuPont-Columbia U. award pub. service in broadcasting, 1969; Roman Cath. Broadcasters Gabriel award pub. service, 1970; Lincoln U. award significant contbn. human relations, 1971; Racial Justice award Com. for Racial Justice, United Ch. Christ, 1973; Ch. Leadership award Council for Christian Social Action, 1973; Public Service award Black Citizens for a Fair Media, 1979, Pioneer award World Assn. for Christian Communication, 1988, Pres.'s Award for Ecumenical Leadership Nat. Coun. Chs., 2000; Congl. citation, 1993. Mem.: Yale (N.Y.C.). Home: 11 Midland Ave White Plains NY 10606-2828 Office: Fordham University Dept Communications Bronx NY 10458

PARKER, FRED I. federal judge; b. Boston, 1938; BA, U. Mass., 1962; LLB, Georgetown U., 1965. With Lyne, Woodworth & Everts, Boston, 1965—66, Office Atty. Gen., Montpelier, Vt., 1969—72, Langrock and Sperry, Middlebury, 1972—75; ptnr. Langrock, Sperry, Parker & Stahl, 1975—82, Langrock, Sperry, Parker & Wool, Middlebury, 1982—90; fed. judge U.S. Dist. Ct. (Vt. dist.), 1990—91, chief judge, 1991—94; fed. judge U.S. Ct. Appeals (2d cir.), 1994—. Mem. conduct bd. Vt. Supreme Ct., 1975—79, jud. conduct bd., 1982—88. Active Vt. Lawyers Project. With USMC, 1955—62. Mem.: Chittenden County Bar Assn., Vt. Bar Assn. (chair spl. com. reform of judiciary 1988—89). Office: US Dist Ct PO Box 392 11 Elmwood Ave Burlington VT 05402-0392 Also: US Dist CourtFederal Building PO Box 392 11 Elmwood Avenue Burlington VT 05402-0392 Office: Thurogood Marshall US Courthouse 40 Foley Square New York NY 10007*

PARKER, GEORGE, retired pen manufacturing company executive; b. Janesville, Wis., Nov. 9, 1929; s. Russell C. and Eleanor (Jackson) P.; m. Nancy E. Bauhan, Aug. 11, 1951; children: George Safford III, Elizabeth, Martha, Patricia. BA, Brown U., 1951, LLD (hon.), 1986; MA, U. Mich., 1952; LLD (hon.), Milton Coll., 1974. With Parker Pen Co., Janesville, 1952-86, from asst. to gen. mgr. Gilman Engring. Co. subs., successively asst. domestic advt. mgr., fgn. advt. mgr., dir. fgn. sales, dir. domestic sales, v.p., gen. mgr., 1958-60, exec. v.p., 1960-66, pres., 1966-77, 81-82, CEO, 1966-80, 81-82, chmn. bd., 1976-86, Manpower Inc., 1976-86; pres., chmn. Caxambas Assocs. of Fla., Inc., 1986—; ret., 1986. Chmn. bd. BANCWIS Corp., 1971-84; bd. dirs. Bank of Wis.; chmn. bd. Moebius Printing Co., Milw., 1992-93. Chmn. Wis. Rep. Fin. Com., 1971-73, state chmn., 1974-76; mem. Nat. Rep. Fin. Com., 1971-73; mem. Rep. Nat. Com., 1974-76; chmn. bd. dirs., CEO Janesville Found.; bd. dirs., pres. Marco Island Taxpayers Assn., 1993-94; fellow Lake Forest Acad.; trustee emeritus Brown U., Beloit Coll.; chmn. emeritus bd. fellows Beloit Coll.; dir. Wis. Acad. Found., 1994-99, v.p., 1996, pres., 1997-99, councillor Wis. Acad., 1998-99; bd. govs. John Carter Brown Libr., 1997-99; dir. Wis. History Found., 1999-2000; coun. mem. Elvehjem Mus. of Art, Madison, Wis., 2001—.

PARKER, GERALD M. osteopath, researcher; b. Olean, N.Y., Nov. 20, 1943; s. Richard and Kathleen (Manwaring) P.; m. Linda Kay Stuart, Dec. 28, 1968; children: Kimberly, Gerald, Cassandra, Kevin. BA, Western Wash. U., 1965; DO, Kirksville Coll. Osteopathy & Surgery, 1969. Intern Art Centre Hosp., Detroit, 1969-70; ptnr. Doctor's Clinic, Amarillo, Tex., 1970. Dir. S.W. Inst. Preventive Medicine, Amarillo, 1978—, Hyperbaric Oxygen Ctr., Amarillo, 1979—; appeared on That's Incredible TV show, 1982. Contbr. articles to profl. jours. Pres. S.W. Amarillo Little Dribblers Assn., 1979—; coach Girls Nat. Champion Basketball Teams, 1981, 83-87, 89. Fellow Am. Acad. Med. Preventics; mem. S.W. Acad. Preventive Medicine (pres. 1980—), Am. Osteo. Assn. Methodist. Avocation: athletics. Office: Doctors Clinic 4714 S Western St Amarillo TX 79109-5950

PARKER, GERALD WILLIAM, physician, retired medical administrator; b. Susquehanna, Pa., Oct. 22, 1929; m. Susan Emerson, May 4, 1985. BS, Union Coll., Schenectady, 1951; MD, N.Y. Med. Coll., 1955. Diplomate Nat. Bd. Med. Examiners, Am. Bd. Internal Medicine; lic. physician, N.Y., Tex., D.C. Intern Ellis Hosp., Schenectady, 1955-56; resident internal medicine Wilford Hall, USAF Med. Ctr., San Antonio, 1958-61; resident in gastroenterology Water Reed Army Med. Ctr., Washington, 1965-66; commd. capt. U.S. Air Force, 1956, advanced through grades to brig. gen., 1980, retired, 1986; chair dept. medicine USAF Hosp., Clark AFB, Philippines, 1967-69; chief internal medicine Malcolm Grow USAF Med. Ctr., Andrews AFB, Washington, 1969-70, chair dept. medicine, 1970-72, Wilford Hall USAF Med. Ctr., Lackland AFB, Tex., 1972-75, dir. hosp. services, 1975-77; comdr USAF Hosp., Torrejon Air Base, Spain, 1977-78; dep. dir. med. plans and resources Office of Surgeon Gen. USAF, Washington, 1978-80, dir. med. plans and resources, 1980-81; dir. med. inspection AF Inspection and Safety Ctr., Norton AFB, Calif., 1981-83; dep. surgeon gen. for ops. AF Med. Service Ctr., Brooks AFB, Tex., 1983-85; dir. profl. affairs and quality assurance Office of Surg. Gen., USAF, Washington, 1985-86; dep. dir., chief profl. services King Health Ctr., U.S. Soldiers and Airmens Home, 1986-97, ret., 1997. Clin. prof. medicine U. Tex. Health Scis. Ctr., San Antonio, 1972-77; adj. prof. Health Care Scis., George Washington Univ., 1987-97; clinical prof. medicine Uniformed Svcs. Univ. of Health Scis., 1988-97. Trustee, Hampshire Country Sch., 2000—; mem. Rindge (N.H.) Planning Bd., 2000—, Rindge Conservation Commn., 2000—; bd. dirs. Rindge Hist. Soc., 2000—; Rindge health officer, 2001—. Decorated Air Force D.S.M. with oak leaf cluster, Legion of Merit with oak leaf cluster, Bronze Star, Air Medal with oak leaf cluster, ACP Laureate award, 1996, Air Force Civilian Outstanding Svc. medal. Fellow ACP; mem. Soc. AF Physicians, Alpha Omega Alpha.

PARKER, GWENDOLYN D. computer programmer; d. Arthur J. and Juanita (Moore) Oates. BS, Western Conn. State U., 1982. Programmer analyst Am. Cyanamid Corp., Danbury, Conn.; sr. programmer analyst BAR Dun and Bradstreet, Norwalk, sr. tech. support programmer date quality Allentown, Pa.; mgr. statistical profile database, system analyst Dun & Bradstreet, Bethlehem. Mem. NAFE, SAS User Group, SUGI User Group, BMBA (Phila. chpt.), UNCF (eastern Pa. region), NCBI Internat. (Pa. chpt.). Home: 1824 W Chew St Allentown PA 18104-5509

PARKER, H. LAWRENCE, investor, rancher, retired investment banker; b. Portchester, N.Y., June 16, 1926; s. Raeburn H. and Alice (Lawrence) P.; m. Eleanor Sage, Mar. 3, 1951 (div. 1967); children: Katherine, Richard, Michael, Douglas (dec.); m. Regine Hawes, Nov. 15, 1994. BA, Yale U., 1949. With Morgan Stanley & Co., N.Y.C., 1950—, ptnr., 1959-75, mng. dir., 1975-83, adv. dir., 1984—; pres. Morgan Stanley Can. Ltd., 1976-79, chmn., 1979-84. Mem. adv. bd. on edn. and tng. Sec. Navy, 1985-87 Trustee Green Mountain Valley Sch., Waitsfield, Vt., 1981-91. Served with USMCR, 1944-46. Mem. Investment Bankers Assn. Am. (bd. govs. 1966-70, pres. 1969), Nat. Assn. Securities Dealers (gov. 1981-84), Sublette County Hist. Soc. (trustee 1987-91). Clubs: Nat. Golf Links Am., Links (N.Y.C.), Blind Brook, Augusta Nat. Golf (Ga.), Bedford Golf and Tennis, Jupiter Island, Seminole Golf. Home: One Angas Trail Hobe Sound FL 33455 E-mail: thepard@aol.com.

PARKER, HAROLD ALLEN, lawyer, real estate executive; b. Denver, Sept. 14, 1924; s. Hyman and Sophia P.; m. Gertrud Parker; children: David, Rodney, Diana, Jesse, Jonathan. JD, Golden Gate U., 1971. Bar: Calif. 1972. Pvt. practice, San Francisco; gen. ptnr. Harold Parker Properties. Legal cons. San Francisco Craft and Folk Art Mus.; past mem. Bay Area Lawyers for the Arts; spkr. in field; prime developer Union St. Comml. Corridor, San Francisco, 1963—. Pub.: Wolfgang Paalen, His Art and His Writings, 1980, Richard Bowman, Forty Years of Abstract Painting, 1986. Chmn. Fine Arts Commn., Tiburon, Calif., 1976-78. Mem. Family Club (San Francisco). Avocations: music, art, tennis. Office: 1844 Union St San Francisco CA 94123-4308

PARKER, HAROLD TALBOT, history educator; b. Cin., Dec. 26, 1907; s. Samuel Chester and Lucile (Jones) P.; m. Louise Salley, July 9, 1980. PhB, U. Chgo., 1928, PhD, 1934; postgrad., Cornell U., 1929-30. Mem. faculty Duke U., Durham, N.C., 1939—, assoc. prof., 1950-57, prof. history, 1957-77, emeritus, from 1977; adj. prof. U. Ala., Huntsville, 1978-81; faculty U. N.C., Chapel Hill, 1984. Author: The Cult of Antiquity and the French Revolutionaries, 1937, Three Napoleonic Battles, 1944, 83, (with Marvin Brown) Major Themes in Modern European History, 3 vols., 1974, Bureau of Commerce in 1781, 1979, An Administrative Bureau During the Old Regime, 1993, History of St. Philip's Episcopal Church (Durham, N.C.) 1978-1994, 1997, Sermons From St. Philips, 1912-1994, 2000; editor: (with Richard Herr) Ideas in History, 1965, Problems in European History, 1979, (with Georg Iggers) International Handbook of Historical Studies, 1979, Theory and Social History, 1980, (with L.S. Parker) Proc. Consortium of Revolutionary Europe, 1981, 84, 85, 86; assoc. editor Historical Dictionary of Napoleonic France, 1985; regional editor, contbg. author: Great Historians of the Modern Age, 1991; contbr. articles to profl. jours. With USAAF, 1942-45. Recipient Disting. Svc. award Consortium on Revolutionary Europe, 1993, Disting Svc. award So. Hist. Assn. European History Sect., 1993. Mem. Soc. for French Hist. Studies (pres. 1957, Disting. Svc. award 1989), AAUP (pres. Duke U. chpt. 1960), Phi Beta Kappa (pres. Duke chpt. 1961) Episcopalian. Home: West Columbia, SC. Deceased.

PARKER, HARRY JOHN, retired psychologist, educator; b. Sioux City, Iowa, Jan. 18, 1923; AB, Elmhurst Coll., 1947; MA, Northwestern U., 1953, PhD, 1956, postgrad., 1958, Roosevelt U., 1957-58; LittD, Elmhurst Coll., 1990. Lic. psychologist, Okla. Tex.; diplomate bd. cert. in rehab. psychology Am. Bd. Profl. Psychology. Counselor Northwestern U. Counseling Ctr., Chgo., 1952-56, counseling psychologist, 1956-59, asst. dir., 1957-58, dir., 1958-59; pvt. practice counseling psychologist Chgo., 1956-59, Okla., 1959-69, Tex., 1969—; prof. edn. U. Okla., 1959-69; dir. manpower planning, regional med. program and Sch. Health Related Professions U. Okla. Med. Ctr., Oklahoma City, 1967-69, prof. preventive medicine and pub. health, 1966-69, prof. human ecology, 1969; assoc. dean Sch. Allied Health Scis. U. Tex. Southwestern Med. Ctr., Dallas, 1969-74, prof. phys. medicine and rehab. 1969-90, prof. psychiatry, 1969-90, prof. rehab. sci., 1970-90. Adj. prof. rehab. U. N. Tex., 1990; adj. prof. psychology Ill. Inst. Tech., 1990-96, Tex. Woman's U., 1991-99; adj. prof. allied health edn. U. Tex. Southwestern Med. Ctr., Dallas, 1990-98. Contbr. articles to profl. jours. Served with U.S. Army, 1943-46 Fellow Am. Psychol. Assn.; mem. Southwestern Psychol. Assn., Dallas Psychol. Assn., Tex. Psychol. Assn., Sigma Xi, Phi Delta Phi, Alpha Eta. Address: 318 Hidden Valley Trl Sherman TX 75092-7618

PARKER, HARRY LEE, retired army officer, counselor; b. Birmingham, Ala., Feb. 20, 1944; s. Guy Milburn and Grace (Lee) P.; m. Sheri Lynn Pogue (div. Oct. 1973); children: John Lee, Suzanne Grace, Stephen Scott; m. Melanie Louise Cox, Apr. 20, 1979; 1 child, Christopher Robert. BA, Miss. State U., 1966; MS, Johns Hopkins U., 1980; postgrad., U.S. Army Command & Staff Coll, 1982. Commd. 2d lt. U.S. Army, 1966, advanced through grades to lt. col., 1987; maintenance officer 85th Maintenance Bn., Hanau, Fed. Republic of Germany, 1967-69; commanding officer 143d Engr. Co. and A Co. 34th Engr. Bn., Long Binh, Vietnam, 1969-70; chief plans and ops. div. Dir. of Logistics, Ft. Rucker, Ala., 1971-73; supply and maintenance officer 97th Signal Bn. NATO, Mannehim, Fed. Republic of Germany, 1973-76; asst. materiel officer 8th Maintenance Bn., Grossalheim, Fed. Republic Germany, 1977; tng. evaluator HQ 1st US Army, Ft. Meade, Md., 1978-81; logistics coord. Cuban Task Force, Ft. Indiantown Gap, Pa., 1980; project officer Dept. Def., Project Office, Mobile Electric Power, Washington, 1982-85; exec. officer 193d Support Bn., Ft. Clayton, Panama, 1986-87; chief of maintenance U.S. Army South, Ft. Corozol, Panama, 1987-88; prof. mil. Sci. Army ROTC, Miss. State U., Starkville, Miss., 1988-90; ops. officer 101st area support group, Guardian City, Saudia Arabia, logistics officer, 1st Corps Support Command, XVIII Airborne Corps., Damman, Saudi Arabia (Desert Shield and Desert Storm), 1990-91; career/coop. edn. counselor Cen. Fla. C.C., Ocala, Fla., 1992-95; educator Seminole County (Fla.) Pub. Sch. Sys., 2000—. Decorated Bronze Star with oak leaf cluster, Meritorious Svc. medal with two oak leaf clusters, Army Commendation medal with four oak leaf clusters. Mem. Ret. Officers Assn. (life), Am. Legion, Sigma Chi. Presbyterian (Elder). Avocations: woodworking, private pilot, scuba, boating, computers. Home: 895 Palmetto St Oviedo FL 32765 E-mail: hleeparker@att.net.

PARKER, HARRY S., III, museum director; b. St. Petersburg, Fla., Dec. 23, 1939; s. Harry S. Parker and Catherine (Baillie) Knapp; m. Ellen McCance, May 23, 1964; children: Elizabeth Day, Thomas Baillie, Samuel Ferguson, Catherine Allan. AB magna cum laude, Harvard U., 1961; MA, NYU, 1966. Exec. asst., adminstrv. asst. to dir. Met. Mus. Art, N.Y.C., 1963-66, exec. asst. to pres., 1966-67, exec. asst. to dir., 1967, chmn. dept. edn., 1967-71, vice dir.

edn., 1971-73; dir. Dallas Mus. Art, 1974-87, Fine Arts Mus. San Francisco, 1987—. Mem. Am. Assn. Mus. (v.p.) Assn. Art Mus. Dirs., Century Assn., Bohemian Club. Office: Fine Arts Mus San Francisco 233 Post St Fl 5 San Francisco CA 94108

PARKER, HENRY GRIFFITH, III, insurance executive; b. Plainfield, N.J., Oct. 27, 1926; s. Henry Griffith and Ruth Martin (Van Auken) P.; m. Audrey Lansing Turner, May 11, 1957; children: Henry Griffith, IV, Elizabeth Wright. AB, Princeton U., 1948; postgrad., U. Pa. Sch. Law. With Chubb & Son, Inc., 1949-97, v.p., 1968-70, sr. v.p., dir., 1971-92, mng. dir., 1986-92; cons. to chmn., 1992-97; v.p. Fed. Ins. Co., 1968-73, sr. v.p., 1973-91; v.p. Vigilant Ins. Co., 1966-91, mgr. internat. div., 1967-84; chmn. Parker Assocs., Madison, N.J., 1997—. Adv. bd. Firemark Global Ins. Fund II, L.P., 1997—, bd. dirs. Alliance Assurance Co. Am., N.Y.C., Sun Ins. Office Am. Inc., N.Y.C.; mem. industry sector adv. com. on svcs. U.S. Dept. Commerce, Washington; bd. dirs. Nat. Fgn. Trade Coun., chmn. declarations com., 1974-81, chmn. ins. com., 1976-81; chmn. internat. policy com. U.S. C. of C., 1970-73; chmn. U.S. del. XII-XIII-XX-XXII-XXII Hemispheric Ins. Conf., Chile, 1969, Paraguay, 1987, Panama, 1985, Buenos Aires, 1989; chmn. Internat. Ins. Adv. Coun., Washington, 1970-73, 85-90, chmn. Internat. Com. Am. Ins. Assn., 1991-93; mem. N.J. Commn. on Internat. Trade, 1986—; chmn. bus. adv. com. bus. coun. UN, 1988—; mem. adv. bd. Liaison Office Peoples Ins. Co. China, 1986-94. Appeared on numerous TV and radio programs; contbr. articles to profl. jours. Chmn. bd. Overlook Hosp., Summit, N.J., 1973-80; trustee Drew U., Madison, 1974—. Lt. (j.g.) USNR, 1944-46. Recipient Internat. Ins. award U.S. C. of C., 1981, Disting. Service award Internat. Ins. Council, 1988. Mem. Nat. Assn. Ins. Commrs. (chmn. internat. adv. com.), Am. Ins. Assn. (chmn. internat. com.), Downtown Assn. Club (N.Y.C.), Princeton Club (N.Y.C.), River Club (N.Y.C.), Devon Yacht Club, Morris County (N.J.) Golf Club, Hillsboro Club (Fla.), Psi Upsilon. Republican. Episcopalian. Office: Parker Assocs 38 East Ln Madison NJ 07940-2652

PARKER, JACK FREDERICK, photojournalist, media consultant; b. Dayton, Ohio, June 15, 1948; s. Thomas R. and Catherine L. Parker; m. Dianne L. Kattau; children: Christine, Jack Jr. A in Practical Electronics, Purdue U., 1987. Live Eye coord. Sta. WISH-TV, Indpls., 1980—2002; chief news photographer Sta. WTTV News, 1970—80. Media cons. Parker Media Consulting, Indpls., 1988—2002. Author: (amateur radio edn.) Building Better Clubs, 2000, Building Better Clubs in the Future, 2001. Mem.: Mid-State Amateur Radio Club (life; pres.). Methodist. Avocations: amateur radio, sailing, photography. Office: Sta WISH TV 1950 N Meridian St Indianapolis IN Personal E-mail: jparker@iquest.net. Business E-Mail: jparker@wishtv.com.

PARKER, JACK STEELE, retired manufacturing company executive; b. Palo Alto, Calif., July 6, 1918; s. William Leonard and Mary Isabel (Steele) P.; m. Elaine Elizabeth Simons; 1 child, Kaaren Parker Gray. BSME, Stanford U., 1939; DBA (hon.), Southeastern Mass. U., 1970; LLD (hon.), Clark U., 1972, Renssalaer Poly. Inst., 1986. Engr. Western Pipe & Steel Co., San Francisco, 1939-40; marine surveyor Am. Bur. Shipping, Seattle, 1940-42; supt. steel constrn. Todd Shipyards, Houston, 1942-44, supt. outfitting L.A., 1944-46; asst. chief engr. Am. Potash & Chem., Trona, Calif., 1946-50; mgr. separations div. GE, Hanford Works, Wash., 1950-52, div. mgr., v.p. aircraft gas turbines Cin., 1952-57, v.p. corp. rels. N.Y.C., 1957-61, v.p., group exec. aerospace and electronics, 1961-68, vice chmn., exec. officer, dir., 1968-80, dir. emeritus, 1980—. Overseer Hoover Instn., Stanford U., chmn. 1974-76; trustee Monterey Bay Aquarium Found., Heard Mus., Phoenix, Ariz.; hon. trustee Renssalaer Poly. Inst., Troy, N.Y.; bd. dirs. Smithsonian Instn., 1985-91. Fellow AIAA, ASME; mem. NAE, NAS (Pres.'s Circle), The Conf. Bd. (councilor for life, chmn. 1971-73), Aerospace Industries Assn. (chmn. 1966-68, hon. dir.), Augusta (Ga.) Nat. Golf Club, Desert Forest Golf Club, Desert Mountain Club, Bohemian Club, Boone & Crocket Club, Conquistadores del Cielo, Forest Highlands Club. Avocations: fishing, shooting, golf. Home: 6972 Stage Coach Pass Carefree AZ 85377 Office: GE 260 Long Ridge Rd Stamford CT 06902-1627

PARKER, JACQUELINE YVONNE, lawyer, educator; b. Urbana, Ill., Jan. 14, 1947; d. Melvin M. and Florence L. (Katz) Pick; m. Bruce Richard Parker, May 30, 1969; children: Kenneth R.L., Michael P., Deborah M. BA, Tufts U., 1969; student law, U. Calif., Berkeley, 1976-77; JD, New Eng. Sch. Law, 1977; LLM, Harvard U., 1981. Bar: Mass. 1978, U.S. Ct. Appeals (1st cir.) 1978, U.S. Supreme Ct. 1990. Asst. prof. law New Eng. Sch. Law, Boston, 1978-81, Albany (N.Y.) Law Sch., 1981-84; assoc. Parker Coulter Daley & White, Boston, 1984-92; atty. Connelly & Norton P.C., 1992—2000. Author, co-author (4 vol. treatise) Contemporary Family Law: Principles, Policy & Practice, 1988; contbr. articles to law revs. Mem. Children's Adoption & Foster Care Coalition, Boston, 1991—. United Way scholar, 1975, New Eng. Sch. Law Trustee's scholar, 1975-76. Mem. ABA (com. for pub. counsel svcs., bd. dirs.), Nat. Assn. of Counsel for Children (bd. dirs. 1991—), Mass. Bar Assn. (family law legis. subcom.). Avocations: hiking, jogging, tennis. Office: Law Office of Jacqueline Y Parker Box 554 Newton Center MA 02459 E-mail: jyparker@worldnet.att.net.

PARKER, JAMES WESLEY, former career naval officer, investment company executive; b. Portsmouth, Va., July 31, 1917; s. Charles Wesley Parker and Dempsey Elizabeth Darden; m. Mary Elizabeth Mara, Oct. 12, 1946; children: Diane Marie Wright, Susan Gertrude Kennelly. BA, Elon Coll., 1939; MBA, Stanford U., 1951. Registered securities broker, life ins. agent, Calif., real estate agt., Calif., registered fin. cons.; accredited estate planner. Commd. ensign USN, 1940, advanced through grades to capt., 1959, ret., 1962; v.p., gen. mgr. so. divsn. Montgomery Bros., Inc., L.A., 1962—66; dir. comm. Master Charge, Western States Bancard Assn., 1967; ops. mgr. Nat. BankAmericard, 1971—73; v.p. Bank of Am., 1974—87, Bank of Calif., 1987—92, Pacific Trust Co., 1992—94, Comerica Bank, 1994—95, Kelmoore Investment Co., Palo Alto, Calif., 1996, exec. v.p., 1997—. Bd. dirs. Diablo Valley Estate Planning Coun., Walnut Creek, Calif., 1986-95, Planned Giving Coun. Santa Cruz County, Calif., 1993-94, Tri-Valley Estate Planning Coun., Pleasanton, 1989-2002; active Santa Clara County Estate Planning Coun., 1988-2002, Estate Planning Coun. So. Alameda County, 1988-92, Santa Cruz County Estate Planning Coun., 1989-2002, San Mateo County Estate Planning Roundtable, 1989-98, Silicon Valley Planned Giving Coun., 1992-, No. Calif. Planned Giving Coun., 1997-2002, Fin. Planning Forum, 1988-, Peninsula Estate Planning Coun., San Mateo, Calif., 1980-, pres., 1996-98, Tri-Valley Estate Planning Coun., 1996; active East Bay Estate Planning Coun., Oakland, Calif., 1991-, pres. 1997-98; bass Calvarymen Gospel Quartet; big band saxaphonist, clarinetist Elon Coll and USS Kasaan Bay; violinist Norfolk Symphony Orch., 1934-35, Bethel Ch. Orch., San Jose, Calif. Mem. Fin. Planning Assn. (bd. dirs. Silicon Valley chpt. 1997-99), Nat. Assn. Estate Planners Couns., Inst. Cert. Investment Mgmt. Cons., Alameda County Bar Assn. (estate planning probate sect. 1988-93), San Mateo County Bar Assn. (estate planning probate sect. 1983-95), Santa Clara County Bar Assn. (estate planning probate sect. 1988-2002), Pi Gamma Mu, Alpha Pi Delta. Avocations: golfing, photography, music. Home: 20278 Kilbride Dr Saratoga CA 95070 Office: Kelmoore Investment Co 2471 E Bayshore Rd # 501 Palo Alto CA 94303

PARKER, JAMES AUBREY, federal judge; b. Houston, Jan. 8, 1937; s. Lewis Almeron and Emily Helen (Stuessy) P.; m. Florence Fisher, Aug. 26, 1960; children: Roger Alan, Pamela Elizabeth. BA, Rice U., 1959; LLB, U. Tex., 1962. Bar: Tex. 1962, N.Mex. 1963. With Modrall, Sperling, Roehl, Harris & Sisk, Albuquerque, 1962-87; judge U.S. Dist. Ct. N.Mex., 1987—2000, chief judge, 2000—. Mem. Standing Commn. on Rules of Practice and Procedures of U.S. Cts., 1993-99, N.Mex. Commn. on Professionalism, 1986—; bd. visitors U. N.Mex. Law Sch., 1996—. Articles editor Tex. Law Rev., 1961-62. Mem. Fed. Judges Assn., Am. Judicature Soc., Am. Bd. Trial Advocates, N.Mex. Bar Assn. (Outstanding Judge award 1994), Albuquerque Bar Assn. (Outstanding Judge award 1993, 2000), Order of Coif, Chancellors, Phi Delta Phi. Avocations: ranching, fly fishing, running, skiing. Office: US Dist Ct 333 Lomas Blvd NW Ste 770 Albuquerque NM 87102-2277 Fax: 505 348-2225. E-mail: jparker@mncourt.fed.us.

PARKER, JAMES JOHN, engineering and marketing manager; b. June 16, 1947; s. John J. and Marjorie (Grohmann) P.; m. Mary P. Nash, Oct. 21, 1972; children: Elizabeth Ann, John James, Patricia Mary. BSEE, Marquette U., 1971; BSBA, Elmhurst Coll., 1981; MBA, U. Chgo., 1987. Student engr. Motorola Consumer Products, Franklin Park, Ill., 1968-70, engring. assoc., 1972-74; co-op engr. Warwick Electronics, Niles, 1971-72; sr. engr. R&D Quasar Electronics, Inc., Franklin Park, 1974-76; sr. project engr. Motorola Data Products, Carol Stream, Ill., 1976-79, Zenith Electronics Co., Glenview, 1979-82, market rsch. mgr., 1982-85, sect. mgr., 1985-86, program mgr., 1988-95; mgr. displays Zenith Data Sys./Groupe Bull, Buffalo Grove, 1995-96; v.p. mktg. AVC Tech, Niles, 1996-97; product mgr. Visiontek, Gurnee, Ill., 1997; dir. product planning Telular, Inc., Vernon Hills, 1997-98; mgr. product meeting Motorola BCS/SBNS, Schiller Park, 1998—2001. Faculty Wright Jr. Coll., Chgo., 1975-80. Mem. editl. bd. Electronic Products Mag., 1976-77. Adviser Jr. Achievement, Chgo., 1972-78; treas. I.C. Christian Svc. Commn., 1988-91; vol. Pub. Action to Deliver Shelter, 1987—; alderman 5th ward Elmhurst, 1993—; vice-chmn. fin. com. City of Elmhurst, 1995—, vice-chmn. telecom. and tech. adv. group. Mem. IEEE Midcon. (vice-chmn. pub. rels. 1979, chmn. spl. exhibits 1981, vice-chmn. spl. exhibits 1983), Delta Mu Delta. Home: 421 Berkley Ave Elmhurst IL 60126-3706 E-mail: jimparker@ameritech.net.

PARKER, JAMES ROGER, chemist; b. L.A., July 19, 1936; BS, Pomona Coll., 1958; PhD, Iowa State U., 1964. Lab. asst. Ames (Iowa) Lab Atomic Energy Commn., 1958-64; analytical supr. PPG Industries, Natrium, W.Va., 1964-73, Corpus Christi, Tex., 1973-82, agrl. chemist Barberton, Ohio, 1982-89, infrared spectroscopist Monroeville, Pa., 1989-96, scientist, 1996—. Contbr. articles to profl. jours. Mem. Am. Chem. Soc., Soc. for Applied Spectroscopy, Spectroscopy Soc. Pitts., Soc. for Analytical Chemists Pitts., Phi Lambda Upsilon. Achievements include research in analytical chemistry of metal halides, iodine compounds, alkali metal oxides, coordination chemistry of phosphine oxides, qualitative identifications with proton magnetic resonance spectroscopy and polymer analyses with photoacoustic infrared spectroscopy. Office: PPG Industries 440 College Park Dr Monroeville PA 15146-1553

PARKER, JAMES TERRY, counselor, consultant; b. Dallas, Mar. 1, 1958; s. Paul J. and Dora Mae (Turner) P. BS, Tex. A&M U., 1980; MS, East Tex. State U., 1985; grad. Drug and Alcohol Studies, Rutgers U., 1986; PhD, Tex. Woman's U., 1990. Cert. health edn. specialist, sch. health educator, Tex.; cert. profl. counselor; lic. athletic trainer, Tex. Classroom tchr., athletic trainer Plano (Tex.) Ind. Sch. Dist., 1981-87; grad. Sch. Drug and Alcohol Studies Rutgers U., 1986; head athletic trainer U.S. Nat. Youth Soccer Team, 1988-89; cons. Adolescent Health Promotion Consultants Ltd., Tex., 1984—; sch. counselor, tchr. health Waxahachie (Tex.) Ind. Sch. Dist., 1989—. Adj. instr. div. social scis. Cedar Valley Coll., 1991—. Contbr. articles to profl. jours. Nat. peer reviewer Comprehensive Sch. Health Edn. Programs U.S. Dept. of Edn. Mem. AACD (cert. profl. devel. counseling at-risk youth, nat. disting. svc. registry counseling and devel.), Sexuality Edn. Coun., Rsch. Coun., Am. Sch. Counselor Assn., Am. Sch. Health Assn. (coun. health behaviors, coun. sexuality edn., chmn. com. gay youth in schs.), Tex. Sch. Health Assn. (bd. govs. 1992—), Nat. Athletic Trainers Assn. (cert.), Chi Sigma, Eta Sigma Gamma, Phi Delta Kappa. Avocations: reading, cooking, entertaining, profl. writing.

PARKER, JANET, entrepreneur; b. Boston, June 9, 1958; d. Theodore B. and Lucy T. P. BA, Cornell U., 1980. Lic. real estate. Sales rep. McGraw-Hill Co., 1981-82; office mgr. Chestnut Hill (Mass.) Psych. Assn., 1982-85; adminstrv. dir., internat. educator The Parker Acad., Sudbury, Mass., 1985-93; dir. pub. rels. IRG/Computer Tune-Up Ctr., Sitka, Alaska, 1994—. Owner, mgr. gifts/exec. gifts UnCommon WhatNot, Needham, Mass., 1991-93. Cable TV prodr., host children's interactive storytime "Talking Story Time", Acton, Mass., 1987-90. Mem. Soc. for the Preservation of the Integrity of the Word "Unique". Avocation: writing children's stories. Office: PO Box 1222 Edgewood MD 21040-0522

PARKER, JEFFREY SCOTT, law educator; b. Alexandria, Va., Sept. 6, 1952; s. Clarence Franklin and Mary Florence (Partlow) P. B in Indsl. Engring., Ga. Inst. Tech., 1975; JD, U. Va., 1978. Bar: N.Y. 1979, U.S. Dist. Ct. (ea. and so. dists.) N.Y. 1979, U.S. Ct. Appeals (3d cir.) 1981, U.S. Ct. Appeals (2d cir.) 1984, U.S. Supreme Ct. 1984, U.S. Ct. Appeals (fed. cir.) 1985, U.S. Ct. Appeals (4th cir.) 1992, U.S. Ct. Appeals (D.C. cir.) 1997. Assoc. Sullivan & Cromwell, N.Y.C., 1978-86, Sacks Montgomery, N.Y.C., 1986-87; dep. chief counsel U.S. Sentencing Commn., Washington, 1987-88; of counsel Sacks Montgomery, N.Y.C., 1988-90; assoc. prof. law George Mason U Sch. Law, Arlington, Va., 1990-94; prof. George Mason U. Sch. Law, 1994—, assoc. dean acad. affairs, 1994-96. Cons. counsel U.S. Sentencing Commn., Washington, 1988-89. Contbr. articles to law revs.; mem. editorial bd. Va. Law Rev., 1976-78. Mem. ABA, Assn. of Bar of City of N.Y., N.Y. State Bar Assn., Am. Law and Econs. Assn., Am. Econs. Assn., Am. Judicature Soc. Office: George Mason U Sch of Law 3401 Fairfax Dr Arlington VA 22201-4411 E-mail: jparke3@gmu.edu.

PARKER, JENNIFER WARE, chemical engineer, researcher; b. Berkeley, Calif., Apr. 18, 1959; d. Raymond Paul and Maureen Christina (Trehearne) Ware; m. Henrik Davidson Parker, July 30, 1983; children: Katherine Joyce, Nathaniel Henrikson. BSChemE, Princeton U., 1980; MSChemE, UCLA, 1983, PhDChemE, 1986. Devel. engr. Am. Pharmaseal, Glendale, Calif., 1980-81; rsch. engr. Crump Inst. Med. Engring, UCLA, 1986-87; sr. engr. The BOC Group, Murray Hill, N.J., 1987-90, lead engr., 1990-92; sr. rsch. engr. CFM Techs., Inc., West Chester, Pa., 1993-97; v.p. CFMT Inc., Wilmington, Del., 1997-99, pres., 1999—2001, Mattson Tech. IP, 2001—. Contbr. articles to profl. jours. Mem. Am. Inst. Chem. Engrs., N.Y. Acad. Scis. Avocations: sports, music, gardening. Home: 201 W Country Club Ln Wallingford PA 19086-6507

PARKER, JOHN OSMYN, management consultant; b. Denver, May 31, 1919; s. George Lindsey and Marie (Bloedorn) P.; m. Judith Fehr, July 20, 1942; children: Craig Steven, John Fehr, Diane, Newton Lindsey. BS in Bus., U. Colo., 1942. Jr. indsl. engr. U.S. Steel Corp., Gary, Ind., 1942-43; mgr. pers. rsch. TWA, Kansas City, Mo., 1945-55; mgmt. cons. Douglas Williams Assocs., N.Y.C., 1955-56; dir. pers. Cen. Hudson Gas & Electric Corp., Poughkeepsie, NY, 1956—69, United Hosp., Port Chester, N.Y., 1969-78; v.p. human resources Mountainside Hosp., Montclair, N.J., 1978-83; mgmt. cons., 1983—. Instr. mgmt. Rutgers U., Ocean County Coll. Author: A Genealogical History of the Parker Family, 1996. Chmn. budget divsn., bd. dirs. United Way, Dutchess County, NB.Y., 1963-69; mem. adv. bd. Montclair Salvation Army; pres. Fellowship Club, Presbyn. Ch., 1985, elder, trustee, deacon; mem. Garden State Philharm. Chorus. With U.S. Army, 1943-45, ETO. Mem. Soc. for Human Resources Mgmt. (accredited exec. in pers.), Am. Soc. Tng. Dirs., Am. Mgmt. Assn., Am. Legion (trustee 1990-92, chaplain 1991-95), DAV (comdr. 1988-90, trustee 1990—), Rotary (bd. dirs. Rye, N.Y. 1975-78, pres. 1977-78, bd. dirs. Montclair 1978-83, bd. dirs. Ctrl. Ocean, Toms River, N.J. 1985-88, 94-95), Phi Kappa Psi. Republican. Home: 2751 Meadow Lake Dr Toms River NJ 08755-2546 E-mail: jparker55@compuserve.com.

PARKER, JOHN CARLYLE, retired librarian and archivist, editor; b. Ogden, Utah, Oct. 14, 1931; s. Levi and Marietta (Parkinson) P.; m. Janet C. Greene, May 31, 1956; children: Denise, Nathan, Bret. BA, Brigham Young U., 1957; MLS, U. Calif., Berkeley, 1958. Cert. jr. coll. life credential, Calif. Spl. svcs. libr. Humboldt State U., 1958-60; cataloger, reference libr. Ch. Coll. Hawaii, 1960-62, acting libr., 1962-63; head Pub. svcs. Calif. State U. Libr., Stanislaus, 1963-68, head pub. svcs., asst. libr. dir., 1968-83, 84-90, acting libr. dir., 1983-84, univ. archivist, 1990-94, libr. and univ. archivist emeritus, 1994—. S ctr. reference svc. for genealogists and geneal. rsch. for genealogists, 1966-98; cons. Bailey's Moving and Storage Co., Allied Van Lines, Bountiful, Utah, 1983-85, Gale Rsch. Co., Detroit, 1986, 92, E & J Gallo Winery, Modesto, Calif., 1990; editor Marietta Pub. Co., 1985—. Author: Library Service for Genealogists, 1981, Going to Salt Lake City to Do Family History Research, 3d rev. and expanded edit., 1996; compiler numerous books, including Directory of Archivist and Librarian Genealogical Instructors, 2d edit., 1990, Rhode Island Biographical and Genealogical Sketch Index, 1991; contbr. articles and book revs. to profl. jours. Founder, vol. libr. Modesto Family History Ctr., 1968-90, Turlock (Calif.) Family History Ctr., 1990-97; chmn. Stanislaus County United Way campaign Calif. State U., Stanislaus Campus, 1980-81; sec. bd. dirs. Turlock Centennial Found., 1971-75; pres. Turlock Cmty. Concert Bd., 1973-75; trustee Turlock Libr., 1969-70; merit badge counselor Yosemite coun. Boy Scouts Am., 1973—. With U.S. Army, 1953-55. Fellow Utah Geneal. Assn., 1984. Mem. ALA (chmn. genealogy com. 1989-92, award reference and adult svcs. divsn., history sect.-Geneal. Pub. Co. award 1994, fellow 1965), AAUP, Nat. Geneal. Soc. (award of merit 1984), Calif. Libr. Assn. (pres. Redwood dist. 1959-60, state coll. librs. divsn. 1969, chmn. geneal. librs. round table 1994, 96-97), Calif. State Geneal. Alliance (historian 1991—), Stanislaus County Hist. Soc. (v.p., program chmn. 1972-73), Geneal. Soc. Stanislaus County (hon.), Turlock Hist. Soc. Democrat. Me. LDS Ch. Avocations: birding, travel, singing solos and duets and in choirs. Home: 2115 N Denair Ave Turlock CA 95382-1821

PARKER, JOHN MALCOLM, management and financial consultant; b. Halifax, N.S., Can., June 13, 1920; came to U.S., 1936, naturalized, 1942; s. Charles Fisher and Mabel (Hennigar) P.; m. Irene Wilson Davis, Oct. 11, 1942 (dec. Nov. 1987); 1 child, Elane Parker Jones; m. Kathryn Harvey Smithey, Apr. 22, 1989. Cert. internal auditor. With Standard Oil Co. N.J., Charlotte, N.C., 1941, Duke Power Co., Charlotte, 1941-42, Do. Bell Tel. & Tel. Co., Charlotte, 1946-50, Atlanta, 1950-68, South Ctrl. Bell Telephone Co., Birmingham, Ala., 1968-83, asst. v.p., gen. internal auditor; pres. Omega Assocs. Inc., 1983—. Commr. gen. assembly Presbyn. Ch. of U.S., 1980, 81. With AUS, 1942-46. Mem. Inst. Mgmt. Accts. (pres. local chpt. 1972-73, nat. dir.), Am. Mgmt. Assn., Inst. Internal Auditors (pres. chpt. 1978-79, dist. dir. 1979-81, regional dir. 1981-83, internat. vice chmn. 1983-84, internat. bd. dirs. 1979-87, v.p. found. 1984-85), Internat. Platform Assn. Republican. Home and Office: 4509 Clairmont Ave S Birmingham AL 35222-4438

PARKER, JOHN MARCHBANK, consulting geologist; b. Manhattan, Kans., Sept. 13, 1920; s. John Huntington and Marjorie Elizabeth (Marchbank) P.; m. Agnes Elizabeth Potts, Mar. 17, 1978; m. Jan Goble, July 18, 1941 (div. 1968); children— Susan Kelly, Elizabeth Douglass, Deirdre Parker, John Eric; m. Nancy Booth, Jan. 24, 1970 (div. 1974). Student U. Minn., 1937, U. Wyo., 1938; B.S., Kans. State U., 1941. Cert. petroleum geologist Am. Inst. Profl. Geologists. Geologist, U.S. Pub. Roads Adminstrn., Alaska Hwy., Can., 1942-43; Field geologist Imperial Oil Ltd., Northwest Ter., Can., 1943-44; dist. geologist Stanolind Oil & Gas Co., Casper, Wyo., 1944-52; v.p. exploration Kirby Petroleum Co., Houston, 1952-74; v.p. exploration Northwest Exploration Co., Denver, 1974-75; cons. geologist Denver, 1975— . Contbr. articles to profl. jours. Recipient Disting. Service in Geology award Kans. State U., 1983. Fellow AAAS, Geol. Soc. Am.; mem. Am. Assn. Petroleum Geologists (pres. 1982-83, adv. council Tulsa 1983-84, Hon. Mem. award), Rocky Mountain Assn. Geologists (explorer of yr. 1979; pres. 1980-81). Home: 25422 Sea Bluffs Dr Unit 207 Dana Point CA 92629-2192

PARKER, JOHN RANDOLPH, pathologist, educator; b. Rochester, Minn., Apr. 29, 1967; s. Joseph Corbin and Patricia (Singleton) P. BA, U. Mo., Kansas City, MD, 1993. Diplomate Am. Coll. Forensic Medicine, Am. Bd. Anatomic Pathology, Forensic Pathology, and Neuropathology. Rsch. asst. U. Tenn. Meml. Hosp., Knoxville, 1985; pathology student fellow U. Mo. Sch. Medicine, 1989-90; intern in diagnostic radiology U. Okla. Health Scis. Ctr., Oklahoma City, 1993-94, resident in anatomic pathology, 1994-96; fellow in forensic pathology office of chief med. examiner State of Okla., 1996-97; chief fellow in surg. pathology U. Tex.-M.D. Anderson Cancer Ctr., Houston, 1997-98, mem. faculty dept. pathology, 1998-99; neuropathology fellow dept. pathology Baylor Coll. Medicine, 1999-2000, Vanderbilt U. Med. Ctr., Nashville, 2000-01, mem. faculty dept. pathology, 2001—. Contbr. articles to Annals of Clin. and Lab. Sci., Archives of Pathology, Jour. Okla. State Med. Assn., Gynecologic Oncology, others. Organizer 4-H Summer Scholars Med. Terminology, Lakewood Hosp., 1989-91; co-chmn. Impaired Med. Student Coun., 1990-91. Recipient Richardson K. Noback Clin. Excellence award, 1993, Gov.'s commendation State of Okla., 1995, cert. of appreciation Office of Chief Med. Examiner, State of Okla., 1995, U. Okla. Lloyd and Ruth Rader Trust Scholarship award, 1995-96, AMA/Glaxo Wellcome Leadership award, 1997. Mem. AMA, Am. Coll. Forensic Examiners, Coll. Am. Pathologists, Am. Soc. Clin. Pathologists, Nat. Assn. Med. Examiners, U.S. and Can. Acad. Pathology, Mortar Board, Golden Key, Alpha Omega Alpha, Omicron Delta Kappa. Office: Vanderbilt U Med Ctr Dept Pathology C-3321 Medical Center North Nashville TN 37232-2562 E-mail: winoglue@aol.com.

PARKER, JOHN RICHARD, mechanical engineer, consultant; b. Cleve., May 2, 1935; s. Walter Coleman Parker and Irene Margaret King; m. Sandra L. Heinzerling, June 16, 1956 (div. Nov. 1988); children: Elisabeth Anne, Susan Lee, Penelope Jane; m. Marilyn Anne Matthessen, Oct. 6, 1990. BSME, Case Inst. Tech., 1956; MSME, U. Conn., 1959; MBA, NYU, 1986. Registered profl. engr., Ohio. Supervising engr. Electric Boat Divsn., Groton, Conn., 1956-69; dept. head Stanley Consultants, Muscatine, Iowa, 1969-72; dir. engring. Air Correction Divsn. Universal Oil Products, Darien, Conn., 1972-74; project mgr. Sanderson and Porter, N.Y.C., 1974-79; fin. mgr. Ebasco Svcs., Inc. (later Raytheon Engrs. and Constrns.), 1979-88; cons., 1998—. Mem. Engrs. Pub. Policy Coun., Washington, 1994-97; mem. steering com. Engrs. Week, Washington, 1994-97; elder Noroton Presbyn. Ch., Darien, 1995-99; tubist New Canaan (Conn.) Town Band, 1985—. Fellow ASME (sr. v.p. 1994-97, v.p. 1995-97, gov. 1997-2000, pres. 2000-01, Disting. Svc. award 1994); mem. Am. Assn. Engring. Socs. (vice chmn. 2001), United Engring. Found. (bd. dirs. 2001), Alpine Club of Can., Roton Point Club. Avocations: hiking, cross country skiing, sailing, music. Home: 30 Wilson Ave Norwalk CT 06853 Office: ASME Internat 3 Park Ave New York NY 10016 E-mail: parkerj@asme.org.

PARKER, JOHN VICTOR, federal judge; b. Baton Rouge, Oct. 14, 1928; m. Mary Elizabeth Fridge, Sept. 3, 1949; children: John Michael, Robert Fridge, Linda Anne. BA, La. State U., 1949, JD, 1952. Bar: La. 1952. Atty. Parker & Parker, Baton Rouge, 1954-66; asst. parish atty. City of Baton Rouge, Parish of East Baton Rouge, 1956-66; atty. Sanders, Downing, Kean & Cazedessus, Baton Rouge, 1966-79; chief judge U.S. Dist. Ct., Middle Dist. La., 1979—. Vis. lectr. law La. State U. Law Sch. Served with Judge Adv. Gen.'s Corps U.S. Army, 1952-54. Mem. ABA, Am. Judicature Soc., Am. Arbitration Assn., La. State Bar Assn. (past mem. bd. govs.), Baton Rouge Bar Assn. (past pres.), Order of Coif, Phi Delta Phi. Clubs: Baton Rouge Country. Lodges: Masons (32 deg.); Kiwanis (past pres.). Democrat. Office: Russell B Long Fed Bldg & Courthouse 777 Florida St Ste 355 Baton Rouge LA 70801-1717

PARKER, JOHN WILLIAM, pathology educator, investigator; b. Clifton, Ariz., Jan. 5, 1931; m. Barbara A. Atkinson; children: Ann Elizabeth, Joy Noelle, John David, Heidi Susan. BS, U. Ariz., 1953; MD, Harvard U., 1957. Diplomate Am. Bd. Pathology. Clin. instr. pathology U. Calif. Sch. Medicine, San Francisco, 1962-64; asst. prof. U. So. Calif. Sch. Medicine, L.A., 1964-68, assoc. prof., 1968-75, prof., 1975-98, prof. emeritus, 1998—, dir. clin. labs., 1974-94, vice chmn. dept. pathology, 1985-97, dir. pathology reference labs., 1991-94, assoc. dean sci. affairs, 1987-89, prof. emeritus, 1998—. Co-chmn. 15th Internat. Leucocyte Culture Conf., Asilomar, Calif., 1982; chmn. 2d Internat. Lymphoma Conf., Athens, Greece, 1981; v.p. faculty senate U. So. Calif., 1991-92; bd. dirs. ann. meeting Clin. Applications of Cytometry, Charleston, S.C., 1988-97. Founding editor (jour.) Hematological Oncology, 1982-93; assoc. editor Jour. Clin. Lab. Analysis, 1985-98; co-editor: Intercellular Communication in Leucocyte Function, 1983; founding co-editor (jour.) Communications in Clin. Cytometry, 1993-97; contbr. over 200 articles to profl. jours., chpts. to books. Named sr. oncology fellow Am. Cancer Soc., U. So. Calif. Sch. Medicine, 1964-69, Nat. Cancer Inst. vis. fellow Walter and Eliza Hall Inst. for Med. Research, Melbourne, Australia, 1972-73. Fellow Coll. Am. Pathologists, Am. Soc. Clin. Pathologists; mem. Am. Assn. Pathologists, Am. Soc. Hematology, Internat. Acad. Pathology, Clin. Cytometry Soc. (v.p. 1994-95, pres. 1995-97), Phi Beta Kappa, Phi Kappa Phi. Avocations: gardening, reading, hiking. Office: Csc 108 2250 Alcazar St Los Angeles CA 90089-0107

PARKER, JOSEPH CORBIN, JR. pathologist, educator; b. Richmond, Va., Aug. 1, 1937; s. Joseph Corbin and Alice Cabell (Horsley) P.; m. Patricia Singleton, June 24, 1961; children: John Randolph, Nancy Jordan. BA, Va. Mil. Inst., 1958; MD, Med. Coll. Va., 1962; MS in Pathology, U. Minn., 1968. Fellow Mayo Clinic, Rochester, Minn., 1963-68; asst. prof. Duke U., Durham, N.C., 1969-70, Harvard U., Boston, 1970-71; assoc. prof. U. Ky., Lexington, 1971-75; prof. U. Miami, Fla., 1975-81; assoc. dean, prof. U. Tenn., Knoxville, 1981-86; prof. pathology, chmn. U. Mo., Kansas City, 1986-92;

chair dept. pathology U. Louisville Sch. Medicine, 1992—96, A.J. Miller prof., 1996—2001, prof. pathology and lab. medicine, 2002—. Bd. dirs. Truman Med. Ctr., Kansas City, Mo., Hosp. Hill Health Svc., Kansas City. Author 4 chpts. in books; contbr. 100 articles to profl. jours. Bd. dirs. Multiple Sclerosis Soc., Knoxville, Tenn., 1985, Alzheimers Assn., Kansas City, 1988-91, U. Louisville Med. Sch. Fund. 1st lt. USAR, 1958-67. Recipient 1st Jackson -Hope medal Va. Mil. Inst., 1958; Caldwell award Alzheimers Assn., 1986. Fellow Am. Asns. Neuropathology, Am. Soc. Clin. Pathology, Coll. Am. Pathology, Assn. Clin. Scientists; mem. So. Med. Assn., Am. Acad. Neurology, Am. Soc. Neurol. Surgeons, Univ. Pathologists (pres.). Democrat. Unitarian Universalist. Achievements include discovery of autosomal recessive neonatal adrenal leuko-distrophy. Home: 4606 Wolf Creek Pky Louisville KY 40241-5502 Office: U Louisville Sch Medicine Dept Pathology Louisville KY 40292-0001

PARKER, JOSEPH MAYON, printing and publishing executive; b. Washington, Oct. 11, 1931; s. James Mayon and Mildred (Poe) P.; m. Lauretta Owen Dyer, Mar. 23, 1957; children: Katherine Suzanne, Joseph Wilbur. Student, Davidson Coll., 1949-51; BA, U. N.C., 1953, MPA, 1992; postgrad., Carnegie Inst. Tech., 1955-56. From mgr. print divsn. to pres. Parker Bros., Inc., Ahoskie, NC, 1956—77, pres., CEO, 1977—2001; dir. Gov.'s Hwy. Safety Program, 1993—2001. Treas. Chowan Graphic Arts Found., Murfreesboro, N.C., 1971-90, pres. 1990-92. Editor, columnist five community newspapers, N.C.; panelist: (TV talk show) North Carolina This Week, 1986-89. Mem. Ind. Devel. Commn., 1974-86; vice chmn. N.C. Goals and Policy Bd., Raleigh, 1977-84; trustee Pitt County Meml. Hosp., 1980-88; pres. Com. of 100, Winton, N.C., 1984-87; chmn. Northeastern N.C. Tomorrow, Elizabeth City, 1981-84, sec., 1984-90; del. Dem. Nat. Conv., N.Y.C., 1980, platform com., 1988; dist. chmn. N.C. Dem. Ctrl. Com., 1980-82. With U.S. Army, 1953-54, col. USAR, 1954-88. Mem. Soc. Profl. Journalists, East N.C. Press Assn. (past pres.), N.C. Press Assn., Nat. Newspaper Assn. (state chmn. 1976-83), Roanoke Island Hist. Assn. (vice-chmn. 1987-89), Ea. N.C. C. of C. (past chmn.), Rotary, Raleigh Exec. Club. Democrat. Methodist. Avocations: golf, reading. Home: 4500 Connell Dr Raleigh NC 27612-5600 Office: 215 E Lane St Raleigh NC 27601-1035 E-mail: jpark4173@aol.com.

PARKER, JOYCE STEINFELD, social worker; b. Neptune, N.J., Dec. 11, 1946; d. Milton Donald and Lillian (Sonia) Steinfeld; m. Lawrence Neil Parker, Sept. 18, 1970 (div. Sept. 1990); children: Jill Monica, Gregory Robert. MEd, Boston U., 1969; MSW, UCLA, 1976; PhD, U.S.C., 1992. Lic. social worker. Tchr. spl. edn. Dearborn Sch., Boston, 1969-70, Christ Ch. Child Ctr., Bethesda, Md., 1970-71; tchr. 1st grade Hiroshima (Japan) Internat. Sch., 1971-72; clin. social worker Orange County Mental Health, Westminster, Calif., 1976-80; employee asst. affiliate Human Affairs Internat., L.A., 1987—; instr. U. So. Calif. Sch. Social Work, 1988-90; pvt. practice clin. social work Torrance, Calif., 1981—. Community speaker parenting, marriage, psychol. topics, So. Bay of La., 1983—. Fellow NASW, Soc. Clin. Social Work (cert. employee assistance profl.). Avocations: gourmet cooking, skiing, tennis, golf.

PARKER, KAREN F. sociology educator; b. Monroe, N.C., Apr. 6, 1967; d. Judy Draughon and Sammy Frank Parker; m. Aaron D. Griffin, Nov. 15, 1997. BA in Sociology, U. N.C., Wilmington, 1989; MS, N.C. State U., 1992, PhD, 1996. Asst. prof. sociology U. Fla., Gainesville, 1996—2001, assoc. prof. sociology, 2002—. Contbr. chpts. to books and articles to profl. jours. Mem. Am. Sociol. Assn., Am. Soc. Criminology, So. Sociol. Soc., Homicide Rsch. Working Group. Office: Univ Fla Criminology & Law Box 115950 Gainesville FL 32611-5950 Office Fax: 352-392-5065. E-mail: karenp@ufl.edu.

PARKER, KEITH DWIGHT, sociology educator; b. Phila., Oct. 15, 1954; s. Emery Woodruff, June 20, 1981; children: Narroyl, Malcolm. BA, Delta State U., Cleveland, Miss., 1978; MA, Miss. State U., 1982, PhD, 1986. Asst. dean students Delta State U., 1979-82; asst. prof. sociology Auburn (Ala.) U., 1986-89, U. Nebr., Lincoln, 1989-94, assoc. prof., 1994—, dir. African Am. studies, 1993—. Mem. editl. adb. bd. Jour. Social and Behavioral Scis., 1990—; cons. editor Internat. Jour. Contemporary Sociology, 1991-95; contbr. articles to profl. jours. Bd. dirs. Lincoln-Lancaster Drug Project, 1992—, Salvation Army, Lincoln, 1993—. Recipient Barbara Jordan award Big 8 Conf. on Student Govt., 1991. Mem. Midwest Sociol. Soc., Am. Soc. Criminology. Democrat. Baptist. Office: U Nebr 730 Oldfather Hall Lincoln NE 68588-0324

PARKER, KEVIN JAMES, electrical engineer educator; BS in Engring. Sci. summa cum laude, SUNY, Buffalo, 1976; MSEE, MIT, 1978, PhD, 1981. Rsch. assoc. lab. for med. ultrasound MIT, Cambridge, 1977-81; asst. prof. dept. electrical engring. U. Rochester, N.Y., 1981-85, assoc. prof., 1985-91, assoc. prof. dept. radiology, 1989-91, prof., 1992—, chair, 1992-98, dean sch. engring. & applied scis., 1998—. Dir. Rochester Ctr. Biomedical Ultrasound, 1990—; com. mem. Internat. Symposium on Ultrasound Imaging, 1989—. Editorial bd. Ultras. Med. Biology, 1989—; contbr. numerous articles to profl. jours., chpts. to books. Fellow NIH, 1979, Lilly Teaching fellow, 1982; named IBM Supercomputing Contest Finalist, 1989; recipient Ultrasound in Medicine and Biology prize World Fed., 1991, Outstanding Innovation award Eastman Kodak Co., 1991. Fellow IEEE, Am. Inst. Ultrasound in Medicine (ethics com. 1987-90, standards com. 1990-93, bd. govs. 1996-99, Joseph P. Holmes Pioneer award 1999), Acoustical Soc. Am. Achievements include 13 patents in field. Office: Univ of Rochester Sch Engring & Applied Scis Lattimore Bldg Rm 306 Rochester NY 14627-0076

PARKER, KIMBERLY JANE, nonprofit association executive, paralegal; b. Ann Arbor, Mich., Sept. 24, 1958; d. John Richard and Jane Eleanor (Twichell) P. BA in Polit. Sci., U. Redlands, 1980; Cert. in Legal Assistantship, U. Calif. Irvine, 1983, Cert. in Non-Profit Exec. Mgmt., 1990; Cert. in Adminstrn. Non-Profit Programs, Calif. State U. Long Beach, 1991; MA in Psychol. Studies, Trinity Coll. Grad. Studies, 1996. Hostess Disneyland, Anaheim, Calif., 1976-80; legal sec., asst. John R. Parker Law Corp., Orange, 1976-81; legal asst. C.D. Daly Law Corp., Newport Beach, 1981-83; exec. dir. Christian Conciliation Svc., Anaheim, 1983—. Editor: Peacemaker's Handbook; contbr. articles to profl. jours. Grad. Leadership Orange, 1993. Recipient Cert. of Appreciation, County of Orange, 1992; grantee Christian Conciliation, 1985. Mem. Calif. Assn. Marriage & Family Therapists, Christian Legal Soc., Christian Ministry Mgmt., So. Calif. Mediation Assn., County Assn. Dispute Resolution, Christian Conciliation Svc. (bd. dirs. 1983—), Assn. Christian Therapists, Christian Assn. Psychol. Studies, Vol. Ctr. of Orange County, Christian Arbitrator and Mediation Svcs., Inc. Republican. Presbyterian. Avocations: theology, snow skiing, reading, hiking.

PARKER, LARRY LEE, electronics company executive, consultant; b. St. Paul, Oct. 21, 1938; s. Clifford Leroy and Evelyn Elaine (McArtor) P.; m. Esperanza Victoria Delgado, Aug. 7, 1965; children: Sean Lawrance, Nicole Kathleen. AA in Engring., Antelope Valley Coll., Lancaster, Calif., 1964; BS in Indsl. Engring., U. Calif., Berkeley, 1966, MS in Ops. Rsch., 1968. Prin., cons. Ted Barry & Assocs., L.A., 1968-73; v.p. mfg. Pacific divsn. Mark Controls, Long Beach, Calif., 1973-79; v.p. world ops. ARL divsn. Bausch & Lombe, Sunland, 1979-84; pres. control products divsn. Leach Corp., Buena Park, 1984-88, exec. v.p., chief operating officer parent co., 1988-90, pres., COO, 1990-96; pres. bd. dirs. Leach Internat., Asia-Pacific, 1996—2001; chmn. bd. Leech-Tianyi China Joint Venture, 2001—. Advisor engring. coun. U. Calif., Long Beach, 1990—2001; bd. dirs. So. Calif. Tech. Exec. Network. Bd. dirs. Calif. Coalition Internat. Trade, L.A. Transp. Found., 1990—2001. With USN, 1956—59. Recipient Outstanding Achievement award Los Angeles County Bd. Suprs., 1964. Mem. Am. Prodn. Inventory Control Soc. (mem. exec. com. mfg.), Am. Electronics Assn. (pres.'s roundtable), Calif. Coalition U.S.-China Rels. Avocations: fishing, supporting world glass manufacturing, international trade. Home: 2711 Canary Dr Costa Mesa CA 92626-4747 Office: Leach Corp PO Box 5032 Buena Park CA 90622-5032

PARKER, LARRY MAYNARD, television producer; b. Moline, Ill., Sept. 29, 1951; s. David Cecil and Fern Mary (Wendstrom) P. Cert., Germain Sch. Photography, N.Y.C., 1970; student, Black Hawk Coll., 1970-72. Dir. Sta. WQAD-TV, Moline, 1972-73, news photographer, 1978-79; TV specialist Black Hawk Coll., 1973-77; prodn. mgr. Videography, Inc., Chgo., 1977-78; news photographer, promotion producer Sta. WESH-TV, Orlando, Fla., 1979-83; dir., designer on-air advt. Sta. WJXT-TV, Jacksonville, 1983-86, dir. creative services, 1986-87, creative dir., 1987-89, Sta. WTSP-TV, St. Petersburg, 1989-93, WREG-TV, Memphis, 1993-94; dir. advt. and promotion KPRC-TV, Houston, 1994—99; v.p. creative svc. and programming KRIV-TV, 1999—2002; v.p. creative svcs. KRIV-TV/KTXH-TV, 2002—. Recipient Fla. Emmy award Nat. Acad. TV Arts and Scis., 1984, 86, 87. Mem. Broadcast Promotion and Mktg. Execs. (Gold award 1986), Am. Film Inst. Democrat. Lutheran. Avocations: films, writing, graphic design. Home: 10027 Spice Ln Apt 1502 Houston TX 77072-5030

PARKER, LEA JANE, communications educator; b. Moline, Ill., Nov. 17, 1947; d. James Elden and Margaret Lorraine Mecum; m. Gary Allen Lundburg, June 10, 1967 (div. Nov. 1983); children: Jessica Ann, Jaina Lorraine; m. Richard Anthony Parker, June 3, 1985. BA, Ariz. State U., 1972; MA, No. Ariz. U., 1983. Science tchr. Deer Valley Jr. H.S., Phoenix, 1972-75; pub. rels. specialist Marifarms, Inc., Panama City, Fla., 1969-70; from staff reporter to Cmty. News editor The Ariz. Daily Sun, Flagstaff, 1985-89; from lectr. to asst. prof. environ. comm. & journalism No. Ariz. U., 1989—. Author: Kidnapped in Canyonlands, 1994, (textbook) Environmental Communication: Messages, Media & Methods, 1995, 97; regional editor, columnist Ariz. Living Mag., 1979-84; freelance writer, photographer Spirit Eagle Studio, Flagstaff, 1978—. Recipient Facilitator Svc. award Women's Polit. Caucus & NAV Leadership Program, 1993, Cmty. Svc. Reporting award Citizen's Against Substance Abuse, 1988. Mem. Nat. League of Am. Pen Women (treas. Flagstaff chpt.), Nat. Comm. Assn. Avocations: camping, hiking, photography, water sports. Office: No Ariz U Sch Comm PO Box 5619 Flagstaff AZ 86011-0001

PARKER, LEE FISCHER, sales executive; b. Chgo., Nov. 28, 1932; d. Meyer Louis and Lena (Raphael) Fischer; m. Joseph Schwartz, Mar. 18, 1950 (div. Jan. 1986); 1 child, Steven Darryl; m. Robert K. Parker, Jan. 13, 1991. Student, Mallinkrodt Coll., Wilmette, Ill., 1976. Freelance fashion model, Chgo., 1958-78; sales assoc. Neiman-Marcus, Northbrook, Ill., 1978-79; owner Keystone Svcs., Woodale, 1969-82; sales assoc. Marshall Field's, Skokie, 1986-94, Jacobson's, Boca Raton, Fla., 1996-99. Fashion coord. Arnie's Restaurant, Chgo., 1964-68, Blackhawk Restaurant, Chgo., 1964-66, Jim Conway TV Show, Chgo., 1968-70. Appeared in movie, 2000. Mem. Brandeis Women's Aux., Holocaust Mus. Democrat. Jewish. Avocations: golf, dancing, reading.

PARKER, MARY ANN, lawyer; b. Pitts., Jan. 6, 1953; d. Harry N. Sr. and Mary (Sperl) P.; 1 child, Nickolas Parker Palacios. BS cum laude, SUNY, Buffalo, 1975; JD, U. Tenn., 1977. Bar: Tenn. 1978, U.S. Dist. Ct. (mid. dist.) Tenn. 1978, U.S. Ct. Appeals (5th cir.) 1980, U.S. Supreme Ct. 1982, U.S. Ct. Appeals (6th cir.) 1987. Asst. Dist. Atty. Gen., Ashland City, Tenn., 1977-78; sole practice Nashville, 1978—. Instr. Nat. Trial Advocacy Coll., 1983-84. Cmty. svcs. vol. St. Henry's Women's Club, Nashville, 1984-90; mem. stewardship com. Holy Family, 1993—; mem. Women's Polit. Caucus, Nashville, 1986—, Tenn. Dem. Polit. Com., 1988—, Tenn. Dem. Fin. Com., 1991—; mem. Dem. Leadership Coun., 1991—, bd. dirs., 1992-96; bd. dirs. Monroe Harding Children's Home, 2000—. Mem. ABA, ATLA (del. 1983-86, sec. 1985-86, young lawyer's sect. sec. 1982-83, 2d vice chair 1983-84, 1st vice chair 1984-85, chair 1985-86, women's caucus sec. 1981-83, 1st vice chair 1983-84, chair motor vehicles, accidents, premises and govtl. liability sect. 1989-90, sec. torts sect. 1988-89, named Del. of Yr. 1986), Tenn. Trial Lawyers Assn. (bd. govs. 1978-86, chair consumer and victims coalition com. 1986-87), Trial Lawyers Pub. Justice (bd. govs. 1982—, treas. 1990-92, v.p. 1992-93, pres.-elect 1993-94, pres. 1994-95), Nashville Bar Assn. (ethics com. 1983—, chancery and cir. ct. com. 1993—), Tenn. Bar Assn., Pa. Trial Lawyers Assn., Alliance Franciase de Nashville (bd. dirs. 1998-2001), So. Ice Youth Hockey Assn. (bd. dirs. 2000—). Roman Catholic. Avocations: snow and water skiing, tennis, Scuba diving. Home: 5113 Fountainhead Dr Brentwood TN 37027-5809 Office: Parker & Crofford 209 10th Ave S Ste 511 Nashville TN 37203-0795

PARKER, MEL, editor; b. N.Y.C., Feb. 11, 1949; s. David Parker and Mollie (Kantorowicz) Lederman; m. Diane Nancy Goldberg, June 27, 1971; children: Emily, David. AB, Rutgers U., 1971; AM in English, NYU, 1973. Editl. rschr. Esquire Mag., N.Y.C., 1973; grad. asst. NYU Dept. English, 1974-77; adj. lectr. CUNY, 1977-78; editor Leisure Books, N.Y.C., 1978-81; sr. editor Playboy Paperbacks, 1981-82, Berkley Pub. Group, N.Y.C., 1982-85, exec. editor, 1985-86, editor-in-chief, 1986-87; v.p. editor-in-chief Warner Paperbacks, 1987-90, pub., 1990-96; sr. v.p. Warner Books, N.Y.C., 1996-98, sr. v.p., editor-in-chief Book-of-the-Month Club, 1999-2000; editl. dir. Bookspan, 2000—. Co-chair exec. pub. com. United Jewish Appeal Fedn.; mem. faculty Stanford Pub. Course, 1997-98. Mem. Jerusalem Book Fair Com., 1997—. Mem. Assn. Am. Publs. (chmn. trade exec. com. 1997-99), Book Table, Pub. Lunch Club (sec.-treas. 2000—, v.p. 2001-02). E-mail: mel.parker@bookspan.com.

PARKER, MICHAEL (MIKE PARKER), federal agency administrator; b. Laurel, Miss., Oct. 31, 1949; m. Rosemary Prather; children: Adrian, Marisa, Thomas. BA, William Carey Coll., 1970. Operator various businesses; mem. U.S. Congress from 4th Miss. dist., 1989-99; prin. Parker Malvaney Consulting, Brookhaven, Miss., 2000—01; asst. secy. civil works U.S. Dept. Defense, Washington, 2001—. Presbyterian. Office: US Dept Defense Civil Works 108 Army Pentagon Washington DC 20310-0108 Office Fax: 703-697-3366.*

PARKER, MICHAEL D. chemicals executive; BSChemE, U. Manchester (Eng.); MBA, Manchester Bus. Sch. With organics R & D Dow Internat., Freeport, Tex., 1968, prodn. engr., field sales position Birmingham, Eng., 1972-75, dist. sales mgr., 1975-77; product mktg. mgr. Epoxy resins Dow Europe, 1977, dir. mktg. inorganic chems., dir. mktg. organic chems., comml. dir. functional products dept., 1983-84; gen. mgr. splty. chems. dept. Dow U.S.A., Midland, Mich., 1984-87, group v.p. chems. and hydrocarbons, 1993-95; comml. v.p. Dow Pacific, Hong Kong, 1987-88, pres., 1988-93; pres., bus. v.p. chems. Dow N.Am., Midland, 1995—96; exec. v.p. Dow Chem. Co., 1996—2000, pres., CEO, 2000—, also bd. dirs. Bd. dirs. Dow Corning Corp. Bd. dirs. Nat. Legal Ctr. Pub. Interest. Mem. Nat. Assn. Mfrs. (bd. dirs.), Am. Plastics Coun. (bd. dirs.), Am. Chemistry Coun. Office: The Dow Chem Co 2030 Dow Ctr Midland MI 48674*

PARKER, MICHAEL G(EORGE), management consultant; b. N.Y.C., Jan. 26, 1950; s. Al and Florence (Samuels) P.; m. Linda M. Prager, June 2, 1985; 1 child, Stephanie Danielle. BA, SUNY, Buffalo, 1970; postgrad., U. N.C., Chapel Hill, 1970-74; cert. in health svcs. adminstrn., NYU, 1977; MBA, Baruch Coll., CUNY, 1981. Prodn. editor Acad. Press, Inc., N.Y.C., 1974-75; grants adminstr. Meml. Sloan-Kettering Cancer Ctr., 1975-78, pers. adminstr., 1978-79; planning analyst Mt. Sinai Med. Ctr., 1979-82; founder, project mgr. The Cybertec Cons. Group, Inc., 1982-90, v.p., 1991-93; mgr. KPMG Cons., 1993-94, sr. mgr., 1994-96, ptnr., 1996-99; v.p. for healthcare and life scis. Razorfish, 2000—01; dir. ISO Healthcare Cons., 2002—. Vice chmn. bd. trustees UN Internat. Sch.; pres. 101 W. 23 Apt. Inc., 1985—86; v.p. 244-246 Owners Corp., 1986—90, pres., 1990—. Mem. evaluation com. programs ARC, N.Y.C., 1980—82. Walter E. Heller fellow, 1981. Mem. Am. Soc. for Quality Control, Drug Info. Assn., Nat. Assn. for Health Care Quality, N.Y. Soc. for Health Planning (treas. 1996-97), N.Y. Acad. Scis., SUNY Buffalo Scis. Alumni Assn. (bd. dirs.), Beta Gamma Sigma. Home: 244 W 23d St Apt 5-b New York NY 10011-2330 Office: ISO Healthcare Cons 641 6th Ave New York NY 10011- E-mail: MiParker1@aol.com.

PARKER, MICHAEL J. editor, writer, researcher; b. Camden, N.J., Apr. 21, 1959; s. Harry J. and Charlotte D. Parker. BA, Glassboro State Coll., 1981. Mng. editor, regional editor Suburban Newspaper Group, Cherry Hill, N.J., 1980-82; database sketch editor Lehigh Press, Pennsauken, 1983; copy control editor, assoc. supr. Datapro, Delran, 1984-95, sr. data quality adminstr., 1996-98; editor Gartner Datapro, 1998—. Article writer, columnist Silent Film Monthly, Silent Film Annual, 1993-2000; freelance writer, 2001—; contbr. articles to The Grapevine. Assoc., coord. Homeless Hospitality Network, Merchantville, N.J., 1995—; rep. Echelon Mall Ministry, Voorhees, N.J., 1975-76; asst. to clergy First Presbyn. Ch., 1992—. Recipient cert. Borough of Haddonfield Commrs., 1981. Avocations: writing to members of the arts, collecting autographed items, exhibits, stamps, coins. Home: 2642 Union Ave Pennsauken NJ 08109-3671 Office: Gartner Datapro 600 Delran Pkwy PO Box 7001 Delran NJ 08075-0700 E-mail: mike.parker@gartner.com.

PARKER, NANCY CULBERTSON, small business owner, embroidery specialist; b. Ft. Worth, Oct. 17, 1951; d. Willis James and Kathryn (Griffin) C.; m. Gene Arrington, Jr., Jan. 4, 1975 (div. Oct. 1974); m. James Clyde Parker, Sept. 3, 1980; 1 stepchild, James Richard. Grad. high sch., Ft. Worth. Sec. Ft. Worth Fat Stock Show, 1979-80; intake sec. Edna Gladney Home, Ft. Worth, 1980-81; owner, mgr. P.D.Q. Monogramming Shop, 1981-85; owner, ptnr. P.D.Q. Monograms, Austin, Tex., 1986—. Freelance embroider for films Heartbreak Hotel, Hot Spot, TV film Two Aces, country music acts, TV network. Mem. Austin Volkswagen Club, Catalina 25 Boat Club. Democrat. Episcopalian. Avocations: sailing, dog shows, music. Office: PDQ Monogram Shop 3636 Bee Caves Rd Ste 109 Austin TX 78746-5376

PARKER, NANCY KNOWLES (MRS. CORTLANDT PARKER), publishing executive; b. Buffalo, Aug. 30, 1929; d. Ward Emerson and Barbara Louise (Bull) Knowles; m. Cortlandt Parker, Sept. 8, 1951; children: Elizabeth, Cortlandt, Stephen, Nancy Gray. Student, Chevy Chase Jr. Coll., 1949. Copy girl Washington Evening Star, 1947-49; reporter Newark Evening News, 1949-51; asst. pub. rels. dir. Newark Cmty. Chest, 1951-52; writer Suburban Life mag., Summit, N.J., 1952-55; co-founder, assoc. editor, then editor Observer Tribune, Mendham, 1955-59; cmty. living editor Recorder Pub. Co., Bernardsville, 1959-84, v.p., 1960—; editor, co-pub. New Eng., Finger Lakes, L.I. and Va. Wine Gazettes, 1988—. V.p. Greenvale Vineyards, Portsmouth, R.I. Former trustee Somerset Hills Cmty. Chest, North Jersey Tng. Sch., Totowa, Morris-Somerset chpt. UN Assn., Bonnie Brae Ednl. Ctr., Millington, N.J. Vis. Homemaker Svc. of Somerset County (N.J.); now trustee, bd. dirs. Camp Brett-Endeavor, Clinton, N.J., N.J. Hist. Soc., Newark, Morristown (N.J.) Meml. Hosp.; mem. Glen Manor House Com., Portsmouth, R.I. Mem. Bus. and Profl. Women, Nat. Soc. Arts and Letters, Southeastern New Eng. Grape Growers Assn., Jr. League, Pen and Brush N.Y.C., New Eng. Wine Coun. (sec.), Friends of Whitehall, Colonial Dames in Am. (former bd. dirs. R.I. chpt.), Newport (R.I.) Garden Club (bd. dirs., past pres.), English Speaking Union. Home: 582 Wapping Rd Portsmouth RI 02871-5306 also: Greenvale Farm & Vineyard 582 Wapping Rd Portsmouth RI 02871-5306 Office: 17 Morristown Rd Bernardsville NJ 07924-2312

PARKER, NANCY WINSLOW, artist, writer; b. Maplewood, N.J., Oct. 18, 1930; d. Winslow Aurelius and Beatrice (Gaunt) P. BA, Mills Coll., 1952; student, Sch. Visual Art, N.Y.C., Art Students League. Pub. relations exec. N.Y. Soccer Club, N.Y.C., 1961-63; with RCA, 1964-67; art dir. Appleton-Century-Crofts, 1968-70; staff designer Holt Reinhart & Winston, 1970-73; free lance writer, illustrator, 1974—. Author, illustrator: The Man with the Take-Apart Head, 1974, author, illustrator: The Party at the Old Farm, 1975, author, illustrator: Mrs. Wilson Wanders Off, 1976, author, illustrator: Love from Uncle Clyde, 1977, author, illustrator: The Crocodile Under Louis Finneberg's Bed, 1978, author, illustrator: The Presiden't's Cabinet, 1978, author, illustrator: rev. edit., 1991, author, illustrator: The Ordeal of Byron B. Blackbear, 1979, author, illustrator: Puddums, The Cathcarts' Orange Cat, 1980, author, illustrator: Poofy Loves Company, 1980 (ALA Notable Book, 1980), author, illustrator: The Spotted Dog, 1980, author, illustrator: The President's Car, 1981, author, illustrator: Cooper, The McNally's Big Black Dog, 1981, author, illustrator: Love from Aunt Betty, 1983, author, illustrator: The Christmas Camel, 1983, author, illustrator: The United Nations from A to Z, 1985; co-author: Bugs, 1987, Frogs,Toads, Lizards and Salamanders, 1990, Working Frog, 1992, Money, Money, Money, 1995, Locks, Crocs and Skeeters, The Story of the Panama Canal, 1996, Land Ho! Fifty Glorious Years in The Age of Exploration with 12 Important Explorers, 2001, (Christopher award, 1976), , (Christopher award, 1981), , , , . Sec. East 74th St. Block Assn., 1974-83. Recipient various awards, 1974— ; Jane Tinkham Broughton fellow, Breadloaf, Vt., 1975 Mem. Author's Guild, Mills Coll. Club of N.Y., Mantoloking Yacht Club. Home: Apt 3R 51 E 74th St New York NY 10021-2717 E-mail: nwparker52@aol.com.

PARKER, NORMAN NEIL, JR. software systems analyst, mathematics educator; b. Chgo., June 23, 1949; s. Norman Neil and Sarah Anne Parker; m. Rowena Robles, June 27, 1987. BS with honors, Iowa State U., 1971, MS with honors, 1974. Cert. secondary math. tchr., Ill. Grad. teaching asst. math. dept. Iowa State U., Ames, 1971-72; tchr. math. dept. Thornwood High Sch., South Holland, Ill., 1972-81; software system analyst, space shuttle software IBM, Houston, 1981-94; software system analyst Loral Space Info. Systems, 1994-96; sr. software sys. analyst Lockheed Martin Space Mission Systems & Svcs., 1996-98, chmn. software architecture rev. bd. for onboard shuttle, 1994—; computer scientist staff IV United Space Alliance, 1998—. Cons. Atomic Energy Commn., Iowa State U., Ames, 1970-72; Iowa State U. rep. NSF Regional Conf., Northfield, Minn., 1972. Contbr. articles to profl. jours. Life mem. Order of Demolay, 1963—; gymnastic judge Ill. High Sch. Assn., Nat. Gymnastics Judges Assn., Internat. Gymnastics Fedn., 1971-81; gymnastics coach Thornwood High Sch., South Holland, Ill., 1972-80; gymnastics program dir. South Holland Park Dist., 1976-80; devel. coord Spaceweek Corp., Houston, 1983-87; officer Filipino-Internat. Families Tex., Houston, 1989-93; mem. retreat team Christ Renews His Parish, 1994-2000, eucharistic min., 2001—, min. to the sick, 2001—; active Christian Action program, 1998-2001; active foster-adoption program Assoc. Cath. Charities, 2000—. Recipient Achievement award, NASA, 1994. Mem. AIAA (sr.), Clear Lake Area Spl. Interest Group Ada, Space Ctr. Object-oriented Projects and Engring. (charter), Johnson Space Ctr. Employees Activities Assn. (assoc.), Gong Yuen Chuan Fa Fedn. (sr.). Republican. Roman Catholic. Home: 4307 Alysheba Ln Friendswood TX 77546-2464 Office: United Space Alliance 1st Fl-1H3 600 Gemini St Houston TX 77058-2783 E-mail: norman.n.parker@usahq.unitedspacealliance.com.

PARKER, OLIVIA, photographer; b. Boston, June 10, 1941; d. Harvey Perley and Barbara Ellen (Churchill) Hood; m. John Otis Parker, Apr. 4, 1964; children: John Otis, Helen Elizabeth. BA, Wellesley Coll., 1963. Tchr. photog. workshops, 1975—. Photographer, 1969— ; author: (monographs) Signs of Life, 1978, Under the Looking Glass, 1983, Weighing the Planets, 1987; portfolios of black and white photographs Ephemera, 1977, Lost Objects, 1980; one-woman shows include, Vision Gallery, Boston, 1976, 77, 79, 82, 83, 86, 87, Friends of Photography, Carmel, Calif., 1979, 81, Marcuse Pfeifer, N.Y.C., 1980, 83, George Eastman House, Rochester, N.Y., 1981, Art Inst. Chgo., 1982, Photo Gallery Internat., Tokyo, 1983, 84, 87, Fotografie Forum Gallery, Frankfurt, Germany, 1985, Lieberman and Saul, N.Y.C., 1988, Mus. Photgraphic Arts, San Diego, 1988, Photographers' Gallery, London, 1990, Brent Sikkema, N.Y.C., 1990, 91, Parco, Tokyo, 1991, ICAC/Weston, Tokyo, 1992, Vision, San Francisco, 1993, Robert Klein, Boston, 1993, 96, 99, Wooster Gardens, N.Y.C., 1996, (with Jerry Velsmann) Isabella Stewart Gardner Mus., Boston, 1997, Huntington (W.Va.) Mus. of Art, 2000, Lancaster (Pa.) Mus. of Art, 2000, Toledo (Ohio) Art Mus., 2002; group shows include, Mus. Fine Arts, Boston, 1978, 92, 93, 96, 99, Chgo. Art Inst., 1978, Internat. Ctr. Photography, N.Y.C., 1985, 87, Fogg Art Mus. Harvard U., 1989; represented in permanent collections, Mus. Modern Art, N.Y.C., Art Inst. Chgo., Boston Mus. Fine Arts, Victoria and Albert Mus., London, (TV documentary) Africans in America, 1998. Bd. dirs. MacDowell Colony, 1988—; trustee Art Inst. Boston, 1992—. Artists Found. fellow, 1978; recipient Wellesley College Alumnae Achievement award, 1996. Mem. Soc. for Photog. Edn. Clubs: Chilton. Office: Robert Klein 4th Fl 38 Newbury St Fl 4 Boston MA 02116-3210 *I am interested in the way people think about the unknown. New ideas form, the old are shattered, and sometimes old ideas pop up among the new like graffiti on a wall. All is uncertainty and change, but optimists and bingo players are on the look out for moments of perfect knowledge and perfect cards.*

PARKER, PATRICK STREETER, manufacturing executive; b. Cleve., 1929; BA, Williams Coll., 1951; MBA, Harvard U., 1953. With Parker-Hannifin Corp. and predecessor, Cleve., 1953—, sales mgr. fittings div., 1957-63, mgr. aerospace products div., 1963-65, pres. Parker Seal Co. div., 1965-67, corp. v.p., 1967-69, pres., 1969-71, pres. and chief exec. officer, 1971-77, chmn. bd. and chief exec. officer, 1977-84, chmn. bd., 1984-99, pres., 1982-84, also bd. dirs., 1982-99, chmn. emeritus, 1999—. Bd. trustees Case Western Res. U.; With USN, 1954-57. Mem. Union Club, Country Club, Pepper Pike Club. Office: Parker Hannifin Corp 6035 Parkland Bvld Cleveland OH 44124-4141

PARKER, PAYUINA ERNEST, accountant, business consultant; b. Monrovia, Liberia, Sept. 28, 1959; s. Payuina Ernest and Johnet Claudia (Whitfield) P. BBA, U. Liberia, Monrovia, 1985; AA, Ricks Jr. Coll., 1980. CPA, Va. Mgr. Price Waterhouse, London and Monrovia, 1983-89, Nat. Bank of Washington, 1989-90, Gardiner, Kamya & Assoc., Washington, 1990-92; chmn., CEO Summit Fin. Ptnrs., Arlington, Va., 1993—; mng. ptnr. Parker Whitfield CPAs, 1992—. Mem. adv. bd. Summit Fin. Ptnrs., Arlington, 1994—. Author: (booklet) Strategies on Marketing to the Federal Government, 1993. Mem. Assn. Govt. Accts., Project Mgmt. Inst., Va. Bd. Accountancy. Presbyterian. Avocations: racquetball, golf, skiing, photography, dancing, reading. Office: Parker Whitfield & Co 1655 Fort Myer Dr Ste 700 Arlington VA 22209-3199

PARKER, R. JOSEPH, lawyer; b. St. Louis, June 29, 1944; s. George Joseph and Ann Rosalie Parker; m. Theresa Gaynor, Aug. 26, 1967; children: Christa Michele, Kevin Blake. AB, Georgetown U., 1966; JD, Boston Coll., 1969. Bar: Ohio 1969. Law clk. to judge U.S. Ct. Appeals (6th Cir.), Akron, Ohio, 1969-70; assoc. Taft, Stettinius & Hollister, Cin., 1970-78, ptnr. 1978—. Arbitrator Am. Arbitration Assn., Cin., 1980—; faculty Nat. Inst. for Trial Advocacy, 1990—; faculty advanced trial advocacy program IRS, 1993. Editor Law Rev. Ann. Survey Mass. Law, 1967-69; contbg. author: Fed. Civil Procedure Before Trial-6th Circuit. Bd. dirs. West End Health Ctr., Inc., Cin., 1972-76, Legal Aid Soc. Cin., 1982-85; chmn. bd. dirs. Vol. Lawyers for Poor Found., Cin., 1986-88; master Am. Inn of Court, 1984—. Fellow Am. Coll. Trial Lawyers; mem. Ohio State Bar Assn., Cin. Bar Assn., Cin. Country Club, Order of Coif. Democrat. Roman Catholic. Office: 1800 Star Bank Bldg 425 Walnut St Cincinnati OH 45202-3923

PARKER, RHONDA WALKER, clinical pathway coordinator; b. Laurel, Miss., June 2, 1955; d. Tom Ben and Darlene (McEachern) Walker; m. Michael Parker, Jan. 2, 1976; children: Holly, Noel, Caleb. Student, Jones County Jr. Coll., Ellisville, Miss., 1973-74, U. So. Miss., 1975; BSN, Miss. Coll., 1977; cert. in cons., Breast Feeding Support Cons., 1988. RN, Miss.; cert. lactation cons. Staff nurse, team leader Miss. Bapt. Med. Ctr., Jackson, 1977-81; staff nurse float pool Hinds Gen. Hosp., 1985-86; childbirth educator Childbirth Edn. Assn. of Met. Jackson, 1982-85; perinatal nurse educator Hinds Gen. Hosp., Jackson, 1986-90, Meth. Med. Ctr., Jackson, 1990-99; clin. pathway coord. Ctrl. Miss. Med. Ctr., 1999—. Home: 63 Springview Dr Brandon MS 39042-2308

PARKER, RICHARD BORDEAUX, writer, educator; b. The Philippines, July 3, 1923; s. Roscoe Stuart and Marguerite Helen (Blossom) P.; m. Jeanne Jaccard, June 23, 1944; children: Alison, Jeffrey, Jill, Richard. BS, Kans. State U., 1947, MS, 1948; postgrad., Princeton U., 1964-65. With U.S. Fgn. Svc., 1949—80, amb. Algeria, Lebanon, Morocco, 1975—79; diplomat-in-residence U. Va., Charlottesville, 1980-82; editor Mid. East Jour., Washington, 1981-87; pres. Assn. for Diplomatic Studies, Arlington, Va., 1986-89; fellow Wilson Ctr. Smithsonian Inst., Washington, 1989-90; writer, lectr., 1990—; scholar in residence Middle East Inst., 1994—. Vis. prof. Lawrence (Wis.) U., 1992-93; instr. Johns Hopkins U., Washington, 1994. Author: Guide to Islamic Monuments in Cairo, 1974, Guide to Islamic Monuments in Morocco, 1981, North Africa, 1984, Miscalculation in the Middle East, 1993 (Choice award 1994); editor: Six-Day War: A Retrospective, 1996, The October War: A Retrospective, 2001. John Adams fellow Fulbright Commn., 1990; recipient Fgn. Svc. Cup Diplomatic and Consular Officer Ret., 1989, Grande Cordon of Order Cedars, Lebanon, 1978. Mem. Mid. East Inst., Coun. Fgn. Rels., Am. Acad. Diplomacy, Assn. for Diplomatic Studies, Cosmos Club, Delta Tau Delta. Avocations: photography, gardening. Home: 3317 P St NW Washington DC 20007-2702 Office: Middle East Inst 1761 N St NW Washington DC 20036-2882

PARKER, RICHARD WILSON, lawyer, rail transporation executive; b. Cleve., June 14, 1943; s. Edgar Gael and Pauline (Wilson) P.; m. Helen Margaret Shober, Jan. 3, 1998; children from previous marriage: Brian Jeffrey, Lauren Michelle, Lisa Christine. BA in Econs. cum laude, U. Redlands, 1965; JD cum laude, Northwestern U., 1968. Bar: Ohio 1968, Va. 1974. Assoc. Arter & Hadden, Cleve., 1968-71; asst. gen. atty. Norfolk & Western Ry. Co., Cleve. and Roanoke, Va., 1971-74, asst. gen. solicitor Roanoke, 1974-78, gen. atty., 1978-84, Norfolk So. Corp., 1985-88, sr. gen. atty., 1988-93, asst. v.p. real estate, 1993-99, v.p. properties, 1999-2000, v.p. real estate, 2000—. Mem. ABA, Va. State Bar, Norfolk-Portsmouth Bar Assn. Presbyterian. Office: 3 Commercial Pl Norfolk VA 23510-2108

PARKER, ROBERT ALLAN RIDLEY, federal agency administrator, astronaut; b. N.Y.C., Dec. 14, 1936; s. Allan Elwood and Alice (Heywood) P.; m. Joan Audrey Capers, June 14, 1958 (div. 1980); children: Kimberly Ellen, Brian David Capers; m. Judith S. Woodruff, Apr. 2, 1981. AB, Amherst Coll., 1958; PhD, Calif. Inst. Tech., 1962. NSF postdoctoral fellow U. Wis., 1962-63, asst. prof., then assoc. prof. astronomy, 1963-74; astronaut NASA Johnson Space Ctr., 1967-91; dir. policy plan Office Space Flight, NASA Hdqs., Washington, 1991, dir. space ops. utilization program, 1992-97; dir. NASA Mgmt. Office, JPL, Pasadena, Calif., 1997—. Mem. support crew Apollo XV and XVII, mission scientist Apollo XVII, program scientist Skylab program, mission specialist for Spacelab 1, 1983, ASTRO-1, 1990. Mem. Am. Astron. Soc., Phi Beta Kappa. Office: NMO 180 801 JPL 4800 Oak Grove Dr Pasadena CA 91109-8001 E-mail: rparker@nmo.jpl.nasa.gov.

PARKER, ROBERT CHAUNCEY HUMPHREY, clergyman, publishing executive, psychic; b. N.Y.C., Apr. 6, 1941; s. Robert Humphrey and Edith Louise (Corya) P. Student, U. Va., 1960-61, 62-63; diploma, Inst. Psychorientology, Laredo, Tex., 1973. Ordained to ministry Ch. of Antioch-Malabar Rite, 1975. Law clk. Shearman & Sterling, N.Y.C., 1961-62; owner Parker's Pronto-Pups Inc., 1962-64; asst. to pres. U.S. Packaging, 1964-66; asst. nat. sales mgr. Elliott Svc. Co. Inc., Mt. Vernon, N.Y., 1966-67; pres., cons. Lenfield Assocs. & Cons., N.Y.C. and Washington, 1967-71; founder, pres. Occult Comm. Corp., N.Y.C., Washington, and Danbury, Conn., 1971-76, New Awareness Corp., London and Mpls., 1973-81; dir., resident minister The Healing Ctr. at St. Patricia's, Inver Grove Heights, Minn., 1975; lectr., minister Ch. of Antioch-Malabar Rite, 1975—; editor New Awareness News, 1975—; founder, pres. Parker/Tofte Comm., Robert Parker Assocs., Minnetonka, Minn., 1977—; pres., CEO Am. Energy & Alcohol Corp., Mpls., 1981-84. Cons. Boat Owners Assn. U.S., Washington, 1967-70, Durance Co., 1994-95; rschr., cons. Am. Marine Corp., Marblehead, Mass.; new product devel., venture capital and cons. investment, banking houses, N.Y.C. and Washington, 1967-71; dir., cons. to regional and nat. healing orgns. and publs., 1973-81; pres. Field Harmonics Rsch. Group Inc., 1993-97, New Awareness Spkrs. and Pub. Group, Inc., 1997—; spkr., tchr. numerous orgns. Author: Watergate Flight 553, 1974, Reabsorption Energy, 1975, Finding Your Own Four-Leaf Clover, 1993; author Telsa Newsletter, 1979; editor New Awareness Mag., 1973-75, (newsletter) Sunbeams; editor, pub. New Awareness News and Book News, 1977—, New Awareness Computer News, 1995—, psychic/parapsychology internat. trade jours., 1971-75; designer, pub.: Henry's Hilarious One Liners, 1991, Henry's Just a Chuckle, 1992, Henry's Just a Laugh, 1992, Henry's Just a Witticism, 1992; contbr. articles to profl. jours.; guest spkr. various radio, TV and Internet programs, including Dimension, Sta. WCCO-AM-FM; featured on Dimension WCCO-TV (CBS), 1991, 93, Forbes Mag., 1996; host cable TV program Astrology and Mind, Etc., 1994-96; syndicated columnist. Bd. dirs. Toutorsky Ednl. Found., Washington, 1988-91. Mem. Nat. Press Club (Washington), Internat. Telsa Soc. Inc., Knickerbocker Greys Vet. Corps (N.Y.C.), Browning Sch. Alumni Assn. (N.Y.C.), Lenox (Mass.) Sch. Alumni Assn. Avocations: sailing, reading, gardening, travelling, golf. Home and Office: 15310 Hwy 7 Minnetonka MN 55345-3520 E-mail: rchparker@aol.com.

PARKER, ROBERT DALE, civil engineer; b. Watertown, N.Y., July 21, 1951; s. Edson Adelbert Parker and Marjorie Lois (Goheen) Parker-Clark; m. Daphne Quinta, Aug. 25, 1978; children: April Beth, Amy Lynn. AAS, Canton Agrl. & Tech. Inst., 1972; B Tech., Rochester Inst. Tech., 1975. Registered profl. engr., Mich., N.Y. Process operator Monroe County Pure Waters, Rochester, N.Y., 1975-77; process ops. engr. Consoer, Townsend & Assocs., Chgo., 1978-79; engr. Rist Frost Assocs., Watertown and Glens Falls, N.Y., 1980-81; project rep. Stearns & Wheler Engrs., Cazenovia, 1979, 82, 83; design engr. Bernier Carr & Assocs., P.C., Watertown, 1983-90, sr. design engr., 1990-92, assoc. engr., 1992—. Author wastewater treatment facilities operation and maintenance manuals. Mem. bd. edn. Faith Fellowship Christian Sch., Watertown, 1987-94; elder River of Life Fellowship Ch., Copenhagen, N.Y., 1994—. Recipient cert. Nat. Coun. Examiners for Engring. and Surveying, 1991. Mem. NSPE, ASCE, Water Environ. Fedn., N.Y. State Soc. Profl. Engrs. Republican. Achievements include design of innovative alternative technology wastewater collection and treatment facilities. Home: 13825 County Route 156 Watertown NY 13601-5735

PARKER, ROBERT FREDERIC, university dean emeritus; b. St. Louis, Oct. 29, 1907; s. Charles T. and Lydia (Gronemeyer) P.; m. Mary L. Warner, June 20, 1934; children: David Frederic, Jane Eleanor (Mrs. Howard H. Hush, Jr.). BS, Washington U., St. Louis, 1925, MD, 1929. Diplomate: Am. Bd. Microbiology. Asst. radiology Washington U. Med. Sch., 1929-30, instr. medicine, 1932-33; asst. Rockefeller Inst., 1933-36; mem. faculty Case Western Res. U., 1936—, prof. microbiology, 1954-77, prof. emeritus, 1977—, assoc. dean, 1965-73, dean, 1973-76, dean emeritus, 1976—. Mem. Cleve. Acad. Medicine (past bd. dirs.), Am. Soc. Clin. Investigation, Central Soc. Clin. Research, Am. Acad. Microbiology, Sigma Xi, Alpha Omega Alpha. Achievements include spl. research virus immunology, quantitative aspects virus infection, tissue culture, action of antibiotics. Home: 1890 E 107th St Apt 226 Cleveland OH 44106-2242

PARKER, ROBERT LEE, SR. petroleum engineer, drilling company executive; b. Tulsa, July 16, 1923; s. Gifford Clevel and Gladys Carolyn (Baker) P.; m. Catherine Mae McDaniel, Dec. 16, 1944; children: Robert Lee, Carolyn Louise, Debra Ann. BS, U. Tex., 1944; LL.D. (hon.), John Brown U., 1967, Oral Roberts U., 1977. With Parker Drilling Co., 1947—, owner, mgr., 1953—, pres., 1954-92, chmn. bd., 1967—. Bd. dirs. CWI, Inc.; dir. Bank Okla.; chmn. Nat. Energy Task Force, 1981-82. Chmn. St. Francis Hosp., Tulsa, U. Tex. Engring. Found.; trustee U. Tulsa, 1st Methodist Ch., Tulsa; bd. dirs. Tulsa YMCA, Jr. Achievement, So. Meth. U.; active Boy Scouts Am. Served with U.S. Army, 1945-47. Named Distinguished Engring. Grad. U. Tex., 1969 Mem. Am. Petroleum Inst., Internat. Assn. Drilling Contractors, Okla. Ind. Petroleum Assn., Soc. Profl. Engrs. Clubs: So. Hills Country, Tulsa, Houston. Republican. Office: Parker Drilling Co 2021 S Lewis Ste 600 Tulsa OK 74104 *A discipline of character and work, an enthusiasm for life and an awareness of God's constant help have all had positive impacts on my life.*

PARKER, ROBERT M. federal judge; b. Longview, TX, Oct. 19, 1937; BBA, U. Tex., 1961, JD, 1964. Bar: Tex. 1964. Ptnr. Parish & Parker, Gilmer, Tex., 1964—65, Kenley & Boyland, Longview, 1965, Roberts, Smith & Parker, Longview, 1966—71, Rutledge & Parker, Ft. Worth, 1971—72, Nichols & Parker, Longview, 1972—79; judge U.S. Dist. Ct. (ea. dist.) Tex., 1979—94, chief judge, 1990—94; judge U.S. Ct. Appeals (5th Cir.), Tyler, Tex., 1994—. Mem.: Tex. Bar Assn. Office: US Courthouse 221 W Ferguson St Ste 400 Tyler TX 75702-7200*

PARKER, RONALD CARLYLE, transpersonal psychologist; b. Colón, Republic of Panama, Nov. 6, 1942; s. Horace Vaz and Emily Estella (Alleyne) P.; m. Ann Wilson, July 5, 1969 (div. Oct. 1979); 1 child, Temple Anouk. BSc in Physics, L.I. U., 1973; MA in Anthropology, New Sch. for Social Rsch., 1975; diploma, Am. Acad. of Dramatic Arts, 1989; PhD in Transpersonal Psychology & Comms., The Union Inst., 1994. Cert. master practitioner in neuro-linguistic programming. Sr. electronic technician Sony Corp., N.Y.C., 1969-72; electronic technician Loral Electronic Systems, 1972-74; instr., lectr. Bklyn. Coll., 1974-80; systems cons. Met Life Corp., N.Y.C., 1980-99; consultant, writer, actor, 2000—. Author: Transform Node, 1990, Traveller On The Path, 1994. Sgt. USAF, 1965-69. Mem. Assn. for Transpersonal Psychology, The Soc. for Sufi Studies, Inst. for the Study of Human Knowledge, Himalayian Inst for Yoga Sci. and Philosophy. Avocation: martial arts.

PARKER, ROSS GAIL, lawyer; b. Council Bluffs, Iowa, July 13, 1948; s. Gail Francis and Mildred Julia P.; m. Deborah Jo LeVan, May 5, 1984; children: Sarah LeVan, Alexander LeVan. BS, Iowa State U., 1970; JD, U. Pitts., 1974. Bar: U.S. Dist. Ct. (ea. dist.) Mich. 1975, U.S. Ct. Appeals (6th cir.) 1975. Law clk. to Hon. Michael Cavanagh Mich. Ct. Appeals, Lansing, 1974-75; atty. Fink and LaRene, Detroit, 1975-78; asst. U.S. atty. U.S. Attys. Office, U.S. Dist. Ct. (ea. dist.) Mich., 1978—, chief criminal divsn., 1981-89, chief asst. U.S. atty., 1989-94. Adj. prof. Detroit Coll. Law, 1980-82. Editor-in-chief U. Pitts. Law Rev., 1973-74. Coach Neighborhood Club, Grosse Pointe, Mich., 1998; mgr. SCH Hockey Assn., St. Clair Shores, Mich., 1998—. Recipient Dirs. award U.S. Dept. Justice, 1990. Mem. FBA (Leonard R. Gilman award 1997). Presbyterian. Avocations: reading, coaching, volunteering in church activities. Office: US Attys Office 211 W Fort St Detroit MI 48226-3202

PARKER, SARA ANN, librarian, consultant; b. Cassville, Mo., Feb. 19, 1939; d. Howard Franklin and Vera Irene (Thomas) P. BA, Okla. State U., 1961; M.L.S., Emporia State U., Kans., 1968. Adult svcs. librarian Springfield Pub. Libr., Mo., 1972-75, bookmobile dir., 1975-76; coord. S.W. Mo. Libr. Network, Springfield, 1976-78; libr. developer Colo. State Libr., Denver, 1978-82; state librarian Mont. State Libr., Helena, 1982-88, State Libr. Pa., Harrisburg, 1988-90; Pa. commr. librs., dep. sec. edn. State of Pa., 1990-95; state libr. State of Mo., Jefferson City, 1995—. Cons. and lectr. in field. Author, editor, compiler in field; contbr. articles to profl. jours. Sec., Western Coun. State Librs., Reno, 1984-88, mem. Mont. State Data Adv. Coun., 1983-88, Mont. Telecommunications Coun., 1985-88, WLN Network Coun., 1984-87, Kellogg ICLIS Project Mgmt. Bd., 1986-88; mem. adv. com. Gates Libr. Initiative, 1998—; mem. OCLC Strategic Directions and Governance Study Adv. Coun., 2000-01. Recipient Pres.'s award, Nature Conservancy, 1989, Friends award, Pa. Assn. Ednl. Comms. and Techs., 1989, Friend of Sch. Librs. award, Mo. Sch. Librs. Assn., 2000, Bohley Libr. Cooperation award, 2001; fellow Inst. Ednl. Leadership, 1982. Mem. ALA, Chief Officers State Libr. Agys. (pres. 1996-98), Mont. Libr. Assn. (bd. dirs. 1982-88), Mountain Plains Libr. Assn. (sec. chmn. 1980, pres. 1987-88). Home: PO Box 554 Jefferson City MO 65102-0554 Office: Mo State Libr PO Box 387 600 W Main St Jefferson City MO 65101-1532

PARKER, SARAH JESSICA, actress; b. Nelsonville, Ohio, Mar. 25, 1965; m. Matthew Broderick May, 1997. Actress: (theatre) The Innocents, 1976, The Sound of Music, 1977, Annie, 1978, The War Brides, 1981, The Death of a Miner, 1982, To Gillian on Her 37th Birthday, 1983, 84, Terry Neal's Future, 1986, The Heidi Chronicles, 1989, How to Succeed in Business Without Really Trying, 1996, Once Upon a Mattress, 1996—, (films) Rich Kids, 1979, Somewhere Tomorrow, 1983, Firstborn, 1984, Footloose, 1984, Girls Just Want to Have Fun, 1985, Flight of the Navigator, 1986, L.A. Story, 1991, Honeymoon in Vegas, 1992, Hocus Pocus, 1993, Striking Distance, 1993, Ed Wood, 1994, Miami Rhapsody, 1995, If Lucy Fell, 1996, Mars Attacks!, 1996, The First Wives Club, 1996, Extreme Measures, 1996, 'Til There Was You, 1997, The Substance of Fire, 1996, (voice) A Life Apart: Hasidism in America, 1997, 'Til There Was You, 1997, Isn't She Great, 1999, Dudley Do-Right, 1999; (TV movies) My Body, My Child, 1982, Going for the Gold: The Bill Johnson Story, 1985, A Year in the Life, 1986, The Room Upstairs, 1987, Dadah Is Death, 1988, The Ryan White Story, 1989, Twist of Fate, 1989, In the Best Interest of the Children, 1992, (TV series) Square Pegs, 1982-83, A Year in the Life, 1987-88, Equal Justice, 1990-91, Sex and the City, 1998- (Best Supporting Actress Golden Globe award 1999, 2000 and 2001), (TV pilots) The Alan King Show, 1986; guest appearances The Ben Stiller Show, 1992, The Larry Sanders Show, 1992; co-exec. prodr. Sex and the City. Nat. amb. U.S. Fund for UNICEF. Recipient, Am. Civil Liberties Union award, 1995. Office: CAA care Jane Berliner 9830 Wilshire Blvd Beverly Hills CA 90212-1804*

PARKER, SCOTT JACKSON, theatre manager; b. Ft. Bragg, N.C., July 28, 1945; s. John William and Darice Lee (Jackson) P. MA, U. N.C., 1971; MFA, U. Va., 1978. Mng. dir. Duke U. Theatre, Durham, N.C., 1970-76; gen. mgr. East Carolina U. Theatre, Greenville, 1980-85; producer The Lost Colony Outdoor Drama, Manteo, N.C., 1986-89; dir. Inst. of Outdoor Drama U. N.C., Chapel Hill, 1990—. V.p. Paul Green Found., nationwide, 1989—. Producer, mgr., dir., scene designer. With U.S. Army, 1969-70. Mem. Nat. Theatre Conf. (pres. 1999-2000), Assn. for Theatre in Higher Edn. (founding mem. 1987), Coll. of Fellows of the Am. Theatre (bd. dirs.), Southeastern Theatre Conf. (pres. 1982), Arts Advs. of N.C. (pres. 1993-94), The Players Club N.Y.C. Democrat. Baptist. Avocations: white water Kayaking, camping, hiking. Office: U NC Inst Outdoor Drama Cb # 3240 Chapel Hill NC 27599-0001

PARKER, STEPHEN ANTHONY, psychologist, educator; b. McCook, Nebraska, Dec. 19, 1950; s. Frank Richard, Jr. and Marjorie Jean (Anthony) P.; life ptnr. Scott Marlow Schroeder, Sept. 8, 1993. BA summa cum laude, U. Minn., Minneapolis, 1975; MA, Coll. St. Thomas, St. Paul, Minn., 1982; Psy D in psychology, U. St. Paul, Minn., 1994. Licensed Psychologist Nat. Register Health Svc. Providers in Psychology. Psychologist, clin. dir. Northland Therapy Ctr., St. Paul, 1985—; asst. prof. adj. U. St. Thomas, 1997—; adj. asst. sch. prof. St. Mary's U. Minn., Minneapolis, 1987—. Contbg. editor Am. Jour. Orthopsychiatry, Jour. Men's Studies; contbr. to articles to profl. jours. Coun. Rep. Spirit of the Lakes, U.C.C., Minneapolis, Meditation Ctr. faculty; del. World Parliment of Religions, Capetown, South Africa. Recipient Phi Betz Kappa Alpha Minn. Chpt. Minneapolis, 1975, Outstanding Vol. Cmty. Mental Health Walk-in Counseling Ctr., 1991. Fellow Am. Orthopsychiatric Assn., Assn. for Transpersonal Psychology, Minn. Soc. Clin. Hypnosis, Int. Himalayan Yoga Tchrs' Assn. (faculty exam bd.), Minn. Psychological Assn; assoc. mem. Am. Psychological Assn. Avocations: music and dance of British Isle, creative writing, gardening, cooking, wilderness sports. Office: Northland Therapy Ctr 2324 University Ave W Ste 104 Saint Paul MN 55114-1843

PARKER, SUSAN ANN, law office executive; b. Marblehead, Mass., May 29, 1951; d. Thomas Edward and Elizabeth Rose (Wheeler) Flaherty; m. Michael McMillan Parker, July 31, 1976 (div. 1985. AS with honors, Marian Ct. Jr. Coll., Swampscott, Mass., 1972; student in bus. adminstrn. Northeastern U., 1980—. Lic. real estate broker; notary public. Exec. sec. R.M. Bradley & Co., Inc., Boston, 1972-78; adminstrv. asst. to treas. Boston Mortgage Co., 1978-79; office mgr. MB Mgmt. Corp., Boston, 1979-81; founder Parker Assocs., Boston, 1981—; law office mgr. Goodwin, Procter & Hoar, Boston, 1982—. Bd. dirs., clk. 1070 Beacon St. Tenants' Coop. Corp., Brookline, Mass., 1982-84, 86-87; mktg. researcher Com. to Elect William B. Golden State Senator, 1984; mem. Friends of Hall Pond, Inc., Brookline. Mem. Am. Mgmt. Assn., Greater Boston C. of C., Marian Ct. Jr. Coll. Alumnae Assn. Democrat. Roman Catholic. Avocations: sailing, skiing, collecting antiques, ballet. Home: 1070 Beacon St Brookline MA 02446-3981 Office: Goodwin Procter & Hoar Exchange Pl Boston MA 02109-2803

PARKER, SUSAN BROOKS, healthcare executive; b. Newport, N.H., Nov. 7, 1945; d. Ronald Elliott and Elizabeth Louise (Wiggins) P.; married; children: Jeffrey Roberts Avery, Mark Brooks Avery. BS in English and French, U. Vt., 1968; MSW in Social Planning, Boston Coll., 1978. EMT, Vt., 1973-76. Resort hotel mgr. and retail buyer Avery Vt. Inns, various cities, 1967-75; aftercare psychiatric worker Orange County Mental Health, Bradford, Vt., 1974-76; adminstrn. asst. Mass. Assn. for Mental Health, Boston, 1976-77; mental health planner Tri-City Area Office, Malden, Mass., 1977-78; exec. dir. Grafton County Planning Coun., Lebanon, N.H., 1978-80, N.H. Developmental Disabilities Planning Coun., Concord, 1980-87; commr. Dept. of Mental Health, Augusta, Maine, 1987-89; assoc. commr. U.S. Social Security Adminstrn., Balt., 1989-93; sec. gen. Rehab. Internat., N.Y.C., 1994—. Cons. Nat. Gov.'s Assn., Washington, 1985-86, Office of Health and Developmental Services, Washington, 1987; directorship Nat. Assn. of Devel. Disabilities, Washington, 1983-87, Ctrl. N.H. Mental Health Ctr., Concord, 1985-87, world com. on disability, Washington, 1997—, Roehrer Inst., Toronto, Ont., Can., 1997—; cons. in field. Author: (poetry collection) Scheme, 1965, Jamaican Collection, 1973; contbr. articles to newspapers and profl. jours. Pres. Parent Tchr. Orgn., Fairlee, Vt., 1972-73; founder and dir. Ford Sayre Ski Program, Dartmouth Coll. Skiway, Fairlee, 1972-76, United Way, Concord, 1983-86; bd. dirs. PTO Rundlett Jr. H.S., Concord, 1982-85; pres. U.S. Coun. for Internat. Rehab., 1993. Recipient Assn. Retarded Citizens Children's Disability Pub. Policy award, 1992, Kathryn C. Arneson award from People to People, 1992, Commr.'s citation for outstanding efforts in developing policy U.S. Social Security Adminstrn., 1992, Commn.'s citation for outstanding exec. leadership, 1993; named Outstanding Alumnus Boston Coll., 1991. Mem. Am. Assn. Mental Retardation, Nat. Assn. State Mental Health Program Dirs., Nat. Assn. Retarded Citizens. Avocations: skiing, gardening, canoeing, mountain climbing, reading. Office: PO Box 38 574 Main St Contoocook NH 03229-0038 Address: 120 route de Ferney 1202 Geneva Switzerland

PARKER, SUSAN JOELLYN, controller; b. Hobbs, N.Mex., July 4, 1967; d. John Edward and Patricia Ivene Parker. BA in Acctg., Southwestern U., Georgetown, Tex., 1989. CPA. Auditor Fed. Energy Rebulatory Commn., San Francisco, 1989-95; audit mgr. Tenet Healthcare, Dallas, 1995—2000, audit dir. Fla., 2000—02; contr. Piedmont Healthcare Sys., 2002—. Mem. AICPA. Methodist. Avocations: boating, reading, travel. E-mail: susan.parker2@tenethealth.com.

PARKER, THEODORE CLIFFORD, electronics engineer; b. Dallas, Sept. 25, 1929; s. Theodore Clifford and Virginia Bernice (Rumsey) P.; m. Janet Ruby Barnes, Nov. 28, 1970; children: Sally Odette, Peggy Claudette. BSEE magna cum laude, U. So. Calif., 1960. V.p. engring. Telemetrics, INc., Gardena, Calif., 1963-65; chief info. sys. Northrop-Nortronics, Anaheim, 1966-70; pres. AVTEL Corp., Covina, 1970-74, Aragon, Inc., Sunnyvale, 1975-78; v.p. Teledyne McCormick Selph, Hollister, 1978-82; sr. staff engr. FMC Corp., San Jose, 1982-85; pres. Power One Switching Products, Camarillo, 1985-86, Condor D.C. Power Supplies, Inc., 1987-88, Intelligence Power Tech. Inc., Camarillo, 1988—. Mem. IEEE (chmn. autotestcon '87), NRA (life), Am. Prodn. and Inventory Control Soc., Am. Def. Preparedness Assn., Armed Forces Comm. and Electronics Assn., Tau Beta Pi, Eta Kappa Nu. Home: 250 E Telegraph Rd Spc 47 Fillmore CA 93015-2145 Office: Intelligence Power Tech Inc PO Box 3158 Camarillo CA 93011-3158 E-mail: parkerted@ieee.org.

PARKER, THERESA ANN BOGGS, special education educator, music educator; b. Spencer, W.Va., Jan. 16, 1947; d. Harry Clay and Betty Jean (Richards) Boggs; m. Larry Glen Parker, Apr. 29, 1967; children: Carey Ann, Jill Renee, Timothy Preston, Jeremy David, Leanna Michelle. AA in Secretarial Studies, Glenville (W.Va.) State Coll., 1967, BA in Music Edn., 1970; MA in Spl. Edn., Coll. of Grad. Studies, 1991; EdS in Ednl. Leadership, W.Va. Grad. Coll., 1996. Cert. tchr. Pvt. practice piano teacher, Spencer, 1967—; sub. tchr. Roane County Schs., 1970-71, tchr. spl. edn., 1987-2001, tchr. music K-8, 2001—, educator team mem.-parent/educator resource ctr., 1989—; sub. tchr. Marietta (Ohio) City Schs., 1986; administrator Sand Hill Day Care Ctr., Reno, 1986-87. Spl. edn. rep. W.Va. Dept. Edn., Charleston, 1995-98; dir. Safetytown Roane County, Spencer, 1989-93. Author: (with others) Selected Teaching Models Integrated with West Virginia's Academic Model for Gifted Education, 1991; poet with works appearing in Echoes of Yesteryear, America at the Millennium, 2000, Enlightened Shadows, Miracles of Nature, Best Poems and Poets of 2001, Internat. Libr. Poetry. Chmn. Cub Scout Pack Boy Scouts Am., Reno, 1983-87, dist. trainer, Parkersburg, W.Va., 1986-87, chmn. Boy Scout Troop, Spencer, 1987-91; organizer First Bapt. Ch. Diabetes Sup. Group, 1995—. Safetytown grantee W.Va. Dept. Edn., Roane County, 1989, W.Va. Edn. Fund, Roane County, 1992; Dental Health grantee W.Va. Edn. Fund, Clover Sch., 1992; Diabetes Support Group grantee Benedium Found., Roane and Calhoun/Jackson Counties, 1995, youth and edn. grantee for Spencer Mid. Sch., Tri-County Partnership, Inc., 1998, W.Va. Humanities Coun. grantee Roane County Schs., 2000-01; named Tchr. of Yr. Spencer Middle Sch., 1999-2000. Mem. MENC, ASCD, W.Va. Profl. Educators, Blue Grass Riding Club, Lions (program chmn., pres. 1997-98, dist. Leo chmn. 1998-00, dist. Flag Day/Peace Poster contest 2000-2001), Roane Arts and Humanities Coun. (charter mem., pres. 2000—). Democrat. Baptist. Avocations: reading, sewing, playing piano, attending children's activities, grandchildren. Home: PO Box 478 Spencer WV 25276-0478 Office: Roane County Schs 102 Chapman Ave Spencer WV 25276-1310 E-mail: partheresa@netscape.net.

PARKER, THOMAS LEE, business executive; b. Ft. Worth, Aug. 23, 1921; s. J.T. Parker and Frances Gertrude (Rogers) Heer; m. Frances N. Newlon, Dec. 14, 1943 (dec. 1981); children: Richard T. (dec.), Pamela Parker Gartin. BSBA, Ohio State U., 1943. Sales rep. Frozen Drumstick Sales Co., Columbus, Ohio, 1946-47; sec.-treas., gen. mgr. Cream Cone Machine Co., 1948-57; pres. Drumstick Inc., 1958-62, Big Drum, Inc., Columbus, 1962-83, chmn. bd., 1983-86. Bd. dirs. Ohio Semitronics, Delta Tau Delta Ednl. Found. Mem. nat. adv. coun. Boy Scouts Am., Dallas. Maj. U.S. Army, 1943-46, ETO. Decorated Bronze Star; recipient Service to Mankind Columbus Sertoma

Club, 1975, Silver Beaver Boy Scouts Am., 1975, Silver Antelope Boy Scouts Am., 1977, Silver Buffalo Boy Scouts Am., 1986; Baden Powell fellow World Scouts, Geneva, 1982 Mem. Scioto Country Club (pres. 1977), Athletic Club (pres. 1971), Masons, Delta Tau Delta. Republican. Address: 2321 Yorkshire Rd Columbus OH 43221-3761

PARKER, TOM F. nephrologist; b. Shreveport, La., Oct. 21, 1949; s. Tom F. and Margery (Henderson) P.; m. Joanne Elizabeth McNeely, Apr. 28, 1990; children: Cynthia Kirby, Wendi, Christie. BS, Okla. U., 1962; MD, La. State U., New Orleans, 1966. Intern, then resident La. State U. Hosp., Shreveport, 1966-70; fellow in nephrology Southwestern Med. Sch., Dallas, 1972-74, clin. prof. medicine, 1974—; nephrologist Dallas Nephrology assocs., 1974-94. Cons. in field. Contbr. over 90 articles to profl. jours., chpts. to books; Seminar in Dialysis, 1990—. Bd. dirs. Tex. Renal Network, Dallas, 1989-96. Recipient Donald Seldin award, 1997. Fellow ACP; mem. Am. Soc. Nephrology, Nat. Kidney Found. (Best Physician 1996), Tex. Soc. Internal Medicine (pres.). Avocations: sailing, piano. Home: 4208 Versailles Ave Dallas TX 75205-3009 Office: Dallas Nephrology Assocs 6010 Forest Park Rd Dallas TX 75235-6408

PARKER, VINETA, social worker; b. N.C., Aug. 17, 1964; d. Benny Dunbar and Betty Lou Cousins. BA, N.C. Ctrl. U., 1987; MSW, So. Conn. State U., 1995. Social worker Cmty. Children and Family Svcs., New Haven, 1987-91, Dept. Children and Family Svcs., New Haven, 1993—; counselor Cornerstone Group Home, 1987-93; social worker, case mgr. New Haven Family Alliance, 1991-93. Dir. ops. Love Ctr. Ministry, Hamden, Conn., 1990—; social work cons. Leila Day Nursery, New Haven, 1992—. Mem. Alpha Kappa Alpha. Home: 62 Frederick St New Haven CT 06515-1521

PARKER, VIRGINIA MARIE, English language educator; b. Boston, Aug. 31, 1950; d. Thomas Gurney Sr. and Marguerite Mary (O'Sullivan) P. BA, Emmanuel Coll., 1972; postgrad. studies in English, Lincoln Coll. U. Oxford, (Eng.) Bread Loaf Sessions, summers 1987-89; MA, Middlebury Coll., 1989. Cert. secondary English tchr., Mass. Vol. Jesuit Vol. Corps N.W., Seattle, 1972-73; tchr. English Blue Hills Regional Tech. Sch., Canton, Mass., 1973—. Editl. cons. competency-based vocat. ednl. curriculum Dept. Edn./Occupl. Divsn., Commonwealth of Mass., 1984-88; nat. honor soc. advisor, screening com. mem. William A. Dwyer Chpt., Blue Hills, Canton, 1986-88, 1994-97; mediation trainee, advisor Sch. Mediation Assocs., 1993—. Ch. lector, religious educator, youth retreat facilitator various parishes, 1970—; grad. master tchr. program Office of Religious Edn., Archdiocese of Boston, 1977. Mem. NEA, Nat. Coun. Tchrs. English, Mass. Vocat. Assn., Mass. Tchrs. Assn., Blue Hills Ednl. Assn. (sec. 1977-78), Alden Kindred Am. Democrat. Roman Catholic. Avocations: traveling, theater-going, beach walking, genealogical research, cemetery haunting. Home: 80 Parks St Duxbury MA 02332-4831 Office: Blue Hills Regional Tech Sch 800 Randolph St Canton MA 02021-1358

PARKER, WALTER BRUCE, arctic research specialist, consultant; b. Spokane, Wash., Aug. 11, 1926; s. Bruce Velorus and Lucille Kathryn (Chessman) P.; m. Patricia Isabelle Ertman, Jan. 28, 1946; children: Sandra Wassilie, Patrick B., Jeffrey K., Douglas S., Lisa M. BA in History, U. Alaska, Fairbanks, 1964; DSc, U. Alaska, Anchorage, 1998. Air traffic controller FAA, 1946-64, evaluation officer, 1964-66, analyst Washington, 1966-68, planner Anchorage, 1968-70; sr. planner Fed. Field Com. for Alaska, 1970-71; rsch. assoc. U. Alaska, 1971-74; commr. Alaska Dept. Hwys., Juneau, 1974-76; chmn. Alaska Fed./State Land Use Planning Commn., 1976-79; disting. practioner in residence U. Alaska, Anchorage, 1979-80; chmn. Alaska Oil Spill Commn., 1989-90; pres., cons. transp. and telecom. sys. Parker Assocs., Inc., 1971—; commr. U.S. Arctic Rsch. Commn. Mem. marine bd., com. on advances in pilotage and navigation NRC, 1991-94; chmn. Alaska Hazardous Substance Spill Coun., 1991-95. Author: Alaska and The Law of the Sea, 1974, Alaska People's and Alaska Lands, 1977; contbr. reports to profl. publs. Chmn. Alaska Conservation Soc., Anchorage, 1969-71, Alaska Humanties Forum, Anchorage, 1987-93, Anchorage Parks and Recreation Coun., 1971-74; active Alaska Bd. Fish and Game, Juneau, 1971-74; chmn. Prince William Sound Sci. Ctr., 1996—, chmn.; assemblyman Anchorage Borough, 1971-74. With USN, 1944-46. Mem. Am. Soc. Pub. Adminstrn. (chmn. Alaska chpt. 1971-73). Democrat. Avocations: skiing, dog mushing and breeding, gardening. Home: 3724 Campbell Airstrip Rd Anchorage AK 99504-4422

PARKER, WALTER GEE, pediatrician; b. Branchville, Va., Feb. 11, 1933; s. Theodore Roosevelt and Theresa Cecil (Harris) P.; m. Henri Mae Smith, Sept. 15, 1960; three children. BS, Hampton U., 1955; MD, Meharry Med. Coll., 1962; MPH, U. Mich., 1967. Diplomate Am. Bd. Pediatrics. Rsch. assoc. U. Mich. Sch. Pub. Health, Ann Arbor, 1967-69; instr. in pediatrics U. Mich. Med. Sch., 1966-69, clin. instr. pediatrics, 1969-96; med. dir. Southwest Detroit Hosp., 1975-86, Western Wayne Correctional Facility, Plymouth, Mich., 1986-2000, ret., 2000. Fellow Am. Acad. Pediats.; mem. APHA, Mich. State Med. Soc., Wayne County Med. Soc., Alpha Phi Alpha. Home: 3626 Deerfield Pl Ann Arbor MI 48103-1711

PARKER, WARREN ANDREW, public health dentist, consultant; b. Swedesboro, N.J., May 31, 1932; s. Warren Henry and Mary Jane (Morrison) P.; m. Eileen Frances Grabosky, Oct. 12, 1957; children: Denise, Warren A., Gail Lamb, Stephen. DDS, U. Md., Balt., 1958; MPH, U. Calif., Berkeley, 1966. Diplomate Am. Bd. Dental Pub. Health. Pvt. practice dentistry, Swedesboro, 1958-60; resident in dental pub. health USPHS, San Francisco, 1967; asst. chief div. preventive dentistry Inst. Dental Rsch., Walter Reed Army Med. Ctr., Washington, 1967-74; chief health care studies divsn. Acad. Health Scis./U.S. Army, San Antonio, 1974-78, chief dental studies office, 1978-81; assoc. prof. grad. sch. Baylor U., Waco, Tex., 1978-92; prof. dept. cmty. health Baylor Coll. Dentistry, Dallas, 1981-88, prof., chmn. dept. cmty. health, 1988-92; dental pub. health cons. in pvt. practice, San Antonio, from 1992. Cons. Agy. for Children and Families, Dept. HHS, Dallas, 1984—; cons. divsn. dental health Tex. Dept. Health, Austin, 1987-92; cons. Inst. for Family Studies, Tex. Tech. U., Lubbock, 1992—; mem. adv. com. Dental Health Programs, Inc., Dallas, 1989-92. Contbr. articles to profl. jours. Mem. exec. com. St. Vincent DePaul Soc., Lancaster, Tex., 1990-95; mem. com. Vis. Nurses Assn., Dallas, 1988-95; rep. Tex. Cancer Coun., Austin, 1989-90; vol. Habitat for Humanity. Col. U.S. Army, 1959-81. Decorated Legion of Merit; recipient Cert., Tex. Agy. on Aging, 1987. Fellow APHA, Am. Coll. Dentists, Tex. Pub. Health Assn. (chair oral health 1990-91, exec. dir. 1992—); mem. ADA, Am. Assn. Pub. Health Dentistry, Delta Omega. Avocations: fishing, gardening. Home: San Antonio, Tex. Died Oct. 15, 2001; Sam Houston National Cemetery.

PARKER, WILLIAM DALE, management consultant, political and presidential adviser; b. Portsmouth, Va., Apr. 13, 1925; s. Otis Durie and Eva Estelle (Dempsey) P.; m. Frances Ross Jennings, Feb. 2, 1946 (dec.); children: Frances Lea, Elizabeth Dale, Kim Carolyn, Penny Jo Ann, Jacquelyn Susan; m. Boots Lee Farthing, 1968. Student, Coll. William and Mary, 1946; grad. indsl. engring., Internat. Corr. Schs., 1956; student, U. Del., 1959-60, Calif. Western U., 1961-62, U. Calif., 1964, Stetson U., 1969; DSc, James Balmes U., Saltillio, Mex., 1968; PhD in Edn., Fla. Inst., 1970. Layout, process and prodn. engr. GM, Wilmington, Del., 1949-59, asst. dir. salaried personnel pub. rels., 1959-61; mfg. engr., lectr. Gen. Dynamics/Astronautic, San Diego, 1961-64; dir. Internat. Inst. Human Rels., LaJolla, Calif., 1964—; family and marriage counselor Titusville, Fla., 1967-71, Boone, N.C., 1996—; mgmt. cons., v.p. Multiple Services, Inc., Titusville and Boone, 1969—. Bd. dirs., v.p. Spangler TV, N.Y.C., 1969-73; chmn. bd. Travel Internat., Inc., Titusville, 1971-74, presdl. advisor, 1972-76, 72-76, 98—; v.p. Pictorial Gravesite Creations, Inc., Boone and Titusville, 1989—. Author: Philosophy of a Genius: American Values, Solutions to Family and Marriage Problems, Gutless America, 1973, God Knows I Want to Come Home, 1989, Prose and Poetry-9 to 90, 1990, Geography 101, 1992, A Political Candidate Guide, 1995, A Selection of Writings, 1992-95, 1995, The Parker Faily, 1616-1996, 1996, Your Personal Angel, 1997—98; spkr. in field; columnist: Sentinal Newspapers, 1963—64, asst. editor : Campers Illus. Mag., 1964—65, asst. editor: Star Adv., 1968, asst. editor: Insight, 1969—72, asst. editor: Challenge, 1970—, asst. editor: Mountain Times, 1981—84, hon. mem. editl. adv. bd: Am. Biog. Inst., 1975—; patentee Amy Carter peanut dolls, inventor process to keep B/W and color pictures from aging in sunlight. Founder Monroe Park CD, 1951; mem. Wilmington coun. Boy Scouts Am., 1953—55; chmn. Varions Agy. Fund, 1954—60; co-chmn. Del. Dept. CD TV Shows, 1956—57; mem. Middle Atlantic States Conf. Correction, 1956—60; chmn., pres. Del. Md. Pa. Tri-State Hosp. Com., 1957—59; mem. Wilmington Inner City Study Commn., 1957—60; chmn. Del. CD Evacuation Commn., 1958—59, Del. Hwy. Safety Campaign, 1959—60; active PTA; bd. advisors Salvation Army, Va. Tech. U., 1999; friend of the libr. Legacy Soc., 2000; Mem. Nat. Dem. Com., 1980—; ind. candidate for gov. Fla., 1976; mem. Dem. Exec. Com., 1975—77; polit. cons. Congress; advisor to U.S. Pres., 1974—; bd. dirs. Boys and Girls Aid Soc. San Diego, 1962—64; traveler Arctic Circle, 1990, 2000. With USCGR, USN, SSII. Named Del. Outstanding Young Man of Yr., Wilmington/U.S. Jr. C. of C., 1957; recipient Silver award Del. Vol. Bur., 1957, ann. awards Va. Jr. Achievement, inc., 1959; speech award U.S. Jr. C. of C., 1960, Gemini award NASA, 1967, Internat. Disting. Svc. to Humanity award, 1971, Keys to City, wilmington, 1959, 61, 72, Titusville, 1970, Miami, 1973; named Hon. Sheriff, Portsmouth, Va., 1973; named White Ho. Vet., White Ho. Chief Staff, 1997; named on on the Gen. Dynamics-Atlas and on Gemini monuments with Mercury, Gemini and Apollo Spacewalk Hall of Fame, Titusville; papers, books and awards are in Librs. Space Archives, Va. Poly. and State U., Blacksburg. Mem.: SAR, NRA, DAV (life), VFW (life), Wilmington Indsl. Mgmt. Club, Am. Assn. Polit. Consultants, Accomack, Va., First Family of Va. (1616 William Parker), Authors League Am., Mus. of Flight (life), Mensa (life), Nat. Space Soc. (life; charter), Monroe Park Civic Assn. (pres. 1952—53), Universal Space Assn. (co-founder 1992), Vols. Spkrs. Bur. (San Diego), Coll. William and Mary Alumni Soc. (pres., rep.), Authors Guild, Mexican Turf Club, Royal Oak Golf and Country Club, S.Am. Turf Club (life), Masons, Moose (life), Elks (life), Am. Legion (life). Address: PO Box 246 Boone NC 28607-0246 also: PO Box 1441 Titusville FL 32781-1441 E-mail: wdp246@webtv.net.

PARKER, WILLIAM H., III, federal official; b. Westbrook, Maine, May 4, 1937; s. William H. II and Anne Marney (Delaney) P.; m. Joan Moody Currier, June 17, 1959; children: Laurie Jean, Michael Currier, Suzan Elizabeth, Julie Ann. BS, U. Maine, 1960; MS, Northeastern U., 1966; MEM, U. Detroit, 1981, MBA, 1982; postgrad., Nova U. Diplomate Am. Acad. Environ. Engrs. Project engr. Camp Dresser & McKee, Boston, 1962-72, v.p., 1972-75, E.C. Jordan, Portland, Maine, 1975-77; sr. v.p., reg. mgr. Camp Dresser & McKee, Detroit, 1977-87, bd. dirs., 1982-87; sr. v.p. CDM Fed. Programs Corp., Washington, 1987-88, bd. dirs., 1987-88; dep. asst. sec. Dept. of Def., 1988-90; dir. environ. health and safety programs, dir. chem programs EG&G Inc., Wellesley, Mass., 1990-98; founder, pres. Global Mgmt. & Tech. Solutions, 1999—. Bd. dirs. Parker Currier Inc., Brunswick, Maine; fin. cons. VMI, treas., pres., 1993—, White River Junction, Vt., 1987-90; presenter Congl. test, 1988-90; keynote speaker tech. and profl. socs., 1988—. Contbr. articles to profl. jours. Mem., chmn. planning bd. Town of Reading, Maine, 1968-73; mem. Town Meeting, Reading, 1969-75, Mcpl. Light Bd., Reading, 1974-75. 1st lt. U.S. Army, 1960-62. Recipient Outstanding Pub. Svc. medal Sec. of Def., 1989, Environ. Svc. award Nat. Def. Industries Assn., 2000. Fellow ASCE; mem. NSPE, Mass. Soc. Profl. Engrs (Young Engr. of Yr. award 1971), Am. Def. Preparedness Assoc., Engring. Socs. New Eng. (New Eng. award 1990), Soc. Am. Mil. Engrs., Nat. Security Industries Assn. (hon.), Water Pollution Control Fedn., Am. Water Works Assn., Mass. Jaycees (Reading) (local pres., state v.p. 1970-72, Econ. Club Detroit, Detroit Club, Sigma Xi, Tau Beta Pi, Alpha Kappa Psi, Beta Gamma Sigma, Phi Kappa Phi, Chi Epsilon. Republican. Roman Catholic. Avocations: reading, writing, traveling. Home and Office: 15 Montclair Rd West Newbury MA 01985-2216 E-mail: w.parker@mediaone.net.

PARKER-CONRAD, JANE E. nursing consultant; m. Daniel E. Conrad. RN, Meth. Hosp. Sch. Nursing, Madison, Wis.; BSN, U. Wis., 1969, MS, 1976; PhD, Loyola U., Chgo., 1987. Chief occupl. health nurse cons. Divsn. of Health State of Wis., Madison, 1975-79, dep. dir. occupl. health sect. Divsn. of Health, 1975-79; program dir. Occupl. Health Nursing U. Ill., Chgo., 1979-86; acting asst. dean Office of Internat. Studies U. Ill. Coll. Nursing, 1984-86; Joanna Johnson chair in Occupl. Health Nursing U. Wis., Milw., 1990-92; dean Health Programs divsn. Walters State Coll., Morristown, Tenn., 1994-96; ednl. cons. Conrad & Conrad Cons., Knoxville, 1996—. Contbr. articles profl. jours.; rsch. on leadership in nursing, health promotion-cost containment programs and occupational health nursing. Recipient Schering award for excellence in occupational health nursing. Mem. ANA, Am. Assn. Occupl. Health Nurses, Internat. Coun. Occupl. Health, Phi Delta Gamma. Home and Office: 11409 Berryhill Dr Knoxville TN 37931-2804

PARKER-FAIRBANKS, DIXIE, artist; b. Cedar Rapids, Iowa, Aug. 1, 1936; d. James N. and Mary Louise (Mussell) Parker; m. Richard Fairbanks, Aug. 26, 1966 (dec. Mar. 1989). BFA, Drake U., 1958, MFA, 1959. Craft instr. State of Wis., Waukesha, 1960-61; asst. dir. dept. edn. Des Moines Art Ctr., 1961-66; art lectr. Ctrl. Wash. U., Ellensburg, 1967-69; dir. Jr. Art Mus., Des Moines, 1965—66, dir. docent program, 1963—66; dir./avd. Cmty. Art Gallery, Ellensburg, 1968—72. Coord./dir. Richard Fairbanks Project, Ellensburg, 1991-95; guest curator, Richard Fairbanks Retrospective, nordic hertiage Mus., Ballard, Wash., 1995; guest spkr., Networks in Ceramics, U. of Art and Design, Helsinki, Finland, 1966. Prodr./editor: (biography) Richard Fairbanks, American Potter, 1993; exhibited in one-person shows, 1962-96, two-person shows, 1970-95; gallery affiliations include Galerie Pelin, Helsinki, Finland, City of Sanda, Japan, Galerie Prisma, Vienna, C.G. Rein, Scottsdale, Ariz., Maxwell Galleries, Inc., San Francisco, Des Moines Art Ctr., Percival Galleries, Inc., Des Moines, Greenwood Galleries, Seattle, PANACA, Bellevue, Wash., Louise Matzke Gallery, Seattle, N.W. Craft Ctr., Bellevue, Lynn McAllister Gallery, Seattle, Seattle Art Mus., Richard White Gallery, Seattle, Gallery One, Ellensburg, Allied Arts, Yakima, Wash., Oak Hollow Gallery, Yakima, Larson Gallery, Yakima. Address: 19111 SE 47th Pl Issaquah WA 98027-9315

PARKERSON, HARDY MARTELL, lawyer; b. Longview, Tex., Aug. 22, 1942; s. James Dee and Winifred Lenore (Robertson) P.; m. Janice Carol Johnson, Aug. 3, 1968; children: James Blaine, Stanley Andrew, Paul Hardy. BA, McNeese State U., Lake Charles, La.; JD, Tulane U., 1966. Bar: La. 1966, U.S. Supreme Ct. 1971. Assoc. Rogers, McHale & St. Romain, Lake Charles, 1967-69; pvt. practice, 1969—. Chmn. 7th Congl. Dist. Crime and Justice Task Force, La. Priorities for the Future, 1980; asst. prof. criminal justice La. State U., 1986. Bd. dirs. 1st Assembly of God Ch., Lake Charles, 1980—; bd. regents So. Christian U., Lake Charles, 1993—; mem. La. Dem. State Ctrl. Com., 1992-96, Calcasieu Parish Dem. Com., 1988—, past sec.-treas., exec. com.; former mem. Gulf Assistance Program, Lake Charles; 7th Congl. Dist. La. mem. Imports and Exports Trust Authority, Baton Rouge, 1984-88. Mem. Fed. Bar Assn. (chmn. fed. cts. com., sr. lawyers divsn.), Pi Kappa Phi Housing Corp. of Lake Charles (bd. dirs., sec.-treas. 1985—), Pi Kappa Phi. Democrat. Mem. Assembly of God Ch. Avocations: political activism, hosting television talk show. Home: 127 Greenway St Lake Charles LA 70605-6821 Office: # B 3309 Common St Lake Charles LA 70601-8603

PARKERSON, JOHN E. (SANDY), art dealer; b. New Orleans, Oct. 16, 1942; s. Emmet Parkerson, Jr. and Rosemary Folse Parkerson; m. Marjorie Genevieve Crain, Sept. 9, 1968 (dec. Mar. 2001); children: Eliza P., John A.C. BA, Rice U., 1965; MA, U. Va., 1970. V.p., painting dept. head Sotheby Parke-Bernet, L.A., 1970—80; owner Parkerson Gallery, 19th/20th Century Art, Houston, 1980—. Bd. mem. Alley Theatre, Houston, 1986—96; bd. mem., v.p. Cultural Arts Coun., 1992—96, Fotofest, Inc., Houston, 1990—97. Mem.: Appraisers Assn. Am., Inc. (cert.). Roman Catholic. Avocations: travel, languages, tennis. Office: Parkerson Gallery 3510 Lake St Houston TX 77098

PARKHURST, CHARLES, retired museum director, art historian; b. Columbus, Ohio, Jan. 23, 1913; s. Charles Percy and Isabella (Woodbridge) P.; m. Elizabeth Huntington Rusling, June 15, 1938 (div. 1962); children: Andrew, Christopher, Bruce; m. Rima Zevin Julyan, Sept. 1, 1962 (div. 1972); 1 child, Brooke; m. Carol Canda Clark, July 18, 1986. BA, Williams Coll., 1935; AM, Oberlin Coll., 1938; MFA, Princeton U., 1941. Rd. and bridge constrn. worker Danali Park Alaska Rd. Commn.; tchr. music, coach basketball Wasilla, Alaska, 1935-37; asst. curator (registrar) Nat. Gallery of Art, Washington, 1942-43; dep. chief, monuments, fine arts and archives sect. Allied Mil. Govt. in both U.S. Zones, Germany, 1945-46; asst. curator Albright Art Gallery, Buffalo, 1946-47; asst. prof. art and archaeology Princeton (N.J.) U.; asst. dir. Princeton (N.J.) Art Mus., 1947-49; head dept. fine arts, dir. Art Mus., prof. history and appreciation of art Oberlin (Ohio) Coll., 1949-62; dir. Balt. Mus. Art, 1962-70; asst. dir., chief curator Nat. Gallery Art, Washington, 1971-83, ret., 1983; co-dir. Mus. Art Williams Coll., 1983-84, mem. vis. faculty, 1980, Clark vis. prof., 1985-86, acting dir. grad. program in art history, 1986-87, dir. M.B. Prendergast Systematic Catalogue project, 1983-87; interim dir. Smith Coll. Mus. Art, 1991-92, emeritus dir., 1992. Faculty fellow Fund for Advancement Edn., 1952-53; Fulbright rsch. scholar U. Utrecht, Netherlands, 1956-57; vis. faculty U. Minn., 1953, UCLA, 1964, Johns Hopkins U., 1971, U. Wis., 1979, Williams Coll., 1980-92; lectr. on art, color theory of Roger Bacon and Giotto and vernacular Italian drama ca. 1300; chmn. Md. Arts Coun., 1967-68; chmn. Md. Revolutionary War Bicentennial Commn., 1968-70, Gov.'s Coun. on Arts in Md., 1966-68; trustee, officer Williamstown Regional Art Conservation Lab., 1983-90; ind. cons. Asian Art Mus., 1993-94; vis. lectr. Mass. Coll. Liberal Arts, 2001. Contbr. articles to profl. jours. Commr. Nat. Mus. Am. Art, 1983-93; overseer Case Western Res. U., Cleve., 1982-86; trustee Amon Carter Mus., 1977-85, Hill-Stead Mus., Farmington, Conn., 1994-96. With USNR, 1943-62. Decorated chevalier Legion d'Honneur de la République Française, 1947; recipient research grants Am. Council Learned Socs. and Am. Philos. Soc., 1961 Mem. Coll. Art Assn. (pres. 1958-60, bd. dirs.), Intermus. Conservation Assn. (co-founder), Assn. Art Mus. Dirs., Am. Assn. Mus. (pres. 1966-68, founder, mem. mus. accreditation com. 1970-76). Among draughters and signers of the Wiesbaden Manifesto, 1945. Office: 33 Dana Pl Amherst MA 01002-2212

PARKHURST, CHARLES LLOYD, electronics company executive; b. Nashville, Aug. 13, 1943; s. Charles Albert Parkhurst and Dorothy Elizabeth (Ballou) Parkhurst Crutchfield; m. Dolores Ann Oakley, June 6, 1970; children: Charles Thomas, Deborah Lynn, Jere Loy. Student, Hume-Fogg Tech. Coll., 1959-61; AA, Mesa Community Coll., 1973; student, Ariz. State U., 1973-76. Mem. design staff Tex. Instruments, Dallas, 1967-68; mgr. design Motorola, Inc., Phoenix, 1968-76; pres. LSI Cons., Inc., Tempe, Ariz., 1976-85, LSI Photomasks, Inc., Tempe, 1985-94, Charles Parkhurst Books, Inc., Prescott, Ariz., 1994—. Designer 1st digital watch chip, 1973. Mem. Rep. Congl. Leadership Coun., Washington, 1988; life mem. Rep. Presdl. Task Force, 1990. Served as cpl. USMC, 1961-64. Mem. Ariz. State U. Alumni Assn. (life), Antiquarian Booksellers Assn. Am. Baptist. Achievements include design of the world's first digital watch chip. Avocations: genealogy, coin collecting, scuba diving, book collecting. Office: Charles Parkhurst Books Inc PO Box 10850 Prescott AZ 86304-0850

PARKHURST, EDWIN WALLACE, JR. healthcare management consultant; b. Waukegan, Ill., June 17, 1943; s. Edwin W. Sr. and Marie Violet (Wolf) P.; m. Grace Ann Dovemuehle, July 6, 1963; children: John Edward, Janet Lynn, Jeanine Marie, Julie Ann. BA, Carthage Coll., 1965; MBA, U. Chgo., 1968. Adminstrv. asst. West Allis (Wis.) Meml. Hosp., 1965—66; asst. dir., asst. prof. U. Mo. Med. Ctr., Columbia, 1968—71; from assoc., prin., to ptnr. Herman Smith Assoc., Hinsdale, Ill., 1971—88; ptnr. Herman Smith Assocs. Internat., Glen Ellyn, 1976—; ptnr. Herman Smith Assoc. divsn. Coopers & Lybrand, Chgo., 1988—93; mng. prin. MEDCO, Inc., Hatboro, Pa., 1997—, PRISM Healthcare Cons., Glen Ellyn, 1993—; assoc., dept. of health studies, lectr. Sch. of Social Svcs. Adminstrn. U. Chgo., 2000—, dir. grad. program in health adminstrn. and policy, 2001—. Spkr. in field; bd. dirs. Clin. Benchmaking. Contbr. articles to profl. jours. Bd. dirs., past pres. Lisle (Ill.) Cmty. Dist. 202 Bd. Edn., 1985—; scout leader Boy Scouts Am., Lisle, 1974-93. Named Disting. Alumni, U. Chgo., 1997; recipient Alumni Svc. citation U. Chgo., 1999. Fellow Am. Assn. Healthcare Cons. (bd. dirs., past pres., Chester A. Minkalis Svc. award 1999); mem. Health Issues Study Soc. (sec.-treas. 1972—), Am. Hosp. Assn., Am. Coll. Healthcare Execs. (cert. healthcare exec.), Soc. Healthcare Planning and Mgmt., Chgo. Health Exec. Forum. Avocations: fishing, hunting, hiking, camping, photography. Home: 4239 White Birch Dr Lisle IL 60532-1252 Office: PRISM Healthcare Cons 799 Roosevelt Rd # B4s317 Glen Ellyn IL 60137-5908 E-mail: eparkhurst@consultprism.com.

PARKHURST, TODD SHELDON, lawyer; b. Evanston, Ill., Mar. 8, 1941; s. Don A. and Ruth Ellen (Sheldon) P.; m. Karen Judy Huckleberry, Sept. 2, 1968 (dec. Sept. 1969); m. Beverly Ann Susler, Aug. 15, 1976. BS in Gen. Engring., U. Ill., 1963; JD, U. Pa., 1966. Bar: Ill. 1968, U.S. Dist. Ct. (no. dist.) Ill. 1968, U.S. Dist. Ct. (ea. dist.) Wis. 1989, U.S. Ct. Appeals (7th cir.) 1977, U.S. Ct. Appeals Fed. Cir. 1978, U.S. Ct. Mil. Appeals, 1968, U.S. Patent and Trademark Office, 1973, U.S. Supreme Ct. 1973. Assoc. Wolfe, Hubbard, Voit & Osann, 1968-72; assoc. and ptnr. Trexler, Wolters, Bushnell & Fosse, Chgo., 1972-84; ptnr. Jenner & Block, 1984-87; ptnr., mgr. intellectual property practice Schiff Hardin & Waite, 1987-96; ptnr. Gardner, Carton & Douglas, 1996-98, Hill & Simpson, Chgo., 1998-2000; ptnr., mgr. intellectual property practice Holland & Knight, 2000—. Adj. prof. John Marshall Law Sch., Chgo., 1980-84, Ill. Inst. Tech.-Chgo. Kent Law Sch., 1989—. Contbr. articles to profl. jours. Mem. Lifeline Pilots, Inc., pres. 1994-96; hearing officer Ill. Pollution Control Bd., 1972-96. Mem. Am. Intellectual Property Law Assn., Licensing Execs. Soc., Chgo. Bar Assn., Patent Law Assn. Chgo., Chgo. Lit. Club (pres. 1989-90), Adventurers Club Chgo. (sec. 1988). Methodist. Avocations: flying, scuba diving, photography, theatrical acting. Home: 260 E Chestnut St Apt 4301 Chicago IL 60611-2474 Office: Holland & Knight 55 W Monroe St Ste 800 Chicago IL 60603-5004 E-mail: tparkhur@hklaw.com.

PARKHURST, VIOLET KINNEY, artist; b. Derby Line, Vt., Apr. 26, 1926; d. Edson Frank and Rosa (Beauchiene) Kinney; student Sch. Practical Arts, Boston, 1941-42, Baylor U., Waco, Tex., 1943, Calif. State U., Los Angeles, 1950-51; m. Donald Winters Parkhurst, Apr. 10, 1948. Fgn. corr. 5 Brazilian mags., 1946-53; tech. illustrator, 1954-55; owner five galleries including Ports of Call, San Pedro, Calif.; artist, specializing in seascapes; work included in permanent collection of Stockholm Mus., many pvt. collections including Presidents Richard M. Nixon, Ford, Reagan, Bush, Gov. Wilson, Mayor of Kobe, Japan, Mayor Yorty of L.A., Rory Calhoun, Barbara Rush, Jim Arness, David Rose; one-shows shows at prominent galleries; numerous paintings published. Winner 30 blue ribbons for art. Fellow Am. Inst. Fine Arts. Mem. Ch. of Religious Sci. Author: How to Paint Books, 1966; Parkhurst on Seascapes, 1972. Paintings reproduced on covers South West Art, Arizona Living; ltd. edit. prints published, also ltd. edit. plates. Office: Parkhurst Gallery Ports of Call Village San Pedro CA 90731

PARKHURST, WILLIAM MICHAEL, media consultant; b. Manchester, N.H., July 29, 1945; s. John Theodore and Anna Agnes (Padden) P.; m. Doreen Carney, Mar. 16, 1968 (div. July 1975); children: Carolyn; stepchildren: Christopher Katz, Terry Katz. BA, U. N.H., 1970. Newscaster Sta. WLKW Radio, Providence, 1970-73; prodr. Sta. WOR Radio-TV, N.Y.C., 1973-74; assoc. dir. publs. Simon & Schuster, 1974-77; dir. pub. Putnam Pub. Group, 1977-80; dir. of publicity Avon Books Hearst Corp., 1980-81; pres. H.K. Simon Co., Yonkers, N.Y., 1992—, Parkhurst Comm., Inc., N.Y.C., 1981—. Chmn. publicity com. Nat. Book Awards, N.Y.C., 1980-81; lectr. Yale U., New Haven, Conn., 1993—; cons. 20-20 ABC-TV, True Detectives CBS-TV, 1991-93. Author: How to Get Publicity, 1985, rev., 2000, The Eloquent Executive, 1988, True Detectives, 1989. With USN, 1967-69. Mem. Pubs. Publicity Assn. (exec. bd. dirs. 1979-82). Democrat. Avocation: marathons. E-mail: BillParkhurst@Parkhurstcom.com.

PARKIN, GERARD FRANCIS RALPH, chemistry educator, researcher; b. Middlesbrough, Cleveland, Eng., Feb. 15, 1959; s. Ralph and Clementine (Gill) P.; m. Rita K. Upmacis. BA with honors, Oxford (Eng.) U., 1981, MA, 1984, PhD, 1985. NATO/SERC (U.K.) postdoctoral rsch. fellow Calif. Inst. Tech., 1985-88; asst. prof. Columbia U., N.Y.C., 1988-91, assoc. prof., 1991-94; prof., chmn. chemistry dept., 1994—; chmn. dept. chemistry. Contbr. numerous articles to profl. jours. Recipient Camille and Henry Dreyfus Tchr.-Scholar award, 1991, award in pure chemistry Am. Chem. Soc., 1994, Corday Morgan medal Royal Soc. Chemistry, 1995; A.P. Sloan rsch. fellow; NSF Presdl. faculty fellow, 1992—. Roman Catholic. Achievements include discovery that bond stretch isomerism is an artifact. Office: Columbia U 116th St And Broadway New York NY 10027

PARKIN, STUART STEPHEN PAPWORTH, materials scientist; IBM fellow IBM Almaden Rsch. Ctr., San Jose, Calif., 1983—. Recipient Internat. prize for new materials Am. Phys. Soc., 1994, C.V. Boys prize Inst. Physics, London, 1991, Inaugural Outstanding Young Investigator award Materials Rsch. Soc., 1991, Europhysics prize Hewlett-Packard, 1997, Indsl. Applications of Physics prize Am. Inst. Physics, 1999-2000; named Innovator of Yr.,

R&D Mag., 2001. Fellow Am. Phys. Soc., Royal Soc. London, Inst. Physics (London). Office: IBM Almaden Rsch Ctr K11 D2 650 Harry Rd San Jose CA 95120-6099 E-mail: parkin@almaden.ibm.com.

PARKINS, FREDERICK MILTON, dental educator, university dean; b. Princeton, N.J., Sept. 8, 1935; s. William Milton and Phyllis Virginia (Plyler) P.; m. Carolyn V. Rude; children: Bradford, Christopher, Eric. Student, Carleton Coll., 1953-56; D.D.S., U. Pa., 1960; MSD. in Pedodontics, U. N.C., Chapel Hill, 1965; PhD in Physiology, 1969. Instr. pedodontics U. N.C., 1965-67; asst. prof. pedodontics U. Pa., 1967-68, dir. Dental Aux. Utilization program, chmn. pedodontics, 1968-69; assoc. prof., head pedodontics U. Iowa, Iowa City, 1969-72, prof., head pedodontics, 1972-75; asst. dean acad. affairs U. Iowa (Coll. Dentistry), 1974-75, asso. dean acad. affairs, 1975-79, dir. continuing edn., 1975-77; prof. pedodontics, dean Sch. Dentistry, U. Louisville, 1979-85, prof. pediatric dentistry, 1985—. Mem. Hillenbrand Fellowship adv. com. Am. Fund Dental Health, 1980-85; cons. Div. Dental Health USPHS, 1969-72; dental cons., med. staff Children's Hosp. Phila., 1968-71; med. staff Kosair Children's Hosp. Louisville, 1983—; cons., mem. pedodontic adv. com. Council Dental Edn., 1974-80, chmn. pedodontic adv. com., 1978-80, cons. council on legislation, 1978-79; dental cons. Aux. Utilization VA, 1968-69; cons. Bur. Health Resources Devel., 1974-76, Dept. Army, 1980— , numerous others Assoc. editor: Jour. Preventive Dentistry, 1973-79; editorial bd., 1980-83; editorial reviewer: Jour. Pediatrics, 1969— , Jour. Dental Edn, 1978— , Jour. AMA, 1979— ; asso. editor: Jour. Clin. Preventive Dentistry, 1979-84; Contbr. chpts. to textbooks, articles to profl. publs. Bd. govs. Youth Performing Arts Coun., Louisville-Jefferson County Sch. Dist., 1980-89, pres., 1986-88; bd. govs. Regional Cancer Ctr., U. Louisville, 1979-84, Univ. Hosp., 1979-84; mem. human studies com. U. Louisville, 1988-90. Robert Wood Johnson Congl. fellow Inst. of Medicine, 1977-78; USPHS postdoctoral fellow, 1963-67; NIH grantee, 1971-75; Recipient Earle Banks Hoyt Teaching award, 1969 Fellow AAAS, Am. Acad. Pediat. Dentistry (chmn. rsch. com. 1972-73, Ann. Rsch. award 1968, chmn. advanced edn. com. 1974-75, chmn. dental care programs com. 1978-80); mem. ADA, Am. Coll. Dentistry, Am. Soc. Dentistry for Children (exec. bd. Iowa unit 1969-75, award com. 1973-76, edn. com. 1974-77, chmn. rsch. adv. com. 1973-76), Biophys. Soc., Internat. Assn. Dental Rsch., N.Y. Acad. Dentistry, Ky. Dental Assn. (exec. bd. 1979-84), Am. Assn. Dental Schs. (coun. deans 1979-85, chmn. pedodontics sect. 1976, chmn. continuing edn. sect. 1979, legis. com. 1978-83), Louisville Dental Alumni Assn. (bd. govs. 1979-84), Am. Assn. Dental Rsch. (nat. affairs com. 1978-85), Acad. Laser Dentistry (co-chmn. rsch. and edn. 1997, chair 1998—, bd. dirs. 1997—, cert. com., T.H. Maiman award for excellence in dental laser rsch.), U.S. Power Squadron (bd. govs. 1987-93, sec. 1989, adminstrv. officer 1990, exec. officer 1991, comdr. 1992), Aircraft Owners and Pilots Assn., Omicron Kappa Upsilon (pres. Wa. chpt. 1991-92), Rotary. Unitarian Universalist. Home: 6424 Marina Dr Prospect KY 40059-8846 Office: U Louisville Sch Dentistry Dept Orth Pediatric & Geriatric Dent Rm 306 Louisville KY 40292 E-mail: fmpark01@louisville.edu.

PARKINSON, BRADFORD WELLS, astronautical engineer, educator; b. Madison, Wis., Feb. 16, 1935; s. Herbert and Metta Tisdale (Smith) P.; m. Virginia Pinkham Wier, Nov. 26, 1977; children: Leslie, Bradford II, Eric, Ian, Bruce, Jared Bradford. BS, U.S. Naval Acad., 1957; MS, MIT, 1961; PhD, Stanford U., 1966; grad. (disting.), USAF Command and Staff Coll., 1969, Naval War Coll., 1972. Commd. 2d lt. USAF, 1957, advanced through grades to col., 1972; divsn. chief AF Test Pilot Sch., 1966-68; chair dept. astronautics and computer sci. USAF Acad., 1969-71; dir. engring. ABRES, 1972; program mgr. NAVSTAR GPS, 1972-78; ret. USAF, 1978; prof. mech. engring. Colo. State U., Ft. Collins, 1978-79; v.p. advanced engring. Rockwell Internat., Downey, Calif., 1979-80; gen. mgr., v.p. Intermetrics, Inc., Cambridge, Mass., 1980-84; prof. emeritus, assoc. dir. gravity probe-B Stanford (Calif.) U., 1984—; CEO, pres. Trimble Navigation Ltd., 1998-99; prof. emeritus aerospace & astronautics Stanford U. Chair adv. coun. NASA; dir. Trimble Navigation Ltd., Sunnyvale, Calif., Draper Lab., Cambridge, Palo Alto, Calif., Aerospace Corp., El Segundo, Calif. Decorated Def. Superior Svc. medal, AF Commendation medal with oak leaf cluster, Meritorius Svc. medal, Presdl. Unit citation, Bronze Star, Legion of Merit, Air medal with oak leaf cluster; recipient Pub. Svc. award, Disting. Pub. Svc. award, NASA, 1984, Thurlow award Inst. Navigation, 1986, Burka award, 1987, Kepler award, 1991, von Karman Lectureship Am. Inst. of Aeronautics and Astronautics, 1996, Magellan Premium, Am. Philos. Soc., 1997, Gold medal Space Tech. Hall of Fame of U.S. Space Found., 1998, Williams Space medal Soc. Logistics Engrs., 1996. Fellow AIAA, Royal Inst. Navigation (Gold medal 1983), Inst. Navigation; mem. IEEE (Kirchner award 1986, Pioneer award 1994, Sperry award 1999, Sr. Remo medal), AAS, NAE, Internat. Acad. Astronautics, Sigma Xi, Tau Beta Pi. Avocations: hiking, skiing, sailing. Home: 1359 Cuernavaca Circulo Mountain View CA 94040-3570 Office: Stanford U 4085 Mail Code Stanford CA 94305

PARKINSON, CLAIRE L. climatologist; b. Bay Shore, N.Y., Mar. 21, 1948; d. C. V. and Virginia (Hafner) P. BA, Wellesley Coll., 1970; MA, Ohio State U., 1974, PhD, 1977. Rsch. asst. Inst. Polar Studies, Columbus, 1972-74; tchg. asst. Ohio State U., 1973-76; rsch. asst. Nat. Ctr. Atmospheric Rsch., Boulder, Colo., 1976-78; rsch. scientist Goddard Space Flight Ctr., NASA, Greenbelt, Md., 1978-87, sr. scientist, 1987—. Sci. colloquium com. mem. Goddard Space Flight Ctr., 1986-99; project scientist Earth Observing System Aqua Mission, NASA, 1993—; sci. exec. com. Earth Observing Sys., 1996-2000; adv. panel climate and global change NOAA, 1990-95; climate rsch. com. Nat. Acad. Scis., 1994-96; sci. advisor Earth & Sky radio series, 1998—, sci. adv. radio series Soundprint Media Ctr., 1998—2001; lead scientist NASA expedition to Resolute Bay and the North Pole, 1999. Author: Breakthroughs, 1985, Gospel Cryptograms, 1994, Earth from Above, 1997 (Spl. Act award 1997); co-author: Antarctic Sea Ice, 1983 (Group award 1982), Three-Dimensional Climate Modeling, 1986; lead author: Arctic Sea Ice, 1987 (Peer award 1988); co-editor: Atlas of Satellite Observations Related to Global Change, 1993 (Group award 1993); lead editor EOS Data Products Handbook, vol. 2, 2000; mem. editl. bd. Internat. Glaciological Soc., —, IEEE Transactions, 2002-, GCambridge, Eng., 1989-92, Earth Obs. Website, 1999—; contbr. articles to profl. jours. Vol. Spl. Olympics, Annapolis, Md., 1989, College Park, Md., 1998—; tutor Greenbelt Cares, 1989-94; sci. speaker, sci. fair judge local schs., 1989—. Recipient Exceptional Svc. medal, NASA, 2001. Fellow Am. Meteorol. Soc. (history com. chmn. 1990); mem. IEEE Geosci. and Remote Sensing Soc. (mem. editl. bd.), Am. Polar Soc., Assn. for Philosophy of Math., Oceanography Soc., Phi Beta Kappa, Phi Beta Kappa Fellows. Achievements include research in global change, satellite remote sensing, sea ice/climate connections, climate modeling, history of science. Home: 8345 Canning Ter Greenbelt MD 20770-2701 Office: Code 971 NASA Goddard Space Flight Ctr Greenbelt MD 20771-0001 E-mail: claire.parkinson@gsfc.nasa.gov.

PARKINSON, HOWARD EVANS, insurance company executive; b. Logan, Utah, Nov. 3, 1936; s. Howard Maughan and Valeria Arlene (Evans) P.; m. Lucy Kay Bowen, Sept. 2, 1960; children: Blake, Gregory, Dwight, Lisa, David, Rebecca. BS, Brigham Young U., 1961; MBA, U. Utah, 1963. CLU. Chartered fin. cons. Mgmt. intern AEC, Richland, Wash., 1963-65; v.p. Belstar, Inc., Rexburg, Idaho, 1965-71, dir., 1966-76, pres., 1971-76; v.p., dir. Grand Targhee Resort, Inc., Rexburg, 1967-69; v.p. Fargo-Wilson-Wells Co., Pocatello, Idaho, 1974-76; equity qualified agt. Equitable Life Assurance So. U.S., Idaho Falls, Idaho, 1977-80, mem. nat. coun. sales group, 1978; dist. mgr. Mass. Mut. Life Ins. Co., Idaho Falls, 1980—; fin. cons. small bus. Bd. dirs. Little League Baseball, 1974-75; coach Little League Basketball, 1975-76; high councilman Rexburg Stake, Ch. of Jesus Christ of Latter-day Saints, 1976-77, bishop, 1977—; mem. Pres.'s Coun., 1988. Recipient Bronze award Mass. Mut. Life Ins. Co., Gold award, 1984. Mem. Million Dollar Roundtable, Toastmasters (past pres.). Republican. Address: Massachusetts Mutual 1970 E 17th St Ste 202 Idaho Falls ID 83404-8048

PARKINSON, JAMES THOMAS, III, investment consultant; b. Richmond, Va., July 10, 1940; s. James Thomas and Elizabeth (Hopkins) P.; m. Molly O. Owens, June 16, 1962 (div. June 1998); children: James Thomas, Glenn Walser; m. Caroline Smith Pyle, Oct. 10, 1998. BA, U. Va., 1962; MBA, U. Pa., 1964. Trainee Chem. Bank, N.Y.C., 1964-66; assoc., corp. fin. dept. Blyth & Co., Inc., 1968-69; v.p., corp. fin. dept. Clark Dodge & Co., Inc., 1969—72; pvt. practice investment mgmt. N.Y.C., Va., 1972—85, 1987—; v.p. Pleasantville Advisors, Inc., N.Y.C., 1986-87. Instr. corp. fin. Ind. U., 1966-68. Sr. warden Ch. of Holy Trinity, N.Y.C., 1978-79; trustee Am. Bible Soc., 1980—, Funds, Episcopal Diocese of Va., 2000—; dir. Bowles Fluidics corp., Columbia, Md., 1998—. With AUS, 1966-68. Mem. Univ. Club (N.Y.C.), Va. Country Club. Republican. Episcopalian. Home and Office: PO Box 2247 Middleburg VA 20118-2247

PARKINSON, PAUL K. lawyer, judge; b. Durango, Colo., Feb. 8, 1952; s. Philip Fulton and Ruth Eloise (Knight) P.; m. Amy Lee Dunham, May 17, 1975; children: Calista R., Karen S. BSE in Psychology, Truman State U., 1977; JD, U. Mo., Kansas City, 1979; LLM in Estate Planning, U. Miami, 1981. Bar: Mo. 1980, U.S. Dist. Ct. (we. dist.) Mo. 1980, U.S. Tax Ct. 1981, Kans. 1989. Assoc. Polsinelli, White, Vardeman & Shelton, Kansas City, Mo., 1981-83; pvt. practice, 1984-85; dir. Van Hooser, Olsen & Parkinson, P.C., 1986-89; pvt. practice Overland Park, Kans. and Kansas City, 1989-90; with Hess & Parkinson, Macon, Mo., 1990-2000; pros. atty. Macon County, 1999-2000, assoc. circuit judge Mo., 2001—. Adj. prof. U. Mo., Kansas City, 1982-85. Pres., dir., program com. chmn. Mid-Am. Planned giving Coun., Kansas City, 1990. Mem. ABA (real property, probate and trust sect. 1980-94), Mo. Bar Assn. (lectr. 1983-90, probate and trust com. 1981—, hosp. law com., banking law com., pres. 41st jud. cir. 1992-94). Office: 101 E Washington Bldg # 2 PO Box 491 Macon MO 63552 Fax: 660-385-3132. E-mail: Paul_Parkinson@osca.state.mo.us.

PARKINSON, WALLACE BRADFORD, music educator, staff sargeant; b. Lubbock, Tex. , Dec. 25, 1941; s. Raoul Bradford and Mary Grace Parkinson; m. Kathleen Cowperthwaite Hatch (div.); 1 child Jennifer Lynn. BS Edn., U. Mo., 1963; M Music Edn., 1965. Instr. music Minot State Coll. , Minto, ND, 1964—66; bandsman U.S. Army, N.Y.C., Vietnam, 1966—69, staff sargeant Vietnam, 1966—69; instr. music Interlochen Arts Acad., Mich., 1969—76; tchr. music Remidji Pub. Schs., Remidji, Minn., 1976—2001; staff sargeant Nat. Guard, 1977—94. Contbr. instrnl. manual. Staft seargent eb US Army, and N.G., 1966—94, New York, NY, and Vietnam. Home: 4201 S Washington St Amarillo TX 79110

PARKINSON, WILLIAM CHARLES, physicist, educator; b. Jarvis, Ont., Can., Feb. 11, 1918; came to U.S., 1925, naturalized, 1941; s. Charles Franklin and Euphemia Alice (Johnston) P.; m. Martha Bennett Capron, Aug. 2, 1944; children: Martha Reed, William Reid. BSE, U. Mich., 1940, MS, 1941, PhD, 1948. Physicist Applied Physics Lab., Johns Hopkins U., 1942-46, OSRD, 1943-44; mem. faculty U. Mich., 1947—, prof. physics, 1958-88, prof. emeritus physics, 1988—, dir. cyclotron lab., 1962-77; mem. subcom. nuclear structure NRC, 1959-68; mem. nuclear physics sub panel mgmt. and costs nuclear program, 1969-70; adv. panel physics NSF, 1966-69. Cons. grad. sci. facilities, 1968, chmn. postdoctoral fellowship evaluation panel, 1969, cons. to govt. and industry, 1955— Quondam mem. Trinity Coll., Cambridge, Eng. Recipient Ordnance Devel. award Navy Dept., 1946; Fulbright research scholar Cavendish Lab., Cambridge U., 1952-53 Fellow Am. Phys. Soc.; mem. N.Y. Acad. Scis., Biophys. Soc., Grad. "M" Club (awarded hon. "M" 1991), Sigma Xi, Phi Kappa Phi, Kappa Kappa Psi. Achievements include invention of automatic judging and timing for swim meets, fast neutron spectroscopy using cyclotrons; development of high resolution nuclear spectroscopy with cyclotrons. Home: 1600 Sheridan Dr Ann Arbor MI 48104-4052 Office: Univ Mich Dept Physics Ann Arbor MI 48109 E-mail: wcpark@umich.edu.

PARKISON, JAMES MAX, trial court administrator, educator; b. Kansas City, Mo., Jan. 12, 1943; s. Amherst Max and Agnes Lorraine (St. George) P.; m. Anne Ruth Hale, Nov. 1, 1969; 1 child, Christopher Hale. BA, Grinnell Coll., 1965; JD, U. Mo., Kansas City, 1968. Bar: Mo. 1968, U.S. Dist. Ct. (ea. dist.) Mo. 1969. Vol. VISTA, 1969-70; staff atty. St. Louis Legal Aid Soc., 1970-71; cts. program chief Mo. Law Enforcement Assistance Coun., Jefferson City, 1971-73; state ct. adminstr. State of Mo. Supreme Ct., 1973-81; asst. dir. Inst. Jud. Adminstrn., N.Y.C., 1981-83; trial ct. adminstr. Burlington County, State N.J., Mt. Holly, 1983-91; clk. of ct. so. dist. N.Y. U.S. Dist. Ct., N.Y.C., 1991—. Mem. nat. adv. com. Nat. Inst. Law Enforcement and Criminal Justice, Dept. Justice, Washington, 1977-81, nat. adv. com. Inst. for Econ. and Policy Studies, Inc., A Comparative Study of State Ct. Orgns., 1980-83; mem. Nat. State Jud. Info. Sys. Com., 1973-81, chmn. sys. documentation com., 1976-77, mem. long range planning com. and sys. devel. com. Nat. Ctr. for State Cts., Williamsburg, Va., 1976-80; mem. exec. com. Coordinating Coun. of Nat. Ct. Orgns., 1983-84; cons. Koba Assocs., 1975-83; adj. asst. prof. law NYU Sch. Law, 1982-83; adj. assoc. prof. NYU Sch. Pub. Adminstrn., 1983-85; adj. instr. Rutgers Sch. Law, Camden, 1986-91; cons. Asian Coun. for Law and Devel., Colombo, Sri Lanka, Ministry of Justice Sri Lanka, 1982; internat. rapporteur Commn. on Juries, Conf. on Independence of Justice, 1983. Mem. editl. bd. The Justice Sys. Jour., 1983-91; exec. prodr. Little Theatre, Jefferson City, 1980-81, bd. dirs., 1979-81; bd. dirs. Burlington Co. Footlighters, 1986-91. U. Mo.-Kansas City Law Sch. scholar, 1965. Mem. ABA (mem. criminal justice sect. 1981-84), Am. Judicature Soc. (life), Conf. State Ct. Adminstrs. (nat. exec. com. 1976-81, nat. vice chmn. 1978-79, nat. chmn. 1979-80), Internat. Bar Assn. (vice chmn. com. on adminstrn. of justice sect. gen. practice 1982-84), Sigma Delta Chi, Phi Alpha Delta. Methodist. E-mail: jparki@aol.com.

PARKLEE, LEE See PARK, LEE

PARKMAN, CYNTHIA ANN, medical and surgical nurse, nursing educator; b. Mpls., Nov. 7, 1957; d. Byron F. and Carolyn M. (Waltenen) Bray; m. Russell O. Parkman, Mar. 15, 1980; children: Theodore Owen, Thomas Edward, Elizabeth Ann. BSN cum laude, Point Loma Coll., San Diego, 1980; MSN, U. San Diego, 1988. Project nurse Sharp Meml. Hosp., San Diego, 1987-91, clin. nurse specialist, mgr. ambulatory care, program mgr., clin. specialist, 1992-93. Instr. Point Loma Nazarene Coll., San Diego, 1991—92; free-lance writer, 1993—; house supr. Suttr Davis Hosp., 1996—98; educator Mercy Healthcare Sacramento, Calif., 1996—99; asst. prof. Calif. State U., Sacramento, 1997—; cons. quality managed care/leadership. Contbr. articles to profl. jours. Manchester scholar, 1988, grad. fellow, 1987-88. Mem.: ANA, Am. Holistic Nurses Assn., Case Mgmt. Am. Soc., Point Loma Nazarene Coll. Nursing Honor Soc. (charter), Zeta Eta, Zeta Mu, Sigma Theta Tau. E-mail: capwriter@hotmail.com.

PARKMAN, HENRY PAUL, medical educator; b. Sept. 6, 1955; AB, Harvard U., 1977; MD, Case Western Res. U., 1982. Assoc. prof. medicine Temple U. Sch. Medicine, Phila., 1991—. Office: Temple U Hosp Dept Medicine 3401 N Broad St Philadelphia PA 19140-5103 E-mail: hparkman@nimbus.temple.edu.

PARKMAN, LAURA JEAN, real estate agent, writer; b. L.A., Nov. 2, 1948; d. Arthur Jr. Gottlieb; m. Michael David Williamson, Aug. 14, 1965 (div. Jan. 1968); 1 child Brian Michael Williamson ; m. Gordon Wayne Parkman, Dec. 14, 1975. AA, Mesa Coll., 1983; BS, U. Calif., San Diego, 1986. Fashion model, L.A., 1969—72; real estate agt. Parkman Realty, San Diego, 1975—. Author: Dreams Don't Last Forever, 2000; inventor: children's game Send Me an Angel, 2001. Mem.: Daus. of the Nile. Democrat. Mem. Assemblies Of God. Avocation: songwriting.

PARKS, ALBERT LAURISTON, lawyer; b. Providence, July 18, 1935; s. Albert Lauriston and Dorothy Isabel (Arnold) P.; m. Martha Ann Anderson, Jan. 12, 1961; children: Amy Woodward, George Webster, Reed Anderson. BA, Kent State U., 1958; JD, U. Chgo., 1961. Bar: R.I. 1962, U.S. Dist. Ct. R.I. 1963, U.S. Ct. Appeals (1st cir.) 1966, U.S. Supreme Ct. 1980. Assoc. Hanson, Curran, Parks & Whitman, Providence, 1961-65, ptnr., 1966-2000. Town solicitor, North Kingstown, R.I., 1978-80, 97—. Fellow Am. Coll. Trial Lawyers; mem. ABA, Maritime Law Assn., R.I. Bar Assn., Saunderstown Yacht Club. Republican. Episcopalian. Office: 10 Coronado St Jamestown RI 02835 Home: 14 Church Ln North Kingstown RI 02852-5004 E-mail: alp@hcpw.com.

PARKS, AUBURN WESLEY, priest; b. Palmer, Alaska, Sept. 15, 1962; s. Eldon and Elizabeth June Parks. Student Mobile Coll., 1982—85. Ordained priest L.D.S. Ch. 1994. Pharmacy asst. Med. Village Pharmacy, Prichard, Ala., 1981—85; high priesthood quorum sec. Ch. L.D.S., Mobile, 1982, elder's quorum sec. Anchorage, 1996. Editor: The Letter of Auburn W. Parks, 2001. Active Urban Devel., Anchorage, 1999; cmty. counsel Mid Town, 1998. Mem.: Writer's Guild Am. West. Republican. Mem. Lds Ch. Avocations: reading, writing, performing arts. Home: 666 W 34th Ave # 417 Anchorage AK 99503

PARKS, BIFFTON ASHLEY, pneudraulics specialist, researcher; b. Great Bend, Kans. s. Sherwood Race Parks and Madge Elizabeth Lewis. AAS, C.C. of the AF, Maxwell AFB, 1983; B in Applied Sci., Boise State U., 1992. Instrument auto pilot specialist Idaho Air Guard, Civil Svc., Boise, 1983-96, pneudraulics specialist, 1996—; historical rschr. AFV/Panzer Hist. Rsch. Ctr., 1989-93; pvt. investigator B's Investigations, 1994-97. Sgt. USAF, 1972—. Mem. VFW (life), NRA (life), Am. Fedn. of Govt. Employees (sgt. at arms 1997—). Avocations: traveling, scuba diving, foreign cuisine, hunting, fishing. E-mail: ba.parks@lycos.com.

PARKS, DEBORA ANN, private school director; b. Homestead, Fla., July 23, 1954; d. Jack Wesley and Blanche Margaret (Shawver) Hardin; m. Lewis O'Dell Parks, Apr. 12, 1970 (div. May 1980); 1 child, Kerri Shane Parks. BS in Early Childhood Edn., U. Ala., Tuscaloosa, 1983, MA in Spl. Edn., 1984, MA in Early Childhood Edn., 1987, PhD in Elem. Edn., 1991. Kindergarten tchr. Martin Luther King Jr. Elem. Sch., Tuscaloosa, 1983-85; tchr. gifted grades 2-5 Martin Luther King Jr. Elem. Sch. and Univ. Place Elem. Sch., 1985-86; early childhood edn. instr. Shelton State C.C., 1985-88; instr. U. Ala., 1987; elem. tchr. 1st grade Martin Luther King Jr. Elem. Sch., 1988-89; tchr. gifted grades 3-6 Carthay Elem. Sch., L.A. Unified Sch. Dist., 1991; faculty-in-residence Sunset Village Residence Halls UCLA, 1991-95; tchr. gifted grades K-8 Maimonides Acad., L.A., 1992-94; asst. rschr. So. Calif. Injury Prevention Rsch. Ctr. Sch. Pub. Health, UCLA, 1993-95; faculty liaison on campus housing darkroom UCLA, 1993-95, instr. dept. edn., 1994, 95, instr., rschr., 1989-95; tchr. gifted grades 2-8 Maimonides Acad., L.A., 1995, gen. studies prin., 1995—. Chair Yom Iyun Citywide In-Svc. for Tchrs., L.A., 2000; grad. tchg. asst. elem. edn. U. Ala., Tuscaloosa, 1986-87; field coord., instr. Tchr. Edn. Lab., Grad. Sch. Edn., UCLA, 1989-93; enrichment tchr. grades 3-5 The Buckley Sch., Sherman Oaks, Calif., summer, 1991, 92, 93; evaluation coach/cons. Stanford Rsch. Inst., SB 620 Statewide Healthy Start Initiative Program, L.A., 1993-95; spl. faculty advisor UCLA Photographic Soc., 1993-95; evaluator lang. arts program, curriculum and tchrs. Maimonides Acad., L.A., 1994; enrichment tchr. grades 4-5 Buckley Sch., Sherman Oaks, Calif., summer 1994, enrichment tchr., summer 1995; evaluation coach, cons. Stanford Rsch. Inst., L.A., 1993-95; mem. governing bd. Nat. Assn. Creative Children and Adults, Ohio, 1992-94; rsch. adviser Phi Delta Kappa, UCLA chpt., 1992-94; mem. Adopt-A-Sch. Coun., L.A. Unified Sch. Dist., 1990-95; chairperson Tuscaloosa City Sch.'s Kindergarten Math. Com., 1984; presenter confs. and workshops. Author: The Newspaper Workbook, 1983, Pedestrian and Bicyclist Safety Curriculum for Grades K-5, 1994, Adopt-A-School Programs: A Guide for Pre-Service Teachers, 1995, Exercises and Tests in English Grammar, 2000; manuscript asst. editor Am. Mid. Sch. Edn., 1986-87; asst. editor Adopt-A-School Newsletter, 1993; contbr. articles to profl. jours; Photog. Exhib., Paralel 45 Pub. House, Pitesti, Romania, 2001/ Vol. Rebuild L.A., 1992-93 Recipient award NEA and Kodak, N.Y. and Ala., 1985, scholarships Am. Bus. Women's Assn., Ala., 1988, Beta Chi of Delta Kappa Gamma, 1983, Epsilon chpt. Alpha Delta Kappa, 1984, Yewell R. Thompson Endowed scholarship, 1988; designee Ala. Tchr. of Yr. Program, 1984-85, 85-86. Mem. Phi Delta Kappa. Democrat. Avocations: photography, calligraphy, graphic arts, genealogy. Home: 311 Westbourne Dr West Hollywood CA 90048-1909 Office: Maimonides Acad 310 N Huntley Dr Los Angeles CA 90048-1919 E-mail: dparks555@yahoo.com.

PARKS, DONALD LEE, mechanical engineer, human factors engineer; b. Delphos, Kans., Feb. 23, 1931; s. George Delbert and Erma Josephine (Boucek) P.; m. Bessie Lou Schur, Dec. 24, 1952; children: Elizabeth Parks Anderson, Patricia Parks-Holbrook, Donna, Charles, Sandra. Student, Kans. Wesleyan U., 1948-50; BSME, BSBA, Kans. State U., 1957, MS in Psychology, 1959. Cert. profl. ergonomist. Elem. tchr., 1950-51; with Kans. State U. Placement Svc., 1959-57; human factors engr., sys. engr. Boeing Co., Seattle, 1959-90, sr. specialist engr., 1972-74, sr. engring. supr., 1974-90; pres. D-Square Assocs. Engring. Cons., 1990-95, Venture Worlds, 1995—. Adj. lectr. UCLA Engring. Extension, 1989—; cons., lectr. in field; participant workshops on guidelines in profl. areas, NATO, NSF, Nat. Acad. Sci., NRC. Author over 80 publs., 8 book chpts. Mem. Derby (Kans.) Planning Commn., 1961-62, chmn., 1962; del. King County (Wash.) Rep. Conv., 1972. With AUS, 1952-54. Mem. ASME, APA, Human Factors Soc. (Puget Sound Pres.'s award 1969), Elks. Presbyterian. Home: 6232 127th Ave SE Bellevue WA 98006-3943

PARKS, GEORGE BROOKS, land development consultant, university dean; b. Lebanon, Ky., Feb. 18, 1925; s. George W. and Eleanor B. (Brooks) P.; children— Paula, William. Student N.C. Central Coll., 1942-44; LL.B., Howard U., 1948; LL.M., George Washington U., 1949. Bar: U.S. Dist. Ct. D.C. 1948, U.S. Ct. Appeals 1949, Ky. 1951, U.S. Supreme Ct. 1952. Assoc. Coleman, Parks & Washington, Washington, 1948-60; sr. title officer Security Title Ins. Co., 1960-63; founder, pres. Mchts. Title Co., Los Angeles, 1963-69; dir. urban affairs Title Ins. & Trust Co., Los Angeles, 1969-70; exec. dir. Housing Opportunity Ctr., Los Angeles, 1970-73; asst. to councilman David Cunningham, Los Angeles, 1973-74; dep. county supr. Los Angeles County, 1974-76; asst. dean South Bay U. Sch. Law, Carson, Calif., 1976-78, Glendale U. Sch. Law, Los Angeles, 1978— ; cons. Summa Corp., Los Angeles, 1978-84; pvt. practice cons., Los Angeles, 1978— . Appointed to Productivity Adv. com. City of Los Angeles by Mayor Tom Bradley, 1986. Recipient Cert. of Appreciation, City of Los Angeles, 1979, Outstanding Leadership award Lutheran Housing Corp., 1980; named Disting. Lectr., Nat. Soc. Real Estate Appraisers, 1981, Disting. Alumni, Howard U. Alumni Assn., 1982. Mem. ABA. Democrat. Lutheran. Home: 1149 S Alfred St Los Angeles CA 90035-2503 Office: George B Parks & Assocs 1122 S La Cienega Blvd Ste 104 Los Angeles CA 90035-2500

PARKS, GEORGE RICHARD, librarian; b. Boston, Apr. 11, 1935; m. Carol A. Richmond; children: Elizabeth, Jennifer, Geoffrey. AB summa cum laude, U. N.H., 1959; MAL.S., U. Mich., 1962; postgrad., Johns Hopkins, 1959-65; EFM cert. Sch. Theology, U. of the South, 1985. Preprofl. young adult librarian Enoch Pratt Free Library, Balt., 1960-61, ctrl., br. librarian, 1962-65, asst. to asst. dir., 1965-66; asst. dir. for adminstrn., libraries U. Rochester, 1966-68, chief adminstrv. officer, 1968-69; dean of libraries U. R.I., 1969-80; univ. librarian Colgate U., 1980-85, U. So. Maine, Portland, 1985-97; ret., 1997. Lectr. in field, cons. libr. bldg.; cons. antique map collection; mem. exec. bd. Greater Portland Theol. Libr., 1986-88, Maine Community Cultural Alliance, 1992-98; mem. exec. bd. So. Maine Libr. Dist., 1990-97, chmn., 1993. Apptd. Maine State Libr. Commn., 1994-98; asst. treas. St. Ann's Episcopal Ch., 1999—. Recipient Margaret Mann award U. Mich., 1962; Phillips Exeter Acad. scholar, 1952-54; U. N.H. scholar, 1955-59; Enoch Pratt Free Library scholar, 1961-62; Woodrow Wilson fellow, 1959-60. Mem. ALA, Assn. Coll. Rsch. Librs. (pres. New Eng. chpt. 1975, chmn. nat. conf. 1978, coll. librs. sect. planning com. 1994-96), Consortium R.I. Acad. Rsch. Librs. (chmn. 1972-73), Maine Libr. Assn., New Eng. Libr. Assn. (conf. planning com. 1992-97, v.p./pres. elect 1995-96, pres. 1996-97, exec. bd. 1997-99), Libr. Adminstrn. and Mgmt. Assn. (exec. bd. bldgs. and equipment sect., libr. bldg. awards com. 1983-85), Phi Beta Kappa, Phi Kappa Phi, Beta Phi Mu. Home: 4 Pierce St Westbrook ME 04092-2331 E-mail: grparks@aol.com.

PARKS, GRACE SUSAN, bank official; b. N.Y.C., Oct. 14, 1948; d. Marco A. and Gloria (Alvino) Vale; m. Louis Parks, Feb. 14, 1988. BS, Pa. State U., 1970; MA, New Sch. for Social Rsch., 1974; cert. in mgmt., Adelphi U., 1979, MBA, 1980; cert. in entrepreneurship, Hofstra U., 1996. Bus. office rep. N.Y. Tel. Co., Rockville Centre, 1971-74; social worker Children's Aid Soc., N.Y.C., 1974-75; EEO officer Edwin Gould Svcs., 1976-79; v.p. fin. instns. and global markets Bankers Trust Co., 1979-92; v.p. compensation human resources Chase Manhattan Bank, 1992-96; pres. Loodie Prodns., Inc., 1996; instr. mgmt. Adelphi U. Grad. Sch. Bus. Adminstrn., 1981—; notary pub. State N.Y., 1978—. Mem. Human Resource Planning Soc., Assn. MBA Execs., Am. Compensation Assn., Wall St. Compensation and Benefits Assn. (chmn. 1994-96, pres. 1993-94), N.Y. Compensation Assn., Adelphi U. Businesswomen's Alumni Assn. (pres. 1980-82).

PARKS, HAROLD RAYMOND, mathematician, educator; b. Wilmington, Del., May 22, 1949; s. Lytle Raymond Jr. and Marjorie Ruth (Chambers) P.; m. Paula Sue Beaulieu, Aug. 21, 1971 (div. 1984); children: Paul Raymond, David Austin; m. Susan Irene Taylor, June 6, 1985; 1 stepchild, Kathryn McLaughlin. AB, Dartmouth Coll., 1971; PhD, Princeton U., 1974. Tamarkin instr. Brown U., Providence, 1974-77; asst. prof. Oreg. State U., Corvallis, 1977-82, assoc. prof., 1982-89, prof. math., 1989—, chmn. dept. math., 2001—. Vis. assoc. prof. Ind. U., Bloomington, 1982-83. Author: Explicit Determination of Area Minimizing Hypersurfaces, vol. II, 1986, (with Steven G. Krantz) A Primer of Real Analytic Functions, 1992, (with G. Musser, R. Burton, W. Siebler) Mathematics in Life, Society and the World, 1997, 2d edit., 2000, (with Steven G. Krantz) The Geometry of Domains in Space, 1999; contbr. articles to profl. publs. Cubmaster Oregon Trail Coun. Boy Scouts Am., 1990-92. NSF fellow, 1971-74. Mem. Am. Math. Soc., Math. Assn. Am., Soc. Indsl. and Applied Math., Phi Beta Kappa. Republican. Mem. Soc. Of Friends. Home: 33194 Dorset Ln Philomath OR 97370-9555 Office: Oreg State U Dept Math Corvallis OR 97331-4605 E-mail: parks@math.orst.edu.

PARKS, JAMES WILLIAM, II, public facilities executive, lawyer; b. Wabash, Ind., July 30, 1956; s. James William and Joyce Arlene (Lillibridge) P.; m. Neil Ann Armstrong, Aug. 21, 1982; children: Elizabeth Joyce, Helen Frances, James William III. BS, Ball State U., 1978; JD, U. Miami, 1981. Bar: La. 1981, U.S. Dist. Ct. (ea. dist.) La. 1981, U.S. Ct. Appeals (5th and 11th cirs.) 1981. Fla. 1982, U.S. Dist. Ct. (mid. dist. La.) 1982.. Atty. Jones, Walker, Waechter, Poitevent, Carrere et al., New Orleans, 1981-83, Foley & Judell, New Orleans, 1983-88, McCollister & McCleary, pc, Baton Rouge, 1988-95; pres., CEO La. Pub. Facilities Authority, 1995—. Mem. AICPA, Nat. Assn. Bond Lawyers, La. State Bar Assn., Fla. Bar Assn., Assn. for Gifted and Talented Students, Baton Rouge (treas. 1994-96, pres.-elect 1996-97, pres. 1997-98), Soc. La. CPA (govt. acctg. and auditing com. 1994-95), Nat. Assn. Higher Edn. Facilities Authorities (bd. dirs. 1996-2001, v.p. 1997-99, pres. 1999-2001). Avocations: travel, computers. Home: 5966 Tennyson Dr Baton Rouge LA 70817-2933 Office: La Pub Facilities Authority 2237 S Acadian Thruway Ste 650 Baton Rouge LA 70808-2380 E-mail: jameswparks2@hotmail.com., parks@lpfa.com.

PARKS, JANE DELOACH, retired law librarian, legal assistant; b. Atlanta, June 7, 1927; d. John Keller and Martha Lorena (Lee) deLoach; m. James Bennett Parks, Dec. 28, 1951 (dec. Sept. 1983); children: Carrie Anne Parks-Kirby, Susan Jane, Lora Beth Parks-Maury. BA magna cum laude, Vanderbilt U., 1949; postgrad., Emory U., 1950-51; tchr. cert., U. Chattanooga, 1954; postgrad., U. Tenn., Chattanooga, 1971-73. Med. rsch./writing dept. surgery Emory U., Atlanta, 1949-51; sec. to med. dir. Tenn. Tuberculosis Hosp., Chattanooga, 1951-53; tchr. Signal Mountain (Tenn.) Elem. Sch., 1954-55; tchr., dean jr. sch. Cleve. (Tenn.) Day Sch., 1963-70; law firm libr., legal asst. Stophel, Caldwell & Heggie, Chattanooga, 1972-85, Caldwell, Heggie & Helton, Chattanooga, 1985-93, Heiskell, Donelson, Bearman, Adams, Williams & Caldwell, Chattanooga, 1993-94, Baker, Donelson, Bearman & Caldwell, Chattanooga, 1994-99; ret., 1999. Tchr. various seminars on legal rsch. and writing, organizing one-person librs. and ch. librs., Chattanooga Legal Secs. Assn., Chattanooga-Hamilton County Bicentennial Libr. Editor (mag.) The Gadfly, 1947-49; editorial asst.: Studio Collotype, 1988 and to profl. jours., 1949—. Tchr. Chattanooga Area Literacy Movement, 1984-86; exec. coun. Friends of Chattanooga-Hamilton County Bicentennial Libr., 1989-94; del. Gov.'s Conf.-White House Conf. on Librs. and Info. Svcs., Nashville, 1990; libr. vol. Tenn. Aquarium. Environ. Learning Lab.; allocations com. United Way, 1994—, Signal Mountain Cmty. Guild, 1999—; dir. Lit. Dept., 2000—02, pub. chmn., 2002-. Mem. Tenn. Paralegal Assn., Chattanooga Area Libr. Assn. (2d v.p. 1989-90, sec. 1992-93), Non-Atty. Profl. Assn. (chmn. 1989-93), Phi Beta Kappa, Mortar Bd. Republican. Methodist. Avocations: ceramics, reading, storytelling, needlework, genealogy.

PARKS, JOE BENJAMIN, entrepreneur, former state legislator; b. McAlester, Okla., Dec. 17, 1915; s. James Allen and Mary Florence (Youngblood) P.; m. Florence M. Evans, Oct. 25, 1941; children: Anne, Kathryn. BS in Pub. Adminstrn., Okla. State U., 1939. Div. dir. U.S. VA, Washington, 1946-56; spl. asst., cons. U.S. GSA, 1957-58; mgr. dist. EDP div. RCA Corp., 1959-65; mgr. Ea. region Dashew Bus. Machines, Arlington, Va., 1966-68; assoc. adminstr. social and rehab. svc. U.S. Dept. Health, Edn. & Welfare, Washington, 1969-73; dir. mktg. govt. systems div. Booz, Allen & Hamilton, 1974-75; ptnr. Forbes & Parks, Dover, NH, 1976—2002; mem. N.H. State Legislature, Concord, 1985-92, chmn. joint com. on elderly affairs, 1987-92, mem. com. on health, human svcs. and elderly, 1987-90; chmn. subcom. mileage and electronic roll call, 1989-90; vice chmn. legis. adminstrn. com., 1990-91; mem. appropriations com., 1991-92; proprietor Portsmouth (N.H.) Athenaeum, 1992—. Corporator Wentworth Douglas Hosp., Dover, 1980-89; pres. Berr Par, Inc., 1994—. Columnist Nat. Antiques Rev., 1975-77, Boston Globe N.H. Weekly 1987-88, Foster's Daily Democrat (Dover, N.H.), 1988-90; freelance writer, 1990—. Vice-chmn. N.H. State Rep. Com., 1987-88; chmn. Strafford County (N.H.) Reps., 1988; Strafford County campaign mgr. George W. Bush for Pres., 1999-2000; bd. dirs. Coastal Maine Bot. Garden, 2001—. Decorated Bronze Star; recipient Lawmakers award for disting. environ. svc. Sierra Club, 1990, N.H. State award New England Wildflower Soc., 1998; named Norris Cotton Rep. of Yr., 1993; Paul Harris fellow Rotary Internat. Found., 1998. Mem. Am. Rhododendron Soc. (pres. Mass. chpt. 1995-96, Bronze medal 1992). Congregationalist. Avocation: rhododendron hybridizing. Home and Office: 195 Long Hill Rd Dover NH 03820-6108

PARKS, JOHN GORDON, English educator; b. Long Beach, Calif., Sept. 29, 1940; s. Wilbert Gordon and Francine Julie (Dellan) P.; m. Joan E. Berry, Aug. 26, 1967 (div. dec. 1994); children: Lori Lynn, Joel G.; m. Linda J. Sheils, Dec. 16, 1994. BA, U. Calif., Berkeley, 1963; D Religion, Sch. Theology, Claremont, Calif., 1968; PhD, U. N.Mex., 1973. Asst. prof. Miami U., Oxford, Ohio, 1973-81, assoc. prof. English, 1981-91, prof., 1991—. Minister United Meth. Ch., Huntington Park, Calif., 1967-69. Author: The Fiction of E.L. Doctorow, 1991; contbr. ; author: American Short Stories Since 1945, 2002. Pres. bd. dirs. Oxford Area Community Theater, 1986-89; candidate for Congress, 2000. Mem. Modern Lang. Assn., Am. Studies Assn., Conf. Christianity and Lit., Am. Culture Assn. Democrat. Avocations: handball, backpacking, tennis.

PARKS, LLOYD LEE, oil company executive; b. Kiefer, Okla., Dec. 9, 1929; s. Homer Harrison and Avis Pearl (Motes) P.; m. Mary Ellen Scott, Aug. 20, 1948; children: Connie Jo, Karyn Ann, Rebecca Lee. Student, Okla. State U., 1948-50, Tulsa U., 1950-51, Harvard U. Bus. Sch., 1965. Acct. Deep Rock Oil Corp., 1951-54; chief acct. Blackwell Oil & Gas Co., Tulsa, 1954-60, sec. treas., 1960-62; v.p., controller Amax Oil & Gas Inc., Houston, 1962-67, pres., CEO, 1968—92; v.p. Amax, Inc., 1975-92; pvt. practice oil and gas and real estate imvestment Salado, Tex., 1992—. Served with AUS, 1946-48, 50-51. Mem.: Ind. Petroleum Assn. Am. (dir.), Lions Club, Wildflower Country Club (Temple, Tex.). Republican. Office: PO Box 1021 Salado TX 76571-1021 *Work hard, work smart and believe in yourself. You can and will be successful; if you want to be.*

PARKS, MICHAEL CHRISTOPHER, journalist; b. Detroit, Nov. 17, 1943; s. Robert James and Rosalind (Smith) P.; m. Linda Katherine Durocher, Dec. 26, 1964; children: Danielle Anne, Christopher, Matthew. AB, U. Windsor, Ont., Can., 1965. Reporter Detroit News, 1962-65; corr. Time-Life News Service, N.Y.C., 1965-66; asst. city editor Suffolk Sun, Long Island, N.Y., 1966-68; polit. reporter, foreign corr. The Balt. Sun, Saigon, Singapore, Moscow, Cairo, Hong Kong, Peking, 1968-80; fgn. corr. L.A. Times, L.A., Peking, Johannesburg, Moscow, Jerusalem, 1980-95, dpty. fgn. editor, 1995-96, mng. editor, 1996-97, editor, 1997-2000, v.p., 1996-97, sr. v.p., 1997-98, exec. v.p., 1998-2000; v.p. Times Mirror Co., 1998-2000; prof. Annenberg Sch. Comm. U. So. Calif., L.A., 2000—02, dir. Annenberg Sch. Comm., 2002—, prof. journalism, 2002—. Disting. fellow Pacific Coun. Internat. Policy, 2000-02, dir. 2002—; trustee Found. Am. Comms. Recipient Pulitzer Prize, 1987. Mem. Am. Soc. Newspaper Editors, Pacific Coun. on Internat. Policy, Internat. Press Inst., Royal Commonwealth Soc. London, Soc. Profl. Journalists, Fgn. Corr. Club (Hong Kong), City Club (L.A.), Coun. on Fgn. Rels. Office: Annenberg Sch U So Calif Los Angeles CA 90089-0281 E-mail: mparks@usc.edu.

PARKS, ORLANDO ALVIN, II, minister; b. Washington, Mar. 7, 1961; s. Orlando Allen and Minnie Marie (Cabell) P.; m. La Vonne Denyse Rawles, Mar. 25, 1989; 1 child; 6 foster children. Student, Prince George's Community Coll., Largo, Md., 1980-83, Bowie State U., 1984-85, Washington Bible Coll., Lanham, Md., 1985. Ordained to ministry Bapt. Ch., 1985. Min. youth Mt. Enon Bapt. Ch., Washington, 1987—; dir. United for Harvest Outreach Ministeries, Lanham, 1989—; psychotherapist Affiliated Santé Group, Landover & Silver Spring, Md., 1991—. Family counselor So. Area Youth Svcs., Temple Hills, Md., 1994—; counselor, asst. spl. edn. Richardson Elem. Sch., Washington; pres., dir. spl. edn., asst. tchr. Prince George's Cmty. Gospel Choir, Largo, 1981-88, advisor, 1988-90; mem. Bowie State Gospel Choir, 1985-87. Active PTA, Ft. Washington, 1989-91, Glendale Bapt. Ch., Landover, Md., 1995—, mem. hosp. ministry com., revival com., young adult and mass choir Healing Hearts Ministry; counselor Prince George's County ARC, 1991—, Assn. for Retarded Citizens of Prince George's County, 1991—; dir. Richardson Elem. Gospel Choir, boys group leader Champs; cmty. supr. Rock Creek Found.; office mgr., counselor/therapist Oxon Hill Profl. Group, 1998. Named to Outstanding Young Men of Am., 1989-90, Counselor of the Yr., Sta. WYCB, Washington, 1987-88. Mem. Coun. of Exceptional Children, Toastmaster Internat., Phi Beta Sigma. Home: 10011 New Orchard Dr Upper Marlboro MD 20774-2249 *As we endeavor to bring about change by God's word, we in our own lives have to remember to keep the bread fresh.*

PARKS, PATRICIA JEAN, lawyer; b. Portland, Oreg., Apr. 2, 1945; d. Robert and Marion (Crosby) P.; m. David F. Jurca, Oct. 17, 1971 (div. 1976). BA in History, Stanford U., 1963-67; JD, U. Penn., Phila., 1967-70. Bar: N.Y. 1971, Wash. 1974. Assoc. Milbank, Tweed, Hadley & McCoy, N.Y.C., 1970-73, Shidler, McBroom, Gates & Lucas, Seattle, 1974-81, ptnr., 1981-90, Preston, Thorgrimson, Shidler, Gates & Ellis, Seattle, 1990-93; pvt. practice, 1993-99; spl. counsel Karr Tuttle Campbell, 1999—. Active Vashon Allied Arts, Mountaineers. Mem.: ABA, Pension Roundtable, Western Pension Conf., Employee Stock Ownership Plan Assn., Seattle-King County Bar Assn., Washington Women in Tax, Wash. State Bar Assn. (past pres. tax sect., past chair gift and estate tax com.), Vashon Athletic Club, Wash. Athletic Club. Avocations: kayaking, hiking, Contra dancing, bird watching, karate. Office: 1201 3rd Ave Ste 2900 Seattle WA 98101-3284

PARKS, ROBERT HENRY, consulting economist, educator; b. New Orleans, Sept. 20, 1924; s. Charles Samuel and Amelia (England) P.; m. Inta Kondrats, Sept. 20, 1958; children: Karen E., Robert R., Alison J.; m. Annette Fiechter, Dec. 10, 1982 (div.). AB in Econs., Swarthmore Coll., 1949; MA, PhD in Econs., U. Pa., 1958. Economist Econ. Forecasting div. Gen. Electric Co., 1958-61; dir. econ. research Life Ins. Assn. Am., 1961-68; chief economist Maj. Wall St. Investment Firms, 1968-80; pres. Robert H. Parks & Assocs., Inc., N.Y.C., 1980—; cons. to instnl. investment officers; prof. fin., dir. Inst. Internat. Fin. Pace U., Wharton Sch. (U. Pa.), Baruch (CUNY); prof. fin. Lehigh U. Author: The Witch Doctor of Wall Street, 1996, Unlocking the Secrets of Wall Street, 1998, Prometheus; contbr. articles to profl. jours. Democrat. Home: Scarborough Manor 6M-2 PO Box 307 Scarborough NY 10510

PARKS, ROBERT MYERS, appliance manufacturing company executive; b. Nevada, Mo., July 18, 1927; s. Cecil R. and Marcella (Myers) P.; m. Audrey Lenora Jones, June 18, 1955; children— John Robert, Janet M. Parks Huston. BS, U. Mo., 1949; MBA, Harvard U., 1952. Asst. dept. mgr. Jewett & Sherman Co., Kansas City, Mo., 1949-50; staff cons. Harbridge House, Inc., Boston, 1952; v.p. Electronic Splty. Co., Inc., Los Angeles, 1952-57; founder, chmn. bd. Parks Products, Inc., Hollywood, Calif., 1957—; pres. Generalist Industries, Inc., 1960-73. Chmn. bd. Shaver Corp. Am., L.A., 1965—; lectr. mktg. UCLA Extension divsn., 1960-61. Contbr. articles to profl. jours.; patentee in field. Active YMCA; bd. dirs. Hollywood Presbyn. Med. Center Found., Presbyn. Homes Found.; mem. dean's adv. council U. Mo. Bus. Sch., mayor's task force on L.A. River Cahuenga Pass Coalition. With USNR, 1944-45. Named in his honor Grad. Bus. Sch., U. Mo. Mem. Sales and Marketing Execs. Assn., C. of C., Navy League, World Affairs Council, Calif. Caballeros, Rangers, Vaqueros del Desierto, Los Caballeros, Rancheros Visitadores, E Clampus Vitus, Delta Sigma Pi, Sigma Chi. Clubs: Mason (Shriner), L.A. Breakfast, Braemar Country, Saddle and Sirloin. Presbyterian. Home: 7421 Woodrow Wilson Dr Los Angeles CA 90046-1322 Office: 3611 Cahuenga Blvd Hollywood CA 90068-1205

PARKS, SHERRI LOU, ballet dancer, thoroughbred handler; b. Washington, Nov. 11, 1955; d. Joseph Allen and Mary Lu Panerosa. HS, Lowell H.S., San Francisco, CA, 1973. Thoroughbred showperson Summerfield Sales, Unknown, Fla.; thoroughbred handler Taylor Made Sales; admin. asst. Don Mankin, CPA, San Francisco; ballet dancer NYC Ballet, New York, San Francisco Opera Ballet, San Francisco, Colo. Ballet, Indpls. Ballet Theater, Indianapolis, Redwood Empire Ballet, Redwood; jewelry designer Market of Marion, 1998—. Choreographer San Francisco Conservatory of Music, San Francisco, Sacramento Opera, Sacramento; costume designer San Francisco Conservatory of Music, San Francisco. Contbr. articles to profl. jours. Educator, children's program Ocala Civic Theater, Ocala, Fla., 1997. Mem.: Farm Managers Assn. Achievements include codified & illustrated pointe shoe dancing techniques and knessive floor-barre therapy for Pointe Magazine's Web site. Avocations: horse riding, long distance swimming, floral & jewelry designing. Home: 745 NE 142nd Ave Silver Springs FL 34488-4123 Home Fax: 352-625-0921. Personal E-mail: sherrilu-1-p.p.@worldnet.att.net.

PARKS, SUZAN LORI, playwright; BA, Mount Holyoke Coll., 1985. Dir. Theater Projects Calif. Inst. Arts, Valencia. Author (play): The Sinner's Place, 1985, Betting on the Dust Commander, 1988, Devotees in the Garden of Love, 1992, The Death of the Last Black Man in the Whole Entire World, 1992, The America Play, 1993, In the Blood, 1999, Topdog/Underdog, 2001, Imperceptible Mutabilities in the Third Kingdom, 1990 (Obie award, 1990), Venus, 1996 (Obie award, 1996). Fellow, Guggenheim Found., 2000. Office: Calif Inst Arts 24700 McBean Pkwy Valencia CA 91355*

PARKS, SUZAN-LORI, playwright; BA, Mt. Holyoke Coll., 1985. Dir. ASK theater projects writing for performance program Calif. Inst. Arts, Valencia. (playwright): (plays) The Sinner's Place, 1985; Betting on the Dust Commander, 1988; Devotees in the Garden of Love, 1992; The Death of the Last Black Man in the Whole Entire World, 1992; The America Play, 1993; In the Blood, 1999; Topdog/Underdog, 2001; Venus (Obie award); Imperceptible Mutabilities in the Third Kingdom (Obie award). Fellow Guggenheim fellow, 2000. Office: ASK Theater Projects 11845 West Olympic Blvd Ste 1250 Los Angeles CA 90064*

PARK SPENCER, KAREN LYNN, architect, jewelry designer; b. Brookville, Pa., Apr. 30, 1963; d. John Joseph Park, Roselyn Ann Park; m. Michael Vincent Spencer. A Specialized Tech., Triangle Tech. Coll., 1986. Cert. interior design 1995, lic. real estate Pa., 1993, cert. kitchen specialist 1988, quality control mfg. housing 1988. Space planner & cad drafter Pace Design, McLean, Va., 1986—86; cad drafter and quality control Strattan Homes , Strattanville, Pa., 1986—88; store planner Penn-Traffic Riverside Engring., DuBois, 1988—95; designer K.T.H. Architects, 1995—96; drafting coord. C-Cor Elecs., State College, 1996—97; mech. engr. D.L. Martin (for Schindler Elevator Corp.), Mercersburg, 1997—98; sr. project mgr. Noelker & Hull Architects, Chambersburg, 1998—2000. Cons. Park Places, Chambersburg, 1995—2002; drafting shadow Riverside Engring., DuBois, 1988—95; real estate Sarvey, Brookville, 1993—94; elec. tech. Strattan Homes, Strattanville, 1987—88. Author: (Poetry) Aspirations of Pen and Thought, 1997 (Editors Choice Award, 1998), Perceptions in Harmony, 1998 (Editors Choice Award, 1999), Dawn of Silence, 1998 (Editors Choice Award, 1999), Last Good-byes, 1998 (Editors Choice Award, 1999), America at the millenium - The Best Poems and Poets of the 20th Century, 2000 (Editors Choice Award, 2001). Vol. Brookville Civic Club, Brookville, 1992—95, Vols. for Charity, DuBois, 1992—95; asst. Girl Scout of Am., Brookville, 1972—76; helper 4-H, Home & Dairy, Brrokville, 1971—76; tchr. The Presbyn. Ch. Brookville, Brookville, 1991—95; facilitator Alpha program The Presby. Ch. Falling Spring, Chambersburg, 2001—02. Mem.: Order of Ea. Star. Presbyterian. Avocations: poetry, art, swimming, travel. Personal E-mail: www.parkplaces.com. Business E-Mail: www.park-places.com.

PARKYN, JOHN WILLIAM, editor, writer; b. London, Dec. 7, 1931; came to U.S., 1967; citizen, 1973; s. James R. and Eva M. (Dix) P.; m. Sybil (Judy) Hetherington; 1 child, Elaine. Student, Dulwich Coll., 1943-48. Staff writer Bus. Mag., London, 1954-56, Amalgamated Press, London, 1956-58; features editor Woman's Illustrated mag., 1958-60; staff writer Internat. Pub. Corp., 1960-61; editor Westward mag. Daily News Ltd., 1961-64; assoc. editor Daily Telegraph mag., 1964-66; features editor King mag. Europress, Ltd., 1966-67; assoc. editor Tropic mag. Miami (Fla.) Herald, 1967-69; editor Tropic mag., 1969-77; editor Calif. Today mag. San Jose (Calif.) Mercury News, 1977-83; editor Sunshine: The Mag. of South Fla. Sun-Sentinel Co. (subs. Tribune Co.), Ft. Lauderdale, Fla., 1983-96; columnist S. Fla. Sun-Sentinel, 1997—; exec. editor, sr. writer Vero Beach (Fla.) Mag., 1998—. Cons. Het Parool newspaper, Amsterdam, 1965. Contbr. numerous articles to Am. and European mags. Chmn. Sunday Mag. Editors Conf., Louisville, 1973. With RAF, 1950-52. Recipient Outstanding Use of Editl. Color award Editor & Pub. mag., 1974, 75, 77, Nat. Headliner award, 1976, 79; named Editor Best Weekly Mag. in State Fla. Press Club, 1985-93, 95. Office: 505 Beachland Blvd Ste 1 PMB 275 Vero Beach FL 32963-1798 E-mail: johnparkyn@aol.com.

PARLAMIS, MICHAEL FRANK, civil engineer, construction company executive; b. Bklyn., May 29, 1940; s. Frank Michael and Phyllis (Burnago) P.; m. Marguerite Koskinas, Aug. 21, 1966; children: Franklin, Christine, Alexander. BSCE, BS in Indsl. Mgmt., MIT, 1962; MSCE, Stanford U., 1963. Registered profl. engr., N.Y. Engr. Port Authority of N.Y. and N.J., 1963-64; asst. to chief engr. George A. Fuller Co., N.Y.C., 1964-67; pres. Frank Parlamis Inc., Bklyn., 1968—, Parlamis Bros. Inc., Bklyn., 1968—, Hermes Constrn. Corp., Bklyn., 1968—; ptnr. City Path LLC, City Jam LLC, Bklyn. Techs. LLC. Author: CPM/PERT As Basis for Management Information Systems in Building Construction, 1966, Regulation of Building Construction in the City of New York, 1967, Greece and the Panama Canal, 1988. Chmn. expansion program Greek Orthodox Cathedral St. John the Theologian, Tenafly, N.J., 1978—; mem. ednl. coun. MIT; trustee Hellenic Heritage Mus., Washington, Frank Parlamus Sr. Citizens Ctr., Jamaica, NY.; founder St. John the Theologian Peace Meml. Gymnasium; exec. dir. St. John the Theologian World Peace Inst. Recipient Ellis Island medal of honor, 2002. Mem. Am. Hellenic Progressive Assn., Bklyn. Tech. Rsch. Found. (life), Tau Beta Pi, Chi Epsilon. Republican. Avocations: engineering and religious history, peace advocacy, ecumenical religious activities. Home: 128 Downey Dr Tenafly NJ 07670-3006 Office: 328 Atlantic Ave Brooklyn NY 11201-5804

PARLE, BERTHA IBARRA, writer short stories, poetry; b. El Paso, Tex., Nov. 14, 1947; d. Arnulfo and Bertha (Soto) Ibarra; m. Dennis Jerome Parle, Aug. 16, 1969; children: Joseph, Mónica, Angélica. BA in French, Spanish, U. Tex., El Paso, 1968; MA in Spanish, U. Kans., 1970, H.S. tchg. cert., 1971; postgrad. courses in French, U. Houston, 1990-95. Bilingual tchr. Kansas Remedial Edn. Program, Sharon Springs, 1967, 71, 72; Spanish tchr. Ottawa (Kans.) H.S., 1971-74; ESL instr. North Harris Coll., Houston, 1977-83; fgn. lang. prof. N. Harris Montgomery C.C. Dist., 1983-97, head lang. inst., 1997—. Cultural cons., sponsor Hispanic students North Harris Coll. and Montgomery Coll., 1983-97, organizer Hispanic cultural events, 1983—, sponsor Cath. Newman Club, 1985-95; lectr., slide show The Nahua Mexica Legacy, 1994-96; participant in field seminars; NEH and Fulbright Ecuador field experience. Poetess; Spanish poetry publ. in Tejidos, Grito al Sol, 1972-94. Hispanic leader St. Leo's Cath. Ch., Houston, 1982-92; del. People to People Am. Program to S. Africa, 2000. Recipient Tchg. Excellence award North Harris Coll., 1997, Excellence award Nat. Inst. for Staff and Orgn. Devel., 1998; Am. Coun. Tchrs. Fgn. Langs. summer scholar U. Montreal, 1999. Mem. AAUW, Am. Coun. Tchrs. Fgn. Langs., Computer Assisted Lan. Instruction Consortium, Am. Assn. C.C. Women, Tex. Fgn. Lang. Assn., Inst. Hispanic Culture., North Harris United Faculty Avocations: creative writing, study of indigenous language cultures, Hispanic students and Hispanic issues in the community. Office: Montgomery Comty Coll 3200 College Park Dr Conroe TX 77384-4500 E-mail: bertha.parle@nhmccd.edu.

PARLIN, CHARLES C., JR. retired lawyer; b. Trenton, Feb. 12, 1928; s. Charles C. and Miriam (Boyd) P.; m. Joan Bona, June 28, 1948; children: C. Christopher, Robert B., Timothy B. BA, U. Chgo., 1946; LL.B., U. Pa., 1949. Bar: N.Y. 1951. Assoc. firm. Shearman & Sterling, N.Y.C., 1950-59, ptnr., 1959-90, of counsel, 1990-92, ret., 1992. Home: Pudding Ln Silver Bay NY 12874 E-mail: parlinjr@aol.com.

PARLOS, ALEXANDER GEORGE, systems and control engineering educator; b. Istanbul, Turkey, July 12, 1961; came to U.S., 1980; s. George Alexander and Helen (Stavridis) P.; m. Dalila Marcia Vieira, Aug. 25, 1985. BS, Tex. A&M U., 1983; MS, MIT, 1985, DSc, 1986. Rsch. asst. MIT, Cambridge, Mass., 1984-86; sr. rsch. assoc. U. N.Mex., Albuquerque, 1986-87; rsch. asst. Tex. A&M U., College Station, 1982-83, asst. prof., 1987-92, assoc. prof., 1993—. Co-founder, pres. ANN Engring., Inc., 1992-96; co-founder, chmn. Orasis Software, Inc., 1997-99; cons. engr. BDM Internat., Inc., McLean, Va., 1988—; sr. engring. assoc. API, Albuquerque, 1990—; cons. engr. Northrop-Grumman Corp., Bethpage, N.Y., 1994—; cons. engr. Kevin Kennedy & Assoc., Inc., Indpls., 1995—. Contbr. articles to Internat. Jour. Control, IEEE Trans. on Nuc. Sci., AIAA Jour. Guidance, Control and Dyamics, AIAA Jour. Propulsion and Power, Space Nuc. Power Sys., Nuc. Tech., Nuc. Sci. Engring., IEEE Trans. on Neural Networks, IEEE Trans. Automatic Control, IEEE Trans. on Industry Applications, also others. Treas. S.W. Crossing Assn., College Sta., 1990-91; advisor Hellenic Student Assn., College Station, 1988-91. Grantee NASA, 1988—, Dept. Energy, 1989—, Lockheed Missile Co., 1989, Electric Power Rsch. Inst., 1988, Am. Pub. Power Assn., 1993—, Advanced Rsch. Projects Agy., 1993—, Tex. Advanced Tech. Program, 1995—, NSF, 2000—; recipient Tech Brief Invention awards (3), NASA, 1999, Best Paper award Internat. Joint Conf. on Neural Networks, 1999. Mem. IEEE (sr., assoc. editor Trans. on Neural Networks 1994—), AIAA (sr.), ASME, Am. Nuc. Soc. (exec. com. human factors divsn. 1993—, chair tech. program com. human factors divsn. 1993—, chair program planning remote sys. divsn. 1989-90), Internat. Neural Networks Soc. (mem. conf. tech. program com. 1995—, mem. editl. bd. trans. on ctrl. automation and sys. 2000—). Achievements include patents in field; patents pending in field; research in neural information processing. Office: Tex A&M U 116 Engring Phys College Station TX 77843-0001

PARMA, FLORENCE VIRGINIA, magazine editor; b. Kenilworth, N.J., Aug. 30, 1940; d. Howard Frank and Mildred Faye (Lister) von Finkel; m. Wilson Henry Parma, June 15, 1973 (div. Aug. 1986). Studies with pvt. tutor, Chaumont, France, 1961-62; student, NYU, 1962-63. Copywriter Schless & Co., N.Y.C., 1963-65; editor, researcher Barchas Lab., Stanford, Calif., 1969-73; adminstrv. exec. Crater Inc., Honolulu, 1974-79; mgr., editor Off Duty mag., 1979—; mktg. dir. Panda Travel, 2001—. V.p. Mapasa, Inc. (dba The Prides of New Zealand), 1992-2000. Editor: Welcome to Hawaii Guide, 1985—; co-editor: Serotonin and Behavior, 1972; freelance columnist. Republican. Episcopalian. Avocations: scuba diving, stained glass, hiking. Home and Office: Off Duty Hawaii 3771 Anuhea St Honolulu HI 96816-3849 E-mail: fparma@hawaii.rr.com.

PARMA, KAAREN LEE, artist; b. Boston, Dec. 20, 1962; d. Arne and Linda Mary (Bergsman) P. Student, S.W. Tex. Coll., 1981, Cambridge Coll., 1990-91. Dir. Karma Designs, Cambridge, Mass., 1990—; creative dir. Boston Block & Toy Co., Inc., 1996—. Illustrator Under One Sky, 1991. Avocations: photography, travel, music. Home: 8 Norfolk Ter # 6 Wellesley MA 02482-6309 Office: Karma Designs PO Box 77 Cambridge MA 02140-0001

PARMALEE, PATTY LEE, writer, educator; b. New Haven, Mar. 18, 1940; d. Phillips Hawkins and Virginia Butterworth Parmalee; 1 child China Beth. BA, Reed Coll., 1962; MA, U. Chgo., 1964; PhD, U. Calif., Irvine, 1970. Asst. prof. Long Beach (Calif.) State U., 1969-71, Calif. Inst. Arts, Valencia, 1971-73, Ramapo Coll., Mahwah, N.J., 1975-80. Mem. program com. Brecht Forum, NYC, 1985—. Author: Brecht's America, 1981; mem. editl. collective Capitalism, Nature, Socialism, 1999—; newsletter editor: Nicaragua Sister City, 1978—. Head coach Achilles Track Club, N.Y.C., 1984-94; mem. steering com. Union for Radical Polit. Econs., New Haven, Conn., 1996-98. Avocations: competitive running, photography, hiking, musician. Home: # 5B 211 W 102 New York NY 10025 E-mail: publiclp@aol.com.

PARMAN, DEBRA LANETTE, physical therapist; b. Knoxville, Tenn., July 19, 1956; d. Carlos Marion and Laura B. (Self) P. AAS in Elem. Edn., Vol. State C.C., Gallatin, Tenn., 1982; BS in Anatomy and Physiology, Andrews U., Berrien Springs, Mich., 1991, MS in Phys. Therapy, 1992. Registered phys. therapist Ga., Tenn. Phys. therapist Tenn. Christian Med. Ctr., Madison, 1992-96, North Ga. Home Health Agy., Dalton, 1996-98; Gordon Hosp., Calboun, Ga., 1998—. Avocations: reading, music, videos and movies, Civil War and Native American history. Home: 151 Spencer Dr SW Calhoun GA 30701-3278

PARMELEE, ARTHUR HAWLEY, JR. pediatric medical educator; b. Chgo., Oct. 29, 1917; s. Arthur Hawley and Ruth Frances (Brown) P.; m. Jean Kern Rheinfrank, Nov. 11, 1939; children: Arthur Hawley III, Ann (Mrs. John C. Minahan Jr.), Timothy, Ruth Ellen. BS, U. Chgo., 1940, MD, 1943. Diplomate Am. Bd. Pediatrics (examiner 1966—). Intern U.S. Naval Hosp., Bethesda, Md., 1943-44; extern Yale Inst. Child Devel., 1947, New Haven Hosp., 1947-48, L.A. Children's Hosp., 1948-49; mem. faculty UCLA Med. Sch., 1951—, prof. pediat., 1967-88, prof. emeritus, 1988, dir. divsn. child devel., 1964-88; mem. Brain Rsch. Inst., 1966-88, Mental Retardation Rsch. Ctr., 1970-88. Rsch. prof. pediat. U. Göttingen, Germany, 1967-68; mem. com. child devel. rsch. and pub. policy NRC, 1977-81; cons. Nat. Inst. Child Health and Human Devel., 1963-70, Holy Family Adoption Svc., 1949-80. Author articles, chpts. in books. Trustee Los Angeles Children's Mus., 1979. Served with USN, 1943-47. Recipient C. Anderson Aldrich award in child devel., 1975; Commonwealth fellow Centre de Recherches Biologiques Neonatales, Clinique Obstetricale Baudelocque, Paris, 1959-60; fellow Ctr. Advanced Study in Behavioral Scis., Stanford U., 1984-85; hon. lectr. Soc. for Developmental and Behavioral Pediat., 1996. Mem. AMA, Am. Pediat. Soc., Soc. Pediat. Rsch., Western Soc. Pediat. Rsch., Am. Acad. Pediat. (chmn. com. sect. child devel. 1966), Assn. Ambulatory Pediat. (mem. coun. 1966-69), Soc. Rsch. in Child Devel. (pres. 1983-85, Disting. Sci. Contbns. to Child Devel. award 1993), Assn. Psychophysiol. Study of Sleep, Los Angeles County Med. Soc., Phi Beta Kappa. Home: 764 Iliff St Pacific Palisades CA 90272-3927 Office: Univ Calif Dept Pediatrics Los Angeles CA 90024

PARMELEE, WALKER MICHAEL, psychologist; b. Grand Haven, Mich., Apr. 26, 1952; s. Walker Michael and Evelyn Mae (Essenberg) P.; m. Gayle Ann Klempel, Jan. 11, 1975; children: Morgan Christine, Kathryn Ann, Elizabeth Mae. BS, Ctrl. Mich. U., 1974, MA, cert. specialist in psychology, 1977; D in Counseling Psychology, Western Mich. U., 1986. Lic. psychologist, Mich. Sch. psychologist Oakridge Pub. Schs., Muskegon, Mich., 1977—82, Ravenna (Mich.) Schs., Muskegon Heights (Mich.) Schs., 1982—84; sr. staff therapist Steelcase Counseling Svcs., Grand Rapids, 1984—90; prin., psychologist Parmelee and Winebarger Psychol. Cons., Grand Haven, 1989—. Consulting psychologist Cross Rds. Family Ctr., Grand Haven, 1989—2000. Contbr. articles to profl. jours. Bd. dirs. Planned Parenthood, Muskegon, 1979-82, Harbinger Inc., Grand Rapids, 1986-90; elder 2d Ref. Ch., Grand Haven, 1989-92; mem. women and families adv. group Allegan, Muskegon, Ottawa Substance Abuse Agy., 1992-95. Mem. Am. Psychol. Assn., Am. Group Psychotherapy Assn., Nat. Assn. Child Alcoholics, Mich. Psychol. Assn., Mich. Sch. Psychologists. Avocations: woodworking, skiing, running, tennis, camping. Home: 215 Howard St Grand Haven MI 49417-1806 Office: Parmelee Psychology Ctr 321 Fulton Ave Grand Haven MI 49417-1231

PARMELEY, JERRY PAUL, paramedic; b. St. Louis, Sept. 27, 1971; s. Jerry Paul and Sherry Nadine P.; m. Tricia Dawn Clarke, Nov. 1, 1997; 1 child, Katelynn. Cert. of Paramedicine, East Ctrl. Coll., Union, Mo., 1994; BS, Columbia Coll., Mo. Cert. paramedic, Mo. Paramedic Boone Hosp. Ctr., Columbia, Mo., 1995-2000; support specialist PDS, 1999-2000, Paramedic Univ. of Mo., 2001—. Alderman Ward One, City of Centralia, Mo., 1998—. With USAF, 1989-93. Republican. Avocations: computers, model rockets. Office: U Med Ctr 1 Hospital Dr Columbia MO 65212 E-mail: jparmeley@hotmail.com.

PARMENTER, ROBERT HALEY, physics educator; b. Portland, Maine, Sept. 19, 1925; s. LeClare Fall and Esther (Haley) P.; m. Elizabeth Kinnecom, Oct. 27, 1951; children: David Alan, Douglas Ian. BS, U. Maine, 1947; PhD, Mass. Inst. Tech., 1952. Mem. staff solid state and molecular theory group Mass. Inst. Tech., 1951-54; guest scientist Brookhaven Nat. Lab., 1951-52; mem. staff Lincoln Lab., 1952-54, RCA Labs., 1954-66, vis. scientist Switzerland, 1958, acting head solid state research group, 1962-65; prof. physics U. Ariz., 1966-96, chmn. dept., 1977-83, prof. emeritus, 1996—. Mem. NASA rsch. adv. com. electrophysics, 1964-68, chmn., 1966-68, mem. rsch. and tech. adv. com. basic rsch., 1966-68; vis. lectr. Princeton (N.J.) U., 1960-61. Served with USNR, 1944-46. Fellow AAAS, Am. Phys. Soc. (chmn. div. condensed matter physics 1967-68); mem. Sigma Xi, Tau Beta Pi. Achievements include predicting the existence of the acoustoelectric effect, the enhancement of the transition temperature of a superconductor by means of tunneling extraction; demonstration of the conditions under which deterministic chaos occurs in quantum mechanical systems. Home: 1440 E Ina Rd Tucson AZ 85718-1175 Office: U Ariz Physics Dept Tucson AZ 85721-0001

PARMER, DAN GERALD, veterinarian; b. Wetumpka, Ala., July 3, 1926; s. James Lonnie and Virginia Gertrude (Guy) P.; m. Donna Louise Kesler, June 7, 1980; 1 child, Dan Gerald; 1 child from previous marriage, Linda Leigh. Student, L.A. City Coll., 1945-46; DVM, Auburn U., 1950. Gen. practice vet. medicine, Galveston, Tex., 1950-54, Chgo., 1959-83; veterinarian in charge Chgo. Commn. Animal Care and Control, 1974-88; med. dir. food protection divsn., disease outbreak control Chgo. Dept. Health, 1988-93, ret., 1993; dir. Cook County Dept. Animal Control, 1998—. Chmn. Ill. Impaired Vets. Com., 1985-93; mem. Ala. Impaired Vets. Com., 1993-98; chmn. Ill. Wellness Com., 1998—; tchr. Highlands U., 1959; humane officer Elmore County, 1994—; dir. sales for south, southeast and lower midwest Am. Vet. Identification Devices, Norco, Calif., 1993-98, nat. dir. companion animal divsn., 1996—. Pres. Elmore County Humane Soc. Served with USNR, 1943-45, PTO, USAF Vet. Corps, 1954-59. Decorated 9 battle stars; recipient Vet. Appreciation award U. Ill., 1971, commendation Chgo. Commn. Animal Care and Control, 1987. Mem.: AVMA (coun. pub. health and regulatory medicine 1990—, nat. com. animal welfare 1999—, nat. com. for impaired vets.), VFW, Ill. State Vet. Med. Assn. (chmn. bd. govs. 2002—), Ill. Acad. Vet. Medicine, Elmore County Humane Soc. (pres. 1994—98), Am. Assn. Zool. Pks. and Aquariums, Am. Assn. Zoo Vets., Nat. Assn. Professions, Ill. Acad. Vet. Practice (pres. 1994), Am. Animal Hosp. Assn. (dir.), South Chgo. Vet. Medicine Assn. (pres. 1965—66), Chgo. Vet. Medicine Assn. (bd. govs. 1969—72, 1974—81, pres. 1982, treas. 1999, Lifetime Merit award 2000), Ill. Vet. Med. Assn. (chmn. civil def. and package disaster hosps. 1968—71, chmn. bd. 2002—, Pres.'s award 1986), Valley Internat. Country Club, Midlothian Country Club, Kiwanis, Shriners, Masons. Achievements include discovery of Bartonellosis in cattle in N.Am. and western hemisphere, 1951; co-development of bite-size high altitude in-flight feeding program USAF. Home: 5704 W 89th St Oak Lawn IL 60453-1222 Office: Cook County Animal Control 10220 S 76th Ave Bridgeview IL 60455-2427 E-mail: drdog11@aol.com.

PARMER, EDGAR ALAN, retired radiologist, musician; b. N.Y.C., Sept. 14, 1928; s. Nathan and Selma (Benett) Parmer; m. Nina Ash (div. 1964); children: Vicki, Robert; m. Judith Rae Parmer, Nov. 22, 1969. AA in Music, UCLA, 1950, BA, 1951; MD, N.Y. Med. Coll., 1958. Intern Grasslands Hosp., Valhalla, N.Y., 1958-59; resident Vets. Hosp., Bronx, 1959-62; assoc. radiologist Francis Delafield Hosp. Columbia Presbyn. Med. Ctr., 1964-82; assoc. radiologist, dir. nuclear medicine Mt. Vernon (N.Y.) Hosp., 1964-82; pvt. practice New Rochelle, N.Y., 1964-84; assoc. radiologist Union Hosp., 1990-97; dir. radiology Hebrew Home for Aged, Riverdale, N.Y., 1968-97. Instr. radiology Columbia U.; vis. fellow dept. radiology Columbia-Presbyn. Med. Ctr.; cons. tech. affairs HEW; mem. staff Radiol. Technicians Program Westchester C.C., chmn. adv. com.; cons., mem. staff St. Barnabas Radiology, 1987—99; med. dir. Ultrasound Diagnostic Sch., 1985—87; assoc. dir. radiology, dir. ultrasound Strang Clinic; asst. prof. Sch. Osteopathy, Westbury, NY, 1984—; lectr. in field. Contbr. articles to profl. jours.; violin soloist: albums N.Y.C. Symphony Orch., 1946, violin soloist: albums Burbank Orch., violin soloist: albums Glendale Orch., violin soloist: albums MGM Symphony, violin soloist: albums Westchester Symphony Orch., violin soloist: albums Westchester Philharm. Orch. Mem., past pres. Dr.'s Symphony Orch. N.Y.; sec. bd. dirs., pres. Westchester Philharm. Orch.; past dir., mem. Am. Cancer Soc.; pres. bd. dirs. Premium Point Pk. With U.S. Army. Fellow: Royal Soc. Health, Am. Coll. Angiology, Am. Inst. Ultrasound Medicine (sr.); mem.: AAAS, AMA, N.Y. Acad. Sci., Westchester Radiol. Soc. (past pres.), Westchester County Med. Soc., N.Y. State Med. Soc., Soc. Nuc. Medicine, Am. Coll. Med. Imaging, Am. Coll. Nuc. Medicine, Am. Coll. Radiology (past pres. Westchester divsn.), Am. Assn. Advancement Boxing (bd. dirs.), Lions Club (pres.). Avocations: tennis, golf, scuba diving. Home: PO Box 1609 Point Pleasant Beach NJ 08742-1609 E-mail: eparmer@comcast.net.

PARMER, JESS NORMAN, university official, educator; b. Elkhart, Ind., Nov. 23, 1925; s. Jess Noah and Zayda Irene (Tressler) P.; m. Bessie Norma Peterson, September 12, 1948; children: Thomas Norman, Sarah Irene. BA, Ind. U., 1949; MA, U. Conn., 1951; PhD, Cornell U., 1957. Resident in Malaya, Southeast Asia program, Cornell U., 1952-55; instr., then asst. prof. history U. Md., 1956-59; mem. faculty No. Ill. U., 1959-67, prof. history, 1960-67, chmn. dept., 1959-63; assoc. dean Coll. Arts and Scis. Ohio U., also dir. Center Internat. Studies, 1967-69, asst. dean faculties for internat. studies, 1969-75; v.p. acad. affairs Trinity U., San Antonio, 1975-82, prof. history, 1975-92; scholar in residence and dir. of special projects Ohio U., Athens, 1993-96; cons. business, govt., edn. Peace Corps rep. in Malaya, 1961-63, Tanzania, summer 1965, Malawi, summer, 1966, Korea, 1967; lectr. Fgn. Service Inst., 1958, 61, 65; vis. prof. history Nat. U. Malaysia, 1984; cons. social scis. com. Ill. Curriculum Program, 1961; cons. various corps.; vis. fellow Cornell U., 1987-88, vis. prof. 1989; luce scholar in res. Ohio U., 1990-91. Author: Governments and Politics of Southeast Asia, 2d edit., 1964, Colonial Labor Policy and Administration, 1960, Southeast Asia: Documents of Political Development and Change, 1974, People and Progress: A Global History, 1977; contbr. chpts. The World of Asia, 1995. Served with inf. AUS, 1944-46, ETO. Mem. AAUP, ACLU, Assn. Asian Studies (chmn. S.E. Asia regional coun. 1968-72, dir. 1969-72), Midwest Conf. Asian Affairs (chmn. library com. 1960-61), Southwest Conf. Asian Studies (pres. 1982-83), Am. Hist. Assn., Sons of the Am. Revolution, Torch Internat., Soc. of Ind. Pioneers, Tex. Soc. War of 1812. E-mail: bessnjess@cs.com. *I find my life full of opportunity, excitement and satisfaction. Satisfaction comes from seeing ideas find institutional or behavioral expression and influencing people in positive ways. Self-fulfillment, hard work, respect for others, and honesty have been guiding principles and I have found them compatible and rewarding.*

PARMET, HERBERT SAMUEL, historian, writer; b. N.Y.C., Sept. 28, 1929; s. Isaac and Fanny (Scharf) P.; m. Joan Kronish, Sept. 12, 1948; 1 child, Wendy. BS, SUNY, Oswego, 1951; MA, Queens Coll., 1957; postgrad., Columbia U., 1958-62. Prof. history Grad. Sch. CUNY, 1968-95, disting. prof. history, 1983-95, prof. emeritus, 1995—. Cons. ABC-TV, N.Y.C., 1983, KERA-TV, Dallas, 1986-91, WGBH-TV, Boston, 1988-91. Author: Aaron Burr: Portrait of an Ambitious Man, 1967, Never Again: President Runs for a Third Term, 1968, Eisenhower and the American Crusades, 1972, The Democrats, 1976, Jack: The Struggles of John F. Kennedy, 1980, JFK: The Presidency of John F. Kennedy, 1983, Richard Nixon and His America, 1990, George Bush: The Life of a Lone Star Yankee, 1997, Presidential Power: From the New Deal to the New Right, 2001. Cpl. U.S. Army, 1952-54. Grantee, NEH, 1987. Fellow Soc. Am. Historians; mem. Am. Hist. Assn., Orgn. Am. Historians, Authors Guild. Avocation: photography. Home: 36 Marsten Ln Hillsdale NY 12529-5816

PARMET, ROBERT DAVID, history educator; b. N.Y.C., Dec. 11, 1938; s. Isaac and Fanny (Scharf) P.; m. Joan Bernice Parmet, June 8, 1963; 1 child, Andrew Charles. BA, CCNY, 1960; MA, Columbia U., 1961, PhD, 1966. Fellow CCNY, 1960-62, lectr., 1962-65; asst. prof. Newark State Coll., Union, N.J., 1965-67, CUNY, Jamaica, N.Y., 1967-70, assoc. prof., 1971-77, chmn. dept. history, 1972-75, prof., 1978—. Author: Labor and Immigration in Industrial America, 1981, rev. edit., 1986; co-author: American Nativism 1830-1860, 1971, rev. edit., 1979; contbr. articles to encys., profl. jours., etc. Mem. King Manor Assn. L.I., Jamaica, N.Y., 1993—. Fellow Woodrow Wilson Nat. Found., 1960, CUNY, 1994. Mem. Am. Hist. Assn., Orgn. Am. Historians, Acad. Polit. Sci., Conn. Hist. Soc., N.Y. Labor Hist. Assn. (mem. exec. bd. 1990—), So. Hist. Assn., Am. Jewish Hist. Assn., King Manor Assn. L.I., Immigration History Soc., Phi Alpha Theta. Democrat. Jewish. Avocations: photography, travel, musical theater, baseball. Home: 1 Highland Pl Great Neck NY 11020 Office: York Coll CUNY 94-20 Guy R Brewer Blvd Jamaica NY 11451 E-mail: parmet@york.cuny.edu.

PARMLEY, JAY, state official; Assoc. in arts, Northeastern A&M Coll.; B in pub. adminstrn., MPA, U. Okla. Fin. dir. Glen Johnson for Congress campaign; mem. DNC Exec. Com., Okla. Dem. Party Exec. Com.; chmn. Young Dems. Am. Nat. Platform Com. , 1997; dir., pres. nat. Dem. Youth Message campaign Young Dems. of Am. , 2000—02; chmn. Okla. Dem. Party, 2001—. Asst. to pres. U. Okla., 1993—95; chancellor's student rels. liaison Okla. State Regents for Higher Edn. , 1995—97; dir. Okla. City Downtown Coll. Consortium , 1997—2001. Democrat. Office: 4100 N Lincoln Blvd Oklahoma City OK 73105*

PARMLEY, RICHARD TURNER, pediatric hematologist, oncologist; b. Madison, Wis., Sept. 10, 1949; *Richard Parmley's parents are Loren F. Parmley Jr. and Dorothy L. Turner. He and his wife, Janice E. McFadden, have four children; Merri J., Richard T. Jr., Banks M., and Andrew L. Richard's paternal grandparents are Loran F. Parmley Sr. and Hope Bartholomew. His maternal grandparents are Thomas J. Turner and Florence M. Bowman. His wife's parents are James Banks McFadden and Agnus E. Rigby. He also has two siblings, Robert J. Parmley and Katherine Parmley.* BA, U. Va., 1970; MD, Med. U. S.C., 1973. Diplomate in pediatrics and in pediatric hematology/oncology Am. Bd. Pediatrics; diplomate in hematopathology Am. Bd. Pathology. Intern Med. U. S.C., Charleston, S.C., 1973, resident in pediats., 1974-75; fellow in pediat. hematology-oncology St. Jude Children's Rsch. Hosp., Memphis, 1976-77, U. Ala., Birmingham, 1977; clin. fellow in med. oncology bone marrow transplant svc. Fred Hutchinson Cancer Rsch. Ctr., Seattle, 1986; dir. Electron Microscopy and History Unit Inst. Dental Rsch. U. Ala., Birmingham, 1978-83, assoc. scientist Comprehensive Cancer Ctr., 1978-83, asst. prof. pediats. and pathology, 1978-82, instr. pediats. and pathology, 1977, assoc. prof. pediats., 1982-83; assoc. prof. pediats. and pathology U. Tex. Health Sci. Ctr., 1983-88, prof. pediats., 1988-94; dir. divsn. pediat. hematology/oncology Carolinas Med. Ctr., Charlotte, NC, 1994—2000; clin. prof. pediat. U. N.C., Chapel Hill, 1994—2000; mem. pediat. hematologist-oncology staff Greenville (S.C.) Children's Hosp., 2000—; clin. prof. pediat. Med. Univ. SC, Charleston, 2000—. Mem. Am. Soc. Hematology, Am. Soc. Pediatric Hematology/Oncology, Am. Soc. Clin. Oncology, Histochemical Soc., Am. Pediatric Soc., Soc. Pediatric Rsch., Alpha Omega Alpha. Office: Greenville Childrens Hosp 900 W Faris Rd Greenville SC 29605-4255 E-mail: rparmley@ghs.org.

PARMLEY, ROBERT JAMES, lawyer, consultant; b. Madison, Wis., Oct. 23, 1950; s. Loren Francis and Dorothy Louise (Turner) P.; m. Debra Paliszewski, Dec. 23, 1982; children: Michelle Hope, Matthew Turner. BA, U. Va., 1972; JD, U. S.C., 1975. Bar: S.C. 1975, Tex. 1976, U.S. Dist. Ct. (so. dist.) Tex. 1976, U.S. Dist. Ct. (we. and no. dists.) Tex. 1980, U.S. Ct. Appeals (5th cir.) 1978, U.S. Tax Ct. 1976, U.S. Supreme Ct. 1980. Staff atty., Vista vol. Tex. Rural Legal Aid, Inc., Alice, 1975-76, mng. atty. Kingsville, 1976-79, sr. staff atty. Kerrville, 1979-81; sole practice, 1981—. Mem. State Bar Tex., State Bar S.C., Kerr County Bar Assn. Episcopalian. Office: Ste 615 222 Sidney Baker St S Kerrville TX 78028-5900

PARMLEY, VAN SAMUEL, retired anesthesiologist; b. Electra, Tex., 1914; s. Tim Hennesy and Madge Parmley; m. Rose Jean Selzer; children: Tim H. II, Martha Lillian Sjogreen. MD, Tulane U., 1939. Cert. in anesthesiology. Intern Charity Hosp., New Orleans, 1939-40; gen. practice, 1945-54; resident in anesthesiology St. Francis Hosp., Wichita, 1954-56; pvt. practice anesthesiology Kans., 1956—64; tchr. Project Hope, 1964—65, U. Tex. Med. Sch., Galveston, 1965—77. With U.S. Army, 1940—45. Mem. AMA, Am. Soc. Anesthesiologists, Pan Am. Med. Assn. Republican. Episcopalian.

PARNELL, CHARLES L. speechwriter; b. Myrtis, La., Feb. 13, 1938; s. Forrest L. and Dorothy D. (Jones) P. BA, Rice U., 1960; M Bus. and Pub. Adminstrn., Southeastern U., 1977. Commd. ens. USN, 1960, advanced through grades to comdr., 1975, ret., 1987; speechwriter Mead Data Cen., Dayton, Ohio, 1987-89, Nationwide Ins. Co., Columbus, 1989-90; exec. speechwriter Miller Brewing Co., Milw., 1990-96; speechwriter, 1996-98; exec. speechwriter, Dallas, 1998—. Contbr. articles to profl. jours.; frequently quoted in leading speech-related publs.; speeches used as models in 8 college level textbooks in U.S. and Can. Mem. U.S. Naval Inst., Ret. Officers Assn., World Future Soc. Avocations: reading, writing, travel. Home and Office: 1311 Brittany Ln Mansfield TX 76063-4013

PARNELL, FRANCIS WILLIAM, JR. otolaryngologist; b. Woonsocket, R.I., May 22, 1940; s. Francis W. and Dorothy V. (Lalor) P.; m. Diana DeAngelis, Feb. 27, 1965; children: Cheryl Lynn, John Francis, Kathleen Diana, Alison Anne, Thomas William. Student, Coll. Holy Cross, 1957-58; AB, Clark U., 1961; MD, Georgetown U., 1965. Diplomate: Nat. Bd. Med. Examiners, Am. Bd. Otolaryngology. Intern Univ. Hosps., Madison, Wis., 1965-66, resident in gen. surgery, 1966-67, otolaryngology, 1967-70; pvt. practice medicine specializing in otolaryngology San Rafael, Calif., 1972-75, Greenbrae, 1972—75; chmn., pres., CEO Parnell Pharms., Larkspur, 1982—; pvt. prac., 1978—2000. Cons. corp. med. affairs, 1978-82; corp. med. dir. Becton, Dickinson & Co., Rutherford, N.J., 1976-78; clin. instr. U. Calif. at San Francisco, 1972-75, asst. clin. prof., 1975-76; Alt. del., U.S. Del. 27th World Health Assembly WHO, Geneva, 1974. Contbr. articles to profl. jours. Candidate Calif. State Assembly, 1988; bd. dirs. Marin Coalition, 1980-96, 97-01, chmn., 1986-87; trustee Ross (Calif.) Sch. Dist., 1981-89; mem. governing bd. Marin Cmty. Coll. Dist., 1995—, pres., 1999-00. Maj. M.C. AUS, 1970-72, lt. col. M.C., USAR, 1985-93. Fellow ACS (gov. 1988-94), Am. Acad. Otolaryngology. Home: PO Box 998 Ross CA 94957-0998 Office: 1100 S Eliseo Dr Greenbrae CA 94904-2017

PARNELL, THOMAS ALFRED, physicist; b. Lumberton, N.C., Nov. 24, 1931; s. Johnathan Alfred and Lula Beale (Lashley) P.; m. Elizabeth G. Brite, June 4, 1955; children: Marc Thomas, Gina Ann. BS in Physics, U. N.C., 1954, MS in Physics, 1962, PhD in Physics, 1965. Rsch. adj., dept. physics U. N.C., Chapel Hill, 1962-65; ops. analyst U.S. Air Force Europe, Wiesbaden, W. Ger., 1965-66; asst. prof. physics Marshall U., Huntington, W.Va., 1966-67; physicist NASA-Marshall Space Flight Center, Huntsville, Ala., 1978-99, chief astrophysics br., 1969-98; prin. rsch. scientist U. Ala., Huntsville, 1999—. Mem. editorial bd. Radiation Measurements; contbr. articles to profl. jours. Served to capt. USNR, 1954-91. Recipient Exceptional Sci. Achievement medal, Outstanding Leadership medal NASA, U.S. Antarctic Svc. medal. Mem. Am. Phys. Soc., Monte Sano Club (Huntsville). Home: 907 Corinth Cir SE Huntsville AL 35801-2064

PARNES, EDMUND IRA, oral and maxillofacial surgeon, educator; b. Pitts., Apr. 16, 1936; s. David E. and Sara (Engelberg) P.; m. Elizabeth Cameron, Nov. 27, 1977; children: Dana, Mara, Lauren. Student, Vanderbilt U., 1954-55, U. Miami, 1955-56; DMD, U. Pitts., 1960. Diplomate Am. Bd. Oral and Maxillofacial Surgery. Oral surgery intern Jackson Meml. Hosp., Miami, Fla., 1960-61; resident, tchr. fellow in anesthesiology Presbyn. Univ. Hosp., Pitts., 1963-64; sr. resident in oral surgery Ben Taub Gen. Hosp., Houston, 1964-65; pvt. practice oral and maxillofacial surgery, Miami, 1965—. Interim assoc. chief oral surgery Jackson Meml. Hosp., Miami, 1970-72; clin. assoc. prof. U. Miami, 1975—; lectr. in field. Mem. Hist. Preservation Bd., City of Coral Gables, Fla. Capt. U.S. Army, 1961-63. Fellow Am. Coll. Dentists, Am. Assn. Oral and Maxillofacial Surgeons (com. on legis. 1972-73, com. sci. sessions 1979-86, trustee 1991-94, pres.-elect 1994-95, pres. 1995-96), Internat. Coll. Dentists; mem. ADA, Fla. Soc. Oral and Maxillofacial Surgeons (pres. 1974-75), Fla. Dental Assn. (ho. of dels., trustee 1982-95, v.p. 1996, pres.-elect 1998, pres. 1999-2000), S.E. Soc. Oral Surgeons, East Coast Dist. Dental Soc. (chmn. coms. 1980-84, pres. 1981-82), North Dade Dental Soc. (pres. 1971-72), Am. Soc. Dental Anesthesiology (pres. Fla. chpt. 1970), Alpha Omega (pres. 1977-78, regent 1983), Hist. Assn. South Fla. (trustee, bd. dirs. Hist. Mus. South Fla.). Jewish. Office: 8700 N Kendall Dr Ste 221 Miami FL 33176-2206

PARNESS, IRA ALLEN, pediatric cardiologist; b. Lakewood, N.J., Nov. 9, 1953; BA, Touro Coll., 1975; MD, SUNY, Bklyn., 1979. Diplomate Am. Bd. Pediat., Am. Bd. Pediat. Cardiology. Intern then resident in pediat. Brookdale Hosp. Med. Ctr., Bklyn., 1979—81, chief resident pediat., 1981-82; fellow pediat. cardiology Children's Hosp., Boston, 1982-85; asst. cardiology Children's Hosp. Boston, 1985-89, med. dir. heart transplant, 1986-92, assoc. cardiology, 1990-92; assoc. prof. divsn. pediat. cardiology Mt. Sinai Med. Ctr., N.Y.C., 1992—, dir. pediat. echo. lab., 1992-2000, dir. divsn. pediat. cardiology, 1998—. Mem. Am. Heart Assn., Am. Acad. Pediat., Am. Coll. Cardiology, Soc. Pediat. Echocardiography, Am. Soc. Echocardiography. Office: Mt Sinai Med Ctr Box 1201 1 Gustave Levy Pl New York NY 10029

PAROLA, FREDERICK EDSON, JR. county comptroller; b. Jamaica, N.Y., Aug. 29, 1946; s. Frederick Edson Sr. and Angela (DelPapa) P.; m. Norene Nilsen; children: Christine, Frederick. BA, Hartwick Coll., 1968; JD, Union U., 1971. Bar: N.Y. 1972, U.S. Ct. Appeals (2nd cir. and fed. cir.) 1975, U.S. Supreme Ct. 1979. Investigator Dist. Atty. Office, Nassau County, N.Y., 1971-72; ptnr. Scaduto, Levy, Mackston, Feuerstein, Esqs., Carle Place, 1971-74, Parola, Gross & Marino, Esqs., Wantagh, 1974—; mem. N.Y. State Assembly, 1979-93; comptroller Nassau County, 1994—. Tchr. adult edn. Wantagh and Copiague H.S., 1976—. Mem. Nassau County Youth Bd., 1972-80, Town of Hempstead House Authority, Hempstead, N.Y., 1974-79; pres. Wantagh Br. Am. Cancer Soc., 1973-74; chmn. Wantagh Heart Fund Dr., 1975, Wantagh Scouting USA Fundraising Dr., 1978; active Wantagh Scholarship Fund Com.; exec. dir. Town of Hempstead Indsl. Devel. Agy., 1994-2001; bd. dirs. Bide-A-Wee Home Assn. Mem. N.Y. State Bar Assn., Nassau County Bar Assn. (coms. on legislation, mcpl. law and surrogate's ct. estates and trusts), Wantagh Kiwanis, Wantagh C. of C., Marco Polo Lodge Sons of Italy, Wantagh Morton Lodge F&AM, Wantagh Preservation Soc., Wantagh-Seaford Homeowners Assn., Phi Alpha Theta. Presbyterian. Home: 2196 Brookside Ave Wantagh NY 11793-3850 Office: Nassau County Comptroller 240 Old Country Rd Mineola NY 11501-4247

PARR, GRANT VAN SICLEN, surgeon; b. N.Y.C., Dec. 30, 1942; s. Ferdinand Van Siclen and Helene H. P.; m. Helen Mushat Frye, July 1, 1967; children: Kathleen Gage, Helen Johnston. AB with honors, Wesleyan U., 1965; MD, Cornell U., 1969. Diplomate: Am. Bd. Thoracic Surgery, Am. Bd. Surgery. Intern, resident U. Hosps. of Cleve., 1969-71; resident in surgery U. Ala. Hosps., Birmingham, 1971-74, chief resident in surgery, 1974-75, resident in cardiovascular and thoracic surgery, 1975-77; practice medicine specializing in thoracic surgery Hershey, Pa., 1978-82; mem. staff Presbyn.-U. Pa. Med. Ctr., Phila., 1982-88, chief div. Thoracic surgery, 1984-88, acting chmn. Dept. Surgery, 1988, chief cardiovascular surgery, 1984-88; asst. prof. cardiothoracic surgery M.S. Hershey Med. Center, Hershey, Pa., 1987-88; chief cardiovascular surgery Morristown (N.J.) Meml. Hosp., 1988-97, co-chmn. dept. cardiovascular scis., 1997—; asst. prof. Pa. State U., 1978-82; clin. assoc. prof. surgery U. Pa., 1982-89; assoc. prof. clin. surgery Columbia U., 1992—. Chief cardiovascular surgery Overlook Hosp., 1988—, Morristown Meml. Hosp., 1988-98; chmn. cardiovascular surgery Atlantic Health Sys., 1998—, trustee, 1998—. Contbr. articles on thoracic surgery to med. jours. Fellow Am. Coll. Cardiology, ACS, Am. Coll. Chest Physicians, Phila. Coll. Physicians; mem. AMA, Internat. Cardiovascular Soc., Assn. of Acad. Surgeons, Am. Assn. Thoracic Surgery, Phila. County Med. Soc., Soc. Thoracic Surgeons, Soc. Critical Care Medicine Pa., Thoracic Surg. Soc., John W. Kirklin Soc., Pa. Med. Assn., N.J. Soc. Thoracic Surgery, N.Y. Soc. Thoracic Surgery, Morris County Golf Club, NYU Club, Beverkill Trout Club. Office: 100 Madison Ave Morristown NJ 07960-6136 E-mail: gparr@ahsys.org.

PARR, JAMES FLOYD, JR. government official; b. Seattle, Feb. 20, 1929; s. James Floyd and Clara (Kestner) P.; m. Carol C. Parr, Aug. 29, 1964 (div. Nov. 1986); children: Lauren Melissa, James Floyd; m. Sharon B. Hornick, May 22, l987. BS in Agr., Wash. State U., 1952; MS in Agr., Purdue U., 1957, PhD in Agr., l96l. Agr. extension agt. Wash. State U., Ephrata, 1953-54, Mont. State U., Gt. Falls, 1954-55; chemist Calif. Dept. Water Resources, Sacramento, 1957-58; instr. Purdue U., West Lafayette, Ind., 1958-61; postdoctoral fellow U. Mich., Ann Arbor, 1961-63; rsch. microbiologist TVA, Muscle Shoals, Ala., 1963-67; rsch. leader soil and water pollution unit Agrl. Rsch. Svc., USDA, Baton Rouge, 1967-75, supervisory microbiologist for waste mgmt. Beltsville, Md., 1975-84, nat. program leader for dryland agr., 1984—. Cons. on agrl. devel. in semiarid regions AID, Washington, 1984—. Editor: Water Potential Relations in Soil Microbiology, 1981, Land Treatment of

Hazardous Wastes, 1982; patentee fluid metering apparatus. With USN, 1946-48. Recipient cert. of merit USDA, 1969, 81, 88, 90, Superior Svc. award, 1977, Md. Gov.'s citation, 1984. Fellow Am. Soc. Agronomy (assoc. editor 1973-84), Soil Sci. Soc. Am. (assoc. editor 1974-76). Office: USDA Agrl Rsch Svc BARC-W Bldg 005 Rm 414 Beltsville MD 20705

PARR, RICHARD ARNOLD, II, lawyer; b. Edmond, Okla., July 26, 1958; s. Jack Ramsey and Martha (Suttle) P.; m. Becky Fay Stapp, Feb. 28, 1987; 1 child, Victoria Martha. BA cum laude, Vanderbilt U., 1979; JD, Cornell U., 1982. Bar: Okla. 1982, Tex. 1983, U.S. Ct. Appeals (10th cir.) 1983, U.S. Supreme Ct. 1988, Tenn. 1993. Law clk. to chief judge U.S. Ct. Appeals for 10th Cir., Oklahoma City, 1982-83; assoc. Johnson & Swanson, Dallas, 1983-85, Gardner, Carton & Douglas, Dallas, 1986-88; sr. atty. Valero Energy Corp., San Antonio, 1988-89; pres., chief exec. officer Paragon Homecare Corp., 1989-91; assoc. gen. counsel OrNda HealthCorp (formerly Republic Health Corp.), Nashville, 1991-94, v.p., asst. gen. counsel, 1994-96; exec. v.p., gen. counsel Concentra Inc., Dallas, 1996—. Sr. editor Cornell Law Rev., 1981-82, contbr., 1983. Mem. ABA, State Bar Tex., Okla. Bar Assn., Tenn. Bar Assn., Am. Soc. Corp. Secs. (bd. dirs. 2001—), Am. Corp. Counsel Assn., Am. Health Lawyers Assn., Health Care Compliance Assn. Republican. Presbyterian. Home: 5224 Beckington Ln Dallas TX 75287-5418 Office: Concentra Inc 5080 Spectrum Dr Ste 400W Addison TX 75001-6443 E-mail: richard.parr@concentra.com.

PARR, ROBERT GHORMLEY, chemistry educator; b. Chgo., Sept. 22, 1921; s. Leland Wilbur and Grace (Ghormley) P.; m. Jane Bolstad, May 28, 1944; children: Steven Robert, Jeanne Karen, Carol Jane. AB magna cum laude with high honors in Chemistry, Brown U., 1942; PhD in Phys. Chemistry, U. Minn., 1947; D (hon.), U. Leuven, 1986, Jagiellonian U., 1996. Asst. prof. chemistry U. Minn., 1947-48; mem. faculty Carnegie Inst. Tech., 1948-62, prof. chemistry, 1957-62, Johns Hopkins U., 1962-74, chmn. dept., 1969-72; William R. Kenan, Jr. prof. theoretical chemistry U. N.C., Chapel Hill, 1974-90, Wassily Hoeffding prof. chem. physics, 1990—. Vis. prof. chemistry, mem. Ctr. Advanced Study, U. Ill., 1962; disting. vis. prof. SUNY, Buffalo, Pa. State U., 1967; vis. prof. Japan Soc. Promotion Sci., 1968, 79, U. Haifa, 1977, Free U., Berlin, 1977, Duke U., 1996-97; Firth prof. U. Sheffield, 1976; Coochbehar prof. Indian Assn. Cultivation of Sci., 1990; Sandoval Vallarta prof. UAM-Iztapalapa, 1992; chmn. com. postdoctoral fellowships in chemistry NAS-NRC, 1961-63; chmn. panel theoretical chemistry Westheimer com. survey chemistry NAS, 1964; mem. coun. Gordon Rsch. Conf., 1974-76; mem. Commn. on Human Resources, NRC, 1979-82; mem. coun. Inst. for Molecular Sci., Okazaki, Japan, 1986-88; bd. trustees Inst. for Fundamental Chemistry, Kyoto, Japan, 1988—. Author: Quantum Theory of Molecular Electronic Structure, 1963, Density-Functional Theory of Atoms and Molecules, 1989, also numerous articles.; Assoc. editor: Jour. Chem. Physics, 1956-58, Chem. Revs, 1961-63, Jour. Phys. Chemistry, 1963-67, 77-79, Am. Chem. Soc. Monographs, 1966-71, Theoretica Chimica Acta, 1966-69, 92-96; Chinese Chem. Letters, 1998—; bd. editors: Jour. Am. Chem. Soc, 1969-77; adv. editorial bd.: Internat. Jour. Quantum Chemistry, 1967—, Chem. Physics Letters, 1967-79. Recipient Outstanding Achievement award U. Minn., 1968, N.C. Disting. Chemist award, 1982; fellow U. Chgo., 1949; research asso., 1957; Fulbright scholar U. Cambridge, Eng., 1953-54; Guggenheim fellow, 1953-54; NSF sr. postdoctoral fellow U. Oxford (Eng.) and Commonwealth Sci. and Indsl. Research Orgn., Melbourne, Australia, 1967-68; Sloan fellow, 1956-60, N.C. award in sci., 1999. Fellow AAAS, Am. Phys. Soc. (chmn. divsn. chem. physics 1963-64); mem. NAS, AAUP, Am. Chem. Soc. (chmn. divsn. phys. chemistry 1978, Irving Langmuir award in chem. physics 1994), Am. Acad. Arts and Sci., Indian Nat. Sci. Acad., Internat. Acad. Quantum Molecular Sci. (pres. 1991-97), Phi Beta Kappa, Sigma Xi, Phi Lambda Upsilon, Pi Mu Epsilon. Home: 701 Kenmore Rd Chapel Hill NC 27514-2019 Office: U NC Dept Chemistry Chapel Hill NC 27599-0001

PARR, ROYSE MILTON, lawyer, baseball writer; b. Elk City, Okla., Sept. 11, 1935; s. Clinton Riley and Ruth Caroline (Royse) P.; m. Sheila Ann Harshaw, May 28, 1960; children: Clint Howard, Reagan Royse. BS, Okla. State U., 1958; JD, U. Tulsa, 1964. Bar: Okla. 1964. Research scout Jersey Prodn. Research Co., Tulsa, 1960-64; atty. Sun Oil Co., 1964-70, White Shield Corp., 1970-71; sec., atty., asst. gen. counsel MAPCO, Inc., Tulsa, 1971-97; gen. counsel, dir. Seminole Pipeline Co., 1989-97. Lectr. Southwestern Legal Found., 1977 Co-author: Glory Days of Summer: The History of Baseball in Oklahoma, 1999, Allie Reynolds: Super Chief, 2002. Vice chmn. Tulsa County Election Bd., 1973-97; pres. Ret. Sr. Vol. Program, 1982-83. Served to 1st lt. U.S. Army, 1958-60; capt. Res. 1960-63. Mem. Am. Bar Assn., ASME, Soc. Petroleum Engrs., Okla. Bar Assn., Tulsa County Bar Assn., Am. Soc. Corp. Secs. (pres. Okla. chpt. 1983-84), Soc. of Am. Baseball Rsch., The Club at Runaway Bay, Oaks Country Club, Phi Delta Phi. Republican. Methodist. E-mail: crashparr@aol.com.

PARR, SANDRA HARDY, government affairs administrator; b. Atlanta, Dec. 30, 1952; d. Raymond William Hardy and Ruth (Berry) Yancey; m. James Parr Jr., Apr. 14, 1978; 1 child, James Andrew Parr III. Student, Lurleen B. Wallace Jr. Coll., 1972. Sales adminstr. Etec Corp., Hayward, Calif., 1976-77; adminstrv. sec. Cities Svc. Co., Atlanta, 1977-82; sales and planning coord. Intermodal Transp. Co., Norcross, 1982-83; freelance temp. sec. Atlanta met. area, 1983-86; freelance word processor, cons. Amoco Container Co., Norcross, 1986-88; psychiat. rev. asst. Am. Psychiat. Assn., Atlanta, 1988-89; support svcs. mgr. Parkside Health Mgmt. Corp., 1989-90; med. staff coord. C.P.C. Parkwood Hosp., 1991-98; govt. affairs sr. assoc. Bristol-Meyers Squibb, 1998—; pres. Parr Enterprises, Lawrenceville, 2002—. Health svcs. asst. Ciba Vision Corp., 1991-93; govt. affairs liaison Philip Morris Govt. Affairs, Alpharetta, Ga., 1993-98. Del. internat. nursing conf., citizen amb. program to People's Republic China, Seattle Washington People to People, Beijing, 1989; part-time exercise instr. Mem. NAFE. Avocations: creative writing, reading, exercising. Home: 1301 Eugenia Ter Lawrenceville GA 30045-7491 Address: Bristol Meyers Squibb 950 E Paces Ferry Rd NE Atlanta GA 30326-1180 Office: Parr Enterprises 1301 Eugenia Terr Lawrenceville GA 30045-7491

PARR, VIRGINIA HELEN, retired librarian; b. Mansfield, Ohio, May 23, 1937; d. Bernard Franklin and Frances Cole (Downes) P.; m. Marvin E. Lickey, June 14, 1959 (div. 1972); children: Sarah Elizabeth, David Andrew, Rachel Alison; m. Laurence E. Steadman, Nov. 27, 1993. AB, Oberlin Coll., 1959; AM, U. Mich., 1961; MLS, U. Oreg., 1973. English and social studies tchr. Whittier Jr. High Sch., Livonia, Mich., 1961-64; libr. U. Oreg. Libr., Eugene, 1973-79, head edn. and psychology, 1979-80, acting asst. univ. libr. for pub. svcs., 1980-82; head reference, rsch. and instrn. svcs. U. Cin., 1982-89, reference libr., biographer, 1989—2002; ret., 2002. Chair, mem. budget com. Eugene Sch., 1976-79. Founding editor: Behavioral and Social Scis. Libr., 1978; contbr. articles to profl. jours. Bd. dirs. Eugene Jr. Symphony Assn., 1979-82; mem. adv. bd. various mental health groups, Eugene, 1971-79. Mem. Assn. Coll. and Rsch. Librs. of ALA (various offices edn. and behavioral sci. sect. 1977-86, numerous coms. reference and adult svcs. divsn. 1981-92), Beta Phi Mu, Pi Lambda Theta. Democrat. Episcopalian. Avocations: reading, classical music. Home: 880 Rue De La Paix Apt T20 Cincinnati OH 45220-1025 E-mail: virginiaparr23@aol.com.

PARRA, FRANCISCO R. retired economist; b. Caracas, Venezuela, Aug. 30, 1929; s. Alirio Parra and Maria Isabel Malaussena; m. Erica Payson, Oct. 14, 1950; children: Antonio Ricardo, Francisco Alejandr, Christina;1 child Miguel Tomas. Degree in polit. sci., U. Geneva, Switzerland. Economist Creole Petroleum Corp., Caracas, Venezuela, 1951—60, Arthur D. Little, Inc., Cambridge, Mass., 1960—62; adviser to sec. gen. OPEC, Geneva and Vienna, 1962—67, sec. gen. Vienna, 1968; pres. Parra, Ramos & Parra, Ltd., London, 1969—76; mng. dir. Petroleos de Venezuela (U.K., 1976—80; exec. dir. Internat. Energy Devel. Corp., Geneva, 1976—80; pres. Energy Econs. Rsch., Ltd., Reading, England, 1985—92. Author: Immortality Observed, 2002. Recipient Order of Francisco Miranda, Govt. Venezuela, 1968, Order of Merit, 1980. Mem.: Inst. Petroleum. Roman Catholic. Avocations: skiing, hiking. Home: 60 Payson Ln PO 672 East Orleans MA 02643 Home Fax: 508-240-3413. E-mail: frparram@aol.com.

PARRA, RUBEN DARIO, chemist, educator; b. Cali, Colombia, Jan. 7, 1968; arrived in U.S., 1994; s. Carlos Antonio Parra, Lilia Rojas; m. Gloria Patricia Parra; children: Scott, Kevin. BS in hemistry, Universidad del Valle Cali, Colombia; PhD, U.Nebr., 1999. Posdoctoral fellow U. Nebr., Lincoln, 1999—2001; asst. prof. DePaul U., Chgo., 2001—. Pres. Acad. Sci.and Philosophy "Francisco Jose de Caldas", Cali, 1987—92. Contbr. Mem.: Am. Chem. Soc. Office: DePaul Univ 1036 W Belden Ave Chicago IL 60614 Office Fax: 773-321-7421. Business E-Mail: rparra1@depaul.edu.

PARRADO, PETER JOSEPH, real estate executive; b. Tampa, Fla., July 7, 1953; s. Peter and Daisy M. (DeLaVina) P. AA, Hillsborough Community Coll., Tampa, 1972; BA in Design, U. Fla., 1976. Designated MAI, Appraisal Inst., SRA. Right of way agt. Dept. Transp., Mango, Fla., 1976-78, real estate appraiser Bartow, 1978-81; appraiser Buckley Appraisal Services, Inc., Tampa, 1981-82; appraiser, pres. Buckley-Parrado Appraisal Services, 1982-83, Parrado Appraisal Services, Brandon, Fla., 1983—. Mem. experience rev., admissions com. Appraisal Inst., 1997, region X rep., 2000-01. Mem. planning assistance team City of Sarasota, Fla., 1985. Mem. Soc. Real Estate Appraiser (chmn. budget and fin. com. 1983-85, young adviser coun. 1987-88, bd. dirs. 1985-87, sec. 1987, instr., v.p. 1988-89, pres. 1989-90), Urban Land Inst. (assoc.), Appraisal Inst. (mem. ethics and counseling panel 1992-96), Internat. R-W Assn., Internat. Soc. Arborculture, Brandon C. of C. (legis. issues com. 1988). Democrat. Methodist. Home: 2715 Fairway View Dr Valrico FL 33594-5209 E-mail: pparrad1@tampabay.rr.com.

PARRAGUIRRE, RONALD DAVID, judge; b. Reno, July 8, 1959; s. Paul Charles and Iris Mae (Bleick) P. BBA, San Diego State U., 1982; JD, U. San Diego, 1985. Bar: Pa. 1986, Nev. 1986, D.C. 1987. Legis. asst. U.S. Senator Paul Laxalt, Washington, 1985-86; counsel subcom. on criminal law, judiciary com. U.S. Senate, 1986-87; lawyer Parraguirre & Parraguirre, Las Vegas, Nev., 1987-91; mcpl. ct. judge Dept. 6 City of Las Vegas, 1991-99; dist. ct. judge Eighth Jud. Dist. Ct., Clark County, Nev., 1999—. Mem. ABA, ATLA, Am. Judges Assn., Nev. Judges Assn., Clark County Bar Assn. Republican. Lutheran. Avocations: skiing, racquetball, hunting, fishing.

PARRAMORE, BARBARA MITCHELL, education educator; b. Guilford County, N.C., Aug. 29, 1932; d. Samuel Spencer and Nellie Gray (Glosson) Mitchell; m. Lyman Griffis Worthington, Dec. 23, 1956 (div. 1961); m. Thomas Custis Parramore, Jan. 22, 1966; children: Lisa Gray, Lynn Stuart. AB, U. N.C., Greensboro, 1954; MEd, N.C. State U., 1959; EdD, Duke U., 1968. Counselor, thcr. Raleigh City Schs., 1954-59, sch. prin., 1959-65; prof. dept. of curriculum and instrn. N.C. State U., 1970-96, prof. emeritus, 1996—. Acad. specialist Office Internat. Edn., U.S. Info. Svcs., sec. sch. initative program, The Philippines, 1987. Author: The People of North Carolina, 1972, 3rd edit. 1983. Japan Inst. Social and Econ. Affairs fellow, 1980; N.C. AAUW award for juvenile lit., 1973, Holladay medal for excellence N.C. State U., 1994. Mem. ASCD, N.C. ASCD (pres. 1994-96), N.C. Coun. for Social Studies (pres. 1985-87), Assn. Tchr. Educators, Delta Kappa Gamma, Kappa Delta Pi. Home: 5012 Tanglewood Dr Raleigh NC 27612-3135

PARRAVANO, AMELIA ELIZABETH (AMY BETH PARRAVANO), recording industry executive; b. Providence, Apr. 5, 1951; d. Olindo Luigi and Violet Carmella (Russo) Izzo; m. Grimaldo Antonio Parravano, July 4, 1979; children: Peter Paul, Paula Elizabeth. AA, Roger Williams Coll., 1972; student, R.I. Coll., 1972-73, Oral Roberts U., 1986. Owner, operator Aura Arts & Crafts, Cranston, R.I., 1985-88; pres. Peridot and Caprice Rec. Artist, 1990—; president, owner Peridot Records; music pub.; host, prodr. cable TV show Amy Beth Presents!. Freelance artist Artist Letters League, Cranston, 1992—; singer (Amy Beth), songwriter, musician. Active PTA, Cranston, 1991-92; artist mem. R.I. State Coun. on Arts, Providence, 1986-92; active Pawtucket (R.I.) Arts Coun., 1986-92. Named Ky. Col.; named to Rockabilly Hall of Fame. Mem. Am. Soc. Composers, Authors and Pubs., Songwriters Guild Am., Gospel Music Assn., County Music Assn., Country Music Showcase Internat., Broadcast Music Inc. (pub.), Retirement Entertainment Orgn., Internat. Fan Club Assn., Greater So. Country Music Assn. (state rep. for R.I.). Avocations: golf, bicycling, entertaining at children's parties, painting, poetry. Home: 17 Woodbine St Cranston RI 02910-1916 E-mail: amybeth_e@yahoo.com.

PARRAWAY, ANDRÉ TORAN, accountant; b. Glenarden, Md., Jan. 20, 1967; s. Kenneth and Jeta Louise (Chalmers) P.; m. Gayle O. Garmise, May 2, 1997. BS in Acctg., U. Md., 1989. CPA, Md. Staff acct. Thomas Havey & Co., CPAs, Washington, 1990-92; sr. acct. Vietnam Vets. Am., 1992-95, contr., 1995-97, Nat. Parts and Conservation Assn., 1997—. Mem. Episcopal Student Youth, U. Md., College Park, 1987-90; sr. acolyte St. Luke's Episcopal Ch., Washington, 1983-93. Mem. Inst. Mgmt. Accts., U. Md. Alumni Assn. Democrat. Avocations: jogging, spectator sports, going to the theatre, traveling. Home: 3 Hathaway Ct Silver Spring MD 20906-3258

PARRES, CYNTHIA DILLARD, lawyer; b. Columbia, Mo., July 3, 1964; d. Robert Howard and Martha Ann Dillard. Student, Vanderbilt U., 1982-83; BS, S.E. Mo. State U., 1986; JD, U. Mo., Columbia, 1990. Bar: Mo. 1990, Kans. 1991. Assoc. Blackwell Sanders et al, Kansas City, Mo., 1990-92; ptnr. Bryan Cave LLP, 1992—. Adminstrv. asst. Mayor's Fast Forward Com., Kansas City, 1996—; mem. Downtown Coun.; vol. Jr. League Kansas City, Mo., 1991—. Mem.: Kansas City Bankruptcy Bar Assn., Kansas Women Attys. Assn., Ctrl. Exchange (chair membership com. 1992—), Kansas City Met. Bar Assn. (bankruptcy com. 1990—, bankruptcy com. chair 1999), Assn. Women Lawyers (bd. dirs. 1999—), Am. Bankruptcy Inst., Workout Profls. Assn. (pres. of bd.), Kansas City Club (athletic com.), Rotary. Roman Catholic. Office: Bryan Cave LLP 3500 One KC Pl 1200 Main St Kansas City MO 64105-2122 E-mail: cdparres@bryancave.com.

PARRESOL, BERNARD ROSS, research biometrician, statistician; b. Washington, Sept. 15, 1953; s. Thomas and Rita Delores P.; m. Lisa Leigh Morton-Barbé, May 5, 1995; children: Sarah Marie Barbé, Christine Pamela Barbé. BS with honors, Mich. State U., 1977; M of Applied Stats., La. State U., 1983, PhD, 1998. Reg. forester, N.C. Br. mgr. James M. Vardaman & Co. Forestry Cons., Shreveport, La., 1977-80; rsch. assoc. dept. explt. stats. La. State U., Baton Rouge, 1983-86; math. statistician USDA Forest Svc., New Orleans, 1986-95, Asheville, N.C., 1996—. Stats. cons. Internat. Inst. Tropical Forestry, Rio Piedras, P.R., 1987—; guest lectr. Nanjing (China) Forestry U., 1994, 97, U. de Tras-os-Montes e Alto Douro, Portugal, 1998, 2002, Universidad Autonoma Denueva Leon, 2001; adj. prof. U. Fla., 1999—. Guest assoc. editor Forest Sci., 1999-2000; contbr. Encyclopedia of Environmetrics; contbr. articles to profl. jours. Officer La. Indian Heritage Assn., 1988-92. Scholar Rockefeller Found., 1990; grantee Smithsonian Tropical Rsch. Inst., Panama, 1992, U.S. Office Internat. Coop. and Devel., Chile, 1993; recipient Humanities Scholar, La. Endowment for Humanities, 2000, 2002. Mem. Am. Statistical Assn., Soc. Am. Foresters, Internat. Soc. Tropical Foresters. Avocation: Am. Indian culture. Office: USDA Forest Svc PO Box 2680 Asheville NC 28802-2680 Fax: 828-257-4840. E-mail: bparresol@fs.fed.us.

PARRETT, SHERMAN O. lawyer; b. Cin., Jan. 8, 1943; s. Earl and Ruby (Angel) P.; m. Rosalind K. Brooks, Sept. 21, 1985; children: Laura, Samantha. BSEE, U. Cin., 1965; JD with honors, George Washington U., 1969. Bar: Calif. 1970, D.C. 1975, Ariz. 1992. Assoc. Flehr, Hohbach et al., San Francisco, 1970-73; ptnr. Cushman, Darby & Cushman, Washington, 1973-86, Irell & Manella, L.A., 1986-91, Streich Lang, Phoenix, 1991-94, Snell & Wilmer, Phoenix, 1994-98. Address: 111 Honeysuckle Ln Owings MD 20736 E-mail: parretts@aol.com.

PARRETTE, LESLIE JACKSON, lawyer; b. Mt Pleasant, Mo., Aug. 25, 1961; s. Leslie Jackson and Janet Parrette. AB, Harvard Coll., 1983; JD, Harvard Law Sch., 1986. Assoc. Hale & Dorr, Boston, 1986-89, Watson Ess Marshall & Enggas, Kansas City, Mo., 1989-91, Bryan Cave, Kansas City, 1991-92; ptnr. Blackwell Sanders Peper Martin, 1992-2000; gen. coun., sr. v.p., corp. sec. Aquila Inc., 2000—. Mem. Sister City Commn. of Kansas City, Mo., 1999—; bd. dirs. Boys and Girls Club Greater Kansas City, 2000—; dir. Am. Jazz Mus., 2002—. Office: Utilicorp United Inc 20 W 9th St Kansas City MO 64105-1711 E-mail: lparrett@utilicorp.com.

PARRICK, GERALD HATHAWAY, communications and marketing executive; b. Cushing, Okla., Oct. 27, 1924; s. Gerald H. and Phyllis A. (Sheppard) B.; m. Gail V. Straney, Dec. 5, 1984; children: Gerald Hathaway III, Candace Anne. BJ, U. Mo., 1948. Creative account exec. George Knox & Assoc., Oklahoma City, 1948-51; account exec. Batten, Barton, Durstine & Osborn, San Francisco, 1952-60; account dir. McCann-Erickson, L.A., 1960-67, v.p. Portland, Oreg., 1967-72; dir. comm. Pacific Power Co., 1972-77, spl. asst. to chmn. bd., 1977-79; pres. Entreepublic Comm., West Linn, Oreg., 1979—, Bailey/Parrick, Inc., Portland, 1981-84, Parrick/Milpacher, Inc., Portland, 1984-85, The Laugh Clinic, Inc., Portland, 1984-90, K-KOR, Inc., 1990-93. Author: A 20th Century Miracle, 1981, Touched by a Miracle, 1997. Mem. Oreg. Advt. Rev. Bd., 1974-75. Capt. AUS, 1943-45, 51-52, ETO. Named Oreg. Advt. Man of Yr., Oreg. Advt. Club, 1971. Mem. Am. Advt. Fedn. (chmn. edn. western region 1973-74), Portland Advt. Fedn. (pres. 1974-75), Toastmasters (pres. 1966-67) (Encino, Calif.), Kappa Tau Alpha. Home: 17185 Carlson Ct Lake Oswego OR 97034-5802

PARRIGIN, ELIZABETH ELLINGTON, lawyer; b. Colon, Panama, May 23, 1932; d. Jesse Cox and Elizabeth (Roark) Ellington; m. Perry G. Parrigin, Oct. 8, 1975. BA, Agnes Scott Coll., 1954; JD, U. Va., 1959. Bar: Tex. 1959, Mo. 1980. Atty., San Antonio, 1960-69; law libr. U. Mo., Columbia, 1969-77, rsch. assoc., 1977-82; atty. pvt. practice, 1982—. Elder, clk. of session First Presbyn. Ch., Columbia; mem. permanent jud. commn. Presbyn. Ch. U.S., 1977-83, mem. advisory com. on constitution, 1983-90. Mem. ABA, Mo. Bar Assn. (chmn. sub-com. revision of Mo. trust law 1988-92), Columbia Kiwanis Club (pres. 1997-98). Democrat. Presbyterian. Avocations: music, gardening, reading. Home: 400 Conley Ave Columbia MO 65201-4219 Office: 224 N 8th St Columbia MO 65201-4844

PARRILLO, GIOVANNI, lawyer; b. Salerno, Campania, Italy, Mar. 20, 1972; m. Laura Cancedda. Degree in Law, Luiss-Guido Carli, Rome, 1994. Bar: Italy 1997. Local treas. ELSA Rome, Rome, 1993—95; nat. treas. European Law Students’ Association - ELSA Italy, 1996—97; assoc. atty. Baker & McKenzie, 1997—. Author: Legal protection of multimedia works. Avocation: travel. Office: Baker & McKenzie Viale di Villa Massimo 57 Rome 00161 Italy Office Fax: 0039 0644063306. Business E-Mail: giovanni.parrillo@bakernet.com.

PARRINGTON, DIANE J. dietitian; b. Bethpage, N.Y., Nov. 29, 1956; d. Lawrence John and Doris Ann (Deane) Klag; m. Josef Robert Parrington, June 17, 1978 (div. Mar. 24, 1988); children: Diana, Lawrence, Ingrid; m. Steven John Lattanzi, Nov. 10, 1990. BS, SUNY, Oneonta, 1978; MS, U. Md., 1983; postgrad., U. Ariz. Registered dietitian. Adminstrv. dietitian Luth. Ctr. for the Aging, Smithtown, NY, 1986—89; geriatric nutrition specialist Dept. Vets. Affairs, Phoenix, 1989—2001, chair clin. nutrition dept., 2001—; instr. Phoenix C.C., 1994—96; faculty, geriatric medicine fellowship VAMC, 1991—. Mem. ethics adv. com. VAMC, Phoenix, 1989-97, team leader patients with head and neck cancer, 1993—. Editor: Ariz. Geriatrics Soc. Jour., Phoenix, 1994-95; contbr. articles to profl. jours. Recipient scholarship Fed. Employee Edn. Assn., 1996, Ruth R. Cowden scholarship U. Ariz., Tucson, 1997, 98, Human Biomed. Nutrition Rsch. fellow, 1999. Mem. Am. Soc. Parenteral and Enteral Nutrition, Ariz. Geriatrics Soc. (bd. dirs. 1993-97), N.Am. Nursing Diagnostic Assn. Avocations: jogging, hiking, reading. Office: VAMC ACS11C-7 650 E Indian School Rd Phoenix AZ 85012-1892 E-mail: diane.parrington@med.va.gov.

PARRINO, ROBERT, finance educator; b. N.Y.C., Sept. 4, 1957; s. Dominick Paul Parrino and Gertrude (Rainer) Wieczorek; m. Emily Allen Parrino, July 12, 1980. BSChemE, Lehigh U., Bethlehem, Pa., 1979; MBA, Coll. William and Mary, 1980; MS, U. Rochester, 1991, PhD in Fin., 1992. CFA. Sr. analyst Marriott Corp., Bethesda, Md., 1984-85; pres. Sprigg Lane Fin. Corp., Charlottesville, Va., 1985-88; faculty dept. fin. U. Tex., Austin, 1992-96, 97—; faculty U. Chgo., 1996-97. Dir. The Bentley Group, Charlottesville, 1987-88, Hicks, Muse, Tate & Furst Ctr. for Pvt. Equity Fin., Austin, 2000—. Contbr. articles to profl. jours. Capt. U.S. Army, 1981-84, lt. col. USAR. Mem. Assn. for Investment Mgmt. and Rsch. (cand. curriculum com. 1994-99), Am. Econ. Assn., Fin. Mgmt. Assn., Am. Soc. Appraisers 1988-96 (Richmond chpt. treas. 1987-88), Beta Gamma Sigma. Office: U Texas Dept Fin 21st and Speedway Austin TX 78712 E-mail: parrino@mail.utexas.edu.

PARRIS, FRANKLIN OTTO, principal, private school educator; b. Davenport, Iowa, Apr. 6, 1967; s. James and Ruby Elaine Parris; children: Derek, Dawson, David, Daniel. BS, Concordia Coll., 1990, M in Elem. Adminstrn., 1996. Prin., tchr., athletic dir., coach St. Paul Luth. Sch., Latimer, Iowa, 1990—92; tchr., ocach, Sunday sch. supt. Immanuel Luth. Sch., Wisconsin Rapids, Wis., 1992—99; prin., tchr., athletic dir., coach Trinity Luth. Sch., Atchison, Kans., 1999—. V.p. Wisconsin Rapids Youth Soccer Orgn., 1996—99; bd. mem. Atchison Outdoor Youth Soccer Orgn., 2001—; vision bd. mem. Trinity Luth. Ch., 2000—. Mem.: Luth. Edn. Assn.-Luth. Elem. Adminstrs. Dept. Avocations: reading, softball, basketball, soccer. Office: Trinity Luth Sch 611 N 8t5h St Atchison KS 66002

PARRIS, MICHAEL LYNN, academic administrator; b. Spartanburg, S.C., Dec. 17, 1960; s. James William and Daisy Elise Parris; m. Sherry Diane Smith; children: Jeffrey. BS in Indsl. Edn., Clemson U., 1983; M in Edn. Adminstrn., U. S.C., 1988. Cert. in ednl. adminstrn., in indsl. tech. Indsl. tech. instr./ football coach Fairforest (S.C.) Mid. Sch., 1983—93; engring. graphics instr. R.D. Anderson Applied Tech. Ctr., Moore, 1993—99; adj. prof. Converse Coll., Spartanburg, 1997; asst. dir. R.D. Anderson Applied Tech. Ctr., Moore, 1999—. Home: 327 Riddle Rd Pauline SC 29374 Office: RD Anderson Applied Tech Ctr 1151 Moore-Duncan Hwy Moore SC 29369 Personal E-mail: mlparris@msn.com. Business E-Mail: mparris@rdanderson.org.

PARRIS, NINA GUMPERT, curator, writer, researcher, photographer; b. Berlin, Germany, Sept. 11, 1927; came to U.S., 1937, naturalized, 1944; d. Martin and Charlotte (Blaschko) Gumpert; m. Arthur Parris, Feb. 13, 1949 (div. 1974); children: Carl Joseph, Thomas Martin. BA, Bryn Mawr Coll., 1968; MA, U. Pa., 1969, PhD, 1979. Tchg. fellow U. Mich., Ann Arbor, 1969-70; lectr. Phila. Coll. Art, 1970-71; rsch. asst. Phila. Mus. Art, 1970-71; curator, lectr. U. Vt. Robert Hall Fleming Mus., Burlington, 1971-79; chief curator Columbia (S.C.) Mus., 1979-89; resident faculty visual arts Vt. Coll. Norwich U., 1991—; chair visual arts Burlington Coll., 1996-99. Author: Prints, Paintings and Drawings in Collection of Robert Hall Fleming Mus., 1979 (exhbn. catalog) Through a Master Printer, 1985, The South Carolina Collection of the Columbia Museum, 1987; columnist State newspaper, Columbia, 1984-88; solo shows at Meteor Gallery, Columbia, 1993, Living Learning Ctr., U. Vt., 1994, St. Michael's Coll. McCarthy Arts Ctr., 1995, Colburn Gallery, U. Vt., 1996; group shows at Westbeth Gallery, N.Y.C., 1993, Thomas Waterman Wood Gallery, Vt., 1994, 96, 2001, 02, Firehouse Gallery, Burlington, 1996, Box Car Exhbn., Burlington, 1996, 98, Soho 20 Gallery, N.Y.C., 1996, 97, 98. Bd. dirs. Photography Coop., Montpelier, Vt., 1977-79, Chittenden Arts Coun., Burlington, 1976-78. Woodrow Wilson fellow, 1968, Univ. fellow Ford Found., 1968-72; grantee NEA, NEH, S.C. Com. Humanities, Vt. Coun. Arts. Mem. Am. Assn. Museums (pres. curator's com. 1985-87, v.p. 1983-85). E-mail: ninag@together.net.

PARRIS, SALLY NYE, real estate agent; b. Evanston, Ill., Apr. 5, 1946; d. Harry Gale Nye Jr. and Bettye (Herb) Sollitt; m. Thomas Baxter Parris, Mar. 25, 1988 (div. Sept. 1985); 1 child, Samantha Ross. AA, Bradford Jr. Coll., 1966; BS in Secondary Edn., Northwestern U., 1968; cert. real estate, Conn. Real Estate Inst., Norwalk, 1985. Lic. real estate agt., Conn. Dir. girls phys. edn. Latin Sch. of Chgo., 1967-68; dir. Greenwich (Conn.) YWCA, 1972-79; English tchr. Inlingua Sch. Langs., Stamford, Conn., 1981-84; real estate agt. Curtis Assocs., Realtors, Greenwich, 1985—. Chair profl. divsn. United Way, Greenwich, 1995-98, chair real estate sect. profl. divsn., 1993-94, co-chair campaign kickoff Septemberfest, 1985-99, co-chair Greenwich Pro-Am. Lit. Vol. Benefit, 1995—; v.p., bd. dirs. YMCA, Greenwich, 1993—, chair spl. events com., 1994—, co-chair annual campaign, 1998; bd. dirs., benefit chair Cmty. Answers, Greenwich, 1994—; co-chair 350th Yr. parade Town of Greenwich, 1990; mem. benefits com. Literacy Vols., 1991-93. Recipient Vol. Recognition award Literacy Vols. Am., 1996, Town of Greenwich, 1991, United Way of Greenwich, 1985-97, Thomas Shepard award, 1995, 96. Mem. Conn. Assn. Profl. Women, Greenwich Bd. Realtors (advisor pub. rels. 1985-87, grievance com. 1999), Riverside Yacht Club (winter mem., social register 1960—), Greenwich Country Club (paddle tennis com. co-chmn. 1984-86, qur. editor 1982-86). Republican. Episcopalian. Avocations: swimming, racquet sports, golf, sporting clays, needlepoint. Office: Colwell Banker/Curtis Assocs 278 Sound Beach Ave Old Greenwich CT 06870-1626

PARRISH, ALMA ELLIS, elementary school educator; b. Peoria, Ill., Mar. 28, 1929; d. William Edward and Marie (Allton) Ellis; m. Clyde R. Parrish, Jr., Nov. 20, 1949; children: Clyde R. III, Charles, Donald, Royce, Christopher. BS, Bradley U., Peoria. Cert. elem. tchr., S.C., Ill. Tchr. Community Consol. Sch. Dist. 59, Elk Grove Village, Ill., Sipp Sch. Dist., Peoria, Kershaw County Sch. Dist., Camden, S.C. Vol. Guardian ad Litum of S.C. Mem. DAR, ACLU, Unitarian Universalist Assn., AARP, S.C. Ret. Edn. Assn., Tchrs. Coun. Dist. 59 (pres., com.), Ill. Ret. Tchr.'s Assn., Kershaw County Ret. Edn. Assn., S.I. Coun.

PARRISH, BENJAMIN EMMITT, II, insurance executive; b. Statesboro, Ga., Dec. 20, 1945; s. Benjamin E. and Ouida L. (Anderson) P.; m. Sandra Dianne Bragg, July 26, 1964; children: Michelle, Benjamin III, Sonya. Student, Atlanta Art Inst., 1963-65. Cert. ins. agt., Ga., Fla., S.C., N.C., Ala., Va. Art dir. Macy's, Atlanta, 1965-66; sales mgr. Clearbrook Realty, 1966-72; pres., comml. pilot, flight instr. Parrish Enterprises, Statesboro, 1972-77; v.p. Design Concepts, 1977-85; cons., pres. Parrish Assocs., 1985-87; ind. ins. agy. Ga., 1987—; dist. coord. Am. Family Life Assurance Corp., 1987-92, regional coord., 1993-99; pres. Turnstone Properties N.C., Otto, 1999—. Author: Captive Management, 1972; writer/dir. (video) Tax Savings 125, 1991. Bd. dirs. Statesboro-Bulloch County C. of C., Chamber Connection, 1992-93; chmn. Statesboro Main Street Action Commn., 1993-94. Featured in Life & Health Ins. Sales mag., Apr. 1992. Republican. Baptist. Avocations: travel, painting, photography, golf. Home: 5633 Ga Highway 46 Statesboro GA 30458-3520 Office: Parrish and Assocs 846 Big Creek Rd Otto NC 28763 E-mail: bep2@rabun.net., info@turnstonecabins.com.

PARRISH, CARMELITA B. retired secondary school educator; b. Varina, N.C., Mar. 19, 1934; d. James Robert and Nita Mae (Webb) Beal; m. John J. Parrish, July 24, 1953 (dec.); children: Deborah Joy Parrish White, Toni Lynne Parrish Altenburg. AA, Mid. Ga. Coll., 1979; BS in Edn., Ga. So. U., 1981; MEd, Valdosta State U., 1988, U. Ga., 1993. Secondary tchr. English, graphic arts, Spanish Ware County Bd. Edn., Waycross, Ga., 1981-91; tchr. Spanish, English Telfair County Bd. Edn., McRae, 1991-92, Pickens County H.S., Jasper, 1992-98. Co-advisor Spanish Club; advisor yearbook; tchr. Spanish, journalism; adj. instr. Spanish, Macon (Ga.) State Coll., 1999—. Former leader Girl Scouts U.S., Spain; tchr. area Sunday sch.; band chaperone; tour leader student travel in Europe, 1985—. Recipient Star Tchr. award, Waycross-Ware County C. of C., 1987. Mem. ASCD, NEA, Nat. Coun. Tchrs. of English, Ga. Assn. Educators (local assoc. pres., legislator contact team, Ga. Assn. Educators-Polit. Action Com.), So. Assn. Colls. and Schs. (mem. evaluation com.), Phi Kappa Phi. Home: 6229 Thomaston Rd Macon GA 31220-7715 Office: 100 College Station Dr Macon GA 31206-5100

PARRISH, DAVID WALKER, JR. legal publishing company executive; b. Bristol, Tenn., Feb. 8, 1923; BA, Emory & Henry Coll., 1948, LLD, 1978; BS, U.S. Merchant Marine Acad., 1950; LLB, U. Va., 1951. Pres. The Michie Co., Charlottesville, Va., 1969-89, vice chmn., 1989-96; pub. cons., 1996—. Home: 114 Falcon Dr Charlottesville VA 22901-2013 Office: 300 Preston Ave Ste 103 Charlottesville VA 22902-5044

PARRISH, E. JEANNE, social worker; b. Independence, Pa. d. James John and Elizabeth B. (Robison) Sella. BA in Sociology and Psychology, West Liberty State, 1969; MA in Polit. Sci. and Pub. Adminstrn., Ohio U., 1994. Registered profl. counsellor, Ohio. Social worker Dept. Human Svcs., Steubenville, Ohio, 1969-87, social svcs. supr., 1987-88, social program adminstr., 1988-93, dir., 1993-97. Mem. exec. com. Ohio Human Svcs. Dirs. Assn., 1994-97; pres. Canton Dist. Dirs. Assn., 1994-97; mem. bus. & industry bd. Jefferson C.C., Steubenville, 1990—; exec. dir. United Way of Jefferson County, 2000; mem. family com. Ohio Supreme Ct.; bd. dirs. Franciscan U., Steubenville. Bd. dirs. United Way, Steubenville, 1995—. Mem. Ohio Human Svc. Dirs. Assn., Ohio Child Support Dirs. Assn., Bus. & Profl. Women (v.p. 1987-91). Office: Jefferson County Dept Human Svcs 125 S 5th St Steubenville OH 43952-2811

PARRISH, EDGAR LEE, financial services executive; b. Washington, Apr. 11, 1948; s. Frank Jennings Parrish and Lorene (Lomax) Parrish.; m. Katherine Ellen MacLachlan, Sept. 12, 1987; children: Robert Alexander Wilson, Stephen Edgar MacLachlan. BS in Commerce, U. Va., 1970. 1979sr. v.p. Wheat, First Securities, Inc., Washington, 1971—79; v.p. Merrill Lynch, Pierce, Fenner & Smith, Inc., 1979—82, Phila., 1982—85; sr. v.p., fin. cons. Shearson Lehman Bros., Inc., 1985—87, mem. chmn.'s coun., 1987—92, mem. dirs. coun. Washington, 1986; sr. v.p. investments, Parrish Consulting Group UBS/PaineWebber, Inc., 1993—, mem. Pacesetter Coun., 1994—2001, managed account cons., 1998—99, sr. managed account cons., 2000—. Pres. HESCO Corp., Manassas, Va., 1989—, also chmn. bd. dirs.; arbitrator hearing bd.NYSE. Mem. adv. bd. McIntire Sch. Commerce, 2001—; chmn. investment com. Nat. Presbyn. Sch., Washington. Capt. USAFR, 1970-76. Mem. U. Va. Alumni Assn. (life), Investment Mgmt. Cons. Assn., Reserve Officers Assn. (life). Democrat. Episcopalian. Home: 4502 Wetherill Rd Bethesda MD 20816-1813 Office: UBS/PaineWebber Inc Investment Bldg 1501 K St NW Washington DC 20005 E-mail: edgar.parrish@ubspw.com.

PARRISH, EDWARD ALTON, JR. electrical and computer engineering educator, academic administrator; b. Newport News, Va., Jan. 7, 1937; s. Edward Alton and Molly Wren (Vaughn) Parrish; m. Shirley Maxine Johnson, Oct. 26, 1963; children: Troy Alton, Gregory Sinton. BEE, U. Va., 1964, MEE, 1966, DScEE, 1968. Registered Tenn., Va. Group leader Amerad Corp., Charlottesville, Va., 1961—64; asst. prof. elec. engring. U. Va., 1968—71, assoc. prof. elec. engring., 1971—77, prof. elec. engring., 1977—86, chmn. dept. elec. engring., 1978—86; dean, centennial prof. electrical engring. Vanderbilt U., Nashville, 1987—95; pres., prof. elec. and computer engring. Worcester Poly. U., 1995—. Cons. U.S. Army, Charlottesville, Va., 1971—77, ORS, Inc., Princeton, NJ, 1973—74, Sperry Marine Systems, Charlottesville, 1975—76, Hajime Industries Ltd., Tokyo, 1978—84. Contbr. articles to profl. jours. With USAF, 1954—58. Grantee numerous rsch. grants. Fellow: IEEE (bd. dirs. 1990—91, v.p. ednl. activities 1992—93, engring. accreditation commn. 1989—96, exec. com. 1991—96, officer 1993—96, chmn. elect 1994—95, chmn. 1995—96, past chmn. 1996—97, editor-in-chief IEEE Computer 1995—98), ABET (bd. dirs. 2000—); mem.: IEEE Computer Soc. (sec. 1997, v.p. 1978—81, pres. 1988), Tau Beta Pi, Eta Kappa Nu, Sigma Xi. Baptist. Avocations: music, woodworking. Office: Office of Pres Worcester Polytechnic Institue 100 Institute Rd Worcester MA 01609-2247 E-mail: eap@wpi.edu.

PARRISH, FRANK JENNINGS, retired food products executive; b. Manassas, Va., Dec. 29, 1923; s. Edgar Goodloe and Alverda (Jennings) P.; m. Lorene Lomax, Feb. 11, 1944 (div. Apr. 1984); children: Edgar Lee, Julia Lorene; m. Mary Jane Biser, Aug. 25, 1984 Student, Va. Poly. Inst., 1942-43; grad., Indsl. Coll. Armed Forces, 1972. Pres. Manassas Frozen Foods, Inc., 1946—2001; pres., mgr. Cert. Food Buyers Svc., Inc., 1953—2001; pres. First Nat. Acceptance Co., 1966—2001; ret., 2001. V.p. Manassas Ice & Fuel Co. Mem. bus. adminstrn. adv. com. No. Va. Community Coll.; chmn. bd. North Va. coun. Am. Heart Assn., 1987-88; mem. inaugural com., 1961, vice-chmn. inaugural parade com. Maj. USAAF, 1943-46, CBI; ret. brig. gen. comdr. 909th TAC Airlift Group 1969-73, USAF; moblzn. asst. DCS plans and ops. Hdqrs., 1973-79. Maj. USAAF, 1943—46, CBI, comdr. USAF, 1969—73, mobilization asst. USAF, 1973—83, ret. brig. gen. USAF, 1983. Decorated Legion of Merit, Air medal. Mem. Nat. Inst. Locker and Freezer Provisioners Am. (past pres., Industry Leadership award 1968), Va. Frozen Foods Assn. (past pres., dir.), Hump Pilots Assn., Va. Assn. Meat Processors (pres. 1986-90), Kiwanis. Methodist (chmn. bd. trustees 1958-66). Home: 9107 Park Ave Manassas VA 20110-4350 *Do unto others as you would have them do unto you.*

PARRISH, JAY See PIFER, ALAN

PARRISH, JOHN ALBERT, dermatologist, research administrator; b. Louisville, Oct. 19, 1939; Children: Lynn, Susan, Mark. BA, Duke U., 1961; MD, Yale U., 1965. Diplomate Am. Bd. Dermatology. Medicine intern U. Mich., Ann Arbor, 1965-67; dermatology resident Harvard Med. Sch., Boston, 1969-72; dermatologist Mass. Gen. Hosp., 1972-87, dir. Wellman labs., 1975—, dir. cutaneous biology rsch. lab. Harvard, 1987—, chief, dermatology; chmn. dermatology Harvard Med. Sch., Boston, 1987—; prof. health sci. & tech. MIT. Dermatology cons. Beth Israel Hosp., Boston, 1973—; elected mem. Inst. of Medicine, 2000. Author: A Doctor's Year in Vietnam, 1972, Dermatology and Skin Care, 1975, Effects of Ultraviolet Radiation on the Immune System, 1983; co-author: Science of Photomedicine, 1982, Photoimmunology, 1983. Lt. Commdr. USN, 1968-89. Decorated Vietnamese Cross Gallantry with gold; recipient Outstanding Gen. Med. Officer award USN, 1969; Dohi lectr. Japanese Soc. Dermatology, 1990. Mem. Am. Soc. Dermatology (photobiology task force 1972—, Marion B. Sulzberger award 1988), Am. Soc. Lasers in Surgery and Medicine (pres. 1987-88), Am. Soc. Photobiology (coun. 1978-82), Soc. Investigative Dermatology (Wm. Montagna award 1982). Achievements include developing novel and safe effective treatment of psoriasis. Office: Mass Gen Hosp Derm Wel 2 55 Fruit St Boston MA 02114-2696*

PARRISH, KENNETH DALE, treasurer, accountant; b. Grand Rapids, Mich., Jan. 3, 1959; s. Harold O. and Grace E. Parrish; m. Sandra Frost, Aug. 7, 1993; 1 child, Kristen. BA, Mich. State U., 1985; MBA, Grand Valley State U., 2001. CPA, Mich. Dir. program devel. and tng. Jr. Achievement, Chgo., 1981-83, exec. dir. Canton, Ohio, 1983-85; v.p. Parrish Acctg. Svc., P.C., Grand Rapids, 1985-96; treas. Kent County, 1997—. Trustee Cascade (Mich.) Charter Twp., 1988-92; commr. Kent County, Grand Rapids, 1993-96. Mem. AIPCA, Mich. Assn. CPAs, Nat. Assn. County Treas. and Fin. Officers, Mich. Assn. County Treas., Govt. Fin. Officers Assn., Grand Rapids Jaycees (pres. 1992-93, Jr. Chamber Internat. Senatorship 1996). Republican. Avocations: golf, tennis, scuba diving, sailing, travel. Office: Kent County Treas 300 Monroe Ave NW Grand Rapids MI 49503-2206 E-mail: ken.parrish@kentcounty.org.

PARRISH, MARIE MCADAMS, nurse, office manager; b. Efland, N.C., May 5, 1916; d. Eugene Franklin and Nina Brown (Haley) McAdams; m. Albert A. Parrish, Aug. 16, 1940 (dec. June 1985); children: Ann Parrish Torp, James Eugene. Grad. in nursing, Duke U., 1937. RN, N.C. Nurse Duke Hosp., Durham, N.C., 1934-46; nurse with Dr. Albert A Parrish, Ft. Lauderdale, Fla., 1946-85. Republican. Presbyterian. Avocations: art, ball room dancing, English horseback riding. Home: 1036 SE 12th Way Fort Lauderdale FL 33316-1351

PARRISH, MATTHEW DENWOOD, psychiatrist; b. Washington, Apr. 1, 1918; s. Forrest Denwood and Alice Lorena (Flynn) P.; m. Virginia John Bennet, Sept. 24, 1944 (div.); children: Denwood, John, Stephen; m. Marilyn Kay Arney, May 29, 1978; children: Megan, Maxwell. BA, U. Va., 1939; MD, George Washington U., 1950. Diplomate Am. Bd. Psychiatry. Intern Letterman Hosp., San Francisco, 1950-51; resident in psychiatry Walter Reed Hosp., Washingtoin, 1951-54; commd. 2d lt. U.S. Army, 1941, advanced through grades to col., 1967, ret., 1971; chief tng. Ill. Dept. Mental Health, Chgo., 1972-74; supt. Singer Mental Health Ctr., Rockford, Ill., 1974-85, med. dir., 1985-93; child and adolescent psychiatrist, 1986-95; ret., 1996. Clin. prof. psychiatry U. Ill., Chgo., 1972-76; clin. asst. prof. psychiatry Coll. Med., Rockford, 1976—. Editor in chief: U.S. Army Vietnam Medical Journal, 1967-68. Decorated Legion of Merit (2). Fellow Am. Psychiat. Assn. (life); mem. Soc. Med. Cons. in Armed Forces, Assn. Mil. Surgeons U.S. Avocations: writing, photography, painting, linguistics, electronics. E-mail: matthewP@uic.edu.

PARRISH, MAURICE DRUE, museum executive; b. Chgo., Mar. 5, 1950; s. Maurice and Ione Yvonne (Culumns) P.; m. Gail Marie Sims, Sept. 2, 1978; children: Theodore, Andrew, Brandon, Cara. BA in Arch., U. Pa., 1972; MArch, Yale U., 1975. City planner City of Chgo., 1975-81; architect John Hiltscher & Assocs., Chgo., 1981-83, Barnett, Jones & Smith, Chgo., 1983-84; zoning adminstr. City of Chgo., 1984-87, bldg. commr., 1987-89; dep. dir. Detroit Inst. of Arts, 1989-97, interim dir., 1997-99, exec. v.p., 1999—. Bd. dirs. Arts League of Mich., Detroit, 1994-97, Mosaic Youth Theatre Detroit, 2000—, chmn., 2002—; co-chmn. Mayor's Affordable Housing Task Force, Chgo., 1984-89; chmn. Chgo. Elec. Commn., 1988-89; mem. Chgo. Econ. devel. Commn., 1987-89; pres. St. Philip Neri Sch. Bd., Chgo., 1981-85, South Shore Commn., Chgo., 1982-84. King Chavez Parks fellow U. Mich., 1991, H.I. Feldman fellow Yale U., 1972; Franklin W. Gregory scholar Yale U., 1974, Nat. Achievement scholar U. Pa., 1968. Mem. Am. Assn. Mus., Am. Assn. Mus. Adminstrs., Constrn. Specifications Inst., Lambda Alpha. Avocations: golf, chess, reading, astronomy. Office: Detroit Inst of Arts 5200 Woodward Ave Detroit MI 48202-4094 E-mail: mparrish@dia.org.

PARRISH, OVERTON BURGIN, JR. pharmaceutical corporation executive; b. Cin., May 26, 1933; s. Overton Burgin and Geneva Opal (Shinn) P. BS, Lawrence U., 1955; MBA, U. Chgo., 1959. With Pfizer Inc., 1959-74; salesman Pfizer Labs., Chgo., 1959-62, asst. mktg. product mgr. N.Y.C., 1962-63, product mgr., 1964-66, group product mgr., 1966-67, mktg. mgr., 1967-68, v.p. mktg., 1969-70, v.p., dir. ops., 1970-71; exec. v.p. domestic pharm. div. Pfizer Pharms., 1971-72; exec. v.p., dir. Pfizer Internat. Divsn., 1972-74; pres., chief operating officer G.D. Searle Internat., Skokie, Ill., 1974-75, pres., chief exec. officer, 1975-77; pres. Worldwide Pharm./Consumer Products Group, 1977-86; pres., chief exec. officer Phoenix Health Care, Chgo., 1987—; chmn., CEO, bd. dirs. Wis. Pharmiacal Co., Inc., 1990-96; co-chmn. Inhalon Pharms., 1991-95, also bd. dirs.; chmn. ViatiCare Fin. Svcs. LLC, 1993—, also bd. dirs.; chmn., CEO, bd. dirs. The Female Health Co., 1996—. Chair Amreimmune Pharmaceuticals, Inc., 1999—; bd. dirs., chair Miicro Inc., 1999—; bd. dirs. Medic Group. Author: The Future Pharmaceutical Marketing; International Drug Pricing, 1971. Trustee Mktg. Sci. Inst.; trustee Food and Drug Law Inst., 1979-86 , Lawrence U., 1983-87, 98— . Served to 1st lt. USAF, 1955-57. Mem. Beta Gamma Sigma, Phi Kappa Tau. Home: 505 N Lake Shore Dr Chicago IL 60611-3427 Office: Phoenix Health Care 515 N State St Chicago IL 60610- E-mail: oparrish@aol.com.

PARRISH, PATRICK MICHAEL, music educator; b. Valley City, N.D., Apr. 24, 1966; s. Daniel Lyle and Patricia Mary Parrish; m. Elizabeth Joan Feneley, July 15, 1989; children: Sydney, Emily, Daniel. MusB in Edn., Cen. Mich. U., 1988; MusM in Edn., VanderCook Coll. of Music, Chgo., 1992. Cert. tchr. Mich. Music educator Ashley (Mich.) Cmty. Schools, 1989—90, Oxford (Mich.) Area Cmty. Schools, 1990—. Adj. faculty Oakland U., Rochester, Mich., 1997. Mem.: Music Educators Nat. Conf., Mich. Sch. Band and Orch. Assn. (state chair of festival improvements com. 1996—97), Phi Mu Alpha. Roman Catholic. Home: 406 Plum Creek Rd Lapeer MI 48446 Office: Oxford Mid Sch 745 North Oxford Rd Lapeer MI 48446 Personal E-mail: pbparrish@chartermi.net. E-mail: parrip02@oxford.k12.mi.us.

PARRISH, RAMON OLENE, JR. gerontologist; b. Atlanta, June 2, 1955; s. Ramon Olene and Sue (Shelnutt) P.; married, 1978 (div. 1994); children: Christopher, Matthew, Daniel; m. Susan Marie Castle, June 17, 1995. AA, Oxford Coll., 1975; BS, Emory U., 1977, MD, 1981. Diplomate Am. Bd. Family Practice; cert. cert. added qualification in geriat. medicine 1994. Flt. surgeon 21st Tactical Air Support System, Shaw AFB, S.C., 1982-84; resident in family practice Eglin AFB Hosp., Fla., 1984-87, mem. family practice faculty, 1987-88; sr. ptnr. Blue Ridge (Ga.) Med. Svcs., 1989—2000; asst. prof. family and preventive medicine Emory U., Atlanta, 2001—. Office: 478 Peachtree St Ste 818-A Atlanta GA 30308-3154

PARRISH, RICHARD KENNETH, II, medical educator; b. Decatur, Ind., July 18, 1951; s. Richard Kenneth and Cloe Marie (Liniger) P.; m. Marianne Pantin, Oct. 7, 1989; children: Andrés, Felipe, Deanna. BA in Biol. Sci., Ind. U., 1972; MD, Ind. U., Indpls., 1976. Asst. prof. ophthalmology U. Miami (Fla.) Sch. Medicine, 1982-89, assoc. prof., 1989-94, prof., 1994—, chmn. dept. ophthalmology, 1996-99, assoc. dean. med. edn., 2000—; staff surgeon VA Med. Ctr., Miami, 1982-83, 97; dir. grad. med. edn. Jackson Meml. Hosp. Co-author: Clinical Decisions in Glaucoma, 1993, Cirugia de Glaucoma, 2000; editor: University of Miami Bascom Palmer Eye Institute Atlas of Ophthalmology; : mem. editl. bd. Archives of Ophthalmology, 1985—95, : mem. editl. bd. Ophthalmic Practice, Am. Jour. Ophthalmology, 1997—, : mem. editl. bd. Ophthalmic Surgery and Lasers, 1989—, : mem. editl. adv. bd. Ophthalmology Times, Eyenet, 1997—. Mem. Am. Ophthalmol. Soc., Alpha Omega Alpha, Phi Beta Kappa. Avocations: gardening, art collecting. Office: Univ of Miami Sch Medicine Bascom Palmer Eye Inst 900 NW 17th St Miami FL 33136-1119 E-mail: rparrish@med.miami.edu.

PARRISH, ROBERT ALTON, retired pediatric surgeon, educator; b. Augusta, Ga., Sept. 10, 1930; s. Robert Alton and Thelma Elizabeth (Roney) P.; children: Joyce Ann, Cynthia Ann. AB, Mercer U., 1951; MS, U. Ga., 1953; MD, Med. Coll. Ga., 1956. Diplomate: Am. Bd. Surgery. Intern Bapt. Meml. Hosp., Memphis, 1956-57; resident in surgery U. Tenn., 1957-62; gen. surgeon Med. Coll. Ga., Aususta, 1962-64, asst. prof. surgery Augusta, 1964-67, assoc. prof., 1967-70, prof. pediatric surgery, chief pediatric surgery, 1970-93, prof. emeritus pediatric surgery, 1993—. Cons. to hosps. Named Outstanding Tchr. of Yr. Med. Found. Ga., Med. Coll. Ga., 1966 Fellow ACS; mem. Am Assn. Surgery of Trauma, So. Surg. Assn., Am. Acad. Pediatrics, Alpha Omega Alpha, Phi Sigma, Alpha Epsilon Delta Methodist. Home: 433 Scotts Way Augusta GA 30909-3134

PARRISH, THOMAS DENNISON, computer systems engineer; b. Gardner, Mass., Dec. 13, 1935; s. Frank T. and Harriet G. (Wilder) P.; m. Pamela M. Despres, Feb. 20, 1969; children: Michelle, Simone, Denise. B of Engring. Physics, Cornell U., 1958. Commd. ensign USN, 1958, advanced through grades to lt., 1963, resigned, 1967; computer systems scientist, engr. Planning Rsch. Corp., McLean, Va., 1967—. Democrat. Achievements include first known application of Quicksort algorithm in production compiler environment; development of operational context-based message retrieval system for U.S. Navy, of generalized Fibonacci series and applied to computer sorting system; designer automated patent system for U.S. Patent Office. Home: 44 Monadnock Dr Marlborough NH 03455-3001 Office: PRC Inc 1500 Prc Dr Mc Lean VA 22102-5050

PARRISH, THOMAS KIRKPATRICK, III, marketing consultant; b. Richmond, Va., May 18, 1930; s. Thomas Kirkpatrick and Sally Cary (Friend) P.; divorced: children: Linn Cary, Wayne Elizabeth, Susan Scott, Thomas Kirkpatrick IV. AB, Princeton U., 1952. Product mgr. Vick Chem. Co., N.Y.C., 1955-58; v.p. Benton & Bowles Advt. Agy., 1958-65; pres. Am. Chicle Co. div. Warner-Lambert Co., Morris Plains, N.J., 1965-70, Life Savers Inc. div. Squibb Corp., N.Y.C., 1970-73, Lanvin-Charles of Ritz Inc. subs. Squibb Corp., N.Y.C., 1974-76; dir. parent co. Squibb Corp., 1974-77; group dir. new bus. devel. Gillette Co., Boston, 1977-78; exec. v.p. SSC & B, Inc., N.Y.C., 1978-81; sr. assoc. Am. Cons. Corp., 1982-86; prin. The Parrish Co., N.Y.C., 1986—. Mem. N.Y. State Republican Com., 1962-63; bd. dirs. YMCA Ctr. for Internat. Mgmt. Studies, N.Y.C., 1970-85. Served to lt., jr. grade USN, 1952-55. Home: 138 Fiddlers Green Waitsfield VT 05673

PARRISH-ST. JOHN, FLORENCE TUCKER, writer, retired government official; b. Greenville, Miss., Nov. 12; d. Victor Amos and Martha Buchannan (Binkley) Denslow; m. Joseph Nathaniel Tucker Jr., Nov. 9, 1946 (dec. Dec. 1955); children: Joseph Nathaniel III, Frederick Steven, James Denslow; m. Noel Francis Parrish, June 25, 1983 (dec. Apr. 1987); m. Adrian St. John, Jan. 29, 1998. Diploma in piano, Ward-Belmont Coll., Nashville, 1945; studied piano with Michael Field, N.Y.C., 1945-46; B of Music Edn., Delta State U., Cleveland, Miss., 1960; MS in Counseling, U. So. Miss., 1971; EdD in Human Resources, George Washington U., 1983. Tchr. music Gulfport (Miss.) Pub. Schs., 1959-63; recreation therapist VA Hosp., Gulfport, 1964-70; edn. counselor USAF, Miss. and Japan, 1971-74; edn. svcs. officer, 1974-75; asst. dir. sr. tng. CAP nat. hdqrs., 1975-77; EEO officer D.C. Dept. Labor, 1977-80; bur. chief complaints processing and adjudication Office EEO, U.S. Geol. Survey, Reston, Va., 1980-82; mgr. human resources Dept. Interior, 1982-84; internat. forum coord. Inspire 85 Pres.'s Com. on Employment of Handicapped, 1985; commr. Alexandria Commn. on Aging, Va., 1985-88, chmn. edn. and cultural affairs com., 1985-88, sec., 1987-88; lead scholar pilot project Nat. Coun. Aging. Vis. prof. Kunsan Tchrs. Coll., Kunsan Jr. Coll., 1974-75; apptd. mem. del. People-to-People Internat. Amb. Program, Beijing, Peoples Republic China and Hong Kong, 1988; mem. steering com. Va. Home Care Alliance, 1990-92; mem. exec. bd. Washington Opera Guild, 1992-94; chmn. Night in Old Vienna benefit ball Embassy of Austria, Washington, 1993, co-chair, 1994; mem. adv. bd. Inst. Conflict Analysis and Resolution George Mason U., 1993—, vice chair, 1995-97, chmn., 1998-2000; del. to Arms Ctrl. Negotiations in the Middle East, Athens, Greece, 1994; mem. ofcl. delegation 8th Internat. Helicopter Olympic Competition, Moscow, 1994; workshop leader, cons. and lectr. in field; bd. dirs. Wake Assocs., Ltd., Washington, 1980-84. Columnist on aging issues, Alexandria Gazette-Packet, feature writer, 1986-92; contbr. articles to profl. jours. Organizer, pres. Gulfport chpt. Parents-Without-Ptnrs., 1962-64; charter mem. Westminster Presbyn. Ch., Gulfport, 1961; active Nat. Coun. on Aging, Military Classics Seminar; officer, bd. dirs. Stonehurst IV Homeowners Assn., 1994-96. Recipient Outstanding Vis. Prof. award Kunsan Tchrs. Coll., Korea, 1974, Kunsan Jr. Coll. award for promoting tchr. exch. program, also certs. of commendation, estab. Brigadier Gen. Noel F. Parrish award The Nat. Tuskegee Airmen, Inc., commendation for organizing Young at Art show Alexandria Commn. on Aging. Mem. Women in Comm., Washington Opera Guild, USAF Assn. (v.p. for cmty. programs Gen. Charles Gabriel chpt. 1991-98, Woman of Distinction award Thomas Anthony chpt., Pres.'s award 1998), NATO Def. Coll. Anciens Assn., Am. Inst. Wine and Food, World Affairs Coun., Va. Assn. on Aging, Nat. Press Club (events and oral history coms., chmn. oral history com., sr. rep. NPC trip to China and Hong Kong 1998, Vivian award 1998, 99, 2000, 02, presenter 4 panel programs), Miss. Soc. Washington, Ret. Officers Assn., Friends of Kennedy Ctr., Smithsonian Assocs., The Nat. Tuskegee Airmen Inc. Orgn. Home: Stonehurst 9302 Arlington Blvd Fairfax VA 22031-2503 also: 9110 Belvoir Woods Pkwy Apt 118 Fort Belvoir VA 22060-2717

PARR-JOHNSTON, ELIZABETH, academic administrator; b. N.Y.C., Aug. 15, 1939; d. Ferdinand Van Siclen (dec.) and Helene Elizabeth (Ham) Parr (dec.); m. David E. Bond, Dec. 28, 1962 (div. July 1975); children: Peter V.S., Kristina Aline; m. Archibald F. Johnston, Mar. 6, 1982; children: James, Heather, Alexandra, Margaret. BA, Wellesley Coll., 1961; MA, Yale U., 1962, PhD, 1973; postgrad., Harvard U., 1986. Various positions Govt. of Can., Ottawa, Ont., 1973-76, INCO Ltd., Toronto, 1976-79; chief of staff, sr. policy advisor Ministry of Employment and Immigration, Govt. of Can., 1979-80; various positions Shell Can. Ltd., Calgary, Alta., 1980-90; pres. Parr-Johnston & Assocs., 1990-91; pres., vice-chancellor Mt. St. Vincent U., Halifax, Nova Scotia, N.S., 1991-96, The U. New Brunswick, Fredericton, Canada, 1996—2002. Instr. U. Western Ont., London, Ont., 1964-67, U. B.C., Vancouver, 1967-71; vis. scholar Wesleyan U., Middletown, Conn., 1971-72; acad. rsch. assoc. Carleton U., Ottawa, 1972-73; bd. dirs. Nova Scotia Power, Emera Ltd., Bank of Nova Scotia, The Empire Co., Social Rsch. and Demonstration Corp., BioAtlantech Ltd., Can. Found. for Sustainable Devel. Tech.; spkr. and presenter in field. Mem. editorial bd. Can. Econ. Jour., 1980-83; contbr. articles to profl. jours. Planning chmn. John Howard Soc., 1980—84; mem. policy adv. com. C.D. Howe, 1980—85; mem. Ont. Econ. Coun., 1981—84; Bd. dirs. Dellcrest Home, 1980—84, Calgary S.W. Fed. Riding Assn., 1985—91, The Learning Ctr., Calgary, 1989—91, Halifax United Way, 1991—92, North/South Inst., 1992—96, Coun. for Can. Unity, 1993—, Vol. Planning N.S., 1992—93, Social Sci. Rsch. Coun., 1995—98, FPI Ltd., 1996—2001. Woodrow Wilson fellow, 1962. Mem. Assn. Atlantic Univs. (chair 1994-96), Assn. Univs. and Colls. in Can. (bd. dirs., mem. exec. com. 1994-96), Women in Acad. Adminstrn. (adv. bd. 1991-96), Calgary Coun. Advanced Tech. (exec. 1990-91), Can. Econs. Assn., Inst. Pub. Adminstrn. Can., Sr. Women Acad. Adminstrs. Can., Assn. Commonwealth Univs. (former mem. exec. com.), Phi Beta Kappa. Anglican. Avocations: skiing, golf, sailing, travel. Office: U NB Office of Pres PO Box 4400 Fredericton NB Canada E3B 5A3 E-mail: EPJ@unb.ca.

PARROTT, DENNIS BEECHER, retired insurance executive; b. St. Louis, June 13, 1929; s. Maurice Ray and Mai Ledgerwood (Beecher) P.; m. Vivian Cleveland Miller, Mar. 24, 1952; children: Constance Beecher, Dennis Beecher, Anne Cleveland. BS in Econs., Fla. State U., Tallahassee, 1954; postgrad., Princeton U., 1964; MBA, Pepperdine U., 1982. With Prudential Ins. Co. Am., 1954-74, v.p. group mktg., 1971-74; sr. v.p. Frank B. Hall Cons. Co., 1974-83; v.p. Johnson & Higgins, 1983-95; exec. v.p. Arthur J. Gallagher & Co., 1995-98; ret., 1998. Spkr. in field. Chmn. Weekend with the Stars Telethon, 1976-80; chmn. bd. dirs. United Cerebral Palsy/Spastic Children's Found., L.A. County, 1979-82, chmn. bd. govs., 1982-83; bd. dirs. Nat. United Cerebral Palsy Assn., 1977-82, pres., 1977-79; bd. dirs. L.A. Emergency Task Force, 1992; mem. cmty. adv. coun. Birmingham High Sch., Van Nuys, Calif., 1982-85; sect. chmn. United Way, L.A., 1983-84; bd. dirs. The Betty Clooney Found. for Brain Injured, 1986-88; mem. com. to fund an endowed chair in cardiology at Cedars-Sinai Med. Ctr., 1986-88; adv. coun. Family Health Program, Inc., 1986-88; bd. deacons Bel Air Presbyn. Ch., 1990-92, chmn., 1991-92, elder, 1993-96; mem. adv. coun. Blue Cross Calif., 1996-98; chmn. Danny Arnold Meml. Golf Classic at Riviera Country Club benefitting John

Wayne Cancer Inst., 1997. 1st lt. AUS, 1951-53. Mem. Am. Soc. C.L.U.s., Internat. Found. Employee Benefits, Merchants and Mfrs. Assns. 44th Ann. Mgmt. Conf. (chmn. 1986), Employee Benefits Planning Assn. So. Calif., L.A. Club, Woodland Hills Country Club, Jonathan Club (L.A.). Republican. Presbyterian. Home: 17023 Encino Hills Dr Encino CA 91436-4009 E-mail: dparr63374@aol.com.

PARROTT, KEVIN BERNARD, elementary school educator; b. Winston-Salem, NC, June 15, 1964; s. Eloise E. Parrott; children: Terrell, Joel, Sahlia, Shanae. BS Music and Edn., Winston-Salem (N.C.) State U., 1995; postgrad., N.C. Agr. and Tech. U., Greensboro, 1997—99. Cert. N.C. School of The Arts 1987. Theatre dir. United Meth. Children's Home, Winston-Salem, NC, 1981—85, drama instr.; dir. Evangel Theatre Prodn. Co., Upper Marlboro, 2002—. Dir.: (theatre) Summer Heat Cool Music, 1999. Mem.: Alpha Phi Alpha. Home: 2416 Eutaw Pl Baltimore MD 21217 Personal E-mail: maconni@hotmail.com.

PARROTT, NANCY SHARON, lawyer; b. Atoka, Okla., Jan. 11, 1944; d. Albert L. and Willie Jo (Parkhill) Furr. BA, Okla. U., 1967; MA, No. Tex. U., 1974; JD, Okla. City U., 1982. Bar: Okla. 1984, U.S. Supreme Ct. 1984. Ptnr. Champman & Chapman, Oklahoma City, 1984-85; chief legal asst. marshal Okla. Supreme Ct., 1985—. Mem. Leadership Oklahoma, Leadership Oklahoma City; bd. dirs. Youth Leadership Exch., recruitment chmn., mentor. Mem. ABA, Okla. Bar Assn. (awards com., civil procedure com.), Okla. County Bar Assn. (bd. dirs., del., mem. cmty. svc. com., Law Day co-chair), Am. Judicature Soc. Office: Okla Supreme Ct State Capital Bldg 245 Oklahoma City OK 73105

PARROTT, THENA ELIZABETH, nurse educator; b. Amarillo, Tex., Sept. 13, 1950; d. William Duard and Ruth Virginia (Crist) Henry; m. William Jackson Parrott, Dec. 23, 1977; children: William Richard, Cody Spencer. BSN, Baylor U., 1972; MSN, Tex. Woman's U., 1977; PhD in Edn. Curriculum and Instrn., Tex. A&M U., 1993. RN, Tex. Asst. prof. Dallas Bapt. U., 1976-81; part-time charge nurse Dallas Med.-Surg. Hosp., 1979-81; dir. Vocat. Sch. Nursing, Goodall-Witcher Hosp. Found., Clifton, Tex., 1982; part-time home health nurse Girling Health Care, Temple, 1988-89; faculty/course coord. Ctrl. Tex. Coll., Killeen, 1984-89; staff nurse ICU/CCU, St. Joseph Regional Health Ctr., Bryan, Tex., 1989-97; mem. faculty Blinn Coll., 1990-97, ADN program, 1997—, dir. ADN program coord. allied health programs, 1997-2000, divsn. chair, 2000—. Cons. reviewer W.B. Saunders Co., Phila., 1999, J.B. Lippincott, Phila., 1999. Contbr. articles to profl. jours. Sunday Sch. tchr., mem. choir, soloist Northview Bapt. Ch., Bryan, 1989—, Christ's Way Baptist Ch., Bryan, 2000; vol., bd. dirs., program chair, CPR instr.-tr ainer Am. Heart Assn., Bryan, 1975—; mem. Brazos Hist. Commn., Bryan, 1995—. Recipient awards for vol. work. Mem. ANA, Nat. Orgn. for AD Nursing, Nat. League for Nursing, Nat. Soc. DAR (past treas.), Kappa Delta Pi. Republican. Baptist. Avocations: sewing, crafts, gardening, fishing. Office: Blinn Coll ADN Program PO Box 6030 Bryan TX 77805-6030 E-mail: tparrott@acmail.blinncol.edu.

PARROTT, TODD, racing team crew chief; b. Charlotte, NC, Feb. 9, 1964; s. Buddy Parrott; m. Debbie Parrott; children: Tyler, Chandler. Crew mem. Winston Cup teams including Richard Petty, Darrell Waltrip and Rusty Wallace, 1978—95; crew chief for Ernie Irvan Robert Yates Racing, Charlotte, 1995—96, crew chief for Dale Jarrett, 1996—. Office: c/o Robert Yates Racing 115 Dwelle St Charlotte NC 28208-2929*

PARROTT, WANDA SUE, writer, journalist; b. Kansas City, Mo., Feb. 12, 1935; d. William Raymond and Lois Marie (Cain) Childress; m. Edward Anthony Cyriacus Parrott, Dec. 16, 1962 (div. 1971); 1 child, Edward Anthony. AA, Citrus Coll., 1954; journalism cert., L.A. Evening Adult Coll., 1968; PhD in Comms., Colegium Orthogenesis, 1961; DD in Comparative Religion, Universal Life Ch., 1974. Tech. writer aerospace industry, So. Calif., 1965-67; journalist Hearst Corp./L.A. Herald-Examiner, 1967-74, Daily News subs. Chgo. Tribune, 1977-79. Assoc. Valley Publs., 1980-82, Sr. Living Newspapers, 1992-2000. *Wanda Sue Parrott is a victim of flooding from urban development that causes rain and sewage to inundate her property. She challenges "Sovereign Immunity," which protects cities from being sued. In her landmark literary Trail of Tears epic poem, she serves as a spokes voice role model all urban victims may emulate by compiling community reports of victims' stories told in their own words. Using a "pen is mightier than the sword" approach to literary settlement of legal issues, she has been called a new Joan of Arc leading common people to victory through the peaceful power of poetic politics and prose.* Co-prodr. Golden Words, 1993-2002; co-author: How to Try Your Own Case in Court...And Win!, 1997, There's A Spirit in the Kitchen, 2001. Co-founder, prodr. nat. ann. Sr. Poet Laureate Poetry Competition; vol. Salvation Army, Springfield, Mo., 1994-2002; founder Springfield Writers' Workshop, 1992. Recipient Gold Kettle award, Salvation Army, 1994—2002. Fellow Ancient Mystical Order Rosae Crucis (master of lodge 1984-85, Ptah award for creative leadership 1985), Springfield Writers' Guild (bd. dirs., past pres.), Mo. Writers' Guild (past sec.-treas.), Book Publicists of So. Calif., Mo. State Poetry Soc. (hon. life). Avocation: pets. E-mail: wparrott@swbell.net.

PARRY, LANCE AARON, newspaper executive; b. Allentown, Pa., Sept. 4, 1947; s. Harwood Clayton Bachman and Iola Mary (Johnson) P.; m. Virginia Eleanor Ford, Apr. 24, 1971; children: Halloran Lee, Christine Ford. BS in Edn., Kutztown U., 1969; postgrad., W.Va. U., 1970. With Call-Chronicle Newspapers, Allentown, 1970-81, mng. editor, 1979-81; asst. news editor The Phila. Inquirer, 1981-82, systems editor, 1982-84, night news editor, 1984-86, news editor daily edit., 1986-87, news editor Sunday edit., 1987-89, sr. editor/systems and tech., 1989-93, page design dir., 1993-94, features news editor, 1994-96, news editor Sunday edit., 1996-98, features news editor, 1998—. Recipient 1st Place award for front page design Pa. Newspaper Pubs. Assn./Pa. Soc. Newspaper Editors, 1985, 87, 88, Disting. Alumnus award Kutztown U., 1992; Sigma Delta Chi scholar, 1969. Mem. Soc. Profl. Journalists, Pen and Pencil Club. Democrat. Presbyterian. Home: 16 Salisbury Ln Malvern PA 19355-2836 Office: The Phila Inquirer 400 N Broad St Philadelphia PA 19130-4099 E-mail: lparry@phillynews.com.

PARRY, ROBERT WALTER, chemistry educator; b. Ogden, Utah, Oct. 1, 1917; s. Walter and Jeanette (Petterson) P.; m. Marjorie J. Nelson, July 6, 1945; children: Robert Bryce, Mark Nelson. BS, Utah State Agr. Coll., 1940; MS, Cornell U., 1942; PhD, U. Ill., 1946; DSc (hon.), Utah State U., 1985, U. Utah, 1997. Rsch. asst. NDRC Munitions Devel. Lab. U. Ill., Urbana, 1943-45, tchg. fellow, 1945-46; mem. faculty U. Mich., Ann Arbor, 1946-69, prof. chemistry, 1958-69; Disting. prof. chemistry U. Utah, Salt Lake City, 1969-97, prof. emeritus, 1997—. Indsl. cons., 1952—; chmn. bd. trustees Gordon Rsch. Conf., 1967-68. Founding editor Inorganic Chemistry, 1960-63. Recipient Mfg. Chemists award for coll. tchg., 1972, Sr. U.S. Scientist award Alexander Von Humboldt-Stiftung, West Germany, 1980, First Govs. medal of Sci., State Utah, 1987. Mem. AAAS (chmn. chemistry sect. 1983), Internat. Union Pure and Applied Chemistry (chmn. U.S. nat. com., chmn. com. tchg. chemistry 1968-74), Am. Chem. Soc. (bd. editors jour. 1969-80, dir. 1973-83, pres.-elect 1981, pres. 1982, Disting. Svc. to Inorganic Chemistry award 1965, Disting. Svc. to Chem. Edn. award 1977, Utah award Utah sect. 1978, Priestly medal 1993), Sigma Xi. Achievements include research and publications on some structural problems of inorganic chemistry and incorporation results into theoretical models, chemistry of phosphorus, boron and fluorine. Home: 5002 Fairbrook Ln Salt Lake City UT 84117-6205 Office: U Utah Dept Chemistry 315 South 1400 East Rm 2174 Salt Lake City UT 84112-0850 Fax: 801-581-8433. Personal E-mail: rwpmnp1@aol.com. Business E-Mail: parry@chemistry.chem.utah.edu.

PARRY, ROGER GEORGE, entrepreneur, writer; b. London, June 4, 1953; s. George and Margharita (Mitchell) P.; m. Johanna Waterous, Dec. 22, 1990; 1 child, Benjamin. MLitt, Oxford U., 1976; BSc with honors, Bristol (Eng.) U., 1973. Prodr., presenter BBC TV, London, 1979-84; cons. McKinsey & Co., 1984-88; group v.p. Aegis Group, 1988-94; CEO More Group Plc, 1995-98, Clear Channel Internat., 1998—. Founder London Radio, 1993; bd. dirs. Jazz FM Plc, iTouch cpl; non-exec. chmn. future Network Plc, Johnson PREJS Plc; non-exec. dir. New Media Spark Plc. Author: People Businesses, 1991; co-author: City and the Single Market, 1991. Dir. Internat. Globe Ctr., London, 1988—. Recipient Gold award N.Y. Film and TV Festival, 1984. Mem. Marylebone Cricket Club, Oxford and Cambridge Club. Office: Clear Channel Internat 33 Golden Square London WIR 3PA England E-mail: rogerparry@clearchannel.com.

PARRY, SALLY ELLEN, academic administrator, English educator; b. Albany, N.Y., Oct. 11, 1953; d. Idwal and Carolyn Jean (Hardy) P.; m. Robert Leonard McLaughlin, Sept. 26, 1981. BA, Fordham U., 1975, MA, 1982, PhD, 1986. V.p. George Peabody & Assocs., N.Y.C., 1978-85; asst. to exec. dir. MLA, 1986-88; asst. prof. Ill. State U., Normal, Ill., 1988-89, academic advisor, asst. to dept. chair, 1990-2000, dir. undergrad. studies English, 2000—. Adj. asst. prof. Iona Coll., New Rochelle, N.Y., 1986-87; adj. instr. Fordham U., Bronx, N.Y., 1985-88; cons. Popular Press, Bowling Green, Ohio, 1995—. Recipient Herb Sanders award Ill. State Acad. Advisement, 1994, Outstanding Adv. certificate of merit Nat. Academic Advising Assn., 1995. Mem. MLA, Sinclair Lewis Soc. (pres. 1992-94, exec. dir. 1995—, editor newsletter 1992—), Am. Studies Assn., Soc. Study Midwestern Lit., Cmty. Players, Marjorie Rawlings Soc., Democrat. Presbyterian. Avocations: theater, piano playing. Office: Ill State U Dept English PO Box 4240 Normal IL 61790-4240

PARRY, SCOTT BRINK, psychologist; b. Reading, Pa., Sept. 4, 1932; s. George Raymond and Claire (Blackburne) Parry; m. Joan SantAntonio; 1 child Christiana Claire. BA, Princeton U., 1954; MS, Boston U., 1960; PhD, NYU, 1969. Account exec. Hill & Knowlton, Inc., N.Y.C., 1960-62; editor Harcourt, Brace, Jovanovich, 1962-64; ptnr. Parry & Robinson, Inc., 1964-66; mgr. N.Y.C. office Sterling Inst., 1966-71; v.p., pres., chmn. Tng. House, Inc., N.Y.C., Princeton, 1971—; prof. comms. Mercer County (N.J.) C.C., 2000—01. Educ. cons. UNESCO, Paris, Nigeria, Ghana, 1963, Paris, Nigeria, Ghana, 64; mem. adv. bd. Training Mag. Lakewood Publs., Mpls., 1988—92; adj. prof. NYU, 1968—74; spkr. convs. and meetings in 17 countries on 6 continents; cons. to more than 50 Fortune 500 cos. Author: (book) The Story of Handbells, 1957, A Handbell Handbill, 1963, From Managing to Empowering, 1993, The Managerial Mirror, 2 vols, 1997, Evaluating the Impact of Training, 1997, Training for Results, 2000, 46 training books; contbr. articles to profl jours and newspapers. Lt U.S. Army, 1957—59. Named Hon Chmn, 25th Anniversary Am Guild English Handbell Ringers, 1979; named to Human Resource Develop Hall of Fame, 1999; recipient Best Training Product Award, Human Resource Exec, 1990, 1994. Mem.: ASTD (prof. Mercer County Comty. Coll. NJ), Instructional Sys Asn, Int Soc Performance Improvement, Int Fedn Training and Develop Orgns. Republican. Presbyterian. Avocations: music (harpsichord, organ, carillon), collecting and restoring antiques, renovating buildings. Office: Training House 96 Bear Brook Rd Princeton NJ 08540-6246 E-mail: jsparry@erols.com.

PARRY, THOMAS HERBERT, JR. school system administrator, educational consultant; b. Detroit, June 28, 1928; s. Thomas Herbert Sr. and Isabel Constance (Brinsmead) P.; m. Frances Ellen Coley, Aug. 15, 1956; children: Virginia Gilkeson, William Thomas, Robert Brinsmead. BA in Edn., U. Fla., 1950; MEd, U. Va., 1958, EdD, 1967. Lic. profl. supr. of counselors; nat. cert. counselor. Tchr. Broward County Pub. Schs., Ft. Lauderdale, Fla., 1950-51, 54-62; instr. Mary Baldwin Coll., Staunton, Va., 1965-66; psychologist McGuffey Reading Ctr., Charlottesville, 1966-67; prof. Clemson (S.C.) U., 1967-86; pres. Ednl. Horizons, Inc., Clemson, 1986-89, Poquoson, Va., 1989—. Cons. Sch. Desegregation Ctr., Columbia, 1970; cons., counselor Advocacy Bd. S.C., 1980-82; exec. sec. S.C. Pers. and Guidance Assn., Columbia, 1980-81; founder S.C. Assn. Measurement and Evaluation in Guidance, 1974-75. Co-author: Developing a Leisure Learning Program, 1980, Beyond the Book: Activities to Correlate with the Virginia Young Readers, 1990-91, Bibliocounseling with Contemporary Children's Literature: A Resource Book for the Clinical Setting, 1996; editor S.C. Pers. and Guidance Newsletter and Jour., 1969-74; founder, editor S.C. Pers. and Guidance Assn. Jour., 1972-74; contbr. articles to profl. jours. Bd. dirs. Peninsula Agy. on Aging, Inc., 1994-2000; mem. adv. coun., Ret. and Sr. Vol. Program of Va. Peninsula, Inc., Newport News, 2001—; mem. adv. coun. Peninsula Agy. on Aging, Inc., 2001—. Recipient Svc. award S.C. Pers. and Guidance, 1968-81, Nat. Award for Excellence State Publs. and Guidance Assn., 1971, Meritorious Svc. award Am. Pers. and Guidance Assn., 1973, Award of Merit for Svc. to Youth Boy Scouts Am., 1975. Mem. APA, Am. Counseling Assn., S.C. Counseling Assn., Kiwanis (bd. dirs., chmn. community svc. com. 1991—, disting. sec. 1994-96, Kiwanian of Yr. 1995-96, life capital dist. Kiwanis Found., Inc. 1995), Masons (Columbus and Newport News Scottish Rite Bodies), Ft. Benning Lodge # 579, Kappa Delta Pi, Phi Delta Kappa. Presbyterian. Avocations: walking, gardening, photography. Bus. Home and Office: 1 Ebb Tide Lndg Poquoson VA 23662-1334 E-mail: edhorizons@aol.com., TparryCWP@aol.com.

PARRY, WILLIAM DEWITT, lawyer; b. Hartford, Conn., June 4, 1941; s. William Brown and Mary Elizabeth (Caton) p.; m. Andrea Hannah Lewis, June 30, 1973; children: Sara, Jessica. BA, U. Mass., 1963; JD, U. Pa., 1966. Bar: N.J. 1987, Pa. 1967, U.S. Dist. Ct. (ea. dist.) Pa. 1974, U.S. Ct. Appeals (3d cir.) 1980, U.S. Ct. Appeals (9th cir.) 1998, U.S. Supreme Ct. 1980. Assoc. Shapiro, Cook & Bressler, Phila., 1966-67; asst. dir. ABA joint com on continuing legal edn. Am. Law Inst., 1967-73; assoc. Lowenschuss Assocs., 1973-85; of counsel Weiss, Golden & Pierson, 1985-88; pvt. practice, 1988; ptnr. Rubin, Quinn, Moss & Patterson, 1989-93; pvt. practice, 1993—. Author: Understanding and Controlling Stuttering: A Comprehensive New Approach Based on the Valsalva Hypothesis, 1994, 2000; editor U. Pa. Law Rev., 1964-66, The Practical Lawyer, 1967-73. Founder Phila. area chpt. Nat. Stuttering Assn., 1996—, bd. dirs.; trustee Unitarian Soc. Germantown, Phila., 1983-86. Mem. ABA, ATLA, Pa. Bar Assn., Phila. Bar Assn., Pa. Trial Lawyers Assn. Democrat. Avocations: writing, lecturing. Home: 520 Baird Rd Merion Station PA 19066-1302 Office: 1608 Walnut St Ste 900 Philadelphia PA 19103-5451 E-mail: wdparry@aol.com.

PARRY-GILL, BARBARA DREPPERD, retired educational administrator; b. Coral Gables, Fla., Sept. 6, 1935; d. Clarence Hartsel and Mildred (Orme) Drepperd; children: William H. Glassford Jr., Robert K. Glassford. BEd, U. Miami, 1957; MS in Ednl. Leadership, Nova U., 1993. Tchr. Dade County Pub. Schs., Miami, Fla., Montpelier (Vt.) Pub. Schs., Longmeadow (Mass.) Pub. Schs.; prin. Lower Sch. Gulliver Acad., Coral Gables; ret. Mem.: AAUW, Delta Kappa Gamma. E-mail: bdparry@aol.com.

PARRY-ROLAND, ANN, secondary school educator; b. Rockville Centre, N.Y. d. Lester and Mary Ann Parry; m. Leonard Roland; m. Michael Grab; children: Susan Grab, Lauren Grab. BA in Secondary Edn. - English, SUNY, New Paltz, 1973; MA in Secondary Edn. with specialization in reading, Hofstra U., 1976. Tchr. Bellmore-Merrick Cen. H.S. Dist., Bellmore, NY, 1973—. Adviser lit. art jour. Grand Ave. Mid. Sch., Bellmore, NY, 1999—. Adviser: lit.-art mag. Illusions, 1999 (EdPress 2000 Disting. Achievement award Jr. High./Mid. School Student Pub., 2000). Mem.: Columbia Scholastic Press Assn., Nat. Scholastic Press Assn.

PARRY-SOLÁ, CHERYL LEE, critical care nurse; b. Bristol, Pa., Oct. 27, 1960; d. Edmund H. and F. Renee (Platt) P. ADN, Bucks County C.C., 1982. RN, N.J.; CCRN. Formerly asst. head nurse Deborah Heart and Lung Ctr., Browns Mills, N.J.; tng. ctr. coord. Holy Spirit Hosp., Camp Hill, Pa., 1995—. Office: Holy Spirit Hosp Edn/Tng/Devel 503 N 21st St Camp Hill PA 17011-2288

PARSA, BAHMAN, nuclear chemist; b. Tehran, Iran, May 16, 1940; came to U.S. 1984; s. Seifollah and Mahrokhsar (Razmara) P.; m. Sima Kermanshahi, Sept. 15, 1972; children: Pantea, Parham. BS, U. Calif., Berkeley, 1963; PhD, MIT, 1967. Asst. prof. nuclear chemistry Tehran U. Nuclear Ctr., 1967-71, asst. dir. rsch., 1968-69; chmn. dept. nuclear sci. U. Tehran, 1969-71; dir. Tehran U. Nuclear Ctr., 1973-74; dep. minister sci. rsch. Ministry of Sci. and Higher Edn., Iran, 1974-78; assoc. prof. nuclear chemistry U. Tehran, 1971-83; rsch. scientist N.J. Dept. of Environ. Protection, Trenton, 1984-97, N.J. Dept. Health and Sr. Svcs., Trenton, 1997—. Contbr. articles to profl. jours. Fulbright scholar, 1972-73, James Flack Norris fellow, MIT, 1965-66; recipient Founders award Bioassay, Analytical, and Environ. Radiochemistry Conf., Seattle, 2000, Mihan Found. award, 2001. Mem. Sigma Xi, Alpha Gamma Sigma. Achievements include discovery of K-46 (a new nuclide); determination of lead in atmosphere; trace elements analysis via neutron activation analysis; radioactivity in drinking water. Home: 9307 Sheffield Dr Yardley PA 19067-7258 Office: NJ Dept Health and Sr Svcs PO Box 361 Radiol Svcs Trenton NJ 08625 E-mail: bparsa@doh.state.nj.us.

PARSA, BRIAN BAHRAM, surgeon, military officer; b. Kansas City, Mo., Mar. 24, 1959; s. Jalil Parsa, Marly (Johnson) Parsa; m. Katie Sue Parsa; 1 child Jordan David. BA in Biology, U. Kans., 1981; DO, U. Health Sci., 1985. Faculty mem. U. Health Scis., Kansas City, Mo., 1986—88; commd. officer USAF, 1989, advanced through grades to lt. col., 1996, flight surgeon, 1989—; intern. Univ. Hosp., Kansas City, Mo., 1985—86; resident in aerospace medicine Brooks AFB, Tex., 1995—98; comdr. 51st Aerospace Medicine Squadron, Osan Air Base, Republic of Korea, 1998—2000; AF med. liaison Naval Operational Medicine Inst., Pensacola, Fla., 2000—02; chief aerospace medicine Air Edn. and Tng. Command, Universal City, Tex., 2002—. Contbr. article to profl. publ. Named Jolly Green Assn. Rescue Mission of Yr., 1992, 93; recipient Sikorsky Helicopter Rescue award United Techs.-Sikorsky Aircraft Co., various 1992, 93; decorated Air Medal USAF, 1991, Air Force Commendation medal with 5 oak leaf clusters, 1993, S.W. Asia Svc. medal, 1994. Mem. Am. Osteo. Assn., Aerospace Med. Assn., Soc. USAF Flight Surgeons (Air Tng. Command Flight Surgeon of Yr. 1990, Air Combat Command Flight Surgeon of Yr. 1992), Korean Mil. Med. Assn. (hon.). Address: 54 Outer Octagon Universal City TX 78148

PARSAIE, HOUMAN JOHN, management consultant; b. Tehran, Iran, Aug. 3, 1972; s. Iranpour Parsaie and Sakineh Abdollahi; m. Evelyn Parsaie. BCE, U. Hanover, Germany, 1992; MBA in Project Mgmt., U. Hanover, 1995; MCE, U. Berkley, 2000, PhD in Civil Engring., 2001; PhD in Mgmt. (hon.) , Americus U., 2002. Lic. profl. engr.; bar: Calif. 2001. Engring. mgr. PDC, Ltd., Hamburg, Germany, 1990—99; project mgr. PTL/Krazan & Assoc., Woodinville, Wash., 1999—2001; project mgmt. cons. Pacific Design, Bellevue, 2001—. Prof. Concord U., Bellevue, 2001—. Author: (book) Testing & Inspection of Engineering Materials, 2000, Construction Materials for Civil & Structural Engineering, Part 1, Concrete, 2001, Training & Reference Manual for Special Inspectors, 2001, Construction Materials for Civil & Structural Engineering, Part 2, Timber, 2002, Construction Materials for Civil & Structural Engineering, Part 3, Steel, 2002, Project Management (Handbook), 2002, Fundamentals of Materials Science & Engineering, 2002. Fellow: Soc. Am. Mil. Engrs.; mem.: Internat. Conf. Bldg. Officials, Internat. Assn. Bridge & Structural Enging., Nat. Soc. Profl. Engrs. Baha'I. Avocations: travel, sports, reading. Office: Pacific Design 14150 NE 20th St Ste 73 Bellevue WA 98007 Office Fax: 425-255-0554. Personal E-mail: parsaie@aol.com. Business E-Mail: john@pacificdesignco.com.

PARSEGHIAN, GENE, talent company executive, producer; b. Oneonta, N.Y., Dec. 11, 1944; s. Richard and Leona (Spickerman) P.; life ptnr. Michael D. Colberg; 1 child, Rachel Colberg-Parseghian. BA, Antioch Coll., 1967; MFA, Stanford U., 1970. Owner Parseghian Assocs., Inc., N.Y.C., 1977-78; founding ptnr., owner Kimble/Parseghian, Inc., 1978-81, DHKPR, N.Y.C., 1981-84, Triad Artists, Inc., N.Y.C., 1984-92; sr. v.p. William Morris Agy., Inc., 1992-99; founding ptnr., owner Parseghian Planco, 1999—. Bd. dirs. Artsgenesis, N.Y.C. Bd. advisors Ctr. for Family Connections, Cambridge, Mass. Democrat.

PARSELL, ROGER EDMUND, retired educator, civic worker; b. Elkhart, Ind., Feb. 8, 1929; s. Abijah Dunnell and Eula Maud (Golden) P.; m. Hazel Mae Stratton, June 11, 1955; children: Reed Dunnel, Portia Ellen Parsell Hainzelin. BA, Wabash Coll., 1951; MA, Butler U., Indpls., 1956; PhD, U. Denver, 1972. Tchr. The Leelenau Schs., Glen Arbor, Mich., 1954-56; instr. Northwestern Mich. Coll., Traverse City, 1956-57; Fulbright asst. Tulle Schule, Mannheim, Germany, 1957-58; asst. prof. Ill. State U., Normal, 1958-68, Western State Coll., Gunnison, Colo., 1968-69; grad. asst. U. Denver, 1969-73; sr. lectr. James Cook U., Townsville, Australia, 1974-82. Reader Advanced Placement Inst., 1969, 73, 77; adv. bd. Samuel Butler Soc. newsletter, 1985-92. Co-editor: Samuel Butler: An Annotated Bibliography, 1990; author: (monograph) In the Wild with Samuel Butler, 1981, (study guide) Butler's The Way of All Flesh, 1974; guest essayist study guides Denver Ctr. for Performing Arts, 1994-96. Mem. Common Cause, Denver, 1983—, Handgun Control, Washington, 1985—. Fulbright Found. assistantship, 1957-58. Mem. MLA. Avocations: reading, choral groups, golf. Home: 4176 S Reading Way Denver CO 80237-2108

PARSHALL, B. LYNNE, science administrator; Ptnr. Cooley Godward LLP; exec. v.p., CFO, dir. Isis Pharm., Inc., Carlsbad, Calif.; also bd. dirs. Bd. vis. Stanford U. Law Sch. Mem.: ABA, San Diego Bar Assn., Calif. Bar Assn., Licensing Execs. Soc. Office: Isis Pharm Inc 2292 Faraday Ave Carlsbad CA 92008*

PARSHALL, GEORGE WILLIAM, chemist, researcher; b. Hackensack, Minn., Sept. 19, 1929; s. George Clarence and Frances (Virnig) Parshall; m. Naomi B. Simpson, Oct. 9, 1954; children: William, Jonathan, David. BS, U. Minn., 1951; PhD, U. Ill., 1954. Rsch. chemist E.I. duPont de Nemours & Co., Wilmington, Del., 1954—65, rsch. supr., 1965—79, dir. chem. sci., 1979—92, cons., 1992—, mem. com. on environ. mgmt. techs., 1994—97; mem. chem. stockpile disposal com. NRC, Washington, 1992—98, mem. non-stockpile com., 1998—99, 2001—02. Bd. chem. sci. NRC, Washington, 1983—86; Reilly lectr. Notre Dame U., 1980; Ipatieff lectr. Northwestern U., 1994. Author: (book) Homogeneous Catalysis, 1980, Homogeneous Catalysis, 2d rev. edit., 1992; editor: Inorganic Syntheses, 1974, Jour. Molecular Catalysis, 1977—80. Recipient Ballar Inorganic Chemistry medal, U. Ill., 1976. Mem.: NAS, Am. Acad. Arts Scis., Am. Chem. Soc. (award in inorganic chemistry 1983, award leadership in chem. rsch. mgmt. 1989), Inst. Chemists (Chem. Pioneer award 1992, Gold medal award 1995), Guild Episcopal Scholars (treas. 1994—99). Episcopalian. Home: 2504 Delaware Ave Wilmington DE 19806-1220 E-mail: parshallgw@aol.com.

PARSHALL, GERALD, journalist; b. St. Paul, Apr. 24, 1941; s. William Elmer and Evelyn (Steckling) P.; m. Sandra Grant, Dec. 20, 1970. BA, U. Minn., 1963; MA, U. Mich., 1964; grad. fellow, U. Chgo., 1966-67. Reporter York (Pa.) Gazette and Daily, 1968, Balt. Evening Sun, 1968-71; Capitol Hill staff U.S. News & World Report, Washington, 1971-77, sr. editor, 1977-79, asst. mng. editor, 1979-90, sr. writer, 1990-99, contbg. editor, 1999—. Mem. Exec. Com. of Periodical Corrs., U.S. Congress, 1974-80, chmn., 1979-80 Served to 1st lt. U.S. Army, 1964-66. Recipient Front Page award Washington-Balt. Newspaper Guild, 1971, Silver Gavel award ABA, 1983 Home: 1004 Congress Ln Mc Lean VA 22101-2116 E-mail: gparshall@worldnet.att.net.

PARSKY, GERALD LAWRENCE, lawyer; b. West Hartford, Conn., Oct. 18, 1942; s. Isadore and Nettie (Sanders) P.; m. Susan Haas, June 26, 1966; children: Laura, David; m. Robin Cleary, Jan. 27, 1980. AB, Princeton U., 1964; JD, U. Va., 1968. Bar: N.Y. 1969, D.C. 1974, Calif. 1983. Assoc. Mudge Rose Guthrie & Alexander, N.Y.C., 1968-71; spl. asst. to under sec. U.S. Treasury Dept., Washington, 1971-73, exec. asst. to dep. sec. Fed. Energy Office, 1973-74, asst. sec. internat. affairs, 1974-77; sr. ptnr. Gibson, Dunn & Crutcher, Los Angeles, 1977-90; of counsel Gibson, Dunn & Cruther, L.A., 1990-92; chmn. Aurora Capital Ptnrs., 1990—. Bd. govs. Performing Arts Council, Los Angeles Music Ctr. Recipient Alexander Hamilton award U.S. Treasury, 1976 Mem. ABA, Coun. Fgn. Rels., N.Y. Princeton Club, Calif. Club, Racquet Club, Anandale Club, Beach Club. Office: Aurora Capital Group 10877 Wilshire Blvd Ste 2100 Los Angeles CA 90024-4376

PARSLEY, BRANTLEY HAMILTON, librarian; b. Oct. 15, 1927; s. Clarence Elroy and Florence Sally (Barnes) P.; m. Loyce Marie Franklin, Apr. 18, 1951; children: Linda Marie, Brantley Hamilton; m. Bettye Abercrombie, 1996. AA, Balt. Jr. Coll., 1950; BA, U. Md., 1952; BD, New Orleans Bapt. Theol. Sem., 1955, MRE, 1958; M in Librarianship, Emory U., 1965. Ordained to ministry Bapt. Ch., 1956. Pastor Calvary Bapt. Ch., Albany, Oreg., 1955-57; libr. asst. New Orleans Pub. Libr., 1958-61; supt. night circulation and stacks Theology Libr., Emory U., 1961-65; dir. libr. Campbellsville (Ky.) Coll., 1965-82; dir. Genealogy Workshop, Ch. History Writing Workshop. Dir.: (radio broadcast series) Kentucky Authors, 1976, Study of Black Literature, 1978; coll. page editor Ala. Libr., 1985-87. Bd. dirs. Taylor County Comty. Concerts, Mobile (Ala.) Coll., 1982-93; pres. Cen. Ky. Arts Series, 1975-78; dir. Sch. Merger Workshop, 1976; sec. ACTS of Mobile, bd. dirs., 1985-88; mem. Ala. Sch. Libr. Task Force, 1990-93; mem. bd. dirs. Habitat for Humanity, 1993-99, west covenant adv. coun., mem. family selection com. constrn. crew; outreach vol., team leader, workshop trainer Widow Persons Svcs., 1993; mem. Helpline Mobile; mem. adv. coun. Ret. Sr. Vol. Program; tchr. Adult Men's Sunday Sch.; hospice chaplain Mobile Infirmary, 1998—. Recipient Sch. award Am. Legion, 1947. Mem. ALA, Southeastern Libr. Assn., Ky. Libr. Assn. (chmn. coll. and rsch. sect. 1970-71, sec. treas. edn. sect. 1972-73), Ala. Libr. Assn. (chmn. project com. coll., univ. and spl. libr. divsn.), Bay Area Libr. Assn. (pres.-elect 1984), Ala. Assn. Coll. and Rsch. Librs. (chmn. 1986-87), Coun. Ind. Ky. Colls. (chmn. 1970-75), Taylor County Hist. Soc. (dir. 1970), Taylor County Bapt. Assn. (dir. tng. 1968-70), Taylor County Bapt. Sunday Sch. Assn. (supt. 1968-70). Home: 808 Montfort Rd E Mobile AL 36608-3576 E-mail: hamilton53@juno.com.

PARSLEY, ROBERT CHARLES, minister; b. Tulsa, Aug. 11, 1956; s. Victor Bernard and Margery Sue (Mathews) P.; m. Carole Ellen McKenzie, Oct. 2, 1982; children: Robert McKenzie, Timothy James, Kelly Mathews. BA in Religion with high honors, Ouachita Bapt. U., 1978; MDiv, So. Bapt. Theol. Sem., 1982; D Ministry, Southwestern Bapt. Theol. Sem., 1990. Ordained to ministry Bapt. Ch., 1978. Youth minister First Bapt. Ch., Leithfield, Ky., 1979-80; chaplain Bapt. Med. Ctr., Little Rock, 1980-81; pastor Lula (Miss.) Bapt. Ch., 1982-84, First Bapt. Ch., Prescott, Ark., 1984-88, Dardanelle, 1988-93, Waialae Baptist Ch., Honolulu, 1993-95, First Baptist Ch., Smackover, Ark., 1995-99, Crofton, Md., 1999—. Baptist. Home: 2328 Westport Ln Crofton MD 21114-1211 Office: First Baptist Ch PO Box 3425 Crofton MD 21114-0425 E-mail: rcparsley@aol.com. *I refuse to accept the idea that the church and Christianity are irrelevant in the modern world. I find my greatest satisfaction in assisting others in spiritual formation.*

PARSLEY, STEVEN DWAYNE, title company executive; b. Monrovia, Calif., Dec. 31, 1959; BBA magna cum laude, U. Albuquerque, 1985. Lic. agt. to issue title ins., N.Mex. Data processing asst. The Orion Corp., Albuquerque, 1978-79; title searcher N.Mex. Title, 1979; various positions Rio Grande Title Co., 1979-84, v.p., mgr. title ops., 1984-91, sr. v.p., escrow officer, 1992-94, exec. v.p., 1994-99; exec. v.p., shareholder Dona Ana Title Co., Las Cruces, 199—. Bd. dirs. N.Mex. Land Title Trust Fund, 2001—. Mem. state apptd. Title Ins. Task Force State of N.Mex.; mem. Affordable Housing Round Table. Recipient Presdl. scholarship U. N.Mex., Albuquerque, 1978. Mem. N.Mex. Land Title Assn. (past v.p., pres. 1997-98), Las Cruces Homebuilders Assn.(v.p.) Avocation: ragtime piano. Home: 746 Oro Viejo Las Cruces NM 88011-8071 Office: Dona Ana Title Co 425 S Telshor Blvd Ste B Las Cruces NM 88011-8237 E-mail: ssp88@prodigy.net., stevep@donaanatitle.com.

PARSON, BEVERLY A. foundation administrator; b. Saint Louis, Nov. 10, 1952; d. William Porter and Lovie (Woods) West; m. Edward Kenneth Parson, Mar. 25, 1972; 1 child, Leslie Nicole. B Liberal Studies, St. Louis U., 1983. Cons. dental practice mgmt. Dental Directions Svcs., St. Louis, 1983-87; dir. program and svcs. ea. Mo. chpt. Arthritis Found., 1987—; with Aventis Pharm., 1999—, med. sci. specialist St. Louis region Mo. Cons. dental practice mgmt. multi specialty groups, Mo., Ill., 1983-87; developer-medically underserved ednl. programming, St. Louis, 1989-93; cons. Guide to Working with Medically Underserved Populations, Atlanta, 1990-93; creator First Com. for Medically Underserved Population, St. Louis, 1990-93; bd. mem. Mo. State Task Force Arthritis in the Working Years, 1990-93; mem. patient svcs. subcom. Nat. Arthritis Found., 1992-93; mem. adv. bd. Mo. Boothill Edn. Program, 1993. Advocate, speaker St. Louis U.-Geriatric Summer Inst., St. Louis, 1992, United Way, St. Louis, 1990-93, Gov.'s Conf. on Aging, St. Louis, 1993; bd. dirs. Grace Hill Wellness Initiative, 1991-93. Recipient award of excellence Nat. Arthritis Found., Atlanta, 1992, Profl. Achievement award, 1993, Yes I Can award Sentinel Newspaper, St. Louis, 1993. Mem. Arthritis Found. Staff Assn. (grants and recognition com. 1991-93, profl. achievement award 1993). Democrat. Avocations: access to care for medically underserved, motivational speaking, reading. Office: Arthritis Found Ea Mo 8390 Delmar Blvd Saint Louis MO 63124-2117 Home: 1 Clydesdale Rnch Saint Peters MO 63376-7701

PARSON, CHRISTINE JENNIFER N. artist; b. Washington, Nov. 8, 1943; d. John Spies and Cora Maribah (Patterson) Nicole; m. Andrew M. Egeland Jr., Sept. 12, 1964 (div. 1968); m. James Thomas Parson, Feb. 14, 1969 (div. 1994); children: Larissa Nicole, Nathaniel James. BS, U. Va., 1967, MA, 1970. Tchr. of handicapped Montgomery County (Md.) Pub. Schs., 1968-69, Charlottesville (Va.) Pub. Schs., 1967-68, Nat. Children's Ctr., Washington, 1969-73; tchr. art Art League, Alexandria, Va., 1982—; ind. portrait artist Washington, 1974—. One-woman shows include Va. Mus. Art, 1966, Art League, Washington, 1976, Montpelier Cultural Art Ctr., 1981, D.C. Pub. Library, 1982, Capitol Hill Arts Workshop, 1986, City of Alexandria City Hall, 1987, Art League, 1989, Capitol Hill Art League, 1991; represented in pvt. collections. Founder, pres. Friends of S.E. Libr., Washington, 1983; founder Washington Swim Team Booster Club, pres. 1984-85, 88; mem. vestry St. Monica's Ch. Grantee Washington Commn. Arts and Humanities, 1988, 92. Mem. Art League, Capitol Hill Art League, So. Water Color Soc. Episcopalian. Avocations: gardening, synchronized swimming. Studio: 105 N Union St Alexandria VA 22314-3217

PARSON, JASON A. lawyer; b. Madisonville, Ky., Jan. 30, 1963; s. Dewey Allen and Peggy Sue Parson; m. Valerie Ann Schmidt, Mar. 28, 1992; 1 child, Samuel Ayres. BA, Ind. Ctrl. U., Indpls., 1985; JD, Washington U., St. Louis, 1988. Bar: Ill. 1989, U.S. Dist. Ct. (no. dist.) Ill. 1991. Fed. clk. to Hon. John F. Nangle U.S. Dist. Ct. (ea. dist.) Mo., St. Louis, 1988-90; assoc. Lord, Bissell & Brook, Chgo., 1990-98, ptnr., 1998-2000, Anderson, Bennett & Ptnrs., Chgo., 2000—. Editor-in-chief Washington U. Law Quar., 1987-88; contbr. articles to profl. jours. Hagelskamp scholar, 1984. Mem. Ill. State Bar Assn., Def. Rsch. Inst., Ill. Assn. Healthcare Attys., Ill. Assn. Def. Trial Counsel. Avocation: vocal music. Office: Anderson Bennett & Ptnrs 55 E Monroe St Ste 3650 Chicago IL 60603 E-mail: Jason.Parson@ABandPartners.com.

PARSONS, ANDREW JOHN, management consultant; b. Kingston, Surrey, Eng., July 22, 1943; arrived in US, 1968; s. S John and Hylda P (Wili) Parsons; m. Carol Ann Iannucci, June 6, 1970; children: Alexandra, Katherine. BA, MA, Oxford U., 1965; MBA, Harvard U., 1970. Acct. exec. LPE/Leo Burnett, London, 1965—68; from strategic planning dir. to v.p. mktg. Prestige Group Ltd. div. Am. Home Products, N.Y.C. and London, 1970-76; v.p. mktg. Kurzweil Computer Products div. Xerox Corp., Cambridge, Mass., 1979-80; assoc. McKinsey & Co., Inc., N.Y.C., 1976-82, prin., 1982-88, dir. consumer industries sector, mktg. ctr., sr. ptnr., 1988-2000; chmn. Kantar Group of WPP, PLC, 2001—. Underwriting mem Lloyds of London, 1986—; chmn Gulliver Growth Ptnrs LLC, 2001—; adv bd McKinsey Adv Coun, 2001—; adv. bd. Ave. A Inc., 2002—; adv. bd. Avenue A Inc., 2002—; pres. Smithfield Estates LLC, 2002—; bd. dirs. A.T. Cross Co. Contbr. articles to profl jours. Mem. adv. bd. Salvation Army, Greater NY, 1983—; chmn. adv. bd. Salavation Army, 1993—97; bd. dirs. United Way, N.Y.C., 1988—; trustee Sarah Lawrence Coll., Bronxville, NY, 1993—2001. Scholar Baker, Harvard Bus Sch, 1970. Mem.: Shelter Harbor Golf Club, Weekapaug Golf Club, Watch Hill Yacht Club, Siwanoy Country Club. Home: 56 Hereford Rd Bronxville NY 10708-5408 Office: McKinsey & Co Inc 55 E 52d St 18th Fl New York NY 10055-0183 E-mail: andrew_parsons@mckinsey.com.

PARSONS, CHARLES ALLAN, JR. lawyer; b. Mpls., July 16, 1943; s. Charles Allan and Grace Adelaide (Covert) P.; m. JoAnne Ruth Russell, Oct. 16, 1965; children: Charles, Daniel, Nancy. BS, U. Minn., 1965, JD cum laude, 1972. Bar: Minn. 1972, U.S. Dist. Ct. Minn. 1972, U.S. Supreme Ct. 1995. Ptnr. Moss & Barnett, P.A., 1972—. Bd. dirs. Legal Advice Clinics Ltd., Mpls., 1975-93, Legal Aid Soc. Mpls., 1999—, first v.p., 2000-2002, pres., 2002—; bd. dirs. Mid-Minn. Legal Assistance, 2001—; chair steering com. S.E. Asian Legal Assistance Project, Mpls., 1988-93. Named Vol. Atty. of Yr., Legal Advice Clinics, Ltd., Mpls., 1990. Mem. ABA, Am. Coll. Real Estate Lawyers, Minn. State Bar Assn. (co-chair legis. com. real property sec. 1986—, coun. mem. 1986—, chair real property sect. 1993-94), Hennepin County Bar Assn. (chair real property sect. 1988-89). Roman Catholic. Avocations: reading, walking, biking, hiking. Office: Moss & Barnett PA 4800 Wells Fargo Ctr 90 S 7th Minneapolis MN 55402-4129 E-mail: parsonsc@moss-barnett.com.

PARSONS, CYNTHIA, writer, educational consultant; b. Cleve., Jan. 1, 1926; d. Sanford Sherman Clark and Elenore Mann. BA, Principia Coll., 1948; MA, Putney/Antioch Coll., 1956; EdD, Norwich U., 1985. Tchr. various pvt. and pub. schs., 1948-62; edn. editor Christian Sci. Monitor, Boston, 1962-69, 74-82; sr. program office Nat. Inst. for Edn., Washington, 1970-73; founder, dir., coord. SerVermont, Chester, Vt., 1985—2001. Instr. new math Madison Project, Syracuse, N.Y., 1959-61; edn. editor World Bank, Washington, 1969-70; vis. instr. Dartmouth Coll., Hanover, N.H., 1982, 83, 88, U. Vt., Burlington, 1983-88; edn. cons. Robert Coll., Istanbul, Turkey, 1984. Author: Seeds, 1985, Service Learning From A to Z, 1991, George Bird Grinnell, 1992, The Early History of Christian Science in Vermont, 1996, The Discoverer, Mary Baker Eddy, 2000; contbr. newspaper series on edn. Mem. Commn. on Edn. Issues, Boston, 1975-81; bd. mem. Grad. Record Examination, Princeton, N.J., 1978-82, Vt. Coun. on the Humanities, Morristown, 1993-97. Recipient Eleanor Roosevelt medal for pub. svc., Val-kill, N.Y., 1992; grantee Edwin Gould Found. for Children, N.Y. and Vt., 1985-95, MacArthur Found.., Chgo. and Vt. Mem. Edn. Writers Assn. (pres. 1970-71). Democrat. Christian Scientist. Avocations: reading, travel, listening to classical music. Home: 4713 N 77th Pl Scottsdale AZ 85251

PARSONS, DANIEL LANKESTER, pharmaceutics educator; b. Biscoe, N.C., Sept. 10, 1953; s. Solomon Lankester and Doris Eva (Bost) P. BS in Pharmacy, U. Ga., 1975, PhD, 1979. Asst. prof. pharmaceutics U. Ariz., Tucson, 1979-82; asst. prof. Auburn (Ala.) U., 1982-86, assoc. prof., 1986-91, prof., 1991—, chmn. divsn., 1990—. Cons. Wyeth-Ayerst, Phila., 1989-93, Technomics, Ardsley, N.Y., 1990-93, Murty Pharm., Lexington, Ky., 1996—; presenter in field. Author: (with G.V. Betageri and S.A. Jenkins) Liposome Drug Delivery Systems, 1993. Named Disting. Alumni Sandhills Coll., 1990, Tchr. of Yr., Pharmacy Student Coun., 1987, Grad. Faculty Mem. of Yr., Grad. Student Orgn., 1994, Prof. of Yr., Kappa Psi Fraternity, 2000. Mem. Am. Pharm. Assn., Am. Assn. Pharm. Scientists, Phi Kappa Phi, Kappa Psi (advisor 1990-95, nat. grad. devel. com. 1993-95, nat. scholarship com. 1995-99, nat. grand coun. dep. com. 1997—, Svc. award 1990, 95, Advisor award 1992). Achievements include research on plasma protein binding of drugs and effects of perfluorochemical blood substitutes on such binding. Office: Auburn U Sch Pharmacy Auburn AL 36849 E-mail: parsodl@auburn.edu.

PARSONS, DEBRA LEA, elementary school educator; b. Redding, Calif., May 13, 1960; d. Gary Leon and Leta Barbara Cox. BA in Music Edn., Columbia Christian Coll., 1983; M Music Edn., U. Portland, 1989. Cert. tchr. Calif. Music tchr. David Douglas Sch. Dist., Portland, Oreg., 1984—85, Harold Oliver Sch., Portland, 1987—97, Shasta County Schs., Redding, Calif., 1997—; pvt. music instr. Parsons Music Sch., Shasta Lake City, 1997—; pvt. tutor math. and lang. arts Parsons Tutoring Svcs., 1997—. Adj. prof. music Columbia Christian Coll., Portland, 1985—91; adj. music instr. Warner Pacific Coll., Portland, 1990—95; adjudicator music competitions Oreg. Music Educators Assn., Portland, 1989—92; grad. tchr. asst. U. Portland, 1986—87. Contbr. poetry to lit. publs. (Editor's Choice award, 98, Editor's Choice award, 99, Editor's Choice award, 00, Editor's Choice award, 01). Vol. Providence Med. Ctr., Portland, 1984—86; asst. sect. leader, libr. Choral Arts Ensemble; asst. dir. Columbia Christian Band. Recipient award for acad. performance, Bank of Am., John Phillips Sousa Band award. Mem.: MENC/CMEA, Delta Kappa Gamma (music chmn. 1996—). Republican. Mem. Ch. Of Christ. Avocations: collecting sea shells, coins, porcelain dolls, sports cards, needlecrafts. Home and Office: 1988 Cabello St Shasta Lake CA 96019 Fax: 530-274-8587. E-mail: debip@c-zone.net.

PARSONS, DONALD JAMES, retired bishop; b. Phila., Mar. 28, 1922; s. Earl and Helen (Drabble) P.; m. Mary Russell, Sept. 17, 1955; children—Mary, Rebecca, Bradford. BA, Temple U., 1943; M.Div., Phila. Div. Sch., 1946, Th.D., 1951, D.D. (hon.), 1964; postgrad., U. Nottingham, Eng., 1968; D.C.L., Nashotah (Wis.) House, 1973. Ordained priest Episcopal Ch., 1946, consecrated bishop, 1973; curate Immanual Ch., Wilmington, Del., 1946-49; rector St. Peter's Ch., Smyrna, 1949-50; prof. N.T. Nashotah House, 1950-73, pres., dean, 1963-73, Ramsey prof. ascetical theology, 2000—; bishop Diocese of Quincy, Ill., 1973-88. Author: A Life-time Road to God, 1966, In Time with Jesus, 1973, Holy Eucharist: Rite Two, 1976. Home: 6901 N Galena Rd Apt 111 Peoria IL 61614-3158

PARSONS, DONALD LEE, telecommunications executive; b. Charleston, W.Va., July 21, 1947; s. Orel Adair and Edith Irene Parsons; m. Jo Lynn Parsons, Aug. 18, 1973; children: Jennifer Elizabeth Parsons Lawrence, Meredith Victoria Parsons Whittington. BS in Edn., W.Va. State U., 1972. Ops. mgr. Bell South, Atlanta, 1973—2000; pres. Parsons and Assocs., Telecomms., 2000—. State rep. Ga. Ho. of Reps., Cobb County, 1994—. With U.S. Army Res., 1966-87. Mem. Kiwanis Club of Marietta. Republican. United Methodist. Home: 3167 Sycamore Ln Marietta GA 30066-4173 Office: 611 Legislative Office Bldg Atlanta GA 30066 E-mail: don@donparsons.net.

PARSONS, DONALD OSCAR, economics educator; b. Pitts., Oct. 22, 1944; s. Leonard J. and Marion (Williams) P.; m. A. Cristina Cunha; children: Donald Williams, Christopher Milne, Madalena Cunha. AB, Duke U., 1966; PhD, U. Chgo., 1970. Asst. prof. econs. Ohio State U., Columbus, 1970-73, assoc. prof., 1973-77, prof., 1977-95; prof. econs., dir. program labor studies George Washington U., Washington, 1998—. Fulbright disting. prof. econs., Siena, Italy, 1991; vis. prof. Copenhagen Bus. Sch., 1997. Author: Poverty and the Minimum Wage, 1980; bd. editors Jour. Econs. and Bus., 1979-91; contbr. articles to Jour. Polit. Economy, Am. Econ. Rev. Rsch. fellow Nat. Bur. Econ. Rsch., 1975-76; grantee NIH. Mem. Am. Econ. Assn., Soc. Labor Economists, So. Econ. Assn. Achievements include findings in modelling and estimation of relationship between job turnover and training in the employment contract, assessment of job search models of quit behavior, measurement of impact of social insurance programs, on labor force participation and income security. Office: Econs Dept George Washington U 2201 G St NW Washington DC 20052-0001

PARSONS, EDMUND MORRIS, investment company executive; b. Houston, Oct. 19, 1936; s. Alfred Morris and Virgina (Hanna) P. AB, Harvard U., 1958; MBA, U. Pa., 1961; MS, MIT, 1970. Pres. Fredonia Enterprises, Inc., Houston, Tex., 1990—; fgn. service officer U.S. Dept. State, Washington, 1965-90; 1st sec. Am. Embassy, Mexico City, 1973-76; economist Fed. Res. Bank N.Y., N.Y.C., 1976-77; chief food aid div. U.S. Dept. State, Washington, 1977-80, dir. office devel., 1981-82, dir. office econ. policy, 1983-84; dep. chief mission U.S. Mission to FAO, Rome, 1985-86; dir. Office Ecology and Natural Resources U.S. Dept. State, Washington, 1986-88; dir. Office of Internat. Narcotics Control Programs, 1988-89; min.-counselor for econ. affairs Am. Embassy, Mexico City, 1989-90; pres. Fredonia Enterprises, Inc., Houston, 1990—. Co-chmn. Tropical Forest Task Force, Washington, 1986-88; dep. U.S. rep. UN FAO, Rome, 1985-86; alt. U.S. rep. to environ. program U.S. Del. Nairobi, Kenya, 1987. Capt. USAF, 1962-72. Mem. Am. Fgn. Svc. Assn., Houston Restaurant Assn. (bd. dirs. 1992—), Houston World Affairs Coun. (bd. dirs. 1995—), Consular Corps of Houston (hon.), Houston Hispanic C. of C., Coun. Fgn. Rels. (Houston com.), Univ. Club (Houston). Republican. Methodist. Avocation: geneology. Office: 2727 Fondren Rd Ste 2A Houston TX 77063-4114 E-mail: elviaspub@aol.com.

PARSONS, EDWIN SPENCER, clergyman, educator; b. Brockton, Mass., Feb. 16, 1919; s. Edwin Webber and Ethel Faunce (Marsh) P.; m. Eleanor Millard, Nov. 3, 1944; children: William Spencer, Ellen, James Millard, Bradford Delano. AB, Denison U., 1941, D.D., 1967; B.D., Andover Newton Theol. Sch., 1945; D.D., Kalamazoo Coll., 1966; L.H.D., Chgo. Coll. Osteo. Medicine, 1978. Ordained to ministry Am. Baptist Ch., 1944; asst. minister First Bapt. Ch., Newton Centre, Mass., 1945-47; exec. dir. Bapt. Student Found., Inc., Cambridge, 1947-59; pastor Hyde Park Union Ch., Chgo., 1959-65; assoc. prof. ethics U. Chgo. Div. Sch., 1965-78, prof., 1978-81; dir. ministerial field edn., 1977-79; asst. to dean, 1981-88; dean Rockefeller Meml. Chapel, 1965-79; v.p., dir. New Eng. office Health Resources Ltd., Kansas City, Mo., 1979-89. Cons. dept. ch. and soc. Am. Bapt. Chs. of Mass., 1979-86, also editor Mass. Bapt. News, 1983-85; chmn. strategy and action com., bd. dirs. Mass. Council Chs., 1983-85; adj. prof. Andover Newton Theol. Sch., 1981-85 Author: The Christian Yes or No, 1964; contbr.: Belief and Ethics, 1978. Pres. Council Hyde Park-Kenwood Chs. and Synagogues, 1963; chmn. Abortion Rights Assn. Ill., 1974-79; founder, chmn. Ill. Religious Coalition for Abortion Rights, 1975, Ill. Clergy Consultation Services on Problem Pregnancies, 1971-79; bd. dirs., chmn. clergy adv. com. Planned Parenthood Assn., Chgo., 1977-79; bd. dirs. Hyde Park YMCA, Facing History and Ourselves Nat. Found., 1983-87; bd. govs. Internat. House, Chgo., 1969-79; trustee Packard Manse (Mass.), Bapt. Theol. Union, U. Chgo., 1960-70, 81-96, hon. trustee, 1996—; pres., bd. mgrs. Ministers and Missionaries Benefit Bd., 1975-81; mem. policy council Religious Coalition for Abortion Rights of Mass., 1980-86; sec., treas. Bolton Inst. for Sustainable Future, 1983-87; mem. gen. bd., mem. exec. com., mem. commn. on Christian unity Am. Bapt. Chs., 1963-72, 74-81; bd. dirs. Planned Parenthood League of Mass., 1984-92; interim assoc. dir. Mass Coun. Chs., 1988-89. Democrat. Home: 82 Briarwood Cir Worcester MA 01606-1200

PARSONS, ESTELLE, actress; b. Lynn, Mass., Nov. 20, 1927; d. Eben and Elinor (Mattson) P.; m. Richard Gehman, Dec. 19, 1953 (div. Aug. 1958); children: Martha and Abbie (twins); m. Peter L. Zimroth, Jan. 2, 1983; 1 child, Abraham. BA in Polit. Sci., Conn. Coll. Women, 1949; student, Boston U. Law Sch., 1949-50. Stage appearances include Happy Hunting, 1957, Whoop Up, 1958, Beg, Borrow or Steal, 1960, Threepenny Opera, 1960, Mrs. Dally Has a Lover, 1962, Ready When You Are C.B, 1964, Malcolm, 1965, Seven Descents of Myrtle, 1968, And Miss Reardon Drinks a Little, 1971, Mert and Phil, 1974, The Norman Conquests, 1975-76, Ladies of the Alamo, 1977, Miss Margarida's Way, 1977-78, The Pirates of Penzance, 1981, The Shadow Box, 1994; adapted, dir., performer Orgasmo Adulto Escapes from the Zoo, 1983, The Unguided Missile, Baba Goya, 1989, Shimada, 1992, Grace & Glorie, 1996, The Last of the Thorntons, 2000-01, Morning's At seven, 2002; film appearances include Bonnie and Clyde, 1966; Rachel, Rachel, 1967, I Never Sang for My Father, 1969, Dick Tracy, 1990, Boys On The Side, 1995, Looking for Richard, 1996, That Darn Cat, 1997; TV appearances include Roseanne, 1990—, NBC Today, 1951-56; artistic dir. N.Y. Shakespeare Festival Players, 1986, Actors' Studio, 1997—. Recipient Theatre World award, 1962-63, Obie award, 1964; recipient award Motion Picture Acad. Arts and Scis., 1967; Recipient Medal of Honor, Conn. Coll., 1969 Home: 924 West End Ave Apt T5 New York NY 10025-3543 *It's in attempting all, that one succeeds.*

PARSONS, HARRY GLENWOOD, retired surgeon; b. San Bernardino, Calif., Mar. 5, 1919; s. Harry Glenwood and Evelen May (Peris) P.; m. Rubyann Kattenhorn, Sept. 28, 1986. AB, Stanford (Calif.) U., 1942, MD, 1946. Diplomate Am. Bd. Surgery, Am. Bd. Thoracic Cardio-Vascular Surgery. Intern Stanford Hosp., San Francisco, 1941-42, Rockor fellow in surg. rsch., 1944-45, asst. resident in surgery, 1945-52, chief resident in surgery, 1952-53, Boyd fellow in thoracic cardiovasc. surgery, 1953-54; asst. clin. prof. surgery Stanford Med. Sch., 1955-65; med. dir., faculty head Weimar (Calif.) Med. Ctr., 1955-72; ret. Capt. M.C. U.S. Army, 1940-44. Fellow ACS; mem. AMA, Western Thoracic Surg. Soc., Placer Nevada County Med. Assn. (pres. 1979), Calif. Med. Assn. (del.), Alpha Omega Alpha. Avocation: flying. E-mail: parsons@neworld.net.

PARSONS, HENRY MCILVAINE, psychologist; b. Lenox, Mass., Aug. 31, 1911; s. Herbert and Elsie Worthington (Clews) P.; m. Renee Oakman, 1938 (div. 1945); 1 son, Jack; m. Marina Svetlova, 1949 (div. 1957); m. Marjorie Thorson, 1957. BA, Yale U., 1933; MA, Columbia U., 1947; PhD, U. Calif., Los Angeles, 1963. Reporter N.Y. Herald Tribune, 1935-42; organizer N.Y. Newspaper Guild, 1942; asst., then lectr. psychology Columbia U., 1947-52; research asso. N.Y. U., 1951-52; supr. Electronics Research Labs., Columbia U., 1952-58; mem. human factors staff Douglas Aircraft Co., Long Beach and Santa Monica, Calif., 1956-58; sr. human factors scientist, br. head System Devel. Corp., Santa Monica and Falls Church, Va., 1958-68; self-employed cons., 1968-69; 70-73; v.p. research Riverside Research Inst., N.Y.C., 1969-70; exec. dir. Inst. Behavioral Research Inc., Silver Spring, Md., 1974-79; pres. Exptl. Coll. of Inst. Behavioral Research, 1974-80; mgr. human factors projects Human Resources Research Orgn., Alexandria, Va., 1980-83; sr. staff scientist Essex Corp., 1983-90; mgr. Ctr. for Human Factors Rsch. Human Resources Rsch. Orgn., 1990—; adj. prof. Lehigh U., 1983-84. Author: Man-Machine System Experiments, 1972; also chpts. in books, articles in jours. Served with USNR, 1942-45. Fellow AAAS, APA (pres. divsn. 21 1975-76, Franklin V. Taylor award 1992), Human Factors and Ergonomics Soc. (pres. 1968-69, Pres.'s Disting. Svc. award 1993), Washington Acad. Scis., Am. Psychol. Soc.; mem. N.Y. Acad. Scis., Ergonomics Soc., Sigma Xi. Clubs: Century (N.Y.C.); Cosmos (Washington). Home: 1600 S Eads St Apt 1223 Arlington VA 22202 Office: Human Resources Rsch Orgn 66 Canal Center Plz Alexandria VA 22314-1591

PARSONS, IRENE ADELAIDE, management consultant; b. North Wilkesboro, N.C. d. Everett T. and Martha (Minton) P. BS in Bus. Edn. and Adminstrn., U. N.C., 1941, LLD (hon.), 1967; MS in Pub. Adminstrn., George Washington U., 1965. Tchr. Roanoake Rapids (N.C.) High Sch., 1941-42; rep. U.S. Civil Svc. Commn., 1942-43; with VA, 1946-74, asst. adminstr. vets. affairs, dir. personnel, dir. equal employment opportunity, 1965-74; mgmt. cons., 1974—. Exec. com. Pres.'s Study Group Careers for Women. Served to lt. USCGR, 1943-46. Recipient Fed. Woman's Outstanding Achievement award, 1966, Silver Helmet award Amvets, 1971, Career Svc. award Nat. Civil Svc. League, 1972, Disting. Alumni Achievement award George Washington U., 1973; named to Brevard Coll. Hall of Fame, 1984 Mem. Assn. Fed. Woman's Award Recipients (chmn. 1972-76) Address: PO Box 2046 North Wilkesboro NC 28659-2046

PARSONS, IVY, artist, sculptor, educator; b. Balt., Mar. 3, 1955; d. Joseph H. and Geneva Mae (Tabor) P. BFA cum laude, Md. Inst. Coll. of Art, 1977; MFA magna cum laude, Va. Commonwealth U., 1980; postgrad., Skowhegan Sch. Paint/Sculpture, 1980. Artist-in-residence Bklyn. Museum, 1980-81, MacDowell Colony, Peterborough, N.H., 1981, Provincetown (Mass.) Fine Arts Work Ctr., 1981-82, Sculpture Space, Utica, N.Y., 1989, ArtPark, Lewiston, 1991, Va. Ctr. for Creative Arts, Sweet Briar, 1995-96, 99, Tyrone Guthrie Ctr., County Monoghan, Ireland, summer 1997, Hungarian Multicultural Ctr., Budapest, summer 1997; gallery dir. Catonsville C.C. Balt., 1998-99; mem. faculty Md. Inst. Coll. Arts, 1998—. Mem. studio artist selection panel School #33 Art Ctr., Mayor's Com. Art and Culture, Balt., 1987-93; lectr., panelist South Eastern Coll. Art Conf., Georgetown U., Washington, 1995, Md. Inst. Coll. of Art, Balt., Munson-Williams Proctor Inst. Art Museum, Utica, 1995; Alfred and Trafford Klots resident Rochefort En Terre, France, 1999, Polar Circuit Residency, Rovaneimi, Finland, 2000. Exhibits include The Corcoran Gallery of Art, Washington, 1996, The Tyrone Guthrie Ctr., Ireland, 1997, New House Ctr. for Contemporary Art, Snug Harbor Cultural Ctr., S.I., N.Y., 1995-96, Munson-Williams Proctor Inst. Art Museum, 1995, Artist Space, N.Y.C., 1994, Chateau Rochefort-en-terre, 1999. Fulbright-Hays fellow, Washington, 1982-83, NEA fellow, 1983; grantee Pollack Krasner Found., N.Y.C., 1987, 99, Adolph and Esther Gottlieb Found., N.Y.C., 1994, Md. State Arts Coun., 1986, 87, 89, 91, 96. Fellow Mid-Atlantic Arts Found., Ruth Chenven Found., Barbara Deming Meml. Fund, Alpha Delta Kappa. Studio: 513 N Duncan St Baltimore MD 21205 E-mail: iparso1@gl.umbc.edu.

PARSONS, JEFFREY ROBINSON, anthropologist, educator; b. Washington, Oct. 9, 1939; s. Merton Stanley and Elisabeth (Oldenburg) P.; m. Mary Thomson Hrones, Apr. 27, 1968; 1 child, Apphia Hrones. BS, Pa. State U., 1961; PhD, U. Mich., 1966. Asst. prof. anthropology U. Mich., Ann Arbor, 1966-71, assoc. prof., 1971-76, prof., 1976—, dir. mus. anthropology, 1983-86. Vis. prof. Universidad Nacional Autonoma de Mexico, 1987; vis. prof. Universidad Buenos Aires, 1994, Univ. Nac de Catamarca, Argentina, 1996, Univ. Nac de Tucuman, Argentina, 1996, Univ. Mayor de San Andres, Bolivia, 1999. Author: Prehistoric Settlement Patterns in the Texcoco Region, Mexico, 1971; (with William T. Sanders and Robert Stanley) The Basin of Mexico: The Cultural Ecology of a Civilization, 1979; (with E. Brumfiel) Prehispanic Settlement Patterns in the Southern Valley of Mexico, 1982; (with M. Parsons) Chinampa Agriculture and Aztec Urbanization in the Valley of Mexico, 1985; (with Mary H. Parsons) Maguey Utilization in Highland Central Mexico, 1990, The Production of Consumption of Salt During Postclassic Times in the Valley of Mexico, 1994; (with E. Brumfiel and M. Hodge) The Developmental Implications of Earlier Dates for Early Aztec in the Basin of Mexico, 1996; (with C. Hastings and R. Matos) Rebuilding the State in Highland Peru, 1997; A Regional Perspective on Inca Impact in the Sierra Central, Peru, 1998; (with C. hastings and R. Matos) Prehispanic Settlement Patterns in the Upper Mantaro-Tarma Drainage, Peru, 2000, The Last Saltmakers of Nexquipayac, Mexico, 2001. Rsch. grantee NSF, 1967, 70, 72-73, 75-76, 81, Nat. Geog. Soc., 1984, 86, 88. Mem. Am. Anthrop. Assn. (Alfred V. Kidder award 1998), Soc. Am. Archaeology, AAAS, Inst. Andean Rsch., Inst. Andean Studies, Sociedad Mexicana de Antropologia, Sociedad Argentina de Antropologia. Office: Museum of Anthropology U Mich Ann Arbor MI 48109

PARSONS, JUDSON ASPINWALL, JR. lawyer; b. Rochester, N.Y., Dec. 15, 1929; s. Judson A. and Frances (Holsopple) P.; m. Chesley Kahmann, Aug. 8, 1959; children: Ames, Brockett. BA, Amherst Coll., 1951; LLB, Harvard U., 1954. Bar: N.Y. 1954, N.J. 1973. Asst. U.S. atty. So. Dist. N.Y., N.Y.C., 1954-55; assoc. Dewey, Ballantine, Bushby, Palmer & Wood, 1958-65, ptnr., 1966-82; pres. Orbiting Clef Prodns., Inc., Summit, N.J., 1982-86; spl. counsel Laughlin, Markensohn, Lagani & Pegg, P.C., Morristown, 1986-90, Parsons & Pegg, Morristown, 1990-91; sole practice, 1991—. Served to 1st lt. U.S. Army, 1955-58. Office: 108 Woodland Ave Summit NJ 07901-2003

PARSONS, LEONARD JON, marketing educator, consultant; b. Pitts., Sept. 1, 1942; s. Leonard J. and Marion Jane (Williams) P.; m. Julia Grieve, Jan. 23, 1965; children: Lorelei, Leonard Jon Jr. BSChemE, MIT, 1964; MS in Indsl. Adminstrn., Purdue U., 1965, PhD in Indsl. Adminstrn., 1968. Asst. prof. Ind. U., Bloomington, 1968-70; assoc. prof. Claremont (Calif.) Grad. Sch., 1970-77; prof. marketing Ga. Inst. Tech., 1977—. Vis. scholar MIT, Cambridge, fall 1973; Fulbright-Hays sr. scholar Cath. U. Leuven, Belgium, spring 1977; vis. prof. INSEAD, France, fall 1984, Norwegian Sch. Mktg., Oslo, fall 1989, UCLA, spring 1990, Advt. Edn. Found., Anheuser Busch, St. Louis, summer 1993, CREER/FUCAM, Belgium, Fall 1995; mem. rsch. and test devel. com. Grad. Mgmt. Admissions Coun., 1988-90. Author: Using Microcomputers in Marketing, 1986; co-author: Marketing Management, 7th edit., 2000, Market Response Models, 2d edit., 2001, others; edtl. bd. Jour. Mktg. Rsch., 1970-80, 83-85, Jour. Bus. Rsch., 1973-79, Jour. Mktg., 1978-80; assoc. editor: Decision Scis., 1976-79; mktg. dept. editor: Mgmt. Sci., 1980-82; contbr. numerous chpts. to books, articles to profl. jours. Recipient first prize rsch. design contest Am. Mktg. Assn., 1971-72. Mem. Am. Mktg. Assn. (mem. adv. bd. mktg. rsch. spl. interest group 1998), Am. Statis. Assn. (chmn. stats. in mktg. sect. 1995), European Mktg. Acad. (mem. exec. com. 1981-84), Theta Delta Chi, Beta Gamma Sigma, Phi Kappa Phi. Office: Ga Inst Tech Dupree Coll Mgmt Atlanta GA 30332-0520 E-mail: len.parsons@mgt.gatech.edu.

PARSONS, LISA KAY, artist, illustrator; b. Portland, Oreg., Mar. 23, 1955; d. Norman Elliott and Virginia Ruby Parsons. BA in Art History, Portland State U., 1984; MA in Liberal Studies, NYU, 1989. Cert. in mus. studies N.Y. Dir. Littman Gallery Portland State U., 1981—83, dir. White Gallery, 1982—83; intern Isamu Noguchi Garden Mus., L.I., NY, 1988, Mus. of Modern Art, N.Y.C., 1989. Author: (poetry) included in Into the Teeth of the Wind, 2001. Mem.: Soc. of Children's Book Artists and Illustrators, Oreg. State Poetry Assn., Willamette Writers. Home: 0215 SW Gaines St Portland OR 97201

PARSONS, LORRAINE LEIGHTON, nurse, child care professional; b. Albany, Maine, Feb. 7, 1939; d. Alfred Elmer Leighton and Arlene Rachael Winslow; m. Jack Arnol Greig (div. July 1982); children: Scotty, Kim; m. Robert Davis Parsons, Dec. 20, 1991. Student, U. Maine. RN, Maine. Office nurse Charles Hannigan, MD, Auburn, Maine, 1961-64; with Stephens Meml. Hosp., Norway, 1964-69; tchr. spl. edn. W. Paris (Maine) Sch., 1969-73; tchr. reading and math. Buckfield (Maine) Sch., 1974-78; nurse Ledgeview Nursing Home, W. Paris, 1979-80, Central Maine Med. Ctr., Lewiston, 1980-96; child care profl. Marwin Cons. Co., Raymond, Maine, 1996—. Author: Families of the Fox and Geese Quilt, 1997, Homesteads of Hartford, 1997, Quilting is Qumforting, 1999, Town of Hartford, 2000, Military Service, 2000, Marston Homestead, 2000, Crazy Quilt, 2000, Winslow Home, 2001, The Alfred E. Leighton Family, 2001; co-author: Hartford in Pictures, 1984. Pres., founder Hartford (Maine) Heritage Soc., 1976; program chairwoman Hartford Bicentennial, 1997-98. Recipient Cert. of Honor Bicentennial, State of Maine, 1998, Double-Trouble Nature category Internat. Libr. Photography, 2000; grantee Maine Arts, 1998. Avocations: dolls, stamps, town histories. Home: RR 1 Box 207 Canton ME 04221-9714

PARSONS, MARK FREDERICK, college development officer; b. Mpls., Nov. 18, 1950; s. Frederick A. and Margaret C. (Anderson) P. BA, U. Minn., 1972; MDiv, United Theol. Sem., New Brighton, Minn., 1976; JD magna cum laude, William Mitchell Coll. Law, St. Paul, 1987; PhD, U. Minn., 1993. Bar: Minn. 1987; ordained deacon Meth. Ch., 1975, elder, 1978. Assoc. min. First United Meth. Ch., Worthington, Minn., 1976-77; min. Fairfax (Minn.) United Meth. Ch., 1977-78, Gethsemane United Meth. Ch., Lino Lakes, Minn., 1979-83; sr. min. Edgewater Emmanuel United Meth. Ch., Mpls., 1983-92; dir. gift planning Hamline U., St. Paul, 1992—. Assoc. atty. Lange & Anderson, P.A., Bloomington, Minn., 1988-91; sabbatical Mission Resource Ctr., Emory U., Atlanta, 1998. Merrill fellow Harvard Div. Sch., Cambridge, Mass., 1992. Mem. Minn. State Bar, Minn. Planned Giving Coun., Phi Kappa Phi. Avocations: hiking, reading, golf, volunteering, travel. Office: Hamline U 1536 Hewitt Ave Saint Paul MN 55104-1284

PARSONS, MINDY (MINDY ENOS), newsletter editor, publisher, non-profit organization executive; b. Cin., May 18, 1962; d. Max Allen and Margery Ann (White) Enos; m. Judd Lewis Parsons, Sept. 4, 1993; children: Cody Robert and Savannah Anne (twins). AA in Liberal Arts, Brevard Community Coll., 1983; BSBA, Fla. Inst. Tech., 1986; MBA, N.Y. Inst., Boca Raton, Fla., 1992. Mem. adminstrv. support staff IBM, Boca Raton, 1980, 81; dir. mktg. Progressive Pub., Melbourne, Fla., 1986; owner, pub. Echelon Pub. Inc., 1986-87; editor Keuthan Communications Inc., 1987-89; staff writer First Mktg. Corp., Pompano Beach, Fla., 1989-90; assoc. editor Billboard Publs. Inc., Coral Springs, 1990-92, Caribbean Clipper, Inc., Clearwater, 1992-93; reporter South Fla. News Network, Coral Springs, 1993-94; owner Creative Communications, Delray Beach, Fla., 1993-96; newsletter editor, pub., founder Breast Cancer Survivor Network Corp., 1997—. Author: How to Save for Your Child's Education, 1990; editor: Soccer for Children, 1988, History of Bahamas, 1990; editor, pub. Breast Cancer Survivor newsletter, 1997—; contbr. articles to profl. publs. Vol. Humane Soc. of Broward County, Coral Springs, 1990-91; founder Breast Cancer Survivor Network; mem. Palm Beach County Breast Cancer Coalition. Mem. NAFE, Newsletter Publishers Assn. Republican. Methodist. Avocations: volleyball tournaments, U.S. Masters swim meets, reading. Home: 221 SE 34th Ave Boynton Beach FL 33435-8632

PARSONS, RICHARD DEAN, communications company executive; b. N.Y.C., Apr. 4, 1948; s. Lorenzo Locklair and Isabelle (Judd) P.; m. Laura Ann Bush, Aug. 30, 1968; children: Gregory, Leslie, Rebecca. Student, U. Hawaii, 1968; JD, Union U., Albany, N.Y., 1971; LLD (hon.), Adelphi U., 1990, Medgar Evers Coll., N.Y.C., 1991. Bar: N.Y. 1972. Asst. counsel to gov. State of N.Y., Albany, 1971-73, 1st asst. counsel to gov., 1973-74; dep. counsel to v.p. Office of V.P., Washington, 1975; gen. counsel, assoc. dir. domestic coun. White House, 1975-77; ptnr. Patterson Belknap Webb & Tyler, N.Y.C., 1977-88; pres., COO Dime Savs. Bank N.Y., 1988-90, chmn., CEO, 1990-94; pres. Time Warner, 1994-2001; co-COO AOL Time Warner, Inc., 2001—02, CEO, 2002—. Bd. dirs. Fed. Nat. Mortgage Assn., Washington, 1989—, Philip Morris Cos., N.Y.C., Time Warner Inc., N.Y.C. Trustee Rockefeller Bros. Fund, N.Y.C., 1989—, Howard U., Washington, 1989—, Met. Mus. Art, N.Y.C., 1990—. Office: AOL Time Warner Inc 75 Rockefeller Plz New York NY 10019-6990*

PARSONS, ROBERT EUGENE, transportation consultant; b. Cin., Apr. 19, 1931; s. Charles Eugene and Samantha Ellen (Snider) P.; m. Beverly Greenhalgh, Dec. 30, 1949; children: Brian Scott, Barry Lawrence, Robert Stephen, Kimberly Ann. ME, U. Cinn., 1954; MSME, Drexel Inst. Tech., 1959. Registered profl. engr., Calif., Nev., Md., Ohio. Asst. project engr. The Martin Co., Balt., 1956-62, sect. mgr., 1962-64; dep. dir. Supersonic Transp. Office FAA, Washington, 1964-71; dir. rsch. and devel. plans U.S. Dept. Transp., 1971; assoc. adminstr. Fed. RR Adminstrn., 1975-80; dir. ctr. field methods Nat. Bur. Standards, Gaithersburg, Md., 1980-81; dir. RR rsch. and devel. program U. Calif., Berkeley, 1981-84; cons. Walnut Creek, Calif., 1986-90; dir. program on advanced technology for hwy. U. Calif. Berkeley, 1984-93; prin. Parsons Transp. Assocs., Midlothian, Va., 1993—. Cons. Assn. Am. R.R.s, Washington, U. Calif., Calif. Dept. Transp., U.S. Dept. Transp., DKS Assocs., Radar Control Sys., Rand, Sys. Control Tech., Intelligent Vehicle Hwy. Soc. Techs., Inc., Lawrence Livermore Nat. Lab., French Inst. Transp. Safety, Intelligent Transp. Soc. Am., chmn. sys. arch. com.; cons. IMRA Am., Inc. JKH & Assocs., Sci. Atlanta, Va. Tech., Va. Dept. Transp., Viggon Corp.; mem. rsch. adv. bd. Nat. ITS Implementation Rsch Ctr. Contbr. articles to profl. jours. Mem. SAE, Intelligent Transp. Soc. Am. (chair interoperability subcom.), Intelligent Transp. Sys. of Va. (bd. dirs., futures group), ITS World (editorial bd.). Methodist. Avocations: computer work, woodworking. Home: 3106 Cove Ridge Rd Midlothian VA 23112-4354

PARSONS, VINSON ADAIR, retired computer software company executive; b. Frankfort, Ky., Oct. 22, 1932; s. Richard Adair and Nina (Mefford) P.; m. Elizabeth Ann Peltier, June 2, 1956. A.S., Mitchell Coll., 1959; BS, U. Conn., 1960; AMP, Harvard U., 1985. Auditor, Price Waterhouse & Co. (C.P.A.s), Hartford, Conn., 1960-65; controller Pervel Industries Inc., Plainfield, 1965-70; v.p., controller Akzo Am. Inc., Asheville, N.C., 1970-71, 73-83, v.p., chief fin. officer, 1983-86, System Software Assocs. Inc., Chgo., 1986-89, also bd. dirs.; ret., 1990. Dir. Am. Tape Co., BRIntec Co., Control Tech. Corp. Elected commr. Town of Weaverville Bd. Commrs., 1994-2000. With USN, 1953-57. Mem. Am. Mgmt. Assn., Fin. Execs. Inst., Inst. Mgmt. Accts. (pres. local chpt. 1969-70) Clubs: Asheville Country; University (N.Y.C.); Reems Creek Golf. Home and Office: 15 Preston Ct Weaverville NC 28787-8907

PARSONS, WAYNE DOUGLAS, air transportation risk specialist; b. Paintsville, Ky., Dec. 21, 1949; s. Dollberta Parsons; m. Debra Jean Dollar, July 25, 1981; children: Matthew Wayne, Sara Rene. Student, Ea. Mich. U., 1974-75, U. Tex., Arlington, 1985-86, Arlington Police Acad., Ins. Inst. of Am. Cert. constrn. safety specialist, accident reconstructionist; cert. in evacuation safety, occupational safety and health adminstrn., profl. safety; lic. ins. adjustor. Test driver Chrysler Corp., Chelsea, Mich., 1974-80; instr. Nat. Acad. for Profl. Driving, Dallas, 1980-82; asst. risk mgr., loss prevention mgr. City of Arlington, 1982-87; loss control cons. Alexander & Alexander, Richmond, Va., 1987-89; risk specialist Dallas/Ft. Worth Internat. Airport, 1990—. Cons. 1989-90; sr. loss control cons. Wethe & Assocs. Author: Airport Risk Management and Loss Control, 1991, Emergency Driving for Aircraft/Fire Rescue Vehicle Training, 1991 (Risk Mgmt. Achievement award Pub. Risk Mgmt. Assn. 1992), Municipal Loss Control, 1991; co-author, developer: Firefighter Survival and Safety, 1984. With USAF, 1969-73. Recipient award of Honor, Tex. Safety Assn., Dallas, 1984. Mem. Am. Soc. Safety Engrs. Methodist. Avocations: custom knife making, skiing. Home: 3202 Flintridge Ct Arlington TX 76017-2513 Office: Dallas/Ft Worth Internat Airport PO Box 619428 Dallas TX 75261-9428

PARSONS, WILLIAM JONATHAN, cardiologist; b. Apr. 3, 1955; married; 3 children. BA, Dartmouth Coll., 1977, MD, 1980. Diplomate Am. Bd. Internal Medicine, Am. Bd. Cardiovascular Diseases, Am. Bd. Nuclear Cardiology, Nat. Bd. Echocardiography. Resident in internal medicine Strong Meml. Hosp. U. Rochester (N.Y.), 1983-85; cardiology fellow Duke U. Med. Ctr., Durham, 1985-88, asst. prof., 1988-91; asst. prof. medicine Southwestern Med. Ctr. U. Tex., Dallas, 1991-93; attending cardiologist Baylor U. Med. Ctr., 1993—2001, Rex Hosp., Raleigh, NC, 2001—. Contbr. articles to profl. jours. Gen. med. officer USPHS-IHS, 1981-83. Fellow Am. Coll. Physicians, Am. Coll. Cardiology. Office: Carolina Cardiology Cons 3324 Six Forks Rd Raleigh NC 27609 E-mail: wjpdnp@aol.com.

PART, HOWARD M. dean; b. N.Y.C., N.Y. BS, Ohio U.; MD, Ohio State U. Cert. Am. Bd. Internal Medicine. Resident in internal medicine Ohio State U.; chief of gen. medicine consult svc. Wright State U. Sch. Medicine, dir. internal medicine residency program, Dayton V.A. Med. Ctr., dept. vice chair and chair med. edn., assoc. dean faculty and clin. affairs, 1995—98, acting dean, 1998—99, dean, 1999—. Fellow: Am. Coll. Physicians. Office: 115 Med Scis Bldg Wright State U 3640 Colonel Glenn Hwy Dayton OH 45435-0001*

PARTAIN, CLARENCE LEON, radiologist, nuclear medicine physician, educator, administrator; b. Memphis, July 12, 1940; s. Archie Leon and Vergie (Young) P.; m. Judith Stafford, Jan., 1964; children: David Blane, Teri Ellyn, Amy Leigh. BSNE, U. Tenn., 1963; MSNE, Purdue U., 1965, PhD in Nuc. Engring., 1967; MD, Washington U., St. Louis, 1975. Diplomate Am. Bd. Nuclear Medicine, Am. Bd. Radiology; registered profl. engr., Mo. Asst. prof. nuc. engring. U. Mo.-Columbia, 1968-71, assoc. prof., 1971-75; resident N.C. Meml. Hosp., Chapel Hill, 1975-79; assoc. prof. radiology U. N.C.-Chapel Hill, 1978-79; assoc. prof. Vanderbilt U., Nashville, 1980-85, prof. radiology and biomed. engring., 1985—, vice chmn. radiology, 1989-92, dir. nuc. medicine, 1981-85, dir. magnetic resonance imaging, 1983-92, chmn. radiology, radiologist in chief, 1992-2000, dir. Ctr. for Imaging Rsch., 2000—; cons. NIH, Bethesda, Md., 1980—; Carol D. and Henry P. Pendegrass prof. radiology and radiol. scis. Vanderbilt U., 1997—. Author: Nuclear Magnetic Resonance (NMR) Imaging, 1983, NMR Imaging: Clinical Utility and Correlation, 1984, Thyroid and Parathyroid Imaging, 1986, Magnetic Resonance Imaging, 2d edit., 1988, Correlative Image: Nuclear Medicine, Magnetic Resonance, Computer Tomography, Ultrasound, 1988; editl. bd. Acad. Radiology, Magnetic Resonance Imaging, Jour. Magnetic Resonance Imaging, Jour. Nuclear Medicine; editor-in-chief Jour. of Magnetic Resonance Imaging. Scientific adv. coun. Whitaker Found. AEC Spl. fellow, 1964-66; grantee Nat. Inst. Neurosci., Communicative Diseases and Stroke, 1977-78 Fellow Am. Coll. Nuclear Physicians, Am. Coll. Radiology, Soc. Magnetic Resonance Imaging (bd. dirs.), Internat. Soc. of Magnetic Resonance in Medicine, Accreditation Coun. for Grad. Med. Edn., Residency Rev. Com. Nuclear Medicine; mem. AMA, IEEE, Radiol. Soc. N.Am. (chair rsch. devel. com.), Assn. Univ. Radiologists (exec. com.), Soc. Nuclear Medicine (trustee, Benedict Casson lectr. 1981), Am. Roentgen Ray Soc. (exec. coun.), Soc. Magnetic Resonance in Medicine (trustee), Internat. Soc. of Magnetic Resonance in Medicine (governance coun., bd. dirs.), Soc. Chmn. Acad. Radiology Depts. (bd. dirs.), Am. Bd. Radiology (examiner in nuc. medicine), Sigma Phi Epsilon. Baptist. Home: 5471 Pinewood Rd Franklin TN 37064-9235 Office: Vanderbilt U Med Ctr Dept Radiology RM RR-1223 MCN Nashville TN 37232-0001

PARTAN, DANIEL GORDON, lawyer, educator; b. Gardner, Mass., Aug. 2, 1933; s. Toivo Antero and Lempi Sivia (Adamson) P.; m. Doris Liepmann, June 8, 1957; children: Andrew Stewart, Matthew Alexander, Sarah Ruth, Iliana Maria, Juan Carlos. AB, Cornell U., 1955; LLB, Harvard U., 1958, LLM, 1961. Bar: Mass. 1959. Rsch. assoc. Harvard Law Sch., 1961, Rule of Law Ctr., Duke U. Law Sch., 1962-65; assoc. prof. U. N.D., 1964-65; assoc. prof. law Boston U., 1965-68, prof., 1968—. Mem. NAFTA dispute settlement roster and binat. dispute panel U.S.-Can. Free Trade Agreement; mem. dispute settlement panel roster World Trade Orgn.; cons. Dept. State, UN Devel. Program, Am. Acad. Arts and Sci.; pres., chmn. Bd. dirs. UN Assn. Greater Boston, 1969-71, 76-77; chmn. Brookline Selectmen's Com. on Harvard Energy Plant, 1976—; vis. scholar Harvard Law Sch., 1977-78; vis. fellow Cambridge (Eng.) U., 1972; vis. prof. Peking U., Beijing, 2000. Author: Population in the United Nations System, 1973, Documentary Study of the Politicization of UNESCO, 2 vols., 1975, The International Law Process, 1992, Documents Supplement to the International Law Process, 1999; co-author: Legal Problems of International Administration, 1968, The United States and the International Labor Organization, 1980; co-editor: Corporate Disclosure of Environmental Risks: U.S. and European Law, 1990; contbr. articles to books and jours. Mem. ABA (amicus brief com. sect. internat. law and practice), Boston Bar Assn., Bretton Woods Com., Commn. to Study the Orgn. Peace, Am. Law Inst., Acad. Coun. UN System, Am. Soc. Internat. Law, Internat. Law Assn., European Communities Studies Assn., UN Assn., Coalition for a Strong UN. Office: 765 Commonwealth Ave Boston MA 02215-1401

PARTANEN, CARL RICHARD, biology educator; b. Portland, Oreg., Nov. 23, 1921; s. Emil and Ellen (Engstrom) P.; m. Jane Nelson, June 24, 1961; children: Karen, Kirsten, Richard (dec.) Student, Multnomah Jr. Coll., 1946-48; BA, Lewis and Clark Coll., 1950; MA, Harvard, 1951, PhD, 1954. Am. Cancer Soc. postdoctoral research fellow Columbia, 1954-55, Harvard, 1955-57; research asso. Childrens Cancer Research Found., Boston, 1957-61; asso. prof. biology U. Pitts., 1961-64, prof. biology, 1964-86, chmn. biology, 1964-70, prof. emeritus, 1987—; Research fellow U. Edinburgh, Scotland, 1971-72, U. Nottingham, Eng., 1978-79. Contbr. articles to profl. jours. Served with AUS, 1942-45, ETO. Recipient Distinguished Achievement award Lewis and Clark Coll., 1968 Mem. AAAS, Bot. Soc. Am., Soc. for Devel. Biology, Soc. for In Vitro Biology. Home: 1112 Farragut St Pittsburgh PA 15206-1746 Office: U Pitts Dept Biol Scis Pittsburgh PA 15260 E-mail: partanen@pitt.edu.

PARTCH, KENNETH PAUL, editor, consultant; b. Mt. Vernon, N.Y., June 22, 1925; s. Edward Augustus and Grace Jane (Crabb) P.; m. Dorothy Sophia Iversen, July 16, 1953; children— Marjorie, Stephen, Jessica. AB, Bklyn. Coll., 1949. Mng. editor Moore Publishing Co., 1955, Chain Store Age mag., 1955-59, Sales Mgmt. mag., 1961; editor Food Topics mag., 1961-68; dir. mktg. Grocery Mfrs. Am., 1969-70; editor Chain Store Age-Supermarket Group, N.Y.C., 1970-77; cons. to supermarket industry, 1977-80; editor-in-chief Supermarket Bus. mag., 1980-93, editor-at-large, 1993—. Contbr. to Wharton Mag. Served with USAAF, 1943-46. Decorated Air medal; recipient Jesse Neal award Assoc. Bus. Press, 1968, Grand award ABP Points of Light Award, 1991. Mem. Sigma Delta Chi. Home: 20 Devils Gardens Rd Norwalk CT 06854-3315

PARTEE, BARBARA HALL, linguist, educator; b. Englewood, N.J., June 23, 1940; d. David B. and Helen M. Hall; m. Morriss Henry Partee, 1966 (div. 1971); children: Morriss M., David M., Joel T.; m. Emmon Werner Bach, 1973 (div. 1996); m. Vladimir B. Borschev, 1997. BA with high honors in Math., Swarthmore Coll., 1961; PhD in Linguistics, MIT, 1965; DSc (hon.), Swarthmore Coll., 1989, Charles U., Prague, Czechoslovakia, 1992, Russian State Humanities U., Moscow, 2001. Asst. prof. UCLA, 1965-69, assoc. prof., 1969-73; assoc. prof. linguistics and philosophy U. Mass., Amherst, 1972-73, prof., 1973-90, Disting. Univ. prof., 1990—, head dept. linguistics, 1987-93; fellow Ctr. for Advanced Study in Behavior Scis., 1976-77. Mem. bd. mgrs. Swarthmore Coll., 1990-2001. Author: (with Stockwell and Schachter) The Major Syntactic Structures of English, 1972, Fundamentals of Mathematics for Linguists, 1979, (with ter Meulen and Wall) Mathematical Methods in Linguistics, 1990, (with Hajicova and Sgall) Topic-Focus Articulation, Tripartite Structures, and Semantic Content, 1998; editor: Montague Grammar, 1976; co-editor: (with Chierchia and Turner) Properties, Types and Meaning, Vol. I: Foundational Issues, Vol. II: Semantic Issues, 1989, (with Bach, Jelinek and Kratzer) Quantification in Natural Languages, 1995, (with P. Portner) Formal Semantics: The Essential Readings, 2002; mem. editoral bd: Language, 1967-73, Linguistic Inquiry, 1972-79, Theoretical Linguistics, 1974—, Linguistics and Philosophy, 1977— . Recipient Chancellor's medal U. Mass., 1977; NEH fellow, 1982-83; Internat. Rsch. and Exchanges Bd. fellow, 1989-90, 95, Fulbright fellow 2000. Fellow AAAS, NAS (chair anthropology sect. 1993-96), Am. Acad. Arts and Scis., Sigma Xi; mem. Linguistic Soc. Am. (pres. 1986), Am. Philos. Assn., Assn. Computational Linguistics. Home: 50 Hobart Ln Amherst MA 01002-1321 Office: U Mass Dept Linguistics Amherst MA 01003 E-mail: partee@linguist.umass.edu. *In college I studied math, Russian, and philosophy, the three subjects I loved best, with no idea of relating them, and ended up ideally prepared for a field that didn't exist then. I'm also grateful for wonderful parents, teachers, students, colleagues, family.*

PARTEN, PRISCILLA M. medical and psychiatric social worker, educator; b. Lowell, Mass., Dec. 7, 1944; d. Ralph Bailey and Margaret Lillian (McDonagh) Newton; m. Samuel L. Parten, June 27, 1965; children: Delora Parten Power, Edward Bailey, Ethan Rogers. BA, Northeastern U., 1968; MSW, Adelphi U., Burlington, Vt., 1987. Lic. ind. clin. social worker, Mass., lic. clin. social worker, Maine; lic. ind. clin. social worker, N.H.; bd. cert. diplomate NASW. Family support coord. Easter Seal Early Intervention, Derry, N.H., 1988-91; med. and psychiat. social worker Salem (N.H.) Vis. Nurses, 1992-96; home sch. coord. Timberlane Regional Sch. Dist., Plaistow, N.H., 1992—; dir. Priscilla M. Parten, MSW, ACSW, BCD, Londonderry, 1992—. Spkr., author, presenter in field, interviewed on Nat. Pub. TV. Bd. dirs. Norwich U. Parents' Assn., 1st v.p., 1999—2001. Recipient commendation Pres.'s Com. on Mental Retardation, 1968. Mem. NASW, Nutfield Exch. Club (bd. dirs. 1994-96). Democrat. Congregationalist. Avocations: skiing, photography, crocheting, gardening, snorkeling. Office: 40 Nashua Rd Londonderry NH 03053-3444

PARTENHEIMER, ROBERT CHAPIN, emergency physician; b. Springfield, Mass., Feb. 12, 1923; s. Joseph Everad and Leila Ursula (Parker) P.; m. Marion Claire Hill, June 23, 1949 (div. Feb. 1971); children: Barbara Haislip, Robert Hill, Richard Chapin; m. Carol Griffiths, Jan. 1991. BA, Amherst Coll., 1945; MD, Cornell U., 1947. Rotating intern Orange (N.J.) Meml. Hosp., 1947-48; intern in medicine U. Hosp., N.Y.C., 1948-49; resident in internal medicine USPHS, Boston, 1950-52; pvt. practice Summit, N.J., 1954-71; emergency physician Raritan Bay Med. Ctr., Perth Amboy, 1971-77, 84-90, St. Cloud (Fla.) Hosp., 1994-97, Columbia HCA Rauterson Hosp., Okeechobee, Fla., 1992-96. Lt. comdr. USPHS, 1949-54. Em. N.J. Med. Soc., Union County Med. Soc. Methodist. Avocations: golf, boating, fishing, skiing. Home: 5213 Indian Bend Ln Fort Pierce FL 34951

PARTER, SEYMOUR VICTOR, computer science and mathematics educator; b. Chgo., June 9, 1927; s. Peter and Tillie (Dekovetzky) P.; m. Ruth Ghitman, Oct. 9, 1957; children: Paul Jeffry, David William. BS, Ill. Inst. Tech., 1949, MS, 1951; PhD, N.Y.U., 1958. Staff mem. Los Alamos Sci. Lab., 1951-57; instr. math. Mass. Inst. Tech., 1957-58; asst. prof. math. Ind. U., 1958-60, Cornell U., 1960-62; vis. asst. prof. computer sci. Stanford, 1962-63; asso. prof. computer sci. and math. U. Wis., Madison, 1963-65, prof., 1965—, chmn. computer sci. dept., 1968-70. Mem. NRC adv. com. on math. to Office Naval Research, 1970-72; mem. adv. com. on computing to pres. Stanford, 1969-72; mem. ICASE Sci. Council, 1981-87 Contbr. articles to profl. jours. Mem. Math. Assn. Am., Soc. Indsl. and Applied Math. (vis. lectr. 1969-72, mem. council 1978-80, mng. editor Jour. Numerical Analysis 1977-80, pres. 1981-82), Bd. Math. Scis. (chmn. 1984-86), Assn. Computing Machinery Home: 5 S Rock Rd Madison WI 53705-4634

PARTH, FRANK R. e-commerce company executive, educator; b. Eichendorf, Germany, Aug. 26, 1949; came to U.S., 1952. s. Frank and Erna (Framelsberger) P.; m. Jane Hoppe, Dec. 27, 1974 (div. Jan. 1985); children: Katherine, Frank. BS in Physics, Creighton U., 1972; MS in Physics, U. Wyo., 1978; MS in Sys. Mgmt., U. So. Calif., L.A., 1986; MBA, Peter Drucker Inst., 2000. Design engr. Tex. Instruments, Dallas, 1978-81; asst. tech. dir. Martin-Marietta Space Sys., Long Beach, Calif., 1981-92; pres. InterVolve Mgmt. Sys., Mission Viejo, 1993-95; mgr. sys. engring. Experian, Orange, 1995-97; mgr. Deloitte & Touche, Santa Ana, 1997-98; practice mgr. Keane, Inc., Long Beach, 1998-99; v.p. devel. Overstock Market, 2000—. Faculty U. So. Calif. Inst. Safety and Sys. Mgmt., L.A., 1993-97, U. Calif. Irvine, 1996—, Claremont Grad. U., 2000—. Contbr. articles to profl. jours. Bd. dirs. Orange County (Calif.) Search and Rescue, 1996—. Mem. Internat. Coun. Sys. Engring., Mensa Internat. (pres. Orange County chpt. 1993), Project Mgmt. Inst. (Spkr.'s award 1998). Avocations: sailing, skiing, wine. Home: 21901 Palanca Mission Viejo CA 92692-1012 Office: IMS PO Box 80688 Rancho Santa Margarita CA 92688-0688 E-mail: frank@fparth.com.

PARTHASARATHY, GAUTHAM, chemical engineer, researcher; b. Bombay, India; s. K S Parthasarathy; m. Smita Jadhav. PhD, Auburn U., Ala., 2000. Summer intern Lubrizol India Ltd., Bombay, 1994; grad. asst. Auburn (Ala.) U., 1996—99; rsch. assoc. Solutia, Pensacola, Fla., 2000—00, sr. rsch. engr. Springfield, Mass., 2000—02. Cons. Millenium Petrochems., Cin., 1997, BOC Gases, Murray Hills, NJ, 1997—98, Gen. Elec. Plastics, Burkeville, Ala., 1998—99, Farmland Industries, Coffyville, Kans., 1999. Recipient CAST Directors award (Honourable Mention), Computing and Systems Tech., AIChE, 1998. Mem.: AIChE. Office: Solutia Inc. 730 Worcester St Springfield MA 01151 Business E-Mail: smigau@yahoo.com.

PARTHASARATHY, SANJAY, information technology executive; BS in Mech. Engring., Anna U., Madras, India; MS in Mgmt., M in Engring., MIT. From product mgr. to corp. v.p. Microsoft, Redmond, Wash., 1990, corp. v.p. strategy & bus. devel. group. Office: One Microsoft Way Redmond WA 98052-6399*

PARTHASARATHY, SRINIVASAN, computer scientist, educator; b. Cleve., Mar. 22, 1970; s. Thiruvenkatachari Parthasarathy, Ranjani Parthasarathy; m. Lakshmi Srinivasan, Mar. 30, 1998. PhD, U. Rochester, 1999. Software cons. Intel Corp., Santa Clara, Calif., 1997—98; adj. prof. Rochester Inst. Techn., Rochester, NY, 1999; vis. asst. prof. U. Rochester, 1999—2000; asst. prof. computer and info. scis. Ohio State U., Columbus, 2000—, asst. prof. biomedical informatics, 2002—. Co-author: (book) Arithmetic and Logic Operations with DNA, 1997; contbr. articles to profl. jours. Fellow Ameritech Faculty, Ameritech Corp., 2001. Avocations: swimming, racquet sports. Office: Ohio State U 2015 Neil Ave, DL 395 Columbus OH 43210 Office Fax: 614-292-2911.

PARTHUM, CHARLES ALBERT, civil engineer; b. Lawrence, Mass., Sept. 26, 1929; s. Albert and Elsie Ida (Eichner) P.; m. Mary Catherine Wiggin, Oct. 20, 1956; children: Stephen Charles, Julie Elizabeth. BSCE, Northeastern U., 1951. With Camp Dresser & McKee, Inc., Boston, 1951—, ptnr., 1967—, sr. v.p., dir., 1971-92; cons., 1992—. Cons. EPA, 1980 Treas., deacon, moderator, clk. Tabernacle Congl. Ch., Salem, Mass.; chmn. Engr.-Joint Contacts Documents Com., 1980. Recipient Outstanding Civil Engring. Alumnus award Northeastern U., 1989. Mem. NSPE, ASCE (bd. dirs. 1987-90, pres. 1995-96, William H. Wisely Am. Civil Engr. award 1993), Am. Acad. Environ. Engrs. (diplomate), Boston Soc. Civil Engrs. (hon., pres. 1975-76), Water Pollution Control Fedn. (chmn. constrn. and bylaws com. 1972-77), Am. Water Resources Assn., Mass. Soc. Profl. Engrs., Am. Water Works Assn., New England Water Works Assn., New England Water Pollution Control Assn., Chi Epsilon (hon.). Fax: 781-631-3081.

PARTIDA, GILBERT A. executive; b. Nogales, Ariz., July 27, 1962; s. Enrique Gilberto and Mary Lou (Flores) P.; m. Soncee Ray Brown, July 30, 1992. BA with distinction, U. Ariz., 1984; JD cum laude, Pepperdine U., 1987; LLD (hon.), Calif. Western Sch Law, San Diego, 1993. V.p., bd. mem. Partida Brokerage, Inc., Nogales, 1983-91; law clk. Office of Ariz. Atty. Gen., Tucson, 1985; assoc. Gray, Cary, Ames & Frye, San Diego, 1986-89, sr. assoc., 1990-92, chmn. Mex. Practice Group, 1992; pres. Greater San Diego C. of C., 1993-98; pres., CEO Price Smart, San Diego, 1998—. Corp. counsel San Diego Incubator Corp., 1990—. Contbr. articles to profl. jours. Mem. United Way Latino Future Scan Com., 1990; mentor Puente, 1991; leadership tng. mentor Chicano Fedn., 1992; dinner com. Young at Art, 1991; mem. Children's Initiative, 1993, Superbowl Task Force, 1993, San Diego Dialogue, 1993; hon. mem. Sister City, 1993, LEAD, 1993; hon. chair Easter Seals Telethon, 1994; vice chmn. Border Trade Alliance, 1989-91; mem. nat. gala com. HDI Ednl. Svcs., 1990; Calif. state del. U.S.-Mexico Border Govs.' Conf., 1990, 92; exec. com. San Diego Conv. and Visitors Bur. Mem. San Diego County Hispanic C. of C. (chmn. 1991, pres. 1990-91, v.p. 1989-90, internat. com. chair 1989-90, sec. 1989, founding bd. mem. 1988), Consejo Nacional de Maquiladoras, Calif. Hispanic C. of C. (state conv. joint venture com. 1991, spl. projects chair 1991), San Diego/Tijuana Sister Cities Soc. (adv. coun. 1993—), San Diego County Bar Assn. (U.S./Mexico liaison com.), ABA (U.S./Mexico bar liaison com.), Hispanic Alliance for Free Trade, Rotary Club San Diego. Avocations: tennis, running, creative writing. Office: Price Smart Inc 4649 Morena Blvd San Diego CA 92117-3650

PARTIN, DANIEL RAY, secondary school educator; b. Tenn., Sept. 6, 1948; m. Gail Reynolds; 1 child BS in English, Shippensburg U., Pa., 1970; MEd in English, Shippensburg (Pa.) U., 1974; MEd in Reading, Lehigh U., 1976; postgrad., Pa. State U., Harrisburg, 1987-88, U. Md., 1977, Millersville U., 1990, 95, 97, U. Pa., 1994-95. Cert. secondary comprehensive English tchr., K-12 reading specialist, Pa. Tchr. English and reading Dauphin Co. Tech. Sch., Harrisburg, Pa., 1974-77, Anne Arundel Co. Pub. Schs., Annapolis, Md., 1977-79; tchr. English Cornwall-Lebanon (Pa.) Sch. Dist., 1979-80, Steelton-Highspire (Pa.) Sch. Dist., 1981-88; instr. composition and reading Harrisburg Area C.C., 1981-86; adult basic edn. advisor Pa. Dept. Edn., Harrisburg, 1988-93; tchr. English/reading/gifted edn., pub. info. officer Camp Hill (Pa.) Sch. Dist., 1993-97; tchr. of gifted Ctrl. Dauphin Sch. Dist., Harrisburg, 1997—. Presenter ednl. workshops; writer funded ednl. grants. Contbr. articles to ednl. jours. Mem. NEA, Pa. State Edn. Assn. Office: Ctrl Dauphin Sch Dist 600 Rutherford Rd Harrisburg PA 17109-5297

PARTIN, WINFRED, clergyman; b. Whitley County, Ky., Oct. 19, 1946; s. Orville and Mary (Partin) P.; student Am. Sch., Chgo., Buford Ellington Vocat. Sch., Morristown, Tenn.; m. Lucille Davis, Sept. 28, 1966; children: Patsy Gail, Pamela Kaye, Paul Timothy. Ordained to ministry So. Bapt. Ch., 1966; pastor chs. in S.E. Ky. and N.E. Tenn., 1966-77; pastor Anthras Bapt. Ch., Duff, Tenn., 1977-79, King's Settlement Bapt. Ch., Clairfield, Tenn., 1981—; coin collector, 1960—; owner Partin's Coins and Stamps, Morristown, 1970—. Mem. Campbell County Bapt. Assn. Democrat. Writer for various hobby publs.; contbr. publs. including Rural Kentuckian, Scott's Stamp Jour., Stamp World, Pulpit Helps, Farm Life News, Linn's Stamp News, Danville Times-Examiner (Ky.). author poetry, fiction and non-fiction. Address: PO Box 3460 Morristown TN 37815-3460

PARTINGTON, JAMES WOOD, naval officer; b. Omaha, Jan. 16, 1939; s. Lee Edward and Carol Virginia (Wood) P.; m. Barbara Jean Arline, July 15, 1961; children: Jennifer, Kathleen, Mary Elizabeth. BA, U. R.I., 1970; grad., Naval War Coll., 1971. Commd. ensign USN, 1961, advanced through grades to rear adm., 1989; ops. officer Attack Squadron 122, Lemoore, Calif., 1974-77; comdg. officer Attack Squadron 27, 1977-80, Strike Fighter Squadron 125, Lemoore, 1980-82; coord. F/A 18 program Chief Naval Ops., Washington, 1982-84; comdg. officer Naval Air Sta., Lemoore, 1984-86; chief of staff Cruiser Destroyer Group 5, San Diego, 1986-87; dir. Naval Aviation Officer Assignments, Washington, 1987-88; comdr. Strike Fighter Wings Atlantic, Jacksonville, Fla., 1988-90, Naval Tng. Ctr., Great Lakes, Ill., 1990-92; v.p., dir. corp. planning Sr. Technologies Inc., 1992-94; pres. Partington and Associates, Lincoln, 1994—, Riser-Bond Instruments, Lincoln, 1998. Decorated Legion of Merit (5), DFC, Air medal (28), Meritorious Svc. medal. Mem. U.S. Naval Inst., Assn. Naval Aviation, Naval Order of U.S. Roman Catholic. Avocations: sailing, tennis, scuba diving. E-mail: jpartington@riserband.com.

PARTINGTON, MICHAEL DAVID, pediatric neurosurgeon; b. Swansea, Wales, June 6, 1960; came to U.S., 1961; s. Gerard Joseph and Mary Philomena (Andrews) P.; m. Mary Beth Kerwin, Oct. 6, 1984; children: Kevin, Emily. BA, Coll. St. Thomas, 1982; MD, U. Minn., 1986. Diplomate Am. Bd. Neurol. Surgery, Am. Bd. Pediat. Neeurol. Surgery. Resident in neurosurgery Mayo Clinic, Rochester, Minn., 1986-92; fellow in pediat. neurosurgery Children's Meml. Hosp., Chgo., 1992-94; asst. prof. neurosurgery U. Colo., Denver, 1994-98. Office: Gillette Children's Hosp 200 E University Ave Saint Paul MN 55101

PARTLETT, DAVID F. dean, law educator; b. 1947; LLB, Sydney U., 1970; LLM, Mich. U., 1972, 74; SJD, U. Va., 1980. Bar: New South Wales 1971, Australian Cap. Terr. 1978. Vis. asst. prof. U. Ala., 1972-73; legis. officer Australia Atty. Gen.'s Office, 1974—75; dir. rsch. Australian Law Reform Commn. , 1975—78; lectr. Australian Nat. U., 1978-80, sr. lectr., 1980-87, assoc. dean, 1982—85; vis. prof. Vanderbilt U., Nashville, 1987-88, prof. law, 1988-2000, acting dean, 1996-97; v.p., dean, prof. Sch. Law Washington & Lee U., Lexington, Va., 2000—. Sparkman Dist. vis. prof. Ala. U., 1986-87. Office: Washington & Lee U Sydney Lewis Hall Lexington VA 24450

PARTLOW, MARIANNE FAIRBANK, artist, consultant, curator; b. Cleve., May 19, 1947; d. Robert Louis and Dorothy (Tomkinson) Fairbank; m. Kenneth Lawrence Partlow III, Apr. 7, 1973; children: Liza Katherine, Joshua Fairbank. BA in Art History, Cornell U., 1969; MA in Art History, U. Va., 1971. Prodn. asst. Hill Holliday Connors Cosmopulos, Boston, 1966-70; rsch. assoc. Adams Davidson Gallery, Washington, 1971-73; instr. art history U. R.I., Kingston, 1973-74; advt. mgr. Foster Parents Plan, Warwick, R.I., 1973-74; dir. Galerie Royale, Vancouver, B.C., Can., 1974-79; cons. Olympia, Wash., 1978-84; owner, dir. Marianne Partlow Gallery, 1984-92; adj. curator N.W. collection Tacoma Art Mus., 1995-99; painter Olympia; instr. watercolor painting Evergreen State Coll., 1998-99. Bd. dirs. Wash. State Capital Mus., Olympia, 1980, Patrons of South Sound Cultural Activities, Olympia, 1980-95; art commr. City of Olympia Art Commn., 1986-95; drafter preservation ordinance City of Olympia, 1982; bd. dirs. Artist Trust, 1998-2000.

PARTNOY, RONALD ALLEN, lawyer; b. Norwalk, Conn., Dec. 23, 1933; s. Maurice and Ethel Marguerite (Roselle) P.; m. Diane Catherine Keenan, Sept. 18, 1965. BA, Yale U., 1956; LL.B., Harvard U., 1961; LL.M., Boston U., 1965. Bar: Mass. 1962, Conn. 1966. Atty. Liberty Mut. Ins. Co., Boston, 1961-65; assoc. counsel Remington Arms Co., Bridgeport, Conn., 1965-70, gen. counsel, 1970-88, sec., 1983-93; sr. counsel E.I. du Pont de Nemours & Co., Wilmington, Del., 1985-95. Served with USN, 1956-58; to capt. USNR (ret.) Mem.: ABA, Naval Res. Assn. (3d dist. pres., nat. exec. com. 1981—85, 1997—99, 2001—, nat. v.p. 1997—99, 2001—), U.S. Navy League (pres. Bridgeport coun. 1975—77, nat. dir., Conn. pres. 1977—80, v.p. Empire region 1980—85), Am. Judicature Soc., Sporting Arms and Ammunition Mfrs. Inst. (chmn. legis. and legal affairs com. 1971—86), Assn. of Yale Alumni (del. 1997—2000), Yale Club of N.Y.C., Harvard Club of Phila., Harvard Club of Boston, Chancery Club. Home: 616 Bayard Rd Kennett Square PA 19348-2504

PARTON, DOLLY REBECCA, singer, composer, actress; b. Sevier County, Tenn., Jan. 19, 1946; d. Robert Lee and Avie Lee (Owens) P.; m. Carl Dean, May 30, 1966. Country music singer, rec. artist, composer, actress, radio and TV personality. Entrepreneur, owner entertainment park Dollywood, established 1985. Radio appearances include Grand Ole Opry, WSM Radio, Nashville, Cass Walker program, Knoxville; TV appearances include Porter Wagoner Show, from 1967, Cass Walker program, Bill Anderson Show, Wilburn Bros. Show, Barbara Mandrell Show; rec. artist, Mercury, Monument, RCA , CBS record cos.; star movie Nine to Five, 1980, The Best Little Whorehouse in Texas, 1982, Rhinestone, 1984, Steel Magnolias, 1989, Straight Talk, 1991; albums include Here You Come Again (Grammy award 1978), Real Love, 1985, Just the Way I Am, 1986, Portrait, 1986, Think About Love, 1986, Trio (with Emmylou Harris, Linda Ronstadt) (Grammy award 1988), 1987, Heartbreaker, Great Balls of Fire, Rainbow, 1988, White Limozeen, 1989, Home for Christmas, 1990, Eagle When She Flies, 1991, Slow Dancing with the Moon, 1993 (Grammy nomination, Best Country Vocal Collaboration for Romeo (with Tanya Tucker, Billy Ray Cyrus, Kathy Mattea, Pam Tillis, & Mary-Chapin Carpenter), (with Tammy Wynette and Loretta Lynn) Honky Tonk Angels, 1994, The Essential Dolly Parton, 1995, Just the Way I Am, 1996, Super Hits, 1996, (with others) I Will Always Love You & Other Greatest Hits, 1996, Hungry Again, 1998, Trio II, 1998, Grass is Blue, 1999, Best of the Best-Porter & Doll, 1999; composer numerous songs including Nine to Five (Grammy award 1981, Acad. award nominee and Golden Globe award nominee 1981); author: Dolly, 1994. Recipient (with Porter Wagoner) Vocal Group of Yr. award, 1968; Vocal Duo of Yr. award All Country Music Assn., 1970, 71; Nashville Metronome award, 1979; Am. Music award for best duo performance (with Kenny Rogers), 1984; named Female Vocalist of Yr., 1975, 76; Country Star of Yr., Sullivan Prodns., 1977; Entertainer of Yr., Country Music Assn., 1978; People's Choice award, 1980, 88; Female Vocalist of Yr., Acad. Country Music, 1980; Dolly Parton Day proclaimed, Sevier County, Tenn., designated Oct. 7, 1967, Los Angeles, Sept. 20, 1979; recipient Grammy awards for best female country vocalist, 1978, 81, for best country song, 1981, for best country vocal performance with group, 1987; co-recipient (with Emmylou Harris and Linda Ronstadt) Acad. Country Music award for album of the yr., 1987; named to Small Town of Am. Hall of Fame, 1988, East Tenn. Hall of Fame, 1988. Address: RCA 6 W 57th St New York NY 10019-3901*

PARTON, THOMAS ALBERT, speech-language pathologist; b. Decatur, Ill., Aug. 28, 1961; s. Harry Michael Parton and Linda Janette Kite; m. Susan Richelle Feinberg, June 13, 1987; children: Zachary Miles, Joshua Brant. BS in Speech Pathology, Ill. State U., 1984, MS in Speech Pathology, 1986. Speech-lang. pathologist Minonk (Ill.)-Dana-Rutland Ctrl. Unit Sch. Dist. 108, 1986-91, McLean County Unit # 5, Normal, Ill., 1991—. Mem. collective bargaining com. Ill. Edn. Assn., Springfield, 1991, 92, 94, 96, chair, 1997, 98, mem. spl. edn. com., 1995. Mem. Am. Speech-Lang.-Hearing Assn., Ill. Speech-Lang.-Hearing Assn. (spkr.), Ctrl. Ill. Speech-Lang.-Hearing Assn. Avocation: music. Home: 1301 Kern St Normal IL 61761-3325 E-mail: partonta@earthlink.net.

PARTOYAN, GARO ARAKEL, lawyer; b. Toledo, Dec. 6, 1936; s. Garo and Vartoohi Partoyan; children: Garo Linck, Elizabeth Margaret, Martin Joseph. BS in Chem. Engring., Northwestern U., 1959; JD, U. Mich., 1962; LLM, NYU, 1964. Bar: N.Y. 1963, U.S. Dist. Cts. (so. dist.) N.Y. 1964, U.S. Ct. Claims 1966, U.S. Ct. Appeals (2nd cir.) 1966, U.S. Dist. Ct. (ea. dist.) N.Y. 1968. Ptnr. Curtis, Morris & Safford, N.Y.C., 1962-76; gen. counsel mktg. and tech. Mars, Inc., McLean, Va., 1976-98; pres. Mgmt. of Intellectual Property, Inc., Sarasota, Fla., 1998—. Mem. Dobbs Ferry (N.Y.) Bd. Edn., 1972-76, pres., 1975-76; chmn. Fairfax Citizens Group, Fairfax County, Va., 1988-90. Mem. ABA, Am. Intellectual Property Law Assn., N.Y. Intellectual Property Law Assn., Internat. Trademark Assn. (pres. 1990-91, bd. dirs. 1983—), Intellectual Property Owners (bd. dirs. 1992-99). Avocations: sailing, curling. Office: 4756 Sweetmeadow Cir Sarasota FL 34238 Fax: (941) 922-2410. E-mail: partoyanga@aol.com.

PARTRIDGE, BRUCE JAMES, lawyer, educator, writer; b. Syracuse, N.Y., June 4, 1926; arrived in Can., 1969; s. Bert James and Lida Marion (Rice) P.; m. Mary Janice Smith, June 13, 1948 (dec. 1986); children: Heather Leigh, Eric James, Brian Lloyd, Bonnie Joyce; m. May S. Archer, May 28, 1988; stepchildren: Sheila Archer, Laurel Archer. AB cum laude, Oberlin Coll., Ohio, 1946; LLB, Blackstone Coll., Chgo., 1950, JD, 1952; LLB, U. B.C., 1974. Bar: B.C. 1976, N.W.T. 1980. Rsch. physicist Am. Gas Assn., Cleve., 1946-48; bus. mgr. Cazenovia (N.Y.) Coll., 1948—51; bus. mgr., purchasing agt., asst. treas. Rochester Inst. Tech., 1953—58; bus. adminstr. Baldwin-Wallace Coll., Berea, Ohio, 1951-53; v.p. bus. and mgmt. U. Del., Newark, 1958-63; v.p. adminstrn. Johns Hopkins U., Balt., 1963-69; pres. U. Victoria, B.C., Can., 1969-72; assoc. Clark, Wilson & Co., Vancouver, Can., 1975-78; successively solicitor, mng. solicitor, gen. solicitor, v.p. law and gen. counsel, sec. Cominco Ltd., 1978-88; exec. dir. Baker & McKenzie, Hong Kong, 1988-90; v.p. Pacific Creations, Inc., 1990-92; faculty Camosun Coll., 1992-99. Author: Management in Canada: The Competitive Challenges, 2000; co-author: College and University Business Administration, 1968; chmn. editl. com. Purchasing for Higher Education, 1962; contbr. numerous articles to profl. jours. Chmn. commn. on adminstrv. affairs Am. Coun. on Edn., Washington, 1966-69; mem. Pres.'s Com. on Employment of Handicapped, Washington, 1967-69; mem. adv. coun. Ctr. for Resource Studies, Queen's U.; bd. dirs. L'Arche in the Americas; mem. adv. coun. Westwater Rsch. Ctr., U. B.C. Mem. Law Soc. B.C., Law Soc. of N.W. Ters., Assn. Can. Gen. Counsel, Fedn. Ins. and Corp. Counsel, Def. Rsch. Inst. (product liability com.), Am. Corp. Counsel Assn., Vancouver Club, Aberdeen Marina Club, Hong Kong Football Club. Unitarian Universalist. E-mail: brucepart@telus.ca.

PARTRIDGE, MARK VAN BUREN, lawyer, educator, writer; b. Rochester, Minn., Oct. 16, 1954; s. John V.B. and Constance (Brainerd) P.; m. Mary Roberta Moffitt, Apr. 30, 1983; children: Caitlin, Lindsay, Christopher. BA, U. Nebr., 1978; JD, Harvard U., 1981. Bar: Ill. 1981, U.S. Dist. Ct. (no. dist.) Ill. 1981, U.S. Dist. Ct. (ea. dist.) Mich. 1983, U.S. Ct. Appeals (fed. cir.) 1983, U.S. Ct. Appeals (4th cir.) 1986, U.S. Ct. Appeals (5th cir.) 1993, U.S. Ct. Appeals (3rd cir.) 1998. Assoc. Pattishall, McAuliffe, Newbury, Hilliard & Geraldson, Chgo., 1981-88, ptnr., 1988—. Adj. prof. John Marshall Law Sch., Chgo., 1987—; arbitrator Cook County Mandatory Arbitration Program, 1989—; v.p. Harvard Legal Aid Bur., 1980-81; mediator no. dist. Ill. Voluntary Mediation Program, 1997—; panelist World Intellectual Property Orgn., Domain Name Dispute Resolution Svc., 1999—. Contbr. articles to profl. jours.; mem. editl. bd. The Trademark Reporter, 1994-97; adv. bd. IP Litigator, 1995—. Vol. Chgo. Vol. Legal Svcs., 1983—. Mem. ABA (com. chmn. 1989-91, 94-99), Internat. Trademark Assn. (com. vice chmn. 1996), World Intellectual Property Orgn. (experts panel internet domain name process 1998-99), Am. Intellectual Property Law Assn. (com. chmn. 1989-91, 96-98, bd. dirs. 1998-2001), Intellectual Property Law Assn. Chgo. (com. chmn. 1993-96), Brand Names Ednl. Found. (moot ct. regional chmn. 1994-96, nat. vice-chmn. 1997-98, nat. chmn. 1998-99), Legal Club (v.p. 1998, pres. 1999), Lawyers Club Chgo. (pres. 2000, bd. dirs. 2000-01), Union League Club, Boy Scouts Am. Avocations: writing, music, genealogy, travel, internet. Office: Pattishall McAuliffe Newbury Hilliard & Geraldso 311 S Wacker Dr Ste 5000 Chicago IL 60606-6631 E-mail: mpartridge@pattishall.com.

PARTRIDGE, WILLIAM J. military officer, government agency administrator; b. Saugerties, N.Y. Grad., U.S. Mil. Acad., 1975; MS in Space Systems Engring., Naval Postgrad. Sch. Commd. 2d lt. U.S. Army, 1975, advanced through grades to col.; comdr. 2d Bn., 2d Aviation Regiment, 2d Infantry Divsn., Republic of Korea; battery fire direction control officer, battery exec. officer 1-15th Field Artillery, Ft. Carson; flight platoon leader, ops. officer 62d Aviation Co., Germany; co. comdr., brigade exec. officer 4th Aviation Brigade, Ft. Lewis, Wash.; plans officer U.S. Space Command; brigade exec. officer 4th Aviation Brigade, 4th Infantry Divsn., Ft. Carson; dep. chief of staff for ops. Army Space Command; chief current ops. divsn. Hqrs. U.S. Space Command, Peterson AFB, Colo.; comdr. Army Space Forces U.S. Army Space and Missile Def. Command, Colorado Springs, 2001—. Decorated Army Meritorious medal with 3 oak leaf clusters, Army Commendation medal with 1 oak leaf cluster, Army Achievement medal with 1 oak leaf cluster. Office: Pub Affairs Office Army Space Command 1670 N Newport Ste 2111 Colorado Springs CO 80916-2749*

PARTRIDGE, WILLIAM RUSSELL, retired federal executive; b. Torrance, Calif., Jan. 9, 1927; s. Frederick Walter and Dorothy (Keller) P.; m. Phyllis Ruth Squires, Feb. 6, 1949; children: William M., Carol C., Mark F. Student, U. Idaho, W. Va. U., 1944-45; BA, Pomona Coll., 1949; MPA, Syracuse U., 1950; MBA, UCLA, 1963. Various mgmt. positions U.S. AEC, Oak Ridge, 1950-55; staff asst., adminstr. mgmt. devel., ops. analyst Gen. Offices and Rocketdyne div./N.Am. Aviation Co., L.A., 1955-61; mgr. mgmt. systems Gen. Offices, N.Am. Aviation Co., 1961-65; project engr. info. sys. divsn. autonetics N.Am. Aviation Co., Anaheim, Calif., 1965-69; ops. rsch. scientist System Devel. Corp., Santa Monica, 1961; various govt. positions to asst. inspector gen. DOE, 1975-87; staff mem. House Appropriations Com., 1987-90; dep. inspector gen., sr. exec. svc. Fed. Emergency Mgmt. Agy., Washington, 1990-95. With AUS, 1944-46. Mem. Inst. for Opers. Rsch. and the Mgmt. Scis.

PARU, MARDEN DAVID, fundraising executive; b. Belmar, N.J., Nov. 18, 1941; s. Isaac and Edith (Rubin) P.; m. Joan Ellen Kemeny, June 5, 1966; children: Victor Milan, Elana Fay. BA, U. Tulsa, 1963; MA, U. Chgo., 1965; postgrad., Syracuse U., 1968-69, Brandeis U., 1970-73. Dir. spl. svcs. Young Men's Jewish Coun., Chgo., 1965-67; asst. dir. Jewish Community Ctr., Syracuse, N.Y., 1967-68; exec. dir. Onondaga County Assn. for Retarded Citizens, 1968-70; lectr., dir. admissions Hornstein program Brandeis U., Waltham, Mass., 1972-74; exec. dir. Jewish Edn. Coun., Montreal, Que., Can., 1974-76, Jewish Fedns. Poughkeepsie-Kingston (N.Y.), 1976-79; exec. v.p. Jewish Fedn. Greater Clifton (N.J.)-Passaic, 1979-82, Cin. Jewish Fedn., 1982-85; dir. N.Y. met. region Am. Technion Soc., N.Y.C., 1985-87; nat. campaign dir. Am. ORT Fedn., 1987-92; dir. devel. Global Hunger Project, 1992-93; exec. v.p. Keren-Or, Inc. Jerusalem Ctr. for Multi-Disabled Blind Children, 1993-96; exec. dir. Jewish Fedn. Rockland, Rockland County, N.Y., 1997-99; fundraising cons., CEO Marden Paru & Assocs., Inc., Nyack, NY, 1999—. Cantor synagogues, Boston, Cin., N.Y. State, Okla., 1960—; cons. on aging pvt. nursing homes, Mass., 1970-74; cons. pvt. Havurot groups, Framingham, Mass., 1970-74. Mem. NASW, Assn. Jewish Community Orgn. Pers. (v.p. 1984-89), Jewish Communal Svc. Assn., Assn. Fundraising Profls., Acad. Cert. Social Workers, Rotary. Democrat. Avocation: writing poetry. Home: 2729 Goodwood Ct Sarasota FL 34235-0964 E-mail: mardenparu@comcast.net.

PARUCHURI, PHANI K. physician; b. Nizamabad, India, June 2, 1958; s. Koteswara Rao and Vanaja Devi (Kodali) P.; m. Vijayasre Velagapudi, Feb. 7, 1993; children: Venkata, Vishnavi. MB BS, Osmania Med. Coll., 1982, MS, 1991. Diplomate Am. Bd. Anesthesiology, Am. Bd. Pain Medicine, Am. Acad. Pain Mgmt. Resident Gandhi Hosp., Hyderabad, India, 1985-88; intern Bronx (N.Y.) Lebanon Hosp. Ctr., 1989-90; resident in anesthesiology St. Joseph Hosp. and Med. Ctr., Paterson, N.J., 1990-93; attending physician in anesthesiology DMC-Hutzel Hosp., Detroit, 1994-98; attending physician anaesthesiology King Drew Med. Ctr., L.A., 1998—99; pvt. practice in pain mgmt., 1999—. Author: (poetry) Kauyasudha, 1981. Mem. Am. Acad. Pain Mgmt., Soc. Physicians Pain Practice, Am. Soc. Reg. Anaesthesia. Business E-Mail: pkparuchuri.pk@verizon.net.

PARVIZI, YADOLLAH LLOYD, engineer, consultant; b. Azerbayjan, Aran, Iran, Jan. 1, 1937; came to U.S., 1982; s. Ali Parvizi and Jeiran Saleh; m. Parvin Parviz; children: Human, Ramin. MSEE, U. Tehran, Iran, 1960; postgrad., U. Stanford, 1971, U. Santa Clara, 1971. Pres., CEO, chmn. bd. Ministry Energy, Tehran, 1970-82; v.p. engring. Energytech, Inc., Long Beach, Calif., 1982—. Dir. transmission engring. and distbn. projects Ministry Energy, Tehran, 1961-70. Mem. IEEE (sr.), AEE, Assn. Energy Engrs. Achievements include patent for energy saving instructions for commercial and industrial facilities. Avocations: book writing, engineering research. Office: Energytech Inc PO Box 14447 Long Beach CA 90853-4447 E-mail: energyparvizi@aol.com.

PARYANI, SHYAM BHOJRAJ, radiologist; b. Bhavnagar, Gujarat, India, July 18, 1956; came to U.S., 1966; s. Bhojraj Thakurdas and Sarswati (Shewarkanani) P.; m. Sharon Dale Goldman, May 12, 1979; children: Lisa Ann, Jason Bhojraj, Gregory Shyam. BSEE, U. Fla., 1975, MSEE, MD, U. Fla., 1979. Diplomate Am. Bd. of Radiology. Intern U. Tex., M.D. Anderson Hosp., Houston, 1979-80; resident Stanford (Calif.) U. Hosp., 1980-83, chief resident, 1983; dir. Williams Cancer Ctr., Bapt. Med. Ctr., Jacksonville, Fla., 1983—, Fla. Cancer Ctr., Jacksonville, 1985—. Bd. dirs. Bapt. Med. Ctr., Jacksonville, 1986—, Meml. Med. Ctr., Jacksonville, 1987—, Meth. Hosp., Jacksonville, 1988—. Contbr. articles to profl. jours. Pres. Am. Cancer Soc., Jacksonville, 1992; bd. dirs. Jacksonville C. of C., 1991; adv. bd. Boy Scouts, 1990—. Mem. Am. Cancer Soc. (pres. 1992), Rotary Club. Republican. Hindu. Achievements include patent in Scott-Paryani Quick Implanter. Office: Fla Cancer Ctr 3599 University Blvd S Ste 1500 Jacksonville FL 32216-7400

PARZEN, EMANUEL, statistical scientist; b. N.Y.C., Apr. 21, 1929; s. Samuel and Sarah (Getzel) P.; m. Carol Tenowitz, July 12, 1959; children: Sara Leah, Michael Isaac. AB in Math., Harvard U., 1949; MA, U. Calif., Berkeley, 1951, PhD, 1953. Research scientist Columbia, 1953-56, asst. prof. math. statistics, 1955-56; faculty Stanford, 1956-70, asso. prof. statistics, 1959-64, prof., 1964-70; prof. statistics State U. N.Y. at Buffalo, 1970-73, prof. statis. sci., 1973-78; distinguished prof. statistics Tex. A and M U., College Station, 1978—. Guest prof. IMperial Coll., London, 1961-62; vis. prof. MIT, 1964-65, Harvard U., 1976, 88, Ctr. for Advanced Study in Behavioral Scis., 1983-84. Author: Stochastic Processes, 1962, Modern Probability Theory and its Applications, 1960, Time Series Analysis Papers, 1967, also articles. Fellow AAAS, Internat. Statis. Inst., Am. Statis. Assn., Royal Statis. Soc., Inst. Math. Statistics; mem. Am. Math. Soc., Soc. Indsl. and Applied Math., Bernoulli Soc., N.Y. Acad. Scis., Phi Beta Kappa, Sigma Xi. Achievements include research in time series analysis, non-parametric statistical data modeling, change analysis. Office: Tex A&M U Dept Stats College Station TX 77843-3143 E-mail: eparzen@stat.tamu.edu.

PASACHOFF, JAY MYRON, astronomer, educator; b. N.Y.C., July 1, 1943; s. Samuel S. and Anne (Traub) P.; m. Naomi Schwartz, Mar. 31, 1974; children: Eloise Hilary, Deborah Donna. AB, Harvard U., 1963, AM (NSF fellow), 1965, PhD (NSF fellow, N.Y. State Regents fellow for advanced grad. study), 1969. Research physicist Air Force Cambridge Research Labs., Bedford, Mass., 1968-69; Menzel research fellow Harvard Coll. Obs., Cambridge, 1969-70; rsch. fellow Hale Obs., Carnegie Instn., Washington, and Calif. Inst. Tech., Pasadena, 1970-72; dir. Hopkins Obs. Williams Coll., Williamstown, Mass., 1972—, chmn. astronomy dept., 1972-77, 91-92, asst. prof. astronomy, 1972-77, assoc. prof., 1977-84, prof., 1984, Field Meml. prof. of astronomy, 1984—. Adj. asst. prof. astronomy U. Mass., Amherst, 1975-77, adj. assoc. prof., 1977-83, adj. prof., 1986-90; vis. colleague and vis. assoc. prof. astronomy Inst. for Astronomy, U. Hawaii, 1980-81; vis. scientist Inst. d'Astrophysique, Paris, 1988; mem. Inst. Advanced Study, Princeton, 1989-90, Harvard-Smithsonian Ctr. for Astrophysics, 1993-94, 2001-02; total and other solar eclipse expdns., Mass., 1959, Que., Can., 1963, Mex., 1970, asst. dir. Harvard-Smithsonian-Nat. Geog. Expdn., P.E.I., Can., 1972, NSF expdn., Harvard-Smithsonian-Williams Expdn., Kenya, 1973; NSF expdn., Colombia, 1973 (annular eclipse), Australia, 1974, Pacific Ocean, 1977, Man., Can., 1979, NSF expdn., India, 1980, Pacific Ocean, 1981, Java, Indonesia, 1983, Miss., 1984 (annular eclipse), Papua New Guinea, 1984, Sumatra, Indonesia, 1988, Hawaii 1989 (partial eclipse), Finland, 1990, Hawaii, 1991, Calif., 1992 (annular eclipse), Pacific near Africa, 1992, N.H., 1994 (annular eclipse), Chile, 1994, India, 1995, Israel, 1996 (partial eclipse), Mongolia, 1997, Aruba, 1998, Malaysia, 1998 (annular eclipse), Australia, 1999, Romania, 1999, Seattle, 2000, Calif., 2000, Zambia, 2001, Costa Rica, 2001; guest investigator NASA Orbiting Solar Obs.-8, 1975-79, NASA Solar and Heliospheric Obs., 1999-2000; Carter lectr., New Zealand, 1998. Author: Contemporary Astronomy, 1977, 4th edit., 1989, Astronomy Now, 1978, Astronomy: From Earth to the Universe, 1979, 6th edit., 2002, A Brief View of Astronomy, 1986, First Guide to Astronomy, 1988, First Guide to the Solar System, 1990, Journey Through the Universe, 1992; co-author: (with Marc L. Kutner, Naomi Pasachoff) Student Study Guide to Contemporary Astronomy, 1977, (with

Kutner, Pasachoff and N.P. Kutner) Student Study Guide to Astronomy Now, 1978; (with M.L. Kutner) University Astronomy, 1978, Invitation to Physics, 1981; (with N. Pasachoff, T. Cooney) Physical Science, 1983, 2d edit., 1990, Earth Science, 1983, 2d edit., 1990; (with D.H. Menzel) A Field Guide to the Stars and Planets, 2d edit., 1983, 3d edit., 1992, 4th edit., 2000; (with R. Wolfson) Physics, 1987, 2nd edit., 1995, 3rd edit., 1999 (Extended with Modern Physics, 1989, 2nd edit. 1995, 3rd edit. 1999), (with N. Pasachoff, R.W. Clark, M.H. Westermann) Physical Science Today, 1987; (with N. Pasachoff and others) Discover Science, 7 vols., 1989; (with Michael Covington) Cambridge Eclipse Photography Guide, 1993; (with Len Holder and James DeFranza) Calculus, 1994, Single Variable Calculus, 1994, Multivariable Calculus, 1995; (with Edward Cheng, Patrick Osmer and Hyron Spinrad) The Farthest Things in the Universe, 1994; editor (with J. Percy) The Teaching of Astronomy, 1990, (with Leon Golub) The Solar Corona, 1997, (with Roberta J. M. Olson) Fire in the Sky: Comets and Meteors, the Decisive Centuries in British Art and Science, 1998, Astronomy, 1998, Sound and Light, 1999; (with Alex Filippenko) The Cosmos: Astronomy at the New Millennium, 2000; assoc. editor: Jour. Irreproducible Results, 1972-94, Annals of Improbable Rsch., 1994—; abstractor from Am. jours. for Solar Physics, 1968-78; cons. editor McGraw-Hill Ency. Sci. and Tech., 1983—; co-editor-in-chief (with S.P. Parker), McGraw-Hill Ency. of Astronomy, 1993; cons. Random House Dictionary, 1983-86, Nat. Geographic Atlas, 5th edit., 1981, 6th edit., 1990; phys. sci. com. World Book Encyclopedia, 1989-95, cons., 1996—; contbr. articles to profl. jours. and encys., articles and photographs to non-tech. publs. Recipient bronze medal Nikon Photo Contest Internat., 1971, photograph aboard NASA Voyagers, 1977, Dudley award Dudley Obs., 1985; grantee NSF, 1973-75, 79-83, 88—, Nat. Geog. Soc., 1973-86, 91—, Rsch. Corp., 1973-78, 82-88, Getty Found., 1994-95, NASA, 1999-2000. Fellow AAAS (chair sect. D 1987-88, 97-98), Royal Astron. Soc., Am. Phys. Soc. (mem.-at-large Am. Phys. Soc./Am. Assn. Physics Tchrs. Forum on Edn. 1995-98), N.Y. Acad. Sci., Internat. Planetarium Soc.; mem. AAUP (chpt. pres. 1977-80), Internat. Astron. Union (U.S. nat. rep. Commn. on Tchg. Astronomy 1976—, chair Eclipse Working Group 1991—, rep. to Com. on Tchg. Sci. of Internat. Coun. Sci. Unions 1991-93, v.p. com. on edn. and devel. 2000—), Am. Astron. Soc. (astronomy edn. adv. bd. 1990-97, astronomy news com. 1991-96), Astron. Soc. Pacific, Union Radio Sci., Am. Assn. Physics Tchrs. (astronomy com. 1983-87), Sigma Xi (chpt. pres. 1973-74, 95—, nat. lectr. 1993-97), Phi Beta Kappa. Home: 1305 Main St Williamstown MA 01267-2630 Office: Williams Coll Hopkins Obs Williamstown MA 01267-2565 E-mail: jay.m.pasachoff@williams.edu.

PASAHOW, LYNN H(AROLD), lawyer; b. Ft. Eutiss, Va., Mar. 13, 1947; s. Samuel and Cecelia (Newman) P.; m. Leslie Aileen Cobb, June 11, 1969; 1 child, Michael Alexander. AB, Stanford U., 1969; JD, U. Calif., Berkeley, 1972. Bar: Calif. 1972, U.S. Ct. Appeals (9th cir.) 1972, U.S. Dist. Ct. (no. dist.) Calif. 1973, U.S. Dist. Ct. (cen. dist.) Calif. 1974, U.S. Supreme Ct. 1976, U.S. Dist. Ct. (ea. dist.) Calif. 1977, U.S. Ct. Appeals (fed. cir.) 1990. Law clk. judge U.S. Dist. Ct. (no. dist.) Calif., San Francisco, 1972-73; assoc. McCutchen, Doyle, Brown & Enersen, Palo Alto, Calif., 1973-79, ptnr. San Francisco, 1979-2001, Fenwick & West LLP, 2001—. Attys. adv. panel Bay Area Biosci. Ctr., 1993—; mem. adv. bd. Berkeley Ctr. for Law and Tech., 1998—. Author: Pretrial and Settlement Conferences in Federal Court, 1983; co-author: Civil Discovery and Mandatory Disclosure: A Guide to Effective Practice, 1994; contbr. articles to profl. jours. Mem. ABA, Calif. Bar Assn. Democrat. Office: Fenwick & West LLP Two Palo Alto Sq Palo Alto CA 94306 E-mail: lpasahow@fenwick.com. *Notable cases include: Amazon.com v. Barnes and Nobles.com, duPont vs. Cetus, PCR patent litigation, Omega Zip Disk litigation, nicotine patch patent litigation, University of California & Vysis v. Oncor FISH litigation.*

PASCAL, AMY, film company executive; b. 1958; BA, U. of Calif., Los Angeles. V.p. of prod. Fox, 1986—87, Columbia, 1987—89, exec. v.p. of prod., 1989—94; pres. of prod. Turner Pictures, 1994—96; pres. Columbia Pictures, Culver City, Calif., 1996-99, chmn., 1999—. Office: Columbia Pictures 10202 Washington Blvd Culver City CA 90232-3119*

PASCAL, C(ECIL) BENNETT, classics educator; b. Chgo., May 4, 1926; s. Jack and Goldie (Zeff) P.; m. Ilene Joy Shulman, Feb. 1, 1959; 1 child, Keith Irwin. BA, UCLA, 1949, MA, 1950, Harvard U., 1953, PhD, 1956. Instr. U. Ill., Champaign, 1955-56, Cornell U., Ithaca, N.Y., 1957-60; asst. prof., then assoc. prof. U. Oreg., Eugene, 1960-75, prof. classics, 1975-96, prof. emeritus, 1996—, head dept., various years - 1965-85. Author: Cults of Cisalpine Gaul, 1964; contbr. articles to profl. jours. Active Eugene Bicycle Com., 1971-83. Wwith USN, 1944-46. Traveling fellow, Italy, Harvard U., 1956-57, Fulbright-Hays fellow, Rome, 1967-68. Mem. Am. Philol. Assn., Classical Assn. Pacific N.W. (pres. 1965-66), AAUP, Archeol. Inst. of Am. (past pres., sec. Eugene Soc.) Democrat. Jewish. Avocations: skiing, fishing, novel writing. Home: 330 Fulvue Dr Eugene OR 97405-2788 Office: U Oreg Dept Classics Eugene OR 97403 E-mail: cbpasc@darkwing.uoregon.edu.

PASCAL, NAOMI BRENNER, editor-in-chief, publishing executive; b. Bklyn., Mar. 13, 1926; d. Mortimer and Sylvia (Freehof) Brenner; m. Paul Pascal, June 27, 1948; children: David Morris, Janet Brenner. BA, Wellesley Coll., 1946. Editor Vanguard Press, Inc., N.Y.C., 1946-48, U. N.C. Press, Chapel Hill, N.C., 1948-50, 52-53, U. Wash. Press, 1953-75, editor-in-chief, 1976—, assoc. dir., 1985—. Dir. Assn. Am. Univ. Presses, 1976-78; cons. editor Scholarly Pub. jour., Toronto, Ont., Can., 1979— ; del. Wash. State Gov.'s Conf. on Library and Info. Services, Olympia, 1978-79. Co-author: Glossary Typesetting Terms, 1994; contbr. chpts. to books, articles to profl. jours. Durant scholar, 1945; recipient constituency award Assn. Am. Univ. Presses, 1991. Mem. Women in Scholarly Pub., Assn. Asian Am. Studies, Native Am. Art Studies Assn., Phi Beta Kappa (treas. Alpha of Wash. chpt. 1975-78). Office: U Wash Press PO Box 50096 Seattle WA 98145-5096

PASCAL, ROGER, lawyer; b. Chgo., Mar. 16, 1941; s. Samuel A. and Harriet E. (Hartman) P.; m. Martha Hecht, June 16, 1963; children: Deborah, Diane, David AB with distinction, U. Mich, 1962; JD cum laude, Harvard U., 1965. Bar: Ill. 1965, U.S. Dist. Ct. (no. dist.) Ill. 1965, U.S. Ct. Appeals (7th cir.) 1969, U.S. Supreme Ct. 1976, Wis. 1985, U.S. Ct. Appeals (2d, 6th, 9th and 10th cirs.) 186. Assoc. Schiff Hardin & Waite, Chgo., 1965-71, ptnr., 1972—. Adj. prof. law Northwestern U. Law Sch., 1994—. Bd. dirs., mem. exec. com. Chgo. Law Enforcement Study Group, 1975-80, pres., 1978-80; pres. Harvard Law Soc. Ill., 1976-78; bd. dirs. ACLU of Ill., 1984—, gen. counsel, 1986—. Mem. ABA (antitrust, intellectual property, and litigation sects.), Pub. Interest Law Initiative (bd. dirs. 1989—, v.p. 1995-97, pres. 1997-98), Fund for Justice (v.p., bd. dirs. 1986-97), Chgo. Coun. Lawyers (bd. dirs. 1970-74, 80-84), Chgo. Legal Assistance Found. (bd. dirs. 1985-88), Univ. Club, Met. Club, Phi Beta Kappa. Office: Schiff Hardin & Waite 6600 Sears Tower Chicago IL 60606

PASCALE, DANIEL RICHARD, lawyer; b. Racine, Wis., Mar. 22, 1940; s. Domenic and Fannie Colette (Julian) P.; m. Mary Sara McDonald, June 28, 1986; 1 child, Alexander. AB cum laude, Harvard U., 1962; JD, U. Chgo., 1965. Bar: Ill. 1966, U.S. Ct. Appeals (7th cir.) 1967, U.S. Dist. Ct. (no. dist.) Ill. 1969, U.S. Supreme Ct. 1972. Asst. corp. counsel City of Chgo., 1966-72, chief appellate atty., 1972-79, 1st dep. corp. counsel, 1979-84; assoc. Rudnick & Wolfe, Chgo., 1984-87, ptnr., 1987-90; judge Circuit Ct. of Cook County, Ill., 1990-94, 96-98; adminstrv. dir. Adminstrv. Office of Ill. Cts., Chgo., 1995-96; sr. corp. aty. Dean Foods Co., 1999—. Bd. dirs. DeKoven Found., Racine, 1986—, The Church Home/Montgomery Pl., 1998--; adv. bd. Art Resources in Teaching, Chgo., 1987-94; v.p. Episcopal Homes Mgmt., Inc., Milw., 1988-94. Mem. ABA, Fed. Bar Assn., Ill. Bar Assn., Chgo. Bar Assn., Justinian Soc., Union League Club Chgo., English-Speaking Union. Independent. Episcopalian.

PASCALE, JANE FAY, pathologist; b. New Haven, May 20, 1932; d. John Adam and Madeline J. (Pompano) P.; m. Joseph H. Kite Jr., Aug. 6, 1970. BA, Mount Holyoke Coll., 1954; MD, U. Chgo., 1959. Cert. anat. and clin. pathology Am. Bd. Pathology; diplomate Nat. Bd. Med. Examiners. Intern, resident in pathology Yale-New Haven Hosp., 1959-63; NIH-NCI spl. fellow dept. microbiology Yale U. Sch. Medicine, 1963-64; NIH-NCI spl. fellow Inst. de Recherches Scientifiques sur le Cancer, Villejuif, France, 1964-66; asst. in pathology Mass. Gen. Hosp. and Harvard Med. Sch., Boston, 1966-68; asst. prof. clin. pathology Yale U. Sch. Medicine, New Haven, 1968-69; attending pathologist Erie County Med. Ctr., Buffalo, 1969-95; clin. asst. prof. pathology SUNY, 1969-90, clin. asst. prof. microbiology, 1991—. Mem. scientific adv. bd. Infectech, Inc., Sharon, Pa., 1995—; scientific del. Citizen Amb. Program People-to-People Internat. Contbr. articles to profl. jours. Recipient Physician's Recognition award AMA, 1981-99. Fellow Am. Soc. Clin. Pathologists, Coll. Am. Pathologists; mem. AMA, N.Y. Acad. Scis., Am. Soc. Cytology, Assn. Clin. Scientists. Methodist. Achievements include research in immunopathology of tuberculosis and autoimmune disease.

PASCARELLA, HENRY WILLIAM, lawyer; b. New Haven, Aug. 15, 1933; s. John Manlio and Mary (Iannotti) P.; m. Tessa Peruzzi, Jan. 28, 1967; children: Averardo, Leonora, Cassandra. BS in Econs., U. Pa., 1955; LLB, Yale U., 1958. Bar: Conn. 1958, U.S. Supreme Ct. 1963. Ptnr. Badger, Fisher, Cohen & Barnett and predecessors, Greenwich, Conn., 1959-73; sr. counsel to Taylor Cooper & Alcorn, 1978—. Pres., dir. The Timber Trails Corp. Sherman, Conn.; dir. Nine West Group, Inc., 1995-99. Author column, theater critic Greenwich Times, 1964-67. Dir. Planned Parenthood League of Conn., Greenwich coun. Boy Scouts Am., 1990-96. Served to lt. (j.g.) USCG, 1959. Me.m ABA, Greenwich Bar Assn. (pres. 1967), Conn. Bar Assn., Yale Club (N.Y.C.), Belle Haven Club (Greenwich). Home: 675 Steamboat Rd Greenwich CT 06830-7140 E-mail: henry@pascarellalaw.com.

PASCARELLA, PERRY JAMES, author, editor, speaker; b. Bradford, Pa., Apr. 11, 1934; s. James and Lucille Margaret (Monti) P.; m. Carol Ruth Taylor, May 4, 1957; children: Cynthia, Elizabeth. AB, Kenyon Coll., 1956; Coll. William and Mary, William and Mary Coll., 1957; postgrad., George Washington U., 1958. Credit reporter Dun & Bradstreet, Cleve., 1956, 60; from asst. editor to mng. editor Steel mag., 1961-69; mng. editor Industry Week mag., 1970-71, exec. editor, 1971-86, editor-in-chief, 1986-89; v.p. editorial Penton Pub. Inc., 1989-96. Lectr. in field. Author: Technology-Fire in a Dark World, 1979, Humanagement in the Future Corporation, 1981, The New Achievers, 1984, The Purpose-Driven Organization, 1989, The Ten Commandments of the Workplace, 1996, Leveraging People and Profit, 1998, Christ-Centered Leadership, 1999; co-author: Optimistic Outlooks, 1982, Creating a Global Agenda, 1984, Leadership in a New Era, 1994, The New Bottom Line, 1996. Lt. comdr. USNR, 1957-60. Recipient Disting. Service award Kenyon Coll., 1975, 81, Am. Bus. Press Crain award, 1992; Carnegie scholar, 1952-56 Mem. World Future Soc., U. Akron Inst. for Future Studies (bd. advisors). Presbyterian (elder). Home: 30413 Winsor Dr Cleveland OH 44140-1143

PASCASIO, ANNE, health science educator; b. Pitts., Dec. 29, 1924; d. Anthony and Filomena (DiPippa) P. BS, U. Pitts., 1946, M.Ed., 1950, PhD, 1966; cert. of proficiency, D.T. Watson Sch. Phys. Therapy, 1953. Tchr. health and phys. edn. Turtle Creek Pub. Schs., 1946-52; staff phys. therapist Children's Hosp. Pitts., 1953-56; chief phys. therapist Hosp. U. Pa., Phila., 1956-59; cons. div. edn. Am. Phys. Therapy Assn., 1959-62; instr. D.T. Watson Sch. Phys. Therapy, part time, 1962-66; assoc. research prof. Sch. Nursing U. Pitts., 1967, asst. to vice chancellor health professions, 1967-68, dean Sch. Health Related Professions, 1969-82, prof. health related professions, 1982—. Cons. Kuwait Ministry Pub. Health, 1985— ; mem. nat. adv. allied health professions Council NIH, 1971-73; cons. rehab. services adminstrn. HEW, 1971-72; mem. Nat. Commn. for Study Accreditation Selected Health Ednl. Programs, 1970-72; chmn. Gov.'s Com. on Health (Manpower) Edn., 1974-76; mem. adv. com. on accreditation and instl. eligibility U.S. Office Edn.; Bd. dirs., mem. exec. com. Hosp. Council Western Pa.; mem. profl. adv. com. to bd. dirs. Nat. Easter Seal Soc. for Crippled Children and Adults, 1978-81; Florence Strattom lectr. Boston Bouve' Coll., Northeastern U., 1968; mem. Nat. Adv. Council on Health Professions Edn., 1980-84, Pa. State Bd. Med. Edn. and Licensure, 1981-83 Editorial bd. Topics in Geriatric Rehabilitation. Contbr. articles to profl. lit., chpts. to books. Fellow Am. Soc. Allied Health Professions; Mem. Am. Assn. Higher Edn., Am. Soc. Allied Health Professions, AMA (adv. com. edn. allied health professions and services Council Med. Edn. 1969-72), Pi Lambda Theta. Republican. Rooman Catholic. Address: 1290 Boyce Rd Apt C223 Pittsburgh PA 15241-3948

PASCH, ALAN, philosopher, educator; b. Cleve., Dec. 1, 1925; s. P. Jerome and Esther (Broverman) P.; m. Eleanor Kudlich Berna, Dec. 27, 1950; 1 child, Rachel. BA, U. Mich., 1949; MA, New Sch. Social Research, 1952; PhD, Princeton U., 1955; Bamford fellow, 1955-56. Instr. philosophy Ohio State U., 1956-59, asst. prof., 1959-60; assoc. prof. philosophy U. Md., College Park, 1960-67, prof., 1967-97, prof. emeritus, 1997—. Author: Experience and the Analytic, 1958; also articles, revs. Active ACLU. Served with AUS, 1944-46, PTO. Mem. AAUP, Am. Philos. Assn. (exec. dir. 1969-72, sec.-treas. Eastern div. 1965-68), Metaphys. Soc. Am., Washington Philosophy Club (pres. 1978-79), Washington Rare Book Group. Office: U Md Dept Philosophy College Park MD 20742-0001

PASCHAL, BETH CUMMINGS, journalist, editor; b. Lohrville, Iowa, June 26, 1917; d. Harry Ross and Agnes (Baird) Cummings. m. George Washington Paschal Jr., Dec. 20, 1944 (dec. Feb. 1995); children: George Washington III, Laura Huston, Robert Cummings. BS, Iowa State U., 1939. Assoc. editor Farm Jour., Phila., 1939-45; bd. dirs. N.C. Art Soc., Raleigh, 1959-69, v.p., pres., 1961-68; bd. dirs. N.C. Mus. Art, 1964—, vice chmn. new bldg. campaign, 1977-78, works of art com., 1983—2002, docent, 1955-87, donor, 1970, docent emeritus, 1987—, trustee emeritus, 1995—. Chmn. 1st N.C. Mus. of Art Beaux Arts Ball, 1973. Editor: A Celebration of Art and Cookery, 1976; columnist Trident Mag., 1940-43; editor State Med. Aux. Newsletter, 1955-63. Arch. selection com. Fine Arts Ctr. Wake Forest U., Winston-Salem, N.C., 1975; chmn. mus. com. Gov. Cultural Adv. Coun., Raleigh, 1980; hon. chmn. N.C. Mus. Art 50th Anniversary Gala, 1997; pres. N.C. State U. Friends of the Libr., 1979-80. Named Tarheel of Week, Raleigh News and Observer, 1965; named to YWCA Acad. of Women, 1983, North Caroliniana Soc., 1998; recipient honor, N.C. Mus. Art, Acquisition of Art, 1974, Lifetime Achievement award, N.C. Mus. Art and N.C. Art Soc., 2001, Alumni Merit award, Iowa State U., 1980, Raleigh medal of Arts, 1986, Phi Beta Kappa award, 1995. Mem. Jr. League Raleigh, Nat. Humanities Ctr. (dir. coun.), Carolina Country Club, Nine O'Clock Cotillion, Mortar Bd., Delta Delta Delta, Theta Sigma Phi. Avocations: reading, tennis, travel, bread baking, sewing. Home: 3334 Alamance Dr Raleigh NC 27609-6902

PASCHAL, JAMES ALPHONSO, counselor, educator secondary school; b. Americus, Ga., Aug. 11, 1931; s. Bouie L. and Mary L. (Jackson) P.; widower Mar. 24, 1988; 1 child, Maret E. BA, Xavier U., New Orleans, 1957; MS, Ft. Valley State Coll., 1963; EdD, U. S.C., 1977. Cert. adminstr., tchr. counselor, social worker, S.C. Tchr. grade 5 East View Elem. Sch., Americus, Ga., 1957-59; libr., counselor Staley Jr. H.S., 1959-65; sch. social worker Americus City System, 1965-67; coord. student svcs. Augusta (Ga.) Tech., 1967-78; dir. student affairs Benedict Coll., Columbia, S.C., 1978-82; coord. facilities S.C. Commn. on Higher Edn., 1982-89; counselor Swainsboro (Ga.) H.S., 1990-91, Monroe H.S., Albany, Ga., 1991—. Vol. Caritas, New Orleans, 1953-57, Friendship House, New Orleans, 1955-56. With U.S. Army, 1951-53, Korea. Recipient scholarship Ft. Valley (Ga.) State Coll., 1948, grad. assistantship, Ft. Valley State Coll., 1962-63. Mem. NEA, ACA. Ga. Counseling Assn., Alpha Phi Alpha (v.p. 1972-74). Republican. Roman Catholic. Avocations: reading, walking, helping others. Home: PO Box 5523 Albany GA 31706-5523

PASCHALIDIS, IOANNIS, engineering educator; b. Athens, Greece, Apr. 27, 1968; came to U.S., 1991; m. Georgia Mourtzinou; 1 child, Aris. Diploma, Nat. Tech. U. Athens, 1991; MS, MIT, 1993, PhD, 1996. Assoc. prof. engring. Boston U., 2000—. Office: Boston U Coll Engring 44 Cummington St Boston MA 02215

PASCHALL, LEE MCQUERTER, retired communications consultant; b. Sterling, Colo., Jan. 21, 1922; s. Lee McQuerter and Agnes (Woldridge) P.; m. Bonnie Jean Edwards, Oct. 24, 1942; children: Patricia Ann Grillos, Stephen Lee, David Edward. BA, U. Ala., 1957; MA, George Washington U., 1964. Served with U.S. Army, 1940-46; communications engr. Colo. Air N.G., Denver, 1946-51; commd. maj. U.S. Air Force, 1951, advanced through grades to lt. gen., 1974, ret., 1978; ind. cons. Springfield, Va., 1978-81; pres., chief exec. officer Am. Satellite Co., Rockville, Md., 1981-84, chmn., 1984-85. Dir. Gen. Data Comm. Industries. Contbr. numerous articles to profl. publs. Mem. com. rev. nat. communications system initiatives NRC, 1982-88. Decorated Legion of Merit with oak leaf cluster; decorated disting. service medals; recipient Eascon IEEE, 1979 Mem. Armed Forces Comms.-Electronics Assn. (chpt. pres., nat. bd. dirs. Disting. Svc.), Air Force Assn., Phi Beta Kappa. Mem. Christian Ch. (Disciples Of Christ). Home and Office: 1513 Hampton Hills Cir Mc Lean VA 22101-6018

PASCHKE, JERRY BRYAN, lawyer; b. Palmdale, Calif., Aug. 6, 1965; s. Donald Joseph and Diana Marie (Scott) P. BS, St. John's U., Collegeville, Minn., 1988; JD, Hamline U., St. Paul, 1991. Bar: Minn. 1991, Army Ct. Mil. Rev. 1992, U.S. Magistrates Ct. 1993. Commd. 1st lt. U.S. Army, 1992, advanced through grades to capt., 1992; post judge advocate U.S. Army-Sierra Army Depot, Herlong, Calif., 1992-94; brigade trial counsel U.S. Army-Camp Stanley, Uijongbu, South Korea, 1994-95; legal instr. U.S. Army-Ft. Huachuca, Sierra Vista, Ariz., 1995-97, chief criminal law, 1997-98, mil. magistrate, 1995-97; acct. Accts.-On-Call, Mpls., 1998—; adminstrv. law officer USAR, Ft. Snelling, Minn., 1998—. Mem. landlord-tenant hotline Minn. Pub. Interest Rsch. Group, Mpls., 1989; advisor DeMolay, Reno, 1992-94. Decorated Army Commendtion medal, Meritorious Svc. medal. Mem. Masons, Order St. Barbara. Avocations: hiking, chess, travel, bowling. Home: Apt 212 14625 Portland Ave Burnsville MN 55306-6704

PASCHKE, TERESA ANN, artist, educator; b. Mpls., Dec. 1, 1962; d. Kenneth George and Joan Marie (Schreader) P. BFA, Mpls. Coll. Art and Design, 1985; MFA, U. Kans., 1998. Instr. art and design U. Kans., Lawrence, 1995-97, asst. to grad. dir., 1995-98; asst. prof. Iowa State U., Ames, 2000—. Homebound vol. Mpls. Pub. Libr., 1992; Homeward vol., 2002--. Dendel scholar Handweavers Guild Am., 1996, Nolte scholar U. Minn., 1991, Allis scholar North Hennepin C.C., 1982; grad. honors fellow U. Kans., 1996; Miller Faculty fellow. Mem. Foundns. in Art: Theory and Edn., Nat. Honor Soc., Surface Design Assn., Am. Craft Coun. Democrat. Avocations: camping, bicycling. Address: 225 S Hazel Ames IA 50010 E-mail: tpaschke@iastate.edu.

PASCHOUD, FRANÇOIS, university educator; b. Bern, Switzerland, Jan. 11, 1938; s. Maurice and Nelly (Suter) P.; m. Anne-Marie Chêne, July 24, 1978; children: Jerôme, Urbain. Lic. Letters, U. Lausanne, 1960, Litt.D., 1967. Mem. Swiss Inst., Rome, 1962-64; Wissenschaftlicher Mitarbeiter Thesaurus linguae Latinae, Munich, Fed. Republic of Germany, 1965-67; prof. extraordinarius, ordinarius U. Geneva, Switzerland, 1969-74, 1974— ; vis. mem. Inst. for Advanced Study, Princeton U., N.J., 1976-77, 83-84. Author: Roma aeterna, 1967; Translation, Commentary of Zosimus I, 1971, II 1 and II 2, 1979, III 1, 1986, III 2, 1989. Historia Agusta, V 1, 1996. Mem. Internat. Fedn. of Socs. of Classical Studies (sec. gen. 1974—), Soc. Latin Studies Paris, Groupe Romand des Etudes Grecques et Latines (pres. 1978-81), Fondation Hardt pour l'étude de l'antiquité Vandoeuvres Geneva (pres.), Real Academia Barcelona (corr. mem.).

PASCIUTO, JOSEPH DORIA, priest; b. Bklyn., June 27, 1945; s. Carmine Michael Pasciuto, Rose Marie (Doria) Pasciuto. BA, St. John's U., 1968, MBA, 1981; MDiv, Immaculate Conception Sem., Huntington, N.Y., 1991; MA in Theology, Immaculate Conception Sem., 1999. Ordination Roman Cath. Diocese Bklyn., 1991. CFO Local 371 AFSCME, N.Y.C., 1981—84; mgr. pers./labor rels Child Welfare Adminstrn., 1984—87; vicar Our Lady Help of Christians, Bklyn., 1991—99, Our Lady of Hope, Middle Village, Nebr., 1999—2000, St. Brendan, Bklyn., 2000—. Chaplain Boy Scouts Am., Bklyn., 2000—, Internat. Firefighters Assn., N.Y.C., 2001. Mem.: KC (chaplain 1995—, 4th degree L.I. Assembly 2001), Montauk Club. Democrat. Avocation: Avocations: music, reading, cooking. Home: 1525 E 12th St Brooklyn NY 11230 Office: Saint Brendan's Ch 1525 E 12th St Brooklyn NY 11230

PASCO, ALLAN HUMPHREY, literature educator; b. Nashville, Aug. 29, 1937; s. Ray Edwin and Bernedine May (Humphrey) P.; m. Dallas Marlene Christiansen, Dec. 29, 1960; children: Schuyler, Teague, Brandt, Chandar. BA, Whitman Coll., Walla Walla, Wash., 1960; MA, Northwestern U., 1961; PhD, U. Mich., 1968. Asst. prof. French U. Chgo., 1967-73; assoc. prof. French Purdue U., West Lafayette, Ind., 1973-79, prof. French, 1979-89; Hall disting. prof. 19th century lit. U. Kans., Lawrence, 1989—. Vis. prof. French UCLA, 1979; editorial bd. Purdue U. Press, 1975-78. Author: The Color Keys, 1976, Novel Configurations, 1987, Balzacian Montage, 1991, Allusion: A Literary Graft, 1994, Sick Heroes: French Society and Literature in the Romantic Age, 1997; editor: Purdue U. Monographs, 1977-87, Summa, 1990—, French Rev., 1989—, Nineteenth-Century French Studies, 1995—; co-editor: The Play of Terror in 19th Century France, 1996; contbr. articles to profl. jours. With U.S. Army, 1961-63. Recipient Cramer Teaching award, U. Kans., 1996, 99, 2000; Ctr. for Humanistic Studies fellow Purdue U., 1985, Lilly Libr. summer rsch. fellow, 1976, various rsch. fellow, 1969-88, Hall Ctr. Humanities fellow, U. Kans., 1996. Mem. MLA, Assn. Am. Tchrs. of French, Am. Soc. 18th Century Studies, Phi Sigma Iota, Phi Kappa Phi. Lutheran. Office: Hall Ctr for Humanities 105 Watkins Home 1540 Sunflower Rd Lawrence KS 66045-7618 E-mail: apasco@ku.edu.

PASCO, HANSELL MERRILL, retired lawyer; b. Thomasville, Ga., Oct. 7, 1915; s. John and Katherine (Merrill) P.; m. Williamine Carrington Lancaster, June 28, 1941; children: Hansell Merrill, Dabney, Robert, Elizabeth, Carrington. BA, Va. Mil. Inst., 1937; LL.B., U. Va., 1940. Bar: Va. bar 1939. Ptnr. Hunton & Williams, Richmond, Va., 1948-81, sr. counsel, 1981—, mng. partner, 1968-76. Chmn. State Counsel Higher Edn. for Va., 1978-80; trustee Protestant Episcopal Sem., Alexandria, Va., 1980-85. Served with U.S. Army, 1940-45. Office: Hunton & Williams Riverfront Plz E Tower PO Box 1535 Richmond VA 23218-1535

PASCOE, E(DWARD) RUDY, insurance sales executive; b. Sioux Falls, S.D., Oct. 13, 1948; s. Marvin E. Pascoe and Celesta M. (Heaton) Hymore; m. Janice A. Kistler, Sept. 2, 1967; children: Jennifer L., Matthew R., Stephen J. BE, U. S.D., 1972; postgrad., U. Iowa, 1972-74. CIC; cert. life underwriter. Tchr. Jo-Daviess Area Vocat. Ctr., Elizabeth, Ill., 1972-74; pvt. practice ins. sales, 1974—; personal line mgr. Herrling & Schmitt, Inc. Multi Line Ins. Agy., Freeport, Ill., 1981—. Vice coordinator Elizabeth Ambulance Corp., 1981—; fin. sec. Elizabeth United Meth. Ch., 1977—, others. Named one of Outstanding Young Men Am., Jaycees Am., 1969. Mem. Life Underwriters Assn. (sec./treas. 1976-77). Lodges: Lions (pres., v.p., sec./treas. 1973-81), Masons. Republican. Avocation: reading. Office: Herrling & Schmitt Inc PO Box 300 Freeport IL 61032-0300 E-mail: rudy.pascoe@wmanny.com.

PASCOE, PATRICIA HILL, state legislator, writer; b. Sparta, Wis., June 1, 1935; d. Fred Kirk and Edith (Kilpatrick) Hill; m. D. Monte Pascoe, Aug. 3, 1957; children: Sarah, Edward, William. BA, U. Colo., 1957; MA, U. Denver, 1968, PhD, 1982. Tchr. Sequoia Union High Sch. Dist., Redwood City, Calif. and Hayward (Calif.) Union High Sch. Dist., 1957-60; instr. Met. State Coll., Denver, 1969-75, Denver U., 1975-77, 81, research asst. bur. ednl. research, 1981-82; tchr. Kent Denver Country Day, Englewood, Colo., 1982-84; freelance writer Denver, 1985—; mem. Colo. Senate, Dist. 32, 1989—93, 1995—2003; chair minority caucus Colo. Senate, 1996-2000, chair policy and planning com., 2000—02, chair edn. com., 2002. Commr. Edn. Commn. of the States, Denver, 1975-82, 2001—. Contbr. articles to numerous publs. and jours. Bd. dirs. Samaritan House, 1990-94, Cystic Fibrosis Found., 1989-93; pres. East H.S. Parent Tchr. and Student Assn., Denver, 1984-85; mem. Moore Budget Adv. Com., Denver, 1966-72; legis. chmn. alumni bd. U. Colo., Boulder, 1987-89; del. Dem. Nat. Conv., San Francisco, 1984, N.Y.C., 1992; mem. Denver Woman's Press Club, 1986—, Colo. Arts Coalition, 1988-97; bd. dirs. Opera Colo., 1996-02. Mem. Soc. Profl. Journalists, Common Cause (bd. dirs. Denver chpt. 1986-88), Phi Beta Kappa. Presbyterian.

PASCOE, PERCY WILLARD, newspaper publisher; b. Little Rock, Jan. 31, 1930; s. Percy Willard and Oma Mae (Grizzle) P.; m. Delma Lucille Huff, Sept. 27, 1967. Student, Beaumont H.S., St. Louis, 1945-48. Pub. Cuba (Mo.) Free Press, 1960—, Steelville (Mo.) Star-Crawford Mirror, 1980—. Pres. bd. dirs. Retirement Homes, Inc., Cuba, 1975-97, v.p. bd. dirs., 1998-2000; sponsor Explorer Scouts, Bourbon, Mo., 1995, 96, 97; active Crawford County Historical Soc. (v.p. 2000-01); vol. Meals on Wheels; pres. Viva Cuba, 2000-01, Staff sgt. USAF, 1951-55. Named Small Bus. Advocate, Small Bus. Adminstrn., Mo., 1988; recipient 88 awards for journalistic work Mo. Press

Assn., Mo. State Tchrs. Assn., Nat. Newspaper Assn., Mo. Advt. Mgrs. Assn., 1960-77. Mem. Soc. Profl. Journalists. Democrat. Church of Christ. Avocation: woodworking. Office: Cuba Free Press 110 S Buchanan St Cuba MO 65453-0568

PASCOTTO, ROBERT DANIEL, cardiovascular/thoracic surgeon; b. N.Y.C., Nov. 16, 1940; s. Sarah Poscotto; m. Joan Posocotto, May 15, 1968; children: Tara, Robert Jr., Lea. BA in Medicine, Manhattan Coll., 1962; MD, Creighton U., 1966. Diplomate Nat. Bd. Med. Examiners, Am. Bd. Surgery, Am. Bd. Thoracic Surgery. Intern St. Vincent's Hosp. and Med. Ctr., N.Y.C., 1966-67, resident, 1967-71, resident in thoracic and cardiovascular surgery, 1973, resident in cardiothoracic surgery, 1974-75; cardiac surgeon Ind. U. Med. Ctr., Indpls., 1974-75, Cardiac Surg. Assn. of S.W. Fla., Fort Myers, Fla., 1975—. Clin. instr. surgery NYU Med. Sch., 1970-71; med. alumni adv. bd. admissions com. Creighton U. Sch. of Medicine, Omaha, 1993—; hosp. staff Lee Meml. Health System, Fort Myers, Fla., Cape Coral (Fla.) Hosp., Naples (Fla.) Cmty. Hosp., Columbia Regional Med. Ctr. of S.W. Fla., Fort Myers; spkr. in field. Maj. USAF, 1971-73. Recipient Man of Yr. award 1993, Appreciation award Lee County Med. Sch., 1988. Fellow Am. Coll. Cardiology, Am. Coll. Chest Physicians, ACS (mem. Fla. chpt.), mem. Soc. of Thoracic Surgeons, Am. Bd. of Thoracic Surgery, Am. Coll. of Cardiology (Fla. chpt.), Am. Coll. of Chest Physicians (mem. So. chpt., Fla. chpt.), Southern Thoracic Surg. Assn., The Creighton U. Surg. Soc., Fla. Thoracic Soc., Internat. Soc. of Cardiovascular Surgery (N.Am. chpt.), Fla. Soc. of Cardiovascular and Thoracic Surgeons, Am. Heart Assn. (cardiovascular surgery mem.), Internat. Soc. for Heart Transplant, Fla. Med. Assn., Lee County Med. Soc., Collier County Med. Soc., Michael E. DeBakey Internat. Surg. Soc. Office: Cardiac Surg Assocs of SW Fla 2675 Winkler Ave Ste 440 Fort Myers FL 33901-9329

PASCRELL, WILLIAM J., JR. congressman; b. Paterson, N.J., Jan. 25, 1937; s. William J. Sr. and Roffie (Loffredo) P., m. Elsie Marie Botto; children: William III, David, Glenn. BS, Fordham U., 1959; MA, Montclair State Coll., 1961; postgrad., Fairleigh Dickinson U. Tchr. Jr. High Sch., Clifton, N.J., 1962, Paramus (N.J.) High Sch., 1962-74; adult sch. tchr. Dwight Morrow High Sch., Englewood, N.J., 1969-70; prof. Fairleigh Dickinson U., Madison, 1963-68; dir. Dept. Pub. Works City of Paterson, 1974-77, dir. Dept. Policy Planning and Mgmt., 1977-87; mem. N.J. Gen. Assembly, 1988-97, chmn. higher edn. com., 1988-97, vice chmn. edn. com., 1988-97, mem. appropriations com., 1988-97; mayor City of Paterson, 1990-97; mem. U.S. Congress from 8th N.J. dist., 1997—; mem. small bus. com., transp. and infrastructure com. Pres. Paterson Bd. Edn., 1979-82; campaign coord. Robert A. Roe for Gov., N.J., 1977; regional coord. James Florio for Gov., Hudson County, N.J., 1981; active County Chairmen for Sen. Frank Lautenberg, N.J., 1982—; chmn. Passaic County Democrats, N.J., 1982—. With U.S. Army, 1961-67. Named Man of Yr., Mother Cabrini Soc., 1978, Am. Legion (John Road Post), 1983, St. Gerard's Parish, 1988, Assn. Retarded Citizens, 1991. Mem. N.J. Math. Coalition (bd. govs. 1991—), UNICO (Paterson chpt. Man of Yr., 1981), Italian Sport Club. Democrat. Roman Catholic. Office: US Ho of Reps 1722 Longworth House Office Bldg Washington DC 20515-0001*

PASCU, DAN, astronomer; b. Arad, Romania, July 20, 1938; came to U.S., 1941; s. Danila and Maria (Pojar) P.; m. Julia Fay Stephens, Aug. 28, 1965; children: David, Mark, Adam. BS in Astronomy, Case Western Res. U., 1961, MS in Astronomy, 1964; PhD in Astronomy, U. Va., Charlottesville, 1972. Astronomer U.S. Naval Obs., Washington, 1963—. Specialist in planetary satellite studies and solar sys. astrometry. Co-discoverer 14th moon of Saturn, Calypso, 1980; contbr. rsch. articles and review articles to profl. jours. Recipient NASA Group Achievement award, 1981, 86, Inaugural Newcomb award U.S. Naval Obs., 1983. Mem. Internat. Astron. Union, Am. Astron. Soc., Sigma Xi. Baptist. Achievements include developing techniques for astrometric observation of the planetary satellites. Office: US Naval Obs 3450 Massachusetts Ave NW Washington DC 20392-5420

PASCUAL, CARLOTA, painter; b. Cartagena, Murcia, Spain, Feb. 2, 1947; came to U.S., 1990; d. Carlos Pascual and Lucia Garcia; divorced; children: Eva Pineda, Carlos Pineda; m. Guillermo Saez. Student, Inst. Parramont Barcelona, Spain, 1971, Mus. Picasso, Barcelona, 1977, Mus. Modern Art, 1977, Dali Mus. Figueras, Spain, 1978, U. Complutense, Madrid, 1980, Mus. Prado, 1980, Mus. Modern Art, 1980. Represented by Ward Nasse Gallery, N.Y.C., 1997—. Creative cons. R.A. Jaquez Assocs., N.Y.C., 1995-97. Creator art style Fantastic Expressionism (copyright 1996); exhibited in group shows at Ariel Gallery, N.Y.C., 1992 (prize E), Agora Gallery, N.Y.C., 1994 (Soho Internat. Competition prize 1992, 94), Fla. Mus. Hispanic and L.Am. Art, Miami, 1995-96, Ward-Nasse Gallery, 1997-98, Internat. Salon 197, 1997, Howland Cultural Ctr., Beacon, N.Y., 2000, Highland Cultural Ctr. Art Gallery, 2001; one-woman shows include Nat. Ctr. Visual Art and Spanish Embassy, Buenos Aires, 1986, Sec. of Culture, Municipality of Buenos Aires, 1987, Immaculate Conception Ctr., Douglastown, N.Y.C., 1999; contbr. cover illustration to Palabras, 1994, Shame: Emotion that Limits Latinos, 1996, Venti d'Amore and L'Emersa Mediocrita, Trento, Italy; contbg. artist: New Art International, 1997; featured in Art in America Annual 1998-99 Guide to Museums, Galleries, Artists. Recipient Talent Spectrum Competition prize, Artis Spectrum Mag., N.Y., 1996; named Author of the Yr., Trento, Italy, 1999. Mem. Allied Artists Am. Inc., Audubon Artists, Inc. Roman Catholic. Avocations: writing poetry, sculpture, theatrical performance. Home: 431 W 204th St 2F New York NY 10034

PASCUAL, JUAN MANUEL, scientist, physician; b. Malaga, Spain, May 19, 1967; came to U.S., 1990; s. Juan and Guadalupe (Fernandez) P. MD, U. Granada, 1990; PhD in Molecular Physiology & Biophys., Baylor Coll. Medicine, 1995. Rsch. assoc. Baylor Coll. of Medicine, Houston, 1995; rsch. scientist Columbia U., N.Y.C., 1995-97; assoc. faculty dept. pediats. and neurology Columbia-Presbyn. Med. Ctr., 1997—; clin. tng. in pediatrics Washington U. Sch. Medicine, St. Louis, 1998. Mem. sci. adv. bd. Alzheimer's Assn.; spkr. in field. Contbr. articles to profl. jours. Recipient Rsch. award Regional Govt. of Andalucia, 1988, Pregradnate Rsch. award Cajap Inst., Madrid, 1988-89, Neurol. Scis. Academic Devel. award NIH, 1997. Mem. Soc. for Neurosci., Biophys. Soc., Soc. Gen. Physiologists, Am. Acad. Pediatrics. Avocations: ancient literature, philosophy of science, epistemology. Home: 61 W 62d St 21H New York NY 10023 Office: Columbia Univ Neurol Inst of NY 710 W 168th St New York NY 10032-2603

PASCUCCI, MARY FRANCES, pathologist; b. Pittston, Pa., Mar. 30, 1963; d. Secondo and SaraFine (Abate) P.; m. Donald George Francis, Oct. 5, 1991. BS cum laude, U. Scranton, 1985; DO, Phila. Coll. Osteo. Medicine., 1989. Rotating intern Lewiston Hosp., 1989-90; med. intern Geisinger Med. Ctr, Danville, Pa., 1990-91, resident in pathology, 1992-96. Mem. AMA, Pa. Med. Soc. (commn. on women physicians 1995-98), Coll. Am. Pathologists (rep.), Am. Soc. Clin. Pathologists (liaison), Pa. Assn. Pathologists, N.E. Path. Soc., Pa. Osteopathic Med. Assn., Kiwanis. Home: 133 Klinger Dr Sugarloaf PA 18249-9534 Office: Hazleton Pathology PC 101 W Broad St Hazleton PA 18201

PASE, MARILYN NELSEN, nurse, educator; b. Brigham City, Utah, Feb. 13, 1943; d. Daniel Clarence Nelsen and Aldine (Anderson) Nelsen Johns. BSN with high honors, U. Ala., Huntsville, 1974, BS in Biology with high honors, 1984; MSN, Vanderbilt U., 1975. RN, Ala., Utah, N.Mex. Staff nurse Med. Ctr. Hosp., Huntsville, 1974-77, LDS Hosp., Salt Lake City, 1977 summer; clin. preceptor for grad. students U. Ala., Birmingham, 1978, instr. nursing, then asst. prof. Huntsville, 1975-83; mem. nursing faculty Oakwood Coll., 1985-86; infection control nurse, employee health nurse Crestwood Hosp., 1984-86; staff nurse Meml. Med. Ctr., Las Cruces, N.Mex., 1987-91; asst. prof. dept. nursing N.Mex. State U., 1988-97, assoc. prof., 1997—, chair grad. program, 1998—. Cons., reviewer; contbr. articles to profl. jours., chpt. to textbook. Mem. APHA, ANA (cabinet (pres. 1991-92), N.Mex. Nurses Assn. (exec. bd. Dist. 14 1994, dist. pres. 1990-93, Nurse Rschr. award 1994), Sigma Theta Tau, Sigma Theta Tay, Pi Omega (pres.-elect 2002). Mem. Lds Ch. Avocations: organ, piano, reading, swimming. Office: Dept Nursing N Mex State U Las Cruces NM 88003

PASEK, JEFFREY IVAN, lawyer; b. Pitts., Apr. 4, 1951; m. Kathryn Ann Hirsh, Aug. 17, 1975; children: Joshua, Benjamin, Michael. BA, U. Pitts., 1973; JD, U. Pa., 1976. Bar: Pa. 1976, U.S. Dist. Ct. (ea. dist.) Pa. 1976, U.S. Ct. Appeals (3d cir.) 1976, U.S. Dist. Ct. (we. dist.) Pa. 1977, U.S. Supreme Ct. 1980, U.S. Dist. Ct. (mid. dist.) Pa. 1984, N.Y. 1988, N.J. 1988, U.S. Dist. Ct. N.J. 1988, U.S. Dist. Ct. (so. and ea. dists.) N.Y. 1989, U.S. Dist. Ct. (no. dist.) N.Y. 2000, U.S. Ct. Appeals (2d cir.) 1989, U.S. Dist. Ct. Vt. 1990, U.S. Dist. Ct. (no. dist.) Ill. 2000. Assoc. Cohen, Shapiro, Polisher, Shiekman & Cohen, Phila., 1976-84, ptnr., 1985-95; sr. mem. Cozen and O'Connor, 1995—. Lectr. Pa. Bar Inst., Harrisburg, 1980-83, 86, 95-2001, course planner, 1986, 2000-01; instr. Inst. for Paralegal Tng., Phila., 1981-82. Mem. nat. governing coun. Am. Jewish Congress, N.Y.C., 1985, 88-96, pres. Pa. region, 1992-95; co-chmn. Commn. on Law and Social Action, Phila., 1985-92; bd. dirs. Jewish Employment and Vocat. Svc. Phila., 1982—, asst. treas., 1986-87, v.p., 1987-95, pres., 1995-98; bd. dirs. Fairmount Geriatric Ctr., 1986-88, sec., 1985-87, v.p., 1987-88; bd. dirs. Pa. Legal Svcs. Ctr., 1987-88, treas., 1988. Mem. ABA (equal employment opportunity law com., labor law sect.), Pa. Bar Assn., Phila. Bar Assn. (co-chmn. labor and employment law com. 1997), Indsl. Rels. Rsch. Assn., Pa. Chamber of Bus. and Industry (exec. com. 1991-96, bd. dirs. 1988—, chmn. indsl. rels. com. 1984-87, chmn. edn. com. 1988-91). Office: Cozen and O'Connor 1900 Market St Philadelphia PA 19103-3527

PASETTI, LOUIS OSCAR, dentist; b. Tampa, Fla., Dec. 27, 1916; s. Joseph G. and Carmen (Gonzalez) P.; m. Mary Mendez, Jan. 11, 1942; children: Louis M., Arleen Pasetti Mariotti. BS, U. Fla., 1937; DDS, Emory U., 1941; postgrad., U. Pa., 1978. Capt. U.S. Army, 1942-46; dentist pvt. practice Tampa, Fla., 1947—. Past. pres. Tampa Civitan Club, 1953; past lt. gov. Civitan Clubs of Tampa, 1962; past dep. gov. Civitan Internat., Tampa, 1964; fin. officer Am. Legion Post 248. Named Fla. Dentist of the Yr., Fla. Acad. Gen. Dentistry, 1983; recipient meritorious Svc. award Fla. Acad. Gen. Dentistry, 1989, Disting. Svc. award, 1985. Fellow Acad. Gen. Dentistry, Am. Coll. Dentists, Internat. Coll. Dentists, Acad. Dentistry Internat.; mem. ADA, Fla. Dental Assn., Fla. Acad. Gen. Dentistry (pres. 1981, Lifetime Achievement award 1996), Tampa Bay Acad. Gen. Dentistry (pres. 1977-78), Elks, Round Table of Civic Clubs of Tampa (sec. 1953), Palma Ceia Golf and Country Club. Democrat. Roman Catholic. Avocations: photography, orchid culture. Home: 10023 Hampton Pl Tampa FL 33618-4227 Office: 10023 Hampton Pl Tampa FL 33618-4227

PASH, TERESA A. piano teacher, performer; b. Hastings, Mich., May 27, 1963; d. Patrick Joseph Gilmore and Norma Violet Hammond Gilmore Earl; m. Robert Christopher Pash, May 10, 1983; children: Sara, Kyle, Anna. Student, Olivet (Mich.) Coll., 1981-83; BA, U. Puget Sound, Tacoma, 1986. Tech. writer, desktop pub. H/H Effective Mgmt. Sys., Battle Creek, Mich., 1990-95; pvt. piano tchr. Nashville. Keyboardist, vocal arranger Holy Smoke Band, Kent, Wash., 1985-88; keyboardist, leader Matthew's House Band, Nashville, Mich., 1996—; keyboardist Yesterday's Gospel Band, Hastings, Mich., 1999—. Artist/producer CD Classical Alloy & Christmas Memories, 1999. Music dir. Cornerstone Cmty. Ch., Kent, 1986-90; band dir. Grace Cmty. Ch., Nashville, 1995-99. Mem.: Battle Creek Area Music Tchrs. Assn. (chair student achievement testing program 1998—2001), Mich. Music Tchrs. Assn., Music Tchrs. Nat. Assn. Christian. Avocations: music, songwriting, reading, computers, family. Home: PO Box 495 Nashville MI 49073-0495

PASHER, VICTORIA SONSHINE, journalist; b. Paterson, N.J., Sept. 29, 1968; d. Richard M. and Jayne Sonshine; m. Matthew C. Pasher, Oct. 11, 1992 (div. Sept. 1999). BA in Journalism, Mass Media, Russian, Rutgers U., 1990. Editl. asst. Cmty. Life Newspaper, Westwood, N.J., 1990-91, copy editor, 1991-92; assoc. editor Kitchen & Bath Design News, Hackensack, 1992-93; freelance asst. editor various mags., N.Y.C., 1993; editl. asst. Pvt. Label mag., Ft. Lee, N.J., 1993-95; staff writer Nat. Underwriter, Hoboken, 1995-98; sr. editor KPMG LLP, N.Y.C., 1998-2000, mgr. internal comm. Montvale, NJ, 2000—02, mgr. Audit Com. Inst., 2002—. Times Mirror fellow Journalism Resources Inst. Rutgers Inst., 1989-90, George H. Cook scholar Rutgers, 1989-90. Mem. Soc. for Profl. Journalists. Avocations: piano, travel.

PASHGIAN, MARGARET HELEN, artist; b. Pasadena, Calif., Nov. 7, 1934; d. Aram John and Margaret (Howell) P. BA, Pomona Coll., 1956; MA in Fine Arts, Boston Univ., 1958; student, Columbia U., 1957. Art instr. Harvard-Newton Program Occidental Coll., 1977-78; artist in residence Calif. Inst. Tech., 1970-71. Grants panelist Calif. Arts Coun., Sacramento, 1993. Artist: solo shows include Rex Evans Gallery, L.A., 1965, 67, Occidental Coll., 1967, Kornblee Gallery, N.Y.C., 1969-72, U. Calif., Irvine, 1975, U. Calif. Santa Barbara, 1976, Stella Polaries Gallery, L.A., 1981, 82, Kaufman Galleries, Houston, 1982, Modernism Gallery, San Francisco, 1983, Works Gallery, Long Beach, Costa Mesa, Calif., 1986, 87, 88, 89, 90, 91, 92, Malka Gallery, L.A., 1997; group exhibitions include Pasadena Art Mus., 1965, Carson Pirie Scott, Chgo., 1965, Calif. Palace of Legion of Honor, San Francisco, 1967, Esther Bear Gallery, Santa Barbara, 1967, 69, Lytton Ctr. of the Visual Arts, L.A., 1968, Salt Lake Art Inst., Salt Lake City, 1968, Mus. Contemporary Crafts, Internat. Plastics Exhibition, 1969, Second Flint (Mich.) Invitational, 1969, Milw. Art Ctr., 1969, U.S.I.S. Mus., N.Y.C., Mus. Contemporary Art, Chgo., 1970, Studio Merconi, Milan, 1970, Calif. Inst. Tech., Baxter Art Galley, 1971, 1980, Calif. Innovations, Palm Springs Dessert Mus., 1981, Calif. Internat. Arts Found. Mus. of Modern Art, Paris, 1982, L.A. Artists in Seoul, Donsangbang Gallery, 1982, An Artistic Conversation, 1931-82, Poland, USA, Ulster Mus., Belfast, Ireland, 1983, Madison (Wis.) Art Ctr., 1994, Calif. State U., Fullerton, 1995, Oakland (Calif.) Mus., 1995; represented in pub. collections at River Forest (Ill.) State Bank, Atlantic Richfield Co., Dallas, Frederic Weisman Collection, L.A., Security Pacific Bank, L.A., Singapore, Andrew Dickson White Mus. of Art, Cornell U., Ithaca, N.Y., L.A. County Mus. of Art, Santa Barbara Art Mus., Laguna Beach Mus. of Art. Trustee, Pomona Coll, Claremont, Calif., 1987—; parade judge Tournament of Roses Centennial Parade, Pasadena, 1987; bd. dirs. L.A. Master Chorale, 1992—. NEA grantee, 1986. Home: 731 S Grand Ave Pasadena CA 91105-2424

PASHMAN, SUSAN ELLEN, writer; b. N.Y.C., Dec. 17, 1942; d. Jonas Charles and Pearl (Steinberg) Greenfield; m. Louis Jonathan Pashman, Sept. 17, 1964 (div. Feb. 1978); children: Joshua, Benjamin. BA, NYU, 1963; JD, Bklyn. Law Sch., 1982. Bar: N.Y. 1983. Tch. fgn. langs. N.Y.C. Pub. Schs., 1963-65; instr. philosophy Adelphi U., Garden City, N.Y., 1965-77; dir. humanities project N.Y. Coun. Humanities, N.Y.C., 1977-79; dean coll. rels. Douglass Coll., New Brunswick, N.J., 1978-79; assoc. atty. Proskauer, Rose, Goetz & Mendelsohn, N.Y.C., 1982-84, Moses & Singer, N.Y.C., 1984-86, Cravath, Swaine & Moore, N.Y.C., 1986-91; freelance writer, 1991—. Bd. dirs. Pub. Access Continuing Edn., N.Y.C., 1991—. Author: The Speed of Light, 1997. Mem. Ashawagh Hall Writers' Circle. Jewish. Avocations: gardening, cooking, tennis. Home: PO Box 2530 57 Pheasant Rd Sag Harbor NY 11963-0116

PASHOLK, PAUL DOUGLAS, retail executive, government official; b. Columbus, Ohio, Mar. 24, 1968; s. Jerome Joseph and Norma Anne (Weigand) Pasholk; m. Rebecca Jean Eaton, June 10, 1995; children: Rachel Marie, Victoria Elizabeth. BA in History, BA in Polit. Sci., Ohio State U., 1990. Dept. supr. Kohl's Dept. Stores, Columbus, 1991-96; market news reporter U.S. Dept. of Agriculture, Fruit and Vegetable Division, Phoenix, 1996—. Author: The Columbus Public Schools and 75 Years of School Board Elections, 1992; co-author (with Rebecca Pasholk): U.S. Senate Elections: The Numbers, and the Story Behind Them; author: King of the Hill - U.S. Presidential Elections, 1992. Vol., rschr. Bill Moss for Columbus Sch. Bd., 1985, 1989, 1991, 1997, Bill Buckel for Columbus Sch. Bd., 1987, treas., 1989, 1991, 1993; presdl. elector cand. Eugene McCarthy for Pres., Columbus, 1988; vol. Bruce Babbitt for Pres., Cedar Rapids, Iowa, 1988, Jesse Jackson for Pres., Columbus, 1988, Richard Letts for Judge, Columbus, 1989, Jerry Brown for Pres., Columbus, 1992; local organizer Hands Across Am., 1986; vol. recruiter AFL-CIO Support Group Frontlash, 1988—90; mem. Indsl. Workers of the World, San Francisco/Ypsilanti, 1991—; organizer, chmn. West H.S. Class Reunion, Columbus, 1991; Ohio state campaign chmn. Ray Rollinson for Pres., 1992; non-voting del. Libertarian Nat. Conv., Salt Lake City, 1993, Nat. Market News Assn. Conf., Austin, Tex., 1997, Oakland, Calif., 1999, Myrtle Beach, SC, 2001; mem. Friends of Freedom and Justice, Columbus, 1998—; contact Ariz. state John B. Anderson for Pres., 2000; mem. We The People, 2000—; contbr. Kirtland Reorganized LDS Ch. Temple Restoration, Kirtland, Ohio, 1996. Republican. Methodist. Avocations: collecting buffalos, political election statistics, public speaking, editorial letters, religious collectibles. Office: 522 N Central Ave Ste 106 Phoenix AZ 85004-2168 E-mail: ilovejesus@buffalo.com., Paul.Pasholk@usda.gov.

PASICH, KIRK ALAN, lawyer; b. La Jolla, Calif., May 26, 1955; s. Chris Nick and Iva Mae (Tormey) P.; m. Pamela Mary Woods, July 30, 1983; children: Christopher Thomas, Kelly Elizabeth, Connor Woods. BA in Polit. Sci., UCLA, 1977; JD, Loyola Law Sch., L.A., 1980. Bar: Calif. 1980, U.S. Dist. Ct. (no., so., ea. and cen. dists.) Calif. 1981, U.S. Ct. Appeals (9th cir.) 1982, U.S. Ct. Appeals (1st cir.) 1992. Assoc. Paul, Hastings, Janofsky & Walker, L.A., 1980-88, ptnr., 1988-89, Troop Steuber Pasich Reddick & Tobey, LLP, L.A., 1989-2000, Howrey Simon Arnold & White LLP, L.A., 2001—. Author: Casualty and Liability Insurance, 1990, 2000; co-author: Officers and Directors: Liabilities and Protections, 1996, 2000, The Year 2000 and Beyond: Liability and Insurance for Computer Code Problems, 2000; contbg. editor: West's California Litigation Forms: Civil Procedure Before Trial, 2000; entertainment law columnist, ins. law columnist L.A. and San Francisco Daily Jour., 1989—; contbr. articles to profl. jours. Active bd. dirs. Nat. Acad. Jazz, L.A., 1988-89, chmn. bd. dirs. Woody Herman Found., L.A., 1989-92, Constnl. Rights Found., 2000; active L.A. City Atty's. Task Force for Econ. Recovery, 1992-93. Named to Calif's. Legal Dream Team as 1 of state's top 25 litigators, Calif. Law Bus., 1992, as one of the nation's top 45 lawyers under age 45, The Am. Lawyer, 1995. Mem. ABA (mem. Task Force on Complex Insurance Coverage Litigation). Home: 10419 Lindbrook Dr Los Angeles CA 90024-3323 Office: Ste 2100 1925 Century Park E Los Angeles CA 90067 E-mail: pasichk@howrey.com.

PASIENZA, JOANNE MARIE, dental hygienist; b. Toledo, June 12, 1954; d. Richard James and Ethel Maybelle Waldeck; m. Peter John Pasienza, Sept. 20, 1975; children: Michelle, Joel, Amanda. Cert. in dental hygiene, Owen's Tech. Coll., 1986. Registered dental hygienist. Dental hygienist Office of Drs. Pero and Glinka, Maumee, Ohio, 1979—83, Office of Dr. Robert Bice, Birmingham, Mich., 1986—88, Office of Dr. Hallet and Wiley, Toledo, 1988—90, Office of Dr. Gary Breymeier, Toledo, 1988—90, Office of Dr. Roger Blank, Waterville, 1990—92, Office of Dr. Donald Kerr, Brighton, Mich., 1992—94, Office of Dr. Charlick, Springstead & Wilson, Dental Assoc., Brighton, 1994—. Author: (children's book) P is for Patience, 2002; contbr. poetry to lit. publs. Charity fund-raiser St. Loius Ctr. Parents Assn., Chelsea, Mich., 1996—. Recipient Citizenship award, St. Louis Ctr., 1998. Mem.: Mich. Dental Hygienists Assn., Internat. Libr. Poetry, Nat. Writers Union. Roman Catholic. Avocations: reading, writing, cake decorating, water skiing, illustrating. Office: 5710 Whitmore Lake Rd Brighton MI 48116

PASINETTI, PIER MARIA, author; b. Venice, Italy, June 24, 1913; came to U.S., 1946, naturalized, 1952; s. Carlo and Maria (Ciardi) P. Dottore in Lettere, U. Padua, Italy, 1935; PhD in Comparative Lit., Yale U., 1949. Fellow La. State U., 1935-36, U. Calif. at Berkeley, 1936-37; lectr. U. Stockholm, 1942-46; prof. Italian and comparative lit. UCLA, 1949—. Author: L'ira di Dio, 1942, Venetian Red, 1960, The Smile on the Face of the Lion, 1965, From the Academy Bridge, 1970, Suddenly Tomorrow, 1971, Dall' Estrema America, 1975, Il Centro, 1979, Dorsoduro, 1983, Life for Art's Sake: Studies in the Literary Myth of the Romantic Artist, 1985, Melodramma, 1993, Piccole Veneziane Complicate, 1996, Astolfo, 1999; also articles, revs., film scripts. Recipient Fiction award Nat. Inst. Arts and Letters, 1965, Prix Écureuil Li. Etrangère, 1996. Mem. Authors Guild. Clubs: Elizabethan Yale. Office: 1259 Dorsoduro Venice Italy 30123

PASK, SCOTT, lighting designer; Grad., Yale Sch. Drama. (lighting designer): Atlantic Theater Co.; Playwrights Horizons; Chgo. Opera Theatre; Yale Rep; Alliance Theater Co.; Roundabout Theater Co. (Lucille Lortel award, 1999, Am. Theatre Wing Henry Hewes award); N.Y. Stage and Film; Lincoln Ctr. New Visions, 1999. Office: 73-75 E 7th St #5E New York NY 10003*

PASKAWICZ, JEANNE FRANCES, pain specialist; b. Phila., Mar. 3, 1954; d. Alex and Lillian (Pyluck) P. BSc, Phila. Coll. Pharmacy; MA, Villanova U., 1973; postgrad., St. Joseph U., 1979; PhD, Kensington U., 1984. Mem. anesthesiology staff Einstein Med. Ctr., Phila., 1990-94, Temple U. Hosp., 1994—; mem. detox./rehab. staff Presbyn. Med. Ctr., Phila., 1984—; house officer Tenet Hosps., Elkins Park, Pa., 1990—; mem. psychiatry staff Hahnemann U. Hosp., Phila., 1984-90; hostage negotiator Office of Mental Health, 1984-90; mem. surgery/anesthesiology staff Mt. Sinai Hosp., 1989-91. Bd. dirs. Phila. Coll. Pharmacy, St. Joseph U. Mem. NAFE, Am. Pain Soc., Nat. Parks Conservation Assn., North Shore Animal League, Amvets, DAV Comdrs. Club, Lambda Kappa Sigma.

PASKER, DEBBIE ANN, protective services official; b. Homestead AFB, Fla., Nov. 25, 1960; d. Wayne Chandler and Sharon Kaye (Boke) Gainey; m. Michael Harold Pasker, Dec. 31, 1988; children: Matthew Michael, Daniel Chandler. BS in Pub. Adminstrn., Fla. Atlantic U., 1998. Police sgt., grant specialist City of Sunrise, Fla., 1982—. Bd. dirs. Broward chpt. Fla. Informed Parents, Ft. Lauderdale, 1988-89; pres. Broward County D.A.R.E. Officers Assn., 1996. Named officer of yr. Sawgrass Optimists Club, 1996. Mem. Nat. Drug Abuse Resistance Edn. Officer's Assn. (Most Outstanding Student award 1991), Fla. Drug Abuse Resistance Edn. Officer's Assn., Fla. Assn. Sch. Resource Officers (treas. Broward chpt. 1988-89), Fla. Juvenile Officers Assn., Broward Crime Prevention Officers Assn. (sec.-treas. 1988-89). Democrat. Roman Catholic. Avocations: writing children's stories, quilting, reading. Office: 10440 W Oakland Park Blvd Sunrise FL 33351-6822

PASKIN, NANCY C. rehabilitation education director; b. Dearborn, Mich., 1947; D. Carl E. and Ruth H. (Olds) Miller; m. Samuel M. Paskin, June 1973. BA, Western Mich. U., 1969, MA, 1971. Rehab. tchr. Cen. Assn. for the Blind, Utica, N.Y.; dir. rehab. svcs. Ctr. for Ind. Living., N.Y.C.; dir. rehab. teaching svcs. Westchester Lighthouse, White Plains, N.Y.; dir. vision rehab. therapies The Lighthouse, Inc., N.Y.C.; dir. rehab. tchg. agy.-wide Lighthouse Internat. Adj. instr. grad. program tchr. edn. Hunter Coll., N.Y.C., 1999—2001; adj. instr. Pa. Coll. Optometry, 1999—2002, Dominican Coll., Blauvett, NY; adj. instr. rehab. tchr. UALR, 1994. Author: Sensory Development: An Instructor's Manual, 1979; co-author: Whatever Works, 1994, Take Charge of Your Life, 2001. Recipient Charlyn Allen award, Mid-Am. Conf. Rehab. Tchrs., 1996, Rehab. Tchr. of the Yr. award, N.Y. State Assn. Edn. and Rehab. of Blind and Visually Impaired, 1997. Mem.: AER (chair membership N.Y., bd. dirs., cert. rehab. tchr. of the blind, chair nat. cert. com. divsn. 11 1994, bd. dirs. N.Y. chpt. 1995, sec.-treas. divsn. 11 2002—, Meritorious Achievement award 1994, Bruce McKenzie Lifetime Achievement in Rehab. Therapy award 1996). Address: 3771 Valleyview St Mohegan Lake NY 10547-1034 E-mail: npaskin@lighthouse.org.

PASKOW, MARC LEE, environmental consultant; b. Newark, Dec. 10, 1947; s. Herbert L. and Anita A. Paskow; m. Susan F. Bialkowicz, Jan. 19, 1974. MS, Nova U., 1976; BEd, U. Miami, 1973. Cert. profl. environ. auditor, Nat. Assn. Safety and Health Profls.; lic., cert. N.J. Dept. Environ. Protection Underground Storage Tank Removal and Remediation. Environ. cons. Analyt Testing Lab., Kenilworth, N.J., 1986—; supr. OSHA, 1992; auditor Nat. Assn. Safelty Health, 1994. Mem. N.J. Small Bus. Assn., Assn. Electroplaters. Republican. Jewish. Office: Analytical Testing Lab PO Box 368 840 Colfax Ave Kenilworth NJ 07033-2006 E-mail: marcpaskow@aol.com.

PASLES, PAUL C. mathematician, educator; BA, U. Pa., 1990; MA, Temple U., 1994, PhD, 1997. Vis. asst. prof. St. Joseph's U., Phila., 1997—99, Villanova (Pa.) U., 1999—2002, asst. prof., 2002—. Contbr. scientific papers to profl. jours. Mem.: Spl. Interest Group of the Math. Assn. Am., Mathematical Assn. Am., Am. Math. Soc.

PASNICU, CORNEL, mathematician, educator; b. Bucharest, Romania, Sept. 6, 1953; arrived in U.S., 1992; s. Tanasa Pasnicu, Xenia Adina Pasnicu; m. Adina Melania Truta; 1 child Nastasia Laura. BA, U. Bucharest, 1976, MS, 1977, PhD, 1987. Rsch. fellow INCREST (IMAR), Bucharest, Romania, 1980—91; vis. scholar U. Copenhagen, 1991—91; vis. assoc. prof. U. Toronto, Canada, 1992—92; assoc. prof. U. P.R., San Juan, 1992—97, full prof., 1997—. Mem. operator algebras/operator theory panel NSF , Arlington, Va., 2002. Contbr. articles to profl. jours. Grantee, NSF, 1994—96,

1996—2000, 2001—. Mem.: Am. Math. Soc. Avocations: reading, music, sports. Office: Univ PR Math Dept San Juan PR 00931 Home: Calle Juan B Huyke 122 San Juan PR 00918 Office Fax: 787-281-0651. Business E-Mail: cpasnic@upracd.upr.clu.edu.

PASOTTI, ELEONORA, researcher; b. Milan, Italy, May 12, 1972; d. Gino Pasotti, Rita Massarotto; m. Roger Julius Edmund Schoenman. MPhil, Columbia University, New York, 1996—98; MSc, London School of Economics, London, UK, 1994—95, BSc, 1991—94. PhD researcher Columbia University, New York, NY, 1996—2002. Mentor Brainstorm, New York, NY, 2001—02. Avocation: Pilot. Office: Dept of Pol. Science Columbia University 420 West 118th Street New York NY 10027 Office Fax: 212 222 3001. Personal E-mail: ep159@columbia.edu. Business E-Mail: ep159@columbia.edu.

PASOUR, ERNEST CALEB, JR. economics educator; b. Dallas, Sept. 12, 1932; s. Ernest Caleb and Hazel (Carpenter) P.; m. Adaline Armstrong, Dec. 17, 1967; children: Virginia Barton, Ernest Caleb III. BS, N.C. State U., 1954, MS, 1959; PhD, Mich. State U., 1963. Agrl. economist U.S. Dept. Agr., East Lansing, Mich., 1962-63; asst. prof. econs. N.C. State U., Raleigh, 1963-67, assoc. prof. econs., 1967-73, prof. econs., 1973—99, prof. emeritus, 1999—. Acad. advisor John Locke Soc., Raleigh, 1989—. Author: Agriculture and the State, 1990; contbr. articles to profl. jours. With U.S. Army, 1954-56. Recipient Leavy award Freedoms Found., 1989; NSF faculty fellow U. Chgo., 1970-71. Mem. Am. Econ. Assn. Lutheran. Avocations: gardening, reading. Home: 4215 Galax Dr Raleigh NC 27612-3713 Office: NC State U Dept Agr and Resource Econs PO Box 8109 Raleigh NC 27695-0001

PASQUALETTI, MARTIN J. geographer; b. San Francisco, Feb. 5, 1945; s. Joseph and Phyllis L. Pasqualetti; m. Mari Anne Williams; 1 child Erika. BA, U. Calif., Berkeley, 1967; MA, La. State U., 1969; PhD, U. Calif., Riverside, 1977. Instr. Crafton Hills Coll., Yucaipa, Calif., 1973—75; cons. Albert A. Webb Assocs., Riverside, 1974—77; prof. Ariz. State U., Tempe, 1977—; co-founder OnPoint Sys., Inc. Cons. EcoGroup, Tempe, 1990—93; prin. Energy Planning Cons., Tempe, 1990—96. Editor: (book) Wind Power in View, 2002, The Evolving Landscape, 1997, Nuclear Decommissioning and Society, 1990, Nucear Power: Assessing and Managing Hazardous Technology, 1984; contbr. Pres. Rural/Geneva Neighborhood Assn., Tempe, 1990—92; mem. Bd. Adjustment, 1996—2001, Ariz. Solar Energy Adv. Coun., Phoenix, Ariz. Geographic Names, Phoenix; bd. dirs. Ariz. Solar Ctr., 1998—2002. Named Environ. Educator of Yr., Assn. Environ. Engrs., 1993. Mem.: Am. Geog. Soc., Assn. Am. Geographers Energy and Environment Specialty Group (pres. 1996—99). Avocations: tennis, photography, travel. Office: ArizState U Dept Geography Tempe AZ 85287-0104 Business E-Mail: pasqualetti@asu.edu.

PASQUARIELLO, JULIUS ANTHONY, pharmacist; b. Schenectady, N.Y., Aug. 3, 1960; s. Julius and Maria (Cervera) P. BS in Pharmacy, Albany Coll. of Pharmacy, 1983. Cert. geriatric pharmacy Commn. Certification Geriatric Pharmacy, 2001. Supervising pharmacist Brooks Pharmacy # 727, Schenectady, 1983-88, NRX Svcs. Inc., Guilderland, N.Y., 1988-90, Cmty. Health Plan, Delmar, 1990-93; staff pharmacist, oncology pharmacist Kaiser Permanente, Latham, 1993-99, Familiy Meds. Pharmacy, 1999-2000, Albany (N.Y.) Med. Ctr. Hosp. Pharmacy, 2000—. Cons. pharmacy edn. com. Am. Cancer Soc., Albany, 1993—, N.Y. State Dept. Health, Medicaid Mgmt. Bur., Albany, N.Y. Avocations: golf, weightlifting, saxophone. Home: 345 Dolan Dr Schenectady NY 12306-1012 Office: 1 Commerce Plz Albany NY 12210

PASQUERELLA, FRANK MATTHEW, music educator; b. Morehead, Ky., Mar. 26, 1967; s. Frank Michael and Janice Ann Pasquerella; m. Maria Rachel Edstrom, Dec. 30, 1995. MusB Edn., Cleve. State U., 1991. Cert. K-12 music tcjr. Minn. Dir. of bands Rocori H.S., Cold Spring, Minn., 1993—97, Eastview H.S., Apple Valley, 1997—. Trumpet player Minn. Symphonic Winds, Edina, 1999—. Mem.: NEA, Internat. Trumpet Guild, Minn. Educators Assn., Minn. Music Educators Assn. Dfl. Avocations: music, antiques, cooking, golf, stock car racing, biking. Home: 15656 Gateway Path Apple Valley MN 55124-5159 Office: Eastview HS 6200 W 140th St Apple Valley MN 55124 Personal E-mail: frankandmaria@netzero.net. E-mail: frank.pasquerella@district196.org.

PASQUIER, JOËL, music educator; b. Montmorency, France, Sept. 25, 1943; arrived in Can., 1967; s. Jean and Raymonde (Gourdin) P.; m. Anne Vachon, Nov. 28, 1970; 1 child, Ariane. Grad. in piano and chamber music, Conservatoire Nat. Superieur de Musique, Paris, 1962. Prof. Conservatoire de Musique de St. Germain-en-Laye, France, 1964-65; grad. asst. Sch. Music, Ind. U., Bloomington, 1965-67; tchr. piano Ecole de Musique, U. Laval, Quebec, Can., 1967—, dir., 1988-91. Appeared as solo pianist concert halls, radio, TV, with chamber and symphony orchs. in France, U.S., Can., The Netherlands. Fulbright scholar Ind. U., 1965. Mem. Que. Yacht Club. Office: U Laval Sch Music Pavillon Casault Sainte Foy QC Canada G1K 7P4

PASS, CAROLYN JOAN, dermatologist; b. Balt., May 14, 1941; d. Isidore Earl and Rhea (Koplowitz) P.; m. Richard Malcolm Susel, June 23, 1963; children: Steven, Gary. BS, U. Md., 1962; MD, U. Md., 1966. Diplomate Am. Bd. Dermatology. Rotating intern USPHS Hosp., Balt., 1966-67; med. resident St. Agnes Hosp., 1967-68; dermatology resident and fellow U. Md. Sch. Medicine Hosps., 1968-71; pvt. practice specializing in dermatology Balt. and Ellicott City, Md., 1971—. Mem. staff St. Agnes Hosp.; vol. dermatology clinics U. Md., St. Agnes hosps.; asst. clin. prof. dermatology U. Md. Sch. Medicine, 1978—; mem. exec. com. adv. bd. Nat. Program in Dermatology, 1975. Mem. AMA, Med. and Chirurgical Soc. State Md. (del.), Balt. City Med. Soc. (del 1974, pub. rels. com., 1992-94, alternate del. 1994—), Am. Women's Med. Assn., Am. Acad. Dermatology (award exhibit 1970), Soc. Investigative Dermatology, Md. Dermatology Soc. (sec.-treas. 1974-76, pres. 1976-77), Soc. Contemporary Medicine and Surgery, U. Md. Sch. Medicine Alumnae Assn. (bd. dirs. 1987—), Woodholme Country Club, Country Garden Club. Jewish. Avocations: gourmet cooking, gardening, golf. Home: Timberlane 8410 Park Heights Ave Baltimore MD 21208-1716 Office: Pine Heights Med Ctr 1001 Pine Heights Ave Ste 301 Baltimore MD 21229-5285

PASSAGE, DAVID, diplomat; b. Charlotte, N.C., June 16, 1942; s. John T. and Virginia (Beam) P. BA in Internat. Rels., U. Denver, 1964; MS in Internat. Econs., Georgetown U., 1966; student, Nat. War Coll., Ft. McNair, Washington, 1981-82. With U.S. Dept. State, 1966-99; politico-mil. affairs officer U.S. Embassy, London, 1966; pacification program analyst U.S. Mil. Command, Saigon, Vietnam, 1968; with U.S. State Dept. Ops. Ctr., 1970; officer Secretariat Staff, 1971; special asst. to Asst. Sec. State Politico-Mil. Affairs, 1972-74; pol. officer Quito, Ecuador, 1974-76; spl. asst. to Sec. of State Henry Kissinger U.S. State Dept., Washington, 1976; polit. counselor Am. Embassy, Canberra, Australia, 1977-79; dir. Press Office and Assoc., 1979; from. dep. to acting spokesman U.S. Dept. State, dep. dir. So. African Affairs, 1982-84; dep. chief mission/charge d'affairs U.S. Embassy, 1984-86; dir. Office Regional Affairs Africa Bur., 1986; dir. for Africa, Nat. Security Coun. for Africa The White House, Washington, 1989; U.S. amb. to Botswana, 1990-93; polit. adviser to U.S. Spl. Opers. Command MacDill AFB, Fla., 1993-96; dir. Andean affairs Dept. State, Washington, 1996-99; ret., 1999—. Lectr. Nat. War Coll., John F. Kennedy Spl. Warfare Ctr., USAF Spl. Ops. Sch., Armed Forces Staff Coll., others. Contbr. chpt.: Managing Contemporary Conflict, 1996, The U.S. and Colombia, 2000; contbr. articles to profl. jours. Recipient Chuong My Boi Tinh medal (Vietnam), Sec. of State Career chievement Medal, State Dept. Superior Hon. Awd.; Gen. James Doolittle Educator of Yr. Awd., U.S. Air Force Def. Disting. Civilian Svc. medal Dept. Def.; Centennial scholar U. Denver. Avocations: environment and conservation. Home: 2416 Chain Bridge Rd NW Washington DC 20016-3304

PASSAGE, STEPHEN SCOTT, energy company executive; b. Miami, Oct. 10, 1946; s. John Thompson and Virginia Frances (Beam) P.; m. Ellen Shapiro, Aug. 21, 1988. BS in Civil Engring., Polit. Sci., MIT, 1969; MA in Polit. Sci., New Sch. Soc. Rsch., 1972, MA in Econs., 1975. Cer. Profl. Engr. Mem. engring. dept. Port Authority N.Y. and N.J., 1969-86; pres. Montenay Power Corp., N.Y., 1986—. Chmn. IWSA. Contbr. articles to profl. jours. Chmn. 607 West End Ave Corp., 1991—. Mem. ASME, NSPE. Avocations: chess, hiking, tennis, canoeing, reading. Office: Montenay Power Corp 800 3rd Ave New York NY 10022-7604

PASSANO, E. MAGRUDER, JR. strategic planning consultant; b. Balt., Oct. 2, 1942; s. Edward M. and Mildred P. (Nelson) P.; m. Helen C. Marikle, Sept. 4, 1971; children: Catherine, Tammy, Sarah. BS, Johns Hopkins U., 1967, MA, 1969. With Waverly Inc., Balt., 1965-98, salesman, 1970-73, v.p., 1973-75, v.p. adminstrn., sec., 1975-90, vice chmn., sec., 1990-98; pres., CEO One Waverly LLC, 1998—. Pres. Passano Found., Balt., 1982—, Am. Lung Assn., Md., 1982-84; mem. exec. com. Vol. Coun. Equal Opportunity, Balt., 1978—, chmn., 1995—; bd. dirs. Combined Health Appeal Am., 1994-97; pres. (CHA) Combined Health Agys., Md., 1985-87, chmn. exec. com., 1987-95; pres. 12:30 Club Balt., 1981-83; mem. exec. com. Balt. City Life Mus., 1982-93, v.p. 1987-93; trustee emeritus, 1993-98; mem. adv. coun. Johns Hopkins U. Sch. Continuing Studies, 1984—, exec. chair alumni chpt., 1986-89, chair edn. cmty. devel. iniative, 1995—; mem. Md. Gov.'s Commn. on High Blood Pressure and Related Cardiovascular Risk Factors, 1986—; bd. govs. Md. New Directions, Inc., 1987-94; bd. dirs., mem. exec. com. YMCA Ctrl. Md., 1988-96; bd. dirs., chair edn. com. Pride of Balt., 1990—; bd. dirs. Ind. Coll. Fund Md., 1994—; bd. vis. Towson State U., 1994—, chmn. 1997—, Sch. Medicine U. Md., 1995—; mem. planning com., bd. vis. Md. Bus. Responsive Govt., 1994—. With USN, 1963-65. Recipient Prince Hall Bicentennial award Masons, 1975; citations Mayor of Balt., 1976, City of Balt., 1977, Vol. of Yr. award for outstanding svc. to CICHA, 1984-85, Presdl. award for outstanding svc. to Am. Lung Assn. Md., 1985, Outstanding Vol., 1988, Disting. Svc. award Soc. Profl. Journalists, 1987, Outstanding Svc. award Am. Heart Assn., 1988, Outstanding Vol. Svc. award Balt. Assn. Retarded Citizens, 1990, Vol. of Yr./Outstanding Leadership and Dedication award Combined Health Agys., 1991-92. Mem. Purchasing Mgmt. Assn. Md. (chmn. com. 1968-70), Balt. Jaycees (v.p. 1974-76, internat. senator 1975), Greater Balt. Minority Purchasing Coun. (Svc. award 1978), Soc. Colonial Wars (chpt. gov. 1989-91), Johns Hopkins U. Alumni Assn. (pres. Balt. 1984-86, Univ. Heritage award 1987). Democrat. Episcopalian. Home: 3925 Linkwood Rd Baltimore MD 21210-3001 Office: One Waverly LLC 100 N Charles St Ste 640 Baltimore MD 21201-3805

PASSANTINO, BENJAMIN ARTHUR, business/marketing executive; b. Bklyn., Feb. 26, 1956; s. Anthony Frank and Ann Marie (Ruggerio) Passantino. Mgr. pub. rels. AT&T, N.Y.C., mgr. mktg. comm. and new techs.; pres. B. Arthur Comm., Morristown, N.J., 1984-89; sr. v.p. bus. devel. IMEDIA Creative Corp. Mktg., 1989-94, also dir.; mng. ptnr., CEO, Tribeca Global, Inc., Hackettstown, NJ; dir. media and comms. onProject.com, Morristown, 2000—01; pres. Avid Records, Inc., N.Y.C., 2002—; chief oper. officer Avid Listener, Inc., 2002—. Bd. dirs. Dieknowligist, Inc., N.Y.C., One World Botanicals, Inc., Red Bank, N.J., Lasercomb Am., Inc., N.Y.C., The Perfect Supply Co., Inc., N.Y.C., Imedia, Morristown, N.J. Co-author: One with the Flame, NFL Quarterbacks; contbr. articles to mags. Bd. dirs. Am. Cancer Soc., Morristown, Jr. Achievement, Basking Ridge, N.J.; mem. Washington Twp. (Morris County) Planning Bd., chairperson econ. devel. com.; trustee Drakestown United Meth. Ch. Mem. IEEE, Internat. Assn. Bus. Communicators, Am. Mktg. Assn., Bus. Profls. of Advt. Assn., Conf. Bd. Office: 375 Mt Prospect Ave Ste 7BE Newark NJ 07104

PASSANTINO, RICHARD J. architect; b. N.Y.C., Apr. 4, 1934; s. Charles V. and Ruth M. (Defina) P.; m. Erika F. Dethlefs, Sept. 1, 1962; children: Stefan C., Fiona R. BS in Architecture, U. Cin., 1957. Registered arch., D.C., Md., Va., Ga., Miss., Fla., Ky., Mo., N.J., S.C.; cert. Nat. Coun. Archtl. Registration Bds. Rsch. assoc. McLeod, Ferrara, Ensign, Washington, 1960-70; founding prin. Richard J. Passantino, AIA Architects, Bethesda, Md., 1970-80; pres. SAIC Architects, McLean, Va., 1980-90, LEA/Passantino & Bavier, Arlington, 1990-94, Passantino & Bavier subs. Facility Holding Corp. Smyrna, Ga., Bethesda, Md., 1995—. Spkr. to various ednl. instn. in U.S., AIA rep. Union Internat. Archs., 1985-88, nat. chmn. com. architecture edn., 1998; mem. nat. archtl. juries throughout U.S., 1975—. Co-author: Urban Schools in Europe, 1963; contbr. numerous articles to profl. jours.; designer 7 earthquake resistant schs. in So. Italy, 1985-88, Project Dir., for design of multiple U.S. Navy projects in Greece, 11 locations, 1985-89, Early Childhood Ctr., Buffalo, 1995, psychiat. hosp., Leesburg, Va., 1979, Haile Selassie U., Addis Ababa, Ethiopia; designer modifications Am. Consulate Gen., Ecuador, Am. embassies, Papua-New Guinea, The Philippines, Liberia, Ghana, others. Bd. dirs. Nat. Child Rsch. Ctr., Washington, 1969-74. 1st lt. USAF, 1958-60; capt. USAFR, 1960-62. Recipient award for sch. architecture exhbn. Am. Assn. Sch. Bd. Adminstrs., 1984. Mem. v.p. chmn., architecture for edn. 1994), Coun. for Ednl. Facilities Planners (co-recipient Projects of Distinction award 1993), recipient of Coun. of Ednl. Facility Planners Internat., 1996, recipient of the James D, MacConnell award for Ednl. Facility Planning Excellence, Assn. for Childhood Edn. Internat., Assn. Sch. Bus. Ofcls. Internat. (award of excellence 1986), Nat. Hist. Trust, Soc. Am. Mil. Engrs. Avocations: tennis, photography, travel. Office: Passantino & Bavier Archs 2233 Lake Park Dr SE Ste 450 Smyrna GA 30080-8856

PASSARO, ERASMO ANDRE, physician, neurologist; b. Bayonne, N.J., Dec. 5, 1961; s. Vincent and Nicolina P.; m. Velicia Ann Passaro, Aug. 8, 1998. BA with honors, U. Chgo., 1984; MD, Robert Wood Johnson Med. Sch., 1988. Diplomate Am. Bd. Psychiatry and Neurology, Am. Bd. Clin. Neurophysiology, , Am. Bd. Clin. Neurophysiology. Resident in neurology UCLA Sch. of Medicine, 1990-93, clin. neurophysiology and epilepsy, 1993-95; clin. asst. prof. U. South Fla., Tampa, 1995-98; asst. prof. U. Mich. Med. Ctr., Ann Arbor, 1998—. Dir. Adult Epilepsy Lab., U. Mich. Health System, Ann Arbor, 1998—; epileptologist/brain mapping U. Mich. Epilepsy Surgery program, 1998—. Recipient Rsch. award Epilepsy found. of Am., 1994-95. Mem. Am. Epilepsy Soc., Am. Acad. Neurology, Am. Clin. Neurophysiology Soc. Office: U Mich Med Ctr UH1B300 1500 E Medical Ctr Dr Ann Arbor MI 48109-0036 E-mail: epassaro@umich.edu.

PASSARO, PAUL CHARLES, business executive; b. Ridgewood, N.J., June 6, 1967; s. Richard Paul and Barbara (Brown) Passaro; m. Kristi-Anne Tolo, June 25, 1994; children: Peter James, Anne Marie. BA in History cum laude, Williams Coll., Williamstown, Mass., 1989; MBA, U. N.C., 1993. Mcpl. bond trader and salesman Roosevelt & Cross, Inc., N.Y.C., 1989-91; v.p. The Fraser Co., Hilton Head, S.C., 1992-94; CFO, Pine Needles and Mid Pines Resorts, Southern Pines, N.C., 1994—. Bd. dirs. small bus. adv. bd. N.C. Citizens for Bus. and Industry, Raleigh, 1999—. Vice-pres. The Toppers, N.Y.C., 1991; founder, Habitat for Humanity Charity Golf Classic, Chapel Hill, 1992—; mem. fin. com. Trinity Sch., Durham and Chapel Hill, 1999—; audit com. mem. N.C. Rep. Party, Raleigh, 1999—, chmn. 2001—; bd. dirs. Leadership N.C., 1999—. Elder Ch. of the Good Shepherd, Durham, 1994—. Mem. Theodore Roosevelt Assn., Durham County Wildlife Club, Christmas Fore Moore (treas. 1997—, Charity Golf Tourney). Republican. Avocations: Bible study, golf, reading history, bird hunting. Office: Pine Needles and Mid Pines Resorts 1005 Midland Rd Southern Pines NC 28387-3121 E-mail: pcpassaro@yahoo.com.

PASSER, GARY LOUIS, college president; b. Ft. Madison, Iowa, May 28, 1946; s. Louis Jacob and Helen Naomi Passer; m. Suzanne Bartsch, July 24, 1984; children: Jamie Ryan, Tammy Hildebrand; m. Patrice Coleman, Nov. 4, 2001. BA, Iowa Wesleyan Coll., 1969; MA, U. Iowa, 1972, PhD, 1992. Mem. faculty Nicolet Area Tech. Coll., Rhinelander, Wis., 1972-85, divsn. chair, 1985-87; dean instrn. Ellsworth C.C., Iowa Falls, Iowa, 1987-92; v.p. instrn. Northland Pioneer Coll., Holbrook, Ariz., 1992-97, pres., 1997—. Mem. Foster Grandparents, Flagstaff, Ariz., 1998—, Ariz. Commn. for Postsecondary Edn., 2001. Wis. health care policy coun. U. Wis., Madison, 1984; bd. dirs. Cmty. Counseling Ctr., Holbrook, 1995—, C.C. Inst./U. Ariz., Tucson, 1994-98; gen. plan com. City of Show Low, Ariz., 1998-99; bd. dirs. Silver Creek Symphony, 1999—, Navajo County Workforce Devel. Bd. Mem. Am. vocat. Assn., Nat. Coun. Instnl. Adminstrs., Nat. Coun. Occupl. Edn., Mountain States Pres.' Assn., Rotary. Avocations: mountaineering, golf. Office: Northland Pioneer Coll PO Box 620 Holbrook AZ 86025-0620 E-mail: dcglp@northland.cc.az.us.

PASSER-MUSLIN, JULIETTE MAYABELLE, lawyer; b. USSR; MusB, Manhattan Sch. Music, 1981, MA in Music Edn., 1984; postgrad., NYU, 1985-86, Columbia U., 1988-89; JD cum laude, Yeshiva U., 1990. Bar: N.Y. 1990. Solist, music dir. mus. theater cos. in U.S. and Europe, 1977-87; dir. admissions and pub. rels. St. Sergius Sch., N.Y.C., 1981-83; tchg. asst. edn. dept. NYU, 1985-86; assoc. Debevoise & Plimpton, 1990-94, Patterson, Belknap, Webb & Tyler, LLP, N.Y.C., 1994-96; pres., gen. counsel Internat. Project Devel. Group, LLC, 1996—. Adj. lectr. Hunter Coll. CUNY, and Hunter Coll. H.S., 1981-82; tchg. asst., substitute lectr. Manhattan Sch. Music, N.Y.C., 1981-83; judge numerous music competitions, including Bklyn. Acad. Music, 1985, 86. Contbr. numerous articles to law and other publs.; performer, dir. musicals, including Camelot, Sound of Music, Fantasticks, Grease, West Side Story, Show Boat, Little Night Music, Carousel, King and I, and Jewus Christ Superstar; spl. guest 3d Internat. Festival Contemporary Music, Leningrad, USSR, 1988. Bd. dirs. Coun. for Trade and Econ. Cooperation, U.S.-Uzbekistan Coun., St. Petersburg Found. Scholar Jewish Found. for Edn. Women, 1977-78, Manhattan Sch. Music. Mem. Internat. Law Soc., N.Y. State Bar Assn., Bar Assn. City N.Y., Women in Internat. Trade, Coun. on Fgn. Rels. Office: Internat Project Devel Group 730 5th Ave 9 flr New York NY 10019 Fax: 212-541-2486.

PASSETTI, LORA LINDA, alcohol/drug abuse services professional, researcher; b. Englewood, N.J., Dec. 2, 1972; BA, Wittenberg U., 1994; MS, Ill. State U., 2002. Rsch. asst. Wittenberg U., Springfield, Ohio, 1993—94; rsch./tchg. asst. Ill. State U., Normal, 1994—95, grad. asst. Univ. Rsch. Office, 1995—96, practicum counselor, 1995—96, Decatur (Ill.) Mental Health Ctr., 1995—96; rsch. project asst. Chestnut Health Sys., Bloomington, 1996—97, data collection coord., 1997—99, rsch. projects mgr., 1999—. Presenter in field. Contbr. articles to profl. jours. Mem.: Am. Evaluation Assn., Am. Psychiat. Assn. (assoc.), Psi Chi. Avocations: puzzles, creative writing, gardening, decorating, crossword puzzles. Office: Chestnut Health Systems 720 W Chestnut Bloomington IL 61701 Personal E-mail: lpassetti@chestnut.org.

PASSEY, GEORGE EDWARD, psychology educator; b. Stratford, Conn., Sept. 28, 1920; s. Henry Richard and Elizabeth (Angus) P.; m. Algie Aldridge Ashe, Nov. 18, 1950; children— Richard Ashe, Elizabeth Aldridge, Mary Louise. BS, Springfield Coll., 1942; MA, Clark U., 1947; PhD, Tulane U., 1950. Asst. prof. U. Ala., Tuscaloosa, 1952-55, assoc. prof., 1955-56, 57-59, prof., 1959-63, prof. psychology, chmn. div. social and behavioral scis., 1967-73, prof. engring., 1969-84, Disting. Service prof. psychology, 1984-85, Disting Service prof. emeritus, 1985—; dean U. Ala. (Sch. Social and Behavioral Scis.), 1973-84. Research scientist Lockheed Ga. Co., Marietta, Ga., 1956-57, 63-65, cons., 1965-67; prof. Ga. Inst. Tech., 1965-67 Served with USNR, 1942-46, PTO; with USAF, 1951-52. Fellow Am. Psychol. Assn.; mem. So. Soc. for Philosophy and Psychology, Southeastern Psychol. Assn., Ala. Psychol. Assn., Pine Harbor Golf and Racquet Club, Coosa Pines Golf Club, Sigma Xi. Home: 7141 Skyline Dr Pell City AL 35128-6936 *Whatever success I have enjoyed ought to be attributed to the attempt I have made to carry out the admonitions of my parents to make choices only after having appraised the alternatives in terms of their consequences, to weigh ethical considerations above all others, never to demand of others what one is unwilling to give of himself, and to work untiringly for those causes to which one is committed.*

PASSEY, MARK LYMAN, sports association executive; b. Healdsburg, Calif., Mar. 4, 1947; s. Lyman E. and Lois L. (Marcantonio) P.; m. Charlene A. Carlsen, Jan. 26, 1968; children: Allison Edmondson, Hilary Walton. Student, Utah State U., Logan, 1965-68. Mgmt. (various) Smith's Mgmt. Corp., Salt Lake City, 1966-85; exec. dir. Utah Golf Assn., 1985-90; dir. regional affairs U.S. Golf Assn., 1990—. Bd. directors Utah Jr. Golf Association, 1985-90, Univ. Hosp. Utah Open, 1985-90, Showdown at Jeremy Ranch PGA Sr. Tour, 1985-90. Bd. dirs. Alliance for the Varied Arts, Logan, 1980-85. Avocations: arts, skiing, music. Office: US Golf Assn 1121 Loch Lomond Way Salt Lake City UT 84117-4974 E-mail: mpassey@usga.org.

PASSIAK, KAREN MARIE, business executive; b. Highland Pk., Mich., July 4, 1958; d. Alexander and Helen E. (Lisowski) P. BS in Edn., Mich. State U., 1980. Secondary tchr. home econs. North Adams (Mich.) Pub. Schs., 1981-82, Farmington (Mich.) Pub. Schs., 1981-82; customer svc. rep. Hertz Corp., Detroit, 1982-83, mgr. customer svc., 1983-84, mgr. tng. and communications, 1984-87, software adminstr. Oklahoma City, 1987-89, mgr. ops. tng., 1989—. Mem. Young Reps., Oklahoma City, 1988—. Olive Goodrich Sophomore scholar Mich. State U., 1977. Mem. ASTD, Nat. Trust Hist. Preservation, Okla. Hist. Soc., Williamsburg Found. Roman Catholic. Avocations: culinary art, American history, historic preservation, architecture. Office: Hertz Corp 5601 NW Expressway St Oklahoma City OK 73132-5297

PASSLACK, MATTHIAS, electrical engineer, researcher; b. Dippoldiswalde, Saxony, Germany, May 24, 1959; came to U.S., 1993; s. Guenter and Christa (Klemm) P.; m. Gudrun Schwartz, Feb. 16, 1985; children: Katrin, Jessica. MS in engring., Tech. U. Dresden, Germany, 1984, D. in Engring., 1988. Asst. prof. U. Dresden, 1989-91; vis. scientist U. Ulm, Germany, 1992, AT&T Bell Labs., Murray Hill, N.J., 1993-95; disting. mem. tech. staff Motorola, Tempe, Ariz., 1995—. Contbr. articles to IEEE Trans., Applied Physics Letters, Phys. Rev. Letters. Grantee German Rsch. Assn., 1992. Mem. IEEE (sr.), Am. Phys. Soc. Achievements include patents and patents pending in field; pioneer in field of GaAs metal-oxide-semiconductor technology. Office: Motorola 2100 E Elliot Rd # 720 Tempe AZ 85284-1806 E-mail: m.passlack@motorola.com.

PASSLOF, PAT, artist, educator; b. Brunswick, Ga. m. Milton Resnick. Student, Black Mountain Coll., 1948, Willem de Kooning, 1948-50; BFA, Cranbrook Coll., 1951. Prof. art Coll. of Staten Island, CUNY, 1972—. One woman show Elizabeth Harris Gallery, 1993, 96, 98, 2000. Fellow John Simon Guggenheim Meml. Found., 1999-00; recipient award of Merit for painting, Am. Acad. of Arts and Letters, 2000, award for achievement in the arts Coun. on Arts and Humanities for S.I., 2001.

PASSMAN, DONALD STEVEN, mathematician, educator; b. N.Y.C., Mar. 28, 1940; m. Marjorie Ann Mednick; children: Barbara Brownsword, Jonathan. BS, Bklyn. Poly. Inst., 1960; MA, Harvard U., 1961, PhD, 1964. Asst. prof. UCLA, 1964—66, Yale U., New Haven, 1966—69; mathmatician Inst. for Def. Analysis, Princeton, NJ, 1969—70; assoc. prof. U. Wis., Madison, 1969—72, prof. math., 1972—. Author: (book) Permutation Groups, 1968, Infinite Group Rings, 1971, Algebraic Structure of Group Rings, 1977, Group Rings, Crossed Products, and Galois Theory, 1986, Infinite Crossed Products, 1989, A Course in Ring Theory, 1991. Mem.: Math. Assn. Am. (Lester R. Ford award 1976, Haimo award for disting. univ. tchg. 2000), Am. Math. Soc. Home: 3118 Todd Dr Madison WI 53713 Office: Univ Wis 480 Lincoln Dr Madison WI 53706 Office Fax: 608-263-8891. Business E-Mail: passman@math.wisc.edu.

PASSMAN, STEPHEN LEE, physical scientist; b. Suffolk, Va., Sept. 3, 1942; s. Milton Lawrence and Jean (Lehrman) P.; married; children: Michael, Rebecca, Sara, Rachel. BSEM, Ga. Inst. Tech., 1964, MSEM, 1966, PhD, 1968. Instr. U.S Naval Acad., Annapolis, Md., 1968-70; postdoctoral fellow Johns Hopkins U., Balt., 1970-71; from asst. to assoc. prof. Ga. Inst. Tech., Atlanta, 1971-78; prin. mem. tech. staff Sandia Nat. Labs., Albuquerque, 1978-99; assoc. Booz-Allen & Hamilton, 1999—. Lectr. George Washington U., Washington, 1969-70; vis. mem. Math. Rsch. Ctr., U. Wis., Madison, 1972, Inst. Math. and Its Applications, U. Minn., Mpls., 1984, 89, Math. Sci. Inst., Cornell U., 1987-90; cons. Bell Labs., Norcross, Ga., 1975-78; vis. scientist Pitts. Energy Tech. Ctr., 1988-90, cons., 1990-96; vis. scientist U.S. Dept. Energy, Washington, 1995-99; vis. scholar Carnegie Mellon U., 1988-90; assoc. editor, Particulate Sci & Tech.; adj. prof. engring. U. Pitts., 1990-96; U.S. rep. multiphase flow com., Internat. Energy Agy., 1992-96; U.S. rep. G-7 Nuclear Experts Meeting, Paris, 1996; mem. steering com. U.S.-Russian Plutonium Disposition Program, 1995—. Author, Theory of Multicomponent Fluids, 1999. Contbr. articles to profl. jours. Served to capt. U.S. Army, 1968-70. Recipient Monie A. Ferst Rsch. award, 1968, awards from Dept. Energy and Dept. Def.; Johns Hopkins U. scholar, 1990. Mem. ASME (elasticity com. 1987-99, multiphase flow com. 1990-96), Soc. Natural Philosophy (treas. 1977-78, dir. 1978-96, chmn. bd. dirs. 1985-86), Soc. Engring. Sci. (bd. dirs. 1986-96, treas. 1987-96), Am. Acad. Mechanics, Am. Phys. Soc., Soc. Rheology, Sigma Xi. Office: Booz Allen & Hamilton 8283 Greensboro Dr Ste 700 Mc Lean VA 22102-3838

PASSMORE, DELORES SHARON, social worker; b. Bklyn., Mar. 31, 1961; d. Jake and Dessie Lee (Murph) P.; m. Clifford Tyrone Crosby, Oct. 13, 1989; 1 child, Christine Desiree. BS, York Coll., 1983; MSW, U. S.C., 1988. Caseworker N.Y. Cath. Guardian Soc., N.Y.C., 1983-85; teaching parent Cedar

Grove (N.J.) Residential Ctr., 1985-86; social worker Dept. Youth Svcs., Columbia, S.C., 1986-87, Wil Lou Grey Opportunity Sch., Columbia, 1987-88; sr. social worker Urban Family Svcs. Ctr., Bklyn., 1988-89; psychiat. social worker Exec. Health Group, Bronx, 1989-90; casework supr. St. Vincent's Svcs., Bklyn., 1990—. Mem. NASW, Nat. Assn. Black Social Workers. Home: 24016 149th Ave Jamaica NY 11422-3218 Office: St Vincent's Svcs 66 Boerum Pl Brooklyn NY 11201-5705

PASSON, RICHARD HENRY, English language educator, former administrator; b. Hazleton, Pa., Aug. 18, 1939; s. Henry Richard and Grace Miriam (Bernstein) P.; m. Margaret Rose Ferdinand, Aug. 14, 1965; children—Michael, Rebecca, Christopher. BA (Bishop Hafey scholar), King's Coll., Pa., 1961; MA, U. Notre Dame, 1963, PhD (NDEA fellow), 1965. From instr. to prof. English U. Scranton, 1964-73, chmn. English dept., 1970-73, fgn. student adviser, 1965-67; dean Coll. Arts and Scis., Creighton U., Omaha, 1973-77; acad. v.p. St. Joseph's U., Phila., 1977-84; provost U. Scranton, 1984-2000, prof. English, 2000—02; interim acad. v.p. St. Joseph's U., Phila., 2002—. Contbr. articles profl. jours. Recipient grant Nat. Assn. Fgn. Students, 1966 Mem. Modern Lang. Assn., Am. Assn. Higher Edn., Am. Assn. Acad. Deans, Nat. Coun. Tchrs. English. Democrat. Roman Catholic. Office: U Scranton 402 Brennan Hall Scranton PA 18510 E-mail: passonr1@scranton.edu.

PASSOS, NELSON LUIZ, computer science educator; b. Santos, Brazil, Mar. 29, 1952; s. Oscar and Norma (Rodrigues) P.; m. Inah Passos, Apr. 19, 1975; children: Alexandre, Katia. BSEE, U. Sao Paulo, 1974; MS in Computer Sci., U. N.D., 1992; PhD in Computer Sci./Engring., U. Notre Dame, 1996. Systems analyst Control Data Corp., Sao Paulo, 1974-79, systems mgr., 1979-90; assoc. prof. Midwestern State U., Wichita Falls, Tex., 1996—. Cons. Biobras S/A, Belo Hor, Zonte, Brazil, 1992-96, Steps Tech., Bello Horizonte, 1997—. Contbr. articles to profl. jours. Rsch. grantee NSF, 1997-2000. Mem. IEEE, Assn. Computing Machinery, Internat. Soc. for Computers and Their Applications, Upsilon Pi Epsilon. Avocations include the development of the theoretical founds. of multi-dimensional re-timing. E-mial. Office: Midwestern State U 3410 Taft Blvd Wichita Falls TX 76308-2096

PASSTY, JEANETTE NYDA, English language educator, writer; b. L.A., Jan. 19, 1947; d. Walter Isaac and Mollie Sarah Nyda; m. Gregory Bohdan Passty, June 18, 1976; 1 child, Benjamin. AA, L.A. Valley Coll., 1966; BA, UCLA, 1968; MA, U. So. Calif., 1974, PhD, 1982. Cert. c.c. instr., Calif. Tchg. asst., lectr., assoc. dir. freshman English program U. So. Calif., 1971-78; lectr. English dept. U. Tex., Austin, 1983-85; vis. asst. prof., adj. assoc. prof. Tex. Luth. U., Seguin, 1983, 85-87; from instr. to asst. prof. St. Philip's Coll., San Antonio, 1988-92, assoc. prof., 1992—. Lectr. UCLA, U. Tex., Austin, Western Mich. U., U. Louisville, Salisbury State U., Morehead State U., Tex. Tech. U., U. Wales, Bangor; humanities book reviewer CHOICE (ALA Jour.), 1985—86; manuscript reviewer Fairleight Dickinson U. Press, 1991—; editl. cons. CONNECTIONS: Online Distance Learning Faculty Forum, 2002—. Author: Eros and Androgyny: The Legacy of Rose Macaulay, 1988, The Lion Tells Her Story: A Biography of the Honorable N.P. Brooks Hinton, 1998, Bringing Denis Home: The Hero from Hope, Kansas, 2001; annotator: Alice Crawford's Paradise Pursued, 1995; contbr. articles to encyclopedia and profl. jours.; guest Sta. KSPL Radio In Touch With, 1989; appearance Sta. KENS-TV, 1992, Channel 12 Morehead, KY, 1998, CNN, 1995, Roadside (entr'acte with G.S. Bailey), 2000. Mem. Nat. Abortion Rights Action League, Tex. Abortion Rights Action League, Greenpeace, Environ. Def. Fund, The Nature Conservancy, Sierra Club, Handgun Control Inc., Orgn. Internat. Conf. on the Holocaust, San Antonio, 2000. Vierling Kersey scholar L.A. Valley Coll., 1964-66; NEH grantee Tex. Luth. U., 1986; recipient Elizabeth K. Pleasants Teaching award U. So. Calif., 1974, Outstanding Acad. Book award ALA, 1989, Women Honoring Women award Am. Assn. Women in Cmty. Colls., 1997, Katherine Anne Porter Lit. prize, 1999; Letters of Appreciation, Lord Bonham-Carter, 1987, HRH Princess Margaret, 1989-90. Mem. AAUW, NOW, MLA, Nat. Coun. Tchrs. of English, South Ctrl. Soc. 18th Century Studies, Virginia Woolf Soc. Avocations: academic decathlon, taekwondo, Arctic travel. Office: St Philip's Coll English Dept 1801 Martin Luther King Dr San Antonio TX 78203-2098

PASSWATER, RICHARD ALBERT, biochemist, author; b. Wilmington, Del., Oct. 13, 1937; s. Stanley Leroy and Mabel Rosetta (King) P.; m. Barbara Sarah Gayhart, June 2, 1964; children: Richard Alan, Michael Eric. BS, U. Del., 1959; PhD, Bernadean U., 1976. Cert. firefighter. Supr. instrumental analysis lab. Allied Chem. Corp., Marcus Hook, Pa., 1959-64; tech. svcs. rep. F&M Sci. Corp., Avondale, 1965; dir. applications lab. Am. Instrument Co., Silver Spring, Md., 1965-77; dir. Am. Gen. Enterprises, Minn.; former daily broadcaster Sta. WMCA, N.Y.C., 1980-88, Sta. WRNG, Atlanta, 1982-85; rsch. dir. Solgar Nutritional Rsch. Ctr., 1978—. Corp. v.p. Solgar Co., Inc.; chmn. Worcester County Emergency Planning Com., 1995-96; bd. dirs. Worcester Meml. Hosp., Atlantic Gen. Hosp., River Run Assn.; pres. 1989-92, Subaqueous Exploration and Archeology Ltd.; apptd. Md. State One Md. Com. and the Eastern Shore Econ. Task Force, Md. Gov. Glendenning, 1999, 2000. Author: Guide to Fluorescence Literature, vol. 1, 1967; vol. 2, 1970, vol. 3, 1974, Supernutrition, 1975, Supernutrition for Health Hearts, 1977, Super Calorie, Carbohydrate Counter, 1978, Cancer and Its Nutritional Therapies, 1978, 83, 93, The Easy No-Flab Diet, 1979, Selenium as Food and Medicine, 1980, The Slendernow Diet, 1982, (with Dr. E. Cranton), Trace Elements, Hair Analysis and Nutrition, 1983, The New Supernutrition, 1991, The Longevity Factor, 1993, Cancer Prevention and Nutritional Therapy, 1993, (with Ben Friedrich and Hans Kugler) Heart Health, 1994, Pycnogenol: The Super Protector Nutrient, 1994, Lipoic Acid: The Metabolic Antioxidant, 1995; contbg. author: Fire Protection Guide to Hazardous Materials, 1991; editor Fluorescence News, 1966-77, Jour. Applied Health Scis., 1982-83; mem. editl. bd. Nutritional Perspectives, 1978-96, The Body Forum, 1979-80, Jour. Holistic Medicine, 1981-88, VIM Newsletter, 1979—; contbg. Firehouse Mag., 1988-94, Jour. Applied Nutrition; contbr. over 400 health articles to mags.; co-editor booklet series Your Good Health; sci. adv. and columnist Whole Foods mag.; patentee in field. Bd. dirs. Sci. Documentation Ctr., Dunfermline, Eng.; Am. Found. Firefighter Health and Safety; chief Ocean Pines Vol. Fire Dept., 1984-93; active Emergency Med. Tech.; adviser Nat. Inst. Nutrition Edn.; past adv. bd. Stephen Decatur High Sch., Worcester County Dept. Edn. Cubmaster, 1975-79. Named Citizen of Yr. Ocean Pines, Md., 1987; recipient 5th Ann. Achievement award, 1989, VFW Cert. of Commendation, 1988, Industry award Nat. Inst. Nutritional Edn., 1991, Pres.'s award Nat. Nutritional Foods Assn., 1999; inducted into Delmarva Fireman's Hall of Fame, 1993. Fellow Internat. Acad. Preventive Medicine, Am. Inst. Chemists; mem. ASTM, AAAS, Am. Chem. Soc., Gerontology Soc., Am. Geriatric Soc., Am. Aging Assn., Internat. Found. Preventive Medicine (v.p.), Internat. Union Pure and Applied Chemistry, Royal Soc. Chemistry (London), Internat. Acad. Holistic Health and Medicine, Capital Chem. Soc., Nutrition Today Soc., Am. Acad. Applid Health Sci. (pres., bd. dirs.), Internat. Found. Preventive Medicine (v.p., dir.), Inst. Nutritional Rsch., N.Y. Acad. Scis., Nat. Fire Protection Assn. (cert. firefighter level III, com. on properties of hazardous chemicals), Pi Kappa Alpha. Office: 11017 Manklin Meadows Ln Berlin MD 21811-9340

PASSY, CHARLES, arts critic; b. N.Y., Jan. 9, 1964; s. Victor and Beverly (Green) P.; m. Leslie M. Olsen, Dec. 15, 1989; two children: Jacob E., Emma F. BA, Columbia U., 1985. Assoc. Jay K. Hoffman and Assocs., N.Y., 1983-87; sr. editor, mng. editor Ovation Mag., 1988-89; editor Classical Mag., 1989-91; editor-in-chief Musical Am. Pub., 1991-92; staff writer The Palm Beach Post, West Palm Beach, 1992—. Announcer, prodr. WNYC FM, N.Y., 1984-85; entertainment stringer N.Y. Newsday, 1987-92. Author (with others): New Voices: Selected University and College Prize Winning Poems, 1989, The New Grove Dictionary of Jazz, 1988, The New Grove Dictionary of American Music, 1986, The New Grove Dictionary of Music and Musicians, 2d edit., 2001; editor: The Letters of Virgil Thomson, 1988; contbr. numerous articles to publs. in field, The Wall St. Jour. Recipient Poetry award Acad. Am. Poets Columbia U., 1985, Criticism awards Soc. Profl. Journalists, 1995, 97, 99, 2001, Fla. Press Club, 1993, Fla. Soc. Newspaper Editors, 1993, 2001, Cox Newspapers, 2001; fellow Knight Ctr. for Specialized Journalism, 1993. Home: 180 Bent Tree Dr Palm Beach Gardens FL 33418-3597 Office: Palm Beach Newspapers Inc 2751 S Dixie Hwy West Palm Beach FL 33405-1298 E-mail: chazpbg@aol.com., charles_passy@pbpost.com.

PASTAN, LINDA OLENIK, poet; b. N.Y.C., May 27, 1932; d. Jacob L. and Bess (Schwartz) Olenik; m. Ira Pastan, 1953; children: Stephen, Peter, Rachel. BA, Radcliffe Coll., 1954; MLS, Simmons Coll., 1955; MA, Brandeis U., 1957. Author: (poetry) A Perfect Circle of Sun, 1971, On the Way to the Zoo, 1975, Aspects of Eve, 1975, The Five Stages of Grief, 1978 (Alice Fay di Castagnola award Poetry Soc. Am. 1978), Setting the Table, 1980, Waiting for My Life, 1981, PM/AM: New and Selected Poems, 1982 (Am. Book award nomination 1982), A Fraction of Darkness: Poems, 1985, The Imperfect Paradise, 1988, Heroes in Disguise, 1991, An Early Afterlife, 1995, Carnival Evening: New and Selected Poems, 1968-98 (nat. Book award nomination 1998), The Last Uncle, 2002. Recipient Dylan Thomas Poetry award Mademoiselle, 1958, Virginia Faulkner award Prarie Schooner, 1992, Charity Randall citation Internat. Poetry Forum, 1996; NEA fellow; grantee Md. Arts Coun.; poet laureate of Md., 1991-95. Jewish. Office: 11710 Beall Mountain Rd Potomac MD 20854-1105 E-mail: lpastan@att.net.

PASTEN, LAURA JEAN, veterinarian; b. Tacoma, May 25, 1952; d. Frank Larry and Jean Mary (Slavich) Brajkovich. Student, Stanford U., Davis, 1970; BA in Physiology, U. Calif., Davis, 1970, DVM, 1974; postgrad., Cornell U., 1975. Veterinarian Nevada County Vet. Hosp., Grass Valley, Calif., 1975-80; pvt. practice vet. medicine, owner Mother Lode Vet. Hosp., 1980-96; veterinarian for Morris the 9-Lives cat (of TV comml. fame), 1985-94. Veterinarian for Morris the 9-Lives cat (of TV comml. fame) 1985-94; lectr. in field; spokesperson Nat. Cat Health Month; guest Today Show on wildlife. Author: Malignant, Tarantula Whisperer, Rocky Point Murders; contbg. author: Rocky Point Murders; pub. video How Smart is Your Puppy? Bd. dirs. Aguajito Property Owners Assn., Sierra Svcs. for the Blind. Mem.: AOPA, AVMA, ASPCA, Bay Area Vet. Assn., Monterey Bay Vet Assn. (Carmel wildlife ednl. com., vet. coord. Monterey County Animal Disasters), Carmel Wildlife Edn. Com., Citizens Against Raccoon Extermination, Monterey SPCA, Denver Area Med. Soc., Am. Animal Hosp. Assn. (Mother Lode Hosp. cited for excellence), Mother Lode Vet. Assn., Calif. Vet. Med. Assn., Fund Animals Defenders Wildlife, Def. Animals, Inst. Protection Animals, In Def. of Animals, Humane Soc. U.S., Nature Conservancy, Am. Intenrat. Fund Animal Welfare, Internat. Vet. Med. Assn., Sierra Club, Big Sur Land Trust, Nat. Assn. Underwater Instrs., Rep. Womens Found. (bd. dirs.), Ninety-Nines Pilots Assn., Mensa. Republican. Lutheran. Home and Office: 5125 Paso Venado Carmel CA 93923-9477 E-mail: lpasten@aol.com.

PASTER, BARRIE, family practice physician; b. Cambridge, Mass., Sept. 24, 1942; s. Eugene and Evelyn (Rosenthal) P.; m. Barbara Ann Braveman, Dec. 24, 1972; children: Aren Yale, Sara Rachael, Noah Elon. BS, U. Vt., 1964, MD, 1968. Diplomate Am. Bd. Family Practice. Med. dir. Gould Corp., Newburyport, Mass., 1987-99, Harbor Schs., Amesbury and Newburyport, 1975—, Maplewood Manor Nursing Home, Amesbury, 1985—; pvt. practice, 1973-95; mem. staff Lahey Clinic, 1995—. Capt. U.S. Army, 1969-71. Named Mass. Family Practitioner of Yr., 2000. Fellow Am. Acad. Family Physicians (nat. del. 1984-99); mem. Mass. Acad. Family Physicians (pres.), Mass. Med. Soc. (Essex North Dist. Cmty. Clinician of Yr. 2001), Pentucket Assn. Physicians. Home: 100 Front St Exeter NH 03833-2626 Office: Lahey/Greenleaf Med Assocs 24 Morrill Pl Amesbury MA 01913-3530

PASTER, HOWARD G. public relations, public affairs company executive; b. N.Y.C., Dec. 23, 1944; BA with honors, Alfred U., 1966; MS in Journalism, Columbia U., 1967. Legis. dir. UAW, 1977-80; exec. v.p. Timmons & Co., 1980-92; asst. to pres. and dir. Office Legis. Affairs White House, Washington, 1993; chmn., CEO Hill and Knowlton, Inc., N.Y.C., 1994—. Office: Hill and Knowlton Inc 466 Lexington Ave Lbby 3 New York NY 10017-3140

PASTERNAC, ANDRÉ, cardiologist, educator; b. Toulouse, France, July 22, 1937; came to Can., 1971, naturalized, 1978. s. Jacques and Règine P. Adv. math., Lycée Henri IV, Paris, 1956; BA in Polit. Sci., Toulouse U., 1963, MD Med. Sch., 1968. Cert. Ins. and Disability Assessment U. Montreal, 2002. Intern Toulouse Univ. Hosp., 1962-63, resident, 1963-64, Edouard-Herriot Hosp., Lyon, France, 1965-66; Fulbright scholar in cardiology Harvard U., 1968-71; research fellow Peter Bent Brigham Hosp., Boston, 1968-69; Milton fellow Children's Hosp., 1969-71; fellow in cardiology Toronto (Ont., Can.) U., 1971-72; staff cardiologist Montreal (Que., Can.) Heart Inst., 1972—; asst. prof. medicine U. Montreal, 1972-78, clin. assoc. prof., 1978—, clin. prof. medicine, 1994—. Vis. lectr. U. Liège (Belgium), 1977, U. Madrid, 1977, U. Warsaw, 1979, 83; cons. Harley St. Clinic, Cromwell Hosp., Wellington Hosp., London; vis. assoc. prof. McGill U., Montreal, Can., 1975-76. Contbr. articles to profl. jours. Bd. dirs. Heart-Brain Rsch. Found. Inc., N.Y.C., Cardiostat Inc., Montreal. Am. Field Svc. grantee, Oreg., 1954-55. Mem. French Cardiac Soc., European Soc. Cardiology, Canadian Cardiovasc. Soc., Am. Coll. Cardiology, Am. Heart Assn., Internat. Soc. Heart Rsch., Am. Fedn. Clin. Rsch., N.Y. Acad. Scis. Research in stress-related myocardial ischemia and dysfunction, mitral valve prolapse, cardiovascular drugs, cardiomyopathies, catecholamines, neuroendocrine control of the heart, stress and the heart, prevention. Home: Port Royal 1455 Sherbrooke St W # 703 Montreal QC Canada H3G 1L2 Office: Montreal Heart Inst 5000 Belanger E Montreal QC Canada H1T 1C8

PASTERNACK, ROBERT FRANCIS, chemistry educator; b. N.Y.C., Sept. 20, 1936; 2 children. BA, Cornell U., 1957, PhD in Chemistry, 1962. Research assoc. in chemistry U. Ill., Champaign, 1962-63; from asst. to prof. chemistry Ithaca Coll., N.Y., 1963-66, Charles A. Dana Endowed prof. chemistry, 1976-82; Edmund Allen prof. chemistry Swarthmore Coll., Pa., 1984—. Invited speaker seminars, colls., univs., nat., internat. meetings, confs. including Bioinorganic Chem., Italy, Portugal, Gordon Rsch. Confs., Spanish Royal Soc. Chem., many others; lectr. series Nankai U., China, U. Messina, Italy; mem. adv. com. Rsch. Corp.; mem. sci. & art com. Franklin Inst.; co-organizer, chmn. workshop on rsch. at undergrad. instn. NSF, mem. undergrad. curriculm chem.; vis. prof., vis. rschr. U Messina, U. Paris, Nakai, Rome, King's Coll., London, Fritz Haber Inst., Berlin, Doshisha U., Kyoto; co-developer A Unified Lab. Program; initiator, chmn. C.P. Snow Lectr. Series. Author, co-author more than 100 sci. publs. Mem. com. on sci. and the arts Franklin Inst., 1992-98. Grantee NSF, 1965-66, 69-72, 77-78, 83-84, 86-94, 95—; Petroleum Rsch. Fund, 1967-74, 86-88, NIH, 1971-89, Monsanto Corp., 1986-92, Rsch. Corp., 1974-75, 78-79, 84-85, Danforth Assocs., 1978-84, Camille and Henry Dreyfus Found., 1981, 95, NATO, 1979, 88-89, 95-96; recipient Camille and Henry Dreyfus Tchg./Scholar award, 1987-89, NSF Manpower Improvement award, King's Coll., U. London, 1977-78, Commemorative medal for sci. contbns. U. Catania, 1994; NSF sci. faculty fellow U. Rome, 1968-70. Mem. AAAS, Am. Inst. Chemists (Hon. Scroll award 1998), Am. Chem. Soc. (award for rsch. at an undergrad. instn. 2001), N.Y. Acad. Sci., Sigma Xi. Office: Swarthmore Coll Dept Chemistry Swarthmore PA 19081 E-mail: rpaster1@swarthmore.edu.

PASTERNACK, ROBERT HARRY, school psychologist; b. Bklyn., Nov. 30, 1949; s. William and Lillian Ruth (Levine) P.; m. Jeanelle Livingston, Apr. 10, 1980; children: Shayla, Rachel. BA, U. South Fla., 1970; MA, N.Mex. Highlands U., 1972; PhD, U. N.Mex., 1980. Dir. Eddy County Drug Abuse Program, Carlsbad, N.Mex., 1972-73; adminstrv. intern U.S. Office Edn., Washington, 1975-76; exec. dir. Villa Santa maria, Cedar Crest, N.Mex., 1976-78; clin. dir. Ranchos Treatment Ctr., Taos, 1978-79; sch. psychologist N.Mex. Boys Sch., Springer, 1980—, supt., 1991; pres. Ensenar Health svcs., Inc., Taos, 1980—; CEO Casa de Corazon, N.Mex., 1994-98; state dir. spl. edn. N.Mex. State Dept. Edn., Santa Fe, 1998—. Instr. N.Mex. Highlands U., Las Vegas, 1980—, U. N.Mex., Albuquerque, 1980—; cons. N.Mex. Youth Authority, Santa Fe, 1988—, N.Mex. Devel. Disabilities Bur., Santa Fe, 1986—, various sch. dists.; state dir. spl. edn., N.Mex., 1998—. Author: Growing Up: The First Five Years, 1986; contbr. articles to profl. publs. Pres., bd. dirs. Children's Lobby, N.Mex., 1978, N.Mex. Spl. Olympics, 1986-88, Child-Rite, Inc., Taos, 1990; mem. Gov.'s Mental Health Task Force, Albuquerque, 1988—. Mem. Nat. Assn. Sch. Psychologists, Correctional Edn. Assn., Nat. Alliance Mentally Ill, N.Mex. Coun. on Crime and Delinquency. Avocations: tennis, racquetball, skiing, cooking. Home and Office: 6235 5th St NE Apt 14 Washington DC 20002*

PASTERNACK, STEFAN ALAN, psychiatrist, psychoanalyst; b. Jersey City, Nov. 5, 1939; BA, Cornell U., 1961; MD, Georgetown U., 1965. Diplomate in psychiatry Am. Bd. Neurology and Psychiatry; lic. physician, D.C., Md. Resident in psychiatry U. Cin. Gen. Hosp., 1966-69; psychiat. cons. North Cmty. Mental Health Ctr., Washington, 1971-97; asst. prof. psychiatry Georgetown U. Sch. Medicine, 1971-79, assoc. clin. prof. psychiatry, 1979-86, clin. prof. psychiatry, 1986—, co-dir. advanced studies prog. in psychiatry/psychoanalysis, 1995—. Pvt. practice psychiatry and psychoanalysis, Washington, 1978—. Editor: Violence and Victims, 1975; contbr. articles to profl. jours. Bd. dirs. Nat. Capital Med. Found., Washington, 1973-76, Forum for Psychoanalytic Study of Film, Washington, 1989—. Lt. comdr. USN, 1969-71. Fellow: Am. Psychiat. Assn.; mem.: Washington Psychiat. Soc. (mem. coun. 1987—99), Am. Psychoanalytic Assn., Cosmos Club. Avocations: motorboating and yachting, piano, writing. Office: 2121 Wisconsin Ave NW Ste 280 Washington DC 20007-2297 E-mail: sp39@aol.com.

PASTERNAK, GAVRIL WILLIAM, neurologist, neuropharmacologist; b. Bklyn., June 29, 1947; m. Sandra F. Pasternak, Nov. 12, 1977; children: Katie, David, Anna. BA, Johns Hopkins U., 1969, MD, 1973, PhD, 1974. Diplomate Am. Bd. Psychiatry and Neurology. Asst. mem. Meml. Sloan Kettering Cancer Ctr., N.Y.C., 1979-85, assoc. mem., 1985-89, mem., 1989—; asst. prof. Cornell U. Med. Coll., 1979-83, assoc. prof., 1983-89, prof., 1989—. Bd. scientific counselors Nat. Inst. on Drug Abuse, 1987-92. Editor: The Opiate Receptors; co-editor: Analgesics: Neurochemical Behavioral and Clinical Perspectives; contbr. numerous articles to profl. jours.; patentee in field. Recipient Boyer Young Investigator award Meml. Sloan Kettering Cancer Ctr., N.Y.C., 1987. Fellow Am. Acad. Neurology (S. Weir Mitchell award 1980); mem. AAAS, Am. Neurol. Assn., N.Y. Acad. Scis. (conf. com.), Soc. Neurosci., Johns Hopkins Soc. Scholars, Phi Beta Kappa. Office: Memorial Sloan Kettering 1275 York Ave New York NY 10021-6094

PASTERNAK, JOANNA MURRAY, humanities educator; b. Houston, Feb. 9, 1953; d. Lee Roy and Evelyn Mary (Kirmss) Murray; children: Sheila Ann Tanner, Lawrence Ross Tanner IV; m. Allen Pasternak, Jan. 9, 1993. BA in Liberal Arts with honors, Our Lady of the Lake, San Antonio, 1990; MA in Liberal Arts, U. St. Thomas, Houston, 1998. Acctg. clk. Houston Post, 1981-85; owner, art cons. Tanner Fine Art, Houston, 1985-92; spl. edn. tchr. Houston Ind. Sch. Dist., 1991-94, dept. chmn., 1994—, secondary social studies tchr., 2000—02; prof. humanities U. Phoenix, Houston, 2001—, chair dept. humanities, 2001—. Art cons. Plz. Gallery, Houston, 1985; mem. benefits com. Houston Ind. Sch. Dist., 1992-2001; presenter Am. Fedn. Tchrs. Nat. Edn. Conf., 1994. Contrb. articles to profl. jours. Vol. legis com. nat. health care campaign AFL-CIO; bd. dirs. PTA, SDMC; Dem. campaign worker, 1993—; precinct and state del. Dem. Senate, 1994-96, 98; sec. Dist. 13 Dem. Com., 1998; v.p. Houston Ind. Sch. Dist. Elem. Chess League, 1996-99; mem. edn. com. Harris County Dem. Com., mem. exec. com.; sec.-treas. Coalition of Cmty. and Commerce, 1997-2000; commr. Houston Bldg. and Stds. Commn., 1999-2002; precinct judge, chmn. precinct 139, Houston. Recipient Vick Driscoll award Tex. Commerce Bank, 1996. Mem. Am. Assn. Children with Learning Disabilities, Tex. Fedn. Tchrs. (bd. dirs. quality ednl. stds. in tchg. 1993, legis. com., chmn. 1993-99), Houston Fedn. Tchrs. (chmn. legis. liaison com. 1993-99, v.p. 1992-99), River Oaks Roadwomen, Delta Mu Delta. Democrat. Avocations: civic and political activities. Home: 2141 Colquitt St Houston TX 77098-3310 Office: Houston Ind Sch Dist 7405 Bissonnet Houston TX 77074

PASTIN, MARK JOSEPH, association executive; b. Ellwood City, Pa., July 6, 1949; s. Joseph and Patricia Jean (Camenite) Pastin; m. Joanne Marie Reagle, May 30, 1970 (div. Mar. 1982); m. Carrie Patricia Class, Dec. 22, 1984 (div. June 1990); m. Christina M. Brecto, June 15, 1991. BA summa cum laude, U. Pitts., 1970; MA, Harvard U., 1972, PhD, 1973. Asst. prof. Ind. U., Bloomington, 1973-78, assoc. prof., 1978-80; founder, bd. Compliance Resource Group, Inc., 1983—; chmn., CEO, pres. Coun. Ethical Orgns., Alexandria, Va., 1986—; prof. mgmt., dir. Ariz. State U., Tempe, 1988-92, prof. emeritus, 1996—; chair Health Ethics Trust, 1995—. Mem. adv. bd. Aberdeen Holdings, San Diego, 1988-90; dir. Learned Nicholson, Ltd., 1990-91; bd. Japan Am. Soc. Phoenix, Found. for Ethical Orgns.; cons. GTE, Interim Healthcare, 1997—, Tex. Instruments, MicroAge Computers, Med-Tronic, Blood Sys., Inc., Opus Corp., GTE, NyNex, Am. Express Bank, Kaiko Bussan Co., Japan, Arex Co., Japan, Century Audit Co., Japan, Scottsdale Meml. Hosp., Consanti Found., Lincoln Electric Co., Tenet Healthcare Corp., The Williams Co.; vis. faculty Harvard U., 1980; invited presenter Australian Inst. Mgmt., Nippon Tel. & Tel., Hong Kong Commn. Against Corruption, 1984, Young Pres.'s Orgn. Internat. U., 1990, Nat. Assn. Indsl. & Office Parks, 1990, ABA, 1991, Govt. of Brazil, 1991. Author: Hard Problems of Management, 1986 (Book of Yr. Armed Forces Mil. Comtrs. 1986, Japanese edit. 1994), Power by Association, 1991, The Hotline Handbook, 1996, Planning Forum, 1992; editor: Public-Private Sector Ethics, 1979; mem. editl. bd. Report on Medicine Compliance; pub. Pastin Report on Healthcare Compliance, 1998—, Guerin Lect. on Philanthropy, 1996. Founding bd. mem. Tempe Leadership, 1985-89; bd. mem. Ctr. for Behavioral Health, Phoenix, 1986-89, Tempe YMCA, 1986—, Valley Leadership Alumni Assn., 1989-92; mem. Clean Air Com., Phoenix, 1987-90. Nat. Sci. Found. fellow, Cambridge, Mass., 1971-73; Nat. Endowment for the Humanities fellow, 1975; Exxon Edn. Found. grant, 1982-83. Mem.: Found. Ethical Orgns. (chmn. 1988, pres.), Bus. Ethics Soc., Am. Soc. Assn. Execs. (invited presenter 1987—97), Univ. Club D.C., Harvard Club D.C., Mt. Vernon Country Club, Phi Beta Kappa, Golden Key. Avocations: golf, running. Office: 214 S Payne St Alexandria VA 22314-3530 Home: 7205 Regent Dr Alexandria VA 22307-2044 E-mail: councile@aol.com.

PASTIZZO, GARY F. physician assistant; b. Hartford, Conn., Jan. 18, 1968; s. Anthony F. and Dolores (Arico) P.; m. Shannon L. Bayreuther, June 27, 1992; children: Mitchell Robert, Lexi Lee. BS, Union Coll., Schenectady, N.Y., 1990; MS, U. Conn., 1992; M.Health Sci., Quinnipiac Coll., Hamden, Conn., 1996. Lic. physician asst. Physician asst. cardiovascular surgery St. Francis Hosp., Hartford, 1996—; rsch. asst. III U. Conn. Health Ctr., Farmington, 1992-94; figure skating coach ISCC, Simsbury, Conn., 1992—. Fellow Am. Acad. Physician Assts., Conn. Acad. Physician Assts.; mem. U.S. Figure Skating Assn., Soc. Critical Care. Republican. Roman Catholic. Avocations: figure skating, drumming.

PASTOR, EDWARD, congressman; b. Claypool, Ariz., June 28, 1943; m. Verma Mendez; children: Yvonne, Laura. BA, Ariz. State U., 1966, JD, 1974. Mem. Maricopa County Bd. Suprs., Phoenix, 1976-91; mem. U.S. Congress from 2d Ariz. dist., Washington, 1991—; mem. appropriations com. Democrat. Office: Ho Reps 2465 Rayburn HOB Washington DC 20515*

PASTOR, MILLIE A. interior designer, consultant; d. Martin Joseph and Bessie B. Kloka; m. Robert Henry Pastor, Sept. 29, 1951; children: Robert Henry, George H., Patricia C., Karen M. BSN, RN, Mercy Coll., 1951. Founder, pres. Pastor Interiors, Inc., Bloomfield Hills, Mich., 1965—. Cons. URI, Nashville; cons., speaker, mem. nat. women's bd. Northwood Inst. Pres., Project Hope, 1973-75. Commr. Mich. Am. Recolution Bicentennial, 1972-78; bd. dirs. March of Dimes, 1980-82, Christ Child Soc., 1960-68, Mich. Artrain, Women's Com. of Detroit Symphony Orch., Mich. Opera, Mich. Bach Festival, Ford Hospice, I.F.D.A., Henry Ford Hospice Health Sys.; pres. Am. Lung assn., Southeastern Mich.; active Boys and Girls Club Met. Detroit; active Mich. Opera Thetare, Mich., Cancer Found. Recipient Outstanding Contbn. award March of Dimes, 1977-79, Outstanding Fund Raising Vol. award Nat. Soc. Fund Raising Execs., 1982, Matilda R. Wilson award Boys & Girls Club, 1998; named Woman of Yr., Boys Town Italy, 1980. Mem. Internat. Furnishings and Design Assn. (v.p., Image Maker award Mich. chpt. 1979), Design Lighting Inst., Detroit Zool. Soc., Orch. Hall Assn. Founders Soc. Republican.

PASTORE, THOMAS MICHAEL, telecommunications sales executive; b. Bronx, N.Y., Jan. 25, 1959; s. Philip J. and Olga E. (DeGenito) P.; m. Kimberly A. Coppersmith, Dec. 13, 1986; children: Gabriela Maria, Thomas John. BA in Bus., Western State Coll., 1981. Sales rep. Victor Technologies Inc., Denver, 1981-84; account mgr. No. Telecom Inc., 1984-87, v.p. sales coun., 1985—, sales engr., 1987-92, dist. sales mgr., 1992-99; nat. acct. mgr. Nortel Networks, 2000—. Mem. Better Air Campaign, 1990—; sec. Warren Sq. Homeowners Assn., Denver, 1987-92; player, contbr. Dale Tooley Tennis Tournament, 1991-92; fundraiser Am. Cancer Soc., Denver, 1991—; mem. Denver Art Mus., 1991-92, 99, Colo. Ocean Jour., 1999. Republican. Roman Catholic. Avocations: skiing, tennis, biking. Home and Office: Nortel Networks 16095 Quarry Hill Dr Parker CO 80134-9553

PASTORE, VINCENT, actor; b. 1946; Night club mgr., N.Y.C. Actor: (films) Black Roses, 1988, True Love, 1989, Goodfellas, 1990, Awakenings, 1990, Backstreet Dreams, 1990, Men of Respect, 1991, Who Do I Gotta Kill?, 1992, Who's the Man?, 1993, Carlito's Way, 1993, Italian Movie, 1993, The Ref, 1994, It Could Happen to You, 1994, Hand Gun, 1994, The Jerky Boys, 1995, The Basketball Diaries, 1995, Money Train, 1995, Pictures of Baby Jane Doe, 1995, The Dutch Master, 1995, Sunset Park, 1996, Walking and Talking, 1996, Joe's Apartment, 1996, Gotti, 1996, West New York, 1996, Night Falls on Manhattan, 1997, All Over Me, 1997; (TV miniseries) The Last Don, 1997; (films) The Deli, 1997, Six Ways to Sunday, 1998; (TV films) Witness to the Mob, 1998; (films) Jane Austen's Mafia!, 1998, No Exit, 1998, Mickey Blue Eyes, 1999, The Hurricane, 1999; (TV films) A Slight Case of Murder, 1999; (films) The Rules for Men, 1999, 18 Shades of Dust, 1999, Blue Moon, 2000, Two Family House, 2000, Under Hellgate Bridge, 2000, Made, 2001, Corky Romano, 2001, Riding in Cars With Boys, 2001, Dating Service, 2001, After the Storm, 2001, Deuces Wild, 2002, Serving Sara, 2002, Return to Sleepaway Camp, 2002; (TV films) Last Laugh, 2002; (TV series) Law & Order, 1990, New York Undercover, 1994, For Your Love, 1998, Son of the Beach, 2000, The Sopranos, 1999—2000, Bull, 2000, Ed, 2000, Emeril, 2001. Mem.: AFTRA, SAG. Office: Abrams Artists Agy 275 7th Ave 26th Fl New York NY 10001*

PASTOREK, NORMAN JOSEPH, facial plastic surgeon; b. Moline, Ill., Feb. 8, 1939; s. Joseph Andrew and Rose (Faurone) P.; m. Janice Marie Gloss, Apr. 27, 1986; children: Kate Haviland, Kelly Taylor. AB, Augustana Coll., 1960; MD, U. Ill., Chgo., 1964. Diplomate Am. Bd. Otolaryngology. Intern San Francisco Gen. Hosp., 1964-65; resident U. Ill. Hosps., Chgo., 1965-69; pvt. practice medicine specializing in facial plastic surgery N.Y.C; clin. asst. prof. N.Y. Hosp. Cornell Med. Coll., 1971-83, dir. div. facial plastic surgery dept. otolaryngology, 1977—, clin. assoc. prof., 1983-91, clin. prof., 1991—. Examiner Am. Bd. Otolaryngology, 1971, 91-93; mem. bd. surgen dirs. Manhattan Eye, Earr and Throat Hosp., N.Y.C., 2001. Author: Blepharoplasty, 1983, 3d edit., 1994; editor: Aesthetic Facial Surgery, 1990; editor for beauty: Archives of Facial Plastic Surgery, 1999. Lt. comdr. USN, 1969-71. Fellow Am. Acad. Otolaryngology, Am. Bd. Otolaryngology (examiner 1991—), Am. Acad. Facial Plastic and Reconstructive Surgery (v.p. eastern region 1982-86, pres.-elect 1989-90, pres. 1990-91, pres. founders club 1996—), ACS; mem. Alpha Omega Alpha. Republican. Episcopalian.

PASTOREK, PAUL, federal agency administrator; Gen. counsel NASA, Washington, 2002—; ptnr. Adams and Reese, New Orleans. Pres. La. State Bd. Elem. and Secondary Edn.; mem. various state bds. and commns. Office: NASA Hdqrs Mail Code A 300 E St SW Washington DC 20546

PASTORIZA, JULIO, lawyer; b. Havana, Cuba, Sept. 22, 1948; came to U.S., 1960; s. Julio S. and Emilia (Bardanca) P.; m. Gloria M. Alvarez-Pedroso, Jan. 5, 1974; 1 child, Gloria Cristina. AA, Miami Dade C.C., 1967; BA, U. Fla., 1969; JD, U. Miami, 1973. Bar: Fla. 1973, U.S. Tax Ct. 1974, U.S. Supreme Ct. 1977. Assoc. Miguel A. Suarez P.A., Miami, Fla., 1973-77; ptnr. Sulli, Pastoriza & Hill, 1977-82; shareholder Julio Pastoriza, P.A., Coral Gables, Fla., 1982-85; ptnr. LaCapra & Wiser, Miami, 1985-87; pvt. practice Coral Gables, 1987—. Agent Attys. Title Ins. Fund, Miami, 1979—; instr. Biscayne Coll., Miami, 1972-76. Spkr. pre-marital conf. St. Theresa Cath. Ch., Coral Gables, 1981-88, mem. adv. bd., 1987-89; mem. adv. bd. Our Lady of Lourdes Acad., Miami, 1991-95; counselor St. Robert Bellarmine Cath. Ch., 2000-01. Democrat. Avocations: fishing, photography. Home: 2601 San Domingo St Coral Gables FL 33134-5534 Office: 7101 SW 99 Ave Ste 109B Miami FL 33173-4661

PASTRANA, RONALD RAY, Christian ministry counselor, Biblical theology educator, former school system administrator; b. N.Y.C., Sept. 5, 1939; s. Anthony and Mildred Pastrana; m. Josephine Pastrana; children: Christine, Therese. BA in History/Sci. Edn., Queens Coll., 1963; advanced sci. cert., Pace U., 1964-68; MS in Counseling Edn., St. John's U., 1967; diploma, U.S. Acad. of Health Sci., 1975, U.S. Army Command and Gen. Staff Coll., 1979; D Ministry, Sch. Bible Theology Sem., 1996, ThD, 2000. Lic. min. Pentecostal Assemblies of God of Am.; cert. life support sys. in internat. space NOAA, NASA. Tchr. sci. Marie Curie Jr. High Sch., Bayside, N.Y., 1963-68; guidance counselor Half Hollow Hills High Sch., Dix Hills, 1969-71, Walt Whitman High Sch., Huntington Station, 1968-69, coord. occupational svcs., 1971-74; guidance coord. Dutchess County Bd. Coop. Ednl. Svcs. Tech. Edn. Ctr., Poughkeepsie, 1974-86; coord. guidance and related acads. Dutchess County BOCES Tech. Edn. Ctr., 1986-96; asst. dir. Reach Out Sch. of Ministry, Hyde Park, 1996—; prof. Biblical theology Sch. Bible Theology Sem., San Jacinto, Calif., 1999—. Ednl. cons. N.Y. State Edn. Dept., Albany, 1975-83, Armed Forces Vocat. Testing Group, Dept. of Def., Washington, 1975-77; cert. educator Lunar Edn. Project, NASA, 1986-87, Asteroids, Lunar Rocks, Meteorites Edn. Projects, 1999—; sci., math. and tech. cons., 1998; pub. Reach Out Ministries. Author: Career Guidance in the Classroom, 1974, A Curriculum Guide to the Study of the Seven Dispensations and Eight Covenants, 1996, Dispensational Theology, 1997, Pentecostal Doctrine and Theology, 1998, Student Guide to the Seven Dispensations and Eignt Covenants, 1999, The Greek Fathers of the Early Christian Church, 2000, The Latin Fathers of the Early Christian Church, 2000, The Reformers of the Christian Church, 2001, Reach Out Ministries. Lt. col. USAR, ret. 1992. NSF sci. study grantee, 1964-68, grantee NASA and Nat. Ocean. and Atmos. Adminstrn., 1999; recipient: Dutchess County Counselor of the Year award, 1995; decorated Joint Svc. Commendation medal, Army achievement medal, Selective Svc. Meritorious medal, Army Res. Components Achievement medal, Nat. Def. Svc. medal, N.Y.S. medal for Meritorious Svc., Meritorious Svc. award for civilian svc. USN, 2000. Mem. Am. Counselors Assn., Am. Mental Health Counselors Assn., Nat. Career Devel. Assn., Am. Assn. Christian Counselors, N.Y. Acad. Scis., N.Y. State Assn. for Counseling and Devel., Sch. Adminstrs. Assn. N.Y. State, Dutchess County Counseling Assn. (exec. bd. 1989-96), Phi Delta Kappa. Avocations: rock and mineral collecting, fitness activities, canoeing, hiking. Office: Wappingers Ctrl Sch Dist Office of Sci & Tech 6 Hillside Lake Rd Wappingers Falls NY 12590 Home: 23 North Loop Rhinebeck NY 12572-1920

PASTRICK, HAROLD LEE, aeronautical engineer; b. Ambridge, Pa., June 28, 1936; s. Samuel and Mary (Makara) P.; m. Vivienne Lee Nusser Heinricher, June 3, 1961; children: Tracy Lee, Gregory Harold, Michael Joseph Samuel. BSEE, Carnegie-Mellon U., 1958; postgrad., Rutgers U., 1959-61, CCNY, 1961-63, U. Ala. Huntsville, 1964-66, 68-73; student, MIT, summers 1961-63; MS in Aeronautics & Astronautics, Stanford U., 1967, engr. in Aeronautics & Astronautics, 1972; PhD in Engring., Calif. Western U., 1977. Registered prof. engr., Ala. Metallurgical engring. aide Jones & Laughlin Steel Corp., Aliquippa, Pa., 1955-56; asst. engr., designer Am. Bridge Divsn., U.S. Steel Corp., Ambridge, 1957; electronics engr. Avionics Divsn., U.S. Army Signal R&D Labs., Ft. Monmouth, N.J., 1958-63; aerospace engr., Inertial Systems Team Missile R&D Labs., Redstone Arsenal, Ala., 1963-64; tech. dir. Army Inertial Guidance & Tech. Ctr., 1964-66; project engr. Inertial Guidance Br., 1967-71; rsch. aerospace engr. Guidance & Control Br., 1971-73; group leader Terminal Homing Missile Analysis, 1973-79; staff specialist, asst. to dir., land warfare Office of Under Sec. Def., Rsch. and Engring., Washington, 1979-80; chief, guidance and control analysis U.S. Army Missile Command, Redstone Arsenal, Ala., 1980-81; v.p. engring. Control Dynamics Co., Huntsville, 1981-83; asst. v.p., engring. analysis divsn. Sci. Applications Internat. Corp., 1983-86; v.p. theater missile def. and system analysis operation, 1986-91; corp. v.p., gen. mgr. SRS Technologies, Huntsville, 1991—. Acting pres. and COO SRS Techs., 1994, mem. corp. exec. mgmt. com., 1991—, mem. profit sharing and 401(k) com., 1993—; lectr. Sch. of Sci. and Engring., U. Ala., Huntsville, 1967-83; lectr. dept. continuing edn. George Washington U., 1985-87; engring. seminar dir. Applied Tech. Inst., Frankfurt, Germany, 1984, Singapore, 1986; tech. tng. dir. Tech. Tng. Corp., Tel Aviv, 1988; lectr. Advanced Tech. Internat., Ltd., London, 1985; guidance and control cons. various labs Dept. of Def., Washington, 1971-2001; lectr., rsch. advisor Southeastern Inst. Tech., Huntsville, 1978-84; lectr., seminar leader Guidance and Control Technologies, U.S., Europe, Asia, Mex., 1980-94. Contbr. over 120 articles to profl. jours. Chmn. combined fed. campaign ARDEC United Way, Redstone Arsenal, 1976; mem. Huntsville Econ. Devel. Com., 1994; chmn. indsl. contbns. Armed Forces Week C. of C. Huntsville-Madison County, 1993—96, 1999, vice chmn. mil. affairs. com., 1994—95, chmn. mil. affairs com., 1996; program chmn. tech. and bus. symposium and exhbn. Huntsville, 1994—95; gen. chmn., 1995—96; chmn. adv. com., 1997—98; founding trustee Ala. Constn. Village Found., 2001—; mem. All-Peoples Meml. for All Vets., Madison County, 2001—; mem. elec. and computer engring. adv. bd. The Citadel, Charleston, SC, 2001—; pres. Greek Orthodox Ch., 1967, 1973, chmn. planning com., 1993—2000. Capt. U.S. Army, 1958—64. Recipient Eminent Engr. Disting. Tau Beta Pi, 1998. Fellow: AIAA (assoc.; vice-chmn. Huntsville chpt. 1979, guest editor Jour. Guidance and Control 1981, missile tech. com. 1989—91); mem.: Ala. Acad. Sci. (vice chmn. 1978—79, engring. chmn. 1979—81), Inst. Navigation, Assn. U.S. Army, IEEE (sr.; chpt. program chmn. 1972—73), Soc. Computer Simulation, Am. Def. Preparedness Assn. (vice-chmn. Huntsville chpt. 1974—75), Huntsville Assn. Tech. Socs. (adv. com. 1997—98, pres. 1998—99, chmn.), Burning Tree Country Club, Redstone Golf Club, Greenwhyche Club (v.p. 1979), Heritage Club, Rotary (sec. 1994—95, pres.-elect. 1995—96, pres. 1996—97, asst. gov. dist. 6860 1997—2000, dist. task force dir. 2000—01), Greater Huntsville Rotary Found. (dir. internat. svc. 1992—94, CEO 1998—2000). Achievements include pioneering hardware in the loop simulations for testing laser semi-active guided missiles. Avocations: golf, weight tng., choral music, reading, running. Home: 2624 Trailway Rd SE Huntsville AL 35801-1474 Office: SRS Technologies 500 Discovery Dr NW Huntsville AL 35806-2810 E-mail: hpastrick@stg.srs.com.

PASTUCH, BORIS MAX See MAX, BUDDY

PASTUSZAK, WILLIAM THEODORE, hematopathologist; b. Stamford, Conn., Feb. 18, 1946; m. Patricia Marie Nelson, June 14, 1969. BS, Tufts U., 1968; MD, U. Conn., 1972. Cert. in anatomic pathology and hematology, Am. Bd. Pathology. Asst. dir. hematology Hartford (Conn.) Hosp., 1976-81, dir. hematology, 1981-94, asst. dir. pathology and lab. medicine, 1986-94, dir. pathology and lab. medicine, 1994—; pres. Hartford (Conn.) Pathology Assocs., P.C., 1992—. Fellow Am. Soc. Clin. Pathology, Am. Soc. Hematology, Coll. Am. Pathologists (vice chmn. 1991-93, mem. govt. affairs com. 1986-96, chmn. state adv. com. 1994-96), Conn. Soc. Pathologists (pres. 1983-84, exec. com. 1985—). Office: Hartford Hosp Dept Pathology 80 Seymour St Dept Hartford CT 06102-8000

PASUPULETI, VENUMADHAV, business executive, consultant; b. Hyderabad, India, Mar. 24, 1969; s. Srinivas Rao and Rama Kumari P.; m. Marilyn L. Miller, May 7, 1992; 1 child, Teja. Grad., Bur. of Data Processing Sys., Hyderabad, 1985; student, Wright State U., 1988-92. Info. tech. cons., 1984-93; mgr. Info. Horizons, Parsippany, N.J., 1993-95; exec. v.p. Globe Tech. Exch., Dayton, Ohio, 1995; COB/CEO Megasoft Corp., 1995—. Pres. Indian Student Assn. Wright State U., Dayton, 1989-92; vol. India Literacy Project, Dayton, 1990-95, Ohio India Project, Dayton, 1990-95, Day of Caring, Dayton, 1990-95; coun. mem. Dayton Minority Supplier Devel. Coun., 1997—. Mem. IEEE, South Ctrl. Ohio Minority Bus. Coun. (coun. mem. 2000—), Assn. for Computing Machinery, Math. Assn. of Am., Dayton Area C. of C., Beavarcreek C. of C. Office: Megasoft Corp PO Box 20271 Dayton OH 45420-0271 E-mail: venup@megasoft-corp.com.

PASURKA, JR. CARL A. economist; b. Elgin, IL, Sept. 15, 1953; s. Carl A. Pasurka, Sr., Lorraine Pasurka. AA, Harper Jr. Coll., Palatine, Ill., 1973; BS, No. Ill. U., 1975; MS, PhD, U. Ill., 1981. Vis. asst. prof. dept. econs. So. Ill. U., Carbondale, 1981—85, vis. asst. prof. dept. fin., 1983; asst. prof. dept. econs. Loyola U., Chgo., 1985—92; economist U.S. EPA, Washington, 1992—. V.p. Chgo. Energy Economists, 1988—89, pres., 1989—90, bd. advisors, 1990—91. Assoc. editor: Jour. Environ. Econs. and Mgmt., 1994—96; contbr. chapters to books, articles to profl. jours. Grantee, U.S. EPA, 1991—92. Mem.: Internat. Input-Output Assn., Productivity Analysis Rsch. Network, Assn. Environ. and Resource Economists, Am. Econs. Assn. Independent. Home: 320 23rd St S Apt 623 Arlington VA 22202-3806 Office: EPA 1301 Constitution Ave NW Washington DC Business E-Mail: PASURKA.CARL@EPA.GOV.

PASVOLSKY, RICHARD LLOYD, parks, recreation, and environment educator; b. Englewood, N.J., Feb. 16, 1924; s. Valentine and Ellen Isabel (Stoughton) P.; m. Jo Anne Evans, June 16, 1968. BEd, Panzer Coll., 1950; MA in Edn., NYU, 1955; D in Recreation, Ind. U., 1973. Asst. supt. recreation City of Rutland, Vt., 1951-53; supt. recreation City of Montpelier, 1953-55; dir. parks and recreation Twp. of Parsippany-Troy Hills, N.J., 1955-62; asst. prof. outdoor and environ. edn. N.J. State Sch. Conservation, Branchville, 1962-71; assoc. prof. edn. Ramapo Coll. N.J., Mahwah, 1972-84, coach archery, 1973-84; adj. prof. Kean Coll. N.J., Union, 1985—. Instr. archery, dir. dance and recreation World Archery Ctr., Pomfret, Conn., 1964-92; dir. N.J. State Coll. divsn. Nat. Archery Assn., 1978-84. Advisor to choreographer, cons. prodn. office closing ceremonies Statue of Liberty Centennial Celebration, 1986; rec. artist: Square Dances, 1961, 91, mag. articles, 1954-66; columnist Lines About Squares, 1983—. Instr. dance camp staff Lloyd Shaw Found., 1981—, bd. dirs., 1982-88; bd. trustees Sussex County Sr. Legal Resources Ctr., 1992-94. With U.S. Army, 1943-46, ETO. Recipient Alumni award Panzer Coll. N.J., 1979, Spl. Alumni award, 1987; named to Ramapo Coll. Athletic Hall of Fame, 1993, Lakewood (N.J.) H.S. Hall of Fame, 1998. Mem. AAHPERD (Recreator of Yr. Ea. Dist. 1977), N.J. Alliance Health, Phys. Edn., Recreation and Dance, Callers Coun. N.J., Callerlab, Phi Delta Kappa. Avocations: calling square dances, ballroom dancing, skiing, golf, tennis. Home: 31 Newton Ave Branchville NJ 07826-4203 Office: Kean U NJ Phys Edn Dept Union NJ 07083

PASYK, KRYSTYNA ANNA, dermatologist; b. Cracow, Poland, Feb. 26, 1929; came to U.S., 1979; d. Antoni and Jadwiga Macalka; m. Stanislaw Pasyk, Nov. 18, 1951; children: Stanislaw-Andrzej, Maria-Małgorzata. MD, Med. Acad. Cracow, 1954, PhD, 1964. 2d degree of specialization Polish Bd. Dermatology and Venerology. From instr. to asst. prof. dept. dermatology Univ. Hosp., Cracow, 1955-65; asst. prof., head dermatology svc.ry sect. Inst. Pediats., Cracow-Prokocim, Poland, 1965-79; postdoctoral scholar plastic surgery sect. U. Mich., Ann Arbor, 1979-82, rsch. investigator plastic surgery sect., 1982-86, asst. rsch. scientist plastic surgery sect., 1986-92, sr. rsch. assoc. Inst. Gerontology, 1992—. Cons. hemangioma clinic, plastic surgery U. Mich., Ann Arbor, 1979-88; acting dir. Plastic Surgery Rsch. Lab., Ann Arbor, 1982-88; rschr. Dow Corning Corp., Midland, Mich., 1984, Biomed. Rsch., U. Mich., Ann Arbor, 1988-90; investigator Barbara Piasecka-Johnson Found., Atlanta, 1989-90, Herrick Found., Detroit, 1989, NIH, 1992. Contbr. numerous articles to med. jours., 13 chpts. to books. Mem. Am. Soc. for Aesthetic Plastic Surgery (rschr. 1982-83, grantee 1982), Am. Assn. Plastic Surgeons (rschr. 1982-83, grantee 1982), Nat. Vascular Malformation Found. (investigator 1992, chmn. med. and sci. adv. bd. 1990-98, grantee 1992), Plastic Surgery Ednl. Found. (rschr., 1981-82, grantee 1981), Polish Dermatol. Soc. (hon. sec. 1956-60), Reed O. Dingman Soc. (hon. mem.), Dean Club, U. Mich. Avocations: music, biographical and historical movies, traveling. Home: 2730 Heather Way Ann Arbor MI 48104 Office: Inst Gerontology U Mich 300 N Engalls Ann Arbor MI 48109

PATAKI, GEORGE E. governor; b. Peekskill, N.Y., June 24, 1945; m. Elizabeth (Libby) Rowland; children: Emily, Teddy, Allison, George Owen. BA, Yale U., 1967; JD, Columbia U. Sch. Law, 1970. Mayor City of Peekskill, NY, 1981—84; elected mem. State Assembly, N.Y., 1985-92, State Senate, NY, 1993—95; assoc. Law Firm of Dewey, Ballantine, Bushby, Palmer & Wood, 1970-74; ptnr. Law Firm Plunckett & Jaffe, P.C., N.Y.C., White Plains, Albany and Peekskill, 1974-89; co-proprietor Pataki Farm, Peekskill, N.Y.; gov. State of NY, 1995—. Advanceman Friends of Rockefeller Team, 1970; upstate campaign Coord. Com. to Elect Gov. Wilson, 1974; mem. Peekskill Rep. City Com., 1974—, chmn. 1977-83; mem. N.Y. State Rep. Com., 1980-85. Address: Office of the Gov Exec Chambers/State Capitol Albany NY 12224*

PATAKY, PAUL ERIC, ophthalmologist; b. Phila., May 19, 1945; s. Andrew and Helen (Koffler) P.; m. Aimee Janet Margoles, June 13, 1971; Meryl Corinne, Lisa Ann. BS, Trinity Coll., 1966; MD, Pa. State U., 1971. Diplomate Am. Bd. Ophthalmology. Resident ophthalmology Mass. Eye and Ear Infirmary, Boston, 1972-76; asst. in ophthalmology Harvard Med. Sch., 1976-79; ophthalmologist Dedham (Mass.) Med. Assocs., 1976-79, Paul E. Pataky M.D. P.A., Boynton Beach, Fla., 1979—. Chmn. dept. surgery Bethesda Meml. Hosp., Boynton Beach, 1988-89; pres. med. staff, 1990-91, chmn. credentials chmn., 1992-93, chmn. surg. care com., 1993-97. Fellow Am. Acad. Ophthalmology; mem. Fla. Soc. Ophthalmology, AMA, Pan-Am. Assn. Ophthalmology, Palm Beach County Med. Soc., Fla. Med. Assn. Avocations: cycling, travel. Office: 2623 S Seacrest Blvd Ste 102 Boynton Beach FL 33435-7531 E-mail: ppataky2@earthlink.net.

PATAN, SYBILL PETRA, research scientist; b. Wetzlar, Germany, Feb. 8, 1955; arrived in U.S., 1994; d. Walter Wilhelm and Ingeborg Ursula Schmidt; m. Ulrich Helmut Patan, Sept. 2, 1983; 1 child Maximilian Patan. MD, Justus-Liebig U., Giessen, Germany, 1980, Dr.med., 1988. Postdoctoral fellow Inst. Anatomy U. Bern, Switzerland, 1989—94; postdoctoral fellow dept. radiation oncology Gen. Hosp., Boston, 1994—99; postdoctoral fellow dept. medicine Albert Einstein Coll. Medicine, Bronx, NY, 1999—2001, instr. dept. medicine, 2001—02. Asst. prof. anatomy and cell biology SUNY, 2002—. Contbr. Recipient Gian Töndury award, Swiss Soc. Anatomy, 1990; grantee, Swiss and German Rsch. Founds., 1994—95, 1996—98. Mem.: Am. Heart Assn. (Scientist Devel. grantee 2001—04), Am. Assn. for Cancer Rsch., Union of Swiss Socs. for Exptl. Biology. Achievements include research in analysis of cellular mechanisms of intussusceptive microvascular growth in development and different states of disease; analysis of function of Tie-1 and Tie-2 Angiopoietin growth factor/receptor system. Office: SUNY Downstate Med Ctr 450 Clarkson Ave Brooklyn NY 11203-2098

PATANKAR, NEELESH ASHOK, mechanical engineer, educator; b. Pune, Maharashtra, India, Sept. 8, 1971; s. Ashok Dattatraya Patankar, Neela Ashok Patankar; m. Dyuti Neelesh Durve; children: Tanvee. BS in Tech., Indian Inst. Tech., Mumbai, 1993; MS, U. Pa., 1995, PhD, 1997. Postdoctoral rschr. U. Minn., Mpls., 1997—98, rsch. assoc., 1999—2000; asst. prof. Northwestern U., Evanston, Ill., 2000—. Sr. vis. fellow Stanford (Calif.) U., 2000. Contbr. articles to profl. jours. Recipient Career award, NSF, 2002—; fellow Searle Jr. fellow, Searle Ctr. for Tchg. Excellence, Northwestern U., 2002; grantee, DARPA, 2001—; scholar Nat. Talent scholar, Nat. Coun. for Edn. Rsch. and Tng., 1987. Mem.: ASME, Am. Phys. Soc. Hindu. Avocation: reading. Office: Northwestern Univ 2145 Sheridan Rd B224 Evanston IL 60208-3111 Office Fax: 847-491-3915. Business E-Mail: n-patankar@northwestern.edu.

PATASHINSKI, ALEXANDER Z. physicist, materials science consultant; b. Vitebsk, Russia, Aug. 8, 1936; came to U.S., 1992; s. Zakhar Shepshelevich Patashinski and Sofia Lipovna Bensman; m. Nadejda A. Duboshina, Sept. 20, 1958; children: David, Ilya, Tanya. MS in Phys. Engring., Moscow Inst. Physics and Tech., 1960; PhD in Physics and Math., Siberian Sci. Ctr., Novosibirsk, Russia, 1963; D of Phys. and Math. Scis., Ukrainian Inst. Physics and Tech., Kharkov, 1968. Rsch. fellow Inst. Thermal Physics, Novosibirsk, 1960-68; prof. Novosibirsk State U., 1968-92; from sr. to chief rsch. scientist Budker Inst. Nuc. Physics, Novosibirsk, 1968-97; vis. prof. Northwestern U., Evanston, Ill., 1992-94, rsch. prof., 1994—. Cons. NASA Glenn Ctr., Cleve., 1994—, Dow Chem., Midland, Mich., 1995—. Co-author: Fluctuation Theory of Phase Transitions, 1974, 82, English edit., 1979, Italian edit., 1983; contbr. over 100 articles to profl. jours. Recipient Landau prize Russian Acad. Scis., Moscow, 1983, rsch. award NASA, 1994, microgravity rsch. award, 1996; recipient polymer rsch. award Dow Chem. Co., Midland, 1995, 96, 97, 98, 99, 2000, 01, 02. Mem. AAAS, Am. Phys. Soc., Materials Rsch. Soc. Home: 721 Simpson St Apt 2 Evanston IL 60201-6106 Office: Northwestern U 2145 Sheridan Rd Evanston IL 60208-0834

PATCHETT, ANN, writer; b. Los Angeles, Calif., 1963; BA, Sarah Lawrence College. Author: (novels) The Patron Saint of Liars, 1992 (James A. Michener/Copernicus award for a book in progress, 1990), Taft, 1994 (Janet Heidinger Kafka prize for the best work of fiction, 1994), The Magician's Assistant, 1997 (Nashville Banner Tennessee Writer of the Year Award), Bel Canto , 2001 (PEN/Faulkner prize, 2002); contbr. articles The New York Times Magazine, Chicago Tribune, Boston Globe, Vogue, GQ, Elle, Gourmet. Fellow, Fine Arts Work Center in Provincetown, Mass., Bunting Fellowship, Mary Ingrahm Bunting Institute at Radcliffe College, 1993, Guggenheim, 1994. Mailing: c/o HarperCollins Publishers 10 East 53rd Street New York NY 10022*

PATCHETT, ARTHUR ALLAN, medicinal chemist, pharmaceutical executive; b. Middletown, N.Y., May 28, 1929; s. Arthur Allan and Anna Gertrude (Vossler) P.; m. Lois Rhoda Mc Neil, Aug. 18, 1962; Thomas John, Steven Edward. BA, Princeton U., 1951; PhD, Harvard U., 1955; DSc (hon.), Bloomfield Coll., 2001. Rsch. assoc. NIH, Bethesda, Md., 1955-57; rsch. chemist Merck Rsch. Labs., Rahway, N.J., 1957-62, dir. synthetic chem. rsch., 1962-69, sr. dir. synthetic chem. rsch., 1969-71, sr. dir. new lead discovery, 1971-76, exec. dir. new lead discovery, 1976-88, v.p. exploratory chemistry, 1988-95, v.p. medicinal chemistry, 1995-2000, cons., 2000—. Contbr. over 170 papers to profl. jours., sci. confs. Named to, N.J. Inventors Hall of Fame, N.J. Inst. Tech., 1990; recipient Discoverers award, Pharm. Mfrs. Assn., 1992, Smissman Bristol-Myers Squibb award, 2001. Fellow AAAS; mem. Am. Chem. Soc. (chmn. div. medicinal chemistry 1971, E.B. Hershberg Important Discoveries in Medicinally Active Substances award 1993, Alfred Burger award in medicinal chemistry 2002). Achievements include 180 U.S. patents (co-holder); co-inventor antihypertensive drug Vasotec; key contbr. to discovery of cholesterol lowering drug Mevacor. Office: Merck Rsch Labs PO Box 2000 Rahway NJ 07065-0900

PATCHIS, PAULINE, handwriting expert, consultant; b. Pawtucket, R.I., Apr. 17, 1940; d. Alexander P. Patchis and Rose E. (Acquaviva) Jankowski. Grad., Warwick Police Acad., 1967. Bd. cert. document examiner, U.S., Can. and Europe; diplomate Am. Bd. Forensic Examiners. Exec. sec. to pers. dir. Ciba-Geigy Pharm. Co., Cranston, R.I., 1963-65; adminstrv. detective Warwick (R.I.) Police Dept., 1967-71; cons. jury selection, handwriting analyst Patchis and Wayne, Warwick, 1971—. Lectr., instr. in field. Contbr. articles to profl. jours. Fellow Am. Coll. Forensic Examiners; mem. Nat. Forensic Ctr., New Eng. Fraud Investigators Assn., Study Group of R.I. (co-founder), Coun. Graphol. Socs. (v.p.), Internat. Assn. for Identification (New Eng. divsn.), R.I. Police Chief Assn., R.I. Fraud Investigators Assn., Soc. of Govtl. Accts. and Auditors, R.I. Criminalist Assocs. Home and Office: 67 S Fair St Warwick RI 02888-1651

PATE, A. J. financial services advisor; b. Palestine, Tex., Dec. 2, 1937; s. Harlen JayVan and Nannie Faye (Hamilton) P.; m. Martha Gomez; children: John Harlen, Debra Darlene Russo. BBA, Sam Houston State U., 1959. CPA, Tex. Auditor Arthur Andersen & Co., Houston, 1959-61; chief acct. Tenneco Inc., 1961-92; v.p. Omega Resource Group, 1992-94; v.p., CFO Career Visions, Inc., 1994-95; account exec. Lincoln Investment Planning, Inc., 1996-97, H.D. Vest Investment Securities, Inc., Irving, 1997—. Redistricting cons. Tex. State Legislature, Houston/Austin, 1990-91, 95-96, 2000-2001; treas., mem. exec. com. Tenneco Employees Good Govt. Fund, Houston, 1983-92. Contbr. poetry to anthology, landmark case briefs to U.S. Supreme Ct. Texas for Edn., Austin, 1991-92, Pachyderm Club, Houston, 1989-92; del. Rep. Party, 1976-88. With U.S. Army, 1956. Named Outstanding Bus. Student, Wall St. Jour., 1959. Republican. Mem. Assembly of God. Avocations: traveling, reading, music, collectibles, political research. Home: 15118 Terrace Oaks Dr Houston TX 77068-3040 Fax: 281-444-4035. E-mail: a12j02@houston.rr.com.

PATE, BROOKS, chemist; BS, U. Va., 1987; PhD, Princeton U., 1992. NRC postdoctoral fellow Nat. Inst. Stds. and Tech., Gaithersburg, Md., 1992—93; prof. chemistry U. Va., Charlottesville, 1993—. Recipient CAREER award, NSF, 1996. Office: U Va Dept Chemistry McCormick Rd Charlottesville VA 22903*

PATE, JACQUELINE HAIL, retired data processing company executive; b. Amarillo, Tex., Apr. 7, 1930; d. Ewen and Virginia Smith (Crosland) Hail; children: Charles (dec.), John Durst, Virginia Pate Edgecomb, Christopher. Student, Southwestern U., Georgetown, Tex., 1947-48; grad., Real Estate Inst., 1998. Exec. sec. Western Gear Corp., Houston, 1974-76; adminstr., treas., dir. Aberrant Behavior Ctr., Personality Profiles, Inc., Corp. Procedures, Inc., Dallas, 1976-790; mgr. regional site svcs. programs Digital Equipment Corp., 1979-92; ret., 1992. Realtor Keller Williams Realty, Austin, Tex., 1996—. Active Austin Bd. Realtors, PTA, Dallas, 1958-73. Mem. Daus. Republic Tex. (treas. French Legation state com. 1996). Methodist. Home: 6501 Brush Country #118 Austin TX 78749 E-mail: jacpate@aol.com.

PATE, JOHN LOUIS, educational consultant; b. Tageu, South Korea, Aug. 18, 1970; came to U.S., 1970; s. James Leon and Ok Nam (Jung) P. BA in English and Philosophy, U. Tex., El Paso, 1996. Writing tutor/instr. U. Tex., El Paso, 1992-95; adult basic edn. instr. Ysleta Pub. Schs., 1997-99; ednl. cons. Scholastic Inc., 1999-2000, Zaner-Bloser Pub., Seattle, 2000—. Author/contbr. poetry to jours. Avocations: fishing, outdoors. Office: Apt M203 31500 33rd Pl SW Federal Way WA 98023-2223

PATE, MICHAEL LYNN, lawyer; b. Ft. Worth, July 9, 1951; s. J.B. and Mary Anna (Hable) P.; m. Barbara Ann Linch, May 28, 1977. AA, Schreiner Coll., 1971; BS, Tex. Wesleyan Coll., 1973; JD, U. Tex., 1975. Bar: Tex. 1976, D.C. 1983, U.S. Tax Ct. 1986, U.S. Supreme Ct. 1987. Adminstrv. asst. to Senator Sherman, counsel natural resources com. Tex. Senate, 1976-77; adminstrv. asst. to Lt. Gov. Bill Hobby, Austin, Tex., 1977-79; legis. asst. Senator Bentsen, Washington, 1979-81, legis. dir., 1981-86; ptnr., head Washington office Bracewell & Patterson, 1986—. Trustee Schreiner U. Mem. ABA, Tex. Bar Assn., D.C. Bar Assn. Democrat. Methodist. Avocations: basketball, tennis, golf. Office: Bracewell & Patterson 2000 K St NW Ste 500 Washington DC 20006-1872 E-mail: mpate@bracepatt.com.

PATE, PATRICIA ANN, women's health nurse; b. Columbus, Ohio, Dec. 23, 1944; d. Wayne E. and Oneitta M. (Craig) Ballentine; m. Daniel B. Pate, July 1, 1989; children: Kimberly Ann Van Horn, Kellie Lynn Van Horn; stepchildren: Tracy Scott, Ronnie Pate, Richard Pate. BSN, Tex. Woman's U., 1979. Nurse ob./gyn. office Dr. Mary Alice Cowan, Houston, 1983-87; charge nurse post-anesthesia recovery rm. Green Park Surgery Ctr., 1987-88; nurse Bellaire Gen. Hosp., 1987-89; clin. rsch. coord. Rsch. for Health, 1988-89; nurse ob./gyn. dept. Dr. Ivor Safro, 1989-91; nurse/day surgery Sam Houston Meml. Hosp., 1991-95; nurse West Houston Surgicare, 1995-97, Breath of Life Rsch., Houston, 1997-98; nurse/day surgery Physicians SurgiCare of Houston, 1999—. Mem. peer rev. com., 1991-93. Home: 10402 Shadow Wood Dr Houston TX 77043-2822

PATE, PAUL DANNY, mayor; b. Ottumwa, Iowa, May 1, 1958; s. Paul Devern and Velma Marie (McConnell) P.; m. Jane Ann Wacker, July 15, 1978; children: Jennifer Ann, Paul Daniel III, Amber Lynn. AA in Bus., Kirkwood Coll., 1978; cert. fin. mgmt. program, U. Pa., 1990. Exec. dir. Jr. Achievement, Cedar Rapids, Iowa, 1978-82; pres. PM Systems Corp., 1982—; senator Iowa State Senate, Des Moines, 1989-93; Sec. of State State of Iowa, 1994-98; mayor City of Cedar Rapids, 2002—. Chmn. Iowa Young Reps., Des Moines, 1989-93, Rep. Senate Campaign Com., 1990. Recipient Guardian Small Bus. award Nat. Fedn. Independent Bus., 1990; named Young Entrepreneur of Yr. U.S. Small Bus. Adminstrn., Iowa, 1988, Alumnus of Yr. Kirkwood Coll., Cedar Rapids, 1990. Methodist. Avocation: water skiing. Home: 6801 Bowman Ln NE Cedar Rapids IA 52402-1575 Office: PM Sys Corp 850 Robins Rd Hiawatha IA 52233-1320

PATE, ROBERT HEWITT, JR. counselor educator; b. Abingdon, Va., Apr. 5, 1938; s. Robert Hewitt and Esther Frances (Kirk) P.; m. Ellen O'Neal Pope, Dec. 11, 1960; children: Robert Hewitt III, Mary Ellen Pate Barton. AB, Davidson Coll., 1960; MEd, U. Va., 1965; PhD, U. N.C., 1968. Lic. prof. counselor, Va. Marketer Sinclair Refining Co., Abingdon, Va., 1960-61, 63-64; counselor St. Andrews Presbyn. Coll., Laurinburg, N.C., 1965-66; prof. counselor edn. U. Va., Charlottesville, 1968—, interim dean, 1994-95, assoc. dean, 1995—. Mem. adj. faculty Fed. Exec. Inst., Charlottesville, 1978—. Author: Being A Counselor, 1983. Elder local Presbyn. ch. 1st lt. U.S. Army 1961-63. Mem. Am. Counseling Assn., Va. Counselors Assn. (pres. 1983-84), Nat. Bd. Cert. Counselors (chair 1996-97). Avocation: reading. Home: 552 Dryden Pl Charlottesville VA 22903-4666 Office: Curry Sch Dean's Office 405 Emmet St S PO Box 400260 Charlottesville VA 22904-4260

PATE, STEPHEN PATRICK, lawyer; b. Beaumont, Tex., May 6, 1958; s. Gordon Ralph and Shirley Jean (Riley) P.; m. Jean Janssen; 1 child, Teddy. BA, Vanderbilt U., 1980, JD, 1983. Bar: Tex. 1984, U.S. Dist. Ct. (ea. dist.) Tex. 1984, U.S. Dist. Ct. (so. dist.) Tex. 1985. Law clk. to judge Joe J. Fisher U.S. Dist. Ct. Tex., Beaumont, 1983-84; ptnr. Fulbright & Jaworski, Houston. Contbr. articles to profl. jours. Fellow Houston Bar Found., Tex. Bar Found.; mem. ABA (vice chmn. property ins. com. tort and ins. practice sect. 1994—, chmn. 1999-2000), Fedn. Ins. and Corp. Counsel, Tex. Bar Assn., Tex. Young Lawyers Assn. (bd. dirs. 1992-94), Houston Young Lawyers Assn. (bd. dirs. 1990-92, sec. 1992-93, chmn. professionalism com., mem. sunset rev. com. 1990), Sons of the Republic Tex., SAR (sec. Paul Carrington chpt. 2001—), Soc. Colonial Wars, Manitoba Master Angler, Billfish Found. (Top Angler 1993), Knight of Momus, The Briar Club, Phi Beta Kappa. Republican. Roman Catholic. Avocations: hunting, fishing. Home: 2740 Arbuckle St Houston TX 77005-3932 Office: Fulbright & Jaworski 1301 Mckinney St Houston TX 77010-3031 E-mail: spate@fulbright.com.

PATE, VIRGINIA FRANCES, artist, educator; b. Athens, Tex., Dec. 16, 1927; BA, U. Evansville, 1974; MA in Edn., Psychology, Southwestern Bapt. Theol. Sem., 1976. Cert. art instr., 1994, Grumbacher cert. instr., 1997. Artist, owner Pate Art and Ceramics, Stanville, Ky., 1977-82, owner, artist Ft. Worth, 1982-88; owner, artist, art instr. PATE Art Studio/Gallery, Lehigh, Fla., 1988—. One-woman shows include First Nat. Bank, Pikeville, Ky., 1980, Cultural Ctr., Prestonsburg, Ky., 1980, PATE Art Studio/Gallery, Lehigh, Fla., 1980—, Tessier Galleries, Paris, Limoges, France, 1996—; group exhibits include S.W. Fla. Art Coun., Ft. Myers, 1994, Charlotte County Art Guild, Punta Gorda, Fla., 1995, Lee County Art Alliance, Ft. Myers, 1997, Robb & Stucky, Fort Myers, Fla., 1999, Am. Impressionist Soc. Nat. Exhibit, 2000 (award, charter/signature mem.), Spring Festival, Lehigh, Fla., 2001 (awards); represented in permanent collections France, Germany, Can., U.S.

PATE, WILLIAM AUGUST, lawyer; b. Selma, Ala., Dec. 9, 1942; s. William Herbert and Shirley Rosemary (DeMattie) P.; m. Wanda Arlene Whaley, Feb. 2, 1973. BA in Polit. Sci., Citadel, 1964; JD, U. Miss., 1972. Bar: Miss. 1972, U.S. Dist. Ct. (no. dist.) Miss. 1972, U.S. Dist. Ct. (so. dist.) Miss. 1973. Sole practice, Gulfport, Miss., 1972—. Mem. Saucier (Miss.) Vol. Fire Dept., Harrison County Pk. Commn., 1980-88, Harrison County Fire Commn.; bd. dirs. Harrison County Mental Health Assn., Christmas in April, Miss. Coast. Capt. USAF, 1965-69. Mem. ABA, Miss. State Bar, Harrison County Bar Assn., Miss. Trial Lawyers Assn., Gulfport Yacht Club, F and AM. Home: 23179 Saucier Lizana Rd Saucier MS 39574-9147 Office: 2017 20th Ave Gulfport MS 39501-3041

PATE, WILLIAM PATRICK, city manager; b. Duplin County, N.C., July 30, 1962; s. William Atlas and Bonny Lou (O'Leary) P.; m. Sandra Martin, Aug. 17, 1985; children: William Glenn, Andrew Patrick. BA in Polit. Sci. and Religion, U. N.C., 1984, MPA, 1986. Budget and evaluation analyst intern City of Winston-Salem, N.C., 1985-86, budget and evaluation analyst, 1986-87, lead budget and evaluation analyst, 1987; budget and rsch. mgr. City of Greensboro, 1987-90, budget and evaluation dir., 1990-99; asst. city mgr. City of High Point, 1999—. Inst. of Govt. intern N.C. Office Coastal Mgmt., Raleigh, N.C., 1984; rsch. asst. U. N.C., Chapel Hill, 1984-85. Mem. Chmns. Soc. United Way of High Point, 1998—; mem. Leadership Greensboro, 1993-99, Leadership High Point, 2000—; elder, clk. session Faith Presbyn. Ch., Greensboro; mem. Salem Presbyn. World Ministries Cluster, 1997-99. Recipient Disting. Svc. award Alpha Phi Omega, 1984. Mem. Internat. City Mgrs. Assn., Am. Soc. Pub. Adminstrn. (pres. Piedmont Triad chpt. 1994), Gov. Fin. Officers Assn. U.S. and Can. (exec. bd. 1998—, nat. com. on govtl. budgeting and mgmt. 1993-98, nat. com. on debt and fiscal policy 1998-2001, pres. 2002--, Disting. Budget Presentation award reviewer, Disting. Budget Presentation award 1992-98), N.C. Local Govt. Budget Assn. (bd. dirs. 1990-92, 95, 1st v.p. 1992-93, pres. 1993-94), N.C. City/County Mgrs. Assn., U. N.C. MPA Alumni Assn. (program chmn. 1992, pres-elect 1993, pres. 1994, Scholarship award 1985), U. N.C. Gen. Alumni Assn. (bd. dirs. 1994-95), Kiwanis Club. Presbyterian. Home: 4509 Calabria Ct High Point NC 27265-9595 Office: City of High Point PO Box 230 High Point NC 27261-0230 E-mail: pat.pate@ci.high-point.nc.us.

PATEL, ANEEL N. psychiatrist; b. Bombay, Aug. 12, 1935; s. Nathoobhai Dajalsi and Laxmibai Patel; m. Jean Claire Byrne, Mar. 23, 1973; 1 child David S. B Medicine and Surgery, G.S. Med. Coll., Bombay, 1958, MD, 1962. Fellow in neurology Bowman Gray Sch. Medicine, Winston-Salem, NC, 1964—65; assoc. prof. neurology Hahnemann Med. Coll., Phila., 1970—73; chief neurology svc. Phila. Gen. Hosp., 1970—73; assoc. prof. neurology Albany (NY) Med. Coll., 1973—74; asst. prof. clin. psychiatry East Carolina Med. Coll., Greenville, NC, 1992—93; pvt. practice neuropsychiatry Goldsboro and Wilmington, 1994—. Cons. neurologist Warren (Pa.) State Hosp., 1974—86, Eastern State Hosp., Williamsburg, Va., 1988—91. Fellow: ACP, Royal Coll. Physicians Can., Royal Coll. Physicians Edinburgh.

PATEL, ANIL S. biomedical engineer, researcher, medical products executive; b. Baroda, India, June 28, 1939; came to U.S., 1961; s. Shankerbhai S. and Gangaben T. Patel; children: Ravi, Sunil; m. Asha Rairkar, Aug. 22, 1992. BS, U. Baroda, 1960; MS, Purdue U., 1963; PhD, Northwestern U., 1966; postgrad., Stanford U., 1993. Sr. rsch. scientist Baxter Travenol Labs. Inc., Morton Grove, Ill., 1968-74; chief scientist Cavitron Corp., N.Y.C., 1974-79; chief scientist, mgr. advanced prodcts rsch. Cooper Vision Sys. divsn. Cooper Vision Inc. (formerly Cavitron Corp.), Irvine, Calif., 1979-83, Bellevue, Wash., 1983-86; dir. advanced product rsch., chief scientist Cooper Vision CILCO divsn. Cooper Cos., Inc., 1986-89; dir. rsch. intraocular lens Alcon Labs., Inc., Ft. Worth, 1989-92, sr. dir. rsch. surg. products, 1993-2000, v.p. rsch. surg. products, 2001—. Contbr. articles to profl. jours.; patentee in field. Organizer Highland Park (Ill.) Chess Club, 1970-74, White Plains (N.Y.) Chess Club, 1974-77. Recipient free passage from India to U.S., Indian Ministry Sci. and Cultural Affairs, 1961; NIH postdoctoral fellow Northwestern U., 1966-67. Fellow Am. Soc. Laser Medicine and Surgery (founder); mem. AAAS, IEEE, Assn. for Advancement Med. Instrumentation (chmn. infrared warmers and incubators stds. com. 1978-80, pulmonary function devices-spirometer stds. subcom. 1978-80), Am. Nat. Stds. Inst. (com. intraocular lenses std. 1988-94, viscoelastic ophthalmic devices 1992—, apptd. tech. expert del. U.S.A. tech. adv. group Internat. Stds. Orgn. tech. com. 1992—), Am. Soc. Cataract and Refractive Surgery, Assn. Rsch. in Vision and Ophthalmology, Internat. Soc. Refractive Keratoplasty, Soc. Biomaterials, Sigma Xi. E-mail: anilasha@alo.com.

PATEL, ARUN PARMANAND, physician; b. Mombasa, Kenya, Sept. 12, 1952; came to U.S., 1977; s. P.R. and K.P. P.; m. Sandhya Shah, Aug. 18, 1978; children: Rajan, Amit. MBBS, U. Bombay, 1976. Diplomate Am. Bd. Family Practice, Am. Bd. Geriatrics, Am. Bd. Addiction Medicine. Pvt. practice, Little Valley, N.Y., 1984—. Med. staff Erie County Med . Ctr., Buffalo, 1982—84; med. dir. Salamanca (N.Y.) Dist. Authority, 1990—97, Cattaraugus County Nursing Home, Olean, NY, 1997—, Woodlawn Park Nursing Home, Salamanca, 1997—; asst. med. dir. Cornstock Hospice, Olean, 1992—; pres. med. staff Olean Gen. Hosp., 2000—. Mem.: Cattaraugus County Med. Soc. (pres. 1995), Am. Acad. Family Practice. Avocations: woodworking, skiing. Office: 449 Broad St Salamanca NY 14779-1455

PATEL, CHANDRA KUMAR NARANBHAI, communications company executive, educator, researcher, entrepreneur; b. Baramati, India, July 2, 1938; came to U.S., 1958, naturalized, 1970; s. Naranbhai Chaturbhai and Maniben P.; m. Shela Dixit, Aug. 20, 1961; children: Neela, Meena. B.Engring., Poona U., 1958; MS, Stanford U., 1959, PhD, 1961. Mem. tech. staff Bell Telephone Labs., Murray Hill, N.J., 1961-93, head infrared physics and electronics rsch. dept., 1967-70, dir. electronics rsch. dept., 1970-76, dir. phys. rsch. lab., 1976-81, exec. dir. rsch. physics and acad. affairs div., 1981-87, exec. dir. rsch., materials sci., engring. and acad. affairs div., 1987-93; trustee Aerospace Corp., L.A., 1979-88; vice chancellor rsch. UCLA, 1993-2000, prof. dept. physics and astronomy, dept. chemistry, 2000—, prof. dept. elec. engring., 2000—; chmn., CEO Pranalytica, Inc, Santa Monica, Calif., 2001—. Mem. governing bd. NRC, 1990-91; bd. dirs. Newport Corp.; chmn. bd. Calif. Accuwave Corp., 1994-98; founder, chmn. bd. Pranalytica, Inc., Santa Monica, Calif.; co-founder Photuris, Inc. Contbr. articles to tech. jours. Chmn. Calif. Biomed. Found., 1994-2000; mem. exec. bd. Calif. Healthcare Inst., 1995-2000; mem. L.A. Regional Tech. Alliance, 1997—. Recipient Ballantine medal Franklin Inst., 1968, Coblentz award Am. Chem. Soc., 1974, Honor award Assn. Indians in Am., 1975, Founders prize Tex. Instruments Found., 1978, award N.Y. sect. Soc. Applied Spectroscopy, 1982, Schawlow medal Laser Inst. Am., 1984, Thomas Alva Edison Sci. award N.J. Gov., 1987, William T. Ennor Manufacturing Technology award ASME, 1995, Nat. Medal of Sci., 1996. Fellow AAAS, IEEE (Lamme medal 1976, medal of honor 1989, Millennium medal 2000), Am. Acad. Arts and Scis., Am. Phys. Soc. (coun. 1987-91, exec. com. 1987-90, George E. Pake prize 1988, pres. 1995), Optical Soc. Am. (Adolph Lomb medal 1966, Townes medal 1982, Ives medal 1989), Indian Nat. Sci. Acad. (fng.); mem. NAS (coun. 1988-91, exec. com. 1989-91), NAE (Zworykin award 1976), Gynecol. Laser Surgery Soc. (hon.), Am. Soc. for Laser Medicine and Surgery (hon.), Third World Acad. Scis. (assoc.), Calif. Biomed. Found. (pres. 1994-2000), Calif. Healthcare Inst. (exec. com. 1995-2000), Sigma Xi (pres. 1994-96). Home: 1171 Roberto Ln Los Angeles CA 90077-2302 Office: Pranalytica Inc 1101 Colorado Ave Santa Monica CA 90401 E-mail: patel@pranalytica.com.

PATEL, GAVISH N. surgeon, educator; b. Nairobi, Kenya, May 11, 1969; came to U.S., 1986; s. Navin and Ranjan Patel. BS in Biochemistry, U. Ill., 1991, MD, 1995. Resident in surgery U. Ill., Peoria, 1995-2000, clin. asst. prof. surgery, 2000—. Mem. Acad. Laparendoscopic Surgeons. Hindu. Office: Associated Surg Group SC 7303 N Knoxville Ave Peoria IL 61614 E-mail: gpatel2@uic.edu.

PATEL, HOMI BURJOR, apparel company executive; b. Bombay, June 28, 1949; s. Burjor Ratan and Roshen Burjor (Marfatia) P.; married; children: Neville H., Cyrus H., Natasha E. BS in Stats., U. Bombay, 1973; MBA in Fin. and Mktg., Columbia U., 1975. Exec. asst. to pres. Corbin Ltd., N.Y.C., 1976, dir. mktg., 1978; with subs. Hartmarx Corp., Chgo., 1979—; v.p., gen. mgr. Fashionaire Apparel Inc., 1979-81; exec. v.p. Austin Reed of Regent St., 1981-82, M. Wile and Co., Buffalo, 1982-84; pres., chief exec. officer M. Wile & Co., Johnny Carson Apparel, Intercontinental Apparel, 1984—; group exec. v.p. Hartmarx Mens Apparel Group Corp., 1987-91, chmn., ceo Chgo., 1991-92; pres., COO Hartmarx Corp., 1992—, bd. dirs., 1994—2001, CEO, 2002—. Mem. Clothing Mfrs. Assn. Am. (bd. dirs. 1984—, chief labor negotiator for U.S. tailored clothing industry), Univ. Club N.Y., Chgo. Club. Office: Hartmarx Corp 101 N Wacker Dr Fl 23 Chicago IL 60606-1718

PATEL, MAHENDRA RAMBHAI, electronics executive; b. Ndeje, Uganda, Nov. 5, 1939; came to U.S., 1980; s. Rambhai Chaturbhai and Savita G. Patel; m. Kapila M. Patel, Oct. 30, 1965; children: Manisha, Naimish. BSEE with honors, U. Manchester, 1961; PhD, U. Cambridge, 1964. Lectr. elec. engring. U. East Africa, Nairobi, Kenya, 1964-66; researcher Nelson Rsch. Labs., Stafford, Eng., 1966-67; sr. engr. English Electric Computers, Kidsgrove, Eng., 1967-68, Internat. Computers Ltd., West Gorton, Eng., 1969-70, prin. engr. Newcastle-under-Lyme, Eng., 1971-74, chief engr. Bracknell, Eng., 1974-80; corp. cons. A.B. Dick Co., Niles, Ill., 1980-82; tech. dir. Digital Equipment Corp., Nashua, N.H., 1982-84, Littleton, Mass., 1984-92, v.p. systems engring., 1993-98; v.p., gen. mgr. Industry Solutions Divsn. Compaq Computer Corp., 1998-2000. Bd. dirs. New Eng. Office Supplies, Washington Tech. Ptnrs. Bd. dirs. Spryance, Entcomm, Banqit. Mem. IEEE. Home: 32 Monteiro Way North Andover MA 01845-5327 E-mail: mahendrapatel@attbi.com.

PATEL, MAHENDRAKUMAR P. plastic surgeon; b. Por, Gujarat, India, Aug. 1, 1935; came to U.S., 1964; s. Purushottomdas M. and Maniben P. Patel; m. Vasumati M. Patel, May 26, 1959; children: Vilas, Vikas, Vinyas, Vihas. MBBS, M.S. U. Baroda, India, 1959, DLO, 1962, MS in Gen. Surgery, 1964; MD, U. State of N.Y., N.Y.C., 1986. Diplomate Am. Bd. Plastic Surgery. Attending plastic surgeon Montefiore Med. Ctr., Bronx, N.Y., 1977-2000; asst. prof. plastic surgery Albert Einstein Med. Coll., 1977-89, asst. prof. anatomy and structural biology, 1978-91, assoc. prof. plastic surgery, 1989-2000, assoc. prof. anatomy and structural biology, 1992-2000; ret. from active clin. practice, 2000. Dir. Burn Ctr., Jacobi Med. Ctr., Bronx, 1981-84, 94-95. Contbr. articles to profl. jours. Mem. Cmty. Planning Bd. # 11, Bronx, 1995—; mem. Neighborhood Adv. Bd. # 11, Bronx, 1996-2001. Recipient several prizes. Fellow ACS (life); mem. Am. Soc. Plastic Surgeons (life), Am. Burn Assn., Internat. Soc. Burn Injuries, Am. Assn. Clin. Anatomists.

PATEL, MANISH M. physiatrist; b. Bhavnagar, India, June 22, 1967; s. Manubhai H. and Anandvilas M.; m. Parul M., June 17, 1991. MBBS, NHL Mcpl. Med. Sch., Ahmedabad, India, 1991. Bd. cert. Am. Bd. Physical Medicine and Rehab., Am. Bd. Electrodiagnostic Medicine, Am. Bd. Pain Medicine, Am. Bd. Pain Mgmt. House physician V.S. Gen. Hosp., Ahmedabad, 1991-92; intern Bklyn. Hosp. Ctr., 1993-94; resident Kingsbrook Jewish Med. Ctr., Bklyn., 1994-97; pvt. practice Assocs. in Phys. Medicine, Hollywood, Fla., 1997—. Mem.: Am. Acad. Disability Evaluating Physicians, Am. Acad. Pain Mgmt., Am. Assn. Phys. Medicine and Rehab. Home: 13037 NW 14th St Pembroke Pines FL 33028-2720

PATEL, MULCHAND SHAMBHUBHAI, biochemist, researcher; b. Sipor, India, Sept. 9, 1939; came to U.S., 1965; s. Shambhubhai J. and Puriben (Patel) P.; m. Kankuben M. Patel; children: Sumitra, Yashomati, Mayank. BS, Gujarat U., 1961; MS, U. Baroda, 1964; PhD, U. Ill., 1968. Asst. prof. pediat. rsch. Sch. Medicine Temple U., Phila., 1970-72, rsch. asst. prof. medicine, 1972-75, rsch. asst. prof. biochemistry, 1970-75, rsch. assoc. prof. biochem. medicine, 1975-78; assoc. prof. biochemistry Sch. Medicine Case Western Res. U., Cleve., 1978-86, prof., 1986-93; prof., chmn. biochemistry SUNY, Buffalo, 1993-98, prof. assoc. dean biomed. rsch. edn., 1999—. Mem. NIH biochem. study sect. 2, 1984-88; mem. editl. bd. Jour. Biol. Chem., 1991-97, 99—. Author, co-author research articles. Contbr. articles to profl. jours. Recipient gold medal in biochemistry U. Baroda, 1973, Fulbright Rsch. Scholar award to India, 1987; prin. investigator, rsch. grantee NIH. Mem. Am. Soc. for Biochemistry and Molecular Biology, Am. Soc. Nutritional Scis. Office: SUNY-Dept Biochemistry Sch Medicine 140 Farber Hall 3435 Main St Buffalo NY 14214-3001 E-mail: mspatel@buffalo.edu.

PATEL, TARUN R. pharmaceutical scientist; b. Borsad, Gujarat, India, Feb. 18, 1952; s. Ramesh C. and Savitaben R.; m. Nilima T. Patel, Feb. 17, 1981; children: Vishal, Shalini, Neha. BS in Pharmacy, Tex. So. U., 1975; PhD in Pharmaceutics, U. Iowa, 1980. Registered pharmacist Tex., Ill., Ind. Scientist Ortho Pharm. Corp., Raritan, N.J., 1980-82, sr. scientist, 1982; group leader, mfg. engr. Bristol Labs., Syracuse, N.Y., 1982-83, mgr. process engring., 1983-84, dir. process engring., 1984-86; assoc. dir. process engring. Bristol Myers-USPNG, Evansville, Ind., 1986-90; dir. pharm. devel. Schering-Plough Corp., Memphis, 1990-94, sr. dir. pharm. devel., 1994-96; mgr. mfg. Bayer Pharm. Corp., West Haven, Conn., 1996—. Adj. prof. U. Tenn., Memphis, 1991—. Contbr. articles to profl. jours. Recipient Remington award Tex. So. Univ., 1975. Mem. Am. Assn. Pharm. Scientists, Am. Pharm. Assn. Office: Bayer Pharm Corp 400 Morgan Ln West Haven CT 06516-4140

PATEL, VINOD MOTIBHAI, accountant; b. Kilosha, Tanzania, Mar. 1, 1944; came to U.S., 1971; s. Motibhai R. and Lalitaben M. (Lalitaben C.) P.; m. Surekha J. Patel, Dec. 6, 1969; children: Chirag, Roshni. BComm., U. Baroda, India, 1964. Chartered acct., India; CPA, Md. Acct. Dalal, Desai & Kumana, Bombay, 1964-70, Bellman, Atlas & Co., London, 1970-71, Garbelman, Winslow & Co., Upper Marlboro, Md., 1971-79; prin. Vinod M. Patel, CPA, Fairfax, Va., 1979—. Hon. auditor Shri Mangal Mandir, 1981—, Gujarati Samarj, 1999—. Mem. AICPA, Md. Assn. CPA's, Inst. Chartered Accts. India. Hindu. Home and Office: 10829 Lee Hwy Fairfax VA 22030-4365

PATEL, VIRENDRA CHATURBHAI, mechanical engineer, educator; b. Mombasa, Kenya, Nov. 9, 1938; arrived in U.S., 1969, naturalized, 1975; s. Chaturbhai S. and Kantaben N. (Rai) Patel; m. Manjula Patel, May 29, 1966; children: Sanjay, Bindiya. BSc with honors, Imperial Coll., London, 1962; PhD, Cambridge (Eng.) U., 1965; Doctor honoris causa, Tech. U. Civil Engring., Bucharest, Romania, 1994. Sr. asst. in rsch. Cambridge U., 1965-69; vis. prof. Indian Inst. Tech., Kharagpur, 1966; cons. Lockheed Ga. Co., Marietta, 1969-70; mem. faculty U. Iowa, Iowa City, 1971—, prof. mech. engring., 1975—, chmn. div., 1976-82, chmn. mech. engring., 1978-82, U. Iowa Found. Disting. prof., 1990—, Edwin B. Green chair in hydraulics, 2000—, 2000—; research engr. Iowa Inst. Hydraulic Rsch., 1971—, dir., 1994—; hon. prof. Dharamsinh Desai Inst. Tech., 2002—. Mem. Iowa Gov. Sci. Adv. Coun., 1977—83; mem. resistance com. Internat. Towing Tank Conf., 1978—87; vis. prof. U. Karlsruhe, Germany, 1980—81, Ecole Nationale Superieure de Mechanique, Nantes, France, 1984, Nantes, 96; jubilee prof. Chalmers Inst. Tech., Goteborg, Sweden, 1988; cons. in field. Author: (book) Three Dimensional Turbulent Boundary Layers, 1972; contbr. articles to profl. jours.; assoc. editor: AIAA Jour., 1987—90. Recipient Sr. Scientist award, Alexander von Humboldt Found., 1980, 1993. Fellow: ASME (Fluids Engring. award 1997), AIAA (assoc.); mem.: Soc. Naval Archtl. Marine Engrs., Am. Soc. Engring. Edn., Pi Tau Sigma, Sigma Xi. Home: 60 Kennedy Pkwy Iowa City IA 52246-2780 Office: IIHR Hyrdoscience and Engring U Iowa 404 Hydraulics Laboratory Iowa City IA 52242-1585

PATER, MICHAEL JOHN, lawyer; b. Natrona Heights, Pa., Aug. 22, 1957; s. Clifford Donald and Alice (Lehmann) P.; m. Kathy Jo Pollack, Apr. 17, 1982. BA in Acctg., BA in Bus. Adminstrn., Grove City (Pa.) Coll., 1979; MSBA, Robert Morris Coll., 1983; JD, Duquesne U., 1988. Bar: Pa. 1988, U.S. Dist. Ct (we. dist.) Pa. 1988. Credit and fin. mgr. Penreco divsn. Pennzoil, Butler, Pa., 1981-88; tax atty. Arthur Young, Pitts., 1988-89; ptnr. Hergenroeder & Heights P.C., Butler, Pitts., 1989—. Campaign treas. Pa. State Senator Melissa A. Hart, 1990—; bd. dirs. Am. Cancer Soc., Four Corners unit, Pitts., 1989-96, New Dirs. Am. Cancer Soc., Pitts., 1988—. Mem. ABA, Pa. Bar Assn., Butler County Bar Assn. (treas. 1991—), Allegheny County Bar Assn. Republican. Avocation: sports. Home: 3128 Primrose Ln Natrona Heights PA 15065-1830 Office: Hergenroeder & Heights 101 E Diamond St Ste 202 Butler PA 16001-5944

PATERSON, ANDREW HOFFMAN, geneticist; b. Lansdale, Pa., Sept. 18, 1960; s. Paul Martin and June Bartholemew (Hoffman) P. BS, U. Del., 1982; MS, Cornell U., 1986, PhD, 1988. Rsch. biochemist E.I. duPont de Nemours, Wilmington, Del., 1989-91; asst. prof. Tex. A&M U., College Station, 1991-95, assoc. prof., 1995-99; prof., dir. Ctr. Applied Genetic Techs. U. Ga., Athens, 1999—. Mem. USDA Crucifier Adv. Com., 1990—, USDA-Series 258-Cotton, 1992—; mem. editorial bd. Brazilian Jour. Genetics, Sao Paulo, 1995—. Mem. editl. bd. JQTL, 1995, Crop Sci., 2001—, Plant Physiology, 2001—, Genetics, 2002—; contbr. rsch. papers to profl. publs. Postdoctoral fellow Cornell U., Ithaca, N.Y., 1988-89; grantee numerous orgns., 1991-2001. Mem. Crop Sci. Soc. Am., Genetics Soc. Am., Phi Kappa Phi, Sigma Xi. Republican. Achievements include seminal work in application of molecular biology to complex measures of agricultural productivity and quality; documentation of genetic/evolutionary processes in plants. Avocations: fishing, hunting, horseback riding, reading, chess. Office: U Ga Ctr Applied Genetic Techs 110 Riverbend Rd Athens GA 30602

PATERSON, BASIL ALEXANDER, lawyer; b. N.Y.C., Apr. 27, 1926; s. Leonard J. and Evangeline (Rondon) P.; m. Portia Hairston, 1953; children: Daniel, David. BS, St. John's Coll., 1948; JD, St. John's U., 1951. Bar: N.Y. 1952. Ptnr. Paterson, Michael, Jones and Cherot, N.Y.C., 1956-77, Meyer, Suozzi, English & Klein, P.C., Mineola, N.Y., 1983—; mem. N.Y. State Senate, 1965-70; dep. mayor for labor rels. City of N.Y., 1978; sec. of state State of N.Y., 1979-82. Pres. Inst. Mediation and Conflict Resolution, 1971-77; chmn. 2d Jud. Screening Com., 1985-95; assoc. chmn. N.Y. State Sentencing Guidelines Com.; commr. Port Authority N.Y. and N.J., 1989-95. Bd. dirs. St. Benedict's Day Nursery, 1999—; vice chmn. Dem. Nat. Com., 1972-78, mem., 1972-78. Recipient Eagleton Inst. Politics award, Disting. Svc. award Guardians Assn. N.Y. Police Dept., City Club N.Y. award, Black Expo award, Excellence medal St. John's U., Kibbe award CUNY. Roman Catholic. Office: Meyer Suozzi English & Klein PC 1505 Kellum Pl Ste 3 Mineola NY 11501-4824

PATERSON, BRUCE FOOTE, internist, allergist; b. San Francisco, July 1, 1952; MD, Loyola U., Maywood, Ill., 1980. Diplomate Am. Bd. Internal Medicine, Am. Bd. Allergy and Immunology. Fellow in allergy and immunology Northwestern U. Med. Sch., Chgo., 1983-85; asst. clin. prof. Stanford U. Sch. Med., U. Calif., Davis. Mem. ACP, Alameda-Contra Costa Med. Assn. Office: 2485 High School Ave # 123 Concord CA 94520-1812 also: 1844 San Miguel Dr Ste 304C Walnut Creek CA 94596-4963

PATERSON, KATHERINE WOMELDORF, writer; b. Huaiyin, China, Oct. 31, 1932; came to U.S., 1940; d. George Raymond and Mary Elizabeth (Goetchius) Womeldorf; m. John Barstow Paterson, July 14, 1962; children: Elizabeth Polin, John Barstow, David Lord, Mary Katherine Nah-he-sah-peche-a. AB, King Coll., Bristol, Tenn., 1954, Litt.D. (hon.), 1978; MA, Presbyn. Sch. Christian Edn., 1957; postgrad., Kobe Sch. Japanese Lang., 1957-60; MRE, Union Theol. Sem., 1962; LHD (hon.), Otterbein Coll., 1979; LittD (hon.), U. Md., 1982, St. Mary's of the Woods, 1981, Shenandoah Coll., 1982; LHD (hon.) , Norwich U., 1990; LHD (hon.) , Mount St. Vincent U., Halifax,

N.S., Can., 1994; LittD, Hope Coll., 1997, Washington and Lee U., 1982; DLitt (hon.) , Prebyn. Coll., 2002. Tchr. Lovettsville (Va.) Elem. Sch., 1954-55; missionary Presbyn. Ch., Japan, 1957-61; master sacred studies and English Pennington (N.J.) Sch. for Boys, 1963-65. Author: The Sign of the Chrysanthemum, 1973, Of Nightingales That Weep, 1974, The Master Puppeteer, 1976, Bridge to Terabithia, 1977, The Great Gilly Hopkins, 1978, Angels and Other Strangers, 1979, Jacob Have I Loved, 1980, Rebels of the Heavenly Kingdom, 1983, Come Sing, Jimmy Jo, 1985, (with John Paterson) Consider the Lilies, 1986, Park's Quest, 1988, The Tale of the Mandarin Ducks, 1990, The Smallest Cow in the World, 1991, Lyddie, 1991, The King's Equal, 1992, Who Am I?, 1992, Flip-Flop Girl, 1994, A Midnight Clear: Stories for the Christmas Season, 1995, A Sense of Wonder, 1995, The Angel and the Donkey, 1996, Jip: His Story, 1996, Marvin's Best Christmas Present Ever, 1997, (with John Paterson) Images of God, 1998, Parzival, 1998, Celia and the Sweet, Sweet Water, 1998, Preacher's Boy, 1999, The Wide-Awake Princess, 2000, The Field of the Dogs, 2001, Marvin One Too Many, 2001, The Invisible Child, 2001; translator: The Crane Wife, 1981, The Tongue-Cut Sparrow, 1987. U.S. nominee for Hans Christian Andersen award, 1979, 89, 97; recipient Nat. Book award, 1977, 79, Newbery medal, 1978, 91, Newbery honor, 1979, New Eng. Book award New Eng. Booksellers Assn., 1982, Union medal Union Theol. Sem., 1992, Scott O'Dell award for hist. fiction, 1997, May Hill Arbuthnot Lectr. award, 1997, Hans Christian Andersen award, 1998, Lion award N.Y. Pub. Libr., 1998, Literary Light award Boston Pub. Libr., 2000, Living Legend award Libr. of Congress, 2000, Jefferson cup Va. Libr. Assn., 2000, Vt. Gov.'s award for excellence in arts, 2001. Mem. Authors Guild, Children's Book Guild Washington. Democrat. Office: Clarion Books 215 Park Ave S New York NY 10003-1603

PATERSON, PAUL CHARLES, retired private investigator, security consultant; b. Bethlehem, Pa., Dec. 31, 1927; s. Thomas and Ida (Weiss) P.; m. Estelle Marie Nabors; children: Linda Ann, Thomas Scott, Terry Maurice Leard. Grad., Inst. Applied Sci., Chgo., 1950. Jr. credit analyst Bethlehem Steel Corp., Pa., 1947-50; inspector claim spec., claim dir., field supr. Equifax Svcs., Inc., Allentown, 1953-61, field claim supr. St. Louis, 1961-63, regional claims mgr. Phila., 1963-71, spl. claim sales, sales exec.-claims Atlanta, 1971-89; pvt. investigator, pres. Paterson Investigations, Inc., Douglasville, Ga., 1989-2001. Editor CFE newsletter The Ga. Examiner, 1994-95. With U.S. Army, 1950-53. Mem. VFW, Am. Legion, Life, Accident and Health Claims Assn. Phila. (life, pres. 1969-70), Mktg. Ins. Claims Assn. (life, v.p. 1985—, pres. 1989-90), So. Loss Assn., Nat. WWII Meml. Assn. (charter), Atlanta Claims Assn., Ga. Assn. Profl. Pvt. Investigators (chair ethics com. 1999, treas. 2000), Assn. Cert. Fraud Examiners (cert., past pres. Ga. chpt. 1990, 93, bd. dirs. 1991-92, faculty 1995-96, bd. regents 1996, Disting. Achievement award 1994, 95, Regent Emeritus, life mem.), Criminal Investigation Divsn. Agts. Assn. Inc., Ga. Sheriffs' Assn., Ga. Claims Assn., Ga. Fire Investigators Assn., Ret. Mil. Police Assn. (assoc.), Am. Legion, Chapel Hills Golf Club. Republican. Avocations: golf, music, swimming, physical conditioning. Home: 6703 Live Oak Ln Douglasville GA 30135-1625 E-mail: paulpaterson@earthlink.net.

PATERSON, RICHARD DENIS, financial executive; b. Ottawa, Ont., Can., Oct. 13, 1942; m. Antoinette Paterson; children: Christopher, Russell, Kathlyn, Victoria, Connor. B in Commerce, Concordia U., Montreal, Que., Can., 1964. Auditor Coopers & Lybrand, Montreal, 1964-67; acct. Genstar Corp., 1967-69; dir. fin. and adminstrn. Industa Corp. (subs. Genstar Corp.), N.Y.C., 1969-73; v.p., comptroller Genstar Corp., Montreal and San Francisco, 1973-83, sr. v.p., CFO San Francisco, 1983-87; exec. v.p. Genstar Investment Corp., 1987-95; mng. dir. Genstar Capital LLC, 1996—. Bd. dirs. Gentek Bldg. Products, Inc.; chmn. bd. dirs. Prestolite Electric Inc.; chmn. Andros Inc. Mem. Order Chartered Accts. Que. Office: Genstar Capital LLC 555 California St Ste 4850 San Francisco CA 94104-1700 E-mail: rpaterson@gencap.com.

PATERSON, ROBERT E. trading stamp company executive; b. Kearny, N.J., Nov. 30, 1926; s. Robert McKinley and Ethel (Brookes) P.; m. Eileen Josephine Connolly; children: Carol, Joan, Robert, Richard, Donald, Jeffrey. MBA, Columbia U., 1971. Sr. v.p. fin., treas. The Sperry & Hutchinson Co., Inc., N.Y.C., 1952-87, also bd. dirs. Mem. Nat. Assn. Accts., 1954-89, nat. treas., 1985-88; bd. dirs. Govt. Obligations Fund, 1986-87. Elected mem. Borough Coun., 1991-98, 2002--, coun. pres., 1995-98, 2002. Served with U.S. Army, 1944-45, PTO.

PATERSON, TONY RALPH, sculptor, educator; b. Albany, N.Y., Dec. 17, 1934; s. Ralph Duncan and Mary Rose P.; m. Eleanor Cohen, Nov. 13, 1962; children: Robert, David. Grad. diploma, Sch. Mus. Fine Arts, 1966, diploma, 1983; attended, U. Guadalajara, Mex., 1953, MIT, La Grand Chaumiere Sch., Paris. Prof. SUNY, Buffalo, 1968—, head sculpture dept., 1995—, dir. Casting/Welding Inst., 1996—. One-man shows include William and Mary Coll., Williamsburg, Va., Tragos Gallery, Boston; group exhbns. include over 100 nat. and internat. shows; represented in permanent collections Brandeis U., Kalamazoo Inst. Arts, Sch. Mus. Fine Arts, Boston. Dir. Rumsey Restoration project, Buffalo, 1968—; overseer restorations for City of Buffalo Arts Commn., 1968—; bd. dirs. Ashford Hollow Found., 1999—. MacDowell Colony fellow; fellow Sch. Mus. Fine Arts, Boston; recipient award NAD, N.Am. Sculpture Exhbn.. Home: 530 Norwood Ave Buffalo NY 14222-1319 Office: SUNY Art Dept 202 Center For The Arts Buffalo NY 14260-6000 E-mail: arp3@acsu.buffalo.edu.

PATHAK, SUNIT RAWLY, business owner, consultant, journalist; b. Calcutta, India, Feb. 14, 1953; came to U.S., 1973. s. Santosh K. and Bira (Laharry) P.; m. Koruna Dutt; 1 child, Arit. BA, Calcutta U., 1972; BBA, U. Ga., 1975; MBA, U. Ark., 1978. Sr. analyst Norton-Christensen, Oklahoma City, 1981-84; bus. cons. Cactus Feeders, Inc., Dumas, Tex., 1984-85; analyst, controller Grindwell-Norton, Calcutta, 1985-87; prin. Tech. Venture Cons., Inc., Amarillo, Tex., 1985-93, Venture Mktg. Cons., Inc., Santa Barbara, Calif., 1985—; journalist Morris Communications, Amarillo, 1987-92; ptnr. Internat. Mktg. Inc./Venture Mktg. Cons., Inc., 1989-93; assoc. N.W. Environ. Tng. Inst., 1992-93; mng. editor Claude (Tex.) News, 1992-93; contr. Khameleon Software, Clearwater, Fla., 2000—. Adj. faculty econs. and acctg. Allan Hancock Coll., Santa Maria, Calif.; adj. faculty internat. bus. and acctg. sys. Concordia U. Wis., 1997-2000; adj. faculty acctg. sys. Ind. Inst. Tech.; assoc. Dameron Petroleum, Midland, Tex., Cease Fire, Inc., Southfield, Mich.; sr. sys. educator Brittania, Inc., Arroyo Grande, Calif., Eco-Adventures, USA, Santa Maria; assoc. Pre-Med, Inc., Santa Monica, Calif. Fund raiser United Way, Oklahoma City, 1983; benefactor Robert Duval Children's Fund, Nitish Laharry Children's Libr., Calcutta, India, 1984—. Recipient English Lit. prize Brit. Coun., 1969; Rotary Dist. 690 scholar, 1973. Mem. Inst. Mgmt. Accts. (v.p. membership Amarillo chpt. 1989-90), Meeting Planners Internat., Tex. Press Assn., Santa Barbara C. of C., Petroleum Club (Bakersfield, Calif.), Calcutta Cricket Club, Indian Polo Assn., Tower Club, Calcutta Club, Santa Barbara Polo & Racquet Club, Pine Valley Country Club, Houston Polo Club, East Lake Woodlands Country Club. Hindu. Avocations: polo, tennis, international air travel. Office: Po Box 17652 Clearwater FL 33762 E-mail: sunit1@hotmail.com.

PATHE, PETER, information technology executive; BS in Engring. & Applied Sci., Calif. Inst. Tech.; MS, MIT. From mgr. to corp. v.p. Microsoft, Redmond, Wash., 1991, corp. v.p. Office: One Microsoft Way Redmond WA 98052-6399*

PATIN FALINI, NANCY MARIE, dietitian; b. Fullerton, Calif., Oct. 26, 1961; d. Patrick Marcellus and Margie Elizabeth (Waltzer) Patin; m. Tullio John Falini Jr., May 31, 1991; children: Francesco Gerardo, Analisa Helen Marisol, Teresa Rose Aisha, Patrick Michael Le. AA in Dietetic Assistance, Santa Rosa (Calif.) Jr. Coll., 1981; student, U. Ariz., Guadalajara, Mex., 1985; BS in Dietetics, Calif. State U., Chico, 1984, MA in Nutrition Edn., 1988. Receptionist, swim instr., lifeguard Wikiup Racquet and Swim Club, Santa Rosa, Calif., 1979-83; lab. asst. intern NIH, Bethesda, Md., 1983; instr. nutrition Kids Country Daycare, Chico, 1984; office/med. asst. Dr. Donald Mangus, 1985; cons. pediat. nutritionist Frank Gladen, 1986; nutrition health aide Women-Infant-Children program Chico Dept. Pub. Health, 1988; dietary technician Chico Cmty. Hosp., 1984-86, 87-88; clin. dietitian Nazareth Hosp., Phila., 1989-91; cons. renal dietitian Biomed. Applications, 1990-91; clin. dietitian Fitzgerald Mercy Hosp., Darby, Pa., 1991-95; pvt. practice dietitian, specializing in celiac disease West Chester, 1995—; homeschool tchr., 1999—. Guest spkr. TV NewsChannel 3 on experience with Mother Theresa of Calcutta, 1997; spkr. ednl. conf. Am. Celiac Soc., Dietary Support Coalition and NIH, Washington, 1990; spkr. U. Md. Sch. Medicine Med. Conf., 1995, Johns Hopkins Hosp. Dept. Nutrition Conf., 1996, Mount Sinai Med. Ctr. Med. Conf., 1996, Am. Celiac Soc. Dietary Support Coalition, 1997, Phila. Pediatric Nutrition Practice Group, 1997, Pa. State Coop. Extension, 1998, 9th Internat. Symposium Celiac Disease, 2000, Am. Soc. Parenteral and Enteral Nutrition, 2001, Advances in Perinatal and Pediatric Nutrition, 2001; nutrition advisor Celiac Spruce Support Group, Phila., 1988—; dietitian adv. bd. For Gluten Free Living, 2000—. Contbg. author: Kids with Celiac Disease: A Family Guide to Raising Happy, Healthy, Gluten-Free Children, 2001, contbg. author: Wheat-Free and Worry Free, 2002; contbg. editor: Gluten Free Living, 1998—99; contbr. articles to profl. and layperson's jours., publs., newsletter. Vol. nutritionist Calvary Commn., Mex., 1990, Verbo Ministries, Guatamala, 1992; gen. vol. Mother Teresa's Missionaries of Charity, India, 1994; missionary Sisters of the Holy Redeemer, Huntingdon Valley and Phila., 1988-89; vol. Spanish speaking interpreter St. Agnes Nurses Ctr., 2000. Mem. Am. Dietetic Assn. (registered; product display presenter ann. meeting 1988), Pediat. Nutrition Practice Group (pres. 1996-97). Roman Catholic. Avocations: skiing, hiking, making crafts, travel, cross country. Home: 437 Sharpless St West Chester PA 19382-3538

PATINKIN, TERRY ALLAN, physician; b. Oak Park, Ill., Feb. 1, 1950; s. Lester D. and Marcella Jaqueline (Steynburg) P.; m. Sandra Lee Friedman, Apr. 21, 1985; children: Jonathan, Zachary. BS, U. Ill., 1971; MD, U. Calif., San Francisco, 1975; MPH in health care mgmt., Harvard U., 1996. Diplomate Am. Bd. Emergency Medicine, Am. Bd. Family Medicine; cert. physician exec., 2002. Intern, resident in family practice U. Calif. San Francisco/Natividad Med. Ctr., Salinas, Calif., 1975-78, assoc. dir. family medicine residency program, 1978-90; dir. emergency dept. Natividad Med. Ctr., 1985-91, dir. continuing med. edn., 1978-91, dir. undergrad. edn., 1978-90, emergency physician, 1979-91, Sturdy Meml. Hosp., Attleboro, Mass., 1991-94; dir., chmn. emergency dept. Roger Williams Hosp., Providence, 1994-99, Landmark Med. Ctr., Woonsocket, 2000—02; dir. urgent care East Boston Neighborhood Health Ctr., 2002—. Asst. clin. prof. U. Calif., San Francisco, 1981-88, assoc. clin. prof., 1988-91; clin. asst. prof. Stanford U., 1990-93; asst. clin. prof. Brown U., Providence, 1995—, Boston U., 1999—. Fellow Am. Coll. Emergency Physicians; mem. Am. Coll. Physician Execs., U. Ill. Alumni Assn. (life), U. Calif. San Francisco Alumni Faculty Assn. Office: 10 Gove St East Boston MA 02128

PATINO, DOUGLAS XAVIER, foundation, government agency, and university administrator; b. Calexico, Calif., Apr. 11, 1939; s. Jose Luis and Maria Teresa (Seymour) P.; m. Barbel Wilma Hoyer, Aug. 13, 1970; 1 child, Viktor Xavier. AA, Imperial Valley Coll., 1960; BA, Calif. State U., San Diego, 1962, MA, 1966; PhD, U.S. Internat. U., 1972. Deputy dir. Sacramento (Calif.) Concilio, Inc., 1968-69; v.p. student affairs U. So. Colo., Pueblo, 1973-75; dep. dir. for planning and rev. svc. br. to dir. Calif. Employment Devel. Dept., dir.; sec. Calif. Health & Welfare Agy., 1975-83; dir. Ariz. Dept. of Econ. Security, Phoenix, 1983-87; pres., chief exec. officer Marin Community Found., Larkspur, Calif., 1987-91; pres. New Partnership Found. and Patino Group, San Rafael, 1991-93; vice chancellor Calif. State U. Sys., Long Beach, 1993—2002; prof. social welfare Calif. State U., L.A., 1998—. Commr. W.T. Grand Found., 1986—88, Enterprize for the Ams., Washington, 1994—; trustee C.S. Mott Found., Flint, Mich., 1995—, Calif. Wellness Found., Woodland Hills, 1997—; bd. dirs. Marguerite Casey Found.; chair, treas. Hispanics in Philanthropy, 1993. Mem. Sec. of U.S. Dept. of Labor Task Force, Ariz., 1985-86, Staff Adv. Com. of the Human Resource Com., Nat. Gov. Assn., Washington, 1983-86; bd. dirs. Calif. Leadershp, Santa Cruz, Calif., 1985-95, No. Calif. Grantmakers, 1990-91, Ariz. Assn. Bus., 1984; chair U.S. Savs. Bond Dr. for State of Calif., 1982; trustee Nat. Hispanic U., Oakland, Calif., 1987-90, Hispanic Community Fund, San Francisco, 1989-95, bd. dirs. Calif. Sch. Profl. Psychology, 1989-94, Coun. on Found., Washington, 1990-96, Found. Ctr., N.Y., 1993; pres. Calif. State U. Found. Recipient The Monty Disting. Alumni award San Diego State U., 1997, Simon Bolivar award for cmty. leadership award Hispanic Cmty. Found. and Bay Area United Way, 1996, Azteca award Human Devel. Corp., 1991, Leadership award Nat. Concilors of Am. and United Way of Bay Area, 1990, Disting. Performance award, Nat. Alliance of Bus., Washington, 1985, Superior Svc. Mgmt. award, Am. Soc. Pub. Adminstrn., 1985, Humanitarian award, Los Padrinos, Inc., 1981, Small and Minority Bus. award for the State of Calif. 1982, Disting. Alumni award, Calif. Jr. Community Coll. Assn., Sacramento, 1982, Silver Spur award, Nat. Fedn. of Charros in Guadalajaro, Jalisco, Mex., 1974, Calif. Community Svc. award, Former Gov. Ronald Reagan, Sacramento, 1973; named to 100 Most Influential Hispanics, Hispanic Bus., 1995, 97. Mem. Am. Pub. Welfare Assn. (bd. dirs., Leadership award 1987), Rotary, 1987-93. Office: The Patino Group Sacramento CA 95822 E-mail: dpatino@earthlink.net.

PATINO, ISIDRO FRANK, law enforcement educator; b. San Antonio, Mar. 10, 1943; s. Isidro F. and Maria (Narro) P.; children: Michael, Rebecca, Karleen. BS, Calif. State U., L.A., 1973; MBA, U. Redlands, 1995. Records comdr. Placentia (Calif.) Police Dept., 1980-85; asst. dean Criminal Justice Tng. Ctr. Golden West Coll., Huntington Beach, Calif., 1986-89, assoc. dean instrn., 1989-92; divsn. dean dept. pub. svc. Rio Hondo Coll., Whittier, 1992—. Pres., mem. State Chancellors Adv. Com. Pub. Safety Edn., 1991—, chmn., 1998—; chmn. So. Calif. Pub. Safety Tng. Consortium, 1994—, active, 1993—; bd. suprs. L.A. County Spl. Task Force on Pub. Safety Tng., 1995—; mem. Hispanic male adv. com. Dept. Edn. Connections Project. Kellogg C.C. Diversity Leadership fellow, 1996-97. Mem. Calif. Law Enforcement Assn. Records Suprs. (pres. so. chpt. 1985-87, state pres. 1986-87), Calif. Acad. Dirs. Assn. (chmn. 1988-89), Am. Soc. Criminologists, Acad. Criminal Justice Scis., Western and Pacific Assn. Criminal Justice Educators, Calif. Assn. Adminstrn. of Justice Educators (v.p. 1996-97, state pres. 1997-99), Calif. Peace Officers Stds. and Tng. Basic Course Consortium (chmn. instrn. com. 1987-88),World Future Soc. (pres. Orange County-Long Beach chpt. 1988-92), Nat. Assn. Field Tng. Officers (nat. pres. 1992-93), Nat. Assn. Chiefs of Police, Internat. Assn. Chiefs of Police, Soc. Law Enforcement Trainers. Roman Catholic.

PATMAN, PHILIP FRANKLIN, lawyer; b. Atlanta, Nov. 1, 1937; s. Elmer Franklin and Helen Lee (Miller) P.; m. Katherine Sellers, July 1, 1967; children: Philip Franklin, Katherine Lee. BA, U. Tex., 1959, LLB, 1964; MA, Princeton U., 1962. Bar: Tex. 1964, U.S. Supreme Ct. 1970, U.S. Dist. Ct. (so. dist.) Tex. 1971, U.S. Dist. Ct. (we. dist.) Tex. 1975. Atty. office of legal adviser Dept. State, Washington, 1964-67; dep. dir. office internat. affairs HUD, 1967-69; pvt. practice Austin, Tex., 1969—. Contbr. articles to legal jours. Ofcl. rep. of Gov. Tex. to Interstate Oil Compact Commn., 1973-83, 87-91. Woodrow Wilson fellow, 1959. Fellow Tex. Bar Found. (life); mem. ABA, State Bar Tex., Tex. Ind. Prodrs. and Royalty Owners Assn., Tex. Oil and Gas Assn., Tex. Law Rev. Assn., Austin Club, Headliners Club, Westwood Country Club, Rotary, Phi Beta Kappa, Phi Delta Phi. Office: Patman & Osborn 515 Congress Ave Ste 1704 Austin TX 78701-3503

PATMAN, RALPH DONALD, surgeon; b. Greenville, Tex., 1933; MD, U. Tex. SW, 1958. Diplomate Am. Bd. Surgery. Intern Parkland Meml. Hosp., Dallas, 1958-59, resident in gen. surgery, 1959-63; pvt. practice, 1963—. Fellow Am. Coll. Surgeons; mem. AMA, Internat. Cardiovascular Soc., Soc. Vascular Surgeons, Alpha Omega Alpha. Address: PO Box 140309 Dallas TX 75214-0309

PATMOS, ADRIAN EDWARD, university dean emeritus; b. Paterson, N.J., June 29, 1914; s. Adrian and Myra (Van Splinter) P.; m. Pearl Van Den Heuvel, Apr. 25, 1942; children: Adrian Edward III, Bruce Douglas. AB magna cum laude, N.Y.U., 1935, A.M., 1936; LLD, Wittenberg U., 1996; Penfield scholar, 1937-38; grad. study, Am. U., 1936-37. Asst. prof. econs. Wittenberg U., 1938-47, assoc. prof., head dept., 1947-50, prof. econs., 1950—, head dept., 1950-64, dir. mgmt. devel. program, 1952-79, eve. sessions, 1952-78; dean Wittenberg U. (Sch. Community Edn.), 1955-79, prof. and dean emeritus, 1979—. Jr. accountant Def. Plant Corp., Curtiss-Wright Corp., summer 1943; vis. instr. Ohio Wesleyan U., summer 1944; spl. field rep. NLRB, 1946; vis. lectr. econs. N.Y.U., 1946-47, summer 1948; vis. prof. econs. USAF Inst. Tech., 1949, 50; cons. Clark C.C., 1982-84, Urbana U., 1983-94. Chmn. Clark County Health Facilities Planning Com., 1965-66, City commr., Springfield, Ohio, 1958-62, mayor, 1960-62; Trustee United Way, Springfield and Clark County, 1960-74; trustee Clark Tech. Coll., 1965-78, chmn., 1969-71; trustee Springfield Community Hosp., 1975-84, Elderly United, 1979-92. Recipient Wittenberg award for meritorious svc. to univ., 1964, Silver Knight award Nat. Mgmt. Assn., Sta. WIZE award for outstanding cmty. svc., Cmty. Svc. award C. of C., 1979, award of distinction Bd. of Realtors, Outstanding Svc. in Cmty. Labor-Mgmt. Relationships award Fed. Mediation Svc., citation as one of Ohio's foremost educators Ohio Senate, Medal of Honor for leadership in liberal arts edn., 1987; named Jr. Achievement Hall of Fame laureate, 1996. Mem. Ohio Coll. Assn. (pres. adult edn. sect. 1959-60), Am. Econs. Assn., Kiwanis (Disting. Svc. to Cmty. award), Phi Beta Kappa, Phi Gamma Delta, Blue Key. Baptist.

PATNAIK, KUNKUN, systems analyst; b. Orissa, India, Nov. 16, 1964; came to U.S., 1970; s. Rabindra Nath and Sobha (Das) P. BS in Info. Systems, U. Md., 1986; M. Adminstrv. Sci. in Info. Tech., Johns Hopkins U., 1989. Programmer Overseas Mktg. Group, Balt., 1985; systems analyst Syscon Corp., Washington, 1986—. Republican. Hindu.

PATNAUDE, ANN MARIE TRUDEL, nurse; b. Nashua, N.H., Mar. 24, 1958; d. Alban Aurelien and Eda Juliette (Simoneau) Trudel; m. Neal Francis Patnaude, May 25, 1985; children: Andrew P., Laura E. Diploma in nursing, Mary Hitchcock Meml. Hosp., Hanover, N.H., 1979; BSN, Curry Coll., 1984. Staff nurse Mass. Gen. Hosp., Boston, 1979-80, Brigham and Women's Hosp., Boston, 1980-83; nurse mgr. Lowell (Mass.) Gen. Hosp., 1984; staff nurse Brigham and Women's Hosp., Boston, 1984-94; staff nurse labor deliver recovery postpartum So. N.H. Regional Med. Ctr., 1994-2000, parent educator, 1994-98; triage nurse Manchester Cmty. Health Ctr., 2000—01; RN team leader Dartmouth Hitchcock Clinic, 2002. Co-leader Girl Scouts USA, Merrimack, N.H.; parent rep. program evaluation and review com. Merrimack, N.H. Sch. Dist., 1997-98; vol. Merrimack Sch. Dist., 1995—. Mem. Am. Can. Geneal. Soc. Roman Catholic. Avocations: needlework, genealogy. Home: 30 Constance St Merrimack NH 03054-2871 E-mail: atrupat@aol.com.

PATNAUDE, WILLIAM EUGENE, architect, writer; b. Sanger, Calif., Sept. 24, 1937; s. Eugene Joseph Patnaude and Vera Mae (Giles) Patnaude Fagan; m. Mary Esther Simerly, Aug. 22, 1971 (div. 1987); children: Nathaniel, Matthew BArch, U. Calif., Berkeley, 1961; postgrad., Calif. State U., Fresno, 1968-72. Registered arch., Calif., Wash., Idaho, Nev., N.Mex., Colo., Utah, Ariz., Mont., Ind., Nebr., Ohio, N.Y., N.J. Draftsman, arch. Robert Stevens Assoc., Santa Cruz, Calif., 1963-66; arch. Llewelyn Davies, Weeks & Ptnrs., London, 1966, Allen Y. Lew, Fresno, Calif., 1967-69, assoc., 1969-74; v.p., arch. Lew & Patnaude, Inc., 1978-84, pres., 1985—. Instr. Calif. State U., Fresno, 1968-81 Constn. arbitrator Am. Arbitration Assn., 1976-96; chair ctrl. area plan citizen's adv. com. City of Fresno, 1991-93, chair gen. plan update com., 1994-97; bd. dirs. Fresno Arts Ctr., 1971-74, Fresno County Alliance for the Arts, 1986-88, 91-94. With USNR, 1961-63. Recipient Award of Merit, Calif. Hist. Preservation Conf., Orange County, 1983; Award of Excellence, Woodwork Inst. Calif., 1982 Fellow AIA (nat. dir. 1983-85, pres. Calif. Coun. 1982, San Joaquin chpt. 1978, Awards of Excellence, 1972-95); mem. Constrn. Specifications Inst. (pres. Fresno chpt. 1977). Democrat. Avocations: photography, fine wines. Home: 4190 N Van Ness Blvd Fresno CA 93704-4213 Office: Lew & Patnaude Inc 1050 S St Fresno CA 93721-1497 E-mail: billp@osufresno.edu.

PATNODE, DARWIN NICHOLAS, academic administrator, professional parliamentarian; b. Mpls., June 20, 1948; s. Arthur T. and Agnes M. P. BA, St. Mary's U., Winona, Minn., 1968; MA, U. Minn., 1970, PhD, 1974. Cert. profl. parliamentarian. Corp. rels. coord. Stanford (Calif.) U., 1983-87; dir. of devel. Foothill Coll., Los Altos Hills, Calif., 1987-94; assoc. dean West Valley-Mission C.C. Dist., Saratoga, 1994-96; exec. dir. San Mateo County C.C. Found., 1996-01. Vis. lectr. in English, Santa Clara (Calif.) U., 1982-83, dir. Major Gifts, Calif. State U., Hayward, 2001—. Author: History of Parliamentary Procedure, 1982; co-author: Robert's Rules of Order, Modern Edition, 1989. Bd. dirs. Nonprofit Devel. Ctr., San Jose, Calif., 1993-96. Mem.: Nat. Assn. Parliamentarians, Am. Inst. Parliamentarians (pres. 1994—95), San Carlos Tennis Club (pres. 2002—). Avocations: tennis, music, reading. Home: 3353 Brittan Ave Apt 13 San Carlos CA 94070-3431 Office: Calif State U Hayward 25800 Carlos Bee Blvd Hayward CA 94542

PATNODE, GERALD RUFUS, marketing professional; b. Balt., Mar. 9, 1945; s. Gerald Rufus Sr. and Mary June (Tolson) P.; m. Donna Lee Babb, Mar. 2, 1968 (div. June 1988); children: Pamela Elizabeth Patnode Eherenrich, Stephanie M. Patnode; m. Nancy Jane Stauffer, June 8, 1991; 1 child, Christian Alexander. BS, Old Dominion, 1968; MBA, U. Md., 1975; MS, Temple U., 1979, ABD, 1980. Asst. prof. mktg. Loyola Coll., Balt., 1974-79; CEO, pres. Delta Comm., Columbia, Md., 1978-82; exec. dir. The Mgmt. Inst. at Catsonville Coll., Balt., 1982-84; v.p., gen. mgr. Loverde/Comml. Realty, 1984-88, Ctrl. Comml. Realty, Columbia, Md., 1988-91; exec. v.p. Data Chromatics, Towson, 1991-93; CEO The Mktg. Advantage Co., Balt., 1993-96; pres., CEO Tastee Foods Corp., Balta, Md., 1996-98; dir. Inst. Enterprise Devel., 1998—. Dir. fed. adv. SBA, Balt., 1975-80; chairperson Balt. County Govt. Pers. Bd., Towson, 1995—; adj. prof. Johns Hopkins U., 1990—, York Coll. of Pa., 1998—; dean Balt. Internat. Coll. Sch. Bus., 2000-. Author: (with others) Household Marketing, 1980; contbr. articles to profl. jours. Mem. Econ. Devel. Commn., Adams County, Pa., 1988, Econ. Devel. Task Force, Balt., 1995; advisor bus. matters Balt. County Exec., 1995. Mem. Am. Mktg. Assn. (past dir., Meritorious Svc. to Acad. 1984, 96, 88), C. of C. (chair edn. com. 1985), Sales and Mktg. Execs. Republican. Lutheran. Avocation: sports. Home: 7 Manor Brook Rd Monkton MD 21111-1606 Office: U Balt Mount Royal Blvd Baltimore MD 21203 E-mail: grpatnode@home.com.

PATNODE, MARK W. artist, graphic designer; b. Apr. 29, 1956; s. Edward M. Patnode and Arlene D. (Bull) Smith; m. Judith R. Abrams, June 21, 1980; children: Rebekah, Benjamin. BFA, SUNY, Purchase, 1978. Graphic designer, illustrator Sonalysts, Inc., Waterford, Conn., 1984-86, sr. graphic designer, 1986-97, COMSUBDEVRON-12/Sonalysts/Subbase N. London, Groton, 1997—. Exhibited in Lyman Allyn Mus., New London, Conn. 1989, 93, 95; graphic designer Devron 12 logo redesign, SubtacDev 50th Anniversary logo, USS Springfield (SSN 761) logo redesign, 1999. Mem.: Purchase Coll. Alumni Assn. (bd. dirs., comms. dir., designer, sec.), Gideons Internat. New London Camp. Avocations: skiing, hiking. Home: 33 Granite St New London CT 06320-5946 Office: Sonalysts Inc 215 Parkway N Waterford CT 06385-1209 E-mail: mpatnode@99main.com.

PATON WALSH, JILL, author; b. London, England, Apr. 29, 1937; d. John Llewelyn and Patricia (Dubern) Buss; m. Antony Edmund Paton Walsh, Aug. 5, 1961; Children: Edmund, Margaret, Clare. Author: Hengest's Tale, 1966, The Dolphin Crossing, 1967, Fireweed, 1969, (World Book Festival award 1970), Wordhoard, 1969, Goldengrove 1972, Farewell Great King, 1972, Toolmaker, 1973, The Dawnstone, 1973, The Emporer's Winding Sheet, 1974 (Whitbread prize 1974), The Huffler, 1975, The Island Sunrise: Preshistoric Culture in the British Isles, 1975, Unleaving, 1976 (Boston Globe, Horn Book award 1976), Children of the Fox: Crossing to Salamis, 1977, The Walls of Athens, 1978, Persian Gold, 1978, A Chance Child, 1978, The Green Book, 1981, Babylon, 1982, Parcell of Patterns, 1983 (Universe prize 1984), Lost and Found, 1984, Gaffer Samson's Luck, 1984 (Smarties Grand prix 1984), Lapsing, 1985, A School for Lovers, 1989, Birdy and the Ghosties, 1990, "Grace", 1991, Matthew and the Sea Singers, 1992, When Grandma Came, 1992, The Wydham Case, 1993, Knowledge of Angels, 1994, A Piece of Justice, 1995, Connie Came to Play, 1995, Thomas and the Tinners, 1995, The Serpentine Cave, 1997, When I Was Little Like You, 1997, (with Dorothy L. Sayers) Thrones, Dominations, 1998, A Desert in Bohemia, 2000. Fellow Royal Soc. of Lit. (CBE award 1996). Address: care David Higham Assocs 5-8 Lower John St Golden Sq London W1R 3PE England

PATOSKY, JAMES VINCENT, JR. financial planner; b. Hamilton, Bermuda, Dec. 23, 1955; s. James V. and Gladys Darlyne (Anderson) P.; m. Renee M. Patosky, Aug. 19, 1978; 1 child, Kristen. BS, Slippery Rock State U., 1977. CFP, ChFC, CLU. Regional dir. Am. Express Fin. Advisors, Clearwater, Fla., 1992-96; fin. planner Provise Mgmt. Group, 1996-99; dir. high net planning AXA Fin. Advisors LLC, 1999—2001; field dir. N.Y. Life, 2001—. Golf coach

East Lake H.S., Tarpon Springs, 1995-99; lectr. in field. Contbr. articles to profl. jours. Mem. Fin. Counseling Svcs. of Morton Plant Mease Found. Mem. Fin. Planning Assn. Republican. Roman Catholic. Avocations: golf, reading, sports.

PATREI, JAMES GILDO, otolaryngologist; b. Ilion, N.Y., Jan. 15, 1948; s. Gildo Paul and C. Katherine (Campagna) P.; m. Sharon Antonucci, Aug. 21, 1971; children: Matthew James, Jonathan Louis. BA, Hamilton Coll., 1970; MD, SUNY, Syracuse, 1974. Intern Albany Med. Ctr. Hosp., 1974-76; resident SUNY Upstate Med. Ctr., Syracuse, N.Y., 1976-79; with St. Josephs Hosp. Health Ctr., Cmty. Gen. Hosp., Syracuse, Crouse-Irving Meml. Hosp., Syracuse, HArrison Ctr. Outpatient Surgery, Syracuse. Mem. med. adv. bd. HMO-CNY, Syracuse, 1992-00. Deacon Grace Assembly of God, Syracuse, 1980-86, 94-98. Fellow Am. Acad. Otolaryngology Head & Neck Surgery; mem. AMA, Am. Acad. Otolaryngologic Allergy. Republican. Office: 406 University Ave Syracuse NY 13210-1803

PATRICAN, RICHARD A. federal agency administrator; BS in Aeronautical Engring., Embry-Riddle Aeronautical U. Lead safety engr. Gen. Elec. Astro-Space Div., 1984—90; ops. safety mgr. Space Station Freedom Program Office NASA, 1990—94; mgr. Internat. Space Station Safety and Mission Assurance NASA Enterprise Safety and Mission Assurance Div., Office of Safety and Mission Assurance, 1994—. Recipient Silver Snoopy award, NASA, 1996. Office: NASA Hdqrs Mail Code Q 300 E St SW Washington DC 20546*

PATRICK, ALAN K. artist; b. Richmond, Ind., June 16, 1942; s. Paul and Edythe (Kackley) P.; m. Dianne Childers, Apr. 5, 1966 (div. June 1977); m. Cynthia Hope Gill, Oct. 12, 1985. Owner Bethel Pottery, Albany, Ind., 1966—. Represented in permanent collections Ball State U., Minnetrista Cultural Ctr., Richmond Art Mus., others. Recipient Best of Show award Minn. Cultural Ctr., 1972, Hoosier Salon, 1991, Richmond Art Mus., 1996. Mem. Ind. Artist Craftsmen, Ind. Artists Club (Best of Show 2000), Ind. Potters Guild. Home: 5809 E Pottery Rd Albany IN 47320-9714

PATRICK, BRENDA JEAN, educational consultant; b. Dallas, Aug. 24, 1955; d. Gene Everett and Peggy Rose (Tanzy) Patrick; 1 child Michael Everett. BS in Elem. Edn., Tex. A&M U., Commerce, 1981, MS, 1984, postgrad., 1989—. Cert. profl. supr., mid-mgmt. adminstr. Tchr. Garland Ind. Sch. Dist., 1982-87, acad. coach, 1983-86; with Austin Acad. for Excellence, 1987-88; program coord., master cons. Region 10 Edn. Svc. Ctr., 1988—. Coord. Tchr. Expectation Student Achievement; trainer Devel. Capable People, Tex. A&M-Commerce/Profl. Devel. Ctr. Project; trainer of trainers Profl. Devel. and Appraisal Sys.; developer, presenter workshops and seminars in field. Author: Better Teaching, Texas Secretary. Bd. dirs. Dallas Arboretum's Fan Club. Recipient Tex. History Tchr. award Daus. of Republic of Tex., Am. History Tchr. award DAR; named Vol. with a Heart, YWCA. Mem. Tex. PTA (hon. life), Tex. Staff Devel. Coun., Phi Delta Kappa.

PATRICK, CHARLES WILLIAM, JR. lawyer; b. Monroe, N.C., Oct. 9, 1954; s. Charles William and Louise (Nisbet) P.; m. Celeste Hunt, June 5, 1976; children: Laura Elizabeth, Charles William III. BA magna cum laude, Furman U., 1976; JD, U. S.C., 1979. Bar: S.C. 1979, U.S. Dist. Ct. S.C. 1981, U.S. Ct. Appeals (11th cir.) 1981, U.S. Ct. Appeals (10th cir.) 1983, U.S. Ct. Appeals (4th cir.) 1986. Law clk. to presiding judge 9th Cir. Ct. State of S.C., Charleston, 1979—80; assoc. Ness, Motley, Loadholt, Richardson and Poole and predecessor firm Blatt and Fales, 1980—2002, 1980—84, ptnr., 1984—2002, Richardson, Patrick, Westbrook & Brickman, LLC, Charleston, 2002—. Exec. editor S.C. Law Review, 1978; contbr. articles to profl. jours. Mem. ABA, Assn. Trial Lawyers Am., S.C. Assn. Trial Lawyers, Trial Lawyers for Pub. Justice, Phi Beta Kappa. Democrat. Presbyterian. Avocations: boating, skiing, jogging. Home: 38 Church St Charleston SC 29401-2742 Office: Richardson Patrick Westbrook & Brickman LLC PO Box 879 174 East Bay St Charleston SC 29402-0879

PATRICK, DANE HERMAN, lawyer; b. San Antonio, Oct. 18, 1960; s. Kae Thomas and Joyce Lynn (von Scheele) P.; m. Kelly Marie Carlson, May 17, 1986. BA in Econs. with honors, U. Tex., 1983; JD, So. Meth. U., 1987. Assoc. Law Office of Earl Luna, Dallas, 1987-88, Veitch & Davis, San Antonio, 1988-91; pvt. practice, 1991—. Mem. ATLA, San Antonio Trial Lawyers Assn. (bd. dirs.), San Antonio United Shareholder Assn. (chmn. 1988-92). Democrat. Methodist. Avocations: weight lifting, hunting, martial arts. Office: 111 Soledad St Ste 300 San Antonio TX 78205-2298

PATRICK, DAVID BRUCE, chiropractor; b. Harrisburg, Pa., Apr. 30, 1952; s. Gerald Vance, Sr. and Barbara Louise (Neff) P.; m. Sylvia Ann McHenry, Mar. 17, 1984; children: David, Laurie, Christopher, Colleen. AA, Harrisburg (Pa.) Area C.C., 1990; BS, D Chiropractic, Palmer Coll. of Chiropractic, 1993. Diplomate Nat. Bd. Chiropractic Examiners. Mgr., instr. Weninger Kung Fu Inst., Harrisburg, 1976-82; truck driver Sygma, 1983-90; assoc. doctor Blake Chiropractic, 1993-94; treating doctor Chiro Plus of York, Pa., 1994-95; owner, treating doctor Patrick Chiropractic Ctr., Elizabethtown, 1995—. Recipient Guy and Helen Swope Leadership award Harrisburg Area C.C., 1990; Pres.'s Freshman scholar, 1987-88. Mem.: Lancaster County Chiropractic Soc., Chiropractic Leadership Alliance, Chiropractic Fellowship Pa., Norlanco-Rheems Club (pres. 2000—01), Kiwanis (club pres. 2000—01), Phi Theta Kappa (chpt. pres. 1989—90, Disting. Student Scholar award 1990). Republic. Mormon. Avocations: Chinese martial arts, bicycling, reading, fishing, hiking. Home: 2735 N 4th St Harrisburg PA 17110-2011 Office: Patrick Chiropractic Ctr 505 N Market St Elizabethtown PA 17022-1516

PATRICK, DEVAL LAURDINE, lawyer; b. Chgo., July 31, 1956; s. Laurdine Kenneth and Emily Mae (Wintersmith) P.; m. Diane Louise Bemus, May 5, 1984; children: Sarah Baker, Katherine Wintersmith. AB cum laude, Harvard Coll., 1978, JD, 1982, Dist. Columbia Law Sch., 1994, Morris Brown Coll., 1996, Curry Coll., 1997, Clark U., 1999, New Eng. Sch. of Law, 1999, Suffolk U., 2000, Northeastern U., 2002. Bar: Calif. 1983, D.C. 1985, Mass. 1987, U.S. Dist. Ct. Mass. 1987, U.S. Dist. Ct. (cen. dist.) Calif. 1983, U.S. Ct. Appeals (1st and 5th cirs.) 1984, U.S. Ct. Appeals (9th and 11th cirs.) 1984, U.S. Supreme Ct. 1988. Law clk. to Hon. Stephen Reinhardt U.S. Ct. Appeals (9th cir.), L.A., 1982-83; asst. counsel NAACP Legal Def. Fund, N.Y.C., 1983-86; ptnr. Hill & Barlow, Boston, 1986-94; asst. atty. gen. civil rights divsn. U.S. Dept. Justice, Washington, 1994-97; ptnr. Day, Berry & Howard, Boston, 1997-99; v.p., gen. counsel Texaco Inc., White Plains, N.Y., 1999-2001; exec. v.p., gen. counsel The Coca-Cola Co., Atlanta, 2001—. Herman Phleger disting. vis. prof. Stanford Law Sch., 1997; lectr. Boston Coll. Sch. Law, 1997, Harvard Law Sch., 1998; mem. various corp. bd. dirs.; bd. overseers Harvard U., 1998—; dir. UAL Corp., 1997-2001, Reebok Internat. Ltd., 2001--, Coca-Cola Enterprises Inc., 2001--. Dir., mem. exec. com., chmn. New Eng. steering com. NAACP Legal Def. and Edn. Fund., Inc., 1991-94, vice chmn. Mass. Jud. Nominating Coun., 1991-93; trustee, mem. exec. com. Milton Acad., 1985-97; overseer WGBH, 1993-94; trustee Nathan Cummings Found., 1998-2000, Ford Found., 2000--. Recipient George Leisure award Harvard Law Sch., 1981; Rockefeller Traveling fellow, 1978. Mem. ABA (numerous bds. and coms.), Mass. Bar Assn., Mass. Black Lawyers Assn., Boston Bar Assn. (coun. mem. 1993), Harvard Alumni Assn. (dir. 1993-96). Avocations: squash, cooking, gardening. Office: The Coca-Cola Co One Coca-Cola Plz Atlanta GA 30301

PATRICK, DONALD LEE, social scientist, health services researcher; b. Eugene, Oreg., Sept. 23, 1944; s. Lawrence Leonard and Marie Esther (Bell) P.; m. Shirley Anne Alexander Beresford, May 31, 1980; children: Alistair Lawrence Beresford, Mira Yvonne Bell. AB with distinction, Northwestern U., 1966; MSPH, Columbia U., 1968, PhD, 1972. Rsch. assoc. U. Calif., San Diego, 1970-72; lectr. Yale U., New Haven, 1972-76; sr. lectr. U. London, 1976-82; assoc. prof. U. N.C., Chapel Hill, 1982-87; prof. and dir. social and behavioral scis. program U. Wash., Seattle, 1987—. Adj. prof. sociology, U. Wash., 1988—, dept. rehab. medicine, 1987—. Author: Health Status and Health Policy, 1993; editor: Sociology as Applied to Medicine, 1976, Disablement in Community, 1989. Mem. APHA (mem. coun. 1993-96), Spina Bifida Assn. Am. (chair profl. adv. bd. 1990-93, Pres.' award 1995), Internat. Soc. for Quality of Life Rsch. (pres. 1994-96, Pres. award 2001), Inst. Medicine. Democrat. Unitarian Universalist. Avocations: gardening, music, travel. Home: 5427 43rd Ave W Seattle WA 98199-1061 Office: U Wash PO Box 357660 Seattle WA 98195-7660

PATRICK, ERLINE M. federal agency administrator; BA in Biology, Talladega Coll., 1960; MEd in Urban Edn., U. Hartford, 1971, 6th yr. cert. adminstrn. and supervision, 1974; PhD, U. Conn., 1992. Secondary sch. math. and sci. tchr., Pa., N.C. and Conn., 1960-71; vice prin. Hartford (Conn.) Bd. Edn., 1971-78, prin., 1978-84; exec. asst. program devel. Sys. Mgmt. Am. Corp., Arlington, Va., 1984-85; profl. staff mem. U.S. Senate Small Bus. Com., Washington, 1985-89; assoc. adminstr. minority small bus. devel. program U.S. Small Bus. Adminstrn., 1989-91, dir. office program rev., 1991-94, agy. liaison to Dept. HUD for Pres.' Empowerment Initiative, 1994, dep. assoc. adminstr. small bus. devel. ctrs., 1994-95, asst. adminstr. OEO Civil Rights, 1995—. Contbr. articles to profl. jours. Corporator Hartford Sem. Found., 1978—; active various civic and charitable orgns. NSF grantee Columbia U., 1963, Franklin and Marshall Coll., 1965; Nat. Edn. Policy fellow George Washington, 1978-79; apptd. Adm. Great Navy of State of Nebr., 1989-91; recipient Svc. award Nat. Urban League, 1981, citations for Outstanding Ednl. Leadership, City of Hartford and State of Conn., 1982-84, Disting. Alumni award U. Hartford, 1978-84, Charlotte Jazz Club award, 1962, various trade assn. awards for leadership and svc., 1989—. Mem. NAACP, Exec. Women in Govt., Greater Washington Talladega Alumni Assn. (pres. 1993—). Address: 417 S 96th St Omaha NE 68114-4968

PATRICK, GEORGE FREDERICK, agricultural economics educator; b. Warsaw, Dec. 1, 1942; s. Louis George and Louise Agnes (Fuess) P.; m. Judith Anne Waters, June 12, 1965 (div. 1980); children: George C., Anne L., Michael F.S.; m. Katherine Jellison, Aug. 25, 1984. Student, U. Buenos Aires, 1962; BS in Agr., Cornell U., 1964; MS in Agrl. Econs., Purdue U., 1966, PhD in Agrl. Econs., 1970. Rsch. assoc. Purdue U., West Lafayette, Ind., 1967-69, asst. prof., 1973-81, assoc. prof., 1981-88, prof. agrl. econs., 1988—. Project specialist Ford Found., Brazil, 1970-73; sr. researcher Brazilian Ministry of Planning, Rio de Janeiro, 1973; vis. prof. U. Sao Paulo, Brazil, 1974-75, U. Fed. Vicosa, Brazil, 1982; Roper vis. rsch. fellow U. Melbourne Australia, 1985; cons. USDA, Washington, 1979, NAS, Washington, 1983; sr. assoc. Tactical Decision Group, Cleve., 1988-98. Author: Agricultural Development in Northeast Brazil, 1972; contbr. articles to profl. jours. Pres., bd. dirs. Land Grant U. Tax Edn. Found., 2001—. Mem. Am. Agrl. Econs. Assn. (chair quality of comm. com. 1983-85, extension com. 1990-92, dir. extension sect. 1999-2001, pres., 2002—), Western Agrl. Econs. Assn., So. Agrl. Econs. Assn., Internat. Soc. Agrl. Economists (co-chair nat. farm income tax adv. com. 1993-1999). Office: Purdue U 1145 Dept Agrl Econs West Lafayette IN 47907

PATRICK, GEORGE MILTON, dentist; b. Accoville, W.Va., Sept. 27, 1920; s. Milton Michael and Martha Mary (Mullins) P.; m. Shirley Ann Rutherford, Mar. 22, 1952 (div. June 1966); 1 child, Geoffrey Milton (dec.); m. Jane Lee Austin, Oct. 1, 1971; stepchildren: Duke Anthony-Spencer Austin, T.L.C. Spencer. BS, Capital U., 1950; DDS, Ohio State U., 1955; postgrad., U. N.C., 1972. Gen. practice dentistry, Columbus, Ohio, 1956-67; dir. mktg. and rsch. Kirkman Labs., Portland, Oreg., 1968; gen. practice dentistry specializing in orthodontics Columbus, 1968; pub. health dentist Ohio Dept. Health, Bowling Green, Ohio, 1968-80; practice dentistry specializing in pedodontics, 1980-82; pvt. practice computer cons. Columbus, 1982-87; mgmt. cons., 1987—. Pres. Shamrock Patrick Cons., 1991—. Contbr. poetry to profl. publs. Prodn. mgr. Vaud-Vilities, Columbus, 1979-86; singer First Community Ch., Columbus, 1972-90, Opera/Columbus Chorus, 1984-86. 2d lt. U.S. Army, 1942-46, ETO, battlefield commn. Decorated Soldier's medal, Bronze Star, Purple Heart with oak leaf cluster. Mem. ADA, Ohio Dental Assn., Columbus Dental Soc. (chmn. children's dental health week), Columbus Coun. World Affairs, Pub. Rels. Soc. (membership com. 1986), Career Execs. of Columbus (pres. 1987-91). Avocations: cooking, poetry, camping, singing. Home and Office: 2620 Love Dr Columbus OH 43221-2645 E-mail: GNJP27@aol.com.

PATRICK, GEORGIA O'BRIEN LAKAYTIS, communications executive; b. Dallas, July 2, 1945; d. Jack Dallas and Jane (Childs) O'Brien; m. Thomas Donald Patrick, Oct. 23, 1981. BJ, U. Mo., 1967. Tech. writer Mo. Regional Med. Programs, Columbia, Kansas City, 1967-69; with Ctr. for Student Life, U. Mo., Columbia, 1969-76; comm. dir. Am. Assn. Family and Consumer Sci., Washington, 1976-81; exec. v.p. The Communicators, Inc., 1981-92, CEO, 1992—. Founder Internat. Managed HealthCare Inst., 1996; Washington office dir. NetCertification, 1999—; Washington bur. chief Profl. Cert. Mag., 2001—; cons. and leader seminars and workshops for nat. and internat. orgns.; expert on Internet relevance to nat. assns. Contbr. articles to profl. jours. Mem.: Nat. Orgn. Competency Assurance, Greater Washington Soc. Assn. Execs. (Leadership Team), Am. Soc. Assn. Execs. Office: The Communicators Inc 10072 Vista Ct Myersville MD 21773-8138 E-mail: georgia@communicators.com.

PATRICK, H. HUNTER, judge; b. Gasville, Ark., Aug. 19, 1939; s. H. Hunter Sr. and Nelle Frances (Robinson) P.; m. Charlotte Anne Wilson, July 9, 1966; children: Michael Hunter, Colleen Annette. BA, U. Wyo., 1961, JD, 1966. Bar: Wyo. 1966, U.S. Dist. Ct. Wyo. 1966, Colo. 1967, U.S. Supreme Ct. 1975. Mcpl. judge City of Powell (Wyo.), 1967-68; sole practice law Powell, 1966-88; atty. City of Powell, 1969-88; justice of the peace County of Park, Wyo., 1971-88; bus. law instr. Northwest Community Coll., Powell, 1968-98; dist. judge State of Wyo. 5th Jud. Dist., 1988—. Mem. Wyo. Dist. Judges Conf., sec.-treas., 1993-94, vice chair, 1994-95, chair, 1995-96. Editor: Bench Book for Judges of Courts of Limited Jurisdiction in the State of Wyoming, 1980-90. Dir. cts. Wyo. Girls State, Powell, 1982-85, 89-99; elder, deacon, moderator of deacons Powell Presbyn. Ch., 1997; mem. Wyo. Commn. Jud. Conduct & Ethics, 1997—. Recipient Wyo. Crime Victims Compensation Commn. Judicial award, 1995. Fellow Am. Bar Found., Wyo. Jud. Adv. Coun.; mem. ABA (Wyo. state del. to ho. of dels. 1994-2001, Wyo. del. judicial adminstrn. divsn., exec. com. nat. conf. trial ct. judges representing Wyo., Colo., Kans., Nebr., N.Mex. 1996-2000, bd. govs. 2001—, Pub. Svc. award for ct.-sponsored Law Day programs 1990, 92), Wyo. Bar Assn. (Cmty. Svc. award 1999, Ann. Pub. Svc. award 1999), Colo. Bar Assn., Park County Bar Assn. (sec. 1969-70, pres. 1970-71), Wyo. Assn. Cts. Ltd. Jurisdiction (pres. 1973-80), Wyo. Dist. Judges Conf. (chair 1996), Am. Judicature Soc. Avocations: photography, travel, fishing, reading, writing. Home: PO Box 941 Powell WY 82435-0941 Office: PO Box 1868 Cody WY 82414-1868 E-mail: hpatrick@parkco.wtp.net.

PATRICK, HUGH TALBOT, economist, educator; b. Goldsboro, N.C., Feb. 22, 1930; s. Talbot and Paula (Miller) P.; children: Stephen, Matthew, Catherine. BA, Yale U., 1951; MA in Far Eastern Studies, U. Mich., 1955, MA in Econs., 1957, PhD in Econs., 1960; MA (hon.), Yale U., 1968; PhD (hon.), Lingnan U., 2000. Econ. analyst U. S. Govt., 1951-52; lectr. econs. U. Mich., 1958-60; asst. prof. econs. Yale U., New Haven, 1960-64, assoc. prof., 1964-68, prof. Far Eastern econs., 1968-84; dir. Yale U. Econ. Growth Ctr., 1976-79, 80-83; R.D. Calkins prof. internat. bus. Columbia U., N.Y.C., 1984—2001. Vis. prof. U. Bombay, 1961-62; mem. Japan-U.S. Econ. Rels. Group, 1978-81, U.S. Com. for Pacific Econ. Coop.; dir. Ctr. on Japanese Econ. and Bus., Columbia U., 1986—. Editor: Japanese Industrialization and Its Social Consequences, 1976, Japanese High Technology Industries-Lessons and Limitations of Industrial Policy, 1986; contbr. chpt. and co-editor (with Henry Rosovsky): Asia's New Giant-How the Japanese Economy Works, 1976; contbr. chpt., co-editor (with Masahiko Aoki): The Japanese Main Bank System: Its Relevance for Developing and Transforming Economies, 1994, co-editor (with Larry Meissner): Pacific Basis Industries in Distress: Structural Adjustment and Trade Policy in Nine Industrialized Economies, 1991 (Masayoshi Ohira Meml. prize 1992), (with Yung Chul Park) The Financial Development of Japan, Korea nad Taiwan: Growth, Repression and Liberalization, 1994, (with Takeo Hoshi) Crisis and Change in the Japanese Financial System, 2000. Ford Found. fellow 1957-58; grantee Am. Coun. Learned Socs., 1962; Guggenheim fellow, 1964-65; Fulbright rsch. prof., 1964-65; Fulbright-Hays NDEA fellow, 1968-69; Assn. Asian Studies Disting. lectr., 1977. Mem. Japan Soc. (dir. 1973-79, 81-2000), Social Sci. Rsch. Coun. (dir., chmn. 1985-88), Pacific Trade and Devel. Confs. (chmn.). Democrat. Office: Columbia U 320 Uris Hall 3022 Broadway New York NY 10027-6945

PATRICK, JAMES NICHOLAS, SR. radio, television, newspaper commentator, consultant; b. Spokane, Wash., Oct. 5, 1950; s. Robert L. and Mamle R. (Canino) P.; m. Rita Irene Roelker, June 13, 1969; children: Stephanie, James Jr., Justin Tood. BA, U. Louisville, 1973. With GE Info. Svcs., Greensboro, N.C., 1975-85; v.p. Am. Airlines, Dallas, 1986-88; v.p., gen. mgr. AMR Gen. Computing, 1988-89; pres., profl. speaker, cons. James N. Patrick Group, Richardson, Tex., 1989—; chmn., CEO, pres. Millennium Prodns., Inc., 1991—; v.p. Paramount Comms. Affiliate, 1993; v.p. worldwide divsn. Computer Assocs., Richardson, Tex., 1998-2001; chmn., chief exec. officer, pres. Millennium Prodns., Inc., 1991—. Bus. news analyst; radio spokesperson. Founder Am. Airlines "Think Tanks", 1986; freelance corres. U.S., Europe for maj. radio and TV networks including #10 Downing St. Bombing, 1991, World Econ. Summit, 1990, Presdl. Election - Channel 5 Australia, 1992; social, econ. and polit. prognostications published in maj. newspapers and TV and radio programs. Named Amb. of Goodwill City of Louiseville, 1969; recipient Ky. State Senate Resolution for Outstanding Contbns. to youth Causes, 1996. Mem. Tex. Computing Industry Coun. (pres. 1988-89), Tex. Innovation Info. Network (bd. mem. 1988-89), El Centro Coll. Bus. Adv. Bd. (bd. mem. 1988-89), Commodore Lavon Yacht Club, Mill Cree Yacht Club (vice commador 1998). Roman Catholic. Avocations: boating, political button collecting. Home: 7005 Oxford Ct Mc Kinney TX 75070-5571 Office: Millennium Prodns Inc PO Box 831830 Richardson TX 75083-1830 E-mail: jpatrick@airmail.net.

PATRICK, JANE AUSTIN, association executive; b. Memphis, May 27, 1930; d. Wilfred Jack and Evelyn Eudora (Branch) Austin; m. William Thomas Spencer, Sept. 11, 1952 (div. Apr. 1970); children: Duke Anthony-Spencer Austin, ToniLee Candice Spencer; m. George Milton Patrick, Oct. 1, 1971. Student, Memphis State U., 1946-47; BSBA, Ohio State U., 1979. Svc. rep. So. Bell Tel. and Tel., Memphis, 1947-52; placement dir. Mgmt. Pers., 1965-66; pers. dir. E & E Ins. Co., Columbus, Ohio, 1966-69; Ohio exec. dir. Nat. Soc. for Prevention of Blindness, 1969-73; regional dir. Ohio and Ky. CARE and MEDICO, 1979-87; v.p. Career Execs. of Columbus, 1987-91; owner, pres. Patricks Distbn., 1994—. Lectr., cons. in field. Author of poetry. Mem. choir 1st Cmty. Ch., Columbus, 1972--, Ohio State U. Med. Ctr. Svc. Bd.; bd. dirs. Columbus Coun. on World Affairs, 1980-92, sec., 1983-91, chmn. devel. com.; chmn. pers. com. Ohio Hunger Task Force, 1989-90; founder Ctrl. Ohio Lions Eye Bank. Recipient commendation Nat. Soc. Prevention Blindness, commendation Ctrl. Ohio Lions Eye Bank, 1973, Svc. award plaque Upper Arlington Pub. Schs., 1986. Mem. Non-Profit Orgn. Mgmt. Inst. (pres.), Nat. Soc. Fund-Raising Execs. (cert., nat. dir., v.p.), Pub. Rels. Soc. Am. (cert., membership com. chairperson), Ins. Inst. Am. (cert.), Mensa Internat., Columbus Dental Soc. Aux. (historian and publicity chair), Alpha Gamma Delta (undergrad. editor Gamma Zeta chpt.), Epsilon Sigma Alpha (pres.). Home: 2620 Love Dr Columbus OH 43221-2645 E-mail: jgnjp27@aol.com.

PATRICK, JANET CLINE, personnel company executive; b. June 30, 1934; , 1981-89; pres. Med. Personnel Svcs., Inc., Washington, 1989—. Chmn. area 2 planning com., Montgomery County Pub. Schs., 1974-75; mem. vestry, corr. sec., Christ Ch., Kensington, Md., chair long-range planning com., 1989. Office: Med Personnel Svcs Inc 1707 L St NW Ste 250 Washington DC 20036-4215 Home: 7800 Glenbrook Rd Bethesda MD 20814-1302

PATRICK, JOHN JOSEPH, social sciences educator; b. East Chicago, Ind., Apr. 14, 1935; s. John W. and Elizabeth (Lazar) P.; m. Patricia Grant, Aug. 17, 1963; children— Rebecca, Barbara AB, Dartmouth Coll., 1957; Ed.D., Ind. U., 1969. Social studies tchr. Roosevelt High Sch., East Chicago, 1957-62; social studies tchr. Lab. High Sch., U. Chgo., 1962-65; research assoc. Sch. Edn., Ind. U., Bloomington, 1965-69, asst. prof., 1969-74, assoc. prof., 1974-77, prof. edn., 1977—, dir. social studies devel. ctr., 1986—, dir. ERIC clearinghouse for social studies, social sci. edn., 1986—. Bd. dirs. Biol. Scis. Curriculum Study, 1980-83; ednl. cons. Author: Progress of the Afro-American, 1968, The Young Voter, 1974; (with L. Ehman, Howard Mehlinger) Toward Effective Instruction in Secondary Social Studies, 1974, Lessons on the Northwest Ordinance, 1987; (with R. Remy) Civics for Americans, 1980, rev. edit. 1986; (with Mehlinger) American Political Behavior, 1972, rev. edit. 1980, (with C. Keller) Lessons on the Federalist Papers, 1987; America Past and Present, 1983; (with Carol Berkin) History of the American Nation, 1984, rev. edit., 1987; Lessons on the Constitution, 1985, James Madison and the Federalist Papers, 1990, How to Teach the Bill of Rights, 1991, Ideas of the Founders on Constitutional Government: Resources for Teachers of History and Government, 1991, Young Oxford Companion to the Supreme Court of the United States, 1994, Founding the Republic: A Documentary History, 1995, (with Gerald Long) Constitutional Debates on Freedom of Religion: A Documentary History, 1999, (with Richard M. Pious and Donald A. Ritchie) The Oxford Essential Guide to the U.S. Government, 2000, The Bill of Rights: A History in Documents, 2002. Bd. dirs. Law in Am. Soc. Found., 1984-88, Social Sci. Edn. consortium, 1984—; mem. Gov.'s Task Force on Citizenship Edn., Ind., 1982-87; active Ind. Commn. on Bicentennial of U.S. Constn., 1986-92; bd. dirs. Coun. for the Advancement of Citizenship, Nat. History Edn. Network, 1994-96; mem. Natr. Coun. for History Standards, 1991-94. Recipient John W. Ryan award for disting. svc. in internat. programs and studies, Ind. U., 2002. Mem. ASCD, Nat. Coun. Social Studies, Social Sci. Edn. Consortium (v.p. 1985-87), Coun. for Basic Edn., Am. Polit. Sci. Assn., Am. Hist. Assn., Orgn. Am. Historians, Phi Delta Kappa. Home: 1209 E University St Bloomington IN 47401-5045 Office: Ind U 2805 E 10th St Bloomington IN 47408-2601

PATRICK, LESLIE DAYLE, hydrologist; b. Grand Island, Nebr., Nov. 20, 1951; d. Robert Norman and Charlotte Ruth (Thomas) Mayfield; m. Jeffrey Rogan Patrick, July 1, 1972 (div. Feb. 1996). BA in Geology, U. Alaska, Anchorage, 1975, MS in Mgmt., 1991. Data base mgr. U.S. Geol. Survey, Anchorage, 1975-78, with digital modeling, 1980-85, with water use studies, 1978-91, chief computer sect., systems analyst, 1985-91, asst. dist. chief mgmt. ops., 1991-97, asst. dist. chief programs, 1997—. Mem. NAFE, Am. Mgmt. Assn., Am. Soc. Quality Control, Alaska Groundwater Assn. (sec., treas. 1980). Office: US Geol Survey Water Resources Div 4230 University Dr Ste 201 Anchorage AK 99508-4650 E-mail: lpatrick@usgs.gov. *Personal philosophy: Greet each day with a stretch and a smile.*

PATRICK, LYNN ALLEN, lawyer, corporate governance and land development; b. Stettler, Alta., Can., Dec. 7, 1935; s. Allen Russell and Florence Lorene (Lynn) P.; m. Roberta Colleen Hughes, May 9, 1959; children: Diane Elizabeth, Ross Gordon. BSc, U. Alta., Edmonton, Can., 1957, LLB, 1960. Bar: Alta. Ptnr. Cormie Kennedy, Edmonton, Alta., Can., 1961-83; sr. v.p., gen. counsel Mutual Fund Group, Can., 1983-88; pres. Stuart Olson Constrn., Inc., Can., 1989-92; v.p., corp. counsel, sec. The Churchill Corp., 1992-98. Mem. Real Estate Coun. Alta., subdivsn. and devel. appeal bd. City of Edmonton; bd. dirs. HomeBank Techs., Inc., Mosaic Mapping Sys. Inc. Past pres., trustee Minerva Found., Edmonton; adv. coun. mem. Minister of Edn., Alta.; gov. Banff Ctr. Mem. Can. Bar Assn., Edmonton Bar Assn., Law Soc. Alta., Royal Glenora Club (Edmonton). Progressive. Home: 64 Quesnell Rd Edmonton AB Canada T5R 5N2 Office: 2500 10104 103rd Ave Edmonton AB Canada T5J 1V3 E-mail: lpatrick@telusplanet.net.

PATRICK, MARTY, lawyer; b. N.Y.C., May 10, 1949; s. Harry and Evelyn (Beroza) P.; m. Yolande Andree, Feb. 26, 2000; 1 child, Jason. BS, L.I. U., 1971; cert., Inst. for Leadership Devel., Jerusalem, 1974; JD, Nova Southeastern U., 1981. Exec. dir. Zionist Orgn. Am., Miami Beach, Fla., 1975-78; pres. Enigma Enterprises, Inc., Miami, 1978-82; ptnr. Martin Howard Patrick, P.A., Miami Beach, 1982—. Pres. Patrick Law Ctr., Miami Beach, 1983-89; pres. First Fla. Title & Abstract Co., Boca Raton, Fla., 1983—; CEO Atlantic Coast Title Co., 1989—; founding ptnr. Patrick & Schwartz, P.A, Boca Raton, 2001—; CEO Laughing in the Dark Prodns., 1994—. Contbr. articles to profl. jours. Pres. United Orthodox Cmty. Coun. of So. Fla., Miami Beach, 2001—. Horovitz scholar, 1980. Mem. ABA, Ga. Bar Assn., Fla. Bar Assn., Mensa. E-mail: mpatrick@dirtlaw.com.

PATRICK, MARY KATHLEEN, freelance/self-employed writer, food service executive; b. Daytona Beach, Fla., Aug. 19, 1976; d. William Minor and Mary Kathleen Hawk; m. Mark Andrew Patrick, June 20, 1998. BA in Pub. Adminstrn., BA in Sociology, U. Ctrl. Fla., 2001. Mgmt. trainee Boston Market, Orlando, 2002—. Poet: www.poetry.com, 2001. Mem.: ASPA, Internat. Soc. of Poets, Nat. Writer's Union. R-Consevative. Avocations: swimming, hiking, reading, writing, cooking. Personal E-mail: kathleenpatrickm@yahoo.com.

PATRICK, MICHELE MARY, government official; b. Phila., Apr. 18, 1963; d. George Robert and Mary Elizabeth (Pristic) P. BA with honors in Econs., La Salle U., 1985; M in Govt. Adminstrn., U. Pa., 1990. Intern Phila. Water Dept.,

1987; intern, asst. to exec. dir. Global Interdependence Ctr., Phila., 1988-89; intern, asst. to dep. dir. Phila. Fin. Dept., 1989, asst. to fin. dir., 1990; asst. mng. dir. City of Phila., 1990-91, 93-96; speechwriter to U.S. Senator Frank R. Lautenberg, 1996-97; speechwriter to Hon. Donna Shalala U.S. Sec. Health and Human Svcs., 1997—. Speaker in field. Author: Haunted Prague; co-author: sect. of Municipal Dept. Handbook; trivia writer Merit Inds., Bensalem, Pa., 1993-95; monthly columnist Global Stamp News, 1994-96. Recipient Fulbright fellowship, U.K., Bd. Fgn. Scholarships, Washington, 1985, Nat. Resource fellowship, Pacific-Asian Mgmt. Inst., U. Hawaii, 1984, Lindback award, La Salle U., Phila., 1985, Pa. Forensic Assn., State Championships, 1982, 83, 85, Nat. Forensic Assn. Nat. championship, 1985, Meyerson fellowship, U. Pa., Phila., 1987, Pres. Classroom scholarship, Pres. Classroom for Young Ams., Washington, 1982, James and Helen Hovorka scholarship, Coun. Higher Edn., Brookfield, Ill., 1982, 83, 84. Mem. Amnesty Internat., Am. Friends of Czech Republic, Fulbright Alumni Assn., Omicron Delta Epsilon. Avocations: historical travel, classical music, British and Russian studies.

PATRICK, NICHOLAS J.M. astronaut; b. North Yorkshire, Eng., 1964; , naturalized, U.S., 1994; s. Stewart Patrick, Gillian Patrick; married. BA in Engring., U. Cambridge, Eng., 1986; MA in Engring., U. Cambridge, 1990; SMME, MIT, 1990, PhDME, 1996. Registered profl. engr. Astronaut, mission specialist candidate NASA, Johnson Space Ctr., Houston, 1998—; mem. Cambridge U. Air Squadron RAF; civil engr. (summers) NY, Conn.; engr. divsn. aircraft engines GE, Boston; tchg. and rsch. asst. Human-Machine Sys. Lab. dept. mech. engring. MIT, Cambridge; statistician, programmer med. and robotic products co.; sys. and human factors engr. Boeing Comml. Airplane Group, Seattle. Flight instr. Hanscom Field's E. Coast Aero Club, Boeing Field's Galvin Flying Svc., Seattle; bd. stockholders Harvard Cooperative Soc. Recipient Project award, GE Aircraft Engines Devel. Program, 1988; scholar, U. Cambridge, 1983. Mem.: Nat. Space Soc., Aircraft Owners and Pilots Assn. Achievements include patents for telerobotics, display design and integrated aircraft alerting systems; logged over 1600 hours as a pilot, 750 hours as a flight instructor in over 20 types of airplanes and helicopters. Avocations: flying, reading, automotive work, hiking, skiing. Office: Astronaut Office/CB NASA Johnson Space Str Houston TX 77058*

PATRICK, PAMELA ANN, research consultant; b. Mesquite, Tex., June 10, 1963; d. Gene Everett and Peggy Rose (Tanzy) P. AAS, Eastfield Coll., 1982; BA in English, Tex. A&M U.-Commerce, 1987, MS in Edn., English, 1988. Tex. provisional cert. 1990. Sales clk. Sears, Mesquite, 1982-84; substitute tchr. various Ind. Sch. Dists., Tex., 1988—. Contbr. articles to profl. jours. Mem. UDC, DAR, Daus. Republic Tex., Daus. Union Vets. Civil War, Dallas County Heritage Soc., Dallas Geneal. Soc., Nat. Trust for Historic Preservation, Dallas Hist. Soc., Green County Hist. Geneal. Soc., Snyder Kennedy Cemetery Preservation Soc. (pres.), Robert Morris Hist. Soc. (pres.), Humane Soc. U.S., DAV Aux., Phi Delta Kappa, Sigma Tau Delta. Republican. Methodist. Avocations: photographer, gardener, genealogist, corvette enthusiast. Home: PO Box 870668 Mesquite TX 75187-0668

PATRICK, PHILIP HOWARD, lawyer; b. Bridgend, Wales, Aug. 12, 1946; s. Frederick Harry and Phyllis Mair (Vaulters) P.; m. Rosalind Elizabeth Davies, Aug. 5, 1969. MusB, U. Wales, 1969; MFA, Princeton U., 1971, PhD, 1973; JD, Washington (D.C.) Coll. Law, 1980. Bar: D.C. 1980, Md. 1981. Asst. prof. Am. U., Washington, 1973-77; cons., 1978-81; pvt. practice, Silver Springs, Md., 1980-89; pres. Computing Community Services Corp., 1980-89; gen. counsel The Orcutt Group Ltd., Rockville, Md., 1989-92; dir. contracts FileTek, Inc., 1992—. Founder, sec. Nat. Welsh-Am. Found., Washington, 1981-84, mem. adv. coun., 1984—. Home: 2523 Oakenshield Dr Potomac MD 20854-2926 Office: FileTek Inc 9400 Key West Ave Rockville MD 20850-3322 E-mail: php@filetek.com.

PATRICK, ROBERT, playwright; b. Kilgore, Tex., Sept. 27, 1937; s. Robert and Beulah (Goodson) O'Connor. Author numerous plays produced off-off Broadway, off-Broadway, Broadway, also abroad including Robert Patrick's Cheep Theatricks (23 plays), 1972, Simultaneous Transmissions, 1973, Play-By-Play, 1975, The Golden Circle, 1975, Kennedy's Children, 1975, Let Me Tell It To You, Dr. Paroo, 1976, One Man, One Woman (6 plays), 1978, T-Shirts, 1979, Mutual Benefit Life, 1980, Mercy Drop and Other Plays (5 plays), 1980, My Cup Ranneth, 1984, Big Sweet, 1985, Untold Decades (7 plays), 1988, Drowned Out, 1990, Connie, 1991, Michaelangelo's Models, 1994, Bread Alone, 1994, The Trial of Socrates, 1994, Evan on Earth, 1995, Pouf Positive (CD), 1996; author: (novels) Temple Slave, 1986, Echo, 1990, (films) Resident Alien, 1990, The O Boys Documentary, 1999; teleplays include: High Tide, 1994, Robin's Hoods, 1995, Ghost Story, 1997, (essay) Film Moi, 1999; contbr. poems, articles, stories to profl. jours. Rockefeller grantee, 1974, N.Y. State CAPS grantee, 1975; recipient Show Bus. Best Playwright award 1968-69, Glasgow Citizens' Theatre Best World Playwright award, 1974, Omni-Act One award, 1975, Robbie award, 1976, Founders award Internat. Thespians Soc., 1980, Blue is for Boys weekends in Manhattan, 1983, 86, Lifetime Achievement award for Gay Playwriting Robert Chesley Found., 1996, Robert Chesley Found. Lifetime Achievement in Gay Playwrighting award, 1996. Home: 1837 N Alexandria Ave Apt 211 Los Angeles CA 90027-4068 E-mail: rbrtptrck@aol.com. *No object or action has any meaning except that given to it by a writer. Writers create the consciousness of humanity, which in turn creates our world. Writers write the world.*

PATRICK, ROBERT HERBERT, JR. economist, educator; BA magna cum laude, Blackburn Coll., 1978; PhD in Econs., U. N.Mex., 1985. Mgr. Burroughs Corp., Fairbanks, Alaska, 1978-80; rsch. assoc. Purdue U., West Lafayette, Ind., 1985-87; asst. prof. Colo. Sch. Mines, Golden, 1987-91, assoc. prof., 1991-93; project mgr. Electric Power Rsch. Inst., Palo Alto, Calif., 1992-94. Vis. scholar Stanford (Calif.) U., 1992-94, assoc. prof. Rutgers U., 1994—; reviewer U.S. EPA, U.S. Dept. Energy, Calif. Energy Commn., NSF, N.Y. Mec. Exch.; coun. of acad. policy advisors N.J. Legis. Contbr. articles to profl. jours. and chpts. to books.; mem. editorial bd. Jour. Regulatory Econs., Jour. Environ. Econs. and Mgmt. Grantee Elec. Power Rsch. Inst., 1994-98, NSF, 1994-96, Gas Rsch. Inst., 1991-92, 90-91, EPA, 1989-92, USDA, 1987, 85-87. Mem. Am. Econ. Assn., Assn. Environ. and Resource Econs., Econometric Soc., Internat. Assn. for Energy Econs. (v.p. Rocky Mountain chpt. 1992, bd. dirs. 1990-91), Mineral Econs. and Mgmt. Soc. (bd. dirs. 1992), N.J. Coun. Acad. Policy Advisors. Home: 7805 Wagon Mound Ct NW Albuquerque NM 87120-2870 Office: Grad Sch of Mgmt Rutgers U Newark NJ 07102

PATRICK, RUTH (MRS. RUTH HODGE VAN DUSEN), limnologist, diatom taxonomist, educator; b. Topeka; d. Frank and Myrtle (Jetmore) Patrick; m. Charles (IV) Hodge, July 10, 1931; 1 child Charles (V). BS, Coker Coll., 1929, LLD, 1971; MA, U. Va., 1931, PhD, 1934; DSc, Beaver Coll., 1970, PMC Colls., 1971, Phila. Coll. Pharmacy and Sci., 1973, Wilkes Coll., 1974, Cedar Crest Coll., 1974, U. New Haven, 1975, Hood Coll., 1975, Med. Coll. Pa., 1975, Drexel U., 1975, Swarthmore Coll., 1975, Bucknell U., 1976, Rensselaer Poly. Inst., 1976, St. Lawrence U., 1978; LHD, Chestnut Hill Coll, 1974; DSc, U. Mass., 1980, Princeton U., 1980, Lehigh U., 1983, U. Pa., 1984, Temple U., 1985, Emory U., 1986, Wake Forest U., 1986, U. S.C., 1989, Clemson, 1989, Glassboro State Coll., 1992. Assoc. curator microscopy dept. Acad. Natural Scis., Phila., 1939-47; curator Leidy Micros. Soc., 1937-47, curator limnology dept., 1947—, chmn. limnology dept., 1947-73; occupant Francis Boyer Research Chair Acad. Natural Scis., Phila., 1973—, chmn. bd. trustees, 1973-76, hon. chmn. bd. trustees, 1976—; lectr. U. Pa., 1950-70, adj. prof., 1970—; guest Fellow of Saybrook Yale, 1975. Participant Am. Philos Soc. limnology expdn. to Mexico, 1947; leader Catherwood Found. expdn. to Peru and Brazil, 1955; del. gen. assembly Internat. Union Biol. Scis., Bergen, Norway, 1947; bd. dirs. E.I. Du Pont, Pa. Power and Light Co.; chmn. algae com. Smithsonian Oceanographic Sorting Ctr., 1963—68; mem. panel on water blooms Pres. Sci. Adv. Com., 1966; mem. panel on water resources and water pollution Gov.'s Sci. Adv. Com., 1966; mem. nat. tech. adv. com. on water quality requirements for fish and other aquatic life and wildlife Dept. Interior , 1967—68; mem. citizen's adv. coun. Pa. Dept. Environ. Resources, 1971—73; mem. hazardous materials adv. com. EPA, 1971—74, exec. adv. com., 1974—79; chmn. com.'s panel on ecology, 1974—76; mem. Pa. Gov.'s Sci. Adv. Coun., 1972; mem. exec. adv. com. nat. power survey FPC, 1972—75; mem. coun. Smithsonian Instn., 1973—; mem. Phila. Adv. Coun., 1973—76; mem. energy R&D adv. coun. Pres.s Emergy Policy Office, 1973—74; mem. adv. coun. Renewable Nat. Resources Found., 1973—76, Elecric Power Rsch. Found., 1973—77; mem. adv. com. for rsch. NSF, 1973—74; mem. gen. adv. com. ERDA, 1975—77; mem. adv. bd. Sec. Energy, 1975—89; mem. com. on human resources NRC, 1975—76; trustee Biological Abstracts, 1974—76; mem. adv. coun. dept. biology Princeton U., 1975—80; mem. com. on sci. and arts Franklin Inst., 1978—; mem. univ. coun. com. Yale Sch. Forestry and Environ. Studies, 1978—80; mem. sci. adv. coun. World Wildlife Fund-US, 1978—80; trustee Aquarium Soc., Phila., 1951—58, Henry Found.; bd. dirs. Wissahickon Valley Watershed Assn.; bd. govs. Nature Conservancy; bd. mgrs. Wistar Inst. Anatomy and Biology. Author: (series of volumes) Rivers of the United States Vol. 1, 1994, Rivers of the United States Vol. 2, 1997, Chemical and Physical Characteristics Vol. 3, 1995, Rivers of Atlantic and Eastern Gulf Drainage Vol. 4, The Mississipi River and Major Tributaries; co-author (with C.W. Reimer): Diatoms of the United States Vol. 1, 1966, Vol. II, Part 1, 1975; co-author: (with others) (books) Ground Water Contamination in the United States, 1983, 2nd edit.; co-author: (with others) (book) Surface Water Quality: Have the Laws Been Successful?, 1992; mem. editorial bd.with C. W. Reimer: sci. jours. Science, 1974—76, mem. editorial bd.: sci. jours. American Naturalist; contbr. articles over 150 to profl. jours. Recipient Disting. Dau. of Pa. award, 1952, Richard Hopper Day Meml. medal, Acad. Nat. Scis., 1969, Gimbel Phila. award, 1969, Gold medal, YWCA, 1970, Lewis L. Dollinger Pure Environment award, Franklin inst., 1970, Pa. award for excellence in sci. and tech., 1970, Eminent Ecologist award, Ecol Soc. Am., 1972, Phila. award, 1973, Gold medal, Pa. State Fish and Game Protective Assn., 1974, Internat. John and Alice Tyler Ecology award, 1975, Gold meda;, Phila. Soc. for Promoting Agr., 1975, Pub. Svc. award, U.S. Dept. Interior, 1975, Iben award, Am. Water Resources Assn., 1976, Outstanding Alumna award, Coker Coll., 1977, Francis K. Hutchinson medal, Garden Club of Am., 1977, Golden medal, Royal Zool. Soc., Antwerp, 1978, Green World award, N.Y. Bot. Garden, 1979, Hugo Black award, U. Ala., 1979, Sci award, Gov. Pa., 1988, Founders award, Soc. Environ. Toxicology and Chemistry, 1982, Environ. Regeneration award, Rene DuBois Ctr., 1985, Disting. Citizen award, Pa., 1989, Excellence award, N. Am. Benthological Soc., 1993, Benjamin Franklin medal, Am. Philosophical Soc., 1993, U.S. medal of svc., Pres. Bill Clinton, 1996, Nat. medal for sci., 1997, Nat. Wetlands award, 2000, Sci. Edn. Ctr. named in her honor, U. S.C., 1989. Fellow: AAAS (com. environ. alternatives 1973—74); mem.: Internat. Phycol. Soc., Am. Inst. Biol. Scis., Ecol. Soc. Am., Am. Soc. Naturalists (pres. 1975—76), Am. Soc. Limnology and Oceanography (Lifetime Achievement award 1996), Am. Soc. Plant Taxonomy, Internat. Soc. Plant Taxonomists, Internat. Limnological Soc., Phycol Soc. Am. (pres. 1954), Bot. Soc. Am.. (mem. Darbarker prize com. 1956, Merit award 1971), Am. Acad. Arts and Scis., Assn. Metro. Sewage Agys. (Environ. award 1995), Am. Philos. Soc. (Benjamin Franklin Outstanding Sci. Achievement award 1993), Nat. Acad. Engring. (com.environ. engr. study explicit criteria for power plant siting 1973), Nat. Acad. Scis. (chmn. panel com. on pollution 1966, mem.environ. measures panel com. remote sensing earth resources survey 1973—74, mem. nominating com. 1973—75, mem. com. sci. and public policy 1973—77), Water Pollution Control Fedn. (hon.), Soc. Study Evolution, Sigma Xi. Presbyterian. Office: Acad Natural Scis 19th at Benjamin Franklin Pkwy Philadelphia PA 19103

PATRICK, VICTOR PHILLIP, lawyer; b. Lake Forest, Ill., Jan. 7, 1958; s. Rodger Ralph Patrick and Phyllis Elaine Bachler; m. Elizabeth Fletcher, Aug. 9, 1985; children: Kathryn Elaine, Stephen James, Diane Elizabeth, Marie Christine, Thomas Grant, John Wallace. AB in Politics magna cum laude, Princeton U., 1982; JD cum laude, Harvard U., 1985. Bar: D.C. 1986, N.Y. 1986, U.S. Ct. Appeals (10th cir.) 1986. Law clk. U.S. Ct. Appeals 10th Cir., Denver, 1985-86; assoc. Cleary, Gottlieb, Steen & Hamilton, Washington, 1986-88, 92-94, Brussels, 1988-91; from asst. gen. counsel to assoc. gen. counsel Honeywell Internat. Inc. (formerly AlliedSignal Inc.), Morristown, N.J., 1994-97; v.p., gen. counsel AlliedSignal Aerospace Equipment Sys., Torrance, Calif., 1997-99; from dep. gen. counsel to v.p., dep. gen. counsel, sec. Honeywell Internat. Inc., Morristown, N.J., 1999—. Officer, dir. Honeywell subsidiaries, 1994—; asst. sec. Honeywell Internat., Inc., 1994-2001. Mem. ABA. Mem. Lds Ch. E-mail: victor.patrick@honeywell.com.

PATRICK, WILLIAM HARDY, JR. wetland biogeochemist, educator, laboratory director; b. Johns, Miss., Nov. 9, 1925; s. William Hardy and Alma (Webb) P.; m. Ruth Martin, Dec. 21, 1951; children: Terry Lynn, William Hardy, Carol Ann, Henry Carr. BS, La. State U., 1950, MS, 1951; PhD, La State U., 1954; D.Honoris Causa, U. Ghent (Belgium), 1979. Asst. prof. agronomy dept. La. State U., Baton Rouge, 1953-56, assoc. prof., 1956-61, prof., 1961-76, prof. marine scis., 1977-78, Boyd prof. marine scis., 1978—; dir. Wetland Biogeochemistry Inst. Moore lectr. in ecology U. Va., 1985, York lectr. U. Fla., 1989; cons. numerous govt., indsl. orgns. Contbr. articles to sci. jours. Organizer, dir. La. Methodist World Hunger Scholarship Program, Baton Rouge, 1979— . Served with AUS, 1944-46. Grantee numerous research orgns., 1963— Fellow AAAS, Am. Soc. Agronomy, Soil Sci. Soc. Am. (Internat. award 1992, Rsch. award 1993); mem. Sigma Xi, Phi Kappa Phi. Republican. Methodist. Home: 888 Dubois Dr Baton Rouge LA 70808-5008 Office: Louisiana St Univ Wetland Biogeochemistry Baton Rouge LA 70803-0001

PATRICKS, EDWARD JOHN, elementary education educator; b. Chgo., Jan. 19, 1958; s. John Anthony and Marion Nora (Kinnavy) P. Ed, Ill. Benedictine, Lisle, Ill., 1981. Cert. tchr., Ill. Sci. tchr. St. Pius X, Stickney, Ill., 1981-84; dept. chair, sci. tchr. St. Giles Junior High, Oak Park, 1984-98; sci. tchr. Hyde Park Mid. Sch., Las Vegas, 1998—, coach boys' basketball. Commr. City of Berwyn, 1991—, North Berwyn Pk. Dist., 1995—; past commr. St. Mary of Celle Little League; sponsor Berwyn Playground and Recreation Commn., Berwyn Blazers Taveling Soccer; coach Redrock Little League, Las Vegas; bd. dirs. Dem. Orgn. Berwyn, St. Mary of Celle, St. Vincent De Paul Conf. Mem. ASCD, NSTA, Nat. Cath. Educators Assn., Ill. Assn. Pk. Dists., Ill. Sheriffs Assn., Suburban Pks. and Recreation Divsn., Nat. Recreation and Pk. Assn., Berwyn Devel. Corp., KC (4 degree). Home: 1344 Angel Falls St Las Vegas NV 89142-1323 Office: Hyde Park Mid Sch 900 Hinson St Las Vegas NV 89107-4452 E-mail: ejpcommish@msn.com.

PATRIQUIN, EDWARD LEROY, JR. software developer, computer architect; b. Upland, Calif., Sept. 30, 1958; s. Edward Leroy Sr. and Margaret Winifred (Robertson) P.; m. Linda Susan King, Mar. 30, 1985; 1 child, Thomas Edward. Grad. high sch., Bishop, Calif. Computer operator U. So. Calif., L.A., 1978-79; software engr. Moss Motors, Santa Barbara, Calif., 1979-80, RKA, Sacramento, 1980; pvt. practice cons., 1980-82; sr. engr. Convergent Techs., San Jose, Calif., 1982-85; mgr. operating systems Valid Logic, 1985-86; prin. engr. Cydrome, Milpitas, Calif., 1986-88; mgr. sotfware devel. Plus Devel., 1988-91; mgr. software devel. Quantum Comml. Products, 1990-92, mgr. devel. engring., 1992—. With USN, 1976-78. Republican. Avocations: basketball, reading, travel, history. Office: Quantum Comml Products 500 Mccarthy Blvd Milpitas CA 95035-7908 Address: 3718 Smallwood Ct Pleasanton CA 94566-7554

PATRON, JUNE EILEEN, former government official; b. N.Y.C., May 15; d. Irving B. and Mollie Patron. BA in Govt. with honors, Clark U., Worcester, Mass., 1965; MA, Am. U., 1967. With U.S. Dept. Labor, 1966-95, dir. Black Lung benefits program, 1976-79, asst. adminstr. pension and welfare benefit programs, 1979-84, assoc. dir. pension and welfare benefit programs, 1984-88, dir. program svcs., 1988-95; ret., 1995. Mem. Sr. Exec. Svc.; ind. contractor, mgmt. cons., 1997—. Vol. alumni admissions program Clark U., 1998—. Recipient various awards Dept. Labor. Mem. Nat. Assn. Ret. Fed. Employees, Sr. Execs. Assn. Home: 3001 Veazey Ter NW Washington DC 20008-5454 E-mail: jpdcny@aol.com.

PATRON, SUSAN HALL, librarian, writer; b. San Gabriel, Calif., Mar. 18, 1948; d. George Thomas and Rubye Denver Hall; m. René Albert Patron, July 27, 1969. BA, Pitzer Coll., 1969; MLS, Immaculate Heart Coll., 1972. Children's libr. LA Pub. Libr., 1972-79, sr. children's libr., 1980—. Reviewer Sch. Libr. Jour., 1980-90, Pubs. Weekly, 1986-91, The Five Owls, 1987-95. Author: (with Christopher Weiman) Marbled Papers, 1979, Burgoo Stew, 1991, Five Bad Boys, Billy Que, and the Dustdobbin, 1992, Maybe Yes, Maybe No, Maybe Maybe, 1993 (ALA Notable Book 1994), Bobbin Dustdobbin, 1993, Dark Cloud Strong Breeze, 1994. Mem. ALA (Caldecott award com. 1988, Laura Ingalls Wilder award com. 2001—), PEN (mem. West Lit. awards jury 1997), Calif. Libr. Assn. (Patricia Beatty award com. 1987-89, 91-92), Internat. Bd. on Books for Young Children, Soc. Children's Book Writers and Illustrators, So. Calif. Coun. on Lit. for Children and Young People (awards com. 1985), Authors Guild, Friends of Children and Lit. (mem. award com. 1984). Office: LA Pub Libr Childrens Svcs 630 W 5th St Los Angeles CA 90071-2002

PATROV, VITALIY, artist; b. Kemerovo, Siberia, USSR, May 14, 1936; s. Konstantin and Antonina (Nikolskaia-Michailova) Patrova; m. Regina Prozhegurina, June 7, 1972; 1 child, Andrey. MA, Art Inst., Kharkov, The Ukraine, USSR, 1964; MA in Sculpture, Kharkov Acad. Art, 1964. Art tchr. Art Inst., Odessa, USSR, 1964-95; sculptor Art Union USSR, 1966-95; pres., 1976-86. Chairperson Gen. Grekov Art Coll., Odessa, 1976-90 Prin. works include 7 memorials, 3 monuments. Mem. Nat. Sculpture Soc., Russian Unit of Artists (hon.). Home: Apt # 502 3099 Brighton 6th St Brooklyn NY 11235

PATROW, KRISTINE LYDAL, television news anchor, reporter, producer; b. Camp LeJuene, N.C., Oct. 1, 1963; d. Lelon LaVerne and Marjorie Lucille (Peterson) Patrow. BA magna cum laude, Lawrence U., 1986. Intern, reporter Sta. WQOW-TV, Eau Claire, Wis., 1987; reporter, prodr. Sta. KTTC-TV, Rochester, Minn., 1987-88; freelance field prodr. Cable News Network, Chgo., 1988-89; anchor, prodr., writer, reporter Orbis Broadcast Group/CNBC, 1989-95; on-camera reporter, anchor Sta. KARE-TV, Mpls., 1995-96; nat. health/med. reporter Everyday Living, 1996-97; reporter KSTP-TV, St. Paul, 1997—. Recipient Harriet Averill music scholarship, 1982, Miss Wis. Pageant scholarship, 1982, Miss Chippewa Valley scholarship, 1982, Good Citizenship award DAR, 1982, U.S. Constitution award, 1982, voice performance award Wis. State competition, 1977-83. Mem. Athena Women's Group, Kappa Kappa Gamma (marshall 1984-85), Phi Beta Kappa. Lutheran. Avocations: creative writing, singing, traveling, weight lifting, aerobics. Office: KSTP-TV 3518 University Ave Saint Paul MN 55114

PATSEL, E. RALPH, JR. retired registrar, research director; b. Roanoke, Va., June 25, 1935; s. Elmer Ralph and Wynnie (Blosser) P.; m. Jane Neel Wells, Jan. 19, 1962; 1 child, Ralph Neel. AA, Bluefield (Va.) Coll., 1957; BA, Baylor U., 1959; MA, U. N.C., 1964; postgrad., U. Va., 1966-67. Dir. pub. rels. and devel. Bluefield Coll., 1961-65; dir. admissions King Coll., Bristol, Tenn., 1965-66; prof. history Bluefield Coll., 1966-72; registrar Bluefield State Coll., 1990-98, registrar, dir. instnl. rsch., 1998—2001, BANNER projects specialist, 2001—; asst. prof. history S.W. Va. C.C., Richlands, Va., 1972-75; computer software cons. Systems, Software & Svc., Bluefield, 1988-94; real estate agt. Ball Realty, 1983-96; owner, mgr. Neel's - The Fashion Pl., 1975-94. Acting acad. dean Bluefield Coll., 1968-69; acting dean of students Bluefield State Coll., 1995. Chmn. merchant com. Downtown Devel. Corp., Bluefield, 1976-85; councilman, vice mayor Town of Bluefield, 1974-78; vote/poll ofcl. Tazewell County, Va., 1982-91. Named Citizen of the Yr., Kiwanis of Bluefield, 1986, 79. Mem. W.Va. Assn. Collegiate Registrars Admission Officers (pres. 1999-2000), Phi Theta Kappa. Republican. Baptist. Avocation: church music. Office: Bluefield State Coll 219 Rock St Bluefield WV 24701-2100 E-mail: rpatsel@bluefield.wvnet.edu.

PATSTONE, CHERYL, public relations executive; b. Boston, May 4, 1955; d. Harold E. and Anna M. Brown; m. Walter Patstone, Nov. 10, 1979. BA in Econs. and French, Tufts U., 1977. Sr. economist, editor electronic bus. forecast Cahners Pub. Co., San Jose, Calif., 1977-87; mgr. pub. rels. Nat. Semiconductor Corp., Santa Clara, 1987-91, Marcom team leader comm. and computing group, 1991-96, dir. product pub. rels., 1996-99, dir. strategic Marcom programs, 1999—; v.p. comm. Autoweb.com, Inc., 2000—; dir. corp. comm. Atheros Comms., Inc., Sunnyvale, Calif., 2001—. Mem. Internat. Assn. Bus. Communicators, No. Calif. Bus. Mktg. Assn. (bd. dirs., v.p. programs 1999-2000). Office: Atheros Comms 529 Almanor Ave Sunnyvale CA 94085 E-mail: cheryl@atheros.com.

PATT, ANTHONY GOODING, environmental economist, geography educator; b. Boston, Aug. 18, 1965; s. Donald Irving and Gail Rachelle Patt. BA, Yale U., 1987; JD, Duke U., 1991; PhD, Harvard U., 2000. Bar: Vt. 1991. Atty. Langrock Sperry & Wool, Middlebury, Vt.; rsch. fellow Harvard U., Cambridge, Mass., 1997—2000; vis. scientist Internat. Inst. Applied Sys. Analysis, Laxenburg, Austria, 1998; asst. prof. geography Boston U., 2000. Vis. scientist Potsdam Inst. Climate Impact Rsch., Brandenburg, Germany, 2002—. Bd. dirs. Addison County Cmty. Action Group, Middlebury, 1991—94. Named Jr. Nat. Champion, U.S. Modern Pentathlon Assn., 1985. Mem.: New Eng. Paragliding and Hang Gliding Club (pres. 2001—02). Avocations: competition paragliding, mountaineering, running, skiing. Home: 273 Upland Rd Cambridge MA 02140 Office: Boston Univ 675 Commonwealth Ave Boston MA 02215 Office Fax: 617-353-5986. Personal E-mail: tony@advance-usa.com. Business E-Mail: apatt@bu.edu.

PATT, HERBERT JACOB, lawyer; b. Chgo., Feb. 12, 1935; s. Abraham and Esther Blanch (Kuchinsky) P.; m. Yvonne Phyllis Shavell, Oct. 9, 1958 (dec. Mar. 1986); children: Aldon Wayne, Bradley Earl, Colette Emile; m. Lynn Cheryl Feingold, December 26, 1993. BA, Northwestern U., 1956, JD, 1958; Diploma, Indsl. Coll., Johannesburg, South Africa. Bar: Ill. 1959, U.S. Dist. Ct. (no. dist.) Ill. 1959, U.S. Supreme Ct. 1977, Calif. 1986, U.S. Dist. Ct. (ctrl. and so. dists.) Calif. 1987, U.S. Ct. Appeals (9th cir.) 1987. Assoc. Andres & Andres, Santa Ana, Calif. Pres. Jewish Nat. Fund Orange Co., Santa Ana, 1994-95, chmn., 1996-98, nat. bd. dirs., N.Y., 1994-98; pres. Temple Judea, Laguna Hills, Calif., 1992-93. Office: Andres & Andres 2041 N Main St Santa Ana CA 92706 E-mail: pattlaw@aol.com.

PATTANAIK, PRASANTA KUMAR, economics educator; b. Cuttack, Orissa, India, Apr. 5, 1943; s. Kshetramohan and Krishnapriya (Devi) P.; m. Geeta Pattanaik, June 11, 1968; 1 child, Swaha. BA (hons.), S.C.S. Coll., Puri, Orissa, India, 1963; MA, Delhi Sch. Econs., 1965, PhD, 1968; PhD (hon.), U. Caen, France, 2000. Lectr. Delhi Sch. Econs., 1967-68, vis. fellow, 1971, reader, 1972, prof. econs., 1972-75; asst. prof. Harvard U., Cambridge, Mass., 1968-70; sr. rsch. fellow Nuffield Coll., Oxford, Eng., 1970-71; prof. LaTrobe U., Bundoora, Vic., Australia, 1975-77; prof. econs. So. Meth. U., Dallas, 1977-78, U. Birmingham, Eng., 1978-91, U. Calif., Riverside, 1991—. Author: Voting and Collective Choice, 1971, Strategy and Group Choice, 1978; co-editor: Social Choice and Welfare, 1983, Choice, Welfare and Development, 1995. Recipient Mahalanobis Meml. Nat. award Indian Econometric Soc., 1986. Fellow Econometric Soc. Avocations: classical Indian music, literature.

PATTEN, BEBE HARRISON, minister, chancellor; b. Waverly, Tenn., Sept. 3, 1913; d. Newton Felix and Mattie Priscilla (Whitson) Harrison; m. Carl Thomas Patten, Oct. 23, 1935; children: Priscilla Carla and Bebe Rebecca (twins), Carl Thomas. D.D., McKinley-Roosevelt Coll., 1941; D.Litt., Temple Hall Coll. and Sem., 1943. Ordained to ministry Ministerial Assn. of Evangelism, 1935; evangelist in various cities of U.S., 1933-50; founder, pres. Christian Evang. Chs. Am., Inc., Oakland, Calif., 1944—, Patten Acad. Christian Edn., Oakland, 1944—, Patten Bible Coll., Oakland, 1944-83; chancellor Patten Coll., 1983—; founder, pastor Christian Cathedral of Oakland, 1950—. Held pvt. interviews with David Ben-Gurion, 1972, Menachim Begin, 1977, Yitzhak Shamir, 1991; condr. Sta. KUSW world-wide radio ministry, 70 countries around the world, 1989-90, Stas. WHRI and WWCR world coverage short wave, 1990— Founder, condr.: radio program The Shepherd Hour, 1934— ; daily TV, 1976— , nationwide telecast, 1979— ; Author: Give Me Back My Soul, 1973; Editor: Trumpet Call, 1953— ; composer 20 gospel and religious songs, 1945— . Mem. exec. bd. Bar-Ilan U. Assn., Israel, 1983; mem. global bd. trustees Bar-Ilan U., 1991. Recipient numerous awards including medallion Ministry of Religious Affairs, Israel, 1969; medal Govt. Press Office, Jerusalem, 1971; Christian honoree of yr. Jewish Nat. Fund of No. Calif., 1975; Hidden Heroine award San Francisco Bay coun. Girl Scouts U.S.A., 1976, Golden State award Who's Who Hist. Soc., 1988; Ben-Gurion medallion Ben-Gurion Rsch. Inst., 1977; Resolutions of Commendation, Calif. Senate Rules Com., 1978, 94, Disting. Leadership award Ch. of God Sch. of Theology, 1996; hon. fellow Bar-Ilan U., Israel, 1981; Dr. Bebe Patten Social Action chair established Bar-Ilan U., 1982. Mem. Am. Assn. for Higher Edn., Religious Edn. Assn., Am. Acad. Religion and Soc. Bibl. Lit., Zionist Orgn. Am., Am. Assn. Pres. of Ind. Colls. and Univs., Am. Jewish Hist. Soc., Am.-Isreal Pub. Affairs Com. Address: 2433 Coolidge Ave Oakland CA 94601-2630 *He that labors in any great or laudable* *undertaking has his fatigues first supported by hope, and afterwards rewarded by joy. To strive with difficulties, and to conquer them, is the highest human felicity. I am not afraid of tomorrow for I have seen yesterday and I love today.*

PATTEN, BERNARD MICHAEL, neurologist, writer, educator; b. N.Y.C., Mar. 23, 1941; s. Bernard M. and Olga (Vaccaro) P.; m. Ethel Doudine, June 18, 1964; children: Allegra, Craig. AB summa cum laude, Columbia Coll., 1962; MD, Columbia U., 1966. Med. intern N.Y. Hosp. Cornell Med. Ctr., N.Y.C., 1966-67; resident neurologist Columbia Presbyn. Med. Ctr., 1967-69, chief resident neurologist, 1969-70; assoc. prof. neurology Baylor Coll. Medicine, Houston, 1973-95; ret., 1995. Asst. chief med. neurology NIH, Bethesda, Md., 1970-73; mem. med. bd. Nat. Myasthenia Gravis Found., 1973—, Nat. AmyoTrophic Lateral Sclerosis Found., 1982—, Nat. Myositis Assn., 1995—; invited faculty Rice U., 1999—. Author: One or Two Things I Remember About Her, 1999, Tristan and Iseult: Modern Version, 2000, Investment Pearls for Modern Times Expressed in Meter and in Rhymes, 2000, The Great Cotzias, 2001, Ascent to Heaven, 2001, Quia Imperfectum, 2001; contbr. more than 200 articles to profl. jours. With USPHS, 1970-73. Rsch. grantee NIH, pvt. founds., nat. health orgns. Fellow ACP, Royal Coll. Physicians, Tex. Neurol. Soc. Roman Catholic. Achievements include discoverer (with others) L-Dopa for Parkinson's disease; pioneered use of immune suppression for myasthenia gravis, diagnosis and treatment of medical and neurologcal complications of breast implants. Home: 1019 Baronridge Dr Seabrook TX 77586-4001 E-mail: DADPATTEN@aol.com.

PATTEN, BRENDA L. lawyer, urban planner; b. Long Beach, Calif., Feb. 15, 1948; d. Benjamin Joseph and Evelyn Jeanette Lott; m. Louis Alan Valla, Jan. 10, 1971 (div. July 1975); m. Robert Bruce Patten, Oct. 9, 1993; 1 child, Ariel Solomon. BA in Polit. Sci., U. Fla., 1970, JD with honors, 1983; M in Urban Planning, Mich. State U., 1978. Bar: Fla. 1983; cert. in city, county and local govt. law; lic. pvt. pilot. Urban planner North Ctrl. Fla. Regional Planning Coun., Gainesville, 1974-76, City of Jacksonville, Fla., 1978-79, State of N.Y., Albany, 1979-80; atty. Winderweedle, Haines, Ward & Woodman, Orlando, Fla., 1983-86; gen. counsel The Emmer Group, Gainesville, 1988-89; dep. county atty., acting gen. counsel Sarasota County Govt., Sarasota, Fla., 1989-97; shareholder, atty. Kirk-Pinkerton, P.A., 1997—. Bd. dirs. Sarasota Coastal Credit Union, 1990-97; legal counsel Gov.'s Growth Mgmt. Adv. Com., 1986-87. Contbg. author: Perspectives on Florida's Growth Management Act of 1985, 1986; contbr. articles to profl. jours. Bd. dirs. Marie Selby Bot. Gardens, Sarasota, 1998-2001; mem. corp. bd. dirs. Ringling Sch. Art and Design, Sarasota, 1997-1998. Mem. Am. Planning Assn., Fla. Planning and Zoning Assn., Sarasota C. of C. (bd. dirs., com. for econ. devel. 1997-1998), Sarasota Film Festival (bd. dirs.). Avocation: flying. Office: Kirk-Pinkerton PA 720 S Orange Ave Sarasota FL 34236-7773

PATTEN, CHARLES ANTHONY, management consultant, retired manufacturing company executive, author; b. Allentown, Pa., May 12, 1920; s. Charles Henerie and Mae (Doyle) P.; m. Kathleen Marie Breene, Jan. 6, 1951 (dec. 1999); children: Charles Anthony Jr., Amy Elizabeth Goddard, Nancy Kathleen Hansen. BSM.E., Lehigh U., 1942. With Joy Mfg. Co., 1947-63, works mgr., 1956-63; v.p. mfg. White Motor Corp., 1963-68, Colt Industries, 1968-69; With Dravo Corp., Pitts., 1942-47, 69-85, gen. mgr. engring. works div., 1970-71, corp. v.p., gen. mgr. engring. works div., 1971-75, corp. group v.p., chief exec. officer Dravo Mfg. Group, 1975-81, corp. sr. v.p., mem. corp. policy com., chief exec. officer Dravo Mfg. Group, 1981-83, corp. sr. v.p., asst. to pres. and chief exec. officer, mem. exec. com., 1984-85; pres. C.A. Patten Enterprises, 1985—. Bd. dirs., v.p. Dravo (Can.) Ltd., 1975-85; dir., pres. Dravo-Okura Co. Ltd., 1974-79; dir. Dravo Mfg. (Can.) Ltd., 1975-83, Tru Weld Grating Inc., 1983-85; v.p. Dravo Internat., Inc., 1974-85; adv. com. Nat. Mgmt. Assn., 1973-85; chief devel. officer Western Pa. Model Rd. Mus., 2001-. Seminar spkr. in field. Trustee Ohio Valley Gen. Hosp., McKees Rocks, Pa., 1975-82, Marietta (Ohio) Coll., 1979-89, emeritus trustee, 1989—; bd. dirs. Vocat. Rehab. Center of Allegheny County, 1972-79, Jr. Achievement of S.W. Pa., 1975-80. Recipient Silver Knight of Mgmt. award Nat. Mgmt. Assn., 1976. Mem. ASME, Neville Island Mfrs. Assn. (pres. 1975-85), Am. Arbitration Assn. (panel of arbitrators, 1989-95), Duquesne Club. Republican. Roman Catholic. Home and Office: 2304 Clearvue Rd Pittsburgh PA 15237-1632 E-mail: cpatten512@aol.com. *The successful manager is a time-oriented goal setter. Without waiting for others to ask, envisions things that should happen and thinks through possible paths to reach the goals. When the goals are reached, is quick to laud and praise people for their accomplishments.*

PATTEN, CHRISTINE TAYLOR, artist, writer; b. L.A., Oct. 17, 1940; d. Malcolm Clark and Virginia (Strong) Patten; children: Robert Roy Powell Jr., Jonathan Taylor Powell, Matthew Clark Powell, Michael Neal Powell; m. Gendron Jensen, Aug. 15, 1987. Student, Pasadena City Coll., 1958-59, 70-72, U. Oreg., 1959-60; BFA, Otis Art Inst., L.A. County, 1974. Tchr. drawing and painting Pacificulture-Asia Mus., Pasadena Art Mus., 1973-74. Author: O'Keeffe at Abiquiu, 1995, Miss O'Keeffe, 1992; Exhibited in group shows at SITE/Santa Fe, Calif. Mus. Sci. and Industry, L.A., Armory for the Arts, Santa Fe, Mus. N.Mex., Mus. Fine Arts, Santa Fe, Santa Barbara (Calif.) City Coll., Pepperdine U., Malibu, Calif., Ctr. for Contemporary Arts, Santa Fe, Addison-Ripley Gallery, Washington, Albuquerque Mus., Horwitch LewAllen Gallery, Santa Fe, Coll. Santa Fe, Knoedler Gallery, N.Y.C., Exit Art, others, Represented in permanent collections L.A. County Mus. Art, Albuquerque Mus., U. N.Mex., Mus. N.Mex., Mus. Fine Arts, Harwood Mus., The Old Jail Mus., James Kelly Contemporary, Santa Fe, pvt. collections. Santa Fe Arts Coun. grantee, 1985. Home: PO Box 194 Vadito NM 87579-0194 E-mail: murasaki@laplaza.com.

PATTEN, DUNCAN THEUNISSEN, ecologist educator; b. Detroit, Oct. 13, 1934; s. Marc T. and Doris (Miller) P.; m. Eva Chittenden, July 27, 1957; children: Michael, Marc, Robin, Scott. BA, Amherst Coll., 1956; MS, U. Mass., Amherst, 1959; PhD, Duke U., 1962. Asst. prof. ecology Va. Poly. Inst., Blacksburg, 1962-65, Ariz. State U., Tempe, 1965-67, assoc. prof., 1967-73, prof., 1973-95, prof. emeritus, 1995—, dir. ctr. environ. studies, 1980-95. Rsch. prof. Mont. State U., 1995—. Contbr. articles to profl. jours. Fellow AAAS, Ariz.-Nev. Acad. Sci.; mem. Ecol. Soc. Am. (bus. mgr. 1979-95), Brit. Ecol. Soc., Soc. Range Mgmt., Am. Inst. Biol. Scis., Soc. Wetland Scientists (pres. 1996-97), Am. Water Resource Assn., Am. Geophys. Union, Soc. Conservation Biology, Sigma Xi. Office: Mont State U Big Sky Inst Box 173490 Bozeman MT 59717-3490 E-mail: dtpatten@starband.net.

PATTEN, EILEEN DUNLEVY, painter, writer, editor, consultant; b. Paterson, N.J. d. Robert P. and Julia (Hennessy) Dunlevy; m. Grant A. Patten Jr., Sept. 30, 1950; children: Kathleen Burke, Margaret Alexandra. AB, Coll. New Rochelle; postgrad., Harvard U., 1954, Rutgers U., 1963. Dir. cmty. rels. Valley Hosp., Ridgewood, NJ, 1959-80; dir. spl. projects Am. Heart Assn. N.J. Affiliate, 1980-84; dir. pub. affairs and fundraising Hosp. Ctr. the Oranges, 1984-91; pres. Patten PR Assocs., 1991—. Pub. rels. and fundraising cons. Rep. Nat. Com., 1979—80; mem. Action Com. Newark Mus.; fine arts cons., 1995—. Vol. Am. Heart Assn., ARC, United Way; co-chair Roukema for Congress Campaign, NJ, 1978; bd. dirs. Hermitage Mus.; founder Ridgewood Sch. Sys. Field Trip Enrichment Program, 1979—82. Mem.: Am. Hosp. Assn. Mktg. and Pub. Rels. Coun., Nat. Fedn. Press Women, N.J. Press Women, Ridgewood Arts Coun., N.J. Advt. Club. Avocations: chamber music, community service. Home and Office: 31 Ridge Rd Ridgewood NJ 07450-3165 E-mail: EileenPatten1@aol.com.

PATTEN, LANNY RAY, industrial gas industry executive; b. St. Joseph, Mo., July 31, 1934; s. E.L. and Sarah Catherine (Langner) P.; m. Ann Rogers Hall, Oct. 26, 1957; children: David, John, Jeffrey, Mark. BS in Engring., Iowa State U., 1956; AMP, Harvard U., 1976. Field engr. Carrier Corp., Kansas City, Mo., 1957; sales engr. Air Products and Chems., Inc., Allentown, Pitts., Chgo., 1960-63, dist. mgr. Cleve., 1964-66, region mgr. Pitts., 1966-68, div. gen. sales mgr. Allentown, Pa., 1969-75, v.p., div. gen. mgr., 1975-88, sr. v.p., gases and equipment, 1988-90; pres., COO Airgas Inc., Radnor, Pa., 1990-91; founder, pres. CylServ, Inc., West Conshohocken, 1992—. Chmn. Lehigh U. Parents Assn., Bethlehem, Pa., 1977-90; campaign com. chmn. Good Shepherd Home, Allentown, 1989-90; mem. Boy Scouts Am., Allentown, 1978-90; pres., coach Youth Baseball Assn., Allentown, 1970-83. USAF Officer, 1957-60. Recipient PACE award for Engring. Achievement Iowa State U., 1990, Friend of Lehigh award, 1991. Mem. SAR, Compressed Gas Assn. (exec. bd. dirs. 1977-91), Internat. Oxygen Mfg. Assn. Allentown C. of C. (exec. bd. dirs. 1978-82), Kappa Sigma. Republican. Episcopalian. Avocations: baseball, golf, reading. Home: 1306 Club House Rd Gladwyne PA 19035-1006

PATTEN, NICHOLAS FREDERICK, artist; b. Troy, N.Y., June 16, 1953; s. Mark B. and Rozamond Patten; m. Amy J. Aden, Aug. 19, 1989. BS in Art, Coll. of St. Rose, Albany, N.Y., 1977. Artist and art frame cons., N.Y.C., 1984—92; artist The Patten Gallery, Chatham, Mass., 1992—. Juror Cape Cod Art Assn., Barnstable, Mass., 2001, 02. One-man shows include Frame Gallery, Brookline, Mass., 1989, The Marlborough Galleries, Boston, 1995, Julie Heller Gallery, Provincetown, Mass., 2000, 2001, exhibited in group shows at Picotte Gallery, Albany, 1977, Gallery 410, Burlington, Vt., 1978, Dillons, Burlington, 1979, Albany Psych Ctr. Gallery, 1980, Art in Pub. Places, Albany, 1981, Schenectady (N.Y.) Mus., 1982, Rennsselaer County Coun. for the Arts, Troy, 1983, Wetherholt Gallery, Washington, 1991, 1992, Elfworks Gallery, Wellfleet, Mass., 1993, Cummaquid Fine Arts, Barnstable, 1994, Burd House Gallery, Nyack, N.Y., 1994, Danforth Mus., Framingham, Mass., 1996, Barret Ho. Galleries, 1997, Frasier Gallery, Washington, 1997, 1999, Fla. Printmakers Nat. Print Exhibit Catalogue, 1997, Print Club of Albany, 1997, 1998 (Purchase prize), Salmagundi Club, N.Y.C., 1997, 1998, Cortland Jessup Gallery, Provincetown, 1998, Silvermine Gallery Nat. Print Exhbn., 1998, U. Wis., 1998, Soc. Am. Graphic Artists Mems. Show, 1999 (Purchase prize), Allied Artists of Am. Ann. Exhbn., 1999 (Gold medal of honor), Represented in permanent collections N.Y. Pub. Libr., Print Club of Albany, Boston Pub. Libr., Zimmerli Art Mus., Rutgers U., Mohawk Paper Corp., Rembrandt Graphic Arts, numerous pvt. collections. Avocation: tennis. Office: The Patten Gallery 459A Main St Chatham MA 02633 Fax: 508-945-5817. E-mail: nickpatten@attbi.com.

PATTEN, RICHARD E. personnel company owner; b. Seattle, May 17, 1953; s. Donald Wesley and Lorraine Louise (Kienholz) P.; m. Monica Rose Bourg, Mar. 20, 1976; children: Richard Douglas, Wesley Bourg, Melinda Rose. BA, U. Wash., 1976. Exec. v.p. Microfilm Svc. Co., Seattle, 1976-84, gen. mgr., 1985-87, chmn. bd., 1988-90; pres. Express Pers. Svcs., 1990—. Candidate for U.S. Ho. of Reps., 1982; deacon Bethany Bapt. Ch., Seattle, 1983-86; co-chmn. fin. com. Wash. State Billy Graham Crusade, 1990-91; chmn. Wash. State Coalition toEliminate Death Tax. Mem. Nat. Micrographics Assn. (pres. N.W. chpt. 1979-80, bd. dirs. 1978-79), Assn. Image and Info. Mgmt. (chmn. svc. co. 1987), Assn. Records Mgrs. and Adminstrs., Wash. Athletic Club, Rotary (bd. dirs. 1996-98). Republican. Baptist. Home: 7012 NE 161st St Kenmore WA 98028-4265 E-mail: dickpatten@expresspersonnel.com.

PATTEN, ROBERT LOWRY, English language educator; b. Oklahoma City, Apr. 26, 1939; s. Charles H. and Helen (Lowry) P.; m. Faith L. Harris, June 12, 1960 (div. 1974); children: Jocelyn S., Christina S. BA, Swarthmore Coll., 1960; MA, Princeton U., 1963, PhD, 1965. Lectr. Bryn Mawr (Pa.) Coll., 1964-66, asst. prof. English, 1966-69; asst. prof. Rice U., Houston, 1969-71, assoc. prof., 1971-76, prof. English, 1976-96, chair, dept. of English, 1991-92, master Grad. House, 1992-95, Lynette S. Autrey prof. humanities, 1996—. Pres. PEN S.W., Houston, 1989-92. Author: Charles Dickens and His Publishers, 1978, George Cruikshank's Life, Times and Art, vol. 1, 1992, vol. 2, 1996 (best biography of the decade Guardian); editor: (book by Charles Dickens) Pickwick Papers, 1972, George Cruikshank: A Revaluation, 1974, 2d edit., 1992, (with John O. Jordan) Literature in the Marketplace, 1995; editor SEL: Studies in English Lit., 1978-84, 90—. Bd. dirs. Cultural Arts Coun., Houston, 1979-80, Tex.Com. for the Humanities, 1979-80; pres., bd. dirs. Houston Ctr. for the Humanities, 1976-84. NEH fellow, 1968-69, 77-78, 87-88; Guggenheim fellow, 1980-81; Nat. Humanities Ctr. fellow, 1987-88; Nat. Gallery of Art Assoc., 1988-89. Mem. AAUP, MLA, PEN Am. Ctr., Dickens Fellowship, Dickens Soc., Phi Beta Kappa (pres. Beta chpt. Tex. 1991-94, 97-2002, senator 2002--). Episcopalian. Avocations: travel, opera. Office: Rice U Dept English MS 30 PO Box 1892 Houston TX 77251-1892 E-mail: patten@rice.edu.

PATTEN, RONALD JAMES, retired university dean; b. Iron Mountain, Mich., July 17, 1935; s. Rudolph Joseph and Cecelia (Fuse) Pataconi; m. Shirley Ann Bierman, Sept. 5, 1959; children: Christine Marie, Cheryl Ann, Charlene Denise. BA, Mich. State U., 1957, MA, 1959; PhD, U. Ala., 1963. Acct. Price Waterhouse & Co., Detroit, 1958; instr. No. Ill. U., 1959-60; asst. prof. U. Colo., 1963-65; assoc. prof. Va. Poly. Inst. and State U., 1965-67, prof., 1967-73, head dept. accounting, 1966-73; dir. research Financial Accounting Standards Bd., Conn., 1973-74; dean Sch. Bus. Adminstrn., U. Conn., Storrs, 1974-88; chief of party-Eastern Caribbean Arthur D. Little Internat., 1988-89; dean Coll. Commerce and Kellstadt Grad. Sch. Bus. De Paul U., Chgo., 1989-99. Individual investors adv. com. N.Y. Stock Exch., 1993-98; cons. in field. Contbr. chapters to books, articles to profl. jours. Bd. dirs. U.S. com. UNICEF, Chgo., 1996—99. Recipient Nat. Quartermaster award Nat. Quartermaster, Assn., 1956; Earhart Found. fellow, 1962-63. Mem. AICPA, Am. Acctg. Assn., Inst. Mgmt. Accts., Acad. Internat. Bus. (Internat. Dean of Yr. award 1987), Internat. Assn. for Acctg. Edn. and Rsch., Ill. Coun. Econ. Edn. (Chgo., trustee 1989—, chmn. bd. trustees 1997-2000), Pacioli Soc., West Towns Chorus, Heidelberg Club Internat., Scabbard and Blade, Golden Key, Beta Gamma Sigma (mem. bd. govs. 1975-90, nat. sec.-treas. 1980-82, nat. v.p. 1982-84, nat. pres. 1984-86), Beta Alpha Psi (bd. dirs. 1992-94), Delta Sigma Pi, Phi Kappa Phi, Delta Mu Delta. Avocations: hiking, skiing, golf, travel, softball. Home: 334 N Montclair Ave Glen Ellyn IL 60137-5253 E-mail: rpatten@depaul.edu.

PATTEN, THOMAS HENRY, JR. management, human resources educator; b. Cambridge, Mass., Mar. 24, 1929; s. Thomas Henry and Lydia Mildred (Lindgren) Patten; m. Rosalie Medina, May 23, 2002. AB, Brown U., 1953; MS, Cornell U., 1955, PhD, 1959. Dir. program planning Ford Motor Co., Dearborn, Mich., 1957-65; prof. mgmt. and sociology U. Detroit, 1965-67; prof. orgnl. behavior and personnel mgmt. Sch. Labor and Indsl. Relations, Mich. State U., E. Lansing, 1967-84; prof. mgmt. and human resources Calif. State Poly. U., Pomona, 1984—. Cons. in field. Author: The Foreman: The Forgotten Man of Management, 1968, Manpower Planning and the Development of Human Resources, 1971, OD-Emerging Dimensions and Concepts, 1973, A Bibliography of Compensation Planning and Administration, 1960-1974, 2d rev. edit., 1981, 3d rev. edit., 1987, Pay: Employee Compensation and Incentive Plans, 1977, Classics of Personnel Management, 1979, Organizational Development Through Teambuilding, 1981, A Manager's Guide to Performance Appraisal, 1982, Fair Pay: The Managerial Challenge of Comparable Job Worth and Job Evaluation, 1988, Exercises for Developing Human Resources Management Skills, 1996. Served with USMC, 1946-51. Mem. ASTD (chmn. orgn. devel. div. 1972), Indsl. Rels. Rsch. Assn. (chpt. pres. 1970-71), Am. Sociol. Assn., Internat. Pers. Mgmt. Assn., Internat. Indsl. Rels. Assn., Inst. Applied Behavioral Sic., Am. Compensation Assn. Home: 2540 King Way Claremont CA 91711-1719 Office: Calif State Poly U Dept Mgmt & Human Resources 3801 W Temple Ave Pomona CA 91768-2557 E-mail: thpatten@csupomona.edu. *Human values come first.*

PATTENAUDE, RICHARD LOUIS, university administrator; b. Seattle, Feb. 22, 1946; s. Joseph Arthur and Alice June (Vrooman) P.; m. Michele Arlen Stevenson, May 31, 1975; children: Lauren, Lisa, Dylan, Joshua. BA with honors in Econs., Calif. State U., San Jose, 1968; PhD in Polit. Sci., U. Colo., 1974. Assoc. prof. Drake U., Des Moines, 1974-80, assoc. dean liberal arts, 1976-80; asst. v.p. acad. affairs SUNY-Binghamton, 1980-82, assoc. v.p., 1982-86; v.p. acad. affairs, prof. polit. sci. Ctrl. Conn. State U., New Britain, 1986-91; pres., prof. polit. sci. U. So. Maine, Portland, 1991—. Cons. in field; panelist, presenter various nat. higher edn. meetings. Contbr. numerous articles to profl. jours., chpts. to books in field. Commr. Occupational and Licensing Commn., Iowa, 1978-80; mem. Gov.'s Com. Efficiency, 1979; mem. adv. coun. planning dept. City of Binghamton, 1984—; bd. dirs. Broome County United Way, 1985, Greater Hartford Red Cross, 1991-93, Mercy Hosp., Portland, 1992-94, Portland Symphony Orch., Maine Devel. Found., 1991-97, Maine Sci. & Tech. Found., 1992-98, Portland Mus. Art, 1993-99, Inst. Civic Leadership, 1992-94, Greater Portland United Way. With U.S. Army, 1969-71, Vietnam. Fanny W. Ames scholar, 1965; Title II fellow, 1970. Mem. Assn. Instl. Rsch. and Planning Officers (v.p. 1983-84, pres. 1984-85), Am. Assn. State Colls. and Univs. (state rep. 1995—, bd. dirs. 1999—), Greater Portland C. of C. Office: U So Maine Office of Pres 707 Law Building 96 Falmouth St Portland ME 04103-9300 Address: University of Southern Maine P.O. Box 9300 Portland ME 04104-9300*

PATTEN-VAN SERTIMA, JACQUELINE L. academic program director, photographer; b. N.Y.C., Jan. 6, 1948; d. Bernard Philip and Sarah Elizabeth (Gay) P.; children: LaCheun LaVette, LaSarah Renata; m. Ivan Van Sertima; stepchildren: Michael E. and Lawrence J. Van Sertima. BS in Psychology and Sociology, Hunter Coll., 1980, MS in Edn., 1982. Asst. theatre and dance photographer for Max Waldman, N.Y.C., 1978-80; free lance photographer and cons., N.Y.C., 1976—; art dir., cover designer Jour. African Civilizations, New Brunswick, N.J., also established audio div., Legacies, Inc., producer companion audio cassettes to vols., 1981—; dir. job location and devel. L.I. U., Bklyn., 1983-85, dir career svcs. 1985-87. Photog. exhbns. include Mus. City N.Y., 1976, Columbia U., 1979, Lincoln Ctr., 1980, Black Artists in Am., 1980, Nat. Urban League, 1980, NYU, 1981, Hunter Coll., 1981. Recipient Lincoln Ctr. photography award Womanart Galleries, 1980; 1st prize award Mademoiselle's 14th Ann. Photography Competition, 1980; internationally known for hand-painted photography and its significant contbn. to social awareness. Mem. Collective Black Photographers, Photog. Soc. Am., Am. Soc. Media Photographers. Home and Office: 347 Felton Ave Highland Park NJ 08904-2217

PATTERSON, ALEXANDER CANNING (XANDER PATTERSON), business and political consultant, activist; b. N.Y.C., Jan. 16, 1963; s. Russel Hugo Jr. and Juliet Boyd Patterson; life ptnr. Teresa Catherine Keane. BA in Anthropology, Reed Coll., 1986; MBA, Portland (Oreg.) State U., 1999. Radio broadcast journalist KBOO, Portland, 1987-89; freelance print and radio journalist Managua, Nicaragua, 1989-91; owner-worker Sunflower Recycling Coop., Portland, 1991-92; owner, operator Pacific Bottle Regeneration, 1992-93; co-chair Pacific Green Party of Oreg., 1999—. Author: Terrasquirma and the Engines of Social Change in 1970s Portland, 2000, Pay Your Way, 2000; columnist The Oregonian. Treas., co-mgr. Victory 2000 PAC, Portland; minister Universal Life Ch., Modesto, Calif., 1996; dir. East Multnomah Soil and Water Conservation Dist., 2000—. Mem.: Physicians for Social Responsibility (dir. Oreg. chpt.). Avocation: deep wilderness backpacking. Home: 2833 NE Couch # 6 Portland OR 97232 E-mail: xman@imagina.com.

PATTERSON, AUBREY BURNS, JR. banker; b. Grenada, Miss., Sept. 25, 1942; s. Aubrey Burns and Elizabeth (Staten) P.; m. Ruby Kathryn Clegg, Dec. 12, 1964; children: Aubrey B. III, Clayton H., Jennifer L. BBA, U. Miss., 1964; MBA, Mich. State U., 1969. With Bancorp South (formerly Bank of Miss.), Tupelo, 1972—, pres., 1983-99, chmn., chief exec. officer, 1990—. Chmn., CEO BancorpSouth, Inc. Former chmn. bd. dirs. Salvation Army, Tupelo, 1978—; bd. dirs. Cmty. Devel. Found., chmn. bd., 1994-95; bd. dirs. Columbia Theol. Sem., Decatur, Ga., Miss. Univ. for Women Found., Presbyn. Ch. U.S.A. Found., New Covenant Trust Co., Bankers' Roundtable; vice-chmn. CREATE, Inc.; bd. dirs. Miss. Econ. Coun., Jackson, 1986—, chmn., 1994; chmn. bd. dirs. North Miss. Health Svcs. Inc., 1987—, also exec. com.; bd. dirs. Miss. Partnership Econ. Devel.; moderator St. Andrews Presbytery Presbyn. Ch. USA; chmn., bd. dirs. U. Miss. Found.; laureate Miss. Bus. Hall of Fame; bd. dirs. Journal Pub. Co.; mem. exec. com. Miss. Pub. Edn. Forum. Capt. USAF, 1965-72. Decorated Air Force Commendation medal, Meritorious Svc. medal, Nat. Def. Svc. medal. Mem. ABA (govt. rels. coun.), Am. Bankers Assn. (chmn. 2002-), Miss. Bankers Assn. (pres. 1995—), Soc. Internat. Bus. Fellows, Conf. of State Bank Supr., Bankers Adv. Coun. (chmn.), Tupelo Country Club, Univ. Club, Kiwanis (pres. Tupelo 1987), Beta Gamma Sigma, Beta Alpha Psi. Presbyterian. Office: BancorpSouth PO Box 789 Tupelo MS 38802-0789

PATTERSON, BEVERLEY PAMELA GRACE, accountant; b. London, Feb. 6, 1956; came to U.S., 1975; d. Ernest Charles and Barbara (Wiseman) Patterson; children: Tamara, Russell, Stuart. AAS with honors, Tacoma C.C., 1978; BBA with honors, U. Puget Sound, 1980. CPA, Wash. Accounts payable clk. Hillhaven Corp., Tacoma, 1975-76, staff acct., 1980-83, acquisition analyst, 1984-86; contr., CFO Tacoma Luth. Home and Retirement Cmty., 1987-97; contr. Nat. Med. Mgmt., Bellevue, Wash., 1998-99, Samis Land Co., Seattle, 1999-2000. Cons. in field; cons. Merrill Lynch, 1997-98. Bd. dirs., treas. YWCA, 1992-94; bd. dirs. Tacoma Farmers Market, 1995, Boys and Girls Club, 1996-97. Mem. AICPA, Wash. Soc. CPAs (healthcare com. 1993-95, comm. com. 1995-97), Am. Soc. Women Accts. (bd. dirs. Tacoma chpt., editl. bd. The Woman CPA mag. 1989-92, pres. 1991-92), Grace Heffernan Arnold Guild/Fred Hutchinson Cancer Rsch. Ctr., Rotary. Avocations: tennis, golf, skiing, horseback riding. Home: 2600 2nd Ave Apt 1501 Seattle WA 98121-1240 E-mail: bpatterson7711@aol.com.

PATTERSON, BEVERLY ANN GROSS, fund raising consultant, grant writer, federal grants administrator, social services administrator, poet; b. Pauls Valley, Okla., Aug. 5, 1938; d. Wilburn G. Jack and Mildred E. (Steward) Gross; m. Kenneth Dean Patterson, June 18, 1960 (div. 1976); children: Tracy Dean, Nancy Ann Patterson-McArthur, Beverly Jeanne Patterson-Wertman. AA, Modesto (Calif.) Jr. Coll., 1958; BA in Social Sci., Fresno (Calif.) State U., 1960; M in Community Counseling, Coll. Idaho; postgrad., Stanislaus State Coll., Turlock, Calif., U. Idaho, Boise (Idaho) State U. Cert. secondary tchr., Calif., Idaho, lic. real estate agt., Idaho. Secondary tchr., Ceres and Modesto Calif., Payette and Weiser Idaho, Ontario Oreg., 1960-67; dir. vol. svcs. mental retardation and child devel. State of Idaho, 1967-70, cons. dir. vol. svcs. health and welfare, 1970-72; dir. Ret. Sr. Vol. Program, Boise, 1972-74; exec. dir. Idaho Nurses Assn., 1974-76; community svcs. adminstr. City of Davis, Calif., 1976-78; dir. devel. and fundraising Mercy Med. Ctr., Nampa, Idaho, 1978-85; exec. dir. St. Alphonsus Med. Ctr. Found., Boise, 1985-87; dir. devel. and gift planning Idaho Youth Ranch, 1989-94; fund devel. cons. Mercy Housing, Nampa, Idaho, 1994-96, Pratt Ranch Boys Home, Emmett, 1994-96, Northwest Childrens Home, Lewiston, 1994-96, Idaho Spl. Olympics, Boise, 1994-95, Idaho Found. for Parks and Lands, Boise, 1994-95, St. Vincent de Paul, Inc., Boise, 1995-96, Nampa Shelter Found., Inc., 1994-95, Turning Point Inc., Nampa, 1994-95, Port of Hope Treatment Ctr. Inc., Boise, 1994-97, Idaho Theater for Youth, Inc., Boise, 1995-96, Boise Tennis Coalition, Inc., 1995-2000, El Ada Cmty. Action Ctr., Boise, 1995, Hemophilia Found. Idaho, 1995-96, Boise YWCA, 1996, Marsing (Idaho) Sch. Dist., 1996-98; and many more. Founder Fellowship Christian Adult Singles, Boise, 1974; cons., exec. dir. Boise Hotline, 1988-90; co-dir. ACOA workshop leader Child Within Concepts, Inc., Boise, 1987—; cons. coord. Rural Hosp. Edn. Consortium, 1988; cons. hosp. fund devel. and cmty. resources Gritman Meml. Hosp., Moscow, Idaho, 1987-88; cons., conf. coord. State of Idaho, 1987-88; counsel Adult Children of Alcoholics, 1991; pres. Nonprofit Solutions, Inc., Boise, 1995—; co-dir. Child Within Concepts, Inc., Meridian, 1996—; cmty. resource devel. specialist Idaho Dept. Health and Welfare, 1997-2000, United Way Portland, 2000; chmn., pres. Creative Solutions P.A., 2000—; grant writing cons. sch. dist. # 3JT, Oreg., Tillamook Sch. Dist., Oreg., Banks Sch. dist., Oreg., North West Regional Ednl. Svcs. Dist., Oreg. Contbr. articles to profl. jours. Coord. Idaho Golf Angels Open Pro-Am Tournament, Boise, 1989-91; founding exec. v.p. Coll. Fund for Students Surviving Cancer, 1993-96; bd. dirs. Arthritis Found., Idaho, 1984-86, Idaho Mental Health Assn., 1978-97; founder Ctrl. Vol. Bur., Boise, 1971. Named Idaho Statesman Disting. Citizen, 1985. Mem. Nat. Assn. for Hosp. Devel. (accredited, treas. 1980, accreditation chmn. 1984-86, conf. chmn. 1982, 85), Assn. Healthcare in Philanthrophy (accredited), Nat. Soc. Fund Raising Execs., Idaho Devel. Network, Choices in Giving, Inc. Mem. Community Christian Ch. Avocations: golf, family activities. Address: PO Box 40629 Portland OR 97240

PATTERSON, BRADLEY HAWKES, executive; b. Wellesley, Mass., Dec. 5, 1921; s. Bradley Hawkes and Helen Gilman P.; m. Shirley DoBos, Dec. 26, 1943; children: Dawn Marie, Bruce DoBos, Glenn Gilman, Brian Brease. BA, MA, U. Chgo., 1943. Prof. asst. Dept. of State, Washington, 1954; asst. cabinet sec. The White House, 1954-61; exec. sec. The Peace Corps, 1961-62; nat. security affairs asst. Treasury Dept., 1962-65; exec. dir. Presdl. Adv. Commn., 1966-68; exec. asst. The White House, 1969-76; sr. staff mem. The Brookings Inst., 1977-88; ret. Author: The Ring of Power, 1988, The White House Staff: Inside the West Wing and Beyond, 2000. Elected mem. nat. bd. trustees Unitarian/Universalist Assn., Boston, 1995-99. Recipient The ARthur S. Flemming award, 1960, Profl. Achievement award, U. Chgo. Alumni Assn., 1994, Disting. Svc. award, River Rd. Unitarian Ch., Bethesda, Md., 1996.

Fellow Nat. Acad. Pub. Adminstrn.; mem. Am. Soc. Pub. Adminstrn., Am. Polit. Sci. Assn., Ctr. Study Presidency (nat. adv. coun.), Potomac Crral Westerners (sheriff 1992). Avocations: mountaineering, table tennis, wildlife cinematography. Home: 6705 Pemberton St Bethesda MD 20817 E-mail: bradshirl@aol.com.

PATTERSON, BRYAN DEL, civil engineer; b. Atlantic, Iowa, Jan. 8, 1953; s. Delmar Dean and Betty Lou Patterson; m. Diann Hunter, Mar. 18, 1978; children: Brianna, Heather. BS in Urban Planning, Iowa State U., 1975; MPA, Ariz. State U., 1981. Registered profl. engr., Ariz.; cert. profl. planner; cert. pub. mgr., Ariz. Transp. planner Iowa Dept. Transp., Ames, 1975-78; transp. and air quality mgr. Maricopa Assn. Govts., Phoenix, 1979-85; planning program mgr. Ariz. Dept. Transp., 1985-90, resident constrn. engr., 1990-92; transp. dir. City of Chandler, Ariz., 1993-97, city engr., 1997-99, dep. pub. works dir., 1999—. United Way coord. Ariz. Dept. Transp., Phoenix, 1987; treas. YMCA Indian Princesses and Trailmates, Tempe, Ariz., 1988-96; bd. dirs. Potato Patch (Ariz.) Homeowners Assn., 1998-99. Transp. fellow Fed. Hwy. Adminstrn., 1977, 84. Mem. Am. Pub. Works Assn., Am. Inst. Cert. Planners, Inst. Transp. Engrs., Ariz. Soc. Cert. Pub. Mgrs., Phi Alpha. Methodist. Avocations: tennis, fishing, hiking. Home: 935 E Vinedo Ln Tempe AZ 85284-1526 Office: City of Chandler PO Box 4008 Chandler AZ 85244-4008 Fax: 480-782-3415.

PATTERSON, CHARLES DAROLD, librarian, educator; b. Wahpeton, N.D., Aug. 8, 1928; s. Charles Irwin and Inez Fern (Slagg) P. B.Sc., Bemidji State U., 1950; MA, U. Minn., 1956; M.Music, W.Va. U., 1964; advanced cert., U. Pitts., 1968, PhD, 1971. Tchr. music Fargo (N.D.) public schs., 1950; jr. reference librarian U. Minn. Libraries, 1954-55; head librarian Bemidji (Minn.) State U., 1955-58; dir. libraries, asst. prof. Glenville (W.Va.) State Coll., 1958-62; asst. prof. W.Va. U., 1962-66; instr. Grad. Sch. Library and Info. Scis. U. Pitts., 1966-71, asst. prof., 1971-72; assoc. prof. Sch. Library and Info. Sci. La. State U., Baton Rouge, 1972-78, prof., 1978-93; prof. emeritus, 1993. Del. La. Gov.'s Conf. on Library and Info. Services, 1978 Author: Analysis of Library of Congress Music Subject Headings, 1971, JEL Cumulative Index, 1979, supplement, 1982, (with D.G. Davis) ARBA Guide to Library Science Literature, 1987; editor: W.Va. Libraries, 1963-66; mem. editorial bd.; Jour. of Edn. for Librarianship, 1975-79, editor, 1980-84; editor: Jour. Edn. for Library and Info. Sci., 1984-88; asst. editor Reference Services Review, 1986-93; contbr. articles to profl. jours. Served with U.S. Army, 1950-52. Recipient La. State U. Faculty Excellence award, 1984, ALA/Beta Phi Mu award, 1989. Mem. ALA (chmn. scholarship jury 1972-73), W.Va. Library Assn. (chmn. coll. and univ. library sect. 1960-61, exec. bd. 1960-61, 64-66), Assn. Coll. and Research Libraries (pres. Tri-state chpt. 1972), Assn. Am. Library Schs. (exec. bd. 1980-88), La. Library Assn., Southeastern Library Assn., AAUP (pres. chpt. 1985-86), Am. Guild Organists (dean chpt. 1985-86), Pitts. Bibliophiles, Univ. Chamber Music Soc. (pres., dir. 1979-80), La. Sinfonietta (exec. bd. 1994—), Beta Phi Mu. (dir.-at-large 1982-85). Methodist. Home: 1480 Kenmore Ave Baton Rouge LA 70808-1130 also: Birchmont Beach Bemidji MN 56601 Office: La State U Sch Libr And Info Sci Baton Rouge LA 70803-0001 *When one is confident in his own mind that he has, with given abilities, done his very best, then perhaps he has paid for his niche in eternity.*

PATTERSON, CHRISTOPHER NIDA, lawyer; b. Washington Courthouse, Ohio, Apr. 17, 1960; s. Donis Dean and JoAnne (Nida) O.; m. Vicky Patterson; children: Travis, Kirsten. BA, Clemson U., 1982; JD, Nova U., 1985. Bar: Fla. 1985, U.S. Dist. Ct. (mid. dist.) Fla. 1985, U.S. Ct. Mil. Rev. 1986, U.S. Ct. Mil. Appeals 1987, U.S. Dist. Ct. (ea. dist.) Va. 1987, U.S. Supreme Ct. 1990, U.S. Ct. Appeals (11th cir.) 1992, U.S. Dist. Ct. (no. dist.) Fla. 1992, U.S. Dist. Ct. (so. dist.) Tex. 1995; cert. criminal trial lawyer Fla. Bar. and Nat. Bd. Trial Advocacy. Pros. Fla. State Attys. Office, Orlando, Fla., 1985; spl. asst. U.S. Atty. U.S. Dist. Ct. (ea. dist.) Va., 1987-90; ptnr. Patterson & Hauversburk, Panama City, Fla., 1992—. Adj. prof. law Gulf Coast Coll.; mem. Fla. Supreme Ct. Mediators Qualifications Bd.; family law mediator Fla. Supreme Ct., dependency law mediator, county ct. mediator, mem. mediators qualifications bd.; mediator County Ct.; on-air legal analyst Nex Media-WYOO-FM. Author: Queen's Pawn, 1996, Treasure Trove, 1997; contbr. Nat. DAR Mag., Fla. Defender mag. Chancellor St. Thomas Episcopal Ch. Capt. JAGC, U.S. Army, 1986-92, Desert Storm. Recipient U.S. Army Chief of Staff award for legal excellence, 1989, Guardian ad litem commendation, Fla. Supreme Ct., 1999. Mem. ABA, ATLA, FBA, SAR, NACDL (life), Am. Coll. Barristers, Fla. Assn. Criminal Def. Lawyers, Acad. Fla. Trial Lawyers, Assn. Fed. Def. Attys., Fla. Acad. Profl. Mediators, Fla. Bar Spkrs. Bur. (criminal law sect., mil. law standing com., del. 11th cir. jud. conf. 1999, Pro Bono Svc. award, nominee Jefferson award for pub. svc. 1999), Bay County Bar Assn., The Ret. Officers' Assn., Christian Legal Soc., Am. Legion, Fellowship of Christian Athletes, Nat. Triathlon Fedn., Soc. Colonial Wars, Mil. Order Fgn. Wars. Episcopalian. Avocations: athletics, triathlons. Office: PO Box 9474 415 Beckrich Rd Ste 290 Panama City Beach FL 32417

PATTERSON, COLEMAN E.P. management educator; b. Stamford, Conn., Aug. 31, 1966; s. Benton Rain and Patricia Jane (Roberts) P.; m. Tracy Lynne Potts, Aug. 1, 1992. BSBA in Fin., U. Fla., 1988, MEd, 1990; EdS, U. Ala., Tuscaloosa, 1995, PhD in Mgmt., 1996. Fin. aid officer U. Fla., Gainesville, 1990; fin. aid specialist Santa Fe C.C., Fla., 1988-90, acad. adviser, 1990, assessment specialist, 1991; rsch. asst. U. Ala., Tuscaloosa, 1991-92, 94-95, teaching asst., 1992-94, 95—, ind. study instr., 1992—. Co-author mgmt. course. Mem. Acad. of Mgmt., So. Mgmt. Assn., S.W. Acad. Mgmt., Pinnacle Honor Soc. Baptist. Avocations: racquetball, softball, canoeing. Home: 1002 Amarillo St Abilene TX 79602-2308 Office: U Ala Mgmt/Mktg Dept PO Box 870225 Tuscaloosa AL 35487-0154

PATTERSON, COLLIS DELANO, secondary school educator; b. Balt., Aug. 29, 1950; s. William Phillip Patterson and Lucille Mini Patterson-Wheeler. BS, Towson U., 1973; MEd, Loyola Coll., Balt., 1988. Cert. tchr. grades 5-12 Md. State Dept. Edn. Tchr. Balt. City Schs., 1973—. Instr. Sojourner-Douglass Coll., Balt., 1990—92. Editor: Dr. Samuel L. Banks Speaks, 1995. Vol. Am. Friends, Balt., 1978—. Grantee Geography grant, Md. Geog. Alliance, Balt., 1988, Tchg. grant, NEH, Washington, 1990. Mem.: Third World Coalition (rep. 1995—98, Honor award 1997), Am. Friends Svc. Com. (clk. 1978—). Democrat. African Methodist. Avocations: gardening, collecting.

PATTERSON, DANIEL WILLIAM, dentist; b. Minot, N.D., Aug. 12, 1948; s. Girdell William and Fern Lemay Patterson. DDS, Northwestern U., 1972; Alumnus degree (hon.), U. Colo., 1977; BS in Biology, U.N.Y., 1993; M in Healthcare, U. Denver, 1994. Cert. health industry orgn., ops. U.Denver, 1993, cert. gerontology, 1996. Dentist Dan L. Hansen, DDS, P.C., Lakewood, Colo., 1974-75; pvt. practice dentistry Littleton, 1975-88; clin. instr. dept. applied dentistry U. Colo., Denver, 1981-83, lectr., 1983, clin. asst. prof. depts. restorative and applied dentistry, 1989-91, dir. advanced dentistry program, 1989-90, asst. prof. clin. track dept. restorative dentistry, 1991—. Mem. editorial adv. panel Dental Econs. Jour., 1981; also articles. Active Chatfield Jaycees, Littleton, 1976-81; vocal soloist, mem. Denver Concert Chorale, 1978-82. Lt. USN, 1968-74. Fellow Acad. Gen. Dentistry; bd. eligible Am. Bd. Gen. Dentistry; mem. ADA, Met. Denver Dental Soc., Colo. Dental Assn. (Pres.'s Honor Roll 1982-84), Mensa, Sedalia Wild Game Club. Lutheran. Avocations: reading, fishing, photography. Home: 6984 N Fargo Trl Littleton CO 80125-9270 Office: U Colo Health Scis Ctr Sch Dentistry Box C 284 4200 E 9th Ave Denver CO 80262-0284

PATTERSON, DAVID HIBBERT, controller, corporate financial executive; b. Teulon, Man., Can., July 28; s. Howard L. and Helen A. (Hibbert) P.; m. Ivy Luus, June 8, 1963; children: Sylvia, Vivian, Steven. BASc in Engring., U. Toronto, Ont., Can., 1960; MBA, U. Western Ont., 1964. Registered profl. engr., Ont. Asst. treas. McIntyre Mines Ltd., Toronto, 1966-72, Procor Ltd. subs. Union Tank Car Co., Oakville, Ont., 1972—, also bd. dirs. Bd. dirs. Procor and 28 subs. of Marmon Group, Chgo. Bd. dirs. Halton Region Conservation Authority, Oakville, 2001—; bd. dirs. Oakville Cmty. Homes Inc., 1994—, pres., 1997—. Mem. Toronto Soc. Fin. Analysts, Ont. Assn. Profl. Engrs., Rotary. Avocations: tennis, golf, canoeing. Home: 1379 Amber Crescent Oakville ON Canada L6J 2P1 Office: Procor Ltd 2001 Speers Rd Oakville ON Canada L6J 5E1

PATTERSON, DAVIE JEAN ETTA, elementary school educator, artist; b. Hugo, Okla., Jan. 9, 1941; d. Henry McDonald and Esther Berniece Patterson; m. Wilburn Augustine Jenkins, June 17, 1988; m. Jimmie Glen Branson, June 17, 1957 (div.); children: Desiree Yvonne Branson Eakle, Jim Glen Branson, Sherri Kathleen Branson Johnson. BS, Ea. State Coll., 1984; BS Edn., Southeastern Okla. State U., 1986; M, Northeastern State U., 1999; degree in edn. Cert. tchg. Okla. State Dept. Edn., agr. lab. technician State of Okla. Fashion merchandiser Mont. Ward, Shawnee, Okla., 1970—71; salesperson Okla. Tire and Supply Co., Shawnee, 1971; lab technician agr. Okla. State Fed. Lab., Oklahoma City, 1972; with William Henry Ryan, AIA Arch. and Assocs., Pryor, 1987; elem. tchr. 4th grade Grant Pub. Sch., Grant, 1988—90; art tchr., tchr. 5th grade Claremont Christian Sch., 1999—2000; with U.S. Census Bur. Fed. Govt., 2000. Ho. spkr. OEA-NEA, Grant, Okla., 1988—90, Okla. Edn. Assn., NEA. Oil painting, collage (award, 1984), project. Mem. Dept. Lost Cherokee Tribe, Marshall, Ark., 2001—02. Recipient Leadership Scholarship Award, SOSU Durant Okla., 2001-2002. Mem.: Kappa Delta Pi (Beta Delta chpt. 1985). Democrat. Protestant. Avocations: art, writing, agriculture. Home: Rt 2 Box 1030 Ew Co Rd Rose OK 74364

PATTERSON, DENIS W. economic development official; b. Mannheim, Germany, Dec. 5, 1956; s. George W. III and Elisabeth Patterson. BA, U. Conn., 1979; MLA, So. Meth. U., 1982; M in Internat. Mgmt., Am. Grad. Sch. Internat. Mgmt., 1984. With Gen. Reinsurance, Dallas, 1979-83, Am. Express, Madrid, 1976, Phoenix, 1983-84; prin., ptnr. P.L.Z., Inc., Stamford, Conn., 1984-89; dir. mktg. Dusseldorf Trade Shows, N.Y.C. and Chgo., 1989-94; sr. exec. office of econ. devel. City of Stamford, Conn., 1997—. Rep. dist. 8 Town Meeting, Greenwich, Conn., 1985—91, 1995—97; bd. dirs. Chgo. Area Project, 1992—94. Named Col. La. State Militia, Gov. Edwards. Mem.: SAR, Chgo. Coun. on Fgn. Rels., Mayflower Soc., World Affairs Forum (Amb.'s Roundtable), Landmark Club, Young Grand Old Party, Univ. Club. Chgo., Sigma Chi (Carlisle scholar 1979, Balfour nominee 1979). Republican. Avocations: travel, literature, civic affairs, vineyard. Home: 114 Strawberry Hill # 110 Stamford CT 06902

PATTERSON, DENNIS JOSEPH, management consultant; b. Honolulu, Apr. 13, 1948; s. Joseph John and Dorothy Elizabeth (Snajkowski) P.; divorced; children: Valerie Jean, Christina Elizabeth. BA, Elmhurst (Ill.) Coll., 1970; MA, George Washington U., 1973. Asst. dir. Vancouver (B.C.) Gen. Hosp., 1973-76, dir., 1975-76; v.p. Shaugnessy Hosp., Vancouver, 1976-79; pres. Westcare, 1979-84; mgr. Ernst & Whinney, Chgo., 1984-86, sr. mgr., 1986-88, ptnr., 1988-93; pres. FHP Internat. Cons. Group, Inc., Fountain Valley, Calif., 1993-95; ptnr. KPMG Peat Marwick, 1996-97; sr. cons. Hay Group, 1997-98; chmn., CEO IMC Rsch. Inst. (now Healthcare Net); ptnr. Wellspring Ptnrs. Author: Indexing Managed Care, 1997; contbr. articles to profl. jours. Fin. mgr. Electoral Action Movement, Vancouver, 1978; trustee George Washington U., 1992-96, Calif. Sch. Profl. Psychology, 1993-96, Alliant U., 1999—. Fellow Am. Coll. Healthcare Execs.; mem. Royal Vancouver Yacht Club, East India Club, Phi Gamma Mu. Republican. Anglican. Avocation: sailboat racing, golf. E-mail: djp@wp-ltd.com.

PATTERSON, DONALD EUGENE, research scientist; b. El Paso, Tex., Feb. 7, 1958; s. Donald M. Patterson and Beverly Lee (Viles) McElroy; m. Mary Jane Ingram, May 6, 1989. BS, U. Tex., 1982, MS, 1984; MA, Rice U., 1987, PhD, 1989. Rsch. scientist Rice U., Houston, 1989-91; sr. rsch. scientist Houston Advanced Rsch. Ctr., The Woodlands, Tex., 1989-93; sr. scientist SI Diamond Tech. Inc., Houston, 1991-95; sr. rsch. scientist TSA, Inc., The Woodlands, 1991-95; dir. R & D SI Diamond Tech. Inc., Houston, 1995-96; edn. supr. ITT Tech. Inst., 1996-97; prin. scientist Systems & Processes Engring. Corp., Austin, 1997-98; founder, sr. v.p. product devel. Extreme Devices, Inc., 1998—. Contbr. articles to profl. jours. Recipient Harry B. Wieser award Rice U., 1988; Rice U. Graduate fello, 1984; UTEP Grad. scholar, 1983, Davis and Bertha Green scholar, 1982, VFW Voice Democracy scholar, 1974. Mem. AAAS, Materials Rsch. Soc., Am. Chem. Soc., N.Y. Acad. Sci., Phi Kappa Phi, Sigma Xi. Achievements include 7 patents in field. Home: 4728 Interlachen Ln Austin TX 78747 Office: Extreme Devices Inc 3500 Consouth Dr Austin TX 78744 E-mail: patterson@extremedevices.com.

PATTERSON, DONALD LEE, music educator; b. Colorado Springs, Colo., Aug. 14, 1947; s. Thurman Alvin and Bernice Eileen (May) P.; m. Janet Louise Andrews, Feb. 19, 1971. MusB, U. Denver, 1969; MusM, Manhattan Sch. Music, 1972; MusD, U. North Tex., 1977. Staff accompanist Harlem Sch. Arts, N.Y.C., 1970-72, Manhattan Sch. Music, N.Y.C., 1970-72; instr. music Angelo State U., San Angelo, Tex., 1972-74; tchg. fellow U. North Tex., Denton, 1974-76; prof. music U. Wis., Eau Claire, 1976—. Co-author: Vincent Persichetti: A Bio-bibliography, 1989; author: One Handed: A Guide to Piano Music for One Hand, 1999, (sound rec.) EDUCO, Inc., Contemporary Rec. Soc. Mem. Am. Liszt Soc., Music Tchrs. Nat. Assn. (cert.), Recs. for Contemporary Rec. Soc., Educo, Hemera Music, Kappa Kappa Psi, Phi Mu Alpha Sinfonia, Pi Kappa Lambda. Home: 3504 W Country Club Ln Altoona WI 54720-1055 Office: U Wis Music Dept Eau Claire WI 54702 E-mail: patterdl@uwec.edu.

PATTERSON, DONALD ROSS, lawyer, educator; b. Sept. 9, 1939; s. Sam Ashley and Marguerite (Robinson) P.; m. Peggy Ann Schulte, May 1, 1965; children: D. Ross, Jerome Ashley, Gretchen Anne. BS, Tex. Tech U., 1961; JD, U. Tex., 1964; LLM, So. Meth. U., 1972. Bar: Tex. 1964, U.S. Ct. Claims 1970, U.S. Ct. Customs and Patent Appeals 1970, U.S. Ct. Mil. Appeals 1970, U.S. Supreme Ct. 1970, U.S. Dist. Ct. (ea. dist.) Tex. 1982, U.S. Ct. Appeals (5th cir.) 1991, U.S. Ct. Appeals (D.C. cir.) 1994; bd. cert. in immigration and naturalization law, Tex. Commd. lt. (j.g.) USN, 1964, advanced through grades to lt. comdr., 1969; asst. officer in charge Naval Petroleum Res., Bakersfield, Calif., 1970-72; staff judge adv. Kenitra, Morocco, 1972-76; officer in charge Naval Legal Svcs. Office, Whidbey Island, Wash., 1976-79; head mil. Justice divsn., Subic Bay, The Philippines, 1979-81; ret. USN, 1982; pvt. practice Tyler, Tex., 1982—. Former instr. U. Md., Chapman Coll., U. LaVerne, Tyler Jr. Coll., Jarvis Christian Coll., U. Tex., Tyler. Mem. East Tex. Estate Planning Coun. Mem. Coll. of State Bar of Tex., Tex. Bar Assn., Smith County Bar Assn., Am. Immigration Lawyers Assn., Masons, Rotary (past pres.), Shriners, Toastmasters (past pres.), Phi Delta Phi. Republican. Baptist. Home: 703 Wellington St Tyler TX 75703-4666 Office: 777 S Broadway Ave Ste 106 Tyler TX 75701-1648 E-mail: oneworld2gether@cs.com.

PATTERSON, DOUGLAS MACLENNAN, finance educator; b. Jan. 16, 1945; s. Thomas and Ruth (MacLennan) P.; m. Sara Louise Lucas; children: Cara Beth, John Douglas. BSEE, U. Wis., 1968, MBA, 1972, PhD, 1978. Elec. engr. Westinghouse Electric, Balt., 1968-71; asst. prof. U. Mich., Ann Arbor, 1976-80, Va. Tech., Blacksburg, 1980-86, dir. PhD program in fin., 1991-95, assoc. prof., 1986-98, prof., 1998—. Vis. prof. U. Calif., Santa Barbara, 1989; vis. scholar U. Tex., Austin, 1994; presenter numerous seminars; participant Fin. Time Series Conf., Isaac Newton Inst. for Math. Scis., Cambridge, Eng., 1998. Co-author: A Nonlinear Times Series Workshop: A Tool Kit for Detecting and Identifying Nonlinear Serial Dependence; contbr. articles to profl. jours. Mem. ad hoc com. Detroit Area Hosp. Assn., 1978-79. Recipient Tchg. Excellence award Va. Tech., 1983; U. Mich. fellow, 1979; USN grantee, 1984, 85, 90. Mem. Am. Fin. Assn., Am. Econ. Assn., Fin. Mgmt. Assn., Beta Gamma Sigma. Methodist. Home: 702 Crestwood Dr Blacksburg VA 24060-6006 Office: Va Poly Inst Dept Finance 0221 Blacksburg VA 24061 E-mail: amex@vt.edu.

PATTERSON, D(OUGLAS) REID, pharmaceutical scientist; b. Port Arthur, Tex., July 30, 1945; s. Howard Hilliard and Rosa Nell (McPhail) P.; m. Mary Emilee Martin, Aug. 16, 1969; children: Keli Anne, Christopher Reid. BS, Tex. A&M U., 1968, DVM, 1969; PhD, U. Mo., 1976. Diplomate Am. Coll. of Lab. Animal Medicine, Am. Coll. Vet. Pathology, Am. Bd. Toxicology, Fellow Internat. Acad. Toxicologic Pathology, Acad. Toxicological Scis. Sr. staff pathologist Hazleton Labs. Am., Vienna, 1975-78; head pathology Hazleton Labs. Europe, Harrogate, Eng., 1978-80; dir. medicine Hazleton Labs. Am., Vienna, 1980-81; supr. pathology/reproductive toxicology Shell Devel. Co., Houston, 1981-84; dir. pathology/toxicology Abbott Labs., Abbott Park, Ill., 1984-87, dir. drug safety, 1987-90; v.p. drug safety Abbott Labs, 1990—2001; interim head neurosci. venture Abbott Labs., 1992-93; v.p. Global Preclinical Safety, 2002—. Adj. asst. prof. U. Tex. Med. Sch., Houston, 1983-84; asst. nat. program dir., bd. dirs. 2000—, Charles L. Davis, DVM Found., Sayre, N.Y., 1981-86. Contbr. articles to profl. jours. Mem. Lions Internat., Columbia, Mo., Houston, 1970-75; mem., v.p. Jaycees, Reston, Va., 1976-78; ruling elder Presbyn. Ch., Reston, Houston, 1976-78, 80-81. Named one of Outstanding Young Men of Am., Jaycees, 1977. Mem. Pharm. Mfg. Assn. (chmn. drug safety subsect. 1992-93), Soc. Toxicologic Pathologists (pres. 1998-99), Soc. Toxicology Regulatory and Safety Evaluation Specialty Sect. (pres. 1997-98), Am. Coll. Vet. Pathologists (fin. com. 1985-91, councilor 1992-96, v.p. 1998, pres. 1999, chmn. bd. 2002—), Gamma Sigma Delta, Phi Kappa Phi, Phi Zeta, Sigma Xi. Republican. Achievements include co-development of numerous health care products of anti-infectives, anti-hypertensives, anti-convulsants, anti-inflammatory, anti-AIDS, and anti-Parkinsonian agents; determination of potential hazards of numerous industrial and environmental toxicants and carcinogents; establishment of safe levels of exposure to chemicals for workers and consumers of various products; research in disease mechanisms. Office: Abbott Labs D-46G AP13A 100 Abbott Park Rd North Chicago IL 60064-3502

PATTERSON, EDWARD, investment banker; b. N.Y.C., Oct. 16, 1920; s. Arthur C. and Evelyn (Crimmins) P.; m. Joan Metzger, Jan. 10, 1947 (div. 1972); children: Patricia Kean, Lucinda, Elizabeth, Christina P. Fay. BA, Yale U., 1943. Mem. N.Y. Stock Exch., N.Y.C., 1950-56; exec. v.p. Allen & Co., 1956—, also bd. dirs. Dir. Teleprompter, 1980-82 Guest writer News Leader, Richmond, W.Va.; contbr. articles to N.Y. Times. Trustee Citizens Budget Commn., N.Y.C., 1957-80; trustee Garvan Collection, Yale U., 1968; mem. Fordham U. Council, N.Y.C., 1975; mem. Cardinal's Com. of the Laity. Lt. USNR, 1942-46, ETO. Mem.: Deepdale (Manhasset, N.Y.) (pres. 1970-75); Piping Rock (Locust Valley, N.Y.); Friendly Sons of St. Patrick. Roman Catholic. Office: Allen & Co 711 5th Ave Fl 8 New York NY 10022-3111

PATTERSON, EDWARD PALMER, retired physical scientist; b. Kansas City, Kans., Sept. 5, 1921; s. Sidney Edward and Dura (Palmer) P.; m. Eula Mae Bennett, Oct. 15, 1945; children: Nona Marie, Wilma Jean Patterson Graham. BS in Metall. Engring., U. Mo., Rolla, 1944, MS in Metall. Engring., 1947, prof. degree of engring., 1957. Registered profl. engr., Kans. Instr. Nat. Sch. Aeronautics, Kansas City, Mo., 1947-50; metall. engr. Boeing Airplane Co., Wichita, Kans., 1950-51; sr. rsch. engr. GM Corp., Kansas City, 1951-52; sr. staff engr. White Motors Co., Cleve., 1952-54; sr. engr. Westinghouse Elec. Co., Kansas City, Mo., 1954-59; sr. staff rschr. Cessna Aircraft Corp., Wichita, 1959-60; project engr., project leader Bendix Corp./Allied Signal Corp., Kansas City, Mo., 1960-87; ret., 1987. Vol. Hospice Mesquite Med. Ctr., 1997-98, Nat. Hospice Orgn., Dallas, 1998. With USAF, 1944-46. Mem. AIME, Am. Soc. Materials Internat., Am. Rocket Soc., Am. Phys. Soc., Masons (master, York Rite Cross of Hon. & Red Cross of Constantine, High Priest), Knights of Kadosh (comdr. 1968). Republican. Mem. Lds Ch. Achievements include discovery that the so called gravitational constant is not a constant; all properties are related by one or more universal constants; there are numerous equations of the type E=MC2, nine dimensions; discovered the unitron, basic command unit for life and non-life; established new values for the Planck time, mass, and length. Avocations: travel, reading, genealogy, computing, family gatherings. Home: 3513 Bermuda Dr Rowlett TX 75088-5364 E-mail: unitron9@attbi.com.

PATTERSON, EDWIN, minister; b. Andalusia, Ala., Sept. 6, 1921; s. Walter Levi and Kate Edline (Aughtman) P.; m. Margaret Alice Hall, May 14, 1966. Degree, Brennan Bus. Sch., 1940; postgrad., Samford U., 1950-57. Ordained to ministry So. Bapt. Conv., 1947. Pastor various chs., Ala., 1947—; including Hopewell, 1949-67, Harmony Bapt. Ch., Andalusia, 1967-80, Searight Bapt. Ch., Dozier, Ala., 1980—; acct. C.G. Tomberlin, M.D., Andalusia, 1985—. Mem. bd. regents Liberty U., Lynchburg, Va. Home: 407 Lakeview Dr Andalusia AL 36420-3542 Office: PO Box 486 Andalusia AL 36420-0486 *In Him, we live and move and have our being. Therefore, my heart's desire is to honor Christ in all things, for He is the way, the truth, and the life.*

PATTERSON, ELIZABETH JOHNSTON, former congresswoman; b. Columbia, SC, Nov. 18, 1939; d. Olin DeWitt and Gladys (Atkinson) Johnston; m. Dwight Fleming Patterson, Jr., Apr. 15, 1967; children: Dwight Fleming, Olin DeWitt, Catherine Leigh. BA, Columbia Coll., 1961; postgrad. in polit. sci., U. S.C., 1961, 62, 64; LLD (hon.), Columbia Coll., 1987; D Pub. Svc. (hon.), Converse Coll., 1989, M in Liberal Arts, 1999; LLD (hon.), Wofford Coll., 1999. Pub. affairs officer Peace Corps, Washington, 1962-64, VISTA, OEO, Washington, 1965-66; D Pub. Svc. Head Start and VISTA, OEO, Columbia, 1966-67; tri-county dir. Head Start, Piedmont Community Actions, Spartanburg, S.C., 1967-68; mem. Spartanburg County Coun., 1975-76, S.C. State Senate, 1979-86, 100th-102nd Congresses from 4th S.C. dist., 1987-93; dir. continuing edn., converse II program Converse Coll., 1993—. Adj. prof. Spartanburg Meth. Coll., 1993—. Trustee Wofford Coll., 1978-90; bd. dirs. Charles Lea Ctr., 1978, Spartanburg Coun. on Aging; pres. Spartanburg Dem. Women, 1968; v.p. Spartanburg County Dem. party, 1968-70, sec., 1970-75; trustee Columbia Coll., 1991—; chmn., bd. dirs. Bethlehem Cmty. Ctr., 1998—; bd. dirs. S.C. Ind. Colls. and Univs., 1995-99. Mem. Bus. and Profl. Women's Club, Alpha Kappa Gamma. Methodist. Office: PO Box 5564 Spartanburg SC 29304-5564 E-mail: liz.patterson@converse.edu.

PATTERSON, ELLMORE CLARK, banker; b. Western Springs, Ill., Nov. 29, 1913; s. Ellmore Clark and Harriet Emma (Wales) P.; m. Anne Hyde Choate, Sept. 28, 1940; children: Michael Ellmore, Arthur Choate, Robert Ellmore, David Choate, Thomas Hyde Choate. Grad., Lake Forest Acad., 1931; BS, U. Chgo., 1935. With J. P. Morgan & Co., Inc., N.Y.C., 1935-39, 39-41, 46-59, v.p., 1951-59; exec. v.p. Morgan Guaranty Trust Co. N.Y. (merger J.P. Morgan and Guaranty Trust Co.), 1959-65, dir., chmn. exec. com., 1967-68, pres., 1969-71, chmn., 1971-77, chmn. exec. com., 1978. With Morgan Stanley & Co., 1939; chmn. dirs. adv. coun. Morgan Guaranty Trust Co.; mem. Presdl. Com. on Fin. Structure and Regulation, 1970-72. Bd. mgrs. Meml. Hosp. Cancer and Allied Diseases, N.Y.C.; Sloan-Kettering Inst. Cancer Center, N.Y.C., U. Chgo., Mass. Inst. Tech. Served from ensign to lt. comdr. USNR, 1941-46. Mem. Meadowbrook Club, Piping Rock Club, Jupiter Island Club (Hope Sound, Fla.), Fishers Island Country Club, Seminole Golf Club (Palm Beach, Fla.). Episcopalian. Office: 1 Chase Manhattan Plz Fl 36 New York NY 10005-1401

PATTERSON, EUGENE CORBETT, retired editor, publisher; b. Valdosta, Ga., Oct. 15, 1923; s. William C. and Annabel (Corbett) P.; m. Mary Sue Carter, Aug. 19, 1950; 1 child, Mary Patterson Fausch. Student, North Ga. Coll., Dahlonega, 1940-42; AB in Journalism, U. Ga., 1943; LL.D., Tusculum Coll., 1965, Harvard U., 1969, Duke U., 1978, Stetson U., 1984, Ind. U., 1990; Litt.D., Emory U., 1966, Oglethorpe Coll., 1966, Tuskegee U., 1966, Roanoke Coll., 1968, Mercer U., 1968, Eckerd Coll., 1977, U. South Fla., 1986, Dillard U., 1992, Colby Coll., 1994, North Ga. Coll. & State U., 1999. Reporter Temple (Tex.) Daily Telegram and Macon (Ga.) Telegraph, 1947-48; mgr. for S.C. United Press, 1948-49, N.Y. night bur. mgr., 1949-53, mgr. London bur., also chief corr. U.K., 1953-56; v.p., exec. editor Atlanta Journal-Constitution, 1956-60; editor Atlanta Constitution, 1960-68; mng. editor Washington Post, 1968-71; prof. polit. sci. Duke U., 1971-72; editor, pres. St. Petersburg (Fla.) Times, 1972-84, chmn., chief exec. officer, 1978-88, editor emeritus, 1988—; editor, pres. Congl. Quar., Washington, 1972-86, chmn., chief exec. officer, 1978-88. Chmn. bd., chief exec. officer Fla. Trend mag., 1980-88, Ga. Trend mag., 1984-88, Ariz. Trend mag., 1986-88, Governing mag., 1987-88, Modern Graphic Arts, Inc., 1978-88, Poynter Inst. Media Studies, 1978-88, Poynter Fund, 1978-88. Vice chmn. U.S. Civil Rights Commn., 1964-68; mem. Pulitzer Prize Bd., 1973-84; trustee ASNE Found., 1981-84, U. Ga. Found., 1982-88, North Ga. Coll. Found., 1991-93, Am. Press Inst., Reston, Va., 1983-88, Duke U., 1988-94, Fla. Bar Found., 1992-93, LeRoy Collins Ctr. for Pub. Policy, 1990-93. Decorated Silver Star, Bronze Star with oak leaf cluster in 10th Armored Divsn., Gen. Patton's 3rd Army; recipient Pulitzer prize for editl. writing Columbia U., 1967, William Allen White Nat. Citation award U. Kans., 1980, Elijah Parish Lovejoy award Colby Coll., 1994; inducted into Fla. Newspaper Hall of Fame Fla. Press Assn., 1997. Fellow Soc. Profl. Journalists; mem. Am. Soc. Newspaper Editors (pres. 1977-78), St. Petersburg Yacht Club. Home: Snell Isle 1967 Brightwaters Blvd NE Saint Petersburg FL 33704-3007 E-mail: Ecp1015@aol.com.

PATTERSON, FRANCINE G. P. foundation administrator; b. Chgo., Feb. 13, 1947; d. Cecil H. and Frances L. (Spano) P. AB in Psychology, U. Ill., 1970; PhD in Devel. Psychology, Stanford U., 1979. Rsch. asst. U. Ill.

Children's Rsch. Ctr., Urbana, 1969-70; pres., rsch. dir. The Gorilla Found., Woodside, Calif., 1976—. Adj. rsch. assoc. dept. anthropology and ctr. anthrop. rsch. San Jose (Calif.) State U., 1982—; adj. assoc. prof. dept. psychology U. Santa Clara (Calif.), 1984—; bd. consultants Ctr. for Cross-Cultural Communications, Washington. Author: Koko's Kitten, 1985 (Tex. Bluebonnet award 1987), Koko's Story, 1987 (N.J. Libr. Assn. award 1990); co-author: The Education of Koko, 1981. Grantee for gorilla lang. rsch. Nat. Geog. Soc., 1976-83, 85; recipient Rolex award for enterprise Rolex, Geneva, 1978, Award for Outstanding Profl. Svc., Preservation of the Animal World Soc., 1986. Mem. Am. Soc. Primatologists, Am. Ednl. Rsch. Assn. Am. Assn. Zool. Parks and Aquariums, Am. Assn. Zookeepers, Animal Behavior Soc., Phi Beta Kappa. Avocations: swimming, snorkling, cooking, horseback riding. Office: The Gorilla Found PO Box 620530 Woodside CA 94062-0530

PATTERSON, FURNIFOLD SIMMONS, JR. cardiologist; b. Phila., June 27, 1945; s. Furnifold Simmons and Ruth Read Patterson; m. Charlotte Keith, May 21, 1981; 1 child, Cressie Patterson Tambling. BA, U. N.C., 1967; MD, U. Pa., 1971. Diplomate Am. Bd. Internal Medicine, Am. Bd. Hematology, Am. Bd. Cardiology. Intern George Washington U. Hosp., 1971-73, resident to chief resident, 1974-76; resident Duke U. Med. Ctr., Durham, N.C., 1973-74; cardiology fellow U. N.C., Chapel Hill, 1976-78; cardiologist Pinehurst (N.C.) Med. Clinic, 1979—. Pres. med. staff First Health Meml. Regional Hosp., Pinehurst, 1998-99, bd. trustees, 1999-2000; mem. N.C. Med. Bd., 1986-92, pres. 1990-91. Fellow ACP, Am. Coll. of Cardiology, Am. Coll. of Chest Physicians; mem. Country Club of N.C., Phi Beta Kappa, Alpha Omega Alpha. Presbyterian. Avocations: skiing, walking, reading.

PATTERSON, GRACE LIMERICK, library director; b. N.Y.C., Nov. 21, 1938; d. Robert and Frieda (Zeiontz) Limerick; m. Joseph Nathaniel Patterson (dec.); children: Lorrayne Carole, Joseph Nathaniel Jr. BA in Sociology, Edn., CUNY, 1971; MLS, Columbia U., 1975; MS in Comm., Coll. New Rochelle, 1989. Cert. libr. N.J. Exec. dir. Manhattanville Community Outreach, N.Y.C., 1971-74; br. and outreach svcs. Paterson (N.J.) Pub. Libr., 1975-79; media specialist II Passaic County C.C., Paterson, 1979-81; coord. outreach svcs. Irvington (N.J.) Pub. Libr., 1981-84; assoc. prof. libr. Rockland C.C., Suffern, N.Y., 1984-89; libr. dir. Hudson County C.C., Jersey City, 1989—. Editor jours. in field. Exec. bd. dirs. IFLA/CPRT, sec.-treas., 1996—; vol. Ridgewood (N.J.) Schs., 1981-83; Ridgewood Centennial Com. First Night, 1993. U.S. Dept. Edn. fellow, 1974-75. Mem. ALA (com., chairperson Black Caucus pub. rels. 1990-92), Am. Coll. and Rsch. Librs., N.J. Libr. Assn. Avocations: photography, oral history, travel, geneology, public speaking. Office: Hudson County CC 25 Journal Sq Jersey City NJ 07306-4012 E-mail: gpatterson@mail.hudson.cc.nj.us.

PATTERSON, HAROLD DEAN, retired superintendent of schools; b. Alexander City, Ala., May 29, 1932; s. Obed Howard and Sara Bell (Joiner) P.; m. Shirley Bryant, May 31, 1958; children: Lisa Jane, Anne Leslie, Harold Dean Jr. BS, Auburn U., 1954; MA, Vanderbilt U., 1957, EdD, 1964. Cert. sch. adminstr., Ala., S.C., Ill. Tchr. Bessemer (Ala.) H.S., 1957-63; asst. prin., 1959-62; prin. North Hall, Evanston (Ill.) Twp. H.S., 1964-66; prin. Mountain Brook (Ala.) H.S., 1966-71; assoc. supt. Greenville County Schs., Greenville, S.C., 1971-74; supt. schs. Sumter County Sch. Dist. 17, Sumter, 1974-82, Spartanburg County Sch. Dist. 7, Spartanburg, 1982-88, Guntersville (Ala.) City Schs., 1988-95, legis. liaison, 1995-98; ret., 1998. Mem. S.C. Gov.'s Com. on Financing Edn., Columbia, 1983, S.C. Pvt. Industry Coun., Columbia, 1984-88, S.C. Legis. Oversight Com., Columbia, 1984; pres. Peabody alumni bd. Vanderbilt U., Nashville, 1989-90. 2d lt. U.S. Army, 1954-56. Recipient Outstanding Educator award Florence chpt. Phi Delta Kappa, 1981, The Exec. Educator 100 award The Exec. Educator mag., 1987. Mem. Am. Assn. Sch. Adminstrs. (chmn. legis. corp. 1985-95, mem. exec. com. 1988-91, James R. Kirkpatrick award 1987, Disting. Svc. award 2000), Ala. Assn. Sch. Adminstrs., Nat. Assn. Secondary Sch. Prins., Rotary (dist. 6860 gov. 1995-96). Methodist. Avocation: golf. Home: 5020 Neely Ave Guntersville AL 35976-8102 E-mail: hpatterson@netnav.com.

PATTERSON, IRANIA MACIAS, newswriter, language educator; b. Caracas, Venezuela, July 14, 1969; arrived in U.S., 1993; d. Yran Asdrubal Macias and Juanita Mercedes Osuna; m. James Patterson, Jan. 28, 1995; children: Samuel, Isabella. Pub. rels. cert., Jose Capriles Inst., Caracas, 1991; student, Andres Bello Cath. U., Caracas, 1992; Spanish tchg. cert., U. N.C., 1997. Asst. coord. comm. Corinon Internat. Chem. Corp., Caracas, 1992; host interviewer Pub. Access TV, Charlotte, NC, 1993—95; prodr., writer, host WNCW FM, 1995; freelance journalist NBC News Ch., 1995; Spanish tchr. Charlotte Christian Sch., 1995—97; writer cultural and children pages La Noticia Newspaper, 1997—; bilingual children specialist Pub. Libr. Charlotte and Mecklenburg County, 1998—. Actress Skenna, Caracas, 1987—92; founder, actress Tablas Teatro de Arte, Charlotte, 1999; children cons. Bilingual Children Resources, Charlotte, 2001—02. Author: No Hiding Place, 2000, Creando Nuestro Libro, 2002; editor: Ventana Magica, 1998. Mem. adv. bd. L.Am. Coalition, Charlotte, 1995—96; mem. comm. com. N.C. Gov. Coun., 1999. Avocations: reading, dancing, beach.

PATTERSON, JAMES, former mayor; b. San Mateo, Calif., Feb. 18, 1948; m. Sharon LeTourneau, 1968; children: B.J., Jason, Lindsay. BA in Polit. Sci. summa cum laude, Calif. State U., Fresno, 1992. Radio broadcasting exec. Sta. KIRV-AM, Fresno, Calif., 1968—; mayor City of Fresno, 1993—2000; now consultant Valley Investment Group. Mem. San Joaquin River Conservancy, Calif. Ten Largest Cities Mayor's Coalition, 1993—; vice chair Fresno County Transp. Authority; bd. mem. Fresno County Coun. Govts.; chmn. NO on Measure H Com., 1989, Criminal Justice and Law Enforcement Commn., 1990-91; vice chmn. YES on Measure E Com., 1988; mem. Human Rels. Commn., City of Fresno, 1987-91; bd. dirs. Leadership Fresno Alumni Assn., 1989-91, Fresno County YFC/Campus Life, 1984-88. Mem. Fresno City and County C. of C. (chmn. local govt. affairs com. 1990-91, bd. dirs. FRESPAC 1990-91, city budget rev. com. 1989-91, privatization task force 1988-89, charter sect. 809 rev. task force 1987-88).*

PATTERSON, JAMES WILLIS, pathology and dermatology educator; b. Takoma Park, Md., Dec. 29, 1946; s. James Clark and Helen (Hendricks) P.; m. Julie Wyatt, Dec. 30, 1989; 1 child, James Wyatt. BA, Johns Hopkins U., 1968; MD, Med. Coll. Va., 1972. Diplomate Am. Bd. Dermatology, Am. Bd. Dermatopathology, Nat. Bd. Med. Examiners; recert. in dermatology. Fellow dermatopathology Armed Forces Inst. Pathology, Washington, 1979-80; rotating intern in medicine Med. Coll. Va., Richmond, 1972-73, resident in dermatology, 1973-76, assoc. prof. pathology and dermatology, 1982-89, prof., 1989-92, dir. dermatopathology, 1982-92; with Dermatology Assocs. of Va., 1992-96, Va. Dermatopathology Svcs., Richmond, 1992-96; clin. prof. pathology Med. Coll. of Va., 1992—; prof. pathology and dermatology U. Va., 1996—. Clin. instr. dermatology U. Colo. Med. Ctr., Denver, 1980-82; cons. in pathology McGuire VA Hosp., Richmond, 1982-92; cons. in pathology and dermatology Kenner Army Hosp., Ft. Lee, Va., 1982-95. Author: Dermatology: A Concise Textbook, 1987; contbr. over 100 articles on dermatology and pathology to med. jours.; asst. editor Jour. Cutaneous Pathology, 1989-94. Mem. nat. alumni schs. com. Johns Hopkins U., 1986—. With M.C., U.S. Army, 1976-82, col. Res. (ret.). Recipient Stuart McEwen award Assn. Mil. Dermatologists, 1980, 82. Fellow: ACP, Am. Soc. Dermatopathology (sec.-treas. 2001—), Am. Acad. Dermatology; mem.: Va. Dermatol. Soc. (sec.-treas. 1984—88, v.p. 1988—89, pres. 1989—90), Johns Hopkins U. Alumni Assn. (pres. ctrl. Va. chpt. 1989), Res. Officers' Assn. (life), Tau Epsilon Phi (life). Republican. Presbyterian. Avocations: American history, baseball, golf.

PATTERSON, JAMES HARDY, entertainer, conductor, musician, educator, arranger, composer; b. Kingston, Ga., Oct. 12, 1935; s. Hardy and Laura (Cargile) P.; m. Lois Gartrell; children: Adonica Patterson Carson, Phillippa G. AB, Clark Coll., 1957; MusM, U. Mich., 1965; postgrad., Atlanta U., 1962, U. Wis., Lacrosse, 1978. Tchr., dept. chmn. (ret.) Fulton County Bd. Edn., Atlanta, 1957-84; instr. to asst. prof., dir. Jazz Orch. Clark Atlanta U., 1962—; entertainer Motown Band, Detroit, 1962-73; profl. condr. Freda Payne Show, Fairmont Hotel, Atlanta, 1975; musician Atlanta Pops Orch., 1970—; leader James Patterson Jazz Quartet, Atlanta and abroad, 1960—. Profl. musician Lionel Hampton and Dizzy Gillespie Small Group, Duke Pearson's Big Band, Ringling Bros., Barnum and Bailey Circus, Ice Shows, Broadway mus. including Sophisticated Ladies, 1970; substitute, extra, soloist Atlanta Symphony, 1971; music panelist Ga. Coun. for the Arts, Atlanta, 1986—, Bur. Cultural Affairs, Atlanta, 1986—; cons. Fulton County Arts Coun., Atlanta, 1987; mem. adv. bd. So. Music Conf., Atlanta. Composer music including Song for Mr. H.P., 1976, Reminiscence, 1986; author: Jazz And the Young Black Audience, 1982; asst. project dir. film In Search of Imporvision, The Essence of Virtuosity in Jazz, 1983; performer "Gillespiana" IAJE Conv., 1996; performed Montreux, Switzerland, Northsea, Den Hague, Holland, Grande Parade de Jazz, Nice, France, Kool Jazz Festivals, Avery Fisher, Lincoln Ctr.,, IAJE Conv., Atlanta; performed at Trumped Awards, CNN; author essay. Served with 7th U.S. Army Band, 1958-60, Germany. Named one of Outstanding Young Men of Am., 1970; recipient Bronze Jubilee award Sta. WETV, 1983. Mem. AAUP, ASCAP, NARAS (nat. edn. com.), Nat. Flute Assn., Internat. Assn. Jazz Educators, N.Am. Saxophone Alliance World Saxophone Congress, Atlanta Fedn. Musicians (v.p. 1994—, bd. dirs. 1969—), Internat. Double Reed Soc., Internat. Clarinet Soc., Duke Ellington Soc., Optimists, YMCA, Alpha Phi Alpha. Democrat. Methodist. Home: 413 Fielding Ln SW Atlanta GA 30311-2020 Office: Clark Atlanta U James P Brawley Fair St SW Atlanta GA 30314

PATTERSON, JAMES MILTON, marketing specialist, educator; b. DeQueen, Ark., Oct. 15, 1927; s. Charles Edward and Phoebe Allene (Steel) P.; m. Della Jeanne Hays, July 3, 1964; children— J. Marshall, Julia M.; children by previous marriage— Robert T., Donald A. BS, U.S. Mcht. Marine Acad., 1948; MBA (Teagle Found. fellow), Cornell U., 1954, PhD (Ford Found. dissertation fellow), 1961. Third mate Esso Shipping Co., 1948-52; instr. in bus. adminstrn. Northwestern U., 1957-60; lectr. Center for Programs in Govt. Adminstrn., U. Chgo., 1959; asst. prof. mktg. Ind. U., 1960-63, asso. prof., 1963-69, prof., 1969—, chmn. dept. mktg., 1972-78, asso. dir. Poynter Ctr., 1980, acting dir., 1981, co-sec. U. Faculty Coun., pres. Bloomington Faculty Coun.; dir. Ind. U. Inst. for Advanced Study, 1994-97. Bd. dirs. Inst. Advanced Study; cons. petroleum mktg.; expert witness on antitrust and mktg. Author: Marketing: The Firm's Viewpoint, 1964, Highway Robbery: An Analysis of the Gasoline Crisis, 1974, Competition Ltd.: The Marketing of Gasoline, 1972. With USNR, 1945-48. Mem. Assn. for Practical & Profl. Ethics. Democrat. Home: 1303 Dreams Landing Way Annapolis MD 21401-1035 Office: Ind U Inst Advanced Study Bloomington IN 47405 E-mail: tartan33@aol.com.

PATTERSON, JAMES RANDOLPH, physician; b. Lancaster, Pa., Jan. 30, 1942; m. Linda Lewis Patterson, Nov. 22, 1969. AB, U. Pa., 1964; MD, Columbia U., 1968. Diplomate Nat. Bd. Med. Examiners, Am. Bd. Internal Medicine, Subspecialty of Pulmonary Disease. Pulmonary and critical care specialist The Oregon Clinic, Portland, 1975—; clin. prof. medicine Oreg. health Scis. U., 1978—. Mem. Am. Bd. Internal Medicine, Phila., 1995—, sec.-treas., 2002--; trustee Collins Med. Trust, Portland, Oreg., 1992—, chair subsplty. bd. pulmonary disease, 1998—. Contbr. numerous articles to profl. jours. Recipient Class of 1964 award U. Pa., Van Loan award Am. Lung Assn. Oreg., 1990, Meritorious Achievement award Oreg. Health Scis. U., 1991; named Class Pres. Coll. Physicians and Surgeons of Columbia U., 1968, Tchr. of Yr. Providence Med. Ctr., Portland, Oreg., 1976, Internist of Yr., 1983, Best Doctors in Am., 1992—. Mem. AMA, Am. Thoracic Soc., Am. Coll. Chest Physicians, Oreg. Lung Assn., North Pacific Soc. of Internal Medicine, Pacific Interurban Clin. Club, Multnomah County Med. Soc., Oreg. Med. Assn., Oreg. Soc. Ctirical Care Medicine. Office: The Oregon Clinic 507 NE 47th Ave Ste 103 Portland OR 97213-2236 E-mail: jpatterson@orclinic.com.

PATTERSON, JANICE PAULINE, community and geriatrics health nurse; b. Riobamba, Ecuador, Oct. 7, 1941; d. Michael James and Ella Catherine (Patzsch) Ficke; m. Michael Milton Patterson, June 11, 1966; children: Michael Shane, Shad Milton. Diploma, West Suburban Hosp., Oak Park, Ill., 1963; BSN, U. Iowa, 1968. Emergency rm., ICU staff nurse Bloomington (Ind.) Hosp.; operating rm. staff nurse VA Hosp., Iowa City; operating rm. supr. Kirksville (Mo.) Osteo. Hosp., 1973-77; clinic coord. Cancer Screening Clinic County Health Dept., Athens, Ohio, 1987-93; supr. Hickory Creek Nursing Ctr., The Plains, 1989-90; dir. nursing Arcadia Nursing Ctr., Coolville, 1990-93; staff nurse Med. Splty. Unit of Kansas City at Alpine North, Riverside, Mo., 1993-2000; mgr. medicine unit West Broward Care Ctr., Plantation, Fla., 2000—. Mem. Ohio Dir. Nursing Assn., Sigma Theta Tau (Lambda Omega chpt. 1990—). Home: 237 NW 100th Ave Plantation FL 33324-7060

PATTERSON, JEFFERY ALLEN, business owner; b. Albertville, Ala., Sept. 17, 1961; Children: Tamara Jesse, Madeline Paige and Victoria Autumn (twins). Founder, pres. Marshall County Young Dem., Albertville, 1996; exec. com. mem. Marshall County Democratic Club, 1999; Masons; v.p. Lions Club, Albertville, 1999, pres., 2000; mem. Albertville C. of C., Guntersville C. of C., Boaz C. of C., Sand Mt. Saddle Club, Beulah vol. Fire Dept., Marshall County Bd. of Realtors; Albertville Future Farmers of Amer. (pres. 1978-79); Marshall County Bd. of Realtors; pres. Albertville Jaycees, 2000; elected constable Marshall County, 1996; formed Marshall County Sheriffs Posse, CAP, 2000. Recipient Senate award, 1997, Alabama Jr. C. of C. Outstanding Young Alabamian award, 1998, commendation Marshall County Citizen of Yr. Com., 1997, Knights of Kings Heroes, DAR award, 1999. Home: 107 Auburn Ave Albertville AL 35951-7437 E-mail: jpatterson@go.com.

PATTERSON, JOHN DE LA ROCHE, JR. lawyer; b. Schenectady, N.Y., July 8, 1941; s. John de la Roche Sr. and Jane C. (Clay) P.; m. Michele F. Demarest, Nov. 28, 1987; children: Daniel C., Sara R., Amy C. BA, Johns Hopkins U., 1963; LLB, Harvard U., 1966. Bar: Mass. 1968. Vol. Peace Corps, Chad, 1966-67; assoc. Foley, Hoag & Eliot, Boston, 1967-73, ptnr., 1974—, exec. com., 1989-97. Chmn. Kodaly Ctr. Am. Inc., Newton, Mass., 1977-87. Mem. ABA, Boston Bar Assn. Democrat. Avocations: sailing, tennis, travel, reading. Office: Foley Hoag LLP 155 Seaport Blvd Boston MA 02210-E-mail: jpatters@fhe.com.

PATTERSON, JOHN KEITH, civil engineer, consultant; b. Homestead, Pa., Apr. 9, 1953; s. Charles Dewey and Rosemarie Joan (Cerveny) Patterson; m. Karen Marilyn Scibetta, June 17, 1972 (div. 1993); children: Eric, Erin; m. Donna Louise Bish, Oct. 9, 1994. AS in Gen. Studies, Community Coll. Allegheny County, Pitts., 1977; BSCE, U. Pitts., 1980. Registered profl. engr., Pa. Project engr. Urban Engrs. Inc., Erie, Pa., 1980-85, Lake Engring., Edinboro, 1985—. Mem.: ASCE (br. pres. 1988—90, br. bd. dirs. 1984—91, treas. 1992—), Erie Engring. Socs. Coun. (chmn. engring. week seminar 1990—2002, treas. 2001—). Democrat. Office: Lake Engring 140 Meadville St Edinboro PA 16412-2508

PATTERSON, JOSEPH FLANNER, JR. surgeon, anesthesiologist; b. New Bern, N.C., Feb. 12, 1917; MD, Harvard U., 1942. Diplomate Am. Bd. Surgery, Am. Bd. Anestesiology. Intern Abington (Pa.) Meml. Hosp., 1942-43; resident in neurol. surgery Med. Coll., Va., 1946-47; resident in surgery Lankenau Hosp., Phila., 1947-50; resident in anesthesiology N.C. Meml. Hops., Chapel Hill, 1961-63; fellow in anesthesiology Children's Hosp. Med. Ctr., Boston, 1963-64; staff anesthesiology dept. Balt. City Hosp., 1964-66, N.C. Meml. Hosp., Chapel Hill, 1966-77; surveyor Joint Commn. Accreditation Hosps., Chgo., 1978-90; prof. emeritus Univ. N.C., Chapel Hill, 1977—. Mem. Am. Acad. Pediat., Am. Soc. Anesthesiologists, N.C. Surg. Assn. E-mail: jpatfeb12@aol.com.

PATTERSON, LILLIAN STANTON, museum specialist; b. Alexandria, Va., June 22, 1927; d. N. Howard and Esther Naomi (Gray) Stanton; m. Edward Lloyd Patterson, June 27, 1956 (dec. Feb. 1979); children: Marilyn Esther Patterson Wilson, Valerie Lisa. BA in Social Studies, Storer Coll., 1950; postgrad., Am. U., 1951-52, U. Va., Alexandria, 1967, 69, 70. Cert. tchr., Va. Field dir. N.W. Fla. coun. Girl Scouts U.S., Pensacola, 1954-56; substitute tchr., 1952-67; travel counselor, mus. specialist City of Alexandria, 1976&; travel counselor Va. State Travel, 1981-82; state asst. to Congressman Stan Parris Alexandria, 1983-86; adminstrv. asst. McEnearney Assoc. Realtors, 1986-92; mus. specialist Alexandria Black History Resource Ctr., 1992—. Bd. dirs. Arlington (Va.) Vets. Meml. YMCA, Alexandria Civic Symphony Orch., Alexandria Cmty. Y, Alexandria Human Rels. Coun., Alexandria United Way, Project Discovery; bd. dirs., sec. Alexandria Vol. Bur.; v.p. MacArthur Sch. PTA; v.p., then pres. Alexandria Cmty. Mental Health Ctr. Adv. Bd.; pres. Quettes of No. Va.; charter mem., treas., v.p. Alexandria-Mt. Vernon chpt. Jack & Jill of Am., Inc.; pres. Semin. Civic Assn.; mem., ch. historian Shiloh Bapt. Ch. Recipient Outstanding Cmty. Svc. award United Way of Nat. Capitol Area, 1980, Cmty. Svc. award Hopkins House Assn., 1981, Cmty. Svc. award Alexandria Br. NAACP, 1998, Recipient Women-to-Women, Making a Difference award The Alexandria Commn. for Women Salute to Women Awards, 2001. Mem. Seminary Hill Assn., Inc. (bd. dirs.). Avocations: genealogy. Home: 1034 Woods Pl Alexandria VA 22302-3014 Office: Alexandria Black History Resource Ctr 638 N Alfred St Alexandria VA 22314-1823

PATTERSON, MADGE LENORE, elementary education educator; b. Vandergrift, Pa., Nov. 9, 1925; d. Paul Warren and Lucy Mae (Lemmon) Schaeffer; m. Stanley Clair Patterson, June 19, 1948 (dec.); 1 child, Stanley Kent. BS in Edn., Indiana State Tchrs. Coll., Pa., 1946, MEd, 1971. Elem. tchr. New Kensington (Pa.) Pub. Schs., 1946-49, Armstrong Sch. Dist. Schs., Ford City, Pa., 1951-52, kindergarten tchr., 1967-93, Rural Valley (Pa.) Presbyn. Ch., 1957-67; vol. tutor Adult Lit., Kittanning, Pa., 1993—; co-owner dairy farm. Sunday sch. tchr., choir mem., 1949—; sec. Rural Valley Presbyn. Ch. Women's Assn., 1988-92. Mem. NEA, Pa. Assn. Sch. Retirees, Clara Cockerille Reading Coun. (treas. 1994-98), Pa. State Edn. Assn., Internat. Reading Assn. (Literacy award 2000), Keystone Reading Assn., Assn. Early Childhood Edn., Rural Valley Bus. and Profl. Club, Women's Civic Club (Woman of Yr. 1994), Am. Assn. Ret. Persons, Rural Valley Grange (lectr.). Democrat. Avocations: dancing (line, square, ballroom), reading, camping, music, travel. Home: RR 2 Box 182 Dayton PA 16222-8813

PATTERSON, MARC CLAYTON, pediatric neurologist, researcher, educator; b. Brisbane, Queensland, Australia, Feb. 19, 1959; s. Rex and Constance Patterson; m. Robin Elizabeth Cook, May 5, 1984; children: Caitlin, Claire, Benjamin. MB, BS with honors, U. Queensland, 1981. Diplomate with spl. qualifications Am. Bd. Neurology, cert. in neurodevelopmental disabilities. Clin. lectr. in neurology U. Queensland, 1986-87; sr. clin. fellow in child neurology Mayo Clinic and Found., Rochester, Minn., 1988-90; vis. assoc. NIH, Bethesda, Md., 1990-92; spl. clin. fellow in pediat. Mayo Clinic and Found., 1993; asst. prof. neurology Mayo Med. Sch., Rochester, 1993—97, assoc. prof. neurology and pediat., 1997-2000; prof. clin. neurology and clin. pediat., dir. pediatric neurology Columbia U. Coll. Physicians and Surgeons, N.Y.C., 2001—. Mem. sci. adv. bd. Nat. Niemann-Pick Disease Found., Ft. Atkinson, 1991—, Ara Parseghian Med. Rsch. Found., Tucson, 1994; mem. med. adv. bd. CDG Family Network, Orangeville, Ill., 1997—; mem. profl. adv. bd. CVSA, Canal Winchester, Ohio, 1994—. Contbr. chapters to books, articles to profl. jours. Recipient Charles Mitford Lilley prize U. Queensland, 1981, Fulbright award U.S. Dept. of State, 1988. Fellow Royal Australasian Coll. Physicians (prize 1981); mem. Internat. Child Neurology Assn., Am. Acad. Neurology, Child Neurology Soc., Soc. for Study of Inborn Errors of Metabolism. Avocations: cycling, reading, music, travel, swimming. Office: Harkness Pavilion HP-542 180 Ft Washington Ave New York NY 10032-3791 Office Fax: 212-305-1253.

PATTERSON, MARIA JEVITZ, microbiology-pediatric infectious disease educator; b. Berwyn, Ill., Oct. 23, 1944; d. Frank Jacob and Edna Frances (Costabile) Jevitz; m. Ronald James Patterson, Aug. 22, 1970; children: Kristin Lara, Kier Nicole. BS in Med. Tech. summa cum laude, Coll. St. Francis, Joliet, Ill., 1966; PhD in Microbiology, Northwestern U., Chgo., 1970; MD, Mich. State U., 1984. Diplomate Am. Bd. Med. Examiners, Am. Bd. Pediatrics Gen. Pediatrics, Am. Bd. Pediatrics Infectious Diseases. Lab. asst., instr. med. microbiology for student nurses Med. Sch. Northwestern U., Chgo., 1966-70; postdoctoral fellow in clin. microbiology affiliated hosps. U. Wash., Seattle, 1971-72; asst. prof. microbiology and pub. health Mich. State U., East Lansing, 1972-77, assoc. prof., 1977-82, assoc. prof. pathology, 1979-82, lectr. dept. microbiology and pub. health, 1982-87, resident in pediatrics affiliated hosps., 1984-85, 86-87, clin. instr. dept. pediatrics and human devel., 1984-87, assoc. prof. microbiology-pub. health-pediatrics-human devel., 1987-90, prof., 1990—. Staff microbiologist dept. pathology Lansing Gen. Hosp., 1972-75; dir. clin. microbiology grad. program. Mich. State U., 1974-81, staff microbiologist, 1978-81; postdoctoral fellow in infectious diseases U. Mass. Med. Ctr., Worcester, 1985-86; asst. dir. pediatrics residency Grad. Med. Edn. Inc., Lansing, 1987-90; med. dir. Pediatrics Health Ctr. St. Lawrence Hosp., Lansing, Mich., 1987-90, Ingham Med. Ctr., 1990-94; cons. clin. microbiology Lansing Gen. Hosp., 1972-75, Mich. State U., 1976-82, Mich. Dept. Pub. Health, 1976—, Ingham County Health Dept., 1988—, Am. Health Cons., 1993, State of Mich. Atty. Gen. Office, 1994-98, Lansing Sch. Dist., 1998—, Mich. Antibiotic Residence Reduction, 1998—; cons. to editl. bd. Infection and Immunity, 1977, Mich. State U. AIDS Edn. Tng. Ctr, 2001—; presenter seminars. Contbg. author: Microbiology: Principles and Concepts, 1982, 4th edit., 1995, Pediatric Emergency Medicine, 1992, Principles and Practice of Emergency Medicine, 1997, Rudolph's Pediatrics, 2000; item writer certifying bd. examination Bd. Am. Acad. Pediats., 1990—, Am. Bd. Osteopathy, 1997—; contbr. articles to profl. jours. and publs. Mem. hon. com. Lansing AIDS Meml. Quilt, 1993. Recipient award for tchg. excellence Mich. State U. Coll. Osteo. Medicine, 1977, 78, 79, 80, 83, Disting. Faculty award Mich. State U., 1980, Woman Achiever award, 1985, excellence in pediatric residency tchg. award, 1988, Alumni Profl. Achievement award Coll. of St. Francis, 1991, excellence in diversity award Mich. State U., 2000, Weil Endowed Disting. Pediat. Faculty award, 2001; grantee renal disease divsn. Mich. Dept. Pub. Health 1976-82. Fellow Pediatric Infectious Diseases Soc., Infectious Diseases Soc. Am., Am. Acad. Pediatrics; mem. Am. Coll. Physician Execs., Am. Soc. Microbiology, Am. Soc. Clin. Pathologists (affiliate, bd. registrant), South Ctrl. Assn. Clin. Microbiology, Mich. Infectious Diseases Soc., N.Y. Acad. Scis., Kappa Gamma Pi, Lambda Iota Tau. Roman Catholic. Home: 1520 River Ter East Lansing MI 48823-5314 Office: Mich State Univ Microbiology/Pub Health East Lansing MI 48824-1101

PATTERSON, MARTHA ELLEN, artist, art educator; b. Anderson, Ind., Mar. 12, 1914; d. Clarence and Corrine Ringwald; m. John Downey, Nov. 27, 1935 (div. 1946); 1 child, Linda Carol; m. Raymond George Patterson, May 6, 1947. Student, Dayton Art Inst., Bendell Art Sch., Bradenton, Fla. Beauty operator WRENS, Springfield, Ohio, 1932-40; co-owner Park Ave. Gallery, Dayton; window decorator, art tchr. Tchr. art; judge art shows. One-woman shows Springfield (Ohio) Mus. Art, 1998, as well as N.C.R. Country Club, Bill Turner Interiors, U. Dayton, High Street Gallery, Trails End Club, The Designerie, Riverbend Park, Statesman Club, State Fidelity Bank, Wegerzyn Hort. Ctr., Pebble Springs, Backstreet, First City Fed. Bank, Bradenton, Fla., Alley Gallery, Merrill Lynch, Miami U., Gem. City Bank, Dayton, Ohio, Winters Bank, Dayton, Sherwin Williams, Howard Johnsons, Dayton Woman's Club, Bergamo, Dayton Meml. Hall, Bob and Arts, Del Park Med. Soc., The Dayton Country Club, Christ Methodist Ch., Unitarian Ch., The Metropolitan, Rikes, Dr. Pavey's, Dr. Chaney's, Dayton Convention Ctr., The Yum Yum, Jan Strunk Interiors, Park Avenue Gallery, Ohio Mus. of Art, Springfield, 1997; artist: (water colors, oils, acylics, inks and pastels) group exhbns. include: Dayton Art Inst., Meml. Hall of Dayton, Dayton Country Club, Bergamo, Women's Club of Dayton, Am. Watercolor Soc., Sarasota Art Ctr., Art League of Manatee County, Butler Inst., Riverbend Park, First City Fed., NCR Country Club, Springfield (Ohio) Mus., Longboat Key Art Ctr., others; represented in permanent collections of Mr. and Mrs. Richard Nixon, Virginia Graham, Les Brown, Paul Lynde, Air Force Mus. at Wright Patterson, U. Dayton-Ohio, Dr. Stephen House, Doug Yeager and others. Vol. Christian Woman's Soc. of Am., Twig Children's Hosp., Dayton, The Utopians; mem. Tri Art Dayton, Long Boat Key Art Ctr., Fla. Recipient first prize Dayton Soc. Painters and Sculptors Show Rikes, First Prize, 1976, 77, First Prize, Best in Show, 1978, Beavercreek Art Assn. First Place, Best in Show, Artist and Sculpture Yearly Show, 1966, 68 2d place, Dayton Art Inst. 2d prize, Tri County Hon. Mention, Walker Motor Sales 2d place, Bendell Art Gallery 2d and 3d, Montgomery County Fair Best in Show. Mem. Art League of Manatee County (Fla.), Nat. Mus. Women in Art, Am. Watercolor Soc., Springfield Mus. Art, Dayton Soc. Painters, Long Boat Key Art League, Tri Art. Republican. Methodist. Avocations: art mus., books, music, travel, gourmet cooking. Home: 3853 Lawrenceville Dr Springfield OH 45504-4459

PATTERSON, MICHAEL MILTON, neuropsychologist, educator; b. Muscatine, Iowa, Mar. 17, 1942; s. Harvey Milton and Vivienne Doris Ann (Bridgeman) P.; m. Janice Pauline Ficke, June 11, 1966; children: Michael Shane, Shad Milton. BA, Grinnell (Iowa) Coll., 1964; PhD, U. Iowa, 1969. Postdoctoral fellow U. Calif., Irvine, 1969-71; from asst. to assoc. prof. Kirksville (Mo.) Coll. of Osteo. Medicine, 1971-77; assoc. prof., prof. Ohio U Coll. Osteopathy, Athens, 1977-93, dir. rsch., prof. dept. psychology, 1977-90; prof., dir. basic sci. rsch. Coll. Osteo. Medicine U. Health Scis., Kansas City,

Mo., 1993-2000; prof. Nova Southeastern U. Coll. Osteo. Medicine, Ft. Lauderdale, Fla., 2000—. Editor: Bioelectric Recording, 1974, Jour. Am. Osteo. Assn., Chgo., 1988—; contbr. articles to profl. jours. Scoutmaster Boy Scouts Am., Athens, 1982-92; trustee 1st Christian Ch., Athens, 1990-93, Parkville, Mo., 1994-2000 Fellow APA, Am. Psychol. Soc.; mem. Am. Acad. Osteo. (life, vis. scholar Indpls. 1990—), Soc. for Neurosci., Rotary (bd. dirs. Athens 1991-93, Parkville 1995-2000), Sigma Sigma Phi, Sigma Pi. Avocations: mechanics, camping, reading. Home: 237 NW 100th Ave Plantation FL 33324 Office: Nova Southeastern U Coll Osteo Medicine Fort Lauderdale FL 33128-2015

PATTERSON, MILDRED LUCAS, retired teaching specialist; b. Winston-Salem, N.C., Jan. 24, 1937; d. James Arthur and Lula Mae (Smith) Lucas; m. James Harrison Patterson Jr., Mar. 31, 1961; children: James Harrison III, Roger Lindsay. BA, Talladega Coll., 1958; MEd, St. Louis U., 1969; postgrad., Webster U., 1970. Classroom tchr. Winston-Salem (N.C.) Pub. Schs., 1959-61, St. Louis Bd. Edn., 1961-72, reading specialist, 1972-88, co-host radio reading show, 1988-91; tchr. specialist Reading to Achieve Motivational Program, St. Louis, 1991-99; ret., 1999—. Bd. dirs. Supt.'s Adv. Com., University City, Mo., 1994—; presenter Chpt. I Regional Conf. Co-author: Wearing Purple, 1996. Bd. dirs. Gateway Homes, St. Louis, 1989-93; mem. com. University City Sch. Bond Issue, 1994; mem. Univ. City Arts and Letters Commn., 1998-99. Recipient Letter of Commendation, Chpt. I. Regional Conf., 1991, Founders' award Gamma Omega chpt. Alpha Kappa Alpha, 1985. Mem. Internat. Reading Assn. (Broadcast Media award for radio 1990, Bldg. Rep. award St. Louis chpt. 1990). Avocations: reading, arts and crafts, storytelling, motivational speaking. E-mail: mildred9@bellsouth.net.

PATTERSON, OSCAR, III, university program administrator; b. July 25, 1945; s. Oscar Jr. and Frances (Killian) P.; m. Kathy E. Gibson, June 6, 1966 (div. Apr. 1979); 1 child, Elizabeth Anne Patterson Cassel; m. Julie Ann Holmes, Dec. 28, 1990. BA, Pfeiffer U., 1967; MFA, U. Ga., 1973; PhD, U. Tenn., 1982. Asst. prof. architecture and fine arts Auburn (Ala.) U., 1972-75; chairperson BFA in Theatre program Western Carolina U., Cullowhee, N.C., 1975-79; dir. telecom. U. N.C., Pembroke, 1984-88; chair comm. and visual arts U. North Fla., Jacksonville, 1998—. Juvenile probation officer Cleveland Ct. Sys., Shelby, N.C., 1967-68; gen. mgr., news dir. WNCP-TV, N.C., 1984-98. Contbr. articles to profl. jours.; host pub. tv program, 1989-98. U.S. Army, 1968-75, Vietnam. Mem. AEJMC, Soc. Profl. Journalists, Phi Kappa Phi. Republican. Avocations: historical reenactment, beach exploration. Home: 248 Patrick Mill Cir Ponte Vedra Beach FL 32082-4013 E-mail: opatters@unf.edu.

PATTERSON, PATRICIA LYNN, applied mathematician, physicist, inventor; b. Kearny, N.J., Feb. 25, 1946; AA, St. Petersburg (Fla.) Jr. Coll., 1965; BA magna cum laude in Physics, U. South Fla., Tampa, 1966; MS in Geophys. Scis., Ga. Inst. Tech., Atlanta, 1976; PhD in Geophysics, Ga. Inst. Tech., 1980. Elec. engr. Burns & McDonnell Engrng. Co., Miami, Fla., 1967-69; tchr. biology and physiology Orange County Bd. Edn., Orlando, 1969-70; acoustical cons. Bolt Beranek & Newman Inc., Downers Grove, Ill., 1971-72; geophysicist Exxon Co., U.S.A., New Orleans, 1976-77; comm. systems engr. E-Systems, St. Petersburg, Fla., 1980-85; pres. Solitonics (Rsch. & Cons.), Clearwater, 1985—; image-processing engr. E-Systems, Garland, Tex., 1991-93. Contbr. articles to profl. jours. and confs.; patentee in field. Recipient Sigma Xi research awards, 1977, 81, others; Ga. Inst. Tech. Pres.'s fellow. Mem. IEEE (reviewer tech. papers), Bioelectromagnetics Soc., Am. Geophys. Union, Engrng. in Medicine and Biology Soc. Achievements include research in remote sensing and image processing, biophysics, nonlinear systems, data compression, coding and information theory, numerical modeling and parallel distributed processing. Avocations: U.S. Masters swimming competitor, holder of 2 state records Fla. Sr. Games, 4 records in Good Life Games; past ranked in top-10 in U.S. for Butterfly.

PATTERSON, PATRICIA LYNNE, artist, educator; b. June 13, 1946; BA in Visual Arts, Chatham Coll., 1996; cert. in art edn., Carlow Coll., 1999, postgrad., 1999—. Owner/operator Pat's Deli, Someplace Else, Butler, Pa., 1981-90; instr. Butler County C.C., 1984-88; tchr. Seneca Valley Schs., 1997—. Cons., pub. spkr., Butler, 1978—. Exhibited paintings in numerous shows, 1992—; co-author: (play) A Whole New Ballgame, 1994. Stephen min., mem. choir St. Andrews Presbyn. Ch., 1988—; v.p. bd. dirs. Downtown Butler Assn.; bd. dirs. YWCA, Soroptomists, Christian Conciliation Svc., Butler, 1984—92, Grapevine Ctr. (Mental Health Assn. of Butler), 1999—2000, Associated Artists of Butler County. Recipient Disting. Svc. award Butler C. of C., 1986. Mem. Nat. Art Educators Assn. Home: 118 Germaine Rd Butler PA 16001-1917

PATTERSON, PAULA JEANNE, secondary education educator; b. Sewickley, Pa., June 13, 1944; d. James Enos and Jeanne Pauline (Watts) Stanyard; m. John J. Patterson, Apr. 6, 1968; children: Barry Jay, Mandee Jeanne. BA, Geneva Coll., 1966; MEd, Kent State U., 1985. Tchr. East Liverpool (Ohio) Schs., 1966-68, Bradford Middle Sch., Starke, Fla., 1968-70, Bohemia Manor H.S., Chesapeake City, Md., 1970-72, Crestview Local H.S., Columbiana, Ohio, 1974—. Mem. early English composition assessment com. Crestview Schs./YSU, Columbiana, 1989-94; mem. prin.'s adv. com. Crestview High, Columbiana, 1995-97. Sec. East Palestine (Ohio) Band Parents, 1988-90; sec. stewardship com. First Presbyn. Ch., East Palestine, 1992-95; bldg. improvement com. Crestview H.S., 1998—. Recipient Best Practices award, 2001, 02, STAR Tchr. award, 2000, 02; Martha Holden Jennings scholar, 1987, 93. Mem. NCTE, OCTELA, NEA, Ohio Edn. Assn., Crestview Edn. Assn. (sec.), Am. Legion Aux., Phi Delta Kappa, Delta Kappa Gamma. Avocations: reading, gardening. Home: 1851 SR 165 East Palestine OH 44413

PATTERSON, RICHARD NORTH, novelist, writer, lawyer; b. Berkeley, Calif., Feb. 22, 1947; s. Richard Wallace and Marjorie Frances (North) P.; m. Laurie Anderson, Apr. 13, 1993; children: Shannon Heath, Brooke North, Adam Chandler, Chase Kenyon, Katherine Jeanne Blunt, Stephen Thomas Blunt. BA History, Ohio Wesleyan U., 1968; JD, Case Western Reserve, 1971. Bar: Ohio, 1971, D.C., 1973, Ala., 1975, Calif., 1984. Asst. atty. gen. State of Ohio, 1971-73; with divsn. enforcement SEC, Washington, 1973-75, San Francisco, 1878-81; assoc. atty. Berkowitz, Lefkovits & Patrick, Birmingham, Ala., 1975-77, ptnr., 1978; assoc. McCutchen, Doyle, Brown & Enerson, San Francisco, 1985-87, ptnr., 1987-93, of counsel, 1993-94. Author: The Lasko Tangent, 1979, The Outside Man, 1981, Escape the Night, 1983, Private Screening, 1985, Degree of Guilt, 1993, Eyes of a Child, 1995, The Final Judgement, 1995, Silent Witness, 1997, No Safe Place, 1998, Dark Lady, 1999, Protect and Defend, 2000. Trustee Ohio Wesleyan U.; mem. regional panel for the selection of White House fellows; bd. dirs. Family Violence Prevention Fund, Common Cause, Brady Campaign to Prevent Gun Violence, National Partnership for Women and Families. Named Man of Yr., WWRAP, 2001; recipient Edgar Allan Poe award for best 1st novel, Mystery Writers Am., 1979, Grand Prix de Literateur Policiere, 1995, Pres.'s award for Disting. Alumni, Case Western Res. U., 1997, Maggie award, Planned Parenthood, 2001.

PATTERSON, RICKEY LEE, clergyman; b. Indpls., Sept. 24, 1952; s. William Irving and Wanda (Calbert) P.; m. Sharon Rose Leonard, May 4, 1974; children: Rachel L., Rickey L. BA, Ind. U., 1976; postgrad., U. Miami, 1976-80; ThM, Internat. Bible Inst. and Sem., 1983; ThD, Christian Leadership U., 1995; PhD, Miami Christian U., 1997. Pres. Pat-Cat Enterprises, Inc., Miami, 1977-81; pastor, 1972—; founder, pres. Jesus Students Fellowship, Inc., 1973—; pastor, 1979—; radio broadcast spkr., 1978—; dir. J.S.F. Cassette Ministries, 1978—; pres. Jesus Fellowship, Inc., 1981—, Miami Christian U., 1982—; with Metanet Mktg. Grp., Inc., 1993—; ceo Churches Dot Network, 1995—, Christian Internet Radio Network, 1996—, Christian Internet TV Network, 1997—. Ordained to minstry Internat. Conv. Faith Chs. and Ministers, Inc., 1980; coll. unit dir., Northwestern Mutual Life Ins. Co., Milw., 1980-83; founder, supt. Jesus fellowship Christian Sch., 1983—, CEO, pres., Metanet Mktg. Grp., Inc., pres. Dade County Pvt. Sch. Sys., Inc., 1983—; instr. Bible, Ind. U., 1973-76; instr. Bible, U. Miami, 1976—, also guest lectr., dept. religion; pres. Miami Bible Inst., 1984—, pres., Christian Internet Radio; guest lectr. Miami North Community Correctional Ctr., Dade County Correctional Inst., Fed. Inst. Corrections; adv. Miami chpt. Women Aglow, 1980-82; campus minister Ind. U., Miami, Fla. internat. U., Miami-Dade C.C., U. P.R.; exec. bd. mem. Internat. Congress of Local Chs., 1988—; dir. Christian Benefactor, 1990—, charter mem. Rep. Presdl. Task Force; sustaining mem. Rep. Nat. Com.; bd. govs. Am. Coalition Traditional Values, 1984—. Mem. Bur. Bus. Practice, Aircraft Owners and Pilots Assn., Nat. Audubon Soc., Am. Entrepreneurs Assn., Inst. Cert. Fin. Planners, Am. Security Counc., U.S. Senatorial Club, Zool. Soc. Fla., Adult Congregate Living Facility (pres. Naples chpt. 1988-90), Christian Booksellers Assn., Nat. Assn. Life Underwriters, Am. Mktg. Assn., Full Gospel Businessman's Fellowship Internat. Coalition of Local Chs. (mem. exec. bd. 1988-99), Ind. U. Alumni Assn., Sigma Pi. Editor: Spirit of Life Mag., 1980-82; chief editor: Miami Jour., 1984—. Home and Office: 9775 SW 87th Ave Miami FL 33176-2954

PATTERSON, ROBERT ARTHUR, physician, health care consultant, retired health care company executive, retired air force officer; b. Palestine, Ill., Sept. 3, 1915; s. Robert Bruce and Nera (McColpin) P.; m. Judith Scheirer, May 15, 1961; children: Mary Kay, Elaine Alice Mills, Robert Arthur II, Victoria Patterson Goodrum. Student, U. Ill., 1933-35; MD, U. Louisville, 1939. Diplomate: aerospace medicine Am. Bd. Preventive Medicine. Intern Detroit Receiving Hosp., 1939-40; joined Mich. N.G., 1940; commd. USAAF, 1946; advanced through grades to lt. gen. USAF, 1972; rated chief flight surgeon and command pilot; assigned U.S. and ETO, 1940-45; assigned U.S., Spain, Japan, Philippines, 1945-63; dep. dir. plans and hospitalization Office Surgeon Gen., USAF, Washington, 1963-65, dir. plans and hospitalization, 1965-68; surgeon Hdqrs. USAFE, Lindsey Air Sta., Germany, 1968-71, Hdqrs. SAC, Offutt AFB, 1971-72; surgeon gen. USAF, 1972-75, ret., 1975; health care cons. Arlington, Va., 1975; sr. v.p. sci. affairs Baxter Travenol Labs., Inc., Deerfield, Ill., 1976-86, health care cons., 1987—. Decorated D.S.M. with oak leaf cluster, Legion of Merit with two oak leaf clusters, Air Force Commendation medal; recipient citation of honor Air Force Assn., citation of distinction Fed. Hosp. Execs., citation of distinction Am. Hosp. Assn. Fellow Am. Coll. Preventive Medicine, Aerospace Medicine Assn., Am. Coll. Physician Execs. (founder); mem. Assn. Mil. Surgeons (pres. 1972), AMA, Am. Acad. Med. Dirs., Ret. Officers Assn., Soc. Mil. Cons. to Armed Forces, Soc. Armed Forces Med. Labs. Scis., NIH Alumni, U. Ill. Alumni Assn., Aircraft Owners and Pilots Assn., Order Daedalians, Assn. for Advancement of Med. Instrumentation, Exptl. Aircraft Assn., Deutsch Kurzhaar Verband, N.A. Versatile Hunting Dog Assn., Uniformed Services U. Health Scis. Alumni Assn., Air Safety Found., Mid-America (Chgo.), Cen. Fla. Conservation and Hunt (Lake Wales, Fla.), Yacht and Country (bd. govs., 1993-95, pres., 1996-97, Stuart, Fla.), Sunshine Gun, Yacht (Stuart), Willoughby Golf Club (Stuart). Home and Office: Yacht & Country Club 3474 SE Fairway E Stuart FL 34997-6160

PATTERSON, ROBERT CAMPBELL, JR. civil engineer; b. Sharon, Pa., May 2, 1966; s. Robert Campbell and Maxine Evelyn (Dickey) P.; m. Patricia Stapley Wagner, May 31, 1997. BS in Civil Engrng., U. Pitts., 1989; MS in Civil Engrng., Youngstown State U., 1996. Registered profl. engr., Pa., N.C. Hwy. constrn. inspector T.W. Cons., Pitts., 1989; staff engr. Kurtanich Engrs. & Assocs., Inc., Hermitage, Pa., 1990-93; project engr. Consumers Pa. Water Co., Sharon, 1995-97; engr. II City of Burlington, N.C., 1997—. Recipient grad. scholarship Youngstown State Grad. Sch., 1995. Mem. ASCE (bd. dirs. Pitts. sect., N.W. Br., 1995-97, v.p. 1996-97, pres. 1997, sec.-treas. no. br. N.C. sect. 1999-2000, 150th Anniversary champion N.C. sect. 1999—), NSPE, Am. Water Works Assn., Kiwanis. Home: 365 S Sixty Ct Graham NC 27253-9463 Office: City of Burlington Engrng Dept 425 S Lexington Ave Burlington NC 27215-4200 Fax: 336 222-5018. E-mail: bpatterson@ci.burlington.nc.us.

PATTERSON, ROBERT EDWARD, lawyer; b. Los Angeles, Sept. 14, 1942; s. Ellis Elwood and Helen (Hjelte) P.; m. Christina Balboni, Oct. 2, 1971; 1 child, Victor Ellis. BA, UCLA, 1964; JD, Stanford U., 1972, grad. bus. exec. program, 1986; vis. scholar, Amos Tuck Sch. Dartmouth Coll., 1998. Bar: Calif. 1972. Ptnr. Squire Sanders & Dempsey LLP, Palo Alto, Calif., 1972—. Bd. dirs. Procyte Corp., Peninsula Equity Ptnrs., Foster Ctr. for Pvt. Equity, Amos Tuck Sch., Dartmouth Coll., Sumida Corp., HK Pharmaceuticals, Inc, Synzyme Techs., LLC, Wealth Cycle Inc., Acuity Ventures; mem. adv. bd. Borealis Ventures. Served to lt. comdr. USN, 1964-69. Mem. Rotary, Palo Alto Club, Menlo Circus Club, Bohemian Club, Band of Angels. Democrat. Office: Squire Sanders & Dempsey 600 Hansen Way Ste 100 Palo Alto CA 94304-1043 E-mail: rpatterson@ssd.com.

PATTERSON, ROBERT EUGENE, insurance company executive; b. Lancaster, Pa., June 13, 1932; s. Blanchard S. and Lydia L. (Wert) P.; m. Dorothy J. Shenk, May 26, 1951; children: Craig Robert, Tracy Ann. BS in Econs. magna cum laude, Franklin and Marshall Coll., 1959; postgrad., Temple U., 1960, Harvard U., 1977. CPA, D.C. With Armstrong World Industries, Lancaster, 1950-69, Hamilton Watch Co., Lancaster, 1969-71; v.p. fin., treas. K-D Mfg. Co., 1971-76, dir., officer and dir. subs., 1972-76; sr. v.p. fin., CFO, Blue Shield, Camp Hill, Pa., 1976-95, sr. v.p. cons., 1996-97; chief investment officer Commonwealth of Pa., 1997—. Vice chmn., sec., corp. sec., bd. dirs. Healthguard of Lancaster, Inc.; bd. dirs. Millerville Univ. Found. Served with U.S. Army, 1952-54. Mem. Fin. Execs. Inst. (chpt. pres., area dir., nat. v.p.), Inst. Mgmt. Accts., AICPAs, Pa. Soc. CPAs, Meadia Heights Country Club, Hamilton Club. Episcopalian. Office: Commonwealth of PA Treasury Dept 121 Finance Building Harrisburg PA 17120-0018

PATTERSON, ROBERT HUDSON, research library consultant; b. Alexandria, La., Dec. 11, 1936; s. Hubert Hudson and Beth (Jones) P.; m. Diana E. Sellers; 1 child, Jennifer Bookhart Peters. BA, Millsaps Coll., Jackson, Miss., 1958; MA, Tulane U., 1963; M.L.S., U. Calif., Berkeley, 1965. Mem. profl. staff Tulane U. Libr., New Orleans, 1965-69, 73-76, asst. dir. collection devel., 1973-76; head spl. collections cataloging U. Tex., Austin, 1970-73; dir. librs. U. Wyo., Laramie, 1976-81, U. Tulsa, 1981-98. Chmn. exec. bd. Wyo. State Libr. Adv. Com., 1976-81; mem. bd. Okla. State Libr. Adv. Com., 1981-84; mem. adv. coun. Bibliog. Ctr. for Rsch., Denver, 1978-81; past mem. exec. bd. S.E. La. Libr. Network; bd. dirs. Amigos Bibliog. Coun., 1983-86; cons. NEH, Harry Ransom Humanities Rsch. Ctr., U. Tex., Austin. Editor Conservation Adminstrn. News, 1979-93; contbr. articles to profl. jours. Pres. Western Conservation Congress, 1981-82. Sr. fellow CLR/UCLA, 1989. Fellow Internat. Boswell Inst.; mem ALA (various offices), Okla. Libr. Assn. (various offices). E-mail: rpatterson1@austin.rr.com.

PATTERSON, ROBERT PORTER, JR. federal judge; b. N.Y.C., July 11, 1923; s. Robert Porter and Margaret (Winchester) P.; m. Bevin C. Daly, Sept. 15, 1956; children: Anne, Robert, Margaret, Paul, Katherine. AB, Harvard U., 1947; LLB, Columbia U., 1950. Bar: N.Y. 1951, D.C. 1966. Law clk. Donovan, Leisure, Newton & Lumbard, N.Y.C., 1950-51; asst. counsel N.Y. State Crime Commn. Waterfront Investigation, 1952-53; asst. U.S. atty. Chief of Narcotics Prosecutions and Investigations, 1953-56; asst. counsel Senate Banking and Currency Com., 1954; assoc. Patterson, Belknap, Webb & Tyler, N.Y.C., 1956-60, ptnr., 1960-88; judge U.S. Dist. Ct. (so. dist.) N.Y., 1988—. Counsel to minority select com. pursuant to house resolution no. 1, Washington, 1967; mem. Senator's Jud. Screening Panel, 1974-88, Gov.'s Jud. Screening Panel, 1975-82, Gov.'s Sentencing Com., 1978-79. Contbr. articles to profl. jours. Chmn. Wm. T. Grant Found., 1974-94, Prisoners' Legal Services N.Y., 1976-88; dir. Legal Aid Soc., 1961-88, pres., 1967-71; chmn. Nat. Citizens for Eisenhower, 1959-60, Scranton for Pres., N.Y. State, 1964; bd. mgrs. Havens Relief Fund Soc., 1994—, Millbrook Sch., 1966-78, Vera Inst. Justice, 1981-99, New Sch. for Social Rsch., 1986-94, George C. Marshall Found., 1987-93; mem. exec. com. Lawyers Com. for Civil Rights Under Law, 1968-88; mem. Goldman Panel for Attica Disturbance, 1972, Temporary Commn. on State Ct. System, 1971-73, Rockefeller U. Council, 1986-88, exec. com. N.Y. Vietnam Vets. Meml. Commn., 1982-85, Mayor's Police Adv. Com., 1985-87. Served to capt. USAAF, 1942-46. Decorated D.F.C. with cluster, Air medal with clusters. Mem. ABA (ho. of dels. 1976-80), N.Y. State Bar Assn. (pres. 1978-79), Assn. Bar City N.Y. (v.p. 1974-75), N.Y. County Lawyers Assn., Am. Law Inst., Am. Judicature Soc. (bd. dirs. 1979). Republican. Episcopalian. Home: Fair Oaks Farm 1657 Route 9D Cold Spring NY 10516-3543 Office: US Dist Ct So Dist NY US Court House 500 Pearl St New York NY 10007-1316

PATTERSON, ROGER LEWIS, psychologist; b. Opelika, Ala., Oct. 30, 1939; s. Homer Lee and Ruby (White) P.; m. Maritza Nunez de Gracia, Dec. 21, 1967; children: Anne Marie, Richard Allen. BA, Auburn U., 1963, MS, 1965; PhD, Fla. State U., 1971. Coord. clin. rsch. Camarillo/UCLA Rsch. Unit, 1969-72; psychologist and dir. day treatment Mental Health Ctr. of Escambia County, Pensacola, Fla., 1972-73; psychology U. Ala. and Montgomery Police Dept., 1974-75; prof. faculty Fla. Mental Health Inst., Tampa, 1975-84, prof., chmn. dept. aging and mental health, 1977-84; adj. assoc. prof. dept. psychology U. South Fla., 1977-84, clin. assoc. prof. dept. psychiatry Coll. Medicine, 1982-84; assoc. project dir. Suncoast Gerontology Ctr., 1984; dir. geriatric psychosocial rehab. program VA Med. Ctr., Tuskegee, Ala., 1984-86; clin. coord. combined adult day healthcare and day treatment VA Outpatient Clinic, Daytona Beach, Fla., 1986—. Internat. speaker in field. Author, editor books; contbr. chpts. to books, articles to profl. jours. Mem. APA, Am. Bd. Med. Psychotherapists (profl. adv. coun.), Behavior Therapy and Rsch. Soc. (clin. fellow). Office: VA Outpatient Clinic 1900 Mason Ave Daytona Beach FL 32117-5103 E-mail: rpatterson@rr.cfl.com.

PATTERSON, RONALD PAUL, publishing company executive, clergyman; b. Ashland, Ohio, Dec. 4, 1941; s. Donald Edward and Mildred (Niswender) P.; m. Marlene Pfahler, Sept. 1, 1962; children: Paul Edward, Mark Loren. BA, Malone Coll., 1963; MDiv, United Theol. Sem., Dayton, Ohio, 1967; MA, Syracuse U., 1970; DD, Cen. Meth. Coll., 1988. Ordained to ministry United Methodist Ch., 1967. Editor youth publs. Otterbein Press, Dayton, 1964-68; assoc. editor The Upper Room, Nashville, 1970-74; editor Word Books, Waco, Tex., 1974-77; editorial dir. Abingdon Press, Nashville, 1977-88; book editor United Meth. Ch. Pub. House, 1977-88, v.p., 1984-88, sr. editor Ch. Resources, 1988-92; pub., CEO United Meth. Reporter, Dallas, 1992—. V.p. Religious Pub. Rels. Coun. Nashville, 1970-74; jr. coll. instr. creative writing, Waco; leader writers' workshops Author: (with others) The Kyle Rote Story, 1975; editor: Come On, Let's Pray, 1972; compiler: The Coming of Easter, 1973; founding editor Alive Now! devotional publ.; editorial dir. Quar. Rev., 1980-87; contbr. articles to mags. Tchr. Tenn. State Prison, Nashville, 1984-88; mem. exec. bd. Perkins Sch. Theology, 1996—; charter mem. Perkins Circle. Recipient George Washington Honor medal Nat. Freedom Found., Valley Forge, Pa., 1960, Paul M. Hinkhouse award Religious Pub. Relations Council, N.Y.C., 1973; named one of Outstanding Young Men Am., 1972. Mem. Am. Acad. Religion, Religion Pub. Group, Christian Publs. Assn., Southeastern Pubs. Assn. (exec. com. 1985-88), Pubs. Assn. of South (treas.), Evang. Christian Pubs. Assn. (bd. dirs. 1987-88), Protestant Ch.-owned Pubs. Assn. (bd. dirs., chmn. biennial planning com. 1999—), Internat. Pubs. Assn. World Meth. Coun., Hogan Quality Roundtable (Dallas), CEO Inst., Dallas Press, Rotary. Democrat. Methodist. Avocations: cycling, refinishing furniture, golf. Home: 1563 Waterside Ct Dallas TX 75218-4488 Office: 2400 Lone Star Dr Dallas TX 75212-6309

PATTERSON, RONALD R(OY), health care systems executive; b. Baton Rouge, Mar. 4, 1942; BS, U. Houston, 1965; MS, Trinity U., San Antonio, 1973. Asst. adminstr. Med. Br. Tex. U., Galveston, 1972-75; asst. v.p. Hosp. Affiliates Internat., Nashville, 1975-81; chief oper. officer Affiliated Hosp. Systems, Houston, 1981-82; sr. v.p. Republic Health Corp., Dallas, 1982-88; pres. Miller Patterson Inc., Plano, Tex., 1988-89; ind. healthcare mgmt. cons., 1989-90; sr. v.p. Harris Meth. Health System, Ft. Worth, 1990-91; exec. v.p., COO Champion Healthcare Corp., Houston, 1991-96; exec. v.p., pres. healthcare ops. Paracelsus Healthcare Corp., 1996-99; pres. R. Patterson Assocs., Inc., 1999—. Bd. dirs. Tarrant County Hosp. Dist., 2001—. Fellow Am. Coll. Healthcare Execs., Tex. Hosp. Assn. (vice chmn. multi-hosp. constituency 1987), Fedn. Am. Health Sys. (bd. govs. 1996-99, bd. dirs. 1997-99, sec. 1997-99). Avocation: photography. Office: R Patterson Assocs Inc PO Box 1826 Keller TX 76244-1826

PATTERSON, SALLY JANE, government affairs consultant; b. Ontario, Calif., May 28, 1948; d. James Lowell and Barbara Verle (Griffin) Swain; 1 child, Robert Elias Sandoval. BA, Calif. State U., Fullerton, 1970, MA, 1974. Adminstrv. asst. Congressman Jerry Patterson, U.S. House of Reps., Washington, 1978-81; v.p. Pub. Response Assocs., 1981-87, Hamilton & Staff, Washington, 1987-90; v.p. pub. affairs Planned Parenthood Fedn. of Am., N.Y.C., 1990-93; internat. cons. Mgmt. Systems Internat., Washington, 1993—; v.p. Wagner & Assocs. Pub. Affairs Cons., Inc., N.Y.C., Washington, 1994-99; pres. Radiant Comms. Inc., 2000—. Cons. Nat. Dem. Inst., Washington, 1994—. Author: Supporting Democracy in The Newly Independent States of The Former Soviet Union, 1994, Women in Government Relations: 20 Years of Vision, Leadership, Education and Networking, 1995, Pursuing a Paradox: Public Attitudes vs. Public Action on Campaign Finance Reform, How does Congress Approach Population and Family Planning Issues?, 1999. Trainer Nat. Women's Campaign Fund. Recipient Gold Key award PR Soc. Am., 1992; named one of 74 Women Shaping Am. Politics, Campaigns and Elections, 1993. Mem. Women in Govt. Rels., Inc. (disting. mem., chair leader found. 1985-87, v.p. 1987-88, pres. 1988-89), Coun. Excellence in Govt. (prin.), NARAL (chair, bd. dirs.). Democrat. Episcopalian. Office: Radiant Comms Inc 2121 K St NW Ste 800 Washington DC 20037-1829

PATTERSON, SAMUEL CHARLES, political science educator; b. Omaha, Nov. 29, 1931; s. Robert Foster and Garnet Marie (Jorgensen) P.; m. Suzanne Louise Dean, June 21, 1956; children— Polly Ann, Dean Foster, Grier Edmund BA, U. S.D., 1953; MS, U. Wis., 1956, PhD, 1959. Asst. prof. polit. sci. Okla. State U., Stillwater, 1959-61; asst. prof. U. Iowa, Iowa City, 1961-64, assoc. prof., 1964-67, prof., 1967-85, Roy J. Carver prof., 1985-86; prof. Ohio State U., Columbus, 1986-98, prof. emeritus, 1998—. Vis. prof. U. Wis., 1962, U. Okla., 1968-78, U. Essex, Colchester, Eng., 1969-70, U. S.D., 2001. Author: (with others) Representatives and Represented, 1975, A More Perfect Union, 4th edit., 1989; co-author: The Legislative Process in the United States, 4th edit., 1986, Comparing Legislatures, 1979; editor: American Legislative Behavior, 1968; co-editor: Comparative Legislative Behavior: Frontiers of Research, 1972, Handbook of Legislative Research, 1985, Political Leadership in Democratic Societies, 1991, Parliaments in the Modern World, 1994, Great Theatre: The American Congress in the 1990s, 1998, Senates: Bicameralism in the Contemporary World, 1999; editor Am. Jour. Polit. Sci., 1970-73; co-editor Legis. Studies Quar., 1981-85; mng. editor Am. Polit. Sci. Rev., 1985-91. Served with U.S. Army, 1953-55 Recipient Disting. Scholar award Ohio State U., 1990; fellow social Sci. Rsch. Coun., 1961, 67, Guggenheim, 1984-85; vis. fellow Brookings Instn., 1984-85, Ctr. Advanced Study in Behavioral Scis., 1993-94; Fulbright Bologna chair, 1995. Mem. Internat. Polit. Sci. Assn., Am. Polit. Sci. Assn. (Frank J. Goodnow award, 2000), Midwest Polit. Sci. Assn. (pres. 1980-81), Phi Beta Kappa, Phi Kappa Phi, Pi Sigma Alpha. Office: Ohio State U Dept Polit Sci 2140 Derby Hall 154 N Oval Mall Columbus OH 43210-1330 E-mail: patpat851@aol.com.

PATTERSON, SCOTT PAUL, civil engineer, consultant; b. Coronado, Calif., Mar. 5, 1948; s. Warren Nelson and Mary Lemoyne (Herbert) P.; m. Jane Pocoroba, Apr. 23, 1972; children: Christopher, Timothy, Sara, Joanna. BSCE, U. Cin., 1971. Lic. profl. engr., 3 states; lic. gen. contractor, Fla. Asst. engr. Ebasco Svcs., N.Y.C., 1971-72; project engr. Conduit and Found. Corp., Elmwood Park, N.J., 1972-79, project mgr., 1979-85; v.p. Bellemead Devel. Corp., Roseland, 1985—. Prin. Civil and Constrn. Engrng. Svcs., Long Valley, N.J., 1990—; pres. Profl. Solar Consultants, Pompton Lakes, N.J., 1977-78; instr. County Coll. of Morris, Randolph, N.J., 1975-79. Coach twp. and recreation teams Pompton Lakes, Long Valley, 1972—; mem. St. Mark's Parish Life Coun., Long Valley, 1990-92. Mem. ASCE (younger mem. of yr. 1972, dir. N.J. sect. 1978-79), NSPE Profl. Engrs. in Constrn. (regional vice chmn. 1990-92, sec. 1993—), N.J. Profl. Engrs. in Constrn. (chmn. 1987-88, regional v.p. 1989-91), N.J. Soc. Profl. Engrs. (pres. 1992-93). Republican. Home: 78 Winay Ter Long Valley NJ 07853-3575 Office: Bellemead Devel Corp 4 Becker Farm Rd Ste 10 Roseland NJ 07068-1734

PATTERSON, STEVE, professional football team executive; b. Beaver Dam, Wis., Sept. 21, 1957; BBA with honors, U. Tex., 1980, JD, 1984. Bar: Tex. 1984. Gen. mgr., profl. basketball team counsel Houston Rockets, 1984-89, profl. basketball mktg. exec. group ticket sales, mgr., bus. ops. exec., gen. mgr., 1989-94; pres. profl. hockey team Houston Aeros, 1994-97; pres. Arena Oper. Co., Houston, 1995-99; exec. v.p. Houston NFL Holdings, 1997—. Exec. v.p. Houston Texans Office: Houston Texans 33rd Fl 711 Louisiana Houston TX 77002-2716 E-mail: spatterson@houstontexans.nfl.com.

PATTERSON, TRUDY JENKINS, librarian; b. Eunice, La., Feb. 2, 1951; d. Jack Gordon and Bettie (Brunson) Jenkins; m. Donald Ray Patterson, Feb. 9, 1979; children: Daniel Alan, Abby Elizabeth. BA in English Edn., U.

Southwestern La., 1972; MLS, La. State U., 1974. Adminstrv. libr. Richland Parish Libr., Rayville, La., 1974-77, Webster Parish Libr., Minden, 1978-79; head reference dept. Lafayette (La.) Pub. Libr., 1979-80; tech. svcs. libr. Calcasieu Parish Pub. Libr., Lake Charles, La., 1981-82; adminstrv. libr. Jefferson Davis Paris Libr., Jennings, 1982-2000; systems libr. Allen Parish Libr., 2001—. Mem. Preservation Resource Ctr. New Orleans. Mem. ALA, La. Libr. Assn., Nat. Trust for Historic Preservation, Pub. Libr. Assn., La. Preservation Alliance. Democrat. Methodist. Home: PO Box 127 Elton LA 70532-0127 Office: PO Box 400 320 S 6th St Oberlin LA 70655 E-mail: tpatters@pelican.state.lib.la.us.

PATTERSON, VALERIE, art educator, artist; b. Sidney, N.Y., July 12, 1963; d. Thomas Taylor and Terry Ann (Herter) Patterson. BA, Potsdam (N.Y.) Coll., 1985, MA, 1990. Cert. tchr. art K-12, elem. edn. K-6, N.Y. Art tchr. Brushton-Moira Ctrl. Sch., Brushton, N.Y., 1985-96, Saranac Lake (N.Y.) Ctrl. Sch., 1996—. Mem. edn. adv. bd. Adirondack Park Visitors Ctr. Paul Smiths, N.Y., 1988-92; educator Nat. Spruce-up Am. Program, Paul Smiths, 1992; workshop presenter. Exhibited in solo shows Ogdensburg (N.Y.) Pub. Libr., 1995, Paul Smith's Coll., 1997, North Country Cmty. Coll., Saranac Lake, 1997, Pendragon Theater, Saranac Lake, 1997, Schoharie County Arts Coun., Cobleskill, N.Y., 1999, others; group shows include Cooperstown (N.Y.) Art Assn., CERES Gallery, N.Y.C., Fowler Gallery Provinceton, Mass., Stage Gallery, Merrick, N.Y., Parkersburg (W.Va.) Art Ctr., Morningside Gallery, Latham, N.Y., Edward Hopper House Art Ctr., Nyack, N.Y., N.E. Watercolor Soc., Kent, Conn., Am. Profl. Artist Profl. League, 1999, numerous others; cover illustrations for Manhattan Arts Internat., The Archer. Recipient 1st Place award State. of N.Y. for Utilizing TV in Edn., 1991, numerous awards for art. Mem. Balt. Watercolor Soc. Home: PO Box 34 Whippleville NY 12995

PATTERSON, W. MORGAN, college president; b. New Orleans, Oct. 1, 1925; s. E. Palmer and Jess Margaret (Wood) P.; m. Ernestine North, June 10, 1948; children— W. Morgan, II, Jay North BA, Stetson U., 1950, D.D. (hon.), 1979; M.Div., New Orleans Baptist Theol. Sem., 1953, Th.D., 1956; postdoctoral, Oxford U., 1965-66, 72-73. Prof. ch. history New Orleans Bapt. Theol. Sem., 1956-59; prof. ch. history, David T. Porter prof. ch. history, dir. grad. studies So. Baptist Theol. Sem., Louisville, 1959-76; dean acad. affairs Golden Gate Bapt. Theol. Sem., Mill Valley, Calif., 1976-84; pres. Georgetown Coll., Ky., 1984-91. Vis. prof. Midwestern Bapt. Theol. Sem., Kansas City, Mo., La. Coll., Pineville, 1991—92, Golden Gate Bapt. Theol. Sem., Mill Valley, Calif., 1992—94, Mill Valley, 1997, Fla. Bapt. Theol. Coll., 1998—99, New Orleans Bapt. Sem., 1998; vis. scholar Campbellsville U., Ky., 2000—02; chmn. hist. commn. So. Bapt. Conv., Nashville, 1969—72; honored guest 2d Vatican Coun., Rome, 1965. Author: Baptist Successionism: A Critical View, 1969; co-editor: Professor in the Pulpit, 1963; contbr., editor: Ency. Southern Baptists; book rev. editor Review and Expositor, 1965-70 Served as flight officer USAF, 1943-46 Recipient Disting. Alumnus award Stetson U., 1992, Disting. Svc. award for outstanding contbn. to Bapt. history Hist. Commn., So. Bapt. Conv., 1993; Am. Assn. Theol. Schs. fellow, 1965-66. Mem. Am. Soc. Ch. History, So. Bapt. Hist. Soc. (pres. 1979-80), William H. Whitsitt Bapt. Heritage Soc., Conf. on Faith and History, Commn. on Bapt. Heritage of Bapt. World Alliance. Avocations: travel, philately, collecting books. Home: 7 Pierce Dr Novato CA 94947-4450

PATTERSON, WILLIAM BROWN, university dean, history educator; b. Charlotte, N.C., Apr. 8, 1930; s. William Brown and Eleanor Selden (Miller) P.; m. Evelyn Byrd Hawkins, Nov. 27, 1959; children: William Brown Patterson, Evelyn Byrd Donatelli, Lucy Patterson Murray, Emily Patterson Higgs. BA, U. South, 1952; MA, Harvard U., 1954, PhD, 1966, cert. ednl. mgmt., 1982; BA, Oxford (Eng.) U., 1955, MA, 1959; MDiv, Episc. Div. Sch., Cambridge, Mass., 1958. Ordained to ministry Episcopal Ch. as deacon, 1958, as priest, 1959. Asst. prof. history Davidson (N.C.) Coll., 1963-66, assoc. prof., 1966-76, prof. history, 1976-80, U. of South, Sewanee, Tenn., 1980—, dean Coll. Arts and Scis., 1980-91. Author: (with others) Discord, Dialogue, and Concord, 1977-93, This Sacred History: Anglican Reflections for John Booty, 1990, King James VI and I and the Reunion of Christendom, 1997; mem. bd. editors St. Luke's Jour. Theology, Sewanee, 1982-90; contbr. numerous articles to profl. jours. Trustee U. South, 1968-71; mem. internat. adv. com. U. Buckingham, Eng., 1977-93; pres. So. Coll. and Univ. Union; organizer Associated Colls. of South, 1988-89. Danforth Found. grad. fellow, 1952, Mellon Appalachian fellow U. Va., 1992-93, rsch. fellow NEH, 1967, Folger Shakespeare Libr., Washington, 1975, Inst. for Rsch. in Humanities, U. Wis., Madison, 1976, Newberry Libr., Chgo., 1979; Rhodes scholar, 1953. Mem. Am. Hist. Assn., Am. Soc. Ch. History (Albert C. Outler prize for best book in ecumenical ch. history 1999), N.Am. Conf. on Brit. Studies, Eccles. History Soc. Eng., Royal Hist. Soc. Eng., Renaissance Soc. Am., So. Hist. Assn., Soc. for Values in Higher Edn., Episcopal Div. Sch. Alumni/ae Assn. (mem. exec. com. 1984-87), Phi Beta Kappa, Beta Theta Pi. Avocations: gardening, tennis. Home: 195 N Carolina Ave Sewanee TN 37375-2040 Office: U of South Dept History Sewanee TN 37383-0001 E-mail: bpatters@sewanee.edu.

PATTERSON DEHN, CATHLEEN, pediatrics administrator; b. Akron, Feb. 25, 1958; d. James Edward and Doris Elizabeth (Boyd) P.; m. James Keith Dehn, June 27, 1981. BSN, U. Akron, 1980; MSN, Case Western Res. U., 1988; MA Applied Psychology, NYU, 1995, postgrad., 1995—. RN, N.Y.; cert. PNP, ANCC. Nurse technician Children's Med. Ctr. Akron, 1979-80, staff nurse, 1980-81; pediatric and advanced clin. nurse, asst. head nurse, clin. nurse specialist Rainbow Babies and Children's Hosp., Cleve., 1981-91, edn. coord., 1991-93; PNP, project coord. divsn. nursing, NYU The Child Health Ctr., Brooklyn, 1994-96; PNP dept. pediat. Inst. for Neurology and Neurosurgery Beth Israel Med. Ctr., N.Y.C., 1996-2000; case mgr. dept. pediats. St. Vincent's Hosp. and Med. Ctr., 2001—. Lectr., clin. instr. Frances Payne Bolton Sch. Nursing, Case Western Res. U., Cleve., 1990-93; mem. adj. faculty divsn. nursing NYU, 1994-96; project coord. Dance Cleve., 1990-91; regional instr. Neonatal Resuscitation Program, Am. Heart Assn., Am. Acad. Pediatrics. Exec. prodr. videos: Getting to Know the Unique Behavioral Capabilities of the Newborn, 1987, One Step at a Time: A Family's Guide to the Neonatal Intensive Care Unit, 1991. Co-founder Sick Kids Need Involved People, Cleve., 1987; team-walk capt. March of Dimes, Cleve., 1989-92 (Edn. grantee 1991); mem. Nat. Mus. Women in Arts. Recipient Samuel E. and Rebecca Elliott award for Cmty. Svc. Case Western Res. U., 1988; named One of Outstanding Young Women of Am., 1988; Fed. Profl. Nurse Trainee scholar, 1986-87. Mem. APA, Am. Ednl. Rsch. Assn., Kappa Delta Pi, Sigma Theta Tau, Pi Lambda Theta. Avocations: health outcomes research, teaching, educational evaluation. Home: 1 University Pl Apt 10L New York NY 10003-4518

PATTESON, CHARLES LYNN, musician, retired music educator; b. Dallas, Mar. 20, 1923; s. James Nelson and Eula Lee (Jolly) P.; children: Lisa Ann Patteson Kennedy, Charles Lynn Jr. BA, Tex. Christian U., 1948. Band dir. Poly. High Sch., Ft. Worth, 1948-50, Handley High Sch., Ft. Worth, 1948-50; owner TV store, 1951-61; band dir. McLean Mid. Sch., 1961—84; leader Charlie Patteson Dance Orch., 1950—. Composer (band) March 200, 1974; (orch.) Two Minute Waltz, 1976, Fantasy, 1991, Paris In June, October in London, November in Rome, Starlight Waltz, Opus in Eb, Dreamer's Waltz, Stardust Waltz, Meadowbrook Waltz, others. With USAF, 1943-46. Recipient ten 1st place Concert Competition award (dir. McLean Middle Sch. Band), Ft. Worth., 1974-84. Mem. Am. Fedn. Musicians, Musician's Fed. Credit Union (life, v.p.), Lions, Elks, Masons, Shriners (50 yr. mem., 1st chair clarinet in band 1950-91). Republican. Avocations: water skiing, recording, music arranging. Home: 5101 Westhaven Dr Fort Worth TX 76132-2036 E-mail: clpatteson@aol.com.

PATTI, MARCO GIUSEPPE, surgeon, educator; b. Catania, Italy, Apr. 15, 1956; came to U.S., 1983; s. Francesco P. and Ada (Travali) P.; m. Verna C. Gibbs, Nov. 30, 1985; 1 child, Verna Ada. MD, U. Catania, 1981. Resident in gen. surgery U. Calif., San Francisco, 1986—93, dir. swallowing ctr., assoc. prof. surgery, 1994—. Fellow ACS, Assn. Acad. Surgery, Internat. Soc. Diseases of Esophagus, San Francisco Surg. Soc., Italian Surg. Assn., Esophageal Club. Avocations: classical music, swimming, languages, travel. Office: Univ Calif San Francisco 533 Parnassus Ave Rm U-122 San Francisco CA 94122-2722

PATTILLO, MANNING MASON, JR. academic administrator; b. Charlottesville, Va., Oct. 11, 1919; s. Manning Mason and Margaret (Camblos) P.; m. Martha A. Crawford, June 8, 1946; children: Manning Mason III (dec.), Martha Crawford, John Landrum. Student, Johns Hopkins U., 1937-38; BA with highest honors, U. of South, 1941, DCL, 1993; student, U. Calif. at Berkeley, 1941-42; AM, U. Chgo., 1947, PhD, 1949; LLD, LeMoyne Coll., 1967, St. John's U., 1968, Oglethorpe U., 1994; LHD, U. Detroit, 1968, Coll. New Rochelle, 1967, Park Coll., 1973; LittD, St. Norbert Coll., 1967. From instr. to assoc. prof. higher edn. U. Chgo., 1949-56; assoc. dir. Lilly Endowment, Inc., Indpls., 1956-60, exec. dir. for edn., 1961-62; dir. Danforth commn. on ch. colls. and univs., 1962-66; assoc. dir. The Danforth Found., 1964-66, v.p., 1966-67; pres. The Found. Center, N.Y.C., 1967-71; adj. prof. N.Y. U., 1968-71; dir. spl. projects U. Rochester, 1972-75; pres. Oglethorpe U., Atlanta, 1975-88, chancellor, 1988—. Cons. in field; tech. asst., then assoc. sec. commn. on colls. and univs. North Ctrl. Assn. Colls. and Secondary Schs., 1948-56; cons. USAF Acad., 1952, Phillips Exeter Acad., 1974; chmn. IBM Incentive awards com., 1970-75; adv. com. Brookings Instn., 1970-71; vis. prof. Inst. Higher Edn., U. Ga., 1988-90; bd. dirs. Fidelity Nat. Bank. Author: (with D.M. Mackenzie) Church Sponsored Higher Education in the United States, 1966, (with D.M. Mackenzie) Eight Hundred Colleges Face the Future, 1965, Private Higher Education in the United States, 1990, The Episcopal Church: Diagnosis and Reform, 1989; contbr. articles to profl. jours. Mem. pres.'s adv. coun. Wellesley Coll., 1969-72; trustee Seabury Press, Japan Internat. Christian U., 1970-72, Le Moyne Coll., 1970-83, Sacred Heart U., 1968-75, U. of South, 1984-88, St. Martin's Episc. Sch.; bd. dirs., interim pres., chmn. Atlanta Coll. Art, 1984-95, Howard Sch.; trustee Greater Rochester Cmty. Found., 1973-75, pres., 1975; trustee, chmn. Nat. Coun. on Philanthropy, 1968-80; trustee, chmn. bd. trustees Park Coll., 1967-74; bd. visitors Salvation Army Coll. for Officer Tng., 1997—; provost St. Mary's Coll. of Md., 1975; bd. visitors Kanuga Confs., Inc.; pres., life trustee Ga. Found. for Ind. Colls., 1977—; chmn. Univ. Center in Ga., 1978-79; pres. Assn. Pvt. Colls. and Univs. of Ga., 1980-81; trustee, chmn. Ga. Spl. Olympics; trustee, mem. exec. com. Nat. Assn. Ind. Colls. and Univs., Ind. Coll. Funds of Am., 1982-86; co-dir. Coll. Cons. Network, So. Assn. Colls. and Schs., 1988-96; mem. De Kalb County Cmty. Rels. Commn.; chmn. De Kalb Cmty. Coun. on the Aging; mem. commn. on colls. and steering com. on revision accrediting procedures So. Assn. Colls. and Schs.; vice-chmn bd. and life trustee, Woodruff Arts Ctr.; mem. adv. coun. ARC. With AUS, 1942-46. Mem. Nat. Assn. Scholars, Assn. for Higher Edn., Nat. Assn. Ind. Schs. (bd. dirs.), Guild of Scholars, English Speaking Union (dir., pres. br., nat. bd. dirs.), Country Day Sch. Headmasters Assn. U.S. (hon.), Phi Beta Kappa Assn. of Atlanta (pres., chmn., fellow nat. soc.), Atlanta Hist. Soc., High Mus. of Art, Am. Anglican Coun., Dekalb C. of C. (dir., chmn.), Omicron Delta Kappa, Kappa Sigma. Episcopalian (vestryman, sr. warden, mem. cathedral chpt., diocesan council, standing com.). Clubs: Century (N.Y.C.); Commerce, Capital City. Lodge: Rotary.

PATTIS, S. WILLIAM, publisher; b. Chgo., July 3, 1925; s. William Robert and Rose (Quint) P.; m. Bette Z. Levin, July 16, 1950; children: Mark Robert, Robin Quint Himovitz. BS, U. Ill., 1949; postgrad., Northwestern U., 1949-50. Exec. v.p., pub. United Bus. Publs., 1949-59; chmn., CEO 3M/Pattis, 1959-88; pres. NTC Pub. Group, Lincolnwood, Ill., 1961-96, Next Chapter Holdings, L.P., Highland Park, 1996—; dir. P-B Comm., Winnetka, 1978-98; vice-chmn. Profl. Media Group, Norwalk, Conn., 1999—. Bd. dirs. 1st Colonial/Highwood; mem. book and libr. com. USIA, Washington, 1986-89, chmn., 1989-93; mem. exec. com. Pub. Hall of Fame, 1987—; chmn. U.S.-USSR Bilateral Info. Talks, Moscow, 1990. Mem. Pres.'s Coun. Youth Opportunity, 1968-70; bd. dirs. Photography Youth Found., 1970-73, Expt. in Internat. Living, 1970, Inst. Human Creativity, 1983—, Fund for Am.'s Libraries, 1996-99; vice chmn. bd. dirs. Annenberg Ctr. for Health Scis., 1991—, vice chmn., 1996-99; trustee Eisenhower Med. Ctr., Rancho Mirage, Calif., 1989—, exec. com. mem., 1996—, chmn. investment com., 2000—; trustee Am. Coun. Tchrs. Russian, 1992-96; bd. dirs. Nat. Security Edn. Act, Washington, 1993-94; lord of manor, Kirkbride, Eng., 1989—. Recipient Human Rels. award Am. Jewish Com., 1971, Paul Simon award Ctrl. States Conf. on Tchg. Fgn. Langs., 1992. Mem. Standard Club (Chgo.), Club Internat. (Chgo.), Northmoor Country Club (Highland Park, Ill.), Tamarisk Country Club (Rancho Mirage). Home: 195 Elder Ln Highland Park IL 60035-5368 Office: Next Chpt Holdings Port Clinton Sq 600 Central Ave Highland Park IL 60035-3211 Home (Winter): 70843 Tamarisk La Rancho Mirage CA 92270 E-mail: bpattis@nextchapterholdings.com.

PATTISON, DELORIS JEAN, retired counselor, university official; b. Logansport, Ind., Oct. 3, 1931; d. John R. and Grace I. Gallagher (Yocum) Taylor; m. John A. Pattison, July 3, 1952; children: Traci (dec.), John A. II, Scott, Becky. BS in Secondary Edn., Goshen Coll., 1973; MA in Edn., Ball State U., 1977. Life cert. vocat. edn. tchr., Ind. Tchr. home econs. Marion (Ind.) H.S., 1973-78; dir. youth employment Logansport Cmty. Schs., 1979-83; substitute tchr. Ft. Wayne (Ind.) Cmty. Schs., 1983-87; employment counselor Ind. Dept. Employment, Marion, 1987-90; counselor, coord. adminstrv. career svcs. Ind. Wesleyan U., 1990-95; ret., 1995. News reporter Woodridge News, United Meth. Meml. Home Newsletter. Editor: A Teen Trace, 1971; also articles. Bd. dirs. Ind. Christian Coll. Consortium, 1990—. Named Outstanding Employee, Ind. Dept. Employment and Tng., 1989. Mem. Nat. Assn. Colls. and Employers, Midwest Coll. Placement Assn., Great Lake Assn. for Sch., Coll. and Univ. Staffing, Dist. Min. Spouse Assn. (sec. 1987-89), Am. Legion Aux., Elegant Dames (charter), Red Hatters Assn. Methodist. Avocations: reading, walking, writing, travel. Home: 801 N Huntington #47 Hippensteel Dr Warren IN 46792

PATTISON, GEORGE EDGAR, lawyer; b. Beaver Falls, Pa., May 25, 1944; s. John Norwood and Rosemary (Smith) P.; m. Marsha Wildermuth, June 8, 1968; children: Geoffrey, Megan. BS, Ohio State U., 1967; JD, U. Cin., 1972. Bar: Ohio 1972, U.S. Dist. Ct. (so. dist.) Ohio 1973, U.S. Supreme Ct. 1980. Legal editor W.H. Anderson Legal Pub., Cin., 1972-75; asst. pros. County of Clermont, Batavia, Ohio, 1975-80, pros. atty., 1981-89; pvt. practice, 1975—. Bd. dirs. Mental Retardation and Developmental Disabilities, 1998—; chmn. S.E. Ohio Developmental Ctr. Citizen Adv. Coun., 1984—. Mem. ABA, Assn. Trial Lawyers Am. (winner environ. law essay 1972), Ohio State Bar Assn., Clermont County Bar Assn., Ohio Trial Lawyers Assn., Clermont County Citizens Law Enforcement Assn., Clermont County C. of C., Masons. Republican. Methodist. Home: 1091 Raintree Dr Milford OH 45150-9653 Office: 285 E Main St Batavia OH 45103-3072

PATTISON, JOHN CURTIS, business owner, researcher; b. Cin., Mar. 1, 1951; s. Paul Joseph and Eunice Evelyn (Curtis) P.; m. Kathleen Robinson, 1980 (div. 1986); 1 child, Brent Curtis; m. Erin Prell, Apr. 12, 1992 (div. Nov. 1993). Student, Calif. Polytech., 1973-74. Tchr. various sch. dists., 1973-78; bus. owner Lefthanded Leather, Monrovia, Calif., 1973-77, Pasadena, 1977-80, Burbank, 1981-83; rsch. for film bus. Ellis Mercantile, L.A., 1984-89; property master various film cos., 1989—; rsch. for film and leather work Pattison Props & Studio Leather, Simi Valley, Calif., 1993—. Pres. Leathercraft Guild, Rosemead, Calif., 1975-76. Crafted leather items used in over 100 films; contbr. articles to profl. jours. Mem. Gene Autry Western Heritage Mus. (charter), Smithsonian Am. Indian Mus. Avocations: leather carved wall hangings, baseball. Office: Pattison Props & Studio Leather PO Box 556 Lake Hughes CA 93532-0556 Address: PO Box 556 Lake Hughes CA 93532-0556

PATTISON, JON ALLEN, computer scientist, consultant; b. Sturgis, Mich., July 18, 1960; s. Jerome and Karen Pattison; m. Nandini Pattison, July 14, 1990; children: Nisha Lynn, Christopher Anand. Student, Glen Oaks C.C., 1978-79, U. Tex., Arlington, 1987. Mgr. Magic City Hardware, 1978-79; engring. technician Quazon Corp., 1983-84, Sci. Machines Corp., 1984; design engr. Tex. Arrays, 1984-86, EMS Group, Inc., 1986-89; hardware project leader Vortech Data, 1990; systems engr. Computer Task Group, 1991; cons. Decision Cons. Inc., 1992; self-employed cons., 1989, 91-92, 93; cons. Oxford and Assocs., Inc., 1992-94, R.S. Internat., 1993-94; devel. mgr. Teknekron InfoSwitch, Fort Worth, 1994-2000, e-talk Corp. (formerly Teknekron Infoswitch), Irving, Tex., 2000—; chief technology officer Lanvera, Ltd., Carrollton, 2000—. Author design papers and system design documents; patentee in field. Served to sgt. USMC, 1979-83. Avocations: woodworking, gardening. E-mail: jpattison@lanvera.com.

PATTON, ALTON DEWITT, electrical engineering consultant; b. Corpus Christi, Tex., Feb. 1, 1935; s. Alton G. and Civilia Louise (Taylor) P.; m. Nancy Jo Elder, Mar. 1, 1959; children: Elizabeth, Carolyn. BEE, U. Tex., Austin, 1957; MEE, U. Pitts., 1961; PhD in Elec. Engring., Tex. A&M U., 1972. Registered profl. engr., Tex.; diplomate Am. Bd. of Forensic Engring. and Tech. Engr. Westinghouse Electric Corp., Pitts., 1957-65; prof. elec. engring. dept. Tex. A&M U., College Station, 1965-79, 82-2000, head elec. engring. dept., 1992-96, Brockett prof., 1986, Dresser prof., 1987, dir. Electric Power Inst., 1976-79, 85-92; rsch. fellow Tex. Engring. Expt. Sta., 1985, dir. Ctr. for Space Power, 1987-92; pres. Associated Power Analysts Inc., College Station, Tex., 1973—. Mem. panel for assessment of NIST Elec. and Electronics Engring. Lab., 1995-2000, NRS. Contbr. articles to elec. engring. jours., 1960—. Fellow IEEE (life, tech. com., aerospace policy com., prize paper award 1975, 94, Richard Harold Kaufmann award 2000); mem. NSPE. Republican. Presbyterian. Avocations: fishing, hunting, photography, stamp and coin collecting. Home: 8411 Spring Crk College Station TX 77845-4608 Office: Associated Power Analysts Inc 303 Anderson St College Station TX 77840-3114 E-mail: adpatton@myriad.net.

PATTON, BOB J. oil industry executive; b. Whitt, Tex., Nov. 5, 1925; s. John Elmer and Dora Althia (Davis) P.; m. Glenda Nell Colbert, May 30, 1950; children: Eva Diane, Elaine Gay, John Carl. BS in Physics, U. North Tex., 1949, MS in Physics, 1950. Instr. U. North Tex., Denton, 1950-51; rschr. Gulf R & D, Pitts., 1951-53; rsch. assoc. Mobil R & D, Dallas, 1953-80; mwd mgr. Gearhart Industries, Ft. Worth, 1980-82; pres. Patton Cons., Inc., Dallas, 1982—. Patentee in field. With USN, 1945-46. Mem. Soc. Petroleum Engrs., Aircraft Owners & Pilots Assn., Sigma Pi Sigma. Republican. Avocations: inventing, woodworking, flying. Home and Office: 2436 Monaco Ln Dallas TX 75233-2826

PATTON, BRUCE M. law educator, management consultant; b. Terre Haute, Ind., Oct. 14, 1956; s. William Eugene and Carol Ann P.; m. Diana McLain Smith, Oct. 21, 1994. AB, Harvard U., 1977, JD, 1984. Bar: Mass. Co-founder, assoc. dir. Harvard Negotiation Project, Cambridge, Mass., 1979-84, dep. dir., 1984—; co-founder, assoc. dir. Program on Negotiation at Harvard Law Sch., 1983—2002; co-founder, ptnr. Vantage Partners, LLC, 1997—. Co-founder, prin. Conflict Mgmt. Inc., Cambridge, 1984—; co-founder, dir. Conflict Mgmt. Group, Cambridge, 1984-2000; Thaddeus R. Beal lectr. Harvard Law Sch., Cambridge, 1985-99. Co-author: The Mainstream of Alegbra and Trigonometry, 2d edit., 1980, Getting To Yes, 2d edit., 1991, Difficult Conversations, 1999; contbr. articles to profl. jours. Avocations: squash, hiking, tennis. Office: Harvard Negotiation Project Harvard Law Sch Pound Hall 524 Cambridge MA 02138 also: Vantage Ptnrs Brighton Landing W Ste 350 10 Guest St Boston MA 02135 E-mail: bpatton@post.harvard.edu.

PATTON, CARL ELLIOTT, physics educator; b. San Antonio, Sept. 14, 1941; s. Carl Elliott and Geraldine Barnett (Perry) Patton. BS, MIT, 1963; MS, Calif. Inst. Tech., 1964, PhD, 1967. Sr. scientist Raytheon Co., Waltham, Mass., 1967-71; assoc. prof. physics Colo. State U., Ft. Collins, 1971-75, prof., 1975—. IEEE Magnetics Soc. Disting. lectr., 1993; chair Am. Phys. Soc. Topical Group on Magnetism and its Applications, 1998-99. Editor-in-chief IEEE Transactions on Magnetics, 1987-91. Fellow IEEE (Third Millenium medal 2000), Am. Phys. Soc. Office: Colo State Univ Dept Physics Fort Collins CO 80523-0001

PATTON, CARL VERNON, academic administrator, educator; b. Coral Gables, Fla., Oct. 22, 1944; s. Carl V. and Helen Eleanor (Benkert) Patton; m. Gretchen West, July 29, 1967. BS in Community Planning, U. Cin., 1967; MS in Urban Planning, U. Ill.-Urbana, 1969, MS in Pub. Adminstrn., 1970; MS in Pub. Policy, U. Calif.-Berkeley, 1975, PhD in Pub. Policy, 1976. Instr. to prof. U. Ill., 1968—83, dir. Bureau of Urban and Regional Planning Rsch., 1977—79, prof., chmn. dept., 1979—83; prof., dean Sch. Architecture and Urban Planning U. Wis., Milw., 1983—89; v.p. acad. affairs, prof. polit. sci., geography and urban planning U. Toledo, 1989—92; pres. Ga. State U., Atlanta, 1992—. Co-author (with others): Academia in Transition, 1979; co-author: (novels) The Metropolitan Midwest, 1985; co-author: (with David Sawicki) Basic Methods of Policy Analysis and Planning, 1986, rev. 2d edit., Chinese translation, 2001, 1993; co-author: (with Kathleen Reed) Guide to Graduate Education in Urban and Regional Planning, 1986, 1988; editor Spontaneous Shelter: International Perspectives and Prospects, 1988; co-editor (with G. William Page) Quick Answers to Quantitative Problems: A Pocket Primer, 1991; editor (assoc.): (jour.) Jour. of Planning Edn. and Rsch., 1983—87; editor: (editl. bd.) Habitat International, 1993—99, Intertrade and Investment (formerly Atlanta Internat. Mag.), 1993—2000; contbr. articles. Fellow NIMH, 1973—75; Chmn. Community Devel. Commn., Urbana, 1978—82; mem. Civic Design Ctr., Milw., 1983—87, City of Milw. Art Commn., 1988—89, Toledo Vision, 1989—92, City of Toledo Bd. Cmty. Rels., 1990—92; chair Centennial Olympic Park Area Inc., 1998—2000, Ctrl. Atlanta Progress, 2000—; mem. Ga. Rsch. Alliance, Atlanta Convention and Vis. Bur., Woodruff Art Ctr., Fox Theatre; chair Grady (Hosp.) Healthcare, Inc., 1998—2000, Atlanta Reg. Consortium for Higher Edn., 1998—; mem. Ga. Coun. on Econ. Edn., Atlanta neighborhood Devel. Ptnrship., U.S. Disabled Athletes Fund Bd.; fellow U. Ill. Ctr. for Advanced Studies, 1973—74; bd. dirs., chair The Atlanta Downtown Partnership, 1997—2000. Mem.: Met. Atlanta C. of C., Assn. Collegiate Schs. of Planning (v.p. 1985—87, pres. 1989—91), Am. Inst. Cert. Planners, Am. Planning Assn. Avocation: racquetball, photography, travel.. Home: 90 Fairlie St NW Apt 801 Atlanta GA 30303-2145 Office: Ga State U Office of Pres University Plz Atlanta GA 30303-3083

PATTON, CHARLES HENRY, lawyer, educator; b. Asheville, N.C., Jan. 13, 1953; s. Charles Robert and Sarah (Gulledge) P. BA, Memphis State U., 1975, JD, 1979. Bar: Tenn. Assoc. Holt, Bachelor, Spicer & Ryan, Memphis, 1979-80; fin. exec. Felsenthal Planning Service Co., 1980-81; sole practice, 1981—; prof. Memphis State U., 1982—. Planned giving dir. Christ United Meth. Ch., Memphis, 1986; mem. Planned Giving Coun. Memphis. Mem. S.E. Regional Bus. Law Professors Assn., Memphis Bar Assn., Estate Planning Coun. Memphis. Republican. Avocations: classic automobile restoration, model trains. Office: 5100 Poplar Ave Ste 2701 Memphis TN 38137-4000

PATTON, DENNIS DAVID, radiologist, educator; b. Oakland, Calif., Aug. 4, 1930; s. Owen and Norma Rose (Barnes) P.; m. Pamela Ruth Patton, Feb. 14, 1965 (div. Jan. 1992); children: James Patrick, William Christopher. Cert., Heidelberg (Germany) U., 1951; AB in Physics, U. Calif., Berkeley, 1953; MD, UCLA, 1959. Diplomate Am. Bd. Radiology, Am. Bd. Nuc. Medicine. Mgr. biomed. group Planning Rsch. Corp., L.A., 1959-68; asst. prof. radiology U. Calif., Irvine, 1968-70; prof. radiology Vanderbilt U., Nashville, 1970-75, U. Ariz., Tucson, 1975—. Author: (slide set) History of Nuclear Medicine, 1980; co-author: Imaging for Medicine, 1980, Public Exposure from Nuclear Medicine Procedures, 1996; composer: Elegy for Orchestra, 1999. Recipient Top Man award City of Santa Monica, Calif., 1961, U.S. Sr. Scientist award Alexander von Humboldt Found., Germany, 1985; disting. fellow Am. Coll. Nuc. Medicine, 1975. Fellow Am. Coll. Nuc. Physicians (del.), Am. Coll. Radiology; mem. Soc. Nuc. Medicine (historian), Am. Bd. Radiology (examiner, Disting. Svc. award 2000), Am. Bd. Nuc. Medicine (life), Alexander von Humboldt Assn. of Am. (bd. dirs.), Med. Soc. of U.S. and Mex., European Assn. Nuc. Medicine. Republican. Methodist. Avocations: history of medicine, composing, travel, languages, philately. Office: U Ariz Med Ctr Tucson AZ 85721

PATTON, GEORGE SMITH, retired military officer; b. Boston, Dec. 24, 1923; s. George Smith, Jr. and Beatrice Banning (Ayer) P.; m. Joanne Holbrook, June 14, 1952; children: Margaret, George, Robert, Helen, Benjamin. BS, U.S. Mil. Acad., 1946; M in Internat. Affairs, George Washington U., 1965. Commd. 2d lt. U.S. Army, 1946, advanced through grades to maj. gen., 1973; parachutist Germany, 1947-51; assigned Armor Br., 1949; instr. tank offense sect. Armored Sch. Fort Knox, Ky., 1952-53; comdr. Co. A, 140th Tank Bn. Korea, 1953; exec. officer I, Corps Reconnaissance Bn. Korea, 1953-54; co. tactical officer dept. tactics U.S. Mil. Acad., 1954-56; officer exec. dept. U.S. Naval Acad., 1956-57; assigned Command and Gen. Staff Coll., Fort Leavenworth, Kans., 1957-58; a.d.c. comdg. gen. 7th Army and comdr. in chief U.S. Army, Europe, 1958-60; exec. officer 1st squadron 11th Armored Cav. Regt. Straubing, Germany, 1960-61; assigned Armed Forces Staff Coll. Norfolk, Va., 1961-62; assigned U.S. Army War Coll. Carlisle

Barracks, Pa., 1964-65; spl. forces ops. officer Mil. Assistance Command Vietnam, 1962-63; comdr. 2/81 Armor, 1st Armored Div. Fort Hood, Tex., 1963-64; chief Mainland S.E. Asia br. Far East-Pacific div. Office Dep. Chief Staff for Mil. Ops., Dept. Army, 1965-67; chief force devel. div. U.S. Army, Vietnam, 1967-68; comdg. officer 11th Armored Cav. Regt. Vietnam, 1968-69; assigned U.S. Army Primary Helicopter Ctr., Ft. Wolters, Tex., 1969-70, Ft. Rucker, Ala., 1969-70; asst. div. comdr. for support 4th Armored div. Hdqrs. U.S. Army, Europe, 1970-71; comdt. U.S. Army Armor Sch. Fort Knox, 1971-73; dir. security assistance Hdqrs. U.S. European Command, 1973-74; comdr. Army Readiness Region, 1974-75; comdr. 2d Armored Div. Fort Hood, 1975-77; dep. comdg. gen. U.S. VII Corps, 1977-79; dir. readiness Hdqrs. Dept. Army Materiel Devel. and Readiness Command Alexandria, Va., 1979-80; ret., 1980; owner Green Meadows Farm, Hamilton, 1980—. Owner Green Meadows Farm, Hamilton, Mass., 1980—; instr. history U. Md., 1960-61. Mem. West Point Fund, Alexandria, Va.; trustee Essex Agrl. and Tech. Inst., Hathorne, Mass. Decorated D.S.C. with oak leaf cluster, Silver Star with oak leaf cluster, Legion of Merit with two oak leaf clusters, D.F.C., Bronze Star with oak leaf cluster, Purple Heart; Cross of Gallantry with gold, silver and bronze stars Vietnam; Army Forces Honor medal 1st class. Mem. Assn. U.S. Army, Armor Assn., Blackhorse Assn., Ducks Unltd., N.E. Farm Bur., Legion of Valor, Am. Legion. Home: 650 Asbury St South Hamilton MA 01982-1321

PATTON, JACK THOMAS, family practice physician; b. Rogers, Ark., Feb. 18, 1941; s. Jack Marcus and Jewell Selah (Pense) P.; m. Lynette Anne Carr, Sept. 2, 1960; children: Robert, John, Mark, Christopher. BA in History, Calif. State U., Long Beach, 1963; MD in Medicine, U. So. Calif., L.A., 1967; MA in Bib. Studies, Mennonite Brethren Bib. Sem., Fresno, Calif., 1980; MA in History, Calif. State U., Fresno, 1993. Cert. Bd. Med. Examiners, Calif., Hawaii. Intern Tripler Army Med. Ctr., Honolulu, 1967-68; resident in gen. practice Walson Army Hosp., Ft. Dix, N.J., 1968-70; med. supt. Nazarene Hosp., Papua New Guinea, 1973-80; chmn. family practice dept. Sharp Rees-Stealy, San Diego, 1981-86; chmn. occupational medicine Kaiser Permanente, Fresno, 1986-87; assoc. med. dir. Sharp Rees-Stealy, San Diego, 1987-92; med. dir. Summer Inst. Linguistics, Papua New Guinea, 1993-94; with family practice dept. Sharp Rees-Stealy Med. Group, San Diego, 1994-97, Northwest Med. Group, Fresno, 1997—; chmn. dept. family practice St. Agnes Med. Ctr., 2002—. Family practice residency liaison Tripler Army Med. Ctr., Honolulu, 1972-73; chief medicine, dep. commr. Schofield Army Med. Clinics, Wahiawa, Hawaii, 1970-72; lectr. Calif. State U., Fresno, 1978-79, Pt. Loma Nazarene Coll., 1982-85, San Jose Christian Coll., 1997—. Mem. med. sch. support Salerni Collegium, U. So. Calif. Sch. Medicine, 1967-85; lectr. Ch.-Mission Inst., Mennonite Brethren Bib. Sem., 1984-92; sec. S.E. Asian task force Mennonite Brethren Ch. Fresno, 1990-93. Maj. U.S. Army, 1966-73. Mackenzie scholar U. So. Calif. Sch. Medicine, 1966-67; decorated Meritorious Svc. medal. Fellow Am. Acad. Family Physicians; mem. Am. Bd. Family Practice (diplomate), Calif. Acad. Family Physicians, Royal Soc. Medicine (assoc., London). Avocations: history, travel, hiking. Home: 1566 S Adler Ave Fresno CA 93727-5101 Office: 4770 W Herndon Ave Fresno CA 93722-8401

PATTON, JAMES EDWARD, school psychologist; b. Clinton, Iowa, Aug. 14, 1949; s. Edward Arthur and Margaret Emma P.; m. Janis Norine Gaass, Dec. 23, 1967; children: Jill Monson, Benjamin. BA, Ctrl. Coll., Pella, Iowa, 1968; MS, Iowa State U., 1970; PhD, Purdue U., 1976. Cert. permanent tchg. profl., sch. psychologist, Iowa. Grad. tchg. asst. Iowa State U., Ames, 1968-70; sch. psychologist Joint County Sch. Sys., Mason City, Iowa, 1970-73; grad. rsch. asst. Purdue U., West Lafayette, Ind., 1974; grad. instr. U. Iowa, Iowa City, 1982; sch. psychologist Grant Wood Area Edn. Agy., Cedar Rapids, Iowa, 1976—. Psychology intern site supr. U. Iowa, Iowa City, 1977-99. Contbr. articles to profl. jours. Councilman City of Bertram, Iowa, 1982—84, mem. land use com., 2001, subdivsn. ordinance com., 2001, planning com., 2001, bd. adjustment, 2002—; rsch. grant project dir. Iowa Dept. Pub. Instrn., Divsn. Spl. Edn., 1985—86, 1986—87. Mem. Soc. Rsch. Child Devel., Nat. Assn. Sch. Psychologists. Avocations: history of Am. west, physical fitness tng., golf, hiking, skiing. Office: Grant Wood Area Edn Agy 4401 6th St SW Cedar Rapids IA 52404 E-mail: jpatton@aea10.k12.ia.us.

PATTON, JAMES RICHARD, JR. lawyer; b. Durham, N.C., Oct. 27, 1928; s. James Ralph and Bertha (Moye) P.; m. Mary Margot Maughan, Dec. 29, 1950; children: James Macon, Lindsay Fairfield. AB cum laude, U. N.C., 1948; postgrad., Yale U., 1948; JD, Harvard U., 1951. Bar: D.C. bar 1951, U.S. Supreme Ct. 1963. Attache of Embassy; spl. asst. to Am. ambassador to Indochina, 1952-54; with Office Nat. Estimates, Washington, 1954-55; atty. Covington & Burling, 1956-61; founding ptnr., chmn. exec. com. Patton Boggs, LLP, 1962—. Lectr. internat. law Cornell Law Sch., 1963-64, U.S. Army Command and Gen. Staff Coll., 1967-68; Mem. Nat. Security Forum, U.S. Air War Coll., 1965, Nat. Strategy Seminar, U.S. Army War Coll., 1967-70, Global Strategy Discussions, U.S. Naval War Coll., 1968, Def. Orientation Conf., 1972; mem. Com. of 100 on Fed. City, Washington; mem. adv. council on nat. security and internat. affairs Nat. Republican Com., 1977-81; bd. dirs. Security Nat. Bank (Wash.), Signet, N.A., Madeira Sch., Greenway, Va., 1975-81, Lawyers Com. for Civil Rights Under Law, Washington, Legal Aid Soc. Washington; mem. Industry Policy Adv. Com. for Trade Policy Matters, 1984-87; mem. visiting com. Ackland Art Mus. U. N.C., 1987—, Nat. Coun. Anderson Ranch Arts Ctr., 1987—. Adv. coun. mem. Johns Hopkins U. Sch. Advanced Internat. Studies, 1989-92; nat. bd. dirs. Aspen Mus., 1987-90; nat. coun. mem. Whitney Mus., 1992—; bd. dirs., exec. com. Nat. Mus. Natural History, Smithsonian, 1992—; bd. dirs. Smithsonian Nat. Bd., 1999—; trustee Aspen Music Festival and Sch., 1993—. Fellow U.N.C. Wilson Library, 1996—. Mem. ABA (past com. chmn.), Inter-Am. Bar Assn. (past del.), Internat. Law Assn. (past com. chmn.), Am. Soc. Internat. Law (treas., exec. coun.), Washington Inst. Fgn. Affairs, Nat. Gallery (collectors com. 1988-91), Gerrard Soc., Met. Club (Washington), Phi Beta Kappa, Alpha Epsilon Delta.

PATTON, JOHN S. pharmaceutical executive; PhD in Biology, U. Calif., San Diego; postgrad., Harvard Med. Sch., U. Lund, Sweden. Prof. U. Ga.; leader drug delivery group Genentech, Inc.; co-founder, v.p. rsch. Inhale Therapeutic Systems. Presenter in field. Contbr. articles to profl. jours. Office: Inhale Therapeutic Systems Inc 150 Industrial Rd San Carlos CA 94070*

PATTON, JOSEPH DONALD, JR. management consultant; b. Washington, Jan. 4, 1938; s. Joseph Donald and Priscilla Ann (Johnson) P.; m. Susan Oertel, June 3, 1967; children: Jennifer Ann, Joseph Donald III. BS in Phys. Scis. and Math. Edn., Pa. State U., 1959; MBA in Mktg., U. Rochester, N.Y., 1970. Registered profl. quality engr., Calif.; cert. profl. logistician; cert. quality engr.; cert. reliability engr. Tchr. Aschaffebburg (W.Germany) Am. Sch., 1963-64; with Xerox Corp., Rochester, 1964-75, mgr. field engring., 1975-93; CEO Patton Cons., Inc., N.Y., 1993—, Hilton Head, SC, 1993—. Chmn., Mgmt. Metrics Svcs., Inc., 1996-2001; mem. adj. faculty Rochester Inst. Tech., SUNY, Geneseo. Author 8 textbooks; contbr. over 100 articles to profl. jours. Capt. U.S. Army, 1959-63. Recipient Leadership and Svc. award Pa. State U. Coll. Edn., 1999. Fellow Am. Soc. Quality Control (reliability and maintainablity tech. award 1982), Soc. Logistics Engrs. (Sole Armitage medal 1980, 82, 97); mem. Instrument Soc. Am. (sr.), Assn. Field Svc. Mgrs. (publs. award 1981), Nat. Assn. Svc. Mgrs. (life cert. svc. exec.). Republican. Presbyterian (elder). Office: Patton Consultants Inc 36 Blue Heron Pt Hilton Head Island SC 29926-1209 E-mail: JDPatton@aol.com.

PATTON, JUDITH WOOD, computer science educator; b. Sanford, N.C., Aug. 30, 1953; d. James Gordon and Nellie Ruth (Kelly) Wood; m. George Ronald Patton, Aug. 22, 1987. BS, U. N.C., Greensboro, 1975, MS in Bus. Edn., 1976, cert. advanced study in bus. edn., 1987. Instr. bus. Halifax Community Coll., Weldon, N.C., 1976-78, chmn. dept. of mktg., 1978-87; instr. bus. computer programming Vance-Granville Coll., Henderson, N.C., 1987—. Co-chmn. faculty senate Halifax C.C., Weldon, 1976-77; mem. curriculum com. Weldon City Schs., 1980-87, mem. adv. com. for mktg. edn., 1985-87, libr. com., 1985; mem. profl. adv. com. Vance-Granville C.C., Henderson, 1987-88, 93-94, mem. curriculum com., 1988-90, student affairs com., 1991-92, scholarship com., 1994-95. Mem. Computer Instrs. Assn., N.C. Bus. Edn. Assn., Delta Pi Epsilon, Phi Theta Kappa (hon. advisor 1991-94). Democrat. Methodist. Avocation: stained glass. Office: Vance-Granville Comm Coll PO Box 917 Henderson NC 27536-0917

PATTON, LISA DARLENE, urban planner; b. Port Huron, Mich., Apr. 15, 1964; d. William David and L. Jean (Burns) Hooper; m. Jeffrey Scott Bitzinger, June 28, 1986 (div. July 1994); children: Anna Leigh, Zachary Alex, Emily Louise; m. Larry Arnold Patton, Nov. 18, 1995; 1 child, Elizabeth Ann Patton. BA in Urban Policy, Mich. State U., 1986. Cert. AICP. Planner I/II St. Clair County Met. Planning Commn., Port Huron, Mich., 1986-96; cmty. devel. dir. Monroe (Mich.) Charter Twp., 1997-99, planning/zoning mgr., 1999-2000; planning and zoning adminstr. City of Garden City, Mich., 2000; dir. downtown devel. authority Milan (Mich.) Devel. Office, 2000—; dir. Milan Pub. Transit, 2001—. Co-chair Olde Town Revitalization Coun., Port Huron, 1989-96; treas. Port Huron Neighborhood Alliance, 1989-94. Editor/pub. Olde Town newsletter, 1989-94. Mem. Exeter Twp. Zoning Bd. Appeals, Monroe County, 1998, 1999—2000; mem. Exeter Twp. Planning Commn., 2000—; bd. dirs. Automobile Nat. Heritage Area, River Rouge Corridor. Mem.: Mich. Downtown and Financing Assn. (bd. dirs. 2000—), Mich. Soc. Planning, Am. Planning Assn., Am. Inst. Cert. Planners. Avocations: Nascar, stamp collecting, gardening. Office: Milan Devel Office 108 E Main St Milan MI 48160-1250 E-mail: countrypatton@mail.com.

PATTON, NICKI, former political organization executive; BA, MA, U. Ky. Childcare cons.; campaign worker Ky. Dem. Party, 1996-98, exec. dir., 1998-99, chmn., 2000—02. Chair Early Childhood Task Force, Govt. of Ky., 1999—. Office: Early Childhood Task Force 700 Capital Ave Ste 100 Frankfort KY 40601*

PATTON, ORIN CLYDE, real estate executive, retired military officer; b. Miami, Fla., Jan. 14, 1933; s. Orin Fitzhugh and Mary Clyde Patton; m. Kathleen Ellis, Feb. 19, 1958 (div.); children: Gregory O., Clyde E., Kenner M.; m. Patricia Mary Patton, Nov. 24, 1972. BA, U. Fla., 1954, MS, 1960; PhD, U. N.C., 1973. Commd. 2d lt. USAF, 1954, advanced through grades to col., 1974; chief U.S. bases br. HQ. USAF Budget and Programs, The Pentagon, 1975-77; prof. aerospace studies Colo. State U., Fort Collins, 1977-79; dir. analysis and studies USAF Mil. Pers. Bd., San Antonio, 1979-83; pers. mem. USAF Phys. Evaluation Bd., 1983-85; sales assoc. Tillman and Tillman Realty, New Braunfels, Tex., 1986-95; assn. exec. New Braunfels/Canyon Lake Area Assn. of Realtors, 1995-2001; owner Patton Properties, 1973—. Tree ordinance adv. com. City of New Baunfels, 1989-99; dir. River Bend Property Owners Assn., 1997-99. Decorated Legion of Merit; named Realtor of Yr. New Braunfel Bd. of Realtors, 1992. Mem. Tex. Assn. of Realtors (edn. task force 1992, tech. task force 1993, polit. action com.). Home: 2080 Partnership Rd Seguin TX 78155-8381 Office: Patton Properties 2080 Partnership Rd Seguin TX 78155

PATTON, PAUL E. governor; b. Fallsburg, Ky., May 26, 1937; Grad. in mech. engring., U. Ky., 1959. With coal bus., until 1979; dep. sec. transp., 1979; judge-exec. Pike County, 1981; lt. gov., sec. econ. devel., pres. senate State of Ky., Frankfort, 1991-95, gov., 1995—. Served on Ky. Crime Commn., Ky. Tourism Commn., Task Force for Workplace Literacy; former mem. Prichard Com. for Acad. Excellence; chmn. Econ. Devel. and Commerce Com.; co-chair Task Force on Transp., Nat. Gov's. Assn.; chmn. Edn. Commn. of the States; former chmn. Southern Regional Edn. Bd., Southern Growth Policies Bd.; former exec. com. mem. Southern Gov's. Assn.; former chmn. Southern Tech. Coun.; mem. Appalachian Regional Commn., Southern States Energy Bd. Mem. bd. overseers Bellarmine Coll., bd. trustees Pikeville Coll.; chmn. Ky. Dems., 1981-83; del. Dem. Nat. Conv.; served numerous terms Pike County Dem. Exec. Com. Office: Office of the Governor State Capitol 700 Capitol Ave Frankfort KY 40601-3410*

PATTON, PETER MARK, lawyer; b. Chgo., Dec. 23, 1955; s. James T. and Dorothy R. Patton; m. Anne E. Castimore, Oct. 12, 1985; 1 child, William James. AB, Harvard Coll., 1977; JD, U. Calif., Berkeley, 1985. Bar: Pa. 1987, U.S. Dist. Ct. (ea. dist.) Pa. 1987, U.S. Ct. Appeals (4th cir.) 1986, U.S. Ct. Appeals (3rd cir.) 1988. Law clk. U.S. Ct. Appeals (4th cir.), Richmond, Va., 1985-87; assoc. Galfand, Berger, Phila., 1987-93, ptnr., 1993—. Committeeman Dem. Orgn., Delaware County, 1998. Reciient Profl. Responsibility award Am. Jurisprudence, 1985. Mem. Pa. Trial Lawyers Assn., Phila. Trial Lawyers Assn., Million Dollar Advocates Forum. Avocation: running. Office: Galfand Berger 1818 Market St Ste 2300 Philadelphia PA 19103-3648

PATTON, RAY BAKER, financial consultant, real estate broker; b. Jan. 24, 1932; s. Dwight Lyman Moody and Opal (Hembre) P.; m. Gloria Ruth Chambers, June 6, 1954; children: David Baker, Dayna Erin. BA, U. Okla., 1955, MRCP, 1960, MAPA, 1969. Asst. dir. planning San Joaquin, Calif., 1959-61; dir. planning City of Norman, Okla., 1961-65, Oklahoma City, 1965-67, St. Louis County, Mo., 1967-71; pres. Creative Environs., Inc., Clayton, 1972-74; prin. Raymond B. Patton & Assocs., Ballwin, 1975-81; investment broker, ins. planner A.G. Edwards & Sons, Inc., Clayton, 1981-83; fin. planning coord., dir. seminars E.F. Hutton & Co., Inc., St. Louis, 1983-84; securities prin. Westport Fin. Group, Inc., 1984-86; securities products coord., agy. edn. coord., fin. planner Equitable Fin. Cos., 1986-91; bus. and fin. cons. Mo. Automative Svc. Assn., 1991-93; broker, sales assoc. Coldwell Banker Real Estate, Chesterfield, Mo., 1994-95. Pres. Patton Real Estate, Inc., 1975-81, Success Power, Inc., St. Louis, 1975-81, chmn. bd., CEO, 1989-93; dir. pub. works and planning, health commr., zoning enforcement officer City of Des Peres, Mo., 1977-79; zone mgr. Investors Diversified Svc.'s, Chesterfield, 1980-81; securities prin. The Patton Fin. Group, Inc., St. Louis, 1984-86; chmn. bd., CEO Body Works, St. Louis, 1989-93; faculty mem. Nat. Inst. Farm and land Brokers, 1971-76; motivational spkr.; cons. in field. Contbr. articles to profl. jours. Scoutmaster St. Louis Area coun. Boy Scouts Am., 1976-80, vice chmn. adult tng., 1977-83; mem. Christian Bus. Men's Com., Chesterfield; mem. adv. bd. Cleveland County (Okla.) Child Welfare, 1963-64; min. music Ballwin, 1978-83, choir cir. E. Free Ch., Ladue, Mo., 1986; vol. tutor OASIS, 1994-96; former choir dir. E. Free, Manchester, Md.; tutor O.A.S.I.S.. Parkway, S.D., 1993-96. Served with USMC, 1955-58. Named Outstanding Mcpl. Employee State of Okla., 1963, Woodbage staff Outstanding Adult Scout Leader Pioneer Dist. Boy Scouts Am., 1978, 79; recipient IDS Mercury award, 1980, A.G. Edwards & Sons Crest award, 1982, Outstanding Exec. award E.F. Hutton, 1983, Blue Chip award, 1983, designated fin. advisor award, 1984. Mem. Am. Inst. Cert. Planners, Am. Inst. Planners (pres.-elect Mo., Kans., Okla. chpt. 1957, co-founder St. Louis Metro sect. 1969), Inst. Cert. Fin. Planners, Internat. Platform Assn., Internat. Assn. Fin. Planners, Eagle Scout Assn. (life), Fellowship Christian Fin. Advisors, Lambda Chi Alpha (pres. 1953-54). also: 2612 87th Ter E Palmetto FL 34221-8374 Home: 2612 87th Ter E Palmetto FL 34221-8374

PATTON, RICHARD WESTON, retired mortgage company executive; b. Evanston, Ill., Sept. 26, 1931; s. Robert Ferry and Sue Buckley P.; m. Lynda A. Kruse, Feb. 2, 1971; 1 child, Robert Weston BA, Amherst Coll., 1954. Sales engr. Thermo Fax Sales Corp., Chgo., 1958-60; account exec. Nat. Mortgage Investors, Inc., 1960-61, sales mgr. Pasadena, Calif., 1962-66, asst. v.p., 1966-67, v.p., 1967-69, exec. v.p., 1969-73, pres., chief exec. officer, dir., 1973-84, vice-chmn. bd., 1984-90; pres. Richard W. Patton Enterprises, Pasadena, 1990—. Pres., chmn. exec. com., dir. Ocean Park Restaurant Corp., Santa Monica, Calif., 1977-88; dir. Cenfed Bank, Cenfed Fin. Corp. Bd. dirs. Pasadena Boys' Club, 1963-66, Opera Assocs., 1984-90; mem. steering com. Amherst Coll. Capital Fund Drive, 1963-66. 1st lt. USMCR, 1955-58. Mem. Amherst Coll. Alumni Assn. (bd. dirs. 1963—, pres. 1977-79, 86-89), Overland Club (sec., bd. dirs.), Kroenstadt Ski Club (past pres.). Office: Rich W Patton Enterprises 3644 San Pasqual St Pasadena CA 91107-5419

PATTON, STUART, biochemist, educator; b. Ebenezer, N.Y., Nov. 2, 1920; s. George and Ina (Neher) P.; m. Colleen Cecelia Lavelle, May 17, 1945; children— John, Richard, Gail, Thomas, Mary Catherine, Patricia, Joseph. BS, Pa. State U., 1943; MS, Ohio State U., 1947, PhD, 1948. Chemist Borden Co., 1943-44; rsch. fellow Ohio State U., Columbus, 1946-48; faculty Pa. State U., University Park, 1949-80, prof., 1959-80, Evan Pugh rsch. prof. agr., 1966-80; adj. prof. neuroscis. Sch. Medicine U. Calif., San Diego, 1981—. Vis. scientist Scripps Instn. Oceanography; cons. in field. Author: (with Robert Jenness) Principles of Dairy Chemistry, 1959; (with Robert G. Jensen) Biomedical Aspects of Lactation, 1975. Lt. (j.g.) USNR, 1944-46. Recipient Borden award chemistry milk Am. Chem. Soc., 1957, Agrl. and Food Chemistry award, 1975, Alexander von Humboldt sr. scientist award, 1981, Macy-Gyorgy award Internat. Soc. for Rsch. on Human Milk and Lactation, 1997, Distinguished Alumnus award Sci. Assn., Pa. State U., 2002, Distinguished Svc. award Am. Dairy Sci. Assn., 1999. Fellow Am. Dairy Sci. Assn.; mem. Am. Chem. Soc., Am. Soc. Biochemistry and Molecular Biology, Am. Soc. Cell Biology. Home and Office: 6208 Avenida Cresta La Jolla CA 92037-6510 E-mail: spatton@ucsd.edu.

PATTON, SUSAN OERTEL, clinical social worker, educator; b. Syracuse, N.Y., May 18, 1946; d. Robert William and Jane (VanWormer) Oertel; m. Joseph D. Patton, Jr., June 3, 1967; children: Jennifer, Joseph D. III. BA, SUNY, Geneseo, 1984; MSW, SUNY, Buffalo, 1987. Cert. social worker, N.Y.; lic. ind. social worker, S.C.; cert. employee assistance profl.; qualified clin. social worker; bd. cert. fellow in managed mental health care; diplomate in clin. social work. Counselor Profl. Counseling Svc., Gowanda, N.Y., 1987-88, Mental Health Mgmt., Rochester, 1988-93, The Health Assn., Rochester, 1988-89, sr. counselor, 1989-90, asst. dir. mktg. and tng., 1990-92; pvt. practice, 1988-93; employee assistance program dir. Recovery Ctr. EAP, Hilton Head, S.C., 1993-95; pres., dir. Employee Assistance Program, Inc., Hilton Head Island, 1995-2001. Instr. Medaille Coll., Buffalo, 1990-93. Co-author: Treating Perpetrators of Sexual Abuse, 1990. Mem.: NASW, Employee Assistance Profls. Assn., Employee Assistance Soc. N.Am., S.C. Counselors Assn., Acad. Cert. Social Workers.

PATTON, THOMAS EARL, lawyer; b. Nov. 25, 1940; s. Thomas E. and Alice F. (Rodarmel) P.; m. Patricia Mann, Aug. 12, 1965 (dec.); m. Barbara Wood, Sept. 21, 1974; 1 child, David Earl AB, Cath. U. Am., 1962, JD summa cum laude, 1965. Bar: N.Y. 1966, D.C. 1966, Va. 1982. Assoc. Sullivan & Cromwell, N.Y.C., 1965-69; mem. Williams Connolly & Califano, Washington, 1970-75; asst. gen. counsel U.S. Dept. Energy, 1977-78; ptnr. Schnader, Harrison, Segal & Lewis, 1979-94. Disting. lectr. Cath. U. Am., 1970-90, 95—, bd. regents; nat. arbitrator Am. Arbitration Assn.; bd. dirs. Elcotel, Inc., IXI, Inc., Vanguard Found. Author: Securities Litigation, 1989, Federal Procedure Casebook, 1990; contbr. articles to profl. jours.; editor in chief Cath. U. Am. Law Rev. Mem. Washington World Affairs Coun., 1980—. Mem. ABA, D.C. Bar (founder and chair litigation sect.), Cosmos Club. Roman Catholic. Office: Tighe Patton Armstrong Teasdale 1747 Pennsylvania Ave NW Washington DC 20006-4688

PATTON, THOMAS EDWARD, artist, educator; b. Sacramento, May 17, 1954; s. Edward Clyde and Joan (Dall) P. BFA, San Francisco Art Inst., 1976; MA, U. New Mex., 1977, MFA, 1982. Instr. Millersville (Pa.) State Coll., 1979, New Mex. Inst. Mining & Tech., Socorro, 1981-82, Skidmore Coll., Saratoga Springs, N.Y., 1982-83; prof. U. Mo., St. Louis, 1983—. Author: (monograph) The Isolation and Intrusion Series, 1979, (catalogue) New Views: Photgaphs from Two Continents, 1985; one-man shows include Blue Sky Gallery, Portland, Oreg., 1982, U. N.Mex. Art Mus, 1982, Brockton (Mass.) Art Mus., 1984, UCLA, 1987, Mitchell Mus., Mt. Vernon, Ill., 1991, Kansas City Art Inst., 1994; exhibited in group shows at San Francisco Mus. Modern Art, 1985, St. Louis Art Mus., 1989, Mus. Photographic Art, San Diego, 1991, Downey Mus. Art, 1992, Wright State U., 1994; represented in public collections at Australia Nat. Gallery, Milw. Art Mus., Okland Mus., Portland Art Mus., Seattle Art Mus., St. Louis Art Mus., San Francisco Mus. Modern Art, U. N.Mex. Recipient Visual Artists fellowship NEA, Washington, 1990-91, James D. Phelan award, 2001-02. Mem. Soc. for Photographic Edn. Office: Calif State U Chico CA 95929

PATTON, THOMAS JAMES, sales and marketing executive; b. Cleve., Nov. 2, 1948; s. Michael Anthony and Delores (Bammerlin) P.; m. Thomasina Bernadette Cavallaro, Aug. 9, 1969; children: Thomasina, Thera V. A in Transp., Cleve. State U., 1971, BA in Mktg., 1973; BA, SUNY, Empire State, 1994. CLU; ChFC; registered health underwriter; registered employee benefit cons. Ins. salesman Manulife, Cleve., 1972-75, Mass. Mut., Cleve., 1976-80, Patton Ins. Assn., Inc., Avon Lake, Ohio, 1976—; ins. cons. Diversified Benefit Plans, Inc., 1978-93, dir. sales and mktg., 1993—; pres. commerce Benefits Group, Inc. and Ins. Mktg. Group, Inc., 1995; prin. Cmty. Health Ptnrs., Ltd., Ill., 1994. Pres. Commerce Benefits Group, Inc.; cons. Regional Sch. Consortium, Lorain County, Ohio, 1986—, County of Lorain, 1984—, City of Lorain, 1986—, County of Lorain, 1984—, City of Lorain, 1984—; prin. Comty. Health Ptnrs. Ltd.; bd. Italian Cultural Found.; founder 1-888 Ohiocomp w/c MCO-Ohio, 1997; co=founder VocRehabOne, Ltd., w/c Vocat. Rehab. Co. Pres. Lake Erie Rate Coun., Cleve., 1970-71; mem. Lorain County Dem. Ctrl. Com., Avon Lake, Ohio, 1986—; mem. com. Cleve. Leukemia Soc., 1985; bd. dirs. Villa Serena Sr. Housing, St. Francis Soc., Italian Cultural Found. Mem. Nat. Assn. Life Underwriters, Profl. Ins. Agts. Assn., Cert. Profl. Ins. Agts. Soc., Soc. Benefit Plan Adminstrn., Lorain County Life Underwriters, Irish Heritage, Order Italian Sons and Daus., Profl. Assn. Dive Instrs./Nat. Assn. Underwater Instrs. (SCUBA diving instr.). Roman Catholic. Avocations: fishing, skin and scuba diving, soccer, photography. Office: Commerce Group PO Box 900 Elyria OH 44036-0900

PATTON, WARREN ANDRE, public relations executive, journalist; b. Chgo., Oct. 15, 1954; s. Willie Roosevelt and Adriana Ultima (Rhodes) P.; m. Annie Yolanda Thomas, Nov. 19, 1981 (div. May 1988); 1 child, Thomas; m. Olga Enid Ostalaza, July 31, 1993 (div. May 1996); children: Rafaela, Jennifer, Christopher, Michael. B in Criminal Justice, Chaminade U., 1986; MBA, Chadwick U., 1992; MPA, Troy State U., 1993. Enlisted USN, 1978, advanced through grades to chief, 1991. Journalist USN, 1978—. Fundraiser Combined Fed. Campaign, Pensacola, Fla., 1991, Waterfront Mission, Pensacola, 1993. Mem. ASPA, Nat. Assn. Black Journalists, Conf. of Minority Pub. Adminstrs., Fleet Res. Assn., Hannibal Masonic Lodge No. 1. Avocations: reading, bowling, chess, poetry, jogging.

PATTY, ANNA CHRISTINE, middle school educator; b. Atlanta, Aug. 25, 1937; d. Henry Richard and Gertrude Johnson; children: Robert E., C. Wayne Jr., Christine E. BS in Math., U. Ga., 1959; MA in Curriculum and Instrn., Va. Poly. Inst. and State U., 1991. Cert. tchr., Va. Mgr. Steak and Ale Restaurants, Inc., Dallas, 1982-84; bus. mgr. Nova Plaza Corp., Charlotte, N.C., 1984-86; asst. mgr. WoodLo, Inc., 1986-87; food activity mgr. Army and Air Force Exch. Svc., Schweinfurt, Germany, 1987-89; substitute tchr. Montgomery County Schs., Christiansburg, Va., 1989-91; rsch. asst. Va. Poly. Inst. and State U., Blacksburg, 1990-91; mid. sch. tchr. math. and sci. Hampton (Va.) City Schs., 1991-93, mid. sch. tchr. sci., 1993-97, mid. sch. tchr. Advancement Via Individual Determination, 1997-98. Mem. NSTA/APST Summer Inst., U.Md., 1992, NSTA Summer Inst., Sci. and Tech., SUNY, Stoney Brook, N.Y., 1995; EXCEL coach Christopher Newport U., 1993-95. With Operation Path Finders, Sandy Hook, N.J., 1994. Mem. NEA, Va. Educators Assn., Nat. Sci. Tchrs. Assn. (summer inst. participant 1992), Va. Middle Sch. Assn., Va. Sci. Tchrs., Nat. Coun. Tchrs. Math. Republican. Unitarian Universalist. Avocations: hiking, camping, herbs, wine tasting, cooking. Home: 3327 Springview Dr Christiansburg VA 24073-6867

PATTY, CLAIBOURNE WATKINS, JR. lawyer; b. Cleve., Feb. 19, 1934; s. Claibourne Watkins and Eleanor (Todd) P.; m. Barbara Benton, May 4, 1968; children— Claibourne Watkins III, William Jordan. BA, U. of South, 1955; JD, U. Ark., 1961. Bar: Ark. 1961. Law clk. U.S. dist. judge, Ft. Smith, 1961-63; pvt. practice Little Rock, 1963-68; asst. ins. commr. State of Ark., 1968-69; trust officer Union Nat. Bank of Little Rock, 1969-77; asst. dean U. Ark. Sch. Law, Little Rock; also exec. dir. Ark. Inst. for Continuing Legal Edn., 1977-86; law clk. 2d Div. Chancery Ct., Pulaski County, 1986-89; of counsel Gruber Law Firm, North Little Rock, 1989-2001; prin. Patty Law Firm, 2001—. Lectr. law Ark. Sch. Law, 1965; bd. dirs., chmn. Pulaski County Legal Aid Bur., 1966-69; mem. com. on civil practice Ark. Supreme Ct., 1998—. Bd. dirs., pres. Family Svc. Agy. of Ctrl. Ark., 1976-81, 86-93, 99—; bd. dirs., pres. Good Shepherd Ecumenical Retirement Ctr., 1975—; bd. dirs. Am. Diabetes Assn., Ark. Affil., 1996—, Ark. Gerontol. Soc. 1996—; mem. Ark. adv. com. U.S. Commn. on Civil Rights, 1985-89. With AUS, 1955-57. Mem. Beta Theta Pi, Phi Alpha Delta. Office: Patty Law Firm 315 N Broadway St North Little Rock AR 72114-5379 E-mail: clairgpm@swbell.net.

PATTY, WILLIAM ROBERT, educator, administrator; b. El Paso, Tex., July 31, 1940; s. Jim Lane and Blanche Helen Patty; m. Sandra Jean Marlin, June 4, 1972 (dec. June 2001); 1 child, Mary Madeline. BS, U. Tex., El Paso, 1969. Cert. elem. and secondary tchr., Tex. Tchr., coach Dolphin Terrace Sch., El Paso, 1966-85; tchr., asst. prin., track coach N.E. Christian Acad., 1985-90, 92—. Diabetes edn. asst. VA Clinic, El Paso, 1999—. ärack coach Northeast

Christian Acad., El Paso, 1963-89;äV.p. PTA, El Paso, 1969-71. With USAF, 1958-59. Mem. DAV, Am. Legion. Baptist. Avocations: coins, fast pitch softball. Home: 3409 Volcanic El Paso TX 79904

PATTYN, SUE, publishing executive; b. Sept. 1, 1958; Owner Guides for Living, Longmont, Colo., 1995—. Home: 7363 Nebraska Way Longmont CO 80504-8419 Office: PO Box 1104 Longmont CO 80502-1104 E-mail: spattyn@guides4living.com.

PATULA, RODNEY RICHARD, lawyer; b. Berwyn, Ill., Nov. 19, 1949; s. Henry Biel and Irene Patricia Patula; m. Judith A. Brey, June 10, 1972 (div. Dec. 1977); m. Marilyn K. Thieme, Apr. 25, 1982; 1 stepchild, Aaron M. Thieme. AB, U. Chgo., 1970; JD, U. Denver, 1973. Bar: Colo. 1974, U.S. Dist. Ct. Colo. 1974, U.S. Ct. Appeals (10th cir.) 1977, U.S. Supreme Ct. 1981, U.S. Ct. Appeals (5th cir.) 1989, U.S Ct Appeals (9th cir.) 1993, Calif., 1996, U.S. Dist. Ct. (no., ctrl. and ea. dists.) 1996, U.S. Ct. Appeals (4th cir.) 2000. Sr. law clk. to chief judge U.S. Dist. Ct. for Colo., Denver, 1974-75; assoc. Davis Graham & Stubbs, 1975-79; shareholder, dir. Pryor Carney & Johnson P.C., Englewood, Colo., 1979-95; ptnr., chmn. nat. litigation practice group Graham & James, LLP, San Francisco, 1995-2000; ptnr., dep. practice area coord., adv. No. Calif. Squire Sanders & Dempsey, LLP, 2000—. Contbr. articles to law jours. Bd. dirs. Mile High United Way, Denver, 1990-92; mem. Lawyers' Com. for Civil Rights, San Francisco, 1995—. Named Top Laywers in Silicon Valley, San Jose Mag., 2000, 2001. Mem. ABA, Colo. Bar Assn. (ethics com. 1987-89), State Bar Calif., Denver Bar Assn. (Vol. Lawyer of Yr. award 1986), Bar Assn. San Francisco. Avocations: hiking, wines. Office: Squire Sanders & Dempsey LLP One Maritime Plz 3d Fl San Francisco CA 94111 E-mail: rpatula@ssd.com.

PATULOT, JUN J. R. insurance company executive; b. Manila, Oct. 30, 1947; came to U.S., 1975; s. Silvino M. and Sotera P. Patulot; m. Connie Castro, Sept. 2, 1950; children: Patrick, Aires. BS in Fgn. Svc., Lyceum of Philippines, Manila, 1968; postgrad. in Law, San Sebastian Coll., Manila, 1972; postgrad. in Mgmt. and Supervision, Seattle C.C., 1980. Fgn. svc. staff officer Ministry of Fgn. Affairs, Manila, 1970-74, Philippine Consulate Gen., Seattle, 1975-84; spl. supr. Gt. Am. Res. Ins. Co., 1985-87; exec. sales dir. Surety Life Ins. Co., 1987-91; mng. gen. agt. N.W. Life Assurance of Am., Belligham, 1991—, Conseco Life Ins. and Investing Brokerage, Carmel, 2001—. Pvt. practice ins. brokerage, Seattle, 1987—. Recipient Nat. Sales Achievement award Nat. Assn. Life Underwriters, Nat Quality award Life Ins. Mktg. and Rsch. Assn. Mem. Million Dollar Round Table. Office: Jun Patulot & Co 1415 2nd Ave Ste 1701 Seattle WA 98101-2042 Home: 11813 SE 75th Pl Newcastle WA 98056-1768 E-mail: junpatulot@hotmail.com.

PATUREAU, ARTHUR MITCHELL, chemical engineer, consultant; b. Beaumont, Tex., Nov. 22, 1913; m. Clara Davis, Dec. 24, 1934. BSChemE, U. Tex., 1943, postgrad., Pa. State U., 1946. Chief process engr. Gasoline Plant Constrn. Co., Corpus Christi, Tex., 1944-46, McCarthy Chem. Co., Houston, 1946-48; chief application engr. Fisher & Porter Co., Hatboro, Pa., 1948-50; cons. reactor coolant controls Nautilus nuc. submarine Westinghouse Atomic Power Divsn., Pitts., 1950-53; chief application engr. chem. industry Brown Instrument Divsn., Phila., 1953-55; western sales mgr. Barksdale Valves, L.A., 1955-74; western divisional mgr. Pa. Indsl. Chem. Co., 1974-75; divisional mgr. Hercules, Inc., 1973-75; cons. to chem. industry Temple, Tex., 1975—; pres. Artgraphics, Inc., 1975—. Editor: (tech. book) Resins in Rubber, 1975; contbg. author to Ency. Chem. Engring.; contbr. articles to profl. jours. Mem. engring. fund adv. coun. U. Tex. Coll. Engring., 1970—75. Mem. AIChE, L.A. Rubber Group, River Art Group, Elks, Rotary. Episcopalian. Avocations: flying, art work, camping, travel, computer work. Home and Office: 4312 S 31st St Apt 55 Temple TX 76502-3359 Fax: 254-899-0353. E-mail: artpatu@aol.com.

PATURIS, E(MMANUEL) MICHAEL, lawyer; b. Akron, Ohio; s. Michael George and Sophia (Manos) P.; m. Mary Ann Toompas, Febr. 28, 1965. BS, U. N.C., 1954, JD with Honors, 1959, student, 1959-60. Bar: N.C. 1959, D.C. 1969, Va. 1973; CPA. Acct., Charlotte and Wilmington, N.C., 1960-63; assoc. Poyner, Geraghty, Hartsfield & Townsend, Raleigh, 1963-64; atty. advisor Chief Counsel's Office, Washington, 1964-66, sr. trial atty. Richmond, Va., 1966-69; ptnr. Reasoner, Davis & Vinson, Washington, 1969-78; sole practitioner Alexandria, 1978—. Acctg. instr. U. N.C., Chapel Hill, 1959-60; acctg., econs. lectr. N.C. State U., Raleigh, 1963-64; business law lectr. George Mason U., Fairfax County, Va., 1978-79. Mem. bd. editors U. N.C. Law Rev. With U.S. Army, 1954-56. Recipient U. N.C. Law Sch. Block award, 1959. Mem. Phi Beta Kappa., Beta Gamma Sigma. Home: 6326 Stoneham Ln Mc Lean VA 22101-2345 Office: Law Offices of E Michael Paturis 431 N Lee St Alexandria VA 22314-2301

PATY, DONALD WINSTON, neurologist, educator; b. Peking, China, Sept. 25, 1936; s. Robert Morris and Katherine (Behenna) P.; m. Jo Anne Haymore, Dec. 28, 1958; children: Morris Britten, Beverly Behenna, Breay Winston, Donald Blake. BA, Emory U., 1958, MD, 1962. Intern Duke U., 1962-63; resident in medicine and neurology Emory U., 1965-70; fellow in immunology MRC Demyelinating Diseases Unit, U. Newcastle-upon-Tyne, Eng., 1970-72; asst. prof., then prof. neurology U. Western Ont. (Can.) Med. Sch., 1972-80; prof. neurology, head div. U. B.C. Med. Sch., Vancouver, 1980-96. Sec.-gen. XV World Congress of Neurology, Vancouver, B.C., 1993; advisor London (Ont.) chpt. Multiple Sclerosis Soc. Can., 1972-80; sec. exec. com., med. adv. bd. Internat. Fedn. Multiple Sclerosis Socs., 1980—; mem. WHO working Group in Multiple Sclerosis, 1998. Author articles in field.; Mem. editorial bds. profl. jours. Bd. dirs. London Symphony, 1978-80; chmn. grants rev. com. Multiple Sclerosis Soc. of Can.; mem. exec. com. med. adv. bd., chmn. med. mgmt. com. Internat. Fed. Multiple Sclerosis Soc., 1983-97. With USPHS, 1963-65. Fellow Can. Life Ins. Assn., 1972-77; grantee Multiple Sclerosis Soc. Can.; grantee Med. Rsch. Coun. Can.; recipient John Dystel Rsch. award Multiple Sclerosis Soc./Am. Acad. Neurology, 1995, Sir Richard Cave award Multiple Sclerosis Soc. Gt. Britain and No. Ireland, 1995, Charcot award Internat. Fedn. of Multiple Sclerosis Socs., 1995. Fellow: ACP, Am. Acad. Neurology, Royal Coll. Physicians and Surgeons Can. (chmn. com. in neurology 1982—86); mem.: World Fedn. Neurology (Can. rep. coun. of dels., chmn. multiple sclerosis rsch. group 1993—98, mem. pub. awareness com., com. on structure and function 2001), Brit. Assn. Neurologists (hon.), Am. Neurol. Assn., Can. Neurol. Soc. (pres. 1989—90), Alpha Omega Alpha. Unitarian Universalist. Home: 3657 W 24th Ave Vancouver BC Canada V6S 1L7 Office: UBC Hosp 2211 Wesbrook Mall Rm S 195 Vancouver BC Canada B6T 2B5 E-mail: paty@interchange.UBC.ca.

PATZ, EDWARD FRANK, retired lawyer; b. Balt., Aug. 25, 1932; s. Maurice A. and Violet (Furman) P.; m. Betty Seldner Levi, Nov. 18, 1956; children— Evelyn Anne, Edward Frank, Thomas L. BS, U. Md., 1954, LLB, 1959. Bar: Md. 1959, U.S. Dist. Ct. Md. 1959, U.S. Ct. Appeals (4th cir.) 1959, U.S. Supreme Ct. 1980. Ptnr. Weinberg and Green and predecessor firms, Balt., 1959-97; ret., 1997. Bd. dirs. Jewish Family and Children's Service, 1965-71; regional bd. dirs. NCCJ; pres. Suburban Club Balt. County, 1977-79; bd. trustees, exec. com. Flagler Ecumenical Social Svcs. Ctr., Inc., 1999—. Mem. Hammock Dunes Club. Home: 39 Island Estates Pkwy Palm Coast FL 32137-2203 E-mail: efpatz@pcfl.net.

PATZAKIS, MICHAEL J. orthopaedic surgeon, educator; b. Campbell, Ohio, Nov. 6, 1937; m. Susan Patzakis, 1961; children: Michele, Theresa, John, Peter. BA, Ohio State U., 1959, MD, 1963. Diplomate Am. Bd. Orthopaedic Surgery. Intern L.A. County-USC Med. Ctr., 1963-64, resident, 1964-68; fellow rheumatoid surgery U. Colo. Med. Ctr., 1968-69; instr. U. So. Calif. Sch. Medicine, 1967-68, asst. prof., 1969-75, assoc. prof., 1975-88, prof., 1988—, interim chmn., 1990-91, chmn., 1991—, The Vincent and Julia Meyer chair, 1996—; chief orthop. surgery U. So. Calif. Univ. Hosp., 2000—, L.A. County-U. So. Calif. Med. Ctr., 2000—. Instr. U. Colo., 1968-69; vis. prof. U. Calif., Irvine, 1969, 70, Case Western Res. U., 1976, Cleve. Clinic, 1976, U. Tex., Dallas, 1977, UCLA, 1977, Northwestern U., 1981, Stanford U., 1981, Northeastern Ohio Sch. Medicine, 1983, U. Calif., San Diego, 1985, Drew Med. Sch., L.A., 1988, Martin Luther King Drew Med. Sch., 1989, Athens Hellenic Trauma Soc., 1990, Walter Reed Army Med. Ctr., Washington, 1996, U. Thessalia, Greece, 1998, many others; mem. med. and sci. com. Arthritis Found. So. Calif., 1974-80; lectr., presenter, cons. in field. Assoc. editor Jour. Clin. Orthopaedics and Related Rsch., 1979—, guest editor, 1983, 84; assoc. editor, mem. editl. bd. Contemporary Orthopaedics, 1980— Mem. festival com. St. Anthony's Greek Orthodox, Pasadena, Calif., 1970—, festival chmn., 1971, dir. youth program, 1971-84, mem. ch. bldg. com., 1976-81; basketball commr. Greek Orthodox Youth League So. Calif., 1984-84; active AXIOS Found. of Worthiness-Greek Ams. So. Calif., 1984—; bd. dirs. L.A. Concert Open, 1994—. Named Greek Orthodox Person of the Yr., So. Calif. St. Nectarios Ch., Covina, Calif., 1986; rsch. grantee Am. Arthritis Found., 1968-69, Eli Lilly and Co., 1970-71, 71-72, 72-73, 73-74, 76-77, Bristol Myers Co., 1971-72, Galaxo, 1984, Merck-Germany, 1984, Merrell-Dow, 1987-88, Miles Lab., 1990, R.W. Johnson, 1994, Genetics Inst., 1993-94, 94-95, Abbott Labs., 1996—, Merck Rsch. Labs., 1998-99, Synercid, 1998—, 98—, 99—, others. Mem. AAUP, Am. Acad. Orthopaedic Surgeons (faculty summer inst. 1980-84, mem. com. on evaluation 1986—), Am. Orthopaedic Assn., Assn. Bone and Joint Surgeons, Am. Rheumatism Assn., Western Orthopaedic Assn. (program chmn. 1983-84), Hellenic-Am. Med. Soc. (bd. dirs. 1982-86, Physician of Yr. 2000), Acad. Orthopaedic Soc (mem.-at-large 1995-97), Musculoskeletal Infection Soc. (pres. 1992-93), Calif. Orthopaedic Assn., Calif. Med. Assn., Hippocratic Orthopaedic Soc., L.A. County Med. Assn., U. So. Calif. Grad. Orthopaedic Soc. (program chair 1977-86, pres. 1988-89), Wilson Bost Interurban Club (com. mem. So. Calif. chpt. 1992—), Alpha Epsilon Delta (pres. 1958-59). Office: LA County & USC Med Ctr GNH 3900 1200 N State St Los Angeles CA 90033-1029

PAUCA, JANET FRANCES, lawyer; b. Hemel Hempstead, Eng., June 13, 1941; came to U.S., 1968; d. Leonard and Kathleen Emily (Finnemore) Thearle; m. Alfredo Lazo Pauca, Aug. 28, 1965; children: Leonard, Rosemary, Deanna. BA, Wake Forest Univ., 1979, JD, 1982. Bar: N.C., 1983. Sr. library asst. Royal Postgrad. Med. Sch., London, 1961-67; sole practice law Winston-Salem, N.C., 1983—. Mem. Winston-Salem Conv. Ctr. Commn., 1984-89. Mem. N.C. Bar Assn. (Hispanic lawyers com.), N.C. Assn. Women Attys. Democrat. Jewish. Avocations: ice skating, reading, music.

PAUCIULO, JOHN WILLIAM, lawyer; b. N.Y.C., Nov. 6, 1965; m. Johanna Choate; children: Michael, Nina. BA, Villanova U., 1987; JD, Temple U., 1990. Staff atty. U.S. Securities and Exch. Commn., N.Y.C., 1990-92; assoc. Lamb, Windle & McErlane, West Chester, Pa., 1992-96; assoc. counsel Pep Boys, Phila., 1996-98; assoc. White & Williams, 1998—. Judge of elections Chester County, Pa., 1995-2001. Mem. Pa. Bar Assn. Home: 22 Hickory Ln Malvern PA 19355-3005 Office: White & Williams 1800 One Liberty Pl Philadelphia PA 19103 E-mail: pauciuloj@whitewms.com.

PAUER, JAMES J. environmental engineer, consultant; b. Bloemfontein, Free State, South Africa, Feb. 22, 1962; m. Lynne Rogers, Apr. 1, 2000. BSc in Chemistry with hons., U. Orange Free State, S. Africa, 1983; MSc in Chemistry, U. Pretoria, S. Africa, 1988; PhD, Mich. Technol. U., 1996. Project leader Coun. for Sci. and Indsl. Rsch., Pretoria, South Africa, 1990-91; chief water quality modeler Welso, Grosse Ile, Mich., 1996—. Office: Welso 9311 Groh Rd Grosse Ile MI 48138 E-mail: pauer.james@epa.gov., iemand@comcast.net.

PAUGH, NANCY ADELE, elementary and secondary education educator; b. Aug. 10, 1953; BS, N.Y. U., 1975, MA, 1978. Tchr. H.S. math. Woodbridge (N.J.) Schs., 1975-87, supr. math. and music, 1987—. Co-contbr. articles to mag. Organist, choir dir. St. Paul's United Methodist Ch., Tottenville, N.Y., 1967-71, 75—; mem. Ocean Grove (N.J.) Auditorium Choir, 1984—. Grantee, NSF, 1995—2001. Mem. ASCD, Am. Assn. Sch. Adminstrs., Nat. Assn. Secondary Sch. Prins., Nat. Assn. Elem. Sch. Prins., Math. Assn. Am., Am. Math. Soc., Music Educators Nat. Conf., Am. Guild Organists, Pi Lambda Theta. Office: Woodbridge Schs PO Box 428 Woodbridge NJ 07095-0428 E-mail: nancy.paugh@woodbridge.k12.nj.us.

PAUGH, PATRICIA LOU, business consultant; b. Pitts., Oct. 30, 1948; d. Marshall Franklin and Helen Jeanne (Graham) P. BA in English, Columbia U., 1982. Adminstrv. asst. Katz, Robinson, Brog & Seymour, N.Y.C., 1972-75; office mgr. Michael D. Martocci, 1975-80; adminstrv. mgr. O'Melveny & Myers, 1982-85, Latham & Watkins, N.Y.C., 1985-88; mgr. Nationwide Legal Svcs., 1988-89; mgr. legal adminstrn. Aluminum Co. of Am., Pitts., 1990-93; ptnr. Domestic & Overseas Countertrade and Consulting Svcs., Ltd., 1986—; pres. Domestic & Overseas Trading Corp., Pitts., 1993—; mng. dir. Gen. Comml. Svcs., Ltd., 1994—. Mem. Am. Mgmt. Assn., Pitts. C. of C. Republican. Episcopalian. Office: Apt 20F 320 Fort Duquesne Blvd Pittsburgh PA 15222-1133

PAUKEN, STEPHEN J. town administrator; b. Maumee, Ohio, Sept. 19, 1955; s. Joseph C. and Margaret A. (Harrigan) P.; m. Margaret M. Feck, Jan. 18, 1974; children: Jennifer L., S. Gregory, John J. AS in Civil Engring., Michael J. Owens Tech. Coll., 1977; BS in Bus. Adminstrn. magna cum laude, Heidelberg Coll., 1999—. Regional sales mgr. Mattei Compressors, Columbia, Md., 1988-93, Powerex Air Techs., Harrison, Ohio, 1987-88; sales engr. Daniel L. Bowers Co., RoyalOak, Mich., 1984-87; dist. sales mgr. Optibelt Corp., Addison, Ill., 1981-83; mem. coun. City of Maumee, Ohio, 1984-93, pres. coun., 1990-93, mayor, 1993-99; town adminstr. Berthoud, Colo., 1999—. Trustee Ohio Mcpl. League, Columbus, 1996-99; chair Toledo Met. Area Coun. Govts., 1997-98. Editor (newsletters) NOMMA News, 1994, 96-97, Mattei Memo, 1990-93. Trustee Lucas County Improvement Corp., Toledo, 1993-99, St. Lukes Hosp., Maumee, 1993-99; chair Lucas County E-911 Com., 1996. Mem. Northwest Ohio Mayors and Mgrs. Assn. (treas. 1995-99). Democrat. Roman Catholic. Office: PO Box 1229 Berthoud CO 80513-2229 E-mail: spauken@prodigy.net.

PAUKEN, THOMAS WEIR, venture capital executive, lawyer, mediator; b. Victoria, Tex., Jan. 11, 1944; s. Thomas N. and Patricia (Weir) P.; m. Ida Ayala; children: Thomas II, Michelle, Angela, Elizabeth, Daniel, Victoria, Monica. AB in Polit. Sci., Georgetown U., 1965, postgrad., 1966-67; JD, So. Meth. U., 1973. Bar: Tex., 1975. White House staff asst., dep. dir. White Ho. fellows, Washington, 1970-71; pvt. practice atty. Dallas, 1974-80; dir. ACTION, Washington, 1981-85; pres. Sta. KRZI-Radio, Waco, Tex., 1985-86; v.p., corp. counsel Garvon, Inc., Dallas, 1986-91; pres. TWP, Inc., 1991—. Chmn., bd. dirs. Tutogen Med., Inc.; bd. dirs. TOR Minerals, Inc. Author: The Thirty Years War - The Politics of the 60s Generation, 1994. Mem. Reagan transition team Counsel's Office, Washington, 1980-81; Tex. Rep. State chmn., 1994-97. 1st lt. U.S. Army, 1967-70, Vietnam. Recipient Drug Edn. Leadership award PRIDE, 1985, Dir.'s award U.S. Office of Personnel Mgmt., 1985; Weaver fellow 1965. Mem. State Bar Tex. Roman Catholic. Avocation: reading. E-mail: twpauken@t-speed.net.

PAUKER, SUSAN PERLMUTTER, clinical geneticist, pediatrician; b. N.Y.C., May 16, 1945; d. Henry Irwin Perlmutter and Sylvia Perlmutter Bailus; m. Stephen G. Pauker, Sept. 2, 1967; children: Sheridan J., Scott Gregory. BS, Tufts U., 1967, MD, 1971. Diplomate Am. Bd. Pediat., Am. Bd. Med. Genetics. Resident in pediat. Mass. Gen. Hosp., Boston, 1971-73, fellow in genetics, 1973-75; chief genetics dept. Harvard Cmty. Health Plan (now Harvard Vanguard), 1975—; dir. Genetics Clinics Mass. Gen. Hosp., 1981—. Chief pediatrics Harvard Cmty. Health Plan, 1978-84, dir. health ctr., 1984-86; pres., CEO Harvard Pilgrim Health Care Found., 1986-99; assoc. prof. pediats. Harvard Med. Sch., Boston, 1999—. Bd. dirs. March of Dimes, 1989-95, Mass. Coalition Against Violence, 1991—; bd. overseers Mus. Sci., Boston, 1990—; violinist Longwood Symphony Orch. Fellow Am. Coll. Med. Genetics (founding). Office: Harvard Vanguard Med Assn Kenmore Office Genetic Dept 133 Brookline Ave Boston MA 02215-3904 E-mail: Susan_Pauker@vmed.org.

PAUL, ALIDA RUTH, arts and crafts educator; b. San Antonio, May 30, 1953; d. Richard Irving and Anne Louise (Holman) Paul. B.S. in Edn., Southwest Tex. State U., 1975; M.Ed., U. Houston, 1984. Cert. tchr., Tex. Tchr. art and crafts Houston Ind. Sch. Dist., 1975—. Republican. Episcopalian. Home: 16830 Grampin Dr Houston TX 77084-1945

PAUL, ANDREW ROBERT, defense and telecommunications consultant; b. N.Y.C., Aug. 14, 1938; s. Andrew B. and Maria (Filotas) P.; m. Britt-Marie Hagelbrant, Feb. 6, 1988. AB in French, Dartmouth Coll., 1960; MS in Fgn. Svc., Georgetown U., 1967. Dir. govt. rels. Motorola, Inc., Washington, 1968-75, Paramount Communications, Washington, 1975-90; sr. v.p. Satellite Broadcasting and Communications Assn., Alexandria, Va., 1990—2001; def. and telecom. cons. Mem. Gatt adv. com. on Intellectual Property, Washington, 1988-94; mem. adv. and admissions coms. MS in Fgn. Svc. program Georgetown U., Washington, 1981—. Presdl. campaign advance man Rep. Nat. Com., 1964; pres. chpt. XI Spl. Forces Assn., Washington, 1981-82; chmn. Alternative House Crisis Intervention Ctr., Vienna, Va., 1983-84. Capt. U.S. Army, 1960-65. Roman Catholic. Home: 1013 Heather Hill Ct Mc Lean VA 22101-2024

PAUL, ARA GARO, university dean; b. New Castle, Pa., Mar. 1, 1929; s. John Hagop and Mary (Injejikian) P.; m. Shirley Elaine Waterman, Dec. 21, 1962; children: John Bartlett, Richard Goyan. BS in Pharmacy, Idaho State U., 1950; MS, U. Conn., 1953, PhD in Pharmacognosy, 1956. Cons. plant physiology Argonne (Ill.) Nat. Lab., 1955; asst. prof. pharmacognosy Butler U., Indpls., 1956-57; faculty U. Mich., Ann Arbor, 1957—, prof. pharmacognosy, 1969—; dean U. Mich. Coll. Pharmacy, 1975-96; dean emeritus, prof. pharmacognosy. Vis. prof. microbiology Tokyo U., 1965-66; mem. vis. chemistry faculty U. Calif., Berkeley, 1972-73; del. U.S. Pharmacopeial Conv., 1980, 90; scholar-in-residence Am. Assn. Colls. Pharmacy, 1996; bd. grants Am. Found. Pharm. Edn., 1997—, chmn., 1999, co-chmn. endowment com., 2002--; mem. organizing com. Millennial World Congress Pharm. Scis., 1996-2000; mem. FIP Found., 2000—, chmn. bd. trustees, 2001--. Contbr. articles to profl. jours. Recipient Outstanding Tchr. award Coll. Pharmacy, U. Mich., 1969, Outstanding Alumnus award Idaho State U., 1976, Profl. Achievement award Coll. Pharmacy, Idaho State U., 1990; G. Pfeiffer Meml. fellow Am. Found. Pharm. Edn., 1965-66, Disting. Svc. Profile award Am. Found Pharm. Edn., 1992; fellow Eli Lily Found., 1951-53, Am. Found. Pharm. Edn., 1954-56, NIH, 1972-73. Fellow AAAS; mem. Am. Pharm. Assn., Am. Soc. Pharmacognosy, Acad. Pharm. Scis., Am. Assn. Colls. Pharmacy, Am. Assn. Pharm. Scientists, Phi Lambda Upsilon, Sigma Xi, Phi Delta Chi, Phi Sigma Kappa, Rho Chi. Home: 1415 Brooklyn Ave Ann Arbor MI 48104-4496 Office: U Mich Coll Pharmacy Ann Arbor MI 48109-1065 E-mail: arapaul@umich.edu.

PAUL, ARTHUR, artist, graphic designer, illustrator, art and design consultant; b. Chgo., Jan. 18, 1925; m. Beatrice Miller, Dec. 24, 1949 (div. 1973); children: William Warren, Fredric; m. Suzanne Seed, Mar. 8, 1975; 1 dau., Nina. Student, Inst. Design, 1947-51. Vice-pres., art dir. HMH Pub. Co., Playboy, Chgo., 1953-82; also sr. art dir., corp. art dir. Playboy mag.; pres. Art Paul Design; freelance artist Chgo., 1984—. Lectr. in field. Free lance illustrator, designer, 1951-53; designer 1st issue: Playboy mag, 1953, Playboy Rabbit symbol, 1953; one-man shows include Etc. Gallery, 1949, 500D Gallery, 1965, U. Ill., 1965, Chgo. Cultural Ctr., 1997-98; organizer, exhibitor: travelling exhbn. Beyond Illustration-The Art of Playboy; museums, Europe, Asia, U.S., 1971-73, Can., 1976-77; author: Vision-Art Paul, 1983, Art of Playboy, 1986, Sex Appeal, 2000; designer PBS-TV title Sence of Humor for humorous feature film presentations on American Playhouse; prodn. design cons. (PBS-TV movie) Who Am I This Time?. Trustee Chgo. Mus. Contemporary Art, 1970-86; apptd. trustee by Gov. of Ill. U. Ill. Summer Sch. of Arts, 1987—. With USAAF, 1943-46. Recipient numerous art awards, including Outstanding Achievement in Trademark Design for Playboy Mag. award Soc. Typographic Arts, 1970, Polycube award Art Dirs. Club Phila., 1975, Art Direction Mag. award, 1975, Gold medal for Chgo. Film Festival poster Art Dirs. Club N.Y., 1980, Top Midwest Mktg. award Playboy TV Subscription Ad, 1979, 82, Gold medal for exhbn. Beyond Illustration City of Milan, 1971, Profl. Achievement award IIT Inst. Design Alumni Assn., 1983; Art Inst. scholar, 1943; named to Art Dirs. Hall of Fame, 1986. Mem. Alliance Graphique Internat. Home: 175 E Delaware Pl Apt 7511 Chicago IL 60611-7740 *Design is more than a sense of order for me. It is beauty and common sense. To draw, to paint and to look at art is in the fabric of my life. I enjoy working with ideas and seeing them develop into a reality, after which I am fortunate enough to learn whether they have performed as intended.*

PAUL, BENJAMIN DAVID, anthropologist, educator; b. N.Y.C., Jan. 25, 1911; s. Phillip and Esther (Kranz) P.; m. Lois Fleischman, Jan. 4, 1936; children: Robert Allen, Janice Carol. Student, U. Wis., 1928-29; AB, U. Chgo., 1938, PhD in Anthropology, 1942. Lectr., rsch. dir. Yale U., 1942-44; community orgn. expert Inter-Am. Ednl. Found., 1946; from lectr. to assoc. prof. anthropology Harvard U., 1946-62, dir. social sci. program Sch. Pub. Health, 1951-62; prof. anthropology Stanford (Calif.) U., 1963—, chmn. dept., 1967-71, dir. program in medicine and behavioral sci., 1963-70. Cons. NIH, 1957—. Editor: Health, Culture and Community: Case Studies of Public Reactions to Health Programs, 1955, Changing Marriage Patterns in a Highland Guatemalan Community, 1963, The Maya Midwife as Sacred Professional, 1975, Mayan Migrants in Guatemala City, 1981, The Operation of a Death Squad in San Pedro la Laguna, 1988. 2d lt. AUS, 1944-46. Travelling fellow Social Sci. Rsch. Coun., 1940-41, Ctr. Advanced Study Behavioral Scis. fellow, 1962-63. Mem. Am. Anthropol. Assn. (Disting. Svc. award 1994), Phi Beta Kappa, Sigma Xi. Achievements include ethnographic field rsch. in Guatemala, 1941, 62, 64-65, 68-69, 73-79, 83-95, 97-98. Home: 622 Salvatierra St Palo Alto CA 94305-8538 Office: Stanford U Dept Anthropology Stanford CA 94305

PAUL, CAROL ANN, retired academic administrator, biology educator; b. Brockton, Mass., Dec. 17, 1936; d. Joseph W. and Mary M. (DeMeulenaer) Bjork; m. Robert D. Paul, Dec. 21, 1957; children: Christine, Dana, Stephanie, Robert. BS, U. Mass., 1958; MAT, R.I. Coll., 1968, Brown U., 1970; EdD, Boston U., 1978. Tchr. biology Attleboro (Mass.) High Sch., 1965-68; asst. dean., mem. faculty biology North Shore Community Coll., Beverly, Mass., 1969-78; master planner N.J. Dept. for Higher Edn., Trenton, 1978-80; assoc. v.p. Fairleigh Dickinson U., Rutherford, N.J., 1980-86; v.p. acad. affairs Suffolk Community Coll., Selden, N.Y., 1986-94, prof. biology, 1994-98; ret. Faculty devel. cons. various colls., 1979-98, title III evaluator, 1985-98. Author: (lab. manual and workbook) Minicourses and Labs for Biological Science, 1972 (rev. edit., 1975); (with others) Strategies and Attitudes, 1986; book reviewer, 1973-77, 94-98. V.p. LWV, Beverly, 1970—74, Cranford, NJ, 1982—83; alumni rep. Brown U., 1972—92; mem. Cape Cod Area LWV, 2001—; bd. dirs. YMCA of Cape Cod, clk. of bd., 1998—. Commonwealth Mass. scholar, 1954-58; recipient Acad. Yr. award NSF, 1968-69, Proclamation for Leadership award Suffolk County Exec., 1989. Mem.: AAUW, AAWCC, AAHE, Nat. Coun. for Staff (nat. exec. bd. 1979—80), Profls. and Orgn. Developers (planning com. 1977—79), Brown Alumni Club of Cape Cod (bd. dirs. 2001—, sec. 2001—), Pi Lambda Theta, Phi Theta Kappa. Roman Catholic. Avocation: swimming. Address: 7 Legend Dr South Yarmouth MA 02664-1315

PAUL, CHARLOTTE PATRICIA PEGGRAM, nursing educator; b. Clarendon, Tex., Jan. 13, 1941; d. William Clyde Peggram and Sibyl (Rattan) Jones; m. Robert M. Paul, Apr. 4, 1964; children: Peter, Lauraine. Diploma, St. Anthony's Hosp. Sch. Nursing, Amarillo, Tex., 1961; student, Amarillo Coll., 1958-65; BS, Syracuse U., 1972, MS, 1973, PhD in Edn. Adminstrn., 1979; postgrad., Wright State U., 1977-79, U. Tex., El Paso, 1983-86. Nurse St. Anthony's Hosp., Amarillo, Tex., 1961-65; evening charge nurse Upstate Med. Ctr. SUNY, Syracuse, 1966-68, VA Hosp. Gen. Hosp., Syracuse, 1965-66; asst. to head nurse Meml. Hosp., 1966-68; nurse IV therapy Cmty.-Gen. Hosp., 1968-72; instr. Syracuse Cen. Sch. Sys., 1972; asst. dir. insvc. edn. House of Good Samaritan Hosp., Watertown, N.Y., 1973-74; instr. SUNY Sch. Nursing, Syracuse, 1974-75, Syracuse U. Sch. Nursing, 1975-76; asst. dean Wright State U., Dayton, Ohio, 1977-79; assoc. prof. Edinboro U. Pa., 1979-86, prof., 1986—, chairperson dept. grad. studies, 1980-82, chairperson dept. nursing, 1987-89. Coord. quality assurance William Beaumont Army Med. Ctr., Fort Bliss, Tex., 1982—85; adj. assoc. prof. U. Tex. El Paso, 1982—85; cons. in field. Contbr. bd. dirs. ARC, Syracuse, 1970—77, Erie County Emergency Mgmt. Agy., cons., 1987—; mem. Coun. on Aging Com. on Long Term Care, Dayton, 1977—78. Lt. col. USAR. Named Hall of Fame, Internat. Bus. and Profl. Women, 1994; recipient Unit Citation award, CAP, 1968, Excellence in Nursing Edn. award, 1992, Comdr. Commendation award, 1995, Leadership and Svc. award, Lake Area Health Edn. Ctr., 1994; fellow Nightingale Soc. fellow, 1988; grantee, HEW, 1977, Wright State U., 1977—78, William Beaumont Army Med. Ctr., 1986, Edinboro U., 1979—80; scholar Gladys Post scholar, 1958—61, Rodney Horle scholar, 1971—72, Nellie Hurly scholar, 1971—72. Mem.: U.S. Nightingale Soc., Assn. Mil. Surgeons (life), Syracuse U. Alumni Assn., St. Anthony's Hosp. Sch. Nursing Alumni Assn., Res. Officers Assn. (life), Nat. Ski Patrol (life), Kiwanis (bd. dirs. Edinboro chpt.

1987—95, pres. 1988—89, v.p. 1987—88), Sigma Theta Tau (advisor 1987—94), Pi Lambda Theta (life; pres. local chpt. 1973—75). Republican. Office: Edinboro U Pa 139 Centennial Hall Edinboro PA 16412 E-mail: peggram_01@yahoo.com.

PAUL, CHRISTOPHER DONALD, carpenter, author; b. Danville, Pa., Sept. 20, 1955; s. Clyde Robert and Helen Elizabeth (Cook) P.; m. Karen Nester, Oct. 14, 1989. Student, Pa. State U., 1973-76. Park maintenance and ride operator Knoebels Amusement Resort, Elysburg, Pa., 1984-85; supr. roller coaster Wild World, Mitchelville, Md., 1986; carpenter Dinn Corp., Cin., 1985-89, Kitchen Spltys., Elmira, N.Y., 1990—. Author: Tracks Through Time, 1984; also articles. Bd. dirs. Eldridge Pk. Preservation Soc., 1988—89; regional rep. Am. Coaster Enthusiasts, Chgo., 1982—85; active Chemung County Hist. Soc., Elmira, 1990—, Tioga Point Mus., Athens, Pa., 1989—92; vice-comdr. Diven Camp, Elmira Sons of Union Vets. Republican. Presbyterian. Avocations: amusement park history research, riding roller coasters, attending local hockey and NY Mets baseball games. Home: 511 Davis St Elmira NY 14901-2422

PAUL, COURTLAND PRICE, landscape architect, planner; b. Pasadena, Calif., Mar. 11, 1927; s. Charles Price and Ethyle Louisa (Stanyer) P.; m. Kathryn Nadine Knauss, July 5, 1947; children: Pamela Kathryn, Courtland Scott, Kimberly Carol, Robyn Annette, Sanford Elliott. AA, John Muir Coll., 1948; student, Calif. Poly. U., 1948-49. Lic. landscape architect Ariz., Nebr., Nev., Calif. Founder, sr. prin., landscape architect Peridian Group, P.C., Pasadena, 1951-96; ret., 1996. Apptd. Calif. State Bd. Landscape Architects, 1960, 1964, pres., 1964; lectr. Calif. Poly. U., Pomona, Tex. A&M U., UCLA, Orange Coast Coll. Bd. dirs. Landscape Architecture Found., 1981-85 (pres. 1983). Served with USN, 1944-46. Recipient Achievement award Calif. Landscape Contractors Assn., 1963, citation award Pasadena Beautiful Found., 1969, Landscape Architecture award of merit Calif. Garden Clubs, 1970, commendation resolution Calif. State Senate Rules Com.,1 986, Profl. of Yr. Life Mem. award, 1986, 1st outstanding svc. to industry and environ. award Long Beach/O.C., Meridian award Landscape Contractors Assn., Max Tipton Meml. award, 1993; named Man of Yr. Landscape and Irrigation mag., 1987. Fellow Am. Soc. Landscape Archs. (at-large coun. fellows); mem. Calif. Coun. Landscape Archs. (pres. 1958, Outstanding Svc. citation 1984). Home and Office: 27605 Avenida Larga San Juan Capistrano CA 92675-3805 *People!! A career must be based on people - family, friends, friends of friends, friends of your clientele. They have shaped and made my career!! Always be there for them! Be on time, produce more than is expected and always, ALWAYS be fair!!!.*

PAUL, DARRELL FREDERICK, state trooper; b. Cairo, Sept. 26, 1949; s. Alvin Luther and Gertrude (Jones) P.; m. Sandra Justine Merideth Paul, Aug. 7, 1970; 1 child, Darrell F. Paul Jr. AA, Eastern Ky. U., 1981, BS, 1997. Sr. trooper Ky. State Police, Frankfort, 1973—. Fire arms tng. and tactics instr.; officer survival instr.; police use of force instr. Lance cpl. USMC, 1968-74. Decorated Purple Heart, Navy Commendation medal with combat v. Mem. Ky. Peace Officers Assn., Ky. State Police Profl. Assn. Baptist. Avocations: target shooting, travel. Home: 1024 W Hebron Ln Shepherdsville KY 40165-7418 Office: Ky State Police PO Box 1297 Elizabethtown KY 42702-1297 E-mail: ksp844@aol.com.

PAUL, DONALD ROSS, chemical engineer, educator; b. Yeatesville, N.C., Mar. 20, 1939; s. Edgar R. and Mary E. (Cox) P.; m. Sally Annette Cochran, Mar. 28, 1964 (wid. Jan. 1995); children: Mark Allen, Ann Elizabeth. BS, N.C. State Coll., 1961; MS, U. Wis., 1963, PhD, 1965. Rsch. chem. engr. E.I. DuPont de Nemours & Co., Richmond, Va., 1960-61; instr. chem. engring. dept. U. Wis., Madison, 1963-65; rsch. chem. engr. Chemstrand Rsch. Ctr., Durham, N.C., 1965-67; asst. prof. chem. engring. U. Tex., Austin, 1967-70, assoc. prof., 1970-73, prof., 1973—, T. Brockett Hudson prof., 1978-85, Melvin H. Gertz Regents chmn. chem. engring., 1985—, chmn. dept. chem. engring., 1977-85, dir. Ctr.'for Polymer Rsch., 1981—, dir. Tex. Materials Inst., 1998—. Turner Alfrey vis. prof. Mich. Molecular Inst., 1990-91; cons. in field. Author: (with F.W. Harris) Controlled Release Polymeric Formulations, 1976, (with S. Newman) Polymer Blends, 2 vols., 1978, (with Y.P. Yampolskii) Polymeric Gas Separation Membranes, 1994, (with C.B. Bucknall) Polymer Blends: Formulation and Performance, 2 vols., 2000. Recipient award Engring. News Record, 1975, Ednl. Svc. award Plastics Inst. Am., 1975, awards U. Tex. Student Engring. Coun., 1972, 75, 76, award for engring. tchg. Gen. Dynamics Corp., 1977, Joe J. King Profl. Engring. Achievement award, 1981, Holcott Engring. Rsch. award, 1994, Disting. Engring. Alumnus award N.C. State U., 1994, Outstanding Grad. Tchg. award U. Tex., 1994, Malcolm E. Pruitt award Coun. Chem. Rsch., 1998, Disting. Svc. citation U. Wis., 2000; named Donald L. Katz lectr. U. Mich., 2000. Fellow AIChE (South Tex. best fundamental paper award 1984, Materials Engring. and Scis. Divsn. award 1985, William H. Walker award 1998); mem. NAE, Mex. Acad. Scis. (corr. mem.), Am. Chem. Soc. (Doolittle award 1973, Phillips award in applied polymer sci. 1984, E.V. Murphree award in indsl. and engring. chemistry 1999), Soc. Plastics Engrs. (Outstanding Achievement in Rsch. award 1982, Internat. Edn. award 1989, Internat. award 1993), Fiber Soc., Nat. Materials Adv. Bd., Phi Eta Sigma, Tau Beta Pi, Phi Kappa Phi, Sigma Xi. Home: 7001 Valburn Dr Austin TX 78731-1818 Office: U Tex Ctr Polymer Rsch Dept Chem Engring Austin TX 78712

PAUL, DWAYNE GLENN, information systems company executive; b. Beaumont, Tex., Aug. 1, 1962; s. James Madison and Mildred Eula (Tatum) P. BA in phil., U. Chgo., 1985. Project mgr. Daystar Computer Systems, Chgo., 1986-88; application devel. cons. Altos Computer Systems, San Jose, Calif., 1988-89; project mgr. cons. Sequent Computer Systems, Santa Clara, 1989-93; exec. dir. info. systems UniHealth, Burbank, 1993-95, v.p. info. svcs., 1995—. Founding mem. Progressive Coalition of Cen. Ky., Lexington, 1980. Mem. ACLU, Healthcare Info. and Mgmt. Systems Soc., Am.'s United for the Separation of Ch. and State. Democrat. Avocations: songwriter, musician, film collector, music collector, student of political sci. Office: UniHealth 3400 W Riverside Dr Fl 8 Burbank CA 91505-4673

PAUL, ELIZABETH HUMPHREY, public health educator; b. N.Y.C. BA, Denison U., 1989; MPH, Columbia U., 1995, MS, 1998; EdD, Columbus U., 1999. Intern N.Y. Health & Hosps. Corp., 1993-94; cons. Ctrs. Disease Control & Prevention, Granville, Ohio, 1994; dir. pub. health interventions Centercare, N.Y.C., 1995-96; program mgr. Oxford Health Plans, White Plains, N.Y., 1996-99; v.p. Nat. Health Promotion Assocs., Hartsdale, NY, 1999—2001; sr. mgr. customer mktg. Pfizer, Inc., 2001—. Founder, exec. dir. Adolescent Health Alliance, N.Y.C., 1996—; pres., founder Sah Wha Dee Silver and Boutique Accessories, N.Y.C., Thailand, 1989-95 Mem.: SOPHE, APHE, Soc. Pub. Health Edn. E-mail: elizabeth.paul@pfizer.com.

PAUL, EVE W. lawyer; b. N.Y.C., June 16, 1930; d. Leo I. and Tamara (Sogolow) Weinschenker; m. Robert D. Paul, Apr. 9, 1952; children: Jeremy Ralph, Sarah Elizabeth. BA, Cornell U., 1950; JD, Columbia U., 1952. Bar: N.Y. 1952, Conn. 1960, U.S. Ct. Appeals (2nd cir.) 1975, U.S. Supreme Ct. 1977. Assoc. Botein, Hays, Sklar & Herzberg, N.Y.C., 1952-54; pvt. practice Stamford, Conn., 1960-70; staff atty. Legal Aid Soc., N.Y.C., 1970-71; assoc. Greenbaum, Wolff & Ernst, 1972-78; v.p. legal affairs Planned Parenthood Fedn. Am., 1979—, v.p., gen. counsel, 1991—. Bd. dirs. Ctr. for Gender Equality, Inc. Contbr. articles to profl. jours. Trustee Cornell U., Ithaca, N.Y., 1979-84; mem. Stamford Planning Bd., Conn., 1967-70; bd. dirs. Stamford League Women Voters, 1960-62, Ctr. for Gender Equality, 1995—. Harlan Fiske Stone scholar Columbia Law Sch., 1952. Mem. ABA, Conn. Bar Assn., Assn. of Bar of City of N.Y., Stamford/Norwalk Regional Bar Assn., U.S. Trademark Assn. (chair dictionary listings com. 1988-90), Phi Beta Kappa, Phi Kappa Phi. Office: Planned Parenthood Fedn 810 7th Ave New York NY 10019-5818 E-mail: eve.paul@ppfa.org. *The ability to plan the number and timing of my children has made it possible for me to enjoy career, marriage and family.*

PAUL, EVELYN ROSS, critical care nurse; b. New Bern, N.C., May 10, 1953; d. Robert Austin and Sadie Marie (Simpson) P. BSN, U. N.C., 1975. Cert. critical care nurse, ACLS. Staff nurse Beaufort County Hosp., Washington, 1975-79; chief nurse, nurse clinician, staff nurse surg. ICU Med. U. S.C., Charleston, 1979-85; staff/charge nurse cardiac surgery Pitt County Meml. Hosp., Greenville, N.C., 1985-89, asst. nurse mgr. cardiac surgery, 1989-95, RN IV, 1995-96, asst. nurse mgr. cardiac surgery ICU, 1996—, acting nurse mgr. cardiac surgery, ICU/IU, 2001—02. Mem. AACN (pres. elect Heart of the East chpt. 1991-92).

PAUL, FRANK, retired consulting company executive; b. Germany, Apr. 13, 1924; came to U.S., 1947, naturalized, 1953; s. Georg and Hedwig (Muenz) P.; m. Trudy Maier, Apr. 9, 1947; 1 son, Robert. BBA summa cum laude, Baruch Coll., CCNY, 1960. Acctg. supr. S. Augstein Co., College Point, N.Y.C., 1953-58; controller Werner Mgmt. Cons., N.Y.C., 1958-61, v.p. fin. adminstrn., 1961-67; exec. v.p. Werner Assocs., N.Y.C., 1968-84; also dir.; pres. ORU Group Inc., 1973-84. Bd. dirs. Treasurer Reliance Cons. Group Inc; cons., 1983-84.

PAUL, FRANK ALLEN, physician; b. Joshua Tree, Calif., Oct. 30, 1958; s. Louis Marion and Vivian Anne Paul. AA in Pharmacy and Marine Biology, Fullerton Coll., Calif., 1979; BA in Biochemistry and Biology, Calif. State U., Fullerton, 1982; DO, U. New Eng., 1990. Cert. Physician Emergency Medicine, Neuro Muscular Skeletal Medicine, 2001. Store mgr. Alpha Beta Markets, La Habra and Industry, Calif., 1977-81; constrn. supr. Louis M. Paul Constrn. Co., La Habra, 1977-82; co-owner Finecraft Jewelers, Claremont, Calif., 1978—; tchg. fellow U. New Eng., Biddeford, Maine, 1988-89; intern Mt. Clemens (Mich.) Gen. Hosp., 1990-91, resident in emergency medicine, cons. staff, 1991-94; rsch. dir. Herpetol. and Ichthyol. Infectious Disease Rsch. Assocs.; clin. faculty mem. U. New Eng. Coll. Osteo. Medicine, 1994—; dir. edn. and rsch. staff St. Johns Hosp., Springfield, Ill., 1997-2000; clin. asst. prof. So. Ill. U. Sch. Medicine, 1997—, problem based learning tutor; EMS med. dir., base sta. med. dir. Tucson Heart Hosp., 2000—02; base sta. med. dir. El Dorado Hosp., 2002—. Med. dir. Ill. Soc. Respiratory Care, 1998—; bd. dirs. Ariz. chpt. Am. Coll. Emergency Physicians. Contbr. Fellow fellow award, Am. Coll. Emergency Physicians, 1999, Am. Coll. Osteo. Emergency Physicians, 1999. Mem.: Am. Coll. Osteo. Emergency Physicians (fellow 1999), Am. Coll. Emergency Physicians (fellow 1999), Am. Acad. Osteopathy, Am. Osteo. Assn. Republican. Roman Catholic. E-mail: icemanco@yahoo.com.

PAUL, FRANK WATERS, mechanical engineer, educator, consultant; b. Jersey Shore, Pa., Aug. 28, 1938; BSME, Pa. State U., 1960, MSME, 1964; PhD in Mechanical Engring., Lehigh U., 1968. Registered profl. control engr., Calif. Control engr. Hamilton Standard div. United Techs. Corp., 1961-64; instr. mechanical engring. Lehigh U., Bethlehem, Pa., 1964-68; asst. prof. mechanical engring. Carnegie-Mellon U., Pitts., 1968-73, assoc. prof., 1973-77, Clemson (S.C.) U., 1977-79, prof., 1979-83, McQueen Quattlebaum prof., 1983—. Cons. numerous cos. including Westinghouse Electric, 1969, 82-83, Alcoa Rsch. Labs., 1976-80, State of N.J., Dept. Higher Edn., 1986, Dunlop Sports, Inc., 1988, BPM Tech.; hon. prof. engring. Hull U. Eng., 1990-93; Dora Jones vis. prof. of electronic engring., 1993; vis. prof. mech. engring. U. Newcastle Upon Tyne, Eng., 1999-00; dir. Ctr. for Advanced Mfg., 1982-99; lectr. to colls. and univs., U.S. and abroad. Contbr. chpt. to books and articles to IEEE Control Systems mag., Jour. of Engring. for Industry (ASME), Jour. of Dynamic Systems Measurement and Control (ASME), and other scholarly publs. Sabbatical United Techs. Rsch. Ctr., 1985-86, Hull U., 1993. Fellow ASME (participant and paper reviewer Dynamic Systems and Control divsn. 1968—, chmn. panel on robotics 1985-87); mem. Am. Soc. Engring. Educators, Soc. Mech. Engrs. (charter mem. Robotics Internat.), Pi Tau Sigma, Tau Beta Pi, Sigma Tau, Sigma Xi. Achievements include patents related to manufacturing automation. Office: Clemson U Fluor Daniel Bldg Rm 204 Clemson SC 29634-0001 E-mail: fwpaul@clemson.edu.

PAUL, GLENN, tile company executive, artist; b. n.Y.C., Feb. 25, 1942; s. Les and Florence Paul; m. Suzanne Starr; children: blair Jonathan, Carla Suzanne, Ian Starr, Arom David. BA, Calif. State U., Fullerton, 1969, MA, 1971. CEO Ken Mason Tile, Long Beach, Calif., BCIA, Long Beach. Artist custom tiles. With U.S. Army, 1961. Avocations: travel, skiing.

PAUL, GORDON LEE, behavioral scientist, psychologist; b. Marshalltown, Iowa, Sept. 2, 1935; s. Leon Dale and Ione Hickman (Perry) P.; m. Joan Marie Wyatt, Dec. 24, 1954; children: Dennis Leon, Dana Lee, Joni Lynn. Student, Marshalltown Community Coll., 1953-54, San Diego City Coll., 1955-57; BA, U. Iowa, 1960; MA, U. Ill., 1962, PhD, 1964. Social sci. analyst VA Hosp., Danville, Ill., 1962; counseling psychologist U. Ill., Urbana, 1963; clin. psychologist VA Hosp., Palo Alto, Calif., 1964-65; pvt. practice clin. psychology, 1964-65; asst. prof. psychology U. Ill., Champaign-Urbana, 1965-67, assoc. prof., 1967-70, prof., 1970-80; Cullen disting. prof. psychology U. Houston, 1980—; pvt. practice psychology Champaign, 1965-80, Houston, 1980—. Psychotherapy rsch. cons., Palo Alto, 1964-65; cons. Ill. Dept. Mental Health, 1965-73, 78-82, NIMH, 1968-78; adviser Ont. (Can.) Mental Health Found., 1968-69, NSF, 1968-69, Can. Coun., 1969-75, VA, 1972, 80—, APA, 1970—, UCLA/VA Med. Ctr./Camarillo Schizophrenia Rsch. Ctr., 1978-93, Alliance for Mentally Ill, 1980—. Author: Insight vs. Desensitization in Psychotherapy, An Experiment in Anxiety Reduction, 1966, Anxiety and Clinical Problems, 1973, Psychosocial Treatment of Chronic Mental Patients, 1977, Assessment in Residential Treatment Settings, Part 1, 1986, Observational Assessment Instrumentation for Service and Research, Part 2, 1987, Part 3, 1988; mem. editl. bd. Behavior Therapy, 1969-75, Behavior Therapy and Exptl. Psychiatry, 1969—, Schizophrenia Bull., 1971-99, Jour. Abnormal Psychology, 1972-76, Jour. Residential Treatment, 1983—, Jour. Psychopathology and Behavioral Assessment, 1985—; cons. editor Jour. Applied Behavior Analysis, 1966-77, 81—, Psychol. Bull., 1967-99, Jour. Abnormal Psychology, 1970-72, 76—, Psych osomatic Medicine, 1971-77, Psychophysiology, 1972—, Archives Gen. Psychiatry, 1973-74, Behavior Therapy, 1976-87, Profl. Psychologist, 1977-87, Hosp. Cmty. Psychiatry, 1980-94, Biobehavioral Revs., 1980-84, Jour. Cmty. Psychology, 1983, Am. Psychologist, 1983—, Brit. Jour. Clin. Psychology, 1985-87, Nervous and Mental Disease, 1992, Current Directions in Psychol. Sci., 1992—; contbr. articles to profl. jours. Served with USN, 1954-58. Recipient Creative Talent award Am. Inst. Rsch., 1964, Teaching award U. Ill., 1968, 75; rsch. award Mental Health Assn., 1985; listed among 353 best mental health experts in nation Good Housekeeping, 1994; NIMH fellow, 1963-64. Fellow Am. Psychol. Assn. (corr. com. 1965-70, pres. sect. III div. 12 1972-73, exec. com. div. 12 1974-77, Disting. Scientist award sect. III, div. 12 1977, Disting. Sci. Contbns. to Clin. Psychology award Soc. Clin. Psychology divsn. 12 1999), Am. Psychol. Soc., Assn. Clin. Psychosocial Rsch., Am. Assn. Applied and Preventive Psychology; mem. Midwestern Psychol. Assn., Tex. Psychol. Assn., Houston Psychol. Assn., Assn. for Advancement Psychology, Phi Beta Kappa, Chi Gamma Iota. Achievements include being subject of NIMH sci. report monograph, 1981: Treating and Assessing the Chronically Mentally Ill: The Pioneering Research of Gordon L. Paul. Home: 6239 S Braeswood Blvd Houston TX 77096-3715 Office: U Houston Dept Psychology 126 Heyne Bldg Houston TX 77204-5022 E-mail: gpaul@uh.edu.

PAUL, GREGORY MARSHALL, motion picture and television executive; b. Hartford, Conn. s. Justus Williams and Lillias (Marshall) P.; m. Ellen Fuchs, Aug. 27, 1989; 1 child, Jesse Justus. AB, Harvard U., 1970; JD, Columbia U., 1973. Bar: Calif. Assoc., then ptnr. O'Melveny & Myers, L.A., 1973-86; pres., COO Castle Rock Entertainment, Beverly Hills, Calif., 1987—. Bd. dirs. UCLA Entertainment Law Symposium, L.a., 1985-98. Mem. Acad. Motion Picture Arts and Scis. (exec. com.), Harvard Club of So. Calif. (bd. dirs. 1983-86), Regency Club. Avocations: history, reading, sports, gardening, antiques. Office: Castle Rock Entertainment 335 N Maple Dr Ste #135 Beverly Hills CA 90210

PAUL, HERBERT MORTON, lawyer, accountant, taxation educator; b. N.Y.C. s. Julius and Gussie Paul; m. Judith Paul; children: Leslie Beth, Andrea Lynn. BBA, Baruch Coll.; MBA, LLM, NYU; JD, Harvard U. Ptnr. Touche Ross & Co., N.Y.C., assoc. dir.-tax, dir. fin counseling; mng. ptnr. Herbert Paul, P.C., N.Y.C., 1983—. Prof. taxation, trustee NYU. Author: Ordinary and Necessary Expenses; editor: Taxation of Banks; adv. tax editor The Practical Acct.; mem. adv. bd. Financial and Estate Planning, Tax Shelter Insider, Financial Planning Strategist, Tax Shelter Litigation Report; bd. dirs. Partnership Strategist, The Business Strategist; cons. Profl. Practice Mgmt. Mag.; mem. panel The Hot Line; advisor The Partnership Letter, The Wealth Formula; cons. The Insider's Report for Physicians; mem. tax bd. Business Profit Digest; cons. editor physician's Tax Advisor; bd. fin. cons. Tax Strategies for Physicians; tax and bus. advisor Prentice Hall; contbg. editor. Jour. of Accountancy; mem. editl. bd. Family Bus. Advisor. Trustee NYU, mem. bd. overseers Grad. Sch. Bus.; mem. com. on trusts and estates Rockefeller U.; trustee Alvin Alley Am. Dance Theatre, Assoc. Y's of N.Y.; mem. accts. divsn. Fedn. Philanthropies; mem. adv. bd. Family Bus. Advisor. Mem. NYU Alumni Assn. (pres., bd. dirs.). Mem. ABA, Inst. Fed. Taxation (adv. com. chmn.), Internat. Inst. on Tax and Bus. Planning (adv. bd.), Assn. Bar City N.Y., NYU Tax Soc. (pres.), Bur. Nat. Affairs-Tax Mgmt. (adv. com. on exec. compensation), Am. Inst. CPAs (com. on corp. taxation), Tax Study Group, N.Y. County Lawyers Assn., N.Y. State Soc. CPAs Dir. (chmn. tax div. com. on fed. taxation, gen. tax com., furtherance com., com. on rels. with IRS, bd. dirs.), Nat. Assn. Accts., Assn. of Bar of City of N.Y., Accts. Club of Am., Pension Club, Nat. Assn. Estate Planners (bd. dirs.), N.Y. Estate Planning Coun. (bd. dirs.), N.Y. C. of C. (tax com.), Grad. Sch. Bus. of NYU Alumni Assn. (pres.), NYU Alumni Assn. (pres.). Clubs: Wall St., City Athletic (N.Y.C.), Inwood Country. Office: Herbert Paul PC 470 7th Ave Ste 3000 New York NY 10123

PAUL, HERMAN LOUIS , JR. valve manufacturing company executive; b. N.Y.C., Dec. 30, 1912; s. Herman Louis and Louise Emilie (Markert) P.; student Duke, 1931-32, Lehigh U., 1932-33; m. Janath Powers (dec. Jan. 1996); children— Robert E., Charles Thomas, Herman Louis III. Power plant engr. Paul's Machine Shop, N.Y.C., 1935-43; pres., chief engr. Paul's Machine Shop, N.Y.C., 1943-48; v.p., chief engr. Paul Valve Corp., East Orange, N.J., 1948-54; pres., chief engr. P-K Industries, Inc., North Arlington, N.J., 1954-59; v.p., dir. research Gen. Kinetics, Englewood, N.J., 1959-62; engring. cons., N.Y.C., 1962-65; v.p., dir. Hydromatics, Inc., Bloomfield, N.J., 1965-67; with P.J. Hydraulics, Inc., Myerstown, Pa., 1967— , pres., chief engr., 1968-80, dir. and stockholder, 1980-81; pres. Flomega Industries, Inc., Cornwall, Pa., 1982— ; cons. to Metal Industries Devel. Center, Taiwan, 1979; engring. cons. valves and complimentary equipment, 1980— ; valve cons. Continental Disc Corp., Kansas City, Mo., 1980-98. Vice chmn. Nat. UN Day Com., 1977, 78, 79, 80. Mem. ASME, Instrument Soc. Am., Am. Soc. Naval Engrs., The Navy League, The Naval Inst. Club: Heidelberg Country (Bernville, Pa.), Quentin (Pa.) Riding. Patentee in field. Home: RD 5 370 Dogwood Ln Lebanon PA 17042-9503

PAUL, JACK DAVIS, retired state official, addictions consultant; b. Bismarck, N.D., Mar. 16, 1927; s. Harry Ernest and Bernice Ambert (Davis) P.; m. Mary Ann Langness, Aug. 23, 1955; children: Steven, William. BSc in Law, U. N.D., 1956, LLB, 1957, JD, 1969. Bar: N.D. 1957; cert. master addiction counselor, addictions clin. supr., profl. educator; lic. social worker, N.D.; diplomate Internat. Orgn. for Treatment of Sex Offenders, 1986. Pvt. practice law, Bismarck, 1957-71; exec. sec., gen. counsel N.D. Trade Commn., 1965-69; master addiction counselor N.D. Corrections Dept., Bismarck, 1972-79, dir. programs, 1980-89; ret., 1989; acting warden, 1986, 88. Instr. alcohol and drug edn. St. Mary's Ctrl. High Sch., Bismarck, 1977-87; dir. penal family treatment N.D. State Penitentiary, 1976-89; lectr. psychology, sociology Bismarck State Coll., 1992-99; cons. additions, sex therapist and sex offender rehab. programs, prison treatment programs, Mandan, N.D., 1974—; lectr. on addictions, 1974—; mem. faculty N.D. Internat. Alcohol Studies, Grand Forks, 1980-83; cons. Internat. Orgn. for Treatment of Sex Offenders and Violence, 1979—, Johnson Inst., 1978-83. Mem. Mandan City Citizens Planning Com. for Law Enforcement, 1984; del. Nat. Conf. on Corrections Policy, Washington, 1986. With USN, 1945-46, PTO; capt. U.S. Army, 1949-53. Recipient citation for nat. flood relief Govt. of Netherlands, 1953. Mem. N.D. Social Workers Assn., N.D. Lic. Addiction Counselors (v.p. 1980). Democrat. Congregationalist. Avocations: volleyball, racquetball, golf, volunteering, reading. Home: 701 3rd Ave NW Mandan ND 58554-2810

PAUL, JAMES WILLIAM, lawyer; b. Davenport, Iowa, May 3, 1945; s. Walter Henry and Margaret Helene (Hillers) P.; m. Sandra Kay Schmid, June 15, 1968; children: James William, Joseph Hillers. BA, Valparaiso U., 1967; JD, U. Chgo., 1970. Bar: N.Y. 1971, U.S. Ct. Appeals (2d cir.) 1971, U.S. Dist. Ct. (so. and ea. dists.) N.Y. 1972, U.S. Supreme Ct. 1977, U.S. Ct. Appeals (6th cir.) 1981, Ind. 1982, U.S. Dist. Ct. (no. dist.) Ind. 1982, U.S. Claims Ct. 1989, U.S. Dist. Ct. (ea. dist.) Mich. 1989, U.S. Ct. Appeals (fed. cir.) 1991. Assoc. Rogers & Wells, N.Y.C., 1970-78, ptnr., 1978—. Dir., officer Musica Sacra, Inc., 1972-81 Bd. dirs. Turtle Bay Music Sch., Am. Lutheran Publicity Bur. Recipient Disting. Alumnus award Valparaiso U., 1994. Mem. ABA (antitrust sect. ins. com.), Assn. Bar City N.Y. (com. on legal and jud. ethics, com. on civil ct.), Fed. Bar Council. Democrat. Home: 360 E 72nd St Apt A-710 New York NY 10021-4755 also: 5 Curtis Dr Sherman CT 06784-1220 Office: Clifford Chance US LLP 200 Park Ave Ste 5200 New York NY 10166-0005

PAUL, JAMES ALBERT, public policy organization executive, author; b. N.Y.C., June 10, 1941; s. James Albert and Jean (Lithgow) P.; m. Susanne Schilling, Aug. 24, 1969; children: Timothy Schilling, Jonathan Summers. BA, Harvard U., 1963; postgrad., U. Vienna, 1964; MA, Oxford (Eng.) U., 1969; PhD in Polit. Sci., NYU, 1975. Instr. Empire State Coll., SUNY, Old Westbury, 1972-75, asst. prof., 1975-76; mem. editorial staff Middle East Report, N.Y.C., 1976-82, pub., 1982-86; exec. dir. Middle East Rsch. and Info. Project, 1986-89; cons. Paul & Assocs., 1989-93; exec. dir. Global Policy Forum, 1993—. Cons. John Hay Whitney Found., N.Y.C., 1972-73, Human Rights Watch, N.Y.C., 1989-90, Physicians for Human Rights, Boston, 1992; consulting editor Oxford U. Press, N.Y.C., 1989-92.; bd. dirs. Computer Mailworks, Phila., 1978-87, Brecht Forum, N.Y.C., 1988-91, chair, 1988-91; chair NGO Working Group on Security Coun., 1995—. Author: Syria Unmasked, 1991, Humanity Comes of Age, 1994, The Road to the Global Compact, 2000, Making Corporations Accountable, 2001, Global Taxes for Global Priorities, 2002; cons. editor Oxford Companion to Politics of the World, 1993; mem. editorial com. Peuples Méditerranéens, 1981-85; editor Oxford Companion to Politics of the World, rev. edit., 2001; also over 100 articles. Bd. dirs. World Fellowship, Conway, N.H., 1993-95, chair 1995; permanent rep. Internat. Fed. of Human Rights to U.N. Hdqtrs., 1995-99. Recipient book prize Christ Church Coll., Oxford U., 1965, media award World Hunger Yr., 1987. Mem. Acad. Coun. on UN Sys., Soc. for Internat. Devel. Avocations: swimming, reading, sailing, classical music. Office: Global Policy Forum 777 Un Plz Ste 7G New York NY 10017-3521 E-mail: james.paul@globalpolicy.org.

PAUL, JAMES CAVERLY NEWLIN, law educator, former university dean; b. Chestnut Hill, Pa., Apr. 30, 1926; s. William Allen Butler and Adelaide Sims (Newlin) P.; m. Margaret Morris Clausen, June 25, 1948; children: Nicholas Newlin, Martha Morris, Adelaide Sims. BA, Princeton U., 1948; JD, U. Pa., 1951. Bar: Pa. 1952. Legal sec. to Chief Justice U.S., 1951-53; asst. prof. U. N.C., 1953-55; asst. dir. Inst. Govt., U. N.C., 1953-55; prof. law, dir. Inst. Legal Research, U. Pa., 1955-63; prof. law, dean and founder of faculty of law Haile Selassie U., Ethiopia, 1963-67, v.p. acad. affairs, 1967-69; exec. v.p. Ednl. and World Affairs, N.Y.C., 1969-70; dean Sch. Law, Rutgers U., Newark, 1970-74, prof. law, 1970-96, Newhouse scholar in law, 1984-88, William J. Brennan prof., 1988-96; exec. sec., trustee Internat. Ctr. for Law in Devel., N.Y.C., 1974—. Founding mem., sec.-treas. Internat. Third World Legal Studies Assn., N.Y.C., 1980—96; adj. prof. Columbia U., 1973—95; cons. Constl. Commn. Transitional Govt. of Ethiopia, 1992—93, UN Devel. Programme, 1994—96; mem. Internat. Eritrean-Ethioplan Claims Commn., The Hague. Author: Rift in the Democracy, 1951, (with others) Federal Censorship, 1961, Ethiopian Constitutional Development, 1969, Lawyers in the Third World, 1981, The International Context of Rural Poverty in the Third World, 1986, Incorporating Human Rights Into the World Summit for Social Development, 1995. Candidate for U.S. Congress from 9th Dist. Pa., 1958; del. Dem. Nat. Conv., 1960. Served with USNR, 1943-46, PTO. Recipient spl. medal for distinguished service to univ. edn. in Ethiopia, 1969 Mem. Am., N.J., Pa. bar assns., Internat. Third World Legal Studies Assn. (sec.-treas. 1980—), Order of Coif. Clubs: Princeton (N.Y.C.). Home: 1352 Chancellor Pt Trappe MD 21673-1540 Office: 15 Washington St Newark NJ 07102-3105 *My life in law and teaching about law gives satisfaction because it enables me to direct my energies towards thinking about social justice, individual dignity, and the possibilities of attaining more of the conditions enabling these ideals. But that satisfaction is tempered by constant realization of my own frailities and the failure everywhere of people, particularly those most fortunately endowed, to be guided by principled thinking.*

PAUL, JEROME L. mathematician, educator; b. St. Paul, Sept. 3, 1937; BS in Math., U. Minn., 1959, MS in Math., 1962; PhD in Math., Case Western Res. U., 1965. Asst. prof. Purdue U., West Lafayette, Ind., 1965—70; assoc. prof. U. Cin., 1970—80, prof., 1980—. Contbr. articles. Mem.: IEEE Computer Soc., ACM. Home: 6632 Ridgeview Ct Loveland OH 45140

PAUL, JODY, computer information scientist; b. Bklyn., June 22, 1955; BS in Math., UCLA, 1978, MS in Computer Sci., 1980, PhD in Computer Sci., 1988. Mem. tech. staff Hughes Research Labs., Malibu, Calif., 1978-80; rsch. scientist Bell Labs., N.J., 1980-82; computing specialist Hughes Aircraft, L.A., 1982-83, cons. knowledge engr., 1983—; computer scientist The Rand Corp., Santa Monica, Calif., 1984—. Lectr. computer sci. dept., UCLA, 1988—, instr. UCLA extension, 1986—. Contbr. articles to profl. jours. Mem. IEEE, Assn. for Computing Machinery, Am. Assn. Artificial Intelligence, Assn. for Computers and Humanities, Upsilon Pi Epsilon (computer sci. honor soc.), Phi Mu Epsilon (math. honor soc.). Home: 1777 Larimer St Apt 1002 Denver CO 80202-1545 Office: The Rand Corp 1700 Main St Santa Monica CA 90401-3297

PAUL, JOSEPH B. executive; b. Bklyn., Jan. 21, 1961; s. Samuel and Ruth (Bassin) P.; m. Rose Jacklyn Futterman, Apr. 1, 1984. BS in Computer Sci., CUNY, S.I., 1983; MBA, Nova U., 1988; postgrad., Calif. Coast U. Computer programmer Office of Mgmt. and Budget, N.Y.C., 1981-83; programmer, analyst Harris Corp., Melbourne, Fla., 1983-84; sr. analyst AT&T, Maitland, 1984-85; project leader Fla. Power and Light, Miami, 1985-90; project mgr. S.E. Toyota Distbr., Deerfield Beach, Fla., 1990-93; dir. customer svcs. Data Net Corp., Miramar, 1993-95; v.p. PC support Citizens Fed. Bank, Ft. Lauderdale, 1995-96; v.p. info. tech., CIO Compass Health Sys., North Miami, 1996-97; pres, CEO The Bulldog Group, Inc., Sunrise, 1997—. Pres. S.E. Area Focus Users Group, Miami, 1986-89, Co-Log Users Group, Miramar, 1993-94. Mem. agy. rels. sub-com. United Way South Fla., Miami, 1988-90; pres. Archtl. Control Com., Sunrise, Fla., 1991-93; Logistics Chmn. Am. Cancer Soc. Relay for Lifve, 1999—; bd. dirs. Plantation C. of C., 1999—. Mem. Health Info. Mgmt. Systems Soc., Am. Mgmt. Assn., Am. Mktg. Assn., Coll. Healthcare Info. Mgmt. Execs., Toastmasters, Tau Alpha Pi (pres. 1982-83). Republican. Jewish. Avocations: photography, woodworking, computers. Home: 13120 NW 11th Dr Sunrise FL 33323-2951 Office: The Bulldog Group Inc 12717 W Sunrise Blvd Ste 175 Sunrise FL 33323-0902

PAUL, KENNETH, newspaper editor; b. N.Y.C., June 7, 1948; s. Samuel D. and Rose (Markoff) P.; m. Sevara Jeleva, Dec. 5, 1993; 1 child, Kathryn Hannah. BA in English, Dartmouth Coll., Hanover, N.H., 1969; spl. diploma in social studies, Oxford (Eng.) U., 1973. Tchr. Concord (N.H.) H.S., 1969-71; dep. European editor L.A. Times/Washington Post News Svc., London, 1972-73; reporter, news editor Riverside (Calif.) Press Enterprise, 1973-76; specialists editor, copy editor, asst. nat. and day nat. editor Newsday, NY, 1976—87; mng. editor N.Y. Observer, N.Y.C., 1987-91; editor The Litchfield County Times, New Milford, Conn., 1993—, Housatonic Pubs., New Milford, 2001—; 2204. Office: The Litchfield County Times 32 Main St New Milford CT 06776-2888

PAUL, LAURENCE EDWARD, investment company executive; b. Chgo., Nov. 16, 1964; s. Robert Arthur and Donna Rae (Berkman) P. AB, Harvard Coll., 1986; MD, Harvard Med. Sch., 1990; MBA, Stanford U., 1992. Investment banker James D. Wolfensohn, Inc., N.Y.C., 1992-94, Donaldson, Lufkin & Jenrette, N.Y.C., 1994-97, investment banker, mng. dir. L.A., 1997-2000; mng. dir. CS First Boston, 2000-01; v.p. Louis Berkman Co., Santa Monica, Calif., 2001—. Co-mgr. Harvard Med. Sch. Capital Campaign, 1996—; adv. bd. Clarity Healthcorp, 1997-99; bd. dirs. Ampco Pitts. Corp., Biovail Corp.; presenter in field. Bd. dirs. Keimei Fund for Edn., 1995-2001; mem. bd. of fellows Harvard Med. Sch., 2002—. Mem. Ampco Pittsburgh Corp. (bd. dirs.), 1998—. Office: 1620 26th St Ste 300S Santa Monica CA 90404

PAUL, LAURENCE JOHNSON, retired journalist; b. Lancaster, N.H., June 29, 1933; s. Laurence James and Ida Mae (Johnson) P.; m. Barbara Anne Phillips, Oct. 24, 1959 (dec. July 1988); children: David, Andrea; m. Sylvia Mayer Helbert, Aug. 4, 1990. BA in English Lit., U. N.H., 1955; MA in Polit. Sci., U. Ill., 1958. Reporter Utica (N.Y.) Daily Press, 1958-66; editorial writer Buffalo News, 1966-99, dep. editor editorial page, 1989-99; ret., 1999. With U.S. Army, 1955-57. Mem. Soc. Profl. Journalists (local chpt. pres. 1976, chmn. Greater Buffalo Scholarship Fund 1989—). Mem. United Ch. of Christ. Home: 172 Chaumont Dr Amherst NY 14221-3534

PAUL, LOIS, public relations company executive; BA in Journalism summa cum laude, Temple U.; MS in Computer Info. Systems, Bentley Coll. Former sr. editor/software Computerworld; former exec. editor/features, founding mem. PC Week; founder, pres. Lois Paul & Ptnrs., Burlington, Mass., 1986—. Chmn. Bentley Coll. Grad. Sch. Mktg. Adv. Coun; bd. on Fleishman-Hillard, 2000. Recipient Disting. Sch. of Comm. and Theater Alumnus award Temple U. Office: Lois Paul and Ptnrs 150 Presidential Way Woburn MA 01801-1179 Fax: 781-782-5999.*

PAUL, M(ALCOLM) LEE, psychology educator; b. Shreveport, La., July 13, 1951; s. Francis Malcolm and Ava Aileen (Boyles) P.; m. Stephanie Maxfield, July 23, 1994; children: Ryan Lee, Cameron Scott; 1 stepchild, Blake Wayne. BS, Abilene Christian U., 1974, MS, 1977; EdD, Nova Southeastern U., 1986. Lic. profl. counselor, Tex., lic. marriage and family therapist, Tex. Entertainer Six Flags Over Tex., Arlington, 1965-78; dir. univ. svcs. and rsch. Abilene Christian U., Dallas, 1977-82; v.p. for psychol. svcs. Security Rsch. Cons., 1980-82; prof. of psychology Amber U., Garland, Tex., 1980—; assoc. prof. psychology Southwestern Christian Coll., Terrell, 1991—. Pvt. practice psychotherapy, Dallas, 1982—; mem. ethics com. Baylor Hosp., Garland. Co-author: The Parable of Man, 1980. Named one of Outstanding Young Men of Am., 1979, named Disting. Alumnus Dallas Christian Sch., 1998. Mem. APA, ACA. Mem. Ch. of Christ. Avocations: scuba diving, hunting, music. Office: Dr M Lee Paul 9535 Forest Ln Ste 200 Dallas TX 75243-6101

PAUL, MARY MELCHIOR, human resources professional; b. Tipton, Ind., Apr. 29, 1952; d. John A. and Inez Marie (Clark) Meyer; 1 child, Regina. BS, U. Evansville, 1974; MBA, So. Ill. U., 1987. Mgr. The Children's Shops, St. Louis, 1980-86; cons., trainer Edison Bros. Stores, 1987; program mgr. Anheuser-Busch Cos., 1988-94; human resources devel. mgr. Campbell Taggart, Inc. (divsn. Anheuser-Busch Cos. Inc.), St. Louis, 1994-96; from orgnl. devel. and tng. mgr. powertrain ops. to corp. sr. mgr. Harley Davidson, Inc., Milw., 1996—2002, corp. sr. mgr. orgnl. devel., 2002—. Active Coro Found. Mem. ASTD, Profl. Woman Network, Profl. Dimensions, Women in Leadership Alumnae. Home: 5801 S Oak Rd West Bend WI 53095 Office: Harley Davidson Motor Co 3700 W Juneau Ave Milwaukee WI 53208-2865 E-mail: mary.paul@harley-davidson.com.

PAUL, MICHAEL GREGORY, public relations executive, educator; b. Bklyn., Mar. 6, 1964; m. Anthony Albert Paul and Jessie Mae Hamilton; m. Jody Tattar Paul, Sept. 9, 2000. MPA, Columbia U., 1992. Dep. rsch. dir. Friends Senator D'Amato, N.Y.C., 1991-92; sr. assoc. Burson-Marsteller, 1992-94; v.p. Hill & Knowlton, 1994-96; pres., CEO MGP & Assocs. PR, 1994-2001; exec. v.p. comm., mktg., and advt. N.Y.C. Econ. Devel. Corp., 1998-99. Spl. asst. Senator Alfonse M.D'Amato, Washington, 1990-91; bd. mem. African Film Festival, Inc., N.Y.C., 1995-2001; adj. prof. comms. NYU, 1999--, Columbia U., 2001--; pub. rels. analyst crisis situations; guest on TV, radio, print news, outlets worldwide. Woodrow Willson fellow Woodrow Wilson Found., 1990-92, Patricia Roberts Harris fellow U.S. Dept. Edn., 1990-92. Mem. Nat. Assn. Ind. Pub. Rels. Firms, Internat. Assn. Bus. Communicators, Coun. Fgn. Rels., Black Pub. Rels. Soc. Greater N.Y. Avocations: working out, soccer, football, swimming, scuba diving. Office: MGP & Assocs PR 244 Fifth Ave Ste 2620 New York NY 10001-7604 Office Fax: 212-504-7964. Business E-Mail: mpaul@mgppr.com.

PAUL, NORMAN LEO, psychiatrist, educator; b. Buffalo, July 5, 1926; s. Samuel Joseph and Tannie (Goncharsky) P.; m. Betty Ann Byfield, June 6, 1951 (dec. May 1994); children: Marilyn, David Alexander. MD, U. Buffalo, 1948. Fellow pharmacology U. Cin. Coll. Medicine, Ohio, 1949-50; resident psychiatry Mass. Mental Health Ctr., Boston, 1952-55; fellow child psychiatry James Jackson Putnam Children's Ctr., 1957-59, Mass. Gen. Hosp., Boston, 1958-59; chief psychiatrist Day Hosp. Mass. Mental Health Ctr., 1960-64; dir. conjoint family therapy Boston State Hosp., 1964-65, cons. in family psychiatry, 1965-70; assoc. clin. prof. dept. neurology Boston U. Sch. Medicine, 1977—. Cons. Mental Health Ctr., Alaska Native Hosp., Anchorage, 1967-68; cons. in family psychiatry Boston VA Hosp., 1967-71, Mass. Soc. for the Prevention of Cruelty to Children, Boston, 1993—; vis. family therapist St. George's Med. Sch., London, 1996-97; lectr. in psychiatry Harvard Med. Sch., Boston, 1976—; faculty assoc. Mgmt. Analysis Corp., Cambridge, Mass., 1979-82; presenter paper Internat. Conf. on Telemedicine and Telecare, London, 1996. Family therapist: (tv documentary) PBS-Trouble in the Family, 1965 (George Foster Peabody award 1965); co-author A Marital Puzzle, 1977, 86, German edit., 1987, French edit., 1995, Chinese edit., 1997. Sponsor Mass. Orgn. to Repeal Abortion Laws, Boston, 1965-70; chair Audio Unit of Child Devel. and Mass Media, White House Conf. on Children and Youth, Washington, 1970; bd. trustees Cambridge (Mass.) Coll., 1977-89; bd. dirs. Let's Face It, 1990—, Ctr. for Family Connections, 1998—. Capt. USAF, 1950-52. Recipient Edward A. Strecker, M.D. award for young psychiatrist of yr., 1966, Cert. of Merit, Mass. Coun. on Family Life, Boston, 1967, Cert. of Commendation, Mass. Assn. for Mental Health, Boston, 1967, Disting. Achievement award Soc. for Family Therapy and Rsch., Boston, 1973, Lifetime Achievement award Mass. Assn. for Marriage and Family Therapy, 1998, Disting. Svc. award Physician Health Svcs., 1998. Fellow Royal Soc. Medicine, Am. Psychiat. Assn. (life); mem. Am. Assn. Marriage and Family Therapy (bd. dirs. 1983-86), Am. Family Therapy Assn. (v.p. 1982-83, Disting. Contbn. award 1984), Assn. for Rsch. in Nervous and Mental Disorders, Group for the Advancement Psychiatry (chair com. on the family 1982-84). Avocations: study of codes, travel. Office: 394 Lowell St Ste 6 Lexington MA 02420-2549 E-mail: nlpaul@aol.com.

PAUL, OGLESBY, cardiologist, educator; b. Villanova, Pa., May 3, 1916; s. Oglesby and Laura Little (Wilson) P.; m. Marquerite Black, May 29, 1943 (dec. Jan. 1979); children: Rodman, Marquerite; m. Jean Lithgow, Jan. 17, 1981. AB, Harvard Coll., 1938; MD, Harvard Med. Sch., 1942. Intern Mass. Gen. Hosp., Boston, 1942-43, resident, 1946-48; prof. medicine Northwestern U., Evanston, Ill., 1963-77; sr. physician emeritus Brigham & Womens Hosp., Boston, 1977—; prof. medicine emeritus Harvard Med. Sch., 1977—. V.p. health scis. Northwestern U., Evanston, 1974-75; dir. admissions Harvard Med. Sch., Boston, 1977-82. Author: Take Heart, 1986, The Caring Physician, 1991. Pres. Am. Heart Assn., Dallas, 1960-61. Lt. USNR. Home: 10 Longwood Dr Apt 322 Westwood MA 02090-1142 Office: Harvard Med Sch Countway Libr 10 Shattuck St Boston MA 02115-6011 E-mail: oleypaul@aol.com.

PAUL, OUIDA FAY, music educator; b. Deatsville, Ala., Jan. 18, 1911; d. Elza Bland and Martha Eleanor (Hinton) P. AB in Math. and English, Huntingdon Coll., 1930, BS in Music Edn., 1933; MA in Music and Music Edn., Columbia U., 1943, EdD in Music and Music Edn., 1957; postgrad., U. Ill., 1968. Tchcr. math., English and music pub. schs., Ala., 1930-42; tchr. math. Sacred Heart Convent Sch., N.Y.C., 1942-43; tchr. h.s. choral music Kingsport, Tenn., 1943-45; instr., asst. prof. music edn. Greensboro (N.C.) Coll., 1945-49; asst. prof. U. Fla., Gainesville, 1949-61, U. Hawaii, Honolulu, 1961-68; tchr. musicology and voice Leeward C.C., Pearl City, Hawaii, 1968-77; pvt. tchr. voice, Honolulu, 1977-95, Gainesville, 1996—. Choir dir. 1st Presbyn. Ch., Gainesville, 1950-61, Protestant Chapel, USN, Honolulu, 1962-68, Cmty. Ch., Honolulu, 1969-78, Wesley United Meth. Ch., Honolulu, 1978-94; contralto soloist various chs., 1950-94; adjudicator solo and choral auditions and festivals, 1945-94. Exhibited oil paintings in solo shows at Honolulu Cmty. Theatre, 1980, 84, First United Meth. Ch., 1980; group shows with Honolulu Artists, others; work in permanent collection of René Malmezac in Tahiti; contbr. articles to profl. jours. Cons. to com. on edn. Hawaii Gov.'s Commn. on Status of Women, 1965; English lang. tutor Hawaii Literacy, Inc., Honolulu, 1978-95. Recipient Alumni Achievement award, Huntingdon Coll. Alumnae Assn., 1998. Mem. Music Educators Nat. Conf. (1st v.p. Hawaii 1969-70), Am. Choral Dirs. Assn. (Hawaii chmn. 1963-66), Nat. Assn. Tchrs. Singing, Common Cause, Altrusa (pres. Gainesville 1960-61, past pres. Honolulu), Delta Kappa Gamma (pres. Hawaii Theta chpt. 1963-64, past state music chmn.). Methodist. Avocation: oil painting. Home: 8015 NW 28th Pl Apt B210 Gainesville FL 32606-8607 E-mail: weefae@webtv.net.

PAUL, PAMELA MIA, concert pianist; b. N.Y.C., Nov. 9, 1949; d. Charles F. Paul; m. Richard John Dufallo, June 19, 1988. BM, Juilliard Sch. of Music, 1970, MM, 1972, DMA, 1976. Prof. U. North Tex., 1987—. Debuted Vienna Symphony; appeared with Vienna ORF Orch., Orchestre de la Suisse Romande, RTE Orch., Dublin, Berlin Stadtskappelle, Stuttgart Chamber Orch., Dutch Radio Symphony, Krakow Philharm., Orchestre Philharm. de Monte Carlo, N.Y. Philharm., Detroit, St. Louis, Pitts. and Houston Symphonies, others. Office: Univ North Tex College of Music Denton TX 76203

PAUL, PETER ANDREW, academic administrator; b. Holland, Mich., Oct. 3, 1964; arrived in Japan, 1990; s. Daniel L. and Joan C. (Ten Hoeve) P. AB summa cum laude, Hope Coll., Holland, 1989; student in Politics and Edn., Tchrs. Coll. Columbia Univ., 1997—. Cert. elem. tchr., Mich., N.Y. Intern Adminstrv. Office U.S. Cts. & D.C. Pub. Defender Svc., Washington, 1989; substitute tchr. Holland and Grand Haven (Mich.) Schs., 1989; tchr. ESL NCA Schs., Shiraoi, Hokkaido, Japan, 1990, acad. dir. Tomakomai, Japan, 1991-93; pres. NCA Internat. Schs., 1994—; grad. intern Tchrs. Network, N.Y.C., 1998; tchr. N.Y.C. Pub. Schs., 1998-99; program assoc. Tchrs. Network, N.Y.C., 1999-00, asst. dir., 2000—. Pub. spkr./cons. Northern Japan. Named Outstanding Coll. Student Am., 1989; awarded membership Nat. Polit. Sci. Honors Soc., 1989; selected as participant UNESCO regional conf., Hokkaido, 1998—; fellow (hon.) Nat. Tchr. Policy Inst., 1999; named Outstanding Person of 20th Century Internat. Biographical Ctr., England, 2000. Home: 350 Richmond Ter Apt 5H Staten Island NY 10301-1524 Office: NCA Internat Schs 3 Chome 2 Omotemachi NCA Tomakomai 053 Japan E-mail: ppaul@teachersnetwork.org.

PAUL, RICHARD WRIGHT, lawyer; b. Washington, May 23, 1953; s. Robert Henry Jr. and Betty (Carey) P.; m. Paula Ann Coolsaet, July 25, 1981; children: Richard Haven, Timothy Carey, Brian Davis. AB magna cum laude, Dartmouth Coll., 1975; JD, Boston Coll., 1978. Bar: Mich. 1978, U.S. Dist. Ct. (ea. dist.) Mich. 1978, U.S. Ct. Appeals (6th cir.) 1982, U.S. Supreme Ct. 1989, U.S. Dist. Ct. (we. dist.) Mich. 1991. Assoc. Dickinson, Wright, Moon, Van Dusen & Freeman, Detroit, 1978-85, ptnr., 1985—. Mediator Wayne County Cir. Ct., Oakland County Dist. Ct. Co-author, Barbarians At The Gate: Daubert Two Years Later, 1995; contbr. articles to profl. publs. Trustee Bloomfield Village Assn., Birmingham, Mich., 2001—; bd. dirs. Little League, Birmingham, 2000—. Mem. ABA, State Bar of Mich. (treas. litig. sect. 1998-99, sec. litig. sect. 1999-2000, chmn. elect litig. sect. 2000-01, chairperson litigation sect. 2001-02), Def. Rsch. Inst., Detroit Bar Assn., Mich. Def. Trial Counsel, Dartmouth Lawyers Assn., Oakland County Bar Assn., Assn. Def. Trial Counsel, Alumni Coun. Dartmouth Coll., Dartmouth Detroit Club (pres. 1980—). Avocations: tennis, cycling. E-mail: rpaul@dickinson-wright.com.

PAUL, ROBERT, lawyer; b. N.Y.C., Nov. 22, 1931; s. Gregory and Sonia (Rijock) P.; m. Christa Holz, Apr. 6, 1975; 1 child, Gina. BA, NYU, 1953; JD, Columbia U., 1958. Bar: Fla. 1958, N.Y. 1959. From assoc. to ptnr. Paul Landy Beiley & Harper, P.A., Miami, 1964-94; ptnr. Sacher Zelman Van Sant Paul Beiley Hartman & Waldman, P.A., 1964-94; counsel Republic Nat. Bank, 1967-95; chmn. internat. affiliation of law firms TerraLex, 1990—. Past pres. Fla. Philharm., Inc., 1978-79; trustee U. Miami. Mem. ABA, N.Y. Bar Assn., Fla. Bar Assn., Fla. Zool. Soc. (past pres.), French-Am. C. of C. of Miami (pres. 1986-87). Home: 700 Alhambra Cir Coral Gables FL 33134-4808 E-mail: rpaul@terralex.com.

PAUL, ROBERT GREGORY, electronic company executive; b. Rockford, Ill., Mar. 5, 1942; s. George A. and Leona (Mueller) P.; m. Margaret Kennedy, June 22, 1984; children: Katherine, Robert, Andrew. BSM.E., U. Wis., 1964; MBA, Stanford U., 1966. From asst. treas. to v.p.-treas. The Allen Group Inc., Melville, NY, 1971—76; v.p. fin. Antenna Specialists Co., Cleve., 1976-77, v.p. ops., 1977-78, pres., 1978—90; from v.p. fin. to pres. Allen Telecom, Inc., 1987—91, pres., CEO, 1991—. Home: 1965 Mornington Ln Apt 14 Cleveland OH 44106-2871 also: Allen Group Inc 25101 Chagrin Blvd Ste 350 Beachwood OH 44122-5687

PAUL, ROBERT ARTHUR, steel company executive; b. N.Y.C., Oct. 28, 1937; s. Isadore and Ruth (Goldstein) P.; m. Donna Rae Berkman, July 29, 1962; children: Laurence Edward, Stephen Eric, Karen Rachel. AB, Cornell U., 1959; JD, Harvard U., 1962, MBA, 1964. With Ampco-Pitts. Corp. (formerly Screw & Bolt Corp. Am.), 1964—, v.p., 1969-71, treas., 1973-79, exec. v.p., 1972-79, pres., COO, 1979-94, pres., CEO, 1994—, dir., 1969—. Exec. v.p., bd. dirs. Louis Berkman Co.; bd. dirs. Nat. City Corp.,; gen. ptnr. Romar Trading Co.; instr. Grad. Sch. Indsl. Adminstrn. Carnegie Mellon U., 1966-69; trustee Cornell U. Bd. trustees H.L. and Louis Berkman Found., U. Pitts. Med. Ctr. Sys.; trustee, pres. Fair Oaks Found.; vice chmn. Jewish Healthcare Found. Pitts. Mem. ABA, Mass. Bar Assn., Harvard Club (N.Y.), Concordia Club, Pitts. Athletic Club, Duquesne Club, Williams Country Club, Laurel Valley Golf Club. Republican. Jewish. Office: Ampco-Pitts Corp 600 Grant St Pittsburgh PA 15219-2702 E-mail: rpaul@ampcopgh.com.

PAUL, ROBERT CAREY, lawyer; b. Washington, May 7, 1950; s. Robert Henry and Betty Jane (Carey) P. AB, Dartmouth Coll., 1972; JD, Georgetown U., 1978. Assoc. Milbank, Tweed, Hadley & McCloy, N.Y.C., 1978-85; ptnr. Dechert Price & Rhoads, 1986-89, Kelley Drye & Warren, Brussels, 1989-93; counsel Rockefeller & Co., Inc., N.Y.C., 1995—. Home: 310 E 46th St Apt 19E New York NY 10017-3029 Office: Rockefeller & Co Inc 30 Rockefeller Plz 55th Fl New York NY 10112-0256 E-mail: rpaul@rockco.com.

PAUL, ROBERT DAVID, management consultant; b. N.Y.C., Nov. 1, 1928; s. Joseph Wolf and Freda (Sturm) P.; m. Eve Weinschenker, Apr. 9, 1952; children: Jeremy Ralph, Sarah Elizabeth. BS in Engring., U. Mich., 1950. Administrv. asst. Martin E. Segal Co., N.Y.C., 1950; naval architect Gibbs & Cox, 1951; with The Segal Co., 1953—, pres., 1967-76, vice chmn., 1977-91, chmn., 1991-94, dir., 1994-99, ret. chmn., 2000—. Trustee Employee Benefit Rsch. Inst., Washington, 1978-94, fellow, 1994; fellow Human Resource Policy Inst., Boston U. Sch. Mgmt.; bd. dirs. Wiss, Janney, Elstner Assocs., Northbrook, Ill., Empire Blue Cross Blue Shield. Contbr. articles to profl. jours. Cpl. U.S. Army, 1951-53. Mem. Soc. Human Resources Mgmt., Am. Compensation Assn., Internat. Found. Employee Benefit Plans (past chmn. corp. com.), Univ. Club. Avocations: naval and mil. history, jazz piano. Office: The Segal Co 1 Park Ave New York NY 10016-5802 E-mail: rpaul@segalco.com.

PAUL, ROBERT MILTON, personnel executive; b. Richmond, Va., Aug. 1, 1942; s. Milton Alexander Paul and Ruth (Smith) Davis; m. Priscilla Cunningham, June 15, 1964 (dec. 1964)); m. Anna Macklen, Oct. 2, 1965; children— Robert Anthony, Michele Kristine, Nicole Marie. Student Lees-McRae Jr. Coll., 1960; B.S., Va. Poly. Inst., 1964; M.S., U. So. Calif., 1971. Employment supr. Owens-Corning Fiberglas, Aiken, S.C., 1972-73, plant personnel mgr., Huntingdon, Pa., 1973-76, personnel mgr. textile and indsl. operating divs., Toledo, 1976-79, personnel mgr. roofing div., 1979-82, dir. compensation and benefits, 1982-86, mgr. supply ops., 1986, dir. compensation benefits, personnel services, 1986-87; v.p. personnel The Ryland Group, Inc., 1987— ; corp. program com. Internat. Found. Employee Benefit Plans, Wis., 1983-86, sec. corp. bd., 1986, vice chmn. corp. bd., 1987, chmn. corp. bd., 1988, adv. dir., 1987-88 . Served to lt. col. USAFR, 1965— . Mem. Internat. Found. Employee Benefit Plans, Council Employee Benefits, Am. Soc. Personnel Adminstrn., Am. Compensation Assn., Benefits Planning Council. Republican. Methodist. Lodge: Masons. Avocations: golf, tennis, hunting, woodworking. Office: Ryland Group Inc 11000 Brokenland Pkwy Columbia MD 21044-3541

PAUL, ROCHELLE CAROLE, special education educator; b. East Liverpool, Ohio, July 8, 1951; d. Homer Neil and Dolores Elizabeth (Seiler) P. BS, Clarion State Coll., 1973; MS, Clarion U., 1987; MDiv, Trinity Luth. Sem., Columbus, Ohio, 1992. Cert. tchr., Pa., Ohio. Spl. edn. tchr. Dorchester County Bd. Edn., Cambridge, Md., 1973-78, Forest Area Sch. Dist., Tionesta, Pa., 1979-88; edn. coord. juvenile-probate divsn. Common Pleas Ct. of Licking County, Newark, 1993-95; instr. Ctrl. Ohio Tech. Coll., 1994—, program dir. for early childhood assoc. degree, 1999-2000; prevention specialist Ctr. Alternative Resources, 1996-98; program dir. early childhood devel. Ctrl. Ohio Tech. Coll., 1999-2000; exec. dir. Literacy Network Ctrl. Ohio, 2000—. Rep. Pres.'s adv. bd. Trinity Luth. Sem., 1991-92; active St. Paul's Evang. Luth. Ch., Newark, Ohio; mem. head start cmty. assessment com., LEADS, 1999—, trustee, 2000—, policy coun. chair head start, 2000—. Mem. ASCD, AAUW, Coun. Exceptional Children (chpt. pres. 1972-73, 98—), Nat. Assn. Edn. of Young Children, Alcohol and Drug Abuse Prevention Assn. Ohio, Ohio Coalition of Assoc. Degree Early Childhood Programs. Avocations: Tai Chi, reading, writing, vocal and instrumental music, travel. Home: 164 Newton Ave Newark OH 43055-4758 Office: Literacy Network Ctrl Ohio COTC Baker House 1179 University Dr Newark OH 43055-1707 E-mail: rcpaulteacher@netscape.net.

PAUL, ROLAND ARTHUR, lawyer; b. Memphis, Jan. 19, 1937; s. Rol and Hattye (Mincer) P.; m. Barbara Schlesinger, June 10, 1962; children: Deborah Lynn, Arthur Eliot. BA summa cum laude, Yale U., 1958; LL.B. magna cum laude, Harvard U., 1961. Bar: N.Y. 1962, Mich. 1978, Conn. 1989. Law clk. to judge U.S. Ct. Appeals, 1961-62; fgn. affairs officer, spl. asst. to gen. counsel Dept. Def., 1962-64; assoc. firm Cravath, Swaine & Moore, N.Y.C., 1964-69; counsel fgn. relations subcom. security commitments U.S. Senate, 1969-71; assoc. firm Simpson Thacher Bartlett, N.Y.C., 1971-73; v.p., gen. counsel Howmet Corp., Greenwich, Conn., 1976-2000, Howmet Internat. Inc., 1997-2000; v.p., gen. counsel, dir. Pechiney Corp., Greenwich, Conn., 1984-95; counsel Day, Berry & Howard, Stamford, 2000—. Author: American Military Commitments Abroad. Mem. Council Fgn. Relations, Am. Bar Assn., Mich. Bar Assn. Home: 8 Ellery Ln Westport CT 06880-5202 Office: Day Berry & Howard One Canterbury Green Stamford CT 06901

PAUL, RON, congressman; b. Pitts., Aug. 20, 1935; m. Carol Paul; five children. Grad., Gettysburg Coll., Duke U. Sch. Medicine. Pvt. practice medicine; mem. U.S. Congress from 14th Tex. dist., 1977-85, 97—. Mem. fin. svcs. com., internat. rels. com. Author: Challenge to Liberty, The Case for Gold, others. With USAF. Recipient Taxpayer's Best Friend award, National Taxpayers Union, Mises Inst. Groseclose Prize and Leadership award, Leadership award Coalition for Peace Through Strength, Disting. Svc. award Am. Constl. Action, Torch Freedom award Young Conservatives Tex., Guardian Freedom award Young Am. Freedom.*

PAUL, RONALD NEALE, management consultant; b. Chgo., July 22, 1934; s. David Edward and Frances (Kusel) P.; m. Nona Maria Moore, Dec. 27, 1964 (div. Oct. 1981); children: Lisa, Karen, Brenda; m. Georgeann Elizabeth Lapkoff, Apr. 10, 1982. BS in Indsl. Engring., Northwestern U., 1957, MBA, 1958. Asst. to pres. Victor Comptometer Co., Chgo., 1958-64; cons. Corplan, 1964-66; pres. Technomic Inc., 1966—. Mng. ptnr. L/P Ptnrs., Chgo., 1978-84; bd. dirs. Summit Restaurants, Salt Lake City, 1990-96. Co-author: The 101 Best Performing Companies in America, 1986, Winning the Chain Restaurant Game, 1994. Mem. Am. Mktg. Assn., Am. Mgmt. Assn., Planners Forum, Pres.'s Assn., Product Devel. Mgmt. Assn., Beta Gamma Sigma. Avocations: reading, racquetball. Office: Technomic Inc 300 S Riverside Plz Ste 1940 Chicago IL 60606-6613 E-mail: rpaul@technomic.com.

PAUL, RONALD STANLEY, research institute executive; b. Olympia, Wash., Jan. 19, 1923; s. Adolph and Olga (Klapstein) P.; m. Margery Jean Pengra, June 5, 1944; children: Kathleen Paul Crosby, Robert S., James N. Student, Linfield Coll., 1940-41, Reed Coll., 1943-44, Harvard U., 1945; BS, U. Oreg., 1947, MS, 1949, PhD, 1951. Physicist, research mgr. Gen. Electric Co., Richland, Wash., 1951-64; asso. dir. Battelle N.W. Labs., 1965-68, dir., 1971-72, Battelle Seattle Research Ctr., 1969-70; v.p. ops. Battelle Meml. Inst., Columbus, Ohio, 1973-76, sr. v.p., 1976-78, exec. v.p., 1978-81, pres., 1981-87, chief exec. officer, 1984-87, assoc. trustee, 1986-92. Lectr. modern physics Ctr. for Grad. Studies, Richland, 1951-62; IAEA cons. to, Japan, 1962; bd. dirs. MicroPlanet Ltd. Contbr. articles to profl. jours. Trustee Linfield Coll., 1970-73, Denison U., 1982-88, Oreg. Mus. Sci. and Industry, 1971-72, Columbus Ctr. Sci. and Industry, 1973-87, Columbus Cancer Clinic, 1974-87, Columbus Children's Hosp. Research Found., 1975-87, Franklin U., 1987;

trustee Pacific Sci. Ctr., 1969-74, Found. assoc., 1989—; v.p. exec. bd. Cen. Ohio council Boy Scouts Am., 1976-87; mem. exec. bd. of fellows Seattle-Pacific Coll., 1970-73; bd. overseers Acad. for Contemporary Problems, 1971-75; mem. nat. adv. bd. Am. U., 1982-86, Ohio State U. Found., 1985-87; bd. dirs. Edward Lowe Found., 1985-98, advisor, trustee emeritus, 1999—. Served with USAAF, 1943-46. Recipient Silver Beaver award Boy Scouts Am., 1986 Mem. Am. Phys. Soc., Am. Nuclear Soc., Sigma Xi, Sigma Pi Sigma, Pi Mu Epsilon. Republican. Presbyterian. Home: 7706 173rd St SW Edmonds WA 98026-5018

PAUL, SINDY MICHELLE, preventive medicine physician; b. Phila., Feb. 13, 1957; d. Gerson Stanly and Phyllis (Ostrum) P.; m. Oren Leonard Friedman, Mar. 8, 1986; children: Melissa, Rebecca. AB in Biology hons., magna cum laude, Bryn Mawr (Pa.) Coll., 1979; MD with hons., Temple U., 1983; MPH, N.J. Grad. Program Pub. Health, Piscataway, N.J., 1993. Diplomate Am. Bd. Gen. Preventive Medicine and Pub. Health. Med. dir. N.J. Dept. Health and Sr. Svcs., Trenton, 1988-96, residency program dir., 1995—; asst. clin. prof. U. Medicine and Dentistry N.J., Piscataway, N.J., 1995—; clin. cons. state labs. N.J. Dept. Health and Sr. Svcs., Trenton, 1995—, med. dir., 1996—. Mem. exec. com. preventive medicine, pub. health sect. Coll. Physicians of Phila., 1995-2001, exec. com. n.e. regional infection control course N.J. chpts. APIC, 1989—. Editor and co-author: (books) Infection Control for Long Term Care Facilities, 1992, HIV/AIDS, 1997; contbr. 150 chpts., abstracts and articles to profl. jours.; mem. editl. adv. bd. (jour.) Infection Control and Hosp. Epidemiology, 1985—, N.J. Medicine., Nursing Spectrum, 2000. Divsn. rep. United Way Campaign, Trenton, N.J., 1988-89. Grantee Ctrs. for Disease Control and Prevention, Atlanta, 1994-98; recipient Disting. Alumnae award U. Medicine and Dentistry N.J. Mem. Am. Coll. Prevention Medicine (chair joint coun. of residency program dirs.), Assn. for Profls. in Infection Control and Epidemiology, N.J. Pub. Health Assn. (pres.-elect, v.p 1996-2000, mem. exec. bd., pres. 2001-2003, pres. elect Ezra Mundy Hunt award, Pres. award for Tb, Pres. award for pub. health), Soc. Healthcare Epidemiology Am. (working group 1995—), Ctrs. for Disease Control and Prevention (5 working groups, 1996—), Acad. Medicine N.J. (Med. Educator of Yr.). Office: NJ Dept Health and Sr Svcs 50 E State St Ste 4 Trenton NJ 08608-1715

PAUL, STEPHEN HOWARD, lawyer; b. Indpls., June 28, 1947; s. Alfred and Sophia (Nahmias) P.; m. Deborah Lynn Dorman, Jan. 22, 1969; children: Gabriel, Jonathan. AB, Ind. U., 1969, JD, 1972. Bar: Ind. 1972, U.S. Dist. Ct. (so. dist.) Ind. 1972. Assoc. Baker & Daniels, Indpls., 1972-78, ptnr., 1979—. Mem. bd. visitors Ind. U. Sch. Law, Bloomington. Editor in chief Ind. U. Law Jour., 1971. Pres. Belle Meade Neighborhood Assn., Indpls., 1974-78; v.p., counsel Brentwood Neighborhood Assn., Carmel, Ind., 1985-88, pres., 1988-91. Mem. ABA (state and local tax com. 1985—, sports and entertainment law com.), Am. Property Tax Counsel (founding mem.), Ind. State Bar Assn., Order of Coif. Office: Baker & Daniels 300 N Meridian St Ste 2700 Indianapolis IN 46204-1782

PAUL, THOMAS DANIEL, lawyer; b. Butte, Mont., June 10, 1948; s. Thomas Anthony and Helen (O'Brien) P.; m. Carolyn Hicks, Dec. 20, 1976; children: Thomas Richard, Jennifer Ann. AB, Carroll Coll., 1970; MS, Ind. U., 1975, PhD, 1977; JD, U. Houston, 1987. Diplomate Am. Bd. Med. Genetics. Asst. prof. SUNY, Buffalo, 1977-84; assoc. Fulbright & Jaworski, Houston, 1987-90, participating assoc., 1990-94, ptnr., 1994—. Staff cons. N.Y. State Dept. Mental Hygeine, Perrysburg, 1978-84. Contbr. articles to profl. jours. Named to Order of Coif U. Houston, 1987. Mem. Tex. Bar Assn., Houston Bar Assn., Am. Intellectual Property Law Assn., Houston Intellectual Property Law Assn. Home: 1400 Hermann Dr Apt 9FG Houston TX 77004-7142 Office: Fulbright & Jaworski 1301 Mckinney St Ste 5100 Houston TX 77010-3031 Fax: 713-651-5105. E-mail: tpaul@Fulbright.com.

PAUL, THOMAS FRANK, lawyer; b. Aberdeen, Wash., Sept. 23, 1925; s. Thomas and Loretta (Ounstead) P.; m. Dolores Marion Zaugg, Apr. 1, 1950; chilren: Pamela, Peggy, Thomas Frank. BS in Psychology, Wash. State U., 1951; JD, U. Wash., 1957. Bar: Wash. 1958, U.S. Dist. Ct. (no. and so. dists.) Wash. 1958, U.S. Ct. Appeals (9th cir.) 1958, U.S. Supreme Ct. 1970. Ptnr., shareholder, dir. LeGros, Buchanan & Paul, Seattle, 1958—. Lectr. on admiralty and maritime law. Mem. ABA (chmn. com. on admiralty and maritime litigation 1982-86), Wash. State Bar Assn., Maritime Law Assn. U.S.A. (com. on nav. and C.G. matters 1981-82, com. on U.S. Mcht. Marine program 1981-82, com. on practice and procedure 1982-86, com. on limitation of liability 1982-86, com. on maritime legislation 1982—, nom. com. 1998-99), bd. Adv. U. San Fransisco Law Journ. Republican. Home: 1323 Willard Ave W Seattle WA 98119-3460 Office: LeGros Buchanan & Paul 701 5th Ave Ste 2500 Seattle WA 98104-7051 E-mail: tpaul@legros.com.

PAUL, THOMAS WAYNE, psychotherapist; b. Vallejo, Calif., Mar. 25, 1950; s. Thomas Birdsall and Shirley Mae (Osterheld) P. BA, Goddard Coll., 1980, Ma, 1989. Diplomate Am. Psychotherapy Assn.; cert. alcohol, drugs counselor, employee assistance profl.; nationally cert. addictions counselor; nat. cert. group psychotherapist. Civilian program coord., dir. community counseling ctr. Seneca Army Depot, Romulus, N.Y., 1981-85; svcs. mgr. Finger Lakes Alcoholism Counseling and Referral Agy., Seneca Falls, 1985-86; dir. outpatient svc. dept., FLACRA, Clifton Springs, 1985; dir. employee assistance program Maxwell Hall, 1985-86; regional svcs. coord. MEDIPLEX Group, Rochester, N.Y., 1986-87; co-owner Human Progress Enterprises, Newark, 1986—; chem. dependency program coord. Hobart & William Smith Colls., 1985-88; pvt. practice in psychotherapy Geneva and Rochester, N.Y., 1985-88; dir., founder Adult Child & Co-dependency Ctr., Rochester, 1988—. Pres. Finger Lakes Alcoholism Counseling & Referral Agy., Clifton Springs, 1983-84, Coun. on Alcoholism of Finger Lakes, Geneva, 1986—; treas. N.Y. State Coalition for Children of Addictions, 1987—, chmn. Rochester chpt., 1986—. Chmn. Combined Fed. Campaign United Way, Romulus, N.Y., 1983-84. Mem. Nat. Assn. Alcohol and Drugs Counselors, Nat. Assn. Children of Alcoholics, Am. Group Psychotherapy Assn., N.Y. Fedn. Alcoholism Counselors, Am. Psychotherapy Assn. Home: 246 Grace Ave Newark NY 14513-2151 Office: 625 Cross Keys Office Park Fairport NY 14450-3508

PAUL, VERA MAXINE, mathematics educator; b. Mansfield, La., Dec. 14, 1940; d. Clifton and Virginia (Smith) Hall; m. Alvin James Paul III, June 14, 1964; children: Alvin J., Calvin J., Douglas F. BS, So. U., 1962; MS, Roosevelt U., 1975. Tchr. Shreveport (La.) Bd. Edn., 1962-64, Chgo. Bd. Edn., 1964-81, asst. prin., 1981—; tchr. South Bend (Ind.) Cmty. Sch., 1967-68. Mem. Chgo. Bd. Edn., 1964-92. Recipient Disting. Vol. Leadership award March of Dimes, Chgo., 1982, Mayoral Tribute award City of Pontiac (Mich.), 1987, Disting. Svc. award City Coun. Detroit, 1988, Svc. award City Coun. Cleve., 1990, State of Mich. Cert. of Merit Sen. Jackie Vaughn III, Great Lakes Svc. award, 1992, Svc. award Mich. Senate, 1992, Outstanding Svc. award U. Ill., Chgo., Women Connecting Project, 1997, Outstanding Leadership and Dir. award Chgo. Women Connecting-U. Ill. Chgo. Ctr. for Rsch. on Women and Gender, 1997. Mem. NAACP, Am. Fedn. Tchrs., Chgo. Tchr. Union, Ill. Coun. Affective Reading Edn., Ill. Coun. Tchrs. Math., Nat. Coun. Tchrs. Math., Nat. Alliance Black Sch. Educators, Zeta Phi Beta (regional dir. 1986-90, Zeta of Yr. 1988, Disting. Svc. award 1992, 95, Outstanding Svc. award 1996), RTAC (bd. dirs. 2002). Lutheran. Avocations: reading, computer games, walking, piano.

PAUL, VIVIAN, lawyer; b. N.Y.C., July 3, 1925; d. A. Spencer and Simonson Feld; m. M.B. Paul, Sept. 10, 1966; children: Leslie Vivian, Melissa Beth. BA, U. Miami, 1944; LLB, U. So. Calif., 1949. Bar: Calif. 1949, U.S. Dist. Ct. (so. dist.) Calif. 1950. Pvt. practice, Cathedral City, Calif., 1949—. Editor-in-chief U. So. Calif. Law Rev., 1944. Los Angeles County Bar Assn. Democrat. Home and Office: 69864 Via Del Norte Cathedral City CA 92234-1726 E-mail: ranchovillage@aol.com.

PAUL, WILLIAM, physicist, educator; b. Deskford, Scotland, Mar. 31, 1926; came to U.S., 1952; s. William and Jean (Watson) P.; m. Barbara Anderson Forbes, Mar. 28, 1952; children: David, Fiona. MA, Aberdeen U., Scotland, 1946; PhD, Aberdeen U., 1951; A.M. (hon.), Harvard U., 1960; D Honoris Causa, Paris, 1994. Asst. lectr., then lectr. Aberdeen U., 1946-52; mem. faculty Harvard U., 1953—, Gordon McKay prof. applied physics, 1963-91, Mallinckrodt prof. applied physics, 1991-2000, prof. physics, 1980-2000, Mallinckrodt rsch. prof. applied physics, 2000—, rsch. prof. physics, 2000—. Professeur associé U. Paris, 1966-67; cons. solid state physics, 1954—; Ripon prof., Calcutta, 1984 Author: Handbook on Semiconductors: Band Theory and Transport Properties, 1982; co-editor: Solids Under Pressure, 1963, Amorphous and Liquid Semiconductors, 1980, Physics of Semiconductor Materials and Applications, 1986, High Pressure in Semiconductor Physics, Vols. 1 and 2, 1998. Carnegie fellow, 1952-53; Guggenheim fellow, 1959-60; Humboldt awardee, 1990; fellow Clare Hall Cambridge U., 1974-75. Fellow Am. Phys. Soc., Brit. Inst. Physics, N.Y. Acad. Scis., Royal Soc. Edinburgh; mem. AAUP, Sigma Xi. Home: 2 Eustis St Lexington MA 02421-5612 Office: Harvard U Pierce Hall Cambridge MA 02138 E-mail: paul@deas.harvard.edu.

PAUL, WILLIAM DEWITT, JR. artist, educator, photographer, videographer, museum director; b. Wadley, Ga., Sept. 26, 1934; s. William DeWitt and Sonoma Elizabeth (Tinley) P.; m. Dorothy Hefling, Sept. 2, 1962; children: Sarah Elizabeth, Barbara Susan, Dorothy Ann. Student, Emory U., summer 1952, U. Rome, summer 1953, Ga. State Coll. Bus. Adminstrn., Atlanta, 1953—, summer 1956; B.F.A., Atlanta Art Inst., 1955; AB, U. Ga., 1958, M.F.A., 1959. Instr. art and art history Park Coll., Parkville, Mo., 1960-61; dir. exhbns., instr. art history Kansas City (Mo.) Art Inst., 1959-64, curator study collections, asst. prof. art, 1964-65; coordinator basic courses dept. art, asst. prof. art U. Ga., Athens, 1965-67; curator Ga. Mus. Art, assoc. prof. art, 1967-69, dir., asso. prof., 1969-80, prof., 1997—2002, gen. Sandy Beaver tchr. prof., 2000—02. Lectr. Boston, L.A., New Orleans, San Antonio, Memphis, Birmingham; chmn. visual arts rev. panel Ga. Council for Arts and Humanities, 1976-77; v.p. Arts Festival Atlanta, 1982, 84, 85, trustee, 1982-93; guest artist Arts Festival Atlanta, 1987; mem. parents council Randolph-Macon Woman's Coll., Lynchburg, Va., 1986-87. Exhibited in one man shows at Ga. Mus. Art, 1959, Atlanta Art Assn., 1959, Unitarian Gallery, Kansas City, 1960, Palmer Gallery, Kansas City, 1965, Heath Gallery, Atlanta, 1976, Hunter Mus. Art, Chattanooga, 1976, Forum Gallery, N.Y.C., 1977, Madison (Ga.) Morgan Cultural Ctr., 1980, Columbus (Ga.) Mus. Arts and Scis., 1980, Macon (Ga.) Mus. Arts and Sci., 1980, Banks Haley Gallery, Albany, Ga., 1980, Augusta Richmond County (Ga.) Mus., 1980, Heath Gallery 1982, Moon Gallery, Berry Coll., Rome, Ga., 1983, Bathhouse Gallery, Atlanta, 1987, MIA Gallery, Seattle, 1988, Valencia C.C., Orlando, Fla., 1991, Gasperi Gallery, New Orleans, 1993, Contemporary Arts Ctr., New Orleans, 1994; numerous site-specific installations, 1986-97; exhibited group shows, New Arts Gallery, Atlanta, 1961, Kansas City Art Inst., 1960-64, Park Coll., 1960, Mulvane Art Ctr., Topeka, 1965, Palazzo Venezia, Rome, 1984, Elaine Benson Gallery, Bridgehampton, L.I., N.Y., 1986, Dulin Gallery Art, Knoxville, Tenn., 1986, 1987 Atlanta Biennale, Nexus Contemporary Art Ctr., Atlanta, Valencia C.C., Orlando, 1988, Greg Kucera Gallery, Seattle, 1992, King Plow Arts Ctr., Atlanta, 1994, Leslie-Lohman Found., N.Y.C., 1995, Mus. Fine Arts, Tallahassee, 1996, Art Ctr., Miami Beach, Fla., 1997, Lebanon Valley Coll., Annville, Pa., 1998, others; represented in permanent collections Gen. Mills, Inc., Mpls., Hallmark Cards, Kansas City, Little Rock Arts Ctr., Ga. Mus. Art, U. Ga., The Kinsey Inst., Ind. U., Calif. State U., Tom of Finland Found. Ford Found. faculty enrichment grantee, 1978; recipient numerous awards for paintings. Mem. Am. Fedn. Arts (trustee 1969-81), Coll. Art Assn., Am. Assn. Museums (council 1981), Lovis Corinth Meml. Found., Ga. Alliance Arts Edn. (dir. 1975-77), Phi Kappa Phi. Home: 150 Bar H Ct Athens GA 30605-4702 Office: 4900 Barnett Shoals Rd Athens GA 30605

PAUL, WILLIAM ERWIN, immunologist, researcher; b. Bklyn., June 12, 1936; s. Jack and Sylvia (Gleicher) Paul; m. Marilyn Heller, Dec. 25, 1958; children: Jonathan M. Carmel, Matthew E. AB summa cum laude, Bklyn. Coll., 1956; MD cum laude, SUNY, Bklyn., 1960, DSc (hon.) , 1991. Intern, then asst. resident Mass. Meml. Hosp., Boston, 1960—62; clin. assoc. Nat. Cancer Inst., NIH, Bethesda, Md., 1962—64; postdoctoral fellow, instr. NYU Sch. Medicine, N.Y.C., 1964—68; sr. investigator Lab. Immunology Nat. Inst. Allergy and Infectious Diseases, NIH, Bethesda, 1968—70, chief Lab. Immunology, 1970—; dir. Office of AIDS Rsch. NIH, assoc. dir. AIDS rsch., 1994—97. Mem. sci. adv. bd. Suntory Pharm. Rsch. Labs; chmn. selection com. Irene Diamond Fund Professorhips in Immunology; bd. dirs. Aaron Diamond AIDS Rsch. Ctr.; Sackler sr. prof. Tel-Aviv U. Editor: Fundamental Immunology, 1984, Fundamental Immunology, 4th edit., 1999, Ann. Rev. Immunology, Vols. 1-20, 1983—; adv. editor Jour. Exptl. Medicine, 1974—; assoc. editor Cell, 1985—96, transmitting editor Internat. Immunology, 1989—96, corr. editor Procs. Royal Soc. Series B, 1989—93, mem. editl. bd. Molecular Biology of Cell, 1990—93, Immunity, 1993—; contbg. editor: Procs. NAS U.S.A., 1992—94; contbr. Bd. dirs. Trudeau Int. USPHS, 1962—64 USPHS, 1975—96. Recipient Founders' prize, Tex. Instruments Found., 1979, Alumni medal, SUNY Downstate Med. Ctr., 1981, Disting. Svc. medal, USPHS, 1985, 3M Life Scis. award, 1988, Tovi-Comet-Wallerstein prize, CAIR Inst., Bar-Ilan U., 1992, 6th ann. award for excellence in immunologic rsch., Duke U., 1993, Alumni honors, Bklyn. Coll., 1994, Abbott Labs. award in clin. and diagnostic immunology, Am. Acad. Microbiology, 1998. Fellow: Am. Acad. Arts and Scis.; mem.: Assn. Am. Physicians, Am. Assn. Immunologist (pres. 1986—87), Am. Soc. Clin. Investigation (pres. 1980—81), Scandinavian Soc. Immunology (hon.), Inst. Medicine NAS, NAS. Office: NIH Bldg 10 Rm 11n311 Bethesda MD 20892-0001

PAUL, WILLIAM GEORGE, lawyer; b. Pauls Valley, Okla., Nov. 25, 1930; s. Homer and Helen (Lafferty) P.; m. Barbara Elaine Brite, Sept. 27, 1963; children: George Lynn, Alison Elise, Laura Elaine, William Stephen. BA, U. Okla., 1952, LL.B., 1956. Bar: Okla. bar 1956. Pvt. practice law, Norman, 1956; ptnr. Oklahoma City, 1957-84; with Crowe & Dunlevy, 1962-84, 96—; sr. v.p., gen. counsel Phillips Petroleum Co., Bartlesville, Okla., 1984-95; ptnr. Crowe & Dunlevy, Oklahoma City, 1996—. Assoc. prof. law Oklahoma City U., 1964-68; adv. bd. Martindale Hubbell, 1990—. Author: (with Earl Sneed) Vernon's Oklahoma Practice, 1965. Bd. dirs. Nat. Ctr. for State Cts., 1993-99, Am. Bar Endowment, 1986—. 1st lt. USMCR, 1952-54. Named Outstanding Young Man Oklahoma City, 1965, Outstanding Young Oklahoman, 1966 Fellow Am. Bar Found. (chmn. 1991), Am. Coll. Trial Lawyers; mem. ABA (bd. govs. 1995—, pres. 1999), Okla. Bar Assn. (pres. 1976), Oklahoma County Bar Assn. (past pres.), Nat. Conf. Bar Pres. (pres. 1986), U. Okla. Alumni Assn. (pres. 1973), Order of Coif, Phi Beta Kappa, Phi Delta Phi, Delta Sigma Rho. Democrat. Presbyterian. Home: 13017 Burnt Oak Rd Oklahoma City OK 73120-8919 Office: Crowe & Dunlevy Mid-Am Tower 20 N Broadway Ave Ste 1800 Oklahoma City OK 73102-8273

PAUL, WILLIAM J. film studies educator, writer; b. New Haven, Apr. 5, 1944; s. Ernest B. and Edna Rosalind (Kaufman) Paul; m. Rafia Margaret Zafar, Oct. 18, 1990; 1 child Nathan. BA in German Lit., Columbia Coll., 1966; MA in Russian Lit., Columbia U., 1969, PhD in Film Studies, 1982. Instr. Haverford (Pa.) Coll., 1971—75, 1977—80; preceptor, instr. Columbia U., N.Y.C., 1976—77, 1979—80; asst./assoc. prof. MIT, Cambridge, Mass., 1980—89; assoc. prof. U. Mich., Ann Arbor, 1989—98, dir. film and video studies, 1991—92; prof., dir. film and media studies Washington U., St. Louis, 1998—. Reviewer NIH and Fulbright fellowships, Washington, 1988—91, 1992, 1995—96; cons. Am. Cinema Project N.Y. Ctr. for Visual History, N.Y.C., 1988—93; alt. mem. Nat. Film Preservation Bd., Washington, 1993—94. Author: Ernst Lubitsch's American Comedy , 1983, Laughing Screaming, 1994; contbr. articles to profl. jours. Fellow Kellett fellow, MIT, 1985; grantee Nat. Endowment for the Humanities, 1974—75, OVPR grant, U. Mich., 1992, 1993. Mem.: Soc. for Cinema Studies (chair com. on preservation and access 1992), Am. Studies Assn. Avocation: bicycling. Home: 6631 Pershing Ave Saint Louis MO 63103 Office: Washington Univ One Brookings Dr Saint Louis MO 63130

PAUL, WILLIAM MCCANN, lawyer; b. Cambridge, Mass., Feb. 9, 1951; s. Kenneth William and Mary Jean (Lamson) P.; m. Janet Anne Forest, Feb. 25, 1984; children: Emily L'Engle, Andrew Angwin, Elizabeth Seton. Student, U. Freiburg, Fed. Republic of Germany, 1971-72; BA, Johns Hopkins U., 1973; JD, U. Mich., 1977. Bar: D.C. 1978, U.S. Dist. Ct. D.C. 1978, U.S. Ct. Claims 1984, U.S. Ct. Appeals (4th cir.) 1980, U.S. Ct. Appeals (fed. cir.) 1983, U.S. Tax Ct. 1990. Law clk. to judge U.S. Ct. Appeals (5th cir.), Austin, Tex., 1977-78; assoc. Covington & Burling, Washington, 1978-87, ptnr., 1987-88, 89—; dep. tax legis. counsel U.S. Treasury Dept., 1988-89. Mem. ABA (asst. sec. tax sect. 1995-97, sec. 1997-99, coun. mem. 1999-2002), D.C. Bar Assn., Am. Law Inst., Am. Coll. Tax Counsel, Order of Coif. Presbyterian. Home: 5604 Chevy Chase Pkwy NW Washington DC 20015-2520 Office: Covington & Burling PO Box 7566 1201 Pennsylvania Ave NW Washington DC 20004-2401 E-mail: wpaul@cov.com.

PAUL, YVONNE C. retired elementary educator, administrator; b. Chgo., July 9, 1934; d. Reuben Douglas Adams and Gladys Winters Bacot; m. William Ralph Paul, Nov. 13, 1962; adopted children: Vanessa, Jonathan. BA, U. Ill., Chgo., 1956; MA in Counseling, San Francisco State U., 1976; MA in Adminstrn., 1983. Classroom tchr. Chgo. Pub. Schs., 1956-59; sch. tchr. Dep. Schs. Europe, Eritrea, East Africa, 1959-60, Stuttgart/Ludwigsburg, Germany, 1960-62; dir. pre-sch. AFB, Killeen, Tex., 1962-63; classroom tchr. Jericho (N.Y.) Sch. Dist., 1964-65; sch. tchr. middle grades Balt. County Schs., Towson, Md., 1965-69; vice prin., tchr. Pittsburg (Calif.) Unified Sch. Dist., 1969-99; ret., 1999. Resource mgr., reading and sci. leadership; classroom tchr., lead math., leader Pittsburg Unified Sch. Dist., 1969-99. Cadet leader Girl Scouts Am., Killeen, 1962; hosp. vol. Killeen Gen. Hosp., 1963; Parent's Booster Club. Technol. Edn. Contra Costa Sch. grantee Alameda/Contra Costa Office Edn., Hayward, Calif., 1985; grant writer awards Technol. Edn. Contra Costa. Mem. No. Calif. Math. Assn., Assn. Calif. Sch. Adminstrs., Artist Guild, Phi Delta Kappa. Roman Catholic. Avocations: writing for publication, reading, gardening, interior design, children's science theater.

PAULEY, BRUCE FREDERICK, history educator; b. Lincoln, Nebr., Nov. 4, 1937; s. Carroll Righter and Blanche Marie (Hulsebus) P.; m. Marianne Barbara Utz, Dec. 21, 1963; children: Mark Allan, Glenn Hamilton. BA, Grinnell Coll., 1959; MA, U. Nebr., 1961; PhD, U. Rochester, 1966. Instr. history Coll. of Wooster (Ohio), 1964-65, U. Nebr., Lincoln, 1965-66; asst. prof. history U. Wyo., Laramie, 1966-71; from assoc. prof. to prof. history U. Ctrl. Fla., Orlando, 1971—, chmn. faculty senate, 1978-79. Cons., expert witness war crimes divsn. Can. Justice Dept., 1998-99. Author: The Habsburg Legacy, 1867-1939, 1972, Hahnenschwanz und Hakenkreuz: Steirischer Heimatschutz und österreichischer Nationalsozialismus, 1918-1934, 1972, Hitler and the Forgotten Nazis: A History of Austrian National Socialism, 1981, Der Weg in den Nationalsozialismus: Ursprünge und Entwicklung in Österreich, 1988, From Prejudice to Persecution: A History of Austrian Anti-Semitism, 1992 (Charles Smith prize So. Hist. Assn. best book European history 1991-92, best book Austrian studies Austrian Cultural Inst. 1992-93), Eine Geschichte des österreichischen Antisemitismus: Von der Ausgrenzung zur Auslöschung, 1993, Hitler, Stalin, and Mussolini: Totalitarianism in the Twentieth Century, 1997, 2d edit., 2002. Chmn. parents' adv. com. Oviedo (Fla.) High Sch., 1981-82. Fulbright fellow, 1963-64, rsch. fellow NEH, 1972, 87. Mem.: Soc. Austrian and Habsburg Historians, German Studies Assn. (exec. com. 1986—89), Am. Hist. Assn. Avocations: traveling to historical sites, photography, golf. Office: U Ctrl Fla Orlando FL 32816-1350 E-mail: bpauley@pegasus.cc.ucf.edu.

PAULEY, JANE, television journalist; b. Indpls., Oct. 31, 1950; m. Garry Trudeau; 3 children. BA in Polit. Sci, Ind. U., 1971; D of Journalism (hon.), DePauw U., 1978. Reporter Sta. WISH-TV, Indpls., 1972-75; co-anchor WMAQ-TV News, Chgo., 1975-76, The Today Show, NBC, N.Y.C., 1976-90; from co-anchor to corr. NBC News, 1976—; prin. writer, reporter NBC Nightly News, 1980-82, substitute anchor, 1990—; co-anchor Early Today, NBC, 1982-83; prin. corr. Real Life With Jane Pauley, NBC, 1991; co-anchor Dateline NBC, N.Y.C., 1992-99, prin. anchor, 1999—; anchor Time & Again MSNBC, 1999—. Adv. bd. Childrens Health Fund, Internat. Coun. Freedom from Hunger; bd. dirs. Publ. Edn. Needs Civic Involvement in Learning. Recipient Emmy award, Edward R. Murrow award, Gabriel award, Nancy Susan Reynolds award, Maggie award, Humanitas award, Commendation award Am. Women in Radio and TV, Gracie Allen award, Clarion award Assn. for Women in Comm., Wilbur award Religious Pub. Rels. Coun., Salute to Excellence award Nat. Assn. Black Journalists, Leonard Zeidenberg First Amendment award Radio TV News Dirs. Found., Paul White award RTNDA; named to Broadcasting and Cable Hall of Fame; named Broadcaster of Yr., Internat. Radio and TV Soc., 1986, Best in Bus., Washington Journalism Rev., 1990. Fellow Soc. for Profl. Journalists (hon. chair Jane Pauley task force on mass comm. edn.). Office: NBC News-Dateline 30 Rockefeller Plz New York NY 10112-0036*

PAULEY, MATTHEW ALFRED, law educator; b. N.Y.C., Oct. 24, 1959; s. Adam R. and Lucile Pauley. BA summa cum laude, Williams Coll., 1981; MA, Harvard U., 1987, PhD, 1990, JD cum laude, 1993. Tchg. asst. Harvard U., Cambridge, Mass., 1983-85, pre-grad. tchg. fellow, 1985-89, instr., 1989-90, postgrad. tchg. fellow, 1990-96; adj. prof. law So. New Eng. Sch. Law, 1996-2000; vis. prof. law Univ. Coll. Galway, Ireland, 2000—. Author: I Do Solemnly Swear: The President's Constitutional Oath, 1999, Criminal Law: Nature and Sources, 1999; contbr. articles to profl. jours. Mem. Phi Beta Kappa. Avocations: American politics and history, Gilbert and Sullivan operettas, English and Irish history, travel. Home: 800 Pleasant St Apt 1501 New Bedford MA 02740 E-mail: mpauley@altansta.com.

PAULEY, SHIRLEY STEWART, religious organization executive; b. Boston, Sept. 13, 1938; d. Charles Norris and Nellie Consuelo (Yorke) Stewart; m. Edward Haven Pauley, May 29, 1964; children: David Stewart, Deborah Jeanne. BA, Gordon Coll., 1960; postgrad., Ariz. State U., 1961, Boston U., 1963. Sec./receptionist Atwell Co., Boston, summer 1956; sec., typist Kelley Girl, 1956-60; asst. office mgr. Radiator Chem. Corp., Scottsdale, Ariz., 1960-62; sec., clerical worker GM, Westwood, Mass., 1962-64; v.p. Truth Alive Ministries, Dallas, 1995—. Spkr. At Large, Boston, 1956-60; Sunday sch. tchr. Blaney Meml. Bapt. Ch., Boston, 1956-60; choir dir. Sherwood Bapt. Ch., Phoenix, 1961-62, co-youth dir., 1961; co-youth dir. Blaney Meml. Ch., Boston, 1964-66; mem. book store com. Prestonwood Bapt. Ch., Dallas, 1994—; messenger Bapt. Gen. Conv. Tex., Ft. Worth, 1996. Republican. Avocations: photography, reading, music. Office: Truth Alive Ministries PO Box 794945 Dallas TX 75379-4945

PAULHUS, NORMAN GERARD, JR. aerospace engineer; b. Washington, May 19, 1950; s. Norman Gerard and Kathryn Frances (Schwartz) P. BS Aerospace Engrng. with high honors, U. Md., 1970. Transp. intern U.S. Dept. Transp., Washington, 1970-71, aerospace engr. Office of Sec., 1971-72, gen. engr., 1972-82, dep. dir. Office Tech. and Planing Assistance, 1982-87, program devel. officer Rsch. and Tech., 1987-91, sr. tech. advisor Office Rsch. and Tech. Transfer, 1991—2002; transp. specialist Fed. Highway Adminstrn., 2002—. Editor: (with D. McKelvey and D. Ewing) Procs. of 4th Nat. Conf. Rural Pub. Transp., 1979, Technology Sharing, 1979, (with A. Brecher, R. Stevens and others) Effective Global Transportation in the Twenty-First Century, 1999; contbr. articles to profl. jours. Recipient Sec.'s award U.S. Dept. Transp., 1974, Meritorious Achievement award, 1979, Spl. Achievement award, 1984, Superior Achievement award, 1989, Cert. Appreciation, Coun. Stat Govts., 1990, Way to Go award Dept. Transp., 1991, Cert. Appreciation, USCG Commandant, 1991, Sec.'s Find Good and Praise It award, 1999, Exemplary Achievemnt (Eagle) award, 2000, Commandant's Pub. Svc. medal USCG, 2002. Mem. AAAS, Nat. Space Inst., U.S. Naval Inst., Navy League U.S., Planetary Soc., Inst. Noetic Scis., Tau Beta Pi, Sigma Gamma Tau, Phi Kappa Phi. Roman Catholic. Home: 18816 Muncaster Rd Rockville MD 20855-1430 Office: 400 7th St SW Washington DC 20590-0001 E-mail: otterx@erols.com., norman.paulhus@fhwe.dot.gov.

PAULHUS, THOMAS A. educator; b. Paterson, N.J., Oct. 8, 1953; s. Albert Richard and Shelby Ann Paulhus; m. Mary C. Fedigan, Aug. 28, 1988 (div. 1996). BA, Heidelberg Coll., Tiffin, Ohio, 1975; MA, Seton Hall U., 2022. Cert. tchr. social studies, N.J. Cons. The Triad Group, Boston, 1984-90, Toma Assocs., Little Falls, N.J., 1990—; tchr. Blessed Sacrament, Paterson, 1999—. Democrat. Roman Catholic. Avocation: golf. Home: 275 6th Ave NW Paterson NJ 07524 E-mail: tpaulhus@hotmail.com.

PAULI, JOSEF FREDERICK, accountant; b. Hammond, La., Nov. 11, 1963; s. Joseph Henry and Cheryl Loraine (Wilcox) P.; m. Lora Lynn Gottlick, July 30, 1988; children: Joshua, Kaitlyn, Meredith, Jenna. Assoc. in Computer Sci., Purdue U., 1985, BS in Acctg., 1987; MBA, Ind. U., South Bend, 1995. Cost acct. Uniroyal Plastics Co., Mishawaka, Ind., 1987-90; sr. acct. Uniroyal Engineered Products, Port Clinton, Ohio, 1990-91; fin. resource/sr. acct. I/N Tek, Inc., New Carlisle, Ind., 1991-97; plant contbr. Philips Med Sys, Charlotte, NC, 1997—. Bus. cons. 8th grade Jr. Achievement, South Bend, 1993-97. Roman Catholic. Office: Philips Med Sys 1301 Westinghouse Blvd Ste A Charlotte NC 28273-6393

PAULIKAS, GEORGE ALGIS, retired physicist; b. Pagegiai, Lithuania, May 14, 1936; came to U.S., 1949, naturalized, 1955; s. George and Olga (Pacas) P.; m. Joan Marie Gross, Sept. 7, 1957; 1 child, Nancy Marie. BS in

Engring. Physics, U. Ill., Chgo. and Urbana, 1957, MS (univ. fellow 1957-58), 1958; PhD in Physics (NSF fellow 1958-61), U. Calif., Berkeley, 1961. With Aerospace Corp., El Segundo, Calif., 1961-98; ret., head space particles and fields dept., 1968, dir. space scis. lab., 1968-81, v.p. labs., 1981-85, sr. v.p. devel., 1985-89, sr. v.p. programs, 1989-94, exec. v.p., 1992-98. Mem. various ad hoc coms. NAS, 1970, 73, 79, 80, ann., 1984-87, 91-92, 99-2001, mem. com. solar and space physics, 1977-80; mem. adv. coun. geophysics U. Calif., 1973-75, exec. com. space scis. lab., Berkeley, 1978-81; mem. sci. adv. bd. USAF, 1975-82, 91-95; cons. Lawrence Berkeley Lab., 1961-66, Office Space Scis., NASA, 1975-82, Los Alamos phys. divsn. adv. com., 1983-96, Naval Rsch. Adv. Com., 1984-86, Naval Studies Bd., 1989-95, Inst. Def. Analysis, 1998—; mem. def. space tech. com. NRC, 1987-92; mem. NAS/NRC Space Studies Bd., 1999—. Author papers in field; asso. editor: Jour. Geophys. Research, 1972-75. Trustee Calif. Sci. Ctr., 1994-2000, Boy Scouts Am., L.A., 1996-2000. Recipient Aerospace Corp. Trustees Disting. Achievement award, 1980, Meritorious Civilian Svc. award USAF, 1982, 95, U. Ill. Alumni Disting. Engring. award, 1992, Nat. Reconnaissance Office Gold Medal, 1998; named U. Ill. (Navy Pier) Hall of Fame, 1996. Fellow AIAA (chmn. tech. com. space sci. and astronomy 1976-77), Am. Phys. Soc.; mem. Am. Geophys. Union, Sigma Xi. Home: 1537 Addison Rd Palos Verdes Estates CA 90274 E-mail: george.a.paulikas@aero.org.

PAULIN, AMY RUTH, civic activist, consultant; b. Bklyn., Nov. 29, 1955; d. Ben and Alice Lois (Roth) P.; m. Ira Schuman, May 25, 1980; children: Beth, Sarah, Joseph. BA, SUNY, Albany, 1977, MA, 1978, postgrad., 1979—. Instr. SUNY, Albany, 1978, Queens (N.Y.) House of Detention, 1979; fundraiser United Jewish Appeal Fedn., N.Y.C., 1979-83; dir. devel. Altro Health & Rehab., Bronx, N.Y., 1983-86; fundraising cons. N.Y.C., 1986-88; pres. LWV, Scarsdale, N.Y., 1990-92, Westchester, 1992-95; trustee Scarsdale (N.Y.) Village, 1995-99; exec. dir. My Sisters' Place, 1999—. Mem. adv. coun. Family Ct.; co-chair woman Westchester Womens Agenda, Westchester Dept. Social Svcs.; mem. adv. com. Fund for Women & Girls; bd. dirs. Mid. Sch. PTA, , 1995-97, Westchester Coalition for Legal Abortion, Scarsdale Open Soc. Assn., 1992-95, United Jewish Appeal Fedn. Scarsdale Women's Campaign; v.p. Westchester Children's Assn.; troop leader Girl Scouts U.S., 1992-96; mem. Town Club Edn. Com., 1983-89; mem. Scarsdale Bowl com., 1992-95, chair, 1994-95; mem. Scarsdale Japanese Festival, 1992-93; mem. Westchester Women's Equality Day, 1987-92; mem. nominating com. Heathcote Neighborhood Assn., 1991-92; bd. advisors Westchester County Found., 1994—; mem. Scarsdale Village Youth Bd., 1992-95; mem. U.S. legislators task force on families at risk Westchester County Bd., 1994—; mem. Updating Voting Equipment Com., 1994; mem. Tobacco Free Westchester, 1993-95, chair 1995—; co-chair Parent Tchr. Coun. Sch. Budget Study, 1991-94; planning chair Kids Base Bd., 1992-95, dir. 1992-94chair parking and traffic subcom. Village Downtown Devel. Com., 1994-95; mem. Westchester Commn. Campaign Fin. Reform, Westchester Commn. Child Abuse, 1996-87; exec. com. Westchester Mcpl. Offcls. Assn., 1996-97; adv. com. Jr. League, 1996-99. Named Westchester County Woman of Yr., 1995, Bridge Fund award, 1998, Women's Health NNetwork Ann. award, 1999. Mem. LWV (bd. dirs. women and children's issues Westchester chpt., dir. social policy N.Y. state), State Communities Aid Assn. (econ. securities com.), N.Y. State Pub. Health Assn. (bd. dirs. Lower Hudson Valley chpt.), N.Y. State Coalition Choice, New Yorkers Against Gun Violence (bd. dirs.). Avocations: swimming, dancing. Home: 12 Burgess Rd Scarsdale NY 10583-4410

PAULISON, R. DAVID, federal agency administrator; b. Miami; BA, Fla. Atlantic U.; postgrad., Harvard U. Rescue firefighter, lt., battalion comdr., dist. chief ops., divsn. chief, asst. chief, deputy dir. adminstrn. Miami-Dade Fire Rescue Dept., chief, 1992—2001; adminstr. U.S. Fire Adminstrn., Fed. Emergency Mgmt. Agy., Emmitsburg, Md., 2001—. Office: FEMA 16825 S Seton Ave Emmitsburg MD 21727*

PAULISSEN, JAMES PETER, retired physician, county official; b. Chgo., Aug. 14, 1928; s. Joseph Edward and Louise Catherine (Muno) P.; m. Lorraine Antoinette Polly, Sept. 11, 1954; children: Linda, Steven, Mark, Daniel. Student, Loyola U., 1946-49, MD cum laude, 1953; MPH, Johns Hopkins U., 1966. Diplomate Am. Bd. Pediat. Intern Milw. County Hosp., 1953-54; resident Milw. Children's Hosp., 1957-58; practice medicine specializing in pediats. Wauwatosa Children's Clinic, Wis., 1959-65; chief Bur. Maternal and Child Health Ill. Dept. Pub. Health, Springfield, 1966-70, chief Divsn. Family Health, 1970-76; exec. dir. DuPage County Health Dept., Wheaton, Ill., 1976-93. Bd. dirs., mem. exec. com. Suburban Cook-DuPage Health Sys. Agy., Oak Park, Ill., 1976-82; bd. dirs., past pres. Comprehensive Health Coun. Met. Chgo., 1977-87; dir. Sr. Home Sharing, Inc., Wheaton, 1981-83; mem. Ill. Commn. on Children, 1971-85, vice chmn., 1983-85; chmn. Ill. Perinatal Adv. Com., 1981-84, mem., 1981-92; mem. Ill. Sch. Health Adv. Com., 1982-93, Gov.'s Adv. Coun. on Devel. Disabilities, 1973-76, Ill. Med. Determinations Bd., 1985-93; vice chmn. Ill. Pub. Health Advisors, 1988-91; mem. adv. bd. divsn. Svcs. Crippled Children U. Ill., 1986-94; trustee DuPage County Med. Found., 1976-82, 86-92, 99—, treas. 2002—; bd. dirs. DuPage Cmty. Clinic, 1993—, Cmty. Nursing Svc. of DuPage, 1993-99, vice chair, 1997-99; mem. cmty. health com. Ctrl. DuPage Health Sys., 1993-98; del. White House Conf. for Children, 1970. Capt. USAF, 1954-56. Recipient Dir.'s award for Sustained Excellence Ill. Dept. Pub. Health, 1988, Ill. Pediatrician of Yr. award, 1992, Humanitarian award DuPage County Health Planning Coun., 1994. Fellow Am. Acad. Pediats. (exec. com. Ill. chpt. 1978-81, sec. 1988-92), APHA, Am. Coll. Preventive Medicine; mem. Ill. Pub. Health Assn. (pres. 1977-78, Disting. Svc. award 1983), Ill. Assn. Maternal and Child Health (pres. 1975-76). Avocation: model railroading. Home: 28w660 Hawthorne Ln West Chicago IL 60185-2472

PAULK, DAVID ALAN, physician assistant, educator; b. Albany, Ga., Oct. 4, 1954; s. Leonard David and Mary Alice (Cheatham) Paulk; m. Donna Folenta, Nov. 7, 1987; children: Margaret, Cassandra, Alanna. AS in Emerg. Med. Svc., Albany Jr. Coll., 1979; BS in Med. Sci., Alderson-Broaddus Coll., 1985; MS in Health Edn., W.Va. U., 1996; postgrad. doctoral candidate Rutgers U. Cert. physician asst. Paramedic, shift capt. Crisp County Emergency Med. Svcs., Cordele, Ga., 1975-81; surg. physician asst. Shady Grove Adventist Hosp., Rockville, Md., 1986-88; physician asst. Potomac Valley Orthopaedics, Olney, 1988-89, Winchester (Va.) Surg. Clinic, 1989-90; head Valley Health Care Inc., Millcreek, W.Va., 1990—91; asst. prof., clin. coord. Univ. Medicine and Dentistry N.J./Rutgers U.; asst. prof. dept. med. sci. and cmty. health Arcadia U., Glenside, Pa., 2000—. Substitute tchr. health occupations Crisp County H.S., Cordele, 1976—81; mem. Ctrl. Jersey Child Protection Com., ; dist. adv. com. Hunterdon County Bd. Edn.; nat. and regional spkr. in field. Contbr. articles to profl. jours. Chmn. safety ARC, Cordele, 1976-81. Mem.: Mem. Am. Acad/. Physician Assts. Presbyterian. Avocation: whitewater rafting. Office: Arcadia U Dept Med Sci & Cmty Health 450 S Easton Rd Glenside PA 19038

PAULL, RICHARD ALLEN, geologist, educator; b. Madison, Wis., May 20, 1930; s. Ethra Harold and Martha (Schaller) P.; m. Rachel Kay Krebs, Mar. 6, 1954; children: Kay Marie, Lynn Ellen, Judith Ann. BS, U. Wis., 1952, MS, 1953, PhD, 1957. Party chief Pan Am. Petroleum Co., 1955-57; research group leader Jersey Prodn. Research Co., 1957-62; mem. faculty U. Wis.-Milw., 1962-97, chmn. dept. geol. scis., 1962-66, prof., 1966-97, prof. emeritus, 1997—. Cons. in field, 1966— Author books, papers in field. Colo. vol. Naturalist Roxborough State Park; co-exec. sec. NAGT/USGS/AASG-Coop. Summer Field Tng. Program, 1994-99. Served with USAF, 1953-55. Hon. curator Milw. Museum; recipient Amoco Distinguished Teaching award, 1975 Fellow Geol. Soc. Am. (chmn. ann. meeting 1970, tech. program com. 1970, 77, membership com. 1977-80, chmn. 1980); mem. Am. Assn. Petroleum Geologists (chmn. sci. fair award com. 1980, membership com. 1981-87, vis. petroleum geologists com. 1982-87, pub. affairs com. 1982-85), Soc. Econ. Paleontologists and Mineralogists, Nat. Assn. Geology Tchrs. (v.p. 1976-77, pres. 1977-78), Am. Geol. Inst. (governing bd. 1977-79, sec. and exec. com. 1986-88), Nature Conservancy, Sigma Xi. Home: 5146 Black Bear Run Littleton CO 80125-9011 E-mail: roc.dox@worldnet.att.net.

PAULOSE, ANIL CHIRAMEL, financial market data/trading systems software infrastructure consultant; b. Kerala, India, Aug. 24, 1965; came to U.S., 1989; s. C.J. Paulose; m. Lata Anil. BS in Electronics, Bangalore (India) U., 1988; MS in Computer Engring., La. State U., 1992. Software arch. IGT, Reno, 1992-94; mem. tech. staff Tibco Software Inc., Palo Alto, Calif., 1994-96; prin. cons. J.P. Morgan, N.Y.C., 1996-98, Greenwich (Conn.) Capital, 1998-2001; sr. architect Bloomberg Tradebook LLC, N.Y.C., 2001—. Cons. bus. strategy Sharp Decisions Inc., N.Y.C., 1997-2000; founder, pres. Marketcube Inc., N.J., 1999-2001, epasse.com, N.J., 2000—. Inventor tibscript/passage software architecture framework. Mem. World Future Soc., N.Y. Acad. Scis. E-mail: anil@chiramel.com.

PAULSEN, DARLYNE EVELYN, artist, residential and commercial architectural designer, interior decorator; b. Delaplaine, Ark., Feb. 16, 1936; d. Chacy Rudolph Sr. and Mary Edith (Rice) Eveland; m. Henry Stevens Paulsen, Feb. 22, 1960 (div. 1969); children: Sherry Lee, Pamela Fay. BFA in Art, Ark. State U., 1968; BSE, U. Ark., Little Rock, 1970. Systems analyst, acct. Wurlitzer Co., DeKalb, Ill., 1954-63; acct. Eugene Stifani CPA, 1957; secondary art and drama instr. Westside H.S., Jonesboro, Ark., 1968-69; secondary art instr. Poplar Bluff Pub. Schs., Poplar Bluff, Mo., 1969-70; owner, mgr. Paulsen Studios, N. Little Rock, Ark., 1970—; art supr. and instructional specialist Pulaski County Spl. Sch. Dist., Little Rock, 1970-79; office mgr., acct. Hardy L. Gage Co., Wichita Falls, Tex., 1980-84; computer acct. Gen. Properties, N. Little Rock, 1984-85; office mgr., acctg. supr. Carrier AR (br. UTC), Little Rock, 1985-86. Guest lectr. U. Mex., Mexico City, 1973; producer, dir. 3 theatre prodn., WHS, Ark. State U., Jonesboro, Ark., 1968-69; mem. panel com. leading art educators in U.S., 1975; lectr. in field. Editor, co-author: Art in Secondary Schools Curriculum Guide for Pulaski County School District, 1977 Coord., hostess Ark. Annual Arts Patron's Christmas Ball, Little Rock, 1971-79; Ark. state com. chmn. Gifted and Talented Children, Little Rock, 1978-79; decorator Ark. Gov.'s Inaugural Ball, Little Rock, 1979; mem. Nat. Mus. for Women of the Art, Washington, 1988; affiliate Lahaima Art Gallery, Michael Angelo Gallery, Tex. Art Gallery, Roughton Galleries, Jay Hudson Gallery. Recipient cert. of recognition Gov. Clinton, Ark., 1989; NEA grantee, 1973. Mem. Ark. Art Edn. Assn. (treas. 1972-76), Nat. Art Edn. Assn. (v.p. Ark. chpt. 1969, workshop instr. 1973-75, Ark. voter rep. nat. level 1975), Ark. Alliance for the Arts. (chmn. constitution & legis.), Kappa Pi (sec. 1967-68), Beta Sigma Phi (Valentine Queen Wichita Falls, Tex. 1981). Home and Office: 3619 Lakeview Rd North Little Rock AR 72116-9022 E-mail: paulsenartstudios@msn.com.

PAULSEN, FRANK ROBERT, college dean emeritus; b. Logan, Utah, July 5, 1922; s. Frank and Ella (Ownby) P.; m. Marye Lucile Harris, July 31, 1942; 1 son, Robert Keith; m. Lydia Ransier Lowry, Nov. 1, 1969. BS, Utah State U., 1947; MS, U. Utah, 1948, Ed.D., 1956; Kellogg Found. postdoctoral fellow, U. Oreg., 1958; Carnegie Found. postdoctoral fellow, U. Mich., 1959-60. High sch. prin., Mt. Emmons, Utah, 1948-51; supt. schs. Cokeville, Wyo., 1951-55; from asst. prof. to assoc. prof. edn. U. Utah, 1955-61; prof. edn., dean Sch. Edn. U. Conn., 1961-64; dean Coll. Edn. U. Ariz., Tucson, 1964-84, dean emeritus, prof. emeritus higher edn., 1984—. Scholar-in-residence Fed. Exec. Inst., Charlottesville, Va., 1970; Disting. prof. edn. U. Bridgeport, summer 1972; dir. Am. Jour. Nursing Pub. Co., N.Y.C., Am. Capital Growth Fund, Am. Series Portfolio Stock Co., Houston, Am. Gen. Equity Fund, Am. Capital Bond Fund, Am. Capital Convertible Securities Fund, Am. Capital Exchange Fund, Am. Series Portfolio Co., Am. Capital Income Trust; exec. com. New Eng. Council Advancement Sch. Adminstrn., 1962-64; trustee Common Sense Trust Co., Houston. Author: The Administration of Public Education in Utah, 1958, Contemporary Issues in American Education, 1966, American Education: Challenges and Images, 1967, Changing Dimensions in International Education, 1968, Higher Education: Dimensions and Directions, 1969, also numerous articles. Trustee Joint Council Econ. Edn., 1962-70; v.p., dir. Southwestern Coop. Ednl. Lab., 1965-67; bd. dirs. Nat. League for Nursing, 1967-69, mem. com. on perspectives, 1966-72; dir., chmn. exec. com. ERIC Clearinghouse on Tchr. Edn., 1968-70; bd. dirs. Tucson Mental Health Center, 1968-70. Served with AUS, 1942-46, PTO. Mem. Aerospace Med. Assn., Am. Assn. Sch. Adminstrs., Am. Acad. Polit. and Social Sci., John Dewey Soc., Utah Acad. Letters, Arts and Scis., Ariz. Acad., Am. Assn. Colls. Tchrs. Edn. (Conn. liaison officer 1962-64, mem. studies com. 1962-68, dir.), Ariz. Assn. Colls. Tchr. Edn. (pres. 1972-80), AAAS, Am. Ednl. Research Assn., Kappa Delta Pi, Pi Sigma Alpha, Pi Gamma Mu., Phi Delta Kappa. Lodges: Rotary.

PAULSEN, JAMES WALTER, law educator; b. Eau Claire, Wis., Feb. 17, 1954; s. Walter Henry and Doris Antoinette (Babington) P.; m. Robin Russell, Apr. 23, 1988 BFA, Tex. Christian U., 1976; JD, Baylor U., 1984.; LLM, Harvard U., 1992. Bar: Tex. 1984, U.S. Dist. Ct. (no. dist.) Tex. 1985, U.S. Dist. Ct. (so. dist.) Tex. 1986, U.S. Ct. Appeals (5th cir.) 1985. Asst. debate coach U. Utah, Salt Lake City, 1976-78; acting debate coach Brigham Young U., Provo, Utah, 1978-79; briefing atty. Supreme Ct. Tex., Austin, 1984-85; assoc. Liddell, Sapp, Zivley, Hill & LaBoon, Houston, 1985-91; prof. law South Tex. Coll. Law, 1992—. Editor-in-chief Baylor Law Rev., 1984; contbr. articles to legal jours. Mem. ABA, State Bar Tex. (vice chmn. legal svcs. com. 1987-88, 90-91), Tex. Bar Found., Tex. Assn. Bank Counsel (bd. dirs. 1990-93), Houston Bar Assn., Houston Vol. Lawyers Assn., Tex. State Hist. Assn., Nat. Order Barristers. Lutheran. Avocations: writing, hiking. Home: 2815 Wroxton Rd Houston TX 77005-4022

PAULSEN, SERENUS GLEN, architect, educator; b. Spooner, Wis., July 27, 1917; s. Serenus Justin and Edna Anne (Dalton) P.; m. Virginia C. Habel, Jan. 26, 1944; children: Thomas J., Nancy Lee (Mrs. John Marshall). Student, U. Ill., 1938-42; B.Arch. cum laude, U. Pa., 1947; Diploma in Architecture and City Planning, Royal Acad. Art, Stockholm, 1948. With Carroll, Grisdale & Van Alan (Architects), Phila., 1946-47, Eero Saarinen & Assos., Bloomfield Hills, Mich., 1949-51, 53-57; chief designer Reisner & Urbahn (Architects), N.Y.C., 1951-52; archtl. coordinator Knoll Assos., 1952-53; prin. Glen Paulsen Assos., Birmingham, Mich., 1958-69; prin., v.p. Tarapata-MacMahon-Paulsen Assos., Inc. (Architects), Bloomfield Hills, 1969-77; pres. Cranbrook Acad. Art, head dept. architecture, 1966-70; prof., chmn. Masters Program in Architecture U. Mich., 1976-78, Emil Lorch prof. architecture, 1982-85, prof. emeritus, 1985—. Mem. Nat. Com. on Urban Planning and Design, 1971-72; archtl. commn. U. Wash., Seattle, 1968-76 (Recipient 3d prize Bi-Nat. Competition for Design Rainbow Center Plaza, Niagara Falls, N.Y. 1972). Gov. emeritus Cranbrook Acad. Art. Served with C.E. USAAF, 1942-46. Fellow AIA (honor awards Detroit chpt. for Shapero Hall of Pharmacy 1965, Our Shepherd Lutheran Ch. 1966, Ford Life Sci. Bldg. 1967, Birney Elementary Sch., Detroit 1971, Fed. Bldg., Ann Arbor, Mich. 1978, gold medal for 1980 Detroit chpt.); mem. Mich. Soc. Architects, (Robert F. Hastings award 1985). Home: 1101 Silver Maples Dr Chelsea MI 48118-1187

PAULSON, ARMOND ORVILLE, nonprofit executive and consultant; b. Mpls. s. Paul Theodore and Minnie Josephine Paulson; m. Judy Ann Zittel, Aug. 13, 1987; children: Mark, Ann, Kate Trimble, David Trimble. BA in Social Psychology, St. Olaf Coll., Northfield, Minn., 1958; MS in Behavioral Scis. highest honors, George Williams Coll., Chgo., 1960. Exec. YMCA, 1960-71, Nat. Offices of Luth. Ch., Mpls., 1971-86; devel. cons. Ward, Dreshman, Reinhart, Columbus, Ohio, 1987-98; devel. exec. S.D. Heritage Fund, Pierre, 1999—. Orgnl. devel. trainer Luth. Ch., Mpls., 1971-80, camp exec., 1984-88, therapist, Green Bay, Wis., 1980-83; youth worker YMCA, Mpls. and St. Louis, 1960-71; fundraising cons. in pvt. practice, Austin, 1988-99. Author: Board Competence, 1974, (tng. manual) Visitation in Fund Raising, 1990, (resource guide) Exercises in Group Development, 1980. Named Disting. Alumnus George Williams Coll., 1966. Mem. Assn. Fund Raising Execs. Democrat. Lutheran. Avocations: wilderness camping, reading, creative writing. Home: 5505B Oakwood Cove Austin TX 78731-4875 Office: 1900 Governors Dr Pierre SD 57501

PAULSON, BERNARD ARTHUR, oil company executive, consultant; b. Lakeview, Mich., July 12, 1928; s. Arthur Bernard and Genevieve Talbard (Bushley) P.; m. Joan Lee Curtiss, Dec. 4, 1954; children: James, Joseph (dec.), Ann, Thomas (dec.), Bernadette, Patricia, Steven. BS in Chem. Engring., Mich. State U.-East Lansing, 1949. Registered profl. engr., Tex. Process engr. Mid-West Refineries Inc., Alma, Mich., 1949-57; plant mgr. Kerr-McGee Corp., Cleve. and Wynnewood, Okla., 1957-66; v.p. Coastal States Petrochemical, Corpus Christi, Tex., 1966-71, Koch Industries Inc., St. Paul and Wichita, 1971-88, cons. Corpus Christi, Tex., 1988-94; pres. Koch Refining Co., Wichita, 1981-88; chmn. bd. dirs. The Automation Group Inc.; chmn., CEO The Inspection Group Inc. CEO Tor Minerals Internat., 1997, also bd. dirs; dir. Orion Refining Corp., 1999—. Chmn., pres. Cleve. Area Hosp. Corp., 1962; dir. Ada Wilson Hosp. Found.; pres. Corpus Christ Bd. Trade; commr. Port of Corpus Christi Authority, sec., 1997. 1st lt. USAF, 1955-57. Recipient Claud R. Erickson Disting. Alumnus award Mich. State U., 1994. Mem. AIChE (fuels and petrochem. award 1989), Nat. Petroleum Refiners Assn., Refining Am. Petroleum Inst., Wichita Area C. of C. (bd. dirs.), Bd. Trade, Corpus Christi Town Club (bd. dirs.), Elks. Home and Office: Tor Minerals 3 Ocean Park Dr Corpus Christi TX 78404-1600

PAULSON, BOYD COLTON, JR. civil engineering educator; b. Providence, Mar. 1, 1946; s. Boyd Colton and Barbara (McKinstry) P.; m. Jane Margaret Kingdon, Feb. 12, 1970; children: Jeffrey Boyd, Laura Jane. BS, Stanford U., 1967, MS, 1969, PhD, 1971. Asst. prof. U. Ill., Urbana, 1972-73; asst. prof., assoc. prof. civil engring. Stanford (Calif.) U., 1974, prof., 1984-89, Obhayashi prof. engring., 1989-91, Charles Leavell prof. civil engring., 1991—. Mem. civil engring. adv. com. NSF, 1983-84; mem. U.S. Nat. Com. on Tunneling, 1986-89; mem. com. on constrn. superconducting supercollider in Tex., NAS, 1988-89; presenter in field. Author: Computer Applications in Construction, 1995; co-author: Professional Construction Management, 1978, 2d edit., 1984, 3d edit., 1992; also articles. Bd. dir. Peninsula Habitat for Humanity, 1996—2002. Fellow Humboldt Found., Munich, 1983, Brit. Coun., Glasgow, Scotland, 1990-91, Fulbright fellow, 1990-91. Mem. ASCE (chmn. constrn. divsn. 1986-87, Huber Rsch. prize 1980, Constrn. Mgmt. award 1984, Peurifoy Rsch. award 1993), Am. Soc. for Engring. Edn., Urban Land Inst., Nat. Acad. Constrn. Achievements include research on human-computer systems for project management, in analytical modeling and simulation of construction operations, in tunneling in urban environments, in low-cost housing. Office: Stanford U 4020 Civil Engring Stanford CA 94305-4020

PAULSON, DONALD ROBERT, chemistry educator; b. Oak Park, Ill., Sept. 6, 1943; s. Robert Smith and Florence Teresa (Beese) P.; m. Elizabeth Anne Goodwin, Aug. 20, 1966; children: Matthew, Andrew. BA, Monmouth Coll., 1965; PhD, Ind. U., 1968. Asst. prof. chemistry Calif. State U., Los Angeles, 1970-74, assoc. prof., 1974-78, prof., 1979—, chmn. dept., 1982-90. Vis. prof. U. B.C., Vancouver, Can., 1977-78, U. Sussex, Brighton, Eng., 1984-85. Author: Alicyclic Chemistry, 1976; contbr. articles to profl. jours. Named Outstanding Prof., Calif. State U., Los Angeles, 1978, 84, 96. Mem. Am. Chem. Soc., Chem. Soc. (London), InterAm. Photochem. Soc., Nat. Assn. Sci. Tchrs., Sigma Xi. Democrat. Episcopalian. Avocations: photography, hiking, soccer. Home: 497 E California Blvd Apt 203 Pasadena CA 91106-3789 Office: Calif State U Dept Chemistry 5151 State University Dr Los Angeles CA 90032-4226 E-mail: dpaulso@calstatela.edu.

PAULSON, GWEN O. GAMPEL, government relations consultant; b. Detroit, Mar. 16, 1945; d. Maurice V. and Lilyan Victor; divorced; children: Jill Susan, Mindy Beth; m. Jerome A. Paulson, July 2, 1989. BA, Mich. State U., 1966; MA, Wayne State U., 1974; postgrad., U. Mich., 1981. Lectr. Oakland (Mich.) U., 1979-80, U. Mich., Ann Arbor, 1981; legis. asst. U.S. Rep. Pete Stark, Washington, 1982-85; mem. profl. staff, ways and means health subcom. U.S. House Reps., 1985-89; v.p. for health Capitol Assocs., 1989-90; pres. Congressional Cons., 1990—. Author: Women and the Structure of Society, 1984. Mem. Nat. Dem. Com., Washington, 1988—. Edward S. Beck fellow U. Mich., Ann Arbor, 1978-79; Rackham Dissertation grant U. Mich., Ann Arbor, 1980. Mem. Women in Govt. Rels., Bus. and Profl. Women, Fedn. Am. (co-chair 1999—2001), Am. League Lobbyists, Phi Alpha Theta, Tau Sigma. Avocations: collecting contemporary glass, travel, history, politics, reading. Office: Congressional Consultants 444 N Capitol St NW Ste 532 Washington DC 20001-1512 E-mail: ccgampel@sso.org.

PAULSON, HENRY MERRITT, JR. venture capitalist, investment company executive; b. Palm Beach, Fla., Mar. 28, 1946; s. Henry Merritt and Marianna (Gallaeur) P.; m. Wendy Judge, Sept. 6, 1969; children: Henry Merritt III, Amanda Clark. BA in English, Dartmouth Coll., 1968; MBA, Harvard U., 1970. Staff asst. to the asst. sec. def. (comptroller) Pentagon, Dept. Def., Washington, 1970-72; staff asst. to the Pres. Domestic Council, The White House, 1972-73; assoc. Goldman Sachs & Co., Chgo., 1974-77, v.p., 1977-82, ptnr. investment banking dept., 1982—, ptnr. in charge investment banking Midwest region, 1984-90; mgmt. com. co-head investment banking div., vice chmn., COO, 1994—98; CEO, chair Goldman Sachs & Co., Chgo., 1999—. Bd. dirs. NY Stock Exch., Peregrine Fund Inc.; mem. exec. com. N.Y.C. Investment Fund. Mem. adv. bd. J.L. Kellogg grad. sch. of mgmt.; chmn. adv. bd. Tsinghua U. Sch. Econs. and Mgmt.; mem. governing bd. Indian Sch. Mgmt. NCAA Scholar Athlete, 1967; named to 1st team All-Ivy, All New Eng., All-East; New Eng. Football Coaches' Selection as Outstanding Coll. Lineman, Div. I, New England, 1967 Mem. The Commercial Club (Chgo.), The Econ. Club (Chgo.), Chgo. Club, Phi Beta Kappa. Republican. Mem. Christian Science Ch. Avocations: skiing; fishing; canoeing; tennis. Office: Goldman Sachs Group 85 Broad St New York NY 10004-2434*

PAULSON, JAMES MARVIN, engineering educator; b. Wausau, Wis., Jan. 1, 1923; s. Gustav Victor and Susanna (Dracy) P.; m. Marjorie Beulah Burton, May 11, 1946; children— Vicki Rae, Michael James. BS in Civil Engring, The Citadel, 1947; MS in Civil Engring, Ill. Inst. Tech., 1949; PhD, U. Mich., 1958. Registered profl. engr., Mich. Draftsman Wausau Iron Works, 1946; engr. Charles Whitney Cons. Engr., Milw., 1948-49; faculty Wayne State U., Detroit, 1949—, prof., 1961-85, chmn. dept. civil engring., 1967-72, assoc. dean Coll. Engring., 1973-83, prof. emeritus, 1985—. V.p. Civil Engrs., Inc., 1954— ; cons. in field. Served with AUS, 1943; Served with USMCR, 1943-46. Mem. ASCE (life), Mich. Soc. Profl. Engrs. (life), Am. Soc. for Engring. Edn., Sigma Xi, Tau Beta Pi, Chi Epsilon. Presbyterian. Home: PO Box 23 Greenbush MI 48738-0023

PAULSON, JEROME AVROM, pediatrician; b. Balt., July 31, 1949; s. Robert R. and Edna (Brenner) P.; m. Susan Miller, 1973 (div. 1986); m. Gwen Victor Gampel, July 2, 1989. BS in Biochemistry, U. Md., 1971; MD, Duke U., 1974. Diplomate Am. Bd. Pediatrics, Nat. Bd. Med. Examiners. Resident in pediatrics Johns Hopkins Hosp., Balt., 1974-76, Sinai Hosp., Balt., 1976-77, fellow in ambulatory pediatrics, 1977-78; asst. prof. pediatrics Case Western Res. U., Cleve., 1978-86; dir. sci. rsch. and pub. policy devel. Joseph P. Kennedy Jr. Found., Washington, 1986-87; dir. pediatrics Regional Inst. for Children and Adolescents, Rockville, Md., 1987-89; clin. assoc. prof. pediatrics Georgetown U., Washington, 1987—; exec. dir. Research!America, Alexandria, Va., 1989-90; assoc. prof. medicine (formerly healthcare scis.) George Washington U., Washington, 1990—, fellow Ctr. Health Policy Rsch., 1991—, assoc. prof. prevention and cmty. health, 1997—; co-dir. Mid-Atlantic Ctr. for Children's Health and the Environment George Washington U. Med. Ctr., 2000—. Mem. conf. on methodology and std. definitions for childhood injury rsch. Nat. Inst. Children & Human Devel., 1989; mem. health adv. com. Congressman James Moran, 8th Congl. Dist., Va., 1992—94; mem. benefits working group Nat. Drinking Water Adv. Coun. EPA, 1989—99; adv. Health Pages, 1994—97; spl. asst. to dir. Nat. Ctr. for Environ. Health, Ctrs. for Disease Control, Washington, 1999—2001; Soros advocacy fellow Children's Environ. Health Network. Author: Pediatrics: Review for New National Boards, 2000; contbr. articles to profl. jours., chpts. to books. Profl. adv. bd. Nat. Safety Town Ctr., Cleve., 1981-85; bd. dirs., pres. James Renwick Alliance, Washington, 1986-93, 95-98. Recipient Cert. for Ednl. and Pub. Policy Activity, Ohio State Senate/Ho. of Reps., 1985; Robert Wood Johnson Health Policy fellow, 1985-86, Soros Advocacy fellowship 2000-01. Fellow Am. Acad. Pediatrics; mem. Ambulatory Pediatric Assn. Jewish. Avocation: collecting contemporary American crafts. Office: George Washington U 2150 Pennsylvania Ave NW Washington DC 20037-3201 E-mail: hcsjap@gwumc.edu.

PAULSON, KENNETH ALAN, journalist, lawyer, foundation executive; b. Chgo., Dec. 3, 1953; s. Knut Norman and Helen Elizabeth (Beardsley) P.; m. Peggy Jean Foot, June 12, 1976; children: Carrie Ann, David. BA in Journalism, U. Mo., 1975; JD, U. Ill., 1978. Bar: Ill., 1978, Fla. 1979. Exec. editor, v.p. news Gannett Suburban Newspapers, White Plains, N.Y., 1992-97; exec. dir. 1st. Amendment Ctr. Vanderbilt U., Nashville. Sr. v.p. Freedom Forum, Arlington, Va., 1997—; adj. prof. Vanderbilt U. Law Sch.; host Speaking Freely, TV show.

PAULSON, LORETTA NANCY, psychoanalyst; b. L.A., Nov. 5, 1943; d. Frank Morris and Rose (Kaufman) Fargo; m. Maurice Krasnow; 1 child, Kira. BA, U. So. Calif., 1966; MS in Social Work, Columbia U., 1969; cert. psychoanalyst, C.G. Jung Inst., N.Y.C. Cert. clin. social worker, N.Y., Conn., N.J. Pvt. practice psychoanalysis, N.Y.C., 1976—. Vice- chmn. CGJ Inst. Tng. Bd. Mem. NASW (diplomate in clin. social work), Internat. Assn. for

Analytical Psychology (past del., bd. dirs.), N.Y. Assn. for Analytic Psychology (past pres., past chair program com.), Conn. Soc. Clin. Social Work (com. on psychoanalysis), C.G. Jung Inst. Address: 334 W 86th St Apt 1A New York NY 10024-3130

PAULSON, PAUL JOSEPH, advertising executive; b. White Plains, N.Y., Sept. 25, 1932; s. Paul and Ann (Loughlin) P.; m. Kathryn P. Keeler, June 30, 1962; children: Thomas, Mark, Kathryn, John, Clifford. BSBA, Ohio State U., 1954; MBA, U. Pa., 1959. With Compton Advt. Inc., N.Y.C., 1959-78, mgmt. supr., 1965-78, sr. v.p., 1968-78, also dir.; pres., dir. Doyle Dane Bernbach Inc., N.Y.C., 1978-83; pres., chief exec. officer Isidore & Paulson, Inc., 1983-93; chmn., pres., CEO Paulson & Co. Mktg. Svcs., Greenwich, 1993—. Chmn. Mktg. Exec. Networking Group, 2000; mem. Ohio State U. Alumni Adv. Coun., 1982—; pres. coun. mem. Ohio State U., 1993—. Author: Fundamentals of Consumer Goods Marketing, 1966. Chmn. Christmas for Underprivileged Children, N.Y.C., 1963—. Served to lt. (j.g.) USNR, 1955-58, MTO, ETO. Mem. Wharton Grad. Bus. Sch. Alumni Assn. (pres. N.Y.C. club 1963-65, dir. 1972—), Ohio State U. Alumni Assn., Wharton Grad. Bus. Sch., Milbrook Owners Assn. (pres.). Clubs: N.Y. (dir.), Milbrook, Sigma Chi. Roman Catholic. Home: 45 W Brother Dr Greenwich CT 06830-6726

PAULSON, PETER JOHN, librarian, publishing company executive; b. N.Y.C., Jan. 30, 1928; s. Peter John and Lillian Agnes Elaine (Neuman) P.; m. Josephine C. Bowen, Dec. 5, 1953; children: David, Debora. B.Social Scis. cum laude, CCNY, 1949; MA in History, Columbia, 1950; MA in L.S, SUNY, Albany, 1955. Library asst. N.Y. State Library, Albany, 1952-55, head, gift and exchange sect., 1955-65, head catalog sect., 1965-66, prin. librarian tech. services, 1966-71, dir., 1972-85; exec. dir. OCLC Forest Press, 1985-98. Adj. asst. prof. library sci. State U. N.Y. at Albany, 1960-71; Adv. com. Ohio Coll. Library Center, 1970-71; adv. council to pub. printer depository libraries, 1972-77, chmn., 1975-77; com. fed. depository library service N.Y. State, 1960-70, chairperson, 1960-70; bd. dirs. Capital Dist. Libr. Coun., Nat. Info. Standards Orgn., N.E. Document Conservation Ctr. Mem. ALA (chmn. com. on legislation 1980-82, pres. state library agy. sect. 1982-83), N.Y. Library Assn. (pres. 1975), Hudson-Mohawk Library Assn. (v.p. 1964), SUNY-OCLC Network (governing bd. 1980-82), Phi Beta Kappa. Home: 24 Tillinghast Ave Albany NY 12204-2312

PAULSON, ROBERT I. social work educator; b. N.Y.C., Dec. 10, 1945; s. Philip A. and Rose (Max) P.; m. Phyllis Spaulding (div.). BA, Brandeis U., 1968; MSW, U. Calif., Berkeley, 1972; PhD, U. Calif., 1977; MA in Health Planning, U. Cin., 1983. Lic. social worker. Vol. Vista, Washington, 1965-66; community devel. trainer Ctr. for Community Action Svcs., U. N.Mex., Albuquerque, 1966-67; vol. Peace Corps, Washington, 1968-70; research asst. U. Calif., Berkeley, 1971-73; assoc. prof. social work U. Cin., 1974-90, prof., 1990—, dir. spl. edn. mental health tng. program Sch. Social Work, 1986—92; prof. Portland State U., 1992—; dir. Ctr. Mental Health Policy Resources, 1996—2001; vis. rsch. prof. Fla. Mental Health Inst., U. S. Fla., 2001—. Cons. in field. Contbr. articles to profl. jours. Bd. dirs. Nat. Council of Community Mental Health Ctrs., Rockville, Md., 1988—, Mental Health Corp. Hamilton County, Cin., 1986-88. Grantee NIMH, 1986, 88, 89, 95-2001, Ohio Dept. Mental Health, 1984, 86-91. Mem. Coll. Healthcare Execs., Am. Soc. Pub. Adminstrn. (chpt. council 1982-84), Council on Social Wk. Edn., Nat. Assn. Social Workers, Assn. Mental Health Adminstrs., Am. Publ. Health Assn., Am. Edn. Assn. Avocations: photography, travel, hiking. Office: Fla Mental Health Inst Univ S Fla 13301 Bruce B Downs Blvd Tampa FL 33612-3899 Home: 15905 Brockway Pl Tampa FL 33647-1404

PAULSON-CRAWFORD, CAROL, conservator, educator; b. Ashland, Ohio, Jan. 15, 1961; d. Donald Howard Paulson and Mary Katherine (Dafoe) Paulson Harris; m. Craig Alan Crawford, May 6, 1995; 1 child, Cole Monroe. BFA, Ohio State U., 1984; MA, U. Wis., 1987, MFA, 1989. Book and paper conservator Wis. Hist. Soc., Madison, 1987-91; conservator Libr. of Congress, Washington, 1992-99; book and paper conservator S.C. Dept. Archives and History, Columbia, 1999-2000; lab. dir., sr. conservator U. S.C., State Park, 2000—. Author, editor: Boxes for the Protection of Books, 1994; also articles; exhibited at Rockville (Md.) Manson, 1996. Mem. Coll. Art Assn., S.C. Archivists Assn., S.E. Regional Conservation Assn., Am. Inst. for Conservation (profl. assoc.), Guild Book Workers, Washington Conservation Guild. Avocations: biking, gardening. Home: 2305 Cardington Dr Columbia SC 29209-3209 Office: U SC Conservation Facility 750 Hinton St State Park SC 29147 E-mail: ccrawfd@gwm.sc.edu.

PAULSON-EHRHARDT, PATRICIA HELEN, sales executive; b. Moses Lake, Wash., June 10, 1956; d. Luther Roanoke and Helen Jane (Baird) Paulson; m. Terry Lee Ehrhardt, Mar. 12, 1983. Student, Pacific Luth. U., 1974-76; BS in Med. Tech., U. Wash., 1976; BS in Biology, MS in Biology, Eastern Wash. U., 1982. Med. technologist Samaritan Hosp., Moses Lake, 1979-81; lab. supr. Moses Lake Clinic, 1982-88; med. technologist Kalispell Regional Hosp., 1987; hosp. bus. devel. mgr. Pathology Assocs. Med. Lab., Spokane, Wash., 1988—. Mem. med. lab. tech. adv. com. Wenatchee (Wash.) Valley Coll., 1984-85, chmn., 1985-86; spkr. in field. Mem. Flathead Valley Community Band, 1987-90. Mem.: Clin. Lab. Mgmt. Assn. (pres. Mont. state chpt. 1999—, nat. bd. mem. 2001—), Am. Soc. Clin. Pathologists, Am. Soc. Clin. Lab. Scientists, Kappa Delta. Republican. Lutheran. Avocations: tennis, volleyball, flying, fishing, playing flute. Home: 26 Cub Dr Great Falls MT 59404-6480

PAULSTON, CHRISTINA BRATT, linguistics educator; b. Stockholm, Sweden, Dec. 30, 1932; came to U.S., 1951; d. Lennart and Elsa Bratt; m. Rolland G. Paulston, July 26, 1963; children: Christopher-Rolland, Ian Rollandsson. BA, Carleton Coll., 1953; MA in English and Comparative Lit., U. Minn., 1955; Ed.D., Columbia U., 1966. Cert. tchr., Minn. Tchr. Clara City and Pine Island High Schs., Minn., 1955-60, Am. Sch. of Tangier, Morocco, 1960-62, Katrineholm Allmanna Laroverk, Katrineholm, Sweden, 1962-63, East Asian Library, Columbia U., N.Y.C., 1963-64; asst. instr. Tchrs. Coll., Columbia U., 1964-66; instr. U. Punjab, Chandigarh, India, summer 1966, Pontificia Universidad Catolica Del Peru, Lima, 1966-67; cons. Instituto Linguistico de Verano, 1967-68; asst. prof. linguistics U. Pitts., 1969-75, prof., 1975-99, prof. emerita, tchg. pro bono, 1999—, asst. dir. English Lang. Inst., 1969-70, dir. English Lang. Inst., 1970-97, acting dir. Lang. Acquistion Inst., fall 1971, acting chmn. dept. gen. linguistics, 1974-75, chmn., 1975-89. Apptd. internat. advisor in sociolinguistics to Summer Inst. of Linguistics, 1997. Author numerous books and articles on linguistics. Recipient research award Am. Ednl. Research Assn., 1980; Fulbright-Hays grantee, Uruguay, 1985. Mem. Assn. Tchrs. of English to Speakers of Other Langs. (2d v.p., conv., chmn. 1972, exec. com. 1972-75, rsch. com. 1973-75, 78-80, chmn. 1973-75, 1st v.p. 1975, pres. 1976), Linguistics Soc. Am. (com. linguistics and pub. interest 1973-77), Internat. Assn. of Tchrs. of English as a Fgn. Lang., Am. Council on Teaching of Fgn. Langs., MLA (exec. com. lang. and soc. 1975-76), Ctr. Applied Linguistics (trustee 1976-81, exec. com. 1980, publs. com. 1981, research com. 1981), Eastern Competitive Trailriding Assn. Democrat. Episcopalian. Office: U Pitts Linguistics Pittsburgh PA 15260

PAULU, FRANCES BROWN, international center administrator; b. Hastings, Minn., June 22, 1920; d. Thomas Andrew and Florence Ida (Tuttle) Brown; m. Burton Paulu, June 29, 1942; children: Sarah Leith Paulu Boittin, Nancy Jean Paulu Hyde, Thomas Scott. BA magna cum laude, U. Minn., 1940. Case worker Family Welfare Assn., Mpls., 1943-45; interviewer Cmty. Health and Welfare Coun., 1963; sch. social worker Project Head Start, 1966; program dir. Minn. Internat. Ctr., 1970-72, exec. dir., 1972-89; mem. tourism adv. com. City of Mpls., 1976-83; mem. adv. coun. Minn. World Trade Ctr., 1984-86. Pres. UN Rally, 1970—72; chmn. Mpls. Charter Commn., 1972—74; dir. Minn. World Trade Week, 1977—81; del. Nat. Coun. World Affairs, Taipei-Manila, 1988; coord. Voices from Around the World, 1996—2000; bd. dirs. Urban Coalition of Mpls., 1967—70, Becketwood Coop., 2001—; participant Intercultural Comm. Project Japan, 1974; mem. mgmt. team Minn. Awareness Project, 1982—89; dir. Elder Learning Inst., 1995—2000. Recipient Nat. People to People Disting. Membership award, 1987; DeWitt Jennings Payne scholar, 1939-40; fellow U. Minn. Sch. Social Work, 1942-44. Mem. Nat. Coun. Internat. Visitors (officer, mem. exec. com. 1975-81, leader fact-finding team North Africa, Middle East, India 1978, conf. chair 1989), People to People Internat., LWV (pres. Mpls. chpt. 1967-69), UN Assn. Minn. (adv. coun. 1979-92, 96—, sec. 1994-96), Alliance Française (bd. dirs. 1991-94), U. Minn. Women's Club (pres. 1992-94), Phi Beta Kappa, Alpha Omicron Pi, Lambda Alpha Psi. Home: 4300 W River Pkwy Apt 444 Minneapolis MN 55406-3681 E-mail: paulu001@tc.umn.edu.

PAULUS, ELEANOR BOCK, professional speaker, author; b. N.Y.C., Mar. 12, 1933; d. Charles William Bock and Borghild (Nelson) Garrick; m. Chester William Paulus Jr., Sept. 6, 1952; children: Chester W. III, Karl Derrick, Diane Paulus Henricks. Student, Smith Coll., 1952-53. Owner, founder Khan-Du Chinese Shar-Pei, Somerset, N.J., 1980—; dir. Pet Net, Santa Fe, 1992—; co-owner, CFO Am. Dream TV Prodns., Washington, 1993—; co-owner, exec. prodr. Capitol Ideas, 1995-2001, Pierre Salinger's Round Table, 1997; pets and animals columnist www.goodnewsbroadcast.com, 2000—. Lectr., cons. on Chinese Shar-Pei and canine health, 1980—; internat. con., lectr. on pet care and health. Author: Health Care Handbook for Cats, Dogs and Birds, The Proper Care of Chinese Shar-Pei; contbr. articles to mags. and jours. including Dog Fancy, chpts. to books, including The World of the Chinese Shar-Pei; creator, prodr. World of Dogs, 1996—. Dir. bd. trustees Rutgers Prep. Sch., Somerset, 1970-76, v.p. bd. trustees, 1976-81, pres. PTA, 1966-76; chmn. Raritan River Festival, New Brunswick, N.J., 1980-91. Named Woman of Yr., City of New Brunswick, 1982. Mem. Dog Writers Am. Assn., Dog Fanciers N.Y.C., Bonzai Clubs Internat., Koi Internat. N.Y., Raritan Valley Country Club, Chinese Shar-Pei Club of Am. (v.p. 1982-86, bd. dirs. east sect. 1980-82, Humanitarian award 1986). Avocations: travel, dog related activities, gardening. Home: 321 Skillman Ln Somerset NJ 08873-5325 Office: E B Paulus 20 Sutton Pl S # 5A New York NY 10022-4165

PAULUS, MICHAEL DAMIEN, computer engineer; b. Ottawa, Ill., June 7, 1965; s. Robert John and Angela Elaine (Kasten) P.; m. Kimberly Ann Heinberg, Oct. 7, 1989; children; Christopher Michael, Benjamin Michael. Student, Waubonsee Community Coll., 1988; BS in Computer Sci., Aurora U., 1990, MS in Computer Sci., 1993. Dir. info. systems Arcar Graphics, Inc., West Chgo., Ill. Cons., owner Paulus & Assocs., 1990—. Mem. IEEE, Am. Soc. for Quality Control, Fox Valley Radio Relay League, Internat. Soc. for Weighing & Measurement. Avocations: bike racing, tennis, travel, boats and cars, amateur radio. Address: 122 Arbor Ave Sugar Grove IL 60554-5404 Office: Arcar Graphics Inc 450 Wegner Dr West Chicago IL 60185-2694

PAULUS, MICHAEL JOHN, government official, bank executive, economist; b. Port Washington, Wis., Feb. 18, 1957; s. John Peter and Elizabeth Jane (Streff) P.; m. Christine H. Kwon, Apr. 29, 2000. BA, U. Wis., Milw., 1980; cert., U. Freiburg, Fed. Republic Germany, 1979-80; M Internat Affairs, Columbia U., 1982. Economist Fed. Res. Bank, N.Y.C., 1982-85, sr. fgn. exchange trader, 1985-87, dep. chief fgn. exchange trader, spl. asst., 1987-88, mgr., chief fgn. exchange trader, 1988-90; asst. v.p. capital markets group 1st Nat. Bank Chgo., 1990-91, v.p. capital markets group, 1991-92; v.p. treasury dept. Dresdner Bank, N.Y.C., 1992-94; v.p., mgr. instnl. mktg. desk Bank of Am., 1994-97, v.p., mgr. sales and mktg., 1997-98, prin., mgr. mktg. and bus. devel. U.S. Fgn. Exch., 1998-2000; dep. asst. sec. for fed. fin. U.S. Dept. Treasury, Washington, 2000—01; dir. FX sales mgr., U.K. investors Citibank, N.A., London, 2001—. Fgn. Student scholar U. Freiburg, 1979; Sch. of Internat. Affairs fellow Columbia U., 1980-81, Internat. fellow Columbia U., 1981. Mem. Mortar Bd., Phi Beta Kappa, Phi Kappa Phi. Roman Catholic. Avocations: sports, history. Office: Citigroup Ctr Canary Warf 33 Canada Sq London E14 5LB England Home: 106 Sassex Mansions 65-69 Old Brompton Rd London SW7 3JT England Fax: 44-0-207-986-1345. E-mail: michael.paulus@citi.com.

PAULUS, NORMA JEAN PETERSEN, lawyer; b. Belgrade, Nebr., Mar. 13, 1933; d. Paul Emil and Ella Marie (Hellbusch) Petersen; m. William G. Paulus, Aug. 16, 1958; children: Elizabeth, William Frederick. LL.B., Willamette Law Sch., 1962; LL.D. (hon.), Linfield Coll., 1985; LittD (hon.), Whitman Coll., 1990; LHD (hon.), Lewis & Clark Coll., 1996. Bar: Oreg. 1962. Sec. to Harney County Dist. Atty., 1950-53; legal sec. Salem, Oreg., 1953-55; sec. to chief justice Oreg. Supreme Ct., 1955-61; of counsel Paulus and Callaghan, Salem; mem. Oreg. Ho. of Reps., 1971-77; sec. of state State of Oreg., Salem, 1977-85; supt. pub. instrn., 1990-99; of counsel Paulus, Rhoten & Lien, 1985-86. Mem. Oreg. exec. bd. U.S. West, 1985-97; adj. prof. Willamette U. Grad. Sch., 1985; mem. N.W. Power Planning Com., 1986-89. Mem. adv. com. Def. Adv. Com. for Women in the Svc., 1986, Nat. Trust for Hist. Preservation, 1988-90; trustee Willamette U., 1978—; bd. dirs. Oreg. Grade Instn. Sci. and Tech., 1985-2001, Edn. Commn. States, 1991-99, Coun. Chief State Sch. Officers, 1995-98, Nat. Assessment Governing Bd., 1996-99, Oreg. Garden Found., 1997—, Oreg. Coast Aquarium, 1999—; bd. dirs., adv. bd. World Affairs Coun. Oreg., 1997—; overseer Whitman Coll., 1985—; bd. cons. Marion-Polk Boundary Commn., 1970-71; mem. Presdl. Commn. to Monitor Philippines Election, 1986; dir. Oreg. Hist. Soc., 2001—. Recipient Disting. Svc. award City of Salem, 1971, LWV, 1995, Path Breaker award Oreg. Women's Polit. Caucus, 1976; named One of 10 Women of Future, Ladies Home Jour., 1979, Woman of Yr. Oreg. Inst. Managerial and Profl. Women, 1982, Oreg. Women Lawyers, 1982, Woman Who Made a Difference award Nat. Women's Forum, 1985; Eagleton Inst. Politics fellow Rutgers U. Mem. Oreg. State Bar, Nat. Order Women Legislators, Women Execs. in State Govt., Women's Polit. Caucus Bus. and Profl. Women's Club (Golden Torch award 1971), Delta Kappa Gamma.

PAULUS, RONALD ALAN, health executive, physician; b. Carlisle, Pa., July 19, 1962; s. John E. Jr. and Margaret M. (Messinger) P.; m. Lori Nadine Griffie, Dec. 27, 1986; children: Kirsten Nadine, Madison Leigh, Alexander John. BS summa cum laude, U. Pa., 1984, MBA with distinction, MD, U. Pa., 1988. Diplomate Nat. Bd. Med. Examiners. Health econs. rsch. specialist N.J. Hosp. Rate Setting Commn., Trenton, N.J., 1984-85; cons. Economed Svcs. Corp., Phila., 1987-88; med. resident dept. internal medicine UCLA Med. Ctr., 1988-89; v.p. opers, mng. dir. Salick Health Care, Inc., L.A., 1989-93; co-founder, pres., dir. Care Sci. Inc., Phila., 1993—. Lectr. and presenter in field. Contbr. articles to profl. jours. Mem. Am. Coll. Physician Execs. Presbyterian. Avocations: running marathons, snow and waterskiing, reading, sports. Office: Care Sci Inc 3600 Market St Philadelphia PA 19104-2650

PAULY, JOHN EDWARD, anatomist, educator; b. Elgin, Ill., Sept. 17, 1927; s. Edward John and Gladys (Myhre) P.; m. Margaret Mary Oberle, Sept. 3, 1949; children: Stephen John (dec.), Susan Elizabeth, Kathleen Ann, Mark Edward. BS, Northwestern U., 1950; MS, Loyola U., Chgo., 1952, PhD, 1955. Grad. asst. gross anatomy Stritch Sch. Medicine, Loyola U., Chgo., 1953-54; rsch. asst. anatomy Chgo. Med. Sch., 1952-54, research instr., 1954-55, instr. in gross anatomy, 1955-57, assoc. in gross anatomy, 1957-59, asst. prof. anatomy, 1959-63, asst. to pres., 1960-62; asso. prof. anatomy Tulane U. Sch. Medicine, 1963-67; prof., head dept. anatomy U. Ark. for Med. Scis., Little Rock, 1967-83, prof., head dept. physiology and biophysics, 1978-80, vice chancellor for acad. affairs and sponsored rsch., 1983-92, assoc. dean Grad. Sch., 1983-92, prof. anatomy, 1992-95, prof. emeritus, 1995—. Flight instr. Ctrl. Flying Svc., Little Rock, 1997—; tech. adviser Ency. Brit. Films, 1956; mem. safety and occupl. health study sect. Nat. Inst. Occupl. Safety and Health, Ctr. for Disease Control, 1975—79; vis. prof. faculty medicine Kuwait U., 1993, 94; vis. prof. anatomy U. Nev., 1996. Author: (with Hans Elias) Human Microanatomy, 1960, 3d edit. 1966, (with Elias and E. Robert Burns) Histology and Human Microanatomy, 1978; editor: (with Lawrence E. Scheving and Franz Halberg) Chronobiology, 1974, (with Heinz von Mayersbach and Lawrence E. Scheving) Biological Rhythms in Structure and Function, 1981, The American Association of Anatomists, 1888-1987. Essays on the History of Anatomy in America and a Report on the Membership-Past and Present, 1987, (with Lawrence E. Scheving) Advances in Chronobiology, 1987, (with Dora K. Hayes and Russel J. Reiter) Chronobiology: Its Role in Clinical Medicine, General Biology and Agriculture, 1990; editor Am. Jour. Anatomy, 1980-92; co-mng. editor Advances in Anatomy, Embryology and Cell Biology, 1980-95; mem. adv. editorial bd. Internat. Jour. Chronobiology, 1973-83; contbr. articles to profl. jours. Chief of staff, mission pilot, instr. pilot and check pilot Ark. Wing Civil Air Patrol, 2002. With USNR, 1945—47. Recipient merit certificates AMA, 1953, 59; Bronze award Ill. Med. Soc., 1959; Lederle Med. Faculty award, 1966 Fellow AAAS; mem. Am. Assn. Anatomists (sec.-treas. 1972-80, pres. 1982-83, Centennial award 1987, Henry Gray award 1995), So. Soc. Anatomists (pres. 1971-72), Assn. Anatomy Chmn. (sec.-treas. 1969-71), Am. Physiol. Soc., Internat. Soc. Chronobiology, Pan-Am. Assn. Anatomy, Internat. Soc. Electrophysiol. Kinesiology, Internat. Soc. Steriology, Consejo Nacional de Profesores de Ciencias Morfologicas (hon.), Sigma Xi, Sigma Alpha Epsilon. Roman Catholic. E-mail: flydoc27@aol.com.

PAUP, MARTIN ARNOLD, real estate and securities investor; b. Seattle, Aug. 30, 1930; s. Clarence Jacob and Emaline Ethel (Lodestein) P.; m. Mary Jean Iske, Apr. 4, 1959; children: Barbara Ann Paup Soriano, Jennifer Marie, Elizabeth Paup-Byrnes. BS, U. Wash., 1952. Indsl. engr. Boeing Airplane Co., Seattle, 1954-60; owner Coopers Unfinished Furniture, 1960-63; claims rep. Unigard Ins., 1963-66; asst. benefits mgr. Equitable Life Assurance, 1966-85; owner Paup Ventures, 1974—, Paup Investment Co., Seattle, 1963—, Ella Paup Properties, Seattle, 1963—. Bd. dirs. Denny Regrade Property Owners' Assn., Seattle, Denny Regrade Bus. Assn., Seattle, First Ave. Assn., Seattle. Seattle Dept. Community Devel. grantee, 1980. Mem. Greenwood C. of C., Seattle Opera Guild. Democrat. Roman Catholic. Avocations: opera, travel, lit., history.

PAUPP, TERRENCE EDWARD, research associate, educator; b. Joliet, Ill., Aug. 10, 1952; s. Edward Theodore and Mary Alice (Combs) P. BA in Social Scis., San Diego State U., 1974; ThM, Luth. Sch. Theology, 1978; JD, U. San Diego, 1990. Instr. philosophy San Diego City Coll., 1983-86, Southwestern Coll., Chula Vista, Calif., 1980-83; law clerk Sch. Law U. San Diego, 1987-88; law clerk Office of Atty. Gen., San Diego, 1988-89; rsch. assoc. Frank & Milchen, 1989, Dougherty & Hildre, San Diego, 1990-95; sr. rsch.-assoc. Inst. for Ctrl. and Ea. European Studies, San Diego State U., 1996-98; sr. policy analyst Nuc. Age Peace Found., Santa Barbara, Calif., 2001—. Cons. Cmty. Reinvestment Act, San Diego, 1993-95; sr. rsch. assoc. Inst. Ctrl. and Ea. European Studies San Diego State U., 1994-95; adj. faculty in criminal justice and polit. sci. Nat. U.; cons., contbr. Inst. for Policy Studies, Washington, Interhemispheric Resource Ctr., N.Mex., The Ctr. of Concer, Washington, Global Exch., San Francisco. Author: Achieveing Inclusionary Governance: Advancing Peace and Development in First and Third World Nations, 2000; contbr. articles to law jours. Appointed National Chancellor of the USA Internat. Assn. of Educators for World Peace, 2001; cons. Neighborhood House 5th Ave., 1994—95, PBS Frontline documentary The Nicotine Wars, 1994, Bethel Baptist Ch., 1994—95. Mem. ATLA, N.Y. Acad. Scis. Democrat. Lutheran. Avocation: tennis. E-mail: tpaupp@aol.com.

PAUSA, CLEMENTS EDWARD, electronics company executive; b. South Gate, Calif., Oct. 18, 1930; s. Oscar Clements and Kathleen Patricia (O'Toole) P.; m. Janice Mary Hanson, Jan. 22, 1955; children: Geoffrey Clements, Ronald Edward. Student, UCLA, 1948-50; BS, U. Calif., Berkeley, 1953, MS, 1954, cert. in bus., 1960. Product mgr. Fairchild Semiconductor Corp., 1959-62, mgr. plant, 1962-64; gen. mgr. Fairchild Hong Kong Ltd., 1964-67, dir. plant group, 1967-68; dir. internat. mfg. Nat. Semiconductor Corp., Santa Clara, Calif., 1968-70, gen. mgr. Far East ops., 1970-73, v.p. internat. mfg., 1973-86, corp. v.p. internat. mfg., 1986-90, corp. v.p. internat. mfg. emeritus, 1991—. Dir. Price Waterhouse Coopers STS; v.p. ops. Power Integrations, Inc., 1997-99; bd. dirs. 8 subs. cos., 2 J.V. cos. Mem. internat. adv. bd. U. Santa Clara, 1984—. Capt. USNR, 1952-81. Mem. Naval Res. Assn., Res. Officer's Assn., Calif. Alumni Assn., Delta Chi Alumni Assn. (v.p., pres. 1978-86). Republican. Roman Catholic. Office: 68 Willow Rd Menlo Park CA 94025-3653 E-mail: clements.e.pausa@us.pwcglobal.com.

PAUSTENBACH, DENNIS JAMES, environmental toxicologist; b. Pitts., Oct. 29, 1952; s. Albert Paustenbach and Patricia Jean Iseman; m. Louise Dunning, Feb. 23, 1985; children: Mark Douglas, Anna Louise. BSChemE, Rose-Hulman Inst. Tech., 1974; MS in Indsl. Hygiene, U. Mich., 1977; MS in Indsl. Psychology, Ind. State U., 1978; PhD in Environ. Toxicology, Purdue U., 1982. Diplomate Am. Bd. Toxicology, Am. Bd. Indsl. Hygiene, Bd. Cert. Safety Profls.; cert. indsl. hygienist, safety profl., environ. assessor. Chem. process engr. Eli Lilly & Co., Clinton, Ind., 1974-76, indsl. hygiene engr. Lafayette, 1977-80; prof. toxicology and indsl. hygiene Purdue U., West Lafayette, 1979-82; risk assessment scientist Stauffer Chem. Co., Westport, Conn., 1982-84; mgr. indsl. and environ. toxicology Syntex Corp., Palo Alto, Calif., 1984-87; v.p. McLaren/Hart Environ. Engring., Alameda, 1987-95, chief tech. officer, 1991-96, pres., CEO, 1996—; group v.p. Exponent, Menlo Park, 1998—. Cons. IBM, Kodak, Hercules, Exxon, Ga.-Pacific, Weyerhauser, 1980—82, 1995, Hewlett-Packard, San Diego, 1984—86, Hughes Aircraft, L.A., 1987—92, Dow, 1995—2000, Brush, 1999—2002; com. mem. nat. coun. on radiol. protection and sci. adv. bd. U.S. EPA; vis. prof. Harvard Sch. Pub. Health , 2991. Contbr. over 200 articles to profl. jours., 20 chpts. to books; author coll. textbook on environ. risk assessment. Recipient Kusnetz award in Indsl. Hygiene. Fellow Am. Acad. Toxicological Scis.; mem. AICE, Am. Indsl. Hygiene Assn., Soc. Toxicology (award for excellence), Soc. Risk Analysis (Best Practioner award), Soc. Environ. Toxicology and Chemistry, Soc. Exposure Assessment, Am. Conf. Govtl. Indsl. Hygienists, N.Y. Acad. Scis., Sigma Xi. Roman Catholic. Avocations: antique furniture, jogging, golf, baseball. Home: 65 Roan Pl Woodside CA 94062-4229 Office: Exponent Enviro & Health 149 Commonwealth Dr Menlo Park CA 94025-1133 Fax: (650) 688-1799. E-mail: dpaustenbach@exponent.com.

PAUTLER, MARIA CHRISTINE SADUSKY, environmental scientist; b. Wilmington, Del., June 20, 1963; d. Joseph Anthony and Concetta Marie (Simeone) S.; m. Philip Mark Pautler, June 29, 1996; 1 child, Nicholas Anthony. BS in Plant Sci. with distinction, U. Del., 1985, MS in Plant Sci., 1987. Scientist III, site mgr. Geo-Ctrs., Inc., Ft. Washington, Md., 1987-96; rsch. assoc. dept. plant and soil scis. U. Del., Newark, 1996—. Contbr. articles to Soil Sci. Soc. Am. Jour., Jour. Environ. Quality, Environ. Toxicology and Chem., Comms. in Soil Sci. and Plant Analysis. Recipient Potash and Phosphate Inst. Fellowship award, 1986. Mem. ASTM (coms. D-18 on soil and rock and E-47 on biol. effects and environ. fate), Soc. Environ. Toxicology and Chem., Am. Soc. Agronomy, Soil Sci. Soc. Am., Assn. Women Soil Scientists (chair 1998-99), U. Del. Agrl. Alumni Assn. (bd. dirs. 1998-2002, sec.-treas. 2001—), Alpha Zeta (pres. 1983-85). Republican. Roman Catholic. Achievements include rsch. on nutrient transport via agrl. drainage and developing environ. test sys. to obtain toxicological fate and effects data on chems. and materials and their impact on the terrestrial ecosystem. E-mail: mpautler@udel.edu.

PAUTLER, STANISLAV, retired anesthesiologist; b. Prague, Czechoslovakia, Oct. 27, 1929; came to U.S., 1969; s. Stanislav and Blazena (Miller) P.; m. Milena Uhrova, Nov. 27, 1954; children: Romana Alexandra Pautler-Kerr, Simona Veronica Pautler-Gibbons. MD, Charles U., Prague, 1953, PhD (hon.), 1962. Diplomate Am. bd. Anesthesiology; lic. physician, Pa. Staff physician Sanatorium for Thoracic Diseases, Pilzen, Czechoslovakia, 1954-55; anesthesiolog Charles U., Prague, 1957-68; resident in anesthesiology U. Pitts., 1968-70, asst. prof., 1970-74, assoc. prof. clin. anesthesiology, 1974-97; dir. dept. anesthesiology St. Francis Med. Ctr., Pitts., 1979-97, ret., 1997. Contbr. articles to profl. jours. Mem. Heritage Found., Washington, 1971—, Am. Security Coun., Washington, 1973—. Capt. Med. Corps., 1955-57. Fellow Am. Bd. Anesthesiology, Am. Coll. Chest Physicians; mem. Am. Soc. Anesthesiology, Am. Med. Soc., Pa. Med. Soc. Avocations: literature, skiing, gardening. Home: 445 Miranda Dr Pittsburgh PA 15241-2037

PAVA, ESTHER SHUB, artist, educator; b. Hartford, Conn., June 29, 1921; d. Jacob H. and Rose (Rietkop) Shub; m. Jacob Pava, June 16, 1946; children: David Lauren, Jonathan Michael, Daniel Seth, Nathaniel Alexander. BFA, R.I. Sch. of Design, 1944; MA, San Francisco State U., 1971. Artist New Eng. Roto Engraving Co., Holyoke, Mass., 1944-46, Wyckoff Advt. Agy., San Francisco, 1947-48; tchr. San Francisco Unified Sch. Dist., 1963-66, Laguna Salada Sch. Dist., Pacifica, Calif., 1966-83; artist, educator Belmont, 1983—. Tchr. pvt. students. Bd. dirs. Belmont Arts Commn. Recipient numerous awards for artwork. Mem. AAUW, Burlingame Art Soc. (pres. 1983-84), Thirty and One Artists (pres. 1992-93), Soc. Western Artists (signature mem. and juror, 2d v.p. and program chmn. 1997-98, pres. 1999-2001) Calif. Watercolor Assn., Nat. League Am. Pen Women, Belmont Arts. Commn. Avocations: world travel, book discussion groups, sketching on location, painting in studio. Home: 2318 Hastings Dr Belmont CA 94002-3318 E-mail: JPava@1opener.net.

PAVALON, EUGENE IRVING, lawyer; b. Chgo., Jan. 5, 1933; m. Lois M. Frenzel, Jan. 15, 1961; children: Betsy, Bruce, Lynn. BSL, Northwestern U., 1954, JD, 1956. Bar: Ill. 1956. Sr. ptnr. Pavalon, Gifford, Laatsch & Marino,

Chgo., 1970—. Adj. prof. Northwestern U. Sch. Law; mem. com. on discovery rules Ill. Supreme Ct., 1981—; lectr., mem. faculty various law schs.; bd. dirs. ATLA Mut. Ins. Co.; 01740982. Author: Human Rights and Health Care Law, 1980, Your Medical Rights, 1990; contbr. articles to profl. jours., chpts. in books. Former mem. state bd. dirs. Ind. Voters Ill. bd. overseers Inst. Civil Justice, Rand Corp., 1993-99; mem. vis. com. Northwestern U. Law Sch., 1990-96. Capt. USAF, 1956-59. Fellow Am. Coll. Trial Lawyers, Internat. Soc. Barristers, Internat. Acad. Trial Lawyers, Roscoe Pound Found. (life, pres. 1988-90); mem. ABA, Chgo. Bar Assn. (bd. mgrs. 1978-79), Ill. Bar Assn., Ill. Trial Lawyers Assn. (pres. 1980-81), Trial Lawyers for Pub. Justice (founding mem., v.p. 1991-92, pres.-elect 1992-93, pres. 1993-94), Assn. Trial Lawyers Am. (parliamentarian 1983-84, sec. 1984-85, v.p. 1985-86, pres.-elect 1986-87, pres. 1987-88), Am. Bd. Profl. Liability Attys. (diplomate), Am. Bd. Trial Advocates, Inner Circle of Advocates, Chgo. Athletic Assn., Std. Club. Home: 1540 N Lake Shore Dr Chicago IL 60610-6684 Office: Pavalon Gifford et al 2 N La Salle St Chicago IL 60602-3702 E-mail: pavalon@pglmlaw.com.

PAVAROTTI, LUCIANO, lyric tenor; b. Modena, Italy, Oct. 12, 1935; s. Fernando and Adele (Venturi) P.; m. Adua Veroni, Sept. 30, 1961; children— Lorenza, Cristina, Giuliana. Diploma magistrale, Istituto Magistrale Carlo Sigonio, 1955; studies with, Arrigo Pola, Ettore Campogalliani. Formerly tchr. elem. schs.; salesman ins. Debut as Rodolfo in La Bohème, Reggio Emilia, Italy, 1961; roles include Edgardo in debut Lucia di Lammermoor, Amsterdam, 1963, the Duke in debut Rigoletto,Carpi, 1961, Rodolfo in La Bohème, Covent Garden, 1963, Tonio in debut The Daughter of the Regiment, Covent Garden, 1966, appeared in Lucia di Lammermoor, Australia, 1965, Am. debut, Miami, Fla., 1965; numerous European performances including Italy, Vienna Staatsoper, Paris; performed with San Francisco Opera, 1967, debut, Met. Opera, N.Y.C., 1968; appeared in The Daughter of the Regiment, Met. Opera, 1971, Elisir d'Amore, Met. Opera, 1973, La Bohème, Chgo. Opera, 1973, La Favorita, San Francisco Opera, 1973, Il Trovatore, San Francisco Opera, 1975, Bellini I Puritani, Met. Opera, 1976, Ponchielli La Gioconda, San Francisco Opera, 1979, Aida, San Francisco Opera, 1981, Mozart, Idomeneo, Met. Opera, 1982, Verdi, Ernani, Met. Opera, 1983, Tosca, Met. Opera, 1995; numerous internat. performances including La Scala, Milan, Hamburg, Teatro Colon, Buenos Aires, Australian Opera, Sydney; concert series of Am. and internat. cities, including Carnegie Hall, 1973, Buenos Aires, Moscow, Beijing, Hong Kong, Tokyo, including arena concerts, Madison Square Garden, 1984, and major cities in America, Europe, South America; appeared in film Yes, Giorgio, 1983; established Opera Co. of Philadelphia/Luciano Pavarotti Vocal Competition, 1980; rec. artist on Winner Concorso Internazionale, Reggio Emilia, 1961, Amore, 1992, Pavarotti and Friends, 1993, Ti Amo-Puccini's Greatest Love Songs, 1993, Pavarotti and Friends 2, 1995; appeared in PBS TV spl. (with Placido Domingo & Jose Carreras) The Three Tenors, 1994. Named Artist of Yr. Gramophone, 1992; recipient Grammy award, 1981, 1988. Office: care Herbert Breslin 119 W 57th St New York NY 10019-2303

PAVEK, CHARLES CHRISTOPHER, information scientist; b. Torrington, Conn., Jan. 15, 1955; s. Charles Hansen and Veronica (Donder) P.; m. Bryn Carpenter, Dec. 18, 1977. Cert de la Civilisation Française, U. Paris, 1977; BA, U. So. Calif., 1978. Asst. archivist U.S. Senate Staff, Washington, 1978-81; sr. researcher Fulbright & Jaworski, 1981-86; owner, operator Data Base Data, 1986-87; dir. libr. Nat. Econ. Rsch. Assocs., 1987-92; info. officer Putnam, Hayes & Bartlett, Inc., 1992—. With USN, 1974-75. Mem. Am. Assn. Law Librs., Spl. Librs. Assn., Law Librs. Soc. D.C. (v.p. 1982-85), Am. Legion. Democrat. Unitarian Universalist.

PAVELIC, ZLATKO P. physician, pathologist; b. Slavonski Brod, Croatia, Aug. 14, 1943; Med. dr. degree, U. Zagreb, 1969, MS, 1969-71, D of Sci., 1974. Intern. Teaching Hosps. U. Zagreb, Gen. Hosp. Pakrac Surgical Dept., 1969-71; resident in pathologic anatomy U. Zagreb, 1971-74, med. faculty, 1974, asst. prof. dept. pathology, 1975, assoc. prof., 1975; assoc. cancer rsch. scientist Dept. Experimental Therapeutis Roswell Park Meml. Inst., Buffalo, 1976-83; asst. clin. rsch. prof., med. sch. dept. Pharmacology SUNY, 1978-81, asst. rsch. prof. dept. Pathology, 1978-89; assoc. cancer rsch. scientist V, Lab. for Toxicol. Pathology Roswell Park Meml. Inst., 1983-89, mem. appointment and promotion com. Grace Cancer Drug Ctr., 1986-89; assoc. prof. Coll. Medicine U. Cin., 1989-91, assoc. prof. dept. otolaryngology head and neck surgery, 1991-92, prof. dept. otolaryngology head and neck surgery, 1992—. Rsch. fellow Med. Sch. Oxford (Eng.) U., 1975; cons. Ruder Boskovic Inst. Dept. Exptl. Biology and Medicine, Zagreb, 1970-75; chmn. tumor procurement com. pathology and lab. medicine U. Cin., 1989-90, mem. rsch. com. otolaryngology, head and neck surgery, 1991—, com. on rsch. Med. Coll., 1994—, dir. divsn. molecular oncology, otolarygology, head and neck surgery, 1991—; cons. E-Z-EM Inc., Westbury, N.Y., 1987-92, Molecular Oncology Inc., Gaithersburg, Md., 1992-94, Med. Ctr. Info. and Comm. U. Cin., 1992—, Centocor Inc., Malvern, Pa., 1992—; spkr. in field; keynote spkr. 4th Internat. Congress on Oral Cancer, Ogaki, Japan, 1995; mem. organizing com. 5 Internat. Congress on Anticancer Rsch., 4th Internat. Congress on Oral Cancer, Internat. Conf. on Epithelial Hyperplastic Lesions of the Larynx. Mem. editl. bd. Libri Oncologici, 1991—; contbr. more than 200 articles to profl. jours. NIH grantee 1984-93. Mem. Med. Assn. Croatia, Croatian Assn. Immunology, Croatian Assn. Pathology, Am. Assn. Cancer Rsch., Am. Soc. for Clin. Oncology, Am. Assn. for Pathology, The N.Y. Acad. Scis., Am. Assn. for the Advancement Sci., Sigma Xi. Home: 2200 Victory Pkwy Apt 1505 Cincinnati OH 45206-2824 Office: U Cin Coll Medicine 231 Bethesda Ave # 528 Cincinnati OH 45229-2827

PAVESE, JACQUELINE MARIE, librarian; b. Plattsburgh, N.Y., Oct. 16, 1942; d. George Earle and Georgiana (Jones) Ladd; m. Alfonso Mario Pavese, Aug. 3, 1968; children: Lori Ann, Kelly Elizabeth. BA, SUNY, Plattsburgh, 1965; MLS, Syracuse (N.Y.) U., 1966. Mid. sch. media specialist Liverpool (N.Y.) Ctrl. Schs., 1966-72; substitute tchr. Cazenovia (N.Y.) Ctrl. Schs., 1985—; story hour libr. Cazenovia Pub. Libr., 1991—; reference libr. Cazenovia Coll. Libr., 1997—2001. Mem. pastor-parish com. Cazenovia Meth. Ch., 1985-2000, gen. chmn. marketplace, 1994-99, mem. worship com., 1985—, membership com., 2000—. Named Vol. of Yr., Cazenovia Pub. Libr., 1994. Republican. Avocations: needlework, crafting, cooking, reading, swimming. Home: 5260 Owera Point Dr Cazenovia NY 13035-9340 E-mail: Pavejack@hotmail.com.

PAVIA, GEORGE M. lawyer; b. Genoa, Italy, Feb. 14, 1928; s. Enrico L. and Nelly (Welisch) P.; m. Ellen Salomon, June 15, 1952; children— Andrew, Alison; m. 2d, Antonia Pearse, Dec. 2, 1976; children— Julian, Philippa. B.A., Columbia U., 1948, LL.B., 1951; postgrad. U. Genoa, 1954-55. Bar: N.Y. 1951, U.S. Supreme Ct. 1956, U.S. Dist. Ct. (so. and ea. dists.) N.Y. 1956. Assoc., Fink & Pavia, N.Y.C., 1955-65; sr. ptnr. Pavia & Harcourt, N.Y.C., 1965— . Served to capt. JAGC, U.S. Army, 1951-54. Mem. ABA, Internat. Law Soc., Consular Law Soc. Home: 18 E 73rd St New York NY 10021-4130 Office: 600 Madison Ave New York NY 10022-1615

PAVIA, LOUIS, JR. consulting company executive; b. Newark, Nov. 21, 1950; s. Louis Sr. and Grace (Montefuseo) P.; m. Jayme Donna Morgan, June 17, 1973; children: Jessica G., Jayme M., Louis J. III. BS in Commerce, U. Va., 1972; MBA, So. Ill. U., 1981. Registered security dealer. Cons. Robert Strong Assoc., Princeton, N.J., 1973-75; stockbroker Todd & Co., Brickteon, 1975-76; cons. The Fantus Co., South Orange, 1976-78, McManis Assocs., Inc. (an MMI Co.), Washington, 1978—, sr. v.p., exec. v.p., COO. Mem. faculty Am. Coll. Physician Execs., Tampa, Fla., 1990; expert testimony FDIC, N.J. Dept. Fin., Trenton, N.J., 1976. Contbr. chpt. to book. Office: McManis Assocs Inc An MMI Co 1900 K St NW Ste 700 Washington DC 20006-1112

PAVIET-HARTMANN, PATRICIA, chemist, researcher; b. Cormeilles, France, June 8, 1964; came to U.S., 1997; d. Roland Jean and Josette Juliette (Camus) Paviet; m. Thomas Hartmann, Apr. 27, 1996; 1 child, Josephine Caroline. BS, U. Nice, France, 1986, MS, 1988; PhD in Chemistry, U. Paris XI, 1992. Rsch. scientist Commissariat a l'Energie Atomique, Cadarache, France, 1990-92; postdoctoral fellow Lawrence Livermore Nat. Lab., Livermore, Calif., 1992-93; mem. staff Forschungszentrum, Karlsruhe, Germany, 1993-97, Los Alamos Nat. Lab., 1997—. Project leader in actinide chemistry, 2000—. Contbr. articles to profl. jours.; patentee in field. Mem. Am. Chem. Soc., Am. Nuclear Soc. Roman Catholic. Avocations: painting, piano, languages (French, English, German, Italian, Spanish). Office: Los Alamos Nat Lab Environ Sci MS A141 Carlsbad NM 88220 E-mail: ppaviet-hartmann@lanl.gov.

PAVILANIS, VYTAUTAS, microbiology educator, physician; b. Kaunas, Lithuania, June 7, 1920; s. Kazys and Antonina (Eimontas) P.; m. Irene Stencelis, Mar. 8, 1947; children: Alain, Christine Gaputis, Marina Pavilanis Branigan, Ingrid. MD, U. Kaunas, 1942; diploma in microbiology, Institut Pasteur, Paris, 1947, diploma in serology and hematology, 1948; hon. doctorate, U. Que., 1988, 89. Asst. prof. pathology U. Kaunas, 1942-44; resident physician Siegburg, Germany, 1944-45; asst. Institut Pasteur, Paris, 1945-48; asst. prof. U. Montreal, Can., 1948; head virus dept. Institut Armand-Frappier, Ville de Laval, Que., Can., 1948-75, sci. dir., 1970-75, research coordinator, 1975-78, dir. quality control, 1976-79, asst. dir. teaching and research, 1978-82; assoc. prof. U. Montreal, 1956-85, prof. emeritus, 1985—; prof. U. Que., 1974-85, prof. emeritus, 1985—. Cons. in field. Contbr. articles to profl. jours. Recipient Queen's Jubilee medal Can., 1977, Prix d'excellence Province of Que., 1993. Fellow Royal Soc. Can., Royal Coll. Physicians (Can.); mem. Can. Soc. Microbiology (2d v.p. 1966, award 1984), Can. Public Health Assn. (chmn. lab. sect. 1969), Virology Club Montreal (pres. 1969), Coll. Physicians and Surgeons P.Q., Can. Med. Assn., Can. Assn. Med. Microbiologists, Soc. Microbiology P.Q., N.Y. Acad. Sci. Home: 4742 The Boulevard Westmount QC Canada H3Y 1V3 Office: PO Box 100 Laval QC Canada H7N 4Z3

PAVIN, COREY ALLEN, professional golfer; b. Oxnard, Calif., Nov. 16, 1959; Winner Mastercard Colonial, 1996. Mem. Ryder Cup Team, 1991, 93, 96; mem. Pres.'s Cup, 1994, 96. PGA Tour top U.S. golfer, leading money winner, 1991, 6th on PGA Tour 1992; Tour Wins include: Houston Coca-Cola Classic, 1984, Colonial Nat. Invitation Tournament, 1985, Hawaiian Open, 1986, 87, Greater Milw. Open, 1986, Bob Hope Chrysler Classic, 1987, 91, Tex. Open, 1988, Bell South Atlanta Golf Classic, 1991, Honda Classic, 1992, L.A. Open, 1994, Nissan Open, 1995, U.S. Open, 1995, Mastercard Colonial, 1996. Address: care PGA Tour 112 Tpc Blvd Ponte Vedra Beach FL 32082-3046

PAVLAKIS, STEVEN GEORGE, medical educator, physician; b. Portland, Maine, Dec. 2, 1953; s. George Stavros and Despina (Pallioes) P.; m. Kathleen Mary Tucker; children: Alexandra, Ariadne. BS in Biology, Brown U., 1976, MD, 1979. Bd. cert. pediatrics, neurology and child neurology; bd. cert. in neurodevel. medicine. Asst. prof. Columbia U., N.Y.C., 1970-89, assoc. prof., 1989; assoc. prof. neurology, pediat. N. Shore U. Hosp. Cornell U., Manhasset, N.Y., 1989-99; dir. devel. medicine and child neurology Beth Israel Med. Ctr., N.Y.C., 1999—2000, attending physician, Maimonides Med. Ctr., Bklyn., Mt. Sinai Med. Ctr. , Mt. Sinai Sch. Medicine, Bklyn. Attending physician North Shore Univ. Hosp., N.Y. Hosp.; prof. neurology and pediat. Mt. Sinai Sch. Medicine, 2000—; mem. coms. NIH. Mem. Child Neurology Soc. Office: Ctr Devel Medicine 977 48th St Brooklyn NY 11219-3314 also: NY Hosp Divsn Pediat Neurology PO Box 91 New York NY 10021-0005 Fax: 718-283-8669. E-mail: spavlakis@maimonidesmed.org.

PAVLAKOS, ELLEN TSATIRI, sculptor; b. Athens, May 25, 1936; d. Andrew and Katherine (Fliskanopoulou) Tsatiri; m. Andrew George Pavlakos, Nov. 2, 1952; children: James, John Andrew. Student, Arsakeion, Athens, 1952, Norton Sch. Art, West Palm Beach, Fla., 1975-79, Nat. Acad. Design, N.Y.C., 1980-81. Solo shows include Brevard Art Mus., 1981, Hess Galleries, Allentown, Pa., 1983, Cultural Ctr. Athens, 1990, 5th Ave. Art Gallery, Melbourne, Fla., 1994, 98; group shows include Le Salon des Nations, Paris, 1984, Nat. Exhbn. of Contemporary Realism in Art, Springfield, Mass., 1984, Springville Mus. Art, Utah, 1985, Capitol Gallery, Fla. Dept. Cultural Affairs, Tallahassee, 1988, Outstanding Am. Women Artists Invitational, Sarasota, 1993, Chamber of fine Arts and Min. of Edn. and Civilization Symposium, Nicosia, Cyprus, 1994, Mus. of Art and Sci., Melbourne, 1996, Appleton Mus. Art, Ocala, Fla., 1997, Sculpture '97, Thessaloniki, Greece, 1997, Dunedin (Fla.) Fine Arts Ctr., 1998, Orlando City Hall Gallery, 1998, 621 Gallary, Tallahassee, Fla., 1999, Lee County Alliance of the Arts, Fort Myers, Fla., 1999, La. State U., Shreveport, 2000, Mt. Dora (Fla.) Art Ctr., 2000, U. Fla. Arts Ctr., Gainesville, 2001, DeLand (Fla.) Mus. Art, 2001, Oceola Art Ctr., Kissimmee, 2002; bronze sculpture commd. The Harry T. Moore Monument, Titusville Social Svcs. Ctr., 1985, wall relief Knowledge, Brevard Libr., 1993, bronze sculpture Mother Earth, Penakotheke, Athens, 1990, painting Interlude, Penakotheke, Hydrostone sculpture The Flame Keeper, Kennedy Space Ctr., Fla., 1992, Stephen Girard relief Girard Coll., Phila., 1999. Recipient best of Show award Brevard Art Mus., 1980; grantee Brevard County Art in Pub. Places, 1990, 93. Mem. Acad. Artists Assn., Medalic Sculpture Assn., Chamber of Visual Arts in Greece, Nat. League of Am. Pen Women, Ten Women in Art. Greek Orthodox. Avocation: art collecting, gardening. Studio: 331 Coral Way W Indialantic FL 32903-4401 Fax: 407-773-2266.

PAVLATH, ATTILA ENDRE, research chemist; b. Budapest, Hungary, Mar. 11, 1930; came to U.S., 1958; s. Eugene Rudolph and Yolanda Elizabeth (Hortobagyi) P.; m. Katalin Wappel, July 27, 1951; children: George, Grace. Diploma in chem. engring., Tech. U., Budapest, 1952; D in Chemistry, Hungarian Acad. of Sci., Budapest, 1955. Asst. prof. Tech. U., Budapest, 1952-56; group leader Cen. Chem. Rsch. Inst., 1954-56; rsch. fellow McGill U., Montreal, Can., 1957-58; sr. group leader Stauffer Chem. Co., Richmond, Calif., 1958-67; project leader Western regional rsch. ctr. USDA, Albany, 1967-78, rsch. leader Western regional rsch. ctr., 1979—. Author three books; contbr. articles to profl. jours; patentee in field. Fellow Am. Inst. Chemists (councilor 1985-95, dir. 1993-95); mem. Am. Chem. Soc. (councilor 1973-90, dir. 1991-99, pres.-elect 2000, pres. 2001, immediate past pres. 2002), Royal Chem. Soc. Great Britain, Internat. Union of Pure and Applied Chemistry. Avocations: flying, tournament bridge, tennis, table tennis, computers. Office: USDA Western Regional Rsch Ctr 800 Buchanan St Berkeley CA 94710-1105

PAVLICK, PAMELA KAY, nurse, consultant; b. Topeka, Aug. 16, 1944; d. Cy Pavlick and June Lucille (Arnold) Dull. Diploma nursing, St. Luke's Hosp., Kansas City, Mo., 1966; BA in Psychology magna cum laude, U. North Fla., 1982, MS in Health Adminstrn. summa cum laude, 1987. RN, Mo., Ill., Fla.; cert. ins. rehab. specialist; lic. rehab. providor, Fla. Clin. instr. St. Luke's Hosp., Kansas City, 1966—70; instr. lic. practical nursing Springfield (Ill.) Sch. Bd., 1970—72; nursing supr. Jacksonville Beach (Fla.) Hosp., 1972—74; pub. health nurse State of Fla., Ocala, 1974—76; dir. nursing Upjohn Health Care, Jacksonville, Fla., 1976—77, mem. adv. com.; med. rep. Travelers Ins. Co., 1977—84; rehab. cons. Aetna Life & Casualty, 1985—, rep. nurse cons. adv. coun., 1988—90. Mem. ANA., Am. Assn. Rehab. Nurses, Nat. Assn. Rehab. Providers, Phi Kappa Phi. Republican. Episcopalian. Avocation: boating. Home: 14023 Tontine Rd Jacksonville FL 32225-2025 Office: Aetna Life & Casualty PO Box 2200 Jacksonville FL 32203-2200

PAVLIK, ELSA M. civic worker; b. Cleve., Apr. 6, 1943; d. Heinrich Sebastian and Olga Mary (Trampush) Felgemacher; m. Thomas Chester Pavlik Sr., Nov. 19, 1966; 1 child, Thomas Chester, Jr. BA, Case Western Res. U., 1967. V.p. Glor-el Real Estate Devel. Corp., Cleve., 1983-86, chief operating officer, 1991—; relocation transition cons. Realty One, 1986-91. Editor On Cue, 1982—. Mem. adv. bd. Fairmount Theatre of the Deaf, Cleve., 1982—, Cath. Social Svcs. Cleve., 1986—; trustee Cath. Charities Corp., 1989—, United Way Assembly Allocations Panel, 1989—, Cleve. Heritage Parks Assn., 1974-76, Beck Ctr. for the Cultural Arts, Lakewood, Ohio, 1985—, Hist. Sites Found., Cleve., 1985—. Named one of 100 Women of Achievement New Cleveland Woman Jour., 1988-89; recipient Mather Centennial award Case Western Res. U., Margaret Ireland award for community svc., 1992. Mem. Susan B. Anthony Soc. Women Space, Internat. Platform Assn., Gt. Lakes Shakespeare Festival (pres. women's com. 1979-81, I Will award 1982, 86), Women's City Club (pres. 1987-89, Elsa M. Pavlik Vol. of Yr. Cleve. chpt.), Coll. Club West, Trout Club of Mus. Natural History, Edgewater Yacht Club. Republican. Roman Catholic. Avocations: antiques, travel, theater, cooking, reading.

PAVLIK, JAMES WILLIAM, chemistry educator; b. Chgo., Sept. 22, 1937; s. Victor William and Rose (Jaros) P.; m. children— Claire, David, Anne AB, Carthage Coll., 1959; MS, Va. Poly. Inst. and State U., 1961; PhD, George Washington U., 1970. Asst. prof. chemistry Haile Sellasie I U., Addis Ababa, Ethiopia, 1967-69; research scientist George Washington U., Washington, 1969-70; from asst. prof. to assoc. prof. chemistry U. Wis., River Falls, 1970-74; prof. chemistry Worcester Poly. Inst., Mass., 1974—. Cons. in field Contbr. articles to profl. jours. Recipient Award for Outstanding Teaching, Worcester Poly. Inst., 1981 Mem. Am. Chem. Soc., Inter-Am. Photochem. Soc., Sigma Xi Home: 11 Sawyer Rd Northborough MA 01532-1353 Office: Dept Chemistry Worcester Poly Inst Institute Rd Worcester MA 01609-2706

PAVLIK, JOHN MICHAEL, performing arts association executive; b. Melrose, Iowa, Dec. 3, 1939; s. Michael and Suzanna (Majersky) P.; m. Susan Catherine Haysel, Aug. 14, 1971; children: Paige, Blythe. BA, U. Minn., 1963. Reporter Jour.-Times, Racine, Wis., 1964-66, Sun-Telegram, San Bernardino, Calif., 1966; news writer Pacific Telephone, L.A., 1966-68; asst. dir. pub. rels., dir. pub. rels., then v.p. Assn. Motion Picture and Television Producers, 1968-79; exec. adminstr. Acad. Motion Picture Arts and Scis., Beverly Hills, Calif., 1979-82; exec. dir. Motion Picture and Television Fund, Woodland Hills, 1982-88; prin. John M. Pavlik Co., Thousand Oaks, 1988-89; dir. endowment devel. Acad. Found./Acad. Motion Picture Arts and Scis., Beverly Hills, 1989-92; dir. comm. Acad. Motion Picture Arts and Scis., Calif., 1992—. Mem. pub. rels. coordinating com. Acad. Motion Picture Arts and Scis., 1969-82; exec. com. L.A. Film Devel. Com., 1974-85, v.p., 1977-78; spl. cons. Calif. Motion Picture Coun., L.A., 1974-79; instr. U. So. Calif. Sch. of Journalism, 1994-96. Bd. dirs. Permanent Charities Com. of Entertainment Industries, L.A., 1979-84. Mem. Acad. Motion Picture Arts and Scis., Assn. Film Commrs. Internat. (adv. bd. 1988-94, chmn. ad hoc com. on exec. mgmt. 1988-89), Conejo Future Found., Hollywood C. of C. (bd. dirs. 1979-85, Walk of Fame com. 1985-89), Soc. of L.A. Pub. Rels. Counselors, Air Force Office of Pub. Affairs Western Region (adv. bd. 1998—). Avocations: reading, photography, travel. Office: Acad Motion Picture Arts and Scis 8949 Wilshire Blvd Beverly Hills CA 90211-1972

PAVLIK, WILLIAM BRUCE, psychologist, educator; b. Cleve., Feb. 29, 1932; s. William Frank and Mary (Maco) P.; m. Mary Katherine Findley, May 22, 1979; children by previous marriage: William James, Heather Ann, Russell Matthew, James Clark; 1 child, Amelia Katherine. BS, Western Res. U., 1953; MA, Ohio State U., 1955, PhD, 1956. Asst. prof. psychology Western Mich. U., 1956-60; asst. prof., then asso. prof. Rutgers U., 1960-68; prof. psychology Va. Poly. Inst. and State U., 1968-77, chmn. dept., 1968-72; prof. psychology U. Ga., Athens, 1977-94; ret., head dept., 1977-84. Author articles in field. Mem. Eastern Psychol. Assn., Southeastern Psychol. Assn. (pres. 1985-86), Psychonomic Soc. Home: 2509 Heidi Loop Flagstaff AZ 86004-1843

PAVLOSKI, VERONICA THERESA, corporate communications specialist; b. Bklyn., June 23, 1966; d. John W. and Veronica Theresa (Bartelotti) P. BA magna cum laude, Seton Hall U., 1988. Lic. FCC operator. Rsch. analyst Katz Comm., Inc., N.Y.C., 1988; rsch. assoc., multimedia designer CMRA, Emerson, N.J., 1990—. Staff, engr. WSOU-FM, South Orange, N.J., 1986. Computer graphics exhbns. include Images '88 Communication Arts Festival, 1988. Avocations: sketching, videography, claymation, reading, French cooking. Office: CMRA 134 E Ackerman Ave Emerson NJ 07630-1923 E-mail: vtp@cmraassociates.com.

PAVLOV, VALERIY ARKADJEVICH, chemist; b. Kazan, Tatarstan, Russia, Nov. 4, 1949; s. Arkadiy Aleksandrovich Pavlov and Anastasija Stepanovna Zorova; m. Rausa Samigullina, Sept. 24, 1971; children: Oleg, Igor. BSc in Organic Chemistry, Kaszan Inst. Chem. Tech., Russia, 1972, PhD in Organophosphorus Chemistry, 1978, DSc in Organoelement Chemistry, 1999. Rschr. dept. organic chemistry Kazan Inst. Chem. Tech., 1972—74, postdoctoral rschr., 1978—79, asst. prof., 1979—84, assoc. prof., 1985—89, rsch. prof., 1989—99; rsch. prof. dept. chemistry UCLA, Loma Linda U. Sch. Medicine, 2000—01; scientist Human BioMolecular Rsch. Inst., San Diego, 2001—02; sr. rsch. scientist NAEJA Pharm., Inc., Edmonton, Canada, 2002—. Head of dept. internat. rels. dept. Kazan U. Tech., 1989-91; postgrad. fellow Moscow State U., 1976-77; postdoctoral fellow Queen Elizabeth Coll./U. London, 1984-85; vis. prof. chemistry Inst. Organ Chemistry, U. Gottingen, Germany, 1997. Author: Practical Organic Chemistry, 1993; patentee in field; contbr. papers to profl. jours. Recipient Soros award Internat. Sci. Found., Washington, 1993, 99, INTAS award Internat. Assn., Brussels, 1995; named Soros prof. Internat. Soros Sci. Edn. Program, Washington, 1999. Mem. Am. Chem. Soc., N.Y. Acad. Scis. Avocations: touring, football, skiing. Office: NAEJA Pharmaceutical Inc #2 4290-91A St Edmonton Canada T6E 5V2 Home: 11265 31st Ave Apt G5 Edmonton AB Canada T6J 3V7 E-mail: valeriy_pavlov@hotmail.com.

PAVLOVA, SYLVIA I, geneticist, researcher; b. Dobrich, Bulgaria, July 6, 1957; d. Ivan P. and Hriska D. Ivanova. MS, Higher Inst. of Food Industry, Plovdiv, Bulgaria, 1980; PhD, Inst. of Gen. Genetics, Russian Acad. of Scis., Russia, 1985. Rsch. assoc. Bulgarian Acad. of Scis., Sofia, Bulgaria, 1986—94; post doctoral rsch. assoc. UMKC, Kansas City, 1994—98; rsch. asst. prof. Univ. Ill., Chicago, 1998—. Contbr. articles to journals. Grantee Rsch. Grant, Truman Med. Ctr. Charitable Found., Kans. City, 1996, Travel Ednl. Grant, Pharmacia-Upjohn Pharm. Co., 1998; scholar Scholarship For Grad. Study, Bulgarian govt., 1980. Mem.: Internat. Infectious Diseases Soc., Am. Soc. for Microbiology. Home: 211 S Kenilworth Ave Oak Park IL 60302 Office: Uic 801 S Paulina St Chicago IL 60612

PAVONE, JOSEPH ANTHONY, designer, display; b. N.Y.C., Apr. 19, 1953; s. Joseph F. P. Student, Sch. Visual Arts Manhattan, 1979-81, Art Students League Manhattan, 1985-91. Freelance display designer, N.Y.C., 1976—. Mem. Amateur Astronomers Assn. Avocations: astronomy, fine arts, body-building. Home and Office: 812 W 181st St New York NY 10033-4543

PAVONY, WILLIAM H. retail executive, consultant; b. Bklyn., Mar. 1, 1940; s. Harry and Mollie (Leibel) Pavony; m. Geraldine Rice, June 10, 1961; 1 child Sheryl. BBA cum laude, Hofstra U., 1960. CPA, N.Y., Tex. Mgr. Arthur Andersen & Co. Inc., N.Y.C., 1960-73; group sr. v.p. Purolator Svcs. Inc., New Hyde Park, N.Y., 1973-75; v.p., contr. Purolator Inc., Piscataway, N.J., 1975-78; sr. v.p. Zale Corp., Dallas, 1978-85; sr. v.p. fin., chief fin. officer Alexander's Inc., N.Y.C., 1985-88, exec. v.p., chief fin officer, 1988-89; exec. v.p. adminstrn. The Kobacker Co., Columbus, Ohio, 1989-93; also bd. dirs.; exec. v.p. Arthur Rutenberg Homes, Clearwater, Fla., 1993-94; CFO Color Tile, Inc., Ft. Worth, 1994-95; pres. Pavony Assocs., Corona Del Mar, Calif., 1995-99, Newport Coast, 1999, 2001—; exec. bus. cons. The Netplex Group, Calif., 1999-2001; pres. Pavony Assocs., 2001—. Treas., bd. dirs. Tex. Vis. Nurses Assn., Dallas, 1984-85. Mem AICPA, Fin. Execs. Internat. (past bd. dirs. North Tex. chpt., sec. Columbus chpts.), N.Y. Soc. CPAs, Inst. Mgmt. Accts. Home: 5 Adriana Newport Coast CA 92657-1224 E-mail: Bpavony@aol.com.

PAVSEK, DANIEL ALLAN, banker, educator; b. Cleve., Jan. 18, 1945; s. Daniel L. and Helen A. (Femec) P. AB, Maryknoll Coll., Glen Ellyn, Ill., 1966; MA, Maryknoll Sch. Theology, Ossining, N.Y., 1971, Cleve. State U., 1972; PhD, Case Western Res. U., 1981; MS, George Washington U., 2000. Pres. Coun. Richmond Heights, Ohio, 1972-75; lectr. econs. Cleve. State U., 1972-75; asst. prof. Baldwin-Wallace Coll., Berea, Ohio, 1975-81; v.p., economist Ameritrust Co., Cleve., 1981-91; dean, prof. econs. Harry F. Byrd Jr. Sch. Bus. Shenandoah U., Winchester, Va., 1992-99, Durell prof. money and banking H.F. Byrd Jr. Sch. Bus., 1999—. Adj. prof. bus. adminstrn. Baldwin-Wallace Coll., Berea, Ohio, 1981-91 Mem. Am. Econ. Assn., Nat. Assn. Bus. Econs. Democrat. Home: 21343 Sawyer Sq Ashburn VA 20147-4728 E-mail: dpavsek@su.edu.

PAVY, ROBERT D. medical supply company executive; b. Rensselaer, Ind., Sept. 17, 1945; s. Robert L. and A. Lucille (Shera) P.; m. Terri L. Bassett, Dec. 29, 1979 (div. May 1993); children: Angela M., David C., Robert C. BA in Zoology, So. Ill. U., 1970. Mktg. dir. Damon Corp., Louisville, 1974-77; br. dir. Affiliated Pathology, Denver, 1977-79; lab. dir. Metpath Inc., 1979-82; gen. mgr. Internat. Medicine, Englewood, Colo., 1982-83; pres. Unified Med. Supply, Littleton, 1983—, PMC Leasing, Littleton, 1984-87, CliniMark, Littleton, 1991-96, Am. Svc., Littleton, 1989-93. Cons. Roche Biomed., Burlington, N.C., 1985. Mem. Young Reps., Carbondale, Ill., 1969. Mem. Mason, Shriners. Methodist. Avocations: scuba, fly fishing, hunting, photography. Home: 8837 S Cactus Flower Way Highlands Ranch CO 80126-2622

PAWELCZYK, JAMES A. astronaut, educator; b. Buffalo, Sept. 19, 1960; s. Joseph A. and Rita M. Pawelczyk; m. Ruth A. Anderson; 2 children. D of Pub. Svc.(hon.) , Tex. Coll. of Osteo. Medicine, Fort Worth, Tex.; BA in Biology, BA in Psychology, U. Rochester, 1982; MS in Physiology, Pa. State U., 1985; PhD in Physiology, U. of North Tex., Denton, 1989. Postdoctoral fellow in cardiovasc. neurophysiology U. Tex. Southwestern Med. Ctr., 1989—92; vis. scientist dept. anaesthesia Rigshospitalet, Copenhagen, 1990; asst. prof. medicine cardiology U. Tex. Southwestern Med. Ctr., 1992—95; dir. autonomic and exercise physiology labs. Inst. Exercise and Environ. Medicine, Presbyn. Hosp. Dallas, 1992—95; asst. prof. bioengring. U. Tex. Southwestern Med. Ctr., 1995; asst. prof. physiology and kinesiology Pa. State U., University Park, 1995—; astronaut, payload specialist NASA, STS-90 (Neurolab), Houston, 1996—98. Rsch. scientist U.S. Olympic Swimming Trials, 1984. Co-editor: Blood Loss and Shock, 1994; contbr. articles to profl. jours., chapters to books. Recipient Predoctoral tng. award, NIH, 1988—89, Rsch. award, Tex. chpt. Am. Coll. Sports Medicine, 1988, Postdoctoral tng. award, NIH, 1989—92, Young Investigator award, Life Scis. Project Divsn., NASA Office of Life and Microgravity Sci. Applications, 1994, Space Flight medal, NASA, 1998. Mem.: Soc. Neurosci., Am. Coll. Sports Medicine, Am. Physiol. Soc., Am. Heart Assn. Avocations: bicycling, swimming, woodworking, philately, outdoor activities. Address: Astronaut Office/CB NASA Johnson Space Ctr Houston TX 77058*

PAWELEC, WILLIAM JOHN, retired electronics company executive; b. Hammond, Ind., Feb. 15, 1917; s. John and Julia (Durnas) P.; m. Alice E. Brown, May 30. 1041 (dec. Dec. 1970); children: William John, Betty Jane Pawelec Conover; m. June A. Shepard, Nov. 27, 1976 (div. June 1980). BS in Acctg., Ind. U., 1939. Statistician Ind. Bd. Accounts, 1939-41; with RCA, 1941-81, mgr. acctg. and budgets internat. divsn., 1957-61, contr. internat. divsn., 1961-68, corp. mgr. internat. fn. ops. and controls, 1968-75, mgr. corp. acctg., 1975-77, dir. internat. acctg., 1977-81, ret., 1981. Contr. RCA Internat., Ltd., Electron Ins. Co., 1977, RCA Credit Corp., 1979; ret., 1981. Active Westfield United Fund, 1967—. Mem. Nat. Assn. Accts. (past nat. v.p.), Watchung Power Squadron, N.J. C. of C., Commerce and Industry Assn. N.Y., Stuart Cameron McLeod Soc., Ind. U. Alumni Assn. (pres. N.J. chpt.), Echo Lake Country Club, Beta Gamma Sigma, Sigma Epsilon Theta. Home: 86 New England Ave Summit NJ 07901-1828

PAWL, RONALD PHILLIP, neurosurgery educator; b. Chgo., July 26, 1935; s. Phillip Joseph and Ruby Helen (Graham) P.; m. Mary M. Rohner, July 11, 1959; children: Mary, Linda, Diane, Julie, Matthew, Michael. BS in Neurosurgery, Loyola U., Chgo., 1957, MD, 1961. Diplomate Am. Bd. Neurol. Surgery. Intern Resurrection Hosp., 1961-62; resident in gen. surgery and orthopedics Hines VA Hosp., 1962-63; resident in neurology and neurosurgery U. Ill., Chgo., 1963-66, asst. prof. neurosurgery, 1968-73; asst. chief neurosurgery Tripler Army Med. Ctr., Honolulu, 1966-68; assoc. prof. neurosurgery U. Ill., Chgo., 1973—; dir. pain treatment ctr. Lake Forest (Ill.) Hosp., 1978—. Pres. Am. Bd. Pain Medicine, 1995, residency rev. com. chmn., 1997—. Author: Chronic Pain Primer, 1979; editor Seminars in Neurology, 1989; editor Clin. Jour. Pain, 1988—, Surg. Neurology, 1994—, Clin. Rev. of Pain, 1997—, Currant Rev. of Pain, 1995—; contbr. articles to profl. jours. Capt. U.S. Army, 1966-68. Named Physician of Yr., Ill. Masonic Med. Ctr., Chgo., 1973. Mem. Ctrl. Neurosurg. Soc. (pres. 1979), Midwest Pain Soc. (pres. 1986), Am. Acad. Pain Medicine (treas. 1990), Ill. Neurosurg. Soc. (pres. 1982). Roman Catholic. Office: 900 N Westmoreland Rd Lake Forest IL 60045-1674 E-mail: ron@pawl.com.

PAWLEY, CARL JOHN, laser engineer, physicist; b. Milw., Feb. 28, 1956; s. James Arthur and Janet (Vogel) P.; m. Kimberly Moran, June 29, 1985; children: Conor M., Kathryn E. BSEE, Purdue U., 1977; MS in Applied Physics, UCLA, 1982, PhD in Applied Physics, 1986. Scientist Sci. Applications Internat. Corp., McLean, Va., 1986-88, Naval Rsch. Lab., Washington, 1989—. Mem. Joint Ctrl. Diagnostics Team, Livermore, Calif., 1998—. Contbr. articles to profl. jours. Mem. Am. Phys. Soc. (spkr. divsn. plasma physics 1986, 96). Democrat. Roman Catholic. Avocations: hiking, sports, science fiction. Office: Naval Rsch Lab 4555 Overlook Ave SW Washington DC 20375-0001

PAWLEY, RAY LYNN, zoological park consultant, real estate developer; b. Midland, Mich., Nov. 7, 1935; s. Lynn Richard and Alice Marie (Skelton) P.; m. Ethel Marie Condon, Feb. 19, 1955 (div. 1974); children: Ray Allyn, Shanna Sue, Cynthia Ann, Dawn Marie, Brandon Earl, Dareen Joy; m. Hedda P. Saltz, Mar. 16, 1997. Student, Mich. State U., 1954-57. Asst. curator, lectr. Black Hills Reptile Gardens, Rapid City, S.D., summers 1952-53; owner, adminstr. Reptile Exhibit, St. Ignace, Mich., 1957-59; animal coord. Marlin Perkin's Wild Kingdom (Don Meier Prodns.), Chgo., 1961-62; zoologist Lincoln Park Zool. Gardens, 1961-64; curator Brookfield (Ill.) Zoo, 1964-97; ret., 1997. Assoc. dept. zoology Field Mus. Natural History, Chgo.; internat. zoo and conservation cons., Russia, Latvia, Mex., Kenya, China, Ecuador, Galapagos Islands; past instr. herpetology Field Mus., Coll. of DuPage, Triton Coll.; assoc. zoologist Moscow Zool. Pk., Russia; info. resource for fed. and state wildlife agys.; lectr., cons. in field. Contbr. over 100 articles to profl. jours. and popular mags.; co-creator money bench Chgo. Children's Mus. Past v.p. Ill. Endangered Species Protection Bd., Springfield; liaison Endangered Species Tech. Adv. Com., Springfield. Mem. Am. Zoo Assn. (3d Outstanding Svc. awards), Chgo. Acad. Scis. (life), Chgo. Herpetological Soc. (life), Mensa. Avocations: hiking, archaeology, art, mechanics, paleontology. Home and Office: PO Box 218 Hinsdale IL 60522-0218 E-mail: raypawley@core.com.

PAWLICZKO, ANN MARIA, demographer; b. N.Y.C., Aug. 14, 1954; d. Wasyl Lencyk and Lydia Myroslawa Szuchewycz; m. George I. Pawliczko, June 10, 1978. BA magna cum laude, Coll. New Rochelle, 1976; MA, Fordham U., 1978, PhD, 1985. Adj. instr. sociology Fordham U., Bronx, N.Y., 1978-81, rsch. assoc. N.Y.C., 1984-86, asst. prof. sociology, 1988-90; rsch. asst. Population Coun., N.Y.C., 1980-84; population affairs officer UN Population Divsn., 1992-95; resource flows officer UN Population Fund, 1996—. Editor: Ukraine and Ukrainians Throughout the World, 1994. Mem. Am. Sociol. Assn., Population Assn. Am., Shevchenko Sci. Soc. (bd. dirs. 1996-2000), Alpha Kappa Delta. Office: UN Population Fund 220 E 42nd St New York NY 10017

PAWLICZKO, GEORGE IHOR, academic administrator; b. Rochester, N.Y., Oct. 26, 1950; s. Roman and Irene Olha (Zubryckyj) P.; m. Ann Maria Lencyk, June 10, 1978. BA, St. John Fisher Coll., 1972; MA, Fordham U., 1974, MBA, 1986, PhD, 1989. Admissions counselor Fordham U., Bronx, N.Y., 1977-78, asst. dean Grad. Sch. of Bus. N.Y.C., 1978-81; asst. to pres., dir. mgmt. info. systems Marymount Coll., Tarrytown, N.Y., 1981-82; exec. dir. N.Y. Inst. Credit, N.Y.C., 1982-94, The Global Inst. Fin. and Banking (formerly Am. Inst. Banking Greater N.Y.), N.Y.C., 1994—. Trustee St. Andrew's Ch., Hamptonburgh, N.Y., 1986—2002. Mem. Shevchenko Scientific Soc., Beta Gamma Sigma, Phi Alpha Theta. Office: The Global Inst Fin and Banking 80 Maiden Ln New York NY 10038-4811

PAWLIGER, CARYN R. think tank executive; b. N.Y. d. Richard and Nancy Pawliger. BA in Spanish & Social Psychology magna cum laude, Tufts U., 1992. Program specialist Am. Diabetes Assn., Alexandria, Va., 1992-95; dir. program devel. Pub. Affairs Coun., Washington, 1995—. Cons. Women Govt. Rels., Washington. Vol. Greater D.C. Cares, 1995—; chairperson Washington Tufts Alliance, 1997-2000. Mem. Am. Soc. Assn. Execs., Tufts U. Alumni Assn. (mem. alumni coun. 2000—), Greater Washington Soc. Assn. Assn. Execs. Avocation: photography. Office: Pub Affairs Coun 2033 K St NW Ste 700 Washington DC 20006-1019 Fax: 202-835-8343. E-mail: cpawliger@pac.org.

PAWLIK, JAMES DAVID, lawyer, historian; b. Cleve., May 26, 1958; s. Eugene Joseph and Eleanor Therese Marie (Gorzelanczyk) P. BA cum laude, Ohio State U., 1980, MA, 1991; JD cum laude, Harvard U., 1983. Bar: Calif. 1984, Ohio 1990, U.S. Dist. Ct. (no. dist.) Calif. 1984, U.S. Dist. Ct. (ctrl. and ea. dists.) Calif. 1986, U.S. Dist. Ct. (no. and so. dists.) Ohio 2001, U.S. Ct. Appeals (9th cir.) 1985, U.S. Ct. Appeals (6th cir.) 1994, U.S. Supreme Ct. 2002. Intern Dept. Def., Washington, 1980; assoc. Chandler, Wood, Harrington & Maffly, San Francisco, 1983-87, ptnr., 1988-89; teaching assoc. Ohio State U., 1990-91; pvt. practice Law Offices of James D. Pawlik, Cleve., 1991-93; ind. contractor Gallagher, Sharp, Fulton & Norman, 1992-93; jud. law clk. to Hon. Robert J. Krupansky U.S. Ct. Appeals (6th cir.), 1993—. Instr. dept. history Cuyahoga C.C., Parma, Ohio, 1993—; instr. dept. polit. sci. Lourdes Coll., Sylvania, Ohio, 1993; co-founder, co-owner The Vicar Sauce Co. Ltd., 2000—. Mem. staff Harvard Internat. Law Jour., 1981-83. Campaign mgr. for city coun. candidate, Westerville, Ohio, 1977; bd. trustees Midpark H.S. Alumni Assn., 1999—, vice chair, 2000—. William Green Meml. scholar 1979, Kosciuszko scholar 1989-91; Ohio State U. fellow, 1989-90; named Midpark H.S. Acad. Hall of Fame, 1997. Mem. AAUP, State Bar Ohio, Fed. Bar Assn., Mensa, Ohio State U. Alumni Assn., Harvard Alumni Assn., Ohio State U. Undergrad. Student Govt. Alumni Assn., Phi Beta Kappa, Phi Kappa Phi, Phi Alpha Theta. E-mail: jdpesq546@msn.com.

PAWLITSCHEK, DONALD PAUL, business consultant; b. Heron Lake, Minn., Aug. 5, 1941; s. Paul P. and Marion (Erickson) P.; student Southwest Tech. Inst., 1960, Mankato State Coll., 1965-66; m. Korrine Kunerth, Oct. 9, 1965; children: Andrew, Jennifer, Heidi, Sarah, Benjamin. Farmer, Heron Lake, 1967-73; pres. Dundee Steel Inc., 1973-75, Alpha Prime Inc., Heron Lake, 1975-80, Prime Ventures, Inc., 1980—; dir. Am. Search and Referral Co. Served with AUS, 1960. Mem. Nat. Assn. Fin. Cons., Am. Entrepreneurs Assn., Am. Legion. Conservative. Roman Catholic. Club: Elks. Patentee livestock flooring. Home and Office: Prime Ventures Inc RR 1 Box 144A Lake Crystal MN 56055-9700

PAWLOSKI, SCOTT JACOB, civil engineer; b. Farmington, Mich., Aug. 6, 1966; s. Alger John and Sharon Ruth (Schumacher) P.; 1 child, Alicia Rene. BSCE cum laude, Mich. Tech. U., 1988. Registered profl. engr., Mich. Asst. engr. Alcona County Rd. Commn., Lincoln, Mich., 1986-87, Sanilac County Rd. Commn., Sandusky, 1989-93; staff engr. R.S. Scott Assocs., Inc., Alpena, 1993-94, project mgr., 1994—. County hwy. engr. Montmorency County Rd. Commn., Atlanta, Mich., 1994—. Judge awards presentation Jr. Achievement N.E. Mich., Alpena, 1995. Mem. NSPE, Mich. Soc. Profl. Engrs., Chi Epsilon. Home: 6751 Truckey Rd Alpena MI 49707-9703 Office: R S Scott Assocs Inc 405 River St Alpena MI 49707-2434

PAWLOWSKI, NICHOLAS ALEXANDER, pediatrician, allergist; b. New Brunswick, N.J., Feb. 7, 1950; s. Alexander Peter and Helen (Pekarski) P.; m. Carol Anne Fritz, June 23, 1973; children: Peter Nicholas, Kathryn Fritz, Thomas Wallace. BS in Biology, Religion, Dickinson Coll., 1972; MD, Georgetown U., 1976. Diplomate Am. Bd. Pediatrics, Am. Bd. Allergy and Immunology. Resident in pediats. N.Y. Hosp.-Cornell, N.Y.C., 1976-78, chief resident in pediats., 1978-79, clin. fellow, 1979-80; postdoc. fellow Rockefeller U., 1980-82, asst. prof., 1982-86; chief allergy Children's Hosp. Phila., 1986—; assoc. prof. pediats. U. Pa., Phila., 1994—. Infectious Diseases Soc. Am. fellow, 1979; grantee NIH, 1980-91. Fellow Am. Acad. Pediats., Am. Acad. Allergy, Asthma, Immunology; mem. Am. Coll. Allergy, Asthma, Immunology, Am. Thoracic Soc., Am. Fedn. Clin. Rsch. Avocations: sports, photography, music, art. Office: Childrens Hosp Phila One Childrens Ctr Philadelphia PA 19104-4399 E-mail: pawlowski@email.chop.edu.

PAWSEY, STUART FREDERICK, structural engineer, retired; b. London, Apr. 20, 1939; came to U.S., 1964; s. Joseph Lade and Greta Lenore (Nicoll) P.; m. Glenda Jean Powell, Dec. 14, 1968; children: Chris, Warwick. BS, U. Sydney, Australia, 1959; B in Engring., U. Sydney, 1961; MS, U. Calif., Berkeley, 1967; PhD, U. Calif., 1970. Reg. profl. engr., Calif. Structural engr. McDonald, Wagner & Priddle, Sydney, 1961-64; asst. prof. Middle East Tech. U., Ankara, Turkey, 1970-72, U. New South Wales, Sydney, 1972-75; structural engr. P.M.B. Engring., San Francisco, 1975-82, Bechtel Corp., San Francisco, 1982-2000, ret., 2000. Mem. ASCE. Home: 1127 Fresno Ave Berkeley CA 94707-2519 E-mail: pawsey@attbi.com.

PAXTON, ALAN HUGH, physicist; b. Phila., Feb. 27, 1946; s. Hugh Campbell and Jean (Thompson) P.; m. Merideth Eileen Daniel, Aug. 1, 1967. BS, U. N.Mex., 1968, PhD, 1981. Rsch. physicist Air Force Weapons Lab., Albuquerque, 1974-82; sr. scientist Mission Rsch. Corp., 1982-93; sr. rsch. scientist U. N.Mex., 1993-96; rsch. physicist Air Force Rsch. Lab., 1996—. Contbr. articles to profl. jours. Mem.: SPIE. Achievements include development of high-energy gas lasers, free-electron lasers, fiber amplifiers, and semiconductor lasers, new concepts and designs for coherence control in these lasers, studies of degradation of photonic components by ionizing radiation; patentee in field. Office: Air Force Rsch Lab/DELO 3550 Aberdeen Ave SE Kirtland AFB NM 87117 E-mail: alan.paxton@kirtland.af.mil.

PAXTON, GLENN GILBERT, composer; b. Chgo., Dec. 7, 1931; s. Glenn G. and Florence A. (Nosek) P.; m. Leslie H. Davis, Dec. 8, 1962; children: Alexandra, Eben. BA, Princeton U., 1953. Freelance composer Broadway, opera, TV and film, 1959—. Composer: (theater prodns.) First Impressions, 1959, The Adventures of Friar Tuck, 1983 (Pulitzer prize nomination 1984), (opera) Monticello, 2000, (film) When the Legends Die, 1972, (concert pieces) Four Character Pieces for Piano, 1962, The Evening Sing, 1981, Harmonizing, Ca. 1940, 1986, (TV movies) Charlie and the Great Balloon Chase, 1981, Vital Signs, 1986, Dark Night of the Scarecrow, 1981, Isobel's Choice, 1981, The Two Worlds of Jenny Logan, 1979, The Clone Master, 1978, (TV shows) Amazing Stories, 1986, Willa Cather's America, 1976, Andy Rooney Takes Off, 1983, An American Christmas: Words and Music, 1971, The Hill Country: Lyndon Johnson's Texas, 1967, The Stately Ghosts of England, 1968, Barry Goldwater's Arizona, 1968, New World Visions, 1984, The American Image, 1969, others; (multi-media) Walking Home, 1991; (CD) Prairie Indigo, 1995. Served to lt. (j.g.) USCG, 1953-56. Mem. ASCAP, Dramatists Guild, Am. Music Ctr., Am. Fedn. Musicians. Home and Office: 230A Saddle Ln Ojai CA 93023-4204 E-mail: gpaxton@alumni.princeton.edu.

PAXTON, HAROLD WILLIAM, former steel company executive, educator; b. Yorkshire, Eng., Feb. 6, 1927; came to U.S., 1953, naturalized, 1961; s. John Wilfrid and Hilda Annie (Vasey) P.; m. Ann Dorothy Davies, May 13, 1953; children: Jane Elizabeth, Sally Patricia, Anthony Charles, Nigel John. B.Sc. with lst class honours, U. Man., 1947, M.Sc., 1948; PhD, U. Birmingham, Eng., 1952. Univ. fellow U. Birmingham, 1950-53; mem. faculty Carnegie-Mellon U., 1953-74, prof. metall. engring., 1962-74, Firth Sterling prof. metall. research, 1958-63; head dept. metallurgy and materials sci., dir. Metals Research Lab., 1966-71, dir. research, 1973-74; adj. sr. fellow Mellon Inst., 1965-67; dir. div. materials research NSF, 1971-73; v.p. research U.S. Steel Corp., 1974-85; USS U. prof. materials sci. and engring. Carnegie Mellon U., 1986-98, univ. prof. emeritus, 1998—. Vis. prof. Mass. Inst. Tech., 1970; Campbell meml. lectr., 1978, cons. to industry, 1953-74, 86—; Chmn. Internat. Conf. High Velocity Deformation, 1960, Internat. Conf. Fracture, 1962 Author: (with E. C. Bain), 3d edit.) Alloying Elements in Steel, 1966, also numerous articles. NSF sr. postdoctoral fellow Imperial Coll., London, Eng., 1962-63 Fellow AAAS, Am. Soc. Metals (Bradley Stoughton Young Tchrs. award 1960, Gold medal advancement research 1983), Metall. Soc. of AIME (pres. 1976-77, v.p inst. 1977-78); mem. AIME (hon.1991, pres. 1982), NAE, Iron and Steel Inst. Japan (hon.), Inst. Metals (Harold Moore lectr. 1987). Home: 115 Eton Dr Pittsburgh PA 15215-1701 Office: Carnegie Mellon MSE Dept Pittsburgh PA 15213 E-mail: paxton@cmu.edu.

PAXTON, JUANITA WILLENE, retired university official; b. Birmingham, Ala. d. Will and Elizabeth (Davis) P. AB, Birmingham So. Coll., 1950; MA, Mich. State U., 1951; EdD, Ind. U., 1971; postgrad., U. Tex., summer 1965. Dormitory dir. Tex. Tech U., Lubbock, 1951-53; counselor Mich. State U., East Lansing, summer 1951; dir. univ. ctr. and housing SUNY, Fredonia, 1953-56, assoc. dean of students, 1956-57; asst. dean of women U. N.Mex., Albuquerque, 1957-63; dean of women East Tenn. State U., Johnson City, 1963-68, 70-78, dir. Counseling Ctr., 1978-93. Tng. dir. CONTACT Teleministries, Tenn., 1984-92, chmn. bd. dirs., 1986, 95. Chmn. social concerns Munsey United Meth. Ch., 1989-92, sec. adminstrv. bd., 1980-84, vice chairperson, 1993, chair, 1994, mem. coun. on ministries, 1980-94, chair stewardship campaign, 1995, chair promotion and publicity subcom. building campaign, 1996—, chair scholarship com., 1997—, lay leader, 2001—, sec. staff parish rels. com., 2001, nominations com., 2001, Circle tchr., 2000—. U.S. Ednl. Profl. Devel. Act grantee, 1968-69. Mem. Am. Coll. Pers. Assn. (mem. media com. 1977-79, newsletter editor com. XVI 1977-79), Asbury Retirement Ctrs. Tenn. and Va. (bd. dirs. 1991-96, policy com. 1991-96, chair 1995-96, mem. fin. com. 1996, mem. nomination com. 1994-96), Univ. Women's Club (pres. 1994-96), Tenn. Coll. Pers. Assn. (legis. chair 1974), Tenn. Assn. Women Deans Counselors (pres. 1966-68), Gen. Federated Womans Club, Monday Club Aux. (pres. 1980-81, 88-89, 95-96, 99-2000, v.p. 1993-95, 96-99, corr. sec. 1979-80), Watauga Pers. and Guild Assn. (pres.-elect 1967-68, chair ETEA guidance divsn. 1968), Delta Kappa Gamma Soc. Internat. (internat. chair rules com. 1992, mem. exec. bd. 1989-91, internat. rsch. com. 1982-84, constn. com. 1992-94, state rec. sec. 1975-77, state v.p. 1977-79, state pres. 1989-91, chpt. pres. 1972-74, chair state nominating com. 1979-81, chair state ad hoc com. to study feasibility exec. sec. 1987-89, mem. pers. com. 1995-97, 2000--, chair 1997-99, mem. archives com. 1999—2001, State Achievement award 1987), E. Tenn. State U. Retiree's Assn. (bd. dirs. 1993-2000, program com. 1994, 95, pres. elect 1995, pres. 1996, sec. 2000). Avocations: reading, bridge, travel, needlework. E-mail: willenepj@aol.com.

PAXTON, MATTHEW WHITE, IV, newspaper publisher; b. Lexington, Va., May 28, 1954; s. Matthew White and Mary Raine Paxton; m. Margaret Ann Paxton, Oct. 14, 1978; children: Ann Courtney, Sarah Macon. BA in Econs., U. Va., 1976. Loan officer Ctrl. Fidelity Bank, Lynchburg, Va., 1976-80; advt. sales The News-Gazette, Lexington, 1980, advt. mgr., 1980-86, bus. mgr., 1986-94; pub., pres. The News-Gazette Corp., 1994—. Bd. dirs., Stonewall Jackson Hosp., Lexington, 1990-99, Lexington Downtown Devel. Assn., 1996-99, D.S. Lancaster Coll. Found., Clifton Forge, Va., 2000—; pres. Rockbridge Concert Theater Series, Lexington, 1988-91. Mem. Nat. Newspaper Assn. (bd. dirs. 1999—), Va. Press Assn. (bd. dirs. 1989-2000, pres. 1998-99, Raymond Bottom award 1999), Exptl. Aircraft Assn. (sect. chpt. 646 2000—), Springwood Soaring Assn. (dir. 1998—). Avocations: flying, soaring, building airplanes, skiing, reading. Home: 12 Jordan St Lexington VA 24450 Office: The News-Gazette Corp PO Box 1153 Lexington VA 24450 E-mail: publisher@thenews-gazette.com.

PAXTON, ROBERT, literature educator; b. Midland, MI, Nov. 1, 1972; BA in Creative Writing and Am. Lit., U. Ariz., 1995. Dir. Casa Peregrino Homeless Shelter Annunciation House, El Paso, Tex., 1995—96; English tchr. Freedom Inst., San Pedro Sula, Honduras, 1997—98. Non-Partisan. Roman Catholic. Personal E-mail: robpaxton@yahoo.com.

PAXTON, ROBERT OWEN, historian, educator; b. Lexington, Va., June 15, 1932; s. Matthew W. and Nell B. (Owen) P.; m. Sarah Plimpton, Dec. 9, 1983 BA, Washington and Lee U., 1954, LittD (hon.), 1974; BA, Oxford (Eng.) U., 1956, MA, 1961; PhD, Harvard U., 1963; DHL (hon.), SUNY, Stony Brook, 1994; DL (hon.), U. Caen, France, 1994. Instr. history U. Calif., Berkeley, 1961-63, asst. prof., 1963-67; asso. prof. SUNY, Stony Brook, 1967-69; prof. history Columbia U., 1969—, chmn. dept., 1980-82, dir. Inst. on West Europe, 1991-95. Author: Parades and Politics at Vichy, 1966, Vichy France: Old Guard and New Order, 1940-44, 1972, 2nd edit., 2001, Europe in the Twentieth Century, 1975, 4th edit., 2001, French Peasant Fascism, 1997; co-author: Vichy France and the Jews, 1981, 2nd edit., 1995; co-editor: De Gaulle and the U.S., 1995. Served with USNR, 1956-58. Decorated comdr. Ordre National des Arts et des Lettres (France), officer Ordre National du Mérite (France); Rhodes scholar, 1954-56; Am. Coun. Learned Socs. fellow, 1974-75; Rockefeller Found. fellow, 1978-79; German Marshall Fund fellow, 1986. Fellow Am. Acad. Arts and Letters (Scholarly Distinction award 1998); mem. Am. Philos. Soc., Linnaean Soc. N.Y. (pres. 1978-80) Home: 460 Riverside Dr Apt 72 New York NY 10027-6801 Office: Columbia U Dept History New York NY 10027 E-mail: rop1@columbia.edu.

PAYANT, V. ROBERT, legal association administrator, educator, judge; b. Iron Mountain, Mich., June 25, 1932; s. Vital Alexander and Anna Jane (Freele) P.; m. Virginia Henneberry, June 23, 1956; children: Margaret, Thomas More, Mary Adele, Ned, Robert. BS in English, Marquette U., 1954, JD, 1956. Bar: Wis. 1956, Mich. 1957, Nev. 1985. Atty. City of Iron Mountain (Mich.), 1959-63; probate judge County of Dickinson, Iron Mountain, 1963-68; 95th dist. judge State of Mich., 1968-77, 41st cir. judge., 1977-82, ct. adminstr. Lansing, Mich., 1985-88; assoc. dean Nat. Jud. Coll., Reno, 1982-85, dean, 1990-94, pres., 1994-98, pres. emeritus, 1999—, mem. faculty, 1973—. Bd. dirs. Nev. Cath. Conf., 2000—. Mem. ABA, Nev. Bar Assn., Mich. Bar Assn., Am. Judicature Soc., K.C. Republican. Roman Catholic. Avocations: amateur theatrics, swimming, camping. Office: U Nevada Nat Judicial Coll Nat Jud College Reno NV 89557-0001 E-mail: veets3@aol.com.

PAYDARFAR, ALI AKBAR, sociology and demography educator; b. Tehran, Iran, Nov. 22, 1928; came to U.S., 1958; s. Mohammad and Robabeh (Faragh) Zoolehe; m. Lila Yazdi, July 18, 1953; children: Amir Ahmad, David, Joseph. BA in Theology, Tehran U., 1950, BLL, 1954; MA in Sociology, U. Ky., 1960, PhD in Sociology, 1962. Asst. prof. Cornell U., Ithaca, N.Y., 1962-63, St. Lawrence U., Canton, N.C., 1963-65; assoc. prof. George Washington U., Washington, 1965-67, Shiraz (Iran) U., 1967-69, prof. sociology, 1976-82; sr. rsch. scientist Am. Rsch. Inst., Washington, 1979-70; sr. rsch. assoc. U. N.C., Chapel Hill, 1970-75, vis. scholar IRSS, 1975-76, adj. prof., 1982—; vis. prof. N.C. Ctrl. U., Durham, 1987-88. Cons. UN Funds for Population Activity, World Bank, 1971-77, UNESCO, Paris and Tehran, 1967-69, WHO, Geneva, 1968-69. Contbr. numerous articles ot profl. publs. Grantee U.S. AID, NSF, WHO; Population Coun. fellow. Mem. Am. Sociol. Assn., Population Assn. Am., Internat. Union for Sci. Study of Population, Alpha Kappa Delta (pres. local chpt. 1962). Home: 1909 S Lakeshore Dr Chapel Hill NC 27514-2029 Fax: 919-967-0193. E-mail: paydarfa@email.unc.edu.

PAYNE, ANCIL HORACE, retired broadcasting executive; b. Mitchell, Oreg., Sept. 5, 1921; s. Leslie L. and Pearl A. (Brown) P.; m. Valerie Dorrance Davies, Apr. 6, 1959; children: Anne Sparrow, Alison Louise, Lucinda Catherine. Student, Willamette U., 1939-41, U. Oreg., 1941, U. Notre Dame, Ohio State U., 1943; BA, U. Wash., 1947; postgrad., Am. U., 1950-51; hon. PhD, Willamette Univ., 1991. Adminstrv. asst. to congressman, Washington, 1949-52; gen. mgr. Martin Van Lines, Anchorage, 1952-56; mgr. Frontiers-Oreg. Ltd., Portland, Oreg., 1956-59; asst. v.p. bus. div. King Broadcasting Co., Seattle, 1959-63, v.p., 1963-70, exec. v.p., 1970-71, pres., 1971-87. Chmn. bd. affiliates NBC, 1975-80. Mem. Oreg. Bd. Higher Edn., 1966-70; bd. trustees Whitman Coll,. 1985-90; Lt. (j.g.) USNR, 1942-45, PTO. Fellow Phi Beta Kappa; mem. Monday Club, Rainier Club, Alpha Delta Sigma. Episcopalian. Office: Ancil H Payne & Assocs 1107 1st Ave Apt 606 Seattle WA 98101-2944

PAYNE, ANITA HART, reproductive endocrinologist, researcher; b. Karlsruhe, Baden, Germany, Nov. 24, 1926; came to U.S., 1938; d. Frederick Michael and Erna Rose (Hirsch) Hart; widowed; children: Gregory Steven, Teresa Payne-Lyons. BA, U. Calif., Berkeley, 1949, PhD, 1952. From rsch. assoc. to prof. U. Mich., Ann Arbor, 1961-96, prof. emeritus, 1996—; assoc. dir. U. Mich. Ctr. for Study Reprodn., 1989-94; sr. rsch. scientist Stanford (Calif.) U. Med. Ctr., 1995—. Vis. scholar Stanford U., 1987-88; mem. reproductive biology study sect. NIH, Bethesda, Md., 1978-79, biochem. endocrinology study sect., 1979-83, population rsch. com. Nat. Inst. Child Health and Human Devel., 1989-93. Assoc. editor Steroids, 1987-93; contbr. book chpts., articles to profl. jours. Recipient award for cancer rsch. Calif. Inst. for Cancer Rsch., 1953, Acad. Women's Caucus award U. Mich., 1986, Mentor award Women in Endocrinology, 1999. Mem. Endocrine Soc. (chmn. awards com. 1983-84, mem. nominating com. 1985-87, coun. 1988-91), Am. Soc. Andrology (exec. coun. 1980-83), Soc. for Study of Reprodn. (bd. dirs. 1982-85, sec. 1986-89, pres. 1990-91, Carl G. Hartman award 1998). Office: Stanford U Med Ctr Dept OB GYN Divsn Reproductive Biology Stanford CA 94305-5317

PAYNE, ARLIE JEAN, parent education administrator; b. Priest River, Idaho, Oct. 9, 1920; d. Charles Ross and Novella (Person) Randall; m. Edgar E. Payne, July 18, 1942; children: Randy, Nancy, Kathleen, Charles, Stacy. BA, East Washington U., 1942, MEd, 1968. Tchr. Rainier (Wash.) Pub. Schs., 1941-42; tchr. phys. edn. George Dewey Jr. High Sch., Bremerton, Wash., 1946; coll. dir. nursery sch. Farragut, Idaho, 1946-47; tchr. kindergarten West Valley Pub. Schs., Dishman, Washington, 1951-52, Mercer Island, 1952-53; active devel. and op. pvt. child care ctr., 1957-63; tchr. pvt. nursery sch. Community Colls. of Spokane, 1964-65; developer 1st program for presch. age handicapped children Lake Washington Spl. Edn. Ctr., Kirkland, 1965-67; cons. parent edn. Lake Wash. Sch. Dist., 1967-68; legis. chairperson A.H.E., 1970-72; coord. family life Shoreline Community Coll., Seattle, 1968-72; dir. parent cooperative program Community Colls. of Spokane, 1973-85; mem. Gov.'s Commn. for Child Care, 1985; owner Whimisical Jean's Books. Author: We're Driving Our Kids Crazy, 1993; editor, publisher Lake Spokane News Forum. Recipient Crystal Apple award for Support for Edn. Wash. State

Pub. Rels. Assn., 1995. Home: 16094 N Saddlebrook Rd Nine Mile Falls WA 99026-9352 Office: Lake Spokane News Forum/ Whimsical Jean's Books 5978 Hwy 291 # 3 Nine Mile Falls WA 99026

PAYNE, DAVID EMER, university administrator; b. Salt Lake City, Mar. 29, 1944; s. John W. and Sara (Harris) P.; m. Grettle Haglund, Nov. 17, 1973; children: Sara, John, Samuel, Daniel, James, David. BS, Brigham Young U., Provo, Utah, 1968; MS, U. N.C., 1970, PhD, 1972. Asst. prof. U. Iowa, Iowa City, 1972-76; assoc. prof. U. N.D., Grand Forks, 1976-80, prof., 1980-81; fellow Am. Coun. Edn., New Orleans, 1981-82; dean social sci. S.E. Mo. State U., Cape Girardeau, 1982-88; v.p. acad. affairs Sangamon State U., Springfield, Ill., 1988-89, Emporia (Kans.) State U., 1989-96, Sam Houston State U., Huntsville, Tex., 1997—. Vis. prof. U. Iceland, Reykjavik, 1974-75. Contbr. articles to profl. jours. Dist. commr. Boy Scouts Am. Am. Coun. Edn. fellow, 1981-82, Bush Found. sr. fellow, 1982. Mem. Coun. Fellows Am. Coun. Edn., Am. Sociol. Assn., C. of C., Renaissance Group (exec. bd. dirs.), Alliance of Univs. for Democracy (exec. bd. dirs.), Rotary, Sigma Xi. Mem. Lds Ch. Home: 837 Elkins Lk Huntsville TX 77340-7322 Office: Sam Houston State U Huntsville TX 77340

PAYNE, DEBORAH ANNE, medical company officer; b. Norristown, Pa., Sept. 22, 1952; d. Kenneth Nathan Moser and Joan (Reese) Dewhurst; m. Randall Barry Payne, Mar. 8, 1975 (div.). AA, Northeastern Christian Jr. Coll., 1972; B in Music Edn., Va. Commonwealth U., 1979. Driver, social asst. Children's Aid Soc., Norristown, Pa., 1972-73; mgr. Boddie-Noell Enterprises, Richmond, Va., 1974-79; retail food saleswoman Hardee's Food Systems, Inc., Phila., 1979-81; supr., with tech. tng. and testing depts. Cardiac Datacorp., 1981-95; tng. supr. Raytel Cardiac Svcs., Forest Hills, N.Y., 1995-98, supr. tech. support Haddonfield, N.J., 1998—. Mem. bd. advisers Am. Biog. Inst., 1989—. Mem. NAFE, Delta Omicron (pres. Alpha Xi chpt. 1978-79, pres. Epsilon province 1980-85, chmn. Eastern Pa. alumni 1986-88, Star award 1979), Am. Soc. Profl. and Exec. Women. Democrat. Avocations: music, sports. Home: 7400 Roosevelt Blvd Apt A10 Philadelphia PA 19152-4324 Office: Raytel Cardiac Svcs 56 Haddon Ave Haddonfield NJ 08033 E-mail: Deborah.A.Payne@att.net.

PAYNE, DONALD M. congressman; b. Newark, July 16, 1934; BA, Seton Hall U. Freeholder Essex County, 1973-78; ins. co. exec., prior to 1989; former v.p. computer forms mfr.; mem. Newark Mcpl. Coun., 1982-89, U.S. Congress from 10th N.J. dist., 1989—; mem. internat. rels. com. edn. and workforce com. Chmn. World YMCA Refugee and Rehab. Com., 1973-81; pres YMCA's of USA. Democrat. Office: US Ho of Reps 2209 Rayburn House Office Bldg Washington DC 20515-0001 also: 50 Walnut St Ste 1016 Newark NJ 07102-3506*

PAYNE, FLORA FERN, real estate broker; b. Carrollton, Mo., Sept. 25, 1932; d. George Earnest and Bernadine Alice (Schaefer) Chrisman; m. H.D. Matticks, Oct. 20, 1950 (div. Oct. 1959); children: Dennis Don, Kathi D.; m. S.L. Freeman, Nov. 25, 1960 (div. Jan. 1973); 1 child, Gary Mark; m. Vernon Ray Payne, Mar. 18, 1988. Student, S.E. C.C., Burlington, Iowa, 1976-77; cert. stenographer, Corr. Sch., Chgo., 1960-61; student, Career Visions Real Estate Sch, 1999. Social svc. designee Mo. League Nursing, 1991. Sec. to v.p. Moore Co., Marceline, Mo., 1973-75; steno to trainmaster A.T. & S.F. Rlwy. Co., Fort Madison, Iowa, 1975-88; with social svc. Brookfield (Mo.) Nursing Ctr., 1990-95; 97-98; candidate for Linn County Pub. Adminstr., 1996; real estate agt. Marceline Realty, Mo., fall 1999; real estate broker Payne Realty, 2000—. Republican. Avocations: writing poetry, dancing, interior decorating. Home: 603 Hickory St Bucklin MO 64631-7282

PAYNE, FRANCES ANNE, literature educator, researcher; b. Harrisonburg, Va., Aug. 28, 1932; d. Charles Franklin and Willie (Tarvin) P. BA, B.Mus., Shorter Coll, 1953; MA, Yale U., 1954, PhD, 1960. adj. fellow St. Anne's Coll., Oxford Eng. Instr. Conn. Coll., New London, 1955-56, U. Buffalo, 1958-60, lectr., 1960, asst. prof., 1960-67; assoc. prof. SUNY, 1967-75, prof. English and medieval lit., 1975—. Adj. fellow St. Anne's Coll., Oxford, Eng., 1966—. Author: King Alfred and Boethius, 1968; Chaucer and Menippean Satire, 1981. Contbr. articles to scholarly publs. AAUW fellow, Oxford, 1966-67; Research Found. grantee SUNY Central, Oxford, 1967, 68, 71, 72; recipient Julian Park award SUNY-Buffalo, 1979. Mem. Medieval Acad. Am., Internat. Arthurian Soc., New Chaucer Soc., Internat. Soc. Anglo-Saxonists, Pi Kappa Lambda. Office: SUNY-Buffalo 306 Clemens Hall Buffalo NY 14260-4600 E-mail: fapayne@buffalo.edu., fapayne@buffalo.edu.

PAYNE, FRANK VALENTINO, information technology company executive; b. Natchez, Miss., Dec. 29, 1950; s. Frank and Hattie (Johnson) P.; m. Cordelia Manuel, Aug 21, 1971; children: Nichelle, Ledevon, Krishna. BSME, Tuskegee Inst., 1974. Group mgr. Procter & Gamble, Cin., 1974-1985; pres., chief exec. officer USTEP Corp., 1985—, also bd. dirs. Bd. dirs. Techsoft Systems, Cin. Vol. United Appeal, Cin., 1981; mem. Cin. Community Devel. Commn., 1982; spl. mem. U.S. Congl. Adv. Bd., Washington, 1983; bd. dirs. Ctr. for Cardiac Support, Cin., 1985—; advisor Drug and Poison Ctr., Cin., 1985—. Served to capt. U.S. Army, 1974-78. Named Black Achiever Cin. YMCA, 1982. Mem. Nat. Assn. Tax Practioners, Inst. Cert. Fin. Planners, Internat. Assn. of Fin. Planning. Avocations: running, tennis, chess, reading.

PAYNE, FRED J. physician, educator; b. Grand Forks, N.D., Oct. 14, 1922; s. Fred J. and Olive (Johnson) P.; m. Dorothy J. Peck, Dec. 20, 1948; children: Chris Ann Payne Graebner, Roy S. William F., Thomas A. BS, U. Pitts., 1948, MD, 1949; MPH, U. Calif., Berkeley, 1958. Diplomate Am. Bd. Preventive Medicine. Intern St. Joseph's Hosp., Pitts., 1949-50; resident Charity hosp., New Orleans, 1952-53; med. epidemiologist Ctr. Disease Control, Atlanta, 1953-60; prof. tropical medicine La. State U. Med. Ctr., New Orleans, 1961-66; dir. La. State U. Internat. Ctr. for Med. Rsch. and Tng., San Jose, Costa Rica, 1963-66; exec. sec. 3d Nat. Conf. on Pub. Health Tng., Washington, 1966-67; epidemiologist Nat. Nutrition Survey, Bethesda, Md., 1967-68; chief pub. health professions br. NIH, 1971-74; med. officer, sr. rsch. epidemiologist Nat. Inst. Allergy and Infectious Diseases, 1974-78; asst. health dir. Fairfax County (Va.) Health Dept., 1978-94; dir. HIV/AIDS case mgmt. program, 1988-94; cons. epidemiologist, 1994—; med. advisor Ams. for Sound AIDS Policy, 1996—, Childrens AIDS Fund, 1997—. Clin. prof. La. State U., 1966-79; cons. NIH, 1979-81; leader WHO diarrheal disease adv. team, 1960. Contbr. articles to profl. jours. Served with AUS, 1942-46, 49-52. Decorated Combat Medic Badge. Fellow Am. Coll. Preventive Medicine, Am. Coll. Epidemiology; mem. AAAS, AMA, Am. Soc. Microbiology, Internat. Epidemiology Assn., Soc. Epidemiol. Rsch., USPHS Commd. Officers Assn., Sigma Xi. Home: 2945 Ft Lee St Herndon VA 20171-1813 Office: PO Box 16433 Washington DC 20041 E-mail: jjiyd@ibm.net., fdpayne6@email.msn.com.

PAYNE, GARELD GENE, vocal music educator, medical transcriptionist; b. Colony, Okla., Aug. 27, 1931; s. Eugene A. and Agnes D. (Chastain) P.; children: Gareld, S. Raymond, Lynn Dita, Jana Lee. MusB, Oklahoma City U., 1965; MusM in Edn., North Tex. State U. (name change to U. North Tex.), 1969; ednl. specialist, Pitts. State U., 1989; postgrad., Okla. State U. Ind. organist, pianist numerous nightclubs, nationwide, 1956-64; instr. vocal, instrumental music Muenster (Tex.) Ind. Sch. Dist., 1965-69; tchr. vocal music Dallas Ind. Sch. Dist., 1966-74, Carrizo Springs (Tex.) Ind. Sch. Dist., 1976-79, Coffeyville (Kans.) Unified Sch. Dist., 1979-91; tchr. elem. vocal music Oklahoma City Pub. Schs., 1996—. Rec. artist (album) Evening With Gareld, 1984; composer publ. anthems. With USAF, 1950-53. Scholar Oklahoma City U., 1949. Mem. Am. Fedn. Musicians, NEA, Am. Orff-Schulwerk Assn., Am. Recorder Soc., Am. Theater Organ Soc., Am. Guild Organist Orgns. of Am. Kodaly Educators, Phi Mu Alpha Sinfonia Frat., Phi Delta Kappa. Republican. Methodist. Avocations: astrology, oil and water color painting, cooking, reading, computers. Home: 3643 NW 15th St Oklahoma City OK 73107-4423 E-mail: pgareld_osu@ionet.net.

PAYNE, GEORGE FREDERICK, educational administrator; b. Summerville, S.C., Jan. 29, 1941; s. Fred N. and Lota (Griffith) P.; m. Kay Martin, June 23, 1963; children: John F., Mark C., Janet E. Student, Ga. Inst. Tech., 1959-60, U.S. Naval Acad., 1960-62; BS, U. S.C., 1963, MA, 1966; MRE, Luth. Theol. Sem., 1968; postgrad., U. Ga., 1969-71; LLD (hon.), Lincoln Meml. U., 1988. Cert. Fund Raising Exec., 2000. From instr. to asst. prof. Ga. So. Coll., Statesboro, 1966-78; dir. admission Brewton-Parker Coll., Mt. Vernon, Ga., 1978-80; v.p. for devel. North Greenville Coll., Tigerville, S.C., 1980-86; pres. Limestone Coll., Gaffney, 1986-91, dir. various grants, 1976-91; spl. agt., registered rep. Prudential Fin. Svcs., 1991-92; dir. ITT Tech. Inst., Greenville, S.C., 1992-95; exec. dir. Inst. Adv. Greenville Tech. Coll./ Greenville Tech. Found., 1996—. Author: An Introduction to the Principles of Geography: Facts, Skills, Concepts, and Models, 1973; also articles. Active Leadership Greer, S.C., 1980-81, regent, 1982-84; active AACTion Consortium, 1980-82, Leadership Greenville, S.C., 1982-83; bd. dirs. Greenville County unit Am. Cancer Soc., 1985-86; advisor Cherokee County Arts Coun., 1986-91, bd. trustees Rolling Green Village Continuing Care Ret. Cmty., 1996—, sec. 1998—, bd. trustees Baptist Found. S.C., 2001—. With USN, 1960-62. Recipient Disting Svc. award Brewton-Parker Coll., 1980, Disting. Svc. award North Greenville Coll., 1986. Mem. Nat. Soc. Fund Raising Execs., Greater Greer C. of C. (bd. dirs. 1981-84). Lodges: Rotary. Baptist. Avocation: reading. Office: Greenville Tech Coll PO Box 5616 Greenville SC 29606-5616 E-mail: paynegfp@GulTec.edu.

PAYNE, GERALD OLIVER, retired elementary education educator; b. East St. Louis, Ill., July 17, 1930; s. Amos Oliver and Suzanne Louise (Goussery) P.; m. Nancy Louise Ecklund, Aug. 8, 1959; children: Paul Clifton, Christopher Amos, Scott Eric, Miriam Louise, Susan Jeannette. BA, Yale U., 1953; MusB, U. Dubuque, Iowa, 1957; PhD, U. Wis., 1969. Tchr. pub. schs., Aspen, Colo., 1959-61; tchr. pub. schs. Madison, 1961-65; coord. fgn. langs., 1964-69; asst. dir. curriculum, 1967-69; assoc. prof. edn. SUNY, Buffalo, 1969-71, prof. edn., 1971-86, chmn. dept. curriculum and supervision, 1975-78, coord. cert. advanced studies in adminstrn. and supervision, 1969-75, 78-86, assoc. chmn. dept. elem. edn. and reading, 1985-86; chmn. dept. edn. and psychology Warren Wilson Coll., N.C., 1986-90, chmn. div. social sci. and profl. studies, 1987-90; tchr. Hendersonville (N.C.) County Schs., Hendersonville, 1990-96. Contbr. articles to profl. jours. Chmn. troop com. Greater Niagara Frontier coun. Boy Scouts Am., Lewiston, N.Y., 1974-76, scoutmaster, 1976-79; advisor Explorer Post, 1979-83, Order of Arrow, 1978-83; elder 1st Presbyn. Ch., Lewiston, 1978-83, 1st Presbyn. Ch., Hendersonville, N.C., 1991-94; leader Stephen Ministries. Mem. NEA (life), Western N.Y. Yale Alumni Assn. (mem. schs. com. 1972-83, dir. 1977-83), Nat. Middle Sch. Assn., Assn. for Supervision and Curriculum Devel., Phi Delta Kappa (exec. com. 1978-81, sec. 1985-86, pres.-elect 1986) Republican. Home: 316 Ridgemount Forest Trail Hendersonville NC 28739-9442 E-mail: ridgemount@ioa.com.

PAYNE, GORDON DOUGLAS, lawyer, researcher; b. Washington, Nov. 28, 1950; s. Gordon Ronald and Marrilee (Gibbs) P.; m. Janet Louise Lynch, June 23, 1984. A.B., Franklin and Marshall Coll., 1971; A.M., Rutgers U., 1973; J.D., Chgo. Kent Coll. Law, Ill. Inst Tech, 1979. Bar: Ill. 1979, U.S. Dist. Ct. (no. dist.) Ill. 1979, Wis. 1983, U.S. Dist. Ct. (we. dist.) Wis. 1983. Loan officer Cragin Fed. Savs. and Loan, Chgo., 1973-74, Skokie Trust and Savs. Bank, Ill., 1974-76; asst. v.p. Olympic Savs. and Loan, Berwyn, Ill., 1976-78; v.p. Gary-Wheaton Bank, Ill., 1978-80; mgr. product devel. div., atty. U.S. League Savs. Instn., Chgo., 1980-82; assoc. gen. counsel Credit Union Nat. Assn./CUNA Service Group, Madison, Wis., 1982— ; dir. H.B., Inc., Milw. Treas., bd. dirs. Boys Club, Hoffman Estates, Ill., 1975-77; committeeman Republican Committeeman Orgn., Downers Grove, Ill., 1978-82, mem. exec. com., 1980-82. Recipient Lord Strathcona medal Govt. of Can. Mem. ABA, Wis. Bar Assn., Chgo. Bar Assn., Co. Mil. Historians. Baptist. Home: 7738 Ox Trail Way Verona WI 53593-9640

PAYNE, HARRY MORSE, JR. architect; b. Norwood, Mass., Nov. 3, 1922; s. Harry Morse and Edna May (Beardsley) P.; m. Helen Marion Beasley, Aug. 29, 1946; children: Harry Morse, Thomas Beasley, Amelia Morse. Student, Boston Archtl. Center, 1946-49, MIT, 1949-50. Draftsman William G. Upham, Norwood, 1946-47; designer William Riseman Assos., Boston, 1947-49, Harry J. Korslund, Norwood, 1949-51, William Hoskins Brown, Boston, 1951-52; designer, prin. dir. The Architects Collaborative, Cambridge, Mass., 1952-86, pres., 1975-77, emeritus, 1986—, Boston Archtl. Center, 1963-65, 71-73; asst. prof. Harvard U. Grad. Sch. Design, 1954-63. Prin. works include U.S. Embassy, Athens, Greece, U. Baghdad, Iraq, Temple Israel, Boston, Quincy Sch., Boston, Nauset Regional H.S., Cape Cod, Mass.; author: The Survey System of the Old Colony, 1985, Name Change--Paine to Payne, 1992, Cape Cod Land Strategy, 1994, New England 17th Century Land Strategy, 1997, America's Stonehenge As Architecture, 1998, Payne Paine Family—England and Cape Cod, 1999. Served with USN, 1943-46. Fellow AIA; mem. Soc. Archtl. Historians, N.E. Antiquities Rsch. Assn., Boston Soc. Architects, Mass. State Assn. Architects, New Eng. Hist. and Geneal. Soc., The Colonial Soc. Mass., Mass. Soc. Genealogists (pres. 1986-88), Lincoln Hist. Soc. (pres. 1990-92). Home: 303 Winthrop Terr Bedford MA 01730

PAYNE, HOWARD JAMES, retired insurance company executive; b. Des Moines, Oct. 22, 1940; s. James W. and Wilma F. (Kever) P.; m. Mary J. Kellam, June 8, 1963; children: Scott D., Steven M. MBA, U. Iowa, 1986. CPCU; assoc. in underwriting, assoc. in mgmt. Underwiter Allied Ins. Co., Des Moines, 1963-70, br. underwriting mgr. Phoenix, 1973-75, asst. br. mgr. Santa Rosa, Calif., 1975-77; casualty underwriting mgr. Am. States Ins. Co., Indpls., 1970-73; asst. v.p. underwriting Lumberman's Mut. Ins. Co., Mansfield, Ohio, 1977-80; asst. v.p., underwriting mgr. Hastings (Mich.) Mutual Ins. Co., 1980-82; v.p. underwriting John Deere Ins. Co., Moline, Ill., 1982-86, v.p., regional mgr., 1986-90; v.p. credit ins. mgr. John Deere Ins. Co, Des Moines, 1990-93; v.p., spl. program mgr. John Deere Transp., Brookfield, Wis., 1993-99. Ins. instr. Am. States Ins. Co., Indpls., 1971-73, CPCU chpt., Phoenix, 1973-75; ins. instr. and adviser C.C. Mansfield, Ohio, 1978-80; pres. Am. States Credit Union, Indpls., 1973. Mem. CPCU Soc., West Des Moines C. of C. Republican. Avocations: tennis, physical fitness, reading. Home: PO Box 847 Cherokee Village AR 72525

PAYNE, JAMES RICHARD, environmental chemist; b. Anaheim, Calif., Sept. 3, 1947; s. Theodore L. and Laura P. (Schutz) P.; m. Marinee J. Pavlovich, June 29, 1968; children: Clayton Bennett, Taylor Sierra. BA with honors, Calif. State U., Fullerton, 1969; PhD, U. Wis., 1974. Chemist in engrng. coll. unit N.Am. Rockwell Corp., Downey, Calif., 1968-69; tchg. asst., rsch. asst., and NIH predoctoral fellow U. Wis., Madison, 1969-74; postdoctoral scholar Woods Hole (Mass.) Oceanographic Inst., 1974-75; asst. rsch. chemist U. Calif. Bodega Marine Lab., Bodega Bay, 1975-78; sr. chemist, asst. v.p., v.p. Sci. Applications Internat. Corp., La Jolla, Calif., 1978-91; sr. v.p., dir. rsch. SOUND Environ. Svcs., Inc., Carlsbad, 1991-96; mgr. chem. tech. br. Ogden Environ. & Energy Svcs. Co., Inc., San Diego, 1996; founder J.R. Payne Environ. Cons., $Drlsbad, 1997; pres. Payne Environ. Cons., Inc., Encinitas, 1998—, 1998—. Mem. exec. sci. and tech. coun. Sci. Applications Internat. Corp., La Jolla, 1985-91; mem. NAS/NRC Marine Bd.: Com. on Effectiveness of Oil Spill Dispersants, Washington, 1985-88. Co-author: Fate and Weathering of Petroleum Spills in the Marine Environment: A Literature Review and Synopsis, 1980, Petroleum Spills in the Marine Environment: The Chemistry and Formation of Water-in-Oil Emulsions and Tar Balls, 1985, Oil Spill Dispersants: Mechanisms of Action and Laboratory Tests, 1993; contbr. over 25 articles to profl. jours. Achievements include participant in two NAS/NRC studies and coms. on oil pollution in the marine environment and the use of oil spill dispersants; research on oil weathering, oil/ice interactions, remediation of hazardous waste sites. Home: 1651 Linda Sue Ln Encinitas CA 92024-2427 Office: Payne Environ Cons Inc Ste 201 317 N El Camino Real Encinitas CA 92024 Fax: 760-942-1036. E-mail: jamesrpayne@compuserve.com.

PAYNE, JEAN L. writer; b. Quincy, Mass., Jan. 13, 1932; d. Louis Pierre and Blanche Istella Lemire; m. Gregory D. Payne, June 28, 1954 (dec. Aug. 6, 1968); children: Douglas, Dwight. BA, Bates Coll., Lewiston, ME, 1953. Office worker Oldtown H.S., Old Town, Maine, 1946—49; bus. asst. Morin's, Old Towne, 1948—49; speech asst. Bates Coll., Lewiston, 1950—53; ins. writer Aetna Life Ins., Hartford, 1953—54; educator/libr. Lewiston H.S., Lewiston, 1954—55; libr., acquisitions Bates Ladd Libr., 1970—90; writer Free-lance Writer, 2002—. Mem.: Women's Lit. Union (pres. 1967), Art/Lit. Club (pres. 2002), LA Coll. Club (pres. 1956). Independent. Avocation: writing poetry. Home: 94 Marble Street Lewiston ME 04240-5344

PAYNE, JOHN ROSS, rare books, archives and photographs appraisal consulting company executive, library science educator; b. Clarksville, Tex., Dec. 4, 1941; BA, Tex. Christian U., 1963; MLS, North Tex. State U., 1967. Successively acting dir., asst. to dir., assoc. libr. for acquisitions, assoc. libr. for ops., rsch. assoc. Harry Ransom Humanities Rsch. Ctr. U. Tex., Austin, 1969-85, prof. Grad. Sch. Libr. and Info. Sci., 1988-89, 91-93, tchr. course in rare books and lit. manuscripts; dir. Payne Assocs., 1978—. Author: A Bibliography of W. H. Hudson, 1977, Modern British Fiction: An Exhibit, 1972; co-author: (with Elizabeth Johnson) Katherine Mansfield: An Exhibit, 1973, (with Adrian Goldstone) A Bibliographical Catalogue of John Steinbeck, 1975; contbr. articles to profl. jours. Lilly fellow Ind. U., 1967-68. Mem. ALA, Am. Soc. Appraisers (state dep. dir.), Appraisers Assn. Am., Soc. Am. Archivists (hon., speaker at Atlanta meeting 1988), Manuscripts Soc., Tex. Libr. Assn., Tex. State Hist. Assn., Book Club of Tex., Tex. and Southwestern Collectors' Assn., Grolier Club, Book Collectors of L.A. Address: 2309 Camino Alto Austin TX 78746-2404 E-mail: payne@payne-associates.com.

PAYNE, KEVIN, professional soccer organization executive; m. Pamela Payne; children: Ashley, Rebecca. Tourism mktg. exec. Vail, Avon and Beaver Creek, Colo., 1983-89; dir. mktg., dep. exec. dir. U.S. Soccer, 1989-91; exec. v.p. sales and mktg. Soccer USA Ptnrs./API Soccer, Herndon, Va., 1991-94; pres., CEO API Soccer, 1994—, Washington Soccer, N.Y.C., 1994—, DC United, 1994—2001; sr. v.p., mng. dir. AEG Soccer, 2001—. Bd. dirs. Washington Soccer, L.P., US Soccer Found., US Soccer, Soccer 94, Washington, D.C. Soccer; exec. prodr. ceremonies World Alpine Ski Championships, Vail, Colo., 1989; exec. com. U.S. Soccer Found. Office: DC United 1412 Newbrook Dr Ste 170 Chantilly VA 20151 Fax: 703-378-5145.

PAYNE, LADELL, retired college president; b. Birmingham, Ala., Dec. 6, 1933; s. Clyde Ladell and Martha Gerusia (McBrayer) P.; m. Mary Jean Taylor, Aug. 23, 1954; children: Lisa, Jennifer BA with honors, Samford U., 1955; MA in English, La. State U., 1956; PhD in English, Stanford U., 1966; LittD, Samford U., 1996; DHL, Randolph-Macon Coll., 1998. From instr. to prof. English, chmn. dept. lit. and presdl. asst. Claremont McKenna Coll., Calif., 1960-79; pres. Randolph-Macon Coll., Ashland, Va., 1979-97, prof. emeritus, 1997—, pres. emeritus, 1998—. Fulbright lectr. U. Vienna, Austria, 1971-72; nat. cons. Ctr. for Study So. Culture, U. Miss., Oxford, 1980—; adminstrv. assoc. Am. Coun. on Edn., Washington, 1979, mem. nat. panel, commn. on women in higher edn., 1981-97; founding mem. pres.'s commn. Nat. Collegiate Athletic Assn., 1984-97. Author: Thomas Wolfe, 1969, Black Novelists and the Southern Literary Tradition, 1981; contbr. articles on William Faulkner, Robert Penn Warren, Thomas Wolfe, and Ellen Glasgow to profl. jours. Mem. Va. bd. dirs. NCCJ, 1980-92, chmn. Va. region, Richmond, 1982-85; trustee, mem. exec. com. The Collegiate Schs., Richmond, 1986-89; bd. dirs. Music in the Mountains, Nevada City, Calif., 2000-02. NEH fellow, 1973. Mem. Nat. Assn. Ind. Colls. and Univs. (bd. dirs. 1990-93), Coun. on Postsecondary Accreditation (bd. dirs. 1991-93), Pi Kappa Phi, Phi Beta Kappa. Methodist. Avocation: classical music.

PAYNE, LUCY ANN SALSBURY, law librarian, educator, lawyer; b. Utica, N.Y., July 5, 1952; d. James Henry and Dorothy Eileen (Seavy) Salsbury; m. Albert E. Payne, June 2, 1973 (div. 1983); 1 child, Joni Eileen. MusB, Andrews U., 1974; MA, Loma Linda (Calif.) U., 1979; JD, U. Notre Dame, Ind., 1988; MLS, U. Mich., 1990. Bar: Ind. 1988, Mich. 1988, U.S. Dist. Ct. (no. and so. dists.) Ind. 1988, U.S. Ct. Appeals (7th cir.) 1992. Rsch. specialist Kresge Libr. Law Sch. U. Notre Dame, 1988—90, asst. libr., 1990—91, assoc. libr., 1991—96, libr., 1996—2002. Vis. prof. Notre Dame London Law Programme, 2001. Contbr. articles to profl. jours. Recipient Rev. Paul J. Foik award, 2001. Adventist. Home and Office: 4420 Barrett NW Albuquerque NM 87114

PAYNE, MARGARET ANNE, lawyer; b. Aug. 10, 1947; d. John Hilliard and Margaret Mary (Naughton) P. Student, Trinity Coll., Washington, 1965-66; BA magna cum laude, U. Cin., 1969; JD, Harvard U., 1972; LLM in Taxation, NYU, 1976. Bar: N.Y. 1975, U.S. Dist. Ct. (so. dist.) N.Y. 1975, Calif. 1979, U.S. Dist. Ct. (so. dist.) Calif. 1979. Assoc. Mudge, Rose, Guthrie, and Alexander, N.Y.C., 1972-75, Davis, Polk and Wardwell, N.Y.C., 1976-78, Seltzer, Caplan, Wilkins and McMahon, San Diego, 1978-79, Higgs, Fletcher and Mack, San Diego, 1980-82, ptnr., 1983-90, of counsel, 1991—. Adj. prof. grad. tax program U. San Diego Sch. Law, 1979-89, Calif. Western Sch. Law, San Diego, 1980-82; judge pro tem Mcpl. Ct., San Diego Jud. Dist., 1983, 92. Bd. dirs. Artist Chamber Ensemble, Inc., 1983-86, Libr. Assn. La Jolla, Calif., 1983-86, San Diego County Crimestoppers, Inc., 1993-95, San Diego Crime Commn., 1994-95, St. Augustine's H.S., 1994-95, San Diego Hist. Soc., 1993-95. Mem. ABA, Calif. State Bar Assn., San Diego County Bar Assn., Mortar Bd., Guidon Soc., Charter 100, Phi Beta Kappa. Office: Higgs Fletcher & Mack 401 W A St Ste 2600 San Diego CA 92101-7913

PAYNE, MARILYN ANN, physical therapist; b. Adams, Mass., Aug. 9, 1952; d. Leonard Robert Hamlin and Dorothy Mabel Gebauer; m. Robert Allen Payne, May 31, 1975; children: Michael, Kevin. BS, U. Conn., 1974. Registered phys. therapist, Mass. Phys. therapist Northampton (Mass.) VA Hosp., 1974-76, Easter Seal Rehab. Ctr. Fairfield County, Bridgeport, Conn., 1976-78; phys. therapist level II, clin. coord. edn. Cooley Dickinson Hosp., Northampton, 1978—. Asst. instr. cross-country skiing Bill Koch Youth Ski League, Worthington, Mass., 1996-97. Avocations: softball, biking, cross-country skiing, gardening, volleyball. Home: Goss Hill Rd Worthington MA 01098 Office: Cooley Dickinson Hosp 30 Locust St Northampton MA 01060-2093

PAYNE, MARY ALICE MCGILL, behavior management healthcare quality consultant; b. Centreville, Miss., Jan. 2, 1936; d. Robert Malcolm and Alice (Brannon) McGill; m. Donald R. Payne, Aug. 8, 1958; children: Patricia Alice, Margaret Jean, Donald Paul. Diploma, So. Bapt. Hosp. Sch. Nursing, New Orleans, 1958; BSN, Northwestern State U., 1962. Psychiat. nursing instr. McNeese U., Lake Charles, La., 1964-67; drug rsch. nurse dept. psychiatry Med. Sch., Tulane U., New Orleans, 1969-79; psychiat. nurse East La. State Hosp., Jackson, 1959-80; acting CEO Feliciana Forensic Facility, 1989, quality assurance dir., 1984-91, med. staff quality coms., 1991—. Mem. ANA, Am. Psychiat. Nurses Assn., Am. Coll. Healthcare Execs. (assoc.), Am. Coll. Med. Quality, La. State Nurses Assn., Nat. Assn. Healthcare Quality, La. Assn. Healthcare Quality, Bapt. Nursing Fellowship, Feliciana Dist. Nurses Assn., Am. Soc. Quality Control, Nat. League for Nursing. Home: 3226 E College St PO Box 144 Jackson LA 70748-0144 E-mail: payne144@worldnet.att.net.

PAYNE, MARY LIBBY, retired judge; b. Gulfport, Miss., Mar. 27, 1932; d. Reece O. and Emily Augusta (Cook) Bickerstaff; m. Bobby R. Payne; children: Reece Allen, Glenn Russell. Student, Miss. U. for Women, 1950-52; BA in Polit. Sci. with distinction, U. Miss., 1954, LLB, 1955. Bar: Miss. 1955. Ptnr. Bickerstaff & Bickerstaff, Gulfport, 1955-56; sec. Guaranty Title Co., Jackson, Miss., 1957; assoc. Henley, Jones, & Henley, 1958-61; freelance rschr. Pearl, 1961-63; solo practitioner Brandon, 1963-68; exec. dir. Miss. Judiciary Commn., Jackson, 1968-70; chief drafting & rsch. Miss. Ho. Reps., 1970-72; asst. atty. gen. State Atty. Gen. Office, 1972-75; founding dean, assoc. prof. Sch. Law Miss. Coll., 1975-78, prof., 1978-94; judge Miss. Ct. Appeals, 1995—2001; ret., 2001. Mem. bd. disting. alumnae Miss. U. Women, 1988—2000. Contbr. articles to profl. jours. Founder, bd. dirs. Christian Conciliation Svc., Jackson, 1983-93; bd. dirs. Exchange Club's Child Abuse Prevention Ctr. of Jackson, 1999—; counsel Christian Action Com. Rankin Bapt. Assn., Pearl, 1968-92; advisor Covenant Ministerial Fellowship, 1995—. Named Miss. Coll. Lawyer of Yr., Miss. Coll. Sch. Law Alumni Assn., 1998, Outstanding Woman Lawyer, Miss. Women Lawyers Assn., 1999, Susie Blue Buchanan award, Women in Profession Com. of Miss. Bar, 2000; recipient Book of Golden Deeds award, Pearl Exch. Club, 1989, Excellence medallion, Miss. U. Women, 1990, Woman of Yr. award, Miss. Assn. Women Higher Edn., 1989, Power of One award, Miss. Govs. Conf., 1996. Fellow Am. Bar Found.; mem. Miss. Bar Found., Christian Legal Soc. (nat. bd. dirs. 1992-2001, Skeeter Ellis Svc. to Law Students award 1999), Margaret Brent League. Baptist. Avocations: public speaking, travel, needlepoint, sewing, reading.

PAYNE, MAXWELL CARR, JR. retired psychology educator; b. Nashville, Feb. 9, 1927; s. Carr and Mary Evans (Tarpley) P.; m. Juanita Campbell, Oct. 17, 1958; children: Maxwell Carr III, Elizabeth Campbell McKinney, Mary Allison Klausner. AB, Vanderbilt U., 1949; AM, Princeton U., 1950, PhD, 1951. Rsch. assoc. U. Ill., Urbana, 1951-54; asst. prof. psychology Ga. Inst. Tech., Atlanta, 1954-60, assoc. prof., 1961-65, prof., 1965-90, ret., 1991. Cons. Lockheed-Ga. Co., Marietta, 1963; testing dir. Aircrew Ctr., Am. Insts. Rsch., Atlanta, 1960-75; faculty Atlanta Sch. Art, 1970; mem. Ga. State Bd.

Examiners of Pyschologists, 1970-74. Contbr. articles to profl. jours. Sunday Sch. tchr. Northside United Meth. Ch., Atlanta, 1989—. With USNR, 1944-46. Recipient Disting. Tchr. award Ga. Inst. Tech., 1970. Fellow AAAS; mem. Am. Psychol. Assn., Ga. Psychol. Assn. (Cert. of Merit), Southeastern Psychol. Assn., So. Soc. Philosophy and Psychology (treas. 1971-74, pres. 1985-86), Ga. Inst. Tech. Faculty Club (pres. 1970), Phi Beta Kappa, Sigma Xi, Phi Kappa Phi, Omicron Delta Kappa, Beta Theta Pi. Avocation: gardening. Home: 3035 Farmington Dr NW Atlanta GA 30339-4704

PAYNE, MEREDITH JORSTAD, physician; b. St. Louis, Feb. 7, 1927; d. Louis Helmar and Cleone Gladys (Branian) Jorstad; m. Spencer Payne, 1948 (div. 1959); m. James McGarity, 1965 (div. 1977); children: Maureen Meredith, James Louis. AB, Washington U., St. Louis, 1947, MD, 1950; MBA, Lindenwood U., 1999. Diplomate Am. Bd. Surgery, Am. Bd. Plastic Surgery. Intern gen. surgery St. Louis City Hosp., 1950-51, asst. resident surgery, 1951-54; chief surg. resident Roswell Park Meml. Hosp., Buffalo, 1954-55; chief plastic surgery resident Allentown (Pa.) Gen. Hosp., 1955-57; clin. instr. surgery Washington U. Med. Sch., 1957-70; vis. surgeon Homer G. Phillips Hosp., St. Louis, 1957-70; staff St. Luke's, St. Louis and Bethesda, 1957—, St. Mary's, 1988—; chief plastic surgery Vets. Hosp., 1986-98; assoc. prof. plastic surgery (clin.) St. Louis U. Sch. Medicine, St. Louis, 1986—. Med. dir. Unity Clft Palate Clinic; asst. dir. Bethesda Delworth Nursing Home, 1997—. Contbr. articles to profl. jours. Fellow ACS; mem. AMA, Am. Soc. Plastic and Reconstructive Surgery, Mo. Med. Assn. (del., councillor 1988X), St. Louis Met. Med. Soc. (councillor 1983-86, sec. 1998-99, v.p. 1999-00), Am. Cleft Palate Assn., Roswell Park Surgery Assn., So. Med. Assn., Washington U. Med. Alumni Assn., Am. Geriatrics Soc., Midwestern Assn. Plastic Surgeons, Pan Am. Med. Assn., City Hosp. Alumni Assn., Soc. Head and Neck Surgeons, St. Louis Area Soc. Plastic Surgeons (pres. 1990-93), City Hosp. Alumni Assn. (v.p. 1995-97, pres. 1997), Mo. Assn. Plastic and Reconstructive Surgery (treas. 1995X, v.p. 1997, pres. 1998), St. Louis Surg. Soc. (v.p. 1998), AMWA (treas. St. Louis chpt. 1995), Order Eastern Star, Zonta (St. Louis pres. 1968-69), College Club (bd. dirs. St. Louis 1983-85). Avocations: skiing, tennis, sewing, knitting, gardening. Home: 7314 Westmoreland Dr Saint Louis MO 63130-4240

PAYNE, MICHAEL LEE, association management executive; b. Monroe, N.C., Aug. 6, 1948; s. Robert H. and Martha (Brooks) P. BA in History, U. S.C., 1970, BA in Journalism, 1971; BA in Polit. Sci., 1972. Program dir. Coastal Plains Reg. Commn., Washington, 1972-75; dir. fed. rels. Office Coastal Zone Mgmt. NOAA, 1975-80; investment specialist Econ. Dirs. Adminstrn. U.S. Dept. Commerce, 1980-82; dep. to asst. sec. for congl. affairs Office of Sec. U.S. Dept. Commerce, 1982-84; exec. v.p. Smith-Bucklin Assoc., 1984—. Bd. dirs. Smith-Bucklin Assoc., PCMA, CEIR, INCOW; mem. worldwide adv. bd. Hilton; presenter to hospitality industry. Author: Complete Guide to Non-Profit Management, 1993; contbr. numerous articles to profl. publs. Mem. Am. Soc. Assn. Execs., Profl. Convention Mgrs. Assn., Meeting Profls. Internat. Avocations: travel, tennis, fishing, handball, biking. Office: Smith-Bucklin Assoc 2025 M St NW # 800 Washington DC 20036-3309

PAYNE, MYRNA CARLEEN, communications executive; b. Lindsay, Calif., June 24, 1938; d. Carl and Olivia Maude (Smith) Main; m. Charles Aubrey Payne, Oct. 20, 1956 (div. Feb. 1985); children: Diane Lynn Payne Monti, Alan Kent. AA, Va. Intermont Coll., 1956; AS, Victor Valley Coll., Victorville, Calif., 1977; student in Engring., Coll. of the AF, USAF, Dept. of Def., 1978, Antelope Valley Coll., Lancaster, Calif., 1985. Cert. USAF journeymay electrician, 1975, electronic technician 1981, flight status mil. test aircraft, 1988. Supr. billeting Dept. of Def. USAF, Travis AFB, Calif., 1965-68, supr. med. records MacDill AFB, Fla., 1970-72, supr. adminstrn. George AFB, Calif., 1973-74, electrician, 1974-79, electrician/engr. technician Rocket Propulsion Lab. Edwards AFB, 1980-87, electronic integrated specialist, air crew, test aircraft, 1988-95, electronic technician, spl. instr., 1989-95; dir. Exec. Security & Communication, Sydney, Australia, 1995—. Owner C&M Enterprises, Lancaster, Calif., 1987-89; cons. World Airlines, 1995—; chair Civilian of Month bd., George AFB, 1974-88; mem. com. civilian adv. bd., Rocket Propulsion Lab., 1980-87. Active Fed. Women's Orgn., USAF Edwards AFB, 1980-95. Recipient Best Photo prize State of Calif., 1990; recipient numerous awards USAF, worldwide. Mem. NAFE. Republican. Methodist. Avocation: photography. Home: 428 W Avenue J # 22 Lancaster CA 93534-3661 Office: Exec Security & Comm PO Box 162 Flemington Markets NSW 2129 Australia also: 428 W Avenue J Ste 22 Lancaster CA 93534-3661

PAYNE, NANCY SLOAN, retired visual arts educator; b. Johnstown, Pa., Aug. 5, 1937; d. Arthur J. and Esther Jenkins (Ashcom) Sloan; m. Randolph Allen Payne, Nov. 19, 1970; 1 child, Anna Sloan. BS in Art Edn., Pa. State U., 1959; MFA in Sculpture, George Washington U., 1981. Visual arts tchr. Alexandria (Va.) Schs., 1960-61; art tchr. sch. program Corcoran Gallery of Art, Washington, 1962; visual arts tchr. Montgomery County Schs., Rockville, Md., 1965-67; instr. No. Va. C.C., Alexandria, 1971-73, Mt. Vernon Coll., Washington, 1971-73; visual arts tchr. Arlington (Va.) County Schs., 1967-79; edn. coord. The Textile Mus., Washington, 1982-87; mid. sch. visual arts tchr., K-12 dept. chair St. Stephen's and St. Agnes Sch., Alexandria, 1988-97; ret. Co-founder Fiber Art Study Group, Washington, 1988—; co-owner Art Gallery, Chincoteague Island, Va., 1989—. Exhibited in group shows at Craftsmen's Biennial Va. Commonwealth U. (Excellence in Textiles award), 1973, Va. Craftsmen Biennial The Va. Mus., 1980, Creative Crafts Coun. 15th Biennial, 1982, Alexandria's Sculpture Festival, 1983, 84, 13 Fiber Artists Exhbn. Foundry Gallery, Washington, 1985. Founding mem. Alexandria Soc. for Preservation Black Heritage, Alexandria, 1982—. Mem. Nat. Art Edn. Assn. Democrat. Avocations: growing flowers, collecting hub caps, McDonald toys, and polit./campaign items. Home: 6258 Circle Dr Chincoteague VA 23336-2222 Office: Clouds/Folly Gallery Chincoteague VA 23336

PAYNE, NELLETON SWITZER, II, neurosurgeon; b. Kansas City, Mo., Dec. 22, 1940; s. Nettleton S. and Mildred Alice (Mitchell) P.; m. Elizabeth Penn Hammond, Dec. 29, 1964; children: Elizabeth Alice, Nettleton S. III. Postdoctoral, U. Rochester, N.Y., 1972; BA, Stanford U., 1963; MD, U. Kans., 1967. Diplomate Am. Bd. Neurol. Surgery (examiner 1987). Intern, resident in neurosurgery Strong Meml. Hosp./U. Rochester, N.Y., 1967-72; chief neurosurgeon Atlanta VA Hosp., 1974-79; asst. prof. neurosurgery Emory U., Atlanta, 1974-79; ptnr. Emory U. Clinic, 1977-79; pres. Peachtree Neurosurgery, 1979—. Contbr. articles to med. jours. Donor Juvenile Diabetes Found., 1992—. Maj. U.S. Army, 1972-74, Republic of Korea. Mem. Am. Assn. Neurol. Surgeons, Congress Neurol. Surgeons, Neurol. Soc. Am. (bd. dirs. 1996-98), Neurosurg. Sect. Soc. (pres. 1989), So. Neurosurg. Soc., Ga. Neurosurg. Soc. (pres.), Capital City Club, Mauna Kea Club. Republican. Avocation: golf. Office: Peachtree Neurosurgery PC 993 Johnson Ferry Rd NE # F Atlanta GA 30342-1620

PAYNE, PAULA MARIE, minister; b. Waukegan, Ill., Jan. 13, 1952; d. Percy Howard and Annie Maude (Canady) P. BA, U. Ill., 1980; MA, U. San Francisco, 1986; MDiv, Wesley Theol. Sem., 1991, student, 1995—. Ordained to ministry United Meth. Ch., 1990. Chaplain for minority affairs Am. U., Washington, 1988-89; chaplain, intern NIH, Bethesda, Md., 1989-90; pastor Asbury United Meth. Ch., Charles Town, W.Va., 1990—. Supt. ch. sch. United Meth. Ch., Oxon Hill, Md., 1989-90; mem. AIDS task force Wesley Theol. Sem., Washington, 1988-89; mem. retreat. com. Balt. Conf., 1990—; chair scholarship com. Asbury United Meth. Ch., 1990—. Bd. dirs. AIDS Task Force Jefferson County, Charles Town, 1991—, Cmty. Ministries, Charles Town, 1991—; formerly N.H. state v.p. Ch. Women United, now pres.; mem. ethics com. Concord Hosp. Tech. sgt. USAF, 1984-88; chaplain Army N.G., Md., 1994-96, Mass. 2001; chaplain USAFR, 1997. Recipient Cert. of Recognition, Ill. Ho. of Reps., 1988, 20th Century award of Achievement Internat. Biog. Ctr., Cambridge, Eng., 1993, 1st Five Hundred, Cambridge, 1994, Citizen's citation, City of Balt., 1994, others; Ethnic Minority scholar United Meth. Ch., 1988-89, Brandenburg scholar, 1988-89, Tadlock scholar, 1989-90, Calvary Fellow scholar Calvary United Meth. ch., 1989-90. Mem. AAUW, U. Ill. Alumni Assn. (bd. dirs. 1987-88), Alpha Kappa Alpha (pres. local chpt. 1974-76, v.p. 1973). Republican. Home: PO Box 356 Contoocook NH 03229-0356 E-mail: revpmpumc@aol.com., revpmpumc@hotmail.com. *Education can be as deep as the ocean.*

PAYNE, RICHARD EARL, physical oceanographer; b. Holyoke, Mass., Apr. 2, 1936; s. Lester Earl Payne and Marjorie Stead Peterson; m. Sheila Tulk Payne, Aug. 25, 1988; children: Heather, Stephanie; m. Deborah Siegal, Oct. 9, 1988. BS, Bowdoin Coll., 1958; MS, U. Md., 1962; PhD, U. R.I., 1971. Physicist Nat. Bur. of Stds., Washington, 1961—93; rsch. asst. Woods Hole Oceanographic Instn., Mass., 1963—67, postdoctoral investigator, 1971—72, rsch. assoc., 1973—99, rsch. specialist, 1999—2001, emeritus, 2001—. Contbr. articles to profl. jours. Fellow NATO postdoctoral fellow, U. Southampton, Eng., 1972—73. Mem. Am. Meteorol. Soc., Am. Geophys. Union. Avocations: folk musician, bicyclist. Office: Woods Hole Oceanographic Instn MS 30 Woods Hole MA 02543

PAYNE, RICHARD HAROLD, university research administrator; b. Lowell, Mass., Apr. 30, 1941; s. Calvin Lee and Helen Josephine (Hennessey) P.; m. Harriett Gean Rowan, Feb. 4, 1961 (dec. Feb. 1977); children: James Richard, Deloria Linn; m. Kathy Leigh Freydenfeldt, Mar. 20, 1978. ABJ, U. Ga., 1965, MA, 1966, PhD, 1970. Asst. prof. polit. sci. The Citadel, Charleston, S.C., 1966-72; prof. polit. sci. Sam Houston State U., Huntsville, 1972—, chair dept., 1972-99, assoc. v.p. rsch. and grad. studies, 1999—. Editor Tex. Jour. Polit. Studies, 1988-90; contbr. articles to profl. jours. Bd. dirs. Tex. Rsch. Inst. for Environ. Studies, Huntsville, 1991-97; mem., vol. positions Boy Scouts Am., Huntsville and Houston, 1974-94. Mem. Aubudon Soc. (pres. Huntsville chpt. 1978-79, 84-85), Tex. Ornithol. Soc., Okla. Ornithol. Soc., Am. Birding Assn. (bd. dirs. 1998—, pres. 1999—), Internat. Ecotourism Soc., Ecotourism Assn. Australia, Nat. Coun. Univ. Res. Adminstrs., Policy Studies Orgn., S.W. Assn. for Can. Studies, Western Social Sci. Assn., Wildlife Mgmt. Inst., Watchable Wildlife, Inc. (vice chmn. bd. dirs. 1999—), Phi Kappa Phi, Pi Sigma Alpha, Kappa Tau Delta, Phi Eta Sigma. Avocations: birding, camping, hiking. Office: Sam Houston State U Office Rsch and Sponsored Huntsville TX 77341

PAYNE, ROGER LEE, geographer; b. Winston-Salem, N.C., Oct. 26, 1946; s. Irvin Lee and Gladys Odel (Binkley) P.; m. Sara Lucinda Parker, Aug. 16, 1970 (div. Feb. 1992); 1 child, Jennifer Nicole; m. Anne F. Remen, June 11, 1995. BA, East Carolina U., 1969, MA, 1972. Geographer, chief geog. names U.S. Geol. Survey, Reston, Va., 1974—; instr. geography and history Pan Am. Inst./U.S. Geog. Survey, 1989—; exec. sec. U.S. Bd. Names, U.S. Geol. Survey, Washington, 1990—. Instr. East Caroline U., Greenville, N.C., 1969-71, George Washington U., Washington, 1977-90, George Mason U., Fairfax, Va., 1979-83, 98—, Benjamin Franklin U., Washington, 1985-87; del. UN, N.Y.C., 1987—, instr., 1995—; mem. scientist exch. Geol. Survey, Beijing, 1989; instr. Nat. Black Colls., Howard U., 1985; book reviewer AAAS, 1975—; mem. Antarctica Sci. Field Program, 1999-2000; cons. in field. Author: Urban Development in South Africa, 1972, Place Names of Outer Banks, 1985, Manuals on Auto Names, 1987, 89, 97; coord., editor: (book series) National Gazetter U.S., 1982—; contbr. articles to profl. jours. Chmn. E. Carolina Blood Dr., Greenville, 1969. Lt. USAF, 1970-72. Recipient Guy Buzzard award Gamma Theta Upsilon, 1970; Superior Svc. award Geol. Survey, 1988, Outstanding Achievement award, 1997. Fellow Explorers Club; mem. Assn. Am. Geographers (various coms. 1969-95, pres. mid-Atlantic divsn. 1981-82, treas., sec.), Am. Name Soc. (pres. 1989), Am. Nat. Std. Inst. (rep. 1986—), Cosmos Club. Avocation: hiking. Home: 47762 Hammerstone Way Sterling VA 20165-4769 Office: US Geol Survey 523 National Ctr 12201 Sunrise Valley Dr Reston VA 20192-0523 E-mail: rpayne@usgs.gov.

PAYNE, ROGER SEARLE, zoology researcher and administrator, conservationist; b. N.Y.C., Jan. 29, 1935; m. Katy Boynton, 1960 (div. 1985); children: John, Holly, Laura Sam; m. Lisa Harrow, Aug. 18, 1991. AB in Animal Behavior, Harvard U., 1957; PhD, Cornell U., 1961. Rsch. zoologist Inst. for Rsch. in Animal Behavior N.Y. Zool. Inst., N.Y.C., 1968-71; asst. prof. biology Rockefeller U., 1968-71; founder, pres. Ocean Alliance, Lincoln, Mass., 1971—. Author: Among Whales, 1995; host (TV documentary) In the Company of Whales, 1992 (series) Ocean Planet, 1994-95; co-writer, co-dir. (film) Whales, 1995. Co-recipient Albert Schweitzer medal Animal Welfare Inst., 1980; recipient Joseph Wood Krutch medal Humane Soc. U.S., 1989, Lyndhurst prize Lyndhurst Found., 1984; genius grantee John D. and Catherine T. MacArthur Found., 1984, Global 500 award UN, 1988; knighted, Netherlands, 1977. Home: 2141 Biscuit Hl South Woodstock VT 05071-9530 Office: Ocean Alliance 191 Weston Rd Lincoln MA 01773-4516 E-mail: rpayne@oceanalliance.org.

PAYNE, RONALD DEAN, h band director; b. Shelby, N.C., May 5, 1953; s. Marion Dean and Melba George Payne; m. Gail Kistler, July 9, 1993; children: Heather Hope, Alex, Adam. MusB in Edn., East Carolina U., 1975, MusM, 1983. Cert. music N.C. Dir. bands Ayden (N.C.) -Grifton H.S., 1976—84, Independence H.S., Charlotte, 1984—98; dir. bands, fine arts dept. chair Providence H.S., 1998—. Mem.: N.C. Bandmasters Assn. (pres. 1994—96, award of excellence 1993), Music Educators Nat. Conf. (cert., registered 1991), Am. Sch. Band Directors Assn., Phi Mu Alpha, Phi Kappa Lambda, Phi Kappa Phi. Home: 13335 Mint Lake Dr Matthews NC 28105-3697 Office: Providence H S 1800 Pineville-Matthews Rd Charlotte NC 28270-0330 Office Fax: 704-343-3956. Personal E-mail: rpayne5@carolina.rr.com. Business E-Mail: phsmband@juno.com.

PAYNE, ROY STEVEN, judge; b. New Orleans, Aug. 30, 1952; s. Fred J. and Dorothy Julia (Peck) P.; m. Laureen Fuller, Sept. 8, 1973; children: Julie Elizabeth, Kelly Kathryn, Alex Steven, Michael Lawrence. BA with distinction, U. Va., 1974; JD, La. State U., 1977; LLM, Harvard U., 1980. Bar: La. 1977, U.S. Dist. Ct. (we. dist.) La. 1980, U.S. Ct. Appeals (5th cir.) 1980, U.S. Supreme Ct. 1983. Law clk. to judge U.S. Dist. Ct., Shreveport, La., 1977-79; assoc. Blanchard, Walker, O'Quin & Roberts, 1980-83, ptnr., 1984-87; U.S. Magistrate judge We. Dist. La., 1987—. Instr. New Eng. Sch. Law, Boston, 1979-80. Contbr. articles to profl. jours. Chmn. Northwest La. Legal Svcs. Assn., Shreveport, 1984-85. Mem. 5th Cir. Bar Assn., 5th Cir. Jud. Coun. (magistrate judges com. 1992—), La. State Bar Assn. (editorial bd. Forum jour., 1983-87, legal aid com.), Fed. Magistrate Judges Assn., Shreveport Bar Assn., La. Assn. Def. Counsel (bd. dirs. 1987), Harry V. Booth Am. Inn of Ct. (pres. elect 1994-95, pres. 1996-98), Order of Coif, Rotary, Phi Kappa Phi, Phi Delta Phi. Republican. Methodist. E-mail: Roy. Home: 12494 Harts Island Rd Shreveport LA 71115-8505 Office: US Courthouse 300 Fannin St Ste 4300 Shreveport LA 71101-3122 E-mail: Payne@lawd.uscourts.gov.

PAYNE, R.W., JR. lawyer; b. Norfolk, Va., Mar. 16, 1936; s. Roland William and Margaret (Sawyer) P.; m. Gail Willingham, Sept. 16, 1961; children: Darrell, Preston, Darby, Clinton. BA in English, U. N.C., 1958, LLB, 1961, Stetson U., 1962. Bar: Fla. 1963, U.S. Dist. Ct. (so. dist.) 1964, U.S. Ct. Appeals (11th cir.) 1965, U.S. Supreme Ct. 1970. Assoc. Roney & Beach, St. Petersburg, Fla., 1963-64, Nichols, Gaither, Beckham, Colson & Spence, Miami, 1964-67; ptnr. Spence, Payne, Masington, 1967-95, Payne, Leeds, Colby & Robinson, P.A., Miami, 1995-97; pvt. practice, 1997, 98; ptnr. McLuskey, McDonald & Payne, P.A., 1999-2001; lawyer R.W. Payne Jr. P.A., 2001—. Presenter numerous profl. convs. and seminars. Contbr. articles to legal jours., legal edn. books. Mem. Ottawa Roughriders, Can. Football League, fall 1958; capt. football team U. N.C., 1957, bd. dirs., v.p. alumni bd., 1984-92, bd. dirs. edn. found., 1988-92; bd. dirs. Chem. Dependency Tng. Inst.; past pres. Coral Gables (Fla.) Sr. H.S. Athletic Boosters Club; past bd. dirs. Coral Gables War Meml. Youth Ctr., bd. trustees 1st United Meth. Ch. Coral Gables; past mem. gov.'s coun. on phys. fitness and sports, Fla.; past assoc. mem. Jr. Orange Bowl Com. With USMC, 1959. Fellow Am. Coll. Trial Lawyers, Internat. Acad. Trial Lawyers; mem. ABA, ATLA, Am. Bd. Trial Advocates, Fla. Bar Assn., Acad. Fla. Trial Lawyers (past mem. bd. govs.), Dade County Bar Assn. (past bd. dirs.), Dade County Trial Lawyers Assn. (founder, past pres.), Bankers Club, Miami Club, Univ. Club, Coral Reef Yacht Club, Order of Golden Fleece, Order of Old Well, Sigma Chi, Phi Delta Phi. Avocations: boating, golf, diving. Office: RV Payne Jr 2645 S Bayshore Dr Ate 1503 Miami FL 33133 E-mail: paynerw@bellsouth.net.

PAYNE, SIDNEY STEWART, retired archbishop; b. Fogo, Nfld., Can., June 6, 1932; m. Selma Carlson, 1962; children: Carla Ann, Christopher Stewart, Robert Clement, Angela Marie Louise. BA, Meml. U., St. John's, Nfld., 1958; lic. of theology, Queen's Coll., St. John's, 1958; BDiv, Gen. Synod, 1968; DDiv (hon.), King's Coll., Halifax, N.S., Can., 1981. Ordained priest Anglican Ch., 1958, bishop, 1978, archbishop, 1990. Deacon Mission of Happy Valley, Goose Bay, Labrador, Nfld., Can., 1957-65; rector Parish of Bay Roberts, Can., 1965-70, Parish of St. Anthony, 1970-78, 1976-78; bishop Diocese of Western Nfld., 1978-90, archbishop of Western Nfld. and Met. Eccles. Province of Can., 1990-97; ret., 1997. Pres. Diocesan Synod, chmn. exec. com., mem. ex-officio diocesan coms.; pres. Provincial Synod, Provincial Coun.; chair Provincial House of Bishops; mem. long range planning com., ministry com., mem. nat. exec. coun. Partners in World Mission, Stewardship and Fin. Devel. Com.; mem. Anglican/Roman Cath. Bishops' Dialogue, Can.; active Provincial and Nat. House of Bishops. Mem. Internat. Grenfell Assn. (past bd. dirs.). Avocations: reading, walking, gardening, cross-country skiing. Home: PO Box 2255 R R 1 Stn Main Corner Brook NF Canada A2H 2N2

PAYNE, STEVEN LAWRENCE, priest; b. Ames, Iowa, July 25, 1950; s. Lawrence Edward and Ruth Marian (Winterstein) P. BA in Philosophy magna cum laude, Cornell U., 1972, MA in Philosophy, 1976, PhD in Philosophy, 1982; MA in Theology, Cath. U. Am., 1981. Ordained priest Roman Catholic Ch., 1982. Asst. instr. Cornell U., Ithaca, N.Y., 1974-75; instr. Weston Sch. of Theology, Cambridge, Mass., 1983-84, De Sales Sch. Theology, Washington, 1988-90; editl. dir. ICS Publ., Brighton, Mass., 1990-95, editor-in-chief Washington, 1995—. Lectr. Washington Theol. Union, 1998—. Contbr. articles to ch. publs. Mem. N.Am. Carmelite Inst., Inst. Carmelite Studies. Home: 2131 Lincoln Rd NE Washington DC 20002-1151

PAYNE, THOMAS L. university official; b. Bakersfield, Calif., Oct. 17, 1941; s. Harry LeRoy and Opal Irene (Ansel) P.; m. S. Alice Lewis, Feb. 1, 1963; children: Jacob, Joanna. AA in Liberal Arts, Bakersfield (Calif.) Jr. Coll., 1962; BA in Zoology, U. Calif., Riverside, 1965, MS in Entomology, 1967, PhD in Entomology, 1969. Asst. prof. entomology and forest sci. Tex. A&M U., College Station, 1969-73, assoc. prof., 1973-78, prof., 1978-87, rsch. coord. USDA so. pine beetle program, 1974-78; prof. entomology, head dept. Va. Poly. and State U., Blacksburg, 1987-92; dir. Ohio Agrl. R & D Ctr., Wooster; assoc. dean rsch., assoc. v.p. agrl. adminstrn. Ohio State U. Coll. Agr., 1993—99; vice chancellor, dean agr., food and natural resources. U. Mo. Coll. Agr., Columbia, 1999—. Sec. protection sect. Nat. Planning Conf. for Rsch. in Forestry and assoc. Rangelands, 1977; bd. dirs. Urban Pest Control Rsch. Ctr. Endowment Fund, 1988—; dean's rep., ex officio mem. Va. Pesticide Control Bd., 1989—; vis. prof. Forest Zoology Inst., U. Freiburg, Germany, 1978. Editor: (with Birch and Kennedy) Mechanisms in Insect Olfaction, 1986; mem. editorial bd. Jour. Ga. Entomol. Soc., 1979-83; co-editor Jour. Insect Behavior, 1987—; contbr. chpts. to books. Pres., co-founder Brazos County Firefighters Assn., 1979-81; v.p., co-founder Precinct 2 Vol. Fire Dept., 1979-80, pres., 1982-86; author grant to build Edge Tex. Sr. Citizens Ctr., 1979; mem. Friends of Blacksburg Master Chorale. Recipient numerous awards, 1976—, including cert. of appreciation for svc. as rsch. coord. expanded so. pine beetle rsch. USDA, 1976, 78, 80, rsch. award Tex. Forestry Assn., 1977, awards Am. Registry Profl. Entomologists, 1979, Alexander von Humboldt Stiftung sr. U.S. scientist award, 1982, Faculty Disting. Achievement award in rsch. Assn. Former Students Tex. A&M U., 1985, A.D. Hopkins award for outstanding rsch.-adminstrn. in forest entomology, 1991; Volkswagenwerk fellow U. Freiburg, 1978. Mem. AAAS, Entomol. Soc. Am. (CIBA-GEIGY agrl. recognition award 1982), Internat. Soc. Chem. Ecology, Internat. Chemoreception Workshop on Insects, Internat. Union Forest Rsch. Orgns., Nat. Corn Growers Assn., So. Forest Insect Work Conf., Va. Agribus. Coun., Va. Agrl. Chem. and Soil Fertility Assn., Va. Hort. Soc. (exec. coun. 1989), Va. Corn Growers Assn., Va. Soybean Assn., Va. Pest Control Assn, Western Forest Insect Work Conf., Coll. Agr. and Life Scis. Agr. Faculty Assn., Sigma Xi, Gamma Sigma Delta. Office: Univ Missouri Coll Agr Food/Nat Resource 2-69 Agrl Bldg Columbia MO 65211-0001 E-mail: cafnr@missouri.edu.

PAYNE, TIMOTHY E. management consultant; b. Valdosta, Ga., Oct. 12, 1948; s. Ernest Elbert and Lorraine (Tomlinson) P. BS, Valdosta State U., 1971. Profl. safety cert. Nat. Safety Coun.; cert. assoc. in rsk mgmt. and assoc. in loss control mgmt. Ins. Inst. Am.; cert. safety and health mgr. Sr. cons. Kent Watkins & Assocs., Miami, Fla., 1975-80; mgmt. engring. coord. U. Fla., Gainesville, 1980-86; adminstrv. sys. mgr. Amelia Island (Fla.) Co., 1986-89; CEO, pres. Payne & Assocs., Gainesville, Fla., 1989—; exec. v.p./COO Nat. Audit & Safety Co., Lake Waler. Cons. Grace Com., Gainesville, 1991; teaching asst. La. State U., New Orleans, 1971. Author: Industrial Location Survey, 1971, (workbook) Bonus Calculation Procedures, 1977; contbr. articles to Indsl. Mgmt. Jour., Compete, Jour. Competitive Techs. Internat. Gov.'s intern State Ga., Atlanta, 1971. Mem. Am. Soc. Safety Engrs., Nat. Safety Mgmt. Soc. (state v.p. 1994—, cert. safety and health mgr.). Avocations: golf, tennis.

PAYNE, TYSON ELLIOTT, JR. retired insurance executive; b. Dallas, May 25, 1927; s. Tyson Elliott and Winnie Claris (Denman) P.; m. Billie Jane Spears, Aug. 28, 1948; children: David Tyson, Sally Jane. B.J., U. Tex., 1949. CLU, ChFC. Sports editor Lufkin (Tex.) News, 1949-51, Tyler (Tex.) Courier Times, 1951-53; with Am. Nat. Ins. Co., Galveston, Tex., 1953-88, v.p. health ins. ops. St. Louis, 1965-1970, v.p. mktg. Galveston, 1970-86; pvt. practice ins. agt. Austin, Tex., 1987-88; exec. v. p., dir. Sch. of Ins. & Fin. Svcs. at U. Houston, 1988-92; ret., 1992. Elder Presbyn. Ch. With USNR, 1945-46. Home: 8110 Cardin Dr Austin TX 78759-8704 E-mail: tpaynejr@aol.com.

PAYNE, WILLIAM JACKSON, microbiologist, educator; b. Chattanooga, Aug. 30, 1925; s. Henry Frederick and Maude (Fonda) P.; m. Jane Lindsey Marshall, June 16, 1949; children: William Jackson, Marshall, Lindsey. BS, Coll. William and Mary, 1950, DSc (hon.), 1996; MS, U. Tenn., 1952, PhD, 1955. Instr. bacteriology U. Tenn., 1953-54; mem. faculty U. Ga., 1955-95, prof. microbiology, head dept., 1962-77, Alumni Found. Disting. prof., 1982-95, acting dean Franklin Coll. Arts and Scis., 1977-78, dean Franklin Coll. Arts and Scis., 1978-88. Vis. professorial fellow U. Wales, Cardiff, 1975, hon. professorial fellow, 1977-87; cons. U. Ala., 1959, 68, 70, 85, Philip Morris Co., 1981, Iowa State U., 1988, Howard U., 1989, U. Ctrl. Fla., 1992, U. Tenn., 1994-96, Auburn U., 1995, 98; summer rsch. participant Oak Ridge Nat. Lab., 1960; chmn. Com. Nat. Registry Microbiologists, 1966-72; cons. U.S. EPA, 1971; mem. biol. oceanography panel NSF, 1976-77; mem. nitrogen-fixation panel CRGO U.S. dept. Agr., 1982; mem. vis. com. So. Assn. Colls., Miss. State U., 1983; vis. lectr. Ctr. for Environ. Biotech., Danish univs.-Copenhagen, Aarhus, Aalborg, 1989; co-chair 1st Gordon Rsch. Conf. on nitric oxide in biochemsitry and biology, 1995. Author: (with D.R. Brown) Microbiology: A Programmed Presentation, 1968, 2d edit., 1972, (transl. to Spanish, 1975), Denitrification, 1981, also articles; mem. editl. bd. Applied and Environ. Microbiology, 1974-79, Environ. Ethics, 1982-95, U. Ga. Press, 1975-78, 88-91. Founding trustee Athens Acad., 1967-72. Served with USNR, 1943-46. Recipient M.G. Michael award 1960, creative rsch. award U. Ga., 1982, Alumni Achievement award McCallie Sch., 1993. Fellow Am. Acad. Microbiology; mem. Am. Soc. Microbiology (pres. southeastern br. 1963, found. lectr. 1972-73, dir. found. 1973-76, chmn. found. com. 1977-82, com. undergrad. and grad. edn. 1974-77, steering com. undergrad. faculty-mentor enhancement program 1988-90, P.R. Edwards award southeastern br. 1972, R.G. Eagon award 1995), Ga. Acad. Sci., Athens City Club, Sigma Xi (pres. U. Ga. chpt. 1963, rsch. award U. Ga. chpt. 1973), Phi Kappa Phi (pres. U. Ga. chpt. 1983), Sigma Alpha Epsilon. Episcopalian. Home: 111 Alpine Way Athens GA 30606-4002 E-mail: wjpayne@arches.uga.edu.

PAYNE, WILLIAM SANFORD, insurance company executive; b. Lynchburg, Va., July 1, 1946; s. William Armistead Jr. and Katherine Christian (Marks) P.; m. Donna Faye McNutt, June 14, 1969; children: Cybill Katherine, Kyle Oniel. BA, Randolph-Macon Coll., 1968; M in Fin. Svcs., Am. Coll. of CLU, 1988. CLU, LUTCF. Dist. mgr. N.Am. Assurance Co., Richmond, Va., 1977-80; life brokerage cons. Comml. Union Life Ins. Co., 1980-87; v.p., groups ins. mgr. Tabb, Brockenbrough & Ragland, 1987—. Bd. dirs. Gayton Forest Assn., Richmond; coach Tuckahoe Little League, Richmond, 1988—; soccer referee Richmond Striker League, 1986-90; fund raiser Boy Scouts Am., Richmond, 1991. With U.S. Army Res., 1968-74. Mem. Va. Assn. Life Underwriters (bd. dirs.), Richmond Assn. Life Underwriters (bd. dirs.), Richmond chpt. CLU, Richmond Jaycees. Republican. Baptist. Avocations: jogging, gardening, cooking. Home: 1905 Pump Rd Richmond VA 23233-3501 Office: Tabb Brockenbrough Ragland 4900 Augusta Ave Richmond VA 23230-3626

PAYNE, WINFIELD SCOTT, national security policy research executive; b. Denver, Jan. 20, 1917; s. Winfield Scott and Mildred (Hulse) P.; m. Barbara P. Reid, Nov. 18, 1945; children: Judith P. Beland, Patricia P. Dominguez. AB, U. Colo., 1939, MA (grad. scholar), 1941; postgrad. (fellow) Syracuse U., 1942; MPA, Harvard U., 1948, PhD, 1955. Economist, Bur. Budget, Washington, 1944-46; staff Inter-Univ. Case Program, Washington, 1948-50; indsl. analyst Pres.'s Materials Policy Commn., Washington, 1950-52; project leader Ops. Research Office, Johns Hopkins U., Bethesda, Md., 1952-63; sr. research staff, panel dir. Inst. for Def. Analyses, Arlington, Va., 1963-72; asst. to pres. System Planning Corp., Arlington, 1972-86; cons. 1986-88; adj. rsch. staff Inst. Def. Analyses, 1989-98; assoc. prof., lectr. George Washington U., Washington, 1963-65; cons. Def. Advanced Research Project Agy., 1972-76; guest lectr., various univs. Mem. Cabin John (Md.) Fire Bd., 1955-65. Served with USMC, 1942. Littauer fellow, 1946-48. Mem. AAAS, Cosmos Club, Phi Gamma Delta, Pi Gamma Mu. Contbr. articles to profl. jours.; contbr.: Public Administration and Policy Development: A Case Book, 1951. Home: 8820 Walther Blvd Apt 1304 Parkville MD 21234-9038

PAYNTER, HARRY ALVIN, retired trade association executive; b. Miami, Ariz., July 22, 1923; s. Harry and Mabel Vera (Moore) P.; m. Betty Clarice Wilkins, Dec. 3, 1944; children: Harry Alvin, Steven Wilkins, Barbara Elizabeth, Susan Moore. BS, Okla. State U., 1948; MBA, Harvard U., 1954; postgrad., Air Command and Staff Coll., 1957, Armed Forces Staff Coll., 1961, Nat. War Coll., 1969. Commd. 2d lt. AC U.S. Army, 1943; advanced through grades to col. USAF, 1968; service as flight comdr. 8th Air Force, World War II and Berlin airlift; asst. air attache (Am. embassy), Karachi, Pakistan, 1958-60, air attache Quito, Ecuador, 1965-67, Vietnam, 1969; prof. aerospace studies Dartmouth, 1967-68; ret., 1970; mng. dir. Gas Appliance Mfrs. Assn., Inc., N.Y.C., 1970-73, pres. Arlington, Va., 1973-88. Decorated D.F.C., Air medal with 3 oak leaf clusters, Purple Heart, Joint Services Commendation medal with oak leaf cluster U.S.; Abdon Calderon Ecuador; recipient Am. Bankers award, 1947; named Ecuador Hon. Command Pilot. Mem. Can. Gas Assn. (life), Guild Ancient Supplers (hon.), Am. Soc. Gas Engrs. (hon.), Air Force Assn., Ret. Officers Assn., Am. Soc. Assn. Execs., Nat. Press Club. Phi Kappa Phi. Presbyterian. Home: 1416 N Inglewood St Arlington VA 22205-2735

PAYNTER, VESTA LUCAS, pharmacist; b. Aiken County, S.C., May 29, 1922; d. James Redmond and Annie Lurline (Stroman) Lucas; m. Maurice Alden Paynter, Dec. 23, 1945 (dec. 1971); children: Sharon Lucinda, Maurice Alden, Doyle Gregg. BS in Pharmacy, U. S.C., 1943. Lic. pharmacist. Owner, pharmacist Cayce Drug Store, S.C., 1944-52, Dutch Fork Drug Store, Columbia, 1955-60, The Drug Ctr., Cayce, 1963-81; pharmacist Lane-Rexall, Columbia, 1952-55; dist. pharmacist S.C. Dept. Health and Environ. Control, 1983-90, ret., 1990. Vol. pharmacist Free Med. Clinic, Columbia, 1987-90. Named Preceptor of Yr., Syntex Co./Student Body of U. S.C., 1981. Fellow S.C. Pub. Health Assn., S.C. Pharm Assn., 5th Dist. Pharm. Assn.; mem. CBI VA Assn. (assoc.), 14th Air Force Assn. (assoc.), Order Eastern Star, White Shrine of Jerusalem, Amaranth Trinity Ct. # 6, Am. Legion Aux. (Post 130). Baptist. Avocations: travel, art, oenology, Lowery organ. Home: 2351 Vine St Cayce SC 29033-3000 E-mail: MPaynter@sc.rr.com .

PAYRI, JOEL, pharmaceutical marketing executive; b. Sidi-Bel-Abbes, Algeria, Nov. 29, 1961; s. Rene and Marie P. DVM, Nat. Vet. Sch., Toulouse, France, 1985, diploma of anatomo-pathology, 1988; diploma of med. stats., U. Paris VI, 1989; MBA, INSEAD, Fontainebleau, France, 1991. Pvt. vet. practice, St. Gaudens, France, 1985-86; study dir. Searle Rsch. and Devel., Sophia Antipolis, France, 1986-87; head exptl. cardiology Rhone Poulenc Sante, Vitry sur Seine, France, 1988-90; mktg. mgr. Parmuka-Rhone Poulenc, Paris, 1991-92; worldwide product mgr. Taxotere Rhone Poulenc Rorer, 1992-96; internat. mktg. dir. GlaxoSmithkline, London, 1996—2001; sr. dir. internat. mktg. Biogen, Paris, 2001—. Surg. asst. Nat. Vet. Sch., Toulouse, 1984-85; pres. new mgmt. team Rhone Poulenc Sante, Paris, 1989-91; interviewer INSEAD MBA cands. Biogen, Paris, 1995—. Author: Telemetry and Gastric pH Measurements, 1985 (gold medal 1985); contbr. to websites and pubs. for Internat. Herpes Alliance. Capt. French Army, 1987-90, Paris. Grantee Ministry Agr., 1985. Mem. Am. Social Health Assn., Infectious Disease Soc. Am. Home: La petite Ourse Anse de Maldorme Bouches du Rhone 13007 Marseilles France Office: Biogen 55 Av Des Champs Pierreux 92012 Nauterre France Fax: 33-147-217535. E-mail: joel_payri@biogen.com.

PAYSON, JANET HARSHA, association administrator, retired; b. Montgomery, Ala., Oct. 2, 1948; d. Joseph Allen and Dorothy Phillips (Spratlan) Harsha; children: Lara Meriwether, Amy Brooks; m. Richard O. Payson, Sr. BS, Huntingdon Coll., 1971; MS, Troy State U., 1987. cert. paralegal. Tchr. Montgomery (Ala.) County Bd. Edn., 1971-88, sch. counselor, 1988-98; newspaper columnist, 1994-95, 99—; asst. dir. VTC Montgomeray Assn. Retarded Citizens, 1998-99; ret., 1999. Counselor Sta. WSFA-TV Counseling Hotline, Montgomery, 1989—. Vol. Montgomery Area Coun. on Aging, 1978-81; mem. YMCA, 1986-89, Montgomery Mus. Fine Arts, 1988-91, ednl. docent, 1988-90. Montgomery Bus. and Profl. Women's Assn. scholar, 1967. Mem. Capital City Club. Republican. Methodist. Avocations: reading, writing, gardening.

PAYSON, MARTIN F. lawyer; b. Bklyn., Dec. 25, 1940; m. Rhoda Shapiro, Oct. 8, 1961; children: Jacqueline, Marla. BBA, CCNY, 1961; JD, Bklyn. Law Sch., 1966. Bar: N.Y. 1967, Pa. 1989, U.S. Ct. Appeals (1st cir.) 1971, U.S. Ct. Appeals (2d and 3d cirs.) 1968, U.S. Ct. Appeals (4th cir.) 1969, U.S. Supreme Ct. 1970. Gen. ptnr. Jackson, Lewis, Schnitzler & Krupman, White Plains, N.Y., 1967—. Lectr. in field. Contbr. articles to various publs. With U.S. Army, 1961-62. Mem. N.Y. State Bar Assn. (labor and employee rels. sects.), Soc. for Human Resource Mgmt. Avocations: photography, cycling, model railroading, gardening. Office: Jackson Lewis Schnitzler & Krupman One N Broadway White Plains NY 10601 E-mail: Paysonm@JacksonLewis.com.

PAYSON, MARTIN SAUL, secondary school educator, mathematician; b. N.Y.C., May 18, 1945; s. Harry and Beatrice Clare (Garber) P.; m. Joan Patricia Thompson, Sept. 11, 1969 (div. 1983); 1 child, Susan Elizabeth; m. Ilene Debbie Gellman, Apr. 10, 1983; 1 child, Howard Jeffrey. BA in Philosophy, Monmouth Coll., 1969; MS in Elem. Edn., CUNY, 1975. Tchr. math. Frederick Douglass Intermediate Sch., N.Y.C., 1970-84, John Philip Sousa Jr. H.S., Bronx, N.Y., 1984-91; leader math. team John Philip Souxa Jr. H.S., 1990-91; tchr. math. Michael Angelo Mid. Sch., 1991—, Pub. Sch. #89, Bronx, 1998—2002; ret., 2002. Asst. head philosophy dept. Monmouth (Ill.) Coll., 1968-69. N.Y. State Edn. Dept. Regents scholar, 1963. Mem. Assn. Math. Tchrds. N.Y. State, Nat. Coun. Tchrs. Math., United Fedn. Tchrs. N.Y.C. Avocations: sports, camping, fishing, gardening, duplicate bridge. Home: 42 Chief Nimham Dr Carmel NY 10512-3624 Office: Michael Angelo Mid Sch 2545 Gunther Ave Bronx NY 10469-6105

PAYSON, NORMAN C. healthcare services company executive; MD, Dartmouth U., 1973; grad., MIT, 1970. Physician; founder, pres., CEO Healthsource, Inc., 1985—97; CEO Oxford Health Plans, Inc., Norwalk, Conn., 1998—, chmn., 1999—. Mem. bd. of dir. American Assoc. of Health Plans, Washington; mem. of faculty Dartmouth Med. Sch. Office: Oxford Health Plans Inc PO Box 7081 Bridgeport CT 06601-7081*

PAYTON, BENJAMIN FRANKLIN, college president; b. Orangeburg, S.C., Dec. 27, 1932; s. Leroy Ralph and Sarah (Mack) P.; m. Thelma Louise Plane, Nov. 28, 1959; children: Mark Steven, Deborah Elizabeth. BA, S.C. State U., 1955; BD (Danforth grad. fellow 1955-63), Harvard U., 1958; MA, Columbia U., 1960; PhD, Yale U., 1963; LLD (hon.), Eastern Mich. U., 1972; LHD (hon.), Benedict Coll., 1972; LittD (hon.), Morgan State U., 1974, U. Md., 1987; LLD, Morris Brown Coll., 1975, Lehigh U., 1990; LLD (hon.) , S.C. State U., 2001. Asst. prof. sociology of religion and social ethics Howard U., Washington; also dir. Howard U. (Community Rsch.-Svc. Project, 1963-65; exec. dir. dept. social justice and Commn. on Religion and Race Nat. Coun. Chs. of Christ in U.S.A., 1965-67; pres. Benedict Coll., Columbia, S.C., 1967-72; program officer higher edn. and rsch. Ford Found., 1972-81; pres. Tuskegee (Ala.) U., 1981—. Mem. nat. rev. bd. Ctr. for Cultural and Tech. Exch. between U.S. and Asia; mem. commn. on Pre-Coll. Edn. in Math., Sci. and Tech. NSF; ednl. advisor to V.P. George Bush during Seven-Nation Tour of Africa, 1982; team leader U.S. Presdl. Task Force on Agrl. and Econ. Devel. to Zaire ; bd. dirs. AmSouth Bancorp.; mem. vis. com. dept. humanities MIT, 1988—90; vis. com. bd. overseers Harvard U., 1989—95. Author: (with Dr. Seymour Melman) A Strategy for the Next Stage in Civil Rights: Metropolitan-Rural Development for Equal Opportunity, 1966. Mem. nat. commn. on higher edn. issues Am. Coun. Edn.; bd. dirs. Ala. Shakespeare Festival. Named South Carolinian of Yr., statewide TV-Radio, 1972; recipient Billings prize, 1st Pl., Harvard U., 1957, Gold medal award, Napoleon Hill Found., 1987, Benjamin E. Mays award, 1988, Centennial Alumnus award, S.C. State U., 1988. Mem. NAACP, Am. Soc. Scholars, Soc. for Religion, Higher Edn. (dir.), Assn. Governing Bds. (pres.'s adv. coun.), Phi Beta Kappa, Alpha Phi Alpha, Alpha Kappa Mu, Sigma Pi Phi. Home: Grey Columns 399 Old Montgomery Rd Tuskegee AL 36083-1519 Office: Office Pres Tuskegee U Tuskegee AL 36088

PAYTON, GARY DWAYNE, professional basketball player; b. Oakland, Calif., July 23, 1968; m. Monique Payton; children: Raquel, Gary Dwayne. Grad., Oreg. State U., 1990. Drafted NBA, 1990; guard Seattle Supersonics, 1990—. Named mem. All-Am. First Team, The Sporting News, 1990, Pacific-10 Conf. Player of Yr., 1990, NBA All-Star, 1994, 95, NBA Player of the Week; named to NBA All-Def. 1st Team, 1994, 95. Office: Seattle Supersonics 351 Elliott Ave W Seattle WA 98119-4101*

PAYTON, GARY E. astronaut; b. Rock Island, Ill., June 20, 1948; BS in Astronautical Engring., USAF Acad., 1971; MS in Astronautical and Aeronautical Engring., Purdue U., 1972; grad. Pilot Tng., Craig AFB, Ala., 1973. Commd. 2d lt. USAF, 1971, advanced through grades to maj.; instr. pilot Craig AFB; spacecraft test contr. Cape Canaveral AFS, Fla., 1976—80; astronaut NASA, Houston. Achievements include logged over 1,080 hours in different aircraft; logged over 73 hours in space; payload specialist STS-51C Discovery (1985). Office: Astronaut Office/CB NASA Johnson Space Ctr Houston TX 77058*

PAYTON, ROBERT See PROUD, ROBERT DONALD

PAYTON, ROGER LOUIS, consultant; b. London, Oct. 18, 1930; s. Leonard Joseph and Vera Mary (Crepin) P.; m. Geraldine Eyre Farley, May 10, 1958; children: Jane Geraldine Lyons, Christopher Charles. LLB, London U., 1958. Solicitor. Mgr. corp. fin. dept. Baring Bros. & Co. Ltd., London, 1958-69; dir. Baring Bros. Co. Ltd., 1969-84; cons. Roger Payton Assoc., 1984—. Chmn. Jarvis Plc, Hertford, Eng., 1994-2000, Richardsons Westgarth Plc, Worcestershire, Eng., 1988-2000, Rothsay Holdings Ltd., Surrey, Eng., 1993-2002; dep. chmn. Great Portland Estates Plc, London, 1990-2000. Chmn. Met. Pub. Gardens Assn., Surrey, 1991—; master Worshipful Co. of Gardeners, London, 1981-82, 98; pres. Bishopsgate Ward Club, London, 1982-83; trustee City Parochial Found., London, 1984—. Fellow Royal Soc. Arts, Inst. Dirs.; mem. Law Soc. Avocations: gardening, tennis. Home and Office: Little Bedwell Essendon Hatfield AL9 6JA England E-mail: RogerLPayton@aol.com.uk.

PAYTON, THOMAS WILLIAM, corporate finance consultant executive; b. Toronto, Ont., Can., Sept. 7, 1946; With Can. Imperial Bank of Commerce, Toronto; dir. Bramalea Ltd., 1981-82, v.p., 1982-88, sr. v.p., 1988-90, sr. v.p., treas., 1991-93; pres. DelLyn Advisors Inc., 1993—; dir. Cadillac Fairview, Inc., 1994-95; pres. Sunnybrook Properties Inc., 1997-2000. E-mail: dellynadvinc@aol.com.

PAYTON-WRIGHT, PAMELA, actress; b. Pitts., Nov. 1, 1941; d. Gordon Edgar and Eleanor Ruth (McKinley) Payton Wright; m. David Arthur Butler, May 8, 1978 (div. 1989); 1 child, Oliver Dickon Hedley. Grad., St. Mary's Jr. Coll., 1961; BA, Birmingham So. Coll., 1963; postgrad., Royal Acad. Dramatic Arts, London, 1963-65. Theatre debut Diary of a Scoundrel, 1965, Broadway debut The Show-Off, 1968, Broadway appearances Exit The King, The Cherry Orchard, 1968, Jimmy Shine, 1969, The Crucible, 1972, Mourning Becomes Electra, 1972, All Over town, 1975, Glass Menagerie, 1976, Romeo and Juliet, 1977, A Streetcar Named Desire, 1988, Night of the Iguana, 1988, M. Butterfly, 1988-90, Something Unspoken, 1995, Off-Broadway appearances The Effect of Gamma Rays on Man-In-The Moon Marigolds, 1970-71, Jesse and the Bandit Queen, 1975, The Seagull, 1980, Don Juan, 1982, Hamlet, 1982, Mrs. Warren's Profession, 1992, The Replacement, 1995, Richard III, 'Til the Rapture Comes, 1998, What You Get and What You Expect, 2000, regional theater appearances Skin of Our Teeth, 1972, Aimee, 1973, Othello, Troilus and Cressida, As You Like It, 1976, Lunch Girls, 1977, Summerfolk, 1978, The Greeks, 1982, The Misanthrope, 1982, Tobacco Road, 1984, Passion, 1984-85, Cat on a Hot Tin Roof, 1985, Little Eyolf, 1985, On the Verge, 1986, Our Town, 1987, The Road to Mecca, 1990, Picnic, 1991, The Way of the World, 1991, Quartermaine's Terms, 1993, Misalliance, 1993, Six Degrees of Separation, 1993, Ghosts, 1994, Sea Gull, 1994, The Show-Off, 1995, The Rivals, 1996, Touch of the Poet, 1996, Glass Menagerie, 1997, Voir Dire, 1997, She Stoops to Conquer, 1997, Blithe Spirits, 1998, Transit of Venus, 1998, Seagull, 1999, Long Day's Journey Into Night, 1999, Sweet Bird of Youth, 1999, A Fair Country, 2000, Philadelphia Story, 2001, Long Days Journey Into Night, 2002, Seascape, 2002, Outward Bound, 2002, others, film appearances At the Dark End of the Street, 1980, Going in Style, 1981, Starlight, 1985, My Little Girl, 1985, Ironweed, 1987, The Freshman, 1989, In Dreams, 1999, TV appearances Look Homeward Angel, 1972, The Haunting of Rosalind, 1973, The Prodigal: Brother to Dragons, 1973, The Adams Chronicles, 1976. Recipient Fulbright award, 1963, Spl. medal, Edmund Gray prize for high comedy, Herbert Beerbohm Tree citation, Royal Acad. Dramatic Art, 1963—65, Obie award, 1970, 1975, Clarence Derwent award, Variety Critics' Poll citation, 1970, Drama Desk award, 1972, Best Actress citation, Dallas Theater Critics' Forum, 1994, Balt., 1997, Dean Goodman award, 1999; fellow Fox Grant fellow, 1999. Mem. Actors Equity Assn., AFTRA, Screen Actors Guild. Episcopalian. Office: Bauman & Assocs 250 W 57th St New York NY 10019-3741

PAYUK, EDWARD WILLIAM, elementary education educator; b. St. Louis, July 19, 1948; s. Stanley Eli and Lillian (Bluestein) P.; m. Pamela Karen Miller, Sept. 5, 1970 (div. Oct. 1986); children: Stacy Lynne, Lori Michelle; m. Judith Ann Cohen, Dec. 4, 1986; stepchildren: Jeffrey Alan Kieffer, Kimberly Beth Kieffer. AA, Meramec C.C., St. Louis, 1969; BS, U. Mo., St. Louis, 1971; MA, Webster U., 1973, postgrad., 1976. Tchr. Ferguson-Florissant Sch. Dist., St. Louis, 1971-2001, mem. lang. arts com. dist. level, 1997-2001; prof. geology St. Charles CC, St. Peters, Md., 2001—. Tutor, St. Louis, 1984-91. Contbr. articles to profl. jours. Sci. literacy com. St. Louis Sci. Acad., 1991—; rep. Tchrs., Industry & Environment Conf., Jefferson City, Mo., 1995; mem. Little Creek Nature Study Adv. Com., 1997. With U.S. Army, 1969-70. Mem. NEA, Mo. Edn. Assn., Ferguson-Florissant Edn. Assn. Jewish. Avocation: collector of Einsteinia. Home: 13660 Amiot Dr Saint Louis MO 63146-3608 Office: St Charles CC PO Box 76795 4601 Mid Rivers Mall Dr Saint Peters MO 63376 E-mail: epayuk@yahoo.com., epayuk@swbell.net.

PAZ, HAROLD LOUIS, dean, medical educator, internist; b. N.Y.C., Jan. 3, 1955; BA in Biology and Psychology, U. Rochester, 1977, MD, 1982; MS in Life Sci. Engring., Tufts U., 1979. Diplomate subspecialty in pulmonary medicine and critical care medicine Am. Bd. Internal Medicine . Intern in internal medicine Northwestern U. Med. Ctr., Chgo., 1982—83, resident in internal medicine, 1983—85, chief med. resident, 1985—86; instr. clin. medicine Northwestern U., 1985—86; fellow in pulmonary and critical care Johns Hopkins U., Balt., 1986—88, fellow in environ. health scis., 1986—88; asst. prof. medicine Hahnemann U., Phila., 1988—92, asst. prof. anesthesia, 1989—92, assoc. dean grad. med. edn., 1992—94, assoc. prof. medicine, 1992—94, dir. med. ICU, 1988—94, assoc. hosp. med. dir., 1992—94, dir. Ctr. for Clin. Outcomes, 1992—94; med. dir., assoc. dean for clin. affairs, assoc. prof. U. Medicine and Dentistry N.J. Robert Wood Johnson Med. Sch., New Brunswick, 1994—95, dean, CEO, assoc. prof. medicine, 1995—. Editor: Jour. Undergrad. Rsch., 1976, Med. Staff News newsletter, 1992—94; cons.: Annals Internal Medicine, cons.: Clin. Immunology and Immunopathology, cons.: Chest, cons.: Intensive Care Medicine, cons.: Physician Execs., cons.: N.Y. State Med. Jour., mem. editl. bd.: Jour. Disease Mgmt. and Clin. Outcomes, 1996—, mem. editl. bd.: Chest, 1998—. Recipient Disting. Svc. award, Motolinsky Rsch. Found., 1998, Cmty. Leaders of Distinction award, County C. of C., 1999; fellow Endowood fellow, Johns Hopkins U., 1987—88; scholar, U. Rochester, 1979. Fellow: ACP, Am. Coll. Chest Physicians; mem.: AMA, Laennec Soc. (pres. 1994—95), Philip Drinker Soc. for Critical Care (pres. 1992—94), Am. Thoracic Soc. Office: UMDNJ Robert Wood Johnson Med Sch 125 Paterson St New Brunswick NJ 08901-1962

PAZANDAK, CAROL HENDRICKSON, liberal arts educator; b. Mpls. d. Norman Everard and Ruth (Buckley) Hendrickson; m. Bruce B. Pazandak (dec. 1986); children: David, Bradford, Chris, Eric, Paul, Ann; m. Joseph P. O'Shaughnessy, May 1991 (dec. Feb. 2000). PhD, U. Minn., 1970. Asst. dir. admissions U. Minn., Mpls., 1970-72, asst. dean liberal arts, 1972-79, asst. to pres., 1979-85, office of internat. edn., acting dir., 1985-87, asst. prof. to assoc. to prof. liberal arts, 1970-96, prof. emerita, 1996—; ptnr. Hollrad-Pers. Consulting, Reykjavik, Iceland, 1999—. Vis. prof. U. Iceland, Reykjavik, 1984, periods in 1983, 86-99; vis. rsch. prof. U. Oulu, Finland, 1993; exec. sec. Minn.-Iceland Adv. Com., U. Minn., 1984—; cons. U. Iceland, 1983-98; co-chair Reunion of Sisters-Minn. and Finland Confs., 1986-98; sec. Icelandic Assn. of Minn., 1995-97. Editor: Improving Undergraduate Education in Large Universities, 1989. Past pres. Minn. Mrs. Jaycees, Mpls. Mrs. Jaycees; formerly bd. govs. St. John's Preparatory Sch., Collegeville, Minn.; former bd. trustees Coll. of St. Teresa, Winona, Minn.. Recipient Partnership award for contbn. to advancing shared interests of Iceland and Am., 1994; named to Order of the Falcon, Govt. of Iceland, 1990, Coll. Liberal Arts Alumna Notable Achievement, 1995, Pres.'s Club, U. Minn., 1996. Mem. APA, Waikoloa Village Outdoor Cir. Home: 4505 Harry's Ln Dallas TX 75229 Office: U Minn N 218 Elliott Hall 75 E River Rd Minneapolis MN 55455-0280 E-mail: carolpz@umn.edu.

PAZDERA, JOHN PAUL, regulatory services executive; b. Jersey City, June 9, 1948; s. Albert Frederick and Helen Katherine (Momat) P.; m. Yolanda Lourdes Lopez, May 26, 1973. BS, Stevens Inst. Tech., 1970; MBA, Fairleigh Dickinson U., 1979. Cert. quality engr. Sales engr. Westinghouse Electric Co., Bloomfield, N.J., 1970-71; tech. dir. Ungerer & Co., N.Y.C., 1972-75; group leader quality control Airwick Industries, Carlstadt, N.J., 1975-78, regulatory affairs specialist, 1979-80; tech. documentalist Am. Home Products, N.Y.C., 1981-91; mgr. regulatory svcs. Lonza Inc., Fair Lawn, N.J., 1991-96; mgr. regulatory affairs Courtaulds Coatings Inc., Union, 1996—. Adj. prof. advt. Fairleigh Dickinson U., 1982, Rutherford, N.J.; polt. writer Herald-News, Passaic, N.J., 1982-85. Mem. Am. Chem. Soc., Regulatory Affairs Profls. Soc., Am. Soc. for Quality Control. Republican. Roman Catholic. Avocation: golf.

PAZIRANDEH, MAHMOOD, rheumatologist, consultant; b. Hamadan, Iran, Jan. 1, 1932; came to U.S., 1966; naturalized U.S. Citizen, 1977; s. Rahim and Zahra (Shoushtar) P.; m. Parvin Danesh, Apr. 19, 1961; children: Bruce, Justin, Navid. MD, U. Tehran, 1958; postgrad., Eng., 1959-64, Pitts. U., 1967-68. Diplomate Am. Bd. Internal Medicine and Rheumatology. Asst. prof. Tehran U., Iran, 1964-67; clin. assoc. Cleve. Clinic Found., 1969-70; clin. instr. Case Western Res. U., Cleve., 1970-72, sr. clin. instr., 1972-78, clin. asst. prof., 1979-93, clin. assoc. prof., 1993—. Dir. med. edn. Lake Hosp., Cleve., 1984-2001, pres. med. staff, 1990-93; mem. CME com. Case Western Res. U. Sch. Medicine, 1994-01; dir. med. edn. Euclid Hosp., Cleve., 1971-73, dir. quality assurance, 1989-93. Contbr. articles to profl. jours. Speaker pub. edn. radio, TV and seminars, Cleve., 1984—; chmn. pub. forums Arthritis Found., Cleve., 1985—, trustee, 1986-99, chmn. pub. edn. com., 1987—; vol. physician Lake County Free Med. Clinic, 1993-99. Recipient recognition svc. award Arthritis Found., 1976, Robert Stecher Vol. award, 1988, Nat. Vols. Svc. citation, 1989; Eng. and Iranian Govt. scholar, 1959-63. Fellow ACP, Am. Coll. Rheumatology; mem. Ohio State Med. Assn. (del. 1989-2002, State Ohio accreditation com. on continuing med. edn. 1996-2002), Lake County Med. Soc. (pres. 1988—), Cleve. Rheumatism Soc. (pres. 1974). Republican. Avocations: arts, antiques, gardening. Home: 124 Pheasant Ln Chagrin Falls OH 44022-4043 Office: Case Western Res U 36100 Euclid Ave Willoughby OH 44094-4456

PAZLAMATCHEV, IVAN GUEORGUIEV, artist, art restorer; b. Yambol, Bulgaria, May 7, 1968; s. Georgi Kolev and Stoyanka Ivanova Pazlamatchev; m. Jeannette Kristine Weiss; children: Sky Nasir. Diploma in Arts, Sch. for Fine and Applied Arts, Sofia, Bulgaria, 1987; BFA, Nat. Acad. of Fine Arts, Sofia, 1992; Diploma in Tchg., Sunbridge Coll., Chestnut Ridge, N.Y., 1995. Cert. Cert. in Painting State Commn., Sofia, 1992. Artist Union of Bulgarian Artists, Sofia, Bulgaria, 1988—92; art curative educator Lehenhof, Deggenhausen, Germany, 1992—93; design artist Decorating With Fabric, Nanuet, NY, 1993—95; artist Nyack, 1995—; artist/restorer Furniture Medic, Pearl River, 1998—. Prin. works include mural Legends, 1992, painting (National Palace of Culture Award, 1997). Recipient Best in Show award, Rockland Ctr. for the Arts, Nyack, NY, USA, 1995, Award of Excellence, NAT-Ednl. Ctr.N.Y.C., 1997, Third Millennium Sculpture award, Angelicum, Milan, Italy, 2000, Special Opportunity Stipend, N.Y. Found. for the Arts, N.Y.C., 2000. Mem.: Coll. Art Assn. Personal E-mail: igp@bellatlantic.net.

PAZMIÑO, PATRICIO AUGUSTO, physician, scientist, consultant; b. Quito, Ecuador, Nov. 7, 1943; came to U.S., 1967; s. Manuel Eduardo and Angela Alicia (Narvaez) P.; m. Lydia Zulema Bohorquez, 1970; children: Patricio, Pablo, Carlos, Katherine. BS, Gonzaga U., 1968; PhD, U. Ill., 1971; D in Medicine and Surgery, Ctrl. U. Ecuador, 1974. Diplomate Am. Bd. Internal Medicine, Am. Bd. Nephrology. Asst. prof. pharmacology Ctrl. U. Sch. Medicine, Quito, Ecuador, 1971-74; staff nephrologist, internist Nat. Naval Med. Ctr., Bethesda, 1979-84; asst. prof. medicine Uniformed Svcs. U. Health Scis., Md., 1980-83; head nephrology divsn. Nat. Naval Med. Ctr., 1983-84; med. dir. El Paso (Tex.) Dialysis Ctr., 1986-89, Nephrology, Internal Medicine & Hypertension Ctr., El Paso, 1987—; asst. prof. medicine Tex. Tech. Sch. Medicine, 1989—; med. dir. BMA Dialysis Ctr., 1989-95; dir. Total Renal Care, 1995-99, DaVita West, 1999—. Staff internist, nephrologist Las Palmas Med. Ctr., Del Sol Med. Ctr., Sierra Med. Ctr., Southwestern Gen. Hosp., R.E. Thomason Gen. Hosp., Rio Vista Rehab. Ctr., Providence Meml. Hosp., William Beaumont Army Med. Ctr. Author: Farmacologia Hormonal, 1974; contbr. articles to profl. jours. and books. With USN, 1979-84. Fellow ACP, Interam. Coll. Physicians and Surgeons; mem. ACP, AMA, Interam. Coll. Physicians and Surgeons, Nat. Kidney Found., Am. Soc. Nephrology, Tex. Med. Assn., El Paso County Med. Assn., Am. Heart Assn. (pres. 1996-97, bd. dirs. El Paso divsn. 1994—, Sun Country Regional Vol. of Yr. 1996-97, Disting. Svc. award 1997-98), S.W. Renal Soc. (pres. 1991-92), S.W. Assn. Hispanic Am. Physicians (pres. 1993, Outstanding Pres. award 1993), Ecuadorean Acad. Medicine, Mayo Clinic Alumni Assn., El Paso County Med. Soc. (del. 1994-98). Avocations: photography, scientific research, travel, chess, sports cars. Office: NIH Ctr 1701 N Mesa St Ste 101 El Paso TX 79902-3503 E-mail: drppazmino@msn.com.

PAZNOKAS, LYNDA SYLVIA, elementary and middle school education educator; b. Portland, Oreg., Feb. 19, 1950; d. Marley Elmo and Undine Sylvia (Crockard) Sims. BA, Wash. State U., 1972; MS, Portland State U., 1975; EdD, Oreg. State U., 1984. Cert. tchr., Oreg. Tchr. 5th grade, outdoor sch. specialist Clover Park Sch. Dist. 400, Tacoma, 1971-72; tchr. 6th grade, outdoor sch. specialist Hillsboro (Oreg.) elem. Dist. 7, 1972-78, Bend (Oreg.)-La Pine Sch. Dist., 1978-82, elem. curriculum specialist, 1983-85, tchr. 4th grade gifted and talented, 1985-90; grad. teaching asst. Oreg. State U., Corvallis, 1982-84; asst. prof., assoc. prof. No. Ariz. U., 1990-99, chair instnl. leadership, 1997-98; Boeing disting. prof. sci. edn. Wash. State U., Pullman, 1999—. Ednl. cons., tchr. workshops, 1973—; presenter workshop Soviet-Am. Joint Conf., Moscow State U., 1991, Meeting of Children's Culture Promoters, Guadalajara, Mex., 1994, Internat. Conf. Sci., Tech. and Math. Edn. for Human Devel., UNESCO, Panaji, India, 2001, and others; faculty Ariz. Journey Schs. for Math. and Sci. Tchg. Improvement; coord. Odyssey of the Mind, Bend, 1985-89, tchr.-mentor program for 1st-yr. tchrs., Beaverton, Oreg., 1982-83; presenter Social Edn. Assn. of Australia, 1997. Author: Pathways of America: Lewis and Clark, 1993, Pathways of America: The Oregon Trail, 1993, Pathways of America: The California Gold Rush Trail, 1994, Pathways of America: The Santa Fe Trail, 1995, Fifty States, 1997, U.S. Presidents, 1997, U.S. Map Skills, 1997, Human body, 1998, National Parks and Other Park Service Sites, 1999, Our National Parks, 1999, Pathways of America: The California Mission Trail, 2000, Circling the World: Festivals and Celebrations, 2000, Endangered Species, 2001; contbr. articles to profl. jours. Vol., leader, bd. dirs. Girl Scouts U.S., 1957—; elder First Presbyn. Ch., Bend, 1980—; vol. hist. interpretation High Desert Mus., Bend, 1987-91; docent Mus. No. Ariz.; pres. bd. dirs. The Arboretum at Flagstaff; sec. bd. dirs. Palouse Discovery Sci. Ctr., 2000—. Recipient Excellence in Teaching award Bend Found., 1985-86, 86-87; named Tchr. of Yr. Oreg. Dept. Edn., 1982; Celebration Teaching grantee Geraldine Rockefeller Dodge Found., 1989, 90, 91, 92, 93, 94, 95, EPA grantee, 1997-99, Eisenhower Math and Sci. Edn. Act grantee, 1997, 99, Grand Canyon Assn. grantee, 1996, 97,

98; commd. Ky. Col., 1993. Mem. NEA, Internat. Coun. Assns. Sci. Edn. (newsletter advisor), Nat. Coun. Tchrs. Math., NSTA (internat. com.), Nat. State Tchrs. of Yr. (nat. pres. 1988-90), Nat. Assn. Rsch. in Sci. Tchg., Oreg. Coun. Tchrs. Math. (bd. dirs. 1981-82), Oreg. Coun. Tchrs. English (bd. dirs. 1981-82), Ariz. Reading Assn. (bd. dirs.), Nat. Coun. for Social Studies, Coun. for Elem. Sci. Internat. (bd. dirs. 1995-98, 99—, chair informal edn. com.), Internat. Reading Assn., Oreg.-Calif. Trails Assn., Nat. Sci. Edn. Leadership Assn., Assn. for Edn. of Tchrs. in Sci., Nat. Assn. for Rsch. in Sci. Tchg., S.W. Oreg.-Calif. Trails Assn., Lewis and Clark Trail Heritage Found., Delta Kappa Gamma (1st v.p.), Phi Delta Kappa (found. rep. 1991-92, v.p. programs 1992-93, historian 1993-94, v.p. membership 1994-95), Golden Key Hon., Pi Lambda Theta, Phi Kappa Phi, Kappa Delta Pi (past chpt. counselor, mem. spkrs. bur.), others. Avocations: cross-country skiing, photography, hiking, researching immigrant trails, gardening. Home: 720 SE Pheasant Run Pullman WA 99163 E-mail: lpaznokas@wsu.edu.

PAZUNIAK, GEORGE, lawyer; b. Phila., Jan. 15, 1952; s. Roman and Natalia Pazuniak; m. Maria Bilynsky, Aug. 3, 1974; children: Maksym, Andriy, Markian. BA, Temple U., 1973; JD, Duke U., 1975. Bar: Del. 1976. Lectr. law Widener U. Sch. Law, Wilmington, Del., 1979-80; v.p. Assn. Patent Law Firms, Washington, 1997-99. Cons. Smolosky, Inc., 1978—. Home: 216 Sorrel Dr Wilmington DE 19803 Office: 1220 N Market St Wilmington DE 19801-2535 Office Fax: (302) 658-5614. E-mail: gp@cblhlaw.com.

PEABODY, ARLENE L. HOWLAND BAYAR, nurse; b. Deposit, N.Y., June 26, 1931; d. Burt and Olive (Oralls) Howland; m. Atilla C. Bayar, Dec. 8, 1956 (div.); m. Norman R. Peabody, Feb. 1, 1975 (dec.); children: Tildy Anne Bayar Sparrow, Carol A. Digilio. Diploma, Harrisburg Hosp. Sch. Enterostomal Therapy, 1971; AAS, Empire State Coll., 1985; BS in Edn., SUNY, Oneonta, 1990. RN, N.Y.; cert. therapeutic touch practitioner, natural force healing practitioner, enterostomal nurse. Sec. pres.'s office Cornell U., Ithaca, N.Y., 1949-55; exec. sec. to Rudolph Lang Office Execs. Assn. N.Y. and Prestige Expositions Inc., N.Y.C., 1955-69; enterostomal therapy nurse M.I. Bassett Hosp., Cooperstown, N.Y., 1972-89; pvt. practice enterostomal therapy nurse Oneonta, 1989—2002. Vol. Am. Cancer Soc., 1972-2002, Catskill Area Hospice, 1990-02, Glimmerglass Opera, 1975-2002; bd. dirs. Del. Heritage Inc., 1996-2002; mem. Unitarian Universalist Soc., trustee; mem. Storytelling Ctr. of Oneonta, Oneonta Concert Assn., Oneonta Contradance. Mem. AARP (bd. dirs. 1986-2002), Order of Ea. Star, N.Y. State Hist. Assn., Del. Co. Hist. Assn., Wound Ostomy and Continence Nurses Soc., United Ostomy Assn. (N.Y. state field svcs. rep.). Avocations: heirloom quilting, traditional folk music, coutourier clothing, costuming, dancing. Home: 13511 Pebblebrook Dr Houston TX 77079-6023

PEABODY, MARYANNE, management consultant; b. N.Y.C. d. Robert F. and Helen (Reilly) P.; m. Laurence J. Stybel, May 19, 1973; 1 child, Jennifer. Diploma in nursing, Bellevue Hosp. Sch. of Nursing, 1967; BS, Hunter Coll., 1971; MBA, So. Meth. U., 1974. RN. Dir. of clinics Planned Parenthood Assn. of N.E. Tex., Dallas, 1972-73; home health care coord. City of Boston Health and Hosps. Corp., 1974-75; profl. svcs. cons. Hillhaven, Inc., Lexington, Mass., 1975-81; v.p. Stybel, Peabody & Assocs., Inc., Boston, 1981—. Columnist Boston Bus. Jour.; contbr. articles to bus. and profl. jours. Elected mem. Wayland (Mass.) Bd. Health, 1985-89, chmn., 1986-88; mem. Wayland Pers. Bd., 1999—, chmn., 2002; bd. dirs. League Sch. of Boston, Newton, Mass., 1981-84, 90—, Newton, Wellesley, Weston, Needham Area Mental Health/Mental Retardation Bd., 1977-81, Christopher House, Worcester, Mass., 1996—. Hoblitzelle Found. scholar So. Meth. U., 1974. Office: Stybel Peabody and Assocs 60 State St Boston MA 02109-1800

PEABODY, SYLVIA ROCKWOOD, retired community health nurse, agency administrator; b. Chester, Vt., June 12, 1919; d. Arthur Cochrane and Gladys Ina (Davis) P. Student, Wellesley Coll., 1937-40; BS, Columbia U., 1946; RN, Children's Hosp. Sch. Nursing, Boston, 1943; MS, Simmons Coll., 1954; postgrad., Harvard U., 1974. RN, R.I., Mich., Mass., N.Y. Staff nurse, team leader Vis. Nurse Svc. N.Y., N.Y.C., 1944-47, Barry County Health Dept., Hastings, Mich., 1947-49; pediatric nursing cons. Mich. Crippled Children's Commn., Marquette, 1949-50; pub. health instr. Children's Hosp. Sch. Nursing, Boston, 1950-53; sr. nurse, supr., asst. dir. Vist. Nurse Assn. Met. Detroit, 1954-64, exec. dir., 1964-78, Vis. Nurse Svc. Newport (R.I.) County, 1979-85; part-time charge nurse John Clarke Nursing Ctr., Middletown, RI, 1989-93. Incorporator, bd. dirs. Island Hospice, Newport, 1982-85. Pres. Newport County, Lit. Vols. Am., 1986—93; vol. Island Hospice, Newport, 1985—2001; buddy Project AIDS of R.I., 1986—95; tutor ESL, 1986—2001; docent Newport Art Mus., 1997—2001. Mem.: APHA (chmn. pub. health nursing sect. 1958—64, newsletter editor 1958—64, v.p. 1968—72), Am. Assn. Ret. Persons (vol. tax counselor 1985—2001), Nat. League for Nursing (v.p. 1973—75, pres. 1975—77), Sigma Theta Tau. Democrat. Episcopalian. Avocations: eucharistic minister, quilting, swimming, theatre, charcoal, pastel and watercolor drawing. Home: 50 Broadlawn Park Apt 111 Chestnut Hill MA 02467-3524 E-mail: sylviarp@att.net.

PEABODY, WILLIAM TYLER, JR. retired paper manufacturing company executive; b. Melrose, Mass., Mar. 17, 1921; s. William Tyler and Dorothy (Atkinson) P.; m. Florence Marshall, July 27, 1946 (dec.); children: Carol Peabody Mathews, William Tyler III, Janet Peabody Barrow, Marshall R.; m. Kay Nolan Giffen, Sept. 18, 2000. AB cum laude, Harvard U., 1942, postgrad. Grad. Sch. Arts and Scis., 1946-47, LL.B., 1949. Bar: N.Y. 1950. Asso. firm Root, Ballantine, Harlan, Bushby & Palmer, N.Y.C., 1949-54; with law div. Scott Paper Co., Phila., 1954-62, 67-85, asst. to gen. mgr. Everett, Wash., 1962-67, asst. sec., 1965-71, corp. sec., 1971-83, asst. sec., 1983-84, ret., 1985. Pres. Knollwood Terrace Civic Assn., Carle Place, N.Y., 1952-53; pres. Carle Place Taxpayers Assn., 1953-54; bd. dirs. Nether Providence Cmty. Assocs., Inc., Wallingford, Pa., 1969-75, pres., 1969-70, operator neighborhood social svcs. ctr.; bd. dirs. Ethel Mason Day Care Ctr., Wallingford, 1976-81, pres., 1979-80; vestryman St. Mary's Episc. Ch., Carle Place, N.Y., 1953-54; vestryman, jr. warden Trinity Episc. Ch., Everett, Wash., 1965-67; chmn. Rose Valley Folk, 1977-78; bd. dirs. Helen Kate Furness Free Libr., Wallingford, 1984-87, v.p., 1986-87; bd. dirs. Chester-Wallingford chpt. ARC, 1991-98, 99—, exec. com., 1992-98, 2000—, 1st vice chmn., 1994-95, chmn., 1995-98, sec., 2000—; bd. dirs. Everett, Wash. Area C. of C., 1965-67; Snohomish County Family Counseling Svc., Everett, 1962-67, pres., 1965; pres. Wallingford, Pa. Swim Club, 1960-61. Lt. USNR, 1942-46. Mem. ABA, Am. Soc. Corp. Secs. (dir. 1977-81, pres. Middle Atlantic group 1976-77), Harvard Club (Phila., sch. com. 1959-62, 76-90). Home: 971 Putnam Blvd Wallingford PA 19086-6762

PEACE, H. W., II, oil company executive; b. Clinton, Okla., May 21, 1935; s. Herman Wilbern and Bernice (Mitchell) P.; m. Norma June Williams; children: Hugh William, Susannah Lee. BS in Geology, U. Okla., 1959, MS in Geology, 1964; postgrad., U. S.W. La., 1968. Jr. geologist Union Oil Co. Calif., Houston, 1964-65, area geologist Lafayette, La., 1965-70, geologist dist. exploration Oklahoma City, 1970-77, mgr. Rocky Mountain exploration Casper, Wyo., 1977-80; mgr. div. exploration Cotton Petroleum Corp., Tulsa, 1980-83; v.p. exploration Hadson Petroleum Corp., Oklahoma City, 1983-85, exec. v.p., chief operating officer, 1985-88, also bd. dirs.; exec. v.p., chief ops. officer Mosswood Oil and Gas Co., 1985-88, Anadarko Supply Co., Oklahoma City, 1986-88, also bd. dirs.; mng. ptnr. EXAD, 1988-91; pres., CEO dir. Panhandle Royalty Co., 1991—; pres., CEO Wood Oil Co. subsitiary Panhandle Royalty Co., 2001—. Mem. mgmt. com. PLC Energy Data, LLC, 1994-2001; dir. OIL Law Recs. Corp., 2001-. Dir. sch. geology adv. com. U. Okla., Norman, 1984—, vice chmn. 1988-89, chmn. 1989-90, exec. com. 1990—. Lt. USN 1959-63, capt. USNR, 1963-82, retired list 1995. Mem. Am. Assn. Petroleum Geology (rep. del. or alt. 1984—), Soc. Exploration Geophysicists, Soc. Econ. Paleontologists and Mineralogists, Petroleum Assn. Wyo. (v.p. 1979-80), Tulsa Geol. Soc., Oklahoma City Geol. Soc. (chmn. profl. affairs 1976-77), Naval Res. Assn., Cherokee Hills Homeowners Assn. (pres. 1971-73), Fieldstone Homeowners Assn. (pres. 1983), Navy League, Okla. Corp. Commn. (mem. royalty adv. com. 1998—). Lodges: Civitan. Republican. Avocations: golf, swimming, hiking. Office: Panhandle Royalty Co 5400 N Grand Blvd Ste 210 Oklahoma City OK 73112-5688

PEACH, PAUL E. physician, medical facility administrator; b. Owensboro, Ky., June 2, 1943; s. Elbert B. and Ermal M. (Bennett) P. Student, So. Meth. U., 1961-63; BS, Ind. U., 1965, JD, 1969; student, U. New Orleans, 1977-79; MD, La. State U., 1983. Bar: Ind., 1970; diplomate Am. Bd. Phys. Medicine and Rehab. Atty. pvt. practice, Indpls., 1970-72; staff atty La. Dept. Health & Human Svcs., New Orleans, 1972-77; resident La. State U. Charity Hosp., 1983-84, Wadsworth VA Hosp., Cedars-Sinai Hosp., L.A., 1984-86; med. dir. Roosevelt Warm Springs (Ga.) Inst. for Rehab., 1986-97, Palmyra Post-Polio Clinic, Albany, Ga., 1997—. Pvt. practice atty., New Orleans, 1972-77; clin. assoc. prof. Ctr. for Rehab. Medicine Emory U., Atlanta, 1987—. Author: (with others) Late Effects of Poliomyelitis, 1991, Effect of Compliance in Treatment Outcomes in Patients with Post-Polio Syndrome, 1991. Fellow Am. Acad. Phys. Medicine and Rehab.; mem. Med. Assn. Ga., Tri-County Med. Assn. Ga. (pres. 1990-91, 93-96), Ga. Soc. Phys. Medicine and Rehab. (pres. 1989-90, 95-96), Am. Acad. Electrodiagnostic Medicine (assoc.), Am. Hosp. Assn. (governing bd. 1988-91, del. rehab. sect. 1990), So. Soc. Physical Medicine & Rehab. (pres. 2001—). Avocations: photography, music. Home: 1230 Rawson Dr Albany GA 31701-1852 Office: 810 13th Ave Ste 103 Albany GA 31701-1333

PEACHEY, LEE DEBORDE, biology educator; b. Rochester, N.Y., Apr. 14, 1932; s. Clarence Henry and Eunice (DeBorde) P.; m. Helen Pauline Fuchs, June 7, 1958; children: Michael Stephen, Sarah Elizabeth Keating, Anne Palmer Lorenz. BS, Lehigh U., 1953; postgrad., U. Rochester, 1953-56; PhD (Leitz fellow), Rockefeller U., 1959; MA (hon.), U. Pa., 1971. Research asso. Rockefeller U., 1959-60; asst. prof. zoology Columbia U., 1960-63, asso. prof., 1963-65; asso. prof. biochemistry and biophysics U. Pa., Phila., 1965-70, prof. biology, 1970-2000, prof. emeritus, 2000—; adj. prof. molecular, cellular and developmental biology U. Colo., 1969-84; mem. molecular biology study sect. NIH, 1969-73. Internat. vis. prof. Ministry Edn., Sci. and Culture Gunma (Japan) U. Med. Sch., Maebashi, 1992-95; mem. Biomed. Rsch. Tech. Rev. Com., NIH, 1994—; mem. Mayor's Sci. and Tech. Adv. Coun., Phila., 1972—; chmn. Gordon Rsch. Conf. on Muscle, 1983; mem. ext. evaluation com. Nat. Inst. Physiol. Sci., Okazaki, Japan, 1997—. Editor: Third and Fourth Conferences on Cellular Dynamics, N.Y. Acad. Scis., 1967, First and Second Confs. on Cellular Dynamics, 1968, Am. Physiol. Soc. Handbook on Skeletal Muscle, 1983; mem. editorial bd. Tissue and Cell, 1969—, Jour. Cell Biology, 1970-73, Pitman Series in Cellular and Development Biology, 1977—, Microscopy Rsch. and Technique, 1982-93, Advances in Optical and Electron Microscopy, 1983—, Neuroimage, 1991—, Jour. Microscopy, 1992-96, Bioimages, 1993—; contbr. articles to sci. jours. Trustee Keith R. Porter Endowment for Cell Biology, Merion Station, Pa., 1981— . Guggenheim and Fulbright-Hays fellow, 1967-68, Overseas fellow Churchill Coll., Cambridge, Eng., 1967-68, Fogarty Sr. Internat. fellow, 1979-80, hon. rsch. fellow U. Coll., London, 1979-80; Royal Soc. (London) guest rsch. fellow, Cambridge, 1986; grantee NSF, 1960-72, NIH, 1973—, Muscular Dystrophy Assn. Am., Inc. 1973-91. Fellow AAAS, Electron Microscopy Soc. Am. (council 1975-78, pres. 1982), Am. Soc. Cell Biology (program chmn. 1965, coun. 1966-69), Biophys. Soc. (program chmn. 1976, coun. 1976-80, exec. com. 1976-82, pres. 1981-82), Internat. Union Pure and Applied Biophysics (coun. 1978-84, v.p. 1984-87, pres. 1987-90, chmn. commn. on cell and membrane biophysics 1981-84, hon. v.p. 1990-93), Physiol. Soc. (Eng.).; mem. Internat. Soc. Stereology (internat. stereology software com. 1982-94), Soc. Gen. Physiologists. Achievements include research in mechanisms of muscle cell contraction; development of methods in light and electron microscopy; development of computer graphic methods for three-dimensional image analysis and reconstruction. Home: 524 Revere Rd Merion Station PA 19066-1033 Office: U Pa Dept Biology Philadelphia PA 19104-6018 E-mail: lee@peachey.net.

PEACOCK, A(LVIN) WARD, textile company executive; b. Durham, N.C., June 17, 1929; s. Erle Ewart and Vera Louise (Ward) P.; m. Barbara Sheppard White, July 2, 1955; children: Alvin Ward, Stephen White, Nancy Lay. BS in Commerce, U. N.C., 1950; MBA, Harvard U., 1952. Asst. to v.p. Erwin Mills, Inc., Durham, 1953-55, sec., 1957-62, sec.-treas., 1962-64; v.p. Dixie Yarns, Inc., Chattanooga, 1964-76, sr. v.p., 1976-81, Springs Industries, Fort Mill, S.C., 1981-86, exec. v.p., 1986-92. Bd. dirs. Palmetto Seed Capital Corp.; regional dir. First Wachovia Corp., Charlotte, N.C., 1988-92. Trustee Holston Conf. Colls., Tenn., 1968-79, Sci. Mus. Charlotte, 1990-94; bd. dirs. Chattanooga Meml. Hosp., 1979-81, Charlotte Symphony, 1990-94, Greater Carolinas chpt. ARC, 1988-94; dir. Allied Arts Fund, 1978-81, Metrolina Food Bank, 1994—; mem. Chattanooga Wastewater Regulation Bd., 1978-81. 1st lt. USAF, 1955-57. Mem. Tenn. Mfrs. Assn. (chmn. bd. dirs. 1980-81), Chattanooga Mfrs. Assn. (pres. 1968-69), Am. Textile Mfrs. Inst., Univ. Club, River Hills Club, Phi Beta Kappa, Alpha Kappa Psi, Sigma Nu. Republican. Methodist. Home: 6618 Seton House Ln Charlotte NC 28277-4520

PEACOCK, CHRISTOPHER A. investment company executive; b. 1946; Student, Wellington Coll., Berkshire, Eng. With Jones Lang Wooten (now Jones Lang LaSalle Inc.), Eng., 1972—, ptnr. Eng., 1974, mem. exec. bd. continent of Europe, 1985—, mng. ptnr. continent of Europe, chmn. leasing agy., 1992-96, European CEO, 1996-97, internat. CEO, 1997-99, pres., dep. CEO, COO, chmn. mgmt. exec. com., dir., 1999—2002, CEO, 2002—. Fellow Royal Instn. Chartered Surveyors. Office: Jones Lang LaSalle Inc 200 E Randolph Dr Chicago IL 60601 Fax: 312-782-4339.

PEACOCK, ERLE EWART, JR. surgeon, lawyer, educator; b. Durham, N.C., Sept. 10, 1926; s. Erle Ewart and Vera Louise (Ward) P.; m. Mary Louise Lowrey, Apr. 17, 1954; children: James Lowrey, Susan Louise, Virginia Gayle. Cert. in medicine, U. N.C., 1947, BS, 1990; MD, Harvard U., 1949; JD, U.N.C., 1993. Bar: N.C. 1993. Intern, asst. resident surgery Roosevelt Hosp., N.Y.C., 1949-51; from asst. resident gen. surgery U. N.C. Hosps., Chapel Hill, 1953-54, chief resident gen. surgery, 1954-55; resident in plastic surgery Barnes Hosp., St. Louis, 1955-56; mem. faculty dept. surgery U. N.C., Chapel Hill, 1956-69, prof. surgery, head div. plastic surgery, 1965-69; prof., chmn. dept. surgery U. Ariz., Tucson, 1969-77; prof. surgery Tulane U., New Orleans, 1977-82; pvt. practice surgery Chapel Hill, N.C., 1982-93; vis. prof. surgery U. Va., Charlottesville, 1988-97; clin. prof. surgery U. N.C., Chapel Hill, 1996—. Chief hand surgery Valley Forge Army Hosp., Phoenixville, Pa., 1951-53; pres. Am. Bd. Plastic Surgery, 1975 Author: Wound Repair, 1977, 3d edit., 1982; assoc. editor: Am. Jour. Surgery, 1967—, Surgery Yearbook, 1970-89, Plastic and Reconstructive Surgery, 1972-78; asst. editor: Jour. Surg. Rsch., 1970-76. With USN, 1945-46; capt. M.C., U.S. Army, 1951-53. Served with U.S. Navy, 1945-46; served to capt. M.C. U.S. Army, 1951-53. Recipient Yandell medal Louisville Surg. Soc., 1972, McGraw medal Detroit Surg. Soc., 1973, Disting. Svc. award U. N.C., 1979, Jacob Markowitz award Acad. Surg. Rsch., 1993, Lifetime Achievement award Wound Healing Soc., 1994. Mem. AMA, ACS, ABA, Womack Sur. Soc. (pres. 1979-80), Soc. U. Surgeons (treas. 1965-68), Plastic Surgery Rsch. Coun. (pres. 1966), Am. Surg. Assn., Am. Bd. Plastic Surgery (pres. 1976), Am. Bd. Gen. Surgery, Am. Assn. Plastic Surgeons (Clinician of Yr. 1985), Am. Soc. Surgery Hand, Internat. Soc. Surgeons, So. Surg. Assn., Am. Coll. Legal Medicine, Rotary, Alpha Omega Alpha. Republican. Methodist. Home: 645 Rock Creek Rd Chapel Hill NC 27514-6714 Office: Hollowell Peacock & Meyer PO Box 31208 Raleigh NC 27622-1208 E-mail: helthlaw@aol.com.

PEACOCK, GEORGE ROWATT, retired life insurance company executive; b. Lakeland, Fla., Aug. 27, 1923; s. Robert and Annie Keane (Rowatt) P.; m. Virginia Jenkins, June 7, 1952; 1 child, Robert George. BA, U. Fla., 1948, postgrad., 1948-49, U. N.C., 1949-50, 51, Ind. U., summers 1966, 67. With Equitable Life Assurance Soc. U.S., 1952-88, v.p., head real estate dept., 1974-77, sr. v.p., head equities sector, 1977-80, sr. v.p., head real estate sector, 1980-84; chmn., chief exec. Equitable Real Estate Investment Mgmt., Inc., 1984-88; pres., chief exec. officer Carluke Inc., 1988—2002. Past pres. Planters Redevel. Corp., St. Louis, 1984-87; trustee Equitable Life Mortgage & Realty Investors, 1981-83; emeritus mem. adv. bd. govs. Wharton Real Estate Ctr., U. Pa., 1985—. Author papers in field. Trustee Urban Land Inst., 1982-88; bd. dirs. Urban Land Found., 1994-99; bd. govs. Ctrl. Atlanta Progress, 1984-86. With USAAF, 1942-45, with USAF, 1950-51. Decorated Purple Heart. Mem. Am. Soc. Real Estate Counselors, Urban Land Inst., Am. Inst. Real Estate Appraisers, Real Estate Bd. N.Y. (past gov.), Phi Beta Kappa, Phi Kappa Phi, Phi Gamma Delta. Democrat. Office: GR Peacock PO Box 420979 Atlanta GA 30342

PEACOCK, JUDITH ANN See ERWIN, JUDITH ANN

PEACOCK, LAMAR BATTS, retired physician; b. Albany, Ga., Sept. 21, 1920; s. Herbert A. and Helen Marian (LeVan) P.; m. Jane Bonner, June 7, 1947; children: Helen Lee (Mrs. Richard Paul Wade), Linda Jane (Mrs. Mathew Gossage), Lamar Bonner. BA, Emory U., 1941; MD, Med. Coll. Ga., 1946. Diplomate: Am. Bd. Internal Medicine. Intern Univ. Hosp., Augusta, 1946-47, resident, 1947-48; fellow internal medicine U. Va. Hosp., Charlottesville, 1948-49; resident Univ. Hosp., Augusta, 1949-50; practice medicine specializing in internal medicine and allergy Atlanta, 1950-91. Mem. staff St. Joseph's Hosp., Crawford Long Hosp., Piedmont Hosp., Grady Meml. Hosp., Hughes Spalding Pavilion, Northside Hosp., All Atlanta, Cobb Gen. Hosp., Austell, Ga., Douglasville (Ga.) Hosp.; instr. internal medicine Ga. Bapt. Hosp., Atlanta, 1950-58, chief medicine, 1958-72; mem. faculty Emory U. Sch. Medicine, Atlanta, 1950— , asst. clin. prof. medicine, 1962— ; instr. internal medicine Sch. Dentistry, 1958— Chief med. br., health services Atlanta Met. Area Civil Def., 1960-63; mem. Ga. Pub. Health Assn., 1967-69, Ga. Bd. Health, 1966-72, Ga. Vocational Rehab. Council, 1973— ; Pres. trustees Med. Coll. Ga. Found., 1963. Recipient Physicians Physician award, MCG, 1984. Fellow ACP, Am. Coll. Allergy, Asthma and Immunology (nat. pres. 1972-73), Am. Acad. Allergy and Immunology; mem. AMA, Am. Heart Assn., Ga. Heart Assn., Am. Soc. Internal Medicine, Ga. Soc. Internal Medicine, 5th Dist. Med. Soc., Ga. Thoracic Soc., Med. Assn. Atlanta (prs. 1965), Med. Assn. Ga. (1st v.p. 1966-67), Southeastern Allergy Assn. (pres. 1963-64), So. Med. Assn., Cherokee Town and Country Club. Episcopalian. Home: 3120 Verdun Dr NW Atlanta GA 30305-1940 E-mail: strutjbp@webtv.net.

PEACOCK, MARILYN CLAIRE, primary education educator; b. Harvey, Ill., Aug. 2, 1952; d. Carmen Anthony and Helen Elaine (Welch) R. AA with high honors, Thornton C.C., 1972; BS in Edn. with high honors, Ill. State U., 1974; MEd, Nat.-Louis U., 1990. Cert. K-9, Ill. Tchr. kindergarten Primary Acad. Ctr., Markham, Ill., 1976-91, tchr. K-3, 1991—. Ill. State scholar, 1969. Mem. Ill. Edn. Assn. (assn. rep. 1976-88), Kappa Delta Pi, Phi Theta Kappa. Republican. Avocations: music, travel. Home: 2447 Clyde St Homewood IL 60430-3103 Office: Prairie-Hills Prim Acad Ctr 3055 W 163rd St Harvey IL 60426-5626 E-mail: mcrpeacock@aol.com.

PEACOCK, MARY WILLA, magazine editor; b. Evanston, Ill., Oct. 23, 1942; d. William Gilbert and Mary Willa (Young) P. BA, Vassar Coll., 1964. Assoc. lit. editor Harper's Bazaar mag., N.Y.C., 1964-69; staff editor Innovation mag., 1969-70; editor in chief, co-founder Rags mag., N.Y.C., San Francisco, 1970-71; co-founder, features editor Ms. mag., N.Y.C., 1971-77; pub., pres. Rags mag., 1977-80; sr. editor Village Voice, 1980-85, style editor, 1985-89; editor-in-chief Model mag., 1989—, editorial cons., 1991—; fashion dir. Lear's Mag., 1992-93; dep. editor In Style Mag., 1993-94, Mirabella mag., 1994-95; cons., 1995—. Contbg. editor InStyle, InStyle.com; writer and cons. in field.

PEACOCK, MOLLY, poet, educator; b. June 30, 1947; d. Edward Frank and Pauline Ruth (Wright) P. BA magna cum laude, Harpur Coll., Binghamton, N.Y., 1969; MA with hons., Johns Hopkins U., 1977. Adminstr., lectr. in english SUNY, Binghamton, 1970-76; lectr. Johns Hopkins U., Balt., 1977-78; instr. english Friends Sem., N.Y.C., 1981-92; poet-in-residence Bucknell U., 1993-94, Cathedral St. John the Divine, 2000. Author: And Live Apart, 1980, Raw Heaven, 1984, Take Heart, 1989, Original Love, 1995, Paradise, Piece by Piece, 1998, How To Read A Poem and Start A Poetry Circle, 1999, The Private I: Privacy in A Public World, 2001, Cornucopia: New and Selected Poems, 2002; contbg. writer House and Garden mag., 1996; contbr. poems to The New Yorker, The New Republic, The Nation Danforth Found. fellow, 1970, Yaddo fellow, 1980, 82, 89, Ingram Merrill Found. fellow 1981, 86, Lila Wallace/Woodrow Wilson fellow 1994, 95, 96, 2001; grantee Creative Artists Pub. Svc. Program, 1977, N.Y. Found. for Arts, 1985, NEA, 1991; Regents scholar U. Calif., Riverside, 1998. Mem. PEN, Poetry Soc. Am. (governing bd. 1988—, pres. emeritus). Home: 505 E 14th St Apt 3G New York NY 10009-2903 also: 109 Front St Apt 1041 Toronto ON Canada M5A 4P7 E-mail: peacockmol@aol.com.

PEACOCK, VALERIE LYNN, paralegal; b. Tallahassee, Nov. 6, 1962; d. William Stanley and Valerie Jo (Tate) P. AA with honors, Tallahassee C.C., 1982; BS in Bus. Communication, Fla. State U., 1986. Cert. legal asst., Ga. With Fla. House of Reps., Tallahassee, 1980-84; with office of registrar Fla. State U., 1984-85; tchr. Leon County Sch. Bd., 1986-87; legal asst. Dept. of Ins.-Receivership, 1987-88, B.K. Roberts, Baggett, LaFace & Richard, Tallahassee, 1988; paralegal specialist criminal div. Fla. Atty. Gen., 1988—. Mem. adv. bd. Nat. Ctr. Paralegal Tng., Miami and Ft. Lauderdale, Fla., 1990—; with paralegal studies program Rollins Coll. Ctr. for Lifelong Edn., 1992—; lobbyist Fla. Peace Officers Assn., 1995—, Fla. Condo. Assn., 1997—; dir. govt. affairs Kids Against Crime Online. Editor-in-chief Fla. Condominium Resource Guide, 1998. Mem. Jr. League of Tallahassee, 1992—, bd. dirs. 1993—, cmty. pub. rels. chmn., 1993—, chmn. internat. pub. rels. com. 1992-93; vol. missionary local ch. to Port-au-Prince, Haiti, 1985, mem. adminstrv. bd. local ch., Tallahassee, 1988—; atty gen. rep. Ptnrs. in Excellence, Tallahassee, 1990; bd. dirs. Am. Heart Assn., 1992— (v.p., 1996-97, pres., 1997—, chmn. public advocacy state task force com., pub. rels. comms. com.); chmn. Children's Miracle Network, 1993, mem. cmty. bd. 1994—, chmn. pub. advocacy, 1996-97; Olympic torchbearer, cmty. hero, 1996; pres. Call Care of Fla., 1996; mem. That Art Group Mus. of Art Tallahassee, 1997—. Recipient Pres.'s award Am. Heart Assn., 1996, Editor's Choice award Nat. Libr. of Poetry, 1998, Publ. Outstanding Achievement in Poetry, 1998; finalist Vol. of Yr., Tallahassee and Leon County, 1994; named Cmty. Hero and Olympic Torchbearer, 1996 Olympics in Atlanta. Mem. Fla. Supreme Ct. Hist. Soc., Tallahassee C. of C. (com. on pub. rels. 1996-97, Disting. Leader award com. 1997, 98, Leadership Tallahassee grad. class X), Friends of Maclay Gardens, Pi Kappa Phi, Phi Sigma Soc., Phi Theta Kappa. Republican. Avocations: fgn. and domestic travel, govt., modeling, recreational sports. Office: Atty Gen Criminal Div The Capitol Tallahassee FL 32399-1050

PEAGLER, OWEN F. retired college dean; b. New Milford, Conn., Nov. 28, 1931; s. Robert James and Myrtle (Gary) P.; m. Joyce Hancock (div. 1983); children: Catherine, Robert; m. Teresa Balough, Mar. 20, 1985; 1 child, Kirin. BS, Western Conn. State U., 1956; MA, NYU, 1959, profl. diploma, 1964. Tchr. New Milford Pub. Schs., 1955-56; dir. guidance White Plains (N.Y.) Pub. Schs., 1957-69; dean Sch. Continuing Edn., Pace U., N.Y.C., 1969-78, Ea. Conn. State U., Willimantic, 1978—. Chmn. bd. WAVE, Inc., Washington, 1976-95; cons., V.I., 1970-73. Sec. dept. community affairs State of Del., Wilmington, 1982-83; asst. to N.Y. Rep. State Chmn. N.Y. Rep. State Com., Albany, 1970-78; chmn. Pres'. Adv. Coun. on Edn. Disadvantaged Children, Washington, 1973-78. Named N.Y. State Young Man of Yr. N.Y. Jr. C. of C., 1964; recipient Outstanding Coll. Programs award Conn. Nat. Guard, 1988. Home: 57 Boughton Rd Old Lyme CT 06371-1321 E-mail: owpeag@aol.com.

PEAK, JAMES MATTHEW, fundraising executive; b. Canton, Ill., Feb. 21, 1936; s. Merle Harry and Hilda (Sepich) P.; m. Julia Lord, Nov. 22, 1962; children: Cynthia, Matthew, Mark, Katherine. BA, U. Tex., El Paso, 1958. Cert. fund raising exec. Agt. trainer Penn Mut. Life Ins., El Paso, 1965-70; gen. agt. Albuquerque, 1970-73, Mass. Mut. Life Ins., El Paso, 1973-76; dir. devel. U. Tex., 1977-89; chief devel. officer, pres. Providence Meml. Hosp. Found., 1989-91; pres., chief devel. officer Mont. Tech. Found., 1998-2000; pres., chief devel. officer Cath. Found. Diocese El Paso, 2001—. With dist. relations Council for Advancement and Support of Edn., Tex., 1984-89, devel. rep. SW dist., 1987-89; fund raising cons., S.W. Dist. IV Case, Tex., 1977-89, conf. dir., 1985—; fund raising cons. Meml. Hosp. Found., 1989-2000. Contbr.: A Handbook of Proven Strategies and Techniques, 1982. Bd. dirs. Am. Cancer Soc., El Paso, 1958-83, El Paso Arts Alliance, 1984-86; mem. El Paso Estate Planning Coun., 1984-2001. Served with U.S. Army, 1958-61. Recipient Outstanding Svc. to Students award, U. Tex.-El Paso, 1980, Disting. Svc. award, 1982, Fund Raising Exec. of the Yr., Assn. Fund Raising Profls., 2000. Mem. Assn. Healthcare Philanthropy, Assn. of Fundraising Profls. (cert., pres. El Paso chpt. 2001—), El Paso Assn. Life Underwriters (v.p. 1973-76), New Eng. Alumni Trust (exec. com. 1987-89). Lodges: K.C. (bd. dirs. 1973-75), Lions (v.p. 1984-87, pres. 1987—). Roman Catholic. Avocations: golf, reading, fishing, sports. Home and Office: 4832 Costa De Oro Rd El Paso TX 79922-1703 E-mail: jimp@elpasodiocese.org.

PEAKE, CANDICE K. LOPER, data processing professional; b. Sublette, Kans., Oct. 29, 1953; d. Robert Franklin and Marion Joyce Loper; m. Eugene E. Peake, Aug. 12, 1993. Student, McPherson (Kans.) Coll., 1971-72; lic. in cosmetology, Crums Beauty Sch., Manhattan, Kans., 1974; student, Garden City (Kans.) Community Coll., 1975-76, Diablo Valley Coll., 1988-89. ICCP cert. data processor. Owner, operator Candi's For Beautiful Hair, Garden City, 1974-78; systems project librarian Bank of Am., San Francisco, 1980, analyst, 1981, systems analyst, 1981-82, sr. systems analyst, 1982-83, cons., 1983-84, systems cons., team leader, 1984; project mgr. Wells Fargo Bank, Concord, Calif., 1984-86; systems analyst 1st Nationwide Bank, San Francisco, 1986-88; adv. systems engr. Bank Am., Concord, Calif., 1988-89; owner Candi's Visions, Independence, Mo., 1988—; sr. mgr. Computer Scis. Corp., 1989—. Home: 3419 S Home Ave Independence MO 64052-1239 Office: Computer Scis Corp 3419 S Home Ave Independence MO 64052-1239 E-mail: candace@go4thevision.com., cpeake@csc.com.

PEAKE, CHARLES FRANKLIN, economist, educator; b. Erwin, Tenn., Feb. 4, 1933; s. Carl Rockard and Vista (Miller) P.; divorced; children: Mary Elizabeth Peake Coppolino, Lilian Ruth Peake Mancuso. BS in Econs., East Tenn. State U., 1956; MS in Econs., U. Tenn., 1958; postgrad., London Sch. Econs. and Oxford, 1960-64; PhD in Econs., U. Md., 1968. Chartered fin. analyst; cert. cost analyst. Instr. econs. Arkansas State U., Jonesboro, 1957-58; assoc. prof. U. Md., Balt., 1964—, chmn. dept. econs., 1967-74, dean div. social sci., 1970-71; mgmt. analyst U.S. Dept. Justice LEAA, Washington, 1978, U.S. Consumer Product Safety Commn., Washington, 1979-81; spl. asst. U.S. Bur. Census Dept. of Commerce, Suitland, Md., 1983-86. Cons. Regional Planning Coun., Balt., 1968-69, Whitfield Russell Assocs., Washington, 1981-83; expert witness various utility rate cases. Contbr. articles to profl. jours. Chmn. bd. trustees Omicron Delta Epsilon Scholarship Fund, 1978-99, Walter V. Hohenstein Scholarship Fund, 1988—. Harold Stonier fellow Am. Bankers Assn.; Fulbright Rsch. Scholar, 1960-61; Fulbright Group Study grantee, 1975. Mem. Am. Econ. Assn., Royal Econ. Soc., Inst. Chartered Fin. Analysts, Assn. Investment Mgmt. and Rsch., Phi Kappa Phi (pres. U. Md. chpt. 1986-88, mem. nat. investment com. 1986-89, chmn. 1989-92, mem. nat. budget adv. com. 1992—), Sigma Phi Epsilon. Democrat. Lutheran. Home: 9331 Mellenbrook Rd Columbia MD 21045-1819 Office: U Md Dept Econs 5401 Wilkens Ave Baltimore MD 21250-1000

PEAKE, FRANK, middle school educator; b. Elgin, S.C., Oct. 25, 1939; s. Barney and Elrie (Branham) P. AA, Anderson Coll., 1966; BS, U. S.C., 1968; MA in Teaching, The Citadel, 1976. Cert. tchr., S.C. Classroom tchr. Berkeley Jr. High, Moncks Corner, S.C., 1968-70, Berkeley Middle Sch., Moncks Corner, 1970-85, 90-95, ret., 1995; classroom tchr. Macedonia Middle Sch., 1986-88, North Ctrl. High, Kershaw, S.C., 1988-89. With S.C. Air Nat. Guard, 1959-65. Mem. Nat. Coun. Tchrs. Math., Mensa. Republican. Baptist. Avocations: reading, gardening. Home: 1201 Peake Rd Elgin SC 29045

PEAL, CHRISTOPHER JOHN, educational administrator; b. Moline, Ill., Dec. 17, 1963; s. Gerald J. and Annette M. Peal. BA, Olivet Nazarene U., 1986; MA, U. Mich., 1989; PhD, Loyola U., 1996. Cert. supt., adminstr., tchr., Ill., Mich. English, lang. arts, speech, journalism tchr., newspaper advisor Plymouth-Canton High Sch., Mich., 1986-90; asst. prin. Muskegon Catholic Ctrl. Jr./High Sch., 1990-91; dean students Canton Mid. Sch., Streamwood, Ill., 1991-94; prin. North Elem. Sch., Watervliet, Mich., 1994-97, Mary Helen Guest Elem. Sch., Walled Lake, 1998—. Mem. Watervliet Sch. Improvement Team, 1994-97; mem. Elgin (Ill.) Sch. Dist. U-46 Mid. Sch. Task Force, 1991-94; advisor to student newspaper, adj. instr. Lake Mich. Coll., 1997; mem. Mary Helen Guest Elem. Sch. PTA, 1998—; mem. Walled Lake Consolidated Schs. Adminstrs. Assn., 1998—, Mary Helen Guest Elem. Sch. North Ctrl. Accreditation Team, 1998—. Mem. Watervliet PTO, 1994-97; short-term missionary work, Turkey, 2000, China, 2001. Recipient Spl. Tribute award State of Mich., 1987, Gold Apple Teaching Excellence award Wayne County (Mich.) Intermediate Sch. Dist., 1987, 88, 89; dean's merit fellow U. Mich., 1987, 88, Dow Jones Newspaper Fund fellow, 1988. Mem. ASCD, Mich. Elem. and Mid. Sch. Prins. Assn., Nat. Assn. Elem. Sch. Prins., Mich. Interscholastic Press Assn. (judge 1988-90), Columbia Scholastic Press Assn. (bd. judges 1987-90, conv. speaker), Gt. Lakes Interscholastic Press Assn. (judge 1988-90), Journalism Edn. Assn., U. Mich. Alumni Assn. (life), Walled Lake Colson. Schs. Adminstrs. Assn. (exec. bd. 2000—). Avocations: antiquing, computers, golf. Office: Mary Helen Guest Elem Sch 1655 Decker Rd Walled Lake MI 48390-2627

PEALE, RUTH STAFFORD (MRS. NORMAN VINCENT PEALE), religious leader; b. Fonda, Iowa, Sept. 10, 1906; d. Frank Burton and Anna Loretta (Crosby) Stafford; m. Norman Vincent Peale, June 20, 1930; children: Margaret Ann (Mrs. Paul F. Everett), John Stafford, Elizabeth Ruth (Mrs. John M. Allen). AB, Syracuse U., 1928, LLD, 1953; LittD, Hope Coll., 1962; LHD (hon.), Judson Coll., 1988. Tchr. math. Cen. High Sch., Syracuse, NY, 1928—30; nat. pres. women's bd. domestic missions Ref. Ch. Am., 1936-46; sec. Protestant Film Commn., 1946-51; chmn. Am. Mother's Com., 1948-49; pres., editor-in-chief, gen. sec., CEO, chmn. bd. dirs. Peale Ctr. for Christian Living, 1940—; nat. pres. bd. domestic missions Ref. Ch. in Am., 1955-56; mem. bd. N. Am. Missions, 1963-69, pres., 1967-69; mem. gen. program council Ref. Ch. in Am., 1968—; mem. com. of 24 for merger Ref. Ch. in Am. and Presbyn. Ch. U.S., 1966-69; v.p. Protestant Council N.Y.C., 1964-66; co-founder, pub. Guideposts, N.Y.C., 1945—, pres., 1985-92, chmn. bd., 1992—; pres. Fleming H. Revell, Tarrytown, N.Y., 1985-92. (appeared on): (nat. TV program) What's Your Trouble, 1952—68; author: I Married a Minister, 1942, The Adventure of Being a Wife, 1971, Secrets of Staying in Love, 1984, A Lifetime of Positive Thinking, 2001; founder, pub. (with Dr. Peale) Guidepost mag., 1945—, co-subject with husband (film) One Man's Way, 1963. Named N.Y. State Mother of Yr., 1963, Disting. Woman of Yr., Nat. Art Assn., Religious Heritage Am. Ch. Woman of Yr., 1969, Woman of Yr., AAUW, 2000; recipient Cum Laude award Syracuse U. Alumni Assn. N.Y., 1965, Honor Iowans award Buena Vista Coll., 1966, Am. Mother's com. award for religion, 1970, Disting. Svc. award Coun. Chs., N.Y.C., 1973, Disting. Citizen award Champlain Coll., 1976, Disting. Svc. to Cmty. and Nation award Gen. Fedn. Women's Clubs, 1977, Horatio Alger award, 1977, Religious Heritage award, 1979, joint medallion with husband Soc. for Family of Man, 1981, Soc. Family of Man award, 1981, Alderson-Broaddus award, 1982, Marriage Achievement award Bride's mag., 1984, Gold Angel award Religion in Media, 1987, Adela Rogers St. John Roundtable award, 1987, Disting. Achievement award Am. Aging, 1987, Paul Harris award N.Y. Rotary, 1989, Leader's award Arthritis Found. Dutchess County, 1992, Dave Thomas Well Done! award, 1994, Norman Vincent Peale award for positive thinking, 1994, Master of Influence award, 1995, The Leadership award Worldwide Leadership Coun., 1998, Cert. for Disting. Svc., N.Y. State Fedn. Women's Clubs, 1999, Light award CANDL Found., 2000, Woman of Distinction awd RCA Women, 2001. Mem. Blanton-Peale Inst. (bd. exec. com.), Am. Bible Soc. (trustee 1948-93, hon. trustee 1993—, bd. dirs.), Nat. Bible Assn. (bd. dirs.), United Bible Soc., Interch. Ctr. (bd. dirs. 1957-92, chmn. 1982-90), Nat. Coun. Chs. (v.p. 1952-54, gen. bd.; treas. gen. dept. United Ch. Women, vice chmn. broadcasting and film commn. 1951-55, program chmn. gen. assembly 1966), N.Y. Fedn. Women's Clubs (chmn. religion 1951-53, 57-58), Home Missions Coun. N.A. (nat. pres. 1942-44, nat. chmn. migrant com. 1948-51), Internat. Platform Orgn. (bd. govs. 1994-2000), Ccmty. Action Network (adv. bd. 1998—), PEO, Sorosis (pres. 1953-56, hon. pres.), Alpha Phi (Frances W. Willard award 1976). Republican. Office: Peale Ctr Christian Living 66 E Main St Pawling NY 12564-1409

PEAPPLES, GEORGE ALAN, retired automotive executive; b. Benton Harbor, Mich., Nov. 6, 1940; s. Arthur L. and Kathleen C. (Peters) P.; m. Rebecca Dean Sowers, June 27, 1962; children: Lucia Christine, Sarah Bouton. BA in Econs., U. Mich., 1962, MBA in Fin., 1963. Fin. analyst GM Corp., Detroit, 1964-68; dir. capital analysis and investment N.Y.C., 1968-73; asst. divsn. comptr. Delco Moraine divsn. Dayton, Ohio, 1973-75; asst. treas. bank rels. Detroit, 1975-77; asst. comptr., 1980-82; v.p. fin. mgr. GM of Can. Ltd., Oshawa, Ont., 1982-84; group dir. strategic bus. planning Chevrolet-Pontiac-Canada group Warren, Mich., 1984-86; v.p. GM Corp., pres., gen. mgr. GM of Can., Oshawa, Ont., Can., 1986-94; v.p. pub. policy Washington, 1994-99; retired, 2000—; asst. sec. of Navy U.S. Dept. Def., 1977-80. Recipient Disting. Pub. Svc. award Washington, 1980. E-mail: gapeapples@aol.com.

PEAR, BERTRAM LINCOLN, radiologist, educator; b. Balt., Feb. 12, 1919; m. Martha Jean Butler, July 3, 1945; 1 child, Melissa. BA, George Washington U., 1941, MD, 1950. Diplomate Am. Bd. Radiology. Intern Fitzsimons Gen. Hosp., Denver, 1950-51; resident George Washington U. Hosp., Washington, 1951-52, U. Colo. Med. Ctr., 1952-54, clin. prof. radiology. Contbr. chpts. to 2 books, more than 30 articles to profl. jours. Served with 93d Bomb Group, USAAC, 1941-45. Fellow Am. Coll. Angiology, Am. Coll. Radiology; mem. AMA, Colo. Med. Soc., Denver Med. Soc., Colo. Radiol. Soc. (pres. 1972-73), Rocky Mountain Radiol. Soc. (pres. 1967-68), Colo. Soc. Nuclear Medicine (founding mem., past pres.), Am. Roentgen Ray Soc., Soc. Nuclear Medicine (pres. chpt. 1969-70), others. Home: 260 S High St Denver CO 80209-2628 E-mail: pearmd217@pol.net.

PEAR, CHARLES E., JR. lawyer; b. Macon, Ga., June 18, 1950; s. Charles Edward and Barbara Jane P.; m. Linda Sue King; children: Jennifer Sue, Charles Edward III, Stephanie Sue. BA, U. Hawaii, 1972 with honors; JD, U. Calif., Berkeley, 1975. Bar: Hawaii 1976, Fla. 1977, Colo. 1994, U.S. Ct. of Appeals (9th cir.). Assoc. Rush, Moore, Craven, Sutton, Morry & Beh, Honolulu, 1976-77, of counsel, 1987-90; assoc., ptnr. Carlsmith & Dwyer, 1977-82; ptnr. Burke, Sakai, McPheeters, Bordner & Gilardy, 1983-87; vis. prof. law and computers U. British Columbia, 1990-93; of counsel Holland & Hart, Denver, 1993-96; counsel, ptnr. McCorriston, Miller, Mukai, MacKinnon, Honolulu, 1996—. Mem. Hawaii Real Estate Commn. com. on condominium and resort real estate legis., 1978-79; spl. counsel to consumer protection com. Hawaii State Ho. of Reps., 1981-82; chair real property and fin. svcs. sect. Hawaii State Bar Assn., ABA. Editor-in-Chief Hawaii Conveyance Manual II, 1987; editor Hawaii Commercial Real Estate Manual, 1988; bd. editors Hawaii Inst. of Continuing Legal Edn.; co-author: Nat. Assn. of Real Estate Licensing Law Officials and Nat. Timesharing Coun. Model Timesharing Act, 1981-82; contbg. author: Winning With Computers, 1992, Hawaii Real Estate Manual, 1997; lectr. in field, 1981—. Mem. ABA .

PEARCE, BETTY MCMURRAY, manufacturing company executive; b. Hastings, Nebr., Oct. 11, 1926; d. Frank Madry and Scereta (Mudd) McMurray; BS in Aerospace, U. Tex., Austin, 1949; 1 child, Karen A. Harsley. Draftsman, Koch & Fowler, Civil Engrs., Dallas, 1945-47; with Ling Temco Vought-Aircraft Products Group-Aircraft Maintenance and Support Group, Dallas, 1949—, project engr., 1955-77, engrng. project mgr., 1977-83, dir. engrng., 1983-89, engrng. mgr. advanced sys. concepts, 1989-90; program mgr. PAMPA 2000, 1990-92; ret., 1992; dir. LTV Fed. Credit Union, v.p. LTV Mgmt. Club; cons. Active Aux. St. Joseph's Hosp.; pres. St. Andrews Catholic Ch. Coun., Fort Worth, 1977-78; mem. Bishop's Adv. Coun. Fort Worth Diocese, 1980-87, chmn. svc. com., 1980-81, pres., 1981-82, 84-85; mem. Allied Cmtys. of Tarrant, 1982— . Mem. AIAA, Tech. Mktg. Soc. Am. Home: 3613 W Biddison St Fort Worth TX 76109-2704

PEARCE, DAVID HARRY, biomedical engineer, consultant; b. Newport News, Va., July 20, 1943; BSEE, Va. Poly. Tech. and State U., 1966; PhD, U. Va., 1972. Registered profl. engr., Miss. Asst. prof. dept. physiology U. Miss. Med. Sch., Jackson, Miss., 1972-74, E. Tenn. State U. Sch. Medicine, JohnsonCity, Tenn., 1974-75; biomed. engr. Miss. Meth. Rehab. Ctr., Jackson, Miss., 1975-82; v.p. Bobby J. Hall & Assocs., McComb, 1982-87. Grant adminstr. HUD Block Grant, Magnolia, Miss., 1985-87; dir. biomed. engrng. Miss. Meth. Rehab. Ctr., Jackson, 1987-99; cons. engr., 1999—. Contbr. articles to profl. jours. Young Investigator Pulmonary award NIH, 1973. Mem. IEEE, Am. Soc. Hosp. Engrs., Assn. Advancement of Med. Instrumentation, Jackson Photo Soc. (pres. 1980), Miss. Writers Assn. (treas. 1992). Avocations: photography, woodworking, writing. Address: PO Box 5336 Brandon MS 39047-5336 E-mail: DHPearce89@aol.com.

PEARCE, DONALD JOSLIN, retired librarian; b. Southampton, Eng., May 31, 1924; came to U.S., 1949, naturalized, 1952; s. Alfred Ernest and Constance May (Jeffrey) P.; m. June Inez Bond, Dec. 7, 1946; children—Kristin, Kim. Student, Sch. Oriental and African Studies, U. London, 1942-43; AB, George Washington U., 1953; MS in L.S, Cath. U. Am., 1954. Part-time library asst. U.S. Dept. Agr., 1949-54; student asst. George Washington U. Library, 1950-53; circulation librarian Denison U., 1954-56; staff Ohio State U. Library, 1956-59, asst. acquisition librarian, 1958-59; head librarian, asst. prof. U. N.D., 1959-69, chief bibliographer, 1969-73, asst. dir. libraries, 1973-75, asst. prof. Oriental philosophy, 1969-75; library dir., asst. prof. philosophy U. Minn., Duluth, 1975-88, ret., 1988. Chmn. staff orgn. round table Ohio Library Assn., 1958-59 Served with Brit. Army, 1943-47. Mem. ALA, N.D. Library Assn. (pres. 1965-67), Minn. Library Assn. (sec. 1978-80, v.p. 1985, pres. 1986), Assn. Coll. Reference Librarians, Mountain Plains Library Assn. (v.p. 1968-69), Buddhist Assn., Phi Beta Kappa, Beta Phi Mu. Home: 70 E St Marie St Apt 127 Duluth MN 55803 E-mail: dpearce@d.umn.edu.

PEARCE, ELI M. chemistry educator, administrator; b. Bklyn., May 1, 1929; s. Samuel and Sarah (Reitzen) Perlmutter; m. Maxine I. Horowitz, Feb. 21, 1951 (div. 1978); children:Russell Gane, Debra Nore; m. Judith Handler, May 29, 1980. BS, Bklyn. Coll., 1949; MS, NYU, 1951; PhD, Poly. Inst. Bklyn, 1958. Research chemist NYU-Bellevue Med. Ctr., N.Y.C., 1949-53, DuPont, Wilmington, Del., 1958-62; sec. mgr. J.T. Baker, Phillipsburg, N.J., 1962-68; tech. supr. Allied Corp., Morristown, 1968-72, research cons., 1972-73; dir. Dreyfus Lab. Research Triangle Inst., Research Triangle Park, N.C., 1973-74; prof. polymer chemistry and chem. engrng. Poly. Inst. N.Y., Bklyn., 1974—, dir. Polymer Research Inst., 1981-96, Univ. prof., 1990-99, head dept. chemistry, 1976-82, dean arts and scis., 1982-90, univ. rsch. prof., 1999—. Cons. AMP, Inc., Harrisburg, Pa., Arco, Newton Square, Pa., Colgate, Piscataway, N.J., Dupont, Richmond, Va., Texaco, Beacon, N.Y. Co-author: Laboratory Experiments in Polymer Synthesis and Characterization, 1982, High Performance Thermosets; editor: Macromolecular Synthesis, Vol. 1, 1982; co-editor: Fiber Chemistry, 1983, Contemporary Topics in Polymer Science, vol. 2, 1977, Flame Retardance of Polymeric Materials, vols. 1-3, Jour. Polymer Sci.; mem. editl. bd. Ency. Materials Sci., 1983; contbr. over 230 articles on polymers to profl. jours. Bd. dirs. Petroleum Research Fund, 1982-84; bd. dirs. Nat. Materials Adv. Bd., 1975-77. Served with U.S. Army, 1953-55. Recipient Edn. Service award Plastics Inst. Am., 1973; recipient Disting. Faculty citation Poly. Inst. N.Y., 1980, Disting. Alumnus citation, 1997, Paul J. Flory Polymer Edn. award, 1992, Kaufman Lectr. award Ramapo Coll., 1992, Gold Medal award N.Y. Inst. Chemists, 1992, Reed-Lignin Lectr. award U. Wis., 1987, Oscar Foster award Chemistry Tchrs. Club, 2000, Henry Hill award, 2002. Fellow AAAS, Am. Inst. Chemists, N.Am. Thermal Analysis Soc., N.Y. Acad. Scis. (chmn. polymer sect. 1972-73), Soc. Plastics Engrs. (Internat. Edn. award 1988); mem. Am. Chem. Soc. (councilor 1978—, chmn. polymer divsn. 1980, coun. policy com. on coms., chmn. com. sci., bd. dirs. 1999—, pres. 2002), Sigma Xi. Home: 2 Fifth Ave New York NY 10011 Office: Polytech U Polymer Rsch Inst 6 Metrotech Ctr Brooklyn NY 11201-3840 E-mail: epearce@poly.edu.

PEARCE, JACK BODELL, marine biologist, educator; b. Dearborn, Mich., Sept. 20, 1930; s. Lloyd William P. and Helen Bodell; m. Ruth Elizabeth Howlett, Mar. 14, 1953; children: Wendy Helen, Scott Anthony. BA, Humboldt State Coll., 1957; MS, U. Wash., 1960, PhD, 1962. Postdoctoral fellow U. Copenhagen NIH, 1962-63; postdoctoral fellow Marine Biol. Lab. NSF, Woods Hole, Mass., 1963-65; assoc. prof. Humboldt State U., Arcata, Calif., 1965-67; officer in charge Sandy Hook Marine Lab Nat. Oceanic and Atmospheric Adminstrn., Highlands, N.J., 1967-84, dir. Nat. Estuarine Program Washington, 1984-85, dep. dir. sci. and rsch. Woods Hole, Mass., 1985-95; editor Fishery Bulletin NOAA and NMFS, 1995-99; N.Am. editor Marine Pollution Bull., 1994—. Chair Marine Environ. Quality Conf. Internat. Coun. Exploration of Sea, 1975-87, N.J. Gov.'s Blue Ribbon Com. on Marine Poll, Trenton, 1988-89, Conf. on Gulf of Maine, Dartmouth Coll., Hanover, N.H., 1995; mem. working group Gulf of Maine Coun. on the Marine Environment, Augusta, 1987—. Co-author: UN Report on Health of World's Oceans, 1989-90; co-editor: Seas at the Millennium, 2000; contbr. articles to profl. jours. Bd. dirs. The Three Hundred Com., Falmouth, Mass., 1984-99; mem. Falmouth (Mass.) Recycling Com., 1986-93, Woods Hole Cmty. Task Force, 1987-98, Woods Hole Libr., 1998—, Rumson-Fair Haven (N.J.) School Bd., 1970-73; mem. Unitarian Ch. Sgt. U.S. Army, 1953-55. Recipient: Gold Medal U.S. Dept. Commerce, 1983, U.S. EPA award for Outstanding Sci., 1982. Fellow AAAS; mem. Am. Fisheries Soc., Scottish Assn. Marine Sci., EStuarine Rsch. Fedn., World Mariculture Assn., Nat. Shellfish Assn., Crustacean Soc. Democrat. Avocations: outdoor photography, hiking, traveling, biking, reading. Home: 54 Upland Ave Falmouth MA 02540-2324 Office: Buzzards Bay Lab 54 Upland Ave Falmouth MA 02540-2324

PEARCE, JANET DINKEL, foundation administrator; b. Toledo, Oct. 26, 1943; d. J. Edward and Betty (Richardson) Dinkel; m. James Erwin Pearce, Mar. 15, 1986. BA, Wittenberg U., 1965; MA, Ohio State U., 1968. Economic analyst Fed. Reserve Bank, Cleve., 1967-76; regional campaign dir. United Way Nat. Capital Area, Washington, 1976-79; exec. dir. United Way Adams County, Quincy, Ill., 1979-83; exec. v.p. United Way L.I., Melville, N.Y., 1983—. Contbr. articles to profl. jours. Mem. Jr. League, L.I. Episcopalian. Home: PO Box 375 Gales Ferry CT 06335-0375

PEARCE, JASON ALEXANDER, communications administrator, content architect, editor; b. Raleigh, N.C., Mar. 22, 1972; s. Irvin Alexander P. BA in Corp. Comm. cum laude, BA in Broadcast Comm., Elon Coll., 1994. Ednl. leadership cons. Lambda Chi Alpha Fraternity, Indpls., 1994-95, dir. comm. and alumni rels., 1995-98, dir. comm. and web devel., 1998-99; content arch. WeAlumni.com, Arlington, Va., 1999-2001; midwest regional mgr. Carden Jennings Pub., Indpls., 2001—02; instr. cmty. info. tech. Peace Corps., Guyana, 2001—. Bd. dirs. Coll. Fraternity Editors Assn., Indpls., 1998-2001. Editor mag. Cross & Crescent, 1998 (3d pl. award 1998, Marilyn S. Ford award 2000-01); webmaster LambdaChi.org, 1998-99 (1st pl. award 1998, 99). Mem. Coll. Fraternity Editors Assn. (chmn., editor The Fraternity Editor 1997-98, chmn. 1998-99, dir. 1998-99), Lambda Chi Alpha, Lambda Pi Eta, Omicron Delta Kappa. Home: 3809 Midlakes Dr Raleigh NC 27612 Personal E-mail: jason@pearce.net.

PEARCE, JENNIFER SUE, real estate appraiser; b. Jacksonville, Fla., Nov. 1, 1954; d. Marvin William and Betty Mae (White) Robinson; m. James Zenous Pearce Jr., Mar. 30, 1974; children: Keith Bryan, Kevin Patrick. Student, Baylor U., 1983, U. Ga., 1985; cert., Jacksonville U., 1986. Cert. residential and comml. real estate appraiser, Fla. Broker, sales Watson Realty Corp., Jacksonville, 1979-82; sr. resdl. appraiser Page Aspinwall Appraiser, 1982-90; owner Jennifer Pearce Appraiser, 1991—. Instr. real estate appraisal Fla. Community Coll., 1987; commissioned by Ednl. Testing Svc. to establish exam for certification of appraisers in state of Fla. Mem. Appraisal Inst. (sec. Jacksonville chpt.), Am. Acad. State Cert. Appraisers (charter), Daus. of the Nile. Home: 4807 Avon Ln Jacksonville FL 32210-7505 Office: 4556 Lexington Ave Jacksonville FL 32210-2038

PEARCE, JOAN DELAP, research company executive; b. Oakland, Calif., June 13, 1930; d. Robert Jerome and Wilhelmina (Reaume) DeLap; m. Gerald Allan Pearce, June 18, 1953; 1 child, Scott Ford. Student. U. Oreg., 1948-55. Rsch. assoc. deForest Rsch., L.A., 1966-78, assoc. dir., 1978-92; dir. rsch. Walt Disney Prodns., Burbank, Calif., 1978; pres., bd. dirs. Joan Pearce Rsch. Assocs., L.A., 1992—. Research company executive; b. Oakland, Calif., June 13, 1930; d. Robert Jerome and Wilhelmina (Reaume) DeLap; m. Gerald Allan Pearce, June 18, 1953; 1 child, Scott Ford. Student, U. Oreg., 1948-55. Rsch. assoc. deForest Rsch., L.A., 1966-78, assoc. dir., 1978-92; dir. rsch. Walt Disney Prodns., Burbank, Calif., 1978; pres., bd. dirs. Joan Pearce Rsch. Assocs., 1992—; lighting dir. Wilcoxen Players, Beverly Hills, Calif., 1955-60, Theatre 40, L.A., 1960-66. Bd. advisors Living History Ctr., Marin County, Calif., 1982-89, bd. dirs., 1989-94. Mem. Am. Film Inst. Democrat. Avocations: photography; travel; theater; swimming. Lighting dir. Wilcoxen Players, Beverly Hills, Calif., 1955-60, Theatre 40, L.A., 1960-66; bd. adv. Living History Ctr., Marin County, Calif., 1982-89, bd. dirs., 1989-94. Mem. Am. Film Inst. Democrat. Avocations: photography, travel, theater, swimming. Home: 2621 Rutherford Dr Los Angeles CA 90068-3042 Office: Joan Pearce Rsch Assocs 8111 Beverly Blvd Ste 308 Los Angeles CA 90048-4525 E-mail: joan@pearceresearch.com.

PEARCE, JOHN Y. lawyer; b. New Orleans, Mar. 26, 1948; s. John Young II and Marina (Harris) P.; m. Marjorie Pamela Doyle, May 22, 1971 (div.); children: Andrea Elizabeth, Roger Wellington. BA, La. State U., 1973, JD, 1976. Bar: La. 1977, U.S. Dist. Ct. (ea., mid. and we. dists.) La., U.S. Ct. Claims, U.S. Ct. Appeals (5th and 11th cirs.). Assoc. Doyle, Smith & Doyle, New Orleans, 1977-79, ptnr., 1979-80, mng. ptnr., 1980-84; ptnr. Montgomery, Barnett, Brown, Read, Hammond & Mintz, 1984—. Pres. New Orleans Legal Assistance Corp., 2000—. Sgt. U.S. Army, 1969—71. Mem.: ABA (ho. of dels. 1998—2002), New Orleans Bar Assn. (exec. com., pres. 1997—98), La. Bar Assn. (chmn. mineral law coun. 1994—95). Republican. Episcopalian. Office: Montgomery Barnett Brown Read Hammond & Mintz 1100 Poydras St New Orleans LA 70163-1101

PEARCE, MALLORY, artist, educator, ecologist; b. Geneva, Apr. 6, 1935; s. George W. and Sally Mallory P.; m. Marcia Berman, Aug. 24, 1963 (div. 1974); children: Peter and James (twins); m. Julia Hill, Aug. 26, 2000; stepchildren: Sierra Wilkinson, Simone Wilkinson. Student, U. Ga.; BS in Zoology, U. Chgo., 1957; MFA in Theatre Arts, UCLA, 1966. Animator, film dir. Wexler Films, L.A., 1971—81, Comms. Group West, L.A., 1971—, Learning Garden, L.A., 1971—80, Sutherland Prodns., L.A., 1980—84, Pyramid Films, Santa Monica, Calif., 1986—87; adj. prof. art Armstrong Atlantic State U., Savannah, Ga., 1992—. Asst. prof. motion pictures Calif. State U., L.A., 1981—82. Author: Celtic Borders on Layout Grids, 1990, Decorative Celtic Alphabets, 1992, Easy to Duplicate Celtic Borders, 1993, Celtic Stickers and Seals, 1995, Celtic Designs, 1996, Celtic Animals Coloring Book, Celtic Animals Iron-on Tranfer Patterns, Celtic Frames and Borders, Celtic Animals Stain Glass Coloring Book, 1999, Celtic Stained Glass Pattern Book, 1999, Seashore Life Illustrations, 1999. Mem. L.A. County Mosquito Abatement Dist., L.A., 1981-91; coun. mem. Tybee Island (Ga.) City Coun., 1996—. Recipient CINE Golden Eagle, 1975, 78, 79. Mem. Ga. Mcpl. Assn., Nat. League of Cities, Tybee Island Land Trust (pres. 1995—). Democrat. Avocation: birdwatching. Home: 8 Fifth St Tybee Island GA 31328

PEARCE, PATSY BEASLEY, elementary education educator; b. Dunn, N.C., Apr. 13, 1945; d. Marvin Franklin and Christine (Bryant) Beasley; m. Robert Michael Cole, Aug. 15, 1970 (div.); 1 child, Matthew Bryant Cole; m. Elwood Glenn Pearce, Mar. 1, 1980. BSEd, E. Caroline U., 1966. Cert. collegiate profl., Va. Primary tchr., 1st and 2d grade Va. Beach (Va.) City Schs., 1966-75; primary tchr., 1st. and 3rd grade Jasper County Schs., Hardeeville, S.C., 1976-78; tchr., 4th grade Campbell County Schs., Lynchburg, Va., 1979; kindergarten tchr. Aesop Acad., Portsmouth, 1981-84; primary tchr., 1st grade Chesapeake (Va.) City Schs., 1984—2001; ret., 2001. Mem. social studies adoption com. Chesapeake City Schs., 1996-98, colleague mentor, 1997-98, Pizza Hut Book-It chairperson, 1997-2001; United Way chair, 1995-97; sch. rep. Chesapeake Reading Coun., 1986-95, colleague mentor, 1988-90; equity tutor Camelot Elem. Sch., Chesapeake, 1994, grade level chmn., 1990-95, coop. tchr., 1990-91; mem. tech. tng. Va. Stds. Learning Tng., 1999-2001, 2001. Sunday sch. tchr. Cradock United Meth. Ch., Portsmouth, Va., 1982, worship com. chmn. 1990-91, Acolyte chmn., 1984-89; vacation Bible sch. tchr. Thail United Meth. Ch., Virginia Beach, 1969; com. chmn., treas. Cub Scout Pack 251, Portsmouth, Va., 1980-91; roundtable commr. Merrimac Dist. Boy Scouts Am., Portsmouth, 1989-90, dist. chmn. Scouts Ann. Mall Show and Pinewood Derby Race, 1987-89; children's choir dir. Kempsville Ch. of Christ, Virginia Beach, 1979-80. Named Camelot's Tchr. of Yr., 1995-96. Mem. NEA, Va. Edn. Assn., Chesapeake Edn. Assn., Chesapeake Reading Coun., Internat. Reading Coun., PTA (corr. sec. 1997-98). Avocations: gardening, needlework crafts, travel, granddaughter. Home: 2233 Ferndale Rd Chesapeake VA 23323-5016

PEARCE, PAUL FRANCIS, retired aerospace electronics company executive; b. Boston, Sept. 17, 1928; s. George Hamilton and Marie Louise (Duval) P.; m. Gilda Troisi, Apr. 11, 1953; children: Janet, Theresa, Diane. BSEE (Edwards scholar), MIT, 1950; MS, Mass. Inst. Tech., L.A., 1952; postgrad. (Hughes fellow), U. Calif., Los Angeles, 1957-58, U. So., Calif., 1958-59, Inst. Mgmt. Northwestern U., 1966. Project engr. Trans-Sonics, Inc., Burlington, Mass., 1952-55; sect. head application engrng., strategic systems Hughes Aircraft Co., Culver City, Calif., 1955-59; with Lockheed Electronics Co., Plainfield, N.J., 1959-67, gen. mgr. div. mil. systems, 1964-65, v.p., gen. mgr., 1965-67; v.p., div. mgr. Tele-Dynamics div. AMBAC Industries, Inc., Ft. Washington, Pa, 1967-74; group v.p. comml. and aerospace electronics group AMBAC Industries, Inc., Carle Place, N.Y., 1973-80; pres. James G. Biddle Co., Blue Bell, Pa., 1980-93, ret. Bd. dirs. AVO Internat. Ltd., 1987-91. Mem. Armed Forces Communications and Electronics Assn. (pres. 1969-71), Inst.

Nav., Delaware Valley Mfrs. Assn. (sr. vice chmn. 1987-89, chmn. 1990-92—), Greater Phila. C. of C., Ft. Washington Indsl. Park Mgmt. Assn. (gov. 1973-74), Sigma Xi. Clubs: Mfrs'. Golf and Country (Oreland, Pa.) (handicap chmn. 1987-90), St. David's Golf Club (Wayne, Pa.).

PEARCE, RICHARD LEE, lawyer; b. Racine, Wis., Apr. 11, 1959; s. John Wallace and Betty Jane P.; m. Cynthia Diane Davis, June 11, 1983; 1 child, Melissa Lauren. BS in Chemistry, U. S.C., 1981, JD, 1984. Bar: S.C. 1984, U.S. Dist. Ct. S.C. 1985, U.S. Ct. Appeals (4th cir.) 1985. Law clk. to resident cir. judge Edward B. Cottingham, 1984-85; assoc. Fox, Zier, Burkhalter & Verenes, Aiken, S.C., 1985-86; ptnr. Toole & Toole, 1986-96; asst. pub. svcs. dir., legis. liaison S.C. Bar, 1996-98; city solicitor, staff atty. City of Aiken, 1998—. Instr. Am. Banking Inst., Nat. Advocacy Ctr., Nat. Dist. Attys. Assn.; guest lectr., adj. instr. U. S.C., Aiken; legal advisor Bd. of Zoning Appeals, Hist. Preservation Commn., Neighborhoods Com., City Dept. Heads, Soc. Prevention of Cruelty to Aminals, 2000-01; U.S. Dept. Justice Operation Cease Fire. Emcee Sch. Bd. Acad. Tournament, Aiken, 1986; bd. dirs. Tri-Devel. Ctr., Aiken, 1985-86; spl. events com. Downtown Aiken Devel. Corp.; fundraiser com. Am. Cancer Soc., 1985-2000, Am. Heart Assn., 2000-01; legal advisor Children's Place, Inc.; judge mock trial high sch. competition, 1991-96; trustee Aiken, Barnwell, Bamberg, and Edgefield Libr. Sys.; organizer, coord. Aiken Youth Ct. Mem. S.C. Bar Assn. (ho. of dels. 1989-95, pro bono program 1989-97, resolution of fee disputes bd., lawyers' fund for client protection, task force on justice for all, ethics adv. com., unauthorized practice law com., co-editor Legis. Update, editor Ethics Adv. Opinion Summaries, coord. annual jud. evaluation, sec. govtl. law sect.), Aiken County Bar Assn. (pres. 1990-92), Aiken C. of C. (legal liaison 1986), Internat. Mcpl. Lawyers Assn., Nat. Dist. Attys. Assn., S.C. Solicitors Assn., Rotary Internat. (bd. dirs. 1994-96, pres.-elect 1994-95, pres. 1995-96, group study exch. coord., Aiken-Llandrindod, Wales, U.K., Exch. Program, Paul Harris fellow, Sustaining Paul Harris fellow), Omicron Delta Kappa, Hitchcock Woods Axe Club. Presbyterian (vice-chair bd. deacons 1999-2000, chair 2000-02). Avocations: camping, outdoor activities, historical research, cycling. Office: City of Aiken PO Box 1177 Aiken SC 29802-1177 E-mail: rpearce@aiken.net.

PEARCE, RONALD, retired cosmetic company executive; b. Apr. 29, 1920; s. Fernley Charles and Medora Kate (Lissenden) P.; m. Olive Stacey, Apr. 4, 1942; children: David Fernley, Jane Ryding Robertson. Cambridge matriculation, Lindisfarne Coll., Ruabon, North Wales, U.K., 1937. Chief cashier Westminster Bank, Croydon, Eng., 1947-48; comml. officer Brit. Consulate, Dallas, 1949-52; v.p. World Gift Co., 1953-63, Nelson Electronics, Dallas, 1963-68; stockbroker Walston & Co., 1968-73; dir. purchasing Mary Kay Cosmetics, Inc., 1973-85; pres. Global Water Techs., Inc., 1992-95; chmn. bd. Alpha Aqua, 1996—. Chmn. bd. Dallas Lighthouse for the Blind, 1987. Flight lt. RAF, 1940-46. Republican. Episcopalian. Home: 3362 Forest Ln Apt 302 Dallas TX 75234-7001

PEARCE, STEPHEN LAMAR, management consultant; b. Bryan, Tex., Nov. 25, 1950; s. Stephen D. and Mabel Louise (Rawls) P.; m. Rhonda Dee Greig, Mar. 24, 1982; 1 child, Joshua Davis Gray (dec.). BS in Indsl. Tech., Tex. A&M U., 1978, MBA, 1985, PhD in Bus. Adminstrn., 1995. Svc. engr. Dresser Titan, Laredo, Tex., 1981-83; owner Pearce Fabrications, Anderson, 1983-87; pres. Stephen L. Pearce Assocs., Bryan, 1986—; asst. prof. indsl. distbn., asst. dir. rsch. Tex. A&M U., College Station, 1991-95. Vis. asst. prof. Tex. A&M U., College Station, 1986-91. Contbr. articles to profl. jours. With U.S. Army, 1971-72. Mem. Distbn. Rsch. and Edn. Found. (panel 1991-95). Republican. Roman Catholic. Avocation: reading, aviation. Home and Office: Stephen L Pearce Assocs 3709 Valley Oaks Dr Bryan TX 77802-4856

PEARCY, LEE THERON, secondary education educator, writer; b. Little Rock, Aug. 20, 1947; s. Lee Theron and Janet Gillum (Jackson) P.; m. Kathryn Ellen Eyre, Aug. 15, 1970; children: Benjamin Theron, Sarah Gillum. BA, Columbia U., 1969, MA, 1971; PhD, Bryn Mawr Coll., 1974. Tchr. Englewood (N.J.) Sch. for Boys, 1969-71; asst. prof. St. Olaf Coll., Northfield, Minn., 1973-77, U. Tex., Austin, 1977-85; tchr., chmn. dept. classics Episcopal Acad., Merion, Pa., 1985-2001, dir. curriculum, 2001—. Author: Mediated Muse, 1984, Shorter Homeric Hymns, 1989, New First Steps in Latin, 2000; asst. editor Classical World, 1993—; founding editor Ancient Medicine/Medicina Antiqua, 1996—; contbr. articles, revs. and poetry to scholarly jours. Fellow Am. Coun. Learned Socs., 1979; tchr.-scholar NEH, 1990-91. Mem. Am. Philol. Assn., Soc. for Promotion Roman Studies, Classical Assn. Atlantic States (pres. 1996-97), Soc. for Ancient Medicine. Methodist. Avocations: tennis, squash, fishing, cycling, walking. Home: 223 Upland Rd Merion Station PA 19066-1821 Office: Episcopal Acad 376 N Latches Ln Merion Station PA 19066-1797 E-mail: lpearcy@ea1785.org.

PEARCY, SUSAN BETH DUE, artist, printmaker; b. St. Louis, May 6, 1945; d. Waldemar Bernard Henry and Doris Jewel (Hoeger) Due; m. Glen Johnston Pearcy, July 7, 1944; children: Noah Johnston, Rebecca Due. Student, Art Student's League, N.Y.C., 1970; BS in Painting, Graphics and Sculpture, NYU, 1969; student, S.E. Mo. State U., 1963-66. Tchr. various pub. schs., various locations, 1970—, Montgomery County, MD; reviewer The New Art Ctr., Washington, 1987; juror Torpedo Factory Arts Ctr., Alexandria, Va., 1988; pres. Washington Printmakers Gallery, Washington, 1988-90. Tchr. Women's Studio Workshop, N.Y.; bd. dirs. Washington Printmakers Gallery; co-chmn. Internat. prints I, Washington, 1989; chmn. Washington Area Printmakers, 1982. Exhibited in group shows include Hudson River Mus., Yonkers, N.Y., 1987, Mus. Modern Art, Buenos Aires, 1987, U. Miss. Mus., 1990, Museu de Arte do Rio Grande do Sul, Brazil, 1989, Visual Arts Ctr., Anchorage, 1989, D.C.&B. Gallery, Brussels, Belgium, 1988, Knoxville Mus. Art, 1988, Nat. Mus. Am. Art, 1988, Silvermine Guild Galleries, New Canaan, Conn., 1988, John Szoke Gallery, N.Y.C., 1988, U. Hawaii at Hilo, 1988, Parkersburg (W.Va.) Art Ctr., 1988, State Tretyakov Gallery, Moscow, 1990, Del. Ctr. for the Comtemporary Arts, Wilmington, 1990, Printmaking Coun. of N.J. Nat. Exhibit, 1999, Newman Gallery, Washington, DC, many others; represented in permanent collection at Nat. Mus. Am. Art, Nat. Gallery Art, Pushkin Mus., USSR, Nat. Mus. Women in Arts, 1994, 96, Corcoran Gallery of Art, 1997, Janner 81 Gallery, N.Y.C., 1998, Nat. Print Biennial and Non-Toxic Prints, Richmond, Va., 1998, FACET, Taos, N.Mex., 1998, others. Co-chair Inclusive Lang. Task Force, Silver Spring, Md., 1989; mem. Stephen's Ministry, 1990. Md. State Arts Coun. grantee, 1989, 1987, Calif. State Arts Coun. grantee, 1977, 79; recipient Equal Merit awards, Art League Gallery, Alexandria, Va., 1987, 86, 85, 84, 83, others. Mem. Md. Printmakers, So. Graphics Coun., Gomez Gallery. Democrat. United Ch. of Christ Avocations: gardening, canoeing. Home: PO Box 63 Barnesville MD 20838-0063

PEARE, DAN C. lawyer; b. Wichita, Kans., Nov. 9, 1960; s. Robert E. and Helen A. (Kraft) P.; m. Valory S. Innes, Sept. 12, 1992; children: Robert Jordan, Regan Elizabeth, Reilly Nicole. BS in Fin., Wichita State U., 1982, MBA, 1985; JD, U. Kans., 1988. Bar: Kans. 1988; U.S. Ct. Appeals (10th cir.). Mem. Hinkle Elkouri Law Firm, LLC, Wichita, 1988—. Dir., trustee The Morrison Found., Wichita, 1993—; chair planned giving coun. Wichita State U. Found., 2000—. Author: (with others) Kansas Estate Adminstration Handbook, 1992. Recipient award for top paper, Am. Jurisprudence, U. Kans. Sch. of Law, 1988. Mem. Wichita Estate Planning Coun., Wichita Estate Planning Forum, Kans. Bar Assn. (exec. com. mem. 1996—). Roman Catholic. Avocations: sports, photography. Home: 1420 N Sport Of Kings Ct Wichita KS 67230-7151 Office: Hinkle Elkouri Law Firm 301 N Main St Ste 2000 Wichita KS 67202-4820 E-mail: dpeare@hinklaw.com., dpeare@aol.com.

PEARL, B. MICHAEL, business owner; b. Cleve., July 21, 1957; s. Raymond Albert and Adele Gertrude (Waxman) P.; m. Patricia Marie Marotta, Oct. 7, 1978; 1 child, Tyler Michael. Cert. pers. cons. Gen. mgr. Pearl Carpet Stores, Cleve., 1979-82; exec. v.p. J.B. Brown & Assocs., 1982-89; pres., owner The Pearl-Waxman Co., Chagrin Falls, 1990—; founder, mng. ptnr. Cruises on Sail Travel, LLC, 1994—. Columnist, Two if By Sea DCI Comm., 2001—. Editor Aware - The Jour. for Inner Devel., 1983-89; author: The Path and the Power, 1988; columnist Chagrin Valley Times, Solon Times and Geauga Times, 1995-2001; talk show host: Becoming Aware, 1989-90. Exec. dir. The A.W.A.R.E. Found., Cleve., 1985-89; mem. spkrs. Bur., 1982—; faculty advisor Cleve. Clinic Ctr. for Health Edn., Rocky River, Ohio, 1986—. Recipient No. Ohio's 88 Most Interesting People, Cleve. Mag., 1988, Spkr. award Masonic Srs., Cleve., 1997, Circolo d'Amici Platinum award, Costa Cruise Lines, Captain's award, Norwegian Cruise Line. Mem. Greater Cleve. Assn. Pers. Cons. (membership chmn. 1985-87), Chagrin Valley C. of C. (corp. sponsor), Cruise Lines Internat. Assn., Vacation.com. Avocations: travel, theater, food and wine, antique collecting, parapsychology.

PEARL, HARVEY, rehabilitation psychologist; b. N.Y.C., July 11, 1930; s. Louis and Blanche (Birnbaum) P.; m. Dorothy Morrison, June 20, 1953; children: Stuart Ray, Lesley, Andrea. BS, NYU, 1953, MA, 1957; PhD, Syracuse U., 1970. Tchr. indsl. arts Pub. Schs. Elizabeth (N.J.), 1955-56; workshop supr. United Cerebral Palsy Assn., Roosevelt, N.Y., 1956-58; workshop dir. Jewish Vocat. Service, Cin., 1958-61; dir. work tng. center Assn. Retarded Children, Rochester, N.Y., 1961-63; asst. exec. dir. Consol. Industries Greater Syracuse (N.Y.), 1965-96, rehab. cons., 1996—. Instr. Cornell U., Ithaca, NY, 1970—; cons. Social Security Adminstrn., 1962—2000. Author: (with A. Speiser, A. Staniec) Bibliography of Work Evaluation in Vocational Rehabilitation, 1966; Comparison of Personal Values and Worker Assessments of Work Evaluators in Rehabilitation and Industrial Settings, 1970. Pres. Jewish Family Service Bur., 1974-82; adv. council Cazenovia Coll., 1977—, Occupational Edn., Syracuse City Sch. Dist., 1971—. Served with U.S. Army, 1953-55. Recipient citation of merit Syracuse U. Sch. Social Work, 1972; cert. rehab. counselor. Mem. Nat. Rehab. Assn., Am. Counseling Assn., Am. Rehab. Counseling Assn., Nat. Career Devel. Assn., Am. Psychol. Assn., Am. Wine Soc. Home and Office: 227 Wellington Rd De Witt NY 13214-2225 E-mail: hndpearl@worldnet.att.net.

PEARL, HELEN ZALKAN, lawyer; b. Washington, Sept. 12, 1938; d. George and Harriet (Libman) Zalkan; m. Jason E. Pearl, June 27, 1959; children: Gary M., Esther H., Lawrence J. BA with honors, Vassar Coll., 1959; JD, U. Conn., 1978. Bar: Conn. 1978, U.S. Dist. Ct. Conn. 1978. Mkt. rsch. analyst Landers, Frary & Clark, New Britain, Conn., 1960-61, managerial statistician, 1961-62; real estate salesperson Denuzze Co., 1966-70; property mgr. self-employed, 1970-75; legal asst. Atty. Gen. Office, State of Conn., Hartford, 1978; assoc. Weber & Marshall, New Britain, 1978-83, ptnr., 1983-99, Weber & Carrier, New Britain, 1999—. Hearing officer Commn. on Human Rights and Opportunities, State of Conn., 1980-98, Dept. Mental Retardation, 2001—; spl. master State of Conn. Judicial Dept., 1986—. New Britain rep. to Cen. Conn. Regional Planning Agy., 1973-75, 84—, chmn., 1990-92; mem. New Britain Bd. Fin. and Taxation, 1973-77; founder, mem. Conn. Permanent Commn. on Status of Women, 1975-82, others. Recipient Women in Leadership award, YWCA of New Britain, 1988, Book award for torts, Am. Jurisprudence, 1976. Mem. AAUW (pres. 1970-72), Conn. Bar Assn., New Britain Bar Assn., LWV (Conn. specialist 1997—, local pres. 1995-97), Hartford Vassar Club, Phi Beta Kappa. Democrat. Jewish. Avocations: travel, theater, reading, cooking. Home: 206 Hickory Hill Rd New Britain CT 06052-1010 Office: Weber & Carrier 24 Cedar St New Britain CT 06052-1302 E-mail: pearlh.wbc@snet.net.

PEARL, JUDEA, computer scientist, educator; b. Tel-Aviv, Sept. 4, 1936; U.S. citizen; married; 3 children. BSc, Israel Inst. Tech., 1960; MSc, Newark Coll. Engring., 1961; PhD in Elec. Engring., Poly. Inst. Bklyn., 1965. Rsch. engr. Dental Sch., NYU, 1960-61; mem. tech. staff RCA Rsch. Labs., 1961-65; dir. advanced memory devices Electronic Memories, Inc., Calif., 1966-69; prof. Sch. of Engring./Dept. Computer Scis. UCLA, 1969—. Instr. Newark Coll. Engring., 1961; cons. Rand Corp., 1972, Integrated Sci. Corp., 1975, Hughes Aircraft, 1989. Recipient Outstanding Achievement award RCA Labs., 1965, Rsch. Excellence award, ISCAI, 1999. Fellow IEEE, Am. Assn. Artificial Intelligence (classical paper award 2000, Iaratos award 2001); mem. Nat. Acad. Engring. Office: UCLA Dept Computer Sci 4532 Boelter Hl Los Angeles CA 90095-0001

PEARL, LAURENCE DICKSON, retired federal government executive; b. Phila., Mar. 2, 1934; s. Simon and Dorothy (Lichtig) P.; m. Ruth Switzer, Dec. 22, 1959 (div. Apr. 1972); children: Natasha, Lisa Talbott, Thomas Simon; m. Anne Womeldorf, Dec. 20, 1972. AB, Antioch Coll., 1955; postgrad., Harvard U., 1955-56; LLB, Yale U., 1959. Bar: D.C. 1959, U.S. Supreme Ct. 1983. Assoc. Trammell, Rand & Nathan, Washington, 1960-61; rsch. assoc. George Washington U., 1961, exec. asst. to gen. counsel, 1967-69; atty., advisor HUD, 1961-67, spl. asst. to asst. sec. for equal opportunity, 1969-72, dir. program standards and data analysis, 1972-74, dir. program compliance, 1974-86, dir. program standards and evaluation, 1986-98; ret., 1998. Pres. Capitol Hill Restoration Soc., Washington, 1990-92. Ford Found. fellow, 1955-56. Mem. ABA, D.C. Bar Assn., Sr. Execs. Assn. (pres. HUD chpt. 1990-91). Avocations: music, gardening, cross country skiing.

PEARL, NANCY LINN, librarian; b. Detroit, Jan. 12, 1945; d. Sidney and Anne Linn; m. Joseph Harold Pearl; children: Eily Raman, Katie. MLS, U. Mich., 1967. Exec. dir. Washington Ctr. Book Seattle Pub. Lib., 1993—; head collection devel. Tulsa City County Libr., Okla. Author: Now Read This: A Guide to Mainstream Fiction, 1978-1998, 1999, Now Read This II: A Guide to Mainstream Fiction, 1990-2001, 2002. Named Fiction Reviewer of Yr., Libr. Jour. Magazine, 1998; recipient Allie Beth Martin award, Pub. Libr. Assn., 2001, Open Book award, Pacific Northwest Writer's Conf., 1997. Office: Seattle Pub Libr 800 Pike St Seattle WA 98101 Office Fax: 206 386 4672. Business E-Mail: nancy.pearl@spl.org.

PEARL, RICHARD ALAN, neurologist, educator; b. N.Y.C., Feb. 2, 1943; s. Sam and Edith (Friedman) P.; m. Barbara Goldstein, Mar. 28, 1971; children: Laurie, Caroline, Jennifer. BA, U. Pa., 1964; MD, Georgetown U., 1968. Diplomate Am. Bd. Psychiatry and Neurology. Intern Mt. Sinai Hosp., N.Y.C., 1968-69, resident in neurology, 1969-70, 72-74; pvt. practice Smithtown, N.Y., 1974—; chief neurology St. John's Hosp., 1980—, Community Hosp. West Suffolk, Smithtown, 1980-90; asst. clin. prof. neurology Stony Brook (N.Y.) U. Hosp., 1980—, chief of staff, 1980—2000. Lt. comdr. M.C., USN, 1972-74. Fellow Am. Acad. Neurology; mem. Assn. for Rsch. in Nervous and Mental Diseases, Alpha Omega Alpha. Office: 307 Middle Country Rd Smithtown NY 11787-2829

PEARL, WILLIAM RICHARD EMDEN, pediatric cardiologist; b. N.Y.C., Nov. 1, 1944; s. William Emden and Sara (Gilston) P.; m. Karlyn Katsumoto, July 9, 1978; children: Jeffrey, Kristine. BA, Queens Coll., 1966; MD, SUNY, Bklyn., 1970. Diplomate Am. Bd. Pediatrics, Am. Bd. Pediatric Cardiology. Intern Roosevelt Hosp., N.Y.C., 1970-71; resident N.Y. Hosp.-Cornell Med. Ctr., 1971-72; fellow Albert Einstein Coll. Medicine, 1972-74; asst. prof. U. Hawaii, Honolulu, 1974-76, Tex. Tech. Med. Sch., El Paso, 1976-82, assoc. prof., 1982-92; chief pediatric cardiology William Beaumont Army Med. Ctr., 1976-94; dir. pediatric cardiology U. Tex. Med. Br., Galveston, 1994—. Cons. Miami (Fla.) Children's Hosp., 1988, Driscol Children's Hosp., Corpus Christi, Tex., 1992, Thomason Hosp., El Paso, 1976-92. Contbr. articles to profl. jours. Col. USAR, 1974-92. N.Y. State Bd. Regents scholar, 1962-66, Fed. Health Careers scholar, 1967-70; NIH fellow, 1972-73; recipient Dept. of Army Commendation for outstanding sci. achievement, 1984. Fellow Am. Acad. Pediatrics, Am. Coll. Cardiology; mem. Am. Heart Assn. (coun. on cardiovascular disease in the young 1982). Office: U Tex Med Br Children's Hosp 301 University Blvd Galveston TX 77555-5302

PEARLMAN, AMALIA CECILE, artist, educator; b. Zborov, Czechoslovakia, Oct. 10, 1918; d. Charles David and F. Rachel (Weissman) Rappaport; m. Lester S. Pearlman, June 18, 1939 (dec. 1992); children: Leslie Ellen, Austin Cecil, Lise Ann, Jared Salom, Justin Dana. BA, Bklyn. Coll., 1939; MFA, NYU, 1965, PhD, 1970. Sr. rsch. scientist curriculum devel. for creative arts NYU Sch. Edn.; adj. prof. art De Anza Coll., Calif.; prof. art So. Conn. Coll.; docent in great literature Bridgeport (Conn.) Engring. Inst.; prof. art and art history Western Conn. Coll. Panelist, spkr. in field. One-person shows at Creative Gallery, N.Y., Silvermine Guild Artists, Mystic Art Assn. Gallery, Western Conn. Coll., Mali's Gallery, Rocky Neck Gloucester, San Francisco Open Studios; exhibited in group shows at Collectore of Am. Art, Bloomfield Hills, Ill. (Purchase prize), Hartford (Conn.) Atheneum (Berthe Dion Tucker award), Alameda (Calif.) Fairgrounds (1st Hon. Mention award), Norton Gallery, Palm Beach, Fla. (1st Hon. Mention), Courtyard Mexico City (1st Hon. Mention), Ligoa Duncan Galleries, Paris (Prix de Paris), Silvermine Guild of Artists (Best New Eng. Landscape award), Riverside Mus., N.Y.C., Norwich (Conn.) Art Assn.; represented in archives Nat. Mus. for Women in the Arts, Washington; prodr. audiovisual documentary: Jerusalem, The Living Past, The Emerging Future. Dir. urban evaluation and planning program at Harlem Sch., AIA. Grantee Kress Found., 1975-77, Vinmount Found., 1972, 73. Mem. Rocky Neck Art Assn. (annual demonstrations), Mechanics Inst. Chess Club, Commonwealth Club, Sierra Club. Avocations: reading, gardening, chess, great-grandchildren, theater. Home: Apt 720 2180 Post St San Francisco CA 94115 E-mail: amaliap@pacbell.net.

PEARLMAN, BARBARA, artist, educator; b. N.Y.C., Apr. 25, 1938; d. Henry and Edith (Stein) P.; 1 child, Alexandre Yulish. BA, Parsons Sch. Design, 1960. Illustrator Neiman Marcus, Dallas, 1960-61, Vogue, Marie Claire, France, Eng., Germany, 1961-65, Galey & Lord, N.Y.C., 1965-78, Vogue, Harpers, N.Y. Mag., Glamour, N.Y. Art, N.Y.C., 1965-78; tchr. Parsons Sch. Design, 1975-79, Fashion Inst. Tech., N.Y.C., 1979-95, Nassau Fine Arts Mus., 1980-81. Spkr. NYU Phenomenology in the Arts. Exhbns. N.Y.C., Germany, 1978-95; featured in Russian and Polish mags.; works featured in History of Fashion (Eunic Sloane), numerous others; contbr. articles to Gebracht Graphic mag. Recipient award Soc. Illustrators, 1976, 69, 70. Mem. Nat. Orgn. Women Artists. Home: 2259 Edsall Ave Bronx NY 10463-6202

PEARLMAN, DAVID SAMUEL, allergist; b. Syracuse, N.Y., Jan. 20, 1934; s. Benjamin Norman and Sylvia Rene (Karp) P.; m. Doris Ann Greenberg, Apr. 16, 1966; children: Michael, Melanie. Student, Cornell U., 1951-54; MD, SUNY, Syracuse, 1958. Diplomate Am. Bd. Allergy and Immunology (dir. 1973-78). Intern, then asst. resident in pediatrics Univ. Hosps., Cleve., 1958-60; chief resident in pediatrics U. Colo. Med. Center, Denver, 1960-61, mem. faculty, 1962—, clin. prof. pediatrics, 1978—, dir. pediatric allergy tng. program, 1964-66, co-dir., 1966-73; practice medicine specializing in allergy Denver, 1972—. Assoc. Colo. Allergy and Asthma Clinic, 1972—; acting chief dept. pediatric allergy Nat. Jewish Hosp. and Rsch. Ctr., 1972-73, sr. staff physician pediatrics allergy, 1973-92; mem. allergy and infectious disease tng. grant com. NIH, 1970-72. Contbr. articles to med. jours. Served to maj. M.C. AUS, 1967-69. U. Colo. Med. Ctr. fellow, 1961-62, NIH fellow, 1963-66, 69-72; recipient Disting. Clinician award Am. Acad. Allergy, Asthma, and Immunology, 1999. Fellow Am. Acad. Pediatrics (chmn. sect. on allergy and Clin. Immunology, 1992-94, Bret Ratner award 1998), Am. Acad. Allergy, Asthma and Immunology (exec. com. 1978-81), Am. Coll. Allergy, Asthma and Immunology (Disting. Svvc. award 1999); mem. AAAS, Am. Soc. Cert. Allergists, Am. Thoracic Soc., Am. Coll. Chest Physicians, Colo. Allergy Soc., Joint Council Allergy and Immunology (bd. dirs. 1985-92, pres. 1988-90), Colo. Med. Soc., Denver Med. Soc., Adams-Aurora County Med. Soc., Friends of Chamber Music (dir. 1965-81). Jewish. Address: 6029 E Prentice Pl Englewood CO 80111-1415 Office: Colo Allergy & Asthma Ctrs PC 125 Rampart St Ste 150 Denver CO 80230-6405 E-mail: ds.pearlman@coloradoallergy.com.

PEARLMAN, JERRY KENT, electronics company executive; b. Des Moines, Mar. 27, 1939; s. Leo R. Pearlman; married; children: Gregory, Neal. BA cum laude, Princeton U., 1960; MBA, Harvard U., 1962. With Ford Motor Co., 1962-70; v.p. fin. dir. Behring Corp., 1970-71; from contr. to chmn. Zenith Electronics Corp., Glenview, Ill., 1971-95. Bd. dirs. Smurfit-Stone Container Corp, Ryerson-Tull Corp., Nanophase Techs., Evanston Northwestern Healthcare. Bd. dirs. Northwestern U. Office: 21 Linden Ave Wilmette IL 60091-2837 E-mail: jpearl@nwu.edu.

PEARLMAN, LOUIS JAY, aviation and entertainment company executive; b. Flushing, N.Y., June 19, 1954; s. Herman and Reenie (Nevler) P. BA, Queens Coll., 1976; MBA, Century U., 1980; Degree in Sales Mgmt., SUNY, Buffalo, 1980; PhD in Bus. Adminstrn., Century U., 1983. Pres. Commuter Helicopter Corp., N.Y.C., 1974-75; pres., COO Trans Continental Airlines, Inc., 1975—, Trans Continental Records, Orlando, Fla., 1991—. Gen. mgr. U.S. Westdeutsche Luftwerbung GmbH, N.Y.C., 1976-85; chmn., pres., CEO Airship Internat. Ltd., N.Y.C., 1982—, bd. dirs., 1985—; pres., CEO Trans Continental Records, Inc., 1992—; pres. Backstreet Boys, Inc., 1993-99; CEO Chippendales, Inc., 1996-2000, Entertainment Internat. Ltd., 1997—, Planet Airways Inc., 1998—, bd. dirs.; cons. Queens Coll., CUNY, 1977—. Author: Survey and Analysis of the Airline Industry, 1983; song writer. Active Mitchell-Linden Civic Assn., Flushing, 1980-82, Kissimmee (Fla.) Mcpl. Airport, 1985—. Recipient Govs. award NARAS, 2000. Mem. U.S. Power Squadron, Wings Club (disting., recipient Lighter-than-Air award 1987), Lighter-than-Air Soc. (hon.), Young Entrepreneurs Am., Young Millionaires Club, Internat. Air Transport Assn., Blimp Port U.S.A. (pres. 1987—), Friar's Club (N.Y.C.). Avocations: flying airplanes, helicopters and blimps, swimming, bowling, music, boating. Office: Trans Continental Cos Inc 7380 Sand Lake Rd Ste 350 Orlando FL 32819-5257

PEARLMAN, MICHAEL ALLEN, lawyer; b. Phila., Sept. 22, 1946; s. William and Mary (Stark) Pearlman; m. Ann Gerald, June 1, 1969; children: Benjamin, Amy. BA, Duke U., 1968, JD, 1970. Bar: N.C. 1970, D.C. 1971, U.S. Dist. Ct. (mid. dist.) N.C. 1973, N.Y. 1982, Ct. Internat. Trade 1982. Atty. FTC, Washington, 1970-73; assoc. gen. counsel, asst. sec. Fieldcrest Mills, Inc., Eden, NC, 1973-81; counsel GE, Syracuse, NY, 1981-85; corp. counsel Eastman Kodak Co., Rochester, 1985-96, internat. counsel, 1997-98, dir. legal affairs L.Am. region, 1998-2001; v.p., gen. counsel PictureVision, Inc., 2001—02, dir. licensing, 2002—. Pres. ctrl. and western N.Y. chpt. Am. Corp. Counsel Assn., 1992—93. Pres. Rockingham County Arts Coun., NC, 1979—80. Mem.: Duke Law Sch. Alumni Assn. (bd. dirs. 1994—97). Home: 71 Bristol View Dr Fairport NY 14450 Office: Eastman Kodak Co 343 State St Rochester NY 14650-0211 E-mail: michael.pearlman@kodak.com.

PEARLMAN, MICKEY LOU, writer; b. Miami Beach, Fla. d. Louis and Marcella (Richardson) Heiman; children: Ted Louis, Mia Bess. BA, CCNY, 1965; MA, CCNY, 1966; MPhil, PhD, CUNY, 1987. Bd. dirs. mentorship program cons. Split Rock, U. Minn.; organizer, dir. A Celebration of Readers Mohonk Mountain House; guest lectr. various univs. Author: What to Read, the Essential Guide for Reading Group Members and Other Book Lovers, 1999, Listen to Their Voices, 1993; co-author (with Katherine Usher Henderson): A Voice of One's Own, 1992; co-author: (with Abby H.P. Werlock) Tillie Olsen, 1991; editor: American ing Fiction: Memory, Identity, Family, Space, 1989, Mother Puzzles: Daughters and Mothers in Contemporary American Literature, 1989, The Anna Book: Searching for Anna in Literary History, 1992, Canadian Women Writing Fiction, 1993, Between Friends, 1994, A Place Called Home, 1996, 1997, A Few Thousand Words About Love, 1998, 1999. Mem.: Authors Guild, Nat. Book Critics Cir. Democrat. Jewish. Avocations: reading, baseball, quilting, raising geraniums. Home: 200 Winston Dr Apt 219 Cliffside Park NJ 07010

PEARLMAN, PETER STEVEN, lawyer; b. Orange, N.J., June 11, 1946; s. Jack Kitchener and Tiela Josephine (Fine) P.; m. Joan Perlmutter, June 19, 1969; children: Heather, Christopher, Megan. BA, U. Ill., 1967; JD, Seton Hall U., 1970. Bar: N.J. 1970, U.S. Dist. Ct. N.J. 1970, U.S. Tax Ct. 1973, U.S. Supreme Ct. 1974, U.S. Ct. Appeals (2d cir.) 1981, U.S. Ct. Appeals (3d cir.) 1983, U.S. Ct. Appeals (7th cir.) 1985, U.S. Ct. Appeals (D.C. cir.) 1998, U.S. Ct. Appeals (4th cir.) 1999, U.S. Ct. Claims 2000; cert. civil trial atty., 1982. Assoc. Cohn & Lifland, Esquires, Saddle Brook, N.J., 1970-72; ptnr. Cohn, Lifland, Pearlman, Herrmann & Knopf, 1972—. Lectr. Nat. Inst. Trial Advocacy, Hempstead, N.Y., 1988—; active trial advocacy program Widener Law Sch.; adj. faculty mem. trial advocacy program Hofstra Law Sch.; master C. Willard Heckel Inn of Ct.; guest lectr. appellate advocacy Roger Williams Law Sch., 1995—; mem. panel arbitrators Am. Arbitration Assn.; lectr. for Inst. Continuing Legal Edn. for State of N.J. Mem. ABA, ATLA, N.J. Bar Assn. Home: 9 Harvey Dr Short Hills NJ 07078-1122 Office: Cohn Lifland Pearlman Herrmann & Knopf 1 Park 80 Plz W Ste 4 Saddle Brook NJ 07663-5808 E-mail: psp@njlawfirm.com.

PEARLMAN, RONALD ALAN, lawyer, educator; b. Hamilton, Ohio, July 10, 1940; AB with honors, Northwestern U., 1962, JD cum laude, 1965; LL.M. in Taxation, Georgetown U., 1967. Bar: D.C. 1991, U.S. Tax Ct. 1969, U.S. Supreme Ct. 1968. Atty. office chief counsel IRS, Washington, 1965-69; assoc. Thompson & Mitchell, St. Louis, 1969-70, ptnr., 1970-83; dep. asst. sec. for tax policy Dept. Treasury, Washington, 1983-84, asst. sec. tax policy, 1984-85; ptnr. Bryan, Cave, McPheeters & McRoberts (now Bryan Cave), St. Louis, 1986-88; chief of staff joint com. on taxation U.S. Congress, Washington, 1988-90; ptnr. Covington & Burling, 1991-99; prof., dir grad. tax program Georgetown U. Law Ctr., 1999—. Adj. prof. Sch. Law Wash. U., St. Louis, 1972-83; vis. instr. Sch. Law U. Va., Charlottesville, 1995-98; mem. BNA Tax Mgmt. Adv. Bd., 1986-88, 93—; participant ednl. seminars; vis. prof.

Georgetown U. Law Ctr., Washington, 1998. Mem. bd. editors Northwestern U. Law Rev.; contbr. articles to various publs. Trustee Am. Tax Policy Inst., 1998—, v.p., 2001—. Fellow Am. Coll. Tax Counsel; mem. ABA (vice chair govt. rels. 1997-99, chair govt. rels. com. 1996-97, mem. coun., tax sect. 1986-88), Am. Law Inst. (tax adv. group, cons. pass-through entities project and tax integration project), Order of Coif. Office: Georgetown U Law Ctr 600 New Jersey Ave NW Washington DC 20001-2022 E-mail: pearlmar@law.georgetown.edu.

PEARLMAN, SAMUEL SEGEL, lawyer, educator; b. Pitts., May 28, 1942; s. Merle Maurice and Bernice Florence (Segel) P.; m. Cathy Schwartz, Aug. 16, 1964; children: Linda P. Kraner, Caren E. AB, U. Pa., 1963, LLB magna cum laude, 1966. Bar: Pa. 1966, Ohio 1967, U.S. Ct. Appeals (3d cir.) 1967. Law clk. U.S. Dist. Ct. for Ea. Dist. Pa., Phila., 1966-67; assoc. Burke, Haber & Berick, Cleve., 1967-72, prin., 1973-86, Berick, Pearlman & Mills, Cleve., 1986-99; ptnr. Squire, Sanders & Dempsey L.L.P., 2000—. Lectr. law Case Western Res. U. Sch. Law, 1978-82; mem. registration com. Ohio Div. Securities, 1979-89; adv. dir. Midland Title Security, Inc.; trustee Realty ReFund Trust, N.Y. Stock Exch., 1990-98. Author: Cases, Forms and Materials for Modern Real Estate Transactions, 1978, 82. Mem. ABA, Ohio Bar Assn., Greater Cleve. Bar Assn. (chmn. securities law sect. 1985-86), Order of Coif. Republican. Jewish. Office: Squire Sanders & Dempsey 4900 Key Tower 127 Public Sq Ste 4900 Cleveland OH 44114-1304 E-mail: spearlman@ssd.com.

PEARLMAN, SETH LEONARD, civil engineer; b. Steubenville, Ohio, Aug. 6, 1956; s. Abraham and Rita Joy (Morov) P.; m. Pamela Diane Bretton, Mar. 29, 1987; children: Isaac Joseph, Julian Brett. BSCE, Carnegie Mellon U., 1978, MSCE, 1979. Registered profl. engr., Pa., Va. Sr. engr. GAI Cons., Pitts., 1979-82; v.p. mktg. Belot Concrete Industries, Tiltonsville, Ohio, 1982-86; chief design engr. Nicholson Constrn. Co., Bridgeville, Pa., 1986-93, regional mktg. mgr., 1993-95, dir. bus. devel., 1995-99, v.p., 1999—. Speaker, lectr. in field. Author conf. publs. Active United Jewish Fedn., Pitts., 1988—; bd. dirs. Beth El Congregation of the South Hills, Pitts., 1991-97. Mem. ASCE (mem. geotech. sect. com. Pitts. chpt. 1990-94), NSPE (pres. Wheeling W.Va. chpt. 1986), GeoInst. (awards com. 2001--), Am. Concrete Inst. (fiber reinforced concrete com. 1982-96, co-chmn. state of art report, mem. concrete piling com. 1989-95, bd. dirs. Pitts. chpt. 1984-87), Deep Founds. Inst. (nat. bd. trustees 1998—, micro piles com. 1996—, treas. 2000—), Internat. Assn. Found. Drilling (earth retention com. 1991-96), Geo Inst. (awards com. 2001—), Engrs. Soc. We. Pa., Chartiers Country Club. Democrat. Home: 266 Twin Hills Dr Pittsburgh PA 15216-1108 Office: Nicholson Constrn 12 McClane St Cuddy PA 15031-0098 E-mail: spearlman@nicholson-rodio.com.

PEARLSTEIN, ARNE JACOB, engineer, educator; b. Los Angeles, Mar. 18, 1952; s. Benjamin Jacob and Fanny (Lilienthal) P.; m. Elizabeth Jane Stern, 1991. BS in Engring., MS in Engring., UCLA, 1977, Engr., 1979, PhD in Engring., 1983. Asst. prof. mech. engring. U. Ariz., 1983-89; assoc. prof. mech. engring. U. Ill., Urbana-Champaign, 1989—2000, prof. mech. engring., 2000—. Contbr. articles to profl. jours. Recipient Presdl. Young Investigator award NSF, 1985. Mem. ASME, Am. Inst. Chem. Engrs. Office: U Ill Dept Mech & Indsl Engring 1206 W Green St Urbana IL 61801-2906

PEARLSTEIN, PAUL DAVIS, lawyer; b. Berlin, Jan. 3, 1938; s. Victor and Sophia (Davis) Pearlstein; m. Patricia Hurston, June 1964 (div.); children: Laura Sue, David Seth; m. Marilyn Mills, Jan. 11, 1981; children: Adam Lowell, Susanna Lee. AB, U. Pa., 1959; LLB, U. Va., 1962. Bar: Va. 1962, D.C. 1963, Md. 1990, U.S. Supreme Ct. 1970, cert.: Comml. Law League Am. Acad., Am. Arbitration Assn. (arbitrator), Nat. Assn. Securities Dealers, Am. Bd. of Cert. (bus. bankruptcy specialist). Atty. HUD, Washington, 1964-66; adminstr. contrn. and purchasing activities Cafritz Co. and affiliated cos., 1966-68; pvt. practice, 1968-96; ptnr. Pearlstein & Jacques, 1989—, Pearlstein & Assocs., Washington, 1997—. Chair adv. rules com. U.S. Bankruptcy Ct. D.C., Washington; bankruptcy trustee Washington and Va., 1973—90; spkr. in the field. Editor, contbg. author: Real Estate Practice in DC, Md. and Va., 1995, contbg. author, editor: articles and books revs. to legal jours. Mandolinist, guitarist Takoma Mandoleers, 1971—, Orgn. Anacostia Rowing and Scullings, Coun. Ct. Excellence; bd. dirs., sec. Met. Washington, DC Trial Lawyers Found., 1991—96; bd. dirs. DC shpt. Am. Diabetes Assn., 1987—89; mem. Capitol Rowina Club, 2001—02; pres. The Counsellors, 2001—02; pres. brotherhood Washington Hebrew Congregation, 1974—75, bd. mgrs., 1979—85; mem. inter group rels. com. Jewish Cmty. Coun., 1973—90. Capt. U.S. Army, 1962—64. Fellow: Am. Bar Found.; mem.: ABA (real property and probate sects.), D.C. Land Title Assn. (v.p. 1989—90), Washington Estate Planning Coun., Washington Assn. Realtors, Jud. Conf. D.C. cir., The Counselors (pres. 2001—02), Bar Assn. D.C. (chmn. real property law com. 1976—78, pres. rsch. found., Chmn. of the Yr. 1977, Spl. Projects award 1987). Democrat. Avocations: kayaking, hiking, mandolin, guitar, rowing. Office: Ste 505 1730 Rhode Island Ave NW Washington DC 20036-3101 Fax: 202-223-8737. E-mail: merraul@aol.com.

PEARLSTEIN, SEYMOUR, artist; b. Bklyn., Oct. 14, 1923; s. Morris Lazarus and Anna (Bassiur) P.; m. Toby Tessie Rubinstein, Mar. 21, 1943; children: Judith Helene, Lawrence Jonathan. Cert., Pratt Inst., Bklyn., 1950, Art Students League N.Y., 1954; student of Jack Potter. Owner, illustrator, designer Sy Pearlstein Advt. Art Studio, N.Y.C., 1946-71; artist-painter rep. by Far Gallery, 1969-81; prof. N.Y.C. Tech. Coll., CUNY, Bklyn., 1971-94, prof. emeritus, 1994—, chmn. art and advt. design dept., 1985-88. One-man shows Silvermine Guild of Artists, New Canaan, Conn., 1973, Far Gallery, 1973, 75, 78, Klitgord Ctr., N.Y.C., C.C., 1974, De Mers Gallery, Hilton Head, S.C., 1975, Adelphi U., Garden City, N.Y., 1979, Grace Gallery, N.Y.C. Tech. Coll., 1992; group shows A.M. Sachs Gallery, N.Y.C., 1971, Springfield (Mo.) Art Mus., 1971, Am. Acad. Arts and Letters, N.Y.C., 1975, 76, 77, NAD, N.Y.C., 1986, 87, 89, 91, 92, Butler Inst. Art, Ohio, 1975, Ball State U., Queens Mus., N.Y.C., 1978, 81, Dept. State Art in Embassies Program, N.Y. Hist. Soc., 1981, Colo. Heritage Mus., Denver, 1981, 82, 86, Am. Watercolor Soc., N.Y.C., Ingber Gallery, N.Y.C., 1985, Audubon Artists, N.Y.C., 1990, 92, 97, Allied Artists Am., N.Y.C., 1990, 91, 95, Phila. Mus. Sales and Loan Gallery, Nat. Arts Club, N.Y.C., 1989, Grace Gallery, N.Y.C. Tech. Coll., CUNY, 1998, 99, 2000, others; represented in permanent collections Mus. N.Mex., Santa Fe, Mint Mus. Art, Charlotte, N.C., NAD, N.Y.C., Fine Arts Gallery, San Diego, Adelphi U., Queens Mus., N.Y.C., Munson-Williams-Proctor Inst., Utica, N.Y., N.Y.C. Tech. Coll., Bklyn. Served with AUS, 1942-46. Recipient Gold medal Nat. Acad. Design, 1969, Hassam Fund Purchase award Am. Acad. Arts and Letters, 1969, 77, Gold medal of honor Nat. Arts Club, 1970, Ranger Fund Purchase award NAD, 1971, 82, Gold medal Soc. Illustrators, 1972, Nat. Inst.-Am. Acad. Arts and Letters grant, 1975 Mem. NAD (sec. coun.) 1980-84, W.H. Leavin prize 1985), Am. Watercolor Soc. (bd. dirs. 1979-80, Watercolor U.S.A. award 1971), Art Students League of N.Y. (life), Allied Artists Am. (bd. dirs. 1976-79, E. Lowe award 1969, gold medal 1980, George Tweed Meml. award 1989, 92), Audubon Artists (bd. dirs. 1986-89, 91-93, Grumbacher award 1971, Fabri medal 1980), Alliance Figurative Artists (c0chmn. 1976-77), Profl. Staff Congress. Home: 52 Dartmouth St Forest Hills NY 11375-5142 Office: NYC Tech Coll AD Dept CUNY 300 Jay St Brooklyn NY 11201-1909 E-mail: sntp52@aol.com.

PEARLSTEIN, STEPHANIE LILIENTHAL, social worker, consultant, therapist; b. N.Y.C., May 6, 1915; d. Jacob and Rose (Adlerstein) Lilienthal; m. Benjamin Jacob Pearlstein, May 30, 1946; 1 child, Arne J. BA, Hunter Coll., CUNY, 1940; MSS, Smith Coll., 1942. Lic. clin. social worker. Social worker Jewish Bd. of Guardians, N.Y.C., 1942-45; asst. field dir. overseas hosp. svc. Army Gen. Hosp.-ARC, France, 1945-46; psychiat. social worker VA Brentwood (Calif.) Psychiat. Hosp., 1946; social worker, student supr. Jewish Family Svc., L.A. and Santa Monica, Calif., 1946-48; mental health cons. L.A. County Dept. of Mental Health, 1965-68; social worker Harbor Gen. Hosp., Torrance, Calif., 1968-69, supr. psychiat. social svc., 1969-77; oncology svc. social worker Daniel Freeman Hosp., Inglewood, 1977-78; ind. after care cons. L.A., 1978-87; ret. Community cons. head start and elem. schs., L.A., 1968-69. Mem. Nat. Assn. Social Workers, Acad. Cert. Social Workers, Plato Soc. Avocations: current events, gardening, sewing, reading, concerts and theater.

PEARLSTINE, NORMAN, editor; b. Phila., Oct. 4, 1942; s. Raymond and Gladys (Cohen) P.; m. Nancy Colbert Friday, 1988. AB, Haverford Coll., 1964; LLB, U. Pa., 1967. Staff reporter Wall Street Jour., Dallas, Detroit, L.A., 1968-73, Tokyo bur. chief, 1973-76; mng. editor Asian Wall Street Jour., Hong Kong, 1976-78; exec. editor Forbes Mag., L.A., 1978-80; nat. news editor Wall Street Jour., N.Y.C., 1980-82; editor, pub. Wall Street Jour./Europe, Brussels, 1982-83; mng. editor, v.p. Wall Street Jour., N.Y.C., 1983-91, exec. editor, 1991-92; pres., CEO Friday Holdings, L.P., 1993-94; editor-in-chief Time Inc., 1994—. Pres. Atsuko Chiba Found.; bd. dirs. Sundance Inst.; bd. councilors USC Annenberg Sch. Comm. Recipient Editor of Yr. award Nat. Press Found., 1989. Mem. ABA, D.C. Bar Assn. (trustee), N.Y. Hist. Soc. (former chmn.), Coun. Fgn. Rels. Office: Time Inc 1271 Avenue Of The Americas New York NY 10020-1300

PEARSALL, GEORGE WILBUR, materials scientist, mechanical engineer, educator, consultant; b. Brentwood, N.Y., July 13, 1933; s. Milo Dickerson and Margaret Elizabeth (White) P.; m. Patricia Louise Stevens, Oct. 11, 1962. B. Metall. Engring., Rensselaer Poly. Inst., 1955; Sc.D. (Am. Soc. Metals fellow), MIT, 1961. Registered profl. engr., N.C. Research engr. Dow Chem. Co., Midland, Mich., 1955-57; research asst. MIT, 1959-60, asst. prof. metallurgy, 1960-64; assoc. prof. mech. engring. Duke U., 1964-66, prof., 1966-81, prof. mech. engring. and materials sci., 1981—2001, prof. pub. policy studies, 1982—, acting dean Sch. Engring., 1969-71, dean, 1971-74, 82-83, prof. emeritus, 2001—. Trustee Triangle Univs. Ctr. for Advanced Studies, 1976-92, chmn. exec. com., 1983-88; dir. Duke-IBM Product Safety Inst., 1979-90. Author: (with W.G. Moffatt and J. Wulff) The Structure and Properties of Materials, 1964; mem. editl. bd. Jour. Products Liability, 1977-96, Proceedings of the IEEE, 1994-96; contbr. articles to profl. jours. Served with AUS, 1957. Mem. ASME (Triodyne Safety award 2001), Am. Soc. Metals (life), Sigma Xi, Phi Lambda Upsilon, Tau Beta Pi, Pi Tau Sigma. Home: 2941 Welcome Dr Durham NC 27705-5555

PEARSALL, GLENN LINCOLN, brokerage house executive; b. Huntington, N.Y., June 19, 1949; s. Alan W. and Jean (Doubrava) Pearsall; m. Carol Ann Ciesla, June 19, 1971; children: Adam, Heather. BA in English, SUNY, Oswego, 1971; cert. investment mgmt. analyst, U. Pa., 1994. V.p. Pearsall Realty Inc., Wevertown, N.Y., 1975-85; investment exec. E.F. Hutton, Glens Falls, 1985-87; fin. cons. Shearson, Lehman, Hutton, Glens Falls, Saratoga, 1987-90; fin. advisor PaineWebber, Glens Falls, 1990—, br. mgr., 1990—2002, divsnl. v.p., 1994—. Mem. 1991 stock pickers coun. Capital Dist. Bus. Rev., Albany, N.Y., 1991; fin. commentator TV 8 Monday Night News, Glens Falls, 1988—; daily stock market reporter Stas. WLPW-FM, WIRD-AM, Lake Placid, N.Y., 1985-90, WKBE-FM, Glens Falls, N.Y., 1992-95, WWSC-AM, 1995, WCKM-FM, 1995—. Fin. columnist several weekly newspapers, 1988—. Pres. bd. dirs. North Creek (N.Y.) C. of C., 1978-86; mem. Assemblyman Glenn Harris Legis. Adv. Coun., Assembly Dist. 109 N.Y. State, 1985-90, Cornell Coop Extension Adv. Coun., 1982-91; bd. dirs. Warren County Coop. Extension, pres., 1985, 86; bd. dirs. Adirondack coun. Girl Scouts U.S., fund-raising chmn., 1990; bd. dirs., v.p. Lake George Opera Festival; bd. dirs. Adirondack Emsemble, 1997—, v.p. 1999, chair, fin. com. 1998—, pres. Adirondack Civil War Round Table, 1997—; trustee Town of Johnsburg Libr. Found., Adirondack Mus. at Blue Mountain Lake; pres. Adirondack Ensemble, 2000-01. Mem. Investment Mgmt. Cons. Assn. Republican. Avocations: white water canoeing, skiing, fishing, reading. Office: PaineWebber One Broad St Pla Glens Falls NY 12801 E-mail: glenn.pearsall@ubspainewebber.com.

PEARSALL, GREGORY HOWARD, naval officer; b. Riverhead, N.Y., Nov. 2, 1951; s. Smith Gregory and Betty Irene (Tuthill) P.; m. Barbara Jean Hesler, June 28, 1970; children: Christopher, Andrew, Kevin. BS in Mgmt., U.S. Naval Acad., Annapolis, Md., 1974; MS in Bus., Naval Postgrad. Sch., Monterey, Calif., 1986; MA in Fgn. Affairs, Naval War Coll., Newport, R.I., 1994. Supply officer USS Hermitage, Virginia Beach, Va., 1978-80, Naval Ordnance Sta., Indian Head, Md., 1980-83; asst. supply officer USS Shenandoah, Norfolk, Va., 1983-85; ADP project officer, comptroller Navy Fleet Material Support Office, Mechanicsburg, Pa., 1987-90; comptroller U.S. Naval Acad., Annapolis, 1990-92; supply officer USS Sierra, Charleston, S.C., 1992-93; dir. fleet/indsl. support group Navy Ships Parts Control Ctr., Mechanicsburg, 1994-95; exec. officer Navy Fleet Material Support Office, 1995-98; site mgr. Sci. Applications Internat. Corp., 1998-2000; CFO Jack Gaughen Realtor ERA, 1999—. Dir. Charles County Econ. Devel. Commn., Waldorf, Md., 1980-83. Coach St. Andrews Little League, Charleston, 1993, King Phillip Little League, Bristol, R.I., 1994, Bristol Youth Soccer Assn., 1994, Hampden Youth Soccer Assn., Mechanicsburg, 1995-2000; treas. Cumberland Valley Lacrosse Boosters. Recipient Meritorious Svc. medal Pres. of the U.S., 1983, 90, 92, 93, Hammer award Nat. Performance Review, 1995, Mil. Outstanding Vol. Svc. medal, 1996. Avocations: gardening/landscaping, woodworking, coin/card collecting, sports. Office: Jack Gaughen Realtor ERA 3915 Carlisle Pike Camp Hill PA 17011 E-mail: ghpearsall@aol.com.

PEARSALL, THOMAS ARMSTRONG, educator; b. Burlington, NC, July 31, 1959; s. John Sanders Pearsall, Mary Mason Pearsall. DMA-Piano Performance and Pedagogy, University of Oklahoma, Norman, OK, 1990—96; MM-Piano Performance, Bowling Green State University, Bowling Green, OH, 1982—84; BM-Piano Performance, University of Kentucky, Lexington, KY, 1977—82. Associate Professor Georgia Southern University, Statesboro, GA, 1993—2002; Artist/Instructor Wausau Conservatory of Music, Wausau, WI, 1985—90; Associate Lecturer/Instructor University of Wisconsin-Marathon County, 1986—88; Instructor University of Toledo, Toledo, 1984—85, Bowling Green State University, Bowling Green, 1984—85. Vice-President, Publicity Georgia Music Teachers Association, Statesboro, GA, 2000—02, Vice-President, In-State Spring Auditions, GA, 1998—2000. Faculty Advisor Phi Mu Alpha Sinfonia, Statesboro, GA, 1994—2001; Member University of Oklahoma Graduate Council, Norman, OK, 1991—92, University of Oklahoma Graduate Student Senate, Norman, 1991—92. Mem.: Music Teachers National Association, Music Educators National Conference. Avocation: Fitness, Reading, Travel. Office: Georgia Southern University Department of Music, P.O. Box 8052 Statesboro GA 30460-8052 Office Fax: 912-681-0583. Business E-Mail: tompear@gasou.edu.

PEARSON, ANNA BELLE, business executive; b. Selma, Ala., July 6, 1934; d. William Franklin Jr. and Margueriete (Rawls) Talbert; m. Rufus Shanks Pearson Sr., June 29, 1952; children: Rufus Shanks Jr., William Edward, Anna Marie. Student, U. Ala., 1958, Trentholm Jr. Coll., Montgomery, 1976. Cert. EMT. Book-keeper Fidelity Balto Fin. Co., Balt., 1954-56; sec., book-keeper Drs. Hutchinson & McBryde, Montgomery, 1957-59; sec., treas., ptnr. Pearson Industries, Inc., Prattville, Ala., 1985—. Pres. Women Meth. Ch., Autaugaville, Ala., 1953-60, Sunday sch. tchr., 1962-80; bd. dirs. Autauga County Farm Bur., Prattville, 1962-86, S.E. Ala. Emergency Med. Coun., 1976—, sec.-treas., 1980—, Pat McMaham Scholarship Fund, 1987—, Am. Cancer Soc., Prattville, 1989—; conf. officer Ala. West Fla. Conf. Meth. Ch., 1962-69; pres. Autauga County Home Demonstration Club, Prattville, 1967-70; bd. dirs. Mental Health, 1988—. Crowned Autauga County Farm Bur. Queen, 1963. Mem. St. Margaret's Found. Guild (bd. dirs. 1988—), Autauga County Cow Bells, Autauga County Heritage Assn., Autaugaville Rescue Squad, Bridge Clubs. Democrat. Methodist. Avocations: bridge, ceramics, antiques, bicycling, crafts. Home: PO Box 129 Autaugaville AL 36003-0129

PEARSON, APRIL VIRGINIA, lawyer; b. Martinsville, Ind., Aug. 11, 1960; d. Clare Grill and Sheila Rosemary (Finch) Rayner; m. Randall Keith Pearson, Dec. 10, 1988; children: Randall Kyle, Austin Finch, Autumn Virginia. BA, Calif. State U., Long Beach, 1982; JD, Pepperdine U., 1987; cert. indsl. fire brigade, HAZWOPER Tex. A&M U. Bar: Calif. 1987, Idaho 1993, D.C. 1989. Assoc. counsel Union Oil Co. Calif., L.A., 1988-2001; owner Avrilex, Chino Hills, Calif., 2001—. V.p. Pa's Bier, Long Beach, Calif., 1988—98, Ammonia Safety Tng. Inst., sec., 1995—98, gen. counsel, 1997—; mem. pub. works commn. City of Chino Hills, 1999—. Mem.: Chem. Industry Coun. Calif. (chair regulatory affairs com. 1995), Am. Corp. Counsel Assn., Women Lawyers Long Beach (v.p. 1990—93). Avocations: running, Tae Kwon Do. Office: Avrilex 13462 Montserrat Ct Chino Hills CA 91709-1327 E-mail: april@avrilex.com.

PEARSON, BARBARA JOY, small business owner; b. St. Louis, Oct. 1, 1942; d. Emerson Maness and Marie (Barlett) Elgin; m. Herby Otto Pearson, Mar. 26, 1963; children: Herby, Christina. Student, Roosevelt U., St. Louis; Diploma, Revlon Sch. Make Up Artistry, 1977; Advanced Facial Tng., Repechage, 1987. Lic. cosmetologist; cert. makeup technician, Am. Bd. Permanent Make Up Tech., Calif. Mgr. safety equipment Reis Equipment, St. Louis, 1958-65; makeup artist Revlon Cosmetics, N.Y.C., 1969-73; facialist, makeup artist Saks Fifth Ave., St. Louis, 1973-85; owner, operator James Pearson Beauty Salon & Day Spa, Frontenac, Mo., 1985—. Mem. Nat. Assn. Women Bus. Owners, Alstisition Profls. St. Louis. Republican. Lutheran. Avocations: investing, watercolor painting, writing poetry, reading, studying makeup artistry. Home: 1949 Lanchester Ct Chesterfield MO 63017-7906 Office: James Pearson Beauty Salon Le Chateau Village 10411 Clayton Rd Saint Louis MO 63131-2928

PEARSON, CAROL ANN, chemistry educator, science resource manager; b. Racine, Wis., Jan. 23, 1952; d. Richard E. and Beverly J. (Adler) Kirchner; m. Dale C. Pearson, Oct. 8, 1977; children: Peter, Greta. BS, U. Wis., Parkside, 1974. Chemist Jos. Schlitz Brewing Co., Milw., 1974-77, McCormick & Co., South Bend, Ind., 1978-80, Donohue, Sheboygan, Wis., 1981-82; instr. chemistry Lakeshore Tech. Coll., Cleveland, 1980-91, Northeast Wis. Tech. Coll., Green Bay, 1993—; sci. resource ctr. coord. Einstein Project, 1998—. Pres. Women of Evang. Luth. Ch. Am., Green Bay Conf., 1990—92; adminstr. sci. fair Langlade Elem. Sch., Green Bay, 1991—96; leader Girl Scouts U.S. Mem. AAUW (pres. Green Bay br. 1992-94, gift honoree), Bayshore Bicycle Club, Nat. Sci. Tchrs. Assn., Green Bay Botanical Garden Assn., Brown County Civic Music Assn. Avocations: gourmet cooking, cross country skiing, bicycling, sewing. Office: Einstein Project 3100 Market St Green Bay WI 54304-5612

PEARSON, CHARLES THOMAS, JR. lawyer, director; b. Fayetteville, Ark., Oct. 14, 1929; s. Charles Thomas and Doris (Pinkerton) P.; m. Wyma Lee Hampton, Sept. 9, 1988; children: Linda Sue, John Paddock. BS, U. Ark., 1953, JD, 1954; postgrad., U.S. Naval Postgrad. Sch., 1959; A.M., Boston U., 1963. Bar: Ark. bar 1954. Practice in Fayetteville, 1963—. Dir. officer N.W. Comms., Inc., Dixieland Devel., Inc., Jonlin Investments, Inc., World Wide Travel Svc., Inc., Okliania Farms, Inc., N.W. Arl. Land & Devel., Inc., Garden Plaza Inns, Inc. Word Data, Inc., M.P.C. Farms, Inc., Fayetteville Enterprises, Inc., NWA Devel.Co., Delta Comm., Inc.; past. dir., organizer N.W. Nat. Bank. Adviser Explorer Scouts, 1968— ; past pres. Washington County Draft Bd.; past pres. bd. Salvation Army. Served to comdr. Judge Adv. Gen. Corps USNR, 1955-63. Mem. ABA, Ark. Bar Assn., Washington County Bar Assn., Judge Advs. Assn., N.W. Ark. Ret. Officers Assn. (past pres.), Methodist Men (past pres), U. Ark. Alumni Assn. (past dir.), Sigma Chi (past pres. N.W. Ark. alumni, past chmn. house corp.), Alpha Kappa Psi, Phi Eta Sigma, Delta Theta Phi. Clubs: Mason (32 deg., K.T., Shriner), Moose, Elk, Lion, Metropolitan. Republican. Methodist. Office: 9 N College Ave Fayetteville AR 72701-5301 E-mail: tpesq1101@aol.com.

PEARSON, CLARENCE EDWARD, management consultant, educator; b. Chgo., Apr. 22, 1925; s. Edward and Irene (Silander) P.; m. June Waldhe, Apr. 21, 1951 (dec. 1967); 1 child, Scott (dec.); m. Laurie Norris, Apr. 25, 1995. BS, No. Ill. U., 1950; MPH, U. N.C., 1952. Instr. Mt. Prospect (Ill.) Pub. Schs., 1950-51; dir. health edn. DuPage County Health Dept., Wheaton, Ill., 1952-55; chief health edn. St. Louis Health Dept., 1955-57; dir. health and hosps. Health and Welfare Council, St. Louis, 1957-61; dir. health and safety Met. Life Ins. Co., N.Y.C., 1961-87. Prof. edn. Columbia Tchrs. Coll., 1975—; pres. Universal Health Concepts, N.Y.C., 1984-87. Coun. Internat. Health, Washington, 1981-84; bd. dirs. AARP, Nat. Coun. Internat. Health, Washington, 1981-84; chmn. Profl. Exam. Svc., N.Y.C., 1996-99; v.p. Peter Drucker Found. for Nonprofit Mgmt., 1994-96; mem. adv. bd. C. Everett Koop Inst.; bd. overseers Dartmouth Med. Sch., 1992-96, 99—; adj. prof. cmty. health Rober Wood Johnson Med. Sch., 1996—; pres., CEO Nat. Ctr. for Health Edn., 1997—; sr. adv. The Who office, U.N; bd. dirs. Am. Assn. Ret. Persons, 2002—. Co-author: Managing Health Promotion, 1982; co-editor: (with C. Everett Koop) Critical Issues in Global Health, 2000; contbr. chpts. to books in field. Co-chmn. Scandinavian-Ams. for Rockefeller presdl. campaign, N.Y., 1968; co-dir. Salzburg Seminar Spl. Session: Critical Issues in Global Health. Served as staff sgt. U.S. Army, 1943-46. Recipient Disting. Career award Am. Pub. Health Assn., Washington, 1981, Gold Medal for Achievement, Columbia U., N.Y.C., 1984, Internat. Health award Asia Pacific Consortium, Honolulu, 1984, Porter Prize, Pitts. Health Ctr., 1986, Disting. Alumni award Sch. Pub. Health, U. N.C., 2001. Fellow APHA (governing coun. 1970-78), AARP (bd. dirs. 2002), Advt. Coun. (adv. bd.), The Univ. Club (N.Y.C.). Home: 530 E 23rd St New York NY 10010-5022 Office: WHO at the UN 2 UN Plz New York NY 10017 E-mail: nyvikings@aol.com., pearsonc@un.org.

PEARSON, DANA BART, librarian; b. San Francisco, Feb. 15, 1948; s. Kenneth W. Pearson and Carlette Tipton. BA, U. Ariz., 1991; M in Libr. and Info. Sci., U. North Tex., Denton, 1993. Prodr., dir., editor Ea. Okla. TV Co., Denison, Tex., 1985-92; dir. libr. Ranger (Tex.) Coll., 1993-95; dir. learning resource ctr. Cisco (Tex.) Jr. Coll., 1995-98; dir. libr. svcs. South Plains Coll., Levelland, Tex., 1998-99; libr. Moreno Valley (Calif.) Pub. Libr., 1999-2000; dir. libr. svcs. North Ctrl. Tex. Coll., Gainesville, 2000—. Cons. distance edn., Cisco, 1995-98. Sgt. U.S. Army, 1968-70, Vietnam. Decorated Purple Heart, U.S. Army, Vietnam, 1970, Bronze Star, 1970. Mem. ALA, Am. Soc. Info. Sci., Assn. Computing Machinery, Tex. Libr. Assn., Tex. Coun. Cmty./Jr. Coll. Librs. (vice-chair 1996-98, chair 1998—). Avocations: running, weightlifting, tennis, basketball. Office: North Central Tex Coll 1525 W California Gainesville TX 76240 E-mail: dpearson@nctc.cc.tx.us.

PEARSON, DAVID PETRI, chemist; b. Oct. 24, 1926; s. Brewer Petri and Laura Alvine (Johnson) P.; m. Patricia Margaret Cowan, June 4, 1949; children: Kathryn A., James P., Rebecca L., Kristine R., Judith G. BA in Chemistry, Reed Coll., 1949; MS in Phys. Chemistry, Oreg. State U., 1953; PhD in Phys. Chemistry, U. So. Calif., 1960. Rsch. chemist Phillips Petroleum Co. (AEC), Idaho Falls, Idaho, 1957-62, Bartlesville, Okla., 1962-69; lectr. in chemistry Portland State U., 1969-71; asst. prof. chemistry So. Oreg. State Coll., Ashland, 1971-72; rsch. assoc. Oreg. Grad. Ctr., Beaverton, 1972-74; sr. chemist Portland Gen. Electric Co., 1975-87, ret., 1987. Patentee in field. Cpl. USAAF, 1946-47. Mem. Am. Chem. Soc. (treas. Portland sect. 1979-82, chmn. 1983). Clubs: Am. Alpine, Idaho Alpine (sec. Idaho Falls 1961, pres. 1962). Republican. Presbyterian. Home: 6324 SW Radcliffe St Portland OR 97219-5749

PEARSON, GARY DEAN, dentist; b. Rockford, Ill., Dec. 25, 1952; s. Miles Addison and Pauline (Hammond) P.; m. Marcea Lou Schlensker, Dec. 4, 1981 (div. 1989); 1 child, Grant Addison; m. Menchu Nagal Caperocho, Apr. 22, 2000; 1 child, Mia Caperocho. BS cum laude, Rockford Coll., 1974; DDS, U. Ill., Chgo., 1978. Lic. dentist, Ill., Mich., N.H., Wis., Ariz. Pvt. practice dentistry, Rockton, Ill., 1978-93; group practice dentistry Tucson, 1993—; dentist in charge Prin. Fin. Group's Dental-Net Family Dental Ctr., 2000—; dental dir. Luth. Med. Ctr. Tucson Cmty. Clinic, 2001—. Recipient Gen. Assembly Scholarship, State of Ill., 1977. Mem. Am. Dental Assn., Ill. State Dental Soc., Winnebago County Dental Soc., U. Ill. Alumni Assn., Rockton C. of C., Phi Theta Kappa. Clubs: Rockford Coll. Alumni. Lutheran. Avocation: flying, photography, motorcycling, tennis, basketball. Home: 5622 N Placita Paisaje Tucson AZ 85750-6078 Office: Dental Net Group 1057 N Kolb Rd Tucson AZ 85710-1328

PEARSON, GAYLE MARLENE, writer, editor; b. Chgo., July 12, 1947; Student, Taylor U., 1965-67; BS in Edn., No. Ill. U., 1970. Asst. news editor Vance Pub., Chgo., 1970-71; child care specialist Ming Quong Children's Ctr., Los Gatos, Calif., 1974-75; area dir. Santa Clara County Info. and Referral, San Jose, 1977-81; edn. writer, editor free lance San Francisco, 1982-97; author children and young adult lit., 1980—. Author: (books) Fish Friday, 1986 (Best Children's Book 1986 Bay Area), The Coming Home Cafe, 1988, One Potato Tu, 1992, The Fog Doggies and Me, 1993, The Secret Box, 1997, Don't Call it Paradise, 1999. Bd. dirs. Bethany United Meth. Ch., San Francisco, Calif., 1991-92. Mem. Soc. Children's Book Writers and Illustrators. Democrat. Avocations: hiking, painting, sculpting, gardening. Home and Office: 16 Marlborough St East Greenwich RI 02818-3830 E-mail: Pearbert@crocker.com.

PEARSON, GERALD LEON, food company executive; b. Mpls., June 24, 1925; s. Perry and Lillian (Peterson) P.; m. Beverly Mary Schultz, Nov. 10, 1946; children: Steven, Perry, Liecia. Grad., Trimont (Minn.) High Sch., 1943. Treas. Trimont Packing Co., 1946-52; v.p. Spencer Foods, Iowa, 1952-68, pres., chief exec. officer, 1969-80, chmn. bd., chief exec. officer, 1972-80; chmn. Beef Specialists of Iowa Inc., 1983-94. Bd. dirs. Graffaloy, Inc., El Cajon, Calif., dir. applied mem. tech., Minnetonka, Minn.; chmn., CEO World Champions of Golf Inc.; owner Brooks Golf Club, Okoboji, Iowa. Pres. Pearson Art Found.; bd. dirs. Bethany Coll., Lindsborg; commr. Nat. Mus. Am. Art-Smithsonian Instn., 1995-99; founder Internat. Ctr. for Jazz Found. With USN, 1943-46. Mem. Swedish Royal Roundtable, Swedish Council Am. (bd. dirs.). Home: Desert Highlands # 444 10040 E Happy Valley Rd Scottsdale AZ 85255-2395 Office: Brooks Golf Club PO Box 948 Okoboji IA 51355-0948 E-mail: brooksgolfclub@aol.com.

PEARSON, GREGORY DAVID, publisher, media specialist; b. Douglas, Ariz., Apr. 28, 1944; s. William Howard and Ruthanna (Knoff) P.; m. Myrna G. Pearson, May 22, 1972 (div. 1984); m. Della Griffith, June 22, 1989; 1 child, Ashley Brooke Klein. BA, DePauw U., 1966. V.p. Rust Comm., Richmond, Va., 1977-81, Capitol Broadcasting Co., Raleigh, N.C., 1982; sr. v.p. mktg. and advt. S&K Famous Brands, Richmond, Va., 1983-89; pres. Media Buying Assocs., Midlothian, 1990-97; owner, pub., editor The Observer, 1995—. 2d v.p. bd. dirs. Brandermill Cmty. Assn. Capt. USAF, 1966-71. Mem. Richmond Ad Club (bd. dirs. 1985-87). Office: The Observer PO Box 1616 Midlothian VA 23113-1616 E-mail: theobserver@mindspring.com.

PEARSON, HARRIET D. information technology executive; b. N.Y.C. married; 2 children. Degree in engring. with honors, Princeton U.; JD with highest honors, UCLA. Engr. major oil co., La., Tex.; environ. lawyer Washington; dir. pub. affairs, govtl. programs group IBM, 1993, chief privacy officer, 2000—. Active Online Privacy Alliance, BBB's Online Privacy Program; bd. dirs. Internet Edn. Found.; mem. exec. com. Privacy Leadership Initiative; co-chairperson privacy com. Info. Tech. Industry Coun.; keynote spkr. several nat. industry confs. Named Best Thinker, Fast Company mag., 2001; recipient W.E.S.T. award, Working Woman mag., 2001. Office: IBM 1133 Westchester Ave White Plains NY 10604*

PEARSON, HENRY CHARLES, artist; b. Kinston, N.C., Oct. 8, 1914; s. A. Louis and Estelle P. BA, U. N.C., 1935; MFA, Yale U., 1938; postgrad., Art Students League, 1953-56. Stage scene designer, 1937-42; instr. art New Sch. Social Research, N.Y.C., 1965—, Pa. Acad. Fine Arts, Phila., 1973-88. Exhbns. include Workshop Gallery, N.Y.C., 1958, Stephen Radich Gallery, N.Y.C., 1960-70, The Responsive Eye, Mus. Modern Art, 1965, 29th Biennial Exhbn., Corcoran Gallery Art, Washington, 1965, Retrospective N.C. Mus. Art, Raleigh, N.C., 1968, Drawings USA, Minn. Mus. Art, St. Paul, 1971-73, Betty Parsons Gallery, N.Y.C., 1971-76, Art Students League Centennial, 1975, Truman Gallery, N.Y.C., 1976-79, Marilyn Pearl Gallery, N.Y.C., 1980—; retrospective Columbia (S.C.) Mus. Art, 1988, Henry Pearson and Friends Arts Ctr., Kinston, N.C., 1993, Seamus Heaney & Henry Pearson, Gordon College, Wenham, Ma., 1996, Native Son, East Carolina U., Greenville, N.C., 1998, Am. Painting, Yale U. Art Gallery, New Haven, Conn., 1998, Gordon Coll., Wenham, Mass., 1999, Looking East, DIALOGUE, Ctrl. Conn. State U., New Britain, Conn., 2001, Palmer Mus. Art, Pa. State U., 2001; represented in permanent collections Mus. Modern Art, N.Y.C., Met. Mus. Art, N.Y.C., Whitney Mus. Am. Art, N.Y.C., Albright-Knox Gallery, Buffalo, N.C. Mus. Art, Raleigh; represented in commd. works include List Art Posters, 1965, N.Y. Film Festival poster, 1968; illustrator: Rime of the Ancient Mariner, 1964, Five Psalms, 1969, Seamus Heaney's Sweeney Praises the Trees, 1981, Seamus Heaney's Poems and a Memoir, 1982, Seamus Heaney's Three Short Poems, 1993-94. With AUS, 1942-48, USAF, 1948-53. Ford Found. fellow, 1964; Recipient gold medal for achievement in the fine arts N.C. Gov., 1970 Mem. Am. Abstract Artists, Century Assn. Studio: 58 W 58th St New York NY 10019-2502

PEARSON, HENRY CLYDE, judge; b. Ocoonita Lee County, Va., Mar. 12, 1925; s. Henry James and Nancy Elizabeth (Seals) P.; m. Jean Calton, July 26, 1956; children: Elizabeth, Frances, Timothy Clyde. Student, Union Coll., 1947-49; LLB, U. Richmond, 1952. Bar: Va. 1952, U.S. Ct. Appeals (4th cir.) 1957, U.S. Supreme Ct. 1958. Sole practice, Jonesville, Va., 1952-56; asst. U.S. atty. Western Dist. Va., Roanoke, 1956-61; ptnr. Hopkins, Pearson & Engleby, 1956-61; judge U.S. Bankruptcy Ct. Western Dist. Va., 1970-98; ret., 1998. Participant Va. Continuing Edn. Seminars; mem. adv. com. fed. rules bankruptcy procedure; mem. Va. Ho. of Reps., 1954-56, Va. Senate, 1968-70; Republican nominee Gov. of Va., 1961. Editl. bd. Am. Survey Bankruptcy Law, 1979. Served with USN, 1943-46, PTO. Mem. Va. State Bar, ABA, Va. Trial Lawyers Assn., Assn. Trial Lawyers Am., Am. Judicature Soc., Am. Judges Assn., Fed. Bar Assn., Delta Theta Phi, Tribune Jefferson Senate, Am. Legion, VFW, Masons, Shriners. Methodist. Office: 1910 Mcvitty Rd Salem VA 24153-7406

PEARSON, JACK WILLIAM, pharmaceutical executive; b. Orleans, France, Oct. 28, 1960; Came to U.S., 1961; BA in Psychology, Chemistry, Biology, Ind. U., 1983; MBA, Nat. U., Las Vegas, Nev., 1987. Sales rep. Glaxo, Inc., Las Vegas, 1985-88, dist. mgr. Sacramento, 1988-92, product mgr., mktg. adminstr. Durham, N.C., 1992-94; sr. mgr. health systems mktg. Glaxo Wellcome, Inc., 1994—. Nat. adv. coun. Nat. Bus. Coalition Health, 1996—; mem. Midwest Bus. Group on Health, 1994—, users com. Nat. Commn. on Quality Assurance, 1994—; com. mem. Employer Purchasing Alliance, Tampa, 1995—. Mem. Am. Mgmt. Assn., Am. Coll. Healthcare Execs., Internat. Soc. for Econ. Evaluation of Medicines, Internat. Found. for Employer Benefit Plans, Soc. for Human Resource Mgmt. Office: Glaxo Wellcome Inc 5 Moore Pl Durham NC 27701-4613

PEARSON, JENNIE SUE, retired government administrator; b. Washington, Jan. 26, 1928; d. Orville Louis and Jennie (Rogers) Ganbin; m. Eugene Ryder Pearson, Feb. 3, 1945 (div. 1955); 1 child, Ronald Eugene. AA, Frederick (Md.) C.C., 1987. Title examiner Md. Motor Vehicle Adminstrn., Glen Burnie, 1970-74, title advisor, 1975-80, title supr., 1980-84, asst. br. mgr., 1984-91; ret., 1991. Pres. Rebekah Assembly Md., 1968-69, Internat. Assn. Rebekah Assemblies, Winston-Salem, N.C., 1973-74; v.p. Citizens Nursing Home Aux. Vols., 1997-98, pres., 1999—; vice chmn. bd. dirs. Md. Odd Fellows Home, 1991-92; mem. Srs. and Law Enforcement Together Coun.-Frederick City Police Dept.; mem. adv. bd. Inst. Learning in Retirement Frederick Cmty. Coll., bd. dirs.; trustee Schuyler Colfax Mus., Winston Salem, N.C.; bd. dirs. Frederick Cmty. Coll. Found., Inc. Recipient Outstanding Alumni award for significant contbns. Coll. Mission and Alumni Assn., 1991, 98, Meritorious Jewel Rebekah Assembly of Md. Outstanding Svc. in Fraternal Order and Cmty., Vol. of Month, Frederick Sr. Mag.; inductee Md. Sr. Citizens Hall of Fame, Inc. Mem. AARP (pres. Frederick chpt. 1997-99), Frederick C.C. Alumni Assn. (pres. 1991-98), Montgomery County Agrl. Ctr., Inc. (life), Frederick County Commn. for Women, Rebekah Lodge (past noble grand mem. 1997-98, Meritorious Jewel award 2000), Frederick Woman's Civic Club, Inc. (mem. com. 1992-98). Republican. Methodist. Avocations: volunteer work, travel, ice skating, walking. Home: 30 Vienna Ct Frederick MD 21702-3907

PEARSON, JIM BERRY, JR. human resources specialist; b. Wichita Falls, Tex., Sept. 25, 1948; s. Jim Berry and June Louise (Young) P.; m. Cynthia Ann Medlin, Nov. 9, 1985 (div. Jan. 1999). Cert. mediator. Community organizer VISTA, Pitts., 1969-71; youth dir. East Liberty YMCA, 1971-72; aide, therapist technician Austin (Tex.) State Sch., 1972-80; labor organizer Comm. Workers Am., Austin, 1980-90; employee resource officer Austin State Hosp., 1990-96; human resource dir. Capital Area State-Operated Cmty. MHMR Svcs., Austin, 1996-97; human resources dir. Bluebonnet Trails Cmty. Mental Health/Mental Retardation Ctr, Round Rock, Tex., 1997-2001; employee rels. specialist Tex. Dept. Mental Health and Mental Retardation, Austin, 2001—. Exec. bd. rep. Communications Workers Am./Tex. State Employees Union, Austin, 1987-90; trustee Austin Cen. Labor Coun. AFL-CIO, Austin, 1983-84. Vol. AFL-CIO Polit. Action Com., 1980—; del. founding conv. Labor Party, 1996. Recipient Vols. in Politics award Nat. ALF-CIO, Washington, 1984, Peacemaker award Travis County Dispute Resolution Ctr., 1993. Mem. Comm. Workers Am./Tex. State Employees Union Local 6186 (founding mem.). Avocations: pre-Colombian archaeology. Home: 1118 Mclain St Taylor TX 76574-2343 Office: Tex Dept Mental Health and Mental Retardation PO Box 12668 909 W 45th St Austin TX 78711-2668 E-mail: dzul@texas.net., jim.pearson@mhmr.state.tx.us.

PEARSON, JOHN MARK, civil engineer; b. Eugene, Oreg., June 15, 1950; s. Robert Lowell and Virginia Dale (Burt) P.; m. Donna Faye Bowman, June 19, 1976; children: David Andrew, Virginia Ruth, Elizabeth Rose, Sarah Lanelle, Abigail Michele, Daniel Joseph. BSCE, Oreg. State U., 1973. Registered profl. engr. Wash., Oreg., Idaho, MIch., Ala. Design engr. Chgo. Bridge and Iron Co., Houston, 1973-81; sr. design engr. Wyatt Industries, Inc., 1981-82; chief engr. GH Progressive Metals, 1982-83; v.p., gen. mgr. Security Concepts, Inc., 1983-87; civil/structural dept. mgr. Evergreen Engring., Inc., Eugene, 1987-91; project engr. Appel Engring. Svcs., 1991; mgr. engring. Bergeson-Boese & Assocs., Inc., 1991-97; sr. project engr. Branch Engring., Springfield, Oreg., 1997—. Alt. chmn. Lane County Rep. Party, 1998—; Rep. candidate Oreg. Ho. of Reps., 1998. Mem. NSPE, ASCE, ASME, Profl. Engrs. Oreg. (bd. dirs. 1992-94). Republican. Baptist. Office: Bergeson Boese & Assocs Inc 65 Centennial Loop Eugene OR 97401-7904

PEARSON, JOHN YEARDLEY, JR. lawyer; b. Norfolk, Va., July 23, 1942; BA, Washington & Lee U., 1964; JD, U. Va., 1971. Bar: Va. 1971. Atty. Willcox & Savage P.C., Norfolk, Va. Bd. editors: Va. Law Rev., 1969-71. Fellow Am. Coll. Trial Lawyers; mem. ABA (mem. litigation, tort and ins. practice sects.), Va. Assn. Def. Attys., Order of Coif. Office: Willcox & Savage PC 1800 Bank of America Ctr Norfolk VA 23510-2197

PEARSON, LARRY LESTER, journalism educator, internet presence provider; b. Sioux Falls, S.D., Sept. 27, 1942; s. Lester Loren and Lois Ursula (Cochran) P.; m. Alice Marie Simons, Sept. 15, 1979; children: Gregory Eric, Hillary Yvette, Andrew Todd. BA cum laude, U. Minn., 1964, PhD, 1990; MA, U. Wis., 1969. Newsman UPI, Mpls., 1962-63; newsman Daily American, Rome, Italy, 1964-65; instr. Journalism Sch., U. Wis., 1965-67; with Mpls. Tribune, 1967-85, wire editor, 1970-72, news editor, 1972-82, Mpls. Star & Tribune, 1982. Asst. prof. U. Alaska, Anchorage, 1985-92, assoc. prof., 1992-99, dir. Ctr. for Info. Tech., 1990-92; spl. cons. to Alaska Ho. Com. on Telecomm., 1985-90; proprieter Online Design, 1995—. Lutheran. Home: 2410 E 16th Ave Anchorage AK 99508-2906 E-mail: design@alaska.net.

PEARSON, MARGARET DONOVAN, former mayor; b. Nashville, Oct. 29, 1921; d. Timothy Graham and Nelle Ligon (Schmidt) Donovan; m. Jimmie Wilson Pearson, Aug. 2, 1946 (dec. Oct. 1978). BS, Vanderbilt U., 1944, MA, 1950; MS, U. Tenn., 1954. Cryptanalysist Army Signal Corps, Washington, 1944-45; phys. edn. tchr. Nashville Bd. Edn., 1945-46; tchr. English, phys. edn. White County Bd. Edn., Sparta, Tenn., 1946-57; spl. edn. supr. Tenn. Dept. Edn., Cookeville, 1957-65, staff devel. dir. Nashville, 1965-84; ret., 1984; 1st woman alderman City of Sparta, 1987-91, 1st woman mayor, 1991-95. Mem. U.S. Ret. Sr. Vol. Program, 1985—; dist. dir. Tenn. Mcpl. League, 1987-94, 2000-02, 1st woman elected as v.p.; mem. Tenn. Gov.'s Com. Employment of Disabled, 1989—; chmn. White County Health Coun. Recipient Cmty. Leader award Wal-Mart; Am. Speech, Lang. and Hearing Assn. fellow, 1971; Ky. Col.; Tenn. Col.; named Unsung Hero, 1998, Citizen of Yr. Sparta Expositor, 2001. Mem. Sparta C. of C., Rotary (1st woman elected pres.). Methodist. Avocations: reading, knitting, needlepoint. Home: PO Box 22 Sparta TN 38583-0022

PEARSON, MARGIT LINNEA, investment manager, technology company executive; b. Weymouth, Mass., Nov. 6, 1950; d. Eric Gustav and Evelyn (Forest) P. BA, Simmons Coll., 1972; MBA, Harvard U., 1975. With McKinsey & Co., Inc., N.Y.C., 1975-83; pres. Berkey, Inc., Greenwich, Conn., 1987-89, APC Corp., Hawthorne, N.J., 1990-91, Sunset Mgmt., Charleston, S.C., 1993-97; prin. CFN, N.Y.C., 1998—; CEO Neoptis, Inc., 2000, Hipn-Tasty, Inc., N.Y.C., 2001—. Bd. dirs. theguystore.com, 1999—. Bd. dirs. Desert Chorale, Santa Fe, 1994—, Tchrs. Network, N.Y.C., 1996—. Avocations: art, skiing, travel. Home: 9 E 96th St New York NY 10128-0778 Office: 14 W 95th St New York NY 10025-6706

PEARSON, NATHAN WILLIAMS, investment management executive; b. N.Y.C., Nov. 26, 1911; s. James A. and Elizabeth (Williams) P.; m. Kathleen P. McMurtry, Apr. 9, 1947; children: James S. (dec.), Nathan Williams. AB, Dartmouth Coll., 1932; MBA, Harvard U., 1934; LLD, Thiel Coll., 1972. With U.S. Steel Corp., 1939-42; mgr. research Matson Navigation Co., 1946-47; controller Carborundum Co., 1947-48; with T. Mellon and Sons, Pitts., 1948-70, v.p., gov., 1957-70; chmn., chief exec. officer, chmn. emeritus Mellon Bank N.A. & Mellon Bank Corp., Pitts., 1987—. Fin. exec. for Paul Mellon, 1948-99. Chmn. Pitts. Theol. Sem., 1987. Served from lt. (j.g.) to comdr. USNR, 1942-46. Mem. Allegheny Country Club, Harvard-Yale Princeton Club, Duquesne Club, Edgeworth Club, Rolling Rock Club (Ligonier, Pa.). Republican. Presbyterian. Home: 10 Woodland Rd Sewickley PA 15143-1123 Office: Mellon Bank Corp Three Mellon Bank Ctr 525 William Penn Pl # 3903 Pittsburgh PA 15219-1711

PEARSON, NATHAN WILLIAMS, communications and investment executive; b. Sewickley, Pa., Aug. 1, 1951; s. Nathan Williams Sr. and Kathleen Patricia (McMurtry) P.; m. Jane Ruth Wallace, Oct. 12, 1985; children: Nathan McMurtry, Howe Quinn, Henry Wallace. BA and MA in Music, Conn. Wesleyan U., 1974; MBA, Columbia U., 1982. Pvt. practice cons., N.Y.C. and Washington, 1974-82; with McKinsey & Co., N.Y.C. and L.A., 1982-88; exec. v.p., chief fin. officer, mng. prin., sec., treas. Broadcasting Ptnrs., Inc., N.Y.C., 1988-95; chmn. Broadcasting Ptnrs., L.L.C., Rye, NY, 1995—; pres., CEO and chmn. RadioWave.com Inc., Chgo., 1999—2001; mng. dir. Manursing Group, Rye, NY, 2002—; with Broadcasting Ptnrs., LLC. Vice chmn. No. Light Comms., Reykjavik, 1995--; mng. dir. Commonwealth Holdings, Inc., N.Y.C., 1996-99; operating affiliate McCown DeLeeuw & Co., N.Y.C., 1997-99. Author: "Goin' to Kansas City," 1987; producer LP records, TV and radio programs; contbr. articles to profl. jours. Sec., bd. dirs. CityLore, Inc., N.Y.C., 1986—, pres., 1990-92; pres. Young Audiences/N.Y.C., 1995-96; bd. dirs. Young Audiences, 1986—, Young Audiences, Inc., 1995—. Mem. Soc. for Ethnomusicology, Am. Folklore Soc., Wadawanuck Club, Nat. Assn. Broadcasting, Manursing Island Club, Hillsboro Club, Beta Gamma Sigma. Avocations: boardsailing, river running, hiking. Home: 3 Holly Ln Rye NY 10580-3953 Office: Broadcasting Ptnrs Rye NY 10580 E-mail: bili_pearson@prodigy.net.

PEARSON, NORMAN, urban and regional planner, administrator, academic and planning consultant, writer; b. Stanley, County Durham, Eng., Oct. 24, 1928; arrived in Can., 1954; s. Joseph and Mary (Pearson) P.; m. Gerda Maria Josefine Riedl, July 25, 1972. BA in Fine Arts with honors in Town and Country Planning, U. Durham (Eng.), 1951; PhD in Land Economy and Ecol. Planning, Internat. Inst. Advanced Studies, 1979; MBA, Pacific Western U., Colo., 1980, DBA, 1982; PhD In Mgmt., Calif. U. for Advanced Studies, 1986; PhD (hon.) in Environ. Planning, Internat. U. Found., 1987. Cons. Stanley Urban Dist. Coun., U.K., 1946-47; planning asst. Accrington Town Plan and Bedford County Planning Survey, U. Durham Planning Team, U.K., 1947-49, Allen and Mattocks, cons. planners and landscape designers, Newcastle upon Tyne, U.K., 1949-51; adminstrv. asst. Scottish Div., Nat. Coal Bd., Edinburgh, Scotland, 1951-52; planning asst. London County Coun., Westminster, U.K., 1953-54; planner Ctrl. Mortgage and Housing Corp., Ottawa, Ont., Can., 1954-55; planning analyst City of Toronto (Ont.) Planning Bd., 1955-56; dir. planning Hamilton Wentworth Planning Area Bd., Hamilton, Ont., 1956-59, Burlington (Ont.) and Suburban Area Planning Bd., Can., 1959-62; commr. planning City of Burlington, Ont., 1959-62; pres. Tanfield Enterprises Ltd., London, Can., 1962—, Norman Pearson & Assocs. Ltd., London, Can., 1962—, Internat. Planning Mgmt. Cons., London, Can., 1962—, Leahy, Pearson, Toll & Assocs. Ltd., London, Can., 1993-95; chmn., CEO The Tanfield Group, 1995—. Pres. Greenleaf Collaborative, Inc., 1997-98; cons. in urban, rural and regional planning, 1962—; life mem. U.S. Com. for Monetary Research and Edn., 1976—; spl. lectr. in planning McMaster U., Hamilton, 1956-64, Waterloo (Ont.) Luth. U., 1961-63; asst. prof. geography and planning U. Waterloo (Ont.), 1963-67; assoc. prof. geography U. Guelph (Ont.), 1967-72, chmn., dir. Ctr. for Resources Devel.; prof. polit. sci. U. Western Ont., London, 1972-79; chmn. bd. dirs. Alma Coll., St. Thomas, Ont., 1990-96; adj. prof. of ecological planning and land econs. Internat. Inst. for Advanced Studies, Clayton, Mo., 1980-89; core faculty Doctoral Program in Adminstrn/Mgmt. Walden U., Mpls., 1985-96, chair adminstrn.-mgmt., 1989-96, mem. acad. coun., 1992-96; prof. bus. adminstrn. and mgmt. Greenwich U., Australia and Hawaii, 1995—, mem. acad. adv. coun., 1995—, chair, 1998—, dean Coll. Bus. and Polit. Sci., 1997—; mem. bd. regents Calif. U. for Advanced Studies, Petaluma, 1987-94; assoc. faculty bus. and orgn., prof. orgn. and mgmt. Capella U., 1996—, prof. human svcs., 2000—; prof. 21st century studies Greenleaf U., St. Louis, 1996-99, bd. govs., 1996-98; mem. Social Scis., Econ. and Legal Aspects Com. of Rsch. Adv. Bd. Internat. Joint Commn., 1972-76; cons. to City of Waterloo, 1973-76, Province of Ont., 1969-70; advisor to Georgian Bay Regional Devel. Coun., 1968-72; real estate appraiser, province of Ont., 1976—; pres., chmn. bd. govs. Pacific Western U., Canada, 1983-84; dir. Advance Lomon, Inc., 1997, sec., 1999—. Author: Administration Management: New Needs and New Opportunities, 1992, Franchise & Partnership: A New Concept of Urban Development, 1995, Pipelines & Farming, 1995, Resources Development Policies in Canada, 1995, Planning for Eastern Georgian Bay, 1996, Vision 2020: The Littoral Concept for Eastern Georgian Bay - The Georgian Bay Association, 1998; (with others) An Inventory of Joint Programmes and Agreements Affecting Canada's Renewable Resources, 1964, An Emerald Light, 1994, Light Beyond the Craft in Canada, 1994, 2d edit., 1998; editor, co-author: Regional and Resource Planning in Canda, 1963, rev. edit., 1970; editor (with others): The Pollution Reader, 1968, Leadership-Phoenix: Principles of Contemporary Leadership, 1998; contbr. numerous articles on town planning to profl. jours., chpts. to books. Pres. Unitarian Ch. of Hamilton, 1960-61. With RAF, 1951-53, RAFVR, 1953-68. Decorated knight of grace Sovereign Order St. John of Jerusalem, 1979, knight Order St. Lazarus of Jerusalem, 1991, Internat. Order of Merit, 1991, Order Internat. Fellowship, 1995, knight of the Order of the Temple of Jerusalem, 1996; recipient Friend of the Escarpment award Province of Ont., 1992; named Disting. Faculty mem. Sch. Bus., Capella U., 1999, 2000. Fellow Royal Town Planning Inst. (Bronze medal 1957), Royal Econ. Soc., Lambda Alpha Internat.; mem. Am. Inst. Planners, Can. Inst. Planners, Can. Polit. Sci. Assn., Internat. Soc. City and Regional Planners, Internat. Assn. Engrs. and Drs. Indsl. Applied Scis., Bruce Trail Assn. (founding pres., chmn., hon. mem., Founder's Plaque 1995), Ont. Club, Empire Club, Univ. Club (London), Baconian Club. Office: PO Box 5362 Station A London ON Canada N6A 4L6

PEARSON, NORMAN RALSTON, librarian; b. Johnsonburg, Pa., Dec. 9, 1939; s. Axel Enoch and Ella Odessa (Bowers) P.; m. Ann Rose Davis, June 22, 1963; 1 child, Sean Ralston. BS, Waynesburg (Pa.) Coll., 1962; MLS, U. Pitts., 1969; EdS, Bowling Green State U., 1976. Tchr. Bradford (Pa.) Area Schs., 1962-69; libr. asst. U. Pitts., Bradford, 1967-69; assoc. libr. tech. svcs. Findlay (Ohio) Coll., 1969-75; editor N.W. Ohio Consortium, Bowling Green, 1975-76; intern Bowling Green State U., 1975-76; assoc. dir. librs. Indiana U. Pa., 1976-77; asst. libr. tech. svcs. Wright State U., Dayton, Ohio, 1977-81; head serials dept. U. Del., Newark, 1981-85; head tech. svcs. Wittenberg U., Springfield, Ohio, 1985—. Editor, mng. editor Dayton Miami Valley Consortium, 1978-81. Corning Glass Works grantee, 1968. Mem. ALA, Am. Soc. Info. Sci., Assn. Coll. and Rsch. Librs., Assn. Libr. Collections and Tech. Libr. Svcs., Lutheran Historic Conf. Roman Catholic. Avocations: antiques, collectibles, book collecting, genealogy. Home: 31 W Hebble Ave Fairborn OH 45324-4901 Office: Wittenburg U Thomas Libr PO Box 7207 Springfield OH 45501-7207

PEARSON, PAUL DAVID, lawyer, mediator; b. Boston, Jan. 22, 1940; s. Bernard J. and Ruth (Bayla) Horblit; m. Carol A. Munschauer; children: David Todd, Lisa Kari, Grant M. BA, Bucknell U., 1961; LLB, U. Pa., 1964. Bar: Mass. 1966, N.Y. 1987. Staff atty., tech. assoc. lab. cmty. psychiatry dept. psychiatry Med. Sch. Harvard U., Boston, 1966-68; assoc. Snyder Tepper & Berlin, 1968-71; ptnr., 1971-77; ptnr., chmn. family law dept. Hill & Barlow, 1977-87; ptnr. chmn. family law dept. Hodgson, Russ, Andrews, Woods and Goodyear, Buffalo, 1987-96; of counsel Sullivan Oliverio & Gioia, 1996—. Lectr. Mass. Con. Legal Edn., New Eng. Law Inst., dept. psychiatry SUNY Sch. of Medicine, Buffalo, 1989—; instr. law and mental health Boston Psychoanalytic Soc. and Inst., 1975-87; lectr. in law, mental health, alternative dispute resolution. Contbr. articles to profl. jours. Founding mem. Alliance for Dispute Resolution, 1996; bd. dirs. Jewish Cmty. Ctr. Greater Buffalo, 1991-96, Am. Jewish Com. Buffalo, 1991—, pres., 1995-97, nat. bd. govs., 1997—; bd. dirs. Arts Coun. Buffalo and Erie County, 1992-99; legal coord. Parent Edn. And Custody Effectiveness program N.Y. 8th jud. dist.; pres., trustee, legal counsel Wayland (Mass.) Townhouse; trustee Family Counseling Svc. (region West); mem., chmn., clk. Wayland Zoning Bd. Appeals, 1970-80; v.p., counsel Arts Wayland Found., 1982-87; vis. fellow Woodrow Wilson Found., 1985-87, Mass. Gov.'s Spl. Commn. on Divorce, 1985-87. Capt. Mil. Police Corps USAR. Fellow Am. Acad. Matrimonial Lawyers (pres., bd. mgrs. Mass); mem. Mass. Bar Assn. (chmn. family law sect.), Assn. Conflict Resolution (advanced practitioner), N.Y. State Coun. on Divorce Mediation, Assn. Family and Conciliation Cts., Boston Bar Assn. (family law com., legis. chmn.), N.Y. Bar Assn. (family law com., ADR com.), Erie County Bar Assn. (chmn. alternative dispute resolution com. 1992-96, family law com.). Home: 605 Lebrun Rd Amherst NY 14226-4232 Office: 600 Main Place Tower Buffalo NY 14202-3706 Fax: 716-854-5299. E-mail: ppearson@soglawny.com.

PEARSON, PAUL HAMMOND, physician; b. Bolenge, Belgian Congo; s. Ernest B. and Evelyn (Utter) P. BS, Northwestern, 1944, B.Medicine, 1946, MD, 1947; M.P.H., UCLA, 1963. Diplomate: Am. Bd. Pediatrics. Intern Los Angeles County Gen. Hosp., 1946-47; resident Cin. Children's Hosp., 1949-51; fellow convulsive disorders and electroencephalography Johns Hopkins Hosp., Balt., 1951-53; resident in child psychiatry U. B.C., Can., Vancouver, 1976-77; practice medicine specializing in pediatrics L.A., 1953-62; chief mental retardation br. USPHS div. chronic disease, 1963-65; asst. dir. mental retardation program Nat. Inst. Child Health and Human Devel., NIH, 1965-66; spl. asst. to surgeon gen. USPHS, 1966-67; C.L. Meyer prof. child health, prof. pub. health and preventive medicine, dir. Meyer Children's Rehab. Inst., 1967-81, McGaw prof. adolescent medicine, dir. adolescent medicine, 1982-89, prof. emeritus dept. pediatrics, 1989—; mem. grad. faculty U. Nebr. Coll. Medicine, Omaha, 1967—, med. dir. Univ. Hosp. Eating Disorder Program, 1983-89, sr. cons. Univ. Hosp. Eating Disorder Program, 1989—. From instr. to asst. clin. prof. U. So. Calif. Med. Sch., 1953-62; from assoc. clin. prof. pediatrics to clin. prof. pediatrics Georgetown U. Sch. Medicine, Washington, 1963-67; Cons., mem. profl. services program com. United Cerebral Palsy Assn., 1969-72, mem. nat. awards com., 1971; Am. Acad. Pediatrics liaison rep. to Am. Acad. Orthopedic Surgery, 1969-73; apptd. to Nat. Adv. Council Services and Facilities for Developmentally Disabled Dept. Health. Edn. and Welfare, 1971-75; councilor Accreditation Council Facilities for Mentally Retarded, Joint Commn. on Accreditation Hosps., 1973-74; fellow adolescent medicine Boston Children's Hosp. Med. Center, 1981 Cons. editor: Am. Jour. Mental Deficiency, 1970-72; Contbr. articles to profl. jours. Mem. com. on accessible environments Nat. Acad. Scis., 1974-77. Served to capt. MC AUS, 1947-49. Mem. Am. Acad. Pediatrcs (com. on children with handicaps 1969-75, com. sect. on child devel. 1974—), Am. Assn. Mental Deficiency, Nat. Assn. for Retarded Children, Greater Omaha Assn. for Retarded Children (dir.), Am. Pub. Health Assn., Am. Acad. Cerebral Palsy and Developmental Medicine (exec. com. 1971-76, chmn. sci. program com. 1972-74, sec. 1974-77, mem. research and awards com. 1977-78, pres. 1981-82, bd. dirs. 1982-84), Assn. Univ.-Affiliated Facilities (exec. com. 1973— , v.p. 1974-75, pres. 1975-76, dir. 1971-78), Soc. Adolescent MedicineAlpha Omega Alpha. Home: 3247 N Boulder Cyn Mesa AZ 85207-1846 Office: U Nebr Med Ctr Dept Pediatrics Omaha NE 68198-0001

PEARSON, PAUL HOLDING, insurance company executive; b. Worcester, Mass., Feb. 14, 1940; s. Malcolm D. and Myra L. (Holding) P.; m. Judith N. Howe, July 13, 1958 (div. June 1974); children: Scott D., Todd E.; m. Anne Beck, July 26, 1974. BA in Bus. and Econs., U. Maine, 1961. C.L.U., 1971. Jr. life underwriter State Mut. Am., Worcester, 1961-63, life underwriter, 1963-67, sr. life underwriter, 1967-69; dir. life underwriting Security Mut. Life Ins. Co., Binghamton, N.Y., 1969, 2d v.p. underwriting, 1970, v.p., 1971-75, sr. v.p. ins. services div., 1975-79, exec. v.p., 1979-81, pres., 1981-96, chief exec. officer, 1987-97; chmn. Security Mutual Life Ins. Co. of N.Y., 1996-97. Chmn., CEO, bd. dirs. SML Properties corp., Binghamton, Security Equity Life Ins. Co., Binghamton, 1987-93; vice chmn. Generalife, 1997-99. Trustee, treas. Lourdes Meml. Hosp., Binghamton, 1978-92; mem. SUNY Found.,

Binghamton, 1982-89; trustee, chmn. fin. com. Elmira Coll., 1983-87; bd. dirs. Broome C.C. Found., 1982-91, pres. 1985-86; pres. New Industries for Broome, Binghamton, 1985-95, N.Y. State Bus. Devel. Coun., 1987-96; bd. dirs. Valley Devel. Found., 1987-91, Bus. Coun. N.Y., 1988-97, Am. Coun. Life Ins., 1990-96; bd. dirs., treas. Fiddlesticks C.C., 2002-; bd. dirs., treas. Fiddlesticks CC, 2002-. Mem. Assn. for Advanced Life Underwriting, Nat. Assn. Life Underwriters, Broome County C. of C. (bd. dirs. 1980-88, chmn. 1986), Binghamton C/C Live Wire Club. Office: PHP Consultants 15520 Greenock Ln Fort Myers FL 33912-2411

PEARSON, R. SCOTT, investment advisor, editor; b. Putnam, Conn., Aug. 27, 1961; s. Walter Donald and Elsa Viola (Swanson) P. BA, Samford U., 1985; MBA, U. South Fla., 1992. Editor Pearson Investment Letter, Dover, Fla., 1990-98; instr. fin. U. South Fla., Tampa, 1993-95, 2002; counselor Consumer Credit Counseling Svcs., 1996-98; editor, pub. Investor's Value View, Winter Park, Fla., 1999—; instr. fin. Webster U., Altamonte Springs, 1999—; investment advisor Value View Fin. Corp., Winter Park, 1999—, 2002. Market commentator Investor's TV News Mag., Orlando Fla., 1999-2000; columnist Englewood Sun-Herald/Venice Gondolier, Fla., 1997-2000. Mem. Fla. Fedn. Young Reps. (platform com. chair 2000-01, mem. Orange County chpt.), Greater Orlando C. of C. Christian. Avocations: tennis, skiing, travel, music, beach. Office: Value View Fin Corp Ste 2000 2254 Winter Woods Blvd Ste B Winter Park FL 32792-1928 E-mail: ValueView@aol.com.

PEARSON, RALPH GOTTFRID, chemistry educator; b. Chgo., Jan. 12, 1919; s. Gottfrid and Kerstin (Larson) P.; m. Lenore Olivia Johnson, June 15, 1941 (dec. June 1982); children: John Ralph, Barry Lee, Christie Ann. BS, Lewis Inst., 1940; PhD, Northwestern U., 1943. Faculty Northwestern U., 1946-76, prof. chemistry, 1957-76, U. Calif., Santa Barbara, 1976-89, prof. emeritus, 1989—. Cons. to industry and govt., 1951— Co-author 5 books. Served to 1st lt. USAAF, 1944-46. Recipient Chemical Pioneer award Am. Inst. Chemists, 1995; Guggenheim fellow, 1951. Mem. Am. Chem. Soc. (Midwest award 1966, Inorganic Chemistry award 1969), Nat. Acad. Sci., Phi Beta Kappa, Sigma Xi, Phi Lambda Upsilon (hon.) Lutheran. Achievements include being originator prin. of hard and soft acids and bases.

PEARSON, RICHARD JOSEPH, archaeologist, educator; b. Kitchener, Ont., Can., May 2, 1938; s. John Cecil and Henrietta Anne (Wallwin) P.; m. Kazue Miyazaki, Dec. 12, 1964; 1 child, Sarina Riye. BA in Anthropology with honours, U. Toronto, 1960; PhD, Yale U., 1966. Asst. prof., then assoc. prof. archaeology U. Hawaii, 1966-71; mem. faculty U. B.C., Vancouver, 1971-2000. Author: The Archaeology of the Ryukyu Islands, 1969, Higashi Ajia no Kodai Shakai to Kokogaku, 1984, Windows on the Japanese Past, Studies in Archaeology and Prehistory, 1986, Ancient Japan, 1992; contbr. articles to profl. jours. Guggenheim fellow. E-mail: pearsonrj@shaw.ca.

PEARSON, ROBERT GREENLEES, writing services company executive; b. Kansas City, Mo., Feb. 19, 1917; s. Ridley Stillson and Agnes (Greenlees) P.; m. Laura Gray Betsy Dodge, Jan. 3, 1945; children— Bradbury, Wendy, Robert Ridley. AB with honors, U. Kans., 1938. Mgr. corp. pub. rels. Shell Oil Co. (N.Y. Head Office), 1938-71; v.p. pub. rels. Council Better Bus. Bur. (N.Y. Hdqrs.), 1971-73; writer pub. affairs dept. Mobil Oil Corp., N.Y.C., 1973-74; sr. advisor Alcoholics Anonymous World Services, Inc., 1974-85; pres. Robert Pearson Assocs., Writing Svcs., Riverside, Conn., 1985—. Bd. dirs. Nat. Safety Council; pres. Fairfield County (Conn.) Council on Alcoholism, 1962 Author: Oil for Victory, 1946, The J.C. Nichols Chronicle, 1994; contbr. articles to profl. jours. Served to lt. comdr. USNR, 1941-45. Mem.: Riverside (Conn.); Yacht, Dutch Treat. Congregationalist. Home and Office: 38 Fox Hollow Rd Bellevue ID 83313

PEARSON, ROBERT LAWRENCE, executive recruiter; b. Chgo., Apr. 19, 1939; s. Jonas Peter and Caroline Margaret (Reilly) P.; m. Norma Eloise Dale, April 27, 1963; children: Jill C., Keith D. BSEE, Mich. State U., 1961; MS, MIT, 1963. Cons. McKinsey and Co., Inc., Chgo., 1964-68; v.p. Raymond James and Assoc., St. Petersburg, Fla., 1968-70; pres. Pearson Wade and Co., Inc., Ft. Lauderdale, 1970-71, Pearson, Inc., Racine, Wis., 1971-81; exec. dir. Russell Reynolds Assoc., Inc., Dallas, 1981-83; mng. dir. Lamalie Assoc., Inc., 1984-89, chmn., 1989-94; pres. Lamalie Amrop Internat., 1994-98, chmn., CEO, 1994—. Mem. fund raising com. Dallas Mus. of Art, 1983-85; mem. Dallas Mus. Natural History, 1985—, bd. dirs., 1988-90; mem. YMCA, Dallas; speech writer Gov.'s Campaign, Chgo., 1968. Contbr. articles to profl. jours. Mem. MIT Enterprise Forum, Dallas C. of C., Phi Delta Theta (pres. 1959-61). Clubs: Tower (Dallas); MIT (pres.) (Dallas). Republican. Episcopalian. Avocations: squash, jogging, deep sea fishing, hunting, marathon running. Home: 3843 Maplewood Ave Dallas TX 75205-2828 Office: LAI Worldwide 1601 Elm St Ste 4150 Dallas TX 75201-4721

PEARSON, ROGER, organization executive; b. London, Aug. 21, 1927; s. Edwin and Beatrice May (Woodbine) P.; m. Marion Primrose Simms, June 3, 1959; children: Edwin, Sigrid, Emma, Rupert BS with honors, U. London, 1951, MS, 1954, PhD, 1969. Chmn. Pakistan Tea Assn., 1963-64; mng. dir. Octavius Steel & Co. of Pakistan Ltd., Chittagong, East Pakistan, 1959-65; chmn. Plummer Bros., Ltd., East Pakistan, 1959-65, Chittagong Warehouses, Ltd., Chittagong, East Pakistan, 1960-65; chmn. dept. sociology and anthropology Queens Coll., Charlotte, N.C., 1970-71; chmn. dept. anthropology U. So. Miss., Hattiesburg, 1971-74; dean acad. affairs, dir. research Mont. Coll. Mineral Sci. Tech., Butte, 1974-75; exec. dir. Council for Econ. and Social Studies, Washington, 1975—. Author: (novels) Eastern Interlude, 1954, Introduction to Anthropology, 1978, Anthropological Glossary, 1985, Race, Intelligence and Bias in Academe, 1991, Shockley on Eugenics and Race, 1992, Heredity and Humanity, 1996; editor Ecology and Evolution, 1982, (jour.) Social Polit. and Econ. Studies, 1976—; author: (novels) Cultural Anthropology, 2002. Trustee, Benjamin Franklin U., Washington, 1984-87. Served to lt. Brit. Indian Army, 1945-48. Mem. Oriental Club, Reform Club (London), Army and Navy Club (Washington). Office: Coun Econ and Social Studies 1133 13th St NW Washington DC 20005-4203

PEARSON, ROGER LEE, library director; b. Galesburg, Ill., Dec. 7, 1940; s. Clifford Emmanuel and Lillian Louise (Fisher) P. BA, Knox Coll., 1963; MA in Sociology, U. Nebr.-Omaha, 1968; MA in Library Sci., Rosary Coll., 1974. Vol. U.S. Peace Corps, Brazil, 1964-66; extension service supr. Brown County Libr., Green Bay, Wis., 1974-75; system adminstr. Nicolet Libr. System, 1976-77; exec. dir. South Central Libr. System, Madison, Wis., 1977-81; dir. Corpus Christi Pub. Librs., Tex., 1981-84, Naperville (Ill.) Pub. Librs., 1984-95, Sonoma County Libr., Santa Rosa, Calif., 1996-2001; interm dir. Spokane (Wash.) Pub. Libr., 2001, Coll. of Marin, Kentfield, Calif., 2002. Lectr. Grad. Sch. Libr. and Info. Sci., Rosary Coll., River Forest, Ill., 1991-95. Mem. ALA, Train Riders Assn. Calif., Am. Assn. Ret. People, Calif. Libr. Assn., Wine Libr. Assocs. Sonoma County. Avocations: power walking, travel research, train travel. Home: 1451 Country Manor Dr Santa Rosa CA 95401

PEARSON, RONALD EARL, educator, researcher; b. Worcester, Mass., Dec. 21, 1944; s. Earl Leon and Hilma (Dahlberg) P.; m. Joanne Miller, June 19, 1965; children: Stacey Lynne, Thomas Alan. BS, U. Mass., 1966; MS, Iowa State U., 1970, PhD, 1971. Rsch. geneticist USDA/ARS, Beltsville, Md., 1971-79; assoc. prof. Va. Poly. Inst. and State U., Blacksburg, 1979-84, prof., 1984—. Cons. Holstein Assn. Am., Brattleboro, Vt., 1986-91, Select Sires, Inc., Plain City, Ohio, 1987—, Jersey Catile Club, Reynoldsburg, Ohio, 1990—, vis. scientist dept. animal breeding Wageningen Agrl. U., 1994-95. Contbr. articles to profl. jours. Elder Northside Presbyn. Ch., Blacksburg, 1984-87; chair budget and fin. com. Presbytery of the Peaks, Lynchburg, Va., 1989-91, chair div. adminstrn., 1992. Recipient Rsch. award Nat. Assn. Animal Breeders, 1992. Mem. Am. Dairy Sci. Assn. (J.L. Lush Animal Breeding Rsch. award 1994). Avocation: raising dairy cattle. Office: Va Polytech Inst & State U Dept Dairy Sci 2100 Litton Reaves Hall Blacksburg VA 24061-0315

PEARSON, ROY LAING, business administration educator; b. Victoria, Hong Kong, Oct. 18, 1939; s. Roy Ross and Martha Ann L.; m. Louise Elliott Johns, June 11, 1960; 1 child, Cynthia Laing. BS in Commerce, U. Va., 1961, PhD in Econs., 1968. Asst. prof. U. Ark. Sch. Bus. Adminstrn., Fayetteville, 1964-68; assoc. prof. Centenary Coll. La., Shreveport, 1968-71; assoc. prof. bus. adminstrn. Coll. William and Mary, Williamsburg, Va., 1971-76, prof. bus. adminstrn., 1976-87, dir. Bur. Bus. Rsch., 1985-98, Chancellor prof. bus. adminstrn., 1987—. V.p. Mid-Atlantic Rsch., Inc., Williamsburg, Va., 1979—; sec.-treas. McKinley land Co., Inc., Williamsburg, 1969—. Editor, author: (newsletter) Virginia Business Report, Virginia Outlook, 1984-99. Bd. dirs. Williamsburg Community Hosp., 1985-90; gov.'s adv. bd. economists Commonwealth of Va., Richmond, 1984-98; mem. trust fund adv. com. Va. Employment Comm., 1984—. NSF fellow, 1963. Mem. Va. Assn. Economists (pres. 1990-91, bd. dirs. 1985-91, disting. fellow 1998), Assn. for Univ. Bus. and Econ. Rsch. (bd. dirs. 1991-92, v.p. 1992-94, pres. 1994-95, hon. mem. 1999—), Nat. Assn. Bus. Economists, Internat. Inst. Forecasters, Richmond Assn. Bus. Economists, Nat. Economists Club. Avocations: scuba diving, underwater photography, science fiction. Office: Coll William & Mary Sch Bus Adminstrn Williamsburg VA 23185 Home: 4400 Chickasaw Ct Williamsburg VA 23188-8020

PEARSON, SELA, poet, speaker; b. Bklyn., Aug. 10, 1952; d. Thomas Turner and Thelma (Brown) Razor; m. Nassar Anwar Jonathan. BS, St. Joseph's Coll., Bklyn., 1988. LPN. Psychiat., pediat. nurse Syosset (N.Y.) Hosp., 1974-78; sales agent Combined Life Ins. Co. N.Y., Albany, 1978-80; med., surg. nurse Bapt. Med. Ctr., Bklyn., 1980-86; nurse counselor Riker's Island Prison Hosp., Queens, N.Y., 1986-88; clinic nurse St. Christopher Ottilie, 1988-90; intensive case mgr. AIDS Ctr. Queens County, 1990-92; quality assurance, utilization rev. nurse Vanderbilt U. Med. Ctr., Nashville, 1992-94; program dir. Boys and Girls Club, Franklin, 1994-95; spkr., writer, nurse Akanke Creations, Brentwood, 1996—; ind. health contractor Clayton County Crisis Unit, 1997-98; nurse Phoenix Program FHC of Nashville, 1998-99; nurse Murci Homes, 1999—. Cons. Murphy Alternative Ctr., Nashville, 1996, Serendipity House, Nashville, 1996, Family and Ednl. Adv. Assocs., Inc., Nashville, 1996, Growing In Grace Leadership Sch., Nashville, 1996; storyteller, presenter poetry recitals; ind. contractor Crisis Group Home, Riverdale, Ga. Author: New York Poetry Foundation Anthology, 1986, Beyond the Stars, 1995 (Editors Choice 1995), Sela's Sounds of Silence, 1995, A Soulful Journey, 2000; performer (video) A Soulful Journey, 1995, The Magic of Peace, 1996, Our Voices, 1996; contbr. articles, poetry to jours., mags. Vol. Williamson County Libr., Franklin, 1995—, Boys and Girls Club, Franklin, 1996—; bd. dirs. Nashville Peace Action, 1996—; mem. New Gospel Singers Choir, 1995—; storytelling del. to South Africa People to People Amb. Programs, invited Women in Soc. rep., Egypt, 2000—. Recipient Vol. Svc. award Berksheire Nursing Ctr., West Babylon, N.Y., 1977. Mayor's award for svc. in cmty. in the arts, 2001; icluson of poem Faith to Wm. Kings Regl. Art Ctr., 1999. Mem. Nat. Spkrs. Assn., Brentwood Early Risers Toastmasters (v.p. membership 1996—, recipient various awards), Tenn. Writers Alliance, Harpeth Storytelling Group, Nat. Storytelling Assn., Internat. Soc. Poets (Poets Choice award 1995, Internat. Poet of Merit award 1995), Tenn. Writers Group Franklin, Tenn. Assn. Perpetuation Preservation Storytelling, Ga. Writers Group, Creative Artists Tenn., Tenn. Spkrs. Assn., Women Vision Enhancing Network (cert.). Avocations: piano playing, travel, reading. Address: PO Box 111341 Nashville TN 37222-1341 E-mail: akankec@aol.com.

PEARSON, SUSAN ROSE, psychotherapist, fine arts educator, artist; b. Elmhurst, Ill., June 14, 1950; BA in Psychology, Calif. State U., 1992, MS in Ednl. Psychology & Counseling, 1995. Cert. pupil pers. svcs., cert. hypnotherapists. Art tchr., master artist Susan Rose Fine Art Gallery, Santa Rosa, Calif., 1979—; therapist Lifestyle with Dignity, Canoga Park, 1985-93. Author, speaker, cons., inventor; fear of flying expert. Mem. ACA, Am. Sch. Counselor Assn., Calif. Assn. Marriage and Family Therapists, Nat. Bd. for Cert. Clin. Hypnotherapists (cert. diplomate), Internat. Soc. Speakers, Authors and Cons., Am. Hypnosis Assn., Internat. Platform Assn., Psi Chi (life).

PEARSON, SUSAN WINIFRED, dean, consultant; b. Wasco, Calif., Oct. 8, 1941; d. Gerald Thomas and Maxine (Jensen) P. BS, Tex. Christian U., 1963, MEd, 1971; EdD, U. Houston, 1982. Tchr. history, chmn. dept. Spring Br. Ind. Sch. Dist., Houston, 1963-68; personnel asst. Tenneco, Inc., 1969-70; grad. asst. Tex. Christian U., 1970-71; dir. student activities Navarro Jr. Coll., Corsicana, Tex., 1972-73; dir. counseling svcs. Horth Harris County Coll., Houston, 1973-84, divsn. head bus., comm. & fine arts, devel. studies, 1984-86, dean instrn./student svcs., 1986—. Ednl. cons., 1994—. Contbr. articles to profl. jours. Mem. Am. Pers. & Guidance Assn., Am. Coll. Pers. Assn., Nat. Assn. Women Deans, Adminstrs. and Counselors, So. Coll. Pers. Assn., Tex. Assn. Women Deans, Adminstrs. and Counselors, Tex. Assn. Coll. and Univ. Student Pers. Adminstrs., Tex. Assn. Jr. Coll. Instructional Adminstrs., Tex. Assn. C.C. Chief Students Pers. Adminstrs., Phi Kappa Phi, Delta Gamma. Presbyterian. E-mail: spea445025@aol.com.

PEARSON, TIMOTHY ALFRED, newspaper circulation executive; b. Meriden, Conn., May 29, 1955; s. Howard Lukens and Fran (Felchner) P.; m. Nancy Marie Zachary, May 10, 1986 (div. June 1989); children: Daniel, Andrew, Kevin, Shellie, Kelly. BS, So. Ill. U., Carbondale, 1977. Ind. cons., Fla., Mont., Colo., 1989-92; circulation mgr. motor rt. and single copy sales The Columbian, Vancouver, Wash., 1992-94; dir. circulation The Sentinel, Howard Publs., Carlisle, Pa., 1994-95; mgr. sales devel. Ctrl. Maine Newspapers divsn. Guy Gannett Inc., Augusta, 1995-96; sales and mktg. mgr. So. Conn. Newspapers divsn. Times-Mirror, Stamford, 1996-98; circulation sales mgr. Hartford (Conn.) Courant, 1998; dir. mem. sales and svc. Seacoast divsn. Dow Jones, Inc., Portsmouth, NH, 1998—2001; with Times Herald-Record, Middletown, NY, 2001—. Contbr., spkr. Anti-Defamation League World of Differnce Diversity Project, New Haven, 1996—. Mem. Dem. Nat. Com., Washington, 1972-2000. Mem. Nat. Wildlife Fedn., Nature Conservancy, Sierra Club, New Eng. Assn. Circulation Execs. Episcopalian. Avocations: travel, history, Native American studies. Home: 26 Black Rock Trail Port Jervis NY 12771 Office: Times Herald-Record 40 Mulberry St Middletown NY 10940

PEARSON, WALTER DONALD, editor, columnist; b. Pittsfield, Mass., Feb. 5, 1916; s. Edgar C. and Edna (Scott) P.; divorced; children: Florence, Donald, Sharon; m. Elsa Swanson (dec.); 1 child, Richard Scott. Student, Dartmouth Coll., 1941-43. Advt. salesman, 1935-41; securities broker Charles A. Day Co., Boston, 1947-55; founder, owner, mgr. First New Eng. Securities Co., Inc., Southbridge, 1955-71; now owner, editor Pearson Investment Letter, Dover, Fla.; ptnr. Pearson Capital Inc.; fin. columnist World Intelligence Rev., CDL Report, Nationalist Times; free-lance columnist various publications; fin. advisor, investment mgr. Author: Investing for the Millions, 1990, Bridge Made Easy, 1995 With inf. U.S. Army, 1943-45, ETO. Decorated Bronze star, Croix de Guerre (France), Combat Infantry badge. Home: 1628 White Arrow Dr Dover FL 33527-5741 E-mail: PearsonCap@aol.com.

PEARSON, WALTER HOWARD, marine biologist, researcher; b. Troy, N.Y., Mar. 25, 1946; s. Howard Stevenson and Mazel Mott (Brownhill) P.; m.. Cynthia-Ruth Egan, June 16, 1972 (div. Oct. 1989); children: Kristin Turnbull, Jeffrey Mott; m. Terri L. Sumner, Nov. 28, 1992. BS in Biology, Bates Coll., 1967; MS in Biology, U. Alaska, 1970; PhD in Oceanography, Oreg. State U., 1977. Fishery biologist, rschr. Nat. Marine Fisheries Svc., Sandy Hook Lab., Highlands, N.J., 1975-78; sr. rsch. scientist Battelle Marine Rsch. Lab., Sequim, Wash., 1978-88, tech. group leader marine scis. lab., 1988-91, mgr. tech. devel. program, 1991-93, sr. rsch. scientist, 1993-95, staff rsch. scientist, 1995-97, staff scientist, 2000—. Program dir. environ. studies program Western Wash. U., Port Angeles Ctr., 1993-98; head marine environ. rsch. ctr. Environ. Rsch. and Wildlife Devel. Agy., Abu Dhabi, United Arab Emirates, 1998-2000; tech. leader large multidisciplinary studies of oil spill effect. Contbr. articles on behavior of marine organisms and effects of pollution and human activity to jours. Sgt. U.S. Army, 1969-71. NSF grantee, 1967-69. Mem. AAAS, N.Y. Acad. Sci., Animal Behavior Soc. Episcopalian. Avocations: hiking, aidiko, canoeing. Home: 332 Viewcrest Ave Port Angeles WA 98362 Office: Battelle Marine Scis Lab 1529 W Sequim Bay Rd Sequim WA 98382-8415 E-mail: walter.pearson@pnl.gov.

PEARSON, WALTER STEPHEN, adult learning educator; b. Ft. Worth, July 15, 1952; s. Walter Joseph Pearson and Virginia Mae Davis; 1 child, Ryan. BA, Antioch U., 1984; MA, U. Mo., Kansas City, 1986; PhD, Iowa State U., 2000. Organizer United Farm Workers, AFLCIO, St. Louis, 1970-71; bus. agt. Organizer Svc. Employees Internat. Union, 1971-77, asst. to gen. organizer Washington, 1977-78; exec. dir. Svc. Employees Internat. Union, Kansas City, Mo., 1978-84; dir. inst. for Labor Studies U. Mo., 1985-88; dir. edn. Bakery Workers, Kensington, Md., 1989-94; dir. adult learning Simpson Coll., Indianola, Iowa, 1995—. Cons. AFL-CIO, Silver Spring, Md., 1995, Retail Wholesale Union, Transp. Workers, 1995-99, Agy. for Internat. Devel., Suva, Fiji Islands, 1996. Bd. dirs. Desegregation Monitoring Com., Kansas City, 1987-88, Kansas City Labor Coun., 1979-84; sec.-treas. Area Food Coun., Kansas City, 1980-84; precinct com. chair Dem. Party, Des Moines, 1998-99. Mem. Assn. for Continuing Edn. (chair awards com.), United Assn. for Labor Edn., Am. Fedn. Tchrs. Unitarian Universalist. Avocations: fishing, woodworking, biking. Office: Simpson Coll 701 N C St Indianola IA 50125-1264 E-mail: pearsonw@simpson.edu.

PEARSON, WILLIAM ROWLAND, retired nuclear engineer; b. New Bedford, Mass., Sept. 30, 1923; s. Rowland and Nellie (Hilton) P.; BS, Northeastern U., 1953; postgrad. U. Ohio, 1960; m. Arlene Cole Loveys, June 14, 1953; children: Denise, Robert, Rowland, Nancy. Engr., Goodyear Atomic Corp., Portsmouth, Ohio, 1953-63, Cabot Titania Corp., Ashtabula, Ohio, 1963-64; supr. United Nuclear, Wood River, R.I., 1964-72; sr. engr. Nuclear Materials and Equipment Co., Apollo, Pa., 1972-74; engr. U.S. Nuclear Regulatory Commn., Rockville, Md., 1974-90, ret., 1990. Served with USNR, 1942-45. Decorated Air medal. Mem. AAAS, Am. Nuclear Soc., Am. Inst. Chem. Engrs. (chmn. 1966-67). Republican. Baptist. Clubs: Masons, Elks. Home: 60 Meeting Hill Rd Hillsboro NH 03244-4856

PEART, LAVERNE T. retired nursing assistant, poet; b. Petersburg, Va. d. Paul Ernest and Gertrude Gay (Nunnally) Pickhardt; m. Thurman Curtis Talley, Mar. 17, 1973 (dec. Jan. 1979); children: Barbara Marie Talley, Patricia Laverne Talley, Paul Ernest Talley; m. Clifford Peart, Apr. 30, 1993. CNA cert., Southwestern Coll., 1982. Nurse asst. Med. Pers. Pool, Silver Spring, Md., 1981-85, Kelly's Health Care, Rockville, 1985-95. Author (poetry): Echoes From Calvary, 1994 (hon. mention, 1994); contbr. Home and Office: 930 Farragut St NW Apt 501 Washington DC 20011-3992

PEASE, DAVID GORDON, artist, educator; b. Bloomington, Ill., June 2, 1932; s. Gordon A. and June (Stephens) P.; m. Julie Jensen, Mar. 29, 1956; children: Lisa Kay, Kerry Susan. BS, U. Wis., 1954, MS, 1955, M.F.A., 1958. Instr. art Mich. State U., 1958-60; mem. faculty Tyler Sch. Art, Temple U., Phila., 1960-83, prof., 1970-83, chmn. painting dept., 1968-77, dean, 1977-83; prof. of painting Yale U. Sch. Art, New Haven, 1983-2000, Street prof., dean emeritus, 2000—, dean, 1983-96, dir. grad. studies/painting, 1997-2000. Vis. faculty mem. Yale U. Summer Sch. Music and Art, 1970-72, Ohio State U., spring 2001. One-man shows include Baylor U., 1972, U. Wis., 1972, Pa. Acad. Fine Arts, 1977, Terry Dintenfass Inc., N.Y.C., 1969, 71, 76, Phila. Art Alliance, 1961, 70, Vassar Coll., 1999, Ohio State U., 2001; group exhbns. include Carnegie Internat., Pitts., 1961, Corcoran Biennial, Washington, 1961, 63, Whitney Annual, N.Y.C., 1963; represented in permanent collections Whitney Mus. Am. Art, Phila. Mus. Art, Pa. Acad. Fine Arts, Des Moines Art Center, Pa. State U., U. Wis., Temple U., Hallmark Cards Inc., Columbia Pictures, Yale U. Art Gallery, others. Trustee Louis Comfort Tiffany Found., 1988-97, 98—; bd. trustees Lyme Acad. Coll. Fine Arts, 1999—. With U.S. Army, 1955-57. Recipient William A. Clark award Corcoran Biennial, 1963, Lindbeck Found. Disting. Teaching award, 1968, Disting. Alumni award U. Wis., 1991; Guggenheim Found. fellow, 1965-66; Tiffany Found. grantee, 1975-76 Mem. Assn. Ind. Colls. Art and Design (trustee 1992-96). Home: 95 Thankful Stow Rd Guilford CT 06437-2529 E-mail: david.pease@yale.edu.

PEASE, ELEANOR JEANNE, humanities educator; b. Phila., Apr. 28, 1935; d. Harold Chandler and Elizabeth (Wright) Hill; m. Richard Bruce Pease, May 26, 1956; children: Richard Bruce Jr., Sharon Pease Andrews. BA in English, Gordon Coll., 1970; MEd in English, Westfield State U., 1973. Educator Gateway Regional Schs., Huntington, Mass., 1970-74; missionary in Japan Christian & Missionary Alliance Hdqrs., Colorado Springs, Colo., 1963-68, 74-93; educator Pasadena (Calif.) Unified Schs., 1989-95; prof., head dept. TESOL, Nyack (N.Y.) Coll., 1995—. Guest lectr. Caransebes Bible Sch., 1996; co-chair Support a Mother project com., 2001--. Contbr. articles to profl. publs. Dir. Womens Ministries, Pasadena Alliance Ch., 1991-95, English Tchrs. Seminar, Hiroshima, 1980-82, 85, 86; coord. homework assistance program Pasadena Schs., 1990-95; vice chmn. Hiroshima (Japan) Internat. Sch. Bd., 1980-83; pres. South Pacific Alliance Women, Pasadena, 1991-93. Mem. TESOL. Avocations: reading, travel. Home: 61 Summit Ave Spring Valley NY 10977-5351 Office: Nyack Coll 1 S Boulevard Nyack NY 10960-3604

PEASE, ELLA LOUISE, elementary education educator; b. Kokomo, Ind., May 31, 1928; d. James E. and Carrie Alice (Ringer) Earnest; m. Harold Edwin Pease, Aug. 10, 1985; children: Charles Miller, James Miller, Ricky Ensley, Wanda Cisna. BS, Ball State U., 1956, MA, 1959; postgrad., Ind. U., Ft. Wayne. Tchr. 1st grade Union Twp. (Ind.) Pub. Schs., 1953-56, Wells City (Ind.) Pub. Schs., Forest Park Sch., Ft. Wayne, Ind., 1956-93. Docent Ft. Wayne Art Mus. Mem. NEA-Ret., Ret. Ind. Tchrs. Assn., Ft. Wayne Ret. Tchrs. Assn. Methodist. Home: 5108 E State Blvd Fort Wayne IN 46815-7467

PEASE, JOHN ALAN, sociology educator; b. Grand Rapids, Mich., Mar. 8, 1936; s. Homer R. and P. Leola (Dulyea) P.; m. Barbara Ann Limpus, Feb. 22, 1958 (dec. 1980); children: Leah Kay, Jay Robert. BS in Sociology, Western Mich. U., 1960; MA in Sociology, Mich. State U., 1963, PhD in Sociology, 1968. Asst. prof. U. Md., College Park, 1967-71, assoc. prof. sociology, 1971—. Part-time faculty Hood Coll., 1975-84, Md. Coll. of Art and design, 1977, Mich. State U., 1961-68, Western Mich. U., 1960; reader/cons. Allyn and Bacon, William C. Brown Pub., Gordon and Breach Pub., Harper and Row, Harper Collins, F.E. Peacock Pub., Macmillan Co., McGraw-Hill Book Co., Oxford U. Press, D. Van Nostrand Co., Wadsworth Pub. Co., West Pub. Co.; program cons./referee Acad. Ednl. Devel., Am. Sociol. Assn., NSF, Social Scis. and Humanities Rsch. Coun. of Can., others. Contbr. numerous articles to profl. jours.; co-author: Sociology and Social Life, 1973, 2d edit. 1979; co-author monograph: Attrition of Graduate Students at the PhD Level in the Traditional Arts and Sciences, 1964; referee, reviewer Am. Jour. Sociology, Am. Sociol. Rev., Am. Sociologist, Housing Educator's Jour., Social Problems, Sociol. Focus, The Sociol. Quar., The Sociologist, Teaching Sociology. Recipient numerous campus teaching awards various orgns.; assoc. Danforth Found., 1980-86. Mem. Am. Sociol. Assn., D.C. Sociol. Soc. (pres. 1974-75). Office: Univ of Maryland Dept Sociology College Park MD 20742-0001 E-mail: jpease@socy.umd.edu.

PEASE, ROBERT BARNARD, civil engineer; b. Atkinson, Nebr., May 10, 1925; s. Clarence I. and Erdine A. (Barnard) P.; m. Rose Mary Wallace, Dec. 20, 1947 (div. Apr. 1974); m. Bessie Carasoulas Economou, Oct. 1, 1976; children: Robert W., Richard B. BS, Carnegie Inst. Tech., 1949; D Social Sci. (hon.), Duquesne U., 1969. Registered profl. engr., Pa. Engr. asst. Carnegie Inst. Tech., Pitts., 1949-53; chief engr. Urban Redevel. Authority, 1953-55, asst. exec. dir., 1955-58, exec. dir., 1958-68, Allegheny Conf. on Cmty. Devel., Pitts., 1968-91; sr. v.p. Nat. Devel. Corp., 1968—. Cons. Ford Found., Calcutta, 1967. Trustee Alaska Pacific U., Anchorage, 1965-91; mem., dir. numerous civic agys., Pitts.; past bd. dirs. DQE and Duquesne Light Co. 1st lt. USAAC, 1943-45, ETO. Mem. ASCE, Duquesne Club, Edgewood Country Club. Avocations: golf, woodworking. Home: 326 Dewey Ave Pittsburgh PA 15218-1412 Office: Nat Devel Corp 4415 5th Ave Pittsburgh PA 15213-2654

PEASE-PRETTY ON TOP, JANINE B. community college administrator; b. Nespelam, Wash., Sept. 17, 1949; d. Benjamin and Margery Louise (Jordan) Pease; m. Sam Vernon Windy Boy, July 30, 1975 (div. Jan. 1983); children: Rosella L. Windy Boy, Sam Vernon Windy Boy; m. John Joseph Pretty On Top, Sept. 15, 1991. BA in Sociology, Anthropology, Ctrl. Wash. U., 1970; MEd, Mont. State U., 1987, EdD, 1994; HHD (hon.), Hood Coll., 1990; LLD (hon.), Gonzaga U., 1991; DHL (hon.), Teikyo/Marycrest U., 1992; EdD (hon.), Whitman Coll., 1993; HHD (hon.), Rocky Mountain Coll., 1998. Dep. dir. Wash. State Youth Commn., Olympia, 1971; tutor student svcs. Big Bend C.C., Moses Lake, Wash., 1971-72, upward bound dir., 1972-75; women's counselor Navajo C.C., Many Farms, Ariz., 1972; dir. adult & continuing edn. Crow Ctrl. Edn. Commn., Crow Agy., Mont., 1975-79; ednl. cons. Box Elder, 1979-81; dir. Indian career svc. Ea. Mont. Coll., Billings, 1981-82; pres. Little Big Horn Coll., Crow Agency, 1982—. Exec. com. Am. Indian Higher Ednl. Consortium, Washington, 1983—; bd. dirs. Am. Indian Coll. Fund, N.Y.C., 1988—; sec. Indian Nations at Risk U.S. Dept. Edn., Washington, 1990-91, collaborator task force, 1990-91; 2d vice chmn. Nat. Adv. Coun. Indian Edn., Washington, 1994—. Chmn. Bighorn County Dem. Ctrl. Com., Hardin, Mont., 1983-88; mem. coun. First Crow Indian Bapt. Ch., 1989—; bd. dirs. Ctr. for Rocky Mountain West, 1998—; chmn. Mont. State Reappt. an dDistructing

Commn., 1999—. MacArthur fellow John D. & Catharine MacArthur Found., 1994. Mem. Nat. Indian Edn. Assn. (Indian educator of yr. 1990), Mont. Assn. Chs. (bd. dirs. 1997—), Crow Tribe Nighthawk Dance Soc. Office: Little Big Horn Coll PO Box 370 Crow Agency MT 59022-0370

PEASLEE, JAMES M. lawyer; b. Scranton, Pa., Sept. 1, 1952; s. Robert Victor and Jean (Mark) P. BA, MA, Yale U., 1973; JD, Harvard U., 1976; LLM in Taxation, NYU, 1979. Bar: N.Y. 1977. Assoc. Cleary, Gottlieb, Steen & Hamilton, N.Y.C., 1976-84, ptnr., 1984—. Office: Cleary Gottlieb Steen & Hamilton 43d Fl 1 Liberty Plz Fl 43D New York NY 10006-1404

PEASLEE, MARGARET MAE HERMANEK, zoology educator; b. Chgo., June 15, 1935; d. Emil Frank and Magdalena Bessie (Cechota) Hermanek; m. David Raymond Peaslee, Dec. 6, 1957; 1 dau., Martha Magdelena Peaslee-Levine. AA, Palm Beach Jr. Coll., 1956; BS, Fla. So. Coll., 1959; med. technologist, Northwestern U., 1958, MS, 1964, PhD, 1966. Med. technologist Passavant Hosp., Chgo., 1958-59; med. technologist St. James Hosp., Chicago Heights, 1960-63; asst. prof. biology Fla. So. Coll., Lakeland, Fla., 1966-68; asst. prof. of biology U. S.D., Vermillion, SD, 1968-71, assoc. prof., 1971-76, prof., 1976, acad. opportunity liaison, 1974-76; prof., head dept. zoology La. Tech. U., Ruston, La., 1976-90, assoc. dean, dir. grad. studies and rsch., prof. biol. scis. Coll. Life Scis., 1990-93; v.p. for acad. affairs U. Pitts. at Titusville, Titusville, Pa., 1993—. Contbr. articles to profl. jours. Fellow AAAS; mem. AAUP, Am. Inst. Biol. Scis., Am. Soc. Zoologists, S.D. Acad. Sci. (sec.-treas. 1972-76), N.Y. Acad. Scis., Pa. Acad. Sci., La. Acad. Sci. (sec. 1979-81, pres. 1983), Sigma Xi, Phi Theta Kappa, Phi Rho Pi, Phi Sigma, Alpha Epsilon Delta. E-mail: peaslee@pitt.edu.

PEASNALL, BRIAN LEE, archaeologist, educator; b. Northridge, Calif., June 13, 1960; s. Richard Clark and Darlene Peasnall, Dennis Monroe Peasnall (Stepfather); m. Mary Margaret White, Mar. 8, 1986; children: Sean, Jennifer. BA, Temple U., Phila., 1989; MA, U. Pa., Phila., 1992, PhD in Anthropology, 2000. Instr. C.C. Phila., 1993—2001; Robert H. Dyson postdoc. fellow U. Pa. Mus. Archaeology and Anthropology, 2001—. Vis. lectr. U. Del., Dover, 1995, Bloomsburg (Pa.) U., 1997. Contbr. articles, chapters to books. Served with USN, 1979—85, USS Forestal. Decorated Letter of Commendation USN; recipient USN academic award, 1979. Mem.: East Coast Archaeol. Soc., Archaeol. Inst. Am., Soc. Am. Archaeology, Am. Anthropol. Assn., Phi Beta Kappa, Eta Sigma Phi (pres. 1988—89). Avocation: photography. Home: 2713 Levick St Philadelphia PA 19149 Office: U Pa Mus 33rd and Spruce Sts Philadelphia PA Personal E-mail: peasnall@earthlink.net. Business E-Mail: peasnall@mail.sas.upenn.edu.

PEASPANEN, JEANETTE HELEN, education educator, educator; b. Cleve., Feb. 5, 1946; d. Robert and Helen (Pachkoski) Hare; m. Carl Peaspanen, May 20, 1967; children: Sarah, Lydia, Matther. BA, Kent State U., 1969; MEd, Edinboro U. of Pa., 1990. Tchr. Ashtabula Area City Sch., Ohio, 1988—, Washington Elem. Sch., Ashtabula, 1988—. Recipient Action Rsch. grant, Internat. Reading Assn., 1994, Nat. Gardening ASsn. grant, 1997.

PEAT, RANDALL DEAN, defense analysis company executive, retired air force officer; b. Chicago, July 6, 1935; s. Thomas R. and Lulu M. (Ray) P.; m. Joyce Enid Hunter, Sept. 15, 1956; children— Brian James, Sondra Lee Peat Gadell BS in Journalism, Medill Sch. Journalism Northwestern U., Evanston, Ill., 1956, MS in Journalism Mgmt., 1957. Commd. officer U.S. Air Force, 1957, advanced through ranks to maj. gen.; pilot, instr. Strategic Air Command, Westover AFB and Clinton-Sherman, Okla., 1958-66; asst. air attache Am. Embassy, Djakarta, Indonesia, 1967; pilot Pacific Command Airborne Command Post, Hickam AFB, Hawaii, 1968-70; staff officer 7th Air Force, Saigon, Vietnam, 1971, Hdqrs. U.S. Air Force, Pentagon, D.C., 1972-75, SHAPE, Belgium, 1976-79, Hdqrs. U.S. Air Force, Pentagon, D.C., 1980-81; dep. dir. plans Office Joint Chief of Staff, 1982-84; asst. chief of staff ops. Supreme Hdqrs. Allied Powers Europe, Belgium, 1984-87; chief of staff Strategic Air Command, Offutt AFB, Nebr., 1987-89; v.p. R&D Assocs., Europe, 1989—. Decorated Air medal, Bronze Star, Meritorious Service medal, Def. Superior Service medal, Def. Disting. Service medal; Republic of Vietnam Cross of Gallantry with Palm, Republic of Vietnam Campaign medal Mem. Daedalians (vice flight capt. 1976), Air Force Assn., Pi Alpha Mu Avocations: cooking; hiking; painting; British mystery writers. Home: Rue des Allies 43 B-7870 Lens Belgium also: LOGICON AT PO Box 471 San Pedro CA 90733-0471

PEATTIE, LISA REDFIELD, urban anthropology educator; b. Chgo., Mar. 1, 1924; d. Robert and Margaret (Park) Redfield; m. Roderick Peattie, June 26, 1943 (dec. 1962); children: Christopher, Sara, Miranda, Julia; m. William A. Doebele, 1973 (div.). MA, U. Chgo., 1950, PhD, 1968. Faculty mem. dept. urban studies MIT, Cambridge, 1965—, prof. urban anthropology, 1968-85, now prof. emeritus, sr. lectr. Cons. World Bank, 1975, 76, 81, UN, 1980 Author: The View from the Barrio, 1968, Thinking About Development, 1982, (with W. Ronco) Making Work, 1983, (with Martin Rein) Women's Claims, 1983, Planning: Rethinking Ciudad Guayana, 1987. Recipient Paul Davidoff award Am. Soc. Collegiate Schs. of Planning, 1989. Mem. Am. Anthrop. Assn., Soc. Applied Anthropology

PEATTIE, MARK ROBERT, humanities educator; b. Nice, France, May 3, 1930; s. Donald Culross and Louise (Redfield) P.; m. Alice Richmond, June 21, 1955; children: Victoria Helm, Caroline, David. BA, Pomona Coll., Claremont, Calif., 1951; MA, Stanford (Calif.) U., 1952; PhD, Princeton U., 1972. Asst. cultural affairs officer U.S. Info. Svc., Phnom Perh, 1955-57, br. pub. affairs officer Sendai, Japan, 1958-60, fgn. svc. lang. officer Tokyo, 1960-62, br. pub. affairs officer Kyoto, 1962-67; Japan-Korea desk officer USIA, Washington, 1967-68; asst. prof., assoc. prof. Pa. State U., State College, 1972-73; vis. assoc. prof. UCLA, 1973-82; assoc. prof., prof. U. Mass., Boston, 1982-92; prof. Hoover Instn. on War, Revolution and Peace, Stanford, 1992—. Author: Ishiwara Kanji and Japan's Confrontation With the West, 1975, Nan'yo: The Rise and Fall of the Japanese in Micronesia 1885-1945, 1988; co-author: (with David Evans) Kaigun: Strategy, Tactics, and Technology in the Imperial Japanese Navy 1857-1941, 1997 (disting. book of yr. Soc. Mil. Historians 1999), Sunburst: The Rise of Japanese Naval Air Power, 1909-1941, 2001. Cpl. U.S. Army, 1952-54. Democrat. Office: Hoover Instn on War Revolution and Peace Stanford CA 94305 E-mail: peattie@hoover.stanford.edu.

PEAVY, HOMER LOUIS, JR. real estate executive, accountant; b. Okmulgee, Okla., Sept. 4, 1924; s. Homer Louis and Hattie Lee (Walker) P.; m. children: Homer Martin, Daryl Mark. Student, Kent State U., 1944-49; grad., Hammel-Actual Coll., Ohio, 1962. Sales supr. Kirby Sales, Akron, Ohio, 1948-49; sales mgr. Williams-Kirby Co., Detroit, 1949-50; area distributor Peavy-Kirby Co., Phila., 1953-54; salesman James L. Peaby Realty Co., Akron, 1964-65; owner Homer Louis Peavy Jr., Real Estate Broker, 1965—; pvt. practice acctg., 1962—. Fin. aid officer Buckeye Coll., Akron, 1982. Author: Watt Watts, 1969; poet: Magic of the Muse, 1978, P.S. I Love You, 1982; contbr. poetry to Am. Poetry Anthology, 1983, New Worlds Unlimited, 1984, Treasures of the Precioys Moments, 1985, Our World's Most Cherished Poems, 1985; songs: Sh...Sh, Sheree, Sheree, 1976, In Akron O, 1979; teleplay: Revenge, 1980. Bd. dirs. Internat. Elvis Gold Soc., 1978—; charter mem. Statue of Liberty-Ellis Island Found., 1984, Nat. Am. Indian, U.S. Holocaust Meml. Mus.; mem. Nat. Trust Hist. Preservation, Ohio Hist. Soc., Preservation/N.C., Japanese Am. Nat. Mus.; charter mem. USS Constn. Recipient Am. Film Inst. Cert. Recognition, 1982, Merit cert. World Poetry 10th ann. contest, 1985, Golden Poet award World of Poetry, 1985, 87-89. Mem. NAACP (mem.-at-large), Ohioana Libr. Assn., Internat. Black Writers Conf., Acad. Am. Poets, Poetry Soc. Am., Smithsonian Nat. Assocs., Manuscript Club Akron, Ohio Theatre Alliance, Kent State U. Alumni Assn. Democrat. Home and Office: 1160 Cadillac Blvd Akron OH 44320-2858

PEAY, J.H. BINFORD, III, retired army officer; b. Richmond, Va., May 10, 1940; m. Pamela Jane Pritchett; children: James, Ryan. BS, Va. Mil. Inst., 1962; MA, George Washington U., 1975; grad., U.S. Army Command and Gen. Staff Coll., U.S. Army War Coll. Commd. 2d lt. U.S. Army, 1962, advanced through grades to gen., 1993, ret., 1997, commd. gen., 101st Airborne Divsn., 1989—91, vice chief staff, 1993; comdr. in chief U.S. Ctrl. Command, MacDill AFB, Fla., 1994-97; ret., 1997; chmn. bd., CEO, Allied Rsch. Corp., 2001—. Served in Viet Nam, 1967-68, 71-72, Desert Storm, 1991. Decorated Silver Star, Legion of Merit with oak leaf cluster, D.S.M. with three oak leaf clusters, Def. D.S.M., Purple Heart, Bronze Star medal with three oak leaf clusters. Home: 7014 Redlac Dr Clifton VA 20124-1937 Office: Allied Rsch Corp Ste 260 800 Towers Crescent Dr Vienna VA 22182

PECA, MICHAEL, professional hockey player; b. Toronto, Ont., Can., Mar. 26, 1974; Center Vancouver Canucks, 1993-95, Buffalo Sabres, NC, 1995—2000; player NY Islanders, 2001—. Recipient Gold medal with Can. team World Jr. Champaionships, 1994, Can. Games gold medal. Office: New York Islanders Nassau Veterans Memorial Coliseum Uniondale NY 11553*

PECANO, DONALD CARL, automotive manufacturing executive; b. L.A., Dec. 2, 1948; s. Domenick Lawrence and Carlotta Noble (Martello) P.; m. Sandra Ann Tuminello, Apr. 26, 1969; children: Julia Ann, Melissa Ann, Donald Carl. BS in Acctg, Pa. State U., 1970; MBA in Mktg., Youngstown State U., 1981. CPA, Pa.; cert. mgmt. acct., cert. fin. mgr. Contr. Atlas Guard Svc. subs. SERVISCO, East Orange, N.J., 1974-76; asst. to pres. SERVISCO, Hillside, 1976-77; v.p. fin. Columbus Svcs., Inc. subs. SERVISCO, New Castle, Pa., 1977-82; dir. fin. East Mfg. Corp. and subs. cos., 1982-88, v.p. fin. and adminstrn., 1988-99, also mem. exec. com., exec. v.p., CFO, 1999—; v.p. fin. Intermodal Techs. Inc., 1991—. Bd. dirs. Intermodal Techs. Inc. Weatherhead fellow Case Western Res. U., 1995. Republican. Roman Catholic. Office: 1871 State Route 44 Randolph OH 44265 *Placing the best interests of the company ahead of your own is ultimately in your own best interest.*

PECCARELLI, ANTHONY MARANDO, lawyer; b. Newark, Apr. 12, 1928; s. Adolph and Mary (Marano) P.; m. Mary Dearborn Hutchison, Dec. 23, 1953; children: Andrew Louis, David Anthony, Laura Elizabeth. BS, Beloit Coll., 1953; JD, John Marshall Law Sch., 1959; M in Jud. Studies, U. Nev., 1990. Bar: Ill. 1961, U.S. Dist. Ct. (no. dist.) Ill., U.S. Supreme Ct. Supr. real estate and claims Gulf Oil Corp., Chgo., 1956-61; asst. state's atty. DuPage County, Wheaton, Ill., 1961-65; first asst. state's atty. DuPage County State's Atty., 1965-69; mem.-del. Ill. Constnl. Conv., Springfield, 1969-70; exec. dir. Ill. State's Atty. Assn., Elgin, 1970-71; ptnr. Barclay, Damisch & Sinson, Chgo., 1971-79; assoc. cir. judge 18th Jud. Cir. Ct., Wheaton, 1979-82, cir. judge, 1982-93, chief judge, 1989-93, presiding judge domestic rels. divsn., 1982-83, presiding judge law divsn., 1987-89, chief judge, 1989-93; justice 2nd dist. Ill. Appellate Ct., 1993-94; state's atty. DuPage County, Ill., 1995-96; assoc., of counsel Ottosen Trevarthen Britz Kelly & Cooper, Ltd., 1996—. Exec. Conflict Resolution Ltd.; chair Ill. Jud. Conf. Ill. Supreme Ct., Springfield, 1987-89. Contbr. articles to profl. jours. Bd. dirs., treas. DuPage Coun. for Child Devel.; bd. dirs. Ctrl. DuPage Pastoral Counseling Ctr.; chair Wheaton Com. for Jud. Reform, 1962; trustee Midwestern U., 1993—, vice chmn., bd. trustees 1997-99. Cpl. USMC, 1946-48. Mem. DuPage County Bar Assn. (pres. 1972-73), DuPage County Legal Assistance Fedn. (pres. 1973-74), DuPage County Lawyer Referral Svc. (pres. 1972).

PECE, ROBERT FRANK, filmmaker; b. Pasadena, Calif., June 7, 1950; s. Otto and Marie Grace Pece; m. Charlene Loree Tullis, July 31, 1971 (div.); children: Andrew Jeffrey. AA, Pasadena City Coll., Pasadena,CA, 1971. Film festival curator ASU Short Film Festival, Tempe, Ariz., 1996—; curator Raid Projects, Santa Ana, Calif., 2000—01. Dir.: (film) The Legend Unlikely, Fossils 'N Stuff;one-man shows include Calif. State U., Fullerton, 2002. Avocations: bird watching, fossil hunting. Home: 26445 Woodcrest San Juan Capistrano CA 92675

PECHILIS, WILLIAM JOHN, lawyer; b. Brockton, Mass., May 13, 1924; s. John and Kaleroe (Karmeris) P.; m. Kay Dillon, June 7, 1958; children: Julie W., Karen P., John D. BA, Harvard U., 1946, LLB, 1951. Bar: Mass. 1951. Law clk. to assoc. justice Supreme Judicial Ct., Boston, 1951-52; assoc. Goodwin, Procter and Hoar LLP, 1952-61, ptnr., 1961-94, of counsel, 1995—. Trustee Concord (Mass.) Acad., 1978-80, Wang Inst. Grad. Studies, Tyngsboro, Mass., 1979-87, Wang Ctr. for Performing Arts, 1983—, Anatolia Coll., Boston, 1984-91; mem. fin. com. Weston, Mass., 1972-74. With USNR, 1943-46, PTO. Fellow Am. Coll. Trust and Estate Counsel; mem. ABA, Mass. Bar Assn., Boston Bar Assn., Harvard Club, Weston Golf Club, Woods Hole Golf Club, Phi Beta Kappa. Avocation: golf. Home: 59 Jericho Rd Weston MA 02493-1209 Office: Goodwin Procter and Hoar LLP Exchange Pl Boston MA 02109-2803

PECHMANN, CORNELIA ANN RACHEL, marketing professional; b. Binghamton, N.Y., May 22, 1959; d. Karl and Helen (Guley) P. BA, Bucknell U., 1981; MS, MBA, Vanderbilt U., 1985, PhD in Mktg. Mgmt., 1988. Asst. prof. mktg. Calif. State U., Fullerton, 1986-88, U. Calif., Irvine, 1988-95, assoc. prof. mktg., 1995—. Rsch. asst. Vanderbilt Diabetes Rsch. & Tng. Ctr., Nashville, 1982-83, Neighborhood Housing Svcs., Nashville, 1982-83, Nashville Cons. Group, 1984-86. Contbr. articles to profl. jours. Recipient Alden G. Clayton Doctoral Dissertation award Mktg. Sci. Inst., 1987; grantee Tobacco Related Disease Rsch. Program. Mem. Assn. for Consumer Rsch., Am. Mktg. Assn., Am. Acad. of Advt., Soc. for Consumer Psychol., Phi Beta Kappa, Beta Gamma Sigma. Democrat. Office: U Calif Grad Sch Mgmt 350 Gsm Irvine CA 92697-3125

PECHUKAS, DIANA GISOLFI **See GISOLFI, DIANA**

PECHUKAS, PHILIP, chemistry educator; b. Akron, Ohio, Oct. 30, 1942; s. Alphonse and Evelyn (Grebenak) P.; children: Rolf Birkhoff, Maria Berenson, Sarah Landau, Fiona Veronese, Amy Hayes. BS, Yale U., 1963; PhD, U. Chgo., 1966. Asst. prof. chemistry Columbia U., N.Y.C., 1967-72, assoc. prof., 1972-78, prof., 1978—, chmn. dept. chemistry, 1984-87. Contbr. articles to profl. jours. Fellow Nat. Bur. Standards, 1966-67, Alfred P. Sloan Found., 1970-74, J.S. Guggenheim Found., 1975, Haverford Coll., 1985; Rockefeller Found. resident fellow Bellagio Study Ctr., 2000. Fellow Am. Phys. Soc.; mem. Am. Chem. Soc. (chmn. theoretical chemistry subdivision 1985-86), Humboldt Sen. Scientist, 1993-94. Office: Columbia Univ Dept Chemistry 3000 Broadway New York NY 10027-6941 E-mail: pechukas@chem.columbia.edu.

PECK, ABRAHAM, editor, writer, educator, magazine consultant; b. N.Y.C., Jan. 18, 1945; s. Jacob and Lottie (Bell) Peckolick; m. Suzanne Wexler, Mar. 19, 1977; children: Douglas Benjamin, Robert Wexler. BA, NYU, 1965; postgrad., CUNY, 1965-67; Cert. Advanced Exec. Program, Northwestern U., 1997. Engaged in community organizing and tutoring, 1962-64; with N.Y.C. Welfare Dept., 1965-67; free-lance writer, 1967—; writer, organizer Chgo. Action Youth Internat. Party, 1968; editor Chgo. Seed, 1968-70; treas. Seed Pub., Inc., 1968-70; mem. coordinating com. Underground Press Syndicate, 1969; assoc. editor Rolling Stone mag., San Francisco, 1975-76, contbg. editor, 1976-2001; cons. various mags., 1984—; edn. cons. Asian Sources Media Group, Hong Kong, Manila, 1989-97; editl. co-auditor Advanstar Comm., 1999—; feature writer Chgo. Daily News, 1977-78; with features dept. Chgo. Sun-Times, 1978-81; from asst. prof. to prof. Medill Sch. Journalism, Northwestern U., 1981—2001, Theodore R. & Annie Laurie Sills prof. journalism, 2001—; dir. mag. programs Media Mgmt. Ctr./Northwestern U., 2002—. Critic at large Sta. WBBM, 1979-82; editor, co-founder Sidetracks, alt. newspaper supplement, Chgo. Daily News, 1977-78; mem. exec. com. Assn. for Edn. in Journalism and Mass Communication, mag. divsn., 1987-89, 92-96, pres., 1994-95; mem. adv. bd. Academe mag., Am. Assn. Univ. Profs., 1990-2000, Heartland Jour., 1990—, Technos, 1992—, chair ethics subcom., Am. Bus. Media, 2002; adv. bd. Asian Am. Journalists Assn., 2002. Editor: Dancing Madness, 1976; author: Uncovering the Sixties: The Life and Times of the Underground Press, 1985, 91; cons. editor, contbr.: The Sixties, 1977; contbr.: The Eighties: A Look Back, 1979, Voices From the Underground, 1993. Served with AUS, 1967. Office: Northwestern U Medill Sch Journalism 1845 Sheridan Rd Evanston IL 60208-0815 E-mail: a.peck@northwestern.edu.

PECK, ANDREW JAY, federal judge; b. 1953; AB, Cornell U., 1974; JD, Duke U., 1977. Bar: N.Y. 1978, U.S. Dist. Ct. (so. dist.) N.Y., U.S. Ct. Appeals (2d thru 11th cirs.), U.S. Supreme Ct. Law clk. to Hon. Paul Roney, U.S. Ct. Appeals for 5th Circuit, St. Petersburg, Fla., 1977-78; assoc., then prin. atty. (counsel) Paul, Weiss, Rifkind, Wharton & Garrison, N.Y.C., 1978-95; magistrate judge for so. dist. N.Y., U.S. Dist. Ct., 1995—. Editor Duke Law Jour., 1976-77. Mem. ABA, Fed. Magistrate Judges Assn., Order of Coif. Office: 1370 US Courthouse 500 Pearl St New York NY 10007-1316

PECK, ANNETTE BIEMOND, retired social worker, writer; b. Amsterdam, Netherlands, Nov. 11, 1928; d. Cornelis Biemond and Maria Johanna Kam; m. Claude J. Peck Jr. (dec. 2001). Advanced MSW, Sch. Social Work, Amsterdam, 1968. Home visiting social worker Royal Sch. for the Blind, Huizen, Netherlands, 1954—63; program dir. Sch. Drop-outs Program, Amsterdam, Netherlands, 1963—68; exec. dir. Coun. Internat. Programs, Chgo., 1976—81. Bd. mem. The Experiment in Internat. Living, Amsterdam, 1965—69. Author: Our Father's House, 2000; contbr. articles to publs. Cons. The Exec. Svc. Corps Chgo., 1988—. Grantee Travel grant, Fulbright Assn., 1969. Mem.: The Winnetka Fortnightly (pres. 1998—99). Episcopalian. Avocations: writing, painting. Home: 589 Sunset Rd Winnetka IL 60093

PECK, ARTHUR JOHN, JR. diversified manufacturing executive, lawyer; b. Trenton, N.J., Mar. 2, 1940; s. Arthur John and Mary Ellen (Kelly) P.; m. Susan Williams Lodge, July 18, 1970; children: David A., Margaret E. BA in Hist., Yale U., 1962; LLB, Washington & Lee U., 1968. Admissions officer Lawrenceville Sch., N.J., 1962-65; atty. Shearman & Sterling, N.Y.C., 1968-72; asst., assoc. counsel Corning (N.Y.), Inc., 1972-81, asst. sec., 1981—88, sec., v.p., 1988—, sr. v.p., 2000-01; ret., 2001. Sec. Teddington Co., Ltd., 1989-2001, Corning Inc. Found. 1981-01, Corning Europe, Inc., 1989-97, Corning Inc., 1988-2001, Corning Internat. Corp., 1991-2001; dir., sec. Corning Inc. Fgn. Sales Corp., 1992-01, Corning Classic Charities, Inc., 1978—; asst. sec. Corning Enterprises, Inc., 1974-97, Corning Mus. Glass, 1981-2001, Market St. Restoration Corp., 1974-01; trustee The Rockwell Mus., sec., 1983-01; trustee, sec. Corning Classic Charities, 1977--; bd. dirs. Wisland, S.A., Guthrie Healthcare Sys., Guthrie Health.

PECK, AUSTIN H., JR. lawyer; b. Pomona, Calif., Dec. 25, 1913; s. Austin H. and Helen (Templeton) P.; m. Jean Albertson, Nov. 9, 1939 (dec. Aug. 1997); children: Julie (dec.), Francesca, Lisa; m. Janice Galloway, Apr. 3, 1998 (dec. May 2001). AB with distinction, Stanford, 1935, JD, 1938. Bar: Calif. 1938. Practiced in, L.A., from 1938; mem. Latham & Watkins, 1946-76, of counsel, 1976-92. Mem. nat. coun. House Ear Inst. Mem. ABA, Calif. Bar Assn., L.A. Bar Assn., Calif. Club, L.A. Country Club, Birnam Wood Club (Montecito, Calif.), Valley Club (Montecito), Zeta Psi, Phi Delta Phi. Home: 2159 Boundary Dr Santa Barbara CA 93108-2262 Office: 633 W 5th St Los Angeles CA 90071-2005

PECK, CAROL FAULKNER, poet, educator, writer, publishing executive; b. Detroit, June 20, 1934; d. Edward Carroll and Barbara Ann (Fite) Faulkner; m. Lawrence David Peck, Dec. 18, 1954; children: David Edward, Wendy Carol Peck Webster. BA in English, U. Mich., 1958; MA in English, U. Md., 1964; postgrad., U. Denver, 1977. Artist-in-edn. Md. State Arts Coun., Balt., 1971—; lectr. in English U. Md. Univ. Coll., College Park, 1971—; writer in residence Sidwell Friends Sch., Washington, 1978-91; poetry workshop leader Montgomery County Pub. Schs. Alternative Programs, Rockville, Md., 1978—. Leader numerous poetry and writing workshops for ednl. and other audiences, 1971—; owner carolpeck prodns., pacem Press. Author: (poetry) From Deep Within, 1989, One World: A Cantata for Peace, 1992, Why the Chimes Rang (musical), 1992, I Ain't Gonna Write No Pome!, 1997; contbr. articles and poems to publs.; mem. editl. bd.: Md. English Jour., 1968—84, mem. editl. bd.: , 1995—. Vol. poetry workshop leader Bethesda Retirement and Nursing Ctr., Chevy Chase, Md., 1978—91; judge numerous sch. and lit. groups poetry and writing contests; vol. Hospice Caring, Inc., 1994—. Recipient 1st prize sonnet divsn., Alexandria Br., Nat. League Am. PEN Women, 1984, Disting. Achievement award, Ednl. Press Assn. Am., 1989, Excellence Tchg. award, U. Md./U. Coll., 1993, Spl. award, Hospice Network Md., 2001, Hopwood award, 1953; scholar Assembly, U. Mich., 1953. Mem.: Internat. Women's Writing Guild (exec. bd.), Md. Coun. Tchrs. English Lang. Arts (exec. bd.), Nat. Coun. Tchrs. English, Writers Ctr., Phi Kappa Phi, Phi Beta Kappa, Alpha Lambda Delta. Home and Office: 14910 Brownstone Dr Burtonsville MD 20866-1849

PECK, CHARLES EDWARD, retired construction and mortgage executive; b. Newark, Dec. 1, 1925; s. Hubert Raymond and Helen (White) P.; m. Delphine Murphy, Oct. 15, 1949; children: Margaret Peck Iovino, Charles Edward, Katherine Peck Koustmer, Perry Anne Peck Flanagan. Grad., Phillips Acad., 1943; student, MIT, 1944; BS, U. Pa., 1949; PhD in Pub. Svc. (hon.), Univ. Md. Univ. Coll., 1995. With Owens-Corning Fiberglas Corp., 1949-81, from sales mgr. home bldg. products to exec. v.p., 1975-81, bd. dir.; co-chmn. The Ryland Group, Columbia, Md., 1981-82, chmn., CEO, 1982-91; dir. The Delaware Group of Funds, 1991-2000; sec. Enterprise Homes, Inc., 1992-2000, New Homes by Enterprise, Inc., 2000-01. Mem. statutory vis. com. U.S. Nat. Bur. Standards, 1972-77; mem. adv. com. Fed. Nat. Mortgage Assn., 1977-78, 85-86; mem. vis. com. MIT-Harvard Joint Ctr. for Urban Studies; chmn. Prodrs. Adv. Forum, 1977-81. Vis. com. Harvard U. Grad. Sch. Design, 1981-86; chmn. Howard County United Way Campaign, Md., 1987, chmn. Cmty. Partnerships, 1991-94; bd. dirs. Nat. Inst. for Urban Wildlife, 1986-90, United Way Ctrl. Md., 1987-91, Howard County Gen. Hosp., 1988-94, Columbia Festival, Inc., 1988-91, NAHB Rsch. Found., 1989-92, Alliance to End Childhood Lead Poisoning, 1990-93; adv. bd. U. Md. Engring. Sch., 1990—, Continuing Edn. Johns Hopkins U., 1988-91; policy adv. bd. Harvard Joint Ctr. Housing Studies, 1984-94; mem. Chancellor's Adv. Comm. U. Md. Sys., 1988-2001, chmn., 1988-99; chmn. Univ. Md. Found., 1990-94, bd. dirs., 1990—; exec. fellow Kennedy Sch., Harvard U., 1990-92; chmn. Affordable Housing Initiative, Columbia, Md., 1990-92; bd. overseers U. Md., College Park, 1994-97; bd. visitors Sch. Law U. Md., Balt., 1996—; mem. vis. com. U. Md. Univ. Coll., 1997—, bd. visitors Ctr. for Environ. Sci., 2002-; bd. dirs. Ctr. for Grant Devel., 1994-98, Victory '94 com. Md. State Rep. party, chmn. election inquiry funding com., 1994-95; chmn. Children of Separation and Divorce Ctr., 1995-2000; pres. adv. coun. Washington Coll., Chestertown, Md., 1997—, chmn., 2000—; mem. Commn. on Future, Howard C.C. bd. visitors, 1999-2002; mem. Howard County Delta Project; pres. Peck Family Found., 1992—; co-chmn. Smart Growth Forum, 2001; bd. visitors Ctr. Environ. Sci., U. Md. System, 2001—; bd. dirs. Columbia Festival of Arts, Md. Mem. U.S. C. of C. (bd. dirs. 1975-81), Ohio C. of C. (bd. dirs. 1975-81), Depression and Related Affective Disorders Assn. (pres. 1986-89, bd. dirs. 1986-2000, pres. 1993-94), Rotary, Talbot Country Club, City Club, Ctr. Club, Caves Valley Golf Club, Phi Gamma Delta. Home and Office: 6855 Pea Neck Rd Saint Michaels MD 21663-2725 E-mail: tpeck@bayserve.net.

PECK, CURTISS STEVEN, organization development consultant, author, educator; b. Kenosha, Wis., May 3, 1947; s. Curtiss Wesley and Frances Helen (Kowalkowski) P.; m. Susan Carol Kostritza, Nov. 3, 1973; children: Jennifer Adel, Stephanie Jean, Curtiss Wesley II, Stacey Marie. BS, U. Wis., Milw., 1976, MS, 1980. Investigator, officer Greendale (Wis.) Police Dept., 1971-80; cons. Nat. Cons. and Tng. Inst., Milw., 1980-83, pres., 1983-92; exec. v.p. Team Mgmt. Sys. (U.S.A.) Inc., Reston, Va., 1994; pres. Assessment Sys. Internat. Inc., Milw., 1992—; prof. Milw. Sch. Engring., 2001—. Instr. Cardinal Stritch Coll., Milw., 1982-89; advisor Booth-Wright, Inc., Boulder, Colo., 1983-87; cons. Howard & Assocs., Chgo., 1985-91, Mgmt. Resources Assn., Brookfield, 1985-91; coord. Trainer's Roundtable Inst. Fin. Edn., 1985-89; mem. adv. com. Milw. Area Tech. Coll., 1988-91; mem. adv. bd. Inst. Team Mgmt. Studies, Queensland, Australia. Author: Guide to Management and Leadership, 1990, Management and Leadership Profile, 1990, Guide to Linking Within and Between Teams, 1990, Management and Leadership Systems, 1992, Team Effectiveness Profile, 1993, Management Candidate Profile, 1996, Union Leadership Profile, 1996, High-Performing Teams Action Planning Workbook, 1996, You Can Teach Old Dogs New Tricks - You Just Need Different Methods, 1998, Selling with Integrity Profile, 2001. Bd. dirs. Multiple Sclerosis Soc., Milw., 1983-89, pres., 1985, 86; bd. dirs. Muskego Scholastic Found., 1993-95; coord. Assn. Adult Educators, Milw., 1984; advisor Goodwill Industries, Milw., 1985, 86. With USAF, 1966-70, USANG, 1970-80. Mem. Nat. Orgnl. Devel. Network, Chgo. Orgnl. Devel. Network, Internat. Soc. Performance Improvement, Internat. Pers. Mgmt. Assn. (assessment coun.), Soc. Human Resource Mgmt., Assn. Quality Participation, Orgnl. Devel. Inst. (cert.), Am. Legion (adjutant Harley-Davidson post 2002-). Lutheran. Avocations: golf, bicycling, gardening, family traveling. Home: 1515 N Van Buren St Milwaukee WI 53202-7500 Office: Assessment Systems Internat 544 E Ogden Ave Ste 700-391 Milwaukee WI 53202-2657

PECK, DALLAS LYNN, retired geologist; b. Cheney, Wash., Mar. 28, 1929; s. Lynn Averill and Mary Hazel (Carlyle) P.; m. Tevis Sue Lewis, Mar. 28, 1951 (dec.); children: Ann, Stephen, Gerritt; m. Carmella M. Benson, Apr. 29,

1995. BS, Calif. Inst. Tech., 1951, MS, 1953; PhD, Harvard U., 1960. With U.S. Geol. Survey, 1954-95, asst. chief geologist, office of geochemistry and geophysics, 1967-72, geologist, geologic div., 1972-77, chief geologist, 1977-81, dir., 1981-93, geologist, 1993-95, emeritus scientist, 1995—. Mem. Lunar Sample Rev. Bd., 1970-71; chmn. earth scis. adv. com. NSF, 1970-72; vis. com. dept. geol. scis. Harvard U., 1972-78; mem. Earthscis. Adv. Bd., Stanford U., 1982-93; chmn. com. earth scis. Fed. Coord. Coun. Sci., Enring. and Tech., 1987-92; mem. sci., tech. com. UN Decade for Nat. Disaster Reduction, 1992-94. Recipient Meritorious Svc. award Dept. Interior, 1971, Disting. Svc. award, 1979; Presdl. Meritorious Exec. award, 1980, Disting. Alumni award Calif. Inst. Tech., 1985, Ian Campbell medal Am. Geol. Inst., 1994. Fellow AAAS (pres. sect. E. 1996-97), Geol. Soc. Am., Am. Geophys. Union (pres. sect. volcancology, geochemistry and petrology 1976-78). Home: 2524 Heathcliff Ln Reston VA 20191-4225 E-mail: dpeck@usgs.gov.

PECK, DANIEL FARNUM, chemical company executive; b. Port Jervis, N.Y., Aug. 6, 1927; s. John Flint and Frances Ann (Farnum) P.; m. Ardyce Chase Hoover, July 14, 1951 (dec. July 1979); children: Cheryl H. Gerber, Daniel Farnum Jr., Laurie A. Peck Perry; m. Barbara Ann Gunning Gillinder, Sept. 5, 1980. BSChemE, Clarkson U., 1950. Field engr. Rsch. Corp., Bound Brook, N.J., 1950-51; process devel. engring. supr. Nat. Starch and Chem. Corp., Plainfield, 1951-55, prodn. dept. head, 1955-60, divsn. supt. Indpls., 1960-67, plant and mfg. mgr. Meredosia, Ill., 1967-72, dir. mfg., 1972-76, divsn. v.p., 1976-80, corp. v.p., 1980-84, group v.p., 1984-89, ret., 1989, also bd. dirs. Bridgewater, N.J. Mem. Envelope Mfrs. Assn., Soc. Chem. Industry, Adhesive Mfrs. Assn., Adhesive Sealant Coun. (pres. edn. found., bd. dirs.). Avocations: boating, golf, bridge, hunting, fishing.

PECK, DAVID BLACKMAN, electrical engineer; b. Whitewater, Wis. s. Clarence Neil and Jean Briese (Blackman) P. BSEE, San Diego State U., 1976. Engrng. specialist Litton Systems, Woodland Hills, Calif., 1977-89; engr., proprietor Cockpit Devices, Edgerton, Wis., 1989—. Mem. NSPE, IEEE. Avocations: private pilot, jazz trumpeter. Home and Office: Cockpit Devices 913 Bliven Rd Edgerton WI 53534-9543

PECK, DIANNE KAWECKI, architect; b. Jersey City, June 13, 1945; d. Thaddeus Walter and Harriet Ann (Zlotkowski) Kawecki; m. Gerald Paul Peck, Sept. 1, 1968; children: Samantha Gillian Gildersleeve, Alexis Hilary. BArch, Carnegi-Mellon U., 1968. Architect P.O.D. R&D, 1968, Kohler-Daniels & Assocs., Vienna, 1969-71, Beery-Rio & Assocs., Annandale, 1971-73; ptnr. Peck & Peck Architects, Occoquan, 1973-74, Peck Peck & Williams, Occoquan, 1974-81; corp. officer Peck Peck & Assocs., Inc., Woodbridge, 1981—. CEO interior design group Peck Peck & Assocs., 1988—; mem. archtl. rev. bd. Prince William County, 1998—, chair 2000—. Work pub. in Am. Architecture, 1985. V.p. Vocat. Edn. Found., 1976; chmn. architects and engrs. United Way, Indsl. Devel. Authority of Prince William, 1976, vice chair, 1977, mem. 1975-79; mem. Health Sys. Agy. of No. Va., commendations 1977, Washington Profl. Women's Coop.; developed rsch. project Architecture for Adolescents, 1987-88; mem. inaugural class Leadership Am., 1988, Leadership Greater Washington, D.C. Coun. Metrication, 1992—, D.C. Hist. Preservation League, Rep. Nat. Com. Recipient commendation Prince William Bd. Suprs., 1976, State of Art award for Contel Hdqrs. design, 1985, Best Middle Sch. award Coun. of Ednl. Facilities Planners Internat., 1989, Creativity award Masonry Inst. Md., 1990, First award, 1990, Detailing award, 1990, Govt. Workplace award for renovations of Dept. of Labor Bldg., 1990, Creative Use of Materials award Inst. of Bus. Designers, 1991, 1st award Brick Inst. Md., 1993, award Brick Inst. Va., 1994, Bull Elephant award Prince William County Young Reps., 1995, Detailing & Craftsmanship award Washington Builder's Congress, 1998; named Best Instl. Project Nat. Comml. Builders Coun.; subject of PBS spl.: A Success in Howard Co. Mem. Soc. Am. Mil. Engrs., Prince William C. of C. (bd. dirs.), Soroptimist Club. Roman Catholic. Research on inner-city rehab., adolescents and the ednl. environ. Office: 2050 Old Bridge Rd Woodbridge VA 22192-2447 E-mail: dpeck@peckandpeck.net.

PECK, EDWARD LIONEL, retired foreign service officer, corporate executive; b. Los Angeles, Mar. 6, 1929; s. Alexander George and Rae (Lee) P.; m. Heather Dianne Hicks-Beach, Jan. 20, 1957 (div. July 1971); m. Ann Day Slevin, May 5, 1974; children— Heather Anne, Brian Michael, Thomas William, Julia Katherine BS, UCLA, 1956; MBA, George Washington U., 1973. Joined Fgn. Service Dept. State, Washington, 1957, intelligence specialist, 1968-71, spl. asst., 1971-74; econ. counselor U.S. Embassy, Cairo, 1974-77; chief of mission U.S. Interests Sect., Baghdad, Iraq, 1977-80; dir. Office of Egyptian affairs Washington, 1980-82; ambassador U.S. Embassy, Nouakchott, Mauritania, 1983-85; dep. dir. Vice Pres.' Task Force on Combatting Terrorism, 1985-86; dir. Office of Career Transition, 1986-88; ret., 1989; pres. Fgn. Svcs. Internat., 1989—; exec. sec. Am. Acad. Diplomacy, 1989-92. Trainer, lectr., cons. on fgn. affairs, internat. bus., 1990—; dir. polit. tradecraft program Nat. Fgn. Affairs Tng. Ctr., Arlington, Va., 1991-96; sr. assoc. Global Bus. Access Ltd., Washington, 1991—; Woodrow Wilson vis. fellow, 1993—. Bd. dirs. Ams. for Middle East Understanding, 1999—; chmn. Coun. for the Nat. Interest Found., 2001. Served to capt. U.S. Army, 1946-49, 50-52 Recipient Meritorious Honor award Dept. State, 1967, 73, 77, 79, Superior Honor award Dept. State, 1974, 88, Wilbur J. Carr award, 1989; Rivkin award Am. Fgn. Svc. Assn., 1973 Home and Office: 106 Grafton St Bethesda MD 20815-3426

PECK, EDWIN RUSSELL, retired real estate management executive; b. Akron, Ohio, Aug. 19, 1931; s. Roy Zola and Mary Susan (Snyder) P.; m. Lou Edith Smith, Oct. 28, 1949; children: Edwin Russell, Lori Rae. BS in Gen. Bus., San Diego State U., 1957. Mortgage trainee South Pacific Corp., San Diego, 1957-58; asst. sec., loan officer Southland Savs., Lamesa, Calif., 1958-60; supr. Phoenix Mut. Life Ins. Co., Hartford, Conn., 1960-63; v.p. comml. loan T.J. Bettes Co., Houston, 1963-68; sr. v.p. comml. loan Am. Mortgage Co., 1968-72; sr. v.p. real estate S.C.I., 1972-87, cons., 1987-97, ret., 1997. Served with USN, 1949-52; Japan/Korea. Republican. Presbyterian.

PECK, ELLIE ENRIQUEZ, retired state administrator; b. Sacramento, Oct. 21, 1934; d. Rafael Enriquez and Eloisa Garcia Rivera; m. Raymond Charles Peck, Sept. 5, 1957; children: Reginaldo, Enrico, Francisca Guerrero, Teresa, Linda, Margaret, Raymond Charles, Christina. Student polit. sci., Sacramento State U., 1974. Tng. svcs. coord. Calif. Divsn. Hwys., Sacramento, 1963-67, tech. and mgmt. cons., 1968-78; expert examiner Calif. Pers. Bd., 1976-78; tng. cons. Calif. Pers. Devel. Ctr., 1978; spl. cons. Calif. Commn. on Fair Employment and Housing, 1978; cmty. svcs. rep. U.S. Bur. of Census, No. Calif. counties, 1978-80; project dir. Golden State Sr. Discount Program, 1980-83; dir. spl. programs Calif. Lt. Gov., 1983-90; ret., 1990; pvt. cons. Sacramento, 1990—. Project dir. SSI/QMB Outreach Project, 1993-94; cons., project dir. nat. sr. health issues summit Congress Calif. Srs. Edn. and Rsch. Fund, 1995; project dir. various post-White House Conf. on Aging seminars and roundtables, 1995-97; coord. Calif. Sr. Legis., 2000-; exec. dir. SMART Coalition Calif., 1997—. Author: Diabetes and Ethnic Minorities: A Community at Risk; mem. editl. adv. bd. Latino Jour. Mag., 1996—. Campaign workshop dir. Chicano/Latino Youth Leadership Conf., 1982—; chmn. ethnic minority task force Am. Diabetes Assn., 1988—90; steering com. Calif. Self-Esteem Minority Task Force, 1990—93; v.p. Comision Femenil Nacional, Inc., 1987—90; del. Dem. Nat. Conv., 1976, White House Conf. Aging, 1995; mem. exec. bd. Calif. Dem. rl. Com., 1977—78; mem. Calif. Dem. Ctrl. Com., 1997—2001; bd. dirs. Sacramento/Sierra Am. Diabetes Assn., 1989—90; trustee Stanford Settlement Inc., Sacramento, 1975—79; bd. dirs. Sacramento Emergency Housing Ctr., 1974—77, Sacramento Cmty. Svcs. Planning Coun., 1987—90, Calif. Advs. for Nursing Home Reform, 1990—96, Calif. Human Devel. Corp., 1995—. Named Dem. of Yr., Sacramento County Dem. Com., 1987, Outstanding Advocate on Aging Issues, Calif. State Senate, 1998; recipient numerous awards including Outstanding Cmty. Svc. award, Comunicaciones Unidos de Norte Atzian, 1975, 1977, Outstanding Svc. award, Chicano/Hispanic Dem. Caucus, 1979, Vol. Svc. award, Calif. Human Devel. Corp., 1981, 1998, Outstanding Advocate award, Calif. Sr. Legis., 1988, 1989, Meritorious Svc. to Hispanic Cmty. award, Comite Patriotico, 1989, Cert. of Recognition award, Sacramento County Human Rights Commn., 1991, Tish Sommers award, Older Women's League/Joint Resolution Calif. Legislature, 1993, Latino Eagle award in govt., Tomas Lopez Meml. Found., 1994. Mem. Hispanic C. of C., Older Women's League, Congress Calif. Srs., Nat. Coun. Sr. Legislators, Nat. Coun. La Raza, Latino Issues Forum, Latino Dem. Club Sacramento County (v.p. 1982-83). Home and Office: 1200 Lakeshore Ave #16-D Oakland CA 94606

PECK, ELSIE HOLMES, museum curator; b. Washington, Oct. 22, 1935; d. Julius Cecil Holmes and Henrietta Allen; m. William Henry Peck, Apr. 8, 1967; children: Alice, Sarah, William. BA, Vassar Coll., 1958; MA, NYU Inst. Fine Arts, 1965. Catalogucr and rschr. Ancient Near East Metro. Mus. Art, N.Y.C., 1963-67; rsch. assoc. ancient and Islamic art Detroit Inst. Arts, 1969-74, asst. curator Near Ea. Art, 1974-80, assoc. curator Near Ea. art, 1980-95, curator Near Ea. art, 1995—. Archaeological excavations include Mendes, Egypt, 1966, Al Hiba, Iraq, 1970, Precinct of Mut, Karnak, Egypt, 1978—; lectr. in field. Contbr. articles to profl. jours. Travel grantee Met. Mus., Iran, 1965; Ford Found. fellow, Iraq, 1970. Mem. Arab Am. Arts Coun. Episcopalian. Office: 5200 Woodward Detroit MI 48202-4008 E-mail: epeck@dia.org.

PECK, FRED NEIL, economist, educator; b. Bklyn., Oct. 17, 1945; s. Abraham Lincoln and Beatrice (Pikholtz) P.; m. Jean Claire Ginsberg, Aug. 14, 1971; children: Ron Evan, Jordan Shefer, Ethan David. BA, SUNY, Binghamton, 1966; MA, SUNY, Albany, 1969; PhM, NYU, 1984; PhD, Pacific Western U., 1984; MS in Edn., Coll. New Rochelle, 1993. Lectr. SUNY, Albany, 1969-70; research asst. N.Y. State Legislature, 1970; sales and research staff Pan Am. Trade Devel. Corp., N.Y.C., 1971; v.p., economist The First Boston Corp., 1971-88; mng. dir. Sharpe's Capital Mkt. Assocs. Inc., 1988-89; pres., chief economist Hillcrest Econs. Group, 1989-93; dir. edn. The Ednl. Advantage, Inc., New City, N.Y., 1990-95. Adj. prof. Hofstra U., Hempstead, N.Y., 1975; lectr. NYU, 1982; mem. faculty New Sch. for Social Rsch., N.Y.C., 1974-94; coord. ednl. tech. N.Y.C. Bd. of Edn., 1990—. Author, editor: (biennial publ.) Handbook of Securities of U.S. Government, 1972-86. Mem. ASCD, Am. Econ. Assn., Ea. Econ. Assn., Econometric Soc., Nat. Assn. Bus. Economists, Am. Statis. Assn., Coun. Exceptional Children, Doctorate Assn. of N.Y. Educators, Beta Gamma Sigma (hon. soc.), Phi Delta Kappa. Lodges: Knights Pythias, Knights Khorassan. Democrat. Jewish. Office: Robert F Kennedy Acad 420 E 12th St New York NY 10009-4019 E-mail: docfnp@bigfoot.com. *March in one place long enough and eventually you will wind up leading the parade of progress...No one grows old. When you tire of learning, of experiencing new things you are old.*

PECK, GAILLARD RAY, JR. defense contractor, aerospace and business consultant, business owner; b. San Antonio, Oct. 31, 1940; s. Gaillard Ray and Lois (Manning) P.; 1 child, Scott; m. Jean Adair Hilger, Dec. 23, 1962 (div. Oct. 1969); children: Gaillard III, Katherine Adair; m. Peggy Ann Lundt, July 3, 1975; children: Jennifer Caroline, Elizabeth Ann. BS, Air Force Acad., 1962; MA, Cen. Mich. U., 1976; postgrad., Nat. War Coll., Washington, 1982-83; MBA, U. Nev., Las Vegas, 1990. Lic. comml. pilot, flight instr. Commd. 2d lt. USAF, 1962, advanced through grades to col., 1983, ret., 1988, air force instr. pilot, fighter pilot, 1963-72, instr. Fighter Weapons Sch., 1972-75; fighter tactics officer Pentagon, Washington, 1975-78; aggressor pilot, comdr. 4477th Test & Evaluation Squadron, Nellis AFB, Nev., 1978-80; mil. advisor Royal Saudi Air Force, Saudi Arabia, 1980-82; dir. ops., vice comdr. Kadena Air Base, Japan, 1983-85; wing comdr. Zweibrucken Air Base, Germany, 1985-87; dep. dir. aerospace safety directorate USAF, Norton AFB, Calif., 1987-88; rsch. asst. U. Nev., Las Vegas, 1988-90; mktg. cons. Ctr. for Bus. & Econ. Rsch. U. Nev., 1990; adminstr. Lung Ctr. of Nev., 1991-93; bus. owner, cons., 1993—; owner Great Western Aircraft Parts, LLC. Acad. instr. USAF. Author: The Enemy, 1973, As Best I Recall, 1994. Recipient Silver Star, Legion of Merit (2), DFC (3), Air Medal (11). Mem. Phi Kappa Phi Nat. Honor Soc., Order of Daedalians, Red River Fighter Pilots Assn., Air Force Assn., U. Nev. Las Vegas Alumni Assn., Air Force Acad. Alumni Assn., The Ret. Officers Assn. Avocations: flying, auto restoration, computer sci., hiking, camping, family activities. E-mail: gaillard.peck@nellis.af.mil; gtwestern@aolcom. Home: 8039 Leather Harness Street Las Vegas NV 89119-2716 E-mail: gaillard.peck@nellis.af.mil.

PECK, GARNET EDWARD, pharmacist, educator; b. Windsor, Ont., Can., Feb. 4, 1930; s. William Crozier and Dorothy (Marentette) P.; m. Mary Ellen Hoffman, Aug. 24, 1957; children: Monique Elizabeth, Denise Anne, Philip Warren, John Edward. BS in Pharmacy with Distinction, Ohio No. U., 1957; MS in Indsl. Pharmacy, Purdue U., 1959, PhD, 1962. Sr. scientist Mead Johnson Research Center, 1962-65, group leader, 1965-67; assoc. prof. indsl. and phys. pharmacy Purdue U., West Lafayette, 1967-73, prof., 1973—, dir. indsl. pharmacy lab., 1975—, assoc. dept. head, 1989-96. Cons. in field. Contbr. articles to profl. jours. Mem. West Lafayette Mayor's Advisory Com. on Community Devel., 1973— ; mem. West Lafayette Citizen's Safety Com., 1974-81; mem. West Lafayette Park Bd., 1981— , pres., 1983-96. Served with U.S. Army, 1951-53. Recipient Lederle Faculty award Purdue U., 1976 Fellow APHA, AAAS, Am. Inst. Chem., Am. Assn. Pharmaceutical Scientists; mem. Am. Chem. Soc., Acad. of Rsch. and Sci. (Sidney Riegelman award 1994), Am. Assn. Colls. of Pharmacy, Cath. Acad. Sci. (founding mem.), KC, Rho Chi, Phi Lambda Upsilon, Phi Kappa Phi, Phi Sigma Lambda, Phi Lambda Sigma. Roman Catholic. Office: Purdue U Sch Pharmacy & Pharm Scis Dept Industrial & Physical Pharm West Lafayette IN 47907

PECK, H. DANIEL, literature educator, educator; b. Milw., July 15, 1940; s. Henry Edward and Carmen (Barbulesco) P.; m. Patricia B. Wallace, Apr. 3, 1982; 1 child, Jennifer Peck. BA, Ohio Wesleyan U., 1962; MA, U. Iowa, 1971, PhD, 1974. Asst. prof. to assoc. prof. U. Calif., Santa Barbara, 1972-80; assoc. prof. Vassar Coll., Poughkeepsie, N.Y., 1980-83, prof. lit., 1983—, dir. Am. Culture program, 1989-92. Dir. NEH conf., 1992, Summer Inst. for Coll. Fac., 1993. Author: Thoreau's Morning Work, 1990, A World by Itself: The Pastoral Moment in Cooper's Fiction, 1977; editor: The Green American Tradition, 1989, New Essays on the Last of the Mohicans, 1992, World's Classics edit. Fenimore Cooper's Deerslayer, 1993, Penguic Classics edit. A Year in Thoreau's Journal: 1851, 1993, Penguin Classics edit. Thoreau's A Week on the Concord and Merrimack Rivers, 1997; contbr. to Columbia Lit. History of the U.S., 1988. Am. Coun. Learned Socs. fellow, 1977-78, NEH fellow, 1984, 94. Mem. MLA (chmn. div. 19th Century Am. lit. 1986), New Eng. MLA, Am. Studies Assn., New Eng. Am. Studies Assn. (coun. 1991-93), Am. Lit. Assn. Home: 26 Sunrise Ln Poughkeepsie NY 12603-4213 Office: Vassar Coll Mail Drop 226 Poughkeepsie NY 12602-0226

PECK, JAMIE ANDREW, geography educator; b. Nottingham, Eng., July 9, 1962; s. Robert Godfrey and Joyce Peck; m. Bryony Jayne Mander, Jan. 3, 1991; children: Holly, Hannah. BA in Geography with honours, Manchester (Eng.) U., 1983, PhD, 1988. Nat. rsch. fellow U. Melbourne, Australia, 1988-89; lectr. geography Manchester U., 1989-95, reader, then prof., 1996-2000; Harkness fellow Johns Hopkins U., Balt., 1995-96; prof. geography U. Wis., Madison, 2000—. Author: Work-Place: The Social Regulation of Labor Markets, 1996 (Choice outstanding acad. book 1996), Workfare States, 2001; editor: Antipode, 1998—, Environ. and Planning A, 1998—; contbr. articles to profl. jours., including Cambridge Jour. Econs., Environ. and Planning A. Mem. Royal Geog. Soc. (Back award 1998). Office: U Wis Madison Dept Geography Madison WI 53706 Fax: 608-265-3991. E-mail: jpeck@geography.wisc.edu.

PECK, KAY CHANDLER, resource development professional; b. Dalhart, Tex., Apr. 19, 1954; d. Raman Leonard and Wilma Fordene (Owens) Chandler; m. Kevin George Peck, Jan. 14, 1978 (div. Nov. 1990). BA, So. Nazarene U., 1976. Cert. fund raiser. Reporter Dalhart (Tex.) Texan, 1976-78; grad. asst. West Tex. State U., Canyon, 1978; asst. editor Boise City (Okla.) News, 1979-83; freelance writer Dalhart, Dumas, Tex., 1983-87; city editor Hereford (Tex.) Brand, 1987-89; informational writer U. Tex., El Paso, 1989-92; owner Flying Pigs Creative Svcs., Amarillo, Tex. and Las Vegas, N.Mex., 1992—. Author: (novel) Folsom Boy, 1989, (play), XIT Trilogy, 1988, (booklet) Walking Tour of Dalhart, 1987; editor: The Coldwater Holdcut mag., 1984; co-pub. Dreamcatcher Books, 2000—. Bd. dirs. OUTstanding Gay Lesbian Support Orgn, 1997; v.p., outstanding mem. Parents, Family and Friends of Lesbians and Gays, Amarillo, 1998-99. Lt. cmmdr. USNR, 1987-96. Decorated Navy Achievement medal USNR; recipient Outstanding Feature Writer award Tex. Assoc. Press, Hereford, 1990. Mem. Nat. Soc. Fund Raising Execs. (Texas Plains chpt. pres.-elect 1996, pres. 1997), Nat. Writers Assn., Assn. Fundraising Profls. (mem. internat. diversity com.). Avocation: advocate of diversity programs. E-mail: FlyingPigs1954@yahoo.com.

PECK, LOUIS MOSES, editor; b. N.Y.C., Apr. 16, 1951; s. Seymour and Susan (Lustig) P.; m. Nancy Jean Schwerzler, Sept. 5, 1987. BA in Am. History, Brown U., 1973. Govt. and politics reporter Frankfort (Ind.) Times, 1974-76, Poughkeepsie (N.Y.) Jour., 1976-78; regional corr. Gannett News Svc., Washington, 1978-82, congl. and polit. corr., 1983-87; editor Campaigns and Elections, 1988-89; freelance writer editor, 1989-91; editor Congress Daily, 1991—; editor-in-chief Nat. Jour.'s Tech. Daily, 2000—. Vis. instr. Medill Sch. Journalism, Northwestern U., Washington, 1988, 90. Editorial cons.: Reform and Reality: The Financing of State and Local Campaigns, 1990, Financing Politics: Money, Elections and Political Reform, 1991. Mem. Washington Ind. Writers. Office: Nat Jour 1501 M St NW Washington DC 20005-1700 E-mail: lpeck@nationaljournal.com.

PECK, MALCOLM CAMERON, educational exchange specialist; b. Boston, Apr. 4, 1939; s. Wilfred Cameron and Ruth Lorriaux (Murdoch) P.; m. Adelaida Boquilon Ravelo, Dec. 30, 1972; 1 child, John Cameron. AB, Harvard U., 1961, AM, 1966; MA, Tufts U., 1963, MALD, 1964, PhD, 1970. Instr. U. Chattanooga (now U. Tenn.), 1967-68; postdoctoral fellow Harvard U., Cambridge, Mass., 1969-70; asst. to the pres., dir. programs Middle East Inst., Washington, 1970-81; Arabian peninsula affairs analyst U.S. Dept. State, 1981-83; program officer Meridian Internat. Ctr., 1984-2000, sr. program officer, 2000—. Pres., bd. dirs. nat. com. to Honor the 14th Centennial of Islam, Washington, 1979-83. Author: The United Arab Emirates: A Venture in Unity, 1986, Historical Dictionary of the Gulf Arab States, 1997; contbr. articles to profl. jours. Pres. Ch. of the Holy City, 1998-00. NDFL fellowship U.S. Govt., 1964-65; postdoctoral fellowship Harvard U., 1969-70. Mem. Middle East Studies Assn., Middle East Inst. (resident fellow 1983), Philippine Arts, Letters, and Media Coun. (sec. 1995—), Soc. for Gulf Arab Studies (co-founder, sec. 1987—). Democrat. Avocations: bicycling, music, reading. Home: 3118 1st St N Arlington VA 22201-1033 Office: Meridian Internat Ctr 1624 Crescent Pl NW Washington DC 20009-4004 E-mail: mpeck@meridian.org.

PECK, MARYLY VANLEER, college president, headmaster, chemical engineer; b. Washington, June 29, 1930; d. Blake Ragsdale and Ella Lillian (Wall) VanLeer; m. Jordan B. Peck, Jr., June 15, 1951; children: Jordan B. III, Blake VanLeer, James Tarleton VanLeer, Virginia Ellaine.; m. 2d, Walter G. Ebert, Sept. 3, 1983 (dec. June 1990); m. 3d Edwin L. Carey, Apr. 13, 1991. Student, Ga. Inst. Tech., 1948, 55-58, Duke U., 1947-48; B.Ch.E., Vanderbilt U., 1951; MSE., U. Fla., 1955, PhD, 1963. Chem. engr. Naval Research Lab., Washington, 1951-52; chem. engr. Med. Field Research Lab., Camp LeJeune, N.C., 1952; asso. research and instr. U. Fla., Gainesville, 1953-55; chem. engr., research asso. Ga. Tech. Expt. Sta., Atlanta, 1956-58; lectr. Ga. State Coll., 1957-58; lectr. math. East Carolina Extension, Camp Lejeune, 1959; sr. research engr. Rocketdyne div. N.Am. Aviation Co., 1961-63; self-employed as lectr., 1963; assoc. prof. Campbell Coll., Buie's Creek, N.C., 1963-66, prof., 1966; acad. dir. St. John's Episcopal Sch., Upper Tumon, Guam, 1966-68; chmn., prof. phys. scis. U. Guam, Agana, 1968-73, dean Coll. Bus. and Applied Tech., 1973-74, dean Community Career Coll., 1974-77; pres. Cochise Coll., Douglas, Ariz., 1977-78; systems planning analyst Urban Pathfinders, Inc., Balt., 1978-79; dean undergrad. studies U. Md. Univ. Coll., College Park, 1979-82; pres. Polk Community Coll., Winter Haven, Fla., 1982-97; headmaster All Saints' Acad., 1997-99. Founder, pres. Guam Acad. Found., 1972-77; bd. dirs. Cochise Coll. Found., 1977-78; charter bd. dirs. Turnaround Inc., 1987-91, chmn. 1990-93; bd. dirs. United Way Ctrl. Fla., 1986-95, vice chmn., 1992, chair elect, 1993, chmn. 1994; founding mem. Prince George's Ednl. TV Cable Coalition; mem. Prince George's Cable TV Ednl. Adv. Group, 1980-82, Polk County Coun. Econ. Edn., 1982; sec. Polk C.C. Found., 1982-97; mem. Polk County Coordinating Coun. Vocat. Edn., 1982-91, PRIDE Adv. Coun.; vice chmn. Fla. Job Tng. Coordinating Coun., 1983-87, Fla. Edn. Fund Bd., 1988-93; mem. Girls Inc. Bd., 1992—, pres., 2000-2001; trustee All Sts.'s Acad. 1994-2002; mem. Vanguard Sch. Bd., 2001-. Named Disting. Alumnus U. Fla., 1992, Woman of Distinction Girls Scouts U.S.A., 1994; fellow NSF, 1961-63; recipient She Knows Where She's Going award Girls Inc. of Winter Haven, 1995. Fellow Soc. Women Engrs. (nat. v.p. 1962-63); mem. AAUW, Am. Inst. Chem. Engrs., Am. Chem. Soc., NSPE, Am. Assn. for Higher Edn., Am. Assn. Community and Jr. Colls., Am. Assn. Univ. Adminstrs., Rotary, Sigma Xi, Tau Beta Pi, Chi Omicron Gamma, Phi Kappa Phi, Delta Kappa Gamma. Episcopalian. Home: 1290 Howard Ter NW Winter Haven FL 33881-3158 E-mail: mpeck@tampabay.rr.com.

PECK, MERTON JOSEPH, economist, educator; b. Cleve., Dec. 17, 1925; s. Kenneth Richard and Charlotte (Hart) P.; m. Mary McClure Bosworth, June 13, 1949; children— Richard, Katherine, Sarah, David. AB, Oberlin Coll., 1949; AM, Harvard U., 1951, PhD, 1954; AM (hon.), Yale U., 1963. Teaching fellow, instr. econs. Harvard U., Boston, 1951-55, asst., then assoc. prof. bus. adminstrn., 1956-61; asst. prof. econs. U. Mich., Ann Arbor, 1955-56; dir. systems analysis Office Sec. Def., Washington, 1961-63; prof. econs. Yale U., New Haven, 1963—, chmn. dept., 1967-74, 77-84, acting dean sch. of orgn. and mgmt., 1987-88. Mem. Council Econ. Advisers, Exec. Office of Pres., 1968-69; cons. in field, 1954— Author: (with others) The Economics of Competition in the Transportation Industries, 1959, Competition in the Aluminum Industry, 1945-58, 1961, (with F. Scherer) The Weapons Aquisition Process, An Economic Analysis, 1962, (with others) Technological Change, Economic Growth and Public Policy, 1967, Federal Regulation of Television, 1973; editor The World Aluminum Industry in a Changing Energy Era, 1988; co-editor: What Is To Be Done? Proposals for the Soviet Transition to the Market, 1991, Competitiveness, The Impact of Public Policy, 1992; contbr. (with others) articles to profl. jours. With AUS, 1944-46. Mem. Am. Econ. Assn., Am. Assn. U. Profs., Lawn Club, Yale Club. Home: 27 Temple Ct New Haven CT 06511-6820 Office: Dept Econs Yale U PO Box 208268 New Haven CT 06520-8268

PECK, MIRA P. lawyer; b. Minsk, USSR, Mar. 31, 1946; d. Wolf and Zofia (Wlaznik) Paszko; m. David O. Peck, May 15, 1971; children: Lena Ruth, Benjamin Jay. BEChemE, RMIT Univ., Australia, 1972; MS in Indsl. Adminstrn., Union Coll., 1976; JD, Rutgers U., 1984. Bar: N.J. 1984, U.S. Dist. Ct. N.J. 1984. Tchr. sci. Victoria Edn. Dept., 1971-72; process engr. GAF Corp., Rensselaer, N.Y., 1974-77; design engr. BASF Corp., Parsippany, N.J., 1977-80, product mgr., 1980-86, mgr. corp. strategic planning, 1986-92, v.p. tech. purchasing Mount Olive, 1993-2000; pvt. law practice Denville, 1984—. Mem., counsel Protect Wildlife Water and Woods, Denville, 1987—; mem. Mus. Modern Art, N.Y.C. Mem. ABA, NOW, N.J. Bar Assn., Am Inst. Chem. Engrs., Am. Humanist Assn., Amnesty Internat., Simon Wiesenthal Ctr., So. Poverty Law Ctr. Democrat. Avocations: art, writing, music, hiking, bicycling.

PECK, PAUL LACHLAN, minister; b. Glens Falls, N.Y., Sept. 11, 1928; s. Paul Lee and Caroline Jeannette (Stanton) Peck; children: Paul Barrett, Kathryn Elizabeth, Gretchen, Kole W. BS, U. Conn., 1952; ThD, Bernadean U., 1976; MEd, Westfield State Coll., 1983. Ordained to ministry Truth Ctr., 1972. With Proctor and Gamble Co., Watertown, N.Y., 1956-60; dir. deferred giving programs Syracuse (N.Y.) U., 1960-68, v.p., 1968-70, Fairleigh-Dickinson U., N.J., 1970-71, Manhattan Coll., Bronx, N.Y., 1971-75; founder, pastor Arete' Truth Ctr., San Diego, 1975—. Author: Footsteps Along the Path, 1978, Inherit the Kingdom, 1978, Milestones of the Way, 1978, Freeway to Health, 1980, Freeway to Work and Wealth, 1981, Freeway to Human Love, 1982, Freeway to Personal Growth, 1982, Your Dreams Count, 1990, Heroic Love Poems, 1990. Bd. dirs. Girl Scouts U.S.A., Syracuse, 1967-70; trustee, bd. dirs. Erickson Ednl. Found., 1970-75; vol. chaplain Auburn (N.Y.) State Prison, 1967-68; mem. chaplains' coun. Syracuse U., 1960-70; co-founder suicide and drug abuse prevention program Syracuse U., 1968-71, Fairleigh-Dickinson U., 1970-71, Manhattan Coll., 1971-75. Staff sgt. USNG, 1947-50. Mem. Internat. New Thought Alliance, SAR, Rotary, Knights of Malta (svc. award 1973), Masons, Shriners, Spiritual Frontiers Fellowship. Avocations: golf, book collecting.

PECK, RALPH BRAZELTON, civil engineering educator, consultant; b. Winnipeg, Man., Can., June 23, 1912; (parents Am. citizens); s. Orwin K. and Ethel Indie (Huyck) Peck; m. Marjorie Elizabeth Truby, June 14, 1937; children: Nancy Jeanne Peck Young, James Leroy. D in Civil Engring., Rensselaer Poly. Inst., 1937; postgrad., Harvard U., 1938; D Eng. (hon.) , Rensselaer Poly. Inst., 1974; DSc (hon.) , Laval U., 1987. Registered Ill., structural engr., Ill., civil engr., Calif. Structural detailer Am. Bridge Co., Ambridge, Pa., 1937; asst. subway engr. City of Chgo., 1939—43; chief engr.

testing Holabird & Root, Scioto Ordnance Plant, Marion, Ohio, 1943; research asst. prof. soil mechanics U. Ill., Champaign-Urbana, 1943—48, research prof. found. engring., 1948—57, prof. found. engring., 1957—74, prof. emeritus, 1974—. Cons. in field. Author (with K. Terzaghi and G. Mesri): Soil Mechanics in Engineering Practice, 1948, 3rd edit., 1996; author: (with T.H. Thornburn and W.E. Hanson) Foundation Engineering, 1953, 2d edit., 1973, Judgment in Geotechnical Engineering: The Professional Legacy of Ralph B. Peck, 1984; contbr. articles to profl. jours. Named to Hall of Fame, Renssalaer Poly. Inst., 1998; recipient Disting. Civilian Svc. award, Dept. of Army, 1973, Moles Non-mem. award, 1973, Nat. Medal Sci., Pres. Gerald Ford, 1974, Golden Beaver award, 1983, Disting. Svc. award, Deep Founds Inst., 1984, Merit award, Am. Cons. Engrs. Coun., 1988. Fellow: Geol. Soc. Am. (sr.); mem.: NSPE (award 1972), ASCE (hon.; nat. dir. 1962—65, Norman medal 1944, Wellington prize 1965, Terzaghi award 1969, Washington award 1976, Pres.'s award 1986, John Fritz medal 1987, Rickey medal 1988, Outstanding Projects and Leaders award 2001), NAE, Internat. Soc. Soil Mechanics and Found. Engring. (pres. 1969—73), Am. Acad. Arts and Scis., Mexican Soc. Soil Mechanics (hon.), Japanese Soc. Soil Mechanics (hon.), Southeast Asian Soc. Soil Mechanics (hon.), Phi Kappa Phi, Tau Beta Pi, Chi Epsilon, Sigma Xi. Home: 1101 Warm Sands Dr SE Albuquerque NM 87123-4328

PECK, RAYMOND CHARLES, SR. driver behavior research specialist and research consultant; b. Sacramento, Nov. 18, 1937; s. Emory Earl and Margaret Helen (Fiebiger) P.; m. Ellie Ruth Enriquez, sept. 5, 1957; children: Teresa M. Peck Montijo, Linda M. Peck Heisler, Margaret V. Peck Henley, Raymond C., Christina M. Peck Reich. BA in Psychology, Calif. State U., Sacramento, 1961, MA in Exptl. Psychology, 1968. Rsch. analyst Calif. Dept. Motor Vehicles, Sacramento, 1962-71, sr. rsch. analyst, program mgr., 1971-80, rsch. program splst. II, 1980, 81-84, acting, chief rsch., 1980-81, chief rsch., 1984-2000; pres. R.C. Peck & Assocs. Chmn. com. on operator regulation Transp. Rsch. Bd., NAS, 1976-82; statis. cons. in field. Past editl. adv. bds. Traffic Safety Evaln. Rsch. Review, Alcohol, Drugs and Driving; mem. editl. bd. Jour. Safety Rsch., Accident Analysis and Prevention; contbr. articles to profl. jours. Recipient Met. Life award of honor. Nat. Safety Coun., 1970, Met. Life cert. of comendation Nat. Safety Coun., 1972, A.R. Lauer award Human Factor Soc., 1981, Award of Honor, Award of Merit, Nat. Hwy. Traffic Safety Adminstrn., 1982. Mem. APHA, AAAS, Am. Statis. Assn. Am. Assn. Automotive Medicine, Internat. Coun. Alcohol, Drugs and Traffic Safety, Human Factors Soc., Soc. Epidemiologic Rsch. Democrat. Home and Office: 1200 Lakeshore Ave Apt 16D Oakland CA 94606

PECK, RICHARD WAYNE, novelist; b. Decatur, Ill., Apr. 5, 1934; s. Wayne Morris and Virginia (Gray) P. Student, Exeter (Eng.) U., 1954-55; BA, DePauw U., 1956; MA, So. Ill. U., 1959; DHL, DePauw U., 1999. Mem. faculty Sch. Edn., Hunter Coll., 1965-71. Lectr. in field; adj. prof. libr. sci. La. State U., 1996—. Author: books for adolescents, including Are You in the House Alone?, 1977 (Edgar Allen Poe award 1977), Father Figure, 1978, Secrets of the Shopping Mall, 1979, A Long Way from Chicago, 1999 (Newbery silver medal, Nat. Book Award finalist); (poetry anthology) Sounds and Silences, 1970; (novels for adults) New York Time; Contbr. articles on architecture and local history to N.Y. Times. Asst. dir. Council Basic Edn., Washington, 1969-70. Served with U.S. Army, 1956-58. Recipient Nat. Prize for Young People's Lit., ALA, 1990, Newbery Gold medal, 2000, Nat. Humanities medal, 2001; fellow English-Speaking Union fellow, Jesus Coll., Oxford (Eng.) U., 1973. Mem. Authors Guild, Authors League, Delta Chi. Republican. Methodist. Home: 155 E 72nd St New York NY 10021-4371

PECK, ROBERT MCCRACKEN, naturalist, science historian, writer; b. Phila., Dec. 15, 1952; s. Frederick William Gunster and Matilda (McCracken) P. BA in Art History, Princeton U., 1974; MA, U. Del., 1976. Dir. Pocono Lake (Pa.) Preserve Nature Ctr., 1971, 72; asst. to dir. Natural History Mus. Acad. Natural Scis., Phila., 1976-77; tech. dir. Bartram Heritage Study U.S. Dept. Interior and Bartram Trail Conf., Atlanta and Montgomery, Ala., 1977-78; spl. asst. to pres. Acad. Natural Scis., Phila., 1977-82, acting v.p. Nat. History Mus., 1982-83, fellow, 1983—, curator Art and Artifacts, 2000—, editor sci. publs., 2001—. Cons. BBC, Eng., 1987-92; bd. dirs. Phila. Conservationists, Natural Lands Trust, Phila., Libr. Co. of Phila., Phila. City Inst.; mng. editor Frontiers, 1979-82; lectr. in field. Author: A Celebration of Birds: The Life and Art of Louis Agassiz Fuertes, 1982, Headhunters and Hummingbirds: An Expedition Into Ecuador, 1987, Wild Birds of America: The Art of Basil Ede, 1991, Land of the Eagle: A Natural History of North America, 1991, German edit., 1992; author: (with others) John James Audubon in the West: The Last Expedition, 2000, William Bartram's Travels, 1980, John Cassin's Illustrations of the Birds of California, Texas, Oregon, British and Russian America, 1991; author: (foward) The Birds of America by John James Audubon, 1985; editor: Bartram Heritage Report, 1978; author (with others), editor: Philadelphia Wildfowl Exposition Catalog, 1979; contbr. chpts. to books, articles to mags. and newspapers including The New York Times. Trustee Chestnut Hill Acad., Phila.; bd. dirs. RARE Ctr. Tropical Bird Conservation, Mus. Coun. of Phila. Recipient Richard Hopper Day Meml. award Acad. Natural Scis. of Phila., 1991; Eleanor Garvey fellow in printing and graphic arts Houghton Libr., Harvard U., 1995; Yale Ctr. for Brit. Art fellow, 1997. Fellow Royal Geographic Soc., Explorers Club (various coms. 1983—, Explorers award 1988); mem. Soc. History of Natural History, Sigma Xi. Achievements include discovery of of a new species of frog, Eleutherodactylus pecki; research in orthoptera indigenous to the Caribbean; status of invasive African Desert Locust in the West Indies; the Orinoco River and its tributaries, botanical, entomological, ichthyological, herpetological and malacological specimens for the Smithsonian Institution and the Academy of Natural Sciences; participation in expeditions which discovered several new species of fish in Guyana Shield, Venezuela; discovery of several new species of amphibians and insects as well as two new races of birds in Ecuador; investigated the ecological, economic and political impact of instream-flow legislation on the Yellowstone River Bain; current projects include biological and cultural research in Mongolia, the natural history illustrations of Edward Lear; research in 19th century exploration. Office: Academy of Natural Sciences 1900 Benjamin Franklin Pkwy Philadelphia PA 19103-1195 E-mail: peck@acnatsci.org.

PECK, ROBERT A. newspaper publisher, state legislator; b. Riverton, Wyo., Oct. 7, 1924; s. LeRoy E. and Elvira Eugenia (Sostrom) P.; m. Cordelia S. Peck, Oct. 5, 1949 (dec. Feb. 1996); children: Christopher, George, Steven. BA, U. Wyo., 1949. Pub. The Riverton Ranger, 1949—; mem. Wyo. Senate, Dist. 26, Cheyenne, 1991—. Pres. Central Wyo. Coll. Bd., Riverton, 1966-81; sec. CWC Found., Riverton, 1968—. Staff sgt. U.S. Army, 1943-46, ETO. Mem. Soc. Profl. Journalists, Masons, Phi Beta Kappa. Republican. Methodist. Office: The Riverton Ranger 421 E Main PO Box 993 Riverton WY 82501-0993 E-mail: bpeck@wyoming.com., ranger@wyoming.com.

PECK, ROBERT DAVID, educational foundation administrator; b. Devil's Lake, N.D., June 1, 1929; s. Lester David and Bernice Marie (Peterson) P.; m. Lyla June Smith, Sept. 6, 1953; children: David Allan, Kathleen Marie. BA, Whitworth Coll., 1951; MDiv, Berkeley (Calif.) Bapt. Div. Sch., 1958; ThD, Pacific Sch. Religion, 1964; postgrad., U. Calif., Berkeley, 1959-60, 62-63, Wadham Coll., Oxford U., Eng., 1963. Music tchr. pub. schs., Bridgeport, Wash., 1954-55; prof., registrar Linfield Coll., McMinnville, Oreg., 1963-69; asst. dir. Ednl. Coordinating Coun., Salem, 1969-75; assoc. prof. Pacific Luth. U., Tacoma, 1976-79, U. Puget Sound, Tacoma, 1977; v.p. John Minter Assocs., Boulder, Colo., 1979-81, Coun. Ind. Colls., Washington, 1981-84; adminstrv. v.p. Alaska Pacific U., Anchorage, 1984-88; pres. Phillips U., Enid, Okla., 1988-94, chancellor, 1994-95; chmn. The Pres. Found. for Support of Higher Edn., Washington, 1995—; sr. assoc. InterEd, Phoenix, 1998—. Pres. Phillips U. Ednl. Enterprises Inc., 1994-95; cons. Higher Edn. Exec. Assocs., Denver, 1984—; owner Tyee Marina, Tacoma, 1975-77; yacht broker Seattle, 1977-79. Author: Future Focusing: An Alternative to Strategic Planning, 1983, also articles. Dem. county chmn., McMinnville, 1968, Dem. candidate for state Ho. of Reps., McMinnville, 1969; pres. McMinnville Kiwanis, 1965-69. Cpl. Signal Corps, U.S. Army, 1952-54. Carnegie Corp. grantee, 1982, 84. Mem. Okla. Ind. Coll. Assn. (sec. 1989—). Mem. Christian Ch. Avocation: sailing, sculpting. E-mail: robertpeckb@cs.com.

PECK, ROBERT STEPHEN, lawyer, educator; b. Bklyn., Dec. 11, 1953; s. Irwin and Edith Rose (Welt) P.; m. Terre Garcia; 1 child, Zachary Madison. BA in Polit. Sci., George Washington U., 1975; JD, Cleve.-Marshall Law Sch., 1978; postgrad., NYU, 1978; LLM, Yale U., 1990. Bar: N.Y. 1979, U.S. Dist. Ct. (so. and ea. dists.) N.Y. 1979, D.C. 1989. Congl. aide U.S. Ho. of Reps., Washington, 1972-74; divsn. dir. Automated Correspondence, 1974-75; law clk. to presiding justice Cleve. Mcpl. Ct., 1976; editor Matthew Bender & Co., N.Y.C., 1977-78; legal dir. Pub. Edn. Assn., 1978-82; staff dir. ABA, Chgo., 1982-87, Washington, 1987-89; jud. fellow U.S. Supreme Ct., 1990-91; legis. counsel ACLU, 1991-95; adj. prof. Am. U., Washington, 1991—, George Washington U., Washington, 2000—; dir. legal affairs Assn. Trial Lawyers Am., 1995-98, sr. dir. legal affairs, 1998—; pres. Ctr. for Constl. Litigation, 2001—. Legal advisor Freedom to Read Found., Chgo., 1986—, exec. com. bd. trustees, 1987-90, 93-97, pres., 1988-90, v.p., trustee, 1993-97; bd. dirs. Nat. Constl. Ctr., 1990-93; bd. overseers RAND Inst. Civil Justice, 2001-; lectr. on constl. law, legal ethics. Author: We the People, 1987, The Bill of Rights and the Politics of Interpretation, 1991, Libraries, the First Amendment and Cyberspace, 1999; co-author: Speaking and Writing Truth, 1985; editor: Understanding the Law, 1983, Blessings of Liberty, 1986, To Govern A Changing Society, 1990; contbr. numerous articles on constl. law to law revs. Mem. N.Y. State Edn. Adv. Bd., Albany, N.Y., 1979-81; bd. dirs. Nat. Com. on Pub. Edn. and Religious Liberty, 1995-97, Ams. for Religious Liberty, 1995-2000, Citizens for Constitution, 1997—; nat. chair Lawyers for Librs., 1996—; chair legal adv. com. Nat. Ctr. for Sci. Edn., 1996-2000; mem. first amendment adv. coun. Media Inst., 1996—. NEH grantee 1983, 85. Mem.: ABA (chmn. pub. election law com. 1983—85, 1987—90, vice chmn. access to justice com. 1997—98, chmn. 1998—99, program chmn. consumer and personal rights litigation com. 1997—2000, chmn. first amendment com. 1999—, chmn. appellate adv. com. 2001—). Democrat. Jewish. Avocations: tennis, music, travel. Office: Ctr for Constl Litigation 1050 31st St NW Washington DC 20007-4499 E-mail: robert.peck@atlahq.org.

PECK, SUSAN NELL, pediatric nurse; b. Dayton, Ohio, July 21, 1951; d. D. Bradley and Helen Louise (DePree) P. BSN, Northeastern U., Boston, 1974; MSN, U. Va., 1981. Cert. registered nurse practitioner. Sr. staff nurse Tufts-New Eng. Med. Ctr., Boston, 1974-79; staff nurse U. Va. Med. Ctr., Charlottesville, 1980-81, grad. teaching asst., 1980-81; clin. nurse specialist in gastroenterology The Children's Hosp. of Phila., 1981—. V.p. profl. edn. Delaware Valley chpt. Crohn's and Colitis Found. Am., Phila., 1992—. Contbr. articles to profl. jours.; author videotape: Facts From Your Friends, 1991. Bd. dirs. Phila. chpt. Am. Liver Found., 1988—. Named Woman of the Yr., Crohn's and Colitis Found. of Am., 1995, Nurse Profl. of Yr., Am. Liver Found., 1997; inducted into Northeastern U. Nursing Hall of Fame, 1998. Mem. ANA, Nat. Assn. Pediatric Nurse Practitioners and Assocs., Soc. Gastroenterology Nurses and Assocs. (editl. bd. 1986-92), Assn. Pediatric Gastroenterology and Nutrition Nurses (founder, sec.-treas. 1989-94, sec. 1994-95, treas. 1996), Sigma Theta Tau. Avocations: travel, reading. Office: Childrens Hosp of Phila 34th And Civic Center Blvd Philadelphia PA 19104

PECK, THOMAS, newspaper publishing executive; BS in Acctg., U. Conn.; MS Wharton Sch. Bus., U. Pa. CPA. Audit mgr. and computer audit specialist Ernst & Young, 1969-75; v.p. fin. and adminstrn. Orba Corp., 1975-83; controller and chief acctg. officer Esprit Systems, 1983-85; v.p. PRD Property Devel., 1985-89; asst. v.p. Mac Andrews & Forbes, 1989-90; CFO Daily News, L.P., 1990—, U.S. News & World Report, Fast Company Media Group, LLC. Office: NY Daily News Office of the CFO 450 W 33rd St Fl 3 New York NY 10001-2681

PECK, WILLIAM ARNO, physician, educator, university official and dean; b. New Britain, Conn., Sept. 28, 1933; s. Bernard Carl and Molla (Nair) P.; m. Patricia Hearn, July 10, 1982; children by previous marriage: Catherine, Edward Pershall, David Nathaniel; stepchildren: Andrea, Elizabeth, Katherine. AB, Harvard U., 1955; MD, U. Rochester, N.Y., 1960; DSc (hon.), U. Rochester, 2000. Intern, then resident in internal medicine Barnes Hosp., St. Louis, 1960-62; fellow in metabolism Washington U. Sch. Medicine, 1963; mem. faculty U. Rochester Med. Sch., 1965-76, prof. medicine and biochemistry, 1973-76, head divsn. endocrinology and metabolism, 1969-76; John E. and Adaline Simon prof. medicine, co-chmn. dept. medicine Washington U. Sch. Medicine, St. Louis, 1976-89; physician in chief Jewish Hosp., 1976-89; prof. medicine and exec. vice chancellor med. affairs, dean sch. medicine, pres. univ. med. ctr. Washington U., 1989—. Chmn. endocrinology and metabolism adv. com. FDA, 1976-78; chmn. gen. medicine study sect. NIH, 1979-81; chmn. Gordon Conf. Chemistry, Physiology and Structure of Bones and Teeth, 1977; chmn. Consensus Devel. Conf. on Osteoporosis, NIH, 1984; co-chmn. Workshop on Future Directions in Osteoporosis, 1987; chmn. Spl. Topic Conf. on Osteoporosis, U.S. FDA, 1987; dir. Angelica Corp., Allied Healthcare Products, Hologic, Reinsurance Group of Am., TIAA-CREF Trust Co. Editor Bone and Mineral Rsch. Anns., 1982-88. Pres. Nat. Osteoporosis Found., 1985-90. Served as med. officer USPHS, 1963-65. Recipient Lederle Med. Faculty award, 1967, career program award NIH, 1970-75, commr.'s spl. citation FDA, 1988, Humanitarian award Arthritis Found. Ea. Mo., 1995, Founders award Nat. Osteoporosis Found., 1996, Humanitarian award Crohn's and Colitis Fedn. Am., 1999; Paul Harris fellow Rotary Found., 2001. Fellow AAAS, ACP; mem. Internat. Bone & Mineral Soc., Royal Soc. Medicine, Am. Assn. Clin. Endocrinologists, Am. Geriatrics Soc., Am. Soc. Biochemistry & Molecular Biophysics, Am. Soc. Bone and Mineral Rsch. (councilor 1978-81, pres.-elect 1982-83, pres. 1983-84), Am. Soc. Clin. Investigation, Am. Soc. Internal Medicine, Assn. Am. Med. Colls. (coun. deans adminstrv. bd. 1992—, chmn. 1996-97, chair elect 1997-98, chair 1998—, immediate past chair 1999), Assn. Am. Physicians, Endocrine Soc., Orthopaedic Rsch. Soc., Soc. Med. Adminstrs., St. Louis Metro. Med. Soc., St. Louis Soc. Internal Medicine (pres. 1986), Inst. Medicine Nat. Acad. Sci., Washington U. Health Adminstrn. Program Alumni Assn. (hon.), Research! Am. (vice chair 1999—), Pi Theta Epsilon (hon.), Sigma Xi, Alpha Omega Alpha (bd. dirs 1992-95). Home: 32 Huntleigh Downs Saint Louis MO 63131 Office: Washington U Sch Medicine 600 S Euclid Ave Saint Louis MO 63110-1010

PECK, WILLIAM HENRY, museum curator, art historian, archaeologist, author, lecturer; b. Savannah, Ga., Oct. 2, 1932; s. William Henry Peck and Mildred (Bass) Peck Tuten; m. Ann Amelia Keller, Feb. 2, 1957 (dec. 1965); children: Alice Ann, Sarah Louise; m. Elsie Holmes, July 8, 1967; 1 child, William Henry IV. Student, Ohio State U., 1950-53; BFA, Wayne State U., 1960, MA, 1961. Jr .curator Detroit Inst. Arts, 1960-62, asst. curator, 1962-64, assoc. curator, 1964-68, curator ancient art, 1968—, acting chief curator, 1984-88, sr. curator, 1988—. Lectr. art history Cranbrook Acad. Art, Bloomfield Hills, Mich., 1963-65; vis. lectr. U. Mich., Ann Arbor, 1970; adj. prof. art history Wayne State U., Detroit, 1966—; excavations in Egypt, Mendes, 1964-66, Precinct of Mut, Karnak, 1978—. Author: Drawings from Ancient Egypt, 1978, The Detroit Institute of Arts: A Brief History, 1991, Splendors of Ancient Egypt, 1978; co-author: Ancient Egypt: Discovering its Splendors, 1978, Mummies, Diseases and Ancient Cultures, 1980, also articles. With U.S. Army, 1953-55. Recipient award in the arts Wayne State U., 1985; Ford Motor Co. travel grantee, 1962; Am. Rsch. Ctr. Egypt fellow, 1971; Smithsonian Instn. travel grantee, 1975. Mem. Archaeol. Inst. Am., Am. Rsch. Ctr. Egypt, Internat. Assn. Egyptologists, Soc. Study Egyptian Antiquities, Am. Assn. Mus., Oriental Inst.-U. Chgo. Democrat. Episcopalian. Avocations: origami, performance of early music, collecting T.E. Lawrence material. Office: Inst Arts 5200 Woodward Ave Detroit MI 48202-4008 E-mail: wpeck@dia.org.

PECKENPAUGH, ROBERT EARL, investment advisor; b. Potomac, Ill., July 17, 1926; s. Hilery and Zella (Stodgel) P.; m. Margaret J. Dixon, Sept. 21, 1945; children: Nancy Lynn, Carol Sue, David Robert, Daniel Mark, Jeanne Beth, Douglas John. Student, Ind. U., 1946-47; BS, Northwestern U., 1949, MBA with distinction, 1952. Chartered fin. analyst. With First Nat. Bank Chgo., 1949-52; pres. Security Suprs., Inc., Chgo., 1952-73; v.p. Chgo. Title & Trust Co., 1973-77; pres. Hotchkiss & Peckenpaugh, Inc., Chgo., 1977-84; v.p. Morgan Stanley Asset Mgmt. Inc., 1984-86, Morgan Stanley & Co., Inc., Chgo., 1986-91; pres. Peckenpaugh Asset Mgmt. Inc., 1991—. Chmn., Evang. Covenant Ch. of Hinsdale, Ill., 1981-84. Served with USNR, 1944-46. Mem. Investment Analyst Soc. Chgo. (pres. 1963-64), Mid-Day Club, Hinsdale Golf Club. Home: 429 S County Line Rd Hinsdale IL 60521-4724 Office: Peckenpaugh Asset Mgmt 429 S County Line Rd Hinsdale IL 60521-4724

PECKERMAN, BRUCE MARTIN, lawyer; b. Milw., Sept. 28, 1949; s. Joseph and Doris (Kassel) P.; m. Jeanette Chrustowski. BA, U. Wis., 1971; JD, Washington U., St. Louis, 1973. Bar: Wis. 1974, U.S. Dist. Ct. (we. dist.) Wis. 1974, U.S. Ct. Appeals (7th cir.) 1977. Sole practice, Milw., 1985—. Recipient young leadership award Milw. Jewish Fedn. Mem. ABA, Wis. Bar Assn. (past chmn. family law sect.), Milw. Bar Assn. (bench/bar com. 1987-88), Am. Acad. Matrimonial Lawyers (past pres.). Office: 920 E Mason St Milwaukee WI 53202-4015 E-mail: bruce_pec@execpc.com.

PECKHAM, BRUCE BARTLETT, mathematician; b. Canton, N.Y., Oct. 20, 1954; s. Donald Charles and Elizabeth Doolittle Peckham; m. Kathryn Elizabeth Lenz; children: Matthew, Gregory;1 child Stella. PhD, U. Minn., 1988. Asst. prof. U. Minn., Duluth, 1990—95, assoc. prof., 1995—. Cons., collaborator Los Alamos Nat. Lab., 1987—95. Contbr. Grantee rsch. grantee, NSF, 1990—2002. Mem.: Soc. for Indsl. and Applied Math., Am. Math. Assn., Math. Assn. Am., Soc. Actuaries (assoc.). Home: 2530 E 6th St Duluth MN 55812 Office: U Minn Duluth MN 55812 Business E-Mail: bpeckham@d.umn.edu.

PECKHAM, DONALD, computer company executive; b. Aberdeen, S.D., Feb. 8, 1932; s. Donald Seth and Crystal (Maytum) P.; m. Jeanette G. Mackenzie, June 20, 1967 (div. Jan. 1995); children: Dean, Deanna Jean. BSEE, U. Wash., 1957; MSEE, Calif. Inst. Tech., 1958. Engr. Hughes Aircraft Co., Culver City, Calif., 1957-60; sr. engr. Nortronics divsn. Northrup Corp., Hawthorne, 1960-61, rsch. scientist Nortronics divsn., 1965-67, tech. dir. Aircraft divsn., 1985-92; v.p. Digitek Corp., Inglewood, 1961-63, v.p., gen. mgr. L.A., 1963-65; mem. staff Decade Computer Corp., Huntington Beach, 1967-71; mgr. software Pertec Computer Corp., Santa Ana, Calif., 1971-81; mgr. software tools CXC Corp., Irvine, 1981-85; instr. U. So. Calif., 1960-61; pres. Modern Computer, Carlsbad, Calif., 1992-2001, Modern.net, Oceanside, 2001—. With USN, 1950-54. Mem. IEEE, Assn. Computing Machinery, Tau Beta Pi. Home and Office: Unit 85 3890 Vista Campana S Oceanside CA 92057-8160 also: Unit 85 3890 Vista Campana S Oceanside CA 92057-8160 E-mail: donaldpeckham@msn.com.

PECKHAM, DONALD EUGENE, retired utilities company executive; b. Willis, Kans., Nov. 28, 1922; s. Rolland Claude and Winona Maude (Lewis) P.; m. Evelynn Darlene Dodson, Dec. 20, 1949 (dec.). BA cum laude in Acctg, Eastern N.Mex. U., 1953; MBA, U. Ariz., 1954. Acct. Ill. Power Co., Decatur, Ill., 1954-57; with Public Service Co. of N.Mex., Albuquerque, from 1957, sec., 1968-70, sec., asst. treas., 1970-74, sec., treas., 1974-79, sec., asst. treas., from 1979; sec. Paragon Resources, Inc., 1972-75, sec., asst. treas., from 1975; sec. Sunbelt Mining Co., Inc., 1980-81, sec., asst. treas., from 1981; sec. Meadows Resources, Inc., from 1981; now ret. Served with USMC, 1943-46. Mem.: Elks. Republican.

PECKHAM, ELLEN, artist, poet; b. Rochester, N.Y., Sept. 28, 1938; d. Walter Fredrick and Florence Albertina (Schmanke) Stoepel; m. Anson Wheeler Peckham, Sept. 10, 1976. Exhibitions include Atelier A/E Enterprises, N.Y.C., 1994—, Instituto Cultural Peruano Norteamericano, Peru, 1997—, Art Internat., N.Y.C., 1998, Boston Printmakers, 1999—, Katonah (N.Y.) Mus., 1999—, Collage/Assemblage Soc., N.Y.C., 2000—02, Matrix, Sacramento, 2000—, Think Ink, N.Y., 2001—, Brand Libr. and Art Ctr., Glendale, Calif., 2001—, Springfield (Mo.) Art Mus., 2001, Stocker Ctr., Elyria, Ohio, 2001, U. Richmond, Va., 2002, N.W. Arts Coun./Ill. Arts Coun., Woodstock, Ill., 2002, Sothebeys, N.Y., 2002, Sumei Multidisciplinary Arts Ctr., Newark, 2002, No. Ariz. U., Flagstaff, 2002; , author numerous poems. Avocations: gardening, theatre.

PECKHAM, EUGENE ELIOT, surogate judge, lawyer; b. Stamford, Conn., Aug. 11, 1940; s. Joseph E. and Margaret (Nabors) P.; m. Judith Alice Chamberlain, Dec. 19, 1964; children: Margaret, Joseph, Elizabeth. BA with honors, Wesleyan U., Middletown, Conn., 1962; JD, Harvard U., 1965. Bar: N.Y. 1965, Fla. 1981, U.S. Tax Ct. 1974, U.S. Ct. Appeals (2d cir.) 1975, U.S. Dist. Ct. (no. dist.) N.Y. 1965. Assoc. Hinman, Howard & Kattell, Binghamton, N.Y., 1965-72, ptnr., 1972-2000; surrogate judge Broome County, 2001—. Instr. Broome C.C., Binghamton, 1968-69, Am. Coll. Life Underwriters, Bryn Mawr, Pa., 1969-70, Am. Coll. Property and Casualty Underwriters, Bryn Mawr, 1970-71; adj. lectr. SUNY, Binghamton, 1972-77, adj. asst. prof., 1977-81, adj. assoc. prof., 1981-87, adj. prof. acctg., 1987—; vis. lectr. Cornell U., Ithaca, N.Y., 1978, adj. prof., 1984. Author: Warren's Heaton Surrogate's Courts, Federal and New York Estate Taxes, vol., revised, 1988, 89, Bender's Federal Tax Service " Income Taxation of Estates & Trusts", 1989; mem. bd. editors Warren's Heaton on Surrogate Courts, 2001-; contbr. articles to profl. jours. Peace Corps vol. tchr. Santa Maria U., Arequipa, Peru, 1966-67, treas. Joint Legis. Adv. Com. on Estates, Powers and Trusts Law and The Surrogates Ct. Procedure Act, 1990—; pres. Binghamton Girls Club, N.Y., 1974-76, bd. dirs., 1970-77; chmn. bd. Binghamton Boys and Girls Club, 1977, trustee, 1987-2000, chmn. bd. trustees, 1996-2000; bd. dirs. A. Lindsay and Olive B. O'Connor Found., 1982—, Dr. G. Clifford and Florence B. Decker Found., 1984-2001; bd. dirs. Comty. Found. South Ctrl. N.Y., 1996-; mem. trust fund. com. Broome County United Way, N.Y., 1979-94; pres. SUNY Found., Binghamton, 1977-79, bd. dirs., 1975-82; bd. dirs. Estate Planning Coun. So. Tier, 1983-87, treas., 1983, sec., 1984, v.p., 1985, pres., 1986; bd. dirs. Samaritan Counselling Ctr. So. Tier, Inc., 1982-87, v.p., 1986, pres., 1987; co-chmn. sta. WSKG-TV auction, 1983; treas. Roberson Ctr. Arts & Scis., 1980, bd. dirs., 1977-80, 87-95; bd. dirs. Twin Tier Home Health, Inc., 1990-97, v.p., 1991-93, pres., 1993-95; chmn. Broome County Cmty. Ambassador Project, 1970-71; mem. Broome Bd. Ethics, 1985-89, chair, 1999-2000; mem. Broome County Arena Bd., 1987-89; deacon 1st Presbyn. Ch., Binghamton, 1971-74, moderator, 1974, elder, 1975-78, 87-90, trustee, 1980-83, 92-95; exec. conm. Broome County Rep. Com., 1980-83, 96-2000, co-chmn. fin. com., 1982-83, vice chmn., 1996-2000; pres. Broome County Young Rep. Club, 1969-70. Recipient SUNY-Binghamton Alumni Recognition award, 1984. Fellow Am. Coll. Trust & Estate Coun.; mem. N.Y. State Bar Assn. (exec. com. trusts & estates sect. 1980-84, 86-92, treas. 1986, sec. 1987, chmn. elect 1988, chmn. 1989, tax sect. 1972-2000, chmn. spl. commn. on alt. sources funding legal svcs. 1976-78, action unit 6 1984-86, ethics com. 1979-82, bd. editors N.Y. State Bar Jour. 1998—, v.p. 1999—, ho. dels. 1990-94, 95—), Fedn. Bar Assns. 6th Jud. Dist. (pres. 1984-85), Broome County Bar Assn. (chmn. prepaid legal ins. com. 1976-80, ethics com. 1981-87, chmn. jud. rating com. 1988-90). Home: 12 Campbell Rd Binghamton NY 13905-4304 Office: Broome County Surrogate Ct PO Box 1766 Binghamton NY 13902-1766

PECKHAM, JEFFREY WILLIAM, music educator; b. Albuquerque, Aug. 3, 1961; s. Vernon Dale and Patricia Mae Peckham; m. Kristin Kaye Goodwin, June 27, 1992; children: Ethan, Mackenzie. MusM, U. of No. Colo., 1987. Vocal music dir. East Mid. Sch., Colorado Springs, 1995—99, Jenkins Mid. Sch., Colorado Springs, 1999—. Vocal dir. Woodmen Valley Chapel, Colorado Springs, 2000—01. Composer (musician): (song) The Final Act, 1985 (Colo. Composer's Classic, 1986). Vocal dir. Show Choir, Colorado Springs, 1995—2002. Recipient Best Mid. Sch. Program award, Colorado Springs C. of C., 1997. Mem.: ASCAP, Music Educator's Nat. Conf., Colo. Music Educator Assn., Am. Choral Director's Assn., Pi Kappa Lambda, Kappa Delta Pi. Republican. Avocation: reading, golf, films, concerts. Home: 8053 Scarborough Dr Colorado Springs CO 80920 Office: Jenkins Mid Sch 6410 Austin Bluffs Pkwy Colorado Springs CO 80918 Office Fax: 719-266-5276. Personal E-mail: jeffpeck@peoplepc.com. E-mail: peckhjw@d11.org.

PECKHAM, JOYCE WEITZ, foundation administrator, former secondary education educator; b. Rochester, N.Y., Oct. 11, 1937; d. Clarence Christian and Mildred Emma (Knapp) Weitz; m. Lauren Augustus Peckham, Dec. 20, 1958; children: David, Kent. BS, Elmira Coll., 1959, MS, 1967. Tchr. science Horseheads (N.Y.) Cen. Sch., 1959-71; sec.-treas. Peckham Pipe Organs, Breesport, N.Y., 1971—. Trustee and sec. electronic coms. Antique Wireless Assn., Bloomfield, N.Y., 1986—, sec. and mem. sec. 1986—, mem. bd. dirs. 1981—. Mem. Horseheads Hist. Soc., Internat. Majolica Soc., First United Methodist Ch. (trustee, choir mem.). Avocations: collecting antiques, reading, travel. Home: 194 Ormiston Rd Breesport NY 14816-9702

PECKHAM, KENDALL I. music educator; b. Boise, Idaho, Oct. 28, 1951; s. Charles Clifford Peckham and Rosalie Mae Jensen; m. Deborah Lynn Mills, Aug. 17, 1973; 1 child Mary Kathryn. BS in Mech. Engring., Boise State U., 1975; M of Mech. Engring., Western Oreg. U., 1981. Cert. music tchr. Oreg. Instrumental music tchr. Harney County Sch. Dist. # 3, Burns, Oreg., 1975—89, 1992—. Pep band dir. Burns H.S., 1992—, sr. class advisor, 1995—2001, curriculum reform com., 2000. Orch. dir. Chamber Music Soc., Harney County, 1979—, treas., 1979—84. Named Outstanding Educator,

Harney County C. of C., 1999; grantee Meyer Meml. Trust, Computer Music Implementation, 1995. Mem.: Ctrl. Oreg. Music Educators (treas. 1999—), Oreg. Music Edn. Assn., Music Educators Nat. Conf. Nazarene. Achievements include 1st pl. World of Music Festival, 1998; concert performance Nat. Festival of States, Washington, 2000. Avocations: fly fishing, astronomy, fly tying. Office: Burns HS 1100 Oregon Ave Burns OR 97720

PECKOL, JAMES KENNETH, consulting engineer; b. Cleve., Oct. 24, 1944; s. William John and Elinor Elizabeth (Bustard) P.; children: Erin, Robyn. BS Engring., Case Inst. Tech., 1966; MSEE, U. Wash., 1975, PhDEE, 1985. Cons. GE, Raytheon, Ling Temco Vought, RCA, Boeing Co., 1966-72; sr. staff engr. indsl. products bus. unit John Fluke Mfg. Co., Seattle, 1972-83, sr. staff engr. automated systems bus. unit, 1983-86, sr. staff engr. MR&D Bus. unit, 1986-93; founder Oxford Cons., Edmonds, Wash., 1987—. Affiliate asst. prof. dept. elec. engring., affiliate asst. prof. dept. computers and software sys. U. Wash., Seattle, 1984-87, 95—, prof. dept. elec. engring., 1997—; sr. lectr., assoc. prof. dept. elec. engring. U. Aberdeen, Scotland, 1987; lectr. dept. math. and sci. Shoreline C.C., Seattle, 1989—; lectr. dept. computer sci. Edmonds (Wash.) C.C., 1992—; assoc. prof. dept. engring./computer sci. U. Nantes, Frances, 1993, 96; mem. computer sci. and elec. engring. curriculum adv. bd. Wash. State U., 1990—; lectr. various confs. and univs. Contbr. articles to profl. jours.; patentee in field. Mem. IEEE, Am. Assn. Artificial Intelligence, Assn. Computing Machinery, Tau Beta Pi. Home and Office: Oxford Cons Ltd 859 14th St SW Edmonds WA 98020-6611

PECKOLICK, ALAN, painter, graphic designer; b. N.Y.C., Oct. 3, 1940; s. Charles and Belle (Binenbaum) P.; m. Jessica Margot Weber, June 3, 1984. AAS, Pratt Inst., Bklyn., 1968. Art dir. McCann-Erickson, 1964-68; graphic designer Herb Lubalin, 1968-72; v.p., creative dir. Lubalin, Smith, Carnase, Inc., N.Y.C., 1972-74, LCS & P Design Group, Inc., N.Y.C., 1974-76; pres. Lubalin Peckolick Assoc., 1976-81, Pushpin, Lubalin, Peckolick, N.Y.C., 1981-86, Peckolick and Ptnrs., N.Y.C., 1986-89; design dir. Addison Design Cons., 1989-91; chmn. Peckolick Inc., 1991—; painter, 2000—. Bd. advisors Designworld mag., Victoria, Australia, 1983—, Herb Lubalin Study Ctr., N.Y.C.; lectr. Pratt Inst., Parsons Sch. Design, Sch. Visual Arts, also various orgns. Co-author, designer Herb Lubalin Graphic Designer, 1986;exhibitions include Sony Gallery, Tokyo, 1989, one-man shows include , N.Y.C., 2000, 2002, Key West, Fla., 2001, Salamagundi Club Invitational, 2002, Gallery 468, N.Y.C., 2002. Bd. dirs. Glaucoma Found., 1993, Whale Conservation Inst., 1994. Recipient awards AIGA, Art Directors Club awards. Mem. N.Y. Art Dirs. Club (6 gold medals, over 50 awards), N.Y. Type Dirs. Club (bd. dirs.), Alliance Graphique Internationale, Art Dirs.Club Bergen (Norway) (hon.). Avocations: automobile racing, sculpting, collecting art and prints, cooking, travel. Home: 30 E 10th St New York NY 10003-6202

PECORARO, STEVEN JOHN, lawyer; b. N.Y.C., Apr. 27, 1961; m. Frances P. Ferraro, Feb. 18, 1996. BA in Polit. Sci., CUNY, Flushing, 1982; JD, St. John's U., Jamaica, N.Y., 1985. Bar: N.Y. 1986, U.S. Dist. Ct. (so. and ea. dists.) N.Y. 1993. Asst. dist. atty. Dist. Atty.'s Office, Queens County, N.Y., 1985-87; sr. staff atty. Law Offices of Stewart H. Friedman, Lake Success, 1987-91; sr. trial atty. Alio & Caiati, N.Y.C., 1991-95; ptnr. Pecoraro & Schiesel, 1995—. Mem. N.Y. State Bar Assn. Avocations: hunting, fishing, outdoor activities. Office: Pecoraro & Schiesel Ste 1800 One Whitehall St New York NY 10004

PECORINO, LAUREN TERESA, biologist; b. Bronx, N.Y., June 17, 1962; d. Joseph Salvatore and Raffaela (Rapillo) P. BS in Biology, SUNY, Stony Brook, 1984, PhD, 1990. Postdoctoral fellow Ludwig Inst. for Cancer Rsch., London, 1991-96; sr. lectr., biochemistry program leader U. Greenwich, 1996—. Cons. for cogent neurosci., 2001. Contbr. articles to profl. jours. Postdoctoral fellow European Molecular Biology Orgn., 1991-93, NATO, 1993-95. Mem. AAAS, N.Y. Acad. Scis., Brit. Soc. for Devel. Biology, Biochem. Soc., Sigma Xi. Home: 1422 San Mateo Ave Lady Lake FL 32159-8661 Office: U Greenwich Woolwich Campus Wellington St Woolwich London SE18 6PF England E-mail: lpecorino@compuserv.com.

PECSOK, ROBERT LOUIS, chemist, educator; b. Cleve., Dec. 18, 1918; s. Michael C. and Katherine (Richter) P.; m. Mary Bodell, Oct. 12, 1940 (dec. Apr. 1996); children: Helen Pecsok Wong, Katherine, Jean Pecsok Nagle, Michael, Ruth Pecsok Hughes, Alice Pecsok Tominaga, Sara Pecsok Lima; m. Marcella Beeman, Apr. 23, 1997. SB summa cum laude, Harvard U., 1940, PhD, 1948. Prodn. foreman Procter & Gamble Co., Balt., 1940-43; instr. chemistry Harvard U., 1948; asst. prof. chemistry U. Calif., L.A., 1948-55, assoc. prof., 1955-61, prof., 1961-71, vice-chmn. dept., 1965-70; prof., chmn. dept. U. Hawaii, Honolulu, 1971-80, dean natural scis., 1981-90. Sci. adviser FDA, 1966-69. Author: Principles and Practice of Gas Chromatography, 1959, Analytical Methods of Organic and Biochemistry, 1966, Modern Methods of Chemical Analysis, 1968, 2d edit., 1976, Modern Chemical Technology, 1970, rev. edit. 1989, Physicochemical Applications of Gas Chromatography, 1978. Lt. USNR, 1943-46. Recipient Tolman medal, 1971; Guggenheim fellow, 1956-57, Petroleum Rsch. Fund Internat. fellow, 1963-64. Mem. Am. Chem. Soc., Am. Inst. Chemists, Phi Beta Kappa, Alpha Chi Sigma, Phi Lambda Upsilon. Home: 13903 Amber Sky Ln San Diego CA 92129-3101

PECZE, DAVID EMERY, marketing professional; b. South Bend, Ind., Mar. 19, 1958; s. Geza David and Yolanda Joan (Batiz) P. BA in Telecommunications, Ind. U., 1980; BS in Bus. Mktg., Ind. U., South Bend, 1984. Sales mgr. LaPorte County Broadcasting, Ind., 1980-82; mktg. analyst St. Joseph Bank & Trust Corp., South Bend, 1984-85; campaign assoc. United Way St. Joseph County, 1985-88; mgr. sales adminstrn. CTS Corp., Elkhart, Ind., 1988-91; market analyst Nat. Steel Corp., Mishawaka, 1992-94; mktg. mgr. Filter Specialists, Inc., Michigan City, 1995—. Mem. LaPorte Jaycees (bd. dirs. 1981-82, Rookie Yr. award 1981), Adams Alumni, Image Club, Am. Mktg. Assn. (bd. dirs. Michiana chpt. 1994-96), Masons, Kiwanis (bd. dirs. 1986-88). Avocations: racquetball, tennis, golf, swimming, boating. Office: Filter Specialists Inc PO Box 735 Michigan City IN 46361-0735 Home: 1118 W Jefferson Blvd South Bend IN 46601-2617 E-mail: hoosieralum@juno.com.

PEDDICORD, ROLAND DALE, lawyer; b. Van Meter, Iowa, Mar. 29, 1936; s. Clifford Elwood and Juanitas Irene (Brittain) P.; m. Teri Linn O'Dell; children: Erin Sue, Robert Sean. BSBA with honors, Drake U., 1961, JD with honors, 1962. Bar: Iowa 1962; cert. civil trial specialist Nat. Bd. Trial Advs. Asst. atty. gen. State of Iowa, 1962-63; assoc. Steward, Crouch & Hopkins, Des Moines, 1962-65; ptnr. Peddicord, Wharton, Spencer & Hook, 1965—. Lectr. in law Drake U., 1962-68; lectr. law Coll. Osteo. Medicine, Des Moines, 1965-72 Editor and chief Drake Law Rev., 1961-62 Past mem. nat. bd. dirs., nat. coun. YMCA of U.S.A., past vice chmn. nat. bd.; bd. dirs., past chmn. Greater Des Moines YMCA, 1968-89. With USMC, 1954-57. Mem. ABA, ATLA, Iowa Bar Assn., Polk County Bar Assn., Iowa Trial Lawyers Assn., Iowa Acad. Trial Lawyers, Am. Bd. Trial Advs. (mem. nat. bd., past pres. Iowa chpt.). Republican. Methodist. Office: 405 6th Ave Ste 700 Des Moines IA 50309-2415 also: Peddicord Wharton Spencer & Hook PO Box 9130 Des Moines IA 50306-9130 E-mail: Dale.Peddicord@Peddicord-Law.com.

PEDDY, JULIE ANN, administrative officer; MPA, Ind. U., Gary, 1984. Lic. foster parent, Washington, 2000—. Benefit authorizer trainee U.S. HHS, Chgo., 1979-80; investigator U.S. Office of Personnel Mgmt., 1980-81, Def. Investigative Svc., Chgo., 1981-83, investigator, sr. resident agt. Hammond, Ind., 1983-84, supervisory investigator, team chief Chgo., 1984-89; spl. agt. in charge Def. Security Svc. (formerly Def. Investigative Svc.), Seattle, 1989-98; adminstr. officer Northwest Fisheries Sci. Ctr., 1998—. Mem. Seattle Fed. Exec. Bd., 1990-98, chairwoman, 1995-96. Bd. dirs. Lynwood (Ill.) Terr. Condominium Assn., 1982—89, Civic Light Opera, Seattle, 1996—99, treas., CFO, 1997—98; bd. dirs. Hearthstone Homeowners, 2002—; foster parent Wash. State, 2000—. Mem. ASPA, Ind. U. Alumni Assn. (life), Pi Alpha Alpha. Protestant. Avocations: fishing, cooking, quilting, music, crafts. Office: Northwest Fisheries Sci Ctr 2775 Montlake Blvd E Seattle WA 98112-2013 E-mail: juliepeddy@aol.com.

PEDEN, KATHERINE GRAHAM, industrial consultant; b. Hopkinsville, Ky., Jan. 2, 1926; d. William E. and Mary (Gorin) P. Student pub. schs. Vice pres. radio sta. WHOP-CBS, Hopkinsville, 1944-68; owner sta. WNVL, Nicholsville, Ky., 1961-71; commr. commerce, 1963-67; mem. Gov. Ky. Cabinet, Frankfort, 1963-67; pres., cons. Katherine G. Peden & Assocs. Inc., Louisville, indsl. and community developers. Bd. dirs. Westvaco Corp.; mem. adv. bd. Norfolk So. Corp. Chmn. Louisville and Jefferson County Riverport Authority, 1975-80; civilian aide to Sec. of Army, 1978-82; mem. com. Pres.'s Commn. on Status of Women, 1961-62; mem. Pres.'s Commn. on Civil Disorders, 1967; pres. Ky. Derby Festival, 1979-80; Dem. nominee U.S. Senate, 1968; mem. adv. coun. U. Ky. Coll. Bus.; trustee Spalding U., 1980-86. Named Woman of Year Hopkinsville, 1952 Mem. Fedn. Bus., Profl. Women's Clubs (pres. state 1955-56, 1st nat. v.p. 1960-61, nat. pres. 1961-62). Mem. Christian Ch. (deaconess 1956-59, 60-63). Home: 3818 Washington Sq Louisville KY 40207-1954 Office: PO Box 6268 Louisville KY 40206-0268

PEDEN, LYNN ELLEN, marketing executive; b. L.A., Mar. 1, 1946; d. Orlan Sidney and Erna Lou (Harris) Friedman; m. Ernest Peden, Aug. 1994. Student, UCLA, 1963-65, 71-72, Willis Bus. Coll., 1965-66, Fin. Schs. Am., 1982, Viewpoints Inst., 1970-71. Office mgr. Harleigh Sandler Co., L.A., 1965-67; customer svc. Investors Diversified Svcs., West L.A., Calif., 1968-76; exec. sec. McCulloch Oil Corp., 1976; mgr. publs. Security 1st Group, Century City, Calif., 1976-80; office mgr. Morehead & Co., 1980-81; dir. mktg., mgr. customer svc. Inst. Mktg. Svcs., Santa Monica, Calif., 1981-82; v.p. Decatur Petroleum Corp., 1982-83; asst. v.p., broker svcs., dir. Angeles Corp., L.A., 1984-87; asst. to pres. Pacific Ventures, Santa Monica, 1988-90, La Grange Group, West L.A., 1990-95; property mgmt. asst. Desert Resort Mgmt., Palm Desert, Calif., 1997-99, bus. mgr., 1999—. Fin. and ins. writer; contbr. poetry to UCLA Literacy Mag., 1964. Mem. Migi Car Am. Club (sec., newsletter editor). Home: 78580 Villeta Dr La Quinta CA 92253-3856

PEDERSEN, DARLENE DELCOURT, publishing executive; b. Westbrook, Maine; 1 child, Jorgen David. BSN, U. Conn., 1967; postgrad., U. B.C., 1974-75; MSN, U. Pa., 1997. RN Pa., N.J., cert. clinical specialist in adult psychiatric and mental health nursing, ANCC. Various nursing positions, psychiat.-comty health, 1967-79; assoc. editor JB Lippincott Co., Phila., 1979-84; acquisition editor WB Saunders Co., 1984-88, v.p., editor in chief, 1988-91, sr. v.p., editorial dir. books divsn., liaison to London office, 1991-95; domestic and internat. cons. in pvt. practice, 1995—; psychotherapist pvt. practice, 1997—. Team leader Northwestern Human Svcs. Delaware County, 1998-99; dir. PsychOptions, 2000—; v.p. editl. ops. MedCases, Phila., 2000—. Author: (with others) Canadian Nurse, 1976; acquisition editor: Saunders Manual of Medical Practice; contbr. Basic Nursing Skills, 1977. Mem. ANA, Am. Group Psychotherapy Assn., Am. Psychiat. Nurses Assn., Am. Group Psychotherapy Assn., Am. Med. Pubs. Assn., Am. Med. Writers Assn., Med. Mktg. Assn., Assn. Am. Pubs. (med. mktg. assoc.), Internat. Soc. Psychiat. Mental Health Nurses (web editor, membership com.), Forum Exec. Women, The Manuscript Soc., Assn. Profl. Comm. Cons., Internat. Platform Assn., Emily's List, Am. Orthopsychiat. Assn., U.S. Dressage Fedn., Inc., Internat. Soc. Traumatic Stress Studies, Montgomery County C. of C., Sigma Theta Tau (Xi chpt.). Avocations: autograph and art collection, travel, francophile, French music, reading. Office: Medcases 1401 Walnut St Philadelphia PA 19102-3128 E-mail: ddped@aol.com., psychoptions@aol.com., ddpubnet@aol.com.

PEDERSEN, KAREN SUE, electrical engineer; b. Indianola, Iowa, Apr. 27, 1942; d. Donald Cecil and Dorothy Darlene (Frazier) Kading; m. Wendell Dean Pedersen, May 6, 1961; children: Debra Ann Pedersen Schwickerath, Michael Dean. AA, Grand View Coll., Des Moines, 1975; BSEE, Iowa State U., 1977; MBA, Bentley Coll., Waltham, Mass., 1989. Registered profl. engr., Mass., Iowa, Ill. Engr. Iowa Power & Light Co., Des Moines, 1978-80, rate engr., 1980-84; sr. rsch. engr. Boston Edison Co., Boston, 1984-87, sr. engr., 1987-94, prin. rsch. analyst, 1994-98; sr. engr. Mid Am. Energy Co., Davenport, Iowa, 1998—. Ops. chmn. Old South Ch., Boston, 1989-98. Mem. IEEE (chmn. Iowa ctrl. sect. 1983-84, sec. Iowa-Ill. sect., exec. bd.), NSPE, Mass. Soc. Profl. Engrs. (pres. 1992-93, NSPE/PEI vice chair northeast region 1995-97, sec. 1997-98, chair elect 1998-99, v.p. NSPE/PEI, v.p NSPE 1999-2000, v.p. NSPE/North Ctrl. region 2001—), Eta Kappa Nu. Republican. Congregationalist. Office: Mid Am Energy Co 106 E 2nd St # D Davenport IA 52801-1502 E-mail: KSPedersen@midamerican.com.

PEDERSEN, KNUD GEORGE, economics educator, academic administrator; b. Three Creeks, Alta., Can., June 13, 1931; s. Hjalmar Neilsen and Anna (Jensen) P.; m. Joan Elaine Vanderwarker, Aug. 15, 1953 (dec. 1988); children: Greg, Lisa; m. Penny Ann Jones, Dec. 31, 1988. Diploma in Edn., Provincial Normal U., 1952; BA, U. B.C., 1959; MA, U. Wash., 1964; PhD, U. Chgo., 1969; LLD (hon.), McMaster U., 1996. Asst. prof. econs. of edn. U. Toronto; asst. prof. econs. of edn., assoc. dir. U. Chgo., 1970-72; dean, assoc. prof., then prof. U. Victoria, B.C., 1972-75, acad. v.p., prof., 1975-79; pres., vice-chancellor, prof. Simon Fraser U., Vancouver, B.C., 1979-83; pres., prof. U. B.C., 1983-85; pres., vice-chancellor U. Western Ont., London, Can., 1985-94, prof. econs. of edn. Can., 1985-96; interim pres. U. No. B.C., 1995; founding pres., vice-chancellor Royal Roads U., 1995-96; chancellor U. No. B.C., 1998—. Bd. dirs. Assn. Univs. and Colls., Canada, 1979—84, chmn., Canada, 1989—91; bd. dirs. Vancouver Bd. Trade, 1983—85; pres. Can. Club Vancouver, 1983—84; mem. coun. trustees Inst. for Rsch. on Pub. Policy, Ottawa, Ont., Canada, 1983—89; chmn. Coun. Ont. Univs., 1989—91. Author: The Itinerant Schoolmaster, 1972; contbr. chpts. to books, numerous articles to profl. jours. Apptd. officer Order of Can., Order of Ont., Order of BC; recipient 125th Anniversary of Confedn. of Can. medal, Queen's Jubilee medal; fellow Ford Found., 1965-68, Can. Coll. Tchrs., 1977, Royal Soc. for Encouragement of Arts, 1984; also 11 major scholarships. Mem. Semiahmoo Golf and Country Club. Avocations: golf, fishing, gardening. E-mail: pedersen@sfu.ca.

PEDERSEN, LEE G. chemistry educator; b. Oklahoma City, June 15, 1938; s. Leonard Melnot Pedersen and Naomi Shinn; m. Barbara L. Pedersen; children: Lars, Kurt. B in Chemistry, U. Tulsa, 1961; PhD in Chemistry, U. Ark., 1965. From asst. prof. to prof. chemistry U. N.C., Chapel Hill, 1967—, now M.A. Smith prof. chemistry. Cons. NIEHS, Research Triangle Park, N.C., 1985—. Author: Problems in Quantum Chemistry and Physics, 1974. NSF fellow, Columbia U., N.Y.C., 1965-66, NIH fellow Harvard U., Boston, 1966-67. Office: Dept Chemistry U NC Chapel Hill CB 3290 Chapel Hill NC 27599

PEDERSEN, MICHAEL, research scientist; b. Holbaek, Denmark, Nov. 29, 1969; s. Ib and Anne Pedersen. MSc, Tech. U. Denmark, Lyngby, 1993; PhD, U. Twente, Enschede, The Netherlands, 1997. Cert. elec. engring. Rsch. asst. Micro Electronics/Materials Engring/Sensors/Actuators Inst., Enschede, 1993-97; rsch. engr. Knowles Electronics, Rolling Meadows, Ill., 1997-2000; MEMS designer Corp. Nat. Rsch. Initiatives, Reston, Va., 2000—. Contbr. articles to profl. jours. Mem.: IEEE, Accoustical Soc. Am. Avocations: reading, music, sports. E-mail: pedersen@mems-exchange.org.

PEDERSEN, NORMAN ARNO, JR. retired headmaster, literary club director; b. Harvey, Ill., May 27, 1927; s. Norman Arno and Helen Baker (Reeves) P.; m. Isabel Whitla Braham, June 24, 1950; children: Selina, Norman A. III, Laura. AB, Princeton U., 1949; MA, U. Buffalo, 1958. Tchr., coach Nichols Sch., Buffalo, 1954-69; headmaster Brunswick Sch., Greenwich, Conn., 1969-88; interim headmaster Erie (Pa.) Day Sch., 1989-90, ret., 1989; dir. Chautauqua (N.Y.) Lit. and Sci. Cir., 1992-96. Mem. adv. bd. Braitmeyer Found., Boston, 1987-91. Cmty. divsn. chair United Way Campaign, Greenwich, Conn., 1986-87; bd. dirs. Greenwich Coun. on Youth and Drugs, 1979-88; elder First Presbyn. Ch., Greenwich, 1971-74. Fulbright summer grantee, 1961. Mem. Country Day Sch. Headmasters Assn., Exec. Svc. Corps Manasota. Avocations: reading, fly-fishing, golf, swimming, bicycle riding. Home: 3702 Sun Eagle Ln Bradenton FL 34210-4236

PEDERSEN, PAUL BODHOLDT, psychologist, educator; b. Ringsted, Iowa, May 19, 1936; BA in History and Philosophy, U. Minn., 1958, MA in Am. Studies, 1959; ThM, Luth. Sch. Theology, Chgo., 1962; MA in Ednl. Psychology, U. Minn., 1966; PhD in Asian Studies, Claremont (Calif.) Grad. Sch., 1968. Asst. prof. dept. psychoednl. studies, psychologist U. Minn., Mpls., 1971-75; sr. fellow Culture Learning Inst. East-West Ctr., Honolulu, 1975-76, sr. fellow coord., 1975-76; assoc. prof. dept. psychoednl. studies, psychologist U. Minn., 1975-79, higher edn. coord., 1976-77; sr. fellow Culture Learning Inst. East-West Ctr., 1979-81; prof., chmn. dept. counselor edn. Syracuse (N.Y.) U., 1982-90, prof. edn. dept. counseling and human svcs., 1989—95, adj. prof. dept. internat. rels., 1993—95, prof. emeritus, 2000—; prof. counseling edn. U. Ala., Birmingham, 1996-2001. Vis. lectr. Nommensen U., Medan, Sumatra, Indonesia, 1962—65, U. Malaya, 1969—71; vis. prof. dept. psychology U. Hawaii, 1978—81, 2000—; spkr. in field. Author numerous books, chpts. in books, articles to profl. jours.; mem. editl. bd. Am. Jour. Multicultural Counseling and Devel.; editl. advisor Jour. Profl. Psychology, Jour. Simulation and Games, Internat. Jour. Intercultural Rels. Sr. Fulbright fellow Nat. Taiwan U., Taipei, 1999-2000. Mem. APA, Am. Assn. Counseling and Devel. Internat. (mem. rels. com., editl. bd. Jour. Counseling and Devel., editor Internationally Speaking newsletter, mentor media com.), Internat. Assn. for Cross Cultural Psychology, Internat. Coun. Psychologists, Soc. Intercultural Tng. and Rsch. (exec. com., program chairperson 1977, chairperson Pacific Com. 1977, pres. 1978-80, editl. bd. Jour. Intercultural Rels.).

PEDERSEN, PEDIE, physiology educator; b. Milan, Apr. 12, 1948; d. E.E. and Bettye M. Pedersen. BA, Rhodes Coll., 1970; MS, U. Ala., 1972; BS, U. New Orleans, 1977; PhD, Tulane U., 1986. Tchr. biology Holy Name Sch. and Chapelle H.S., New Orleans, 1978-81; vis. instr., postdoctoral fellow Tulane U., 1986-87; asst. prof. physiology Delgado C.C., 1987-91, assoc. prof., 1991—. Author: Human Anatomy and Physiology: Lecture Outlines and Self Tests I and II, 1995. Mem. Human Anatomy and Physiology Soc., Sweet Adelines, Sigma Xi. Office: Delgado Cmty Coll 615 City Park Ave New Orleans LA 70119

PEDERSEN, RICHARD FOOTE, diplomat and academic administrator; b. Miami, Ariz., Feb. 21, 1925; s. Ralph Martin and Gertrude May (Foote) P.; m. Nelda Newell Napier, May 9, 1953; children: Paige Elizabeth, Jonathan Foote, Kendra Gayle. BA summa cum laude, Coll. of Pacific, 1946; MA, Stanford U., 1947; PhD, Harvard U., 1950; LLD (hon.), George Williams Coll., 1964, U. of Pacific, 1966; DHL (hon.), Am. U., Cairo, 1997. Teaching fellow, tutor Harvard U., Cambridge, Mass., 1949-50; with UN econ. and social affairs Dept. State, Washington, 1950-53; adviser econ. and social affairs U.S. Mission to UN, N.Y.C., 1953—55, adviser polit. and security affairs, 1956-59, sr. advisor polit. and security affairs, 1959-64, minister, counselor, 1964-66, ambassador, sr. adviser to U.S. rep., 1966-67; ambassador, dep. U.S. rep. UN Security Coun., 1967—69; counselor Dept. State, 1969-73; ambassador to Hungary, 1973-75; sr. v.p. internat. U.S. Trust Co., 1975-78; pres. Am. U., Cairo, 1978-90; dir. internat. programs Calif. Poly Pomona U., 1990-95. Mem. adv. bd. Nat. Coun. U.S.-Arab Rels., 1985—; trustee Consortium for Internat. Devel., 1990—95; mem. adv. bd. Ctr. Near Eastern Studies UCLA, 1996—99; adv. bd. Sch. Internat. Studies, U. Pacific, 1997—. Mem. Nat. Coun. YMCAs, 1961-73; bd. dirs. Ctr. for Civic Edn., 1995—, Physicians for Peace, 1988-90; mem. Fulbright bd., Egypt, 1980-82, adv. bd. Fulbright Cultural Enrichment Program, So. Calif., 1991—. With AUS, 1943-45 ETO. Recipient Sumner Peace prize Harvard U., 1950, Outstanding Alumnus award U. Pacific, 1962, Order of Sacred Treasure, Gold and Silver Star, Govt. of Japan, 1987; named One of 10 Outstanding Young Men, U.S. Jr. C. of C., 1956; awarded Order of Scis. and Arts, first class Govt. of Egypt, 1990. Mem. Royal Inst. Internat. Affairs, Coun. Fgn. Rels., Am. Soc. Internat. Law, L.A. World Affairs Coun., Am. Fgn. Svc. Assn., Mid. East Inst., Oriental Inst., UN Assn. Am., Internat. Assn. Univ. Pres., Pacific Coun. Internat. Policy, Asia Soc. Clubs: Harvard (N.Y.); Cosmos (Washington). Democrat. Congregationalist. Avocations: swimming, tennis, Egyptology, local history. Home: 2503 N Mountain Ave Claremont CA 91711-1545 E-mail: rfpdrsn@earthlink.net.

PEDERSEN, WESLEY NIELS M. public relations and public affairs executive; b. South Sioux City, Nebr., July 10, 1922; s. Peder Westergaard and Marie Gertrude (Sorensen) P.; m. Angeline Kathryn Vavra, Oct. 17, 1948; 1 son, Eric Wesley. Student, Tri-State Coll., Sioux City, Iowa, 1940-41; BA summa cum laude, Upper Iowa U.; postgrad., George Washington U., 1958-59. Editor, writer Sioux City Jour., 1941-50; corr. N.Y. Times, Life, Time, Fortune, 1948-50; editor Dept. State, 1950-53, fgn. svc. officer, 1960-63; fgn. affairs columnist, roving corr., counselor summit meetings and fgn. ministers confs. USIA, 1953-60, chief, worldwide spl. publs. and graphics programs, 1963-69; chief Office Spl. Projects, Washington, 1969-78, Office Spl. Projects, Internat. Comm. Agy., 1978-79; v.p. Fraser Assocs., pub. rels., Washington, 1979-80; dir. comm. and pub. rels. Pub. Affairs Coun., 1980—. Lectr. creative comm. Upper Iowa U., 1975; chmn., Europe, Ambassadorial Internat. Affairs Seminar, Fgn. Svc. Inst., 1975; lectr. internat. pub. rels. Pub. Rels. Inst., Am. U., 1976; lectr. bus. and mgmt. divsn. NYU, 1976, 77, 78; cons. pub. rels., editl. and design; del. founding sessions 1st Amendment Congress, Phila. and Williamsburg, Va., 1980, mem. exec. com., 1980. Columnist: (as Paul L. Ford) The World Today, 1952-60; (as Benjamin E. West) Behind the Curtain, 1952-60; White House Report, 1966-69 (as Wesley Pedersen), Washington Report-Pub. Rels. Jour., 1980-85; author: Mr. President: Lyndon B. Johnson, 1964, Legacy of a President, 1964, Journey to the Pacific, 1965, Mr. President: Richard M. Nixon, 1969, American Heroes of Asian Wars, 1969; co-author: Effective Government Public Affairs, 1981; editor: The Imam's Story, 1961, Escape at Midnight and Other Stories (Pearl S. Buck), 1962, Exodus From China (Harry Redl), 1962, Macao, 1962, The Dividing Line (Arturo Gonzalez), 1962, China's Men of Letters (K.E. Priestley), 1963, Children of China (Pearl S. Buck and Margaret Wylie), 1963, Destination the Moon (William Howard), 1964, Man on the Moon, 1964, Nine From Little Rock, 1964, To the Moon and Beyond, 1965, Bounty From the Land, 1965, Workers Paradise Lost (Eugene Lyons), 1967, The Americans and the Arts (Howard Taubman), 1969, The Dance in America (Agnes de Mille), 1969, Getting the Most From Grassroots Public Affairs Programs, 1980, Computer Applications in Public Affairs, 1984, Cost-Effective Management for Today's Public Affairs, 1984, Making Community Relations Pay Off: Tools and Strategies, 1988, Winning at the Grassroots: How to Succeed in the Legislative Arena by Mobilizing Employees and Other Allies, 1989, Leveraging State Government Relations, 1990, Managing the Business-Employee PAC, 1992, Adding Value to the Public Affairs Function, 1994, Winning at the Grassroots (with Tony Kramer), 2000, Managing the Corporate Action Committee, 2001; Pub. Affairs Rev. Mag., 1980-86, 2000, 01, 02, Impact newsletter on nat. and internat. pub. affairs, 1980—; contbr. to The Commissar, 1972, Informing the People: A Public Affairs Handbook, 1981, The Practice of Public Relations, 1984, Pub. Affairs Rev., 2000, 01, 02; mem. editl. bd. Pub. Rels. Quar., 1975—, Washington correspondent, Pub. Rels. quarterly, 1998—, Fgn. Svc. Jour., 1975-81; mem. adv. bd. Pub. Rels. News, 1991-98; author scripts Uncle Walter's Doghouse radio show, 1983; contbr. articles to profl. jours. Founding chmn. bd. dirs. Nat. Inst. for Govt. Pub. Info. Rsch., Am. U., 1977-80. Served with USAAF, 1943-46. Recipient 2 awards A.P. Mng. Editors Assn., Iowa, 1949, Meritorious Svc. award USIA, 1963, Superior Svc. award USIA, 1964, Presdl. commendation, 1964, 70, 1st prizes Fed. Editors Assn., 1970, 74-75, Agy. Dir.'s citation USIA, 1974, 78, 1st prizes Soc. Tech. Comm., 1974, 75-76, Gold award Internat. Newsletter Conf., 1982, Silver award, 1985, Eddi award for design excellence Editor's Workshop, 1983, Gold Circle award for outstanding comm. Am. Soc. Assn. Execs., 1983-89, 97, 98, 99, 2000, Ten Cool award Am. Soc. Assn. Execs., 2001, Editors' Forum award, 1988-90, 94, 95, 96, Assn. Trends award, 1989-2002, 1st ann. Great Assn. Communicator award, Assn. Trends, 1999, Best of Century Comm. award, Assn. Trends, 2001, spl. citation Assn. Trends, 2001; Grand prize Internat. Ann. Report Conf., 1989, Gold award 1997, Comm. Concepts awards, 1989—, Grand awards, 1992, 2000, MerComm awards, 1990-2000, Nat. Media Conf. award, 1989, 90, Internat. Acad. Comm. Arts and Scis. award, 1994, 95, 96, 97, 98, 2000, Grand prize, 1995, awards Printing and Graphic Assn., 1987, 91, 96, 97, 2000, Excell award Soc. of Nat. Assn. Publishers, 2000, Judges award 2000; named Most Outstanding Info. Officer in Exec. Br. Govt. Info. Orgn., 1975, Ky. Col. and Adm. Nebr. Navy, 1984. Mem. DAV, Am. Fgn. Svc. Assn., Am. Legion, Internat. Assn. Bus. Communicators (Communicator of Yr. Washington chpt. 1978, various awards 1973, 76-78, 84, 90, 94, 95, 96, 97, 98, 99, 2000, 01, Winners' Circle awards dist. III 1996-2002), Nat. Assn. Govt. Communicators (pres. 1978-79, Communicator of Yr. 1977, Disting. Svc. award 1978), Pub. Rels. Soc. Am. (mem. Counselor's Acad. 1980—, chmn. 1st Amendment task force 1980-81, co-recipient Thoth award 1980, 81, 94, recipient twin Thoth awards 1995, 96, 97, 3 Thoth awards 1998, 2 Thoth awards 1999, 2 Thoth awards 2000, 01, Bronze Anvil award 2000, 2 Thoth tropies 2001), World Affairs Coun., Soc. of Profl. Journalists, The Acad. Polit. Sci., Fgn. Svc. Club, Nat. Press Club, Overseas Press Club. Episcopalian. Home: 4701 Willard Ave Apt 1007 Chevy Chase MD 20815-4622 Office: Pub Affairs Coun 2033 K St NW Ste 700 Washington DC 20006-1019 E-mail: wpedersen@pac.org. *Keenness of mind and an abundance of luck, it is said, are the key ingredients of personal success. The truth be told, however, I've performed only one act of brilliance* *in my lifetime: the selection of my parents. But I've had an enormous amount of good fortune, a fact manifestly clear to anyone who has ever met my wife, my son and my granddaughters. They, thank goodness, chose me.*

PEDERSEN, WILLIAM FRANCIS, lawyer; b. N.Y.C., Apr. 4, 1943; s. William F. and Priscilla S. (Auchincloss) P.; m. Ellen L. Frost, Feb. 2, 1974; children: Mark Francis, Claire Ellen. BA, Harvard U., 1965, LLB, 1968. Bar: Mass. 1969, D.C. 1978. Assoc. Ropes & Gray, Boston, 1969-72; staff atty. EPA, Washington, 1972-75, dep. gen. counsel, then assoc. gen. counsel, 1976-85; staff counsel Senate Com. on Govt. Ops., Washington, 1975-76; lectr. Harvard Law Sch., 1985-86; of counsel Perkins Coie, Washington, 1987—89, ptnr., 1989-94, Shaw, Pittman, Potts & Trowbridge, Washington, 1994-2001; pvt. practice, 2001—. Vis. prof. Law Sch., U. Mich., 1997-98. Contbr. articles to profl. jours. Mem. ABA (standing com. on environ. law 1987-89). Republican. Episcopalian. Office: William F Pedersen PLLC Ste 800 1752 N St NW Washington DC 20036 E-mail: bill.pedersen@billpedersen.com.

PEDERSON, GORDON ROY, state legislator, retired military officer; b. Gayville, S.D, Aug. 8, 1927; s. Roy E. and Gladys F. (Masker) P.; m. Betty L. Ballard, Mar. 8, 1955; children: James D., Carol A. Pederson Niemann, Nancy G. Pederson Holub, Gary W. Student, Yankton Coll., 1948-50, Fla. State U., 1963; advanced course, Infantry Sch., 1958-59. Drafted U.S. Army, 1945-47, commd. 2nd lt., 1952, advanced through grades to lt. col., 1967, served Korean War, 1950-54, served CONUS World War II, platoon leader 17th infantry regiment, 7th infantry divsn. Korea, 1953-54, rifle co. commdr. 10th mountain divsn. Germany, 1955-58, instr., dir. instrn. U.S. Army Jungle Warfare Tng. Ctr. Canal Zone, 1961-63, comdr. post Canal Zone, 1963-64, 1st brig., 1st infantry divsn. Vietnam, 1965-66, dir. tng. hdqs., 1966-68; advisor Ministry of Nat. Def., Rep. China on Taiwan, 1969-70; retired U.S. Army, 1970; rep. S.D. Ho. Reps., Pierre, 1977-99, 2001—; operator Dairy Queen, Wall, S.D., 1990-95. Chmn. transp. com. S.D. Ho. Reps., 1979-93, vice chair state affairs com., 1996-98, vice chair commerce com., 1998, chmn. budget audit com., 2001—, vice chmn. transp. com., 2001—. Del. S.D. Rep. Conv., 1974-78, 80, 82, 84, 86, 88, 90, 92, 94, 96, 98, 2000, 02, Nat. Rep. Conv., 1976, 80, 84, 88, 92, 96, 2000; bd. dirs. Legis. Rsch. Coun., 1988, 90, 92, 96, 98, 2001—. Decorated Bronze Star, Medal of Merit, U.S. Presdl. Unit Citation, Rep. Korea Presdl. Unit Citation, Rep. Vietnam Presdl. Unit Citation, Combat Infantry Badge with Star, Legion of Merit, Air Medal with 2 Oak Leaf Clusters, Army Accomodation medal with 2 oak leaf clusters, Cross of Gallantry with Palm, Republic Vietnam. Mem. VFW, DAV, Am. Legion, Retired Officers Assn., Wall C. of C., Internat. Lions Club, Sons of Norway. Lutheran. Home: PO Box 312 116 W 7th St Wall SD 57790 Office: SD Ho of Reps State Capitol Bldg Pierre SD 57501 E-mail: bpers@GWTC.net., gordonpederson@state.U.S.S.D.

PEDERSON, JIM, political party official; B in Polit. Sci., 1965, M in Pub. Adminstrn., 1967. Intern City of Tucson, Ariz.; admin. asst. office of rsch. City of Phoenix; with US Senate campaign of Sam Grossman, Westcor; owner devel. co., 1983; chmn. State Dem. Party Ariz., 2001—. Office: 2910 N Central Ave Phoenix AZ 85012 Office Fax: 602-298-7117. Business E-Mail: jpederson@azdem.org.*

PEDERSON, JOHN, music educator, musician; b. Grafton, Nd, Jan. 19, 1955; s. Marvin Victor and Lois Eileen Pederson; m. Marlys Mae Pederson, June 14, 1975; children: Sara, Scott, Ross. BS, Mayville State U., Mayville, ND, 1974—78; MM, U. of ND, Grand Forks, ND, 1990—91. Band dir. Walhalla Pub. Sch., Walhalla, ND, 1982—83, Grafton Pub. Schools, Grafton, 1983—94, Fargo Pub. Schools, Fargo, 1994—. Musician Richard King Big Band, Grand Forks, ND, 1979—89, Fargo-Moorhead Jazz Arts Band, Fargo, ND, 1994—. Recipient Tchr. Of The Yr., Grafton Pub. Schools, 1988. Achievements include released solo album entitled Live Performances of John Pederson; Frequently Play Solo Trumpet On Many Area Album Projects. Home: 2326 25th Avenue South Fargo ND 58103 Personal E-mail: pedersj@i29.net.

PEDERSON, KATHRYN MARIE, human resources professional; b. Minot, N.D., Apr. 28, 1958; d. Clifford Artine and Leona (Schlecht) Lang; m. Robert Norman Pederson, Oct. 11, 1986. BA, Minot State U., 1984; MA, U. Mary, 1989. Mgr. Answer Dakota Answering Svc., Minot, 1980-82; legal sec. Teevens, Johnson, Montgomery, 1982-86; acctg. clk. Interstate Brands Corp., 1986; data input operator N.D. Legis. Coun., Bismarck, N.D., 1986-87; asst. Bismarck Pub. Schs./Tech. Enabling Disabled Individuals, 1987-89; state tech. dir. Dept. Pub. Instrn., 1989-92; instructional tech. adminstr. Prairie Pub. Broadcasting, Fargo, 1992-95; ctr. dir. N.D. State Coll. of Sci., 1995-96; human resource officer First Am. Bank West, Minot, 1996-99; mgr. human resources ReliaStar Svc. Ctr., 1999—. Editor: (newsletter) CEC Newsletter, 1987-89, TEDIgram, 1987-89, Superintendent's Report, 1990-92; author: (newsletter) TecTalk, 1990-92, No. Plains Corvette newsletter, 1995—. Fin. com. Faith United Meth. Ch., Minot, 1986. Named ann. premier performer Bremer Fin., 1996, 97. Mem. N.D. Edn. Assn., N.D. Libr. Assn., Assn. Instrnl. Tech., N.D. Ednl. Telecommunications Coun. (exec. dir. 1989-92), Okla. State U. Satellite Program (adv. coun. 1989-92), Satellite Ednl. Resources Consortium (adv. coun. 1989-92), Jaycees (Outstanding Fundraiser 1989, Jaycee of Month 1989, Outstanding Com. chmn. 1989, Project of Yr. 1989, Top Mem. Recruiter 1990, Bremer Ann. Premier Performer award 1996, 97). Methodist. Avocations: sport related activities. Office: PO Box 5050 Minot ND 58702-5050

PEDERSON, LINDA LUE, epidemiologist, researcher; d. Richard and Lucy (Kouyoumjian) Johnson; m. David R. Pederson, June 12, 1965 (div. 1983); children: Ingrid, Erica, Kristen; m. Frederick D. Hamilton, Dec. 8, 2002. BA, Brown U., 1964; MA, Inst. Child Behavior & Devel., U. Iowa, 1966; PhD, U. Western Ont., London, Can., 1980. Tchr. devel. psychology U. Western Ont., 1968-73, rsch. asst. dept. medicine, 1973-76, tchg. asst. dept. epidemiology and preventive medicine, 1978, asst. prof. dept. medicine, 1980-84, assoc. prof. dept. epidemiology and biostats., 1984-93, prof., 1993-95, prof. cmty. health and preventive medicine, 1995-99, dir. rsch., 1995—. Assoc. dir. Drew-Meharry-Morehouse Consortum Cancer Ctr., 1996-97; sr. staff fellow Office on Smoking and Health, CDC. Contbr. more than 130 articles and revs. to sci. publs. Recipient numerous grants, fellowships and scholarships. Avocations: fitness, cats, music. Office: CDC/OSH NCCDPHP MS K-50 4770 Buford Hwy Atlanta GA 30341-3717

PEDERSON, RENA, newspaper editor; Editor-at-large Dallas Morning News, 1986—. Office: The Dallas Morning News PO Box 655237 508 Young St Dallas TX 75265

PEDERSON, SALLY, lieutenant governor; b. Muscatine, Iowa, Jan. 13, 1951; d. Gerald and Wineva Pederson; m. James A. Autry, Feb. 6, 1982; children: Rick, Jim Jr., Ronald. Grad., Iowa State U., 1973. With Meredith Corp., 1973-84; sr. food editor Better Homes & Gardens mag.; lt. gov. State of Iowa, 1999—. Pres. Polk County Health Svcs.; bast bd. trustees Nat. Alliance for Autism Rsch.; pres. bd. trustees Autism Soc. Iowa; founding pres. The Homestead Living and Learning Ctr. for Adults with Autism; past cmty. bd. svcs. includes Des Moines Cmty. Playhouse, Very Spl. Arts Iowa, YWCA Aliber Child Care Ctr., YMCA Ctr. Br.; parent rep. Heartland AEA Autism Steering Com.; mem. Iowa State Spl. Edn. Adv. Bd; bd. dirs. Blank Children's Hosp., Mid-Iowa Health Found.; gov.'s appointee State Spl. Edn. Adv. Panel. Office: Office of Lt Governor State Capitol Bldg Des Moines IA 50319-0001*

PEDERSON, WILLIAM DAVID, political scientist, educator; b. Eugene, Oreg., Mar. 17, 1946; s. Jon Moritz and Rose Marie (Ryan) P. BS in Polit. Sci., U. Oreg., 1967, MA in Polit. Sci., 1972, PhD in Polit. Sci., 1979. Tchg. asst. polit. sci. dept. U. Oreg., Eugene, 1975-77; instr. govt. dept. Lamar U., Beaumont, Tex., 1977-79; asst. prof. polit. sci. dept. Westminster Coll., Fulton, Mo., 1979-80; asst. prof., head polit. sci. and pre-law Yankton Coll. U. S.D., 1980-81; prof., Am. Studies Chair, dir. Internat. Lincoln Ctr. La. State U., Shreveport, 1981—; program analyst NIH, Bethesda, Md., summer 1973; assoc. prof. jr. state program Am. U., Washington, summer 1984; prof. jr. state program Georgetown U., 1997—; rsch. assoc. Russian and East European Ctr./U. Ill., Urbana, summers 1982—; founding dir. Washington semester La. State U., Shreveport, 1982-91, 96—, with Presdl. Conf. Series, 1992—, with ann. Abraham Lincoln lecture series/Am. Studies program, 1982—. Editl. staff writer: The Times, Shreveport, 1990.; author: The Rating Game in American Politics, 1987; editor: The Barberian Presidency, 1989; Congressional-Presidential Relations: Governmental Gridlock, 1991; co-editor: Grassroots Constitutionalism, 1988; Morality and Conviction in American Politics, 1990, Great Justices of the U.S. Supreme Court: Ratings and Case Studies, 1993, 2d edit., 1994, Lincoln and Leadership: A Model for a Summer Teachers Inst., 1993; Abraham Lincoln: Sources and Style of Leadership, 1994, Abraham Lincoln: Contemporary, 1995, 2d printing, 96; guest editor: Quarterly Jour. Ideology, 1994; co-editor: Jour. of Contemporary Thought, 1997—; editor: FDR and the Modern Presidency: Leadership and Legacy, 1997, Lincoln Forum: Abraham Lincoln, Gettysburg and the Civil War, 1999, George Washington's Image in American Culture, 2001, George Washington and the Origins of the American Presidency, 2000, George Washington: Foundations of Leadership and Character, 2001, Franklin D. Roosevelt and the Shaping of American Culture, 2001, Franklin D. Roosevelt and Congress, 2001; The New Deal and Public Policy, 1998; editor: The Polit. Sci. Educator, 1996-98, Abraham Lincoln Abroad, 1998—; founding editor Washington Semesters and Internships, 1998—, Internat. Abraham Lincoln Jour., 2000—; contbr. articles to profl. jours.; founder La. Lincolnator, 1994. Mem. Mayor's Comm. on the Bicentennial U.S. Constn., 1987; active Barnwell Ctr., Shreveport, 1984, Am. Rose Soc., Shreveport, 1982. Served with U.S. Army, 1968-70. Recipient Tng. award NIH, 1973, Outstanding Prof. award Westminster Coll. 1980, La. State U., 1984, Cultural Olympiad award, 1995, Page Shreveport Rose Shreveport Times Jour., 1995; grantee La. State U., 1982, La. Endowment for Humanities, 1987, 93, 95, 96, 97; fellow NEH, 1981-85. Fellow Am. Polit. Sci. Assn., Am. Judicature Soc.; mem. Abraham Lincoln Assn. (mem. bd. dirs. 1994, Achievement award 1994, dir. conf. in the south, 1992, dir. 1st summer Inst. on Abraham Lincoln, 1993, grantee 1992, 93), Ctr. Study Presidency, Internat. Soc. Polit. Psychology, Washington Semesters and Internship Assn., Internat. Lincoln Assn. (bd. dirs. 1994-95, pres. 1990-93, chair bd. dirs. 1998—), La. Hist. Assn. (bd. dirs. 2001—). Office: La State U Internat Lincoln Ctr 1 University Pl # 148 Bh Shreveport LA 71115-2301 E-mail: wpederso@pilot.lsus.edu.

PEDESCLEAUX-MUCKLE, GAIL, financial consultant, writer, poet; b. Cleve., June 20, 1949; d. Alfonso Pedescleaux and Belle Pinkard Pedescleaux; m. Kirk Muckle, Oct. 24, 1997; 1 stepchild Christopher Cor Muckle. BA in English Lit., Ctrl. Mich. U., 1971. Acct. asst. Travelers Ins. Co., Southfield, Mich., 1972—79, underwriter Garden City, NY, 1979—81, Commerce and Industry, N.Y.C., 1981—83; sr. underwriter Firemans' Fund, 1983—85; bus. analyst Am. Internat. Group, 1985—94, sr. quality assurance analyst Livingston, NJ, 1994—2000, sr. bus. analyst Parsippany, 2000—. Author: (anthology) America at the Millennium, 2000 (Editor's Choice, 2000), Poetry's Elite: The Best Poets of 2000, 2001 (Editor's Choice, 2001), Nature's Echoes, 2001 (Editor's Choice, 2001). Mem. DAV: Comdr.'s Club, 1993—, Nat. Multiple Sclerosis Soc., 1994—, Nat. Trust, 1993—. Avocations: writing poetry, writing children's stories, jazzercise, photography, attending plays. Home: 54 Rainford Rd Edison NJ 08820-2903 Office: Am Internat Group 9 Entin Rd Parsippany NJ 07054

PEDINI, EGLE DAMIJONAITIS, radiologist; b. Kaunas, Lithuania, July 22, 1943; d. Vytautas and Elena Damijonaitis; m. Kenneth Pedini, June 4, 1966; children: David Durand, Julian Adam. BA cum laude, MD, Boston U., 1967. Diplomate Am. Bd. Radiology. Intern St. Elizabeth's Hosp., Brighton, Mass., 1967-68; resident in radiology Boston City Hosp., 1968-71; radiologist St. John's Hosp., Lowell, Mass., 1972, Chelmsford (Mass.) X-Ray, 1979-80, Amesbury (Mass.) Hosp./Amesbury Health Ctr., 1973-98, New Eng. Meml. Hosp./Boston Regional Med. Ctr., Stoneham, Mass., 1973-98, Anna Jacques Hosp., Newburyport, 1973-98. Ptnr. NE Radiology Assocs., Brockton, Mass., 1980-98; chief radiology Anna Jacques Hosp., Newburyport, Mass., 1984, Amesbury Hosp., 1988, 89, 90. Founder, bd. dirs. Andover Sch. Montessori, Mass., 1974-79; parent ann. fundraising com. Phillips Exeter (N.H.), 1985, 86, 87. Mem. Am. Coll. Radiology, Mass. Radiol. Soc., New Eng. Roentgen Ray Soc., Stonehorse Yacht Club, Wychmere Harbor Club, Hyannis Yacht Club, Chatham Women's Club.

PEDINI, KENNETH, radiologist; b. Hartford, Conn., Mar. 19, 1940; s. Daniel Victor and Elizabeth Catherine Pedini; m. Egle Damijonaitis; children: David D., Julian A. AB in Philosophy, Trinity Coll., 1962; MD, Boston U., 1966. Diplomate Nat. Bd. Med. Examiners, Am. Bd. Radiology. Resident in radiology Boston City Hosp., 1967-70, chief resident in radiology, 1969-70, jr. staff radiologist, 1970-71, U. Hosp., Boston, 1970-71; ptnr. Shawsheen Radiology, Andover, Mass., 1971-98; sr. radiologist Lawrence (Mass.) Gen. Hosp., 1971—, dir. radiology, 1976-87; sr. radiologist Melrose (Mass.)-Wakefield Hosp., 1971-99, chief radiologist, 1993-97, emeritus staff, 1999; pres. L & M Radiology Inc, Andover, Mass., 1994-98. Bd. trustees Lawrence Gen. Hosp., 1984-89, fin. com., 1986—. Trustee Lawrence Gen. Hosp. Health Enterprises, Inc., 1990-93; fin. com. Lawrence Gen. Regional Health Sys., 1996—; co-founder Andover Sch. of Montessori, 1975—; alumni adv. com. Trinity Coll., 1995; mem. Harwich Water Quality Mgmt. Task Force, 2001-. Fellow Am. Coll. Radiology (councilor 1979-81); mem. New England Roentgen Ray Soc., Mass. Radiol. Soc. (pres. 1985-86, pres.-elect 1984-85, v.p. 1983-84, exec. com. 1977-87), Mass. Med. Soc., Stonehorse Yacht Club, Algonquin Club. E-mail: wychview@aol.com.

PEDLEY, JOHN GRIFFITHS, archaeologist, educator; b. Burnley, Eng., July 19, 1931; arrived in U.S., 1959, naturalized, 2002; s. George and Anne (Whitaker) Pedley; m. Mary Grace Sponberg, Aug. 30, 1969. BA, Cambridge (Eng.) U., 1953, MA, 1959; postgrad. (Norton fellow), Am. Sch. Classical Studies, Athens, Greece, 1963-64; PhD, Harvard U., 1965. Loeb rsch. fellow in classical archaeology Harvard U., Cambridge, Mass., 1969-70; asst. prof. classical archaeology and Greek U. Mich., Ann Arbor, 1965-68, assoc. prof., 1968-74, acting chmn. dept. classical studies, 1971-72, 75-76; dir. Kelsey Mus. Archaeology, 1973-86, prof., 1974—2002, prof. emeritus, 2002—. Guest scholar J. Paul Getty Mus.; mem. staff excavations, Sardis, Turkey, 1962—64, Pylos, Greece, 1964; co-dir. excavations, Apollonia, Libya, 1966—68; field dir. Corpus Ancient Mosiacs, Tunisia, 1972—73; co-prin. investigator excavations, Carthage, North Africa, 1975—79; dir. excavations, Paestum, Italy, 1982—85, Paestum, 1993, Paestum, 95, Paestum, 1997—98; vis. scholar UCLA, 1989; resident in archaeology Am. Acad., Rome, 1990. Author: (book) Sardis in the Age of Croesus, 1968, Sardis in the Age of Croesus, reprint, 1999, Ancient Literary Sources on Sardis, 1972, Greek Sculpture of the Archaic Period: The Island Workshops, 1976, Paestum: Greeks and Romans in Southern Italy, 1990, Greek Art and Archaeology, 1992, Greek Art and Archaeology, 3d edit., 2002; co-author: Apollonia, the Port of Cyrene, 1977, The Sanctuary of Santa Venera at Paestum, Vol. 1, 1993, Corpus des Mosaiques de Tunisie, Vol. III, 1996; editor: New Light on Ancient Carthage, 1980; co-editor: Studies Presented to GMA Hanfmann, 1971. Fellow Am. Coun. Learned Socs., 1972—73, NEH, 1986; grantee, Am. Philol. Soc., 1979, Nat. Endowment Arts Mus., 1974, 1977, 1979, 1980, NEH, 1967, 1975, 1983, 1984. Home: 1720 Morton Ave Ann Arbor MI 48104-4522 Office: Dept Classical Studies Univ Mich Ann Arbor MI 48109 E-mail: jpedley@umich.edu.

PEDLEY, LAWRENCE LINDSAY, lawyer; b. Hopkinsville, Ky., May 27, 1932; s. Gracean McGoodwin and Elizabeth (Lindsay) Pedley; m. Ellen Mack, Oct. 9, 1957 (div. 1981); children: Lawrence Lindsay Jr., David M., Joan Elizabeth; m. Jill Flick, 1981 (div. 1991); 1 child Jill Katharine ; m. Wanda Polk, Feb. 3, 1995. BA, The Citadel, S.C., 1955; JD, Yale U., 1959. Bar: Ky. 1959, Fla. 1980, U.S. Dist. Ct. Ky. 1959, U.S. Ct. Appeals (6th cir.), 1975, U.S. Supreme Ct. 1981. Prin. atty. Ky. Dept. of Hwys., Frankfort, 1960; v.p. Nat. Industries, Louisville, 1964-66; gen. counsel, v.p., dir. Life Ins. Co. Ky., 1966-69; ptnr. Goldberg & Pedley, 1970-80, Pedley, Zielke & Gordinier, Louisville, 1980—. Owner Exec. Express, Louisville, 1969—80. Capt. JAGC, 1967. Mem. ABA, Ky. Bar Assn., Fla. Bar Assn., Filson Club, Harmony Landing Country Club, Pendennis Club. Office: Pedley Zielke & Gordinier 455 S 4th St Ste 1150 Louisville KY 40202-2512

PEDLEY, TIMOTHY ASBURY, IV, neurologist, educator, researcher; b. Phoenix, Aug. 31, 1943; s. Timothy Asbury Pedley III and Mary Adele (Newcomer) Melis; m. Barbara S. Koppel, Mar. 17, 1984. BA, Pomona Coll., 1965; MD, Yale U., 1969. Cert. neurology, electroencephalography, clin. neurophysiology; diplomate Am. Bd. Psychiatry and Neurology. Intern Stanford U. Hosp., 1969-70; resident in neurology Stanford U., 1970-73, postdoctoral fellow, 1973-75, asst. prof. neurology, 1975-79; from assoc. prof. neurology to prof., vice chmn. Columbia U., 1979-98, Henry and Lucy Moses prof., chmn. neurology, 1998—; neurologist-in-chief Columbia-Presbyn. Med. Ctr., N.Y.C., 1998—. Dir. comprehensive epilepsy ctr. Columbia-Presbyn. Med. Ctr., 1983-97. profl. adv. bd. Epilepsy Found Am., 1984-98, chmn. profl. adv. bd., 1985-87, pres. bd. dirs., 1991-93, chmn. 1993-95. mem. rev. com. NIH Nat. Inst. Neurol. and Chronic Diseases and Strokes, 1985-89, chmn., 1988-89; various adv. coms. NIH/NINDS, 1990—; vis. fellow in exptl. neurology Inst. Psychiatry, London, 1978-79; mem. merit rev. bd. neurobiology rsch., VA, 1992-96, chmn., 1995-96; vis. prof. various univs., U.S. and abroad. Editor-in-chief: Epilepsia, 1993—2001; contbr. articles to profl. jours. Recipient various honors and awards. Fellow Am. Acad. Neurology, Am. Electroencephalographic Soc. (pres. 1989-90, bd. dirs. 1981-85); mem. Am. Neurol. Assn. (coun. 1992-94, treas. 1995-98), Am. Epilepsy Soc. (treas. 1980-83, pres. 1991-92), Soc. for Neurosci., Internat. League Against Epilepsy (exec. com. 1994-2002), Yale Club, Met. Opera Club, Shenorock Shore Club (Rye, N.Y.), Alpha Omega Alpha. Office: The Neurological Inst 710 W 168th St New York NY 10032-2603 Fax: 212-305-6978. E-mail: tap2@columbia.edu.

PEDOTO, GERALD JOSEPH, supplier quality analyst; b. Jersey City, Jan. 5, 1948; s. Salvatore Joseph and Rosalie (Benigno) P.; m. Karen Sue Knutty, June 28, 1975; children: Deborah Louise, Donald Lee, Timothy Scott. BS, Bowling Green (Ohio) State U., 1970; MBA, U. Akron, 1976. Cert. mgr., quality engr., quality auditor. Trainee indsl. engring. Timken Co., Canton, Ohio, 1970, assoc. indsl. engr., 1972-73, supervisory candidate, 1973-74, foreman product inspection, 1974-75, supr. indirect labor, 1975-80, supr. heat treatment, 1980-82, sr. product acceptence engr., 1982-96, sr. supplier quality engr., 1996-97, prin. supplier quality advancement analyst, 1997—. Active United Way, YMCA fund dirs.; region and automotive divsn. councilor. With U.S. Army, 1970-72. Mem. Nat. Mgmt. Assn., Assn. MBA Execs., Am. Soc. for Quality (bd. dirs. 1992-2000), Alpha Tau Omega, Beta Gamma Sigma, Omicron Delta Kappa. Home: 5596 Brookstone St NW Canton OH 44718-1280 Office: The Timken Co GNW-35 1835 Dueber Ave SW Canton OH 44706-2798 E-mail: pedoto@timken.com.

PEDRETTI, ANTHONY D. information systems specialist; b. Maywood, Ill., Aug. 12, 1976; s. Dennis Andrew and Gail Ann Pedretti. AS, Morton Coll., 1996, A in Liberal Studies, 1997; BS, Ill. State U., 1999. Microcomputer support specialist Morton Coll., Cicero, Ill., 1996-99; tech. support specialist Ill. State U., Normal, 1997-99; PC/LAN technician TransUnion LLC, Chgo., 1999-2000, LAN engr., 2000—. Mem. Mortar Bd. (Chgo., life). Avocation: personal fitness. Home: Apt 5 303 E Plainfield La Grange IL 60525-6916 Office: TransUnion LLC 555 W Adams St Chicago IL 60661-3696 Fax: 312-466-7944. E-mail: ynotpe@hotmail.com.

PEDRETTI, MICHAEL A. performing company executive, artistic director, festival director; b. LaCrosse, Wis., Apr. 17, 1942; s. William C. and Agnes M. (Venner) P.; m. Nancy Bradly Hill, Oct. 27, 1990; children: Bruce, Dean, Leann, Victoria. BS, U. Wis., 1965; MA, U. Kans., 1969. Tchr. Oakfield (Wis.) H.S., 1967-68; dir. BerryPlayers Berry Coll., Mount Berry, Ga., 1969-71; co-chair U. Dayton Players, Ohio, 1971-74; chair theater dept. Davis and Elkins (W. Va.) Coll., 1974-84; dir. Sch. for Movement Theater, Elkins, W. Va., 1979-84; pres., artistic dir. Movement Theatre Internat., Phila., 1985—; sr. lectr. theater U. of the Arts, 1997—; lectr. Bucks County C.C., 2000—. Co-chair Performing Arts League of Phila., 1990-93; chair prodrs. round table Dance Now, Phila., 1992-93; first v.p. West Phila Ptnrs. for the Arts, 1993-98; mng. dir. Am. Music Theatre Festival, Phila., 1985; artistic dir. Internat. Clown Theatre Congress, 1992, New Mime Festival, 1993; dir. MTI Little Circus, 1991; lectr. theatre Pa. Stat U., 1998-99. Dir. (play) "Riffs" with Cathy Crimmins and Flash Rosenberg, 1994. Dir. Greater Phila. Cultural Alliance, 1990-93; panelist NEA Theater Program, Washington, 1991—, N.J. Arts Coun., 1996, 99, 2000, Mid-Atlantic Arts Found., 1995; evaluator N.J. State Arts Coun., 1995, 96, 97, 2000. Recipient Travel award Danish Ministry, 1993, Dutch Govt., 1993. Mem. Nat. Movement Theater Assn. (founding dir., patron), Theatre Assn. Pa., Citzen for the Arts, Roundtable African Prodrs. Democrat. Avocations: writing poetry, novels and essays, travel.

PEDROTTI, LENO STEPHANO, physics educator; b. Zeigler, Ill., May 21, 1927; s. Celeste Louis and Dolores (Galeaz) P.; m. Wilma Jean Sullivan, June 23, 1951; children— Daro Stephano, Michael Louis, Sandra Maria, Laura Jean, Catherine Ann, Leno Matthew, Mary Ann, John Owen. BS in Edn, Ill. State U., 1949; MS in Physics, U. Ill., 1951; PhD, U. Cin., 1961. Teaching asst. U. Ill., Urbana, 1949-51; prof. physics, chmn. dept. Air Force Inst. Tech., Wright-Patterson AFB, Ohio, 1951-82, prof. emeritus, 1982—; cons., editor Ctr. Occupational Rsch. & Devel., Waco, Tex., 1975-82, sr. v.p., 1982—. Presenter in field, 1982—; author, editor, lectr. laser and electro-optics Engring. Tech., Inc., Waco, 1978—; mem. indsl. adv. com. laser electro-optics program Cin. Tech. Coll., 1981-82; tech. cons. Univ. Eye Surgeons, Inc., Ohio State U., 1979-82; mem. exec. com. joint svcs. optical program Optical Scis. Ctr., U. Ariz., 1975-82. Author: Principles of Technology, 1986, Introduction to Optics, 1987, rev. edit., 1993, Applied Mathematics, 1988, Optics and Vision, 1998; contbg. author: Technical Prep Associate Degree: A Win/Win Experience, 1991, The Science Technology, Society Movement, 1993; contbr. articles to profl. jours. Fellow Faculty fellow, NSF, 1959. Fellow Optical Soc. Am.; mem. Am. Nuclear Soc., Am. Phys. Soc. (vice chmn. then chmn. Ohio sect. 1974-76), Laser Inst. Am. (bd. dirs. 1974-84), Am. Assn. Physics Tchrs., Am. Soc. Engring. Edn., Am. Vocat. Assn. (Outstanding Mem. award 1988 vocat. instrnl. materials affiliate Ednl. Exhibitor Assn.-SHIP citation for outstanding commitment to vocat.-tech. edn. 1994), Nat. Coun. Tchrs. Math., Sigma Xi, Tau Beta Pi (Outstanding Tchr. award 1961, 62, 63, 68), Sigma Pi Sigma. Home: 11006 Trailwood Dr Waco TX 76712-3131 Office: Cord 601 Lake Air Dr Waco TX 76710-5841

PEDUTO, RALPH, actor, author, producer; b. Jersey City, Mar. 9, 1942; s. Vincent Peduto, Helen Peduto; m. Laura Patalano; children: Maro Littletree, Oceanna Ceja. High School, Dickinson High School, Jersey City, NJ, 1959—61. Announcer/ DJ KICO-AM, Calexico, CA, 1973—74; Radio Announcer/DJ KRML-FM, Carmel, 1974—76; Assistant Film Editor Cinquegrano Productions, San Francisco, 1977—79; Director/Photographer KSBW-TV, Salinas, 1980—81; Owner/Creative Director Ralph Peduto Advertising Associates, Santa Cruz, 1981—2001; Owner/Producer/Director The Reel Works Film Production Company, 2001—; Assistant Film Editor Cinquegrano Productions, San Francisco, 1977—79; Director/Photographer KSBW-TV, Salinas, 1980—81; Actor/Director/Producer Los Angeles, San Francisco, 1981—. Board of Directors Santa Cruz Actors Theatre, Santa Cruz, 1996—98. Actor: (Feature Film) Kung Phooey!, 2002, Just one Night, 2000, Patch Adams, 1998, Metro, 1997, Rock, The, 1996, (TV Movie) Psychic Detective, 1994, (Feature Film) Getting Even with Dad, 1994, Mrs. Doubtfire, 1993, (Made for TV Movie) Visions of Murder, 1993, (Feature Film) True Believer, 1989, (Made for TV Movie) Splash Too, 1988, Brotherhood of Justice, 1986, Nitti, 1988, (TV Series) Action, 1999, Norm, 1999, Party of Five, 1994, Jesse Hawks, 1989, Nash Bridges, 1996, Cheers, 1982. Performer/ Fund Raiser Resource Center for Non Violence, Santa Cruz, CA, 1996—96, Performer/Fund Raiser, 1996—96; Radio Spot Writer/Producer/Director Anti Nuclear Initiative, 1981—82; Fund Raiser/Performer Resource Center for Non Vilence, 1996—96. Specialist 4th Class U.S. Army, 1964—66, Korea. Mem.: International Brotherhood of Electronic Workers, American Federation of Television and Radio Artist, Screen Actors Guild. Home: P.O. Box 685 Capitola CA 95010 Personal E-mail: Peduto@jps.net.

PEEBLES, ALLENE KAY, manufactured housing company executive; b. Waukegan, Ill., Feb. 9, 1938; d. Allan Laverne and Kathryn Bernice (McGill) Sedlmayr; m. William Ross Peebles, July 9, 1960; children: Ross William, Robb Allan, Raymond John, Renda Kay (Mrs. Christopher Sivak). BS with high honors, U. Wis., 1960, MS, 1967; grad., Realtors Inst., 1968. Cert. home economist. Tchr. Horicon (Wis.) High Sch., 1960-61, Oconomowoc (Wis.) High Sch., 1961-67; freelance writer, 1967-70; v.p. Luxury Homes, Inc., Watertown, Wis., 1970-93, Land Devel. Plus Devel. Inc., Watertown, 1970—; co-developer Hidden Meadows Condominium Community, 1976-96; gen. ptnr. W and A Elderly Housing Ltd. Partnership, 1988—; pres. Housing Am., Inc., 1991—. Gen. ptnr. Sunrise Housing Ltd. Ptnrship., 1990—; builder new and rehab low-income housing, 1983—. Mem. Wis. Gov.'s Conf. on Family, 1980, mem. long range planning team, 1996—; membership chmn. Boy Scouts Am., 1984—90; chmn. Ams. Abroad Am. Field Svc., Oconomowoc, 1982—87; del. Wis. Rep. Conv., 1997—; chmn. adminstrv. bd. United Meth. Ch., Oconomowoc, 1974—77, 1996—99, lay leader, 2000—, pres. United Meth. Women, chmn. family ministry Wis. Conf. Recipient Dist. award of Merit Potawatomi Area coun. Boy Scouts Am., 1986. Mem.: AAUW (pres. Oconomowoc 1983—85, pres. Oconomowoc br. 1981—83, officer's bd. 1984—93, fin. advisor 1995—), NAFE, Wis. Assn. Family and Consumer Scis. (state bd. 1999—, state housing chmn. 2000—02), Met. Builders Assn. Greater Milw., Internat. Fedn. Home Economists (USA internat. del. 1997—), Wis. Manufactured Housing Assn. (bd. dirs. 1979—90, chmn. bd. 1985—88, Mem. of Yr. award 1986), Wis. Builders Assn., Waukesha Bd. Realtors, Wis. Assn. Realtors, Am. Assn. Family and Consumer Scis., Nat. Assn. Realtors, Wis. Home Economists in Bus. (internat. rep. 1998—, state chmn. 1987—88, Home Economist in Bus. of Yr. 1987), Internat. Profl. and Bus. Women, Nat. Assn. Home Builders, Nat. Home Economists in Bus. (internat. com. 1985—87, regional U.S. advisor 1990—92), Wis. Home Econs. Assn. (parliamentarian 1988—90), Am. Home Econs. Assn., Phi Lambda Theta, Kappa Omicron Nu, Phi Upsilon Omicron, Phi Kappa Phi. Republican. Avocation: writing. Home: 37788 Mapleton Rd Oconomowoc WI 53066 Office: Housing Am Inc W1140 Marietta Ave Ixonia WI 53036-9748 E-mail: peebles@execpc.com.

PEEBLES, CAROL LYNN, immunology researcher; b. Wellington, Kans., Jan. 20, 1941; d. Harry Alexander and Phyllis Dorothy (Pyle) P. BA, Kans. State Coll. of Pittsburg, 1962, MS, 1964; cert. med. technology, St. Francis Hosp., Wichita, Kans., 1965. Med. technologist St. Francis Hosp., Wichita, 1965-74; lab. supr. allergy and immunology Scripps Clinic and Rsch. Found., La Jolla, Calif., 1974-77, sr. rsch. asst. Autoimmune Disease Ctr., 1982—2001; lab. supr. rheumatology lab. U. Colo. Health Scis. Ctr., Denver, 1977-82; scientist Inova Diagnostics, Inc., San Diego, 2001—. Author workshop manual; contbr. articles to sci. publs. Mem. Am. Coll. Rheumatology, AAAS, Am. Soc. Microbiology, Am. Soc. Clin. Lab. Sci., Am. Soc. Clin. Pathology. Avocation: photography. Office: Inova Diagnostics Inc 10180 Scripps Ranch Blvd San Diego CA 92131-1234 E-mail: cpeebles@inovadx.com.

PEEBLES, CHRISTOPHER SPALDING, anthropologist, dean, academic administrator; b. Clearwater, Fla., May 26, 1939; s. Frederick Thomas and Corinne deGarmendia (Stephens) P.; m. Laura Ann Wisen, Oct. 6, 1993. AB, U. Chgo., 1963; PhD, U. Calif., Santa Barbara, 1974. Asst. prof. U. Windsor, Ont., Can., 1970-74; asst. curator U. Mich., Ann Arbor, 1974-81; prof. prehistory U. Amsterdam, The Netherlands, 1981-82; prof. Ind. U., Bloomington, 1983—, dean acad. computing, assoc. v.p., 1992—. Author: Excavations at Moundville, 1974, Representations in Archaeology, 1992. With USAF, 1956-60. Mem. Cosmos Club. Avocation: flying. Office: Ind U 116 Franklin Hall Bloomington IN 47405-1223 E-mail: peebles@indiana.edu.

PEEBLES, E(MORY) B(USH), III, lawyer; b. Hattiesburg, Miss., May 3, 1943; s. E.B. Jr. and Lee (Baldwin) P.; m. Celeste H. Hodges; children: E.B. IV, Catharine Celeste, Thomas Hill. BA, Vanderbilt U., 1965; JD, U. Ala., 1967. Bar: Ala. 1967, U.S. Dist. Ct. (so. dist.) Ala., U.S. Ct. Appeals (5th and 11th cirs.), U.S. Supreme Ct. Assoc. Armbrecht, Jackson, DeMouy, Mobile, Ala., 1967-72, ptnr., 1972—. Bd. dirs. South Ala. area bd. Am. South Bank. Mem. Ala. Securities Commn., 1989-93; chmn. sports com. Mobile Area C. of C., 1988-90; bd. dirs. Am.'s Jr. Miss Orgn., Mobile, 1983-90; active Mobile area coun. Boy Scouts Am., 1979—; mem. Sr. Bowl Com., Mobile, 1978—; chmn. trustees Maritime Mus. of Mobile. Mem. ABA (chmn. fin. svcs. com., tort and ins. practice sect. 1989-90, comml. fin. svcs. com. bus. law sect. 1984—), Ala. Bar Assn., Maritime Law Assn. U.S., Southea. Admiralty Law Inst., Internat. Bar Assn., Am. Soc. Internat. Law, Inter-Am. Bar Assn., Ala. Law Inst. (mem. governing coun. 1975—, corp. law com., letters of credit com.), Mobile Touchdown Club (pres. 1987-88), Mobile Area C. of C. (bd. dirs. 2000—). Office: 1300 Riverview Plz Mobile AL 36602

PEEBLES, JULIAN T. health education administrator; b. Mpls., Feb. 16, 1946; s. Wilford W. and Helen Margaret Peebles; m. Mary S. Peebles, Nov. 27, 1969 (div. June 1999); children: William, Mollie, Terry, Katie. BS, Butler U., 1969. Pres. Peebles Dairy Products, Indpls., 1973-83; v.p. Indpls. Alliance For Jobs, 1983-85; pres. Associated Consulting and Tng., Indpls., 1985-89, Cathedral H.S., Indpls., 1989-2000, Ruth Lilly Health Edn. Ctr., Indpls., 2000—. Vol. coach Cath. Youth Orgn., Indpls., 1972-96; v.p. Fall Creek Little League, Indpls., 1972-84; chmn. St. Matthew Athletic Com., Indpls., 1974-82; active St. Matthew Cath. Ch., officer, 1974-85. Recipient St. John Bosco award Cath. Youth Orgn., Indpls., 1985; named Outstanding Alumnus, CAthedral H.S. Alumni Assn., Indpls., 1999. Mem. Nat. Assn. Health Edn. Ctrs., Ind. Assn. Ind. Schs. (pres. 1989-2000), Ind. Non Pub. Edn. Assn. (bd. mem. 1996-2000), Ind. Sch. Assn. Ctrl. States (bd. mem. 1998-2000), Indpls. Athletic Club, Indpls. C. of C., Rotary Club Indpls., Lambda Chi Alpha (officer 1967-69). Avocations: golf, reading, spectatur sports, boating, traveling. Office: Ruth Lilly Health Edn Ctr 2055 Senate Ave Indianapolis IN 46202

PEEBLES, PEYTON ZIMMERMANN, JR. electrical engineer, educator; b. Columbus, Ga., Sept. 10, 1934; s. Peyton Zimmermann Peebles Sr. and Maida Erlene Dials; m. Barbara Ann Suydam, Sept. 6, 1969; children: Peyton Zimmermann III, Edward Arlen. BSEE, Evansville Coll., 1957; MSEE, Drexel Inst., 1963; PhD, U. Pa., 1967. Design engr. RCA, Moorestown, N.J., 1958-64, systems engr., 1966-69; prof. U. Tenn., Knoxville, 1969-75, 76-81; vis. prof. U. Hawaii, Honolulu, 1975-76; prof. U. Fla., Gainesville, 1981-84, 90-96, assoc. chmn., 1984-90, prof. emeritus, 1996—. Cons. in field. Author: Communication System Principles, 1976, Probability, Random Variables and Random Signal Principles, 1980, 4th edit., 2001, Digital Communication Systems, 1987; prin. author: Principles of Electrical Engineering, 1991, Radar Principles, 1998; contbr. articles to profl. jours.; patentee in field. Capt. USAFR, 1957-61. David Sarnoff fellow, 1964-66. Fellow IEEE (life); mem. Sigma Xi, Eta Kappa Nu, Tau Beta Pi, Sigma Pi Sigma, Phi Beta Chi. Methodist. Avocations: fishing, painting, woodworking. Office: U Fla Dept Elec& Computer Engring Gainesville FL 32611 E-mail: ppeeb@ece.ufl.edu.

PEEK, DAVID LOWELL, music educator, conductor; b. Alton, Ill., Oct. 10, 1950; s. Herman Leroy and Elizabeth Ginn Peek; m. Marsha Jane Pepmeier. MusB in Performance & Edn., So. Ill. U., 1972; MusM in Orchestral Conducting, Colo. State U., 1973; student, Ball State U., 1974—77. Musical dir. Interlochen Music Camp, Theatre Dept., Interlochen, Mich., 1976—77; condr. Marion H.S., Marion, Ind., 1977—83; asst. condr. Marion Philharm. Orch., 1979—83; music dir. Brentwood Symphony, Brentwood, Mo., 1983—99; founder, music dir. St. Charles County Youth Symphonies, St. Peters, 1996—99; music dir. Symphony Soc. of St. Charles County, St. Charles, 1998—, Town & Country Symphony Orch., Town & Country, 1999—. Invited condr. Villa-Lobos Internat. Conducting Competition, Rio de Janiero, 1975; music dir. Brentwood Symphony Tours to Europe, 1987, 94. Mem.: NEA, Am. String Tchr. Assn., Phi Eta Sigma (v.p. 1973—74), Phi Delta Kappa (hon.). Avocation: golf. Home: 1024 Orchard Lakes Drive Saint Louis MO 63146 Office: Ritenour High School 9100 St Charles Rock Road Saint Louis MO 63114 Personal E-mail: conductor@ezl.com. Business E-Mail: peekd@ritenour.k12.mo.us.

PEEK, ROBIN PATRICIA, library and information science educator; b. San Francisco, Jan. 10, 1958; d. Duane Edwin and Geneve Ellen (Purvis) Geer; m. Gerald Paul Miller, Aug. 15, 1992. BS, U. Oreg., 1980; MS, Syracuse U., 1988, PhD, 1997. Asst. prof. Simmons Coll., Boston, 1992-98, assoc. prof., 1998—. Lectr. Syracuse (N.Y.) U., 1988-89, grad. asst. 1988-91; vis. prof. SUNY, Albany, 1989. Author, editor: Scholarly Publishing: The Electronic Frontier, 1996; columnist Info. Today, 1997—. Mem. Am. Soc. Info. Sci. (mem. edtl. bd. Jour. Am. Soc. Info. Sci.), Assn. for Computing Machinery. Office: Simmons Coll Grad Sch Libr and Info Sci 300 Fenway Boston MA 02115-5820 E-mail: rpeek@simmons.edu.

PEEL, HARRIS, art gallery owner, retired diplomat; b. Decatur, Ill., Nov. 14, 1923; s. Wilbur David Peel and Ruth Harris; m. Margaret Backus, Oct. 11, 1946 (dec. Nov. 1990); children: Susan Harris, Jane Peel Fuller, David Harris, Josh Criss. BS, Columbia U., 1950; MS, George Washington U., 1967. Editor War Dept., Frankfurt, Germany, 1946; writer Holiday Mag., Europe, 1947-48; fgn. svc. officer U.S. Dept. State and USIA, various locations, 1950-74; owner Peel Gallery Fine Art, Danby, Vt., 1976—. Author: (book) History of 254th Infantry Regiment, 1945. Advisor on psychol. warfare U.S. Army and USN, Ft. Bragg, N.C., 1971-74. Cpl. U.S. Army, 1943-45. Decorated Bronze star U.S. Army, 1945; 4-yr. scholar Chgo. Tribune, 1941. Mem. Vt. Assn. Galleries (pres. 1978-98), Overseas Press Club. Avocation: astronomy. Home: 1 Peel Rd Danby VT 05739 Office: Peel Gallery Peel Rd Danby VT 05739 E-mail: hpeel@earthlink.net.

PEEL, JAMES E. engineering executive; b. Lonaconing, Md., Dec. 26, 1924; s. Thomas Roscoe and Agnes Ferguson (Kirkpatrick) Peel; m. Camilla Ellen Macaluso, June 25, 1955; children: James E. Peel Jr., David Thomas. BSChemE, Carnegie Inst. Tech., 1953. Registered profl. engr., Pa. Rsch. engr. Diamond Alrali Co., Painesville, Ohio, 1953—59; devel. engr. PGH Coke & Chem., Neville Island, Pa., 1960—65; owner Peel Engring. & Constrn., Pitts., 1962—; owners rep. PPG Industries, 1965—86. With U.S. Army, 1942—46. Avocation: collecting stamps & coins. Home: 1028 Benton Ave Pittsburgh PA 15212-1607

PEEL, VICTORIA, elementary educator; b. Phila., July 31, 1971; d. Edward Timothy P. and Barbara Ann Peel Swonger. B, Pa. State U., 1993. Tchr. mid. sch. sci. and health Balt. City Pub. Schs., 1995-99, 5th grade tchr., 1999—. Mem. sci. acad. program Morgan State U., Balt., 1995; advisor for gifted and talented program Md. State Dept. Edn., 1997—, co-chair budgeting com., 1997—, 8th grade class adv., 7th/8th grade team leader, mem. sch. improvement team, 1997-02; dir. Gifted and Talented Summer Inst. Md. State Dept. Edn., mem. core knowledge writing team, attendance com. chairperson, mem. sch. improvement team, direct instrn. coach, 1999-2002. Mem. planning com. Dream Catchers program, Port Discovery Children's Mus. and Jr. League Balt.; Balt. Harbor Oyster Corps., Balt. Ecosystem Study. Mem. Pa. State Alumni Assn. (Greater Balt. chpt.), Golden Key, Dream Catcher Club, Pi Lambda Theta. Avocations: field hockey, tennis, softball, swimming, skiing.

PEELE, ANNE MARIE, government agency administrator; b. Durham, NC, June 30, 1968; d. Robert Louis and Brabara (Davis) P. BA, N.C. A&T State U., 1996; MPA, N.C. Ctrl. U., 1996; postgrad., High Point Univ. Cert. human resources mgr. Legis. com. clk. N.C. Ho. of Reps., Raleigh, 1993-2001; mgmt. intern Caswell County Govt., Yanceyville, N.C., 1997-98; employment recruiter Triangle Communities, Durham, 2000-01; v.p. Durham Chamber Commerce, 2002—. Mem. ASPA, Soc. Human Resources Mgmt., Am. Polit. Sci. Soc., Nat. Black MBA Assn., Nat. Forum Black Pub. Adminstrs., Internat. City/County Mgmt. Assn., Multi Jurisdictional Adv. Bd. Transporatation. Home: 3601-F Highgate Dr Durham NC 27713

PEELE, PAMELA BONIFAY, economics educator; b. Pensacola, Fla., 1953; d. Jack Edward Bonifay; m. James Peele, Nov., 1974. BA magna cum laude, Roanoke Coll., Salem, Va., 1989; MA, Va. Tech., Blacksburg, Va., 1990, PhD, 1994. Technologist VA Med. Ctr., Gainesville, Fla., 1974-75, technologist EEG Salem, Va., 1975-87; prof. health econs. U. Pitts., 1994—. Mem. Omega Delta. Office: U Pitts 130 DeSoto St Pittsburgh PA 15216 Office Fax: 412-624-3146.

PEELE, ROGER, hospital administrator; b. Elizabeth City, N.C., Dec. 24, 1930; s. Joseph Emmett and Catherine (Groves) P.; m. Diana Egan, June 15, 1963 (dec.); children: Amy, Rodney, Holly; m. Gail Nelson Oct. 15, 1992. AB, U. N.C., 1955; MD, U. Tenn., 1960. Cert. adminstrv. psychiatry, 1970 cert. forensic psychiatry, 1982. Intern St. Elizabeths Hosp., Washington, 1960-61, resident in psychiatry, 1961-64, tng. officer, 1964-67, chief of service William A. White div., 1967-69; dir. Area D Community Mental Health Center, 1969-73, asst. supt., 1974-75, 77-79, acting supt., 1975-77, chmn. dept. psychiatry, 1979-95. Clin. prof. George Washington U., 1979—; asst. dir. NIMH, 1978-79; chief clin. officer D.C. Commn. on Mental Health, 1987-91; med. dir. Northern Va. Mental Health Ctr., 1996-98; attending George Washington U., 1998-2001; chief psychiatrist Montgomery County, Md. Contbr. articles on clin., forensic and adminstrv. issues in Am. psychiatry to profl. jours. Served with USAF, 1950-53. Superior Service award HEW, 1967. Fellow Am. Coll. Psychiatry, Am. Psychiat. Assn. (speaker 1986-87, Adminstr. of Yr. 1989); mem. AMA, D.C. Med. Soc., Am. Assn. Psychiat. Adminstrs. (past pres.), Group for Advancement Psychiatry, Med. Soc. St. Elizabeth's Hosp. (past pres.), Fed. Physicians Assn. (past pres.). Episcopalian. Home: 8002 Lions Crest Way Gaithersburg MD 20879-5637 E-mail: RogerPeele@aol.com. *A key to effective treatment is not to allow the seductiveness of logic to narrow one's observations.*

PEELER, BOB, lieutenant governor; b. Gaffney, S.C., 1952; s. Smith and Sally (Bratton) P.; m. Bett Carter; children: Caroline, Robert, Jr. V.p. Peeler's Milk now Peeler Bros. Dairy Cattle Co.; former chmn. Cherokee County Sch. Bd., S.C. State Bd. Edn.; lt. gov. State of S.C., 1995—. Founding mem. advancement bd. Coll. Commerce, Clemson U. Mem. S.C. Dairy Assn. (past pres.), Cherokee County C. of C. (past pres.), Sertoma Internat. (life), Rotary (Gaffney chpt.), Masons, York Rite. Republican. Methodist. Office: Office Lt Gov PO Box 142 Columbia SC 29202-0142*

PEELER, STUART THORNE, petroleum industry executive and independent oil operator; b. Los Angeles, Oct. 28, 1929; s. Joseph David and Elizabeth Fiske (Boggess) P.; m. Sylvia Frances Townley, Nov. 5, 1985. BA, Stanford U., 1950, JD, 1953. Bar: Calif. 1953. Ptnr. Musick, Peeler & Garrett, L.A., 1958-73; with Santa Fe Internat. Corp., Orange, Calif., 1973-81, v.p., sec., assoc. gen. counsel, 1973-74, sr. v.p., gen. counsel, dir., 1975-81; vice-chmn. bd., chmn. exec. com. Supron Energy Corp., 1978-82; chmn. bd., CEO Statex Petroleum, Inc., 1982-89; chmn., pres., CEO Putumayo Prodn. Co., Tucson, 1989—. Bd. dirs. Chieftain Internat. Inc. Trustee J. Paul Getty Trust, 1963-99; mem. U.S. Tuna Team, 1957-67, capt., 1966. Served with U.S. Army, 1953-55. Decorated Army Commendation medal. Mem. AIME, State Bar Calif., Am. Judicature Soc., Theta Chi, Phi Delta Phi, Skyline Country Club. Republican. Congregationalist. Office: PO Box 35852 Tucson AZ 85740-5852 Fax: 520-544-0632.

PEEPLES, RUFUS RODERICK, JR. (RODDY PEEPLES), farm and ranch news radio broadcaster; b. Tehuacana, Tex., July 3, 1932; s. Rufus Roderick and Josephine (Gray) P.; m. Bettimae Scrivener, Aug. 8, 1953; children: James Roderick, Deidre Lynn. BA, Tex. A&M Coll., 1953. Farm dir. KADA Radio, Ada, Okla., 1953-56, KGNO Radio, Dodge City, Kans., 1956-59, KLIK Radio, Jefferson City, Mo., 1959; assoc. farm dir. KWFT Radio, Wichita Falls, Tex., 1959-64; sr. farm broadcaster, former owner Voice of S.W. Agt. Radio Network, San Angelo, 1964—. Mem. adv. bd. Tex. Agrl. Lifetime Leadership Program, College Station, 1987—, West Tex. Boys Ranch, San Angelo, 1966—. Named Man of Yr. in Tex. Agr., Tex. Assn. County Agrl. Agts., 1984, Disting. Alumnus, Coll. Agr. and Life Scis. Tex. A&M U., 1995; recipient Ann. Comms. award, Tex. Profl. Agrl. Workers, 1982, Tex. Farm Bur. Agr. Journalism award, 1997. Mem.: Nat. Assn. Farm Broadcasters (pres. 1982, Farm Broadcaster of Yr. 1992, Farm Broadcasters Hall of Fame 2001). Republican. Methodist. Avocations: flying, music, photography.

PEEPLES, WILLIAM DEWEY, JR. mathematics educator; b. Bessemer, Ala., Apr. 19, 1928; s. William Dewey and Thelma Jeannette (Chastain) P.; m. Katie Ray Blackerby, Aug. 30, 1956; children: Mary Jeannette, William Dewey III, Gerald Lewis, Stephen Ray. BS, Samford U., 1948; MS, U. Wis., 1949; PhD, U. Ga., 1951. Rsch. mathematician Ballistics Rsch. Lab., Aberdeen, Md., summer 1951; mem. faculty Samford U., Birmingham, Ala., 1951-56, prof. math., 1959-95, head dept., 1967-95; prof. emeritus, 1995; mem. faculty Auburn U., 1956-59. Cons. Hayes Internat. Corp. Co-author: Modern Mathematics for Business Students, 1969, Finite Mathematics, 1974, Modern Mathematics with Applications to Business and the Social Sciences, 4th edit, 1986, Finite Mathematics with Applications to Business and the Social Sciences, 1981, 2d edit., 1987; Contbr. articles to profl. publs. Served to 1st lt. AUS, 1954-56. Mem. Am. Math. Soc., Math. Assn. Am., Nat. Council Tchrs. Math., Ala. Coll. Tchrs. Math. (pres. 1969), Sigma Xi, Pi Mu Epsilon, Phi Kappa Phi (pres. 1977), Lambda Chi Alpha. Baptist (deacon, chmn. 1986). Club: Mason (Shriner). Home: 419 Poinciana Dr Birmingham AL 35209-4129 E-mail: wdpeeples@peoplepc.com.

PEER, GEORGE JOSEPH, metals company executive; b. St. Louis, Aug. 26, 1925; s. George J. and Melba (Rahning) P.; m. Mary Jane Hazlewood, Feb. 14, 1948; children— Linda, Gary, Steven, Scott. BS, Purdue U., 1945, MS, 1948; postgrad., Advanced Mgmt. Program, Harvard, 1967. Operating supr. Republic Steel Corp., Canton, Ohio, 1948-54; various sales positions to v.p. sales Basic, Inc., Chgo., Cleve., 1954-63; v.p. marketing Handy & Harman, N.Y.C., 1963-71, dir., 1971-75, group v.p. precious metals, 1972-75; chmn., pres., chief exec. officer Multi-Metal Wire Cloth, Inc., 1975-88; pres. Holyoke Wire Cloth Co., 1975-88, Multi-Wedge Corp., 1976-88, United-Holyoke Corp., 1980-86; pres., chief exec. officer Liquid-Solids Separation Corp., 1988-93, dir., 1988-96; retired. Bd. dirs. Handy & Harman Refining Group Inc.; chmn. Phillips Steel Fabricators, Inc., 1989-93. Chmn. bd. Lucas Milhaupt, Inc., Cudahy, Wis., 1967-75. Served with USNR, 1943-46, 51-53. Mem. Am. Mgmt. Assn., Nat. Indsl. Conf. Bd., Am. Inst. Mining and Metall. Engrs., Tau Beta Pi, Kappa Delta Rho. Clubs: Landings Club (Savannah, Ga.), First City Club (Savannah), Cornell of N.Y. Republican. Congregationalist. Home: 9 Springpine Ln Savannah GA 31411-3080

PEERADINA, SALEEM, English educator, poet; b. Bombay, India, Oct. 5, 1944; came to U.S., 1988; s. Habib and Noorunnisa Peeradina; m. Mumtaz Peeradina, May 11, 1978; children: Shoneizi, Lail. MA, Bombay (India) U., 1969, Wake Forest U., 1973. Lectr. in English St. Xavier Coll., Bombay, India, 1976-77, Sophia Coll., Bombay, 1977-80, dir. open classroom, 1978-84; copywriter Hindustan Thompson, 1984-87; vis. prof. Adrian/Alma (Mich.) Colls., 1988-89; assoc. prof. Siena Heights U., Adrian, Mich. Revs. editor Express Mag., Bombay, 1982-88; poetry readings East West Ctr., Univ. Hawaii, Third World Arts Festival, London, The Commonwealth Inst., London, U. Sussex and Milan, as well as numerous readings at instns. in continental U.S. Author: (poetry) First Offence, 1980, Group Portrait, 1992; editor: (poetry anthology) Contemporary Indian Poetry in English: An Assessment and Selection, 1972; contbr. poetry to many anthologies. Mem. MLA. Avocations: cooking, photography, travel, walking. Home: 1110 Bent Oak Ave Adrian MI 49221-1509 Office: Siena Heights U 1247 E Siena Heights Dr Adrian MI 49221-1755 E-mail: speerad2@sienahts.edu.

PEERMAN, DEAN GORDON, magazine editor; b. Mattoon, Ill., Apr. 25, 1931; s. Staley Jacob and Irene (Monen) P. BS with highest distinction, Northwestern U., 1953; postgrad., Cornell U., 1953-54; B.D., Yale, 1959; D.D., Kalamazoo Coll., 1967. With Christian Century Found., 1959—; copy editor Christian Century mag., 1959-61, assoc. editor, 1961-64, mng. editor, 1964-81, exec. editor, 1981-85, sr. editor, 1985-98, contbg. editor, 1998—. Author: (with M.E. Marty) Pen-ultimates, 1963, (with Marty, L.M. Delloff, J.M. Wall) A Century of The Century, 1987; editor: Frontline Theology, 1967; co-editor: (with Marty) New Theology 1-10, 1964-73, A Handbook of Christian Theologians, 1965, enlarged edit., 1984, (with Alan Geyer) Theological Crossings, 1971. Contbr.: Chile: Under Military Rule, 1974; editor, contbr. Faithful Witness, 2002. Active Chgo. community theater groups. Recipient award for distinction in lay ministry within the church Yale Div. Sch., 1995. Mem. ACLU, Fellowship of Reconciliation, Amnesty Internat., Chgo. Religious Leadership Network on Latin Am., Phi Beta Kappa. Democrat. Baptist. Office: Christian Century Mag 104 S Michigan Ave Ste 700 Chicago IL 60603-5901

PEERSCHKE, ELLINOR IRMGARD BARBARA, hematopathologist, educator; b. Braunschweig, Fed. Republic of Germany, May 7, 1954; came to U.S., 1965; d. Heinz Herbert Otto and Barbara (Halberkann) P. BA, Rutgers U., 1975; PhD, NYU, 1980. Head clin. hematology labs U. Hosp., Stony Brook, N.Y., 1980-96; asst. prof. pathology SUNY, 1980-86, assoc. prof., 1986-93, prof., 1993-96, dir. grad. program in pathology, 1987-90; prof. Weill Med. Coll. Cornell U., N.Y.C., 1996—; chief clin. hematology lab. svc. N.Y. Hosp.-Presbyn. Hosp./Cornell Med. Ctr., 1996—. Vis. scientist Weizmann Inst. Sci., Rehovot, Israel, 1980, 81; with hematology study sect. NIH, Washington, 1990-94; faculty advisor undergrad. rsch. and creative activities Stony Brook; advisor Bd. Continuing Edn. Svc., Stony Brook. Editor: Hematology Tech Sample, 1985-89, Thrombosis Research, 1990-94; mem. editl. bd. Thrombosis & Hemostasis, 2002-; contbr. articles to profl. jours. NIH grantee, 1980-. Mem. Am. Soc. Hematology (platelet coun. 1987-90, edn. com. 2000—), Am. Soc. Clin. Pathologists (edn. com. 2000—), Internat. Soc. for Thrombosis and Hemostasis, N.Y. Acad. Scis. (faculty advisor), Soc. for Exptl. Biology and Medicine, Am. Heart Assn. (peer review ctr. 1986-93, 2000—, rsch. coun. 1990-94, grantee 1984-85, 90-92), Harvey Soc., Sigma Xi, Phi Beta Kappa. Office: NY Presbyn Hosp Weill-Cornell Med Ctr f 707 525 E 68th St New York NY 10021-4870 E-mail: epeersch@med.cornell.edu.

PEET, AMANDA W. science educator; BSc with honors, U. Canterbury, New Zealand, 1990; PhD, Stanford U., 1994. Rsch. assoc. Princeton U., Princeton, 1994—97; fellow U. Calif. Inst. for Theoretical Physics, Santa Barbara, 1997—2000; asst. prof. physics dept. U. Toronto, Canada, 2000—. Lectr. in field. Contbr. articles to profl. jours. Fellow Radcliffe fellow, 2001, Sloan Rsch. fellow, 2002; scholar, CIAR, 2000—. Office: Univ Toronto Dept Physics 60 St George St Toronto M5S 1A7 Canada*

PEET, CHARLES D, JR. lawyer; b. N.Y.C., Sept. 3, 1935; s. Charles D and Margaret Louise (Sherman) P.; children: Alisa, Amanda. BA, Yale U., 1957; JD, Harvard U., 1960. Bar: N.Y. 1962. Assoc. Milbank, Tweed, Hadley & McCloy, N.Y.C., 1960-68, ptnr., 1969-98; of counsel Freshfields Bruckhaus Deringer LLP (and predecessor firm), 1998—. Mem. Assn. Bar N.Y.C. Office: Freshfields Bruckhaus Deringer LLP 520 Madison Ave Fl 34 New York NY 10022-4213 E-mail: charles.peet@freshfields.com.

PEET, HOWARD DAVID, English educator, writer; b. Fargo, N.D., Oct. 7, 1930; s. Howard Morrison and Beatrice Katherine (Gunness) P.; m. Jacquelyn Marie Hegge, June 20, 1953; children: Terry H., Pamela Peet Astrup. BA, Macalaster Coll., St. Paul, 1956; BS, MS, Moorhead State U., 1965; postgrad., U. Minn., 1970. Ride trumpet Ray Palmer Orch., Chgo., 1950-52; lead trumpet Kliff Riggs Orch., Omaha, 1954-55; ins. investigator Retail Credit Assn., St. Paul, 1955-60; prof. English N.D. State U., Fargo, 1965-86, prof. emeritus, 1986—, dir. concentrated approach program, 1970-80. Author and co-author 85 books including The English Book: A Complete Course, 1980, Wordskill for The Micro Computer, 1982, MacMillan Spelling, 1983, Vocabulary for College Reading and Writing, 1984, Linguistics For Teachers, 1993, Wordskills, 1993, (audio tapes) Words to Success, 1998; co-author 4 lang. arts grad courses for the Internet, N.D. State U., 1999-2002, Spelling for Writing, 2001. Pres. Young Reps., Wilkin county, Minn., 1970's, PTA, Barnesville, Minn., 1970's; treas. Presbyn. Ch., Deerhorn, Minn., 1970's. With USN, 1952-54, Korea. Named Red River Valley Educator, Red River Valley Heritage Soc., 1992. Mem. Nat. Coun. Tchrs. English, Writers of the Purple Sage, Am. Legion, La. Soc. Des 40 Hommes Et 8 Chevaux. Avocations: music, reading, traveling, writing poetry and short stories. Home: 25 Prairiewood Xing Fargo ND 58103-4667

PEET, NORTON PAUL, science administrator; b. Fargo, N.D., June 14, 1944; s. Theodore Fredrick and Tenie Lyla Peet; m. Patricia Lee Peet, June 17, 1967; children: Dustin Paul, Dulcie Lee, Andrea Holly. BA, U. Minn., 1966; PhD in Chemistry, U. Nebr., 1970. Instr. Concordia Coll., Moorhead, Minn., 1967; rsch. assoc. MIT, Cambridge, 1970-71, U. S.C., Columbia, 1971-72; sr. rsch. chemist Dow Chem. Co., Midland, Mich., 1972-76, rsch. specialist Indpls., 1976-79; rsch. leader, group leader Merrell Dow Rsch. Inst., 1979-84, rsch. assoc., group leader Cin., 1984-91; sr. rsch. scientist, dir. Marion Merrell Dow, 1991-96; head medicinal chemistry Hoechst Marion Roussel, Inc., 1996-98, disting. scientist Bridgewater, N.J., 1998-2000; head med. chemistry Aventis Pharms., Inc., 2000; v.p. discovery alliances ArQule, Inc., Woburn, Mass., 2000—02; CEO Aurigene Discovery Tech., North Andover, 2002—. Contbr. articles to profl. jours., chpts. to books; mem. editl. bds.; 55 patents in field. NIH-PHS predoctoral fellow, 1968-70; recipient award for outstanding rsch. Merck, Sharpe and Dohme, 1969. Mem. AAAS, Am. Chem. Soc., Internat. Soc. Heterocyclic Chemistry. Presbyterian. Avocations: piano, woodworking, writing. Office: Aurigene Discovery Tech 50 Blue Ridge Rd North Andover MA 01845 E-mail: norton_p@aurigene.com.

PEET, RAYMOND EDWARD, consultant; b. Oneonta, N.Y., Jan. 27, 1921; s. Ursil Lee and Hannah Thomas P.; m. W. Dian Hutchinson, July 13, 1945; 1 child, Gary Raymond. BSEE, U.S. Naval Acad., 1942; MSEE, MIT, 1948. Commd. ensign USN, 1939, advanced through grades to vice admiral, retired, 1974; v.p. internat. Teledyne Ryan Aeronautical, San Diego, 1974-82; dir. Cubic Corp., 1985—; chmn. The Price Reit, 1994-98. Mem. adv. bd. U.S. Gen. Acctg. Office, Washington, 1982-98. Chmn. San Diego Dialogue, 1997-2001. Decorated Bronze star, Presdl. Unit. citation, Dept. of Def. and Navy Disting. Svc. medals. Mem. Rotary. Avocation: golf. Home: 7433 Fairway Rd La Jolla CA 92037-5629 E-mail: vadmraypeet@prodigy.net.

PEET, RICHARD CLAYTON, lawyer, consultant; b. N.Y.C., Aug. 24, 1928; s. Charles Francis and Florence L. (Isaacs) P.; m. Barbara Jean McClure, Mar. 17, 1956 (div. July, 1988); children: Victoria Clementine, Alexandra Constance, Elizabeth Erica, Clarissa Barbara. JD, Tulane U., 1953. Bar: La. 1955, D.C. 1955. Law clk. Melvin M. Belli, San Francisco, 1954; with The Calif. Co., Standard Oil of Calif., 1955; atty. appellate sect. Lands div. Dept. Justice, Washington, 1956; asst. to dep. gen. counsel Dept. Commerce, 1957; legis. asst. Republican policy com. U.S. Senate, 1958; legis. asst. U.S. Senate minority leader William F. Knowland, 1958; asso. counsel House Judiciary Com., 1959-62; asso. minority counsel House Pub. Works Com., 1969-74; pres. Citizens for Hwy. Safety, 1978-84; practiced in Washington, 1962-68; prin. Richard Clayton Peet & Assos., 1972—; ptnr. Anderson, Pendleton, McMahon, Peet & Donovan, 1977-80, Anderson, Peet & Co., 1980-84. Pres., mng. dir. Lincoln Rsch. Ctr., 1965-72; v.p. Oil East Corp., 1978-83. Author: Goals for a Constructive Opposition, 1966; contbg. editor: Congressional Digest, 1960-61, Jour. Def. and Diplomacy, 1983-86, Senate Rep. Week, 1991; (weekly radio show) Across the Aisle, 1992; composer: song Stand Up For America, 1971 (George Washington medal Freedom's Found. 1971), A Monologue With God, 1996, Remembrance House. Chmn. bd. Workshop Library on World Humor; Rep. candidate Pres. of U.S., 1999-2000. With U.S. Army, 1946-47, with USAFR, 1950-55. Nominated for Rockefeller Public Svcs. Awd. Mem. Phi Delta Phi, Pi Kappa Alpha. Achievements include conceiving Highway Safety Act of 1973 with Cong. Wm. Harsha, OH, establishing road safety improvement programs, created (with congress) Natl. Bicentennial Highway Safety Year to promote, organized and chaired (with Pres. Ford) White House Conf. on Highway Safety, 1976, Rep. candidate for U.S. Pres., 1999-2000. Home: Remembrance House Inc Ste 186-184 4200 Wisconsin Ave NW Washington DC 20016 E-mail: Dick079@aol.com.

PEETE, RUSSELL FITCH, JR. aircraft appraiser; b. Memphis, June 15, 1920; s. Russell Fitch and Louise Gift (Edmondson) P.; m. Esther Eletha Mosley, Feb. 7, 1942 (dec. Jan. 1987); children: Miriam, Russell III, William; m. Margery May George, Sept. 2, 1988. BS in Aerospace Engring., Miss. State U., 1942. Dredge hand U.S. Corp. Engrs., West Memphis, Ark., 1937, rodman Mobile, Ala., 1939; rsch. engr. Chicago & Southern Airlines, Memphis, 1941-51; tech. sales rep. Lockheed Corp., Burbank, Calif., 1951-82; ops. analyst Flying Tiger Line, L.A., 1982; dir. sales engring. Cammacorp, El Segundo, Calif., 1982-85, Anacorp, Marina Del Rey, 1987-89. Cons. Avcons, Camarillo, Calif., 1985-86, Marana, Ariz., 1997—. Sec. Conejo Y's Mens Clubs, Thousand Oaks, Calif., 1960-63. With U.S. Army, 1944-46. Mem. Soc. Automotive Engrs., Exptl. Aircraft Assn., Aircraft Owners and Pilots Assn., Confederate Air Force, Internat. Aerobatic Club. Republican. Lutheran. Avocations: flying, photography, golf, travel.

PEETZ, MICHAEL E. surgeon; b. Omaha, Dec. 18, 1950; s. John Peter Peetz and Constance Irene Copenhaver; m. Shelley Lynn Hanson, Dec. 28, 1974; children: Elizabeth, Joseph, John. BS, U. Nebr., 1973; MD, U. Nebr., Omaha, 1976. Gen. surgeon Greeley (Colo.) Med. Clinic, 1982—; asst. adminstr. North Colo. Med. Ctr., 2001. Committeeman Greeley Independence Stampede, 1984—88. Fellow: ACS (pres. Colo. chpt. 1994, gov. 1995—2000); mem.: Soc. Gastrointestinal Surgeons (exec. com. 1986). Avocations: poetry, photography, mountain climbing, golf. Home: 1855 Frontier Rd Greeley CO 80634-3412 Office: Greeley Med Clinic 1900 16th St Greeley CO 80631

PEFKAROS, KYRIACOS C. internist, cardiologist; b. Limassol, Cyprus, 1948; MB ChB, U. Leeds, 1972. Diplomate Am. Bd. Internal Medicine, Am. Bd. Cardiology. Intern Leeds Gen. Infirmary, England, 1972-73; resident Prince of Wales Hosp., 1973-74, Sinai Hosp. Balt., 1974-77; fellow in cardiology Jackson Meml. Hosp., Miami, 1977-79; asst. prof. U. Miami, 1979-83; chief divsn. cardiology Mercy Hosp., Miami, 1991-95; pvt. practice, 1983—. Assoc. clin. prof. medicine U. Miami, 1984—. Fellow Am. Coll. of Cardiology. Office: 3661 S Miami Ave Ste 603 Miami FL 33133-4214

PEFLEY, CHARLES SAUNDERS, real estate broker; b. Portsmouth, Va., Sept. 4, 1943; s. William R. and Dorothy (Everett) P.; m. Audrey Diane Bennett, Aug. 15, 1977 (div. Sept. 1983). BA in Polit. Sci., Old Dominion U., 1967; JD, U. Balt., 1971; postgrad., Johns Hopkins U., 1972. Lic. real estate broker. V.p. Saxis Island Devel. Corp., Virginia Beach, Va., 1965-72, Pefley, Inc., Virginia Beach, 1972-77; ptnr. Pefley Realty Co., 1977—; pres. Pefley Realty Corp., Camden, N.C., 1983—; ptnr. Mickey Properties, Virginia Beach, 1983-87, C.J.S. Enterprises, Virginia Beach, 1986—, Pefzar Realty, Rockville, Md., 1986—, Kelben Properties, Rockville, 1983—. Pres. Pefley Realty Corp., Camden, N.C., Bold Realty and Realty Co., Inc., Fair Rental Group, Inc., Centurian Residential Realty Corp., Ava Corp., Budget Realty Devel. Corp. Served with U.S. Army, 1968-69. Mem. Tidewater Bd. Realtors. Democrat. Lutheran. Avocations: boating, camping. Home: 2021 Pefley Ln Virginia Beach VA 23457-1223 Office: Pefley Realty Corp 1808 Arctic Ave Virginia Beach VA 23451-3306

PEFLEY, NORMAN GORDON, consultant; b. Eugene, Oreg., Dec. 15, 1955; s. Gordon Vergne Pefley and Jean Pefley (Lee) Hawley; m. Emma Ginete Lacuesta, July 5, 1986. BA, U. Calif., Davis, 1977; MA, Johns Hopkins U., 1979; MBA, U. Chgo., 1981; MA, Golden Gate U., 2001. CFA. Rsch. analyst Chgo. Bd. Options Exch., 1981-83; sr. fin. analyst Bank of Am., San Francisco, 1983-89, v.p., 1989-99. Referee Jour. Futures Markets, N.Y.C., 1984-87. Mem. Am. Fin. Assn., Am. Soc. for Tng. and Devel., Assn. for Investment Mgmt. and Rsch., Internat. Soc. for Performance Improvement, The Security Analysts of San Francisco, Toastmasters Internat., Phi Beta Kappa, Delta Phi Alpha, Omicron Delta Epsilon. Avocation: foreign languages.

PEGELS, C. CARL, management science and systems educator; b. Barendrecht, Holland, The Netherlands, Feb. 26, 1933; came to U.S., 1962, naturalized, 1968; s. Bertus and Adriana Maria (Denotter) P.; children: Janice Joy, Kevin Carl. BS in Mech. Engring., Detroit Inst. Tech., 1961; MS, Purdue U., 1963, PhD in Mgmt., 1966. Prodn. engr. Ford Motor, Windsor, Can., 1955-62; instr. Purdue U., W. Lafayette, Ind., 1962-66; prof. SUNY, Buffalo, 1966—. V.p. Ctr. Mgmt. Sys., Buffalo, 1978-91. Author: Basic for Business, 1973, Health Care & Elderly, 1980, Japan vs The West, 1984, Q.C. in Health Care, 1985, Decision Support Systems for Production and Operations Management, 1986, Management and Industry in China, 1987, Strategic Management for Hospitals and Health Care Corporations, 1987, Health Care and the Older Citizen, 1988, Decision Support Systems for Management Science/Operations Research, 1989, Strategic Information Systems, 1993, Total Quality management, 1995, Strategies and Tools for the Learning Company, 1998. Krannert fellow, 1966; Krannert scholar Purdue U., 1963. Mem. Ops. Rsch. Soc. Am., Inst. Mgmt. Sci., Am. Inst. Decision Scis. Avocation: long distance running. Home: 150 Arielle Ct Apt D Buffalo NY 14221-1969 Office: Sch of Mgmt Suny At Buffalo Buffalo NY 14260-0001

PEGUES, JUNE ALLEN, social work educator; b. Alexandria, Va., Mar. 2, 1943; d. Millard Randolph and Lottie Sue (Armstrong) Allen; m. James Cary Pegues Jr., Mar. 22, 1975; children: Susan Scott, James Allen. BA, U. Miss., 1965; MSW, Fla. State U., 1967; D of Social Work, U. Ala., 1990. Lic. clin. social worker; cert. social worker. Social worker in tng. Miss. Dept. Pub. Welfare, Jackson, 1965-67, child welfare worker, 1967, county supr., 1967-68, adoption worker, 1968-69, cons., family and children's svcs., 1969-72; asst. prof., coord. social work program Delta State U., Cleveland, Miss., 1972-78, assoc. prof., dir. social work program, 1978-90, prof., dir. social work program, 1990-91; assoc. prof. U. Okla., 1991-97, assoc. prof., coord. undergrad. social work program, 1993-97; vis. prof. U. So. Miss., Hattiesburg, 1997—2001. Site visitor Coun. Social Work Edn., Alexandria, Va., 1986—.

PEHLIVANOV, NONKO DIMITROV, gastroenterologist, researcher; b. Sliven, Bulgaria, Aug. 25, 1961; came to U.S., 1997; s. Dimitar Noykov and Bogdana Georgieva Pehlivanov; m. Daniela Nikolaeva Mitreva, Feb. 16, 1985; 1 child, Plamena. MD, Med. Acad., Sofia, Bulgaria, 1985, specialist in internal medicine, 1991, specialist in gastroenterology, 1993. Asst. prof. Transport Med. Inst., Sofia, 1987-97; rsch. assoc. U. Va., Charlottesville, Va., 1997; postgrad. fellow U. Calif., San Diego, 1998-99; rsch. assoc. U. Kans. Med. Ctr., 1999—. Contbr. rsch. articles and studies to profl. jours.; patentee in field. Mem. Am. Gastroenterol. Assn. Avocation: classical music. Office: U Kans Med Ctr DELP 4035 3901 Rainbow Blvd Kansas City KS 66160 Office Fax: 913-588-6951. E-mail: npehl@hotmail.com., npehlivanov@kumc.edu.

PEHLKE, ROBERT DONALD, materials and metallurgical engineering educator; b. Ferndale, Mich., Feb. 11, 1933; s. Robert William and Florence Jenny (McLaren) P.; m. Julie Anne Kehoe, June 2, 1956; children: Robert Donald, Elizabeth Anne, David Richard. BS in Engring, U. Mich., 1955; S.M., Mass. Inst. Tech., 1958, Sc.D., 1960; postgrad., Tech. Inst., Aachen, Ger., 1956-57. Registered profl. engr., Mich. Mem. faculty U. Mich., 1960—, prof. materials sci. and engring., 1968—, chmn. dept., 1973-84. Cons. to metall. industry; vis. prof. Tohoku U., Sendai, Japan, 1994; Campbell Meml. lectr., 2001. Author: Unit Processes of Extractive Metallurgy, 1973; Editor, contbr. numerous articles to profl. jours. Pres. Ann Arbor Amateur Hockey Assn., 1977-79. NSF fellow, 1955-56; Fulbright fellow, 1956-57 Fellow Am. Soc. Metals (tech. divsn. bd. 1982-84, sec. metals acad. com. 1977), Minerals, Metals and Materials Soc. of AIME (Gold Medal award extractive metallurgy divsn. 1976), Alpha Sigma Mu (disting. life, pres. 1977-78); mem. Iron and Steel Soc. of AIME (Disting. life mem., chmn. process tech. divsn. 1976-77, dir. 1976-79, Howe meml. lectr. 1980), Germany, London, Japan Socs. Iron and Steel, Am. Foundrymen's Soc., Am. Soc. Engring. Edn., Sigma Xi, Tau Beta Pi. Home: 9 Regent Dr Ann Arbor MI 48104-1738 Office: U Mich Materials Sci & Engring Dow Bldg 2300 Hayward St Rm 2098 Ann Arbor MI 48109-2136 E-mail: rdpehlke@engin.umich.edu.

PEI, MING L. civil engineering educator; b. Peking, China, Apr. 17, 1923; came to U.S., 1944; s. I. Hsiang and Chao H. (Wu) P.; m. Yen Fen Kiang, Sept. 2, 1951; children: Victor C., Daniel C. BS, Oreg. State U., 1945; MS, Cornell U., 1946, PhD, 1948. Asst. prof. civil engring. Nat. Central U., Nanking, China, 1948-49; mem. faculty City Coll. CUNY, 1950—, prof. civil engring., 1963-86, prof. emeritus, 1986—, chmn. dept., 1965-68, chief Computation Ctr., 1963-71, chmn. dept. computer sci. Computation Ctr., 1968-71. Cons. to govt. and industry, 1951— Home: 7004 Boulevard E # 37A Guttenberg NJ 07093-5029

PEIFFER, ARTHUR LEROY, health services executive; b. Borger, Tex., July 30, 1942; s. Clifton Lee and Eloise Mae (Brown) P.; m. Susan Jean Munn, Apr. 7, 1969 (div. 1973); children: Gregory Lloyd, Rochelle Jean. BS in Psychology and Sociology, Eastern N.Mex. U., 1965; MA in Counseling Psychology, U. N.Mex., 1968, postgrad., 1969-77; PhD in Behavioral Sci., Clayton U., 1978; grad. Sarus Inst. Biofeedback Tech. Lic. chem. dependency counselor, clin. social worker, marriage and family therapist, Tex.; cert. chem. dependency specialist, stress mgmt. educator, Tex. Psychol. counselor, div. vocat. rehab. N.Mex. Dept. Edn., Albuquerque, 1965-66; dir. counseling and testing Home Edn. Livelihood Program, OEO Project, N.Mex. Council of Chs., Albuquerque, 1966-67; instr. Western State Coll., Gunnison, Colo., summer 1968; doctoral intern, Nazareth Psychiat. Hosp., Albuquerque and U. N.Mex., 1968-69; psychometrist, U. N.Mex., Albuquerque, 1967-69; cons. psychologist, div. vocat. rehab., Inmate Program, N.Mex. State Penitentiary, Santa Fe, 1969-70, dir. placement, instr. psychology, Coll. of Santa Fe, 1969-70; cons. psychologist, div. vocat. rehab. Patient Program, Alcoholism Treatment Program, Albuquerque, 1970-71, chief clin. psychologist, 1971-72; program psychologist, adminstr. Alcohol Safety Action Program, Albuquerque, 1970-71; adj. prof. for internship programs, Eastern N.Mex. U., Portales, 1971-72; dir. clin. services La Hacienda Alcoholism Rehab. Facility (br. Nat. Living Ctrs., Inc.), Hunt, Tex., 1972-74, exec. dir. La Hacienda Alcoholism Treatment Ctr., Inc., Hunt, 1974-75; instr. psychology Schreiner Coll., Kerrville, Tex., 1972-75; founder-clin. dir. Stress, Tension, & Anxiety Tng. Clinic, Inc., Houston, 1975-77; dir. clin. services program for alcoholisms, addictions, stress and anxiety Houston Internat. Hosp. and Med. Ctr. Del Oro Hosp., East Dallas Hosp., Shoal Creek Hosp., Austin, 1975-77; v.p. Positive Alternatives to Anxiety, Stress, and Addictions, Inc., Houston, 1977-78; corp. staff specialist Hosp. Affiliates Internat., Inc., Gulf Coast Region, Houston, 1977-78; exec. v.p., full ptnr. Contemporary Health, Inc., nat. hdqrs., Houston, 1978-82; founder, exec. dir. Stress Mgmt. Research Assocs., Inc., Houston, 1978— ; pres. Vista Health, Inc. of Calif., San Diego, 1981—; pres. Med. Programs, Inc., nat. hdqs., Houston, 1982—; pres. Vista Health Programs, Inc., nat. hdqrs., Houston, 1982—, Internat. HealthNet, Inc., Houston, 1986—; prin. Dr. Arthur L. Peiffer and Assocs., Inc., Houston. Charter mem. Republican presdl. task force; mem. Nat. Rep. Congl. Com.; campaign mem. Rep. Nat. Com., 1982. Mem. Tex. Assn. Alcoholism Counselors, Nat. Assn. Alcoholism Counselors and Trainers, Biofeedback Soc. Am., Am. Assn. Biofeedback Clinicians, Biofeedback Soc. Tex., Nat. Rehab. Counselors Assn., Council for Exceptional Children, Am. Personnel and Guidance Assn., Am. Group Psychotherapy Assn., World Congress Profl. Hypnotists, Am. Assn. Marriage and Family Therapy, Sigma Alpha Epsilon (founder mem. N.Mex.). Author: Alcohol, The Individual and the Automobile, 1972, cassette tape series: Stress Management Tng. Program, 1980; contbr. papers to profl. publs. and confs. Office: 6251 Corporate Dr Houston TX 77036-3411

PEIFFER, GERALDINE M. anesthesiologist; b. Hammond, Ind., Nov. 18, 1923; MD, Loyola U., Chgo., 1949. Diplomate Am. Bd. Anesthesiology. Intern Little Co. Mary Hosp., Evergreen Park, Ill., 1949-50; gen. practice, 1950-55; resident in anesthesiology Mass. Gen. Hosp., Boston, 1955-57; resident Charity Hosp., New Orleans, 1957; staff anesthesiologist St. Margaret Mercy Healthcare Ctr., North Campus, North Hammond, Ind.; former staff anesthesiologist Cmty. Hosp., Munster; pvt. practice, Hammond and Munster, 1957—. Past. instr. respiratory therap Ind. U., Gary. Recipient Stritch medal of medicine Loyola U. Stritch Med. Sch., 1984. Mem. AMA, Am. Surg. Assn., Am. Soc. Anesthesiology.

PEIFFER, RANDEL AARON, agricultural sciences educator, researcher; b. Ligonier, Pa., Aug. 4, 1944; s. Tony and Emma E. (Leighty) P. BS, Delaware Valley Coll., 1968; MS, Pa. State U., 1970, PhD, 1976. Rsch. asst. prof. Del. State U., Dover, 1986; asst. prof. Del. State Coll., 1986-93, assoc. prof., 1993—. Vis. prof. Farmers Home Adminstrn. Advisor carpentry adv. com. Vocat. Tech. Sch., Kent County, Del., 1987—; mem. Del. Agr. Mus., Dover, 1986—; mem. tech. com. NE-SARE, 1994—. Recipient First Pl. Sci. Poster in Plant and Soil Sci., 9th Biennial Rsch. Symposium, Assn. Rsch. Dirs. 1890 Land-Grant Colls. and Univs., Atlanta, 1992—. Mem. Am. Soc. Agronomy, Crop Sci. Soc. Am., Fraternal Order Police, Silver Lake Fishing Club (editor newsletter Dover chpt. 1984—). Achievements include research inforage management and utilization, biological control of gypsy moth in urban forest and crop ecology. Office: Del State U Dept Agr Natural Resources Dover DE 19901

PEIMBERT, MANUEL, astronomer; b. Mexico City, June 9, 1941; s. Gonzalo Peimbert and Catalina Sierra; m. Silvia Torres, Aug. 25, 1962; children: Antonio, Mariana. BS, U. Nacional Autónoma de Mex., 1962; PhD in Astronomy, U. Calif., Berkeley, 1967. Fellow U. Calif., Berkeley, 1967-68; prof. astronomy U. Nat. Autónoma Mex., Mexico City, 1968—; mem. El Colegio Nacional, Mex., 1993—; mem. acad. bd. govs. U. Nat. Autónoma, Mexico, 2000—. Editor Revista Mexicana de Fisica, 1981-85; contbr. articles to profl. jours. Recipient Guillaume Budé medal Coll. de France, Paris, 1974, Nat. Prize of Scis. Govt. of Mex., 1981. Fellow Third World Acad. Scis. (v.p. 1998—); mem. NAS (fgn. assoc.), Am. Astron. Soc. (councilor 1975-78), Internat. Astron. Union (v.p. 1982-88), Royal Astron. Soc. U.K. (fgn. assoc.), Acad. Mexicana Sci. (Scis. prize 1971), Latinamerican Acad. Scis., Soc. Mexicana de Fisica. Office: Inst de Astronomia APDO Postal 70-264 04510 Mexico City Mexico

PEIPERL, ADAM, kinetic sculptor, photographer; b. Sosnowiec, Poland, June 4, 1935; came to U.S., 1953, naturalized, 1958; s. Jacob and Fanny (Alster) P.; m. Martha Rose Dorf, June 15, 1958; children: Maury, Laurence, Linda. Grad., Cours Complementaire Gen, Paris, 1952; BS in Chemistry, George Washington U., 1957; postgrad., Pa. State U., 1959. Cons. in Russian sci. lit. Libr. Congress, Washington, 1959-61, 66-67; chemist Nat. Bur. Standards, 1961-63; sci. translator Am. Inst. Physics, N.Y.C., 1973-94, Plenum Pub., 1993-98. One-man shows include Balt. Mus. Art, 1969, Pa. Acad. Fine Arts, 1969, Marlborough Gerson Gallery, N.Y.C., 1969, Smithsonian Mus. History and Tech., 1972, Electric Gallery, Toronto, Ont., Can., 1975, Phila. Art Alliance, 1978; group shows include Washington Gallery Modern Art, 1968, Corcoran Gallery Art, 1968, Kent State U., McKay Art Inst., San Antonio, 1969, NASA Manned Spacecraft, Houston, 1970-71, Nat. Mus. Am. Art, 1972-82, Meml. Art Gallery, U. Rochester, 1978, Foster Harmon Galleries Am. Art, Sarasota, Fla., 1982-83, Artworks Gallery, Santa Barbara, Calif., 1989, Art of the Sixties, Fred Jones Jr. Mus. of Art, U. Okla., 2002; represented in permanent collections Pa. Acad. Fine Arts, Mus. Boymans-van Beuningen, Rotterdam, The Netherlands, John F. Kennedy Ctr. for Performing Arts, Hirshhorn Mus. and Sculpture Garden, Kreeger Mus.; made first kinetic polarized-light sculpture in water, 1968; designed polarized-light kaleidoscope interiors, 1989; kaleidoscope photographs pub. on book covers for Prentice-Hall/Simon & Schuster, 1991, 92, 97, Mayfield Pub. Co., 1992, 95, 98, 2000, Modern Curriculum Press, 1993; poster for Elektra Entertainment Deee-Lite, 1990 (reproduced in book 1995); art for Andersen Consulting brochure, 1995, Time-Life Book-of-the-Month brochures, 1995-96; collaborated with choreographer Maida Rust Withers on UTAH * Spirit Place * Spirit Planet * Tukuhnikivatz, 1996, multimedia dance theater commd. by Lincoln Ctr. for Lincoln Ctr. Out-of-Doors; work featured in Kaleidoscopes: Wonders of Wonder, 1999; photography represented by The Stock Market Photo Agy. Home: 1135 Loxford Ter Silver Spring MD 20901-1130

PEIPERT, JAMES RAYMOND, journalist; b. Alton, Ill., Nov. 15, 1942; s. Lawrence George and Virginia Pauline (Sieve) P.; m. Mary Ellen Finney, Aug. 1, 1970; children: Benjamin, Matthew, Thomas. BA, So. Ill. U., 1965. Reporter, editor AP, Chgo., 1965-68, N.Y.C., 1968-70, corr. Moscow, 1970-74, London, 1974-80, news editor Johannesburg, South Africa, 1980-81, East Africa bur. chief Nairobi, Kenya, 1981-86; nat.-fgn. editor Fort Worth Star-Telegram, 1986-2001, mem. editl. bd., 2001—. With U.S. Army, 1965-67. Roman Catholic. Avocations: bicycling, maintaining 1967 Mustang, reading. Office: Fort Worth Star Telegram PO Box 1870 Fort Worth TX 76101-1870 E-mail: jpeipert@star-telegram.com.

PEIRANO, LAWRENCE EDWARD, civil engineer; b. Stockton, Calif., May 13, 1929; s. Frank Lloyd and Esther Marie (Carigiet) P.; m. Mary Ellen Alabaster, July 26, 1952; children: Thomas Lawrence, Ellen Marie. BSCE, U. Calif., Berkeley, 1951, MSCE, 1952. Registered profl. engr., Calif.; diplomate Am. Acad. Environ. Engrs. Assoc. civil engr. Calif. Div. Water Resources, 1952-53; with Kennedy Engrs., Inc., San Francisco, 1955-94, project mgr., 1960-79, v.p., chief environ. engr., 1974-79; dir. ops. Kennedy/Jenks Engrs., Inc., 1979-86; sr. v.p., regional mgr. Kennedy/Jenks/Chilton, Inc., 1986-90; exec. v.p., chief tech. officer Kennedy/Jenks Cons., Inc. (formerly Kennedy Engrs., Inc.), 1990-94, also bd. dirs., chmn. bd., 1972-94; ret., 1994. Spl. lectr. san. engring. U. Calif., Berkeley, 1976. Served in U.S. Army, 1953-55, Korea, Okinawa. James Monroe McDonald scholar, 1950-51; recipient Trustees' citation U. Calif., Berkeley, 1996. Fellow ASCE (life); mem. Water Environ. Fedn., U. Calif. Alumni Assn., Sierra Club, Tau Beta Pi, Chi Epsilon. Republican. Roman Catholic. Home: 3435 Black Hawk Rd Lafayette CA 94549-2326 *Focus on serving clients and rewards will follow.*

PEIRCE, BROOKE, English language educator; b. Washington, Jan. 2, 1922; s. Charles Brooke, Jr. and Nancy Ley (Bass) P.; m. Carol Emily Marshall, July 12, 1952. BA, U.Va., 1943; MA, Harvard U., 1947, PhD, 1954. Teaching fellow Harvard U., 1948-51; instr. English U. Va., 1951-54; mem. faculty Goucher Coll., 1954-85, prof. English, 1966-85, prof. emeritus, 1985—, chmn. dept. English and dramatic arts, 1964-69, 72-75, chmn. faculty humanities, 1964-66, 72-73, 79. Vis. prof. English SUNY, Oswego, 1985—87; lectr. Villa Julie Coll., 1989—2000; adj. prof. U. Md., Baltimore County, 2001. Author: (with Carol Peirce) Introduction to English Literature, 2 vols., 1954. Treas. Edgar Allan Poe Soc., Balt., 1959-66, mem. bd., 1959—, Phi Beta Kappa Alumni Assn. Greater Balt., 1995—. Served with U.S. Army, 1943-45. Nat. Endowment for Humanities fellow, 1977-78; recipient Disting. Tchr. award, 1979 Mem. Modern Lang. Assn., Raven Soc. of U. Va., Classical Assn., Phi Beta Kappa. Democrat. Home: 705 Warren Rd Cockeysville MD 21030-2824

PEIRCE, CAROL MARSHALL, English educator; b. Columbia, Mo., Feb. 1, 1922; d. Charles Hamilton and Helen Emily (Davault) Williams; m. Brooke Peirce, July 12, 1952. AB, Fla. State U., 1942; MA, U. Va., 1943; PhD, Harvard U., 1951. Head English dept. Fairfax Hall, Waynesboro, Va., 1943-44; instr. English Cedar Crest Coll., Allentown, Pa., 1944-46; instr. Harvard U., 1952-53; asst. dean Radcliffe Coll., Cambridge, 1950-53; head English extension home study U. Va., Charlottesville, 1953-54; asst. dir. admissions Goucher Coll., Towson, Md., 1956-62; prof. English and comm. design U. Balt., 1968—, chmn. dept., 1968-94, gen. edn. core coord., 1985-87, Disting. teaching prof. Coll. Liberal Arts, 1981-82, chmn. humanities div., 1972-79; gen. edn. dir., 1995-97; chmn. bd. New Poets Series, 1975—. Vis. scholar Lucy Cavendish Coll., U. Cambridge, Eng., 1977-78; co-coord. On Miracle Ground: The Internat. Lawrence Durrell Conf., 1980, 82, 90, 2000; co-coord. conf. Evermore! Celebrating the 150th Anniversary of Edgar Allan Poe's "Raven," 1995. Author: (with Brooke Peirce) A Study of Literary Types and an Introduction to English Literature from Chaucer to the Eighteenth Century, 1954, A Study of Literary Types and an Introduction to English Literature from the Eighteenth Century to the Present, 1954; editor: (with Lawrence Markert) On Miracle Ground: Second Lawrence Durrell Conference Proceedings, 1984; guest editor: (with Ian S. MacNiven) Lawrence Durrell Issue, Parts I and II, Twentieth Century Literature, Fall, Winter, 1987; contbr. essays to: Poe and Our Times, 1986, Critical Essays on Lawrence Durrell, 1987, Into the Labyrinth: Essays on the Art of Lawrence Durrell, 1989, On Miracle Ground: Essays on the Fiction of Lawrence Durrell, 1990, Dictionary of Literary Biography Yearbook, 1990, St. James Reference Guide to English Literature, 1991, Poe's Pym: Critical Explorations, 1992, Selected Essays on the Humor of Lawrence Durrell, 1993, Lawrence Durrell: Comprehending The Whole, 1994, D.H. Lawrence: The Cosmic Adventure, 1996, Anais Nin: A Book of Mirrors, 1996, others; assoc editor: Deus Loci: The Lawrence Durrell Jour., 1990-92, co-editor, 1993—. McGregor fellow, DuPont fellow U. Va., 1943; Harvard tutor, Anne Radcliffe traveling fellow Harvard U., 1951. Mem. MLA, Edgar Allan Poe Soc. of Balt. (bd. dirs. 1973-89, pres. 1989—), Lawrence Durrell Soc. (nat. pres. 1980-82, internat. pres. 1994-98), Md. Assn. Depts. English, Phi Beta Kappa, Chi Delta Phi, Phi Alpha theta, Phi Kappa Phi. Home: 705 Warren Rd Cockeysville Hunt Valley MD 21030-2824 Office: Univ Balt Divsn English/ Comm Dsgn Baltimore MD 21201 E-mail: cpeirce@ubmail.ubalt.edu.

PEIRCE, CAROLE, elementary school educator; b. Oshkosh, Wis., June 11, 1943; d. Charles J. and Bernadette (Graf) P.; m. Jack McDowell, Nov. 18, 1982. BS, U. Wis., Oshkosh, 1965; MA, U. Wis., Madison, 1966. Instr. U. Wis. Ctr. System, Marinette & Fond Du Lac, 1966-70, Concordia Coll., Milw., 1970-71; tchr. of French Behavioral Rsch. Labs., Palo Alto, Calif., 1971-73; elem. tchr. Nido De Aguilas Internat. Sch., Santiago, Chile; elem. bilingual tchr. Alum Rock Sch. Dist., San Jose, Calif., 1978-87; elem. tchr. Huntsville (Ark.) Sch. Dist., 1987-95; French, Spanish, and ESL tchr. Huntsville (Ark.) H.S., 1995-2000. Presenter Bay Area Sch. Dists. Calif., 1984-87, Springdale Tchrs. Co-op, Little Rock, Arkadelphia, Ark., Dallas, Albuquerque, St. Paul, Dominican Republic; tchr., cons. Nat. Geog. Soc., 1990-96. Author Social Studies Review Article 1985. Grantee Environ. Edn. State of Calif., 1986, NSTA to Internat. Geographical Congress, Washington, 1992, NASA Ednl. Workshop for Elem. Sci. Tchrs., 1993; Christa McAuliffe fellow, 1993-94; recipient Nat. Disting. Teaching award Nat. Achievement Coun. Geographic Edn., 1993. Mem. NEA, Nat. Coun. for Social Studies, Nat. Coun. for Geog. Edn., Ark. Geog. Alliance (newsletter editor, Geography Tchr. of Yr., 1993-94), Ozark Soc. Avocations: global studies, geography, outdooring, travel. Home: 2046 Madison 8325 Hindsville AR 72738-9727

PEIRCE, FREDERICK FAIRBANKS, lawyer; b. Torrington, Conn., Jan. 28, 1953; s. Everett L. and Frederica (Fairbanks) P.; m. Sandra Marie MacMillan, Dec. 16, 1989. BS with high honors, Colo. State U., 1975; JD, U. Colo., 1979. Bar: Colo. 1979, U.S. Dist. Ct. Colo. 1979. Assoc. Bratton & Zimmerman, Gunnison, Colo., 1979-80; staff atty. Holland & Hart, Aspen, 1980-82; assoc. Austin, McGrath & Jordan, 1982-84, Austin & Jordan, Aspen, 1984-87; ptnr. Austin, Jordan, Young & Peirce, 1987-89, Austin & Peirce, Aspen, 1989-92, Austin, Peirce & Smith, P.C., Aspen, 1992—. Bd. dirs. Aspen Nordic Coun. Inc., 1985-88, Aspen Velo Club Inc., 1986-88, Aspen Cycling Club, Inc., 1988-93, Kids First, 1997—, pres., 2000—; bd. dirs. Aspen Ctr. for Environ. Studies, 1991-97, v.p., 1992-94, pres., 1994-97; bd. dirs. Pitkin County Pks. Assn., Inc., 1990-98, v.p., 1991-92, pres., 1992-95; mem. Aspen Valley Land Trust, 1990-98, v.p., 1991-92, pres., 1992-95; mem. bd. edn. Aspen Sch. Dist., 1997—. NSF grantee, 1975. Mem. Colo. Bar Assn. (bd. govs. 1989-93, exec. coun. 1993-95, v.p. 1995-96, ethics com., 1995-97), Pitkin County Bar Assn. (v.p. 1985-86, pres. 1986-88, bd. govs. rep. 1989-93),

Phi Kappa Phi. Avocations: skiing, hiking, fly fishing, cycling, flying. Office: Austin Peirce & Smith PC Ste 205 600 E Hopkins Ave Aspen CO 81611-2933 E-mail: fpeirce@aps-pc.com., feircto@rof.net.

PEIRCE, GEORGIA WILSON, public relations executive; b. Newton, Mass., Jan. 6, 1960; d. Norris Ridgeway and Anne (McCusker) P. BA, Duke U., 1982. Intern to Speaker of Ho. of Reps., Washington, 1981; prin. PR, etc., Quincy, Mass., 1987-94; dir. media rels. and info. sys. The Mass. Gen. Hosp., Boston, 1994—. Cons. Mass. Group Insur. Commn., 1985. Contbr. articles to profl. jours. Mem. community rels. com. Vis. Nurse Assn./Hospice of South Shore; mem. com. to elect Mondale-Ferraro, Mass., coord. speakers bur., 1984; mem. charitable trust com. Maj. John F. Regan; com. mem. City of Quincy Recycling Com.; del. Mass. Dem. Conv., 1982, 83; v.p. South Shore Ad Club, 1990-91, mem.-at-large, 1991-92. Recipient 9th Wave awards 1989, 1st pl. in Pub. Rels. award, 1989, merit awards, 1992. Mem. NAFE, South Shore C. of C., Small Bus. Assn. New Eng., Women's Golf Assn. Mass., Publicity Club New Eng. (v.p. media rels. 1989, Merit Bell Ringer award 2000, 01), Rotary Internat., Eastward Ho! Country Club Chatham (club champion 1977-81, 83, 91, 93). Democrat. Roman Catholic. Avocation: golf (many awards including state titles). Home: 71 Bayfield Rd North Quincy MA 02171-2007 Office: Mass Gen Hosp Office of Pub Affairs Fruit St Boston MA 02114

PEIRCE, JAMES WALTER, retired secondary school educator; b. Aug. 8, 1933; s. Kenneth Adelbert and Helen Virginia Peirce; married, Apr. 14, 1962; 1 child Mary Andrew. Cert. social studies tchr., secondary prin. Md. Tchr., adminstr. Prince George's County Bd. Edn., Upper Marlboro, Md., 1957—89, ret., 1989. Vol. fireman Chillum-Adelphi (Md.) Fire Dept., 1960—65; vol. ranger Pasapsco River Valley State Pk., Ellicott City, Md., 1994—99. Author: Pasapsco Valley Mill Sites, 1995, Four Hundred Years of Dicken, 2001, (poems) The People Call it Chesapeake, 1999. Life mem. Md. Congress of Parents and Tchrs., Hyattsville, 1976—. With USN, 1951—56. Named Outstanding Educator of Am., Acad. Am. Edn., 1974. Mem.: U. Md. Alumni Assn., Nat. Arbor Day Found., Am. Legion (life; historian 1995—2001). Democrat. Avocations: history, genealogy, research, poetry, writing. Home: 3119 Beltsville Rd Beltsville MD 20705

PEIRCE, NEAL R. journalist; b. Phila., Jan. 5, 1932; s. J. Trevor and Miriam deS. (Litchfield) P.; m. Barbara von dem Bach-Zelewski, Apr. 18, 1959; children: Celia, Andrea, Trevor. BA, Princeton U., 1954; postgrad., Harvard U., 1957-58. Polit. editor Congl. Quar., 1960-69; co-founder, contbg. editor Nat. Jour., Washington, 1969-97. Cons. and commentator elections CBS News, 1962, 67-76, NBC News, 1964-66; lectr. in field; syndicated newspaper columnist Washington Post Writers Group; chmn. The Citistates Group; mem. faculty Salzburg (Austria) Seminar, 1980, 84, 97; 1st Weinberg prof. Princeton U.'s Woodrow Wilson Sch. Pub. and Internat. Affairs, 1992. Author: The People's President, 1968, 2d edit., 1981, The Megastates of America, 1972, The Pacific States of America, 1972, The Mountain States of America, 1972, The Great Plains States America, 1973, The Deep South States of America, 1974, The Border South States, 1975, The New England States, 1976, The Mid-Atlantic States of America, 1977, The Great Lakes States of America, 1980, The Book of America: Inside Fifty States Today, 1983, Citistates: How Urban America Can Prosper in A Competitive World, 1993, Breakthroughs: Recreating The American City, 1993; Corrective Capitalism, 1987; editor Peirce Report series on 21 regions' Citistate futures starting with Phoenix Republic and Gazette, 1987. Founder, chmn. S.W. Neighborhood Assembly, Washington, 1963-65; mem. exec. com. Nat. Civic League, 1990-95; trustee German Marshall Fund U.S., 1987-97. With CIC, U.S. Army, 1954-57. Fellow Woodrow Wilson Internat. Center Scholars, 1971-74 Fellow Nat. Acad. Pub. Adminstrn.; mem. Newfound Lake Region Assn. (v.p. 1989-92), Phi Beta Kappa. Episcopalian. Home and Office: 610 G St SW Washington DC 20024-2440 E-mail: npeirce@citistates.com.

PEIRIS, SUHITHI MAHESICA, research chemist; b. Colombo, Sri Lanka, Nov. 23, 1965; d. Suran A. and Marguerite M. Peiris; m. Brett M. Goodman, Apr. 28, 2001. BS with honors, U. Mich., 1991; PhD in Inorganic Chemistry, U. Chgo., 1996. Postdoctoral fellow U. Chgo., 1996-97; staff scientist Nova Rsch. Inc., Alexandria, Va., 1997-98; rsch. chemist Naval Rsch. Lab., Washington, 1998-2000, Naval Surface Warfare Ctr., Indian Head, Md., 2000—. Contbr. articles to profl. jours. Sci. fair judge, Washington, 1999, Indian Head, 2000. Recipient award for Outstanding Young Scientist, Gordon Rsch. Conf., 2000. Mem. Am. Chem. Soc. Avocations: swimming, reading.

PEISER, JOHN GEORGE, accountant, consultant; b. Chgo., June 2, 1944; m. Liora Rappaport, June 29, 1969; children: Daniela Jacqui, Gary Dean. BSc, U. Witwatersrand, South Africa, 1965, BSc (hon.), 1969; M in Bus. Leadership, U. South Africa, Pretoria, 1977. CPA; cert. valuation analyst. Researcher Nat. Inst. for Pers. Rsch., Johannesburg, South Africa, 1966-69; various mgmt. positions Lindsay Saker, South Africa, 1970-76, bd. dir. pers. South Africa, 1976 -78; mgr. human resource planning & devel. Fox & Jacobs, Dallas, 1978-83, regional sales dir., 1984-85; pres. Sidran, Inc., 1985-90; CPA, ptnr., exec. cons. Peiser & Peiser, CPAs, 1990-93; ptnr., exec. cons. bus. valuations Goldin Peiser & Peiser, CPAs, L.L.P., 1993—. Bd. dirs. Solomon Schechter Acad. Dallas, chmn., 1984-86. Bd. dirs. Shearith Israel Congregation, Dallas, 1983-86, Zionist Orgn. Am., Dallas; pres. Yavneh Acad. of Dallas, 1993—, pres./treas. Zionist Mvmt./Bnai, Zion. Mem. AICPA, Am. Inst. Tng. and Devel., Nat. Assn. Cert. Valuation Analysts, Tex. Soc. CPA, Inst. Personnel Rsch. (branch chair, 1974-75). Avocations: reading, squash, tennis, bridge, travel. Office: 17742 Preston Rd Dallas TX 75252

PEISER, ROBERT ALAN, financial executive; b. N.Y.C., Apr. 17, 1948; s. Donald Edward and Natalia (Phillips) Peiser; children: Karyn, Brian, Craig, Scott. BA, U. Pa., 1969; MBA, Harvard U., 1972. Dir. corp. fin. TWA, N.Y.C., 1972-77, sr. v.p. fin., CFO, 1983-86, exec. v.p. fin., CFO, 1994-96; treas. Hertz Corp., 1977-80; staff v.p., treas. ops. RCA Corp., 1980-81; v.p., treas. Trans World Corp., 1981-83; sr. v.p., CFO ALC Comm. Corp., Birmingham, Mich., 1986-88; sr. v.p. fin., CFO Borman's Inc., Detroit, 1988-89; pres., CEO Orange-Co. Ic., Bartow, Fla., 1989-92; with BBK, Ltd., Southfield, Mich., 1992-94; vice chmn., CEO FoxMeyer Drug Co., Carrollton, Tex., 1996; pres., CEO Western Pacific Airlines, Colorado Springs, Colo., 1996-98; chmn. CVSI, Inc., Bedford, Mass., 1998-99; chmn., CEO Vitality Beverages, Tampa, Fla., 1999—. Bd. dirs. Ascent Assurance, Inc., Microware, Inc., Tampa Bay Partnership. Trustee Mich. chpt. Leukemia Soc. Am. Mem. Birmingham Athletic Club, The Wyndgate Country Club. Home: 831 Normandy Trace Rd Tampa FL 33602 Office: Ste 2000 400 N Tampa St Tampa FL 33602

PEITLER, ARTHUR JOSEPH, mayor, lawyer; b. N.Y.C., Dec. 2, 1948; s. Arthur Joseph and Dorothy Virginia Peitler; m. Mary Elizabeth Fitzpatrick, July 1, 1972; children: Daniel Joseph, Maureen Elizabeth, James Fitzpatrick. BS, St. Johns U., Jamaica, N.Y., 1970, MBA, 1973; JD, U. Conn., 1983. Bar: Conn. 1983, U.S. Dist. Ct. Conn. 1984. Acctg. mgr. J.C. Penney Co., N.Y.C., 1970-75; fin. analyst AMF, White Plains, N.Y., 1975-78; fin. mgr. Timex, Middlebury, Conn., 1978-83; pvt. practice, New Milford, 1983-95; mayor Town of New Milford, 1995—. Pres. New Milford Bar Assn., 1987. Treas., asst. treas. New Milford Jaycees/Conn. Jaycees, 1975-78; vice chmn. Childrens Ctr. Inc., New Milford, 1984-95; treas. Merryall Ctr. for Arts, New Milford, 1986—; chmn. Rep. Town Com., New Milford, 1988-89, 93-95; active Fin. Coun. St. Francis, New Milford, 1990-94. Roman Catholic. Office: Town of New Milford 10 Main St New Milford CT 06776-2831

PEITZMAN, ANDREW BERTRAM, surgeon; b. Phila., Feb. 3, 1949; m. Debra Shaffer; children: Elizabeth, Jonathon, Emily, David. BS, U. Pitts., 1971, MD, 1976. Intern U. Pitts., 1976-77, resident, 1977-79, 81-84; fellow Cornell Med. Ctr. N.Y. Hosp., 1979-81; asst. prof. surgery U. Pitts., 1984-89, assoc. prof., 1989-96, prof. surgery, 1996—. Dir. trauma and emergency svcs. U. Pitts. Med. Ctr., 1984—2001, med. dir. referral communication ctr., 1989—; chief divsn. gen. surgery; co-dir. trauma/neurosurg. ICU Presbyn. U. Hosp., Pitts., 1992—; dir. surg./critical care fellowship U. Pitts., 1992—96, vice-chmn. clin. svcs. for dept. surgery. Author: Trauma, 1993, Pathophysiologic Foundations of Critical Care Medicine, 1993; editor: UPMC Trauma Manual, 1994, The Trauma Manual, 1998. Recipient Nat. Rsch. Svc. award NIH, 1980-81. Fellow ACS; mem. Assn. for Acad. Surgery, Soc. Critical Care Medicine, Soc. Univ. Surgeons, Surg. Infection Soc., Ctrl. Surg. Assn. Shock Soc. Office: U Pitts Med Ctr F1264 Presbyn Univ Hosp Pittsburgh PA 15213

PEIXOTO NETO, JOSE ULYSSES, internist, researcher; b. Crato, Ceará, Brazil, Aug. 29, 1930; s. Adérito de Aquino Silva and Adelite Alencar Peixoto; m. Maria Isolda Teles Cartaxo, May 23, 1958; children: Jose Ulysses Peixoto Filho, Eunice Ulysséia Peixoto Maia, Jorge André Cartaxo Peixoto. 1st degree, State Coll. Goias, Brazil, 1942, postgrad., 1942-49; 2d degree, St. John Coll., Fortaleza, Brazil, 1949; postgrad., Fed. U., Recife, Brazil, 1955; Laurel, Cearense Med. Ctr., 1994. Med. resident St. Michael Hosp., Rio de Janeiro, 1956; intern St. Anthony Hosp., Iguatú, Ceará, 1957; founder Social Providence, Crato, 1958-64; attendent St. Frances Hosp., 1958-69; founder St. Michael Hosp., 1967-93, pres., dir., 1983-93, internist, researcher, 1993—; founder Faculty of Law, 1977-78. Lectr. faculty of medicine The Fed. U. of Ceará, 1976—. Recipient Good Svc. award Lyons Club, 1992, Laurel Cearense Med. Ctr., 1994, Cert. Merit Health Care Profls. Juazeiro North Profl. Health Assn., 1998, Gold Medal of Profl. Merit, Ceara Estate Regional Coun. Medicine, 1999. Fellow Brazilian Med. Assn. (specialist); mem. AAAS, ACP, Brazilian Soc. Clin. Medicine (specialist), N.Y. Acad. Sci. Roman Catholic. Avocations: reading, walking in woods, cinema, farming.

PEKARSKY, MELVIN HIRSCH, artist; b. Chgo., Sept. 18, 1934; s. Abe and Inda (Levin) P. Student, Sch. of Art Inst., Chgo., 1951-52; BA, Northwestern U., 1955, MA, 1956. Faculty Northwestern U., 1955-56; faculty Kendall Coll., 1960-67, chmn. art dept., 1965-67; asst. dean Sch. Visual Arts, N.Y.C., 1967-68, assoc. dean, 1968-69; grad. faculty NYU, 1970-71; assoc. prof. art SUNY, Stony Brook, 1975-84, prof. art, 1984—, chmn. dept., 1977-78, 84-89, dir. MFA and studio programs, 1990—2002. One-man shows include Gimpel and Weitzenhoffer, N.Y.C., 1974, Lehigh U., 1975, Ball State U. Gallery, Muncie, Ind., 1975, G.W. Einstein Co., Inc., N.Y.C., 1975, 77, 78, 80, 81, 82, 84, 86, 88, 91, 95, 97, Hull Gallery, Washington, 1978, Centro Colombo-Americano, Bogotá, Colombia, 1980, 112 Greene St. Gallery, N.Y.C., 1980, 82, Marianne Deson Gallery, Chgo., 1987, Butler Inst. Am. Art, Youngstown, Ohio, 1990, The Mus. at Stony Brook, 1993, Nev. Mus. Art, Reno, 2001; group shows include Chgo. Art Inst., 1966, Whitney Mus., N.Y.C., 1971, Bklyn. Mus., 1974, Cleve. Mus., 1978, Cooper-Hewitt Mus., 1971, Mus. Modern Art Corp.,Lending and Adv. Svc. Exhbns., Kuznetsky-Most Galleries, Moscow, 1989, NAD, N.Y.C., 1990, Fogg Mus. Art/Harvard U., 2000, Am. Acad. Arts and Letters, N.Y.C., 2001, Nielsen Gallery, Boston, 2001, public murals commns., Houston and Crosby Sts., N.Y.C., 1972, Lafayette and Bleecker Sts., N.Y.C., 1969; represented in permanent collections, Cleve. Mus., Fogg Mus. Art, Harvard U., Indpls. Mus., Nev. Museum of ARt, Westinghouse Corp., Corcoran Gallery Art, Yale U., Notre Dame U., AT&T, Chase Manhattan Bank, other pub. and corp. collections, also pvt. collections. Founding mem., v.p., bd. dirs. City Walls, 1969-77. Served with Combat Engrs. AUS, 1957-59. Recipient grants in public art through City Walls Kaplan Fund, 1969, City Walls Bernhard Found., 1971, City Walls N.Y. State Council on Arts, 1970, City Walls Nat. Endowment for the Arts, 1971 Mem. Coll. Art Assn. Am. Home: PO Box 1575 Stony Brook NY 11790-0875 Office: Suny Art Dept Stony Brook NY 11794-0001 E-mail: pekarsky@aol.com., mpekarsky@ms.cc.sunysb.edu.

PEKER, ELYA ABEL, artist; b. Moscow, June 15, 1937; came to U.S. 1972; s. Aba Z. and Frieda I. (Warshavsky) P.; m. Katrina Friedman, May 19, 1977; 1 child, Benjamin E. Diploma of Artist for Theater Decoration, Art Inst., Moscow, 1956. Comml. artist, N.Y.C., 1972-88. One-man shows include Nakhamkin Fine Art Gallery, N.Y.C., 1980-85; exhibited in group shows in Basel, Switzerland, Hong Kong, others; represented in permanent collections of Kennedy-Onassis family, Emil Wolf, Frank L'Angella, Campbell family, Benjamin family, others; contemporary flower and still-life poster series published 1991, reproductions published worldwide. Mem. Am. Biog. Inst. (dep. gov., order internat. ambs., Gold Record Achievement 1995, 20th Century Achievement award 1995, Internat. Cultural Diploma Honor 1996), Internat. Platform Assn., Licensing Industry Merchandiser's Assn. Address: 1673 E 16th St Ste 164 Brooklyn NY 11229-2901 E-mail: pekerelya@webtv.net.

PEKLO, KAREN SUE, retail executive; b. Rocky Mount, N.C., June 1, 1961; d. Joseph William and Marilyn Janelda (Murdoch) P. BS in Mktg., U. West Fla., 1987. Dept. mgr. trainee Gayfers, Pensacola, Fla., 1984-88, asst. sr. buyer Mobile, Ala., 1988-89, dept. mgr. and buyer Ridgeland, Miss., 1989-92; dept. mgr. Marshall Fields, Schaumburg, Ill., 1992-95; dep. mgr. Sears, Pensacola, Fla., 1995-98, mdse. analyst Hoffman Estates, Ill., 1998-2000, dist. mktg. mgr. N.Y.C., 2000—01, 2002—. Mem. Jr. League of N.Y.C., Pensacola Ski Club. Republican. Roman Catholic. Avocations: golf, tennis, skiing. Home: 195 Wellington Ct Ste 3C Staten Island NY 10314 Office: Sears 195 N Broadway Hicksville NY 11801 E-mail: ksp12345@aol.com .

PEKOZ, EROL A. finance educator; b. N.Y.C., Jan. 1, 1965; s. Teoman and Regina Pekoz. PhD, U. Calif., Berkeley, 1995. Assoc. prof. Boston U., 1999—. Mem.: Applied Probability Soc., Inst. for Ops. Rsch. and Mgmt. Scis.

PÉLADEAU, MARIUS BEAUDOIN, art consultant, retired museum director; b. Boston, Jan. 27, 1935; s. Marius and Lucienne (Beaudoin) P.; m. Mildred L. Cole, Feb. 26, 1972. BA cum laude, St. Michael's Coll., 1956; MS, Boston U., 1957; MA, Georgetown U., 1962. Assoc. editor Public Utilities Fortnightly, Washington, 1962-66; adminstrv. asst., press sec. to U.S. Congressman J. P. Vigorito, 1967-72; dir. Maine League Hist. Socs. and Mus.'s, Monmouth, 1972-76, William A. Farnsworth Library and Art Mus., Rockland, Maine, 1976-87; gen. mgr. The Theater at Monmouth, 1989; cons. in field, 1990—. Author: The Verse of Royall Tyler, 1968, The Prose of Royall Tyler, 1972, Chansonetta: The Life and Photographs of Chansonetta Stanely Emmons, 1858-1937, 1977, Charles Daniel Hubbard, 1876-1951: American Impressionist, 1996, John Francis Sprague: Chronicler of Maine History, 1998, Burnished Rows of Steel: The Role of Vermont Troops at the Battle of Gettysburg, July 1-3 1963, 2002 Trustee Mus. Glass and Ceramics; guest curator L.C. Bates Mus., Hinckley, Maine, 1993-2000. Fellow Co. Mil. Historians; mem. Vt. Hist. Soc. Democrat. Roman Catholic. E-mail: peladeau@g.w.i.net.

PELAEZ, ROLANDO FEDERICO, economics educator, consultant; b. Washington, May 5, 1940; s. Rolando Juan and Maria Gertrudis (Bringuier) P. BS, La. State U., 1962, MA, 1964; PhD in Econs., U. Houston, 1973; postgrad., Rice U., 1978-79. Teaching fellow U. Houston-Univ. Park, 1970-71, instr., 1971-73; asst. prof. N.Mex. State U., 1973-74, Southeastern La. U., 1976, U. Houston-Downtown, 1977-80, assoc. prof. fin. Coll. Bus., 1987—; assoc. prof. U. St. Thomas, 1980-87. Expert witness forensic economist; vis. asst. prof. U. Houston-Univ. Park, 1974-75; spkr., presenter confs. in field. Contbr. articles to profl. jours. OAS doctoral fellow, 1970. Mem. Am. Econ. Assn., Am. Statis. Assn., So. Finance Assn., Southwestern Econ. Assn., Southwestern Finance Assn., Western Econ. Assn., Nat. Assn. Forensic Economists. Home: 8318 Daycoach Ln Houston TX 77064-8202 E-mail: pelaezr@uhd.edu.

PELAGALLI, JAMES A. surgeon; b. Bedford, Ohio, Mar. 10, 1931; MD, Loyola U. - Stritch Sch. Med., 1955. Diplomate Am. Bd. Surgeons. Intern St. Vincent Charity Hosp., Cleve., 1955-56, resident, 1956-57, 59-62; surgeon Parma Comm. Gen. Hosp., Ohio, U.S. Army Med. Corp., 1957-59. Fellow Am. Coll. Surgeons; mem. AMA. Office: 3666 Forest Run Dr Richfield OH 44286-9408

PELANT, BARNEY FRANK, international business consulting executive; b. L.A., Mar. 4, 1942; s. Barney William and Marie Bohumila (Riha) P.; m. Judith Ann Proctor, May 23, 1970; 1 child, Nicole Marie; 1 step-child, Dalina Lynn DuBois. AA, El Camino Coll., 1962; BS, U. So. Calif., L.A., 1969, MBA, 1970. Cert. Master Bus. Continuity Professional, Disaster Recovery Planner. Engr., scientist McDonnell Douglas Corp., Culver City, Calif., 1963-70; sect. mgr., officer Continental Bank, Chgo., 1970-84; dir. contingency svcs. SunGard Recovery Svcs., Northbrook, Ill., 1984-89; dir. cons. Harris Devlin Assocs., 1989-90; sr. mgr. Ernst & Young, Chgo., 1990-91; owner, prin. Barney F. Pelant & Assocs., Bloomingdale, Ill., 1991—. Bd. dirs. Disaster Recovery Inst. Internat., St. Louis, 1992-93, 95-96, exec. dir., 1992-93, certification bd. dirs., 1991-96, chmn., 1995-96; bd. dirs. Can. Ctr. Emergency Preparedness, Hamilton, Ont., 1993—. Contbr. articles to profl. jours. Chmn. Plan Commn., Bloomingdale, 1984-96, Zoning Bd. Appeals, Bloomingdale, 1984-96, Sesquicentennial Landmark Com., Bloomingdale, 1983-86. With U.S. Army NG, 1964-70. Mem. U. So. Calif. Midwest Alumni Club, Beta Gamma Sigma. Avocations: swimming, tennis. Office: Barney F Pelant & Assocs 243 Harvard Ln Bloomingdale IL 60108-2141

PELAVIN, DIANE CHRISTINE, science administrator; m. Sol H. Pelavin, Aug. 14, 1966. BA, So. Ill. U., 1965; MS, San Jose (Calif.) State U., 1979. Tchr., 1965—68; planning analyst EPRI, Palo Alto, Calif., 1977—78; rsch. analyst NTS Rsch. Corp., Durham, NC, 1978—82; v.p., co-founder Pelavin Assocs., Inc., Washington, 1982—94; pres., co-founder Chesapeake Inst., 1991—94; sr. v.p. Am. Insts. for Rsch., 1994—. Contbr. articles to profl. jours. U. Chgo. fellow, 1966, NSF fellow, 1968. Mem. Am. Edn. Rsch. Assn. Office: 1000 Thomas Jefferson St NW Washington DC 20007-3835

PELAVIN, SOL HERBERT, research company executive; b. Detroit, Dec. 16, 1941; s. Norman J. and Alice A. Pelavin; m. Diane Christine Blakemore, Aug. 14, 1966; 2 children. BA in Math., U. Chgo., 1965, MAT in Math., 1969; MS in Stats., Stanford U., 1974, PhD candidate in mathematical models of edn. research, 1975. Tchr. pub. schs., 1965-70. teaching rsch. asst. Stanford (Calif.) U., 1972-74; cons. Rand Corp., Santa Monica, Calif., 1975; policy analyst SRI Internat., Menlo Park, Calif., 1975-78; exec. officer NTS Research Corp., Durham, N.C., 1978-82; pres. Pelavin Assocs., Inc., Washington, 1982-94; exec. v.p., COO Am. Inst. Rsch., 1994-2001, pres., CEO, 2001-; dir. Data Analysis and Tech. Support Ctr., Washington, 1989-93, Policy Analysis Support Ctr., Washington, 1993—; expert witness to U.S. Congress, 1977, 79, Cabinet briefing, 1983; cons. Frank, Bernstein, Conway and Goldman, Balt., 1980-81; dir. Ednl. Analysis Ctr., Washington, 1982-85. Author: (with others) Investigation of the Impact of the Emergency School Assistance Programs on Black, Male 10th Grade Student Achievement, 1975, (with P. Barker) A Study of the Generalizability of the Results of Standardized Achievement Tests, 1976, (with J.L. David) Research on the Effectiveness of Compensatory Education Programs: A Reanalysis of Data, 1977, (with others) Federal Expenditures for the Education of Children and Youth With Special Needs, 1981, (with D.C. Pelavin) An Evaluation of the Fund for the Improvement of Postsecondary Education, 1981, 83, (with others) Evaluation of the Commodity Supplemental Food Program, 1982, An Evaluation of the Bilingual Education Evaluation, Dissemination and Assessment Centers, 1984, A Study of a Year-Round School Program, 1978, Teacher Preparation: A Review of State Certification Requirements, 1984, Analysis of the National Availability of Mathematics and Science Teachers, 1983, Minority Participation in Higher Education, 1988, Changing the Odds, 1990, others; contbr. articles to profl. jours. NSF fellow U. Chgo., 1968-69; Cuneo fellow Stanford U., 1973. Mem. Am. Ednl. Research Assn., Am. Psychol. Assn. Democrat. Jewish. Office: American Inst Rsch 1000 Thomas Jefferson Washington DC 20007-3500 E-mail: spelavin@air.org.

PELC, KAROL IGNACY, engineering management educator, researcher; b. Czestochowa, Poland, July 29, 1935; came to U.S., 1985; s. Stanislaw Pelc and Kamilla (Hecko) Pelc-Kosna; m. Ryszarda Lidia Ryglewicz, Sept. 24, 1959; 1 child, Dariusz. MScEE, Tech. U. Wroclaw, Poland, 1958, PhD in Econs., 1976; PhD in Electronics, U. Uppsala, Sweden, 1968. Prodn. & engrng. mgr. Energopomiar Co., Wroclaw, 1960-65; rsch. asst. dept. electronics U. Uppsala, 1961-62; assoc. dir. divsn. Inst. Electric Power Industry, Wroclaw, 1966-68; founder, dir. Forecasting Rsch. Ctr., 1971-81; electronic design engr. Rsch. Inst. Tech. U. Wroclaw, 1957-60, rsch. dir., 1968-77, lectr., dir. Jelenia Gora Coll. br., 1982-85; prof. Mich. Technol. U., Houghton, 1985—; dir. Ctr. for Technol. Innovation, Leadership & Entrepreneurship, 2001—. Vis. prof. Indian Inst. Tech., Bombay, 1981, Stevens Inst. Tech., Hoboken, N.J., 1993; vis. scholar Japan Ctr. for Mich. Univs., Hikone, 1992; mem. innovation task force Internat. Inst. for Applied Systems Analysis, Laxenburg, Austria, 1983-84; chmn. forecasting seminar Polish Acad. Scis., Warsaw, 1974-81; v.p. divsn. Soc. Mgmt. and Orgn., Wroclaw, 1979-80. Author: Planning of Research and Development, 1981; co-author: Technological Challenges, 1999; mem. editl. bd. Technol. Forecasting and Social Change, U.S. R&D Mgmt., Eng., Transformations, Poland; contbr. over 100 articles to scholarly jours.; patentee in field. Mem. Internat. Assn. Mgmt. Tech., Internat. Assn. for Rsch. and Devel. Mgmt., Am. Soc. Engrng. Mgmt., Engrng. Mgmt. Soc. of IEEE, Acad. Mgmt. Roman Catholic. Avocations: classical music, tourism, cross-country skiing, bicycling, swimming. Office: Mich Technol Univ Sch Bus & Econ Houghton MI 49931

PELCYGER, IRAN, retired principal; b. Bklyn., Feb. 26, 1937; s. Jacob and Yetta (Nabridge) P.; m. Elaine Morley, June 4, 1956; children: Stuart Lawrence, Gwynne Ellice, Wayne Farrol. BS, CCNY, 1959, MA in Sci. and Edn., 1962; postgrad., Yeshiva U., 1963, Adelphi U. and NYU, 1964-67, 68-74. Cert. tchr., ednl. adminstr., N.Y. Tchr., adminstr. various pub. schs., Bklyn., 1959—; tchr., acting chmn. sci. dept., chmn. program dept. Jr. High Sch. 265, 1959-66; tchr. aerospace and gen. sci., chmn. sci. dept. Jr. High Sch. 111, 1966-71, asst. prin., 1971-74; prin. Frances E. Carter Sch., 1974-98; ret., 1998. Adj. instr. Sch. Edn., CCNY, 1988—; mem. ad-hoc com. elem. edn., N.Y. Dept. Edn., 1987, mem. organizing com., moderator edn. conf., 1986—; adj. prof. York Coll., 1998, Bronx C.C., 1998—, Iona Coll., New Rochelle, N.Y., 2000—. Contbg. editor: A Guide for Elementary Sch. Prins., 1985, Proceedings of the Mainstream Conf.: Opening Doors to a Brighter Future, 1988; co-writer: Mainstreaming Handbook: A Guide to Implementing. Mem. N.Y.C. Elem. Sch. Prins. Assn. (past pres.), Coun. Suprs. and Adminstrs. (past v.p., exec. bd. 1983—, trustee Welfare Fudn 1986—), N.Y. Acad. Pub. Edn., Nat. Assn. Elem. Sch. Prins., Network for Effective Schs., ASCD, Phi Delta Kappa. Home: 79 Sheryl Cres Smithtown NY 11787-1321

PELEG, ILAN, political science educator; b. Tel Aviv, Oct. 5, 1944; came to U.S., 1971; d. Jochanan and Eva (Doppler) Popper; m. Sima Ashkenazy Peleg, Oct. 24, 1968; children: Gil, Talia. BA, Tel Aviv U., 1969, MA, 1971, Northwestern U., 1972, PhD, 1974. Asst. prof. Lafayette Coll., Easton, Pa., 1974-80, chmn. internat. affairs program, 1977-85, assoc. prof. polit sci., 1980-88, head govt. and law dept., 1985—, prof., 1988-90, Charles A. Dana prof. govt. and law, 1990—. Author: Begin's Foreign Policy, 1977-83, Israel Move to the Right, 1987; editor: Patterns of Censorship Around the World, 1993; co-editor: The Emergence of Binational Israel, 1989; contbr. articles to profl. jours. Mem. Internat. Studies Assn., Atlantic Council USA (bd. assocs.). Jewish. Avocations: chess, classical music.

PELFREY, D. PATTON, lawyer; b. Ky., 1941; BA, Calif. State U., L.A., 1963; JD, U. Louisville, 1968. Bar: Ky. 1968. Trial atty. region 9 NLRB, Cin., 1968-72; mem. Frost Brown Todd LLC, Louisville, 1972—. Prof. labor law sch. law U. Louisville. Fellow Coll. Labor and Emloyment Lawyers; mem. ABA (sect. labor and employment law), Ky. Bar Assn. (labor sect.), Louisville Bar Assn. (mem. labor com. 1983—), Delta Theta Phi. Office: Frost Brown Todd LLC 400 W Market St Ste 3200 Louisville KY 40202-3363

PELIKAN, JAROSLAV JAN, history educator; b. Akron, Ohio, Dec. 17, 1923; s. Jaroslav Jan and Anna (Buzek) P.; m. Sylvia Burica, June 9, 1946; children: Martin, Michael, Miriam. Grad. summa cum laude, Concordia Jr. Coll., Ft. Wayne, Ind., 1942; BD, Concordia Theol. Sem., St. Louis, 1946; PhD, U. Chgo., 1946; MA (hon.), Yale U., 1961; DD (hon.), Concordia Coll., Moorehead, Minn., 1960, Concordia Sem., 1967, Trinity Coll., Hartford, Conn., 1987, St. Vladimir's Orthodox Theol. Sem., 1988, Victoria U., Toronto, 1989, U. Aberdeen, Scotland, 1995; LittD (hon.), Wittenberg U., 1960, Wheeling Coll., 1966, Gettysburg Coll., 1967, Pacific Luth. U., 1967, Wabash Coll., 1988, Jewish Theol. Sem., 1991; HHD (hon.), Providence Coll., 1966, Moravian Coll., 1986, Jewish Theol. Sem., 1991; LLD (hon.), Keuka Coll., 1967, U. Notre Dame, 1979, Harvard U., 1998, U. Regina, 1998; LHD (hon.), Valparaiso U., 1966, Rockhurst Coll., 1967, Albertus Magnus Coll., 1973, Coe Coll., 1976, Cath. U. Am., 1977, St. Mary's Coll., 1978, St. Anselm Coll., 1983, U. Nebr.-Omaha, 1984, Tulane U., 1986, Assumption Coll., 1986, LaSalle U., 1987, Carthage Coll., 1991, U. Chgo., 1991, So. Meth. U., 1992, SUNY, Albany, 1993, Fla. Internat. U., 1997; ThD (hon.), U. Hamburg, 1971, St. Olaf Coll., 1972, Charles U., Prague, 1999; STD, Dickinson Coll., 1986; DSc in Hist., Comenius U., Bratislava, 1992; ScD (hon.), Loyola U., Chgo., 1995. Faculty Valparaiso (Ind.) U., 1946-49, Concordia Sem., St. Louis, 1949-53, U. Chgo., 1953-62; Titus Street prof. eccles. history Yale U., 1962-72, Sterling prof. history, 1972-96, William Clyde DeVane lectr., 1984-86, dir. div. humanities, 1974-75, chmn. Medieval studies, 1974-75, 78-80, dean Grad. Sch., 1973-78; Joseph chair Boston Coll., 1996-97; prof. Annenberg Sch. U. Pa., 1998-2001; Disting. Vis. Scholar Libr. Congress,

Washington, 2001—02. Vis. prof. Boston Coll., 1996-97, Annenberg Sch. Comm., U. Pa., 1998—; Gray lectr. Duke U., 1960, Ingersoll lectr. Harvard U., 1963, Gauss lectr. Princeton U., 1980, Jefferson lectr. NEH, 1983, Richard lectr. U. Va., 1984, Rauschenbusch lectre. Colgate-Rochester Divinity Sch., 1984, Gilson lectr. U. Toronto, 1985, 98, Hale lectr. Seabury-Western Sem., 1986, Mead-Swing lectr. Oberlin Coll., 1986, Gross lectr. Rutgers U., 1989; bd. dirs. Nat. Humanities Ctr., 1984-90, Univ. Support Svcs. Inc., 1992-94; adv. bd. Ctr. Theol. Inquiry, 1984-90; mem. coun. The Smithsonian Instn., 1984-90; U.S. chmn. U.S. Czechoslovak Commn. on Humanities and Social Scis., 1987-92. Author: From Luther to Kierkegaard, 1950, Fools for Christ, 1955, The Riddle of Roman Catholicism, 1959 (Abingdon award 1959), Luther the Expositor, 1959, The Shape of Death, 1961, The Light of the World, 1962, Obedient Rebels, 1964, The Finality of Jesus Christ in an Age of Universal History, 1965, The Christian Intellectual, 1966, Spirit Versus Structure, 1968, Development of Doctrine, 1969, Historical Theology, 1971, The Christian Tradition, 5 vols., 1971-89, Scholarship and Its Survival, 1983, The Vindication of Tradition, 1984, Jesus through the Centuries, 1985, The Mystery of Continuity, 1986, Bach Among the Theologians, 1986, The Excellent Empire, 1987, The Melody of Theology, 1988, Confessor Between East and West, 1990, Imago Dei, 1990, Eternal Feminines, 1990, The Idea of the University: A Reexamination, 1992, Christianity and Classical Culture, 1993, Faust the Theologian, 1995, The Reformation of the Bible/ The Bible of the Reformation, 1996, Mary through the Centuries, 1996, The Illustrated Jesus Through the Centuries, 1997, What Has Athens to do with Jerusalem?, 1997, also introductions to works of others; editor, translator: Luther's Works, 22 vols., 1955-71, The Book of Concord, 1959; editor: Makers of Modern Theology, 5 vols., 1966-68, The Preaching of Chrysostom, 1967, Interpreters of Luther, 1968, Twentieth-Century Theology in the Making, 3 vols., 1969-70, The Preaching of Augustine, 1973, The World Treasury of Modern Religious Thought, 1991, Sacred Writings, 7 vols., 1992; mem. editorial bd. Collected Works of Erasmus, Classics of Western Spirituality, Evangelisches Kirchenlexikon, Emerson's Nature, 1986, The World Treasury of Modern Religious Thought, 1990; departmental editor Ency. Britannica, 1958-69; adminstrv. bd. Papers of Benjamin Franklin; chmn. publs. com. Yale Univ. Press, 1979-90, 92—, v.p. bd. govs., 1988—; contbr. to many symposia, jours., encys. Pres. 4th Internat. Congress for Luther Research, 1971, New Eng. Congress on Grad. Edn., 1976-77. Recipient Abingdon award, 1959; Pax Christi award St. John's U., Collegeville, Minn., 1966, Colman J. Barry award, 1995; John Gilmary Shea prize Am. Cath. Hist. Assn., 1971, nat. award Slovak World Congress, 1973, religious book award Cath. Press Assn., 1974, Christian Unity award Atonement Friars, 1975, Bicentennial award Czechoslovak Soc. Arts and Scis., 1976, Wilbur Cross medal Yale U. Grad. Sch. Assn., 1979, Profl. Achievement award U. Chgo. Alumni Assn., 1980, Shaw medal Boston Coll., 1984, Comenius medal Moravian Coll., 1986, Alumnus of Yr. award U. Chgo. Div. Sch., 1986, Bicentennial medal Georgetown U., 1989, award for excellence Am. Acad. Religion 1989, Umanità award Newberry Libr., 1990, Jacques Barzun award Am. Acad. for Liberal Edn., 1997, Festschriften: Schools of Thought in the Christian Tradition, 1984, The Unbounded Community, 1996; sr. fellow Carnegie Found. for Advancement Tchg., 1982-83. Fellow Medieval Acad. Am. (councillor, Haskins medal 1985); mem. Am. Hist. Assn., Am. Soc. Ch. History (pres. 1965, Achievement award 1998), Internat. Congress Luther Rsch. (pres. 1971), Am. Acad. Arts and Scis. (v.p. 1976-94, pres. 1994-97), Am. Philos. Soc. (councillor 1984-87, Moe prize 1997), Am. Acad. Polit. and Social Sci. (pres. 2000—), Coun. Scholars of Libr. of Congress (founding chmn. 1980-83), Elizabethan Club, Mory's, Phi Beta Kappa (senator United chpts. 1985-90). Home: 156 Chestnut Ln Hamden CT 06518-1604

PELINO, DAVID FRANKLIN, psychiatrist, writer; b. Providence, Nov. 12, 1952; s. Pasco and Angelina Pelino; m. Sonia Grineva, Jan. 1, 1996. BS, Boston Coll., 1974; MS, U. of Ga., 1977; MD, Med. Coll. of Ga., 1984; Cert. in Psychoanalytic Medicine, Columbia U., 1994. Diplomate Nat. Bd. Med. Examiners, 1986, American Board of Psychiatry and Neurology. Resident in psychiatry U. of South Fla. Hospitals, Tampa, 1985—86; asst. psychiatrist NY Hosp., White Plains, 1986—89; staff and rsch. psychiatrist New York-Cornell Hosp., Westchester Divsn., 1989—91, asst. psychiatrist, 1986—89; pvt. practice of psychiatry N.Y.C., 1991—; lectr. in psychoanalysis Columbia U., 1994—; clin. asst. prof. of psychiatry Cornell U., 2000—. Psychotherapy supr. Lincoln Hosp. and Med. Ctr., N.Y.C., NY, 2000—; psychopharmacology supr. Payne Whitney Psychiat. Clinic, N.Y.C. Author: (novel) One Good Deed, 2001; contbr. numerous articles to profl. jours. Mem.: ABA (assoc. 2001—02), Med. Soc. State of NY (mem. 1992—2002), Am. Med. Writers Assn. (mem. 2001—02), Internat. Soc. of Polit. Psychology (mem. 2000—02), Am. Psychiat. Assn. (mem. 1986—2002). Independent. Office: 1100 Park Ave #1B New York NY 10128 Office Fax: 212-828-4109.

PELIZZO, RICCARDO, political scientist; b. Verona, Italy, Dec. 31, 1971; came to U.S., 1997; s. Carlo Pelizzo and Vittoria Elisabetta Benedetti. Laurea, U. Bologna, Italy, 1995; diploma, Sch. Adv. Internat. Studies, Bologna, 1997. Polit. scientist Johns Hopkins U., Balt. Bd. dirs. Azienda Municipalizzata di Igiene Ambientale, Verona, 1994-96. Roman Catholic. Office: Johns Hopkins U 3400 N Charles St Baltimore MD 21218

PELIZZONI, VIRGINIA MATKO, writer, editor, consultant; b. East Orange, N.J., July 2, 1951; d. Edward Martin and Dorothy (Pohorelli) Matko; m. Joseph A. Pelizzoni, May 10, 1975. BA in Journalism and Art, Rutgers U., 1973; postgrad., Union County Tech. Inst., 1974, DuCret Sch. of the Arts, Plainfield, N.J., 1980. Pub. rels. asst. Mutual Benefit Life Ins. Co., Newark, 1973-75, publs. supr., 1975-84, comms. mgr., 1984-85; pub. rels. dir. Welkind Rehab. Hosp., Chester, N.J., 1985-87; prin., owner VMP Comm., Warren, 1987—. Contbr. articles to profl. publs. Mem. pub. rels. com. Am. Cancer Soc., Somerset County, Raritan, N.J., 1997-98. Recipient First Pl. award United Way of Tri-State, 3 awards for merit Life Advertisers Assn., award of excellence Bus. Mktg. Assn. of N.J., Internat. Assn. of Bus. Communicators, 2 awards of excellence, 3 1st pl. U.S. Savs. Bond campaign newsletter awards U.S. Dept. Treasury, 1st pl. award editl. writing, 2 awards of merit newsletters. Mem. Internat. Assn. of Bus. Communicators. E-mail: vpelizzo@bellatlantic.net.

PELL, ARTHUR ROBERT, human resources specialist, consultant, author; b. N.Y.C., Jan. 22, 1920; s. Harry and Rae (Meyers) P.; m. Erica Frost, May 19, 1946; children— Douglas, Hilary. AB, NYU, 1939, MA, 1944; PhD, Calif. Coast U., 1977; diploma, Cornell U., 1943. Personnel dir. Eagle-Electric Mfg. Co., Long Island City, N.Y., 1946-50, North Atlantic Constructors, N.Y.C., 1950-53; v.p. Harper Assos., Inc., 1953-75; cons. Human Resources Mgmt., Hempstead, N.Y., 1975—. Adj. assoc. prof. mgmt. NYU Sch. Continuing Edn., 1962-84, St. John's U. Coll. Bus. Adminstrn., 1971-76; lectr. Baruch Sch. Bus. and Pub. Adminstrn. Coll. City N.Y., 1948-67. Author: (with W.B. Patterson) Fire Officer's Guide to Leadership, rev. edit., 1963, Placing Salesmen, 1963, Placing Executives, 1964, Police Leadership, 1967, How to Get the Job You Want After 40, 1967, Recruiting and Selecting Personnel, 1969, (with M. Harper) Starting and Managing an Employment Agency, 1970, Recruiting, Training and Motivating Volunteer Workers, 1972, Be a Better Employment Interviewer, 1972, rev. edits., 1978, 86, 94, The College Graduate Guide to Job Finding, 1973; (with Wilma Rogalin) Women's Guide to Executive Positions, 1975; (with Albert Furbay) College Student's Guide to Career Planning, 1975; (with Dale Carnegie Assocs.) Managing Through People, 1975, rev. edits., 1978, 1987, Choosing a College Major: Business, 1978, Enrich Your Life: The Dale Carnegie Way, 1979, The Part Time Job Book, 1984, Making the Most of Medicare, 1987, rev. edit., 1990; (with Gregor Sadek) Resumes for Engineers, 1982, Resumes for Computer Professionals, 1984, How to Sell Yourself on an Interview, 1982, The Job Finder's Kit, 1989, Getting the Most from Your People, 1990, Diagnosing Your Doctor, 1991, The Supervisor's Infobank, 1994, The Complete Idiot's Guide to Managing People, 1995, 2d edit., 1999, The Pocket Idiot's Guide to One Minute Management, 1999, The Complete Idiot's Guide to Team Building, 1999, The Complete Idiot's Guide to Recruiting The Right Stuff, 2000, The Complete's Idiot Guide to Human Resources Management, 2001, (with Franklin C. Ashley) Embracing Excellence, 2001; editl. cons. for revision Dale Carnegie's How to Win Friends and Influence People, 1981; author syndicated feature The Human Side; contbr. articles to profl. jours. With AUS, 1942-46. Office: 111 Dietz St Hempstead NY 11550-7625 E-mail: arpell@aol.com.

PELL, CLAIBORNE, former senator; b. N.Y.C., Nov. 22, 1918; s. Herbert Claiborne and Matilda (Bigelow) P.; m. Nuala O'Donnell, Dec. 1944; children: Herbert Claiborne III, Christopher T. Hartford, Nuala Dallas Yates, Julia L.W. Student, St. George's Sch., Newport, R.I.; AB cum laude, Princeton U., 1940; AM, Columbia U., 1946; 51 hon. degrees. Enlisted USCGR, 1941; served as seaman, ensign North Atlantic sea duty, Africa, Italy; hospitalized to U.S., 1944; instr. Navy Sch. Mil. Govt., Princeton, 1944-45; capt. USCGR; ret.; on loan to State Dept. at San Francisco Conf., 1945, State Dept., 1945-46, U.S. embassy, Czechoslovakia, 1946-47; established consulate gen. Bratislava, Czechoslovakia, 1947-48; vice consul Genoa, Italy, 1949; assigned State Dept., 1950-52; v.p., dir. Internat. Rescue Com.; senator from R.I., 1961-96; U.S. del. to UN, 97—. Ranking minority mem. Fgn. Rels. Com., Labor and Human Resources Subcom. on Edn., Arts, and Humanities; mem. Rules and Adminstrn. Com., Joint Com. on Libr. and Congl. Intern Program, Senate Dem. Policy Com.; U.S. del. Internat. Maritime Consultative Orgn., London, 1959, 25th Gen. Assembly, 1970; disting. vis. prof. Salve Regina U., Newport, R.I., 1997—. Author: Megalopolis Unbound, 1966, (with Harold L. Goodwin) Challenge of the Seven Seas, 1966, Power and Policy, 1972. Hon. bd. dirs. World Affairs Council R.I.; trustee St. George's Sch.; trustee emeritus Brown U.; Cons. Democratic Nat. Com., 1953-60; exec. asst. to chmn. R.I. State Dem. Com., 1952-54; chmn. R.I. Dem. Fund drive, 1952, Dem. nat. registration, chmn., 1956, co-chmn., 1962; chief delegation tally clk. Dem. Nat. Conv., 1956, 60, 64, 68. Decorated knight Crown of Italy, Grand Cross Order of Merit Italy, Red Cross of Merit Portugal, Legion of Honor France, comdr. Order of Phoenix Greece, Grand Cross Order of Merit Liechtenstein, Grand Cross Order of Christ Portugal, Order of Henry the Navigator, Portugal, Grand Cross Order of N. Star Sweden, Grand Cross of Merit Knights of Malta, Grand Officer of Merit Luxembourg, Grand Comdr. Lebanon; recipient Caritas Elizabeth medal Cardinal Franz Koenig, Grand decoration of honor in silver with sash Austria, Gold medal of St. Barnabas (Cyprus), recipient Pres.'s Fellow award R.I. Sch. Design, medal Nat. Order of Cedar, Hugo Grotius Commemorative medal The Netherlands, recipient Harold W. McGraw, Jr. Prize in Education, McGraw-Hill, 1988. Mem. Soc. Cin. Clubs: Hope (Providence); Knickerbocker (N.Y.C.), Racquet and Tennis (N.Y.C.), Brook (N.Y.C.); Metropolitan (Washington); Travellers (Paris); Reading Room (Newport); White's (London). Episcopalian. *I have a seven word definition of my job and of my life: "Translate ideas into events, and help people".*

PELL, JONATHAN LAURENCE, artistic administrator; b. Memphis, Oct. 20, 1949; s. Burton Marshall and Eleanor (Leopold) P. BA, U. So. Calif., 1971. Interior designer Gene Morse Assocs., Wichita, Kans., 1971-77; mgr. Internat. Artists Mgmt., N.Y.C., 1977-79, Robert Lombardo Assocs., N.Y.C., 1979-80; TV producer Sta. WNET, 1980-83; dir. publicity John Curry Skating Co., 1983; prodr. Jerome Kern Centennary Gala Town Hall, 1984; dir. artistic administration The Dallas Opera, 1984—. Vocal competition judge Met. Opera Nat. Coun. Audutions, Pavarotti Competition, George London Awards, Ctr. for Contemporary Opera, Dallas Opera Guild, Denver Lyric Opera Guild, Ft. Worth Opera, Marguerite McCammon Competition, San Antonio Opera Guild, Richard Tucker Award, others; tchr. master classes for young singers Opera Am., Nat. Opera Assn., Can. Opera Co., S.W. Chpt. NATS, Performing Arts Assistance Corp., U. North Tex., So. Meth. U.; host Dallas Opera Radio Hour, WRR, 1994—97; advisor singer svcs. com. Opera Am. Bd. dirs., chmn. nat. auditions com., mem. award selection com. Richard Tucker Music Found.; mem. adv. bd. Awards Recognizing Individual Artistry; advisor to singer svcs. com. Opera Am. Office: Dallas Opera Campbell Ctr I LBI-11 8350 N Central Expy Ste 210 Dallas TX 75206-1601

PELL, SIDNEY, epidemiologist; b. N.Y.C., Dec. 13, 1922; m. Lola May, July 2, 1950. MBA, CCNY, 1952; PhD, U. Pitts., 1956. Biostatistician E.I. Du Pont de Nemours and Co., Wilmington, Del., 1955-76, mgr. epidemiology sect., 1976-82, sr. cons., 1982-85; epidemiology cons., 1985—. Epidemiology cons. Del. Divsn. Pub. Health, Dover, 1986-95. Contbr. articles to New Eng. Jour. Medicine, Jour. Occupational Medicine, Jour. AMA. With U.S. Army, 1943-45, ETO. Recipient Merit in Authorship Hon. Mention, Inds. Med. Assn., 1959. Fellow Am. Coll. Epidemiology, Am. Heart Assn., Am. Pub. Health Assn. Home: 1416 Emory Rd Wilmington DE 19803-5120

PELLA, MILTON ORVILLE, retired science educator; b. Wilmot, Wis., Feb. 13, 1914; s. Charles August and Ida Marie (Pagel) P.; m. Germaine Marie Reich, Dec. 9, 1944. B.E., Milw. State Tchrs. Coll., 1936; MS, U. Wis., 1940, PhD, 1948. Tchr. sci. and math. Wyler Mil. Acad., 1937-38; tchr. elementary sch. Delavan Pub. Schs., 1938-39; tchr. sci. U. Wis. High Sch., 1939-42; prof. sci. edn. U. Wis., Madison, 1946-80, prof. emeritus, 1980—; With Fgn. Ednl. Service, Turkey, 1959, Iran, Turkey, Jordan, Syria, Lebanon, 1961, 62, Jordan, Lebanon, 1963, 64, 65, 66, 68, Costa Rica, 1967, Saudi Arabia, 1969, Nigeria, 1968, 69, Lebanon and Egypt, 1971-81. Author: Physical Science for Progress, 3d edit, 1970, Science Horizons— The Biological World, (with Branley and Urban), 1965-70. Served with AUS, 1942-46. Fellow A.A.A.S.; mem. Central Assn. Sci. and Math. (pres. 1955), Nat. Assn. for Research in Sci. Teaching (pres. 1966), Nat. Sci. Tchrs. Assn. (dir. 1950, 60) Clubs: Masons. Home: 5518 Varsity Hl Madison WI 53705-4652

PELLE, EDWARD GERARD, biochemist; b. N.Y.C., Jan. 20, 1950; s. Enrico and Maria Donata (Cello) P.; m. Evangeline Solero, June 23, 1973; children: Edward G., John L., Gina M., Anthony C. BS, Fordham U., 1972; MS, NYU, 1978, PhD, 2002. Rsch. asst. Rockefeller U., N.Y.C., 1972-78, NYU Med. Ctr., N.Y.C., 1978-82; prin. scientist Estee Lauder Rsch. Lab., Melville, N.Y., 1982—. Peer rev. com. Am. Inst. Biol. Scis., Washington, 1989—. Author: RNA: Biological Aspects, 1980, (with others) Antioxidant Protection Against Ultraviolet Light-Induced Skin Damage, 1993; contbr. articles to Archives Biochem. & Biophysics, Annals-N.Y. Acad. Scis., Cancer Rsch., Proceedings of the Nat. Acad. Scis. Recipient N.Y. State Regents scholarship N.Y. State Regent, 1968-72, Fordham U. scholarship, 1968-72. Mem. Soc. Investigative Dermatology, N.Y. Acad. Scis., AAAS. Achievements include patents in Cu-DIPS, an antioxidant used in sunscreen composition; in an L-Tocopherol derivative molecule with antioxidant properties; in a derivative molecule with UVA sunscreen ability. Office: Estee Lauder Rsch Labs 125 Pinelawn Rd Melville NY 11747-3135

PELLECCHIA, EVE WASSALL, management consultant; b. Columbus, Ohio, Dec. 7, 1956; d. Robert Byron Wassall and Constance Leona (Windey) Moult; m. Dennis John Pellecchia, Oct. 29, 1983; children: Kevin Patrick, Kara René. BS, Lebanon Valley Coll., 1978; MBA, Lehigh U., 1983. CFP. Ops. rsch. analyst Air Products & Chems., Inc., Trexlertown, Pa., 1978-83, ops. rsch. mng. analyst, 1984-87, ops. rsch. mgr. gas. div., 1987-88; pvt. practice Wyomissing, Pa., 1990—. Mem. Reading Hosp. Aux., Wyomissing, Pa., 1987—; fundraiser Am. Heart Assn., 1991—97; pres. Cross Keys Wranglers 4-H Club, 1997—98, Wyomissing Hills Shade Tree Commn., 1997, Consistory Bausman Meml. United Ch. of Christ, 2000—. Avocations: skiing, tennis, photography, horseback riding, golf. Home: 102 Robert Rd Wyomissing PA 19610-3116

PELLECCHIA, JOHN MICHAEL, lawyer; b. Orange, N.J., Dec. 6, 1958; BA, Lafayette Coll., 1980; JD cum laude, Tulane U., 1983. Bar: N.J. 1983, U.S. Dist. Ct. N.J. 1983, U.S. Supreme Ct. 1994. Assoc. Pitney, Hardin, Kipp & Szuch, Morristown, N.J., 1983-86; asst. counsel to gov. Thomas H. Kean State of N.J., Trenton, 1986-88; ptnr. Riker, Danzig, Scherer, Hyland & Perretti, LLP, Morristown and Trenton, 1988—. Mem. mgmt. com. Riker, Danzig, Scherer, Hyland & Perretti LLP, Morristown and Trenton, 1995-98; jud. extern to fed. dist. ct. judge, U.S. Dist. Ct., New Orleans, 1982-83; sr. fellow Tulane Law Sch., 1982-83, mem. N.J. Supreme Ct. Com. on Tax Ct., 1993-96, 2000-2002; mem. bus. and fin. svcs. task force of Gov. Whitman's Econ. Master Plan Commn., 1994. Trustee, v.p. Leukemia Soc. Am. North Jersey chpt., 1991—; trustee N.J. Shakespeare Festival, 1996—. Vol. of Yr., Leukemia Soc. Am. North Jersey chpt., 1994. Office: Riker Danzig Scherer Hyland & Perretti LLP 50 W State St Ste 1010 Trenton NJ 08608-1220

PELLEGRENE, THOMAS JAMES, JR. editor, researcher; b. Wilmington, Del., Dec. 26, 1959; s. Thomas J. and MaryBelle (McGowan) P.; m. Pamela Heinecke, Apr. 5, 1986. BS in Journalism, Northwestern U., 1981, MS in Journalism, 1982. Staff writer Ft. Wayne (Ind.) Journal-Gazette, 1982-87, bus. editor, 1987-95, asst. metro editor, 1995-98, mgr. news techs., 1998—. Mem. Soc. Profl. Journalists, Spl. Librs. Assn. Office: Fort Wayne Journal-Gazette 600 W Main St Fort Wayne IN 46802-1408 E-mail: tpellegrene@jg.net.

PELLEGRINO, EDMUND DANIEL, physician, educator, academic administrator; b. Newark, June 22, 1920; s. Michael J. and Marie (Catone) Pellegrino; m. Clementine Coakley, Nov. 17, 1944; children: Thomas, Virginia, Michael, Andrea, Alice, Leah. BS, St. John's U., 1941, DSc (hon.), 1971; MD, NYU, 1944; 39 hon. degrees. Diplomate Am. Bd. Internal Medicine. Intern Bellevue Hosp., N.Y.C., 1944—45, asst. resident medicine, 1948—49; resident medicine Goldwater Meml. Hosp., N.Y.C., 1945—46; fellow medicine NYU, 1949—50; supervising Tb physician Homer Folks Hosp., Oneonta, NY, 1950—53; dir. internal medicine Hunterdon Med. Center, Flemington, NJ, 1953—59, med. dir., 1955—59; prof., chmn. dept. medicine U. Ky. Med. Center, 1959—66; prof. medicine SUNY, Stony Brook, 1966—72, v.p. for health scis., dir. Health Scis. Center, 1968—73, dean Sch. Medicine, 1968—72; v.p. health affairs U. Tenn. System; chancellor U. Tenn. Med. Units, Memphis, 1973—75; prof. med. Yale U., New Haven, 1975—78; pres. Yale-New Haven Med. Center, 1975—78, Cath. U. Am., Washington, 1978—82, prof. philosophy and biology, 1978—82; John Carroll prof. medicine and med. ethics Georgetown U., Washington, 1982—; dir. Kennedy Inst. Ethics, 1983—88; dir. Ctr. for Advanced Study Ethics Georgetown U., 1988—94, dir. Ctr. for Clin. Bioethics, 1991—, acting chief Divsn. Gen. Internal Medicine, 1993—94, chief Gen. Internal Medicine, 1995. Founding editor: Jour. Medicine and Philosophy, 1983—. With USAAF, 1946—48. Master: ACP; fellow: N.Y. Acad. Medicine; mem.: Inst. Medicine of NAS, AMA, Am. Clin. and Climatol. Assn., Assn. Am. Physicians. Office: Georgetown U Ctr for Clin Bioethics Washington DC 20007

PELLEGRINO, JAMES WILLIAM, college dean, psychology educator; b. N.Y.C., Dec. 20, 1947; s. Vincent and Emily (Nicosia) P.; m. Barbara Jo Sposato, June 6, 1970 (div. 1975); 1 child, Christopher Michael; m. Susan Rosen Goldman, Dec. 23, 1978; children: Joshua Goldman, Seth Goldman. BS in Psychology, Colgate U., 1969; MS in Experimental, Quantitative Psychology, U. Colo., 1970, PhD in Experimental, Quantitative Psychology, 1973. Asst. prof. U. Pitts., 1973-78, assoc. prof., 1978-79, U. Calif., Santa Barbara, 1979-83, prof., 1983-89; Frank Mayborn prof. Vanderbilt U., Nashville, 1989—2001, dean Peabody Coll. Edn. and Human Devel., 1991-98; disting. prof. cognitive psychology and edn. U. Ill., Chgo., 2001—, co-dir. Ctr. for Study of Learning, Instrn. and Tchr. Devel., 2001—. Co-dir. Learning Tech. Ctr. Vanderbilt U., 1989-91; proposal reviewer NSF, Can. Rsch. Coun., Australian Rsch. Coun.; chmn. com. on evaluation of nat. assessment of ednl. programs, Nat. Acad. Scis., com. on found. of assesment, com. on learning rsch. and ednl. practice; presenter in field. Author: (with others) Cognitive Psychology and Instruction, 1978, Handbook of Semantic Word Norms, 1978, Memory Organization and Structure, 1979, Aptitude, Learning and Instruction: Cognitive Process Anayses, How Much and How Can Intelligence Be Increased, 1982, Advances in Instructional Psychology, vol. II, 1982, Handbook of Research Methods in Human Memory and Cognition, 1982, Advances in the Psychology of Human Intelligence, 1982, Individual Differences in Cognition, 1983, Human Abilities: An Information Processing Approach, 1984, Test Design: Developments in Psychology and Psychometrics, 1985, International Encyclopedia of Education, 1985, What is Intelligence?, 1986, Arthur Jensen: Consensus and Controversy, 1987, Intelligence and Cognition: Contemporary Frames of Reference, 1987, Metacognition, Motivation and Understanding, 1987, Test Validity, 1988, Learning and Individual Differences: Abilities, Motivation and Methodology, 1989, The Psychology of Learning and Motivation, 1989, The Proceedings of the 22nd Annual Hawaii International Conference on System Sciences, 1989, Vision and Action: The Control of Grasping, 1990, Learning Disabilities: Theoretical and Research Issues, 1990, Intelligence: Reconceptualization and Measurement, 1991, Philosophy of Science, Cognitive Psychology, and Educational Theory and Practice, 1992, New Approaches to Testing: Rethinking Aptitude, Achievement and Assessment, 1992, Cognitive Approaches to Automated Instruction, 1992; co-author: Human Intelligence: Perspectives and Prospects, 1985, Testing: Theoretical and Applied Perspectives, 1989, Instruction: Theoretical and Applied Perspectives, 1991, Jasper Project: Lessons in Curriculum, Instruction, Assessment and Professional Development, 1997, Grading the Nation's Report Card, 1999, How People Learn: Building Research and Practice, 1999; contbr. numerous articles to profl. jours. Named Lifetime Nat. Assoc., NAS; recipient Austen Colgate award, Phil R. Miller award, Outstanding Young Men in Am. award. Mem. AAAS, NRC, Am. Ednl. Rsch. Assn. (various coms.), Midwestern Psychol. Assn., Rocky Mountain Psychol. Assn., N.Y. Acad. Sci., European Assn. Rsch. on Learning and Instrn., Cognitive Sci. Soc., Soc. Multivariate Experimental Psychology, Computers in Psychology, Soc. Mathematical Psychology, Soc. Rsch. and Child Devel., Psychonomic Soc., Sigma Xi, Phi Beta Kappa, Psi Chi. Avocations: sports, gardening, music. Home: 175 N Harbor Dr # 4703 60601 Office: U Ill at Chgo Dept Psychology (MC285) 1007 W Harrison St Chicago IL 60607 E-mail: pellegjw@uic.edu.

PELLEGRINO, MARY MADELINE, speech language pathologist; b. N.Y.C., Oct. 9, 1953; d. Joseph and Gwen (LaPrairie) Fennelly; m. Matt Pellegrino, Aug. 17, 1974; children: David, Joseph, Chris, Daniel, Mary. BA, Immaculata Coll., 1975; MA, Cath. U. Am., 1977. Cert. clin. competence speech lang. pathologist. Owner, dir. Mary Pellegrino and Assocs., Tallahassee. Speech cons. Active Good Shepherd Cath. Ch. Mem. Am. Speech and Hearing Assn., Fla. Speech and Lang. Assn. Avocations: scuba diving, swimming. Office: 3215 Capital Medical Blvd Tallahassee FL 32308-4413

PELLER, ANDREW MARTIN JOSEPH, artist; b. Toronto, Ont., Can., Feb. 28, 1953; came to U.S., 1985; s. Joseph Andrew and Constance Shirly (Martin) P.; m. Eugenia Alberta Everett, July 19, 1985. Ed., Banff (Alta., Can.) Sch. Fine Arts, 1972-73, U. Toronto, 1974-78, Art Students League N.Y., 1985-86, NAD Sch., 1987. Artist, Toronto, 1982-84, N.Y.C., 1985—. Sculpture design cons. Phillip Carter Architect, 1993; guest lectr. Mt. Holyoke Coll., South Hadley, Mass., 1994; artist/collaborator to choreographer Fausto Matias, N.Y.C., 1992. Exhibited in group shows at NAD, 1994, St. John's U., N.Y.C., 1995; one-man shows, N.Y.C., 1994, Toronto, 1988. Revson Found. grantee Art Students League N.Y., 1985. Mem. Orgn. Ind. Artists, Art Initiatives, Pastel Soc. Am. (Bd. Dirs. award 1991), Allied Artists Am. (Len G. Everett Meml. award 1994), Knickerbocker Artists Am. (Nat. Sculpture Soc. award 1992). Avocations: sailing, hiking, rock climbing, jazz and classical music. Office: 85 N 3rd St Brooklyn NY 11211-3944

PELLER, MARCI TERRY, realtor; b. Upland, Pa., Nov. 5, 1949; d. Max Maclyn and Lucille Eugenia (Zucker) P. AA, Harcum Jr. Coll., Bryn Mawr, Pa., 1971; student, Villanova U., 1971-73. With sales dept. William H. Cartwright Real Estate, North Palm Beach, Fla., 1985-91; realtor-assoc. Fin. Realty Group, Lake Park, 1991—. Owner, Cards By Marci divsn. Atlas Co. Republican. Jewish. Avocations: theater, football, golf, attending concerts. Office: Fin Realty Group 9498 Alternate A1A Lake Park FL 33403-1439 E-mail: mpell@bellsouth.net.

PELLET, PEDRO FERNANDO, economist, educator, consultant; b. Havana, Cuba, May 19, 1943; came to U.S., 1965; s. Fernando Pellet-Pons and Maria Luisa (Acosta) Pellet. BA in Econs./Polit. Sci. summa cum laude, U. P.R., 1971, MA in Econs., 1976; PhD, U. Miami, 1986; BSc in Biology summa cum laude, U. Sacred Heart, 1981. Instr. U. P.R., Rio Piedras, 1976-78; asst. prof. U. Sacred Heart, Santurce, P.R., 1974-81; prof. Nova Southeastern U., Ft. Lauderdale, Fla., 1982—. Vis. prof. Broward Community Coll., Hollywood, Fla., 1984-85, Fla. Internat. U., Miami, 1990; cons. various orgns., Miami, 1984-88. Contbr. articles to profl. jours. U.S. Army, 1966-72. Roman Catholic. Avocatons: airplane flying, chess, judo, sailing, classical music. Home: 911 Columbus Blvd Coral Gables FL 33134 Office: Nova Southeastern U FSBE 3301 College Ave Fort Lauderdale FL 33314-7721

PELLETIER, ARTHUR JOSEPH, state legislator, educator; b. Dec. 13, 1946; s. Joseph Telesphor and Elsie Jane (Dillon) P.; m. Marsha Lynn Mingle, May 19, 1973; 1 child, John. Diploma, N.H. Vocat. Tech. Inst., 1966; BA, Kans. State U., 1970, MS, 1972. Asst. to dir. Kans. State U. Divsn. Contg. Edn., Manhattan, N.Y., 1971-74; tchr. drafting Portsmouth (N.H.) H.S., 1974-86; tchr. computer programming McIntosh Coll., Dover, N.H., 1982-84; assoc. prof. N.H. Vocat.-Tech. Coll., Stratham, 1986-87; kitchen designer Area Kitchen Ctr., Portsmouth, 1987; mem. N.H. Ho. of Reps., 1993—. Mem. legis. sci., tech. and energy com., N.H. Ho. Reps., 1993-96, mem. legis. edn. com., 1997-2000; co-founder N.H. Coalition for Edn.; mem. Dover Ready to Learn Task Force, 1995-2001; mem. evaluation and review com., Dover Schs., curriculum com., 1997-2001, facilities com., 1997-98; bd. advs. Hub Family Support Ctr., 1996-97. Mem. Partnership Healthier Cmty., 1995-97, Ams. for Non-Smoker's Rights, 1996—. Mem. World Future Soc., Friends of Dover Libr. Avocations: radio-controlled model aircraft, tennis, photography. Home: 94 Back River Rd Dover NH 03820-4411

PELLETIER, LOUIS CONRAD, surgeon, educator, health facility administrator; b. Montreal, Que., Can., Mar. 15, 1940; s. Conrad L. and Lucienne (Rochette) P.; m. Louise Montpetit, June 26, 1965; children: Conrad R., Marie-Helene. BA, Brébeuf Coll., Montreal, 1959; MD, U. Montreal, 1964, MBA, 1996. Resident in cardiovascular and thoracic surgery U. Montreal, 1964-70, chmn. dept. surgery, 1986-94; rsch. asst. Mayo Clin. Found., Rochester, Minn., 1970-72; mem. dept. surgery Maisonneuve-Rosemont Hosp., Montreal, 1972-76, Sacré-Coeur Hosp., Montreal, 1972-80, Montreal Heart Inst., 1979—2000, head dept. surgery, 1979-87; dir. rsch. Ctr. Sacre-Coeur Hosp., 1998—2002; pres. Cardianove, Inc., 1998—; dir. med. affairs Sacrè-Coeur hosp., 2000—02; cons. in health adminstrn. and mgmt. of emergency wards, 2002—. Contbr. articles to profl. jours. Mem. adminstrv. bd. College Stanislas, Montreal, 1979-86, Que. Heart Found., 1980-84, regional healthcare bd., 1991-92, Hotel-Dieu Hosp., 1993-95. Recipient Young Investigator's award Am. Coll. Cardiology, 1972; Med. Rsch. Coun. Can. scholar U. Montreal, 1973-78. Fellow Royal Coll. Physicians and Surgeons Can.; mem. ACS, Association des Medecins de Langue Francaise du Canada, Can. Med. Assn., Royal Coll. Can., Assn. Cardiovascular and Thoracic Surgery Que., Can. Cardiovascular Soc., Montreal Cardiac Soc., Clin. Rsch. Club Que., Soc. Thoracic Surgeons, Can. Assn. Clin. Surgeons, Sociedad de Cardiocirujanos, Coun. on Cardiovasular Surgery, Am. Heart Assn., Internat. Soc. for Heart Transplantation, Can. Soc. Cardiovascular and Thoracic Surgeons, Am. Assn. Thoracic Surgery, Am. Surgical Assn. Roman Catholic. Avocations: skiing, bicycling.

PELLETIER, MARSHA LYNN, secondary school educator, state legislator, poet; b. Mt. Pleasant, Mich., July 29, 1950; d. Eugene Russell and Mary Ellen (Edde) Mingle; m. Arthur Joseph Pelletier, May 19, 1973; 1 child, John Frederick. BS in Home Econs. and Edn., Kans. State U., 1971, MS in Edn. Guidance and Counseling, 1972. Lic. rela estate broker, N.H. Conf. coord., guidance counselor Kans. State U., Manhattan, 1971-73; tchr. home econs. Franklin (Mass.) H.S., 1974, Exeter (N.H.) H.S., 1974-75, Barrington (N.H.) Mid. Sch., 1975-81, Pentucket Regional Jr. H.S., West Newbury, Mass., 1981-82; realtor assoc. Century 21 Ocean and Norword Realty, Portsmouth, N.H., 1983-86; tchr. interior design, cons. U. N.H., Durham, 1986-87; tchr. family and consumer sci. Dover Middle Sch., 1983-2001; tchr. Dover H.S., 2001—; mem. legis. adminstrn. com. N.H. Ho. of Reps., Concord, 1992-94, 96-98, 99—; ind. real estate broker Dover, 1986-2000. Bd. dirs. N.H. State Profl. Bd. Standards. Bd. dirs. Dover Adult Learning Ctr., 1995-98; mem. Health Task Force, Dover and Concord, 1993-94; trustee St. John's Meth. Ch., 1995-97; mem. Dover Friends of the Pub. Libr., 1996—. Mem. NEA (local pres., negotiator, v.p., membership chair, leadership exec. com., bldg. rep. 1979—, N.H. del. to nat. conv.), Nat. Coalition for Consumer Econ., Alpha Delta Kappa. (v.p. historian altruistic chmn. 1984-89). Democrat. Avocations: gardening, aerobics, poetry, sewing, cooking. Home: 94 Back River Rd Dover NH 03820-4411

PELLETIER, NANCY ANNE, obstetrical and gynecological nurse, educator; b. St. Louis, June 16, 1951; d. David Cooper Hill and Cenith Lorraine Gore; m. Russell Dean Pelletier, June 16, 1972; children: Kyle, Lindsay, Bradley. Cert. in practical nursing, Alexandria Hosp. Sch. of Practical Nursing, 1971; cert. in health edn., U. Md., 1973; AAS magna cum laude, No. Va. C.C., 1984. LPN, Va.; RN, Va.; Lamaze Cert. Childbirth Educator. LPN in pediatrics Alexandria (Va.) Hosp., 1971-72, LPN in medications, 1972-73, LPN in post partum and intensive care nursery, 1977-84, nurse post partum and float pool, 1984-85, childbirth educator, 1978—; sch. nurse, tchr. health edn. Alexandria City Pub. Schs., 1973-76; lead nurse Ob-Gyn Assocs. No. Va., Alexandria, 1984-91; lead ob-gyn nurse Kaiser Permanente of Mid-Atlantic Region, Woodbridge, Va., 1991—. Advisor Vocat. Edn. Clubs Am., Washington, 1974. Author: (pamphlet) A Nurse Discusses Your Cesarean Delivery, (teaching tool) Test Your Pregnancy Knowledge. Recipient Nurse of Yr.-Kaiser Woodbridge/Meade Johnson award, 1997. Mem.: NAACOG, Am. Soc. for Psychoprophylaxis in Obstetrics (Lamaze cert. childbirth educator), Phi Theta Kappa. Avocations: interior design, reading, children's interests.

PELLETIER, S. WILLIAM, chemistry educator; b. Kankakee, Ill., July 3, 1924; s. Anthony Amos and Estella Edith (Hays) P.; m. Leona Jane Bledsoe, June 18, 1949; children: William Timothy, Jonathan Daniel, Rebecca Jane, Lucy Ruth, David Mark, Sarah Lynn. BS in Chem. Engring. with highest honors, U. Ill., 1947; PhD in Organic Chemistry, Cornell U., 1950. Instr. chemistry U. Ill., 1950-51; mem. staff Rockefeller Inst., 1951-62, assoc. prof. organic chemistry, 1961-62; prof. chemistry, head dept. U. Ga., 1962-69, Alumni Found. disting. prof., 1969—, provost, 1969-76, Univ. prof., 1976—; dir. Inst. for Natural Products Research, 1976—. Gordon lectr., New Hampton, N.H., 1955, 59, 69; lectr. German Acad. Agrl. Scis., 1959; Am. Swiss Found. lectr., Zurich, Basel, Bern, Geneva, Switzerland, 1960; Commemorative dedication lectr. Shionogi Rsch. Lab., Osaka, Japan, 1961; Victor Coulter lectr. U. Miss., 1965; Nason-Piston lectr. Boston Pub. Libr., 1982; Plenary lectr. 32d Internat. Congress on Medicinal Plant Rsch., Antwerp, Belgium, 1984; lectr. for internat. symposia in Berlin, Melbourne, Hong Kong, Latvia, Prague, Stockholm, London, Riga, Latvia, Varna, Bulgaria, Istanbul, Turkey, Cairo also other lectures in Eng., Italy, India, Israel, Taiwan, Japan; mem. health medicinal chemistry study panel NIH, 1968-72. Author: Chemistry of the Alkaloids, 1970, 7 monograms on am. etcher John Taylor Arms, 1975—93, Alkaloids: Chemical and Biological Perspectives vols. 1-15, 1983—2001, catalog of etchings of Charles Meryon and Jean-Francois Millet, 1994, Adriaen van Ostade, Etchings of Peasant Life in Holland's Golden Age, 1994, From Rembrandt and his Studio: Two Paintins from the Bader Collection, 1998, Sir Muirhead Bone: His Etched and Drypointed Portraits and Figure Studies, 1999; mem. editl. bd.: Jour. Organic Chemistry, 1966—70, mem. editl. bd.: Heterocycles, 1979—, mem. editl. bd.: Jour. Natural Products, 1980—2001, mem. editl. bd.: Phytochem. Analysis, 1989—99, mem. editl. bd.: Trends in Heterocyclic Chemistry, 1994, mem. editl. bd.: Recent Rsch. Devel. in Heterocyclic Chemistry, 1994, mem. editl. bd.: Turkish Jour. Chemsitry, 1996—; contbr. articles to profl. jours.; author: Everyday Life in Holland's Golden Age: The Complete Etchings of Adriaen van Ostade, 1998. Pres. bd. Flushing Christian Day Sch., 1956-60; bd. advisers Ga. Mus. Art, 1968— ; bd. dirs. Center for Research Libraries, Chgo., 1975-81. With USNR, 1944-46. Fellow AAAS, Royal Soc. Arts (London), Royal Soc. Chemistry (London); mem. Am. Chem. Soc. (chmn. N.E. Ga. sect. 1968, Charles Herty medal 1971, So. Chemists award 1972), Am. Soc. Pharmacognosy (hon. life, Rsch. Achievement award 1991, v.p. 2000, pres. 2001), Worldwide Discipleship Assn. (bd. dirs. 1980-88), Sigma Xi, Phi Eta Sigma, Tau Beta Pi, Sigma Tau. Presbyn. (elder). Achievements include research in structure and stereochemistry diterpenoid alkaloids, applications of carbon-13 nuclear magnetic resonance to structure determination, synthesis of terpenes, X-ray crystallographic structures of natural products. Office: U Ga Dept Chemistry Athens GA 30602-2556 E-mail: pelletier@sunchem.chem.uga.edu. *I have been working in the field of natural products for over forty years now. As we unravel the structures of complex natural products and illuminate their fascinating chemistry. I am impressed over and over with the marvelous design and handiwork of the Creator. In a certain real sense, as I explore and discover new truth about the part of the universe in which I work, I believe that I am thinking God's thoughts after him.*

PELLETT, JON MICHAEL, lawyer; b. Orlando, Fla., Nov. 16, 1961; s. Milton Francis and Jean Ellen (Avery) P.; m. Karen Walker, July 21, 1984 (div. Sept. 1990). BS in Biology, U. Ctrl. Fla., Orlando, 1984, BS in Stats., 1985; JD, Fla. State U., 1993. Bar: Fla. 1995, U.S. Dist. Ct. (mid. dist.) Fla. 1996. Legal trainee Dept. Bus. and Profl. Regulation, Tallahassee, 1993-95; staff atty. Agy. for Health Care Adminstrn., 1995-96; assoc. Freeman, Hunter & Malloy, Tampa, Fla., 1996-2000, Barr, Murman, Tonelli et al, Tampa, 2000—. Vol. guardian ad litem Guardian ad Litem Program, Tallahassee, 1991-95. Bd. dirs. Friends of Arboretum, Orlando, 1998—. Mem. ABA, ATLA, Hillsborough County Bar Assn. Avocations: racquetball, beach volleyball. Office: Barr Murman Tonelli Et Al 201 E Kennedy Blvd Ste 1750 Tampa FL 33602-5829

PELLEY, PATRICIA MARIE, Asian history specialist; b. Spokane, Wash., June 2, 1955; d. Thomas R. and Irene N. P. BA, Cornell U., 1985, MA, 1989, PhD, 1993. Vis. fellow Nat. U. Singapore, 1993-94; vis. asst. prof. Wittenberg U., Springfield, Ohio, 1994-95; asst. prof. Tex. Tech. U., Lubbock, 1995—2002, assoc. prof., 2002—. Author: Postcolonial Vietnam: New Histories of the National Past, 2002. Mem.: World History Assn., Am. Hist. Assn., Assn. Asian Studies. Office: Tex Tech U History 41013 Lubbock TX 79409-1013 E-mail: patricia.pelley@ttu.edu.

PELLI, CESAR, architect; b. Tucuman, Argentina, Oct. 12, 1926; arrived in U.S., 1952, naturalized, 1964; s. Victor V. and Teresa S. Pelli; children: Denis G., Rafael A. BArch cum laude, U. Tucuman, 1949; MS in Architecture, U. Ill., 1954. Assoc. firm Eero Saarinen & Assocs., 1954-64, Daniel, Mann, Johnson & Mendenhall, 1964-68, Gruen Assocs. Inc., L.A., 1968-77, Cesar Pelli & Assocs., New Haven, 1977—; dean Sch. Architecture, Yale U., 1977-84. Works include Pacific Design Ctr. and Expansion, L.A. (Honor award So. Calif. chpt. AIA 1976), U.S. Embassy, Tokyo, Mus. Modern Art Expansion, N.Y.C., World Fin. Ctr. and Winter Garden, N.Y.C. (Bard award 1992), Cleve. Clinic (Honor award AIA 1986), Herring Hall, Rice U., Houston (Honor award AIA 1986), Carnegie Hall Tower, N.Y.C. (Honor award AIA 1994, Design award AIA/Conn. 1991), Boyer Ctr. Molecular Medicine Yale U. (Design award AIA/Conn. 1991), Bank of Am. Corp. Ctr., Charlotte, NTT Corp. Hdqrs., Tokyo (Design award AIA/Conn. 1997), New Terminal, Washington Nat. Airport (Design award AIA/Conn. 1998, NE Design award 1999, Design for Transp. award 2000), Aronoff Ctr. for the Arts, Cin. (USITT honor award 1996, Design award AIA/CIN 1996, Design award AIA/Conn. 1997), Petronas Towers, Kuala Lumpur, Malaysia (Design award AIA/Conn. 1999, NE Design Award 2000, Honor award AIA 2000), Frances Lehman Loeb Art Ctr. Vassar Coll., Poughkeepsie, N.Y. (Design award AIA/Conn. 1996), Internat. Fin. Ctr., Hong Kong, Nat. Mus. Contemporary Art, Osaka, Japan, Performing Arts Ctr. of Greater Miami, Fla.; editor Yale Seminars on Architecture, 1981-82; author Observations for Young Architects, 1999. Fellow AIA (Firm award 1989, named to top ten list of living Am. archs. 1991, Gold medal 1995); mem. NAD (Arnold M. Brunner Meml. prize 1978), Am. Acad. Arts and Letters (academician), Internat. Acad. Architecture (academician). Office: Cesar Pelli Assocs Pub Rels 1056 Chapel St New Haven CT 06510-2402 E-mail: mailroom@cesar-pelli.com.

PELLICONE, WILLIAM, artist, sculptor, writer, architect; b. Phila., Apr. 12, 1915; s. Emilio and Amelia (Practico) P.; m. Marle Guzzette, July 1964 (div. 1992); m. Ilka Bartel, Aug. 5, 1992. Student, Temple U., Pa. Acad. Fine Arts. Lectr. art Phila. Parkway Mus., Queens Settlement, N.Y., U. Iowa, Iowa City, Delaware Sch. Sys., Converse Coll., S.C., Ednl. Alliance, N.Y. One-man shows include Allen Stone Gallery, N.Y., Beryl Lush Gallery, Phila., Trylon Gallery, Southampton, N.Y., Capricorn Gallery, Bethesda, Md., Opus 127 Gallery, Soho, N.Y.C., Harpers Coll., Binghamton, N.Y., Phoenix Gallery, N.Y., Creighton Univ., Nebr., Gallery East, East Hampton, N.Y., Frederick Spratt Gallery, San Jose, Calif., Cheltenham (Pa.) Gallery, Goodman Gallery, South Hampton, N.Y., Woodmere (Pa.) Mus., Frederick Spratt Gallery, San Jose; group shows include Allan Stone Gallery, N.Y., Egan Gallery, N.Y., Alan Gallery, N.Y., Betty Parsons Gallery, N.Y., Tanager Gallery, N.Y., Phoenix Gallery, N.Y., M & L Gallery of Fine Art, N.Y., Arsenal Gallery, N.Y., Camino Gallery, N.Y., Trylon Gallery, N.Y., March Gallery, N.Y., Capricorn Gallery, Bethesda, Md., Brata Gallery, N.Y., Art Alliance, Phila., Landmark Gallery, N.Y., Tenth St. Days, N.Y., Profile Gallery, N.Y., Noho Gallery, N.Y., Gallery East, East Hampton, N.Y., Marie Pellicone Gallery, N.Y., Parish Mus., Southampton, N.Y., Elaine Benson Gallery, Bridgehampton, N.Y., Belanthi Gallery, A Retrospective, Bklyn., Lombardi Gallery, Retrospective, Austin, Tex., 1997; represented in permanent collections, including Met. Mus. Art, N.Y.C., Boston Mus., Smithsonian Inst., Washington, Am. Broadcasting Collection, Iowa Mus., Iowa City, Bayonne (N.J.) Mus., Martin-Rathburn Gallery, San Antonio. With Merchant Marines, 1943-45, France. Grantee Barnes Found., Temple U., Pa. Acad. Fine Arts, Greek Govt., others; exhibited first in Pa. Acad. Fine Arts, Phila. Republican. Avocations: musician, sailing, carpentry, writing. Home and Office: 101 Myers Creek Rd Dripping Springs TX 78620-3302

PELLINO, CHARLES EDWARD, JR. lawyer; b. Chgo., May 2, 1943; s. Charles Edward Sr. and Ella Pellino; m. Melinda Poorman, Aug. 20, 1966; children: Charles, Tracy, William. BA, Drake U., 1965; JD, U. Wis., 1968. Bar: Wis. 1968, U.S. Dist. Ct. (we. dist.) Wis. 1972, U.S. Tax Ct. 1984, U.S. Dist. Ct. (ea. dist.) Wis. 1985, U.S. Ct. Appeals (7th cir.) 1985, U.S. Supreme Ct. 1985, U.S. Dist. Ct. Hawaii, 1996, U.S. Dist. Ct. Del. 1997. Assoc. McAndrews, Fritschler & Huggett, Madison, Wis., 1968-70; ptnr. Fritschler, Ross, Pellino & Protzman, 1970-73, Fritschler, Pellino & Assocs., Madison, 1973-76, Fritschler, Pellino, Schrank & Rosen, Madison, 1976-88, Fritschler, Pellino, Rosen and Mowris, Madison, 1988—. Contbr. articles to profl. jours. Mem. ABA, Wis. Bar Assn., Nat. Assn. Criminal Def. Lawyers, Wis. Acad. Trial Lawyers, Wis. Assn. Criminal Def. Lawyers (sec.-elect 1987—). Avocations: flying, golf. Office: Pellino Rosen Mowris & Kirkhuff PC 131 W Wilson St Ste 1201 Madison WI 53703-3243

PELLMAN, JAMES CARL, artist; b. Superior, Wis., Jan. 4, 1947; s. Carl John and Delores Mary Ann (Pollari) P. BA, BFA, U. Minn., 1974. Counselor White Bear Lakes (Minn.) Schs., 1978-79; electronics technician Control Data Corp., Edina, Minn., 1979-81; self-employed artist, writer Finnworks, Maple, Wis., 1981—, owner, 1990—. Author: Faithful, Finn & Free, 2000; artist numerous paintings, drawings and sculptures, 1960—. Pres., newsletter editor Old-Brule Heritage Soc. Inc., Maple, Wis., 1998—; mem. bldg. recreation com. Town of Maple, Wis., 1998—, mem. long range planning com., 2000—. With USMC, 1967-71. Avocations: outdoors, photography, book collecting, Finnish culture.

PELLMAR, TERRY C. neurophysiologist, researcher; b. Bklyn., Nov. 4, 1951; d. Ruben and Frances (Freilich) P.; m. Howard Louis Leikin, Jan. 4, 1981. ScB in biology magna cum laude, Brown U., 1973; PhD, Duke U., 1977. Fellow Marine Biological Lab., Woods Hole, Ma., 1978, Armed Forces Radiobiology Rsch. Inst., Bethesda, Md., 1977-80, Nat. Inst. Alcohol Abuse & Alcoholism, Rockville, 1980-82; rsch. physiologist physiology dept. Armed Forces Radiobiology Rsch. Inst., 1982-84; adj. asst. prof. physiology dept. Georgetown U., Washington, 1983-90; project mgr. neurophysiology physiology dept. Armed Forces Radiobiology Rsch. Inst., Bethesda, Md., 1984-95, chmn. radiation pathophysiology and toxicology dept., 1995—99; dir. neuroscience & behavioral health Inst. of Medicine, Washington, 1999—. Mem. VA Merit Rev. Bd. in Neurobiology, 1991-94; mem. neurology disorders program rev. A com., NIH, 1995—. Contbr. articles to profl. jours. Rsch. Peer Review Com. mem. Am. Heart Assn., 1989-92. Mem. N.Y. Acad. Scis., Soc. Neurosci., Oxygen Soc., Assn. Women in Sci., Oxygen Club Washington (councilor 1988-91, sec. 1991-94, pres. elect 1994, pres. 1995), Sigma Xi. Office: Board on Neuroscience and Behavioral Hlth Inst of Med 500 5th St, NW Washington DC 20001*

PELOFSKY, JOEL, lawyer; b. June 23, 1937; s. Louis J. and Naomi (Hecht) Pelofsky; m. Brenda L. Greenblatt, June 19, 1960; children: Mark, Lisa, Carl. AB, Harvard U., 1959. Bar: Mo. 62, U.S. Dist. Ct. (we. dist.) Mo. 62, U.S. Ct. Appeals (8th cir.) 68, U.S. Ct. Appeals (10th cir.) 70. Law clk. to judge U.S. Dist. Ct. (we. dist.) Mo., 1962—63; mem. Miniace & Pelofsky, Kansas City, Mo., 1962—63; asst. pros. atty. Jackson County, 1967—71; mem. Kansas City (Mo.) City Coun., 1971—79; judge U.S. Bankruptcy Ct. Western Dist. Mo., Kansas City, 1967—71; mem. Kansas City (Mo.) City Coun., 1971—79; ptnr. Shughart, Thomson & Kilroy P.C., 1986—95; appd. U.S. trustee Ark., Mo., Nebr., 1995—. Intermittent lectr. in law U. Mo.; mem. Region I Law Enforcement Assistance Adminstr. Mem. adv. bd. Urban League, Kansas City, Mo.; chmn. human resource devel. com. Mo. Mcpl. League; bd. dirs., mem. exec. com. Truman Med. Ctr., Kansas City, Mo., pres. bd., 1988—90, chmn. bd., 1990—92; bd. dirs. Greater Kansas City Mental Health Found. Lt. U.S. Army, 1963—65. Mem.: ABA, Am. Coll. Bankruptcy, Comml. Law League, Kansas City Bar Assn., Mo. Bar. Office: US Trustee 400 E 9th St Ste 3440 Kansas City MO 64106-2625

PELOSI, MARCO ANTONIO, obstetrician and gynecologist; b. Lima, Peru, Oct. 5, 1942; came to the U.S., 1968; m. Luisa Garcia-Pacheco, 1962; children: Marco, Carla, Monica. BS, U. Peruana Mayor de San Marcos, Lima, 1962; MD, U. Peruana Cayetano Heredia, Lima, 1968. Cert. Am. Bd. Ob-Gyn. Intern Navy Med. Ctr., Lima, 1967-68; intern dept. ob-gyn. U. Medicine and Dentistry of N.J., Martland Hosp., Newark, 1968-69; resident dept. ob-gyn. CMDNJ-NJMC/Martland Hosp., 1969-72, fellow oncology dept. ob-gyn., 1972-74; pvt. practice, 1975—. Instr. dept. ob-gyn. UMDNJ-N.J. Med. Sch., Newark, 1972-75, clin. asst. prof., 1975-80, 80—; clin. asst. prof. dept. ob-gyn. Hahnemann Med. Coll. Phila., Pa., 1980—; attending physician dept. ob-gyn. UMDNJ-N.J. Med. Sch., Newark, 1972—, Bayonne (N.J.) Hosp., 1974—, St. Joseph Hosp., Paterson, N.J., 1974—, St. Elizabeth Hosp., Elizabeth, N.J., 1979-87, Meadowlands Hosp., Secaucus, N.J., 1979—, Greenville Hosp., Jersey City, N.J., 1980—; dir. dept. ob-gyn. Bayonne (N.J.) Hosp., 1987—; presenter; pres. Bayonne Hosp. Med. Staff, 1996—. Contbr. chpts. to books and articles, abstracts to profl. jours. Recipient 1st prize The Female Patient's 1st Annual Photo Contest, The Female Patient Mag., 1988, Physician's Recognition award AMA, 1979, 81, 84, 87, 90, 93, 96, 99, Sci. Exhibit Recognition award, Sci. Exhibit Achievement award 83rd Annual Sci. Assembly, So. Med. Assn., Washington, 1989, Physician's Recognition award Med. Soc. N.J., 1999. Fellow ACS, AGOG (Philip F. Williams award 1972, Continuing Edn. award 1972, 79, 82, 84, 87, 90, 93, 96, 99, 2nd prize winner film festival 1999), Internat. Coll. Surgeons, Am. Fertility Soc., N.J. Ob-Gyn. Soc., Am. Inst. Ultrasound in Medicine; mem. Am. Soc. Profs. Ob.-Gyn., Soc. for Minimally Invasive Surgery, Soc. Laparoendoscopic Surgeons, N.J. Med. Soc., Passaic County Med. Soc., Am. Soc. Cytology, Pan Am. Cancer Cytology Soc., Gynecol. Urology Soc., Med. Collectors Assn., Am. Assn. for the History Medicine, Internat. Soc. Physicians Historians, Am. Assn. Gynecol. Laparoscopists (best surgical videos of 1995-2nd place, 1st place best video prodn., 1st place best surgical videos 1996, winner of golden laparoscope award 1996, 3rd place best surgical videos 1997, first place/golden laparoscope award best surgical video 1998), Royal Soc. Medicine, Med. History Soc. N.J. Office: Pelosi Womens Med Ctr 350 Kennedy Blvd Bayonne NJ 07002-1313

PELOSI, NANCY, congresswoman; b. Balt., Mar. 26, 1940; d. Thomas J. D'Alesandro Jr.; m. Paul Pelosi; children: Nancy Corinne, Christine, Jacqueline, Paul, Alexandra. Grad., Trinity Coll. Former chmn. Calif. State Dem. Com., 1981; committeewoman Dem. Nat. Com., 1976, 80, 84; fin. chmn. Dem. Senatorial Campaign Com., 1987; mem. U.S. Congress from 5th Calif. dist., 1987-93, U.S. Congress from 8th Calif. dist., 1993—; mem. appropriations com., intelligence com.; mem. House Dem. Whip, 2002—. Office: US Capitol H-307 Washington DC 20515-0508

PELOSO, JOHN FRANCIS XAVIER, lawyer; b. N.Y., Oct. 7, 1934; s. Rocco C. and Victoria P.; m. Elizabeth Byrne Peloso, Oct. 7, 1961; children: Alycia, John, Matthew. BA, Fordham U., 1956, LLB, 1960. Bar: N.Y. 1960, U.S. Dist. Ct. (so. dist.) N.Y. 1962, U.S. Ct. Appeals (2nd cir.) 1967, U.S. Supreme Ct. 1968. Law clk. to judge U.S. Dist. Ct. (so. dist.) N.Y., 1960-61; asst. U.S. Atty. U.S. Atty.'s Office, N.Y., 1961-65; assoc. Carter Ledyard & Milburn, 1965-70; chief trial counsel NYRO-SEC, 1970-75; ptnr. Sage Gray Todd & Sims, 1975-87; ptnr. to mng. ptnr. Morgan, Lewis & Bockius, LLP, N.Y.C., 1987-95, 95-99, sr. counsel, 2000—. Adj. prof. law Fordham Law Sch., 2000—; speaker in field. Contbr. articles to profl. jours. Capt. inf. USAR, 1956-64. Mem. ABA (sect. corp., banking and bus. law, com. fed. regulation securities 1975—, com. bus. and corp. litigation, chair subcom. securities litigation 1993-99, litigation co-chmn. com. securities 1983-87, com. on liaison with jud. 1987-88, coun. 1989-91, co-chmn. com. trial evidence 1994-95, co-chmn. task force on the ind. lawyer 1995-99), Assn. of Bar of City of N.Y. (arbitration com. 1970-73, fed. legis. com. 1975-78, fed. cts. com. 1982-86), Nat. Assn. Securities Dealers (nat. panel arbitrators 1975—, nat. arbitration com. 1982-85), CPR Inst. for Dispute Resolution (Disting. Neutral). Office: Morgan Lewis & Bockius LLP 101 Park Ave Fl 44 New York NY 10178-0060

PELOU, PIERRE MARIE, librarian; b. Espalion, Rouergue, France, Aug. 24, 1941; s. Gaston and Odette (Serres) P.; divorced; children: Nathalie, Jean-Philippe; m. Marie Thérèse Moyon, May 27, 1972; 1 child, Frédéric-Vincent. MPhil, Claude Bernard U., Lyon, France, 1965, diplôme d'études supérieures de philosophie, 1966; diplôme supérieur de bibliothécaire, Ecole Nat. Supérieure des Bibliothèques, Paris, 1968. Libr. U. Libr., Lyon, 1968-70; head programme Del. for the Constrn. of the Beaubourg Centre, Paris, 1970-71; libr. Nat. Libr., 1971-75; chief co-operation and automation div. Ministry of Univs., 1975-77; chief libr., dep. dir. La Documentation Francaise, 1977-88; chief libr. UN Libr., Geneva, 1988—. Chmn. CIMAB-Micrographie, Paris, 1975-80; dep. sec. gen. Groupement francais des producteurs de bases de données, Paris, 1979-82. Author: (book) L'Europe de l'information, 1990; editor: (books) Les nouvelles technologies de la documentation et de l'information, 1985, Innovation et nouvelles technologies de l'information, 1987, documentation administrative, 1989, la gestion des publications officielles, 1989, International Documentation, 1991, Les Bibliothèques ministérielles, 1992. Decorated chevalier de l'Ordre Nat. du Mérite Premier Ministre (France), chevalier de l'Ordre des Palmes académiques (France). Fellow Internat. Micrographic Congress; mem. Internat. Fedn. Libr. Assns. and Instns. (The Netherlands). Avocation: jazz. Home: Ave Blanc 46 1202 Geneva Switzerland Office: UN Palais des Nations 1211 Geneva 10 Switzerland

PELTASON, JACK WALTER, foundation executive, educator; b. St. Louis, Aug. 29, 1923; s. Walter B. and Emma (Hartman) P.; m. Suzanne Toll, Dec. 21,1946; children: Nancy Hartman, Timothy Walter H., Jill K. BA, U. Mo., 1943, MA, 1944, LLD (hon.), 1978; AM, Princeton U., 1946, PhD, 1947; LLD (hon.), U. Md., 1979, Ill. Coll., 1979, Gannon U., 1980, U. Maine, 1980, Union Coll., 1981, Moorehead (N.D.) State U., 1980; LHD (hon.), 1980, Ohio State U., 1980, Mont. Coll. Mineral Scis. and Tech., 1982, Buena Vista Coll., 1982, Assumption Coll., 1983, Chapman Coll., 1986, U. Ill., 1989. Asst. prof. Smith Coll., Mass., 1947-51; asst. prof. polit. sci. U. Ill., Urbana, 1951-52, assoc. prof., 1953-59, dean Coll. Liberal Arts and Scis., 1960-64, chancellor, 1967-77; vice chancellor acad. affairs U. Calif., Irvine, 1964-67, chancellor, 1984-92; pres. U. Calif. System, Oakland, 1992-95, Am. Coun. Edn., Washington, 1977-84; prof. emeritus dept. politics and soc. U. Calif., Irvine, 1995—; pres. Bren Found., 1997—. Cons. Mass. Little Hoover Commn., 1950 Author: The Missouri Plan for the Selection of Judges, 1947, Federal Courts and the Political Process, 1957, Fifty-eight Lonely Men, 1961, Understanding the Constitution, 15th edit., 2000, orig. edition, 1949, (with James M. Burns) Government By the People, 1952, 19th edit., 2002; contbr. articles and revs. to profl. jours. Recipient James Madison medal Princeton U., 1982 Fellow Am. Acad. Arts and Scis.; mem. Am. Polit. Sci. Assn. (council 1952-54), Phi Beta Kappa, Phi Kappa Phi, Omicron Delta Kappa, Alpha Phi Omega, Beta Gamma Sigma. Home: 18 Whistler Ct Irvine CA 92612-4069 Office: U Calif Dept Politics & Society Social Sci Plz Irvine CA 92697-0001 E-mail: jwpeltas@uci.edu.

PELTIER, EUGENE JOSEPH, civil engineer, former naval officer, business executive; b. Concordia, Kans., Mar. 28, 1910; s. Frederick and Emma Helen (Brasseau) P.; m. Lena Evelyn Gennette, June 28, 1932 (dec.); children: Marion Joyce, Eugene Joseph (dec.), Carole Josephine, Kenneth Noel, Judith Ann. BS in Civil Engring., Kans. State U., 1933, LL.D., 1961. Registered profl. engr., Mo., N.Y., Kans., Fla., Va., Calif. Commd. lt. (j.g.) U.S. Navy, 1936, advanced through grades to rear adm., 1957; asst. public works officer Great Lakes, Ill., 1940-42; sr. asst. supt. civil engr. Boston, 1942-44; officer in charge 137th Constrn. Bn. Okinawa, 1945; officer in charge 54th Constrn. Regt., 1945; officer various public works assignments Pensacola, Fla., 1945-46, Memphis, 1946-49, Jacksonville, Fla., 1949-51; dist. public works officer (14th Naval Dist.), 1951-53; asst. chief maintenance and materials Bur. Docks Washington, 1953-56; comdg. officer Pt. Hueneme, 1956-57; chief Bur. Yards and Docks, Navy Dept. Washington, 1957-62; chief of civil engrs., 1957-62; ret., 1962; instrumentman, resident engr. Kans. Hwy. Commn., Norton, Topeka, Chanute, 1934-40; v.p. Sverdrup & Parcel & Assocs., Inc., St. Louis, 1962-64; sr. v.p. Sverdrup & Parcel & Assos., Inc., 1964-66, exec. v.p., 1966-67, pres., dir., 1967-75, chief exec. officer, 1972-75, ptnr., 1966-75, cons., 1975-82; pres., dir. Sverdrup & Parcel & Assos., N.Y., Inc., 1967-75; dir. Sverdrup & Parcel Internat., Inc., 1967-75; v.p., dir. ARO, Inc., Tullahoma, Tenn., 1966-75; cons. EPA, 1976-80. Dir. Merc. Trust Co., St. Louis, 1971-81 Mem. emeritus Civic Progress, Inc.; bd. dirs. YMCA, St. Louis, 1972-76. Decorated Legion of Merit; recipient citation Am. Inst. Steel Constrn., 1973 Mem. ASCE (hon.), Am. Public Works Assn. (1 of Top Ten Public Works Men of Year 1960), Soc. Mil. Engrs. (pres. 1960-61), Am. Concrete Inst., Am. Road and Transp. Builders Assn. (pres. 1972-73), Nat. Soc. Profl. Engrs., Mo. Soc.

Profl. Engrs., Public Works Hist. Soc. (pres. 1977-78, trustee 1975-79), Nat. Acad. Engring., Cons. Engrs. Council (award of Merit 1962), Sigma Tau, Phi Kappa Phi. Clubs: Army-Navy Country (Washington); Old Warson Country (St. Louis). E-mail: pel32810@aol.com.

PELTIN, SHERWIN CARL, lawyer; b. Milw., Aug. 2, 1929; s. Alvin Leonard and Rebecca (Weisfeldt) P.; m. Julie Marion Stern, Mar. 15, 1953; children: Laurie Peltin Merar, Steven, William. BBA, U. Wis., 1950, LLB, 1952; LLM in Taxation, NYU, 1955; SJD, George Washington U., 1962. Bar: Wis. 1952, U.S. Tax Ct. 1958, U.S. Fed. Claims Ct. 1960; CPA, Wis. Atty.-advisor U.S. Tax Ct., Washington, 1955-58; atty. Offices of Louis L. Meldman, Milw., 1958-62; ptnr. Laikin, Swietlik & Peltin, 1962-68, Peregrine, Marcuvitz & Peltin, SC, Milw., 1968-87, Weiss, Berzowski, Brady, LLP, Milw., 1987—. Elected trustee Village Bd. Trustees, Bayside, 1967-73. Capt. U.S. Army, 1952-54, Korea. Mem. ABA, State Bar Wis., Milw. Bar Assn., Estate Counselors' Forum, Profl. Inst. Tax Study. Office: Weiss Berzowski Brady LLP 700 N Water St Milwaukee WI 53202-4206

PELTO, GRETEL H. nutritional anthropologist, educator; b. Mpls., May 6, 1940; d. Isaac L. and Deana (Harris) Hoffman; m. Pertti J. Pelto, July 27, 1968 (div. Dec. 1995); children: Jonathan, Dunja, Ari; m. Jean-Pierre Habicht, June 13, 1997. Student, Bennington Coll., 1957-60; BA, U. Minn., 1963, MA, 1967, PhD, 1970; DSc (hon.), U. Helsinki, 1996. Clin. assoc. U. Conn. Sch. Medicine, Farmington, 1970-74; asst. prof. anthropology U. Conn., Storrs, 1974-77, prof. nutritional scis., 1977-92; scientist, child health divsn. WHO, Geneva, 1992-98; prof. nutritional scis. Cornell U., Ithaca, N.Y., 1998—. Mem. adv. bd. divsn. diarrheal disease control WHO, 1987-92; mem. adv. bd. subcom. on maternal and infant nutrition NAS, Washington, 1980-83; cons. UN U., Washington and Tokyo, 1985, Population Coun., N.Y.C., 1980-82. Co-author: Anthropological Research, 1978, Community Assessment of Natural Food rces of Vitamin A; co-editor: Nutritional Anthropology, 1999. Bd. dirs. Parent-Child Rsch. Ctr. for Eastern Conn., 1974-79; mem. task force Hartford (Conn.) Area Health Edn. Ctr., 1980-82; mem. adv. com. Travelers Ctr. on Aging, Hartford, 1988-89. Fulbright grantee, 1984; hon. rsch. fellow U. Birmingham, Eng., 1994-97; U.S. AID rsch. grantee, Mex., 1982-87. Fellow Soc. for Applied Anthropology; mem. Soc. for Internat. Nutritional Rsch. (bd. dirs. 1989-92), Coun. on Nutritional Anthropology (pres. 1982-84, v.p. 1998-00), Am. Soc. Nutritional Scis., Soc. for Med. Anthropology (bd. dirs. 1980-82). Avocations: photography, cooking. Home: 129 Eastlake Rd Ithaca NY 14850-9700 Office: Cornell U Div Nutritional Sci MVR 3M1 Ithaca NY 14853 E-mail: gp32@cornell.edu.

PELTON, HAROLD MARCEL, mortgage broker; b. Montreal, Que., Can., Jan. 24, 1922; s. Grover Cleveland and Denise (Pigeon) P.; m. Frances Farley, June 1947 (div. 1968); children: Mary Virginia Joyner, Diane Jean Slagowski; m. Virginia L. King, July 11, 1970. Student, L.A. City Coll., 1948-49, Anthony Schs., Van Nuys, Calif., 1966. Lic. real estate real broker, Calif. Stockbroker, agt. Mitchum, Jones, Templeton Assurance Co., L.A., 1957-60; owner Assurance Investment Co., Van Nuys, Calif., 1960-65; sales syndicator TSI Investment Co., L.A., 1965-69; pres., owner Univest Co., Beverly Hills, Calif., 1970-72, Am. Oil Recovery, L.A., 1973-79; v.p. Newport Pacific Funding Co., Newport Beach, Calif., 1979-81; chmn. bd. dirs. TD Publs., El Toro, 1981-83; pres., broker HP Fin., Inc., Laguna Hills, 1983--. Contbg. editor Am. Oil Recovery newspaper, 1973-79; editor Trust Deed Jour., 1981-83. Served with U.S. Army, 1942-46, PTO. Mem. L. A. Mus. Art, Laguna Hills C. of C., Kiwanis, Toastmasters. Republican. Avocations: photography, travel, reading, computers. Office: HP Fin Inc 24942 Georgia Sue Laguna Hills CA 92653-4323

PELTON, JAMES RODGER, librarian; b. St. Louis, Mar. 21, 1945; s. Norman C. and Leona V. (Schulte) P.; m. Sandra Lee Birdsell, Mar. 29, 1969; 2 daus., Joni Lee, Vicki Sue. B.A., U. Mo., 1967, M.L.S., 1969. Br. librarian Scenic Regional Library, Union, Mo., 1968-71; adminstr. Daniel Boone Regional Library - Columbia Center, Columbia, Mo., 1971-78; cons. La. State Library, Baton Rouge, 1978-80; dir. Shreve Meml. Library, Shreveport, La., 1980— . Mem. ALA, La. Library Assn. Home: 3201 Old Mooringsport Rd Shreveport LA 71107-3926 Office: 424 Texas St Shreveport LA 71101-3522

PELTON, LEROY HOWARD, social work educator; b. N.Y.C., Apr. 30, 1940; s. Myer and Rose (Stein) P. BS in Math. and Psychology, CUNY, 1961; MA in Psychology, New Sch. for Social Rsch., 1963; MSW, Rutgers U., 1985; PhD in Psychology, Wayne State U., 1966. Asst. prof. SUNY, Albany, 1966-73, Susquehanna U., Selinsgrove, Pa., 1973-75; program devel. specialist N.J. Div. Youth and Family Svcs., Trenton, 1975-79, spl. asst. to dir., 1979-81; rsch. assoc. Assn. for Children N.J., Newark, 1981-82; dir. child welfare Vera Inst. Justice, N.Y.C., 1982-83; policy and planning specialist N.J. Commn. for Blind and Visually Impaired, Newark, 1984-86; vis. lectr. Rutgers U., New Brunswick, N.J., 1985-86; vis. assoc. prof. U. Tenn., Knoxville, 1986-87; prof. social work Salem (Mass.) State Coll., 1987-97; prof., dir. Sch. Social Work U. Nev., Las Vegas, 1997—. Author: The Psychology of Nonviolence, 1974, For Reasons of Poverty, 1989; editor: The Social Context of Child Abuse and Neglect, 1981; cons. editor Arete, 1989-97; assoc. editor Children and Youth Svcs. Rev., 1990—; contbr. articles to profl. jours. Office: U Nev Sch Social Work Box 455032 4505 S Maryland Pkwy Las Vegas NV 89154-9900

PELTON, RUSSELL GILBERT, lawyer; b. Monticello, N.Y., July 23, 1914; s. William and May (Morgan) P.; m. Marion Gosart, Dec. 14, 1940; children: William, Marjorie, Marilyn Pelton Barringer. BS, Syracuse U., 1935; JD, George Washington U., 1944. Bar: D.C. 1944, N.Y. 1947, U.S. Supreme Ct. 1948, U.S. Dist. Ct. N.Y. 1947; U.S. Dist. Ct. (fed. dist.). Ptnr. Darby & Darby, N.Y.C., 1945-56; sr. v.p. N.Am. Philips Corp., 1956-75; exec. v.p. U.S. Philips Corp., 1968-75; of counsel Rogers, Hoge & Hills, 1976-78; ptnr. Spellman, Joel & Pelton, White Plains, N.Y., 1979-81, Eslinger & Pelton, N.Y.C., 1983-85. Officer, dir. Tech. Container Corp., N.Y.C., 1977-95; former dir. Ferroscube Corp., Savgerties, N.Y., Polyseal Corp., N.Y.C.; lectr. Practising Law Inst., 1953-69; arbitrator, mediator Am. Arbitration Assn., 1985—. Patentee in field. V.p. Siwanoy coun. Boy Scouts Am., 1948-53; v.p. Rye Neck Bd. Edn., Mamaroneck, N.Y., 1952-62; mem. Zoning Bd. Appeals, 1966-70; town justice, 1970-85; trustee Syracuse U., 1967-73. Served with Signal Corps, U.S. Army, 1941-45. Mem. ABA, Am. Patent Law Assn. (past chmn. antitrust com.), N.Y. State Bar Assn. (ethics com., Iola com.), N.Y. Patent Law Assn. (past bd. govs.), State Magistrates Assn., County Magistrates Assn. (treas., v.p., pres.), Westchester County Bar Assn. (dir., chmn. ethics com., alternative dispute resolution com.), Assn. Bar City N.Y. (patent com.), IEEE, Am. Radio Relay League, Aircraft Owners and Pilots Assn., Wings Club, Cloud Club, Winged Foot Golf Club, Waccabuc Country Club, Masons, Elks. Home: 3 Oxford Rd Larchmont NY 10538-1428

PELTON, RUSSELL MEREDITH, JR. lawyer; b. Chgo., May 14, 1938; BA, DePauw U., 1960; JD, U. Chgo., 1963. Bar: Ill. 1963, U.S. Supreme Ct. 1979. Assoc. Peterson, Ross, Schloerb & Seidel, Chgo., 1966-72, ptnr., 1972-90, Oppenheimer, Wolff & Donnelly, Chgo., 1990-2000, Chgo. mng. ptnr., 1992-95, 98-2000; ptnr. Ross & Hardies, 2000—. Co-founder, gen. counsel Chgo. Opportunities Industrialization Ctr., 1969—83; gen. counsel Delta Dental Plann Ill., 1979—96, Am. Assn. Neurol. Surgeons, 1983—. Pres. Wilmette Jaycees, 1970; chmn. Wilmette Sch. Bd. Caucus, 1970-71; Wilmette Dist. 39 Bd. Edn., 1972-80; bd. dirs. Wilmette United Way, 1980-86, campaign chmn., 1983-85, pres., 1985-86; Wilmette Zoning Bd. Appeals, 1989-2000, chmn., 1990-2000. Served to capt. USAF, 1963-66. Mem.: ABA, Soc. Trial Lawyers, Chgo. Bar Assn., Ill. Bar Assn., Ill. State Dental Soc. (hon.). Office: Ross & Hardies 150 N Michigan Ave Ste 2500 Chicago IL 60601-7567 E-mail: russell.pelton@rosshardies.com.

PELTON, TERRY LYNN, computer programmer; b. Orange, Calif., Nov. 6, 1950; d. John William and Billie Lou (Bomhoff) Bryant; m. R. Ballard, Oct. 10, 1976 (annulled 1982); m. Jeffery Scot Pelton, May 2, 1982; 1 child, Ida Yvonne. Student, Butte Coll., Oroville, Calif., 1972-77, Yuba Coll., Marysville, Calif., 1979-80; grad., Ctr. Ind. Living/Computer Tng., Berkeley, Calif., 1980; student, U. N.H., Burnwick, Maine, 1988. Cert. computer programmer, Calif. Computer operator U. Calif., Chico, 1976-78; key punch operator Beal AFB, Marysville, 1978-79; computer programmer U. Calif., Berkeley, 1980, Disabled Programmers Inc., San Jose, Calif., 1980-82; cons. Informatics Inc., Palo Alto, 1982-83; computer programmer Keystone Orgn., Phila., 1984-85; tech. support specialist Applied Data Rsch., Princeton, N.J., 1985-86; computer programmer, Supr. Shipbldg. USN, Brunswick, 1987-90; retrospace resource scheduler satelite tracking group Onizuka US AFB, Sunnyvale, Calif., 1990—. Recipient Letter of Commendation, Am. Pres. Lines, San Mateo, Calif., 1983, cert. of appreciation and numerous other awards Disabled Programmers Inc., 1981. Mem. Am. Legion Aux., Navy Patrol Squad Spouse Club, Ctr. for Ind. Living/Computer Tng. Project, Epilepsy Found. Republican. Avocations: puzzles, guitar, ceramics, camping, fishing.

PELTON, VIRGINIA LUE, small business owner; b. Utica, Kans., Apr. 15, 1928; d. Forrest Selby and Nellie (Simmons) Meier; m. Theodore Trower King Jr., Oct. 27, 1956 (div.); m. Harold Marcel Pelton, July 11, 1970; children: Mary Virginia Joyner, Diana Jean. Student, Kans. State U., 1946-47, Ft. Hays U., 1947-48, Washington U., St. Louis, 1950-51. Instr. Patricia Stevens Modeling Sch., Kansas City, Mo., 1948-50; model various cos., Calif. and N.Y., 1951-53; fashion cons. Giorgio, Beverly Hills, Calif., 1967-68, Charles Gallay, Beverly Hills, 1975-77, Dorso's, Beverly Hills, 1977-79; buyer, mgr. giftware Slavick's, Laguna Hills, Calif., 1980-83; owner P.J. Secretarial Svcs., 1980—; v.p. H.P. Fin. Inc., 1983—. Editor Profl. Network newsletter, 1980—. Sec. Leukemia Soc. Am., Santa Ana, 1985—; mem. Laguna Beach Art Mus., 1986—. Mem. Profl. Network Assn. (sec. 1986-96), Market Plus The Consumer Network, Saddleback C. of C., Laguna Hills Club, Kappa Delta. Republican. Methodist. Avocations: gourmet cooking, sewing. Home: 24942 Georgia Sue Laguna Beach CA 92653-4323

PELTZ, ALAN HOWARD, manufacturing company executive; b. July 16, 1944; s. Harry and Rachel (Hammer) P.; m. Frieda Wichter, Nov. 16, 1968; children: Jason, Elissa. BBA in Acctg., CCNY, 1966; MBA in Fin., Pace U., 1971; grad. advanced mgmt. program, Harvard U., 1988. Corp. auditor RCA, N.Y.C., 1966-69; sr. fin. analyst Celanese Chem. Co., 1969-70; asst. treas. Baker Industries, Inc., Parsippany, N.J., 1970-74; v.p. fin., adminstrn., human resources, mgmt. info. sys. Burndy Corp., Norwalk, Conn., 1974-93, v.p., CFO, 1993-97, chmn. bd., CEO, 1997—. V.p. fin. Framatome Connectors Internat., Paris, 1993—; mem. faculty Fairfield (Conn.) U., 1979-80; mem. exec. adv. com. Western Conn. State Coll., 1979-80. Bd. dirs. Elderhouse, 1985, Friends of Norwalk Coll., 1986, Hallbrook Hosp. Served as sgt. USMC, 1967-68. Fellow Internat. House Columbia, 1965; mem. Fin. Execs. Inst. Internat. Treasury Orgn., Norwalk C. of C. (bd. dirs. 1984—), Nat. Assn. Corp. Treas., Mfrs. Alliance Productivity and Innovation Inc. (fin. coun. II), Nat. Elec. Mfrs. Assn. (human resources). Republican. Jewish. Avocations: skiing, golf. Office: Framatome Connectors Internat 825 Old Trail Rd Etters PA 17319-9392

PELTZ, ALICE JEAN, bacteriologist; b. Astoria, N.Y., Apr. 7, 1950; d. John Christopher and Alice Rose (Faltin) Rauth; m. Lowell J. Peltz, Oct. 12, 1974 (dec. Mar. 1987); adopted children: Laura Jean Scruggs, Randall Michael, James Julius. AAS in Biol. Tech., SUNY, Farmingdale, 1970; BA in Natural Sci., Adelphi U., 1989; MPA, L.I. U., 1992, cert. in gerontology, 1994. Lab. technician toxicology lab. drug abuse sect. Suffolk County Dept. Health Svcs., Hauppage, N.Y., 1973-81, bacteriologist pub. & environ. health lab. water bac. sect., 1981—. Presenter confs. and workshops Adelphi U., Garden City, N.Y., 1992, 93, Hofstra U., Hempstead, N.Y., 1993, N.Y. Inst. Tech., Old Westbury, 1993, Suffolk Acad. Law, 1993, 94, Suffolk County C.C., Brentwood campus, 1994. Active Suffolk County Rep. Women, 1993, Huntington Breast Cancer Action Coalition, Family Svc. League Suffolk County, Inc.; intern Cath. Charities Meals on Wheels Program, 1994; mem. Nassau Assn. Continuing Cmty. Edn. Mem. NAFE, Am. Soc. for Pub. Adminstrn. (mem. environ. and natural resources sect.), Soc. Forensic Toxicologists, Inc., N.Y. State Pub. Health Assn., Suffolk County Assn. Mcpl. Employees (mem. polit. action com., sec.-treas., med. examiners' unit), Pi Alpha Alpha. Lutheran. Avocations: needlepoint, crafts. Home: 114A Wells Rd Northport NY 11768-3450 Office: Suffolk County Med Examiner Bldg 487 North Complex Smithtown NY 11787

PELTZER, DOUGLAS LEA, semiconductor device manufacturing company executive; b. Clinton, Iowa, July 2, 1938; s. Albert and Mary Ardelle (Messer) P.; m. Nancy Jane Strickler, Dec. 22, 1959; children: Katharine, Eric, Kimberly. BA, Knox Coll., 1960; MS, N.Mex. State U., 1964; MBA, U. Phoenix, 1990. Rsch. engr. Gen. Electric Co., Advanced Computer Lab., Sunnyvale, Calif., 1964-67; large scale integrated circuit engr. Fairchild Camera & Instrument, Rsch. & Devel. Lab., Palo Alto, 1967-70, bipolar memory divsn. Mountain View, 1970-83, tech. dir., 1977-83; v.p. tech. ops. Trilogy Systems Corp., Cupertino, 1983-85; pres. Tactical Fabs, Inc., 1985-89; v.p. process devel. Chips and Techs. Inc., 1989-92; pres., CEO Camlan, Inc., San Jose, 1992-94; staff Chip Express, Santa Clara, 1994-98; prin. Corp. Tech. Devel., 1994—. Inventor, patentee in field. NSF fellow, 1962-63; recipient Sherman Fairchild award for tech. excellence, 1980, Semiconductor Equipment and Materials Inst. award, 1988; Inventor of Yr. award Peninsula Patent Law Assn., 1982. Mem. IEEE, Sigma Pi Sigma. Home: 340 San Marco Dr Fort Lauderdale FL 33301

PELTZMAN, SAM, economics educator; b. Bklyn., Jan. 24, 1940; s. Benjamin Raphael and Ceil (Heller) P.; m. Nancy Virginia Bradney, Sept. 7, 1952; children: Shira Malka, Talya Rose. BBA, CCNY, 1960; PhD, U. Chgo., 1965. Prof. econs. UCLA, 1964-73; sr. staff economist Coun. Econ. Advisers, Washington, 1970-71; prof. econs. grad. sch. bus. U. Chgo., 1973-87, Sears, Roebuck prof., 1987-2001, dir. George J. Stigler Ctr. Study of Economy and the State, 1992—, Ralph and Dorothy Keller disting. svc. prof., 2001—. Vis. fellow Inst. for Advanced Study Hebrew U., Jerusalem, 1978; dir. CMP Industries LLC, 1995—; mem. coun. acad. advisers Am. Enterprise Inst., 1995—. Author: Political Participation and Government Regulation, 1998; co-author: Public Policy Toward Mergers, 1967; editor Jour. Law and Econs.; contbr. articles to profl. jours. Mem. Am. Econ. Assn., Mt. Pelerin Soc. Jewish. Office: U Chgo Grad Sch Bus 1101 E 58th St Chicago IL 60637-1511

PELZ, HERMAN H. physician; b. N.Y.C., May 28, 1931; s. Elias and Sima (Mansterman) P.; m. Janice G. nee Gersten, Mar. 1, 1958; children: Ellen, Daniel. BS, L.I. U., 1952; MD, SUNY, Bklyn., 1956. Diplomate Am. Bd. Allergy and Immunology. Intern Mt. Sinai Hosp. of N.J., 1956-57; medicine residency VA Hosp., Bronx, 1957-58; fellowship in allergy Bklyn. Jewish Hosp., 1960-61; pvt. practice specializing in internal medicine/allergies Elmhurst, N.Y., 1961—; chief allergy VA Hosp., Bklyn., 1962—, Wyckoff Hts. Hosp., Bklyn., 1963—; intern Mt. Sinai Hosp. of N.J., 1956-57; medicine residency VA Hosp., Bronx, 1957-58; fellowship in allergy Bklyn. Jewish Hosp., 1960-61; chief resident in medicine Bklyn. Jewsih Hosp., 1961-62. Author: Primer in Allergy, 1978. Lt. USN 1958-60. Fellow Am. Acad. Allergy, Internat. Acad. Allergology, Am. Genetics Soc. Republican. Jewish. E-mail: jgpelz@aol.com.

PELZER, CHARLES FRANCIS, molecular geneticist, biologist, educator, research scientist; b. Detroit, June 5, 1935; s. Francis Joseph and Edna Dorothy (Ladach) P.; m. Veronica Ann Killeen, July 7, 1972; 1 child, Mary Elizabeth. BS in Biology, U. Detroit, 1957; PhD in Human Genetics, U. Mich., 1965. Postdoctoral fellow Wabash Coll., Crawfordsville, Ind., 1965-66; instr. U. Detroit, 1966-68; asst. prof. biology dept. Saginaw Valley State U., University Center, 1969-74, assoc. prof., 1974-79, prof., 1979—. Rsch. fellow Henry Ford Hosp., Detroit, 1982-83, 88-92; v.p. Saginaw Valley Retinitis Pigmentosa Found., Mich., 1979-81; vis. scientist Am. Inst. Biol. Scis., Washington, 1975-78; grant reviewer U.S. Dept. Edn., Washington, 1984-87, 91. Contbr. articles to profl. jours. Recipient Alumni award Saginaw Valley State U. Alumni Assn., 1971, Outstanding Svc. award Mich. Assn. Biology Tchrs., 1995; grantee Kellogg Found., 1961, NIH, 1961-64, Kettering Found., 1965-66, Mich. State U., 1977, Saginaw Valley State U. Found., 1979-82, 83-85, 86-89, Fund for Ford Hosp., 1983, Dow Chem. Co., 1988, 89, Dow Corning Co., 1988, 89, Mich. Rsch. Excellence Fund, 1993, rsch. grantee Monsanto Co., 1987. Mem. Am. Soc. Human Genetics, Genetics Soc. Am., Nat. Assn. Biology Tchrs. (dir. for Mich. Outstanding Biology Tchr.'s award), Internat. Electrophoresis Soc., Coun. for Undergrad. Rsch., N.Y. Acad. Scis., also others. Home: 43 Sawmill Creek Trail Saginaw MI 48603 Office: Saginaw Valley State U Dept Biology 7400 Bay Rd University Center MI 48710-0001

PELZER, LINDA LEE, English language educator; b. South Bend, Ind., Mar. 31, 1952; d. William Joseph and Lois May (Wilburn) Claycomb; m. John David Pelzer, Mar. 16, 1974 (dec. Apr. 1997). BA, Ball State U., 1974; MA, U. Notre Dame, 1976, PhD, 1984. Asst. prof. English Ball State U., Muncie, 1980-82, 83-88; prof. English Wesley Coll., Dover, Del., 1988—. Author: Mary Higgins Clark, 1995, Erich Segal, 1997, Student Companion to F. Scott Fitzgerald, 2000. Mem. Del. Humanities Coun., Wilmington, 1990-95. Collaborative Rsch. grantee Fulbright Commn., Eng., 1986. Mem. MLA, N.E. MLA. Avocations: travel, herb gardening, needlework. Office: Wesley Coll 120 N State St Dover DE 19901-3835 E-mail: pelzerli@mail.wesley.edu.

PEMBER, JOHN BARTLETT, social worker, educator; b. White Plains, N.Y., June 24, 1951; s. John Raymond and Allyn Marie (Case) P.; m. Deborah Ann Dudley, June 9, 1973; children: John Scott, Matthew Bartlett, Jenna Lynne. BA, Houghton (N.Y.) Coll., 1973; MSW, SUNY, Buffalo, 1978. Cert. social worker, N.Y. Social work asst. Cuba (N.Y.) Meml. Hosp. and Skilled Nursing Facility, 1973-76; staff social worker Wyoming County Mental Health, Warsaw, 1978-80, supervising social worker, 1980-85; parole officer N.Y. State Div. Parole, Rochester, 1985-87; team supr., social worker II, Capital Dist. Psychiat. Ctr., Albany, N.Y., 1987—; pvt. practice Capital Area Christian Counseling Svc., Delmar, 1988—. Social work cons., Warsaw, 1978-87; instr. field work SUNY, Buffalo, 1982-85, SUNY, Albany, 1987—; clin. instr. dept. psychiatry Albany Med. Coll., 1991—. Mem. NASW. Avocations: fishing, hiking, gardening, softball, camping. Office: Capital Area Christian Cons PO Box 313 Delmar NY 12054-0313

PEMBER, JOHN SCOTT, poet; b. Jackson Heights, N.Y., June 3, 1940; s. Gordon Franklin and Marion Louise (Burt) P.; m. Patricia Ann Farley, Nov. 10, 1965; 1 child, John Scott Jr. BA, Trenton State Coll., 1963; EdM, Rutgers U., 1979, postgrad., 1979-81, 88, U. Va., 1987. Cert. secondary tchr., N.J. Tchr. Hammarskjold Jr. H.S., East Brunswick, N.J., 1963-69, East Brunswick H.S., 1969-94, Rutgers U., New Brunswick, N.J., 1992; vis. poet Geraldine R. Dodge Found., Morristown, 1994—; tchr. Green Mountain Coll. Acad., Dorset, Vt., 2000—. Journalism evaluator Columbia U., N.Y.C., 1993-94; mem. poetry adv. bd. Geraldine R. Dodge Found., 1986-94; panelist Piscataway (N.J.) Pub. TV, 1992; presenter, cons. in field. Author: Rope to the Barn, 1993 (Poetry award), (anthology) Under a Gull's Wing, 1996; contbr. poetry to lit. jours. Docent Pember Mus. Natural History, Granville, N.Y., 1996—. Grantee East Brunswick Bd. Edn., 1972, 90-93; Va. Coun. on Arts fellow, 1987; recipient Gov.'s award for outstanding tchg. N.J. Bd. Edn., 1992. Mem. Acad. Am. Poets, Am. Philatelic Soc., Equinox Poetry Soc. Manchester, Vt., Poets' House, Kappa Delta Pi. Avocations: philately, golf, reading, cinema. Home: 276 Dorset West Rd Dorset VT 05251-9426 also: PO Box 185 Dorset VT 05251-0185

PEMBERTON, BRADLEY POWELL, lawyer; b. Ft. Scott, Kans., June 15, 1952; s. Howard Duane and Juanita Lucille (Powell) P.; m. Kathleen Frances Querrey, May 22, 1976 (div. Feb. 1984); m. Lori Scott, June 18, 1994. BSBA, U. Mo., Columbia, 1974; JD, U. Mo., Kansas City, 1977. Bar: Mo. 1977, U.S. Dist. Ct. (we. dist.) Mo. 1981, U.S. Tax Ct. 1981; CPA, Mo. Tax acct. Alexander Grant & Co., Kansas City, Mo., 1977-79; shareholder Polsinelli, Shalton & Welte, 1979—; also bd. dirs. Polsinelli, White, Vardeman & Shalton. Active Vol. Atty. Project, Kansas City, 1984—; bd. dirs. Synergy House Inc., Kansas City, 1985-88, Youth Vol. Corps of Am., 1991—, March of Dimes, 1995—. Mem. ABA, Internat. Entrepreneurs Coun. (bd. dirs.), Mo. Bar Assn., Kansas City Bar Assn., AICPAs, Mo. Soc. CPAs, Kansas City C. of C., Entrepreneurs Club of Kansas City (bd. dirs.), KC. Avocations: tennis, golf, water skiing, snow skiing, private aviation. Home: 5806 W 131st St Shawnee Mission KS 66209-3639 Office: Polsinelli Shalton & Welte 700 W 47th St Ste 1000 Kansas City MO 64112-1805 E-mail: bpemberson@pswlaw.com.

PEMBERTON, CYNTHIA LEE A. educational leadership educator; b. Portland, Oreg., Oct. 2, 1958; d. Ronald E. and Patricia E. (Schars) Pemberton. BS in Biology and Psychology, Willamette U., 1980; MS in Interdisciplinary Studies, So. Oreg. State U., 1983; EdD in Ednl. Leadership-Higher Edn. Adm., Portland State U., 1996. Instr. Trucker Meadows C.C., Nev., 1985-87; instr., swimming coach U. Nev., Reno, 1984-89; asst. athletic dir. women's sports Linfield Coll., McMinnville, Oreg., 1989-95, assoc. prof., aquatics dir., sr. women adminstr., 1989-98; asst. prof. grad. faculty dept. sport sci., phys. edn. and dance Idaho State U., 1998—2001, assoc. prof. grad. faculty, dept. chmn. edn. leadership, 2001—. Hannah Kennan scholar, Peck scholar. Mem. AAUW, NOW, AAHPERD, NAGWS, NASPE, AERA, Women's Sports Found., Alpha Chi Omega, Omicron Delta Kappa, Psi Chi, Kappa Delta Pi, Pi Kappa Phi. Avocations: exercise, reading. Office: Idaho State U Dept Edn Leadership PO Box 8059 Pocatello ID 83209-8059 Fax: 208-282-5324. E-mail: pembcynt@isu.edu.

PEMBERTON, MERRI BETH MORRIS, educator; b. Tahlequah, Okla., July 26, 1959; d. Roger C. and Evelyn A. (Mercer) Morris; m. Larry Jay Pemberton, Nov. 22, 1986; children: Eric Michael, Ciara Elise, Andrew Levi. BS, Midwestern State U., 1986, MEd, 1989. Receptionist YMCA, Wichita Falls, Tex., 1984-91; tchr. resource spl. edn. Petrolia (Tex.) Ind. Sch. Dist., 1986-89; tchr. spl. edn. emotionally disturbed Wichita Falls Ind. Sch. Dist., 1989-91; diagnostician Cookson Hills Christian Schs., Kansas, Okla., 1991-92, spl. edn. cons., 1992—. Contbr. article to profl. jour. Named to Outstanding Young Women of Am., 1991. Mem. Coun. for Exceptional Children (pres. 1989-90), Tex. Coun. for Exceptional Children (sec. 1990-91), Kappa Delta Pi. Home: RR 3 Box 200 Kansas OK 74347-9533

PEMBERTON, RYAN, race car driver; b. Saratoga Springs, N.Y., June 1, 1969; m. Andrea Pemberton. Grad. H.S., So. Guilford, N.C/. Tire specialist to mechanic Roush Racing, 1988—91; tire specialist and mechanic Robert Yates Racing, 1991—93; tire mechanic, tire carrier Team SABCO, 1993—95; crew chief Martin Motor Sports Busch Series Team, 1995—96, NASCAR Winston Cup Series various drivers, 1995—2000; crew chief for #77 Jaspar Ford Jaspar Motorsports, 2000—. Mem.: Crew Chief Club. Office: Jaspar Motorsports 110 Knob Hill Rd Mooresville NC 28115

PEMBROOK, RICHARD CHARLES, internist, cardiologist; b. Lincoln, Nebr., May 12, 1930; MD, U. Minn., 1963. Intern USPHS Hosp., Balt., 1963-64; resident U. N.Mex. Hosps., Albuquerque, 1965-67, U. Mo. Hosps., Columbia, 1967-68, Maine Med. Ctr., 1971-72; asst. med. dir. Las Vegas (N.Mex.) Med. Ctr., 1991—2001. Clin. asst. prof. medicine U. N.Mex. Sch. Medicine, 1995—2001. Fellow: ACP, Am. Heart Assn. Address: 876 Middlebridge South Kingstown RI 02879 E-mail: r.pembrook@cox.net.

PENA, ANTONIO FRANCISCO (TONY PENA), professional athletics coach; b. Monte Cristy, Dominican Republic, June 4, 1957; m. Amaris Pena; children: Tony, Jennifer Amaris. Profl. baseball player Pitts. Pirates, Nat. League, 1980-86, St. Louis Cardinals, 1986-89, Boston Red Sox, 1989—93, Cleveland Indians , 1994—97; mgr. Astros AAA farm club , New Orleans, 1997—2001; mgr. Kansas City Royals , 2002—. Player Major League All-Star Game, 1982, 84; winner Gold Glove. Office: Kansas City Royals One Royal Way Kansas City MO 64129*

PEÑA, ELIZABETH, actress; b. Elizabeth, N.J., Sept. 23, 1961; d. Mario Peña and Margarita Toirac. Grad., Sch. of the Performing Arts. Actress: (stage prodns.) Romeo and Juliet, Antigone, Blood Wedding, Night of the Assassins, Italian-American Reconciliation, Cinderella, Blood Wedding, Act One and Only, (feature films) El Super, 1979, Times Square, 1980, They All Laughed, 1981, Crossover Dreams, 1984, Down and Out in Beverly Hills, 1985, La Bamba, 1986, Batteries Not Included, 1987, Vibes, 1988, Blue Steel, 1989, Jacob's Ladder, 1990, The Waterdance, 1991, Across the Moon, 1992, Free Willy II, 1994, Dead Funny, 1995, Lone Star, 1996, The Pass, 1997, Strangeland, 1997, Rush Hour, 1998 (ALMA award for outstanding actress in a feature film 1998), Seven Girlfriends, 1999, Impostor, 2000, Tortilla Soup, 2001, Ten Tiny Love Stories, 2001, Zig-Zag, 2001; (made for TV movies) Fugitive Among Us, 1992, It Came From Outer Space II, Contagious, 1996, Dead Man's Gun, 1997, Aldrich Ames: America Betrayed, 1998, Border Line, 1999; (TV mini-series) Drug War: The Camarena Story, The Invaders; (TV episodes) Saturday Night Live, Hillstreet Blues, Cagney and Lacey, Dellaventura; regular (TV series) I Married Dora, 1987—, Shannon's Deal, Tough Cookies, Resurrection Blvd., 2000-2002. Mem. Actors' Equity Assn., Screen Actors Guild, AFTRA. Office: Paradigm care Joel Rudnick 10100 Santa Monica Blvd Fl 25 Los Angeles CA 90067-4003

PENA, GUILLERMO ENRIQUE, lawyer; b. Miami Beach, Fla., Aug. 16, 1963; s. Gustavo A. and Rosa Amelia (LeRiverend) P.; m. Jacqueline Torre, Sept. 11, 1993; children: Justin Jake, Allison Lee. BBA, Austin Peay State U., Clarksville, Tenn., 1988; JD, Fla. State U., 1991. Bar: Fla. 1991, U.S. Dist. Ct. (no. and so. dists.) Fla. 1991, U.S. Ct. Appeals (11th cir.) 1991, U.S. Supreme Ct. 1996; cert. in criminal trial law Criminal Trial Law Found., Middle Dist. of Fla., 1998, Dist. of Utah, 1999, Western Dist. of Tex., 1998. Assoc. Boehm, Brown, Rigdon & Seacrest, P.A., Tallahassee, 1990-92, Raia & Preira, Miami Beach, Fla., 1992-95, Jeffrey S. Weiner, P.A., Miami, 1995-96; pvt. practice, 1996—. Guest judge U. Miami Sch. Law-Moot Ct. Camp, 1996-99. Sgt. U.S. Army, 1984-86, ETO. Young pres. Mt. Sinai Hosp., Miami Beach, Fla. Recipient Recognition award Legal Svcs. Greater Miami, 1996, Pro Bono Svc. award Dade County Bar Assn., Miami, 1995, Young Pres. Mt. Sinai Hosp., 1999. Mem. ABA (criminal justice sect.), Cuban Am. Bar Assn. (Pro Bono Project 1996), Nat. Assn. Criminal Def. Lawyers, Am. Judicature Soc., Am. Inns of Ct. (barrister), Fla. Assn. Criminal Def. Lawyers, Fla. Bar (cert. as specialist in criminal law), Young Pres. Club. Office: 1101 Brickell Ave Ste 1801 Miami FL 33131-2407 E-mail: gepena@yahoo.com.

PEÑA, JUAN JOSÉ, interpreter; b. Hagerman, N.Mex., Dec. 13, 1945; s. Rosa Peña; m. Petra Cervantes, Dec. 22, 1974 (div. 1982); children: Federico Ezequiel, Margarita María Blea. BA, N.Mex. Highlands U., 1968, MA, 1972, postgrad. With Albert Garcia Gen. Contr., Las Vegas, N.Mex., 1955-67; teaching asst. N.Mex. Highlands U., 1971-72, prof. Spanish, Chicano studies, 1972-78; teaching asst. U. N.Mex., Albuquerque, 1978-79; attendant N.Mex. State Mental Hosp., Las Vegas, 1982-83; staff and supervisory interpreter U.S. Dist. Ct. N.Mex., Albquerque, 1983—. Head Raza Unida del to PLO in Lebanon, 1981, head negotiator with Iranians for release of 2 Chicanos and 1 Indian; supr ct. interpreters and reporters sect. U.S. Dist. Ct. N.Mex.; co-chmn. Cuatro-Centennial Com., Inc.; mem. exec. com. N.Mex. Human Rights Coalition. Author collection of poetry: Angustias y Remembranzas; contbr. articles to profl. jours.; author play: Canto a La Raza, 1978. Pres. Dads Against Discrimination, Albuquerque, 1993—; chmn. bd. trustees No. N.Mex. Legal Svcs., Las Vegas, 1972-81; mem. exec. com. Ind. Socialist Parties of Latin Am.; exec. commn. N.Mex. Human Rights Coalition; vice chmn. Barelas Cmty. Devel. Corp.; Barelas rep. Hist. Neighborhoods Alliance; mem. cmty. coun. on equity Albuquerque Pub. Schs.; mem. N.Mex. Cmty. Loan Fund; bd. dirs. Albuquerque Downtown Action Team, N.Mex. Land Grant Forum; mem. textbook rev. commn. N.Mex. Dept. Edn., mem. bilingual edn. adv. com.; commr. N.Mex. Textbook Selection Commn., 2001—; nat. sec. Am. GI Forum of U.S., 2000-01. Decorated Bronze Star; recipient Human Rights award City of Albuquerque Human Rights Bd., N.Mex. State Coun. Profile of Courage award Vietnam Vets. Am., 1995, N.Mex. Nat. Guard Cinco de Mayo award, 1995, Hispanics for U N.Mex. Achievement award, 1999, Human Rights award Albuquerque Human Rights Bd., 2000. Bd. dirs. Albuquerque Downtown Action Team; mem. N.Mex. Translator and Interpreters Assn. (pres. 1984-86), Nat. Assn. Judiciary Interpreters (sec. 1986-88), Nat. Partido Raza Unida (pres. 1976-81), N.Mex. Partido Raza Unida (pres. 1972-75, 77-78), Vietnam Vets. Am. (vice chmn. chpt. 1993—), Vietnam Vets. N.Mex., Am. GI Forum (Albuquerque chpt. 1 comdr. 1993—, vice comdr. 1997-98, sec.), N.Mex. GI Forum (comdr. 1996), Nat. Assn. Chicano Studies (founding mem.), N.Mex. Chicano Studies Assn. (pres. 1972-78), Hispanic Round Table of N.Mex. (chmn. 1995, 98), Barelas Neighborhood Assn. (pres.), Historic Neighborhoods Assn., Barelas Cmty. Devel. Corp. (rep.), Phi Sigma Iota. Democrat. Roman Catholic. Avocations: weight lifting, swimming, ice skating, hiking, camping. office), (home). Home: 1115 9th St SW Albuquerque NM 87102-4027 Office: US Dist Ct Dist NMex 333 Lomas Blvd NW Albuquerque NM 87102-2272 Fax: 505-764-8527. E-mail: jpena71@comcast.net., jjp3000@aol.com.

PENA, MARIA GEGES, academic services administrator; b. Torrance, Calif., Nov. 27, 1964; d. Nicholas John and Dina Connie (Vengel) Geges; m. Vicente Gregorio Pena, June 22, 1991. AA, El Camino Coll., 1985; BA, U. Calif., San Diego, 1987; MS, San Diego State U., 1989, postgrad., Claremont Grad. Sch., 1990—, Western State U., 1995—. Peer counselor El Camino Coll., Torrance, Calif., 1982-85; peer advisor U. Calif., San Diego, 1985-87, vice chancellor student affirmative action rsch. intern, 1986-87, outreach asst. disabled student svcs., 1986-89; coord. student svcs. Mira Costa Coll., Oceanside, Calif., 1989—. Contbr. articles to profl. jours. Mem. Calif. Assn. Postsecondary Educators of Disabled. Democrat. Greek Orthodox. Avocations: law, education, CD collecting, collecting Beatles memorabilia. Office: Mira Costa Coll 1 Barnard Dr Oceanside CA 92056-3820

PENA, MODESTA CELEDONIA, retired principal; b. San Diego, Mar. 3, 1929; d. Encarnacion E. and Teofila (Garcia) P. BA, Tex. State Coll. for Women, 1950, MA, 1953. Cert. sch. supr., prin., supt., Tex. Tchr. English San Diego H.S., 1950-76; asst. supt. curriculum and instrn. San Diego Ind. Sch. Dist., 1976-80; gifted edn. resource tchr. William Adams Jr. H.S., Alice, Tex., 1980-83, asst. prin. for instrn., 1983-88; ret., 1988. Faculty Bee County Coll., 1975-76. V.p. San Diego PTA, 1963; charter mem. Duval County Hist. Commn., 1975—; reporter Duval Co. Hist. Com., 1988—; chmn. Com. to Establish Local Pub. Libr., 1993; trustee Duval County-San Diego Pub. Libr., pres., 1993-98, mem., 1999—, dir. Duval County literacy program, 1994—; cmty. rep. site-based dist. mgmt. com. San Diego Ind. Sch. Dist., 1995-97. Newspaper Fund Inc. fellow, 1964; recipient Adolfo Arguijo Day award, 1990; named Outstanding Sr. of Duval County, Grayfest, 1992; named to San Diego Hall of Honor, 1995. Mem. Tex. State Tchrs. Assn. (rec. sec. 1952-53, 63-64, 1st v.p. 1957-58, 66-67, pres. 1961), Delta Kappa Gamma (rec. sec. chpt. 1972-74, 1st v.p. 1974-76, pres. 1976-78, chpt. parliamentarian 1984-88, state com. constn./bylaws, state com. Eula Lee Carter Meml. Fund, area coord. state com. pers., state rec. sec., state com. nominations 1995-97, chmn. 1997-99, state conv. chair 1999-2000, state com. necrology 2001—, Chpt. Achievement award 1985, Internat. Golden Gift award 1994, State Achievement award 1996), Phi Delta Kappa (treas. chpt. 1978-79, rec. sec. chpt. 1983-84). Home: PO Box 353 306 W Gravis St San Diego TX 78384-2604

PENA, RAYMUNDO JOSEPH, bishop; b. Corpus Christi, Tex., Feb. 19, 1934; s. Cosme A. and Elisa (Ramon) P. D.D., Assumption Sem., San Antonio, 1957. Ordained priest Roman Catholic Ch., 1957; asst. pastor St. Peter's Ch., Laredo, Tex., 1957-60, St. Joseph's-Our Lady of Fatima, Alamo, 1960-63, Sacred Heart, Mathis, 1963-67, Christ the King and Our Lady of Pillar Parishes, Corpus Christi, 1967-69; pastor Our Lady of Guadalupe Parish, 1969-76; v.p. Corpus Christi Diocesan Senate of Priests, 1970-76; aux. bishop of San Antonio, 1976-80; bishop El Paso, 1980-95, Brownsville, Tex., 1995—. Mem. secretariat to Prep. Synod of Bishops for Am., 1996-97, Synodal Father, Synod of Bishops for Am., 1995. Mem. U.S. Conf. Cath. Bishops (chmn. bishops' com. for hispanic affairs 1987-90, bishops' com. for ch. in L.Am. 1994-97, 2000). Home: 741 Bowie Alamo TX 78516 Office: PO Box 2279 Brownsville TX 78522-2279 E-mail: rjpena@cdob.org.

PENA, RICHARD, lawyer; b. San Antonio, Feb. 13, 1948; s. Merced and Rebecca (Trejo) P.; m. Carolyn Sarah Malley, May 25, 1979; 1 stepchild, Jason Charles Schubert. BA, U. Tex., 1970, JD, 1976. Bar: Tex. 1976, Colo. 1986. Pvt. practice, Austin, Tex., 1976—. Instr. bus. law St. Edwards U., Austin, 1983, Austin C.C., 1981-82; broker Tex. Real Estate Commn., 1980—; sports editor Austin Light, 1982. Bd. dirs. Ctr. for Battered Women, Austin, 1979-82, Austin Assn. Retarded Citizens, 1980-82; chmn. Austin Travis County Mental Health/Mental Retardation Pub. Responsibility Com., 1979-84; chmn. pvt. facilities monitoring com. Austin Assn. Retarded Citizens, 1981; bd. dirs. Boys Club of Austin, 1987-88; chair Homeless Task Force Austin, 1999—. Named to Outstanding Young Men. of Am., 1982. Fellow Tex. Bar Found. (sustaining life; trustee 1994, sec., treas. 1994, vice-chmn. 1995, chmn. 1996); mem. ABA (ho. dels., nominating com. 1998—, vice chair credentials com. 2001), Am. Bar Found. (bd. dirs. 2000, immigration bono com. 2000—, state del. 2002), Nat. Conf. Bar Pres. (exec. com. 2001—), State Bar Tex. (bd. dirs. Dist. 9 1991—, exec. com. 1992—, chmn. minority representation com. 1991-92, chair James Watson Inn 1997-98, pres. 1998-99, chmn. profl. devel. com. 1991-92, policy manual com. 1993, fed. jud. appts. com. 1984-86, opportunities for minorities in the profession com. 1990-91, mem. advt. rev. com., pres.-elect 1997, pres. 1998-99), Travis County Bar Assn. (trustee lawyer referral svc. 1984-85, bd. dirs. 1986-88, sec. 1988, pres. 1990-91, chmn. jud. screening com. 1987, chmn. 1988-89, ins. com. 1988, 89, chmn. law day banquet com. 1988-89, lawyer referral svc. com. 1983-84, trustee 1984-86, membership com. 1989), Capitol Area Mex. Am. Lawyers (pres. 1985, Outstanding Hispanic Lawyer Austin 1989), Legal Aid Soc. Ctrl. Tex. (bd. dirs. 1984), Austin Young Lawyers Assn., Tex. Trial Lawyers Assn., Austin C. of C. (Leadership Austin 1985-86). Democrat. Home: 107 Top O The Lake Dr Austin TX 78734-5234 Office: 2028 E Ben White #220 Austin TX 78741

PENACHIO, ANTHONY JOSEPH, JR. psychotherapist, hypnotherapist, behavioral therapist; b. Stamford, Conn., Apr. 3, 1953; 1 child, Ariana. Cert. in psychotherapy, Am. Sch. Med. Hynotherapy, 1978; DD, Aquarian Ch. of Jesus, 1978; PSD, Neotharian Sch. of Philosophy, 1980. Cert. clin. registered med. hypnotherapist, psychotherapist, behavioral therapist, biomed. electronics, psychophysiologist; ordained counseling min. Aquarian Ch.; diplomate Am. Psychotherapy Assn. Counseling min., exec. dir. Inst. Clin. Tricotomy, Stamford, 1978—. Author, emotional investment profiler Wall St., corps. and govts.; lectr., radio and cable TV talk show seminar presenter. Contbr. articles profl. jours., corps. and govts. Mem. Am. Coun. Hypnotherapist-Psychotherapist (bd. examiners), N.Y. Acad. Sci. (lectr.).

PENALTA, C. RICHARD, prosecutor; b. Matanzas, Cuba, May 27, 1959; m. Carol Ann Sogan, Nov. 14, 1992; children: Lance Alexander, Gabrielle Alexa. Student, Brunel U. West London, 1991, U. Madrid, 1991; JD, Washburn Sch. Law, 1991. Bar: U.S. Dist. Ct. (no., mid. and so. dist.) Fla., U.S. Ct. Appeals (11th cir.), U.S. Ct. Internat. Trade, U.S. Ct. Appeals (armed forces cir.); lic. real estate agt., Fla. Adminstrn. specialist IBM, Boca Raton, Fla., 1985, Miami, 1985-86, Gainesville, 1986-88; assoc. comml. litigation divsn. Kinsey Vincent Pyle, P.A., Daytona Beach, 1992; asst. state atty. Office of State Atty. 7th Jud. Cir. Fla., 1992-96, Office of State Atty. 15th Jud. Cir. Fla., West Palm Beach, 1997—; assoc. Eubank, Hassel & Assocs., P.A., Daytona Beach, 1996-97. Instr. Penalta & Assocs., P.A., Fla., 1994—; dir., owner Knights of Neptune, Dive & Travel, 1988—; adj. faculty, instr. U. Fla., Gainesville, 1987-88; corp. instr. Unemployment Ins. Corp., Boca Raton, Fla., 1999—; lectr. in field. Mem. Volusia County Domestic Violence Task Force,1 993-94. Recipient Outstanding Instr. award U. Fla. Mem. ABA, ATLA, Nat. Dist. Attys. Assn., Fla. Bar Assn., Palm Beach County Bar Assn., Hispanic Bar Assn., Fla. Pros. Attys. Assn. (DUI trial sch. staff), Fla. Def. Lawyers Assn., Def. Rsch. Inst., Aircraft Owners and Pilots Assn., World Underwater Fedn., Nat. Assn. Underwater Instrs., Profl. Assn. Diving Instrs., Nat. Assn. Cave Diving, U.S. Navy League. Avocations: flying, scuba diving, golf, tennis, running. Home: 2128 Tarpon Lake Way West Palm Beach FL 33411-5766 Office: Office of State Atty 401 N Dixie Hwy West Palm Beach FL 33401-4209

PENALVER, ANGELICA MARIA, research scientist; b. Bklyn., Sept. 9, 1972; d. Pablo Hugo and Lucy E. Penalver. BA in Cell Biology, CUNY, 1997; postgrad. MBA, U. Phoenix. Rsch. study asst. radiology Meml. Sloan-Kettering Cancer Ctr., N.Y.C., 1995-97, clin. rsch. asst., data mgr., 1997-98; clin. data coord. Pfizer Pharms., Inc., 1998-99; clin. rsch. assoc. Quintiles CNS Therapeutics, Cranford, N.J., 1999-2000, Forest Labs., Inc., N.Y.C., 2000—; clin. study mgr. Pfizer Pharmaceuticals, 2000—. Queens Coll. Mayor scholar, 1990-91. Mem. Assn. of Clin. Rsch. Profls., Soc. Clin. Rsch. Assocs., Golden Key Nat. Honor Soc. Avocations: running, piano, equestrianship, travel. Office: Pfizer Pharm Inc 235 E 42nd St New York NY 10017

PENASHUE, PETER, political organization worker; Pres. Innu Nation Sheshatshing, Labrador, 1990—. Office: Innu Nation PO Box 119 Sheshatshin, Labrador Canada A0P 1M0*

PENBERTHY, STANLEY JOSIAH, JR. publisher; b Des Moines, Sept. 3, 1921; s. Stanley Josiah and Beatrice Ann (Voith) P.; m. Dorothea Oehmke, July 7, 1945; 1 child, Robert Bruce. Student, Drake U., Des Moines, 1940-43. Engaged in broadcasting WJR, Detroit, 1941-56; freelance radio, TV, motion picture, actor, narrator, 1956—95. V.p. Fed. I-D Equipment Corp., Dearborn, Mich., 1951-62; pres. Publishers, Inc., Detroit, 1976-99. Author, prodr., narrator nat. radio series These Were Our Presidents, 1975; contbr. Mich. Sesquintennial hist. articles; author: Living Under Cover, Episodes of Life and other Relatives, Cottage Industry, The Photographs of William A. Roeser: A Talent Unfulfilled, . . .From the Golden Tower of the Fisher Building. Past mem. bd. dirs. Sleeping Bear Dunes Citizens Coun., Traverse City, Mich., 1968-72, Cass Park Area Devel. Corp., City of Detroit, 1989; pres. Heritage Village Condominium Assn.; trustee Detroit Masonic Temple Assn.; mem. Founders Soc. Detroit Inst. Arts. Mem. AFTRA (past dir.), Adcraft Club Detroit, Detroit Execs. Assn. (dir.), Am. Film Inst., Detroit Prodrs. Assn., Broadcast Pioneers, Masons (33rd degree), Alpha Tau Omega (past alumni pres.). Home: 35560 Heritage Ln Farmington MI 48335-3136

PENCE, IRA WILSON, JR. material handling research executive, engineer; b. Pontiac, Mich., June 18, 1939; s. Ira Wilson and Fern Elizabeth (Fraser) P.; m. JoAnna Springer, Sept. 5, 1959; children: Ira W. III, Teresa Ann, Deidre Lynn. BS, U. Mich., 1962, MSEE, 1964, PhD, 1970. Rsch. engr. Willow Run Labs., Ypsilanti, Mich., 1960-67, Dow Lab., Ann Arbor, 1967-70, GE, Schenectady, N.Y., 1970-80, enging. mgr. Charlottesville, Va., 1980-83; v.p. enging. Unimation, Inc., Danbury, Conn., 1983-87; dir. MHRC Ga. Inst. Tech., Atlanta, 1987-97, dir., pres. Intelligent Integrated Info. Sys., 1999—. Cons. Superior Motor, Hartford, 1987-89; bd. dirs. Wesley Found.; mem. adv. coun. Westinghouse, Pitts., 1983-87, treas. Wesley Comm. Ctrs., Inc., 1999—; dir. 21iii.com, 2000—; exec. pres. Intelligent Integrated Info. Sys., 1999. Editor: Progress in Material Handling and Logistics, 1988; Material Handling for 90's, 1990. Trustee United Meth. Ch., 1988—, Camp Wesley, 1998—. Recipient New Product of Yr. award Innovation Today, 1985. Mem. IEEE (sr., sect. chmn. 1978), ASME (Materials Handling Engring. divsn. chair 1994). Republican. Methodist. Avocations: cabinet making, golf. Office: Ga Inst Tech 765 Ferst Dr Atlanta GA 30332-0001 Fax: (770) 435-0493. E-mail: ipence@isye.gatech.edu.

PENCE, MIKE, congressman; b. Columbus, Ind. m. Karen; three children. Grad., Hanover Coll., 1981; JD, Ind. U. Sch. Law, 1986. Radio broadcaster The Mike Pence Show, 1992; host public affairs TV show, Indpls., 1995-99; mem. U.S. Congress from 2nd Ind. dist., 2001—. Named Asst. Majority Whip; mem. Congressional judiciary com. House Agriculture; subcom. chmn. House Small Bus. on Reg. Reform and Oversight. Republican. Office: 1605 Longworth House bldg Washington DC 20515

PENCE, ROBERT DUDLEY, biomedical research administrator, hospital administrator; b. Hillsboro, Ohio, June 16, 1928; s. Glenn Roush and Mildred (Wright) P. BA cum laude, Miami U., Oxford, Ohio, 1950; postgrad., U. Montpellier, France, 1950-51. Mktg. rep. Tex. Petroleum Co., West Africa, 1956-58; mgr. lab. and office svcs. Sloan-Kettering Inst. for Cancer Rsch., N.Y.C., 1958-68; bus. mgr., cancer rsch. inst. New Eng. Deaconess Hosp., Boston, 1968-72, adminstr. Shields Warren Radiation Lab., 1970-78, asst. dir., 1972-86, adminstrv. dir., cancer rsch. inst., 1974-88, adminstrv. dir. Shields Warren Radiation Lab., 1978-88, dir. div. of rsch., 1986-88, cons., 1988—. Field liaison fellow ACS, Chgo., 1981-88. Pres. Am. Cancer Soc., Brookline, Mass. Served to lt. (j.g.) USN, 1951-55. Fulbright scholar, Montpellier, 1950. Mem. Assn. Community Cancer Ctrs. (del.), Internat. Union Against Cancer (U.S. standing com.), Assn. Am. Cancer Insts., Soc. Rsch. Adminstrs. (charter), Nat. Coun. Univ. Rsch. Adminstrs., Nat. Tumor Registrars Assn. (advisor 1980—), Tumor Registrars Assn. New Eng. (bd. dirs. 1975—), Phi Beta Kappa. Home: 30 Driftwood Cir Norwood MA 02062-5505

PENCEK, CAROLYN CARLSON, treasurer, educator; b. Appleton, Wis., June 13, 1946; d. Arthur Edward and Mary George (Notaras) Carlson; m. Richard David Pencek, July 10, 1971; children: Richard Carlson, Mallory Barbara Rowlands. BA in Polit. Sci., Western Coll., 1968; Ma in Polit. Sci., Syracuse U., 1975; EdD, Temple U., 1999. Investment analysts asst. Bankers Trust Co., N.Y.C., 1969-71; substitute tchr. Lackawanna Trail Sch. Dist., Factoryville, Pa., 1971-81; instr. polit. sci. Keystone Coll., La Plume, 1972-73; USGS coding supr. Richard Walsh Assocs., Scranton, 1975-76; instr. polit. sci. Pa. State U., Dunmore, 1976-77; treas. Creative Planning Ltd., 1988—. Bd. trustees Lourdesmont Sch., Clarks Summit, Pa., 1989—, v.p., 2000—. Bd. dirs. Lackawanna County Child and Youth Svcs., Scranton, 1981—, pres., 1988-90; founding mem., sec. Leadership Lackawanna, 1982-84; bd. dirs. N.E. Pa. Regional Tissue and Transplant Bank, Scranton, 1984-88, Vol. Action Ctr., Scranton, 1986-91; founding mem. Women's Resource Ctr. Assn., Scranton, 1986—, pres., 1986-87; v.p. sch. improvement coun. Lackawanna Trail Sch. Dist., 1995-96, sec., 1996-97; mem. adv. bd. Pa. State U., Worthington Scranton, 1998—. Named Vol. of Yr. nominee, Vol. Action Ctr., 1985; Temple U. fellow, Phila., 1991-92. Mem. AAUW (sec. 1973-75, state sel. com. 1979-81), Assn. Jr. Leagues Internat. (area II coun. mem. 1978-79), Jr. League Scranton (v.p. 1980, pres. 1981-83, Margaret L. Richards award 1984), Philharmonic League (v.p. 1976, pres. 1977). Episcopalian. Home: RR 2 Box 2489 Factoryville PA 18419-9649 Office: Creative Planning Ltd 1100 Dunham Dr Dunmore PA 18512-2653 E-mail: spot717@aol.com.

PENDER, MICHAEL ROGER, engineering consultant; b. Feb. 18, 1926; s. Horace Gibson and Lilian Frances (Higgins) P.; m. Francina Joan Krosschell, June 4, 1949; children: Michael Roger, Jr., William J., Robin Jane, Richard A., John A. AB, Dartmouth Coll., 1949, MS in Civil Engring., 1950. Registered profl. engr., Fla., N.Y., N.H.; diplomate Am. Acad. Environ. Engrs. Project engr. Madigan-Hyland, Inc., L.I., 1950-60; dir. state exhibits N.Y. World's Fair, Flushing, 1960-65; commr. pub. works Town of Hempstead (N.Y.), 1966-77, Nassau County, Mineola, N.Y., 1978-82; supt. pub. works Village of Valley Stream (N.Y.), 1982-85; tech. advisor N.Y. State Assembly, Albany, 1985-86; cons. engr. Boyle Engring. Corp., Sarasota, Fla., 1987—. Exec. dir. World's Fair Collectors Soc., 1968—. Contbr. articles to profl. jours. Treas. Town of Hempstead Local Devel. Corp., 1967-86, Town of Hempstead Ind. Devel. Agy., 1973-86, Nassau County Local Devel. Corp., 1978-83; mem. adv. bd. Sarasota County Pub. Utilities, 1986-87; chmn. adv. bd. Solid Waste Mgmt., 1992—, Sarasota County Water & Sewer, 1995—. Sgt. U.S. Army, 1945-46. Named Profl. Enging. Mgr. of Yr., N.Y. State Soc. Profl. Engrs., 1979. Fellow ASCE (life), Inst. Transp. Engrs. (life), Fla. Engring. Soc.; mem. NSPE (life, v.p. 1982-84), Am. Pub. Works Assn. (life, pres. 1984-85, chmn. Suncoast br. 1993-94, named one of Top Ten Pub. Works Ofcls. in U.S. 1973), Dartmouth Club of Sarasota (pres. 1991-93), Sarasota Sister Cities Assn. (treas. 1990-01), Am. Water Works. Assn. (life), Univ. Club L.I. (pres. 1985-86), Rotary (pres. Sarasota Bay 1992-93). Republican. Presbyterian. Avocation: photographing railroad depots. Home: 6639 Waterford Ln Sarasota FL 34238-2639 Office: Worlds Fair Collectors Soc PO Box 20806 Sarasota FL 34276-3806 E-mail: wfcs@aol.com.

PENDER, RICHARD F. communications executive, consultant, theater critic; b. Akron, Ohio, May 7, 1949; s. Franklin B. and Merle C. Pender; m. Joan M. Kaup; children: Geoffrey. BA, Oberlin Coll., 1971; MA, Case Western Reserve U., 1972, PhD, 1980. Accredited in pub. rels. Asst. dir. publs. Hiram (Ohio) Coll., 1976—78; dir. comms. Walsh Coll., Canton, 1978—80; pub. info. officer WGUC-FM, U. Cin., Cin., 1980—84; gen. mgr. WNKU-FM, No. Ky. U., Highland Heights, 1984—85; dir. corp. comm. ChoiceCare, Cin., 1985—90; v.p. Dan Pinger Pub. Rels. Inc., 1991—98; asst. editor arts and entertainment Cin. CityBeat, 1998—. V.p. mktg. comm. The Jewish Hosps., Cin., 1995—97. Author: (Book) Studies in the Writings of Sir Thomas Malory, 1980. Sec. Over-the-Rhine Foundation, Cin., 1999—; arts and culture panel chair Cincinnatus, 2001—; bd. mem. Women Helping Women, 1993—95; pres. Leadership Cin. Alumni Assn., 2002, Pub. Rels. Soc. Am., Cin. Chpt., 1985—86. Named to Coll. of Fellows, Pub. Rels. Soc. Am., 1996. Mem.: Found. Am. Theatre Critics Assn. (treas. 2001—02), Am. Theatre Critics Assn. (exec. com. 2001—), Pub. Rels. Soc. Am. (pres. 1985—86, Werner-VonderHaar award 1991). Office: Cincinnati CityBeat Fifth Fl 811 Race St Cincinnati OH 45202

PENDERECKI, KRZYSZTOF, composer, conductor; b. Debica, Poland, Nov. 23, 1933; s. Tadeusz and Zofia P.; m. Elzbieta Solecka; children: Lukasz, Dominique. Grad., State Acad. Music, Krakow, 1958; student, Arthur Malawski and Stanislaw Wiechowicz; Dr. honoris causa, U. Rochester, St. Olaf Coll., Northfield, Minn., Cath U., Leuven, Belgium, U. Bordeaux, France, Georgetown U., Belgrade U., Madrid U., Spain, Adam Mickiewicz U., Warsaw U., Poland, 1993, U. Catolica Argentina, Buenos Aires, 1994, Acad. Music, Cracow, 1994, Acad. Music, Warsaw, 1994, U. Glasgow, 1995, Beijiung Conservatory, 1998, U. Pitts., 1999. Prof. composition Krakow State Sch. Music, 1959-65, Folkwang Hochschule für Musik, Essen, Fed. Republic Germany, 1966-68; composer-in-residence Sch. Music, Yale U., alternate years; guest condr. London Symphony Orch., Polish Radio Orch., Berlin Philharm. Orch. Composer: Psalms of David for chorus and percussion, 1958, Emanations for 2 string orchs., 1959, Strophes for soprano, narrator and 10 instruments, 1959, Dimensions of time and silence, 1959-61, Anaklasis, 1959-60, Threnody for the Victims of Hiroshima, 1960, Psalmus for tape, 1961, Polymorphia, 1961; Fluorescences, 1961, Stabat Mater, 1962, Canon, 1962, Sonata for cello and orch., 1964, St. Luke Passion, 1965, De Natura Sonoris I, 1966, Dies Irae, 1967, Capriccio for violin and orch., 1967, Capriccio for cello Solo, 1968; opera The Devils of Loudun, 1968-69; Utrenja for double chorus, soloists and orch., 1969-71, Cosmogony, 1970, Utrenja II-Resurrection, 1971, Actions for jazz ensemble, 1971, Partita for harpsichord, 4 solo instruments and orch., 1971-72, Cello Concerto, 1967-72; for double chorus, soloists and orchestra Ecloga VIII for 6 male voices, 1972; Symphony 1, 1972-73, Canticum Canticorum Salomonis for 16 voices and chamber orch., 1970-73, Magnificat, 1973-74, When Jacob Awoke for orch., 1974, Violin Concerto, 1976-77, Paradise Lost (rappresentazione), 1976-78, (Christmas) Symphony No. 2, 1980, Te Deum, 1979-80, Lacrimosa, 1980, Agnus Dei for a cappella chorus, 1981, Cello Concerto No. 2, 1982, Requiem, 1983, Concerto per Viola, 1983, Polish Requiem, 1983-84, The Black Mask, 1986, Der Unterbrochene Gedanke, 1987, Adagio, 1989, Ubu Rex, 1991, Sinfonietta for orchestra, 1990-91, Symphony No. 5 for orchestra, 1991-92, Partita for orchestra, rev. edit., 1991, Flute concerto, 1992-93, Quartet for Clarinet and String Trio, 1993, Divertimento per Cello solo, 1994, Violin Concerto No. 2, 1992-95, Agnus Dei, 1995, Symphony No. 3, Seven Gates of Jerusalem, 1997, Hymn to St. Daniel, 1997, Hymn to St. Adalbert, 1997, Credo, 1998, Sonata No. 2 for violin and piano, 2000, Sextet for violin, viola, piano, clarinet, and french horn, 2000, also other works; prin. guest condr. NDR Symphony Orch., Hamburg, and MDR Symphony Orch., Leipzig; artistic dir. Casals Festival, PR. Recipient 1st prize for Strophes Polish Composers Assn., 1959, UNESCO award, Fitelberg prize and Polish Ministry Culture award all for Threnody, 1960, Krakow composition prize for Canon, 1961, grand prize State N. Rhine-Westphalia for St. Luke Passion, 1966, Pax prize Poland, 1966, Jurzykowski prize Polish Inst. Arts and Scis., 1966, Sibelius award, 1967, Prix d'Italia, 1967-68, Polish 1st Class State award, 1968, Gottfried von Herder prize, 1977, prix Arthur Honegger, 1978, Sibelius prize Wihouri Found., 1983, Wolf Found. prize, 1987, 3 Grammy awards, Gamma prize Acad. Rec. Arts and Scis., 1988, Manuel de Falla Gold medal Accademia de Bellas Artes, Granada, 1989, Das Grosse Verdienstkreuz des Verdienstordens der Bundesrepublik Deutschland, 1990, 2 Grammy nominations, 1992, Grawermeyer Music award, 1992, Österreichische Ehrenzeichen für Wissenschaft und Kunst, 1994, 2 Primetime Emmy awards, 1995, 96, Crystall award, Davos, 1997, 2 Grammy awards, 1999, Musikpreis Duisburg, 1999, Cannes Classical award Composer of Yr., 2000, Principe de Asturias, 2001; grantee several founds., govts., insts. Mem. AAAL (hon.), Royal Acad. Mus. London (hon.), Nat. Acad. of Santa Cecilia (Rome) (hon.), Royal Swedish Acad. Music, Acad. of Kuenste West Berlin (extraord. mem.), Nat. Acad. of Bellas Artes (Buenos Aires) (corr.), Internat. Acad. Philosophy and Art (Berne), Nat. Acad. Scis., Belles-lettres et Arts (Bordeaux), Acad. Scientiarium et Artium Europaea (Salzburg), L'Ordre de Saint Georges de Bourgogne (officer, Brussels), Am. Acad. Arts and Letters, Bay. Acad. des Schönen Künste. Achievements include creating original notational system allowing aleatory freedom for performer within sects. of precise duration. Home: ul Cisowa 22 30229 Cracow Poland Office: ICM Artists Ltd c/o Jenny Vogel 8942 Wilshire Blvd Beverly Hills CA 90211-1934 also: Panstwowa Wyzsza Szkola Muzyczna ul Starowislna 31 038 Cracow Poland also: Am Daubhaus 6 D 55276 Oppenheim Germany Fax: 49-6133/92 63 56.

PENDERGAST, JOHN JOSEPH, III, lawyer; b. Lewiston, Maine, Jan. 29, 1936; s. John Joseph and Grace (McCarty) P.; m. Joan Shaw Cole, June 14, 1958; children: John Joseph IV, Timothy S., Terrence B., Mary R., Michael C., Joan M. BA, Yale U., 1957, LLB, 1960. Bar: R.I. 1961, U.S. Dist. Ct. R.I. 1961, U.S. Ct. Appeals (1st cir.) 1963. Assoc. Hinckley, Allen & Snyder, Providence, 1960-66, ptnr., chmn. labor dept., 1966—; instr. U. R.I., Kingston, 1984-88. Adj. prof. Providence Coll., 1984—86, Roger Williams Law Sch., 1998—. Author: (with others) The Developing Labor Law, 2d edit., 1983, Labor and Employment Arbitration, 1988, NLRA Law and Practice, 1992. Mem. Cath. Charities panel Diocese of Providence, 1976-94; bd. dirs. Smith Hill Ctr., Providence, 1978-93; v.p. Providence Boys Clubs, 1970-72, bd. dirs., 1990—, sec., 1996—. Mem. ABA (labor law sect.), Am. Coll. Hosp. Attys.,

Indsl. Rels. Rsch. Assn., R.I. Bar Assn., Sakonnet Yacht Club, Yale Club of R.I. (Providence). Avocations: antiques, fly fishing. Home: 21 Elmhurst Ave Providence RI 02908-2802 Office: Hinckley Allen & Snyder 1500 Fleet Ctr Providence RI 02903-2319

PENDERGHAST, THOMAS FREDERICK, business educator; b. Cin., Apr. 23, 1936; s. Elmer T. and Dolores C. (Huber) P.; m. Marjorie Craig, Aug. 12, 1983; children: Brian, Shawna, Steven, Dean, Maria. BS, Marquette U., 1958; MBA, Calif. State U., Long Beach, 1967; D in Bus. Adminstrn., Nova U., 1987. Cert. in data processing. Sci. programmer Autonetics, Inc., Anaheim, Calif., 1960-64; bus. programmer Douglas Missile & Space Ctr., Huntington Beach, 1964-66; computer specialist N.Am. Rockwell Co., 1966-69; asst. prof. Calif. State U., 1969-72; prof. Sch. Bus. and Mgmt. Pepperdine U., L.A., 1972—; spl. adviser Commn. on Engring. Edn., 1968; v.p. Visual Computing Co., 1969-71; founder, pres. Scoreboard Animation Systems, 1971-77; exec. v.p. Microfilm Identification Systems, 1977-79; pres. Data Processing Auditors, Inc., 1981—. Data processing cons. designing computer system for fin. health and mfg. orgns., 1972—; mem. Orange County Blue Ribbon Com. on Data Processing, 1973; mem. Orange County TEC Policy Bd., 1982-87; mgmt. and organization devel. cons. Assn. Psychological Type, 1993—. Author: Entrepreneurial Simulation Program, 1988, Journey to Couples' Conflict Resolution Using Game Theory, 1999. Served to lt. USNR, 1958-60. Mem. Users of Automatic Info. Display Equipment (pres. 1966). Home: 17867 Bay St Fountain Valley CA 92708-4443 E-mail: tpenderg@pepperdine.edu.

PENDERGRAFT, JANICE GAYLE, volunteer; b. San Antonio, Mar. 9, 1950; d. Janice Gayle and John Joseph Pendergraft(Stepfather); m. Pete E. Kraus, Nov. 3, 1973 (dec. Aug. 3, 1987); 1 child Heather Kraus ; m. John Joseph Pendergraft, June 18, 1988 (dec.). Cert. dental asst., L.A. Coll. Med. and Dental Assts., San Bernardino, Calif., 1969. Cert. dental asst. Vol. M.A.D.D., San Bernardino, 1995—, Ronald McDonald House, Loma Linda, 1998—. Author poetry. Active Yucaipa Edn. Bd., Calif., 1980—98. Recipient several poetry awards, 1998—2002. Office: Ronald Mcdonald House Barton Rd Loma Linda CA 92353

PENDERGRASS, EWELL DEAN, communications executive; b. Houston, Dec. 24, 1945; s. Ewell Burl and Mary LaVerne (Sharp) P.; m. Linda Jo Williams, 1973; children: William Dean, Douglas Aaron, Nagaya Jo. AAS, Westark C.C., 1979. Comm. technician Murdock Comm., Ft. Smith, Ark., 1966-73; electronics technician City of Ft. Smith, 1973—, now electronics supr.; co-owner LED Comms., 1975—. Broadcast engr. Sta. KWHN, 1972-73, Sta. KFSA, 1975-76; mem. Ark. Dept. Pollution and Ecology Wastewater Licensing Bd.; mem. Ark. Licensing Commn. Mem. Am. Water Works Assn., Ark. Water Works and Pollution Control Assn. (chmn., Western dist. dir.), Border Amateur Radio Club (prs. 1974-75). Democrat. Methodist. Home: 1106 Country Meadow Ln Cedarville AR 72932-9524 Office: 3900 Kelley Hwy Fort Smith AR 72904-5610

PENDERGRASS, HENRY PANCOAST, physician, radiology educator; b. Bryn Mawr, Pa., Jan. 29, 1925; s. Eugene Percival and Rebecca (Barker) P.; m. Carol Lowe Dodson, Aug. 27, 1960 (dec. Aug. 1993); children: Sharon (dec. Aug. 1993), Lisa (dec. Aug. 1993), Deborah, Margaret; m. Carol Minster Roberts, Oct. 2, 1994. Student, U.S. Naval Acad., 1944-46; AB, Princeton U., 1948; MD, U. Pa., 1952; MPH, Harvard U., 1969. Diplomate: Am. Bd. Radiology, Am. Bd. Nuclear Medicine. Intern Pa. Hosp., 1952—53; resident Hosp. U. Pa., 1953—56; mem. staff and faculty U. Pa. Med. Sch. and Univ. Hosp., Phila., 1956—58, U. Pa. Med. Sch. & U. Hosp., 1960—61; clin. asst. in neuroradiology Inst. Neurology Queen Sq., London, 1959-60; mem. staff and faculty Harvard U. Med. Sch. and Mass. Gen. Hosp., Boston, 1958-59, 61-76; prof. radiology Vanderbilt U. Sch. Medicine, Nashville, 1976-95, prof. emeritus, 1995—, vice chmn., 1976-89; adj. prof. radiology U. Pa. Sch. Medicine, Phila., 1996—. Mem. editorial bd. Am. Family Physician, 1980-94, Jour. Digital Imaging, 1987-96; contbr. chpts. to books, articles to med. jours. Mem. cancer control rev. com. Nat. Cancer Inst., 1975-79; Bd. dirs. state and local div. Am. Cancer Soc., 1976-85; mem. Project Hope Med. Mission, Peru, 1962; trustee Harpeth Hall Sch., Nashville, 1983-88. With U.S. Army, USN, 1943-46. Am. Cancer Soc. grantee, 1956-57; Nat. Cancer Inst. grantee, 1957-58; Nat. Inst. Neurol. Disease and Blindness grantee, 1959-60; Nat. Inst. Gen. Med. Scis. grantee, 1968-69. Fellow: AMA (sect. coun. on radiology 1979—99, sect. on med. schs. 1979—99, sec. 1986—97, mem. ho. of dels. 1986—99, specialty and svc. sect. 1986—99, grad. med. edn. adv. com. 1994—97, chair 1996, chair 1997—99, Gold medal 1994), Tenn. Radiol. Soc. (exec. com. 1984—88, pres.-elect then pres. 1985—86, Disting. Svc. award 1993), Soc. Magnetic Resonance in Medicine, Soc. Thoracic Imaging, Mid. Tenn. Radiol. Soc. (pres. 1984—85), Tenn. Med. Assn., Am. Soc. Emergency Radiology, Radiol. Soc. N.Am. (bd. dir. 1972—77, chmn. 1975—76, pres.-elect then pres. 1977—78, appointee to AMA ho. dels. 1986—97, sec.-treas. 1988—90, trustee RSNA rsch. and edn. found., Gold medal 1984), Nashville Acad. Medicine (chmn. com. on ethics 1981—82), Mass. Med. Soc. (counselor 1968—76), Mass. Radiol. Soc. (v.p. 1967—68, 1975—76, sec.-treas. 1985—94), Assn. U. Radiologists, Ea. Radiol. Soc. (sci. program chmn. 1964, pres. 1968—72, trustee 1968—72), Coun. on Med. Specialty Socs., Brit. Inst. Radiology, Am. Roentgen Ray Soc., Am. Coll. Radiology (life; coun. steering com. 1968—73, bd. chancellors 1977—81, appointee to AMA ho. of dels. 1997—99, benefactor, coun.); mem.: Belle Meade Country, Merion Golf, Merion Cricket, Amateur Ski (N.Y.), Cap and Gown (Princeton, N.J.), Merion Cricket Club, Merion Golf Club, Belle Meade Country Club, Amateur Ski Club NY, Cap & Gown Club (Princeton, NJ), Delta Psi, Sigma Xi.

PENDLETON, ANDREW H. optical cabling executive; b. Dallas, Sept. 9, 1965; s. Frederick A. and Patricia A. Pendleton. BA, Tex. A&M U., 1989; MBA, NYU, 1992. Auditor Coopers & Lybrand, N.Y.C., 1989-92; internal auditor Pepsi Co., Purchase, N.Y., Dallas, 1992-95; mgr. fin. reporting Cott Beverages, Dallas, 1995-98; dir. planning and analysis Apio, Inc., Guadalupe, Calif., 1998-2001; chief oper. officer Optical Cabling Systems, Dallas, 2001—.

PENDLETON, BARBARA JEAN, retired banker; b. Independence, Mo., Aug. 14, 1924; d. Elmer Dean and Martha Lucille (Friess) P. Student, Cen. Mo. State Coll., 1942; D of Bus. Adminstrn. (hon.), Avila Coll., 1986. V.p. Grand Ave. Bank, Kansas City, Mo., 1962-76, exec. v.p., 1976-79; vice chmn. City Bank & Trust Co., 1979-82, chmn., 1982-83; exec. v.p. United Mo. Bank of Kansas City, 1983-93, United Mo. Bancshares, Inc., 1990-93. Bd. dirs. Shepherd Ctrs. of Am., Inc., 1992—. Vice chmn., mem. Dept. Def. adv. com. Women in Svc., Washington, 1967-69; chmn. City of Kansas City Employee Retirement Fund, 1985-99; bd. dirs. YMCA USA, 1996—; commr. Kansas City Tax Increment Fin. Commn., 1996—. Recipient Matrix award Press Women, 1963, Wohelo award Campfire, Inc., 1979. Mem. Fin. Women Internat. (nat. pres. 1972-73), Am. Humanics, Inc. (chmn. 1987-88). Clubs: Cen. Exchange (Kansas City) (pres. 1983-84).

PENDLETON, GAIL RUTH, newspaper editor, writer, educator; b. Franklin, N.J., May 8, 1937; d. Waldo A. and Ruby (Bonnett) Rousset; m. John E. Tyler, Mar. 10, 1956 (div. 1978); children: Gwenneth, Victoria, Christine; m. Jeffrey P. Pendleton, Oct. 1, 1978 (dec. 1992). BA, Montclair (N.J.) State Coll., 1959; M in Div., Princeton (N.J.) Theol. Sem., 1973; MA in English, William Paterson Coll., 1998. Ordained minister Presbyn. Ch., 1974. Tchr. Epiphany Day Sch., Kaimuki, Oahu, Hawaii, 1956-58; editor Women's Sect. Daily Record, Morristown, N.J., 1959-62, reporter, 1963-65; tchr. Hardystown Twp. Sch., Franklin, 1968-69; asst. pastor 1st Presbyn. Ch., Sparta, N.J., 1973-74; reporter N.J. Herald, Newton, 1976-78, editor lifestyle sect., 1978-93, editor Friday entertainment sect., 1993-95, editor spl. sect., 1995-97; pres. Crystal Palce Networking Inc., 1995—. Adj. prof. Ramapo Coll. of N.J., Mahwah, 1998, County Coll. of Morris, Randolph, N.J., 1998, Sussex County C.C., Newton, N.J., 1998-99, Centenary Coll., Hackettstown, N.J., 1999—; tchr. Univ. H.S., Newark, 1999-2000. Recipient Ruth Cheney Streeter award Planned Parenthood N.W. N.J., 1985. Mem. N.J. Press Assn. (family sect. layout award 1985, 87, 88, 89, 91, 2d feature columns award 1986).

PENDLETON, JOAN MARIE, microprocessor designer; b. Cleve., July 7, 1954; d. Alvin Dial and Alta Beatrice (Brown) P. BS in Physics, Elec. Engring., MIT, 1976; MSEE, Stanford U., 1978; PhDEE, U. Calif., Berkeley, 1985. Sr. design engr. Fairchild Semiconductor, Palo Alto, Calif., 1978-82; staff engr. Sun Microsystems, Mountain View, 1986-87; cons., designer Computer Sci. Dept. U. Calif., Berkeley, 1988-90; dir. engring. Silicon Engring. Inc., Scotts Valley, Calif., 1994-95; CEO Harvest VLSI Design Ctr., Inc., San Jose, 1988—; dir. ASIC devel. Poseidon Tech., 1997-98. Founder Aurora VLSI, Inc., Santa Clara, Calif., 1998—. Contbr. articles to profl. jours.; inventor, patentee serpentine charge transfer device. Recipient 1st, 2d and 3d place awards U.S. Rowing Assn., Fairchild Tech. Achievement award, 1982, 1st place A award Fed. Internat. Soc Aviron, 1991. Mem. IEEE, Assn. for Computing Machinery, Los Gatos Rowing Club, U.S. Rowing Assn. Avocations: rowing, skiing, backpacking.

PENDLETON, MARY CATHERINE, foreign service officer; b. Louisville, June 15, 1940; d. Joseph S. and Katherine R. (Toebbe) Pendleton. BA, Spalding Coll., 1962; MA, Ind. U., 1969; cert., Nat. Def. U., 1990; D (hon.) , U. N. Testemitanu, Moldova, 1994. Cert. secondary tchr. Ky. Tchr. Presentation Acad., Louisville, 1962-66; vol. Peace Corps, Tunis, Tunisia, 1966-68; employment counselor Ky. Dept. for Human Resources, Louisville, 1969-75; gen. svcs. Am. Embassy, Khartoum, Sudan, 1975-77, counsular officer Manila, 1978-79, adminstrv. officer Bangui, Central African Republic, 1979-82, Lusaka, Zambia, 1982-84; post mgmt. officer Dept. of State Bur. European and Can. Affairs, Washington, 1984-87; adminstrv. counselor Am. Embassy, Bucharest, Romania, 1987-89; dir. adminstrv. tng. divsn. Fgn. Svc. Inst., Arlington, Va., 1990-92; ambassador Am. Embassy, Chisinau, Moldova, 1992-95, adminstrv. counselor Brussels, 1995-98; consul gen. U.S. Consulate Gen., Montreal, 1998-2001; adminstrv. counselor Am. Embassy, Cairo, 2001—. Bd. dirs. Cairo Am. Coll., 2001—, Am. Sch. Bucharest, 1987—89. Named to, Hon. Order Ky. Cols., 1988. Democrat. Roman Catholic. Avocations: family history research, outdoor activities. Home: Unit 64900 Box 3 APO AE 09839-4900 Office: 8 Kamel El-Din Salah St Garden City Cairo Egypt E-mail: pendletonmc@state.gov.

PENDLETON, MILES STEVENS, JR. diplomat; b. Montclair, N.J., Mar. 22, 1939; s. Miles Stevens and Lucille (Bond) P.; m. Elisabeth Morgan, Aug. 13, 1967; children: Constance Morrow, Nathaniel Palmer. BA magna cum laude, Yale U., 1961; MPA, Harvard U., 1967; diploma, Nat. War Coll., 1980. Tchr. Ghana Secondary Sch., Koforidua, 1962-63, Adisadel Coll., Cape Coast, Ghana, 1963-64; vice consul Am. Embassy, Tel Aviv, Israel, 1968-70, polit. and econ. officer Bujumbura, Burundi, 1970-72; watch officer Ops. Ctr. Dept. State, Washington, 1972-73, staff officer Secretariat Staff, 1973-74, spl. asst. to Dep. Sec. of State Office Dep. Sec., 1974-76; polit. officer U.S. Mission to NATO, Brussels, 1976-79; dep. dir. Office of No. European Affairs Dept. State, Washington, 1980-82, dir. Office of Israel and Arab-Israel Affairs, 1982-83, exec. asst. to under sec. of state for polit. affairs, 1983-85; min.-counselor for polit. affairs Am. Embassy, London, 1985-89, min., counselor for polit. affairs Paris, 1989-93; prof. strategy Indsl. Coll. Armed Forces Nat. Def. U., Washington, 1993-95; dir. Office of Ecology and Terrestrial Conservation Dept. of State, 1995-97. Mem. Am. Fgn. Svc. Assn., North Haven (Maine) Yacht Club, Met. Club (Washington), Phi Beta Kappa. Avocations: sailing, reading. Home: 3410 Lowell St NW Washington DC 20016-5023

PENDLETON, OTHNIEL ALSOP, fundraiser, clergyman; b. Washington, Aug. 22, 1911; s. Othniel Alsop and Ingeborg (Berg) P.; m. Flordora Mellquist, May 15, 1935; children: John, James (dec.), Thomas, Ann, Susan. AB, Union Coll., Schenectady, N.Y., 1933; BD, Eastern Bapt. Theol. Sem., 1936; MA, U. Pa., 1936, PhD, 1945; postgrad., Columbia U., 1937-38. Ordained to ministry Bapt. Ch., 1936. Pastor chs., Jersey City, 1935-39, Phila., 1939-43; dean Sioux Falls Coll., S.D., 1943-45; fund raiser Am. Bapt. Ch., N.Y.C., 1945-47; fund-raiser Mass. Bapt. Ch., Boston, 1947-54, Seattle, Chgo., Boston, Washington, N.Y.C. and Paris, France, 1955-64, Westwood, Mass., 1971-84; staff mem. Marts & Lundy, Inc., N.Y.C., 1964-71. Lectr. Andover-Newton (Mass.) Sem., 1958, Boston U. Sch. Theology, 1958, Harvard U., Cambridge, Mass., 1977-84; cons. Grant MacEwan Coll., Edmonton, Alta., Can. Author: New Techniques for Church Fund Raising, 1955, Fund Raising: A Guide to Non-Profit Organizations, 1981; contbr. articles in field to profl. jours. Address: 627 Leyden Ln Claremont CA 91711-4236

PENDLETON, ROBERT GRUBB, pharmacologist; b. Kansas City, Mo., Apr. 24, 1939; AA, Kansas City Jr. Coll., 1959; AB in Chemistry, U. Mo., 1961; PhD in Pharmacology, U. Kans., 1966. Sr. scientist SmithKline and French, Phila., 1966-67, assoc. sr. investigator, 1967-69, sr. investigator, 1969-74, asst. dir., 1974-79, assoc. dir., 1977-80, dir. pharmacology, 1980-81; dir. gastroenterology Merck, West Point, 1981-86; sr. dir. biology Rper Ctrl. Rsch., King of Prussia, 1986-90; cons. dir. pharmacology Sepracor, Marlborough, Mass., 1991—96; sr. rsch. scholar Temple U., Phila., 1993—. Chief sci. officer Biopharm Cons., 1996—; lectr. pharmacology Thomas Jefferson U., 1991—; lab. sci. cons. Office of the Surgeon Gen., U.S. Army, Washington, 1989-96, Ft. Detrick, Md., 1996-99. Col. AUS (ret.). Decorated Legion of Merit. Mem. Am. Soc. Pharmacology Exptl. Therapy, Am. Chem. Soc. (divsn. med. chem.), Soc. of Armed Forces Med. Lab. Scientist. Achievements include U.S. patents describing dopamine receptor agonists (SK&F 38393) and PNMT inhibitors; discovery of new drugs to activate dopamine reactors in CNS and kidney, to inhibit epinephrine biosynthesis PNMT in adrenal gland and CNS and to block histamine receptors insurmountably in stomach; discovered that tricyclic antidepressants act in CNS to decrease gastric acid secretion and new approaches to treat ischemia via rightward shifts of hemoglobin/oxygen dissocation curve; research on role of catecholamines in developmental biology and Parkinson's disease; pharmacology of chiral molecules. Avocation: ballroom dancing. Home and Office: 1312 Sumneytown Pike Lower Gwynedd PA 19002-1303

PENDLETON, WINSTON KENT, III, aerospace engineer, physics educator; b. Jacksonville, Fla., Nov. 30, 1940; s. Winston Kent II and Pauline Crouch (Hall) P.; m. Judith McCutcheon, Aug. 26, 1964; children: Winston Kent IV, Scott Everett, Wendy Pendleton McPhillips. BS in Sci. Engring., U. Mich., 1962; MS in Nuclear Engring., Air Force Inst. Tech., 1964, PhD in Aerospace Engring., 1971. Commd. 2d lt. USAF, 1962, advanced through grades to col., 1984; prof. physics USAF Acad., Colorado Springs, Colo., 1973-80, chief scientist European Office Aerospace R&D London, 1980-82; nuclear rsch. officer Air Force Weapons Lab., Albuquerque, 1982-85; prof. aerospace studies Ga. Inst. Tech., Atlanta, 1985-88; prof. physics North Ga. Coll., Dahlonega, 1988-94; ret. Laser rschr. Air Force Weapons Lab., 1969-73; radiation rschr. Armed Forces Radiobiology Rsch. Inst., Bethesda, Md., 1964-67. Contbr. articles to profl. jours. Bd. dirs. W.T. Bland Libr., Mount Dora, Fla., 1997-99, Riparian Inst.; docent Mount Dora Ctr. for the Arts, 1994-99. Decorated Legion of Merit. Mem. East Valley Astronomy Club, Rotary, Omicron Delta Kappa, Phi Kappa Phi, Sigma Pi. Achievements include research on the laser triggered switch; developed techniques for density and temperature measurement on laser-produced plasmas. Home: 1225 N Crystal Shores Gilbert AZ 85234-2702 E-mail: pendleton1@juno.com.

PENDLEY, DONALD LEE, association executive; b. Jersey City, Nov. 5, 1950; s. Donald L. and Loretta M. (Purcell) P.; m. Donna Lynn Meade, Oct. 14, 1984; 1 child, Katelyn. BA, Montclair State Coll., 1972; MA, Syracuse U., 1974. Reporter/rewriter The Herald-News, Passaic, N.J., 1969-72; reporter The Dispatch, Union City, 1973; writer Keep America Beautiful, Inc., N.Y.C., 1974-75, comm. dir., 1976-78, v.p. comm. program devel., 1979-84; sr. v.p. comm. Greater Newark C. of C., 1985-86; dir. pub. rels. Internat. Coun. Shopping Ctrs., N.Y.C., 1987-92; exec. dir. N.J. Hospice and Palliative Care Orgn., Scotch Plains, N.J., 1993-97, pres., 1997—. Creator, dir. theatre composer series William Carlos Williams Ctr., 1987-91; creator, dir. SRO Cabaret Series, 1991-99. Pres. State Repertory Opera, South Orange, N.J., 1981-85, 92-99, Ars Musica Chorale, Englewood, N.J., 1979-81; mem. steering com. Coun. of States, 1999—, chmn. 2000—; bd. dirs. Nat. Hospice Orgn., 2000—. Recipient Award of Excellence Am. C. of C. Execs. 1986, Gold Key awards, Pub. Rels. News, 1982, 86. Mem. PRSA (accredited, sec.-treas. assn. sec. 1989-90, vice-chmn. assn. sect. 1990-91, chmn. 1991-92), Am. Soc. Assn. Execs. (cert., Gold Circle award 1988, comm. sect. coun. 1994-96, dean Sch. Pub. Rels. 1998-2000), Am. Mensa, Ltd. (nat. devel. officer 1985-89, 96—, regional tng. officer 1989-93), Intertel. Avocations: music, photography. Home: 32 Hamilton Rd Glen Ridge NJ 07028-1109

PENDLEY, REX DALE, systems engineer; b. Dallas, June 18, 1954; s. J. D. and Nelda Louise (Armstrong) P.; m. Diane Carol Satin, May 29, 1976 (div. Dec. 1982); m. Bonnie Jean Quearry, Dec. 17, 1982 (separated Sept. 2001); 1 child, Elizabeth Amelia. BA in Chemistry, Rice U., 1976; PhD in Chem. Physics, Ind. U., 1981. Postdoctoral fellow Harvard U., Cambridge, Mass., 1982; mem. tech. staff Computer Scis. Corp., Rockville, Md., 1983-85, sect. mgr., 1985-88, dept. mgr., 1988-95, cons. engr., 1995-96, sr. prin. engr., 1996-98, sr. consulting engr., 1998—2000, mgr. advanced programs for satellite command and control sys., 2001—. Mem. NASA project teams, including Earth Radiation Budget Explorer Project Team, 1985, Cosmic Background Explorer Project Team, 1989, Gamma Ray Obs. Project Team, 1990, Upper Atmosphere Rsch. Satellite Project Team, 1991; chief system architect Global Positioning System Control Segment Block IIF, USAF, 1997—. Contbr. rsch. articles to profl. publs. Recipient awards for successful launches of spacecraft, NASA, 1985, 90, 92. Mem. Am. Chem. Soc., Am. Phys. Soc., Inst. Nav. Episcopalian. Home: 2120 Clark Pl Silver Spring MD 20910- Office: Computer Scis Corp 15245 Shady Grove Rd Rockville MD 20850-3222

PENDLEY, WILLIAM TYLER, naval officer, international relations educator; b. Paris, June 21, 1936; s. Louis Tyler and Virginia Lorene (Poplin) P.; m. Anne Carrol Cooke, Dec. 13, 1958; children: Stephen Tyler, Robert Randolph, Lisa Carrol, Leslie Brooks. BS in Engring., U.S. Naval Acad., 1958; MA, Am. U., Washington, 1965. Commd. ens. USN, 1958, advanced through grades to rear adm., 1983; comdg. officer Patrol Squadron 45, Jacksonville, Fla., 1975-76; ops. officer Patrol Wing 11, U.S. Atlantic Fleet, 1976-78, commdr., 1979-81; exec. sec. for joint chief of staff matters Chief Naval Ops., Washington, 1978-79, planner for joint chief of staff matters, 1981-82, dir. plans policy and strategy div., 1985-86; exec. asst. to comdr. in chief U.S. Pacific Fleet, Pearl Harbor, Hawaii, 1982-83; commdr. patrol wings U.S. Atlantic Fleet, Brunswick, Maine, 1983-85; commdr. Naval Forces Korea, Seoul, 1986-89; sr. mem. UN Mil. Armistice Commn., 1986-89; dir. strategic plans and policy USCINCPAC, Camp H. M. Smith, Hawaii, 1989-91; dep. asst. sec. def. for East Asia and Pacific affairs Dept. Defense, Washington, 1992-93; prof. internat. rels. Air War Coll., Maxwell AFB, Ala., 1993-98. Lectr. and cons., 1998—; fellow Georgetown U. Leadership Seminar, Washington, 1985. Co-author: Nuclear Coexistence, 1994; contbr. articles to profl. jours. Decorated Def. D.S.M. with oak leaf cluster, Legion of Merit with 4 gold stars; named hon. Ky. Col., 1975; recipient Def. medal for disting. pub. svc., 1993. Mem. Internat. Inst. Strategic Studies, Phi Kappa Phi, Pi Gamma Mu. Methodist. Avocations: flying, golf, tennis, skiing. Home: 10 Walden Ln Bluffton SC 29910-5026 E-mail: pendleyw@aol.com.

PENDRAGON, MICHAEL M(ALEFICA), writer, poet; b. Vineland, N.J., Oct. 23, 1963; s. Michael Leroy and Lillian Ruth Scarpa; m. Jeannette Melinda Sassiver, Dec. 1, 1997; children: Cassandra Lily, Raphael Aryeh. BA in media Arts, Jersey City State U., 1992. Editor-in-chief, pres. Excaliber, Jersey City, 1988-90; with Pendragonian Publs., N.Y.C., 1996—, Songs of Innocence, 1999—, Penny Dreadful, 1996—, The Oracle, 2000—, The Bible of Hell (anthology), 2001. Columnist The Gothic Times, N.J., 1988-90. Author: Much of Madness, Magic Shadow Show, Pendragonia, Nocturne, plays including Night Magic, The Damned, (screenplays) Children of the Night, The Mark of Cain, (short story collection) Nightscapes, 1999, (short story collection) Nocturne, 2001; prodr./dir. films including The Vampyre, 1991, Love's Philosophy, 1992; co-writer/actor: The Priest's Chamber, 1992, Paranoia, 1989; actor The Chess Game, 1992; contbr. articles to profl. jours., short stories and poetry to popular mags. Mem. Doppelgänger Soc., Soc. Terror Scribes (Supreme Terror Scribe award 1998, 99), The Paradoxist Lit. Movement Assn. (Disting. Achievement award 1998, hon. mention Yr.'s Best Fantasy and Horror 1999), The Wicked Verses Poetry Cir. Avocations: music, piano, trumpet, photography, sketching, cooking. Office: PO Box 719 New York NY 10101-0719 E-mail: mmpendragon@aol.com.

PENDYGRAFT, GEORGE WILLIAM, lawyer; b. Jeffersonville, Ind., Nov. 3, 1946; s. George Benjamin and Norma Jean (Hall) P.; m. Melissa Ann Pendygraft, 1977 (div. Sept. 1990); children: Alexandrea Jean, Ryan Samuelson; m. Jacqueline Sue Samuelson, Jan. 15, 1991 (div. Mar. 2001). AB in Chemistry, Franklin Coll., 1968; PhD in Phys. Organic Chemistry, U. Ky., 1972; JD, Columbia U., 1975. Bar: N.Y. 1976, Ind. 1976, U.S. Patent and Trademark Office 1976, U.S. Dist. Ct. (ea. and so. dists.) N.Y. 1980, U.S. Ct. Appeals (D.C. cir.) 1980. Lectr. in chemistry U. Ky., Lexington, 1968-70; assoc. Watson, Leavenworth, Kelton & Taggart, N.Y.C., 1975-76; ptnr. Baker and Daniels, Indpls., 1976-88, Pendygraft, Plews & Shadley, Indpls., 1988-90; prin., pres. George W. Pendygraft, P.C., 1990—. Contbr. articles to profl. jours. Bd. trustees Franklin Coll., 1982-86, nat. chmn. ann. fund, 1981. NDEA fellow, NSF fellow; Franklin Coll. scholar. Office: 1000 Waterway Blvd Indianapolis IN 46202-2155 also: 10414 Muir Ln Fishers IN 46038

PENEZINA, OKSANA P. biochemist; b. Kiev, Ukraine, Sept. 11, 1965; d. Petr Dmitrievich and Svetlana Vasil'evna Levchuk; 1 child, Anastasia. B in Chemistry, Kiev State U., 1987; M in Biochemistry, Nat. Acad. Scis. Ukraine, 1990, PhD in Biochemistry, 1991. Jr. rschr. Palladin Inst. Biochemistry Nat. Acad. Scis. Ukraine, Kiev, 1991-96; rsch. fellow U. Mich. Med. Sch., Ann Arbor, 1996-97; staff scientist Whatman Inc. Healthcare, 1997-2000, sr. scientist Newton, Mass., 2000—. Judge Internat. Sci. Fair, Detroit, 2000-2001; invited judge South Eastern Mich. Sci. Fair, Ann Arbor, 1997-2000. Contbr. articles to profl. jours.; inventor in field. Recipient travel grant Am. Assn. Cancer Rsch. Conf. Modern Devel. in Cancer Therapeutics Internat. Sci. Found., 1994, travel grant Keystone Symposia Molecular Basis Cancer Devel. Resnaissance Found. Kiev, Ukraine and Nat. Cancer Inst., 1994, travel grant Am. Assn. Cancer Rsch. Conf. Signal Transduction of Normal and Tumor Cells Internat. Sci. Found., 1995. Mem. Am. Soc. Cell Biology, Am. Assn. Blood Banks. Office: Whatman Inc 200 Wells Ave Newton MA 02459-3304

PENFIELD, PAUL LIVINGSTONE, JR. electrical engineering educator; b. Detroit, May 28, 1933; s. Paul Livingstone and Charlotte Wentworth (Gilman) P.; m. Martha Elise Dieterle, Aug. 24, 1956 (dec. Apr. 1988); children: David Wesley, Patricia Jane, Michael Baldwin; m. Barbara Jean Buehrig Lory, July 22, 1989. BA, Amherst Coll., 1955; ScD, MIT, 1960. Asst. prof. elec. engring. MIT, Cambridge, 1960-64, assoc. prof., 1964-69, prof., 1969—, head dept. elec. engring. and computer sci., 1989-99. Author: Frequency-Power Formulas, 1960, MARTHA User's Manual, 1971; co-author: Varactor Applications, 1962, Electrodynamics of Moving Media, 1967, Tellegen's Theorem and Electrical Networks, 1970. Sr. postdoctoral fellow NSF, 1966-67. Fellow IEEE (chmn. Boston sect. 1971-72, Darlington award 1985, Centennial medal 1984, Golden Jubilee award 1999); mem. Nat. Acad. Engring., Am. Phys. Soc., Assn. for Computing Machinery, Audio Engring. Soc., Sigma Xi. Avocation: field identification of ferns and fern hybrids. Office: MIT Dept EECS Cambridge MA 02139

PENG, FANG ZHENG Z. engineering educator; b. Daye, Hubei Province, China, Feb. 18, 1963; s. Yiren Peng and Xuemei Quan; m. Qing Fang Ye; 1 child YeZi. PhD, Nagaoka U. Tech., Japan, 1990. Rsch. scientist Toyo Electric Mfg. Co., Yokohama, Japan, 1990—92; rsch. asst. prof. Tokyo Inst. Tech., Tokyo, 1992—94; lead scientist Oak Ridge (Tenn.) Nat. Lab., 1994—2000; assoc. prof. Mich. State U., East Lansing, 2000—. Assoc. editor IEEE Transactions on Power Electronics, Piscataway, NJ, 1997—; chair tech com. rectifiers and inverters IEEE Power Electronics Soc., Piscataway, 2001—, mem. adminstrn. com., 2001—. Contbr. articles to profl. jours. Recipient Best Paper award, Transactions of IEE of Japan, 1990, Promotion award, Elec. Acad., 1990, 1st prize paper award, IEEE Transactions on Industry Applications, 1991, 2d prize paper award, Indsl. Power Converter Com., IEEE Industry Applications Soc., 1995, 1st prize paper award, 1996, Advanced Tech. award, Inventors Clubs Am., Inc., Internat. Hall of Fame, 1996, Tech. Achievement award, Lockheed Martin Corp., 1998. Mem.: IEEE (sr.). Achievements include invention of voltage balanced multilevel voltage source converter system. Home: 1968 Belwood Dr Okemos MI 48864 Office: Mich State U 2120 Engring Bldg East Lansing MI 48824 Home Fax: 517-349-3419; Office Fax: 517-353-1980. Business E-Mail: fzpeng@egr.msu.edu.

PENG, LIANG-CHUAN, mechanical engineer; b. Taiwan, Feb. 6, 1936; came to U.S., 1965, naturalized, 1973; s. Mu-Sui and Wang-Su (Yang) P.; m. Wen-Fong Kao, Nov. 18, 1962; children: Tsen-Loong, Tsen-Hsin, Lina, Linda. Diploma, Taipei Inst. Tech., 1960; MS, Kans. State U., 1967. Registered profl. engr., Tex., Calif. Project engr. Taiwan Power Co., 1965-66; asst. engr. Carlson & Sweatt, N.Y.C., 1966-67, Pioneer Engrs., Chgo., 1967-68; mech. engr. Bechtel, San Francisco, 1969-71; sr. specialist Nuc. Svcs. Co., San Jose, Calif., 1971-75; sr. engr. Brown & Root, Houston, 1975; stress engr. Foster Wheeler, 1976; staff engr. AAA Technologists, 1977; prin. engr. M.W. Kellogg,

1978-82; pres., owner Peng Engring., 1982—. Instr. U. Houston; condr. piping tech. seminars. Developer: (computer programs) SIMFLEX. Chmn. South Bay Area Formosan Assn., 1974, No. Calif. Formosan Fedn., 1975. Mem. ASME, NSPE. Buddhist. Home: 3010 Manila Ln Houston TX 77043-1312 E-mail: lepeng@pipestress.com.

PENG, MIKE W. business educator; b. Shanghai, China, July 5, 1968; BSc, Minn. State U., 1991; PhD, U. Wash., 1996. Asst. prof. U. Hawaii, Honolulu, 1995-97, Chinese U. of Hong Kong, Shatin, 1997-98, Ohio State U., Columbus, 1999—. Author: Business Strategies in Transition Economies, 2000, Behind the Success and Failure of U.S. Export Intermediaries, 1998; contbr. articles to profl. jours. Mem. Acad. of Mgmt., Acad. of Internat. Bus., Strategic Mgmt. Soc. Office: Fisher Coll of Bus Ohio State U 2100 Neil Ave Columbus OH 43210

PENG, XIAOYUAN, optical engineer; b. Xiaogan, Hubei, China, Nov. 14, 1967; s. Zhenguo Peng and Xiaozhi Zhou; m. Lei Xu, Aug. 11, 1969. BS, Huazhong U. of Sci. and Tech., Wuhan, China, 1989, MS, 1997; PhD, Nanyang Technol. U., Singapore, 2001. Engr. Wuhan Rsch. Inst. of Optical Sci. & Tech., 1989—93; lectr. Huazhong U. of Sci. and Tech., 1993—98; rsch. staff Nanyang Technol. U., Singapore, 1998—2001; sr. engr. Photonics Industries Internat., Bohemia, NY, 2001—. Mem.: IEEE, Optical Soc. Am., Internat. Soc. for Optical Engring. (grantee 2001). Office: Photonics Industries Internat 390 Central Ave Bohemia NY 11716

PENGRA, LILAH, anthropologist, consultant; b. Bettendorf, Iowa, Nov. 26, 1946; d. Robert I. Morton, Virginia Morton; m. Roy W. Pengra. BA, Grinnell (Iowa) Coll., 1969; MA, U. Wis., Madison, 1971, PhD, 1975. Exec. dir. So. Hills Develpmental Svcs., Hot Springs, SD, 1988—93; cultural specialist Multicultural Consulting Svcs., Buffalo Gap, 1993. Author: Your Values, My Values: Multicultural Services in Developmental Disabilities, 2000 (Bettendorf High School Hall of Honor, 2001), (exhibition guide) African American History in the Black Hills, 1999; contbr. articles, chapters to books. Mem. (life) Girl Scouts USA, trainer, leader, 1969—99; bd. dirs. Fall River County Elderly and Handicapped Svcs., Hot Springs, SD, 1984—93. Mem.: Am. Anthropol. Assn. Avocations: creating art jewelry, photography, birdwatching. Office: Multicultural Consulting Svcs PO Box 126 Buffalo Gap SD 57722 Personal E-mail: lilah@rapidnet.com. Business E-Mail: lilah@rapidnet.com.

PENHOET, EDWARD, medical association administrator, biochemicals company executive, former dean; b. Oakland, Calif., Dec. 11, 1940; AB, Stanford U., 1963; PhD, U. Wash., 1968. Dean Sch. Pub. Health U. Calif., Berkeley, 1998—2002, dean emeritus, 2002—; sr. dir., Sci. & Higher Education Gordon and Betty Moore Found., 2002—. Bd. dirs., sr. adv. to CEO Chiron Corp. Mem.: Inst. Medicine. Office: Chiron Corp 4560 Horton St Emeryville CA 94608-2900*

PENICHEIRO, TICHA NUNES, professional basketball player; b. Portugal, Sept. 18, 1974; d. Joao Penicheiro. Degree comm. and interdisciplinary studies, Old Dominion. Profl. basketball player Sacramento Monarchs, 1998—. Named 3d Rookie of Yr., 1998, All-WNBA 1st Team, 1999, All-WNBA 2nd Team, 2001. Mem.: Portuguese Nat. Team. Avocation: music. Office: Arco Arena 1 Sports Pkwy Sacramento CA 95834 Office Fax: 916-928-8109. Business E-Mail: monarchs@arcoarena.com.*

PENICK, ELIZABETH C. psychologist; b. New Orleans, July 17, 1934; d. Rawley M. Penick and Marie G. Sells. BA, Newcomb Coll., 1957; MS, Tulane U., 1960; PhD, Washington U., St. Louis, 1975. Diplomate clin. psychology Am. Bd. Profl. Psychology. Prof. dept. psychiatry Kans. U. Med. Ctr., Kansas City, 1980—, dir. divsn. psychology. Rsch. grantee Nat. Assn. Alcohol Abuse and Alcoholism, Washington, 1980-97. Mem. APA, Kans. Psychol. Assn. (dir.). Home: 12231 Charlotte Kansas City MO 64146 Office: Kans U Med Ctr Dept Psychiatry 3901 Rainbow Blvd Kansas City KS 66160 E-mail: epenick@kumc.edu.

PENICK, GEORGE DIAL, pathologist; b. Columbia, S.C., Sept. 4, 1922; s. Edwin Anderson and Caroline Inglesby (Dial) P.; m. Marguerite Murchison Worth, Feb. 7, 1947; children: George Dial, Hal Worth, David Williams, Anderson Holladay, Marguerite Worth. Student, U. N.C, 1939-42, BS, 1944; MD, Harvard U., 1946. Intern in pathology Presbyn. Hosp. City Chgo., 1946-47; instr. pathology U. N.C., Chapel Hill, 1949-53, asst prof. pathology, 1953-56, assoc. prof. pathology, 1956-63, prof. pathology, 1963-70; prof., head dept. pathology U. Iowa, Iowa City, 1970-81, prof. pathology and dermatology, 1981-93. Cons. Watts Hosp., Durham, N.C., 1949-70; attending pathologist N.C. Meml. Hosp., Chapel Hill, 1953-70; dir. Nat. Heart Inst. Program, Project U. N.C.,1962-70; cons. lab. svc. VA Med. Ctr., Iowa City, 1970-93. Contbr. articles to profl. jours. Capt. U.S. Army, 1947-49. Med. Sci. scholar John and Mary Markle Found., N.Y.C., 1953-58; recipient Disting. Svc. award Sch. of Med. U. N.C., 1979. Fellow Coll. Am Pathologists; mem. AMA, Am. Soc. Clin. Pathologists, Am. Assoc. Pathologists, Internat. Acad. Pathology, Phi Beta Kappa. Democrat. Episcopolian. Avocations: bicycling, tennis, computing, Christian education. Home: 3712 Reston Ct Apt C Wilmington NC 28403-6175 E-mail: gpenick@aol.com.

PENICK, JOHN E. education educator; b. Langley, Va., Jan. 2, 1944; s. Edgar Cohen and Bessie (Beene) P.; m. Nell Inman, July 23, 1966; children: Lucas T., Megan J. Penick. BS, U. Miami, 1966, MA, 1969; PhD, Fla. State U., 1973. Sci. dept. head Miami (Fla.) Jackson High Sch., 1967-70; instr. Miami-Dade Community Coll., 1968, Fla. State U., Tallahassee, 1970-73; dir. tchr. edn. Loyola U., Chgo., 1973-75; prof. U. Iowa, Iowa City, 1975-97, head Sci. Edn. Ctr., 1982, 89-93; prof., head dept. math., sci. and tech. edn. N.C. State U., Raleigh, 1998—. Editor monograph series Focus on Excellence, 1983-89; author: Biology: A Community Context, 1998; contbr. numerous articles to profl. jours. Named Disting. Alumnus Fla. State U., 1987; recipient Burlington No. award for outstanding career achievement U. Iowa, 1992; Fulbright fellow USIA, Portugal, 1985. Fellow Iowa Acad. Sci.; mem. ASCD, NSTA (bd. dirs. 1986-88, pres.-elect 2002, Ohaus award), Nat. Assn. for Rsch. in Sci. Tchg. (assoc. editor 1979-84), Coun. Sci. Soc. Prs. (sec. 1991-92), Nat. Assn. Biology Tchrs. (pres. 1989), Assn. for Edn. of Tchrs. in Sci. (Outstanding Sci. Educator 1987, Outstanding Mentor 1997, pres. 2002), Phi Delta Kappa. Office: NC State U 326 Poe Hl Raleigh NC 27695-0001

PENIKETT, ANTONY DAVID JOHN, producer, writer, politician; b. Nov. 14, 1945; s. Erik John Keith and Sarah Ann (Colwell) P.; m. Lula Mary Johns, 1974 (div. 1997); children— John Tahmoh, Sarah Lahlil, Stephanie Yahsan Exec. asst. to nat. leader New Dem. Party, Ottawa, Ont., Canada, 1975-76, nat. pres. Canada, 1981-85, fed. councillor Canada, 1973—, leader Whitehorse, Y.T., Canada, 1980—, campaign mgr. N.W.T., Canada, 1972; city councillor City of Whitehorse, Y.T., Canada, 1977-79; elected mem. Yukon Legis. Assembly, 1978-95, opposition leader Y.T., Canada, 1982-85, 92-95, elected govt. leader Yukon Terr., 1985-92; sr. policy advisor, exec. coun. Govt. of Saskatchewan, 1995-97; dep. min. negotiations Ministry of Fin. and Corp. Rels., Govt. of B.C., Victoria, 1997-2000, dep. min. labor, 2000—01; propr. Tony Penikett Negotiations Inc., Vancouver, Canada, 2001—. Author (film): The Mad Trapper, 1972; La Patrouille Perdue, 1974. Mem. Christian Socialist Ch. Office: Tony Penikett Negotiations INc PO Box 2494 Vancouver BC V6B 3W7 Canada

PENIN, LINDA MARGARET, elementary education educator; b. N.Y.C., May 18, 1946; d. Santos Rodriquez and Dorothea May (Fink) P. BA, Jersey City State Coll., 1969, MA, 1973. Cert. elem. tchr., reading tchr., reading specialist. Tchr. elem. Leonia (N.J.) Bd. Edn., 1969—. Recipient Gov.'s Tchr. Recognition award State of N.J., 1989. Mem. NEA, N.J. Edn. Assn., Bergen County Edn. Assn., Leonia Edn. Assn., Order Ea. Star N.J. (officer, sec. local chpt.). Republican. Methodist. Avocations: reading, bike riding, relaxing at beach. Home: 24 Kimble Ct Pompton Plains NJ 07444-1656 Office: Leonia Bd Edn 500 Broad Ave Leonia NJ 07605-1598

PENISTEN, GARY DEAN, entrepreneur; b. Lincoln, Nebr., May 14, 1931; s. Martin C. and Jayne (O'Dell) P.; m. Nancy Margaret Golding, June 3, 1951; children: Kris D., Janet L., Carol E., Noel M. BS in Bus. Adminstrn., U. Nebr., Omaha, 1953; LLD (hon.), Concordia Coll., 1993. With Gen. Electric Co., 1953-74, mgr. fin. ops. power generation group, 1973-74; asst. sec. navy fin. mgmt., 1974-77; sr. v.p. fin., chief fin. officer, dir. Sterling Drug Inc., N.Y.C., 1977-89; sr. v.p. fin., health group Eastman Kodak Co., 1989-90. Bd. dirs. Foster Ptnrs. Inc., chmn. bd. dirs. Acme United Corp. Mem. corp. adv. bd. U. Nebr. Coll. Bus., Omaha. Recipient Disting. Public Service award Navy Dept., 1977; Alumni Achievement citation U. Nebr., Omaha, 1975. Mem. Fin. Execs. Inst., Navy League of U.S., Army and Navy Club (Washington), Rotary, Union League (N.Y.), Ft. Lauderdale (Fla.) Country Club, White Eagle Golf Club (Naperville). Republican. Unitarian Universalist. Home and Office: 1409 Aberdeen Ct Naperville IL 60564-9787 E-mail: asnfm@aol.com.

PENKAVA, ROBERT RAY, radiologist, educator; b. Virginia, Nebr., Jan. 30, 1942; s. Joseph Evert and Velta Mae (Oviatt) P.; m. Kathy Bennett Secrest, Apr. 6, 1973; children: Ashley Secrest, J. Carson Bennett. AB BS, Peru State Coll., Nebr., 1963; MD, U. Nebr., Omaha, 1967. Intern Lincoln Gen. Hosp., Nebr., 1967-68; resident Menorah Med. Cen., Kansas City, 1968-71; chief resident Menorah Med. Ctr., 1970-71; adj. faculty U. Mo., 1970-71; staff radiologist Ireland Army Hosp., Ft. Knox, Ky., 1971-72, chief, dept. radiology & nuclear med., 1972-73; staff radiologist Deaconess Hosp., Evansville, Ind., 1973-99; mem. faculty U. So. Ind., 1973—; assoc. faculty Ind. U. Coll. Med., Bloomington, 1973—; med. dir. Sch. Radiol. Tech. U. So. Ind., Evansville, 1978—; dep coroner Vanderburgh County, 1991—; med. dir. Deaconess Breast Ctr., 1999—. Chmn. So. Ind. Health Sys., 1980-83; pres. Vanderburgh County Med. Soc. Svc. Bur., 1979—; mem. roentgen soc. liaison com. Ind. Bd. Health, 1968. Author numerous articles on med. ultrasound, nuclear med., angiography, and computed tomography. Chmn. profl. div. United Way of So. Ind., 1983; bd. dirs. S.W. Ind. Pub. Broadcasting, 1978-84, S.W. Ind. PSRO, 1982; v.p. Mesker Zoo Found., bd. dirs., 1991-95; mem. Evansville Pub. Safety Bd., 2000—. Maj. U.S. Army, 1971-73. Named Sci. Tchr. of Year, Lewis & Clark Jr. High Sch., 1963. Mem. AMA, Evansville Med. Radiol. Assn. (treas. 1987-98), Am. Soc. Breast Disease, Internat. Soc. Clin. Dosimetry, Tri-State Radiology Assn. (pres.), Vanderburgh County Med. Soc. (pres.), Physicians Svc. Bur. (treas.), Magnetic Resonance Imaging, Inc. (treas. 1995-98), Am. Coll. Radiology, Radiol. Soc. N.Am., Am. Roentgen Ray Soc., Am. Inst. Ultrasound in Medicine, Soc. Cardiovascular and Interventional Radiology. Avocations: golf, boating, flying. Office: 520 Mary St Ste #140 Evansville IN 47710

PENKE, CYNTHIA MARIE, critical care nurse; b. Omaha, Jan. 8, 1963; d. Gary and Barbara K. (Ulrich) Toman; children: Jason, Stephanie Jo, Alexis Grace. ASN, U. Nebr. Med. Ctr., 1984. Charge nurse rehab. unit Irving (Tex.) Community Hosp., 1984-87; BCLS instr., home health nurse Health Force, Dallas, 1987-88; staff nurse med./surg. unit Baylor U., 1987-88; nurse ICU, ethics com. St. Joseph Hosp., Omaha, 1988-92; home health nurse Tabitha Home Health Agy., 1990-92; home health resource nurse We Care Nursing Svcs., Milw., 1992-93, asst. dir. nursing, 1993-95; ICU staff and recovery rm. nurse Fst Trac Heart com. St. Joseph Hosp., Omaha, 1995—; clin. supr. NurseFinders, 1996-97, 99-01, on call nurse, 1997-99; dir. facility Wood-Bridge Assisted Living, 1997-98; IV/staff nurse Chelation Clinic, 2001—.

PENLAND, JAMES GRANVILLE, psychologist; b. Dallas, Mar. 1, 1951; s. James Marr and Katherine (Lindsley) P.; m. Michelle Elizabeth Stahl, Aug. 13, 1977; children: Abraham Christopher, Simon Peter, Zachary James. BA summa cum laude, Met. State Coll., 1977; MA, U. N.D., 1979, PhD, 1984. Instr. U. N.D., Grand Forks, 1978-83, statistician, 1981-84, psychologist, 1984-85; rsch. psychologist USDA, Agrl. Rsch. Svc., 1985—. Adj. prof. U. N.D., 1984—; mem. panel on micronutrients Inst. of Medicine/Food and Nutrition Bd.; mem. Commn. Mil. Nutrition Rsch.; cons. in field. Mem. editl. bd. Nutritional Neurosci.; contbr. articles to profl. jours. Met. State Coll. scholar, 1977. Mem. APA, Am. Inst. Nutrition, Midwestern Psychol. Assn., N.D. Acad. Sci., Nat. Acad. Scis., Am. Statis Assn., Sigma Xi. Home: 1804 S 36th St Grand Forks ND 58201-5740 Office: USDA ARS GFHNRC Box 9034 2420 2nd Ave N Grand Forks ND 58202-9034 E-mail: jpenland@gfhnrc.ars.usda.gov.

PENLAND, JOHN THOMAS, retired import and export and development companies executive; b. Guntersville, Ala., Mar. 31, 1930; s. James B. and Kathleen (Bolding) P.; m. Carolyn Joyce White, May 30, 1961; children—Jeffrey K., Mark A., Michael J. BA, George Washington U., 1957. Vice pres., dir. Rouse, Brewer, Becker & Bryant, Inc., Washington, 1957-63; staff mem. SEC, 1963-67; pres., dir. INA Trading Corp., Phila., 1968-69; v.p. INA Security Corp., 1967-69; from v.p. to pres. Shareholders Mgmt. Co., L.A., 1969—75; v.p. Shareholders Capital Corp., 1972-73; v.p., dir. several mut. funds managed by Shareholders Mgmt. Co., 1970-75; pres., chmn., CEO, HMO Internat. and its subs., L.A., 1975; founder, pres., chmn. Pendlar Corp., Atlanta, 1977-97; chmn., pres. Bella Vista Developers, Inc., Albuquerque, 1977-98; chmn. CompuComp Corp., Atlanta, 1977-81; chmn., pres. Fran Stef Corp., N.Y.C., 1982-89; pres., chmn. Engineered Products Corp., Dandridge, Tenn., 1983-90; founder, chmn., CEO Am. Accessories Inc., Covington, Ga., 1983-98; founder, pres., chmn. United Am. Products Corp., Dandridge, 1983-89; founder, chmn. Chamisa Properties, Inc., Albuquerque, 1988-94, Glorieux Ltd., Atlanta, 1988-96, Ga. Ptnrs. Ltd., Covington, 1988-94, Premier Trading Internat., Inc., Atlanta, 1989—98, Chamisa Enterprises, Inc., Covington, 1990—2001; founder, mng. ptnr. Ft. Hill Ptnrs., Knoxville, Tenn., 1990-93; chmn. Einson Freeman & Detroy Corp., Fair Lawn, N.J., 1978-83; founder, dir., pres. West Point Contract Packaging, Inc., Martinsville, Va., 1991-98; founder, mng. ptnr. Harbor View, Ltd., Fernandina Beach, Fla., 1992-94; founder, chmn. West Point Tech. Assembly, Inc., Winston-Salem, NC, 1993—2002; dir., pres. BKP Industries, Inc., Monroe, Ga., 1995-97. Served with AUS, 1948-55. Republican. Episcopalian. Home: PO Box 549 Social Circle GA 30025-0549

PENLEY, JULIE ANNE, psychologist, researcher, educator; b. Chicago, Ill., July 13, 1967; d. John and Marcheta Isabelle Dietzen; m. Howard Lawson n/a; m. Howard Lawson Penley. PhD, U. Tex., 2001. Tchg. asst. U. Tex., El Paso, 1995—96, rsch. asst., 1996—2001; instr. Dona Ana C.C., Sunland Park, N.Mex., 1999; part-time instr. El Paso C.C., 2000—02, full-time instr., 2002—; evaluation coord. U. Tex., El Paso, 2001—02. Mem.: APA, Soc. Behavioral Medicine, Am. Edn. Rsch. Assn., Am. Evaluation Assn. Lutheran. Personal E-mail: japenley@utep.edu. Business E-Mail: japenley@aol.com.

PENLIDIS, ALEXANDER, chemical engineering educator; b. Kozani, Greece, Feb. 12, 1957; Diploma in engring., U. Thessaloniki, 1980; PhD in Chem. Engring., McMaster U., 1986. Rsch. assoc. Polymer Prodn. Techs., McMaster Inst., Can., 1985-86; from asst. prof. to assoc. prof. chem. engring. U. Waterloo, Ontario, Can., 1986-90, assoc. prof., 1990-95, prof., 1995—, assoc. dir. Inst. Polymer Rsch. Ont., Can., 1990-95, dir. Can., 1995—, assoc. dean rsch. & grad. studies, faculty engring. Can., 1998—. Cons. in field, 1985—. Founding co-editor Polymer Reaction Engring. Jour., 1990—. Fellow Chem. Inst. Can.; mem. AIChE, Am. Chem. Soc., Can. Soc. Chem. Engring. Office: Univ Waterloo Inst Polymer Rsch Chem Engring Dept Waterloo ON Canada N2L 3G1

PENN, AUDREY S. federal agency administrator; Prof. neurology Coll. Physicians and Surgeons, Columbia U.; neurologist Columbia Presbyn. Med. Ctr.; dir. Am. Bd. Psychiatry and Neurology; deputy dir. Nat. Inst. Neurological Disorders and Stroke, acting dir. Mem.: AAAS, Assn. Rsch. in Nervous and Mental Disease, Harvey Soc., Am. Acad. Neurology, Am. Neurological Assn. (former pres.). Office: 6001 Executive Blvd Rm 8184 Bethesda MD 20892*

PENN, DAWN TAMARA, entrepreneur; b. Knoxville, Tenn., July 22, 1965; d. Morton Hugh and Virginia Audra (Wilson) P. AS, Bauder Fashion Coll., Atlanta, 1984; postgrad., U. Tenn., 1986; grad., Rasnic Sch. Modeling, Knoxville, 1986. Gen. mgr. Merry-Go-Round, Knoxville, 1984-86; mgr., dancer Lady Adonis Inc. Performing Arts Dance Co., 1987-90; owner, pres. Lady Adonis, Inc. Performing Arts Dance Co., 1990—, also chmn.; owner, pres. Penn Mgmt. and Investment Co. Comml. Real Estate, 1989—; deputized bonded rep. Knox County Sheriff's Dept., 1989-90. Fgn. dance tours include Aruba, Curacao, Caracas, Barbados, Ont., Que., Montreal, Nfld., Labrador, N.S., New Brunswick; cons. The John Reinhardt Agy., Winston-Salem, N.C., 1987—, Gen. Talent Agy., Monroeville, Pa., 1990—, Xanadu, Inc., Myrtle Beach, S.C., 1991—. Author, editor: Lady Adonis Performing Arts promotional mag., 1988; TV and motion picture credits include: Innocent Blood, 1992, The Phil Donahue Show, N.Y.C., 1989, 91. Coord. bridal fair Big. Bros./Big Sisters Knox County, Knoxville, 1985, 86; judge Southeastern Entertainer of Yr. Pageant, Knoxville, 1992—, Miss Knoxville U.S.A. Pageant, Knoxville, 1990—; active Knoxville Conv. and Visitors Bur., 1993-94. Recipient 1st Pl. award for swimsuit TV comml. and runway modeling Internat. Model's Hall of Fame, 1986, 1st Pl. award for media presentation Modeling Assn. Am. Internat., 1986; nominee The Pres.'s Commn. on White House Fellowships, U.S. Office Pers. Mgmt., 1994-95. Mem. Internat. Platform Assn., Profl. Assn. Diving Instrs. (cert.). Methodist. Avocations: scuba diving, racquetball, horseback riding, piano, theology. Home: 7320 Old Clinton Pike Apt 9 Knoxville TN 37921-1064 Office: Lady Adonis Inc/Penn Mgmt Ste 9 7320 Old Clinton Hwy Knoxville TN 37921-1064 E-mail: ldyadonis1@aol.com.

PENN, GERALD MELVILLE, pathologist; b. Toledo, Mar. 24, 1937; s. Melville Delroy and Hildegarde Agnes (Wammus) P.; m. Joyce Earl, June 5, 1965; children: Gerald Bradley, David Joshua. MD, Ohio State U., 1964, PhD, 1975. Cert. Am. Bd. Pathology. Head hematology sect. Bethesda (Md.) Naval Hosp., 1970-72; chief clin. pathology Children's Hosp., Columbus, Ohio, 1972-81; dir. lab. medicine Grant Med. Ctr., 1981-96; med. dir. Cytometry Assocs., 1996-99. V.p. med. affairs Wendt Bristol Health Svcs., Columbus, 1998—; chmn. Am. Bd. Med. Lab. Immunology, Washington, 1982-85. Author: Interpretation of Immunoelectrophoretic Patterns, 1978, The Clinical Use and Interpretation of Agarose Gel Electrophoresis Patterns, 1982; editor: Manual of Clinical Laboratory Immunology, 1992. Chmn. med. coun. Health Coalition of Ctrl. Ohio, Columbus, 1991-96. Lt. comdr. USN, 1970-72. Recipient Commendation for Meritorious Svc., USN Nat. Naval Med. Ctr., Bethesda, 1972. Fellow Am. Soc. Clin. Pathology (dep. sec. 1973-88, CCE Meritorious Svc. award), Coll. Am. Pathologists; mem. Acad. Medicine Columbus (sec.-treas. 1992-96), Columbus Med. Assn. (pres. 2000-01), Columbus Med. Assn. Found. (trustee 1992-2002, v.p. 1992-98, sec.-treas. 1998-2000). Republican. Roman Catholic. Office: Wendt Bristol Oncology 921A Jasonway Columbus OH 43214-2330 E-mail: penn.2@osu.edu.

PENN, HUGH FRANKLIN, JR. psychology educator; b. Hartselle, Ala., Jan. 28, 1941; s. Hugh Franklin and Marynelle (Walter) P.; m. Susan Irwin Adams, June 5, 1976; children: Charles Bracken, Caryn Elizabeth. BS, Florence State Coll., 1964, MA, Florence State Univ., 1967; grad. ednl. specialist, U. Ala., 1972, PhD, 1982. Psychology tchr. Hartselle (Ala.) H.S., 1964-89, sch. counselor, 1989-91, spl. svcs. counselor, 1991—; psychology instr. Calhoun C.C., Decatur, Ala., 1970—; counseling psychologist/disabilities coord. Hartselle City Schs., 1996—. Chmn. bd. North Ctrl. Ala. Mental Health Bd., 1984-87, v.p. bd. dirs., 1998—, pres., 2001—; pres. of advisors Ala. Assn. Student Couns., 1970; ea. states head advisor So. Assn. Student Couns., 1973-74; mem. adv. bd. Mental Health Assn. Morgan County, 1996—. Named Outstanding Young Educator of Ala., Ala. Jaycees, 1973; recipient Georgia Valley award for outstanding svc. in cmty. mental health State of Ala., 2000. Mem. APA, ACA, Coun. for Exceptional Children, Learning Disabilities Assn., Am. Sch. Counselor Assn., Autism Soc. Am., Internat. Dyslexia Assn., Hartselle C. of C. (Thomas Guyton Humanitarian award 1994). Methodist. Home: 412 Aquarius Dr SW Hartselle AL 35640-4000 Office: Hartselle City Schs 305 College St NE Hartselle AL 35640-2357

PENN, LEE, information technology consultant, journalist; b. Midland, Tex., Jan. 19, 1953; s. Rhesa and Dorothy Penn. BA, Harvard U., 1976; MBA, MPH, U. Calif., Berkeley, 1986. Freelance journalist Oregon mag. and others, Portland, 1975-79; rsch. asst. Kaiser Permanente Ctr. for Health Rsch., 1979-83; sys. planner Alta Bates Corp., Berkeley; sr. fin. analyst St. Mary's Hosp., San Francisco, 1987; mgr. assoc., cons. JDA/SAIC, 1992-96; prin. Penn Cons., 1988—. Mem. adj. faculty, lectr. Goden Gate U., San fRancisco, 1990-98. Contbr. articles to profl. jours. and mags., including Jour. Ambulatory Care Mgmt., also chpts. to books. Vestryman, chmn. fin. com., mem. search coms. Episcopal Parish St. John the Evangelist, San Francisco, 1989-94. Edgar F. Kaiser sr. fellow U. Calif., 1983-84, Regents fellow, 1984-85. Mem. IEEE Computer Soc., Soc. Profls. in Healthcare, Am. Coll. Health Care Execs., Phi Beta Kappa. Office: Penn Cons 131 Corwin St Ste 3 San Francisco CA 94114-2343 Fax: 4250255-1381. E-mail: leepenn@aol.com.

PENN, MAGGIE SCOTT, school counselor, mental health therapist, small business owner; b. Columbia, S.C., Jan. 1, 1940; d. Walter Lee and Ruby Lee (Seawright) Scott; m. Luther Penn (dec. Oct. 1977); 1 child: Cydni Charise. BS, Eastern Mich. U., 1963, MA, 1966; PhD, U. San Jose, 1998. Diplomate Am. Assn. Forensic Counselors; lic. profl. counselor, Mich.; notary, Mich. Bus. tchr. Highland Park (Mich.) Bd. Edn., 1963-70, 1971-96, high sch. counselor, mental health therapist, 1999—; pres. Bramblewood Enterprises, Detroit, 1978—; owner Penn Hardware; mental health therapist Detroit Ctrl. City Mental Health Agy., 1999—. Sec. Detroit br. NAACP, 1978-84, bd. dirs. 1978-84; sec. Sr. Citizens of Detroit Com., 1980-90, Cotillion Wives Aux., Detroit, 1979-85; mgr. state senate pol. campaign, Detroit, 1980; supr. Peoples Cmty. Ch. Credit Union, Detroit, 1978-84. Recipient Disting. Service award City of Detroit, 1984, Outstanding Membership award Detroit NAACP, 1970, 80-85, Spl. Tribute award State of Mich., 1987. Mem. ACA, Am. Assn. Christian Counselors, Internat. Assn. Counselors and Therapists, Am. Fedn. Tchrs. Assn., Devel. Ass., Am. Bus. Profl. Assn., Nat. Assn. Counselors and Female Execs., Mich. Fedn. Tchrs., Highland Park Fedn. Tchrs., Mich. Guidance Assn., Mich. Career Devel. Assn., Am. Bus. Educators, New Metro Detroit Bus. and Profl. Women (editor newsletter, appreciation award 1982), Devel. Assn., Landlords Assn. Mich., Tots 'n Teens, Delta Sigma Theta, Phi Delta Kappa. Mem. Cmty. Ch. Avocations: writing, speaking, organizing, decorating, wedding consulting. Home: PO Box 21010 Coll Park Sta Detroit MI 48221 also: Penn Hardware 7300 Puritan St Detroit MI 48238-1206

PENN, PHILIP JULIAN, lawyer; b. Anchorage, May 11, 1955; s. Percy Junius and Jeanne Naomi (Johnson) P.; m. Rita Elaine Edwards, Feb. 20, 1993. AB, Duke U., 1977; JD, N.C. Ctrl. Law Sch., 1981. Bar: N.C. 1981. Law clerk Henry E. Moss/Paul C. Bland, Durham, N.C., 1981; pvt. practice, 1981, 83-84; ptnr. Sloan, Moss & Penn, 1982; assoc. atty. Malone, Brown & Matthewson, P.A., 1982; fed. jud. law clk. to Hon. Richard C. Erwin U.S. Dist. Ct., Greensboro, NC, 1982-83; appeals referee N.C. Employment Security Commn., Winston-Salem, N.C., 1984-87; asst. pub. defender 26th Defender Dist., Charlotte, 1987-92; asst. atty. gen. Virgin Islands Govt., St. Croix, 1992-93; mgr. Know Bookstore, 1995; pvt. practice Charlotte, 1996-98; staff atty. Children's Law Ctr., 1998—. Bd. dirs. chmn. legis. and legal issues com. N.C. Gov's. Waste Mgmt. Bd., Raleigh, N.C., 1991-92; adv. bd. mem. Mecklenburg Community Corrections, Charlotte, 1992. Author: Colorblind is a Spiritual State of Mind, 1993. Bd. dirs. Neighborhood Justice Ctr., Winston-Salem, 1987, Recovery Inc., Charlotte, 1994, Portraits of Color, 1996; mentor Queens Coll., Charlotte, 1990-92; facilitator New Options for Violent Actions, Mecklenburg County, N.C., 1992; bd. dirs. Mecklenburg County Juvenile Crime Prevention Coun., 2000--. Recipient African-Am. Image award Queens Coll., 1992; named to Outstanding Young Men of Am., 1983, 86. Mem. N.C. Bar Assn. (bd. dirs.), Tuskegee Airmen, Inc., Kappa Alpha Psi (lt. strategus 1990). Democrat. Roman Catholic. Avocations: aviation, photography, art, sports, history. Address: PO Box 34204 Charlotte NC 28234-4204

PENN, RICHARD DEREN, neurosurgeon, educator; b. Chgo., Mar. 11, 1941; m. Frances; children: Anna, Katharine. BA, Haverford Coll., 1962; MD, Columbia U., 1966. Intern Rush Presbyn.-St. Lukes, Chgo., 1966-67; fellow NIH, 1967-69; assoc. in neurosurgery Rush Presbyn.-St. Luke's Med. Ctr., Chgo., 1973-99; resident in neurosurgery Neurol. Inst. N.Y., Columbia Presbyn. Med. Ctr., 1969-73; assoc. attending Rush Presbyn. St. Luke's Med. Ctr., Chgo., 1976-99, sr. attending, 1996—; prof. dept. neurosurgery Rush Med. Coll., 1984-99; prof. neurosurgery Mt. Sinai Med. Sch., N.Y.C., 1999-00, U. Chgo., 2001—. Cons. bur. med. devices, 1980—; panel neurol. peripheral nervous sys., 1992—95, 1999; med. adv. bd. divsn. svcs. crippled children U. Ill., 1980—99. Recipient Pub. Health Svc. award, 1991; named amont Top 5% Physicians, Chgo. Mag., 1996. Fellow ACS. Avocations: photography, tennis. Office: U Chicago Divsn NeuroSurg MC 3026 5841 S Maryland Ave MS3026 Chicago IL 60637-9935

PENN, RONALD HULEN, manufacturing executive; b. Pocahontas, Ark., Dec. 31, 1951; s. Hulen and Isabell (Smith) P.; m. Janieca Ann Thielemier, May 31, 1975; children: Alicia, Candace, Dustin. BS in Mktg., Ark. State U., 1973. Office mgr. Brown Shoe Co., Houston, 1973-76, overseas technician South America, 1976-77, asst. plant mgr. Ill., 1978-79, plant mgr., 1979-84, mgr. tech. svcs., 1984-88, dir. tech. svcs., 1989-93, dir. tech. svc. sourcing, coord. internat. ops., 1994—. Advisor Pikeland Cmty. Unit Sch., Pittsfield,

1980; coach Little League Baseball, Union, Mo., 1986-92, sec., 1987-91; coach Little Basketball, 1987-93, pres., 1991-93; bd. dirs. Union Pks., 1992-93, treas., 1990-91, pres., 1991-94, co-chmn. aquatic/civic ctr. project; v.p. RII Athletic Booster Club, 1995-98. Named All-Conf. and Regional Football Player N.E. Ark. Athletic Assn., 1969. Mem. Alpha Kappa Psi. Republican. Mem. Ch. of Christ. Avocations: golf, fishing. Office: Meramec Group Sullivan MO 63080

PENN, SHERRY EVE, communication psychologist, educator; b. Jersey City, Nov. 25, 1941; d. Herman Joseph and Ida (Eventoff) P.; m. Donald Eugene Crawford, Aug. 15, 1987; stepchildren: Dan, Helen, David. BA in Psychology and Theatre, U. Louisville, 1963; MA in Theatre and Music History, U. Fla., 1967; PhD in Communication Psychology, Performing Arts, Union Inst., 1975. Dir. dance, assoc. prof. Miami (Fla.)-Dade Community Coll., 1967-78; assoc. dean baccalaureate program World U., Miami, 1978; press sec., dir. comm. Jefferson County (Ky.) Judge Exec. A. Mitch McConnell, 1979-81; assoc. dean, asst. v.p. Union Inst. Grad. Sch., 1984-87, core faculty prof., 1984—; v.p. communication Penn-Crawford Assocs., 1987—. Chair program policy bd., external masters degree program in psychology Lone Mountain Coll., Miami, 1975-76; cons. in pub. rels., comm., 1970—; vis. prof. U. Fla., 1969, Calif. State U., San Francisco, 1973, 74, Fla. Internat. U., 1975-76, U. Louisville, 1982-84, Webster U., 1983-84; presenter, speaker in field. Artistic dir., producer Miami Jazz Dance Ensemble, Miami Mime Artists, 1967-79; writer, producer pub. TV programs, 1980; exec. producer weekly pub. affairs series Consumer Corner, 1980-81; choreographer for various dance, mime and operatic prodns. Fellow Ford Found., 1961. Mem. ASTD, Pub. Rels. Soc. Am., Am. Women in Radio and TV, Women in Communication. Home: 100 Uno Lago Dr Apt 405 Juno Beach FL 33408-2699

PENN, STANLEY WILLIAM, journalist; b. N.Y.C., Jan. 12, 1928; s. Murray and Lillian (Richman) P.; m. Esther Aronson, July 12, 1952; children— Michael, Laurel. Student, Bklyn. Coll., 1945-47; B. Journalism, U. Mo., 1949. With Wall St. Jour., 1952-90; investigative reporter N.Y. bur., 1957-90. (Co-recipient Pulitzer prize for nat. reporting 1967). Home: 380 Riverside Dr New York NY 10025-1858

PENN, SUSAN BERLAND, community volunteer; b. N.Y.C. d. Harry and Sherle Joy (Peters) Berland; m. Deane Arnold Penn, Mar. 28, 1970; children: Jonathan Jay, Stacey Helene. BA in Psychology and Sociology, U. Pa., 1969; MBA in Marketing and Finance, Columbia U., 1971. Sr. research analyst NBC, N.Y.C., 1971-74; media cons. polit. polling Penn & Schoen, Inc., 1984-86; assoc. realtor Schlott Realtors, Alpine, N.J., 1986-87. Arbitrator Better Bus. Bur., Paramus, N.J., 1986-87; trustee Alpine Bd. Edn., 1985—, co-chmn. curriculum and pub. relations coms.; program chmn. Young Leadership United Jewish Appeal, Bergen County, N.J., 1987, 88, nat. cabinet mem. 1987, 88; co-chmn. after sch. enrichment programs Alpine Sch., 1981-88; chmn. Alpine Recreation Com., St. Jude's Bikeathon, 1983-84; pres. Alpine Home and Sch. Assn. (PTA), 1983-86, Bergen County Med. Soc. Aux., 1980-81, v.p. fashion show com., 1979-80; mem. Alpine Environ. Commn., 1987, 88; bd. dirs. women's div. United Jewish Community, Bergen County, 1986-88, co-chmn. spring luncheon women's div., 1986. Mem. Orgn. for Rehabilitation through Tng. (v.p. membership 1975-77), Sisterhood Temple Sinai (v.p. programming 1988). Clubs: Alpine Country, U. Pa. Metro N.J. (bd. dirs.). Republican. Avocation: tennis. Home: Buckingham Dr Alpine NJ 07620

PENNA, DAVID ROCCO, educator; b. Rutherford, N.J., Aug. 5, 1960; s. Rocco Frank and Ann Lucy P.; m. Vickie Rae D'Andrea, Dec. 24, 1956; children: Lesedi, Gina. BA, Duquesne U., MA, 1982; JD, U. Denver, 1985, PhD, 1993. Bar: Colo. 1985. Head math. & sci. dept. Sefhare Cmty. Jr. Secondary Sch., Botswana, 1986-87; assoc. editor Africa Today, Denver, 1991-93; dir. publs. Ctr. Rights Devel., 1990-93; assoc. prof. govt. Gallaudet U., Washington, 1993—. Chair instl. rev. bd. protection human subjects Gallaudet U., 2001—. Co-author: (chpt.) Democratization and the Protection of Human Rights, 1998; editor: Racism and the Underclass, 1991, Africa, Human Rights and the Global System, 1994; contbr. articles to profl. jours. Mem. spl. edn. adv. bd. Frederick County (Md.) Pub. Schs., 2000, mem. social studies curriculum audit, 1999-2000. Mem. Am. Polit. Sci. Assn., Am. Soc. Internat. Law, Internat. Studies Assn., African Studies Assn. Office: 800 Florida Ave NW Washington DC 20001-3018 E-mail: david.penna@gallaudet.edu.

PENNACCHIO, LINDA MARIE, secondary school educator; b. Boston, Oct. 8, 1947; d. Antonio and Florence (Delano) P. BA in Math., U. Mass., 1969; MEd in Guidance, Boston State Coll., 1974, cert. advanced study in adminstrn., 1976. Cert. math., guidance counselor, prin. Math. tchr. Abraham Lincoln Sch., Revere, Mass., 1969-91; office asst. Mass. Gen. Hosp., Bunker Hill Health Ctr., Charlestown, 1982-96; computer tchr. grades K-8 Abraham Lincoln Sch., Revere, 1985-91; math. tchr. Beachmont Middle Sch., 1991-97, guidance counselor, equity coord., mentor tchr., 1995-98; dean of students Revere H.S., 1998—. Adviser Nat. Jr. Honor Soc., Revere, 1985-94; mem. math. Curriculum Revision Com., Revere, 1985-86, 94-95, Com. to Establish Gifted and Talented Program, Revere, 1988; participant U.S. Dept. Edn. Tech. Grant, Revere, 1989-92; mem. math. portfolio pilot study Commonwealth of Mass. Dept. Edn., 1992-98, mem. palms leadership team, chair textbook selection com. for elem. sch. math., coach advisor-advisee program; co-adviser Beachmont Sch. Aspirers Club. Mem. ASCD, Nat. Coun. Tchrs. Math., Mass. Tchrs. Assn., Assn. Tchrs. Math. in Mass., Nat. Assn. Student Activity Advisers. Democrat. Roman Catholic.

PENNAMPED, BRUCE MICHAEL, lawyer; b. Kearney, Nebr., July 16, 1948; s. Matthew Paul and Betty Fern (Harper) P.; m. Victoria A. Crull, May 13, 1972 (div. Dec. 1980); 1 child, Katheryn A.; m. Melissa J. Barth, July 22, 1985. BS in Mgmt., Ind. U., 1970, JD, 1972. Bar: Ind. 1972, U.S. Dist. Ct. (no. and so. dists.) Ind. 1972, U.S. Ct. Appeals (7th cir.) 1978. Assoc. Rocap Rocap Reese & Young, Indpls., 1972-76; pvt. practice, 1976-78, 88-91; ptnr. Forbes & Pennamped, 1978-88, Lowe Gray Steele & Hoffman, Indpls., 1991-96, Lowe Gray Steele & Darko, Indpls., 1996—2000, Pennamped $ Assocs., Indpls., 2000—. Chair and panelist Ind. Continuing Legal Edn. Forum; mem. Ind. Child Custody and Support Adv. Commn. Contbr. articles to profl. jours. Majority atty. Ind. Ho. of Reps., Indpls. Cpl. USMCR, 1967-69. Fellow Am. Acad. Matrimonial Lawyers. Home: 9662 Decatur Dr Indianapolis IN 46256-9654 Office: Pennamped & Associates 3925 River crossing Parkway Ste 280 Indianapolis IN 46240 Fax: 317-843-0718. E-mail: bruce@pennamped-associates.com.

PENNANT-REA, RUPERT LASCELLES, banker, economist; b. Harare, Zimbabwe, Jan. 23, 1948; came to Britain, 1966; s. Peter Athelwold and Pauline Elizabeth (Creasy) Pennant-Rea; m. Louise Greer, Oct. 3, 1970 (div. 1976); m. Jane Trevelyan Hamilton, Aug. 18, 1979 (div. 1986); children: Emily Trevelyan, Rory Marcus; m. Helen Jay, June 24, 1986; 1 child, Edward Peter. B.A. with honors, Trinity Coll., Dublin, 1970; M.A., U. Manchester, 1972. Economist, Confedn. Irish Industry, Dublin, 1970-71, Gen. and Mcpl. Workers Union, Eng., 1972-73, Bank of Eng., 1973-77; journalist The Economist, London, 1977-93, editor, 1986-93; dep. gov. Bank of Eng., London, 1993-95; chmn. Plantation and General Investments, London, 1997—, chmn. The Stationery Office, London, 1996—. Author: Gold Foil, 1979; The Pocket Economist, 1983; The Economist Economics, 1986. Recipient Wincott prize for fin. journalism Wincott Found., London, 1984. Mem. Ch. of Eng. Clubs: Marylebone Cricket, Reform (London), Harare (Zimbabwe). Avocations: music; tennis. Office: The Stationery Office 51 Nine Elms Lane London SW8 5DR England

PENNEL, MARIE LUCILLE HUNZIGER, retired elementary education educator; b. Oregon, Mo., Jan. 16, 1934; d. William Henry and Milree (Huff) Hunziger; m. Berres H. Pennel, Mar. 6, 1955; children: Patricia Lu Pennel Wolfe, Pamela Cille Pennel Ginther. BS, Northwest Mo. State U., 1954; MS, Kans. U., 1959; postgrad., Kans. State U. Cert. elem. tchr., Kans. 1st grade tchr., Lawrence, Kans.; kindergarten tchr. Atchison, Unified Sch. Dist. 415, Hiawatha, 1972-94. Recipient Outstanding Svc. award, Lawrence Jaycees, 1958, 59. Mem. ASCD, NEA, Kans. Edn. Assn., Assn. for Childhood Edn. Internat., PEO, Kappa Delta Pi, Delta Kappa Gamma. Home: 403 Woodbury Ln Hiawatha KS 66434-1525 E-mail: 403lnml@jbntelco.com.

PENNELL, DANNY JOE, social worker; b. Aug. 31, 1945; s. Donald Louis and Lela Geneva (Murray) P.; m. Janis Evelyn Reynolds, Dec. 26, 1984; children: Joel, Jason, Jaime, Chad, Colter. BA, U. Ill., 1970, MSW, 1972. Social worker Dept. Child and Family Svcs., Danville, Ill., 1971-72, social worker supr. Rockford, 1972-74; instr. Rockford Coll., 1977-78; pres., CEO Goldie B. Floberg Ctr., Rockton, Ill., 1974—. Exec. dir. Found. Ft. Lewis Coll., Durango, Colo., 1986-87; bd. dirs. Winnebago County Child Protection Assn., Rockford, 1974-76; bd. dirs., mem. legis. affairs com., chmn. mental health devel. disabilities com., spl. edn. com. Child Care Assn. Ill., Springfield, Ill., 1980—; mem. child welfare adv. com. Ill. Dept. Children and Family Services; mem. devel. disabilities adv. com. Dept. Mental Health, mem. children's svcs. subcom.; cons. in field. Grantee Ill. Dept. Children and Family Svcs., 1970-72. Mem. Nat. Soc. Fund Raising Execs. (bd. dirs., sec. 1984-85, v.p. 1986-87), Nat. Soc. Fund Raising Dirs. (pres. bd. dirs. 1988, v.p. 1987, v.p. 1986, bd. mem. various coms. 1984, 85), Am. Assn. Mental Deficiency, Nat. Assn. Retarded Citizens, Coordinating Council for Handicapped Children, Nat. Assn. Devel. Disabilities Mgrs., Roscoe C. of C. (bd. dirs. 2000—). Home: 12080 N Ledges Dr Roscoe IL 61073-9600 Office: Goldie B Floberg Ctr PO Box 346 Rockton IL 61072-0346 E-mail: dpenn58@aol.com.

PENNELL, WILLIAM BROOKE, lawyer; b. Mineral Ridge, Ohio, Oct. 28, 1935; s. George Albert and Katherine Nancy (McMeen) P. AB, Harvard U., 1957; LLB cum laude, U. Pa., 1961; m. Peggy Polsky, June 17, 1958; children: Katherine, Thomas Brooke. Bar: N.Y. 1963, U.S. Dist. Ct. (so. dist.) N.Y. 1964, U.S. Dist. Ct. (ea. dist.) N.Y. 1964, U.S. Ct. Appeals (2d cir.) 1966, U.S. Ct. Claims 1966, U.S. Tax Ct. 1967, U.S. Supreme Ct. 1967. Clk. U.S. Dist. Ct., (so. dist.) N.Y., N.Y.C., 1961-62; assoc. Shearman & Sterling, N.Y.C., 1962-71, ptnr., 1971-91. Recent case editor U. Pa. Law Rev., 1960-61. Bd. govs. Bklyn. Heights Assn., 1964-74, pres., 1969-71; chmn. bd. Willoughby House Settlement, 1972-95. Served with U.S. Army, 1957. Fellow Salzburg Seminar Am. Studies, 1965. Mem. Rembrandt Club. Office: PO Box 249 Canaan NY 12029-0249

PENNELLO, GENE ANTHONY, statistician; b. Huntsville, Ala., Nov. 23, 1962; s. Julian Joseph and Betsy Pennello; m. Chung-Chin Sun, Sept. 18, 1993; children: Julian, Chelsie. BS in Computer Sci. & Math., BS in Statis., U. Calif., Davis., 1985, MS in Statis., 1989; PhD in Statis., Oreg. State U., 1993. Math. statis. Food and Drug Adminstrn., Rockville, Md., 1998—. Lectr. George Washington U., 1996-97. Author: Atlas of Cancer Mortality: 1950-1994, 1999; contbr. articles to profl. jours. Postdoctoral fellow Nat. Cancer Inst., Bethesda, Md., 1994-98. Mem. Am. Statis. Assn. Republican. Roman Catholic. Avocations: origami, tennis. Office: Food & Drug Adminstrn 1350 Piccard Dr Rockville MD 20850 E-mail: gxp@cdrh.fda.gov.

PENNER, KEITH, Canadian government official; b. Sask., Can., May 1, 1933; BA, U. Alberta, Can., 1955; MDiv, Toronto U., 1959; MEd, U. Ottawa, Can., 1971. Secondary sch. tchr., Dryden, Ont., Can., 1961-68; mem. parliament Cochrane-Superior, 1968-88; mem. Can. Transp. Agy., Ottawa, 1988—. Past parliamentary sec. to Min. of State for Sci. and Tech., past parliamentary sec. to Min. of Indian Affairs and No. Devel., past chmn. Standing Com. on Indian Affairs and No. Devel.; vis. fellow Sch. of Polit. Sci., Queen's U., 1987-88. Fellow: Chartered Inst. of Transport. Office: Can Transp Agy Ottawa ON Canada K1A 0N9

PENNER, RUDOLPH GERHARD, economist, educator; b. Windsor, Ont., Can., July 15, 1936; s. Jacob Gerhard P. and Agnes (Dyck) Bremsteller; m. Alice Braeker, June 27, 1959; children: Eric, Brian. Vis. asst. prof. Princeton U., 1965-66; sr. staff economist Council Econ. Advisers, Washington, 1970-71; prof. U. Rochester, N.Y., 1970-75; asst. dir. econ. Office Mgmt. and Budget, Washington, 1975-77; resident scholar Am. Enterprise Inst., 1977-83; dir. Congl. Budget Office, 1983-87; dep. asst. sec. econ. HUD, 1973-75; sr. fellow Urban Inst., 1987-92; dir. econ. studies KPMG Peat Marwick, 1992-97; sr. fellow Urban Inst., 1997—. Washington editor BCA Pubs., Montreal, 1987; author: (with Alan Abramson) Broken Purse Strings, (with Isabel Sawhill and Timothy Taylor) Updating America's Social Contract. Mem. Nat. Economist Club (chmn. 1980-81, pres.), Am. Econ. Assn., Nat. Tax Assn., Nat. Assn. Bus. Economists (bd. dirs.), Manpower Demonstration Rsch. Corp. (bd. dirs.). Republican. Mennonite. Office: Urban Inst 2001 M St NW Washington DC 20036-3310

PENNER, STANFORD SOLOMON, engineering educator; b. Unna, Germany, July 5, 1921; came to U.S., 1936, naturalized, 1943; s. Heinrich and Regina (Saal) P.; m. Beverly Preston, Dec. 28, 1942; children: Merilynn Jean, Robert Clark. BS, Union Coll., 1942; MS, U. Wis., 1943, PhD, 1946; Dr. rer. nat. (hon.), Technische Hochschule Aachen, Germany, 1981. Research asso. Allegany Ballistics Lab., Cumberland, Md., 1944-45; research scientist Standard Oil Devel. Co., Esso Labs., Linden, N.J., 1946; sr. research engr. Jet Propulsion Lab., Pasadena, Calif., 1947-50; mem. faculty Calif. Inst. Tech., 1950-63, prof. div. engring., jet propulsion, 1957-63; dir. research engring. div. Inst. Def. Analyses, Washington, 1962-64; prof. engring. physics, chmn. dept. aerospace and mech. engring. U. Calif. at San Diego, 1964-68, vice chancellor for acad. affairs, 1968-69, dir. Inst. for Pure and Applied Phys. Scis., 1968-71, dir. Energy Ctr., 1973-91. Bd. dirs. Optodyne Corp.; U.S. mem. adv. group aero. rsch. and devel. NATO, 1952-68, chmn. combustion and propulsion panel, 1958-60; mem. adv. com. engring. scis. USAF-Office Sci. Rsch., 1961-65; mem. subcom. on combustion NACA, 1954-58; mem. rsch. adv. com. on air-breathing engines NASA, 1962-64; mem. coms. on gas dynamics and edn. Internat. Acad. Astronautics, 1969-80; nat. lectr. Sigma Xi, 1977-79; chmn. fossil energy rsch. working group Dept. Energy, 1978-82, chmn. advanced fuel cell commercialization working group, 1993-95; mem. assembly engring. NAE, 1978-82; chmn. NAS-NRC U.S. Nat. Com. IIASA, 1978-82; mem. commn. engring. tech. sys. NRC, 1982-84; spl. guest Internat. Coal Sci. Confs., 1983, 85, 87, 89, 91; mentor Def. Sci. Studies Group, 1985-93; chmn. studies mcpl. waste incineration NSF, 1988-89, Calif. Coun. Sci. Tech., 1992; pub. info. adv. com. Nat. Acad. Engring., 1994-98, Independent Commn. on Environ. Edn., 1995-97, Environ. Literacy Coun., 1998—; sci. adv. bd., San Diego County, 1997—; divsn. advisor, bds. of the divsn. on engring. and phys. scis. The Nat. Acads., 2001—. Author: Chemical Reactions in Flow Systems, 1955, Chemistry Problems in Jet Propulsion, 1957, Quantitative Molecular Spectroscopy and Gas Emissivities, 1959, Chemical Rocket Propulsion and Combustion Research, 1962, Thermodynamics, 1968, Radiation and Reentry, 1968; sr. author: Energy, Vol. I (Demands, Resources, Impact, Technology and Policy), 1974, 81, Energy, Vol. II (Non-nuclear Energy Technologies), 1975, 77, 84, Energy, Vol. III (Nuclear Energy and Energy Policies), 1976; editor: Chemistry of Propellants, 1960, Advanced Propulsion Techniques, 1961, Detonations and Two-Phase Flow, 1962, Combustion and Propulsion, 1963, Advances in Tactical Rocket Propulsion, 1968, In Situ Shale Oil Recovery, 1975, New Sources of Oil and Gas, 1982, Coal Combustion and Applications, 1984, Advanced Fuel Cells, 1986, Coal Gasification: Direct Applications and Syntheses of Chemicals and Fuels, 1987, CO2 Emissions and Climate Change, 1991, Commercialization of Fuel Cells, 1995, Advanced Nuclear Techs., 1998, energy and Power Systems: Encyclopedia of Physical Science and Technology, 1998-02; assoc. editor Jour. Chem. Physics, 1953-56; founding editor Jour. Quantitative Spectroscopy and Radiative Transfer, 1960-92, Jour. Def. Rsch., 1963-67, Energy-The Internat. Jour., 1975-98; sect. editor Energy and Power Systems, Ency. Phys. Sci. and Tech., 1998-2002. Recipient spl. award People-to-People Program, pub. svc. award U. Calif., Sn Diego, N. Manson medal Internat. Colloquia on Gasdynamics of Explosions and Reactive Systems, 1979, internat. Columbus award Internat. Inst. Comm., Genoa, Italy, 1981, disting. assoc. award U.S. Dept. Energy, 1990, Edward Teller award for def. of freedom, 1997. Fellow Am. Phys. Soc., Optical Soc. Am., AAAS, N.Y. Acad. Scis., AIAA (dir. 1964-66, past chmn. com., G. Edward Pendray award 1975, Thermophysics award 1983, Energy Systems award 1983), Am. Acad. Arts and Scis.; mem. Nat. Acad. Engring., Internat. Acad. Astronautics, Am. Chem. Soc., Sigma Xi. Home: 5912 Avenida Chamnez La Jolla CA 92037-7402 Office: U Calif San Diego 9500 Gilman Dr La Jolla CA 92093-0411

PENNEY, CHARLES RAND, lawyer, civic worker; b. Buffalo, July 26, 1923; s. Charles Patterson and Gretchen (Rand) P. BA, Yale U., 1945; JD, U. Va., 1951; DFA (hon.), SUNY, 1995. Bar: Md. 1952, N.Y. 1958, U.S. Supreme Ct. 1958. Law sec. to U.S. Dist. Ct. Judge W.C. Coleman, Balt., 1951-52; dir. devel. office Children's Hosp., Buffalo, 1952-54; sales mgr. Amherst Mfg. Corp., Williamsville, N.Y., 1954-56, also; Delevan Electronics Corp., East Aurora; mem. firm Penney & Penney, Buffalo, 1958-61; pvt. practice, Niagara County, N.Y., 1961—. Numerous contemporary art collection exhbns. include Mus. Modern Art, N.Y.C., 1962, Whitney Mus. Am. Art, N.Y.C., 1963, 79, 80, Burchfield-Penney Art Ctr., 1973, 92-2001, Meml. Art Gallery, Rochester, 1976, 78, 83, 88, U. Iowa, 1978, Columbus Bd. dirs. Buffalo State Coll. Found.; hon. life trustee Burchfield-Penney Art Ctr.; active Peterson Soc. of Buffalo State Coll.; adv. bd. Found. Study of Arts and Crafts Movement at Roycroft. 2d lt. U.S. Army, 1943-46. Recipient Pres.'s Disting. Svc. award Buffalo State Coll., 1991, Disting. Svc. to Culture award Coll. Arts and Scis., SUNY, Potsdam, 1983; named Disting. fellow Cultural Studies of the Burchfield-Penney Art Ctr., 1994, Outstanding Individual Philanthropist, Nat. Soc. Fund Raising Execs. Western N.Y., 1996, Individual Patron of the Arts award Buffalo and Erie County Arts Coun. and Buffalo C. of C., 1997, Citation for Outstanding Achievements and Svc. to Lockport Cmty., N.Y. State Assembly, 1997; awarded Key to City of Lockport, 1997; inductee Lockport Historic Walk of Fame, 1999. Fellow The Explorers Club: mem. AARP, YWCA Niagra (life), Albright-Knox Art Gallery Buffalo (life), Buffalo Mus. Sci. (Life), Buffalo and Erie County Hist. Soc. (life, Red Jacket award 2000), Niagara County Hist. Soc. (life), Old Ft. Niagara (life), Buffalo Soc. Artists (hon. trustee), Hist. Lockport (life), Landmark Soc. Western N.Y. (life), Nat. Trust Hist. Preservation, Am. Ceramic Cir., Hist. Lewiston (life), Friends of U. Rochester Librs. (life) Meml. Art Gallery U. Rochester (hon. bd. mgrs., hon. life), Winslow Homer Soc. of Dirs. Cir. (hon. life), Smithsonian Instn. (benefactors cir.), Rochester Hist. Soc. (life), Am. Hist. Print Collectors Soc. (life), Burchfield Homestead Soc. (hon. life), Charles E. Burchfield Nature and Art Ctr., Archives Am. Art, Mark Twain Soc. (hon.), U. Rochester's Pres.'s Soc. (hon. life), U. Iowa's Pres.'s Club (hon. life), Va. Law Found., Nat. Geog. Soc. (life), World's Fair Collectors Soc., Hist. Soc. of Tonawandas (life), Pres.'s Cir. Buffalo State Coll. (hon. life), Peanut Pals, Grolier Club, Pan Am. Expo Collectors Soc., Buffalo Indsl. Heritage Com., Roycrofters-at-Large Assn. (life), Arctic Circle Club, Order of the Alaska Walrus, Chi Psi, Phi Alpha Delta. Clubs: Automobile (Lockport); Niagara County Antiques (hon.); Rochester Art (hon. life). Office: 538 Bewley Building Lockport NY 14094-2944 *I have tried to strive for excellence in whatever I undertake, be it small or large. What success I may have achieved has required initiative, imagination, and dedication to the task at hand. Satisfaction comes from the hard work that leads to an objective. In all that I do I adhere to the Golden Rule and to fairness, honesty, and understanding in human relationships. I try to maintain a sense of humor at all times. And I enjoy living in a small community because it is from such areas that the strength of America comes.*

PENNEY, SHERRY HOOD, university president, educator; b. Marlette, Mich., Sept. 4, 1937; d. Terrance and B. Jean (Stoutenburg) Hood; m. Carl Murray Penney, July 8, 1961 (div. 1978); children: Michael Murray, Jeffrey Hood; m. James Duane Livingston, Mar. 30, 1985. BA, Albion Coll., 1959, LLD (hon.), 1989; MA, U. Mich., 1961; PhD, SUNY, Albany, 1972; hon. degree, Quincy Coll., 1999. Vis. asst. prof. Union Coll., Schenectady, N.Y., 1972-73; assoc. higher edn. N.Y. State Edn. Dept., Albany, 1973-76; assoc. provost Yale U., New Haven, 1976-82; vice chancellor acad. programs, policy and planning SUNY System, Albany, 1982-88; acting pres. SUNY, Plattsburgh, 1986-87; chancellor U. Mass., Boston, 1988-95; pres. U. Mass. Sys., 1995; chancellor U. Mass., 1996-2000, endowed prof., 2001—. Chmn., bd. dirs. Nat. Higher Edn. Mgmt. Sys., Boulder, Colo., 1985-87; mem. commn. on higher edn. New Eng. Assn. Schs. and Colls., Boston, 1979-82, Mid. States Assn. Schs. and Colls., Phila., 1986-88; mem. commn. on women Am. Coun. Edn., Washington, 1979-81, commn. on govt. rels., 1990-94; bd. dirs. NSTAR, Boston Edison Co., Carnegie Found. for Advancement of Teaching. Author: Patrician in Politics, 1974; editor: Women and Management in Higher Education, 1975; contbr. articles to profl. jours. Mem. Internat. Trade Task Force, 1994-96; mem. exec. com., Challenge to Leadership, 1988, chair, 1995-98; mem. Mid-Am. adv. bd. HERS, 1992—, Mary Baker eddy Libr., Boston, 2001—; trustee Berkeley Div. Sch., Yale U., 1978-82, John F. Kennedy Libr. Found., 1988-2001; bd. dirs. Albany Symphony Orch., 1982-88, U. Mass. Found., 1988-2000, Mcpl. Rsch. Bur., Boston, 1990-2001, New Eng. Coun., 1990-2000, Greater Boston C. of C., Met. Affairs Coalition (chair 1999-2001), New Eng. Aquarium, Greater Boston One to One Leadership Coun., 1990-2000, NASULGC Commn. Urban Affairs, 1990-2000, The Ednl. Resource Inst., chair, 1996—, The Environ. Bus. Coun., 1991-97; nat. adv. com. Nat. Initiative for Women in Higher Edn. Recipient Disting. Alumna award Albion Coll., 1978, Disting. Citizen award for racial harmony Black/White Boston, 1994, Am. Coun. on Edn./Nat. Identification Program Mass. Leadership award, 1995, New Eng. Women's Leadership award, 1996, Pinnacle award for Lifetime Achievement Greater Boston C. of C., 1998. Mem. Am. Assn. Higher Edn., Orgn. Am. Historians, St. Botolph Club, Comml. Club (Boston). Unitarian Universalist. Office: U Mass Boston 100 Morrissey Blvd Boston MA 02125-3300 E-mail: sherry.penney@umb.edu.

PENNIMAN, NICHOLAS GRIFFITH, IV, retired newspaper publisher; b. Balt., Mar. 7, 1938; s. Nicholas Griffith Penniman III and Esther Cox Lony (Wight) Keeney; m. Linda Jane Simmons, Feb. 4, 1967; children: Rebecca Helmle, Nicholas G. V. AB, Princeton U., 1960; MA, Washington U., 1999. Asst. bus. mgr. Ill. State Jour. Register, Springfield, 1964-69, bus. mgr., 1969-75; asst. gen. mgr. St. Louis Post-Dispatch, 1975-84, gen. mgr., 1984-86, pub., 1986-99; sr. v.p. newspapers ops. Pulitzer Pub. Co., 1986-99; pres., CEO Pulitzer Comm. Newspapers Inc., 1997-99; chmn. bd. Penniman & Browne, Inc., Balt., 2001—. Chmn. Downtown St. Louis, Inc., 1988-90, Mo. Health and Ednl. Facilities Adminstrn., 1982-85, Ill. State Fair Bd., Springfield, 1973-75, Parks and Open Space Task Force St. Louis 2004, 1996-2000; pres. Caring Found. for Children, 1988-91, Forest Park Forever, 1991-93, St. Louis Sports Com., 1992-93, Gateway Parks and Trails 2004, 1999—; trustee St. Louis Country Day Sch., 1983-86, Mercantile Libr. of St. Louis, 1997-2000; bd. dirs. Mo. Coalition for the Environment, 1997-2000, Randall Rsch. Ctr., Pineland, Fla., 2001--; 1st vice chair Am. Rivers, 2002—. With U.S. Army, 1962—67. Mem.: Lake Champlain Yacht Club, St. Louis Country Club, Noonday Club (pres. 1994), Grey Oaks Country Club. Home: 611 Portside Dr Naples FL 34103-4118 E-mail: ngpiv@aol.com.

PENNIMAN, W. DAVID, information scientist, educator, consultant; b. St. Louis, Dec. 19, 1937; s. William Leon and Laura Mae (Van Winkle) P.; m. Charlotte Ann Meder, Mar. 17, 1973; children: Kara, Rachel, John; 1 child by previous marriage, Jessica. BS in ME, U. Ill., 1960, MS in Journalism, Communications, 1962; PhD in Communication Theory, Ohio State U., 1975. Registered profl. engr., Ohio. Assoc. dir. engring. publs. U. Ill. Coll. Engring., Urbana, 1965-66; research scientist info. systems Battelle Columbus Labs., Columbus, Ohio, 1966-69, assoc. mgr. info. systems, 1969-77; research scholar Internat. Inst. Applied Systems Analysis, Laxenburg, Austria, 1977; mgr. research Online Computer Library Ctr., Dublin, 1978-79, dir. software devel., 1979-82, v.p. planning and research, 1982-84; dir. libraries and info. systems AT&T Bell Labs., Murray Hill, N.J., 1984-90, dir. info. svcs. group, 1990-91; pres. Coun. on Libr. Resources, Inc., Washington, 1991-95; dir. Ctr. for Info. Studies, 1995-99; prof. sch. of Info. Scis. Univ. Tenn., 1995-99; private cons., 1999—2001; prof. sch. informatics U. Buffalo, Buffalo, 2001—, dean sch. informatics, 2001—. Bd. dirs., chmn. Engring. Info. Inc., N.Y.C., 1983-91, Planet Connect, 1997—; governing com. Forest Press Inc., Albany, N.Y., 1985-88; adv. com. info. sci. Rutgers U., 1982-91. Author numerous book chpts. and articles in profl. jours. Advisor United Way, Columbus, 1981-83. Served with U.S. Army, 1963-65. Named Tech. Person of the Yr. Columbus Tech. Council, 1982, U.S. Del. to Internat. Inst. for Applied Systems Analysis, 1977. Fellow AAAS; mem. IEEE (sr.), Am. Soc. Info. Sci. (pres. 1988-89), Assn. for Computing Machinery. Avocations: antique automobiles, hiking. Office: U Buffalo Sch of Informatics Buffalo NY 14260 Business E-Mail: penniman@buffalo.edu.

PENNING, PATRICIA JEAN, elementary education educator; b. Springfield, Ill., Sept. 3, 1952; d. Howard Louis and Jean Lenore (Hartley) P. AA, Lincoln Land C.C., Springfield, 1972; BA, Millikin U., 1975. Cert. tchr. grades K-9. Receptionist Drs. Penning, Marty & Teich, Springfield, 1968-72; child care asst. La Petite Acad., 1970-72; tchr. St. Agnes Sch., 1975—. Mail clk. St. John's Hosp., Springfield, 1977-88; mem. dir. instrnl. tv St. Agnes Sch., Springfield, 1981—, sec. primary level, 1993—, mem. reading com., 1994—, mem. social com., 1994—. Mem. St. Agnes Folk Choir, Springfield, 1976—; cantor, St. Agnes Ch., Springfield, 1976—, creator butterfly garden. Recipient Outstanding Tchr. award Office Cath. Edn., Springfield, 1988,

Golden Apple award Ch. 20 and Town and Country Bank, Springfield, 1993; named Apprentice Cathechist, Diocese of Springfield, Ill., 1992. Mem. Internat. Reading Assn., Nat. Coun. Math., Nat. Cath. Edn. Assn. (Grad. award 1991), Ill. State Assn. Curriculum and Devel. Roman Catholic. Avocations: reading, crafts, gardening, classical music. Home: 22 Westminster Rd Chatham IL 62629-1254 Office: St Agnes Sch 251 N Amos Ave Springfield IL 62702-4792

PENNINGER, FRIEDA ELAINE, retired English language educator; b. Marion, N.C., Apr. 11, 1927; d. Fred Hoyle and Lena Frances (Young) P. AB, U. N.C., Greensboro, 1948; MA, Duke U., 1950, PhD, 1961. Copywriter Sta. WSJS, Winston-Salem, N.C., 1948-49; asst. prof. English Flora Macdonald Coll., Red Springs, 1950-51; tchr. English Barnwell, S.C., 1951-52, Brunswick, Ga., 1952-53; instr. English U. Tenn., Knoxville, 1953-56; instr., asst. prof. Woman's Coll., U. N.C., Greensboro, 1956-58, 60-63; asst. prof., assoc. prof. U. Richmond (Va.), 1963-71; chair., dept. English Westhampton Coll., Richmond, 1971-78; prof. English U. Richmond, 1971-91, Bostwick prof. English, 1987-91; ret., 1991. Author: William Caxton, 1979, Chaucer's "Troilus and Criseyde" and "The Knight's Tale": Fictions Used, 1993, (novel) Look at Them, 1990; compiler, editor: English Drama to 1660, 1976; editor: Festschrift for Prof. Marguerite Roberts, 1976. Fellow Southeastern Inst. of Mediaeval and Renaissance Studies, 1965, 67, 69. Democrat. Presbyterian. Home: 2701 Camden Rd Greensboro NC 27403-1438

PENNINGTON, BEVERLY MELCHER, financial services company executive; b. Vermillion, SD, Feb. 8, 1931; d. Cecil Lloyd and Phyllis Cecelia (Walz) M.; m. Glen D., Sept. 1, 1965 (dec. Aug. 1986); 1 child, Terri Lynn. BS, U. S.D., Vermillion, 1952. Enrolled agt. cert. IRS 1989. Sec. budget dept. Bur. of Indian Affairs, Aberdeen, S.D., 1952-53, pvt. sec., 1953-54, U.S. P.H.S. Indian Health, Aberdeen, 1954-55; adminstr. asst. U.S. Pub. Health Svc., Anchorage, 1955-58, U.S. Pub. Health, Dental Pub. Health, Washington, 1958-61; grant adminstr. Dental Pub. Health, 1961-65; co-owner Penn Mel Marina, Platte, S.D, 1965-74, Pennington Tax Service, Platte, 1974-86, owner, 1986-93; pres., CEO, White Tiger Fin. Svc., Inc., 1994—. Contbr. articles to profl. jours. Mem. Platte Women's Club, sec., 1965-68, pres., 1968-70, 89-91; mem. Libr. Bd., sec., 1982-85, treas., 1995—. Fellow Am. Soc. Tax Profls. (sec. 1989-91, 2d v.p. 1995, 1st v.p. 1996, pres. 1997); mem. NAFE, Platte C. of C. (v.p. 1989, pres. 1990), Lyric Theatre Mus. Soc. (pres. 1988-92), U.S. C. of C., Washington Dakota Cen. Com. Republican. Presbyterian. Avocations: collecting jewelry, reading, dress designing, gourmet cooking. Office: White Tiger Fin Svc Inc 420 Main St Platte SD 57369

PENNINGTON, DONALD HARRIS, musician, retired physician; b. Clarksville, Ark., Sept. 13, 1945; s. John Powers and Verna Olive (Harris) P.; m. Susan Myree Snyder, Aug. 27, 1966 (div. Aug. 1982); children: Thomas Walter, Aimee Myree, John Herrick. BA, U. of the Ozarks, 1968; MD, U. Ark., 1972; wine diploma, Calif. Dept. Agr., 1973. Intern St. Vincent Infirmary, Little Rock, 1973; physician, founding ptnr. Clarksville Med. Group, P.A., 1972-93; physician Mercy Med. Svcs., Inc., Ft. Smith, Ark., 1993-98; ret., 1998. Cons. family planning svcs. Ark. State Bd. of Health, 1973-93; mem. physician adv. bd. Mercy Med. Group, 1996—. Founding mem., musician Ft. Douglas (Ark.) Backporch Bluegrass Symphony, 1976-91; acoustic double bassist River Valley Jazz Union, Russellville, Ark., 1991-97. Active ACLU, Planned Parenthood Fedn., The League to Make a Difference, Sierra Club Legal Defense Fund, The Nature Conservancy; mem. Nat. Trust for Hist. Preservation, 1982—, Clarkesville Planning and Zoning Commn.; mem. governing bd. Oakland Cemetery Assn., 1997—; mem. vol. United Meth. Com. on Relief; asst. ch. organist 1st United Meth. Ch., Clarksville, 1968—; full time organist 1st Presbyn. Ch., 1994—; bd. dirs. Johnson County Regional Hosp., Clarksville, 1973—82, Johnson County Cmty. Found. Mem. AMA, Assn. Am. Physicians for Human Rights, Nat. Trust for Historic Preservation, Ark. Med. Soc. (county del. 1972-96), Ark. Acad. Family Practice, Religious Coalition for Abortion Rights, Johnson County Hist. Soc. (life mem., pres. 2000—), Nat. Orgn. for Reformed Marijuana Laws, Nat. Drug Policy Task Force, Nat. Gay and Lesbian Task Force, 90-Yr. Old's Friday Bridge Club (chauffeur), Tuesday Culture and Bridge Club. Democrat. Avocations: restoration of historic homes, antiques, family history, music, historical preservation. Home: 317 N Johnson St Clarksville AR 72830-2953 E-mail: donpen@arkansas.net.

PENNINGTON, KENNETH JAMES, history and law educator; b. Salem, N.J., Oct. 6, 1941; s. Kenneth James and Grace Elaine Pennington; m. Marlene Ann Carlson, Dec. 30, 1994; children: Kenneth James III, Alison. BA, U. Wis., 1965, MA, 1967; PhD, Cornell U., 1971. Prof. medieval history Syracuse (N.Y.) U., 1971—2001; Kelly Quinn prof. ecclesiastical and legal history Cath. U. Am., Washington, 2001—. Author: Johannis Teutonici Apparatus glossarum in Compilationem tertiam, 1981. Fellow Alexander von Humboldt Stiftung, 1969, 83, 93, 93-96, NEH, 1974, Am. Coun. Learned Socs., 1980, Fulbright fellow, 1985, Gerda-Henkel Stiftung, 1986; rsch. grantee NEH, 1989-96, Werner Reimers Stiftung, 1990, 92. Fellow Medieval Acad. Am.; mem. Am. Hist. Assn., Internat. Soc. Medieval Canon Law (life, pres. 2000-01). Home: 142 E Street SE Washington DC 20003-2613 Office: Cath U Am Columbus Sch Law Washington DC 20064 Fax: 315-44305876. E-mail: pennington@cua.edu., kenneth.pennington3@verizon.net.

PENNINGTON, ROBERT EDGAR, music educator; b. West Line, Mo., Nov. 27, 1931; s. William Ray Pennington, Edna Marie Johnson. BMus, Northwestern U., 1953, M in Music, 1955, DMus, 1966. Instr. Howard Coll., Birmingham, Ala., 1955—56; prof. piano Drury Coll., Springfield, Mo., 1959—65, West Chester (Pa.) U., West Chester, 1966—. Mem.: Mo. Tchrs. Assn. (editor notes 1962—63), Music Tchrs. Nat. Assn., Pi Kappa Lambda. Avocation: Travel. Home: Apt D 4 S Brandywine St West Chester PA 19382 Office: West Chester Univ West Chester PA 19383 Office Fax: 610-436-2873. Business E-Mail: rpennington@wcupa.edu.

PENNINGTON, ROBERT MICHAEL, marketing communications consultant; b. Chgo., Oct. 22, 1948; s. Charles Sheldon and Marcella Mary (Crossen) P.; m. Carol Sue-Chen Chang, Jan. 29, 1994. BA, U. Wis., Whitewater, 1981, MS, 1984; PhD, U. Wis., 1991. Advt. coord. Johnson Hill Press, Fort Atkinson, Wis., 1984-85; cons., 1985—; project asst. U. Wis., Madison, 1986-90; asst. prof. U. Okla., Norman, 1990-92, U. Tex., Arlington, 1992-98, N.Mex. State U., Las Cruces, 1998-2001. Mem. adv. com. Polit. Comm. Ctr., U. Okla., 1990-92. Bus. mgr. Jour. of Advt., 2001—; contbr. articles to profl. jours. Vice chmn. Bd. Adjustment, Duncanville, Tex., 1995-98. With U.S. Army 1973-74. Mem. Am. Acad. Advt. (rsch. com. 1992, internat. com. 1993—), Assn. Edn. Journalism and Mass Comm. (jour. com. 1994-96), Soc. for Consumer Psychology, Am. Soc. Competitiveness, Phi Kappa Phi, Phi Beta Delta. Avocations: competitive sailing, photography, music. E-mail: pennington@zianet.com.

PENNINGTON, RODNEY LEE, engineer; b. Bloomsburg, Pa., Oct. 17, 1946; s. Ernest Eli and Ellen M. (Albertson) P.; m. Patricia Ann Bond, Sept. 4, 1965 (div. 1983); 1 child, Denise Rene; m. Linda Rae Petruna, Aug. 8, 1984. Engring. Tech. Cert., Williamsport Tech. Inst., Pa., 1965; AS in Engring., Williamsport Area Coll., 1972; BS in Engring. Sci., Pa. State U., 1974. Registered profl. engr. N.J. Design engr. Piper Aircraft, Lock Haven, Pa., 1965-66; staff engr. Armstrong World Ind., Lancaster, 1974-75; project mgr. REECO, Morris Plains, N.J., 1975-78, sales mgr., 1978-80, sales adminstr., 1980-81, engring. mgr., 1981-82, mktg. devel. mgr., 1982-84, v.p. engring. and R&D, 1982—. Dir ARTCO, Inc., Morristown. Patentee in field; contbr. articles to profl. jours. With USAF, 1966-70. Recipient Alcan Engring. Sci. award, 1972. Mem. Nat. Coil Coaters Assn. (bd. dirs. 1991-94, chmn. environ. com. 1989-91). Avocations: computers, hunting, landscaping. Office: REECO PO Box 1500 Somerville NJ 08876-1251

PENNINGTON, WILLIAM LANE, manufacturing executive; b. Vinita, Okla., Sept. 15, 1955; m. Susan W., June 19, 1982; children: Clay, Anne, Sarah. B, Okla. State U., 1977; JD, U. Tulsa, 1980. Lawyer Holliman, Langholz, Runnels & Dorwart, Tulsa, Okla., 1980-85, ptnr., shareholders, bd. dirs., 1985-88; v.p. legal Hilti Western Hemisphere; pres. Hilti Can., Toronto, Ont., 1993-94, Hilti Asia Ltd., Hong Kong, 1994-97, Lennox Asia Pacific, Dallas, 1998-2000; pres. worldwide heat transfer Lennox Internat. Inc., 1999—2001; pres. IMCO Internat., Irving, 2001—. Bd. dirs. Tulsa Boys Home, Tulsa, 1992-93, Tulsa Philharm. Soc., 1988-93, exec. com., 1988-92. Mem. Young Pres. Orgn. Avocations: fly fishing, running, horseback riding, ranching. Home: 4205 Amherst Dallas TX 75225 Office: IMCO Internat 5215 N O'Connor Blvd Ste 1500 Irving TX 75039

PENNISI, LIZ, women's health nurse; b. Bklyn., Nov. 20, 1953; d. Alexander and Marjorie (Soviero) Perillo; m. Stephen Crain Pennisi, Jan. 17, 1976; children: Stephen, Scott, Greg. Diploma, Beth Israel Sch. Nursing, N.Y.C., 1974. RN, N.Y.; cert. ambulatory women's health nurse. Staff nurse Montefiore Hosp., Bronx, N.Y., 1974-75; mem. staff Beth Israel Med. Ctr., N.Y.C., 1975-77; office nurse Martin Kurman, M.D., 1977-80, Adam Romoff, M.D. and Suzanne Yale, M.D., P.C, 1984—. Mem. AWHONN. Avocations: tennis, horseback riding, reading. Office: Drs Romoff and Yale 768 Park Ave New York NY 10021-4153 E-mail: liz@exgen.net.

PENNISTEN, JOHN WILLIAM, computer scientist, linguist, actuary; b. Buffalo, Jan. 25, 1939; s. George William and Lucy Josephine (Gates) P. AB in Math. and Chemistry with honors, Hamilton Coll., 1960; postgrad., Harvard U., 1960-61, U.S. Army Lang. Sch., 1962-63; MS in Computer Sci. with honors, N.Y. Inst. Tech., 1987; cert. in taxation, NYU, 1982; cert. in profl. banking, Am. Inst. of Banking of Am. Bankers Assn., 1988.; cert. Asian Langs., NYU, 1992. Actuarial asst. New Eng. Mut. Life Ins. Co., Boston, 1965-66; asst. actuary Mass. Gen. Life Ins. Co., 1966-68; actuarial assoc. John Hancock Mut. Life Ins. Co., 1968-71; asst. actuary George B. Buck Cons. Actuaries, Inc., N.Y.C., 1971-75, Martin E. Segal Co., N.Y.C., 1975-80; actuary Laiken Siegel & Co., 1980; cons. Bklyn., 1981—; timesharing and database analyst banklink corp. cash mgmt. div. Chem. Bank N.Y.C., 1983-85; programmer analyst Empire Blue Cross and Blue Shield, N.Y.C., 1986-88, Mt. Sinai Med. Ctr., N.Y.C., 1988-89, French Am. Banking Corp. (subs. Banque National de Paris), N.Y.C., 1989; sr. programmer analyst Dean Witter Reynolds, Inc., 1989-92; computer specialist for software N.Y.C. Dept. Fin., 1992-97; sr. cons. Pinkerton Computer Cons., Inc., N.Y.C., 1997-99; tech. officer J.P. Morgan Chase & Co., 1999—. Enrolled actuary U.S. Fed. Pension Legis. Bklyn., 1976—. Contbr. articles to profl. jours. With U.S. Army, 1961-64. Fellow: Soc. Actuaries; mem.: IEEE Computer Soc., MLA, AAAS, Harvard Grad. Soc., Am. Friends of Covent Garden, Bklyn. Heights Assn., Nat. Ry. Hist. Soc., Am. Chem. Soc., Math. Assn. Am., Nat. Model R.R. Assn. (life), Ry. and Locomotive Hist. Soc. (life), Am. Math. Soc., Assn. Computational Linguistics, Linguistic Soc. Am., Am. Assn. Artificial Intelligence, Assn. Computing Machinery, Met. Opera Guild, Am. Legion, Phi Beta Kappa. Home: 135 Willow St Brooklyn NY 11201-2255

PENNOYER, PAUL GEDDES, JR. lawyer; b. N.Y.C., Feb. 11, 1920; s. Paul G. and Frances (Morgan) P.; m. Cecily Henderson, Feb. 5, 1949; children: Jennifer, Deidre, Paul T., Sheldon K., William M. BS, Harvard U., 1942, LLB, 1948. Bar: N.Y. 1949, U.S. Dist. Ct. (so. and ea. dists.) N.Y. 1952, U.S. Supreme Ct. 1972, U.S. Ct. Appeals (2d cir.) 1964, U.S. Ct. Appeals (4th cir.) 1986, U.S. Ct. Appeals (11th cir.) 1987. Assoc. Bingham Englar Jones & Houston, N.Y.C., 1949-55, ptnr., 1955-63, Chadbourne & Parke, N.Y.C., 1963-89; of counsel, 1989—. Trustee Frick Collection, 1975—, L.I. U., 1975-85, Morgan Meml. Park, 1970—, North Shore Wildlife Inc., 1980—. Lt. USN, 1942-45. Decorated Navy Cross, Air Medal (2) Mem. ABA, N.Y. State Bar Assn., Assn. Bar City N.Y., N.Y. Bar found., Am. Coll. Trial Lawyers, N.Y. Yacht Club. Republican. Episcopalian. Office: Chadbourne & Parke 30 Rockefeller Plz Fl 31 New York NY 10112-0129

PENNOYER, ROBERT M. lawyer; b. N.Y.C., Apr. 9, 1925; BA, Harvard U., 1946; LL.B., Columbia U., 1950. Bar: N.Y. 1951, U.S. Supreme Ct. 1971. Asst. U.S. atty. criminal div. So. Dist., N.Y., 1953-55; asst. to gen. counsel Office of Sec. of Def., Dept. Def., Washington, 1955-57, spl. asst. to asst. sec. of def. for internat. security affairs, 1957-58; ptnr. Patterson, Belknap, Webb & Tyler, N.Y.C., 1962-95, of counsel, 1995—. Trustee Carnegie Instn., Washington, 1968-79, John Merck Fund, 1982—, Mrs. Giles Whiting Found., 1970—, Met. Mus. Art, 1966—, Pierpont Morgan Libr., 1969—, Columbia U., 1982-88, Boyce Thompson Inst. for Plant Rsch., Cornell U., 1974-97, Inst. Democracy Studies, 1999—. Lt. (j.g.) USNR, 1944-46. Mem. ABA, N.Y. State Bar Assn., Assn. Bar City N.Y., Century Assn. Office: Patterson Belknap Webb & Tyler Rm 2200 1133 Ave of the Americas New York NY 10036-6731 E-mail: rmpennoyer@pbwt.com.

PENNY, BRENT ANTHONY, career officer; b. Beckley, W.Va., Jan. 2, 1964; s. Skip and Leigh Penny; m. Sonjia D. Napper, June 14, 1986; children: Brent Anthony, Matthew. BS in Acctg., Va. Commonwealth U., 1986; postgrad., Syracuse U., 2002—. Cert. Def. Fin. Mgr., Am. Soc. Mil. Compt. Advanced through ranks to maj. U.S. Army; co. comdr. 19th Corps Material Mgmt. Ctr., Wiesbaden, Germany, 1993-95; logistics officer 3rd Regl. Tng. Brigade, Ft. Hood, Tex., 1995-97; comptroller 13th Corps Support Command, 1997-99; program analyst Hdqtrs. U.S. Army, Pentagon, Washington, 1999-2000; comptr. assignments officer U.S. Total Army Pers. Command, Alexandria, Va., 2000—02. Contbr. articles to profl. jours. Coord. Adopt-a-Hwy., Va. Dept. Transp., Springfield, Va., 2000-01; children's Bible sch. tchr., Christian House of Prayer, Copperas Cove, Tex., 1995-99. Mem. Am. Soc. Mil. Comptrollers, Am. Soc. Pub. Adminstrs., Am. Assn. Program and Budget Analysts.

PENNY, PAUL BALDWIN, artist; b. Lawrence, Kans., July 27, 1925; s. Myrl Nuzum and Addie (Underwood) P.; m. Virginia Rae Alburty, Nov. 20, 1949; children: Alan Dean, Michael Paul, Gary Russell, Christopher Ray, Melissa Lynn Penny Swanson. Student, Bethany Coll., 1948-49; BFA in Drawing and Painting, U. Kans., 1952. Prodn. illustrator, engring. educator Boeing Aircraft, Wichita, 1952-55; supt. Penny Ready-Mix Concrete Co., 1955-60; artist Wichita, 1952-55, Lawrence, Kans., 1968—. Oil painting tchr. Adult Edn., Lawrence, 1976-78; guest lectr. H.S. Art Class, Perry, Kans., 1973, 76. One-man shows include Muchnic Gallery, Atchison, Agriculture Hall of Fame, Bonner Springs; artist numerous paintings, commnd. works. Instnl. rep. Boy Scouts Am., Lecompton, Kans.; mem. website Post Rock Opportunities Found., 1997-99, Kans. Originals Market, Wilson. Mem. Lawrence Art Guild (exhbn. mem., contbr. paintings to ann. art auction). Avocations: swimming, fishing, camping, nature walks, historial record. Home: 638 Ohio St Lawrence KS 66044-2356

PENNY, SUSAN CAROLINE VOELKER, investment manager; b. N.Y.C., July 26, 1949; d. Friedrich and Anna Voelker; m. Ralph E. Penny, Aug. 31, 1974 (div. 1989); m. Radomir Stevanovic, Mar. 14, 1992. BA, Syracuse U., 1970; MBA, Columbia U., 1972. CFA. Securities analyst Shearson, Hammill & Co., Inc., N.Y.C., 1972-73; investment analyst, v.p. The Equitable Life Assurance Soc. of the U.S., 1973-85; mng. dir. Equitable Capital Mgmt. Corp., 1985-91, sr. v.p., 1991-93, Alliance Corp. Fin. Group, Inc., N.Y.C., 1993-96; prin. August Ptnrs., LP, 1996-98, corp. fin. cons., 1998-2000; mng. ptnr. Associated Mezzanine Investors LLC, New Canaan, 2000—. Vice-chair trustees Syracuse U., N.Y., 1997—, chair trustees investment and endowment com., 1996—, trustee exec. com., 1994—, acad. affairs com., 1995-2000, mem. bd. orgn. and nominating com., 2000—, mem. adv. bd. Maxwell Grad. Sch. of Citizenship and Pub. Affairs, 1991—; bd. dirs. Elderhostel Inc., 2001—. Mem. AIMR. Republican. Lutheran. Avocations: reading, hiking, opera. Office: 436 Frogtown Rd New Canaan CT 06840-4411 E-mail: scpenny@aol.com.

PENNY, WILLIAM LEWIS, lawyer; b. Memphis, Sept. 4, 1953; s. Charles B. and Dorothy R. (Rivers) P.; m. Linda Brown, Sept. 8, 1979; 1 child, Joseph Martin. BA, U. Tenn., 1975; JD, Nashville Sch. Law, 1981. Bar: Tenn. 1981, U.S. Ct. Appeals (6th cir.) 1981. Program evaluator Office of Comptroller, State of Tenn., Nashville, 1975-80; mgr. compliance and audit Tenn. Dept. Edn., 1980-82; chief environ. counsel Tenn. Dept. Health and Environment, 1982-84, asst. commr., gen. counsel, 1984-91; gen. counsel Tenn. Dept. Environment and Conservation, 1991-92; prin. Law Firm of Manier, Herod, Hollabaugh & Smith, 1992-98; ptnr. Wyatt, Tarrant & Combs, 1998—, 1999—. Prof. environ. law Nashville Sch. Law. Bd. dirs. Hosp. Hospitality House, chmn., 1993. Mem. ABA (vice chair of programs, solid waste com., sect. energy environments and resources), Tenn. Bar Assn. (chmn. environ. law sect. 1991, 92, exec. com. 1992—), Nashville Bar Assn. (chair environ. law com.), Assn. Govt. Accts. (editor newsletter, Nashville 1977-79, sec. Nashville chpt. 1979-80, bd. dirs. chpt. 1980-84). Methodist. Avocations: music, bluegrass guitar, hiking, coaching little league sports. Home: 6501 Cornwall Dr Nashville TN 37205-3041 Office: Wyatt Tarrant & Combs LLP 2525 West End Ave Nashville TN 37203-1423 E-mail: wpenny@wyattfirm.com.

PENROSE, CHARLES, JR. professional society administrator; b. Phila., Oct. 9, 1921; s. Charles and Beatrice (d,Este) P.; m. Ann Lucille Cantwell, Apr. 17, 1943; children: James, Thomas, John. Grad., Episcopal Acad., Overbrook, Pa., 1940. Exec. sec. Newcomen Soc. N.Am. (N.A.), Phila., 1946-48; dist. sales mgr. Fitchburg Paper Co., Mass., 1948-50, 52-53; from sales mgr. to v.p. sales A.M. Collins Mfg. Co., Phila., 1953-55; sales mgr. A.M. Collins divsn. Internat. Paper Co., N.Y.C., 1955; asst. to sales mgr. fine paper and bleached bd. divsn., 1956-57; sr. v.p., CEO Newcomen Soc. in N.Am., Downingtown, Pa., 1957-61, also bd. dirs.; pres., CEO Newcomen Soc. U.S., 1961-87, chmn., 1987-89, chmn. emeritus, 1989—; sr. v.p. N. Am. Newcomen Soc., London, 1957-89, hon. v.p., 1989—. Pres., CEO Newcomen publs. in N. Am., Inc., 1958-61, trustee, 1948-61; pres., dir. Rocaton, Inc., Darien, Conn., 1960-61. Author: They Live on a Rock in the Sea The Isles of Shoals in Colonial Days, 1957. Sec., asst. treas. Chester County Investment Fund Assn., Phila., 1959-64; v.p. Brit. Am. Ednl. Found., Inc., N.Y.C., 1968-70, pres., 1970-75, trustee, 1968-81; trustee Stanley Mus., Kingfield, Maine, 1995-2000; sec. Stanley Mus., Maine, 1996-98, 1999-2000, trustee. Capt. USAAF, 1940-46, PTO; capt. U.S. Army, 1950-2. Mem. Most Venerable Order Hospice of St. John of Jerusalem (London). Mem. Newcomen Soc. U.S., Newcomen Soc. London, Royal Soc. Arts (Benjamin Franklin fellow 1980), Pilgrims of U.S., First Troop Phila. City Calvary (hon.), Nat. Inst. Social Scis., Soc. Am. Historians, Marine Hist. Assn., N.H. Hist. Soc., Mt. Washington Obs., Sandwich (N.H.) Hist. Soc. (trustee 1992-94, v.p. 1994-98), Chi Psi Omicron. Clubs: Tokeneke (Darien); Tamworth Outing (N.H.); Wonalancet Outdoors (N.H.). Republican. Episcopalian. Home: Briar Farm 232 Quaker Whiteface Rd North Sandwich NH 03259 also: 11 Mansfield Ave Darien CT 06820-4714

PENROSE, CYNTHIA C. retired health care consultant; b. Manila, Philippines, Nov. 24, 1939; d. Douglas Lee Lipscomb Cordiner and Jane (Sturgeon) Edises; m. Douglas Francis Penrose, July 11, 1959 (div. 1981); children: Vicki Flores, Lee Douglas; m. Alan Harrison Magazine, Aug. 30, 1984. BA, U. Calif., Berkeley, 1963; MBA, U. Santa Clara, 1977. Cert. social svcs. V.p., dir. employment Resource Ctr. for Women, Palo Alto, Calif., 1973-78; bus. planner Raychem Corp., Menlo Park, 1979; adminstrv. mgr. Electric Power Rsch. Inst., Palo Alto, 1979-83; sr. ptnr. MB Assocs., Washington, 1983-88; dir. ops. Utility Data Inst., 1984-85, Randmark, Inc., 1986-87; coord. market devel. for Mid-Atlantic states Kaiser Found. Health Plan, Washington, 1987-88, asst. to assoc. regional mgr., 1988-94; market planner MetraHealth, Vienna, 1995; exec. staff asst. United HealthCare, 1995, dir. strategic planning, splty. cos., 1996-97; dir. spl. projects MetraComp subs. United HealthCare, 1995, v.p. regulatory affairs and compliance, 1997-99; ptnr. Penrose Mag. LLC, 2000-01; ret., 2001. Bd. dirs., treas. Unique Enterprises, Washington, 1985-87; sec. Wesley Property Mgmt. Co., 1987-89; bd. dirs. Wesley Housing Devel. Corp., 1988-89. Chair vol. com. Habitat for Humanity, No. Va., 2002—; mem. Affirmative Action Adv. Com., Palo Alto, 1975—76; bd. dirs., sec. Am. Hospice Found., 1995—97, treas., 1998—2000; bd. dirs. Nat. Inst. for Med. Options, 1999—2001; bd. dirs., v.p. LWV, Berkeley and Palo Alto, 1966—73; chmn. program adv. com. Resource Ctr. for Women, Palo Alto, 1980—83. Mem. Peninsula Profl. Women's Network (v.p. 1981-82), U. Calif. Alumni Assn., AAUW (Bicentennial br. sec. 1986-88), Capitol Area Soc. Healthcare Planning and Mktg., Nat. Capital Healthcare Execs., LWV. Democrat. Episcopalian. Avocations: swimming, nutrition and health, reading. Home and Office: 322 S Fayette St Alexandria VA 22314-5903 E-mail: ccpenrose@comcast.net.

PENROSE, GILBERT QUAY, financial planning company executive; b. Robinson, Pa., Sept. 8, 1938; s. Albert Snyder and Olive Jeanette (Boring) P.; m. Anna Mae Riffle, Aug. 22, 1959; children: Kim Denise, Kevin Lee, Kara Lynn. BS in Chem. Engring., Pa. State U., 1960. Registered investment advisor SEC. Registered rep. Investors Diversified Services, 1969-70, div. mgr. W.Va., 1972-73, Miami, 1973-76; mgr. South Fla. region Westam. Fin. Corp., Miami Lakes, from 1976; pres. Gilbert Penrose & Assocs., Inc., Miami, from 1976. Pres., chmn. bd. dirs. Three K Investments, Inc., Swank Mgmt. Co., Inc., G & K Constrn. Co., Inc., West Fla. Mgmt. Co. Inc., Penrose Internat., Inc., Western Pa. Mgmt. Co., Inc., New Dimension Constrn. Co., Inc., New Dimension Mgmt. Co., Inc., New Expectations Realty Co., Inc., New Expectations Mortgage Co., Inc., Multi-State Mgmt. co., Inc. Chmn. bd. dirs. Miami Lakes Civic Assn., 1975-76. Mem. Internat. Assn. Fin. Planners, Assn. Cert. Fin. Planners, Palm Beach Social Club Inc. (chmn., pres. 1991—). Died Dec. 26, 2001.

PENSACK, SUSAN, elementary education educator; b. Somerville, N.J., Mar. 13, 1956; d. Charles Florence and Eloise Joyce Green; m. Rodney Drew Pensack, June 25, 1977; children: Heather, Ryan. BA in Edn., Rider Coll., 1978; MS in Edn., E. Stroudsburg U., 1991. Cert. elem. tchr. K-8, tchr. handicapped K-12, N.J. Dir. nursery sch. Surprise House, Belvidere, N.J., 1978-79; head tchr. NORWESCAP, Phillipsburg, 1979-81; impaired tchr. Washington Nursery, Washington, 1981-90; tchr. intermediate perceptually Washington Schs., 1990-91; tutor Masons/Allentown Learning Ctr., Allentown, Pa., 1998—; resource ctr. tchr. Hope Twp. Sch., Hope, NJ, 1991—2001; supr. trainee Masons-Allentown Learning Ctr., Allentown, 1999—; tchr. Lebanon Twp. Valley View Sch., 2001—; resource ctr. tchr. Lebanon Twp. Sch., Califon, NJ, 2001—. Learning disabilities tchr. cons. Lebanon Twp. Sch. Svc. unit dir./leader Girls Scouts Great Valley Coun., Allentown, 1983—; sec. Lower Mt. Bethel Sports Assn., Martins. Creek., Pa., 1986-94, treas. 1994—. Recipient Outstanding Vol. Leadership award, Girl Scouts, Allentown, 1992, Outstanding Leader, Valley Coun., 1990, Great Valley award, 2000. Mem. NEA, Coun. Exceptional Children, Internat. Dyslexia Assn., N.J. Edn. Assn., Assn. Learning Cons. Democrat. United Meth. United Methodist. Avocations: girl scouts, reading, fitness, walking. Home: 10317 Upper Little Creek Rd Bangor PA 18013-4447 E-mail: pens@epix.net.

PENSADO, OSVALDO, research scientist; b. Xalapa, Veracruz, Mex., May 31, 1971; s. Faustino Pensado and Ana María Rodríguez; m. Esperanza Ortiz-Pensado; children: Edna. BS in Physics and Math., U. de las Américas, Puebla, Mex., 1994; PhD in Engring. Sci., Pa. State U., 1998. Contbr. rsch. articles to sci. jours. Mem.: Materials Rsch. Soc., Electrochem. Soc. Avocation: playing soccer and tennis. Office: S W Rsch Inst 6220 Culebra Rd San Antonio TX 78238 Office Fax: 210-522-6081. Business E-Mail: opensado@swri.org.

PENSE, ALAN WIGGINS, metallurgical engineer, academic administrator; b. Sharon, Conn., Feb. 3, 1934; s. Arthur Wilton and May Beatrice (Wiggins) P.; m. Muriel Drews Taylor, June 28, 1958; children— Daniel Alan, Steven Taylor, Christine Muriel. B.Metall. Engring., Cornell U., 1957; MS, Lehigh U., 1959, PhD, 1962. Research asst. Lehigh U., Bethlehem, Pa., 1957-59, instr., 1960-62, asst. prof., 1962-65, asso. prof., 1965-71, prof., 1971-96, chmn. dept. metallurgy and materials engring., 1977-83, assoc. dean Coll. Engring. and Applied Scis., 1984-88, dean, 1988-90, v.p., provost, 1990-96, prof. emeritus, 1996—. Assoc. dir. Ctr. Advanced Tech. for Large Structural Systems NSF, 1986-89; cons. adv. com. on reactor safeguards NRC, 1965-86; rsch. engr., 1997—; cons. Lehigh U., 1997—. Author: (with D. Henkel) Structure and Properties of Engineering Materials, 5th edit, 2001; also articles. Recipient Robinson award Lehigh U., 1965, Stabler award, 1972, Hillman award 1997; Danforth fellow, 1974-86. Fellow Am. Soc. Metals, Am. Welding Soc. (William Spraragan award 1963, Adams Membership award 1966, Jennings award 1970, Adams lectr. 1980, William Hobart medal 1982, Plummer lectr. 1995); mem. ASTM, Am. Soc. Engring. Edn. (Western Elec. award 1986), Internat. Inst. Welding, Nat. Acad. Engring. Republican. Evang. Congregationalist (bd. trustees Evang. Sch. Theology). Home: 2586 Lynhurst Dr Bethlehem PA 18017-3940 Office: The ATLSS Rsch Ctr 117 Atlss Dr Bethlehem PA 18015-4728 E-mail: awp0@lehigh.edu. *Achievement of significant goals in our life must be balanced by the quality of that life itself, for what we are is as important as what we do.*

PENSINGER, JOHN LYNN, lawyer; b. Hagerstown, Md., June 5, 1949; s. Linford Snider and Marguerite Joan (McNeal) P.; m. Eileen Sue Howard, Nov. 7, 1972. BA, U. Md., 1971; JD, U. Balt., 1976; LLM, George Washington U., 1987. Bar: Md. 1976, D.C. 1977, U.S. Ct. Claims 1977, U.S. Tax Ct. 1977, U.S. Dist. Ct. Md. 1978, U.S. Dist. Ct. D.C. 1978, U.S. Ct. Appeals (4th cir.) 1978, U.S. Ct. Mil. Appeals 1978, U.S. Ct. Appeals (D.C. cir.) 1978, U.S. Customs Ct. 1979, U.S. Supreme Ct. 1980, U.S. Ct. Internat. Trade 1981, U.S. Ct. Appeals (fed. cir.) 1982, U.S. Ct. Appeals (5th cir.) 1986, U.S. Ct. Appeals (3d cir.) 1988, U.S. Army Ct. Mil. Rev. 1989. Mgr. E.M. Willis & Sons,

Washington, 1977-79; pvt. practice Rockville, Md., 1978-79; atty. Amalgamated Casualty Ins. Co., Washington, 1979-86; asst. gen. counsel Legal Svcs. Corp., 1986-88, sr. litigation counsel, 1988-95; atty. Office Justice Programs, U.S. Dept. Justice, 1995-96, assoc. gen. counsel, 1996—. Mem. ABA, Am. Soc. Internat. Law, Fed. Bar Assn., Med. Bar Assn. Roman Catholic. Home: 4 Stratton Ct Rockville MD 20854-6227

PENSIS, HENRI BRAM, music educator, conductor; b. Luxembourg, Mar. 18, 1927; came to U.S., 1940; s. Henri Paul and Marielouise (Deltgen) P.; m. Patricia Adams Robinson, June 14, 1951; children: Henri Paul, Claude Norris. Student, Morningside Coll., 1944-45; MusB, Northwestern U., 1950, MusM, 1951, postgrad., 1952. Conductor Chamber Orch., Evanston, Ill., 1947-51; prof., chair music dept. Salem (W.Va.) Coll., 1952-55; asst. prof., conductor orch. Cen. Meth. Coll., Fayette, Mo., 1955-65; prof., conductor emeritus U. Wis., Oshkosh, 1965-95; music dir., conductor, mem. exec. com. Oshkosh Symphony Orch., 1967-96, music dir. laureate, 1998. Guest conductor Radio Luxembourg Symphony Orch., 1964, 72, 76, 78, 82, 84, 88; conducted Orchestre Philharmonique de Luxembourg Gala Concert in honor of father's death anniversary, October 1998; mus. dir., condr. CD: 20th Century Contracts, 2002. Recipient Key to City of Oshkosh, 1976, cert. of appreciation U.S. Amb. to Luxembourg, 1976, cert. of commendation Gov. of Wis., 1988: Henri B. Pensis Day declared in his honor, 1988, Maestro Pensis Week declared in his honor, 1996; selected as an influential citizen The Oshkosh Northwestern, 1993. Mem. Assn. Wis. Symphony Orchs. (exec. com. 1976—, past pres.; hon. life mem., Outstanding Svc. award 2002), Am. Symphony Orch. League (hon.), Conductors Guild, Grand Ducal Inst. Arts and Letters Luxembourg, Phi Mu Alpha Sinfonia (life), Pi Kappa Lambda. Avocations: photography, collecting records, stereo equipment. E-mail: hbpensis@northnet.north.

PENSKAR, MARK HOWARD, lawyer; b. Detroit, Mar. 4, 1953; s. Sol Leonard and Frances (Rosenthal) P.; m. Carol Ann Stewart, Aug. 7, 1977; children: David, Rebecca. BA, U. Mich., 1974, M in Pub. Policy, 1975, JD cum laude, 1977. Bar: Calif. 1977, U.S. Dist. Ct. (no. dist.) Calif. 1977, (ea. and cen. dists.) Calif. 1983, (so. dist.) 1988, U.S. Ct. Appeals (9th cir.) 1987, U.S. Tax Ct. 1993. Assoc. Pillsbury, Madison and Sutro, San Francisco, 1977-84, ptnr., 1985-96; sr. bus. litigation atty. Pacific Gas and Electric Co., 1996—, acting sect. head comml. and contracts sect., 2001—. Mediator Superior Ct. early settlement program, San Francisco; mediator and early neutral evaluator U.S. Dist. Ct. Alternative Dispute Resolution Program; bd. dirs. Legal Aid Soc. of San Francisco Employment Law Ctr. Mem. bd. dirs. Orindawoods Assn. Mem. ABA, San Francisco Bar Assn., Commonwealth Club, Phi Gamma Delta (past pres. Bay Area grad. chpt.). Avocations: camping, golf, wine collecting. Home: 29 E Altarinda Dr Orinda CA 94563-2415 Office: Pacific Gas & Electric Co Law Dept B30A PO Box 7442 San Francisco CA 94120-7442 E-mail: MHP5@pge.com.

PENSKE, ROGER S. manufacturing and transportation executive; b. 1937; married. Grad., Lehigh U., 1958. With Alcoa Aluminum, Pitts., 1958-63, George McKean Chevrolet, Phila., 1963-65; prin. Penske Corp., Red Bank, N.J., pres., chmn. bd.; chmn. bd. dirs., pres., CEO Penske Transp. Inc., Detroit; chmn. bd. dirs., pres. Pa. Internat. Raceway, Nazareth, 1986—; CEO Detroit Diesel Corp., chmn. bd. dirs.; pres. Competition Tire West, inc., Brooklyn, Mich.; chmn., CEO United Auto Grp. Chmn. bd. dirs. Penske Truck Leasing Corp., Penske Speedway, Inc., Detroit, Penske Automotive Group, Detroit, Outer Drive Holidays, Inc., Detroit, D Longo, Inc., El Monte, Calif.; sec. Ilmore Engring., Inc., Redford, Mich. Office: Penske Corp 8801 N Haggarty Rd Ann Arbor MI 48107*

PENSLER, JAY MICHAEL, plastic surgeon, educator; b. Detroit, Apr. 29, 1954; s. Paul and Joyce (Keywell) P.; m. Laurie Ellen Olson, May 1985; children: Arielle, Alexander. BS Microbiology, U. Mich., 1976; MD, U. Chgo., 1980. Diplomate Am. Bd. Plastic Surgeons, Nat. Bd. Med. Examiners; lic. N.Y., Calif., Mass., Ill. Resident gen. surgery NYU Med. Ctr., 1980-83; resident plastic surgery U. Tex. Med. Br., Galveston, 1983-86; fellow craniofacial surgery Harvard U., Boston, 1986-87; plastic surgeon Northwestern Meml. Hosp., Chgo., 1987—. Assoc. prof. surgery Northwestern U., Chgo., 1987-93; plastic surgeon Children's Meml. Hosp., Chgo., 1987—; surf. staff Columbus-Cabrini Med. Ctr., Chgo., 1990—, Evanston (Ill.)-Glenbrook Hosps., 1992—. Contbr. articles to profl. jours. Fellow Am. Coll. Surgeons (Met. Chgo. chpt.), Internat. Coll. Surgeons (Plastic Surgery); mem. AMA, Am. Acad. Pediatrics, Am. Assn. Pediatric Plastic Surgeons, Am. Burn Assn., Am. Cleft Palate-Craniofacial Assn., Am. Fedn. Clin. Rsch., Am. Soc. Bone and Mineral Rsch., Am. Soc. Maxillofacial Surgeons, Am. Soc. Plastic and Reconstructive Surgeons, Bioelec. Repair and Growth Soc., Blocker-Lewis Plastic Surgery Soc., Midwestern Assn. Plastic Surgeons, Chgo. Med. Soc., Chgo. Soc. Plastic Surgery. Office: 680 N Lake Shore Dr Ste 1125 Chicago IL 60611-8701

PENSMITH, SHARYN ELAINE, communications executive; b. Washington, Mar. 22, 1945; d. Alfred Munk and Helen Victoria (Sollers) Lawson; m. Charles Lee Pensmith, Oct. 18, 1986. BA in Psychology, U. Md., 1967. Sales/acct. rep. GE, Bethesda, Md., 1967-75; sr. sales Nat. CSS, Arlington, Va., 1975-79, Itel Corp., McLean, 1978-80; br. mgr. On-Line Systems, 1980-82; dist. sales support AT&T, Rosslyn, 1982-84; dir. bus. devel. Govt. Systems Inc., Fairfax, 1984-96; v.p. Fed. Sources Inc., 1996-98; sr. v.p. CACI, Arlington, Va., 1998—2000; v.p. bus. devel. and sales Global Crossing, 2000—01; v.p. fed. sys. Sigaba, 2001—. Pres. ARI Consulting Group, Fairfax, 1993—. Founder Migration Methodology strategy. Annual recipient pres.'s award Infonet, 1986-96, Best of the Best Infonet award, 1992, 93, 94, 96. Mem. NAFE, Women in Tech., Inter Agy. Com., Armed Forces Comm. and Electronics Assn. Avocations: cooking, investments. Home: 775 Bon Haven Dr Annapolis MD 21401-7107 Office: CACI 1100 N Glebe Rd Ste 200 Arlington VA 22201-4797

PENSO, CHRISTINE ARETY, obstetrician-gynecologist; b. Ft. Lauderdale, Fla., Feb. 5, 1952; BS, Fla. Atlantic Univ., 1974; MD, U. Miami, 1979. Diplomate Am. Bd. Ob-Gyn., Am. Bd. Maternal and Fetal Medicine. Intern Jackson Meml. Hosp., Miami, 1979-80, resident ob-gyn., 1980-83, fellow maternal and fetal medicine, 1983-85; fellow in ultrasound and prenatal diagnosis Yale-New Haven (Conn.) Hosp., 1995-96; mem. staff St. Elizabeth's Hosp., Boston. Mem. ACOG, Am. Inst. Ultrasound in Medicine, Soc. Maternal-fetal Med., Internat. Soc. Ultrasound in Ob-gyn.

PENSON, CHARLIE FREDERICK, member of parliament; b. Grande Prairie, Alta., Can. m. Bernice Penson; 4 children. Owner, operator 2,000-acre grain and oilseed farm; M.P. for Peace River House of Commons, 1993—; ofcl. opposition industry critic, 1999—; mem. standing com. on fgn. affairs and internat. trade House of Commons, vice chmn. standing com. on industry, sci., and tech., 1999—2002; ofcl. opposition fin. critic, 2002—. Critic for internat. trade Reform Party, 1993-99. Bd. dirs. LaGlace Savs. and Credit Union. Mem. No. Alta. Rapeseed Processors (chmn.), Rural Elec. Assn. (dir.), LaGlace and Dist. Agrl. Soc. (dir., past pres.). Office: House of Commons 925 Confederation Bldg Ottawa ON Canada K1A 0A6

PENSON, EDWARD MARTIN, management consulting company executive; b. N.Y.C., Aug. 30, 1927; s. Michael and Cecile (Cohan) P.; m. Georgann Ellen McCune, June 25, 1975; children: Jeffery, Albert, Cynthia. BA cum laude, U. Fla., 1950, PhD, 1955; MA, Ohio U., 1951. Prof. communication Ohio U., Athens, 1955-75, dean, 1965-68, v.p., 1969-75; pres., prof. Salem State Coll., Mass., 1975-78; prof., chancellor U. Wis.-Oshkosh, 1978-89, chancellor emeritus, 1989—; pres. Penson-Strawbridge, Mgmt. Cons., Tallahassee, 1989—. Cons. Royal McBee, Litton Industries, Ohio Credit Union, Battelle Meml. Inst., 1963-66, U. Nev., 1980-81, OshKosh B'Gosh, Inc., 1987, Akron U., 1988, universities and sys., 1989—; bd. dirs. Valley Bank, Wis. Contbr. numerous articles to profl. jours., chpts. to books. Bd. dirs. Assn. Retarded Citizens, Salem, Mass., 1975-78; bd. dirs. Econ. Devel. Council, North Shore, Mass., 1976-78, Ohio student loan commr., Columbus, 1971-75. Mem. Communication Assn. Am., Internat. Communication Assn., Am. Assn. State Colls. and Univs., Nat. Assn. Student Personnel Adminstrs., Sigma Alpha Eta, Phi Kappa Phi, Alpha Lambda Delta, Psi Chi, Rotary (Salem, Mass. and Oshkosh, Wis.). Home and Office: 924 Summerbrooke Dr Tallahassee FL 32312-6729

PENTELÉNYI, THOMAS JOHN, neurosurgeon; b. Budapest, Hungary, Feb. 25, 1939; s. László and Anna Maria (Bohuniczky) P.; m. Mary P. Pálfalvy, Dec. 19, 1947; children: Marianne, Kinga. MD, Semmelweiss Medical Sch., Budapest, 1963, specialist of surgery, 1967; specialist of neurosurgery, Haynal Imre Univ., Budapest, 1974; PhD, Hungarian Acad. of Scis., 1978. Resident of surgery Szovetség Hosp., Budapest, 1964-66, Bajcsy Hosp., Budapest, 1966-68; resident of neurosurgery Nat. Inst. of Traumatology, 1968-73, scientific co-worker, 1974-86, head of neurosurgery, 1986-96; prof., chmn. of neurosurgery Nat. Inst. of Traumatology, Haynal Imre Univ., 1987-96; head, chmn. dept. neurosurgery Nat. Inst. of Traumatology, 1986—; prof. of neurotraumatology Semmelweis U., 1986—. Pres. Internat. Conf. on Lumbar Fusion and Stabilization/ICLFS Movement, Budapest, 1995—; mem. internat. adv. bd. Paraplegia and Spinal Cord, 1992—, mem. editorial bd. Clinical Neuroscience, 1992—; vis. prof. Univ. Chgo. Medical Sch., 1990, Univ. Tenn., 1989, Temple U., Phila., 1990, Thomas Jefferson U., Phila., 1990, U. Calif., Davis, 1990, U. Calif., Sacramento, 1990, U. Xaveriana, Bogota, Columbia, 1990; coord. Ctrl.-European Internat. Brain Injury Data-Base, 1997—; sr. cons. bd. Memphis Neuroscis. Ctr., 1989-96. Hungarian coord. Ctrl. European Internat. Brain Injury Data Base. Recipient Highest Medical Profl. award Min. of Health, 1987, Budapest, Felicitation Medalist of Indian Neurology Soc., 1994. Mem. WHO (steering com.), World Fedn. Neurosurg. Socs. (neurotraumatology com., chmn. subcom. edn.), Internat. Med. Soc. of Paraplegia, Scientific Program Com. (coun. mem.), European Fedn. Neurol. Soc. (scientist panel 1994—), Euroacad. Multidisciplinary Neurotramatology (exec. com.), Hungarian Spine Soc. (pres. 1993-95), U. Padova (hon.), Purkinje Med. U. (hon.), N.Y. Acad. Scis. (diploma), Indian Neurology Soc. (hon.). Avocations: music, philosophy, fine arts, history of family, ethical problems. Office: Nat Inst of Traumatology Dept Neurosurgery VIII Fiumei ut 17 1081 Budapest Hungary E-mail: pentelenyi@freemail.hu., atri@mail.matav.hu.

PENTKOWSKI, RAYMOND J. principal; Former supt. Battenkill (Vt.) Valley Supervisory Union, Addison-Rutland (Vt.) Supervisory Union; prin. Ludlow (Vt.) Elem. Sch. Named state finalist Nat. Supt. of Yr. award, 1989. Office: Ludlow Elem Sch Ludlow VT 05149 E-mail: rayp@ludlowelementary.org.

PENTLAND, KAREN JEAN, mental health facility administrator; b. Mich. d. Eddie and Barbara Pentland. BSW, No. Mich. U., 1997, MPA, 1999. Alcohol/substance counselor No. Mich. U., Marquette, 1992-94; rape counselor Women's Ctr., 1994-95, domestic violence shelter worker, 1995-96; direct care worker North Woods Hospice, Manistique, Mich., 1996-97; cmty. dir. March of Dimes, Marquette, 1997-99; adminstrv. intern Pathways, 1999. Author: Youth Psychiatric Directory, 1997. Mem. ASPA. Avocations: photography, sculpture, painting. Home: 1414 Gray St Marquette MI 49855-1538

PENTLETON, CAROL JUNE, visual communications designer; b. New Bedford, Mass., June 8, 1952; d. Stanley Ivan and Bertha Caroline (Best) P.; m. Eric Neil Robinson, Aug. 24, 1980; 1 child, Brett Ivan. BFA, R.I. Sch. of Design, 1974; MFA, Syracuse U., 1982. Art dir. Maxfield Advt., Providence, 1974-75, R. J. LaChance Advt., Providence, 1975-76; creative dir. Carol Pentleton & Others, Design, 1976-80; art dir. R. I. Mag., Newport, 1980; creative dir. Pentleton Advt./Design, Glocester, R.I., 1980-97; pres. Third Planet, Inc., 1993-98; sr. designer Image Makers, Providence; sr. designer, owner, creative dir. The Digital Artist, Glocester, R.I., 1998—. Adj. assoc. prof. Sacred Heart Univ., Fairfield, Conn., 1980; sec. Glocester Econ. Devel. Commn., 2001. Mem. Glocester Planning Bd., 1986-91, 93-97, chair, 1991-92, vice chair, 1993-97; mem. Glocester Comprehensive Comty. Plan Commn., 1990-94; bd. dirs. No. R.I. Comty. Child Care Assn., Glocester, 1989-91, Puppet Workshop, Providence, 1979-81; co-chair religious edn. com. 1st Unitarian Ch. Providence, 1995, chair com. on coms. 1996-98, chair adult edn. com., 2001. Mem. N.W. Art Assn. R.I. (bd. dirs., v.p. 1993, pres. 1995-98), Warwick Arts Found. (bd. dirs.), Women's Advt. Club R.I. (founding dir. Supershow), Preservation Group (co-founder, sec. 1995-96, v.p. 1996-97, pres. 1997—), Citizens for Glocester (exec. bd.). Unitarian Universalist. Avocations: genealogy, gardening. Office: 685 Chestnut Hill Rd Chepachet RI 02814-1833 E-mail: the_digital_artist@compuserve.com.

PENWELL, DEREK LEE, minister; b. Michigan City, Ind., May 18, 1965; s. Dan Lee and Gloria Louise Penwell; m. Susan Michele Parks, Sept. 26, 1967; children: Samuel Parks-Penwell, Mary Grace Parks-Penwell. MA in Religion, Emmanuel Sch. Religion, Johnson City, Tenn., 1990; MDiv, Lexington (Ky.) Theol. Sem., 1993, DD, 2000. Ordained to ministry Christian Ch. (Disciples of Christ), 1996. Min. 1st Christian Ch., Middlesboro, Ky., 1993-2001, Hurstbourne Christian Ch., Louisville, 2001—. Pres. Coop. Christian Ministries, Middlesboro, 1997-98; chair Human Concerns Com., Lexington, Ky., 2000—. Recipient Peace award Christian Appalachian Project, 2000. Mem. Middlesboro Ministerial Assn. (pres. 2000—). Avocation: reading, weight lifting, travel, writing. Office: Hurstbourne Christian Ch 601 Nottingham Pky Louisville KY 40222

PENZER, MARK, lawyer, editor, corporate trainer, former publisher; b. Bklyn., Nov. 22, 1932; s. Ed and Fay (Weinberg) P.; m. Eileen Malen, Aug. 12, 1962; children: Matthew, Nicole; m. Nydia A. Rey, Nov. 25, 1984. BBA, CCNY; JD, Fordham U. Bar: N.Y. 1968, D.C. 1973, Fla. 1982, U.S. Dist. Ct. (ea. dist.) N.Y. 1976, U.S. Dist. Ct. (so. dist.) Fla. 1991; cert. instr. DMA, 1986. Free-lance writer, 1950-83; editorial asst. Hearst mags., N.Y.C., 1955, asst. editor, 1956, assoc. editor, 1957-66; columnist N.Y. Jour.-Am., 1960-62; editor in chief Rudder mag., 1967-69, editorial dir., 1970-74; editor in chief True, 1970-73, editor at large, 1973-75; pub., editor in chief Jour. Energy Medicine, 1978-81; Medicare hearing officer Miami, Fla., 1981-82; pres. Success Internat., Inc., Coral Gables, 1984-85; adj. prof. bus. and tech. writing Fla. Internat. U., small bus. mgmt., U. Miami, 1986-89; pres. Heroica, Inc., Miami Lakes, Fla., 1989-90; pvt. practice Law Offices of Mark Penzer, Hialeah and Miami Lakes, 1991—. Tchr. creative writing Dade County Off Campus Edn. Author: The Motorboatman's Bible, 1965, The Powerboatman's Bible, 1977; asst. editor: The Path of Least Resistance, 1989, Do It!, 1991. Served with AUS, 1953-55. Mem. Hialeah-Miami Lakes Bar Assn. (pres. 1990-92). E-mail: mpenz@aol.com.

PENZIAS, ARNO ALLAN, astrophysicist, technology consultant, research scientist, information systems specialist; b. Munich, Germany, Apr. 26, 1933; arrived in U.S., 1940, naturalized, 1946; s. Karl and Justine (Eisenreich) Penzias; m. Sherry Chamove Levit, Aug. 2, 1996; children: David Simon, Mindy Gail, Laurie Shifra. BS in Physics, CCNY, 1954; MA in Physics, Columbia U., 1958, PhD in Physics, 1962; DHC (hon.) , Observatoire de Paris, 1976; ScD (hon.) , Rutgers U., 1979, Wilkes Coll., 1979, CCNY, 1979, Yeshiva U., 1979, Bar Ilan U., 1983, Monmouth Coll., 1984, Technion-Israel Inst. Tech., 1986, U. Pitts., 1986, Ball State U., 1986, Kean Coll., 1986, U. Pa., 1992, Ohio State U., 1988, Iona Coll., 1988, Drew U., 1989, Lafayette Coll., 1990, Columbia U., 1990, George Washington U., 1992, Rensselaer Univ., 1992, U. Pa., 1992, Bloomfield Coll., 1994, Rankin Tech. U., 1997, Hebrew Union Coll., 1997, Oxford U., 2002. Mem. tech. staff Bell Labs., Holmdel, NJ, 1961—72, head radiophysics rsch. dept., 1972—76, dir. radio research lab., 1976—79, exec. dir. rsch., communications scis. div., 1979—81, v.p. rsch., 1981—85; v.p., chief scientist Lucent Technologies, 1995—98, sr. tech. adv., 1998—2000; venture ptnr. New Enterprise Assocs., 1998—. Bd. dirs. Alien Tech. Corp.; sr. advisor New Enterprise Assocs., 1997—98; adj. prof. earth and scis. SUNY, Stony Brook, 1974—84, Univ. Disting. lectr., 1990; lectr. dept. astrophys. Scis. Princeton U., 1967—72, vis. prof., 1972—85; rsch. assoc. Harvard Coll. Obs., 1968—80; Edison lectr. U.S. Naval Rsch. Lab., 1979; Kompfner lectr. Stanford U., 1979; Gamow lectr. U. Colo., 1980; Jansky lectr. Nat. Radio Astronomy Obs.1983, 1983; Michelson Meml. lectr., 85; Grace Adams Tanner lectr., 87; Klopsteg lectr. Northwestern U., 1987; grad. faculties alumni Columbia U., 1987—89; Regents' lectr. U. Calif., Berkeley, 1990; Lee Kuan Yew Disting. vis. Nat. U. Singapore, 1991; mem. astronomy adv. panel NSF, 1978—79, mem. indsl. panel on sci. and tech., 1982—92, disting. lectr., 1987; affiliate Max-Planck Inst. for Radioastronomy, 1978—85; chmn. Fachbeirat, 1981—83; rschr. in astrophysics, info. tech., its applications and impacts. Patentee auction-based selection of telecom. carriers, participant tracking in conference call, remote card game using ordinary playing cards, computer-based transportation system, fraud prevention in calling cards, identifying telephone extensions in residence environment, double-encrypted identity verification sys.; author: Ideas and Information Managing in a High-Tech World, 1989, Harmony-Business, Technology and Life After Paperwork, 1995; editl. bd. Ann. Rev. Astronomy and Astrophysics, 1974—78, AT&T Bell Labs. Tech. Jour., 1978—84, chmn., 1981—84, assoc. editor Astrophys. Jour., 1978—82, contbr. over 100 articles to tech. jours. Trenton (N.J.) State Coll., 1977—79; bd. overseers U. Pa. Sch. Engring. and Applied Sci., 1983—86; mem. vis. com. Calif. Inst. Tech., 1977—77; mem. Com. Concerned Scientists, 1975—, vice chmn., 1976; mem. adv. bd. Unioin of Couns. for Soviet Jews, 1983—; bd. dirs. Coun. on Competitiveness, 1989—92. With U.S. Army, 1954—56. Named to N.J. Lit. Hall of Fame, 1991; recipient Herschel medal, Royal Astron. Soc., 1977, Nobel prize in Physics, 1978, Townsend Harris medal, CCNY, 1979, Newman award, 1983, Joseph Handleman prize in the scis., 1983, Grad. Faculties Alumni award, Columbia U., 1984, Achievement in Sci. award, Big Bros. Inc., N.Y.C., 1985, Priestly award, Dickinson Coll., 1989, Pender award, U. Pa., 1992, N.J. Sci. and Tech. medal, 1996, Internat. Eng. Cons. Fell. award, 1997, Indsl. Rsch. Inst. medal, 1998. Mem.: AAAS, NAS (Henry Draper medal 1977), IEEE (hon.), NAE, World Acad. Arts and Sci., Internat. Astron. Union, Am. Phys. Soc. (Pake prize 1990), Am. Astron. Soc. Office: New Enterprises Assocs 2490 Sand Hill Rd Menlo Park CA 94025-6940*

PENZIEN, JOSEPH, structural engineering educator; b. Philip, S.D., Nov. 27, 1924; s. John Chris and Ella (Stebbins) P.; m. Jeanne Ellen Hunson, Apr. 29, 1950 (dec. 1985); children: Robert Joseph, Karen Estelle, Donna Marie, Charlene May; m. Mi-jung Park, June 16, 1988. Student, Coll. Idaho, 1942-43; BS, U. Wash., 1945; Sc.D., Mass. Inst. Tech., 1950. Mem. staff Sandia Corp., 1950-51; sr. structures engr. Consol. Vultee Aircraft Corp., Fort Worth, 1951-53; asst. prof. U. Calif. at Berkeley, 1953-57, asso. prof., 1957-62, prof. structual engring., 1962-88, prof. emeritus, 1988—; dir. Earthquake Engring. Research Center, 1968-73, 77-80. Cons. engring. firms; chief tech. adv. Internat. Inst. of Seismology and Earthquake Engring., Tokyo, Japan, 1964-65; chmn. bd. Ea. Internat. Engrs., Inc., 1980-90, Internat. Civil Engring. Cons., Inc., 1990—. NATO Sr. Sci. fellow., 1969 Fellow Am. Acad. Mechanics; hon. mem. ASCE (Walter Huber Rsch. award, Alfred M. Freudenthal medal, Nathan M. Newmark medal, Ernest E. Howard award), Earthquake Engring. Rsch. Inst. (hon., Hausner medal), IAEE (hon.), EERI (Alfred E. Alquist award, Dist. Lectr. 2000); mem. Am. Concrete Inst., Structural Engrs. Assn. Calif., Seismol. Soc. Am., Nat. Acad. Engring. Home: 800 Solana Dr Lafayette CA 94549-5004 Office: Int Civil Engr Cons Inc 1995 University Ave Berkeley CA 94704

PEOPLES, ESTHER LORRAINE, elementary education educator, writer, publisher; b. Ames, Iowa, Sept. 18, 1933; d. Henry Francis and Hildred Cecile (Jacques) Gulliver; m. Ralph William Hill, Dec. 1951; m. Graydon Peoples, Dec. 11, 1970; children: Cathryn Louise Hill, Charles Henry Hill, Stephen Edward Hill; 6 stepchildren. BS in Elem. Edn., Drake U., 1962, MS in Edn., Curriculum and Instruction, 1967, postgrad., 1978. Cert. elem. tchr., Iowa; cert. elem. tchr., elem. prin., Ariz. Primary tchr. Glick Elem., Marshalltown, 1962-63, Grant Elem., Des Moines, 1963-65, Fisher Elem. Sch., Marshalltown, 1965-78, student tchr., coop. tchr., 1966-77, 90, intern prin., 1978; elem. tchr. Phoenix Country Day Sch., Paradise Valley, 1978-88, acting head lower sch. K-5, 1985; elem. program dir. Tesseract, 1988-91, tchr. grade 2, 1988-96; ret., 1996. Spkr. in field. Author: You Can Teach Someone to Read, A How-To Book for Friends, Parents and Teachers, 2000; contbr. articles to profl. jours. Honored by Paradise Valley Tesseract named sci. bldg. The Lorraine Peoples Sci. Ctr. Mem. NEA, Ariz. Edn. Assn., Iowa State Edn. Assn., Assn. Childhood Edn., Ariz. Pub. Assn., Small Pubs. Assn. N.Am., Ariz. Book Pubs. Assn., Mobile In Svc. Tng. Lab., Mortar Bd. Home: PMB 333 7760 E Hwy 69 C-5 Prescott Valley AZ 86314 E-mail: gelpeoples@aol.com., globkspub@aol.com.

PEOPLES, JAMES HOWARD, JR. economist, educator; b. L.A., May 14, 1959; s. James Howard Sr. Peoples, Martha Evelyn Peoples; m. Joyce Denise Coverson, Nov. 26, 1956; children: Langston. PhD, U. Calif., Berkely, 1984. Asst. prof. econs. Rutgers U., Newark, 1984—90; prof. econs. U. Wis., Milw., 1990—. Vis. assoc. prof. Northwestern Univ., Evanston, Ill., 1996—97; L'Institute fellow L'Institute, U. Ferrara, Italy, 2000—. Author: Regulatory Reform and Labor Markets, 1998; author: (with Edwin Mansfield) Microeconomic Problems: Case Studies and Exercises for Review, 10th edit., 2000. Grad. student mentor Ford Found., Washington. Fellow postdoctoral fellow, Ford Found., 1988—89; grantee, NSF, 1991—92. Mem.: Nat. Econs. Assn. (bd. mem. 1998—2001, grad. student mentor). Office: U Wis-Milw Bolton Hall PO Box 413 Milwaukee WI 53201 Office Fax: 414-229-3860. Business E-Mail: peoples@uwm.edu.

PEOPLES, JOHN ARTHUR, JR. former university president, consultant; b. Starkville, Miss., Aug. 26, 1926; s. John Arthur and Maggie Rose (Peoples) P.; m. Mary E. Galloway, July 13, 1951; children: Kathleen, Mark Adam. BS, Jackson State U., 1950; MA, U. Chgo., 1951, PhD, 1961. Tchr. math. Froebel Sch., Gary, Ind., 1951-58; asst. prin. Lincoln Sch., 1958-62; prin. Banneker Sch., 1962-64; asst. to pres. Jackson (Miss.) State U., 1964-66, v.p., 1966-67, pres., 1967-84; Trustees disting. prof. Univs. Ctr. of Jackson, 1984-85; asst. to pres. SUNY, Binghamton, 1965-66; cons. in higher edn., 1985—. Lectr. summers numerous univs. and colls. Contbr. articles to profl. jours. Active Boy Scouts Am.; bd. govs. So. Regional Edn. Bd.; bd. visitors Air U.; adv. com. U.S. Army Command and Gen. Staff Coll.; mem. Commn. Excellence Am. Assn. State Colls. and Univs.; bd. commrs. Jackson Airport Authority. Served with USMCR, 1944-47. Recipient Disting. Am. award Nat. Football Found., Presdl. citation, Lifetime Achievement award Nat. Black Coll. Alumni Found., 1993—; named to Southwestern Athletic Hall of Fame. Mem. Am. Council Edn. (chmn. dir. 1975), Am. Assn. Higher Edn. (dir. 1971-74), NEA, Miss. Tchrs. Assn., Jackson C. of C. (econ. council), Alpha Kappa Mu, Phi Kappa Phi, Phi Delta Kappa, Omega Psi Phi (Man of Year, Sigma Omega chpt. 1966), Sigma Pi Phi. Lodges: Masons (33 deg.).

PEOPLES, LINDA ERWIN, psychotherapist; b. Mobile, Ala., Mar. 29, 1954; d. James H. and Jean (Rossman) Erwin; m. Joel Davis, 1975 (div. 1980); m. Terry W. Peoples, June 1980. BA, U. Ala., Birmingham, 1979; MS in Psychology, P.W. U., New Oleans, 1993. Cert. addictions counselor, prevention mgr., clin. supr. Head counselor Birmingham Women's Med. Clinic, 1979-80; dir. pub. rels. and counselor Summit Med. Ctr., Birmingham, 1979-80; therapist, counselor, social worker Pearson Hall, 1980-83; assessments, intervention and referral counselor, 1984-87; social worker, counselor Jefferson County Nursing Home, 1987; dir. social svcs. The Nursing Home of Boaz (Ala.), 1987-88; primary counselor Bradford Adolescent Ctr., Pelham, Ala., 1988-89; counselor, aftercare supr. Pearson Hall, Birmingham, 1989-95. Author/editor: Let's Do Something (A Guide to leisure Time Activities for the Elderly of Jefferson County), 1979. Mem. Nat. Assn. Alcoholism and Drug Counselors (assn. sec. 1982-83), Ala. Alcohol and Drug Abuse Assn. (bd. dirs., Ala. state oral case evaluator for state certification), Alpha Lambda Delta. Republican. Roman Catholic. Avocations: skiing, horseback riding, handcrafts, reading. Home: Exodus Farm 664 House Rd Remlap AL 35133 E-mail: pferd@earthlink.net.

PEPE, FRANK A. cell and developmental biology educator; b. Schenectady, May 22, 1931; s. Rocco and Margherita (Ruggiero) P. BS, Union Coll., 1953; PhD, Yale U., 1957. Instr. anatomy U. Pa., Phila., 1957-60, assoc. in anatomy, 1960-63, asst. prof., 1963-65, assoc. prof., 1965-70, prof., 1970-92, chmn. dept. anatomy, 1977-90, prof. cell. and devel. biology, 1992-96, emeritus prof., 1996—. Editor: Motility in Cell Function, 1979. Recipient Rsch. Career Devel. award USPHS, 1968-73, Raymond C. Truex Disting. Lecture award Hahneman U., 1988. Fellow AAAS; mem. Am. Assn. Anatomists, Am. Chem. Soc., Biophys. Soc., Microscopy Soc. Am., Sigma Xi. Home: 4614 Pine St Philadelphia PA 19143-1808 E-mail: fpepe@cellbio.med.upenn.edu.

PEPE, JOY, art history educator; b. New Haven, Aug. 8, 1953; d. William Vito and Terese Joan (Carofano) P. Student, Sacred Heart U., Fairfield, Conn., 1971-72, U. Hartford, 1972-75; BA, Charter Oak Coll., Newington, Conn., 1985; M of Liberal Arts, Wesleyan U., Middletown, Conn., 1988; postgrad., Rutgers U., 1995—. Curatorial asst., painting and sculpture Yale Ctr. for Brit. Art, New Haven, 1980-91; assoc. prof. Lyme Acad. Fine Arts, Old Lyme, Conn., 1992—. Adj. faculty art history U. Hartford, West Hartford, 1988-98, St. Joseph Coll., West Hartford, 1989-95, U. Bridgeport, Conn., 1991-92, Albertus Magnus Coll., New Haven, 1992-94; vis. faculty Wesleyan U., 1993—, Hartford Coll. for Women, 1996; sr. advisor Lyme Acad., 1996—, chair liberal arts and scis., 1997—, chair ednl. outcomes com., 1997—. Author articles and revs. Lectr. So. Conn.Libr. Coun., Hamden, 1989—, NEH,

Groton, Conn., 1992. Recipient Pres.'s award for excellence in tchg. Lyme Acad. Fine ARts, 1996. Mem. Coll. Art Assn., Renaissance Soc. Am. Democrat. Home: 120 Front St New Haven CT 06513-3928 Office: Lyme Acad Fine Arts 84 Lyme St Old Lyme CT 06371-2333 E-mail: joypepe@aol.com., jpepe@lymeacademy.edu.

PEPE, LOUIS ROBERT, lawyer, educator; b. Derby, Conn., Mar. 7, 1943; s. Louis F. and Mildred R. (Vollaro) P.; m. Carole Anita Roman, June 8, 1969; children: Marissa Lee, Christopher Justin, Alexander Drew. B in Mgmt. Engring., Rensselaer Poly. Inst., 1964, MS, 1967; JD with distinction, Cornell U., 1970. Bar: Conn. 1970, U.S. Dist. Ct. Conn. 1970, U.S. Ct. Appeals (2d cir.) 1971, U.S. Supreme Ct. 1975, U.S. Ct. Claims 1978. Assoc. Alcorn, Bakewell & Smith, Hartford, Conn., 1970-75, ptnr., 1975-82; sr. ptnr. Pepe & Hazard, 1983—. Adj. assoc. prof. Hartford Grad. Ctr., 1972-87; dir. BayBank Conn., 1987-93; Adv. coun. Cornell Law Sch., 1990—. Mem. New Hartford Housing Authority, 1971-72, New Hartford Planning Zoning Commn., 1973-84, chmn., 1980-84, New Hartford Inland Wetlands Commn., 1975-78; mem. adv. coun. Cornell Law Sch., 1990—; dir. Capitol Area Found. Equal Justice, 1993—, pres., 1999-2001. 1st lt. U.S. Army, 1964-66. Decorated Army Commendation medal. Fellow Am. Bar Found., Am. Coll. Constl. Lawyers; mem. ABA, Am. Coll. Trial Lawyers, Am. Bd. Trial Advocates, Conn. Bar Assn. (chmn. constrn. law sect. 1989-92, chmn. standing com. on professionalism), Conn. Trial Lawyers Assn., Hartford County Bar Assn., Phi Kappa Phi. E-mail; (office). Home: 3 Metacom Dr Simsbury CT 06070-1851 Office: Pepe & Hazard Goodwin Sq Hartford CT 06103-4300 E-mail: lpepe@pepehazard.com.

PEPE, STEPHEN PHILLIP, lawyer; b. Paterson, N.J., Oct. 30, 1943; s. Vincent Attilio and Emma (Opletal) P.; m. Catherine B. Hagen, Dec. 8, 1990. BA, Montclair (N.J.) State U., 1965; JD, Duke U., 1968. Bar: Calif. 1969, J.S. Dist. Ct. (no., so., ea. and cen. dists.) Calif. 1975, U.S. Ct. Appeals (9th cir.) 1975, U.S. Sup. Ct. 1978. Assoc. O'Melveny & Myers, L.A., 1968-75, ptnr., 1976—, chmn. lab. and employment law dept., 1989-92. Co-author: Avoiding and Defending Wrongful Discharge Claims, 1987, Privacy in the Work Place, 1993, Corporate Compliance Series: Designing an Effective Fair Hiring and Termination Compliance Program, 1993, The Law of Libel & Slander, 1994; co-editor: Guide to Acquiring and Managing a U.S. Business, 1992, Calif. Employment Law Letter, 1990-94. Bd. visitors Duke Law Sch., 1992-96; bd. trustees Montclair State U. Found., 1991; bd. govs. Coll. of Labor and Employment Law, 1996—, pres., 2000—; pres. Inst. Indsl. Rels. Assn., 1989-91; bd. advisors UCLA Sch. Medicine, 2001--. With USAR, 1969-75. Fellow Coll. of Labor and Employment Law, 1996—. Mem. Am. Hosp. Assn. (labor adv. com. 1975-90), The Employers Group (bd. dirs., chmn. legal com. 1989-93), Calif. Club (chmn. employee rels. com. 1980—). Democrat. Roman Catholic. Avocations: wine collecting, wine making, wine judging, vineyard owner. Office: O Melveny & Myers 610 Newport Center Dr Newport Beach CA 92660-6419

PEPE, STEVEN DOUGLAS, federal magistrate judge; b. Indpls., Jan. 29, 1943; s. Wilfrid Julius and Roselda (Gehring) P.; m. Janet L. Pepe. BA cum laude, U. Notre Dame, 1965; JD magna cum laude, U. Mich., 1968; postgrad., London Sch. Econs. and Polit. Sci., 1970-72; LLM, Harvard U., 1974. Bar: Ind. 1968, U.S. Dist. Ct. Ind. 1968, D.C. 1969, U.S. Dist. Ct. D.C. 1969, mass. 1973, Mich. 1974, U.S. Dist. Ct. (ea. dist.) Mich., 1983. Law clk. Hon. Harold Leventhal U.S. Cir. Ct. Appeals, Washington, 1968-69; staff atty. Neighborhood Legal Svcs. Program, 1969-70; cons. Office of Svcs. to Aging, Lansing, Mich., 1976-77, Adminstrn. Aging, Dept. Health and Human Svcs., 1976-78; U.S. magistrate judge Eastern Dist., Ann Arbor, Mich., 1983—. Mem. Biregional Older Am. Advocacy Assistance Resource and Support Ctr., 1979-81; cons., bd. dirs. Ctr. Social Gerontology (1988-93); clin. prof. law, dir. Mich. Clin. Law Program, U. Mich. Law Sch., 1974-83; adj. prof. law Detroit Mercy Sch. Law, 1985; lectr. U. Mich. Law Sch., 1985-97. Editor Mich. Law Rev.; contbr. articles to profl. jours. Recipient Reginald Heber Smith Cmty. Lawyer fellowship, 1969-70; Mich.-Ford Internat. Studies fellow, 1970-72, Harvard Law Sch. Clin. Teaching fellow, 1972-73. Mem. State Bar Mich., State Bar Ind., Fed. Bar Assn., Washtenaw County Bar Assn., Am. Inn Court XI, U. Detroit Mercy, Pi Sigma Alpha, Order of Coif. Office: US District Court PO Box 7150 Ann Arbor MI 48107-7150 E-mail: Steven_Pepe@mied.uscourts.gov.

PEPELEA, KIMBERLI RAE, activities director; b. Clinton, Ind., Sept. 14, 1963; d. Charles W. and Sally Luft; m. Rockie Gene Pepelea, Sr., Jan. 19, 1990. AA, Southeastern C.C., West Burlington, Iowa, 1999; BA in Psychology and Criminal Justice, Iowa Wesleyan Coll. Cert. activity dir. Nurses aide Clinton (Ind.) Nursing Home, 1982-87; asst. activity dir. BMC Klein Unit, Burlington, Iowa, 1992-98. Avocations: cross-stitch, computers.

PEPER, CHRISTIAN BAIRD, lawyer; b. St. Louis, Dec. 5, 1910; s. Clarence F. and Christine (Baird) P.; m. Ethel C. Kingsland, June 5, 1935 (dec. Sept. 1995); children: Catherine K. Peper Larson, Anne Peper Perkins, Christian B.; m. Barbara C. Pleiter, Jan. 25, 1996. AB cum laude, Harvard U., 1932; LLB, Washington U., 1935; LLM, Yale U., 1937. Bar: Mo. 1934. Pvt. practiced, St. Louis; of counsel Blackwell Sanders Peper Martin LLP. Lectr. various subjects Washington U. Law Sch., St. Louis, 1943-61; ptnr. A.G. Edwards & Sons, 1945-67; pres. St. Charles Gas Corp., 1953-72; bd. dirs. El Dorado Paper Bag Mfg. Co., Inc. Editor: An Historian's Conscience: The Correspondence of Arnold J. Toynbee and Columba Cary-Elwes, 1986. Mem. vis. com. Harvard Div. Sch., 1964-70; counsel St. Louis Art Mus. Sterling fellow Yale U., 1936. Mem. ABA, Mo. Bar Assn., St. Louis Bar Assn., Noonday Club, Univ. Club, Harvard Club, East India Club (London), Order of Coif, Phi Delta Phi. Roman Catholic. Home: 1454 S Mason Rd Saint Louis MO 63131-1211 Office: Blackwell Sanders Peper Martin LLP 720 Olive St Saint Louis MO 63101-2338 E-mail: cpeper@ospmlaw.com.

PEPI, VINCENT, artist; b. Boston, June 25, 1926; s. Frank and Marie (DeFelice) P.; m. Teresa Gigantino, Apr. 30, 1928; children: Leonard, Diana. Student, Cooper Union Coll., 1947; cert. in painting, Pratt Inst., 1948; diploma in painting, Meschini Inst., rome, 1951. Asst. to Pericle Fazzini, sculptor, Rome, 1950-51; art dir., book designer NYU Press, 1952-54. Exhibited in one-man shows at Fordham U., Bronx, N.Y., 1962, Adelphi U., Garden City, N.Y., 1962, Hofstra U., 1979, Allene Lapides Gallery, Santa Fe, Sid Deutsch Gallery, N.Y.C., Staller Ctr., Univ. Art Gallery/SUNY, Stony Brook, 1996; exhibited in group shows at Stable Gallery, 1953, Allene Lapides Gallery, Santa Fe, 1989, Lowe Art Mus., U. Miami, Fla., Terra Mus. Am. Art, Chgo., Whitney Mus., N.Y.C., 1989-90, Katonah Art Mus, N.Y., 1990, Sid Deutsch Gallery, N.Y.C, 1990, Gallery at Bristol Myers Squibb, Princeton, N.J., 1992, Zimmerli Art Mus. Rutgers U., N.J., 1992, 93, Rosenfeld Gallery, 1992, Montclair Art Mus., N.J., 1996, Gallery at Bristol Myers Squibb, Princeton, N.J., 1992, Montclair (N.J.) Art Mus.; represented in permanent collections at David W. Bell Gallery/Brown U., Grey Art Gallery, NYU, N.Y.C., Heckscher Mus., Huntington, N.Y., Montclair Art Mus., Nat. Mus. Am. Art, Smithsonian Instn., Washington, N.J. State Mus., Trenton, San Francisco Mus. Modern Art, Tufts U. Art Gallery, Medford, Mass., Weatherspoon Art Gallery, U. N.C., Greensboro, Zimmerli Art Mus., Rutgers U., New Brunswick, N.J. Served with U.S. Navy, 1944-46, USNR, 1947-79. Home: 307 E 44th St Apt 1509 New York NY 10017 Studio: Unit C 7 Country Club Dr Coram NY 11727 E-mail: vince2526@yahoo.com.

PEPIN, JOHN NELSON, materials research and design engineer; b. Lowell, Mass., June 5, 1946; s. Nelson Andre and Leanne Florine (Boucher) P. BS in Mech. Engring., Northeastern U., 1968; MS in Aerospace Engring., MIT, 1970. Aero. engr. Bradway STOL Amphibian Ltd., Raymond, Maine, 1979; staff engr. Fiber Materials, Inc., Biddeford, 1979-84; pres. Pepin Assocs., Inc., Greenville, 1984—. Cons. Foster-Miller Engrs., Waltham, Mass., 1985-95, Johnson & Johnson Orthopedic Divsn., Braintree, Mass., 1984-86, Allied Signal Aerospace, South Bend, Inc., 1985-93, B.F. Goodrich, Akron, Ohio and Marlboro, Mass., 1986-87. Patentee in field. U.S. Dept. Transp. grantee, 1989-94, U.S. Dept. of Energy grantee, 1990-93; NIH grantee, 1994-96; U.S. Dept. Commerce grantee, 1996-99, U.S. Dept. Def. grantee, 2000—. Mem. Soc. for Advancement of Materials and Process Engring., Seaplane Pilots Assn., MIT Club of Maine. Achievements include research contributions in lightweight structures to contain turbine engine rotor failures, process to recycle plastics into automotive structures, and advanced bone replacement materials. Home: PO Box 143 Greenville ME 04441-0143

PEPIN, YVONNE MARY, artist, writer; b. San Francisco, May 28, 1956; d. Arthur Henry and Mary Alice (Ratté) P. BA, Antioch U., 1982; postgrad., Fielding Inst., 1989—, MA in Human Orgn. and Devel., 1991, PhD in Human Orgn. and Devel., 1992. Arts adminstr. Mendocino (Calif.) Art Ctr., 1978-85; founder, dir. Port Townsend (Wash.) Art Edn. Ctr., 1986—. Presenter Am. Inst. of Med. Edn. Confs., 1987, 89-94, 2000-01. Author: Cabin Journal, 1984, Three Summers, 1986. Recipient Fulbright Meml. Fund scholarship. Mem. AAUW, Am. Ednl. Rsch. Assn.. Avocations: painting, teaching, writing. E-mail: hjcarrol@olypen.com.

PEPLOWSKI, CELIA CESLAWA, librarian; b. Montreal, June 4, 1918; came to U.S., 1923; d. Stanley and Wladyslawa (Fabisiak) P. BA and BS with honors, Tex. Woman's U., 1953; MALS, U. Wis., 1955. Substitute libr. Shorewood (Wis.) Pub. Libr., 1955; cataloger, libr. periodical svcs. Arlington (Tex.) State Coll., 1955-56; head libr. English sect. U. of the Sacred Heart, Tokyo, 1956-57; base libr. Sioux City (Iowa) AFB/53rd Fighter Group, USAF, 1957-59; substitute libr. Milw. Sch. Bd., 1959-61; head tech. svcs. Milw. Downer Coll., 1961-63; cataloger, reference libr. Sterling Mcpl. Pub. Libr., Baytown, Tex., 1964-67, acting city libr., 1964-65; asst. extension supr. Mobile (Ala.) Pub. Libr., 1967-68, adminstrv. asst., pers. officer, 1968-69, internat. trade ctr. libr., 1969-70, supr. main libr., 1970-87, substitute libr., 1995—. Mem.: AAUW (historian Mobile br.), ALA, Tex. Woman's U. Alumni Assn., Wis. U. Alumni Assn., Polish Heritage Alliance Wis., Mobile Opera Guild, Beta Phi Mu, Pi Lambda Theta. Avocations: research, writing, reading, volunteer work, travel. Home: 217 Berwyn Dr W Apt 209 Mobile AL 36608-2119

PEPONIS, HAROLD ARTHUR, insurance agent, broker; b. Chgo., Dec. 12, 1928; s. Arthur Harold and Ethel (Karambis) P.; m. Toula H. Preketes, Mar. 1, 1952 (dec. Dec. 1984); 1 child, Arthur Harold II; m. Aphrodite E. Stavros, May 26, 1990. BS, Loyola U., Chgo., 1950, postgrad., 1991—. Treas. Plaza Cleaners & Dyers, Inc., Chgo., 1950-58; owner Exch. Cleaners, 1958-63; ins. agt. Aetna Life & Casualty, Lisle, 1969—95; owner Park West Plaza Cleaners, Chgo., 1963-69; ptnr. lecture series/pub. co. Images of Orthodoxy; instr. religion Plato Acad., Chgo., 1998-99; independent broker registered rep., 1995—. Pres. Tesera Assoc., Evanston, Ill., 1973—. Mem. editl. bd. Christianity and Arts mag., 1996-98. Pres. parish coun. United Greek Orthodox Chs. of Chgo., 1963—64, Annunciation Cathedral, 1991—92, 1994; archon Order of St. Andrew, Greek Orthodox Ch., state comdr., 1994—2001, regional comdr., 2001—. Recipient medal of St. Paul, Greek Orthodox Archdiocese, 1999. Mem. Pan Arcadian Fedn. Am. (nat. pres. Chgo. 1963-64), Du Page Life Underwriters Assn.. Home: 2626 N Lakeview Apt 2503 Chicago IL 60614-1821 Office: 2956 Central St Evanston IL 60201-1246

PEPPAS, NIKOLAOS ATHANASSIOU, chemical and biomedical engineering educator, consultant; b. Athens, Greece, Aug. 25, 1948; s. Athanassios Nikolaou Peppas and Alice Petrou Rousopoulou; m. Lisa Brannon, Aug. 10, 1988; 1 dau., Katherine. Diploma in Engring., Nat. Tech. U., Athens, 1971; ScD, MIT, 1973; D hon. causa, U. Parma, Italy, 1999, U. Ghent, Belgium, 1999, U. Ghent, U. Athens, 2000. Asst. prof. chem. engring. Purdue U., West Lafayette, Ind., 1976-78, assoc. prof., 1978-81, prof., 1981—, Showalter Disting. prof. of chem. and biomed. engring., 1993—. Vis. prof. U. Geneva, 1982-83, Calif. Inst. Tech., Pasadena, 1983, U. Paris, 1986, Hoshi U., Japan, 1994, Hebrew U., Jerusalem, 1994, U. Naples, 1995, U. Berlin, 2001, Complutense U. Madrid, 2001; adj. prof. U. Parma, Italy, 1987; cons. in field; mem. adv. bd. several cos. Author: Biomaterials, 1982, Hydrogels in Medicine and Pharmacy, 1987, One Hundred Years of Chemical Engineering, 1989, Pulsatile Drug Delivery, 1993, Biopolymers, 1993, Superabsorbent Polymers, 1994, Polymer/Inorganic Interfaces, 1995, Biomaterials for Drug and Cell Delivery, 1994; contbr. over 845 articles and over 300 abstracts to jours. Active Indpls. Symphony Orch., Indpls. Mus. Arts, Holy Trinity Orthodox Ch. Indpls. Recipient APV medal, Herbert McCoy award Purdue U., 2000. Fellow: AIChE (chmn. materials divsn. 1988—90, dir. bioengring. divsn. 1994—97, bd. dirs. 1999—, Materials Engring. Sci. award 1984, Bioengring. award 1994, Best Paper award 1994), Am. Phys. Soc., Italian Soc. Medicine and Scis., Am. Phys. Soc., Am. Assn. Pharm. Scientists (Rsch. Achievements Pharm. Tech. award 1999, Dale Wurster award 2002), Am. Inst. Med. Biol. Engrs., Soc. Biomaterials (pres.-elect 2002, 2002—); mem.: numerous others, Polymer Pioneer, Am. Soc. Engring. Edn. (AT&T award 1982, Curtis McGraw award 1988, G. Westinghouse award 1992), Soc. Biomaterials (Clemson award 1992), Controlled Release Soc. (pres. 1987—88, Founders award 1991, Eurand award 2002), N.Y. Acad. Scis., Am. Chem. Soc. (Newsmaker of Yr. award 2002), Sigma Xi. Avocations: linguistics (conversant in 8 langs.), opera, rare maps, classical record collecting, wine collecting. Office: Purdue U Sch Chem Engring West Lafayette IN 47907

PEPPER, ALLAN MICHAEL, lawyer; b. Bklyn., July 5, 1943; s. Julius and Jeanette (Lasovsky) P.; m. Barbara Benjamin, Aug. 30, 1964; children—Leslie Anne, Joshua Benjamin, Adam Richard, Robert Benjamin BA summa cum laude, Brandeis U., 1964; LL.B. magna cum laude, Harvard U., 1967. Bar: N.Y. 1968, U.S. Dist. Ct. (so. and ea. dists.) N.Y. 1968, U.S. Ct. Appeals (2d cir.) 1968, U.S. Supreme Ct. 1988. Law clk. U.S. Ct. Appeals for 2d Circuit, N.Y.C., 1967-68; assoc. Kaye, Scholer, Fierman, Hays & Handler LLP, 1968-74, ptnr., 1975—. Lectr. in field. Mem. exec. com., assoc. nat. chmn. Brandeis U. Alumni Fund, 1979-82, nat. chmn., 1982-85, chmn. 25th Reunion gift com., 1989, devel. com., trustee, 1982-85, pres., councillor, 1980—, mem. 35th Reunion gift com., 1999; trustee Brandeis U., 1985-95, sec., 1992-93, budget and fin. com., 1988-95, chmn. com. strategic plan, 1990-91, acad. affairs com., 1985-92, student life and phys. facilities com., 1985-89, vice chmn. ad hoc by-laws com., 1988-89, long range planning com., 1989-91, chmn. audit com., 1991-95, exec. com., 1990-91, mem. 35th Reunion gift com., 1999; bd. dirs. Styles Brook Homeowners Assn., 1990—, exec. com., 1994—; nominating com. Edgemont Sch. Bd., 1992-93; trustee Edgemont Sch. Found., 1994—; mem. 30th reunion gift com. Harvard Law sch., 1996-97, class agt., 1998-2001. Recipient Henry Jones-Golda Meier Bnai Brith Youth Services award, 1986, L.I. Press Valedictory medal, 1960; Felix Frankfurter scholar Harvard U. Law Sch., 1964-65; Louis D. Brandeis hon. scholar Brandeis U., 1964 Mem. ABA, Assn. of Bar of City of N.Y. (mem. law firm mgmt. com. 1987-91, litigation com, 1998-2001), N.Y. State Bar Assn. (comml. and fed. lit. sect., vice chmn. com. on discovery 1993-97), Brandeis U. Alumni Assn. (exec. com. 1982-87, alumni giving strategic planning com., 1992, Alumni Svc. award 1988), Phi Beta Kappa (L.I. Alumni award 1960). Lodges: B'nai B'rith (pres. Henry Jones Lodge 1982-84, mem. Westchester-Putnam council 1982-85, bd. govs. dist. 1, 1985-86). Democrat. Jewish. Office: Kaye Scholer 425 Park Ave New York NY 10022-3506 E-mail: apepper@kayescholer.com.

PEPPER, DAVID M. writer, physicist, educator, physicist, inventor; b. L.A., Mar. 9, 1949; s. Harold and Edith (Kleinplatz) P.; m. Denise Danyelle Koster, Mar. 19, 1992. BS in Physics summa cum laude, UCLA, 1971; MS in Applied Physics, Calif. Inst. Tech., 1974, PhD in Applied Physics, 1980. Mem. tech. staff Hughes Rsch. Labs., Malibu, Calif., 1973-87, sr. staff physicist, 1987-91, head nonlinear and electro-optic devices sect., 1989-91, sr. scientist, 1991-94; sr. rsch. scientist HRL Labs. (formerly Hughes Rsch. Labs.), 1994—. Adj. prof. math. and physics Pepperdine U., Malibu, 1981—; mem. adv. panel NSF, Washington, 1997, mem. U. Va. panel on advanced signal processing, 1999; mem. DARPA Def. Scis. Rsch. Coun., U.S. Govt., Washington, 1999; presenter in field. Co-author: Optical Phase Conjugation, 1983, Laser Handbook, Vol. 4, 1985, Optical Phase Conjugation, 1995, Spatial Light Modulator Technology, 1995, CRC Handbook of Laser Science and Technology, 1995; tech. referee profl. jours.; ; contbr. articles to tech. jours. including Sci. Am.; (patents) 26 U.S. patents. Mem. Sons and Daughters of 1939 Club, 2d Generation of Martyrs Meml., Mus. Holocaust. Recipient Rudolf Kingslake award Soc. Photo-Optical Instrumentation Engrs., 1982, Publ. of Yr. award Hughes Rsch. Lab., 1986, Patent award of excellence HRL Labs., 1997, 98, 99, 2000; NSF trainee Calif. Inst. Tech., 1971; Howard Hughes fellow Hughes Aircraft Co., 1973-80. Fellow Optical Soc. Am. (conf. session chair 1996, 97, 98, 99, 2000, 2001, mem. adv. bd. topical conf. on nonlinear optics, Hawaii 1996, 98, 2000, invited tutorial annual meeting laser ultrasound 2001); mem. AAAS, IEEE (guest editor, assoc. editor, mem. program com. lasers and electro-optics 1997—, instr. laser tech. 1994-2000, invited tutorial laser tech. 2001, Europeal Cleo laser conf. program com. 2003), SPIE (guest editor, conf. co-chmn. 1998, 99, 2000), N.Y. Acad. Scis., Am. Phys. Soc., Laser Inst. Am., Internat. Coun. Sci. Unions (com. on sci. and tech. in developing countries), Sigma Xi (v.p. 1986-87, chpt. pres. 1987-88, 90-91, 91-92), Sigma Pi Sigma. Jewish. Achievements include patents in field of holder 26 patents. Avocations: classical music, travel, sports, astronomy. Office: HRL Labs 3011 Malibu Canyon Rd Malibu CA 90265-4797 E-mail: dmpepper@hrl.com. *Personal philosophy: We all have a profound, meaningful purpose and mission in life—the challenge is to identify, appreciate, realize and embrace our dreams and goals.*

PEPPER, DOROTHY MAE, nurse; b. Merill, Maine, Oct. 16, 1932; d. Walter Edwin and Alva Lois (Leavitt) Stanley; m. Thomas Edward Pepper, July 1, 1960; 2 children, including Walter Frank. RN, Maine Med. Ctr. Sch. Nursing, Portland, 1954. RN, Calif. Pvt. duty nurse, Lafayette, Calif.; staff nurse Maine Med. Ctr., Portland, 1954-56, Oakland (Calif.) VA Hosp., 1956-58; pvt. duty nurse, dir. RN's Alameda County, Oakland. Mem. Profl. Nurses Bur. Registry, Maine Writers and Pubs. Alliance. Avocation: writing.

PEPPER, FLOY CHILDERS, educational consultant; b. Broken Arrow, Okla., Mar. 14, 1917; d. James Alexander and Louise Lena (Barber) Childers; m. James Gilbert Pepper, Mar. 23, 1940; children: James G., Suzanne Pepper Henry. BS, Okla. State U., Stillwater, 1938; MS, Okla. State U., 1939; postgrad., Oreg. U. Home econs. tchr. Bur. Indian Affairs, Ft. Sill, Okla., 1939-40, Chemawa, Oreg., 1940-42, Portland (Oreg.) Pub. Schs., 1945-65; instr. Portland State U., 1967-85; supr. spl. edn. Multnomah Ednl. Svc. Dist., Portland, 1965-83; orientation specialist N.W. Regional Ednl. Lab., 1983-85; curriculum writer Oreg. State Bd. Edn., Salem, 1987-90; evaluator Native Indian Tchr. Edn. Program U. B.C., Vancouver, 1987-89; cons. Indian edn. Portland Pub. Sch., 1989—. Co-author: Maintaining Sanity in the Classroom, 1971, revised edit., 1982; contbr. articles to profl. jours. Recipient Ed Elliot Human Rights award Oreg. Edn. Assn., 1996 Mem. Indian Curriculum Com. (alternative chmn. 1990-99), Oreg. Soc. of Individual Psychology, Multicultural Task Force (co-chmn. 1990-99, Dist. Svc. award 1990-91). Republican. Avocations: writing, reading, dancing, presenting workshops. Home and Office: Remembrance LLC 2200 SW Scenic Dr Portland OR 97225-4015

PEPPERS, JERRY P. lawyer; b. Cleve., Mar. 8, 1946; s. Jerry P. and Katherine M. Peppers; m. Sue E. Schafer, June 14, 1969; children: Amy E., Erica K., Christina A., Michele S. BBA, Ohio U., 1968; JD, Duke U., 1971. Bar: N.Y. 1972, U.S. Dist. Ct. (so. dist.) N.Y. 1972, U.S. Ct. Appeals (2nd cir.) 1972. Assoc. Pillsbury Winthrop LLP, N.Y.C., 1971-81, ptnr., 1982—. Bd. dirs. Firth Rixson, Inc., Rochester, NY, Monroe Forgings, Inc., Rochester, Viking Metall. Corp., Reno; mem. N.Am. pension com. The Morgan Crucible Co., Windsor, England. Editor (booklet): Outline of Mergers and Acquisitions in the United States, 15th edit., 2002. Trustee emeritus, mem. investment com. Ohio Univ. Found., Athens, 1991—; trustee Scarsdale Youth Soccer Club, Inc.; bd. dirs. Scarsdale Maroon and White Club, Atheneum Venture Fund, Athens, 1996—. Mem.: ABA, Soc. Automotive Engrs., Assn. Bar City NY, Internat. Bar Assn., India House, Fox Meadow Tennis Club (Scarsdale, NY). Avocation: coaching soccer (lic. FIFA). Office: Pillsbury Winthrop LLP 1 Battery Park Plz New York NY 10004-1490 Business E-Mail: jpeppers@pillsburywinthrop.com.

PEPPET, RUSSELL FREDERICK, accountant; b. Chgo., Oct. 3, 1939; s. George Russell and Elizabeth (Foster) P.; m. Rosemary Meyer, June 18, 1960 (dec. 2000); children— Cynthia, Jeffrey, Scott; m. Sandra S. Wharton, Feb. 2, 2002. BS in Math, Mich. State U., 1960; MBA, Northwestern U., 1963. C.P.A., Ill., Minn. Cons. Peat, Marwick, Mitchell & Co., Chgo., 1961-68, head mgmt. cons. dept. Mpls., 1968-72, partner, 1969-88; sr. cons. partner for Continental Europe, Paris, 1972-78, partner-in-charge mgmt. cons. dept., N.Y. office, 1978-81, vice chmn. mgmt. cons., 1981-86; mng. ptnr. San Jose Bus. Unit, 1986-88; v.p. internat. devel. Towers Perrin, N.Y.C., 1989-90; vice-chmn. Quirk Carson Peppet Inc., 1990-98; prin. Churchill Capital Inc., 1999—2001. With U.S. Army, 1962-64. Mem. AICPA, Country Club of Darien (Conn.). Home and Office: 15 Wildcat Rd Darien CT 06820

PEPPIN, RICHARD JOSEPH, engineer; b. Bklyn., Feb. 18, 1943; s. Harry Edmund and Betty H. Peppin; m. Cynthia E. Harrison, July 9, 1970 (div.); Melanie, Scarlett, Ashley. BS in Engring., CCNY, 1965; MSME, Rensselaer Poly., 1969; MS in Theoretical Mechanics, W.Va. U., 1966. Registered profl. engr., N.Y., N.J., Md., Ont. Sr. engr. Sci. Applications, McLean, Va., 1975-77; county noise control engr. Montgomery County Md., Rockville, 1977-79; sr. engr. Jack Faucett Assocs., Chevy Chase, Md., 1979-81; sr. scientist OSHA, Washington, 1981-85; acting chief, safety mgmt. Nat. Park Svc., 1983-85; head acoustics group Bruel & Kjaer Instruments, Marlboro, Mass., 1983-85; pres. Scantek, Inc., Silver Spring, Md., 1985-95; v.p. Indsl. Acoustics Co., Rockville, 1995—; mgr. ea. region Larson Davis Labs., 1995—. Cons. Battelle Meml. Labs., NIST, IAC, Fairfax County, State of Md. Editor: Noise Control, 1979, Community Noise, 1980. Treas. Nat. Women's Symphony, Washington, 1989-94; trustee Washington Ethical Soc., 1990-91. Fellow Soc. Automotive Engrs.; mem. ASHRAE, ASTM (chair subcom. 1982—, Wallace Waterfall awrd 1993), ASME (chair safety divsn. 1979-80, Centennial medal 1980, Dedicated Svc. award 1990), Inst. Environ. Sci. (sr.), Inst. Noise Control Engring. (bd. dirs. 1980-94, v.p. 1984-94), Acoustical Soc. Am. (working group chair 1988—). Avocations: music, dance.

PEPPLER, WILLIAM NORMAN, aviation executive; b. Hanover, Ont., Can., June 29, 1925; Student public shcs., Hanover. Can. rep. Aircraft Owners and Pilots Assn., Internat. Coun. Aircraft Owner and Pilot Assns., Ottawa, 1998—. E-mail: billpeppler@igs.net.

PEPYNE, EDWARD WALTER, lawyer, psychologist, former educator; b. Springfield, Mass., Dec. 27, 1925; s. Walter Henry and Frances A. (Carroll) P.; m. Carol Jean Dutcher, Aug. 2, 1958; children— Deborah, Edward, Jr., Susan, Byron, Shari, Randy, David, Allison, Jennifer BA, Am. Internat. Coll., 1948; MS, U. Mass., 1951, Ed.D., 1968; postgrad., NYU, 1952-55; prof. diploma, U. Conn., 1964; JD, Western New Eng. Coll., 1978. Bar: Mass. 1978, U.S. Supreme Ct. 1981. Prin., tchr. Gilbertville Grammar Sch., Hardwick, Mass., 1948-49; sch. counselor West Springfield High Sch., 1949-53; instr. NYU, 1953-54; supt. schs. New Shoreham, R.I., 1954-56; asst. prof. edn. Mich. State U., 1956-58; sch. psychologist, guidance dir. Pub. Sch. System, East Long, Mass., 1958-62; lectr. Westfield State Coll., 1961-65; dir. pupil services Chicopee Pub. Sch., 1965-68; assoc. prof. counselor edn. U. Hartford, West Hartford, Mass., 1968-71, prof., 1971-85, dir. Inst. Coll. Counselors Minority and Low Income Students, 1971-72, dir. Div. Human Services, 1972-77; cons. Aetna Life & Casualty Co., Hartford, 1962-75; hearing officer Conn. State Bd. Edn., 1980-99; exec. dir. Sinapi Assocs., 1959-78; pvt. practice, Ashfield, Mass., 1978—. Co-author: Better Driving, 1958; assoc. editor: Highway Safety and Driver Education, 1954; chmn. editorial com.: Man and the Motor Car, 5th edit., 1954; contbr. numerous articles to profl. jours. Chief Welfare Svcs. Civil Def., Levittown, N.Y., 1953-54; chmn. Ashfield Planning Bd., Mass., 1979-83; moderator Town of Ashfield, 1980-81, town counsel, Charlemont, Mass., 1983-84; mem. jud. nominating coun. Western Regional Com., 1993-99; mem. Mohawk Regional Sch. Com., 1999-2000. Mem. ABA, APA, Mass. Bar Assn., Mass. Acad. Trial Attys., Am. Pers. and Guidance Assn., New Eng. Pers. and Guidance Assn. (bd. dirs.), New Eng. Ednl. Rsch. Orgn. (pres. 1971), Am. Assn. Sch. Adminstrs., Am. Ednl. Rsch. Assn., Mt. Tom Amateur Radio Assn., Franklin County Amateur Radio Club, Elks, Kiwanis (pres. 1988-89, lt. gov. div. 12, 1991-92), Masons (master 1994-96), Shriners, Phi Delta Kappa. Home: PO Box 31 134 Ashfield Mountain Rd Ashfield MA 01330-9505 Office: PO Box 345 134 Ashfield Mountain Rd Ashfield MA 01330-9505 Home: 3808 Airport Rd Coventry VT 05855 E-mail: pepyne@shaysnet.com.

PERADOTTO, JOHN JOSEPH, classics educator; b. Ottawa, Ill., May 11, 1933; s. John Joseph and Mary Louise (Giacometti) P.; m. Noreen Doran, Aug. 29, 1959 (div. 1982); m. Marlene Rosen, Aug. 29, 1992; children: Erin, Monica, Noreen, Nicole. BA, St. Louis U., 1957, MA, 1958; PhD, Northwestern U., 1963. Instr. classics and English Western Wash. U., Bellingham, 1960-61; instr. Georgetown U., 1961-63, asst. prof. classics, 1963-66, SUNY, Buffalo, 1966-69, assoc. prof., 1969-73; prof., chmn. classics U. Tex., Austin, 1973-74; prof. classics SUNY-Buffalo, 1974-2000, Andrew V.V. Raymond prof. classics, 1984-99, Disting. tchg. prof., 1990-2000, Disting. tchg. prof. emeritus, 2000—, chmn. dept., 1974-77, dean div. undergrad. edn., 1978-82. Martin lectr. Oberlin Coll., 1987; dir. summer seminar for coll. tchrs. NEH, 1976, for secondary sch. tchrs., 1984 Author: Classical Mythology: An Annotated Bibliographical Survey, 1973, Man in the

Middle Voice: Name and Narration in the Odyssey, 1990, also articles and revs.; founding assoc. editor: Arethusa, editor-in-chief: , 1974—95, mem. bd. editors: SUNY Press, 1978—81; editor: SUNY Press Classical Series, 1981—2000, Classical Literature and Contemporary Literary Analysis, 1977, Women in the Ancient World, 1978, 1983, Studies in Latin Literature, 1984, Under the Text; co-editor: Population Policy in Plato and Aristotle, 1975, The New Archilochus, 1976, Augustan Poetry Books, 1980, Indo-European Roots of Classical Culture, 1980, Vergil: 2000 Years, 1981, Texts and Contexts: American Classical Studies in Honor of J.P. Vernant, 1982, Semiotics and Classical Studies, 1983, Audience-oriented Criticism and the Classics, 1986, Herodotus and the Invention of History, 1987, Gonimos: Neoplatonic and Byzantine Studies Presented to L.G. Westerlink at 75, 1988, The Challenge of Black Athena, 1989, Pastoral Revisions, 1990, Reconsidering Ovid's Fasti, 1992, Bakhtin and Classical Studies, 1993, Rethinking the Classical Canon, 1994, Horace: 2000 Years , 1995, The New Simonides, 1996, The Iliad and its Contexts, 1997. Fellow Center for Hellenic Studies, 1972-73; recipient Chancellor's award for teaching excellence State U. N.Y., 1975, Disting. Retiring Editor award Coun. of Editors of Learned Jours., 1995. Mem. Am. Philol. Assn. (dir. 1974-77, pres. 1990), Classical Assn. Atlantic States (exec. com. 1976-78) Office: Dept Classics State U Ny Buffalo NY 14261-0011 E-mail: peradott@buffalo.edu.

PERAHIA, MURRAY, pianist; b. N.Y.C., Apr. 19, 1947; m. Naomi Shohet, 1980; 2 children. MS, Mannes Coll. Music; student, Jeannette Haien, Artur Balsam, Mieczyslaw Horszowski; Doctorate (hon.), U. of Leeds, United Kingdom. Appeared with Berlin Philharm., Chgo. Symphony Orch., English Chamber Orch., Boston Symphony Orch., N.Y. Philharm., Cleve. Orch., Los Angeles Philharm., Phila. Orch., others; performed with Budapest, Guarneri and Galimir string quartets; frequent performer, artistic dir.: Aldeburgh Festival, 1983-89; apptd. prin. guest condr. Acad. St. Martin in the Fields, 2000; past participant: Marlboro Music Festival; recital tours in U.S., Can., Europe and Japan; recs. for SONY Classical; 1st Am. to record the Complete Mozart Concertos as condr. with English Chamber Orch., recorded complete Beethoven concertos with Haitink concertgebouw Orch. Recipient Kosciusko Chopin prize, 1965, Avery Fisher prize, 1975, Gramophone Record award, 1997, Grammy award, 1999, numerous maj. rec. awards including Leeds Competition, 1972. Office: c/o Edna Landau IMG 825 7th Ave New York NY 10019-6014

PERAINO, SHARON ANN, social worker; b. Belleville, N.J., May 26, 1961; d. Richard and Corinne Fitzsimmons; m. John Peraino III, Feb. 23, 1990; 1 child, Nathan. BSW, Kean Coll., Union, N.J., 1983; MSW, Columbia U., N.Y.C., 1989. Lic. Social Worker, N.J., Sch. Social Worker, N.J. Staff counselor, case mgr. Project Youth Haven, Paterson, N.J., 1984-88; case mgr. PSI Creative Instrn., East Orange, 1989-90; sch. social worker Bayonne (N.J.) Bd. Edn., 1990—. Active Big Brother/Big Sister, Belleville, 1982-83; vol. probation counselor Union County, N.J., 1983-85; mem. CONTACT Morris/Passaic, N.J., 1984-85. Recipient award of Merit Garden State Coalition Rsch. Project, 1987; named Sch. Social Worker of Yr. N.J. Assn. Sch. Social Workers, 1998. Office: Bayonne HS Ave A & 29th St Bayonne NJ 07002

PERAIRE, JAUME, aeronautical engineering educator; b. Barcelona, Spain, June 26, 1960; came to U.S., 1993; s. Jaime and Concepcion (Guitart) P.; m. Anna Bueno, June 26, 1993. Ingeniero de Caminos, U. Poly. de Catalunya, Barcelona, 1983; PhD, U. Wales, 1986, DSc, 1997. Lectr. U. Coll. Swansea, Eng., 1986-89, Imperial Coll. London, 1989-92, reader computational aerodynamics, 1992-93; assoc. prof. aeros. and astronautics, dir. lab. MIT, Cambridge, 1993-99, prof. aeros. and astronautics, 1999—. Dir. Computational Dynamics Rsch. Ltd., Swansea, 1987—. Contbr. articles to profl. jours. Recipient Young Rschr. award Rsch. Corp. Trust, London, 1987, Group Achievement award NASA Langley, Hampton, Va., 1989, Exceptional Achievement award NASA, 1997. Mem. Internat. Assn. Computational Mechanics (Young Rschr. award for outstanding contbns. 1998). Achievements include development of unstructured gnd methods for computational aerodynamics. Office: MIT Rm 37-451 77 Massachusetts Ave Cambridge MA 02139-4307 E-mail: peraire@mit.edu.

PERALTA, JOSEPH SORIANO, financial planner; b. Davao City, Philippines, Mar. 11, 1962; came to the U.S., 1984; s. Edward Embry and Rosamar Marfori (Soriano) P.; m. Leslie Sison-Aquino. BS in Commerce with honors, BA in Econs., De La Salle U., 1983; grad. profl. edn. program, Coll. for Fin. Planning, 1992. CFP; registered prin. series 24, registered rep. series 7; enrolled agt., lic. to practice before IRS; cert. sr. advisor. Gen. mgr. RSP Enterprises, Davao City, 1983-84; market rsch. supr. Sheer Communications, Albertson, N.Y., 1985-86; dir. fin. Apex Health Svcs./Kidney Ctr. of Vernon, Tex., 1987-89; CFP FFP Securities, Inc., Orange, Calif., 1990—; pres. Retirement Distbn. and Wealth Mgmt. Strategies, Inc., 1998—, founder, pres. Co-author: Econometric Investigation of the Debt Service Capacity of the Philippines, 1982, Role of Government in the Development of Private Investment Houses, 1983. Mem. Fin. Plannig Assn., Calif. Soc. Enrolled Agts. Democrat. Roman Catholic. Avocations: reading, travel, performing arts, basketball, swimming. Home: 737 Lakewood Pl Pasadena CA 91106-3923 Office: Retirement Distbn and Wealth Mgmt Strategies Inc 2501 E Chapman Ave Ste 230 Fullerton CA 92831-3108

PERATT, ANTHONY LEE, electrical engineer, physicist; b. Belleville, Kans., Feb. 26, 1940; s. Galvin Ralph and Arlene Frances (Friesen) P.; m Glenda Delores White, Dec. 19, 1966; children: Sarah, Galvin, Mathias. BSEE, Calif. State Poly. U., 1963; MSEE, U. So. Calif., L.A., 1967, PhD, 1971. Staff The Aerospace Corp., El Segundo, Calif., 1971-72, Lawrence Livermore (Calif.) Nat. Lab., 1972-79; guest scientist Max Planck Inst. for Plasma Physics, Garching, Germany, 1975-77; sr. scientist Maxwell Labs., San Diego, 1979-81; staff Los Alamos (N.Mex.) Nat. Lab., 1981—; sci. advisor U.S. Dept. Energy, Office of Rsch. and Inertial Fusion, Washington; vis. scientist Royal Inst. Tech., Stockholm, 1985, 88. Adv. bd. Mus. Sci. and Industry, Chgo., 1990—. Author: Physics of the Plasma Universe, 1992, Plasma Astrophysics and Cosmology, 1995; editor IEEE Transactions on Plasma Sci. Jour., 1986, 89, 90, 92, Laser and Particle Beams, 1988; co-editor Advanced Topics on Astrophys. and Space Plasmas, 1997. Recipient Award of Excellence, Dept. of Energy, 1987, Birkeland award Norwegian Acad. Sci. and Letters, 1995. Felllow IEEE, Nuc. and Plasma Soc. of IEEE (mem. exec. com. 1987-90, vice chmn. 1997, gen. chmn. internat. conf. on plasma sci. 1994); mem. Am. Phys. Soc., Am. Astron. Soc., Eta Kappa Nu. Achievements include coining of term "plasma universe"; research in modeling magnetic fields in galaxies with 3D particle-in-cell simulations and prediction of bisymmetric magnetic fields in spiral galaxies. Office: Los Alamos Nat Lab Assoc Lab Directorate F630 Los Alamos NM 87545-0001 E-mail: alp@land.gov.

PERAZA, RICHARD A. corporate communications specialist; b. Fontana, Calif., Jan. 23, 1951; s. Tony Ordaz Peraza and Helen Lopez; m. Vickie Leah Raub, July 22, 1978; children: Jennifer, Joshua. BA in Comms., Calif. Poly., Pomona, 1974. Reporter The Daily Report, Ontario, Calif., 1974—83, asst. city editor, 1983—86, polit. reporter, 1984—87; assoc. news editor So. Calif. Gas. Co., L.A., 1989—97, mktg., pub. rels. coord. Downey, Calif., 1997—98; comms. mgr. Sempra Energy, 1998—99, comms. advisor, 1999—. Vol. bd. Eagles bd. rev. troop 105 Boy Scouts Am., Fontana, 2001. Mem.: Internat. Assn. Bus. Communicators, Soc. Profl. Journalists. Avocation: camping. Office: Sempra Energy 9240 Firestone Downey CA 90239 Fax: 562-803-7534. E-mail: rperaza@sempra.com.

PERCAS DE PONSETI, HELENA, foreign language and literature educator; b. Valencia, Spain, Jan. 17, 1921; came to U.S., 1940, naturalized, 1950; m. Ignacio V. Ponseti, 1961. Baccalaureat, Paris, France, 1939; BA, Barnard Coll., 1942; MA, Columbia, 1943, PhD, 1951. Tchr. lang. and lit. Barnard Coll., 1942-43, Russell Sage Coll., 1943-45, Columbia U., 1945-47, Queens Coll., 1946-48; mem. faculty Grinnell Coll., 1948—, prof. lang. and lit., 1957—, Roberts Honor prof. modern fgn. langs., 1961-62, Richards prof. modern fgn. langs., 1963-82, prof. emerita, 1982—. Author: La Poesia Femenina Argentina, 1810-1950, 1958, Cervantes y su concepto del arte, 1975, Cervantes the Writer and Painter of Don Quijote, 1988. Mem.: Hispanic Soc. Am. (hon. assoc.), Asociacion de Cervantistas Alcala de Henares Spain (charter 1987), Cervantes Soc. Am. (founding mem.). Home: 110 Oakridge Ave Iowa City IA 52246-2935

PERCHIK, BENJAMIN IVAN, operations research analyst; b. Passaic, N.J., May 3, 1941; s. Morris and Frances (Antman) P.; m. Ellen Mae Colwell, Aug. 25, 1963 (dec. Oct. 1993); children: Joel, Dawn; m. Mary L. Westcott, Jan. 25, 1994 (div. Mar. 1997). BA, Rutgers U., 1964; postgrad., N.Y. Inst. Tech., 1964-65. Quality control rep. E.R. Squibb Corp., New Brunswick, N.J., 1964-67; edn. specialist Signal Sch., Ft. Monmouth, 1967-74, Armor Sch., Ft. Knox, Ky., 1974-75, ops. rsch. analyst, 1975-78, HQ TRADOC, Fr. Monroe, Va., 1978-80, Army Material Command, Alexandria, 1980—; exec. officer USAREUR ORSA Cell, 1988-90, chmn. supervisory com. credit union, 1985-88, 91—. Cons. Delta Force, Carlisle Barracks, Pa., 1982-84, Internat. Policy Inst., 1983-85, World Future Soc., 1982—; nat. coord. Mansa investment SIG, 1983—; coord. econ. forecasting group Met. Washington Mensa, 1983-99; chmn. security com. Watergate at Landmark, 1985-88. Author: ADP Program and Repair, 1972; writer, editor, pub. internat. newsletter Speculation and Investments, 1983—. Chmn. credit com. ComonWealthOne fed. Credit Union, 1982-85; vol. Crisis Link Hot Line; mentor offender aide and restoration Arlington County. Mem. Inst. Mgmt. Scis., Ops. Rsch. Soc. Am., Nat. Integrative Health Congress (treas.), Prayer Vigil for Earth (treas.). Office: 5001 Eisenhower Ave Alexandria VA 22333-0001 E-mail: perchikb@hqamc.army.mil.

PERCIOUS, JACQUELIN MARLYN, musician, travel writer; b. Oak Park, Ill., July 5, 1934; d. Adolph F. Krauss and Helen (Richardson) Grove-Blake; m. Donald J. Percious, June 18, 1970 (div. 1986); 1 child, Wendi. BFA in Music, U. Ariz., 1987. Radio announcer Sta. KCUB, Tucson, 1969-70; TV talk show hostess Ramey Air Force Base, P.R., 1970; dir. pub. rels. Trader Vics, St. Thomas, USVI, 1971-72; program dir. South Branch YMCA, Tucson, 1975-76; exec. dir. Mulcahy YMCA, 1976-80; spl. svcs. dir. Point Sur (Calif.) Naval Facility, 1980; exec. dir. (interim) Ott YMCA, Tucson, 1976-87; profl. musician, 1984—; sales-travel writer Worldwide Travel, 1988-99; v.p. mktg. Ariz. Backroad Touring Co., Inc., Sonoita, 1992—; asst. exec. dir. Sonoita/Elgin (Ariz.) C. of C., 1992—; exec. dir. Santa Cruz Humane Soc., Nogales, Ariz., 2000—. Freelance writer Tucson Newspapers Inc., 1993-94; bd. dir. Animal Ctrl., Zanta Internat. Contbr. travel articles to publs. Avocations: Arabian horses, riding, scuba diving, music, camping. Home: PO Box 565 Sonoita AZ 85637-0565 Office: 232 E Patagonia Hwy Nogales AZ 85621-1418

PERCIVAL, DARRYL LEE, health care executive; b. Phila., Nov. 15, 1951; s. Robert I. and Betty-Jane (Allen) P.; m. Kathleen Reynolds; children: Alexis, Dean. BS in Pharmacy, Phila. Coll. Pharm. and Sci., 1975. Registered pharmacist Pa., R.I. Mgr. bus. devel. Hook-SuperX-Brooks Drug, Pawtucket, 1989-95; sr. v.p. Pequot Pharm Network divsn. Mashantucket Pequot Tribal Nation, Ledyard, Conn., 1991-96; exec. v.p., sr. ptnr. Solutions for Health Care Group, West Greenwich, R.I., 1996-97; nat. dir. pharamcy Mariner Health Svcs., New London, Conn., 1997—. Mem. adv. bd. Novartis Co. Asst. coach Little League, West Greenwich, R.I., 1995. Grantee USPHS, 1994. Fellow Am. Soc. Cons. Pharmacists, Am. Health Info. Mgrs. Assn. Office: 125 Eugene Oneill Dr New London CT 06320-6410

PERCUS, JEROME KENNETH, physicist, educator; b. N.Y.C., June 21, 1926; s. Philip M. and Gertrude B. (Schweiger) P.; m. Ora Engelberg, May 20, 1965; children: Orin, Allon. BSE.E., Columbia U., 1947, MA, 1948, PhD, 1954. Instr. elec. engring. Columbia U., N.Y.C., 1952-54; asst. prof. Stevens Inst. Tech., Hoboken, N.J., 1955-58; assoc. prof. NYU, N.Y.C., 1958-65, prof. physics, 1965—. Dir. Nat. Biomed. Research Found. Author: (book) Many-Body Problem, 1963, Kinetic Theory and Statistical Mechanics, 1969, Combinatorial Methods, 1971, Combinatorial Methods in Developmental Biology, 1977, Mathematical Methods in Developmental Biology, 1978, Mathematical Methods in Enzymology, 1984, Lectures on the Mathematics of Immunology, 1986, Mathematics of Genome Analysis, 2001; editor: (Jours.) Pattern Recognition, Jour. Statis. Physics. With USN, 1944-46. Recipient Pregel Chemistry Physics award N.Y. Acad. Scis., 1975, Joel Henry Hildebrand award in the Theoretical and Exptl. Chemistry of Liquids, Am. Chem. Soc., 1993, Pattern Rec. Soc. award, 1992. Fellow AAAS, Am. Phys. Soc.; mem. Am. Math. Soc., Sigma Xi. Office: NYU 251 Mercer St New York NY 10012-1110 E-mail: percus@cims.nyu.edu.

PERCY, LEE EDWARD, motion picture film editor; b. Kalamazoo, Feb. 10, 1953; s. Richard Noyes and Helen Louise (Sheffield) P. Student, Goodman Sch., Chgo., 1971, Juilliard Sch., 1972; AB, U. Calif., Santa Cruz, 1977. Radio news reporter McGovern Campaign, Chgo., 1972; cons. Kjos Pub. Co., 1973-74; dir. VisArt, Ltd., San Francisco, 1977; ind. film editor L.A., 1978—. Editor: motion pictures: Re-Animator, 1984, Kiss of the Spiderwoman, 1985 (Acad. award Best Actor), Slam Dance, 1987, Checking Out, 1988, Blue Steel, 1989, Reversal of Fortune, 1990 (Acad. award Best Actor), Year of the Gun, 1991, Single White Female, 1992, Against the Wall, 1993 (Eddie award 1995, nominated for Cable ACE award), Corrina, Corrina, 1994, Kiss of Death, 1995, Before and After, 1996, Desperate Measures, 1997, "54", 1998, Boys Don't Cry, 1999 (Acad. award Best Actress), The Center of the World, 2001, Lift, 2001 (ofcl. selection Sundance Film Festival), The Believer, 2001 (winner Sundance Film Festival), Our Lady of the Assassins (La Virgen de los Sicarrios), 2001, Murder by Numbers, 2002. Mem. Am. Cinema Editors, Motion Picture Editors N.Y., Motion Picture Editor's Guild.

PERDEW, JOHN PAUL, physics educator, condensed matter and density functional theorist; b. Cumberland, Md., Aug. 30, 1943; BS, Gettysburg Coll., 1965; PhD, Cornell U., 1971. Postdoctoral fellow U. Toronto (Ont., Can.), 1971-74, Rutgers U., New Brunswick, N.J., 1974-77; prof. physics Tulane U., New Orleans, 1977—, chair physics dept., 1991-94, 2001—. Vis. scientist Nordita, Copenhagen, Argonne Nat. Lab., ETH Zurich, ITP Santa Barbara, Naval Rsch. Lab., Washington; invited lectr. more than 55 internat. confs. Contbr. more than 170 sci. articles to profl. jours. NSF Rsch. grantee, 1978—, Petroleum Rsch. Fund grantee 1998-2000; recipient Tulane LAS award for excellence in rsch., 1990. Fellow Am. Phys. Soc.; mem. Am. Chem. Soc., Am. Assn. Physics Tchrs., Phi Beta Kappa. Office: Tulane U Dept Physics New Orleans LA 70118 E-mail: perdew@tulane.edu.

PERDUE, BEVERLY E. state lieutenant governor, geriatric consultant; b. Grundy, Va., Jan. 14; d. Alfred P. and Irene E. (Morefield) (dec.) Moore; m. Robert W. Eaves, Jr.; children: Garrett, Emmett. BA, U. Ky., 1969; MEd, U. Fla., 1974, PhD, 1976. Pvt. lectr., writer, cons., 1980-86; pres. The Perdue Co., New Bern, N.C., 1985—; rep. N.C. State Gen. Assembly, Raleigh, 1986-90; senator N.C. Gen. Assembly, 1990-2001; lt. gov. State of N.C., 2001—. Bd. dirs. Nations Bank, New Bern. Bd. dirs. N.C. United Way, Greensboro, 1990-92; exec. mem. N.C. Dem. Party, Raleigh, 1989—; mem. N.C. travel bd. Nat. Conf. State Legislators. Named Outstanding Legislator, N.C. Aging Network, 1989, 92, Toll fellow Nat. Conf. State Legislators, Lexington, Ky., 1992. Mem. Nat. Coun. on Aging, Bus. and Profl. Women, Rotary. Episcopalian. Home: 211 Wilson Point Rd New Bern NC 28562-7519 : Hawkins-Hartness House 310 North Blount Street Raleigh NC 27603 E-mail: bperdue@ncmail.net.*

PERDUE, CHARLES L., JR. anthropology and English educator; b. Panthersville, Ga., Dec. 1, 1930; s. Charles L. Sr. and Eva Mae (Samples) P.; m. Nancy J. Martin; children: Martin Clay, Marc Charles, Kelly Scott, Kevin Barry (dec.). Student, North Ga. Coll., 1948-49, Santa Rosa (Calif.) Jr. Coll., 1953; AB in Geology, U. Calif., Berkeley, 1958, postgrad., 1958-59; MA in Folklore, U. Pa., 1968, PhD in Folklore, 1971. Engring. writer Convair Astronautics, Vandenberg AFB, Calif., 1959-60; geologist, mineral classification branch U.S. Geological Survey, Washington, 1960-67; asst. prof. English dept. U. Va., Charlottesville, 1971-72, asst. prof. English and sociology, anthropology depts., 1972-73, asst. prof. English and anthropology depts., 1973-76, assoc. prof., 1976-92, prof., 1992—. Cons. in field. Author: Outwitting the Devil: Jack Tales from Wise County, Virginia, 1987, Pig's Foot Jelly and Persimmon Beer: Foodways from the Virginia Writers' Project, 1992, (with others) Weevils in the Wheat: Interviews with Virginia Ex-Slaves, 1976, (with Nancy J. Martin-Perdue) Talk about Trouble: A New Deal Portrait of Virginians in the Great Depression, 1996; contbr. articles to profl.jours. With U.S. Army, 1951-54. Univ. Predoctoral fellow U. Pa., 1967-71; Wilson Gee Inst. Rsch. grant U. Va., 1974, 75; Rsch. grant NEH, 1980-81, 84; Sesquicentennial Assoc. award Ctr. for Advanced Studies U. Va. 1978-79, 87-88, 98—, Nat. Oral History Assn. award for Outstanding Book Using Oral History, 1997. Mem. Am. Folklore Soc. (exec. bd. 1980-83, book rev. editor jour. 1986-87), Mid Atlantic Folklore Assn. (founding mem., bd. dirs.), Nat. Coun. for Traditional Arts (bd. dirs. 1971-87, pres. 1973-79), Va. Folklore Soc. (archivist/editor 1974-89, archivist 1990-94, archivist/pres. 1995-96, archivist 1997—). Office: U Va Dept Anthropology PO Box 400120 Charlottesville VA 22904-4120 E-mail: clp5a@virginia.edu.

PERDUNN, RICHARD FRANCIS, management consultant; b. Trenton, N.J., Dec. 12, 1915; s. Francis R. and Edith (Nogle) P.; m. Eugenia E. Morel, June 7, 1941; 1 child, Justine Reneau; m. Doris D. Andrus, Jan. 30, 1993. BS, Lehigh U., 1939; postgrad. student, U. Pitts., 1939-40, Johns Hopkins, 1941-42. With U.S. Steel Co., also Glenn L. Martin, 1939-43, supt. machine and assembly, 1941-43; partner Nelson & Perdunn (engrs. and cons., also); v.p. Penco Corp., 1947-49; with Merck & Co., 1949-54, mgr. adminstrn., 1951-54; with Stevenson, Jordan & Harrison (mgmt. engrs.), N.Y.C., 1954-68, exec. v.p., 1962-64, pres., 1964-68; pres., chief exec. officer Bachman-Jacks, Inc., Reading, Pa., 1968-71; sr. v.p. Golightly Internat., N.Y.C., 1971—, also dir. Chmn. Perdunn Assocs., Inc., 1979— , dir. West Point & Annapolis Text Book Pub. Co., 1948— , Indsl. Edn. Films Inc., 1966— , Eldun Corp., 1964— , Security Nat. Bank, Newark, 1964— , Surburban Life Ins. Co., 1966— , Mainstem Inc., 1965— , Greenhouse Decor Inc., 1961— , Neuwirth Mut. Fund Inc., 1975— ; Lectr. on finance and mfg. in, U.S., Can., Eng., Sweden. Assoc. editor: Systems and Procedures Quar, 1948-51; Contbr. articles to profl. publs. Bd. dirs. Inst. Better Confs., Internat. Inst. Bus. Devel., Inst. Urban Affairs, People Care, Inc.; dir. finance Assn. Help for Retarded Children. Served with USAAF, 1942-47. Mem. N.Y.C. C. of C., Council Econ. Devel., Am. Mgmt. Assn., AIM (pres.'s council), Newcomen Soc. N.Am., Systems and Procedures Assn. Am., Soc. Advanced Mgmt. Address: 28 Bay Point Harbour Point Pleasant NJ 08742-5504

PEREIRA, ANTHONGY FRANCIS, priest, writer; b. Rangoon, Burma, Mar. 13, 1952; s. Harold and W. Periera. M in Theology, Grad. Theol. Union, Berkeley, 1981. Dir., chaplain Salesian Boys & Girls Club, East L.A., 1982—88; parochial vicar St. John Vianney Ch., San Jose, 1988—92, St. Simon Ch., Los Altos, 1992—96, St. Mary's Ch., Los Gatos, 1996—99, St. Martin Ch., Sunnyvale, 1999—. Singer: (albums) Celebrate Faith, 1998 (BEST CLERGY OF LOS GATOS, 1998); author: (book) Oh! For Heaven's Sakes, 2000, Comfort Those Who Grieve, 1999, Walk with Jesus Through Lent, 2000, Lord Teach Us to Pray, 2001. Named Most Oustanding Person of the Yr., East L.A. Jaycees, 1985. Home: 864 Kathryne Ave San Mateo CA 94401 Office: St. Martin Ch 590 Central Ave Sunnyvale CA 94086 Personal E-mail: padreet@cs.com. Business E-Mail: padreet@cs.com.

PEREIRA, EDGARD LUIZ, physician; b. Porto Alegre, Brazil, July 20, 1955; s. Edgard Ferreira and Lays Ramos P.; m. Dulce Beatriz Lunardon, Dec. 24, 1990; children: Nicholas Lunardon Pereira, Lucas Lunardon Pereira. MD, Fund. Fac. Fed. Ciencias, Med., Brazil, 1982. Med. staff Pronto Socorro Hosp., Porto Alegre, Brazil, 1986-94; med. dir. U.S. Gravatai/Health Dept. of Rio Grande, Brazil, 1989-91; asst. prof. radiology and neurol. surgery Neurointerventional Svc./U. Louisville Hosp., 1991—. Mem. coun. Old Town Assn., Winchester, Va., 2000—. Mem. Brazilian Acad. Neurology (mem. coun. 2000—). Achievements include being the first neurologist in U.S. to perform endovascular neurosurgery. Avocation: photography. Office: U Louisville Hosp 530 S Jackson St Louisville KY 40202

PEREIRA, JOSÉ VICENTE, theologian, educator, art historian; b. Bombay, Jan. 22, 1931; s. Aleixo Francisco Pereira and Esmeralda Rosa Monteiro; m. Maria Ângela Diniz Pereira, Aug. 5, 1965; children: Sofia, Teresa, Paulo, Mário, Carmela. BA in Sanskrit with honors, Siddharth Coll., Bombay, 1951; PhD in Ancient Indian History and Culture, St. Xavier's Coll., Bombay, 1959. Vis. prof. Instituto Superior de Estudes Ultramarinos, Lisbon, Portugal, 1959—60; rsch. asst. in the history of Indian art Sch. Oriental and African Studies, London, 1961, rsch. fellow in the history of Indian art, 1962—66; rsch. assoc. in the history of Indian art Am. Acad. Benares, Varanasi, India, 1967—69; prof. theology Fordham U., Bronx, NY, 1970—2001; ret., 2001. Author: Hindu Theology, 1976, Islamic Sacred Architecture, 1994, Baroque India, 2000. Roman Catholic. Home: 339 Hawthorne Ave Yonkers NY 10705-1831 Office: Dept Theology 441 E Fordham Rd Bronx NY 10458

PERENYI, TAMAS, internist; b. Budapest, Hungary, May 1, 1952; came to U.S., 1990; s. Bela Perenyi and Margit Godar; m. Ágnes Perenyi; children: Sofia, Gabor. MD, Semmelweis U. Medicine, Budapest, 1976. Bd. cert. diplomate in internal medicine. Intern and resident Lenox Hill Hosp., N.Y.C., 1993-96; pvt. practice, 1996—. Hospital affiliations Lenox Hill Hosp., Beth Israel Med. Ctr., Cabrini Hosp.

PERERA, LAWRENCE THACHER, lawyer; b. Boston, June 23, 1935; s. Guido R. and Faith (Phillips) P.; m. Elizabeth A. Wentworth, July 5, 1961; children: Alice V. Perera Lucey, Caroline F. Perera Barry, Lucy E., Lawrence Thacher. BA, Harvard U., 1957, LL.B., 1961. Bar: Mass. 1961, U.S. Supreme Ct. 1973. Clk. Judge R. Ammi Cutter, Mass. Supreme Jud. Ct., Boston, 1961-62; assoc. Palmer & Dodge, 1962-69, ptnr., 1969-74; judge Middlesex County Probate Ct., East Cambridge, Mass., 1974-79; ptnr. Hemenway & Barnes, Boston, 1979—. Mem. faculty and nat. coun. Hon. Nat. Jud. Coll., Reno, prof./pres. Mass. Continuing Legal Edn., Inc., 1988-90. Chmn. Boston Fin. Commn., 1969-71; overseer Brigham and Women's Hosp., Boston, Boston Lyric Opera; chmn. bd. overseers Boston Opera Assn.; chmn. Back Bay Archtl. Commn., 1966-72; trustee emeritus Sta. WGBH Ednl. Found., Boston Athenaeum, Wang Ctr. Performing Arts; trustee Social Law Libr., Boston. Fellow Am. Acad. Matrimonial Lawyers, Am. Coll. Trust and Estate Counsel; mem. ABA, Am. Bar Found., Am. Law Inst., Mass. Bar Assn., Mass. Bar Found., Boston Bar Assn.. Home: 18 Marlborough St Boston MA 02116-2101 Office: 60 State St Boston MA 02109-1800

PERES, JUDITH MAY, journalist; b. Chgo., June 30, 1946; d. Leonard H. and Eleanor (Seltzer) Zurakov; m. Michael Peres, June 27, 1972; children: Dana, Avital. BA, U. Ill., 1967; M Studies in Law, Yale U., 1997. Acct. exec. Daniel J. Edelman Inc., Chgo., 1967-68; copy editor Jerusalem (Israel) Post, 1968-71, news editor, 1971-75, chief night editor, 1975-80, editor, style book, 1978-80; copy editor Chgo. Tribune, 1980-82, rewriter, 1982-84, assoc. fgn. editor, 1984-90, nat. editor, 1990-95, nat./fgn. editor, 1995-96, specialist writer, 1997—; Yale Law fellow, 1996-97. Recipient Media award, U. Mich., 2000. Office: Chicago Tribune 435 N Michigan Ave Chicago IL 60611-4066 E-mail: jperes@tribune.com.

PERESS, MAURICE, symphony conductor, musicologist; b. N.Y.C., Mar. 18, 1930; s. Haskell Ben Ezra and Elka (Tygier) P. BA, N.Y.U., 1951; postgrad., Mannes Coll. Music, NYU Grad. Sch. Musicology. Asst. condr. Mannes Coll. Music, 1957-60; music dir. NYU, 1958-61; asst. condr. New York Philharmonic, 1961-62; music dir. Corpus Christi (Tex.) Symphony, 1961-74, Austin Symphony, 1970-72, Kansas City Philharm., 1974-80; dir. Bur. Indian Affairs pilot project Communication through Music, 1968; faculty Queens Coll., 1969-70, 83—; mus. dir. world premiere Bernstein Mass, J.F. Kennedy Center, Washington, 1971. Pub.: musical adaptation and devel. Ellington Opera, Queenie Pie; orchestrations: Ellington, New World 'a Comin', Black Brown and Beige, Bernstein West Side Story Overture; reconstrn. Gershwin's "Strike Up the Band", 1929, Paul Whiteman's Historic Aeolian Hall concert of 1924 (recorded Musical Heritage Soc.), Duke Ellington's First Carnegie Hall concert, 1944; George Antheil's 1927 Carnegie Hall "Ballets Mécanique" concert (recorded Musical Heritage Soc.); James Reese Europes Clef Club concert, 1912, First "All Negro" concert composed and performed by African Ams. in Carnegie Hall; author: Some Music Lessons for American Indian Youngsters, 1968; contbr. articles profl. jours. Served with AUS, 1953-55. Named Millicent James fellow NYU, 1955; Mannes Coll. scholar, 1955-57. Mem. ASCAP, Conductor's Guild, The Friends of Earl Robinson (pres.), Dvorak Am. Soc. (bd. dirs.), Am. Soc. for Jewish Music (bd. dirs.). Jewish. Home: 310 W 72nd St New York NY 10023-2675

PERET, KAREN KRZYMINSKI, health service administrator; b. Springfield, Mass., Mar. 8, 1950; d. Edward S. and Doris L. (Beaudry) Krzyminski; m. Robert J. Peret, June 19, 1971; children: Heather, James, Kaitlin, Matthew. BSN, St. Anselm's, 1972; MS in Nursing Adminstrn., Boston U., 1980; EdD in Orgnl. Devel., U. Mass. Amherst, 1993. RN, Mass. Staff nurse Boston VA's Hosp., 1972-73; staff nurse pediatrics Harrington Meml. Hosp., Southbridge, Mass., 1973-74, instr. edn., 1974-75, relief day asst. dir. nursing, 1975;

coordinator continuing edn. Cen. Maine Med. Ctr., Lewiston, 1975-76; asst. dir. nursing Monson Devel. Ctr., Palmer, Mass., 1977-83, DON, 1983-94; exec. nursing cons. Liberty Healthcare, Waltham, 1994-98, v.p. ops. Phila., 1998—; dir. nursing W.E. Fernald Ctr., Waltham, 1994-98; ind. mgmt. cons., 1993—. Instr. Quinsigamond Cmty. Coll., Worcester, Mass., 1972-73. Contbr. articles to profl. jours. Mem. ANA, Mass. Nurses' Assn., Am. Assn. on Mental Retardation, Sigma Theta Tau. Home: 79 Sturbridge Rd Holland MA 01521-3123 Office: 401 E City Ave Ste 820 Bala Cynwyd PA 19004-1130 E-mail: karenperet@aol.com.

PERETTI, MARILYN GAY WOERNER, human services professional; b. Indpls., July 30, 1935; d. Philip E. and Harriet E. (Meyer) Woerner; children: Thomas A., Christopher P. BS, Purdue U., 1957; postgrad., Coll. DuPage, 1980—, U. Wis., 1981—. Nursery sch. lab. asst. Mary Baldwin Coll., Staunton, Va., 1957-58; tchr. 1st grade, nursery sch. No. Ill. area schs., 1958-61; asst. tchr. of blind Glenbard E. H.S., Lombard, Ill., 1978-80; adminstrv. asst. Elmhurst Coll., 1980-81; dir. vol. svcs. DuPage Convalescent Ctr., Wheaton, 1981-95; dir. cmty. outreach Sr. Home Sharing, Inc., Lombard, Ill., 1996-97; asst. to dir. of Career Vision, graphic designer The Ball Found., 1997-98; adminstrv. asst. Christ Ch. of Oak Brook, 1998-99; asst. for comms. Lombard Mennonite Peace Ctr., 2000—02; owner freelance computer bus. Pages by Peretti, 2002—. Developer new vol. pos. for vis. the non-verbal handicapped, 1994, for Christian Svc., 2001, vol. computer tech. asst., 2001; prodr. ednl. slide programs on devel. countries, 1988-98; initiator used book collection for library project U. Zululand, S. Africa, 1997-98. Author, pub. (poetry): Poems of a Woman, 1999, Crack the Rifle in Two, 1999, To Love Cranes, 2000; editor/designer (newsletters) Our Developing World's Voices, 1994-98, The Leaflet, Nature Artists' Guild of the Morton Arboretum, 1997—, Ill. State Poetry Soc., 1997-98. Bd. dirs. Lombard YMCA, 1977-83, pres., 1980; vol. Chgo. Uptown Ministry, 1979; participant fact finding trips El Salvador, 1988, Honduras, 1989, Nicaragua, 1989, Republic of South Africa, 1991, Guatemala and El Salvador, 1997; mem. Nature Artists Guild of Morton Arboretum, exhibitor, 1992—; vol. homeless shelter, 1994-97. Recipient 1st prize for poetry, Current, Ann Arbor, Mich., 2001. Avocations: swimming, poetry writing, desktop publishing, Third World concerns, botanical watercolors.

PERETZ, CAROL, fashion designer; BFA, Parsons Sch. Design, N.Y.C., 1973. Designer Priscilla of Boston, 1973-74; owner, designer Carol Peretz, New Hyde Park, N.Y., 1974—. Mem. Fashion Group Internat. Avocations: ballet dancer, antiques collector, painter. Office: 121 Lakeville Rd New Hyde Park NY 11040-3003

PERETZ, EILEEN, interior designer; b. N.Y.C., Oct. 29, 1934; d. Leo and Mary Miller; m. David Peretz, Aug. 28, 1955; children: Deborah, Adam. BA in Fine Art, CCNY, 1956; Cert. in Interior Design, N.Y. Sch. Interior Design, N.Y.C., 1964. Interior design asst. Narden & Radoszy, N.Y.C., 1956; assoc. interior designer Renee Ross Interiors, 1964-70; chief interior designer Peretz & Marks Interiors, 1972-82; sole propr. Eileen Peretz Interiors Inc., 1970-72, pres., 1982—. Cons., mentor, lectr. Marymount Coll., N.Y.C., 1980; lectr. Fashion Inst. Tech.; cons., Paris. Publ.: Great Designers of the World, 1998; columnist for weekly newspaper Our Town, N.Y.C., 1976-79; contbr. articles to profl. pubs.; featured in Great Designers of the World. Mem. ASID (assoc.), Allied Bd. Trade. Home and Office: 300 Central Park W New York NY 10024-1513 also: 32 Rue de Varenne Paris 75007 France E-mail: epicpw@aol.com.

PEREY, ARNOLD, anthropologist, consultant; b. N.Y.C., Sept. 23, 1940; s. Samuel and Rose Lillian P.; m. Barbara Lee Allen, May 29, 1977. BA, U. Chgo., 1962; PhD, Columbia U., 1973; study of esthetic Realism with Eli Siegel, N.Y.C., 1968—78, study with Ellen Reiss, 1977—. Mem. faculty Aesthetic Realism Found., N.Y.C., 1973—. Lectr. Seton Hall U., S. Orange, N.J., 1970-71, Drew U., Madison, N.J., 1971, Bklyn. Coll. CUNY, N.Y.C., 1971; instr., assoc. prof. Queensborough Cmty. Coll., N.Y.C., 1971-76. Author: Oksapmin Society and World View, 1973; contbr. articles to profl. jours. and newspapers. Grantee NSF, 1964, 67-68; fellow USPHS, 1964-69. Mem. Am. Anthrop. Assn. Office: Aesthetic Realism Found 141 Greene St New York NY 10012 E-mail: waverly@gis.net., aperey@aestheticrealism.org.

PEREY, RON, lawyer; b. Cleve., Feb. 2, 1943; s. John Perecinsky and Anne (Nagy) Disman; 1 child, Page Suzanne; m. Janice Ash, Aug. 19, 1995. BA in Polit. Sci., Miami U., Oxford, Ohio, 1965; JD cum laude, Ohio State U., 1968. Bar: Wash. 1968, U.S. Dist. Ct. (we. dist.) Wash. 1968, U.S. Ct. Appeals (9th cir.) 1973, U.S. Supreme Ct. 1985. Assoc. Reed McClure, Seattle, 1968-71, ptnr., 1971-82, Perey & Smith, Seattle, 1982-86, Perey Langley, Seattle, 1986-92; owner Law Offices of Ron Perey, 1992—. Lectr. in field of personal injury and trial practice. Contbr. articles to profl jours. Fellow Roscoe Pound Found.; mem. ATLA (state del. 1989-90), ABA (litigation sect.), King County Bar Assn. (chmn. med.-legal com. 1989-90), Wash. State Trial Lawyers Assn. (bd. govs. 1983-85, 89-91), Am. Bd. Trial Advs. (diplomate; nat. bd. rep. 1996—, treas. 1998, v.p. 1999), Wash. State Bar Assn. (bd. govs. 1994-97), Damage Attys. Round Table. Democrat. Avocations: travel, reading, weight lifting, tennis, hiking, jogging. Office: Market Place Tower 2025 1st Ave Ste 250 Seattle WA 98121-2147

PEREZ, ANA VERONICA, developmental biology researcher; b. Lima, Peru, Jan. 27, 1962; came to U.S., 1986; d. Cesar Antonio and Ines Gladys (Marquina). BS, Cayetano Heredia U., Lima, 1984, licentiate in chemistry and biology, 1985; MA, Columbia U., 1988, MPhil, 1990, PhD in Microbiology, 1992. Jr. prof. dept. chemistry Cayetano Heredia U., 1985-86; teaching asst. dept. microbiology U. Ga., Athens, 1987, Columbia U., N.Y.C., 1989; postdoctoral fellow life scis. div. Los Alamos (N.Mex.) Nat. Lab., 1992-95; rsch. assoc. dept. biology U. N.Mex., Albuquerque, 1996-99, rsch. asst. prof., 2000-01; dir. mouse transgenic facility Ctr. for Comparative Functional Genomics, U. Albany, SUNY, 2001—. Spkr. in field; adj. faculty SUNY, 2001—. Contbr. articles to sci. jours. Recipient young scientist award Fedn. Am Socs. for Exptl. Biology, 1992; Nat. Coun. Sci. and Tech. grad. fellow Cayetano Heredia U., 1985-86; Fieger predoctoral scholar Norris Comprehensive Cancer Ctr., U. So. Calif., 1991-92. Mem. AAAS, Am. Soc. Microbiology, Am. Soc. Human Genetics. Office: One University Pl Rensselaer NY 12144-3456 Home: 39 The Crossway Delmar NY 12054

PEREZ, BERTIN JOHN, investment banker; b. Havana, Cuba, Feb. 5, 1939; s. Bertin Porfirio and Otilia Maria (Padron) P.; m. Maria Luisa Miranda, Aug. 5, 1960; 1 child, Bertin Henry. Student, U. Havana, 1958; BBA in Acctg., U. Villanova, 1960; MBA, U. Miami, Fla., 1967. CPA. Fla. Auditor/analyst Hilton Hotels, N.Y.C., 1961-63; ptnr. Laventhol Howarth, Miami, 1964-68; treas. Caesar's World, Inc., 1969-72, v.p. fin., CFO, 1973-78, group v.p., 1979-82; cons. B.P. Assocs., 1983-87; mng. dir. Perlman Enterprises, Atlantic City, 1988-89; v.p., CFO Continental Health Affiliates, Englewood Cliffs, 1990-93; sr. v.p. Printon Kane Group, Short Hills, 1993-94; pres. Brtin J. Peres & Assocs., N.Y.C., 1994—. Spkr.-lectr. Wash. State U., 1974-75. Mem. Republican Nat. Party, Washington, Nat. Geog. Soc., Washington, 1970-85, Nat. Rifle Assn., Washington. Mem. Financial Exec. Inst., Smithsonian Inst. Roman Catholic. Avocations: hunting, fishing, tennis. Home: 715 Escobar Ave Coral Gables FL 33134-7013 Office: Bertin J Perez & Assocs Rm 316 10 Rockefeller Plz Ste 1120 New York NY 10020-1903

PEREZ, CARLOS A. radiation oncologist, educator; b. Colombia, Nov. 10, 1934; came to U.S., 1960, naturalized, 1969; children: Carlos S., Bernardo, Edward P. BS, U. de Antioquia, Medellin, 1952, MD, 1960. Diplomate: Am. Bd. Radiology (trustee 1985-97). Rotating intern Hosp. U. St. Vincente de Paul, Medellin and Caldas, 1958-59; resident Mallinckrodt Inst. Radiology Barnes Hosp., St. Louis, 1960-63, mem. faculty, 1964—; prof. radiation oncology Mallinckrodt Inst. Radiology Washington U., 1972—, dir. radiation oncology ctr., 1976—. Fellow radiotherapy M.D. Anderson Hosp. and Tumor Inst., U. Tex., Houston, 1963-64. Co-editor: Principles and Clinical Practice of Radiation Oncology, Principles and Practice of Gynecologic Oncology; mem. editl. bd. Internat. Jour. Radiation and Physics, 1975—, Cancer, 1993—; contbr. articles to med. jours. Recipient Am. Coll. of Radiology Gold Medal award, 1997. Fellow Am. Coll. Radiology; mem. AAAS, AMA, Am. Soc. Clin. Oncology, Am. Soc. Therapeutic Radiologists (pres. 1981-82, Gold medal 1992), Am. Radium Soc., Am. Assn. Cancer Rsch., Am. Assn. Cancer Edn., Radiol. Soc. N.Am., Mo. Radiol. Soc., Mo. Acad. Sci., Mo. Med. Soc., St. Louis Med. Soc., Greater St. Louis Soc. Radiologists, Radiation Rsch. Soc. Office: Washington U Radiation Oncology Ctr 4511 Forest Park Ave Ste 200 Saint Louis MO 63108-2190 Home: # 1204 8025 Bonhomme Ave Saint Louis MO 63105-3501 E-mail: perez@radonc.wustl.edu., caperez2@mehsi.com.

PEREZ, CARLOS F. health facility administrator; BS, Hobart Coll., 1974; MPA, NYU, 1974-76. Adminstrv. intern Kings County Hosp., NYU Med. Ctr., Bronx Psychiat. Ctr., 1973-75; adminstrv. asst. to dep. commr. N.Y.C. Dept. Health, 1975-76; adminstrv. resident Met. Hosp. Ctr., N.Y.C., 1975-77; night-weekend adminstr. Bronx Psychiat. Ctr., 1975-77; assoc. dir. Queens Hosp. Ctr., Jamaica, N.Y., 1977-78; sr. mental health program analyst Health and Hosp. Corp., N.Y.C., 1981-83; dep. area adminstr. N.Y. State Dept. Health, 1983-89, dir. hosp. surveillance, 1988-89, area adminstr. N.Y.C. Office Health Sys. Mgmt., 1988-95, v.p. for network devel. mental health divsn., 1995—; sr. v.p., exec. dir. N.Y.C. H.H.C. Bellevue Hosp., 1997—. Presenter numerous papers. Recipient Peter B. Schwab Meml. trust fund scholarship, 1973-74, 75-76; Martin Luther King fellow, 1974. Mem. Nat. Assn. Health Svcs. Execs., Hispanic Assn. Health Svcs. Execs., Assn. Univ. Programs in Hosp. Adminstrn., P.R. Health Svcs. Fedn. Office: Bellevue Hosp Ctr 462 1st Ave New York NY 10016-9196*

PEREZ, CAROL ANNE, rehabilitation services professional, consultant; b. N.Y.C., Dec. 9, 1935; d. Paul Nesnow and Lillian (Nesnow) Oxhandler; m. Charles Clift Perez, Mar. 11, 1956; children: Rosanne Perez Sterne, Daniel Paul. AA, Queen's Coll., 1956; BS, Northeastern U., 1970, MEd, 1972. Cert. rehab. counselor. Rehab. counselor Middlesex Hosp., Waltham, Mass., 1972-73, Mass. Rehab. Commn., Cambridge, 1973-75, supr. Concord and Newton, 1975-77, area dir. Cambridge, 1977-89, Malden, 1989-92; exec. dir. Facioscapulo Humeral Soc., Lexington, Mass., 1992—; pvt. rehab. cons., 1992—. Mem. Pvt. and Industry Coun., Cambridge, 1987-92; chair Human Svc. Commn., Lexington, 1980-82, Interagy. Group, Cambridge, 1977-89, Malden, 1989-92. Author, editor (newsletter) FSH Watch. Pres. MIT Dames, Cambridge, 1960-62; support group leader Muscular Dystrophy Assn., Waltham, 1989—. Avocations: swimming, travel. Office: FSH Society Inc 3 Westwood Rd Lexington MA 02420-1833

PEREZ, EDDIE A. mayor; b. 1957; m. Maria Perez; 2 children. AAS in Liberal Arts, Capital Cmty. Coll.; BA in Econs., Trinity Coll. Assoc. v.p. cmty. and govt. rels. Trinity Coll.; mayor City of Hartford, Hartford , Conn., 2002—. Exec. dir., chmn. Southside Instns. Neighborhood Alliance, Inc. (SINA); vol. VISTA, 1978; founder, dir. O.N.E./C.H.A.N.E., Inc., North Hartford; dir. program MASH (Make Something Happen), Urban League Greater Hartford, Conn. Puerto Rican Forum; former commr. Met. Dist.; established teen pregnancy program Breaking the Cycle; MetroHartford Regional Econ. Alliance. Office: 550 Main St Hartford CT 06103*

PEREZ, ERNEST R. librarian; b. San Marcos, Tex., May 10, 1943; s. Guadalupe Sebastian and Susie Gonzalez Perez; m. Sandra Jean Meredith, Dec. 3, 1983; children: Alecia Spillman, Elaine Howard, Alison May. BA in Journalism, U. Tex., El Paso, 1964; MLS, U. Tex., Austin, 1969; PhD, Tex. Woman's U., 1991. Libr. dir. Houston Chronicle, 1971-78, Chgo. Sun-Times, 1978-88; program group leader Oreg. State Libr., Salem, 1992—. Sr. cons. Access Info. Assocs., Inc., Houston, 1991-92. Bd. dirs. Unitarian Universalist Congregation, Salem, Oreg., 1999—. 1st lt. U.S. Army,1965-67, Fed. Rep. of Germany. Mem. ALA, Spl. Libraries Assn. (Henebry Roll of Honor 1987). Office: Oreg State Libr 250 Winter St NE Salem OR 97301

PEREZ, FELIPE PABLO, physician; b. Arequipa, Peru, Jan. 15, 1958; s. Julio Justo and Blanca Cecilia Perez; m. Magali Nancy Chumbiauca, Jan. 22, 1989; children: Felipe, Cristina, Carmen, Nancy. MD, Villarreal U., Lima, Peru. Bd. cert. internal medicine and geriat. medicine. Physician West Suburban Hosp., Oak Park, Ill.; fellow Loyola U., Maywood; attending physician Mercy Hosp., Chgo.; faculty U. Ill. E-mail: fperez04@uic.edu.

PEREZ, JORGE LUIS, retired manufacturing executive; b. Jaguey Grande, Matanzas, Cuba, Nov. 29, 1945; came to U.S., 1960; s. Adalberto Aquileo and Esther Mireya (Haedo) P.; children: Jorge Alejandro, Ricardo Javier, Ruben Luis. BS in Commerce & Engring. Sci., Drexel U., 1969, MBA, 1981. Jr. indsl. engr. IBM Corp., East Fishkill, N.Y., 1969-70, assoc. indsl. engr., 1970-71, sr. assoc. indsl. engr., 1972-75, staff indusl. engr., 1976-77, ops. rsch. analyst Princeton, N.J., 1977-80, fin. program adminstr. Franklin Lakes, N.J., 1980-82, mgr. production control Boca Raton, Fla., 1983-85, project mgr. div., 1986-88, program mgr., 1988-92, ret., 1992. Pres. Presch. Mgmt., Inc., 1999; ind. cons. Eclipse Group. Author: (manuals) Machine Tooling, Transportation Forecasting, Workload Planning, Measurement, 1972-81. Exec. com. Palm Beach (Fla.) County Rep. Party, 1989; pres., bd. dirs. Palm Beach Farm Workers Coun., 1989; pres. presch. Mgmt., Inc. Mem. Am. Prodn. & Inventory Control Soc. (v.p. membership com. 1984-85), Inst. Indsl. Engrs. (sr. mem., pres. 1974-75, excellence award, 1975). Republican. Roman Catholic. Avocations: boating, fishing, scuba diving, reading. Home and Office: 10920 Paso Fino Dr Lake Worth FL 33467 E-mail: jlph55@cs.com.

PEREZ, JOSEPHINE, psychiatrist, physician, educator; b. Tijuana, Mex., Feb. 10, 1941; came to the U.S., 1960, U.S. citizenship, 1968. BS in Biology, U. Santiago de Compostela, Spain, 1971, MD, 1975. Nuc. medicine technician, EEG technician, supr. Electrographic Labs., Encino, Calif., 1963-71; clerkships in internal medicine, gen. surgery, otorhinolaryngology, dermatology and venereology Gen. Hosp. of Galicia, Spain, 1972-75; resident in gen. psychiatry U. Miami, Jackson Meml. Hosp. and VA Hosp., Miami, Fla., 1976-78; practice medicine specializing in psychiatry, marital and family therapy, individual psychotherapy, 1979—. Emergency room physician Miami Dade Hosp., 1975; attending psychiatrist Jackson Meml. Hosp., 1979—, asst. dir. adolescent psychiat. unit, 1979-83; mem. clin. faculty U. Miami Sch. Medicine, 1979—, clin. instr. psychiatry, 1979—. Mem. AMA (Physicians' Recognition award 1980, 83, 86, 89, 98, 2000), Am. Assn. for Marital and Family Therapy (cert. clin. mem., treas. 1982-84, pres.-elect 1985-87, pres. 1987-89), Am. Psychiat. Assn., Am. Med. Women's Assn., Assn. Women Psychiatrists, Fla. Psychiat. Soc., South Dade Women Physicians Assn. Office: 420 S Dixie Hwy Ste 4A Coral Gables FL 33146-2228

PEREZ, JULIE ANNA, audio engineer; b. Miami, Fla., Sept. 2, 1961; d. Miguel Angel and Dorothy Elizabeth (Headford) P. Student, U. Miami, 1979-83. Audio engr. NBC, Inc., N.Y.C., 1984—; pres. BDC Prodns. Ltd. Asst. music mixer (TV shows) Saturday Night Live, 1987-93, Late Night with David Letterman 7th Anniversary Spl., 1989; music mixer Late Night with David Letterman, summer 1989, Late Night in L.A. with Conan O'Brien, 1993—; audio engr. Later with Bob Costas, Friday Night Videos, Brokaw Reports; co-founder TECHNET, Nabet Diversity Com.; sem. chair AES Women in Audio, 1991, Saturday Night Live, 1993. Editor: Music Engring. Tech. newsletter, 1983; audio engr. TV talk-show Donahue, 1985-87 (Emmy nomination); recorded and mixed Live from 6A, CD music performances from Late Night with Conan O'Brien; music mixer (NBC Millennium Spl.) Sting Concert Live from Studio 8H. Contbr. Planned Parenthood Fedn. Am., 1986—, Women in the Arts. Recipient Down Beat award Down Beat mag., 1982, Best Engineered Live Performance award Down Beat mag. Mem. NARAS, NOW, ACLU, NATAS, (Emmy nomination for sound mixing 1986), Acad. TV Arts and Scis. (Emmy nomination for sound mixing 1993), Audio Engring. Soc., Nat. Assn. Broadcast Employees and Technicians (co-chair local diversity com.), Women in Music. Democrat. Office: NBC Inc 30 Rockefeller Plz Rm 901W2 New York NY 10112-0002

PEREZ, LEYANNE C. nutritionist, consultant; b. Habana, Cuba, Dec. 7, 1966; d. Andres and Teresa Perez; m. Guillermo Jose Cuevas, Mar. 9, 1996; children: Fernando J. Cuevas. Assoc. Arts, Miami Dade CC, Miami, FL, 1989; BS, Fla. Internat. U., Miami, FL, 1992. Cert. RDLD Am. Dietetic Assn. Nutritional specialist NutriSystem, Miami, Fla., 1990—92; cons. dietitian Med. Offices Miami Lakes, 1992—95; clin. dietitian Cedars Med. Ctr., 1993—95; clininical dietitian Hialeah Hosp., 1995—96; cons. dietitian and corp. mem. Nutrition & Wellness Consultants, 1995—99; regional cons. to chief clin. cons. Integrated Health Services, 1996—2001; owner, mgr. The Floridian Day Spa Salon & Nutritional Inst., 2001—, dietitian, 2001—. Author: (book) The Ultimate Diet - A Journey into the new Millennium. Mem.: Am. Fedn. Astrologers, Am. Dietetic Assn. R-Consevative. Avocations: reading, writing, stydying, decoration. Office: The Foridian Day Spa 7160 W 20th Avenue Suite M 133 Hialeah FL 33016 Office Fax: 305-828-0554.

PEREZ, LILLIAN, Spanish language educator; b. N.Y.C., Mar. 3, 1957; d. Gilberto and Aida Luz (Velazquez) P. BA Polit. Sci., Spanish, Rutgers U., 1979; MPA in Pub. Fin. Mgmt., Am. U., 1985, MBA in Mgmt. and Industrial Rels., 1988; postgrad. advanced studies, Catholic U., 1995—. Cert. budget analyst. Community devel. intern Met. Washington Coun. Govts., Washington, 1983-84; fin. mgmt. intern IRS, 1984-85; program evaluator U.S. GAO, 1985-88; legis. and grants officer D.C. Commn. on the Arts and Humanities, 1988—. Chmn. D.C. Congl. Art Competition Panel, 1989; mem. ann. conf. planning com. Nat. Assembly State Arts Agys., Washington, 1989-90, Inter-DC. Grants-making Task Force, Washington, 1989; mem. benefit com. Capitol Women's Network; keynote speaker IMF Visitors' Ctr.; guest lectr. George Washington U. Author: Directory of Special Transportation Services, 1984, Information of EPA's Proposal to Delete Chemicals from Groundwater Monitoring USGAO, 1987; former co-editor, contbr. Guernica (Rutgers U. fgn. lang. publ.); contbr. to Art Lines, NPRC Reports, El Foro. Mem. Nat. Conf. Puerto Rican Women, Washington, 1992, Humane Soc.of U.S., Nat. Coun. of Hispanic Women, D.C. Hispanic Employees Assn.; mgr. Flute Ensemble; panel Mem. Loy Krathong Festival Competition; John R. Rischer Jr. pub. affairs speaker, 1991; D.C. Mayor's com. on Persons with Disabilites Journalism Scholastic Competition, 1992; bd. dirs. XXIII Hispanic Festival of Washington, The WashingtonArea Coun. Alcoholism and Drug Abuse, Inc. 1993-94, La Luna Theatre, 1992; mem. Latino adv. com. Nat. Mus. Women in Arts, 1994, 95—, Aids Walk Found.; mem. steering com. and host com. OAS Mus. Art Auction, 1994; mem. planning com. Washington Salsa and Jazz Festival, 1993; mem. Latino Bus. Leaders Fighting AIDS, Latino adv. com. Whitman-Walker Clinic, 1994, mem. adv. com. Dare to Dream Career Prospects Nat. Mus. Women in the Arts. Recipient cert. of merit Office of D.C. Mayor, Cert. Appreciation, Nat. Coun. Hispanic Women; Am. U. scholar, 1984-86. Mem. NAFE, Am. Soc. for Pub. Adminstrs., Nat. Network Grantsmakers, Coun. Govtl. Ethics Laws, Cultural Alliance Greater Washington. Avocations: writing poetry, painting ceramics. Office: Cath U Am Dept Modern Langs McMahon Hall Washington DC 20064

PEREZ, LOUIS ANTHONY, radiologist; b. N.Y.C., June 11, 1939; s. Salvatore Lawrence and Valvadina Rose (Ruscillo) P.; divorced, 1988; children: Lisa, Gregg, Nicole; m. Patricia Ann McVey, May 19, 1990; 1 child, Kelsey. BEE, Manhattan Coll., 1962; MD, SUNY, Bklyn., 1966. Diplomate Am. Bd. Radiology (oral examiner), Am. Bd. Nuclear Medicine. Chief nuclear medicine Misericordia Hosp., Bronx, 1973-75; cons. Manhattan Coll., Radiology Inst., Riverdale, N.Y., 1974-81; chief nuclear medicine Norwalk (Conn.) Hosp., 1975-82; dir. radiology Lawrence Hosp., Bronxville, N.Y., 1982—; asst. clin. prof. radiology Columbia U. Coll. Physicians and Surgeons, N.Y.C., 1995—. Contbr. articles to profl. jours., chpts. to books. Lt. comdr. USN, 1963-77. Grantee, Am. Cancer Soc., 1968-70, USPHS, 1974-75. Fellow Am. Coll. Radiology; mem. Soc. Nuclear Medicine (trustee 1985-89, 92—, chmn. sci. subcom. 1988—, chpt. pres. 1982), Am. Coll. Physician Execs., N.Y. State Med. Soc., Explorers Club, Alpine Club. Republican. Roman Catholic. Office: Diagnostic Imaging Svcs of Bronxville 700 White Plains Rd Ste 244 Scarsdale NY 10583-5063 also: Lawrence Hosp Dept Radiology 55 Palmer Ave Bronxville NY 10708-3403

PEREZ, LUZ LILLIAN, psychologist; b. Ponce, P.R., Aug. 7, 1946; d. Emiliano and Maria D. (Torres) P.; children: Vantroi, Maireni. BA, Herbert H. Lehman Coll., 1974; PhD, NYU, 1989. Lic. bilingual (Spanish and English) psychologist, N.Y. Staff psychologist Soundview Throgs Neck Community Mental Health Ctr., Bronx, 1980-88; coord. early childhood program Crotona Park Cmty. Mental Health Ctr., 1988-91; cons. psychologist Highbridge Adv. Coun. Presch. Program, N.Y., 1991-93, Coalition for Hispanic Family Svcs., Bklyn., 1991-95, Marathon Child Devel. Ctr., Queens, 1993-94, Bronx Orgn. for Learning Disabled, 1993—, Village Child Devel. Ctr., N.Y.C., 1994-97, Graham-Windham Svcs. to Families and Children, 1994-95, Jackson Child Devel. Ctr., Jackson Heights, N.Y., 1996-97, Leake & Watts Svcs., Inc., Yonkers, 1996—. Grantee NIMH, 1974-77. Mem. Assn. Hispanic Mental Health Profls. Avocation: flamenco dancing.

PEREZ, MANUEL, engineering educator; b. N.Y.C., Nov. 9, 1939; s. Jose and Manuela Perez; m. Maria Alda Vagos; m. Carol Ann Wanagel, Sept. 2, 1961 (div. Apr. 15, 1980); children: Kiera, Lisa. BME, CCNY, 1961; MME, NYU, 1963; PhD, CUNY, 1968. Engr. Arde Inc., Paramus, NY, 1961—64, St. Regis, West Nyack, 1964—71; prof. N.J. Inst. Tech., Newark, 1971—. Contbr. Mem. Bd. of Health, River Vale, NJ, 1968. Achievements include patents for wet scrubber. Avocation: computers. Office: NJ Inst Tech 323 King Blvd Newark NJ 07102

PEREZ, MARY CHRISTINE, guidance counselor, small business owner; b. Miami, Fla., Dec. 5, 1967; d. Marta Miranda Perez. BA, Fla. Internat. U., 1989, MS, 1995. Cert. K-12 tchr., sch. guidance counselor, Fla. Tchr.'s aide Dade County Pub. Schs., Miami, 1986-87, tchr.'s asst., 1987-89, elem. tchr., 1989-95, guidance counselor, 1995—, chmn. student svcs. dept. Ruben Dario Mid. Sch., 1996—, mem. curriculum coun., 1996—. Sec.-treas., part owner K Lucky Transp. Svc., Miami, 1997—. Active Young Rep. Club, Miami, 1997. Named Role Model, 1st Union Nat. Bank and Hot Wheels Skating Ctr., 1997. Mem. Fla. Counseling Assn., Dade County Counseling Assn. Roman Catholic. Avocations: animals, music, sports, creative writing. Home: 14855 SW 39th Ct Miramar FL 33027-3324 Office: Ruben Dario Mid Sch 350 NW 97th Ave Miami FL 33172-4107

PEREZ, REINALDO JOSEPH, electrical engineer; b. Palm River, Cuba, July 25, 1957; came to U.S., 1975; s. Reinaldo I. and Palminia Ulloa (Rodriguez) P.; m. Madeline Kelly Reilly, Mar. 11, 1989; children: Alexander, Laura-Marie, Richard Kelly, Ella-Dean, Ray-Reilly. BSc in Physics, U. Fla., 1979, MSc in Physics, 1981; MScEE, Fla. Atlantic U., 1983, PhD, 1989. Comms. engr. Kennedy Space Ctr., NASA, Cape Canaveral, Fla., 1983-84; chief reliability engr. jet propulsion lab. JPL Calif. Inst. Tech., Pasadena, 1988—, chief engr. Mars surveyor program, 1994—. Instr. engring. UCLA, 1990-94, U. Denver, 2000-; owner M.R. Rsch. Inc., a telecomm. and aerospace cons. co.; mem. U.S. Engring. Accreditation Com. for Computer Engring. Author, editor: Handbook of Electromagnetic Compatibility, 1994, Noise and Interference Issues in Wireless Communications, 3 vols., Wireless Communications Handbook, 1998, Medical Electronics Design Book, 2002; designer Med. Electronics Devices, 2002; contbr. articles to profl. publs. Mem. AAAS, IEEE (sr. mem., book rev. editor 1990—), NSPE, Electromagnetic Compatibility Soc. (assoc. editor jour.), Am. Soc. Physics Tchrs., N.Y. Acad. Scis., Applied Computational Electromagnetic Soc. (assoc. editor jour., chief editor newsletter, bd. dirs., v.p.), Phi Kappa Phi. Republican. Baptist. Avocations: flying, skiing, fishing. Office: JPL Calif Inst Tech 4800 Oak Grove Dr # 301460 Pasadena CA 91109-8099

PEREZ, SHABAZZ, literature educator; b. Memphis; s. J.D. and Dovie Wandick. BA, Northeastern Univ., Chicago, IL, 1974. Mental health technician Read Zone Ctr., Oak Park, Ill., 1972—72; mental health specialist Madden Mental Health Zone Ctr., 1974—87; english lang. educator Chgo. Pub. Sch. Sys., Chicago, 1974—2002. Avocations: poetry, theater . Home: 10300 South Corliss Ave #2R Chicago IL 60628-3039

PEREZ-ABREU, JAVIER, lawyer; b. Havana, Cuba, Aug. 20, 1960; came to U.S., 1961; s. Gustavo and Martha (Caballero) Perez-Abreu; m. Dulce Maria Fernandez, Jan. 25, 1986; children: Carla, victor. BA in English and Bus. Adminstrn., Fla. State U., 1982; JD, U. Miami, 1985. Bar: Fla. 1985; cert. in marital and family law, family mediator, civil mediator, arbitrator. Atty./law clk. Antonio J. Pineiro, Jr., P.A., Miami, Fla., 1982-85; assoc. Manuel Alonso-Poch, P.A., Coral Gables, 1986-87; ptnr. Perez-Abreu, & Martin-Lavielle, PA, 1987—. Vice chmn. fla. Bar grievance Com. 11-B, Miami, 1993-97; barrister First Family chpt. Inns of Ct., Miami, 1995—; panel mem. Mediator qualifications Adv. Panel, Miami, 1994—. Author/editor: (seminar materials) Temporary Support Middle Income Divorce, 1994. Guardian ad litem pro-bono Dade County Bar, Miami, 1985—, pro-bono project mem., 1985—. Mem. Cuban Am. Bar Assn. (former v.p. and dir.), Dade County Bar Assn., Fla. Trial Lawyers Assn. Republican. Avocations: tennis, jogging, gym, cycling. Office: Perez-Abreu & Martin-Lavielle 901 Ponce De Leon Blvd Ste 502 Miami FL 33134-3073

PEREZ-BORJA, CARLOS M. neurologist, hospital executive; b. Quito, Ecuador, Oct. 24, 1927; came to U.S., 1959; s. Manuel V. Perez and Margot Borja; m. Rosa Enriquez, Sept. 6, 1954; children: Carmen, Patricia, Maria,

Helena, Carlos. MD, U. Quito, 1952. Diplomate Am. Bd. Psychiatry and Neurology; Am. Bd. Electroencephalography. Asst. prof. neurology Wash. Med. Sch., Seattle, 1965-66; chief of medicine Macomb Hosp. Ctr., Warren, Mich., 1982-84, chief of neurology, 1969-96, vice chief of staff, 1995-96. Dir. bd. dirs Detroit Macomb Hosp. Corp., 1985-87, 89-91. Contbr. numerous rsch. papers to profl. jours. Fellow ACP, Am. Acad. Neurology, Am. EEG Soc., Pan Am. Coll. Physicians. Roman Catholic. Avocations: reading, foreign languages. E-mail: capebo@worldnet.att.net.

PEREZ-CRUET, JORGE, physician, psychiatrist, psychopharmacologist, psychophysiologist, educator, psychiatrist, educator, addictionologist, geropsychiatrist; b. Santurce, P.R., Oct. 15, 1931; s. Jose Maria Perez-Vicente and Emilia Cruet-Burgos; m. Anyes Heimendinger, Oct. 4, 1958; children: Antonio, Mick, Graciela, Isabelle. BS magna cum laude, U. P.R., 1953, MD, 1957; diploma in psychiatry, McGill U., Montreal, Que., Can., 1976. Diplomate Am. Bd. Psychiatry and Neurology, Nat. Bd. Med. Examiners, Am. Bd. Geriat. Psychiatry; lic. Can. Coun. Med. Examiners, Med. Coun. Canada; cert. in quality assurance; cert. CHPQ by HQCB92; cert. specialist in psychiatry RCPC. Rotating intern Michael Reese Hosp., Chgo., 1957-58; fellow in psychiatry Johns Hopkins U. Med. Sch., 1958-60, instr., then asst. prof. psychiatry, 1962-73; lab. neurophysiology and psychomatic lab. Walter Reed Army Inst. Rsch., Washington, 1960-62, cons., 1963-65; rsch. assoc. lab. chem. pharmacology NHI, NIH, Bethesda, Md., 1969-71; adult psychiatry sect. lab. clin. sci. NIMH, 1971-73; psychiatry resident diploma course in psychiatry McGill U. Sch. Medicine, Montreal Gen. Hosp., 1973-76, Montreal Children's Hosp., 1975; prof. psychiatry U. Mo.-Mo. Inst. Psychiatry, St. Louis, 1976-78; chief psychiatry svc. San Juan (P.R.) VA Hosp., pharmacy and therapeutic com., 1978-92; also prof. psychiatry U. P.R. Med. Sch., 1978-92; prof. psychiatry U. Okla. Health Sci. Ctr., Oklahoma City VA Med. Ctr., 1992—. Spl. cons. NASA, 1965-69; cons. divsn. narcotic addition and drug abuse NIDA, 1972-73; mem. drug adv. com. FDA/NIDA, 1977-80, mem. pharmacy and therapeutic com., 1992—; local organizer Internat. Coll. Neuropsychiatry, San Juan, P.R., 1986; spl. advisor mental health P.R. Senate, P.R. sec. health, 1989; prin. investigator NASA biosatellite project JH Sch. Med., 1963-65.; staff psychiatrist mental health svcs., VAM, Oklahoma City, 1992-. Editor: Catholic Physicians Guild Archiocese of Okla., 1997-98. Mem. Rep. Nat. Com., 1995; mem. Eisenhower Commn., 2001. Capt. M.C. USAR, 1960-62; sr. surgeon USPHS, 1969-71, med. dir., 1971-73. Recipient Coronas award, 1957, Ruiz-Arnau award, 1957, Diaz-Garcia award 1957, Geigy award, 1975, 76, AMA Recognition award 1971, 76, 81, Horner's award 1975, 76, Pavlovian award, 1978, Recognition cert. VA Svc. awards and commendations, 1980-98, Senate of P.R., 1986, Cert. of Merit Gov. of P.R., 1986, Cert. Recognition, Sec. Health, San Juan, Puerto Rico, Appreciation plaque Fifth World Congress or Irma, Manila, Philippines, Eisenhower Commn., 1995. Fellow Interam. Coll. Physicians and Surgeons, Royal Coll. Physicians and Surgeons Can. (sr., cert.), Am. Psychiat Assn. (life 2002); mem. Am. Coll. Med. Quality, Am. Physiol. Soc., Am. Coll. Psychiatrists, Pavlovian Soc., Am. Fedn. Clin. Rsch., Am. Fedn. Med. Rsch., Am. Assn. Geriat. Psychiatry, Am. Soc. Clin. Pharmacology and Therapeutics, Am. Soc. Pharmacology and Exptl. Therapeutics, Am. Soc. Addiction Medicine (cert. 1998), Am. Acad. Addiction Psychiatry, Soc. Neurosci., Am. Coll. Med. Quality, Nat. Assn. Healthcare Quality, Internat. Soc. Rsch. Aggression, Okla. Psychiat. Assn., Am. Soc. Clin. Psychopharmacology, Menninger Found.; Charles F. Menninger Soc., Okla. Assn. Health Care Quality, Alumni, UPR Sch. Med., Johns Hopkins Med. Surg. Inst., NIH, McGill, Okla. Hist. Soc. Roman Catholic. Home: 3304 Rosewood Ln Oklahoma City OK 73120-5604 Office: Oklahoma City VA Med Ctr 921 NE 13th St Oklahoma City OK 73104-5007 Fax: 405-270-1566. E-mail: jperezcrue@aol.com.

PEREZ-CRUET, MICK JORGE, neurological surgeon, educator; b. Washington, May 3, 1961; s. Jorge Fortunato and Anyes Lilly (Heimendinger) Perez-Cruet; m. Donna Jeanne Roggenbuck, July 9, 1994; children: Kristin Magdalene, Joshua Michael, Rachel Elizabeth, David Gabriel. BA, Grinell Coll., 1983; MSc in Chemistry, U. South Fla., 1986; MD, Tufts U., 1991. Intern surg. svc. Baylor Coll. Medicine, Houston, 1991-92, resident in neurosurgery, 1992-97; attending neurosurgery, v. chmn. Wilford Hall Med. Ctr., San Antonio, 1997—2001; spinal fellow Rush U./CINN, Chgo., 2001—02; asst. prof., dir. minimally invasive spine surgery Rush U., 2002—; assoc. dir. Inst. Spine Care/CINN. Prin. investigator clin. trials; presenter in field; appointee to Coun. of State Neurosurg. Socs., 1997; chmn. young physicians com. Editor: (textbook) Outpatient Spinal Surgery; asst. editor: Neurosurgery News; contbr. chapters to books, articles to profl. jours. Chmn. class reunion Tufts Sch. Medicine, 1995-96; dir. class fund Grinnell Coll., 1999—. Air Force Health Professions scholar, 1987-91. Mem. AMA, ACS, AAAS, Congress Neurol. Surgeons, Am. Assn. Neurol. Surgeons, Mass. Med. Soc., Tex. Med. Assn., Maj. USAF Med. Corp, Fla. Acad. Sci., Am. Fedn. Clin. Rsch., Sigma Xi (grantee 1985). Avocations: hunting, fishing, scuba diving, underwater photography, biking. Home: 70 Old Creek Rd Palos Park IL 60464 Office: Rush-Presbyn St Lukes Med Ctr Dept Neurosurgery 1653 W Congress Pkwy Chicago IL 60612 Office Fax: 312-942-2176. Business E-Mail: mpcruet@neurosource.com. E-mail: perezcruet@yahoo.com.

PEREZ-MENDEZ, VICTOR, physics educator; b. Guatemala, Aug. 8, 1923; came to U.S., 1946; m. 1949; 2 children MS, Hebrew U., Israel, 1947; PhD, Columbia U., 1951. Rsch. assoc. Columbia U., N.Y.C., 1951-53, staff physicist, 1953-61; sr. scientist Lawrence Berkeley Lab., U. Calif., Berkeley, 1960—. Vis. lectr. Hebrew U., 1959—; prof. physics dept. radiology U. Calif., San Francisco, 1968— Fellow IEEE, AAAS, Am. Phys. Soc., N.Y. Acad. Sci.; mem. Soc. Photo Instrumentation Engrs. Office: U Calif Lawrence Berkeley Lab Berkeley CA 94720-0001 E-mail: vpm@lbl.gov.

PEREZ-REYES, EDWARD, molecular physiologist; b. Cheverly, Md., Feb. 18, 1957; s. Mario Perez-Reyes and Maria Gispert; m. Emilia Aranda Ripoll, June 15, 1984 (div. June 1989); m. Deborah Lynn Benuska, Apr. 13, 1991. PhD, U. Colo., 1986. Technician Nat. Inst. Environ. Health Scis., Research Triangle Park, N.C., 1978-80; postdoctoral fellow Baylor Coll. Medicine, Houston, 1986-91, asst. prof., 1991-92, Loyola U. Med. Ctr., Maywood, Ill., 1993-98, assoc. prof., 1998-99, U. Va., Charlottesville, 1999—. Contbr. articles to profl. jours. Recipient Nat. Rsch. Svc. award NIH, 1988, Established Investigatorship award Am. Heart Assn., 1996; fellow NSF, 1980. Mem. Biophys. Soc. Achievements include molecular biophys. characterization of dihydropyridine sensitive L-type and T-type calcium channels. Office: 1300 Jefferson Park Ave Charlottesville VA 22908-0735

PÉREZ-RIVERA, FRANCISCO, writer; b. Vertientes, Cuba, Oct. 3, 1938; came to U.S., 1968, naturalized, 1974; s. Francisco Daniel Pérez and María Eloísa Rivera. BA, Camagüey Coll., Cuba, 1955; MA in Romance Langs., U. Munich, 1967. Newsman, script writer Bavarian Radio, Munich, 1964-68; newsman AP, N.Y.C., 1968-92, arts and entertainment editor, 1992—; dir. Spanish programs for lang. labs., 1987. *Francisco Pérez-Rivera has single-handedly created the arts and entertainment section of the AP's Latin American Desk. Since he was named as the first entertainment editor ever of that desk in 1992, his work has given the AP's Spanish Service an unusually high profile in the cultural field. Of his fiction, professor Carol Wasserman writes: "The dominant elements of (his) stories are the consistency of style and the versatility of the genre. Behind each word we can trace an unrelenting course towards a revelation that is always cunning and often hair-raising." As a fiction writer, his byline is Frank Rivera.* Author: (poetry) Construcciones, 1979, (novel) Las sabanas y el tiempo, 1986, (short stories) Cuentos cubanos, 1992, (short stories) Varadero y otros cuentos cubanos, 1998; co-author: Introducción a la literatura española, 1982; short stories in the anthologies New Cuban Storytellers, 1961, Cuba: Nouvelles et contes d'aujourd'hui, 1985, Narrative and Liberty: Cuban Tales of the Dispersion, 1996, Prosa moderna del mundo hispánico, 1997; (narrator audio tape) El Siglo de Oro Español, 2002. Grantee German Academic Exchange Svc., Munich, 1961-67; fellow Cintas Found., N.Y., 1980; 1st prize Círculo de Escritores y Poetas Latinoamericanos Short Story Contest, N.Y., 1997, 1st prize Círculo de Cultura Panamericano Short Story Contest, N.J., 1997. Home: 212 E 77th St Apt 1G New York NY 10021-2111 Office: AP 50 Rockefeller Plz New York NY 10020-1605

PÉREZ-STABLE, MARIA ADELAIDA, librarian; b. Havana, Cuba, Nov. 2, 1954; came to U.S. 1960; d. Diego Javier and Maria Luisa (Dominguez) Perez-Stable. BA magna cum laude, Miami U., Oxford, Ohio, 1976; MSLS, Case Western Res. U., Cleve., 1977; MA in History with honors, Western Mich. U., 1986. Catalog libr. Western Res. Hist. Soc., Cleve., 1977-79, Western Mich. U., Kalamazoo, 1979-84, edn. libr., 1984-91, social scis. libr., 1991-97, head ctrl. reference, 1997—. Co-author: Peoples of the American West, 1989, Understanding American History Through Children's Literature: Instructional Units and Activities for Grades K-8, 1994; editor: Directory of Michigan Academic Libraries, 1984. Mem. ALA, Mich. Library Assn., Orgn. Am. Historians, Nat. Trust for Historic Preservation, Phi Beta Kappa, Phi Kappa Phi, Beta Phi Mu. Democrat. Roman Catholic. Avocations: reading, movies, gardening, bicycling, dance, travel. Office: Waldo Libr Western Mich U Kalamazoo MI 49008

PERFETTI, ROBERT NICKOLAS, educational consultant; b. Staples, Minn., Jan. 8, 1937; s. Nickolas Albert and Lila Bertha (Beurge) P. BS, St. Cloud State U., 1960; postgrad., Bemidji State U., 1961-62, Calif. State U., L.A., 1964-68, Pepperdine U., 1967-68; MA, La Verne U., 1970; postgrad., U. So. Calif., 1972-73, Point Loma U., Pasadena, Calif., 1974-75; EdD, Pacific States U., 1975. Cert. admistr., counselor, secondary, community coll., jr. high sch., adult, and elem. edn. Calif. Prin. Richmond (Minn.) Pub. Schs., 1960-62; elem. tchr. Sebeka (Minn.) Sch. Dist., 1962-63; team leader lang. arts, social sci. and summer sch. Rowland Unified Sch. Dist., Rowland Heights, Calif., 1965-76, coord. math. lab., 1976-79, secondary counselor, 1979-81, coord. work experience edn., career edn. and career ctr., 1981-95, home ind. study coord., ednl. cons., 1992-95; mental health counselor St. Gabriel's Hosp., Little Falls, Minn., 1999. Coord. Gender Equity, 1980-95, Job Tng. Partnership Act, 1980-95; advisor Nat. Vocat. Tech. Honor Soc., 1991-95; alumni dir. Sacred Heart Sch., Staples. Editor: (profl. newspaper) Reaction. Officer parish coun. Our Lady of the Assumption Ch., Claremont, Calif., chmn. edn. com.; chmn. PTA, Rowland Heights; rep. fed. project, Rowland Heights; scoutmaster, chmn. troop com. Boy Scouts Am. Recipient Svc. Commendation Rowland Unified Sch. Dist., 1978; named. L.A. County Tchr. of Yr. Calif. State Dept. Edn., 1975, Outstanding Secondary Educator of Am., 1974, Giano Tchr. of Yr. Giano Intermediate Sch., 1973, Tchr. of Yr. Rowland Unified Sch. Dist., 1974. Mem. NEA (life), Calif. Tchrs. Assn., Assn. Rowland Educators (v.p.), Calif. Assn. Work Experience Educators (Alpha chpt. v.p.), Alpha Phi Omega (pres.), Pi Delta Epsilon (pres.), KC (3d degree). Roman Catholic. Avocations: water sports, traveling, research, writing. Home: 4318 320th St Cushing MN 56443-2115 E-mail: perfetti@brainerd.net., drnickolas@yahoo.com.

PERFETTO, ELEANOR MARIE, health outcomes/economic research consultant; b. Providence, Sept. 12, 1958; d. Ralph J. and Carolyn Ann (Ferri) P.; m. Ralph R. Wenzel, Jan. 2, 1987. BS in Pharmacy, U. R.I., Kingston, 1980, MS in Pharmacy Adminstrn., 1988; PhD in Pub. Health, U. N.C., 1992. Registered pharmacist, R.I. Chief of pharmacy svcs., staff pharmacist USPHS Indian Health Svc., Pine Ridge, S.D., 1980-85, Talahina, Okla., 1985-86; cons. pharmacist Long Term Care Pharmacy Svcs., West Warwick, R.I., 1986-88; project mgr. U. N.C. Ctr. for Health Promotion and Disease Prevention, Chapel Hill, 1988-91; sr. pharmacoepidemiologist, project officer USPHS Agy. for Health Care Policy and Rsch., Rockville, Md., 1991-94; dir., health outcomes assessment Wyeth-Ayerst Rsch., Radnor, Pa., 1994-97; chief exec. officer MEDTAP sys., LLC, Bethesda, Md., 1997-99; exec. v.p. QualityMetric, Inc., Lincoln, R.I., 1999-2000; mng. ptnr. Healthcentric Assocs., 2000—01; mng. cons. The Weinberg Group, 2002—. Mem. tech. adv. group Health Care Financing Adminstrn. Drug Utilization Rev. Demonstrations, Balt., 1992—98; steering com. Drug Info. Assn., Amber, Pa., 1994—, bd. dirs., Pa., 1999—2002, pres.-elect, 2002—; mem. health outcomes work group Pharm. Rsch. and Mfrs. Assn., Washington, 1996—97; panel mem. U.S. Pharmacopeial Conv., Rockville, Md., 1997—2000. Author: Pharmacoepidemiology, 1991, 2nd edit., 1998; contbr. articles to profl. jours. Vol. Am. Diabetes Assn., 1986—. Fellow: Am. Pharm. Assn. (chair 1997—98, mem. exec. com. 1998—), Rsch. and Edn. Found. (trustee 1996—2000), Am. Soc. Cons. Pharmacists. Avocations: cooking, kayaking, wine, gardening, travel. E-mail: elpe@weinberggroup.com.

PERGANTIS, CONSTANTINE GEORGE, lighting contractor; b. Washington, Apr. 1, 1964; s. Constantine Peter and Evangeline (Stamatiades) P.; m. Elaine Maria Santorios, Oct. 8, 1994; children: Christina Elaina, Evangeline Maria. Student, Montgomery Coll., Rockville, Md., 1982-84. Gen. mgr. Constantine's Kitchens, Inc., Bethesda, Md., 1981-83; agt. supr. USA Today, Washington, 1983-85; mfrs. rep. Al Kraus Assocs., Inc., Kensington, Md., 1985-87; East Coast regional mgr. Luma Lighting Industries, Inc., Santa Ana, Calif., 1987-88; owner, pres. Nite Lites, North Potomac, Md., 1988—. Cons., seminar spkr. Hinkley Lighting, Cleve., 1992-94; cons., spkr. Focus Lighting Industries, Inc., Lakeforest, Calif., 1990-2001; bd. dirs. Fore All, Inc., Kensington, Mo.; EPA Green Lights Surveyor Ally. Author: (monthly column) California Landscaping Mag., 1993-94. Umpire Montgomery County (Md.) Umpires Assn., 1981—92; com. mem. Am. Heart Assn.-Hot Hoops, College Park, Md., 1995; vol. Ft. Stanton Park Cmty. Ctr., 1997; organizer Operation Smile Basketball Classic, 1995—2001; bd. dirs. Heritage Walk HOA, 1998—2001, Forg All Inc.; cons. elec. lighting renovation Bartman Sch. Painting, Glen Echo Park, 1994. Recipient Pepco Silver Club award, 1994, 1st Pl. ENCOMP award, 1996. Home: 10613 Montrose Ave #2 Bethesda MD 20814 Office: Nite Lites 10636 Chisholm Landing Ter North Potomac MD 20878-4263 E-mail: nitelitescgp@hotmail.com.

PERGOLA, PABLO EZEQUIEL, internist, nephrologist; b. Buenos Aires, Sept. 21, 1963; came to U.S., 1988; s. Oscar Ruben and Elba Norma P.; m. Gabriela M., Mar. 13, 1987; children: Francisco Jose, Tomas Ezequiel. MD, U. del Salvador, 1988; PhD in Pharmacology, U. Kans. Med. Ctr., 1991. Postdoctoral fellow dept. physiology U. Tex. Health Sci. Ctr., San Antonio, 1991-93, intern in internal medicine, 1994, resident in internal medicine, 1995-96, nephrology fellow, 1997-99, asst. prof. medicine--nephrology, 1999—. Contbr. articles to profl. jours. Mem. Internat. Soc. Nephrology, Am. Physiol. Soc., Am. Soc. Nephrology, Nat. Kidney Found. Home: 1510 Thrush Rdg San Antonio TX 78248-1713

PERGOLIZZI, ROBERT GEORGE, molecular biologist, educator; b. Bklyn., Feb. 21, 1950; s. Santo Joseph and Marian Pergolizzi; m. Camille Roxanne Kotowski, Apr. 8, 1972; children: Christopher Dylan, Alexander Joseph, Zachary Taylor. BS in Chemistry, Hofstra U., 1971, MA in Biology, 1974; MA, Columbia U., 1976, MPhil, 1978, PhD in Biochemistry, 1979. Rsch. asst. Waldemar Med. Rsch. Found., Plainview, N.Y., 1971-73, North Shore U. Hosp., N.Y.C., 1973-75; grad. rsch. asst. Columbia U., 1975-79, postdoctoral fellow dept. human genetics and devel., 1980-82; dir. mfg. Enzo Biochem, Inc., 1982-86, dir. Recombinant DNA Lab., 1982-86; dir. molecular genetics rsch. North Shore U. Hosp.-Cornell U. Med. Coll., 1986-2000; dir. Genotyping Ctr., North Shore Hosp.-NYU, 1994-2000; asst. prof. pathology Cornell U. Med. Coll., 1988-93, assoc. prof. pathology, 1993-2000; dir. Good Mfg. Practice Viral Vector Lab., North Shore U. Hosp., 1994-2000; dir. molecular genetics and gene therapy North Shore-L.I. Jewish Health Sys., 1998-2000; assoc. dir. Belfer Gene Therapy Core Facility, Weill Med. Coll. of Cornell U., 2000—; faculty mem. dept. genetic medicine Weill Cornell Med. Coll., 2000—. Adj. prof. L.I. U., Brookville, N.Y., 1988-2000; dir. transgenic animal facility North Shore U. Hosp./NYU Med. Coll., Manhasset, N.Y., 1990-2000; instr. liaison N.Y. State Ctr. for Biotech., 1990-2000, L.I. Rsch. Inst., 1991-2000; dir. rsch. apprentice program for minority students NIH, 1987-95, mem. study sect., 1992—; pres. Starship Enterprises rec. studio, 1989—, Pergolizzi GMP Consulting, 1999-; sec.-treas. Camille prodns., Inc., 1989—. Editor: Genetic Engineering, 1982; patentee in field; contbr. articles to profl. jours. Trustee Bergen County Mental Health Ctr. (Compcare), 1994—98. Recipient Waldemar Found. award Waldemar Med. Rsch. Found., 1972, Brookdale Found. award, 1978; fellow Columbia U., 1975-79, NIH, 1979-82. Fellow Harvey Soc.; mem. Am. Assn. Cancer Rsch., Am. Soc. Hematology, Am. Soc. Gene Therapy, N.Y. Acad. Scis., N.Y. Biotech. Assn., Am. Soc. Human Genetics. Republican. Roman Catholic. Office: Belfer Gene Therapy Core Facility Weill Cornell Med Coll 515 E 71st St New York NY 10021

PERHAC, RALPH MATTHEW, institute administrator; b. Bklyn., July 29, 1928; s. George and Irene (Harpas) P.; m. A. Constance Main, Feb. 4, 1950 (dec. Feb. 1973); children— Ralph Matthew, Jr., Janet I. A.B., Columbia U., 1949; A.M., Cornell U., 1952; Ph.D., U. Mich., 1961. Mining engr. Anaconda, Butte, Mont., 1952-53; dist. geologist U.S. AEC, Albuquerque, 1953-55; geologist Caltex, Australia, 1955-57; sr. researcher Exxon, Houston, 1960-67; prof. U. Tenn., Knoxville, 1967-74; program mgr. NSF, Washington, 1974-76; dept. dir. Electric Power Research Inst., Palo Alto, Calif., 1976— ; lunar investigator NASA, Oak Ridge, Tenn., 1972-74. Contbr. articles to profl. jours. Fellow Geol. Soc. Am.; mem. Geochem. Soc., Am. Assn. Petroleum Geologists, Internat. Assn. Geochemistry and Cosmochemistry (editor 1970-73), Soc. Geochemistry and Health. Home: 675 Sharon Park Dr Menlo Park CA 94025-6938 Office: Electric Power Research Inst PO Box 10412 Palo Alto CA 94303-0813

PERHACH, JAMES LAWRENCE, pharmaceutical company executive; b. Pitts., Oct. 26, 1943; s. James Lawrence and Elizabeth Louise (Hoffman) P.; m. Judith Irene Selter, Apr. 15, 1967; children: Laura Anne, Amy Elizabeth. BS, U. Dayton, 1966; MS, U. Pitts., 1969, PhD, 1971. Sr. scientist dept. pharmacology Mead Johnson Rsch. Ctr., 1971-74, sr. investigator dept. biol. rsch., 1974-76, sr. rsch. assoc. dept. biol. rsch., 1976-77, sr. rsch. assoc. dept. pathology and toxicology, 1977-78, prin. rsch. assoc. dept. pathology and toxicology, 1978-80; from dir. pharmacology to dir. biol. rsch. to dir. clin. investigation Wallace Labs. Divsn. Carter-Wallace, Inc., Cranbury, NJ, 1980—87, v.p. clin. pharmacology and pharmacokinetics, 1987—2001; sr. dir. clin. pharmacology Purdue Pharma, L.P., 2001—. Vis. asst. prof. dept. pharmacy practice and adminstrn. Coll. Pharmacy Rutgers U., 1993—; adj. prof. toxicology Phila. Coll. Pharmacy and Sci., 1981-87; assoc. faculty Evansville Ctr. Med. Edn., Ind. U., 1973-80; lectr. grad. physiology U. Evansville, 1973-79; mem. adv. bd. clin. rsch. ctr. U. Medicine and Dentistry N.J. Robert Wood Johnson Med. Sch., 1995—; mem. Drug Utilization Rev. Coun., State of N.J., 1983—, med. pharmacologist, 1983, sec., 1984, chmn., 1985-87; mem. substance abuse com. Tri-State Area Health Planning Coun., Evansville, 1972-75; mem. addictions mem. edn. program Evansville Ctr. for Med. Edn., 1972-78. Fellow: Am. Coll. Clin. Pharmacology; mem.: AAAS, Drug Info. Assn., N.Y. Acad. Sci., Soc. Neurosci., Soc. Exptl. Biology and Medicine, European Soc. Toxicology, Am. Coll. Toxicology, Am. Soc. Clin. Pharmacology and Therapeutics, Sigma Xi. Achievements include research in drug discovery, elucidation of mechanism of action and safety evaluation of new therapeutic agents. Home: 6 Highfield Ct Lawrenceville NJ 08648-1077 Office: Purdue Pharma LP 201 College Rd East Princeton NJ 08540 E-mail: james.perhach@pharma.com.

PERHACS, MARYLOUISE HELEN, musician, educator; b. Teaneck, N.J., June 15, 1944; d. John Andrew and Helen Audrey (Hosage) P.; m. Robert Theodore Sirinek, Jan. 27, 1968 (div. Jan. 1975). Student, Ithaca (N.Y.) Coll., 1962-64; BS, Juilliard Sch., 1967, MS, 1968; postgrad., Hunter Coll., 1976, St. Peter's Coll., Jersey City, N.J., 1977. Cert. music tchr., N.Y., N.J. Instr. Carnegie Hall, N.Y.C., 1966-69; program developer, coord., instr. urban edn. program Newburgh (N.Y.) Pub. Sch. System, 1968-69; adj. prof. dept. edn. St. Peter's Coll., Jersey City, 1976-92; tchr. brass instruments Indian Hills High Sch., Oakland, N.J., 1976; tchr. Jersey City Pub. Schs., 1976-77, N.Y.C. Pub. Sch., Bronx, 1980-84; pvt. tchr. Cliffside Park, N.J., 1976—; vocal music tchr. East Rutherford, 1990; tchr. music Bergen County Spl. Svcs. Sch. Dist., 1990-91; tchr. gen. music Little Ferry (N.J.) Pub. Schs., 1991-92; tchr. mid. sch. instrumental Paramus (N.J.) Pub. Schs., 1993-94; tchr. vocal music West New York (N.J.) Pub Schs., 1995—. Tchr. music summer enrichment program, West New York, NJ, 1999, 2000, summer instrumental music program Park Ridge (N.J.) H.S., 1995, 96; tchr., singer, trumpeter Norwegian Caribbean Lines, 1981-82, Jimmy Dorsey Band, Paris and London, 1974; music and edn. lecture cir., 1992—. Singer with Original PDQ Bach Okay Chorale, 1966, Live from Carnegie Hall Recordings, 1970, St. Louis Mcpl. Opera, 1970, Ed Sullivan Show, 1970; singer, dancer, actress (Broadway shows) Promises, Promises, 1969-71, Sugar, 1971-72, Lysistrata, 1972; trumpeter (Broadway shows) Jesus Christ Superstar, 1973, Debbie!, 1976, Sarava!, 1979, Fiddler on the Roof, Lincoln Ctr., 1981, Sophisticated Ladies, 1982; writer, host series on women in music Columbia Cable/United Artists, 1984; recordings: Carnegie Hall Live, Avery Fisher Hall, Lincoln Ctr. Cons. to cadette troop Girl Scouts U.S., Jersey City, 1967-68, Bergen County N.J. Coun., 1995—. Mem. NEA, AFTRA, Actors Equity Assn., Am. Fedn. Musicians (mem. theatre com. local 802 N.Y.C. 1972—, chmn. 1973), Music Educators Nat. Conf., N.J. Music Educators Assn., N.J. Sch. Music Assn., N.J. Edn. Assn., Internat. Women's Brass Conf. (charter mem.), Internat. Trumpet Guild, Women of Accomplishment (charter mem. 1992), Mu Phi Epsilon. Democrat. Episcopalian. Avocations: cats, cake decorating, food sculpting, horticulture, sewing. Home and Office: 23 Crescent Ave Cliffside Park NJ 07010-3003

PERHAM, ROY GATES, III, industrial psychologist; b. Hackensack, N.J., Apr. 22, 1958; s. Roy Gates Jr. and Titania Joan (Robbitts) P. BA with honors, Bates Coll., 1980; MS, Stevens Inst. Tech., 1982, PhD, 1989. Intern Sen. Edmund S. Muskie, Washington, 1978; psychometrician Lab. Psychol. Studies Stevens Inst. Tech., Hoboken, N.J., 1981-83, instr., 1985, adj. asst. prof., 1990—, Fairleigh Dickinson U., Rutherford, 1986; sr. assoc. AAI Orgnl. Performance Cons., Florham Park, 1990-94; assessment projects mgr. Tech. Employee Selection and Tng. Inc., Hasbrouck Heights, 1995—. WordStar coord. N.Y. Computer Soc., N.Y.C., 1985-88. Chmn. Juvenile Conf. Com., Hasbrouck Heights and Wood-Ridge, N.J., 1985-95; mem. N.J. State Juvenile Delinquency Commn., Trenton, N.J., 1988-91; county exec.'s rep. Bergen County Youth Svcs. Commn., 1990—, chair, 1994-96; chair Bergen County Task Force on Youth Violence, 1993—; asst. Bergen County Exec. for Juvenile Justice, N.J., 1999—; mem. N.J. Juvenile Justice and Delinquency Prevention Adv. Com., 2001—. Named Citizen of Yr., Lions Club of Hasbrouck Heights, N.J., 1988. Mem. APA, Am. Psychol. Soc., Met. N.Y. Assn. for Applied Psychology, Soc. for Indsl./Orgnl. Psychology, Inc., Phi Beta Kappa, Psi Chi. Home: 269 Raymond St Hasbrouck Heights NJ 07604-1723 Office: Technical Employee Selection & Tng Inc The Profl Bldg 248 Blvd Hasbrouck Heights NJ 07604 E-mail: Rperham@compuserve.com.

PERHINSCHI, MARIO GEORGE, aerospace engineer; b. Bucharest, Romania, May 4, 1959; s. Mimail and Maria P.; m. Gabriela Cristina Radoi, Sept. 10, 1982; 1 child, Andrei. B, Politechnica U., Bucharest, Romania, 1984; M, Georgia Inst. Tech., Atlanta, 1994; PhD, Politechnica U., 1999. Prin. rschr. Inst. Fluid Mechanics & Flight Dynamics, Bucharest, 1986-93; tchg. asst. Politechnica U., 1988-93, 98-99; engr. Aircraft Enterprise, 1984-86; design leader Nat. Aerospace Rsch. Inst., 1996—. Grantee Swiss NSF, Zurich, 2001, GAMM, Regensbud, Germany, 1997, ANSTI, Romania, 1996-00. First Romanian rschr. to perform rsch. and pub. results in: applications of artificial intelligence tech. to solve aerospace problems, use of human pilot models for aircraft handling qualities evaluation, autonomous aerial vechicles. Office: WV Univ Dept Mech & Aero Engring Morgantown WV 26506 E-mail: mperhinschi@pcnet.pcnet.ro.

PERI, JOSEPH SILVIO JULIUS, physicist, mathematician; b. Palermo, Italy, Mar. 28, 1948; s. Concetta Giuseppa Bagnera and Gerlando Peri; m. Marcia Owings Frank, Nov. 28, 1981; children: Alexander, Rachel, Julian. PhD, Cath. U. of Am., 1978. Programmer analyst Computer Scis. Corp., Silver Spring, Md., 1978—79, Andrulis Rsch. Corp., Bethesda, 1979—81; physicist The Johns Hopkins U. Applied Phys Lab, Laurel, 1981—. Mem.: Am. Math. Soc. Roman Catholic. Office: The Johns Hopkins U Applied Physics Lab 11100 Johns Hopkins Rd Laurel MD 20723-6099 Office Fax: 443-778-6587. E-mail: joseph.peri@jhuapl.edu.

PERI, LINDA CAROL, librarian; b. Johnsville, Pa., Sept. 8, 1943; d. Willard and Ethel F. (Furness) Hinkle. BA, Juniata Coll., 1965; MA, Columbia U., 1967; MLS, Emporia State U., 1995. Sr. lectr. Oslo Inst. Bus. Adminstrn., Norway, 1967-72; Fulbright sr. lectr. Tech. U . Wroclaw, Poland, 1972-75; acad. dir. Inlingua Sch. Langs., Singapore, 1975-82; nat. accts. coord. United Van Lines, Denver, 1982-94; libr. Arapahoe Libr. Dist., Littleton, Colo., 1995-99; libr. Bus. Resource Ctr. Aurora (Colo.) Ctrl. Libr., 1999—. Editor: Mystery in Malacca, 1981. Mem. Am. Libr. Assn., Colo. Libr. Assn., Beta Phi Mu. Avocations: skiing, tennis, book discussion, travel. E-mail: lperi@ci.aurora.co.us.

PERI, WINNIE LEE BRANCH, educational director; b. Dallas; d. Floyd Hamilton and Eula Dee (Richardson) Branch; m. Fred Ronald Peri; children: Kenneth Michael, Michael Anthony, Desiree Denise. BA in Psychology, Calif. State U., Long Beach, 1978, English teaching credential, 1988; social sci. teaching credential, Calif. State U., Northridge, 1979. Republic of South Africa tchr. Internat. Sch. Svcs., Princeton, N.J., 1980-82; tchr. English, St.

Jeanne de Lestonnac Sch., Tustin, Calif., 1988-91; dir. edn. Sylvan Learning Ctr., Mission Viejo, 1993-94; self-employed as tutor, 1995-97; ESL tchr. Capistrano Unified Sch. Dist., San Juan Capistrano, Calif., 1998-2000. Facilitator Rainbows for All God's Children, 1989; mem. team experience sch. evaluation com. WASC/WCEA. Mem. adv. bd. Thomas Paine Sch. PTA; dep. sheriff Los Angeles County. Mem. Psi Chi.

PERICH, TERRY MILLER, secondary school educator; b. Greensburg, Pa., Sept. 22, 1948; s. Miller and Eleanor Ann (Schmuck) P.; m. Kathleen Ann Ferrari, July 26, 1975. BA in Elem. Edn., Edinboro U., 1970; elem. cert., Pa. State U., 1973; Masters equivalency degree, U. Pitts., 1994; postgrad., Carlow Coll., 1994. Trained student assistance profl., Pa.; cert. tchr. elem. edn. Tchr. sci. and math. Penn Trafford Schs., Harrison City, Pa., 1970—. Mentor, tchr. Tchr. Enhancement Inst. St. Vincent Coll., Latrobe, Pa.; selected tchr. Watershed Restoration St. Vincent Coll., Latrobe. County committeeman Dem. Party, Penn Twp., Pa., 1994—; lion tamer Bushy Run Lions Club, Claridge, Pa., 1993—, 3rd v.p., 1995, 2d v.p., 1996, 1st v.p., 1997—. Recipient Commendation, Pres.-elect Clinton, Student Assistance Program award for working with students at risk St. Vincent Coll. Prevention Projects, 1991. Mem. NEA, ASCD, PACE, Nat. Sci. Tchrs. Assn., Pa. Tchrs. Edn. Assn., Pa. Sci. Tchrs. Assn., Westmoreland County Assn. Student Assistance Profls. (bd. dirs. 1992-94, mem. Westmoreland county student assistance team 1995-96, 96-97), Penn Trafford Edn. Assn. (exec. bd. dirs. 1990-91). Roman Catholic. Avocations: travel, education. Home: 13 Rizzi Dr Irwin PA 15642-8902 Office: Penn Mid Sch PO Box 368 Watt Rd Claridge Pa 15623

PERICH, TONI ANNETTE, sales executive; b. Galveston, Tex., Sept. 22, 1946; d. Daniel John Jr. and Adelaide Lucia (Lopez) Traverso; m. Thomas Joseph Perich, June 3, 1978 (div.); children: Matthew John, Stephen Christopher. Designated assoc. in surety and fidelity bonding Ins. Inst. Am.; CPCU. Comml. svc. rep. various ins. agys., Houston, 1965-87; field rep., outside sales Old Republic Surety, 1987-90; owner Galerie d'Alexandria, Galveston, Tex., 1990-92; ins. cons. various law firms, Houston, 1990-91; comml. svc. rep. The Houston Agys., Inc., 1992-94; field rep., outside sales Universal Surety of Am., Houston, 1994-95; field rep., sales exec. RLI Ins. Co., Dallas, 1995—. Tchr. piano pvt practice Sugarland, Tex., 1994—. Editor Surety Newsfacts, 1996—, The Reporting Cover, 1999—. Schoolsite liaison Am. Heart Assn., Upper Pinellas County, 1996-98; dir. Upper Pinellas divsn. Am. Heart Assn., 1997-98. North Tex. State U. Music scholar, 1964; recipient Gold medal Internat. Piano Recording Festival, 1956, 1st Pl. Contestant, 1963, Paderweski Gold medal Nat. Guild Piano Tchrs., 1964. Mem.: Houston Surety Assn., Fla. Surety Assn. (v.p. 1998—99), Ins. Women St. Petersburg (treas. 1997—98, v.p. 1998), Nat. Assn. Ins. Women (mem.-at-large 1995—96, mem. tech. panel 1998—99, pres.-elect 2000—, legis. liaison Tex. coun. 2000—, pres. 2001—02, edn. found. amb. Tex. coun. 2002, chair pub. rels. Houston NAIW, Inc., Profl. of the Yr. Tex. Coun. 2001, Profl. of Yr. 2002), Am. Coll. Musicians, Blue Bird Circle. Roman Catholic. Avocations: reading, handwork, golf, crossword puzzles. Office: RLI Surety Ste 1020 3010 Lyndon B Johnson Fwy Dallas TX 75234-7006 E-mail: Tonitp@aol.com.

PERIC-KNOWLTON, WLATKA, nurse practitioner; b. Nürnberg, Germany, Oct. 29, 1955; came to U.S., 1957; d. Vladimir and Zlata (Mihaljevic) Peric; m. Gregory Dean Knowlton, May 1, 1983. BSN, Ariz. State U., 1977, MSN, 1986. RN, Ariz.; cert. adult nurse practitioner CCRN, CDE; CEN. Gen. surgery staff nurse St. Joseph's Hosp., Phoenix, 1977-78, staff nurse cardiovascular oper. room, charge nurse, 1978-80; staff nurse surg. ICU, charge nurse Carl Hayden VA Med. Ctr., 1980-83, dir. anti-coagulation clinic, 1984-94; primary care nurse practitioner dept. Vet. affairs S.E. Ext. Clinic, Carl Hayden VA Med. Ctr., 1983-94, primary care provider, 1994—. Mem. adj. clin. faculty Ariz. State U., Tempe, 1986-93. Editor-in-chief newsletter VA Nurse Practitioner News, 1989-91; guest editor Nurse Practitioner Forum; contbr. articles to nursing jours. Named Nat. Nurse Practitioner of Yr., Syntex, 1989, Fed. Employee of Yr., Phoenix Fed. Exec. Assn., 1989; recipient award for excellence in nursing western region VA, 1991. Mem. ANA (Search for Excellence award 1991), Am. Acad. Nurse Practitioners (Ariz. rep. 1991-93, bd. dirs., region 9 dir. 1993-95), Ariz. Nurse Practitioner Coun. (treas. 1985-87, v.p. 1989-90, pres. 1990-91, legis. chmn. 1992-95), Ariz. Nurses Assn. (vice chmn. legis. com. 1985-87, bd. dirs. 1982-83), Am. Heart Assn. (coun. on thrombosis 1989—, cmty. spkr. Phoenix 1989—), Sigma Theta Tau. Democrat. Roman Catholic. Avocations: folk dancing, scuba diving, hiking, white water rafting, travel. Office: Carl Hayden VA Med Ctr 650 E Indian School Rd Phoenix AZ 85012-1839

PERILSTEIN, FRED MICHAEL, electrical engineer, consultant; b. Phila., Oct. 25, 1945; s. Paul Pincus and Adeline Sylvia (Schneyer) P.; m. Abigail Siff, June 13, 1971. BS in Econs., CCNY, 1968; BSEE, Newark Coll. Engring., 1972; MSEE Power, N.J. Inst. Tech., 1977. Registered profl. engr., N.J., Pa., N.Y., Calif. Applications engr. Fed. Pacific Electric Corp., Newark, 1972-78; cons. in field, 1978-82, 97—; pres. Tramlec Corp., Cons. Engrs., Springfield, N.J., 1982-97. Seminar instr. Multi-Amp Corp., Springfield, N.J., 1980; mem. IEEE Cons.' Network, no. N.J., 1992-96; lectr. IEEE Montech 86, Montreal, 1986, ASME/IEEE joint railroad conf., Chgo., 1994, Boston, 1997, Newark, 2000. Contbr. articles to IEEE Transactions, Cons.-Specifying Engr., and EC&M Mag.; cons. in field. Regents scholar N.Y. Bd. Regents, 1963; recipient 3d prize trophy World Wide Inventor Expo '82, 1982. Mem. IEEE (power engring., vehicular tech., indsl. application socs., and stds. assn., mem. rail transit vehicle interface stds. com., 1996—). Achievements include U.S. patent for Polyphase Variable Frequency Inverter. Office: 30 Benjamin Dr Springfield NJ 07081-3019

PERIN, DONALD WISE, JR. former association executive; b. Newton, Mass., Feb. 28, 1915; s. Donald Wise and Beatrice Franklin (Cobb) P.; m. Jean Newcomb Mulcahy, Dec. 5, 1942; children: William Kirk, Betsy Cobb, Donald Wise. Student, Norwich U., 1932-34; BA, Columbia U., 1936. With Gt. Am. Indemnity Co., N.Y.C., 1936-50, asst. sec., 1946-50; asst. sec.-treas. Nat. Assn. Ins. Agts., N.Y.C., 1950-54; v.p. Alexander & Co., Chgo., 1954-63, Great Am. Ins. Co., N.Y.C., 1964-69; dir. research Ind. Ins. Agts. of Am., 1970-79, exec. v.p., 1979-81, exec. v.p. emeritus, 1981. Served with U.S. Army, 1940-46, PTO. Mem. Am. Soc. Assn. Execs., Soc. C.P.C.U.'s, Sigma Alpha Epsilon. Republican. Home: 2523 Monument Ave Bennington VT 05201-9347

PERINE, MAXINE HARRIET, retired reading educator; b. Worth County, Mo., May 11, 1918; d. Robert Rozwell and Della Dale (Martin) P. BS in Edn., Ctrl. Mo. State U., 1944; MA, Columbia U., 1954, profl. diploma, 1960, EdD, 1977. Tchr. Worth County schs., 1935-44, Kansas City (Mo.) pub. schs., 1944-59, reading cons., 1959-64; editor Holt, Rinehart, Winston, N.Y.C., 1964; mem. faculty U. Mich., Flint, 1964-86, tchr. specializing in reading, ret., 1986. Vis. scholar Columbia U., 1978; program chair World Congress of Reading, Dublin, 1982; spkr. Nat. Coun. Tchrs. English, Honolulu, 1967, World Congress Reading, Hamburg, Fed. Republic Germany, 1978, Hong Kong, 1984, World Congress for the Gifted, Manila, The Philippines, 1983. Author, editor in field. Mem. Internat. Reading Assn., Kappa Delta Pi (chpt. founding counselor 1980—, internat. com. constn. and bylaws 1982-84), Delta Kappa Gamma (Woman of Distinction 1972). Presbyterian.

PERINELLI, MARGUERITE ROSE, women's health nurse, educator; b. Bklyn., Dec. 20, 1947; d. Joseph and Carmela (Conti) Perinelli; children: Joseph, Philip, Kathryn, Thomas, Mary Sarah, Rosemarie. Diploma, St. Vincent Med. Ctr. Richmond, S.I., N.Y., 1968; student, Coll. S.I., 1969-74; BSN, Wagner Coll., 1991. Lamaze certified childbirth educator. Nursery staff nurse St. Vincent's Med. Ctr. Richmond, 1968-72; obstetrics staff nurse S.I. Univ. Hosp., 1973—, maternal child nurse labor and delivery, 1993—; staff nurse Carmel Richmond Nursing Home, 1992-93; per diem nurse U. Hospice, 1995—. Vol. Pax Christi Hospice, 1992—96; sec. CNP SIUH North, 1994—, S.I. chpt. NYCRNA, 1997—99, 2002—. Recipient The Nightingale Soc. Distinguished Leadership award, Nat. Collegiate Nursing award. Mem.: ANA, Internat. Childbirth Edn. Assn., NY State Nurses Assn., Lamaze Internat.

PERIUT, RICHARD, internist, pulmonologist, intensivist; b. N.Y.C., Sept. 21, 1964; MD, U. Ctrl. del Este, Dominican Republican, 1989. Diplomate in internal medicine, pulmonary diseases and critical care medicine Am. Bd. Internal Medicine. Intern Maimonides Med. Ctr., Bklyn., 1993, resident, 1995, fellow pulmonary and critical care medicine, 1995—. Fellow Am. Coll. Chest Physicians. Office: Maimonides Med Ctr 4802 10th Ave Brooklyn NY 11219-2844 E-mail: rperiut@nj.rr.com.

PERKEL, ROBERT SIMON, photojournalist, educator; b. Jersey City, Apr. 23, 1925; s. Louis Leo and Flora Sonia (Levin) P. BS, NYU, 1948; MS, Barry U., 1964; postgrad., Columbia U. Owner, operator Gulfstream Color Labs., Miami Beach, Fla., 1955-61; graphics instr. Dade County Pub. Schs., 1962-66; freelance photojournalist, 1967—. Rep. News Events Photo Svc., Ft. Lauderdale, Fla.; instr. photography Broward Community Coll., 1982-92; rep. Patch Communications, Titusville, Fla., 1985-88; pub. Biograph/Communications, North Miami Beach, Fla., 1987-90; contbr. photo stories, and photographs to numerous mags. and indsl. trade publs. including Women's World, Merck, Sharp & Dohme's Frontline Mag., Gt. Am. Combank News, Nat. Utility Contractor, Mainstream, Nat. Jewish Monthly, Delta Digest, Textile Rental, Sprint Communicator, Rag. the All-Music Mag., DAV Mag., Hallandale Digest, Miami Herald, record jacket C.P. Records, Inc.; exhibited at Met. Mus. and Art Center, Coral Gables, Fla., Mus. of Fine Arts, Boston. Former publicity dir. Coun. for Internat. Visitors of Greater miami; mem. Mus. Art, Ft. Lauderdale. With AUS, 1943-46, ETO. Recipient Comty. Spirit award Zonta Club Greater Miami, 1980, Found. medal Nat. Press Photographers Found., 2000. Mem. World Ocean and Cruise Liner Soc., NYU Alumni Fedn. (Leadership award for 1982-83 fund campaign), Barry U. Alumni Assn., Nat. Press Photographers Assn. (life), Nielsen Media Rsch., DAV (life, Nat. Citation for Disting. Svc. 1969, trustee Jack Schwartz chpt., past comdr. Miami Beach-Surfside chpt. DAV Nat. Svc. plaque, 2000), Steamship Hist. Soc. Am. Found. (life; S.E. Fla. chpt.), Am. Legion, VFW (life), Alpha Mu Gamma. Home: 3619 NE 207th St Apt 2107 Aventura FL 33180

PERKIN, GORDON WESLEY, international health executive; b. Toronto, Ont., Can., Apr. 25, 1935; came to U.S., 1962; s. Irvine Boyer and Jean (Laing) P.; m. Elizabeth Scott, Dec. 21, 1957; children: Scott, Stuart. MD, U. Toronto, 1959. Asst. dir. clin. rsch. Ortho Rsch. Found., Raritan, N.J., 1962-64; assoc. med. dir. Planned Parenthood Fedn. Am., N.Y.C., 1964-66; program advisor Ford Found., 1966-67, regional program advisor Bangkok, 1967-69, Rio de Janeiro, 1973-76, program officer Mexico City, 1976-80; project specialist Ministry Fin. and Econ. Planning, Accra, Ghana, 1969-70; cons. WHO, Geneva, 1971-73; pres. Program for Appropriate Tech. in Health, Seattle, 1980-99; dir. reproductive and child health program Bill and Melinda Gates Found., 1999—. Affiliate prof. pub. health, U. Wash., Seattle. Contbr. numerous articles to profl. jours. APHA fellow, 1970. Mem. Planned Parenthood Fedn. Am. (bd. dirs. 1983-89), Planned Parenthood Seattle-King County (bd. dirs. 1982-96, mem. exec. com. 1983-86), Planned Parenthood Western Wash. (bd. dirs. 1996—), Nat. Coun. for Internat. Health (mem. bd. govs. 1984-95), NAS (com. mem. 1987-90), Alan Guttmacher Inst. (bd. dirs. 1985-90), Assn. Reproductive Health Profls., Alpha Omega Alpha. Office: Bill & Melinda Gates Found PO Box 23350 Seattle WA 98102-0650

PERKIN, HAROLD JAMES, retired social historian, educator; b. Nov. 11, 1926; s. Robert James and Hilda May (Dillon) P.; m. Joan Griffiths, July 3, 1948; children: Deborah Jane, Julian Robert. BA with 1st class distinction, Cambridge U., 1948, MA, 1952. From asst. lectr. to lectr. social history Manchester U., 1951-65; sr. lectr. Lancaster U., 1965-67, prof. social history, 1967-84, dir. ctr. social history, 1975-84, vis. prof., 1984-97, prof. emeritus, 1997—; prof. history Northwestern U., Evanston, Ill., 1985-97, prof. higher edn., 1987-97, prof. emeritus, 1997—. Vis. fellow Princeton U., 1979-80; fellow Nat. Humanities Ctr., N.C., 1982-83; hon. prof. U. Wales, Cardiff, 1997—. Author: The Origins of Modern English Society, 1780-1880, 1969, reprinted, 2002, Key Profession: The History of the Association of University Teachers, 1969, New Universities in the U.K., 1969, The Age of the Railway, 1970, The Age of the Automobile, 1976, The Structured Crowd, 1980, Professionalism, Property and English Society since 1880, 1981, The Rise of Professional Society: England since 1880, 1989, reprinted, 2002, Higher Education and English Society, Japanese transl., 1993, The Third Revolution: Professional Elites in the Modern World, 1996, The Making of a Social Historian, 2002. With RAF, 1948-50. Recipient Gold medal Nat. Inst. Ednl. Rsch., Tokyo, 1982; maj. scholar Cambridge U., 1945-48; John S. Guggenheim fellow, 1989-90. Fellow Royal Hist. Soc.; mem. Social History Soc. U.K. (founder 1976), Econ. History Soc., History of Edn. Soc., Assn. U. Tchrs. (pres. 1970-71). Home: 106 St Mary's Mansions St Mary's Terr London W2 ISZ England E-mail: hjperkin@borwicks.demon.co.uk.

PERKIN, RONALD MURRAY, pediatrician, educator; b. Denver, July 31, 1948; s. Robert Murray and Marion Kathryn (Thompson) P.; m. Susan Renee Sheer; children: Matthew Murray, Jeffrey Jay, Nickolas James, Thomas Mitchell, Benjamin Sheer. BS in Engring., U. Colo., 1970; postgrad., Johns Hopkins U., 1970-71; MD, U. South Fla., 1976; MA, Loma Linda Univ. Diplomate Am. Bd. Pediatrics. Resident in pediatrics Children's Med. Ctr., Dallas, 1976-79, fellow in pediatric intensive care, 1979-81, asst. dir. pediatric intensive care, 1981; clins. asst. prof. pediatrics U. Tex. Health Sci. Ctr. Southwestern Med. Sch., 1981; asst. adj. prof. pediatrics U. Calif. Sch. Medicine, San Diego, 1982-84, co-dir. pediatric intensive care, 1982-84; dir. pediatric ICU attending physician Childrens Hosp. Orange (Calif.) County Hosp., 1984-88; attending physician newborn ICU St. Joseph's Hosp., Orange, 1984-88; assoc. prof. pediatrics Loma Linda Univ., 1988-90, prof. pediactics, 1990-2000; prof., chmn. dept. pediats. Brody Sch. Medicine, East Carolina U., Greenville, NC, 2000—. Cons. Naval Hosp., San Diego, 1983-84; asst. adj. prof. pediatrics U. Calif., Irvine, 1984-88; dir. pediatric intensive care fellowship program U. Calif. Irvine and Children's Hosp. Orange County, 1984-88; mem. critical care adv. com., critical care council, Extra Corporeal Membrane Oxygenation found. So. Calif., emergency dept. com., ethics com., ethics cons. svc. critical care com., resident evaluation sub-com., respiratory care com.; dir. pediatrics critical care Loma Linda Univ. Children's Hosp., 1988-2000, assoc. chair pediatrics Sch. Medicine, 1993-2000; lectr. in field. Editor: (with others) Brain Insults in Infants and Children: Pathophysiology and Management; Emergency Management of the Critically Ill Child; reviewer Capistrano Press, Ltd., 1982-84, Jour. Pediatrics, 1982—; contbr. numerous articles and to profl. jours. Served with USN, 1971-73. Recipient student awards U. South Fla. Coll. Medicine, faculty awards U. Calif., Irvine, Lange Ann. award Lange Book Co., 1974; Mosby scholar Mosby Book Co., 1975-76. Fellow Am. Acad. Pediatrics, Am. Coll. Critical Care Medicine; mem. Soc. Critical Care Medicine, Calif. Children Svcs. (adv. com. rev. pediatric ICU's 1986-2000). Office: 3E-142 Brody Med Scis Bldg Greenville NC 27858-4354 Fax: 252 816 3292. E-mail: perkinr@mail.ecu.edu.

PERKINS, ALFRED LAMONT, transportation company administrator; b. Louisville, Sept. 4, 1949; s. Emmett Perkins and Kathleen (Williams) Logan; m. Dorothy H. Gough, Apr. 7, 1975; children: Sean L., Adrian S. BS in Social Work, U. Louisville, 1976, MS in Social Work, 1977. Cert. clin. social worker, Ind. Mental health cons. Lifespring Mental Health Svcs., Jeffersonville, Ind., 1978-85; mgmt. cons. to industry and bus. Family and Children's Agy., Louisville, 1985-89; coord. drug free workplace and employee assistance program Am. Comml. Barge Line Co., Jeffersonville, 1989—. Instr. Jefferson C.C., Louisville, 1979-85; cons. Urban League, Louisville, 1987-88. With USAF, 1966-70. Avocations: reading, golf, travel. Office: Am Comml Barge Line Co 1701 E Market St Jeffersonville IN 47130-4747

PERKINS, ANTHONY B. editor-in-chief, writer, educator; V.p. bus. devel. Silicon Valley Bank; founder, CEO Upside Pub. Co.; founder, CEO, editor-in-chief Red Herring mag., 1993—. Commentator CNN Fin. Network Digital Jam show, CNN, CNBC, ZDTV's News programs, Silicon Spin, European Bus. News; spkr. in field. Contbr. guest columns for various industry pubs. Founding chmn. Churchill Club , Palo Alto, Calif.; mem. bd. dirs. Am. Entrepreneurs Econ. Growth, Wash. Named one of the top ten tech./bus. journalists, Mktg. Computers mag. Office: Red Herring mag 1550 Bryant St Ste 450 San Francisco CA 94103 Office Fax: 415-865-2280.*

PERKINS, BARBARA M. English educator, editor; b. St. Benedict, Pa., July 9, 1933; d. George Russell and Gladys Annette (Patterson) Miller; m. George B. Perkins, May 9, 1964; children: Laura J., Suzanne C., Alison C. BA, Baldwin-Wallace Coll., 1956; MA, Kent State U., 1959; PhD, U. Pa., 1972. Tchr. Cleve. Pub. Schs., 1956-58; asst. prof. Baldwin-Wallace Coll., Berea, Ohio, 1958-63; tchg. fellow U. Pa., Phila., 1963-64; asst. prof. Fairleigh Dickinson U., Rutherford, N.J., 1964-66; dir. writing improvement Ea. Mich. U., Ypsilanti, 1976-78; mng. editor Journ. of Narrative Tech./Ea. Mich. U., 1977-92. Vis. prof. U. Newcastle, N.S.W., Australia, 1989; adj. prof. U. Toledo, 1992-97. Assoc. editor: Narrative, Columbus, Ohio, 1992—; co-editor: (books) The American Tradition in Literature, 1994, 10th edit., 2002, Women's Work, 1993, Kaleidoscope, 1993, Reader's Encyclopedia of American Literature, 2d edit., 2002. Bd. dirs., program com. chair, sec. HelpSource, Ann Arbor, Mich., 1993—; mem. Airport Adv. Com., Ann Arbor, 1991-97. Recipient Danforth Faculty fellowship Danforth Found., Nat. Libr. of Scotland, 1966-67. Mem. MLA, Soc. for Study of Narrative Lit. (sec./treas.). Home: 1316 King George Blvd Ann Arbor MI 48108-3212 E-mail: eng_perkins@online.emich.edu.

PERKINS, BRADFORD, history educator; b. Rochester, N.Y., Mar. 6, 1925; s. Dexter and Wilma (Lord) P.; m. Nancy Nash Tucker, June 18, 1949 (dec.); children: Dexter III, Matthew Edward, Martha Nash. James Bradford (dec.). AB, Harvard U., 1946, PhD, 1952. From instr. to asso. prof. history U. Calif. at, Los Angeles, 1952-62; prof. history U. Mich., 1962-97, chmn. dept., 1971-72, 80-81, prof. emeritus, 1997—. Commonwealth Fund lectr. Univ. Coll., London, Eng., 1964; vis. prof. history Brandeis U., 1970, Ecole des Hautes Etudes en Sciences Sociales, Paris, 1983; Albert Shaw lectr. Johns Hopkins U., 1979; mem. council Inst. Early Am. History and Culture, 1968-71; program dir. Nat. Endowment for Humanities Fellowships in Residence for Coll. Tchrs., 1974-75 Author: The First Rapprochement: England and the United States, 1795-1805, 1955, Youthful America, 1960, Prologue to War: England and the United States, 1805-1812, 1961, Causes of the War of 1812, 1962, Castlereagh and Adams: England and the United States, 1812- 1823, 1964, The Great Rapprochement: England and the United States, 1895-1914, 1968, The Creation of a Republican Empire, 1993. Served with AUS, 1943-45, ETO. Decorated Bronze Star.; Recipient Bancroft prize, 1965, Disting. Faculty award U. Mich., 1986; Warren fellow, 1969-70; Social Sci. Research Council faculty research fellow, 1957-60; Guggenheim fellow, 1962-63 Mem. Am. Hist. Assn., Soc. Am. Historians, Orgn. Am. Historians (coun. 1969-72), Soc. Historians Am. Fgn. Rels. (coun. 1967-72, pres. 1974, Graebner award 1992), Mass. Hist. Soc., Am. Antiquarian Soc. Home: 827 Asa Gray Dr # 458 Ann Arbor MI 48105 E-mail: bperkins@umich.edu.

PERKINS, BRENDA ELIZABETH, veterinarian; b. Bryn Mawr, Pa., July 26, 1957; d. Edward Betts and Jean Marion (Ashmead) Perkins; m. Mark S. Taylor, June 16, 1984; children: Ian Perkins-Taylor, Colin Perkins-Taylor. BS, Swarthmore Coll., 1979; MS, U. Del., 1982; VMD, U. Pa., 1984. Assoc. veterinarian Stratford (N.J.) Vet. Hosp., 1984-85, Aston (Pa.) Vet. Hosp., 1985-87, West Chester (Pa.) Animal Hosp., 1987-93, veterinarian, owner, 1993—. Mem. governing bd. Westtown Sch., 1993—; treas. Phila. Dog Tng. Club, 1998—; mem. Animal Welfare Com. Swarthmore Coll., 1990—. Home: 913 Strath Haven Ave Swarthmore PA 19081-2221 Office: West Chester Animal Hosp 1140 Pottstown Pike West Chester PA 19380-4138

PERKINS, CHARLES, III, newspaper editor; b. Brockton, Mass., July 25, 1952; s. Charles II and Barbara Perkins; m. Linda C. Burroughs, Jan. 4, 1985. BA, Dartmouth Coll., 1975. Editor Journal-Opinion, Bradford, Vt., 1977-78; reporter, editor The Union Leader and N.H. Sunday News, Manchester, 1978-81; Sunday editor N.H. Sunday News, 1981-84; mng. editor The Union Leader and N.H. Sunday News, 1984-92, exec. editor, 1992-2000, v.p. editl., 2000—. Office: PO Box 9555 Manchester NH 03108-9555

PERKINS, CHARLES THEODORE, real estate developer, consultant; b. Houston, Aug. 16, 1967; s. Charles Abraham and Mary Margaret Perkins. Attended, St. John's Coll., Santa Fe, 1985-86; AB in Psychology, AB in French, Washington U., St. Louis, 1989; MBA, Institut Superieur Des Affaires/Groupe HEC Paris, 1994; postgrad. The Wharton Sch., U. Pa., 1994-95. Lic. broker, N.Y. Asset mgr. A. David Schwarz, III, Inc., Houston, 1989-93; pres. CTP Interests, Inc., 1991—; projet mgr. Washington Sq. Ptnrs., N.Y., 1995—, The Arete Group, N.Y., 1995—; mng. dir. Plymouth Ptnrs. Ltd., 1997—. Broker's lic. Tex. Real Estate Commn., Austin, 1991—. Dir. Washington Crew Classic Regata, St. Louis, 1989; founding coach Rice U. Crew, Houston, 1990; lic. judge referee U.S. Rowing Assn., 1991—, level I coach, 1991—. Recipient Prix De L'excellence BDE, Groupe HEC-ISA, Paris, 1994. Mem. The Penn Club of N.Y., N.Y. Sports Club, Mensa. Episcopalian.

PERKINS, DAVID, English language educator; b. Philadelphia, Pa., Oct. 25, 1928; s. Dwight Goss and Esther M. (Williams) P. AB, Harvard U., 1951, MA, 1952, PhD, 1955. Mem. faculty Harvard U., 1957—, prof. English, 1964-94, chmn. dept. English, 1976-81, chmn. dept. lit., 1987-89, prof. emeritus, 1994—; prof. U. Calif., 1996, 97, 2000. Vis. prof. Goettingen U., 1968-69 Author: The Quest for Permanence: the Symbolism of Wordsworth, Shelley and Keats, 1959, Wordsworth and the Poetry of Sincerity, 1964, English Romantic Writers, 1967, A History of Modern Poetry: From the 1890's to the High Modernist Mode, 1976, A History of Modern Poetry, Vol. 2, Modernism and After, 1987; (with W. Jackson Bate) British and American Poets: Chaucer to the Present, 1986, Is Literary History Possible, 1991; editor: The Teaching of Literature: What is Needed Now, 1988, Theoretical Issues in Literary History, 1991; mem. editorial adv. bd. Keats-Shelley Jour., 1962-89, The Wordsworth Circle, Modern Lang. Quar. Served with AUS, 1955-57. Guggenheim fellow, 1962, 73; Fulbright fellow, 1968-69; Am. Council Learned Socs. fellow, 1977 Mem. Am. Acad. Arts and Scis., Cambridge Sci. Club. Home: 27881 Horseshoe Bnd San Juan Capistrano CA 92675-1523

PERKINS, DAVID L. music educator; s. Dallas and Sagemary Perkins; m. Beth Ellen Kutzner, Nov. 19, 1994; children: Michael, Ellen, Spencer. BS in Music Edn., West Chester U., West Chester, Pennsylvania, 1980—84. Instructional II Commonwealth of Pa, 1989, Instructional I Commonwealth of Pa, 1984. Jr. h.s. choral dir. Lehighton Area Sch. Dist., Lehighton, Pa., 1985—93, h.s. choral dir., 1993—. Dir. of ch. music First Presbyn. Ch. of Panther Valley, Summit Hill, Pa., 1989—. Scenic and lighting designer (off-broadway production (set/lights) Holy Heists; actor: (college musical production) Oklahoma. Elected to music/worship com. Lehigh Presbytery, Allentown, Pa., 1993—96; elected as ch. elder First Presbyn. Ch. of Panther Valley, Summit Hill, 1986—89, pres. of ch. corp. NC, 1988—89. Recipient Kappa Delta Pi, Kappa Delta Pi, 1984, Tchr. of the Yr., Lehighton Area Chamber of Commerce, 1991, Outstanding Music Student, UNICO, 1980, Ministerial Award, Panther Valley Ministerium, 1980; scholar The Swope Found. Scholarship, Swope Found. West Chester U., 1983, Off-Campus Student Assn. Scholarship, Off-Campus Student Assn. West Chester U., 1983, Summer Sch. of the Arts, Lehigh CC, 1977 & 1978, Leadership Camp at Keystone CC, Panther Valley Rotary, 1978, Fred Waring Music Workshop, Panther Valley Chamber of Commerce, 1979. Mem.: Pa, State Educators Assn. (assoc.), Music Educators Nat. Conf. (assoc.), Pa, Music Educators Assn. (assoc.), Kappa Delta Pi (assoc.), Phi Mu Alpha Sinfonia (assoc.; choral dir. 1983—84). R-Consevative. Presbyterian. Achievements include 1991 Educator of the Year; Winner of Talent Search at Easton State Theatre. Avocations: travel, magic, lighting and sets, horse back riding. Office: Lehighton Area High School 1 Indian Lane Lehighton PA 18235 Office Fax: 610-377-1852. Personal E-mail: musiktime@hotmail.com.

PERKINS, DEBORAH ANNE, interior designer; b. Mineola, N.Y., Mar. 8, 1954; d. Arthur Cudner and Maria (Risko) P.; 1 child, Olivia Anne Perkins. AAS in Interior Design magne cum laude, Chamberlayne Sch., Boston, 1975. Cert. fitness instr. YMCA. Film admissions coord. Gen. Cinema Corp., Chestnut Hill, Mass., 1976-78; tchr. adult edn. Kennedy Community Sch., Cambridge, 1976; interior design cons. Jordan Marsh Co., Quincy, 1978-81; freelance interior designer Honduras, Central Am., 1981; sales rep. New Eng. territory LaFrance (S.C.) Fabrics, 1982-84; owner, designer The Design Studio, Watertown, Mass., 1985—. Mem. Boston Soc. Architects Task Force for Homeless, 1988-90; big sister YWCA, Boston, 1985—; participant Grace Chapel Nursing Home Ministry, Lexington, Mass., 1989-90; co-leader Daybreak Single Parent Support Group, 1992-93. Mem. NAFE, Women Entrepreneurs Homebased, Am. Soc. Interior Designers, Alpha Nu Omega. Avocations: skiing. Home and Office: 68 Washington St Natick MA 01760-3521

PERKINS, DEBORAH LOUISE, music educator; b. Redwood City, Calif., Nov. 3, 1953; d. Robert Horace and Louise (Hughes) Walpole; m. Stephen Perkins, July 21, 1979; 1 child, Kayla Michelle. B in Music Edn., SUNY, Potsdam, 1975; M in Music Edn., U. S.C., 1980. Cert. music edn. grades K-12, Tex., Fla., S.C. Music tchr., orch. dir. Charleston (S.C.) City Schs., 1975-76,

Spartanburg (S.C.) Sch. Dist. Seven, 1976-79; grad. asst. U. S.C., Columbia, 1979-80; music tchr., orch. dir. Lexington (S.C.) Sch. Dist. One, 1980-84, Ramblewood Middle Sch., Coral Springs, Fla., 1984-89; tchg. fellow U. North Tex., Denton, 1989-92; music tchr., orch. dir. Wilson Middle Sch., Plano, Tex., 1993—. Pres. S.C. U. Am. String Tchrs. Assn. Orch. Divsn. S.C. Music Educators Assoc., 1982-84; so. divsn. chair Nat. Sch. Orch. Assn., 1985-88, pub. rels. chair, 1985-89; pres. Fla. Orch. Assn., 1987-89. Contbr. articles to profl. jours. Mem. Am. String Tchrs. Assn., Music Educators Nat. Conf., Tex. Music Educators Assn., Tex. Orch. Dirs., Rsch. in Am. Edn., Phi Kappa Lambda. Republican. Episcopalian. Home: 4825 N Meadow Ridge Cir Mc Kinney TX 75070-5236 Office: Wilson Middle Sch 1001 Custer Rd Plano TX 75075-8347

PERKINS, DIANA OTYLIA, psychiatrist; b. Elgin AFB, Fla., Mar. 16, 1958; d. Richard W. and Barbara Anne P.; children: Christopher Walter, Nicholas Walter, Katherine Walter. BS in Psychology with honors, U. Md., 1980; MD, 1984; MPH in Epidemiology, U. N.C., 1992. Diplomate Am. Bd. Psychiatry. Asst. prof. U. N.C., Chapel Hill, 1993-98, assoc. prof., 1998—; inpatient attending U. N.C. Mental Health Clin. Rsch. Ctr., 1993—2001, med. dir. Schizophrenia Treatment and Evaln. Program (STEP), 1993—, dir. clin. assessments and procedures, 1996—2002. Cons. Eli Lilly, Indpls., 2000—; mem. spkrs. bur. Astra Zeneca, 1997—, Janssen, 1997—; mem. adv. bd. Pfizer, 1997. Contbr. articles to profl. jours. Mentor Student Nat. Med. assn., 1999-2001, Health Professions Recruitment exposure Progress, 1999-2001. Grantee Lilly rsch. Labs, 1999-2001; recipient Disting. Profl. Svc. award Mental Health Assn. Orange County (N.C.), 1997, K-23 award NIMH, 2000—. Fellow Am. Psychiat. Assn.; mem. N.C. Psychiat. Assn. (Eugene A. Hargrove Mental Health Rsch. award 2000), Soc. Biol. Psychiatry, Delta Omega Theta. Avocations: windsurfing, biking, skiing. Office: U NC Dept Psychiatry CB # 716D Chapel Hill NC 27599-7160

PERKINS, DWIGHT HEALD, economics educator; b. Chgo., Oct. 20, 1934; s. Lawrence Bradford and Margery (Blair) P.; m. Julie Rate, June 15, 1957; children: Lucy Fitch, Dwight Edward, Caleb Blair. BA, Cornell U., 1956; AM, Harvard U., 1961, PhD, 1964. From instr. to assoc. prof. Harvard U., Cambridge, Mass., 1963-69, prof. econs., 1969-81, assoc. dir. East Asian Rsch. Ctr., 1973-77, chmn. dept. econs., 1977-80, H.H. Burbank prof. polit. economy, 1981—, dir. Asia Ctr., 2002—; dir. Harvard Inst. Internat. Devel., 1980-95. Dir. Nat. Com. on U.S.-China Rels., 1991-2000; trustee China Med. Bd., 1995—, chair, 2000—; cons. permanent subcom. on investigations U.S. Senate, 1974-80; H.M. Jackson vis. prof. Chinese studies U. Wash., 1985, Phi Beta Kappa lectr., 1992-93, Faculty Salzburg seminar, 1996; lectr. Fulbright tchg. policy program, Vietnam, 1997-2002; mem. Internat. Adv. Group to Prime Min. of Papua, New Guinea, 1991-92, 2000-02; cons. Korea Devel. Inst., 1972-80, Govt. Malaysia, 1968-69. Author: (with M. Halperin) Communist China and Arms Control, 1965, Agricultural Development in China, 1368-1968, 1969, Market Control and Planning in Communist China, 1966, China: Asia's Next Economic Giant?, 1986, (with E.S. Mason and others) The Economic Modernization of Korea, 1980, (with S. Yusuf) Rural Development in China, 1984, (with M. Gillis and others) Economics of Development, 1983, 5th edit., 2001; editor: China's Modern Economy in Historical Perspective, 1975, (with M. Roemer) Reforming Economic Systems in Developing Countries, 1991, (with J. Stern and others) Industrialization and the State: The Korean Heavy and Chemical Industry Drive, 1995, (with others) Assisting Development in a Changing World, 1997, (with others: Industrialization and the State: The Changing Role of the Taiwan Government in the Economy, 1945-1998, 2001. Mem. Vis. Com. Far Ea. Studies, U. Chgo., 1973-77; mem. bd. govs. East-West Ctr., Honolulu, 1979-82; co-moderator Aspen Inst. Seminar on Korea, Colo., 1980-83. Lt. (j.g.) USNR, 1956-58. Fgn. Area Tng. fellow Ford Found., N.Y., 1958-62; NSF Sci. Faculty fellow Tokyo, 1968-69 Mem. Am. Philos. Soc., Assn. Asian Studies, Assn. Comparative Econ. Systems (pres. 1999-2000), Am. Econ. Assn., Phi Beta Kappa. Home: 64 Pinehurst Rd Belmont MA 02478-1504 Office: Harvard Univ Dept Econs Cambridge MA 02138-5781 E-mail: dwight_perkins@harvard.edu.

PERKINS, EDWARD J. diplomat; b. Sterlington, La., June 8, 1928; m. Lucy Liu; children: Katherine, Sarah. Student, U. Calif., Lewis and Clark Coll.; BA, U. Md., 1967; MPA, U. So. Calif., 1972, DPA, 1978; studied French, Fgn. Service Inst., 1983; LLD (hon.), U. Md., 1990, St. John's U., 1990, Lewis and Clark Coll., 1988; LHD (hon.), Winston-Salem State U., 1990, Bowie State Coll., 1993; HHD (hon.), St. Augustine Coll., 1991, Beloit Coll., 1990, U. So. Calif., 1995. Chief of pers. Army and Air Force Exch. Svc., Taipei, Taiwan, 1958-62, dep. chief Okinawa, Japan, 1962-64; chief pers. and adminstrn. Army and Air Force Exchange Service, Japan, 1964-66; asst. gen. svcs. officer Far East bur. AID, 1967-69, mgmt. analyst, 1969-70; asst. dir. for mgmt. U.S. Ops. Mission to Thailand, 1970-72; staff asst. Office of Dir. Gen. Fgn. Svc., 1972, personnel officer, 1972-74; adminstrv. officer Bur. Near Eastern and South Asian Affairs, 1974-75; mgmt. analysis officer Office Mgmt. Ops., Dept. State, 1975-78; counselor for polit. affairs Accra, Ghana, 1978-81; dep. chief of mission Monrovia, Liberia, 1981-83; dir. Office of West African Affairs, Bur. African Affairs, Dept. State, 1983-85; U.S. amb. to Liberia, 1985-86; U.S. amb. to South Africa, 1986-89; dir. gen., dir. pers. Fgn. Svc., Dept. of State, Washington, 1989-92; U.S. rep. to UN N.Y.C., 1992-93; U.S. amb. to Australia Canberra, 1993-96. William J. Crowe prof. and exec. dir. Internat. Programs Ctr., U. Okla., Norman 1996—; mem. adv. bd. Inst. Internat. Pub. Policy, 1997—; mem. adv. coun. Univ. Office of Internat. Programs, Pa. State U., 1997—. Contbr. articles to profl. publs.; editor (with David Boren) Preparing American's Foreign Policy for the 21st Century, 1999, with (Joseph Ginat) Palestinian Refugees: Traditional Positions and New Solutions, 2001, (with David Boren) Democracy, Morality, and the Search for Peace in America's Foreign Policy, 2002. Trustee Lewis and Clark Coll., 1994—, Woodrow Wilson Nat. Fellowship Found., 1999—; bd. govs. Joint Ctr. for Polit. and Econ. Studies; mem. steering com. Ctr. for Australian and New Zealand Studies, Georgetown U., 1996—; bd. Cranlana Programme. Recipient Presdl. Meritorious Svc. award, 1987, Presdl. Disting. Svc. award, 1989, Meritorious Honor award AID, 1967, Disting. Alumni award U. So. Calif., 1991, Achievement award So. U., 1991, award for outstanding svc. as fgn. svc. officer Una Chapman Cox Found., 1989, Living Legend award The Links, Inc., 1989, Statesman of Yr. award George Washington U., 1992, Superior Honor award Dept. of State, 1983, Dir. Gen.'s cup Dept. of State, 2001; honoree U. Okla. chpt. Beta Gamma Sigma, 1998. Fellow Nat. Acad. Pub. Adminstrn.; mem. VFW, ASPA, Navy League, Am. Polit. Sci. Assn., Fgn. Policy Assn. (ambassadorial fellow), Internat. Studies Assn., Coun. on Fgn. Rels., Am. Acad. Diplomacy, Am. Consortium Internat. Pub. Adminstrn., Am. Fgn. Svc. Assn., Am. Legion, Ctr. Study of Presidency, Chester A. Arthur Soc., Pub. Svc. Comm., World Affairs Couns. Okla. and Washington, Am. Acad. Diplomacy, Pacific Coun. on Internat. Policy, Assn. for Diplomatic Studies and Tng. (bd. dirs. 1998—), Kappa Alpha Psi (Laurel Wreath award 1993, C. Rodger Wilson Leadership Conf. award 1990, Disting. Svc. award 1989, Outstanding Achievement award for Fgn. Svc. 1986), Phi Kappa Phi. Office: U Okla Internat Programs Ctr 339 W Boyd St Rm 400 Norman OK 73019-5144

PERKINS, FLOYD JERRY, retired theology educator; b. Bertha, Minn., May 9, 1924; s. Ray Lester and Nancy Emily (Kelley) P.; m. Mary Elizabeth Owen, Sept. 21, 1947 (dec. June 1982); children: Douglas Jerry, David Floyd, Sheryl Pauline; m. Phyllis Genevra Hartley, July 14, 1984. AB, BTh, N.W. Nazarene Coll., 1949; MA, U. Mo., 1952; MDiv, Nazarene Theol. Sem., 1952; ThM, Burton Sem., 1964; PhD, U. Witwatersrand, Johannesburg, South Africa, 1974; ThD, Internat. Sem., 1994. Ordained to Christian ministry, 1951. Pres. South African Nazarene Theol. Sem., Florida Transvaal, Africa, 1955-67, Nazarene Bible Sem., Lourenzo Marques, Mozambique, 1967-73, Campinas, Brazil, 1974-76; prof. missions N.W. Nazarene Coll., Nampa, Idaho, 1976; prof. theology Nazarene Bible Coll., Colorado Springs, Colo., 1976-97. Chmn., founder com. higher theol. edn. Ch. of Nazarene in Africa, 1967-74; sec. All African Nazarene Mission Exec., 1967-74; ofcl. Christian Council Mozambique, 1952-74. Author: A History of the Christian Church in Swaziland, 1974. Served with USN, 1944-46. Mem. Soc. Christian Philosophers, Evang. Theol. Soc., Am. Schs. Orientan Rsch., Am. Soc. Missiology, Assn. Evang. Missions Profs. Republican. Avocation: golf. Home: 6355 Oak Ave Apt 21 Temple City CA 91780-1300 *Personal philosophy: Be cheerful, hopeful, courageous, honest, candid, faithful, committed, loyal, and the whole world will be yours!.*

PERKINS, FRANK OVERTON, university official, marine scientist; b. Fork Union, Va., Feb. 14, 1938; s. Frank Otie and Mary Ella (Hughes) P.; m. Beverly Anne Weeks. BA, U. Va., 1960; MS, Fla. State U., Tallahassee, 1962, PhD, 1966. Marine scientist Va. Inst. Marine Sci., Coll. William and Mary, Gloucester Point, 1966-69, sr. marine scientist, 1969-77, asst. dir., 1977-81, dir., dean Sch. Marine Sci., 1981-91, prof. marine sci., 1991-97; asst. v.p. rsch. and grad. edn. U. Hawaii, Honolulu, 1997—. Baptist. Home: 7519 Olowalu Pl Honolulu HI 96825-2950 Office: U Hawaii 105 Bachman Hall Honolulu HI 96822

PERKINS, GEORGE, educator, writer; b. Lowell, Mass., Aug. 16, 1930; s. George Burton Perkins and Gladys Beatrice Jones; m. Barbara Miller Perkins, May 9, 1964; children: Laura, Suzanne, Alison. AB, Tufts U., 1953; MA, Duke U., 1954; PhD, Cornell U., 1960. Instr. Wash. U., St. Louis, 1957-60; asst. prof. Baldwin-Wallace Coll., Berea, Ohio, 1960-63, Fairleigh Dickinson U., Rutherford, N.J., 1963-66; lectr. U. Edinburgh, Scotland, 1966-67; prof. Ea. Mich. U., Ypsilani, 1967-01. Author, editor: The American Tradition in Literature, The Reader's Encyclopedia of American Literature, others. Fellow Inst. for Advanced Studies in the Humanities, U. Edinburgh, 1981; Sr. Fulbright scholar Australia Coun. for Internat. Exch. of Scholars, 1989. Avocations: travel, tennis, literature. Home: 1316 King George Blvd Ann Arbor MI 48108-3212

PERKINS, GEORGE HOLMES, architectural educator, architect; b. Cambridge, Mass., Oct. 10, 1904; s. George Howard and Josephine (Schock) P.; m. Georgia Hencken, June 3, 1933; children— Gray H., Jennifer H. Student, Phillips-Exeter Acad., 1920-22; AB, Harvard U., 1926, M.Arch., 1929; LL.D., U. Pa., 1972. Instr. architecture U. Mich., 1929-30; instr. architecture Harvard, 1930-36, asst. prof., 1936-39, asso. prof., 1939-42, Norton prof. regional planning, chmn. dept., 1945-51; dean, chmn. dept. architecture Grad. Sch. Fine Arts, U. Pa., 1951-71, prof. architecture and urbanism, 1971—; practicing architect and city planner, 1933—. Asst. regional rep., acting dir. urban devel. div. Nat. Housing Agy., 1942-45; cons. Brit. Ministry of Town and Country Planning, 1946, UN, 1946, 55-56; cons. to Govt. Turkey, 1958-60, Balt. Redevel. Authority, Cambridge Redevel. Authority, Worcester Redevel. Authority.; Mem. Cambridge Planning Bd., 1950-51; dir. Phila. Housing Assn., 1951-56, pres., 1953-56; dir. Citizens Council City Planning, 1951-54; chmn. Phila. Zoning Commn., 1955-58, Phila. City Planning Commn., 1958-68; dir. Phila. Port Corp., Old Phila. Devel. Corp., Phila. Indsl. Devel. Corp. Author: Comparative Outline of Architectural History, 1937; editor: Jour. Am. Inst. Planners, 1950-52; contbr. articles to profl. jours. Mem. Phila. Commn. Higher Edn.; Trustee Fairmount Park Art Assn., 1965— . Fellow A.I.A. (chancellor coll. fellows 1964-66); mem. Am. Inst. Planners, Am. Soc. Planning Ofcls., Nat. Assn. Housing Ofcls., World Soc. Ekistics; hon. corr. mem. Royal Inst. Architects Can. Clubs: The Country (Brookline); Franklin Inn (Phila.), Rittenhouse (Phila.), Philadelphia Cricket (Phila.), Art Alliance (Phila.); Century (N.Y.C.). Home: 82 Bethlehem Pike Philadelphia PA 19118-2821

PERKINS, HERBERT ASA, hematologist, educator; b. Boston, Oct. 5, 1918; s. Louis and Anna (Robinson) P.; m. Frances Snyder, Sept. 2, 1942; children: Susan, Deborah, Dale, Karen, Ronnie. AB cum laude, Harvard U., 1940; MD summa cum laude, Tufts U., 1943. Intern Boston City Hosp., 1944, resident, 1947-48; practice medicine specializing in transfusion medicine; clin. instr. Stanford Med. Sch., 1953-57, asst. clin. prof., 1957-58; hematologist Open Heart Surgery Team, Stanford Hosp., San Francisco, 1955-58, Jewish Hosp., St. Louis, 1958-59; dir. rsch. Irwin Meml. Blood Ctrs. (now Blood Ctrs. of the Pacific), San Francisco, 1959-78, med. and sci. dir., 1978-90, exec. dir., 1987-91, pres., 1991-93, sr. med. scientist, 1993—. Asst. prof. medicine Washington U., St. Louis, 1958-59, U. Calif., San Francisco, 1959-66, assoc. prof., 1966-71, clin. prof., 1971—. Co-editor: Hepatitis and Blood Transfusion, 1972. Maj. M.C., U.S. Army, 1944-47. Mem. AAAS, Am. Assn. Blood Banks (chmn. sci. adv. com. 1972-73, chmn. stds. com. 1968-71, chmn. com. on organ transplantation and tissue typing 1970-80, bd. dirs. 1982-86), Am. Soc. Hematology, Internat. Transfusion Soc., Am. Soc. Histocompatibility and Immunogenetics (pres. 1985-86), Nat. Marrow Donor Program (chair bd. dirs. 1995-96, chmn. com. on stds. 1987-94, chmn. fin. com. 1987-94). Home: 520 Berkeley Ave Menlo Park CA 94025-2323 Office: Blood Ctrs of the Pacific 270 Masonic Ave San Francisco CA 94118-4417 E-mail: hperkins@bloodcenters.org.

PERKINS, HOMER GUY, manufacturing company executive; b. New Haven, Oct. 23, 1916; s. Frank W. and Emily (Oesting) P.; m. Dorothy C. Stock, Jan. 24, 1942; children: Maribeth Perkins Grant, Homer Guy Jr., Hazel Mary Perkins Adolphson, Dorothy Catherine, Caroline Ann, Faith Elizabeth Perkins Crotteau, Ruth Emily Perkins Sico. BA in Internat. Rels., Yale U., 1938; LLD (hon.), Westfield (Mass.) State Coll., 1977. With Enesco Group, Inc. (formerly Stanhome, Inc.), Westfield, 1939—, v.p., 1965-66, exec. v.p., 1966-70, pres., CEO, 1970-78, chmn., 1978-81, also bd. dirs. Treas. Stanley Park of Westfield, 1949—; pres. Citizens Scholarship Found., Easthampton, Mass., 1966-67, Easthampton Cmty. Chest, 1960-61; chmn. fin. com., bd. dirs. Western Mass. coun. Girl Scouts U.S., 1966-69; mem. devel. com. Clarke Sch. Deaf, Northampton, 1965-68; mem. fin. com. Town of Easthampton, 1962-70, chmn. fin. com., 1967-68; dir. Frank Stanley Beveridge Found., Westfield, 1956-95, pres., 1986-87; trustee Cooley Dickinson Hosp., Northampton, 1963-70, 84-92, chmn. bd. trustees, 1989-91; pres. bd. trustees Northampton Sch. for Girls, 1964-73; bd. dirs. Porter Phelps Huntington Found., Hadley, Mass., 1960-92, Guild of Holy Child, Westfield, 1969-76; mem. bd. overseers Williston Acad., Easthampton, 1961-64, Old Sturbridge (Mass.) Village, 1970-76; v.p. bd. trustees Williston-Northampton Sch., 1970-75, pres., 1975-78; dir. The Lathrop Communities, 2000, chair fin. com., 2001. With USAAF, 1942-46. Mem. Direct Selling Assn. (chmn. 1975, bd. dirs., mem. Hall of Fame), Paperweight Collectors Assn. (pres. 1991-95), Lions (past pres. Easthampton club). Home: 8 Carol Ave Easthampton MA 01027-1904

PERKINS, HUEL DAVIS, academic administrator; b. Baton Rouge, Dec. 27, 1924; s. John Earl Perkins, Sr. and Velma Davis Perkins; m. Thelma Ovella Smith; 1 child Huel Alfred. BS, So. U., Baton Rouge, LA, 1947; MusM, Northwestern U., 1951, PhD, 1958. Dean coll. of arts & humanities So. U., Baton Rouge, 1968—78; from asst. vice chancellor for academic affairs to spl. asst. to chancellor La. State U., 1980—98, spl. asst. to the chancellor, 1998—. Vis. faculty Havard U., Boston, 1968; chmn. alpha phi alpha edn. found. Alpha Phi Alpha Frat., Balt., 1986—92; nat. chmn. scholars selection com. Coca Cola Found., Atlanta, 1996; invited participant Caribbean-American Scholars Exch. Program, Port-au-Prince, Haiti, 1974; mem. Pres. Clinton's Commn. on Black Coll. and U., Washington, 1994—96. Composer: (musical composition) Southern U. Fight Song, 1953, (songs) Alpha Phi Alpha Sweetheart Song, 1974; book reviewer: Black World Mag., 1973. Pres. Capital Area United Way; torch bearer U.S. Olympics, Baton Rouge, 1995. Named one of 100 Most Influential African Americans, Ebony Mag., 1993; recipient Brotherhood Award, Nat. Conf. of Christian and Jews, 1986, 100 Most Influential African Americans, Ebony Mag., 1994; fellow Humanities fellowship, Nat. Endowment for the Humanities, 1972, Huel D. Perkins Doctoral fellowship, La. State U., 1995; grantee Tchr. grant, Danforth Found., 1957. Mem.: Am. Soc. of Composers, Authors and P:ub., Omicron Delta Kappa, Pi Kappa Lambda, Sigma Pi Phi (grand sire archon 1992—94), Alpha Phi Alpha (chmn. edn. found. 1986—92). Democrat. Baptist. Avocations: tennis, reading, opera. Home: 1923 79th Avenue Baton Rouge LA 70807 Office: Louisiana State University Baton Rouge LA 70803 Home Fax: 225-355-2483; Office Fax: 225-578-5980. Personal E-mail: HDPerk@Bellsouth.net. Business E-Mail: hperkins@lsu.edu.

PERKINS, JACK EDWIN, lawyer; b. Portola, Calif., May 25, 1943; s. Charles James and Vira Almena (Wing) P.; m. Barbara Kay Nielson, Jan. 18, 1969; children: Jill Christy, Kelli Anne. BA, San Jose State Coll., 1966; JD, Hastings Coll. Law, 1972. Bar: Calif. 1972, D.C. 1989. Asst. U.S. atty., Dept. Justice, San Francisco, 1973-74, staff atty. criminal divsn. Washington, 1972, 74-76, staff atty. Office Legis. Affairs, 1976-80, legis. counsel, 1980-86, dep. asst. atty. gen., 1986-90; chief adminstrv. hearing officer Exec. Office for Immigration Rev., Falls Church, Va., 1990—. Served to capt. USMC, 1966-69, Vietnam. Recipient John Marshall award Dept. Justice, 1986. Avocations: tennis, jogging, racquetball. Office: Exec Office Immigration Rev 5107 Leesburg Pike Ste 2519 Falls Church VA 22041-3234

PERKINS, JAMES FRANCIS, physicist; b. Hillsdale, Tenn., Jan. 3, 1924; s. Jim D. and Laura Pervis (Goad) P.; A.B., Vanderbilt U., 1948, M.A., 1949; Ph.D., 1953; m. Ida Virginia Phillips, Nov. 23, 1949; 1 son, James F. Sr. engr. Convair, Fort Worth, Tex., 1953-54; scientist Lockheed Aircraft, Marietta, Ga., 1954-61; physicist Army Missile Command Redstone Arsenal, Huntsville, Ala., 1961-77; cons. physicist, 1977— . Served with USAAF, 1943-46. AEC fellow, 1951-52. Mem. Am. Phys. Soc., Sigma Xi. Contbr. articles to profl. jours. Home and Office: 102 Mountain Wood Dr SE Huntsville AL 35801-1809

PERKINS, JAMES R. manufacturing engineering educator, researcher; b. Urbana, Ill., Sept. 10, 1964; married. BA in Engring. Sci., Harvard U., 1986; MSEE, U. Ill., 1990, PhD in Elec. Engring., 1993. Assoc. prof. mfg. engring. Boston U., Brookline, Mass., 2002—, asst. prof. mfg. engring., 1993—2002; rsch. asst. U. of Ill., Urbana, 1991—93, IBM mfg. rsch. fellow, 1989—91; tchg. asst. Harvard U., Cambridge, 1985—85; programmer Dynamic Sys., Urbana, Ill., 1984. Assoc. editor conf. editl. bd. IEEE Control Sys. Soc., 2000—; departmental editor IIE transactions Inst. of Indsl. Engineers, 1997—99; chmn. working group on control of mfg. networks IEEE Control Systems Soc., 1994—97. Contbr. articles to profl. jours. Recipient Rsch. Initiation award, NSF, 1994—98; grantee Harvard Coll. scholar, 1984—85; scholar John Harvard scholar, Harvard U., 1985—86. Mem.: IEEE. Office: Boston U 15 St. Mary's St Brookline MA 02446 Business E-Mail: perkins@bu.edu.

PERKINS, JAMES WINSLOW, international business consultant, builder, contractor; b. Southington, Conn., Sept. 15, 1955; s. Robert Winslow and Florence Corinne (Angelone) P. Student, Tunxis C.C., Farmington, Conn., 1973-75. Owner Town & Country Club, Smithfield, R.I., 1975-80, Ad Mark of Mass, Inc., Ludlow, Mass., 1980-84, Car Stereo Distbrs., Inc., West Palm Beach, Fla., 1983-85, Internat. Imports, Lauderdale Lakes, 1985-88, Modern Sectional Homes, Inc., Southington, Conn., 1989-93. Mem. Nat. Assn. Realtors, Cen. Conn. Bd. Realtors, Mayflower Soc., 100 Club Conn. Republican. Avocations: sailing, water skiing. Home: 2587 Meriden-Wtby Rd Marion CT 06444 Office: James Perkins and Assocs PO Box 153 Marion CT 06444

PERKINS, JAMES WOOD, lawyer; b. New Bedford, Mass., Oct. 14, 1924; s. Ralph Chamberlain and Louise Bartlett (Allen) P.; m. Margaret Neale Heard, Feb. 3, 1951; children: Charles H., James A., George H. AB, Havard U., 1945, JD, 1948; MTS, Harvard Div. Sch., 1996. Bar: Mass. 1948, U.S. Dist. Ct. Mass. 1948. Engr. Sylvania Electric Products, Inc., Salem, Mass., 1944-45; assoc. Palmer & Dodge LLP, Boston, 1948-54, ptnr., 1955-91, mng. ptnr., 1986-89, of counsel, 1992—. Mem. ABA (chmn. sect. local govt. law 1970-71, sect. del. 1974-78), Nat. Assn. Bond Lawyers (pres. 1985-86).

PERKINS, JOHN ALLEN, lawyer; b. New Bedford, Mass., Sept. 13, 1919; s. Ralph Chamberlain and Louise Bartlett (Allen) P.; m. Lydia Bullard Cobb, Sept. 9, 1944; children: John A., Susan W., Robert C., William B. AB, Harvard U., 1940, LL.B., 1943. Bar: Mass. Of counsel Palmer & Dodge LLP, Boston; clk. Social Law Library, 1961-83; grad. researcher Univ. Coll., Oxford U., 1978. Bd. dirs. Greater Boston Legal Services, Inc., 1972-91. Author: The Prudent Peace— Law as Foreign Policy, 1981; contbr. articles to profl. jours. Mem. Dedham (Mass.) Sch. Com., 1959-65, chmn., 1963-65, town counsel, Dedham, 1971-72. Mem. Am. Law Inst., Am. Coll. Trust and Estate Counsel, Mass. Bar Assn. (dir. 1973-75), Internat. Acad. Estate and Trust Law (exec. coun. 1990-94), Boston Bar Assn. (council 1972-75, v.p. 1981-82, pres. 1982-84). Home: 203 Highland St Dedham MA 02026-5835 Office: Palmer & Dodge LLP 111 Huntington Ave at Prudential Ctr Boston MA 02199-7613

PERKINS, JOSEPH S. medical association administrator; Past corp. retirement mgr. Polaroid Corp.; v.p. AARP, Washington, 1994-96, pres.-elect, 1996-98, pres., 1998-2000. Mem. bd. fin. com., nat. legis. coun., bus. partnerships adv. coun. AARP, trustee Andrus Found. Bd., past vice chair; past mem. exec. com., bd. fin. com., bd. com. human resources, trustee investment program, group health ins. trust, bd. observer pension/welfare trust AARP; bd. councilors Ethel Percy Andrus Gerontology Ctr., U. So. Calif.; mem. bd. Operation ABLE (Abilities Based on Long Experience); mem. adv. coun. Foster Grandparent Program Greater Boston; past mem. Pension Benefit Guaranty Corp. Adv. Com.; past bd. dirs. Alzheimer's Assn., Internat. Soc. Retirement Planning; past founding mem., pres. New England Retirement Planners Coun.; past vol. Project RAP; formerly indsl. engr. Office: AARP 601 E St NW Washington DC 20049-0003*

PERKINS, LEEMAN LLOYD, music educator, musicologist; b. Salina, Utah, Mar. 27, 1932; s. Milton Lloyd and Ida Margaret (Johnson) P.; m. Marianne Suzanne Contesse, Nov. 14, 1956; children: Eric Raymond, Bruce Philippe, Marc Christian (dec.), Patrick Thierry. BFA, U. Utah, 1954; PhD, Yale U., 1965. Instr. Boston U., 1964, Yale U., 1964-67, asst. prof., 1967-71, dir. undergraduate studies in music history, 1969-70; assoc. prof. music history, coord. for musicology U. Tex., Austin, 1971-75, grad. adv. for musicology, 1976; prof. music Columbia U., N.Y.C., 1976—, chmn. dept music, 1985-90. Instr. advanced seminar in Medieval History, Smith Coll., 1968; vis. assoc. prof. music Columbia U., 1975; vis. prof. Boston U., 1978; dir. NEH Summer Seminar, 1977. Editor: Johannes Lheritier Opera Omnia, 1969, (with Howard Garey) The Mellon Chansonnier, 1979, Music in the Age of the Renaissance, 1999; gen. editor: Masters and Monuments of Renaissance Music, 1978—. Chmn. grad. musicology com., Columbia U., 1980-84, 1993-96, 97-2001. Sgt., 7th Army Symphony, U.S. Army, 1957-59. Recipient James Morris Whiton Fund award Yale U., 1965, The Otto Kinkeldey award Am. Musicological Soc., 1980, la Médaille de la Ville de Tours, 1997; Trumbull Coll. fellow Yale U., 1966-71, Lewis-Farmington fellow Yale U., 1962-63, Morse fellow Yale U., 1967-68, Am. Coun. Learned Soc. fellow, 1973-74, NEH fellow, 1979, 1984-85, French Archival Scis. fellow Newberry Libr. Center for Renaissance Studies, 1991; Martha Baird Rockefeller grantee, 1963-64, Paul Mellon Found. grantee, 1972, Am. Coun. Learned Soc., 1972, 82, U. Tex. grantee, 1975, Mem. Am. Musicological Soc. (chmn. program com. 1979, bd. dirs. 1980-81, adv. bd., 1985-86, chmn. ad hoc sub com., 1985-86, exec. com. delegate, 1989-92, mem. fellowship com. 1995-98), Internat. Musicological Soc., The Renaissance Soc. of Am., Amici Thomae Mori, Phi Beta Kappa, Phi Kappa Phi. Mem. Lds Ch. Office: Columbia U Dept Music Mail Code 1826 2960 Broadway New York NY 10027-6902 E-mail: LLP1@columbia.edu.

PERKINS, LINDA GILLESPIE, real estate executive; b. Albany, Calif., Sept. 17, 1944; d. Leonard Leroy and Cloie Vivian (Howard) Gillespie; m. Harold Michael Morgan, Sept. 18, 1965 (div. Oct. 1978); 1 child, Trisha Leigh Morgan Franz; m. Donald Anthony Perkins, June 1, 1996. BA with honors, N.Mex. State U., 1967, MA in English Lit. with honors, 1972. Social worker N.Mex. Human Svcs., Santa Fe, 1967-78, adoption dir., 1978-81, adolscent crisis counselor, 1978-81; exec. Yablon Real Estate, 1981-98, Vista Property Corp., Santa Fe, 1999—. Aerobics instr. Tom Young's Spa, Sante Fe, 1980-85; cons. in field. Author of poems. Foster parent judicial rev. panel Dist. Ct. N.Mex., Santa Fe, 1992-95, permanancy planning project, 1992-95; mem. YMCA. Mem. Planned Parenthood, Mensa, Alpha Chi Omega. Democrat. Methodist. Avocations: reading, travel, foreign languages, snorkeling. Home: 808 Vassar Dr NE Albuquerque NM 87106-2726 Office: Vista Property Corp PO Box 1794 Santa Fe NM 87504-1794

PERKINS, LISA CARDENAS, physician assistant; b. Monterey, Calif., May 24, 1966; d. Carlos Guillermo Cardenas and Mercedes Emma (Shields) Copeland; m. Lawrence Clayton Perkins, Jan. 2, 1993; children: Madison Claire, Clayton Moses. BS, U. Fla., 1988; M Med. Sci., Emory U., 1992. cert. physician asst., Ga., Fla. Physician asst. Grady Health System, Atlanta, 1993-94, Emory Egleston Pediat. Care Found., Atlanta, 1994-96, East Cobb Pediatrics, Kennesaw, Ga., 1997-99. Fellow Am. Acad. Physician Assts Avocations: antiques, waterskiing, aerobics, family recreation. Home: 7606 Willow Bastic Ct Tallahassee FL 32312-6723 E-mail: lisaperkins@email.com.

PERKINS, LUCIAN, photographer; Grad., U. Texas. Intern The Washington Post, 1979, now staff photographer. Founder InterFoto (U.S./Russian photography orgn.). Author: (photography book) Runway Madness, 1998. Named Newspaper Photographer of Yr., Pictures of Yr. competition, 1993; recipient

Pulitzer Prize for explanatory journalism, 1995, Pulitzer price for feature photography, 2000, Photo of Yr. award World Press, 1996. Office: The Washington Post 1150 15th St NW Washington DC 20071-0002

PERKINS, MARILYN JO, civic worker; b. Muscatine, Iowa, Aug. 11, 1944; d. John Bernard and Madge Mariam (Inglish) Vaira; m. Paul Dean Perkins, Mar. 18, 1961; children— Brian Dean, John Joseph. Grad. high sch., Centerville, Iowa. Sec. Bd. Health, Centerville, 1977— . Mem. care rev. com. Centerville Care Ctr., 1980-83; mem. Sch. Bd. Adv. Com., Centerville, 1982-83; bd. dirs. Centerville Sch. Bd., 1983— , Centerville/Appanoose Recreation Bd., 1985— . Mem. Bus. and Profl. Women U.S.A. (state corr. sec. 1983-84, local scholarship chmn. 1984-86), Centerville C. of C. Republican. Home: RR 1 Box 71 Mystic IA 52574-9720

PERKINS, NORRIS LYNWOOD, III, newspaper columnist and writer; b. Smithfield, N.C., Nov. 3, 1947; s. Norris Lynwood Jr. and Mildred Mary (Brate) P.; m. Zoe Katherine Annis, May 1, 1982; children: Molly, Drew. Student, U. N.C., 1965-68; AB in English Lit., So. Ill. U., Edwardsville, 1970, postgrad., 1971-75. Store mgr. Streetside Records, St. Louis, 1975-81, mgr. retail ops., 1981-83; music columnist Riverfront Times, 1983--; music reviewer, feature writer St. Louis Post-Dispatch, 1984--. Freelance bus. and tech. writer, prodr. bus. meetings and promotional events, St. Louis, 1988—; contbg. writer (websites) Office.com, All About Jazz, 1999—; prodr. Busch Creative Svcs., St. Louis, 1985-87; tech. writer McDonnell Douglas Fed. Health Systems Co., St. Louis, 1987-88. Editor Sou'wester, 1972-76; contbr. articles to Post, Riverfront Times, others under name of Terry Perkins. Mem. Jazz St. Louis (bd. dirs. 1988—). Episcopalian. Avocations: baseball, reading. Home and Office: 32 Orchard Ln Saint Louis MO 63122-6945 E-mail: tperkins01@earthlink.net.

PERKINS, RAYMOND LAMONT, retired government official; b. New Rochelle, N.Y., Apr. 8, 1924; s. Raymond Lamont and Dorothy Marie (Porter) P.; m. Margaret Johnson, Aug. 25, 1946; children: Deborah, Doriane, Amy. AB, U. Denver, 1946, LLB, 1948. Bar: Colo. Pvt. practice, Springfield, Colo., 1949-54; fgn. svc. officer Dept. State, various locations, 1954-86; ret., 1986. Lmem. Fgn. Svc. Grievance Bd., Washington, 1990-2000. Contbr. articles to profl. jours. County atty. Baca County, Colo., 1949-54, dep. dist. atty., 1949-52. Capt. USAR. Mem. Kiwanis. Methodist. Home: 1304 Tannery Cir Midlothian VA 23113 E-mail: rperkpeg@aol.com.

PERKINS, ROBERT ANTON, judge; b. Laredo, Tex., Oct. 27, 1947; s. William Anton and Carol (Salisbury) P.; m. Yoland Velasquez, June 7, 1969 (div. 1979); 1 child, Javier; m. Cyndy Allen, Aug. 2, 1980; children: Allen, Ana. BA in Govt., U. Tex., 1970, JD, 1973. Bar: Tex. 1973. Pvt. practice, Austin, Tex., 1973-75; justice of the peace County of Travis, 1975-80, judge county ct., 1980-82; judge 331st Dist. Ct., 1982—. Adminstrv. judge Criminal Dist. Judges, Austin, 1991—. Mem. City Human Rels. Commn., Austin, 1976-79, Austin Mediation Ctr. Bd., 1983-84; mem., pres. Pan-Am. Recreation Ctr., Austin, 1975—; bd. dirs. Ctr. for Battered Women, Austin, 1978-80. Mem. Mex.-Am. Bar Assn., Tex. Bar Assn. (jud. sect.), Travis County Bar Assn. (criminal law and procedure com.), Sierra. Democrat. Roman Catholic. Avocations: jogging, hiking. Home: 2633 Deerfoot Trl Austin TX 78704-2764 Office: PO Box 1748 Austin TX 78767-1748

PERKINS, ROBERT EDWARD, civil engineer; b. Olean, N.Y., Dec. 15, 1952; s. Loren Frank and Thelma Sylvia (Higgins) P.; m. April Sue Moyer, Nov. 29, 1975; children: Justin Edward, Amanda Laureen. AD in Civil Engring., Horry-Georgetown Tech. Coll., Conway, S.C., 1978; AS, U. S.C., Conway, 1984, BA in Interdisciplinary Studies, 1985. Cert. design engr. supr. Mgr. Winn-Dixie Stores, Inc., Myrtle Beach, S.C., 1975-84; engr. technician Sur-Tech, Inc., Murrells Inlet, 1984-88, Grand Strand Water and Sewer Authority, Conway, 1988—. With U.S. Army, 1972-75, Korea. Mem. Water Environment Assn. S.C. (dist. chmn. 2000-01). Republican. Avocations: travel, biking, hiking, gardening, swimming. Home: 905 Fox Hollow Rd Conway SC 29526-1106 Office: Grand Strand Water & Sewer Authority PO Box 2368 Conway SC 29528-2368 E-mail: rperkins@gswsa.com.

PERKINS, ROGER ALLAN, lawyer; b. Port Chester, N.Y., Mar. 4, 1943; s. Francis Newton and Winifred Marcella (Smith) P.; m. Katherine Louise Howard, Nov. 10, 1984; children: Marshall, Morgan, Matthew, Justin, Ashley. BA, Pa. State U., 1965; postgrad., U. Ill., 1965-66; JD with honors, George Washington U., 1969. Bar: Md. 1969, Mass. 1975. Trial atty. Nationwide Ins. Co., Annapolis, Md., 1969-72; assoc. Arnold, Beauchemin & Huber, PA, Balt., 1973; from assoc. to ptnr. Goodman & Bloom, PA, Annapolis, 1973-76; ptnr. Luff and Perkins, 1976-78; pvt. practice Anapolis, 1978—. Temp. adminstrv. hearing officer Anne Arundel County, 1984-99; asst. city atty., Annapolis, 1980-82; atty. Bd. Appeals of City of Annapolis, 1986—; mem. Appellate Jud. Nominating Commn., 1995—. Editl. adv. bd. Daily Record, 1996-97. Mem. Gov.'s Task Force on Family Law, 1991-94; adv. coun. on family legal need of low income persons MLSC, 1991; coach youth sports. Fellow Am. Acad. Matrimonial Lawyers, Am. Bar Found., Md. Bar Found. (bd. dirs. 1992-95); mem. ABA (ho. dels. 1991-93, 94-96, standing com. on solo and small firm practitioners 1993-97, chair 1996-97), Md. State Bar Assn. (pres. 1992-93, treas. 1988-91, bd. govs. 1985-87, chair spl. com. on lawyer profl. responsibility 1994-95, family and juvenile law sect. coun. 1983-89, chair 1987-88), Anne Arundel County Bar Assn. (pres. 1984-85). Home: 503 Bay Hills Dr Arnold MD 21012-2001 Office: The Courtyards 133 Defense Hwy Ste 202 Annapolis MD 21401-8907 E-mail: roger@perkinslaw.com.

PERKINS, RONALD DEE, geologist, educator; b. Covington, Ky., May 18, 1935; s. Stanley E. and Pauline L. (Green) P.; m. Beverly L. Hughes, June 8, 1957; children— Lisa, Debra. BS, U. Cin., 1957; MS, U. N.Mex., 1959; PhD in Geology, Ind. U., 1962. Research geologist Shell Devel. Co., Houston, 1962-63, project leader Coral Gables, Fla., 1963-68; mem. faculty Duke U., Durham, N.C., 1968—, prof. geology, 1975-2000, chmn. dept., 1978-90, prof. emeritus, 2000—. Cons. to industry. Author numerous papers in field. NSF grantee, 1969-80 Mem. Internat. Assn. Sedimentologists, Soc. Econ. Paleontologists and Mineralogists (sec.-treas. 1978-82), Geol. Soc. Am., Am. Assn. Petroleum Geologists. Office: Duke U Dept Geology West Campus Old Chemistry Bldg Durham NC 27708 E-mail: rperkins@eas.duke.edu.

PERKINS, ROSWELL BURCHARD, lawyer; b. Boston, May 21, 1926; AB cum laude, Harvard U., 1945, LLB cum laude, 1949; LLD, Bates Coll., 1988. Bar: Mass. 1949, N.Y. 1949. Assoc. Debevoise, Plimpton & McLean, N.Y.C., 1949-53; ptnr. Debevoise & Plimpton and predecessor firm, 1957-96; of counsel, head rep. office Debevoise & Plimpton LLC, Moscow, 1997-01. Asst. sec. U.S. Dept. Health, Edn. and Welfare, 1954-56; counsel to Gov. Nelson A. Rockefeller State of N.Y., 1959; asst. counsel spl. subcom. Senate Commerce Com. to investigate organized crime in interstate commerce, 1950; chmn. N.Y.C. Mayor's Task Force on Transp. Reorgn., 1966; mem. Pres.'s Adv. Panel on Pers. Interchange, 1968, chmn. adv. com. Medicare Adminstrn. Contracting, Subcontracting HEW, 1973-74; dir. Fiduciary Trust Co., N.Y., 1963—; trustee Bowery Savs. Bank, 1975-82; mem. legal com. to bd. dirs. N.Y. Stock Exch., 1995— Editor Harvard Law Rev., 1948-49. Mem. N.Y. Lawyers Com. Civil Rights, 1970-73; mem. nat. exec. com., 1973—, co-chmn. 1973-75; mem. adv. coun. Woodrow Wilson Sch. Pub. and Internat. Affairs, Princeton U., 1967-69; bd. dirs. The Commonwealth Fund, 1974-97, Sch. Am. Ballet, 1974-85, chmn. bd. 1976-80; dir., sec. N.Y. Urban Coalition, 1967-74; trustee Pomfret Sch., 1961-76; The Brearley Sch., 1969-75; dir. Salzburg Seminar Am. Studies, 1970-80; mem. overseers vis. com. Kennedy Sch. Govt., Harvard U., 1971-77, Harvard and Radcliffe Colls., 1958-64, 1971-77, Davis Ctr. for Russian and Eurasian Studies. Recipient Spl. Merit citation Am. Judicature Soc., 1989, Harvard Law Sch. Assn. award, 1994, 50 Ur. award Fellows of ABA, 2002. Mem. ABA (commn. on law and economy, 1975-79, mem. house of dels. 1980-93), N.Y. State Bar Assn., Assn. of the Bar of the City of N.Y. (chmn. spl. com. on fed. conflict of interest laws 1958-60). Harvard Alumni Assn. (pres. 1970-71), Am. Law Inst. (mem. coun. 1969, pres. 1980-93, chmn. coun. 1993—), Am. Arbitration Assn. (bd. dirs. 1966-71). Home: 1120 5th Ave New York NY 10128-0144 Office: Debevoise & Plimpton 919 3rd Ave 46th Fl New York NY 10022-3904 E-mail: rbperkins@debevoise.com.

PERKINS, RUSSELL ALEXANDER, publisher, consultant; b. N.Y.C., July 31, 1958; s. Thomas F. and Helen P.; m. Susan Chew, Sept. 20, 1991. BA, Sarah Lawrence Coll., 1982. Assoc. editor NBC Pub., N.Y.C., 1982-83; editor Thomas Pub., N.Y.C, 1983-85; cons. AT&T, Morristown, N.J., 1985; pres. Morgan-Rand Pubs., Phila., 1986-94; group pres. N.Am. Pub. Co., 1994-96; v.p. Legal Comm., Ltd., 1996-97; pres. Dorland Healthcare Info., 1998—. Bd. dirs. Univenture Group, Inc., Phila., Charter Info. Corp., Phila., Ctr. for Healthcare Info., Newport Beach., Calif. Author: (book) Directory Publishing, 1986, InfoCommerce, 1999; columnist The Morgan Report newsletter. Mem. Assn. Info. Mgrs., Info. Mktg. Roundtable, Phila. Pubs. Group, Phila. Book Clinic, Info. Industry Assn., Union League Phila. Office: Perkins Group Ltd 1528 Walnut St Philadelphia PA 19102-3606 E-mail: rperkins@perkinsgroup.net.

PERKINS, SHERRIE LYNN, pathologist, educator; b. Los Alamos, N.Mex., Feb. 5, 1956; d. Ralph Hulet Perkins and Marion Patricia McGuire; m. donald Elliot Kohan, Sept. 29, 1984; children: Jessica, Rachel. BA, Colby Coll., 1977; MD, Washington U., 1985; PhD, U. Miami, 1984. Diplomate Am. Bd. Anatomic Pathology, Am. Bd. Pathology, Am. Bd. Hematopathology. Instr. Barnes Jewish Hosp., St. Louis, 1989-90; asst. prof. U. Utah Sch. Medicine, Salt Lake City, 1990-96, assoc. prof., 1996—. Pathology reviewer Children's Oncology Group, Arcadia, Calif., 1993—; mem. Nat. Inst. Aging Study Sect., Behtesda, 1996-2000. Contbr. chpts. to books. Fellow NIH, 1989-91; recipient rsch. award NIH, 1993-98. Fellow Am. Soc. Clin. Pathology (hematology coun. 1998—). Office: U Utah Health Scis Dept Pathology 50 N Medical Dr Salt Lake City UT 84132

PERKINS, TAMMY JEAN, administrative assistant; b. Gettysburg, Pa., July 26, 1962; d. Raymond Smith and Grace Marie Gorsuch; m. Jay Michael Perkins, May 14, 1994; children: Melissa, Nicholas. Writer, 1997—; exec. asst. Sandler Sys. Inc., Stevenson, Md., 2000—. Author: Mystery of the Attic, 2002, Wound Too Tight, 2002. With USN, 1981-85. Avocations: writing, gardening, exercising. Office: 10411 Stevenson Rd Stevenson MD 21153 E-mail: sunbed007@aol.com.

PERKINS, WHITNEY TROW, political science educator emeritus; b. Boston, Feb. 28, 1921; s. Wesley Trow and Hazel Alice (Mason) P; m. Kathryn A. Sylvester, June 28, 1947; children— Rebecca, Mason, Wesley, Rachel AB, Tufts U., 1942; PhD, Fletcher Sch. Law and Diplomacy, 1948. Asst. prof. internat. relations U. Denver, 1948-53; from assoc. prof. to prof. polit. sci. Brown U., Providence, 1953-84. Chmn. Internat. Relations Concentration, Brown U., 1955-84; cons. U.S.-P.R. Commn. on Status of Puerto Rico, 1965 Author: Denial of Empire: The United States and its Dependencies, 1962; Constraint of Empire: The United States and Caribbean Interventions, 1981 Served to capt. USAF, 1942-45, PTO Recipient Fulbright Research award, 1951-52 Mem. Am. Polit. Sci. Assn., Internat. Studies Assn., Phi Beta Kappa Democrat. Avocations: tennis; squash; hiking. Home: 11 Catalpa Rd Providence RI 02906-2614

PERKINS, WILLIAM CLINTON, company executive; b. Decatur, Ill., Mar. 7, 1920; s. Glen Rupert and Frances Lola (Clinton) P.; m. Eunice Cagle, Sept. 7, 1939 (div. 1954); stepchildren: William Rea Cagle, Howard Christy Cagle; 1 child, Clinton Colcord; m. Lillian Wuollet, Sept. 7, 1955 (div. 1965); m. Shirley Thomas, Oct. 24, 1969. BS Mil. Sci. and Meteorology, U. Md., 1954; MS in Bus. and Pub. Adminstrn., Sussex Coll., Eng., 1975. Commd. USAF, 1943-73, advanced through grades to col.; with Ship Systems div. Litton Ind., Culver City, Calif., 1973-75; dir. material Hughes Aircraft Co., Tehran, Iran, 1974-78; mgr. internat. s/c Northrop Corp., Dahran, Saudi Arabia, 1978-81; dir. materiel CRS, Riyadh, Saudi Arabia, 1981-83; head major subcontracts Lear Ziegler Corp., Santa Monica, Calif., 1984-88; pres., chmn. bd., CEO Snowtech, Inc., L.A., 1984—. Bd. dirs. Ice Village Ctrs., Inc., L.A., Forefront Industries, Maywood, Calif. Bd. dirs. World Children's Transplant Fund, L.A., 1987-95; mem. Mayor's Space Adv. Com., L.A., 1970-74; mem. aerospace hist. com. Mus. Sci. and Industry, L.A., 1988-98, Mus. of Flying, 1998—. Mem. AIAA (sec. chmn. 1970), Ret. Officers Assn. (pres. 1992-95), Soc. for Non-destructive Testing (program chmn. 1973), Aerospace Hist. Soc., Am. Soc. Quality Control, Am. Meterol. Soc., Sigma Alpha Epsilon (alumni chpt. pres. 1974-76). Avocations: golf, scuba diving, sailing, flying, gardening. Home: 8027 Hollywood Blvd Los Angeles CA 90046-2510 E-mail: snowtech@pacbell.net.

PERKINS, WILLIAM H., JR. finance company executive; b. Rushville, Ill., Aug. 4, 1921; s. William H. and Sarah Elizabeth (Logsdon) P.; m. Eileen Nelson, Jan. 14, 1949; 1 child, Gary Douglas. Ed., Ill. Coll. Pres. Howlett-Perkins Assos., Chgo. Mem. Ill. AEC, 1963-84, sec., 1970-84; mem. adv. bd. Nat. Armed Forces Mus., Smithsonian Instn., 1964-82 Sgt.-at-arms Democratic Nat. Conv., 1952, 56, del.-at-large, 1964, 68, 72; spl. asst. to chmn. Dem. Nat. Com., 1960; mem. Presdl. Inaugural Com., 1961, 65, 69, 73. Served with U.S. Army, 1944-46. Mem. Ill. Ins. Fedn. (pres. 1965-84), Ill. C. of C. (chmn. legis. com. 1971), Chgo. Assn. Commerce and Industry (legis. com., Raoul Wallenberg Humanitarian award 1993), Sangamo Club, Masons, Shriners. Methodist. Home: 52 N Cowley Rd Riverside IL 60546-2042 Office: 2501 South Des Plaines Ave North Riverside IL 60546-1521 Fax: (708) 795-1349.

PERKINS-CARPENTER, BETTY LOU, fitness company executive; b. Jan. 22, 1931; d. Edward C. and Bertha M. (Loeser) Kalmn; m. Floyd F. Perkins, Jan. 31, 1951 (div. 1979); children: Cheryl Lee Perkins, F. Scott Perkins; m. Marcellus Chipman Carpenter, Oct. 10, 1981. BS in Phys. Edn. Adminstrn., Empire State Coll., N.Y., 1979; MS in Early Childhood Edn. Adminstrn., Nova U., 1983; postgrad., Kennedy Western U. Cert. gerontology St. John Fischer Coll. Tchr., coach Rochester YWCA, NY, 1954-59, Perkins Swimming Sch., Penfield, N.Y., 1959-64; pres. Perkins Swim Club, Inc., Rochester, 1959—94, Penfield Fit By Five, Inc., Rochester, 1969-97, Child Fitness Prodns., Inc. d/b/a Sr. Fitness Prodns., Rochester, 1983—. Diving coach Olympic Games, Montreal, Canada, 1976; mem. adv. com. Cmty. Savs. Bank, Rochester, 1976—79; cons. European sports facilities, 1969—83; mem. adv. com. N.Y. State Task Force Phys. Fitness and Sports, 1978—82; mem. adv. bd. O.A.S.I.S.; bd. dirs. U.S. Olympic Diving Com., 1976—80, Wesley Group, Arthritis Found. Genesee chpt., 1995—; affiliated with Pres.'s Coun. Phys. Fitness and Sports, 1986—89, 1995—; exercise cons. U. Rochester Pepper Study, 1992—95. Author: (book) The Fun of Fitness - A Handbook for the Senior Class, 1988, How to Prevent Falls - Introducint the Balance System, 1989, Stretching in Bed to Look and Feel Better, 1999; Am. editor: book Teaching Babies to Swim, 1979; contbr. articles to profl. jours.; exec. prodr.: audio-visual instrnl. materials. Vice-chmn., bd. dirs. Regional Coun. on Aging; co-chmn. Monroe County Coun. for Elders. With USAF, 1948—51. Named Sports Woman of the Yr., U.S. Olympic Diving Commn., 1979, Citizen of the Yr., Rotary, 1988, Health Fitness Leader, Rochester Small Bus. Person of the Yr., 1990, Citizen of the Yr., Lions Club, 1995; named to Monroe County Athletes Hall of Fame, Rochester, 1979, Frontier Field Walk of Fame, 1999, Nat. Swim Sch. Hall of Fame, 1999; recipient Gold medal, Inst. Achievement of Human Potential, Brazil, 1973, Mike Malone Meml. Diving award, 1977, Cady Diving award, 1977, Honor award, ARC, 1991, Lifespan-Hero award, 2001. Mem.: U.S. Diving Assn. (life; numerous offices), Nova U. Alumnae Assn., Oak Hill Country Club, Order Eastern Star (life), Sigma Phi Omega (Alpha Lamda chpt.). Republican. Avocations: swimming, cross country skiing, reading, travel. Office: Senior Fitness Inc 1780 Penfield Rd Penfield NY 14526-2104

PERKINSON, ROBERT RONALD, psychologist, consultant; b. Richmond, Va., Aug. 8, 1945; s. Gordon Archibald and Sarah (Haskins) P.; m. Elizabeth Godfrey Fly, July 27, 1968 (div. 1984); children: Robert Reps, Nyshie Page, Shane William; m. Angela Kaufman, Sept. 20, 1991. BS, Colo. State U., 1968; MS, Ea. Wash. State U., 1970; PhD, Utah State U., 1974. Lic. psychologist, S.D.; cert. chem. dependency counselor level III, S.D.; nat. cert. gambling counselor; nat. cert. alcohol and drug counselor; lic. marriage and family counselor, S.D. Juvenile ct. psychologist, Cedar City, Utah, 1971-72; psychologist in pvt. practice Jackson, Wyo., 1974-83; dir. psychol. svcs. Western Wyo. Mental Health Assn., 1977-78, psychologist, 1983—; psychologist, clin. dir. Keystone Treatment Ctr., 1988—. Cons. in field; chief psychologist Grand Teton Nat. Pk., Teton County Sheriff's Office and Police Dept. Copyrights: The Yellowstone Park Game, The Good Health Game, The Grizzly Control Team, Communication from God, Chemical Dependency Counseling, The Mystics, God Talks CD, Peace Will Come CD, The Treatment of Pathological Gambling: A Step By Step Approach. Author: Chemical Dependency Counseling: A Practical Guide, 1997, The Chemical Dependency Treatment Planner, 1998, God Talks to You, 2000, The Addiction Treatment Planner, 2001, Chemical Dependency Counseling: A Practical Guide, 2d edit., 2002; contbr. articles to profl. jours. Mem. APA, S.D. Psychol. Assn., S.D. Chem. Dependency Assn., Biofeedback Soc. Am. (bd. dirs. Wyo. br.), Wyo. Bd. Psychologist Examiners (pres. 1997, bd. dirs. S.D. coun. problem gambling), Nat. Registere of Health Svc. Providers in Psychology. Address: PO Box 159 Canton SD 57013-0159

PERKO, KENNETH ALBERT, JR. lawyer, real estate executive, mathematics researcher; b. Iron Mountain, Mich., Feb. 9, 1943; s. Kenneth Albert and Alice Ellen (Hamad) P.; m. Susan Jane Roodenburg, Oct. 5, 1968; children: Kathryn Ann, Kenneth Albert. AB in Math. with honors magna cum laude, Princeton U., 1964; JD, Harvard U., 1967. Bar: Ohio, N.Y.; cert. real estate broker, N.Y. Assoc. Milbank, Tweed, Hadley & McCloy, N.Y.C., 1967-79; asst. sec. The Rockefeller Group, 1979-96, 98—; counsel Radio City Music Hall, 1985-96, Tishman Speyer Properties, 1996-97; pres. Petrarch LLC, 2002—. Lectr. Cambridge U., 1979, U. Paris, 1979; asst. sec. RCPI Trust, Rockefeller Ctr. Properties, Inc., The Rockefeller Ctr. Tower Condominium, 1996-97; reviewer Math. Revs., 1980—. Contbr. aricles to profl. jours. Trustee Princeton Libr., N.Y.C., 1968—, Rockette Alumnae Found., 1992—. Grantee NSF, Blacksburgh, Va., 1982. Mem. Assn. Trial Lawyers Am., Assn. Bar of the City N.Y. (com. profl. and judicial ethics 1994-97, com. profl. discipline 1997-2000). Democrat. Roman Catholic. Home: 325 Old Army Rd Scarsdale NY 10583-2643

PERKO, MIKE A. health education and health promotion educator; b. Ithaca, N.Y., Aug. 22, 1962; s. John Joseph and Elizabeth (Farrell) P. BS, East Stroudsburg U., 1986, MS, 1989; PhD, U. Ala., 1996. Cert. health edn. specialist. Health coord. N.J. Tech. U., Newark, 1988-91; assoc. dir. Good Health Makes Sense Ala. Power Co., Birmingham, 1992-96, prodr. Good Health Makes Sense show, 1992-96; exec. dir. Ctr. for Innovative Health Solutions, Tuscaloosa, Ala., 1994—; prof. health edn. and promotion U. N.C., Wilmington, 1997—. Bd. dirs. N.C. Wellness Coun. Am., Wilmington, 1997—. Author: Making Your Workplace Smoke Free, 1996, Giving New Meaning to the Term "Taking One for the Team": The New Thinking on Dietary Supplements and Young Athletes, 2002; producer 35 health edn. videos; contbr. articles to profl. jours. Recipient Outstanding Alumni Achievement award East Stroudsburg U., 1998, Keystonian of Yr., Keystone Coll., 2000, Jack W. Davis Alumni award U. Ala., 2001. Mem. AAHPERD, APHA (chmn. workplace health 1996-98, mem. governing coun. 1999-01, Early Career award 1997), Am. Assn. Health Edn. (chmn. profl. devel. com. 1998—, bd. dirs., Horizon award 2000), Am. Sch. Health Assn., Soc. Pub. Health Educators. Avocations: soccer, triathlon. Office: U NC Wilmington 601 S College Rd Wilmington NC 28403-3297 E-mail: perkom@uncwil.edu.

PERKO, WALTER KIM, pilot, computer engineer, songwriter, poet; b. Mpls., Dec. 8, 1950; s. Eero Nestor and Margie (Hanson) P. Computer Sci./Aeronautics, U. Minn., 1975. Contract computer analyst/cons. Dept. Def., Dept. Justice, NASA and pvt. industry; owner The Home MultiMedia Hobbyst BBS, San Francisco, 1987—95, Natural Digital Musical Productions, San Francisco. Author: This is America, 1991. With USN, 1968-72, Korea and Vietnam. Lutheran. Avocations: songwriting, flying, computer network interactivity, philanthropy.

PERKOVIC, ROBERT BRANKO, retired international management consultant; b. Belgrade, Yugoslavia, Aug. 27, 1925; came to U.S., 1958, naturalized, 1961; s. Slavoljub and Ruza (Pantelic) P.; m. Jacquelyn Lee Lipscomb, Dec. 14, 1957; children: Bonnie Kathryn, Jennifer Lee. MS in Econs, U. Belgrade, 1954; B.F.T., Am. Grad. Sch. Internat. Mgmt., 1960; grad. Stanford exec. program, Stanford U., 1970. Auditor Gen. Foods Corp., White Plains, N.Y., 1960-62, controller Mexico City, 1962-64; dir. planning Monsanto Co., Barcelona, Spain, 1964-67, dir. fin. Europe, Brussels, 1967-70, dir. fin. planning-internat., 1970-71, asst. treas., 1971-72, Brussels, 1972-74; corp. treas. Fiat-Allis Inc. & BV, Deerfield, Ill., 1974-78; v.p., treas. TRW Inc., Cleve., 1978-88; pres. RBP Internat. Cons., 1988—. Former dir. U.S. Bus. Coun. for Southeastern Europe, Inc. Active Cleve. Commn. on Fgn. Relations. Inc. Served with Yugoslavian Army, 1944-47. Mem. Fin. Execs. Inst., Cleve. Treas. Club (past bd. dirs., pres.), Latin Am. Bus. Assn. (co-founder), Mayfield Village (Ohio) Racquet Club. Office: RBP Internat Cons 26 Pepper Creek Dr Cleveland OH 44124-5248 Office Fax: 216-464-8898.

PERKOWSKI, JAN LOUIS, language and literature educator; b. Perth Amboy, N.J., Dec. 29, 1936; m. Liliana Asenova Daskalova, May 24, 1989. AB, Harvard U., 1959, AM, 1960, PhD, 1965. Asst. prof. U. Calif., Santa Barbara, 1964-65; assoc. prof. U. Tex., Austin, 1965-74; prof. U. Va., Charlottesville, 1974—. Author: A Kashubian Idiolect in U.S., 1969, Vampires, Dwarves & Witches Among the Ontario Kashubs, 1972, Vampires of the Slavs, 1976, Gusle & Ganga Among the Hercegovinians of Toronto, 1978, The Darkling-A Treatise on Slavic Vampirism, 1989; contbr. over 65 articles to profl. jours. Grantee, fellow Ford Found., Harvard U., Kościuszko Found., U. Tex., Am. Philos. Soc., Nat. Mus. Man, U. Va., NEH, Kennan Inst., I.R.E.X., Fulbright, others. Mem. Am. Assn. for the Advancement of Slavic Studies, Am. Assn. Tchrs. of Slavic and East European Langs., Am. Assn. S.E. European Studies. Office: U Va Dept Slavic Langs & Lits 109 Cabell Hall Charlottesville VA 22903

PERKOWSKI, MAREK ANDRZEJ, electrical engineering educator; b. Warsaw, Poland, Oct. 6, 1946; came to U.S., 1981; s. Adam Perkowski and Hanna (Zielinska) Mystkowska; m. Ewa Kaja Wilkowska, Oct. 26, 1974; 1 child, Mateusz Jan. MS in Electronics with distinction, Tech. U. Warsaw, 1970, PhD in Automatics with distinction, 1980. Sr. asst. Inst. Automatics, Tech. U. Warsaw, 1973-80, asst. prof., 1980-81; vis. asst. prof. dept. elec. engring. U. Minn., Mpls., 1981-83; assoc. prof. elec. engring. Portland (Oreg.) State U., 1983-94, prof., 1994—. Co-author: Theory of Automata, 3d edit., 1976, Problems in Theory of Logic Circuits, 4th edit., 1986, Theory of Logic Circuits-Selected Problems, 3d edit., 1984; contbr. 134 articles to profl. jours., 11 chpts. to books. Mem. Solidarity, Warsaw, 1980-81. Recipient Design Automation award SIGDA/ACM/DATC IEEE, 1986-91; Rsch. grantee NSF, 1991, 94, Commn. for Familites Roman Cath. Ch., Vatican, 1981, Air Force Ofice Sci. Rsch., 1995. Mem. IEEE (Computer Soc.), Polish Nat. Alliance, Assn. for Computing Machinery, Am. Soc. for Engring. Edn. Roman Catholic. Avocations: tourism, philosophy, woodcarving. Home: 15720 NW Perimeter Dr Beaverton OR 97006-5391 Office: Portland State U Dept Elec & Comp Engring PO Box 751 Portland OR 97207-0751 E-mail: mperkows@ece.pdx.edu.

PERKOWSKI, PAUL JAMES, accountant; b. Glen Ridge, N.J., Feb. 19, 1956; s. Benjamin and Adele P.; m. Beth Vasselli, Sept. 17, 1978; children: Thomas, Katelyn. BS, Montclair State Coll., 1978. CPA. Auditor, sr. tax mgr. Ernst & Young, Hackensack, N.J.; ptnr. Perkowski & Assocs., CPAs, Spring Lake. Presenter in field. Mem. AICPA, Inst. Mgmt. Accts., N.J. Soc. CPAs, Internat. Assn. Fin. Planning (bd. dirs. 1988-94), Spring Lake C. of C. Roman Catholic. Office: Perkowski & Assocs CPAs 1011 Hwy 71 Spring Lake NJ 07762-2030

PERKS, MICAH EVE, writer, educator; b. N.Y.C., Sept. 30, 1963; d. John Perks and Naomi Tannen; 2 children. BA, Cornell U., 1985, MFA, 1990. Lectr. Cornell U., 1990-93; vis. asst. prof. Hobart & William Smith, Geneva, 1993-96, U. Calif. Santa Cruz, 1996—. Mem. Associated Writing program, 1999—. Author: (novel) We Are Gathered Here, 1997, (memoir) Pagan Time, 2001; contbr. stories to profl. publs. Grantee Saltonstall Found., 1998. Jewish. E-mail: meperks@cats.ucsc.ed.

PERL, JUSTIN HARLEY, lawyer; b. Mpls., Sept. 30, 1957; s. Norman and Addie Perl; m. Lynn Goldman, Feb. 23, 1985; children: Alexandra, Phillip. BA, U. Mich., 1980, JD, 1983. Bar: Minn. 1983, U.S. Dist. Ct., Minn. 1983, U.S. Ct. Appeals (8th cir. 1986, 7th cir. 1994), U.S. Supreme Ct. 1995. Summer assoc. Fried, Frank, Harris, Shriver & Jacobson, N.Y.C., 1982; assoc. Maslon Edelman Borman & Brand, LLP, Mpls., 1983-88, ptnr., 1988—. Adj. faculty Civil Practice Clinic, William Mitchell Coll. Law, St. Paul, 1987-91; presenter in field. V.p., trustee, mem. pers. com. Adath Jeshurun Congregation, Minnetonka, Minn., 1996—. Mem. Am. Arbitration Assn., Hennepin County Bar Assn. (investigator 1991—, dist. IV ethics com. 1991—, lawyers vol. com.

1991—, immigrant projects com. 1996—), Advanced Dispute Resolution, Inc., Conflict Mgmt. and Dispute Resolution. Office: Maslon Edelman Borman & Brand LLP 3300 Wells Fargo Minneapolis MN 55402

PERL, MARTIN LEWIS, chemical engineer; b. N.Y.C., June 24, 1927; children: Jed, Anne, Matthew, Joseph. B in Chem. Engring., Poly. Inst. Bklyn., 1948; PhD, Columbia U., 1955; ScD (hon.), U. Chgo., 1990. Chem. engr. Gen. Electric Co., 1948—50; asst. prof. physics U. Mich., 1955—58, assoc. prof., 1958—63; prof. Stanford, 1963—. Author: High Energy Hadron Physics, 1975, Reflections on Experimental Science, 1996; contbr. articles on high energy physics and on relation of sci. to soc. to profl. jours. With U.S. Mcht. Marine, 1944—45, with U.S. Army, 1946—47. Recipient Wolf prize in Physics, 1982, Nobel prize in Physics, 1995. Fellow: Am. Phys. Soc.; mem.: NAS, Am. Acad. Arts and Scis. Home: 3737 El Centro Ave Palo Alto CA 94306-2642 Office: Stanford U Stanford Linear Accelerator Ctr Stanford CA 94305 E-mail: martin@slac.stanford.edu.

PERLBERG, JULES MARTIN, lawyer; b. Chgo., Jan. 28, 1931; s. Maurice and Louise Mae (Schonberger) P.; m. Dora Ann Morris, Dec. 22, 1968; children: Julia, Michael. BBA with high distinction, U. Mich., 1952, JD with high distinction, 1957. Bar: Ill. 1958, D.C. 1964; C.P.A., Ill. Acct. Arthur Andersen & Co., Chgo., 1954-55; faculty U. Mich. Law Sch., Ann Arbor, 1957-58; assoc. Sidley & Austin and predecessor firm, Chgo., 1958-65, ptnr., 1966-98, sr. counsel, 1998—. Mem. Glencoe (Ill.) Bd. Edn., 1980-87, pres., 1985-86; bd. dirs. Juvenile Diabetes Found., Chgo., 1981-2001, v.p. 1983-85, treas., 1988-90, 96-98; exec. bd. Am. Jewish Com., Chgo., 1978-88, v.p., 1981-83; trustee New Trier Twp. Schs., 1987-91, pres., 1989-91; class co-chairperson parents com. Duke U., 1992-94. 1st lt. U.S. Army, 1952-54. Recipient Gold medal Ill. Soc. C.P.A.s, 1955 Mem. ABA, Chgo. Bar Assn., Lawyers Club, Mid-Day Club (Chgo.), Std. Club. Clubs: Legal, Law; Mid-Day (Chgo.); Standard. Home: 568 Westley Rd Glencoe IL 60022-1071 Office: Sidley Austin Brown & Wood Apt 605 425 W Surf St Chicago IL 60657-6139

PERLBERG, MARK (MYRON), poet, educator; b. Palisade, N.J., Feb. 19, 1929; s. Emanuel Perlberg and Rene Myra Lewisohn; m. Anna Nessy Backer, Feb. 4, 1953; children: Katherine Eve Friedberg, Julie Anna Farwell. BA, Columbia U., 1950; postgrad., Columbia U., 1950-52. Contbg. editor, corr. Time Mag., N.Y.C., Chgo., 1955-60; sr. editor World Book Ency. Yr. Book, Chgo., 1961-66; prin. editor Ency. Britannica, 1967-72; mng. editor text Prism Mag., AMA, 1972-76; mgr. publs. Rotary Internat., Evanston, Ill., 1979-91; instr. poetry workshop Newberry Libr., Chgo., 1982—. Author: The Burning Field, 1970, The Feel of the Sun, 1981; contbr. poetry and translations to publs. Author: The Burning Field, 1970, The Feel of the Sun, 1981, The Impossible Toystore, 2000; contbr. poetry and translations to publs. Sgt. U.S. Army, 1952-54, PTO. Recipient Robert Ferguson Meml. award in poetry Friends of Lit., Chgo., 1971. Mem. PEN, Poetry Soc. Am., Soc. Midland Authors (5 yr. judge/poetry award), Poetry Ctr. Chgo. (co-founder 1974, bd. mem. 1974—, pres. 1980-94, recipient Lannan Writer's Residency, 2002). Home and Office: 612 W Stratford Pl Chicago IL 60657-2632 E-mail: mperlberg@msn.com.

PERLE, EUGENE GABRIEL, lawyer; b. N.Y.C., Dec. 21, 1922; s. Philip and Simme (Meschenberg) P.; m. Ellen Carlotta Kraus, Nov. 26, 1953 (dec. 1964); 1 child, Elizabeth Perle; m. Ruth Friedberg Lerner, May 23, 1972 (div. 1977); m. Patricia Fitzpatrick Sinnott, Jan. 24, 1981. BA, Queens Coll., 1943; JD, Yale U., 1949. Bar: N.Y. 1950, Conn. 1995. Assoc. Cravath, Swaine & Moore, N.Y.C., 1949-53; asst. counsel N.Y. State Moreland Commn. Investigation Harness Racing, 1953-54; assoc. Gordon, Brady, Caffrey & Keller, 1954-56; assoc. gen. atty. Time Inc., 1956-66, pub. counsel, 1966-73, v.p. law, 1973-80, corp. v.p. law, 1980-85; counsel Proskauer Rose Goetz & Mendelsohn, N.Y.C., 1985-92, Chapman & Fennell, 1992-94; mem. Ohlandt, Greeley, Ruggiero & Perle, Stamford, Conn., 1995-97, sr. counsel, 1998—. Co-author: Publishing Law, 1988-2002; mem. editl. bd. Yale Law Jour., 1948-49; mem. adv. bd. Bur. Nat. Affairs Patent, Trademark and Copyright Jour., 1972-86; contbr. to Bull. Copyright Soc. U.S.A. Trustee Baron deHirsch Fund, 1959-87, hon. trustee, 1988—; commr. Nat. Commn. New Technol. Uses Copyrighted Works, 1975-78; bd. dirs. N.Y. Sch. for Circus Arts, Inc., 1979-87, Am. Arbitration Assn., 1979-84; justice of peace City of Norwalk, Conn., 1960-63. Lt. USNR, 1943-46. Mem. ABA (chmn. copyright divsn. 1970-71, 86-87, chmn. com. copyright and new tech. 1971-73, chmn. com. econs. profession 1976, coun. patent, trademark and copyright sect. 1979-83, governing bd. forum com. comms. law 1979-85, chmn. related fields and future devels. divsn. forum com. entertainment and sports industries 1979), Copyright Soc. U.S.A. (trustee 1962-64, 69-70, 71-74, pres. 1976-78, hon. trustee 1978—), U.S. Trademark Assn. (bd. dirs. 1969-72, 74-77, v.p. 1972-73), Assn. of Bar of City of N.Y., Sunningdale Country Club, Century Assn., Banyan Golf Club of Palm Beach. Democrat. Office: Ohlandt Greeley Ruggiero & Perle One Landmark Sq Stamford CT 06901 E-mail: egperle@ix.netcom.com.

PERLE, GEORGE, composer; b. Bayonne, N.J., May 6, 1915; s. Joseph and Mary (Sanders) Perlman; m. Laura Slobe, 1940; m. Barbara Philips, Aug. 11, 1958 (dec.); children: Kathy, Annette; 1 stepchild, Max Massey; m. Shirley Gabis Rhoads, June 6, 1982; stepchildren: Paul Rhoads, Daisy Rhoads. MusB, DePaul U., 1938; MusM, Am. Conservatory of Music, 1942; PhD, NYU, 1956. Faculty U. Louisville, 1949-57, U. Calif., Davis, 1957-61, Juilliard Sch. Music, 1963, Yale U., 1965-66, U. So. Calif., summer 1965, Tanglewood, summers 1967, 80, 87; from asst. prof. to prof. CUNY, 1961-85, prof. emeritus, 1985—; composer-in-residence San Francisco Symphony, 1989-91. Vis. Birge-Cary prof. music SUNY, Buffalo, 1971-72; vis. prof. U. Pa., 1976, 80, Columbia U., 1979, 83; vis. Ernest Bloch prof. music U. Calif., Berkeley, 1989; vis. disting. prof. music NYU, N.Y.C., 1994. Author: Serial Composition and Atonality 1962, 6th edit., 1991, Twelve-Tone Tonality, 1977, 2d edit., 1996, The Operas of Alban Berg, vol. 1, 1980, vol. 2, 1985, The Listening Composer, 1990, The Right Notes, 1995, Style and Idea in the Lyric Suite of Alban Berg, 1995, 2d edit., 2001; contbr. articles in Am., fgn. mus. jours.; composer: Pantomime, Interlude and Fugue, 1937, Little Suite for Piano, 1939, Two Rilke Songs, 1941, Sonata for Solo Viola, 1942, Three Sonatas for Clarinet, 1943, Piano Piece, 1945, Hebrew Melodies for Cello, 1945, Lyric Piece for Cello and Piano, 1946, Six Preludes for Piano, 1946, Sonata for Solo Cello, 1947, Solemn Procession for Band, 1947, Sonata for Piano, 1950, Three Inventions for Piano, 1957, Quintet for Strings, 1958, Wind Quintet I, 1959, Sonata I for Solo Violin, 1959, Wind Quintet II, 1960, Fifth String Quartet, 1960-67, Three Movements for Orchestra, 1960, Monody I for flute, 1960, Music for The Birds of Aristophanes, 1961, Monody II for double bass 1962, Serenade I for Viola and Chamber Ensemble, 1962, Three Inventions for Bassoon, 1962, Sonata II for Solo Violin, 1963, Short Sonata for Piano, 1964, Solo Partita for Violin and Viola, 1965, Six Bagatelles for Orch., 1965, Concerto for Cello and Orch., 1966, Wind Quintet III, 1967, Serenade II for Chamber Ensemble, 1968, Toccata for Piano, 1969, Suite in C for Piano, 1970, Fantasy-Variations for Piano, 1971, Sonata Quasi una Fantasia for Clarinet and Piano, 1972, Seventh String Quartet, 1973, Songs of Praise and Lamentation for chorus and orch. 1974, Six Etudes for Piano, 1976, 13 Dickinson Songs, 1978, Concertino for Piano, Winds, and Timpani, 1979, A Short Symphony, 1980; Ballade for Piano, 1981, Sonata a quattro, 1982, Serenade III for Piano and Chamber Ensemble, 1983, Six New Etudes for Piano, 1984, Wind Quintet IV, 1984, Sonata for Cello and Piano, 1985, Sonatina for Piano, 1986, Sonata a cinque, 1986, Dance Fantasy for Orch., 1986, Lyric Intermezzo for fifteen players, 1987, Lyric Intermezzo for piano, 1987, New Fanfares for brass ensemble, 1987, Sinfonietta, 1987, Windows of Order for string quartet, 1988, Sextet for winds and piano, 1988, Concerto for Piano and Orch., 1990, Sinfonietta II, 1990, Concerto No. 2 for Piano and Orch., 1992, Adagio for Orch., 1992, Transcendental Modulations (commd. for 150 anniversary N.Y. Philharmonic), 1993, Phantasyplay for Piano, 1994, Duos for French horn and string quartet, 1995, Six Celebratory Inventions for Piano, 1995, Critical Moments for Six Players, 1996, Chansons Cachées for Piano, 1997, Musical Offerings for Piano (left hand alone), 1998, Brief Encounters for string quartet, 1998, Nine Bagatelles for Piano, 1999, Critical Moments (2) for Six Players, 2001. Served with AUS, 1943-46, ETO, PTO. Recipient Nat. Inst. Arts and Letters award, 1977, Pulitzer prize, 1986; Guggenheim fellow, 1966-67, 74-75, MacArthur fellow, 1986; grantee Am. Council Learned Socs., 1968-69, Nat. Endowment for the Arts, 1978-79, 85. Fellow Am. Acad. Arts and Scis.; mem. Am. Musicol. Soc., ASCAP (Deems Taylor award 1973, 78, 81), Am. Acad. Arts and Letters. E-mail: gxperle@aol.com.

PERLE, RICHARD NORMAN, government official; b. N.Y.C., Sept. 16, 1941; s. Jack Harold and Martha Gloria P.; m. Leslie Joan Barr, July 31, 1977; 1 child, Jonathan Barr. BA, U. So. Calif., 1964; postgrad. in econs., U. London, 1962-63; MA, Princeton U., 1967. Asst. sec. internat. security policy Dept. Def., Washington, 1981-87; prof. staff mem. subcom. nat. security Senate Com. on Govt. Ops., 1970-72; profl. staff mem. committee on armed services U.S. Senate, 1969-80; resident fellow Am. Enterprise Inst. for Pub. Policy Rsch., 1987—; chmn. Def. Policy Bd., 2001—. Office: Am Enterprise Inst Pub Policy Rsch 1150 17th St NW Washington DC 20036-4603

PERLEGOS, GEORGE, electronic executive; BS Electrical Engring., 1972. Pres., CEO, chmn. Atmel Corp., San Jose, 2002—. Office: Atmel Inc 2325 Orchard Pkwy San Jose CA 95131-1034*

PERLESS, ELLEN, advertising executive; b. N.Y.C., Sept. 9, 1941; d. Joseph B. and Bertha (Messinger) Kaplan; m. Robert L. Perless, July 2, 1965. Student, Smith Coll., 1958-59; BA, Bard Coll., 1962. Copywriter Doyle, Dane Bernbach, N.Y.C., 1964-70, Young & Rubicam, N.Y.C., 1970-74, creative supr., 1974-76, v.p., creative supr., 1977, v.p., assoc. creative dir., 1978, sr. v.p., assoc. creative dir., 1979-84; v.p., assoc. creative dir. Leber Katz Ptnrs., 1984-85, sr. v.p., creative dir., 1986-87; sr. v.p., sr. creative dir. Foote Cone & Belding, N.Y.C., 1987-93, sr. v.p., group creative dir., 1994—. Recipient Clio awards, Andy awards, awards Art Dirs. Club N.Y., N.Y. Festivals, One Club. Home: 37 Langhorne Ln Greenwich CT 06831-2611 Office: Foote Cone & Belding 150 E 42d St New York NY 10017-5612 E-mail: eperless@fcb.com.

PERLESS, ROBERT L. sculptor; b. N.Y.C., Apr. 23, 1938; s. Meyer and Ethel (Glassman) Perless; m. Ellen R. Kaplan, July 2, 1965. Student, U. Miami, Fla., 1955-59. One-man shows include Bodley Gallery, N.Y.C., 1968, 1970, Galerie Simonne Stern, New Orleans, 1969, Bernard Danenberg Gallery, N.Y.C., 1970—72, Bonino Gallery, 1976, exhibited in group shows at Bodley Gallery, 1970, Whitney Mus., 1970, Forum Gallery, N.Y.C., 1975, Bonino Gallery, 1975, Houston Gallery, Aldrich Mus., Ridgefield, Conn., 1978, 1987, 1994, 1997, 1998, Taft Mus., Cin., 1980, Stamford (Conn.) Mus., 1989, Bience Mus., Greenwich, Conn., 1989, 2001, André Emmerich's Top Gllant Farm, 1991—96, Greenwich Art Soc., 2000, Represented in permanent collections Whitney Mus., Aldrich Mus., Chrysler Mus., Norfolk, Va., Okla. Art Ctr., Oklahoma City, Phoenix Art Mus., Stamford Mus., Bard Coll., Annandale-on-Hudson, N.Y., Bucknell U., Lewisburgh, Pa., City of Corpus Christi, Tex., City of Palm Desert, Calif., Syracuse Hancock Internat. Airport, Miami U., Oxford, Ohio, Rusk Inst., N.Y.C., Salt Lake C.C., Town of Port Chester, N.Y., U. Conn., Storrs, U. No. Iowa, Cedar Falls. Address: 37 Langhorne Ln Greenwich CT 06831-2611

PERLGUT, MARK RALPH, public relations executive; b. New Brunswick, N.J., Oct. 4, 1942; s. Louis Eliot and Mildred Ruth (Shapiro) P.; m. Phyllis Norma Hershon, May 21, 1946; children: Lauren, Andrew. AB in History, Rutgers U., 1964; MS in Journalism, Columbia U., 1965. Investigative reporter Atlantic City (N.J.) Press, 1965-67; nat. and local reporter N.Y. Times, 1967-72; assoc. editor McGraw-Hill Inc., 1973-77; dir. new ventures Instnl. Investor, Inc., 1977-78; editl. mgr., personal speechwriter Donald T. Regan Merrill Lynch & Co., Inc., 1978-80; sr. policy writer N.Y. Stock Exch., Inc., 1980-82; v.p., dir. policy comms. Chem. Bank, 1982-84, v.p., dep. head of corp. comms. divsn., 1984-85; pres. Mark Perlgut Pub. Rels., 1985-87; v.p., editorial dir., account group supr. Fin. Rels. Bd., Inc., 1987-90; pres. Perlgut Pub. Rels., Inc., 1990-96, Investor Rels. Co. N.Y., 1992-96; sr. v.p., mng. dir. investor rels. divsn. Lobsenz Stevens, Inc., N.Y.C., 1996-99; exec. prin., mng. dir., investor rels. Publicis Dialog, 1999—2001; mng. dir. Stern & Co. Comm., 2001—. Author: Electricity Across the Border: The U.S.-Canadian Experience, 1978. Chmn. Fair Harbor (N.Y.) Community Assn., 1980-82. Recipient 1st pl. award Fin. World Ann. Report Competition, 1st pl. award ARC awards Ann. Report Competition, 1989. Mem. Nat. Investor Rels. Inst. Office: 460 Park Ave S New York NY 10016-7315 E-mail: mark.perlgut@mail.com.

PERLICK, RICHARD ALLAN, steel company executive; b. Chgo., June 23, 1947; s. Allan Arthur and Lorraine Perlick; m. Sharon Behrendt, Mar. 29, 1969; children: Jill Sharon, Timothy Richard, David Matthew. BS in Metall. Engring., Mich. Tech. U., 1969. Corrosion engr. CarTech Specialty Steel Corp., Reading, Pa., 1969-71, nondestructive test engr. Union, N.J., 1971-75; quality control sr. engr. heavy products AlTech Specialty Steel Corp., Watervliet, N.Y., 1975-78, gen. supt. bar finish Dunkirk, 1978-79, sr. supr. metallurgist rod mill, 1979-86, mgr. product metallurgy, 1986-87, wire mill supt., 1987-89, sr. product metallurgist, 1989-90; gen. mgr. Techalloy Co.-Union (Ill.) Wire Plant, Ill., 1990-94; dir. corp. metall. svcs. Techalloy Co., Inc., Union, 1994-96, v.p. metallurgy, process and quality depts., 1997—. Pub. spkr. and trainer on metallurgy of stainless steels; expert in field. Author, co-patentee in field. Cubmaster, scoutmaster Boy Scouts Am., Fredonia, N.Y., 1982-90; mem. ch. choir St. Paul Luth., Dunkirk, 1980-82. Recipient Pres.'s Scoutmaster's award Boy Scouts Am., 1988. Mem. AIChE, Nat. Assn. Corrosion Engrs., Indsl. Fasterner Inst., Am. Soc. for Materials, Wire Assn. Internat., Am. Soc. Surface Finishing, Kiwanis. Republican. Avocations: vegetable gardening, woodworking, fishing, golfing, family camping. Home: 1758 Woodhaven Dr Crystal Lake IL 60014-1940 Office: Techalloy Co Olson And Jefferson St Union IL 60180 E-mail: Tecaloymet@aol.com., rperlick@techalloy.com.

PERLIK, WILLIAM R. lawyer; b. Pitts., May 20, 1925; s. Charles A. and Teresa Anna (Kraft) P.; m. Annabel Virginia Shanklin, June 16, 1949; children— Ronald A., Lynn C. BA, Oberlin Coll., 1948; JD, Yale U., 1951; LLD (hon.), Oberlin Coll., 2000. Bar: D.C. 1952, Va. 1955, U.S. Supreme Ct. 1974. Law clk. to judge U.S. Ct. Appeals, Washington, 1951-52; assoc., then ptnr. Cox Langford Stoddard & Cutler, 1952-62; ptnr., of counsel Wilmer Cutler & Pickering, 1962-98; adj. prof. politics and econs. Oberlin Coll., Ohio, 1973-1997. Trustee, chmn., mem. exec. com. Oberlin Coll., 1980-2000; pres. Va. Sch. Bd. Assn., 1971-72; mem. and chmn. Fairfax County Sch. Bd., Va., 1964-72; pres. Fairfax County Fedn. Citizens Assns., 1958. Served with U.S. Army, 1943-46; ETO Recipient Edn. award Fairfax Edn. Assn., 1960; Citizen of Yr. award Washington Evening Star, 1961 Mem. ABA, Phi Beta Kappa. Avocations: music, gardening. Home: 1249 Daleview Dr Mc Lean VA 22102-1538 Office: Wilmer Cutler & Pickering 2445 M St NW Washington DC 20037-1487

PERLIN, ARTHUR SAUL, chemistry educator; b. Sydney, N.S., Can., July 7, 1923; s. Benjamin and Eva (Gaum) P.; m. Ruth Laurel Freedman, Nov. 18, 1950; children: Anna, Louise, Deborah, Myra, David BSc, McGill U., Can., 1944, MSc, 1946, PhD, 1949. Rsch. officer Nat. Rsch. Council Can., Ottawa, Ont., Can., 1948-67; E.B. Eddy prof. chemistry McGill U., Montreal, Que., Can., 1967-91, prof. chemistry emeritus Can., 1991—; rsch. scientist Pulp and Paper Rsch. Inst. Can., 1967—. Contbr. articles to profl. jours., chpts. to books; patentee in field Fellow Royal Soc. Can., Chem. Inst. Can.; mem. Am. Chem. Soc. (C.S. Hudson award 1979) Office: McGill U Dept Chemistry Montreal QC Canada H3A 2K6

PERLIN, SEYMOUR, psychiatrist, educator; b. Passaic, N.J., Sept. 27, 1925; s. Samuel and Fanny (Horowitz) P.; m. Ruth Joan Rudolph, Aug. 21, 1958; children: Jonathan Brian, Steven Michael, Jeremy Francis. Student, Johns Hopkins U., 1943-44; BA summa cum laude, Princeton U., 1946; MD, Columbia U., 1950; grad., Washington Psychoanalytic Inst. Diplomate Am. Bd. Psychiatry and Neurology. Intern Univ. Hosp., Ann Arbor, Mich., 1951-52; resident N.Y. State Psychiat. Inst., 1950-51, 53-54, Manhattan State Hosp., 1952; practice medicine specializing in psychiatry and psychoanalysis Bethesda, Md., 1954-59, Stanford, Calif., 1959-60, N.Y.C., 1960-63, Balt., 1964-72, Bethesda, 1974—; chief div. psychiatry Montefiore Hosp., 1960-63; dir. clin. care and tng. Henry Phipps Psychiat. Clinic, Johns Hopkins Hosp., 1964-72; sr. research scholar Ctr. for Bioethics, Kennedy Inst., Georgetown U., Washington, 1974-78; clin. prof. psychiatry UCLA Sch. Medicine, 1973-74, George Washington U. Sch. Medicine, 1974-76, prof. to prof. emeritus, 1977-97, 97—, also dir. residency tng., 1977-93; lectr. psychiatry Columbia U., 1963-64; assoc. prof. psychiatry Johns Hopkins Sch. Medicine, 1964-65, prof., 1966-72, dep. chmn. dept. psychiatry and behavioral scis., 1969-72; program dir. Fellowship Program in Suicidology, 1967-72; adv. council Univ. health services Princeton, 1970-82. Vis. fellow Princeton U., 1973, Oxford U., 1974; Joseph P. Kennedy fellow medicine, law and ethics, 1974-75; chief sect. psychiatry Lab. Clin. Sci., NIMH, 1955-59, mem. clin. program-project com., 1967-70; fellow Ctr. Advanced Study in Behavioral Scis., 1959-60; chmn. mental health study sect. B, div. research grants NIH, 1964-66; cons. Community Mental Health Services, Md. Dept. Mental Hygiene, 1964-72; chmn. bd. dirs. Youth Suicide Nat. Ctr., 1985-87. Cons. editor: Jour. Suicide and Life Threatening Behavior, 1970-89; editorial bd.: Johns Hopkins Med. Jour, 1970-72; editor: Handbook for the Study of Suicide; co-editor: Ethical Issues in Death and Dying; contbr. numerous articles to med. jours. Served with USNR, 1944-46, with USPHS, 1954-58. Recipient Meirhoff award in pathology, 1950, Bicentennial Silver medal for achievement in psychiatry, 1967, both Coll. Phys. and Surg. Columbia. Fellow Am. Psychiat. Assn.; mem. Am. Coll. Psychiatry, Washington Psychoanalytic Soc., Med. Soc. D.C., Washington Psychiat. Soc., Am. Assn. Suicidology (pres. 1969-70, Dublin award 1978, ann. lectureship in suicidology in his name George Washington U. 1995). Home and Office: 5125 Westbard Ave Bethesda MD 20816-1413

PERLIS, HOWARD WILLIAM, computer consultant; b. Paterson, N.J., June 20, 1941; s. Leo and Betty Francis (Gantz) P.; B.A., Adelphi U., 1969; Ph.D., U. Ala., 1978; m. Loretta J. Stodel, Dec. 26, 1965; children— Jonathan Andrew, Melissa Amy. Research asst. Albert Einstein Coll. Medicine, N.Y.C., 1965-67; project engr. MIRU, U. Ala. Med. Center, Birmingham, 1967-70, mgr. obstetrics computer center, 1970-79, asst. prof. biophysics dept. ob-gyn, 1979-84; office automation cons., 1984— ; pres. Compu-Train, Inc. (tng. and custom software), Pelham, Ala., 1984— ; instr. Sch. Bus., U. Ala., Birmingham, 1979-86. Recipient cert. of Merit, Central Assn. Obstetricians and Gynecologists. Mem. So. Repub. Exchange. Home and Office: 8218 De Longpre Ave # B Los Angeles CA 90046-3757

PERLIS, SHARON A. lawyer; b. New Orleans; d. Rogers I. and Dorothy Perlis. BA in French, Principia Coll., 1967; JD, Tulane U., 1970. Officer, dir. Perlis, Inc., New Orleans, 1973—; pres. SILREP Internat. Co., Metairie, 1984—; officer, dir. Internat. Adv. Svcs., Inc., New Orleans, 1985-89; prin. Perlis, Hogg & Reynolds, Metairie, 1985-01. Legal counsel La. Ins. Rating Commn., 1980-84; adminstrv. law judge State of La., 1980-84, mem. Econ. Devel. Adv. Coun., 1982-84; bd. dirs. Bd. of Trade, 1986-96, exec. com. small bus. coun., 1987-89, chmn. small bus. coun., 1988, exec. com. East Jefferson coun., 1989-96; dir. World Trade Ctr., 1985-2002, vice chmn. internat. bus. com.; dir. New Orleans br. Fed. Res. Bank of Atlanta, 1982-88, chmn., 1984, 86, 88; bd. of commr. Port of New Orleans, 1992-96, vice chmn., 1995, chmn. bd., 1996; del. U.S. Def. Dept.'s Joint Civilian Orientation Conf., 1997. Mem. human rels commn. City of New Orleans, 1992-93, Commn. To Reorganize Govt., Leadership La., 2001; mem. exec. bd. La. Coun. Econ. Edn., 1986-89, Pvt. Enterprise Edn. Found., 1986-89; state del. White House Conf. on Small Bus., La. rep. internat. trade issues, 1986; dir. Metro YMCA, 1990-97; exec. com. agy. rels. United Way, 1987-90; mem. exec. com. Jr. Achievement Project Bus., 1987; vice chmn. La. Dist. Export Coun.; bd. dir. Bur. Govermental Rsch.; mem. bd. La. Internat. Trade Commn. Recipient Achiever's award Woman Bus. owners Assn., 1994, Jefferson Econ. Devel. Commn. award, 1994, Advocacy of Yr. award Small Bus. Adminstrn., 1988, 89, Iberville award New Orleans Pub. Group, 1996, Women of the Yr. award New Orleans Pub. Group, 2000, Patty Strong award Jefferson-21, 2000; named Young Leadership Coun. Role Model, 2001. Mem. ABA, Banker's Assn., Am. Arbitration Assn. (arbitrator/mediator), Jefferson Bar Assn., Orleans Bar Assn., Federal Bar Assn., Adv. Coun. Federalist Soc., La. Estate Planning Coun., La. Bar Assn., Gov.'s Commn. on Internat. Trade Devel., New Orleans Regional C. of C. (bd. dirs. 1990—)., New Orleans Regional Leadership Inst., New Orleans Area Polit. Action Coun. (pres.). Avocations: reading, sailing, tennis. Office: Perlis & Reynolds 3421 N Causeway Blvd Ste 404 Metairie LA 70002-3722

PERLISH, HARVEY NEIL (NEIL HARVEY), early education educator, academic administrator, author; b. Phila., Apr. 5, 1921; s. Herman Leonard and Dora (Polay) P.; m. Florence Helen Powell, Mar. 14, 1943 (dec. Apr. 1987); children: Joel, Lillian. BA, U. Pa., 1949, MA, 1965, PhD, 1968. Dir. ednl. projects Triangle Broadcasting Corp., Phila., 1945-71; dean Insts. Achievement Human Potential, 1963—; v.p. Broadcast Pioneers, 1997—. Pres. World Orgn. Human Potential, Phila., 1988—. Author: Kids Who Start Ahead, Stay Ahead, 1994, Of Time's Flight, 2000. Served with USAF, 1943-45, ETO. Named to Broadcasting Hall of Fame, 2001. Fellow Internat. Acad. Child Brain Devel. (sec. 1986—, award 1979); inducted Broadcasting's Hall of Fame, 2001. Avocations: languages, swimming. Office: Insts Achievement Human Potential 8801 Stenton Ave Glenside PA 19038-8151 E-mail: nharveyp@aol.com.

PERLMAN, BARRY STUART, electrical engineering executive, researcher; b. Bklyn., Dec. 5, 1939; s. Harold Wallace and Jane (Cohen) P.; m. Carolyn Amelia Francis; 1 child, David Matthew. BEE, CCNY, 1961; MSEE, Poly. U. N.Y., 1964; PhD in Electrophysics, Poly. Inst. N.Y., 1973. Mem. tech. staff, comms. lab. RCA Corp., N.Y.C., 1961-68; mem. tech. staff RCA Labs., Princeton, N.J., 1968-81, mgr. microwave rsch. lab., 1981-86, head design automation rsch., 1986-88; chief microwave photonic devices br. Electronics and Power Source Directorate, Army Rsch. Lab., Ft. Monmouth, 1988-95; dir. electronics divsn. Phys. Scis. Directorate, Army Rsch. Lab., 1995-96; chief RF and electronics divsn. Sensor and Electron Devices Directorate, Army Rsch. Lab., Ft. Monmouth and Adelphi, Md., 1996-97; R&D Engring. Ctr. staff Comm.-Electronics Command, Ft. Monmouth, 1997-98, chief applied comm., 1998-99; assoc. dir. for tech., prin. scientist Intel and Info Directorate, 1999—, exec. agt. DARPA reconfigurable apertures program, 1999—. Pres., mem. bd. dirs. INTEREX, Los Altos, Calif., 1981—83; rep. adv. group on electron devices, chmn. subpanel on RF Components Office of Undersec. of Def.; chmn. Computational Electronics and Nanoelectronics tech. area HPCMO, 1995—, program mgr. modeling and simulation Electronic Battlefield Environ. Portfolio, 2000—, chmn. Darpa Working Group, program mgr., agent Nanomechanical Array Signal Processors, MTO; mem. sys. study team DARPA FCS Comm. Program, ATO; DARPA agent for intelligent RF front end program (IRFFE), Tech. for Agile Efficient Microsystems program (TEAM) and Meta-Materials program; mem. NASA/JPL adv. com. for SATCOM "sys. on a chip" U. Mich.; mem. tech. adv. bd. Multidisciplinary U. Rsch. Initiative Photonic Band Gap Devices, UCLA, Multidisciplinary U. Rsch. Initiative, low power/low noise electronics UCLA, U. Mich., Multidisciplinary U. Rsch. Initiative quasi optical devices Calif. Tech. U., U. R.I., Ctr. High Frequency Microelectronics, U. Mich., 1990—96, Multidisciplinary U. Rsch. Low Energy Mobile Communications U. Mich., Multidisciplinary U. Rsch. for Nano and Molecular Electronics, Stevens U. and Terahertz Devices for Bio/Chem Sensing, U. Va.; mem. ind. adv. bd. Computer Applications to Electromagnetics Edn. NSF and U. Utah, 1990—94, MIMICAD Ctr., U. Colo., 1989—95; mem. ind. adv. bd. Elec. Engring./WAMI U. So. Fla., Wireless Commns. N.J. Inst. Tech.; Ctr. prof. microwave/lightwave engring. Drexel U., Phila., 1992—. Editor: Advances in Microwaves, 1974; mem. editl. bd. Wiley Jour. MW.MMW CAD, 1992—; contbr. articles to profl. jours.; patentee in field. Bd. dirs. YMCA, Princeton, 1975-78; pres. Home Owners Assn., E. Windsor, N.J., 1976-78; instr. Am. Heart Assn., N.J., 1978-82; chief rescue squad, E. Windsor, 1978-82. Fellow: IEEE (awards and advancement com. 1987—95, tech. program chair Sarnoff Symposium 1999—); mem.: Comm., Antennas & Propagation, Automated RF Techniques Group (treas. 1984—88, v.p. 1990—91), Cirs. and Sys., Ultrasonics, Ferroelectrics and Frequency Control, Microwave Theory and Tech. Soc. of IEEE (IMS tech. program com. 1980—, editl. bd. chmn. CAD com. MTT-1 1985—92, MTT adcom. 1990—94, chmn. Instersoc. Liaison 1995—97, MTT adcom. 2002—, chmn. meetings and symposia com. 2002—). Avocations: woodworking, photography, camping, gardening, gourmet cooking. Office: Army Comm-Electronics Command AMSEL-RD-I2-DE Fort Monmouth NJ 07703-5000 E-mail: b.perlman@ieee.org.

PERLMAN, BURTON, judge; b. Dec. 17, 1924; s. Phillip and Minnie Perlman; m. Alice Weihl, May 20, 1956; children: Elizabeth, Sarah, Nancy, Daniel. BE, Yale U., 1945, ME, 1947; LLB, U. Mich., 1952. Bar: Ohio 1959, N.Y. 1953, Conn. 1952, U.S. Dist. Ct. (so. and ea. dists.) N.Y. 1954, U.S. Dist. Ct. (so. dist.) Ohio 1959, U.S. Ct. Appeals (2d cir.) 1953, U.S. Ct. Appeals (6th cir.) 1959. Assoc. Armand Lackenbach, N.Y.C., NY, 1952—58; pvt. practice Cin., 1958—61; assoc. Paxton and Seasongood, 1961—67; ptnr. Schmidt, Effton, Josselson and Weber, 1968—71; U.S. magistrate U.S. Dist. Ct. (so. dist.) Ohio, 1971—76, U.S. bankruptcy judge, 1976—. Chief bankruptcy judge so. dist. Ohio, 1986—93; adj. prof. U. Cin. Law Sch., 1976—. Served with U.S. Army, 1944—46. Mem.: ABA, Cin. Bar Assn., Am. Judicature Soc., Fed. Bar Assn. Office: US Bankruptcy Ct Atrium 2 8th Fl 221 E 4th St Cincinnati OH 45202-4124

PERLMAN, DAVID, science editor, journalist; b. Balt., Dec. 30, 1918; s. Jess and Sara P.; m. Anne Salz, Oct. 15, 1941; children: Katherine, Eric, Thomas. AB, Columbia U., 1939, MS, 1940. Reporter Bismarck (N.D.) Capital, 1940; reporter San Francisco Chronicle, 1940-41, reporter, sci. editor, 1952-77, city editor, 1977-79, assoc. editor, sci. editor, 1979—; reporter New York Herald Tribune, Paris, N.Y.C., 1945-49; European corr. Colliers mag. and New York Post, 1949-51. Regents prof. human biology U. Calif., San Francisco 1974; vis. lectr. China Assn. Sci. and Tech., Beijing, Chengdu and Shanghai, 1983; sci. writer-in-residence U. Wis., 1989. Contbr. articles to major mags. Founding dir. Squaw Valley (Calif.) Community of Writers; dir. Alan Guttmacher Inst., 1990-99; trustee Scientists Inst. for Pub. Info., 1986-94; chmn. pub. svc. award com. Nat. Sci. Bd., 1998—. Served with inf. USAAF, 1941-45. Recipient Atomic Indsl. Forum award, 1975, AAAS Sci. Writing award, 1976, Exploratorium award 1977, Ralph Coates Roe medal ASME, 1978, Margaret Sanger Cmty. Svc. award, 1981, Fellows' medal Calif. Acad. Scis., 1984, Career Achievement award Soc. Profl. Journalists, 1989, Glenn T. Seaborg award Internat. Platform Assn., 1993, Sustained Achievement award for sci. journalism Am. Geophys. Union, 1997, U. Calif. San Francisco medal, 2000, Columbia U. Journalism award, 2000, San Francisco Med. Soc. award for disting. med. reporting, 2000, Grady-Stack award for sci. journalism Am. Chem. Soc., 2001; Poynter Inst. fellow Yale U., 1984, Carnegie Corp. fellow Stanford U., 1987. Fellow Calif. Acad. Scis.; mem. AAAS (adv. bd. Science-81-86 mag., com. Pub. Understanding of Sci. 1985-90), Coun. for Advancement Sci. Writing (pres. 1976-80), Nat. Assn. Sci. Writers (pres. 1970-71, Disting. Sci. Journalism award 1994), Astron. Soc. Pacific (dir. 1976-78), Sigma Xi. Office: San Francisco Chronicle 901 Mission St San Francisco CA 94103-2905 E-mail: dperlman@sfchronicle.com.

PERLMAN, JAY IRA, ophthalmologist; b. N.Y.C., Dec. 19, 1954; s. Max Perlman and Annabelle (Weber) P.; m. Nancy Allison Estrin, June 27, 1993. BS, Cornell U., 1975; MS, Purdue U., 1977, PhD, 1982; MD, Albert Einstein Coll., Bronx, N.Y., 1986. Diplomate Am. Bd. Ophthalmology. Transitional intern Jersey Shore Med. Ctr., Neptune, N.J., 1986-87; ophthalmic pathology fellow Armed Forces Inst. Pathology, Washington, 1987-88; ophthalmology resident Bronx Lebanon Hosp., 1988-91; ophthalmic pathology fellow U. Ill., Chgo., 1991-93; asst. chief ophthalmology Hines (Ill.) VA Hosp., 1993—; asst. prof. ophthalmology and pathology Loyola U. Med. Ctr., Maywood, Ill., 1993-2000, assoc. prof. ophthalmology and pathology, 2000—. Ophthalmic pathology cons. U. Ill., Chgo., 1994-95. Fellow Am. Acad. Ophthalmology; mem. Assn. Rsch. in Vision and Ophthalmology, Am. Assn. Ophthalmic Pathologists. Office: Edward Hines Jr VA Hosp Dept Ophthalmology Hines IL 60141

PERLMAN, JEFFREY MICHAEL, neonatologist; b. Cape Town, South Africa, Sept. 20, 1950; came to U.S., 1979; s. David Louis and Leah P.; divorced; children: David, Jacqueline. MB ChB, U. Cape Town, 1974; pediatric cert., St. Louis Children's Hosp., 1979-81; neonatal-perinatal medicine, Washington U., St. Louis, 1981-83. Intern in ob-gyn./surgery Groote Schuur Hosp., Cape Town, 1975, sr. intern ob-gyn., 1976; mission hosp. Thafolafee Hosp., Travskei, South Africa, 1976-77; pediatric resident Johannesburg Hosp., 1977-79, St. Louis Children's Hosp., 1979—81, neonatal fellow, 1981—83, med. dir. NICU, 1983—89; prof. pediatrics, med. dir. NICU Parkland Hosp., Dallas, 1989—; prof. pediatrics ob-gyn. U. Tex., Southwestern Med. Ctr., 1995—. Mem. steering com. Neonatal Resuscitation Com. Contbr. chpts. to books and articles to profl. jours.; editl. bd. Scis. in Neonatology, 1999—. Recipient Teen Support Group award March of Dimes, 2000, Chrystal Charity award Crystal Charity Orgn., 1999-2000. Fellow Am. Acad. of Pediatrics; mem. Soc. for Pediatric Rsch., Am. Pediatric Soc., Child Neurology Soc., Dallas County Med. Soc. Democrat. Jewish. Avocations: gardening, jogging, collecting African art. Office: 5323 Harry Hines Blvd Dallas TX 75390-7208 E-mail: Jperlm@mgonet.swmed.edu.

PERLMAN, JERALD LEE, lawyer; b. Baton Rouge, Feb. 25, 1947; s. Ralph Robert and Carol Mayer (Herzberg) P.; m. Francine Evonne McKelvey, May 8, 1984; children: Louise, Lee, Kevin. BA, Washington & Lee U., 1969; JD, La. State U., 1972. Bar: La. 1972, Tex. 1994, U.S. Dist. Ct. (we. dist.) La. 1972, U.S. Dist. Ct. (ea. and we. dists.) Ark. 1991, U.S. Ct. Appeals (5th cir.) 1977, U.S. Supreme Ct. 1990. Assoc. Blanchard, Walker, O'Quin & Roberts, Shreveport, La., 1972-76, ptnr., 1976-83, Walker, Tooke, Perlman & Lyons, Shreveport, 1983-94; regional office chief litigation divsn. La. Dept. Justice, 1994—. Assoc. editor La. State U. Law Rev., 1971-72. Bd. dirs. Broadmoor Southside YMCA, Shreveport, 1984-88, vice chmn., 1986, chmn., 1987; bd. dirs. Shreveport Met. YMCA, 1987; bd. dirs. NW La. chpt. ACLU, 1987-93. Capt. USAR, 1972. Named to La. State U. Law Ctr. Hall of Fame. Mem. La. Bar Assn. (com. on uniform court rules 1998—), Shreveport Bar Assn., La. Assn. Def. Counsel (bd. dirs. 1979-81), Fedn. Ins. and Corp. Counsel, Order of Coif, Phi Beta Kappa, Omicron Delta Kappa. Democrat. Jewish. Avocations: tennis, reading. Office: La Dept Justice Litigation Divsn 330 Marshall St Ste 777 Shreveport LA 71101-3016

PERLMAN, JOHN NIELS, educator, poet; b. Alexandria, Va., May 13, 1946; s. Ellis Sherman and Birthe Elaine P.; m. Janis Lynn, May 26, 1967; 1 child, Nicole Jeanne Kachina. BA, Ohio State U., 1969; MS in Edn., Iona Coll., 1981. Cons. NEA, Washington, 1971-72; tchr. Mamaroneck (N.Y.) Pub. Schs., 1973—. Author: (poetry books) Kachina, 1971, Homing, 1981, The Natural History of Trees, 1995, Edward-John, 1998. Recipient Acad. Am. Poets prize, 1969; N.Y. Found. Arts fellow, 1991. Buddhist. Avocations: hiking, canoeing, gardening. Home: 38 Ferris Pl Ossining NY 10562-3510 E-mail: johnperl@aol.com.

PERLMAN, KALMAN ISADORE, management consultant, pharmacist; b. Chgo., May 27, 1915; s. Morris and Mary Ada (Weiner) P.; m. Ida Faye Bauer, July 2, 1939. BS in Pharmacy, U. Ill., Chgo., 1940; BBA, Northwestern U., 1962; postgrad., Loyola U., Chgo., 1966-69. Registered pharmacist; cert. purchasing mgr. Pharmacist, mgr. various drug stores, Chgo., 1932-44; chief pharmacist various hosp. pharmacies, 1946-70; sr. hosp. procurement specialist Health & Hosps. Governing Commn. of Cook County, 1970-80; assoc. adminstr. Chgo. Specialty Hosp., 1981-84; instr. Northeastern Ill. U., Chgo., 1979-84; cons. mgmt., 1984—. Vol. pharmacist, purchasing agt. The Ark, Chgo., 1985—. Author: Handbook of Purchasing and Materials Management, 1990, The Leasing Handbook, 1992; contbr. articles to profl. jours. Served with U.S. Army, 1944-46. Fellow AAAS; mem. AMA (affiliate), Am. Pharm. Assn., Nat. Assn. Purchasing Mgmt. Lodges: Masons (Master 1958), El Jalla Grotto (Monarch 1967). Jewish. Avocations: philately, photography, writing. Home and Office: 2726 W Catalpa Ave Chicago IL 60625-3216

PERLMAN, KATHERINE LENARD (KATO LENARD), organic chemist; b. Budapest, Hungary, July 18, 1928; came to U.S., 1963; d. Sandor and Lili (Fischer) Lenard; m. David Perlman, Aug. 18, 1968 (dec. 1980). Diploma chemistry, Eotvos U., Budapest, 1950, PhD, 1960. Rsch. chemist CHINOIN Pharms., Budapest, 1950-54; rsch. staff member Rsch. Inst. for Pharm. Industry, 1954-62, Princeton (N.J.) U., 1963-68; rsch. assoc. U. Wis., Madison, 1968-69, assoc. scientist sch. pharmacy, 1969-81, sr. scientist biochemistry dept., 1981—. Contbr. numerous articles to profl. jours.; patentee in field. Mem. Am. Chem. Soc., Chem. Soc. London. Democrat. Avocations: cooking, gardening, hiking, music, Navajo rug weaving. Home: 1 Chippewa Ct Madison WI 53711-2803 Office: U Wis 420 Henry Mall Madison WI 53706-1502

PERLMAN, LAWRENCE, retired business executive, corporate director, consultant; b. St. Paul, Apr. 8, 1938; m. Linda Peterson; children: David, Sara. BA, Carleton Coll., 1960; JD, Harvard U., 1963. Bar: Minn. 1963. Law. clk. for fed. judge, 1963; assoc., ptnr. Fredrikson & Byron, Mpls., 1964-75; gen. counsel, exec. v.p. U.S. pacing ops. Medtronic, Inc., 1975-78; sr. ptnr. Oppenheimer, Wolff & Donnelly, 1978-80; sec., gen. counsel, v.p. corp. svcs. Control Data Corp., 1980-82; pres. Comml. Credit Co., 1983-85; pres., CEO Imprimis Tech., 1985—88; pres., COO Control Data Corp., Mpls., 1989; pres., CEO Control Data Corp. (now Ceridian Corp.), 1990-92, chmn., CEO, 1992—2000; ret., 2000. Dir., chmn. Seagate Tech., 1989-2000; bd. dirs. Amdocs Ltd., Carlson Cos., Inc., The Valspar Corp.; chmn. Arbitron Inc.; trustee Carleton Coll. Bd. dirs. Walker Art Ctr.; regent Univ. of Minn., 1993-95; chmn. 21st Century Workforce Commn., 1999-2000. Address: 343 Union Plaza 333 Washington Ave N Minneapolis MN 55401

PERLMAN, MARK, economist, educator; b. Madison, Wis., Dec. 23, 1923; s. Selig and Eva (Shaber) P.; m. Naomi Gertrude Waxman, June 7, 1953; 1 child, Abigail Ruth Williams. BA, MA, U. Wis., 1947; PhD, Columbia, 1950. Asst. prof. U. Hawaii, 1951-52, Cornell U., 1952-55; asst. prof., then assoc. prof. Johns Hopkins U., 1955-63; prof. econs., history and pub. health U. Pitts., 1963-94, chmn. dept., 1965-70, univ. prof., 1969-94, univ. prof. emeritus, 1994—. Co-chmn. Internat. Econ. Assn. Conf. on Econs. of Health in Industrialized Nations, Tokyo, Japan, 1973, Conf. on Orgn. and Retrieval Econs. Data, Kiel, West Germany, 1975; vis. fellow Clare Hall U. Cambridge, 1977; ofcl. visitor faculty econs. and politics, U. Cambridge, 1976-77; co-chmn., co-editor Internat. Congress on Health Econs., Leyden, The Netherlands, 1980; mem. Princeton Inst. Adv. Study, 1981-82; adj. scholar Am. Enterprise Inst., 1981—; Österreichischer Länderbank Joseph Schumpeter prof. Technische Universität, Vienna, 1982; disting. vis. scholar Beijing Chinese Nat. Acad. Social Scis., 1983; Rockefeller Found. resident scholar Villa Serbelloni, Bellagio, Como, Italy, 1983; vis. prof. Inst. für Weltwirtschaft U. Kiel, 1987, U. Augsburg, 1992, U. Chemnitz, 1996; mem. Internat. Com. for Documentation in the Social Scis., UNESCO, 1988-94, exec. com. 1993-94. Author: Judges in Industry: A Study of Labor Arbitration in Australia, 1954, Labor Union Theories in America, 1958, 2d edit., 1976, The Machinists: A New Study in American Trade Unionism, 1962, (with T.D. Baker) Health Manpower in a Developing Economy, 1967, (with Charles R. McCann, Jr.) Pillars of Economic Understanding: Factors and Markets, 1998; editor: The Economics of Health and Medical Care, 1974, The Organization and Retrieval of Economic Knowledge, 1977, (with G.K. MacLeod) Health Care Capital: Competition and Control, 1978, (with K. Weiermair) Studies in Economic Rationality: X-Efficiency Examined and Extolled, 1990, (with A. Heertje) Evolving Technology and Market Structure: Studies in Schumpeterian Economics, 1990, (with N.H. Ornstein) Political Power and Social Change: The United States Faces a United Europe, 1991; (with C.E. Barfield) Capital Markets and Trade: The United States Faces a United Europe, 1991, Industry, Services, and Agriculture: The U.S. Faces a United Europe, 1991; Political Power and Social Change: The United States Faces a United Europe, 1991; (with F.M. Scherer), Entrepreneurship, Technological Innovation, and Economic Growth: Studies in Schumpeterian Economics, 1992, (with Yuichi Shionoya) Innovations in Technology Industries and Institutions, 1994, Schumpeter in the History of Ideas, 1994, (with Ernst Helmstadter) The Character of Economic Thought, Economic Characters and Economic Institutions, 1996, Behavioral Norms, Technological Progress, and Economic Dynamics, 1996; also articles, essays on health, population change, econ. devel., orgn. econ. knowledge and methodology, econ. productivity, history of econ. discipline; Festschrifts (Sir John Barry, Edgar M. Hoover), 1972; editor: series Cambridge Surveys of Contemporary Economics 1977-94, Cambridge Surveys of Economic Institutions and Policies, 1991-96; cons. editor, later editorial cons. USIA publ., Portfolio on Internat. Econ. Perspectives, 1972-83; mng. co-editor Jour. Evolutionary Econs., 1989-96; corr. Am. editor Revue d'Economie Politique, 1990—; series editor Great Economists of the World, 1990-96. With U.S. Army, 1943-46. Social Sci. Research Council fellow, 1949-50; Ford Found. fellow, 1962-63; Fulbright lectr. Melbourne U., 1968 Mem. Am. Econ. Assn. (founding and mng. editor Jour. Econ. Lit. 1968-81), Royal Econ. Soc., History Econs. Soc. (v.p. 1979-80, pres. elect 1983-84, pres. 1984-85), J.A. Schumpeter Gesselleschaft (editor 1986-96), Phi Beta Kappa. Clubs: Athenaeum (London). Jewish. Home: 5622 Bartlett St Pittsburgh PA 15217-1514

PERLMAN, MATTHEW SAUL, lawyer; b. Washington, Aug. 30, 1936; s. Jacob and Helen (Aronson) P.; m. Julia Gertrude Hawks, June 22, 1966; children— Penelope Leah, Deborah Jane, Sarah Louise, Jacob Henry AB, Brown U., 1957; LLB, Harvard U., 1960. Bar: D.C. 1960, Md. 1960, U.S. Supreme Ct. 1965. Atty. Air Force Gen. Counsel's Office, Washington, 1960-65; mem. Armed Services Bd. of Contract Appeals, 1965-67; gen. counsel Pres.' Commn. on Postal Orgn., 1967; asst. gen. counsel Dept. Transp., 1967-69; ptnr. Arent, Fox, Kintner, Plotkin & Kahn, 1969—2001, arbitrator, 2002—. Mem. Pres. Reagan's Transition Team for GSA, Washington, 1980-81; mem. adv. bd. Fed. Contracts Report, Washington, 1970-97; overseas corr. Internat. Constn. Law Rev., London, 1983—. Contbr. articles to profl. jours. Pres. Civic Assn. River Falls, Potomac, Md., 1975-77; mem. Montgomery County Md. Citizens Adv. Commn. for Rock Run AWT Plant, 1979-85. Served to capt. USAF, 1960-63 Mem. ABA (pub. contracts sect.), Fed. Bar Assn., Cosmos Club. Republican. Jewish. Home: 10517 Stable Ln Potomac MD 20854-3867 Office: Arent Fox Kintner Plotkin & Kahn 1050 Connecticut Ave NW Ste 500 Washington DC 20036-5303 E-mail: perlmanm@arentfox.com., mpjp@erols.com.

PERLMAN, RICHARD BRIAN, lawyer; b. N.Y.C., Aug. 19, 1951; s. William H. and Beryl N. (Cohen) P.; m. Virginia Merrill, Aug. 1, 1976; 1 child, Jason Eric. BA, Franklin and Marshall Coll., 1973; JD, Temple U., 1976. Bar: Pa. 1976, U.S. Dist. Ct. (ea. dist.) Pa. 1977, U.S. Supreme Ct. 1982, Fla. 1999; cert. family mediator Fla. Supreme Ct., 1996. Assoc. Law Offices of Peter N. Harrison, Doylestown, Pa., 1976-77, Zion & Klein, Bryn Mawr, 1977-78; founder, owner The Law Ctr., Norristown, 1978-96, West Chester, 1982-96. Pres. Mothers Against Drunk Driving, Chester and Delaware Counties, Pa., 1987-89, 90-92; bd. dirs. Big Bros./Big Sisters, Montgomery County, Pa., 1979-85. Avocations: music, boating, golf. E-mail: rbpesqlbk@aol.com.

PERLMAN, RICHARD DONALD, orthopedic surgeon; b. Bkyln., Mar. 12, 1938; s. Rubin and Miriam Perlman; m. Patricia Livingston, Sept. 1, 1960; children: Mark H., Kenneth S. BA magna cum laude, Princeton U., 1959; MD, Columbia U., 1963; MPH, San Diego State U., 1997. Diplomate Am. Bd. Orthop. Surgery. Internship Columbia Surg. Divsn. Bellevue Hosp., N.Y., 1963-64; resident in general surgery Hosp. Jt. Diseases, 1964-65, resident in orthop. surgery, 1965-68; fellowship Orthop. and Calif. Luth. Hosp.; instr. orthops. U. So. Calif., 1968-69; asst. clin. prof. orthops. U. Calif., San Diego; chief orthops. Sharp Meml. Hosp., 1984-86. Hosp. affiliations Sharp Meml. Hosp., Mercy Hosp., San Diego, Scripps Meml., San Diego, exec. med. bd. Sharp Meml. Hosp., 1986-95; mem. orthop. supervisory com., 1978-2002; chair med. legal liaison com. San Diego County Med. Soc., chair Problem Foot Clinic Sharp Rehab. Inst., mem. undergrad. sch. com. Princeton U., 1987-89. Contbr. articles to profl. jours. Former bd. dirs. San Diego Hosp. Assn., So. Calif. Health Svcs., Sharp Ind. Physicians Assn., pres.; mem. bd. trustees San Diego Space Theater and Sci. Found. With USN, 1969-71. Fellow ACS; mem. AMA, Soc. Military Surgeons, Western Orthop. Assn., San Diego County Med. Soc., Calif. Med. Assn., Am. Acad. Orthop. Surgeons, Am. Soc. Surgeery of the Hand, Am. Orthop. Foot and Ankle Soc. Office: 770 Washington St Ste 301 San Diego CA 92103-2209

PERLMAN, RICHARD WILFRED, economist, educator; b. Mt. Vernon, N.Y., Dec. 15, 1923; s. Uriel and Annie (Feitelberg) P.; m. Irma Lowenthal, Sept. 18, 1949; children: Abel, David, Laura, Jennifer. AB, Cornell U., 1947; PhD, Columbia U., 1953. Asst. prof. econs. Adelphi U., Garden City, N.Y., 1953-57, assoc. prof., 1957-64; prof. econs. U. Wis., Milw., 1964-97, prof. emeritus, 1997—, chmn. dept., 1965-68, 74-77; NRC prof. Brookings Instn., 1958-59. Fulbright lectr. Inst. Politecnico Nacional, Mexico City, 1964, Autonomous U. Madrid, 1972 Author: Economics of Education, 1973, Labor Theory, 1969, Economics of Poverty, 1976, (with others) An Anthology of Labor Economics, 1972, Economics of Unemployment, 1984, Issues in Labor Economics, 1989, Sex Discrimination in the Labor Market, 1994. Mem. President's Com. on EEO, 1963. Rsch. fellow U. Melbourne, Australia, 1985, hon. rsch. fellow U. Birmingham, 1990-93, sr. fellow, 1993-00; Fulbright rsch. scholar, Australia, 1987, rsch. scholar Victoria U. Tech., Australia, 1997. Mem. Am. Econ. Assn., Indsl. Relations Research Assn., Phi Beta Kappa. Home: 3341 N Summit Ave Milwaukee WI 53211-2930

PERLMUTH, WILLIAM ALAN, lawyer; b. N.Y.C., Nov. 21, 1929; s. Charles and Roe (Schneider) P.; m. Loretta Kaufman, Mar. 14, 1951; children: Carolyn, Diane. AB, Wilkes Coll., 1951; LLB, Columbia U., 1953. Bar: N.Y. 1954. Assoc. Cravath, Swaine & Moore, N.Y.C., 1955-61; ptnr. Stroock & Stroock & Lavan, 1962—. Editor Columbia U. Law Rev., 1952-53. Trustee Aeroflex Found., N.Y.C., 1965—, City Ctr. 55th St. Theater Found., 1995—, Harkness Found. for Dance, N.Y.C., 1976—, Sch. Am. Ballet, 1997—, Wilkes U., Wilkes-Barre, Pa., 1980—, Weininger Found., 1985—. NYU Hosps. Ctr., 1994—, Hosp. for Joint Diseases Orthopaedic Inst., N.Y.C., 1980—, chmn. bd. trustees, 1994—. Mem. N.Y. State Bar Assn., Assn. of Bar of City of N.Y. Jewish. Home: 880 5th Ave New York NY 10021-4951 Office: Stroock & Stroock & Lavan 180 Maiden Ln Fl 34 New York NY 10038-4982

PERLMUTTER, ALVIN HOWARD, television and film producer; b. Poughkeepsie, N.Y., Mar. 24, 1928; s. Fred and Jennie (Albert) P.; children: James F., Stephen H., Tom W. Student, Colgate U., 1945-47; BA, Syracuse U., 1949. Dir. pub. affairs Sta. WNBC, also Sta. WNBC-TV, N.Y.C., 1957-59; program mgr. Sta. WNBC-TV, 1959-61; exec. producer Nat. Ednl. TV, 1961—; v.p. news documentaries NBC, from 1975; pres. Alvin H. Perlmutter Inc., N.Y.C.; instr. TV news and pub. affairs NYU, 1957, Fairleigh Dickinson U., 1962; pres., CEO, Sunrise Media LLC, N.Y.C., 1997—. Cons. John and Mary Markle Found., Pub. Agenda Found.; chmn. Dore Schary Awards for film and TV, Anti-Defamation League. Producer: series Assignment America; Great American Machine, Consumer Reports Presents, Money Matters, Cover Story, Black Journal; various spl. programs including: Native Land, The Primal Mind, Adam Smith's Money World series, Family Computing series, Priceless Treasures of Dresden, The Perpetual People Puzzle; exec. producer: Report From Philadelphia, The Secret Government, The Power of Myth, Muslims (PBS spl. documentary). Chair Dore Schary awards, Anti-Defamation League; bd. dirs. N.Y. Open Ctr., Citizens for Ind. Pub. Broadcasting. 1st lt. AUS, 1950-53. Recipient various citations and awards including 6 Emmy awards, Peabody award, Robert Kennedy award. Mem. Acad. TV Arts and Scis. (gov. N.Y. chpt., nat. trustee, chmn. awards com. 1968), Assn. Pub. TV Producers (chmn. 1969) Clubs: Overseas Press (N.Y.C.), University; Coffee House. Home: 27 W 86th St New York NY 10024-3615 Office: 45 W 45th St New York NY 10036-4602

PERLMUTTER, DIANE F. communications executive; b. N.Y.C., Aug. 31, 1945; d. Bert H. and Frances (Smith) P. Student, NYU Grad. Sch. of Bus., 1969-70; BA in English, Miami U., Oxford, Ohio, 1967. Writer sales promotion Equitable Life Assurance, N.Y.C., 1967-68; bus. adminstr. de Garmo, Inc., 1968-69, asst. account exec., 1969-70, account exec., 1970-74, v.p., account supr., 1974-76; mgr. corp. advt. Avon Products, Inc., 1976-79, dir. communications Latin Am., Spain, Can., 1979-80, dir. brochures, 1980-81, dir. category merchandising, 1981-82, group dir. motivational communications, 1982-83, group dir. sales promotion, 1983-84, v.p. sales promotion, 1984, v.p. internat. bus. devel., 1984-85, area v.p. Latin Am., 1985, v.p. advtg. and campaign mktg., 1985-87, v.p. U.S. operational planning, 1987; cons., 1987-88; sr. v.p. Burson-Marsteller, 1988-90, exec. v.p., mng. dir. consumer products, 1991-93, bd. dirs., 1992—, co-chief operating officer, 1993-94, chief operating officer, 1994-96; chmn. mktg. practice/U.S., 1996-98. Vice chmn., CEO Cohn & Wolfe, N.Y.C., 1998—2000; CEO Gilda's Club Worldwide, 2001—; chair ann. meeting Direct Selling Assn., Washington, 1982; v.p. Nat. Home Fashions League, N.Y.C., 1975—76; adj. instr. SUNY/ Fashion Inst. Tech., 1992—; vice chmn. Columbia-Greene Hosp. Found., 2000—, Olana Partnership, 2000—; bd. dirs. Double L.P. Industries, Inc. Named to YWCA Acad. Women Achievers, 1996. Mem. Pub. Rels. Soc. Am., Advt. Women of N.Y., Women in Communications, Miami U. Alumni Assn. (pres., chair 1986), Publicity Club N.Y. (bd. dirs. 1994-96), YMCA of Greater N.Y. (bd. dirs. 1996—), The Women's Forum (bd. dirs. 1998-2000, pres. 2002—), Women's Econ. Round Table (bd. dirs. 1999-2000), Beta Gamma Sigma. Avocation: interior design. Office: Gilda's Club Worldwide 322 8th Ave 14th Flr New York NY 10001

PERLMUTTER, DONNA, music and dance critic; b. Phila. d. Myer and Bessie (Krasno) Stein; m. Jona Perlmutter, Mar. 21, 1964; children: AAron, Matthew. BA, Pa. State U., 1958; MS, Yeshiva U., 1959. Music and dance critic L.A. Herald Examiner, 1975-84; contbr. L.A. Times, 1984—, N.Y. Times, 1994—. Dance critic Dance Mag., N.Y.C., 1980—; music critic Opera News, N.Y.C., 1981-98, Ovation Mag., N.Y.C., 1983-89, N.Y. Mag., 1995—, L.A. Mag., 1996—, Daily News, L.A., 1996-97, New Times, L.A., 1997—, Performing Arts Mag., 1996—; panelist, speaker various music and dance orgns. Author: Shadowplay: The Life of Antony Tudor, 1991. Recipient Deems Taylor award for excellence in writing on music ASCAP, 1991. Mem. Music Critics Assn. Home: 10507 Le Conte Ave Los Angeles CA 90024-3305

PERLMUTTER, JEROME HERBERT, communications specialist; b. N.Y.C., Oct. 17, 1924; s. Morris and Rebecca (Shiffman) P.; m. Evelyn Lea Friedman, Sept. 19, 1948; children: Diane Muriel, Sandra Pauline, Bruce Steven. AB cum laude, George Washington U., 1949; MA, Am. U., 1957. Chief editor svc., prodn. editor NEA, Washington, 1949-50; editor in chief Jour. AAHPER, 1950-51; editor Rural Elec. News, REA, USDA, 1951-53; publ. writer Agrl. Rsch. Svc., 1953-56; chief, editor br. Office Info., 1956-60; sec. Outlook and Situation Bd., 1960-62; chief econ. reports Econ. Rsch. Svc., 1960-62; chief div. pub. and reprodn. svcs. U.S. Dept. State, Washington, 1962-79; pres. Perlmutter Assocs., 1979—. Writing cons. CSC, 1956, World Bank, 1967—; communication cons. European Investment Bank, Can. Internat. Devel. Agy., Inter-Am. Devel. Bank, Internat. Monetary Fund; faculty agr. grad. sch. U. Md., also Fgn. Svc. Inst.; pub. cons. White House Conf. on Children and Youth, 1971. Author: A Practical Guide to Effective Writing, 1965; Contbr. articles profl. jours. Coord. fed. graphics Nat. Endowment for Arts, 1972-79, graphic designer, conv. of maj. polit. com., 1980. With USNR, 1943-46. Recipient award U.S. Jr. C. of C., 1963, Editors Choice award Nat. Libr. Poetry. Mem. Am. Assn. Agr. Coll. Editors, Assn. Editl. Bus. (bd. dirs.), Fed. Editors Assn., Am. Farm Econ. Assn., Soc. Tech. Comm. (bd. dirs.), Md. Literacy Coun., Soc. Profl. Journalists, Phi Beta Kappa, Phi Eta Sigma, Artus. Home: 15111 Glade Dr Silver Spring MD 20906-1542

PERLMUTTER, LEONARD MICHAEL, concrete construction company executive; b. Denver, Oct. 16, 1925; s. Philip Permutter and Belle (Perlmutter); m. Alice Love Bristow, Nov. 17, 1951; children: Edwin George, Joseph Kent, Cassandra Love. BA, U. Colo., 1948, postgrad., 1948-50. Ptnr. Perlmutter & Sons, Denver, 1947-58; v.p. Prestressed Concrete of Colo., 1952-60; pres. Stanley Structures, Inc., 1960-83, chmn. bd., 1983-87; dir. Colo. Nat. Bankshares, Inc.; adj. prof. Grad. Sch. Pub. Affairs U. Colo., Denver, 1987—; chief exec. officer Econ. Devel. Gov.'s Office State of Colo., 1987-88. Chmn. bd. Colo. Open Lands, 1989. Chmn. bd. U. Colo. Found., Boulder, 1979-81; dir. Santa Fe Opera Assn., N.Mex., 1976-85; v.p. Santa Fe Fedn., 1979-87; chmn. bd. Nat. Jewish Hosp.-Nat. Asthma Ctr., Denver, 1983-86; pres. Denver Symphony Assn., 1983-84, chmn. bd., 1985; trustee Midwest Rsch. Inst., 1989—; pres. Nat. Jewish Ctr. for Immunology and Respiratory Medicine, 1991-93. Recipient Humanitarian Am. Jewish Com., 1981 Mem. Prestressed Concrete Inst. (pres. 1977, dir. 1973-74) Clubs: Rolling Hills Country (Golden) (pres. 1966-68). Home: 15125 Foothill Rd Golden CO 80401-2044 Office: LAP Inc 1515 Arapahoe St Denver CO 80202-3150

PERLMUTTER, LOUIS, investment banker, lawyer; b. Cambridge, Mass., Oct. 3, 1934; s. Kermit H and Rachel P (Ehrlich) Perlmutter; m. Barbara Patricia Sondik, Dec. 11, 1966; children: Kermit, Eric. BA, Brandeis U., 1956; JD, U. Mich., 1959; LHD (hon.), Brandeis U., 1995. Bar: Mass 1959, NY 1961. Law practice, N.Y.C., 1960-65; asst. to pres. New Eng. Industries, 1965-67; pres. Octagon Assocs., 1967-75; sr. v.p. White Weld, 1975-78; mgn. dir. Merrill Lynch, White, Weld, 1978; exec. mng. dir Lazard Freres & Co. LLC, 1978-99, ltd. mng. dir., 2000—. Contbr. articles to profl jours. Mem exec comt, bd gov Am Jewish Comn; dir Charles H Revson Found, UN; exec. comt. of bd. of gov. Am Jewish Committe; mem comt visitor Council on Foreign Relations; chmn bd trustees Brandeis Univ, Waltham, Mass., 1988—95, Am Jewish Cong, New York, NY, 1988—94; chmn exec comt, bd dirs UN Asn US, 1993—96; mem comt visitors Univ Mich Law Sch; bd fellows Harvard Med Sch. Recipient Human Relations Award, Am Jewish Comn, 1995, Pub Serv Award, Phoenix Hs, 1999, Israel Tribute Dinner, 2001. Mem.: Econ Club NY. Home: 39 E 79th St New York NY 10021-0216 Office: Lazard Freres & Co LLC 30 Rockefeller Plz Fl 61 New York NY 10112-5900

PERLMUTTER, MARTIN LEE, interactive media producer, consultant, writer, educator; b. N.Y.C., Sept. 3, 1947; s. Alvin I. and Sylvia Sande P.; m. Miki Raver, July 4, 1977; 1 child, Sara Sasha Perl-Raver. AB, Harvard U., 1968. Pres. Ghost Dance, Cambridge, Mass., 1970-76, San Francisco, 1977-80, N.Y.C., 1980-87, San Francisco, 1986-96, Multisensory Interactive Learning Inst., Oakland, 2001—; ptnr. Hook-Up!, San Francisco, 1995-2000; prin. META-4 Prodns., 1996—; sr. prodr. LookSmart Ltd., 1998-2001. Cons.

Harvard U., 1971-72, MIT, 1973-74, CBS Labs., 1974, RCA, 1975, Westinghouse Broadcasting, 1977-79, State of Mass., 1983-84, Xerox, 1991, Kodak, 1991, Hewlett-Packard, 1992, Time Warner, 1993-95, EDS, Providence Jour., 1993, EEN Bus. Network, Sony Signatures, 1994, SBC Comm., 1993, Hands-On Tech., 1995, Strategos, 1996, Pacific Bell, 1996; prodr. Met. Mus. Art, N.Y.C., 1982-83; instr. NYU Tisch Sch. Arts, 1986, San Francisco State U., 1988-89, 99; editor, pub. The Green Sheet, San Francisco, 1989-90; editor Media Letter, 1991-92; bd. dirs. Multimedia Devel. Group, San Francisco, 1993-94; mem. Oakland Telecom. Policy Commn., 1997-98, 98-2000. Prodr. nat. advt. The Student Vote, 1972, Evangelist, Look Smart, broadband and wireless, 1999-2001; designer, prodr. Interactive TV exhibit Vision and Television, 1976-82 (NEA and NSF award 1976); designer interactive video exhibit The Rainbow Machine, 1978 (Lawrence Hall Sci.), The Frog's Eye, 1986 (N.Y. Hall of Sci.); exec. prodr. Teleprompter Corp., Coping with Life Crises, 1980, Videodisc Pub., 1983-84, AT&T Telemktg., 1984; prodr. interactive videodisc Murder, Anyone?, 1982 (Best Interactive Program 1983, Best Dir. 1983, Best Made-for-Home Product 1983, Best Consumer Product 1983), Many Roads to Murder, 1983, Anthology of American Video Art, 1987; prodr. Feldenkrais Profl. Tng. Program, 1982-84, Convergence! Inside the Information Revolution, 1995; multimedia prodr. Video Almanac of 20th Century, 1993-94; author: The Producer's Guide to Interactive Videodiscs, 1991; columnist San Francisco Examiner, 1997-99, Upside mag., 1998, Business 2.0, 1999. Organizer Nat. Student Strike, 1970, Boston Yippies, 1970-71. Recipient medal Internat. Film-Video Festival N.Y., 1981, VIRA awards Video Rev. Mag., N.Y.C., 1983, Nebr. Video Disc Design/Prodn., 1983, Tokyo Audio-Visual Age Software Fair, 1988, Best of Category award Casa de las Ciencias Competition, 1990. Avocations: trumpet, painting. Home: 2866 Mckillop Rd Oakland CA 94602-1503 E-mail: martinperlmutter@yahoo.com.

PERLOFF, JAMES EDWARD, writer, publisher; b. Painesville, Ohio, Oct. 27, 1951; s. John Walton and Dorothy Relyea Perloff; m. Wei-Hsin Chau, June 22, 1991; 1 child, David. Student, Colby Coll., 1969-72; BS, Boston U., 1975. RN, Mass. Staff nurse Spaulding Rehab. Hosp., Boston, 1982-87, Mt. Auburn Hosp., Cambridge, Mass., 1989-93, Deaconess-Waltham (Mass.) Hosp., 1993-99; contbg. editor New Am. mag., Belmont, Mass., 1986-89; rschr. Birth Rsch. Inc., 1988-89; pub. Refuge Books, Arlington, Mass., 1999—. Author: The Shadows of Power, 1988, Tornado in a Junkyard, 1999, The Case Against Darwin, 2002; talk show guest, 1999—. Avocations: Civil War literature. Office: Refuge Books PO Box 191 Arlington MA 02476

PERLOFF, JEAN MARCOSSON, lawyer; b. Lakewood, Ohio, June 25, 1942; d. John Solomon and Marcella Catherine (Borngen) Marcosson; m. Lawrence Storch, Stpe. 8, 1991. BA magna cum laude, Lake Erie Coll., 1965; MA in Italian, UCLA, 1967; JD magna cum laude, Ventura Coll. Law, 1976. Bar: Calif. 1976, U.S. Dist. Ct. (cen. dist.) Calif. 1978. Assoc. in Italian U. Calif.-Santa Barbara, 1967-70; law clk., paralegal Ventura County Pub. Defender's Office, Ventura, Calif., 1975; sole practice, 1976-79; co-prin. Clabaugh & Perloff, A Profl. Corp., 1979-82; sr. jud. atty. to presiding justice 6th divsn. 2d Dist. Ct. Appeals, L.A., 1982-97; comml. property mgr. Santa Barbara, Calif., 1997—. Instr. Ventura Coll. Law, 1976-79. Pres., bd. dirs. Santa Barbara Zool. Gardens, 1987-88; bd. dirs. Montecito Found., 1999—; trustee Lake Erie Coll., 1993—; mem. 19th Agrl. Dist. Bd., 2001—. Named Woman of Yr., 18th Senatorial dist. and 35th Assembly dist. Calif. Legislature, 1993; recipient Disting. Alumnae award Lake Erie Coll., 1996; sesquicentennial fellow Lake Erie Coll., 2001. Mem. Calif. Bar Assn. (appellate ct. com. 1993-95), Fiesta City Club, Kappa Alpha Sigma. Democrat. Avocations: tennis, jogging, biking, reading, music. Home: 1384 Plaza Pacifica Santa Barbara CA 93108-2877

PERLOFF, JEFFREY MARK, agricultural and resource economics educator; b. Chgo., Jan. 28, 1950; s. Harvey S. and Miriam (Seligman) P.; m. Jaqueline B. Persons, Aug. 15, 1976; 1 child, Lisa. BA, U. Chgo., 1972; PhD, MIT, 1976. Asst. prof. U. Pa., Phila., 1976-80, U. Calif., Berkeley, 1980-82, assoc. prof., 1982-89, prof., 1989—. Author: (with Dennis Carlton) Modern Industrial Organization, 1990, 3d edit., 2000, Microeconomics, 1999, 2d edit., 2001; contbr. numerous articles to profl. jours. Office: U Calif Dept Agrl Econs 207 Giannini Hall Berkeley CA 94720-3310 E-mail: perloff@are.berkeley.edu.

PERLOFF, MARJORIE GABRIELLE, English and comparative literature educator; b. Vienna, Austria, Sept. 28, 1931; d. Maximilian and Ilse (Schueller) Mintz; m. Joseph K. Perloff, July 31, 1953; children— Nancy Lynn, Carey Elizabeth. AB, Barnard Coll., 1953; MA, Cath. U., 1956, PhD, 1965. Asst. prof. English and comparative lit. Cath. U., Washington, 1966-68, asso. prof., 1969-71, U. Md., 1971-73, prof., 1973-76; Florence R. Scott prof. English U. So. Calif., Los Angeles, 1976—; prof. English and comparative lit. Stanford U., Calif., 1986—, Sadie Dernham prof. humanities, 1990—, prof. emerita, 2000. Author: Rhyme and Meaning in the Poetry of Yeats, 1970, The Poetic Art of Robert Lowell, 1973, Frank O'Hara, Poet Among Painters, 1977, 2nd edit., 1998, The Poetics of Indeterminacy: Rimbaud to Cage, 1981, 2d edit., 1999, The Dance of the Intellect: Studies in the Poetry of the Pound Tradition, 1985, 2d edit., 1996, The Futurist Moment: Avant-Garde, Avant-Guerre and the Language of Rupture, 1986, Poetic License: Essays in Modern and Postmodern Lyric, 1990, Radical Artifice: Writing Poetry in the Age of Media, 1991, Wittgenstein's Ladder: Poetic Language and the Strangeness of the Ordinary, 1996, Frank O'Hara, 2d edit., 1998, Poetry On and Off the Page: Essays for Emergent Occasions, 1998, Twenty-first Century Modernism, 2001; editor: Postmodern Genres, 1990; co-editor: John Cage: Composed in America, 1994; contbg. editor: Columbia Literary History of the U.S., 1987; contbr. preface to Contemporary Poets, 1980, A John Cage Reader, 1983. Guggenheim fellow, 1981-82, NEA fellow, 1985; Phi Beta Kappa scholar, 1994-95. Fellow Am. Acad. Arts and Scis.; mem. MLA (exec. coun. 1977-81, Am. lit. sect. 1993—), Comparative Lit. Assn. (pres. 1993-94, mem. adv. bd. Libr. of Am.), Lit. Studies Acad. Home: 1467 Amalfi Dr Pacific Palisades CA 90272-2752 Office: Stanford U Dept English Stanford CA 94305 E-mail: mperloff@earthlink.net.

PERLOFF, ROBERT, psychologist, educator; b. Phila., Feb. 3, 1921; s. Myer and Elizabeth (Sherman) P.; m. Evelyn Potechin, Sept. 22, 1946; children: Richard Mark, Linda Sue, Judith Kay. AB, Temple U., 1949; MA, Ohio State U., 1949, PhD, 1951; DSc (hon.), Oreg. Grad. Sch. Profl. Psychology, 1984; DLitt (hon.), Calif. Sch. Profl. Psychology, 1985. Diplomate Am. Bd. Profl. Psychology. Instr. edn. Antioch Coll., 1950-51; with pers. rsch. br. Dept. Army, 1951-55, chief statis. rsch. and cons. unit., 1953-55; dir. R & D Sci. Rsch. Assos., Inc., Chgo., 1955-59; vis. lectr. Chgo. Tchrs. Coll., 1955-56; mem. faculty Purdue U., 1959-69, prof. psychology, 1964-69; field assessment officer univ. Peace Corps Chile III project, 1962; Disting. Svc. prof. bus. adminstrn. and psychology U. Pitts. Joseph M. Katz Grad. Sch. Bus., 1969-90, Disting. Svc. prof. emeritus, 1991—; dir. rsch. programs U. Pitts. Grad. Sch. Bus., 1969-77; dir. Consumer Panel, 1980-83. Bd. dirs. Book Ctr.; cons. in field, 1959—; adv. com. assessment exptl. manpower R & D labs. Nat. Acad. Scis., 1972-74; mem. rsch. rev. com. NIMH, 1976-80, Stress and Families rsch. project, 1976-79; mem. adv. bd. Cornell Inst. for Rsch. on Children, 2002—. Contbr. articles to profl. jours.; editor Indsl. Psychologist, 1963-65, Evaluator Intervention: Pros and Cons; book rev. editor Personnel Psychology, 1952-55; co-editor: Values, Ethics and Standards Sourcebook, 1979, Improving Evaluations; bd. cons. editors Jour. Applied Psychology; bd. advs. Archives History Am. Psychology, Psychol. Svc. Pitts., Recorded Psychol. Jours.; guest editor Am. Psychologist, 1972, Edn. and Urban Soc., 1977, Profl. Psychology, 1977; adv. editor Contemporary Psychology, 1994—. Bd. dirs., v.p. Sr. Citizens Svc. Corp., Calif. Sch. Profl. Psychology; bd. dirs. Greater Pitts. chpt. ACLU, sec., 1997-98; chmn. nat. adv. com. Inst. Govt. and Pub. Affairs, U. Ill., 1986-89, sec. nat. adv. com., 1997—. Decorated Bronze Star; named in his honor, Robert Perloff Grad. Rsch. Assistantship in Inst. Govt. and Pub. Affairs, U. Ill., 1990, in his honor, Robert Perloff Career Achievement award, Knowledge Utilization Soc., 1991; recipient Legacy award, Greater Pitts. Psychol. Assn., 2001, Hist. Preservation award, City of Pitts., 2002. Fellow: APA (mem.-at-large exec. com. divsn. consumer psychology 1964—67, coun. reps. 1965—68, pres. divsn. 1967—68, chmn. sci. affairs com., divsn. consumer psychology 1968—69, edn. and tng. bd. 1969—72, mem.-at-large exec. com. divsn. consumer psychology 1970—71, coun. reps. 1972—74, dir. 1974—82, chmn. fin. com., treas. 1975—84, chmn. investment com. 1977—82, pres. 1985, adv. bd., bd. sci. affairs 1994—96, task force intelligence and Intelligence Tests, author column Std. Deviations in jour., pres. address selected as one of 50 over 50 yrs.), AAAS, Ea. Psychol. Assn. (dir. 1977—80, pres. 1980—81); mem.: Coun. of Sci. Soc. (found. alumnus, pres. 1998—), Knowledge Utilization Soc. (pres. 1993—95), Soc. Psychologists in Mgmt. (pres. 1993—94, Disting. Contbn. to Psychology Mgmt. award 1989), Am. Evaluation Assn. (pres. 1977—78), Am. Psychol. Found. (v.p. 1988—89, pres. 1990—92, trustee 1995—98, Lifetime Achievement in Psychology Gold Medal award 2000), Assn. for Consumer Rsch. (chmn. 1970—71), Pa. Psychol. Assn. (Disting. Svc. award 1985), Internat. Assn. Applied Psychology, Am. Psychol. Soc., Phi Beta Kappa, Psi Chi, Beta Gamma Sigma, Sigma Xi (pres. U. Pitts. chpt. 1989—91). Home: 815 Saint James St Pittsburgh PA 15232-2112 E-mail: rperloff@katz.pitt.edu. *Experiment. Innovate responsibly. Take risks judiciously. Do not shrink from new ventures for fear of failure. No one is immune from adversity. The hallmark of a successful achieving person is his or her ability to snap back after misfortune, and to benefit from and not be immobilized by failure.*

PERLONGO, BOB, writer; b. Chgo., Dec. 24, 1933; s. Dominic Perlongo and Caroline Hoffman; m. Carol Pearson, May 23, 1968 (div. Apr. 28, 1980); 1 child Ingrid. BS in Journalism, U. Ill., 1955; MA in English Lit., NYU, 1960. Assoc. editor Metronome, N.Y.C., 1967—68; instr. U. Iowa, Ames, 1967—68; staff editor N.Y. Times Almanac, N.Y.C., 1969—72; publs. editor Chgo. State U., 1975—79; exec. editor TriQuarterly Northwestern U., Evanston, 1981—97; freelance writer, editor, 1997—. Editor: The Everyday Almanac, 2 edits., 1979, ; compiler: Early American Advertising, 1985; author: All Hours of the Night, 1998. With U.S. Army, 1956—58. Democrat. Avocations: photography, sculpture, music. Home and Office: 820 Reba Pl Evanston IL 60202-2691 Fax: 847-475-6645 . E-mail: xyzzo@aol.com.

PERLONGO, DANIEL JAMES, composer, educator; b. Gaastra, Mich., Sept. 23, 1942; s. James and Camille (Fittante) P. Mus.B. in Composition, U. Mich., 1964, Mus.M., 1966; Corso di Perfezionamento, Accademia di S. Cecilia, Rome, 1968. Assoc. prof. music Indiana (Pa.) U., 1968—. Composer (for orch.) Myriad, 1968, Ephemeron, 1972, Concertino, 1980, Lake Breezes, 1990, Concerto for Piano and Orchestra, 1992, Shortcut from Bratislava for Piano and Orch., 1994, Sunburst for Clarinet and Orch., 1995, Two Movements, 1996, Millennium Overture, 2000, Symphony No. 1, Millennium Voyage, 2001, (chamber orch.) Variations 1973, Voyage, 1975, Ariadne's Thread for string orchestra, 2002, (chamber music) Improvision for Four, 1965, Improvisation 2, 1966, Eufonia, poetica e sonora, 1966, (string trio) Intervals, 1967, (ensemble pieces) Movement for 8 Players, 1967, Semblance for string quartet, 1969-70, String Quartet II, 1983, (percussion quartet) For Bichi, 1968, Movement in Brass, 1969, (various works) Process 7, 5, 3 for 6 in 12, for flute, oboe, clarinet, 3 percussions, 1969, Tre Tempi for flute, oboe, clarinet, violin, cello, 1971, Fragments for flute and cello, 1972, Structure, Semblance and Tune for tuba and percussion, 1973, (wind ensemble) Changes, 1970, (violin) Violin Solo, 1971, (double bass) Episodes, 1966, (for oboe, clarinet and bassoon) Ricercar, 1976, (solo piano) Piano Sonata, 1965, Suite for Piano, 1988, Serenade, 1977, First Set, 1990, (saxophone quartet) Aureole, 1978, (brass quintet) Summer Music, 1979, (solo bass clarinet) Soliloquy, 1980, (soprano voice and piano) Six Songs, 1980, (solo organ) Tapestry, 1981, (winds, percussion and piano) Montalvo Overture, 1984, (piano and woodwind quintet) A Day At Xochimilco, 1987, (trombone and organ) Novella, 1988, (mezzo soprano, violin, clarinet and piano) By Verse Distills, 1989, (wind ensemble) Preludes and Variations, 1991, (horn and harp) Arcadian Suite, 1993, (cello and piano) Poppies with Butterflies, 1997, (woodwind quintet) Groznjan Souvenir, 1998, (violin, cello, piano) Breezes at Yellow Creek, 1999, Aubade, Morning Songs, for wind trio and string trio, 2002, Sunday Afternoon at the Ghost Ranch for Violin, Trumpet and Alto Sax, 2002. Fulbright fellow Italy, 1966; Italian Govt. grantee, 1967; recipient Joseph Bearns prize Columbia U., 1966; Rome prize, 1971, 72; award Nat. Inst. Arts and Letters, 1975, Internat. Double Reed Soc. prize, 1979, New Music for Young Ensembles prize, 1979, Nebr. Sinfonia prize, 1981; Nat. Endowment Arts grantee, 1981, 95; Guggenheim fellow, 1982. Office: Indiana U of Pa 101 Cogswell Hall Music Dept Indiana PA 15705-0001

PERLOV, DADIE, management consultant, consultant; b. N.Y.C., June 8, 1929; d. Aaron and Anna (Leight) Heitman; m. Norman B. Perlov, May 29, 1950; children— Nancy Perlov Rosenbach, Jane, Amy Perlov Schenkein BA, NYU, 1950; postgrad., Adelphi U., 1963, Vanderbilt U., 1973. Cert. assn. exec., N.Y. Exec. dir. ops. Open City, N.Y.C., 1962-64; field svcs. dir. Nat. Coun. Jewish Women, 1968-74; exec. dir. N.Y. Libr. Assn., 1974-81, Nat. Coun. Jewish Women, N.Y.C., 1981-90; founder, prin. Consensus Mgmt. Group, N.Y.C. and Washington, 1989—. Cons. HEW 1975-76; pres.-elect Internat. Coun. Libr. Assn. Execs., 1979-80; exec. mem. Conf. of Pres., 1981-90; strategic planner, lectr., merger facilitator; mgmt. cons. ABA, Am. Bankers Assn., ALA, Nat. Assn. Home Builders, Am. Coll. Healthcare Execs., Nat. Assn. Ind. Insurers, and more than 500 other maj. trade and profl. assns. Co-author: The Ultimate Association Diet: How to Stay Fit and Trim in the 21st Century; author monthly column Dear Dodie for Assoc. Trends; contbr. articles to profl. jours. Dem. committeewoman, 1966; mem. N.Y. Zool. Soc., 1959—, adv. bd. Nat. Inst. Against Prejudice and Violence, 1985-89, profl. adv. com. for Hornstein program in Jewish communal svc. Brandeis U., 1986-90; bd. visitors Pratt Inst., Bklyn., 1980-84; bd. dirs. Pres. Coun. on Handicapped, 1981—; facilitator Nursing Summit, 1994. Recipient Recognition award N.Y. Libr. Assn., 1978, BUDDY award NOW Legal Def. and Edn. Found., 1989, cert. N.Y. State Legislature, 1978; named N.Y. State Exec. of Yr., 1980, One of Am.'s 100 Most Important Women, Ladies' Home Jour., 1988. Fellow Am. Soc. Assn. Execs. (cert. 1978, evaluator 1980-91, bd. dirs. 1987-90, bd. found. 1990-92, Excellence award 1983); mem. LWV (chpt. pres. 1960-62), N.Y. Soc. Assn. Execs, (pres. 1985, Outstanding Assn. Exec. 1989, Outstanding Svc. award 1991), Global Perspectives in Edn. (bd. dirs.), Nat. Orgn. Continuing Edn. (coun.), Audubon Soc., N.Y. Citizens Coun. on Librs. (bd. dirs. 1981-84), Am. Arbitration Assn. (mem. panel). Avocations: writing, mycology, history, music, art. Fax: 212-874-8068. E-mail: dadie@virtualcmg.com.

PERLSTEIN, ABRAHAM PHILLIP, psychiatrist, educator; b. N.Y.C., Apr. 15, 1926; s. Benjamin William and Pauline (Gittler) P.; m. Shirley Anne Rubenstein, July 10, 1949; children: Judith Paula, Susan Carol, Bernard William. BS, U. Oreg., 1949; MD, NYU, 1953. Diplomate Am. Bd. Psychiatry and Neurology with added qualifications in Geriat. Psychiatry. Cons. alcoholism dir. SUNY, Bklyn., 1958—, clin. asst. prof. psychiatry, 1957—; med. dir. Peninsula Counseling Ctr., Woodmere, N.Y., 1973-78, psychiat. cons. geriatrics, 1978-90; pvt. practice Elmont, 1957-90; assoc. psychiat. dir. Frankling Gen. Hosp., Valley Stream, 1980-82; clin. asst. prof. psychiatry Oregon Health Scis. U., Portland, 1997—. Attending psychiatrist Kings County Hosp. Ctr., Bklyn., 1957-90, SUNY, U. Hosp. Bklyn., 1963-90, Franklin Gen. Hosp., Valley Stream, 1969-90; adj. clin. asst. prof. psychiatry Cornell U. Med. Coll., N.Y.C., 1978-90; assoc. attending psychiatrist North Shore U. Hosp., Manhasset, N.Y., 1978-90; clin. asst. prof. psychiatry Oreg. Health Scis. U., Portland, 1997—. Sgt. U.S. Army, 1944-46. Fellow Am. Psychiat. Assn. (life). Avocations: music, art, literature, sports. Office: Columbia River Mental Health Svcs PO Box 1337 Vancouver WA 98666-1337 Fax: 360-993-3176.

PERLSTEIN, WILLIAM JAMES, lawyer; b. N.Y.C., Feb. 7, 1950; s. Justin Sol and Jane (Goldberg) P.; m. Teresa Catherine Lotito, Dec. 20, 1970; children: David, Jonathan. Student, London Sch. Econs., 1969-70; BA summa cum laude, Union Coll., 1971; JD, Yale U., 1974. Bar: Conn. 1974, D.C. 1976, U.S. Dist. Ct. D.C. 1977, U.S. Ct. Appeals (D.C. cir.) 1978, U.S. Supreme Ct. 1993, N.Y. 2000. Law clk. to judge Marvin Frankel U.S. Dist. Ct., N.Y.C., 1974-75; assoc. Wilmer, Cutler & Pickering, Washington, 1975-82, ptnr., 1982—, mem. mgmt. com., 1995—, chmn., 1998—. Mng. editor Yale Law Jour., 1973-74; contbg. author The Workout Game, 1987. Dir. Neighborhood Legal Svcs. program. Mem.: Am. Bar Found., Am. Coll. Bankruptcy (gen. counsel), Am. Law Inst., Am. Bankruptcy Inst. (chmn. legis. com. 1986—89, bd. dirs. 1989—93, 1997—), ABA (bus. bankruptcy com 1983—, v.chmn. executory contracts subcom. of bus. bankruptcy com. 1988—90, bankruptcy cts. subcom. 1990—97, chmn. legislation subcom. 1997—), Phi Beta Kappa. Jewish. E-mail: wperlstein@wilmer.com.

PERMAN, CARRIE LEE, artist, educator; b. Cin., Oct. 28, 1959; d. Daniel Theodore and Ann Weller Owczarczak; m. Ralph Eugene Perman Jr., July 2, 1982; children: Stephen, Christina. AA, Daytona Beach C.C., 1996; BA, Stetson U., 1998. Gen. technician art dept. Stetson U., DeLand, Fla., 1996-98; arts and crafts instr. African Am. Mus. Arts, 1998—. Art camp instr. DeLand Mus. Art, 1997, 98, Harris House, New Smyrna Beach, Fla., 1999; art tchr. Discovery Days Acad., Edgewater, Fla., 1999; graphic designer Gary's Quality Signs, Holly Hill, Fla., 1999—; cert. framer, framing assoc. Michael's Arts & Crafts, Daytona Beach, 2000, frame dept. mgr., 2000—. Exhibited shows at Harris House of the Atlantic Ctr. for the Arts, New Smyrna Beach, Fla., 1998, 2001, Stetson U./Duncan Gallery Art, DeLand, Fla., 1999, Palms Gallery, Daytona Beach, Fla., 1999, Ormond Meml. Mus. and Garden, Ormond Beach, Fla., 1999, Art League of Daytona Beach, 2000, others. Mem. Art League Daytona Beach. Avocation: collecting religious objects. Home: 1224 Deneece Ter Holly Hill FL 32117 E-mail: clop@worldnet.att.net.

PERMAN, JAY ALLAN, pediatrician, educator; b. Chgo., Aug. 14, 1946; s. Ma and Rose (Fishbein) P.; m. Andrea Merle Mittelman, Aug. 31, 1969; children: Corey, Marissa, Chad, Saranne. BA, Northwestern U., 1968, MD, 1972. Resident Northwestern U., Children's Meml. Hosp., Chgo., 1972-75; asst. prof. pediatrics U. Calif., San Francisco, 1977-82, assoc. prof., 1982-84; dir. pediatric gastroenterology and nutrition Johns Hopkins U., Balt., 1984-96, assoc. prof. pediatrics, 1984-92, prof., 1992-96; pres. Johns Hopkins Pediatrics at Home, Balt., 1992-96; Jessie Ball du Pont prof., chmn. dept. pediatrics Med. Coll. Va./Va. Commonwealth U., Richmond, 1996-99; prof., chmn. dept. pediatrics, chief of pediatrics med. sys. U. Md. Sch. Medicine, Balt., 1999—. Contbr. articles to profl. jours. and chpts. to books. Trustee Har Sinai Congregation, Balt., 1987-90. Grantee NIH, numerous pvt. founds. and industry. Mem. N.Am. Soc. for Pediatric Gastroenterology and Nutrition (pres. 1988-90). Avocations: walking, singing. Office: U Md Med Ctr 22 S Greene St # N5e14 Baltimore MD 21201-1544 E-mail: jperman@pedrumaryland.edu.

PERMUT, STEPHEN ROBERT, physician, lawyer; b. Olympia, Wash., Sept. 24, 1945; s. Max L. and Ruth E. (Epstein) P.; m. Marylene Quiambao, Apr. 20, 1974; children: Laura Q., Irene Q. AB, U. Pa., 1967; MD, Temple U., 1972; JD, Widener U., 1985. Bar: Pa. 1985. Program dir. St. Francis Hosp., Wilmington, Del., 1976-85; med. dir. Blue Cross and Blue Shield of Del., 1985-90; special counsel Saul, Ewing, Remick & Saul, Phila., 1990-93; v.p. med. affairs St. Francis Hosp., Wilmington, 1993-96; prof., chmn. dept. family and cmty. medicine Temple U., Phila., 1994—, asst. dean academic affiliations, 1999—. Pres. Children's Bur. Del., Wilmington, 1986-89. Fellow ACP, Am. Acad. Family Physicians, Am. Coll. Legal Medicine, Coll. Physicians Phila.; mem. ABA, AMA (coun. legislation 1999—, vice chmn. task force on E&M Coding 1999—), Pa. Bar Assn., New Castle County Med. Soc. (bd. trustees 1979—), Med. Soc. Del. (bd. trustees 1979—, v.p. 1990-91, pres.-elect 1991-92, Disting. Svc. award 1987, Pres.'s award 1989). Home: 32 Beethoven Dr Wilmington DE 19807-1923 Office: 3400 N Broad St Philadelphia PA 19140-5104

PERNA, MICHAEL LEWIS, language educator; b. Hampton, Va., Oct. 3, 1941; s. Michael Archangel and Rita M. (Kocher) Perna. AB, Wash. Coll., Chestertown, Md., 1963; MA, Duke U., PhD, 1977. Spanish tchr. St. Mary's County Schs., Chaptico, Md., 1964—68; instr. Spanish U. N.C., Chapel Hill, 1968—70, Duke U., Durham, 1970—73; acting asst. prof. U. Va., Charlottesville, 1973—76; Spanish tchr. The Tandem Sch., 1977—78; asst. prof. Spanish U. Maine, Orono, 1978; assoc. prof. Romance langs. Hunter Coll., N.Y.C., 1979—. Editor, contbr.: Twentieth-Century Spanish Poets, 1991; contbr.: Dictionary of Literary Themes and Motifs, 1988. Mem., activist Harlem Peacemakers, N.Y.C., 1986—96; chair South Africa com. Ch. of Heavenly Rest, 1987—92; mem., activist Episcopal Peace Fellowship, Chgo., 1981—. Recipient Summer Rsch. Stipend, U. Va., 1976; scholar, Md. State Senate, 1959—63. Mem.: Am. Assn. Tchrs. Spanish and Portuguese, Northeast Modern Lang. Assn. (exec. dir. 1988—90). Episcopalian. Avocations: camping, music, sailing. Home: 1601 Third Ave New York NY 10128 Office: Hunter Coll Dept Romance Langs 695 Park Ave New York NY 10021 Office Fax: 212-772-5093. Business E-Mail: mperna@hunter.cuny.edu.

PERNASETTI, FLAVIA MERCER, molecular biologist; b. Sao Paulo, Dec. 13, 1964; d. Paulo Edison Coimbra Pernasetti and Maria Helena Paes de Barros Mercer. PhD in Biochemistry, U. Liege, Belgium, 1996; MS in Biochemistry, U. Sao Paulo, 1991. Postdoctoral fellow U. Calif., San Diego, 1996—2001; rsch. scientist Targeted Molecules Corp., 2001—. Postdoctoral fellowship Am. Heart Assn., 1998-2000, Lalor Found., 2000. Mem.: Endocrine Soc., Am. Assn. Cancer Rsch. Office: Targeted Molecules Corp 6605 Nancy Ridge San Diego CA 92121

PERNG, JESSICA, interior designer; b. Taiwan, May 1969; d. John and Vicki Perng. BA, Calif. State U., Long Beach, 1994. Receptionist, sec. Yamaha, Cypress, Calif., 1990; interior design intern Green St. Interiors, Los Alamitos, 1993; accounts receivable rep., sec. Med. Office, Oxnard, 1993-95; accounts receivables rep. Apria Pharmacy Network, 1995-98; CAD designer Creative Design Cons., Inc., Costa Mesa, Calif., 1998—2000; project designer Facilities Resource Group, Irvine, 2000—01; CAD designer, drafter Hart Interior Design Ltd., Tempe, Ariz., 2001—. Mem. Am. Soc. Interior Design. Office: Alley CAD and Interior Design 3960 S Hollyhock Pl Chandler AZ 85248-4122

PERNICIARO, CHARLES VINCENT, dermatologist, educator, entrepreneur; b. New Orleans, June 15, 1957; s. Ernest Gabriel and Phereby Sheppard (Eagan) P.; children: Jamie Lynn, Kelly Gabrielle. BS, U. La., Lafayette, 1979; MD, La. State U., New Orleans, 1983. Diplomate Am. Bd. Dermatology, Am. Bd. Dermatology and Pathology. Staff physician Ochsner Clin. of Baton Rouge, La., 1987-90; sr. assoc. cons. and staff dermatologist Mayo Clinic, Jacksonville, Fla., 1990-93, cons., staff dermatologist and dermatopathologist, 1993-99; pvt. practice dermatology Brunswick, Ga., 1999—, Neptune Beach, Fla., 1999—. Pres., CEO Holiday Lighting Concepts, Inc., 1996-2000; lectr., presenter in field; adj. clin. assoc. prof. pathology U. Fla. Shands Jacksonville Med. Ctr., 1999-2001. Contbr. articles to profl. jours. Founder, bd. dirs. S.W. La. Skin Cancer Found., 1987. Recipient Resident-in-Tng. award So. Med. Assn., 1994, Outstanding Paper award Noah Worcester Dermatol. Soc., 1993, First Place Poster award 17th Internat. Colloquium Dermatopathology, 1996. Fellow: Am. Soc. Dermatopathology (chair membership com. 2000—01, bd. dirs. 2000—01), Am. Acad. Dermatology (com. on preventive dermatology 1988—90, task force on dermatologic oncology 1990—93, environ. coun. 1994—96, adv. coun. 1995—2001); mem.: So. Med. Assn. (vice chair sect. dermatology 1995—96, chair-elect 2001—02), Fla. Soc. Dermatology (bd. dirs. 1998—, chair membership com. 1999—2002, v.p. 2002—), Jacksonville Dermatology Soc. (sec.-treas. 1995, pres. 1996), Lions (charter, bd. dirs. Ponte Vedra Beach 1997—98). Avocations: tennis, computers. Home: 514 Midway St Neptune Beach FL 32266 Office: Brunswick Dermatology Clinic 3008 E Park Ave Brunswick GA 31520-4241

PERO, JANICE, molecular biologist; b. Lowell, Mass., June 11, 1943; d. Henry Leland and Helen Elizabeth P.; m. Richard Marc Losick, Aug. 8, 1970; children: Eric Pero Losick, Vicki Pero Losick. BA summa cum laude, Oberlin Coll., 1965; PhD, Harvard U., 1971. Asst. prof. Harvard U., Cambridge, Mass., 1975-78, assoc. prof., 1978-83; program dir. Biotechnia Internat., 1982-85, v.p. rsch. and devel., 1985-91, OmniGene, Inc., Cambridge, 1991-95; pres./CEO OmniGene Bioproducts, Inc., 1995—. Contbr. articles to profl. jours.; patentee in field. Mem. Phi Beta Kappa. Office: OnmiGene Bioproducts Inc 763D Concord Ave Cambridge MA 02138-1044 E-mail: jpero@omnigenebioproducts.com.

PEROTTI, ROSE NORMA, lawyer; b. St. Louis, Aug. 10, 1930; d. Joseph and Dorothy Mary (Roleski) Perotti. BA, Fontbonne Coll., St. Louis, 1952; JD, St. Louis U., 1957. Bar: Mo. 1958. Trademark atty. Sutherland, Polster & Taylor, St. Louis, 1958-63, Sutherland Law Office, 1964-70, Monsanto Co., St. Louis, 1971-85, sr. trademark atty., 1985-91, assoc. trademark counsel, 1991-94, trademark counsel, 1994-96, Polster, Lieder, Woodruff & Lucchesi, 1996—. Honored with dedication of faculty office in her honor, St. Louis U. Sch. Law, 1980. Mem. ABA, Mo. Bar, Bar Assn. Met. St. Louis, Am. Judicature Soc., Smithsonian Assocs., Friends St. Louis Art Mus., Mo. Bot. Garden. Office: Polster Lieder Woodruff & Lucchesi 763 S New Ballas Rd Ste 160 Saint Louis MO 63141-8750 E-mail: rperotti@patpro.com.

PEROTTO, GREGORY TODD, public relations professional; b. Pitts., July 13, 1974; s. Richard Daniel and Linda Lou Perotto. BA in Bus. Adminstrn. and Mktg., U. Puget Sound, 1996. Advt. intern Esco Corp., Portland, Oreg.,

1992-95, Ad Mark Svcs., Seattle, 1995; mktg. coord. Simon Mktg., Oak Brook Terrace, Ill., Seattle, summer 1995; corp. comms. mgr. Esco Corp., Portland, 1996-99; tactical marketing coordinator ESCO Corporation, 1999; e-commerce marketing manager ESCO Steel Distrubtion, 2000; sr. account exec. KVO Pub. Rels./Fleishman-Hillard, 2000. Mem. Internat. Assn. Bus. Communicators, Pub. Rels. Soc. Am., Puget Sound Mktg. Assn. (dir. publicity), Portland Advt. Fedn., Phi Kappa Phi. Democrat. Lutheran. Avocations: scuba diving, traveling, hiking, biking. Office: KVO Pub Rels 200 SW Market St Ste 1400 Portland OR 97201 E-mail: greg_perotto@kvo.com., gtperotto@excite.com.

PERPER, MICHAEL JOSEPH, federal agency administrator; b. Washington, Mar. 5, 1941; s. Harold Perper; 2 children. BBA in Acctg. and Fin., George Washington U., 1962, M in Hospital Svcs. Adminstrn., 2000; JD, Washington Coll. Law, 1966; MBA, Am. U., Washington, 1969; M in Resource Mgmt. and Internat. Rels., Indsl. Coll. Armed Forces, 1991. Lic. realtor, Md., Va. Sr. tax. atty. IRS, Washington, 1967—81; exec. asst. to U/sec. DOE, 1982—87, dir. internat. affairs, 1991-95; dir. Internat. Programs Emergency Ops., 1987-89; cons. on homeland security and transp. security issues Contingency Mgmt. Svcs., 1987—; prof. Indsl. Coll. Armed Forces, Nat. War Coll., 1989-91; capt. USCG, N.Y., 1995-96. Bd. dirs. Nat. Children's Hosp., Washington, Econ. & Trade Devel. Com. Contbr. articles to profl. jours. Active Landlord Tenant Commn., 1989, orgns. for disabled vets.; fundraiser Am. Cancer, 1995-. Mem. DAV (cert. appreciation), VA (cert. appreciation), Heart, Lung and Diabetes Assn., Am. Legion, Nat. War Coll. Alumni Assn., Phi Alpha Delta. Avocations: collecting sports memorabilia, art, painting, golf, civic activities. Home: 9408 Wooden Bridge Rd Potomac MD 20854-2421 Office: DOE 1000 Independence Ave SW Washington DC 20585

PERRAUD, PAMELA BROOKS, human resources professional; m. Jean-Marc Francois Perraud; children: Marc Alexander, Andrea Elizabeth. BA, Conn. Coll., 1970; MA in Urban Studies, Occidental Coll., 1972; MA in Indsl. Rels., U. Minn., 1977. Cert. sr. profl. in human resources, compensation profl., benefits profl., relocation profl., global renumeration profl. Dir. personnel Mpls. Housing and ReDevel. Authority, Mpls., 1973-75; dir. adminstrn. United Svcs. Orgn., Paris, 1976-78; dir. office svcs. Pechiney Ughine Kuhlmann, Greenwich, Conn., 1979-80; lectr., trainer Monodnock Internat., London, 1981-85; personnel recruiter IBM Europe, Paris, 1989; prof. bus. Am. Bus. Sch., 1988-92; pres. Women's Inst. for Continuing Edn., 1992-93; human resource cons. N.Y.C., 1994-97; pres. Global Transitions, 1998—. Chair Women on the Move, Paris, 1990-93; v.p. Women's Inst. for Continuing Edn., Paris, 1988-92; Non-govtl. Orgn. rep. at UN for Fedn. Am. Women's Clubs Overseas, 1998—; bd. dirs. METRO Internat., Assn. Am. Residents Overseas. Co-author: Living in France, 1994. Co-founder Focus Info. and Referral, London, 1982, Women in Mgmt., Mpls., 1973; trustee Conn. Coll., New London, 1970-72. Fellow in Pub. Affairs, Coro Found., L.A., 1970. Mem. Friends of WICE, World at Work Assn., Soc. for Human Resources Mgmt., Soc. for Intercultural Edn., Tng. and Rsch., Mayflower Soc. of Minn. Avocations: tennis, skiing. E-mail: pperaud@aol.com.

PERRAULT, JACQUES, educator; b. Montreal, Quebec, Can., June 25, 1944; s. Jean-Paul and Irene (Girard) P.; m. Katherine Hampton Rhodes, May 4, 1996; 1 child, Juliette. BSc, McGill U., 1964; PhD, U. Calif., San Diego, 1972. Asst. prof. dept. microbiology and immunology Washington U. Sch. Medicine, St. Louis, 1977-84; assoc. prof. biology San Diego State U., 1984-87; prof. dept. of biology prof., 1987—. Contbr. articles to profl. jours. Recipient Research Career Devel. award, NIH, 1980-85; grantee, NIH, NSF, March of Dimes Defects Found., 1977—. Mem. AAAS, Am. Soc. Microbiology, Am. Soc. Virology, Gen. Soc. for Microbiology. Avocations: karate (Shotokan Japanese style). Office: San Diego State U Dept Biology San Diego CA 92182 E-mail: jperrault@sunstroke.sdsu.edu.

PERREAULT, WILLIAM DANIEL, JR. business administration educator; b. N.Y.C., Apr. 7, 1948; s. William Daniel Sr. and Barbara Louise (Peckham) P.; m. Pamela Pittard, May 27, 1972; children: Suzanne Elizabeth, William Daniel III. BS, U. N.C., 1970, PhD, 1973. Asst. prof. U. Ga., Athens, 1973-76, U. N.C., Chapel Hill, 1976-79, assoc. prof., 1979-81, prof., 1981-83, Hanes prof., 1983-88. Vis. prof. Stanford (Calif.) U., 1986-87, assoc. dean, 1988-92. Kenan prof., 1988—; vis. prof. Cambridge (Eng.) U., 1997. Co-author: Essentials Marketing, 2000, The Marketing Game, 2001, Basic Marketing, 2002; editor: Jour. Mktg. Rsch., 1982-85; contbr. articles to profl. jours. Chmn. adv. com. Bur. Census, Washington, 1982-86. Mem. Am. Mktg. Assn. (v.p. 1986, 95, bd. dirs. 1986-89, 94-95, Odell award 1985, Disting. Educator award 1997, Churchill award 1997), Acad. Mktg. Sci. (Outstanding Edn. award 1995), Decision Scis. Inst. (coun. 1977), Assn. Dir. Consumer Rsch. Conf. (chmn. 1976—), Mktg. Sci. Inst. (trustee 1989-94), Phi Beta Kappa. Republican. Presbyterian. Office: U NC CB 3490 Mccoll Bldg Chapel Hill NC 27599-3490

PERRECA, MICHAEL ANDREW, artistic director, freelance editor; b. Freeport, N.Y., Jan. 13, 1961; s. Fred and Rose (Murasso) P. BA magna cum laude, Seton Hall U., 1983. Asst. editor Nat. Jeweler/Gralla Publs., N.Y.C., 1983-84; assoc. editor Giftware Bus./Gralla Publs., 1984-85; sr. editor Food and Beverage Mktg., U.S. Bus. Press, 1985-87; journalist, 1987-90; mng. editor Network Computing/CMP Media, Manhasset, N.Y., 1990-97; theatrical dir., 1989-99; artistic dir. Bristol Valley Theatre, Naples, N.Y., 1999—. Public spkg. coach; guest spkr. in schs. Actor, Off Broadway Theaters. Adv. bd. TADA!, N.Y.C.; bd. dirs. Bristol Valley Theater. Mem. Actors Equity Assn., Soc. Stage Dirs. and Choreographers. Office: Bristol Valley Theatre PO Box 218 Naples NY 14512-0218 E-mail: mperreca@bvtnaples.org.

PERRELLA, ANTHONY JOSEPH, electronics engineer; b. Boulder, Colo., Sept. 16, 1942; s. Anthony Vincent and Mary Domenica (Forte) P.; m. Pamela Smith, July 19, 1980; 1 child, Kathleen. BS, U. Wyo., 1964, postgrad., 1965, U. Calif., San Diego, 1966-67, U. Calif., Irvine, 1968-70. Flight engr. US Naval Tng. Devices Ctr., San Diego, 1965-67; rsch. engr. Collins div. Rockwell Internat. (formerly Collins Radio Co.), Newport Beach, 1967-69, electromagnetic interference and TEMPEST group head, 1969-74, supr., 1974-75, mgr., 1975-77, mgr. sys. integration, 1977, mgr. space comm. sys., 1977-78; sr. mem. tech. staff ARGOSys. Inc., Sunnyvale, 1978-81, program mgr., 1978-81, dep. mgr. EW sys., 1980-83, divsn. EW staff engr., 1983-84, dept. mgr., 1984-87, Sun Microsys. Inc., Mountain View, 1987-89; prin. A.J. Perrella-Cons., Las Vegas, Nev., 1989—. V.p. rsch. and devel. Things Unlimited, Inc., Laramie, Wyo., 1965-72, pres., 1972-75; bd. dirs., v.p. Columbian Credit Union, 1994-97. Bd. dirs. Bay Area Found. Mentally Retarded Children, 1994-2002, treas., 1996-2002; bd. dirs. Columbian Retirement Home Inc., 1999—. Mem. IEEE, AAAS, Am. Mgmt. Assn., N.Y. Acad. Scis., Assn. Old Crows (treas. San Jose chpt. 1992-93, sec. 1993-94, v.p. 1994-95, pres. 1995-96, trustee 1996—, dep. dist. 22 1993-94, dist. 21 1994-97, Calif. youth dir. 1997-98, 2000-01, Calif. dist. sec. 1996-2000, Calif. dist. master 2000-02, Calif. ch. dir. 2001-02), KC, Tau Kappa Epsilon. Roman Catholic. Office: 2550 Garcia Ave Mountain View CA 94043-1109 Home: 22 Cascade Lake St Las Vegas NV 89148-2791

PERRELLA, JAMES ELBERT, former manufacturing company executive; b. Gloversville, N.Y., May 30, 1935; s. James E. and A. Irene (Ferguson) P.; m. Diane F. Campesi; 1 child, Joy. BSME, Purdue U., 1960, MSIM, 1961. Gen. mgr. Centac div. Ingersoll-Rand Co., Mayfield, Ky., 1972-75, gen. mgr. Air Compressor Group Woodcliff Lake, N.J., 1975-77, corp. v.p., pres. Air Compressor Group, 1977-82, exec. v.p., 1982-92, pres., 1992—, chmn., CEO, 1993-99, chmn., 1999-2000, also dir. Bd. dirs. Becton Dickinson and Co., Milacron Inc., ArvinMeritor Inc., Bombardier Inc. Named Disting. Alumnus Sch. Mech. Engring., Purdue U., 1982; named Disting. Alumnus Krannert Mgmt. Sch., Purdue U., 1982 Office: Ingersoll-Rand Co 200 Chestnut Ridge Rd Woodcliff Lake NJ 07677-7700

PERRENOD, DOUGLAS ARTHUR, astronautical engineer; b. Sept. 13, 1947; s. George Edward and Eunice Lillian (Cohn) P. Student, Fla. Inst. Tech., 1968-72; BA in Interdisciplinary Sci., U. South Fla., 1973; postgrad., Calif. State U., 1982—; grad. engr. mgmt. cert. program, Calif. Inst. Tech., 1987; bioenvironmental engr., USAF Sch. Aerospace Medicine, 1992. Cert. glider flight instr. FAA. Engr. trainee NASA Kennedy Space Ctr., Fla., 1969-73; quality control engr. Pelletech Corp., Fontana, Calif., 1976-77; electronics specialist Gen. Telephone Co., San Bernardino, 1977-79; aerospace and project engr. Rockwell Internat., Downey, 1979-85, Lockheed Corp., Ontario, 1986-87, Lockheed Engring. Mgmt. Svc. Co., 1987, Eagle Engring., 1988—, Eagle Tech. Svcs., 1989—. Aviation cons., owner-founder Flight Unltd., Long Beach, Calif.; mission pilot, project engr. Flight Level 500 High Altitude Soaring Project. Developed concept for and co-authored unprecedented Inter-agency agreement between USAF and NASA for exchange of advanced environmental technology, 1994; designer telescope mount for 1st astronomy obs. Fla. Inst. Tech., 1969. Vol. mem. Orange County Human Svcs. Agy., 1981-86; active Big Bros. of Am., 1978. Lt. col. USAFR, 1973—. Recipient Amelia Earhart award CAP, 1968, Manned Flight Awareness Apollo 11 medallion NASA, 1971, 1st Shuttle Flight award NASA, 1981, Aerospace Maintenance Officer of Yr. award USAFR, 1979; named to Engr. Honor Roll, Rockwell Internat., 1982, 83, 85. Mem. AIAA, Assn. Mil. Surgeons U.S., Res. Officers Assn., Officers Assn., Air Force Assn., Soc. Flight Test Engrs., Assoc. Glider Soc. of So. Calif., Long Beach Navy Aero. Club.

PERRET, GARY WILLIAM, priest, educator; b. Sioux City, Iowa, May 20, 1947; s. William Joseph and Geraldine Marie (Maurice) Perret. BA in Secondary Edn., U. Ariz., Tucson, 1970; ThM, St.Mary's U., San Antonio, Tex, 1991. Asst. pastor St, Albert the Great, Compton, Calif., 1976—77; asst. pastor St. Joseph, Granite City , Ill., 1977—78; dir. vocations Misssionaries of Holy Family, Overland, Mo., 1978—82; pastor St. Joseph, Granite City, 1982—86; dir. adult religious edn. Our Lady of Guadalupe, Seguin, Tex., 1986—92, St. Joseph Parish, Donna, 1993—96, Brownsville (Tex.) Diocese, 1993—96. Dir. R.C.I.A. Various Parishes, San Antonio, 1986—92; instr. sacred scriptures Parishes and Diocese , Tex. Valley, 1993—96. Mem.: KC. Home: 3601 E. Seneca Tucson AZ 85716

PERRET, GERARD ANTHONY, JR. orthodontist; b. New Orleans, Feb. 13, 1959; s. Gerard A. and Marie M. (Gamino) P.; m. Catherine J. McMahon, 1996; 1 child, Caroline Marie. BS in Chemistry, U. N.C., 1981; DDS, La. State U., 1986, cert. orthodontics, 1989. Clin. asst. prof. La. State U. Sch. Dentistry, New Orleans, 1986-87; pvt. practice dentistry Lakeside Dental Group, Metairie, 1986-87; pvt. practice orthodontics Jacksonville, Fla., 1989-91, Tampa, 1991—; founder, pres. Orthogap, Inc., 1993—2001, Rodent Realty, Inc., 2001—. Patentee in field. Active New Tampa Cmty. Coun. Mem. ADA, Am. Assn. Orthodontists, Fla. Assn. Orthodontists, Hillsborough County Dental Soc., Hillsborough County Dental Rsch. Clinic, So. Assn. Orthodontists, Rotary (pres. New Tampa chpt. 1997-98), Omicron Kappa Upsilon. Avocations: sailing, fishing, music, golf. Office: 15281 Amberly Dr Tampa FL 33647

PERRI, AUDREY ANN, lawyer; b. Oxnard, Calif., Feb. 2, 1936; d. Zafon A. and Francis M. (Sandblom) Hartman; m. Frank M. Perri, Aug. 10, 1958; children: Michael H., Michelle F. Conte. BA, U. Redlands, 1958; JD, U. La Verne, 1976. Bar: U.S. Dist. Ct. (ctrl. dist.) 1977, Calif., 1976. Tchr. Corona (Calif.) Unified Sch. Dist., 1958-60, Chaffey H.S. Dist., Upland, Atta Loma, Calif., 1960-64, 70-71, Claremont (Calif.) H.S. Dist., 1967-68, Oak Park (Ill.)-River Forrest H.S., 1971-72; dep. dist. atty. Dist. Atty.'s Office, San Bernardino, Calif., 1976-81, with career criminal prosecution unit, 1979-81; assoc. Civington & Crowe LLP, Ontario, Calif., 1981-85, ptnr., 1986—; dept. mgr. family law, 1995—. Tchr. ESL, Reykjavik, Iceland, 1961-62; judge pro tem, mediator San Bernardino County Superior Ct., 1983—, L.A. County Superior Ct. East Dist., 1983—; seminar panelist. Aricles editor Jour. Juvenile Law, 1977. Bd. dirs. Am. Field Svc., 1965-69, Nat. Conf. Christians and Jews, 1977-82; trustee U. LaVerne Law Sch. Found., 1990-95; mem. state ctrl. com. Dem. Party, 1981-82. Recipient Boss of Yr. award, Ontario-Inland Valley Legal Secs. Assn., 1989, Susan B. Anthony Women of Yr. award San Bernardino County Commn. Status of Women, 1992, Disting. Alumnus of Yr. award U. La Verne Law Sch., 1993. Mem. ABA, AAUW (past-pres. chpt., Disting. Cmty. Svc. award 1983), Calif. Bar Assn. (family law sect. 1977—, del. conf. dels. 1977-96, exec. com. conf. dels. 1985-88, commr. legal svc. fund 1993-95, commr. jud. nominees evaluation commn. 1995-98), San Bernardino County Bar Assn. (trustee 1981-83, 84-86, chair legis., resolution com. 1980-81, mem. bench, bar, media com. 1980-85, mem. jud. evaluation com. 1986-95), Western San Bernardino County Bar Assn. (bd. dirs. 1992-95), Assn. Cert. Family Law Specialists, Inland County Women at Law (founding pres. 1981-82), Calif. Women Lawyers (bd. dirs. 1980-81, 82-84, first v.p. 1983-84, bylaws com. 1980-81, jud. evaluation com. 1981-82, co-chair legis. com. 1982-83), East-West Family Coun. Home: 8373 Camino Sur Cuminosur Rancho Cucamonga CA 91730 Office: Covington & Crowe 1131 W 6th St Ontario CA 91762-1121

PERRI, DOROTHY GRIMMEL, healthcare educator; b. Balt., May 8, 1949; d. Charles Edwin Sr. and Dorothy Viola (Smith) Grimmel; m. Anthony Joseph Perri, May 31, 1975; children: Anthony J. III, Christopher M. BSN, Am. U., 1971; MS, Tex. Woman's U., 1989. Cert. sch. nurse, Tex. Staff nurse gen. surgery, ICU, recovery rm. Georgetown U. Hosp., Washington, 1971-75; utilization rev. coord. Hahnemann Hosp., Phila., 1975-77; office mgr., urological nurse Office of Anthony J. Perri, MD, 1979-82; vis. nurse Tex. Star Health Care/Vis. Nurses East Tex., Corsicana, 1984-86; sch. nurse Dallas Ind. Sch. Dist., 1989-90, Highland Park Ind. Sch. Dist., Dallas, 1990-99; nursing instr. Navarro Coll., Corsicana, 1999—. Mem.: ANA, Tex, C.C. Tchrs. Assn., Tex. Nurses Assn., Sigma Theta Tau. Roman Catholic. Avocations: gourmet cooking, gardening, reading. Home: PO Box 1697 3816 NW CR 0007 Corsicana TX 75151-1697

PERRICCI, JEFFREY MICHAEL, dentist; b. N.Y.C., Apr. 23, 1953; s. Joseph Anthony and Jeannette (Gordon) P. BS, Ramapo Coll., 1975, Rutgers U., 1987; DMD, U. Medicine & Dentistry N.J., Newark, 1991. Registered dentist, N.J. Pvt. practice, Kearny, N.J., 1991—, Newark, 1996—, Bayonne, N.J., 1997—. Contbr. articles to profl. jours.; inventor in field. Commr. Zoning Bd. of Adjustment, Kearny, 1993-96, Bd. of Health, Kearny, 1996. Recipient gold Foil award U. Medicine and Dentistry of N.J., 1988; Nat. Inst. Dental Rsch. Summer Rsch. fellow, 1989-90. Mem. ADA, N.J. Dental Assn., Essex County Dental Soc., Acad. Gen. Dentistry, Acad. History of Dentistry, Hispanic Dental Assn., Rutgers U. Alumni Assn., Rotary Internat. (v.p. 1994, sec. 1993-94), Sports Club Portuguese, Xi Psi Phi. Avocations: writing, geneology, travel, jogging. Home: 38 Feronia Way Rutherford NJ 07070-2008 Office: PO Box 523 Kearny NJ 07032-0523 E-mail: dentaworld@aol.com.

PERRICONE, CHARLES, former state legislator; b. Oct. 10, 1960; Student, Kalamazoo Coll., Western Mich. U.; DPS (hon.) , W. Mich. U. Rep. Mich. State Dist. 61, 1995—; spkr. of the house Lansing, 1999—2001; pres., CEO New Era Consulting. Vice chair tax policy com.; mem. corrections com., house oversight and ethics com., legis. coun.; asst. Rep. leader. Recipient Champion of Commerce, Mich. Chamber of Commerce, Guardian of Small Business, Nat. Fed. of Ind. Bus. Address: 1909 Nichols Rd Kalamazoo MI 49006*

PERRIER, BARBARA SUE, artist; b. Akron, Ohio, Oct. 7, 1937; d. Willis Austin and Mary Gladys (Campbell) Bibler; m. David John Perrier, July 14, 1956 (div. Nov. 1972); children: David John Jr., Kenneth James, Mark Richard. AA in Comml. Art, AA in Liberal Arts, Ventura Coll., 1991. Artist Anointed Brush Studio, Oxnard, Calif., 1987—. One-woman shows at Columbia Arts Ctr., Vancouver, Wash., 1988, Gallery Los Olivos, 1993; exhibited in group shows at Santa Paula Soc. of Arts 3d Annual Fall Show, 1992, Gloria Dei Art Show, Camarillo, Calif., 1991, 92, 13th Annual Nat. Bald Eagle Conf. Art Show, 1992, 53d Annual City of Santa Paula Art Show, 1989, 5th Annual Buenaventura Art Assn. Art Show, Ventura, 1988, Westlake Village 15th Annual Art Show, 1988, Oct. West Wildlife Art Show, Burbank, Calif., 1993, Decoy & Wildfowl Carvers Wildlife Art Show, 1994, Spectacular Monuments Art Show, 1994, Fallbrook Nature Conservancy Art Show, 1995, 96, October West Wildlife Art Show, 1995, numerous others; exhibited in corp. collections at Impact Ministries, Redmond, Wash., The Kid's Pl., Roseburg, Oreg., Trinity, Redding, Calif., Vista, Marina Del Rey, Calif., Century 21 Gold Coast, Port, Hueneme, Calif., Divine Love Internat. Ch., Nigeria, Africa, numerous others. Mem. Calif. Gold Coast Watercolor Soc. (charter, pres. 1992), So. Calif. Wildlife Artist Assn. (pres. 1995, 96), Ventura County Artist Guild. Baptist. Avocations: camping, travel, photography. Home and Office: Anointed Brush Studio 1451 Fathom Dr Oxnard CA 93035-2334

PERRIMAN, WENDY KAREN, poet, educator; b. Stamford, England, July 9, 1958; d. David Wathen Blower and Heather Boulton Unwin; m. Steven Ralph Perriman, Aug. 8, 1981; 1 child. BA, U. Lancaster, Eng., 1979; Postgrad. Cert. Edn., U. Bristol, Eng., 1980; MA, Drew U., 2000, MPhil, 2001. Probationary tchr. Eastbrook Comprehensive Sch., London, 1980-81; English and drama tchr. Cornwall Sch., Dortmund, West Germany, 1981-83, King's Sch., Gutersloh, West Germany, 1983-85; acting head English and drama Weston Park Girls' Sch., Southampton, England, 1989-92; head drama, asst. head English Bitterne Park Sch., 1992-94; freelance poet Madison, N.J., 1994—. Pub., editor Inka Publs., N.J., 1996—. Author: Collected Experience, 1996, Show and Tell, 1997, Free Fall, 1998. Mem. Poetry Soc. Am., Acad. Am. Poets, Modern Poetry Assn. Office: Inka Publs PO Box 53 Madison NJ 07940-0053

PERRIN, ARNOLD STRONG, writer, editor; b. Nov. 26, 1932; B in Edn., Plymouth State Coll., 1965; postgrad., Dartmouth Coll., 1966. Tchr. area h.s., Vt., 1966-71; freelance writer Maine, 1971—. Editor, pub. Wings Press Maine, 1976—; poetry editor New England Sampler, Maine, 1980-84. Home: PO Box 809 720 Barrett Hill Rd Union ME 04862 E-mail: asper@midcoast.com.

PERRIN, BARBARA NELL, editor; b. Bremerton, Wash., Mar. 3, 1952; d. Robert Henry Perrin and Lorna Marie Storgaard Perrin; children: Martin Henry. BA, Hunter Coll., New York, NY, 1973; MA, Goddard Coll., Plainfield, VT, 1983. Asst. Haddon Craftsmen, New York, NY, 1974—76; asst. mktg. dir. Dover Publications, 1976—80; mktg. dir. Human Sciences Press, 1980—88; mktg. coord. NY Acad. Sciences, 1988—96; editor rsch. alert EPM Comm., 1997—. D-Liberal. Elca. Home: 694 De Graw Street Brooklyn NY 11217 Office: EPM Communications 160 Mercer Street New York NY 10012 E-mail: bperrin@epm.com.

PERRIN, EDWARD BURTON, health services researcher, biostatistician, public health educator; b. Greensboro, Vt., Sept. 19, 1931; s. J. Newton and Dorothy E. (Willey) P.; m. Carol Anne Hendricks, Aug. 18, 1956; children: Jenifer, Scott. BA, Middlebury Coll., 1953; postgrad. (Fulbright scholar) in stats, Edinburgh (Scotland) U., 1953-54; MA in Math. Stats., Columbia U., 1956; PhD, Stanford U., 1960. Asst. prof. dept. biostats. U. Pitts., 1959-62; asst. prof. dept. preventive medicine U. Wash., Seattle, 1962-65, assoc. prof., 1965-69, prof., 1969-70, prof., chmn. dept. biostats., 1970-72, prof. dept. health svcs., adj. prof. dept. biostats., 1975-98, chmn. dept., 1983-94, prof. emeritus, 1999—; prof. (hon.) West China U. of Med. Scis., Szechwan, Peoples Republic of China, 1988-98; overseas fellow Churchill Coll., Cambridge U., 1991-92; sr. scientist Seattle Vets. Affairs Med. Ctr., 1994—2001. Clin. prof. dept. cmty. medicine and internat. health Sch. Medicine, Georgetown U., Washington, 1972—75; dep. dir. Nat. Ctr. for Health Stats., HEW, 1972—73, dir., 1973—75; rsch. scientist Health Care Study Ctr. Battelle Human Affairs Rsch. Ctr., Seattle, 1975—76, dir., 1976—78; dir. Health & Population Study Ctr. Battelle Human Affairs Rsch. Ctr., 1978—83; sr. cons. biostats. Wash./Alaska regional med. programs, 1967—72; biometrician VA Co-op Study on Treatment of Esopageal Varices, 1961—73; mem. epidemiology & diesease control study sect. NIH, 1969—73; chmn. health svcs. rsch. study sect. HEW, 1976—79; chmn. health svcs. R&D field program rev. panel VA, 1988—91; chmn. health svcs. info steering com. State of Wash., 1993—94; mem. nat. adv. coun. Agy for Health Care Policy & Rsch. Dept. Health & Human Svc. US Govt., 1994—97; mem. com. on nat. stats. NRC, 1994—2000, NAS, 1994—2000; chmn. scientific adv. com. Med. Outcomes Trust, 1994—99. Contbr. articles on biostats., health services and population studies to profl. publs.; mem. editorial bd.: Jour. Family Practice, 1978-90, Public Health Nursing, 1992-98. Mem. tech. bd. Milbank Meml. Fund, 1974-76, Health Svcs. and Outcomes Rsch. Methodology, 1999—. Recipient Outstanding Service citation HEW, 1975 Fellow AAAS, Am. Pub. Health Assn. (Spiegelman Health Stats. award 1970, program devel. bd. 1971, chmn. stats. sect. 1978-80, governing coun. 1983-85, stats. sect. recognition award 1989), Am. Statis. Assn. (mem. adv. com. to divsn. statis. policy 1975-77); mem. Assn. Health Svcs. Rsch. (pres. 1994-95, bd. dirs. 1991-2000), Inst. Medicine of Nat. Acad. Sci. (chmn. membership com. 1984-86, mem. bd. on health care svcs. 1987-96, forum health stats. 1994-95, chmn. com. on clin. evaluation 1990-93), Biometrics Soc. (pres. Western N.Am. Region 1971), n., Sigma Xi, Phi Beta Kappa. Home: 4900 NE 39th St Seattle WA 98105-5209 Office: U Wash Dept Health Svcs PO Box 358853 Seattle WA 98195-8853 E-mail: perrin@u.washington.edu.

PERRIN, EDWARD PATTERSON, retired lawyer; b. Spartanburg, S.C., Sept. 19, 1925; s. Lewis Wardlaw and Elizabeth (Patterson) Perrin; m. Anne Porcher Zeigler, Apr. 7, 1951; children: Anne Perrin Flynn, Sallie Perrin White, Edward Patterson Jr. BS, U. Va., 1948; JD, U. S.C., 1950. Ptnr. Perrin, Perrin, Mann & Patterson, Spartanburg; ret. Chmn. Spartanburg Bank and Trust Co., 1970—72, 1st State Savs. and Loan Assn., Spartanburg, 1980—86; bd. dirs. Carolina Cash Co., Spartanburg. Trustee Spartanburg County Found., 1982—88, chmn., 1987, trustee, 1992—; deacon 1st Presbyn. Ch., Spartanburg, 1954—65, elder, 1966—. Cpl. Air Corps U.S. Army, 1944—45. Mem.: S.C. Bar Found. (bd. dirs. 1986—91, pres. 1988—89), Country Club Spartanburg (bd. dirs. 1993—95, pres. 1993—94), Spartanburg Rotary Club (pres. 1972—73, cert. of Honor 1988—89). Avocations: tennis, travel, reading history. E-mail: patperrin@charter.net.

PERRIN, JAMES KIRK, lawyer; b. Saginaw, Mich., Feb. 10, 1940; s. Robert Wallace and Elizabeth (Kirk) P.; m. Harriet Halteman, June 12, 1962; children: Mark, Rob, Jane, Jim. BA, Ohio Wesleyan U., 1962; JD, U. Mich., 1965. Bar: Ill. 1965, U.S. Dist. Ct. (no. dist.) Ill. 1965, U.S. Ct. Appeals (7th cir.) 1976, U.S. Supreme Ct. 1977. Assoc. McKenna Storer Rowe White & Haskell, Chgo., 1965-70, ptnr., 1970-75; founding ptnr. Haskell & Perrin, 1975—, sr. ptnr., 1989—. Contbr. over 30 articles to profl. jours.; spkr. in field. Commr. Deerfield (Ill.) Plan Commn., 1970-72. Mem. ABA (trial techniques com., task force on delay in litigation), Internat. Assn. Def. Counsel, Am. Bd. Trial Advocates, Soc. Trial Lawyers, Ill. Assn. Def. Trial Counsel, Phi Beta Kappa. Office: Ste 2440 30 N LaSalle St Chicago IL 60602

PERRIN, LISA C. fiber artist; d. Henry Joseph and Ruth (Tabor) Clarke; 1 child: Gilbert. Student, R.I. Sch. Design, 1952-54; BA, Brown U., 1954. Fiber artist, New London, Conn. Tchr. Embroiderer's Guild of Am., 1972X; designer Cragg Mountain Collection, Granby, Conn., 1974-79 Work in permanent collection of White House (Collection of the Work of Am. Artisans), Washington, 1996, many pvt. collections. Pres. New London County Hist. Soc., 1984-94. Mem. Embroiderers Guild of Am. (founder Pequot Colony chpt. 1986, tchr. 1972X, Master Craftsman), Golden Isles Fiberarts Guild (vice chmn. 1996-98). Avocations: walking, reading.

PERRIN, MICHAEL WARREN, lawyer; b. Cameron, Tex., Nov. 10, 1946; s. Frank W. and Mary Ann (Green) P.; m. Melinda Elizabeth Hill, Aug. 9, 1969; children: Elizabeth, Carter, Hunter. BS, U. Tex., Austin, 1969, JD, 1971. Bar: Tex. 1972, U.S. Dist. Ct. (no., ea., we. and so. dists.) Tex., U.S. Ct. Appeals (5th and 11th cirs.), U.S. Supreme Ct. Assoc. Vinson & Elkins, Houston, 1972-73; assoc. Fisher, Roch & Gallagher, 1973-76; ptnr. Fisher, Gallagher, Perrin & Lewis, 1976-91; sole practice, 1991-96; ptnr. King & Spalding, 1996—. Fellow Am. Coll. Trial Lawyers, Internat. Acad. Trial Lawyers, Internat. Soc. Barristers; mem. Am. Bd. Trial Advocates, Am. Bar Found., Houston Young Lawyers Assn. (sec. 1974-75), Tex. Young Lawyers Assn. (dir. 1976-78, chmn. bd. 1978-79), Houston Trial Lawyers Assn. (pres. 1987-88), Tex. Trial Lawyers Assn. (pres. 1989-90), Tex. Bar Found. (Houston chpt.), U. Tex. Devel. bd. Methodist.

PERRIN, ROBERT, editorial consultant, writer; b. Ann Arbor, Mich., Aug. 21, 1925; m. Barbara J. Groom, June 25, 1949; children: Stephen, Jennifer Perrin Hummel. BS, U. Minn., 1945. Reporter United Press Assn., Detroit, 1948-49, Detroit Free Press, 1949-55; adminstrv. asst. U.S. Senate, Washington, 1955-66; asst. dir. U.S. Office Econ. Opportunity, 1966-68, dep. dir., 1968-70; v.p. Mich. State U., East Lansing, 1970-79; vice-chancellor SUNY System, Albany, 1979-85; exec. v.p. Tchrs. Ins. and Annuity Assn.-Coll. Retirement Equities Fund, N.Y.C., 1987-92; cons. Dept. State, 1993-94. Author: Piggy's Luck and More Tales of Evildoing, 1998, Keeping in Practice, 2001; contbr. articles to mags., newspapers. Mem. U.S.-Mex. Commn. on Border Devel., Washington, 1967-68. Lt. USNR, 1943-46, PTO. Fellow Reid Found., 1954; Pulitzer prize nominee Detroit Free Press, 1956. Home: 2435 Emerald Lake Dr East Lansing MI 48823-7256

PERRIN, RONALD FREDERIC, retired humanities educator; b. Montpelier, Vt. s. Rene George and Ella (Williamson) P.; m. Alexandrine Koutovsky, Sept. 17, 1960; 1 child, Sasha. BA, Northwestern U., 1965; MA, U. Calif. San

Diego, 1967, PhD, 1971. Prof. Philosophy U. Mont., Missoula, 1979-81, prof. Polit. Theory, 1981-97, prof. Philosophy emeritus, 1997—. Author: (book) Max Scheler's Concept of the Person, 1992. Chair Mont. Com. for the Humanities, 1984; mem. bd. dirs. Nat. Fedn. of State Humanities Couns., 1985-88. Hon. Woodrow Wilson fellow Woodrow Wilson Found., 1965; vis. fellow Va. Ctr. for Humanities & Pub. Policy, 1987. Mem. Phi Kappa Phi. Home: 302 Pattee Canyon Dr Missoula MT 59803-1625 Office: Philosophy Dept U Mont Missoula MT 59812-0001 E-mail: ronperrin@mtwi.net.

PERRINE, RICHARD LEROY, environmental engineering educator; b. Mountain View, Calif., May 15, 1924; s. George Alexander and Marie (Axelson) P.; m. Barbara Jean Gale, Apr. 12, 1945; children: Cynthia Gale, Jeffrey Richard. AB, San Jose State Coll., 1949; MS, Stanford U., 1950, PhD in Chemistry, 1953. Cert. environ. profl., 1987. Research chemist Calif. Research Corp., La Habra, 1953-59; assoc. prof. UCLA, 1959-63, prof. engring. and applied sci., 1963-92, prof. emeritus, 1992—, chmn. environ. sci. and engring., 1971-82; prin. Aspen Environ. Group, 1990-93. V.p. Sage Resources, 1988-91; cons. environ. sci. and engring., energy resources, flow in porous media; mem. Los Angeles County Energy Commn., 1973-81; mem. adv. council South Coast Air Quality Mgmt. Dist., 1977-82; mem. air conservation com. Los Angeles County Lung Assn., 1970-84; mem. adv. com. energy div. Oak Ridge Nat. Lab., 1987-90; mem. policy bd. Inst. Environ. and Natural Resource Rsch. and Policy U. Wyo., 1994—. Editor in chief The Environ. Profl., 1985-90. Served with AUS, 1943-46. Recipient Outstanding Engr. Merit award in environ. engring. Inst. Advancement Engring., 1975; ACT-SO award in field of chemistry West Coast region NAACP, 1984. Fellow AAAS; mem. Am. Chem. Soc., Soc. Petroleum Engrs., Am. Inst. Chem. Engrs., Can. Inst. Mining and Metallurgy, N.Am. Assn. Environ. Edn., Nat. Assn. Environ. Profls. (cert.), Air and Waste Mgmt. Assn., Assn. Environ. Engring. Profs., Sierra Club, Wilderness Soc., Audubon Soc., Sigma Xi, Tau Beta Pi, Phi Lambda Upsilon. Home: 22611 Kittridge St West Hills CA 91307-3609 Office: Univ Calif Engring Bldg I Rm 3066D Los Angeles CA 90095-0001 E-mail: rperrine@ucla.edu.

PERRING, CHRISTIAN DAVID, philosophy educator; b. London, Oct. 8, 1962; s. Wyndham Reginald Perring and Myriam Odile Whicheloe. BA, Oxford U.; MSc, King's Coll., London; PhD, Princeton U., 1996. Asst. prof. Dowling Coll., Oakdale, N.Y., 1998—. Editor Metapsychology Online Rev., 1997—. Office: Dowling Coll Dept Philosophy Idle Hour Blvd Oakdale NY 11769 E-mail: cperring@yahoo.com.

PERRIS, ANDREW ARTHUR, real estate company official; b. San Gabriel, Calif., June 28, 1968; s. Andres Flores and Lydia (Guajardo) P. Student, U. San Diego, 1986—; real estate lic., Anthony's Real estate Sch., L.A., 1987. Agt. Century 21 Advantage Real Estate, Alhambra, Calif., 1987—. Campaigner Citizens for Almquist for Congress, Alhambra, 1986, Calif. for Pete Wilson, San Diego, 1988. Mem. Calif. Assn. Realtors, Century 21 Real Estate Million Dollar Sales Club. Republican. Baptist. Avocations: skiing, racquetball, sailing. Home: 2035 Clover Dr Monterey Park CA 91755-6715 Office: Century 21 Advantage RE 115 S Garfield Ave Alhambra CA 91801-3832

PERRIZO, JAMES DAVID, art and sculpture educator, forestry pilot; b. L.A., Dec. 10, 1938; s. Francis John and Mary Ellen Perrizo; m. Helen Martin, Aug. 1, 1964; children: Teva Vaea, Rano Darian, Melia Tiare. AB, U. Calif., Berkeley, 1967, MA, 1969, MFA, 1974. Cert. airline transport pilot, DC-3, BH-47. Prof. art Calif. State U., Hayward, 1970—; forestry pilot Calif. Dept. Forestry, Sacramento, 1983-87; charter capt. Temsco Helicopters, Alaska, 1988-89, Horizon Helicopters, Calif., 1991; forestry pilot Reeder Flying Svc., Twin Falls, Idaho, 1995-96, Landells Aviation, Desert Hot Springs, Calif., 1997-98, Kachina Aviation, Va., Ariz., Md., Idaho, 1999—; news gatering helicopter capt. Helinet, Inc., Oakland and Hayward Airports, 1998—; line capt. Aris Helicopters Ltd., San Jose, Calif. Prin./capt. Air Charter West, Oakland, Calif., 1969—70; chair dept. art Calif. State U., Haward, 1987—91, 1996—97, adj. prof., 1970—98, emeritus, 1999—; pres. Z-Enterprises, Hayward, 1996—. Sculptor First and Last Men, 1974, Five Moon Prairie, 1982, Overhand, 1989, Paradise, 1997, Standing Site, 1999, Ship, 1999, Good Works, 2000, On the Horns of a Dilemma, 2002. Rep.-at-large Calif. Faculty Assn., Calif. State U., Hayward, 1995-97; treas. Sun Gallery, Hayward, 1995-96. Lt. comdr. USNR, 1957-70, naval aviator, 1960-70. Mem. Pacific Rim Sculptors Group, Aircraft Owners and Pilots Assn., Tailhook Assn., Nat. Broadcast Pilots Assn., Yakflight One Nonprofit Assn., Encinal Yacht Club, VFW (life), Silver Wings Fraternity (life), U. Calif. Berkeley Alumni Assn. (life). Democrat. Roman Catholic. Avocation: sailing. Home: 22797 Bayview Ave Hayward CA 94541-3307 E-mail: parizo@pacbell.net.

PERRONE, NICHOLAS, mechanical engineer, business executive; b. Apr. 30, 1930; B. Aero. Engring., Poly. Inst. Bklyn., 1951, MS, 1953, PhD, 1958. Research asst., then assoc. applied mechanics Bklyn. Poly. Inst., 1951-58; asst. prof., then assoc. prof. Pratt Inst., 1958-62; sr. scientist Structural Mechanics br. Office Naval Research, Washington, 1962-67, acting head dept., 1967-68, dir. program, 1968-69, 71-82; pres. CASA Gifts Inc., 1983-85; dep. to pres. Advanced Tech. and Research Inc., 1986-87; pres. Perrone Forensic Cons. Inc., 1987—. Lectr. civil engring. Cath U. Am., 1962-64, adj. prof., 1965-91; spl. research fellow NIH, Georgetown U., 1969-70; participant numerous workshops, confs., symposia; lectr. in field. Contbg. author: Biodynamics, 1980; editor or co-editor numerous monographs; editorial adv. bd.: Advances in Engring. Software, Computers and Structures, Engineering Fracture, Pressure Vessels and Piping; contbr. numerous articles to profl. jours. Fellow AAAS, ASME, Am. Acad. Mechanics; mem. ASCE, AIAA, N.Y. Acad. Sci., Am. Soc. Engring. Edn., Soc. Automotive Engrs., Soc. Mfg. Engrs. Address: 8 Cherry Ln Newtown Square PA 19073-3949 E-mail: NickPerrone@aol.com.

PERRONE, RUTH ELLYN, university administrator; b. Hearne, Tex., July 2, 1951; d. John Paul Perrone and Ellen Gayle (Sullivan) Perrone-Robertson. BS, Stephen F. Austin State U., 1973; MPA, Tex. A&M U., 1986. Social worker Tex. Dept. Pub. Welfare, Nacogdoches, Tex., 1974-76; licensing rep. Tex. Dept. Human Resources, Bryan, 1976-85; spl. asst. to vice chancellor for state affairs Tex. A&M Univ. System, Austin, 1987-90; asst. to pres. Tex. A&M U., College Station, 1990-92, dir. external rels., 1992-99, v.p. govt. affairs, 1999—. Advisor legis. study group Tex. A&M U., 1992—; bd. dirs. Scott & White Hosp. Health Plan, 1995-2000. Chair governing bd. John Ben Shepperd Pub. Leadership Found., Odessa, Tex., 1993-94; bd. dirs. Tex. Lyceum, Austin, 1992-97; assoc. mem. St. Joseph Hosp. Aux., Bryan, 1993—. Named Best of Show, Greater Omaha Am. Mktg. Assn., 2002. Mem.: Assn. Am. Univs., Council of Fed. Relations, Bryan/College Station C. of C. (coun. on govtl. affairs), Assn. Am. Univs. (coun. fed. rels. 2001—), Coun. ADvancement and Support Edn., Nat. Assn. State Univ. and Land Grant Coll. (exec. com. mem., coun. on govtl. affairs). Avocations: ballet, theatre, reading, dinner parties. Office: Texas A&M University 1246 TAMU 805 Rudder Tower College Station TX 77843-0001 E-mail: e-perrone@tamu.edu.

PERRONI, CAROL, artist, painter; b. Boston, July 28, 1952; d. Michael John and Mary Agnes (Collett) P.; m. John Richard Mugford, May 23, 1987; 1 child, Jonathan Perroni. Student, Boston Mus. Sch., 1970-71; BA in Art, Bennington Coll., 1976; student, Skowhegan Sch. Painting and Sculpture, 1978; MFA in Art, Hunter Coll., 1983. Studio asst. for artist Isaac Witkin, Bennington, Vt., 1973-74; libr. asst. Simmons Coll. Libr., Boston, 1977-78; studio asst. for artist Mel Bochner, N.Y.C., 1979; bookkeeper Internat. House, 1979-80; studio asst. for Lee Krasner, East Hampton, N.Y., 1980; rsch. asst. Art News Mag., N.Y.C., 1981; intern Greenespace Gallery, 1982-83; tech. asst. Avery Architectural and Fine Arts Libr. Columbia U., 1981-83; libr., rechr. Kennedy Galleries, Inc., 1984-86; program specialist, art tchr. Swinging Sixties Sr. Citizen Ctr., Bklyn., 1986-87; with Arts in Edn. Program, R.I., 1993-96. One-woman shows include Boston City Hall, 1978, Hunter Coll. Gallery, N.Y.C., 1983, Ten Worlds Gallery, N.Y.C., 1986, Gallery X, New Bedford, Mass., 1993-94, Hera Gallery, Wakefield, R.I., 1995, 98, AS220, Providence, R.I., 1996, C.C. of R.I., Lincoln, 1996, Boyden Libr., Foxboro, Mass., 1997; group shows include Salem State Coll., Mass., 1978, Fuller Mus. Art, Brockton, Mass., 1989-90, Danforth Mus. Art, Framingham, Mass., 1989, Attleboro Mus., Mass., 1989, Gallery One, Providence, 1992, Gallery X, New Bedford, Mass., 1992-98, Grove St. Gallery, Worcester, Mass., 1993, Bell St. Chapel, Providence, 1994-95, AS220, Providence, 1994, 98, Hera Gallery, Wakefield, R.I., 1993-99, 2000, 2001, St. Andrew's Sch., Barrington, R.I., 1994, McKillop Gallery, Salve Regina U., Newport, R.I., 1995, North River Arts Soc., Marshfield Hills Village, Mass., 1995, Providence Art Club, 1995, The Sarah Doyle Gallery, Brown U., Providence, 1995-96, R.I. Watercolor Soc. Slater Meml. Park, Pawtucket, 1995, Fed. Reserve Bank, Boston, 1996, Art Advisory/Boston, Quincy, Mass., 1996, Rotch-Jones-Duff Mus., New Bedford, Mass., 1997, Dryden Galleries, Providence, 1997, Renaissance Gallery, Fall River, Mass., 1997, 98, Island Arts Gallery, Newport, 1997, Harwood Art Ctr., Albuquerque, 1998, Branigan Cultural Ctr., Las Cruces, N.Mex., 1999, 2000, Atrium Gallery, Providence, R.I., 2000, New Haven Pub. Libr., New Haven, 2000, Angelo State U., San Angelo, Tex., 2000, Rockport (Tex.) Ctr. Arts, 2001, Lorain C.C., Elyria, Ohio, 2001, Hiestand Galleries, Miami U., Oxford, Ohio, 2001, South Broadway Cultural Ctr., Albuquerque, 2001, N.Mex. State U. Art Gallery, Las Cruces, 2001, Sedona (Ariz.) Arts Ctr., 2002, Cork Gallery, Avery Fisher Hall, Lincoln Ctr., N.Y., 2002; represented in permanent collection at R.I. Hosp. Art Collection and pvt. collections. Bd. dirs. Hera Ednl. Found., 1994—2001. Grantee Artists Space, 1986, Flintridge Found., 1993, fellow Vt. Studio Ctr., Johnson, 1990, Dorland Mountain Arts Colony, 1993. Mem.: SOHO 20 Gallery (nat. affiliate mem.), Am. Acad. Women Artists (assoc.). Home: 2089 Plaza Thomas Santa Fe NM 87505-5438 E-mail: carolpi56@msn.com.

PERROT, PAUL NORMAN, museum director; b. Paris, France, July 28, 1926; came to U.S., 1946, naturalized, 1954; s. Paul and K. Norman (Derr) P.; m. Joanne Stovall, Oct. 23, 1954; children— Paul Latham, Chantal Marie Claire, Jeannine, Robert. Student, Ecole du Louvre, 1945-46, N.Y. U. Inst. Fine Arts, 1946-52. Asst. The Cloisters, Met. Mus. Art, 1948-52; asst. to dir. Corning (N.Y.) Mus. Glass, 1952-54, asst. dir. mus., 1954-60, dir., 1960-72; editor Jour. Glass Studies, 1959-72; asst. sec. for mus. programs Smithsonian Instn., Washington, 1972-84; dir. Va. Mus. Fine Arts, 1984-91, Santa Barbara Mus. Art, 1991-94, mus. cons., 1995—. Lectr. glass history, aesthetics, museology; past v.p. Internat. Coun. Mus. Found.; past pres. N.E. Conf. Mus.; past pres. Internat. Centre for Study of Preservation and Restoration of Cultural Property, Rome, mem. coun., 1974-88. Author: Three Great Centuries of Venetian Glass, 1958, also numerous articles on various hist. and archael. subjects. Former trustee Winterthur Mus.; former trustee, treas. Mus. Computer Network; former mem. Internat. Cons. Com. for the Preservation of Moenjodaro; former chmn. adv. com. World Monuments Fund; former chmn. vis. com. Getty Conservation Inst. Mem. Am. Assn. Mus. (past v.p., coun. 1967-78), N.Y. State Assn. Mus. (past pres.), Internat. Assn. History Glass (past v.p.) Corning Friends of Library (past pres.), So. Tier Library System (past pres.).

PERRUCCI, ROBERT, sociologist, educator; b. N.Y.C., Nov. 11, 1931; s. Dominic and Inez (Mucci) P.; m. Carolyn Land Cummings, Aug. 4, 1965; children: Mark Robert, Celeste Ann, Christopher Robert, Alissa Cummings, Martin Cummings. BS, SUNY, Cortland, 1958; MS (Social Sci. Research Council fellow), Purdue U., Ph.D., 1962. Asst. prof. sociology Purdue U., West Lafayette, Ind., 1962-65, asso. prof., 1965-67, prof., 1967—, head dept., 1978-87. Vis. Simon prof. U. Manchester (Eng.), 1968-69; Bd. dirs. Ind. Center on Law and Poverty, 1973-76 Author: Sociology, 1983, Circle of Madness, 1974, Divided Loyalties, 1980, The Triple Revolution, 1971, Profession Without Community, 1968, The Engineers and the Social System, 1968, Mental Patients and Social Networks, 1982, Plant Closings: International Context and Local Consequences, 1988, Networks of Power, 1989, Japanese Auto Transplants in the Heartland: Corporatism and Community, 1994, The New Class Society, 1999, Science Under Siege?, 2000; editor: The American Sociologist, 1982—84, Social Problems, 1993-96, Contemporary Sociology, 2000-; contbr. articles to profl. jours. Served with USMC, 1951-53. Recipient grants, NSF, 1966—68, 1976—78, NIMH, 1969—72, Sloan Found., 2002—. Mem. Am. Sociol. Assn., Soc. Study Social Problems (dir. 1980-83, v.p. 1996-97, pres. 1999—), N. Central Sociol. Assn. (pres. 1973-74) Home: 305 Leslie Ave West Lafayette IN 47906-2411 Office: Dept Sociology Purdue U West Lafayette IN 47907

PERRY, ANTHONY FRANK, entertainment company executive, printing company executive, graphic designer; b. L.A., Oct. 23, 1965; s. Frank Guy and Verna Dean Perry. Artist Thunderbird Printing Co., Inc., Reno, 1983-87; pres., chief exec. officer T-Bird Entertainment, Inc., 1987-91; mktg. dir. Thunderbird Printing and Screening Inc., 1991-92; pres., CEO Perri Entertainment Svcs., Inc., 1992—; pres. Internat. Touring Pers. Assn., 2001—. Tour pass security designer Rolling Stones World Tour, 1989-90, Billy Joel Storm Front Tour, 1990, New Kids on the Block, 1990-91, Jimmy Buffett Chameleon Caravan, 1994, Billy Joel River of Dreams, 1994, ZZ Top Antenna World Tour, 1994; designer credentials for San Francisco 49ers, 1995-2000; founder Knotty Baker Pretzel Co.; promoter Big Bang New Years Party, 1987-91; founder Webcarvers Am. Interactive Devel. Co.; creator StreetMagic web site and products. Author: The Expert from Out of Town, Sometimes I Forgot to Look Both Ways; lighting designer Sheep Dip Show, Reno Hilton, 1986, 87, 89; designer tour logo Doobie Brothers and Foreigner Tour 1994; designer Michael Jackson History World Tour, 1996-97, U2 World Tour; credential mfr. for Rolling Stones Bridges to Babylon World Tour, 1997-98, Pavarotti Tour 2000, Rolling Stones No Security Tour, 1999. Mem. Nev. Repertory Co., 1983-89. Recipient Lifetime Achievement award Reed H.S. Theatre Dept., 1983. Mem. Reno Advt. Club, Rotary Internat. Roman Catholic. Office: Perri Entertainment Svcs Inc PO Box 11852 Reno NV 89510-1852

PERRY, ANTOINETTE KRUEGER, pianist, instructor; b. Manhattan, N.Y., Sept. 21, 1954; d. Paul Krueger and Lillian (Haslach) Teddlie; m. John Perry, Dec. 29, 1984; children: Sean Paul, Michael James, Maureen Brigit. Student, Kans. U., 1972-74; MusB, U. Tex., 1976, MusM, 1978; postgrad., Munchen Hochschule Für Musk, 1979-80. Instr. Community Sch. Performing Arts (name changed R.D. Colburn Sch. of the Performing Arts), L.A., 1981—; summer faculty artist Aspen (Colo.) Music Sch., 1985—; mem. summer workshop faculty Idyllwild (Calif.) Sch. Music and the Arts, 1987-92. Concert artist in field; adj. asst. prof. UCLA, 1984-96; faculty U. So. Calif., 1996—. U. Tex. fellow, 1976-79; German-Am. Club Exch. scholar, 1979-80. Mem. Phi Kappa Phi. Avocations: reading, hiking, Yoga. Office: U So Calif Sch Music # Mc0851 Los Angeles CA 90089-0001

PERRY, ARTHUR WILLIAM, plastic surgeon, educator; b. Cornwall, N.Y., Jan. 2, 1957; s. Michael Martin and Harriet (Estrin) P. AB magna cum laude, Rutgers U., 1977; MD with distinction, Albany Med. Coll., 1981. Diplomate Am. Bd. Plastic Surgery. Clin. fellow in surgery Harvard Med. Sch., Boston, 1981-84; fellow in burn surgery Cornell U. Med. Coll., N.Y.c., 1984-85; resident in plastic surgery U. Chgo., 1985-87; clin. asst. prof. surgery U. Medicine and Surgery N.J.-Robert Wood Johnson Med. Sch., New Brunswick, 1987-97, clin. assoc. prof. plastic surgery, 1997—; clin. assoc. in surgery U. Pa., Phila., 1993—. Mem. N.J. Bd. Med. Examiners, Trenton, 1995—, treas., 2002—, mem. exec. com., 2002, chmn. advt. com., 1997—; chmn. preliminary evaluation com., 1997—2001; vice chmn., mem. devel. com. Carnegie Bank, Princeton, NJ, 1990—98; mem. body art steering com. N.J. Dept. health and Sr. Svcs., 1999—2001; designee State Bioterrorism Task Force, 2001. Co-author: Cosmetic Surgery, 1997; contbr. chpt. to books, articles to profl. jours. Mem. health adv. bd. to Congressman Mike Ferguson, 2001—. Recipient Gingrass award Plastic Surgery Rsch. Coun., 1981, best paper award Midwestern Assn. Plastic Surgeons, 1987. Fellow ACS; mem. Am. Soc. Plastic Surgeons, Am. Soc. Aesthetic Plastic Surgery, Alpha Omega Alpha. Office: 3055 State Route 27 Franklin Park NJ 08823-1315

PERRY, BURTON LARS, retired pediatrician; b. Midland, Mich., Dec. 8, 1931; s. Willard Russell and Myrl Alice (Jacobsen) P.; m. Nancy Fawn Towsley, Aug. 24, 1956; children: Ellen, Willard. BS, U. Mich., 1953, MD, 1960. Diplomate Am. Bd. Pediats.; sub-bd. pediat. cardiology. Physician U. Mich., Ann Arbor, 1960-78, Childrens Hosp. Mich., Detroit, 1978-97. 1st lt. infantry, U.S. Army, 1954-56. Home: 1416 Dicken Dr Ann Arbor MI 48103-4417 Office: Childrens Hosp Mich 3901 Beaubien St Detroit MI 48201-2119

PERRY, CHARLES, photo-illustrator, writer, researcher; b. Marshalltown, Iowa, Mar. 20, 1947; s. Cecil Carl and Grace (Verle) P. Cert. profl. photography, Sch. Modern Photography, Little Plains, N.J., 1987; BA, U. Colo., 1989. Mill operator Calco Inc., Colorado Springs, Colo., 1972-81; photographer, 1981-86; outside salesperson Belen, N.Mex., 1990-94; photographer Charles Perry Photographics, 1997—. Photographer, writer Spanish Barb Breeders Assn., Gulfport, Miss.; photographer Horse Trader Mag., Founders Day Com., Finding the Horse, Habitat for Humanities; writer children's ednl. picture books, mag. articles. Mem. Hispano C. of C. Democrat. Avocation: documentary photography. Home: 1215 W Castillo Belen NM 87002

PERRY, CINDA, music educator; b. Hagerstown, Md., Jan. 22, 1947; d. Rowland Clay and Mary (Gaylor) Bradenburg; m. Spence William Perry; children: Dale Mattingly, Tom Colihan. Student, Peabody Inst., 1967-70; BA cum laude, Shepherd Coll., 1995. Music tchr. Kiddie Kampus, Hagerstown, Md., 1971-75, Colonial Music, Hagerstown, 1971-78, Hagerstown Music, Hagerstown, 1979-80, Keyboard Studio, Hagerstown, 1980—. Bd. dirs. Millbrook Orch., Shepherdstown, W.Va; mem. Washington County Hist. Soc., 1995—. Mem. Nat. Music Tchrs. Assn., Md. Music Tchrs. Assn., Shepherd Coll. Alumni Assn. Democrat. Home: 1101 Hamilton Blvd Hagerstown MD 21742-3338

PERRY, CYNTHIA SHEPARD, federal agency administrator; Grad., Ind. State U.; EdD, U. Mass. Chief edn. and human resourcesAfrica Bus. USAID, 1982—86; ambassador Sierra Leone, 1986—89, Burundi, 1990—93; dir. internat. investment adv. svcs. FCA Corp., Houston, 1996—2001; U.S. dir. African Devel. Bank, Abidjan, Cote d'Ivoire, 2001—. N. counsel gen., Senegal. Office: African Devel Bank 01 BP 1387 Abidjan 01 Cote d'Ivoire*

PERRY, DALE LYNN, chemist; b. Greenville, Tex., May 12, 1947; s. Francis Leon and Violet (Inabinette) P. BS, Midwestern U., 1969; MS, Lamar U., 1972; PhD, U. Houston, 1974. NSF fellow dept. chemistry Rice U., Houston, 1976-77; Miller Research fellow dept. chemistry U. Calif.-Berkeley, 1977-79; prin. investigator solid state chemistry and spectroscopy Lawrence Berkeley Lab. U. Calif., 1979—, sr. scientist, 1987—. Lectr. Ana G. Mendez Ednl. Found., 1988; rsch. mem. G.T. Seaborg Inst. for Transactinium Sci. Author, editor: Instrumental Surface Analysis of Geologic Materials, 1990, Applications of Analytical Techniques to the Characterization of Materials, 1992, Applications of Synchrotron Radiation Techniques to Materials Science, 1993, II, 1995, III, 1996, IV, 1998, V, 2001, VI, 2002, Handbook of Inorganic Compounds, 1995, Materials Synthesis and Characterization, 1997; contbr. articles to profl. jours. Recipient Outstanding mentor for Undergrad. Rsch., U.S. Dept. Energy, 2002. Fellow Royal Soc. Chemistry (London); mem. Am. Chem. Soc. (chmn. materials chemistry and engring. subdivsn., indsl. and engring. chemistry divsn., 1992-96), Soc. Applied Spectroscopy, Coblentz Soc., Materials Rsch. Soc. (corp. participation com. 1991-96), Sigma Xi (nat. rsch. award 1974). Office: U Calif Lawrence Berkeley Nat Lab Mail Stop 70A 1150 Berkeley CA 94720-0001

PERRY, DONNY RAY, electrician; b. Amarillo, Tex., Apr. 29, 1959; s. Ernest Elwood and Donnie Mae Perry; m. Tina Marie Conn, Sept. 9, 1988; children: Contessa, Jason, Stephen, Christopher. Cert. in fiber optics, Tex. State Tech. Inst., 1988; student, Amarillo Coll., 1990—. Electrician Mason & Hanger, Amarillo, 1979—. Mem. negotiating com. Mason & Hanger, 1989-90, mem. sick leave and team concept coms., 1991, mem. elec. safety com., 1992, mem. job track analysis and procedure adherence coms., 1993. Mem. Internat. Brotherhood Elec. Workers, Metal Trades Coun. (negotiating com. 1989-90, exec. bd. 1989-90, co-chair elec. safety com. 1995—, team leader Hazard Identification Team 1995—, legis. and polit. action com. 1996—, apprenticeship com. 1996—), Phi Theta Kappa, Nat. Dean's List. Avocations: snow skiing, water skiing, running.

PERRY, DOUGLAS, opera singer; B.M., Wittenberg U.; MA, Ball State U. Made debut as Don Basilio in Marriage of Figaro, with N.Y.C. Opera; appeared as King Kaspar in: Amahl and the Night Visitors; appeared as Timothy in: Help! Help! The Globolinks; appeared as Guillot in: Manon; Dancing Master and Brighella in: Ariadne auf Naxos; Met. Opera debut as scientist/first mate in: The Voyage (Philip Glass); European debut with Netherlands Opera as Mahatma Gandhi in Satyagraha (Philip Glass); appeared as analyst in A Quiet Place (Bernstein), La Scala and Vienna Stadtsoper, as Sailor 1, Scientist 3, Traveler 2 world premier Corvo Bronco, Teatro Camô, Lisbon, Portugal, Teatro Real, Madrid; featured soloist on tours and recs. with Gregg Smith Singers and Camerata Singers; performed with Sante Fe Opera, also performed with Ft. Worth Opera, Chatauqua Opera, N.Y.C. Opera, Opera Co. of Boston, Houston Grand Opera, Balt. Opera., Miami Opera, Chgo. Lyric Opera, Seattle Opera, San Francisco Opera, Opera Co. Phila.; recs. include Satyagraha, Songs from Liquid Days, A Quiet Place, Mother of Us All. Address: 170 W End Ave New York NY 10023-5401 Office: Trawick Artists Mgmt Inc 250 W 57th St Ste 901 New York NY 10107-0999

PERRY, E. EUGENE, communication educator; b. Martins Ferry, Ohio, Dec. 25, 1957; s. Edwin Ray and Sally Lou (Youst) P. BS in Edn., Ohio U., 1979; MDiv, U. Dubuque, 1982, MA in Comms., 2000. Intern chaplain U. Dubuque, Iowa, 1981-82, instr. theater, 1984; intern sem. rels. Theol. Sem., 1982-83; deacon Westminster Presbyn. Ch., Dubuque, 1986-87; instr. N.E. Iowa C.C., Peosta, 1989—. Youth adv. del. Gen. Assembly, United Presbyn. Ch. in U.S.A., 1977; substitute tchr. Dubuque Cmty. Schs., 1982-85; advisor drama and speech dept. Western Dubuque Cmty. Schs., Epworth, Iowa, 1989-91; contest judge Iowa H.S. Speech Assn., 1986—. Author: (plays) It Works for Everybody Else, 1984, Wanted: A Cook, 1990, Just a High School Play, 1991, Once Upon a Beginning, 1994, (textbook) Articulate: a practical handbook for public speakers, 2000; contbr. articles to profl. jours. Chmn. play-selection com. Barn Cmty. Theater, Dubuque, 1981-83; active Dubuque County Dem. Cen. Com., 1984-87, 89-91, office mgr. hdqrs., 1984; del. County Dem. Conv., Dubuque, 1984, 86, 90; del., sec. 2d Dist. Dem. Conv., 1984, 86, 90; mem. 5 Flags City Civic Ctr. Commn., Dubuque, 1989-92, chmn., 1991-92; founding bd. dirs. Dubuque County Habitat for Humanity, 1991; sec., bd. dirs. Dubuque Fine Arts Players, 1993-96; mem. Cmty. Devel. Commn., Dubuque, 1992-94; mem. rezoning rev. com. Dubuque Cmty. Sch. Dist., 1996-97. Individual Artist grantee Iowa Arts Coun., 1993, 96. Home: 1010 W Locust St #3 Dubuque IA 52001 E-mail: perryg@nicc.edu.

PERRY, ESTON LEE, real estate and equipment leasing company executive; b. Wartburg, Tenn., Mar. 16, 1936; s. Eston Lee and Willimae (Heidle) P.; m. Alice Anne Schmidt, Oct. 21, 1961; children: Julie Anne, Jeffrey John, Jennifer Lee. BS, Ind. State U., 1961. With Oakley Corp., 1961—, dir., 1965—. Corp. officer Ind. State Bank, Terre Haute, 1975-80; pres. One Twenty Four Madison Corp., Terre Haute, 1979—, also bd. dirs., chmn. bd., 1981—; bd. dirs. Fifth Third Bank of Ind. Bd. dirs. Salvation Army, Terre Haute, 1975-91, mem. exec. adv. bd., 1979-87; bd. dirs. Vigo County Dept. Pub. Welfare, 1979-82, Jr. Achievement Wabash Valley, 1980-86; bd. dirs. United Way of Wabash Valley, 1984-89, chmn. fund campaign, 1984, bd. dirs. United Way of Ind., 1984-90, v.p., 1986, pres., 1988-89; trustee Oakley Found., 1970—; bd. dirs. Terre Haute Symphony Orch., 1984-87, Ind. State U. Found., 1988—, Goodwill Industries of Terre Haute, 1984-97, Leadership Terre Haute, 1984-88, Cen. Eastside Assocs., 1984-88, pres., 1984-85; mem. exec. com. Ind. State U. Found., 1990-94; bd. dirs. City of Terre Haute Hulman Links Commn., pres., 1986-91; mem. President's Assocs., Ind. State U., adv. bd.; bd. overseers Sheldon Swope Art Gallery of Terre Haute, 1984-87; bd. assocs. Rose Hulman Inst. Tech., 1986—. Served with U.S. Army, 1955-57. Mem. Jaycees Terre Haute (v.p. 1967-69), C. of C. Terre Haute (bd. dirs. 1984-93, vice chmn. 1986-88, chmn. 1990), Wabash Valley Pilots Assn., Aircarft Owners and Pilots Assn., Air Safety Found., Aviation Trades Assn., Country Club of Terre Haute (bd. dirs.), Aero Club of Terre Haute, Sycamore Athletic Scholarship Fund (Ind. State U.), Lions (pres. Terre Haute 1983-84), Elks, Lambda Chi Alpha. Home: 25 Bogart Dr Terre Haute IN 47803-2401 Office: 8 S 16th St Terre Haute IN 47807-4102 E-mail: bperry@oakleyusa.com.

PERRY, EVELYN REIS, communications company executive; b. N.Y.C., Mar. 09; d. Lou L. and Bertl (Wolf) Reis; m. Charles G. Perry III, Jan. 7, 1968; children: Charles G. IV, David Reis. Student, Am. Acad. Dramatic Arts, 1958-59, U. N.Mex., 1963-64; BA, U. Wis., 1963. Lic. real estate broker, N.C. Vol. ETV project Peace Corps, Colombia, 1963-65; program officer-radio/tv Peace Corps, Washington, 1965-68; dir. Vols. in Svc. to Am. (VISTA), Raleigh, N.C., 1977-80; exec. dir. CETA Program for Displaced Homemakers, 1980-81; cons. exec. dir. to Recycle Raleigh for Food and Fuel, Theater in the Park, 1981-83; pres., CEO Carolina Sound Commn., MUZAK, Charleston, S.C., 1984—; pub. rels. account exec. various cos. Washington, Syracuse, N.Y., 1969-71; cons. pub. rels. and orgn. Olympic Organizing Com., Mexico City, 1968; cons. pub. rels., fundraising, arts mgmt. pub. speaking Ill., Pa., N.C., 1971-77; orgnl. and pub. speaking cons. Perry & Assocs., Raleigh,

1980—. Spkr. Nat. Syss. Contrs. Assn., 1993, 95, 97; founder Nat. Assn. Women Bus. Owners, Charleston, S.C., 1998; bd. dirs. Charleston Area Br. Banking and Trust, 1999—; bd. dirs. Branch Banking and Trust Adv. Bd., 1986-98, mem. adv. bd., 1999--. Contbr. articles to Sound and Comm. mag. Mem. adv. bd. Gov.'s Office Citizen Affairs, Raleigh, 1981-85; mem. Involvement Coun. of Wake County, N.C., Raleigh, 1981-84; mem. Adv. Coun. to Vols. in Svc. to Am., Raleigh, 1980-84; mem. Pres.'s adv. bd. Peace Corps, Washington, 1980-82; v.p., bd. dirs. Voluntary Action Ctr., Raleigh, 1980-84, bd. dirs., Charleston, 1988-94; sec. bd. dirs. Temple Kahil Kadosh Beth Elohim, 1987-89, sec. fin., 1989-90, v.p. programming, 1990-93, v.p. adminstrn. 1993-95, v.p. sisterhood, 2001—; bd. dirs. Chopstik Theater, Charleston, 1989-90; del., chmn. S.C. Delegation to White House Conf. Sml. Bus., 1995; S.C. del. Congl. Sml. Bus. Summit, 1998. Named Bus. Women Adv. of Yr., SBA, 2002. Mem. N.C. Coun. of Women's Orgns. (pres., v.p. 1982-84), Charleston Hotel and Motel Assn., N.C. Assn. Vol. Adminstrs. (bd. dirs. 1980-84), S.C. Restaurant Assn., Nat. Assn. Women Bus. Owners (founder lowcountry chpt. 1998, pres. 1998—2001), Internat. Planned Music Assn. (chmn. conf. 1993, adv. bd. Branch Banking & Trust, 1999-), Nat. Fedn. Ind. Bus. (mem. adv. bd. 1987—, chmn. leadership coun. 1994-2000, del. Congl. Summit, Washington), Internat. Platform Assn., Theaterworks (bd. dirs. 1994-96), Internat. Planned Music Assn. (bd. dirs. 2000—, v.p. 2001-). Office: Carolina Sound Comm Inc 1941 Savage Rd Ste 200G Charleston SC 29407-4789 E-mail: evelyn@carolina-sound.com.

PERRY, GAIL WALBORN, human resources executive; b. Wiesbaden, Germany, Mar. 9, 1952; d. William Edward and Eloise (Walborn) P. BA, Tulane U., 1974. Restaurant and personnel mgr. Village Inn Pancake Houses of Tucson, Inc., 1974-78; sr. personnel counselor Temporaries Inc., L.A., San Francisco, 1978-80; human resources mgr. Group Health Med. Assocs., Tucson, 1980-85; personnel dir. The Tucson Nat. Resort and Spa, 1985-86, Northwest Hosp., Tucson, 1986-88; human resources dir. Charter Hosp. of Tucson, 1988-89, Thomas-Davis Med. Ctrs., P.C., Tucson, 1989—. Bd. dirs. Big Bros./Big Sisters of Tucson, 1992—, v.p. planning and program devel., 1993—. Recipient Excellence in Community Svc. award Hosp. Corp. of Am., 1986. Mem. Soc. for Human Resource Mgmt. (Ariz. state coun. dir. 1989, state coun. 1986-91), Soc. for Human Resource Mgmt. of Greater Tucson (pres. 1984-85, bd. dirs. 1982-86), Jr. League of Tucson (v.p. of tng. 1986-87, bd. dirs. 1985-87, exec. coun. 1986-87). Democrat. Episcopalian. Avocations: art history, reading, aerobic dance, theatre. Home: 6006 E West Miramar Dr Tucson AZ 85715-3001

PERRY, GEORGE, neuroscientist, educator; b. Lompoc, Calif., Apr. 12, 1953; s. George Richard and Mary Arlene (George) P.; m. Paloma Aguilar, May 21, 1983; children: Anne, Elizabeth. BA in Zoology with hons., U. Calif., Santa Barbara, 1974; PhD in Marine Biology, U. Calif., San Diego, 1979. Postdoctoral fellow Baylor Coll. Medicine, Houston, 1979-82; from asst. prof. to prof. pathology Case Western Res. U., Cleve., 1982-94, prof., 1994—, interim chmn. dept., 2001—. Tchg. asst. U. Calif., San Diego, 1977, Stanford U., 1978—79; mem. task force on Alzheimer's disease Ohio Gov., 1987, 90; mem. scientific adv. bd. Familial Alzheimer's Disease Rsch. Found., 1988—; mem., chair neurol. scis. study section NIH, Bethesda, Md., 1989—95; vis. scholar Sci.-by-Mail, 1991—94; cons. Nymox, Inc., Panacea Pharms., Inc., Prion Devel. Labs., Voyager, Takada Pharm.; spkr. in field; mem. numerous rev. bds. nationally/internationally. Author: The Neuronal Cytoskeleton, 1992; co-author: (chpt.) Muscle and Cell Motility, 1982, Membranes in Growth and Development, 1982, Electron Microscopy and Alzheimer's Disease, 1986, Banbury Report 27, Molecular Neuropathology of Aging, 1987, Advances in Behavioral Biology, 1987, Fidia Research Series, 1988, Progress in Clinical and Biological Research: Alzheimer's Disease and Related Disorders, 1989, 93, International Congress Series: Molecular Biology and Genetics of Alzheimer's Disease, 1990, Neuroscience Year, 1992, Amyloid and Amyloidosis, 1993, Dementia in Parkinson's Disease, 1994, Non-Neural Cells in Alzheimer's Disease, 1995, Alzheimer's Disease: Aetiological Mechanism and Therapeutic Possibilities, 1996; editor-in-chief Jour. Alzheimer's Disease, 1998—; guest editor Clin. Neurosci., 1993; editor Biomed. Jour., 1994-95; assoc. editor Am. Jour. pathology, 1994-2000; mem. editl. bd. Am. Jour. Pathology, 1992—, Alzheimer Disease and Associated Disorders, 1994—, Alzheimer's Disease Rev., 1995—, Jour. Alzheimer's Disease,1997—, Jour. Exptl. Neurol., 1997-99, Molecular Chem. Neuropathology, 1997—, Jour. Neural Transmission, 1998—, Investigational Drugs Jour., 1998—, Brain Pathology, 1999—, Jour. Molecular Neurosci., 1999—, Antioxidant and Redox Signaling, 2000-2002, Research Signal Post, 2000—, Lab. Investment, 2000-, Fronteirs Biosci., 2000-, Brain Rsch., 2002-; reviewer Acta Neuropathol., Alan Liss Publ. Co., Am. Jour. Pathol., Ann Neurol, others; contbr. articles to Experimental Cell Rsch., Jour Cell Biology, Jour. Leukocyte Biology, Devel. Biology, Brain Rsch., Am. Jour. Pathology, Jour. Neurosci., European Jour. Cell Biology, Nature, Annals Neurology, Lancet, Acta Neuropathology, Jour. Neurochemistry, Neurosci. Letters, Hepatology, Jour. Hirnforsch, Cancer Letters, Neuroreport, Med. Hypotheses, Nature Medicine, Neurodegeneration, Brain Rsch. Protocols, others. Pres. Serra Club, 1995-97. Recipient Bausch and Lomb medal, 1971, Rsch. Career Devel. award, NIH, 1988—93, Temple award, Alzheimer's Assn., 1999, Career Devel. award, NIH, 1988, Disting. American of Portuguese Ancestry award, Portuguese-Am. Hist. Found., Inc., 2001; fellow Kennecott Copper fellow, 1974—75, Muscular Dystrophy Assn. fellow, 1980—82; grantee NIH, 1985—, grantee, Am. Health Assistance Found., 1988—90, 1997—99, Alzheimer's Assn., 1989—90, 1998—, Belgian Nat. Found. Sci. Rsch., 1994—, Neurogeriatrics Fund., 1995—96, 1997—, Britton Fund, 1996. Fellow AAAS; mem. AAUP (exec. com. 1996—, membership chair 1996-98, v.p. 1998-99, pres. 1999—), Am. Soc. Cell Biology (fellow 1992), Electron Microscopy Soc. N.E. Ohio (treas. 1986-88, trustee 1988-90, pres. 1990-91), Soc. Neurosci., Am. Assn. Neuropathologists (awards com. 1992-93, 95-2001, chmn. 2001, internat. congress neuropathology concilator 1995-2000), Am. Soc. Investigative Pathology (BioInfo Net 1996—, program com. 1998-2001), Oxygen Club, Soc. Neuroscientists Africa, Am. Soc. Neurochemistry, Am. Inst. Biol. Scis., Mitochondrion Rsch. Soc., U.S. and Can. Acad. of Pathology, Hispanic Med. Assn. (com. on status of Portuguese in medicine and sci.), Sigma Xi. Democrat. Roman Catholic. Home: 2500 Eaton Rd University Heights OH 44118-4339 Office: Case Western Res U Inst Path 2085 Adelbert Rd Cleveland OH 44106-2622 E-mail: GXP7@po.cwru.edu.

PERRY, GEORGE LEWIS, research economist, consultant; b. N.Y.C., Jan. 23, 1934; s. Lewis G. and Helen L. (Couloumbis) P.; m. Jean Marion West, 1956; children: Elizabeth, Lewis G., George A.; m. 2d, Dina Needleman, 1987. BS, MIT, 1954, PhD, 1961. Editor Brookings Papers on Econ. Activity, 1970—; columnist L.A. Times, 1981-93. Bd. dirs. State Farm Mut. Automobile Ins. Co., Bloomington, Ill., Dreyfus Mut. Funds, N.Y.C.; co-dir. Brookings Panel Econ. Activity. Author: Unemployment, Money Wage Rates and Inflation, 1966, Curing Chronic Inflation, 1978, Economic Events, Ideas and Policies, 2000; contbr. articles to profl. jours. Mem. Am. Econs. Assn. Office: Brookings Instn 1775 Massachusetts Ave NW Washington DC 20036-2103

PERRY, GEORGE WILLIAMSON, lawyer; b. Cleve., Dec. 4, 1926; s. George William and Melda Patricia (Arther-Holt) P. BA in Econs., Yale U., 1949; JD, U. Va., 1953. Bar: Ohio 1953, D.C. 1958, U.S. Supreme Ct. 1958, U.S. Ct. Appeals (D.C. cir.) 1959. Atty. U.S. Dept. Justice, Washington, 1954-56; assoc. Roberts and McInnis, 1957-59; atty. assoc. counsel Com. on Interstate Fgn. Commerce, U.S. Ho. Reps., 1960-65; atty., advisor ICC, 1965-68; assoc. dir. devel. Yale U., New Haven, 1968-70; trust officer The No. Trust Co., Chgo., 1970-71; dir. tax rsch. Pan Am. World Airways, N.Y.C., 1973-75; hearing officer Indsl. Commn. Ohio, Cleve., 1978-81; sole practice, 1981—. With U.S. Army, 1945-46. Mem. Soc. Cin. in State of Conn., Ancient and Hon. Artillery Co. (mem. Boston-hereditary), Concord Coalition, Phi Delta Phi. Episcopalian.

PERRY, GEORGE WILSON, oil and gas company executive; b. Pampa, Tex., July 18, 1929; s. Frank M. and Ruth (Ingersoll) P.; m. Patricia Carberry Bowen, 1950; children: Sally Jett Perry Pemrick, Susan Jeanne Perry Bynder-Schrier, Virginia Anne Perry Haynie, Tobe Jackson Perry. BS in Petroleum Engring., U. Tulsa, 1952. Registered profl. engr., Tex. Engr. Stanolind Oil & Gas Co., Oklahoma City, 1952-53, Parker Drilling Co., Tulsa, 1953-54, Holm Drilling Co., Tulsa, 1954-55; drilling engr. Mobil Oil, Victoria, Tex., Lake Charles, La., Paris, France, 1955-68; drilling mgr. Anaco, Venezuela, N.Y.C., Tehran, Iran, Stavanger, Norway, New Orleans, La., 1968-79; exec. v.p. Loffland Bros. Co., Tulsa, 1979-89; pres., CEO Gas Well Properties, Inc., Dallas, 1989—. Mem. Delta Tau Delta. Office: Gas Well Properties Inc PO Box 795302 5995 Summerside Dr Dallas TX 75248-9992 E-mail: gperry@airmail.net.

PERRY, HAROLD OTTO, dermatologist; b. Rochester, Minn., Nov. 18, 1921; s. Oliver and Hedwig Clara (Tornow) P.; m. Loraine Thelma Moehnke, Aug. 27, 1944; children— Preston, Oliver, Ann, John. AA, Rochester Jr. Coll., 1942; BS, U. Minn., 1944, MB, 1946, MD, 1947; MS, Mayo Grad. Sch. Medicine, 1953. Diplomate Am. Bd. Dermatology with spl. competence in dermatopathology. Intern Naval Hosp., Oakland, Calif., 1946-47; resident in dermatology Mayo Grad. Sch. Medicine, 1949-52; practice medicine specializing in dermatology Rochester, 1953-86; mem. staff Mayo Clinic, 1953-86, mem. emeritus staff, 1987—; instr., asst. prof., assoc. prof. Mayo Med. Sch., 1953-86, prof., 1978-83, Robert H. Kieckhefer prof. dermatology, 1978-83, head dept. dermatology, 1975-83, emeritus prof. dermatology, 1987—. Civilian cons. dermatology to surgeon gen. USAF, 1979-99. Contbr. articles to med. jours. and, chpts. to books. With USNR, 1943-45, 46-49. Inducted into Rochester (Minn.) C.C. Alumni Hall of Fame, 1993; recipient Disting. Alumnus award Mayo Found., 1995. Mem. AMA, Am. Acad. Dermatology (pres. 1981, Sulzberger internat. lectr. 1986, Gold Medal for visionary leadership 1998), Am. Dermatol. Assn. (bd. dirs. 1985-89, pres. 1989-90), Am. Bd. Dermatology (bd. dirs. 1979-90, v.p. 1989, pres. 1990), Noah Worcester Dermatol. Soc. (pres. 1969), Minn. Dermatol. Soc. (pres. 1967), Chgo. Dermatol. Soc., Internat. Soc. Tropical Dermatology, Minn. Med. Assn.; hon. mem. French Dermatol. Soc., Spanish Acad. Dermatology, Brazilian Dermatol. Soc., Ga. Dermatol. Soc., Iowa Dermatol. Soc., Korean Dermatol. Soc., Bolivar Soc. Dermatology, Jacksonville Dermatol. Soc., N.Am. Clin. Dermatol. Soc., Pacific Dermatol. Assn. Home: 3625 SW Bamber Valley Rd Rochester MN 55902 Office: Mayo Clinic Emeritus Staff Ctr 10th Fl Plummer Bldg Ctr Rochester MN 55905-0001

PERRY, HELEN, home care nurse, educator; b. Birmingham, Ala., Mar. 4, 1927; d. Van Mary Ellenol (Thornton) Curry; m. Charlie Pitts, May, 1960; 1 child, Charlenia; m. George Perry (dec. 1989); children: Hattie Mae (dec.), George Jr., Bishop, Jose Sr. Student, LaSalle Extension U., Chgo., 1968, Georgetown U., 1979; Doctorate/Mayanuis Mosaic Soc., Duke Univ., San Antonio, 1979. LPN; cert. paramedic. Tchr. Wenona H.S. City Bd. Edn., Birmingham, 1977—. Notary pub., Ala., 1975—; home health nurse U. Ala. at Birmingham Hosp., 1988—. Vol. ARC, Birmingham, 1970—; mem. crime watch Am. Police, Washington, 1989; mem. Hall of Fame Pres. Task Force, Washington, 1983-91; nominee Nat. Rep. Com., Washington, 1991, 92; selected VIP Guest delegate Rep. Nat. Conv., Houston, 1992, fin. com. fundraiser Middleton for Congress Campaign '94, Dist. # 59 Bd. Reps.; life mem. Rep. Presdl. Task Force, Washington, 1992, mem. Jefferson com., 2001; trustee Nat. Crime Watch, 1989, adv. bd. Am. Security Coun., Va., Washington, 1969-91; mem. Nat. Congl. Com. Adv. Bd., Washington; mem. Nat. Law Enforcement Assn., 1989; min. Greater Emmanuel Temple Holiness Ch., Birmingham, 1957—, ordained elder, vice-champion of mother bd.; mem. exec. com. Jefferson County Rep., chairperson legis. dist. 52; chair Harriet Tubman Rep. Com.; mem. Image Devel. Adv. Bd.; mem. Coalition for Desert Storm, various others; del. Commonwealth of Ky. 2000 So. Rep. Leadership Conf. Recipient cert. of appreciation Pres. Congl. Task Force, 1990, Diamond award U.S.A. Serve Am., 1992, award Ala. Sheriff Assn., 1989, Navy League, 1989-91, Rep. Presdl. award Legion of Merit, 1994, cert. of appreciation Rep. Nat. Commn., 1994, nominated Presdl. Election Registry Rep. Presdl. Task Force, 1992; named God Samaritan Law Enforcement Officers, Royal Proclamation Royal Highness Kevin, Prince Regent of Hutt River Province, 1994, Royal Ceremonial Jewel, svc. award Ala. Bd. Nursing, Outstanding Sr. Citizens' Cert. of Recognition. Mem. Nat. Rep. Women Assn., LaSalle Extension U. Alumni (life mem.), Ala. Nurses Assn., Nat. Assn. Unknown Players. Avocations: singing, writer, speaking, reading, planting flowers. Home: 201 W Ann Dr SW Birmingham AL 35211-4935

PERRY, I. CHET, petroleum company executive; b. Phila., Jan. 18, 1943; s. Irving Chester Sr. and Erma Jackson (McNeil) P.; 1 child, London Schade. BA in Psychology, Bus., Lake Forest Coll., 1965. Lic. real estate broker, Ill. Sr. mgmt. trainee British Overseas Airways Corp., London, Eng., 1968-69; owner Itec Internat. Ltd., Barrington, Ill., 1970—, Itec Refining & Mktg. Co., Ltd., Barrington, 1970—, CEO, mng. dir., 1986—. Lt. U.S. Army, 1965-68, Vietnam. Decorated Bronze Star, Purple Heart. Mem. Am. Petroleum Inst., European Petrochem. Assn., Barrington Bd. Realtors (bd. dirs. 1974-78), Forest Grove Club, Barrington Tennis Club. Republican. Mem. Soc. Of Friends. Avocations: tennis, photography. Home: 444 W Russell St Barrington IL 60010-4123

PERRY, J. WARREN, health sciences educator, administrator; b. Richmond, Ind., Oct. 25, 1921; s. Charles Thomas and Zona M. (Ohler) Perry. BA, DePauw U., 1944, DSc (hon.) (hon.), 1998; postgrad., Harvard U., 1948—49; MA, Northwestern U., 1952, PhD, 1955; DSc (hon.) (hon.) , D'Youville Coll., 1990, Med. Coll. Ohio, 1996, DePauw U., 1998. Instr. St. John's Mil. Acad., Delafield, Wis., 1944—47; counselor, asst. prof. psychology U. Ill.-Chgo., 1953—56; dir. prosthetic-orthotic edn., asst. prof. orthopaedic surgery Northwestern U. Med. Sch., 1957—61; lectr. psychology U. Chgo., 1957—61; asst. chief div. tng. Vocat. Rehab. Adminstrn., HEW, 1961—64, dep. asst. commr. research and tng., 1964—66; prof. health scis. adminstrn. SUNY-Buffalo, 1966—95, founding dean Sch. Health Related Professions, 1966—77, dean and prof. emeritus, 1985—. Mary E. Switzer Meml. lectr., Dallas, 1977, Lexington, 91; mem. Task Force for Legislation for Allied Health Professions, 1966—67; com. edn. allied health professions and svcs., coun. med. edn. AMA, 1968—73; nat. adv. com. Am. Dietetic Assn., 1970—75, chmn., 1972—75; nat. rev. com., regional med. programs HEW, 1969—72; mem. steering com. on manpower policy for primary care bd. health promotion and disease prevention Inst. of Medicine-NAS, 1981—83, sr. advisor com. to study role allied health, com. to study med. manpower in VA, 1988—91; spl. med. adv. com. VA, 1974—77; mem. task force on manpower for prevention Fogarty Internat. Inst., NIH, 1975—76; mem. acad. planning com. Mass. Gen. Hosp. Founding editor Jour. Allied Health, 1972—78, editor emeritus, 1985—; contbr. articles. Mem. Legacy Soc.; charter mem. Cmty. Found. for Greater Buffalo, 1998—; patron of the arts Coun. of Buffalo and Erie County, 2000; bd. dirs., dir. com. opera edn. Lyric Opera Guild, Chgo., 1957—61; chmn. acad. divsn. dr., coun. trustees Buffalo Philharm. Orch., 1987—93; bd. dirs. Goodwill Industries, Buffalo, 1969—76; trustee Cmty. Music Sch. Buffalo, 1977—80; adv. bd., v.p. Sisters of Charity Hosp., Buffalo, 1969—87, pres., 1986—88; bd. visitors U. Pitts., 1977—80; coun. trustees D'youville Coll., Buffalo, 1978—88, trustee emeritus, 1989—95; bd. dirs. Am. Lung Assn. Western N.Y., 1975—92, pres., 1983; bd. dirs. ARC, Buffalo, Artpark State Performing Arts Ctr., Lewiston, 1986—96, Am. Lung Assn. N.Y.State, 1981—85, exec. com., 1989—92; chmn. N.Y. State Coalition Smoking or Health, Albany, NY, 1987—91; trustee Theodore Roosevelt Inaugural Site Found., 1987, pres., 1991—94; bd. advisors Buffalo Coun. on World Affairs, 1987—88; trustee Buffalo Opera Co., 1989—94, chmn. opera adv. coun., 1995—97. Named Outstanding Individual Philanthropist, Nat. Soc. Fundraising Execs. Western N.Y., 1992, Ky. Col., 1969, Nebr. Admn., 1964, Man of the Yr., Opera Found. Buffalo, Inc., 2000; recipient Sustained Superior Svc. award, HEW, 1965, Disting. Svc. award, Am. Orthotics-Prosthetics Assn., 1966, Buffalo Opera Co., 1995, Chancellor's award for adminstrv. svc., SUNY, 1977, 1st Allied Health Leadership award, 1988, Disting. Author award, Jour. Allied Health, 1978, Cert. of Merit, AMA, 1979, Pres. Cir. Pin, Buffalo State Coll., 1993, 50th Anniversary Alumni citation, De Pauw U., 1994, Outstanding Svc. award, Theodore Roosevelt Inaugural Site Found., 1994, Theodore Roosevelt Exemplary Citizenship award, 1997, Brotherhood/Sisterhood award in health, NCCJ Western N.Y., 1995, Christmas Seal Hall of Fame award, ALA N.Y. State, 1995, Disting. Citizenship award, Mayor of Buffalo, 1995, Patron of the Arts award, Arts Coun. of Buffalo and Erie County, 2000, Alumni Achievement award, SUNY-Buffalo, 2000, Wisdom award of honor, 1999, J. Warren Perry Disting. Author award named in his honor, Jour. Allied Health, 1984—, J. Warren Perry Meml. lectr. named in his honor, SUNY-Buffalo, 1990—, J. Warren Perry Outstanding Vol. Leadership award named in his honor, Western N.Y. chpt. ALA, 1994—, Perry Scholarships presented in his honor, U. Buffalo Found., 1991—, Humanitarian award, Coordinated Care Assn., 2002; fellow Wisdom Hall of Fame fellow, Wisdom Soc., 1999. Fellow: Assn. Schs. of Allied Health Professions (pres. 1969—70, Cert. of Merit 1977, Pres.'s award 1978, Honors of Soc. award 1984); mem.: Nat. Rehab. Assn., Am. Pers. and Guidance Assn., Am. Dietetics Assn. (hon.), APA, Phi Beta Kappa, Delta Tau Delta, Phi Delta Kappa (pres. 1955). Home: 83 Bryant St Apt 5A Buffalo NY 14209-1831

PERRY, JAMES ALFRED, b. Dallas, Sept. 27, 1945; BA in Fisheries, Colo. State U., 1968; MA, Western State Coll., 1973; PhD, Idaho State U., 1981. Sr. water quality specialist Idaho Div. Environ., Pocatello, 1974-82; area mgr. Centrac Assocs., Salt Lake City, 1982; H.T. Morse disting. prof. water quality U. Minn., St. Paul, 1982—, head dept. fisheries, wildlife, conservation biol., 2000—, dir. natural resources policy and mgmt., 1985—, dir. grad. studies in water resources, 1988—92, 1999—2001; dep. dir. AID-funded Environ. Tng. Project for Ctrl. and Ea. Europe, 1992-96; spl. asst. to dean grad. sch. U. Minn., St. Paul, 1996-2000. Vis. scholar Oxford U., Green College, Eng., 1990-91; internat. cons. in water quality. Author: Water Quality Management of a Natural Resource, 1996, Ecosystem Management for Central and Eastern Europe, 2001; editor: Jour. Natural Resources and Life Scis. Edn. Charter mem. Leadership Devel. Acad., Lakewood, Minn., 1988; bd. dirs. Minn. Ctr. for Environ. Advocacy. Recipient Richard C. Newman Art of Tchg. award, 1998, Morse-Alumni award, 1999; ACOP/ESCOP nat. leadership fellow, 1995-96; CIC acad. leadership fellow, 2000-01. Mem.: The Soc. for Conservation Biology, The Wildlife Soc., Am. Fisheries Soc., N.Am. Benthol. Soc. (exec. bd. Albuquerque 1990—91), Internat. Soc. Theoretical and Applied Limnology, Internat. Water Resources Assn., Am. Water Resources Assn., Minn. Acad. Scis. (bd. dirs. 1987—90), Gamma Sigma Delta (merit award 2001), Xi Sigma Pi, Sigma Xi. Office: U Minn Dept Fisheries Wildlife amd Cpmservation Biology 204 Hodson Hall 1980 Folwell Ave Saint Paul MN 55108-1037 E-mail: jperry@umn.edu.

PERRY, JAMES DEWOLF, retired management consultant; b. Providence, June 24, 1941; s. James DeWolf and Adela (Daingerfield) P.; m. Velura Flora Fifield, Dec. 10, 1966 (div. 1975); children: James DeWolf VI, Robert Scott, Leigh Daingerfield; m. Shirley M. Dunn, May 17, 1986; 1 stepchild, Andre David Simon Bernier. AB, Harvard U., 1963. Fgn. service officer State Dept., Washington, 1964-70; spl. asst. to chancellor U. Mass., Amherst, 1970-75; dir. devel. New Eng. Home for Little Wanderers, Boston, 1975-76, Wheelock Coll., Boston, 1976-78; mktg. dir. Boston Zool. Soc., 1978-81; exec. dir. Big Bro. Assn., Boston, 1981-85, South Shore Day Care, Weymouth, Mass., 1985-87; mgmt. cons. to non-profit orgns. Lenox, 1978-95. Mem. Soc. of Cin.

PERRY, JAMES E. not-for-profit development executive; b. Franklin, N.J., Dec. 18, 1957; s. Evan and Emeline (Norman) Hendershot. Student, Kansas Wesleyan U., 1975-79. Exec. dir. Hospice Green Country, Tulsa, 1989-92; dir. devel. Stop AIDS, Chgo., 1993-94; pres. Genesis Assocs., 1994-96; dir. devel. Voices for Ill. Children, 1996—. Pres. Tulsa Oklahomans for Human Rights, 1987-88; chair Tulsa Human Rights Commn., 1990-93; trustee, pres. Eagle Condor Inst., 2000—. Mem. Nat. Soc. Fundraising Execs., Am. Mktg. Assn. Democrat. Episcopal. Office: 208 S LaSalle St Ste 1490 Chicago IL 60604

PERRY, JAMES FREDERIC, philosophy educator, writer; b. Washington, Jan. 21, 1936; s. Albert Walter and Helene Anna Maria (Neumeyer) P.; m. Sandra Jean Huizing, Feb. 18, 1957 (div. May 1972); children: Sandra Elaine, James Frederic Jr., Bartholomew; m. Roberta Schofield, June 6, 1984. Student, Princeton U., 1953-56, Marietta (Ohio) Coll., 1958-60; BA with honors in Philosophy, Ind. U., 1962, PhD in Philosophy of Edn., 1972. NDEA fellow in philosophy U. N.C., 1962-65; instr. N.C. State U., Raleigh, 1965-66; Univ. fellow Ind. U., 1971, adj. lectr., 1972-75; prof. philosophy Hillsborough Community Coll., Tampa, Fla., 1975-97, hons. prof. philosophy, 1997—. Adj. prof. philosophy U. South Fla., 2000—. Author: Random, Routine, Reflective, 1989; contbr. articles to profl. jours. Precinct committeeman Dem. Party, Tampa, 1988—. Nat. Def. Edn. Act fellow U. N.C., 1962-65, Univ. fellow Ind. U., 1970-71. Mem. AAUP (pres. Fla. conf. 1986-89, chair com. "A" on acad. freedom 1989-2002), C.C. Humanities Assn. (so. divsn. exec. bd. 1981-89), Am. Philos. Assn., Fla. Philos. Assn., Internat. Soc. Philos. Enquiry, Internat. Congress for Critical Thinking and Moral Critiques (founding mem. S.E. coun. 1991), World Congress Philosophy, Princeton Alumni Assn. of Fla. Suncoast (sec. 1983-86, pres. 1986-95), Mensa, Authors Guild, Textbook and Acad. Authors Assn., Nat. Collegiate Honors Coun. Avocations: travel, foreign travel, genealogy. Office: Hillsborough C C PO Box 10561 Tampa FL 33679-0561 E-mail: philart@gte.net.

PERRY, JON ROBERT, lawyer; b. Kane, Pa., May 14, 1965; s. James Felix and Judith Rose (Zelina) P.; m. Joni Lee Detrick, Aug. 10, 1991; children: Alex Joseph, Trevor James. BA summa cum laude, Pa. State U., 1987; JD magna cum laude, Duquesne U., 1991. Bar: Pa. 1991, U.S. Dist. Ct. (we. dist.) Pa. 1991, U.S. Ct. Apppeals (3d, 6th, 7th and fed. cirs.). Assoc. Reed Smith Shaw & McClay, Pitts., 1990-94; ptnr. Betts & Perry, 1994-97, Meyers Rosen Louik & Perry, Pitts., 1998—. Bd. dirs. Flying Pig Theatre, Pitts., J's Place, Inc., Kane, RBCI, Inc., Cranberry, Pa., CDS, Inc., Pitts. Exec. editor Duquesne Law Rev., 1991. Vol. mentor/spkr. elem. and high schs., Pitts., 1992—; founder Pennies From Heaven Children's Charity. Mem. ATLA, Pa. Trial Lawyers Assn., Pa. Bar Assn., Allegheny County Bar Assn., Allegheny County Acad. Trial Lawyers, Phi Beta Kappa. Office: Meyers Rosen Louik and Perry 437 Grant St Pittsburgh PA 15219-6002

PERRY, JORDAN LEE, music educator; b. Moberly, Mo., Oct. 21, 1962; s. Ray Elmo Perry and Carolyn Sue Jackson; m. Lori Lynn Glasgow, Oct. 26, 1991; children: Kyler Jordan. BS, U. of Mo. Columbia, Columbia, MO, 1981—87, MA, 1988—2001. Teaching Certificate U. of Mo. Music educator Callaway County Schools, New Bloomfield, Mo., 1987—88; asst. band dir. Rolla Pub. Schools, Rolla, 1988—89; police officer U. of Mo. Police, Colombia, 1989—2000; assoc. band dir. Moberly Pub. Schools, Moberly, 2000—. Dir. Moberly H.S. Jazz Band, Moberly, Mo., 2000—. Mem. Moberly Area Arts Coun., Moberly, Mo., 2000; dir. Moberly Area Cmty. Band, 2000. Recipient Cert. Of Excellence, Mo. Fine Arts Acad., 2002. Mem.: Mo. Music Educators Assn., Mo. Bandmasters. Office: Moberly High School 1625 Gratz Brown Drive Moberly MO 65270

PERRY, JOSEPH N. bishop; b. Chgo., Apr. 18, 1948; Ordained priest Roman Cath. Ch., 1975. Pastor All Sts. Parish, Milw.; episcopal vicar Vicariate VI; consecrated aux. bishop, 1998; aux. bishop Archdiocese of Chgo., 1998—. Office: PO Box 733 South Holland IL 60473-0733

PERRY, KATHRYN ABBOTT, telecommunications engineer; b. Mobile, Ala., Mar. 19, 1958; d. Thomas William South and Nancy Jeanne (Abbott) Smith; m. Russell Owen Perry, July 2, 1988. Student, DeVry Tech. Inst., 1997—. Network analyst Trust Co. Bank, Atlanta, 1980-85; network coord. Crawford & Co. Risk Mgmt., 1985-88; telecomm. ops. mgr. First Interstate Bank Tex., Houston, 1988-90; sr. sys. engr. LDDS World Comm. (formerly Wiltel), Atlanta, 1990-98; sr. ops. mgr. Rapid Link USA, Marietta, Ga., 1998—. Co-founder AT&T Sys. 75 User Group. Episcopalian. Avocations: gardening, fishing. Office: Rapid Link USA 1000 Circle 75 Pkwy SE Atlanta GA 30339-3026

PERRY, KENNETH WALTER, retired integrated oil company executive; b. Shamrock, Tex., Feb. 24, 1932; s. Charles Bowman and Sunshine Virginia (Grady) P.; m. Mary Dean Sudderth; children: Mary Martha Ernst, Kathryn Virginia. BSME, U. Okla., 1954. Sales engr. Mid-Continent Oil Well Supply Co., 1954-55; with Cosden Oil & Chem. Co., Big Spring, Tex., from 1957, jr. engr., 1957-59, project engr., 1959-60, chem. salesman, 1960-64, chem. products mgr., 1964-65, mktg. mgr., then v.p. mktg., 1965-69, v.p. chems., 1969-72, sr. v.p., 1972-76, pres., from 1976; group v.p. Am. Petrofina, Inc., Dallas, 1976-85, sr. v.p., 1985—89, pres., CEO, 1989, vice chmn., bd. dirs., 1989-92; CEO Nimir Petroleum Co. Ltd., 1992-96; ret., 1992. CEO United Commerce Bank, Highland Village, Tex., 1990—91. Mem. bd. govs. Dallas Symphony Orch., 1987-93; bd. dirs. Dallas Coun. World Affairs, 1980; mem. engring. com. U. Okla. Aerospace, Nuclear, 1982; bd. dirs. Colo. Mcpl. Water Dist., 1972; bd. visitors Coll. Engring., U. Okla., 1990—. 1st lt. USASC, 1955-57. Mem. Am. Petroleum Inst. (bd. dirs. 1986-90), Nat. Petroleum Coun., Nat. Petroleum Refiners Assn. (chmn. petrochem. com. 1984-87), Ctr. Strategic and Internat. Studies, 25-Yr. Clubs, Petroleum Industry Club, Petrochem. Industry Club, Northwood Club, Dallas Petroleum Club.

PERRY, KENNETH WILBUR, accounting educator; b. Lawrenceburg, Ky., May 21, 1919; s. Ollie Townsend and Minnie (Monroe) P.; m. Shirley Jane Kimball, Sept. 5, 1942; 1 dau., Constance June (Mrs. Linden Warfel). BS, Eastern Ky. U., 1942; MS, Ohio U., 1949; PhD, U. Ill., 1953; LL.D., Eastern Ky. U., 1983. C.P.A., Ill. Instr. Berea Coll., 1949-50, U. Ky., summer 1950; teaching asst. U. Ill. at Champaign, 1950-53, asst. prof. accounting, 1953-55, asso. prof., 1955-58, prof., 1958—, Alexander Grant prof., 1975—. Vis. prof. Northeastern U., summer 1966, Parsons Coll., 1966-67, Fla. A. and M. U., fall 1971; Carman G. Blough prof. U. Va., fall 1975; dir. Illini Pub. Co. Author: Accounting: An Introduction, 1971, Passing the C.P.A. Examination, 1964, (with N. Bedford and A. Wyatt) Advanced Accounting, 1960; contbg. author: Complete Guide to a Profitable Accounting Practice, 1965, C.P.A. Review Manual, 1971; Editor: The Ill. C.P.A, 1968-70; contbg. editor: Accountants' Cost Handbook, 1960. Served to maj. AUS, 1942-46; col. Res. ret. Named outstanding alumnus Eastern Ky. U., 1969 Mem. Am. Accounting Assn. (v.p. 1963, Outstanding Educator award 1974), Am. Inst. C.P.A.'s, Am. Statis. Assn., Nat. Assn. Accountants (dir. 1969-71), Ill. Soc. C.P.A.s (chair in accountancy), Beta Alpha Psi, Beta Gamma Sigma (Distinguished scholar 1977-78), Omicron Delta Kappa. Methodist. Home: 2314 Fields South Dr Champaign IL 61822-9302 Office: Commerce W U Ill Champaign IL 61822

PERRY, LEE ROWAN, retired lawyer; b. Chgo., Sept. 23, 1933; s. Watson Bishop and Helen (Rowan) P.; m. Barbara Ashcraft Mitchell, July 2, 1955; children: Christopher, Constance, Geoffrey. BA, U. Ariz., 1955, LLB, 1961. Bar: Ariz. 1961. Since practiced in, Phoenix; clk. Udall & Udall, Tucson, 1960-61; mem. firm Carson, Messinger, Elliott, Laughlin & Ragan, 1961-99. Mem. law rev. staff, U. Ariz., 1959-61. Mem. bd. edn. Paradise Valley Elem. and H.S. Dists., Phoenix, 1964-68, pres., 1968; mem. bd. edn. Osborn Elem. Sch. Dist., Phoenix, 2002; treas. troop Boy Scouts Am., 1970-72; mem. Ariz. adv. bd. Girl Scouts U.S.A., 1972-74, mem. nominating bd., 1978-79; bd. dirs. Florence Crittenton Services Ariz., 1967-72, pres., 1970-72; bd. dirs. U. Ariz. Alumni, Phoenix, 1968-72, pres., 1969-70; bd. dirs. Family Service Phoenix, 1974-75; bd. dirs. Travelers Aid Assn. Am., 1985-89; bd. dirs. Vol. Bur. Maricopa County, 1975-81, 83-86, pres., 1984-85; bd. dirs. Ariz. div. Am. Cancer Soc., 1978-80, Florence Crittenton div. Child Welfare League Am., 1976-81; bd. dirs. Crisis Nursery for Prevention of Child Abuse, 1978-81, pres., 1978-80; Ariz. dir. Devereux Found., 1996-2000, vice chmn. 1996-98. 1st lt. USAF, 1955-58. Mem. State Bar Ariz. (conv. chmn. 1972), Rotary (dir. 1971-77, 95-96, pres. 1975-76, West Leadership award 1989), Ariz. Club (bd. dirs. 1994-2002, pres.-elect 1997-98, pres. 1998-99), Phoenix Country Club, Phi Delta Phi, Phi Delta Theta (pres. 1954). Republican. Episcopalian. Home: 106 N Country Club Dr Phoenix AZ 85014-5443 E-mail: imlerp@att.net.

PERRY, LEWIS CHARLES, emergency medicine physician, osteopath; b. La Plata, Mo., Apr. 22, 1931; s. Lewis C. and Emily B. Perry; m. M. Sheryl Gupton, Oct. 30, 1953; children: David, Susan, Stephen, John. BS, U. Mo., 1958; postgrad., Louisville Presbyn. Sem., 1958-60; DO, Kirksville Coll. Osteo. Medicine, 1967. Intern Midcities Meml. Hosp., Arlington, Tex.; parish min. Presbyn. Bd. Nat. Missions, Canada, Ky., 1960-62; intern Mid Cities Meml. Hosp., Arlington; pvt. practice, Ingleside, Tex., 1968-72, Tucson, 1972-81; emergency physician Tucson Gen. Hosp., 1981-88, pres. med. staff, 1978-79, clin. instr., 1981-88; emergency physician Meml. Med. Ctr. East Tex., Lufkin, 1988—. Clin. instr. Osteo. Coll. Pacific, Pomona, Calif., 1985-88. Pres. Helping Hands, Ingleside, 1969-72; bd. dirs., pres. Salvation Army, Tucson, 1978-81; commr. Cub Scouts Am., Tucson, 1975-76; bd. dirs. Unity of Tucson, Inc., 1986-88; pres. bd. dirs. Unity of Nacogdoches, 1993-94. 1st lt. USAF, 1952-56. Named Physician of Yr., Tucson Gen. Hosp., 1978; recipient God and Country award Boy Scouts of Am., 1960. Mem. Am. Legion, Rotary (recipient God and Country award), Masons, Scottish Rite, Shrine. Avocations: cooking, gardening. Home: 1 Columbia Ct Lufkin TX 75901-7212

PERRY, LEWIS CURTIS, historian, educator; b. Somerville, Mass., Nov. 21, 1938; s. Albert Quillen and Irene (Lewis) P.; m. Ruth Opler, June 5, 1962 (div. 1970); 1 child, Curtis Allen; m. Elisabeth Israels, Nov. 26, 1970; children: Susanna Irene, David Mordecai. AB, Oberlin Coll., 1960; MS, Cornell U., Ithaca, N.Y., 1964; PhD, Cornell U., 1967. Asst. prof. history SUNY, Buffalo, 1966-72, assoc. prof., 1972-78; prof. Ind. U. Bloomington, 1978-84; Andrew Jackson prof. history Vanderbilt U., 1984-99, dir. Am. Studies, 1992-95; John Francis Bannon prof. history St. Louis U., 1999—. Ampart lectr. U.S. Info. Service, India and Nepal, 1986, France, 1989; vis. prof. U. Leeds, 1988-89; vis. Raoul Wallenberg fellow Rutgers U., 1991-92. Author: Radical Abolitionism, 1973, reissue, 1995, Childhood, Marriage, and Reform, 1980, Intellectual Life in America, 1984, 2nd edit. 1989, Boats Against the Current, 1993; co-author: Patterns of Anarchy, 1966, Antislavery Reconsidered, 1979; co-editor Moral Problems in American Life, 1998; editor: Jour. Am. History, 1978-84, American Thought and Culture Series, 1985—. Pres. Unitarian-Universalist Ch., Bloomington, Ind., 1983-84; mem. Ralph Waldo Emerson prize com. Phi Beta Kappa, 1997-99, chair, 1999. N.Y. State Regents fellow, 1965-66, Am. Coun. Learned Socs. fellow, 1972-73, Nat. Humanities Inst. fellow, 1975-76, John Simon Guggenheim Found. fellow, 1991, NEH fellow, 1987-88. Mem.: Soc. Historians Early Am. Republic, Am. Hist. Assn., Orgn. Am. Historians (editor 1978—84, exec. bd. 1996—99). Office: St Louis U Dept History 3800 Lindell Blvd Saint Louis MO 63156-0907 E-mail: perryl@slu.edu.

PERRY, LILLIAN DUNN, musician; b. New Orleans, Oct. 24, 1914; d. Henderson Hollowell and Lillian Landry Dunn; m. Robert N. Perry, June 25, 1940 (dec. Oct. 1989); children: Robert, Beatrice Perry Stanley. BA, Dillard U., 1940; MusM, Columbia U., 1955. Tchr. music and English Lockett Elem. Sch., New Orleans, 1933-53, Woodson Jr. H.S., New Orleans, 1953-67; vocal music cons. Orleans Parish Schs., 1967-76; tchr. class tchrs. Tulane U., 1969-78; pianist City Coun. New Orleans, 1986—; dir., accompanist Robert Perry TV Singers, New Orleans, 1986—; organist, choir dir. St. Paul's Luth. Ch., 1998—. Musician, choir dir. Dillard U. Alumni Choir, New Orleans. Chaplain Friends of Amistad, New Orleans, 1992—; bd. mem. YMCA, New Orleans, Women in Fellowship, New Orleans, Greater New Orleans Fedn. Chs., Mayor's Elder Action Coalition, New Orleans; co-chairperson Customer Adv. Coun., Post Office, New Orleans, 2001—. Recipient Disting. Alumnus award Dillard U., New Orleans, 1982, Humanitarian award Ctrl. Ch., New Orleans, 1999; named Musician of the Decade, Gov. La., Baton Rouge, 1994, Outstanding Citizen of the Yr., Omega Psi Phi, Rho Phi chpt., 1996. Mem. AARP (chpt. program dir.), Lutheran. Home: 7320 Arbor Dr New Orleans LA 70126-3025

PERRY, LOIS WANDA, safety and health administrator; b. Seattle, Dec. 29, 1937; d. William and Ethel Lenora (Benson) Abrahamson; m. S. Peter Perry, Jan. 12, 1991; stepchildren: Christopher, Tony. BA, Pacific Luth. U., 1962; postgrad., Gonzaga U., 1984. Cert. vocat. rehabilitaton counselor. Claims rep. Social Security Adminstrn., Calif. and Oreg., 1962-69; field rep. Oreg. Dept. of Labor and Industries, Salem, Oreg., 1969-72; safety cons. and trainer, regional safety coord. Wash. Dept. of Labor and Industries, Spokane, 1987—. Guardian Ad Litem Spokane County Juvenile Ct., 1989-98. Mem. AAUW (pres. Spokane Valley Br., membership v.p. Valley br. 1992-94, program v.p., co-chair 1994—, com. chair Downtown br. 1989-90, bd. dirs. 1989-90), ASTD (bd. dirs. Spokane-Inland N.W. chpt. 1992), Spokane Tng. Consortium. Democrat. Lutheran. Avocations: gardening, traveling, textile design. Home: 914 S Mckinzie Rd Liberty Lake WA 99019-9685 Office: Wash State Dept Labor & Industries 901 N Monroe St Ste 100 Spokane WA 99201-2148

PERRY, LOUIS BARNES, retired insurance company executive; b. Los Angeles, Mar. 4, 1918; s. Louis Henry and Julia (Stoddard) P.; m. Genevieve Patterson, Feb. 8, 1942; children: Robert Barnes, Barbara Ann, Donna Lou. BA, UCLA, 1938, MA, 1940, PhD, 1950; fellow in econs., Yale U., 1941; LL.D., Pacific U., 1964; L.H.D., Whitman Coll., 1967, Linfield Coll., 1981; D.C.S., Willamette U., 1977. Teaching asst. UCLA, 1940-41, research teaching asst., 1946-47; faculty Pomona Coll., 1947-59, asst. to pres., 1955-57, prof. econs., 1957-59; pres. Whitman Coll., Walla Walla, Wash., 1959-67; v.p., treas. Standard Ins. Co., Portland, Oreg., 1967-68, exec. v.p., 1968-71, pres., 1972-83, chmn., 1983-85, also bd. dirs. Investment counselor, broker Wagenseller & Durst, L.A., 1951-59; rsch. coord. So. Calif. Rsch. Coun., 1952-54; cons. Carnegie Survey Bus. Edn., 1957-58. Author: (with others) Our Needy Aged, 1954, A History of the Los Angeles Labor Movement, 1963; Contbr. (with others) articles to profl. jours. Mem. Oreg. Bd. Higher Edn., 1975-87, pres., 1975-80. Served to maj. AUS, World War II; lt. col. Res. Mem. Am. Coll. Life Underwriters (trustee 1972-81), Rotary, Phi Beta Kappa, Beta Gamma Sigma, Phi Delta Kappa, Pi Gamma Mu, Alpha Gamma Omega, Artus. Methodist. Home: 1585 Gray Lynn Dr Walla Walla WA 99362-9282 *In looking back over the years, an unspoken and oftentime subliminal guiding principle has been to reach beyond one's realistic grasp. This concept coupled with an interest in treating others as one would like to be treated has made it possible to react to new challenges. Successfully meeting the latter has provided a varied career in a number of different fields of activity.*

PERRY, MALCOLM BLYTHE, biologist, researcher; b. Birkenhead, Cheshire, Eng., Apr. 26, 1930; s. Cyril A. and Hilda P. (Blythe) Perry; m. Eileen M. Perry, Aug. 10, 1956 (dec. Dec. 1981); children: Sara Jane, Judith Anne; m. Philomena C. Kingsley, July 25, 2001. B.Sc., U. Bristol, Eng., 1953; PhD, U. Bristol, 1956, D.Sc., 1969. Banting research fellow Queen's U., Kingston, Ont., Can., 1955, asst. prof., 1956-60, R.S. McLaughlin research prof., 1960-62; sr. research officer Nat. Research Council, Ottawa, Ont., 1962-81, prin. research officer, 1981—. Scientist U. Cambridge, Eng., 1969, U. Paris, 1979; prof. U. Ottawa, 1982 Contbr. articles to profl. jours. Fellow Royal Soc. Can., Royal Inst. Chemistry; mem. Can. Soc. Microbiology (award 1991), Am. Soc. Microbiology. Home: 769 Hemlock Rd Ottawa ON Canada K1K 0K6 Office: NRC 100 Sussex Dr Ottawa ON Canada K1A 0R6 E-mail: malcolm.perry@nrc.ca.

PERRY, MALCOLM OLIVER, vascular surgeon; b. Allen, Tex., Sept. 3, 1929; BA, U. Tex., 1951; MD, U. Tex., Dallas, 1955. Diplomate Am. Bd. Surgery, Am. Bd. Gen. Vascular Surgery. Intern Letterman Army Hosp., San Francisco, 1955-56; resident in surgery Parkland Meml. Hosp., Dallas, 1958-62; fellow in vascular surgery U. Calif., San Francisco, 1962-63; asst. prof. surgery U. Tex., Dallas, 1962-67, assoc. prof. surgery, chief vascular surgery, 1967-71, prof. surgery, chief vascular surgery, 1971-74; prof. surgery U. Wash., Seattle, 1974-77; prof. surgery, chief vascular surgery Cornell U. Med. Coll., N.Y.C., 1978-87, Vanderbilt U. Sch. Medicine, Nashville, 1987-91; chief vascular surgery Tex. Tech U. Health Scis. Ctr., Lubbock, 1991-95; prof. surgery Southwestern Med. Sch., Dallas. Capt. USAF, 1955-58; major Tex. Air N.G., 1960-66. Home: RR 2 Box 830 Jacksonville TX 75766-9815 Office: U Tex Dept Surgery Southwestern Med Sch 5323 Harry Hines Blvd Dallas TX 75390-7208 also: St Paul Med Ctr Dept Surgery 5939 Harry Hines Blvd Dallas TX 75235-6246

PERRY, MARGARET, librarian, writer; b. Cin., Nov. 15, 1933; d. Rufus Patterson and Elizabeth Munford (Anthony) P. AB, Western Mich. U., 1954; Cert. d'etudes Francaises, U. Paris, 1956; MSLS, Cath. U. Am., 1959. Young adult and reference libr. N.Y. Pub. Libr., N.Y.C., 1954-55, 57-58; libr. U.S. Army, France and Germany, 1959-63, 64-67; chief circulation U.S. Mil. Libr., West Point, N.Y., 1967-70; head edn. libr. U. Rochester, 1970-75, asst. prof., 1973-75, assoc. prof., 1975-82, asst. dir. librs. for reader svcs., 1975-82, acting dir. librs., 1976-77, 80; univ. libr. Valparaiso U., Ind., 1982-93; ret., 1993. Mem. Task Force on Coop. Edn., Rochester, 1972; freelance writer Mich. Land Use Inst., 1995—. Author: A Bio-bibliography of Countee P. Cullen, 1903-1946, 1971, Silence to the Drums: A Survey of the Literature of the Harlem Renaissance, 1976, The Harlem Renaissance, 1982, The Short Fiction of Rudolph Fisher, 1987; also numerous short stories; contbr. articles to profl. jours. Bd. dirs. Urban League, 1978-80 Recipient 1st prize short story contest Armed Forces Writers League, 1966; 2d prize Frances Steloff Fiction prze, 1968, 1st prize short story Arts Alive, 1990, 2d prize short story Willow Rev., 1990; seminar scholar Schloss Leopoldskron, Salzburg, Austria, 1956, 3d prize short story West Shore C.C., Scottville, Mich., 1995. Mem. ALA. Democrat. Roman Catholic. Avocations: violin and viola, collecting book marks, gardening, reading, travel. Home: 15050 Roaring Brook Rd Thompsonville MI 49683-9216 E-mail: mperry@aliens.com.

PERRY, MARILYN See PERRY-WIDNEY, MARILYN

PERRY, SIR MICHAEL (SIR MICHAEL SYDNEY PERRY), industrialist; b. Eastbourne, Sussex, U.K., Feb. 26, 1934; s. Sydney Albert and Jessie Kate (Brooker) P.; m. Joan Mary Stallard, Oct. 8, 1958; children: Carolyn Clare, Deborah Anne, Andrew John William. MA, St. John's Coll., Oxford, U.K., 1957. From mem. staff to chmn. Unilever PLC, London, 1957—92, chmn., 1992—96; chmn. Dunlop Slazenger Group Ltd., 1996—2001; chmn. Centrica PLC, 1997—. Non-exec. dir. Bass Plc, London; chmn. Japan Trade Group, London, 1985-98; dep. chmn. Bass PLC, 1991-2001; non exec. dir. Marks & Spencer Ltd., 1996-2001; chmn. Shakespeare Globe Trust, 1993, chmn.; v.p., then pres. Liverpool (Eng.) Sch. Tropical Medicine, 1993-2001; non exec. dir. Brit. Gas, 1992, 1997; mem. supervisory bd. Royal Ahold; pres. Mktg. Coun. Decorated Knight Bachelor; decorated comdr. Brit. Empire, knight grand cross Brit. Empire; award GBE double knighthood, 2002. Mem. Oriental Club. Avocations: golf, music. Office: Centrica Plc Head Office Millstream Maidenhead Rd Windsor Berkshire SL4 5GD England

PERRY, MICHAEL CLINTON, physician, medical educator, academic administrator; b. Wyandotte, Mich., Jan. 27, 1945; s. Clarence Clinton and Hilda Grace (Wigginton) P.; m. Nancy Ann Kaluzny, June 22, 1968; children: Rebecca Carolyn, Katherine Grace. BA, Wayne State U., 1966, MD, 1970; MS in Medicine, U. Minn., 1975. Diplomate Am. Bd. Internal Medicine, Am. Bd. Hematology, Am. Bd. Oncology. Intern in internal medicine Mayo Grad. Sch. Medicine, Rochester, Minn., 1970-71, resident, 1971-72, fellow, 1972-75; instr. Mayo Med. Sch., 1974-75; asst. prof. U. Mo., Columbia, 1975-80, assoc. prof., 1980-85, prof., 1985—, chmn. dept. medicine, 1983-91, sr. assoc. dean, 1991-94, Nellie A Smith chair oncology, dir. div. hematology/oncology, 1994—. Prin. investigator Cancer and Leukemia Group B, Nat. Cancer Inst., Chgo., 1982—, exec. com., 1982-84, 1987-90. Author, co-author 30 book chpts.; editor: Toxicity of Chemotherapy, 1984, The Chemotherapy Source Book, 1992, 96, Comprehensive Textbook of Thoracic Oncology, 1996; contbr. articles to profl. jours. Recipient Faculty Alumni award U. Mo., Columbia, 1985, Disting. Alumnus award Wayne State U., 1995, Disting. Oncologist of Yr. award So. Assn. Oncology, 2000. Fellow ACP; mem. Am. Soc. Hematology, Am. Soc. Clin. Oncology, Cen. Soc. Clin. Research, Am. Soc. Internal Medicine (Young Internist of Yr. 1981), Sigma Xi, Alpha Omega Alpha. Home: 1112 Pheasant Run Columbia MO 65201-6254 Office: U Mo-Columbia 516 Ellis Fischel Cancer Ctr 115 Business Loop 70 W Columbia MO 65203-3244 E-mail: perrym@health.missouri.edu.

PERRY, NANCY ESTELLE, psychologist; b. Pitts., Oct. 30, 1934; d. Simon Warren and Estelle Cecelia (Zaluski) Reichard; children: Scott, Karen, Elaine. BS, Ohio State U., 1956, MA in Psychology, 1969, PhD in Psychology, 1973. Nurse various locations, 1956-63; psychologist Pub. Schs., Columbus, Ohio, 1970-72; human devel. specialist Madison County (Ohio) Schs., 1972-75; pvt. practice clin. psychology; cons. psychology Worthington, Ohio, 1975-80; tchr. U. Wis. Sch. Nursing, Milw., 1980-88, Milw. Devel. Ctr., 1980-83; pvt. practice Assoc. Mental Health Svcs., 1983-87, Glendale Clinic for Stress Mgmt. and Mental Health Clinics, 1987-98, Cambridge Group, 1999—; pvt. practice life transactions therapy Milw. and Santa Fe, 1999—. Mem. faculty Wis. Profl. Schs.; adj. faculty U. Wis., Milw. Ohio Dept. Edn. grantee, 1973-76. Bd. dirs. Youth Shelters & Family Svcs., Santa Fe. EPDA fellow Ohio State U., 1973; Ohio Dept. Edn. grantee, 1973-76. Fellow Internat. Soc. Study of Dissociation (sec.-treas. 1995-98), Wis. Psychol. Assn.; mem. APA, Am. Soc. Clin. Hypnosis, Am. Assn. Marriage and Family Therapists. Home: 2305 Perilla Ct Santa Fe NM 87505 Office: 110 Delgado St Santa Fe NM 87501-2781 also: 6110 N Port Washington Rd Milwaukee WI 53217-4308

PERRY, NANCY TROTTER, former telecommunications company executive; b. Cleve., Jan. 1, 1935; d. Charles Hanley and Mable Dora (Lowry) Trotter; m. Robert Anthony Perry, Apr. 27, 1957. Student, Dunbarton Coll., 1952-53; BA, W.Va. U., 1999. Svc. rep. C&P Telephone Co., Balt., 1956-60, adminstrv. asst., 1960-67, staff supr., 1967-69; staff mgr., 1969-79; mgr. consumer affairs C&P Telephone Co., Balt., 1979-91. Bd. dirs., founding dir. Balt. Mus. Industry, Md., Info. and Referral Providers Coun., 1990—, sec., 1994-98, v.p. 1999-2002; bd. dirs. Learning Ind. Through Computers, Inc., 1991-99, pres., 1994-96; bd. dirs. Md. Gerontol. Assn., 1991, Md. Consumer Coun., 1991-2000, chair, 1994-96; bd. dirs. Fgn.-Born Info. and Referral Network, 1992-96; bd. dirs. Hearing and Speech Agy., 1989-94, exec. v.p. 1991-94; founding dir. Tele-Consumer Hotline, 1986-92; mem. responding to crisis panel United Way, 1995—, vice chmn., 1995-99, 2001—. Mem. Soc. Consumer Affairs Profls. in Bus., Nat. Fedn. of Blind, Alliance for Pub. Tech., Sons of Italy (v.p. 1997-99, 2001—, trustee 1999-2001, editor Il Giornale). Avocations: travel, reading. Home: 3701 Chatham Rd Ellicott City MD 21042-5105 E-mail: ntperry@prodigy.net.

PERRY, NELSON ALLEN, radiation safety engineer, radiological consultant, retired; b. Louisville, Mar. 26, 1937; s. Leslie Irvin and Sue Helen (Harris) P.; m. Sarita Sue Cornn, Apr. 28, 1956; children: Melody S. Doyle, Kimberly D. Horne. AS, Campbellsville (Ky.) Coll., 1954; BS, U. Louisville, 1961; MS, U. Okla., 1966. Cert. hazard control mgr., hazart material mgt.; lic. med. physicist, Tex. Assoc. prof. Ind. Christian U., Indpls., 1974-76; asst. prof. Ind. U., 1971-75; instr. Ind. Voc. Tech. Coll., 1968-76; health physicist Michael Reese Hosp., Chgo., 1966-68; radiation safety officer St. Francis Hosp., Beech Grove, Ind., 1968-76, Ind. U., Indpls., 1971-74, U. South Ala., Mobile, 1976—, assoc. prof., 1981—2001; radiol. cons. Perry Radiol. Cons., Inc., 1974—2001. Radiol. cons., 1974—. Contbr. articles to profl. jours. Named Ky. Col., 1964; USPHS trainee, 1965-66. Mem. Am. Assn. Physicists in Medicine, Health Physics Soc., Ala. Health Physics Soc. (sec. 1977-79, pres. 1980-81). Republican. Baptist. Avocation: collecting miniatures. Office: U South Ala 257 Csab Mobile AL 36688-0001

PERRY, PAUL ALVERSON, utility executive; b. Farwell, Mich., Apr. 19, 1929; s. LaVerne Seneca and Ruth Valeria (McNeal) P.; m. Mildred Mayhew Small, Apr. 13, 1957; children: Patricia Perry Larson, Ruth Perry Watkins, Robert Paul, Donna Jean. BSBA, Ctrl. Mich. U., 1952. With Consumers Power Co., Jackson, Mich., 1954-84, asst. sec., 1960-68, sec., 1968-84; sec., dir. Mich. Gas Storage Co., Jackson, 1969-84. Dir. No. Mich. Exploration Co.; sec. Plateau Resources Ltd.; sec., dir. Mich. Utility Collection Service Co., Inc. Served with U.S. Army, 1952-54. Mem. Am. Soc. Corp. Secs. Home: 9110 42d St Pinellas Park FL 33782

PERRY, RALPH BARTON, III, lawyer; b. N.Y.C., Mar. 17, 1936; s. Ralph Barton Jr. and Harriet Armington (Seelye) P.; m. Mary Elizabeth Colburn, Sept. 2, 1961; children: Katherine Suzanne, Daniel Berenson. AB, Harvard U., 1958; LL.B., Stanford U., 1963. Bar: Calif. 1964. Assoc. and mem. Keatinge & Sterling, Los Angeles, 1963-68; mem. firm Graven Perry Block Brody & Qualls, 1968—. Bd. dirs. Planning and Conservation League, 1968—, Coalition for Clean Air, 1961—, pres. 1972-80, 85-88. Served with U.S. Army, 1956-58. Mem. ABA (ho. of dels. 1975-95), State Bar Calif., L.A. County Bar Assn., Lawyers Club L.A. County (gov. 1968-82), Keep Tahoe Blue, Nat. Wildlife Fedn., Internat. Wildlife Fedn., Sierra Club, L.A. Athletic. Home: 296 Redwood Dr Pasadena CA 91105-1339 Office: Graven Perry 523 W 6th St Ste 723 Los Angeles CA 90014-1223 E-mail: rbp3@earthlink.net.

PERRY, RANDALL A. business executive; b. Furstenfeldbruk, Germany, Nov. 18, 1955; s. Norman Francis and Elfriede Dorothea (Wachter) P.; m. Donna A. Perry, Apr. 9, 1994; 1 child, Christopher; m. Helen A. Perry, Dec. 11, 1977 (div. Dec. 1992); children: Lea, David, Jonathan, Timothy. BSBA, Kennesaw U., 1981. Dir. reimbursement and legis. affairs Healthdyne, Inc., Marietta, Ga., 1983-85, Abbey Health Care, Inc., Fountain Valley, Calif., 1985-88; dir. reimbursement devel. Genentech, Inc., South San Francisco, 1988-93. Biotech. industry rep. Am. Legis. Exchange Coun., Washington, 1990-93; dir. customer devel. Janssen Pharm., Titusville, N.J., 1993-94; v.p. reimbursement Mckesson/HDS, Scottsdale, Ariz., 1994-96; v.p. bus. devel. Bergen Brunswig/ICS, Addison, Tex., 1996-99; prin. Med. Comm. Techs., Atlanta, 1999—. Author: Biopharmaceuticals in Transition, 1990. With USAF, 1973-75. Mem. Nat. Assn. of Med. Equipment Suppliers (bd. dirs. 1983-88), Health Industry Distributors Assn. (co-chmn. health care reform com. 1985-88), Biotech. Industry Orgn. (co-chmn. health care reform com. 1989-93), Republican. Avocations: snow skiing, mountain biking, rollerblading. Home: 234 Picketts Lake Dr Acworth GA 30101-4787

PERRY, RICHARD JOHN, anthropology educator; b. North Tonawanda, NY, June 13, 1942; m. Alice Pomponio, Oct. 14, 1994; children: Charles Gregory Pomponio, Travis Thomas; m. Patricia Ann Murphy, Feb. 25, 1967 (div. July 11, 1994); children: Richard Aaron, Jaya Ann. BA, Harvard U., Cambridge, Mass., 1966; MA, Syracuse U., Syracuse, N.Y., 1966, PhD, 1971. Prof. of anthropology St. Lawrence U., Canton, NY, 1971—. Author: Western Apache Heritage: People of the Mountain Corridor, 1991, Apache Reservation: Indigenous Peoples and the American State, 1993, From Time Immemorial: Indigenous Peoples and State Systems, 1996, Five Key Concepts in Anthropological Thinking, 2002. Pfc N.G., 1964—70, United States (Massachusetts, New York). Fellow: Am. Anthrop. Assn. Democrat-Npl. Avocations: cooking, fishing, camping. Office: St Lawrence U Park St Canton NY 13617

PERRY, RICK, governor; b. Paint Creek, Tex., Mar. 4, 1950; m. Anita Thigpen; children: Griffin, Sydney. B.Animal Sci., A&M U., 1972. Farmer/rancher; mem. Tex. Ho. of Reps., 1985-90, mem. appropriations and calendars com.; commr. of agr. State of Tex., 1991-98, lt. gov., 1999-2000, gov., 2000—. Active Boy Scouts Am. Capt. USAF, 1972-77 Named One of the Most Effective Legislators, Dallas Morning News, 1989. Mem. Am. Legion. Methodist. Office: Office of Governor PO Box 12428 Austin TX 78711*

PERRY, ROBERT MICHAEL, engineering company executive; b. N.Y.C., Dec. 5, 1931; s. Jerome and Rose P.; m. Frances Diane Gross, Feb. 2, 1957; children— Karen, David, Janice. BSE., U. Mich., 1953; postgrad., Columbia U., 1955-57. Engr. Dames & Moore (Cons. Engrs.), L.A., 1955-60, assoc., 1960-65, ptnr., 1965-75, mng. ptnr., 1975-79, CFO, 1980-96, dir., 1981-98, exec. v.p., 1992-99; chmn., CEO, pres. RMP Inc., Palos Verdes Estates, Calif., 1999—. Pres., dir. RMP Inc., 1972—; bd. dirs. Locus Techs., Trinity Cons., SWCA Inc. Served with C.E. U.S. Army, 1953-55. Mem. ASCE (dir., treas. N.Y. sect. 1964-68). Office: RMP Inc 2376 Via Victoria Palos Verdes Estates CA 90274

PERRY, ROBERT PALESE, molecular biologist, educator; b. Chgo., Jan. 10, 1931; s. Robert John and Gertrude Katherine (Hyman) Palese-Perry; m. Zoila Figueroa, Apr. 28, 1957; children— Rocco, Adele, Monique BS, Northwestern U., 1951; PhD, U. Chgo., 1956; PhD (hon.), U. Paris, 1983. From rsch. assoc. to assoc. mem. Inst. for Cancer Rsch., Fox Chase Cancer Ctr., Phila., 1960-69, sr. mem., 1969—; Stanley Reimann chair in rsch. Fox Chase Cancer Ctr., 1994—; assoc. dir. Inst. for Cancer Rsch., Fox Chase Cancer Ctr., 1971-74; prof. biophysics U. Pa., Phila., 1973-95. Contbr. articles to profl. jours. Guggenheim fellow, 1974; Nat. Acad. scholar USA/USSR Exch. Program, 1987. Mem. Nat. Acad. Scis. (com. on human rights 1979-86), Internat. Cell Rsch. Orgn. (pres. 1983-86), European Molecular Biology Orgn. E-mail: RP. Home: 1808 Bustleton Pike Southampton PA 18966-4608 Office: Inst Cancer Research 7701 Burholme Ave Philadelphia PA 19111-2412 E-mail: RP_Perry@fccc.edu.

PERRY, ROBERT TAD, educational official; b. Iowa City, Mar. 11, 1943; s. Thomas Amherst and Lora Margaret (Turner) P.; m. Jane Lynn Martin, 1965 (div. 1983); children: Tod, Jay; m. Carolyn Summers Cross, 1989. AB, Cen. Meth. Coll., Fayette, Mo., 1965; MA, U. Mo., 1967, PhD, 1972. Program dir. YMCA, Kansas City, Mo., 1965-66; asst. instr. U. Mo., Columbia, 1966-70; asst. prof. Ball State U., Muncie, Ind., 1971-76, assoc. prof., 1976-81, chmn. dept. polit. sci., 1973-77, 79-80, prof., 1981-94, exec. asst. for fiscal rels., 1981-87, asst. provost, 1985-87, assoc. v.p., 1987-94; chief oper. officer Ind. Partnership for Statewide Edn., 1992-94; exec. dir. S.D. Bd. Regents, 1994—. Treas. Acad. Pub. Svc., Ind., 1985-91; lectr. Gov.'s Exec. Devel. Inst., Ind., 1985-89, Clk.-Treas.'s Inst.; cons. city, town and county govts., Ind.; dir. rsch. and econ. devel. planning Ind. Dept. Commerce, 1979-80; commr. Edn. Commn. of States. Author: Black Legislators, 1976; co-author: Indiana State Government, 1977, 2d edit., 1982, Politics & Public Policy in Indiana, 1983; producer videotape "Using Contemporary Tech. for State Relations," 1987; co-producer (video tapes) State House, 1990, Making Legislative Decisions, 1990, Legislative Calender, 1990, Law Making, 1990, Citizen Legislature, 1990. Mem. Western Commn. for Higher Edn., 1994—, vice chair, 2000—01, chair, 2001—02; bd. curators Ctrl. Meth. Coll., 2000—; mem. Fayette City Coun., 1966—71, Ind. State Pers. Bd., 1982—84, Gov.'s Citizenship Edn. Task Force, 1983; chmn. Gov.'s Task Force Welfare Reorgn., 1983—84; bd. dirs. Rural Devel. Telecomms. Network, SD, 1994—95, S.D. Pub. Broadcasting, 1994—, S.D. State Libr., 1994—, Rural Econ. Devel. Commn., 1995—. Recipient Sagamore of the Wabash award Gov. of Ind., 1981, 94. Mem. Am. Soc. Pub. Adminstrn. (pres. Ind. chpt. 1981-82), Coun. for Advancement and Support of Edn. (commn. on govt. rels. 1991-94), State Higher Edn. Exec.

Officers (exec. com. 1998-2001), Nat. Assn. Sys. Heads (sec.-treas. 2002--), Rotary, Exch. Club. Methodist. Home: 133 Hyde Dr Pierre SD 57501-4808 Office: Bd Regents AD104 306 E Capitol Ave Pierre SD 57501-2519 E-mail: Tadp@RIS.sdbor.edu., TadP3@pie.midco.net.

PERRY, ROBERT TERRELL, JR. nuclear engineer, consultant; b. Paris, July 19, 1938; s. Robert Terrell and Eleanor Cordia (Endsley) P.; m. Elisabeth Irmina Scherf, July 1, 1976. BS, Tex. A&M U., 1961, MS, 1967, PhD, 1974. Registered prof. engr., Wis. Sr. engr. EG&G Inc., Las Vegas, 1976-78; scientist Interatom Gmbh, Bensberg, Germany, 1972-75; sr. engr. Battelle Lab, Richland, Wash., 1976-79; scientist U. Wis., Madison, 1979-81; asst. prof. Tex. A&M and Pa. State U., Coll. Sta., Univ. Park, 1981-86; tech. staff Los Alamos (N.Mex.) Nat. Lab., 1987—. Vis. sci. Princeton (N.J.) U., 1975-76, Max Plank Inst., Garching, Germany, 1975; adj. prof. nuclear engring. Tex. A&M U., College Station, 1998—. Contbr. over 200 articles to profl. mags., jours., reports. 1st Lt. U.S. Army, 1961-63, Korea. Recipient Best Tech. Article award Tex. A&M U., 1979. Mem. NRA, Am. Nuclear Soc. (co-chair RP&S tech. program com. 1996—, chair stds. com. 1996—), Los Alamos Soc. Profl. Engrs. (pres. 1996-97), Internat. Radiation Physics Soc., Am. Legion, Masonic Lodge. Libertarian. Mem. Universal Life. Avocations: sailing, exploration. Bus. Home: 394 Catherine Ave Los Alamos NM 87544-3565 Office: Los Alamos Nat Lab MS E541 Los Alamos NM 87545-0001 E-mail: rtperry@lanl.gov., rtp@rt66.com.

PERRY, ROBERTA L. graphics designer; b. Hempstead, N.Y., Mar. 14, 1962; d. Alfred S. and Carolyn I. Tucker; m. Ross D. Perry, Feb. 3, 1985; children: Craig, Eric, Brooke. BFA, L.I. U., 1984. Illustrator (children's book series) A is for Adoption..., 2000, B is for Bandages..., 2001, C is for Capable..., 2001. Corr. sec., vol. Primary and Secondary PTA's, Plainview, 1994—2002. Conservative. Avocations: blading, skiing, gourmet cooking, gardening. Home: 7 Wood Ln Plainview NY 11803 Office: Point To Point Graphics 7 Wood Ln Plainview NY 11803 E-mail: pttopt@optonline.net.

PERRY, RONALD WILLIAM, public affairs educator; b. Phoenix, Nov. 13, 1949; s. Hugh and Katherine Elizabeth (Ham) P.; m. Paula Piper, Mar. 3, 1972; 1 child, Elizabeth. BS, Ariz. State U., 1971, MA, 1973; PhD, U. Wash., 1975. Lectr. sociology Pacific Luth. U., Tacoma, 1973-75; asst. prof. sociology U. Hartford, Conn., 1975-77; sr. research scientist Battelle Inst., Seattle, 1977-83; prof. pub. affairs Ariz. State U., Tempe, 1983—. Mem. com. U.S. emergency preparedness Nat. Acad. Scis., Washington, 1978-81, com. emergency mgmt., 1981-83. Author: Disaster Management, 1984, Comprehensive Emergency Management, 1985, Minority Citizens in Disaster, 1986, Living with Mt. St. Helens Volcano, 1990, Behavioral Foundations of Planning, 1992. Human Adjustment to Volcanoes grantee NSF, 1980—, Flood Response Mgmt. grantee NSF, 1978-80. Mem. Am. Sociol. Assn., Internat. Sociol. Assn., Pacific Sociol. Assn., Ariz. Emergency Services Assn. Office: Sch Pub Affairs Ariz State U Tempe AZ 85287 E-mail: ron.perry@asu.edu.

PERRY, ROTRAUD MEZGER, lawyer; b. Berlin, Aug. 29, 1927; came to U.S., 1927; d. Fritz and Luise (Scheuerle) M.; m. John Wilson Perry, Sept. 9, 1950; children: Erik David, Julia Louise, Kathleen Anne, Duncan Gerrit, Ellen Eva. AB, Bryn Mawr Coll., 1948; JD, U. Mich., 1952. Bar: D.C. 1954, Md. 1974, U.S. Supreme Ct. 1962. Various positions Library of Congress, Washington, 1947-50; atty. USN, 1955-56; sole practice, 1957-78; ptnr. Perry & Perry, 1978-97; retired. Mem. Bar Assn. D.C., D.C. Bar Assn., Women's Bar Assn. D.C. (pres. 1975-76). Democrat. Home: 3511 Idaho Ave NW Washington DC 20016-3151

PERRY, RUTH, writer; b. Balt., Jan. 14, 1936; d. John Dean and Julia (Hicks) P.; 1 child. Student, Morgan State Coll., 1948-51, Cortez Peters Bus. Sch., 1951-52. Author: Behold: A Slave Child, Accent on Slavery, Aftermath Desires, Time Spent, I, Nebra; songwriter Give Me This Day, others; author numerous childrens stories; inventor (toy) Princess Sasha; lyricist 10 songs. Recipient poetry awards World of Poetry; Accomplishment of Merit award Creative Arts and Scis. Enterprises, 1992, 96. Mem. Poetry Soc. Am., Poetry Assn. Am., Nat. Libr. Poetry, Poetry Guild.

PERRY, SARAH HOLLIS, artist; b. Framingham, Mass., Mar. 24, 1934; d. Hollis Stratton and Mary (Norris) French; m. John Curtis Perry, Sept. 14, 1957; children: Elizabeth, Margaret, Rachel, Lyman, Maria. BA, Smith Coll., 1956; diploma, Sch. Mus. Fine Arts, Boston, 1999, cert., 2000. Syss. svc. rep. IBM, Boston, 1956-57; photog. aide Polaroid, Cambridge, 1957-74, asst. to chmn., 1974-82; asst. to dir. rsch. Rowland Inst., 1982-92, archivist, 1992-2001, artist in residence, 1992—2002. Mem. teaching faculty Sch. Mus. Fine Arts, Boston, 1999-2000. Recipient Jurors award Hera Gallery, Providence, 1996, 97, Erector Sq. Gallery, New Haven, 1998, Atlanta Paper Mus., 1999-2000; named winner of competition to create sculpture Tufts U. Libr. Lobby, 1997; Travelling scholar Sch. Mus. Fine Arts, 2000. Mem. Phi Beta Kappa (Zeta of Mass. chpt.). Studio: 35 Norwood Heights Gloucester MA 01930-1212 E-mail: shperry@adelphia.net.

PERRY, SARAH TERESA ANDERSON (TERI PERRY), nurse manager, critical care nurse; b. Flushing, N.Y., Jan. 14, 1957; d. John Thomas and Dorothy Reu (James) Anderson; m. Dennis Michael Perry Sr., Oct. 17, 1981; children: John Thomas, Clayton Foster. ADN, Augusta (Ga.) Coll. Sch. Nursing, 1979; BSN, Med. U. S.C., 1985, MSN, 1987. Shift supr. ICU Univ. Hosp., Augusta, Ga.; staff nurse III Roper Hosp., Charleston, S.C.; nurse mgr. Med. U. S.C. Med. Ctr., mem. biomed. ethics com., 1988-94; nurse mgr. CCU Med. Coll. Ga., Augusta, 1994-96, nurse mgr. cardiology svc. line, 1996—, mem. biomed. ethics com., 1995—; registry coord. Nat. Registry of Myocardial Infarction 2, 1994—. Mem. AACN (pres. Charleston chpt. 1989-90, officer Ctrl. Savannah River Area chpt.), S.C. Nurses Assn., Sigma Theta Tau. Home: 4826 Rocky Shoals Cir Evans GA 30809-7037

PERRY, STEPHEN A. federal agency administrator; b. Ohio; m. Sondra Perry; 5 children. B Acctg., U. Akron; M Mgmt., Stanford U. Various acctg. positions including dir. acctg., dir. purchasing, sr. v.p. Timken, 1964; apptd. dir. Dept. Dept. Admintsrv., 1991; v.p. human resources Timken, 1993, sr. v.p., 1997, ret., 2001; adminstr. Gen. Svcs. Adminstrn., Washington, 2001—. Chmn. bd. trustees Canton Urban League; chmn. Canton Scholar Fund; chmn. bd. trustees Trinken Mercy Med. Ctr.; chmn. Stark County Dist. Libr. Bd., United Way Campaign Ctrl. Start County, 1996, Jr. Achievement, 1999. Named Man of Yr., Canton Christian Hall of Fame, 2000; recipient Disting. Svc. award, Jaycees, 1977, Pres. Social Responsibility award, Kent State U., 1995, Disting. Alumni award, 1996, Dr. Frank L. Simonetti Disting. Bus. Alumnus award, U. Akron, 1999, Disting. Alumni award, Trimken High Sch. Alumni Assn., 1999, U. Akron, 2001. Office: Gen Svcs Adminstrn 1800 F St NW Washington DC 20405

PERRY, STEPHEN CLAYTON, manufacturing executive; b. Atlanta, Feb. 9, 1942; s. Clayton Henry and Elizabeth Hill (Staples) P.; m. Bonnie Janet Bentley, Nov. 27, 1965; 1 child, Beverly Elizabeth. B in Indsl. Engring., Ga. inst. Tech., 1964; MBA, Harvard U., 1968; PhD, George Washington U., 1998. Indsl. engr. Union Carbide Corp., Columbia, Tenn., 1964; sys. analyst metals and controls divsn. Tex. Instruments, Attleboro, Mass., 1967; with Exxon Corp., 1968-86; gen. mgr. Toledo Scale Corp. subs. Reliance Electric Co., Worthington, Ohio, 1984-89; pres. Toledo Scale Corp. (subs. Ciba-Giegy), 1989-90; pres., CEO Easco Hand Tools, Inc., 1990; instr. George Washington U., 1991-94, 99; pres. mfg. divsn. Leucadia, Inc., 1995-98; prof. Gardner-Webb U., 1999—, interim dean Sch. Bus., 2002—, Dover Found. chair bus. adminstrn., 2002—. Mem. engring. adv. bd. Ga. Tech., 1996-2001. Bd. dirs. Ctr. Sci. and Industry, Columbus, Ohio, 1984-89; mem. Berkeley Heights Twp. (N.J.) Com., 1977-79; dep. mayor, police commr., 1978, mayor, 1979; mem. Clemson U. Pres.'s Adv. Coun., 1990-93; dir., trustee Mars Hill Coll., 1997-99; adv. bd. Mars Hill Coll., 1999—. Home: 152 Lakemont Dr Shelby NC 28150-8326 E-mail: sperry@gardner-webb.edu.

PERRY, THOMAS EDMUND, novelist, television screenwriter, producer; b. Tonawanda, N.Y., Aug. 7, 1947; s. Richard Edmund and Elizabeth Marie P.; m. Jo Anne Lee Perry, Aug. 31, 1980; children: Alix Eliabeth, Isabel Rose. BA cum laude, Cornell U., 1969; PhD in English, U. Rochester, 1974. Adminstr. Coll. Creative Studies U. Calif., Santa Barbara, 1975-80, U. So. Calif., L.A., 1980-84; tv writer, prodr., staff Universal Studios, Disney Studios, Viacom Entertainment, 1984-90; freelance writer for tv Cannell Prodns., Paramount Studios, others, 1990—. Author: The Butcher's Boy, 1982, Metzger's Dog, 1983, Big Fish, 1985, Island, 1987, Sleeping Dogs, 1992, Vanishing Act, 1995, Dance for the Dead, 1996, Shadow Woman, 1997, The Face-Changers, 1998, Blood Money, 2000, Death Benefits, 2001, Pursuit, 2001. With Air Nat. Guard, 1970-76. Recipient Edgar Allan Poe award for best first novel Mystery Writers Am., 1983. Mem. Writers' Guild Am., Internat. Assn. Crime Writers.

PERRY, TROY D. clergyman, religious organization administrator; divorced; 2 children. Student, Midwest Bible Sch.; D in Ministry (hon.), Samaritan Coll., L.A.; D in Human Svcs., Sierra U., Santa Monica, Calif. Former pastor Ch. of God of Prophecy, Santa Ana, Calif.; founder, moderator Universal Fellowship Met. Community Chs., L.A. Rep. Met. Community Chs. and gay and lesbian rights movement numerous TV shows including 60 Minutes, Phil Donahue, The Mike Douglas Show; author: The Lord is My Shepherd and Knows I'm Gay, Don't Be Afraid Anymore, 1991, (video) God, Gays and The Gospel: This is Our Story; contbg. editor Is Gay Good? Mem. Los Angeles County Commn. Human Rels.; del. 1st White House Conf. on AIDS, 1993; del. 1st White House Conf. on hate crimes, 1997. Recipient Humanitarian award Gay Press Assn., Equality award Human Rights Campaign, 1996. Office: Universal Fellowship Met Comm Chs 8704 Santa Monica Blvd Fl 2 West Hollywood CA 90069-4548 E-mail: revtroyperry@mccchurch.org.

PERRY, VERNON G. research scientist, educator; b. Boaz, Ala., May 8, 1921; s. George and Bertie Orr Perry; m. Imogene Hyatt, July 28, 1948; children: David K, Ronald L. BS, Aubury, Aubury, AL, 1943; MS, Aubura, Aubura,AL, 1949; Phd, U. Md., College Park, MD, 1954—55. Asst.nematologist ARS-WSDA, Sanford, Fla., 1949—54, assoc. nematologist Madison, Wis., 1955—58; prof. U. of Fla., Gainesville, Fla., 1959; asst. dean U. of Flordia, 1976—87, prof. & asst. dean, 1987. Contbr. chapters to books; editor: (book) Tropical Nematology. 21 2t U.S. Army, 1943—46, pto-Japan. Recipient Best Paper, Fla State Hort Soc, 1963, Am. soc. hort sci., 1969, Hon. Award, Congress Italiano dineatologist, 1974. Fellow: Soc. of Nematologist (assoc.; pres. 1966—67). Presbyterian. Achievements include Elected Fellow Amer Assoc. Adv. Science. Avocations: golf, fishing, gardening. Home: 720 Sw 80th Blvd Gainesville FL 32607

PERRY, WILLIAM JAMES, educator, former federal official; b. Vandergrift, Pa., Oct. 11, 1927; s. Edward Martin and Mabelle Estelle (Dunlap) Perry; m. Leonilla Green, Dec. 29, 1947; children: David, William, Rebecca, Robin, Mark. BS in Math., Stanford U., 1949, MS, 1950; PhD, Pa. State U., 1957. Instr. math. Pa. State U., 1951—54; sr. mathematician HRB-Singer Co., State College, Pa., 1952—54; dir. electronic def. labs. GTE Sylvania Co., Mountain View, Calif., 1954—64; pres. ESL, Inc., Sunnyvale, 1964—77; tech. cons. Dept. Def., Washington, 1967—77, under sec. def. for research and engring., 1977—81; mng. dir. Hambrecht & Quist (investment bankers), San Francisco, 1981—85; chmn. Tech. Strategies & Alliances, Menlo Park, 1985—93; prof., co-dir. Ctr. for Internat. Security and Arms Control Stanford U., 1989—93; apptd. Dep. Sec. Def. Pentagon, Washington, 1993—94, appt. Sec. Def., 1994—97; prof. engring.-econ. sys. and ops. rsch. Stanford (Calif.) U., 1997—. With U.S. Army, 1946—47. Recipient Def. Disting. Svc. medal, U.S. Govt., 1980, 1981, Achievement medal, Am. Electronics Assn., 1980, Forrestal medal, 1994, Henry Stimson medal, 1994, Arthur Bueche medal, NAE, 1996, Eisenhower award, 1996, Presdl. Medal Freedom, 1997, Outstanding Civilian Svc. medals, U.S. Army, 1997, USN, 1997, USAF, 1997, USCG, 1997, NASA, 1997, Def. Intelligence Agy., 1997; fellow sr. fellow, Inst. Internat. Studies, Stanford U., 1997—. Fax: 650-725-0920. E-mail: wjperry@stanford.edu.

PERRY, WILLIAM JOSEPH, food processing company executive; b. Sacramento, Nov. 4, 1930; s. Joseph Nasciemeto and Jennie (Nunez) P.; m. Beverly Ann Styles, Dec. 9, 1956 (div. May 1981); children: Katherine, Bill Jr., Kathleen, Barbara; m. Leslie Z. Blumberg, June 30, 1986. BS, U. Calif., Berkeley, 1953; MBA, U. So. Calif., 1995. Quality control supr. Stokely Van Camp, Oakland, Calif., 1953-54; plant mgr. Safeway Stores, Brookside div., Grandview, Wash., 1954-61, Gallo Winery, Modesto, Calif., 1961-62; gen. mgr. Bocca Bella Olive Assoc., Wallace, 1962-65; v.p. Early Calif. Ind., L.A., 1965-74, Fairmont Foods, Santa Ana, Calif., 1974-75; pres. Cal Agra Ind., Stockton, 1975-76; exec. v.p. Food Brokers Internat., L.A., 1976—; pres., co-owner G.F.F., Inc., 1981—. Dir. G.F.F., Inc., L.A., 1981—, Food Brokers, Inc., L.A., 1976—, Cozad & Assoc. Ad Agy., Encino, Calif., 1985-87. Wrestling com., dir. protocol, L.A. Olympic Com., 1981-84; dir. Nat. Kidney Cancer Assn., 1999. Mem. Nat. Food Brokers Assn., Assn. of Dressings and Sauces, Product Mktg. Assn., Nat. Single Svc. Assn., Am. Chem. Soc., Calif. League Food Processors (dir. 1997), U. Calif. Alumni Assn., U. So. Calif. Alumni Assn., L.A. Athletic Club. Republican. Roman Catholic. Avocations: tennis, photography, bicycling, amateur sports associations. Home: 3700 Brigantine Cir Thousand Oaks CA 91361-3816 Office: 5422 Jillson St Los Angeles CA 90040-2118

PERRY-BÖTTINGER, LYNNE VALENCIA, interventional cardiologist; b. Washington, June 1, 1961; d. Levi V. and Eula F. Perry; m. Erwin Paul Böttinger, Nov. 26, 1994; children: Maximilian, Leopold. AB cum laude, Harvard-Radcliffe U., 1982; MD cum laude, Yale U., 1986. Resident in internal medicine Yale-New Haven Hosp., 1986-89, chief med. resident, 1989-90; fellow in cardiology Johns Hopkins Hosp., Balt., 1990-94; instr. medicine Georgetown Univ. Hosp., Washington, 1996-97; asst. prof. medicine Albert Einstein Coll. Medicine, Bronx, 1997-2000; interventional cardiologist N.Y. Hosp. Queens, Flushing, N.Y., 2000—; clin. asst. prof. medicine Cornell U. Weill Med. Coll.; asst. dir. cardiac cath lab., interventional cardiologist N.Y. Hosp., Queens. Fellow: Am. Coll. Cardiology. Democrat. Roman Catholic. Office: NY Hosp Queens Cardiac Cath Lab 56-45 Main St Flushing NY 11355 E-mail: lvp9001@nyp.org.

PERRY-CAMP, JANE, music educator, pianist; b. Durham, N.C., Oct. 5, 1936; d. Harold Sanford and Margrid (Hagelberg) Perry; m. John Barton Camp, Aug. 20, 1960 (div. Sept. 1970); m. Harold Anthony Schiffman, June 10, 1978. AB magna cum laude, Duke U., 1958; MusM in Piano Performance, Fla. State U., Tallahassee, 1960, PhD in Music Theory, 1968; studied piano with, Edward Kilenyi, Ernst von Dohnanyi. Asst. prof. music Brevard C.C., Cocoa, Fla., 1968-69; faculty St. Petersburg (Fla.) Coll., 1969-73; asst. prof., assoc. prof. Sweet Briar (Va.) Coll., 1974-80; assoc. prof., prof. Sch. Music, Fla. State U., Tallahassee, 1980-96, prof. emeritus, 1996—, Orpheus chair musicology, 1999. Mem. adv. bd. Fla. State U., Music Theory Soc., Tallahassee, 1982-88; bd. dirs. Fla. State U. Friends of Libr., Tallahassee, 1985-87. Pianist: (CDs) Schiffman: Spectrum, My Ladye Jane's Booke: Eighteeen Fugues and Postludes for Piano, 1996, Concerto for Piano and Orchestra, 1999, (LPs) Fantasy for Piano, 1986, Chamber Concertino for Piano and Double Wind Quintet, 1987; contbr. articles to profl. jours. and anthologies. Fellow NEH, Paris, London, 1973-74; faculty fellow Sweet Briar Coll., 1979-80; recipient rsch. grants Fla. State U. Found., 1985-86, Internat. Rsch. and Exch. Bd., Krakow, Poland, 1986. Mem. Am. Soc. 18th Century Studies (pres. 1991-92), SE Am. Soc. 18th Century studies (pres. 1987-88), Mozart Soc. Am. (bd. dirs. 1996-2001), Internat. Soc. Study of Time, Am. Musicol. Soc., Coll. Music Soc. Avocations: gardening, hiking, needlework (knitting, crocheting, sewing). Home: 2304 Don Andres Ave Tallahassee FL 32304-1313 E-mail: jperrycp@mailer.fsu.edu.

PERRYMAN, ROBERT G. surgeon; b. Tulsa, Nov. 20, 1922; BS, U. Tulsa, 1943; MD, U. Okla., 1946. Diplomate Am. Bd. Surgery. Intern U. Okla. Hosps., 1946-47; resident in surgery St. Vincent's Hosp., Toledo, 1949-50; fellow in surgery Cleve. Clin. Hosp., 1950-53; mem. staff St. John's Med. Ctr., Tulsa; clin. prof. surgery U. Okla., 1978-86. Fellow ACS; mem. AMA. Home: 2716 E 39th Pl Tulsa OK 74105-8209

PERRY-WIDNEY, MARILYN (MARILYN PERRY), international finance and real estate executive, television producer; b. N.Y.C., Feb. 11, 1939; d. Henry William Patrick and Edna May (Bown) Perry; m. Charles Leonidas Widney (dec. Sept. 1981). BA, Mexico City Coll., 1957. Pres. Marilyn Perry TV Prodns., Inc., N.Y.C., 1970—, C.L. Widney Internat., Inc., N.Y.C., 1977—. Mng. dir. Donerail Corp., N.Y.C., 1980-88, Lancer, N.Y.C., 1980-88, Assawata, N.Y.C., 1980-88. Prodr., host TV program Internat. Byline, series of more than 100 documentaries on the UN; host 80 radio and 200 pages on Internet series regarding environ. and devel. issues; contbr. pages on environ. and devel. issues to radio and Internet sites; internat. byline-mem. nations UN exec. com. HNCA, 1998, PBS, in S.C., N.C., Ga., Tenn. Bd. dirs. UN After Sch. Program; ambassadorial candidate Pres. Bush., 1989; mem. Gibbes Mus., S.C. Recipient U.S. Indsl. Film Festival award, CINE Golden Eagle award, Bronze medal Internat. Film & TV Festival of N.., Bronzenen Urkinde, Berlin, award for superior quality Intercom-Chgo. Internat. Film Festival, Knights of Malta Trophy award for superior programming from Min. of Tourism, Internationales Tourismus award Film festival, Vienna, Manhattan Cable Ten Year award for continuous programming, citations from former pres. Ford and Carter, King Hussein Jordan, Pres. Clinton, pres. Maumoon Gayoon, Maldives, pres. Jacques Chirac, France. Mem. UN Corrs. Assn., UN After Sch. Programs, Rep. Presdl. Task Force (charter mem.), Harbour Club (S.C.), Gibbes Mus. (S.C.). Avocations: music, travel, antiques, collecting the art of David Roberts. Home: 211 E 70th St Apt 3A New York NY 10021-5206

PERSAUD, TRIVEDI VIDHYA NANDAN, anatomy educator, researcher, consultant; b. Port Mourant, Berbice, Guyana, Feb. 19, 1940; arrived in Canada, 1972; s. Ram Nandan and Deen (Raggy) P.; m. Gisela Gerda Zehden, Jan. 29, 1965; children: Indrani Uta and Sunita Heidi (twins), Rainer Narendra. MD, Rostock U., Germany, 1965, DSc, 1974; PhD in Anatomy, U. West Indies, Kingston, Jamaica, 1970. Intern, Berlin, Germany, 1965-66; govtl. med. officer Guyana, 1966-67; lectr., sr. lectr. anatomy dept. U. West Indies, 1967-72; assoc. prof. anatomy dept. U. Man., Winnipeg, 1972-75, prof., 1975—, prof. ob-gyn., reproductive scis., 1979-99, prof. emeritus, 1999—, prof. pediatrics and child health, 1989—, prof., chmn./head dept. human anatomy & cell sci., 1977-93, dir. Teratology Rsch. Lab., 1972-97. Cons. in teratology, Children's Centre, Winnipeg, 1973—; mem. sci. staff Health Scis. Centre, Winnipeg, 1973—. Author, editor 22 med. textbooks, including: Early History of Human Anatomy: From Antiquity to the Beginning of the Modern Era, 1984, (with others) Basic Concepts in Teratology, 1985, Environmental Causes of Human Birth Defects, 1991, History of Human Anatomy: The Post-Vesalian Era, 1997, (with K.L. Moore) The Developing Human, 6th edit., 1998, Before We Are Born, 5th edit., 1998; contbr. numerous chpts. to books, over 200 articles to profl. jours. Recipient Carveth Jr. Scientist award Can. Assn. Pathologists, 1974, Albert Einstein Centennial medal German Acad. Scis., 1975, Dr. & Mrs. H.H. Saunderson award U. Manitoba, 1985, 12th Raymond Truex Disting. Lectureship award Hahnemann U., 1990. Fellow Royal Coll. Pathologists of London; mem. Can. Assn. Anatomists (pres. 1981-83, J.C.B. Grant award 1991), Am. Assn. Anatomists, Teratology Soc., European Teratology Soc. Office: U Man Dept Anatomy & Cell Sci 730 William Ave Winnipeg MB Canada R3E OW3 E-mail: persaud@ms.umanitoba.ca.

PERSAVICH, WARREN DALE, diversified manufacturing company executive; b. Cleve., Dec. 15, 1952; s. Nick and Sophie (Makris) P.; m. Anita Geraldine Zeleznik, Oct. 12, 1974; children: Nicholas, Katherine. BBA, Kent State U., 1975. CPA, Ohio. Staff acct. Price Water House, Cleve., 1975-76; asst. contr. Banner Industries Inc., 1976-79, contr., 1979-86, treas., 1986-88, v.p., treas., 1988-90; sr. v.p., chief fin. officer Banner Aerospace Inc., 1990-98, sr. v.p., chief oper. officer, 1998-99; pres. Banner Aerospace Distbn. Group, 2000—. Mem. AICPA, Ohio Soc. CPAs. Republican. Office: Banner Aerospace Inc 45025 Aviation Dr Ste 400 Dulles VA 20166-7514

PERSCHBACHER, PETER WESLEY, environmental scientist, educator; b. Davenport, Iowa, Nov. 15, 1946; s. Wesley Adolph and Margaret Pohly P.; m. Virginia Brady, Feb. 14, 1986. BS, U. Mich., 1968; MS, Auburn U., 1975; PhD, Tex. A&M U., 1985. Rsch. assoc. U. N.C. Inst. Marine Sci., Morehead City, N.C., 1975-79; grad. rsch. asst. Tex. A&M U., Baytown, 1980-85; Aquaculture Trainer-Peace Corps Rsch. Planning Inst., Ft. Pierce, Fla., 1983; aquaculture biologist Caribbean Marine Rsch. Ctr., Lee Stocking Island, Bahamas, 1985; aquaculture advisor Harza Engring. Internat., Mymensingh, Bangladesh, 1986-87; rsch. biologist Agrl. Rsch. Svc., USDA, Tishomingo, Okla., 1989-93; assoc. prof. U. Ark., Pine Bluff, 1993—. Cons. KTAADIN, Newton, Mass., Norwegian Govt., Trondheim, Norway. Author: (bibliography) Recirculation-Aeration Bibliography for Aquaculture, 1993; contbg. author: Third National Reservoir Symposium, 1997, Am. Chemical Soc. symposium in Agrl., 2002, Third World Fisheries Congress, Beijing, 2000; contbr. article to N.Am. Jour. of Aquaculture, 1998 (named to top ten papers of 1998), others. Chair Clean and Beautiful Commn. Bd., Pine Bluff, 2000; mem. Racial Harmony Task Force, Pine Bluff, 1996-98; organizer and co-chair Environ. Fair Grace Episcopal Ch., Pine Bluff, 1997, 99, 2001; organizer and chair Waste Mgmt. and Specialty Animal Prodn. Workshops, U. Ark., 1999, Sustainable Aquaculture Session World Aquaculture Soc., Tampa, Fla., 1999; chair Rural Life Conf., Univ. Ark., 2003, small-scale Aquaculture Special Session World Aquaculture Soc., San Diego, 2002. Grantee Mgmt. of Environmentally-Derived Off-Flavors in Warmwater, USDA, Stoneville, Miss., 1995-2000, USDA-CSRS, 1999-2004. Mem. Am. Fisheries Soc., Am. Inst. Fisheries Rsch. Biologists, World Aquaculture Soc., Asian Fisheries Soc., Sigma Xi, Xi Sigma Pi. Democrat. Episcopalian. Avocations: native orchids, palms. Office: Univ Ark at Pine Bluff Mail Slot 4912 Pine Bluff AR 71601 E-mail: pperschbacher@uaex.edu.

PERSCHE, HENRY-PETER, art consultant, artist; b. Bklyn., Nov. 21, 1940; s. Henry-Peter and Marie (Gramegna) P. BFA, U. Buffalo, 1973, postgrad., 1973-74, Coll. St. Rose, 1993-94. Installation dir. for artist Ellsworth Kelly, Spencertown, N.Y., 1966-93; archivist, asst., 1966-93. Installation cons. for artist Ellsworth Kelly exhins. at Sidney Janis Gallery, Loe Castelli gallery, Blum/Helman gallery, N.Y.C., 1996-93, Mus. Modern Art, N.Y.C., 1973, Mus. Nat. d'Art Moderne, Paris, 1980, Stedelijk Mus., Amsterdam, 1979, Kunsthalle, Baden Baden, Germany, 1979, Mus. Nat. d'Art Moderne, Paris, 1980. Exhibited in group shows Albany (N.Y.) Inst. Art, 1973, Albright-Knox Art Gallery, Buffalo, N.Y., 1973. Poll inspector Dem. Party, Ghent, N.Y., 1994-95. With fin. corps. U.S. Army, 1963-66. Mem. Mus. Modern Art (N.Y.C.), Met. Mus. Art, Guggenheim Mus., Whitney Mus. Am. Art, Gottschee Heritage Assn., Gottscheer Relief Assn. Democrat. Roman Catholic. Avocations: collecting art publications, stamps, and photographs, travel, music. Home: 127 Oak St Hawley PA 18428-1039

PERSCHETZ, MARTIN L. lawyer; b. Bklyn., Sept. 15, 1952; s. Louis and Edith (Sandhaus) P.; m. Babs D. Hanfling, Mar. 23, 1980; children: Monica, Keith, Evan. BA, U. Md., 1974; JD, SUNY, Buffalo, 1977. Bar: N.Y. 1978, U.S. Dist. Ct. (so. dist.) N.Y. 1978, U.S. Dist. Ct. (ea. dist.) N.Y. 1979, U.S. Ct. Appeals (2d cir.) 1984, U.S. Dist. Ct. (no. dist.) N.Y. 1989, U.S. Dist. Ct. Colo. 1998. Assoc. Obermaier, Morvillo & Abramowitz, N.Y.C., 1977-80; asst. U.S. atty. So. Dist. N.Y., 1980-86, chief major crimes unit, 1985-86; chief counsel N.Y.C. Spl. Commn. to Investigate City Contracts, 1986; dep. commr. N.Y.C. Dept. Investigation, 1986; spl. counsel Schulte, Roth & Zabel, 1986-87; ptnr. Schulte, Roth & Zabel, LLP, 1988—. Contbr. article to profl. jour. Recipient Joseph Halpern award Buffalo Law Rev., 1977. Mem. ABA, N.Y.C. Bar Assn., N.Y. Coun. Def. Lawyers. Home: 271 Clayton Rd Scarsdale NY 10583-1517 Office: Schulte Roth & Zabel 919 3d Ave New York NY 10022-4774 E-mail: martin.perschetz@sri.com.

PERSELL, CAROLINE HODGES, sociologist, educator, author, researcher, consultant; b. Ft. Wayne, Ind., Jan. 16, 1941; d. Albert Randolph and Katherine (Rogers) Hodges; m. Charles Bowen Persell III, June 17, 1967; children: Patricia Emily, Stephen David. BA, Swarthmore Coll., 1962; MA, Columbia U., 1967, PhD, 1971. Sr. assoc., then nat. coord. Nat. Scholarship Svc. and Fund for Negro Students, N.Y.C., 1962-66; project dir. Bur. Applied Social Rsch., 1968-71; asst. prof. NYU, 1971-76, assoc. prof., 1976-86, prof., 1986—, dir. grad. studies dept. sociology, 1984-87, chair dept. sociology, 1987-93, Robin Williams Disting. lectr., 1993-94. Author: Education and Inequality, 1977, Understanding Society, 1984, 3d edit., 1990; author: (with Cookson) Preparing for Power, 1985, Making Sense of Society, 1992; author: (with Maisel) How Sampling Works, 1996; assoc. editor: Tchg. Sociology, 1983—85, assoc. editor: Sociology of Edn., 1991—95, assoc. editor: Gender & Society, 1992—95; contbr. articles to profl. jours. Carnegie scholar Advancement of Tchg., 2000-01; grantee Fund for Improvement of Postsecondary Edn., 1989-92, NSF Equipment Fund, 1993-96; recipient Faculty Devel. award NSF, 1978-79, Women Educators' Rsch. award, 1978. Mem.: Sociologists for Women in Soc., Ea. Sociol. Soc. (pres. 1995—96), Am. Edn. Rsch. Assn., Am. Sociol. Assn. (chair sect. 1983—84, 1988—89, chmn. publs. com. 1987—89). Avocations: visiting, gardening, opera, sports. Office: NYU Dept Sociology 269 Mercer St New York NY 10003-6633

PERSELLIN, ROBERT HAROLD, physician; b. Fargo, N.D., July 3, 1930; s. James Harry and Bessie (Hoffman) P.; m. Bonnie Feibleman, June 27, 1957 (dec. 1983); children: Kathleen, Jamie; m. Diane Cummings, June 14, 1986 BS, Northwestern U., 1952, MD, 1956, MS, 1959. Diplomate: Am. Bd. Internal Medicine, Am. Bd. Rheumatology. Intern Charity Hosp., New Orleans, 1956-57; resident in internal medicine Northwestern U. Med. Center, 1957-60; fellow in rheumatology Southwestern Med. Sch., 1962-64; asst. prof. medicine U. Oreg. Med. Sch., 1964-68; prof. medicine, head div. rheumatology U. Tex. Health Sci. Center, San Antonio, 1968-81; prof. family practice U. Tex. Health Sci. Ctr., 1993—. Cons. rheumatology VA Hosps., U.S. Army, Internat. Med. Corps, Kosovo and Republic of Moldova; vis. prof. rheumatology Kingstown Med. Coll.; vis. scholar Corpus Christi Coll., Cambridge U., 1979-80; vis. scientist Strangeways Rsch. Lab., Cambridge; cons. Eurasian Med. Edn. Program. Contbr chpts. to books, articles to profl. jours. Bd. dirs. San Antonio Chamber Music Soc., 1970-75, 80-96, pres., 1983-85; bd. dirs. Friends of Strings, 1972-75, San Antonio Bot. Soc., 1985-87; Dem. precinct committeeman Washington County, Oreg., 1966-68. Served to capt. M.C. U.S. Army, 1960-62. Fellow ACP, Am. Coll. Rheumatology (exec. com. mem.); mem. Arthritis Found. (chmn. med. and sci. com. South Ctrl. Tex. chpt.), Heberden Soc., Am. Fedn. Clin. Rsch., So. Soc. Clin. Investigation, Tex. Rheumatism Assn. (pres.), Nat. Soc. Clin. Rheumatology, Mex. Rheumatology Soc. (hon.). Office: 635 E Olmos Dr San Antonio TX 78212-2504

PERSHAN, RICHARD HENRY, lawyer; b. N.Y.C., Jan. 4, 1930; s. Benjamin and Sadie (Aronowsky) P.; m. Kathryn Schaefler, June 11, 1952; children: Lee S., Richard H. Jr., Pamela P. Hochman, Julia B. BA, Yale U., 1951, LLB, 1956. Bar: N.Y. 1956, U.S. Supreme Ct.1969. Assoc. Davis, Polk & Wardwell, N.Y.C., 1956-60; ptnr. Finch & Schaefler, 1960-85, LeBoeuf, Lamb, Greene & MacRae, N.Y.C., 1986-94, of counsel, 1995—. Counsel Mcpl. Art Soc., N.Y.C., 1965-70, Fine Arts Fedn., N.Y.C., 1975-80. Served to 1st lt. USAF. Fellow Am. Coll. Trust and Estate Counsel (author, editor, articles and studies 1960—); mem. Assn. of Bar of City of N.Y., Yale Club (N.Y.C.), N.Y. Croquet Club, Newport Casino Croquet Club. Democrat. Avocations: indoor rowing, croquet, body building. Home: 1435 Lexington Ave New York NY 10128-1625 Office: LeBoeuf Lamb Greene & MacRae 125 W 55th St New York NY 10019-5389 E-mail: rpershan@aol.com., rpershan@llgm.com.

PERSHE, EDWARD RICHARD, civil engineer; b. Omaha, July 30, 1924; s. Joseph Edward and Theresa Elizabeth (Mikich) P.; m. Clotilde Amalia (Sintes-Roscelli), Apr. 28, 1954; children: John Charles, Robert Andrew. BS in Civil Engring., U. Ill., 1949; MS in Sanitary Engring., MIT, 1950; PhD in Civil Engring., U. Ill., 1966. Registered profl. engr., Ohio, Fla. Design engr. Gannett Fleming Engrs., Harrisburg, Pa., 1953-56; project engr. Black & Veatch Engrs., Kansas City, Mo., 1956-58; asst. prof. Civil Engring. U. Nebr., Lincoln, 1958-62; assoc. prof. Northeastern U., Boston, 1966-70; dir. rsch. Whitman & Howard, Inc., 1970-84; asst. dist. drainage engr. Dept. Transp. State of Fla., Deland, 1987—. Contbr. articles to profl. jours. Pres. Cranes Roost Homeowners Assn., Altamonte Springs, Fla., 1988; pres. Altamonte Springs Garden Club, 1990-91. 1st. lt. USAF, 1950-53. Recipient NSF Sci. Faculty fellowship U. Ill., 1962, USPHS rsch. fellowship U. Ill., 1963, 64, 65, Ford Found. grant U. Ill., 1964, 65. Fellow ASCE (life mem., chmn. environ. engring. com. 1976-84). Republican. Home: 217 Mallard St Altamonte Springs FL 32701-7666 Office: Fla Dept Transp 719 S Woodland Blvd Deland FL 32720-6834

PERSHING, DAVID WALTER, chemical engineering educator, researcher; b. Anderson, Ind., Oct. 2, 1948; s. Walter L. and Treva B. (Crane) P.; m. Lynn Marie Kennard, Apr. 9, 1977; 1 child, Nicole. BSChemE, Purdue U., 1970; PhDChemE, U. Ariz., 1976. Rsch. asst. Exxon Prodn. Rsch., Houston, 1969; project engr. EPA, 1970-73; asst. prof. chem. engring. U. Utah, Salt Lake City, 1977-82, assoc. prof., 1982-85, prof., 1985—, assoc. dean Grad. Sch., 1983-87, dean Coll. Engring., 1987-98, v.p., 1998-99, sr. v.p. acad. affairs, 2000—; asst. to pres. Reaction Engring. Inc., 1990—. Vis. scientist Internat. Flame Rsch. Found., Ijmuiden, The Netherlands, 1972-73; vis. assoc. prof. chem. engring. U. Ariz., Tuscon, 1976-77; cons. Energy and Environ. Rsch. Ctr., Irvine, Calif., 1974-90, Acurex Corp., Mountain View, Calif., 1974-79, Kennecott Corp., Salt Lake City, 1979-81, Nat. Bur. Standards, Washington, 1976-78, Geneva Steel, 1989-95; assoc. dir. Engring. Rsch. Ctr., NSF, 1986-97. Contbr. articles to profl. publs.; patentee in field. Maj. USPHS, 1970-73. Recipient Disting. Teaching award U. Utah, 1982, Disting. Rsch. award U. Utah, 1990; grantee NSF, PYI, 1984-90. Mem. Am. Inst. Chem. Engrs., Combustion Inst. Methodist. Office: U Utah Coll Engring 201 Presidents Cir Rm 205 Salt Lake City UT 84112-9007 E-mail: david.pershing@utah.edu.

PERSHING, ROBERT GEORGE, telecommunications company executive; b. Battle Creek, Mich., Aug. 10, 1941; s. James Arthur and Beulah Francis P.; m. Diana Kay Prill, Sept. 16, 1961 (div. Jan. 1989); children: Carolyn, Robert; m. Charlene Jean Reed Wallis, Mar. 18, 1989 (div. Dec. 1995). BSEE, Tri-State Coll., 1961. Comm. engr. Am. Elec. Power, Ind., N.Y. and Ohio, 1961-69; design supr. Wescom, Inc., Ill., 1969-74; dir. engring. Tellabs, Inc., Lisle, 1974-78; pres., CEO Teltrend, Inc., St. Charles, 1979-89, chmn. bd., 1979-88; CEO DKP Prodns., Inc., 1986-89; exec. cons. Teltrend, 1979-93; asst. treas. Magnekopy, inc., Villa Park. Bd. dirs. TI Investors, Inc.; advisor entrepreneurial studies U. Ill.; engring. cons. Recipient Chgo. Area Small Bus. award, 1986., INC 500 awards, 1987, 88. Mem. IEEE. Office: 1519 Kirkwood Dr Geneva IL 60134-1659

PERSICO, JOSEPH EDWARD, author; b. Gloversville, N.Y., July 19, 1930; s. Thomas Louis and Blanche (Perrone) P.; m. Sylvia La Vista, May 23, 1959; children: Vanya, Andrea. BA, SUNY-Albany, 1952, PhD (hon.), 1996; postgrad., Columbia U., 1955. Writer on staff of gov. N.Y. State, Albany, 1955-59; commd. fgn. service officer USIA, 1959, served in Argentina, Rio de Janeiro, Brazil, 1959-62; speechwriter Commr. N.Y. State Health Dept., Albany, 1963-66; chief speechwriter for gov. N.Y. State, 1966-74; speechwriter for v.p. U.S., Washington, 1975-77. Author: My Enemy My Brother: Men and Days of Gettysburg, 1977; (novel) The Spiderweb, 1979, Piercing the Reich: The Penetration of Nazi Germany by American Secret Agents during World War II, 1979 (Nat. Intelligence Study Ctr. prize for best book on intelligence 1979), The Imperial Rockefeller: A Biography of Nelson A. Rockefeller, 1982, Murrow: An American Original, 1988, Casey: William J. Casey, From the OSS to the CIA, 1990, Nuremberg: Infamy on Trial, 1994; collaborator: Colin Powell: My American Journey, 1995, Roosevelt's Secret War, 2001; Roosevelt's Secret War: FDR and World War II Espionage, 2001. Served to lt. (j.g.) USN, 1952-55. Recipient Disting. Alumnus award SUNY-Albany, 1982 Mem. Authors Guild, Inc. Home and Office: 222 Heritage Rd Guilderland NY 12084-9314 E-mail: persico@aol.com.

PERSING, CHRISTOPHER ALLEN, secondary school educator; b. Sunbury, Pa., Apr. 28, 1975; s. David Lee Persing, Sr. and Kathaleen Louise Persing; m. Betsy Jean Clark, Oct. 7, 2000; 1 child Peyton Allen. BA History, Susquehanna U., 1997. Instnl. I cert. in secondary social studies grades 7-12 Pa. Sales assoc. First Nat. Trust Bank, Bloomsburg, Pa., 1997—2001; tchr. Muncy (Pa.) Sch. Dist., 2001—. Head baseball coach Muncy Sch. Dist., Pa., 1999—. Asst. baseball coach Susquehanna U., Selinsgrove, Pa., 1997—99; sec. City of Sunbury Parks and Recreation Commn., Sunbury, 2000—01. Mem.: Nat. HS Baseball Coaches Assn., Pa. Coaches Assn.

PERSING, JOHN ARTHUR, surgeon; b. Burlington, Vt., Apr. 16, 1948; s. Raymond Maurice and Natalie (Vespucci) P.; m. Susan Powers Light, June 22, 1971; children: Sarah Merriman, John Scott. BA cum laude, U. Vt., 1970, MD, 1974; MA (hon.), Yale U., 1992. Diplomate Am. Bd. Plastic and Reconstructive Surgery, Am. Bd. Neurol. Surgeons. Resident gen. surgery Hosp. of U. Ariz., Tuscon, 1974-76; resident neurol. surgery Hosp. of U. Va., Charlottesville, 1976-82, resident plastic surgery, 1982-84, dir. cranial base surgery, 1988-92, vice chmn. dept. of plastic surgery, 1988-92, chief divsn. of craniofacial surgery, 1988-92; asst. prof. plastic and neurosurgery U. Va., 1984-87, assoc. prof. of plastic and neurosurgery, 1987-89, prof. plastic and neurosurgery, 1989-92; prof. plastic surgery and neurosurgery Yale U. Sch. of Medicine, New Haven, 1992—, chief sect. of plastic surgery, 1992—; fellow Trumbull Coll. Yale U., 1994—. Editor: Clinics in Plastic Surgery, July, 1995; co-editor Jour. of Craniofacial Surgery, 1992—, Scientific Foundations and Surgical Treatment for Craniosynostosis, 1989, Neurosurgery Clinics of North America, July, 1991; assoc. editor Plastic and Reconstructive Surgery, 1997—; ad hoc reviewer Cancer, Head and Neck Surgery, Jour. of Neurosurgery, Neurosurgery, Plastic and Reconstructive Surgery, Pediatrics, Jour. of Dental Rsch. Recipient Donald D. Matson award Am. Assn. of Neurol. Surgeons, 1981. Mem. Am. Assn. Pediatric Plastic Surgeons (pres.-elect 1993-95, pres. 1995-97), Am. Assn. Plastic Surgeons (membership com. 1994-95), Am. Soc. Plastic and Reconstructive Surgeons (coms.), Am. Cleft Palate-Craniofacial Assn. (coms.), Am. Soc. Maxillofacial Surgeons (coms., v.p. 2000-01, pres.-elect 2001-02, Bernd Speissl award 1991, Maxillofacial Surgeons Found. Rsch. award 1992), Assn. of Acad. Chmn. of Plastic Surgery (plastic surgery residency tng. evaluation com. 1993, chair issues com. 1994, sec.-treas. 1998-2002), Northeastern Soc. Plastic Surgeons (program com. 1995), Plastic Surgery Rsch. Coun. (program com. 1991-94). Office: Yale Plastic Surgery 333 Cedar St # 2 New Haven CT 06510-3206

PERSINGER, DEL LOUIS, pharmaceutical company executive; b. Whiting, Iowa, Aug. 2, 1949; s. Ardell L. and Doris L. Persinger; m. Mary L. Tabor, Sept. 16, 1984; children: Christopher, Benjamin Hammerschlag, Sarah Hammerschlag. BSChemE with distinction, Iowa State U., 1971, MS in Journalism and Mass. Comm., 1975; MBA in Fin., Am. U., 1990. Refinery process engr. Exxon Co., Baton Rouge, 1971-73; environtl. and pub. affairs mgr. Am. Petroleum Inst., Washington, 1975-89, sr. assoc. refining, 1989-92, dep. dir. mfg., distbn. and mktg., 1992-94, dir. mgmt. and budget, 1994-96; v.p. fin. ops. Pharm. Rsch. and Mfrs. of Am., 1996—; pres., CEO PhRMA Found., 1999—. Bd. trustees, past pres. Bethesda Jewish Congregation, 1992—. Mem. Fin. Execs. Inst., Am. Soc. of Assn. Execs., Am. Found. for Pharm. Edn. (bd. dirs. 1999—), Phi Kappa Phi, Tau Beta Pi, Omega Chi Epsilon. Office: Pharm Rsch and Mfrs of Am 1100 15th St NW Ste 900 Washington DC 20005-1763

PERSINGER, JUDITH EILEEN, management plan clerk; b. Weston, W.Va., Aug. 4, 1944; d. William Edward and Pearl Lenna (Blake) Skinner; m. Claude Calvin Persinger, Sept. 4, 1962; children: Lisa, Shawn. Grad. high sch., Burnsville, W.Va. Telephone operator Chesapeake and Potomac Telephone Co., Morgantown, W.Va., 1965-68, plant clk., 1969-71; RAAS clk. Bell Atlantic Va., Culpeper, 1978-79, assignment clk. Fairfax, 1979-86, mgmt. plan clk. Falls Church, 1987—. Pres. Home Owners Assn., Slidell, La., 1975, Cmty. Rel. Bell Atlantic, Warrenton, Va., 1982-89; v.p. Literacy Vol., Warrenton, 1994; pres. Bell Atlantic Pioneers, Richmond, 1995—. Recipient Govs. award, State of Va., 1994. Mem. Eta Sigma (pres. 1989-90). Office: Bell Atlantic Va 2980 Fairview Park Dr Falls Church VA 22042-4525 Home: 189 Youhill Dr Tappahannock VA 22560-5227

PERSOFF, ILENE LEOPOLD, accountant, educator; b. Huntington, N.Y., Sept. 13, 1953; d. Jack H. and Gladys D. (Schwartz) Leopold; 1 child, Stacy Rose. BA in Econs. and Urban Studies, Brandeis U., 1975; MS in Acctg., L.I. U., 1977. CPA, N.Y. Staff acct. Ronald J. Klein, CPA, Huntington, 1978-82; pvt. practice, 1982—. Assoc. prof. L.I. U., Brookville, N.Y., 1993—; lectr. numerous orgnl. meetings. Bd. dirs. Victims Info. Bur. of Suffolk, Hauppauge, N.Y., 1987-95, treas., 1989-92; treas. Huntington Village Bus. Improvement Dist., 1995-97. Mem. AICPA, Acctg. Rsch. Assn., N.Y. State Soc. CPAs (chair various coms., bd. dirs. 1996-99), N.Y. State Bd. Pub. Accountancy. Avocations: tennis, bicycling, reading, rollerblading. Office: 23 Green St Ste 300 Huntington NY 11743-3336

PERSOFF, NEHEMIAH, actor, artist; b. Jerusalem, Aug. 2, 1919; came to U.S., 1929; s. Samuel and Puah (Holman) P.; m. Thia Persov; children: Jeffrey Jonathan, Dan Deckel, Perry Erez, Dahlia. Student, Hebrew Tech. Inst., N.Y.C., 1934-37. Ind. stage, screen and TV actor, 1945—. Actor: (Broadway prodns.) Sundown Beach, Galileo, Richard the 3d, King Lear, Peer Gynt, Peter Pan, Reclining Figure, Flahooly, Montserrat, Tiger at the Gate, Only in America, (local, regional prodns.) Fiddler on the Roof, Man of La Mancha, Oliver, I'm Not Rappaport, 1988, Death of a Salesman (Stratford, Ont.), Two, Drinking America, Rosebloom, Dybbuk (Best Actor L.A. Critics 1975), Glass Menagerie (Israeli prodn.), Volpone, Of Mice and Men, (films) In Search of the Real Jesus, The Harder They Fall, The Wrong Man, This Angry Age, Men in War, Some Like It Hot, Al Capone, Green Mansions, The Commancheros, The Greatest Story Ever Told, Voyage of the Damned, Yentl, The Hook, The Last Temptation of Christ, Twins, numerous TV shows including For Whom the Bell Tolls (Sylvania award for best supporting actor 1958), The Big Knife, Alfred Hitchcock Presents, Rawhide, Twilight Zone, The Untouchables, The Wild, Wild West, I Spy, Gunsmoke, Police Story, Columbo, Barney Miller, Six Million Dollar Man, Delta House, Littlest Hobo, Magnum P.I., Hotel, Adderly; (TV miniseries) The French Atlantic; (one-man show) Aleichem Sholem-Sholem-Alecheim, 1971 (L.A. Critics award, San Francisco Critics Circle award 1979); paintings exhibited at George Krevsky Fine Arts, Cambria, Calif. With U.S. Army, 1942—45. Jewish. E-mail: thiap@thegrid.net.

PERSON, CURTIS S., JR. state legislator, lawyer; b. Nov. 27, 1934; married; 6 children. BS, Memphis State U., 1956; LLB, U. Miss., 1959. Chief legal officer Juvenile Ct. Memphis and Shelby County; former mem. Tenn. Ho. Reps.; mem. Tenn. Senate, 1968—, Senate Rep. whip, 1973-76, minority caucus chmn., 1976-82. Chmn. Senate Judiciary com. 95th - 102d Gen. Assemblies. Pres. Memphis-Shelby County Mental Health Assn., 1969-73, Handicapped Inc., 1972-74; chmn. Memphis Commn. Drug Abuse, 1970-71; charter pres. Memphis State Tiger Rebounders; past trustee Memphis State U.; exec. committeeman St. Jude's Memphis Open Golf Classic; co-chmn. Shelby County Legis. Del., 1973-74, vice chmn., 1970, 75, 76, 85-88; chmn. Shelby Rep. Del., 1977, 83-84; mem. adv. bd. Jr. League Memphis, 1955-98; vice chmn. Select Com. Children and Youth, 1997-2002, ex officio Senate Mem., Juvenile Justice Reform Commn., 1998. Named Memphis and Tenn. Outstanding Young Man of Yr., Jaycees, 1969, Outstanding Legis. of Yr., Govt. Leader Against Drunk Driving, Tenn. MADD, 1988, Legis. of Yr., Tenn. Alcohol and Drug Assn., 1988, Legislator of Yr. Tenn. Juvenile Svcs. Yr., 2001; recipient Liberty Bell Freedom award Memphis/Shelby County Bar Assn., 1969, Tenn. Adv. of Yr. Handicapped Children, 1978, Outstanding Svc. Children award Tenn Coun. Juvenile Ct. Judges, 1981, Pres.' Svc. award Tenn. Juvenile Ct. Svcs. Assn., 1981, Americanism award Memphis Civitan Club, 1986, Disting. Svc. award County Ofcls. Assn. Tenn., 1989, Cmty. Svc. award Tenn. Med. Assn., 1989, Eagle award Eagle Forum, 1994, Bill Bates Legis. award United Tenn. League, 1994, Champion for Children award Tenn. Assn. Child Care, 1995, Outstanding Legis. award County Ofcls. Assn. Tenn., 1996, Tenn. Juvenile Svcs. Assn. Pres. Svc. award, 1997, Tenn. Trial Lawyers Assn. Legis. of Yr. award, 1997, Shelby County Rep. Party Chmn. of Yr. award, 1999, Am. Lung Assn. Tenn. Legis. of Yr. award, 1999, Tenn. Task Force Against Domestic Violence Outstanding Legis. of Yr. award, 1999, Tenn. Dispensing Opticians Assn. Legis. of Yr. award, 2000. Office: War Meml Bldg Rm 308 Nashville TN 37243 E-mail: sen.curtis.person@legislature.state.tn.us.

PERSON, EVERT BERTIL, newspaper and radio executive; b. Berkeley, Calif., Apr. 6, 1914; s. Emil P. and Elida (Swanson) P.; m. Ruth Finley, Jan. 26, 1944 (dec. May 1985); m. 2d, Norma Joan Betz, Mar. 12, 1986. Student, U. Calif., Berkeley, 1937; LHD, Calif. State Univs., 1983, Sonoma State U., 1993. Co-publisher, sec.-treas. Press Democrat Pub. Co., Santa Rosa, Calif., 1945-72, editor, 1972-73, pres., pub., editor-in-chief, 1973-85; sec.-treas. Finley Broadcasting Co., 1945-72, pres., 1972-89, Kawana Pubs., 1975-85; pub. Healdsburg Tribune, 1975-85; prin. Evert B. Person Investments, Santa Rosa, 1985—. Pres. Person Properties Co., Santa Rosa, 1945-70; v.p. Finley Ranch & Land Co., Santa Rosa, 1947-72, pres., 1972-79; pres. Baker Pub. Co., Oreg., 1957-67, Sebastopol (Calif.) Times, 1978-81, Russian River News, Guerneville, Calif., 1978-81; pres. publ. Kawana Pubs., 1978-85; mem. nominating com. AP, 1982-84, mem. auditing com., 1984-85 Bd. dirs Empire Coll., Santa Rosa, 1972-98, Sonoma County Taxpayers Assn., 1966-69, San Francisco Spring Opera Assn., 1974-79; bd. dirs. San Francisco Opera, 1986—, v.p., 1988—; pres. Calif. Newspaperboy Found., 1957-58; chmn. Santa Rosa Civic Arts Commn., 1961-62; pres. Santa Rosa Sonoma County Symphony Assn., 1966-68, Luther Burbank Meml. Found., 1979, Santa Rosa Symphony Found., 1967-77; adv. bd. Santa Rosa Salvation Army, 1959-67; commodore 12th Coast Guard Dist. Aux., 1969-70; trustee Desert Mus., Palm Springs, 1987-92, v.p. Nat. Bd. Canine Companions, Inc., 1989-92. Decorated Knight of the Holy Sepulchre. Mem. Calif. Newspaper Pubs. Assn. (pres. 1981-82), Internat. Newspaper Fin. Execs. (pres. 1961-62), Bohemian Club, Sonoma County Press Club, Santa Rosa Golf and Country club, The Springs Club, Santa Rosa Rotary (past pres.), Masons (33 degree, Legion of Merit), Shriners. Roman Catholic. Home: 775 White Oak Dr Santa Rosa CA 95409-6155 Office: The Oaks 1400 N Dutton Ave Ste 12 Santa Rosa CA 95401-4644

PERSON, PAULA (MRS. P. BARRY PERSON), social skills organization executive, entrepreneur; b. Worcester, Mass., Feb. 19, 1935; d. Leo Joseph and Imelda Mary (Elmore) Barry; married; children: Suzanne Elizabeth Person Tapley, John Lloyd III, Christian Barry. BA in Edn. and Spanish, Marymount Coll., 1957; postgrad., Harrington Inst. Interior Design, 1974-75. Cert. elem. tchr., N.Y. Founder, tchr. Post Nursery Sch. U.S. Forces, Aschaffenbrug, Fed. Republic Germany, 1958, Post Kindergarten Sch. U.S. Forces, Aschaffenbrug, 1959-62; tchr. King Solver Sch., Ft. Knox, 1963-64, Model Sch., Louisville, 1964-66; free lance interior designer Chgo., 1974-79; pres., founder The Children's Spoon, Dinner is Served, Winnetka, Ill., 1979—, The Children's Spoon, London, 1985-92. Co-founder Aschaffenburg Players, 1960-62, creater of cultural events for children U.S./Eng., 1980—; motivational spkr. Designer/author The Children's Spoon Coloring Book of Manners for Boys and Girls, 1984, 2d printing, 1985, Paula Person's Activity Book for Ladies and Gentlemen, 2001; prodr./dir. WCTV series The Style of Social Manners, 2001; creater 9 musical ditties for program and cassette tape. Active presdl. campaigns, 1972, 80; swimming instr. ARC, Milton, Vt. Marymount Coll.; fundraiser UNICEF Children with AIDS, 1992, 93, 94, 95; organizer Mothers United for Manners Soc., 1995. Named Showcase House Designer, Park Ridge Youth Campus Fundraiser, 1982, 84, 85. Mem. Internat. Assn. Culinary Profls., Internat. Women Assocs. Internat. Visitor's Ctr., The English Speaking Union (Chgo. chpt.), Marymount Coll. Alumnae Assn. (pres. 1977-80). Avocations: photography, travel, tennis, restaurant epicure, antiques. Office: PO Box 148 Winnetka IL 60093-0148

PERSON, PHILIP, biomedical consultant, biochemist, dentist; b. N.Y.C., Aug. 6, 1919; s. Barney and Lena (Spindel) P.; m. Bertha Paula Kaufman, Mar. 14, 1953; children: Sarah, Naomi, Matthew. BS, CUNY, 1940; DDS, NYU, 1946; MS, Rutgers U., 1951, PhD, 1952. Lic. dentist. Chief dental research lab. VA Med. Ctr., Bklyn., 1954-86; vis. prof. biochemistry Boston U. Sch. Grad. Dentistry, 1964-74; sr. vis. investigator systematics-ecology Marine Biol. Lab., Woods Hole, Mass., 1966-72; spl. research fellow (NIH) Inst. for Muscle Research, 1967-68; adj. prof. oral biology Columbia U. Sch. Dental and Oral Surgery, N.Y.C., 1969-73; adj. prof. biochemistry and periodontics NYU Coll. Dentistry, 1977—; dir. oral health studies Research Testing Labs., Little Neck, N.Y., 1986—; biomed. cons., 1986—. Mem. NIH Dental Study Sect., Bethesda, Md., 1963-66; cons. NIDR, NIAMD (NIH), Bethesda, 1963-80, Radiation and Solid State Lab., NYU, N.Y.C., 1965-68, dental health, marine biology WHO, Geneva, 1967-68, Coun. on Dental Therapeutics, ADA, Chgo., 1984-89. Editor: Metabolism of Oral Tissues, 1962, Biology of the Mouth, 1968. Investigator Biocore, Mission of Apollo 17, NASA, Ames Research Ctr., Moffet Field, Calif., 1973. Capt. USAR, 1952-54. Fellow AAAS, Am. Inst. Chemists, N.Y. Acad. Sci., The Harvey Soc. Office: 13787 75th Rd Flushing NY 11367-2815

PERSON, ROBERT JOHN, financial management consultant; b. Mpls., Mar. 7, 1927; s. Otto Carl and Alice Kathryn (Kasper) P.; m. Jeanette Haines, Mar. 11, 1948; 1 dau., Julie Ann. BBA, U. Minn., 1947, MS, Columbia u., 1953. Financial analyst Equitable Life Assurance Soc. U.S., N.Y.C., 1947-53; asst. v.p. bus. devel. met. banking dept. Bankers Trust Co., 1953-64; v.p. bus. devel. div. Union Bank, Los Angeles, 1964-67; v.p., dir. mktg. Bank of Calif., San Francisco, 1967-70; sr. v.p. Central Nat. Bank of Chgo., 1970-72, 1st v.p., 1973-76, Central Nat. Chgo. Corp., 1973-76; v.p., regional mgr. Lester B. Knight & Assos., Inc., San Francisco, 1976-77; dir. bank cons. Coopers & Lybrand, 1977-80, partner-in-charge, nat. dir. bank cons. Chgo., 1980-89; exec. v.p. RJP Assocs., Inc., Stockton, Calif., 1989-92. Instr. salesmanship sch. pub. relations N.Y. Bankers Assn., 1960-63; instr. mktg. research Stonier Grad. Sch. Banking, Rutgers U., 1964-65, 73, 75-77, Brown U., 1964; instr. Agrl. Lending Sch., Ill. Bankers Assn., 1973-76, Nat. Comml. Lending Sch., Am. Bankers Assn., 1973-76, Sch. Bank Adminstrn., U. Wis., 1982-85, Nat. Grad. Trust Sch., Northwestern U., 1982-84, Southwestern Grad. Sch. Banking, 1983-84; Vice chmn. mgmt. effectiveness com. Community Fund Chgo. Treas. Sch. Bd., Huntington, N.Y., 1957-59; Bd. dirs. Am. Cancer Soc., Chgo.; chief crusader Crusade of Mercy. Served to lt. comdr. USNR, 1944-46, ret. Recipient Florence McNeil Stanley award Columbia, 1953 Mem. Am. Bankers Assn., Bank Mktg. Assn., Am. Mgmt. Assn. (mktg. planning council), Mgmt. Centre-Europe (fin. mgmt. adv. com. 1971—), Sales and Mktg. Execs. Internat., Stockton Symphony Assn. (bd. dirs. 1989-92), Beta Gamma Sigma. Clubs: Eastward Ho (Cape Cod); Stockton Golf and Country (Calif.). Lodges: Elks. Republican. Presbyterian. Home: 14406 W Trading Post Dr Sun City West AZ 85375-5791 also: PO Box 3659 2734 Ponderosa Cir Pinetop AZ 85935-3659

PERSON, RUTH JANSSEN, academic administrator; b. Washington, Aug. 27, 1945; d. Theodore Armin and Ruth Katherine (Mahoney) Janssen. BA, Gettysburg (Pa.) Coll., 1967; AMLS, U. Mich., 1969, PhD, 1980; MS in Adminstrn., George Washington U., 1974. Head of reference/asst. prof. Thomas Nelson C.C., Hampton, Va., 1971-74; lectr. U. Mich., Ann Arbor, 1975-79, coord. of continuing edn., 1977-79; asst. prof. Cath. U., Washington, 1979-85, assoc. prof., 1985-86, assoc. dean Sch. of Libr. and Info. Sci., 1983-86; dean Coll. Libr. Sci. Clarion (Pa.) U., 1986-88; assoc. vice chancellor U. Mo., St. Louis, 1988-93; v.p. for acad. affairs Ashland (Ohio) U., 1993-95; v.p. acad. affairs, prof. bus. adminstrn. Angelo State U., San Angelo, Tex., 1995-99; chancellor, prof. bus. Ind. U., Kokomo, Ind., 1999—. Reviewer U.S. Dept. Edn., Washington, 1987-89, 92; trustee Pitts. Regional Libr. Ctr., 1986-88; chair publs. com. Assn. of Coll. and Rsch. Librs., Chgo., 1986-90; cons. United Way, Alexandria, Va., 1985; cons.-evaluator North Ctrl. Assn., 1993-95, 2000—; nat. vis. com. Southwest Ctr. Advanced Tech. Edn., 1996-98; Health Profs. Edn. Adv. Com.; faculty workload com. Tex. Higher Edn. Coord. Bd., 1998-99; Higher Edn. Info. Sys. Com. Co-editor: (book) Academic Libraries: Their Role and Rationale in Higher Education, 1995; editor: (book) The Management Process, 1983; editl. bd. Coll. & Rsch. Librs., 1990-96; contr. articles to profl. jours. Mem. Strategic Planning Task Force, Ashland C. of C., 1994; bd. dirs. Alternatives for Living in Violent Environs., Inc., St. Louis, 1992-94, San Angelo Cultural Affairs Coun., 1998-99; commr. Commn. for Women, Anne Arundel County, Md., 1984-86; mem. Citizens Adv. Bd., Clarion, Pa., 1986-88; mem. Olivette, Mo. Human Rels. Commn., 1992-94, San Angelo Bus. and Profl. Women's Club, 1995-99, pres.-elect, 1996-97, pres., 1997—; mem. bldg. design oversight com. San Angelo Mus. Fine Arts, 1995-99; mem. com. Cactus Jazz Festival, 1995-99; bd. dirs. San Angelo Bus. and Edn. Coalition, 1997-99, San Angelo Cultural Affairs Coun., 1998-99; bd. dirs. Ind. Tech. Partnership, 2001—, YWCA, Kokomo, 2000—; mem. adv. bd. St. Joseph's Hosp., 2000, KeyBank, 1999—. Fellow Am. Coun. Edn., 1990, Harvard Inst. Ednl. Mgmt., 1989, Rackham fellow U. Mich., 1976; ACE fellow Ariz. Bd. Regents, 1990-91; recipient Washington Woman award Washington Woman mag., 1986. Mem.: ALA (com. on accreditation 1993—97), Howard County C. of C. (women's bus. coun. 2000—), Coun. for the Preservation of Anthropol. Records (bd. dirs.), Am. Assn. Univ. Adminstrs. (bd. dirs. 1993—95, v.p. elect 2001—), Beta Gamma Sigma, Phi Alpha Theta, Kappa Delta Pi, Pi Lambda Theta, Beta Phi Mu, Psi Chi. Lutheran. Avocations: piano, herb gardening, antiques, cooking, sailing. Office: Ind U Kokomo PO Box 9003 2300 S Washington St Kokomo IN 46904

PERSONS, W. RAY, lawyer, educator; b. Talbottan, Ga., July 22, 1953; s. William and Frances (Crowell) P.; m. Wendy-Joy Mottley, Sept. 24, 1977; children: Conrad Ashley, April Maureen. BS cum laude, Armstrong State Coll., 1975; JD, Ohio State U., 1978. Bar: Ga. 1979, U.S. Dist. Ct. (so. dist.) Ga. 1980, U.S. Dist. Ct. (no. dist.) Ga. 1986, U.S. Ct. Appeals (11th cir.) 1986. Assoc. Troutman, Sanders, Lockerman & Ashmore, Atlanta, 1978-79; atty. Nat. Labor Rels. Bd., 1980-82; legis. counsel U.S Ho. Reps., Washington, 1983-86; atty. Mack & Bernstein, Atlanta, 1986-87; ptnr. Arrington & Hollowell, 1987-95, Swift, Currie, McGhee & Hiers, Atlanta, 1995-99, Hunton and Williams, Atlanta, 1999—2001, King & Spalding, Atlanta, 2001—. Adj. prof. litigation Ga. State U., Atlanta, 1989—; spl. asst. atty. gen. State of Ga., Atlanta, 1988—. Master Am. Inns of Ct. (Lamar chpt.); fellow Am. Coll. Trial Lawyers; mem. ABA, Internat. Soc. Barristers, Am. Bd. Trial Advocates, State Bar Ga., Atlanta Bar Assn., Lawyers Club of Atlanta. Republican. Roman Catholic. Office: Hunton and Williams 600 Peachtree St NE Ste 4100 Atlanta GA 30308-2217

PERSSON, ERIK BONDE, computer engineer; b. Västervik, Sweden, Apr. 15, 1958; s. Folke Lennart and Astrid Ulla Stina (Pamp) P.; m. Gudrun Ingela Ask, July 16, 1983. BA, Lund (Sweden) U., 1983, 88; MS in Computer Engring., degree, Lunds Tekniska Högskola, 1991. Computer cons. Ad Hoc Sys. AB, Lund, 1990-91, Fenestra Data H.B., Harlösa, 1991; sys. cons. Medisys AB/Dialog AB, Lund, 1992-95; sr. cons. Cambridge Tech. Ptnrs., Malmö, 1995-96; computer engr. Lund U., 1996—. Mem. Harlösa Rotary Club (sec. 1994-95), Tessinsällskapet, The Classical Assn., Lärdomshistoriska Samfundet. Avocations: bibliophily, classical studies, gardening. E-mail: Erik.Persson@cs.lth.se.

PERSSON, ERLAND KARL, electrical engineer; b. Soderala, Sweden, Oct. 9, 1923; came to U.S., 1949, naturalized, 1953; m. Elaine Darm; children: Ann Monn, Eric. BSEE, U. Minn., 1955. Registered profl. engr., Minn. Prin. engr. Gen. Mills, Mpls., 1956-61; v.p. engring. Electro-Craft Corp., Hopkins, Minn., 1961-72; v.p. R & D, 1972-83; sr. v.p., chief tech. officer, 1983-86; pres. Erland Persson Co., Mpls., 1987—. Contbr. articles to profl. jours., chpts. to books. Patentee in field. Mem. mech. engring. adv. com. U. Minn.; bd. dirs. Minn. High Tech. Coun., 1984-86, mem., 1987. Fellow IEEE (life, mem. subcom. electric machines com., indsl. drives com.), Audio Engring Soc. (founder Midwest chpt. 1974); mem. Eta Kappa Nu. E-mail: persso002@tc.umn.edu.

PERSSON, IVAR LENNART, military program director; b. Uppsala, Sweden, Oct. 28, 1945; s. Ivar and Anna Marie Elisabet (Soderstrom) P.; m. Ann Mari M. Borjesson, Jan. 2, 1971; children: Katarina, Ulrika. M in Mil. Sci., Swedish Nat. War Coll., Stockholm, 1977. Co. comdr. no. signal regiment Swedish Army Signal Corps, 1969, advanced through grades to lt. col., 1986, co./battalion comdr. no. 3 signal regiment, 1985; program mgr. Def. Material Adminstrn., Stockholm, 1977-84, dep. program dir., 1987-93, program dir. AEW, 1993-94, program dir. internat. air force interoperability, 1994-96, sr. ops. avionics specialist, 1996—. Conservative. Lutheran. Home: S 165 76 Hasselby 5 Krakbarsgr Sweden Office: Def Material Adminstrn MSLS S 115 88 Stockholm Sweden

PERSSON, RONNY ANDERS, accountant, historian; b. Helsingborg, Skane, Sweden, Nov. 19, 1945; s. Oscar Valfrid and Ellen Valborg Persson; m. Eva Gunilla Lindqvist, Oct. 5, 1968; children: Mikael, Thomas, Annika. Economy, Nicolai, 1971. Chief acct. Byggprodukter, Helsingborg, 1970-73, Bilakarna, Helsingborg, 1973-80, Bjuvs Congregation, Bjuv, Sweden, 1980—. Founder, mgr. R.P. Company Service, Bjuv, 1981-85, R.P. Trading, Bjuv, 1985—. Sector pres. World Union Protection Life; founder Internat. Peace, Economy and Ecology, Bjuv, 1982. Environ. Party. Avocations: reading, sports, natural medicine, politics, world history. Home: Vintergatan 1C 267 31 Bjuv Sweden E-mail: kyrkan.bjuv.ronny@swipnet.se.

PERTHOU, ALISON CHANDLER, interior designer; b. Bremerton, Wash., July 22, 1945; d. Benson and Elizabeth (Holdsworth) Chandler; m. A.V. Perthou III, Sept. 9, 1967 (div. Dec. 1977); children: Peter T.R., Stewart A.C. BFA, Cornish Coll. Arts, 1972. Pres. Alison Perthou Interior Design, Seattle, 1972—, Optima Design, Inc., Seattle, 1986-89; treas. Framejoist Corp., Bellevue, Wash., 1973-90; pres. Classics: Interiors & Antiques, Inc., 1988—. Cons. bldg. and interiors com. Children's Hosp., Seattle, 1976—; guest lectr. U. Wash., Seattle, 1980-81. Mem. bd. trustees Cornish Coll. Arts, Seattle, 1973-80, sec. exec. com., 1975-77; mem. procurement com. Patrons of N.W. Cultural and Charitable Orgn., 1985—, mem. antiques com., 1991—. Mem.: Am. Soc. Interior Design, Sunset Club, Seattle Tennis Club (mem. house and grounds com. 1974—75). Fax: 206-322-2335.

PERTSCHUK, LOUIS PHILIP, pathologist, consultant; b. London, July 4, 1925; s. Isaac M. and Rose Pertschuk; m. Andrea Roberts, June 28, 1985; children: Eric, Shawn, Brandy. AB, NYU, 1946; DO, Phila. Coll. Osteo. Medicine, 1950. Diplomate Am. Bd. Pathology. Instr. Downstate Med. Ctr./SUNY, Bklyn., 1974-75, asst. prof., 1975-79, assoc. prof., 1979-86, prof., 1986—. Cons. Corning (N.Y.) Glass Works, 1982-86, Zeus Sci. Co., 1982-94, Abbott Labs., 1982-92, Lifecodes Corp., 1989-93, Oncor, Inc., Gaithersburg, Md., 1994-96, Internat. Bioimmune Sys., Great Neck, N.Y., 1994-96, Bio-Genex, San Ramon, Calif., 1996-99. Author: Immunocytochemistry for Steroid Receptors, 1990; editor: Localization of Putative Steroid Receptors, 1985. Served with U.S. Army, 1943-46. NCI/NIH grantee, 1979, 82, 85, 92. Fellow Coll. Am. Pathologists, Am. Soc. Clin. Pathologists; mem. AAAS, Am. Assn. Pathologists, Internat. Acad. Pathology, N.Y. Acad. Sci., Histochem. Soc. Achievements include identification of steroid hormone binding sites in human neoplasms by histochemical and immunohistological techniques. Office: SUNY Health Sci Ctr at Bklyn 450 Clarkson Ave # 25 Brooklyn NY 11203-2056

PERTSEMLIDIS, DEMETRIUS, surgeon, educator; b. Kavala, Greece, 1929; came to U.S., 1960; MD, U. Hamburg, 1959. Cert. in surgery. Intern Kings County Hosps., Bklyn., 1960-61; resident in surgery Mt. Sinai Hosp., N.Y.C., 1961-65; clin. prof. surgery Mt. Sinai Sch. Medicine. Fellow ACS, Am. Coll. Gastroenterology; mem. AMA, Soc. for Surgery of Alimentary Tract, N.Y. Surg. Soc. Office: 1199 Park Ave New York NY 10128-1711

PERTZSCH, EVELYN MARIA, civic worker; b. La Crosse, Wis., Nov. 6, 1932; m. Dayton Irving Pertzsch, July 5, 1952; children: Patti Pertzsch Virnig, Peggy Pertzsch Chaudhry, Anne Pertzsch Cadd, Kathryn. Reading tutor vol., coord. Onalaska (Wis.) Pub. Schs., 1974-77. Chmn. La Crosse County Housing Authority, 1988—92, La Crosse County chpt. Am. Cancer Soc., 1992—94, pres., 1994—96; past v.p. Wis. PTA; chmn. Book Study Club, Onalaska Libr.; past pres. Onalaska Pub. Libr. Commn.; dir. internal edn. Centering Onalaska Orgn.; mem. sch. bd. Onalaska Pub. Schs., 2000—; chmn. Sias Libr. Trust Fund, 1999—; pres. La Crosse County Rep. Party, 1994—96. Named Pertzsch Manor, elderly manor, named in her honor, Onalaska, 1994; recipient award for dedicated svc., La Crosse County Rep. Party, 1986, Campbell award, Wis. Rep. Com., 1976—2002, svc. award, 1995—97, Cultural Dir. award, Sons of Norway, 1986, Literacy award, Midwest Reading Coun., 1989, Women of Achievement award, Miss Onalaska Pageant, 1998, 15 Yr. Recognition award, Riverland Girl Scouts. Mem.: Learning in Retirement (v.p. 2002), Sons of Norway (sec.), Wis. PTA (life). Home: 229 2d Ave N Onalaska WI 54650 E-mail: epertzsch@aol.com.

PERUCCA, KIRK PAUL, not for profit organization executive; b. Kansas City, Aug. 29, 1955; s. Paul George and Helen (Raney) P.; m. Roxanne Rothrock, May 16, 1981. MPA, U. Iowa, 1982; MDiv, Louisville Seminary, 1982. Ordained minister Presbyn. Ch., 1982. Minister First Presbyn. Ch., Shellsburg, Iowa, 1982-86, Van Brunt Blvd. Presbyn. Ch., Kansas City, 1986-96; pres., CEO Project Equality, 1996—. Bd. dirs. Planned Parenthood, Kansas City, 1991—, Civil Rights Consortium, 1996—. Democrat. Presbyterian. Avocation: collecting road maps. Home: 9920 El Monte St Overland Park KS 66207-3630 Office: Project Equality 7132 Main St Kansas City MO 64114-1406 E-mail: krikp@projectequality.org.

PERUMPRAL, JOHN VERGHESE, agricultural engineer, administrator, educator; b. Trivandrum, Kerala, India, Jan. 14, 1939; came to U.S., 1963; s. Verghese John and Sarah (Geverghese) P.; m. Shalini Elizabeth Alexander, Dec. 27, 1965; children: Anita Sarah, Sunita Anna. BS in Agrl. Engring., Allahabad (UP India) U., 1962; MS in Agrl. Engring., Purdue U., 1965, PhD, 1969. Postdoctoral rsch. assoc. agrl. engring. dept. Purdue U., West Lafayette, Ind., 1969-70; asst. prof. agrl. engring. dept. Va. Poly. Inst. and State U., Blacksburg, 1970-78, assoc. prof., 1978-83, prof., 1983-86, Wm. S. Cross Jr. prof., head dept. biol. systems engring., 1986—. Author more than 100 tech. publis. including articles in scholarly and profl. jours. Mem. Am. Soc. Agrl. Engring. (outstanding faculty award student br. 1976, 81, cert. teaching excellence 1979, assoc. editor, transaction of ASAE 1985-86), Fluid Power Soc., Sigma Xi, Alpha Epsilon. Presbyterian. Office: Va Poly Inst and State U Biol Sys Engring Dept Blacksburg VA 24061

PERUZZO, ALBERT LOUIS, actuary, accountant; b. Chgo., Dec. 27, 1951; s. Anthony L. and Annette Peruzzo. BS in Math., No. Ill. U., 1973, BS in Accountancy, 1974, MBA, 1975. CPA, Ill. Auditor Deloittes CPA's, Chgo., 1976-79; valuation analyst IV CNA Ins., 1979-89, mgr. valuation compliance, 1989-92, valuation analyst, 1992-97, asst. actuary, 1998-2000, actuarial dir., 2000—. Treas., bd. dirs. Dignity/Chgo., 1982-84, Integrity/Chgo., 1988-93; dep. vol. Voter's Registrar Bd. Elections, Chgo., 1984-86; bd. dirs. Colonial Condo, 1990-99. Fellow Soc. Actuaries (mem. edn. and exam. com. 1998-99), Life Mgmt. Inst. (with distinction); mem. AICPA, Am. Acad. Actuaries (participant val. task force 1998-99), Ill. CPA Soc. (Silver medal 1975), Am. Acctg. Assn., Acctg. Rsch. Assn., Beta Gamma Sigma (life charter mem. Chgo. chpt.), Mensa (life mem.), ACLU. Democrat. Roman Catholic.

PERVEZ, YAQUB RAZIQ, telecommunications engineer; b. Peshawar, Pakistan, Dec. 15, 1961; s. Yaqub Masih and Alice (Bibi) Y.; m. Kiran Raziq Gill, Nov. 9, 1989; children: Anita Raziq, Monica Raziq. BSc, U. Peshawar, Pakistan, 1981; BSc in Engring. with hons., N.W. Frontier Province U. Engring & Tech., Peshawar, 1985, MSc. with hons., 1993; PhD, Keio U., Yokohama, Japan, 1998. Aircraft engr. Pakistan Internat. Airlines, Karachi, Pakistan, 1986-87; shift engr. Pakistan Water & Power Devel. Authority, Peshawar, 1987-88; asst. divisional engr. Pakistan Telecomm. Corp., 1988-98; rsch. engr. Nokia Rsch. Ctr., Tokyo, 1998-99; asst. mgr. DDI Corp., Japan, 1999-2001; rsch. dir. Toshiba Am. Rsch. Inc., Morristown, N.J., 2001—. Vis. rschr. Rikkyo U., Tokyo; tech. advisor Initiatives N.W.F.P. Pakistan for Hearing Impaired Children, Pehswar, 1991-93; participant, presenter IEEE Internat. Symposium on Info. Theory and its Applications, Victoria, Can., 1996, IEEE Internat. Conf. Comm., Montreal, 1997, Asia Pacific Symposium on Info. and Telecom. Tech., Vietnam, 1997, Internat. Conf. Telecomm., Melbourne, Australia, 1997, IASTED Applied Informatics, Garmisch, Germany, 1998, Global Summit 3d Generation Mobile Comm., Japan, 1999, Internat. Symposium Computers and Comm., Red Sea, Egypt, 1999, Vehicular Comm. Techs., Houston, Amsterdam, 1999, IEEE Vehicular Tech. Conf., Amsterdam, 1999, Internat. Workshop on Distributed Computing and Comms., Pakistan, 2000; chmn. working group 1 Mobile Wireless Internet Forum, also project mgr.; also others. Contbr. rsch. papers to profl. jours. and conf. proceedings; editor, writer English newspaper Keio U., Tokyo, 1994-95. English tchr. YMCA, Minami Jr. High Sch. Tsurugashima, Saitama, Japan, 1995-98; mem. Anglican Ch. Peshawar, Pakistan. Recipient scholarship Ministry of Edn., Govt. of Japan, 1996-98, Keio U., 1995-96, Rikkyo U., Tokyo, 1993-95. Mem. IEICE, Christian Student Fellowship Pakistan (sec. 1986-93). Anglican. Avocations: teaching, writing articles. Office: Toshiba Rsch Am Inc Ste 1B268B 445 South St Morristown NJ 07960-6454 Home: 15 Cook Ct Stewartsville NJ 08886 Fax: 908-454-7669.

PERVIN, WILLIAM JOSEPH, computer science educator; b. Pitts., Oct. 31, 1930; s. Abraham and Stella (Greenberger) P.; m. Susan P. Chizeck, 1981; 1 child, Hannah; children by previous marriage: Edward, James, Rachel. BS, MS, U. Mich., 1952; PhD, U. Pitts., 1957. Prof. Pa. State U., 1957-63; vis. prof. Heidelberg (Germany) U., 1963-64; prof., chmn. U. Wis.-Milw., 1964-67; dir. Computer Center, prof. math. Drexel U., Phila., 1967-73; dir. Regional Computer Center U. Tex., Dallas, 1973-78, prof. computer scis., 1973—, chmn. elec. engring., computer scis. & math., 1983-85, master sch. engring. and computer scis., 1987-94. Author: Foundations of General Topology, 1964. Mem. Assn. Computing Machinery, Am. Math. Soc., IEEE Computer Soc., Soc. Indsl. and Applied Math., Math. Assn. Am. Office: U Tex Dallas PO Box 830688 M/S EC 31 Richardson TX 75083-0688 E-mail: pervin@utdallas.edu.

PERYON, CHARLEEN D. education educator, consultant; b. Milw., Apr. 29, 1931; d. Raymond James Dolphin and Violet Selma Solheim Dolphin Berendes; m. Robert Edward Peryon, Nov. 21, 1953; children: Anne Marie Peryon Noonan, Robert Louis, Lynne Marie Peryon Lang. BA in Biology, Clarke Coll., Dubuque, Iowa, 1953; cert. med. tech., St. Anthony Hosp. Sch. Med. Technology, Rockford, Ill., 1954; MEd in Clin. Reading, U. Guam, 1972; PhD in Spl. Edn., Utah State U., 1979. Cert. tchr. Ill., Iowa; cert. cons. Iowa; cert. sch. adminstr. Utah. Tchr. sci. LaGrange (Ill.) Schs., 1966-68, Washington Sr. High Sch., Mangiloa, Guam, 1968-70; asst. prof. edn. U. Guam, 1970-71; reading specialist Dept. Edn. Territory of Guam, Agana, 1971-73, state curriculum cons., 1973-75; assoc. prof. reading and spl. edn. U. Guam, Mangiloa, 1975-85; assoc. prof. reading and learning disabilities Clarke Coll., Dubuque, 1985-86; spl. edn. cons. Keystone Area Edn. Agy., 1986-89; prof. spl. edn. U. Dubuque, 1989—. Cons. in field. Author: Distar Teacher Aide's Handbook, 1974; co-auuthor: Reading Specialist's Handbook, 1973; mem. editorial bd. U. Guam Press, Manigloa, 1983-85; contbr. numerous articles to profl. jours. Trustee Cascade Libr. Bd. Recipient spl. award U.S. Dept. Def. Sch. Dist., Manila, 1976, Internat. Reading Assn. of Newark, 1975. Mem. Internat. Reading Assn. (pres. Guam chpt. 1973-74, chmn. Pacific area 1973-75), Coun. for Exceptional Children (pres. 1992-93), Am. Soc. Clin. Pathologists, Phi Delta Kappa (historian 1977-78, 83-84), Chi Omicron Gamma (pres. 1982-84), Kappa Delta Pi (counselor 1993) Roman Catholic. Avocations: reading, music, cooking, camping, tennis, riding. Home: PO Box 127 Cascade IA 52033-0127 Office: U Dubuque 2000 University Ave Dubuque IA 52001-5050

PESCH, LEROY ALLEN, physician, educator, health and hospital consultant, business executive; b. Mt. Pleasant, Iowa, June 22, 1931; s. Herbert Lindsey and Mary Clarissa (Tyner P.); children from previous marriage: Christopher Allen, Brian Lindsey, Daniel Ethan; m. Donna J. Stone, Dec. 28, 1975 (dec. Feb. 1985); stepchildren: Christopher Scott Kneifel, Linda Suzanne Kneifel; m. Gerri Ann Cotton, Sept. 27, 1986; 1 child, Tyner Ford. Student, State U. Iowa, 1948-49, Iowa State U., 1950-52; MD cum laude, Washington U., St. Louis, 1956. Intern Barnes Hosp., St. Louis, 1956-57; rsch. assoc. NIH, Bethesda, Md., 1957-59; asst. resident medicine Grace-New Haven Hosp., New Haven, 1959-60; clin. fellow Yale Med. Sch., 1960-61, instr. medicine, 1961-62, asst. prof. medicine, 1962-63, asst. dir. liver study unit, 1961-63; assoc. physician Grace-New Haven Hosp., 1961-63; assoc. prof. medicine Rutgers U., New Brunswick, N.J., 1963-64, prof., 1964-66, chmn. dept. medicine, 1965-66; assoc. dean, prof. medicine Stanford Sch. Medicine, 1966-68; mem. gen. medicine study sect. NIH, 1965-70, chmn., 1969-70; dean, dir. univ. hosps. SUNY, Buffalo, 1968-71; dep. asst. sec. manpower HEW, 1970-72, spl. cons. to sec. for health, 1970-75; prof. div. biol. scis. and medicine U. Chgo., 1972-77; prof. pathology Northwestern U., 1977-79; health and hosp. cons.; chmn., chief exec. officer Health Resources Corp. Am., 1981-84; chmn. bd. dirs. Republic Health Corp., 1985-88; chmn., chief exec. officer The Bora Health Group, Seattle, 1987-92; pres. Genus Tech. Corp., 1987—; chmn., chief exec. officer The Pesch Group Cos., Sun Valley, Idaho, 1989—. Contbr. articles on internal medicine to profl. jours. Bd. dirs. Buffalo Med. Found., 1969-72, Health Orgn., Western N.Y., 1968-71, Joffrey Ballet, N.Y.C., 1980—; trustee Michael Reese Hosp. and Med. Ctr., Chgo., 1971-76, pres., CEO, 1971-77; mem. exec. bd. Auditorium Theatre Coun., Chgo.; trustee W. Clement and Jessie V. Stone Found.; mem. adv. com. Congressional Awards; pres. Pesch Found. Sr. asst. surgeon USPHS, 1957-59. Mem. AAAS, Am. Assn. Study of Liver Diseases, Am. Fedn. Clin. Rsch., Am. Soc. Biol. Chemists, Quadrangle Club, Acapulco Yacht Club, Sigma Xi, Alpha Omega Alpha. Office: PO Box 6810 Ketchum ID 83340-6810

PESCOSOLIDO, PAMELA JANE, arts and craft supply store owner, graphic designer; b. Chgo., Dec. 28, 1960; d. Carl Albert Jr. and Linda Clark (Austin) P.; m. Larry Carl Vangroningen, Mar. 5, 1994 (div.); 1 child, Harley Austin. BA, Scripps Coll., 1983; JD, Vt. Law Sch., 1990. Bar: Maine 1990. Office mgr., asst. chef The Elegant Picnic, Stockbridge, Mass., 1983; receptionist, sec. Sequoia Orange County, Exeter, Calif., 1983-84; A/R clk. Tropicana Energy Co., Euless, Tex., 1984-85; owner, calligrapher Calligraphic Arts, Great Barrington, Mass., 1986-87; legal intern Pine Tree Legal Assistance, Augusta, Maine, 1989, Office of the Juvenile Defender, Montpelier, Vt., 1990; bookkeeper Badger Farming Co., Exeter, 1991—; owner, legal drafter and researcher Legal Rsch. Svc., Visalia, Calif., 1990—; owner, graphc designer Hourglass Prodns., 1995—; owner, mgr. The Angel Within, Artists, Supplies and Gallery, Exeter, Calif. Rsch. editor Vt. Law Rev., Vt. Law Sch., South Royalton, 1989-90. Designer, graphic artist polit. propaganda for Libertarian Party of Calif.; contbr. poetry to Nat. Coll. Poetry Rev. Mem. county cen. com., chair Valley Libertarians, Libertarian Party of Calif., Visalia, 1996—; candidate Libertarian Party Dist. 19, Calif. U.S. Congress, 1996; candidate Libertarian Party Calif. State Contr., 1998. Chase scholar Vt. Law Sch., 1989. Mem. ACLU, AAUW (newsletter editor 1994-96), ABA, Nature Conservancy. Avocations: artistic endeavors of all kinds. Office: The Angel Within LLC 137 North E St Exeter CA 93221-1728

PESEC, DAVID JOHN, data systems executive; b. Cleve., Apr. 19, 1956; s. Rudolph J. and Martha C. (Kessler) P. BS, Cleve. State U., 1988; MBA, U. Phoenix, 1999; PhD, Trinity Coll., 2000. Pvt. practice cons., Cleve., 1976-78; programmer Champion Svc. Corp., 1978; sr. sys. programmer United Tel. of Ohio, Mansfield, 1978-89; dir. devel. Broderick Data Sys., 1989-97; prin. cons. Keane, Inc., Independence, Ohio, 1997-2000; pres. Pesec Creative Mgmt., Inc., Mansfield, 2000—. Bd. dirs. Park Ave. Pets, Inc. Bd. dirs. ARC, Mansfield, 1989—, Mansfield Emergency Svc., 1986; assoc. pastor Cornerstone Grace Brethren Ch., 1995—; life mem. Rep. Nat. com., 1991—, Rep. Senatorial Inner Circle, 1991—. Recipient Senatoral medal of freedom, 1996. Mem. Am. Mgmt. Assn., Assn. Computing Machinery, Intercity Radio Club (pres. 1987-90), NRA, Gideons (v.p. 1992), Profl. Photographers. Republican. Mem. Grace Brethren Ch. Avocations: flying, auto racing. Office: Pesec Creative Mgmt Inc 1633 Hickory Ln Mansfield OH 44905-2945 E-mail: dpesec@peseccreativemanagement.com.

PESERIK, JAMES E. electrical, controls and computer engineer, consultant, forensics and safety engineer, fire cause and origin investigator; b. Beloit, Wis., Sept. 30, 1945; s. Edward J. and G. Lucille Peserik; m. Elaine L. Peserik, May 6, 1972. BSEE, U. Wis., 1968; MS, St. Joseph's U., 1990. Registered profl. engr., registered profl. land surveyor; cert. fire and explosion investigator, cert. fire investigation instr.; diplomate Am. Coll. Forensic Examiners. Development and instrumentation engr. Square D Co., Milw., 1968-71; product engr. I-T-E Imperial Corp., Ardmore, Pa., 1971-72; project engr. Harris-Intertype Corp., Easton, 1972-74; elec. engr. Day & Zimmerman, Inc., Phila., 1974-76; pvt. practice Coopersburg, Pa., 1976—; sr. elec. engr. S.T. Hudson Engrs., Inc., Phila., 1980-81. Mem. adv. coun. Swenson Skills Ctr., Phila., 1990-95. Treas. Salford-Fraconia Joint Parks Commn., Montgomery County, Pa., 1980-83. Mem. IEEE (sec. indsl. applications group Phila. chpt. 1980, chmn. 1981, chmn. Lehigh Valley computer sect. 1999—), NSPE, Pa. Soc. Profl. Engrs., Del. Assn. Profl. Engrs. (external affairs com. 1995—), Nat. Fire Protection Assn., Internat. Assn. Arson Investigators, Nat. Assn. Fire Investigators. Office: PO Box 181 Coopersburg PA 18036-0181 E-mail: jepeserik@enter.net.

PESETSKY, BETTE, writer, educator; b. Milw., Nov. 16, 1932; d. Louis Block and Rose McKnight; m. Irwin Pesetsky, 1956; 1 child David. BA, Washington U., St. Louis, 1954; MFA, U. Iowa, 1959. Vis. prof., Writers Workshop U. Iowa, Iowa City, 1990-91; vis. prof., dept. English and comparative studies U. Calif., Irvine, 1992-93; vis. prof. dept. English St. Lawrence U., Canton, N.Y., 1994; Disting. vis. fiction writer Wichita (Kans.) State U., 1994; Disting. vis. prof. dept. English U. Miami, 1997. Piaker vis. prof. dept. English, gen. lit. and rhetoric SUNY, Binghamton, 2002. Author: (novels) Stories Up To a Point, 1982 (NY Times Notable Books, 1982), Author from a Savage People, 1983 (NY Times Notable Books, 1983), Digs, 1985, Midnight Sweets, 1988 (NY Times Notable Books, 1988), Confessions of a Bad Girl, 1989 (NY Times Notable Books, 1989), The Late Night Muse, 1991 (NY Times Notable Books, 1991), Cast a Spell, 1993 (NY Times Notable Books, 1993). Recipient Creative Artists Pub Serv Award, NY Coun Arts, 1980—81; fellow Creative Writing, NEA, 1979. Mem.: PEN. Home: Hilltop Park Dobbs Ferry NY 10522

PESHKIN, MURRAY, physicist; b. Bklyn., May 17, 1925; s. Jacob and Bella Ruth (Zuckerman) P.; m. Frances Julie Ehrlich, June 12, 1955; children—Michael, Sharon, Joel. BA, Cornell U., 1947, PhD, 1951. Instr., then asst. prof. physics Northwestern U., 1951-59; physicist, then sr. scientist Argonne (Ill.) Nat. Lab., 1959—, assoc. dir. physics div., 1972-83. Fellow Weizmann Inst. Sci., Rehovoth, Israel, 1959-60, 68-69; sr. scientist SciTech Mus., Aurora, Ill., 1991—. Served with AUS, 1944-46. Home: 838 Parkside Ave Elmhurst IL 60126-4813 Office: Argonne Natl Lab Argonne IL 60439 E-mail: peshkin@anl.gov.

PESHKIN, SAMUEL DAVID, lawyer; b. Des Moines, Oct. 6, 1925; s. Louis and Mary (Grund) P.; m. Shirley R. Isenberg, Aug. 17, 1947; children: Lawrence Allen, Linda Ann. BA, State U. Iowa, 1948, JD, 1951. Bar: Iowa 1951. Ptnr. Bridges & Peshkin, Des Moines, 1953-66, Peshkin & Robinson, Des Moines, 1966-82. Mem. Iowa Bd. Law Examiners, 1970—. Bd. dirs. State U. Iowa Found., 1957—, Old Gold Devel. Fund, 1956—, Sch. Religion U. Iowa, 1966—. Fellow Am. Bar Found., Internat. Soc. Barristers; mem. ABA (chmn. standing com. membership 1959— , ho. of dels. 1968— , bd. govs. 1973—), Iowa Bar Assn. (bd. govs. 1958— , pres. jr. bar sect. 1958-59, award of merit 1974), Inter-Am. Bar Assn., Internat. Bar Assn., Am. Judicature Soc., State U. Iowa Alumni Assn. (dir., pres. 1957) Home: 6445 E Winchcomb Dr Scottsdale AZ 85254-3356

PESICKA, HARLENE NEAVE, therapist; b. Aberdeen, S.D., July 27, 1937; d. Harlan Michael and Margaret Marie (Hatzenbeller) Loye; m. William John Pesicka, Dec. 23, 1956; children: William Michael, Sandra Sue, Charlene Marie, Dennis John. BS, No. State U., 1992, MS in Edn. (Counseling and Guidance), 1997. Clk. J.J. Newberry, Aberdeen, 1955-56, IRS, Aberdeen, 1957-58; staff asst. Office of Environ. Health Indian Health Svc., 1958-90; exec. dir. battered women shelter Resource Ctr. for Women, 1990-92; exec. dir. S.D. Coalition Against Domestic Violence and Sexual Assault, 1992-95; edn. aide May Overby Sch., 1996; grad. asst. dept. psychology No. State U., 1997; therapist, case mgr. Northeastern Mental Health Ctr., 1997—. Bd. dirs. Resource Ctr. for Women; founding mother Aberdeen Area Rape Task Force, 1976, advocate, spkr., 1977—; bd. dirs. S.D. Peace and Justice, v.p., 1996, pres., 1997, 98; mem. S.D. Advocacy Network for Women, 1984—, pres., 1987; mem. various coms. and bd. dirs., Brown County United Way, chmn. bd., 1980; den mother Boy Scouts Am., also instnl. rep.; mem. S.D. NOW, 1974—, state coord., 1980-90; mgr. Fed. Women's Program Com., nat. EEO counselor, 1975-76; vol. mem. 4-person team on sexism and racism Am. Luth. Ch., N.E. S.D. Dist., 1978-80 Named S.D. Vol. of Yr., 1983, Nat. Vol. of the Yr., Dept. Health and Human Svcs., 1983; recipient award U.S. Dept. Justice, 1992, Athena award Aberdeen C. of C., 1997. Mem. AAUW, Phi Beta Kappa, Pi Gamma Mu. Democrat. Home: 13529 386th Ave Aberdeen SD 57401-8754 Office: Northeastern Mental Health Ctr PO Box 550 Aberdeen SD 57402-0550

PESIKOFF, BETTE SCHEIN, lawyer; b. N.Y.C., Oct. 9, 1942; d. Stephen and Ethel (Barrett) Schein; m. Richard B. Pesikoff, June 7, 1964; children: David, Josh, Daniel. BS, NYU, 1963, MA, 1964; JD, U. Houston, 1974. Bar: Tex. 1974, U.S. Dist. Ct. (so. dist.) Tex. 1975, U.S. Patent and Trademark Office 1995. Tchr. N.Y.C. Bd. Edn., 1964-68; pvt. practice Houston, 1977—. Chmn. social action com. Cong. Emam El, Houston, 1985-87, bd. dirs., sec., 1986-88; mem. community rels. com. Jewish Fedn. Houston, 1986-88; mem. Tex. Supreme Ct. Child Support Guidelines Commn., 1986-87. Fellow Tex. Bar Found.; mem. ABA, Houston Bar Assn. (sec. family law sect. 1986-87), Gulf Coast Family Law Specialists. Democrat. Office: 1715 North Blvd Houston TX 77098-5413

PESIN, ELLA MICHELE, journalist, public relations professional; b. North Bergen, N.J., Aug. 29, 1956; d. Edward and Helene Sylvia (Rattner) P. BA, Sarah Lawrence Coll., 1978. Press rep. CBS-TV News and Entertainment, N.Y.C., 1978-80; publicist Newsweek Mag., 1980-81; freelance journalist, 1982-85; publicist Universal Studios MCA Inc., L.A., 1982-83; with publicity and mktg. NBC-TV News, N.Y.C., 1985-86; media exec. Burson Marsteller Pub. Rels., 1986-87; prin. Pesin Pub. Rels., 1987—. Contbg. editor Cable Age mag., TV Radio Age mag., Advt. Forum, Facts Figures & Film, Advt. Compliance Svc.; syndicated newspaper columnist. Active Israel Bonds/United Jewish Appeal, N.Y.C., Rudolph Giuliani for N.Y.C. Mayor campaign. Mem. Pub. Rels. Soc. Am., N.Y. Venture Group, Women in Comm., Publicity Club N.Y., Healthcare Pub. Rels. and Mktg. Soc. Avocations: photography, sculpture, modern dance, tennis, skiing. Home and Office: 303 E 83rd St Apt 27J New York NY 10028-4323 E-mail: eem75-@aol.com.

PESKER, NICK LEO, musician; b. Sewickly, Pa., July 15, 1946; s. Nicholas Leo and Marcella Pesker. Student, Alliance Coll., 1964-69, Point Park Coll., 1969-72. Musician, dancer Kujawaki Dance Troupe, Cambridge Springs, Pa., 1964-68; musician, arranger Potpourri Trio, Pitts., 1969-73; entertainer, bandleader, ptnr. Eddie Stevens Orch., Hollywood, Fla., 1975-94; prin. Music Grams, 1986-94; founder Nick Pesker's Elegant Music and Entertainment, 1994—; keyboard advisor, concert artist Fletcher Music Ctrs., 2000—02; with Elegant Music and Entertainment, 2002—. Pres. Eagle Scout Mus. Troupe, Ambridge, Pa., 1963-64. Mem. Miami Fedn. Musicians, South Palm Beach Bd. Realtors, Boynton Beach C. of C. Lodges: Croatian Fraternal Union (Pitts.), Polish Nat. Alliance (Chgo.). Republican. Roman Catholic. Avocation: selling real estate. Home: 2186 SW Congress Blvd Boynton Beach FL 33426-5321

PESKIN, CHARLES, physicist, educator; b. N.Y.C., Apr. 15, 1946; AB, Harvard U., 1968; PhD in Physics, Albert Einstein Coll. Med., 1972. Prof. math N.Y.U., 1973—. Elected mem. Inst. of Medicine, 2000. McArthur Found. fellow 1982. Mem. Nat. Acad. Sci. Office: Courant Inst 251 Mercer St New York NY 10012-1185*

PESKOV, VLADIMIR DMITRIEVICH, physicist, educator, consultant; b. Karaganda, Russia, Jan. 30, 1947; s. Dmitri S. and Olga D. (Petrova) P.; m. Tatiana R. Zabotina, May 3, 1973; children: Dmitri, Tatiana. MS in Physics, Phys. and Tech. Inst., Moscow, 1971; PhD in Physics, USSR Acad. Sci., Moscow, 1976, DSc, 1981. Rschr. Inst. Phys. Problems, Moscow, 1971-76, sr. rschr., 1976-97, leading scientist, 1981-97, prof., 1998; assoc. scientist European Ctr. for Nuclear Rsch., Geneva, Switzerland, 1986-92; application physicist II Fermi Nat. Accelerator Lab., Batavia, Ill., 1992-95; invited prof. Coimbra (Portugal) U., 1995-98; NRC sr. rsch. assoc. Marshall Space Ctr., Huntsville, Ala., 1995-98; guest prof. Royal Inst. Tech., 1998—; dir. rsch. Inst. Applied Mechanics Russian Acad. Sci., 1998—. Mem. adv. bd. several internat. confs.; org. com. Internat. Conf. Imaging 2000, Stockholm; mem. neutron time of flight experiment European Orgn. for Nuclear Rsch.. Contbr. more than 100 articles to profl. jours. including Nuclear Instruments and Methods, Soviet Physics JETF, Jour. Physics. Participant Internat. Meeting on Chem. Disarmament, Rome, 1989, Internat. Forum di Amore, Italy, 1991, Internat. Meeting Our Nature, Italy, 1991. Recipient Prize of World Fedn. of Scientists, World Lab./Italian Physics Soc., 1991. Mem. Am. Phys. Soc., Italian Phys. Soc. Achievements include invention of device for magnetic field measurement of landing spacecraft, position sensitive gas scintillating detector; invention of new detector and methods for radiation measurement; some of them, for example detectors with gaseous and solid photocathodes are now widely used in experimental techniques; discovery of new type of plasma instability, connected to accumulation of excited atoms and molecules, a flux-induced breakdown, cathode excitation effect. Office: Stockholm Physics Ctr Particle Physics Grp KTH Phys Dept S-10691 Stockholm Sweden

PESMEN, SANDRA (MRS. HAROLD WILLIAM PESMEN), editor; b. Chgo., Mar. 26, 1931; s. Benjamin S. and Emma (Lipschultz) P.; m. Harold W. Pesmen, Aug. 16, 1952; children: Bethann, Curtis. BS, U. Ill., 1952. Reporter Radio and Community News Service, Chgo., 1952-53; wire editor Champaign-Urbana (Ill.) Courier, 1953; reporter, feature writer Lerner Chgo. N. Side Newspapers, 1953-55; stringer corr. Wayne (Mich.) Eagle, 1958-61; reporter, feature writer Chgo. Daily News, 1968-78; features editor Crain's Chgo. Business mag., 1978-89; corp. features editor Crain Communications, Inc., 1989-95; tchr. feature writing Northwestern U. Evening Sch., 1972-81. Author: Writing for the Media, 1983, Dr. Job's Complete Career Guide, 1995; editor: Career News Service; author syndicated column Dr. Job, 1985—. Recipient Golden Key award Ill. Mental Health Dept., 1966, 71, award Inst. Psychoanalysis, 1971, Penny Mo. award, 1978, Stick o'Type award Chgo. Newspaper Guild, 1978, award AP, 1975, Peter Lisagor award Soc. Profl. Journalists, 1991; inductee Chgo. Journalism Hall of Fame, 1997. Home: 2811 Fern Ave Northbrook IL 60062-5809 E-mail: drjob@voyager.net.

PESNER, CAROLE MANISHIN, art gallery owner; b. Boston, Aug. 5, 1937; m. Robert Pesner (dec. 1983); children: Ben, Jonah; m. Martin Cherkasky, 1995 (dec. 1997). BA, Smith Coll., 1959. Asst. dir. Kraushaar Galleries, Inc., N.Y.C., 1959-86, dir., 1986-90, pres., 1991—. Author, editor publs., catalogues in field. Mem. Art Dealers Assn. Am., Internat. Fine Print Dealers Assn. Office: Kraushaar Galleries Inc 724 5th Ave New York NY 10019-4106

PESOLA, GENE RAYMOND, physician, educator; b. Hancock, Mich., Oct. 21, 1952; s. Raymond Lloyd and Helen Eleanor Pesola; m. Helen Rostata, Jan. 5, 1991; children: Gene Richard, Glen Raymond, Gary Roger. BS in Biology magna cum laude, Mich. Technol. U., Houghton, 1974; MD, Wayne State U., 1979; MPH in Biostats. magna cum laude, Columbia U., 1998. Diplomate Am. Bd. Internal Medicine, also sub-bds. pulmonary medicine and critical care medicine; cert. BCLS, ACLS, ATLS, PALS. Intern Harlem Hosp., N.Y.C., 1979-80; resident U. Tenn. Affiliated Hosps., Memphis, 1980-82; fellow in pulmonary medicine Mt. Sinai Hosp. and Affiliates, N.Y.C., 1982-84; fellow in critical care medicine Meml. Sloan-Kettering Cancer Ctr., 1984-85, rsch. fellow, 1985-87; asst. prof. medicine and anesthesia Albert Einstein U., Bronx, N.Y., 1988-89; attending physician Mt. Vernon (N.Y.) Emergency Room, 1989-90; rschr. cell/molecular pharmacology and exptl. therapeutics Med. U. S.C., Charleston, 1991-94; attending physician critical care and emergency medicine N.Y. Cmty. Hosp., Bklyn., 1989—; attending physician dept. emergency medicine St. Vincent's Hosp., N.Y.C., 1994—; asst. prof. emergency medicine N.Y. Med. Coll., 1995-2000, assoc. prof. emergency medicine, 2000; assoc. attending physician Divsn. Pulmonary and Critical Care Medicine Harlem Hosp./Columbia U., NYC, 2001—. Contbr. chpts. to books, numerous articles to profl. jours.; reviewer for numerous jours. including CHEST, Catheterization and Cardiovascular Interventions. Recipient various awards; grantee Am. Fedn. Clin. Rsch., 1992; Pharm. Mfrs. Found. fellow, 1992-94.

PESOLA, WILLIAM ERNEST, restaurant management executive; b. Marquette, Mich., Mar. 2, 1945; s. Ernest Ensio and Janice Mary (LeDuc) P.; m. Kathleen Mary Deschaine, July 9, 1966; children: Christie Lynn, Laurie Anne. BS, No. Mich. U., 1968, MS, 1971. Route driver Coca Cola Co., Marquette, 1963-68; tchr. Gwinn (Mich.) Schs., 1968-78, pub. Sch. News, 1969; pres. Pesola Mgmt., Marquette, 1974—, Humboldt Ridge, Marquette, 1977—; treas. Elite Bar, Inc., 1978—; v.p., dir. Marquette Cablevison, 1981-85; pres. Upper Peninsula Big Boy, Marquette, 1990—. Cons. cable TV, 1985—, Bresnan Comm., 1984—. Pres. Gwinn Edn. Assn., 1975-77; regional pres. Upper Peninsula Edn. Assn., 1977-78; mem. Marquette City Commn., 1977-81. Mem. NEA, Marquette Econ. Club, Mich. Edn. Assn., Marquette C. of C. (Exemplary Citizen award 1990), Rotary. Roman Catholic. Home: 1026 N Front St Marquette MI 49855-3514

PESSES, MARVIN, metal products executive, consultant; b. Bklyn., July 18, 1923; s. I. Aaron and Ann (Deines) P.; m. Elaine Barbara, Oct. 13, 1931; children: Lawrence, Ian, Paul, Michael. BS, Purdue U., 1944; MS, U. Ill., 1946; student, U. Iowa, 1946-48; DSc (hon.), London Coll. Eng., 1966. Registered profl. engr. V.p. Alloy Metal Products, Davenport, Iowa, 1950-64; pres. Mercer Alloys, Greenville, Pa., 1964-71; CEO, chmn. The Pesses Co., Pepper Pike, Ohio, 1971-80; CEO Pentad Group, Boca Raton, Fla., 1980—. Dir. Stainless & Alloy Corp., Greenville, Pa., 1964-1971, Quinten Ptrs., Solon, Ohio, 1971—. Patentee in field. Pres. Tent-at-the-Tower, Moline, Ill., 1960-64. Mem. Am. Soc. Metals (chmn., dir. 1952-68), Am. Foundrymen's Soc. (dir.), Ductile Iron Soc. (dir. 1960-68). Avocations: bicycling, horseback riding, target shooting, hunting, photography. Home: 7234 Francisco Bend Dr Delray Beach FL 33446- E-mail: labelsaver@aol.com.

PESTA, BEN W., II, lawyer, writer; b. Hagerstown, Md., Oct. 15, 1948; s. Ben W. and Ethel Irene (Kirkpatrick) P.; m. Monique Raphel High, Dec. 24, 1987. AB, UCLA, 1969; JD, U. Calif., Berkeley, 1972. Bar: U.S. Supreme Ct., U.S. Ct. Appeals, U.S. Dist. Ct., Calif. Assoc. pub. Weider Health & Fitness, Woodland Hills, Calif., 1984-90; atty. Contbr. Esquire, Playboy, Rolling Stone, Sport, TV Guide, Cosmopolitan,L.A. Times, L.A. Style mags. and profl. jours. Capt. USAF., 1973. Office: Ste 900 1801 Avenue Of The Stars Los Angeles CA 90067-5803

PESTANA, CARLOS, physician, educator; b. Tacoronte, Tenerife, Canary Islands, Spain, June 10, 1936; came to U.S., 1968, naturalized, 1973; s. Francisco and and Blanca (Suarez) P.; m. Myrna Lorena Serrato, Aug. 25, 1966; children— Becky Elizabeth, George Byron. BS, Nat. U. Mex., 1952, MD, 1959; PhD in Surgery, U. Minn., 1965. Intern St. Mary of Nazareth Hosp., Chgo., 1959-60; resident Mayo Clinic, Rochester, Minn., 1961-65; surgeon Hosp. 20 de Noviembre Mexico City; asst. prof. surgery Nat. U. Mex., 1966-67, U. Tex. Med. Sch. at San Antonio, 1968-70, asso. prof., 1970-74, prof., 1974—, asso. dean for acad. devel., 1971-73, asso. dean for student affairs, 1973-86, assoc. dean acad. affairs, 1986-97, clin. prof. surgery, 1998-2000, prof. emeritus, 2000—. Recipient Edward John Noble Found. award, 1965, Piper Prof. award Minnie Stevens Piper Founds., 1972, Nat. Golden Apple award Am. Med. Student Assn., 1999. Mem. Alpha Omega Alpha (Robert J. Glaser Disting. Tchr. award 1997). Home: 10123 N Manton Ln San Antonio TX 78213-1932 Office: 7703 Floyd Curl Dr San Antonio TX 78284-6200

PESTANA-NASCIMENTO, JUAN M. civil, geotechnical and geoenvironmental engineer, consultant; b. Caracas, Venezuela, June 24, 1963; came to U.S., 1986; s. Domingos Pestana and Maria Cisaltina Nascimento; m. Sandra Mattar, Oct. 29, 1988; 1 child, Maria Teresa Pestana. BS summa cum laude, U. Catolica Andres Bello, Caracas, 1985; MS, MIT, 1988, ScD, 1994. Registered civil engr., Venezuela. Teaching asst. U. Catolica Andres Bello, Caracas, 1982-85, instr., lectr., 1986; cons. engr. GEODEC, Geotech. Cons., 1986-92; civil engr. CALTEC, Hydraulic Cons., 1983-86, asst. engr., 1983-85, T.W. Lambe, Inc., Cambridge, Mass., 1990; cons. Portfolio Mgmt., 1990-92; rsch. asst. MIT, Mass., 1992-94; asst. prof. U. Calif., Berkeley, 1994—. Contbr. articles to profl. jours. Gran Mariscal de Ayacucho scholar, 1986-88, INTEVEP scholar, 1989-92. Mem. ASCE, ASTM, Can. Soc. Geotech. Engrs., Internat. Soc. Soil Mechanics and Found. Engring., Sigma Xi. Achievements include development of a model to describe the behavior in compression of cohesionless soils, development of a new effective stress model which united the modelling of clays, sand and silts which is capable of describing shear behavior over a wide range of confining stresses; research in description of stress-strain behavior of soils under monotonic and cyclic loading, time effects, numerical modelling of soil-structure interaction using advanced soil models. Home: 10 San Antonio Ct Walnut Creek CA 94598-4127 Office: U Calif Dept Civil Engring 440 Davis Hl Berkeley CA 94720-0001

PESUT, DANIEL J. nursing educator; b. DeKalb, Ill., Dec. 12, 1951; s. George D. and Donna M. Pesut; m. Susan E. Ziel, Aug. 28, 1981; children: Elliott, Erin. BSN, No. Ill. U., 1975; MSN, U. Tex., San Antonio, 1977; PhD, U. Mich., 1984. RN, Ind.; cert. specialist. Assoc. prof. U. Mich. Sch. Nursing, Ann Arbor, 1978-81; dir. nursing William S. Hall Psychiat. Inst., Columbia, 1984-87; assoc. prof. U. S.C., 1987-93; prof., dept. chair environ. health Ind. U. Sch. Nursing, Indpls., 1997—. Author: Clinical Reasoning: The Art and Science of Critical and Creative Thinking, 1999. Fellow Am. Acad. Nursing; mem. Sigma Theta Tau (pres.-elect 2001--, Creativity award 1993). Avocations: piano, travel, reading. Home: 14144 Blue Heron Dr Carmel IN 46033 Office: Ind Univ Dept Environ Health Sch Nursing Indianapolis IN 46204 E-mail: dpesut@iupui.edu.

PESUT, TIMOTHY SCOTT, investment advisor, professional speaker, life advisor; b. Gary, Ind., June 30, 1956; s. Anton and Virginia Udean (Carahoff) P.; m. Michelle Angela Durdov, May 25, 1985; children: Ariel Fay, Caitlin Michelle. AAS in Elec. Engring. Tech., Purdue U., 1978, AAS Supervision, BS Elec. Engring. Tech., 1980. Cert. fin. planner; cert. funds specialist, trust and estate planning advisor, investment mgmt. cons.; cert. sr. advisor. Cardiology clin. rsch. assoc. Cordis Corp., Miami, Fla., 1980-82, neurosurg. specialist, 1982; investment broker A. G. Edwards Sons, Merrillville, Ind., 1982-86, Shearson Lehman, Sarasota, Fla., 1986-88; portfolio mgr. Prudential Securities, Inc., Venice, 1988-91; resident mgr. First Southeastern Securities Group, Sarasota, 1995-2000; v.p. Wealth Dr., LLC, 2000—. Arbitrator Am. Arbitration Assn., 1992-99; founder Inst. of Cert. Estate Planners. Columnist Money Talks, 1985, Money Mgmt., 1995. Guardian ad litem 12th Dist. Ct., Sarasota, 1985; bd. dirs. Jr. Achievement of Sarasota County; founding mem. Anthony Robbins Found., 1990; fundraising chmn. Jr. Achievement of Sarasota County. Cpl. USMC, 1974-76. Mem. Profl. Assn. Diving Instrs. (Divemaster), Nat. Speakers Assn., Toastmasters Internat. (yr. 2000 conv. chmn., lt. gov. mktg. 1996-97, dist. treas. 1995-96, lt. gov. edn. and tng. 1997-98, disting. dist. 47 gov. 1998-99, Area Gov. of Yr. 1994, Excellence in Edn. and Tng. award 1997-98, Dist. Dist. Gov. award 1998-99, yr. 2000 conv. chmn.). Republican. Methodist. Avocations: scuba diving, skiing, sailing, woodworking, fine arts. Office: Wealth Dr LLC 7061 S Tamiami Trl # 201 Sarasota FL 34231-5559 E-mail: wealthdr@hotmail.com.

PESZKE, MICHAEL ALFRED, psychiatrist, writer; b. Deblin, Poland, Dec. 19, 1932; s. Alfred Bartlomiej and Eugenia Halina (Grebocka) Peszke; m. Alice Margaret Sherman, Sept. 20, 1958; children: Michele Halina Olender, Michael Alexander. BA, Trinity Coll., Dublin, Ireland, 1956; MB, BCh, BAO, Dublin U., 1956. Cert. Bd. cert. psychiatrist. Staff psychiatrist Yale Student Health Svc., New Haven, 1961-64; asst. prof. sch. medicine U. Chgo., 1964-68; cons. psychiatrist Wesleyan U., Middletown, Conn., 1968-70; asst. prof. Sch. Medicine U. Conn., Farmington, 1970-73, assoc. prof., 1973-80, prof. psychiatry, 1980-90; clin. prof. U. Md. Sch. Medicine, Balt., 1991-99; chief Psychiatry Svc. Perry Point (Md.) VA Med. Ctr., 1990-98, co-coord. R&D, 1998-99. Dir. psychiat. clin. svcs. John Dempsey Hosp. U. Conn. Health Ctr., Farmington, 1983—87; chief VA Med. Ctr., Newington, Conn., 1987—90; ind. rschr., 1999—. Author: Involuntary Treatment of the Mentally Ill: The Problem of Autonomy, 1975, Battle for Warsaw, 1939-44, 1995, Poland's Navy: 1918-1945, 1999; co-author (edited by L.A. Pervin, L.R. Reik, W. Dalrymple): The College Drop-out and the Utilization of Talent, 1966; co-author: (edited by J. Zusman, E. Bertsch) The Future of Psychiatric State Hospitals, 1975; contbr. Fellow: APA (Life); mem.: Am. Coll. Psychiatrists, Royal United Svc. Inst. (London), Soc. for Mil. History.

PETACQUE, ARTHUR M. journalist; b. Chgo., July 20, 1924; s. Ralph David and Fay Nora (Brauner) P.; m. Regina Battinus, Dec. 10, 1944; children: Susan Petacque Block, William Scott. Student, U. Ill., 1940-42; PhD (hon.), So. Ill. U., 1987. With Chgo. Sun, 1942-47; with Chgo. Sun-Times, 1947-91, investigative reporter, 1957-91, columnist, 1974-91. Crime editor World Book Ency., 1970-75; lectr. various univs. and civic orgns. Mem. B'nai B'rith. Recipient Page One awards for outstanding journalism Chgo. Newspaper Guild, 1949, 57, 59, 62, 63, 65, 68; Joseph M. Fay Meml. award Chgo. Newspaper Reporters Assn., 1960; Prof. Jacob Scher-Theta Sigma Phi Daily Newswriting award Chgo. chpt. Theta Sigma Phi, 1964; John Baptist Scalabrini award for leadership Am. Community Italian Ancestry, 1966; awards for investigative reporting and spot news AP, 1963, 66, 68, (2) 74, 76; Marshall Field award for outstanding editorial contbn. in behalf of Chgo. Sun-Times, 1968; Pulitzer Prize for gen. reporting, 1974; State of Israel Prime Minister's medal, 1976; Dante award Civic Com. Italian Americans, 1980; UPI award for best spot news coverage Ill., 1980; Emmy award for ABC-TV local news spot reporting, 1984; Award for Long and Dedicated Newspaper Reporting on Crime and the Criminal Justice System, Ill. Acad. Criminology, 1985; named to Chgo. Journalism Hall of Fame Chgo Headline Club, 1990. Mem. Chgo. Newspaper Guild, Jewish War Vets. (hon.), Sigma Delta Chi, Sigma Alpha Mu. Jewish. *Have tried to be fair, careful and objective in my profession, realizing that what we say about the person we write about has not only an effect on the subject but his family and friends.* Died June 6, 2001.

PETAEV, MIKHAIL IVANOVICH, geologist, researcher; b. Kasimov, Russia, May 7, 1957; came to U.S., 1991; s. Ivan M. and Zinaida V. (Ivanova) P.; m. Vera N. Glodina, Mar. 6, 1982; 1 child, Ivan. MS, Moscow State U., 1979; PhD, USSR Acad. Scis., 1985. Staff scientist Lab. Thermodynamics of Natural Processes, Vernadsky Inst., Moscow, 1982-84, head meteorite rsch. group Lab. Comparative Planetology, 1984-91; rsch. assoc. Harvard-Smithsonian Ctr. for Astrophysics, Harvard U., Cambridge, Mass., 1992—. Dir. Precious Stones and Meteorites from the USSR Exhbn., Prague, Czechoslovakia, 1987-88; curator Nat. Meteorite Collection of USSR Acad. Scis., Moscow, 1988-92. Contbr. articles to profl. jours. Mem. Meteoritical Soc., Am. Geophys. Union, Geochem. Soc. Avocations: fishing, outdoor activity, reading, political analysis. Office: Harvard-Smithsonian CFA 60 Garden St Cambridge MA 02138-1516 E-mail: mpetaev@cfa.harvard.edu.

PETAK, WILLIAM JOHN, systems management educator; b. Johnstown, Pa., June 23, 1932; s. Val Andrew and Lola Agatha (Boroski) P.; m. Ramona Janet Cayuela, Dec. 28, 1957; children: Elizabeth Ann Petak-Aaron, William Matthew, Michael David. BS in Mech. Engring., U. Pitts., 1956; MBA, U. So. Calif., 1963, DPA, 1969. Engr. Northrop Corp., Hawthorne, Calif., 1956-59; test engr. Wyle Labs., El Segundo, 1959-63; we. regional mgr. Instrument div. Budd Co., Phoenixville, Pa., 1963-69; v.p., dir. J.H. Wiggins Co., Redondo Beach, Calif., 1969-81; prof. systems mgmt. U. So. Calif., L.A., 1982-98, exec. dir. Inst. Safety and Sys. Mgmt., 1987-98, prof. policy, planning and devel., 1998—. Chmn. earthquake mitigation com. Nat. Com. on Property Ins., Boston, 1990-92; mem. com. on natural disasters NRC, Washington, 1985-91, mem. U.S. nat. com. for the decade for natural disaster reduction, 1989-92. Co-author: Natural Hazard Risk Assessment and Public Policy, 1982, Politics and Economics of Earthquake Hazard Reduction, 1986, Disabled Persons and Earthquake Hazards, 1988; editor spl. issue Pub. Adminstrn. Rev., 1985. Commr. County of Los Angeles, 1994—; mem. policy bd. So. Calif. Earthquake Prep. Project, L.A., 1986-92; trustee Marymount Coll., Palos Verdes, Calif., 1974—. Sgt. U.S. Army, 1950-52. Mem. Soc. for Risk Analysis, Earthquake Engring. Rsch. Inst., Am. Soc. for Pub. Adminstrn., Sigma Xi. Republican. Roman Catholic. Avocations: skiing, fishing, hiking. Office: U So Calif MC 0626 Sch Policy Planning & Devel Los Angeles CA 90089-0001

PETAKOV, DRAGAN SVETOZAR, internist, educator; b. Belgrade, Yugoslavia, June 18, 1962; came to U.S., 1995; s. Svetozar and Miroslava P.; m. Izolda Petakov, Aug. 21, 1992; children: Aleksandar, Luka. MD, U. Belgrade, Yugoslavia, 1990. Diplomate Am. Bd. Internal Medicine. Intern Clin. Ctr. Belgrade, 1990-91; med. intern Elim (South Africa) Hosp., 1992, med. officer, 1993-94; resident Johannesburg (South Africa) Gen. Hosp., 1994-95, NYU Med. Ctr., N.Y.C., 1995-98; attending physician Lowell (Mass.) Cmty. Health Ctr., 1998—. Clin. instr. Harvard Med. Sch., Boston, 1999—. Mem. ACP. Avocations: music, reading, stamp collecting. Office: Lowell Cmty Health Ctr 585 Merrimack St Lowell MA 01854-3908 E-mail: dpetakov@pol.net.

PETCHENEV, ALEX, scientist; b. St. Petersburg, Russia, May 3, 1956; arrived in the U.S., 1993; BS, Poly. U., St. Petersburg, 1977, MS, 1979, PhD, 1987. Engr. Mekhanobr-Tekhnika, St. Petersburg, 1978-85, scientist, 1985-92; engr. Bently Nevada Corp., Minden, Nev., 1993-94, scientist, 1994—. Mem. ASME, Russian Engring. Acad. (fgn.). Office: Bently Nevada Corp 1711 Orbit Way Bldg 1 Minden NV 89423-4114 E-mail: alex.petchenev@bently.com.

PETE, ERIC E. claims representative, writer; b. Seattle, Oct. 1, 1968; s. Earl Joseph Pete and Edna Mae Bushnell; m. Marsha Bluin; 1 child Chelsea. BS, McNeese State U., 1993. Assoc. in mgmt., assoc. in claims, sr. claims liaison assoc. Claim specialist State Farm Cos., 1994—; owner E-fect Pub., Harvey, La., 2000—. Author: (novels) Real for Me, 2000, Someone's In the Kitchen, 2002. With U.S. Army, 1987—89. Mem.: Internat. Assn. Spl. Investigative Units, Romance Writers Am., Young Leadership Coun. Greater New Orleans, Black Writers Alliance, Toastmasters Internat., Delta Sigma Pi. Avocations: reading, travel, dancing, weightlifting, art. Office: PO Box 2425 Harvey LA 70059-2425 Business E-Mail: heyeric@att.net.

PETE, MAHEN CHANDUBHAI, civil engineer; b. Rasnol, India, Jan. 11, 1955; came to U.S., 1983; s. Chandubhai N. and Savitaben C. Patel; m. Jyotsna M. Patel; children: Roshni, Chirag. BE in Civil Engring., Maharaja Sayajirao U., Baroda, India, 1976; MS in Engring. Mgmt., U. So. Fla., 1995. Registered profl. engr., Fla. Civil engr. City of Lakeland, Fla., 1987—. Mem.: ASCE, Fla. Engring. Soc. Achievements include rsch. in problem solving using techniques of both civil and industrial engineering. Office: City of Lakeland 228 S Massachusetts Ave Lakeland FL 33801-5012

PETER, ARNOLD PHILIMON, lawyer, business executive; b. Karachi, Pakistan, Apr. 3, 1957; came to U.S., 1968; s. Kundan Lal and Irene Primrose (Mall) P. BS, Calif. State U., Long Beach, 1981; JD, Loyola U., L.A., 1984; MS, Calif. State U., Fresno, 1991. Bar: Calif. 1985, U.S. Dist. Ct. (ea., so., no. and cen. dists.) Calif. 1986, U.S. Ct. Appeals (9th cir.) 1989, U.S. Ct. Appeals (11th cir.) 1990. Law clk. appellate dept. Superior Ct., L.A., 1984-85, U.S. Dist. Ct. (ea. dist.) Calif., Fresno, 1986-88; assoc. Pepper, Hamilton & Scheetz, L.A., 1988-89, McDermott, Will & Emery, P.A., L.A., 1989-90, Cadwalader, Wickersham & Taft, L.A., 1990-91; labor and employment counsel City of Fresno, Calif., 1991-94; atty. Littler Mendelson, L.A., 1999—. V.p. legal and bus. affairs Universal Studios, Hollywood, Calif., 1994—; adj. prof. law San Joaquin (Calif.) Sch. Law, 1993—; adj. prof. law Calif. State U., Fresno, 1993—, acad. inquiry officer, 1993—. Contbr. articles to profl. jours. Mem. L.A. 2012 Olympic Bd. Com. Mem. ABA, L.A. County Bar Assn. (mem. conf. of dels., com. on fed. cts.), Calif. State Bar Assn. (chmn. com. on fed. cts., chmn. exec. com. labor and employment law sect.), L.A. Athletic Club. Friars Club. Office: Universal Studios 100 Universal City Plz Universal City CA 91608

PETER, PHILLIPS SMITH, lawyer; b. Washington, Jan. 24, 1932; s. Edward Compston and Anita Phillips (Smith) P.; m. Jania Jayne Hutchins, Apr. 8, 1961; children: Phillips Smith Peter Jr., Jania Jayne Hutchins Stone. BA, U. Va., 1954, JD, 1959. Bar: Calif. 1959. Assoc. McCutchen, Doyle, Brown, Enerson, San Francisco, 1959-63; with GE (and subs.), various locations, 1963-94, v.p. corp. bus. devel., 1973-76, v.p., 1976-79, v.p. corp. govtl. rels., 1980-94; counsel, head govt. rels. dept. Reed Smith Shaw & McClay, 1994—. Chmn. bd. govs. Bryce Harlow Found., 1990-92, bd. dirs. Mem. editl. bd. Va. Law Rev., 1957-59. Trustee Howard U., 1981-89; bd. dirs., exec. com. Nat. Bank of Washington, 1981-86; v.p. Fed. City Coun., Washington, 1979-85; bd. dirs. Carlton, 1987-90, 95-98, pres., 1995-96; bd. dirs. Tudor Place Found., 1999—, v.p., 2001-02, pres., 2002--. With transp. corps U.S. Army, 1954-56. Mem. Calif. Bar Assn., Order of Colf, Wee Burn Club, Ea. Yacht Club, Farmington Country Club, Ponte Vedra Club, Lago Mar Club, Landmark Club, Congl. Country Club, Georgetown Club, Chevy Chase Club, Pisces Club, F Street Club, Fairfax Club, Carlton Club (bd. dirs. 1990-98), Coral Beach and Tennis Club, Johns Island Club, The Windsor Club, Omicron Delta Kappa. Episcopalian. Home: 10805 Tara Rd Potomac MD 20854-1341 also: Johns Island 1000 Beach Rd & 690 Ocean Vero Beach FL 32963-3429 E-mail: ppeter@reedsmith.com.

PETER, RICHARD ECTOR, zoology educator; b. Medicine Hat, Alta., Can., Mar. 7, 1943; s. Arthur E. and Josephine (Wrobleski) P.; m. Leona L. Booth, Dec. 27, 1965; children: Jason E., Matthew T.B. BSc with honors, U. Atla., 1965; PhD, U. Wash., 1969. Postdoctoral fellow U. Bristol, Eng., 1969-70; asst. prof. U. Alta., Edmonton, 1971-74, assoc. prof., 1974-79, prof., 1979—, chmn. dept. zoology, 1983-89, 90-92, dean of sci., 1992—2002; v.p. Alta. Rsch. Coun., 2002—. Contbr. over 300 papers to sci. publs. Recipient Outstanding Leadership in Alberta Sci. award Alberta Sci. and Tech. Leadership Awards Found., 1998, Excellence in Mentoring award U. Alberta, 2002; named Disting. Biologist, Can. Coun. Univ. Biology Chairmen. Fellow AAAS, Royal Soc. Can.; mem. Can. Soc. Zoology (pres. 1991-92), Endocrine Soc., Soc. for Study of Reprodn., Internat. Soc. Neuroendocrinology, Can. Coun. of Univ. Biology Chmn. (pres. 1986-87), Internat. Fedn. Comparative Endocrinol. Socs. (pres. 1989-93, Pickford medal 1985), Canadian Conf. of Deans of Sci., 1995-96 (pres.), Western Can. Univs. Marine Scis. Soc. (pres. 2001-02).

PETER, SEBASTIAN AUGUSTINE, endocrinologist; b. St. Georges, Grenada, Jan. 20, 1944; came to U.S., 1975; s. Sidney Augustine and Cisly (Scoon) P.; m. Angela Missouri Sherman, July 18, 1970; children: Sebastian Augustine Jr., Senaka Akalbi. MBBS, U. W.I., 1969. Intern U. W.I., Nassau, 1970; resident in medicine Dalhousie U., Halifax, N.S., Can., 1971-72, U. Ottawa, Ont., Can., 1972-74, resident in endocrinology Can., 1974-75; fellow in endocrinology SUNY Health Sci. Ctr., Bklyn., 1975-76, assoc. clin. prof. medicine, 1992—; chief of endocrinology St. Mary's Hosp., 1992—. Contbr. articles to profl. jours. Recipient Community award Grenada Ex-Students Assn., 1991. Democrat. Avocations: music, jazz, playing musical instrument, reading. Home and Office: Apt 5L 71 Ocean Pkwy Brooklyn NY 11218-1832

PETERA, ANNE PAPPAS, state official; b. Richmond, Va., Feb. 13, 1950; d. Evangel Thomas and Margaret Theresa (McGuire) Pappas; m. Ronald Petera, Sept. 15, 1968; 1 child, Paul Evangel. BS, Va. Commonwealth U., 1980; grad., Realtors Inst. Br. officer Ctrl. Fidelity Bank, Richmond, 1972-79; asst. v.p. Signet Bank, 1979-85; sales assoc. Hermitage Realty, 1985-92; assoc. broker Napier Old Colony, 1992-95, Bowers, Nelms & Fonville & Jefferson-Jones, Richmond, 1995-96; chair Va. Dept. Alcoholic Beverage Control, 1996-97; sec. Commonwealth of Va., 1998—2002; chief of staff to Atty. Gen. of Va., 2002—. Mem. faculty Richmond Assn. Realtors Sch. Real Estate, 1991-96; bd. visitors Va. Commonwealth U., 2001—. Vice-chmn. Hanover (Va.) County Rep. Com., 1990-92, chmn., 1992-94; chmn. 1st Congl. Dist., Rep. Party Va., Richmond, 1994-98, budget dir., 1996-98, treas. 1998-2001; mem. Rep. Nat. Com., 2001—. Named Disting. Achiever, Richmond Assn. Realtors, 1986, 87, 89, 90, 91, 92, 93, 94. Mem. Nat. Alcohol Beverage Control Assn. (dir. 1996-98), Nat. Assn. Realtors, Nat. Assn. Bank Women. Republican. Roman Catholic. Avocations: golf, reading, travel. Office: Office of the Atty Gen 900 E Main St Richmond VA 23219-2725 E-mail: annepetera@aol.com.

PETERKIN, ALBERT GORDON, retired education educator; b. Phila., May 25, 1915; s. Albert Gordon and Eleanor Frances (Fricke) P.; m. Helen Webster, June 14, 1947; children: Eleanor Fricke, Scott Boddington, Mark Webster. BA, U. Pa., 1936; MAT, Harvard U., 1946; EdD, Columbia U., 1954.

Cert. sch. adminstr., N.J., Conn., Ill. Tchr. Arms Acad., Shelburne Falls, Mass., 1938-39, Park Sch. of Buffalo, Snyder, N.Y., 1939-41; asst. prof. Lehigh U., Bethlehem, Pa., 1948-55; founding supt. Watchung Hills Regional H.S., Warren, N.J., 1955-60; supt. Westport (Conn.) Pub. Schs., 1960-70, Winnetka (Ill.) Sch. Dist. 36, 1971-77; prof. edn. Vanderbilt U., Nashville, 1977-81; ret., 1981. Cons. Nat. Assn. Sch. Bus. Officers, Washington, 1968-70, Tenn. State U., Nashville, 1980-81; advisor Coun. Basic Edn., Washington, 1975; trustee Country Sch., Madison, Conn., 1985-91; chmn. master's program Iranian Sch. Devel., 1978-80, assessment instrument student devel., 1974; initiator Cooperative Individualized Reading Project, U.S. Office Edn., 1970-73. Initiator Urban Coalition Sch. Study, Bridgeport, Conn., 1969-70; pres. Friends of Libr., Madison, 1984-85; prodr. cmty. TV, Madison, 1984-90; mem. Madison Inland Wetlands Commn., 1985—, chmn., 1990-92. Lt. comdr. USNR, 1941-45. John Hay fellow Greenwood Found., 1965; Kettering Found. fellow, 1966, 69; Whitehead fellow Harvard Sch. Edn., 1970-71; named to Supt.'s Hall of Fame Sch. Mgmt. Study Group, 1973. Mem. Am. Assn. Sch. Adminstrs., Suburban Sch. Supts., Madison Beach Club, Phi Delta Kappa. Mem. Religious Soc. of Friends. Avocations: garden design, travel, home video, golf, music. Home: 88 Notoh Hill Rd Apt 282 New Branford CT 06471-1851

PETERKIN, GEORGE ALEXANDER, JR. marine transportation company executive; b. Baton Rouge, Apr. 12, 1927; s. George Alexander and Genevieve (Favrot) P.; m. Nancy Girling, Jan. 27, 1965; children— George Alexander III, Julie, John Thomas, Susan, Lynn. BBA, U. Tex., 1948. With Dixie Carriers, Inc., Galveston, Tex., soliciting freight agt. New Orleans, Houston, 1949-50, asst. to pres. Houston, 1953, pres., 1953-73, chmn. bd., 1973-99; pres. Kirby Industries, Inc., 1973-76, Kirby Corp., 1976-95, chmn. bd., 1995-99. Bd. dirs. Tex. Med. Center, 1965—, Living Bank, 1968-86; trustee Tex. Children's Hosp., 1964—. Served with USN, 1945-46. Mem. World Pres. Orgn., Chief Execs. Orgn., Am. Bur. Shipping, Houston Country Club, Bayou Club, Univ. Club N.Y. Avocations: swimming, croquet, golf, shooting. Home: 5787 Indian Cir Houston TX 77057-1302 Office: 5005 Woodway Dr Ste 200 Houston TX 77056-1789 E-mail: gapjr@swbell.net.

PETERLE, TONY JOHN, zoologist, educator; b. Cleve., July 7, 1925; s. Anton and Anna (Katic) P.; m. Thelma Josephine Coleman, July 30, 1949; children: Ann Faulkner, Tony Scott. BS, Utah State U., 1949; MS, U. Mich., 1950, PhD (univ. scholar), 1954; Fulbright scholar, U. Aberdeen, Scotland, 1954-55; postgrad., Oak Ridge Inst. Nuclear Studies, 1961. With Niederhauser Lumber Co., 1947—49, Macfarland Tree Svc., 1949—51; rsch. biologist Mich. Dept. Conservation, 1951—54; asst. dir. Rose Lake Expt. Sta., 1955—59; leader Ohio Coop. Wildlife Rsch. Unit U.S. Fish and Wildlife Svc., Dept. Interior, 1959—63; asso. prof., then prof. zoology Ohio State U., Columbus, 1959—89, prof. emeritus, 1989, chmn. faculty population and environmental biology, 1968—69, chmn. dept. zoology, 1969—81, dir. program in environ. biology, 1970—71; liaison officer Internat. Union Game Biologists, 1965—93; chmn. internat. affairs com., mem. com., ecotoxicology co-organizer XIII Internat. Congress Game Biology, 1979—80; proprietor The Iron Works, 1989—. Pvt. cons., 1989—; mem. com. rev. EPA pesticide decision making Nat. Acad. Scis.-NRC; mem. vis. scientists program Am. Inst. Biol. Scis.-ERDA, 1971-77; mem. com. pesticides Nat. Acad. Scis., com. on emerging trends in agr. and effects on fish and wildlife; mem. ecology com. of sci. adv. council EPA, 1979-87; mem. research units coordinating com. Ohio Coop. Wildlife and Fisheries, 1963-89; vis. scientist EPA, Corvallis, 1987. Author: Wildlife Toxicology, 1991; editor: Jour. of Wildlife Mgmt., 1969-70, 84-85, 2020 Vision Meeting the Fish and Wildlife Conservation Challenges of the 21st Century, 1992. Served with AUS, 1943-46. Fellow AAAS, Am. Inst. Biol. Scis., Ohio Acad. Sci.; mem. Wildlife Disease Assn., Wildlife Soc. (regional rep. 1962-67, v.p. 1968, pres. 1972, Leopold award 1990, hon. mem. 1990, Profl. award of merit North Ctrl. sect. 1993), Nat. Audubon Soc. (bd. dirs. 1985-87), Ecol. Soc., INTECOL-NSF panel U.S.-Japan Program, Xi Sigma Pi, Phi Kappa Phi. Home: 4072 Klondike Rd Delaware OH 43015-9513 Office: Ohio State U Dept Zoology 1735 Neil Ave Columbus OH 43210-1220

PETERMAN, DONNA COLE, communications executive; b. St. Louis, Nov. 9, 1947; d. William H. Cole and Helen A. Morris; m. John A. Peterman, Feb. 7, 1970. BA in Journalism, U. Mo., 1969; MBA, U. Chgo., 1984. Mgr. employee comm. Sears Merchandise Group, Chgo., 1975-80; affairs and mktg. comm. Seraco Real Estate, 1980-82; dir. corp. comm. Sears, Roebuck and Co., 1982-85; sr. v.p., dir. corp. comm. Dean Witter Fin. Svcs. Group, N.Y., 1985-88; sr. v.p., mng. dir. Hill and Knowlton, Inc., Chgo., 1988-94, exec. v.p. N.Y.C., 1994-96; sr. v.p., dir. corp. comm. Paine Webber Group, Inc., 1996-2000; mng. dir., regional head comms. and kmtg. The Americas, UBS Americas Inc., 2000—. Media chair DeKalb County Comm., Ga., 1975; media dir., Mo. Atty. Gen., 1971, Rep. Govs. Conf., 1974; copywriter Govt. fo Mo., 1971. Trustee Securities Industry Found. for Econ. Edn. Mem. Internat. Assn. Bus. Communicators, Pub. Rels. Soc. Am., Univ. Club, Women Execs. in Pub. Rels., Arthur Page Soc., Pub. Rels. Seminar, The Wise Men. Republican. Roman Catholic. Avocations: tennis, golf, sailing, skiing, bridge.

PETERMANN, HANS JÜRGEN, research scientist; b. Vienna, Austria, Feb. 2, 1942; MA in German, Calif. State U., 1971; PhD in Physics, 2d Phys. Inst., Vienna, Austria, 1976; PhD in Botany (hon.), Bot. Inst., Berlin, Germany, 1980. Prof. phys. scis. Coll. of Desert, Palm Desert, Calif.; rsch. scientist Palm Springs, 1991—. Chmn. hot technologies, in charge of mfg. new 10 kw home energy products and devices, 2002; lectr. in field. Author: The Esoteric Scis., 2d edit., 2001, Esoteric Curiosities of Plant Kingdom, 2d edit., 2001, Gravitation and Space Travel, 2d edit., 2002; patentee in field. With U.S. Army, 1963-66. Avocations: hiking, tennis, scuba diving, mountain climbing, swimming. Office: PO Box 4513 362 N Palm Canyon Dr Apt 6 Palm Springs CA 92263-4513

PETERS, AARON SHELDON, monk, priest; b. Hutchinson, Kans., May 13, 1939; s. Raymond Peters and A. Violet Christina Trotter. BA, St. Benedict's/Benedictine Coll., Atchison, Kans., 1972; MDiv, St. Meinrad (Ind.) Sem., 1977; postgrad., U. Ind., 1977, U. San Francisco, 1982. With USN Submarine Svc., 1957—67, St. Benedict's Abbey, Atchison, 1967—; mem. faculty Benedictine Coll., 1977—80; chaplain USN, 1980—82; chaplain, counselor Valley Hope Alcohol Drug Treatment, Atchison, 1983—93; various pastoral positions Archdiocese of Kansas City, Dodge City, Atchison, Topeka, Great Bend, 1983—94; monastery tailer, 1994—; chaplain Ursuline Sisters, Paola, Kans., 1995—. Mem.: Puppetry Guild of Kansas City, Puppeters of Am., Inc., U.S. Submarine Vets., Inc. Republican. Avocations: puppetry, music, winemaking, making herbal vinegars. Office: Ursuline Sisters Inc 901 E Miami St Paola KS 66071 Home: St Benedicts Abbey 1020 N 2d St Atchison KS 66002-1499 also: 913 E Wea St Paola KS 66071 Fax: 913-557-2340. E-mail: aaronosb@hotmail.com.

PETERS, ALAN, anatomy educator; b. Nottingham, Eng., Dec. 6, 1929; came to U.S., 1966; s. Robert and Mabel (Woplington) P.; m. Verona Muriel Shipman, Sept. 30, 1955; children: Ann Verona, Sally Elizabeth, Susan Clare. BSc, Bristol (Eng.) U., 1951, PhD, 1954. Lectr. anatomy Edinburgh (Scotland) U., 1958-66; vis. lectr. Harvard, 1963-64; prof., chmn. dept. anatomy and neurobiology Boston U., 1966-98, Waterhouse prof., 1998—. Anatomy com. Nat. Bd. Med. Examiners, 1971-75; mem. neurology B Study sect. NIH, 1975-79, chmn., 1978-79; affiliate scientist Yerkes Regional Primate Rsch. Ctr., 1984—. Author (with S.L. Palay and H. deF Webster): The Fine Structure of the Nervous System, 1970, The Fine Structure of the Nervous System, 3rd edit., 1991; author: Myelination, 1970; contbr. articles to profl. jours.; mem. editl. bd.: Anat. Record, 1972—81, mem. editl. bd.: Jour. Comparative Neurology, 1981—97, mem. editl. bd.: Neurocytology, 1972—89, mem. editl. bd.: , 1993—, mem. editl. bd.: Cerebral Cortex, 1990—, mem. editl. bd.: Studies of Brain Function, Anat. and Embryology, 1989—92; editor (with E.G. Jones): (book series) Cerebral Cortex, 1984—2000; exec. prodr.(with B. Payne): Cat Visual Cortex, 2001. Served to 2d lt. Royal Army Med. Corps, 1955-57. Recipient Javits neurosci. investigator award NIH, 1986; Henry Gray award, 1998. Mem. Anat. Soc. Gt. Britain and Ireland (Symington prize anatomy 1962, overseas mem. coun. 1969), Assn. Anatomy Chmn. (pres. 1976-77), Am. Anat. Assn. (exec. com. 1986-90, pres. 1992-93, Henry Gray award 1998), Am. Soc. Cell Biology, Soc. Neurosci., Internat. Primatological Soc., Cajal Club (Harman lectr. 1990, Cortical Discoverer award 1991). Home: 16 High Rock Cir Waltham MA 02451-2207 Office: Boston U Sch Medicine Dept Anatomy and Neurobiology 80 E Concord St Roxbury MA 02118-2307 E-mail: cajal-1@bu.edu.

PETERS, ANDREA JEAN, artist; b. Boston, Dec. 27, 1947; d. Andrew A. and Mary M. (Badessa) De Francesco; m. Mark Douglas Peters, Aug. 9, 1970; children: Melissa J., Christine M. Cert. of completion/diploma, Vesper George Sch. Art, 1966; student, Mass. Coll. Art, 1966-68. Drawing and painting tchr. Tewksbury (Mass.) Fine Art Ctr., 1975-76, Wilmington, Mass., 1975-79. Author: (book) The Art of Maine in Winter, 2002; gallery representation Art 3, Inc., Manchester, N.H., 1985—, Diana Levine Fine Art, Boston, 1988—, Gleason Fine Art, Boothbay Harbor, Maine, 1992—, Sandwich Art Gallery, Mass., 1994—, Granite Shore Gallery, Mass., 1997-2000, Penobscot Marine Mus., 2002; (cover illustrations) Community Connection Phone Book, 1993, 94; featured in The Art of Maine in Winter (Carl Little). Recipient Daniel V. Hoye Meml. award Permanent Collection of Hoyt Inst. Fine Art, New Castle, Pa., 1986, Jurors award Whistler Mus., Lowell, Mass., 1987, Madlyn-Ann Woolwich award Pastels 1996 Pastel Soc. of No. Fla., 1996. Mem. Pastel Soc. Am. (master pastelist, Pearl Paint award 1987, J.G. Sher award 1988), Copley Soc. Boston (Jurors award 1988), North Shore Arts Assn. (J.S.G. Saunders Meml. award 1984), Am. Artist Profl. League, Allied Artists Am., Maine Coast Artists. Home: Boothbay Shores PO Box 245 East Boothbay ME 04544-0245

PETERS, ANN LOUISE, accounting administrator; b. Knoxville, Tenn., Jan. 26, 1954; d. William Brown and Louise (Emerson) Nixon; m. Raymond Peters, July 11, 1975. BBA, Miami U., Oxford, Ohio, 1976; MBA, Xavier U., 1985. Cert. internal auditor. Acctg. officer Soc. Bank (formerly Citizens Bank), Hamilton, Ohio, 1977-85; internal auditor Procter & Gamble Co., Cin., 1985-86, audit sect. mgr., 1986-88, sr. cost analyst, beauty care, 1988-90; plant fin. mgr. Procter & Gamble Mfg. Co., Phoenix, 1990-92; sr. fin. analyst, beauty care Procter & Gamble Co., Cin., 1992-93, group mgr., gen. acctg., 1993-96, group mgr. R&D fin., 1996-99, group mgr., global fin., paper divsn., 1999—. Mem. Inst. Internal Auditors, Inst. Mgmt. Accts. Republican. Congregationalist. Avocations: golf, swimming. Home: 7889 Ironwood Way West Chester OH 45069-1623 Office: Procter & Gamble Co PO Box 599 Cincinnati OH 45201-0599

PETERS, BARB WATERMAN, artist, educator; b. Topeka, Nov. 3, 1944; d. L.E. Clifton Bailey and Gertrude Minnie McFarland; m. John Herman Waterman, Dec. 21, 1965 (div. Dec. 1985); m. Larry Dean Peters, May 30, 1986. BFA, Washburn U., 1973; MFA, Kans. State U., 1998. Adj. instr. Washburn U., Topeka, 1985-88, adj. asst. prof., 1989—96, 1999—2001; grad. tchg. asst. Kans. State U., Manhattan, 1997-98. Mus. specialist ednl. svcs. Mulvane Art Mus., Topeka, 1987; faculty advisor Washburn Art Students Assn., Topeka, 1994-96; guest curator Water Marks exhbn. Mulvane Art Mus., Topeka, 1995-96; exhbn. juror in field; spkr., reviewer in field. One-woman shows include Bedyk Gallery, Kansas City, Mo., 1983, 88, Collective Art Gallery, Topeka, 1988-90, 96-97, 1999-2000, 02, Yost Gallery-Highland (Kans.) C.C., 1989, 95, Art Craft Gallery, Denver, 1994, 95, 97, Fourth St. Gallery, Kansas City, 1997, Michael Cross Gallery, Kansas City, 1999-2000, Wichita Ctr. Arts, 2001; group shows include Holman Art Gallery-Trenton State Coll., 1979, N.Mex. Art League, Albuquerque, 1980, Nat. Soc. Painters, N.Y., 1980 (Michael Engle Meml. award), Ball State U. Art Gallery, Muncie, Ind., 1981, Portsmouth (Va.) Cmty. Ctr., 1982, Nelson-Atkins Mus., Kansas City, 1982, Owensboro (Ky.) Mus. Fine Art, 1982 (award), Joslyn Art Mus., Omaha, 1988, others, Women's Conf., Beijing, 1995, Jan Weiner Gallery, Kansas City, 1995, The Columbian Art Gallery, Wamego, Kans., 1997, Topeka and Shawnee County Pub. Libr., 1997, Strecker Gallery, Manhattan, Kans., 1999-2000, Cedar Rapids (Iowa) Mus. Art, 1997, Wichita Ctr. for the Arts, 2000, Birger Sandzen Gallery, Lindsborg, Kans., 2001, U. Kans. Art and Design Gallery, 2002, Strecker-Nelson Gallery, Manhattan, Kans., 2002; contbr. articles to profl. jours. Vol. art gallery Topeka and Shawnee County Pub. Libr., 1986—; panelist Kans. Arts Commn., Kans. Presswomen, 1990—; bd. dirs. Arts Coun. Topeka, 2002. Recipient Outstanding Achievement award, Am. Inst. Banking, Topeka, 1977, assistantship in lithography, Kans. Arts Commn., 1981, Woman of Distinction in the Arts award, Kaw Valley Girl Scouts, Topeka, 1996, Artist's Residency award, The Raymer Soc., 2001—02. Mem. Nat. Mus. Women in the Arts, Chgo. Artists' Coalition, Kansas City Artists Coalition, Mulvane Art Mus., The Collective (charter, treas. 1987-89, v.p. 1990-94, 99-00, pres. 2001, newsletter editor 2000—), Friends of Art Bd. Beach Mus. Art (collections com. 1997—). Avocations: reading, writing, travel. Home: 2223 SW Knollwood Dr Topeka KS 66611-1623 E-mail: barbara.r.peters@att.net.

PETERS, BARBARA AGNES, principal; b. Lockport, N.Y., Aug. 11, 1952; d. Raymond Charles Betsch and Evelyn Mae (Ehmke) Soulvie; m. Victor Waldorf Baker, June 17, 1978 (div.); children: Alexander, Erik; m. Robert Emerson Peters, Nov. 3, 1990; children: Brian, Jennifer. BS in Edn., SUNY, Fredonia, 1974; MEd, U. Wales, Cardiff, 1979; EdD, SUNY, Buffalo, 2002. Cert. tchr. N, K-6, secondary English, reading, CAS-sch. dist. adminstr., N.Y, CAS Ednl. Adminstrn., SAS, SDA. Tchr. English Emmet Belknap Jr. H.S., Lockport, N.Y., 1974-76; exec. dir. Dept. of Youth and Recreation Svcs., 1978-89; instr. Empire State Coll., 1983—; tchr. English Akron (N.Y.) Cen. Sch. Dist., 1989-95; asst. prin. West Seneca East Middle Sch., 1995-97; prin., mem. numerous dist. coms. Winchester Elem. Sch., 1997—. Mem. dist. planning team Akron Sch., 1990-95, mem. tech. long-range planning com., 1992-94. Team owner's mgr. Buffalo Bills Football Club, Orchard Park, N.Y., 1978—; mem. Bd. Performing and Visual Arts,Tonawanda, 1992. Recipient Erie County Youth Best award, 1995; honoree Internat. Women's Decade, 1985; named to Outstanding Young Women of Am., 1986, Educator of Yr. West Seneca C. of C., 2000; Rotary grad. fellow, 1975. Mem. ASCD, N.Y. State Middle Sch. Assn., Swiftwater Power Squadron Advanced Pilot and Bridg eOfficer, LaSalle Yacht Club, Western N.Y. Women in Adminstrn. (treas. 1998, bd. dirs. 1999—, Excellence in Ednl. Leadership award 1996), Phi Delta Kappa (award innovative ednl. program 1996). Avocations: boating, golf. Office: Winchester Elem Sch 350 Harlem Rd West Seneca NY 14224 E-mail: Barbara_Peters@westseneca.wnyric.org.

PETERS, BERNADETTE (BERNADETTE LAZZARA), actress; b. Queens, N.Y., Feb. 28, 1948; d. Peter and Marguerite (Maltese) Lazzara. Student, Quintano Sch. for Young Profls., N.Y.C. Ind. actress, entertainer, 1957—. Appeared on TV series All's Fair, 1976-77; frequent guest appearances on TV; films include The Longest Yard, 1974, Vigilant Force, 1975, W.C. Fields and Me, 1975, Silent Movie, 1976, The Jerk, 1979, Heart Beeps, 1981, Tulips, 1981, Pennies from Heaven, 1982 (Golden Globe Best Actress award), Annie, 1982, Slaves of New York, 1989, Pink Cadillac, 1989, Impromptu, 1990, Alice, 1990, Snow Days, 1999, A Few Good Years, 2002; TV movies include Cinderella, ABC-TV, 1997, Holiday in Your Heart, 1997; stage appearances include This is Google, 1957, The Most Happy Fella, 1959, Gypsy, 1961, Curly McDimple, 1967, Johnny No-Trump, 1967, George M!, 1968, Dames at Sea, 1968, La Strada, 1969, On the Town, 1971, Tartuffe, 1972, Mack and Mabel, 1974, Sally and Marsha, 1982, Sunday in the Park with George, 1983-85 (Tony nomination 1983), Song and Dance, 1985-86, Into the Woods, 1987, The Goodbye Girl, 1992-93, Annie Get Your Gun 1998-1999 (Tony Award, Best Actress, Musical, 1999); TV films: David, 1989, Fall From Grace, 1990, The Last Best Year, 1990, What the Deaf Man Heard, 1997; film Anastasia (voice), 1997, Cinderella, 1997, The Closer, 1998, Prince Charming, 2001, Bobbie's Girl, 2002; video Beauty and the Beast: The Enchanted Christmas (voice), 1997; TV mini-series The Odyssey, 1997; rec. artist: (MCA Records) Bernadette Peters, 1980, Now Playing, 1981; CD's include I'll Be Your Baby Tonight, Angel Records, 1996 (Grammy nomination), Sondheim Etc: Bernadette Peters Live at Carnegie Hall, Angel Records, 1997 (Grammy nomination), solo concert Radio City Music Hall, 2002. Recipient Drama Desk award for Dames and Sea, 1968, Drama Desk award nomination for Into The Woods, 1987, 88, Tony award nominee, 1971, 74, 83, 85, 92, Tony award for Best Actress in Song and Dance, 1986, Theatre World citation for George M!, 1968, Drama Desk award, 1968, 86, Hasty Pudding Theatrical award, 1987 Woman of Yr. award, Sara Siddons Actress of Yr. award, 1993-94, Tony award for best actress in a musical, 1999, Actors Fund medal for artistic achievement, 1999; named Woman of Yr., Police Athletic League, 1999; named to Theatre Hall of Fame.*

PETERS, CARL M., II, minister, choral conductor; b. Carlisle, Ky., Mar. 29, 1965; s. August C. and Betty Sue Peters; m. Renee' Dawn Daulton, June 22, 1991; children: Daulton Jacob, Kendall Carson. BME, Georgetown Coll., 1988; MCM, So. Bapt. Theol. Sem., 1992; postgrad., Inst. for Worship Studies, Orange Park, Fla., 2000—. Min. of youth Hillsdale (Mich.) Bapt. Ch., 1982-83; min. of children's music Georgetown (Ky.) United Meth. Ch., 1984; min. of music and youth Stamping Ground (Ky.) Bapt. Ch., 1985-87; min. of music Edgewood Bapt. Ch., Nicholasville, Ky., 1987-95; min. of music and worship Ancient City Bapt. Ch., St. Augustine, Fla., 1995—. Condr. St. Augustine (Fla.) Cmty. Chorus, 1996—, North Fla. Women's Chorale, Jacksonville Beach, 1998—, St. Augustine Chamber Choir, 1999—. Composer: (choral work) Magnificat, 2000. Recipient Mark Levi award Georgetown Coll. Baseball Team, 1982, Outstanding Sr. Man in Music award Georgetown Coll., 1983. Republican. Avocations: tennis, football, softball, writing, lifting weights. Office: Ancient City Bapt Ch 27 Sevilla St Saint Augustine FL 32084 Home: Apt 101 1005 Bella Vista Blvd Saint Augustine FL 32084-1249 E-mail: goblue@aug.com.

PETERS, CAROL ANN, secondary school educator; b. Ashtabula, Ohio, Feb. 12, 1946; d. Leonard Jay and Anniece Edna Hawkins; m. Robert Lewis Peters, June 12, 1971; children: Brian Jay, Sharon Lynne. BS in Edn., Kent State U., 1968; ESL cert., U. Houston, 1990; postgrad., S.W. Tex. State U., 1999—. Cert. secondary edn. Tex. Tchr. Fairport (Ohio) Exp Village Sch. Dist., 1968—71; substitute tchr. Spring Branch Ind. Sch. Dist., Houston, 1972—74, tchr., 1987—93; substitute tchr. San Marcos (Tex.) Ind. Sch. Dist., 1993—94; tchr. Wackenhut Corrections Corp., Lockhart, 1994—96; tutor, owner Village Sensei, Maxwell, 1998—; tchr. cons. Nat. Evaluation Sys., Inc., Austin, 2000—. Mem. San Marcos H.S. campus improvement team San Marcos Cons. Ind. Sch. Dist., 1999—2002, mem. facilities task force, 2000—02. Troop leader, svc. unit officer Girl Scouts USA, Houston, 1981—93; organizer Ams. Promise Youth Summit City of San Marcos, 1998—99, youth commr., 1998—. Mem.: NEA, TESOL, Internat. Dyslexia Assn., San Marcos Area and Hispanic C. of C. (edn. com.), Tex. PTA (life), Lions Internat. (youth outreach chair). Roman Catholic. Avocations: bridge, playing piano and organ, camping, landscaping, writing. Home: 36 Mill St Maxwell TX 78656 Office: Village Sensei 36 Mill St Maxwell TX 78656

PETERS, CAROL ANN DUDYCHA, counselor; b. Ripon, Wis., Dec. 23, 1938; d. George John and Martha (Malek) Dudycha; m. Milton Eugene Peters, Aug. 27, 1960. AB, Wittenberg U., 1960, MEd, 1963; leadership devel. cert., Ctr. for Creative Leadership, Greensboro, N.C., 1986; postgrad., U. Toledo, 1973-97, U. Findlay, 1997-99. Lic. profl. counselor, Ohio; nat. cert. counselor, nat. cert. career counselor Nat. Bd. Cert. Counselors, Inc.; cert. basic critical incident stress mgmt. Internat. Critical Incident Stress Found., 1999. Tchr. Springfield (Ohio) City Schs., 1960-62, Mad River-Green Local Schs., Springfield, 1962-63; counselor Napoleon (Ohio) Area Schs., 1963-70, Findlay (Ohio) City Schs., 1970-2000; sr. lectr. U. Findlay, 1999—; field counselor Career Relocation Corp. Am., Armonk, N.Y., 1992-95, 98-99. Cons., prin. Peters and Peters, Findlay, 1979—; leader Creative Edn. Found., Buffalo, 1980-91, colleague, 1985—; founder ednl. corp. Career Info. Bur. Hancock County, 1974. Pres. Big Bros./Big Sisters Hancock County, 1982-83; bd. dirs. Citizens Opposing Drug Abuse (C.O.D.A.), Findlay, 1982—; advisor, leader Hancock Addictions Prevention for Youth (H.A.P.P.Y.), 1985-91; mem. Hancock County Community Devel. Found. Edn. Com., 1990-93, Findlay/Hancock County Am. 2000 New Sch. Design Team, 1991-92; mem. Hancock County Crisis Response Team, 1991-97, 99—; mem. assets/needs assessment com. United Way, 1997-98; mem. Findlay Juvenile Diversion Task Force, 1997-98 Named One of Outstanding Young Women of Am., 1967; named Outstanding Woman in Edn., Bus. and Profl. Women, 1983; recipient Outstanding Citizenship award The Lincoln Ctr., Findlay, 1989, Meritorious Svc. award Big Bros./Big Sisters Hancock County, 1988. Mem. ACA, AAUW (Findlay br.), NEA (life), Nat. Career Devel. Assn., Ohio Ret. Tchrs. Assn. (life), Ohio Counseling Assn., Findlay-Hancock County C. of C. (sec. edn. com. 1984-90), Ohio Career Devel. Assn. Lutheran. Avocations: sailing (advanced pilot U.S. Power Squadron), flower arranging, cooking, handicapped accessibility planning.

PETERS, CHARLES GIVEN, JR. editor; b. Charleston, W.Va., Dec. 22, 1926; s. Charles Given and Esther (Teague) P.; m. Elizabeth Bostwick Hubbell, Aug. 3, 1957; 1 child, Christian Avery. BA in Humanities, Columbia U., 1949, MA in English, 1951; LLB, U. Va., 1957; LLD (hon.), U. Charleston, 1979. Bar: W.Va. 1957, D.C. 1981. Atty. Peters, Merrick, Leslie & Mohler, Charleston, 1957-61; mem. W.Va State Legislature, 1960-62; dir. evaluation Peace Corps, Washington, 1962-68; founder, editor in chief The Washington Monthly, 1968—2001; pres. Understanding Govt., 1999—; Times-Mirror David Laventhol vis. prof. Grad. Sch. Journalism, Columbia U., 2002. Delacorte lectr. Columbia U., 1990; Times-Mirror David Laventhol vis. prof., Columbia U. Grad. Sch. Journalism, 2002. Author: How Washington Really Works, 1980, Tilting at Windmills, 1988; editor: (with Taylor Branch) Blowing the Whistle, 1972, (with James Fallows) The System, 1975, (with Michael Nelson) The Culture of Bureaucracy, 1977, (with Jonathan Alter) Inside the System, 5th edit., 1985. Mgr. John F. Kennedy campaign, Kanawha County, W.Va., 1960. Served with inf. U.S. Army, 1944-46. Named West Virginian of Yr., Charleston Gazette-Mail, 1980, Poynter fellow, Yale U., 1980; named to Hall of Fame, Am. Soc. Mag. Editors, 2001; recipient Columbia Journalism award, 1978, Richard S. Clurman award, 1996. Democrat. Presbyterian. Office: Washington Monthly Co 733 15th St NW Washington DC 20005

PETERS, CHARLES WILLIAM, research and development company manager; b. Pierceton, Ind., Dec. 9, 1927; s. Charles Frederick and Zelda May (Line) P.; m. Katharine Louise Schuman, May 29, 1953; 1 child, Susan Kay; m. 2d, Patricia Ann Miles, Jan. 2, 1981; children: Bruce Miles Merkle, Leslie Ann Merkle Sanaie, Philip Frank Merkle, William Macneil Merkle. AB, Ind. U., 1950; postgrad. U. Md., 1952-58. Supervisory rsch. physicist Naval Rsch. Lab., Washington, 1950-71; physicist EPA, Washington, 1971-76; mgr. advanced systems EATON-Consol. Controls Corp., Springfield, Va., 1976-89, v.p. Nuclear Diagnostic Systems, Inc., Springfield, Va, 1989-92, cons. Am. Tech. Inst., 1993—. With U.S. Army, 1945-47. Mem. IEEE, AAAS, Am. Phys. Soc. Home and Office: 5235 N Whispering Hills Ln Tucson AZ 85704-2510

PETERS, DAVID ALLEN, mechanical engineering educator, consultant; b. East St. Louis, Ill., Jan. 31, 1947; s. Bernell Louis and Marian Louise (Blum) P.; children: Michael H., Laura A., Nathan C. BS in Applied Mechanics, Washington U., St. Louis, 1969, MS in Applied Mechanics, 1970; PhD in Aeros. and Astronautics, Stanford U., 1974. Assoc. engr. McDonnell Astronautics, 1969-70; rsch. scientist Army Aeronautics Lab., 1970-74; asst. prof. Washington U., 1975-77, assoc. prof., 1977-80, prof. mech. engring., 1980-85, chmn. dept., 1982-85; prof. aerospace engring. Ga. Inst Tech., Atlanta, 1985-91; dir. NASA Space Grant Consortium Ga. Inst. Tech., 1989-91; dir. Ctr. for Computational Mechanics Washington U., 1992—, prof. dept. mech. engring., 1991—, chmn. dept. mech. engring., 1997—, McDonnell Douglas prof. engring., 1999. Contbr. 65 articles to profl. jours. Recipient sci. contbn. award NASA, 1975, 76. Fellow AIAA, ASME; mem. Am. Helicopter Soc. (jour. editor 1987-90), Am. Soc. for Engring. Edn., Internat. Assn. for Computational Mechanics (charter), Am. Acad. Mechs., Pi Tau Sigma (gold medal 1978). Baptist. Home: 7629 Balson Ave Saint Louis MO 63130-2150 Office: PO Box 1185 Saint Louis MO 63188-1185

PETERS, DENNIS GAIL, chemist; b. L.A., Apr. 17, 1937; s. Samuel and Phyllis Dorothy (Pope) P. BS cum laude, Calif. Inst. Tech., 1958; PhD, Harvard U., 1962. Mem. faculty Ind. U., 1962—, prof. chemistry, 1974—, Herman T. Briscoe prof., 1975—. Co-author textbooks, contbr. articles profl. jours. Woodrow Wilson fellow, 1958-59; NIH predoctoral fellow, 1959-62; vis. fellow Japan Soc. for Promotion Sci., 1980; recipient Ulysses G. Weatherly award disting. teaching Ind. U., 1969, Disting. Teaching award Coll. Arts and Scis. Grad. Alumni Assn. Ind. U., 1984, Nat. Catalyst award for Disting. Teaching Chem. Mfrs. Assn., 1988, Henry B. Linford award The Electrochem. Soc., 2002; grantee NSF. Fellow Ind. Acad. Sci., Am. Inst. Chemists; mem. ACS (grantee, Div. of Analytical Chemistry award for excellence in teaching 1990, James Flack Norris award 2001). Home: 1401 S Nancy St Bloomington IN 47401-6051 Office: Dept Chemistry Ind U Bloomington IN 47405 Business E-Mail: peters@indiana.edu.

PETERS, DOUGLAS ALAN, medical-legal consultant, appeals analyst; b. Portsmouth, Va., Oct. 4, 1968; s. Terrance Gene and Pamela (Haffner) P. BA in Philosophy, Va. Poly. Inst. and State U., 1992; BSN summa cum laude, James Madison U., 1995; postgrad., Johns Hopkins U., 1997, U. Md., Balt., 1998—. RN, Md.; cert. case mgr. Photojournalist CVNI/The Greene County Record, Stanardsville, Va., 1992; nursing asst. Rockingham Meml. Hosp., Harrisonburg, 1993-95; clin. nurse Bapt. Hosp., Pensacola, Fla., 1995-96; neurology nurse Tallahassee Meml. Regional Med. Hosp., 1996; nurse mgr. quality assurance Escambia County Jail Infirmary, Pensacola, 1996-97; case mgr. U.R. Total Health Care, Balt., 1997-98; case mgr. Blue Cross/Blue Shield of Md., 1998-2000, appeals analyst, 2000—01, sr. appeals analyst, 2001—. Quality control team advisor Bapt. Health Care, Pensacola, 1995. Vol. hospice unit Rockingham Meml. Hosp., 1994-95; vol. tourette Syndrome Assn., 1996-2000. Mem.: ABA, Student Health Care Orgn., Nat. League for Nursing, Student Bar Assn., Balt. City Bar Assn., Phi Alpha Delta, Sigma Theta Tau, Phi Sigma Pi, Alpha Chi Sigma. Avocations: biomedical ethics, photography.

PETERS, DOUGLAS CAMERON, mining engineer, geologist; b. Pitts., June 19, 1955; s. Donald Cameron and Twila (Bingel) P. BS in Earth and Planetary Sci., U. Pitts., 1977; MS in Geology, Colo. Sch. Mines, 1981, MS in Mining Engring., 1983. Technician, inspector Engring. Mechanics Inc., Pitts., 1973-77; rsch. asst. Potential Gas Agy., Golden, Colo., 1977-78; geologist U.S. Geol. Survey, Denver, 1978-80; cons. Climax Molybdenum Co., Golden, 1981-82, 1982-84; mining engr., prin. investigator U.S. Bur. Mines, Denver, 1984-96; owner Peters Geoscis., Golden, 1996—. Bur. rep. to Geosat Com., 1984-95; program chmn. GeoTech Conf., Denver, 1984-88, mem. long range planning subcom., 1989-92, gen. chmn., 1991; engr. in tng. #11800, Colo., profl. geologist, Wyo., #367, Pa., #2365, Washington, #396. Author: Physical Modeling of Draw of Broken Rock in Caving, 1984, bur. mines articles and reports; editor COGS computer contbns., 1986-90, Geology in Coal Resource Utilization, 1988-91, Atlas of Coal Geology, 1999, Remote Sensing for Site Characterization, 2000; assoc. editor: Computers & Geosciences, 1991-2000; contbr. articles to profl. jours.; guest editor various jours.; dep. editor: Natural Resources Research, 1999—. Recipient award Am. Inst. Profl. Geologists, 1984, 85, 86, Appreciation award, 1987, Spl. award Denver Geotech Com., 1988, Appreciation award, 1989. Mem. Am. Inst. Profl. geologists (cert. profl. geologist # 8274, sec. Colo. sect. 1997, pres. elect 1998, pres. 1999), Am. Assn. Petroleum Geologists (astrogeology com. 1984-2000, pub. com. 1995—, Energy Mineral divsn. v.p. 1990-91, pres. 1991-92, chmn. pubs. com. 1990-98, remote sensing com. 1990—, dir. environ. geology 1993-, assoc. editor Search and Discovery 2000—, Cert. Merit 1992, 93, 99, Pres.'s award 1993, Disting. Svc. award 1994), Am. Soc. Photogrammetry and Remote Sensing, Nat. Space Soc., Computer Oriented Geol. Soc. (charter, com. chmn. 1983-95, pres. 1985, dir. 1986, contbg. editor newsletter 1985-96), Assn. Exploration Geochemists, Geol. Soc. Am., Rocky Mountain Assn. Geologists, Soc. Mining Metallurgy and Exploration, Planetary Soc., Space Studies Inst., Denver Mining Club. Republican. E-mail: petersdc@petersgeo.com.

PETERS, EDWARD MURRAY, history educator; b. New Haven; BA, Yale U., 1963, MA, 1965, PhD, 1967. Instr. English and history Quinnipiac Coll., Hamden, Conn., 1964-67; asst. prof. history U. Calif., San Diego, 1967-68, U. Pa., Phila., 1968-70, assoc. prof., 1970-81, Henry Charles Lea prof. history, 1981—, curator Henry Charles Lea Library, 1968—; vis. prof. Cath. U. Louvain, Belgium, 1992. Vis. prof. history Yale U., 1998, 2001-02. Author: The Shadow King, 1970, (with A.C. Kors) Witchcraft in Europe, 1100-1750, 1972, 2d edit., 2000, Europe: The World of the Middle Ages, 1977, The Magician, The Witch and The Law, 1978, Europe and the Middle Ages, 1983, 3d edit., 1997, Torture, 1985, expanded edition, 1996, Inquistion, 1988, Limits of Thought and Power in Medieval Europe, 2001, (TV series) The World of the Middle Ages, 1974, The World Around the Revolution, 1977, also articles, revs. and introductions; editor, translator: (with Jeanne Krochalis) The World of Piers Plowman, 1975; editor: Heresy and Authority in Medieval Europe, 1980. Served with AUS, 1956-59. Woodrow Wilson fellow, 1963-64, dissertation fellow, 1966-67, hon. Sterling fellow, 1966-67, ACLS fellow, 1981-82, Guggenheim fellow, 1988-89. Fellow Medieval Acad. Am., Royal Hist. Soc.; mem. Am. Hist. Assn., Medieval Acad. Am., Am. Soc. Legal History, Maiestas, Iuris Canonici Medii Aevi Consociatio, Soc. Jean Bodin, Dante Soc. Am., Renaissance Soc. Am. Office: U Pa Dept History Philadelphia PA 19104-6228 E-mail: empeters@sas.upenn.edu.

PETERS, ELEANOR WHITE, retired mental health nurse; b. Highland Park, Mich., Aug. 11, 1920; d. Alfred Mortimer and Jane Ann (Evans) White; m. William J. Peters, 1947 (div. 1953); children: Susannah J., William J. (dec.). BA, Jersey City State Coll., 1968; postgrad., U. Del., 1969-70; MS, SUNY, New Paltz, 1983. RN, N.J., N.Y. Staff various hosps., N.J., 1941-58; indsl. nurse Abex, Mahwah, 1958-68; nurse Liberty (N.Y.) Ctrl. Sch., 1971-76; coord. practical nurse program Hudson County C.C., Jersey City, 1979-80; cmty. mental health nurse Letchworth Village, Thiells, N.Y., 1981-96; ret., 1996. Historian, Bishop House Found., Saddle River, N.J. Mem. AAUW (pres. Liberty-Monticello br. 1988-92), Am. Sch. Health Assn., Alpha Delta Kappa (sec. Mu chpt. 1973-75), Sigma Theta Tau (Kappa Eta chpt.). Republican. Lutheran. Avocations: antiques, history, traveling, education of children. Home: PO Box 224 Saddle River NJ 07458-0224

PETERS, ELIZABETH ANN HAMPTON, retired nursing educator; b. Detroit, Sept. 27, 1934; d. Grinsfield Taylor and Ida Victoria (Jones) Hampton; m. James Marvin Peters, Dec. 1, 1956; children: Douglas Taylor, Sara Elizabeth. Diploma, Berea Coll. Hosp. Sch. Nursing, 1956; BSN, Wright State U., Dayton, Ohio, 1975; MSN, Ohio State U., Columbus, 1978. Therapist, nurse Eastway, Inc., Dayton, Ohio, 1979-81; therapist, family counseling svc. Good Samaritan-Cmty. Mental Health Ctr., 1981-83; instr. Wright State U. Sch. Nursing, 1983-84; clin. nurse specialist, pain mgmt. program UPSA, Inc., 1983-86; staff nurse Hospice of Dayton, Inc., 1985-86, dir. vol. svcs., 1986-89, dir. bereavement svcs., 1986-87; asst. prof. Cmty. Hosp. Sch. Nursing, Springfield, Ohio, 1990-93, prof., 1993-97; ret., 1997; parish nurse Honey Creek Presbyn. Ch., 1998—. Author: (with others) Oncologic Pain, 1987. Mem. Clark County Mental Health Bd., Springfield, 1986-95; mem. New Carlisle (Ohio) Bd. Health, 1990—. Mem.: Sigma Theta Tau. Home: 402 Flora Ave New Carlisle OH 45344-1329

PETERS, ELIZABETH ANNE, nutrition educator; b. Hebron, Ill., June 9, 1940; d. Tibbets and Ruby Marie (Giddens) Rolls; B.S., U. Ill., 1962, MEd, 1967; postgrad. U. Ill., 1970-74, Iowa State U., 1974, Northwestern U., 1980, 86. Tchr., dept. chair Bremen High Sch., Midlothian, Ill., 1962-65; asst. buyer Carson Pirie Scott, Chgo., 1965-66; tchr. Waller High Sch., Chgo., 1965-67, Evanston (Ill.) High Sch., 1967-70; instr., coordinator food service adminstrn. and hotel mgmt. Coll. DuPage, Glen Ellyn, Ill., 1970-75; clin. dietitian U. Chgo. Hosps. and Clinics, 1975; asst. restaurant mgr. Hyatt Regency, Chgo., summer 1980; prof., coordinator hospitality mgmt. program foodsvc. sanitation program and nutrition Chicago City-Wide Coll., 1975-92, chair campus com. for evaluation of baccalaureate transfer programs; pres. faculty Chgo. City Wide Coll., prof. foodsvc. sanitation and nutrition, 1992-97 ; cons. bds. health, No. Ill. U. adv. com., judge various food contests; mem. Chgo. Council on Fgn. Relations; pres. Near North chpt. Lyric Opera; trustee, treas. Three Arts Club Chgo. Recipient Nat. Restaurant Assn. Fellowship award, 1980; Master Tchrs. Seminar Fellowship award, 1974; Nat. Leadership Devel. Fellowship award, 1975. Registered Dietitan. Mem. Nat. Restaurant Assn., Ill. Restaurant Assn., Chgo. Restaurant Assn., Am. Dietetic Assn. (dietetic tech. com.), Ill. Dietetic Assn., Chgo. Nutrition Assn., Ill. Nutrition Com. (program chair), Chgo. Dietetic Assn. (dir.), Soc. Nutrition Edn., Inst. Food Technologists, Restaurant Women's Club Chgo. (dir.), Am. Pub. Health Assn., Coun. on Hotel-Restaurant Edn., Flossmoor Country Club, Lake Geneva Yacht Club, Canyon Club. Home: 505 N Lake Shore Dr Chicago IL 60611-3427 Office: 30 E Lake St Chicago IL 60601-2403

PETERS, ELLEN ASH, judge, trial referee, retired state supreme court justice; b. Berlin, Mar. 21, 1930; came to U.S., 1939, naturalized, 1947; d. Ernest Edward and Hildegard (Simon) Ash; m. Phillip I. Blumberg; children: David Bryan Peters, James Douglas Peters, Julie Peters Haden. BA with honors, Swarthmore Coll., 1951, LLD (hon.), 1983; LLB cum laude, Yale U., 1954, MA (hon.), 1964, LLD (hon.), 1985, U. Hartford, 1983; LLD (hon.) , Georgetown U., 1984; LLD (hon.), Yale U., 1985, Conn. Coll., 1985, N.Y. Law Sch., 1985; HLD (hon.), St. Joseph Coll., 1986; LLD (hon.), Colgate U., 1986, Trinity Coll., 1987, Bates Coll., 1987, Wesleyan U., 1987, DePaul U., 1988; HLD (hon.), Albertus Magnus Coll., 1990; LLD (hon.), U. Conn., 1992; LLD, U. Rochester, 1994, Detroit Mercy Coll. Law, 2001. Bar: Conn. 1957. Law clk. to judge U.S. Circuit Ct., 1954-55; assoc. in law U. Calif., Berkeley, 1955-56; prof. law Yale U., New Haven, 1956-78, adj. prof. law, 1978-84; assoc. justice Conn. Supreme Ct., Hartford, 1978-84, chief justice, 1984-96; judge trial referee Superior Ct., 2000—. Author: Commercial Transactions: Cases, Texts, and Problems, 1971, Negotiable Instruments Primer, 1974; contbr. articles to profl. jours. Bd. dirs. Nat. Ctr. State Cts., 1992—96, chmn., 1994; bd. mgrs. Swarthmore Coll., 1970—81; trustee Yale-New Haven Hosp., 1981—86, Yale Corp., 1986—92; mem. conf. Chief Justices, 1984—, pres., 1994; hon. chmn. U.S. Constl. Bicentennial Com., 1986—91; mem. Conn. Permanent Commn. on Status of Women, 1973—74, Conn. Bd. Pardons, 1978—80, Conn. Law Revision Commn., 1978—84; bd. dirs. Hartford Found., 1997—. Recipient Ella Grasso award, 1982, Jud. award Conn. Trial Lawyers Assn., 1982, citation of merit Yale Law Sch., 1983, Pioneer Woman award Hartford Coll. for Women, 1988, Disting. Svc. award U. Conn. Law Sch. Alumni Assn., 1993, Raymond E. Baldwin Pub. Svc. award Quinnipiac Coll. Law Sch., 1995, Disting. Svc. award Conn. Law Tribune, 1996, Nat. Ctr. State Cts., 1996; named Laura A. Johnson Woman of Yr. Hartford Coll., 1996. Mem. ABA, Conn. Bar Assn. (Jud. award 1992, Spl. award 1996), Am. Law Inst. (coun.), Am. Acad. Arts and Scis., Am. Philos. Soc. Office: Superior Ct 95 Washington St Hartford CT 06106-4431 Fax: 860-548-2887.

PETERS, ESTHER CAROLINE, aquatic toxicologist, pathobiologist, consultant; b. Greenville, S.C., May 9, 1952; d. Otto Emanuel and Winifred Ellen (Bahan) P.; m. Harry Brinton McCarty, Jr., May 27, 1984; children: Rachel Elizabeth, William Brinton. BS, Furman U., 1974; MS, U. South Fla., 1978; PhD, U. R.I., 1984. Rsch. asst. Environ. Rsch. Lab., U.S. EPA, Narragansett, R.I., 1980-81; grad. rsch. asst. U. R.I., Kingston, 1981-84; assoc. biologist JRB Assocs., Narragansett, 1984-85; postdoctoral fellow Dept. of Invertebrate Zoology, Nat. Mus. Natural History, Washington, 1985-86, resident rsch. assoc., 1986-89; rsch. fellow Registry Tumors in Lower Animals, Nat. Mus. of Natural History, 1987-91; sr. scientist Tetra Tech, Inc., Fairfax, Va., 1991-98, prin. scientist, 1998—. Sci. adv. panel Project Reefkeeper, Am. Littoral Soc., Miami, Fla., 1988—; courtesy asst. prof. Dept. Marine Sci., U. South Fla., St. Petersburg, 1987-96, courtesy assoc. prof. Dept Marine Sci., 1996—; adj. scientist Mote Marine Lab., Sarasota, Fla., 1997—; cons. The Nature Conservancy, Arlington, Va., 1991; adj. faculty George Mason U., Fairfax, Va., 1999—. Author: (with others) Pathobiology of Marine and Estuarine Organisms, 1993, Disease Processes of Marine Bivalve Molluscs, 1988, Life and Death of Coral Reefs, 1997; contbr. articles to profl. jours. Recipient Nat. Rsch. Svc. postdoctoral tng. fellowship NIH, Bethesda, Md., 1987-91. Fellow AAAS (coun. del. biol. sci. divsn. 2001—); mem. Am. Fisheries Soc., Internat. Soc. Reef Studies, Soc. for Environ. Toxicology and Chemistry, Nat. Shellfisheries Assn. Office: Tetra Tech Inc 10306 Eaton Pl Ste 340 Fairfax VA 22030-2201 E-mail: peteres@tetratech-ffx.com.

PETERS, EVELYN JOAN, artist; b. Anchorage, Mar. 25, 1927; d. Algernon Sidney Jones and R. Lee (Bartholf) Jones-Lange; m. Curtis Gordon Chezem, Sept. 29, 1945 (div. Oct. 1956); children: Joanne Lee Chezem, David Gordon Chezem; m. Frederick William Peters Jr., May 30, 1958. *Evelyn Joan Jones can trace her roots back to paternal and maternal ancestors who came into the Carolinas and New Amsterdam in the early 1600's. Evelyn's great-grandfather, mother's side, Frank G. Bartholf, owned most of downtown Loveland, Colorado. On mother's maternal side, Evelyn descended from Josiah Bartlett, a Declaration of Independence signer. Evelyn's mother, R. Lee Bartholf, was graduate nurse at Railroad Hospital in Anchorage where she met Al Jones. They married June 19, 1924. At the time of his death landing a plane in Bethel, Al owned Al Jones Airways. The Alaska Aviation Heritage Museum, Anchorage, owns Evelyn's painting of her father in his plane.* Student, U. Oreg., 1945-50, Oreg. State Coll., 1955-56. Pvt. sec. Pub. Svc. Commn., Las Vegas, Nev., 1957-58; tech. sec. Los Alamos (N.Mex.) Nat. Lab., 1958-70; sr. sec. EG&G, Los Alamos, 1970-71. Chmn. bd. dirs. Buchanan Arts and Crafts, Inc., Buchanan Dam, Tex., 1980, 86. One-woman shows include Frame Corner Gallery, Farmington, 1996, San Juan Coll., 1998, invitational retrospective St. Francis Newman Ctr., Silver City, N.Mex., 1994, exhibited in group shows at Inn of Loretto, Santa Fe, 1982, Capital Rotunda, Austin, Tex., 1983, Golub Gallery, Steamboat Springs, Colo., 1985, Cowtown Invitational, Ft. Worth, 1987, Safari Park Hotel, Nairobi, Kenya, 1990 (Artistic Expressions award, 1990, Gold medal, 1990), St. John's Coll., Cambridge, Eng., 1992 (Bronze medal, 1992), Western N.Mex. U., Silver City, 1993, Sixth Bear River Western Hist. Art Exhbn., Craig, Colo., 1994, Fed. Hall Mus., N.Y.C., 1994, 1997, Ann. COGAP Exhbn., Governor's Island, N.Y., 1994 (George Gray award, 1993), Apples, Aspen and Art, Cedaredge, Colo., 1995 (Most Popular Painting), Western and Wildlife Art Show, Estes Park, Colo., 1995, Sheraton-on-the-Park Hotel, Sydney, Australia, 1995, Colo. Indian Market, Denver, 1995, Art Concepts Gallery, Tacoma, Wash., 1997, Keble Coll., Oxford, Eng., 1997, Sunwest Bank, Farmington, 1997, Rotunda Canon Office Bldg., U.S. Ho. of Reps., Washington, 1997, Alpine Holiday, Ouray, Colo., 1997, 1999, 2000, Durham (Eng.) Art Gallery, Arts for the Parks, 2000, Represented in permanent collections Aviation Heritage Mus., Anchorage, Daystar Found., Oklahoma City, Eleanor Bliss Ctr. Arts, Steamboat Springs, Marble Falls Depot Mus., Mus. N.W. Colo., Craig, Nat. Gallery Rural Art, Bonner Springs, Kans., Pioneer and R.R. Mus., Temple, Tex., San Juan Coll., Farmington, N.Mex., USCG, art. Pres. Highland Arts Guild, Marble Falls, Tex., 1977, 90, 2d v.p., 1989; sec. Highland Lakes Arts Coun., Marble Falls, 1986. Recipient Marine Safety award Olin-Matheson, 1968, cert. of appreciation USCG Aux., 1969, 70, 1st and purchase award Kiwanis Art Competition, Granbury, Tex., 1983, 2d Pl. award Tex. Women Western Artists Show, Cresson, Tex., 1983, 2d and 3d pl. awards Llano Rodeo Art Show, 1986, 1st pl. award 9th Nat. Small Painting Western Show, 1987, 1st and purchase award Gt. Am. Art Competition, 1988, Most Popular Painter award 3d Ann. Invitational Art Show, Waco, Tex., 1988, Best of Show award Bear Valley Hist. Art Show, Craig, 1989, Best of Show, 1st Watercolor, 1st Oil, 1st Sculpture, Highland Lakes Arts Competition, Kingsland, Tex., 1991, Internat. Woman of Yr. in art Internat. Biog. Ctr., 1991-92, Most Popular Painting award Western Colo. Ctr. for Arts, 1996, Purchase award NWNMAC, Farmington, 1997, Purchase award Ouray Coll. 39th Ann. Art Exhibit, 1999, choice award 8th Ann. Nat. Christian Art Show, San Juan Coll., Farmington, N.Mex., 2000, Top 200 Arts for the Parks, 2000, 1st pl. Gateway Regional Art Show, Farmington, N.Mex., 2000, numerous others. Mem. N.Mex. Arts Coun., signature mem. Nat. Acrylic Painters Assn. (US/UK, invitation cover award 5th Internat. Open Exhibit 2000), official Coast Guard Artist, 1987—, Salmagundi Club, 1989-95, World Found. of Successful Women (charter mem.), Am. Biog. Inst. Rsch. Assn. (life, dep. gov. 1989, Gold Cup 1993, Medal of Honor 1992, Woman of Yr. 1994, 95), World Inst. of Achievement (life, Excellence as Painter award 1988), N.W. N.Mex. Arts Coun. (acting exec. dir. 1999—). Avocations: gardening, photography, reading, travel. Studio: Evelyns Studio 3706 San Medina Ave Farmington NM 87401-2328 E-mail: petersart@sprynet.com.

PETERS, FRANK ALBERT, retired chemical engineer; b. Washington, June 3, 1931; s. Charles Albert and Dorothy Lynette (Paine) P.; m. Carol Beattie Taylor, Feb. 25, 1955; children: Thomas, June, Erick, Victor. BSChemE, U. Md., 1955. Devel. engr. Celanese Corp. Am., Cumberland, Md., 1955-58; chem. Engr. U.S. Bur. Mines, College Park, 1958-66, project leader, 1966-70, rsch. supr., 1970-77, chief process evaluation Washington, 1977-94, ret., 1994. Contbr. over 20 articles to profl. jours. Avocations: photography, model railroading. Home: 12311 Glen Mill Rd Potomac MD 20854-1928

PETERS, FREDERICK WHITTEN, lawyer; b. Omaha, Aug. 20, 1946; s. Jordan Holt and Elizabeth (O'Bryant) P.; children: Mary Irvin, Elizabeth Holt, Margaret Etheridge. BA magna cum laude, Harvard U., 1968; MS with distinction, London Sch. Econs., 1973; JD magna cum laude, Harvard U., 1976. Bar: D.C. 1978, U.S. Dist. Ct. D.C. 1978, U.S. Dist. Ct. Md., 1994, U.S. Ct. Appeals (3d and D.C. cirs.) 1979, U.S. Ct. Claims 1981, U.S. Ct. Appeals (11th cir.) 1986, U.S. Ct. Mil. Appeals 1993. Law clk. to Hon. J. Skelly Wright U.S. Ct. Appeals (D.C. cir.), Washington, 1976-77; law clk. to justice William J Brennan U.S. Supreme Ct., 1977-78; assoc. Williams & Connolly, 1978-84, ptnr., 1984-95, 2001—; prin. dep. gen. counsel Dept. of Defense, 1995-97, undersec., acting sec. USAF, 1997-99, sec. USAF, 1999-2001; ptnr. Williams & Connolly LLP, Washington, 2001—. Mem. legal ethics com. D.C. Bar, 1988-94, chmn. rules rev. com., 1991-96; rules com. U.S. Ct. Mil. Appeals, 1993-95. Pres. Harvard Law Rev., 1975-76. Bd. dirs. Cleveland Park Hist. Soc., Washington, 1986-91, 2001—, Washington Area Lawyers for the Arts, 1987-93, Air Force Enlisted Found., 2001—; mem. adv. com. on streamlining procurement laws DOD, 1991-93, adv. com. on future of US aerospace industry. Lt. USNR, 1969-72. Fellow Am. Bar Found.; mem. ABA. Democrat. Episcopalian. Avocations: sailing, tennis, computer science. Home: 3250 Highland Pl NW Washington DC 20008-3231 Office: Williams & Connolly 725 12th St NW Washington DC 20005 E-mail: secaf19@aol.com., wpeters@wc.com.

PETERS, GEORGE NICHOLAS, surgical oncologist; b. Clarksdale, Miss., Apr. 8, 1947; s. Nicholas Emanuel and Lillie (Lemonis) P.; m. Janet Lee Straub, July 28, 1973 (div); children: Nicholas George, Barton Frederick. BA, U. Miss., Oxford, 1970; MD, U. Miss., Jackson, 1974. Diplomate Am. Bd. Surgery. Surg. resident Baylor U. Med. Ctr., Dallas, 1974-79; vis. fellow in surgery Columbia Presbyn. Hosp., N.Y.C., 1979-80; surg. oncology fellow Rosewll Park Meml. Inst., Buffalo, 1980; attending in surgery Baylor U. Med. Ctr., 1980—; attending staff Gaston Episcopal Hosp., Dallas, 1980-88; prof. surgery U. Tex. Southwestern Med. Ctr., 1996—; exec. dir. U. Tex. Southwestern Ctr. for Breast Care, 1996—. Contbr. articles to profl. jours. Mem. parish bd. Holy Trinity Greek Orthodox Ch., 1984-85, bd. v.p., 1985. Named Man of Yr., Susan G. Komen Found., 1988, Best Drs. in Am., Woodward White, 1995—, Ctrl. region, 1996—, Dallas Top Dr., D mag., 1996, Best Med. Spls. 1995, Town and Country, 1995, Top Cancer Drs. Women, Good Housekeeping, 1999, Top Breast Cancer Specialists, Redbook Mag., 2001; recipient award for achievement in pub. edn., Am. Cancer Soc., Tex. divsn., 1984, Sword of Hope award, Am. Cancer Soc., 1987, Leadership award, Zeta Tau Alpha, Honorary award, Holy Trinity Greek Orthodox Ch., 1995, St. George medal, Nat. Am. Cancer Soc., 1996, Local Hero award, Susan B. Komen Breast Cancer Fund BMW Drive for the Cure, 2001. Fellow ASC; mem. Soc. Med. Assn., AMA, Nat. Assembly Am. Cancer, Am. Soc. Clin. Oncology, Dallas Soc. Gen. Surgeons, Dallas Am. Cancer Soc. (bd. dirs., med. v.p. 1985-87, pres. 1987-89), Am. Cancer Soc. (pres. elect 1989-91, pres. 1991-93 Tex. divsn., mem. detection and treatment com., Sherry W. Crow Evergreen award 2001), Am. Soc. Breast Disease (sec., treas. 1989-93, pres. 1993-95), So. Assn. Oncoloyg, S.W. Surg. Congress, So. Med. Assn., Senologic Internat. Soc. (v.p. N.Am. 1996-98), World Soc. Breast Health (treas. 1999—), Titanic Hist. Soc., Roswell Park Surg. Soc., Am. Hellenci Edn. Progressive Assn., Am. Soc. Breast Surgeons. Republican. Greek Orthodox. Avocations: chess, painting, bicycling. Office: UT Southwestern Ctr Breast Care Stop 9161 5323 Harry Hines Blvd Dallas TX 75390-9161 E-mail: george.peters@utsouthwestern.edu.

PETERS, GORDON BENES, retired musician; b. Oak Park, Ill., Jan. 4, 1931; s. Arthur George and Julia Anne (Benes) P.; children: Rénee Kemper, Erica Kemper. Student, Northwestern U., 1949-50; Mus.B., Eastman Sch. Music, 1956, Mus.M., 1962. Founder, dir. Marimba Masters, 1954—59; percussionist Rochester (N.Y.) Philharmonic Orch., 1955-59; prin. percussionist Grant Park Symphony Orch., Chgo., 1955-58; mem. faculty Rochester Bd. Edn., 1956-57, Geneseo State Tchrs. Coll., 1957-58; acting prin. percussionist Rochester Philharm., N.Y., 1958-59; prin. percussionist and asst. prin. timpanist Chgo. Symphony Orch., 1959—2001; condr., adminstr. Civic Orch. Chgo., 1966-87; condr. Elmhurst Symphony Orch., 1968-73; ret., 2001. Instr. percussion instruments Northwestern U., 1963-68, lectr., 1991; guest conductor Bangor (Maine) Symphony, 1993. Author, pub. The Drummer: Man, 1975; arranger-pub. Marimba Ensemble arrangements; composer-pub.: Swords of Moda-Ling; editor: percussion column Instrumentalist mag, 1963-69; contbr. articles to profl. jours. Bd. dirs. Pierre Monteux Sch., Hancock, Maine, 1965-95. With U.S. Mil. Acad. Band, 1950-53. Recipient Pierre Monteux disciple award conducting, 1962, Prin. Timpani chair named GBP, Chgo. Youth Symphony Orch., 2000. Mem. Percussive Arts Soc. (pres. 1962-66), Am. Symphony Orch. League, Condrs. Guild (treas., exec. com. 1979-82, 86-90), Japan Xylophone Assn. Home (Winter): 824 Hinman Ave Apt 2N Evanston IL 60202-5906 Home (Summer): PO Box 403 Hancock ME 04640-0403

PETERS, HENRY AUGUSTUS, neuropsychiatrist; b. Oconomowoc, Wis., Dec. 21, 1920; s. Henry Augustus and Emma N. P.; m. Jean McWilliams, 1950; children— Henry, Kurt, Eric, Mark. BA, MD, U. Wis. Prof. dept. neurology and rehab. medicine U. Wis. Med. Sch., Madison, emeritus prof., 1996—. Mem. med. adv. bd. Muscular Dystrophy Assn. Served to lt. M.C. U.S. Navy. Fellow A.C.P.; mem. Wis. Med. Assn., Am. Acad. Neurology, Am. Psychiatric Assn. Clubs: Rotary. Office: 600 Highland Ave Madison WI 53792-0001

PETERS, HOWARD NEVIN, foreign language educator; b. Hazleton, Pa., June 29, 1938; s. Howard Eugene and Verna P.; m. Judith Anne Griessel, Aug. 24, 1963; children: Elisabeth Anne, Nevin Edward. BA, Gettysburg Coll., 1960; PhD, U. Colo., 1965. Asst. prof. fgn. langs. Valparaiso (Ind.) U., 1965-69, assoc. prof., 1969-75, dir. grad. divsn., 1967-70, acting dean Coll. Arts and Scis., 1970-71, assoc. dean Coll. Arts and Scis., 1971-74, dean Coll. Arts and Scis., 1974-81, prof. fgn. langs., 1975—, prof. fgn. langs. and lits., chair dept. fgn. langs. and lits., 1994—95, prof. emeritus fgn. langs. and lits., 1995—. Author (poetry) Espejo De Son, 1997. NDEA fellow, 1960-63 Mem. Midwest MLA, Phi Beta Kappa, Sigma Delta Pi, Phi Sigma Iota. Lutheran. Home: 860 N Cr 500 E Valparaiso IN 46383 Office: Meier Hall Rm 113 Valparaiso U Valparaiso IN 46383 E-mail: hpeters@exodus.valpo.edu.

PETERS, JACQUELINE MARY, secondary education educator; b. Milw., Oct. 6, 1947; d. Arnold Martin and Rosalie Ellen (Mulherin) Fladoos; divorced; children: Casey Martin, Ann Marie. Student, Clarke Coll., Dubuque, Iowa, 1965-67; BA, Calif. State U., Long Beach, 1970; MA in History and Tchg., LaVerne (Calif.) U., 1973. Reading tchr. Chaffey H.S., Ontario, Calif., 1971-78, tchr. phys. edn., 1976-78, English tchr., 1978-90, tchr. history, 1990—. Mentor AAUW, cmty. schs., 1997-99. State rep. Trans Nat. Golf Assn., 1963-75; bd. dirs. Cmty. Challenge Grants, Ontario, 1996-00. Named to Sports Hall of Fame, Dubuque Sr. H.S., 1996; Med-Cal grantee, 1996, Project Yes grantee, 1997-99. Mem. AAUW (bd. dirs., br. pres. 1995-99, Edn. Foun. Gift Honoree 1998), Calif. Tchrs. Assn. Republican. Roman Catholic. Avocations: golf, fly fishing, pysanka, poetry, bridge. Home: 320 W 21st St Upland CA 91784-1413 Office: Chaffey HS 1245 N Euclid Ave Ontario CA 91762-1923

PETERS, JOHN ADAM, retired pathologist; b. Elizabeth, N.J., Aug. 18, 1925; s. Rudolph Braun and Margaret (Brazinski) P.; m. Lillian Lilburn Clark, July 8, 1950; children: John III, Clark, Lynn, Stacey, Michael. AB, Princeton (N.J.) U., 1950; MD, Harvard U., 1954. Diplomate Am. Bd. Pathology. Vis. pathologist Carney Hosp., Boston, 1958-59; pathologist Plymouth County Hosp., Hanson, Mass., 1962-85, South Shore Hosp., Weymouth, 1958-89, ret., 1989. Pres. active med. staff South Shore Hosp., Weymouth, 1977-78. With U.S. Army, 1943-46. Fellow Norfolk South Dist. Med. Soc. (emeritus), Mass. Med. Soc. (emeritus), Coll. of Am. Pathologists (emeritus); mem. Weymouth Rotary Club. Avocations: weight training, gardening, reading (science and math). Home: 3 Gardiner Rd Scituate MA 02066-1049

PETERS, JOHN DOUGLAS, lawyer, artist; b. Dover, N.H., Jan. 23, 1948; s. John Philip Peters, Helen Irene Hurst; m. Christine K. Consales, June 23, 1973. BA, U. N.H., 1971; JD, U. Toledo, 1975. Exec. dir. PSRO 4th Ohio Area PSP Coun., Toledo, 1974—75; assoc. Charfoos & Christensen, P.C., Detroit, 1975—. Legal dir. Mich. Med. Schs. Coun. of Deans, Ann Arbor, 1978—80; lectr. law U. Toledo, 1978—88; assoc. prof. Sch. Medicine Wayne State U., Detroit, 1978—; cons. Georgetown U. Inst. for Health Policy, Washington, 1989, Office of Tech. Assessment, Washington, 1992—96, Robert Wood Johnson Found., Washington, 1994—98. Author: (book) Anesthesiology and the Law, 1983, Obstetrics/Gynecology and the Law, 1984, Social Security Disability Claims, 2002; actor: (book) The Law of Medical Practice in Michigan, 1981; editor: (book) Legal and Ethical Aspects of Treating Terminally Ill Patients, 1982. Bd. dirs. Am. Lung Assn., Detroit, 1978—83, Vis. Nurse Assn., Detroit, 1987—96, Preservation Wayne, 1992—; violinist Portland Symphony, Maine. Fellow Undergrad. fellow in the arts, U. N.H.; grantee, Health Care Fin. Adminstrn., Rockville, Md., 1978—80. Mem.: Am.

Soc. Hosp. Attys., Am. . of Law and Medicine (exec. coun. 1981—85). Avocations: Persian textiles, folk art, collecting and studying antiquities. Office: Charfoos and Christensen PC 5510 Woodward Ave Detroit MI 48202

PETERS, JOHN DURHAM, speech educator, writer; b. Salt Lake City, May 4, 1958; s. John Milton Peters and Carolyn Widtsoe Durham Person; m. Marsha Paulsen, Oct. 19, 1979; children: Benjamin J.P., Daniel N.P. BA, U.of Utah, Salt Lake City, 1981; MA, U. of Utah, Salt Lake City, Utah, 1981—82; PhD, Stanford (Calif.) U., 1988. F. Wendell Miller disting. prof. Dept. of Comm. Studies, U. Iowa, Iowa City, 2002—. Author: (book) Speaking into the Air: A History of the Idea of Communication, 1999; contbr. articles to profl. jours. including. Recipient Winans-Wichelns Award for Disting. Scholarship in Rhetoric and Pub. Address, Nat. Comm. Assn., 2000; fellow, NEH, 1995-1996, Leverhulme Trust, 1999-2000; grantee Fulbright Professorship (Greece), Fulbright Found., 1998-1999. Mem. Lds Ch. Avocations: basketball, frisbee, languages, music. Office: Dept Comm Studies Univ Iowa Iowa City IA 52242-1498 Office Fax: 319-335-2930.

PETERS, JOHN HENRY, artist; b. Sioux Falls, S.D., Mar. 9, 1953; s. Arnold John and Lorraine Ellen (Oaks) P.; m. Debra Ann Pollock, Sept. 19, 1981; children: Benu, Jonah, Steffan, Skylar. BA in Art, Augustana Coll., 1976; MFA, U. Ill., Champaign, 1990. Asst. sculptor Christiane T. Martens, Sioux Falls, Gregory, Ind., 1976-79; artist S.D. Artists-in-Schs., Madison, Sioux Falls, S.D., 1979-80; tchr. Sioux Falls Coll. and Augustana Coll., 1986-87; dir. of exhibits Augustana Coll./Eide/Dalrymple Gallery, Sioux Falls, 1984-88; tchr. U. Ill. Sch. of Art and Design, Champaign, 1988-90; residential trainer Sioux Vocat. Svcs., 1990-95; tchr. Augustana Coll. Art Dept., Sioux Falls, 1995-97; self-employed artist Archtl. models, 1997—. Lectr., presenter slide presentations regional colls., S.D. and Ill., 1990-95; juror of art competitions, Sioux Falls regional art competitions, 1986-87; chmn., display art work seminar Assn. of S.D. Mus., 1985; exhibitor various schs., 1975-2002. Artist: (steel sculpture) Augustana Coll., 1975, (wood carving) Commn. for St. Michael's Ch., Sioux Falls, 1986, Commn. for Holy Spirit Ch., 1991-2002, (mixed-media sculpture) S.D. Elements Minnehaha County Courthouse, Sioux Falls, 1996, Commn. for St. John Am. Luth. Ch., 1999 (wood relief). Cub scout leader, asst. Boy Scouts Am., 1990-2002, leader, com. mem. Pack 112, Pack 45, Troop 150. Recipient hon. mention for sculpture, 16th Joslyn Biennial/Joslyn Art Mus., Omaha, 1980, 1st place sculpture award Dahl Fine Arts, Rapid City, S.D., 1980, individual artist fellowship S.D. Fine Arts, NEA, Sioux Falls, 1980, Luth. Brotherhood Nat. Student Art Competition, Mpls., 1975. Avocation: swimming. Home: 822 W 3rd St Sioux Falls SD 57104-2610

PETERS, JOSEPH DONALD, filmmaker; b. Montebello, Calif., Mar. 7, 1958; s. Donald Harry and Anna Lucia (Suarez) P. BA in Comm., U. So. Calif., L.A., 1982. Filmmaker Renaissance Prodns., Ltd., San Dimas, Calif., 1986—. Writer, prodr., dir. films, TV, Seniors and Alcohol Abuse, 1986, Eskimo Ice Cream Shoes, 1990 (Gold award 1991), Rachel, 1994 (Silver and Bronze award 1995), The Adventures of Sam and Kathy, 1998, Emotions, 1999 (Gold and Honorable Mention award 1999). Mem. Am. Film Inst., Cinewomen, The Writer's Table.. Avocations: reading film books, collecting videos, sporting events. Office: Renaissance Prodns Ltd Ste 48 301 N San Dimas Canyon Rd San Dimas CA 91773-2734 E-mail: jpeters@directorsnet.com.

PETERS, KAREN HORNE, language educator; b. Norton, Va., July 7, 1951; d. Earl Jackson and Mildred Young Horne; m. Joseph Richard Peters; children: Andrew, Jeremy, Sara. BA, Clinch Valley Coll., 1973; MEd, U. Va., 1992. Freelance writer Streetmail, North Adams, Mass., 2000—01; tchr. English Coeburn H.S., Va., 1979—2002; adj. instr. U. Va., Wise, 1999—2002; ch. musician Tacoma United Meth. Ch., Coeburn, 1966—2002, Coeburn United Meth. Ch., 1998—2002. Site coord. 21st Century-Project SOAR, Coeburn, VA., 2002—02; academic coach Coeburn H.S., 1995—2002, forensics coach, 1997—2002. Merit badge counselor Boy Scouts of Am., Coeburn, VA., 1985—90. Mem.: NEA. Independent. Methodist. Avocation: needlework; reading; genealogy; piano and organ.

PETERS, KURT JAMES, obstetrician, gynecologist; b. N.Y.C., Jan. 10, 1947; s. John Henry and Gertrude Anna (Lang) P.; m. Mahafarin Partovi, Nov. 24, 1974; children: Katherine Amy, Suzanne Elizabeth. AB, U. Pa., 1969; MD, Pahlavi Med. Sch., Shiraz, Iran, 1975; diploma, marine radio operator's permit, Chapman Sch. Seamanship, Stuart, Fla., 1997. Lic. capt. USCG. Intern Boston City Hosp., 1975-76, resident in ob-gyn., 1976-79; clin. instr. ob-gyn. Boston U. Sch. Medicine, 1979-81; pvt. practice, Sparta, N.J., 1981-89; pvt. practice Newton, 1989-97; ret., 1997; obstetrician, gynecologist Women's Health Care Assocs., NJ, 2001—. Mem. attending staff Newton Meml. Hosp., 1981-97, treas. med. staff, 1983-85. Mem. Med. Soc. N.J., Sussex County Med. Soc., Alpha Chi Sigma, Alpha Beta Kappa. Republican. Lutheran. Avocations: boating, scuba diving.

PETERS, LEE IRA, JR. public defender; b. Jamestown, N.Y., Dec. 17, 1946; s. Lee Ira and Carrie Irene (Roberson) P.; m. Mabel Luisa Thompson, June 21, 1969; children: Tammy M., Lee III, Ryan J. BA in Criminology, Fla. State U., 1971; JD, U. Fla., 1984. Bar: Fla. 1984, U.S. Dist Ct. (mid. dist.) Fla. 1989. Sr. intern Pub. Defender State of Fla., Gainesville, Fla., 1983; spl. asst. U.S. Atty No. Dist. Fla., Tallahassee, 1987-89; asst. states atty. 3d cir. State's Atty. Office, Live Oak, Fla., 1984-89; asst. pub. defender, felony divsn. chief 3rd cir. Pub. Defender's Office, 1989—. Spl. agt. crim. investigation Bur. ATF- U.S. Treas., Anniston, Ala., Boise, Idaho, 1971-77, resident agt.-in-charge Portland, Oreg., 1977-81; assoc. counsel (pro bono) Nat. Assn. Treas. Agts., 1993—. With USN, 1965-67, Vietnam, U.S. Army Res., 1981-95. Recipient Disting Svc. award Fla. Coun. Crime & Delinquency, Chpt. XV, 1989; Meritorious Svc. Sec. Army U.S., 1997. Mem. ACLU, Fla. Assn. Criminal Def. Lawyers, Fla. Bar Assn. (3d cir. grievance com. 1993-96), Acad. Fla. Trial Lawyers, 3d Cir. Bar Assn., Am. Legion (fin. officer post 107, Live Oak), McAlpin Comty. Club (pres. 1990-96), Rotary Club, Elks, Phi Alpha Delta. Avocation: cattle and Arabian horse raising. Office: Third Cir Pub Defender 106 Ohio Ave S Live Oak FL 32064-3212 E-mail: pd3liveoak@hotmail.com.

PETERS, LEO FRANCIS, environmental engineer; b. Melrose, Mass., Aug. 14, 1937; s. Joseph Leander and Mary Gertrude (Phalen) P.; m. Joan Catherine Anderson, May 20, 1961; children: Elizabeth M., Susan J., Carolyn A., Jennifer L. BS in Civil Engring., Northeastern U., Boston, 1960, MS in Civil Engring., 1966; postgrad., Harvard U., 1989. Registered profl. engr., Mass., N.H.; diplomate Am. Acad. Environ. Engrs. Jr. engr. N.Y. Dept. Transp., Albany, 1960-61; chief engr. John M. Cashman, Weymouth, Mass., 1961-62; project engr. Metcalf & Eddy, Inc., Boston, 1962-65, Weston & Sampson, Boston, 1965-67, assoc., 1967-70, ptnr., 1970-76; exec. v.p. Weston & Sampson Engrs., Inc., 1976-82, pres., CEO Wakefield and Peabody, Mass., 1982-99, chmn., 1999—. Mem. corp. Northeastern U., 1992, dir. Nat. Coun. of Northeastern U., 1993—; treas. The Engring. Ctr., 1991-93; chmn. The Engring. Ctr. Edn. Trust, 1994-95, treas. 1992-94. Clk., mem. Melrose (Mass.) Planning Bd., 1969-91; bd. dirs. Environ. Bus. Coun. New Eng., 1997—. Named Young Engr. of Yr. Mass. Soc. Profl. Engrs., Outstanding Civil Engr. Nat. Coun. Northeastern U., 1991; recipient Environ. Merit award Environ. Bus. Coun. New Eng., Engring. Ctr. Leadership award, 2001. Fellow Am. Cons. Engrs. Coun. (v.p. 1995-96, sr. v.p. 1996-97, pres.-elect 1998-99, pres. 1999-2000); mem. Am. Water Works Assn., Am. Pub. Works Assn., Water Environ. Fedn., Am. Cons. Engrs. Coun. New Eng. (pres. 1990-91), New Eng. Water Works Assn. (hon., life mem., pres. 1989-90), Mass. Water Works Assn., Boston Soc. Civil Engrs. (hon.). Roman Catholic. Home: 187 E Emerson St Melrose MA 02176-3534 Office: Weston & Sampson Engrs Inc 5 Centennial Dr Peabody MA 01960-7985 E-mail: petersl@wseinc.com.

PETERS, LEON, JR. electrical engineering educator, research administrator; b. Columbus, Ohio, May 28, 1923; s. Leon P. and Ethel (Howland) Pierce; m. Mabel Marie Johnson, June 6, 1953; children: Amy T. Peters Thomas, Melinda A. Peters Todaro, Maria C. Cohee, Patricia D., Lee A., Roberta J. Peters Cameruca, Karen E. Peters Ellingson. BSE.E., Ohio State U., 1950, MS, 1954, PhD, 1959. Asst. prof. elec. engring. Ohio State U., Columbus, 1959-63, assoc. prof., 1963-67, prof., 1967-93, prof. emeritus, 1993—, assoc. dept. chmn. for rsch., 1990-92, dir. electro sci. lab., 1983-94. Contbr. articles to profl. jours. Served to 2d lt. U.S. Army, 1942-46, ETO. Fellow IEEE Home: 2087 Ellington Rd Columbus OH 43221-4138 Office: Ohio State U Electrosci Lab 1320 Kinnear Rd Columbus OH 43212-1156

PETERS, LEROY RICHARD, materials management consulting company executive; b. Milw., June 26, 1943; s. LeRoy Edwin and Eleanor Hedwig (Bensing) Peters; m. Barbara Jean Hackney, Nov. 18, 1964 (div. July 1970); 1 child, Neal; m. Nancy Elizabeth Till, July 17, 1971; children: Richard, Brenda, Eric, Linda. BS, U. Wis., 1966; Grad., U.S. Army/Command and, Gen. Staff Coll., Ft. Leavenworth, Kans., 1977. Cert. fellow in prodn. and inventory mgmt. Inventory supr. Bucyrus Erie, Erie, Pa. and Pocatello, Idaho, ach3-76; inventory mgr. Am. Microsystems, Pocatello, 1976-78; prodn. mgr. Worthington Compressor, Buffalo, 1978-80; mfg. mgr. St. Regis WPM Div., Denver, 1980-82; materials mgr. Robinson Brick Co., 1982-86; prodn. mgr. Merritt Equipment Co., 1986-89; instructional designer Martin Marietta, 1989-90; sr. cons. J.D. Edwards, 1990-93; sr. cons. mgr. AMX Internat., 1993-97; v.p. The Thompson Group, 1997-98; CEO, Enterprise Resource Mgmt., Inc., 1998—. Editorial com.: Aerospace and Defense Dictionary, 1990; contbr. articles to profl. jours. Scoutmaster Boy Scouts Am., Denver, 1989, cubmaster, 1988, outdoor chmn., Denver, 1990; dist. capt. Adams County Colo. Reps., Denver, 1986. Col. U.S. Army, 1966-94, Vietnam, Desert Storm. Decorated Legion of Merit, Bronze Star, Meritorious Svc. medal, Army Commendation medal. Fellow Am. Prodn. and Inventory Control Soc. (bd. dirs. region VI 1990—, pres. Colo. chpt. 1989-90); mem. Am. Def. Preparedness Assn., Moose. Lutheran. Avocations: fishing, reading, music, photography, geology. Home: 1468 W 111th Ave Northglenn CO 80234-3397

PETERS, LINDA ELLEN, interior designer, educator, real estate agent; b. Oak Park, Ill., July 9, 1946; d. Russell C. and Vilma (Janik) Lowry; m. Roger W. Peters, June 24, 1967 (div. Jan. 1982). BS in Nursing with honors, U. Ill., Chgo., 1968; MA, Memphis State U., 1976; PhD, U. Ga., 1983. RN; cert. tchr., Mo., Calif.; lic. real estate agt., Calif. Tchr. Augusta (Ga.) Coll., 1978-80; designer J.T. Interiors, Athens, Ga., 1984, Hallmark Interiors, Los Angeles, 1985; tchr. Woodbury U., 1985—; prin. Intraspace Design, 1986—. V.p. Friends of Hollyhock (Frank Lloyd Wright) Ho., Los Angeles, 1986—. Mem. Am. Soc. Interior Designers, Soc. Archtl. Historians (treas. 1986—), Coll. Art Assn., Alpha Lambda Delta, Sigma Theta Tau. Avocations: growing orchids, jogging, camping. Office: 740 E Green St Pasadena CA 91101-2118

PETERS, LORI SUSAN, human resources executive; b. Balt., Oct. 19, 1958; d. Harry John and Denise (Sfreddo) Peters; m. John Walter Guenther, June 10, 1989. BA, Loyola Coll., Balt., 1980; MA in Human Resource Devel., George Washington U., 1988. Pers. mgmt. specialist Dept. Interior, Nat. Pk. Svc., Washington, 1980-82; human resources mgr. Monumental Corp., Balt., 1982-83, compensation and benefits mgr., 1984-85; asst. v.p., dir. human resources Citicorp, McLean, Va., 1985-88; cons. in human resources Freddie Mac, Reston, 1988-89; dir. tng. and devel. Continuum, Austin, Tex., 1989-90; asst. div. dir. Argonne (Ill.) Nat. Lab., 1990-93. Cons. in field. Vol. George Bush for Pres. Campaign, 1988; fundraising vol. United Way of Md., 1980-85. Mem. ASTD, NAFE, Nat. Assn. Bank Women, Soc. Human Resource Profls., Am. Compensation Assn., OD Network, Alpha Sigma Nu. Republican. Roman Catholic. Home: 12152 Jonathons Glen Way Herndon VA 20170-2349

PETERS, MARCIE LOUANN, financial analyst; b. Salem, Oreg., Oct. 26, 1972; d. Edward Arthur Peters, Melody Jean Winn. AA, Bellevue Coll., 1997; BA, U. Wash. Bothell, 2000. Staff human resources Storage Tek, Bellevue, Wash.; staff mktg. and pers. Diagnostic Ultrasound, Bothell; staff clin. staff mgmt. Icos Corp.; info. tech. bus. analyst Blue Cross Blue Shield, Jacksonville, Fla., Tek Sys., Jacksonville. Author (poetry): Poetry Collection, 2002. Bd. dirs. Multicultural Network, Jacksonville. Mem.: Univ. Club. Avocations: reading, skiing. Home: 1831 Riviera Pkwy #9 Jacksonville FL 32205

PETERS, MARJORIE SPANNINGER, historical society executive; b. Perkasie, Pa., July 14, 1933; m. Kenneth R. Peters; 2 children. Administr. Washington County Hist. Soc., Hagerstown, Md., 1975—. Mem. adv. com. Washington County; mem. steering com. Nat. Pike Festival, Antietam Battlefield Meml. Illumination; mem. Greater Hagerstown Preservation and Urban Renewal Task Force com. Vol. Am. Cancer Soc.; pres. Y-Me of Cumberland Valley, 1998-99. Recipient Resolution of Appreciation, 1998, Senate of Md., Cmty. of Hope award Nat. Cancer Survivors Day, 1994, Portrait of Hope award Am. Cancer Soc., 1998; named One of Washington County's Most Wonderful Citizens, 1993, 94, Woman on the Move, 1992. Methodist. Office: Wash Co Hist Soc PO Box 1281 135 W Washington St Hagerstown MD 21740-4709

PETERS, MARY CATHERINE, journalist, researcher; b. Glen of Aherlow, County Tipperary, Ireland, July 27, 1947; d. Thomas Peters and Agnes Columba Griffin. Cert. pre-coop. devel. Journalist La - The Irish Lang. Newspaper, Belfast, Ireland, 1970—2002, Radio na Gaeltachta, Casla, Ireland; dir. Clann na hEireann USA (Reuniting Irish Am. Families), Naples, Fla., 2001—. Rschr. family surnames Clans of Ireland Office, Tipperary, Ireland; creator, rschr. SBB Show for Telefis Eireann (Irish TV), Dublin. Author: (Poem) Aggie, 1996; contbr. TV show; actor: the TD in Letters of a Successful TD. Named Internat. Writer of Merit.

PETERS, MARY E. federal agency administrator; m. Terry Peters; 3 children. B, U. Phoenix; attended govt. program for state & local govt., Harvard U. Dir. Ariz. Dept. Transp., 1985—2001; fed. hwy. adminstr. U.S. Dept. Transp., Washington, 2001—. Past bd. dirs. Project Challenge, Nat. Guard; past chair adv. bd. Hwy. Expansion Loan Program; mem. Gt. Ariz. Develop. Authority; past mem. Growing Smarter Commn. Named Women of Yr., Women's Transp. Seminar; named one of Most Influential Person in Ariz. Transp., Ariz. Bus. Jour. Mem.: We. Assn. State Hwy. Transp. Officials, Am. Assn. State Hwy Officials (past chair standing com. on planning, assest mgmt. task force, reauthorization steering com. 2001). Office: US Dept Transp Fed Hwy Adminstrn 400 7th St SW Washington DC 20590 Office Fax: 202-366-3244.*

PETERS, MAX STONE, chemical engineer, educator; b. Delaware, Ohio, Aug. 23, 1920; s. Charles Clinton and Dixie Mae (Stone) P.; m. Laurnell Louise Stephens, June 29, 1947; children— Margaret Dixie, M. Stephen. BS in Chem Engring, Pa. State U., 1942, MS, 1947, PhD (Shell Oil Co. grad. fellow 1949-51), 1951. Registered profl. engr., Pa., Colo. Prodn. supr. Hercules Powder Co., 1942-44; research asst. Pa. State U., 1946-47; tech. plant supr. George I. Treyz Chem. Co., 1947-49; mem. faculty U. Ill., 1951-62, prof. chem. engring., 1957-62, head dept., 1958-62; dean engring. U. Colo., 1962-78, prof. chem. engring., 1978-87, chmn. dept., 1981-85, emeritus prof. chem. engring., emeritus dean engring., 1987—. Mem. adv. com. engring. div. NSF, 1962-66; chmn. Pres.'s Nat. Medal Sci. Com., 1969-70, Colo. Environ. Commn., 1970-72 Author: Elementary Chemical Engineering, 1954, rev. edit., 1984, Plant Design and Economics for Chemical Engineers, 1958, rev. edit. 1968, 80, 91; cons. editor: McGraw-Hill series chem. engring, 1960-87. Served with AUS, 1944-46. Recipient Merit award Am. Assn. Cost Engrs., 1969; Distinguished Alumnus award Pa. State U., 1974; Distinguished Alumnus award U. Colo., 1971; Phillips Lecture award Okla. State U., 1980 Mem. Nat. Acad. Engring., Am. Inst. Chem. Engrs. (dir. 1961-64, pres. 1968, Founders award 1974, Lewis award 1979), Am. Soc. Engring. Edn. (chmn. chem. engring. div. 1962, sec. engring. coll. adminstrn. council 1965-67, George Westinghouse award 1959, Lamme award 1973, Merry Field award 1985), Am. Chem. Soc. (adv. bd. jour. 1956-59), Am. Assn. Cost Engring., Sigma Xi, Alpha Chi Sigma, Phi Eta Sigma, Phi Lambda Upsilon, Tau Beta Pi, Sigma Tau. Achievements include spl. research biomass, kinetics, mechanisms. Home: 4875 Sioux Dr No 004 Boulder CO 80303

PETERS, MERCEDES, psychoanalyst; b. N.Y.C. BS, L.I. U., 1945; MS, U. Conn., 1953; tng. in psychotherapy, Am. Inst. Psychotherapy, 1960-70; PhD in Psychoanalysis, Union Inst., 1989. Cert. in psychoanalysis Am. Exam. Bd. Psychoanalysis, mental health cons. Sr. psychotherapist Cmty. Guidance Svc., 1960-75; staff affiliate Postgrad. Ctr. for Mental Health, 1974-76; pvt. practice psychoanalysis and psychotherapy, Bklyn., 1961—; cons. to advanced tng. program Jewish Bd. Family and Children's Svcs., 2000—. Contbr. articles to profl. jours. Bd. dirs. Brookwood Child Care Assn. Fellow: Am. Orthopsychiat. Assn.; mem.: NASW, LWV, NAACP, Postgrad. Psychoanalytic Soc., Nat. Assn. Advancement Psychoanalysis (bd. dirs., chair UN com.), Wednesday Club. Office: 142 Joralemon St Brooklyn NY 11201-4709

PETERS, MICHAEL P. former mayor; m. Jeannette Peters; 3 children. Former firefighter City of Hartford; former owner small bus. Hartford; mayor City of Hartford, 1993—2001. Former chmn Hartford Civic Ctr. Commn., Hartford Redevel. Agy.; former mem. Bushnell Park Found.; founder Hartford Thomas Hooker Day Parade and Festival; mktg. com. Downtown Coun.; mem. Am. Leadership Forum, Dem. Town Com.; vol. neighborhood baseball and football teams; bd. dirs. Cedar Hill Cemetery.*

PETERS, MILTON EUGENE, educational psychologist; b. Anderson, Ind., July 22, 1938; s. Olen A. and Dorothy LaVerne (Lambert) P.; m. Carol Ann Dudycha, Aug. 27, 1960. BA, Wittenburg U., 1960; M in Div., Hamma Sch. Theology, 1963; MA, Bowling Green State U., 1965; PhD, U. Toledo, 1975. Lic. psychologist, Ohio. Pastor Luth. Ch. Am., 1966-69; instr. psychology Defiance (Ohio) Coll., 1969-70, Bluffton (Ohio) Coll., 1970-72; tchr., rsch. asst. U. Toledo, 1973-75, prof., 1975-76; dir. instl. rsch., asst. prof. psychology U. Findlay, Ohio, 1976-85, assoc. prof. psychology, 1985-89, prof., 1989—. Cons., lectr. in field; ednl. rschr. Contbr. articles to profl. and religious jours. Mem. APA, Am. Assn. Univ. Prof. (pres. U. Findlay), Midwestern Psychol. Assn., Creative Edn. Found. (colleague), Findlay Beacon Club, Fostoria Power Squadron. Home: 1130 Country Club Dr Findlay OH 45840-6342 Office: 1000 N Main St Findlay OH 45840-3653 E-mail: peters@findlay.edu.

PETERS, PATRICIA L. elementary education educator; b. Alton, Ill., Oct. 20, 1954; d. Golden D. Jr. and Patricia A. (Elmore) Zike; m. M.L. Peters, Dec. 14, 1979; 1 child, Goldie Lee. BA in Bus., William Woods Coll., Fulton, Mo., 1976; MS in Edn., So. Ill. U., 1987. Cert. elem. and early childhood tchr., Mo. Corp. officer, stockholder Am. Marine Svcs., Inc., Alton, 1980—; elem. tchr. computers, lang. arts and math. Ferguson (Mo.)-Florissant Sch. Dist. Program presenter edn. seminars. Contbr. articles to profl. publs. Lit. sets grantee, Intermediate sci. grantee; recipient William Walter Griffith award, 1991, Citicorp Ednl. award. Mem. NEA, ASCD, Nat. Assn. for Edn. Young Children, Internat. Reading Assn., Ferguson-Florissant Edn. Assn. (rep.), Kappa Delta Pi, Alpha Chi Omega.

PETERS, PEGGY L.S. investment broker; b. Milw., Dec. 28, 1945; d. Carl Frederick and Bernice Ida (Schpatz) Schoenfeldt; m. Michael Harvey Peters, June 5, 1981; 1 child, Lee Michael Peters. BA in Psychology, U. Wis., Milw., 1970. Mgr. Solana Studios Outboard Marine Corp., Milw., 1970-74; real estate broker, salesperson Relocation Realty, 1973-74; investment broker Prudential Bache, Washington D.C., 1975-82; v.p. investments, retirement planning cons. Paine Webber, Vienna, 1982—. Rep. dive team, mem. bd. dirs. Great Falls Swim & Tennis Club, 1995; chmn. PTA, 1995. Mem. Gamma Phi Beta (life). Republican. Avocations: family life, sports. Home: 917 Golden Arrow St Great Falls VA 22066-2520

PETERS, PHILLIP JOSEPH, endocrinologist, educator; b. Columbus, Ohio, Feb. 19, 1945; s. Phillip John and Elisabeth (Baas) P.; m. Janice Kassalow, Mar. 7, 1968; children: Julie Elaine, Jason Todd. BA, Harvard U., 1967; MD, W.Va. U., 1971. Diplomate Am. Bd. Internal Medicine, Am. Bd. Endocrinology and Metabolism. Intern in internal medicine W.Va. U. Med. Ctr., 1971-72, from resident to chief resident in internal medicine, 1974-76; fellow in endocrinology W.Va. U. Sch. Medicine, Morgantown, 1976-78, instr. in endocrinology and internal medicine, 1977-78, asst. prof. endocrinology and internal medicine, 1978-79; clin. asst. prof. endocrinology U. Ark. for Med. Scis., Little Rock, 1979-84, 91—; endocrinologist Little Rock Diagnostic Clinic, 1979—. Med. dir. Diabetic Treatment Ctr. of Am., Little Rock, 1992-95; chairperson dept. medicine Bapt. Med. Ctr., Little Rock, 1996-97, vice chief of staff, 2000-01, chief of staff, 2002-. Pres., bd. dirs. Unitarian Universalist Ch. Little Rock, 1981-84; sec., bd. dirs. Chamber Music Soc. Little Rock, 1984-86. Capr. USAF, 1972-74. Named Outstanding Endocrinologist, Ark. Times, 1994-95, 97, 2000, 02. Fellow ACP, Am. Coll. Endocrinology; mem. Am. Assn. Clin. Endocrinologists, Am. Soc. Internal Medicine, Endocrine Soc., Harvard Club of Ark. (mem. exec. com. 1985—, pres. 1997—), Harvard U. Alumni Assn. (mid south regional dir. 1992-95), Internat. Soc. for Clin. Densitometry. Avocations: skiing, golf, reading, soccer. Home: 11 Shawbridge Ln Little Rock AR 72212-2910 Office: Little Rock Diagnostic Ctr 10001 Lile Dr Little Rock AR 72205-6217

PETERS, R. JONATHAN, lawyer, manufacturing company executive; b. Janesville, Wis., Jan. 6, 1927; m. Ingrid H. Varvayn, 1953; 1 dau., Christina. BS in Chemistry, U. Ill., 1951; JD, Northwestern U., 1954. Bar: Ill. 1954. Chief patent counsel Englehard Industries, 1972-82, Kimberly-Clark Corp., Neenah, Wis., 1982-85; gen. counsel Lanxide Corp., Newark, 1985-87; pvt. practice Chgo., 1985—. Served with CIC, U.S. Army, 1955-57. Patentee in field. Mem. ABA, Am. Intellectual Property Law Assn., Lic. Execs. Soc., Assn. Corp. Patent Counsel, North Shore Golf (Menasha, Wis.), Masons, Scottish Rite, Shriners.

PETERS, RALPH EDGAR, architectural and engineering executive; b. Harrisburg, Pa., Feb. 20, 1923; s. George Edward and Rebecca Flavia (Michener) P.; m. Roberta Jane Shaffer, June 12, 1948; children: Sheila Jane, Gail Marie, Ralph Jr., Bret Edward. Student, U. Pa., 1942; BA in Bus. Adminstrn., Pa. State U., 1948. From payroll supt. to asst. budget supr. Pa. State U., 1948-52; chief acct., pers. officer Haller, Raymond & Brown, State College, Pa., 1952-54; from contr. to CEO and chmn. bd. Benatec Assocs., Inc. (formerly Berger Assocs., Inc.), Camp Hill, 1954—. Chmn. bd. advisors Pa. State U., Harrisburg, 1979—; chmn. bd. dirs. Holy Spirit Hosp., Camp Hill, 1982—; past pres. Tri-County United Way, Harrisburg, 1978—; chmn. Pvt. Industry Coun., Harrisburg, 1982-87. With U.S. Army, 1943-45, ETO, 1952-53, Korea. Recipient Comty. Svc. award Salvation Army, 1980, Disting. Pennsylvanian award Greater Phila. C. of C., 1981, Catalyst award Capital Region Econ. Devel., 1992, James Skelly award for exceptional svcs. to the hwy. program Associated Constructors of Pa., 1993, Alexis de Tocqueville Humanitarian award United Way, 1999; named Transp. Adv. of Yr., Pa. Hwy. Info. Assn., 1994; finalist Cen. Pa. Entrepreneur of Yr., 1996; Paul Harris fellow Rotary Internat., 1997. Mem. Pa. C. of C. (bd. dirs., transp. com. chmn. 1972-90), Harrisburg Area C. of C. (pres., chmn. 1979-83), Ams. for Competitive Enterprise Sys. (pres. 1981-83), Cumberland County Transp. Authority, Susquehanna Valley Regional Airport Authority, Lions, Masons, Pa. Jaycees (pres. 1955-56, nat. v.p. 1956-57), Delta Sigma Pi. Lutheran. Office: Benatec Assocs Inc 200 Airport Rd New Cumberland PA 17070-2467 E-mail: rpeters@benatec-iba.com.

PETERS, RALPH FREW, investment banker; b. Mineola, N.Y., Mar. 21, 1929; s. Ralph and Helen Louise (Frew) P.; m. Ann Marie Haberski, Dec. 31, 1997; children from previous marriage: Louise Frew, Jean Reid, Ralph Frew, Melvyn T., Richard Clayton. BA, Princeton U., 1951; postgrad., Stonier Grad. Sch. Banking, Rutgers U., 1962. With Corn Exchange Bank & Trust Co., 1947-52; chmn. bd., dir. Discount Corp. N.Y., N.Y.C., 1955-93. Bd. dirs. Van Eck Funds, Sun Life Ins. & Annuity of N.Y. Served with USNR, 1948-55. Mem. Pub. Securities Assn. (gov.), Anglers Club, Leash Club, Links Club, North Woods Club. Episcopalian.

PETERS, RALPH IRWIN, JR. biology educator, researcher; b. Tulsa, June 30, 1947; s. Ralph I. and Margenelle M. (MacDowell) P.; m. Marsha A. Lerenberg; 1 child, Caitlin Louise. BS, U. Tulsa, 1969; PhD, Wash. State U., 1975. NIH pre-doctoral trainee Wash. State U., Pullman, 1971-75; rsch. assoc. Tex. A&M U., College Station, 1975-76; NIH post-doctoral fellow Wash. State Coll. of Vet. Medicine, Pullman, 1976-77; asst. prof. Bates Coll., Lewiston, Maine, 1977-80; from asst. to assoc. prof. Wichita (Kans.) State U., 1980-89; prof., chmn. Lynchburg (Va.) Coll., 1989-93; clin. assoc. prof., dir. office analysis and planning U. Mo. Sch. Dentistry, Kansas City, 1993—. Reviewer West Pub. Co., 1983-84, Worth Pubs., 1985, NSF, 1987, Internat. Jour. of Comparative Psychology, 1988. Contbr. articles and abstracts to profl. jours.. With U.S. Army, 1969-71. Summer rsch. fellow USAF, 1987; rsch. grantee NSF, USAF, also others. Mem. AAAS, Sci. Rsch. Soc., Soc. for Neurosci., Internat. Brain Rsch. Orgn., Am. Assn. Dental Schs., Mid-Am. Assn. for Instnl. Rsch. Office: U Mo Sch Dentistry 650 E 25th St Kansas City MO 64108-2716

PETERS, RALPH MARTIN, education educator; b. Knoxville, Tenn., May 9, 1926; s. Tim C. and Alma (Shannon) P.; m. Lorraine Daniel, 1949; children— Teresa, Marta. BS, Lincoln Meml. U., 1949; MS, U. Tenn., 1953, Ed.D., 1960. Tchr. pub. schs, Lincoln Meml. U., 1956-63, prof., dept. chmn., v.p., 1956-63, 92-97, interim pres., 1997-98; prof. edn., dean students, dean

Grad. Sch. Tenn. Tech. U., Cookeville, 1963-89; dean emeritus, 1989. Editor publs. Served with Armed Forces, World War II. Mem. Phi Kappa Phi, Phi Delta Kappa, Omicron Delta Kappa. Clubs: Rotary. Baptist. Home: PO Box 3231 Cookeville TN 38502-3231

PETERS, RAY JOHN, surveyor; b. St. Louis, Feb. 10, 1931; s. John Henry and Pearl Minnie Peters; m. Barbara Mary Linacre, June 18, 1955; children: Alison Elizabeth, Andrew James, Gwendoline Joy. Student, Mo. Sch. Mines, 1952-53. Cert. land surveyor, Calif., Nev., N.D. Surveyor State of Calif., San Francisco, 1955-60; pres. Peters, Verdugo & Hull, Lafayette, Calif., 1960-88; ptnr. Peters & Hull, 1988—. Author: Real Estate Handbook, 1993, The Lafitte Case, 1997. With U.S. Army, 1948-52. Recipient Disting. Cmty. Svc. award Lafayette Sun., 1978; named Citizen of Yr. Lions Club, 1983. Mem. ASCE (Calif. coun.), Calif. Land Surveyors Assn., Calif. Writers club. Republican. Congregationalist. Avocations: travel, hiking, camping. Home: 1324 Martino Rd Lafayette CA 94549-2531

PETERS, RAYMOND EUGENE, computer systems company executive; b. New Haven, Aug. 24, 1933; s. Raymond and Doris Winthrop (Smith) P.; m. Millie Mather, July 14, 1978 (div. Nov. 1983); life ptnr. Mamie L. Romero, 1986—. Student, San Diego City Coll., 1956-61; cert., Lumbleau Real Estate Sch., 1973, Southwestern Coll., Chula Vista, Calif., 1980. Cert. quality assurance engr. Founder, pub. Silhouette Pub. Co., San Diego, 1960-75; co-founder, news dir. Sta. XEGM, 1964-68; news dir. Sta. XERB, Tijuana, Mex., 1973-74; founder, chief exec. officer New World Airways, Inc., San Diego, 1968-77; co-founder, exec. vice chmn. bd. San Cal Rail, Inc.-San Diego Trolley, 1974-77; founder, pres., CEO Ansonia Sta., micro systems, 1986—. Cons. on multimedia and electronic commerce sys., 1995—; co-founder, dir. S.E. Cmty. Theatre, San Diego, 1960-68; commr. New World Aviation Acad., Otay Mesa, Calif., 1971-77; co-founder New World Internat. Trade and Commerce Commn., Inc., 1991-94, New World Airways Inc, 1968-77. Author: Black Americans in Aviation, 1971, Profiles in Black American History, 1974, Eagles Don't Cry, 1988; founder, pub., editor Oceanside Lighthouse, 1958-60, San Diego Herald Dispatch, 1959-60. Co-founder, bd. dirs. San Diego County Econ. Opportunity Commn., 1964-67; co-founder Edn. Cultural Complex, San Diego, 1966-75; co-founder, exec. dir. S.E. Anti-Poverty Planning Coun., Inc., 1964-67; mem. U.S. Rep. Senatorial Inner Circle Com., Washington, 1990—; mem. bus. adv. bd. Value Add Reseller, 1995. With U.S. Army, 1950-53, Korea. Decorated (2) Bronze Svc. stars, UN medal. Mem. Am. Soc. Quality Control, Nat. City C. of C., Afro-Am. Micro Sys. Soc. (exec. dir. 1987—), Negro Airmen Internat. (Calif. pres. 1970-75, nat. v.p. 1975-77), Tuskegee Airmen (charter, bd. dirs. Benjamin O. Davis San Diego chpt. 1995—), Internat. Platform Assn., U.S. C. of C., Greater San Diego Minority C. of C. (bd. dirs. 1974—, past chmn. bd.), Masons (most worshipful grand master, supreme coun.), Shriners (Al Kadosh Disting. Cmty. Svc. award 1975). Republican. Avocations: creative writing, golf, world history. Home: Meadowbrook Estates # 245 8301 Mission Gorge Rd Santee CA 92071-3500 E-mail: ansonia@home.com, author33d@hotmail.com.

PETERS, RAYMOND ROBERT, bank executive; b. Concord, Calif., Sept. 14, 1942; s. Robert V. and Pegi M. (Carr) P.; m. Nancy Tsai; children: Angel, Ray, Matthew. BBA, U. Oreg., 1964. Head customer securities Bank of Am., San Francisco, 1969-71, Eurocurrency and fgn. exch. mgr. London, 1971-72, San Francisco, 1972-76, sr. v.p., head offshore funds, 1985-86, exec. v.p., 1987-92; group exec. v.p., treas. Bank Am. Corp., 1992-98, Charlotte, 1998-2001; mng. sr. ptnr. RNR-MAP, Zephyr Cove, Nev., 2001—. Mem. fgn. exch. com. N.Y. Fed. Res. Bank, 1978-87, chmn., 1984-85; mem. Chgo. Merc. Exch., 1987-2001; mem. Chgo. Bd. Trade, 1987-2001; bd. dirs. Bank Am. Fed. Sav. Bank and other subs.; cons. on internat. interest rate risk mgmt., fgn. currency, offshore banking matters, U.S. regulators, fgn. ctrl. banks, and pension and investment funds mgmt. Office: RNR-MAP PO Box 11879 Zephyr Cove NV 89448 E-mail: RRPETERS@aol.com.

PETERS, RICHARD, lawyer; b. Bklyn., June 6, 1945; s. Edmund Richard and Louise (Parks) P. BA, Tulane U., 1967; MA, Fla. State U., 1968, PhD, 1985; JD, Calif. Western, 1988. Bar: Calif. 1989. Instr. English U. San Diego, 1991, San Diego City Coll., 1989—, San Diego Mesa Coll., 1989—; panel atty. Appellate Defenders, Inc., San Diego, 1989—. Author: (poetry) On Aging, 1991. Mem. ABA, San Diego County Bar Assn. Office: Richard Peters Atty 5690 Greenshade Rd San Diego CA 92121-4230

PETERS, RICHARD SPENCER, musician; b. San Antonio, Feb. 2, 1951; s. Alva Spencer and Lucy Alma Peters; m. Nellie Julia Cruz, June 16, 1990; children: Matthew, Brittany; m. Cynthia Lynn White, Aug. 17, 1975 (div. May 0, 1976). BA, music edn., U. of So. Miss., Hattiesburg, MS, 1973; MA, music, Miss. Coll., Clinton, MS, 1984. Band dir. Mt. Olive Attendance, Mt. Olive, Miss., 1973—75; band dir./supr. Brookhaven H.S., Brookhaven, 1975—78; head band dir. Mendenhall H.S., Mendenhall, 1978—85, Newton City Schools, Newton, 1985—87; asst. band dir. Mission Ind. Sch. Dist. Ctr., Mission, Tex., 1987—91, McAllen Ind. Sch. Dist., McAllen, 1991—92; dist. music coord. East Ctrl. Ind. Sch. Dist., San Antonio, 1992—. Mem., adv. bd. US Achievement Acad., Huntsville, Ala., 1980—85, Salvation Army, McAllen, Tex., 1989—91. Contbg. editor: Bandworld Mag. Vol. Salvation Army, San Antonio, 1992; choir mem. Cornerstone Ch., 1996. Recipient Outstanding Educator, 1985, outstanding young man of Am., 1987, Who's Who Among Am. Teachers, 1998. Mem.: Tex. Music Administrators Conf., Nat. Fedn. Interscholastic Music Assn., Detroit Concert Band Assn., Percy Grainger Soc., Assn. of Tex. Profl. Educators, Nat. Band Assn., Tex. Bandmasters Assn., Tex. Music Educators Assn. Avocations: golf, remote control models. Home: 715 Arch Stone San Antonio TX 78258 Office: East Central Music Department 7173 Fm 1628 San Antonio TX 78263 Office Fax: 210-649-2951. E-mail: rsp6577@aol.com.

PETERS, RITA PUTINS, political scientist, educator; b. Rezekne, Latvia; came to U.S., 1951; BA in Polit. Sci. & Fine Arts, U. Conn., 1961; MA in Polit. Sci., Boston U., 1965, PhD, 1973. Lectr. Boston U., 1968-70, 79-80, Simmons Coll., 1973, Boston State Coll., 1978-78, 81, U. Mass., Boston, 1982—. Vis. lectr. U. Latvia, Riga, 1990, 1993, 1995, Estonian Sch. Diplomacy, Tallin, 1996; cons. U. Latvia, 1993, 1995, Polit. Candidates & others, Riga, 1998, 1999. Author: (with others) The Baltic In International Relations, 1988; book reviewer Choice, 1987—, contr. to Encyclopedia Americana, 1993,94,97 and to profl. jours. Vol. Foster Care Rev. Program, Boston, 1990—; bd. dirs. Baltic Am. Soc. of New England, Boston, 1980—; mem. exec. bd. Am. Nat. Latvian League. Fellow Wm. Joiner Ctr. Study of War U. Mass., 1986, grantee Internat. Rsch. & Exch. Bd., 1992, U. Mass., 1993, 1995. Mem. Harvard U. Davis Ctr. Russian Studies (assoc.), Am. Assn. for Advancement Slavic Studies, Assn. for Advancement Baltic Studies (life). Avocations: skiing, designing hand-knit clothing. Office: U Mass Polit Sci Dept 100 Morrissey Blvd Boston MA 02125-3300

PETERS, ROBERT JAMES, SR. draftsman, assistant manager; b. St. Louis, Dec. 20, 1946; s. Lewis Nathaniel and Thelma (Hudson) P.; m. Sharon Loretta Anderson, May 6, 1963 (div. Apr. 1992); m. Sharon Ann Dungy, July 21, 1992; children: Kimberly Rachele Peters Beck, Robert James Jr., Kelly Yusef. AA in Bus. Adminstrn., Forest Park Coll., St. Louis, 1968; BS in Indsl. Safety, Cen. Mo. State U., 1983; MBA, Lindenwood U., 1999. Polyphase tester AmerenUE, St. Louis, 1972-77, safety coord., 1977-79, safety supr., 1979-86, pers. supr., 1986-89, chief draftsman, 1989-2001, asst. mgr., 2001—. Bd. dirs. Electro Savings Credit Union, 2000. Exec. bd. dirs. United Way, St. Louis, 1997—, St. Louis chpt. Am. Red Cross, mem. exec. com., chmn. vols., 1999; sec. regional bd. Nat. Conf. Cmty. and Justice; chmn. spkrs. bur. ARC, St. Louis, 1998; mem. spkrs. bur. Alzheimer's Assn., St. Louis, 1998; bd. pres. Wesley House Assn., St. Louis, 1998; bd. dirs. Nat. Conf. Cmty. and Justice, 1999, Do The Right Thing, 1999. With U.S. Army, 1970-72, Vietnam. Recipient Cerman F. Mathews award Mathews-Dickey Boys Club, 1994, Exceptional Vol. Svc. award ARC, 1994, Clara Barton award, 1996, Partnership award, 1996. Mem. Nat. Spkrs. Assn. (Gateway chpt.), Powermasters Toastmasters (pres. 1988-89, DTM award 1995), Optimist Club St. Louis (pres. 1985-86). Assemblies of Yahweh. Avocations: racquetball, cycling, running, public speaking. Home: # 12 Bellerive Acres Saint Louis MO 63121 Office: AmerenUE 1901 Chouteau Ave Saint Louis MO 63103-3003 E-mail: rjpsdp@aol.com.

PETERS, ROBERT L(OUIS), retired educator, English, poet, critic; b. Wis., Oct. 20, 1924; m. Jean Powell, 1950 (div. 1971); children: Robert Louis II, Meredith Jean, Richard, Jefferson. BA, U. Wis., Madison, 1948, MA, 1949, PhD, 1952. Teaching asst. U. Wis., Madison, 1950-52; instr. English U. Idaho, 1952-53, Boston U., 1953-55; asst. prof. English Ohio Wesleyan U., 1955-58; assoc. prof. English Wayne State U., 1958-63; prof. English U. Calif., Riverside, 1963-68, Irvine, 1968-92, prof. English emeritus, 1993—. Mem. exec. bd. Ren Hen Press Publs., 1999—. Author: Songs for a Son, 1960, The Sow's Head and Other Poems, 1961, Crunching Gravel: On Growing Up in the Thirties, 1993, Nell: A Sister's Story, 1995, For You Lili Marlene: Memoir of WWII, 1995, Deather: A Child's Death and Life, 1997, (fiction and play) Snapshots for A Serial Killer, 1991, Zapped, 1993; author of poems; contbg. editor: American Book Review, 1976—, Contact II, 1977-92, Poetry Australia, 1989—; co-editor The Letters of John Addington Symonds, 3 vols., 1959-62. Recipient Hilberry Pub. prize, 1965, Borestone Mountain award, 1967, poetry Soc. Am. Hawker de Castagnola prize, 1984, Larry P. Fine Criticism award, 1985; named Outstanding Alumnus U. Wis., 1999; nominee Pulitzer prize, 1993, Pushcart award, 1993; Am. Coun. Learned Socs. grantee, 1963, Nat. Endowment for Arts grantee, 1974; Guggenheim fellow, 1966-67, NEA fellow, 1992. Mem. Pen N.Y., Pen L.A., Authoir Guild, Am. Soc. Aesthetics (trustee 1965-68). Avocations: hiking, gardening, reading, cooking, weight-lifting. Home: 9431 Krepp Dr Huntington Beach CA 92646 E-mail: ptrachrp@aol.com.

PETERS, ROBERT TIMOTHY, judge; b. Memphis, Dec. 28, 1946; s. Rhulin Earl and Bertie Nichols (Moore) P.; m. Ruth Audrey Allen, Dec. 11, 1973; children: Lindsay Elizabeth, Christopher Andrew. AA, St. Petersburg Jr. Coll., 1969; BA, U. Fla., 1971, JD, 1973. Bar: Fla. 1973, U.S. Dist. Ct. (mid. dist.) Fla. 1977, U.S. Ct. Appeals (5th cir.) 1981; cert. real estate lawyer. Ptnr. Goza, Hall & Peters P.A., Clearwater, Fla., 1973-84; sole practice, 1984-95; apptd. cir. judge Fla., 1995—. Gov. Fla.'s appointee Condominium Study Commsn., Clearwater, 1990-91. Columnist Clearwater Sun newspaper, 1985—. 1st Lt. U.S. Army, 1966-68, Vietnam. Decorated Silver Star, Purple Heart, Bronze Star with oak leaf cluster. Mem. Fla. Bar (condominium and planned devel. com.), Clearwater Bar Assn. Avocations: reading, exercise. Office: Pinellas County Courthouse 315 Court St Clearwater FL 33756-5165 Address: PO Box 6316 Clearwater FL 33758-6316

PETERS, ROBERT WAYNE, direct mail and catalog sales specialist; b. LaPorte, Ind., Jan. 2, 1950; s. Harry Carl and Dorothy May (Fischer) P.; m. Frances Kay Cooley, Aug. 21, 1971; children: Carolyn Marie, Angela Lynn. BA, Purdue U., 1972. CLU. Mgr. pension adminstrn. Gen. Life Ins. Corp., Milw., 1973-75; dir. qualified plan devel. Cen. Life Assurance Co., Des Moines, 1976-84; v.p. individual ops. First Farwest Ins. Co., Portland, Oreg., 1984-90; pres. CAF Enterprises, Inc., 1990—. Lectr. various govt. agys. Contbr. articles to profl. jours. Mem. N.W. Vintage Thunderbird (v.p. 1988, pres. 1989-90, exec. bd. 1991, sec. 1992-93, 97-2002, treas. 1995-96, sec.-treas. 2000), N.W. Car Collectors Assn. (treas. 2002). Avocations: reading, woodworking, vintage Thunderbirds, gourmet cooking. Office: CAF Enterprises Inc PO Box 1529 Tualatin OR 97062-1529

PETERS, SARAH WHITAKER, art historian, writer, lecturer; b. Kenosha, Wis., Aug. 17, 1924; d. Robert Burbank and Margaret Jebb (Allen) Whitaker; m. Arthur King Peters, Oct. 21, 1943; children: Robert Bruce, Margaret Allen, Michael Whitaker. BA, Sarah Lawrence Coll., 1954; MA, Columbia U., 1966; student, L'Ecole du Louvre, Paris, 1967-68; diplome, Ecole des Trois Gourmandes, Paris, 1968; PhD, CUNY, 1987. Freelance critic Art in Am., N.Y.C. Lectr.-in-residence Garrison Forest Sch., Owings Mills, Md.; adj. asst. prof. art history C.W. Post, U. L.I.; lectr. Bronxville (N.Y.) Adult Sch., Internat. Mus. Photography, 1979, Tufts U., 1979, Madison (Wis.) Art Ctr., 1984, Meml. Art Gallery, Rochester, N.Y., 1988, 91, Caramoor Mus., Katonah, N.Y., 1988, Yale U. Art Gallery, New Haven, Conn., 1989, The Cosmopolitan Club, N.Y.C., 1977, 91, Sarah Lawrence Coll., Bronxville, 1992, The Phillips Collection, Washington, 1993, Mpls. Inst. Arts, 1993, Whitney Mus. Am. Art, Champion, 1994, U. Wis., Parkside, 1994, Nat. Mus. Wildlife Art, Jackson Hole, Wyo., 1995, The Georgia O'Keeffe Mus., Santa Fe, 1997, Bronxville Pub. Libr., 1998. Author: Becoming O'Keeffe: The Early Years, 1991, 2d edit., 2001; contbr. essays to Portraits of American Women, 1999, The Dictionary of Art, 1996, Frames of Reference; Works from the Whitney Museum of American Art, 1999, Pattern of hte Past: A Kenosha Memoir, 2001; TV appearances include: BBC, London, The Late Show, 1993; radio interview: Art Today, Australia Broadcasting Corp., 1999; contbr. articles to profl. jours. Mem. Coll. Art Assn., Bronxville Field Club, The Cosmopolitan Club. Avocations: horseback riding, rock climbing, tennis, cooking. Home: 14 Village Ln Bronxville NY 10708-4806

PETERS, SHAWNA, political science educator; b. San Diego, May 23, 1968; d. Jason and Rachel Smith; m. Cooper Peters, Dec. 20, 1995; children: Patrick, Markus. BA, Calif State U., 1990. Assoc. prof. Santa Clara U., Calif., 1991—99; prof. Univ. Ctrl. Fla., 2000—; dir. Meriks Learning Ctr, Orlando, Fla., 2001—. Contbr. articles to profl. jours. Mem.: Phi Beta Kappa. Democrat. Avocations: painting, walking, decoupage. Office: Meriks Learning Ctr 7611 S Orange Blossom Trl #161 Orlando FL 32809-6903

PETERS, STEPHEN PAUL, medical educator; b. Johnstown, Pa., Apr. 26, 1949; m. Diane H. Henley. BA magna cum laude, Yale U., 1971; PhD in Biochemistry, U. Pitts., 1976, MD cum laude, 1978. Diplomate Nat. Bd. Med. Examiners, Am. Bd. Internal Medicine, Am. Bd. Pulmonary Disease. Intern, asst. resident in internal medicine Johns Hopkins Hosp., Balt., 1978-80; fellow in medicine Johns Hopkins U. Sch. Medicine, 1980-83, asst. prof., 1982-86, dir. pulmonary consultation svc., 1983-86; assoc. prof. dept. medicine Thomas Jefferson U., Jefferson Med. Coll., Phila., 1986—, assoc. dir. divsn. critical care, pulmonary allergic and immunologic diseases, 1986—, dir. rsch. divsn. pulmonary medicine and critical care, 1989—, prof. divsn. pulmonary medicine and critical care, 1989—. Hosp. staff Johns Hopkins Hosp., 1982-86, Good Samaritan Hosp., Balt., 1982-86, Francis Scott Key Med. Ctr., Balt., 1983-86, Thomas Jefferson U. Hosp., Phila., 1986—, Jefferson Park Hosp., Phi.a, 1989-94; VA merit rev. bd. Respiration Study Sect., 1991, 97—; spl. rev. com. NIH, Nat. Inst. of Allergy and Infectious Diseases, 1991, 97. Author: Practical Enzymology of the Spingolipidoses, 1977, Year Book of Pulmonary Disease, 1986-91, Clinical Studies in Medical Biochemistry, 1987; mem. editl. bd. Jour. of Allergy and Clin. Immunology, 1988-93, Respiratory Medicine, 1991—, Audio Forum on Asthma, 1998, Respiratory Digest, 1999—, Respiratory Rsch., 2000—; contbr. numerous articles to profl. jours. Med. scientists scholar, Ins. Med. Scientist scholarship Fund, Mass. Life Ins. Co., 1975-78; recipient numerous rsch. grants. Fellow ACP, Am. Acad. Allergy and Immunology, Coll. of Physicians of Phila., Am. Coll. of Chest Physicians; mem. Am. Thoracic Soc. (program com. allergy, immunology and inflamation sect. 1992—), Am. Assn. of Immunologists, Am. Fedn. for Clin. Rsch., Soc. for Leukocyte Biology, Pa. Thoracic Soc. (rsch. rev. com. 1990-94), Am. Lung Assn. (rsch. rev. com. 1990—), Sigma Xi. Home: 609 New Gulph Rd Bryn Mawr PA 19010-3650 Office: Thomas Jefferson U Jefferson Med Coll 1025 Walnut St Philadelphia PA 19107-5001 E-mail: stephen.p.peters@mail.tju.edu.

PETERS, THEODORE, JR. research biochemist, consultant; b. Chambersburg, Pa., May 12, 1922; s. Theodore and Miriam (Lenhardt) P.; m. Margaret Campbell, June 9, 1945; children: Theodore D., James C., Melissa Peters Barry, William L. BS in Chem. Engring., Lehigh U., 1943; PhD in Biol. Chemistry, Harvard U., 1950. Diplomate Am. Bd. Clin. Chemistry. Grad. asst. MIT, Cambridge, 1943-44; rsch. fellow Harvard Med. Sch., Boston, 1948-50; instr. U. Pa. Sch. Medicine, Phila., 1950-51; biochemist U.S. VA Hosp., Boston, 1953-55; rsch. biochemist Mary Imogene Bassett Hosp., Cooperstown, N.Y., 1955-88, rsch. scientist emeritus, 1988—; vis. scientist Carlsberg Laboratorium, Copenhagen, Denmark, 1958-59; guest worker NIH, Bethesda, Md., 1971-72; vis. rsch. prof. U. Western Australia, Perth, 1982. Chmn. classification panel FDA, Washington, 1976-79; bd. dirs. Nat. Com. for Clin. Lab. Standards, Villanova, Pa., 1986-87. Author: All About Albumin, Biochemistry, Genetics, and Medical Applications, 1996; chmn. bd. editors Clin. Chemistry, 1979-84; contbr. articles to profl. jours. Chmn. Sewer Bd., Cooperstown, 1975—; mem. Water Bd., Cooperstown, 1973—; chmn. lake com. Otsego County Conservation Assn., Cooperstown, 1972-78. Comdr. USNR, 1944-47, 51-53. Recipient Gold medal Biol. div. Electron Microscope Soc. Am., 1966. Fellow Am. Assn. Clin. Chemistry (pres. 1988, awards 1976, 77, 91); mem. Am. Chem. Soc., Am. Soc. Biol. Chem. Molecular Biology (emeritus), Am. Soc. for Cell Biology (emeritus), Protein Soc., Nat. Acad. for Clin. Biochemistry (diplomate), Acad. Clin. Lab. Physicians and Scientists, Phi Beta Kappa. Avocations: tennis, hiking, music. Home: 85 Lake St Cooperstown NY 13326-1038 Office: Mary Imogene Bassett Hosp Atwell Rd Cooperstown NY 13326-1038 E-mail: tedp@telenet.net.

PETERS, WILLIAM, author, producer, director; b. San Francisco, July 30, 1921; s. William Ernest and Dorothy Louise (Wright) P.; m. Mercy Ann Miller, Oct. 12, 1942 (div. 1968); children: Suzanne Peters Payne, Geoffrey Wright, Jennifer Peters Johnson, Gretchen Peters Daniel; m. Helene Louise Yager White, May 31, 1987. BS, Northwestern U., 1947. Account exec. pub. relations J. Walter Thompson Co., Chgo., 1947-51; mem. fiction staff Ladies' Home Jour., 1951-52; article editor Woman's Home Companion, N.Y.C., 1952-53; freelance writer, Pelham, N.Y., 1953-62; producer CBS Reports, CBS News, N.Y.C., 1962-66; freelance writer, film dir. and TV producer/exec. producer, 1966-82; dir. Yale U. Films, New Haven, 1982-89; freelance writer, film dir., TV producer/exec. producer Guilford, Conn., 1990—. Cons. race relations, 1959—, hist. TV documentaries, 1976—. Author: American Memorial Hospital--Reims, France: A History, 1955, Passport to Friendship--The Story of the Experiment in International Living, 1957, The Southern Temper, 1959, (with Mrs. Medgar Evers) For Us, The Living, 1967, A Class Divided, 1971; A More Perfect Union, 1987, A Class Divided: Then and Now, 1987 (Hollywood Films option 1998); producer, writer, dir. documentaries Storm Over the Supreme Court, Parts II and III, 1963 (George F. Peabody award, Golden Gavel award ABA), (co-producer) After Ten Years: The Court and the Schools, 1964 (Nat. Sch. Bell award NEA), The Eye of the Storm, 1970 (George Foster Peabody award, Christopher award, Cine Golden Eagle award), Suddenly an Eagle, 1976 (George Foster Peabody award, Cine Golden Eagle award), Death of a Family, 1979 (Writers Guild Am. award), A Bond of Iron, 1982, A Class Divided, 1985 (Emmy award, Sidney Hillman award, Cine Golden Eagle award), others; exec. producer dramas Boswell's London Journal, 1986, others. Co-founder North Shore Citizens Com., 1946, bd. dirs., 1946-51; co-founder Pelham Com. Human Relations, 1963, vice chmn., 1963-65, chmn., 1965-66. Served to capt. USAAF, 1942-45, ETO. Decorated Air medal with 2 oak leaf clusters, D.F.C.; recipient Benjamin Franklin mag. award, 1954; Peabody TV award, 1963, 70, 76, Golden Gavel award ABA, 1963, Sch. Bell award NEA, 1964, Emmy award, Sidney Hillman award, 1985. Mem. Dirs. Guild Am., Writers Guild Am. Democrat. Home: 3108 Long Hill Rd Guilford CT 06437-3619

PETERS, WILLIAM FRANK, art educator; b. Oakland, Calif., Nov. 8, 1934; s. Clifford Leslie and Gladys Fay (Parrish) P.; m. Patricia Ann Redgwick, June 3, 1956 (div. 1973); 1 child, David William. B. Art Edn. with honors, Calif. Coll. Arts & Crafts, 1961; postgrad., various schools, various locations. Cert. spl. secondary art edn. life, gen. jr. high life. Summer campus art dir., instr. Richmond (Calif.) Unified Sch. Dist., 1961-66, Sch. of Fine Arts, Mt. Diablo Unified Sch. Dist., Concord, Calif., 1967-74; instr. Liberty Union H.S. Dist., Brentwood, 1961—, chmn. arts & crafts dept., 1976-91, curriculum cons., 1995—. Dist. rep. Pacific Art Assn., East Contra Costa County, Calif., 1967-70, Calif. Art Assn., East Contra Costa County, 1970-74; accreditation team mem. Western Assn. Schs. and Colls., Albany, Calif., 1981; film evaluator Contra Costa County Schs., 1965-84; art cons. Exhibited in group shows at Contra Costa County Fair (oil painting Best of Show 1968, watercolor Best of Show 1990, Collage Best of Show, 1999, 1st pl. photography 1987-95, 98, 99, 2000, 2001, Open Photography Overall Most Popular award 2001), Delta Art Show, Antioch, Calif. (1st pl. jewelry 1979), Festival of Color, Concord, Calif. (1st pl. ceramic 1963). Fundraiser United Crusade, Brentwood, Calif., 1980-83; publicity vol. East Contra Costa County Soroptimist Club, East County Rape/Crisis Ctr., Kappa Beta, John Marsh Meml. Assn., Knightsen 4-H, Delta Rotary Club, Delta Recreation Dept., Oakley Women's Club, Town of Byron, others. Named Contra Costa County Tchr. of Yr. AAUW, 1981; candidate for Tchr. of Yr. State of Calif. Tchr. of Yr., AAUW, 1981; postgrad scholar Calif. Coll. of Arts and Crafts, 1962-63. Mem. NEA, Calif. Tchrs. Assn., Liberty Edn. Assn. (v.p. chmn. salary com., chmn. evaluation com., chmn. pers. policies com., chmn. scholarship com.), Delta Art Assn. (past bd. dirs.), Brentwood C. of C. (dir. Brentwood Christmas decorations 1968-94). Democrat. Avocations: painting, photography, reading, writing poetry, sports. Office: Liberty Union HS Dist 929 2d St Brentwood CA 94513-1335

PETERS, WILLIAM P. oncologist, science administrator, educator; b. Buffalo, Aug. 26, 1950; m. Elizabeth Zentai; children: Emily, Abigail, James. BS, BS, BA, Pa. State U., 1972; MPhil, PhD, Columbia U., 1976, MD, 1978; postgrad., Harvard U., 1984; MBA, Duke U., 1990. Diplomate Am. Bd. Internal Medicine, Am. Bd. Med. Oncology. Prof. medicine Duke U. Med. Ctr., Durham, N.C., 1993-95, assoc. dir. for clin. ops. Duke Comprehensive Cancer Ctr., 1994-95, dir. bone marrow transplant program, 1984-95; pres., CEO, Mich. Cancer Found., Detroit, 1995—2001; pres., dir., CEO Karmanos Cancer Inst., 1995—2001; assoc. dean for cancer programs Wayne State U., 1995—2001, prof. oncology, medicine, surgery and radiation oncology, 1995—; disting. chair of oncology Wayne State U., 2002—; pres., dir., CEO CETAID, Karamanos Cancer Inst., 2001—; pres. Inst. for Strategic Analysis and Innovation, Detroit Med. Ctr., 2001—. Sr. v.p. for cancer svcs. Detroit Med. Ctr., 1995-2001. Office: Karmanos Cancer Inst Rm 437 HWCRC 110 E Warren Ave Detroit MI 48201-1312

PETERSCHECK, WALTER HERMANN, chemical engineer; b. Rockenhausen, Germany, June 25, 1943; came to U.S., 1977; s. Walter Ludwig and Auguste (Gass) P.; m. Vicki Thurson, June 28, 1969 (div. June 1987); m. Erika Peterscheck-Volk, Dec. 27, 1996; children: Walter John, Hermann Karl, Robert Ludwig. BS in Chem. Engring., Inst. of Tech., Darmstadt, 1968; MS in Chemistry/Chem. Engring., Tech. U. Berlin, 1973. Cert. of designation European Engr. R&D engr. Amoco Chem., Naperville, Ill., 1969-71; process design engr. Lummus Tech. Ctr., Broomfield, N.J., 1973-76; process and project mgr. Lurgi, Frankfurt, Germany, 1977-83; v.p. tech. and ops. VerTech Treatment Sys., Denver, Baarn, Netherland, 1984-93; pres., CEO Euro-US, Inc., Longmont, Colo., 1994—; pres. Peterscheck & Soehne, GmbH, Rockenhausen, Germany, 1995—. Cons. European Commn.; advisor new tech. Mannesmann Demag, Duesseldorf, Germany, 1994—. Contbr. articles to profl. jours.; patentee (30) in field. Recipient Mannesmann Fed. award for best environ. process Fed. Republic of Germany. Fellow Am. Inst. Chem. Engrs. (local chair), Verein Deutscher Ingenieure (local chair); mem. Planetary Soc. Achievements include patent and reutilization of 1200m below ground reaction vessle for waste treatment of liquids and slurries as apparatus; processes for the environmental industries of various kinds are patented and in use. Avocations: classical music, singing, politics, philosophy, hiking. Address: Euro-Us Inc Apt 314 14052 E Tufts Dr Aurora CO 80015 Office: Euro-US Inc 10509 Appaloosa Pl El Paso TX 79924-2021

PETERSDORF, ROBERT GEORGE, physician, medical educator, academic administrator; b. Berlin, Feb. 14, 1926; s. Hans H. and Sonja P.; m. Patricia Horton Qua, June 2, 1951; children: Stephen Hans, John Eric. BA, Brown U., 1948, DMS (hon.) , 1983; MD cum laude, Yale U., 1952; ScD (hon.) , Albany Med. Coll., 1979; MA (hon.) , Harvard U., 1980; DMS (hon.) , Med. Coll. Pa., 1982, Brown U., 1983; DMS, Bowman-Gray Sch. Medicine, 1986; LHD (hon.) , N.Y. Med. Coll., 1986; DSc (hon.) , SUNY, Bklyn., 1987, Med. Coll. Ohio, 1987, Univ. Health Scis., The Chgo. Med. Sch., 1987; DSc (hon.) , St. Louis U., 1988; LHD (hon.) , Ea. Va. Med. Sch., 1988; DSc (hon.) , Sch. Medicine, Georgetown U., 1991, Emory U., 1992; DSc (hon.) , Tufts U., 1993; DSc (hon) , Mt. Sinai Sch. Medicine, 1993, George Washington U., 1994; other hon. degrees. Diplomate Am. Bd. Internal Medicine. Intern, asst. resident Yale U., New Haven, 1952—54; sr. asst. resident Peter Bent Brigham Hosp., Boston, 1954—55; fellow Johns Hopkins Hosp., Balt., 1955—59; chief resident, instr. medicine Yale U., 1957—58; asst. prof. medicine Johns Hopkins U., 1958—60, physician, 1958—60; assoc. prof. medicine U. Wash., Seattle, 1960—62, prof., 1962—79, chmn. dept. medicine, 1964—79; physician-in-chief U. Wash. Hosp., 1964—79; pres. Brigham and Women's Hosp., Boston, 1979—81; prof. medicine Harvard U. Med. Sch., 1979—81; dean, vice chancellor health scis. U. Calif.-San Diego Sch. Medicine, 1981—86; clin. prof. infectious diseases Sch. Medicine Georgetown U., 1986—94; pres. Assn. Am. Med. Colls., Washington, 1986—94, pres. emeritus, 1994—; prof. medicine U. Wash., 1994—, disting. prof., sr. advisor to dean, 1998—; disting. physician Vets. Health Adminstrn., Seattle, 1995—98, sr. physician, 1998—. Cons. to surgeon gen. USPHS, 1960—79; cons. USPHS Hosp., Seattle, 1962—79; mem. spl. med. adv. group VA, 1987—94. Editor: Harrison's Principles of Internal Medicine, 1968—90; contbr. With USAAF, 1944—46. Named Disting. Internist of 1987, Am. Soc. Internal Medicine; recipient Lilly medal, Royal Coll. Physicians, London, 1978, Wiggers award, Albany Med. Coll., 1979, Robert H. Williams award, Assn. Profs. Medicine, 1983, Keen award, Brown U., 1980, Disting. Svc. award, Baylor Coll. Medicine, 1989, Scroll of Merit, Nat. Med. Assn., 1990, 2d Ann. Founder's award, Assn. Program Dirs. in Internal Medicine, 1991, Flexner award, Assn. Am. Med. Coll., 1994. Master: ACP (pres. 1975—76, Stengel award 1980, Disting. Tchr. award 1993, Laureate award Wash. chpt.); fellow: AAAS, Execs. Assn. (hon.); mem.: Assn. Am. Physicians (pres. 1976—77, Kober medal 1996), Inst. Medicine of NAS (councillor 1977—80), Rainier Club, Cosmos Club. Home and Office: 8001 Sand Point Way NE C71 Seattle WA 98115

PETERSEN, ANNE C.(CHERYL), foundation administrator, educator; b. Little Falls, Minn., Sept. 11, 1944; d. Franklin Hanks and Rhoda Pauline (Sandwick) Studley; m. Douglas Lee Petersen, Dec. 27, 1967; children: Christine Anne, Benjamin Bradfield. BA, U. Chgo., 1966, MS, 1972, PhD, 1973. Asst. prof., rsch. assoc. Dept. Psychiatry U. Chgo., 1972-80, assoc. prof., rsch. assoc., 1980-82; prof. human devel., head Dept. Individual and Family Studies Pa. State U., University Park, 1982-87, dean Coll. Health and Human Devel., 1987-92, prof. health and human devel., 1987-92; dean grad. sch., v.p. for rsch. throughout state U. Minn., Mpls., 1992-94, prof. adolescent devel. and pediatrics, 1992-96; dep. dir., COO NSF, Arlington, Va., 1994-96; sr. v.p. programs W.K. Kellogg Found., 1996—. Vis. prof., fellow Coll. Edn., R&D Psychology, Roosevelt U., Chgo., 1973-74; cons. Ctr. for Health Adminstrn. Studies U. Chgo., 1976-78, Ctr. for New Schs., Chgo., 1974-78, Robert Wood Johnson Found. Mathtech, Inc., 1987-89; coord. clin. rsch. tng. program Michael Reese Hosp. and Med. Ctr., Chgo., 1976-80, dir. Lab. for Study of Adolescence, 1975-82; mem. faculty Ill. Sch. for Profl. Psychology, 1978-79; statis. cons. Coll. Nursing U. Ill. Med. Ctr., 1975-83; assoc. dir. health program MacArthur Found., 1980-82, also cons. health program, 1982-88; chair sr. adv. bd. NIMH, 1987-88; mem. nat. adv. mental health coun. NIH, 1997—; trustee Nat. Inst. Statis. Scis., 1998—. Author: (books) Sex Related Differences in Cognition Functioning: Developmental Issues, 1979, Promoting Adolescent Health: A Diolog on Research and Practice, 1982, Firls at Puberty: Biological and psychosocial Perspectives, 1983, Brain Maturation and Cognitive Development: Comparative and Cross Cultural Perspectives, 1991, Narrowing the Margins: Adolescent Unemployment and the lack of a social role, 1991, Grofit: A Fortran Program for the Estimation of Parameters of a Human Growth Curve, 1972, Girls at Puberty: Biological and Psychosocial Perspectives, 1983, Adolescence and Youth: Psychological Development in a Changing World, 1984, Youth Unemployment and Society, 1994, Transitions Through Adolescence: Interpersonal Domains and Context, 1996; reviewer Jour. of Youth and Adolescence, 1975-80, Devel. Psychology, 1979—, Sci., 1979—, Jour. of Edn. Psychology, 1979—, Child Devel., 1980—, Jour. Edn. Measurement, 1980, Ednl. Researcher, 1980, Am. Ednl. Rsch. Jour., 1981—, Jour. of Mental Imagery, 1982-92, Sex Roles, 1984—; cons. editor Psychology of Women Quar., 1978-82, assoc. editor, 1983-86; adv. editor Contemporary Psychology, 1985-86; editorial bd. various profl. jours.; contbr. chpts. to books and articles to profl. jours. Bd. overseers Lewis Coll., Ill. Inst. Tech., 1980-82; mem. adv. bd. longitudinal data archive project Murray Ctr., Radcliffe Coll., 1985-91, mem. sci. adv. bd., 1983-91 Fellow: APA (chmn. task force on reproductive freedom 1979—81, program chmn. 1981—82, chmn. task force on long range planning 1986—89, pres. divsn. 7 1992—93), AAAS; mem.: NAS (nat. forum on future children and their families 1987—91, chmn. panel on child abuse and neglect 1991—93, mem. forum on adolescence Inst. of Medicine 1997—2000, chair bd. on behavioral, cognitive and sensory scis. 1997—), Soc. for Rsch. on Adolescence (pres. 1990—92, past pres. 1992—94, chmn. nominations com. 1992—94), Acad. Europaea, Psychometric Soc., Behavior Genetics Assn., Assn. Women in Sci. (bd. dirs. 1996—2000), Am. Ednl. Rsch. Assn. (various offices), Internat. Soc. for the Study of Behavioral Devel. (coun. mem. 1995—2001, pres. elect 2002—04), Inst. for Medicine. Home: 3715 Blackberry Ln Kalamazoo MI 49008-3333

PETERSEN, ARNE JOAQUIN, chemist; b. L.A., Jan. 27, 1932; s. Hans Marie Theodore and Astrid Maria (Pedersen) Petersen; m. Sandra Joyce Sharp, Aug. 12, 1961; children: Christina Lynn, Kurt Arne. AA, Compton Coll., 1957; BS, Calif. State U., Long Beach, 1959; BA, U. Calif., Irvine, 1975. Lic. comml. pilot. Chemist, scientist Beckman Instruments, Inc., Fullerton, Calif., 1959-62, engr., scientist, 1962-65, project, sr. project engr., 1965-74; project/program mgr. Beckman Clin. Ops., Fullerton/Brea, 1974-80; ops. mgr. Graphic Controls Corp., Irvine, 1980-82; engr./rsch. and devel. mgr. Carle Instruments Chromatography, Anaheim, Calif., 1982-84; ops. mgr. Magnaflux/X-Ray Devel., L.A., 1984-85; rsch. and devel. dir., new products Am. Chem. Systems, Irvine, Calif., 1985-86; rsch. assoc. U. Calif., 1987-88; ind. cons., contractor, sales real estate investment, 1989—. Career guidance counselor U. Calif., Irvine, 1976. Contbr. scientific papers. Exec. svc. with AID Internat. Exec. Svc. Corps, Egypt, 1993—94; vol. F.I.S.H., Costa Mesa, Newport Beach, Calif.; basketball coach Boys-Girls Club, Newport Beach, 1975—78; baseball coach Newport Beach Parks, 1975—78; adv. com. Newport/Costa Mesa Sch. Bd., 1974—75. Mem.: Biomed. Engrng. Soc., U. Calif., Irvine Club (bd. dirs.), Kappa Sigma (founder Calif. State U., Long Beach chpt.). Achievements include patents in field. Avocations: flying, photography, swimming, travel, bridge. E-mail: AJPetersen@earthlink.net.

PETERSEN, BARRY REX, news correspondent; b. Norfolk, Va., Jan. 14, 1949; s. Kermit and Mavis Lucille (Sutton) P.; m. Sandra H. Petersen, June 7, 1971 (div. Dec. 1984); children: Emily Jensine, Juliette Rose; m. Jan Chorlton, Feb. 14, 1985. BS in Journalism, Northwestern U., 1970, MS in Journalism, 1972. Sports columnist Sidney (Mont.) Herald, 1964-66; city hall reporter Arlington Heights (Ill.) Day, 1968-69; columnist, copy editor Chgo. Today, 1970-71; pub. Daily Northwestern, Evanston, Ill., 1970-71; reporter Milw. (Wis.) Jour., 1971-72; investigative reporter Sta. WITI-TV, Milw., 1972-74; reporter, anchor Sta. WCCO-TV, Mpls., 1974-78; corr. CBS News, L.A., 1978-81, San Francisco, 1981-85, Tokyo, 1986-88, Moscow, 1988-90, London, 1991-95, Tokyo, 1995—. Pres. AFTRA, Milw., 1973-74; Josephine B. and Newton N. Minow vis. prof. in communications Northwestern U., Evanston, Ill., 1991. Recipient Investigative Reporting award Wis. Press Assn., 1973, Nat. Emmy award, 1994, 97, World gold medal radio breaking news N.Y. Festivals, 1999. Mem. Fgn. Corrs. Club Japan. Lutheran. Avocations: sailing, travel, internat. real estate. Office: CBS News/Tokyo 524 W 57th St New York NY 10019-2924 also: CBS News 5-3-6 Akasaka Minato-ku Tokyo 107 Japan

PETERSEN, BENTON LAURITZ, paralegal; b. Salt Lake City, Jan. 1, 1942; s. Lauritz George and Arleane (Curtis) P.; m. Sharon Donnette Higgins, Sept. 20, 1974 (div. Aug. 9, 1989); children: Grant Lauritz, Tashya Eileen, Nicholas Robert, Katrina Arleane. AA, Weber State Coll., 1966, BA, BA, Weber State Coll., 1968; M of Liberal Studies, U. Okla., 1980; diploma, Nat. Radio Inst. Paralegal Sch., 1991; JD, Monticello U., 1999. Registered paralegal. Announcer/news dir. KWHO Radio, Salt Lake City, 1968-70, KDXU Radio, St. George, Utah, 1970-73, KSOP Radio, Salt Lake City, 1973-76; case worker/counselor Salvation Army, Midland, Tex., 1976-84; announcer/news dir. KBRS Radio, Springdale, Ark., 1984-86; case worker/counselor Office of Human Concern, Rogers, 1986-88; announcer KAZM Radio, Sedona, Ariz., 1988-91; paralegal Benton L. Petersen, Manti, Utah, 1991—. Cons. Sanpete County Srs., Manti, 1992—. Award judge Manti City Beautification, 1992-96; treas. Manti Destiny Com., 1993-98; tourism com. Sanpete County Econ. Devel., Ephraim, Utah, 1993-96. Served with U.S. Army N.G., 1959-66. Mem. Nat. Assn. Attys. in Fact (past pres.). Mem. Lds Ch. Avocation: reading. Home: 470 E 120 N Manti UT 84642-1164 E-mail: bpfreedom@hotmail.com.

PETERSEN, BRET T. gastroenterologist; b. Fargo, N.D., Sept. 14, 1953; s. Arnold Jerome and Mary Junette Petersen; m. Karen Clark. BA summa cum laude, St. Olaf Coll., Northfield, Minn., 1972; MD, Mayo Med. Sch., 1981. Intern Georgetown U. Hosps., Washington, 1981-82, resident in internal medicine, 1982-84; fellow in gastroenterology and hepatology Mayo Grad. Sch. Medicine, 1986-89; cons. in gastroenterology Mayo Clinic, Rochester, Minn., 1989—. Mem. ACP, Am. Soc. Gastrointestinal Endoscopy, Am. Gastroenterol. Assn., Am. Coll. Gastroenterology, Phi Beta Kappa, Alpha Omega Alpha. Office: Mayo Clinic Ei8W 200 1st St SW Rochester MN 55905-0002 E-mail: petersen.bret@mayo.edu.

PETERSEN, BRIAN DOUGLAS, music educator, farmer; b. Brigham City, Utah, Nov. 26, 1956; s. JDell Douglas and Charlene Benson Petersen; m. Carol Jean Funk, Aug. 24, 1979; children: Jaylene, Evelyn, Rebecca, Erica, Carrie, Jennica, Andrea. MEd, Utah State U., 1987, BM, 1982. Cert. secondary sch. tchr. Utah. Music and Spanish tchr. Preston (Idaho) H.S., 1982—85; choral music tchr. Mountain View H.S., Orem, Utah, Bear River H.S., Garland. Mgr., owner Petersen Ponderosa, LLC, Tremonton, Utah, 1999—; mem. Mormon Tabernacle Choir, Salt Lake City, 2001—. Composer: (choral music octavo) Once In Royal David's City, 2000, Joyfully Sing, 2001, Lift Up Your Heart & Rejoice, 2002. Mem.: Am. Choral Dirs. Assn. (state pres. Utah chpt. 1999—2001), Utah Music Educators Assn. (state choral com. 1989—2002). Republican. Mem. Lds Ch. Avocations: singing, composing, farming, tree research. Home: 10055 North 4800 West Tremonton UT 84337 Office: Bear River HS 1450 South Main St Garland UT 84312 Office Fax: 435-257-3899. E-mail: bpeterse@boxelder.k12.ut.us.

PETERSEN, DAVID L. lawyer; AA, Concordia Jr. Coll., Milw., 1963; BA, Concordia Sr. Coll., Ft. Wayne, Ind., 1965; JD, Valparaiso U., Ind., 1968. Bar: Wis. 1968, U.S. Dist. Ct. (ea. dist.) Wis. 1969, U.S. Ct. Appeals (7th cir.) 1972, U.S. Supreme Ct. 1988, Fla. 1989. Ptnr. Quarles & Brady, Milw. and Naples, Fla., 1968—. Author: Wisconsin Condominium Law, 1988, 98; editor Valparaiso U. Law Rev., 1967-68; contbr. articles to profl. jours. Mem. Greater Milw. Com. Cmty. Devel., 1983; bd. dirs. Goals for Greater Milw. 2000, 1982, Broward Com. of 100; mem. nat. adv. bd. Nat. Ctr. for Missing and Exploited Children, Washington, Adam Walsh Children's Fund, Palm Beach, Fla.; dir. Boys and Girls Club Collier County. Lt. col., instr. pilot USAF/Wis. Air N.G., 1970-90. Mem. ABA, Wis. Bar Assn., Milw. Bar Assn., Fla Bar Assn., Broward County Bar Assn., Palm Beach County Bar Assn., Collier County Bar Assn., Wis. Mortgage Bankers Assn., Am. Coll. Real Estate Lawyers, Milw. Yacht Club, Palm Beach Yacht Club. Office: Quarles & Brady LLP 4501 Tamiami Trail N Naples FL 34103-3060 also: Quarles & Brady LLP 411 E Wisconsin Ave Ste 2550 Milwaukee WI 53202-4409 E-mail: dlp@quarles.com.

PETERSEN, DEVI LYNNE, accountant; b. Portland, Oreg., May 10, 1973; d. William Neal and Shirley Jean (Peterkort) Judd; m. Kevin Arnold Petersen, Sept. 10, 1995. BSBA, Walla Walla Coll., 1995. CPA. Acct. Lifetime Women's Health Ctrs., Portland, 1995-97; sr. staff acct. Geffen Mesher & Co., P.C., 1998—. Mem. AICPA, Oreg. Soc. CPAs. Republican. Seventh-Day Adventist. Office: Geffen Mesher & Co PC 888 SW 5th Ave Ste 800 Portland OR 97204-2090 E-mail: dpetersen@gmco.com.

PETERSEN, DONALD SONDERGAARD, lawyer; b. Pontiac, Ill., May 14, 1929; s. Clarence Marius and Esther (Sondergaard) P.; m. Alice Thorup, June 5, 1954; children: Stephen, Susan Petersen Schuh, Sally Petersen Riordan. Student, Grand View Coll., 1946-48; BA, Augustana Coll., Rock Island, Ill., 1951; JD, Northwestern U., 1956. Bar: Ill. 1957. Assoc. Norman & Billick and predecessors, Chgo., 1956-64, ptnr., 1965-78; counsel Sidley & Austin, 1978-80, ptnr., 1980-93, ret., 1993. Pres. Chgo. Exhibitors Corp., Chgo., 1972-85. Bd. dirs. Mount Olive Cemetery Co. Inc., Chgo., 1972-90; bd. dirs. Augustana Hosp., 1983-87, Danish Old People's Home, 1976—; bd. dirs. Luth. Gen. Hosp., Park Ridge, Ill., 1968—, chmn., 1979-81, 89-91; bd. dirs. Luth. Gen. Health System and predecessors, Park Ridge, 1980-95, chmn., 1980-81, 83-85; bd. dirs., chmn. Parkside Health Mgmt. Corp., Parkside Home Health Svcs., 1985-88. With U.S. Army, 1951-53. Mem. Chgo. Bar Assn., Ill. State Bar Assn. Clubs: Union League (Chgo.). Home: 241 N Aldine Ave Park Ridge IL 60068-3009 Office: 55 W Monroe St Ste 2000 Chicago IL 60603-5008

PETERSEN, DOUGLAS ARNDT, financial development consultant; b. Albert Lea, Minn., Sept. 18, 1944; s. Arndt H. and Helen L. (Slater) P.; m. Winnifred K. Taylor, Aug. 14, 1964 (div. July 1970); children: Scott, Jennifer; m. Cynthia L. Schnabel, June 14, 1975; 1 child, Christopher. BS in Edn., Mankato State U., 1966, postgrad., 1966-68. Youth dir. Mankato (Minn.) YMCA, 1965-68; tchr. Mankato State U., 1965-68; exec. dir. YMCA Camp Christmas Tree, Mound, Minn., 1968-72; asst. exec. dir. West Suburban YMCA, Minnetonka, 1968-72; exec. dir. Eastside YMCA, Mpls., 1972-75; program/fin. devel. dir. Eastside Neighborhood Svc., 1975-79; asst. exec. dir. Mpls. Red Cross, 1979-89; dir. major/planned gifts ARC Nat. Staff, Mpls., 1989-91; pres./chief exec. officer/cons. D.A. Petersen Assocs., 1992—. Mem. St. Anthony/New Brighton Found. (chair 1988-92), YMCA Am. (pres. APD 1974), ARC (pres. MFDDC 1988-89). Lutheran. Avocations: travel, community service, scuba, canoeing, backpacking. Home: 3216 Skycroft Dr Minneapolis MN 55418-2552 Office: PO Box 18411 Minneapolis MN 55418-0411 E-mail: dapa@mindspring.com.

PETERSEN, EDWARD SCHMIDT, retired physician; b. Chgo., Nov. 19, 1921; s. William F. and Alma C. (Schmidt) P.; m. Zoe Andre Bakeeff, June 11, 1944; children: Catherine Petersen Mack, Edward B. Student, Harvard U., 1942, MD, 1945. Diplomate Am. Bd. Internal Medicine. Intern St. Luke's Hosp., Chgo., 1945-46, med. practice, 1951-53; resident in medicine U. Chgo., 1948-51; asst. dir. profl. svcs. VA Rsch. Hosp., Chgo., 1953-54; from asst. to assoc. dean, assoc. prof. Northwestern U. Med. Sch., 1954-72, asst. dir. to dir. divsn. undergrad. med. edn., AMA, 1972-88, ret., 1988. Chair Midwest group on student affairs Assn. Am. Med. Colls., Washington, 1967-69; pres. Inst. Medicine, Chgo., 1976; chair com. on hosps. and clinics Ill. Dept. Pub. Aid,Chgo., 1961-70; bd. dirs. Hull House, Chgo., 1962-70; mem. sci. adv. com. Mcpl. TB Sanitarium, Chgo., 1970-74. Capt. Med. Corps., AUS, 1946-48. Fellow ACP; mem. AMA (co-sec. liason com. on med. edn. 1976-87), Geneva Lake Assn. (bd. dirs. 1975-99). Lutheran. Avocations: environmental and historical restoration. Home: W4268 Southland Rd Lake Geneva WI 53147-3957

PETERSEN, ELLEN ANNE, artist; b. N.Y.C., Dec. 18, 1930; d. William George and Dina (Bockmeyer) Heinrich; m. Ralph Lamon Petersen, Dec. 14, 1952; children: William, Bryan. BS, NYU, 1968, MS, 1970. Art educator Paramus (N.J.) High Sch., 1969-85; tchng. artist William Carlos Williams Ctr. for Arts, Rutherford, N.J., 1989-91; studio artist Parrish Mus., Southampton, N.Y., 1988—; artist workshops Guild Hall Mus., East Hampton, 1992—; instr. The Art Barge, Amagansett, NY, 1999—. Video interview "Women in the Arts", Fairleigh Dickinson U., Teaneck, N.J., 1977, LTV-local TV, East Hampton, 1991. Represented in permanent collections Guild Hall Mus., East Hampton, N.Y., Bujese Gallery, Heckscher Mus., Mus. of New Art, Rochester, Minn., Gayle Willson Gallery, Southampton, NY, exhibitions include Islip Art Mus., 2002, A.I.R. Gallery, 2002. Bd. dirs. Jimmy Ernst Artists' Alliance, East Hampton, N.Y., 1985-92; mem. edn. com. Parrish Art Mus., Southampton, 1989-98; curator Springs Invitational Art Exhbn., East Hampton, 1994, 95, 96. Recipient hon. mention, Guild Hall Mus., 1994, 1st prize, N.J. state Exhbn., East Orange, N.J., 1967, award, Springs-Ashawagh Hall Invitational, East Hampton, 1993—2002, Juried Exhbn., Parrish Mus., 1992, Hon. Mention, Salon des Femmes, Southampton Cultural Ctr., 1997, award of merit, Southampton Cultural Ctr., 1999. Mem. Nat. Women's Caucus of Art, Artists' Equity, Jimmy Ernst Artists' Alliance (treas. 1988-90, v.p. 1990-92), Art Students' League (life), Women's Caucus for Art (v.p. Dallas chpt. 1987-88). Avocations: musician/playing the recorder in East End Consort ensemble. Home: 7 S Pond Rd East Hampton NY 11937-3719 E-mail: ellenanne@peconic.net.

PETERSEN, FINN BO, oncologist, educator; b. Copenhagen, Mar. 26, 1951; came to U.S., 1983; s. Jorgen and Ebba Gjeding (Jorgensen) P.; m. Merete Secher Lund, Mar. 7, 1979; children: Lars Secher, Thomas Secher, Andreas Secher. BA, Niels Steensen, Copenhagen, 1971; MD, U. Copenhagen, 1978. Intern U. Copenhagen, Copenhagen, 1978-79, resident in hematology, 1980-83; fellow oncology Fred Hutchinson Cancer Rsch. Ctr. U. Wash., Seattle, 1983-85, assoc. rschr. oncology, 1985-87, asst. mem. in clin. rsch., 1987-91, asst. prof., 1988-91, prof. medicine, 1992—; program dir. U. Utah Blood and Marrow Transplant, 1992—; med. dir. bone marrow transplant program LDS Hosp., 1997—. Author: Hematology, 1977; contbr. articles to profl. jours. Mem. AMA, AAAS, Internat. Soc. Exptl. Hematology, Am. Soc. Clin. Oncology, Am. Soc. Hematology, Assn. Gnotobiology. Office: U Utah Bone Marrow Transplant Program Div Hematology & Oncology Salt Lake City UT 84132-0001

PETERSEN, JEAN SNYDER, association executive; b. N.Y.C., Oct. 16, 1931; d. Peter Eugene and Helyn Brownell (Parker) Snyder; m. Elton Reed Petersen, Sept. 16, 1954; children— Bruce Brownell, Craig Reed. Student, N.Y. U., 1949-51; degree fgn. banking, Am. Inst. Banking, 1952. Fgn. credit investigator Chase Nat. Bank Hdqrs., N.Y.C., 1952-56; nat. exec. dir. Assn. Children and Adults with Learning Disabilities (name changed to Learning Disabilities Assn. of Am.), Pitts., 1972—. Mem. exec. com., treas. Jr. League, Pitts.; bd. dirs. Found. for Children with Learning Disabilities, N.Y.C., Children's Hosp., Pitts., Music for Mt. Lebanon, Vocat. Rehab. Ctr., Pitts.; bd. dirs., v.p., mem. exec. com. Assn. Retarded Citizens Pa.; ptnr. UN Internat. Yr. of Disabled; ruling elder Presbyn. Ch.Assn. Retarded Citizens Pa.; mem. exec. com. Pat Buckley Moss Nat. Children's Charity Found; chmn. bd. dirs. Masonic Learning Ctrs. for Children. Recipient Sustainers award Jr. League, 1977, Recognition award, 1975, Pres.'s award, 1978 Mem. AAUW, Meeting Planners Internat. (treas.), Am. Soc. Assn. Execs. Republican. Presbyterian. Home: 343 Shadowlawn Ave Pittsburgh PA 15216-1239 Office: 4156 Library Rd Pittsburgh PA 15234-1349 Fax: (412) 5634537.

PETERSEN, JOHN LAURENS, future research and strategic planner; b. Omaha, July 11, 1943; s. J. Allan and Evelyn R. (Witt) P.; m. Diane Carter, July 22, 1967; 1 child, John Carter Laurens. BSEE, John Brown U., 1966. Asst. to the pres. Embosograph Display Mfg., Chgo., 1971-72; assoc. Richard S. Latham & Assocs., 1972-74; v.p. Family Concern, Inc., 1974-79; pres. Petersen & Assocs., 1979-90; pres., founder The Arlington (Va.) Inst., 1989—. Co-chmn. Nat. Security Group, Washington, 1987-88; adj. fellow Ctr. for Strategic and Internat. Studies, Washington, 1987-91; mem. vis. com. Ctr. for East Asian Studies, U. Chgo., 1987-90; assoc. scholar Fgn. Policy Rsch. Inst., Phila., 1988; lectr. Joint Mil. Intelligence Coll., Def. Intelligence Agy., 1994—; vis. lectr. Internat. Space U., Stockholm, 1995; vis. prof. Indsl. Coll. Armed Forces, Nat. Def. U., 1995. Author: The Road to 2015: Profiles of the Future, 1994 (Outstanding Acad. Book of 1995), Out of the Blue: Wildcards and Other Big Future Surprises, 1997. Ill. state chmn. Gary Hart for Pres. Campaign, 1984, mem. exec. fin. com., 1984; elected del., vice chmn. Ill. Delegation to Dem. Nat. Conv., 1984; del. candidate Dem. Nat. Conv., 1988. Comdr. USNR, 1962-83. Recipient Writing award U.S. Naval Inst., 1994. Mem. Assn. Naval Aviation (life, former nat. trustee), Aircraft Owners and Pilots Assn., Exptl. Aircraft Assn., Global Bus. Network, U.S. Navy Meml. Found. (vice chmn. bd. dirs.), Soc. for Sci. Exploration. Avocations: flying, building an airplane. Office: The Arlington Inst 1501 Lee Hwy Arlington VA 22209-1109

PETERSEN, JÖRG, software engineering educator; b. Gelsenkirchen, Germany, 1961; D of Engring., Gerhard-Mercator-U., 1996. Cert. computer sci. Asst. lectr. in automotive computing, artificial and computational intelligence Gerhard-Mercator-U., Duisburg, Germany, 1991—. Mem. GI Gesellschaft für Informatik. Office: Gerhard-Mercator-U Fak 5 IIMT IIT 47048 Duisburg Germany Fax: 49 203 379 2205. E-mail: jp@uni-duisburg.de.

PETERSEN, KEVIN, federal agency administrator; b. LeMars, Iowa, Oct. 4, 1951; BS in Aerospace Engring., Iowa State U., 1974; MS , UCLA, 1976; postgrad. in Engring., Stanford U. Rsch. engr. Dryden Flight Rsch. Ctr. NASA, Houston, 1971—74, aerospace engr., 1974, chief flight controls sect., 1982—85, chief engr., 1985—86, chief vehicle tech. br., 1989—90, acting dir., 1998—99, dir., 1999—. Office: Dryden Flight Rsch Ctr PO Box 273 Edwards CA 93523-0273*

PETERSEN, LANCE W. fine arts educator; b. Bay City, Mich., Oct. 11, 1941; s. Bill Petersen and Jean McMaster; m. Barbara L. Bell, Oct. 10, 1969; 1 child, Alexander Sascha. BA, Alaska Meth. U., 1964; MLA, Alaska Pacific U., 1994. Cert. tchr. Alaska. Assoc. prof. humanities U. Alaska, Anchorage, 1994—; theatre mgr. Kenai Peninsula Borough Sch. dist., Homer, Alaska, 1985—. Artistic dir. Pier One Theatre, Homer, 1973—; exec. dir. Alaska Alliance for Arts Edn., Soldotna, Alaska, 1998—. Author: (book) The Kenai Peninsula College History, 1992; author: (plays) The Ballad of Kenai, 1981 (winner Biennial N.W. Regional ACTFEST), The Raven's Place, 1996, The Brown Bear Grill, 1993, others; contbr. articles to profl. jours. Coun. mem. Alaska State Coun. on the Arts, Anchorage, 1994—. Recipient award Best Poems of the Twentieth Century, 2000, others. Mem. Assn. Literary Scholars and Critics, The Manuscript Soc., Stage Dirs. and Choreographers Found., Theatre Comms. Group, Internat. Drama Educators Assn. Office: Kenai Peninsula Coll 34820 College Dr Soldotna AK 99669 Home: PO Box 894 Homer AK 99603-0894

PETERSEN, LARRY J. music educator; b. Mpls., Oct. 18, 1970; s. Larry J. and JoAnn L. Petersen; m. Laura E. Price. B in Music Edn., S.D. State U., 1994. Cert. K-12 music tchr. Band dir. Elk Point-Jefferson Sch. Dist., SD, 1994—96, Huron (S.D.) Sch. Dist., 1996—. Local chmn. all-state band S.C. Bandmasters, 2001—. Mem. First United Meth. Ch., Huron, SD, 1997—, dir. handbell choir, 1999—. Mem.: NEA, Music Educators Nat. Conf. Methodist. Avocations: travel, music. Office: Huron High Sch 801 18th St SW Huron SD 57350 Office Fax: 605-353-7807. Business E-Mail: larry.petersen@k12.sd.us.

PETERSEN, MARTIN EUGENE, curator; b. Grafton, Iowa, Apr. 21, 1931; s. Martin S. and Martha Dorothea (Paulsen) P. BA, State U. Iowa, 1951, MA, 1957; postgrad., The Hague (Netherlands), 1964. Curator San Diego Mus. Art, 1957-96; advisor Olaf Wieghorst Mus., El Cajon, Calif., 1996—. Extension instr. U. Calif., 1958, lectr., 1960 Author art catalogues, books, articles in field. Served with AUS, 1952-54. Mem. So. Calif. Art Historians. Home: 2003 Bayview Heights Dr Spc 138 San Diego CA 92105-5537

PETERSEN, MARTIN ROSS, public affairs executive; b. Bakersfield, Calif., Aug. 14, 1944; s. Peter Arthur and Valerie A. (Swink) P.; m. Geri Gottuso, Nov. 12, 1987; children: Kaitlin Jean, Alexander Ross. BA in Govt., Calif. State U., Sacramento, 1969. Asst. dir. govtl. affairs Calif. State U. and Colls., Sacramento, 1967-72; adminstr. divsn. consumer svcs. Calif. Dept. Consumer Affairs, 1972-75; dir. Office External Liaison The White House Office Consumer Affairs, Washington, 1975-77, 83-85; pres. Knauer & Assocs., Inc., 1977-83; dir. corp. pub. affairs and N.J. ops. adminstrn. Playtex Products, Inc., Allendale, 1985—. Exec. v.p. Trade Net, Washington, 1981-85; chmn. Washington Legis. Group, 1984-85; mem. bd. govs. Ramapo (N.J.) State Coll., 2001—. Editor: Auto Imports, 1979; founding editor Customer Relationship Mgmt., 1980-82. Pub. mem. Voluntary Effort To Contain Health Care Costs in Am., Chgo., 1977-80; sec. subcom. on consumer affairs Rep. Nat. Com., Washington, 1979-80; mem. transition team and inaugural com. Reagan-Bush White House, Washington, 1981; v.p. Nat. Coalition for Consumer Edn., Washington, 1981-91; v.p. Oakland (N.J.) Rep. Club, 1990, 2001; councilman Borough of Oakland, 1991—; author, vol. in pub. svc. Consumer Product Safety Commn., 1977. With USAF, 1962-66. Mem. Soc. Consumer Affairs Profls. in Bus. (nat. bd. dirs. 1979-83, 98—, exec. com. 1980-83, 99—, pres. D.C. chpt. 1977-78, Outstanding Leader of Yr. award 1985), Am. League Lobbyists, Govt. Affairs Profls. (N.Y.C.), Am. Soc. Quality, Internat. Facility Mgmt. Assn., Internat. Bus. Comm. Assn. Avocation: horseback riding. Home: 10 Wichita Path Oakland NJ 07436-3818 Office: Playtex Products Inc 75 Commerce Dr Allendale NJ 07401-1600 E-mail: martin.petersen@usa.net.

PETERSEN, MAUREEN JEANETTE MILLER, management information consultant, former nurse; b. Evanston, Ill., Sept. 4, 1956; d. Maurice James and M. Joyce (Mielke) Miller; m. Gregory Eugene Petersen, July 7, 1984; children: Trevor James, Tatyana Brianne. BS in Nursing cum laude, Vanderbilt U., 1978; MS in Biometry and Health Info. Systems, U. Minn., 1984. Nurse U. Iowa Hosps. and Clinics, Iowa City, 1978-82; research asst. Sch. Nursing, U. Minn., Mpls., 1982-83; mgr. Accenture, 1984—. Mem. Mensa. Methodist. Avocation: travel. Home: 1050 County Rd C2 W Roseville MN 55113-1945 Office: Accenture 333 S 7th St Minneapolis MN 55402-2414 E-mail: peters10500@aol.com., maureen.j.m.petersen@accenture.com.

PETERSEN, ROBERT ALLEN, pediatric ophthalmologist; b. N.Y.C., Dec. 30, 1933; s. Harold Marinus and Elinor Louise (Buckley) P.; m. Veronica Margiana Stinnes, Dec. 22, 1956; children: Anne, Catherine, John. BS, CUNY, 1955; MD, Columbia U., 1959, DrMedSc, 1964. Diplomate Am. Bd. Ophthalmology. Med. resident Presbyn. Hosp., N.Y.C., 1959-61; USPHS postdoctoral fellow Columbia U. Coll. Physicians and Surgeons, 1961-62; USPHS preclin. trainee Howe Lab. of Ophthalmology, MEEI, Boston, 1962-63; resident in ophthalmology Mass. Eye and Ear Infirmary, 1963-66; instr. in ophthalmology to asst. prof. Harvard Med. Sch., 1970—; assoc. in Ophthalmology to sr. assoc. Children's Hosp., 1966—. Contbr. over 40 articles to profl. jours. Cons., vision task force Mass. Dept. Pub. Health, 1981-85. Major U.S. Army, 1967-69, South Vietnam. Various rsch. grants NIH, 1961-63, 94—. Fellow Am. Acd. Ophthalmology, Am. Acad. Pediatrics; mem. Am. Assn. for Pediatric Ophthalmology and Strabismus (bd. dirs. 1974-76, edn. com. 1987-93, Costenbader Lectureship com. 1993-96, 97-2000, chair 1995-96, 99-2000, chair site selection com. 1995-97), New Eng. Ophthal. Soc. Mem. Soc. Of Friends. Achievements include rsch. on the genetics of retinoblastoma; first to describe optic nerve hypoplasia in the children of diabetic mothers, to describe eye findings in a variety of systemic anomalies. Office: Children's Hosp 300 Longwood Ave Boston MA 02115-5737 E-mail: robert.petersen.tch@harvard.edu.

PETERSEN, STEVE ALAN, orthopaedic surgeon; b. Berwyn, Ill., July 9, 1954; s. Richard Alan and Priscilla (Pierce) P.; m. Gail Nelson, July 3, 1976; children: Bryan, Rebecca. BA in Chemistry, Monmouth Coll., 1976; MD, Rush Med. Coll., 1981; MS in Biomed. Scis. Orthopaedics, Mayo Graduate Sch., 1989. Diplomate Am. Bd. Orthop. Surgery. Orthop. resident Mayo Grad. Sch., Rochester, Minn., 1981-86, orthop. rsch. fellow, 1986-87; associate chief orthop. Letterman Army Med. Ctr., San Francisco, 1987-91; asst. prof. Wayne State U., Detroit, 1992-94, assoc. prof., 1995—. Cons. Smith-Nephew Richards Orthop. Divsn., Memphis, 1998—. Author 8 chpts. in books; lectr. in field; contbr. articles to profl. jours.; guest editor Seminars in Arthroplasty, 1995. Hawkins Shoulder fellow, Vail, Colo., 1991-92; Am. Shoulder and Elbow Soc. traveling fellow, Europe, 1999; grantee Orthop. Rsch. Edn. Found., Letterman Army Med. Ctr. Mem.: SICOT, AMA, Detroit Orthop. Acad. (v.p.), Mich. Orthop. Soc. (bd. dirs.), Soc. Mil. Orthop. Surgeons, Euro. Soc. Shoulder and Elbow, Acad. Orthop. Soc., Orthop. Rsch. Soc., Am. Acad. Orthop. Surgeons, Am. Shoulder and Elbow Soc. (assoc.). Avocations: skiing, golf, working out. Office: Univ Orthopaedic Assn. Detroit 4707 Saint Antoine St Detroit MI 48201-1427 Fax: 313-993-0857. E-mail: sapetersen@wayne.edn.

PETERSEN, ULRICH, geology educator; b. Negritos, Peru, Dec. 1, 1927; s. Georg and Harriet (Bluhme) P.; m. Edith Martensen, Apr. 27, 1952 (dec. Aug. 1978); children: Erich, Armin (dec.), Heidi.; m. Eileen Bourque, June 19, 1982. Mining Engr., Escuela Nacional de Ingenieros, Lima, Peru, 1954; MA, Harvard U., 1955, PhD, 1963. Geologist Instituto Geológico del Peru and Instituto Nacional de Investigación y Fomento Mineros, 1946-51; geologist Cerro de Pasco Corp., Peru, 1951-54, asst. chief geologist, 1956-57, chief geologist, 1958-63; lectr. Harvard, 1963-66; assoc. prof. Harvard U., 1966-69, prof. mining geology, 1969-81, Harry C. Dudley prof. econ. geology, 1981-95; cons. geologist, 1963—; prof. emeritus, 1996—. Named comendador de la orden al Merito por Servicios Distinguidos Peru, 1968; recipient A. von Humboldt rsch. award, 1992-93. Mem. Soc. Econ. Geologists (pres. 1988-89), Geol. Soc. Am., Soc. Geologica del Peru (hon.) Home: 414 Marsh St Belmont MA 02478-1109 Office: 20 Oxford St Cambridge MA 02138-2902

PETERSEN, VERNON LEROY, communications and engineering corporations executive; b. Mason, Nev., Nov. 3, 1926; s. Vernon and Lenora Eloise (Dickson) P.; children: Anne C., Ruth F. Cert. naval architecture U. Calif., 1944, cert. in plant engring., adminstrn., and supervision UCLA, 1977; cert. in real estate exchanging Orange Coast Coll., 1978; lic. real estate agent, Calif., 2000. Engr. Philippines Real Estate Office, U.S., C.E., 1950-55; pres., gen. mgr. Mason Merc. Co., 1956-62, Mason Water Co., 1956-62; pres. Petersen Enterprises, Cons. Engrs., Nev. and Calif., Downey, 1962-79, Vernon L. Peterson, Inc., 1980—; pres., CEO Castle Comms. Co., Inc., 1985—, Sta. KCCD-TV, 1985-89; installation mgr. Pacific Architects & Engrs., L.A. and South Vietnam, 1969-72; facilities engr., ops. supr., acting contract mgr. L.A. and Saudi Arabia, 1979-82; bldg. engr. Purex Co., Inc., Lakewood, Calif., 1975-79. Lectr. plant engring., various colls. in Calif., 1975—. Candidate for U.S. Congress, 1956, del. Rep. State Conv., Nev., 1960-64; candidate for U.S. Presidency, 1980. With AUS, 1944-47. Inducted into the Order of the Engrs. Fellow Soc. Am. Mil. Engrs. (life mem., named Orange County Post's Engr. of Yr. 1977, founder Da Nang Post 1969, Orange County Post 1977, pres. 1978-79, Red Sea Post, Jeddah, Saudi Arabia 1980); mem. AIAA, Internat. Platform Assn., Orange County Engr. Coun. (pres. 1978-79), Am. Inst. Plant Engrs. (chpt. 38 Engring. Merit award 1977-78), Soc. Women Engrs. (assoc.). Mem. Lds Ch. Office: Castle Comms Inc PO Box 787 Temecula CA 92593-0787 Fax: 760-731-6250. E-mail: castleint@hotmail.com., castleint@engineer.com.

PETERSEN, WILLIAM OTTO, lawyer; b. Chgo., Nov. 28, 1926; s. William Ferdinand and Alma Schmidt P.; m. Jane Browne, Nov. 25, 1978. AB cum laude, Harvard U., 1949, LLB, 1952. Bar: Ill., 1952. Atty. No. Trust. Co., Chgo., 1952-55; ptnr. Vedder, Price, Kaufman & Kamholz, 1955-2001, of counsel, 2001—. Mem. exec. bd. Ct. Theatre, 1992-97; mem. vis. to U. Chgo. Libr., 1992—; bd. dirs. Chgo. Youth Ctrs., 1958—, pres., 1971, 72; bd. dirs., v.p. Luther I. Replogle Found., Chgo. and Washington, 1986—. With USN, 1944-46. Mem. ABA, Ill. State Bar Assn., Chgo. Bar Assn. (chmn. corp. law com. 1976), Racquet Club of Chgo. (pres. 1981, 82), Univ. Club, Lake Geneva (Wis.) Country Club, Lake Geneva Yacht Club, Caxton Club. Lutheran. Home: 1120 N Lake Shore Dr Chicago IL 60611-1036

PETERSEN-FREY, ROLAND, manufacturing executive; b. Hamburg, Germany, Aug. 17, 1937; arrived in US, 1958; s. Georg and Erna (Coltzau) Petersen-Frey; m. Pamela Susan Mobley, Feb. 2, 1993; children: Martin, Anya, Daniel. BA in Fin., CUNY, 1967, MA in Fin., 1970. Asst. v.p. Mfrs. Hanover, N.Y.C., 1961-70; v.p. gen. mgr. Rusch Inc., 1970-75; CEO, chmn. bd. dirs. Inmed Corp., Atlanta, 1975-89; chmn. bd. Burrellco, Inc., 1989-90; pres., chmn., CEO A4, Inc., 1997—. Bd dirs Albert Int, Gainesville, Ga.; chmn bd dirs A4, Inc, Alpharetta, Ga.; mng ptnr Bunter Holdings Ltd, Atlanta, chmn bd dirs. With U.S. Army, 1959—61. Fellow: Inst Dirs. Republican. Avocations: tennis, hiking, swimming. Office: A4 Inc 2302 Abbey Ct Alpharetta GA 30004 E-mail: r.frey@a4inc.com.

PETERSHACK, RICHARD EUGENE, lawyer; b. Milw., Nov. 17, 1953; s. Richard Victor and Dolores Barbara (Weitzer) P.; m. Michele Elaine Carrier, Aug. 6, 1977; children: Benjamin, Katherine. BA, Oberlin Coll., 1975; JD, U. Wis., 1982. Bar: Wis. 1982, U.S. Dist. Ct. (we. dist.) Wis. 1982, U.S. Dist. Ct. (ea. dist.) Wis. 1992. Legis. aide Wis. State Senate, Madison, 1978-79; exec. dir. Wis. Dist. Atty. Assn., 1980-82; law clk. Wis. Surpeme Ct., 1982-83; assoc. Herz, Levin, Teper, Summer & Croysdale, Milw., 1983-85, Easton & Harms, Madison, 1985-88, Axley Brynelson, Madison, 1988-90; ptnr. Axley Brynelson, LLP, 1991—. Mem. Order of Coif. Home: 307 Farwell Dr Madison WI 53704-6023 Office: Axley Brynelson LLP 2 E Mifflin St Ste 200 Madison WI 53703-2860 E-mail: rpetershack@axley.com.

PETERS-LAMBERT, BETTY A. physical education educator; b. Clifton, Ill., Aug. 24, 1958; d. Clarence Henry and Margaret Pauline (Hebert) P. AA, Kankakee C.C., Ill., 1978; BS, Ill. State U., Normal, 1980, MS, 1990; CAS in Ednl. Adminstrn., U. Ill., Urbana-Champaign, 1998. Cert. tchr. phys. edn., K-12, Ill. Substitute tchr. various schs., Iroquois/Kankakee County, 1981-83; tchr.'s aide for gifted Alan Shepard Sch., Bourbonnais, Ill., 1983-84; phys. edn. tchr. Noel LeVasseur Elem. Sch., 1984—. Bd. dirs. AHA, 1985—, pres. 1993—, mem. Jump Rope for Heart Task Force, AHA, Springfield, Ill., 1994—; mem. PTA, Bourbonnais, 1991; bd. dirs. Bradley Bourbonnais Schs. Fed. Credit Union, 1993—; mem. Jr. League of Kankakee, 1993—. Mem.: Ill. Assn. for Health, Phys. Edn., Recreation and Dance, Kappa Delta Pi. Roman Catholic. Avocation: walking. Home: 5073 Oakridge Dr Saint Anne IL 60964-4462 Office: Noel LeVasseur Elem Sch 601 Bethel Dr Bourbonnais IL 60914-1114

PETERSON, ALFRED EDWARD, family physician; b. Bridgeport, Conn., Mar. 23, 1922; s. Carl Emil Rudolf and Elin Maria (Lindholm) P.; m. June Meadows, May 27, 1944; children: Christina, Elin, Martha, Amy. BA, Dartmouth Coll., 1946; MD, U. Vt., 1950. Diplomate Nat. Bd. Med. Examiners. Intern Binghamton (N.Y.) City Hosp., 1950-51; pvt. practice, Binghamton, N.Y., 1952—; a founding mem. Chenango Bridge Med. Group. Sch. physician Chenango Forks (N.Y.) Ctrl. Schs., 1953-94. Bd. dirs. Chenango Emergency Squad, Binghamton, 1980-85, Robert W. Smith Found., Rotary Club, 1980—; bd. dirs. med. records Broome C.C., Binghamton, 1988—. Capt. USAAF, 1943-45. Fellow Am. Acad. Family Physicians; mem. AMA, N.Y. State Med. Soc., Broome County Med. Soc., N.Y. State Acad. Family Physicians. Democrat. Avocations: cabinet making, environmental and animal welfare causes, travel, history. Office: Chenango Bridge Med Group 1290 Upper Front St Binghamton NY 13901-1043

PETERSON, ANN SULLIVAN, physician, health care consultant; b. Rhinebeck, N.Y., Oct. 11, 1928; A.B., Cornell U., 1950, M.D., 1954; M.S. (Alfred P. Sloan fellow 1979-80), M.I.T., 1980. Diplomate Am. Bd. Internal Medicine. Intern, Cornell Med. Div.-Bellevue Hosp., N.Y.C., 1954-55, resident, 1955-57; fellow in medicine and physiology Meml.-Sloan Kettering Cancer Ctr., Cornell Med. Coll., N.Y.C., 1957-60; instr. medicine Georgetown U. Sch. Medicine, Washington, 1962-65, asst. prof., 1965-69, asst. dir. clin. research unit, 1962-69; assoc. prof. medicine U. Ill., Chgo., 1969-72, asst. dean, 1969-71, assoc. dean, 1971-72; assoc. prof. medicine, assoc. dean Coll. Physicians and Surgeons, Columbia U., N.Y.C., 1972-80; assoc. prof. medicine, assoc. dean Cornell U. Med. Coll., N.Y.C., 1980-83; assoc. dir. div. med. edn. AMA, Chgo., 1983-86, dir. div. grad. med. edn., 1986-89; v.p. Mgmt. Cons. Corp., 1989-93; ind. cons., Chgo., 1993—; mem. bd. regents Uniformed Svcs. U. of Health Scis., 1984-90. John and Mary R. Markle scholar, 1965-70. Fellow ACP; mem. Mortar Board, Alpha Omega Alpha, Alpha Epsilon Delta. Contbr. articles to med. jours.

PETERSON, ARTHUR LAVERNE, foundation administrator; b. Glyndon, Minn., June 27, 1926; s. John M. and Hilda C. (Moline) P.; m. Connie Lucille Harr, June 14, 1952; children: Jon Martin, Rebecca Ruth, Donna Harr, Ingrid Bliss AB, Yale U., 1947; MSPA, U. So. Calif., 1949; postgrad., U. Chgo., 1949-50; PhD, U. Minn., 1962; LLD, Lebanon Valley Coll., 1988. Mem. Wis. State Legislature, 1951-55; from instr. to asst. prof. polit. sci. U. Wis., Eau Claire, 1954-60; assoc. prof. to prof. polit. sci. Ohio Wesleyan U., Delaware, 1961-65, 70-80; pres. Am. Grad. Sch. Internat. Mgmt., Phoenix, 1966-70; dean spl. programs Eckerd Coll., St. Petersburg, Fla., 1980-84, dir. Acad. Sr. Profls., 1987-94; pres. Lebanon Valley Coll., Annville, Pa., 1984-87; pres., CEO Ctr. for the Study of the Presidency, 1997-99; Scott prof. leadership Rocky Mountain Coll., Billings, Mont., 1999—2002; mem. Mont. Ho. Reps., 2001—; pres. Thomas Wathen Found. Acad., Riverside, Calif., 2002—. Bd. dirs. Arnold Industries; asst. to chmn. Rep. Nat. Com., Washington, 1960-61; founding dir. Ctr. Internat. Bus., L.A., 1969-70; cons. Novin Inst. Polit. Affairs, Tehran, Iran, 1973; exec. dir. Fla. Assn. Colls. and Univs., 1988—. Author: McCarthyism: Ideology and Foundations, 1962; co-author: Electing the President, 1968; contbr. articles to profl. jours. Chmn. Ohio Civil Rights Commn., 1963-65; dep. chmn. Republican Nat. Com., 1965-66; mem. Ohio Ethics Commn., 1976-80. Capt. USMC, 1951-52, Korea Citizenship Clearing House Nat. Faculty fellow, 1960; recipient citation for excellence Sigma Phi Epsilon, 1977, Marshall award Ohio Wesleyan Students, 1979. Mem. Am. Polit. Sci. Assn., Am. Judicature Soc. (dir. 1975—), Soc. Polit. Enquiries (pres. 1985—), Acad. Polit. Sci., Rotary, Masons, Pi Sigma Alpha (dir. 1972—), Phi Mu Alpha Sinfonia, Omicron Delta Kappa Republican. Mem. United Ch. of Christ. Avocations: sailing, flying, music. Home: 26555 Chambers Ave Sun City CA 92586-2132 E-mail: apeter333@aol.com. *Give the most you can give, of what you are and what you believe, both talent and treasure - where you are - now!.*

PETERSON, BARBARA ANN BENNETT, history educator, television personality; b. Portland, Oreg., Sept. 6, 1942; d. George Wright and Hope Bennett; m. Frank Lynn Peterson, July 1, 1967. BA, BS, Oreg. State U., 1964; MA, Stanford U., 1965; PhD, U. Hawaii, 1978; PhD (hon.), London Inst. Applied Rsch., 1991, Australian Inst. Coordinated R, 1995. From prof. history to prof. emeritus U. Hawaii, 1967—95, prof. emeritus, 1995—; prof. history Oreg. State U., 2000—. Prof. Asian history and European colonial history and world problems Chapman Coll. World Campus Afloat Semester At Sea, 1974, European overseas exploration, expansion and colonialism U. Colo., Boulder, 1978, Modern China, Modern East Asia, The West in the World U. Pitts., 1999; assoc. prof. U. Hawaii-Manoa Coll. Continuing Edn., 1981; Fulbright prof. history Wuhan (China) U., 1988-89; Fulbright rsch. prof. Sophia U., Japan, 1978; rsch. assoc. Bishop Mus., 1995-98; lectr. Capital Spkrs., Washington, 1987—; prof. world civilization Hawaii State Ednl. Channel, 1993-97; adj. fellow East-West Ctr., Honolulu, 1998—; prof. history U. Pitts. Semester at Sea, fall 1999; adj. prof. Hawaii Pacific U. Co-author: Women's Place is in the History Books, Her Story, 1962-1980: A Curriculum Guide for American History Teachers, 1980; author: America in British Eyes, 1988, John Bull's Eye on America, 1995; editor: Notable Women of Hawaii, 1984, (with W. Solheim) The Pacific Region, 1990, 91, American History: 17th, 18th and 19th Centuries, 1993, America: 19th and 20th Centuries, 1993, Notable Women of China, 2000 (nominated for Pulitzer Prize 2001), Hawaii in the World, 2000, Sarah Childress Polk, 2001; assoc. editor Am. Nat. Biography, 1998 (Dartmouth medal); contbr. articles to profl. publs. Participant People-to-People Program, Eng., 1964, Expt. in Internat. Living Program, Nigeria, 1966; chmn. 1st Nat. Women's History Week, Hawaii, 1982; pres. Bishop Mus. Coun., 1993-94; active mem. Hawaii Commn. on Status of Women; fundraiser local mus. and children's activities. Fulbright scholar, Japan, 1967, sr. tchg. Fulbright scholar, China, 1988-89; NEH-Woodrow Wilson fellow Princeton U., 1980; recipient state proclamations Gov. of Hawaii, 1982, City of Honolulu and Hawaii State Legis., 1982, Outstanding Tchr. of Yr. award Wuhan (China), U., 1988, Medallion of Excellence award Am. Biog. Assn., 1989, Woman of Yr. award, 1991; inducted into the Women's Hall of Fame, Seneca Falls, N.Y., 1991; co-champion Hawaii State Husband and Wife Mixed Doubles Tennis Championship, 1985. Fellow: World Lit. Acad. (Eng.); mem.: AAUW, Am. Studies Assn. (pres. 1984—85), Women in Acad. Adminstrn., Hawaii Found. History and Humanities (mem. editl. bd. 1972—73), Am. Coun. on Edn., Fulbright Assn. (founding pres. Hawaii chpt. 1984—88, mem. nat. steering com. chairwomen ann. conf. 1990), Am. Hist. Assn. (mem. numerous coms.), Maison Internat. des Intellectuals, Phi Kappa Phi, Pi Beta Phi. Avocation: writing, cooking, fund raising for charity and children's organizations and museums, gardening, travel. Office: East West Ctr Burns Hall 1601 East West Rd Honolulu HI 96848-1601 also: Oreg State U History Dept 306 Milam Hall Corvallis OR 97331

PETERSON, BARBARA OWECKE, artist, nurse, realtor; b. Winona, Minn., Nov. 25, 1932; d. Adelbert Paul and Hermanda Gilda Bittner; m. Jerome Francis Owecke, Nov. 28, 1953 (div. 1974); children: Paul Richard Owecke, Michael Jerome Owecke, Margaret Francis Owecke (dec.), Stacy Ann Owecke, Wendy Alane Owecke (dec.), James William Owecke, William Harold Owecke; m. Roy Eugene Peterson, May 28, 1983. RN, St. Francis Sch. Nursing, 1953; B Individualized Study, George Mason U., 1994. RN, Va., Wis., Mich., Ill., Ohio, Fla. Staff nurse Commonwealth Hosp., Fairfax, Va., 1973-74; realtor Century 21 United, 1974-91; telemetry nurse Fairfax Hosp., 1974-76; med. sales rep. CB Fleet Pharm., Lynchburg, Va., 1976-78; territory mgr. Bristol-Myers Squibb, Northern Va., Washington, 1978-92; ret., 1992; artist Warrenton, Va., 1992—98. Bd. dirs. Fauquier Artists' Alliance, Warrenton, Va., 1993-96, pres., 1994-95. Exhibited in group shows at Fauquier Artists' Alliance, Warrentown, 1994—97, Alexandria Art League, 1994—98, Ctr. for Creative Art, Fredricksburg, Va., 1994—98, George Mason U., Fairfax, Va., 1994, Neighborhood Art Show, The Plains, Va., 1994—97, Japanese Embassy, Washington, 1996, The Campagna Ctr., Alexandria, 1996—97, The Torpedo Factory, Alexandria, Va., 1994—98, Petersburg Area Art League, Va., 1998—2001, Brush Strokes Gallery, Ft. Pierce, Fla., 1998—2001, Treasure Coast Art Assn., Ft. Pierce, 1998—2002, Vero Beach Art Ctr., 1999—2002, Waterways Gallery, 2002, Backus Gallery, 2002. RN Fauquier Free Clinic, Warrenton, 1993-98; mem. Goldvein Vol. Fire Dept., 1989-94. Mem. Internat. Registry Artists and Artwork, Nat. Mus. Women in the Arts (charter mem.), Archives of Nat. Mus. Women in the Arts, Vero Beach Art Club, Vero Beach Ctr. for the Arts, Treasure Coast Art Assn., Art Assocs. of Martin County. Roman Catholic. Avocation: tennis. Home: 2400 S Ocean Dr Villa 512 Fort Pierce FL 34949 E-mail: BaMaBi66@aol.com.

PETERSON, BART, mayor; m. Amy Minick; 1 child, Meg. Grad., Purdue U., 1980; JD, U. Mich., 1983. Atty. Ice Miller Donadio & Ryan, Indpls.; from exec. asst. for environ. affairs to chief of staff Ind. Gov. Evan Bayh, 1989-95; pres. Precedent Cos., 1995; mayor City Indpsl., 2000—. Bd. mem. Ind. Nature Conservancy, Regenstrief Found. Office: 2501 City-County Bldg 200 E Washington St Indianapolis IN 46204-3307 E-mail: mayor@indygov.org.*

PETERSON, BRADLEY LAURITS, lawyer; b. Mpls. m. Christine Elizabeth Stoutner, Sept. 16, 1989; children; Alexandra May, Elizabeth K. MBA, U. Chgo., 1982; JD, Harvard U., 1988. Bar: Ill. 1988. Mktg. rep. IBM, Chgo., 1982-85; assoc. Kirkland & Ellis, 1988-93, Wildman & Harrold, Chgo., 1993-95; ptnr. Mayer Brown & Platt, 1995—. Author: The Smart Way to Buy Information Technology: How to Maximize Value and Avoid Costly Pitfalls, 1998. Office: Mayer Brown & Platt 190 S Lasalle St Ste 3100 Chicago IL 60603-3441 E-mail: bpeterson@mayerbrown.com.

PETERSON, CARL ERIC, metals company executive, banker; b. Wareham, Mass., Apr. 8, 1944; m. Frances Harkness, Sept. 7, 1966; children: Robin, Alec Harkness. BA, Brown U., 1966; MA, U. Pa., 1971. With R.I. Hosp. Trust Nat. Bank, Providence, 1971-82; with Engelhard Corp., Iselin, N.J., 1982-85, Dryvit System, Inc., West Warwick, R.I., 1986, Gerald Metals, Inc., Stamford, Conn., 1987—2002.

PETERSON, CAROL POWELL, restaurant owner; b. Seattle, Feb. 15, 1941; d. Benjamin Olaf and Lois Carol (Smith) Michel; m. William Fred Roth, Apr. 8, 1961 (div. Dec. 1972); children: Christine Roth Elliott, Fred Roth, Traci Roth Johnson; m. George Benjamin Powell, Dec. 22, 1972 (dec. 1993); children: Kathy Powell Nickles, George Benjamin. Grad., Franklin H.S., Seattle, 1959. Cert. nurses aide. Dishwasher Happy Chef, Cherokee, Iowa, 1978; dishwasher, waitress Randall's Cafe, 1978-79, mgr., 1979-82; owner, operator The FoodBroker, 1983-92; with Amway Network Mktg., 1988—; health aide Cherokee (Iowa) County Home, 1994—; CNA Mountain Glen Retirement Home, Mount Vernon, Wash. Mem. Cherokee C. of C. Democrat. Avocations: reading, aerobics, piano, hospice. Home and Office: 33745 SR20 Sedro Woolley WA 98284

PETERSON, CHARLENE MARIE, educational administrator; b. Milw., Mar. 30, 1953; d. Clyde Leonard and Marguerite Jean (Taitt) P. BS, U. Wis., Menomonie, 1977; MS, U. Wis., Superior, 1993. Instrnl. materials specialist U. Wis., Menomonie, 1975-77, vocat. edn. program evaluation specialist, 1979-82, 84-85; graphic designer Woodland Arts, Eau Claire, Wis., 1983; Job Tng. Ptnrship. Act specialist Wis. Dept. Pub. Instrn., Madison, 1985-87; vocat. specialist Coop. Edn. Svc. Agy. 10, Chippewa Falls, Wis., 1978-79; dir. vocat. edn. Coop. Edn. Svc. Agy. 12, Ashland, 1987-90; dir. vocat. and alternative edn. Sch. Dist. Superior, 1990-97, prin. Northland Alt. H.S., 1997—. Regional chair Wis. Gender Equity Cadre, 1987-90; divsn. edn. adv. coun. U. Wis., Superior, 1991-93, chair, 1993; mem. N.W. Wis. Tech Prep Curriculum Com., 1992-97, Regional Aerospace Compact, 1992-97, Mcpl. Airport Expansion Com., 1993-97, N.W. Wis. Sch.-to-Work Consortium, 1994-97, Superior Area Bus. Incubation Adv. Com., 1994-95; chair Douglas County Truancy Com., 1993-96. Co-author manuals on vocat. program evaluation process, 1979-85. Bd. dirs. Ctr. for Assault and Domestic Abuse, 1998-2000. Mem. ASCD, Am. Vocat. Assn., Wis. Vocat. Assn., Wis. Assn. Secondary Vocat. Adminstrs. (state pres. 1989, exec. com. 1988-93), Rotary. Avocations: downhill ski racing, sailing, fishing, photography, golf. Office: Sch Dist of Superior 611 24th Ave E Superior WI 54880-3869 E-mail: petersonc@superior.k12.wi.us.

PETERSON, CHARLES HAYES, lawyer; b. St. Louis, May 8, 1938; s. Edmund Herbert and Dorothy Marie (Brennan) P.; m. Auli Irene Ahonen, Nov. 28, 1981; children: Mika, Charles, Michael, Katja. BS, U.S. Naval Acad., 1960; MBA, Stanford U., 1971, JD, 1974. Commd. ensign USN, 1956, advanced through grades to capt., resigned, 1969; with USNR, 1969-89, ret., 1998; counsel Gen. Electric, San Jose, Calif., 1973-79; div. counsel Syracuse, N.Y., 1980-83; v.p. COGEMA, Inc., Washington, 1983-87; pres. NUEXCO Trading Co., 1987-95; of counsel Morgan, Lewis & Bockius, LLP, 1995—2001; ptnr. Shaw Pittman, Washington, 2001—. Recipient Meritorious Service medal State of Calif., 1986. Mem. Calif. and Washington Bar Assns. Lutheran. Office: Shaw Pittman 2300 N Street NW Washington DC 20037 Fax: 202 663 8007.

PETERSON, CHARLES BUCKLEY, III, librarian, geographer; b. Lancaster, Pa., Oct. 3, 1936; s. Charles Buckley Peterson Jr. and Elsie Marie (Prosser) Peterson. BA in Geography, Northwestern U., 1958; MA in Geography, U. Wash., 1962, PhD of Geography, 1969; MLS, Cath. U. Am., 1975. Sr. map cataloguer Geography and Map divsn. Libr. of Congress, Washington, 1975—. Mem.: ALA, Assn. Am. Geographers, Am. Name Soc. Achievements include donated 16,000 piece map collection to Libr. of Congress in 2000. Avocation: Avocations: road map collecting, book collecting. Home: 1030 31st St NW Washington DC 20007-4405 Office: Libr of Congress Geography and Map Divsn 101 Independence Ave SE Washington DC 20540-4650

PETERSON, CHARLES GORDON, retired lawyer; b. Lansing, Mich., May 21, 1926; s. Russell V. and Edna E. (Jones) P.; m. Clara Elizabeth Parmelee, Mar. 8, 1947; children— Wendy, Pamela, Christopher BS, Columbia U. Sch. Gen. Studies, 1954; LL.B., Columbia U. Sch. Law, 1956. Bar: N.Y., 1957. Legal assoc. Beekman & Bogue, N.Y.C., 1956-67; mem. Gaston & Snow, 1967-91; of counsel Reid & Priest, 1991-93; ret., 1993. Trustee The Riverside Ch., N.Y.C., 1968-80, 82-89, mem. bd. deacons, 1960-68; pres. Lincoln Guild Housing Corp., N.Y.C., 1961-62, 84-87, v.p., 1987-89, 94-96, bd. dirs., 1961-62, 84-89, 94-96. Mem. Phi Beta Kappa. Republican. Mem. United Ch. of Christ. Avocations: piano, reading, travel. Home: 303 W 66th St Apt 20ee New York NY 10023-6330

PETERSON, CHRISTINA E. neurologist; b. L.A., Apr. 6, 1952; d. Sherman Earle and Harriet J. Peterson. AS in Nursing, Long Beach City Coll., 1972; BA, Calif. State U., Long Beach, 1978; MD, U. So. Calif., 1982. Intern Huntington Meml. Hosp., Pasadena, Calif., 1982-83; resident in neurology Oreg. Health Scis. U., Portland, 1983-86; pvt. practice Lake Oswego, Oreg., 1986-92, Oregon City, 1992—; med. dir. MedExperts Inc., 1993—, Oreg. Headache Clinic, Oregon City, 1995—2001. Spkr., cons. Merck Human Health, West Point, Pa., 1997—, Astra Zeneca Pharms., 1998—, Cerenex/Glaxo Wellcome, Triangle Park, N.c., 1997-98, Glaxo Smith Kline, 2000-, Pharmacia, 2001-. Author: The Women's Migraine Survival Guide, 1999. Chair women physician task force Multnomah County Med. Soc., 1989-91, mem. pub. policy com. 1989-91, mem. young physician's task force 1989-91, del., 1989-91; mem. head injury adv. bd. Vocat. Rehab. Divsn. State of Oreg., 1989-90. Mem. AMA, Am. Headache Soc., Nat. Headache Found., Internat. Headache Soc., Oreg. Med. Assn. (young physician trustee 1990-92, workers compensation com. 1988-98, trustee 1995—), Clackamas County Med. Soc. (mem. long range planning com. 1990-94, sec.-treas. 1991, grievance com. 1990-91, bd. trustees 1997-, pres. 1994). Avocations: medieval history, fiber arts. Office: 19001 SE Mcloughlin Blvd Portland OR 97267-6727

PETERSON, CLARK C. announcer, writer, poet, speaker; b. Pine City, Minn., Dec. 27, 1947; s. Carl A. and Bernice C. Peterson. AA, U. Minn., 1967, B Econs., 1969; A in Bible, Grace Bible Coll., 1993. Announcer Sta. KOLM/KWWK Radio, Rochester, Minn., 1974-84; pub. affairs specialist U.S. Army, Oklahoma City, 1985-97; announcer, writer Power Zone Wresting Fedn., 1992-97; corr. Pro Wrestling Illustrated Mag., 1992-97; announcer, writer Mid-South Wrestling Fedn., Oklahoma City, 1998—; corr. The Wrestling Tribune, 1993—; host weekly pro wrestling radio talk show "The Three Count" aired throughout one-half of continental U.S., 2001—. Parade announcer Mora's (Minn.) Centennial, 1983; announcer Richards-Gebaur AFB Open House, Kansas City, Mo., 1973, Nat. Drum and Bugle Corps Contest, Stillwater, Minn., early 1980's; announcer, entertainment Rochester's (Minn.) 125th Anniversary, 1983; announcer, writer, entertainment Korn & Klover Karnival, Hinckley, Minn., 1973-87, 90-91; judge Miss Teen Minn. Pageant, St. Paul, 1984. Author: The Great Hinckley Fire, 1978, Blasted Unto a Pile of Rubble, 1995; co-author: In Their Name, 1995, We Will Never Forget, 1996, Forever Changed, 1998; contbg. author: Wrestling Title Histories, 2000. Mem., survivor Apr. 19, 1995 Oklahoma City Bombing, Family and Survivors United, 1995—; pub. rels. and advt. advisor Rep. campaign for Minn. Senate, 2000; bd. dirs. Grace Bible Coll., Morrisville, NC, 2002-. Served with USAF, 1970-74. Recipient Best Coverage of a Local Story in the U.S., AP, 1978, scholarship Fairfax U., 1988, Civil Svc. Achievement medal U.S. Army, 1997, 14 New Idea/Suggestion awards, One of the highest numbers in U.S. Civil Svc., 1997, 5th prize World-Wide Christmas Outdoor Lighting Display Contest, 1997; named among 25 winners Turner Broadcasting Wrestling Announcing Contest, 1992; inducted Profl. Wrestling's Wall of Fame, 1998. Avocations: outdoor Christmas lighting display, state and city flag collections, coin collecting.

PETERSON, COLLIN C. congressman; b. Fargo, N.D., June 29, 1944; children: Sean, Jason, Elliott. BA in Bus. Adminstrn. and Acctg., Moorhead State U., 1966. CPA, Minn. Senator State of Minn., 1976-86; mem. U.S. Congress from 7th Minn. dist., 1991—; mem. agrl. com., subcoms. gen. farm commodities, specialty crops and natural resources, livestock, environ. credit and rural devel.; mem. permanent select Com. Intelligence , 2001—; mem. govt. ops. com., chmn. subcom. employment housing and aviation; mem. resource conservation com., rsch. and forestry subcom., livestock, dairy and poultry subcom., govt. reform and oversight com.; nat. econ. growth com., nat. resources and regulatory affairs com.-ranking minority mem., vet. affairs com. With U.S. Army N.G., 1963-69. Mem. Am. Legion, Ducks Unltd., Elks, Sportsmen's Club, Rural Caucus, Mainstream Forum, Cormorant Lakes Sportsmen Club, Congl. Sportsmen's Caucus, Mainstream Forum, Congl. Rural Caucus. Democrat. Office: US Ho of Reps 2159 Rayburn Hob Washington DC 20515-0001 also: Dist Office 714 Lake Ave Ste 107 Detroit Lakes MN 56501*

PETERSON, COURTLAND HARRY, law educator; b. Denver, June 28, 1930; s. Harry James and Courtney (Caple) P.; m. Susan Schwab, Gisvold, Jan. 28, 1966; children: Brooke, Linda, Patrick. BA, U. Colo., 1951, LL.B., 1953; M.C.L., U. Chgo., 1959; JD, U. Freiburg, Ger., 1964. Bar: Colo. 1953. Mem. faculty U. Colo. Law Sch., 1959—, prof., 1963—, dean, 1974-79, Nicholas Rosenbaum prof., 1991-94, Nicholas Doman prof. emeritus, 1995—. Vis. prof. U. Calif. Law Sch., Los Angeles, 1965, Max Planck Inst., Hamburg, Ger., 1969-70, U. Tex. Law Sch., Austin, 1973-74, Summer Program, Tulane U., Rodos, Greece, 1993, Summer Program, La. State U., Aix-en-Provence, France, 1996; bd. dirs. Continuing Legal Edn. in Colo., 1974-77 Author: Die Anerkennung Auslaendischer Urteile, 1964; Translator: (Bauer) An Introduction to German Law, 1965. Served to 1st lt. USAF, 1954-56. Fgn. Law fellow U. Chgo., 1957-59; Ford Found. Law Faculty fellow, 1964; Alexander von Humboldt Stiftun fellow, 1969-70 Mem. ABA, Colo. Bar Assn. (bd. govs. 1974-79), Boulder County Bar Assn., Am. Soc. Comparative Law (dir., bd. editors, treas. 1978-89, hon. pres. 1996-98), Internat. Acad. Comparative Law, Am. Law Inst., Boulder County Bar Found. (trustee 1995-2000). Home: 205 Camden Pl Boulder CO 80302-8032 Office: U Colo Law Sch Boulder CO 80309-0001

PETERSON, DAVE LEONARD, psychologist; b. Memphis, Nov. 29, 1952; s. Leroy Leonard and Mary Elizabeth (Linker) P.; m. Eleanor M. Hjelvik, Aug. 14, 1980. Student, U. Wis., 1972-74; BA, Sonoma State U., Rohnert Park, Calif., 1976; MA, U.S. Internat. U., San Diego, 1982, PhD, 1989. Diplomate Am. Coll. Forensic Examiners, Am. Bd. Psychol. Specialties. Psychology intern, 1986; forensic psychologist, forensic psychology coord. Ctrl. State Hosp., Milledgeville, Ga., 1995-97; staff sr. psychologist Winnebago (Wis.) Mental Health Inst., 1992-95, ret., 1997. Occasional lectr., 1997—. Mem. Psi Chi. Avocations: philosophy, hunting, long-range rifle shooting. Home: 253 Ivey Dr SW Milledgeville GA 31061-3725 also: PO Box 2233 Sylacauga AL 35150-5233 E-mail: davepe@alltel.net.

PETERSON, DAVID EUGENE, lawyer; b. Ft. Wayne, Ind., Dec. 29, 1957; s. Earl Eugene and Gloria Anne (Richardson) P.; m. Cynthia Elaine Davis, Aug. 5, 1958; children: Sarah Kirsten, Philip Conrad. AB in Econs., U. Mich., 1980, JD, 1983. Bar: Fla. 1983. Atty. Lowndes, Drosdick, Doster, Kantor & Reed, P.A., Orlando, Fla., 1983—. Office: Lowndes Drosdick Doster Kantor & Reed 215 N Eola Dr Orlando FL 32801 Home: 1158 Grove St Maitland FL 32751 Fax: (407) 843-4444. E-mail: depeterson01@msn.com.

PETERSON, DAVID FREDERICK, government agency executive; b. Washington, Apr. 4, 1937; s. Victor Henry and Alice Augusta (Vogle) P.; m. Laurie A. Cadigan, June 11, 1988. AB, Harvard U., 1959; LL.B., Cornell U., 1962. Bar: D.C. 1963. With Metromedia Inc., N.Y.C. and Los Angeles, 1963—70; exec. dir. consumer info. ctr. GSA, Washington, 1970—76, dir. consumer affairs, 1976—82, assoc. archivist for mgmt. Nat. Archives and Records Service, 1982—83; asst. archivist for Fed. Records Ctrs. Nat. Archives and Records Adminstrn., 1983—96; asst. archivist Presdl. Librs., 1996—2002; ret., 2002. Served with U.S. Army, 1963 Home: 1417 NE High Hammock Ct Jensen Beach FL 34957-6507

PETERSON, DAVID ROBERT, lawyer, former Canadian government official; b. Toronto, Dec. 28, 1943; s. Clarence and Laura Marie (Scott) P.; m. Shelley Peterson, Jan. 16, 1974; children: Benjamin David, Chloe Matthews, Adam Drake Scott BA, U. Western Ont., 1964; LLB, U. Toronto, 1967; LLD (hon.), U. Ottawa, Am. U. of Caribbean, U. Tel Aviv, U. Toronto. Bar: Ont. 1969, Queens counsel 1981. Chmn., pres. C.M. Peterson Co. Ltd., 1969-75, Cambridge Acceptance Corp., 1969-75; M.P. Ontario Parliament, Can., 1975—; leader Ont. Liberal Party, 1982; premier Province of Ont., 1985-90; chmn. Cassels Brock & Blackwell LLP, Toronto, 1991—. Bd. dirs. Rogers Comms., Ltd., Nat. Life Assurance Co., Industrielle-Alliance Life Assurance Co., BNP Paribas (Can.), SMK Speedy Inc., Franc-Nev. Mining Corp. Ltd., Rogers AT&T Wireless, others; founding chmn. Chpts. Inc., Cassels-Pouiliot Noriega; mem. strategic adv. bd. Xerox Can. Inc. Leader of the official opposition party, Liberal Party, Ont., 1982-85; dir. Legal Svcs., Yorkville; mem. Kidney Found. Can., Ont., Cystic Fibrosis Found. Fellow McLaughlin Coll., 1985; appointed Knight of Order of Legion of Honor, Govt. France, 1994; recipient Ordre de la Pléiade, Internat. Assembly French-Speaking Parliamentarians, 1995. Mem. Law Soc. U.C., Young Pres. Orgn., London C. of C., London Hunt Country Club, London Racquets Club, Can. Club, Toronto Raptors Basketball Club Inc. (foundg chmn.). Mem. United Ch. Christ. Avocations: theatre, riding, jogging, skiing, tennis. Office: Cassels Brock Blackwell LLP 40 King St W Ste 2100 Toronto ON Canada M5H 3C2

PETERSON, DELAINE CHARLES, lawyer, bank executive; b. Villisca, Iowa, July 28, 1936; s. Reuben Merrill and Margaret Helena (Sederquist) P.; m. Maria Joan Hitchcock, Aug. 18, 1962; children: Robert, Paul, Janet. BBA, U. Iowa, 1963, JD, 1966. Bar: Iowa 1966. Asst. trust officer Security Nat. Bank, Sioux City, Iowa, 1966-73, mgr. trust dept., 1974-82, sr. v.p., 1983-92, sr. v.p., chief trust officer, 1992—2001; assoc. atty. Corbett Anderson Law Firm, 2001—. Bd. dirs. Siouxland Easter Seals, Sioux City, 1983-91, St. Luke's Health Systems, Inc., 1987-2000, chmn. 1989-91; bd. dirs. St. Luke's Regional Med. Ctr., chmn. 1988-89; bd. dirs. St. Luke's Coll. Nursing and Health Scis., 1991-2000, chmn., 1991-93; trustee Prarie Gold coun. Boy Scouts Am., 1987—, pres., 1989-92; mem. Iowa Coll. Found., 1975-85; com. mem. Morningside Coll. Found., 1989-95. Mem. ABA, Iowa Bar Assn., Woodbury Bar Assn., Iowa Trust Assn. (pres. 1978), Rotary (pres. 1984), Masons (past master 1988). Republican. Methodist. Office: Corbett Anderson Law Firm PO Box 3527 Sioux City IA 51102

PETERSON, DONALD FRED, physiologist, educator; b. Great Bend, Kans., Aug. 4, 1941; s. Donald F. and Mary K. (Doerr) P.; m. Bonnie Jean Campbell, July 30, 1967; children: Corilynn, Bailey, Ronald. Student, U. Sorbonne, Paris, 1962-63; BS in Zoology, Kans. State U., 1965, PhD in Physiology, 1970. Postdoctoral fellow U. Utah Med. Ctr., Salt Lake City, 1969-71; instr. U. Tex. Health Sci. Ctr., San Antonio, 1971-73, asst. prof., 1973-77, assoc. prof., 1977-78, Oral Roberts U. Med. Ctr., Tulsa, 1978-88, prof., chmn. physiology, 1988-90; prof., chmn. physiology Kirksville (Mo.) Coll. Osteo. Medicine, 1990—. Mem. extra-curricular task force Kirksville (Mo.) Sch. Dist., 1995, pres. Kirksville Boosters, 1994-95. Recipient Rsch. Career Devel. award NIH, 1976. Fellow Am. Physiol. Soc.; mem. Am. Heart Assn. (chmn. Mo. peer rev. com. 1995-96, chmn. Mo. rsch. com. 1996-97, bd. dirs. and exec. com. Mo. affil. 1996-98, bd. dirs. Heartland affiliate 1998-2000, Heartland rsch. com. 1997-2000), Sigma Xi. Mem. Ch. of Christ. Avocations: road-running races, gardening. Home: 2201 Crestline Dr Kirksville MO 63501-5709 Office: Kirksville Coll Osteo Med Dept Physiology 800 W Jefferson St Kirksville MO 63501-1443 E-mail: fpeterson@kcom.edu.

PETERSON, DONALD K. telecommunications executive; b. Worcester, Mass. m. Maureen Mack; children: Janine, Daniel. BSME, Worcester Poly. Inst., 1971; MBA, Darmouth Coll., 1973. CLU, ChFA. Sr. analyst State Mutual Life Assurance Co., Worcester, 1973-76; with Northern Telecom, 1976-94; pres. NORTEL Comm. Sys., Inc., Nashville, 1994-95; CFO AT&T Comm. Svcs. Group, 1995-96; exec. v.p., CFO Lucent Technologies, Inc., Murray Hill, N.J., 1996-2000; pres., CEO, vice chmn. Avaya, Inc., Basking Ridge, 2000—. Bd. dirs. Reynolds & Reynolds, Dayton, Ohio. Active various repertory theaters, Inroads, Inc., Dallas United loaned exec. programs; bd. trustees Worcester Poly. Inst., Lucent Found. Avocations: karate, travel, woodworking. Office: Avaya Inc 211 Mount Airy Rd Basking Ridge NJ 07920*

PETERSON, DONALD ROBERT, magazine editor, vintage automobile consultant; b. Sandstone, Minn., Apr. 1, 1929; s. Martin Theodore and Margaret Mildred (Dezell) P.; m. Lois Taylor, Dec. 31, 1951 (div. 1975); children: Wyatt A., Winston B., Whitney C. (dec.), Westley D., Webster E.; m. Edie Tannenbaum, Aug. 31, 1975; 1 child, Ryan Kerry. Student, U. Minn., 1947-50; BS, Gustavus Adolphus Coll., 1952. Asst. underwriter Prudential Ins. Co. Am., Mpls., 1953-64; chief health underwriter North Central Life, St. Paul, 1964-66; pres. 1st State Bank Murdock, Minn., 1967-73, EDON, Inc., Roswell, Ga., 1974—; editor Car Collector mag., 1977-91, editor emeritus, 1992—; v.p., dir. Classic Pub. Inc., Atlanta, 1979-97. Contbr. chpt. to book. Councilman, City of Murdock, 1968-72, mayor, 1972-74; del. State Republican Conv., 1970-72; treas. Swift County Rep. Com., 1970-73. Served with U.S. Navy, 1946-47. Recipient citation for disting. service Classic Car Club Am., 1965, Hemmings Motor News Hobby Hero Award, 2002. Mem. Internat. Soc. Philos. Enquiry, Swift County Bankers Assn. (pres. 1970-73), Soc. Automotive Historians, Am. Legion, Mensa (pres. Ga. chpt. 1976-78), Milestone Car Soc., Classic Car Club Am. (chpt. pres. 1959, 60, 63, nat. bd. dirs. 1978-81, 97—), Rolls-Royce Owners Club, Antique Automobile Club, Vet. Motor Car Club Am., Packard Club, Cadillac-La Salle Club, Lincoln and Continental Owner's Club, Horseless Carriage Club Am. Republican. Avocations: automobile collecting, internat. traveling. Home: 1400 Lake Ridge Ct Roswell GA 30076-2869 Office:

PETERSON, DONALD ROBERT, psychologist, educator, university administrator; b. Pillager, Minn., Sept. 10, 1923; s. Frank Gordon and Ruth (Friedland) P.; m. Jean Hole, Feb. 10, 1952 (div.); children: Wendy, Jeffrey, Roger, Lisa; m. Jane Snyder Salmon, Dec. 21, 1974. BA, U. Minn., 1948, MA, 1950, PhD, 1952. Mem. faculty U. Ill., Urbana, 1952-75, prof. clin. psychology, 1963-75, head div. clin. psychology, 1963-70, dir. Psychol. Clinic, 1961-70, dir. D. Psychology program, 1970-75; dean Grad. Sch. Applied and Profl. Psychology Rutgers U., New Brunswick, 1975-89. Pres. Nat. Coun. Schs. of Profl. Psychology, 1981-83. Author: The Clinical Study of Social Behavior, 1968, Educating Professional Psychologists, 1997; co-author: Close Relationships, 1983; also articles; editor Jour. Abnormal Psychology, 1970-72. With AUS, 1943-46. Mem. N.J. Psychol. Assn., Am. Psychol. Assn. (awards for disting. contbns. to practice of psychology 1983, disting. contbns. to edn. and tng. 1989) Office: Rutgers U Grad Sch Applied & Profl Psychology Piscataway NJ 08854-8085 E-mail: drpeters@rci.rutgers.edu.

PETERSON, DONN NEAL, forensic engineer; b. Northwood, N.D., Jan. 1, 1942; s. Emil H. and Dorothy (Neal) Peterson; m. Lorna Jean Kappedal, July 8, 1962 (div. July 1966); m. Donna Sue Butts Daiker, Aug. 26, 1967; children: Barbara Daiker, Elizabeth Plamondon, Phoebe Prathap, Phaedra, Rosalind Ward. BSME, U. N.D., 1963; MSME, U. Minn., 1972. Registered profl. engr. Advanced engrng. courses student GE, Evendale, Ohio, 1963-66; systems engr. GE Aircraft Engine Group, 1963-70; prin. Donn N. Peterson & Assocs., Mpls., 1971-74; pres. Donn N. Peterson & Assocs., Inc., 1974-85, Peterson Engrng., Inc., Mpls., 1985—. Instr. GE Edn. Program, 1968-69; seminar presenter State Bd. of Registration, Mpls., 1980; seminar leader Minn. Fedn. Engrng. Socs., Mpls., 1990-91; speaker in field; expert witness 100 ct. trials and 100 depositions. Del. Minn. 6th Dist. Rep. Conv., Brooklyn Park, Minn., 1982. Fellow Am. Acad. Forensic Scis. (sect. chmn. 1989-90, Founders award 1991), Nat. Acad. Forensic Engrs. (v.p. 1996, sr. v.p. 1997-98); mem. ASME (Young Engr. of Yr. 1976, state chmn. 1979-80), NSPE, Profl. Engrs. in Pvt. Practice (state pres. 1987-88, Svc. award 1988), Soc. of Automotive Engrs., Rotary Club (sec. Brooklyn Park chpt. 1990-93, v.p. 1993-94, pres.-elect 1994-95, pres. 1995-96, Svc. award 1992), Brooklyn Park C. of C. (city hwy. 610 corridor com. 1992-94). Lutheran. Achievements include devel. of successful math. models to simulate jet engine transient performance and wave dynamics in gas flow, computer simulations for vehicle and occupant dynamics during collisions. Home: 15720 15th Pl N Plymouth MN 55447-2405 Office: PO Box 47565 Plymouth MN 55447-0565

PETERSON, DONNA KAY, business consultant; b. Chgo., July 7, 1960; d. Richard Lavern and Donna Kay P. BS in Gen. Engrng., U.S. Mil. Acad., 1982. Commd. 2d lt. U.S. Army, 1982, advanced through grades to capt., 1986, helicopter pilot Tex., 1983-86, chief of protocol, 1986-87, resigned, 1987; freelance author, 1988-90; freelance bus. cons. Orange, Tex., 1991—. Mem. Svc. Acad. Selection Bd., State of Tex., 1992-95. Author: Dress Gray: A Woman at West Point, 1990; contbr. articles to mil. and polit. jours. Rep. candidate for U.S. Congress, 1992, 94. Maj. USAR, 1994—. Named Outstanding Female Vet. of Tex., Tex. Vet.'s Land Bd., 1988; Capt. Donna Peterson Day proclaimed in Orange County, Tex., 1988. Mem. Am. Legion, Vietnam Vets. Am. (life., hon. award 1990), Houston West Point Soc. (1st female mem.), Women Mil. Pilots, Inc., Tex. Bus. and Profl. Women's Club (Young Careerist award 1987). Republican. Avocations: snow skiing, horseback riding, running, raising dogs, judo. Home: PO Box 158 Orange TX 77631-0158

PETERSON, DONNA RAE, marketing professional; b. Wichita, Kans., Aug. 29, 1948; d. Raymond Houston and Edna Brooks (Waddell) Hobbs; m. William E. Peterson, Nov. 7, 1993; 1 child, Shauna Layne Reed. Student, Wichita State U., 1968-70; BS in Mgmt., N.W. Christian Coll., 1996, MA in Interdisciplinary Studies Gerontology, 2000. Adminstrv. asst. postgrad. edn. Med. Sch. U. Kans., Wichita, 1974-80; activity coord. continuing med. edn. Wesley Med. Ctr., 1980-84; mgr. support svcs. 9th dist. Farm Credit Svcs., 1984-88; sales and mktg. mgr. Amb. Travel, Eugene, 1988-93; mktg. dir. Peterson Design Devel., Oreg., 1993-95; pres. Davinci Designs, 1996-2000; owner 2nd Half Dynamics, 2000—02; dir. Alzheimer's program Sunwest Mgmt., Inc., 2002—. Cons. Jr. League Wichita, 1983, Plancon, Inc., Martinsville, N.J., 1987-88, Changing Creatively, 1997; continuing edn. instr. Lane C.C., 2000—; mem. adv. bd. Lane C.C. Ctr. for Leisure and Learning, 2000—. Mem. Wichita Conv. and Visitors Bur., 1987; mem. events com. Wichita Festivals, Inc., 1987; mem. Eugene Conv. and Visitors Bur., 1988—; mem. Eugene Airport Commn., 1991—, chmn., 1992-93; bd. dirs. Campus Life, chmn., 1993-94; mem. steering com. Eugene Celebration, 1991-94, Oreg. Women Bus. Owners Conf., 1997; bd. pres. Of Coun. for Bus. Edn., 1999-2000. Mem. AAUW, Am. Mktg. Assn. (pres. S.W. chpt. 1991—, pres. 1992-94, bd. dirs.), Soc. Travel Agts. in Govt., Adminstrv. Mgmt. Soc., Forum for Exec. Bus. Women, Gt. Plains Bus. Adminstrn. Group, Assn. Travel Execs., Eugene C. of C. (bus. devel. com. 1990-91), The Gerontol. Soc. Am. (campus rep. 1999), Eugene High Ground Assocs. (chmn.), Delta Gamma Alumni Assn. Republican. Avocations: decorating, writing, snow skiing, water skiing, camping. Home: 1460 Olive St Apt 32 Eugene OR 97401-3991 E-mail: gerovision@aol.com.

PETERSON, DOROTHY LULU, artist, writer; b. Venice, Calif., Mar. 10, 1932; d. Marvin Henry and Fay (Brown) Case; m. Leon Albert Peterson, June 21, 1955; 1 child, David. AD, Compton (Calif.) Coll., 1950. Artist Moran Printing Co., Lockport, N.Y., 1955—; caricature artist West Seneca and Kenmore Creative Artist Socs., 1973-86; commd. artist in pvt. practice, 1986—. Comml. artist Boulevard Mall, Kenmore (N.Y.) Arts Soc., 1974—. Works include portraits of Pres. and Mrs. Reagan in Presdl. Libr. Collection, also portraits of Geraldine Ferraro, Presidents Clinton, Bush, Nixon, Ford, also Bette Davis, Lucille Ball, Bing Crosby, Elizabeth Taylor, 1971-94; sculpture of Pres. Bush, Princess Diana; caricature sculptures of Joan Rivers, Erma Bombeck, Lucille Ball; author articles, poems. Recipient awards West. Seneca Art Soc., 1975, Kenmore Art Soc., 1982, 86. Recipient Editors award Nat. Poetry Soc., 1997, Editors Choice award Nat. Libr. of Poetry, 1998, Best Poems and Poets of 2001; named to The Best Poems and Poets of the 20th Century, Internat. Libr. of Poets. Democrat. Baptist. Home: 247 Pryor Ave Tonawanda NY 14150-7407

PETERSON, DOUGLAS ARTHUR, physician; b. Princeton, N.Y., Sept. 13, 1945; s. Arthur Roy William and Marie Hilma (Anderson) P.; m. Virginia Kay Eng., June 24, 1967; children: Rachel, Daniel, Rebecca. BA, St. Olaf, 1966; PhD, U. Minn., 1971, MD, 1975. Postdoctoral fellow U. Pitts., 1971-72; intern Hennepin County Med. Ctr., Mpls., 1975-76, resident in medicine, 1976-78; physician Bloomington Lake Clinic, 1978-82; staff physician Mpls. VA Med. Ctr., 1992—, chief compensation and pension, 1992—2001, emergency physician, 2001—. Asst. prof. U. Minn., 1985—. Bd. dirs. Rolling Acres Home, Victoria, Minn., 1985-2000. Col. M.C., USAR. Mem.: AAAS, Am. Coll. Emergency Physicians. Achievements include introduction of concept of reductive activation of receptors. Home: 5008 Queen Ave S Minneapolis MN 55410-2207 Office: VA Med Ctr One Veterans Dr Minneapolis MN 55417 E-mail: douglas.peterson@med.va.gov.

PETERSON, DOUGLAS KENT, business and management educator; b. Lincoln, Nebr., June 22, 1962; s. David Kent and Hazel Grace P.; m. Frederica Robin Suess, Sept. 29, 2002; children: Simone Ballard, Ellen, Katie Marie. BA in Polit. Sci. and Human Resources Mgmt., U. Kans., Lawrence, 1984, MBA in Gen. Mgmt., 1989; PhD in Organizational Behavior and Mgmt., U. Nebr., Lincoln, 1997. Vis. prof. mgmt. Ohio U., Athens, Ohio, 1998—99; asst., then assoc. prof. mgmt. and internat. bus. Ind. State U., Terre Haute, 1999—. Pres., lead cons. Havamal Cons., Savoy, Ill., 1999—. Author: Managing Organizational Change, 1990, Cross Cultural Franchising Strategy, 1997, Test of Compensation Strategy on Employee Attitudes, 1997. Trainer Terre Haute Human Rels. Commn., 2000—02; expert witness Nebr. Equal Employment Opportunity Commn., Lincoln, 1995. Mem.: S.W. Fedn. Adminstrv. Scis., Acad. Mgmt. Democrat. Avocations: swimming, writing, travel, gourmet cooking. Home: 803 Vista Dr Savoy IL 61874 Office: Ind State U 606 School of Business Terre Haute IN 47809 Office Fax: (812) 237-8129. Personal E-mail: drdoug3@yahoo.com. Business E-Mail: d-peterson3@indstate.edu.

PETERSON, DOUGLAS PETE (PETE PETERSON), ambassador, former congressman; b. Omaha, June 26, 1935; m. Carlotta Ann Neal (dec.); children: Michael, Paula, Douglas (dec.); m. Vi Peterson. Grad., Nat. War Coll., 1975; BA, U. Tampa, 1976; postgrad., U. Ctrl. Mich., 1977. Commd. USAF, 1954, advanced through grades to col., ret., 1980; exec. CRT Computers, 1984-90; mem. faculty Fla. State U., 1985-90; mem. 101st-104th Congresses from 2nd Fla. Dist., 1991-96; mem. appropriation com.-energy and water, agrl.; amb. to Vietnam, 1996—2001; pres. Peterson Internat., Inc., 2001—. Prisoner of war, Vietnam. Mem. DAV, VFW, Am. Legion. Roman Catholic. Office: 905 Hays St Tallahassee FL 32301

PETERSON, E. ANNE, federal agency administrator; married; 3 children. MD, Mayo Med. Sch.; MPH, Emory U. Cert. bd. cert. gen. preventive medicine and pub. health, lic. Va., Ga., Minn., Zimbabwe. Resident Emory U.; commr. health State of Va., 1998—2001; asst. adminstr. bur. global health USAID, Washington, 2001—. Cmty. devel., pub. health tng. and AIDS prevention, Kenya, Zimbabwe. Office: USAID RRB 1300 Pennsylvania Ave NW Washington DC 20523-3900*

PETERSON, EDWARD ADRIAN, lawyer; b. St. Louis, May 19, 1941; s. Adrian J. and Virginia (Hamlin) P.; m. Catherine Frances Younghouse, Dec. 17, 1960; children: Kristin, Kendra. BSBA, Washington U., St. Louis, 1963; LLB, So. Methodist U., 1966. Bar: Tex. 1966, U.S. Dist. Ct. (no. and so. dists.) Tex. Instr. bus. law and acctg. Midwestern U., Wichita Falls, Tex., 1966-67; assoc. Schenk & Wesbrooks, 1966-67, Newman & Pickering, Dallas, 1967-72; ptnr. Moore & Peterson, 1972-89, Winstead Sechrest & Minick P.C., Dallas, 1989—. Speaker in field. Contbr. articles to legal jours. Bd. dirs. Leukemia Soc., 1970-71, North Tex. Commn., 1992-96, South Dallas/Fair Park Trust Fund, 1992. Fellow Tex. Bar Found. (life); mem. ABA, Am. Coll. Real Estate Lawyers (professionalism and practice com., nominating com.), State Bar Tex., Coll. State Bar Tex., Tex. Coll. Real Estate Attys., Dallas Bar Assn., Phi Alpha Delta, Sigma Alpha Epsilon. Lutheran. Home: Ste 617 2808 McKinney Ave Dallas TX 75204-2562 also: 131 Hilton Head Island Dr Mabank TX 75147-9325 Office: Winstead Sechrest & Minick PC 5400 Renaissance Tower 1201 Elm St Dallas TX 75270-2199 E-mail: epeterson@winstead.com.

PETERSON, EDWIN J. retired judge, mediator, law educator; b. Gilmanton, Wis., Mar. 30, 1930; s. Edwin A. and Leora Grace (Kitelinger) P.; m. Anna Chadwick, Feb. 7, 1971; children: Patricia, Andrew, Sherry. BS, U. Oreg., 1951, LL.B., 1957. Bar: Oreg. 1957. Assoc. firm Tooze, Kerr, Peterson, Marshall & Shenker, Portland, 1957-61, mem. firm, 1961-79; assoc. justice Supreme Ct. Oreg., Salem, 1979-83, 91-93, chief justice, 1983-91; ret., 1993; disting. jurist-in-residence, adj. instr. Willamette Coll. of Law, Salem, Oreg., 1994—. Chmn. Supreme Ct. Task Force on Racial Issues, 1992-94; standing com. on fed. rules of practice and procedure, 1987-93; bd. dirs. Conf. Chief Justices, 1985-87, 88-91. Chmn. Portland Citizens Sch. Com., 1968-70; vice-chmn. Young Republican Fedn. Orgn., 1951; bd. visitors U. Oreg. Law Sch., 1978-83, 87-93, chmn. bd. visitors, 1981-83; pres., bd. dirs. Understanding Racism Found., 1999—. 1st lt. USAF, 1952-54. Mem. Oreg. State Bar (bd. examiners 1963-66, gov. 1973-76, vice chmn. profl. liability fund 1977-78), Multnomah County Bar Assn. (pres. 1972-73), Phi Alpha Delta, Lambda Chi Alpha. Episcopalian. Home: 3365 Sunridge Dr S Salem OR 97302-5950 Office: Willamette Univ Coll Law 245 Winter St SE Salem OR 97301-3916 E-mail: epeterso@willamette.edu.

PETERSON, ELAINE GRACE, retired technology director; b. Chgo., Feb. 6, 1943; d. Lincoln and Martha (Guthmiller) Wyman; m. Robert J. Peterson, June 5, 1965; children: Wesley, Christian. Cert. in computer programming, Moraine Valley Coll., Palos Hills, 1975; BA in Edn., MA in Comm. Sci. and Adminstrn., Governors State U., 1981. Computer coord. Dist. 144, Hazel Crest, Ill., 1984-86; adj. prof. Governors State U., University Park, 1986-87; program coord. ISBE-Ednl. Svc. Ctr., Flossmoor, 1986-92; rsch. assoc. Argonne (Ill.) Nat. Lab., 1991-93; dist. tech. dir. Lombard (Ill.) Dist. 44, Lombard, Ill., 1991-92; dir. tech./media svcs. DuPage H.S. Dist. 88, Addison, 1992—, dir. tech./Media Svcs. Villa Park, 1992-2000, dir. cmty. edn. and distance learning, 2000—; grant writer Layne Cons., Addison, 1993-94. Bd. dirs. Audio-Visual Inst. DuPage, Lombard; mem. Bus. Profl. of Am., Flossmoor, 1990-92, Regional Office Edn./Profl. Dev. Ctr., Lombard, 1993—; tech. mem. Addison 2000 Cmty. Orgn. Village and Schs., 1993—; tech. com. adv. Dist. 45-Feeder Sch., Villa Park, 1994—; grant reader Ednl. Svc. Ctr. Ill. Math Sci. Acad., Aurora, Ill., 1992-94, Ill. Bd. Edn., Springfield, 1995—; Du-Page problem-based learning trainer LINC, 1997—. Contbr. articles to profl. jours.; tech. peer reviewer ISBE Tech Plans, 1998—. Mem. Am. Assn. Sch. Adminstrs., Nat. Assn. Investing Clubs (treas. for Carillon Sr. Citizens Pocketbook Investors), Internat. Soc. for Tchr. Edn., Ill. Computing Educators, Tech 2000, Ill. Sch. Libr. Media Assn., Argonne Cmty. Tchrs., Ill. ASCD, Ill. Soc. Bus. Educators (tech. steering com. area 1 1997-98, tech. leadership steering com. 1998, peer reviewer for tech. 1998—), Ill. Tech. Leadership Acad. (devel. com. 1998-99, treas. 1999—, com. to setup orgn. for a tchr. acad. 1999, steering com. 1999—, regional dir. 2000), Phi Delta Kappa (treas. DuPage County chpt. 1999—), Avocations: bowling, investing, computing, golf, shopping. Home: 1680 Piccadilly Cir Port Charlotte FL 33980 E-mail: epeter214@comcast.com.

PETERSON, ERLE VIDAILLET, retired metallurgical engineer; b. Idaho Falls, Idaho, Apr. 29, 1915; s. Vier P. and Marie (Vidaillet) P.; m. Rosemary Sherwood, June 3, 1955; children: Kent Sherwood, Pamela Jo. BS in Mining Engrng., U. Idaho, 1940; MS in Mining Engrng., U. Utah, 1941. Tech. advisor Remington Arms Co., Salt Lake City, 1941-43; constrn. engr. plutonium plant duPont, Hanford, Wash., 1943-44, R & D engr. exptl. sta. Wilmington, Del., 1944-51, plant metallurgist heavy water plant Newport, Ind., 1951-57, rsch. metallurgist metals program Balt., 1957-62, prin. project engr. USAF contracts, 1962-68, devel. engr. Wilmington, 1969-80; ret., 1980. Patentee in field; contbr. articles to profl. jours. Candidate for State Senate-Am. Party, Wilmington, 1974; com. chmn. Boy Scouts Am., Wilmington, 1975-78; treas. Local Civic Assn., Wilmington, 1977-79. Rsch. fellow U. Utah, 1940. Mem. Am. Soc. Metallurgists Internat., Del. Assn. Profl. Engrs. Republican. Avocations: lapidary, jewelry making, photography, prospecting, gardening. Home: PO Box 74 Rigby ID 83442-0074 *It matters not that you grow up on homestead and graduate from a country high school in a class of five during a great depression. With persistence and dedication toward your objectives, you can achieve goals that appear impossible.*

PETERSON, FRANKLIN DELANO, lawyer; b. Braham, Minn., Nov. 11, 1932; s. John Erick and Myrtle M. (Anderson) P.; m. Beverly Ann Crabb, Aug. 2, 1958; children: Heidi, Durward, Heather. Student, Augsburg Coll., 1950-51; BA, St. Cloud State Coll., 1955; LLB, William Mitchell Coll. Law, 1961. Bar: Minn. 1961. Field claims adjuster Farmers Mut. Ins. Co., St. Paul, 1955-57; asst. dist. claims mgr. Minn. Farmers Ins. Group, Mpls., 1957-62; sole practice Kenyon, Minn., 1963—. Atty. City of Kenyon, 1964-82; v.p. Kenyon Devel.

Corp., bd. dirs.; sec. Tri-Valley Constrn. Co., Kenyon, bd. dirs. Chmn. Goldwater for Pres. campaign, Village of Kenyon Reps., 1964, Goodhue County LeVander for Gov., 1966, Goodhue County Reps, 1969-70; sec. Goodhue Selective Service Bd., 1968—; pres. Mineral Springs Chem. Dependency Ctr., 1974-85; mem. Kenyon Pub. Sch. Bd. Edn., 1976-82, treas. 1980-82, Kenyon Booster Club (charter), v.p. 1983; mgr. mgr. Kenyon Legion Baseball, 1979—; bd. dirs. Kenyon Roseview Apts., 1967—, pres. 1985—. Served with USAF, 1950-52. Mem. ABA, Minn. Bar Assn. (jud. dist. del., pres. 1st dist. 1979-80), Goodhue County Bar Assn., Minn. Assn. Plaintiffs Attys., Nat. Assn. Claimants Counsel, Sons of Norway (pres. Kenyon lodge 1969), Kenyon Comml. Club, Kenyon Country Club (pres. Osman Shrine Clowns 1993), Masons, Shriners, Lions (pres. Kenyon chpt.), royal Order Jesters, Ct. of St. Paul and Shriner Clowns. Lutheran. Home: RR Box B Kenyon MN 55946 Office: 634 2nd St Kenyon MN 55946-1334

PETERSON, FRED MCCRAE, retired librarian; b. Mpls., Dec. 29, 1936; BA, U. Minn., 1958, MS, 1960; PhD in L.S., Ind. U., 1974. Asst. to dir. Iowa State U. Library, 1961-64, head catalog dept., 1964-67, asst. dir. library, 1967-69, assoc. dir. library, 1969-70; with Catholic U. Am., Washington, 1970-82, asst. prof., assoc. chairperson, 1973-77, acting dir. libraries, 1977-78, dir., 1978-82; univ. librarian Ill. State U., Normal, 1982-96, univ. libr. emeritus, 1996—. Mem. ALA, Ill. Libr. Assn. (past pes., Libr. of Yr. award 1994). Home: 32792 Via Malaga San Juan Capistrano CA 92675-4455

PETERSON, GALE EUGENE, historian; b. Sioux Rapids, Iowa, May 23, 1944; s. George Edmund and Vergene Elizabeth (Wilson) P. BS, Iowa State U., 1965; MA, U. Md., 1968, PhD, 1973. Instr. dept. history U. Md., College Park, 1971-72, Cath. U. Am., Washington, 1972-73; prin. investigator Gregory Directory project Orgn. Am. Historians, Bloomington, Ind., 1973-75; instr. dept. history Purdue U., West Lafayette, 1975-76; dir. U.S. Newspaper Project, Orgn. Am. Historians, Bloomington, 1976-78; exec. dir. Cin. Hist. Soc., 1978-96, exec. dir. emeritus, 1996—; exec. dir. Ohio Humanities Coun., 1998—. Author: (with John T. Schlebecker) Living Historical Farms Handbook, 1970, Harry S Truman and the Independent Regulatory Commissions 1945-52, 1985. Mem. Cin. Bicentennial Commn., 1983-88. Mem. Orgn. Am. Historians (treas. 1993—), Am. Assn. State and Local History, Am. Hist. Assn., Am. Assn. Mus., Assn. Midwest Museums (v.p.-at-large 1993-95, exec. v.p. 1995-96, pres. 1996-98), Nat. Coun. on Pub. History (bd. dirs. 1992-95). Office: Ohio Humanities Coun Ste 1620 471 E Broad St Columbus OH 43215-3857 E-mail: galep@one.net.

PETERSON, GARY ANDREW, agronomics researcher; b. Holdrege, Nebr., Apr. 30, 1940; s. Walter Andrew and Evelyn Christine (Johnson) P.; m. Jacquelyn Charlene Flick, June 18, 1965; children: Kerstin, Ingrid. BS, U. Nebr., 1963, MS, 1965; PhD, Iowa State U., 1967. Research assoc. agronomy Iowa State U., Ames, 1964-67; prof. U. Nebr., Lincoln, 1967-84; prof. soil and crop scis. Colo. State U., Ft. Collins, 1984—. Assoc. editor AGronomy Jour., 1979-81, tech. editor, 1981-83, editor, 1984-89, editor-in-chief, 1991-96; contbr. articles to profl. jours. Fellow Am. Soc. Agronomy (Ciba-Geigy Agr. Achievement award 1974, Agronomic Achievement award-Soils 1990), Soil Sci. Soc. Am. (Applied Rsch. award 1987); mem. Soil Conservation Soc. Am. Republican. Avocations: reading, hiking, skiing. Office: Colo State U Dept Soil Crop Scis Fort Collins CO 80523-0001 E-mail: gary.peterson@colostate.edu.

PETERSON, GERALD JOSEPH, aerospace executive, consultant; b. Decatur , Ill., Oct. 27, 1947; s. Raymond Gerald (dec.) and Mary Louise (Johnson) P. AA, Lincolnland Community Coll., Springfield, Ill., 1969; student, Schiller Coll., Heidelberg, Germany, 1971, Sangamon State U., Springfield, 1972, U. Minn., 1976. Cert. aircraft pilot, engring. tech. Author LOGIC IV commodities futures trading program, 1996; patentee in field. Served with USAF, 1965, French Foreign Legion, 1979. Mem.: Internat. Platform Assn., U.S. Naval Inst. (life). Avocation: Shaolin Kung Fu. Office: Peterson Aerospace Corp PO Box 1294 Mountain View HI 96771-1294 E-mail: peterson@shaolintemple.zzn.com .

PETERSON, GERALD ALVIN, physics educator; b. Chesterton, Ind., Apr. 12, 1931; s. Gustaf Albert and Esther Josephine (Carlson) P.; m. Doris Lee DeJonge, Dec. 22, 1953; children— Curtis Mark, Thomas Andrew, Anna Beth. BS, Purdue U., 1953, MS, 1955; PhD, Stanford U., 1962. Lectr. Yale U., New Haven, 1962-64; asst. prof., 1964-67; research scientist Inst. voor Kernphysisch Onderzoek, Amsterdam, 1967-68; assoc. prof. physics U. Mass., Amherst, 1968-73, prof., 1973-2000, prof. emeritus, 2000—. Vis. prof. U. Mainz, Fed. Republic Germany, 1975, Japan Soc. Promotion Sci., 1972, 89; U.S.-Israel Binat. Sci. Found. vis. prof. Tel Aviv U., 1983; cons. in field. Contbr. articles to profl. jours. Served with U.S. Army, 1955-57. NATO fellow, 1969, U.K. sr. rsch. fellow, 1970. Fellow Am. Phys. Soc. (chmn. New Eng. sect. 1996); mem. Sigma Xi. Congregationalist. Achievements include research in electron scattering and nuclear structure. Home: 10 Old Briggs Rd Leverett MA 01054-9759 Office: U Mass Nuclear Physics Grad Rsch Ctr Amherst MA 01003 E-mail: peterson@physics.umass.edu.

PETERSON, GRANT MARK, obstetrician, gynecologist; b. Rexburg, Idaho, July 21, 1941; MD, U. Utah, 1969. Diplomate Am. Bd. Ob-gyn. Intern Providence Hosp., Portland, 1969-70; resident in ob-gyn. U. Utah Affiliated Hosps., Salt Lake City, 1970-73; med. staff Bingham Meml. Hosp., Blackfoot, Idaho; pvt. practice. With U.S. Army, 1973-76. Mem. ACOG, AMA, Idaho Med. Assn. Email (business). Office: Blackfoot Med Clin 625 W Pacific St Blackfoot ID 83221-2049 E-mail: drpeterson@bfmed.com.

PETERSON, GWEN ENTZ, artist; b. Newton, Kans., Mar. 8, 1938; BA, No. Colo. U., 1959. Art tchr. pub. schs., Colby, Kans., 1959-61, Denver, 1961-62, Lake Bluff, Ill., 1964-66; studio artist Albuquerque, 1968—. One-woman shows include Jonson Gallery, U. N. Mex., 1975, 77, 79, 81, Thompson Gallery U. N. Mex., 1984, Magnifico's Art of Albuquerque show, 1993, 95; represented in permanent collections Mt. Sinai Med. Ctr., N.Y.C., La Familia Med. Ctr., Santa Fe, U. N. Mex., Albuquerque, Eastern N. Mex. U., Portales, IBM, AT&T, Albuquerque. Recipient Calendar Page award Hist. Soc., Albuquerque, 1975, Poster award N.Mex. Arts & Crafts Fair, 1982, Banner Design award Nat. Presbyn. Mariners, 1997. Mem. Nat. PEN Women, Christians in the Visual Arts. Avocations: hiking, mountain climbing, reading. Studio: 3717 General Patch St NE Albuquerque NM 87111-3253

PETERSON, H. DALE, lawyer; b. Amherst, Wis., Jan. 4, 1951; s. Harold C. and Eva I. (Hansen) P.; m. Julie A. Goplin, Jan. 1, 1995; children: Matt, David, Alex, Ellen. BS with honors, U. Wis., Stevens Point, 1973; JD cum laude, U. Wis., 1978. Bar: U.S. Dist. Ct. (we. dist.) Wis., U.S. Ct. Appeals (7th cir.) Wis. Rsch. analyst U.S. Dept. Justice, Washington, 1973-75; ptnr. Stroud, Willink & Howard, LLC, Madison, Wis., 1978—. Dir. Wis. Farm Bur. Svc. Bd., Inc., Madison, 1994—. Co-author: Contract Law in Wisconsin, 1995. Mem. Dane County Bar Assn. (dir./treas. 1987-91). Office: Stroud Willink & Howard LLC PO Box 2236 Madison WI 53701-2236

PETERSON, H(ARRY) WILLIAM, chemicals executive, consultant; b. Yokohama, Honshu Island, Japan, Mar. 9, 1922; came to U.S., 1924; s. Harry William and Alice (Mateer) P.; m. Doris Jane Howe, Apr. 27, 1946; children: Robert, Christine Fitzpatrick, Janet McMillan. BA in Chemistry and Botany, Colgate U., 1946; postgrad., Princeton U., 1949-50, U. Del., 1982-83. Lic. capt. U.S. inland waters U.S. Coast Guard. Researcher, developer ESSO Standard Oil Co., Bayway, N.J., 1946-51; various positions Enjay Chem. Co., N.Y.C., 1951-65; coord. world-wide chem. Gulf Oil Corp., Pitts., 1965-67; gen. mktg. mgr. Gulf Oil-Eastern Hemisphere, London, 1967-71; corp. v.p. chem. mktg., corp. v.p. mktg. Gulf Oil Can. Ltd., Montreal, Que., Can., 1971-77; CEO chems. divsn., corp. v.p. Golfoil Can., Quebec, Can., 1971-77; chief operating officer Corpus Christi Chem. Co., Wilmington, Del., 1971—; mng. dir. Food Machinery & Chem. Corp. Internat. Chems., Phila., 1979-80; internat. cons. Bozman, Md., 1980—. Patentee in field. Leader Young Christians Assn., 1st Bapt. Ch., Somerville, N.J., 1948-53; lay speaker, mem. adminstrn. bd. Riverview Charge, United Meth. Ch.; chaplain Mil. Order Purple Heart. With USMC, 1942-46, PTO. Decorated Purple Heart, two battle stars. Fellow Am. Inst. Chemists; mem. Am. Chem. Soc. (emeritus). Avocations: writing, philosophy, religion. Home and Office: Quakerneck Rd Mulberry Pt Bozman MD 21612

PETERSON, HOLGER MARTIN, electrical engineer; b. Colman, S.D., Nov. 16, 1912; s. Peter and Karen Marie (Jensen) P.; m. Myrtle Berthine Teigen, Mar. 26, 1939; children: Robert Kent, Janice Marie (Peterson) Priddy. BS in Elec. Engring., S.D. State U., 1933. Chief draftsman bridge dept. S.D. Highway Commn., Pierre, 1935-39; draftsman U.S. Army Corps of Engrs., Tulsa, Okla., 1939-40; tech. instr. Army Air Corps, Rantoul, Ill., 1940-41; supr. Plans & Programming Mgr. USAF Tech. Tng. Command, Biloxi, Miss., 1941-50, Sheppard AFB, Tex., 1950-70; program mgr. Individual Devel. Ctr., Wichita Falls, 1970-72, cons., 1972-80; owner, mgr. Creative Leaded Glass Co., 1981-92. Mem. Commn. on Disability, 1990-93. Editor (tech. manuals, extension courses) Aircraft Maintenance, 1941-42, 1968-70. Recipient Exceptional Civilian Svc. award USAF, 1961. Mem. Elks Lutheran. Avocations: audio equipment, stained glass art, fishing. Home and Office: 4600 Taft Blvd # 315 Wichita Falls TX 76308-4935

PETERSON, HOWARD COOPER, lawyer, accountant; b. Decatur, Ill., Dec. 12, 1939; s. Howard and Lorraine (Cooper) P. BEE, Ill., 1963; MEE, San Diego Sate Coll., 1967; MBA, Columbia U., 1969; JD, Calif. Western Sch. Law, 1983; LLM in Taxation, NYU, 1985. Bar: Calif.; CFP; CPA, Tex.; registered profl. engr., Calif.; cert. neuro-linguistic profl. Elec. engr. Convair divsn. Gen. Dynamics Corp., San Diego, 1963-67, sr. electronics engr., 1967-68; v.p., dirl Equity Programs Corp., 1973-83; gen. ptrn. Costumes Characters & Classics Co., 1979-86; pres., dir. Coastal Properties Trust, 1979-89, Juno Securities, Inc., 1983-96, Juno Real Estate Inc., 1974—, Juno Fin. Svcs., Inc., 1999—, Scripps Mortgage Corp., 1987-90, Juno Transport Inc., 1988-89. CFO, dir. Imperial Screens of San Diego, 1977-96, Heritage Transp. Mgmt. Inc., 1989-91, A.S.A.P. Ins. Svcs. Inc., 1983-85. Mem.: ABA, Am. Assn. Atty.-CPAs, Assn. Enrolled Agts., Internat. Assn. Fin. Planning, Interam. Bar Assn.

PETERSON, JAMES KENNETH, manufacturing company executive; b. Sioux City, Iowa, Oct. 17, 1934; s. David Winfield and Beulah Lillian (Johnson) P.; m. Nanette Kay Olin, Feb. 2, 1957; children: Kimberly, Kristin, David. BA in Econs, Mich. State U., 1956. R & D engr. Reynolds Metals Co., Richmond, Va., 1957-59, sales rep., 1959-61, dist. sales mgr., 1961-65, regional sales mgr., 1965-67, asst. to exec. v.p., 1968, mktg. dir., 1969-71; dir. nat. account sales The Continental Group, Stamford, Conn., 1971, gen. mgr. sales, 1972-73, div. gen. mgr., 1974-78, v.p., corp. officer, 1974-80, v.p., gen. mgr. global bus. devel., 1979; pres., COO, Ludlow Corp., Needham, Mass., 1980-82, also bd. dirs.; pres., CEO, dir. Graphic Packaging Corp., Paoli, Pa., 1982-89; pres., CEO, Peterson Group, Easton, Md., 1989—. Bd. dirs. Jenard Co., Graphic Packaging Corp., South Chester Tube Co.; mem. Pricision Strip, Inc. Served to 1st lt. U.S. Army, 1957. Mem. Merion Golf Club, Merion Cricket Club, Talbot Country Club. Home: 27779 Waverly Rd Easton MD 21601-8121

PETERSON, JAMES ROBERT, engineering psychologist; b. St. Paul, Apr. 16, 1932; s. Palmer Elliot and Helen Evelyn (Carlson) P.; m. Marianna J. Stockvig, June 26, 1954; 1 child, Anne Christine. BA in Psychology cum laude, U. Minn., 1954, MA in Exptl. Psychology, 1958; PhD in Engring. Psychology, U. Mich., 1965. Devel. engr. Honeywell Inc., 1961-65, sr. devel. engr., 1965-67, staff engr., 1967-90, sr. project staff engr., 1990-93, retired, 1993. Honeywell sponsor rep. Shuttle Student Involvement Program, 1982, 84. Contbr. articles to profl. jours. With USMC, 1954-57, USMCR, 1957-62. Mem. Human Factors and Ergonomics Soc. (life), Air & Space Mus. (charter), Smithsonian Inst., Masons. Achievements include invention of Apollo translation hand controller; participation in development work in all U.S. Manned Space Programs (Mercury, Gemini, Apollo, Lunar Excursion Module, Manned Orbiting Laboratory, Space Shuttle and Space Sta.) as member/manager of associated human factors groups. Home: 3303 San Gabriel St Clearwater FL 33759-3341 E-mail: bpeteputt@aol.com.

PETERSON, JAMES ROBERT, retired writing instrument manufacturing executive; b. Momence, Ill., Oct. 28, 1927; s. Clyde and Pearl (Deliere) P.; m. Betty Windham, May 12, 1949; children: Richard James, Lynn Peterson Anderson, Susan Peterson Hanske, John Windham. Student, St. Thomas Coll., 1945, Iowa State U., 1945-46, U. Colo., 1946, Northwestern U., 1946; BS in Mktg. cum laude, U. Ill., 1952; grad. exec. MBA program, Stanford U., 1967. With Pillsbury Co., Mpls., 1952-76, brand mgr. grocery products, 1953-57, brand supr. flour, 1957-61, dir. mktg., 1961-66, v.p. mktg., 1966-68; v.p., gen. mgr. Grocery Products Co., 1968-71, group v.p. consumer cos., 1971-73, pres., dir., 1973-76; exec. v.p., dir. R.J. Reynolds Industries, Inc., Winston-Salem, N.C., 1976-82; pres., chief exec. officer, dir. Parker Pen Co., Janesville, Wis., 1982-85. Dir. Dun & Bradstreet Corp., N.Y.C., 1977-98, Waste Mgmt., Inc., Oak Brook, Ill., 1980-98, IMS. Health, Inc., Westport, Conn., 1996-98. Former mem. bd. dirs. Boy Scouts Am., past pres. Viking coun.; mem. bd. regents St. Olaf Coll., 1974-91. Lt. USN, 1945-50. Recipient Bronze Tablet award U. Ill. Mem. Pilgrims of U.S., Tequesta Country Club, Bear Path Golf & Country Club, Bodega Harbour Golf, Jupiter Hills Club, Beta Gamma Sigma. Methodist. Address: 19750 Beach Rd Unit 505 Tequesta FL 33469-2863 E-mail: jrsonpeter@aol.com.

PETERSON, JAN ERIC, lawyer; b. Seattle, Apr. 28, 1944; s. Theodore Dare and Dorothy Elizabeth (Spofford) P.; children: Nels Andrew, Anne Elizabeth; m. Marguerite Victoria Caggiano, Mar. 31, 1984. AB in History, Stanford U., 1966; JD, U. Wash., 1969. Bar: Wash. 1969, U.S. Dist. Ct. (we. and ea. dists.) Wash. 1970, U.S. Ct. Appeals (9th cir.) 1970. Gen. counsel ACLU, Seattle, 1969-71; assoc. Daniel F. Sullivan, 1972-73; sr. ptnr. Peterson, Young, Putra, Fletcher, Zeder, Massong & Knopp, 1973—. Drafter (state statute) Tap Water Regulation Act, 1983. Fellow Am. Coll. Trial Lawyers; mem. ABA (editor assoc. 1976-78), Damages Attys. Round Table (founding, pres. 1997-98), ATLA (del. 1985-86), Wash. State Trial Lawyers Assn. (bd. 1973-85, pres. 1982-83, Trial Lawyer of Yr. 1999), Wash. State Bar Assn. (jud. selection 1985-87, bd. govs. 1992-95, pres. 2000-01), Am. Bd. Trial Adv. (diplomate, pres. Wash. chpt. 1990), ACLU, Bd. Legal Found. Wash. Democrat. Avocations: piano, baseball, basketball, golf. Office: Peterson Young Putra Fletcher Zeder Massong & Knopp 1501 4th Ave Ste 2800 Seattle WA 98101-1609 E-mail: janeric@pypfirm.com.

PETERSON, JANET ANNE, pharmaceutical executive; b. Jersy City, June 15, 1961; d. Arthur Conrad and Gail Lois (Flury) P.; children: Matthew, Thomas, Andrew. BS cum laude, U. Mass., 1983; MS, Rutgers U., 1988, PhD, 1992. Lab. technician N.Y. Blood Ctr., N.Y.C., 1984-85; adj. prof. Kean Coll., Union, N.J., 1990-91; assoc. med. dir. Roberts Pharmaceutical, Eatontown, NJ, 1992-93; assoc. dir. med. affairs Enzon, Inc., Piscataway, N.J., 1993-94; assoc. dir. safety evaluation and epidemiology Pfizer Inc., N.Y.C., 1994-96; asst. dir. sci. affairs Pfizer Internat. Inc., 1996-97; clin. dir. Pfizer Pharm. Group, 1998-99; global dir. infectious disease Pharmacia Corp., Peapack, NJ, 1999—2001; dir. clin. rsch. Pliva d.d, Zabreb, Croatia, 2001—. Recipient Nat. Rsch. Svc. award, NIH, 1986-91. Roman Catholic. Avocations: reading, travel, foster parenting. Home: 55 Portland Rd Highlands NJ 07732-1910 Office: Pliva d.d Zagrebi Croatia E-mail: janetpeters5@comcast.net.

PETERSON, JOHN E. congressman; b. Titusville, Pa., Dec. 25, 1938; s. Axel Benjamin and Mary Elizabeth (Baker) P.; m. Saundra June Watson, 1968; children: Richard D., Florence Waychoff. Student, Pa. State U. Owner retail food market, Pleasantville, Pa., 1958-84; mem. Pa. Ho. of Reps., 1977-84, Pa. State Senate, 1984-96, U.S. Congress from 5th Pa. dist., 1997—; mem. appropriations com., resources com. Former mem. nat. adv. coun. U.S. Small Bus. Adminstrn.; mem. Pub. Health and Welfare Com., now chmn.;active PENNVEST Bd., Pa. Hardwoods Devel. Coun.; sec. Ctr. Rural Pa. Former dist. asst. U.S. Congressman Albert Johnson; mem. regional adv. coum. Pitts. Cancer Inst.; former lay leader Pleasantville United Meth. Ch., former chmn. pastoral parish com.; bd. advisors Foxview Manor, Inc.; mem. adv. bd. U. Pitts., Titusville and Bradford campuses; mem. adv. coun. Ind. U. of Pa. Culinary Sch.; active Pa. Trauma Ctr. Found., Venango County Indsl. Bd. Served U.S. Army. Recipient John Heinz Meml. award; Presdl. Distinction medal U. Pitts. at Bradford, Recognition award Pa. Acad. Family Physicians, Appreciation award, Better Life award Pa Health Care Assn., Guardian of Small Bus. award Nat. Fedn. Ind. Bus., Spl. Achievement award Pa. Bar Assn., Elected Officials award Pa. Home Health Assn., 1994; named Senator of Yr., Pa. Jewish Coalition, Legislator of Yr., Pa. Assn. County Human Svc. Adminstrs., 1993, Pa. Home Health Care Assn., 1993. Mem. Titusville Area C. of C. (past pres.), Pleasantville Parent-Tchr. Assn. (past pres.), Lions. Republican. Methodist. Home: PO Box 295 248 N Main St Pleasantville PA 16341-9776 Office: US Ho of Reps 307 Cannon Ho Office Bldg Washington DC 20515-0001*

PETERSON, JOHN EDGAR, JR. retired nursing home executive and agricultural executive, textile executive; b. Radford, Va., Mar. 26, 1916; s. John Edgar and Mary Elizabeth (Dolan) P.; m. Mary Jane Crowell, May 8, 1943; children: John Edgar III, Mary Stuart Peterson Henegar, William Early. BSBA, Va. Poly. Inst., 1936. CPA, N.Y., Ga., Tenn., N.C.; cert. internal auditor. Jr. auditor Arthur Andersen & Co., N.Y.C. and Atlanta, 1937-39, sr. auditor, 1939-44; sec.-treas. Magnet Cove Barium Corp., Houston, also Jamestown, Tenn., 1944-46; asst. to contr. Burlington Industries, Inc., Greensboro, N.C., 1946-47; sec.-treas., dir. Burlington Mills Internat. Corp., 1947-48, co-divsn. mgr., 1948-49, divsn. contr., 1949-56, area contr., 1956-58, asst. corp. contr., 1958-70, asst. corp. v.p., from 1970, now ret. Chmn. bd. dirs., pres. Lane Processing, Inc., 1985-86, now ret.; chmn. bd. trustees The Lane Processing Trust, 1985-96, now ret.; bd. dirs., sec.-treas. Everetts Lake Corp., 1958—; examiner, trustee U.S. Bankruptcy Ct., 1982-87; chmn. bd. trustees The Evergreens, Inc., 1980-99, now ret.; former commr. Greensboro Housing Authority. Mem. adv. coun. Pamplin Coll. Bus., Va. Poly. Inst., 1969-99/ Mem. AICPA, N.C. Soc. CPAs, Inst. Internal Auditors, Starmount Forest Country Club, Off Island Gun Club, Three Lake Club Inc. (bd. dirs.), Brush Creek Hunting Club (bd. dirs.), Tar Heel State Sr. Golf Assn., Masons. Presbyterian. Home: 1001 Kemp Rd W Greensboro NC 27410-4517 E-mail: mjjpete@earthlink.net.

PETERSON, JOHN WILLARD, composer, music publisher; b. Lindsborg, Kans., Nov. 1, 1921; s. Peter Ephraim and Adlina Mary (Nelson) P.; m. Marie Alta Addis (Feb. 11, 1944); children: Sandra Lynn Peterson Catzere, Candace Kay Peterson Strader, Pamela Lee Peterson Cruse. Student, Moody Bible Inst., 1947-48; MusB, Am. Conservatory Music, 1952; MusD (hon.), John Brown U., 1967; DD (hon.), West Bapt. Sem., 1970; DFA (hon.), Grand Canyon U., 1979. Radio broadcaster Sta. WMBI, Chgo., 1950-55; editor in chief, pres. Singspiration, Inc., Grand Rapids, Mich., 1955-71, exec. composer Carefree, Ariz., 1977-83; pres. Good Life Prodns., Scottsdale, 1977-83, John W. Peterson Music Co., Scottsdale, 1983-88. Bd. dirs. Gospel Films, Inc., Muskegon, Mich. Co-author: (autobiography) The Miracle Goes On, 1976; composer works include numerous cantatas, musicals, gospel songs, hymns and anthems. 1st lt. USAAF 1942-45, CBI. Decorated Air medal; recipient Sacred Music award Nat. Evang. Film Found., 1966, Music Achievement award Christian Artists, 1985; Honor Cert. Freedoms Found., 1975; winner Internat. Gospel Composition of Yr., Soc. European Stage, Authors and Composers, 1986, Ray DeVries Ch. Music award, 1996; inductee Gospel Music Hall of Fame, 1986. Mem. ASCAP, Hump Pilots Assn. Home: 11668 N 80th Pl Scottsdale AZ 85260-5650

PETERSON, JULIE ANN, media relations executive, consultant; b. Sauk Centre, Minn., June 10, 1962; d. David Alexander and Eleanor (LeMoyne) P.; m. Michael John McBrairty, May 11, 1985 (div. Nov. 1995); children: Nicholas Jon, Mitchell Alan, Alexander Michael. BA, Ind. U., 1984, MBA, 1989. Asst. to dir. comms. Sch. Bus. Ind. U., Bloomington, 1984-86, writer, media liaison, 1986-89, mng. editor News Bur., 1989-94; dir. news and info. svcs. U. Mich., Ann Arbor, 1994-2000, assoc. vice pres. media rels. and pub. affairs, 2000—. Treas., mem. com. Cub Scout Pack 17, Boy Scouts Am., Ann Arbor, 1999—; treas., bd. dirs. Forestbrooke Athletic Club, Ann Arbor, 1996—; mem. adv. coun. Planned Parenthood, Bloomington, 1992-93. Avocation: vocal and instrumental musical performance. Home: 2631 Lillian Rd Ann Arbor MI 48104-5317 Office: U Mich 2026 Fleming Adminstrn Bldg Ann Arbor MI 48109-1340

PETERSON, KENNETH ALLEN, SR. superintendent of schools; b. Hammond, Ind., Jan. 20, 1939; s. Chester E. and Bertha (Hornby) P.; B.Ed. cum laude, Chgo. State U., 1963; M.S., Purdue U., 1970; NSF grantee U. Iowa, 1964-65; postgrad. U. Ill., 1977-81; Vanderbilt U.; m. Marilyn M. Musson, Jan. 3, 1961; children: Kimberly, Kari, Kenneth Allen Jr. Tchr., Markham (Ill.) Sch. Dist. 144, 1961-67; prin. Brookwood Sch., Glenwood (Ill.) Sch. Dist. 1967, 1967-77, prin. Hickory Bend Sch., 1977-78, dir. spl. edn., 1978-80, asst. supt. schs., 1981-83, ret supt schs., 1983-94; prof. Govs. State U., 1994—, now emeritus superintendent of schools; mem. No. Ill. Planning Commn. for Gifted Edn. Chmn. Steger (Ill.) Bicentennial Commn., 1976; vice chmn. Ashkum dist. Boy Scouts Am., 1981-83, lodge advisor, sect. advisor, exec. bd., area advisor Vigil honor mem. Order of Arrow Calumet council Boy Scouts Am.; v.p. Calumet Coun. Boy Scouts of Am., 1989—; program com. South Cook County council Girl Scouts U.S.A., 1971-73, 80-81, mem. fin. com., 1981-86 , also bd. dirs., nat. del.; mem. Steger Community Devel. Commn. Recipient Order of Arrow Service nat. founders award, Silver Beaver award, Dist. award of merit Boy Scouts Am., Disting. Svc. award Nat. Order of Arrow. Mem. ASCD, Coun. Exceptional Children, P.T.A. (life), Am. Assn. Sch. Adminstrs., Kappa Delta Pi. Republican. Lutheran. Home: 3208 Phillips Ave Steger IL 60475-1161 Office: Coll of Edn Governors State Univ University Park IL 60466

PETERSON, KENT WRIGHT, physician; b. Portsmouth, Va., Apr. 16, 1943; s. Gerald Milton and Julia Elizabeth (Hoover) P.; children: Liesl Lynn, Owen Sonne. BA, U. N.C., Chapel Hill, 1964; MD, U. Pa., 1968. Diplomate Am. Bd. Preventive Medicine, Am. Bd. Occupl. Medicine. Intern U. Wis., 1968-69, resident, 1970-71; Robert Wood Johnson clin. scholar George Washington U., 1975-77; family physician E. Madison Clinic, Madison, Wis., 1969; chief med. officer policy devel. U.S. Cost of Living Council, Washington, 1973-74; assoc. dir. Assn. Univ. Programs in Health Adminstrn., 1974-77; exec. v.p. Am. Coll. Preventive Medicine, 1977-81; corp. mgr. preventive and environ. medicine IBM Corp., White Plains, N.Y., 1981-84; corp. med. dir. Am. Standard, N.Y.C., 1984-86; pres. Occupational Health Strategies, Charlottesville, Va., 1984—. Clin. asst. prof. Georgetown U. Sch. Medicine, 1979-85; clin. assoc. prof. NYU dept. environ. medicine, 1985—; rep. to Coun. Med. Specialty Socs., 1980-86; mem. Accreditation Coun. for Continuing Med. Edn., 1981-86; treas. Med. Rev. Officer Cert. Coun., 1992—; v.p. Am. Bd. Ind. Med. Examiners, 1995-98; sr. v.p. Inst. for Health and Productivity Mgmt., 1997-2002. Author of 8 books including Handbook of Occupational Health Informatics, 11th edit., 2000, SPM Handbook of Health Assessment Tools, 4th edit., 1999; contbr. numerous articles to profl. jours. and chpts. in books. Pres. Children of the Americas Found., 1979-84; treas. Alliance for Transforming the Lives of Children, 2000—; bd. dirs., Conserve Va., 1996—. Served to maj. M.C. U.S. Army, 1971-73. Fellow Am. Coll. Preventive Medicine, Am. Coll. Occupl. and Environ. medicine (pres. 1996-97); mem. AMA, APHA, Assn. Tchrs. Preventive Medicine, N.Y. Acad. Medicine, Metadocs (gen. sec. 1984—), Ramazzini Soc., Soc. Prospective Medicine (officer) World Future Soc., Coun. for Liveable World, Va. Occupl. Medicine Assn. (pres. 1988-90). Home: 1059 Blackburn Blf Charlottesville VA 22901-0609 Office: Occupational Health Strategies Inc 901 Preston Ave Ste 400 Charlottesville VA 22903-4491 E-mail: kent@healthyself.org.

PETERSON, KEVIN BRUCE, newspaper editor, publishing executive; b. Kitchener, Ont., Can., Feb. 11, 1948; s. Bruce Russell and Marguerite Elizabeth (Hammond) P.; m. Constance Maureen Bailey, Feb. 11, 1975 (dec. May 1975); m. Sheila Helen O'Brien, Jan. 9, 1981 BA, U. Calgary, Alta., Can., 1968. Chief bur. Calgary Herald, 1972-75, city editor, 1976-77, news editor, 1977-78, bus. editor, 1978, mng. editor, 1978-86, editor, asst. pub., 1986-87, gen. mgr., 1987-88, pub., 1989-96; sr. counsel GPC Comms., 1999—. Pres. Canadian Univ. Press, Ottawa, Ont., Can., 1968-69; dir. New Directions for News. Harry Brittain Meml. fellow Commonwealth Press Union, London, 1979 Mem. Can. Mng. Editors (bd. dirs. 1983-87), Am. Soc. Newspaper Editors, Horsemen's Benevolent and Protective Assn., Alta. Legis. Press Gallery Assn. (v.p. 1971-76), Can. Daily Newspaper Assn. (bd. dirs. 1990-96, vice chmn. , treas 1992, chmn. 1993-96), Alta. Theatre Projects (bd. dirs. 1996—, v.p. 1998—), Calgary Ctr. for Non-Profit Mgmt. (bd. dirs. 1998—), Calgary Petroleum Club, Ranchmen's Club, 100-t-1 Club, (Arcadia, Calif.) Avocations: thoroughbred horse racing; art collecting.

PETERSON, LARRY RICHARD, history educator; b. Denver, May 25, 1947; s. Viola Mercedes Peterson; m. Gail Dorothy Beaton, Apr. 26, 1968 (dec. July 1998); children: Geoffrey, Erik; m. Mary Caroline Struck, Nov. 6, 2000. BA in English, Moorhead (Minn.) State Coll., 1970; MA in Am. Studies,

U. Minn., 1975, PhD in Am. Studies, 1978. Asst. prof. history N.D. State U., Fargo, 1978-83, assoc. prof. history, 1983-94, chair dept. history, 1989—, prof., 1994—. Author: Ignatius Donnelly: A Psychohistorical Study in Moral Development Psychology, 1982; contbr. articles to scholarly jours. Mem. steering com. Equality N.D., Fargo, 1999; advisor Ten Percent Soc., Fargo, 1992—. Recipient Outstanding Svc. award Coll. Humanities and Social Scis./N.D. State U., 1992, Sarah Nelson Friend award FargoMoorhead PFLAG, 1998; Fulbright grantee, 1982-83;Leslie Hewes award Great Plains Rsch., 1999. Mem. Soc. Of Friends. Office: ND State U Minard Hall Fargo ND 58105-5075 E-mail: Larry.R.Peterson@ndsu.nodak.edu.

PETERSON, LEROY, retired secondary education educator; b. Fairfield, Ala., Feb. 15, 1930; s. Leroy and Ludie Pearl (Henderson) P.; m. Theresa Petite, Apr. 6, 1968 (div. Oct. 1984); children: Leroy III, Monica Teresa; m. Ruby Willodine Hopkins, July 21, 1985 (div. Mar. 1996). Cert. in piano, Bavarian State Acad., Wuerzburg, Fed. Republic Germany, 1954; BS in Music Edn., Miami U., Oxford, Ohio, 1957. Life credential music tchr., Calif. Tchr. music Cleve. Pub. Schs., 1957-62, L.A. Unified Schs., 1963-94; retired, 1994. Song composer. With U.S. Army, 1952-54. Mem. Alpha Phi Alpha, Phi Mu Alpha Sinfonia. Republican. Avocations: amateur concert pianist, composing, photography. Home: 13005 Spelman Dr Victorville CA 92392-7239 E-mail: nosretep@bigplanet.com.

PETERSON, LESLIE ERNEST, bishop; b. Noranda, Que., Can., Nov. 4, 1928; s. Ernest Victor and Blanche (Marsh) P.; m. Yvonne Hazel Lawton, July 16, 1953; children— Shauna Peterson Van Hoof, Tom, Jennifer Peterson Glage, Kathryn Peterson Scott, Jonathan BA, U. Western Ont., London, Ont., Can., 1952; L.T.H., Huron Coll., London, Ont., Can., 1954, D.D. (hon.), 1984; tchr.'s cert., North Bay Tchrs. Coll., Ont., 1970. Ordained to ministry Anglican Ch., 1954. Priest Diocese of Algoma, Coniston, Ont., 1954-58, priest Elliot Lake, 1959-63, rural dean, 1961-63, priest North Bay, 1963-78, Parry Sound, Ont., 1978-83, archdeacon, 1980-83, bishop Sault Ste. Marie, 1983-94; tchr. North Bay Elem. Sch., 1970-78; ret., 1994. Avocations: canoeing, woodworking, gardening. Address: 615 Santa Monica Rd London ON Canada N6H 3W2

PETERSON, LESLIE RAYMOND, barrister; b. Viking, Alta., Can., Oct. 6, 1923; s. Herman S. and Margaret (Karen) P.; m. Agnes Rose Hine, June 24, 1950; children: Raymond Erik, Karen Isabelle. Student, Camrose Luth. Coll., Alta., McGill. U., Can., London U., Eng.; LLB, U. B.C., Can., 1949; LLD, Simon Fraser U., Can., 1965, U. B.C., 1993; EdD, Notre Dame U., Nelson, Can., 1966; hon. diploma tech., B.C. Inst. Tech., 1994. Bar: B.C. 1949; called to Queens Counsel, 1960. Pvt. practice barrister, Vancouver, B.C., 1949-52; with Peterson & Anderson, 1952; then with Boughton & Co. (now Boughton Peterson Yang Anderson).; mem. B.C. Legislature for Vancouver Centre, 1956-63, Vancouver-Little Mountain, 1966; min. of edn., 1956-68; min. of labour, 1960-71; atty. gen., 1968-72; bd. govs. U. B.C., Vancouver, 1979-83, chancellor, 1987-93. Bd. dirs. Can. Found. Econ. Edn., Inst. Corp. Dirs. Can., West Vancouver Found., Inst. for Pacific Ocean Sci. and Tech., Peterson Bus. Consultants Inc.; trustee Peter Wall Inst. for Advanced Studies; chmn. U. B.C. Found., 1990—96. Bd. dirs. Portland unit Shriners Hosp. for Crippled Children, 1994-96; past bd. dirs. Western Soc. of Rehab., YMCA, Victoria B.C.; past pres. Twenty Club; hon. mem. Vancouver Jr. C. of C.; former v.p. Normanna Old People's Home; founding mem. Convocation, Simon Fraser U. and U. Victoria; hon. dep. French Nat. Assembly, Paris; hon. commr. labor State of Okla.; gov. Downtown Vancouver Assn. With Can. Army, 1942-46, ETO. Recipient Disting. Alumnus award Camrose Luth. Coll., 1980. Fellow: Royal Soc. Arts; mem.: Internat. Assn. Govt. Labour Ofcls. (chmn. standing com., Can. mins. of edn. 1965—66), Law Soc. B.C., Vancouver Bar Assn., Wesbrook Soc. of U. B.C. (chmn. 1987), Union Club (Victoria), Terminal City Club (pres. 1991—), Scandinavian Bus. Men's Club (past pres.), Hazelmere Golf and Tennis Club (bd. dirs.), Venerable Order of Saint John (comdr.), Order of B.C., Freemason (potentate Gizeh Temple Shrine 1988), Order of St. Lazarus (knight comdr.). Avocations: skiing, golf, fishing, hunting. Home: 814 Highland West Vancouver BC Canada V7S 2G5 Office: Boughton Peterson Yang Anderson 595 Burrard St Ste 1000 Ste 2500 Vancouver BC Canada V7X 1S8 Fax: 604-693-5317. E-mail: lpeterson@bpya.com.

PETERSON, LINDA H. English language and literature educator; b. Saginaw, Mich., Oct. 11, 1948; BA in Lit. summa cum laude, Wheaton Coll., 1969; MA in English, U. R.I., 1973; PhD in English, Brown U., 1978. From lectr. to assoc. prof. Yale U., New Haven, 1977-92, prof., 1992—, dir. undergrad. studies English, 1990-94, chair, 1994-2000, Niel Gray Jr. prof. of English, 2002—. Dir. Bass writing program Yale Coll., 1979-89, 90—; mem. various departmental and univ. coms. Yale U., 1977—; presenter in field. Author: Victorian Autobiography: The Tradition of Self-Interpretation, 1986, Traditions of Victorian Women's Autobiography: The Poetics and Politics of Life Writing, 1999; co-author: Writing Prose, 1989, A Struggle for Fame: Victorian Women Artists and Authors, 1994; co-editor: Wuthering Heights: A Case Study in Contemporary Criticism, 1992, The Norton Reader, 10th edit., 2000, Instructor's Guide to the Norton Reader, 2000; mem. editl. bd. Writing Program Adminstrn., 1983-85, Coll. Composition and Comm., 1986-88, Auto/Biography Studies, 1990—;, Victorian Poetry, 2002—; contbr. articles to profl. jours. Resident fellow Branford Coll., 1979-87, Mellon fellow Whitney Humanities Ctr., 1984-85, fellow NEH, 1989-90, fellow Harry Ransom Humanities Rsch. Ctr., U. Tex., 1997; life fellow Clare Hall, Cambridge, Eng., 1998—. Mem. MLA (del. assembly 1984-86, mem. program com. 1986-89, mem. non-fiction divsn. com. 1988-92, mem. nominating com. 1993-94, mem. teaching of writing divsn. 1993-98), Nat. Writing Program Adminstrs. (mem. cons.-evaluator program 1982-95, mem. exec. bd. 1982-84, 89-90, v.p. 1985-86, pres. 1987-88), Nat. Coun. Tchrs. English (mem. CCCC nominating com. 1985, mem. coll. sect. com. 1987-90). Home: 53 Edgehill Rd New Haven CT 06511-1343 Office: Yale U Dept English PO Box 208302 New Haven CT 06520-8302

PETERSON, LOUIS ROBERT, retired consumer products company executive; b. Racine, Wis., Nov. 11, 1923; s. Edward J. and Effie (Buenning) P.; m. Marian Francis Barber, Nov. 22, 1947; children: Karen Jean, Kathleen Alice, Jill Ann. Student, Utah State Agrl. Coll., U. Wis.-Racine. With Johnson Wax Co., Racine, Wis., 1947—, sales rep., 1970-72, v.p. household sales, 1972-76, exec. v.p. U.S. consumer products, ptnr. in office of the chmn., 1976-80, exec. v.p. internat. consumer products, 1980-86. Past pres., bd. dirs. Racine Area United Way.; bd. dirs. St. Mary's Med. Ctr. With U.S. Army, 1943-46. Mem. Northwestern U. Assocs., Conf. Bd. (internat. coun.), Internat. C. of C. (U.S. coun. internat. bus.), Somerset Club (Racine, Wis.), Pinnacle Peak Country Club (Scottsdale, Ariz.). Republican. Roman Catholic. Home: 10579 N Peninsula Rd Hayward WI 54843-4061

PETERSON, LOWELL, cinematographer; b. L.A., Feb. 1, 1950; s. Lowell Stanley and Catherine Linda (Hess) P.; m. Deanna Rae Terry, Aug. 2, 1981. Student, Yale U., 1968; BA in Theater Arts, UCLA, 1973. Asst. cinematographer, Hollywood, Calif., 1973-83; camera operator, 1983-92; dir. photography, 1992—. Asst. cinematographer various prodns. including Blind Ambition, 1979, Hawaii Five-O, 1979-80, White Shadow, 1980-81, Lou Grant, 1981-82, Two of a Kind, 1982, Remington Steele, 1982-83, Something About Amelia, 1983; camera operator various prodns. including Tourist Trap, 1979, Newhart, 1983, Scarecrow and Mrs. King, 1983-85, Children in the Crossfire, 1984, Stranded, 1986, Knots Landing, 1986-87, 89-92, Like Father Like Son, 1987, Star Trek: The Next Generation, 1987-89, Coupe de Ville, 1990, Show of Force, 1990; dir. photography Knots Landing, 1992-93, Second Chances, 1993-94 (Am. Soc. Cinematographers award nomination), Galaxy Beat, 1994, Hotel Malibu, 1994, Lois and Clark, 1995, The Client, 1995-96, Moloney, 1996-97, Four Corners, 1998, Profiler (Am. Soc. Cinematographers award nomination), 1998-99, Ryan Caulfield, 1999, Bedazzled (2d Unit), 2000, Bubble Boy (2d Unit), 2001, Just Ask My Children, 2001; contbr. articles to Film Comment, 1974, Internat. Photographer, 1984—. Mem. Acad. TV Arts and Scis. (bd. govs. 2001—), Am. Soc. Cinematographers, Soc. Motion Picture and TV Engrs., Internat. Cinematographers Guild, L.A. Music Ctr. Opera League, Friends of UCLA Film Archive, Am. Cinematheque, U.S. Chess Fedn. Home and Office: 11863 Nebraska Ave Los Angeles CA 90025-7400 E-mail: lowell@peterson.net.

PETERSON, M. ROGER, international investment banker, retired manufacturing executive, retired air force officer; b. Chgo., June 7, 1929; s. Milton Albert and LaVergne Geraldine (Andelin) P.; m. Sally Ann Alder, Apr. 25, 1952; children: Bruce Roger, Dale Alder, Drew Alan. BS in Acctg., UCLA, 1955; MS in Mgmt., U. Colo., 1964; grad., Air Command and Staff Coll. Air U., Ala., 1965; grad. Exec. Program for Internat. and Nat. Security, J.F. Kennedy Sch. Govt., Harvard U., 1983. Joined USAF, 1955, advanced through grades to maj. gen., 1981, pilot, 1956-61, mgr. tactical missile site constrn., 1961; air officer comdg. 11th Cadet Squadron, Air Force Cadet Wing USAF Acad., 1961-64; asst. sec. Joint Chiefs of Staff and NSC matters for Hdqrs. Pentagon, 1965-68; transport pilot USAF, Vietnam, 1968, asst. chmn. U.S.-Japan Joint Com., Adminstrn. of Status of Forces Agreement, 1968-73, chief program cost, dir. budget, 1973-76, chief plans, comptroller of Air Force, 1976-78, dir. mgmt. analysis, 1978-79, dir. programs, asst. chief of staff for research and devel., 1979-81; asst. dir. plans, policies and programs Def. Logistics Agy., Alexandria, Va., 1981-82, dep. dir., 1982-83; asst. dep. chief staff for logistics and engring. Hdqrs. USAF, Washington, 1983-84; pres., chief exec. officer advanced tech. factory, 1984-85; strategic planner United Techs. Corp., 1985-88; v.p., chief oper. officer Sikorsky Support Svcs. Inc., 1988-90; exec. asst. to mng. ptnr. O'Connor & Assocs., 1990-92; mng. dir. global ops. and svcs. Swiss Bank Corp., Zurich, 1992-96, chief of staff Chgo., 1996-99, br. mgr. Chgo. N.Am. and S.Am., 1996-99; mng. dir. UBS Warburg Dillon Read (formerly Swiss Bank Corp. N.Am.), NY, 1996-99. Mng. dir. UBS AG, N.Y.C., 1999-2001. Decorated D.S.M., Legion of Merit, Air medal with oak leaf cluster, Joint Service Commendation medal, Air Force Commendation medal with two oak leaf clusters Mem. Air Force Assn., Beta Gamma Sigma, Sigma Iota Epsilon Presbyterian. Achievements include designing and negotiating consolidation of U.S. Air Force bases in Tokyo, 1970-73; negotiating mil. and civil aviation agreement for return of Okinawa to Japan; created global bus. mgmt. system for Swiss Bank Corp. Home: 1602 Deerpath Rd Dothan AL 36303-2173 Office: UBS Warburg c/o Jan Galayda 141 W Jackson Blvd Chicago IL 60604-2992 *Always with honor.*

PETERSON, MARIA CAROLINE, retired telecommunications executive; b. Hackensack, N.J., July 18, 1950; d. Carmine and Rose (Pisano) Zazzaro; m. John Peterson, May 5, 1984; children: Damon, Jessica. Grad. high sch., Orange, N.J. Phone ctr. mgr. AT&T, Parsippany, N.J.; bus. performance mgr., asst. staff mgr. phone ctr. support Lucent Techs., sr. fin. mgr. Mem. NAFE. Home: 47 Curtis Ct Kendall Park NJ 08824-1532 E-mail: jbmc505@att.net.

PETERSON, MARJORIE, mayor; b. Chisholm, Minn., Aug. 16, 1924; d. Martin and Catherine Mihelich Champa; m. Andrew Levchak, July 6, 1946 (dec. Mar. 2, 1975); children: Carol, Andrea, Richard, Lisbeth; m. Walter C. Peterson, Sept. 25, 1976. Bookkeeper Ford Sales & Svc., Chisholm, Minn.; dental asst. Office of Dr. J.E. Hoffman, 1960—65; podiatrist asst. Office of Dr. Larson, Hibbing, 1967; divsn. sec. Fin. Programs, 1967—74; mem. city coun. City of Chisholm, 1977—85, ofcl., 1989—95, mayor, 1996—98. Mem. Pub. Utilities Bd., Chisholm. Pres. Range Assn. Sch. and City, Chisholm; chmn. Chisholm-Hibbing Airport Authority, Hibbing, 1991—2001; v.p. bd. dirs. Mus. Mining, 2002; mem. Friends of Libr.; bd. dirs. League Minn. Cities, St. Paul, 1984. Recipient C.C. Ludwig award, League Minn. Cities, 1984, Silver award, World of Poetry, 1990, Golden Poet award, 1998, Famous Poet, Famous Poet Soc., 2000. Mem.: Moose. Democrat. Roman Catholic. Avocations: reading, volunteer work, travel, cards. Home: 405 7th St NW Chisholm MN 55719

PETERSON, MARK F. finance educator; b. Phila., May 23, 1953; s. Eugene F. Jr. Peterson, June R. Peterson; m. Susan M. Mende; children: Janice M., Daniel F. BA, Duke U., 1975; PhD, U. Mich., 1975. Prof. mgmt. Tex. Tech. U., Lubbock, 1985—96; Internet Coast Adams prof. mgmt. Fla. Atlantic U., Boca Raton, 1996—. Editor: Handbook of Organizational Culture and Climate, 2001 (Outstanding Academic Title, ALA, 2001). Dir. Boca Raton Orchid Soc., 2001—02. Presbyterian. Office: Fla Atlantic U Coll Bus Dept Mgmt Boca Raton FL 33431

PETERSON, MARTHA, artist; b. Flint, Mich., Sept. 26, 1927; d. Carl J. and Addie Amelia Primm; m. Edward Carlyle Peterson, Sept. 9, 1948; children: Mark, Laura, Michelle. Student, Corcoran Art Sch., Washington, 1966-68, Cath. U., 1966-67, Mich. State U., 1974-76. Art tchr. Forsyth C.C., Winston-Salem, N.C., 1995-96. Bd. dirs. Assoc. Arts of Winston-Salem, 1995-97; pvt. tchr. beginning to advanced students, Winston-Salem, 1995—; co-founder Quincy Valley Art Students League. Mem. Surry County Arts Coun., High Point Arts Coun. Davison County Arts Mus. Unitarian Universalist. Avocations: sewing, gardening, reading, travel.

PETERSON, MARTIN LEE, lawyer; b. Lawton, Okla., Jan. 20, 1956; Student, Tarleton State U., 1974-75; BA, U. Tex., Arlington, 1976; JD, U. Tex., 1979. Bar: Tex. 1979, U.S. Supreme Ct. 1991. Staff atty. McMillan & Lewellen, PC, Stephenville, Tex., 1979-89; pvt. practice, 1990-96; asst. dist. atty. 220th Jud. Dist., 1996—. Contbr. articles to profl. jours. Mem. Asst. Dist. Atty. 220th Jud. Dist., 1996—. Avocations: sailing, stamp collecting. Home and Office: 811 N Lydia Stephenville TX 76401 E-mail: 220da@htcomp.net.

PETERSON, MAX RUPERT, JR. chemist, researcher; b. Sampson County, N.C., May 26, 1945; s. Max Rupert Sr. and Mary Lily (Peterson) P.; m. Bonnie Fay Farrell, July 20, 1969; children: Karen Fay, Kathryn Hope. BS in Chemistry, Campbell U., 1966; PhD in Organic Chemistry, N.C. State U., 1971. Tchg. asst. N.C. State U., Raleigh, 1966-70, vis. assoc. prof., 1980-82; instr. Campbell U., Buies Creek, N.C., 1970-71, asst. prof., 1971-75, assoc. prof., 1975-87; rsch. chemist Research Triangle Inst., Research Triangle Park, 1987—. Cons. Natural Energy Rsch., Inc., Lillington, N.C., 1978-80, Geotech. Engring., Raleigh, 1975. Contbr. numerous articles to profl. jours. and ency., chpt. to book. Named Outstanding Educator in Am., Acad. Am. Educators, 1974-75. Mem. Am. Chem. Soc., Air and Waste Mgmt. Assn., Sigma Xi, Phi Kappa Phi. Baptist. Achievements include research in chemical method development, evaluation and validation studies related to measurement of pollutants in stationary source emissions, ambient air, indoor air, hazardous and other wastes, and commercial formulations. Avocations: genealogy, Civil War history, astronomy. Home: 116 Braintree Ct Cary NC 27513-3117 Office: Research Triangle Inst 3040 Cornwallis Rd PO Box 12194 Durham NC 27709-2194

PETERSON, MERRILL DANIEL, history educator; b. Manhattan, Kans., Mar. 31, 1921; s. William Oscar and Alice Dwinell (Merrill) P.; m. Jean Hymphrey, May 24, 1944 (dec. Nov. 1995); children: Jeffrey Ward, Kent Merrill. Student, Kans. State U., 1939-41; AB, U. Kans., 1943; PhD in History of Am. Civilization, Harvard U., 1950. Teaching fellow Harvard U., Cambridge, Mass., 1948-49; instr., then asst. prof. history Brandeis U., Waltham, 1949-55; asst. prof., bicentennial preceptor Princeton U., N.J., 1955-58; mem. faculty Brandeis U., Waltham, Mass., 1958-62, dean students, 1960-62; Thomas Jefferson Found. prof. U. Va., Charlottesville, 1962-87, prof. emeritus, 1987—, chmn. dept. history, 1966-72, dean faculty Arts and Scis., 1981-85; Mary Ball Washington prof. Am. History University Coll., Dublin, Ireland, 1988-89; vol. Peace Corps, Armenia, 1997. Scholar in residence Bellagio Study Ctr., 1974; faculty Salzburg Seminar in Am. Studies, 1975; Lamar lectr. Mercer U., 1975; Fleming lectr. La. State U., 1980; lectr. at 20 European univs., 40 Am. colls. and univs. Author: The Jefferson Image in the American Mind, 1960 (Bancroft prize, Gold medal Thomas Jefferson Meml. Found.), Major Crises in American History, 2 vols., 1962, Democracy, Liberty and Property: The State Constitutional Convention Debates of the 1820s, 1966, Thomas Jefferson and the New Nation: A Biography, 1970, James Madison: A Biography in His Own Words, 1974, Adams and Jefferson: A Revolutionary Dialogue, 1976, Olive Branch and Sword: The Compromise of 1933, 1982, The Great Triumvirate: Webster, Clay and Calhoun , 1987; editor: Thomas Jefferson: A Historical Profile, 1996, The Portable Thomas Jefferson, 1975, Thomas Jefferson Writings, 1984, Thomas Jefferson: A Reference Biography, 1986, The Virginia Statute for Religious Freedom: Its Evolution and Consequences in American History, 1988, Visitors to Monticello, 1989, Lincoln in American Memory, 1994 (History finalist, Pulitzer prize, PBK Book award U. Va.), Coming of Age with the New Republic, 1938-1950, 1999, The John Brown Legend Revisited, 1859-2000, 2002. Bd. dirs. Thomas Jefferson Found.; chmn. Thomas Jefferson Commemoration Commn., 1993-94. Guggenheim fellow, 1962-63, Ctr. for Advanced Study in Behavioral Scis. fellow, 1968-69, NEH and Nat. Humanities Ctr. fellow, 1980-81; recipient 20th Anniversary award Va. Found. for Humanities, 1994, Nat. First Freedom award First Freedom Coun., 1997. Fellow Am. Acad. Arts and Scis.; mem. Am. Hist. Assn., Am. Antiquarian Soc., Mass. Hist. Soc., Phi Beta Kappa. Home: 250 Pantops Mountain Rd Apt 6 Charlottesville VA 22911-8600

PETERSON, MICHAEL J. music educator; b. Fergus Falls, Minn., Sept. 4, 1955; s. Gordon John and Beverly Jane Peterson; m. Lisa Marie Hoehn, Aug. 18, 1984; children: Alicia, Tamara, Todd. BA Music, Bemidji State Univ., Bemidji, MN, 1977. Educator Okabena Pub. Schools, Okabena, Minn., 1977—78, Fulda Pub. Schools, 1978. Mem.: Minn. State H.S. League Region IIIA (exec. com. 1991—95), Fulda Edn. Assn. (head negotiator 1988), Fulda Edn. Assn. (pres. 1987—88), Minn. Band Directors Assn., NEA, MEA, MENC, Minn. Music Edn. Assn., bd. of dirs., band v.p., 1989-1991, Phi Beta Mu, Nat. Bandmasters Frat. Achievements include Band has won over 100 parade and marching band competitions in the past 23 years. Avocations: men's quartet singing, golfing, golfing, golfing, golfing. Home: 410 Baltimore Ave Fulda MN 56131-9508 Office Fax: 507-425-2514.

PETERSON, MICHAEL R. music company executive; b. Des Moines, June 23, 1958; s. Robert Dean and Mildred Catherine Peterson. BMus Edn., Drake U., 1980; MMus, Northwestern U., 1981. Dir. bands Hamilton (Ill.) Pub. Sch., 1981—84, Ottawa Twp. (Ill.) H.S., 1984—87, Osage (Iowa) H.S., 1987—92, Oconomowoc (Wis.) H.S., 1992—2000; nat. mktg. dir. Music Celebrations Internat., Tempe, Ariz., 2000—. Mem. Nat. Bd. Profl. Tchg. Stds., Washington, 1998—2000; mem. task force on publs. Music Educators Nat. Conf., Washington, 1999. Contbr. articles to profl. jours. Mem. coun. Martin Luther Ch., Oconomowoc, 1998—2000. Recipient citation of excellence, Nat. Band Assn., 1998. Mem.: Am. Sch. Band Dirs. Assn. (bd. dirs. 1993—99, pres. 1996—97, author, editor Curriculum Guide 1998, Stanbury award 1989). Republican. Lutheran. Avocations: hiking, travel, music, reading. Home: 17415 N 1st Ave Phoenix AZ 85023 Office: Music Celebrations Internat 1440 S Priest Dr Ste 102 Tempe AZ 85281 Office Fax: 480-894-5137. E-mail: Michael@musiccelebrations.com.

PETERSON, NAD A. lawyer, retired corporate executive; b. Mt. Pleasant, Utah, 1926; m. Martha Peterson, 1948; children: Anne Carroll (Mrs. Stanford P. Darger, Jr.), Christian, Elizabeth (Mrs. Henry G. Ingersoll), Robert and Lane (twins). AB, George Washington U., 1950, JD, 1953. Bar: D.C. 1953, Calif. 1960, U.S. Supreme Ct. 1958. Law practice, Washington, 1953-60; sec., asst. gen. counsel Dart Industries, Los Angeles, 1960-67; chief counsel, 1967-73; gen. counsel Fluor Corp., 1973-79, v.p. law, 1979-82, sr. v.p. law, 1983-84, sr. v.p., sec. Calif., 1984-93; sr. v.p., gen. counsel San Diego Gas & Electric Co., 1993-95. With USNR, PTO, 1944-46. Mem. ABA, Calif. Bar Assn., Phi Delta Phi. Home: PO Box 9101 Rancho Santa Fe CA 92067-4101

PETERSON, OSLER LEOPOLD, lawyer; b. Mpls., Oct. 19, 1946; s. Osler Luther and Delores (Kealy) P.; m. Sandra Ann Freeto, Jan. 2, 1971 (div. Dec. 1983); m. Deborah Jean Bero, July 30, 1989. BA, Brown U., 1969; JD cum laude, Suffolk U., 1976. Bar: Mass. 1976, U.S. Dist. Ct. Mass. 1976. Pvt. practice, Newton, Mass., 1976-84; ptnr. Freeto, Peterson & Scoll, 1984—. Bd. mem. Riverside Cmty. Care (formerly Neww Ctr., Inc.), 1976-96, clk., 1978-84, pres., 1984-89; bd. mem. Lasell Coll. (formerly Lasell Jr. Coll.), 1983-97, 98—, clk., 1984-91; bd. mem. Lasell Village, Inc., 1990-2000, 2001-, chmn., 1992-2000; bd. mem. Medfield Zoning Bd. Appeals, 1993-2000;, Beth Israel Deaconess Hosp.-Needham Campus, 2001—; selectman Town of Medfield, 2000—. Mem. ABA, ATLA, Mass. Bar Assn., Mass. Conveyancers Assn. Home: 10 Copperwood Rd Medfield MA 02052-1034 Office: Freeto Peterson & Scoll 580 Washington St Newton MA 02458-1416 also: 66 North St PO Box 358 Medfield MA 02052-0358 E-mail: opeterson@juno.com.

PETERSON, PAMELA CARMELLE, English language educator; b. Bakersfield, Calif., Sept. 24, 1954; d. Bob Eugene and Carmelita Denyse (Coodey) York; m. Robert Leroy Peterson, Feb. 9, 1979; children: Aimee, Sara, Matthew, Hannah. Assoc., Bakersfield Coll., 1992; BA in History, Calif. State U., Bakersfield, 1994. Exec. adminstr. Kern Bldg. Materials, Bakersfield, 1973-95; prin. Rosewall Christian Acad., 1994—; prin., tchr. Dynasty Christian Schs., 1995-97; instr. ESL, Calif. State U., 1997—; instr. English, Santa Barbara (Calif.) Bus. Coll., 1998—. Pres. bd. Dynasty Christian Schs., 1995; exec. sec. bd. dirs. Kern Bldg. Materials, 1983-95. Mem. Assn. Christian Schs., Inc., Assn. Christian Sch. Adminstrs., Phi Alpha Theta (sec. 1994-95, v.p. 1995-96). Avocations: history, reading, needlework, gardening, baking. Home: 4213 Rosewall St Bakersfield CA 93313-2529 Office: Rosewall Christian Acad 7850 White Ln # E149 Bakersfield CA 93309-7689

PETERSON, PATRICIA ELIZABETH, library network administrator, educator; b. Iowa City, July 25, 1942; d. Gregory Raymond and Ruth Elizabeth (Green) Patterson; m. Sylvan Johnathan Peterson, June 14, 1964; children: Deborah Lynn, Christine Elizabeth. BS, Mayville State Coll., 1963; MS, St. Cloud State U., 1979. Tchr., libr. Nekoma (N.D.) High Sch., 1963-67, Gackle (N.D.) High Sch., 1967-70; tchr. Lester Prairie (Minn.) High Sch., 1971-73; dir. media Kimball (Minn.) High Sch., 1978-83; dir. Cen. Minn. Librs. Exch., St. Cloud, 1983—. Pres. Coun. Coop. Librs., St. Paul, 1987-88, 94-95, 00-01. Mem. ALA, AAUW, Forum of Exec. Women, Friends of the Libr. Devel. and Svcs. Libr., Minn. Libr. Assn., Minn. Ednl. Media Orgn. (v.p. 1992-94), Cold Spring Home Pride Lions Club. Avocations: reading, camping, fishing. Home: 591 Central Ave SE Richmond MN 56368-8117 Office: Ctrl Minn Librs Exch Bldg MC130D St Cloud State U Saint Cloud MN 56301 E-mail: ppeterson@stcloudstate.edu.

PETERSON, PAUL AMES, lawyer, educator; b. Los Angeles, Feb. 17, 1928; s. Ames and Norma (Brown) P.; m. Cynthia Peterson, June 21, 1953 (div.); children: Daniel C., Andrew G., Matthew A., James F.; m. Barbara J. Henderson, Sept. 12, 1976. BS in Econs., U. Calif., Berkeley, 1953, JD, 1956. Bar: Calif. 1956, U.S. Ct. Appeals (9th cir.) 1956, U.S. Supreme Ct. 1964. Assoc. Peterson & Price, San Diego, 1958—. Assoc. prof. Calif. Western Coll. Law, San Diego, 1960—63, U. San Diego Law Sch. , 1958—60, U. Calif., San Diego, 1984—87, chmn. bd. overseers, 1994—, chmn., 2000—02; bd. trustees U. Calif. Found., San Diego, 1988—2002; bd. dirs. Children's Advocacy Inst., San Diego Regional Airport Authority, 2002—. Contbr. articles to profl jours. Bd. dirs. San Diego Conv. Ctr. Corp., 1985—90, San Diego Stadium Authority, 1964—72, San Diego County Water Authority, 1984—90, San Diego Regional Govt. Efficiency Commn., 2001—02. Fellow Am. Judicature Soc.; mem. State Bar of Calif., Phi Beta Kappa, Order of Coif. Democrat. Avocation: hiking. Home: 7020 Neptune Pl La Jolla CA 92037-5328 Office: Peterson & Price 7979 Ivanhoe Ave Ste 520 La Jolla CA 92037-4513 E-mail: ppeterson@price-entities.com.

PETERSON, PETER G. investment company executive; b. Kearney, Nebr., June 5, 1926; s. George and Venetia P.; m. Sally H., May 1953 (div. 1979); children: John, Jim, David, Holly, Michael; m. Joan Ganz Cooney, Apr. 26, 1980. BS, Northwestern U., 1947; MBA, U.Chgo., 1951; PhD (hon.), Colgate U., George Washington U., Northwestern U., Georgetown U., U. Rochester, Southampton Coll. at L.I. Exec. v.p. Market Facts, Chgo., 1948-52; v.p. McCann Erickson, 1952-58; pres. Bell and Howell, 1958-71, exec. v.p., 1958-61, CEO, 1963-71; asst. to Pres. of U.S. for Internat. Econ. Affairs Washington, 1961-63; sec. of commerce U.S. Govt., 1972-73; CEO, chmn. bd. Lehman Bros. and Lehman Bros., Kuhn, Loeb, Inc., N.Y.C., 1973-84; chmn. The Blackstone Group, 1985—. Chmn. Fed. Res. Bank N.Y., 1999-; founding pres. The Concord Coalition Author: Gray Dawn: How the Coming Age Wave Will Transform America--and the World, Will America Grow Up Before it Grows Old, Facing Up: How to Rescue the Economy from Crushing Debt and Restore the American Dream; editor: Readings in Market Organization and Price Policies; co-author: On Borrowed Time: How The Growth In Entitlement Spending Threatens America's Future. Founding mem. Bi-Partisan Budget Appeal; pres. The Concord Coalition; trustee Commn. for Econ. Devel., Mus. Modern Art, N.Y.C.; bd. dirs. Pub. Agenda. Recipient Outstanding Service award, Phoenix House, N.Y.C., 1976, Stephen Wise award, Am. Jewish Congress, 1981, U. Chgo. Alumni medal, 1983, Man of Vision award, 1994, Nebraskalander award, 1994; named to Pres. Clinton's Bi-Partisan Comm. on Entitlement Refirm, 1994. Mem. Coun. on Fgn. Rels. (chmn. bd. 1985—), Inst. Internat. Econs. (chmn. bd 1980), Nat. Bur. Econ. Rsch. (trustee), Japan Soc., Blind Brook Club (Purchase, N.Y.), Deepdale Club (Manhasset, N.Y.), Maidstone Club (Easthampton, N.Y.), Chgo. Club, River

Clib, Links, Augusta Nat. Club, Burning Tree (Washington), Quail Valley Golf Club, Atlantic Club. Republican. Home: 435 E 52nd St Apt 11G New York NY 10022-6445 Office: The Blackstone Group 345 Park Ave Ste 3101 New York NY 10154-0004

PETERSON, PHILLIP KEITH, physician, clinical investigator; b. Chgo., Feb. 10, 1943; s. Frank Martin and Ann dorothea (Engwall) P.; m. Karin Enette Sundquist, June 3, 1967; children: Kirstin, Per. BA, St. Olaf Coll., 1965; MD, Columbia U., 1970. Asst. prof. medicine U. Minn., Mpls., 1977-80, assoc. prof., 1980-85, prof., 1986—; dir. infectious diseases Hennepin County Med. Ctr., 1984—; dir. internat. med. edn. and rsch. program U. Minn., 1998—; dir. Inst. on Brain and Immune Disorders Mpls. Med. Rsch. Found., 1998—. Editor Internat. Jour. Antimicrobial Agts., 1993-99; author med. textbooks; contbr. articles to profl. jours. Grantee NIH, 1986—. Mem. Mpls. Med. Rsch. Found. (pres. 1995-00), Internat. Immunocos. Host Soc. (past pres.). Avocations: travel, angling, hiking, reading, gardening. Home: 4822 Russell Ave S Minneapolis MN 55410-1913 Office: Hennepin County Med Ctr Dept Medicine 701 Park Ave Dept Medicine Minneapolis MN 55415-1623 E-mail: peter137@umn.edu.

PETERSON, RANDALL SCOTT, management educator; b. Fergus Falls, Minn., Apr. 22, 1964; s. David Harold and Betty Louise Peterson. BS, U. Minn., 1986, MA, 1990; PhD, U. Calif., Berkeley, 1995. Asst. prof. Northwestern U., Evanston, Ill., 1995-97, Cornell U., Ithaca, N.Y., 1997—. Contbr. articles to profl. jours. Mem. APA, Am. Psychol. Soc., Acad. Mgmt. Avocation: photography. Home: PO Box 3893 Ithaca NY 14852 E-mail: rsp12@cornell.edu.

PETERSON, RICHARD WILLIAM, retired judge, lawyer; b. Council Bluffs, Iowa, Sept. 29, 1925; s. Henry K. and Laura May (Robinson) P.; m. Patricia Mae Fox, Aug. 14, 1949; children: Katherine Ilene Peterson Sherbondy, Jon Eric, Timothy Richard. BA, U. Iowa, 1949, JD with distinction, 1951; postgrad., U. Nebr.-Omaha, 1972-80, 86. Bar: Iowa 1951, U.S. Dist. Ct. (so. dist.) Iowa 1951, U.S. Supreme Ct. 1991, U.S. Ct. Appeals (8th cir.) 1997. Pvt. practice law, Council Bluffs, 1951—; U.S. commr. U.S. Dist. Ct. (so. dist.) Iowa, 1958-70. U.S. magistrate judge U.S. Dist. Ct. (so. dist.) Iowa, 1970-99; nat. faculty Fed. Jud. Ctr., Washington, 1972-82; emeritus trustee Children's Square, U.S.A.; verifying ofcl. Internat. Prisoner Transfer Treaties, Mexico City, 1977, La Paz, Bolivia, 1980-81, Lima, Peru, 1981. Author: The Court Moves West: A Study of the United States Supreme Court Decision of Appeals from the United States Circuit and District Court of Iowa, 1846-1882, 1988, West of the Nishnabotna: The Experiences of Forty Years of a Part-Time Judicial Officer as United States Commissioner, Magistrate and Magistrate Judge, 1958-1998, 1998; co-author: (with George Mills) No One is Above the Law: The Story of Southern Iowa's Federal Court, 1994; contbr. articles to legal publs. Bd. dirs. Pottawattamie County (Iowa) chpt. ARC, state fund chmn., 1957-58; state chmn. Radio Free Europe, 1960-61; dist. chmn. Trailblazer dist. Boy Scouts Am., 1952-55; mem. exec. coun. Mid-Am. Coun., 1976—. With inf. U.S. Army, 1943-46. Decorated Purple Heart, Bronze Star; named Outstanding Young Man Council Bluffs C. of C., 1959 Fellow Am. Bar Found. (life); mem. ABA, Am. Judicature Soc., Iowa Bar Assn. (chmn. com. fed. practice 1978-80, probate and trust coun. and sect. 1997—), Pottawattamie County Bar Assn. (pres. 1979-80), Fed. Bar Assn., Inter-Am. Bar Assn., Supreme Ct. Hist. Soc., Fed. Magistrate Judges Assn. (pres. 1978-79), Iowa Conf. Bar Assn. (pres. 1985-87), Hist. Soc. of U.S. Cts. Eighth Jud. Cir. (pres. 1989-99, ct. historian U.S. Dist. Ct. S.D. and Iowa 2000-), Kiwanis (pres. Council Bluffs chpt. 1957), Masons, Phi Delta Phi, Delta Sigma Rho, Omicron Delta Kappa. Republican. Lutheran. Home: 1007 Arbor Ridge Cir Council Bluffs IA 51503-5000 Office: PO Box 248 25 Main Pl Ste 200 Council Bluffs IA 51503-0790

PETERSON, RICHARD HERMANN, history educator, retired; b. Berkeley, Calif., Jan. 16, 1942; s. William Martin and Dorothy Jean (Heyne) P.; m. Nora Ann Lorenzo, June 21, 1970; 1 child, Nina Elizabeth. AB, U. Calif., Berkeley, 1963; MA, San Francisco State U., 1966; PhD, U. Calif., Davis, 1971. Calif. community coll. teaching credential. Asst. prof. history Ind. U., Kokomo, 1971-76; instr. social studies Coll. of Redwoods, Ft. Bragg, Calif., 1976-78; assoc. prof. history San Diego State U., 1978-82, prof. history, 1982-96, prof. emeritus, 1996—; freelance writer, 1996—. Author: Manifest Destiny in the Mines, 1975, The Bonanza Kings, 1977, 91, Bonanza Rich, 1991; book rev. editor Jour. of San Diego History, 1978-82, editl. cons., 1980-82; contbr. articles to profl. jours., websites, newspapers. Judge for papers Internat. History Fair, San Diego, Tijuana, Mex., 1983-88. Faculty Summer fellow Ind. U., 1975, 76, San Diego State U., 1980, Meritorious Performance and Prof. Promise award, 1989; rsch. grantee Sourisseau Acad., 1977, Am. Assn. State/Local History, 1988; named Golden Poet of Yr., World of Poetry, 1987-89. Mem. Am. Hist. Assn., Calif. Hist. Soc., Western History Assn., Calif. Studies Assn. Avocations: golf, gardening, writing poetry, travel. Home: 7956 Lake Adlon Dr San Diego CA 92119-3117

PETERSON, ROBERT ALLEN, marketing educator; b. N.Y.C., Mar. 25, 1944; s. Robert A. and Carrol D. (Collins) P.; m. Diane S. Femrite, June 18, 1966; children: Jeffrey, Jennifer, Matthew. BS, U. Minn., 1966, MS, 1968, PhD, 1970. Asst. prof. mktg. U. Tex., Austin, 1970-73, assoc. prof., 1973-77, prof., 1977—, John T. Stuart chair, 1985—, chmn. dept. mktg. adminstrn., 1983-85. Prin. Group Seven Assocs., Austin Author: Marketing Research, 1982, 2d edit., 1988; co-author: Modern American Capitalism, 1990, Strategic Marketing, 9th edit., 2001; editor: Jour. Mktg. Rsch., 1985-88, Jour. Acad. Mktg. Sci., 1991-94; mem. editorial bd. Jour. Mktg., Internat. Mktg. Rev. Recipient rsch. award AMA, 1988, Charles Hurwitz fellow, 1983—. Fellow Southwestern Mktg. Assn. (pres. 1977-78), Am. Mktg. Assn. (v.p. 1980-81), Acad. Mktg. Sci. (bd. govs. 1982-86, chmn. 1994-98, pres. 2000-02), Am. Inst. Decision Scis. (dir. 1974-75). Lutheran. Office: Univ Texas Dept Mktg Austin TX 78712

PETERSON, ROBERT AUSTIN, manufacturing company executive retired; b. Sioux City, Iowa, July 5, 1925; s. Austen W. and Marie (Mueller) P.; m. Carol May Hudy, May 17, 1952; children: Roberta, Richard., Bruce. BS, U. Minn., 1946, BBA, 1947. Credit mgr. New Holland Machine div. Sperry Rand Corp., Mpls., 1952-61; from credit mgr. to treas. Toro Co., 1961-70, v.p., treas. internat. fin., 1970-83; v.p. fin., pres. Toro Credit Co., 1983-93. Chmn. Prior Lake Spring Lake Watershed Dist., 1970-80; chmn., bd. dirs. Prior Lake Bd. Edn., 1965-71; chmn. Scott County Republican Party, 1969-70; bd. dirs. Scott Carver Mental Health Center, 1969-73, Minn. Watershed Assn., 1972-76. Served to ensign USNR, 1943-46. Mem. Prior Lake Yacht Club (bd. dirs.).

PETERSON, ROBERT SCOTT, electrical engineer; b. McKeesport, Pa., Mar. 24, 1930; s. William James and Emma Elizabeth (Scott) P.; m. Betty Louise Oleska, Aug. 11, 1962 (dec. 1995). *Robert Scott Peterson was born in McKeesport, Pennsylvania in 1930, the grandson of immigrants from Europe who came to Pittsburgh to work in the steel mills in the late 1880's. After graduation from high school in 1948, he worked as a laborer in the local mills during the summer vacation while attending college.* BSEE, Pa. State U., 1952; MSEE, U. Pitts., 1961. Lic. profl. engr., Pa. Sr. application, design engr. Westinghouse Elec., Pitts., 1952-63, devel. engr. Buffalo, 1963-85, Pitts., 1985-89, AEG Automation Corp., Pitts., 1989-94; cons. engr. CDI-Ctrl. Corp., 1994—. *Mr. Peterson started his career as an application and design engineer in mining and material handling industries. For the past thirty-nine years, his main responsibilites have been devoted to the development of drives and steel mill automation control. Mr. Peterson functioned as a fellow design and development engineer for Westinghouse Electric Corporation from 1952-89, AEG Automation Corporation from 1990-1995 and is presently a consulting engineer in steel mill automation. There have been 30 U.S. patents granted to Mr. Peterson, as an inventor or co-inventor, pertaining to drive and automation controls. He has expertise in the mathematical analysis of drive system and rolling mill automation control and was a senior member of a team that developed the first microprocessor controlled steel rolling mills in the world.* Patentee in field. Coach Midget Football League, McKeesport, 1953-55. With U.S. Army, 1955-57. Mem. IEEE, N.Y. Acad. Scis., Assn. Iron Steel Engrs. Avocations: gardening, woodworking, oil painting, dancing, sports. Home and Office: 719 Heathergate Dr Pittsburgh PA 15238-1000

PETERSON, ROBIN TUCKER, marketing educator; b. Casper, Wyo., July 31, 1937; s. Walfred Arthur and Mary Lurene Peterson; m. Marjorie K. Greenwald, June 25, 1963; children: Timothy, Kimberly. BS, U. Wyo., 1959, MS in Bus., 1961; PhD, U. Wash., 1967. Mem. faculty Idaho State U., Pocatello, 1963-73; prof. mktg., head mktg. dept. St. Cloud (Minn.) State U., 1973-76, N.Mex. State U., Las Cruces, 1976—. Fulbright lectr., Yugoslavia, 1973; vis. scholar Ea. Mont. State Coll., 1985; Sunwest Fin. Svcs. Disting. Centennial prof. N.Mex. State U., 1991, 92; Norwest Disting. prof. N.Mex. State U., 1999, Wells Fargo Disting. prof., 2002; vis. lectr. Nirma Inst. Ahmedabad, India, 1999, Chiang Moi U., Thailand, 2000; Fulbright lectr. Kathmandu U., Nepal, 2001. Author: Marketing-A Contemporary Introduction, 1976, Forecasting, 1976, edit., 1983, Personal Selling, 1977, Marketing in Action, 1977, Lernbook Marketing, 1984, Marketing: Concepts and Decision Making, 1987, Principles of Marketing, 1989, Argentina, 1990, Managing the Distributor Sales Network, 1990, Business Forecasting, 1992, Getting New Products to Market Rapidly, 1994; exec. editor Bus. Forecaster, 1993-94; editor Jour. Bus. and Entrepreneurship, 1994-98; also contbr. articles to profl. publs. Served with USAR, 1962-63. Fellow Assn. Small Bus. Entrepreneurship; mem. Am. Mktg. Assn., Sales and Mktg. Execs. Internat., Acad. Mktg. Sci. (pres. 1977-78, 80-82), Am. Arbitration Assn. (Outstanding Educators Am. award), S.W. Small Bus. Assn. (pres. 1983-84, Outstanding Mktg. Educators award, Outstanding Educator, Assn. of Small Bus., 2002), S.W. Mktg. Assn., Western Mktg. Educators, Las Cruces C. of C., Las Cruces Sales and Mktg. Club, Beta Gamma Sigma, Phi Kappa Psi, Alpha Kappa Psi, Alpha Mu Alpha. Republican. Presbyterian. Home: 4350 Diamondback Dr Las Cruces NM 88011-7539 Office: NMex State U PO Box 5280 Las Cruces NM 88003-5280

PETERSON, ROBYN GAYLE, museum curator; b. San Francisco, Jan. 17, 1958; BA, UCLA, 1979; MA, U. Wis., 1982, PhD, 1987. Goldsmith, 1974-80; collections acquisition asst. social studies bibliographer Meml. Libr./U. Wis., 1984-86; curator of collections The Rockwell Mus., Corning, N.Y., 1988-99; dir. collections and rsch. Turtle Bay Exploration Park, 1999—. Author: American Frontier Photography, 1993, Edward Borein, 1997, Warp and Weft: Cross-cultural Exchange in Navajo Weavings, 1997, Transforming Trash: Bay Area Fiber Art, 2000; contbg. author: Allgemeines Künstlerlexikon, 1998—; editor/contbr.: Collector's Choice Review: Masterpieces of Glassmaking; Frederick Carder and the Steuben Glass Works, 1993, Brilliance in Glass: The Lost Wax Glass Sculpture of Frederick Carder, 1993; mng. editor: Frederick Carder and Steuben Glass: American Classics (Thomas P. Dimitroff), 1998; contbr. articles to profl. jours.; peer reviewer IMLS. Mem. Coll. Art Assn., Soc. Advancement of Scandinavian Studies, Glass Art Soc., Am. Assn. Mus. Office: Turtle Bay Exploraton Park PO Box 992360 Redding CA 96099-2360 E-mail: rpeterson@turtlebay.org.

PETERSON, RODNEY DELOS, mediator, forensic economist; b. Sioux Falls, S.D., Nov. 10, 1932; s. Severin Ingvald and Vera (Blow) P.; m. Evelyn Koubsky, Dec. 26, 1965; children: Douglas, Russell, Stuart. BA, Huron (S.D.) Coll., 1958; MS in Econs, S.D. State U., 1959; PhD in Econs. and Bus. Orgn, U. Nebr., 1964; JD, U. Denver, 1982. Instr. U. Nebr., Lincoln, 1959-64, vis. asst. prof. agrl. econs., summers 1964-66; instr. adult edn. U. Omaha, part-time 1963-64; asst. prof. econs. Cen. Wash. State U., Ellensburg, 1964-65; asst. prof., then assoc. prof. U. Idaho, Moscow, 1965-68; mem. faculty Colo. State U., Ft. Collins, 1968-91, prof. econs., 1971-91, mediation officer, 1985-91, prof. emeritus, 1991; economist Fla. Dept. Commerce, 1991-96, Fla. Dept. Labor, 1996-98; dir. Ctr. Econ. Edn. Colo. State U., 1976-77. Vis. prof. Simon Fraser U., Vancouver, B.C., Can., 1974-75. Author: Student Guide to Accompany Our Changing Economy, 1976, Economic Organization in Medical Equipment and Supply, 1973, Political Economy & American Capitalism, 1991; contbr. numerous articles to profl. jours. NSF fellow, summers 1971, 73, expert witness personal injury and antitrust cases. Mem. Am. Econ. Assn., Midwest Econs. Assn., Sigma Xi, Delta Sigma Pi, Beta Gamma Sigma, Omicron Delta Epsilon (regional dir. 1975-76) Home: 8479 Manderston Ct Fort Myers FL 33912-6613

PETERSON, ROLAND E. business management company executive; b. Rockford, Ill., Jan. 4, 1955; s. Eugene Alfred Peterson and Ethel Lorraine Saari; m. Camille E.W. Peterson, Nov. 10, 1984; 1 child, Birgitta. BA in Polit. Sci., San Francisco State U., 1976, postgrad., 1976-78. Mgr. Orinda (Calif.) Camera, 1976-95; project supr. Advanced Office Systems, Concord, Calif., 1995-98; with admissions office San Francisco Theolog. Sem., San Anselmo, 1999; exec. dir. Telegraph Property and Bus. Mgmt. Corp., Berkeley, 1999—. V.p. Experience Unltd., San Francisco, 1997-99. Mem. World Affairs Coun., San Francisco, 1998—; mem. Berkeley Dem. Club, 1997—, bd. dirs., 2002-. Mem. Berkelely C. of C. (bd. dirs. 2000—), Calif. Downtown Assn. Democrat. Presbyterian. Avocations: politics, hiking, photography, wine. Office: Telegraph Property & Bus Mgmt 2509 Haste St Berkeley CA 94704

PETERSON, RONALD R. health service administrator; b. New Brunswick, NJ, 1948; m. Elizabeth Rooney; children: Joey, Susie. MA in Hosp. Adminstrn., Johns Hopkins U., Balt., 1970. Adminstrv. resident Johns Hopkins U., Balt., 1973, adminstr. Henry Phipps Psychiatric Clinic, 1974, adminstr. cost improvement program, 1975, adminstr. Children's Ctr., 1978, adminstr. Balt. City Hosps., 1982, exec. v.p., COO Johns Hopkins Health Sys., 1995, acting pres. Hopkins Hosp. and Health Sys., 1996, pres. John Hopkins health Sys., 1997—. Mem. bus. adv. coun., Balt.; vol. ARC, United Way, Am. Heart Assn. Mem. Md. Hosp. Assn. (mem. exec. com.), Md. C. of C. Office: Johns Hopkins Hosp 600 N Wolfe St Baltimore MD 21287-0005 also: Johns Hopkins U 720 Rutland Ave Baltimore MD 21205-2109*

PETERSON, RUDOLPH A. banker; b. Svenljunga, Sweden, Dec. 6, 1904; s. Aaron and Anna (Johannson) P.; m. Patricia Price, 1927 (dec. 1960); children: Linnea Peterson Bennett, R. Price; m. Barbara Welser Lindsay, Dec. 25, 1962; stepchildren: Robert I. Lindsay, Lorna Lindsay, Anne Lindsay, Margaret Lindsay. BS in Commerce, U. Calif., 1925, LLD, 1968; LHD, U. Redlands, 1967. With Comml. Credit Co., 1925-36, successively asst. mgr., v.p., gen. mgr. Mexico City, div. operations mgr. Chgo.; dist. mgr. Bank Am. Nat. Trust & Savs. Assn., Fresno, Calif., 1936-41, v.p. San Francisco, 1941-46; pres., chief exec. officer Allied Bldg. Credits, 1946-52; v.p. Transam. Corp., San Francisco, 1952-55; pres., chief exec. officer Bank of Hawaii, Honolulu, 1956-61; pres., CEO BankAm. Corp., San Francisco, 1961-70, chmn. exec. com., 1970-76, also dir., 1968-98; adminstr. UN Devel. Programme, 1971-76. Bd. dirs. Alza Corp., Asia Found.; chmn. Euro Can. Bank, 1982-94; adminstr. UN Devel. Programme, 1972-76. Mem. adv. coun. Calif. Acad. Scis. Decorated Grand Cross of Civil Merit Spain; Order of Merit Italy; named Swedish-Am. of Year Vasa Order, 1965; U. Calif. Alumnus of Year, 1968; recipient Capt. Robert Dollar Meml. award for contbn. to advancement Am. fgn. trade, 1970, Chancellor's award U. Calif., 1992, Great Swedish Heritage award, 1996. Mem.: Bohemian (San Francisco), Pacific-Union (San Francisco). Home: 86 Sea View Ave Piedmont CA 94611-3519 Office: Bank Am Ctr Mailcode CA5 705-11-01 555 California St Fl 11 San Francisco CA 94104-1502

PETERSON, RUSSELL WILBUR, former association executive, former state governor; b. Portage, Wis., Oct. 3, 1916; s. John Anton and Emma (Anthony) P.; m. E. Lillian Turner, June 30, 1937 (dec. Apr. 28, 1994); children: Russell Glen, Peter Jon, Kristin, Elin; m. June B. Jenkins, Oct. 21, 1995. BS, U. Wis., 1938, PhD, 1942, LL.D. (hon.), 1984; D.Sc. (hon.), Williams Coll., 1975, Butler U.; DSc (hon.), Springfield Coll., Stevens Inst. Tech., 1979, Gettysburg Coll., 1980, Alma Coll., 1981, Ohio State U.; D.Sc. (hon.), SUNY-Syracuse; DSc (hon.), Northland Coll., Fairleigh Dickinson U., 1981; LLD (hon.), Monmouth Coll., 1982, Salisbury State U., 1988; LHD, Meadville-Lombard Theol. Sch., 1992; DHL, Colby-Sawyer Coll., 2000. With E. I. DuPont de Nemours & Co., Inc., 1942-69, rsch. dir. textile fibers dept., 1954-55, 56-59, merchandising mgr. textile fibers, 1955-56, dir. new products divsn. textile fibers, 1959-62, dir. R & D divsn. devel. dept., 1963-69; chmn. exec. com. Textile Research Inst., Princeton, N.J., 1959-61, chmn. bd. dirs., 1961-63, fellow, 1969; gov. of Del., 1969-73; chmn. exec. com. Nat. Commn. Critical Choices for Am., 1973; chmn. U.S. Council on Environ. Quality, 1973-76; pres. Nat. Audubon Soc., 1979-85; mem. Nat. Commn. Critical Choices for Am., 1973-74; dir. Office Tech. Assessment, U.S. Congress, 1978-79. Pres. New Directions, 1976-77; regional v.p. Nat. Mcpl. League, 1968-78; chmn. Edn. Commn. States, 1970; chmn. com. nuclear energy and space tech. So. Govs. Conf., 1970-71; chmn. Nat. Adv. Commn. on Criminal Justice Standards and Goals, 1971-73; chmn. com. law enforcement, justice and pub. safety Nat. Govs. Conf., 1970-73; v.p. Council State Govts., 1970-71; chmn. adv. bd. Solar Energy Research Inst., 1979-83; vis prof. Dartmouth Coll., 1985, Carleton Coll., 1986, U. Wis., Madison, 1987; chmn. Centennial Internat. Symposium, Nat. Geog. Soc., 1986-88. Author: Rebel with a Conscience, 1999, Oral History, Russell W. Peterson, Delaware Heritage Series, 1999, (CD) We Can Save the Earth, 2000. Chmn. Del. River Basin Commn., 1971-72; founding chmn. Bio-Energy Coun., 1976-78; bd. dirs. World Wildlife Fund, 1976-82, Population Action Internat., 1973-97, Alliance to Save Energy, 1979-93, Global Tomorrow Coalition, 1981-91, chmn., 1981-87; regional councillor Internat. Union Conservation Nature and Natural Resources, 1981-88, v.p., 1984-88; mem. Pres.'s Commn. on Accident at Three Mile Island, 1979; pres. Nat. Audubon Soc., 1979-85, Internat. Coun. Bird Preservation, 1982-90; chmn. Ctr. on Consequences of Nuclear War, 1983-87; vice-chmn. Better World Soc., 1985-90, pres., 1985-87; vis. com. John F. Kennedy Sch. Govt., 1979-85; Goodwill amb. UN Environ. Program, 1984-2002, world environ. prize com., 1989—; mem. Gov. Cuomo's Environ. Adv. Bd., 1985-94; adv. bd. Pace U. Sch. Law, 1988-98, Earth Island Inst., 1988—; chmn. bd. Earth Lobby, 1992-96; co-chmn. gov.'s task force on rejuvenating Wilmington waterfront, 1992-95; exe. com. Del. Riverfront Devel. Corp., 1995—. Decorated Order of Golden Ark (The Netherlands); Disting. fellow U. Del., 2000; recipient Ann. award NCCJ, 1966, Gold medal World Wildlife Fund, 1971, Ann. award Comml. Devel. Assn., 1971, Gold Plate award Nat. Acad. Achievement, 1971, Audubon award Nat. Audubon Soc., 1977, Frances K. Hutchinson medal Garden Club Am., 1980, Robert Marshall award Wilderness Soc., 1984, Nat. Conservation medal DAR, 1989, Human and Civil Rights award Del. Human Rights Commn., 1989, Environ. Law Inst. award, 1990, Ann. award Am. Civil Liberties Found. Del., 1992, Lawrence Solid Waste award Assn. N.Am., 1993, Kiwanis Cmty. Svc. award, 1993, Lifetime Achievement award Global Tomorrow Coalition, 1994, Lifetime Achievement award League of Conservation Voters, 1995, Del. Nature Soc., 1997, Liberty Bell award Del. State Bar Assn., 1998, Green Century award Resource Renewal Inst., 1999; named Conservationist of Yr., Nat. Wildlife Fedn., 1972, Swedish-Am. of Yr., Vasa Order of Am. In Sweden, 1982, Lifetime Achievement award Creative Grandparenting, 1999, NAACP, 1999; Del. refuge named in his honor Russel W. Peterson Wildlife Refuge, 2000. Fellow Am. Inst. Chemists (hon.), AAAS (past bd. dirs.); mem. Am. Ornithologists Union, Linnaean Soc., Fedn. Am. Scientists, Am. Chem. Soc. (Parsons award 1974), Del. Acad. Sci., U.S. Assn. for Club of Rome, Cosmos Club, Phi Beta Kappa, Sigma Xi (Proctor prize 1978), Phi Lambda Upsilon, Phi Kappa Phi. Unitarian Universalist. Address: 11 E Mozart Dr Wilmington DE 19807-1942

PETERSON, SHARON L. community health nurse; b. New Castle, Pa., June 26, 1950; d. Paul Lewis and Beatrice Marie (Payne) Zook; m. Mark J. Peterson, Aug. 5, 1972; children: Eric James, Daniel Mark, Krista Marie. BSN, Roberts Wesleyan Coll., 1972. RN, Pa.; cert. comm. health. Comm. health nurse II Pa. Dept. of Health, Seneca, Pa. Facilitator Venango-Forest Prenatal Task Force, Venango-Forest Cmty. Health Action Team. Mem. Sigma Theta Tau (sec. Mu Xi chpt.), Clarion U. Pa. Nursing Honor Soc.

PETERSON, SHARON LYNN CRAIG, medical case manager, cost containment specialist; b. Decatur, Ill., July 7, 1945; d. Corwin Moore and Evelyn Marie (Oye) Craig; 1 child, Karla Christina Johnson Fopiano. Diploma in nursing, Decatur Macon County Hosp., 1967; BS, Gov. State U., 1975, MSN, 1977. RN, Mo., Ill., Ark.; cert. case mgr. Head nurse med./surg. unit St. Mary's Hosp., Kankakee, Ill., 1967-74, part-time emergency rm. staff, 1978-85; mental health adminstr. Manteno (Ill.) Mental Health Ctr., 1974-85; rehab. specialist Intracorp., 1985-87; rehab., med. case mgr. Upjohn Co., Springfield, Mo., 1987-89; rehab. and med. mgr., dist. mgr. Fortis Corp., 1989-93; owner, case mgr., care mgr., cost containment specialist ADVO-CARE, 1993—. Mem. Assn. Rehab. Nurses (past sec. and bd. dirs.), Case Mgmt. Soc. Am., Am. Assn. Occupl. Health Nurses, Nat. Assn. Orthopeadic Nurses, Case Mgmt. Soc. Assn. Springfield Mo. and the Ozarks (bd. dirs. 1997—, chmn. edn. com. 1997—), Acad. Cert. Case Mgrs. Home and Office: 103 Laurel Ln Branson West MO 65737-9296 Fax: 417-338-9112. E-mail: advo-care@juno.com.

PETERSON, SOPHIA, international studies educator; b. Astoria, N.Y., Nov. 24, 1929; d. George Loizos and Caroline (Hofstetter) Yimoyines; m. Virgil Allison Peterson, Dec. 28, 1951; children: Mark Jeffrey, Lynn Marie. BA, Wellesley (Mass.) Coll., 1951; MA, UCLA, 1956, PhD, 1969; DHL (hon.), Wheeling Jesuit U., 1997. Instr. Miami U., Oxford, Ohio, 1961-63; with W.Va. U., Morgantown, 1966—, assoc. prof., 1972-79, prof., 1979-97, prof. emerita, 1997—, dir., internat. studies maj., 1980-92. Dir. W.Va. Consortium for Faculty & Course Devel. in Internat. Studies, Morgantown, 1980-97, founding dir., 1997—. Author: monograph Monograph Series in World Affairs, 1979. Recipient gold medal semi-finalist CASE Prof. of Yr. award Coun. for Advancement and Support of Edn., 1987, Outstanding Tchr. award W.Va. U., W.Va. U. Coll. Arts and Scis., 1988, finalist Prof. of Yr. award W.Va. Faculty Merit Found., 1991, Heebink award for disting. state svc. W.Va. U., 1984. Mem. Internat. Studies Assn. (v.p. Mid-Atlantic chpt. 1978-86), W.Va. Polit. Sci. Assn. (pres. 1984-85), AAAUP (pres. W.Va. U. chpt. 1976-78). Democrat. Avocation: sailing. Home: 849 Vandalia Rd Morgantown WV 26501-6247 Office: WVa U Dept Polit Sci Morgantown WV 26506

PETERSON, STANLEY LEE, artist; b. Viborg, S.D., Mar. 26, 1949; s. Norman and Neva Jean (Harns) P.; m. Katherine Anne Burnett. BFA, U. S.D., 1971. Artist W.H. Over Museum, Vermillion, S.D., 1971-72; graphic artist S.D. Pub. TV, Brookings, 1972-76; freelance artist San Francisco, 1976-77; engrng. technician City of Tracy, Calif., 1977-85; artist Stanley Peterson Graphics, Los Banos, 1985—; contract engrng. technician, system mgr. City of Tracy, 1985-89, system mgr., 1989-90; engrng. technician IV County of Sacramento, 1991, prin. engrng. technician, 1991—. Cons. in field. Artist, designer Nat. History Diorama, W.H. Over Museum, 1972. Democrat. Avocations: bicycling, walking, photography, travel, painting. Home: 427 N Santa Monica St Los Banos CA 93635-3223 E-mail: petersonsta@saccounty.net.

PETERSON, STEVEN A. lawyer; b. Princeton, Minn., Sept. 9, 1953; s. Albin Arthur and Patricia Ann (Samuelson) P.; m. Michelle Behring, Jan. 11, 1980; children: Michael Charles, Stephanie Rose. BA, U. Minn., 1975; JD, Hamline U., 1978. Bar: Minn. 1978, U.S. Dist. Ct. Minn. 1979. Pvt. practice, Milaca, Minn., 1978-92, Chanhassen, 1984—. Mem. Minn. Bar Assn. Republican. Lutheran. Home: 736 Ashley Dr Chaska MN 55318-1536 Office: 80 W 78th St Chanhassen MN 55317-8716

PETERSON, SUSAN M. corporate investigator; b. Flushing, N.Y., May 27, 1951; d. Carlton Douglas and Marion Peterson. BA, MS, Queens Coll., 1972. Cert. fraud examiner; cert. fraud specialist; cert. forensic acct. COO Kessler Internat., N.Y.C., 1994; self-employed as cons., to 1994. Mem. Phi Beta Kappa. Avocation: theater. Office: Kessler Internat 237 Park Ave Fl 21 New York NY 10017-3140

PETERSON, THOMAS CHARLES, minister, pastoral counselor and therapist; b. San Francisco, Mar. 16, 1955; s. Roy Joseph and Grace Jeannette (Burns) P.; m. Melody Rose Clarkson, Aug. 17, 1985; children: Shannon Nicole, Chad Michael. BA, Living Word Sem., Maryland Heights, Mo., 1986; MS, Carolina Christian U., Linwood, N.C., 1990; postgrad., U. Bibl. Studies, Bethany, Okla., 1990; PhD in Counseling Psychology, Carolina U. Theology, Charlotte, N.C., 1995. Ordained to ministry Full Gospel Assemblies, 1984, Internat. Conf. Faith Ministries, 1986, Assn. Evang. Assemblies, 1989; lic. pastoral counselor and temperament therapist, Wash. Elder, tchr. Joy of Lord Fellowship, Buckley, Wash., 1980-81, By His Word Christian Ctr., Tacoma, 1982-88; assoc. pastor Valley Christian Ctr., Sumner, 1988-89; founder, pres. Joyful Life Ministries, Tacoma, 1985-92; pastoral staff Victory Bible Ch., 1992-96; dir., chancellor, acad. dean Tacoma Christian Life Sch. of Theology, 1993-96; pastor Resurrection Christian Life Ctr., 1996—. Chaplain Tacoma Police Dept., 1988-90, Tacoma Gen. Hosp., 1988—; dir. Inst. for Personal Devel., Tacoma, 1991. Mem. Critical Incident Stress Mgmt. Team, Tacoma Gen. Hosp., 1997—. Sgt. USAF, 1973-77. Mem. Nat. Christian Counselors Assn. (profl. clin. mem.). Am. Assn. Christian Counselors (founding mem.), Internat. Assn. Christian Clin. Counselors, U.S. Chaplaincy Assn., United Assn. Christian Counselors. Republican. Home: 5615 S Verde St Tacoma WA 98409-1745 Office: Resurrection Life Ministries Internat PO Box 98198 Tacoma WA 98498-0198 *The human potential is limited only by our ability to believe.*

PETERSON, V. SPIKE, social sciences educator; d. Charles Russell and Mattie Lois (Bird) Peterson. BS in Psychology and Philosophy, U. Ill., 1965—70, MA in Social Scis. and Anthropology, 1974—75; PhD in Internat. Rels., American U., Washington, DC, 1981—88. Adj. asst. prof. U. So. Calif., Los Angeles, 1988—89; asst. prof. American U., Washington, 1989—90, U. Ariz., Tucson, 1990—96, assoc. prof., 1996—. Author: Global Gender Issues, 1999; editor: Gendered States: Feminist (Re)Visions of International Relations Theory, 1992 (Visiting, 2000); contbr. articles. Recipient Provost Gen. Edn. Tchg. award, U. Ariz., 2001, Nat. Mentor award, Soc. for Women in Internat. Polit. Econ., 2000; grantee MacArthur Found. Rsch. and Writing grantee, 1996; scholar Vis. Rsch. scholar, U. of Goteborg, Sweden, 2000, U. of Bristol, Eng., 1998, Australia Nat. U., Canberra, Australia, 1995. Office: Dept Polit Sci U of Arizona 315 Social Scis Tucson AZ 85721

PETERSON, VICTOR LOWELL, aerospace engineer, management consultant; b. Saskatoon, Sask., Can., June 11, 1934; came to U.S., 1937; s. Edwin Galladet and Ruth Mildred (McKeeby) P.; m. Jacqueline Dianne Hubbard, Dec. 21, 1955; children: Linda Kay, Janet Gale, Victor Craig. BS in Aero. Engring., Oreg. State U., 1956; MS in Aerospace Engring., Stanford U., 1964; MS in Mgmt., MIT, 1973. Rsch. scientist NASA-Ames Rsch. Ctr., Moffett Field, Calif., 1956-68, asst. chief hypersonic aerodyns., 1968-71, chief aerodyns. br., 1971-74, chief thermo and gas dynamics div., 1974-84, dir. aerophysics, 1984-90, dep. dir., 1990-94; pvt. mgmt. cons., 1994—. Mem. nat. adv. bd. U. Tenn. Space Inst., Tullahoma, 1984-94. Contbr. numerous articles to profl. jours. Treas. Woodland Acres Homeowners Assn., Los Altos, Calif., 1978—. Capt. USAF, 1957-60. Recipient medal for outstanding leadership NASA, 1982; Alfred P. Sloan fellow MIT, 1972-73. Fellow AIAA. Republican. Methodist. Achievements include development of numerical aerodynamic simulation system for aerospace, of method for reconstructing planetary atmosphere structure from accelerations of body entering atmosphere, of theory for motions of tumbling bodies entering planetary atmospheres. Home: 484 Aspen Way Los Altos CA 94024-7100 E-mail: vlpeterson@worldnet.att.net. *Achievements in life are maximized by creating visions of success and focussing relentlessly on successful accomplishment of intermediate objectives.*

PETERSON, VIRGINIA GUILBERT, artist, educator; b. San Francisco, Apr. 1, 1912; d. Joseph Daniel and Virginia (Guilbert) Loughrey; m. Fritz Waldemar Peterson, Dec. 31, 1938; children: Virginia, Douglas, Ronald, Beverly, Elizabeth. Student, Barnes Found., Merion, Pa., 1970, Art Inst. Chgo., 1970-72, SUNY, Stony Brook, 1997. Cert. art tchr., Pa. Color separation artist Stecher Tng. Lithography Corp., San Francisco, 1931-41; portrait painter Elberon, N.J., 1950-68; art tchr. Huntington Twp. (N.Y.) Art League, 1971-94; pvt. art tchr. Centerport, N.Y., 1994—. Art show judge, Long Branch, N.J., 1960-70. Achievements include 1st woman journeyman color separation artist in U.S.A. Avocations: reading, swimming, traveling, golf, television. Home: 18 Harding Ct Centerport NY 11721-1209

PETERSON, WALLACE CARROLL, SR. economics educator; b. Omaha, Mar. 28, 1921; s. Fred Nels and Grace (Brown) P.; m. Eunice V. Peterson, Aug. 16, 1944 (dec. Nov. 1985); children: Wallace Carroll Jr., Shelley Lorraine; m. Bonnie B. Watson, Nov. 11, 1988 (dec. Oct. 1996). Student, U. Omaha, 1939-40, U. Mo., 1940-42; BA in Econs. and European History, U. Nebr., 1947, MA in Econs. and European History, 1948, PhD in Econs. and European History, 1953; postgrad., Handelshochschule, St. Gallen, Switzerland, 1948-49, U. Minn., 1951, London Sch. Econs. and Polit. Sci., 1952. Lic. pilot. Reporter Lincoln (Nebr.) Jour., 1946; instr. econs. U. Nebr., Lincoln, 1951-54, asst. prof., 1954-57, assoc. prof., 1957-61, prof., 1962—, chmn. dept. econs., 1965-75, George Holmes prof. econs., 1966-92; George Holmes prof. econs. emeritus, 1992—; v.p. faculty senate U. Nebr., Lincoln, 1972-73, pres. faculty senate, 1973-74; S.J. Hall disting. vis. prof. U. Nev., Las Vegas, 1983-84. Author: The Welfare State in France, 1960, Elements of Economics, 1973, Our Overloaded Economy: Inflation, Unemployment and the Crisis in American Capitalism, 1982, Market Power and the Economy, 1988, Transfer Spending, Taxes and the American Welfare State, 1991, Income, Employment and Economic Growth, 8th edit., 1996, Silent Depression: The Fate of the American Dream, 1994; co-author: (with F.R. Strobel) The Coming Class War: Power, Conflict and the Consequences of Middle Class Decline, 1998, The Social Security Primer: What Every Citizen Should Know, 1999, Pylon! The Omaha Air Races, 1931-1934, 2002. Mem. Nebr. Dem. Cen. Com., 1968-74, vice-chmn., chmn. Nebr. Polit. Accountability and Disclosure Commn., 1977-80; chmn. Nebr. Coun. Econ. Edn., 1976-77. Capt. USAAF, 1942-46. Recipient Champion Media award for Econ. Understanding, 1981; Fulbright fellow, 1957-58, 64-65; Mid-Am. State Univs. honor scholar, 1982-83. Mem. ACLU, AAUP (pres. Nebr. 1963-64, nat. coun.), Assn. for Evolutionary Econs. (pres. 1976, Veblen-Commons award 1991), Am. Econs. Assn., Midwest Econs. Assn. (pres. 1968-69), Mo. Valley Econ. Assn. (pres. 1989), Assn. Social Econs. (pres. 1992, Thomas F. Devine award 1995), Fedn. Am. Scientists, Antique Aircraft Assn., Aircraft Owners and Pilots Assn., Exptl. Aircraft Assn., Nat. Assn. R.R. Passengers. Office: U Nebr Dept Econs CBA Lincoln NE 68588-0489 E-mail: wcpeterson@mindspring.com.

PETERSON, WALTER FRITIOF, academic administrator; b. Idaho Falls, Idaho, July 15, 1920; s. Walter Fritiof and Florence (Danielson) P.; m. Barbara Mae Kempe, Jan. 13, 1946; children: Walter Fritiof III, Daniel John. BA, State U. Iowa, 1942, MA, 1948, PhD, 1951; HHD (hon.), Loras Coll., 1983; LHD (hon.), Clarke Coll., 1991; DHum (hon.), U. Dubuque, 1997. Asst. prof. history, chmn. dept. history Milw. Downer Coll., 1952-57, assoc. prof. history, chmn. social sci. div., 1957-64; assoc. prof. history Lawrence U., Appleton, Wis., 1964-67, prof. history, Alice G. Chapman libr., 1967-70; pres. U. Dubuque, 1970-90, chancellor, 1990—. Regional tng. officer Peace Corps, 1965-68; cons. history Allis-Chalmers Mfg. Co., 1959-75, Secura Ins. Group, 1968-92, Wm. C. Brown Pub. Co., 1981-92, bd. dirs. Editor: Transactions of Wis. Acad. Scis., Arts and Letters, 1965-72, The Allis-Chalmers Corporation: An Industrial History, 1977, A History of Wm. C. Brown Cos., 1994, A History of Hawkeye Bancorporation, 1996. Advisor Templeton Prize for Progress in Religion, 1986-91; bd. dirs. Finley Hosp., pres., 1983-84; chmn. Finley Health Found., 1986-95, Finley Health Found. Hall of Fame, 2000; bd. dirs. Dubuque Symphony Orch., Dubuque Art Assn., Jr. Achievement, Nat. River Hall of Fame, 1984; chmn. Iowa Assn. Coll. and Univ. Pres., 1975-76; chmn. Iowa Coll. Found., 1982-83; chair Grand Opera House Found., 1998—. With USAAF, 1942-45, PTO. Recipient Dubuque 1st Citizen award, 1990, Disting. Civic Svc. award, 1991, Benjamin Franklin award Nat. Soc. Fundraising Execs., 1994, Paul Harris fellowship, Duduque Rotary Club, 1993; named to Dubuque Bus. Hall of Fame, 1990 Mem. Iowa Assn. Ind. Colls. and Univs. (chmn. 1988-89), Dubuque County Hist. Soc. (bd. dirs.), Dubuque Golf and Country Club, Phi Alpha Theta, Kappa Delta Pi, Phi Delta Kappa. Office: U Dubuque Office of Chancellor 2000 University Ave Dubuque IA 52001-5050

PETERSON, W(ALTER) SCOTT, ophthalmic surgeon; b. Newton, Kans., Sept. 5, 1944; s. Walter F. and Elizabeth (Wiebe) P.; m. Jean Louise Murray, Dec. 16, 1967; children: James Scott, Hilary Jean. BA summa cum laude, Yale U., 1966, MD, 1971. Diplomate Am. Bd. Ophthalmology. Ophthalmic surgeon OptiCare Eye Health Ctr., 1974—. Mem. tchg. faculty Yale U. Med. Sch., New Haven, 1975—. Author: An Approach to Paterson, 1967. Bd. dirs. Waterbury Found., 1985-2000, pres., 1997-2000; trustee Dickinson Coll., 1993-2000. Recipient Med. Sci. award Am. Diabetes Assn., 1980. Fellow ACS, Am. Acad. Ophthalmology; mem. MLA, New England Ophthal. Soc., William Carlos Williams Soc., Phi Beta Kappa Assocs. Office: OptiCare Eye Health Ctr 87 Grandview Ave Waterbury CT 06708-2563

PETERSON, WILLIAM ALLEN, lawyer; b. Marshall, Mo., Oct. 1, 1934; s. R.O. and Marjorie E. (Mallot) P.; m. Mary Kay Moore, July 26, 1958; children: Laura, Clayton, Mary M., Sarah. BS, Drury Coll., Springfield, Mo., 1958; JD, Washington U., 1963. Bar: Mo. 1963, U.S. Dist. Ct. (ea. dist.) Mo. 1964, U.S. Dist. Ct. (we. dist.) Mo. 1965, U.S. Supreme Ct. 1967. Assoc. Riddle, O'Herin & Newberry, Malden, Mo., 1963-65; asst. atty. gen. State of Mo., Jefferson City, 1965-70; legislator Mo. Ho. Reps., 1970-74; pvt. practice Marshall, 1974—. Atty. City of Marshall, 1976-78, City of Slater, Mo., 1988-89; judge mcpl. divsn. State Cir. Ct., Marshall, 1979-80, 2000—, Slater, 1990-94; pros. atty. County of Saline, Marshall, 1979-80, 84-88. With USN, 1954-56. Mem. ABA, Mo. Bar Assn., Assn. Trial Lawyers Am., Am. Legion, VFW. Methodist. Home: 503 E Eastwood St Marshall MO 65340-1535 Office: 54 W Arrow St PO Box 9 Marshall MO 65340-0009

PETERSON, WILLIAM CANOVA, architect; b. Cleve., Nov. 3, 1945; m. Anne Lee Deitz Vassar, June 3, 1967 (div. Nov. 1981); children: Lisa Peterson Thompson, Amanda Peterson Courtney; m. Patricia Hill, July 4, 1985. BArch, Va. Poly. Inst. and State U., 1968; postgrad., Va. Commonwealth U., 1975-77. Registered architect, Va.; cert. Nat. Coun. Archtl. Registration Bds. Project mgr. R.P. Fox Architects, Newark, 1970-73, Highfill & Assocs., Richmond, Va., 1973, Wright, Jones & Wilkinson, Richmond, 1973-79; pres. Canova Assocs. Arch., Mechanicsville, Va., 1979—. Chmn. Bldg. & Code Appeals Bd., King William County, Va., 1997—; mem. Housing Task Force, Hanover County, Va., 1992; mem. exec. UVB Sr. PGA, Richmond, 1984. 1st lt. U.S. Army, 1968-70. Mem. AIA, Assn. of Cons. for Liturgical Space, Constrn. Specifications Inst. (bd. dirs. 1985-87, 88-90), Greater Richmond C. of C., Hanover County Rotary (pres. 1981-82, Paul Harris fellow). Roman Catholic. Office: Canova Assocs Arch PO Box 429 7277 Hanover Green Dr Mechanicsville VA 23111-1764 E-mail: canova-arch@erols.com.

PETERSON-VITA, ELIZABETH ANN, psychologist; b. Apr. 16, 1955; d. Donald Arthur and Adelphine Rose (Lippman) Peterson; m. James Paul Vita, June 10, 1978. BA, NYU, 1975; MA, L.I. U., 1977, PhD, 1984. Lic. psychologist, N.Y., Va., N.C. Psychology intern Northport VA Med. Ctr., N.Y., 1978-79; clin. psychologist L.I. Cons. Ctr., Rego Park, 1979-85, J.F.K. Med. Ctr., Edison, N.J., 1980, Northport VA Med. Ctr., 1980-85; instr. in clin. psychiatry SUNY, Stony Brook, 1985-89; staff psychologist South Oaks Hosp., Amityville, N.Y., 1985-88, dir. internship tng., 1985-88; pvt. practice psychology Wappingers Falls, 1989-99; clin. dir. program devel. Alternative Behavioral Svcs., Norfolk, Va., 1998—99, 1998—99; clin. dir. Mecklenburg County Mental Health Authority, Charlotte, N.C., 2000—. Cons. to psychology and psychiatry svcs. Northport VA Med. Ctr., 1985-89;exec. dir. Psychol. Cons. Assoc., P.C., South Salem, N.Y., 1989-90; cons. Four Winds Hosp., Katonah, N.Y., 1988-92, clin. dir. Devereux- N.Y., Red Hook, 1993-97, Craig House Hosp., Beacon, N.Y., 1989-99. Mem. APA (accreditation com.), Am. Assn. Mental Retardation, Nat. Assn. for Dual Diagnosis, N.Y. Acad. Sci., Nat. Register of Health Svc. Providers in Psychology. Presbyterian. Avocations: theater, film arts, art history, creative writing. Office: 429 Billingsley Rd Charlotte NC 28211 E-mail: epvita@carolina.rr.com.

PETERZELL, DAVID, psychologist; b. Santa Monica, Calif., Apr. 26, 1961; s. Harry Labe and Joyce Moore P. BA, U. Calif., Berkeley, 1983; MA, U. Colo., 1988, PhD, 1991, Alliant Internat. U., 2001. Undergrad. tchg. and rsch. asst. U. Calif., Berkeley, 1980-83; accreditation supr. L.A. Olympic Organizing Com., 1984; tchg. and rsch. asst. U. Colo., Boulder, 1984-91; NIH postdoctoral fellow The Smith-Kettlewell Eye Rsch. Inst., San Francisco, 1992-94, U. Wash., Seattle, 1994-97, U. Calif. San Diego, La Jolla, 1997-98; psychology intern/clin. svcs. St. Vincent de Paul Village, San Diego, 1999-2000; intern in psychology U. San Diego Counseling Ctr., 2000—01; psychologist Cath. Charities, 2002—. Vis. scholar U. Calif., San Diego, La Jolla, 1998—; lectr. Calif. Sch. Profl. Psychology/Alliant Internat. U., San Diego, 2000—; statis. cons., 1990—. Contbr. articles to profl. jours. Recipient Garland Clay award Am. Acad. Optometry, 1991, Rsch. award NIH, Nat. Eye Inst., 1996-98. Mem. Am. Psychol. Soc., Assn. for Rsch. in Vision and Ophthalmology, Soc. for Rsch. in Child Devel., Internat. Assn. for Cognitive Psychotherapy, Integral Inst. Avocations: meditation, yoga, art glass, running. Office: U Calif Psychology Dept 9500 Gilman Dr La Jolla CA 92093

PETESCH, NATALIE L. MAINES, English language educator, author; BS magna cum laude, Boston U., 1955; MA, Brandeis U., 1956; PhD, U. Tex., 1962. Teaching fellow U. Tex., Austin, 1956-59, spl. instr., 1959-60; asst. prof. dept. English San Francisco State U., 1961-62, Southwest Tex. State U., 1962-65; author short stories, novels. Disting. vis. prof. in creative writing, U. Idaho, 1982; presenter readings and fiction workshops nationwide. Author: After the First Death, There is No Other, 1974 (winner U. Iowa Sch. Letters award for Short Fiction, 1974), The Odyssey of Katinou Kalokovich, 1974, Two Novels: The Leprosarium and The Long Hot Summers of Yasha K., 1979 (winner New Letters Summer Prize book award, 1978), Soul Clap Its Hand and Sing, 1981 (literary fellowship Pa. Coun. on Arts, 1980), Duncan's Colony, 1982, Wild With All Regret, 1986 (winner Swallow's Tale competition, 1985), Flowering Mimosa, 1987, Justina of Andalusia and Other Stories, 1990, The immigrant Train and Other Stories, 1996, biog. essay in Lessons in Persuasion, 2000; short stories included in anthologies. Recipient Pitts. Cultural Trust award for Outstanding Established Artist, 1991, Harvey Curtis Webster award for Best Story, 1989; Main Street Morning included in Best American Short Stories, 1979, other writing awards. Avocations: travel, walking, reading, music. Home: 6320 Crombie St Pittsburgh PA 15217-2511

PETH, HOWARD ALLEN, lawyer, educator; b. Calif., Apr. 20, 1955; s. Howard Allen and Diane Marie (Munyan) P.; m. Gloria Gene Stockton, Aug. 9, 1992; children: Andrew Howard, Rachel Gloria. BA, U. Calif., San Diego, 1980; MD, U. Santiago, 1984; JD, U. Mo., 1991. Bar: Calif. 1993, U.S. Ct. Appeals (9th cir.) 1993, U.S. Ct. Claims, U.S. Ct. Appeals (fed. cir.) 1993, U.S. Dist. Ct. (so. dist.) Calif. 1993, U.S. Supreme Ct. 1997; diplomate Am. Bd. Internal Medicine, Am. Bd. Emergency Medicine; lic. physician, Calif., Mo., Wis. Asst. prof. U. Mo. Sch. Medicine, Columbia, 1997—. Fellow Am. Coll. Legal Medicine; mem. AMA, ABA (health law sect.), ACP, Am. Coll. Emergency Physicians. Republican. Episcopalian. Office: U Mo Hosp and Clinic One Hospital Dr Columbia MO 65212 Business E-Mail: perthh@health.missouri.edu.

PETHICK, CHRISTOPHER JOHN, physicist; b. Horsham, Sussex, Eng., Feb. 22, 1942; s. Richard Hope and Norah Betty (Hill) P. BA, Magdalen Coll., Oxford (Eng.) U., 1962, DPhil, 1965. Fellow Magdalen Coll., Oxford U., 1965-70; research assoc. U. Ill., Urbana, 1966-68, research asst. prof., 1968-69, assoc. prof. physics, 1970-73, prof. physics, 1973-95, Nordita, Copenhagen, 1975—. A.P. Sloan research fellow, 1970-72. Fellow Am. Phys. Soc.; mem. European Phys. Soc. Office: Nordita Blegdamsvej 17 DK-2100 Copenhagen Denmark

PETHLEY, LOWELL SHERMAN, retired management consultant; b. Tacoma, Nov. 14, 1928; s. Sherman and Faye Maude (Newton) P.; m. Agnes Lenore Hudgins, Feb. 21, 1953; children: Lynn Louise, Curtis Sherman, Christopher Lowell, Suzanne Elizabeth. BS, U. Wash., 1956, MBA, 1957. Cert. mgmt. cons., CPA. Sr. acct., cons. prin. Deloitte & Touche, Seattle, 1957-65, San Francisco, 1965-67, ptnr. in charge Midwest cons. Chgo., 1968-86, ptnr., 1968-86; ret. Author, editor: Bank Costing for Planning and Control, 1973; contbr. articles to profl. jours. Mem. AICPA (hon. life; cons.), Inst. Mgmt. Cons. (hon. life.), Ill. Soc. CPA, Wash. Soc. CPA, Inverness Golf Club (treas. 1971-73), PGA, Nat. Golf Club, PGA West Club, Phi Beta Kappa, Delta Upsilon, Beta Alpha Psi. Avocations: computers, art. Home: 55-017 Southern Hills La Quinta CA 92253 Office: Deloitte & Touche 10 Westport Rd Wilton CT 06897-4522 E-mail: pinhigh08@aol.com.

PETILLON, LEE RITCHEY, lawyer; b. Gary, Ind., May 6, 1929; s. Charles Ernest and Blanche Lurene (Mackay) P.; m. Mary Anne Keeton, Feb. 20, 1960; children: Andrew G., Joseph R. BBA, U. Minn., 1952; LLB, U. Calif., Berkeley, 1959. Bar: Calif. 1960, U.S. Dist. Ct. (so. dist.) Calif. 1960. V.p. Creative Investment Capital, Inc., L.A., 1969-70; corp. counsel Harvest Industries, 1970-71; v.p., gen. counsel, dir. Tech. Svcs. Corp., Santa Monica, Calif., 1971-78; ptnr. Petillon & Davidoff, L.A., 1978-92, Gipson Hoffman & Pancione, 1992-93; pvt. practice Torrance, Calif., 1993-94; ptnr. Petillon & Hansen, 1994—. Co-author: R&D Partnerships, 2d edit., 1985, Representing Start-Up Companies, 1992, 9th edit., 2002; contbr. chapters to books. Chmn. Neighborhood Justice Ctr. Com., 1983-85, Middle Income Co., 1983085; active Calif. Senate Commn. on Corp. Governance, State Bar Calif. Task Force on Alternative Dispute Resolution, 1984-85; chmn. South Bay Sci. Found., Inc.; vice-chmn. Calif. Capital Access Forum, Inc.; dir., legal counsel ACE-Net.org, Inc. Recipient Cert. of Appreciation L.A. City Demonstration Agy., 1975, United Indian Devel. Assn., 1981, City of L.A. for Outstanding Vol. Svcs., 1984, Outstanding Vol. award Torrance C. of C., 2000, Small Bus. Adv. of Yr. award Torrance C. of C., 2001; named Small Bus. Adv. of Yr. Calif. C. of C., 2001. Mem.: ABA, Los Angeles County Bar Assn. (chmn. law tech. sect., alt. dispute resolution sect. 1992—94, trustee 1984—85, bus. and corp. law sect. 2000—, Griffin Bell Vol. Svc. award 1993), Los Angeles County Bar Found. (bd. dirs.), Calif. State Bar Assn. (pres., Pro Bono Svcs. award 1983). Avocations: backpacking, reading, music, painting. Home: 1636 Via Machado Palos Verdes Estates CA 90274-1930 Office: Petillon & Hansen 21515 Hawthorne Blvd Ste 1260 Torrance CA 90503-6503 E-mail: lpetillon@corplawp-h.com.

PETINA, DAVID ANTHONY, industry analyst; b. Cleve., Aug. 15, 1969; s. David Francis and Martha Ann (Kosarko) P. BA in Polit. Sci., BS in Math., Ashland U., 1991; postgrad., Ind. U., 1991-93. Sales assoc. Kaufmann's, Mentor, Ohio, 1993-96; corp. analyst The Freedonia Group, Cleve., 1996-98, pvt. co. analyst, 1998-2000; industry analyst, 2000—. Vol. intern State Rep. L. Eugene Byers Office, Columbus, Ohio, 1991. Mem. Ashland U. Alumni Assn. (bd. dirs. 1997), Ashbrook Alumni Assn. Office: The Freedonia Group 767 Beta Dr Cleveland OH 44143-2326

PETINGA, CHARLES MICHAEL, transportation executive; b. Atlantic City, July 9, 1946; s. Thomas Joseph and Rose Marie (Merindino) P.; m. Velna Mae McVicker, June 7, 1969; children: Scott, Jeffery. BS in Geology, Geography, U. Wis., Superior, 1969. Ops. supr. Schneider Transport, Inc., Green Bay, Wis., 1973-74, prodn. mgr., 1974-76, safety dir., 1976-79; dir. safety Schneider Nat., Inc., 1979-82, dir. risk mgmt., 1982-87; gen. mgr. Petinga Candy Co., Atlantic City, 1987-89; sr. v.p., midwest practice leader Transp. Industry , Appleton, Wis., 1989-2000. Cons. local charitable groups, Green Bay, 1985-88; preactice leader freight/logistics Global Transp. Industry; adviser, cons. Small Bus. Execs., Green Bay, 1989; mem. worker compensation task force Wis. Motor Carriers, Madison, 1991; nat.-internat. spkr. at univs., bus. schs., vocat. schs. and high schs.; speaker to motor carrier assns., bd. directors, and industry mgmt. groups, nat. and state assns. Co. liaison Green Bay United Way, 1985, 86. With U.S. Army, 1971-73. Mem. Wis. Coun. Safety Suprs., Nat. Safety Mgmt. Soc., Wis. Motor Carriers Assn., Risk and Ins. Mgmt. Soc., Nat. Safety Coun., Am. Trucking Assn. Avocations: martial arts, physical fitness, weight lifting. Office: Marsh Global Transp Group 59 Park Pl Appleton WI 54914-8230

PETIT, PARKER HOLMES, health care corporation executive; b. Decatur, Ga., Aug. 4, 1939; s. James Percival and Ethel (Holmes) P.; m. Janet Lewis; children: William Wright, Patricia Monique, Meredith Katherine. BS in Mech. Engring., Ga. Inst. Tech., 1962, MS in Engring. Mechanics, 1964; MBA, Ga. State U., 1973. Engr. Gen. Dynamics Corp., Fort Worth, Tex., 1966-67; engring. project mgr. Lockheed-Ga. Co., Marietta, 1967-71; pres., founder, chief exec. officer Healthdyne, Inc., 1971—. Bd. dirs. Atlantic S.E. Airlines, Atlanta, Healthdyne Technologies, Inc., Atlanta, Healthdyne Info. Enterprises, Inc., Marietta, Ga., Matria Healthcare, Inc., Marietta, Logility Corp., Atlanta, Intelligent Sys., Norcross, Ga. Author: Primer on Composite Materials, 1968; patentee in field Chmn. bd. dirs. Sudden Infant Death Syndrome Alliance, Washington, 1986; active nat. adv. coun. Emory U. Med. Sch., Coun. fellows for the Emory, Ga. Tech. Biomed. Tech. Rsch. Ctr.; bd. dirs. Ga. Rsch. Alliance, 1995. 1st lt. U.S. Army, 1964-67. Recipient Humanitarian award La SocieteFrancaise de Bienfaisance, 1981; mem. Tech. Hall of Fame of Ga.; mem. Ga. Tech. Acad. Disting. Alumni, 1994; Internat. Bus. fellow, 1986. Mem. Health Industry Mfrs. Assn., Cobb County C. of C. (bd. dirs. 1980-82), Atlanta C. of C. (bd. dirs. 1997—), Pi Kappa Phi. Republican. Methodist. Avocations: flying, oil painting, golf, tennis. Office: Healthdyne Inc 1850 Parkway Pl SE Marietta GA 30067-4439

PETIT, SUSAN YOUNT, French and English language educator; b. Fairfield, Ohio, Aug. 25, 1945; d. Howard Wesley and Elizabeth R. Yount; m. John M. Gill, June 22, 1984. BA in English, Knox Coll., 1966; MA in English, Purdue U., 1968; MA in French, Coll. of Notre Dame, Belmont, Calif., 1983. Prof. French and English Coll. of San Mateo, Calif., 1968—. Mem. exec. com. Calif. C.C. Acad. Senate, Sacramento, 1984-86; pres. acad. senate San Mateo County C.C. Dist., 1981-82, Coll. of San Mateo, 1978-79. Author: Michel Tournier's Metaphysical Fictions, 1991, Françoise Mallet-Joris, 2001; contbr. articles and revs. to profl. publs., chpts. to books. Mem. MLA, Am. Assn. Tchrs. French, Simone de Beauvoir Soc., Conseil Internat. d'Etudes Francophones, Women in French, Calif. Lang. Tchrs. Assn., F. Scott Fitzgerald Soc., Phi Beta Kappa. Home: 777 San Antonio Rd Apt 64 Palo Alto CA 94303-4843 Office: Coll of San Mateo 1700 W Hillsdale Blvd San Mateo CA 94402-3757 E-mail: petits@pacbell.net.

PETIT, WILLIAM ARTHUR, JR. endocrinologist; b. Southington, Conn., Sept. 24, 1956; AB cum laude, Dartmouth Coll., 1978; MD cum laude, U. Pitts., 1982. Diplomate Am. Bd. Internal Medicine, Am. Bd. Endocrinology, Diabetes and Metabolism. Postdoctoral fellow Sch. Medicine Yale U., New Haven, 1985-87, assoc. rsch. scientist, 1987-89, asst. clin. prof., 1989—; chief sect. endocrinology, dir. Joslin Diabetes Ctr. New Britain (Conn.) Gen. Hosp., 1997—; asst. prof. clin. medicine U. Conn. Sch. Medicine, 1997—. Contbr. articles to sci. jours. Chmn. com. on advt. Am. Diabetes Assn., 1996—, pres. Conn. affiliate, 1991-93, bd. dirs., 1987-97. Named to Hall of Merit, Am. Diabetes Assn., Hartford, Conn., 1994. Fellow ACP, Am. Assn. Clin. Endocrinologists; mem. AMA, Endocrine Soc., Hartford County Med. Soc. (Cmty. Svc. award 1994), Conn. Endocrine Soc. (pres. 1999—). Republican. Roman Catholic. Avocations: golf, horticulture. Office: 36 Whiting St Plainville CT 06062-0886 also: 100 Grand St New Britain CT 06050

PETITAN, DEBRA ANN BURKE, educator, education counselor, design engineer, writer, author; b. Chgo., Mar. 12, 1932; d. James Marcellus and Susan Florence (Hines) Burke; m. Kenneth Charles Petitan, Aug. 9, 1952; 1 child, Susan Florence. AA, Wilson Jr. Coll., Chgo., 1951, N.Y. Inst. Photography, 1952; BS in Primary Edn., Chgo. State U., 1956, MS in Indsl. Edn., 1967; DSc in Applied Sci. and Tech., London Inst. Tech., 1971; postgrad., U. Wis., Bradley U., U. Calif., U. Ill.; grad., Inst. Children's Lit., West Redding, Conn., 1991; cert. in Childrens' Portraiture, North Light Art Sch., 1997. Tchr. Chgo. Bd. Edn., 1958-71, guidance counselor, 1976-84, now tchr., cons.; nat. dir. edn. Nation of Islam, 1971-75; design engr. Fed. Sign and Signal Corp., Chgo., 1975-76; CEO, owner Petitan's Creative Projects, Inc. Nat. adv. bd. Nat. Right to Work Orgn., 1976-85; cons. ednl. devel., 1978; computer libr. cons.; owner, CEO, Fayzah's Fin. Svcs., Instrn. Svcs. in Trading and Investing, Fayzah's Creative Projects, Inc.; participant summer writing festival U. Iowa, 1991. Photographer VISTA News, 1969-70; writer children's lit.; author curriculum introducing computer-aided design techniques in the pub. schs., 1965. Cmty. svc. rec. sec. 9600 Block Club; navigator, pub. rels. officer IL wing Squadron 8, capt. CAP, 1953—56; chmn. Career Women for Johnson/Humphrey, Chgo., 1965; dir. Christian edn. Trinity United Ch. Christ, 1978—81, family counselor, 1978—81; organizer, leader family counseling ministry, lic. lay Eucharistic min. Episcopal Ch. St. Edmund, Chgo. Episc. Diocese, 1989. Named Woman of Yr. Iota Phi Lambda, 1978; recipient 250 Hr. medal Ground Observer Corps, 1952, 25 Yr. Service medal Chgo. Bd. Edn., 1987. Mem. Off-Campus Writer's Workshop (editor newsletter), Soc. of Children's Book Writers, Am. Contract Bridge League, Am. Bridge Assn. (life master, rec. sec.), Children's Reading Roundtable, Green River Writers, Epsilon Pi Tau. Achievements include introduction of CAD curriculum to field of edn. Avocations: computer science, canoeing, water color painting, tournament bridge, lapidary. Office: Chgo Bd Edn 125 S Clark St Chicago IL 60603 E-mail: drdapetitan@cs.com.

PETITO, MARGARET L. public relations executive, consultant; b. Dallas, Sept. 28, 1950; d. Jacob Charles and Eileen (Shank) Loehr; m. John Haven Petito, 1978 (div. 1984); children: John Christian Robert, David Nelson. BA, So. Meth. U., 1972. Mem. Action/Vista Program U.S. Govt., Middlesex, N.Y., 1972-74; prin. Petito & Assocs., Washington, 1994—, 1994—; dir., curator Oliver House Mus., Penn Yan, N.Y., 1975-77; staff asst. Williams & Jensen, P.C., Washington, 1986-89; dir. fed. rels. Chambers Devel. Co., Inc., 1989-92; dir. fed. affairs DSSI-U.S. Biotech., Washington, 1992-94; cons., dir. pub. affairs Embassy Ecuador, Govt. Ecuador, 1994-96. Dir. external events Internat. Cancer Alliance, Bethesda, Md., 1996—97, Sch. of Bus., Georgetown U., Washington, 1998—99; exec. dir. Friends of Rule of Law in Ecuador, Inc., 2001—. Spl. legis. advisor Drugwatch Internat., Chgo., 1993—; mem. Women's Coun. Energy and Environ., Washington, 1990—94; bd. dirs. Nyumbani Orphanage for Kenyan Children with AIDS, 1989—99; dir. Marshall Ho. Mus., Lambertville, NJ, 1980—82; mem. task force Women in Govt. Rels., Washington, 1990—96; founder, co-chair Forum for Environ.,

1989—91; pres. Cultural Partnership of the Ams., 1999—. Mem.: Tex. State Soc., Tex. Breakfast Club. Roman Catholic. Avocations: squash, needlepoint, fishing. Home: 6008 34th Pl NW Washington DC 20015-1607 Fax: 202-362-2414. E-mail: mlp3@starpower.net.

PETITTI, MICHAEL JOSEPH, JR. lawyer; b. Canton, Ohio, July 25, 1955; s. Michael Joseph and Shirley Darlene Petitti; m. Anita Jean Charley, Aug. 27, 1977; 1 child, Michael Joseph III. BA in Edn., Ari. State U., 1982, JD cum laude, 1987. Bar: Ariz. 1987, U.S. Dist. Ct. Ariz. 1987, U.S. Ct. Appeals (9th cir.) 1987. Social worker Tempe (Ariz.) Ctr. for the Handicapped, 1982-84; atty. Evans, Kitchel & Jenckes, P.C., Phoenix, 1987-88, Bevs, Gilbert & Morrill, P.C., Phoenix, 1988-90, Gomez & Petitti, P.C., Phoenix, 1990—. Spkr. in field. Pedrick scholar, 1984, 85, 86. Mem. ABA, State Bar Ariz. (mem. exec. coun. state bar employment and labor law sect. 1997—), Maricopa County Bar Assn., Nat. Employment Lawyers Assn., Ariz. Employment Lawyers Assn. Democrat. Office: Gomez & Petitti PC 2525 E Camelback Rd Ste 860 Phoenix AZ 85016-4279 E-mail: mjp@gomezlaw.net.

PETITTO, BARBARA BUSCHELL, artist; b. Jersey City; d. John Edward and Anna (Barnaba) Buschell; m. Joseph Bruno Petitto; children: Vincent John, Christopher Joseph. Studio art cert., N.J. Ctr. Visual Arts, Summit, 1985; student, Art Students League, N.Y.C., 1980, 89-92, Montclair Art Mus., 1991-93. Artist-in-resident art faculty Acad. St. Elizabeth, Convent Stations, NJ, 1989—91; art faculty Morris County Art Assn., Morristown, NJ, 1989; curator Olcott Studio Gallery Art Show, Bernardsville, NJ, 1985, Color/Divine Madness Ward-Nasse Gallery, N.Y.C., 1996; demonstrator Acad. St. Elizabeth Convent Sta., 1989—90, DuCret Sch. Arts Student Art Exhbn.; organizer for acad. students, 1989; dir. Student's Art Festival WNET/Thirteen, Acad. St. Elizabeth, 1989. One-woman shows include County Coll. Morris, 1989, Allied Corp., N.J., 1989, Corner Gallery, World Trade Ctr., N.Y.C., 1989—90, Ward-Nasse Gallery, 1997—98, Johnson & Johnson World Hdqrs. , New Brunswick, N.J., 1998—, Hanover Twp. Mcpl. Bldg., 1999, Dominion County Club, Tex., 1999, Nexus Gallery , N.Y.C., 1999, 2001—02, N.J. Ctr. Visual Arts, Summit, 2001, exhibited in group shows, Summit, 1985, 1992, 1998, Manhattan Arts Internat., 1994—2000, Meadowlands Cultural Ctr. for Arts, Rutherford, N.J., 1995, New World Art Ctr., Soho, 1995—2001, Nat. Assn. Women Artists, Inc., 420 West Broadway Mems. Exhbn. , Ward-Nasse, N.Y.C., Nexus Gallery, N.Y.C., 1999—2002, Hunterdon Art Mus., 1999, Ward-Nasse Gallery, 1989—99, Jain Gallery, N.Y.C., 1989, 1991, N.J. Assn. Ind. Schs., Gill St., Bernard, 1989, Artworks-Trenton , N.J., 1989, 1992, Montclair Art Mus., Bloomfield Coll., 1990, Morris County Park Commn., 1991, Jain-Marunouchi Gallery, N.Y.C., 1992—93, Ben-Shahn Gallery, William Paterson Coll., 1992, Blackwell St. Gallery, Dover, N.J., 1993, Ben-Shahn Gallery, William Paterson Coll., 1994, Cmty. Arts Assn. , Ridgewood, N.J., 1995, Nat. Assn. Women Artists, Inc. , Soho, 1995—2001, Salmagundi Club, 1996, 1998, 2001, Westwood Arts Coal, N.Y.C., 1997, Hunterdon Art Mus., 1997—98, Nexus Gallery, East Village, 1999—2001, N.A.W.A., Chelsea, N.Y.C., 2000—01, Atelier 14, Chelsea, N.Y., 2000, Internat. Salon, 2000—02, Nat. Soc. Painters in Casein and Acrylic, Balt. Convention Ctr., 2000, Represented in permanent collections Nat. Assn. Women Artists, Inc. , Ethicon Corp., New Brunswick, N.J., Allied Corp., N.J. , Interior Sensations , Marinac, N.Y. , Palisades Amusement Pk. Hist. Soc. , Cliffside Park Libr., ACI Art Communication Internat., The Best Contemporary Art , Chgo. Named Miss Livingston N.J., Livingston C. of C.; recipient Rudolph A. Voelcker Meml. award Art Ctr. N.J., 1982, Excellence award Hunterdon Art Mus., 1988, award for excellence Artists League Ctrl. N.J., 1989, Cornelius Low House, Middlesex County Mus., 1989, Montclair Art Mus., 1990, award for mixed media Millburn-Short Hills Art Assn., 1989, 1st Pl. award N.E. Caldwell Arts Festival, 1989, award Nabisco Brands, Inc., East Hanover, N.J., 1990, Excellence award Ann. Tri-State Artists League Ctrl. N.J., 1991-92, Winsor & Newton plaque, Visual Arts League, Edison, N.J., 1992, Excellence award Manhattan Arts Internat. Cover Art Competition, 1994-2000, Hunterdon Art Mus. award for acrylic/mixed media, 1996, Newark Acad., 1996, Livingston Art Assn., 1996, Midland Gallery, Montclair, N.J., 1998 ADP Corp., 1998, Group Liv. Art Assn., 1998, Mary K. Karasick Meml. award, 2000, award N.J. Ctr. Visual Arts, 2001; juried show Somerset Art Assn., 1997-98. Mem. Nat. Soc. Painters in Casein and Acrylic, Nat. Assn. Women Artists, Inc., N.J. Ctr. Visual Arts, Nat. Mus. Women in Arts, Jersey City Mus., Catherine Lorillaird Wolfe Art Club, World Wildlife Fedn., Ward-Nasse Gallery, N.Y.C., Somerset Art Assn., Nexus Gallery, City Without Walls, Newark, N.J. Avocations: opera, vocalist, piano, concerts, museums. Office: PO Box 515 Whippany NJ 07981-0515

PETIX, STEPHEN VINCENT, lawyer; b. Detroit, Oct. 29, 1942; Honors AB, Xavier U., Ohio, 1964; JD, U. Mich., 1967. Bar: Mich. 1968, Calif. 1972, U.S. Dist. Ct. (ea. dist.) Mich. 1968, U.S. Dist. Ct. (so. dist.) Calif. 1972, U.S. Ct. Claims 1996, U.S. Ct. Appeals (9th cir.) 1974, U.S. Supreme Ct. 1980. Law clk. to Hon. Gordon Thompson Jr. U.S. Dist. Judge for So. Dist. Calif., 1972-73; asst. U.S. atty. criminal divsn. U.S. Atty.'s Office, San Diego, 1974-78, asst. chief civil divsn., 1983—94; ptnr. Quinton & Petix, 1994—. With JAGC USNR, 1968-71. Mem. State Bar Calif. (conf. dels. 1995-2001, litigation sect. 1995-98), San Diego County Bar Assn. (chairperson pub. lawyers com. 1989, vice-chairperson 1987-88, fed. ct. com. 1995-2001), San Diego Trial Lawyers Assn. (environ. law seminar, govtl. immunities seminar), San Diego Bar Assn. (aviation sect., fed. tort claims seminar), Orange County Bar Assn. (aviation sect.), Mission Bay Yacht Club (past dir.). Avocations: youth sports coach (soccer, baseball), golf, yachting. Office: Quinton and Petix Koll Ctr 501 W Broadway Ste 1780 San Diego CA 92101-8567

PETKUS, ALAN FRANCIS, microbiologist; b. Chgo., Feb. 4, 1956; s. Frank Anthony and Valeria (Shimkus) P.; m. Karan Elaine Blakeley, Apr. 21, 1990; children: Sabrina Marie, Alexandra Louise, Emerson Alan. BS, Ill. Benedictine Coll., Lisle, 1979; PhD, Chgo. Med. Sch., North Chicago, 1986. Technologist Palos Community Hosp., Palos Heights, Ill., 1973-79, med. technologist, 1979-86; microbiologist South Bend (Ind.) Med. Found., 1986-91; dir. microbiology and immunology Met. Hosp., Grand Rapids, Mich., 1991—. Mem. AAAS, Am. Soc. Clin. Pathologists, Am. Soc. Microbiology, N.Y. Acad. Sci., Ill. Soc. Microbiology, South Ctrl. Assn. Microbiology (Mich. state dir. 2000). Roman Catholic. Avocations: designing computer programs, fishing, skiing. Office: Met Hosp 1919 Boston St SE Grand Rapids MI 49506-4199

PETOK, SAMUEL, retired manufacturing company executive; b. Detroit, Aug. 12, 1922; s. Harry and Jennie (Weingarten) P.; m. Fayne Joyce Myers, June 26, 1952; children— Carol, Seth, Michael. BA in History, Wayne State U., Detroit, 1945; postgrad., Medill Sch. Journalism, Northwestern U., 1946. Reporter Detroit Free Press, 1946-50; account exec. McCann Erickson, 1950-52; pub. relations exec. Chrysler Corp., 1952-70; Vice pres. public relations and advt. White Motor Corp., Cleve., 1971-76; dir. communications automotive ops. Rockwell Internat. Co., Troy, Mich., 1976-77, corp. staff v.p. public relations Pitts., 1977-78, v.p. communications, 1978-82, sr. v.p. communications, mem. mgmt. com., 1982-88; retired. Former trustee Arthur W. Page Soc.; trustee Hist. Soc. Princeton. Recipient Page One award Newspaper Guild Detroit, 1948 Mem. Pub. Rels. Soc. Am. (Silver Anvil award 1964), Internat. Pub. Rels. Assn., Overseas Press Club Am., The Old Guard of Princeton, Nassau Club, Cherry Valley Country Club.

PETOSA, JANET FRANCES, recruiting executive, publishing executive; b. Hartford, Conn., Sept. 10, 1954; d. Paul and Agnes Casmiras (Kamarauskus) Aiello; m. Frank Joseph Petosa, May 17, 1980; children: Allison Marie, Justin Paul-Charles. BA, Ctrl. Conn. State U., New Britain, 1976, MS in Orgn. and Mgmt., 1995. Mgr. clerical divsn. Hobson Assocs., Southington, Conn., 1978-80; br. mgr. Uniforce Temporary Svcs., Hartford, 1985; exec. dir. Women in World Trade-Conn., Inc., Suffield, 1995-96; pres. Computext, Bristol, Conn., 1996—, Global Recruiters, Bristol, 1996—, Computext, Bristol, 1996—. Editor-in-chief Global Job Bank, 1997. Hon. mem. Permanent Commn. on the Status of Women, Conn., mem. Congl. Dist. 6 adv. coun., 1996-98. Mem. AAUW, NAFE, Am. Entrepreneur's Assn. (charter), Am. Seminar Leaders Assn., Am. Women's Econ. Devel. Corp., Nat. Assn. Women Bus. Owners (congl. adv. coun. 1995-96). Democrat. Roman Catholic. Avocations: piano, statistical research, internet. Office: Global Recruiters 115 Peppermint Ln Bristol CT 06010-2275

PETOSA, JASON JOSEPH, publisher; b. Des Moines, Apr. 26, 1939; s. Joseph John and Mildred Margaret (Cardamon) P.; m. Theodora Anne Doleski, Aug. 12, 1972; 1 son, Justin James. Student, Marquette U., 1957-59, St. Paul Sem., 1959-63, 65-67, Colegio Paolino Internationale, Rome, 1963-65. Asso. editor Cath. Home Mag., Canfield, Ohio, 1965-67, editor, 1968; dir. Alba House Communications, Canfield, 1968-71; with Office of Radio and TV, Diocese of Youngstown, Ohio, 1969-71; dir. pub. relations, instr. Alice Lloyd Coll., Pippa Passes, Ky., 1971-76; writer, cons. Bethesda, Ohio, 1976-79; pres., pub. Nat. Cath. Reporter, Kansas City, Mo., 1979-85; v.p., gen. mgr. Towsend-Kraft Pub. Co., Liberty, 1985-86; pres., pub. Steadfast Pub. Co., Kansas City, 1986—. Bd. dirs. David (Ky.) Sch., 1973-79; mem. Mayor's UN Day Com., Kansas City. Mem. Kansas City Direct Mktg. Assn., UN Assn. (bd. dirs. Met. Kansas City chpt., pres. 2000), Sigma Delta Chi. Roman Catholic. Office: 19 W Linwood Blvd PO Box 410265 Kansas City MO 64141-0265 E-mail: jasonpetosa@steadfastpublishing.com.

PETOSKEY, THOMAS W. secondary school educator; b. Bay City, Mich., Feb. 17, 1955; s. Walton R. and Henrietta (Wesolowski) P. BS, U. Detroit, 1977; MS, Oklahoma City U., 1982, EdD, 1984. Cert. tchr., Okla., Mich., Calif. Tchr. sci. Oklahoma City Pub. Schs.; now tchr. sci. Archdiocese of L.A. Com. mem. Loyola Marymount U. Named Vol. of Yr., Oklahoma City Pub. Schs., 1982, 83, Tchr. of Yr., 1992. Mem. ASCD, Am. Fedn. Tchrs., Calif. Sci. Tchrs. Assn., Nat. Cath. Edn. Assn., Nat. Sci. Tchrs. Assn.

PETOW, JOAN CLAUDIA, orthopedic nurse; b. Spokane, Wash., Mar. 5, 1946; d. August and Ella (McHargue) P. Diploma summa cum laude, Deaconess Hosp. Sch. Nursing, Spokane, 1967; BSN cum laude, Pacific Luth. U., 1969. RN, Wash.; cert. orthopedic nurse. Staff nurse orthopedic unit Deaconess Med. Ctr., Spokane, 1969-70, nurse ICU, 1970-72, asst. head nurse adult surg. unit, 1972-73, head nurse orthopedics unit, 1973-83; orthopedic staff nurse Valley Hosp. and Med. Ctr., 1984-96; nurse N.W. Orthopedic Specialists, 1995—. Orthopedic quality assurance rep. Valley Hosp. and Med. Ctr., Spokane, 1988-90. Chmn. Spokane Coun. Christian Bus. and Profl. Women, 1976-77. Mem. Nat. Assn. Orthopedic Nurses (cert., pres.-elect Inland N.W. chpt. 1998-99, pres. Inland N.W. chpt. 1999-2000), Sigma Theta Tau. Avocations: reading, bicycling.

PETRACCA, MARK PATRICK, political scientist, educator; b. Melrose, Mass., Oct. 6, 1955; s. Pasquale George and Frances (Pavuk) P.; m. Terry B. Schuster, June 24, 1979; children: Gina, Joseph. AB, Cornell U., 1977; AM, U. Chgo., 1979, PhD, 1986. Instr. U. Chgo., 1980-81; asst. prof. Amherst (Mass.) Coll., 1982-84; asst. prof. polit. sci. U. Calif., Irvine, 1984-92, assoc. prof. polit. sci., 1992—. Vis. prof. Beijing (China) U., 1987; panelist Lobdell Group, Cosa Mesa, Calif., 1991—. Editor: The Politics of Interests, 1992; co-author: The American Presidency; columnist Orange Coast Daily Pilot, 1991—; contbg. editor Orange County Metropolitan, Newport Beach, Calif., 1989—. Mem. Com. on Election Reform, City of Irvine, 1991-92; mem. exec. com. Irvine Tomorrow, 1990—; mem. Blue Ribbon Com. on Housing, City of Irvine, 1989-90; trustee Calif. State U. Fullerton Coll. Legal Clinic. Recipient Lauds and Laurels award for disting. teaching U. Calif. Irvine Alumni Assn.; ABA Fund for Justice and Edn. grantee, 1988; U.Calif.-Irvine teaching exch. fellow, 1987. Mem. Am. Polit. Sci. Assn., Midwest Polit. Sci. Assn., Western Polit. Sci. Assn. (editorial bd. 1990), So. Polit. Sci. Assn., Presidency Rsch. Group, Acad. Polit. Sci.

PETRAIT, BROTHER JAMES ANTHONY, secondary education educator, clergy member; b. Phila., May 4, 1937; s. John Joseph and Antonina Frances (Cizek) P. BA, U. Detroit, 1969; MEd, U. Ga., 1971; postgrad. in Scis. and Edn., 8 Univs. and Colls. in U.S., 1971—. Joined Oblates of St Francis de Sales, Roman Cath. Ch., 1957. Sci. tchr. Salesian H.S., Detroit, 1961-70, Judge Meml. H.S., Salt Lake City, 1972-76, Benedictine H.S., Detroit, 1976-82, St. Joseph H.S., Ogden, Utah, 1983-88, Fredriksted, V.I., 1988—; tchr. resource agt. Am. Astron. Soc., 1995—. Pres. Mich. Assn. of Biology Tchrs., 1978-82, Utah Biology Tchrs. Assn., 1985-88; bd. dirs. Utah Sci. Tchrs. Assn., 1985-88; presenter at workshops, speaker in Chgo., New Orleans, Las Vegas, Detroit, Phila., Salt Lake City, Layton, Orlando, Purdue U., Anaheim, Australian Nat. Univ., Canberra; participant in 8 NSF-funded programs: U. Ga., Christian Bros. Colls., Vanderbilt U., St. Lawrence U., Ball State U., W. Va. U., No. Ariz. U. Contbr. article to teacher's mags. and ednl. jours. including The Am. Biology Tchr., The Sci. Tchr., The Cath. Digest., Congrl. Record. Anti nuclear weapons activist, founder and leader Nuclear Free Utah, Ogden, 1986-88; led boycott against Morton Salt Co., maker of nuclear weapons.. Recipient Outstanding Biology Tchr. award Nat. Assn. Biology Tchrs., 1975, Nat. Finalist in Presdl. awards for excellence in sci. and math. tchg. Nat. Sci. Tchrs. Assn./NSF/The White House, 1995, finalist and alt. in the Albert Einstein fellowship for Disting. Educators, 1997; fellow Access Excellence fellow Genentech Inc. program for Outstanding Biology Tchrs., 1996, 97. Mem. AAAS, Nat. Sci. Tchrs. Assn. (cert. in biology and gen. sci., Star award 1976, Ohaus awards, 1980, 84), Am. Astron. Soc. (tchr. resource agt. 1995—, leadership inst. participant U. Tex. and McDonald Observatory 1998), Soc. of Amateur Radio Astronomers, Nat. Sci. Edn. Leadership Assn., Soc. For Sci. Exploration, Inst. of Noetic Scis., Soc. Scientific Exploration, Seti League (V.I. coord.), Nat. Assn. Biol. Tchrs., Phi Delta Kappa. Avocations: radio amateur, computers, photography, videography. Home and Office: Saint Joseph H S Plot 3 Rte 2 Frederiksted VI 00840 E-mail: jpetrait@earthling.net.

PETRAK, CLIFF MATTHEW, secondary school educator; b. Chgo., Sept. 6, 1942; s. Joseph Petrak and Josephine Marcella (Jedlinski) Petrak. BS in Math., De Paul U., Chgo., 1964; MS in Math., Chgo. State U., 1970, MS in Edn. Libr. Sci. and Comms., 1981. Mem. math. faculty Brother Rice H.S., Chgo., 1964—, head libr., 1976—89, asst. libr, 1975—76, 1990—, frosh-soph baseball coach, 1966—89, varsity baseball coach, 1990—2000, varsity and jr. varsity bowling coach, 1987—. Author: (book) The Art and Sci. of Aggressive Base Running, 1986, The Complete Guide to Outfield Play, 1998; contbr. articles to scholastic and athletic jours. Named to Coaches Hall of Fame, Chgo. Cath. League, 2002; recipient Tony Lawless award, Chgo. Cath. League (baseball), 1991, 1993, 1994, 2000. Mem.: Nat. Coun. Tchrs. of Math. Roman Catholic. Avocations: dancing, hiking, bicycling, baseball, white-water rafting. Office: Brother Rice HS 10001 S Pulaski Rd Chicago IL 60655 E-mail: cpetrak1@hotmail.com.

PETRAKIS, HARRY MARK, author; b. St. Louis, June 5, 1923; s. Mark E. and Stella (Christoulakis) P.; m. Diane Perparos, Sept. 30, 1945; children: Mark, John, Dean. Student, U. Ill., 1940-41, L.H.D., 1971, Governor's State U., 1980, Hellenic Coll., 1984, Roosevelt U., 1987. Freelance writer, tchr., lectr.; tchr. workshop classes in novel, short story; McGuffey vis. lectr. Ohio U., Athens, 1971; writer-in-residence Chgo. Pub. Library, 1976-77, Chgo. Bd. Edn., 1978-79; Kazantzakis Prof. San Francisco State U., 1992. Author: Lion at My Heart, 1959, The Odyssey of Kostas Volakis, 1963, Pericles on 31st Street, 1965 (nominated for Nat. Book award), The Founder's Touch, 1965, A Dream of Kings, 1966 (Nat. Book award nomination), The Waves of Night, 1969, Stelmark: A Family Recollection, 1970, In the Land of Morning, 1973, The Hour of the Bell, 1976, A Petrakis Reader, 28 Stories, 1978, Nick the Greek, 1979, Days of Vengeance, 1983, Reflections on a Writer's Life and Work, 1983, Collected Stories, 1986, Ghost of the Sun, 1990, Tales of the Heart, 1999, Twilight of the Ice, 2003; contbr. short stores to mags. including, Atlantic Monthly, Sat. Eve. Post, Harper's Bazaar, Country Beautiful. (Story included in Prize Stories, also O. Henry Award 1966). Recipient awards Friends of Am. Writers, Friends of Lit., Soc. Midland Authors, Carl Sandburg award, Ellis Island medal of honor, 1995. Mem. Authors Guild, PEN, Writers Guild Am.-West. Address: Dune Acres 80 East Rd Chesterton IN 46304-1035 E-mail: hmp801@attbi.com. *"...The older I become, the more clearly I see that there is a stunning purity in the writing of a book that I cannot achieve in my own life with its frailty and desperation. The work takes over with a life of its own. In those moments, I wouldn't trade writing with all its loneliness and sometimes with its pain, for any other profession in the world.*

PETRAKIS, NICHOLAS LOUIS, edidemiologist, medical researcher, educator; b. San Francisco, Feb. 6, 1922; s. Louis Nicholas and Stamatina (Boosalis) P.; m. Patricia Elizabeth Kelly, June 24, 1947; children: Steven John, Susan Lynn, Sandra Kay. BA, Augustana Coll., 1943; BS in Medicine, U. S.D., 1944; MD, Washington U., St. Louis, 1946. Intern Mpls. Gen. Hosp., 1946-47; physician, researcher U.S. Naval Radiol. Def. Lab., San Francisco, 1947-49; resident physician Mpls. Gen. Hosp., 1949-50; sr. asst. surgeon Nat. Cancer Inst., USPHS, San Francisco, 1950-54; asst. research physician Cancer Research Inst., U. Calif., 1954-56; asst. prof. preventive medicine U. Calif. Sch. Medicine, 1956-60, assoc. prof., 1960-66, prof., 1966-91, chmn. dept. epidemiology and internat. health, 1978-88, prof. emeritus, 1991—; prof. epidemiology U. Calif. Sch. Pub. Health, Berkeley, 1981-91. Assoc. dir. G.W. Hooper Edn., U. Calif., San Francisco, 1970-74, acting dir., 1974-77, chmn. dept. epidemiology and internat. health, 1979-89; co-dir. Breast Screening Ctr. of No. Calif., Oakland, 1976-81; cons. Breast Cancer Task Force, Nat. Cancer Inst., Bethesda, Md., 1972-76; chmn. Biometry & Epidemiology Contract Rev. Com., Bethesda, 1977-81; mem. bd. sci. counselors, div. cancer etiology Nat. Cancer Inst., Bethesda, 1982-86; mem. scientific adv. com. Calif. State Tobacco-Related Disease Rsch. Program, 1991-93; cons. U. Crete Sch. Medicine, Heraklion, Greece, 1984; bd. dirs. No. Calif. Cancer Ctr., 1991. Contbr. over 200 research papers on breast cancer, med. oncology and hematology. Eleanor Roosevelt Internat. Cancer fellow Am. Cancer Soc., Comitato Reserche Nucleari, Cassacia, Italy, 1962; U.S. Pub. Health Service Spl. fellow Galton Lab., U. London, 1969-70; recipient Alumni Achievement award Augustana Coll., Sioux Falls, S.D., 1979, Axion award Hellenic-Am. Profl. Soc. of Calif., San Francisco, 1984, Lewis C. Robbins award Soc. for Prospective Medicine, Indpls., 1985, Otto W. Sartorius, MD, award from Susan Love MD Breast Cancer Found., 2001. Mem. Am. Soc. Preventive Oncology (founding, pres. 1984-85, Disting. Achievement award 1992), Soc. for Prospective Medicine (founding), Am. Assn. Cancer Rsch., Am. Epidemiol. Soc., Am. Soc. Clin. Investigation, Am. Bd. Preventive Medicine (cert.). Home: 335 Juanita Way San Francisco CA 94127-1657 Office: U Calif Sch Medicine Dept Epidemiology & Biostats Box 0560 MU420W San Francisco CA 94143-0001 E-mail: petrakis@ix.netcom.com.

PETRALIA, RONALD SEBASTIAN, entomologist, neurobiologist; b. Lawrence, Mass., Nov. 7, 1954; s. Samuel and Rosalie (Zanfagna) P. BS in Entomology summa cum laude, U. Mass., 1975; PhD in Entomology and Biology, Tex. A&M U., 1979. Rsch. asst. Tex. A&M U., College Station, 1975-79, rsch. assoc., 1979-80; asst. prof. biology St. Ambrose Coll., Davenport, Iowa, 1980-85; rsch. fellow dept. anatomy George Washington U., Washington, 1985-90; sr. staff fellow Nat. Inst. Deafness and Other Comm. Disorders, NIH, Bethesda, Md., 1991-97, staff scientist, 1997—. Presenter in field. Contbr. chpts. to books: Excitatory Amino Acids, 1992, The Mammalian Coclear Nuclei: Their Role in Neuroendocrine Function, 1996, The Ionotropic Glutamate Receptors, 1997, Ionotropic Glutamate to Receptors in the CNS, 1999, Handbook of Chemical Neuroanatomy: Glutamate, 2000; contbr. articles to profl. jours. Mem. AAAS, Chesapeake Soc. Microscopy (coun. mem., newsletter editor, past pres.), Soc. Neurosci., Entomol. Soc. Am., Microscopy Soc. Am., Assn. Rsch. Otolaryngology, Cambridge Entomol. Club, Sigma Xi. Roman Catholic. Home: 3 Pooks Hill Rd Apt 218 Bethesda MD 20814-5404 Office: NIDCD NIH Rm 50/4142 9000 Rockville Pike Bethesda MD 20892-8027 E-mail: petralia@nidcd.nih.gov.

PETRASH, JEFFREY MICHAEL, lawyer; b. Cleve., Dec. 14, 1948; s. Robert Anthony and Naomi Marjorie (Close) P.; m. Patricia Ann Early, May 29, 1971 (div. Mar. 1986); 1 child, Michael Stewart; m. Patrice M. Kennard, Nov. 18, 2000. AB, U. Mich., 1969, JD, 1973. Bar: Mich. 1974, D.C. 1975, Md. 1997. Assoc. Dickinson, Wright, McKean, Cudlip & Moon, Detroit, 1973-75, Hamel, Park, McCabe & Saunders, Washington, 1975-78; from assoc. to ptnr. Dickinson, Wright, 1978-99; sr. counsel Am. Gas Assn., 2000—. Capt. U.S. Army, 1973-74. Mem. Soc. Barristers. Episcopalian. Avocation: sailing. Home: 6606 Hillandale Rd Bethesda MD 20815-6406 Office: 400 N Capitol St NW Washington DC 20001-1511

PETRASICH, JOHN MORIS, lawyer; b. Long Beach, Calif., Oct. 13, 1945; s. Louis A. and Margaret A. (Moris) P.; children from previous marriage: Jason, Jacquelyn; m. Mary T. Nevin, Aug. 22, 1997. BA, U. So. Calif., 1967, JD, 1970. Bar: Calif. 1971, U.S. Dist. Ct. (cen. dist.) 1971, U.S. Ct. Appeals (9th cir.) 1973, U.S. Dist. Ct. (no. dist.) Calif. 1974, U.S. Ct. Appeals (ea. dist.) Calif. 1976. Assoc. Fulop, Rolson, Burns & McKittrick, Beverly Hills and Newport Beach, Calif., 1971-74, ptnr., 1975-82; ptnr., head litigation McKittrick, Jackson, DeMarco & Peckenpaugh, Newport Beach, 1983-93; shareholder, head litigation Jackson, DeMarco & Peckenpaugh, 1993—; also bd. dirs. McKittrick, Jackson, DeMarco & Peckenpaugh. Mem. editorial staff U. So. Calif. Law Rev., 1969-70. Mem. ABA, Beverly Hills Bar Assn., L.A. Bar Assn., Assn. Trial Lawyers Am., Orange County Bar Assn., Lawyers Club L.A., Order of Coif. Office: Jackson DeMarco Peckenpaugh PO Box 19704 Irvine CA 92623-9704 E-mail: jpetrasich@jdplaw.com.

PETRELLA, MARY THERESE, community health and women's health nurse; b. Joliet, Ill., Aug. 16, 1957; d. Edward M. and Frances K. (Kolar) Lauric; m. Bradley J. Petrella, July 14, 1979; children: Laurica Antonia, Philip Edward. Diploma, St. Joseph Hosp. Sch. Nursing, Joliet, 1978; BSN with honors, U. Ill., Chgo., 1982; MS, Rush U., Chgo., 1985, Nursing Doctorate, 1997. Cert. childbirth educator, intravenous therapist, family nurse practitioner; CPR instr.-trainer; cert. in scoliosis screening, disaster tng. Staff nurse in nursery/pediatrics St. Joseph Hosp., Joliet, 1979-81; instr. pediatrics and obstetrics Triton Coll., River Grove, Ill., 1985-87; dir. maternal-child svcs. Parkside Profl. Home Health, Park Ridge, 1987-89; pub. health nursing mgr., pub. health nurse Will County (Ill.) Health Dept., Joliet, 1982-84, 89-97; primary care clin. specialist Hines VA Primary Care Clinic, 1997-98; nurse practitioner Hines VA Home Based Primary Care, Maywood, Ill., 1998; family nurse practitioner Hygienic Inst. Cmty. Health Care, LaSalle, 1998—, Joliet (Ill.) Primary Care VA Clinic, 1999—. Bd. dirs. Alvernia Manor; mem. Ill. Maternal-Child Health Coalition; active ARC, Am. Heart Assn., Voices for Ill. Children. Mem. Sigma Theta Tau. Home: 500 David Dr Shorewood IL 60431-9714

PETREQUIN, HARRY JOSEPH, JR. foreign service officer; b. Ste. Genevieve, Mo., July 1, 1929; s. Harry Joseph and Crescentia Ellen (Bechter) P.; m. Katharine McDonnell Drouin, Oct. 7, 1980; children: John Andrew, Marc Christopher, Paul Nicholas. AB, Westminster Coll., 1950; B of Fgn. Trade, Am. Grad. Sch. Internat. Mgmt., 1954; postgrad., Johns Hopkins U., 1960; MA, Tufts U., 1970. Joined U.S. Fgn. Svc., 1955; assigned AID and predecessor agys., 1955—; dep. dir. S.E. Asia Regional Econ. Devel. Office, Thailand, 1970-74; U.S. coord. Senegal River Basin Authority, Dakar, 1975-76; dir. ASEAN and South Pacific Affairs, 1977-80; dir. program devel. and evaluation staff Bur. Internat. Orgn. Affairs State Dept., 1980-81; dep. dir. AID Mission, Morocco, 1981-85; coord. AID Sr. Mgmt. Course, 1985-86, Indsl. Coll. of the Armed Forces, 1986-87; faculty dept. nat. security policy Nat. War Coll., Washington, 1987-89; internat. devel. cons. Black Mountain, N.C., 1989—. Adj. prof. polit. sci. Warren Wilson Coll., Swannanoa, N.C., 1993-94; mem. faculty U. N.C. Coll. Srs., 1995—. Lt. (j.g.) USCGR, 1951-53, comdr. Res. Recipient Superior Honor award AID, 1979, State Dept. Superior Honor award, 1981, Comdrs. award for Civilian Svc., Dept. of the Army, 1989. Mem. Soc. Internt. Devel., World Federalist Assn. (nat. bd. dirs.), Am. Fgn. Svc. Assn., UN Assn. U.S., Acad. Polit. Sci., Cousteau Soc., Common Cause, Inst. Noetic Scis., World Future Soc., Amnesty Internat., Coast Guard Combat Vets Assn., Greenpeace, Vets. for Peace, The Land Inst., Phi Alpha Theta.

PETREY, R. CLAYBOURNE, JR. lawyer; b. Kingsport, Tenn., June 19, 1951; s. Robert C. and Helen Kabrich P.; m. Suzanne Van Zandt, Oct. 22, 1977; children: Caleb Claybourne, Elizabeth Anne. BS, Mich. State U., 1972; MS, U. Tenn., 1976; JD, U. Mich., 1983. Computer systems analyst IRS, Washington, 1977-78; rsch. assoc. NSF, 1978-80; assoc. Dearborn & Ewing, Nashville, 1983-89, ptnr., 1989-92; of counsel Boult, Cummings, Conners, 1992-94; assoc. gen. counsel Am. Health Ctrs., Parsons, Tenn., 1994-97; sec., gen. counsel Ayers Asset Mgmt., 1998—. Bd. dirs. Nashville Bd. Zoning Appeals, 1993—, chmn., 1995; bd. dirs. Nashville Civic Design Ctr., 2001—. Office: Ayers Asset Mgmt Inc Ste 100 200 4th Ave N Nashville TN 37219 E-mail: claypetrey@aol.com.

PETRI, PETER ALEXANDER, economist, educator, director; b. Budapest, Hungary, Oct. 17, 1946; came to U.S., 1959; s. George and Margaret (Fejer) P.; m. Jean H. Lawrence, June 19, 1976; children: Philip, Nicholas. BA, Harvard U., 1968, PhD, 1976. Prof. of Econ. Brandeis U., Waltham, Mass., 1974—; dean Grad. Sch. Internat. Econs. and Fin., 1994—; dir. Lemberg Prog. in Internat. Econ. & Fin., Brandeis U., 1986-94; Carl Shapiro prof. of internat.

fin. Brandeis U., 1989—. Fulbright rsch. scholar Keio U., Tokyo, 1991; cons. World Bank, Washington, OECD, Paris. Author: The Future of the World Economy, 1977, Modeling Japanese-American Trade, 1984, East Asia's Trade and Investment, 1994; editor: Wassily Leontief, 1982, The Economics of the Dollar Cycle, 1990, Regional Co-operation and Asian Recovery, 2000, ASEAN Econ. Bulletin, Jour. of Asian Econs., Singapore Econ. Rev. Grantee Study of Japanese Trade, U.S. State Dept., 1980, Study of U.S. Social Security, Social Security Adminstrn., 1982-83, Internat. Bus. Edn., U.S. Dept. Edn., 1989, 92, 94, Ctr. for Global Partnership, 1995—, NSF, 1995; Econ. Policy fellow Brookings Inst., 1979. Mem. Am. Econ. Assn., Acad. Internat. Bus.

PETRI, THOMAS EVERT, congressman; b. Marinette, Wis., May 28, 1940; s. Robert and Marian (Humleker) P.; m. Anne Neal, Mar. 26, 1983; 1 child, Alexandra. BA in Govt., Harvard U., 1962, JD, 1965. Bar: Wis. 1965. Law clk. to presiding justice U.S. Dist. (we. dist.) Wis., Madison, 1965-66; vol. Peace Corps, Somalia, 1966-67; aide White House, Washington, 1969-70; dir. crime and drug studies Pres.'s Nat. Adv. Coun. on Exec. Orgn., 1969; pvt. practice Fond du Lac, Wis., 1970-79; mem. Wis. State Senate, Madison, 1973-79, U.S. Congress from 6th Wis. dist., Washington, 1979—; mem. edn. and workforce com., trans. and infrastructure com. Editor: National Industrial Policy: Solution or Illusion, 1984. Republican. Lutheran. Avocations: reading, swimming, hiking, biking, skiing. Office: US Ho of Reps 2462 Rayburn Bldg Washington DC 20515-0001

PETRICK, ALFRED, JR. mineral economics educator, consultant; b. Mt. Vernon, N.Y., Dec. 30, 1926; s. Alfred and Ruth (Updike) P.; m. Ruth Goodridge, Jan. 2, 1956; children: Elizabeth, Andrew Wayne. BS, BA, Columbia U., 1952, MS, 1962; MBA, Denver U., 1966; PhD, U. Colo., 1969. Registered profl. engr., Colo. Sales engr. Ingersoll Rand Co., N.Y.C., 1953-54; project engr. U.S. AEC, Grand Junction, Colo., 1954-57; mining engr. Reynolds Metals Co., Bauxite, Ark., 1957-61, Guyana, 1957-61; mineral economist U.S. Bur. Mines, Denver, 1963-70; Coulter prof. Colo. Sch. Mines, Golden, 1970-84, emeritus prof., 1984—; dir. Petrick Assocs., Evergreen, Colo. Author: Economics International Development, 1977, Economics of Minerals, 1980, Preparacion y Evaluacion, 1982. Mem. com. tech. aspects strategic materials Nat. Acad. Sci., Washington, 1973-76, mem. com. surface mining and reclamation, 1979. Served with USAF, 1945-47, PTO. Fulbright research scholar U. Otago, Dunedin, New Zealand, 1986; recipient Edn. award Instituto Para Funcionarios De Las Industrias Minera y Siderurgica, Mexico City, 1981; recipient Service award Office Tech. Assessment, U.S. Congress, 1981. Mem. AIME (chmn. council econs. 1977-78, Henry Krumb lectr. 1986, service award), Profl. Engrs. Colo. Presbyterian. Home: 5544 S Hatch Dr Evergreen CO 80439-7233 Office: Colo Sch Mines Golden CO 80401

PETRICK, ERNEST NICHOLAS, mechanical engineer, researcher; b. Pa., Apr. 9, 1922; s. Aurelius and Anna (Kaschak) P.; m. Magdalene Simcoe, June 13, 1946; children: Deborah Petrick Healey, Katherine, Denise, Victoria Petrick Kropp. BS in Mech. Engring, Carnegie Inst. Tech., 1943; MS, Purdue U., 1948, PhD, 1955. Registered profl. engr., Mich. Faculty Purdue U., 1946-53; dir. heat transfer research Curtiss-Wright Corp., Woodridge, N.J., 1953-56; chief advanced propulson systems Curtiss-Wright Research divsn., Quehanna, Pa., 1957-60; chief research engr. Kelsey-Hayes Co., Detroit, 1960-65; chief scientist, tech. dir. U.S. Army Tank-Automotive Command, Warren, Mich., 1965-82; chief scientist, dir. engring. labs. Gen. Dynamics, 1982-87; engring. cons., 1987—; panel mem. combat vehicles NATO, 1973-82; mem. adv. bd. on basic combustion research NSF, 1973; chmn. advanced transp. systems com. White House Energy Project, 1973; mem. adv. com. NSF-RANN research program Drexel U. Coll. Engring., 1976-78; mem. Army Sci. Bd., 1983-89; cons. Air Force Studies Bd. NRC, 1991-93, cons. Def. Sci. Bd., 1994-95; cons. Nat. Acad. of Scis., 1997-99, 2001—. Adj. prof. engring. Wayne State U., Detroit, 1972-82, U. Mich., Ann Arbor, 1982-83. Contbr. articles on transp., ground vehicles, flight propulsion and project mgmt. to profl. jours. Lt. USNR, 1952—54. Recipient certificate of achievement U.S. Army, 1967, Outstanding Performance awards, 1970, 71, 76, 82, Outstanding Mech. Engring. award Purdue U., 1991; named Disting. Engring. Alumnus Purdue U., 1966 Mem. Soc. Automotive Engrs. (nat. dir. 1978-80), Am. Def. Preparedness Assn. (chmn. land warfare survivability divsn. 1990-95, Silver medal 1992, Recognition award 1992), Assn. U.S. Army, Sigma Xi, Pi Tau Sigma. Home: 1540 Stonehaven Rd Ann Arbor MI 48104-4150 Office: ENP Cons 1540 Stonehaven Rd Ann Arbor MI 48104

PETRICK, MICHAEL JOSEPH, journalism educator; b. Antigo, Wis., Sept. 6, 1942; BS, U. Wis., Milw., 1965, MS, 1967; PhD, U. Wis., Madison, 1970. News editor Milw. South Times Star, 1966-67; disting. teaching fellow U. Wis., Madison, 1969-70; from asst. to assoc. prof. U. Md., College Park, 1970-78; copy editor Evening Star, Washington, 1974-75; chairperson dept. journalism Ctrl. Mich. U., Mt. Pleasant, 1978-84, prof., 1984-2000, prof. emeritus, 2000—. Writing and editing coach Ctrl. Mich. Newspapers, 1984-85; writing and reporting coach Greenville (Mich.) Daily News, 1997-99; chair bd. in control of student media Ctrl. Mich. U., 1997-99. Co-author: Using the Mass Media, 1975; contbr. articles to profl. jours. Mem. Md.-Del.-D.C. Press Assn. (chmn. freedom of info. com. 1972-73), Soc. Profl. Journalists (campus chpt. adviser 1970-99), Nat. Coun. Editl. Writers, Assn. for Edn. in Journalism and Mass Communication. Home: PO Box 6 Mount Pleasant MI 48804-0006 Office: PO Box 6 Mount Pleasant MI 48804-0006 E-mail: michael.petrick@cmich.edu.

PETRICK, PATRICIA A. physician, educator; b. Oak Ridge, Tenn., Dec. 28, 1952; d. Nicholas A. and Irene M. P.; m. William W. Mullins, Feb. 15, 1986; children: Katherine, Thomas. BS, Pa. State U., 1973, MS, 1974; MD, U. Pitts., 1978. Diplomate Am. Bd. Internal Medicine, Am. Bd. Endocrinology and Metabolism. Intern U. Pitts., 1978-79; resident, then chief resident U. Calif., San Diego, 1979-82; fellow Scripps Clinic, La Jolla, Calif., 1982-83, NIH, Bethesda, Md., 1983-85; pvt. practice Endocrine Diabetes Assocs., Ltd., Rockville, 1985—; clin. instr. Georgetown U., Washington, 1988—. Bd. dirs. alumni bd. coll. scis. Pa. State U., University Park, 1994-2001. Fellow ACP; mem. Am. Diabetes Assn. (profl.), Am. Soc. Internal Medicine, Am. Assn. Clin. Endocrinologists. Office: Endocrine Diabetes Assocs 6001 Montrose Rd Ste 211 Rockville MD 20852-4872

PETRICOFF, M. HOWARD, lawyer, educator; b. Cin., Dec. 22, 1949; s. Herman and Neoma P.; m. Hanna Sue, Aug. 11, 1974; children: Nicholas, Eve. BS, Am. U., 1967-71; JD, U. Cin., 1971-74; M in Pub. Adminstrn., Harvard U., 1980-81. Bar: Ohio, U.S. Ct. Appeals (D.C. cir.) 1977, U.S. Ct. Appeals (10th cir.) 1985, U.S. Ct. Appeals (6th cir.) 1989, U.S. Supreme Ct. 1989. Asst. city law dir. City of Toledo (Ohio), 1975-77; asst. atty. gen. Ohio Atty. Gen. Office, Columbus, 1977-82; ptnr. Vorys, Sater, Seymour & Pease, 1982—. Adj. prof. law Capital U. Law Sch., Columbus, 1991—. Contbr. articles to profl. jours. Reginald Heber Smith Found. fellow Washnigton, 1974-75. Mem. Ohio Bar Assn., Columbus Bar Assn., Ohio Oil and Gas Assn. Office: Vorys Sater Seymour & Pease PO Box 1008 52 E Gay St Columbus OH 43215-3161

PETRIDES, CHARLOTTE A. interior designer; b. Miami, Fla. d. Robert Michel and Marguerite (Lively) Ackerman; children: Dana Elizabeth, Stephen James, Laura Amelia. A in Interior Design, Atlanta Area Tech. Sch., 1974; AA, DeKalb Community Coll., Atlanta, 1979; B Visual Arts in Interior Design, Ga. State U., 1981. Cert. profl. interior designer. Owner Forte Interior Design, Atlanta, 1974—92; sr. project designer Designers II, Inc., 1980—92; pres. Phoenix Design Group, Inc., 1992—. Juror Nat. Council for Interior Design Qualification, 1985—. Mem. speakers bur. DeKalb Community Coll., 1986—. Recipient Silver Seal, NAHB Sr. Housing Coun., 1993. Mem. Am. Soc. Interior Designers (1st pl. hospitality design award with Amoco Fibers 1985). Republican. Avocations: art, drawing, nature studies.

PETRIDES, GEORGE ATHAN, ecologist, educator; b. N.Y.C., Aug. 1, 1916; s. George Athan and Grace Emeline (Ladd) P.; m. Miriam Clarissa Pasma, Nov. 30, 1940; children: George H., Olivia L., Lisa B. BS, George Washington U., 1938; MS, Cornell U., 1940; PhD, Ohio State U., 1948; postdoctoral fellow, U. Ga., 1963-64. Naturalist Nat. Park Service, Washington and Yosemite, Calif., 1938-43, Glacier Nat. Park, Mont., 1947, Mt. McKinley Nat. Park, Alaska, 1959; game technician W.Va. Conservation Commn., Charleston, 1941; instr. Am. U., 1942-43, Ohio State U., 1946-48; leader Tex. Coop. Wildlife Unit; assoc. prof. wildlife mgmt. Tex. A. and M. Coll., 1948-50; assoc. prof. wildlife mgmt., zool. and African studies Mich. State U., 1950-58, prof., 1958—; research prof. U. Pretoria, S. Africa, 1965; vis. prof. U. Kiel, Germany, 1967; vis. prof. wildlife mgmt. Kanha Nat. Park, India, 1983; del. sci. confs. Warsaw, 1960, Nairobi and Salisbury, 1963, Sao Paulo, Aberdeen, 1965, Lucerne, 1966, Varanasi, India, Nairobi, 1967, Oxford, Eng., Paris, 1968, Durban, 1971, Mexico City, 1971, 73, Banff, 1972, Nairobi, Moscow, The Hague, 1974, Johannesburg, 1977, Sydney, 1978, Kuala Lumpur, 1979, Cairns, Australia, Mogadishu, Somalia, Peshawar, Pakistan, 1980. Participant NSF Expdn., Antarctic, 1972, FAO mission to, Afghanistan, 1972, World Bank mission to, Malaysia, 1975 Author: Field Guide to Trees and Shrubs, 1958, 2d edit., 1972, Field Guide to Eastern Trees, 1988, 98, Field Guide to Western Trees, 1992, 98, First Guide to Trees, 1993, Trees of the California Sierra Nevada, 1996, Trees of the Pacific Northwest, 1998, Trees of the Rocky Mountains and Intermountain West, 2000, Trees of the American Southwest, 2000; editor wildlife mgmt. terrestrial sect. Biol. Abstracts, 1947-72; contbr. articles to biol. publs. Served to lt. USNR, 1943-46. Fulbright research awards in E. Africa Nat. Parks Kenya, 1953-54; Fulbright research awards in E. Africa Nat. Parks Kenya, Uganda, 1956-57; N.Y. Zool. Soc. grantee Ethiopia, Sudan, 1957; N.Y. Zool. Soc. grantee Thailand, 1977; Mich. State U. grantee Nigeria, 1962; Mich. State U. grantee Zambia, 1966; Mich. State U. grantee Kenya, 1969; Mich. State U. grantee Africa, 1970, 71, 73, 81; Mich. State U. grantee Greece, 1974, 83; Mich. State U. grantee Iran, 1974; Mich. State U. grantee Botswana, 1977; Mich. State U. grantee Papua New Guinea, Thailand, 1979; Iran Dept. Environment grantee, 1977; Smithsonian Instn. grantee India and Nepal, 1967, 68, 75, 77, 83, 85; World Wildlife Fund grantee W. Africa, 1968 Mem. Am. Ornithologists Union, Am. Soc. Mammalogists, Wildlife Soc. (exec. sec. 1953), Wilderness Soc., Am. Comm. Internat. Wildlife Protection, Ecol. Soc., Fauna Preservation Soc., E. African Wildlife Soc., Internat. Union Conservation Nature, Zool. Soc. So. Africa, Sigma Xi. Presbyterian. Home: 4895 Barton Rd Williamston MI 48895-9305 Office: Mich State U Dept Botany East Lansing MI 48824 E-mail: petrides@msu.edu.

PETRIE, BRUCE INGLIS, lawyer; b. Washington, Nov. 8, 1926; s. Robert Inglis and Marion (Douglas) P.; m. Beverly Ann Stevens, Nov. 3, 1950 (dec. Oct. 1993); children: Laurie Ann Roche, Bruce Inglis, Karen Elizabeth Medsger. BBA, U. Cin., 1948, JD, 1950. Bar: Ohio 1950, U.S. Dist. Ct. (so. dist.) Ohio 1951, U.S. Ct. Appeals (6th cir.) 1960, U.S. Supreme Ct. Assoc. Kunkel & Kunkel, Cin., 1950-51, Graydon, Head & Ritchey, 1951-57, ptnr., 1957—. Exec. prodr. (sch. video) Classical Quest, 2000; author: How To Get the Most Out of Your Lawyer, 2002; contbr. articles to legal jours. Mem. bd. Charter Com. Greater Cin., 1952—; pres. Charter Rsch. Inst., 2000; mem. bd. edn. Indian Hill Exempted Village Sch. Dist., 1965-67, pres., 1967; mem. adv. bd. William A. Mitchell Ctr., 1969-86; mem. Green Areas adv. com. Village of Indian Hill, Ohio, 1969-80, chmn., 1976-80; mem. Ohio Ethics Com., 1974-75; co-founder Sta. WGUC-FM; mem. WGUC-FM Cmty. Bd., 1974—, chmn., 1974-76; bd. dirs. Murray Seasongood Good Govt. Fund, 1975—, pres., 1989—; bd. dirs. Nat. Civic League, Cin. Vol. Lawyers for Poor Fund., Linton Music Series, Amernet Chamber Music Soc.; founder Parents as Tchrs. Metro Housing Authority Commn., 1991—; elder, trustee, deacon Knox Presbyn. Ch.; a prin. advocate merit selection judges, Ohio; trustee, mem. bd., Seven Hills Neighborhood Houses, Inst. for Learning in Retirement; mem. bd. Hamilton County Good Govt. League; organizer Late Great Lakes Book Distbn. project. Recipient Pres.'s award U. Cin., 1976, Disting. Alumnus award, 1995. Fellow Am. Bar Found.; mem. ABA, Ohio Bar Assn., Cin. Bar Assn. (pres. 1981, Trustee's award 2000), Am. Judicature Soc. (Herbert Lincoln Harley award 1973, dir.), Nat. Civic League (Disting. Citizen award 1985, coun. 1984—), Am. Law Inst., Ohio State Bar Assn. Found. (Outstanding Rsch. in Law and Govt. award 1986, Charles P. Taft Civic Gumption award 1988, Ohio Bar medal 1988), Cincinnatus Assn., Order of Coif, Lit. Club, Univ. Club, Cin. Club. Avocations: tennis, squash, woodworking, writing, horticulture, music. Home: 2787 Walsh Rd Cincinnati OH 45208-3428 Office: Graydon Head & Ritchey 1900 Fifth 3d Ctr 511 Walnut St Ste 1900 Cincinnati OH 45202-3157

PETRIE, DONALD JOSEPH, banker; b. N.Y.C., Sept. 2, 1921; s. John and Elizabeth (Thomson) P.; m. Jane Adams, Aug. 27, 1949; children: R. Scott, Anne, Elizabeth, Douglas, Susan. BBA, Manhattan Coll., 1950. Personnel mgr. Otis Elevator Co., N.Y.C., 1951-59; personnel dir. Brown Bros. Harriman & Co., 1959-68; exec. v.p. U.S. Trust Co., 1968-79; sr. v.p. Marine Midland Bank, 1979-86, Drake Beam Morin Inc., N.Y.C., 1986-90; chmn., chief exec. officer Webster Corp., 1990—. Lectr. Baruch Sch. Bus., Coll. City N.Y., 1955-58; pres., chmn. exec. and fin. coms., dir. Webster Apts., N.Y.C., 1973—; adj. prof. mgmt. Hofstra U., Hempstead, N.Y., 1986-93. Author: Explaining Pay Policy, 1969, Handling Employee Questions About Pay, 1976. Capt. USAAF, 1942-46. Mem. N.Y.C. Partnership and C. of C. (chmn. mgmt. edn. and adv. com. 1964-98). Home: 11 Fairview Ave Great Neck NY 11023-1462 Office: 419 W 34th St New York NY 10001-1596

PETRIE, FERDINAND RALPH, illustrator, artist; b. Hackensack, N.J., Sept. 17, 1925; s. Archibald John and Bessie (Rutherford) P.; m. Phyllis C. Haddow, Oct. 19, 1951; children: Beth, David. Advt. cert., Parson's Sch. Design, N.Y.C., 1949; student, Art Students League, 1947-49, Famous Artists Course in Illustration, 1958-59. Illustrator J. Gans Assos., N.Y.C., 1950-69. Free lance illustrator, artist, 1969— , owner, Petrie Gallery, Rockport, Mass., 1971-95; represented in permanent collections, U.S. Supreme Ct., Smithsonian Instn., Washington, Indpls. Mus. Art; designer U.S. commemorative stamp design, 2 Zaire commemorative stamps, 1980; Author: Drawing Landscapes in Pencil, 1979; illustrator: The Drawing Book, 1980, The Color Book, 1981, The Alkyd Book, 1982, The Watercolorists Guide to Painting Trees, 1983, The Watercolorists Guide to Painting Skies, 1984; The Watercolorists Guide to Painting Water, 1985, Painting Nature in Watercolor, 1990. Served with U.S. Maritime Service, 1943-46. Mem. Artists Fellowship, Rockport Art Assn., Am. Artists Profl. League, N.J. Watercolor Soc. Presbyterian. Address: 51 Vreeland Ave Rutherford NJ 07070-2227

PETRIE, GREGORY STEVEN, lawyer; b. Seattle, Feb. 25, 1951; s. George C. and Pauline P.; m. Margaret Fuhrman, Oct. 6, 1979; children: Kathryn Jean, Thomas George. AB in Polit. Sci and Econs., UCLA, 1973; JD, Boston U., 1976. Bar: Wash. 1976, U.S. Dist. Ct. (we. dist.) Wash. 1976. Adminstr. Action/Peace Corps, Washington, 1973, Fed. Power Commn., Washington, 1974; assoc. Oles Morrison et al, Seattle, 1976-80; ptnr. Schwabe Williamson Ferguson & Burdell, 1981-94; mng. shareholder Krutch Lindell Bingham Jones & Petrie, 1994—. Mem. Seattle-King County Bar Assn., Profl. Liability Architects and Engrs., Wash. Athletic Club. Avocations: woodworking, skiing. Office: Krutch Lindell Bingham Jones & Petrie 1420 Fifth Ave Ste 3150 Seattle WA 98101 E-mail: gsp@nwlink.com.

PETRIE, HOWARD LANE, engineer, researcher; b. Rockford, Ill., Dec. 26, 1953; s. Ronald Irving and Betty Lou (Lane) P. BS, U. Ill., 1977, MS, 1980, PhD in Mech. Engring., 1984. Rsch. assoc., mem. grad. faculty applied rsch. lab. Pa. State U., State College, 1985-91, sr. rsch. assoc., 1991—. Contbr. articles to profl. jours. Mem. Assn. for Retarded Citizens, nationwide, League Am. Bicyclist. U. Ill. fellow, 1978; nat. rsch. coun. post-doctoral associateship, 1984-85. Mem. AIAA, ASME, ACLU, Internat. Soc. Optical Engring., Iowa Mountaineers, Sierra. Avocations: mountaineering, mountain travel, bicycling, golf, fishing. Home: 214 Fry Dr State College PA 16801-6214 Office: Pa State U Applied Rsch Lab PO Box 30 State College PA 16804-0030

PETRIE, HUGH GILBERT, philosophy of education educator; b. Lamar, Colo., Sept. 21, 1937; s. Charles Albert and Mary Madeleine (Ocsay) P.; m. Patricia Donahoe Bradasich, June 3, 1959 (div. 1978); children: Trent Anthony, Ragan Andrea, Brock Asher; m. Carol Ann Hodges, Aug. 26, 1978; stepchildren: Lara Wardrop, Amy Wardrop. BS in Bus., BS in Applied Math., U. Colo., 1960; Phd in Philosophy, Stanford U., 1965. Asst. prof. Northwestern U., Evanston, Ill., 1965-71; assoc. prof. U. Ill., Champaign/Urbana, 1971-75, prof., 1975-81, assoc. vice chancellor for academic affairs, 1977-80; dean Grad. Sch. Edn. SUNY, Buffalo, 1981-97, prof., 1981-2000; ret., 2000. Coord. N.E. region Holmes Group, 1986-90, bd. dirs.; mem. bd. overseers N.E. Regional Lab., 1986-92, chmn., 1986-87; co-chmn. N.Y. State Task Force on Preparation and Licensure Sch. Adminstrs., 1988-89; mem. N.Y. State Spl. Commn. on Edn., Structure, Policies, and Practices, 1993; bd. dirs. Orgn. Inst. Affiliates, Am. Edn. Rsch. Assn., 1991-93; pres. Tchr. Edn. Conf. Bd., N.Y., 1991-95; mem. N.Y. State Comm. Cert. of Edn. Profl., 1996-97. Author: The Dilemma of Enquiry and Learning, 1981; editor jour. Ednl. Theory, 1980-81; founding mem. bd. editors jour. Ednl. Policy, 1986-98; contbr. numerous articles to profl. jours. Mem. commn. on teaching Nat. Assn. State Univs. and Land Grant Colls., 1988-92. Resident assoc. Ctr. for Advanced Study, U. Ill., 1980-81. Fellow Philosophy of Edn. Soc. (pres. 1984-85, mem. exec. com. 1974-76, 82-83); mem. Am. Ednl. Rsch. Assn., Am. Philos. Assn. E-mail: hgpetrie@acsu.buffalo.edu.

PETRIE, JOHN NOEL, career officer; s. John and Marie Carmelita Petrie; m. Ann Legan, June 22, 1974; children: Alex, Noel, Sean. AB, Villanova U., 1971; MA in Law and Diplomacy, Fletcher Sch., 1984, PhD, 1990. Commd. ensign USN, 1971, advanced through ranks to capt.; navigator USS Talbot, 1971-74; faculty U.S. Naval Acad., Annapolis, Md., 1974-76; ops. officer USS Merrill, 1977-80; ops. and plans officer Destroyer Squadron SEVEN, 1980-81; exec. officer USS Oldendorf, 1986-86; asst. br. chief western hemisphere Joint Chiefs of Staff, Washington, 1986—88; commanding officer USS Doyle, 1990-92; dir. rsch., prof. nat. security policy Nat. War Coll., Washington, 1992-95; exec. asst. Dep. Chief Naval Ops for Plans, Policy & Ops., 1995-96; commanding officer Naval Station Norfolk, Va., 1996-98; exec. dir. CNO Exec. Panel, Washington, 1998-2001; asst. v.p. pub. safety and emergency mgmt. George Washington U. Author: American Neutrality, 1995; editor: Essays in Strategy XI, 1994 (Blue Penci award, 1995); contbr. articles; editor: Essays in Strategy XII, 1994. Recipient Cruz de la Resistencia de Nicaragua Dem. Resistance, 1988, Mentzer award, Villanova U., 1971, Def. Superior Svc. medal, Legion of Merit. Mem.: UN Assn., Acad. Coun. UN Sys., Am. Soc. Internat. Law, Internat. Inst. Strategic Studies. Home: 5325 Stonington Dr Fairfax VA 22032 Office: George Washington Univ Rice Hall Ste 701 2121 Eye St NW Washington DC 20052

PETRIE, PAUL ERIC, interior design educator; b. Clinton, Ont., Canada, Oct. 22, 1943; s. Joseph A. and Lily O. (Reed) P.; m. Margaret A. Ridge, Aug. 28, 1967; children: Alexandra, John, Garth. B in Interior Design with honors, U. Manitoba, 1967; MFA, Syracuse U., 1977. Prof. U. Man., Winnipeg, 1967-84; ptnr. Group 4 Design Cons., 1969-84; prof., chmn. Va. Commonwealth U., Richmond, Va., 1984-95, asst. dean Sch. of Arts, 1995—. Interior design cons. Contbr. articles to profl. jours. Fellow Interior Design Educators Coun., Internat. Interior Design Assn.; mem. Am. Soc. Interior Designers (affiliate), Profl. Interior Designers Inst. of Man. Office: Va Commonwealth U 325 N Harrison St Richmond VA 23284-9057

PETRIE, WILLIAM, physicist, researcher; b. Victoria, B.C., Can., Dec. 30, 1912; s. James and Amelia (Robertson) P.; m. Isabelle Ruth Chodat, May 8, 1944; children: Heather Louise (dec.), Douglas Bruce. BA, U. B.C., Vancouver, Can., 1938; A.M., Harvard U., 1941, PhD, 1944. Assoc. prof. U. Sask., Saskatoon, Can., 1945-51; chief ops. research Def. Research Bd., Ottawa, Ont., Can., 1954-60, dep. chmn. Can., 1966-68, chief Can. def. research staff London, 1968-71. Sci. advisor Apollo Energy, Victoria, 1981-83; mem. numerous sci. bds. and coms. Author: The Story of the Aurora Borealis, 1963, Guide to Orchids of North America, 1981; also numerous articles Recipient Centennial medal Govt. of Can., 1967, numerous research grants and contracts Fellow Royal Soc. Can. Avocations: gardening; fishing. Home: 306-2300 Henry Ave Rural Rt 4 Sidney BC Canada V8L 2B2

PETRIK, GERARD FRANCIS, health care administrator; b. Balt., June 1, 1935; s. Clement William and Ernestine (Bieble) P.; m. Patricia Boothe, June 15, 1957; children: Gerard Francis Jr., Mary Susan Petrik King, Martin. BS in Acctg., Loyola Coll., Balt., 1957. CPA, Md. Acct. Peat Marwick, Balt., 1960-65; CFO Kernan Hosp., 1965-72, Deaton Med. Ctr., Balt., 1972-74; dir. Blue Cross of Md., 1974-86; exec. v.p. Ches. Med. Specialists, 1986—87; ptnr. Yaffe & Co., Inc., 1987—93; program mgr. Health Care Commn., 1993—. Mem. Healthcare Fin. Mgmt. Assn. Home: 7 Airway Cir Apt 2 D Baltimore MD 21286-3465 Office: MHCC 4201 Patterson Ave Baltimore MD 21215-2222 E-mail: gpetrik@mhcc.state.md.us.

PETRIK, GERD, pharmaceutical executive; b. Brno, CSR, Czechoslovakia, Apr. 13, 1943; came to U.S., 1993; s. Wilhelm and Ingeborg (Bittner) P.; m. Feli Schueller, July 10, 1971; children: Sharon, Wendy. Pharmacist, Free U. Berlin, 1968. Pres. Dr. Will Inc., Karlsruhe, Germany, 1968-70; product mgr. Pfizer, Illertissen, Germany, 1970-73; head rsch. Helopharm, Berlin, 1973-85, pres., owner, 1985—. Pres. Berlin Pharm. Assn., 1990-93; owner over 25 rsch. and devel. med. cos., worldwide, 1995—. Inventor chem. compounds. Pres. Harness Racing Assn., Berlin, 1992-96. Named hon. consul Bangladesh, 1986-90, hon. gen. consul, Panama, 1990-94; scholar Columbia U., 1995-97. Roman Catholic. Avocations: harness racing (German champion, world record holder), golf, tennis, classic car collector. Home: 1538 N Casey Key Rd Osprey FL 34229-9770 E-mail: gpetrik@comcast.net.

PETRILA, JOHN PHILIP, health law educator; b. Terre Haute, Ind., June 25, 1951; s. John Joseph and Patricia Ann (McCrisaken) P.; m. Amelia Ann Thompson, Oct. 18, 1953; 1 child, Patrick John. BA, St. Joseph's Coll., Renssalaer, Ind., 1973; JD, U. Va., 1976, LLM, 1977. Bar: Va. 1976. Fellow in mental health law U. Va. Law Sch., Charlottesville, 1976-78; asst. atty. gen. State of Mo., Jefferson City, 1978-79; dir. forensic svcs. Mo. Mental Hygiene Dept., 1979-81; dep. counsel N.Y. Office Mental Health, Albany, 1981-87, counsel, dep. commr., 1987-92; chmn. dept. mental health law and policy Fla. Mental Health Inst./ U. South Fla., Tampa, 1992—. Mem. mental health planning coun. State of Fla., 1993-95, mem. steering com. on managed behavioral health care, 1996; mem. Fla. Gov.'s Task Force on Medicaid Reform, 1996; interim dir. Statewide Pub. Guardianship Office, 2000—. Co-author: Psychological Evaluations for the Courts: A Handbook for Mental Health Professionals and Attorneys, 1987, 2d edit., 1997, Law and Mental Health Professionals: Florida, 1996, Mental Health Services: A Public Health Perspective, 1996; contbr. articles to profl. jours. Mem. Keel Club Hillsborough County United Way, Tampa, 1993—. Recipient Cmty. Svc. award Sch. Social Work U. South Fla., 1995, Saleem Shah award for contbn. to forensic mental health, 1999. Avocations: biking, sailing. Office: U South Fla 13301 Bruce B Downs Blvd Tampa FL 33612-3807

PETRILLO, LEONARD PHILIP, corporate securities executive, lawyer; b. Toronto, Ont., Can., June 20, 1941; s. Philip Ralph and Bernice (Kowalski) P.; m. Linda née Hodgson; children: Larissa, Matthew, Stefanie, Ann-Marie, Karen. BSc, U. Toronto, 1964; LLB, Osgoode Hall Law Sch., Toronto, 1967. Bar: Ont. 1969. Ptnr. Robinson & Petrillo, 1969-79; corp. counsel Seel Enterprises Ltd., 1979-81; gen. counsel Toronto Stock Exch., 1981, corp. sec., sec. to bd. dirs., 1984—, v.p., gen. counsel, sec., 1996—. Bd. dirs. Can. Dealing Network, Inc., TSE CDNX Markets Inc. Office: Toronto Stock Exch Inc 2 1st Canadian Pl Toronto ON Canada M5X 1J2 E-mail: lpetrill@tse.com.

PETRIN, HELEN FITE, lawyer, consultant, mediator; b. Bklyn., June 22, 1940; d. Clyde David and Connie Marie Keaton; m. Michael Richard Petrin, June 29, 1963; children: Jennifer Lee, Michael James, Daniel John. BS, Rider Coll. (now Rider U.), 1962, MA, 1980; postgrad., Glassboro (N.J.) Coll. (now Rowan U.), 1981; JD, Widener U., 1987. Bar: Pa. 1989, N.J. 1990, U.S. Dist. N.J. 1990. Tchr. bus. edn. Pennsville (N.J.) Meml. High Sch., 1962-66; asst. prof. Salem Community Coll., Carney's Point, N.J., 1977-81; asst. prof. Brandywine Coll. Widener U., Wilmington, Del., 1981-87, asst. prof., adminstr., dir. paralegal program, 1987-88; dir. continuing legal edn. Widener U. Sch. Law, Brandywine, 1987-88; pvt. practice computer cons. Del., Pa., N.J., Del., Pa., N.J., 1988—; pvt. practice law Salem, N.J., 1989—; prosecutor Pilesgrove Township, 1990-91; dep. surrogate Salem County, 1991-2000. Word processing cons. New Castle County (Del.) Pers. Dept., 1983; mem. dist. I ethics com. N.J. Supreme Ct., 1993-96; instr. N.J. Inst. for CLE, 1995—; adv. com. on minority concerns Superior Ct. N.J. Vicinage 15, 1995—; judge mock trial N.J. State Bar, 1994—; mem. women's advocacy panel Salem C.C., 1998—. Pres. bd. Salem County YMCA, 1983; dir. mediator Salem County YMCA Mediation Svcs., 1995—2001; vol. atty. Phila. Vols. for Indigent Program, 1990—95, Camden Legal Svcs., Inc. for Salem County, 1990—2001; mem. Hope III com. (Home Ownership and Opportunity for People Everywhere), Salem, NJ, 1992—2001; vol. atty. Salem County N.J. Office Aging Sr. Law Day, 1991—2001; vol. dir. Guardianship Monitoring Program, 1993—2001; sec.-treas. Stand Up for Salem, Inc., 1997—2002; bd. dirs. Salem County YMCA, 1980—98, United Way Salem County, 1991—97, treas., 1994—95; bd. dirs. United Ways of Pa. & N.J., 1994—97, Stand Up for Salem, Inc., 1991—2002, Salem Main St. Program, 2000—, Salem County Hist. Soc., 2002—. Mem. ABA (chmn. young lawyers econs. com. 1990-93, vice chmn. mktg. legal svcs. com. gen. practice sect. 1993-98), N.J. State Bar

Assn. (exec. com. young lawyers divsn. 1990-93, trustee 1998—, pro bono com. 1998-2000), Pa. Bar Assn., Phila. Bar Assn. (probate adv. panel 1992-94), Salem County Bar Assn. (treas. 1991-92, sec. 1992-93, v.p., pres.-elect 1993-94, pres. 1994-95, dir. of Salem County, N.J. YMCA Family Ct. Mediation program 1995-2001), Salem County Hist. Soc. (bd. dirs. 2002--), Delta Pi Epsilon (sec. bd. dirs. 1980-82). Avocations: swimming, music, walking, reading. Home: 99 Marlton Rd Woodstown NJ 08098-2722 Office: 51 Market St Salem NJ 08079-1909

PETRIN, JOHN DONALD, school system administrator; b. Woonsocket, R.I., Feb. 26, 1959; s. Hector Arthur and Claire Jeannette (Dalpe) P.; m. Kimberly Ann Marcotte, May 31, 1986. BA, Stonehill Coll., 1981; MPA, Northeastern U., 1987. Accredited assessor Mass. Assn. Assessing Officers, 1985. Assessor Town of Bellingham, Mass., 1982-85; town adminstr. Town of Pepperell, 1985-88, Town of Harvard, 1988—2001; asst. supt. schs. Marlborough Pub. Schs., 2001—. Vice-chmn. Minuteman-Nashoba Health Group, Concord, Mass., 1990-94, chmn., 95-96; part-time adj. prof. Anna Maria Coll., Paxton, Mass., 1997-98. Pres. Bellingham (Mass.) Youth Baseball, 1979—82, v.p., 1980—85; elected mem. Bellingham (Mass.) Pk. Commn., 1980—85; corporator Boys & Girls Club Metrowest, 1996—, treas., 1996—2000; commr. Mass. Police Accreditation Commn., 1997—2001; elected town com. mem. Dem. Com., Bellingham, 1984—88. Recipient citation, Mass. Ho. of Reps., 1985, 2001, Mass. Senate, 2001. Mem. Internat. City/County Mgmt. Assn., Mass. Mcpl. Assn. (bd. dirs., v.p. 2000, pres. 2001), Mass. Mcpl. Mgmt. Assn. (past pres. 1995). Roman Catholic. Avocations: swimming, woodworking, reading, history. Home: 41 Eager Ct Marlborough MA 01752-2360 Office: Marlborough Pub Schs Dist Edn Ctr 17 Washington St Marlborough MA 01752 E-mail: petrin@mediaone.net., petrin@marlborough.k12.ma.w.

PETRIN, JURIJ, pharmaceutical company executive; b. Ljubljana, Slovenia, Feb. 10, 1956; came to U.S., 1994; s. Ernest and Mira Petrin; m. Vilma Petrin, June 27, 1979; children: Anze, Ziva, Vesna. MD, U. Ljubljana, 1979. Diplomate Am. Bd. Internal Medicine. Intern U. Ljubljana Med. Ctr., Slovenia, 1979-81, resident, 1983-87, staff physician, 1983-92, ZD Ribnica, Slovenia, 1981-83; rsch. fellow U. Mich. Med. Ctr., Ann Arbor, Mich., 1987-88; med. dir. Ea. Europe Bristol-Myers Squibb, Munich, Germany, 1992-94, exec. dir. internat. regulatory affairs Princeton, 1994-96, v.p. intercontinental regulatory sci., 1996—. Asst. prof. internal medicine U. Ljubljana Med. Sch., 1989-91; presenter in field. Author: Emergency Medicine Manual, 1988, 89, 90; contbr. over 40 articles to profl. publs. Mem. ACP, Am. Acad. of Pharm. Physicians, Am. Soc. of Hypertension, Internat. Soc. of Hypertension, Interam. Soc. of Hypertension. Office: Bristol Myers Squibb Rte 206 & Provinceline Rd Princeton NJ 08543

PETRINI, FABRIZIO, computer science researcher; b. Foligno, Italy, May 26, 1964; m. Mariella DiGiacomo, June 22, 1997; 1 child Alessandro DiGiacomo. Laurea in computer sci., U. Pisa, Italy, 1990, PhD in Computer Sci., 1997. Rsch. fellow Hewlett Packard Labs, Pisa, 1990-93, U. Oxford, U.K., 1999; mem. tech. staff Los Alamos (N.Mex.) Nat. Lab., 1999—. Grantee Enidata, 1990; Marie Curie fellowship European Cmty., 1997. Mem. IEEE, Computer Soc. Office: Los Alamos Nat Lab MSB256 CCS-3 Los Alamos NM 87545 E-mail: fabrizio@lanl.gov.

PETRINOVICH, LEWIS FRANKLIN, psychology educator; b. Wallace, Idaho, June 12, 1930; s. John F. and Ollie (Steward) P. BS, U. Idaho, 1952; PhD, U. Calif., Berkeley, 1962. Asst. prof. San Francisco State Coll., 1957-63; from assoc. to prof. SUNY, Stony Brook, 1963-68; prof. U. Calif., Riverside, 1968-91, chmn. psychology, 1968-71, 86-89, prof. emeritus, 1991—. Author: Understanding Research in Social Sciences, 1975, Introduction to Statistics, 1976, Human Evolution, Reproduction and Morality, 1995, Living and Dying Well, 1996, Darwinian Dominion: Animal Welfare and Human Interests, 1999, The Cannibal Within, 2000; editor: Behavioral Development, 1981, Habituation, Sensitization and Behavior, 1984; cons. editor Behavioral and Neural Biology, 1972-90, Jour. Physiol. and Comparative Psychology, 1980-82, Jour. Comparative Psychology, 1983-90. Fellow Am. Psychol. Assn., Am. Psychol. Soc., Calif. Acad. Scis., Human Behavior and Evolution Soc., Western Psychol. Assn.; mem. Am. Ornithological Union (elected), Animal Behavior Soc., Sigma Xi. Home: 415 Boynton Ave Berkeley CA 94707-1701 Office: U Calif Riverside Psychology Dept Riverside CA 92521-0001

PETRO, JAMES MICHAEL, lawyer, politician; b. Cleve., Oct. 25, 1948; s. William John and Lila Helen (Janca) P.; m. Nancy Ellen Bero, Dec. 16, 1972; children: John Bero, Corbin Marie. BA, Denison U., 1970; JD, Case Western Res., 1973. Bar: Ohio 1973, U.S. Dist. Ct. (no. dist.) Ohio 1974, U.S. Ct. Appeals (6th cir.) 1981. Spl. asst. U.S. senator W.B. Saxbe, Cleve., 1972-73; asst. pros. atty. Franklin County, Ohio, 1973-74; asst. dir. law City of Cleve., 1974; ptnr. Petro & Troia, Cleve., 1974-84; dir. govt. affairs Standard Oil Co., 1984-86; ptnr. Petro, Rademaker, Matty & McClelland, 1986-93, Buckingham, Doolittle & Burroughs, Cleve., 1993-95. Mem. city coun. Rocky River, Ohio, 1977-79, dir. law, 1980; mem. Ohio Ho. of Reps., Columbus, 1981-84, 86-90; commr. Cuyahoga County, Ohio, 1991-95; Auditor of State of Ohio, 1995—. Mem. ABA, Ohio State Bar Assn., Cleve. Bar Assn. Republican. Methodist. Home: 1933 Lake Shore Dr Columbus OH 43204-4963 Office: 88 E Broad St Columbus OH 43215-3506 E-mail: petro@auditor.state.oh.us.

PETROCHILOS, ELIZABETH A. writer, publisher; b. Blytheville, Ark., Aug. 11, 1943; d. James Alfred Clark and Macie Lee Burris; m. Cleomenis Matheos Petrochilos, Oct. 26, 1961 (div. Mar. 1966); children: Matthew C., Raquel D. Grad., Fresno H.S. Cashier Family Owned Markets, Fresno, 1961-64; med. receptionist Dr. Floyd E. Lee, Lemoore, Calif., 1964-65; pub., author E.A. Prodns., Fresno, 1965—. Author: (poetry) Stone the Poet, 1964. Avocations: books, music, antiques, swimming. Home: 1155 E Bullard Ave Apt 206 Fresno CA 93710-5527 *Love the Lord your God with all your heart, with all your soul, with all your mind, and with all your strength.*

PETROFF, JOHN, economics educator, software company executive; b. Paris, Feb. 3, 1941; came to U.S., 1958; s. Michael and Emilia (Paberg) P.; m. Christiane Jeanne Relier, Nov. 24, 1964; children: Marc, Anne. Diploma, Sch. Higher Comml. Studies, Paris, 1964; MBA in Fin., NYU, 1972, PhD in Econs. and Internat. Bus., 1980. Buyer Gertz, Allied Store Co., Queens, N.Y., 1969-72; tax researcher Chase Manhattan Bank, N.Y.C., 1972-77; tax and econs. researcher Pan Am. Airways, 1974-76; owner, mgr. Midtown Bicycle, 1976-79; asst. prof. Manhattan Coll., Riverdale, N.Y., 1979-84; assoc. prof. econs. SUNY, Geneseo, 1984-85, N.Y. Inst. Tech., Westbury, 1986-88, Manhattanville Coll., Purchase, N.Y., 1988—. Pres. Acad. Software Corp., Conesville, N.Y., 1983—. Author: How To Choose a Charitable Trust, 1976; patentee in field. Mem. Am. Econ. Assn., Acad. Internat. Bus. Home: Bull Hill Rd Gilboa NY 12076

PETROKUBI, MARILYN, film company executive, researcher, producer; b. Orange, N.J., Oct. 15, 1951; d. Stephen Joseph and Mary L. (Butchkosky) P.; m. Robert A. Lieberman; 1 child, Matthew Alexander. BA, Upsala Coll., 1973; MLS, Rutgers U., 1974. Reference librarian Livingston (N.J.) Pub. Library, 1974-75, Phillipsburg (N.J.) Free Pub. Library, 1975-78; freelance researcher, producer, 1979—; pres., exec. producer TimeSteps Prodns., Inc., West Orange, N.J., 1987—. Library systems cons., 1979—. N.J. State Council on the Arts grantee, 1977. Mem. Media Comms. Assn. Internat., N.Y. Women in Film and TV. Avocations: gardening, hiking, skiing, ice skating, biking. Office: TimeSteps Prodns Inc 2 Glenside Dr West Orange NJ 07052-4709

PETRONE, JOSEPH ANTHONY, business consultant, writer; b. N.Y.C., July 6, 1956; s. Louis Richard and Catherine Amelia (DeVito) P.; m. Deborah Bernice Steele, Sept. 24, 1983. BS in Chemistry, Muhlenberg Coll., 1978. Sales rep. Calgon Corp., San Francisco, 1978-82, mktg. mgr. Pitts., 1982-85; sales engr. Nicolet Corp., 1985-88, regional sales mgr. San Francisco, 1988-91, gen. mgr., 1992-95; bus. author, cons. Joe Petrone & Assocs., Pleasanton, Calif., 1995—. Author: Building the High Performance Sales Force, 1994 (Top Book ranking Soundview Exec. Book Summaries, Fortune & Newgridge Bus. Book Club selection); contbr. articles to profl. publs. Vol. Big Bros./Big Sisters, Oakland, Calif.; hospice vol., Sewickley, Pa., 1985; active Make a Wish Found., 1998-2000; examiner for Calif. Quality awards 1997-99; exec. min. Influencing Influencers; mem. leadership team Men's Bible Study. Recipient award, Family Assistance Ministries. Mem. Inst. Mgmt. Cons. Avocations: tennis, weight training, reading, travel. Home and Office: 5103 Costa Rustico San Clemente CA 92673

PETRONE, WILLIAM FRANCIS, physician, microbiologist, corporate executive; b. Bklyn., Sept. 12, 1949; s. Arthur Carmen and Helen (Kenny) P.; m. Kathleen Anne Baron, Aug. 25, 1979; children: William Gaetano, Katherine Bridget, Jason Daniel. BA, U. Conn., 1972; MS, U. Mass., 1974; PhD, U. R.I., 1978; MD, U. South Ala., 1984. Diplomate Am. Bd. Pediatrics, Pediatric Emergency Medicine, Gen. Pediatrics. Rsch. assoc. Coll. Medicine U. South Ala., Mobile, 1978-80; resident in pediat. Orlando (Fla.) Regional Med. Ctr., 1984-85, W.Va. Univ. Med. Ctr., 1985-87; emergency rm. physician, pediat. emergency svcs. Mercy Hosp., Springfield, Mass., 1987—. Pres. Med. Simulation Software, Cmty. Pediat. Assoc. Contbr. articles on inflamation and white blood cell function to sci. jours. Fellow Am. Acad. Pediat., Am. Coll. Emergency Physicians; mem. AAAS, AMA, N.Y. Acad. Scis., Sigma Xi. Roman Catholic. Office: Mercy Hosp Emergency Unit PO Box 9012 Springfield MA 01102-9012

PETROSKI, CATHERINE, writer, consultant; b. St. Louis, Sept. 7, 1939; d. Robert and Mary S. Groom; m. Henry Petroski, July 15, 1966; children: Karen, Stephen. BA, MacMurray Coll., 1961, DLitt (hon.), 1984; MA, U. Ill., 1962. Writer, 1968—; cons., 1984—. Vis. prof. U. N.C., Chapel Hill, 1984, Duke U., Durham, N.C., 1985-87. Author: Gravity and Other Stories, 1981, Beautiful My Mane in the Wind, 1982, The Summer That Lasted Forever, 1984, A Bride's Passage, 1997. Pres. Friends of Durham Libr. Inc., 1992-93; trustee Durham County Libr. Sys., 1993—, chmn. bd. trustees, 1994—. Mem. Authors Guild, Nat. Book Critics Circle. Home: HC 33 Box 98 Bath ME 04530-9403

PETROSKI, HENRY, engineer educator, writer; b. N.Y.C., Feb. 6, 1942; s. Henry Frank and Victoria Rose (Grygrowych) P.; m. Catherine Ann Groom, July 15, 1966; children: Karen Beth, Stephen James. B Mech. Engring., Manhattan Coll., N.Y.C., 1963; MS, U. Ill., 1964, PhD, 1968; DSc (hon.), Clarkson U., 1990; DHL (hon.), Trinity Coll., Hartford, Conn., 1997; DSc (hon.), Valparaiso U., 1999. Registered profl. engr., Tex.; chartered engr., Inst. of Engrs. of Ireland. Instr. U. Ill., Urbana, 1965-68; asst. prof. U. Tex., Austin, 1968-74; engr. Argonne (Ill.) Nat. Lab., 1975-80; assoc. prof. civil engring. Duke U., Durham, N.C., 1980-87, prof., 1987-93, Aleksandar S. Vesic prof., 1993—, prof. history, 1995—, chmn. dept. civil and environ. engring., 1991-2000, dir. grad. studies, 1981-86. Author: To Engineer is Human, 1985, Beyond Engineering, 1986, The Pencil, 1990, The Evolution of Useful Things, 1992, Design Paradigms, 1994 (Best Book award in engring., Am. Assn. U. Presses , 1994), Engineers of Dreams, 1995, Invention by Design, 1996, Remaking the World, 1997, The Book on the Bookshelf, 1999; writer, presenter: documentary To Engineer is Human, 1987, columnist: Am. Scientist, 1991—, columnist: ASEE Prism, 2000—; author: Paperboy, 2002. Fellow NEH, 1987-88, Nat. Humanities Ctr., 1987-88, Guggenheim fellow, 1990-91; recipient Outstanding Engring. Grad. award Manhattan Coll., 1992, Alumni award for disting. svc. Coll. Engring. U. Ill. at Urbana-Champaign, 1994. Fellow ASCE (Civil Engring. History and Heritage award 1993), ASME (Ralph Coats Roe medal 1991), Inst. Engrs. Ireland, NAE, Soc. History Tech., The Moles (hon.), Sigma Xi. Office: Duke U Sch Engring Durham NC 27708-0287

PETROSKY, SARA LYNN, lawyer, township commissioner; b. Lancaster, Pa., Apr. 18, 1960; d. Joseph Paul and Iona (Piper) P.; m. Stanley Ervin, July 4, 1986; children: Jarek Ervin, Danika Ervin. BA magna cum laude, Messiah Coll., 1982; JD cum laude, Temple U., 1987. Bar: Pa. 1987. Atty. Pepper, Hamilton & Scheetz, Phila., 1987-89, Sprecher, Felix, Visco, Hutchison & Young, Phila., 1989-90, Morgan, Lewis & Bockius, Phila., 1993-95, McCann, Mailey & Geschke, Phila., 1995—. Coord. Delaware County Mock Trial Competition, 1990-91. Mem. fin. com. Wallingford-Swarthmore Sch. Dist., 1992; bd. dirs. Family and Cmty. Svc. of Delaware County, 1995—; commr. Nether Providence Twp., 1994—, pres. 1996; mem. Delaware County Leadership Group, 1994-96. Mem. Pa. Bar Assn. (commn. on women in legal profession 1994—), Phila. Bar Assn. (chancellor's commn. on children at risk 1994-95). Home: 214 Sykes Ln Wallingford PA 19086-6337

PETROU, ANASTASIS D. phd candidate, ucla information studies department, consultant, adjunct faculty; b. Kato Varosi, Famagusta, Cyprus, Oct. 6, 1961; s. Androula and Demetrios Theodotou. B.S, Mankato State U., Mankato, MN, 1981—84; MBA, Mankato State U., Mankato, MN, USA, 1985—89; MA, Polit. Sci., Mankato State Univesity, Mankato, MN, USA, 1989—94; MLIS, UCLA, 1996—2000, doctoral studies, 1996. Faculty mem. / tenured asst. prof. Mankato (Minn.) State U., 1988—94; grad. student rschr. UCLA, Los Angeles, Calif., 1996—99; adj. faculty Woodbury U., Burbank, 2000—01. Author: (manual) PALS Personal Computer Disaster Prevention and Recovery Plan, 1991; contbr. articles to profl. jours. and confs.

PETROU, DAVID MICHAEL, marketing and communications executive; b. Washington, Nov. 3, 1949; s. John and Bebe (Koch) P. BA, U. Md., 1971; MA, Georgetown U., 1973. Assoc. dir. publicity Random House-Ballantine Books, N.Y.C., 1973-75; asst. prodr. Salkind Orgn., London, 1975-78; asst. dir. promotional devel. Warner Bros., L.A., 1978-79; dir. spl. projects Jos. P. Kennedy Jr. Found., Washington, 1980-83; pres., COO Eisner, Petrou & Assoc., 1986—. Author: Crossed Swords, 1977, The Making of Superman, 1978; sr. editor: Regardie's mag., 1983-84. Mem. nat. fundraising com. Dukakis for Pres., Washington, 1988; mem. bd. U. Md. Ctr. Performing Arts, 1996—; mem. adv. bd. Washington Men's Camerata, 1996—. Woodrow Wilson fellow U. Md., 1971. Mem. Am. Film Inst.'s 2d Decade Coun. (chmn. of bd. 1992-96), Found. for Cmty. Mental Health (bd. dirs. 1984—), Choral Arts Soc. Washington (bd. dirs. 1996—). Democrat. Jewish. Avocations: choral singing, music, tennis, film and film criticism. Office: Eisner Petrou & Assoc Inc 927 15th St NW Ste 900 Washington DC 20005-2340

PETROV, NICOLAS, dance educator, choreographer; b. Novia Sad, Serbia, Yugoslavia, Dec. 13, 1933; came to U.S., 1967; s. Sergie Nicolas and Iren Rehorovic (Roboz) P.; m. Marion Freyda Brookes, Apr. 11, 1956. Ed., Govt. Theatrical Acad., Novi Sad, 1945-51; apsolvent, Drzavne Pozorisne Skole Baletski, Otsek, 1951; ed, State Ballet Acad. of Belgrade, Yugoslavia, 1951-54, Belgrade Govt. U. Fgn. Langs., 1951-55, U. de Paris à Sorbonne, 1956-58. Dancer Nat. Popular Theatre Serbi, Belgrade, 1951-54, Ballet de France de Janine Charrat, Paris, 1954-56; prin. dancer Theatre d'Art du Ballet, 1957-59, Balletto Europeo di Nervi, Genova, Italy, 1960-62; dancer, choreographer Radio TV France, Paris, 1960-67; from asst. prof. to prof. dance Point Park Coll., Pitts., 1968-78, prof., 1978—, dir. fine, applied and performing arts dept. and dance div., 1975-87. Founder, artistic dir. Ballet Russe de Nicolas Petrov, Paris, 1962-67, Pitts. Ballet Theatre, Inc., 1967-77, Am. Dance Ensemble, Pitts., 1977-87; choreographer Pitts. Opera, 1967-73, 77-89; guest dancer Leonide Massine Festival, Goteberg, Sweden, 1956-57; guest dancer and actor Theatre de Vervie Belgium, 1956-57; guest star dancer Opera Mcpl. de Marseille, Paris, 1960-62. Appeared in ballets, including Scheherazade, Swan Lake, Romeo and Juliet, Le Carnaval, Nutcracker, Legend of Ohrid, La Valse, Noir et Blanc, Beethoven's 7th Symphony, Blue Danube, Les Amadas de Tervel, Laudes Evangelii, Barber of Seville, Choriartium, many others; choreographer (operas) Aida, Pitts., 1967-68, Carmen, Pitts., 1967-68, 80-81, La Traviata, Pitts., 1977-78; (ballets) Romeo and Juliet, Pitts., 1971-72, Rite of Spring, Pitts., 1971-72, Swan Lake, Pitts., 1971-72, Beethoven's 9th Symphony, Pitts., 1972-73, Cinderella, Pitts., 1973-74, Steel Symphony, Pitts., 1975-76, Fantasia, Pitts., 1976-77, Prince of the Pagodas, Pitts., 1977-78, Nutcracker, Pitts., 1978-79, Bolero, Pitts., 1982-83, Merry Widow, Pitts., 1987-88, Coppelia, Pitts., 1991-92, numerous others; director dance films including Alice in Wonderland, 1972, Carmina Catulli, 1973-74, Romeo and Juliet, 1975; author: The Dance Method, 1967. Asst. mayoral elections, Pitts., 1968, 77; vol. Pitts. Ballet Theatre. Recipient choreography award Nat. Steel Corp., 1976. Mem. AAUP, Am. Guild Music Artists, Rotary, French Masons (N.Y.C.). Avocations: building renovations, skiing, golf, boating. Home: 77 Southern Ave Pittsburgh PA 15211-1913 Office: Point Park Coll 201 Wood St Pittsburgh PA 15222-1984 E-mail: nicolas.petrov@verizon.net., npetrov@ppc.edu.

PETRU, SUZANNE MITTON, health care finance executive; b. Shawano, Wis., Sept. 26, 1947; d. William Wallace and Gertrude Priscilla Mitton; m. W. James Petru, Jan. 2, 1987. BSBA, Northwestern U., 1970, MBA, 1971. CPA, Ill., Wis. Diplomate Am. Coll. Healthcare Execs. Sr. acct. Arthur Andersen & Co., Chgo., 1971-77; v.p. fin. Thorek Hosp. and Med. Ctr., 1977-82; sec./treas. La Grange (Ill.) Meml. Health Sys., 1982-85; v.p. fin. La Grange Meml. Hosp., 1982-85; audit prin. Deloitte & Touche (formerly Touche Ross & Co.), Chgo., 1985-88; sr. v.p. fin., treas. SSM Health Care Sys., St. Louis, 1988-95; pres. healthcare divsn. Am. Home Assurance Co. (subs. Am. Internat. Group, Inc.), 1995-96; v.p., CFO, treas. Group Health Plan (subs. Coventry Corp.), 1996-98; v.p. Petru Enterprises, Petru Internat., 1998—; sr. v.p. fin., CFO Rockford (Ill.) Health Sys., 2000—. Mem. investment com. Sisters of Charity Healthcare Sys., Cin., 1993-96, mem. fin. com., 1994-96; mem. assoc. bd. La Grange Meml. Hosp., 1988-95; advisor Jr. Achievement, 1971-76. Fellow Healthcare Fin. Mgmt. Assn. (bd. dirs. 1989-91, principles and practices bd. 1992-95, nat. matrix 1985-86, 88-89, pres., pres.-elect, sec., bd. First Ill. chpt. 1979-86, compliance officers forum adv. coun. 1998—, Follmer Bronze award 1982, Reeves Silver award 1985, Muncie Gold award 1988, Alice V. Runyan chpt. 1988); mem. Fin. Execs. Inst., Country Club at Legends (adv. bd. 1991-93), St. Louis Club (house com. 1991-95). Republican. Presbyterian. Avocations: golf, travel. Home: 12033 Tindall Dr Saint Louis MO 63131-3135 Office: Rockford Health Sys 2400 N Rockton Ave Rockford IL 61103-3655 E-mail: spetru@rhsnet.org.

PETRUS, ROBERT THOMAS, internet business owner, real estate investor; b. Manchester, Conn., 1957; s. John Joseph and Geraldine Petrus; m. Laura Lee Waggoner, Nov. 22, 1986; children: Elizabeth Ashley, Nicholas Kent. BA with honors, Trinity Coll., Hartford, Conn., 1979. Mgmt. intern Aetna Life & Casualty Co., Hartford, 1979-82, sr. adminstr. data processing ops., 1982-85, cons. Tech. Ctr., 1985-90; pres. Omoo Distbn. Corp., Mansfield, Conn., 1990—; v.p. Cogitore, Inc., 1990—. Author: Get Organized!, 1991. Chmn. Conn. Youth for Pres. Ford, 1976; com. mem. Big Bros.-Big Sisters, Hartford, 1982-83; loaned exec. Greater Hartford United Way-Combined Health Appeals Campaign, 1985. Recipient ofcl. citation Conn. Ho. of Reps., 1985. Mem. Phi Beta Kappa, Pi Gamma Mu, Mu Alpha Theta. Republican. Avocations: photography, golf, skiing. Office: ODI-Omoo Distbn Inc 27 Wormwood Hill Rd Ste 101 Mansfield Center CT 06250-1135

PETRUSKI, JENNIFER ANDREA, speech and language pathologist; b. Kingston, N.Y., Jan. 28, 1968; d. Andrew Francis and Judith (Cruger) Petruski. BS, SUNY, Buffalo, 1990, MSEd, 1992. Cert. tchr. speech-hearing handicapped N.Y., clin. competence, Fast ForWord provider, lic. speech-lang. pathology N.Y. Speech-lang. pathologist Kingston (N.Y.) City Schs., 1992—; clin. practicum supr. SUNY, New Paltz, 1996—. Cooperating tchr. SUNY, New Paltz, 1995—; ind. contr. speech svcs. Ulster County, 1997; cooperating tchr. Coll. St. Rose, 1997. Mem.: Speech and Hearing Assn. Hudson Valley, Bd. Regional PResidents, N.Y. State Speech-Lang. and Hearing Assn., Am. Speech and Hearing Assn., Speech and Hearing Assn. Hudson Valley (corr. sec. 1995—98, newsletter editor 1995—2001, membership com. 1995—, treas. 1997, pres. 1999—2000, nominating com. 1999—2000, legis. chair 2000—, past. pres. 2001—), Bd. Regional Presidents (membership chair 2000—). Home: PO Box 88 Hurley NY 12443 E-mail: jpetruski@aol.com.

PETRY, RUTH VIDRINE, assistant principal; b. Eunice, La., Jan. 20, 1947; d. Adea and Ruth Alice (Fox) Vidrine; m. Carson Clinton Petry, June 19, 1976. BA, La. Coll., 1971; MEd, McNeese State U., 1984. Cert. tchr., La. Tchr. jr. high sch. Jefferson Davis Parish, Jennings, La., 1970-72; tchr. high sch. St. Tammany Parish, Mandeville, 1972-73, Jefferson Parish, Gretna, 1973-81; tchr. jr. high Acadia Parish, Crowley, 1981-90; tchr. lang. arts Crowley Jr. High Sch., 1981-90; master tchr. assessor La. State Dept. Edn., Lafayette, 1990-91; tchr. Crowley Mid. Sch., 1991-94, instrnl. asst., 1994-95; exec. dir. Assoc. Profl. Educators of La., Baton Rouge, 1995-96; asst. prin. Rayne (La.) H.S., 1996—2001, principal, 2001—. Writing assessment coord. Crowley Jr. High Sch., 1984-85, mem. faculty insvc. team, 1986-89, chmn. spelling bee, 1983-90, 92-93, co-chmn. interim self study Crowley Jr. High Sch. So. Assn., 1985-86; mem. state selection com. for La. Tch. of Yr., Students of Yr., 1992-93; mem. Tchr. Evaluation Revision Panels, I, III, IV, 1992-93, Prin.'s Evaluation State Com., 1993; presenter workshops in field. Co-sponsor Nat. Jr. Hon. Soc., 1984-90; mem. La. Gov.-Elect's Edn. Transition Team, 1991-92; mem. La. Goals 2000 steering com. on sch. governance and accountability, 1994-95, mem. sch. fin. comm., 1999-2000. Named Crowley Jr. High Tchr. of the Yr., 1985-86. Mem. ASCD, Assn. Profl. Educators La. (pres. Acadia chpt. 1988-92, mem. dist. VII state exec. bd., 1990-91, state pres.-elect 1991-92, state pres. 1992-94), Nat. Assn. Secondary Sch. Prins., La. Assn. Sch. Execs., La. Assn. Prins., La. Assn. for Retarded Citizens, Delta Kappa Gamma (chpt. pres. 1988-90, state leadership scholar 1993), Phi Delta Kappa. Republican. Baptist. Avocations: music, reading, sewing. Home: 206 Bruce St Lafayette LA 70503-6102

PETRYSHYN, WALTER ALEXIS, otolaryngologist; b. N.Y., 1922; MD, SUNY, 1945. Diplomate Am. Bd. Otolaryngology. Intern Lenox Hill Hosp., N.Y.C., 1945-46; resident otolaryngology NYU Bellevue Med. Ctr., 1948-51; fellow otolaryngology NYU Med. Sch., 1948. Fellow ACS, Am. Acad. Otolaryngology Head and Neck Surgery; mem. AMA, Am. Triol. Assn.

PETRZILKA, HENRY See FILIP, HENRY

PETSKO, GREGORY ANTHONY, chemistry and biochemistry educator; b. Washington, Aug. 7, 1948; s. John and Mary (Santoro) P.; m. Carol Bannister Chamberlain, July 3, 1971 (div. 1982). BA, Princeton U., 1970; DPhil, Oxford U., 1973. Instr. Wayne State U. Med. Sch., Detroit, 1973-75, asst. prof., 1975-78; assoc. prof. MIT, 1979-85, prof. chemistry, 1985-90; Lucille P. Markey prof. biochemistry and chemistry Brandeis U., Waltham, Mass., 1990-96, Gyula & Katica Tauber prof. biochemistry & Pharmacodynamics, 1997—, dir. Rosenstiel Basic Med. Scis. Rsch. Ctr. Mass., 1994—. Founding scientist, cons. Arqule, Inc., Medford, 1993—. Editor. Jour. Protein Engring., 1988—. Recipient Sr. Scientist award Alexander von Humboldt Found., 1989, Max Planck prize Max Planck Gesellschaft, 1992, Sr. Scientist award Ellison Med. Rsch. Found., 1998, Lynen medal Nature Mag., 2001; Rhodes scholar Oxford U., 1970; Alfred P. Sloan fellow MIT, 1978, Danforth fellow 1980, Guggenheim fellow 1995. Mem. NAS, Inst. of Medicine, Am. Acad. Arts and Scis., Am. Crystallographic Assn. (Siddhu award 1981), Am. Chem. Soc. (Pfizer award 1987), Biophys. Soc., Am. Soc. Biochemistry and Molecular Biology, Am. Soc. Microbiology. Avocations: writing essays, poetry and fiction, hiking, travel, old movies, sports cars. Home: 8 Jason Rd Belmont MA 02478-3129 Office: Brandeis U Mail Stop 029 Rosenstiel Ctr Waltham MA 02454-9110 E-mail: petsko@brandeis.edu.

PETT, STEPHEN DONOHOE, cardiovascular surgeon; b. Midland, Tex., July 31, 1945; m. Lisa B. Bendig; children from previous marriage: Elizabeth, Katherine, Margaret. BS, Seton Hall U., 1967; MD, George Washington U., 1971. Intern and resident in thoracic and cardiovascular surgery George Washington U. Sch. Medicine, Washington, 1971-80; pvt. practice Cardiopulmonary and Periperal Vascular Assn., Erie, Pa., 1982—; chief divsn. cardiothoracic surgery St. Vincent Health Ctr., 1991-93, sec.-treas. med./dental staff, 1992-93, v.p. med./dental staff, 1993-94, pres., 1994-96. Fellow ACS; mem. AMA, Am. Coll. Cardiology, Am. Coll. Chest Physicians, Pa. Med. Soc., Chesapeake Vascular Soc. Office: Flagship/CUTS 316 W 23rd St Erie PA 16502-2620

PETTAPIECE, BOB (MERVYN ARTHUR PETTAPIECE), education educator; b. Detroit, May 27, 1941; s. Alvy M. and Thelma M. (Fetterly) P.; children: Lori, Michelle Howe, Erin Howe. BA in Humanities, Mich. State U., 1963, BA in Religion, 1967; MEd, Wayne State U., 1971, EdD, 1980. Cert. tchr. history, humanities, math., religion, Mich. Tchr. Detroit Pub. Schs., 1967-96; instr. tchr. edn. and social studies edn. Wayne State U., Detroit, 1981-96, lectr., 1996—, assoc. mem. grad. faculty, 1990—. Speaker in field. Contbr. articles to profl. jours. Mem. state bd. dirs. ACLU of Mich. Wayne State U. Grad. fellow, 1978. Mem. APA (assoc.), Nat. Coun. Social Studies, Mich. Assn. Computer Users in Learning, Internat. Coun. for Computers in Edn., Alumni Assn. Wayne State U., Phi Delta Kappa. Avocations: squash, photography, computing. Home: 555 Brush St Apt 2206 Detroit MI 48226-4336 Office: Wayne State U 271 Education Detroit MI 48202 E-mail: pettapiece@wayne.edu.

PETTEE, DANIEL STARR, retired neurologist; b. N.Y.C., Feb. 15, 1925; s. Allen Danforth and Helen Marien (Starr) P.; m. Dimetra Marie Peters, June 24, 1961; children: William, Margaret, Allen. BA, Yale U., 1951; MD, Columbia U., 1955. Diplomate Am. Bd. Psychiatry and Neurology, 1965, Am. Bd. Clin. Neurophysiology, 1984. Rotating internship Strong Meml. Hosp. U. Rochester, N.Y., 1955-57, residency neurology, 1957-62; neurologist pvt. practice,

Rochester, 1962-96; clinic dir. Rochester (N.Y.) Area Multiple Sclerosis Chpt., 1962-76; assoc. clin. prof. neurology U. Rochester (N.Y.) Sch. Medicine, 1978-96, emeritus assoc. clin. prof., 1996-97, emeritus clin. prof. neurology, 1997—; clin. assoc. dept. neurology Strong Meml. Hosp., Rochester, 1978-96; head neurology div. dept. medicine The Genesee Hosp., 1972-96; pres. Genesee Neurol. Assocs., 1974-96. Mem. bd. dirs. Rochester (N.Y.) Area Multiple Sclerosis Chpt., 1970-76. Contbr. articles to profl. jours. Mem., singer Rochester Oratorio Soc., 1955—78, bd. dirs., 1960—61. Recipient Purple Heart, Bronze Star U.S. Army, 1944, Bronze Hope Chest for Svc. award Rochester (N.Y.) Area Multiple Sclerosis Chpt., 1976. Mem. N.Y. Acad. Sci., Rochester Acad. Sci. (astronomy sect. 1989-98, bd. dirs. astronomy sect. 1993-94). Home: 1141 S Gaylord St Denver CO 80210-1826

PETTEE, DAVID ALLEN, minister, social worker; b. Huntington, N.Y., Aug. 18, 1957; s. James Lombard Pettee and Mary Loraine Tetlow; m. Mindy Jo Scharlin, June 17, 1990; children: Hannah Scharlin-Pettee, Sophie Scharlin-Pettee. BS, Ithaca Coll., 1975—79; MSW, Boston U., 1981—83; MDiv, Starr King Sch. Ministry, 1985—88. Cert. ministerial fellowship Unitarian Universalist Assn., 1993, Ordination into the Unitarian Universalist ministry 1994. House mgr. Tompkins County Mental Health Assn., Ithaca, NY, 1979—81; clin. social worker Walnut St. Ctr., Somerville, Mass., 1983—84; program developer The Psychol. Ctr., Lawrence, 1984—85, Golden Gate Regional Ctr., San Francisco, 1989—92; hospice social worker Sutter VNA & Hospice, Emeryville, 1993—2001; cmty. min. First Unitarian Universalist Soc. San Francisco, 1994—2001. Pacific Ctrl. Dist. Cmty. Ministry Coun. Pacific Ctrl. Dist. Bd. Unitarian Universalist Assn., Oakland, 1996—99; W. Regional Sub-Committee on Candidacy ministerial fellowship com., Unitarian Universalist Assn., Boston, 1999—2001; vis. prof. ministry Starr King Sch. Ministry, Berkeley, Calif., 2001. Contbr. articles. Pacific Ctrl. Dist. co-chair Bill Sinkford for Pres. UUA, Midland, 2000—01; election officer Bd. Election's, Ithaca, NY, 1980; bd. mem. Sperm Bank Calif., Oakland, 1993—98, Resolve of N. Calif., San Francisco, 1992—94. Nominee Nobel Peace Prize, mem. Great Peace March for Global Nuclear Disarmament, Nobel Com., Oslo, Norway, 1987. Mem.: Starr King Sch. Ministry Grad. Assn., Nat. Assn. Social Worker's, Unitarian Universalist Min. Assn. (Pacific Ctrl.Dist. Chpt. Pres. 1999—2001), Winthrop Soc., Desc. Gov. William Bradford, New England Hist. Geneal. Soc., The Alden Kindred, Soc. Mayflower Desc. State Calif., The Roger Williams Family Assn. (life), Unitarian Universalist Hist. Soc. Unitarian Universalist. Avocations: New England history, genealogy, marathons. Home: 1214 Kains Ave Berkeley CA 94706

PETTENGILL, GORDON H(EMENWAY), physicist, educator; b. Providence, Feb. 10, 1926; s. Rodney Gordon and Frances (Hemenway) P.; m. Pamela Anne Wolfenden, Oct. 28, 1967; children: Mark Robert, Rebecca Jane. BS, MIT, 1948; PhD, U. Calif., Berkeley, 1955. Staff mem. Lincoln Lab. MIT, Lexington, 1954-63, 65-68, prof. planetary physics, dept. earth, atmospheric and planetary scis. Cambridge, 1971—, dir. Ctr. Space Rsch., 1984-90; assoc. dir. Arecibo (P.R.) Obs., 1963-65, dir., 1968-71. Served with inf., Signal Corps AUS, 1944-46. Decorated Combat Inf. badge; recipient Magellanic Premium, Am. Philos. Soc., 1994. Fellow Am. Geophys. Union (Whipple award 1995, Charles A. Whitten award 1997); mem. AAAS, Am. Phys. Soc., Am. Astron. Soc., Internat. Astron. Union, Internat. Radio Sci. Union, Nat. Acad. Sci., Am. Acad. Arts and Sci. Achievements include pioneering several techniques in radar astronomy for describing properties of planets and satellites; discovering 59-day rotational period of planet Mercury. Office: MIT 77 Massachusetts Ave Rm 37-582D Cambridge MA 02139-4307

PETTERCHAK, JANICE A. researcher, writer; b. Springfield, Ill., Sept. 15, 1942; d. Emil H. and Vera C. (Einhoff) Stukenberg; m. John J. Petterchak, Oct. 5, 1963; children: John A., Julie Gilmour, James. AA, Springfield Coll., 1962; BS, Sangamon State U., 1972, MA, 1982. Supr. hist. markers Ill. State Hist. Soc., Springfield, 1973-74, asst. exec. dir., 1985-87; curator photographs Ill. State Hist. Libr., 1974-79, assoc. editor, 1979-83, rep. local history svcs., 1983-85, libr. dir., 1987-95. Project dir. NEH/Ill. newspaper cataloging project. Author: Mapping a Life's Journey: The Legacy of Andrew McNally III, 1995, Jack Brickhouse: A Voice for All Seasons, 1996, Researching and Writing Local History in Illinois: A Guide to the Sources, 1987, Taming the Upper Mississippi, 2000; To Share: The Heritage, Legend and Legacy of Nathan Cummings, 2000, Out To Sea Again: A Naval Armed Guard in World War II, 2002; editor: Illinois History: An Annotated Bibliography, 1995; assoc. editor Illinois Historical Jour.; contbr. articles to profl. jours. Grantee NEH, 1987-95. Mem. Ill. State Hist. Soc., Abraham Lincoln Assn. (co-editor Papers Abraham Lincoln Assn. 1981-82), Stephen A. Douglas Assn., Sangamon County Hist. Soc. (bd. dirs. 1991-94, 99—, v.p. 1996-97, pres. 1995-96), Soc. of Midland Authors. Home: 11381 Mallard Dr Rochester IL 62563-8011 E-mail: petterchak@biogwriter.com.

PETTERSEN, KEVIN WILL, investment company executive; b. Yonkers, N.Y., July 4, 1956; s. Kjell Will and Marilyn Ann (Stevens) P.; m. Mary Elizabeth Murphy, Aug. 30, 1981; children: Kelly, Elizabeth, Erin. Diploma academia, Chaminade, Mineola, N.Y., 1974; BA in Econs., SUNY at Stony Brook, 1978. Buyer JC Penney Co., Inc., N.Y.C., 1979-82; nat. sales mgr. Randa Corp., Inc., 1982-83; dir. sales Wemco, Inc., 1983-86; mng. dir., sr. v.p. D.H. Blair & Co., Inc., 1986-89; exec. v.p. Brean Murray, Foster Securities, Inc., 1989-90; v.p., br. mgr., corp. officer A.G. Edwards and Sons, Inc., Glen Cove, N.Y., 1990—. Cons. Oncor Inc., Gaithersburg, Md., 1987-93, Wedding Info. Network, Inc., Omaha, 1987-91; fin. adviser European banking, ins. and investment industry, 1987-95; mem. Pres. Coun. A.G. Edwards, Million Dollar Club A.G. Edwards, Chmn.'s Coun. A.G. Edwards, 1998; mem. pres.'s adv. coun. The Rochester Funds, exec. coun. The Oppenheimer Funds Group; mem. All=Am. team The Am. Funds Group, 1990-94, mem. Pres. club, 1997, Alliance Premier Coun. Bd. dirs. Harbour Green L.I. Assn., 1990-94, pres., 1991; mem. Oyster Bay Supr.'s Adv. Com. on Crime, 1993-95; del. Rep. Party Planning Com., 1996; basketball coach Cath. Youth Orgn. Girls Team, 1998-2001. Recipient Outstanding Character award Chaminade, 1974. Mem. Chaminade Wall St. Assn., Green Harbour Beach Club (bd. dirs. 1994-98, treas. 1999), Swan Lake Country Club, Chaminade Torch Club. Republican. Roman Catholic. Avocations: golf. skiing, boating. Home: 280 Bay Dr Massapequa NY 11758-8142 Office: AG Edwards and Sons Inc 51 Glen St Glen Cove NY 11542-2738

PETTERSEN, KJELL WILL, stockbroker, consultant; b. Oslo, Norway, June 19, 1927; came to U.S., 1946, naturalized, 1957; s. Jens Will and Ragna O. (Wickstrom) P.; m. Marilyn Ann Stevens, Aug. 16, 1952; children: Thomas W., Maureen, Kevin W., Maryann, Kathleen. Student, Zion Theol. Sch., 1945-49, N.Y. Inst. Finance, 1955-56. Mgr. A.M. Kidder & Co., N.Y.C., 1954-64; sr. v.p., sec., dir. Halle & Stieglitz, Fillor Bullard Co., Inc., 1964-73; sr. v.p., dir. mktg. Parrish Securities, Inc., N.Y.C., 1973-74; cons. Loeb, Rhoades & Co., 1974-79; mng. dir. Prudential Securities, 1979-89; pres. Arbitration Recovery Cons., Marco, Fla., 1992-93; vice chmn. Noddings Investment Group, Inc., Oakbrook Terrace, Ill., 1993-95; mem. City Coun., Marco Island, Fla., 1997—. Dir. Ski for Light Inc., Mpls., Creative Arts Rehab. Ctr. Inc., N.Y.C. Dem. candidate N.Y. State Assembly, Nassau County, 1962; past dir. Guadalupe Ctr., Marco YMCA; pres. Quest for Peace Internat.; co-chmn. Marco Island Celebration 2000. Mem. Nat. Assn. Security Dealers (bd. arbitrators), N.Y. C. of C., Norwegian-Am. C. of C. (dir. Guadalope Ctr.), Scandinavian Found., Bankers Club of Am., Norwegian Club (N.Y.C.), Rotary. Home: 350 Rockhill Ct Marco Island FL 34145-3860 E-mail: marcokjell@aol.com.

PETTERSEN, THOMAS MORGAN, accountant, finance executive; b. Poughkeepsie, N.Y., Nov. 9, 1950; s. Olsen Thomas and Reva Frances (Palmer) P. BS, U. Albany, 1973. CPA, N.Y. Sr. acct. Arthur Andersen and Co., N.Y.C., 1973-76; sr. ops. auditor Gulf and Western Inc., 1977, fin. analyst, 1978; adminstr. auditing NBC, 1979, mgr. auditing Burbank, Calif., 1980, dir. auditing, 1981-88, dir. acctg. systems and ops. analysis, 1988-90; v.p. fin. and adminstrn. Data Dimensions, Inc., Culver City, 1991-92; cons. Westwood One, Inc., 1992-93; CFO Computer Image Sys., Inc., Torrance, Calif., 1993-97; dir. corp. fin. DeCrane Aircraft Holdings, Inc., El Segundo, 1997-2000; bus. cons., 2000—. Mem. AICPA, Fin. Execs. Internat. Republican. Roman Catholic. Avocations: sports, travel. Home: 217 1st Pl Manhattan Beach CA 90266-6503

PETTERSON, MARGO, artist; b. L.A., Jan. 12, 1944; d. Edmund and Helen Smolinski; m. Richard M. Petterson, Apr. 14, 1962; 1 child, Sandra. AA, San Bernardino Valley Coll., 1981; student, Cuesta Coll., 1982-83. Asst. libr. San Bernardino County, Big Bear Lake, Calif., 1975-81; med. records clk. San Luis Obispo (Calif.) Gen. Hosp., 1981-83; adminstrv. asst. Donez Real Estate, Big Bear Lake, 1984-90; owner Petterson's Bear Valley Saw Shop, 1983—; artist Margo Petterson/The Feminine West, 1986—. Instr. Beverly Hills (Calif.) Art Guild, 1997-98, Orange (Calif.) Art Guild, 1998, Corona (Calif.) Art League, 1999, Huntington Beach (Calif.) Art Guild, 1999; dir. publicity Women Artists of the West. Pub. limited edit. lithographs, 1990—; contbr. painting to Art of American West, 1998. Sec. City Spirit, Big Bear Lake, 1977; pres. Big Bear Lake Art Assn., 1977-78, treas., 1979-80, 84-86; fundraiser United We Stand Am., Big Bear Lake, 1992; bd. dirs. Friends of the Libr., Big Bear Lake. Recipient 3d Pl. award George Phippen Meml., 1989, Best of Show, 1st Pl. Big Bear Lake Art Assn., 1992, Excellence in Artisty Ed and Maxine Runci Meml. award, 1993, Best of Show award Snake River Showcase, 1995. Mem. Calif. Art Club, Women Artists of the West, Oil Painters of Am., Soroptimist Internat. Avocations: reading, camping, cooking. E-mail: MargoFemWest@msn.com.

PETTES, ROBERT CARLTON, artist; b. Mpls., May 16, 1922; s. Robert Oscar and Mertez Jennie (Swartwood) P.; m. Gladys Arlene Pettes, July 27, 1922 (div. Feb. 1976); children: Jo Anne, Roberta Gay, Douglas Kent; m. Phyllis Gwen Browne, Apr. 3, 1976. Grad. high sch., Mpls.; student, Oberlin Coll., 1944-45, Mpls. Sch. Art, 1945-48. Artist Brown and Bigelow, St. Paul, 1946-56; illustrator Creative Group, Mpls., 1956-60; studio mgr. Bob Pettes Art For Advt., 1960-67; builder, architect Bob Pettes Rustique Homes; illustrator Design Studios Inc., St. Paul, 1969-70; artist Hallmark Cards, 1972-80, Nostalgic Impressions, Prairie Village, Kans., 1980—. Group precinct leader Rep. Group, Edina 1961-64. With Coast Guard Navy, 1942-45. Mem. Soc. Artists and Art Dirs. (treas. 1962). Avocations: gardening, travelling. Home: 7403 NW Oak Dr Parkville MO 64152-1947

PETTEWAY, SAMUEL BRUCE, college president; b. Fayetteville, N.C., July 18, 1924; s. Walter Bernard and Margaret Maysie (Cole) P.; m. Eleanor Glenn Sugg, Nov. 27, 1948; children— Margaret Petteway Small, Samuel Bruce. BS, N.C. State U., 1949, MEd, 1966, EdD, 1968. Gen. mgr. Homeowners Ins. and Realty Co., 1960-63; engrng. tech. dept. chmn., dean occupational and transfer programs, dir. evening programs Lenoir County Community Coll., 1963-68; pres. Coll. of the Albemarle, Elizabeth City, N.C., 1968-75, N.C. Wesleyan Coll., Rocky Mount, 1975-86. Prof. Va. Poly. Inst. and State U., 1973-75, East Carolina U., 1994-99; pres. Philanthropic Cons., Inc., Kinston, N.C., 1986-96; sec. Coll. Mgmt. Svcs., Inc., Raleigh, N.C., 1989; lic. amateur radio operator, 1992—. Pres. chpt. Am. Cancer Soc., 1960-61, Boys' Club Lenoir County, 1987-91, Westminster Homeowners Assn., 1997; bd. dirs. Rocky Mount Acad., 1979-80, Triangle East, Inc., 1985-86, Cypress Glen Retirement Home, chmn. 1996; chmn. deferred giving com. N.C. Meth. Found., 1979-86; chmn. coun. on ministries 1st United Meth. Ch., Rocky Mount, 1980-81, Westminster United Meth. Ch., 1989-90, chmn. bd. trustees, 1994-99; chmn. bd. trustees Art Edn. Found., 1980; mem. Nash County Bd. Health, 1985-86; bd. trustees United Meth. Retirement Homes, Inc., 1996-99; treas. Meth. Home for Children, 1997-99. Named Tar Heel of Week News and Observer, 1975, Today's Outstanding N.C. Citizen WNCT-TV, 1975; NSF fellow U. Ill., 1963 Mem. Nat. Assn. for Hosp. Devel., N.C. Assn. Colls. and Univs., N.C. Conf. United Meth. Ch. (chmn. bd. trustees 1973-79), Nat. Soc. Fund Raising Execs. (cert.), Rocky Mount C. of C. (bd. dirs. 1980-84), Rotary (scholarship com. dist. 7730 1995-99), Phi Kappa Phi, Theta Alpha Phi. Clubs: Benvenue Country, Galaxy Social; Kinston Country. Lodges: Rotary (pres. 1980-81, bd. dirs. Kinston chpt. 1988-92). Democrat. Office: 708 Westminster Ln Kinston NC 28501-2770 E-mail: petteway@icomnet.com.

PETTIBONE, PETER JOHN, lawyer; b. Schenectady, N.Y., Dec. 11, 1939; s. George Howard and Caryl Grey (Ketchum) P.; m. Jean Kellogg, Apr. 23, 1966; children: Stephen, Victoria. AB summa cum laude, Princeton U., 1961; JD, Harvard U., 1964; LLM, NYU, 1971. Bar: Pa. 1965, D.C. 1965, N.Y. 1968, U.S. Supreme Ct. 1974, Russia (fgn. legal cons.) 1995. Lectr. Heidelberg (Fed. Republic Germany) U., 1965-67; assoc. Cravath, Swaine & Moore, N.Y.C., 1967-74, Lord Day & Lord, Barrett Smith, N.Y.C., 1974-76, ptnr. N.Y.C. and Washington, 1976-94, Patterson, Belknap, Webb & Tyler LLP, N.Y.C. and Moscow, 1994-99, Hogan & Hartson LLP, N.Y.C. and Moscow, 2000—. Pres. 1158 Fifth Ave. Corp., N.Y.C., 1991-94; pres. North Ferry Co., Shelter Island, N.Y., 1987-90; bd. dirs., vice-chmn. N.Y. State Facilities Devel. Corp., N.Y.C., 1983-89. Editor USSR Legal Materials, 1990-92. Trustee, treas. Hosp. Chaplaincy Inc., N.Y.C., 1980-86, Civitas, N.Y.C., 1984-92; mem. Coun. Fgn. Rels., 1993—; trustee Union Chapel, Shelter Island, N.Y., 1990—, CEC Internat. Ptnrs., 1996-2002; bd. dirs., vice chmn. Geonomics Inst., Middlebury, Vt., 1991-98; mem. vestry Ch. of Heavenly Rest, N.Y.C., 1987-93; mem. Nat. Adv. Coun. Harriman Inst. Columbia U., 1996—; mem. Russia com. Episcopal Diocese of N.Y. Capt. U.S. Army, 1965-67, Heidelberg, Germany. Mem. ABA, Assn. Bar City N.Y. (chmn. com. on CIS affairs 1991-94), U.S.-USSR Trade and Econ. Coun. Inc. (U.S. co-chmn. legal com. 1980-92), U.S.-Russia Bus. Coun. (bd. dirs.), Soc. of Cin., Anglers Club N.Y.C., N.Y. Yacht Club, Shelter Island Yacht Club, Moscow Country Club, Amateur Ski Club N.Y. (pres. 1980-82), Canterbury Choral Soc. (pres. 1983-84), Phi Beta Kappa. Episcopalian. Home: 1158 5th Ave New York NY 10029-6917 also: 10 Wesley Ave Shelter Island Heights NY 11965 Office: Hogan & Hartson LLP 885 3rd Ave New York NY 10022-7519

PETTIETTE, ALISON YVONNE, lawyer; b. Brockton, Mass., Aug. 16, 1952. Student Sorbonne, Paris, 1971-72; BA, Sophie Newcomb Coll., 1972; MA, Rice U., 1974; JD, Bates Coll., 1978. Bar: Tex. 1979, U.S. Dist. Ct. (so. dist.) Tex. 1980, U.S. Ct. Appeals (5th cir.) 1981. Ptnr. Harvill & Hardy, Houston, 1979-83; pvt. practice, Houston, 1983-84; assoc. O'Quinn & Hagans, Houston, 1984-86, Jones & Granger, Houston, 1986-88; pvt. practice, Houston, 1988—. Editor Houston Law Rev. U. Houston, 1976-78. Exercise instr. YWCA, Houston, 1976-81, U. St. Thomas, Houston. NDEA fellow Rice U., Houston, 1972-74; Woodrow Wilson scholar, Tulane U., New Orleans, 1972. Mem. ABA, Assn. Trial Lawyers Am., Tex. Trial Lawyers Assn., Houston Trial Lawyers Assn., Phi Delta Phi, Phi Beta Kappa. Home: PO Box 980847 Houston TX 77098-0847

PETTIGREW, CAROLYN LANDERS, theological school official, minister; b. Columbus, Ohio, Sept. 30, 1945; d. Wayman and Mary Gerldine (Lambert) Landers; m. Grady L. Pettigrew, Jr., Jan. 27, 1968; children: Dawn Karima, Grady Landers. BSc in Edn., Ohio State U., 1967; MDiv, Meth. Theol. Sch., Delaware, Ohio, 1987; postgrad., Washington Theol. Union, 1991—, United Theol. Sch., Dayton, Ohio. Ordained to ministry United Ch. of Christ, 1988; lic. speech and hearing therapist, Ohio. Youth min., dir. Christian edn. 1st Congl. Ch., Columbus, 1983-86; assoc. chaplain Grant Med. Ctr., 1987-90; ednl. asst. to acad. dean for MA in alcohol and drug abuse ministry and continuing edn. Meth. Theol. Sch., 1990-94. Trustee United Ch. of Christ House, Chautauqua, N.Y., 1990—, Chautauqua Inst. Arts, 1990-94; chmn. new clergy orientation Met. Area Ch. Bd., Columbus, 1990-91, co-convenor drug abuse task force; sec., tchr. gifted children's program Ohio Wesleyan U.; speaker in field; faculty Ea. Union Bible Coll., 1998—; planning team U.S. Atty. Gen. Drug Abuse Task Force, 1990-94. Compiler, author: African American Spirituality: A Bibliography, 1991. Mem. women's bd. Martin Luther King Ctr. for Performing Arts, Columbus, 1987—; mem. docent alumni group Columbus Mus. Arts; mem. women's agenda on human svcs. Ohio Gov.'s Task Force, Columbus, 1990—; mem. Chgo. Conf. Spiritual Renewal Task Force; exec. bd. United Ch. Christ, Cleve., 1997—. Recipient 11 Kudos, Grant Med. Ctr., 1987-90, Humanitarian award Columbus chpt. Alpha Kappa Alpha, 1990. Mem. Women's Theol. Group, Cen. S.E. Assn. United Ch. of Christ (chair dept. Christian edn. 1985-90), Jr. League Columbus, Zora Lit. Club (founder, convenor), Ladies of Lambda. Home: 1801 E 12th St Apt 301 Cleveland OH 44114-3530 Office: Meth Theol Sch Delaware OH 43015-0931

PETTIGREW, DANA MARY, musician, insurance agent; b. Oklahoma City, Jan. 15, 1951; d. Richard Clester and Alice Butler (Sargent) Pettigrew; children: Marilyn Yvonne Pettigrew-Davenport, Lonnie Dean Dupuis Jr. Student, Oklahoma City U., 1966-68. Cert. profl. ins. agt. Cert. Profl. Ins. Assn. Profl. performance musician, Oklahoma City, 1965—, Seattle, 1989-2000, Colorado Springs, 2000—; ind. agt. Pettigrew Ins. Agy., Oklahoma City, 1974-89, Protection Designs, Seattle, 1989-2000; owner Protection Designs Ins. Agy.; dir., organist Burien Free Meth. Ch., 1995—; dist. life mgr. Farmers Ins., 2000—. Ch. organist Pa. Ave Christian Ch., 1979-89. Life Underwriter Tng. Council fellow, 1984. Mem. Am. Guild Organists, Oklahoma City Health Underwriters Assn. (bd. dirs., pres. 1989), Oklahoma City Life Underwriters Assn. (bd. dirs. 1984-85), Renton-Auburn Musicians Assn., Pikes Peak Musicians Assn., Ind. Ins. Agts. Assn., Profl. Ins. Agts. Assn., Colorado Springs Assn. Life Underwriters, Cascade Assn. Life Underwriters (sec. 1995-96, treas. 1996-98, pres. 1998-99), Renton C. of C., Colorado Springs C. of C., Colorado Springs Conv. Visitors Bur., Kiwanis (sec. Renton chpt. 1988, 89, pianist 1987—). Republican. Methodist. Home and Office: 6973 Cloud Dancer Dr Colorado Springs CO 80918-5126 E-mail: Danasmusic@aol.com.

PETTIGREW, JOHNNIE DELONIA, educational diagnostician; b. Electra, Tex., July 2, 1948; d. John Drew and Dolly Marie (Watkins) Chester; divorced; 1 child, Jan Elise. B Elem. Edn., U. North Tex., 1970, MEd, 1982; postgrad., Tex. Woman's U., 1993—, EdD, 1998. Cert. elem., kindergarten, learning disabilities, spl. edn. early childhood, gifted edn. tchr., ednl. diagnostician, adminstr., Tex. 2d grade tchr. Azle (Tex.) Ind. Sch. Dist., 1969-70; 3d grade tchr. Decatur (Tex.) Ind. Sch. Dist., 1970-72; kindergarten, spl. edn. tchr. Boyd (Tex.) Ind. Sch. Dist., 1972-74, kindergarten, gifted edn., spl. edn. tchr., 1981-93; spl. edn. tchr. Springtown (Tex.) Ind. Sch. Dist., 1977-81; gifted edn. tchr. Denton (Tex.) Ind. Sch. Dist., 1993-94, ednl. diagnostician, 1994—. Cons. in gifted edn., early childhood and drama to various sch. dists., Tex.; rsch. cons. various HeadStrt programs; adj. prof. U. North Tex., Denton, 1993—, Tex. Woman's U., 1997—. Author: (play) The Monks Tale: Romeo and Juliet, 1990, also ednl. materials. Co-founder children's story hour Decatur Pub. Libr., 1970; bd. dirs., dir. Wise County Little Theatre, Decatur, Off 380 Players, Wise County, Tex.; life mem. Boyd Ind. Sch. Dist. PTA, 1989, Tex. PTA. Mem. Am. Assn. for Tchg. and Curriculum, Assn. for Childhood Edn. Internat., Am. Edn. Rsch. Assn., Tex. Assn. for Gifted and Talented, Nat. Assn. for the Edn. of Young Children, So. Early Childhood Assn., Phi Delta Kappa, Phi Kappa Phi. Avocations: theater, needlecraft, sewing. Home: PO Box 91 Decatur TX 76234-0091 Office: 1205 W University Dr Denton TX 76201-1753 E-mail: jpettigrew@denton.isd.org., jpettigrew@twu.edu.

PETTIGREW, PIERRE S. politician, member of parliament; b. Quebec City, Can., Apr. 18, 1951; BA in Philosophy, U. Que., Trois-Rivères, 1972; M in Philosophy in Internat. Rels., Balliol Coll., Oxford, 1976. Dir. polit. com. NATO Assembly, Brussels, 1976-78; exec. asst. to the leader Que. Liberal Party, 1978-81; fgn. policy advisor Prime Min. Can., 1981-84; v.p. Samson Bélair Deloitte & Touche Internat., Montreal, 1985-95; co-chair First Nat. Forum on Can. Internat. Rels., 1994; min. for Papineau-St. Denis, internat. coop. and la Francophonie Ho. of Commons, Ottawa, Canada, 1996—; min. human resources devel. Can. House of Commons, 1996-99; min. for internat. trade Can. Ho. of Commons, 1999—. Author: The New Politics of Confidence, 1999; contbr. articles to profl. jours. Office: House of Commons Min for Internat Trade Rm 507 Confederation Bldg Ottawa ON Canada K1A 0A6

PETTIGREW, RICHARD A. lawyer; b. Charleston, W.Va., June 10, 1930; s. Grady Lewis and Otella Lee Pettigrew; m. Ann Moorhead, Mar. 8, 1954; children: Jill E., Grady BA, U. Fla., 1953, JD, 1957. Bar: Fla. 1957, state cert. mediator and arbitrator;. Assoc., ptnr. Walton, Lantaff, Miami, 1957-67; ptnr. Pettigrew, Hartnett & Gilman, 1967-68, Pettigrew & Bailey, Miami, 1968-75, Pettigrew, Arky, Freed, Stearns, Watson & Green, Miami, 1975-77; asst. to pres. White House, U.S. Govt., Washington, 1977-79; sr. counsel Arky, Freed, Stearns, Watson & Greer, Miami, 1979-81; ptnr. Morgan, Lewis, Bockius, 1981-98; pvt. practice, 1998—. State rep. Fla. Ho. Reps., Tallahassee, 1963-72, spkr., 1970-72; sen. Fla. Senate Tallahassee, 1972-74; mem. Constn. Revision Commn., Tallahassee, 1965-67; chmn. Gov. Commn. for Sustainable South Fla.; chmn. bd. Audubon of Fla., 1999-2002. 1st lt. USAF, capt. res., 1953-55, Korea. Recipient William Sadowski award 1000 Friends of Fla., 1997, Silver Medallion award Greater Miami Region of Nat. Conf. for Cmty. Justice, 1999, Jurisprudence award Anti-Defamation League, 1999, Steward of the Everglades award Everglades Coalition, 2000. Mem. ABA, Fla. Bar Assn., Dade County Bar Assn. Democrat. Congregationalist. Avocations: golf, tennis, fishing, skiing, biking. Home: 1151 Sunset Dr Coral Gables FL 33143

PETTIGREW, THOMAS FRASER, social psychologist, educator; b. Richmond, Va., Mar. 14, 1931; s. Joseph Crane and Janet (Gibb) P.; m. Ann Hallman, Feb. 25, 1956; 1 son, Mark Fraser. AB in Psychology, U. Va., 1952; MA in Social Psychology, Harvard U., 1955, PhD, 1956; DHL (hon.), Governor's State U., 1979. Rsch. assoc. Inst. Social Rsch., U. Natal, Republic South Africa, 1956; asst. prof. psychology U. N.C., 1956-57; asst. prof. social psychology Harvard U., Cambridge, Mass., 1957-62, lectr., 1962-64, assoc. prof., 1964-68, prof., 1968-74, prof. social psychology and sociology, 1974-80; prof. social psychology U. Calif., Santa Cruz, 1980-94, rsch. prof. social psychology, 1994—; prof. social psychology U. Amsterdam, 1986-91. Adj. fellow Joint Ctr. Polit. and Econ. Studies, Washington, 1982—; adv. bd. women's studies program Princeton (N.J.) U., 1985-2001; vis. prof. Westfaelishe Wilhelms-U., Germany, 1993, Philipps U., Germany, 2000; disting. vis. prof. Flinders U., Australia, 1997; sr. fellow Rsch. Inst. for the Comparative Study of Race and Tehnicity, Stanford U., 2001-02. Author: (with E.Q. Campbell) Christians in Racial Crisis: A Study of the Little Rock Ministry, 1959, A Profile of the Negro American, 1964, Racially Separate or Together?, 1971; (with Frederickson, Knobol, Glazer and Veda) Prejudice, 1982; (with Alston) Tom Bradley's Campaigns for Governor: The Dilemma of Race and Political Strategies, 1988, How to Think Like a Social Scientist, 1996; editor: Racial Discrimination in the United States, 1975, The Sociology of Race Relations: Reflection and Reform, 1980; (with C. Stephan & W. Stephan) The Future of Social Psychology: Defining the Relationship Between Sociology and Psychology, 1991; mem. editorial bd. Jour. Social Issues, 1959-64, Social Psychology Quarterly, 1977-80; assoc. editor Am. Sociol. Rev, 1963-65; adv. bd. Integrated Edn, 1963-84, Phylon, 1965-93, Edn. and Urban Society, 1968-90, Race, 1972-74, Ethnic and Racial Studies, 1978-95, Rev. of Personality and Social Psychology, 1980-85, Cmty. and Applied Social Psychology, 1989—, Individual and Politics, 1989-93, Jour. Ethnic and Migration Studies, 1994—, 21st Century Afro Rev., 1994—; contbr. articles to profl. jours. Chmn. Episcopal presiding Bishop's Adv. Com. on Race Relations, 1961-63; v.p. Episcopal Soc. Cultural and Racial Unity, 1962-63; mem. Mass. Gov.'s Adv. Com. on Civil Rights, 1962-64; social sci. cons. U.S. Commn. Civil Rights, 1966-71; mem. White House Task Force on Edn., 1967; mem. nat. task force on desegregation policies Edn. Commn. of States, 1977-79; trustee Ella Lyman Cabot Trust, Boston, 1977-79; Emerson Book Award com. United Chpts. Phi Beta Kappa, 1971-73; com. status black Ams. NRC, 1985-88. Guggenheim fellow, 1967-68, Sr. Scientist fellow NATO, 1974, fellow Ctr. Advanced Study in Behavioral Scis., 1975-76, Sydney Spivack fellow in intergroup rels. Am. Sociol. Assn., 1978, Netherlands Inst. Advanced Study fellow, 1984-85; recipient Kurt Lewin Meml. award Soc. for Psychol. Study of Social Issues, 1987, (with Martin) Gordon Allport Intergroup Rels. Rsch. prize, 1988, Faculty Rsch. award U. Calif., Santa Cruz, 1988; Bellagio (Italy) Study Ctr. resident fellow, Rockefeller Found., 1991. Fellow APA, Am. Sociol. Assn. (coun. 1979-82); mem. Soc. Psychol. Study Social Issues (coun. 1962-66, pres. 1967-68, Disting. Svc. award 1998), Soc. Exptl. Social Psychology (Disting. Scientist award 2002), European Assn. Social Psychology. Home: 524 Van Ness Ave Santa Cruz CA 95060-3556

PETTIJOHN, FRED PHILLIPS, retired newspaper executive, consultant; b. Balt., May 11, 1917; s. Fred and Adelaide Josephine (Phillips) P.; m. Elaine Wilson, Dec. 7, 1946; children: Fred Phillips, Mark Clay. BAE., U. Fla., 1941. Sports editor Tallahassee Democrat, 1946-53; with Fort Lauderdale (Fla.) News, 1953-82, exec. editor, 1960-68, gen. mgr., 1968-77, editorial dir., from 1977; 1st v.p. Gore Newspapers Co., from 1960; now cons. Bd. dirs. Salvation Army, 1975-79, v.p., 1979; bd. dirs. Fla. Council 100, 1976-78. Served with AUS, 1943-45. Recipient Disting. Service award Fla. Press Assn., 1976, Disting. Alumnus award U. Fla., 1977; inducted into Fla. Newspaper Hall of Fame, 1990. Mem. Fla. Press Assn. (pres. 1963-64, 69-70), AP Mng. Editors (bd. dirs. 1964-66), So. Newspaper Pubs. Assn., Lauderdale Yacht Club, Tower Club, Sigma Delta Chi, Theta Chi. Democrat. Presbyterian. Home: 911 N Rio Vista Blvd Fort Lauderdale FL 33301-3037

PETTINE, LINDA FAYE, physical therapist; b. New London, Conn., Nov. 11, 1958; d. Robert Anderson and Pauline Priscilla (Johnson) Erwin; m. H. Louis Pettine Jr., Mar. 6, 1982. BS, U. Conn., 1980; student, Quinnipiac Coll.,

Hamden, Conn., 1989-91. Registered phys. therapist, Conn. Staff phys. therapist Worcester (Mass.) Hahneman Hosp., 1980, Newport (R.I.) Hosp., 1980-82, Middlebury Orthopaedic Group, Waterbury, Conn., 1982, Easter Seal Rehab. Ctr. of Cen. Conn., Meriden, 1982-84, hosp. and rehab. ctr. coord., 1984-86; co-founder Pettine & McDiarmid Phys. Therapy, Cheshire and Wallingford, Conn., 1986-88; pres. Keystone Phys. Therapy & Sports Medicine P.C., 1988-99; facility adminstr. Keystone Phys. Therapy and Sports Medicine, 1999—2001; facility dir. Conn. Physical Therapy LLC, 2001—02, dist. dir., 2002—. Lectr. Diabetes Edn. Program, Meriden, 1985; cons. Waterbury (Conn.) Nursing Ctr., 1986-87. Mem. adv. bd. Waterbury Continuing Edn. program, 1985; guest speaker Conn. chpt. Am. Diabetes Assn., Meriden, 1986, Arthritis Support Group, Meriden, 1986, Meriden Indsl. Mgr. Assn., 1986. Katherine Wyckoff and Margaret Wyckoff Moore Endowed scholar, 1991. Mem. Am. Phys. Therapy Assn., Conn. Phys. Therapy Assn. (program com. chair 1991-92, qualified peer reviewer 1995-98), MD Health Plan (phys. therapist/chiropractor liason com. 1997). Avocations: reading, needle work, quilting. also: 850 N Main Street Ext Wallingford CT 06492-2400 Office: Conn Phys Therapy LLC 85 Barnes Rd Ste 211 Wallingford CT 06492

PETTINELLA, NICHOLAS ANTHONY, financial executive; b. Little Falls, N.Y., Sept. 9, 1942; s. Nicholas and Rose (Zuccaro) P.; m. Nancy C. Whitehouse, Oct. 28, 1978; children: Albert J., Michael A. BS, Bentley Coll., 1968; MBA, Babson Coll., 1975; postgrad., Harvard U., 1979, Stanford U., 1983. CPA. Mass. auditor Coopers & Lybrand, Boston, 1970-76; treas. Courier Corp., Lowell, 1976-80; controller corp. ops. Digital Equipment Corp., Maynard, 1980-81; dir. fin. Intermetrics, Inc., Burlington, 1981-83, sr. v.p. fin., chief fin. officer, treas., 1983-98; sr. v.p. fin., treas. Averstar, Inc., 1999-2000; v.p., CFO Iron Bridge Networks, Inc., Lexington, Mass., 2000—01; CFO ideaLogix, Inc., Framingham, 2001—02, Managing B2B, 2002—. Bd. dirs. The Computer Mus., Boston, treas. 1988-98, bd. overseers 1997-99, Mus. Scis., Boston, 1999—. Chmn. fin. com. Town of Ashland, Mass., 1980-82. Served with U.S. Army, 1964-66. Mem. Fin. Execs. Inst., AICPA, Inst. Mgmt. Accts., Mass. Soc. CPAs, Treas. Club Boston, Pacioli Soc. Roman Catholic. Home: 141 South St Ashland MA 01721-2263 Office: 5 Whittier St Framingham MA 01701

PETTIS, DAVID WILSON, JR. lawyer; b. Montgomery, Ala., Jan. 28, 1945; s. David W. and Mildred R. Pettis; children: Kelly S. Thomas, Amy K. BS in Chemistry, Tulane U., 1966; JD, U. Ga., 1973. Bar: Ga. 1973, Fla. 1974, U.S. Dist. Ct. (mid. dist.) Fla. 1974, U.S. Ct. Appeals (11th cir.) 1981, U.S. Ct. Appeals (fed. cir.) 1983, U.S. Dist. Ct. (no. dist.) Fla. 1987. Assoc. Stein & Orman, PA, Tampa, Fla., 1973-76; shareholder Duckworth, Allen, Dyer & Pettis, PA, 1976-86, Pettis & McDonald, PA, Tampa, 1986-96, David W. Pettis Jr., PA, Tampa, 1997, Pettis & Van Royen, PA, Tampa, 1998—. Lt. USN, 1966-70, Vietnam. Mem. Am. Intellectual Property Law Assn. Office: Pettis & Van Royen PA 501 E Kennedy Blvd Ste 700 Tampa FL 33602-5200 E-mail: david@tampaiplaw.com.

PETTIS, FRANCIS JOSEPH, JR. electrical engineer; b. Portland, Maine, Oct. 2, 1930; s. Francis Joseph and Mida (Pedersen) P. BSEE, U. Maine, 1960. Electronic technician CAA, Burlington, Vt., 1957, CAA/FAA, New Bedford, Mass., 1958-59; electronic engr. FAA, Portland, 1960-65, Boston, 1965-68, N.Y.C., 1968-69, electronic technician Bangor, Maine, 1969-79, gen. engr. Washington, 1979-94, program mgr., 1994-97, gen. engr., 1997—. Cpl. U.S. Army, 1953-54. Mem. IEEE, AAAS, AIAA. Achievements include numerous contributions to the development and improvement of the National Airspace System (NAS). Office: FAA 800 Independence Ave SW Washington DC 20591-0001

PETTIS-ROBERSON, SHIRLEY MCCUMBER, former congresswoman; b. Mountain View, Calif. d. Harold Oliver and Dorothy Susan (O'Neil) McCumber; m. John J. McNulty (dec.); m. Jerry L. Pettis (dec. Feb. 1975); m. Ben Roberson, Feb. 6, 1988; children: Peter Dwight Pettis, Deborah Neil Pettis Moyer. Student, Andrews U., U. Calif., Berkeley; PhD (hon.) , Loma Linda U. Mgr. Audio-Digest Found., L.A., Glendale; sec.-treas. Pettis, Inc., Hollywood, 1958-68; mem. 94th-95th Congresses from 37th Calif. Dist., mem. coms. on interior, internat. rels., edn. and labor. Pres. Women's Rsch. and Edn. Inst., 1979-80; bd. dirs. Kemper Nat. Ins. Cos., 1979-97, Lumbermens Mut. Ins. Co.; bd. dir. Kemper Corp. Mem. Pres.'s Commn. on Arms Control and Disarmament, 1980-83, Commn. on Presdl. Scholars, 1990-93; trustee U. Redlands, Calif., 1980-83, Loma Linda (Calif.) U. and Med. Ctr., 1990-95; chair Loma Linda U. Children's Hosp. Found.; mem. Former Mems. Congress, 1988—. Mem. Morningside Country Club (Rancho Mirage, Calif.).

PETTIT, ALEXANDER DRUMMOND, English language educator; b. Albany, N.Y., Mar. 4, 1958; s. Paul Bruce and Bernice Minker P.; m. Melinda Jean Kerlee, May 24, 1986 (div. Sept. 1994); m. Jacqueline Alice Vanhoutte, July 5, 1997. PhD, U. Wash., 1991, MA, 1998. Asst. prof. English U. North Tex., Denton, 1991-96, assoc. prof. English, 1996-2001, prof. English, 2001—. Author: Illusory Consensus: Bolingbroke and the Polemical Response to Walpole, 1730-1739, 1997; editor: Textual Studies and the Common Reader: Essays on Editing Novels and Novelists, 2000; mem. editl. bd.: 1650-1850: Ideas, Aesthetics, and Inquiries in the Early Modern Era Jour., 1997—, mem. editl. bd.: Studies in the Eighteenth Century Novel Jour., 1997—, mem. editl. bd.: The Eighteenth Century: A Current Bibliography, 1988-2000, —, founding editor, gen. editor, textual editor: Selected Works of Eliza Haywood, 2000—, gen. editor: The Works of Tobias Smollett, 1997—, founding editor, gen. editor: British Ideas and Issues, 1660-1820: A Series of Reprinted Books and Pamphlets , 1997—, book rev. editor: Studies in the Novel Jour., 1991—97, assoc. editor: Studies in the Novel Jour., 1997, mem adv. bd.: , 1999—, co-gen. editor: Eighteenth-Century British Erotica, 2001—02, textual editor: The Cambridge Edition of the Works of Samuel Richardson , 2002. Office: U North Tex PO Box 311307 Denton TX 76203-1307

PETTIT, CLAUD MARTIN, religious organization administrator; b. Okemah, Okla., Sept. 19, 1926; s. Frank Martin and Ruby May (Thompson) P.; m. Margaret Esta Cain, July 30, 1948; children: Ruth Elaine Maenpaa, Paul Martin. Degree, Denver Bible Inst., 1948; BS, Rockmont Coll., 1952; postgrad., Bill Ogden Engring./Radio Sch., 1961; DD, Pioneer Sem., 1954. Ordained pastor Conservative Bapt. Assn., 1952. Pastor First Bapt. Ch., Arvada, Colo., 1952-60, Coal Creek Canyon, 1960; ceo, owner Radio Sta. KEOS, Flagstaff, Ariz., 1960-61; pastor Elmwood Bapt. Ch., Brighton, Colo., 1962-65; ceo, owner Radio Sta. KWIV, Douglas, Wyo., 1965-74; pastor Bethany Bapt. Ch., North Fed. Bapt. Ch., Denver, 1973-95; ceo, owner Radio Sta. KCMP, Brush, Colo., 1976-87; gen. dir. Better Life Ministries, Arvada, 1992—. Trustee Colo. Christian U., Lakewood, 1967-2001, advisor radio network, 1971-2001; chmn. bd. Am. Indian Crusade, Oklahoma City, 1987-2001; dir. Compa Food Ministries, Denver, 1981-91. Mem. Radio Hist. Soc., Broadcast Pioneers of Colo., Broadcasters Found., Model T Ford Club Am. (Mile High chpt. 1969—). Avocations: collecting and restoring antique automobiles, collecting big band music. Home: 8320 W 66th Ave Arvada CO 80004-3327

PETTIT, FREDERICK SIDNEY, metallurgical engineering educator, researcher; b. Wilkes Barre, Pa., Mar. 10, 1930; s. Edwin Humes and Edith Mae (Barnecut) P.; m. Lou-Jean Mary Corso, Aug. 30, 1958; children: Frederick N., Theodore E., John C., Charles A. B in Engring., Yale U., 1952, M in Engring., 1960, D in Engring., 1962. Jr. engr. Westinghouse Electric Corp., Pitts., 1952-54; engr. Avco-Lycoming, Stratford, Conn., 1957-58; postdoctoral student Max Planck Inst. Phys. Chemistry, Gottingen, Fed. Republic Germany, 1962-63; sr. staff scientist Pratt & Whitney Aircraft Co., East Hartford, Conn., 1963-79; prof. metall.-material engring. dept., chmn. U. Pitts., Pa., 1979-88, prof., 1988—, Harry S. Tack prof. materials engring., 1992—; mem. adv. bd. Jour. Oxidation of Metals, Plenum Press, N.Y., 1975—. 1st lt USMC, 1954-57. NSF fellow, 1962-63 Mem. Metall. Soc. (program dir. 1982-83), Electrochem. Soc. (sec.-treas. high temperature materials div. 1979-83), Am. Soc. Metals, Materials Rsch. Soc. Roman Catholic. Home: 201 Ennerdale Dr Pittsburgh PA 15237-4026 Office: U Pitts 848 Benedum Hall Pittsburgh PA 15261-2208 E-mail: pettit@engring.pitt.edu.

PETTIT, GEORGE ROBERT, cancer researcher; b. Long Branch, N.J., June 8, 1929; s. George Robert and Florence Elizabeth (Seymour) P.; m. Margaret Jean Benger, June 20, 1953; children: William Edward, Margaret Sharon, Robin Kathleen, Lynn Benger, George Robert III. BS, Wash. State U., 1952; MS, Wayne State U., 1954, PhD, 1956. Tchg. asst. Wash. State U., 1950-52, lecture demonstrator, 1952; rsch. chemist E.I. duPont de Nemours and Co., 1953; grad. tchg. asst. Wayne State U., 1952-53, rsch. fellow, 1954-56; sr. rsch. chemist Norwich Eaton Pharms., Inc., 1956-57; asst. prof. chemistry U. Maine, 1957-61, assoc. prof. chemistry, 1961-65, prof. chemistry, 1965; vis. prof. chemistry Stanford U., 1965; prof. chemistry Ariz. State U., 1965—, chmn. organic chemistry divsn., 1966-68, disting. rsch. prof., 1978-79, Dalton prof. medicinal chemistry and rsch., 1986—, Regent's prof. chemistry, 1990—. Vis. prof. So. African, Univs., 1978; dir. Cancer Rsch. Lab., 1974-75, Cancer Rsch. Inst., 1975—; lectr. various colls. and univs.; cons. in field. Contbr. articles to profl. jours. Mem. adv. bd. Wash. State U. Found., 1981—85. With Res. USAF, 1949—53. Recipient Alumni Achievement award, Wash. State U., 1984. Fellow: Am. Inst. Chemists (Pioneer award 1989, Ariz. Gov.'s Excellence award 1993); mem.: Am. Soc. Oncology, Am. Assn. Cancer Rsch., Am. Soc. Pharmacognosy (Rsch. Achievement award 1995), Chem. Soc. London, Am. Chem. Soc. (mem. awards com. 1968—71, Guenther award in chemistry of natural products 1998), Phi Lambda Upsilon, Sigma Xi. Office: Ariz State U Cancer Rsch Inst Tempe AZ 85287

PETTIT, GHERY DEWITT, retired veterinary medicine educator; b. Oakland, Calif., Sept. 6, 1926; s. Hermon DeWitt Pettit and Marion Esther (St. John) Menzies; m. Frances Marie Seitz, July 5, 1948; children: Ghery St. John, Paul Michael. BS in Animal Sci., U. Calif., Davis, 1948, BS in Vet. Sci., 1951, DVM, 1953. Diplomate Am. Coll. Vet. Surgeons (recorder 1970-77, pres., chmn. bd. dirs. 1978-80). Asst. prof. vet. surgery U. Calif., Davis, 1953-61; prof. vet. surgery Wash. State U., Pullman, 1961-91, prof. emeritus, 1991—. Mem. Wash. State Vet. Bd. Govs., 1981-88, chmn., 1987; vis. fellow Sydney (Australia) U., 1977. Author/editor: Intervertebral Disc Protrusion in the Dog, 1966; co-author: Centennial History of the Washington State University College of Veterinary Medicine, 1999; cons. editoral bd. Jour. Small Animal Practice, Eng., 1970-88; mem. editoral bd. Compendium on C.E., Lawrenceville, N.J., 1983-86, editoral rev. bd. Jour. Vet. Surgery, Phila., 1984-86, editor 1987-92; contbr. articles to profl. jours., chpts. to books. Elder Presbyn. Ch., Pullman, 1967—. Served with USN, 1944-46. Recipient Norden Disting. Tchr. award Wash. State U. Class 1971, Faculty of Yr. award Wash. State U. Student Com., 1985. Mem.: AVMA, Kiwanis Internat., Am. Legion, Phi Kappa Sigma (chpt. advisor 1981—, 2d v.p. 1993—98, internat. pres. 1998—2000), Phi Zeta, Sigma Xi. Republican. Avocations: camping, small boat sailing.

PETTIT, GHERY ST. JOHN, electronics engineer; b. Woodland, Calif., Apr. 6, 1952; s. Ghery DeWitt and Frances Marie (Seitz) P.; m. Marilyn Jo Van Hoose, July 28, 1973; children: Ghery Christopher, Heather Kathleen. BS in Electrical Engring., Wash. State U., 1975. Nuclear engr. Mare Island Naval Shipyard, Vallejo, Calif., 1975-76; electronics engr. Naval Electronic Systems Engring. Ctr., 1976-79; sr. engr. Martin Marietta Denver Aerospace, 1979-83; staff engr. Tandem Computers Inc., Santa Clara, Calif., 1983-90, mgr. electromagnetic capability Cupertino, 1990-91, electromagnetic compatibility lead engr., 1991-95; electromagnetic compatibility engr. Intel Corp., Hillsboro, Oreg., 1995-96, Dupont, Wash., 1996—. Mem. U.S. tech. adv. group subcom. I, Spl. Com. on Radio Frequency Interferences subcom. Internat. Electrotechnical Commn.; mem. CISPR SC I, WG2, WG3 and WG4. Asst. cubmaster Boy Scouts Am., San Jose, Calif., 1985-86, cubmaster, 1986-88, ast. scoutmaster, 1988-90, scoutmaster, 1990-93. Mem. IEEE (sr.), Nat. Rsch. Coun. (bd. assessment of NIST programs 1999—), EMC Soc. (bd. dirs. 1999—), Electromagnetic Capability Soc. (sec.-treas. Littleton, Colo. chpt. 1983, sec. Santa Clara Valley chpt. 1985-87, vice chmn. 1987-89, chmn. 1989-91, sec. Santa Clara Valley sect. 1991-92, treas. 1992-93, vice chmn. 1993-94, chmn. 1994-95), IEEE Electromagetic Capability Soc. (chmn. Seattle chpt. 1997-2000). Republican. Presbyterian. Avocations: flying, amateur radio, sailing. Office: Intel Corp 2800 Center Dr Dupont WA 98327-9773 E-mail: ghery.pettit@intel.com.

PETTIT, JAMES ROBERT, computer programmer; b. Chattanooga, July 7, 1944; s. Stanley Clyde and Mary Lena (Daves) P.; m. Katherine R. Osteen, May 27, 1978; children: Scott David, Andrea Michelle Pettit Backel. BS in Indsl. Engring., U. Tenn., 1968. Registered profl. engr. Ga., N.C., S.C., Tenn. Plant engr. Wentworth Mfg. Co., Lake City, S.C., 1968-69, chief engr., 1970-71, plant mgr., 1972-75; v.p. Tech. Computer Svcs., Florence, S.C., 1975-84; pres. Summit Systems, Inc., Columbia, 1984—. Dir., vestry St. Francis Episcopal Ch., Chapin, S.C., 1983-87. Sgt. U.S. Army, 1967. Mem. Nat. Assn. Profl. Engrs., Inst. Indsl. Engrs. Avocations: travel, snow skiing. Home and Office: 2163 Amicks Ferry Rd Chapin SC 29036-7926 E-mail: symsys@juno.com.

PETTIT, JOHN DOUGLAS, JR. management educator; b. Alice, Tex., Aug. 19, 1940; s. John Douglas and Vivian Iola (Beaman) P.; m. Suzanne McLeod, Aug. 23, 1964; children: Melanie Ann Wilson, David Bryant. BBA, U. North Tex., 1962, MBA, 1964; PhD, La. State U., 1969. Instr. mgmt. Miss. State U., Starkville, 1964-65; grad. asst. La. State U., Baton Rouge, 1965-67, instr. mgmt., 1967-68; asst. prof. bus. Tex. Tech. U., Lubbock, 1968-69; assoc. prof. mgmt. U. North Tex., Denton, 1969-78, prof. mgmt., 1978-95; chair excellence in free enterprise Austin Peay State Univ., Clarksville, Tenn., 1995-96; interim chair and prof. dept. info. and decision scis. U. Tex., El Paso, 2000-2001; vis. prof. Eslem, Poitier, France, 2002. Cons. various orgns., 1969-98; mgr., co-owner Pettit's Cleaners/Hatters, Alice, 1992-96; vis. prof. mgmt. Wichita State U., Kans., 1994-95; vis. prof. Ecole Superieure de Commerce et de Management, Poitier, France, 2002. Co-author: Business Communication: Theory and Application, 7th edit. 1993, Report Writing for Business, 10th edit. 1998, Lesikar's Basic Business Communication, 8th edit. 1999; mem. editl. bd. Organl. Comm. Abstracts, 1980-85; mem. editl. bd. Jour. Bus. Comm., 1987-90, mng. editor, 1990-94. Mem. choir St. Andrew Pres. Ch., Denton, 1985—, diaconate bd. mem., 1988-91; actor, singer Denton Cmty. Theater Summer Prodn., 1988-95. Recipient Master's Degree award Chgo. Bd. Trade, 1963. Fellow Assn. Bus. Comm. (pres., 1st v.p., exec. dir., 1990-94); mem. Southwestern Fedn. Adminstrv. Disciplines (pres., v.p.), Acad. Mgmt., Denton Country Club (bd. dirs.), Blue Key Nat. Hon. Fraternity, Beta Gamma Sigma (hon.), Phi Kappa Phi (hon.), Delta Sigma Pi. Presbyterian. Avocations: music, tennis. Home: 9122 David Fort Rd Argyle TX 76226-2953

PETTIT, JOHN W. administrator; b. Detroit, Mar. 6, 1942; s. John W. and Clara (Schartz) P.; m. Kathleen Endres, Aug. 8, 1970; children: Julie, Andrew, Michael. BBA, U. Notre Dame, 1964; MBA, Mich. State U., 1974. CPA, Mich.; CFP, 2001. Acct. Ernst & Ernst, Detroit, 1964-67; chief acct. Detroit Inst. Tech., 1967-69; controller, dir. adminstrn. & fin. Mich. Cancer Found., 1969-80; chief adminstrv. officer Dana-Farber Cancer Inst., Boston, 1980-94; exec. v.p., chief oper. officer John Wayne Cancer Inst., Santa Monica, Calif., 1995-97; fin. cons. L.A., 1998—. Grant reviewer Nat. Cancer Inst., Bethesda, Md., 1979-94. Pres. advanced mgmt. program Mich. State U., 1978-79; mem. adv. bd. Arthritis Found. So. Calif. chpt., 1999—; mem. Town Meeting, Wellesley, Mass., 1991-94. Mem.: AICPA, Fin. Planning Assn. Avocations: sailing, woodworking, photography, music. Office: 21031 Ventura Blvd Ste 705 Woodland Hills CA 91364 E-mail: jwpettit@yahoo.com.

PETTIT, LAWRENCE KAY, university president; b. Lewistown, Mont., May 2, 1937; s. George Edwin and Dorothy Bertha (Brown) P.; m. Sharon Lee Anderson, June 21, 1961 (div. Oct. 1976); children: Jennifer Anna, Matthew Anderson, Allison Carol, Edward McLean. BA cum laude, U. Mont., 1959; AM, Washington U., St. Louis, 1962; PhD, U. Wis., 1965. Legis. asst. U.S. Senate, 1959-60, 62; asst. & assoc. prof. dept. polit. sci. Pa. State U., 1964-67; assoc. dir. fed. rels. Am. Council Edn., Washington, 1967-69; chmn. dept. polit. sci. Mont. State U., 1969-72; adminstrv. asst. to gov. State of Mont., 1973; chancellor Mont. Univ. System, Helena, 1973-79; pvt. practice ednl. cons. Mont., 1979-81; dep. commr. for acad. affairs Tex. Coordinating Bd. for Higher Edn., 1981-83; chancellor Univ. System of South Tex., 1983-86; chancellor (now pres.) So. Ill. U., Carbondale, Edwardsville, 1986-91, Disting. svc. prof., 1991-92; pres. Indiana U. Pa., 1992—. Mem. various nat. and regional bds. and coms. on higher edn.; mem. adv. bd. S & T Bancorp., 1997—; mem. regional adv. bd. Nat. City Bank, 1997-99; bd. dirs. Ind. Healthcare Corp. Author: (with H. Albinski) European Political Processes, 2d edit., 1974, (with E. Keynes) Legislative Process in the U.S. Senate, 1969, (with S. Kirkpatrick) Social Psychology of Political Life, 1972, (with J. Goetz and S. Thomas) Legislative Process in Montana, 1975; mem. editl. bd. Ednl. Record, 1985-98. Mem. adv. bd. Leadership Ctr. Ams., 1988-90, Ill. Coalition, 1989-92; candidate for 2d dist. U.S. Ho. of Reps., Mont., 1980; mem. Ill. Gov.'s Com. on Sci. and Tech., 1986-90; bd. dirs. Tex. Guaranteed Student Loan Corp., 1985-86; chmn. Ill.-Niigata Commn. on Edn. and Econ. Devel., 1990-92; chair bd. dirs. Nat. Environ. Edn. and Tng. Ctr., 1994—. U. Wis. fellow 1962-63, Vilas fellow U. Wis., 1963-64. Mem. AAUP (pres. Mont. conf. 1971-72), Nat. Assn. Sys. Heads (pres. 1989), Am. Coun. on Edn. (chmn. leadership commn. 1989-90, sr. fellow 1991-92), Am. Assn. Higher Edn., Am. Assn. State Colls. and Univs. (Disting. Svc. award 1991), Newcomen Soc., Duquesne Club Pitts., Allegheny Club Pitts., World Affairs Coun. Pitts., Univ. Club Pitts., Pa. Soc., Ind. Country Club, Rotary (Paul Harris fellow), Ind. C. of C. (bd. dirs. 1992—), Sigma Chi (Significant Sig award 1988), Phi Kappa Phi. Episcopalian. Office: Indiana U President's Office 201 John Sutton Hl Indiana PA 15705-0001 E-mail: lpettit@iup.edu.

PETTIT, WILLIAM DUTTON, SR. investment executive, consultant; b. Bklyn., May 8, 1920; s. Karl Dravo and Estelle (Fitch) P.; m. Carole Earle Pettit, Dec. 27, 1941 (dec. Dec. 1983); children: Carol Pettit Lovelock, Penelope Pettit Kreinberg, William D. Jr., Jonathan E., Donald S.; m. Elizabeth McChristie Stetson, June 26, 1986. BA, Princeton (N.J.) U., 1941; postgrad., NYU, 1946-51. Co-owner Karl D. Pettit & Co., N.Y.C., 1946-74; pres., dir. Knickerbocker Growth Fund, 1956-76, Knickerbocker Shares inc., N.Y.C., 1960-75; exec. v.p., dir. Schuster Fund, 1975-82, Liberty Fund, N.Y.C., 1975-81; v.p., pres. Manhattan Fund, 1976-81, Hemisphere Fund, N.Y.C., 1982-86; v.p. Morse Williams & Co. Inc., 1986—; exec. v.p. Wall St. Fund, 1986-90. Cons. Morse Williams, 1990—. Class of 1941 pres. Princeton U., 1992-98. Maj. U.S. Army, 1944-46, ETO. Decorated Bronze Star. Mem. Bedens Brook Country Club, Nassau Club, Edgartown Yacht Club, Edgartown Golf Club, Cannon Club. Republican. Episcopalian. Avocations: sports, sailing, gardening. Home: 29 Hedge Row Rd Princeton NJ 08540 Office: Morse Williams & Co Inc 230 Park Ave Rm 1635 New York NY 10169-1602 E-mail: wpettitsr@aol.com.

PETTITE, WILLIAM CLINTON, public affairs consultant; b. Reno, 1937; s. Sidney Clinton and Wilma (Stibal) P.; m. Charlotte Denise Fryer; children: Patrick Keane, William Ellis, Joseph Clinton. Owner Market Lake Citizen & Clark County Enterprise Newspapers, Roberts, Idaho, 1959-70, pub., 1959-61; publicity dir. Golden Days World Boxing Champs, Reno, 1970; pub. Virginia City (Nev.) Legend newspaper, 1970; pub. affairs cons. Fair Oaks, Calif., 1966—. Owner PT Cattle Co., Firth, Idaho; cons. in Ireland, Wales, Korea, Japan, France, Czech Republic, Scotland, Alberta, Brit. Columbia, New Brunswick, Prince Edward Island, Nova Scotia, Can,. Channel Islands, Costa Rica, Belize, Macau, Hong Kong, Italy. Author: Memories of Market Lake, Vol. I, 1965, A History of Southeastern Idaho, Vol. II, 1977, Vol. III, 1983, Vol. IV, 1990; contbr. articles to profl. jours.; dir. TV programs on history Forgotten Pioneers, 1990—. County probate judge Idaho, 1959-61; acting County coroner, 1960-61; sec., trustee Fair Oaks Cemetery Dist., 1963-72; bd. dirs. Fair Oaks Water Dist., 1964-72, v.p., 1967-68, pres., 1968-70; dir., v.p. San Juan Cmty. Svc. Dist., 1962-66, 68-72; exec. sec. Calif. Bd. Landscape Archs., 1976-78, Calif. Assn. Collectors, 1966-68; cons. Senate-Assembly Joint Audit Com. Calif. Legislature, 1971-73; exec. officer Occupational Safety and Health Appeals Bd., 1981-83; mem. regulatory rev. commn. Calif. FabricCare Bd., 1981-82; mem. Sacramento County Grand Jury, 1973-74, 81-82, cons. bd. suprs. Sacramento County, 1985-87; chmn. bus. adv. bd. East Lawn Corp., 1991—; devel. cood. Sacramento Diocese Cath. Cemeteries, 1996-99; election campaign coord. for E.S. Wright, majority leader Idaho Senate, 1968, Henry Dworshak, U.S. Senator, 1960, Hamer Budge, U.S. Rep., 1960, Charles C. Gossett, former Gov. Idaho, 1959-74; asst. sgt. at arms Rep. Nat. Conv., 1956; chmn. Rep. County Ctrl. Com., 1959-61. Recipient Idaho Centennial award, 1967, 68, 69, Promotion of History award Sacramento County Hist. Soc., 1999. Mem. Assn. Sacramento County Water Dists. (bd. dirs. 1967-72, pres. 1970-72), Sacramento County Hist. Soc., Nat. Coun. Juvenile Ct. Judges (com. 1959-61), Antelope/Highlands C. of C. (bd. dirs.). Home: PO Box 2127 Fair Oaks CA 95628-2127 Office: 2631 K St Sacramento CA 95816-5103

PETTITT, JAY S. architect, consultant; b. Redford, Mich., Jan. 6, 1926; s. Jay S. and Florence Marian (Newman) P.; m. Ruth Elizabeth Voigt, June 21, 1947; children— J. Stuart, Laura Ellen, Patricia Lynn, Carol Ann B.Arch., U. Mich., 1951. Registered architect, Mich. Draftsman Frank J. Stepnoski and Son, Fond du Lac, Wis., 1951; project architect Albert Kahn Assocs., Inc., Detroit, 1951-62, chief archtl. devel., 1962-67, v.p., 1967-88, dir. architecture, 1975-88; archtl. cons. Beulah, Mich., 1988—. Active Jr. Athletic Assn., Redford, Mich., 1959-63; com. chmn. Boy Scouts Am., 1960-65; supr. Benzonia Twp. Served with U.S. Army. 1943-46, ETO. Fellow AIA; mem. Mich. Soc. Architects (pres. 1967), Am. Arbitration Assn., Am. Assn. Hosp. Planning, Engring. Soc. Detroit, U. Mich. Pres.' Club Avocations: sailing; skiing. E-mail: jaypettitt@bignetnorth.net.

PETTOELLO-MANTOVANI, MASSIMO, pediatrician, educator, microbiologist, researcher; b. Milan, Dec. 21, 1956; came to U.S., 1989; s. Luciano and Clara (Ghirardi) P.; m. Ida Giardino, July 15, 1985; children: Luciano, Clara. BA, St. John Evangelist Coll., Rome, 1975; MD, La Sapienza U., Rome, 1983; PhD in Pediat. Scis., Federico II U., Naples, Italy, 1989; PhD, State U., Turin, Italy, 1989. Assoc. Albert Einstein Coll. Medicine, N.Y.C., 1990—. Rsch. assoc. dept. pediat. Federico II U., Naples, 1984-85, sr. med. staff assoc. dept. pediat., 1987-89; co-dir. biohazard viral culture and animal study sect. Ctrs. AIDS Rsch., Yeshiva U., N.Y.C., 1994—; cons. Consulate of Italy, N.Y.C., 1996—; prof. pediat. U. Naples, 1997-99, assoc. prof. pediats., 2000—; exec. v.p. Found. Sci. and Tech. Edn. and Rsch., F.O.S.T.E.R. Sci., N.Y., 1998; mem. exec. com. World Health Policy Forum, 2000. Contbr. articles to Lancet, Jour. Immunology, Jour. Exptl. Medicine, Jour. Pediat., Gastroenterology, others. Pres. Villa Contarini Sci. Art Cultural Cr. GHIRARDI Found., Padua, Italy, 1997-98. Recognized as outstanding prof. U.S. Dept. State, 1994; fellow Cath. U. Sacred Hart, 1986; grantee Coun. Nat. Rsch., 1990, Italian NIH, 1992, U.S. NIH, 1996. Fellow Royal Soc. Tropical Medicine Hygiene; mem. N.Y. Acad. Scis., Internat. Soc. Infectious Diseases, European Soc. Clin. Microbiology, Am. Acad. Italian Scientists (v.p. 1996). Achievements include development of a modified humanized-animal model for the study of human immunological diseases and drug development; definition of the role of cryptococco polysaccharide in HIV-1 infection. Office: Albert Einstein Coll Medicine Forch Bldg Rm 401 1300 Morris Park Ave Bronx NY 10461-1926

PETTY, CINDY, music educator; b. Nashville, Oct. 22, 1952; dl John Wilson and Mary Emily (Gathright) Floyd; m. Clifton Frederick Petty, May 18, 1974; children: April, J.C., Bryce. B Music Edn., Ouachita Bapt. U., 1974. Cert. music tchr. Piano tchr., Pine Bluff, Ark., 1974-76; pvt. piano tchr. Nashville, 1976—. Children's choir dir., adult pianist Immanuel Bapt. Ch., Nashville, 1976—; musician for numerous weddings, funerals, cmty. projects, Nashville, 1976—. Mem. Nat. Music Tchrs. Assn., Ark. State Music Tchrs. Assn. (rally chair 1990-94, sec. 1992-94, 2d v.p. 1994-96, 1st v.p. 1996-98, state pres. 1998-2000), Am. Coll. Musicians (judge), Nat. Fedn. Music clubs (dist. pres.). Baptist.. Avocation: decorative painting.

PETTY, DONNA MATTHEWS, middle school educator; b. Charleston, S.C., Nov. 15, 1957; d. Duncan Newton Matthews Jr. and Calista Doris (Chapman) Matthews; m. Michael George Petty, May 31, 1980 (div Mar. 1988); 1 child, Adrian Michael. BA, Columbia (S.C.) Coll., 1990; Interdisciplinary MA in Natural Scis., U. S.C., 2000. Tchr. 7th grade math. and health Ridge Spring (S.C.)-Monetta Mid. Sch., 1990-92; tchr. multigrade levels New Directions/S.C. Dept. Juvenile Justice, Columbia, 1992-96; tchr. 8th grade earth sci. Dent Middle Sch., 1996—. Facilitator PBS Mathline, Alexandria, Va., 1995-96; mem. Curriculum Leadership Inst., Columbia, 1995—. Den leader Boy Scouts Am., West Columbia, S.C., 1992-95, asst. cubmaster, 1995-96, dist. webmaster Chinquapin Dist., 1995-98, pack com. chair, 1996-98. Named Tchr. of Yr., 1996, SC Dept. Juvenile Justice. Baha'i faith. Avocations: computers, camping, environmental efforts. Office: Dent Middle Sch 6950 N Trenholm Rd Columbia SC 29206-1708 E-mail: dpetty@teacher.com.

PETTY, ELIZABETH MARIE, geneticist; b. Chgo., July 13, 1959; d. Ralph David and Joyce Elizabeth (Carlson) P.; life ptnr. Karen Kay Milner, Dec. 15, 1985. BA, Clarke Coll., 1981; MD, U. Wis., 1986. Diplomate Nat. Bd. Med.

Examiners, Am. Bd. Pediats., Am. Bd. Med. Genetics, Molecular Genetics and Clin. Genetics. Pediat. intern and resident U. Wis., Madison, 1986-89; genetics fellow Yale U., New Haven, 1989-93; assoc. prof. U. Mich., Ann Arbor, 1994—, med. dir. genetic counseling program, 1996—, dir. med. genetics outpatient clinic, 1996—. Expert witness DNA testing in State of Ohio and Mich., 1995—; presenter regional, nat. and internat. confs. on genetics, 1991—. Contbr. chpt. to books, articles, editls. to profl. jours.; peer reviewer various jours., 1994—. Participant Gay and Lesbian Health Group, Ann Arbor, 1994—; apptd. to State of Mich.'s Gov.'s Commn. on Genetic Privacy and Progress, 1997-98. Recipient Clin. Investigator award NIH-NCI, 1995-2000, RO1 award, 1997—, Am. Cancer Rsch. Fund award, 1997-98, U. Mich. award for Disting. Pub. Svc., 2000, Breast Cancer award Dept. Def., 2001. Fellow Am. Soc. Human Genetics, Am. Coll. Med. Genetics; mem. AMA, Am. Acad. Scis., European Soc. Human Genetics, Human Genome Orgn., Alpha Omega Alpha. Democrat. Roman Catholic. Avocations: flutist, photographer. Office: U Mich 4301 MSRB III Ann Arbor MI 48109-0638

PETTY, GEORGE OLIVER, lawyer; b. L.A., Mar. 31, 1939; s. Hugh Morton and May (Johnson) P.; m. Sandra Diane Kilpatrick, July 14, 1962; children: Ross Morton, Alison Lee, Christopher Henry. AB, U. Calif., Berkeley, 1961; LLB, U. Calif., 1964. Bar: Calif. 1965, Eng. and Wales 1986, U.S. Supreme Ct. 1976. Atty. Huovinen & White, Oakland, Calif., 1967-69; counsel Bechtel Power Corp., San Francisco, 1969-83; prin. counsel Bechtel Ltd., London, 1983-86; gen. counsel Sun-Diamond Growers of Calif., Pleasanton, Calif., 1987-95; pvt. practice, 1995—. Capt. U.S. Army, 1965-67. Mem. Calif. State Bar Assn., Alameda County Bar Assn., Eng. and Wales Bar Assn., Bar Assn. for Commerce, Fin. & Industry (Eng.), Middle Temple Inn. Office: 843 Arlington Ave Berkeley CA 94707-1926 E-mail: 80petty@aol.com.

PETTY, JAMES ALAN, mathematics educator, consultant; b. Dublin, Dec. 27, 1954; s. Orris Delmar and Blanche Irene Petty; m. Soranee Holasuit, May 17, 1980; 1 child, Krissada Holasuit Petty; m. Christy Foley, Feb. 18, 2001. BS in Math. and Econs., Ball State U., 1977, MS in Math., 1978; PhD, Purdue U., 1996. Instr. math. U. Guam, Mangilao, 1989-92, asst. prof., 1992-94; instr. math./statistics U. Md.-Asia, Andersen AFB, Guam, 1990-94; tchr. educator Western Ky. U., Bowling Green, 1994-95; asst. prof. math. Ind.-Purdue U., Ft. Wayne, 1995-97; asst. prof. edn. U. Tenn., Martin, 1997-00. V.p. mktg. FPA Ednl. Consulting, Martin, 1995-00. Contbg. author: Epistecybernetics, 1997; contbr. articles to profl. jours. Mem. Math. Assn. Am., Nat. Coun. Tchrs. Math., Navy League U.S., Psychology Math. Edn.-N.Am., Tenn. Assn. Math. Educators, Phi Delta Kappa (program coord. N.W. Tenn. chpt. 1998-00). Republican. Office: U Tenn 240 J Gooch Hl Martin TN 38238-0001 E-mail: jpetty@utm.edu.

PETTY, JOHN ROBERT, financier; b. Chgo., Apr. 16, 1930; s. Dewitt Talmage and Beatrice (Worthington) P.; children: L. Talmage, Robert D., George M., Victoria Lee. AB, Brown U., 1951; postgrad., NYU, 1953-54. With Chase Manhattan Bank, N.Y.C. and Paris, 1953-66, v.p., 1964-66; dep. asst. sec. Dept. Treasury, Washington, 1966-68, asst. sec. for internat. affairs, 1968-72; partner Lehman Bros., N.Y.C., 1972-76; pres., dir., chmn. exec. com. Marine Midland Banks, Inc., from 1976, chmn., chief exec. officer, 1976-88; mng. gen. ptnr. Petty-FBW Assocs., Washington, 1989-91; chmn. Fed. Nat. Payables Inc. Fed. Nat. Svcs. Inc., 1992—; chmn. Nippon Credit Trust Co., N.Y.C., 1990-98. Chmn. Hydro-Icona, Inc., chmn. TECSEC Inc., Czech & Slovak Am. Enterprise Fund, 1991-95; bd. dirs. Antec Corp., Magnetic Analysis Corp., Anixter Internat. Corp.; trustee Am. Univ. With USNR, 1951-53. Mem. Council Fgn. Relations, Fgn. Bondholders Protective Council (pres.). Office: Fed Nat Svcs Inc 7315 Wisconsin Ave Ste 820W Bethesda MD 20814-3225

PETTY, MARTY, publishing executive; m. Mark Petty; 2 children. BJ, U. Mo., 1975; MS in Mgmt., Harvard Grad. Ctr., 1989. Asst. mng. editor Kansas City Star and Times; mng. editor The Hartford Courant, 1983-86, v.p., dep. exec. editor, 1986-89, assoc. pub. for projects and planning, 1989, sr. v.p., gen. mgr., pub., CEO, 1997—2000; exec. v.p. St. Petersburgh Times, 2000—. Editor The Electronic Times, 1991-92. Mem. journalism bd. Wm. Randolph Hearst Found., 1987-89; mem. CEO adv. bd. Greater Hartford Arts Coun.; pres. bd. Camp Courant; bd. dirs. Hartford Courant Found., Hartford Hosp. Holding Co.; mem. The MetroHartford Growth Couns. millennium mgmt. com. Mem. Newspaper Assn. of Am. (Ptnrs. 2000 com., Copyright Clearance Ctr. adv. bd.), Soc. Newspaper Design (pres. 1985, active cons.), Am. Soc. Newspaper Editors, Am. Press Inst., AP Mng. Editors, Poynter Inst. Office: St. Petersburg Times 490 First Ave., S Saint Petersburg FL 33701-1121*

PETTY, NILA MARIE, artist; b. Rockford, Ill., Aug. 15, 1969; d. John H. and Judith A. P. BFA, Rockford Coll., 1996; BA in Art History, 2000; MFA, U. Wis., 1999. Curatorial asst. State Hist. Soc., Madison, Wis.; gallery dir. Rockford Coll., 2000. Vis. cons. Beloit Coll., 1996. Exhibns. include Emerging Artists-Figurative Clay, 1999, NCECA Conf., Columbus, Ohio, 1999, Wayne (Pa.) Art Ctr., 2000, Crafts Nat. 34, 2000, Freeport Arts Ctr., 2000, Crafts Nat. 35, 2001, Zoller Gallery, Pa. State U., Gray Gallery, Quincy, Ill., 2001. Scholar Manville Found., 1994, Edith L. Gilbertson scholar, 1998. Mem. Coll. Art Assn., Phi Beta Kappa (Eta chpt.). Avocations: music, playing violin, reader, travel.

PETTY, PRISCILLA HAYES, writer, columnist, producer; b. Nashville, Aug. 22, 1940; d. Anderson Boyd and Margaret Louise Hayes; m. Gene Paul Petty, Jan. 10, 1961; children: Eric, Damon, Boyd. BA in English, Vanderbilt U., 1962; postgrad., Lang. Inst., Dartmouth Coll., 1965. Cert. tchr. Ohio. Tchr. English Cin. Suburban Pub. Schs., 1962-65, head dept. English, tchr., 1971-79; newspaper columnist Cin. Enquirer, 1978-89; also syndicated newspaper columnist Gannett News Svc., Washington, 1982-89, Cons. Arthur Andersen & Co., 1981-82; writer United Western Corp., 1982; exec. producer, on camera interviewer national TV documentary, 1992; commentator nat. bus. TV show, 1992; pres., owner, Petty Cons. Prodns., producer Total Quality Tng. Tapes. speaker W. Edwards Deming Seminars; cons. in field. Author: History of a Boardsman (oral history), 1979, Under a Lucky Star: The Story of Frederick A. Hauck, 1986, What's in It for You and the Firm: CEOs and Presidents Look at Community Involvement. Mem. Cin. Coun. World Affairs; chmn. Cin. Media-Bus. Exch., 1983; founder, pres., bd. trustees Cin. Oral History Found., 1984—. Named Outstanding Tchr., Project Teach, Ohio Edn. Assn., 1978; recipient WICI Great Lakes Regional Communicators' award; Pulitzer Prize nominee for Harvard U. Bus. Rev. article. Mem. Women in Comms. (Outstanding Communicator of Yr. 1985), Oral History Assn., Soc. Profl. Journalist. Home: 229 Oliver Rd Cincinnati OH 45215-2638

PETTY, SCOTT, JR. rancher; b. San Antonio, Apr. 10, 1937; s. Olive Scott and Edwina (Harris) P.; m. Marie Louise James, June 10, 1959 (dec. Dec. 1981); children: Joan Louise Petty, Susan Harris Arnim, Scott James; m. Eleanor Oliver, Apr. 30, 1983; children: Tim A. Weed, Richard Oliver Weed. BS in Petroleum Engring., U. Tex., 1960, MS in Petroleum Engring., 1961. Profl. engr. Tex., La. Asst. to pres. Petty Geophys. Engring., 1961-63, v.p., 1963-65; pres., exec. officer Petty Labs., 1965-67; pres., dir. Petty Geophys. Engring., 1967-73; exec. v.p. Petty-Ray Geophys., 1973-74; cons. Geosource Internat., 1974-76; chmn. bd. C.H Guenther & Son, Inc., San Antonio, 1982—, White Lily Foods Co., Knoxville, Tenn. Mem. chancellor's coun. U. Tex., Austin, devel. bd., San Antonio; bd. dirs. Tex. and Southwestern Cattle Raisers, Ft. Worth, Nat. Cattleman's Beef Assn., N.Am. Deer Farmers Assn. Mem. Am. Assn. Petroleum Geologists, Am. Inst. Mining, Metall. & Petroleum Engrs., Assn. Profl. Engrs., Geologists & Geophysicists of Alberta, Geophys. Soc. Houston, Internat. Assn. Geophys. Contractors, Internat. Oceanographic Found., Soc. Exploration Geophysicists, Soc. Petroleum Engrs., South Tex. Geol. Soc., Tex. Soc. Profl. Engrs., Explorers Club. Republican. Episcopalian. Home: 202 La Jara Blvd San Antonio TX 78209-4444 Office: Petty Ranch Co 711 Navarro St Ste 235 San Antonio TX 78205-1710

PETTY, SUE WRIGHT, library director; b. Kenton, Ohio, May 17, 1953; d. Norman Wilbur and Cynthia Elizabeth (Sapp) W.; m. Raymond O. Petty, Apr. 23, 1983; children: Jeremy Michael, Joshua Matthew. BA, Ohio No. U., 1975; MLS, Ind. U., 1977. Vol. VISTA, Iowa Falls, Iowa, 1975-76; tech. svcs. libr. Bowling Green (Ky.) Pub. Libr., 1978-82; libr. dir. Mary Lou Johnson-Hardin County Dist. Libr., Kenton, Ohio, 1982—. V.p. adv. coun. WORLDS, Lima, Ohio, 1983; exec. com. Dollars for Scholars, 1983—; mem. choir Epworth United Meth. Ch., 1997—, adminstrv. coun., 1998-2001, worship com., 1999—, chmn., 2001-2002; treas. Kenton Band Boosters, 1997—; active Hardin County Women Dems.; vol. polls. Mem. ALA, Ohio Libr. Assn., Kenton Rotary, Fortnightly Literary Club, Newcomers Club (sec. 1983-84). Home: 706 N Wayne St Kenton OH 43326-1344 Office: Hardin County Dist Library 325 E Columbus St Kenton OH 43326-1577 E-mail: pettysu@oplin.lib.oh.us.

PETTY, THOMAS LEE, physician, educator; b. Boulder, Colo., Dec. 24, 1932; s. Roy Stone and and Eleanor Marie (Kudrna) P.; m. Carol Lee Piepho, Aug. 7, 1954; children: Caryn, Thomas, John. BA, U. Colo., 1955, MD, 1958. Intern Phila. Gen. Hosp., 1958-59; resident U. Mich., 1959-60, U. Colo., Denver, 1960-62, pulmonary fellow, 1962-63, chief resident medicine, 1963-64, instr. medicine, 1962-64, asst. prof., 1964-68, assoc. prof., 1968-74, prof. medicine, 1974—; pres. Presbyn./St. Luke's Ctr. for Health Scis. Edn., 1989-95; practice medicine, specializing in internal medicine, pulmonary medicine Denver, 1962—; prof. medicine Rush Univ., 1992—. Cons. Vencor Hosp., 1991-. Author: For Those Who Live and Breathe, 1967, 2d edit., 1972, Intensive and Rehabilitative Respiratory Care, 1971, 3d edit., 1982, Chronic Obstructive Pulmonary Disease, 1978, 2d edit., 1985, Principles and Practice of Pulmonary Rehabilitation, 1993, Enjoying Life With COPD, 1995, 3d edit., others; contbr. articles to profl. jours. NIH and Found. grantee, 1966-88. Master ACP, Am. Coll. Chest Physicians (master, pres. 1982); mem. Assn. Am. Physicians, Assn. of Pulmonary Program Dirs. (founding pres. 1983-84, chmn. nat. lung health edn. program 1995—, co-chmn. 2000—), Am. Bd. Internal Medicine (bd. govs. 1986-92), Am. Thoracic Soc. (Disting. Achievement award 1995), Phi Beta Kappa, Phi Delta Theta, Alpha Omega Alpha, Phi Rho Sigma (pres. 1976-78). Home: 1940 Grape St Denver CO 80220-1353 Office: Presbyn Hosp Dept Internal Medicine Denver CO 80218 E-mail: nlhep@aol.com.

PETTYJOHN, FRANK SCHMERMUND, emergency medicine educator; b. Milford, Del., Sept. 28, 1934; s. James K. and Eloise K. (Kelley) P.; m. Jean A. Rovey, July 1, 1961; children: Elise K. Pettyjohn, Ellen E. Pettyjohn. BCE, U. Del., 1956; MD, Hahnemann U., 1963. Diplomate Am. Bd. Internal Medicine, Cardiovasc. Disease, Am. Bd. Preventive Medicine-Aerospace Medicine, Am. Bd. Emergency Medicine. Commd. 2d lt. U.S. Army, 1957, advanced through grades to col., 1977, intern, resident Madigan Gen. Hosp. Tacoma, 1963-69, chief med. staff aeromed. ctr., Lyster Army Community Hosp. Ft. Rucker, Ala., 1977-80, dir. applied aeromed. rsch. program Aerospace Med. Rsch. Lab., Fla., 1980-82; commdg. officer Winn Army Comty. Hosp. U.S. Army, Ft. Stewart, Ga., 1982-85; retired U.S. Army, 1986; clin. prof. medicine U. So. Ala. Coll. Medicine, Mobile, 1986-89, prof. medicine, 1989—, chmn. dept. emergency medicine, 1992—, dir. divsn. cardiology, 2001—. Med. dir. Southflite, Aeromed. Helicopter Svc., U. So. Ala. Med. Ctr., Mobile, 1990—; med. staff emergency medicine U. South Ala. Med. Ctr., Drs. Hosp., U. South Ala. Children's and Women's Hosp., U. South Ala. Knollwood Park Hosp., Mobile, 1991—; med. staff cardiology and internal medicine West Fla. Regional Med. Ctr., Pensacola, 1982—, Gulf Breeze (Fla.) Hosp., 1985—. Contbr. articles to profl. jours. Decorated Bronze Star, Legion of Merit, Air medal with two oak leaf clusters. Fellow ACP, Am. Coll. Cardiology, Am. Coll. Chest Physicians, Am. Coll. Preventive Medicine, Coun. Clin. Cardiology (Am. Heart Assn.), Aerospace Med. Assn. (exec. coun. 1979-82), Am. Coll. Emergency Physicians; mem. Soc. Acad. Emergency Medicine, Assn. Acad. Chmn. Emergency Medicine, Am. Coll. Physician Execs., Internat. Acad. Aviation and Space Medicine (chancellor). Methodist. Avocations: jogging, fishing, sailing. Home and Office: 607 Silverthorn Rd Gulf Breeze FL 32561-4625 E-mail: fpettyjo@usamail.usouthal.edu.

PETTYJOHN, SHIRLEY ELLIS, lawyer, real estate executive; b. Liberty, Ky., Aug. 16, 1935; d. Wesley Barker and Ada Lou (Bryant) Ellis; m. Flem D. Pettyjohn, Sept. 24, 1955; children: Deena Renee, Ellisa Denise. BS in Commerce, U. Louisville, 1974, JD, 1977. Bar: Ky. 1978, Ind. 1988; lic. real estate broker, Ky., Ind.; cert. mediator. Pres. Universal Devel. Corp., Ky. and Fla., 1984—, Pettyjohn Inc., Ky. and Ind., 1967—. Ind. Mediation Svcs., Inc., 1990—, Ky. Mediation Svcs., Inc., 1991—; v.p. Continental Investments Corp., 1986—; sr. ptnr. Pettyjohn & Assocs., Attys., 1987—. Editor Law-Hers Jour. Vice chmn. Louisville and Jefferson County Planning Commn., 1971-75; mem. Gov.'s Conf. on Edn., 1977, jud. nominee, 1981, Met. Louisville Women's Polit. Caucus, Bluegrass State Skills Corp., 1992-96, Ky. Opera Assn. Guild; elected mem. Ky. State Dem. Exec. Com., 1988-92; del. Nat. Dem. Conv. and Dem. Nat. Platform Com., 1988; bd. dirs. Ky. Dem. Hdqs., Inc., 1988-92, Pegasus Rising, Inc.; chmn. Okolona Libr. Task Force; mem. Clinton-Gore Nat. Steering Com., 1995; hon. mem. Gore 2000 Presdl. Campaign Com. Recipient Mayor's Cert. Recognition, 1974, Mayor's Fleur de lis award, 1969-73, Excellence in Writing award Arts Club Louisville, 1986, 87, 93, 99; inducted into Casey County Alumni Hall of Fame, 1997. Mem. ABA, NAFE, Nat. Assn. Adminstrv. Law Judges, Ky. Bar Assn., Louisville Bar Assn., Women Lawyers Assn. of Jefferson County, Am. Judicature Soc., Clark County Bar Assn., Ind. Bar Assn., Ind. Assn. Mediators, Am. Inst. Planners, Women's C. of C. of Ky. (past bd. dirs., chmn. legis. com.), Am. Legion (aux.), Fraternal Order Police Assn. (award 1982), Louisville Legal Secs. (past pres., editor Law-Hers Jour.), Coun. of Women Pres. (past pres., Woman of Achievement award 1974), Louisville Visual Arts Assn. (past bd. dirs.), Louisville Ballet Guild (chair audience devel. 1989-91), Fern Creek Woman's Club, Ky. Fedn. Women's Clubs, Gen. Fedn. Women's Clubs, Dem. Leadership Coun., Casey County Alumni Assn. (pres. 1998-2000), Poplar Level Area Bus. Assn., Jefferson County Dem. Women's Club (past v.p.), Nat. Fedn. Dem. Women's Clubs, Spirit of 46th Club, Mose Green Club, North End Club, 12th Ward Club, S. End Club, 3rd Ward Club, Highland Pk. Club, Grass Roots Club, Harry S. Truman Club, Beargrass Club, Arts Club of Louisville (past pres.), Sigma Delta Kappa (life), Chi Thi Theta, Century 2000 Democrat Club. Home: 6924 Norlynn Dr Louisville KY 40228-1471 Office: 4500 Poplar Level Rd Louisville KY 40213-2124

PETZ, EDWIN V. real estate executive, lawyer; b. Beatrice, Nebr., May 14, 1935; s. Virgil Leonard and Ruth Elenor (Thomsen) P.; m. Daphne Cross, May 17, 1958 (div. June 1964); 1 dau., Katherine J.; m. Anne Higgins, Dec. 3, 1964 (div. Sept. 1993); 1 son, W. Christopher; m. Louise Loosli, Jan. 9, 1997. BA, Principia Coll., Elsah, Ill., 1955; JD, Harvard U., 1958. Bar: N.Y. 1959, Mass. 1976. Assoc. Chadbourne, Parke, Whiteside & Wolff, N.Y.C., 1958-62; asst. gen. counsel Martin Marietta Corp., Bethesda, Md., 1963-64, 1965-75; gen. atty. sec. Bunker-Ramo Corp., Oakbrook, Ill., 1964-65; asst. gen. counsel United Brands Co., N.Y.C., 1975-82, v.p., gen. counsel, sec., 1982-84; sr. v.p., gen. counsel Milstein Properties Corp., 1985—; sr. v.p., gen counsel The Milstein Group Inc., 1992—. Mem. ABA, Assn. of Bar of City N.Y. Clubs: University (N.Y.C.). Republican. Episcopalian. Office: Milstein Properties Corp Ste 1500 335 Madison Ave New York NY 10017

PETZ, THOMAS JOSEPH, internist; b. Detroit, Feb. 10, 1930; s. Arthur J. and Marie (McCarthy) P.; m. Catherine Crowe, June 13, 1959; children: Thomas Jr., William, David, John, Catherine. BS, U. Detroit, 1951; MD, Wayne State U., 1955. Diplomate Am. Bd. Internal Medicine and Pulmonary Disease. Intern Harper Hosp., Detroit, 1955-56, resident, 1958-59, 60-62, U. Calif., San Francisco, 1959-60; clin. instr. Wayne State U., Detroit, 1962-72, assoc. prof., 1972-76, clin. assoc. prof., 1976-95, clin. prof., 1996-97, prof. emeritus, 1997—; pvt. practice pulmonary disease and internal medicine, 1962-72, St. Clair Shores, Mich., 1977-96; med.-legal cons. Grosse Pointe, 1996—. Chief pulmonary Wayne State U., Detroit, 1974-76, Harper Hosp., Detroit, 1972-79; dir. med. intensive care unit Harper Hosp., Detroit, 1977-83; chmn. dept. medicine Bon Secours Hosp., Grosse Pointe, Mich., 1984-86; chmn. Gen. Motors human rsch. com., 1995. Bd. govs. Wayne State Sch. of Medicine Alumni Assn., Detroit, 1981-85. Fellow Detroit Acad. Medicine (pres. 1982-83), Am. Coll. Chest Physicians; mem. Am. Coll. Physicians, Detroit Med. Club. Republican. Roman Catholic. Avocations: golf, skiing.

PETZAL, DAVID ELIAS, editor, writer; b. N.Y.C., Oct. 21, 1941; s. Henry and Aline Born (Bixer) P.; m. Arlene Anne Taylor, May 29, 1974. BA, Colgate U., 1963. Editor Maco Publs., N.Y.C., 1964-69; mng. editor Davis Publs., 1969-70; features editor Hearst Publs., 1970-72; mng. editor CBS Publs., 1972-79, editor, 1979-83, exec. editor, 1983-2001, Field & Stream Mag., N.Y.C., 1983-2001, mng. editor, 2001—. Author: The .22 Rifle, 1972; editor: The Experts Book of the Shooting Sports, 1972, The Experts Book of Upland Game and Waterfowl Hunting, 1975, The Experts Book of Big-Game Hunting in North America, 1976, The Ency. of Sporting Firearms, 1991. Office: Time 4 Mags 10th Fl 2 Park Ave New York NY 10016-5602 E-mail: david.petzal@time4.com.

PETZEL, FLORENCE ELOISE, textiles educator; b. Crosbyton, Tex., Apr. 1, 1911; d. William D. and Eloise P. PhB, U. Chgo., 1931, AM, 1934; PhD, U. Minn., 1954. Instr. Judson Coll., 1936-38; asst. prof. textiles Ohio State U., 1938-48; assoc. prof. U. Ala., 1950-54; prof. Oreg. State U., Corvallis, 1954-61, 67-75, 77, Corvallis, 77, prof. emeritus, 1975—, dept. head, 1954-61, 67-75; prof., divsn. head U. Tex., 1961-63; prof. Tex. Tech. U., 1963-67. Vis. instr. Tex. State Coll. for Women, 1937; vis. prof. Wash. State U., 1967. Author: Textiles of Ancient Mesopotamia, Persia and Egypt, 1987; contbr. articles to profl. jours. Effie I. Raitt fellow, 1949-50. Mem. Met. Opera Guild, Greenville County Mus. Art, Sigma Xi, Phi Kappa Phi, Omicron Nu, Iota Sigma Pi, Sigma Delta Epsilon. Home: 150 Downs Blvd Apt A206 Clemson SC 29631-2043

PETZOLD, CAROL STOKER, state legislator; b. St. Louis, July 28; d. Harold William and Mabel Lucille (Wilson) Stoker; m. Walter John Petzold, June 27, 1959; children: Ann, Ruth, David. BS, Valparaiso U., 1959. Tchr. Parkwood Elem. Sch., Kensington, Md., 1960-62; legis. aide Md. Gen. Assembly, Annapolis, 1975-79; legis. asst. Montgomery County Bd. Edn., Rockville, Md., 1980; cmty. sch. coord. Parkland Jr. H.S., 1981-87; mem. Md. Ho. of Dels., Annapolis, 1987—, mem. constl. and adminstrv. law com., 1987-93, mem. judiciary com., 1994—, vice chair Montgomery County del., 1995—, dep. majority whip, 1999—. Mem. transp. planning bd. Nat. Capitol Region, 1989—; vice chmn. assembly on fed. issues Nat. Conf. State Legislatures, 1996-97, chair adv. com. on energy, 1997-99, chair energy and transp. com., 1998-99. Editor Child Care Sampler, 1974, Stoker Family Cookbook, 1976. Pres. Montgomery Child Care Assn., 1976-78; mem. Md. State Scholarship Bd., 1978-87, chmn. 1985-87; chmn. Legis. Com. Montgomery County Commn. for Children and Youth, 1979-84; mem., v.p. Luth. Social Services Nat. Capitol Area, Washington, 1980-86; mem. exec. com. coun. Montgomery United Way, 1981-2000. Named Mother of Yr., March of Dimes, 2000; named one of Top 100 Md. Women, Daily Record, 2002; recipient Statewide award, Gov.'s Adv. Bd. on Homelessness, 1994, recognized for outstanding commitment to children, U.S. Dept. HEW, 1980, Award of Excellence, MADD, 2002. Mem. AAUW (honoree Kensington br. 1971, honoree Md. divsn. 1981), Women's Polit. Caucus (chmn. Montgomery County 1981-83), Md. Women Legislators Caucus. Democrat. Lutheran. Home: 14113 Chadwick Ln Rockville MD 20853-2103

PETZOLD, JOHN PAUL, judge; b. 1938; BA, U. Maine, 1961; LLB, Washington & Lee U., 1962. Bar: Ohio 1962, Va. 1962. Pvt. practice law, Ohio, 1962-91; asst. atty. gen. State of Ohio, 1964-71; law dir. City of Miamisburg, Ohio, 1979-91; judge Montgomery County Common Pleas Ct., Dayton, 1991—. Bd. tax appeals City of Kettering, Ohio, 1971-91. Mem. ABA, Ohio State Bar Assn. (bd. govs., former chairperson young lawyers sect., chairperson pub. rels. com., vice chairperson lawyers assistance com., eminent domain com., banking, comml., and bankruptcy law com., pres. 1998-99), Dayton Bar Assn. (pres. 1989-90), Common Pleas Judge Assn. (mem. bd. commrs. on grievances and discipline 1995-97). Avocations: golf, swimming, writing, teaching, reading, genealogy. Office: Montgomery County Common Pleas Ct 41 N Perry St Dayton OH 45402-1431

PETZOLD, LINDA RUTH, numerical analyst, researcher; b. Chgo., Sept. 11, 1954; d. Carl George and Donna Elaine (Webb) P.; m. John Andrew Emerick, Aug. 9, 1978; 1 child, Matthew Ryan. BA in Computer Sci. and Math., U. Ill., 1974, PhD in Computer Sci., 1978. Researcher Sandia Nat. Labs., Livermore, Calif., 1978-85; group leader Lawrence Livermore Nat. Lab., 1985-91; prof. computer sci. U. Minn., Mpls., 1991—. Author: Numerical Solution of Initial-Value Problems in Differential-Algebraic Equations, 1989. Mem. Soc. for Indsl. and Applied Math. (coun. 1987-93, v.p. for publs. 1993—, mng. editor Jour. Sci. Computing 1989-93), Assn. for Computing Machinery (sec.-treas. spl. interest group for numerical analysis 1986-89). Office: U Minn Dept Computer Sci 200 Union St SE Rm 4213 Minneapolis MN 55455-0154

PEUGEOT, PATRICK, insurance executive; b. Paris, Aug. 3, 1937; s. Jacques Louis and Edith (Genoyer) P.; m. Catherine Dupont, 1963; children: Hubert, Thomas, Camille. Degree, Ecole Poly., Paris, 1959, Ecole Nat. D'Adminstrn., 1965. Ins. auditor Ministry of Fin., Paris, 1962-65; auditor Cour des Comptes, 1965-83; spl. asst. Bur. Planning, 1966-70; sr. v.p. EMC, Toulouse, France, 1970-72, Hachette Inc., Paris, 1972-74; exec. v.p. ops. AGF Life, 1974-78; exec. v.p. AGF Reims, 1979-82; pres. Caisse Cen. de Reassurance, 1983-85; chmn., CEO Scor S.A., 1983-94, hon. chmn., 1994, 1994—; dir. SCOR U.S., 1994—; vice-chmn., CEO La Mondiale, Paris, chmn., CEO, 1996—. Home: 82 Rue Notre Dame Champs 75006 Paris France Office: La Mondiale 22 Blvd Malesherbes 75008 Paris France

PEVEAR, ROBERTA CHARLOTTE, retired state legislator; b. Bethel, Maine, July 4, 1930; d. Frank Albert Sr. and Thirza Estella (Hickford) Gibson; m. Edward Gordon Pevear, Aug. 21, 1971. Diploma in Comml. Art, Gould Acad., 1947. Sec. Wilner Wood Products, South Paris, Maine, 1947-50; sec. export dept. Whitaker Cable, North Kansas City, Mo., 1951-56; sec. br. and dist. Anheuser-Busch, Inc., Kansas City, 1957-59; legal sec. Johnson & Johnson, New Brunswick, N.J., 1960-65, St. John, Ronder & Bell, Kingston, N.Y., 1966; sec., adminstrv. asst. Sears-Roebuck & Co., Overland Park, Kans., 1967-70, Exeter, N.H., 1971-77; salesman Avon Products, Hampton Falls, 1978-86; mem. ho. reps. State of N.H., 1979-88, ret., 1988. Commr. Rockingham Planning Commn., N.H., 1979-88, N.H. Planning Com., 1985-88; clk. Environment and Agrl. Com. N.H. Ho. Reps., 1983-88; del. mem. Rockingham County, 1979-88, exec. bd., 1984-88; chmn. Rockingham County Home, 1987-88. Civil Def. dir., Hampton Falls, NH, 1980—88. Recipient Community Citizen award Hampton Falls Grange, 1982, Seacoast Retired Sr. Service award, 1985. Mem. Nat. Order Women Legislators, N.H. Order of Women Legislators, DAR. Avocations: writing, genealogy, travelling.

PEVEC, ANTHONY EDWARD, bishop; b. Cleve., Apr. 16, 1925; s. Anton and Frances (Darovec) P. MA, John Carroll U., Cleve., 1956; PhD, Western Res. U., Cleve., 1964. Ordained priest Roman Catholic Ch., 1950. Assoc. pastor St. Mary Church, Elyria, Ohio, 1950-52, St. Lawrence Ch., Cleve., 1952-53; rector-prin. Borromeo Sem. High Sch., Wickliffe, Ohio, 1953-75; adminstrv. bd. Nat. Cath. Edn. Assn., 1972-75; pastor St. Vitus Ch., Cleve., 1975-79; rector-pres. Borromeo Coll., Wickliffe, 1979-82; aux. bishop Diocese of Cleve., 1982—. Mem. v.p. Slovenian-Am. Heritage Found., Cleve., 1975—. Honoree, Heritage Found., Cleve., 1982; named Man of Yr., Fedn. Slovenian Nat. Homes, Cleve., 1985, Cath. Man of Yr. KC, 1998, Man of Yr., Pioneer Assn., 2001; inducted into Hall of Fame, St. Vitus Alumni Assn., 1989, Wickliffe Hall of Fame, 2000. Mem. Nat. Conf. Cath. Bishops (com. on vocations 1984-86, com. on pro-life activities, 1990-92, com. on sci. and human values 1993-96, com. on priestly formation 1993-95), U.S. Cath. Conf. (nat. adv. coun. 1996-97). Democrat. Roman Catholic. Avocations: reading; music. Home and Office: Diocese of Cleve 28700 Euclid Ave Wickliffe OH 44092-2527 E-mail: bpaepevec@dioceseofcleveland.org. *Ultimately I must always remember that the Lord is totally in control of my life, no matter how complicated it may seem to be. I am here to do the Lord's will, and wherever I go I come to do His will.*

PEW, JOHN GLENN, JR. lawyer; b. Dallas, Apr. 18, 1932; s. John Glenn Sr. and Roberta (Haughton) P. BA, U. Tex., 1954, LLB, 1955. Bar: Tex. 1955, U.S. Dist. Ct. (no. dist.) Tex. 1959, U.S. Supreme Ct. 1959, U.S. Ct. Appeals (5th cir.) 1961, U.S. Ct. Appeals (10th cir.) 1982. Ptnr. Jackson Walker LLP, Dallas, 1964—. With USNR, 1955-58. Mem.: Order of Coif, Phi Beta Kappa. Republican. Presbyterian. Office: Jackson Walker LLP 901 Main St Ste 6000 Dallas TX 75202-3797 E-mail: jpew@jw.com.

PEW, ROBERT ANDERSON, retired real estate and equipment leasing corporation officer; b. Phila., Aug. 22, 1936; s. Arthur Edmund and Mary Elizabeth (Elliott) P.; children from previous marriage: Robert Anderson (dec.), James Cunningham, Glenn Edgar, Joan Elliott; m. Daria S. Decerio, June 19, 1993; 1 child, Richard Westerman. Student, Princeton U., 1954-56; BS, Temple U., 1959; MS in Mgmt. (Alfred P. Sloan fellow), MIT, 1970; LLD (hon.), Widener U., 1982; DPS (hon.), Temple U., 1983; LHD (hon.),

Gettysburg Coll., 1984. Ops. asst. prodn. div. Sun Oil Co., Premont, Tex., 1959-60, ops. asst. prodn. div. Morgan City, La., auditor internal audit dept. Phila., 1960-65, staff asst. treasury dept., 1965-69, asst. to exec. v.p. corp. projects group, 1970-71, sec.-treas., mgr. financial control of products group, 1971-74, corp. sec., 1974-77; pres. Helios Capital Corp., 1977-96; CEO Radnor Corp., 1995-96; chmn. Glenmede Corp., Phila., 1997—. Bd. dirs. Sun Co., Inc., Phila., Pew Charitable Trusts, Phila., Glenmede Trust Co., Phila., Glenmede Trust Co. N.A., Wilmington, Del., 1999—. Trustee Children's Hosp. Phila., vice chmn. 1991—, Bryn Mawr (Pa.) Coll., vice chmn., 1991—, Curtis Inst. Music, 1993—. Served Pa. Air N.G., 1956-59. Recipient R. Kelso Carter award Widener U., 1971 Mem. Aircraft Owners and Pilots Assn. (trustee, chmn. 1974-77, 85-2002, vice-chmn. 1979-85), Am. Hosp. Assn. (hon.), Union League Club, Seal Harbor Club (pres. 1992-96), Phila. Aviation Country Club, Merion Cricket Club, N.E. Harbor Fleet. Republican. Presbyterian. Home: 916 Muirfield Rd Bryn Mawr PA 19010-1921 Office: Sun Co Ten Penn Ctr 17th Flr 1801 Market St Ste Sl Philadelphia PA 19103-1699 E-mail: dungarnem@aol.com.

PEYA, PRUDENCE MALAVA, retired elementary education educator; b. Rochester, Pa., July 27; d. George and Mildred (Tesla) P. BS, Duquesne U., 1965, MEd, 1967, MS, 1977. Permanent substitute tchr. Montour Area Sch. Dist., Coraopolis, Pa., 1965; tchr. elem. Ctr. Area Sch. Dist., Monaca, 1965-76, gifted support tchr., 1977-97, coord. gifted program, 1977-98, coord. spl. edn., 1995-98; ret., 1999. Local coach Odyssey of the Mind, 1985-97; sponsor Beaver County Acad. Games League, 1988—. Author: (handbook) Instructional Areas Appropriate for Gifted Students, 1987. Active Logstown Assocs. Hist. Soc., Ambridge, Pa., 1990—. Mem. AAUW, Greek Cath. Union U.S.A. (life), Pa. Assn. for Gifted Edn. (Elem. Gifted Tchr. of Yr. award 1984), 4th grade tchr., Beaver County Gifted Tchrs. (pres. 1993-94), Alpha Delta Kappa (past pres. Delta chpt.) Democrat. Byzantine Catholic. Avocations: Michael Ricker pewter collector, travel, calligraphy. Home: 341 Beaver Ave West Aliquippa PA 15001-2415

PEYSER, HEDY JEANETTE, social worker; b. N.Y.C. d. Leo and Helen (Friedman) Kuflik; m. Paul Peyser; children: Shoshana, Uri. BA, Bklyn. Coll., 1963; MSW, Howard U., 1966. Lic. social worker, Md. Caseworker Jewish Family and Children's Svc., St. Louis, 1966-67; adminstr., prin. Yeshiva High Sch. Greater Washington, Silver Spring, Md., 1968-69; profl. lectr. Am. U., Washington, 1976-80; dir. vols. Hebrew Home Greater Washington, Rockville, Md., 1971—. Mem. Gov.'s Com. on Volunteerism, Md., 1989—. Contbr. articles to profl. publs. Chmn. bd. edn. Yeshiva High Sch. Greater Washington, 1975-78. Mem. Nat. Assn. Social Workers. Avocations: music, painting, singing. Office: Hebrew Home 6121 Montrose Rd Rockville MD 20852-4856 E-mail: peyser@hebrew_home.org.

PEYSER, IRVING GERALD, surgeon; b. Cambridge, Mass., Nov. 27, 1941; MD, U. Vt., 1967. Intern Montefiore Hosp., Bronx, N.Y., 1967-68, resident surgery, 1968-72; surgeon St. Clares Hosp., Denville, N.J., Morristown Meml. Hosp. Mem. Alpha Omega Alpha. Home: 3699 Hwy 46 Parsippany NJ 07054-1049

PEYSER, JOSEPH LEONARD, educator, author, translator, historial researcher; b. N.Y.C., Oct. 19, 1925; s. Samuel and Sadye (Quinto) P.; m. Julia Boxer, May 30, 1948; children: Jay Randall, Jan Ellen. BA, Duke U., 1947, MA, 1949; profl. diploma, Columbia U., 1955; postgrad., U. Nancy, France, 1949-50; Ed.D., NYU, 1965. Prof., chmn. fgn. langs., adminstr. Nancy (France) École Normale, 1949-50; Tchr., chmn. fgn. langs. Monroe (N.Y.) Pub. Schs., 1951-54, Uniondale (N.Y.) Pub. Schs., 1954-61; asst. high sch. prin. Plainview, N.Y., 1961-63; mem. faculty Hofstra U., Hempstead, 1963-68, assoc. prof. edn., 1966-68; asst. dean, then asso. dean Hofstra U. (Sch. Edn.), 1964-66; interim dean Sch. Edn. Hofstra U., 1966-68; dean acad. affairs, prof. French and edn. Dowling Coll., Oakdale, N.Y., 1968-70, v.p. acad. affairs, dean faculty, 1970-73; prof. French and edn. Ind. U., South Bend, 1973-94, prof. emeritus French, 1994—, dean faculties, 1973-75, chmn. fgn. lang. dept., 1987-89. Vis. asst. prof. NYU, 1964-66; adj. asst. prof. L.I. U., 1961-63; prin. researcher, translator French Michilimackinac Rsch. Project, Mich., 1991—; rsch. reviewer NEH, 1994-98. Author: Letters from New France, 1981; rev. edit. Letters from New France: The Upper Country, 1686-1783, 1992; co-author, Fort St. Joseph, 1691-1781, 1991, The Fox Wars: The Mesquakie Challenge to New France, 1993, Jacques Legardeur de Saint-Pierre: Officer, Gentleman, Entrepreneur, 1996, On the Eve of the Conquest: Chevalier de Raymond's Critique of New France in 1754, 1997, Ambush and Revenge: George Washington's Adversaries in 1754, 1999; translator Fort St. Joseph Manuscripts, 1978, William Henry Harrison's French Correspondence, 1994; contbr. profl. publs. Bd. dirs. South Bend Symphony, 1979-86. Served with USNR, 1943-46. Recipient Founders Day award NYU, 1966, State Hist. Soc. of Wis. Hesseltine award, 1991, French Colonial Hist. Soc. Heggoy Book prize, 1994; tchg. fellow French Ministry Edn., 1949-50, Lilly Endowment faculty fellow, 1985-86, NEH fellow, 1988, 94-95, Lundquist faculty fellow, 1989-90; Newberry Libr. rsch. assoc., 1985-86. Mem. Ind. Hist. Soc. (Thornbrough award 1996), Hist. Soc. Mich., French Colonial Hist. Soc. (v.p. 1988-91, exec. com. 1988-94), Ctr. for French Colonial Studies.

PEYTON, DONALD LEON, retired standards association executive; b. Portland, Oreg., May 5, 1925; s. Bernard Thomas and Nelle (Moses) P.; m. Jane Frances Kirkman, Aug. 26, 1950; children: Patrick Philip, James Allen. Student, Mont. State U., 1946-47; BA, No. Colo. U., 1950. Civilian edn. specialist USAF, 1951-56; engaged in real estate Cheyenne, Wyo., 1956-57; adminstrv. asst. to congressman, 1957-60; with U.S. C. of C., 1960-66, gen. mgr. govt. relations, 1965-66; pres. Am. Nat. Standards Inst., Inc., 1966-89, ret., 1989, Peyton Assocs., Standards Cons., White Plains, N.Y., 1989—. Lectr. govt. bus. relations Am. U., 1965-66, Amos Tuck Sch., Dartmouth, 1965—. Author: Standards and Trade in the 1990's; author monographs. Pres., Cheyenne Jr. C. of C., 1955-56. Mem. Am. Soc. Assn. Execs., Old Guard of White Plains. Home and Office: 2 Beverly Rd White Plains NY 10605-3306 *My personal philosophy of life parallels that of my philosophy regarding voluntary organizations. In personal and professional life there is no hope for the self-satisfied individual or the self-satisfied organization.*

PEYTON, MARY JOHANNA, secondary school educator; b. Salt Lake City, Apr. 15, 1946; d. John Edward and Ellen Bernice (Michaud) P. B in Music, U. Mont., 1968, M in Music Edn., 1970. Cert. secondary tchr., Calif. Elem. instr. music Ceres (Calif.) Unified Sch. Dist., 1969-71, instr. jr. high music, 1971-75, instr. jr. high English, 1975-84, instr. jr. high econs., 1984-86, coordinator career edn., 1984—, instr. ind. study, 1986—. Cons. various edn. orgns., 1984—; trainer career edn. Nat. Diffusion Network, U.S. Dept. Edn., Washington, 1985—. Producer, writer film Project Ceres, 1985; speaker in field. Mem. NEA, Calif. Tchrs. Assn., Calif. Career Edn. Assn., Ceres Unified Tchrs. Assn. (faculty rep. 1969—, negotiations team 1979—, 2nd v.p. 1980, negotiations chair 1984—), Phi Delta Kappa. Republican. Roman Catholic. Avocations: golfing, photography and video. Home: 3128 Scenic Dr Modesto CA 95355-4771

PEYTON, SHARON ANNE REED, geriatrics nurse; b. Lewisburg, W.Va., Mar. 19, 1947; d. Paul Elliott and Millie Anne (Medley) Reed; m. Joseph B. Peyton, Dec. 17, 1965; children: Timothy B., Sarah A. AAS in Nursing, Ohio U., Zanesville, 1987; BSN summa cum laude, cert. gerontology, Ohio U., Athens, 1997. Cert. gerontol. nurse, 1991. Charge nurse Mark Rest Ctr., McConnellsville, Ohio, shift supr., asst. dir. nursing, 1990-92, dir. nursing, 1992-94; staff nurse, supr. Health Care & Retirement Corp., 1994-98; adminstr., DON Morgan County Home Health, 1998; instr. health tech. Morgan H.S., 1999—. Mem. Morgan County Bd. Health, 1989—. Mem. Nat. Assn. Dirs. Nursing Adminstrn. Long-Term Care, Ohio Assn. Nurses, Ohio Assn. Dirs. Nursing Adminstrn. Long-Term Care, Assn. Dirs. Nursing Adminstrn. Long-Term Care, Phi Kappa Phi, Gamma Pi Delta, Sigma Theta Tau. Home: RR 1 Malta OH 43758-9801

PEZESHKI, KAMBIZ A. metallurgical engineer; b. Tabriz, Iran, Sept. 30, 1949; came to U.S., 1970, naturalized; s. Amir Aziz and Azam (Mazi) P.; m. Shiron Cashmir Wisenbaker, Apr. 7, 1976; children: Shahene A., Shahla J. BS in Metall. Engring., U. Utah, 1977; MBA in Mktg. and Human Rels., U. Phoenix, 1983. Cert. tchr., Ariz. Process metallurgist Amax, Inc., Golden, Colo., 1977-79; process, rsch. engr. Cities Svcs. Co./Oxidental, Miami, Ariz., 1979-84; tech. svcs. engr. Am. Cyanamid, Wayne, N.J., 1984-87; mgr. western mining Rhone-Poulenc, Inc., Salt Lake City, 1987-93; sales mgr. mining divsn. Hychem, Inc., 1993—. Polymerization cons. RTZ/Kennecott Copper, Salt Lake City, 1989—. Olympic vol. human rels. specialist, Salt Lake City, 2002; fundraiser, motivator Barry Goldwater for Senate re-election, 1980—81; vol. Ted Wilson for Gov., Salt Lake City, 1988; elder Presbyn. Ch. U.S.A. Mem. Am. Mining Engrs. Soc. Republican. Presbyterian Elder. Avocations: wind surfing, racquetball, tennis, total fitness, cross country skiing, roller skiing.

PEZESHKI, S. REZA, educator; b. Dezful, Iran, Apr. 9, 1948; m. Fataneh Farmani; children: Mona. PhD, U. Wash, 1982. Cert. profl. wetland scientist 1997. Rsch. faculty La. State U., Baton Rouge, 1983—90, assoc. prof., 1990—94, U. Memphis, 1994—98, prof. biology, 1998—. Editor-in-chief: Americas & Australia, Environmental and Experimental Botany, 1998—. Mem.: Soc. Wetland Scientists (mem. exec. bd., pres.-elect, pres. Southcentral chpt. 1995—2000), Am. Soc. Plant Biologists, Sigma Xi. Office: U Memphis Dept Biology 3706 Alumni St Memphis TN 38152

PEZZELLA, JERRY JAMES, JR. investment and real estate executive; b. Chesapeake, Va., Sept. 30, 1937; s. Jerry James Sr. and Mabel (Aydlett) P.; m. Carolyn Blades; children: James M., Stanley J., Julie Pezzella Scanlon. BS, U. Richmond, 1963; MBA, U. Pa., 1964. Asst. v.p. Va. Nat. Bank (now Bank of Am.), Norfolk, 1964-68; chmn. bd., pres. First Am. Investment Corp., First Ga. Investment Corp., Atlanta, 1968-74; v.p. Great Am. Investment Corp., 1974-78; sr. exec. v.p., 1984-85; exec. v.p. Equity Fin. & Mgmt. Co., Chgo., 1978-99; pres., chmn. bd. First Capital Fin. Corp., 1983-85; pres. GAFGI Holdings Inc., 1983-98; chmn. bd. 1st Property Mgmt. Corp., 1990-92. Bd. dirs. Great Am. Mgmt. and Investment, Inc., Chgo., Nat. Multi Housing Coun., 1992-94, mem. exec. com.; real estate cons., 1997—. Bd. dirs., exec. com. Nat. Multi-Housing Coun., 1991-93. Mem. Met. Club (Chgo.), Cherokee Golf and Country Club (Murphy, N.C.), Mountain Harbor Golf and Country Club (hayesville, N.C.). Home: 1240 Village Rd Murphy NC 28906-1763

PEZZULLO, RALPH MICHAEL, writer, playwright; b. N.Y.C., Dec. 27, 1951; s. Lawrence Anthony Pezzullo and Josephine DiMattia; m. Alice Palmisano, Aug. 8, 1980 (div. Jan 1994); children: John Lawrence, Michael Richard; m. Jessica Rae Pezzullo, May 19, 1994; children: Francesca Sophia, Alessandra Sabina. M in Pub. and Internat. Affairs, George Washington U., 1975. Grants specialist Nat. Endowment for the Arts, Washington, 1975-79. Author: (books) At the Fall of Somoza, 1994, (plays) From Behind the Moon, 1984, The Tail of the Tiger, 1985, Eating the Shadow, 1990, Wilderness of Mirrors, 1994, Hide Mother in My Heart, 1996, Gauquin's Parrot, 1997, Spain, 1998, Stakes, 1999, Okeechobee Split, 2000, Murder Sketched Gently, 2000, (radio drama/series) The Life and Times of Swamp Fox, 1985. Recipient Spl. citation Kesselring award, 1986, award Ctr. Theater, 1994, screenwriting award Writer's Guild of Am. East Found., 1987; playwriting fellowship Jerome Found., 1997, 98, 99, 2001. Mem.: Author's League Am., Art Student's League, Dramatists Guild. Avocations: painting, sports. Home: 500 W 111th St New York NY 10025-1904 Office: 927 Columbus Ave New York NY 10025-3704

PFAELZER, MARIANA R. federal judge; b. L.A., Feb. 4, 1926; AB, U. Calif., 1947; LLB, UCLA, 1957. Bar: Calif. 1958. Assoc. Wyman, Bautzer, Rothman & Kuchel, 1957-69, ptnr., 1969-78; judge U.S. Dist. Ct. (ctrl. dist.) Calif., 1978—. Mem. Jud. Conf. Adv. Com. on Fed. Rules of Civil Procedure. Pres., v.p., dir. Bd. Police Commrs. City of L.A., 1974-78. UCLA Alumnus award for Profl. Achievement, 1979, named Alumna of Yr., UCLA Law Sch., 1980, U. Calif. Santa Barbara Disting. Alumnus award, 1983. Mem. ABA, Calif. Bar Assn. (local adminstrv. com., spl. com. study rules procedure 1972, joint subcom. profl. ethics and computers and the law coms. 1972, profl. ethics com. 1972-74, spl. com. juvenile justice, women's rights subcom. human rights sect.), L.A. County Bar Assn. (spl. com. study rules procedure state bar 1974), Ninth Cir. Dist. Judges Assn. (pres.). Office: US Dist Ct 312 N Spring St Ste 152 Los Angeles CA 90012-4703

PFAFF, ROBERT JAMES, lawyer; b. Pitts., Jan. 12, 1943; s. William Michael and Elizabeth (Ludwig) P.; m. Carol Pillich, June 18, 1977. BS in Edn., Slippery Rock U., 1965; JD, Duquesne U., 1973. Bar: Pa. 1973, U.S. Dist. Ct. (we. dist.) Pa. 1973, U.S. Supreme Ct. 1980. Tchr. secondary schs., Norwin and Jeanette, Pa., 1965-66; suit group supr. Liberty Mut. Ins. Co., Pitts., 1966-70; assoc. Egler, McGregor & Reinstadtler, 1973-76; ptnr. Leopold, Eberhardt & Pfaff, Altoona, 1976-80; sr. ptnr. Meyer, Darragh, Buckler, Bebenek & Eck, Pitts., 1980-84, Pfaff, McIntyre, Dugas, Hartye & Schmitt, Hollidaysburg, 1984—2001, Thomson, Rhodes & Cowie, Pitts., 2001—. Bd. dirs. Blair County Legal Services, Altoona. Mem. ABA, Internat. Assn. Def. Counsel, Def. Rsch. Inst., Pa. Bar Assn., Blair County Bar Assn., Allegheny County Bar Assn., Pa. Assn. Mut. Ins. Cos. (claims com.), Pa. Def. Inst., Altoona Area Claims Assn. Republican. Roman Catholic. Avocations: golf, music, licensed pilot. Home: 405 Kingsberry Cir Pittsburgh PA 15234-1065 Office: Thomson Rhodes & Cowie 1010 Two Chatham Ctr Pittsburgh PA 15219-3499 E-mail: rjmpfaff@aol.com.

PFAFF, WILLIAM WALLACE, medical educator; b. Rochester, N.Y., Aug. 14, 1930; s. Norman Joseph and Eleanor Blakesley (Wells) P.; m. Patricia Ann Clark; children: Nancy, Karen, Margaret, Mary Catherine. AB, Harvard U., 1952; MD, SUNY, 1956. Intern U. Chgo., 1956-58; sr. asst. surgeon NIH, Bethesda, Md., 1958-60; resident Stanford U. Med. Ctr., Palo Alto, Calif., 1960-65; asst. prof. U. Fla., Gainesville, 1965-68, assoc. prof., 1968-71, prof. surgery, 1971-95, prof. emeritus, adj. prof., 1995—, dir. organ transplant programs, 1971-95. Bd. dirs. United Network for Organ Sharing, Richmond, Va., pres. elect, 1997-98, pres., 1998-99; pres., com. chmn. Southeastern Organ Procurement Found., Richmond, 1973-95. Fellow Am. Coll. Surgeons; mem. Am. Surg. Assn., Am. Soc. Transplant Surgeons, So. Surg. Assn., Transplantation Soc., Alachua County Med. Soc. (pres. 1977-78). Home: 2445 NW 15th Pl Gainesville FL 32605-5148 Office: U Fla Dept Surgery PO Box 100286 Gainesville FL 32610-0286

PFAFFENROTH, PETER ALBERT, lawyer; b. Mineola, N.Y., Mar. 29, 1941; s. Albert and Genevieve Astrid (Anderson) P.; m. Sara Ann Beekey, June 26, 1966; children: Elizabeth Cartwright, Peter Cyrus, Catherine Genevieve. BS in Engring., Diploma in European Civilization, Princeton U., 1963; JD, U. Mich., 1966; LLM in Taxation, NYU, 1972, LLM in Corp., 1976, LLM in Internat. Law, 1998. Bar: N.J. 1966, U.S. Dist. Ct. (N.J. dist.) 1966. With Daimler-Benz, Stuttgart, Fed. Republic Germany, 1961, B.P. Benzin & Petroleum, Hamburg, Fed. Republic Germany, 1962, Office of Internat. Affairs, U.S. Treasury Dept., Washington, 1963, Office of Export Control, U.S. Commerce Dept., Washington, 1964, Commrs. Office, U.S. Patent Office, Washington, 1965; atty. McCarter & English, Newark, 1966-68, Kentz & Gilson, Esqs., Summit, 1968-69; corp. counsel Tex. Plastics, Maine Sugar Industries, Robbinsville, 1969-70; atty. c/o Lewis Stein, Esq., Netcong, 1970-71; pvt. practice Chester, 1971—. Avocations: antiques, foreign languages, travel, wine. Home: Route 24 At Twin Brooks Trail Chester NJ 07930

PFAFFLE, ANTONY, physician; b. Bklyn. s. Anton Eugene and Rosemary Ellen (Reilly) P.; m. Linda J. Chadwick, July 18, 1992; children: Alexandra, Cameron. BS, CCNY/CUNY, 1987; MD, N.Y. Med. Coll., Valhalla, 1989. Diplomate Am. Bd. Internal Medicine. Intern Lenox Hill Hosp., N.Y.C., 1989-90, resident, 1990-92, chief resident, 19992-93, Siebel fellow, 1993-95; clin. instr. in medicine NYU Sch. Medicine, 1996—, Cornell U. Med. Coll., N.Y.C., 1996—; asst. attending in medicine N.Y. Hosp., 1996—2002, Lenox Hill Hosp., N.Y.C., 1995—2002; cons. in medicine Meml. Sloan-Kettering Cancer Ctr., 1997—2000. Mem. ACP, Am. Soc. Nephrology. Office: 330 Madison Ave New York NY 10017 Fax: 646-495-5597. E-mail: pfaffle@bdrllc.com.

PFAFFLIN, SHEILA MURPHY, psychologist; b. Pasadena, Calif., July 31, 1934; d. Leonard Anthony and Honora (Shields) Murphy; m. James Reid Pfafflin, Sept. 7, 1957. BA, Pomona Coll., 1956; MA, Johns Hopkins U., 1958, PhD, 1959. Mem. tech. staff AT&T Bell Labs., Murray Hill, N.J., 1959-75; dist. mgr. AT&T, Morristown, 1975-98. Chair sub com. on Women-Com. on Equal Opportunities in Sci. and Tech., NSF, Washington, 1981-85; mem. adv. coun. Math/Sci. Tchr. Supply and Demand, N.J. Dept. Higher Edn., 1982-83; mem. adv. bd. for Maths., Sci. and Computer Sci. Teaching Improvement Grants, N.J. Dept. Higher Edn., 1984-89. Co-editor: Expanding the Role of Women in the Sciences, 1978, Scientific-Technological Change & the Role of Women in Development, 1981, Psychology & Educational Policy, 1987; contbr. articles to profl. jours. Trustee Ramapo Coll. of N.J., Mahwah, N.J., 1984-96; adv. bd. Project "SMART", Girls Clubs of Am., N.Y.C., 1984-94, Consortium for Ednl. Equity, Rutgers U., New Brunswick, N.Y., 1983—; pres. Assn. for Women in Sci. Ednl. Found., Washington, 1982-98. Fellow AAAS, N.Y. Acad. Scis., Am. Psychol. Assn.; mem. Assn. for Women in Sci. (pres. 1980-81, Women Scientist award, Met. Chpt., 1987), Phi Beta Kappa, Sigma Xi. Avocation: sailing. Home: 173 Gates Ave Gillette NJ 07933-1719

PFALMER, CHARLES ELDEN, secondary school educator; b. Trinidad, Colo., Aug. 9, 1937; s. Arthur Joseph and Nettie Mildred (Powell) P.; m. Margaret Christine La Duke, June 25, 1964; children: Betholyn Ann, Garret. AA, Trinidad State Jr. Coll., 1957; BA, Adams State Coll., 1959, MA, 1962. Cert. tchr., Colo. Tchr. Olathe (Colo.) H.S., 1959-60, Yuma (Colo.) H.S., 1960-98. Instr. Northeastern Jr. Coll., Sterling, Colo., 1990-97. Precinct chmn. Dem. Orgn., Yuma, 1992-96, del. to state conv., 1984-86, 88-90, 92-94, 96, Dem. county chair, 2001—; ch. treas. Yuma Episcopal Ch., 1985—; v.p. Citizens Action Com., Yuma, 1994. Recipient Outstanding Educator award West Yuma Sch. Dist., 1987, Colo. State Ho. of Reps., 1987, Local Disting. Svc. award Colo. H.S. Activities Assn., 1991, Outstanding Cmty. Svc. award Colo. Athletic Dirs. Assn., 1990; named Citizen of Yr., Yuma C. of C., 1999. Mem. NEA, Am. Polit. Collectors, Nat. Coun. for the Social Studies, Colo. Edn. Assn., Phi Delta Kappa. Avocations: collecting political buttons, antiques, sports. Home: 321 E 10th Ave Yuma CO 80759-3001 E-mail: cmpfalmer@plains.net.

PFALSER, IVAN LEWIS, retired civil engineer; b. Anthony, Kans., July 11, 1930; s. John Lewis and Gladys Evelyn (Murry) P.; m. Viola Florence Pfalser, Apr. 13, 1952 (dec.); children: Ann, John, Jane, Jean. Student, U. Wichita, 1948-50; BS in Civil Engring., U. Kans., 1952. Registered profl. engr., Okla. Structural engr. Boeing Aircraft Co., Wichita, 1954-56, Phillips Petroleum Co., Bartlesville, Okla., 1956-59, geotech. engr., 1959-65, material handling engr., 1965-70, civil/geotech./environ. prin. engr., 1970-92; ret., 1992. Civil and geotech. cons. Alyeska Pipeline Co., Houston, 1970-73, Bonney LNG, Ltd., Lagos, Nigeria, 1980-83; airport engr. City of Bartlesville, 1980-92. 1st lt. C.E. U.S. Army, 1952-54. Mem. ASCE, Okla. Profl. Engrs. Republican. Achievements include patent for groundwater sealing for cathopic protection well uranium mine deep shaft sealing and abandiment closure; development of frozen pit LNG storage facilities; development and testing of construction equipment and methods for Trans-Alaska Pipeline.

PFALTZGRAFF, ROBERT LOUIS, JR. political scientist, educator; b. Phila., June 1, 1934; s. Robert L. and Mary (Warriner) P.; m. Diane A. Kressler, May 20, 1967; children: Suzanne Diane, Robert Louis III. BA with honors, Swarthmore Coll., 1956; MBA, U. Pa., 1958, PhD in Polit. Sci. (Penfield fellow), 1964; MA in Internat. Relations, 1959. Research assoc. Fgn. Policy Research Inst., 1964-71; asst. prof. polit. sci. U. Pa., Phila., 1964-70; dep. dir. Fgn. Policy Research Inst., 1971-73; assoc. prof. internat. politics Fletcher Sch. Law and Diplomacy, Tufts U., Medford, Mass., 1971-78; pres. Inst. for Fgn. Policy Analysis, Cambridge, 1976—; prof. internat. politics Fletcher Sch. Law and Diplomacy, Tufts U., Medford, 1978-83, Shelby Cullom Davis prof. internat. security studies, 1983—. Vis. lectr. Fgn. Service Inst. Dept. State, 1970-71; George C. Marshall prof. Coll. of Europe, Bruges, Belgium, 1970-71; short term acad. guest prof. Nat. Defense Coll., Tokyo, Japan, 1981; pres. U.S. Strategic Inst., Washington, 1977-79; pres. Inst. Fgn. Policy Analysis, Cambridge, Mass. Author: Britain Faces Europe, 1957-1967, 1969, Politics and the International System, 1969, The Atlantic Community: A Complex Balance, 1969, The Study of International Relations, 1977, Power Projection and the Long Range Combat Aircraft: Missions, Capabilities and Alternative Designs, 1981, Contending Theories of International Relations: A Comprehensive Survey, 1981; co-editor: Contrasting Approaches to Strategic Arms Control, 1974, SALT: Implications for Arms Control in the 1970s, 1973, The Other Arms Race: New Technologies and Non Nuclear Conflict, 1975, Arms Transfers to the Third World: The Military Build-up in Less Industrial Countries, 1978, Intelligence Policy and National Security, 1981, Projection of Power: Perspectives, Perceptions and Problems, 1982, The U.S. Defense Mobilization Infrastructure: Problems and Priorities, 1983, International Dimensions of Space, 1984, National Security Policy: The Decision-Making Process, 1984, The Peace Movements in Europe and the United States, 1985, American Foreign Policy: FDR to Reagan, 1986, co-editor: Selling the Rope to Hang Capitalism? The Debate on West-East Trade and Technology Transfer, 1987, Emerging Doctrines and Technologies: Implications for Global and Regional Political-Military Balance, 1987, Protracted Warfare--The Third World Arena: A Dimension of U.S.-Soviet Conflict, 1988, Guerrilla Warfare and Counter-Insurgency: U.S.-Soviet Policy in the third World, 1988, U.S. Defense Policy in an Era of Constrained Resources, 1989, Contending Theories of International Relations: A Comprehensive Study, 1990, 4th edit., 1998, National Security Decisions: The Participants Speak, 1990, The United States Army: Challenges and Missions for the 1990s, 1991, The Future of Air Power in the Aftermath of the Gulf War, 1992, Naval Forward Presence and the National Military Strategy, 1993, Ethnic Conflict and Regional Instability: Implications for U.S. Policy and Army Roles and Missions, 1994, Naval Expeditionary Forces and Power Projection: Into the 21st Century, 1994, Roles and Missions of Special Operations Forces in the Aftermath of the Cold War, 1995, War in the Information Age: New Challenges for U.S. Security, 1997, NATO and Southeastern Europe: Security Issues for the Early 21st Century, 2000, The Role of Naval Forces in 21st Century Operations, 2000, Strategy and International Politics, 2000, Contending Theories of International Relations, 5th edit., 2001, others; contbr. articles to scholarly jours. Guggenheim fellow, 1968-69; Relm Found. grantee, 1969 Mem. Internat. Studies Assn., Coun. Fgn. Rels., Internat. Inst. Strategic Studies, Capitol Hill Club, Army and Navy Club (Washington). Home: 663 Wallace Dr Wayne PA 19087-1911 Office: Inst Fgn Policy Analysis 675 Massachusetts Ave Ste 10 Cambridge MA 02139-3309 E-mail: rlp@ifpa.org.

PFANSTIEL PARR, DOROTHEA ANN, interior designer; b. San Antonio, Nov. 10, 1931; d. Herbert Andraes and Ethel Missouri (Turner) Pfanstiel; m. Thurmond Charles Parr, Jr., Sept. 15, 1951; children: Thurmond Charles, III, Richard Marshall. AA, Coll. San Antonio, 1951. Asst. dean evening divsn. Alamo C.C., San Antonio, 1951; tchr., cons., dir. Humpty Dumpty Early Childhood Devel. Ctr., 1951-58; exec. sec., cons. Thurmond C. Parr, Jr. & Co., 1960-61; founder, pres. Creative Designs, Ltd., 1962—. Liaison, coord. Internat. Students Lang. Sch., Lackland AFB, San Antonio, 1959-65. Adv., cons. Urban Renewal Inner City San Antonio, 1959-61. Named Notable Woman of Tex., Awards and Hons. Soc. Am., 1984-85. Republican. Presbyterian. Avocations: travel, swimming, reading, studying, walking. Office: Creative Designs Ltd PO Box 6822 San Antonio TX 78209-0822

PFANZ, HARRY WILLCOX, historian; b. Columbus, Ohio, Dec. 9, 1921; s. Harry Edwin Pfanz and Marion Adele Wilcox; m. Letitia Louise Earll, May 29, 1952; children: Letitia Elizabeth(dec.), Frederick Willcox, Donald Crittenden, Marion Louise Ake. BS Edn., Ohio State U., 1943, MA History, 1948, PhD History, 1958. Historian Dept. Army, Washington, 1952—56; historian Gettysburg Nat. Mil. Park Nat. Pk. Svc., Gettysburg, Pa., 1956—66, asst. supt., supt. Jefferson Nat. Expansion Meml. St. Louis, 1966—70, chief historian Washington, 1974—80. Author: Gettysburg: The Second Day, 1987, Gettysburg: Culp's Hill and Cemetery Hill, 1993, Gettysburg: The First Day, 2001. 1st lt. U.S. Army, 1943—47, ETO. Decorated Purple Heart medal, Meritorious Svc. award Dept. of Interior, Disting. Svc. award. Mem.: Nat. Park and Conservation Assn., Montgomery County Civil War Round Table (bd. dirs.), 87th Inf. Divsn. Assn. Lutheran. Avocations: church work, historical research and writing, travel, genealogy. Home: 1221 Fallsmead Way Rockville MD 20854-5532

PFAU, GEORGE HAROLD, JR. investment advisor; b. Milw., May 7, 1924; s. George Harold and Elisabeth C. (Hunter) P.; m. Anne Elizabeth Mayhew (dec.); 1 child, George Harold III; children by previous marriage: Mary D., Peter W., Elizabeth C. BS, Yale U., 1948. Tchr., 1948-49; with Fleishhacker Paper Box Co., San Francisco, 1952-54; salesman A.G. Becker & Co., 1954-55; v.p., sec., dir. Carl W. Stern & Co., 1955-57; with White Weld & Co. Inc., 1957-78; 1st v.p. corp. fin. dept. Blyth Eastman Dillon, 1978-79; sr. v.p. UBS Paine Webber, 1979—. Bd. dirs. 1 A Dist. Argl. Assn. Bd. dirs. The Guardsmen, 1966-67, Pathfinder Fund, 1974-82, San Francisco Zool. Soc., 1979-80; trustee Thacher Sch., Ojai, Calif., 1967-76, Town Sch., San Francisco, 1966-70; pres. Planned Parenthood San Francisco-Alameda County, 1968-69, bd. dirs., 1965—; chmn. Lincoln Club of No. Calif,

1993-95, mem., 1982—; chmn. Citizens for Better San Francisco. With C.E. AUS, 1942-44; with Am. Field Svc., 1944-45. Mem. Kappa Beta Phi, San Francisco Bond Club, Bohemian Club (San Francisco), Calif. Tennis Club, Villa Taverna. Office: UBS Paine Webber 555 California St Fl 32D San Francisco CA 94104-1502 E-mail: team.pfav@ubspw.com.

PFAU, RICHARD ANTHONY, college president; b. N.Y.C., Feb. 19, 1942; s. Hugo and Irene Beatrice P.; m. Nancy Ann DiPace, Sept. 12, 1964; children: Bradley Madison, Aleksandra Nicole. AB, Hamilton Coll., 1964; MA, U. Va., 1973, PhD, 1975. Systems analyst Equitable Life Ins. Co., N.Y.C., 1964-66; asst. prof. history Dickinson Coll., Carlisle, Pa., 1975-80; assoc. prof., assoc. dean U. Miami, Coral Gables, Fla., 1980-85; dean of faculty, provost Emory (Va.) and Henry Coll., 1985-93; pres. Ill. Coll., Jacksonville, Ill., 1993—2002, Averett U., Danville, Va., 2002—. Author: No Sacrifice Too Great: The Life of Lewis L. Strauss, 1985. Contbr. articles, book revs. to profl. publs. Vestryman St. Thomas Episc. Ch., Abingdon, Va.; chmn., sec.-treas., exec. com., bd. dirs. Va. Found. for Humanities and Pub. Policy, Exec. Com. Fedn. Ind. Ill. Colls. and Univs.; mem. adv. bd. Salvation Army, Jacksonville. Capt. USAF, 1966-71. DuPont fellow, 1974-75; Hoover fellow, 1982. Mem. Omicron Delta Kappa, Alpha Psi Omega, Pi Delta Epsilon, Union League Club (Chgo.). Home: 500 Hawthorne Drive Danville VA 24541 Office: Averett Univ Pres Office 420 West Main Street Danville VA 24541

PFEFFER, CYNTHIA ROBERTA, psychiatrist, educator; b. Newark, May 22, 1943; d. Edward I. and Ann Pfeffer. BA, Douglas Coll., 1964; MD, NYU, 1968. Assoc. dir. child psychiatry inpatient unit Albert Einstein Coll. Medicine, Bronx, N.Y., 1973-79; chief child psychiatry inpatient unit N.Y. Hosp. Cornell Med. Ctr., White Plains, 1979-95; assoc. prof. clin. psychiatry Weill Med. Coll. Cornell U., N.Y.C., 1984—. Prof. psychiatry Cornell U. Med. Coll., 1989—; pres. N.Y. Coun. on Child and Adolescent Psychiatry, N.Y.C., 1989—; dir. childhood bereavement program Weill Med. Coll. Cornell U., 1999—. Author: The Suicidal Child, 1986, Difficult Moments in Child Psychotherapy, 1988; editor: Youth Suicide: Perspectives on Risk and Prevention, 1989, Intense Stress and Mental Disturbance in Children, 1996; co-editor: Neurologic Disorders: Developmental and Behavioral Sequelae for Child and Adolescent Psychiatric Clinics of North America, 1999. Recipient Erwin Stengel award Internat. Assn. Suicide Prevention, 1987, Wilford Hulse award N.Y. Coun. on Child & Adolescent Psychiatry, 1989, Sigmund Freud award Am. Soc. Psychoanalytic Physicians, 1994. Fellow Am. Psychiat. Assn., Am. Acad. Child and Adolescent Psychiatry (councillor-at-large 1989—, Norbert Rieger award 1988), Am. Psychopathological Assn.; mem. Am. Assn. Suicidology (pres. 1987, Young Contbrs. award 1981, 82). Office: NY Hosp Westchester Div 21 Bloomingdale Rd White Plains NY 10605-1504 also: 1100 Madison Ave New York NY 10028-0327

PFEFFER, DAVID H. lawyer; b. N.Y.C., Mar. 15, 1935; B. Chem. Engring., CCNY, 1956; JD, NYU, 1961, LL.M. in Trade Regulation, 1967. Bar: N.Y. 1961. With patent dept. U.S. Rubber Co., Wayne, N.J., 1957-61; assoc. Watson, Leavenworth, Kelton & Taggart, N.Y.C., 1961-63, Morgan & Finnegan, LLP, N.Y.C., 1963-70, ptnr., 1971—. Village prosecutor Roslyn Harbor, N.Y., 1976-78, village justice, 1979—; panel of arbitrators Am. Arbitration Assn. Mem. ABA (litigation sect.), N.Y. State Bar Assn., Assn. Bar City N.Y., Nassau County Bar Assn. (coms. on patent and trademarks, fed. practice), Am. Intellectual Property Law Assn. (com. alt. dispute resolution), N.Y. Intellectual Property Law Assn. (com. on alt. dispute resolution), N.Y. State Magistrates Assn., Nassau County Magistrates Assn., Order of Coif. Office: Morgan & Finnegan LLP 345 Park Ave Fl 22 New York NY 10154-0053 E-mail: dpfeffer@morganfinnegan.com.

PFEFFER, EDWARD ISRAEL, educational administrator; b. Newark, July 1, 1914; s. Jacob and Fannie Bessie (Fisher) P.; m. Anna Chinich, July 14, 1940; children— Cynthia Roberta, Bruce Paul. BS, N.Y. U., 1937; MA, N.J. State Tchrs. Coll., Montclair, 1942; Ed.D., Rutgers U., 1954. Tchr. Abington Ave. Sch., Newark, 1937-46; vice prin. Warren St. Sch., 1946-53; prin. Monmouth St. and Coes Pl. schs., 1953-57, Robert Treat Jr. High and Elem. Sch., 1957-64; asst. supt. spl. services Newark Dist. Pub. Schs., 1964-67, dep. supt., 1967-72, 73—, acting supt., 1972-73. Contbr. articles profl. publs. Commr. Newark Sr. Citizens Commn., 1967— ; mem. Newark Juvenile Problems Commn., 1958-62; chmn. Children's Resources Commn., Council Social Agys., 1955-60; mem. exec. bd. Family and Children's Div., 1955-62; mem. Newark Commn. for UN Week, 1962— , Newark Disaster Com., 1967— , Bd. Edn., Temple B'nai Abraham, Essex County, N.J., 1964-65; Mem. exec. bd. Newark Central Community Council; mem. adv. bd. Essex County Tech. Sch. Recipient citations Newark Assn. Dirs. and Suprs., 1973, citations Newark Title I Central Parents Council, 1973 Mem. Newark Pub. Sch. Prins. Assn. (pres. 1963-64), N.J. Elementary Sch. Press Assn. (pres.), Congress Parents and Tchrs. (life), NEA (life), Am., N.J. assns. sch. adminstrs., Newark Schoolmens Assn. (bd. govs., named Outstanding Schoolman of Year 1972-73), Columbia Scholastic Press Assn. (v.p., Gold Key 1948), Urban League, NAACP, Phi Delta Kappa. Home: 507 Clinton Pl Newark NJ 07112-1703 Office: 2 Cedar St Newark NJ 07102-3015

PFEFFER, JEFFREY, business educator; b. St. Louis, July 23, 1946; s. Newton Stuart and Shirlee (Krisman) P.; m. Kathleen Frances Fowler, July 23, 1986. BS, MS, Carnegie Mellon U., 1968; PhD, Stanford U., 1972. Tech. staff Research Analysis Corp., McLean, Va., 1968-69; asst. prof. U. Ill., Champaign, 1971-73; from asst. prof. to assoc. prof. U. Calif., Berkeley, 1973-79; prof. Grad. Sch. Bus., Stanford U., Calif., 1979—. Vis. prof. Harvard U. Sch. Bus., Boston, 1981-82; dir., mem. compensation com. Portola Packaging, Inc.; dir. SonoSite, Inc., Audible Magic, Inc., Actify, Inc., Unicru, Inc. Author: The External Control of Organizations, 1978, Organizational Design, 1978, Power in Organizations, 1981, Organizations and Organization Theory, 1982 (Terry Book award 1984), Managing with Power, 1992, Competitive Advantage Through People, 1994, New Directions for Organization Theory, 1997, The Human Equation, 1998, The Knowing-Doing Gap, 1999, Hidden Value, 2000. Fellow Acad. Mgmt. (bd. govs. 1984-86, New Concept award 1979, Richard D. Irwin award for scholarly contbns. to mgmt. 1989); mem. Indsl. Rels. Rsch. Assn. Jewish. Avocations: cooking, music. Home: 425 Moseley Rd Hillsborough CA 94010-6715 Office: Stanford U Grad Sch Bus Stanford CA 94305 E-mail: pfeffer_jeffrey@gsb.stanford.edu.

PFEFFER, LAWRENCE MARC, cell biologist; b. N.Y.C., Nov. 28, 1951; s. Paul and Bess (Wilkins) P.; m. Susan Ritterstein, Sept. 19, 1976; children: Jessica Rachel, Elyssa Danielle. BS (magna cum laude), SUNY, Albany, 1972; PhD, Cornell U., 1977. Undergrad. fellow SUNY, Albany, 1971-72; grad. fellow Cornell U. Grad. Sch. Med. Sci., N.Y.C., 1972-77; postdoctoral fellow Rockefeller U., 1977-80, rsch. assoc., 1981-87, asst. prof., 1981-87, assoc. prof., 1987-91; assoc. prof. dept. pathology U. Tenn. Coll. Medicine, Memphis, 1991-92, prof., 1992—. Ad hoc reviewer for sci. Procs. NAS, Cancer Rsch., Interferon Rsch., Jour. Immunology, Molecular Cellular Biology. Editor: Mechanisms of Interferon Actions, 1989; mem. editl. bd. Jour. Interferon Cytokine Rsch., 1992—. Recipient Jr. Faculty Rsch. award Am. Cancer Soc., 1982-85, Leukemia Scholar award Leukemia Soc. Am., 1986-91. Mem. Harvey Soc., Interferon Soc., Sigma Xi, Am. Soc. for Microbiology. Democrat. Jewish. Achievements include research on signal transduction of cytokines, cytokine receptors, mechanism of interferon action, and regulation of gene expression by interferon. Office: U Tenn Dept Pathology Coll Medicine 800 Madison Ave Memphis TN 38103-3400

PFEFFER, PHILIP ELLIOT, biophysicist; b. N.Y.C., Apr. 8, 1941; s. Charles and Della (Smith) P.; m. Judith Stadlen, Dec. 22, 1962; children: Charles, Ari, Shira. AB, Hunter Coll., 1962; MS, Rutgers U., 1964, PhD, 1966. Rsch. asst. dept. chemistry Rutgers U., New Brunswick, N.J., 1964-66; rsch. fellow dept. chemistry U. Chgo., 1966-68; rsch. scientist Ea. Regional Rsch. Ctr. USDA, Phila., 1968-88, rsch. leader Ea. Regional Rsch. Ctr., 1976-88, lead scientist Ea. Regional Rsch. Ctr., 1988—. Editor-at-large Marcel Dekker, N.Y.C., 1990—; adj. prof. dept. biosci. and biotech. Drexel U., Phila., 1996—; vis. prof. U. Bordeaux, France, 1998. Editor: Nuclear Magnetic Resonance in Agriculture, 1989, Nuclear Magnetic Resonance in Plant Biology, 1996; mem. editl. bd. Jour. Carbohydrate Chemistry, 1985—, Jour. Magnetic Resonance Analysis; contbr. articles to profl. jours. including Plant Physiology, Carbohydrate Rsch., Biochemica Acta, Biophysica, Jour. Magnetic Resonance. Recipient Bond award Am. Oil Chemists Soc., 1976, Fed. Svcs. award Phila. Fed. Assn., 1979, Science and Edn. award USDA, 1982; fellow Orgn. for Econ. Cooperation and Devel., 1989; Agrl. Rsch. Svc. rsch. fellow, 1989; vis. scientist grantee Centre d'Etudes Nucleaires de Grenoble, 1986, Oxford U., 1989. Mem. AAAS, Internat. Soc. for Magnetic Resonance, Am. Chem. Soc. (Phila. sect. Scientist of Yr. 1982), Soc. for Applied Spectroscopy. Achievements include patents and publs. concerning use of alpha-anions; discovery of deuterium isotope shift NMR method for determining carbohydrate structures; development of P-31 NMR in vivo methodology for studying metal ion transport and C-13 NMR for studying plant/microbe interactions in nitrogen fixing plant nodules and symbiotic mycorrhizae. Office: USDA 600 E Mermaid Ln Wyndmoor PA 19038-8598

PFEFFER, PHILIP MAURICE, book publishing executive; b. St. Louis, Jan. 20, 1945; s. Philip McRae and Jeanne (Kaufman) P.; m. Pamela Jean Korte, Aug. 28, 1965; children: John-Lindell Philip, James Howard, David Maurice. BA in Math. and Chemistry, So. Ill. U., 1965, MA in Econs., 1966; postgrad., Vanderbilt U., 1966-68; LHD (hon.), So. Ill. U., 1997. Economist Genesco, Inc., Nashville, 1968, mgr. internat. fin., 1969, asst. treas.; pres. Genesco Export Co., 1970-75; dir. fin. planning Ingram Distribution Group, Inc., 1976-77, v.p. fin. and adminstrn., 1977-78, exec. v.p., 1978, pres. and chief exec. officer, 1978-81, chmn. bd. and chief exec. officer, 1981-96, dir., 1978-96; exec. v.p. Ingram Industries, Inc., 1981-96, dir., 1981-96; pres., dir., chief ops. officer Random House Inc., N.Y.C., 1996—. Bd. dirs. Ingram Micro Inc.; instr. fin. and econs. U. Tenn., Nashville, 1968-77; lectr. corp. fin. Vanderbilt U., 1972-77. Bd. dirs. So. Ill. U. Found., 1982—; mem. exec. bd. mid.-Tenn. coun. Boy Scouts Am., 1982—. Recipient Long Rifle and Silver Beaver award Boy Scouts Am., Nashville, 1981, also Disting. Eagle from Nat. Coun.; Benjamin Gomez award for Disting. Contbns. to the Art of Book Pub. Mem. Fin. Execs. Inst. (pres. 1978-79), Nat. Eagle Scout Assn. (bd. dirs., Silver Wreath award), Nashville Area C. of C. (vice chmn.), Am. Wholesale Booksellers Assn. (past v.p., trustee), So. Ill. U. Alumni Assn. (past bd. dirs.), Young Pres.'s Orgn., World Pres.'s Orgn., Tenn. Assn. Bus., Rotary Internat. Avocations: scouting, sailing, water sports, landscaping. Home: 836 Treemont Ct Nashville TN 37220-1536 Office: Random House Inc 201 E 50th St New York NY 10022-7703

PFEFFER, RICHARD LAWRENCE, geophysics educator; b. Bklyn., Nov. 26, 1930; s. Lester Robert and Anna (Newman) P.; m. Roslyn Ziegler, Aug. 30, 1953; children— Bruce, Lloyd, Scott, Glenn. BS cum laude, CCNY, 1952; MS, Mass. Inst. Tech., 1954, PhD, 1957. Research asst. MIT, 1952-55, guest lectr., 1956; atmospheric physicist Air Force Cambridge Research Center, Boston, 1955-59; sr. scientist Columbia U., 1959-61, lectr., 1961-62, asst. prof. geophysics, 1962-64; assoc. prof. meteorology Fla. State U., Tallahassee, 1964-67, prof. meteorology, 1967-96, disting. rsch. prof., 1997—, Carl-Gustav Rossby prof. meteorology, 1999—; dir. Geophys. Fluid Dynamics Inst., 1967-93. Cons. NASA, 1961-64, N.W. Ayer & Son, Inc., 1962, Ednl. Testing Service, Princeton, N.J., 1963, Voice of Am., 1963, Grolier, Inc., 1963, Naval Research Labs., 1971-76; Mem. Internat. Commn. for Dynamical Meteorology, 1972-76 Editor: Dynamics of Climate, 1960; Contbr. articles to profl. jours. Bd. dirs. B'nai B'rith Anti-Defamation League; chmn. religious concern and social action com. Temple Israel, Tallahassee, 1971-72. Fellow Am. Meterol. Soc. (program chmn. ann. meeting 1963); mem. Am. Geophys. Union, N.Y. Acad. Scis. (chmn. planetary scis. sect. 1961-63), Sigma Xi, Chi Epsilon Pi, Sigma Alpha. Home: 926 Waverly Rd Tallahassee FL 32312-2813

PFEFFER, ROBERT, chemical engineer, academic administrator, educator; b. Vienna, Austria, Nov. 26, 1935; came to U.S., 1938, naturalized, 1944; s. Joseph and Gisela (Aberbach) P.; m. Marcia Borenstein, Dec. 24, 1960; children— Michael, Jacqueline. BChE, NYU, 1956, MChE, 1958, DEngSc, 1962. Mem. faculty CCNY, 1957-92, asst. prof. chem. engring., 1962-66, assoc. prof., 1966-71, prof., 1971-92, chmn. dept. chem. engring., 1973-87, Herbert Kayser prof., 1980-92, dean grad. studies and research, dep. provost, 1987-88, provost, v.p. acad. affairs, 1988-92; v.p. rsch. and grad. studies, prof. chem. engring. N.J. Inst. Tech., Newark, 1992-97, disting. prof. chem. engring., 1997—. Vis. prof. Imperial Coll., London, 1969; Fulbright scholar Technion-Israel Inst. Tech., 1976-77; cons. in field. Contbr. articles to tech. publs. Fulbright Hays awardee, 1976-77; DuPont faculty fellow, 1962; NASA faculty fellow, 1964-65 Mem. AIChE (Particle Tech. Forum Nat. award 1995, Thomas Baron Nat. award 2000), Am. Soc. Engring. Edn., Sigma Xi, Tau Beta Pi, Phi Lambda Upsilon. Jewish. Office: P.O. Box 37 Teaneck NJ 07666 E-mail: pfeffer@njit.edu.

PFEFFER, RUBIN HARRY, publishing executive; b. Bklyn., Oct. 9, 1951; s. Martie and Idell (Treiber) P.; m. Lurie Horns; children: Stephanie, Ian, Rebecca, Vaughn. BFA in Graphic Design, Carnegie-Mellon U., 1973. Dir. art Harcourt Brace Jovanovich, San Diego, 1979-84, corp. art dir. Orlando, Fla., 1984—, dir. children's books San Diego, 1984-85; pres. Harcourt Brace & Co. Trade Books, 1985-98, Harcourt Online, San Diego, 1998—, 1998—2001; sr. v.p., chief creative officer Pearson Educ, Needham, Mass., 2001—. Bd. dirs. Calif. Ballet Co., San Diego, 1986-87, Easter Seal Soc., San Diego, 1988—. Avocation: painting. Office: Pearson Education 20 Park Plaza Boston MA 02216

PFEFFERBAUM, BETTY JANE, b. Seattle, Sept. 7, 1946; d. Lois (Yager) P.; m. Richard L. Van Horn, May 29, 1988. BA, Pomona Coll., 1968; MD, U. Calif., San Francisco, 1972; JD, U. Okla., Norman, 1993. Bar: Okla. 1993; diplomate Am. Bd. Psychiatry and Neurology with subspecialty in child psychiatry. Intern pediatrics Martin Luther King Jr. Gen. Hosp., Compton, Calif., 1972-73; resident in psychiatry Neuro Psychiat. Inst., UCLA, 1973-76, fellow in child psychiatry, 1975-77; pvt. practice psychiatry, L.A., 1977-78; prof. U. Tex. Med. Sch., Houston, 1978-89; v.p. for edn. U. Tex. Health Sci. Ctr., 1987-89; prof., chief child sect. dept. psychiatry U. Okla. Health Scis. Ctr., Oklahoma City, 1989-96, chair dept. psychiatry, 1996—; adj. prof. Oklahoma City U. Sch. Law, 1994-95. Mem. Okla. Indigent Def. Sys. Bd., 1992-93, Okla. Bd. Mental Health and Substance Abuse Svcs., 1993-99. Contbr. over 100 articles to med. jours. Grad. Leadership Tex., 1988, Leadership Okla., 1995. Fellow Am. Psychiat. Assn., Am. Acad. Child and Adolescent Psychiatry, Group for Advancement Psychiatry; mem. ABA, Am. Coll. Psychiatrists, Order of Coif, Phi Beta Kappa, Pi Mu Epsilon. Jewish. Avocation: hiking. Home: 12017 Ashbury Ct Oklahoma City OK 73170-4603 Office: U Okla Health Scis Ctr 920 S L Young Blvd Oklahoma City OK 73104-5020 E-mail: betty-pfefferbaum@ouhsc.edu.

PFEFFERKORN, MICHAEL GENE, SR. secondary school educator, writer; b. Delano, Calif., July 19, 1939; s. E. Michael and N. Ruth (Ervin) P.; m. Sandra J. Carter, June 15, 1963; children: Michael Jr., Patricia. AB, BS in Secondary Edn., S.E. Mo. State, 1961; MEd, U. Mo., 1963. Cert. Eng., life Social Studies tchr., Mo. Tchr. De Soto (Mo.) Pub. Schs., 1961-62, Cleveland H.S., St. Louis, 1963-84, S.W. H.S., St. Louis, 1984-86, tchr., history dept. head, 1987-92; tchr. Gateway Inst. of Tech. H.S., 1992—. Cons. Internat. Edn. Consortium, St. Louis, 1989-92. Co-author: Chits, Chiselers, and Funny Money, 1976; editor Mo. Jour. Numismatics; contbr. articles to numis. jours. Pres. Carondelet Hist. Soc., 1977-78, mem., 1970-90; mem. Landmarks and Urban Design Com., St. Louis, 1976-80. St. Louis Pub. Schs. Secondary Tchr. of Yr., 1999-2000; recipient Emerson Electric's Excellence in Tchg. award, 2000. Mem. ASCD, Am. Fedn. Tchrs., Nat. Coun. Social Studies Tchrs., State Hist. Soc. Mo., Am. Numis. Assn., Mo. Numis Soc. (bd. dirs. 1997—), Numis. Lit. Guild, World Coin Club Mo. Roman Catholic. Avocations: numismatics, writing, genealogy. Home: 6803 Leona St Saint Louis MO 63116-2833 Office: Gateway Inst of Tech 5101 McRee Ave Saint Louis MO 63110-2019

PFEFFERKORN, SANDRA JO, secondary school educator; b. St. Louis, Jan. 14, 1940; d. Albert A. and Alice C. (Lowell) Carter; m. Michael G. Pfefferkorn, June 15, 1963; children: Michael G. Jr., Patricia A. BS in Secondary Edn., S.E. Mo. State Coll., 1961; MEd, U. Mo., 1966. Cert. life English, Spanish, French, and reading tchr., Mo. Tchr. English, head English and fgn. lang. dept. St. Louis Bd. Edn./Cen. H.S., 1961-89; English tchr., head dept. Cleveland Naval Jr. Res. Officer Tng. Corps H.S., St. Louis, 1989—. Asst. editor Mo. Jour. Numismatics. Regents scholar, 1957; fellow Mo. Writing Project, 1981. Mem. AAUW, Nat. Coun. Tchrs. English, Internat. Reading Assn., Mo. Assn. Tchrs. English, Delta Kappa Gamma (pres. Beta Theta chpt.), Phi Delta Kappa. Roman Catholic. Avocations: writing, reading, ceramics. Home: 6803 Leona St Saint Louis MO 63116-2833 Office: Cleve Naval Jr ROTC 4352 Louisiana Ave Saint Louis MO 63111-1046

PFEIFER, HOWARD MELFORD, mechanical engineer; b. St. Louis, Aug. 23, 1959; s. Howard William and Ruth Joyce P. BS in Applied Sci. and Tech., Charter Oak State Coll., 1990; BSME, U. Hartford, 1991; MBA, Rensselaer Poly. Inst., 1997. Engr. in tng., Conn. Engr. asst. Pratt & Whitney, East Hartford, Conn., 1984-89; devel. engr. Chromalloy Rsch. and Tech. Divsn., Orangeburg, N.Y., 1991-93; process devel. engr. Howmet Corp., North Haven, Conn., 1993-95; process engr. Windsor Airmotive, The Barnes Group, East Granby, 1995-98; sr. engr. Pratt & Whitney, 1998—. Mem. U. Hartford Engring. Alumni Adv. Bd., Bloomfield, Conn., 1992-98, chmn., 1996-98; founder, prin., treas. WEMBA5 Investments LLC, Conn. Mem. NSPE, Sigma Xi (assoc.). Republican. Achievements include research, design and construction of a human powered helicopter, and research to map acoustical soundboard characteristics in a Steinway Grand Piano. Home: 83 Buckley Hill Rd Colchester CT 06415-1712 Office: Pratt & Whitney 400 Main St East Hartford CT 06108-0968

PFEIFER, LARRY ALAN, public health service coordinator; b. Rock Springs, Wyo., July 20, 1958; s. Jack Albert and Betty Lee (Ethington) P.; m. Sandra Lynn, June 20, 1986. BS cum laude, So. Oreg. State Coll., 1983, MS in Health Edn., 1989; paramedic diploma, Rogue Community Coll., 1984; postgrad., Columbia Pacific U. Cert. paramedic, Oreg. Cpt., paramedic Tualatin Valley Fire and Rescue, Portland, Oreg., 1991—. Adj. faculty Oreg. Health Scis. U. Sch. of Medicine, Dept. of Emergency Medicine, 1995; lectr. in field. Author (text) Non-Verbal Pre-Hospital Assessment of the Trauma Patient. Mem. Oreg. Paramedic Assn., Phi Kappa Phi, Kappa Delta Pi. Home: 10026 NW Priscilla Ct Portland OR 97229-5273

PFEIFFER, MICHELLE, actress; b. Santa Ana, Calif., Apr. 29, 1957; d. Dick and Donna P.; m. Peter Horton (div.); 1 adopted child, Claudia Rose; m. David Kelley, Nov. 13, 1993. Student, Golden West Coll., Whitley Coll. Actress: (feature films) Falling in Love Again, 1980, Hollywood Knights, 1980, Charlie Chan and the Curse of the Dragon Queen, 1981, Grease II, 1982, Scarface, 1983, Ladyhawke, 1985, Into the Night, 1985, Sweet Liberty, 1986, Amazon Women on the Moon, 1987, Witches of Eastwick, 1987, Married to the Mob, 1988, Tequila Sunrise, 1988, Dangerous Liaisons, 1988 (Acad. award nominee 1989), The Fabulous Baker Boys, 1989 (Achievement award L.A. Film Critics Assn. 1989, D.W. Griffith award Nat. Bd. Rev. 1989, N.Y. Film Critics award 1989, Nat. Soc. Film Critics award 1990, Golden Globe award 1990, Acad. award nominee 1990), The Russia House, 1990, Frankie & Johnny, 1991, Love Field, 1992 (Acad. award nominee 1993), Batman Returns, 1992, The Age of Innocence, 1993, Wolf, 1994, Dangerous Minds, 1995; (TV movies) The Solitary Man,1979, Callie and Son, 1981, The Children Nobody Wanted, 1981, Splendor in the Grass, 1981, Up Close and Personal, 1996, To Gillian on her 37th Birthday, 1996, One Fine Day, 1996, A Thousand Acres, 1997, Privacy, 1997, The Prince of Egypt (voice), 1998, The Story of Us, 1998, A Midsummer Night's Dream, 1999, Deep End of the Ocean, 1999, Being John Malkovich, 1999, What Lies Beneath, 2000, I Am Sam, 2001, White Oleander, 2002; (TV series) Delta House, 1979, B.A.D. Cats, 1980 Named Woman of the Yr., Harvard's Hasty Pudding Theater Club, 1995. Office: care ICM 9830 Wilshire Blvd Beverly Hills CA 90211-1934*

PFEIFER, PAUL E. state supreme court justice; b. Bucyrus, Ohio, Oct. 15, 1942; m. Julia Pfeifer; 3 children. BA, Ohio State U., 1963, JD, 1966. Asst. atty. gen. State of Ohio, 1967-70; mem. Ohio Ho. of Reps., 1971-72; asst. prosecuting atty. Crawford County, 1973-76; mem. Ohio Senate, 1976-92, minority floor leader, 1983-84, asst. pres. pro-tempore, 1985-86; ptnr. Cory, Brown & Pfeifer, 1973-92; justice Ohio Supreme Ct., 1992—. Chmn. jud. com. Ohio Senate, 10 yrs. Mem. Grace United Meth. Ch., Bucyrus. Mem. Bucyrus Rotary Club. Office: Supreme Court of Ohio 30 E Broad St Fl 3 Columbus OH 43215

PFEIFER, PETER MARTIN, physics educator; b. Zurich, Switzerland, Apr. 19, 1946; came to U.S., 1986; s. Max and Eva (Korrodi) P.; m. Therese M. Abgottspon, June 13, 1980; children: Anne, Helen. MS in Chemistry, Swiss Fed. Inst. Tech., 1969, PhD in Natural Scis., 1980. Rsch. assoc., instr. Swiss Fed. Inst. Tech., Zurich, 1975-80; rsch. fellow Hebrew U. Jerusalem, 1981-82; asst. prof. chemistry U. Bielefeld, West Germany, 1982-86, habilitation West Germany, 1986; assoc. prof. physics U. Mo., Columbia, 1986-95; vis. prof. physics Swiss Fed. Inst. Tech., 1993-94; vis. scientist Ecole Poly., Palaiseau, France, 1994; prof. physics U. Mo., Columbia, 1995—; sr. assic. Inst. Phys. Scis., Inc., Los Alamos, 1997—; vis. scientist Los Alamos Nat. Lab., 2000-01. Mem. adv. bd. Symposium on Probability Methods in Physics, Bielefeld, 1984, Symposium on Small Irregular Particles, Cuernavaca, Mex., 1988, Conf. on Fractals in Natural Scis., Budapest, Hungary, 1993, 22d Midwest Solid-State Theory Symposium, Columbia, 1994, 2d Internat. Symposium on Surface Heterogeneity, Zakopane, Poland, 1995, 3d conf. Fractals in Engring., Arcachon, France, 1997; spkr. in field. Mem. editl. bd. Internat. Jour. Fractals, 1992-97, Heterogeneous Chemistry Revs., 1992-98; contbr. over 100 articles to profl. jours. Recipient Gränacher Grad. fellowship Found. of Swiss Chem. Industry, 1970-71, fellowship for jr. scientists Swiss Nat. Sci. Found., 1981-82, Outstanding Rsch. prize U. Bielefeld, 1986; grantee Petroleum Rsch. Fund, 1987-99, Rsch. Leave award U. Mo., 1993-94, Inst. Phys. Sics., Los Alamos, 1999—. Mem. AAAS, N.Y. Acad. Scis., Am. Phys. Soc., Materials Rsch. Soc. Achievements include development of fractal analysis in surface science; discovery of first fractal materials, of numerous structure-function relationships (diffusion, scattering, wetting and transport properties), and of optimal performance of fractal lung; fundamental research in quantum theory: discovery of chiral superselection rule in molecules, unified framework for reduced quantum dynamics, generalized time-energy uncertainty relations, variational bounds for transition probabilities, quantum computing. Office: Univ Mo Dept Physics Columbia MO 65211-0001

PFEIFER, THOMAS J. legislative staff member; b. Copaigue, N.Y., Apr. 5, 1954; married; twin daughters. AS in Journalism, Moorpark Coll., 1983. Reporter, editor-in-chief Simi Valley (Calif.) Mirror, 1983; reporter, news editor, mng. editor Simi Valley Enterprise, 1984-92; city editor, team leader, bur. chief Ventura County (Calif.) Star, 1992-98; press sec., dir. comms. Congressman Elton Gallegly, Washington, 1998—. Office: Hon Elton Gallegly US Ho Reps 2427 Rayburn Hob Washington DC 20515-0001 E-mail: thomas.pfeifer@mail.house.gov.

PFEIFFER, EDWARD J. public and economics affairs specialist, presidential historian, research scientist; b. Gyula, Hungary, May 5, 1936; came to U.S., 1957, naturalized, 1962; s. Edward A. and Judith (Vanyska) P. Student, U. London, 1957, Oxford U., 1962, 85; BA in Internat. Rels., U. So. Calif., 1963; MA in Am. Govt., Claremont Grad. U., 1967, PhD in Am. Govt., 1982; student, U. London, Oxford U. Author, lectr. Nat. Lectr. Bur., 1959-66; prof. polit. sci., Am. govt. Calif. Univs., 1970-79; rsch. specialist U.S. Presdl. Libr., 1971—. Rsch. specialist diplomacy Internat. Olympic Com., 1983—; cons. World Bank, Washington, 1992—; adv. bd. Ctr. Nat. Policy, Washington, 1989—; lectr. in field; prin. organizer State of Am. Soc. symposia Calif. Univ. Sys.; panelist Salzburg Seminars, Austria, Anglo-Am. rels. Woodrow Wilson Ctr., Ditchley Found. symposiums, Oxford U. and Washington, Crans Montana, Geneva econ. and world affairs forums; panelist World Bank Econs. Conf., Oslo, Norway, 2002.. Author: Growing-up in Central Europe Post World War II, 1959; contbr. articles to jours., mags. Vol. Summer Olympic Games, L.A., 1984. With U.S. Army, 1960-66. Rsch. grantee U.S. Presdl. Librs., 1971—. Mem. PEN, Am. Polit. Sci. Assn. (panelist), Internat. Polit. Sci. Assn. (panelist), Delta Phi Epsilon, Phi Sigma Alpha. Home: PO Box 70515 Pasadena CA 91117-7515

PFEIFFER, EDWARD JOSEPH, public relations consultant, photojournalist; b. Phila., Nov. 24, 1926; s. Edward Joseph Jr. and Elizabeth Syra (Fogarty) P.; m. Catherine Anne Roache, Sept. 22, 1956; children: Laura Louise Pfeiffer-Cleinman, Lisa Katherine Pfeiffer-Scott, Edward Thomas Pfeiffer. BS in Econs., Villanova U., 1949; student, Columbia U., 1950. Sr. v.p. advertising and pub. rels. East N.Y. Savings Bank, N.Y.C., 1970-78; sr. v.p. industry rels. Direct Mktg. Assn., 1979-91; spl. adv. direct mktg. Deloitte & Touch L.L.P., 1991—2000; cons., 2000—. Dep. commr. equestrian media Spl. Olympics World Summer Games, Old Lyme, Conn., 1995. With USN, 1944-46. Recipient Silver Anvil Pub. Rels. Soc. Am., 1971. Mem. Am. Soc. Assn. Execs. (chmn. comms. sect. 1992, mem. bd. 1992), Direct Mktg. Assn. (vice chmn. Retail Coun. 1994-96). Avocations: railroad antiques, collectibles. Office: 14 Windcrest Dr Granby CT 06035

PFEIFFER, ERIC ARMIN, psychiatrist, gerontologist, writer; b. Rauental, Germany, Sept. 15, 1935; came to U.S., 1952; naturalized, 1957; s. Fritz and Emma (Saborowski) P.; m. Natasha Maria Emerson, Mar. 21, 1964; children: Eric Alexander, Michael David, Mark Armin. AB, Washington U., 1956, MD, 1960. Intern Albert Einstein Coll. Medicine, Bronx, N.Y., 1960-61; resident in psychiatry U. Rochester, 1961-64; practice medicine specializing in psychiatry Durham, N.C., 1966-76, Denver, 1976-78; asst. prof. Duke U., Durham, 1966-69, assoc. prof., 1969-72, prof., 1973-76, project dir., 1971-76, assoc. dir., 1974-76; dir. Davis Inst. Care and Study Aging, Denver, 1976-77; prof. psychiatry U. Colo., 1976-78; prof. psychiatry, chief div. geriatric psychiatry U. South Fla. Coll. Medicine, Tampa, 1978—, dir. Suncoast Gerontology Ctr., 1980—. Chief psychiatry svc. Tampa VA Med. Ctr., 1979-80; cons. in field; chmn. bd. Social Systems, Inc., 1975-76; chmn. com. on mental health and mental illness of elderly HEW, 1976-77. Author: Disordered Behavior, 1968, (with E.W. Busse) Behavior and Adaptation in Late Life, 1970, 3d edit., 1977, Successful Aging, 1974, Multidimensional Functional Assessment, 1977, Alzheimer's Disease, 1989. With USPHS, 1964-66. Markle Found. scholar acad. medicine, 1968-73; Eric Pfeiffer Chair in Alzheimer's Disease Rsch. named in his honor, U. S. Fla., 1985. Fellow Gerontol. Soc. (chmn. clin. medicine sect. 1975-76), Am. Psychiat. Assn.; mem. Am. Geriatrics Soc. (Allen Gold medal 1977), So. Psychiat. Soc., Phi Beta Kappa. Home: 5140 W Longfellow Ave Tampa FL 33629-7534 Office: 12901 Bruce B Downs Blvd Tampa FL 33612-4742 E-mail: epfeiffe@hsc.usf.edu.

PFEIFFER, JANE CAHILL, former broadcasting company executive, consultant; b. Sept. 29, 1932; d. John Joseph and Helen (Reilly) Cahill; m. Ralph A. Pfeiffer, Jr., June 3, 1975. BA, U. Md., 1954; postgrad., Cath. U. Am., 1956-57; LHD (hon.), Pace Coll., 1978, U. Md., 1979, Manhattanville Coll., 1979, Amherst U., 1980, Babson Coll., 1981, U. Notre Dame, 1991, Bryant Coll., 1995. With IBM Corp., Armonk, N.Y., 1955-76, sec. mgmt. rev. com., 1970, dir. comm., 1971, v.p. comm. and govt. rels., 1972-76, bus. cons., 1976-78; chmn. NBC, Inc., N.Y.C., 1978-80; bus. cons., 1980—. Dir. Ashland Oil Co., Mony Fin. Svcs., Internat. Paper Co., J.C. Penney Co.; trustee The Conf. Bd., 1991. Mem. pres.'s adv. com. White House Fellows, 1966, Pres.'s Gen. Adv. Commn. on Arms Control and Disarmament, 1977-80, Pres.'s Commn. Mil. Compensation; trustee Rockefeller Found., U. Md., Carnegie Hall, 1981-1986, U. Notre Dame; bd. mem., Catholic Univ. of Am., 1973-1978, Rockefeller Found., 1973-1985, White House Fellows, 1976-1981, Kettering Found., 1975-1979. Recipient Achievement award Kappa Kappa Gamma, 1974-80, Eleanor Roosevelt Humanitarian award N.Y. League for Hard of Hearing, 1980, Disting. Alumna award U. Md., 1975, Humanitarian award NOW, 1980, Centennial Alumna medallion U. Md., 1988; White House fellow, Washington, 1966, Making Waves award, Greatest 50 Women in Radio and Television-AWRT, 2002. Mem. Coun. Fgn. Rels., Overseas Devel. Coun., Econ. of N.Y. Club. Office: C/O Jonathan L Smith Chesapeake Asset Mgmt LLC 1 Rockefeller Plz Rm 1210 New York NY 10020-2002 Home: Johns Island 1050 Beach Rd Apt 1G Vero Beach FL 32963-3413

PFEIFFER, LEONARD, IV, executive recruiter, consultant; s. Leonard Jr. and Felicia Pfeiffer; m. Anna Gunnarsson. BA, MBA, Harvard U. Mktg. mgr. Am. Express, N.Y.C., 1970-72; project dir. S.T.I., N.Y.C. and San Francisco, 1972-74; v.p. R. Olivier & Assocs., N.Y.C., 1974-76, A. Kane & Assoc., N.Y.C., 1976-78; v.p., mng. dir. Korn/Ferry Internat., Washington and N.Y.C., 1978-98; sr. ptnr., group leader Heidrick & Struggles, Washington, 1998—2001; pres. Leonard Pfeiffer & Co., 2001—. Bd. dirs. Cmty. Found., Washington, 1982-84, Nat. Ctr. for Missing Children, 1989—, Nat. Blood Found., 1995-97, Nat. Bldg. Mus., 1998—; founding mem. jr. bd. dirs. Washington Opera, 1983-93; mem. men's com. Project Hope; mem. devel. com. Nat. Head Injury Found., Choral Arts Soc., Nat. Symphony Orch. Lt. U.S. Army, 1968-70. Schepp Found. scholar, 1968-70. Mem. Am. Soc. Assn. Execs., Greater Washington Soc. Assn. Execs., Congl. Country Club, Harvard Club (activities com., admissions com. N.Y.C. chpt. 1975-81, 1st v.p. bd. dirs. Washington chpt. 1985-87). Avocations: water and snow skiing, power and sail boating, tennis. Office: Leonard Pfeiffer & Co 1319 F St NW Ste 301 Washington DC 20004-1140

PFEIFFER, MARGARET KOLODNY, lawyer; b. Elkin, N.C., Oct. 7, 1944; d. Isadore Harold and Mary Elizabeth (Brody) K.; m. Carl Frederick Pfeiffer II, Sept. 2, 1968. BA, Duke U., 1967; JD, Rutgers U., 1974. Bar: N.J. 1974, N.Y. 1976, D.C. 1981, U.S. Supreme Ct. 1979. Law clk. to Hon. F.L. Van Dusen U.S. Ct. Appeals 3d cir., Phila., 1974-75; assoc. Sullivan & Cromwell, N.Y.C. and Washington, 1975-82, ptnr., 1982—. Contbr. articles to profl. jours. Trustee Am. Found. for Blind, Nat. Law Ctr. on Homelessness and Poverty; mem. bd. visitors Trinity Coll. Mem. ABA, Internat. Bar Assn., D.C. Bar Assn., N.Y. State Bar Assn., Assn. of Bar of City of N.Y. Avocations: hiking, reading, music. Office: Sullivan & Cromwell 1701 Pennsylvania Ave NW Washington DC 20006-5866

PFEIFFER, PHYLLIS KRAMER, publishing executive; b. N.Y.C., Feb. 11, 1949; d. Jacob N. and Estelle G. Rosenbaum-Pfeiffer; m. Stephen M. Pfeiffer, Dec. 21, 1969; children: Andrew Kramer, Elise Kramer. BS, Cornell U., 1970; postgrad., U. San Diego, 1976-78. Instr. Miss Porter's Sch., Farmington, Conn., 1970; tchr. Dewey Jr. H.S. N.Y.C. Bd. Edn., 1970-73; rschr. Hunter Coll., N.Y.C., 1971-72; account exec. La Jolla (Calif.) Light, 1973-75, advt. dir., 1975-77, gen. mgr., 1977-78, pub., 1978-87; exec. v.p. Harte Hanks So. Calif. Newspapers, 1985-87; gen. mgr. San Diego edit. L.A. Times, 1987-93; pres., pub. Marin Ind. Jour., Novato, Calif., 1993-2000; v.p. advt. and mktg. Contra Costa Times, 2000—. Dir. comm. ctr. San Diego State U., 1980-93. Bd. dirs. La Jolla Cancer Rsch. Found., 1979-82, YMCA, San Diego Ballet, 1980, Dominican Coll., San Rafael, Calif, 1994—, Marin Theater Co., Alvarado Hosp., 1981-88, chmn. fin. com., 1986, sec. bd., 1986; co-chmn. Operation USS La Jolla, USN, 1980—; mem. mktg. com. United Way, 1979-81, chmn., 1983; trustee La Jollan's Inc., 1975-78, Nat. Pk. Trust, 2000-02, Dogs for the Blind, 2001-.; mem. Conv. and Visitors Bur. Blue Ribbon Com. on Future, 1983; mem. resource panel Child Abuse Prevention Found., 1983—; bd. overseers U. Calif., San Diego; mem. violent crimes task force San Diego Police Dept.; dir. Guide Dogs for the Blind, Oveland Mus. Grantee N.Y. Bd. Edn., 1971-72; named Pub. of Yr., Gannet Co., Inc., 1995. Mem. Newspaper Assn. Am., Calif. Newspaper Pubs. Assn. (bd. dirs., exec. com.), Chancellor's Assn. U. Calif.-San Diego, Clairemont Club. Office: Contra Costa Times 2640 Shadelands Dr Walnut Creek CA 94598 E-mail: ppfeiffer@cctimes.com.

PFEIFFER, RAYMOND SMITH, philosophy educator; b. N.Y.C., Oct. 11, 1946; s. Raymond Louis and Gertrude B. (Smith) Pfeiffer; m. Lolita Dawson, June 22, 1968 (div. Feb. 1998); children: Mariah Dawson, Ryan Smith, Caven Dawson; m. Jelica Baotic, Nov. 12, 1999. AB in philosophy cum laude, Kenyon Coll., 1968; AM, Washington U., St. Louis, 1972, PhD, 1974. Prof. philosophy Alma (Mich.) Coll., 1974-75, Delta Coll., University Center, Mich., 1975—. Fellow Exxon Tchg. Workshop, Houston, 1986; univ. fellow, tchg. asst. Washington U., 1971-73; cons., presenter, spkr. in field; mem. U.S. bd. editors Philosophy Now, 1997—; bd. editors Teaching Philosophy, 1987—, manuscript judge, 1984-86. Author: Why Blame the Organization? A Pragmatic Analysis of Collective Moral Responsibility, 1995, (with Ralph P. Forsberg) Ethics on the Job: Cases and Strategies, 2d edit., 2000; contbr. articles to profl. jours. Recipient Svc. award AAUP, 1998, Scholarly Achievement award Delta Coll., Barstow, 1995; grantee NEH, 1977, 79, Oxford U., 1983, 92; fellow NEH, 1977, 87. Mem. Am. Philos. Assn., Mich. Acad. Sci., Arts and Letters, Soc. for Philosophy and Pub. Affairs, Soc. for Health, Ethics and Life Scis., Internat. Assn. for Philosophy of Law and Social Philosophy, Sigma Xi. Office: Delta Coll 1361 Delta Rd University Center MI 48710 E-mail: rspfeiff@alpha.delta.edu.

PFEIFFER, ROBERT JOHN, business executive; b. Suva, Fiji Islands, Mar. 7, 1920; came to U.S., 1921, naturalized, 1927; s. William Albert and Nina (MacDonald) P.; m. Mary Elizabeth Worts, Nov. 29, 1945; children— Elizabeth Pfeiffer Tumbas, Margaret Pfeiffer Hughes, George, Kathleen. Grad. high sch., Honolulu, 1937; DSc (hon.), Maine Maritime Acad.; HHD (hon.), U. Hawaii; DHL (hon.), Hawaii Loa Coll. With Inter-Island Steam Navigation Co., Ltd., Honolulu, (re-organized to Overseas Terminal Ltd. 1950), (merged into Oahu Ry. & Land Co. 1954), 1937-55, v.p., gen. mgr., 1950-54, mgr. ship agy. dept., 1954-55; v.p., gen. mgr. Pacific Cut Stone & Granite Co., Inc., Alhambra, Calif., 1955-56, Matcinal Corp., Alameda, 1956-58; mgr. div. Pacific Far East Line, Inc., San Francisco, 1958-60; with Matson Nav. Co., 1960—, v.p., 1966-70, sr. v.p., 1970-71; pres. The Matson Co., 1970-82; exec. v.p. Matson Nav. Co., San Francisco, 1971-73, pres., 1973-79, 84-85, 89-90, CEO, 1973-92, chmn. bd., bd.dirs., 1978-95, chmn. emeritus, 1995-98, chmn., 1998-99; chmn. emeritus, 1999—; v.p., gen. mgr. Matson Terminals, Inc., San Francisco, 1960-62, pres., 1962-70, chmn. bd., 1970-79, Matson Svcs. Co., 1973-79, Matson Agys., Inc., 1973-78; sr. v.p. Alexander & Baldwin, Inc., Honolulu, 1973-77, exec. v.p., 1977-79, chmn. bd., 1980-95, chmn. emeritus, 1995-98, 99—, chmn., pres., CEO, 1998, chmn. bd. dirs., 1998-99, CEO, 1980-92, pres., 1979-84, 89-91, chmn. emeritus, 1999—; chmn. bd., pres., dir. A&B-Hawaii, Inc., 1988-89, chmn. bd., 1989-95, chmn. emeritus, 1995-98, chmn. bd. dirs., 1998-99. Former mem. Gov.'s commn. on exec. salaries State of Hawaii, com. on jud. salaries. Past chmn. maritime transp. rsch. bd. NAS; former mem. select com. for Am. Mcht. Marine Seamanship Trophy Award; mem. commn. sociotech. systems NRC; mem. adv. com. Joint Maritime Congress; Pacific Aerospace Mus., also bd. dirs.; vice-chmn. Hawaii Maritime Ctr.; former chmn. A. Com. on Excellence (ACE), Hawaii; bd. govs. Japanese Cultural Ctr. Hawaii; hon. co-chmn. McKinley H.S. Found. Lt. USNR, WWII; comdr. Res. ret. Mem. VFW (life), Nat. Assn. Stevedores (past pres.), Internat. Cargo Handling Coord. Assn. (past pres. U.S. Com.), Propeller Club U.S. (past pres. Honolulu chpt.), Nat. Def. Transp. Assn., Containerization & Intermodal Inst. (hon. bd. advisors), 200 Club, Aircraft Owners and Pilots Assn., Pacific Club, Outrigger Club, Oahu Country Club, Maui Country Club, Pacific Union Club, Bohemian Club, World Trade Club (San Francisco), Masons, Shriners. Republican. Home: 535 Miner Rd Orinda CA 94563-1429 Office: Alexander & Baldwin Inc 822 Bishop St Honolulu HI 96813-3925

PFEIFFER, SOPHIA DOUGLASS, state legislator, lawyer; b. N.Y.C., Aug. 10, 1918; d. Franklin Chamberlin and Sophie Douglass (White) Wells; m. Timothy Adams Pfeiffer, June 7, 1941; children: Timothy Franklin, Penelope Mesereau Keenan, Sophie Douglass. AB, Vassar Coll., 1939; JD, Northeastern U., 1975. Bar: R.I. 1975, U.S. Ct. Appeals (1st cir.) 1980, U.S. Supreme Ct. 1979. Editl. rschr. Time, Inc., N.Y.C., 1940-41; writer Officer War Info., Washington, 1941-43, N.Y.C., 1943-45; editl. staff Nat. Geog. Mag., Washington, 1958-59, 68-70; editor Turkish Jour. Pediatrics, Ankara, 1961-63; staff atty. R.I. Supreme Ct., Providence, 1975-76, chief staff atty., 1977-86; mem. Maine Ho. Reps., 1990-94; lectr. U. So. Maine, 1995; bioethics writer, 1996—. Bd. dirs. Death and Dying project. Contbr. in field. Chair bioethics study League Women Voters; pres. Karachi (Pakistan) Am. Sch., 1955-56; chair Brunswick Village Rev. Bd., 1986-89; trustee Brunswick Sewer Dist., 2000—. Home: 15 Franklin St Brunswick ME 04011-2101 E-mail: aminta@gwi.net.

PFEIFFER, STEVEN BERNARD, lawyer; b. Orange, N.J., Jan. 19, 1947; s. Bernard Victor and Elizabeth Sophia (Bissell) P.; m. Kristin Reagan, June 27, 1970; children: Victoria Elizabeth, Rachel Catherine, Emily Dorothea, Stephanie Kristin Bissell, Andrew Steven Bernard. BA in Govt., Wesleyan U., 1969; BA in Jurisprudence, Oxford U., 1971, MA, 1983; MA in African Studies, U. London, 1973; JD, Yale U., 1976. Bar: N.J. 1976, D.C. 1978. Assoc. Fulbright & Jaworski, Houston, London, 1976—83, ptnr. London, Washington, 1983—, ptnr.-in-charge London, 1983—86, 1989—, head internat. dept. Washington office, 1989—, ptnr.-in-charge Washington office, 1998—. Bd. dirs., chmn. internat. com. Riggs Nat. Corp., Washington; bd. dirs., non-exec. chmn. Riggs Bank Europe Ltd., London; bd. dirs. The Africa Am. Inst., N.Y.C., Barloworld Ltd., Johannesburg. Contbr. articles to profl. jours. Alumni-elected trustee Wesleyan U., Middletown, Conn., 1976-79, charter trustee, 1980-92, vice chmn. bd. trustees, 1986-87, chmn. bd. trustees, 1987-92, chmn. emeritus, 1992—; trustee St. Andrews Sch., Middletown, Del., 1995—. With USN, 1969, 72-74; asst. cinceur plans officer, Office of CNO, Washington, 1972-73; spl. asst. to Sec. of Navy, Washington, 1973-74. Rhodes scholar, 1969-72; Thomas Watson Travel fellow, The Watson Found., 1969. Mem. ABA, N.J. State Bar Assn., Soc. Internat. Law, Internat. Bar Assn. (past chmn. sect. energy and natural resources law 1992-94), Naval Res. Assn., Internat. Inst. Strategic Studies (London), Coun. Fgn. Rels. Avocations: tennis, history, fishing, books. Home: 301 N View Ter Alexandria VA 22301-2609 Office: Fulbright & Jaworski LLP 801 Pennsylvania Ave NW Washington DC 20004-2623

PFEIFFER, WERNER BERNHARD, artist, educator; b. Stuttgart, Germany, Oct. 1, 1937; came to U.S., 1961; s. Jakob and Emilie (Nufer) P.; children: Jan-Stephen, Michaela Veronica. Diploma, Grafische Fachschule, Stuttgart, Akademie Fine Arts. Instr. Pratt Inst., Bklyn., 1961-64, prof., 1968-75, adj. prof., 1976—; asst. prof. N.Y. Inst. Tech., Westbury, 1965-67. Dir. Pratt Adlib Press, Bklyn., 1968-75 Exhibited in over 50 one-man shows. Mem. Soc. Am. Graphic Artists Avocations: skiing, travel, music. Address: PO Box 147 Red Hook NY 12571

PFEISTER, RAYMOND LYNN, diversified financial services company executive; b. Cape Girardeau, Mo., May 31, 1946; s. Herman Joe and Imogene Elsie (Groseclose) P.; m. Susan Jane Selby, July 1, 1969; children: Joseph Robert, John Charles. BS, U. Ill., 1969, MBA, 1971; PhD, CUNY, 1978. Sales analyst Koppers Co., Magnolia, Ark., 1969-70; instr. bus. U. Ill., Urbana, 1971; spl. agt. Prudential Ins. Co. Am., Champaign, Ill., 1971, divsn. mgr. Balt., 1971-74, mktg. specialist, mgr. group pension Newark and N.Y.C., 1974; account exec. Alexander & Alexander Inc., N.Y.C., 1974-76, asst. v.p., 1976-78, v.p., 1978-80, Johnson & Higgins, N.Y.C., 1980-83; founder, chmn. bd., CEO, Pfeister Barter Inc., N.Y. Reciprocal Trade Exch., 1979-87; founder, chmn., pres. Pfeister Corp., Wilmington, Del., 1977—; co-founder, pres., treas. Chattan Group, Ltd., N.Y.C., 1983—; co-founder, pres., CEO, Sheffield Assocs., Ltd., 1985—; co-owner Ceramic Design Ltd., Greenwich, Conn., 1987—; vice chmn. Fred Alger Mgmt., N.Y.C. Bd. dirs. U.S. Ceramic Tile Corp., Canton, Ohio, London Pacific Life Ins. Co., Calif.; lectr., cons. in field. Author: The Strategic Planning Process for Alexander & Alexander Services, Inc. and Subsidiaries, 1980; contbg. author: The Practice of Planning—Strategic, Administrative and Operational, 1981. Pres. Jr. Achievement, Denver, 1963-64; active boy Scouts Am., 1964—, United Fund, 1973. Mem. APA, Acad. Mgmt., Nat. Eagle Scout Assn., Soc. Am. Foresters, Forest Products Rsch. Soc., nat. Life Underwriters Assn., Nat. MBA Assn., U. Ill. Alumni Assn. (life, v.p. 1974—), Siwanoy Country Club, Campfire Club Am., Union League Club, Sigma Iota Epsilon. E-mail: rpfeister@alger-ny.com.

PFENDER, EMIL, mechanical engineering educator; b. Stuttgart, Germany, May 25, 1925; came to U.S., 1964, naturalized, 1969; s. Vinzenz and Anna Maria (Dreher) P.; m. Maria Katharina Staiger, Oct. 22, 1954; children: Roland, Norbert, Corinne. Student, U. Tuebingen, Germany, 1947-49; diploma in physics, U. Stuttgart, Germany, 1953, D Ing. in Elec. Engring., 1959. Assoc. prof. mech. engring. U. Minn., Mpls., 1964-67, prof., 1967—. Contbr. articles to profl. jours.; patentee in field. Fellow: ASME; mem.: NAE, IEEE (assoc.). Home: 1947 Bidwell St Saint Paul MN 55118-4417 Office: U Minn Dept of Mech Engrg 111 Church St SE Minneapolis MN 55455-0150 E-mail: pfender@tc.umn.edu.

PFENDT, HENRY GEORGE, retired information systems executive, management consultant; b. Frankfurt, Germany, Sept. 19, 1934; s. Georg and Elisabeth K. (Schuch) P.; m. Jane Ann Gossard, July 15, 1961; children: Katherine Ann, Henry G. Jr., Karen Jane. BS, postgrad., U. Rochester, N.Y., 1972, U. Mich., 1986. Dir. No. info. ctr. Eastman Kodak Internat., Göteborg, Sweden, 1972-73, sr. project mgr. Stuttgart, Fed. Republic of Germany, 1973-75; dir. adminstrv. svcs. Kodak Australasia Party Ltd., Coburg, Australia, 1975-77, dir. customer svcs. div., 1977-81; dir. mktg. Eastman Kodak Co. for Asia, Africa and Australia, 1981-84; dir. architecture devel. Eastman Kodak Info. Systems, Rochester, 1984-86, dir. corp. info. systems, 1986-93; ret., 1993; bus. and info. mgmt. cons., 1993—. Bd. dirs. client adv. coun. Compu Ware, Detroit. Creator concepts and mgmt. processes in field. Mem. indsl. devel. agy. adv. bd. Zoning Bd. Appeals, 2001; chmn. Yates County Fair Taxation Com.; elected town councilman Town Bd. of Barrington, 1999; charter mem. adv. bd. Rochester Inst. Tech. Sch. Computer Sci. and Tech., 1987; bd. dirs. YMCA of Maplewood, Rochester, 1989—; mem. Rep. Nat. Com. With USAF, 1955-59. Recipient Industry Visionary award of 25 Most Influential Communications Execs., 1991, Lectr. of Yr. award Australian Computer Soc., Editor's Choice award Nat. Libr. Poetry. Mem. Soc. for Info. Mgmt., Coun. of Logistics Mgmt., Ctr. for Info. Systems Rsch., Strategic Mgmt. Soc., Internat. Platform Assn., Interact Network (assoc.), C. of C., Am. Legion. Lutheran. Avocations: reading, golf, gardening, jogging, travel. Home: 968 E Lake Rd Dundee NY 14837-9749

PFENING, FREDERIC DENVER, III, manufacturing company executive; b. Columbus, Ohio, July 28, 1949; s. Frederic Denver Jr. and Lelia (Bucher) P.; m. Cynthia Gordon, July 1, 1978 (div. 1999); children: Lesley, Frederic Denver IV; m. Janet Evans, 1999. BA, Ohio Wesleyan U., 1971; MA, Ohio State U., Columbus, 1976. Various positions Fred. D. Pfening Co., Columbus, 1976-88, pres., 1988—. Bd. dirs. Friends of Ohio State U. Librs., 1988-94, 98—, Columbus State C.C. Devel. Found., 1991-99, Hist. Sites Found., Baraboo, Wis., 1984—, pres., 1987-91. Mem. Am. Soc. Bakery Engrs., Orgn. Am. Historians, Bakery Equipment Mfrs. Assn. (bd. dirs. 1985-91), Young Pres.'s Orgn., Circus Hist. Soc. (pres. 1986-89, mng. editor Bandwagon Jour.), Rotary. Office: 1075 W 5th Ave Columbus OH 43212-2629

PFEUFFER, DALE ROBERT, secondary school social studies educator; b. Pitts., May 23, 1955; s. Francis Jerome and Dorothy Jean (Hankey) P.; m. Mary Elizabeth Hunter, June 4, 1983 (div. 1992); 1 child, Elberta Hunter. AA, C.C. Allegheny County, 1976; BA, U. Pitts., 1977, MEd, 1983. Cert. tchr. secondary comprehensive social studies, Pa. Tchr. secondary social studies Sto-Rox Sch. Dist., McKees Rocks, Pa., 1980-81, Avonworth Sch. Dist., Pitts., 1983-84, Harford County Sch. Dist., Bel Air, Md., 1984-86. Tchr. of homebound Penn Hills Sch. Dist., 1979-80, Sto-Rox Sch. Dist., McKees Rocks, Pa., 1980-84, 86-87, Avonworth Sch. Dist., Pitts., 1983-84. Fund raiser Community Redevel. Fund, Ethnic Festival Sponsor, ARC, 1980-81; sponsor Speech and Debate Club, Harford County Sch. Dist., 1985-86. Mem. NEA, Nat. Coun. Social Studies, Assn. Undergrad. Edn. (subcom. student rsch. grants), Pa. State Edn. Assn., Md. State Tchrs. Assn., Coun. Grad. Students Edn., Nat. Geograph. Soc., Nat. Trust Historic Preservation, The Smithsonian Assocs. Democrat. Roman Catholic. Avocations: racquetball, golf, volleyball, softball, swimming. Home: 5703 Kingfish Dr Apt C Lutz FL 33558-5932

PFEUFFER, ROBERT JOHN, musician; b. Cleve., Dec. 25, 1925; s. Henry Vincent and Elmo Alice (Burger) P.; m. Betty June Weller, Sept. 21, 1946; children— Barbara (Mrs. Steven Mosley), Jeanne, Susan, Catherine. B.Mus. in Edn, U. Mich., 1950, M.Mus. in Edn, 1951. Contrabassoonist, bassoonist Detroit Symphony Orch., 1951-61, Phila. Orch., 1962-91; instr. bassoon Wayne State U., 1957-61, New Sch. Music, Phila., 1969—; prin. bassoon Lynchburg Symphony, 1994—, Roanoke Opera, 1996—. Served with AUS, 1942-44. Mem. U.S. Power Squadron, Kappa Kappa Psi, Pi Mu Alpha. Roman Catholic. Home: 1224 Barnhill Ln Moneta VA 24121-6007

PFISTER, CLOYD HARRY, consultant, former career officer; b. State College, Pa., Dec. 20, 1936; s. Rudolf John Pfister and June Ruth (Braun) Pfister Gray; m. Rita Askerc Kracht, Aug. 17, 1962 (div. Mar. 1982); m. Gail Williams, Apr. 24, 1982; children, Gabriele, Catherine, Michael, Romi; Eric Williams, Lori Williams. BA in Philosophy, Oberlin Coll., 1957; MA in Internat. Rels., Am. U., 1964, postgrad., 1964-67. Enlisted U.S. Army, 1957, advanced through grades to maj. gen., 1989; staff officer Nat. Security Agy., Fort Meade, Md., 1965-68; S3 (Ops.) 303d Radio Rsch. Bn., Plantation, Vietnam, 1968-69; instr. JFK Ctr. and Sch., Fort Bragg, N.C., 1969-72; politico-mil. officer, Office Dep. Chief of Staff for Ops. Hdqrs. Dept. Army, Washington, 1972-75; comdr. 307th U.S. Army Security Agy. Bn., VII U.S. Corps, Ludwigsburg, Fed. Republic Germany, 1975-77; asst. chief of staff intelligence 8th Mech. Inf. Div., Bad Kreuznach, Fed. Republic Germany, 1977-79; Mid. East staff officer Office Sec. Def., The Pentagon, 1979-82; comdr. U.S. Army Field Sta., Berlin, 1982-84; chief of staff U.S. Army Intelligence Ctr. and Sch., Fort Huachuca, Ariz., 1984-85, dep. comdt., 1985-86; dir. intelligence (J2), Hdqrs., U.S. Cen. Command, MacDill AFB, Fla., 1986-88; dep. chief of staff intelligence Hdqrs., U.S. Army Europe and 7th Army, Heidelberg, Fed. Republic Germany, 1988-91; asst. dep. chief of staff Intelligence Hdqrs., Dept. Army, Pentagon, 1991-93. Cons. Def. Sci. Bd., 1994, Def. Airborne Reccon Office, 1994-97, Nat. Imagery and Mapping Agy., 1999—; chmn. Cancer Ctr. Adv. Coun., Inova, 2000—. Decorated Def. D.S.M., D.S.M. Def. Superior Svc. medal, Legion of Merit with two oak leaf clusters, Nat. Intelligence D.S.M.; Ehrenkreutz der Bundeswehr (gold) (Fed. Republic Germany); other awards. Mem. Internat. Inst. for Strategic Studies, Middle East Inst., Security Affairs Support Assn., Assn. U.S. Army. Avocations: tennis, photography, gardening, computers. Office: Tech Strategies & Alliances 5242 Lyngate Ct Burke VA 22015-1631 E-mail: pfister@tsanda.com.

PFISTER, GAIL WILLIAMS, economics educator; b. Seattle, May 6, 1936; d. Randall Smallwood Jr. and Jean (Miller) Williams; m. John S. Williams, Aug. 23, 1958 (div. 1979); children: Eric, Lori; m. Cloyd Harry Pfister, Apr. 24, 1982; stepchildren: Gaby, Cathy, Michael, Romi. AA, Marymount Coll., Rome, 1955; BA in Econs., Oberlin Coll., 1957; MA in History magna cum laude, Fairleigh Dickinson U., 1968; MA in Econs., NYU, 1976. Rsch. assoc., then lectr. Fairleigh Dickinson U., Teaneck, N.J., 1973-79; asst. prof. George Mason U., Fairfax, Va., 1979-82; lectr. U. Md., Heidelberg, Germany, 1982-84, U. Ariz., Tucson, 1984-86, U. South Fla., Tampa, 1986-89, Echerd Coll., St. Petersburg, Fla., 1986-89; mem. faculty dept. bus. adminstrn. Marymount U., Arlington, Va., 1989-95; lectr. UCLA Grad. Sch., 1991—95. Mem. rev. panels HHS, 1992—96. Author: Multinational Corporations: Problems and Prospects, 1975, Transborder Data Flows and Multinational Enterprise, 1988. Home: 4653 Kirkpatrick Ln Alexandria VA 22311-4913

PFISTER, HOWARD FREDERICK CARL, retired surgeon; b. Newport, Ky., 1917; BS, U. Cin., 1939, MD, 1943. Diplomate Am. Bd. Surgery. Intern Cin. Gen. Hosp., 1943-44, resident in surgery, 1944-45, 47-52; pvt. practice, Cin., 1951-95; ret., 1995. Former asst. clin. prof. surgery U. Cin. Mem. AMA.

PFISTER, KARL ANTON, industrial company executive; b. Ernetschwil St. Gallen, Switzerland, Oct. 17, 1941; came to U.S., 1966; s. Josef Anton and Paula Pfister; m. Karen Antonie Sievers; children: Kirsten, Marc, Theodore, Alexandra. Student trade sch., Rapperswil, Switzerland, 1957-61; student bus. sch., Zuerich, Switzerland, 1964-65. Tool and die maker H. Schmid, Rapperswil, Switzerland, 1957-61, Neher AG, Ebnat-Kappel, Switzerland, 1962-63; process engr. NCR, Buelach, Switzerland, 1964-66, Gretag, Regensdorf, Switzerland, 1966; tool and die maker Stoffel Fineflow Corp., White Plains, N.Y., 1966-67; mgr. mfg. Finetool Corp., Detroit, 1968; pres. Mich. Precision Ind., Inc., 1969—, MPI Internat. Inc., Rochester Hills, Mich., 1990—; chmn. bd., pres. Kautex N.Am., Inc., 1994; pres. Kloeckner Automotive, Inc., 1996, MPI Internat. Inc., Rochester Hills, 1998—. Dir. Kloeckner Capital Corp., Gordonsville, Va., MPI Internat., Inc. Consul, consulate Switzerland, Detroit, 1984—. Mem. Plum Hollow Club. Republican. Roman Catholic. Office: MPI Internat Inc 2129 Austin Ave Rochester Hills MI 48309-3668

PFISTER, RICHARD CHARLES, physician, radiology educator; b. Ypsilanti, Mich., Nov. 27, 1933; s. Emil Robert and Francis Josephine (LeForge) P.; m. Sally DeAnn Haight, Dec. 31, 1956 (div. 1980); children: Kirk Alan, Gary Raymond, Karen Dawn, James Kevin, William Charles. BS, Ctrl. Mich. U., 1958; MD, Wayne State U., 1962. Assoc. prof. radiology Harvard Med. Sch. and Mass. Gen. Hosp., Boston, 1966-89; med. officer FDA, Washington, 1989-90; prof. radiology U. South Ala., Mobile, 1990-92, La. State U., New Orleans, 1993—. Editor, author: Interventional Radiology, 1982. With U.S. Army Med. Corps, 1953-55. Recipient Investigator award NIH, Washington, 1972. Fellow Am. Coll. Radiology; mem. AMA, Soc. Uroradiology (pres. 1984-85), Radiologic Soc. N.Am., Am. Roentgen Ray Soc., Soc. Cardiovascular Interventional. Avocation: sailing (Trans-Atlantic passages). Office: LSU Med Ctr 1542 Tulane Ave New Orleans LA 70112-2825

PFISTER, TERRI, city official; Grad. high sch., Redfield, S.D., 1984; cert. stenographer, Stenotype Inst. of S.D., 1986. Police pension sec. City of Spokane, Wash., 1991-96, city clk., 1996—. Office: 808 W Spokane Falls Blvd Spokane WA 99201-3342

PFLAGER, GODFREY HOLTERHOFF, tapestry artist; b. St. Louis, Nov. 2, 1938; s. Dorothy (Holloway) F.; m. Susan Denious, June 6, 1964; children: Charles Denious, Dorothy Holloway. AB, Wash. U., St. Louis, 1963; MS, Boston U., 1966. Asst. editor Radio & TV Packagers, Inc., N.Y.C., 1966-68, Inst. Luce, Rome, 1969-70; editor Columbia Pictures, N.Y.C., 1970, The Big Fights, Inc., N.Y.C., 1971-93; tapestry artist, 1970—. One man shows include Avanti Galleries, N.Y.C., 1970, Collector's Cove, Atlanta, 1974, Artreach, Columbus, Ohio, 1983, Washington County Mus., Hagerstown, Md., 1988, Burke Arts, Morgantown, N.C., 1989, Stoner Arts Ctr., Shreveport, La., 1990, The Pyramid Gallery, N.Y.C., 1990; exhibited in group shows Mark A. Gallery, Teaneck, N.J., 1983, A.S.I. Gallery, San Francisco, 1988, Nabisco

World Hqrs., N.J., 1989; represented by Creiger Assocs., Boston, Fay Gold Gallery, Atlanta, Mahler Fine Arts, Seattle, Gallery One, Miami Beach, Fla., Michelson Gallery, Washington, Joan Robey Gallery, Denver; juried No. Platte Art, Scottsbluff, Nebr., 1987, Two Flags Festival, Douglas, Ariz., 1987, Spring Art Show, Steubenville, Ohio, 1988, 25th Art Mart, Greeley, Colo., 1988, Three Rivers Festival, Pitts., 1989, Internat. Art Fair, Houston, 1989, Braille Inst., L.A., 1989; represented in permanent collections William A. Borders, N.Y.C., Ann Ruwitch, St. Louis, Edith McAlpin, Phila., Harriet Hart, Houston, Ann Gillis, N.Y., Judith Fehlig, N.Y.

PFLANZE, OTTO PAUL, history educator; b. Maryville, Tenn., Apr. 2, 1918; s. Otto Paul and Katrine (Mills) P.; m. Hertha Maria Haberlander, Feb. 20, 1951; children: Stephen, Charles, Katrine. BA, Maryville Coll., 1940; MA, Yale U., 1942, PhD, 1950. Historian Dept. State, 1948-49; instr. N.Y. U., 1950-51; asst. prof. U. Mass., 1952-58, U. Ill., 1958-61; prof. history U. Minn., 1961-76, Ind. U., 1977-86, emeritus, 1986; Stevenson Prof. of History Bard Coll., Annandale On Hudson, N.Y., 1987-92, emeritus, 1992. Chmn. Conf. Group Central European History, 1978; mem. exam. bd., grad. record exam Ednl. Testing Service, 1972-76; mem. Inst. Advanced Study, 1970-71, mem. Historisches Kolleg, Munich, 1980-81. Author: Bismarck and the Development of Germany: Vol. 1.-The Period of Unification, 1815-1871, 1963 (Biennal Book award Phi Alpha Theta), rev. edit., 1990, Vol. 2-The Period of Consolidation, 1871-1880, 1990, Vol. 3-The Period of Fortification, 1880-1898, 1990 (3 vols. collectively named Most Outstanding Book in History, Govt. & Polit. Sci. by Assn. Am. Pubs., 1991); translated as Bd. I-Bismarck, Der Reichsgründer, 1997, Bd II-Bismarck, Der Reichskanzler, 1998 (Einhard prize 1999); co-author: A History of the Western World: Modern Times, 3d edit, 1975; editor: Innenpolitische Probleme des Bismarck-Reiches, 1983; co-editor: Documents on German Foreign Policy, 1918-1945, Vols. I-III, 1949-50; editor Am. Hist. Rev., 1976-85; mem. editl. bd. Jour. Modern History, 1971-73, Central European History, 1972-74. Served to 1st lt. U.S. Army, 1942-46. Fulbright research fellow, 1955-57; fellow Am. Council Learned Socs., 1951-52; fellow Guggenheim Found., 1966-67; fellow Nat. Endowment Humanities, 1975-76; fellow Internat. Research and Exchanges Bd., 1976; fellow Thyssen Stiftung, Essen, 1986; recipient Humanities award McKnight Found., 1962. Mem. Am. Hist. Assn., German Studies Assn.

PFLAUM, CHRISTOPHER CHARLES, economist, consultant; b. Bklyn., Oct. 4, 1947; s. Christopher Charles and Eileen Agnes (Dunn) P.; m. Kim Laury; 1 child, Laury Lynn. BA, St. John's U., Jamaica, N.Y., 1969; MBA, U. Miami, 1976; PhD, U. S.C., 1983. Asst. prof. East Tenn. State U., Johnson City, 1978-80; instr. So. Ill. U., Carbondale, 1980-82; sr. fin. economist Ill. Commerce Commn., Springfield, 1982-84; dir. econ. rsch. LMSL, Overland Park, Kans., 1984-86; prin. QED Rsch., 1986-88, Spectrum Econs., Overland Park, 1988-92, pres., 1992—. Contbr. articles to profl. jours. Republican. Avocation: scuba. Office: Spectrum Econs 9401 Indian Creek Pkwy Ste 360 Overland Park KS 66210-2007

PFLOMM, KIRSTEN NELSON, grant writer; b. Norwich, Conn., Sept. 26, 1970; d. Robert Eiriksson and Ruth Matilda (Nelson) P. Student, Three Rivers Coll., Norwich, Conn., 1991-95, Conn. Coll., New London, Conn., 1995—. Grantwriter Eastern Peaquot Tribe, Stonington, Conn., 1994—; adminstr. Hubbel Engring., 1995—. Cons. Eastern Pequot Tribe, Stonington, 1994—. Mem. ACLU, Amnesty Internat.; activities coord. Winthrop Highrise Family Support Ctr., New London, 1995. Mem. NOW, AAUW, Libr. of Congress, Phi Theta Kappa. Democrat. Avocations: tennis, jogging, skydiving, rock climbing.

PFLUEGER, M(ELBA) LEE COUNTS, academic administrator; b. St. Louis, Sept. 2, 1942; d. Pless and Edna Mae (Russell) Counts; m. Raymond Allen Pflueger, Sept. 14, 1963 (div. June 1972); children: Salem Allen, Russell Counts. BS in Home Econs., Univ. Mo., 1969; MEd in Guidance and Counseling, Washington Univ., St. Louis, 1973. Ednl. psychologist Ozark Regional Mental Health Ctr., Harrison, Ark., 1974-75; from account mgr. to mgr. pers. Enterprise Leasing Co., St. Louis, 1977-79; mgr. employee rels. Eaton Corp., Houston, 1979-80; owner Nature's Nuggets Fresh Granola, St. Louis, 1980-83; dir. corp. ednl. svcs. Maryville Coll., 1983-84; adminstr. mgmt. skills devel. McDonnell Douglas, 1984-85, mgr. employee involvement, 1985-86, prin. specialist human resources mgmt., 1988-89, mgr. human resources Houston, 1986-88; dir. devel. sch. engring. U. Mo., Rolla, 1989-93, dir. devel., corp. and found. rels., 1992-93; regional dir. devel., assoc. dir. maj. gifts and capital projects Washington U., St. Louis, 1994—. Part-time leader trainer Maritz Motivation, St. Louis, 1984-89. Chair United Fund Campaign for U. Mo., Rolla, 1991. Mem. PEO. Avocations: reading, theatre, yoga, travel. Office: Washington U Office Maj Gifts and Capital Projects Campus Box 1228 One Brookings Dr Saint Louis MO 63130-4899

PFLUGHAUPT, JANE RAMSEY, secondary school educator; b. Houston, Dec. 19, 1940; Sidney Clarence and Lillian Bess (Melton) Ramsey; m. Louis Elliott Pflughaupt, Aug. 11, 1962; children: Cheryl Diane, Russell Alan. BA, U. Tex., 1962; MA, Stanford U., 1971. Cert. life secondary tchr., Calif., Tex. Tchr. math. Austin (Tex.) Ind. Sch. Dist., 1962-65, San Jose (Calif.) Unified Sch. Dist., 1967—, mentor tchr., 1985-90, dist. math task force, 1985—, prin.'s cabinet, 1997. Pioneer Bay Area Reform Sch. Coalition Leadership Team, 1997—; dist. curriculum adv. com. San Jose (Calif.) Unified Sch. Dist., 1991-93, dist. profl. devel. coach, 2000—; textbook rev. com. State of Calif., Sacramento, 1988-89; writer of textbook correlations for State of Oreg., 1995; chair math. dept. Pioneer H.S., 1990—, cons. McDougal Littel-Houghton Mifflin, 1993—, City of San Juse Math. Coalition, 2000—; profl. devel. coach 2000-02. Author: Integrated Math Teacher's editions, 1, 2, and 3, 1993-95, Algebra I, 1995, Algebra II, 1996, Geometry, 1997, Heath Algebra I, 1997, Algebra II, 1997, D.C. Heath Passport Series grades 6, 7, and 8, 1997. Vol. Indian Guides, Girl Scouts U.S.A., Lyceum, Los Madres, San Jose and Los Gatos, Calif., 1974-88; participant Coll. Bds. Project Equity 2000, 1991-96; demonstration tchr. NSF/Equity 2000, 1992; grant writer Pioneer H.S. Bay Area Reform Sch. Coalition, 1997, mem., 1997—. Named Tchr. of Yr. Pioneer H.S., 1990, 95; grantee Hewlett-Packard Co., 1989, 91, 92, Inst. Computer Aided Math., 1989, Tandy Co., 1994; fellow, grantee Semicondr. Rsch. Corp., 1990; Tandy Tech. Math. nat. scholar, 1994. Mem. NEA, Math. Assn. Am., Nat. Coun. Tchrs. Math., Calif. Math. Coun., Calif. Tchrs. Assn., Santa Clara Valley Math. Assn., San Jose Tchrs. Assn., Beginning Tchrs. Support Assn. (mentor 2001-02). Avocations: calligraphy, graphic design. Office: Pioneer High Sch 1290 Blossom Hill Rd San Jose CA 95118-3193

PFLUM, BARBARA ANN, pediatric allergist; b. Cin., Jan. 10, 1943; d. James Frederick and Betty Mae (Doherty) P.; m. Makram I. Gobrail, Oct. 20, 1973; children: Christina, James. BS, Coll. Mt. St. Vincent, 1967; MD, Georgetown U., 1971; MS, Coll. Mt. St. Joseph, 1993. Cons. Children's Med. Ctr., Dayton, Ohio, 1975—, dir. allergy clinic, 1983-89; dir. allergy divsn. Hopeland Splty. Clinic, 1998-2000. Fellow Am. Acad. Pediatrics, Am. Acad. Allergy and Immunology, Am. Coll. Allergy and Immunology; mem. Ohio Soc. Allergy and Immunology, Western Ohio Pediatric Soc. (pres. 1985-86). Roman Catholic. Office: 207 E Stroop Rd Dayton OH 45429-2825 E-mail: bapflum@hotmail.com.

PFNISTER, ALLAN OREL, humanities educator; b. Mason, Ill., July 23, 1925; s. Ardon Orel and Rose Margaret (Sandtner) P.; m. Helen Edith Klobes, Dec. 18, 1948; children: Alicia Ann, Jonathan Karl, Susan Elaine. AB summa cum laude, Augustana Coll., 1945; MDiv summa cum laude, Augustana Theol. Sem., 1949; AM, U. Chgo., 1951, PhD, 1955; LLD (hon.), U. Denver, 1978. Instr. in religion Augustana Coll., 1946-47; instr. in philosophy and German Luther Coll., Wahoo, Nebr., 1949-52, dean, 1953-54; research asst., univ. fellow U. Chgo., 1952-53, instr., 1954-57, asst. prof., 1957-58; dir. research joint bds. parish edn. Lutheran Ch. Am., 1958-59; vis. asso. prof. U. Mich., 1959-62, asso. prof., 1962-63; dean Coll. Liberal Arts, prof. philosophy Wittenberg (Ohio) U., 1963-67, provost, prof., 1967-69, acting pres., 1968-69; prof. higher edn. U. Denver, 1969-77, 78-90, exec. vice chancellor and acting chancellor, 1977-78, vice chancellor acad. affairs, 1984-87, assoc. provost, 1988-89, prof. emeritus, 1990—. Dir. study grp. study programs Fedn. Regional Accrediting Commns. Higher Edn., 1970-72; cons. in field; bd. dirs. Nat. Ctr. for Higher Edn. Mgmt. Systems Mgmt. Svcs.; trustee Capital U., Columbus, Ohio, 1983, vice chmn. bd., 1987-89, 91-94. Author: Teaching Adults, 1967, Trends in Higher Education, 1975, Planning for Higher Education, 1976; contbr. numerous articles on higher edn. to profl. jours. Bd. visitors Air Force Inst. Tech., 1978-83, chmn. bd. visitors, 1981-83. Recipient Outstanding Achievement Alumni award Augustana Coll., 1963, Outstanding Contributions to the Univ. award Univ. Denver, 1995. Mem. Am. Am. Assn. Higher Edn., Assn. for Study Higher Edn., Comparative and Internat. Edn. Soc., Blue Key, Phi Beta Kappa. Democrat. Home: 7231 W Linvale Pl Denver CO 80227-3556 E-mail: apfnister@cs.com.

PFOUTS, RALPH WILLIAM, economist, consultant; b. Atchison, Kans., Sept. 9, 1920; s. Ralph Ulysses and Alice (Oldham) P.; m. Jane Hoyer, Jan. 31, 1945 (dec. Nov. 1982); children: James William, Susan Jane Pfouts Portman, Thomas Robert (dec.), Elizabeth Ann Pfouts Klenowski; m. Lois Bateson, Dec. 21, 1984 (div.); m. Felicia Sprincenatu, 1993 (div.); m. June St. James, July 14, 2001. BA, U. Kans., 1942, MA, 1947; PhD, U. N.C., 1952. Rsch. asst., instr. econs. U. Kans., Lawrence, 1946-47; instr. U. N.C., Chapel Hill, 1947-50, lectr. econs., 1950-52, assoc. prof. econs., 1952-58, prof. econs., 1958-87, chmn. grad. studies dept. econs. Sch. Bus. Adminstrn., 1957-62, chmn. dept. econs. Sch. Bus. Adminstrn., 1962-68; cons. econs., 1987—. Vis. prof. U. Leeds, 1983; vis. rsch. scholar Internat. Inst. for Applied Systems Analysis, Laxenberg, Austria, 1983; prof. Cen. European U., Prague, 1991. Author: Elementary Economics-A Mathematical Approach, 1972; editor: So. Econ. Jour, 1955-75; editor, contbr.: Techniques of Urban Economic Analysis, 1960, Essays in Economics and Econometrics, 1960; editorial bd.: Metroeconomica, 1961-80, Atlantic Econ. Jour, 1973—; contbr. articles to profl. jours. Served as deck officer USNR, 1943-46. Social Sci. Research Council fellow U. Cambridge, 1953-54; Ford Found. Faculty Research fellow, 1962-63. Mem. AAAS, Am. Statis. Assn., N.C. Statis. Assn. (past pres.), Am. Econ. Assn., So. Econ. Assn. (past pres.), Atlantic Econ. Soc. (v.p. 1973-76, pres. 1977-78), Population Assn. Am., Econometric Soc., Math. Assn. Am., Phi Beta Kappa, Pi Sigma Alpha, Alpha Kappa Psi, Omicron Delta Epsilon. Home and Office: 127 Summerlin Dr Chapel Hill NC 27514-1925

PFOUTS, STEPHEN ALEXANDER, small business owner; b. Pitts., Apr. 21, 1948; s. William Alexander and Barbara Mary (Jackman) P.; m. Judy Kay Horton, Nov. 21, 1980; children: Gypsey A., Barbara A., Stephanie A., Stephen A., Jr. BA, Point Park Coll., 1971. Lab technician Vesuvius Internat. Inc., Pitts., 1971-72, lab mgr., 1972, asst.- v.p. internat. sales, 1972-73, regional sales mgr. Dayton, Ohio, 1972-75; owner Midwest Security, Muncie, Ind., 1975-76, Etienne Inc., Greensleeves Inc., Monroeville, Pa., 1986-94; v.p., owner Brooks Olds, Cad, GMC, Connellsville, 1995—. Exec. legal asst. Galloway, De Bermardo, Antonio, McCabe & Davis, Greensburg, Pa., 1987-91. Active Moon Area Chamber, Moon Township, Pa., 1972; dir. Westmoreland Symphony Orch., Greensburg, Pa., 1993—; mem. Nat. Rep. Legion of Merit and Task Force, 1990—. Mem. Pitts. Athletic Assn., West Penn Antique Car Club. Avocations: classic cars, restoration, metal and woodwork, collections. Home: RR 2 Box 786A Ruffs Dale PA 15679-9409 Office: Brooks Olds Cad GMC 2401 Memorial Blvd Connellsville PA 15425-1414

PFUND, EDWARD THEODORE, JR. electronics company executive; b. Methuen, Mass., Dec. 10, 1923; s. Edward Theodore and Mary Elizabeth (Banning) P.; BS magna cum laude, Tufts Coll., 1950; postgrad U. So. Calif., 1950, Columbia U., 1953, U. Calif., L.A., 1956, 58; m. Marga Emmi Andre, Nov. 10, 1954 (div. 1978); children: Angela M., Gloria I., Edward Theodore III; m. Ann Lorenne Dille, Jan. 10, 1988 (div. 1990). Radio engr., WLAW, Lawrence-Boston, 1942-50; fgn. svc. staff officer Voice of Am., Tangier, Munich, 1950-54; project. engr. Crusade for Freedom, Munich, Ger., 1955; project mgr., materials specialist United Electrodynamics Inc., Pasadena, Calif., 1956-59; cons. H.I. Thompson Fiber Glass Co., L.A., Andrew Corp., Chgo., 1959, Satellite Broadcast Assocs., Encino, Calif., 1982, TRW Inc., Redondo Beach, Calif., 1994; teaching staff Pasadena City Coll. (Calif.), 1959; dir. engring., chief engr. Electronics Specialty Co., L.A. and Thomaston, Conn., 1959-61; with Hughes Aircraft Co., various locations, 1955, 61-89, mgr. Middle East programs, also Far East, Latin Am. and African market devel., L.A., 1971-89, dir. internat. programs devel., Hughes Comm. Internat., 1985-89; mng. dir. E.T. Satellite Assocs. Internat., Rolling Hills Estates, Calif., 1989; dir. programs devel. Asia-Pacific TRW Space and Tech. Group, Redondo Beach, Calif., 1990-93, Pacific Telecom. Coun., Honolulu, 1993—. With AUS, 1942-46. Mem. AIAA, Phi Beta Kappa, Sigma Pi Sigma. Contbr. articles to profl. jours. Home: 25 Silver Saddle Ln Palos Verdes Peninsula CA 90274-2437

PHADKE, ARUN G. electrical engineering educator; b. Gwalior, M.P., India, Aug. 27, 1938; came to U.S., 1959; s. Gajanan G. and Indira G. Phadke; m. Kusum K. Joglekar, Sept. 14, 1964; 1 child, Ajit A. BS, Agra U., India, 1955; B in Tech. with honors, Indian Inst. Tech., 1959; MS, Ill. Inst. Tech., 1961; PhD, U. Wis., 1964. Systems engr. Allis Chalmers, Milw., 1963-67; asst. prof. elec. engr. dept. U. Wis., Madison, 1967-69; cons. engr. Am. Elec. Power Svc. Corp., N.Y.C., 1969-82; univ. disting. prof. Va. Poly Inst. & State U., Blacksburg, 1982—, 2000—. Cons. various electric utilities, equipment mfrs., 1980—. Co-author: Computer Relaying for Power Systems, 1988; patentee in field. Disting. Svc. citation, 1987, Centennial medal U. Wis., 1991. Fellow IEEE (chmn. power sys. relaying com., outstanding educator Power Engring. Soc. 1991, Millennium medal, Halperin award); mem. Edison Elec. Inst. (outstanding educator 1986), Conf. Internat. Grand Reseaux Electrique (chmn. working groups), Nat. Acad. Engring. Avocations: painting, tailoring. Office: Va Poly Inst & State U Elec Engring Dept 426 Whittemore Hall Blacksburg VA 24061-0111 E-mail: aphadke@vt.edu.

PHAIR, JOSEPH BASCHON, lawyer; b. N.Y.C., Apr. 29, 1947; s. James Francis and Mary Elizabeth (Baschon) P.; m. Bonnie Jean Hobbs, Sept. 04, 1971; children: Kelly I., Joseph B., Sean P. BA, U. San Francisco, 1970, JD, 1973. Bar: Calif., U.S. Dist. Ct. (no. dist.) Calif., U.S. Ct. Appeals (9th cir.). Assoc. Berry, Davis & McInerney, Oakland, Calif., 1974-76, Bronson, Bronson & McKinnon, San Francisco, 1976-79; staff atty. Varian Assocs., Inc., Palo Alto, Calif., 1979-83, corp. counsel, 1983-86, sr. corp. counsel, 1986-87, assoc. gen. counsel, 1987-90, v.p., gen. counsel, 1990-91, v.p., gen. counsel, sec., 1991-99; v.p. adminstrn., gen. counsel, sec. Varian Med. Sys., Inc., 1999—. Mem. devel. bd. St. Vincent de Paul Devel. Coun., San Francisco, 1992—. Mem. Bay Area Gen. Counsel, Silicon Valley Assn. Gen. Counsel, The Olympic Culb. Roman Catholic. Office: Varian Med Sys Inc M S V 250 3100 Hansen Way Palo Alto CA 94304-1030

PHALEN, ROBERT FRANKLYNN, environmental scientist; b. Fairview, Okla., Oct. 18, 1940; married, 1966; 2 children. B in Physics, San Diego State U., 1964, M in Physics, 1966; PhD in Biophysics, U. Rochester, 1971. Engring. aide advanced space systems dept. Gen. Dynamics/Astronautics, San Diego, 1962-63; asst. to radiation safety officer, lab. teaching asst. San Diego State U., 1964-66, instr. physics dept., 1966; mem. summer faculty biology dept. Rochester (N.Y.) Inst. Tech., 1970-72; rsch. assoc. aerosol physics dept. Lovelace Found. for Med. Edn. and Rsch., Albuquerque, 1972-74; from adj. asst. prof. to assoc. prof. in residence dept. community and environ. medicine U. Calif., Irvine, 1974-84, prof., dir. Air Pollution Health Effects Lab., 1985—, faculty Ctr. for Occupl. Environ. Health, 1985—. Reviewer Aerosol Sci. and Tech., Am. Rev. Respiratory Disease, Applied Indsl. Hygiene, Bull. Math. Biology, Exptl. Lung Rsch., Jour. Toxicology and Environ. Health, Jour. Toxicology and Applied Pharmacology, Jour. Aerosol Sci., Sci.; reviewer, mem. editl. bd. Fundamental and Applied Toxicology, 1986-92, Inhalation Toxicology, Jour. Aerosol Medicine, 1988-98; mem. safety and occupl. health study sect. NIH, 1988-99, mem. spl. study sects., 1980, 81, chmn. spl. study sects., 1982-84, 87, 88, 92, mem. site visit teams, 1980-2001; mem. expert panel on sulfur oxides EPA, mem. inhalation toxicology divsn. peer rev. panel, 1982, session chmn., 1983, participant workshop on non-oncogenic lung disease, 1984, mem. grants rsch. sci. rev. panel on health rsch., EPA advisor, 1985-88, 93-98; mem. task group on respiratory tract kinetic model Nat. Coun. Radiation Protection, 1978-97; mem. adv. panel on asbestos APHA, 1978; chmn. atmospheric sampling com. Am. Coun. Govtl. Indsl. Hygienists, 1982-92; chmn. NIOSH spl. study sect., 1983; panelist workshop Nat. Heart, Lung and Blood Inst., 1982; sci. advisor Prentice Day Sch., 1986-98. Author: Inhalation Studies: Foundations and Techniques, 1984, (with others) Advances in Air Sampling, 1988, Concepts in Inhalation Toxicology, 1989, Deposition, Retention and Dosimetry of Inhaled Radioactive Substances, 1997; editor: Methods in Inhalation Toxicology, 1997; contbr. numerous articles to profl. jours. Am. Legion scholar. Mem. AAAS, Am. Assn. Aerosol Rsch. (charter, chmn. ann. meeting 1985), Am. Conf. Govtl. Indsl. Hygienists, Am. Indsl. Hygiene Assn. (jour. reviewer, chmn. ann. conf. 1981, 85, 86), Brit. Occupl. Hygiene Soc., Internat. Soc. Aerosols in Medicine, So. Calif. Acad. Scis., Soc. for Aerosol Rsch., Health Physics Soc., Soc. Toxicology (chmn. 20th ann. meeting 1981, dir. 3 internat. confs. on health effects of particulate air pollution, Career Achievement award 2000). Achievements include research in nasal, tracheobronchial and pulmonary transport of inhaled deposited particles and effects of pollutant exposure on transport kinetcs, laboratory simulation and characterization of airborne environmental pollutants, respiratory tract deposition and clearance models for inhaled particles, including species comparisons and body size effects, behavior of highly-concentrated aerosols with respect to deposition in the respiratory tract. Office: U Calif Air Pollution Health Effects Lab Cmty & Environ Medicine Irvine CA 92697-1825 E-mail: rfphalen@uci.edu.

PHAM, DAVID LAN, secondary school educator, writer; b. Binh Chuan, Thudaumot, Vietnam, Feb. 1, 1940; s. Khoai Van Pham and Chuc Thi Le; m. Tam Thi Nguyen, Nov. 22, 1965; children: Albert, Elizabeth, Wellington, An, Victoria. BEd, Faculty of Pedagogy, Saigon Vietnam, 1963; BA in History, Faculty of Letters, Saigon Vietnam, 1965; M in Libr. Sci, Faculty of Pedagogy, Saigon Vietnam, 1973. Tchr., chief libr. Ly Thuong Kiet Comprehensive H.S., Hoc Mon, Vietnam, 1963—75; social svcs. coord. Cath. Social Svcs. Refugee Resettlement Program, Bayou La Batre, Ala., 1987—96. Advisor Binh Duong Bo De Sch., 1968—75; advisor Binh Duong Confedn, Vietnamienne du Travail, 1968—75; vis. Thailand for Libr. Sci. Observation, 1973; advisor, founder Mutual Assistance Assn., Bayou La Batre, Ala., 1988—89. Columnist Thoi Bao Daily, Saigon, Vietnam, 1963—64, columnist Point South, Mobile, Ala., 1991—94; editor: (Bulletin) Bulletin Tin Viet, Dac San Que Huong, 1987—96; author: (Memoirs) Two Hamlets in Nam Bo, 1999, (novels) Earthy Life, 2001, (History 2 vols.) Vietnam History Dictionary, 2002. Gen. sec. Assn. Vietnamese Tchrs. of History and Geography, 1967—69; founder Tutorial Program, Bayou La Batre, Ala., 1992—96. Buddhist. Avocations: reading, travel, walking, writing, zen. Home: 1341 Leith Dr Toledo OH 43614 E-mail: davidlanpham@hotmail.com.

PHAM, HOANG, engineering educator, researcher; b. Vietnam, Nov. 8, 1960; came to U.S., 1980; m. Michelle Pham, June 17, 1989; children: Hoang Jr., David. BS in Computer Sci., BS in Math., Northeastern Ill. U., 1982; MS in Stats., U. Ill., 1984; MS in Indsl. Engring., SUNY, Buffalo, 1988, PhD in Indsl. Engring., 1989. Sr. specialist engr. Boeing Co., Seattle, 1989-90; sr. engring. specialist Idaho Nat. Engring. Lab., Idaho Falls, 1990-93; assoc. prof. Rutgers U., Piscataway, N.J., 1993—. Author: Software Reliability, 1999; editor: Software Reliability and Testing, 1995, Handbook of Reliability Engineering, 2002; editor-in-chief: Internat. Jour. Reliability, Quality and Safety Engring. Recipient Guest Editor award IEEE Comms. Soc., 1994. Mem. IEEE (sr., editor IEEE Trans. on Systems, Man and Cybernetics), Inst. Indsl. Engrs. (sr., divsn. dir. 1997-98, quality control and reliability achievement award 1998). Achievements include contributions to software reliability engineering, leadership in the field of reliability engineering. Office: Rutgers U Coll Engring Dept Indsl Engring 96 Frelinghuysen Rd Piscataway NJ 08854-8018 Fax: 732-445-5467.

PHAM, KINH DINH, electrical engineer, educator, administrator; b. Saigon, Republic of Vietnam, Oct. 6, 1956; came to U.S., 1974; s. Nhuong D. (dec.) and Phuong T. (Tran) P.; m. Ngan-Lien T. Nguyen, May 27, 1985; children: Larissa, Galen. BS with honors, Portland State U., 1979; MSEE, U. Portland, 1982; postgrad., Portland State U., 1988-90. Registered profl. engr., Oreg., Calif., Ariz., Fla., Wash., Mass., Conn., R.I., Tex. Elec. engr. Irvington-Moore, Tigard, Oreg., 1979-80, Elcon Assocs., Inc., Beaverton, 1980-87, from sr. elec. engr., assoc. ptnr., 1987-96, v.p., 1996—. Adj. prof. Portland (Oreg.) C.C., 1982—; mem. adv. bd. Mass Transit System Compatibility, 1994. Co-author: FE/EIT Exam: Electrical Engineering Review and Study Guide, 2000, Electrical Engineering Professional Engineer License Exam Review Handbook, 2001; pub.: Research and Education and Association, 2000; cons. tech. editor Rsch. and Edn. Assn., 1998—; contbr. articles to profl. jours. Recipient Cert. Appreciation Am. Pub. Transit Assn. and Transit Industry, 1987. Sr. mem. IEEE, Industry Applications, Power Engring. and Vehicular Tech. Soc.; mem N.Y. Acad. Scis., Mass Transit Sys. Compatibility Adv. Bd, Eta Kappa Nu. Buddhist. Avocations: reading, teaching; profl. interests include traction power systems simulation, analysis and design, computer systems simulations. Office: Elcon Assocs Inc 12670 NW Barnes Rd Portland OR 97229-9001 E-mail: kinhlien@aol.com., kpham@elconasoc.com.

PHAM, QUANG XUAN, statistics educator; b. Mytho, Vietnam, Apr. 30, 1938; came to U.S., 1985; BS, U. Saigon, Vietnam, 1961; MS, Western Wash. U., Bellingham, 1971; PhD, U. Calif., Berkeley, 1974. Math tchr. Chu Van An High Sch., Saigon, Vietnam, 1961—70; info. analyst Henkel France, Gentilly, France, 1979—85; prof. stats. U. Alaska, Fairbanks, 1985—2001; adj. prof. stats. U. Calif., Berkeley, 2001—. Mem. Am. Statis. Assn., Biometrics Soc. Office: U Calif Berkeley Dept Stats Berkeley CA 94720

PHAM, SI MAI, cardiothoracic surgeon, medical educator; b. Ninh Hoa, Khanh Hoa, Vietnam, Oct. 6, 1955; came to U.S. 1975; s. Tro Pham and Nhung Thi Mai; m. Marie Christine Pham, Sept. 9, 1987; children: Benjamin Bartley, Anthony Ninh, Vivienne Elisabeth, Victoria B.H. Student, U. Saigon, Sch. Pharmacy, Vietnam, 1973-75; BS in Chem. magna cum laude, Lebanon Valley Coll., Annville, Pa., 1979; MD, U. Pitts., 1983. Diplomate Am. Bd. Surgery, Am. Bd. Thoracic Surgery. Intern, resident gen. surgery U. Pitts., 1983-86, rsch. fellow, cardiothoracic surgery, 1986-87, sr. and chief resident, gen. surgery, 1987-89, resident cardiothoracic surgery, 1989-92, asst. prof. surgery, Sch. of Medicine, 1992-97, dir. adult cardiac transplant program, Sch. of Medicine, 1993-97, assoc. dir. heart transplant and artificial heart program, 1997-98, dir. cardiothoracic transplant rsch., 1997-98; dir. extracorporeal membrane oxygenation svc. Presbyn. U. Hosp., Pitts., 1993-98; dir. cardiopulmonary transplantation divsn. cardiothoracic surgery U. Miami Sch. Medicine, 1998—; assoc. prof. surgery U. Miami Sch. Medicine, 1998—2002, prof., 2002—. Prof. surgery U. Miami Sch. Medicine, 2002—. Contbr. chpts. to books, articles to profl. jours. Recipient Am. Chem. award, 1979, Radiology award U. Pitts., 1983, Dalsemer rsch. scholar award Am. Lung Assn., 1997-99; ACS Faculty fellowship award, 1994-96; grantee Children's Hosp. Pitts., 1987, Am. Heart Assn., 1987-89, 94-96, 96-99, Thoracic Surgery Found., 1996-97, 97-98, Am. Lung Assn., 1997—, Presbyn. U. Hosp., 1987-89, NIH, 1999—. Fellow Am. Coll. Surgeons; mem. Am. Soc. Artificial Internal Organs, Internat. Soc. Heart and Lung Transplantation, Soc. Critical Care Medicine, Am. Assn. Advancement of Sci., Am. Soc. Transplant Surgeons, Soc. Thoracic Surgeons, Am. Assn. Thoracic Surgery, Extracorporeal Life Support Organization, Assn. for Acad. Surgery, Phi Alpha Epsilon. Home: 13250 SW 67th Ave Miami FL 33156-6929 Office: U Miami Sch Medicine Divsn Cardiothoracic Surgery PO Box 016960 (R-114) Miami FL 33101 E-mail: spham@med.miami.edu .

PHAM, TAN DIEM, physician; b. Saigon, Vietnam, July 29, 1970; came to the U.S., 1975; BA, Johns Hopkins U., 1992; MD, N.Y. Med. Coll., 1997. Intern, resident North Shore U. Hosp., Manhasset, N.Y., 1997-2000. Mem.: Vietnamese Med. Assn. USA. Roman Catholic. E-mail: tandiempham@hotmail.com.

PHAN, PHILLIP HIN CHOI, business educator, consultant; b. Singapore, Feb. 23, 1963; came to U.S., 1982; s. Bryan K. and Rosaline (Teo) P.; m. Soo-Hoon Lee-Phan, Feb. 13, 1988. BBA with distinction, U. Hawaii, 1984; PhD, U. Wash., 1992. Cost contr. Westin Hotels & Resorts, Dallas and Singapore, 1984—88; assoc. prof. York U., Toronto, 1992—2000; cons. World Bank, 1998—, OECD, 1998—2000; Bruggeman chaired assoc. prof. Rensselaer Poly. Inst., Troy, NY, 1998—. Asst. prof. CUNY, 1997; adj. assoc. prof. Nat. U. Singapore, 1998—; vis. prof. Thammasat U., Thailand, 1997; ptnr. Core Competence Cons., Inc., Toronto, 1993-98; dir. Blood Trac Sys. Internat., Edmonton, 1996-98; mem. Multi-Nat. Enterprises and Investment com. Can. Coun. Internat. Bus., 1993-2000 Mem. editl. bd. Jour. Bus. Venturing, 1998—, Acad. Mgmt. Jour., 2002—; co-editor Asia Pacific Jour. of Mgmt., 1999-2001. Recipient Endowment for Excellence award Boeing Corp., Seattle, 1992, Schulich Sch. Faculty Rsch. award, 1996; Rsch. grantee Social Scis. and Humanities Rsch. Coun. Can., 1997, John Broadbent Rsch. Fund, 2000—, Kauffman Entrepeneur Found., 2002; Edna G. Benson fellow, Seattle, 1992, Michael G. Foster fellow, Seattle, 1992; George W. Tyler scholar, Seattle,

1992. Mem. Acad. Mgmt., Inst. Mgmt. Scis., Acad. Internat. Bus. Republican. Avocations: reading, cycling, tennis, scuba. Office: Lally Sch M&T 110 8th St Troy NY 12180-3522 Home: #47 201 River St Troy NY 12180

PHAN, RICHARD MAN, chemist; b. Saigon, Vietnam, July 30, 1970; came to U.S., 1993; s. Hong Van Phan and Tan Thi Nguyen. BS, U. Utah, 1998, postgrad., 1998—. NIH fellow, 2000. Mem. Golden Key Nat. Honor Soc. (life). Home: 4900 Hellas Dr Salt Lake City UT 84120 Office: Univ Utah 3155 1400E # Dock Salt Lake City UT 84112

PHAN, TÂM THANH, medical educator, psychotherapist, consultant, researcher; b. Hue, Vietnam, June 10, 1949; d. Quê'Dinh and Chánh Thi (Tô) P. BA, Adams State Coll., 1979; MA, Western State Coll., 1980; PhD in Nutrition, Am. Coll. Nutrition, 1983; D of Nutrimedicine, John Kennedy Nutrisci., Gary, Ind., 1986; PhD in Counseling, Columbus Pacific U., 1988; DSc, Lafayette U., 1989. Lic. profl. counselor, marriage and family therapist; cert. nutrimedicine specialist. Counselor Lamar U., Beaumont, Tex., 1980-82; cons. Vietnamese Cmty., Golden Triangle, 1980—, The Wholistic Clinic, Beaumont, 1980—. Mem. adv. bd. Internat. Homeopathic Clearance, Mo., 1993—. Author: How Western Culture..., 1988, Natural Preventive Medicine, The Wholitic Approach, 1992, How to Prevent Mental Illness, 1995, How to Prevent Diabetes, 1996. Fellow Internat. Nutrimedicine Assn., Am. Nutrimedicine Assn.; mem. Interant. Alliance of Nutrimedical Therapists, Internat. Holistic Med. Soc. (bd. dirs. 1996, Cert. of Merit 1996). Avocations: writing, reading, swimming, cooking, knitting. Office: The Wholistic Clinic 1995 Broadway St Beaumont TX 77701-1941

PHANEUF, GERALD JOHN, retired pathologist; b. Woonsocket, R.I., Nov. 13, 1935; s. John Robert and Jessie (Rapko) P.; m. Joanne Marie Borgatti, May 19, 1962; children: Mary Anne, Jill, John, Mark, Eric. BA in Biology, Providence Coll., 1956; MD, Georgetown U., 1960. Diplomate Am. Bd. Clin. & Anatomical Pathology. Assoc. pathologist Truesdale Hosp., Fall River, Mass., 1965-69, chief pathologist, 1969-74; dir. labs. Damon Clin. Lab. Inc., Needham, 1972-79, Ctrl. Maine Med. Ctr., Lewiston, 1979-95; pres. Mgmt. Svcs. Inc., North Conway, N.H., 1976—. Bd. dirs. Ctrl. Maine Healthcare, Lewiston, 1994. Campaign chmn. United Fund Greater Fall River, 1972. Roman Catholic. Avocations: golf, tennis, skiing, airplane pilot. Home: PO Box 646 North Conway NH 03860-0646 E-mail: phan4j@aol.com.

PHANSTIEL, HOWARD G. health care system executive; BA in Political Sci., M in Pub. Adminstrn., Syracuse U. Exec./mgmt. Prudential Bache Internat. Bank/Securities, Marine Midland Banks, Sallie Mae; exec. v.p. fin./info. svcs. WellPoint Health Networks, Inc., Woodland Hills, Calif.; chmn., CEO ARV Assisted Living, Inc., Costa Mesa; exec. v.p., CFO PacifiCare Health Sys., Santa Anna, 2000, pres., CEO, 2000—. Office: PacifiCare Health Sys 3120 W Lake Ctr Dr Santa Ana CA 92704*

PHARES, ALAIN JOSEPH, physicist, educator; b. Beirut, Apr. 20, 1942; came to U.S., 1975, naturalized, 1982; s. Joseph Michel and Renee Cecile (Dommmar) P.; m. Claude Tawa, July 27, 1968; children— Caroline, Denis, Pascal. BS in Engring., St. Joseph U., 1964; Docteur-es-Sciences, U. Paris, 1971; PhD, Harvard U., 1973. Research fellow Nat. Council Sci. Research, Lebanon, 1973-75; assoc. prof. Lebanese U., 1973-75; research fellow Internat. Centre Theoretical Physics, Trieste, Italy, 1974, Harvard U., 1975-76; vis. asst. prof. U. Mont., 1976-77; asst. prof. physics Villanova U., Pa., 1977-79, assoc. prof., 1979-82, prof., 1982—, chmn. dept., 1981-91, dir. secondary sch. sci., 1981-94. Contbr. articles to profl. jours. French Govt. fellwo, 1964-66, IAEA fellow, 1974; grantee Villanova Rsch., 1978, NSF, 1991-98, PSC, 1991—; recipient Outstanding Faculty Rsch. award Villanova U., 1986. Mem. Am. Phys. Soc., Internat. Assn. Math. and Computers in Simulation, Sigma Xi Office: Villanova U Dept Physics Villanova PA 19085 Business E-Mail: alain.phares@villanova.edu.

PHARES, E. JERRY, psychology educator; b. Glendale, Ohio, July 21, 1928; s. Bruce and Gladys (West) P.; m. Betty L. Knost, Aug. 6, 1955; 1 dau., Lisa M. BA, U. Cin., 1951; MA, Ohio State U., 1953, PhD, 1955. Faculty Kans. State U., Manhattan, 1955—, prof. psychology, 1964-91, prof. emeritus, 1991—, head dept., 1967-89. Vis. asso. prof. Ohio State U., Columbus, Ohio Wesleyan U., 1961-62 Author, co-author books.; Contbr. articles to profl. jours. Research grantee NIMH, 1960, 80; Research grantee NSF, 1964-76; Research grantee Population Council, 1971 Fellow Am. Psychol. Assn., Am. Psychol. Soc. Office: 2812 Nevada St Manhattan KS 66502-2330 E-mail: ephares@ksu.edu.

PHELAN, ARTHUR JOSEPH, financial executive; b. N.Y.C., Oct. 26, 1915; s. Arthur Joseph and Josephine Adelaide (Barrett) P.; m. Mary Frances Ryan, Feb. 11, 1939; children— Jane Carolee, Leslie Diane, Sandra Christine. Student, Am. Inst. Banking, 1934-35, NYU, 1935-36. With Guaranty Trust Co. of N.Y., 1933-37; accountant N.Y. Post, 1937-38, Webb & Knapp, Inc., N.Y.C., 1938-41, asst. sec., 1941, comptroller, 1942-44, treas., 1944-53, v.p., treas., 1953-55, sr. v.p., dir., 1955-65; also trustee employees profit sharing plan, exec. v.p. David Greenewald Assocs., Inc., 1965-66; sr. v.p. Lefrak Orgn., Inc., Forest Hills, N.Y., 1966-92. Exec. v.p., dir. LOGO Inc., Tulsa, Okla., 1976-92. Mem.: North Hempstead Country. Roman Catholic. Home: 88 Summit Rd Port Washington NY 11050-3341

PHELAN, CHARLES SCOTT, retired lawyer; b. Saranac Lake, N.Y., Mar. 21, 1926; m. Ruth Rene Kuntzleman, Sept. 4, 1948; children: Susan P. Moser, Donna K. Merrick, Barbara K. Glumac. BSEE, Pa. State U., 1949; LLB, George Washington U., 1954. Bar: N.Y. 1955, U.S. Patent Office, 1956, U.S. Ct. Appeals (fed. cir.) 1982. Elec. engr. GE, Schenectady, N.Y., 1949-52, patent asst., 1950-54; sr. atty. AT&T Bell Labs., Whippany, N.J. and other cities, 1954-86; pvt. practice Millington, N.J., 1987-95; ret., 1995. Active Passaic Twp. (N.J.) Bd. Edn., 1962-64. 2d lt. U.S. Army, 1944-47. Mem. ABA, Am. Intellectual Property Law Assn., N.J. Patent Law Assn. (pres. 1964-65), Tau Beta Pi, Eta Kappa Nu. Avocations: fishing, hiking, sketching. E-mail: volneighbor@aol.com.

PHELAN, JAMES RICHARD, JR. otolaryngologist; b. Montclair, N.J., May 28, 1941; s. James Richard and Ellen Irma (McGeehan) P.; m. Bonnie Gaye Brasfield, Aug. 3, 1974. BA, U. Pa., 1963; MD, U. Medicine Dentistry N.J., 1968. Diplpmate Am. Bd. Otolaryngology. Intern Chgo. Wesley Meml. Hosp., 1968-69; resident in otolaryngology Naval Regional Med. Ctr., Oakland, Calif., 1972-76; with dept. of otolaryngology Sansum Med. Clin., Santa Barbara, 1978-92. With the USN, 1969-78, 93—. Fellow Am. Acad. Otolaryngology, ACS; mem. Aerospace Med. Assn., AMA, Soc. USN Flight Surgeons, Assn. Mil. Surgeons U.S., Soc. Mil. Otolaryngologists, Tailhook Assn. Office: Naval Aeospace Med Inst 340 Hulse Rd Pensacola FL 32508-1092 E-mail: jrphelan@nomi.med.navy.mil., jayphelan@aol.com.

PHELAN, JOHN DENSMORE, insurance executive, consultant; b. Kalamazoo, Aug. 31, 1914; s. John and Ida (Densmore) P.; m. Isabel McLaughlin, July 31, 1937; children: John Walter, William Paul, Daniel Joseph. BA magna cum laude, Carleton Coll., 1935. Reporter New Bedford (Mass.) Std.-Times, 1935-36; with Hardware Mut. Ins. Co., Stevens Point, Wis., 1936-45, Am. States Ins. Co. (name now Safeco Ins.), Indpls., 1945-90, pres., 1963-76, chmn., 1976-79, also bd. dirs. numerous subs. Bd. govs. Internat. Ins. Soc. Author: Business Interruption Primer, 1949, also later edits; contbr. articles to profl. jours. Past pres. Marion County Assn. Mental Health; chmn. emeritus CPCU-Harry J. Loman Found. Named to Hon. Order Ky. Cols., Sagamore of Wabash. Mem. CPCU Soc. (past nat. pres.), CLU Soc., Woodland Country Club (Indpls.), El Conquistador Country Club, Phi Beta Kappa. Presbyterian. Home: 6501 17th Ave W Apt W206 Bradenton FL 34209-7806

PHELAN, MARTHA ARMSTRONG, realtor; b. Shelby, Ohio, July 26, 1927; d. George Woodburn and Anna Louise (Wood) A.; m. Vincent Roche Phelan, Aug. 9, 1952 (dec. July 2000); children: Elizabeth Ann Riley, David Woodburn, Anne Louise. BA, Oberlin Coll., 1949. Sec. U.S. Govt., Washington, 1950-52; adminstrv. officer Com. for Free Asia, N.Y.C., 1952-53; legal sec. Atty. V.R. Phelan, Shelby, Ohio, 1975-79; realtor Mattox Realtors, Mansfield, 1976-93, Hancock Agy., Shelby, 1993—. Precinct committeeman Rep. Orgn., Shelby, 1965—; poll worker Richland County Bd. Elections, Shelby, 1960—; mem. exec. com. Richland County Reps., Mansfield, 1965—; mem. Kingwood Ctr. Gardens. Mem. Nat. Assn. Realtors, Mansfield Bd. Realtors, Rotary, Shelby Garden Club (pres. 1997-99), Shelby Women's Club (sec. 1990-01). Republican. Presbyterian. Avocations: gardening, reading, creative arts and crafts, swimming, music. Home: 26 Woodland Rd Shelby OH 44875

PHELAN, MARY HELEN, artist, educator; b. Laurium, Mich., Sept. 18, 1953; d. Joseph Francis and Florence Mary (LeBlanc) P.; m. Edmund Paul Berlanga, Jan. 25, 1975 (div. Jan. 1982); m. Arthur Plotnik, Dec. 2, 1983. Student, U. Ill., 1971-72; Assocs. in Fine Arts, Am. Acad. Art, 1977; BA, Northeastern U., 1986; student, The Sch. of Art Inst. Chgo., 1987. Drawing tchr. Am. Acad. of Art, Chgo., 1977—, chair drawing dept., 1990—. Guest spkr. Ridge Art Assn., Chgo., 1992, Cmty. Arts Coun. Crystal Lake, Ill., 1992; art exhibit judge Women's Works Nat. Exhibit, Crystal Lake, 1992, LCA Summerfest 1993, Chgo.. Commd. works include Libr. of Congress, 1985, U. Ill., 1988, Mercy Hosp., Janesville, Wis., 1993, U. Ill., Chgo., 1995, Robert Morris Coll., 1997, 2000, 01; contbg. illustrator various mags. including U.S. Fish and Wildlife, Playboy; illustrator (permanent outdoor exhibit) Notebaert Nature Mus., Chgo., 1999, (book) The Urban Tree Club, 2000/ Vol. illustrator The Nature Conservancy, Chgo., 1986-96. Elizabeth T. Greenshields Meml. Found. award, 1976, 77. Mem. Chgo. Artists' Coalition. Avocations: gardening, tennis, yoga, Ayurvedic cooking, traveling. Home: 2120 W Pensacola Ave Chicago IL 60618-1718 E-mail: mhphel@aol.com.

PHELAN, PATRICK JOHN, engineer; b. Upland, Calif., Feb. 16, 1959; BS, U. Calif., Riverside, 1981, MS, 1984, PhD, 1987. Rsch. asst. U. Calif., 1981-87; sr. engr. materials and processing Rohr Industries, Inc., Riverside, 1987-88, sr. rsch. engr., 1988-91, engring. specialist, 1991-92, project engr., 1992-94; mgr. land and water chemistry U. Calif., 1994-96; sr. staff engr. B.F. Goodrich Aerospace Aerostructures Group, Riverside, 1996—. Editor: Materials - Pathway to the Future, 1988; contbr. profl. jours. Rsch. scholar U. Calif., 1981-87. Mem. Am. Chem. Soc., Soc. Advancement Material and Process Engrng. (internat. treas. 1989-91), Newport Sailing Club, Sigma Xi, Gamma Sigma Delta. Avocations: sailing, skiing, softball. Home: 8892 E Crestview Ln Anaheim CA 92808-1663

PHELAN, RICHARD MAGRUDER, mechanical engineer; b. Moberly, Mo., Sept. 20, 1921; s. Frederick William and Ethel Ray (Magruder) P.; m. Olive Bernice McIntosh, May 25, 1951; children— William James, Susan Ray. Student, Moberly Jr. Coll., 1939-41; BS in Mech. Engring, U. Mo., Columbia, 1943; M.M.E., Cornell U., 1950; postgrad., U. Mich., 1956-57. Instr. Cornell U., 1947-50, asst. prof. mech. engring., 1950-56, assoc. prof., 1956-62, prof., 1962-87, prof. emeritus, 1988—. Author: Fundamentals of Mechanical Design, 1957, 3d rev. edit., 1970, Dynamics of Machinery, 1967, Automatic Control Systems, 1977. Served with USNR, 1943-46. Mem. ASME, Am. Soc. Engring. Edn., Soc. Exptl. Stress Analysis, Am. Gear Mfrs. Assn., AAUP, AAAS, N.Y. Acad. Scis., Soc. Exptl. Mechanics, Sigma Xi, Phi Kappa Phi, Pi Tau Sigma, Tau Beta Pi. Home: 4 Cornell Walk Ithaca NY 14850-6145 Office: Cornell U Upson Hall Ithaca NY 14853

PHELAN, ROBIN ERIC, lawyer; b. Steubenville, Ohio, Dec. 28, 1945; s. Edward John and Dorothy (Borkowski) P.; m. JoAnn Keach, June 27, 1970 (dec. May 1994); children: Travis McCoy, Tiffany Marie, Trevor Monroe; m. Melinda Jo Rickets, May 27, 1995; 1 child, Taezja Monet. BSBA, Ohio State U., 1967, JD, 1970. Bar: Tex. 1971, U.S. Ct. Appeals (5th cir.) 1981, U.S. Ct. Appeals (11th cir.) 1981, U.S. Ct. Appeals (6th cir.) 1986, U.S. Ct. Appeals (10th cir.) 1988, U.S. Supreme Ct. Ptnr. Haynes and Boone, Dallas, 1970—. Co-author: Bankruptcy Practice and Strategy, 1987, Cowans Bankruptcy Law and Practice, 1987, Annual Survey of Bankruptcy Law, 1988, Bankruptcy Litigation Manual; contbr. articles to profl. jours. Mem. ABA (chmn. bankruptcy litigation subcom. 1990-95, chmn. unconventional bankruptcy issues), Internat. Bar Assn., Internat. Insolvency Inst., Am. Bankruptcy Inst. (dir., past pres.), Am. Coll. Bankruptcy, State Bar Tex. (chmn. bankruptcy law com. sect. bus. law 1989-91), Dallas Bar Assn. Roman Catholic. Avocation: athletics. Home: 4214 Woodfin St Dallas TX 75220-6416 E-mail: phelanr@haynesboone.com.

PHELAN, THOMAS, clergyman, academic administrator, educator; b. Albany, N.Y., Apr. 11, 1925; s. Thomas William and Helen (Rausch) P. AB (N.Y. State Regents scholar 1942, President's medal 1945), Coll. Holy Cross, Worcester, Mass., 1945; S.T.L., Catholic U. Am., 1951; postgrad., Oxford (Eng.) U., 1958-59, 69-70. Ordained priest Roman Cath. Ch., 1951; pastor, tchr., adminstr. Diocese of Albany, 1951-58; resident Cath. chaplain Rensselaer Poly. Inst., Troy, N.Y., 1959-72, prof. history, 1972—, dean Sch. Humanities and Social Scis., 1972-95, inst. historian, inst. dean, sr. adviser to pres., 1995—. Chmn. architecture and bldg. commn. Diocese Albany, 1968—; cons. in field. Author: Hudson Mohawk Gateway, 1985, Achieving the Impossible, 1995; author monographs, articles, revs. in field. Treas. The Rensselaer Newman Found., 1962—; pres. Hudson-Mohawk Indsl. Gateway, 1971-84, bd. dirs. exec. com. 1984—; mem. WMHT Ednl. Telecomm. Bd., 1966-77, 84-90, chmn. 1973-77; chmn. Troy Hist. Dist. and Landmarks Rev. Commn., 1975-86, chmn. hist. adv. com., 1987—; v.p. Preservation League N.Y. State, 1979-82, mem. trustees coun., 1982-87, 89—, pres. 1987-89; sec. and bd. dirs. Ptnrs. for Sacred Places, 1989—; bd. dirs. Hall of History Found., 1983-87; trustee Troy Pub. Libr., 1992—. With USN, 1943-46. Recipient Paul J. Hallinan award Nat. Newman Chaplains Assn., 1967, Ann. award Albany Arts League, 1977, Disting. Cmty. Svc. award Rensselaer Poly. Inst., 1979, Edward Fox Demers medal Alumni Assn. Rensselaer Poly. Inst., 1986, Disting. Svc. award Hudson-Mohawk Consortium of Colls. and Univs., 1988; named Acad. Laureate of the SUNY Found. at Albany, 1988; Danforth Found. fellow, 1969-70; grantee Homeland Found., 1958-59, Dorothy Thomas Found., 1969-70. Fellow Soc. Arts, Religion and Contemporary Culture; mem. Ch. Soc. Coll. Work (dir., exec. com. 1970—), Am. Conf. Acad. Deans, Liturgical Conf., Soc. Indsl. Archaeology, Assn. Internat. pour l'Etudes des Religions Prehistoriques et Ethnologiques, Cath. Campus Ministry Assn., Cath. Art Assn., Assn. for Religion and the Intellectual Life (bd. dirs. 1987—), Soc. History of Tech. Clubs: Ft. Orange, Troy Country; Squadron A (N.Y.C.). Home: 5 Whitman Ct Troy NY 12180-4732 Office: Rensselaer Poly Inst Troy NY 12180 E-mail: phelan@rpi.edu. *Service and community building have motivated most of my business and personal actions. I received these values from my parents and from the church. I work to make positive contributions towards a world in which there is more justice and consequent hope of peace.*

PHELAN, THOMAS DOUGLAS, power company executive; b. Hattiesburg, Miss., Dec. 6, 1946; s. Douglas Edward and Velma Lee (Wyatt) P.; m. Claire Hennings, Dec. 26, 1966 (div. Feb. 1985); 1 child, Andrew Leonard. BS, SUNY, New Paltz, 1969; MS, SUNY, Albany, 1973, cert. specialist, 1976; DEd, Syracuse (N.Y.) U., 1996. Cert. sch. dist. adminstr., supr., tchr. N-9 English, N.Y. Tchr., dir. adult edn. Red Hook (N.Y.) Ctrl. Sch., 1969-77; acting prin. Boynton Jr. H.S., Ithaca, N.Y., 1977; asst. prin., dir. adult edn. Ichabod Crane Ctrl. Sch., Valatie, 1977-82; prin Tamarac Middle Sch., Troy, 1982-85; prin. Parker Elem. Sch., Cortland, 1985-88; sr. cons. Strategic Tchg. Assocs., Liverpool, 1988—; mgr. emergency planning and employee comms. Niagara Mohawk Power Corp., Syracuse, 1990—. Adv. bd. Public Safety Inst., Syracuse, 1996-97, OCC Tech Prep, Syracuse, 1994-97; pres. Ctrl. N.Y. Coalition of Adult and Continuing Edn., Syracuse, 1996-98. Author: (with others) New Directions in Adult Education, 1994, Current Developments in Self-Directed Learning, 1996; contbr. articles to profl. jours. Bus. rep. Goals 2000 Com., Syracuse, 1996—; founder CNY Workforce Prep. Conf., Syracuse, 1994-95; v.p., bd. dirs. Cortland Repertory Theatre, 1987-88. Recipient Outstanding Adult Edn. Profl. Ctrl. N.Y. Coalition Adult Continuing Edn., 1994, Leadership award, 1999. Mem. Ctrl. N.Y. Coalition for Adult and Continuing Edn. (v.p. 1995-96, pres. 1996-98). Avocation: vocal soloist. Office: Niagara Mohawk Power Corp 300 Erie Blvd W Syracuse NY 13202-4250

PHELAND, EILEEN HOPE, writer; b. Bklyn., July 22, 1965; d. Bernard and Phyllis (Halpern) P. Writer, publ. Happy Hour Newsletter, N.Y.C., 1999—. Author: The Truth About Being Homeless, 1998. Avocations: karaoke singing as street performer. Home: PO Box 18 Beverly Hills CA 90213-0018

PHELIZON, JEAN FRANCOIS, business executive; b. Paris, Apr. 28, 1946; s. Christian and Anne (Camuset) P.; m. Isabelle Delatour, July 3, 1971; children: Camille, Constance, Charlotte. MBA and MS, Paris U., 1970, PhD in Econ. Sci., 1975. Contr. Flat Glass div. St. Gobain, Paris, 1979; CFO St. Gobain Spain, Madrid, 1983-85; CFO paper wood div. St. Gobain, Paris, 1985-89; CEO, Lembacel, Lyon, France, 1988-89; CFO, Compagnie St. Gobain, Paris, 1989-2000, sr. v.p., 1998—; pres., CEO, Saint-Gobain Corp., 2000—; CEO, Certain Teed, 2000—. Editor: Economica, 1970, 2d edit. 1977, 3d edit. 1985, 4th edit. 1998, also 1998, 99, 2001, Masson, 1981, 2d edit. 1984, Decorated chevalier Order of Merit, Legion of Honor. Home: 1315 Wrenfield Way Villanova PA 19085 Office: SG Corp PO Box 860 750 E Swedesford Rd Valley Forge PA 19482 E-mail: jfp@sgcna.com.

PHELPS, ASHTON, JR. newspaper publisher; b. New Orleans, Nov. 4, 1945; s. Ashton Sr. and Jane Cary (George) P.; children— Cary Clifton, Mary Louise, Sanders. BA, Yale U., 1967; JD, Tulane U., 1970. Trainee Times-Picayune Pub. Corp., New Orleans, 1970-71, asst. to pub., 1971-79, pres., pub., 1979-97, pub., 1997—. Bd. dirs. Bur. Govtl. Rsch., New Orleans, 1973-89, Xavier U. of La., New Orleans, 1974-82, Coun. for Better La., 1982-85, Met. Area Com., New Orleans, Ochsner Found. Hosp., New Orleans, 1982—, Internat. House, New Orleans, 1981-83, Pub. Affairs Rsch. Coun., New Orleans, 1982-85, 2000—, La. Children's Mus., New Orleans, 1983-90, Yale Alumni Assn. of La., 1985, Newspaper Advt. Bur. Future of Advt. Com., 1986-89; chmn. Audit Com. of Associated Press, 1986-90, mem. nominating com., 1996—. Mem. So. Newspaper Pubs. Assn. (bd. dirs. 1982-85, found. bd. dirs. 1982-83, pres. 1990-91), La. Press Assn. (bd. dirs. 1984-93, v.p. 1989-90, pres. 1991-92). Avocation: tennis. Office: The Times-Picayune 3800 Howard Ave New Orleans LA 70125-1429

PHELPS, BARTON CHASE, architect, educator; b. Bklyn., June 27, 1946; s. Julian Orville and Elizabeth Willis (Faulk) P.; m. Karen Joy Simonson; 1 child, Charlotte Simonson Phelps. BA in Art with honors, Williams Coll., 1968; MArch, Yale U., 1973. Registered architect, Calif. With Colin St. John Wilson & Ptnrs., London, 1972-73, Frank O. Gehry and Assocs., Inc., Santa Monica, Calif., 1973-76, Charles Moore/Urban Innovations Group, L.A., 1976-78; dir. architecture Urban Innovations Group, 1980-84; prin. Barton Phelps & Assocs., 1984—; asst. prof. architecture Rice U. Sch. of Architecture, Houston, 1977-79; asst. dean Grad. Sch. Architecture and Urban Planning, UCLA, 1980-83; former prof. architecture Sch. Arts and Architecture UCLA. Faculty mem. Nat. Endowment Arts, Mayors Inst. for City Design, 1990, 92. Author, editor Architecture California, 1988-92, mem. editl. bd., 1998; editor: Views From the River, 1998; mem. editl. bd. Archtl. Record, 1998—. Fellow Graham Found. for Advanced Studies in the Fine Arts, 1989, 96, Nat. Endowment for the Arts, 1990, 98. Mem. AIA (Coll. of Fellows, chair nat. com. on design, design excellence program USGSA, recipient design awards for L.A. Pub. Libr., Los Feliz and Woodland Hills, Cabrillo Marine Aquarium, Royce Hall at UCLA, Arroyo House, Kranz House, North Range Clark Libr. UCLA, L.A. Dept. Water and Power Ctrl. Dist. Hdqrs., No. Hollywood Pump Sta., East Bldg. Seeds U. Elem. Sch., UCLA, Inst. Honor for Collaborative Design, Games XXIII Olympiad L.A. 1984), L.A. Conservancy (bd. dirs.). Democrat. Home: 10256 Lelia Ln Los Angeles CA 90077-3144 Office: Barton Phelps & Assocs 5514 Wilshire Blvd Los Angeles CA 90036-3829

PHELPS, CAROL JO, neuroendocrinologist; b. Sendai, Japan, Apr. 20, 1948; d. Harry J. and Helen I. (Davies) P.; m. James B. Turpen, June 13, 1969 (div. Apr. 1982); children: J. Matthew Turpen, John A. Turpen; m. David L. Hurley, Oct. 12, 1985. BS in Zoology, U. Denver, 1969; PhD in Anatomy, La. State U. Med. Ctr., 1974. Postdoctoral fellow NIH, U. Rochester, N.Y., 1974-76; rsch. assoc. Pa. State U., Univ. Park, 1976-77, instr., 1977-80, postdoctoral scholar, 1980-82; asst. prof. neurobiology U. Rochester, 1982-90; assoc. prof. anatomy Tulane U. Sch. Medicine, New Orleans, 1990-94; prof., 1994—. Nat. scientific adv. coun. Am. Fedn. Aging Rsch., N.Y.C., 1988—; rev. coms. Nat. Inst. on Aging, Bethesda, Md., 1993-97; editl. bd. Neuroendocrinology, Paris, 1994—, Endocrinology, 1996—, Jour. of Andrology, 1996-99. Com. sec., chair Otetiana Coun. Pack 10 Boy Scouts Am., Honeoye Falls, N.Y., 1987-89. NIH fellow, 1974-76; grantee NIH, 1983—. Mem. Am. Assn. Anatomists, Soc. Exptl. Biology and Medicine, Endocrine Soc., Soc. Neurosci. (chpt. pres. 1995-96). Avocations: antique restoration, photography. Office: Tulane U Sch Medicine Dept Anatomy 1430 Tulane Ave New Orleans LA 70112-2699

PHELPS, CHARLES ELLIOTT, economics educator; b. N.Y.C., Apr. 20, 1943; s. McKinnie L. and Carolyn (McCleery) P.; m. Dale L. King, Sept. 2, 1967; children: Darin, Teresa. BA in Math., Pomona Coll., 1965; MBA, U. Chgo., 1968, PhD, 1973. Economist RAND Corp., Santa Monica, Calif., 1973-84; prof. econs. U. Rochester, N.Y., 1984—, provost, 1994—. Cons. JUREcon, Inc., L.A., 1977-86; pvt. cons., Rochester, N.Y., 1986—. Author: Health Economics, 3d edit., 2002; also over 70 articles. Fellow Nat. Bur. for Econ. Rsch.; mem. Inst. Medicine, Am. Econ. Assn., Nat. Acad. Social Ins., Soc. for Med. Decision Making (trustee 1991-93), Assn. for Pub. Policy Analysis (sec. 1982-91). Avocations: photography, archery, astronomy, canoeing, woodworking. Office: Office of the Provost U Rochester 200 Wallis Hall Rochester NY 14627-0001

PHELPS, CHARLOTTE DEMONTE, retired economics educator; b. East Orange, N.J., Jan. 26, 1933; d. Robert William and Marian Ethel (Page) DeMonte; m. Edmund Strother Phelps, 1957 (div. 1969). BA magna cum laude, Radcliffe Coll., 1955; MA, Yale U., 1956, PhD, 1961. Instr. Conn. Coll., New London, 1961; rsch. staff economist Cowles Found. and Econ. Growth Ctr., Yale U., 1963-65; postdoctoral rsch. felow com. on econ. stblzn. Social Sci. Rsch. Coun., 1965-68; asst. prof. dept. econs. Temple U., Phila., 1967-68, assoc. prof., 1969-97, prof., 1998-2000. Cons. Hay/McBer, 1999-2000. Author: Unconscious Motivation and Economic Choice, 1981; mem. editl. bd. : Jour. Econ. Behavior and Orgn., 1998—, mem. editl. bd. : Jour. Socio-Econs., 2001—; contbr. Mem. Phila. Cmty. Coordinated Child Care Coun., 1970-72; mem. schs. and scholarships com. Harvard-Radcliffe Clubs Phila., 1977-82. Vis. fellow Yale U., 1998-99; predoctoral grantee Commn. on Money and Credit, 1959-60, grantee Murray Rsch. Ctr., Radcliffe Coll., 1998-2000, Smith Richardson Found., 1998-2000. Mem. Am. Econ. Assn., Assn. Yale Alumni (del. 1994-97), YalClub Phila., Cosmopolitan Club Phila., Harvard Club Phila., Phi Beta Kappa. Home: 604 S Washington Sq Apt 2505 Philadelphia PA 19106-4129 Office: Temple U Dept Econs 879 W Ritter Annex Philadelphia PA 19122 E-mail: cdphelps@astro.temple.edu.

PHELPS, DAVID D. congressman; b. Eldorado, Ill., Oct. 26, 1947; m. Leslie Phelps; 4 children. BS, So. Ill. U. Mem. Ill. Ho. of Reps. from 118th dist., 1985-98; mem., chmn. healthcare com. 106th Congress from 19th Ill. dist., 1999—; mem. agr. com.; mem. small bus. Mem. Transp. and Motor Vehicles, Appropriations I, Energy, Environ. and Natural Resources, Edn. Appropriations, Human Svcs., Elem. and Secondary Edn., Counties and Twp., Econ. Devel. Coms. Ill. Ho. of Reps., vice chmn. Coal Devel. and Mktg., Econ. and Urban Devel. Coms., chmn. Health Care Com. Democrat. Home: RR 1 Box 114 Eldorado IL 62930-9727 Office: Ho of Reps 1523 Longworth Ho Office Bldg Washington DC 20515-1319*

PHELPS, DENNIS LANE, minister, educator, author; b. Monroe, La., July 23, 1955; s. Vaughn Lavelle and Vestal (Humphreys) P.; m. Robbin Jean Loewer, May 27, 1979; children: Kristen Lane, David Loewer. BA, La. Coll., 1978; MDiv, New Orleans Bapt. Theol. Sem., 1981; PhD, Southwestern Bapt. Theol. Sem., 1990. Ordained to ministry Bapt. Ch., 1978; cert. intern supr. Coord. ch. ministries La. Moral and Civic Found., Baton Rouge, 1973-79; staff evangelist Dennis Phelps Evangelistic Ministries, 1979—; pastor Brownfields Bapt. Ch., Baton Rouge, 1981-82; grader/teaching fellow Southwestern Bapt. Theol. Sem., Ft. Worth, 1982-87; pastor St. Francis Village Protestant Fellowship, Crowley, Tex., 1986-88; assoc. prof. of preaching Bethel Theol. Sem., St. Paul, 1988-99; assoc. tchg. pastor, exec. adminstr. Severns Valley Ch., Elizabethtown, Ky., 1998—. V.p. Global Horizons, Inc., 1994--. Editor Jour. of Am. Acad. Ministry, 1995-98. Mem. strategy coun. AD2000: Mission Twin Cities, 1994-98; chmn. resolutions com. Kk. Bapt. Conv., 2000—; bd. dirs. Youth Connection, Inc., 1997—; v.p. Hardin County Ministerial Assn., 2002. Named Southwesterner of Yr., Minn.-Wis. S.W. Bapt. Theol. Sem. Alumni, 1994. Mem. Inst. Bibl. Rsch., Religious Speech Comm. Assn., Acad. Homiletics, Am. Assn. Religion, Soc. Bibl. Lit., Assn. Practical Theology, Am. Acad. Ministry (charter), Nat. Storytelling Assn., Evang. Homiletics Soc. (charter), Southwestern Bapt. Theol. Sem. Alumni Assn. (pres. Ky. chpt. 1999-2000). Office: Severns Valley Ch PO Box 130 Elizabethtown KY 42702-0130

PHELPS, DOROTHY FRINK, civic worker; b. Macon, Ga., June 15, 1906; d. James Richard and Alma (Hall) Frink; m. John Grady Phelps, Feb. 18, 1929 (dec. Oct. 1981); children: Judith Ann Phelps Austin (dec.), John Richard Phelps. Cert. in bus. law, commerce, Fla. State Coll. Women, Tallahassee. Sec. Dir. Pub. Health and Welfare, Miami, 1925-39; ret., 1939. Editor Ch. News Notes, 1st United Meth. Ch., former offices held include chmn. Christian edn.; pres. Silver Bluff Elem. PTA, 1948; v.p. Shennandoah Jr. H.S. PTA; mem. exec. bd., pres. Miami Sr. H.S. PTA; vol. mentor program Milam Elem. Sch., Hialeah, Fla. Recipient award for 76 years serving in Christian edn., 1st United Meth. Ch., 1996. Mem. DAR, Miami Women's Panhellenic Assn. (pres. 1930-31), Miami Woman's Club, Delta Delta Delta Mother's Club, Delta Zeta. Democrat. Home: 5300 W 16th Ave Apt 310 Hialeah FL 33012-2104

PHELPS, EDMUND STROTHER, economics educator; b. Evanston, Ill., July 26, 1933; s. Edmund Strother and Florence Esther (Stone) P.; m. Viviana Regina Montdor, Oct. 1, 1974. BA, Amherst Coll., 1955, DLitt (hon.), 1985; MA, Yale U., 1956, PhD, 1959. Economist Rand Corp., Santa Monica, Calif., 1959-60; asst. prof. Yale U., Cowles Found., 1960-62, assoc. prof., 1963-66; vis. assoc. prof. M.I.T., 1962-63; prof. econs. U. Pa., Phila., 1966-71, Columbia U., 1971-78, 79-82, McVickar prof. polit. economy, 1982—; scholar Russell Sage Found., 1993-94; prof. NYU, 1978-79. Fellow Ctr. for Advanced Study in Behavioral Scis., 1969-70; sr. advisor Brookings Inst., 1976—; econ. advisor European Bank for Reconstrn. and Devel., 1991-94; mem. econ. policy panel Observatoire Francais des Conjonctures Economiques, 1991—. Author: numerous books including Golden Rules of Economic Growth, 1966, Microeconomic Foundations of Employment and Inflation Theory, 1970, Economic Justice, 1973, Studies in Macroeconomic Theory, Vol. I, 1979, Vol. II, 1980, Political Economy, 1985, The Slump in Europe, 1988, Structural Slumps, 1994, Rewarding Work, 1997. Fellow Social Sci. Rsch. Coun., 1966, Guggenheim fellow, 1978. Fellow AAAS, Am. Econ. Assn. (disting., exec. com. 1976-78, v.p. 1983, Kenan Enterprise award 1996), Econometric Soc.; mem. Nat. Acad. Scis., Phi Beta Kappa. Home: 45 E 89th St New York NY 10128-1251 Office: Columbia Univ Dept Economics New York NY 10027

PHELPS, GEORGE GRAHAM, computer systems engineer, consultant; b. Radford, Va., Aug. 13, 1963; s. Eugene Graham and Flora Doris (Baird) P.; m. Vickie St. Claire, Feb. 19, 1994 (div. Feb. 1997); 1 stepchild, Chase Kevin Irby. BA in Polit. Sci., U. Tenn., 1986. Cert. Novell Netware engr.; cert. product specialist Microsoft Windows 3.1 and Windows 95, Microsoft Corp. Pers. clk. U.S. Army Total Army Pers. Agy., Washington, 1987-88, U.S. Army Corps Engrs., Washington, 1988; network sys. engr. U.S. Army RDAISA, Radford, Va., 1988—; computer cons. Acculan Consulting, Pulaski, 1992—; prof. computer sci. New River C.C., Dublin, 1996—. Vol. Habitat for Humanity, Christiansburg, Va., 1994, Montgomery County Xmas Store, Christiansburg, 1994—, Red Cross, Radford, Va., 1995. Methodist. Avocation: home improvement. Office: US Army RDAISA PO Box 4 Radford VA 24143-0004

PHELPS, GERRY CHARLOTTE, economist, minister; b. Norman, Okla., Oct. 15, 1931; d. George and Charlotte LeNoir (Yowell) P.; 1 child, Scott. BA, U. Tex., 1963, MA, 1984; MDiv, San Francisco Theol. Seminary, 1981. Cert. tchr., Calif. Lectr. in econs. U. Houston, 1966-69; pastor United Meth. Ch., Kelseyville, Calif., 1980-82; sr. pastor Bethany United Methodist Ch., Bakersfield, 1982-84; founding exec. dir. Bethany Svc. Ctr., 1982-84; pres., founding exec. dir. Concern for the Poor, Inc., San Jose, Calif., 1985-92; pastor United Meth. Ch., Flatonia, Tex., 1993-97; founding exec. dir. CRISES, Austin, 1994-98, v.p. devel., 1998-99; pvt. practice cons. poverty issues, 1999—. Cons. to programs helping people out of poverty. *Rev. Phelps became a Christian during seven and a half years in prison. Upon parole, she studied for the ministry. After ordination in the United Methodist Church, she pastored three churches, including an Hispanic church. The churches grew rapidly, and later she trained pastors in church-growth methods. She started and ran two homeless shelters in California, 156 and 143 beds respectively. The last one became a national model because of documented 65-75% sucess rate. Using the same "tough love' approach, she began the LIFT project in Austin, organizing churches to help people successfully leave the Welfare System. As an ex-con, she is very grateful for the many opportunities of service.* Co-author: Nutrition for Better Living, 1999, Budgeting for Better Living, 1999. Mem. Task Force on the Homeless, San Jose, 1987, Santa Clara County, 1991. Recipient commendation Mayor of Bakersfield, 1984, Santa Clara County Bd. Suprs., 1992. Avocations: Latin American studies, refugee assistance, homeless assistance, study of connections between economic and social problems. Fax: 512-926-6222. E-mail: gphelps@austin.rr.com.

PHELPS, JAMES FRANKLIN, retired county official; b. Mobile, Ala., May 29, 1940; s. James Carlton and Ela Kate (Hendrix) P.; m. Florence Annette Coley, June 30, 1972; children: Brant Michael, Kenneth Coley. Student, U. Ala., Mobile, 1962-63. Auditor Tax Collector's Office, Mobile, 1971-82, chief clk., 1983-86, chief adminstr., 1987-89; adminstr. collection divsn. Mobile County Revenue Commrs. Office, 1989-96, adminstr., 1997—2002; ret., 2002. Republican. Baptist. Avocations: golf, woodworking, collecting and building die-cast model cars. Home: 9121 Howells Ferry Rd Semmes AL 36575-7207 E-mail: car57man@aol.com., fphelps@mobile-county.net.

PHELPS, JAMES SOLOMON, III, astrodynamic engineer; b. Balt., Mar. 2, 1952; s. James S. Jr. and Rachel (Bruton) P.; m. Suzanne Rowell, July 24, 1975; 1 child, Caroline. BSNE, N.C. State U., 1974, MS, 1977. Nuclear engr. Combustion Engring., Windsor, Conn., 1978-79; sr. engr. Advanced Tech., Reston, Va., 1980-81, Nuclear Power Cons., Rockville, Md., 1981-83; chief engr. GE Space System div. MDSO, Springfield, Va., 1983-89; chief systems engr. Hughes STX, Vienna, 1989-94; sr. scientist Scientific and Tech. Analysis Corp., Fairfax, 1994-96; chief sys. engr. Raytheon STX, Greenbelt, Md., 1996—. Cons. Submarine Maintenance Monitoring Support Office USN, Washington, 1988-90. Contbr. articles to profl. jours. Mem. Am. Nuclear Soc., Sigma Xi (assoc.). Achievements include devel. of a new approach to the use of process error in sequntial estimation.

PHELPS, JOSEPH ALFRED, social services administrator, small business owner; b. Detroit, May 4, 1927; s. Alfred Henry and Laura Etta (Flynn) P.; m. Alberta Johnigan, May 1, 1948 (div. Aug. 1971); children: Wanda M., Linda J., Joey A., David J., Shawn E. AA, Solano Community Coll., 1968; BA, Sonoma State U., 1974; MA, San Francisco State U., 1978. Cert. community coll. instr. (life). Enlisted USAF, 1945, advanced through grades to master sgt., 1965; served at various AFBs Calif., Alaska, Colo., also Fed. Republic Germany, 1946-67; retired USAF, 1967; adminstrv. services officer HHS Marin County, San Rafael, Calif., 1968—; instr. drama Solano Community Coll., Fairfield, 1978, 84-85; owner JAMV Pub. Co., Novato, 1985—. Author: On Being Black in America, 1978, Breaking Out--On Becoming More Than I Was, 1985; writer numerous poems; dir., producer local prodns. (plays) A Medal for Willie, The Amen Corner, A Raisin in the Sun. Active Concerned Parents of Novato, 1986. Recipient Non-fiction Writer's award Santa Barbara (Calif.) Writer's Conf., 1984, Poetry Achievement award Santa Barbara Writer's Conf., 1985, Outstanding Achievement in Writing award Santa Barbara Writer's Conf., 1986. Democrat. Congregationalist. Avocations: tennis organizer of agy. tournaments. Home: 3700 Lyon Rd Ste 265 Fairfield CA 94533-7991

PHELPS, LOUISE WETHERBEE, writing and rhetoric educator; b. Greenville, Miss., Aug. 5, 1940; d. Donald Gist and Virginia (LaRochelle) Wetherbee; m. Frederick Ward Phelps, June 16, 1962; children: Christopher Ward, Alexander Gist, Lon Wetherbee. BA in English summa cum laude, Vassar Coll., 1962; MA in Tchg. English, Johns Hopkins U., 1963; MA in English, Cleve. State U., 1976; PhD in English Composition and Rhetoric, Case Western Res. U., 1980. Instr. English Towson High Sch., Balt., 1963-65; dir. writing lab. Cleve. State U., 1973-77; asst. prof. English U. So. Calif., L.A., 1979-86; prof. writing and English Syracuse (N.Y.) U., 1986—, dir. writing program, 1986-92. Author: Composition as a Human Science, 1988; co-editor: Feminine Principles and Women's Experience in Am. Composition and Rhetoric, 1995, Composition in Four Keys, 1995; guest editor jour. Pre/Text, 1983; contbr. articles to profl. jours. Am. Coun. Edn. fellow, 1993-94. Mem. MLA, Am. Assn. Higher Edn., Nat. Coun. Tchrs. English, Writing Program Adminstrs., Conf. Coll. Composition and Comm., Phi Beta Kappa. Avocation: jazz piano. Office: Syracuse U H B C # 239 Syracuse NY 13244-0001

PHELPS, MICHAEL EDWARD, biophysics educator; b. Cleve., Aug. 24, 1939; s. Earl E. and Regina Bridget (Hines) P.; m. Patricia Emory, May 15, 1969; children: Patrick, Kaitlin. BA, Western Wash. State U., 1965; PhD, Washington U., St. Louis, 1970. Asst. prof. Washington U. Sch. Medicine and Engring., 1970-73, assoc. prof., 1973-75; assoc. prof. dept. radiology U. Pa., Phila., 1975-76; prof. biomath. UCLA, 1976—, prof., chief div. nuclear medicine, 1980—, dir. Crump Inst. for Biol. Imaging, 1990—, chair molecular and med. pharmacology, 1992—; assoc. dir. UCLA/DOE Lab. Structural Biology and Molecular Medicine; dir. UCLA/DOE Inst. Molecular Medicine, 1989—2002. Mem. study sect. NIH, Bethesda, Md., 1974-78. Author: Reconstruction Tomography in Diagnostic Radiology and Nuclear Medicine, 1977, Physics in Nuclear Medicine, 1980, 1987, 2002, Principles of Tracer Kinetics, 1983; contbr. articles to profl. jours. Recipient Von Hevesy Found. award, 1975, Von Hevesy Found. award, 1982, Von Hevesy prize Von Hevesy Found., Zurich, 1978, 82, E.O. Lawrence award Dept. Energy, 1983, Pasarow Found. award, 1992, Enrico Fermi Presdl. award, 1999, GM Kettering prize, 2001; holder Norton Simon endowed chair, 1983-; named Disting. Alumnus Western Wash. State U., 1980 Fellow Am. Heart Assn.; mem. ACP (Rosenthal award 1987), Inst. Medicine NAS (elected), Nat. Acad. Scis. (elected 1999), Soc. Nuclear Medicine (Aebersold award 1983), Internat. Soc. Cerebral Blood Flow and Metabolism (Excellence award 1979), N.Y. Acad. Scis. (Sarah L. Poiley award 1984), Soc. Neuroscis. Roman Catholic. Home: 16720 Huerta Rd Encino CA 91436-3544

PHELPS, MICHAEL EDWARD, publishing executive; b. Terre Haute, Ind., Nov. 9, 1945; s. Bernard Fred and Margaret Leah (Sullivan) P.; m. D. Elizabeth DuVall, Oct. 22, 1966 (div. Jan. 1996); children: Aimee DuVall, Jeremiah Sullivan; m. Louise Dennett Levin-Cutler, Dec. 26, 1996. AB in Econs., Miami U. Ohio, 1966; MA in Journalism, Mich. State U., 1971. Reporter Falmouth (Mass.) Enterprise, 1971-78, news editor, 1978-80, mng. editor, 1980-86, asst. to pub., 1983-86; pres., pub. The Weekly Group, Newspapers of New England, Concord, N.H., 1986-89; mng. prin. Phelps, Cutler & Assocs., Falmouth, 1990-93, Marshfield Hills, Mass., 1993-94, Savannah, Ga., 1995—. Mem. profl. adv. coun. Journalism Sch., Mich. State U., East Lansing. With USNR, 1966-69. Mem. Newspaper Assn. Am., Soc. Profl. Journalists, Assn. Edn. in Journalism and Mass Comm., Nat. Press Club, Rotary (Davenport), Savannah Yacht Club, Kappa Tau Alpha, Phi Delta Theta. Democrat. Roman Catholic. Avocations: fishing, racquetball. Home: PO Box 3828 Davenport IA 52808-3635 Office: 500 E. Third St Davenport IA 52801

PHELPS, ROBIN MCCANN, clinical social worker; b. Cleveland, Tenn., Dec. 7, 1957; d. William Donald and Joyce Ann (Guffey) McC.; m. Neal Harris Phelps III, Dec. 18, 1981; children: Amber Rae, Miranda Brooke, Neal Harris IV. BS, Brigham Young U., 1979; MS, U. Utah, 1983. Lic. social worker. Psychiat. technician Utah State Hosp., Provo, 1980-81, children and youth coord., 1984-86; psychiat. social worker Hiwassee Mental Health Ctr., Cleveland, 1983-86; social svc. cons. Omni Home Health, 1985-87; psychiat. social worker Kenneth E. Shoemaker, M.D., 1985-89, Davidson Clinic, Farmington, Utah, 1989-91, Mountain Heights Clinic, 1991-94, Layton Care Ctr., Utah, 1994—. Presenter in field. Mem. C.A.P.P., Inc., Cleveland, 1985, Child Abuse Rev. Bd., Cleveland, 1985; mem. treatment com. Child Sexual Abuse Investigative Team, Cleveland, 1985. Mem. NASW. Avocations: snow skiing, swimming, outdoor recreations. Home: 1594 E 2475 N Layton UT 84040-7080 Office: PO Box 1253 Layton UT 84041-6253

PHELPS, WAYNE HOWE, educational administrator; b. Potsdam, N.Y., Sept. 2, 1938; s. Elmer R. and Floy E. (Howe) P. BA in English magna cum laude, St. Lawrence U., Canton, N.Y., 1959; MA in English, Princeton U., 1961, PhD in English, 1965. Instr., then asst. prof. English U. Pa., Phila., 1962-72; asst. prof. Va. Poly. Inst. and State U., Blacksburg, 1972-77; rsch. assoc. acad. programs State Coun. Higher Edn. for Va., Richmond, 1978-80, rsch. assoc. instl. approval, 1980, coord. instl. approval, 1980-82; dir. planning and ednl. rsch. W.Va. Bd. Regents, Charleston, 1982-86. Student pers. officer U. Pa., Phila., 1963-66; editl. cons. Univ. Self-Study, Va. Poly. Inst. and State U., 1975-76. Contbr. articles to various profl. publs., 1962-80. Bd. dirs. Friends of Owen D. Young and Launders Librs., St. Lawrence U., 1989—. Woodrow Wilson Nat. fellow Princeton U., 1959-60, jr. fellow, 1960-61, summer fellow, 1961, 62; Charles Scribner jr. fellow, 1961-62. Mem. Phi Beta Kappa, Pi Mu Epsilon. Home: 59 Bird St Canton NY 13617-1232 Office: Saint Lawrence U Owen D Young Libr Park St Canton NY 13617

PHEMISTER, ROBERT DAVID, veterinary medical educator; b. Framingham, Mass., July 15, 1936; s. Robert Irving and Georgia Nora (Savignac) P.; m. Ann Christine Lyon, June 14, 1960; children: Katherine, David, Susan. D.V.M., Cornell U., 1960; PhD, Colo. State U., Ft. Collins, 1967. Diplomate: Am. Coll. Vet. Pathologists. Research assoc. U. Calif., Davis, 1960-61, vis. rsch. pathologist, 1974-75; staff scientist Armed Forces Inst. Pathology, Washington, 1962-64; sect. leader to dir. collaborative radiol. health lab. Colo. State U., 1964-77; mem. faculty Coll. Vet. Medicine and Biomed. Scis., 1968-85, prof. vet. pathology, 1973-85, assoc. dean, 1976-77, assoc. dir. expt. sta., 1977-85, dean, 1977-85, interim acad. v.p. Univ., 1982, interim pres. Univ., 1983-84, spl. counselor to pres., 1984-85; vis. prof. Colo. State U., 1995-96; prof. vet. pathology Cornell U., 1985-99, dean and prof. emeritus, 1999—, dean Coll. Vet. Medicine, 1985-95. Cons. Miss. State U., 1977-81; commr. Colo. Advanced Tech. Inst., 1983-84; mem. governing bd. N.Y. Sea Grant Inst., 1985-95, vice chmn., 1990-92; mem. vet. medicine adv. com. FDA, 1984-88; mem. joint coun. on food and agrl. scis. USDA, 1988-92, mem. exec. com., 1989-92; chmn. Zweig Meml. Fund for Equine Rsch., 1985-95; mem. adv. panel for vet. medicine Pew Health Professions Commn., 1991-93. Author papers in field. Served to comdr. USPHS, 1960-68. Recipient Charles A. Lory award and Disting. Univ. Leadership award Colo. State U., 1984, Disting. Practitioner award Nat. Acad. Practice, 1985, Regional Health Adminstr.'s award, 1985; named Honor Alumnus, Colo. State U., 1989. Mem. AVMA (coun. on edn. 1985-91, adv. bd. vet. specialities 1985-89), Assn. Am. Vet. Med. Colls. (pres. 1982-83), Colo. Vet. Med. Assn. (Disting. Svc. award 1985), N.Y. State Vet. Med. Soc. (Centennial award 1990), Sigma Xi, Phi Zeta, Phi Kappa Phi, Gamma Sigma Delta (Merit award for Adminstrn. 1995). Home: 5110 Hogan Ct Fort Collins CO 80528-8801

PHEMISTER, THOMAS ALEXANDER, lawyer; b. Framingham, Mass., June 2, 1940; s. Robert Irving and Georgia Nora (Savignac) P.; m. Lois Ann Devol, Dec. 28, 1963; children: Michael Anderson, Elizabeth Lynn, Mary Nicole, Virginia Noel. BA, Carleton Coll., 1962; JD, U. Chgo., 1965. Bar: Ill., Colo. 1965. Pvt. practice law, Chgo., 1965—69; gen. atty. Western R.R. Assn., 1969—71; in law practice with Richard J. Hardy, Washington, 1972—73; gen. atty. Assn. Am. R.R.s, 1973—79; dir. Bur. Explosives Assn. Am. Railroads, 1979—85; sole practice Washington, 1985—87; with Office Chief Counsel Fed. R.R. Adminstrn., 1987—2002; sr. hazardous materials specialist Office of Safety, 2002—. Mem. dept. of transp. intermodal hazardous materials attys. group, 1989—; mem. com. on transp. of hazardous materials Transp. Rsch. Bd., 1980-86; mem. nat. motor carrier adv. com. Fed. Hwy. Adminstrn., 1982-86; mem. Can. Nat. Rail Task Force for Movements of Dangerous Commodities, 1985; mem. hazardous materials control course oversight com. Tex. A&M U., 1981-87; mem. bd. correction mil. records USCG, 1992—. Pub.: Emergency Handling of Hazardous Materials in Surface Transportation, 1981, Hazardous Materials Regulations Excerpted for Railroad Employees, 1981, Emergency Action Guides, 1983; author: A Report on Tank Cars: Federal Oversight of Design Construction and Repair, 1990, Forward through the 90s: A Report on Selected Issues in the Transportation by Rail of Hazardous Materials, 1994. Mem. Fairfax County Drug Task Force chpt. Parents Alliance to Neutralize Drug and Alcohol Abuse (PANDAA), 1987—89, Kairos Prison Ministries, 1997—; mem. teams 1, 2, 3, 4, 5, 8, lead percussionist, teams 2, 3, 4, 5, 8 Va. Augusta Correctional Ctr., 1997—99; adult advisor Fairfax County 4-H Horse Forum, 1988—; adult overall advisor Fairfax County 4H Fair Horse Show; treas. Ill. Lawyers for McCarthy, 1968; trustee First Congregational Ch., Western Springs, Ill., 1970—71; mem. program ministries coun. United Christian Parish of Reston, Va., 1980—82, mem. South Lakes vestry, 1984—87, mem. parish bd., deacon, ministries com., 1987—93; bd. dirs. Upper Room Emmaus of nat. capital area, 1989—90, lay leader, 1990. Mem. Hunters Valley Riding Club (bd. dirs., v.p. 1993-94). Home: 10802 Dayflower Ct Reston VA 20191-5110 Office: 1120 Vermont Ave NW MS10 Washington DC 20590-0001 E-mail: wagsdadt@hotmail.com., tom.phemister@fra.dot.gov. *Integrity is an absolute essential - both preserving my own and dealing with other people so that they, too, do not have to compromise on matters of principle.*

PHIBBS, BRENDAN PEARSE, cardiologist; b. N.Y.C., Dec. 3, 1916; s. Harry Clandillon Phibbs and Teresa Ann Kelly; m. Marie-Claire Harle, June 24, 1940 (dec. Sept. 1975); m. Liana Fernandez de Castro, Apr. 10, 1982; children: Susan, Henry, Judith, Hugh. MD, Northwestern U., 1941, MS in Physiology. Diplomate Am. Bd. Internat. Medicine, Am. Bd. Cardiovascular Medicine. Intern St. Luke's Hosp., Chgo., 1941-42, resident, 1946-47, rsch. fellow, 1947-48, preceptor in cardiology, 1948-50; clin. faculty mem. Northwestern U. Med. Sch., 1948-52; pvt. practice Casper, Wyo., 1952-71; dir. No. Wyo. Streptococcal Control Lab., 1954-71; dir. cardiopulmonary unit Natrona County Meml. Hosp., Casper, 1969-71; dir. diagnostic cardiology U. Ariz. Coll. Medicine, 1971-74, clin. assoc. prof. medicine, 1975-78, prof. clin medicine sect. cardiology, 1978—; chief cardiology Pima County Hosp., Tucson, 1975-77; chief medicine, dir. cardiology Kino Cmty. Hosp., 1977-84, chief cardiology, 1983—87; dir. rsch. Wyo. Heart Inst., 1984-87. Instr. Cook County Postgrad. Sch., 1948-50; cons. Papago Streptococcal Project, 1971-82, Navajo Streptococcal Project, 1973-74; dir. Chronic Lung Disease Rehab. Project, 1968-71; asst. clin. prof. medicine dept. cardiology U. Colo. Sch. Medicine, 1967-71; cardiac cons. Ariz. Regional Med. Program, 1971. Author: The Cardiac Arrhythmias, 1961, 3d edit., 1978, The Human Heart, The Layman's Guide to Heart Disease, 1967, 7th edit., 1997, The Human Heart, A Consumer's Guide to Cardiac Care, 1982, Emergency Handbook: Symptomatic Arrhythmias: Emergency Care, 1992, Advanced ECG. Boards and Beyond — What you really need to know about electrocardiography, 1997; contbr. numerous articles to profl. jours. Mag's. Med. Corps U.S. Army, 1942-46. Fellow ACP, Am. Coll. Cardiology (gov. Wyo. chpt. 1968-70, long range planning com., continuing edn. com., peer rev. com., electrocardiographic interpretation com.). Address: 5300 E Camino Bosque Tucson AZ 85718-3813

PHIBBS, CLIFFORD MATTHEW, surgeon, educator; b. Bemidji, Minn., Feb. 20, 1930; s. Clifford Matthew and Dorothy Jean (Wright) P.; m. Patricia Jean Palmer, June 27, 1953; children— Wayne Robert, Marc Stuart, Nancy Louise BS, Wash. State U., 1952; MD, U. Wash., 1955; MS, U. Minn., 1960. Diplomate Am. Bd. Surgery. Intern Ancker Hosp., St. Paul, 1955-56; resident in surgery U. Minn. Hosps., 1956-60; practice medicine specializing in surgery Oxboro Clinic, Mpls., 1962—, pres., 1985—; cons. to health risk mgmt. corps., 1994—. Mem. Children's Hosp. Ctr., Northwestern-Abbott Hosp., Fairview-Southdale Hosp., Fairview Ridges Hosp.; clin. asst. prof. U. Minn., Mpls., 1975-78, clin. assoc. prof. surgery, 1978—; med. dir. Minn. Protective Life Ins. Co. Contbr. articles to med. jours. Bd. dirs. Bloomington Bd. Edn., Minn., 1974— , treas., 1976, sec., 1977-78, chmn., 1981-83; mem. adv. com. jr. coll. study City of Bloomington, 1964-66, mem. community facilities com., 1966-67, advisor youth study commn., 1966-68; vice chmn. bd. Hillcrest Meth. Ch., 1970-71; mem. Bloomington Adv. and Rsch. Coun., 1969-71; bd. dirs. Bloomington Symphony Orch., 1976— , Wash. State U. Found., trustee, 1990—; dir. bd. mgmt. Minnesota Valley YMCA, 1970-75; bd. govs. Mpls. Met. YMCA, 1970—; bd. dirs. Bloomington Heart-Health Found., 1989—, Martin Luther Manor, 1989; pres. Oxboro Clinics, 1985—; bd. dirs. Bloomington History Clock Tower Assn., 1990—; bd. dirs. Fairview Hosp. Clinic, 1994—, Bloomington Sister city Orgn., 1999-, Bloomington Cmty. Found., 1997-, Bloomington Health Adv. Bd., 1999-, Com. on Cult. Competence Minnesota Med. Assn., 19986. Capt. M.C., U.S. Army, 1960-62. Mem. ACS, AMA (Physician Recognition awards 1969, 73, 76, 79, 82, 85, 88, 91, 94), Assn. Surg. Edn., Royal Soc. Medicine, Am. Coll. Sports Medicine, Minn. Med. Assn. (del. 1991-94), Minn. Surg. Soc., Mpls. Surg. Soc., Hennepin County Med. Soc., Pan-Pacific Surg. Assn., Jaycees, Bloomington C. of C. (chmn. bd. 1984, chmn. 1985-86). Home: 9613 Upton Rd Minneapolis MN 55431-2454 Office: 600 W 98th St Minneapolis MN 55420-4773

PHIBBS, HARRY ALBERT, interior designer, professional speaker, lecturer; b. Denver, Jan. 9, 1933; s. Harry Andrew and Mary May (Perriam) P.; m. Alice Conners Glynn, Oct. 23, 1957 (div. Jan. 1988); children: Kathleen Ann Phibbs Pierz, Paul Robert, Mary Alice Phibbs Hettle, Michael John, Peter James, Daniel Edward; m. Nevelle Haley Jones, Feb. 1988. BA, U. Colo., 1954, B.F.A., 1957. Interior designer Howard Lorton, Inc., Denver, 1957-68; interior designer, v.p. Ronald Ansay Inc., Wheatridge, Colo., 1969-71; interior designer, pres. Phibbs Design Assos., Inc., Denver, 1972-78; interior designer, mgr. Howard Lorton, Inc., Colorado Springs, Colo., 1979-93; prin. Phibbs Design, 1993—. Pres. Interior Designers Housing Devel. Corp., 1969-72; chmn. adv. com. interior design program Pikes Peak C.C., 1998—; adj. faculty, Pike's Peak C.C., 2000—. V.p. Arvada (Colo.) Hist. Soc., 1973; bd. dirs. Colo. Opera Festival, also pres., 1986; bd. dirs. Downtown Colorado Springs, Inc., also pres., 1984; chmn. bd. trustees Interior Design Internship Denver, 1991-94. With U.S. Army, 1954-56. Fellow Am. Soc. Interior Designers (nat. pres. 1977); mem. Am. Arbitration Assn., Theta Xi (pres. Denver Area alumni club 1958-64) Democrat. Roman Catholic. Home: 91 W Boulder St Colorado Springs CO 80903-3371 *Each of God's infinite creations was carefully placed on earth with the same responsibility....to grow. Man has the unique role in that plan in that he can help other things and the people around him to grow. This process is contingent upon "loving your neighbor as yourself." Transposing the equation therefore requires that you love yourself. I wish I had learned at an earlier age to take what you do seriously, but not to take yourself too seriously.*

PHIFER, FORREST KEITH, lawyer; b. Port Arthur, Tex., Jan. 3, 1956; s. Ernest Carl and Ollie (Decker) P.; m. Teresa Darlene Jowell, Febr. 20, 1993. BFA, So. Meth. U., 1978; JD, South Tex. Coll. Law, 1988. Bar: Tex. 1989, U.S. Dist. Ct. (ea., no. and so. dists.) Tex. 1990, U.S. Ct. Appeals (5th cir.) 1990, U.S. Supreme Ct. 1994. Briefing atty. 12th Supreme Jud. Dist. Ct. Appeals, Tyler, Tex., 1989-90; assoc. Norman, Thrall, Angle & Guy, Rusk, 1990-95; pvt. practice, 1996—; city atty. City of Rusk, 1996—; alt. judge Mcpl. Ct., Jacksonville, Tex., 1998—; city atty. New Somerfield, 2000—. Active So. Meth. U. TV Guild, Dallas, 1977—78, U.S.A. Film Festival, Dallas, 1978, Cherokee County Civic Theatre, 2001—; pres., co-founder Tyler United Meth. Dist. Singles Coun., 1989—90; bd. dirs. Cherokee County Child and Family Svcs., 1990—93, Cherokee County Health Adv. Bd., 1991—, Cherokee County Indsl. Commn., 1991—; chmn., pres. Rusk Make It Happen, 1991—92. Mem. ABA, ATLA, Tex. Trial Lawyers Assn., Tex. Criminal Def. Lawyers Assn., U.S. Fifth Cir. Bar Assn., Tex. Bar Assn., Coll. State Bar Tex. (pro bono), Cherokee County Bar Assn. (sec.-treas. 1994-95, pres. 1995-96), Cherokee County Dem. Club (pres. 2000-01), Rotary (pres. 1992-93, 2000-01), Phi Delta Phi. Avocations: photography, theatre, fine arts. Office: 509 N Main PO Box 829 Rusk TX 75785-0829

PHILBERT, ROBERT EARL, secondary school educator; b. Anderson, Ind., Nov. 17, 1946; s. James William and Lois Louise (Hartman) P.; m. Cheryl Toney, July 24, 1976. BS, Ball State U., Muncie, Ind., 1969, MA, 1974, EdD, 1987. Cert. social sci. tchr., Ind. Tchr. chair dept. social sci. Marion (Ind.) Cmty. Schs., 1969—; instr. social sci. methods Ball State U., 1983. Cons. St. Paul-Bennett Schs., St. Paul's Sch. Bd., Marion, 1990-93, I.S.T.E.P. validation com., Indpls., 1992; mem. Ind. State Textbook Adv. Bd., Indpls., 1992; participant NASA Tchr. in Space program; Marion Police Dept. candidate interview com., 1997. Mem. Citizen's Amb. Program, Social Studies Delegation to the Republic of Vietnam. Sgt. U.S. Army, 1970-72. Named Outstanding Educator, Marion High Sch., 1977-80. Mem. NEA, VFW, Nat. Coun. Social Studies, Ind. Coun. for the Social Studies, Ind. Tchrs. Assn., Marion Tchrs. Assn. (pres., v.p., award), Vietnam Vets Am., Am. Legion, Elks, Phi Alpha Theta, Pi Gamma Mu, Kappa Delta Pi, Phi Delta Kappa, Delta Tau Delta. Democrat. Roman Catholic. Avocations: white water rafting, traveling, dog training, photography. Home: 1703 W 32nd St Marion IN 46953-3435 Office: 750 W 26th St Marion IN 46953

PHILBIN, ANN MARGARET, brokerage house executive; b. Clinton, Mass., June 15, 1941; d. John J. and Angela J. (O'Flynn) P. AB, Trinity Coll., Washington, 1962. With Paine Webber, Boston, 1963—, v.p. adminstrn., 1985—. Arbitrator N.Y. Stock Exchange, Boston, 1987—. V.p. fundraising

Boston Symphony Assn. Vols., 2000; trustee Trinity Coll., 1992-95. Mem. Trinity Coll. Alumnae Assn. (1st v.p. 1989-92, pres. 1992-95, Alumnae Achievement award 1995). Office: Paine Webber 265 Franklin St Boston MA 02110-3196

PHILBRICK, DONALD LOCKEY, retired lawyer; b. Portland, Maine, May 3, 1923; s. Donald Ward and Ruth (Lockey) P.; children: Deborah Palmer, Sarah Peyton; adopted children: Paul Sloat, Mark Whitfield, Andrew Hunter; m. Janet Mitchell Poole, Aug. 7, 1982. AB, Bowdoin Coll., 1944; JD, Harvard U., 1948. Bar: Maine 1948. Pvt. practice, Portland; ptnr. Verrill & Dana, 1951-82. Selectman, Cape Elizabeth, Maine, 1957-63. Served with AUS, 1943-45; with USAF, 1951-53. Mem. Maine Hist. Soc. (past pres.), N.E. Hist. Gen. Soc., Delta Kappa Epsilon. Clubs: Portland Country. Republican. Congregationalist. Home: 15 Piper Rd Apt J-307 Scarborough ME 04074-7546 E-mail: dphilbr1@maine.rr.com.

PHILBROOK, MAUREEN, small business owner; b. Lowell, Mass., July 3, 1951; d. William Joseph and Mildred Harried (Macomber) Peake; m. Verne Haven Philbrook III, July 7, 1984; 1 child, Shane Michael. Grad. h.s., Billerica, Mass. Assembler Electronic Products Inc., Burlington, Mass., 1967-69; from assembler to mgr. MA-COM, Inc., 1969-88; pres. Wonderful Moments, Woburn, Mass., 1988—. Roman Catholic. Avocations: photography, reading, country music. Home: 90 Maple Ave Woburn MA 01801-2650

PHILIP, A. G. DAVIS, astronomer, editor, educator; b. N.Y.C., Jan. 9, 1929; s. Van Ness and Lillian (Davis) P.; m. Kristina Drobavicius, Apr. 25, 1964; 1 dau., Kristina Elizabeth Elanor. BS, Union Coll., 1951; MS, N.Mex. State U., 1959; PhD, Case Inst. Tech., 1964. Tchr. physics, math. and chemistry Brooks Sch., 1954-59; instr. Case Inst. Tech., 1962-64; asst. prof. astronomy U. N.Mex., 1964-66, SUNY-Albany, 1966-67, assoc. prof., 1967-76, mem. exec. com. Arts and Scis. Coun., 1975-76; rsch. prof. astronomy Union Coll., Schenectady, 1976—, astronomer Dudley Obs., 1967-81, Frank L. Fullam chair astronomy, 1980-81, editor Dudley Obs. Reports, 1977-81; astronomer Van Vleck Obs. Wesleyan U., 1982-94; editor contbns. VVObs., 1982-94; pres. Inst. for Space Observation, 1986—. 76, 86, Acad. Scis. Lithuania, 1973, 76, 79, 86, Stellar Data Ctr., Strasbourg, France, 1978, 79, 80, 82, 85, 86; vis. astronomer Moletai Obs., 1988, 94, 99, 2000, Vatican Advanced Tech. Telescope, 1996—, CASLEO, Argentina, 2000—; bd. dirs., sec.-treas. N.Y. Astron. Corp., 1969-2001; pres., treas. L. Davis Press, Inc., 1982—; trustee, mem. Grants award com. Fund Astrophys. Rsch., 1985—; dir. Shapley Vis. Lectureships Program, 1994—; rsch. bd. advisors Am. Biog. Inst., 1996-. Exhibited: 2d Ann. Photography Regional, Albany, 1980; author: (with M. Cullen and R.E. White) UBV Color - Magnitude Diagrams of Galactic Globular Clusters, 1976; (with A. Robucci, M. Frame, K.W. Philip) Mm, Fractal Series, Vol. 1, Midgets on the Spike, 1991; editor: The Evolution of Population II Stars, 1972, (with D.S. Hayes) Multicolor Photometry and the Theoretical HR Diagram, 1975, (with M.F. Mc Carthy) Galactic Structure in the Direction of the Galactic Polar Caps, 1977, (with D. H. DeVorkin In Memory of Henry Norris Russell, 1977, (with Hayes) The HR Diagram, 1978, Problems in Calibration of Multicolor Systems, 1979, (with M.F. McCarthy and G.V. Coyne) Spectral Classification of the Future, 1979, X-Ray Symposium, 1981, (with Hayes) Astrophysical Parameters for Globular Clusters, 1981, (with A.R. Upgren) The Nearby Stars and the Stellar Luminosity Function, 1983, (with Hayes and L. Pasinetti) Calibration of Fundamental Stellar Quantities, 1985, (with D.W. Latham) Stellar Radial Velocities, Horizontal-Branch and UV-Bright Stars, 1985, Spectroscopic and Photometric Classification of Population II Stars, 1986, (with J. Grindley) IAU Symposium No. 126, Globular Cluster Systems in Galaxies, 1987, (with Hayes and Liebert) IAU Colloquium No. 95, The Second Conference on Faint Blue Stars, (with Hayes and Adelman) New Directions in Spectrophotometry, 1988, Calibration of Stellar Ages, 1988, (with A.R. Upgren) Star Catalogues; A Centennial Tribute to A.N. Vyssotsky, 1989, (with P. Lu) The Gravitational Force Perpendicular to the Galactic Plane, 1989, (with D.S. Hayes and S.J. Adelman) CCDs in Astronomy. II. Precision Photometry: Astrophysics of the Galaxy, 1991, (with Robucci, Frame and Philip K.) Midgets on the Spike, vol. I, 1991, (with A.R. Upgren) Objective-Prism and Other Surveys, 1991, N.Y. State Astronomy, 1992, (with B. Hauck and A.R. Upgren) Workshop on Databases for Galactic Structure, 1993, (with K.A. Janes and A.R. Upgren) IAU Symposium No. 167, New Developments in Array Technology and Applications, 1995, (with V. Straizys) Photometric Systems and Standard Stars, 1996, 30 Years of Astronomy at Van Vleck Observatory, 1997, (with Peter Boyce) Electronic Publishing: Now and the Future, 1997, (with J. Liebert and R. Saffer) The Third Conference on Faint Blue Stars, 1997, (with W. van Alterna and A. Upgren) Anni Mirabiles: A Symposium Celebrating the 90th Birthday of Dorrit Hottleit, 1999, The Kth Reunion, 2000, (with R.A. Koopmann) The Starry Universe: The Cecilia Payne-Gaposchkin Centenary, 2001; mem. editl. bd., 1994—, co-editor, 1998—, Baltic Astronomy, Astrometric and Photometric Group, Wesleyan U., 1997—; lectr. tours (with K.W. Philip) An Introduction to the Mandelbrot Set, 1988-91; contbr. chpts. to books, articles to profl. jours.; worked with Dr. Irving Langmuir on "The Pathology of Science", 1950—. Served with AUS, 1951-53. Yale U. vis. fellow, 1976; rsch. grantee Rsch. Corp., NSF, NASA, Nat. Rsch. Lab., NAS, Am. Astron. Soc. Fellow AAAS, Royal Astron. Soc., Am. Phys. Soc.; mem. Am. Astron. Soc. (Harlow Shapley lectr. 1973—, auditor 1977, 79-85), Am. Math. Soc., Can. Astron. Soc., Internat. Astron. Union (chmn., sec. various coms. and commns., pres. commn. 30 1982-85, chmn. working group on spectroscopic and photometric data 1985-94, chmn. sci. organizing com. symposium # 167, mem. working group on pub. 2000-), N.Y. Acad. Scis., Astron. Soc. Pacific, Astron. Soc. N.Y. (sec.-treas. 1969-2001, editor newsletter 1974-2001), Capital Computer Club (bd. dirs. 1990—, v.p. 1993—), H. Rider Haggard Soc., Sigma Xi. Achievements include being 1st U.S. observer Soviet 6M telescope, 1980. Home: 1125 Oxford Pl Schenectady NY 12308-2913 Office: Union Coll Physics Dept Schenectady NY 12308 E-mail: agdp@union.edu.

PHILIP, BEVERLY KHNIE, anesthesiologist; b. N.Y.C., Dec. 27, 1948; d. Sender and Hilde (Helmreich) K.; m. James Henry Philip, Mar. 12, 1972; children: Noah, Benjamin. BA, Queens Coll., CUNY, 1969; MD, SUNY, Syracuse, 1973. Diplomate Nat. Bd. Med. Examiners, Am. Bd. Anesthesiology. Intern New Eng. Deaconess Hosp., Boston, 1973-74; resident medicine Harvard Med. Sch., 1973-74, resident anaesthesia, 1974-77; jr. asst. resident in anesthesia Peter Bent Brigham Hosp., Boston, 1974-75, sr. asst. resident, 1975-76, resident in anesthesia, 1976-77; instr. anesthesiology Harvard U. Med. Sch., 1977-85, asst. prof. anesthesiology, 1985-93, assoc. prof., 1994—; dir. day surgery unit Brigham & Women's Hosp., 1981—. Clin. fellow in medicine Harvard U. Med. Sch., Boston, 1973-74, clin. fellow in anesthesia, 1974-76, rsch. fellow in anesthesia, 1976-77. Author chpts. to books; contbr. articles to profl. jours. Patroller Nat. Ski Patrol, 1971-74, sr. patroller, 1974—. Fellow Am. Coll. Anesthesiologists; mem. Soc. Ambulatory Anesthesia (dir. 1985—, pres. 1991-92), Federated Ambulatory Surgery Assn. (bd. dirs. 1986-96), Am. Soc. Anesthesiologists (mem. com. on ambulatory surg. care 1990—). Office: Brigham & Women's Hosp 75 Francis St Boston MA 02115-6106

PHILIP, GEORGE MICHAEL, pension fund administrator; b. Kingston, N.Y., June 7, 1947; s. Michael and Margarita Philip; m. Sandra Philip, Aug. 22, 1970; children: Matthew, Michael, Robert. BA, SUNY, Albany, 1969, MA, 1972; JD, Western New Eng. Coll., Springfield, Mass., 1977. Bar: N.Y. 1978, U.S. Dist. Ct. (no. dist.) N.Y. 1978; cert. tchr., N.Y. Tchr. H.S. Schnectady (N.Y.) City Sch. Dist., 1969-71; pub. info. rep. N.Y. State Tchrs. Retirement Sys., Albany, 1971-73, mgr. facilities and adminstrv. svcs., 1973-77, mgr. mem. and employer svcs., 1977-82, chmn. task force, 1982, divsn. mgr. mgmt. and fin., 1982-86, dir. investor rels., pub. info., and budget, 1986-88, chief real estate investment officer, 1988-92, asst. exec. dir., 1992-95, chief investment officer, 1992—, exec. dir., 1995—. Bd. dirs., sec. Pension Real Estate Assn., Glastonbury, Conn., 1989-95; mem. real estate adv. com. Babson Coll., Wellesley, Mass.; mem. exec. com. Nat. Coun. on Tchr. Retirement, Sacramento; mem. State Acad. for Pub. Adminstrn., Albany; chair exec. com. Coun. Instl. Investors, Washington. Chair bd. dirs., chmn. investment com. St. Peter's Hosp., Albany; chmn. investment com. Cath. Health East, Phila.; chmn. univ. coun. SUNY, Albany; bd. dirs. Univ. at Albany Found., Univ. at Albany Alumni Assn.; bd. dirs., chair investment com. Saratoga (N.Y.) Performing Arts Ctr. Office: NY State Tchrs Retirement Sys 10 Corporate Woods Dr Albany NY 12211-2500

PHILIP, JAMES (PATE PHILIP), state legislator; b. Elmhurst, Ill., May 26, 1930; married; 4 children. Student, Kansas City Jr. Coll., Kans. State Coll. Ret. dist. sales mgr. Pepperidge Farm, Inc.; rep. State of Ill., 1967-74, senator, 1975—. Asst. senate minority leader, 1979, senate minority leader, 1981-93, senate pres., 1993—; chmn. DuPage County Rep. Ctrl. Com.; committeeman Addison Twp. Precinct 52; past Jr. Nat. Rep. Committeeman. Past dir. Nat. Found. March of Dimes; past gen. chmn. Elmhurst March of Dimes; spl. events chmn. DuPage Heart Assn.; mem. DuPage Meml. Hosp. Century Club; dir. Ray Graham Assn. Handicapped Children; mem. bd. sponsors Easter Seal Treatment Ctr.; active Lombard YMCA; bd. dirs. Danada Sculpture Garden. With USMC, 1950-53. Recipient Ill. Coun. on Aging award, 1989, Leaders of 90's award Downers Grove Twp., 1989, Man of Yr. award United Hellenic Voters Am., 1989, Legis. of Yr. award Ill. County Treas.'s Assn., 1990, Tax$avers award Ill. Assn. County Auditors, 1990, Statesman of Yr. award Internat. Union of Operating Engrs. Local 150, 1991, Friend of Youth award Assn. Ill. Twp. Com. on Youth, 1991, Spl. Svc. award Serenity House, 1991, Recognition award DuPage Ctr. Independent Living, 1991. Mem. Am. Legion, Ill. Young Reps. (past pres.), DuPage County Young Rep. Fedn. (past chmn.), DuPage County Marine Corps League (life), DuPage Indsl. and Mfg. Assn. (past dir.), Suburban Bus. Mgmt. Coun. (past v.p.), Mil. Order Devil Dogs, Gocery Mgmt. and Sales Exec. Club Chgo., Exec. Club DuPage County, Shriners, Elks, Masons, Order of DeMolay (life), Moose. Office: Ill State Senate 327 Capitol Building Springfield IL 62706*

PHILIP, PETER VAN NESS, former trust company executive; b. N.Y.C., Feb. 23, 1925; s. Van Ness and Lillian (Davis) P.; m. Sabina FitzGibbon, May 3, 1952; children: William Van Ness, Thomas Winslow, Peter Sandys. AB, Yale U., 1945W; MBA, NYU, 1950. With Price, Waterhouse & Co., N.Y.C., 1947-52; W.H. Morton & Co., Inc., 1952-73; pres., CEO Equitable Securities, Morton & Co., Inc., 1970-73; sr. v.p., dir. White Weld & Co., Inc., N.Y.C., 1974-76; v.p. Morgan Guaranty Trust Co., 1977-88, ret. With 86th inf. div. AUS, 1943-45. Decorated Purple Heart, Bronze Star. Mem.: Racquet and Tennis (N.Y.C.); Links; Yale (N.Y.C.), Downtown Assn. (N.Y.C.), Bond (N.Y.C.); Bedford ((N.Y.); Golf and Tennis; Ekwanok (Manchester, Vt.). Home: Box 395 740 Guard Hill Rd Bedford NY 10506-1042

PHILIP, SUNNY KOIPURATHU, municipal official; b. Ranny, Kerala, India, Sept. 3, 1957; came to U.S., 1983; s. Mathai Koipurathu and Sosamma (Ninan) P.; m. Achamma John; children: Sunny K. Jr., Christine. B in Commerce, U. Kerala, India, 1978; M in Commerce, U. Kerala, 1982. Controller St. Thomas Evang. Ch. Hdqtrs., Kerala, India, 1978-81; instr. Minerva Coll., 1981-83; fin. dir. City of La Feria, Tex., 1983-91; exec. dir. La Feria Indsl. Devel. Corp., 1991-93; city mgr. City of La Feria, 1993—. Controller La Feria Indsl. Found. Corp., 1986—. Chmn. Cub Scouts Pack 47. Mem. Tex. City Mgrs. Assn., Tex. Indsl. Devel. Coun., Tex. Assn. Assessing Officers, Govt. Fin. Officers Assn. Tex. Lodges: Lions (treas. La Feria club 1983—). Methodist. Avocations: fishing, travel, reading. Home: PO Box 671 La Feria TX 78559-0671 Office: City of La Feria 115 E Commercial Ave La Feria TX 78559-5002

PHILIPP, ANITA MARIE, computer sciences educator; b. Evergreen Park, Ill., Sept. 7, 1948; d. Benedict Anthony and Anne Therese (Bolf) Butkus; m. Leslie Howard Philipp, Sept. 6, 1975; children: Leslie Aaron, Renée Marie. BA in Elem. Edn., St. Norbert Coll., 1969; MEd in Ednl. Media, U. Okla., 1978; postgrad., Okla. City C.C., 1980-93, U. Ctrl. Okla., 1994-2000. Cert. tchr., Okla., audio-visual specialist, Okla.; Microsoft cert. profl. in visual basic 6.0. Tchr. fifth grade Green Bay (Wis.) Bd. Edn., 1970; social ins. rep. Social Security Adminstrn., Chgo., 1970-73, ops. supr. Evanston, Ill., 1973, employee devel. specialist Chgo., 1973-76, claims rep. Oklahoma City, 1976-77, ops. analyst, 1977-78; adj. instr. computer sci. Okla. City C.C., 1985-96; dir. computer edn. St. James Sch., Oklahoma City, 1987-93; adj. instr. computer sci. U. Ctrl. Okla., Edmond, 1996; prof. computer sci. Okla. City C.C., 1996—, computer sci. votech liaison. Ednl. computer cons., 1989—; faculty advisor St. James Light Newspaper; mem. restaurant evaluation team Dunn-Farley Enterprises, San Marcos, Calif., 1978-85; computer sci. votech liaison Oklahoma City C.C., 1996—. EEO counselor Social Security Adminstrn., Chgo., 1972-73, coord. info. and referral svcs., 1982-83; leader Campfire Girls, Oklahoma City, 1986-89; mem. St. James Sch. Bd. Edn., Oklahoma City, 1987 (St. James sch. devel. com., 1990—, chairperson, interim devel. dir., 1994-96); eucharistic min. St. James Ch. Named among Top 25 Tchrs., Apple Computer/Homeland Stores, 1990; recipient Excellence in Tchg. award Nat. Inst. for Staff and Orgnl. Devel., 1999. Roman Catholic. Avocations: computers, crafts, sewing, shopping. Home: 2209 Laneway Cir Oklahoma City OK 73159-5827 Office: Okla City CC 7777 S May Ave Oklahoma City OK 73159-4419 E-mail: aphilipp@okccc.edu.

PHILIPP, JEANNE, artist; b. Dayton, Mar. 10, 1946; d. Charles Otterbein and Loraine Ida Adams. BFA, Antioch Coll., 1974; MA, Antioch U., 2001. Mem. faculty Univ. Without Walls/Ohio, Dayton, 1975-81; coord. expanding horizons for children Wright State U., 1985-87; ednl. cons. Yellow Springs, Ohio, 1980—. Adj. faculty dept. art Wright State U., Dayton, 1975-80; vis. faculty dept. art Antioch Coll., 1976; guest lectr. Dayton Art Inst., 1976; curator Artists Curate, Dayton, 1990—; presenter in field; artist-in-residence Tech. Ctr., Dayton, 1984. One-woman shows include Antioch Coll., 1976, Wright State U., 1976, The Art Gallery, 1989, Dayton chpt. Nat. Conf. Artists, 1990, Dayton Visual Arts Ctr., 2001, Miami Valley Coop. Gallery, 2001; group shows include Diamond Club, N.Y.C., 1972, Provincetown Invitational, Mass., 1972, 74, Antioch Coll., 1975, 76, Springfield (Ohio) Arts Coun., 1981, Sinclair Coll., 1984, Dayton City Beautiful Coun., Dayton, 1984, Miami Valley Arts Coun., 1987, Miami Valley Coop. Gallery, 1992, 2000, Dayton Visual Arts Ctr., 1992, 99, 2000, Miami U. Art Mus., Oxford, Ohio, 1993, Culture Works, Dayton, 1995, Miami Valley Coop. Group, 1996, Wright State U. Art Mus., Dayton, 1999, Antioch Theater, Yellow Springs, Ohio, 1999. Provincetown (Mass.) Workshop grantee, 1972, 74; Miami Valley Arts Coun. grantee, 1989. Mem. Coll. Art Assn., Dayton Visual Art Ctr., Women's Caucus on Art (regional v.p.). Avocations: music, gardening. E-mail: chimaeramedia@ivillage.com.

PHILIPP, WALTER VIKTOR, mathematician, educator; b. Vienna, Dec. 14, 1936; came to U.S., 1963, naturalized, 1974; s. Oskar and Anna Julie (Krasucky) P.; m. Ariane Randell, Dec. 10, 1984; children: Petra, Robert, Anthony, Andre. MS in Math. and Physics, PhD in Math., U. Vienna, 1960. Asst. U. Vienna, 1960-63, 65-67, dozent, 1967; asst. prof. U. Mont., 1963-64; vis. asst. prof. U. Ill., Urbana, 1964-65, mem. faculty, 1967—, prof. math., 1973—, prof. stats., 1988—, chmn. dept. stats., 1990-95. Vis. prof. U. N.C., Chapel Hill, 1972, 88, MIT, 1980, Tufts U., 1981, U. Göttingen, 1982, 85, Imperial Coll., London, 1985; adv. bd. Monatshefte für Mathmatik, 1994—. Assoc. editor Annals of Probability, 1976-81. Fellow Inst. Math. Stats.; mem. Am. Math. Soc., Austrian Math. Soc., Internat. Statis. Inst., Am. Statis. Assn., Austrian Acad. Scis. (corr. mem.). Avocations: mountaineering. Home: 1922 Maynard Dr Champaign IL 61822-5265 Office: U Ill Dept Math Champaign IL 61821

PHILIPPON, MARC JOSEPH, orthopaedic surgeon; b. Quebec City, Can., May 9, 1965; came to U.S., 1990; s. Pontien Aderville and Micheline (Lortie) P.; m. Senenne Catalina Reid, Mar. 25, 1995; children: Michèle, Marc-Christophe, Mia-Véronique. BA with honors, Fla. Atlantic U., 1987; MD, McMaster U., Hamilton, Ont., Can., 1990. Lic. physician, Fla., Pa.; diplomate Am. Bd. Orthopaedic Surgery. Orthopaedic surgeon Holy Cross Hosp., Ft. Lauderdale, Fla., 1995—, chief orthopaedic surgery, 2000-01; chief orthopaedic surgeon humanitarian mission to Ukraine Kiev Orthopaedic Inst., 1997; orthopaedic surgeon Broward Gen. Hosp., Ft. Lauderdale, 1998—2002; dir. sports medicine/hip disorders dept. orthopaedic surgery U. Pitts. Med. Ctr.; dir. fellowship program U. Pitts. Med. Ctr. for Sports Medicine, dir. hip arthroscopy fellowship, dir. golf medicine program, dir. Fla. site. Cons. Howmedica Inc., Rutherford, N.J., 1996-97, Smith & Nephew Inc., Memphis, 1998-99; clin. adv. bd. Oratec Interventions, Inc., Menlo Park, Calif., 1998-2002; cons. Zimmer (Bristol-Myers Squibb); lectr. in field. Contbr. chapters to books, articles to profl. jours. Bd. dirs. Svc. Agy. for Sr. Citizens, Ft. Lauderdale, 1996-2000. Farquharson scholar Can. Med. Rsch. Coun., 1989. Fellow Internat. Coll. Surgeons, Am. Acad. Orthopaedic Surgeons; mem. AMA, Fla. Med. Assn., Phi Kappa Phi. Roman Catholic. Avocations: skiing, tennis, sailing, hockey, soccer, golf.

PHILIPPS, EDWARD WILLIAM, banker, real estate appraiser; b. N.Y.C., Dec. 19, 1938; s. Edward Charles and Eleanor Elizabeth (Eisenger) P.; m. Diane Rose DiCuffa, June 12, 1960; children: James Michael, Robert Christopher. Appraiser Dry Dock Savs., N.Y.C., 1956-70, Nat. Bank of West, White Plains, N.Y., 1970-72, Aires Real Estate, Yonkers, 1972-74; sr. v.p. Am. Savs. Bank (merger Empire Savs. Bank), N.Y.C., 1974-92; self employed real estate appraiser Yonkers, 1992-93; sr. v.p., chief lending officer LaJolla (Conn.) Bank, 1993-99; cons., 1999—. Mem. mortgage com. Cmty. Preservation Corp., N.Y.C., 1990-92. Mem. Am. Inst. Real Estate Appraisers, Homebuilders Assn. Fairfield County (bd. dirs.). Avocations: wood working, fishing. Home and Office: 261 Kimball Ave Yonkers NY 10704-3030

PHILIPS, ABE L., JR. lawyer; b. Columbus, Ga., Dec. 31, 1934; s. Abram Lewis and Mary Louise (Rice) P.; m. Frances Carolyn Tingen, Aug. 23, 1957; children: A. Lewis III, Sidney Tingen, Scott Rice, L. Bradley. Student, Auburn U., 1953-55; BA, U. Ala., Tuscaloosa, 1957, JD, 1959. Bar: Ala. 1959, U.S. Dist. Ct. (so., mid., no. dists.) Ala. 1961, U.S. Ct. Appeals (5th cir.) 1967, U.S. Supreme Ct. 1970, U.S. Ct. Appeals (11th cir.) 1982. Assoc. Reams, Philips, Brooks et. al., Mobile, Ala., 1959—66, ptnr., 1966—98, mng. ptnr., 1976—98; ptnr. Pierce, Ledyard, Latta, Wasden & Bowron PC, 1998—. Mem. Gov.'s Indsl. Com., Ala.; mem. world trade com. C. of C., Mobile; mem. exec. com. Mobile County Dems., 1963; gen. chmn. Am. Jr. Miss Program, Mobile, 1968; pres. Jr. C. of C., 1969. Mem. Maritime Law Assn. U.S. (proctor), Southeastern Admiralty Law Inst., Mobile Bar Assn. (mem. admiralty com.), Mystics of Time, Soc. Les Bon Vivants. Methodist. Avocations: tennis, scuba diving, quail hunting, youth sports coach. Home: 4160 Carmel Dr N Mobile AL 36608-2405 Office: Pierce Ledyard Latta Wasden & Bowron PC 400 Colonial Bank Centre 41 N Beltline Hwy Mobile AL 36608-1204 Fax: 334-344-9696. E-mail: alp@pllaw.com.

PHILIPS, CHUCK, journalist; Journalist L.A. Times, 1990—. Recipient Pulitzer prize for Beat Reporting, 1999. Office: c/o LA Times Bus Sect Times Mirror Sq Los Angeles CA 90053 E-mail: chuck.philips@latimes.com.

PHILIPS, SUZANNE MARGUERITE See CASEY, SUE

PHILIPSON, HERMAN LOUIS, JR. investment banker; b. Dallas, May 14, 1924; s. Herman Louis and Lillian (Adler) P.; m. Sonia Topletz, July 20, 1955; children: Cynthia Ann, Leslie, Nancy, Julie. BS, Tex. A&M U., 1946; postgrad., Harvard Sch. Bus. Adminstrn., 1947-48. Pres. Philipson's, Inc., 1946-56; pres. Nat. Data Processing Corp., 1957-60, chmn. bd., 1960-61, Techno-Growth Capital Corp., 1962-72; pres. Recognition Internat. Inc., Dallas, 1961-73, chmn. exec. com., 1973-76; vice chmn. Recognition Equipment Inc., 1976-83; pres. Internat. Bus. Devel. Ltd., Dallas, 1973—, IBDL, Inc., Dallas, 1979—. Patentee in field. Former mem. Dallas Citizens Coun., also v.p., mem. exec. com.; bd. dirs. Dallas County Camp Fire Girls; trustee So. Meth. U. Found. for Sci. and Engring.; mem. engring. adv. coun. Tex. A&M U. 1st Lt. AUS, 1943-46. Decorated Bronze Star, Purple Heart with cluster; recipient Dallas Exporter of Yr. award, 1970, Ernest Thompson Seton award, 1975; named to Tex. A&M U. Acad. Disting. Mech. Engring. Grads. Mem. Dallas C. of C. (world trade com.), Japan-Tex. Assn. Lodges: Masons, Shriners. Home: 9100 Rockbrook Dr Dallas TX 75220-3907

PHILIPSON, MORRIS, university press director; b. New Haven, June 23, 1926; s. Samuel and Edith (Alderman) P.; m. Susan Antonia Sacher, Apr. 26, 1961; children: Nicholas, Jenny, Alex. Diploma, U. Paris, 1947; BA, U. Chgo., 1949, MA, 1952; PhD in Philosophy, Columbia U., 1959; L.H.D. (hon.), Coe Coll., 1985. Instr. English lit. Hofstra Coll., 1954—55; instr. philosophy Juilliard Sch. Music, 1955—58; lectr. Hunter Coll., 1957—60; editor Vintage Books, Alfred A. Knopf, Inc., N.Y.C., 1959—61, Modern Library, also trade books Random House, Inc., Pantheon Books, 1961—65; sr. editor Basic Books, N.Y.C., 1965—66; exec. editor U. Chgo. Press, 1966—67, dir., 1967—2000, dir. emeritus, 2000—. Author: Outline of Jungian Aesthetics, 1963, Bourgeois Anonymous, 1964, The Count Who Wished He Were a Peasant: A Life of Leo Tolstoy, 1967, Paradoxes, 1969, Everything Changes, 1972, The Wallpaper Fox, 1976, A Man in Charge, 1979, Secret Understandings, 1983, Somebody Else's Life, 1987; also short stories, articles; editor: Aldous Huxley on Arts and Artists, 1960, Aesthetics Today, 1961, Automation: Implications for the Future, 1962, (with Clapp, Rosenthal) Foundations of Western Thought, 1962. Served with AUS, 1944-46. Decorated comdr. Order Arts and Letters (France). Mem.: Arts (Chgo.), Caxton (Chgo.), Tavern (Chgo.), Quadrangle (Chgo.).

PHILIPSON, TOMAS, economist, educator; b. Uppsala, Sweden; s. Lennart and Malin Philipson. BSc, Uppsala U., East Orange, N.J., 1984; MA, Claremont Grad. Sch., 1985; PhD, U. Pa., 1989. Postdoctoral fellow U. Chgo., 1990; vis. asst. prof. Yale U., New Haven, 1990-95; assoc. prof. U. Chgo., 1996-98, prof. Harris Sch. Pub. Policy Studies, 1998—. Office: Univ of Chicago Harris Sch Pub Policy 1155 E 60th St Chicago IL 60637 E-mail: t-philipson@uchicago.edu.

PHILLABAUM, LESLIE ERVIN, publisher; b. Cortland, N.Y., June 1, 1936; s. Vern Arthur and Beatrice Elizabeth (Butterfield) P.; m. Roberta Kimbrough Swarr, Mar. 17, 1962; children— Diane Melissa, Scott Christopher. BS, Pa. State U., 1958, MA, 1963. Editor Pa. State U. Press, 1961-63; editor-in-chief U. N.C. Press, 1963-70; assoc. dir., editor La. State U. Press, Baton Rouge, 1970-75, dir., 1975—. Served to 1st lt. AUS, 1959-61. Mem. Assn. Am. Univ. Presses (dir. 1978-80, 83-86, pres. 1984-85), So. Hist. Assn., Acacia, Omicron Delta Kappa, Alpha Kappa Psi. Democrat. Home: 769 Castle Kirk Dr Baton Rouge LA 70808-6018 Office: La State U Press PO Box 25053 Baton Rouge LA 70894-5053

PHILLIPE, CHESTER TOLLESON, alcohol/drug abuse services professional, educator, substance abuse facility administrator; b. Long Beach, Calif., Oct. 15, 1929; s. Chester Marion Phillipe and Ethyle Kent Theinhaus; m. Florence Marie Phillipe (dec. July 1998); children: Jeffrey, Patrick, Melissa, Andrew, Aimee. BA in Religion and Bus. Adminstrn., Calif. Bapt. Coll., 1972; MDiv, Golden Gate Bapt. Theol. Sem., 1975. Cert. alcohol and drug abuse counselor; coll. instr. Calif. Alcohol and drug abuse counselor Calif. Assn. Alcohol and Drug Abuse Counselors, Sacramento, 1981—; CEO Family Addictions Ctr. Treatment. Mem. faculty in human svcs. Porterville Coll. Author: (book) Church Under Fire, 1998; editor: (addiction manuals) Substance Abuse, A Physical Disease, 1998. Bd. dirs. Calif. Alcohol and Drug Commn. Edn. Programs, Sacramento. Sgt. Army Security Agy. U.S. Army, 1947—50. Grantee, Idaho Mental Health, 1981. Mem.: Calif. Assn. Alcohol and Drug Abuse Counselors (bd. dirs. 1980—, Excellent Svc. award 1991), Nat. Assn. Alcohol and Drug Abuse Counselors, Internat. Consortium Reciprocity Commn. Republican. Avocations: reading, fishing, travel. Home: 3216 E Cathie Ct Visalia CA 93292-7026 Office: Counseling Addiction Ministries P1015 Visalia CA 93279 E-mail: chetp@psnw.com.

PHILLIPPE, RYAN, actor; b. Sept. 10, 1974; 1 child Ava Elizabeth. Student, New Castle Bapt. Acad., 1992. Co-founder prodn. co. Actor: (TV series) One Life to Live, 1992, The Secrets of Lake Success, 1993; (films) Crimson Tide, 1995, White Squall, 1996, Nowhere, 1996, Little Boy Blue, 1997, I Saw What You Did Last Summer, 1997, 54, 1998, Playing by Heart, 1998, Cruel Intentions, 1999, The Way of the Gun, 2000, Antitrust, 2001, Gosford Park, 2001, Igby Goes Down, 2002. Office: c/o William Morris Agy Attn: John Fogelman 151 El Camino Dr Beverly Hills CA 90212

PHILLIPPI, ELMER JOSEPH, JR. data communications consultant; b. Canton, Ohio, May 31, 1944; s. Elmer Joseph and Rita M. (Tillitski) P.; m. Susan Mary Schrader, July 10, 1971; 1 child, Nathan Audie. AB, Cornell U., 1966; MA, Rice U., 1970. Cert. energy auditor. Tchr. Brackenridge H.S., San Antonio, 1970-71; asst. prof. engring. tech. Muskingum Tech. Coll., Zanesville, Ohio, 1971-80, sec., treas. AAUP chpt.; data comm. analyst Chem. Abstracts Svcs., Columbus, 1980-87; sr. software engr. Control Data Corp., Dayton, 1987-89; analyst computing Boeing Computer Svcs., Huntsville, Ala., 1989; software engr. specxialist Ford Aerospace, Houston, 1989-92; computer sys. analyst Lockheed Engring. and Sci. Co., 1992-93; computer cons. CIBER, 1993-94; comm. cons. Genesis Data Sys., 1994; cons., lead cons. Deloitte & Touche Cons., 1994-98; sr. cons. KPMG, 1998-2000; ebus. arch. IBM, 2000—. Comm. cons. Ala. Supercomputer Network; designer, devel. Tech. Order Tracking System USAF; part-time instr. physics Ohio U.; editl. referee Am. Jour. Physics, 1975-85; network design cons. Aero. Systems div. USAF;

subsystem mgr. for mission control ctr. upgrade, Johnson Space Ctr.; cons. U.S. Senate, 1998; adj. instr. physics San Jacinto Coll., 1992—. Grantee NSF, 1979. Mem. Assn. Computing Machinery (past treas. Ctrl. Ohio chpt., mem. symposium com.), N.Y. Acad. Scis., Rice Bus. Network, Cornell U. Club Houston. Avocations: ham radio, music, bicycling, swimming, volunteer church work. Home: 18618 Prince William Ln Houston TX 77058-4225 Office: IBM Global Svcs 2 Riverway Houston TX 77056 E-mail: elmerp@us.ibm.com., ephillippi@earthlink.net.

PHILLIPS, ADRAN ABNER (ABE PHILLIPS), geologist, oil and gas exploration consultant; b. Feb. 6, 1924; s. James M. and Jennie Elizabeth (Norman) P.; m. Carmel Darlene Pesterfield, Aug. 20, 1949 (div.); 1 child, John David. BS in Geology, U. Okla., 1949. From geologist to pres. Exxon Corp. and affiliates, Chico, Calif., 1949-80, pres., 1980-92. Oil and gas exploration cons., 1992—; bd. dirs. Mountain States Legal Found., 1992—; apptd. Colo. Oil and Gas Conservation Commn., 1999; commr. Interstate Oil and Gas Compact Commn., 1999—. Mem. Colo. Oil and Gas Conservation Commn., 1999—. Mem. Am. Assn. Petroleum Geologists, Ind. Petroleum Assn. Mountain States (pres.), Ind. Petroleum Assn. Am. (dir.). Home and Office: 2194 S Augusta Dr Evergreen CO 80439-8923 E-mail: abephllips@msn.com.

PHILLIPS, ALMARIN, economics educator, consultant; b. Port Jervis, N.Y., Mar. 13, 1925; s. Wendell Edgar and Hazel (Billett) P.; m. Dorothy Kathryn Burns, June 14, 1947 (div. 1976); children: Almarin Paul, Frederick Peter, Thomas Rock, David John, Elizabeth Linett, Charles Samuel; m. Carole Cherry Greenberg, Dec. 19, 1976. BS, U. Pa., 1948, MA, 1949; PhD, Harvard, 1953. Instr. econs. U. Pa., 1948-50, 51-53, asst. prof. econs., 1953-56, prof. econs. and law, 1963-91; Hower prof. pub. policy U. Pa, 1983-91; chmn. dept. econs. U. Pa., 1968-71, 72-73, assoc. dean Wharton Sch., 1973-74, dean Sch. Pub. and Urban Policy, 1974-77, chair faculty senate, 1990-91. Teaching fellow Harvard, 1950-51; assoc. prof. U. Va, 1956-61, prof., 1961-63; vis. prof. U. Hawaii, summer 1968, U. Warwick, London Grad. Sch. Bus. Studies, 1972, Ohio State U., McGill U., 1978, Calif. Inst. Tech, Northwestern U., 1980, Ariz. Coll. Law, 1987, Inst. Européen d'Adminstrn. des Affairs (INSEAD), France, spring 1990; co-dir. Pres.'s Commn. Fin. Structure and Regulation, 1970-71; mem. Nat. Commn. Electronic Fund Transfers, 1976-77; chmn. bd. Econsult Corp., 1990-96. Author: (with R.W. Cabell) Problems in Basic Operations Research Methods for Management, 1961, Market Structure, Organization and Performance, 1962, Technology and Market Structure: A Study of the Aircraft Industry, 1971, (with P. Phillips and T.R. Phillips) Biz Jets: Technology and Market Structure in the Corporate Jet Aircraft Industry, 1994; Editor: Perspectives on Antitrust Policy, 1965, (with O.E. Williamson) Prices: Issues in Theory, Practice and Policy, 1968, Promoting Competition in Regulated Markets, 1975 ; editor Jour. Indsl. Econs., 1974-90; Contbr. articles to tech. lit. Served with AUS, 1943-45. Decorated Purple Heart, Bronze Star. Fellow: AAAS, Am. Statis. Assn.; mem.: Internat. Telecomms. Soc. (bd. dirs. 1990—2002), European Econ. Assn., Econometric Soc., Am. Econ. Assn. Home: 1115 Remington Rd Wynnewood PA 19096-4021

PHILLIPS, ANN Y. art advisor; b. Omaha, July 9, 1955; d. Irvin and Annette Swezey Yaffe; m. Lee Stuart Phillips, Aug. 12, 1984; children: S. Perry, Lucy A. BA, Yale U., 1977; grad., Hunter Coll., 1979-81. Adminstr. Pace Gallery, N.Y.C., 1978-79; asst. dir. Rosa Esman Gallery, 1979-82; dir. Bette Stoler Gallery, 1982-87; assoc. Hirschl & Adler Galleries, 1987-93; v.p., art advisor Citibank Art Adv. Svc., 1993-2000; pvt. art. adv., 2000—. Mem. art com. Montclair (N.J.) Art mus., 1997—. Co-author catalog: Prints of Eugene Delacroix, 1977; co-author, editor catalog: From Architecture to Object--Masterworks from the American Arts and Crafts Movement, 1989; organizer, co-author catalog: Cross Currents: Americans in Paris, 1993. Mem. Am. Assn. Museums, Art Table. Avocations: reading, gardening. Office: Ann Yaffe Phillips Fine Art 329 Park St Upper Montclair NJ 07043-2210

PHILLIPS, ANNA, publisher, editor-in-chief newspaper; b. Oakalla, Tex., Nov. 19, 1936; d. Edward C. and Barbara W. (Roberts) Spinks; 1 child, Kenny E. Phillips. Asst. sales mgr. Am. Legion Newspaper, San Antonio, 1961-68; sales profl. Sta. KLRN-TV Ednl. Broadcasting, 1969-73; sales mgr. Victor Bloom Advt. Agy., L.A., 1973-77, Non-Commd. Officers Assn., Oceanside, Calif., 1977-80; asst. sales mgr. Marshals Assn., San Diego, 1978-81; editor-in-chief, founder World of Entertainment, 1981-90; founder, pub. Associated News of So. Calif., San Bernardino, 1985-93; pub. Sheriff & Police News So. Calif., 1987—; owner Assoc. Native News of U.S.A. News editor, publ. films, Hollywood and Las Vegas, Nev., 1980-94; pub. for Hollywood celebrities and major stage productions, 1984—; pub., editor-in-chief Free Native News. Mgr. pub. rels. dept. Student Coun., Trinity U. for world famous celebrities, jazz musicians, concert news and public relations; news and pub. rels. coord. for Native Am. Indians; fundraiser scholarships for American Indian students, 1989-98. Recipient Nat. Pub. award Nat. Fedn. of Fed. Employees, 1966, Golden Halo Trophy Motion Picture Coun. So. Calif., 1996, Star Sapphire award Motion Picture Coun. So. Calif., 1996. Mem. Associated Press (recipient Hon. Charter Mem. Plaque award, 1997, lifetime charter mem.). Avocations: jogging, bicycling, dancing, playing piano. Office: Associated News PO Box 336 Yucaipa CA 92399-0336 E-mail: associatednativenew@aol.com.

PHILLIPS, ANTHONY FRANCIS, lawyer; b. Hartford, Conn., May 18, 1937; s. Frank and Lena Phillips; m. Rosemary Karran McGowan, Jan. 28, 1967; children: Karran, Antonia, Justin. BA, U. Conn., 1959; JD, Cornell U., 1962. Bar: N.Y. 1964, U.S. Dist. Ct. (so. dist., ea. dist.) N.Y. 1965, (ctrl. dist.) Calif. 1980, U.S. Tax Ct. 1981, U.S. Ct. Appeals (2nd cir.) 1967, (3d cir.) 1985, (4th cir.) 1983, (5th cir.) 1972, (7th cir.) 1987, (9th cir.) 1983, (10th cir.) 1983, U.S. Supreme Ct. 1971. Assoc. Willkie, Farr & Gallagher, N.Y.C., 1963-69, ptnr., 1969—. Mem. adv. com. Cornell U. Law Sch., 1994—. Fellow Am. Bar Found.; mem. ABA, N.Y. State Bar Assn., N.Y. County Bar Assn. (bd. dirs. 1989-95), Assn. of Bar of City of N.Y. Home: 3 Elm Rock Rd Bronxville NY 10708-4202 Office: Willkie Farr & Gallagher 787 7th Ave Lbby 2 New York NY 10019-6018 E-mail: aphillips@willkie.com.

PHILLIPS, ANTHONY GEORGE, neurobiology educator; b. Barrow, Cumbria, Eng., Jan. 30, 1943; came to Can., 1953; s. George William and Mabel Lilian (Wood) P. BA (hon.), U. Western Ont., London, Can., 1966, MA, 1967, PhD, 1970. Asst. prof. psychobiology U. British Columbia, Vancouver, Can., 1970-75, assoc. prof. Can., 1975-80, prof. Can., 1980—, prof. dept. psychiatry, 1994—, head dept. psychology, 1994-99. Founder Quadra Logic Tech., Inc., Vancouver. Contbr. numerous papers to sci. jours. Chair inst. adv. bd. CIHR Inst. for Neurosci. Mental Health & Addiction; chmn. Can.-India Village Aid, Vancouver, 1981—86; bd. dirs. Tibetian Refuge Aid Soc., 1980—. Recipient Killam rsch. prize Can. Coun., 1977, Killam Rsch. prize U. B.C., 1986, D.O. Hebb award Can. Psychol. Assn.; Steacie fellow Nat. Scis. and Engring. Rsch. Coun. (Can.), 1980. Fellow Royal Soc. Can.; mem. Soc. Neurosci., Can. Soc. for Neurosci., Can. Coll. Neuropsychopharmacology. Office: U BC Dept Psych 2255 Wesbrook Mall Vancouver BC Canada V6T 1Z4

PHILLIPS, ARTHUR MORTON, III, botanist, consultant; b. Cortland, N.Y., Jan. 20, 1947; s. Arthur Morton Jr. and Ruth (Mason) P.; m. Diedre Weage, Sept. 3, 1988. BS, Cornell U., 1969; PhD, U. Ariz., 1977. Instr., dept. biol. sci. U. Ariz., Tucson, 1971-73, rsch. asst., dept. geosciences, 1973-76; rsch. botanist Mus. No. Ariz., Flagstaff, 1976-80, curator biology, 1980-89; environ. cons., 1990—. Ariz. plant recovery team U.S. Fish & Wildlife Svc. Endangered Species, Phoenix, 1981—, Natural Areas Adv. Coun. Ariz. State Pks., Phoenix, 1980-89, chmn. 1985-86; adj. prof. No. Ariz. U., Flagstaff, 1984—. Author: Grand Canyon Wildflowers, 2d edit., 1990; co-author: Checklist, Vascular Plants, Grand Canyon National Park, 1987, High Country Wildflowers, 1987, Expedition to San Francisco Peaks, 1989, 5 endangered plants recovery plans, 1984-95. Fellow Ariz.-Nev. Acad. Sci.; mem. Am. Quaternary Assn., Soc. for Conservation Biology, Flagstaff Rotary Club (sec. 1989-92, achievement 1990, pres. 1993-94). Achievements include research in Native American ethnobotany in southwestern U.S., late Pleistocene climate and vegetation change in Grand Canyon, in status evaluation and ecological assessments of 110 species of rare and endangered plants in southwestern U.S. Home and Office: Bot & Environ Cons PO Box 201 Flagstaff AZ 86002-0201

PHILLIPS, BARNET, IV, lawyer; b. New York, N.Y., July 5, 1948; s. Barnet III and Isabelle (Auriema) P.; m. Sharon Walsted Packey, Jan. 2, 1981; children: Victoria Ilonka, Caroline Walsted. BA, Yale U., 1970; JD, Fordham U., 1973; LLM, NYU, 1977. Bar: N.Y. 1974. Assoc. Hughes Hubbard & Reed, N.Y.C., 1973-76, Skadden, Arps, Slate, Meagher & Flom, N.Y.C., 1977-81, ptnr., 1981—. Adj. assoc. prof. Fordham U., N.Y.C., 1987-88; articles editor The Tax Lawyer, 1989-91. Co-author: Structuring Corporate Acquisitions--Tax Aspects. Bd. dirs Student/Sponsor Partnership, N.Y.C., 1990-95; bd. cons. Portsmouth (R.I.) Abbey Sch., 1991-96, chmn.,1997-2002. Republican. Avocations: skiing, opera, triathlons. Home: 6 Hycliff Rd Greenwich CT 06831-3223 Office: Skadden Arps Slate Meagher & Flom Four Times Square 42nd Flr New York NY 10036-6522 E-mail: bphillip@skadden.com.

PHILLIPS, BARRY, lawyer; b. Valdosta, Ga., Feb. 16, 1929; s. W. Otis and Gypsy (Mercer) P.; m. Grace Greer, Aug. 3, 1957; children: Mary Grace, Barry Jr., Greer, Quinton. AB, U. Ga., 1949, LLB, 1954. Bar: Ga. 1951, D.C. 1977. Assoc. Kilpatrick Stockton, Atlanta, 1954-60, ptnr., 1960-97, of counsel, 1997—. Bd. dirs., mem. exec. com., credit com. Bank South Corp., 1978-96. Mem. bd. regents Univ. Sys. Ga., 1988-94, vice chmn., 1991-93, chmn., 1993-94; trustee U. Ga. Found., Atlanta, 1983-87, treas., 1985-87; mem. bd. visitors U. Ga. Law Sch., 1983-87, chmn., 1985; dir. Ctrl. Atlanta Progress, 1985-86; dir. USA-ROC Econ. Coun., 1985-91; bd. dirs. Ga. Coun. Internat. Visitors, Atlanta, 1986-93, sec., 1986-87, pres., 1987-88; bd. dirs. Atlanta Conv. and Visitors Bur., 1986-91, sec., 1986-87, v.p., 1987-88; bd. dirs. Ga. Region NCCJ, 1980-98, co-chair, 1982-83; chmn. Met. Atlanta Olympic Games Authority, 1990-91; bd. dirs. Ga. Sports Hall of Fame, 1990—, vice chmn., 1993-95, chmn., 1995-96; attache Can. Olympic Team for 1996 Olympics, 1995-96. 1st lt. U.S. Army, 1951-53, Korea. Decorated Air medal; recipient Brotherhood-Sisterhood award Ga. Regional NCCJ, 1993. Fellow Am. Coll. Investment Counsel (bd. dirs. 1986-88), Ga. Bar Found., Soc. Internat. Bus. Fellows; mem. Ga. Bar Assn. (chmn. corp. and banking law sect. 1977-78), Atlanta Bar Assn., D.C. Bar Assn., Lawyers Club Atlanta, U. Ga. Law Sch. Alumni Assn. (trustee 1979-84, pres. 1982-83), Can. Am. Soc. (bd. dirs. 1981-90, pres. 1981-83), Brit. Am. Bus. Group (bd. dirs. 1985-95), Sphinx, Gridiron, Phi Beta Kappa, Phi Kappa Phi, Omicron Delta Kappa. Democrat. Methodist. Avocations: reading, travel. Home: 4850 Tanglewood Ct NW Atlanta GA 30327-4558 Office: Kilpatrick Stockton 1100 Peachtree St NE Ste 2800 Atlanta GA 30309-4530 E-mail: bphillips@kilstock.com., bphilatl@aol.com.

PHILLIPS, BARRY, artist, educator; b. Odessa, Tex., Mar. 9, 1960; s. Barry and Sharon (Shaw) P.; m. Glenda Means, May 4, 1984; children: Shanae, Kelsey. BA, Tex. Tech. U., 1983; MFA, East Tex. State U., 1987. Faculty, chmn. dept. art Odessa (Tex.) Coll., 1994—. Artist drawings/prints Sophisto series, 1984-87, mixed media Man Overboard, 1990-97; one-man shows include Cameron U., Lawton, Okla., 1993, St. Edward's U., Austin, 1994, Mus. of Abilene, Tex., 1995; exhibited in group shows Zaner Gallery, Rochester, N.Y., 1986, Fla. State U., Tallahassee, 1987, Clemson (S.C.) U., 1987, Nelson-Atkins Mus., Kansas City, Mo., 1989, Hoyt Inst. Fine Art, New Castle, Pa., 1990, San Diego Art Inst., 1991, Cullen Ctr., Houston, 1993. Recipient Kimbrough award Dallas Mus. Art, 1989; Nat. Endowment for the Arts Visual Artists fellow, 1987. Mem. Coll. Art Assn., Tex. Assn. Schs. of Art, Big Red's Art Groupies. Office: Odessa Coll 201 W University Blvd Odessa TX 79764-7105 E-mail: barryphillips3@aol.com.

PHILLIPS, BERNICE CECILE GOLDEN, retired vocational education educator; b. Galveston, Tex., June 30, 1920; d. Walter Lee and Minnie (Rothsprack) Golden; m. O. Phillips, Mar. 1950 (dec.); children: Dorian Lee, Loren Francis. BBA cum laude, U. Tex., 1945; MEd, U. Houston, 1968. cert. tchr., tchr. coord., vocat. tchr., Tex. Dir. Delphian Soc., Houston, 1955-60; bus. tchr. various private schs., Houston area, 1960-65; vocat. tchr. coord. office edn. program Pasadena (Tex.) Ind. Sch. Dist., 1965-68, Houston Ind. Sch. Dist., John H. Reagan High Sch., 1968-85, ret., 1985. Bd. dirs. Regency House Condominium Assn., 1991-93. Recipient numerous awards and recognitions for vocat. bus. work at local and state levels. Mem. AAUW (life, 50 yr. mem., Houston Br. v.p. ednl. found. 1987-90, pres. 1992-94, bd. dirs. 1987-96, 50-Yr. mem. cert.), NEA, Nat. Bus. Edn. Assn., Am. Vocat. Assn. (life), Tex. State Tchrs. Assn. (life), Tex. Classroom Tchrs. Assn. (life), Tex. Bus. Edn. Assn. (emeritus, Life Mem. award, numerous other awards), Vocat. Office Edn. Tchrs. Assn. Tex. (past bd. dirs.), Greater Houston Bus. Edn. Assn. (reporter), Houston Assn. Ret. Tchrs., Tex. Assn. Ret. Tchrs., Delta Pi Epsilon (emeritus), Beta Gamma Sigma. Avocations: bridge, reading, arts, crafts, travel. Home: 1123 Royston Pl Apt D Bel Air MD 21015-4614

PHILLIPS, BETTY LOU (ELIZABETH LOUISE PHILLIPS), author, interior designer; b. Cleve. d. Michael N. and Elizabeth D. (Materna) Suvak; m. John S. Phillips, Jan. 27, 1963 (div. Jan. 1981); children: Bruce, Bryce, Brian; m. John D.C. Roach, Aug. 28, 1982. BS, Syracuse U., 1960; postgrad. in English, Case Western Res. U., 1963-64. Cert. elem. and spl. edn. tchr., N.Y.; cert. interior designer, Calif. Tchr. pub. schs., Shaker Heights, Ohio, 1960-66. Sportswriter Cleve. Press, 1976-77; spl. features editor Pro Quarterback Mag., N.Y.C., 1976-79; bd. dirs. Cast Specialties Inc., Cleve. Author: Chris Evert: First Lady of Tennis, 1977, Picture Story of Dorothy Hamill , 1978 (ALA Booklist selection), American Quarter Horse, 1979, Earl Campbell: Houston Oiler Superstar, 1979, Picture Story of Nancy Lopez, 1980 (ALA Notable book), Go! Fight! Win! The NCA Guide for Cheerleaders, 1981 (ALA Booklist), Something for Nothing, 1981, Brush Up on Your Hair, 1981 (ALA Booklist), Texas..The Lone Star State, 1989, Provençal Interiors-French Country Style in America, 1998, French by Design, 2000, French Influences, 2001, Villa Décor: Decidedly French and Italian Style, 2002; contbr. articles popular mags. Mem.: Am. Soc. Interior Designers (profl. mem., cert.), Soc. Children's Book Writers, Delta Delta Delta. Republican. Roman Catholic. Home: 4278 Bordeaux Ave Dallas TX 75205-3718

PHILLIPS, CARTER GLASGOW, lawyer; b. Canton, Ohio, Sept. 11, 1952; s. Max Dean and Virginia Scott (Carter) P.; m. Sue Jane Henry, June 5, 1976; children: Jessica, Ryan. BA, Ohio State U., 1973; MA, Northwestern U., 1975, JD, 1977. Bar: Ill. 1977, D.C. 1979, U.S. Dist. Ct. (no. dist.) Ill., U.S. Dist. Ct. (D.C. dist.), U.S. Ct. Appeals (1st, 2d, 3d, 4th, 5th, 6th, 7th, 8th, 9th, 10th, 11th, D.C. and Fed. cirs.). Law clk. U.S. Ct. Appeals (7th cir.), Chgo., 1977—78; law clk. to chief Justice Warren E. Burger U.S. Supreme Ct., Washington, 1978—79; asst. prof. law U. Ill., Champaign, 1979—81; asst. solicitor gen. U.S. Dept. Justice, Washington, 1981—84; ptnr. Sidley & Austin, 1984—; mng. ptnr. Sidley Austin Brown & Wood LLP, 1995—. Contbr. articles to profl. jours. Chief counsel Spina Bifida Assn. Am., Rockville, Md., 1987—; mem. bd. advisors state and local legal ctrs., Washington, 1985-91. Mem.: Am. Coll. Trial Lawyers, Acad. Appellate Lawyers, Am. Law Inst. Republican. Episcopalian. Office: Sidley Austin Brown & Wood LLP 1501 K St NW Fl 10 Washington DC 20005-3705

PHILLIPS, CARYL, writer; b. St. Kitts, West Indies, Mar. 13, 1958; BA with honors, The Queen's Coll., Oxford, Eng., 1979; AM (hon.), Amherst (Mass.) Coll., 1995; DUniv (hon.), Leeds Metro. U., 1997. Writer in residence Factory Arts Ctr. Arts Coun. Great Britain, London, England, 1980-82; writer in residence U. Mysore, India, 1987, U. Stockholm, 1989; vis. writer Amherst Coll., 1990-92, writer in residence, 1992—98, co-dir. creative writing ctr., 1994-97, prof. English, writer-in-residence, 1994-98; prof. English, Henry R. Luce prof. migration and social order Barnard Coll., Columbia U., N.Y.C., 1998—. Vis. lectr. U. Ghana, 1990, U. Poznan, 1991; vis. writer Humber Coll., 1992, 93; writer-in-residence Nat. Inst. Edn., Singapore, 1994; vis. prof. English NYU, 1993; vis. prof. humanities U. W.I., 1999—2000; mem. arts coun. Gt. Britain Drama Panel, 1982—85; mem. prodn. bd. Brit. Film Inst., 1985—88, Bush Theatre, 1985—89; mem. Caribbean Writer bd. U.S. V.I., 1989—; hon. sr. mem. U. Kent, 1988—; cons. editor Faber & Faber, Inc., 1992—94, Caribbean series editor, 1996—2000; participant, keynote spkr 12 ann. confs. German-speaking countries New Lits. in English, Giessen, Germany, 1989; resident writer Hull (Engl.) Internat. Lit. Festival, 1992; instr. writing Arvon Found., summers, 1983—; reader, lectr. in field. Author: The Final Passage, 1985 (Malcolm X prize for lit. 1985), A State of Independence, 1986, Higher Ground, 1989, Cambridge, 1991, Crossing the River, 1993 (James Tait Black meml. prize), The Nature of Blood, 1997, The European Tribe, 1987 (Martin Luther King meml. prize 1987), The Atlantic Sound, 2000, A New World Order: Selected Essays, 2001; editor: Extravagant Strangers: A Literature of Belonging, 1997, The Right Set: A Tennis Anthology, 1999; (plays) Strange Fruit, 1981, Where There Is Darkness, 1982, The Shelter, 1984; (TV documentary screenplays), Welcome to Birmingham, 1983, The Hope and Glory, 1984, The Record, 1985, Lost in Music, 1984, Darker Than Blue: Curtis Mayfield, 1995; (film) Playing Away, 1986, The Final Passage, 1996, The Mystic Masseur, 2001; (radio plays) The Wasted Years, 1984 (Best Radio Play of Yr. award BBC 1984), Crossing the River, 1985, The Prince of Africa, 1987, Writing Fiction, 1991; (radio documentaries) St. Kitts (Pride of Place), 1983, Sport and the Black Community, 1984, No Complaints: James Baldwin at Sixty, 1985; contbr. to documentary programs, including Black on Black, London Weekend TV, 1983, Bookmark, 1984; contbr. articles to periodicals. Recipient Young Writer of Yr. award, London Sunday Times, 1992, award, Lannan Lit., 1994; fellow, Guggenheim, 1992, 50th Anniversary, Brit. Coun., 1984, Royal Soc. Lit., 2000. Office: care G Garrett AP Watt Ltd 20 John St London WC1N 2DR England also: Barnard Coll English Dept 3009 Broadway New York NY 10027-6501

PHILLIPS, CHANDLER ALLEN, biomedical/human factors engineer; b. L.A., Dec. 21, 1942; s. Chandler A. and Ann (Lloyd) P.; m. Jane Draper, Feb. 14, 1980. AB in Biol. Scis., Stanford U., 1965; MD, U. So. Calif., 1969; AB in Classical Langs., Wright State U., 1982; PhD (hon.), U. Human Studies, Las Vegas, 1985. Registered profl. engr., Ohio, Calif. Rsch. physician U. Dayton (Ohio), 1972-74; asst. prof. Wright State U., Dayton, 1975-79, assoc. prof. biomed. engring., 1979-84, prof. biomed. engring., 1984-91, prof. biomed. and human factors engring., 1991—. Mem. editorial bd. Jour. Biomechanics, 1984-87, Jour. Clin. Engring., 1984—, Auto Medica, 1988—, Prosthetics-Orthotics Engring., 1995—. Author: Functional Electrical Rehabilitation, 1991, Human Factors Engineering, 2000; sr. editor: Mechanics of Skeletal and Cardiac Muscle, 1983, Effective Extremity Prostheses, 1989; regional editor Auto Medica, 1997—; mem. editl. bd. Jour. Biomechanics, 1984-87, Jour. Clin. Engring., 1984-98, Prosthetics-Orthotics Engring., 1995-98. Capt. USAF, 1970-72. Fellow IEEE (Harry Rowe Minno award 1984), Am. Inst. for Med. and Biol. Engring., Aerospace Med. Assn. (assoc.), Am. Acad. Neurologic Orthopedic Surgeons (hon.). Avocations: amateur radio, commercial-instrument pilot, fishing. Office: Dept Biomed Indsl Human Factors Engring Wright State U Dayton OH 45435

PHILLIPS, CHARLES ALAN, accounting firm executive; b. Cin., Aug. 12, 1939; s. Charles Stanley and Mary Lucile (Kirkpatrick) P. BS in Bus. Adminstrn., Northwestern U., 1960, MBA, 1961. Cert. systems profl. Investment adviser Continental Ill. Bank, Chgo., 1960-65; asst. to pres. A.S. Hansen, 1965-67; investment adviser Francis I. du Pont, N.Y.C., 1967-70; prof. North Central Coll., Mansfield, Ohio, 1970-73; prin. Peat, Marwick, Mitchell (now KPMG Peat Marwick), Cleve., Tulsa, Houston, 1973-88. Presbyterian. Avocations: classical music, natural history, gardening.

PHILLIPS, CHARLES FRANKLIN, JR. economist, educator; b. Geneva, Nov. 5, 1934; s. Charles Franklin and Evelyn (Minard) P.; m. Marjorie Hancock, June 22, 1957; children: Charles Franklin, Susan Hancock, Anne Davis. BA, U. N.H., 1956; PhD, Harvard U., 1960. Asst. prof. econs. Washington and Lee U., Lexington, Va., 1959-63, assoc. prof., 1963-66, prof., 1966—, Robert G. Brown prof., 1979—. Mem. adv. bd. Shenandoah Valley area, First Union, 1971—; econ. cons. pub. utilities. Author: Competition in the Synthetic Rubber Industry, 1963, The Economics of Regulation, 1965, rev. edit., 1969, The Regulation of Public Utilities, 1984, 3d edit., 1993; editor: Competition and Monopoly in the Domestic Telecommunications Industry, 1974, Competition and Regulation-Some Economic Concepts, 1976, Expanding Economic Concepts of Regulation in Health, Postal and Telecommunications Services, 1977, Regulation, Competition and Deregulation-An Economic Grab Bag, 1978, Regulation and the Future Economic Environment-Air to Ground, 1980. Mem. city coun. Lexington, 1969-71, mayor, 1971-88; mem. Va. Rep. Ctrl. Com., 1974-76, 77-96; trustee Hebron Acad., Maine, 1971-82; mem. Presbyn. Ch., 1959—, elder, 1993-98, trustee, 1994—; mem. Commn. on Rev. of Nat. Policy Toward Gambling, 1972-76; chmn. Valley Program for Aging Svcs., 1993-95, treas., 1996-99; bd. dirs. Rockbridge Area Presbyn. Home, 1973—, Nat. Regulatory Rsch. Inst., 1992-95, Stonewall Jackson Found., 1997-2000, 2001—; pres. United Way of Lexington-Rockbridge County, 1996-98, crusade chmn., 1999; pres. Hist. Lexington Found., 1997-00. Recipient award McKinsey Found., 1962, J. Rhoads Foster award, 1995. Mem. Am. Econ. Assn. (Disting. Mem. award transp. and pub. utility group 1997), , So. Econ. Assn., Am. Mktg. Assn., Kiwanis, Phi Beta Kappa, Omicron Delta Epsilon (pres. 1976-77, 78-79, 96-97, Outstanding Regional Dir. award 1971). Home: 414 Morningside Dr Lexington VA 24450-2739 Office: Washington and Lee U Dept Economics Lexington VA 24450 E-mail: phillipscf@wlu.edu.

PHILLIPS, CHRISTOPHER HALLOWELL, diplomat, consultant; b. The Hague, The Netherlands, Dec. 6, 1920; s. William and Caroline A. (Drayton) P.; m. Mabel B. Olsen, May 11, 1943 (dec. May 1995); children: Victoria A. Phillips Boyd, Miriam O. Phillips Eley, David W.; m. Sydney Watkins Osborne, Nov. 29, 1997. AB, Harvard U., 1943. Reporter, Beverly (Mass.) Evening Times, 1947-48; mem. Mass. Senate, 1948-53; spl. asst. to asst. sec. UN affairs Dept. State, 1953; later dep. asst. sec. of state for internat. orgn. affairs; apptd. U.S. Civil Service commr.; vice chmn. U.S. Civil Service Commn., 1957; U.S. rep. on UN Econ. and Social Council, 1958-61; Chase Manhattan Bank rep. for UN affairs, 2d v.p., mgr. Canadian div., 1961-65; pres. U.S. council Internat. C. of C., 1965-69; ambassador, dep. U.S. rep. UN Security Council, 1969-70; ambassador, dep. permanent U.S. rep. to UN, 1970-73; pres. Nat. Council for U.S.-China Trade, Washington, 1973-86, now hon. mem. bd. dirs.; U.S. ambassador to Brunei Darussalam, 1989-91; presdl. appointee to bd. U.S. Inst. Peace, 1992-97. Trustee Am. Inst. in Taiwan, 1995—; mem. adv. coun. Sch. Advanced Internat. Studies, Johns Hopkins U. Mass. dist. del. Rep. Nat. Conv., 1952, 60. Served to capt. USAAF, 1942-46. Mem. UN Assn. U.S.A., Coun. Fgn. Rels., Asia Soc., Mass. Hist. Soc., Coun. Am. Ambs., Met. Club Washington. Episcopalian. Home: 165 Argilla Rd PO Box 526 Ipswich MA 01938

PHILLIPS, DANIEL ANTHONY, trust company executive; b. Boston, Feb. 24, 1938; s. Lyman Waldo and Harriet Anthony (Carlow) P.; m. Diana Walcott, Aug. 18, 1962; children: Lisa Walcott Phillips, Bradford Lyman, Phillips. AB cum laude, Harvard U., 1960, MBA, 1963. From v.p. to dir. to mem. exec. com. Fiduciary Trust Co., Boston, 1963-92, exec. v.p., dir., trust com. sec., trust officer, 1992—, exec. v.p., dir., trust com., trust officer, 1993-94, pres., CEO, 1993—. Dir., sec., treas. Ways To Work, 1998—. Bd. dirs. Family Svc. Am., chair fin. comn., 1993-95, treas., chair bd. dirs., 1995-97; bd. dirs., mem. exec. com. Am. Meml. Hosp., Reims, France, pres., 1988-98; bd. dirs. Family Found., N.Am., 1993-99, Lend A Hand Soc.; bd. dirs., treas. Grimes-King Found. for the Elderly, Inc.; v.p., treas. Frederick E. Weber Charities Corp.; chair bd. dirs. Families Internat., Inc., 1997-99; founds. chair United Way Mass. Bay, 1996—, dir., 1998—, chair cmty. investments, 2000, vice chmn., bd. dirs., mem. exec. com. Decorated chevalier Legion of Honor (France); recipient Grand medal of Reims Am. Meml. Hosp., 1998, Champagne Ardenne medal Am. Meml. Hosp., 1998. Mem. Boston Soc. Security Analysts, Harvard U. Alumni Assn. (1st v.p. 1996-97, pres. 1997-98, Harvard Alumni Assn. award 1995), Boston Econ. Club, Comml. Club. Home: 975 Memorial Dr Cambridge MA 02138-5753 Office: Fiduciary Trust Co 175 Federal St Boston MA 02110-2210 E-mail: DAPharvard@aol.com.

PHILLIPS, DAVID P. sociologist, educator; b. Capetown, South Africa, Aug. 14, 1943; came to U.S., 1956; s. Harry Tarley and Eva Juliet Phillips; m. Juliet Rapaport, June 13, 1965; children: Rachel, Miranda. BA magna cum laude, Harvard U., 1964; PhD, Princeton U., 1970. Asst. prof. SUNY, Stony Brook, 1970-74; from assoc. prof. to prof. U. Calif., San Diego, 1974—. Cons. GM Rsch. Labs., Warren, Mich. Contbr. numerous articles to profl. jours., including Sci., New Eng. Jour. Medicine, Lancet, Jour. AMA. Recipient Behavioral Sci. prize AAAS, 1983. Mem. Am. Assn. Suicidology (Shneidman award 1983). Avocations: metalwork, cabinetwork, reading poetry. Office: U Calif San Diego Dept Sociology La Jolla CA 92093-0533

PHILLIPS, DOROTHY ALEASE, lay church worker, educator, freelance writer; b. Durham, N.C., May 11, 1924; d. Clarence Robert and Addie Lee (Outen) Hicks; m. Chester Raymond Phillips, Oct. 10, 1942; children: Cynthia Kaye, Dean Hayward, Kent Vincent. BS in Edn. and English, Bob Jones U., 1954; M in Edn., East Carolina U., 1970. Cert. secondary tchr., N.C. Former writer, illustrator Sunday sch. lit. Ayden (N.C.) Press.; former nat. youth chmn.

women's aux. Free Will Bapts.; dir. pub. rels. and Christian edn. Heritage Bapt. Ch., Johnson City, Tenn., 1980-91; tchr. Four Oaks (N.C.) H.S., 1955-56, Smithfield (N.C.) H.S., 1956-61, Farmville (N.C.) H.S., 1963-65, Rose H.S., Greenville, 1965-76, Univ. H.S., Johnson City, Tenn., 1976-78. Participant Blue Ridge Mountain Christian Writers Conf., Black Mountain, N.C.; former thcr. journalism Rose H.S., Greenville, N.C.; mem. choirs, Sunday sch. tchr. various Bapt. chs.; speaker at women's retreats and seminars. Dir. writers group Sr. Citizen's Ctr., Johnson City. Home: 1601 Paty Dr Johnson City TN 37604-7636 Fax: (423) 928-6413. E-mail: daps888@aol.com. *My dual role, as a high school teacher and a minister's wife, has afforded me wonderful opportunities to know and love many people. I have found joy in serving others.*

PHILLIPS, DOROTHY KAY, lawyer; b. Nov. 2, 1945; d. Benjamin L. and Sadye (Levinsky) Phillips; children: Bethann P., David M. Schaffzin. BS inEnglish Lit. magna cum laude, U. Pa., 1964; MA in Family Life & Marriage Counseling, NYU, 1975; JD, Villanova U., 1978. Bar: Pa,=. 1978, N.J. 1978, U.S. Dist. Ct. (ea. dist.) Pa. 1978, U.S. Dist. Ct. N.J., 1978, U.S. Ct. Appeals (3d cir.), 1984, U.S. Supreme Ct. 1984. Tchr. Haddon (N.J.) Twp. H.S., Haddon Heights H.S., 1964-70; lectr., counselor Marriage Coun. of Phila., U. Pa., Hahnemann Med. Schs., Phila., 1970-75; atty. Adler, Barish, Daniels, Levin & Creskoff, 1978-79, Astor, Weiss & Newman, Phila., 1979-80; ptnr. Romisher & Phillips, P.C., 1981-86; prin. Dorothy K. Phillips & Assocs., LLC, 1986—. Faculty Sch.. of Law Temple U.; guest spkr. on domestic rels. issues on radio and TV shows; featured in newspaper and mag. articles; bd. mem. Anti-Defamation League of B'nai B'rith, Nat. Mus. Jewish History; mem. friend's circle, Athenaeum, Phila., shareholder. Contbr. articles to profl. jours. Mem. ABA, ATLA (membership com. 1990-91, co-chair 1989-90), Pa. Trial Lawyers Assn. (chair membership com. family sect. 1989-90, presenter ann. update civil litigators-family law, author procedures practice of family law Phila. County Family Law Litigation Sect. County practiced database 1991) Pa. Bar Assn. (continuing legal edn. com. 1990-92, faculty, lectr. Pa. Bar Inst. Continuing Legal Edn. 1990, panel mem. summer meeting 1991), N.J. Bar Assn., Phila. Bar Assn. (chmn. early settlement program 1983-84, mem. custody rules drafting com. for Supreme Ct. Pa., spl. events spkr. on pensions, counsel fees, eritten fee agreements 1989-91, co-chair and moderator of panel mandatory continuing legal edn. 1994), Nat. Bus. Inst. (lectr. 1997—), Phila. Trial Lawyers Assn., Montgomery County Bar Assn., Lawyers Club. Office Fax: 215-568-1711. E-mail: dphillips@dkphillips.com.

PHILLIPS, DOROTHY LOWE, nursing educator; b. Jacksonville, Fla., June 3, 1939; d. Clifford E. and Dorothy (MacFeeley) Lowe; m. Dale Bernard Phillips, Feb. 14, 1973; children: Francis D., Sean E., Dorothy F. AA in Nursing, Ventura Coll., 1969; BSN, Calif. State U. Consortium, San Diego, 1984; M. Nursing, UCLA, 1987; EdD, Nova Southeastern U., 1995. Cert. community colls. tchr., Calif.; RN, Calif., pub. health nurse, Calif., clin. nurse specialist maternal/child. Staff nurse Cmty. Meml. Hosp., Ventura, Calif., 1969-70; charge nurse women and children's clinic Ventura County Regional Med. Ctr., 1974-76; staff nurse, RN II Pleasant Valley Hosp., Camarillo, Calif., 1978-85; lead instr. cert. nursing asst. program div. adult edn. Oxnard (Calif.) Union H.S. Dist., 1984-89; staff rsch. assoc. UCLA, 1988; clin. instr. Ventura C.C. Sch. Nursing, 1988; college nurse Ventura Community Coll., 1989; lectr. Sch. of Nursing UCLA, 1989, lectr., coord. maternity nursing Sch. of Nursing, 1989-90, 90-91; vocat. nursing dir., health scis. coord. Oxnard Union H.S. Dist., 1990-99; assoc. dean health occupations Allan Hancock Coll., 1999—. Vis. educator health careers unit Calif. Dept. Edn., 1992-94; cons. Oxnard Adult Sch.; mem. adv. com. nursing asst./home health aide program Ventura County Regional Occupational Program; presenter in field. Competitive events judge !st Annual Leadership Conf., Health Occupations Students of Am., Anaheim, Calif.; active St. John's Regional Med. Ctr. Health Fair, 1991, Pleasant Valley Hosp. Health Fair, 1991; seminar leader "Babies and You", March of Dimes, 1988. Grad. Div. Rsch. grantee UCLA, 1986; Calif. State PTA scholar UCLA, 1986, Ventura County Med. Secs. scholar, 1967, Audrienne H. Mosley Grad. scholar, 1987. Mem. Calif. Assn. Health Career Educators (pres. 1994), So. Calif. Dirs. Vocat. Nursing Programs (rec. sec. 1996—), So. Calif. Vocat. Nurse Educators (exec. bd.), Assn. Calif. C.C. Adminstrs., Nat. Coun. Instrnl. Adminstrs., Calif. C.C. Assn. Occupl. Edn., No. Calif. ADN Dirs., Santa Maria Valley Leadership Class, Sigma Theta Tau. Republican. Lutheran. Avocations: skiing, reading, exercise, travel, backpacking. Home: 1448 Oakridge Park Rd Santa Maria CA 93455-4560 Office: Allan Hancock Coll 800 S College Dr Santa Maria CA 93454-6399

PHILLIPS, DOROTHY REID, retired medical library technician; b. Hingham, Mass., Apr. 21, 1924; d. James Henry and Emma Louise (Davis) Reid; m. Earl Wendell Phillips, Apr. 22, 1944; children: Earl W., Jr., Betty Herrera, Carol Coe. Cert., Durham Vocat. Sch., 1952; B.S. in Comml. Edn., N.C. Central U., 1959; postgrad. U. Colo., 1969; M.Human Relations, Webster Coll., 1979; postgrad. Grad. Sch. Library Sci., U. Denver, 1983. Vocat. nurse Meml. Hosp., U. N.C., Chapel Hill, 1955-59; vol. work, Cairo, Egypt, 1965-67; library technician Base Library, Lowry AFB, Colo., 1960-65, Fitzsimons Med. Library, Aurora, Colo., 1976-93; ret. 1993; mem. Denver Mus. Natural History, Denver Art Mus., Mariners. Mem. AARP, NARFE, AAUW (chpt. community rep. 1982-83, state chmn. edn. found. 1982-84, pres. Denver br. 1984-86), Altrusa Internat. (corr. sec. Denver 1982-83, bd. dirs. 1984-85, pres. Denver chpt. 1988), Friends of Library, Peace Links, Colo. Coordinating Coun. of Womens Orgn., Inc. (pres. coun.), Colo. Library Assn., Council Library Technicians, Federally Employed Women, Delta Sigma Theta (corr. sec. Denver 1964-66), Women's Assn. of Peoples Presbyn. Ch., League of Women Voters, Denver Urban League. Democrat. Presbyterian. Home: 3085 Fairfax St Denver CO 80207-2714

PHILLIPS, EARL NORFLEET, JR. diplomat, financial services executive; b. High Point, N.C., 1940; s. Earl Norfleet Phillips and Lillian Jordan; m. Sarah Boyle, Oct. 19, 1971; children: Courtney Dorsett, Jordan Norfleet. BSBA, U. N.C., 1962; MBA, Harvard U., 1965. Security analyst Wertheim & Co., N.Y.C., 1965-67; exec. v.p. Factors Inc., High Point, 1967-71, First Factors Corp., High Point, 1972-81, pres., 1982-98; chmn. GE Capital First Factors, 1998-2000; pres. Phillips Interests, 2000—; U.S. amb. to Eastern Caribbean , 2002—. Bd. dirs. Oakdale Cotton Mills, N.C. Enterprise Corp., Culp Inc. Mem. nat. adv. coun. SBA, 1988—91; trustee High Point Regional Hosp., Asian Inst. Tech., Bangkok; former mem. Piedmont Triad Airport Authority; trustee U. N.C., Chapel Hill, 1983—91, chmn. bd., 1989—91, mem. endowment bd., 1985—2001; mem. U. N.C. Found., 1987—91; bd. govs. U. N.C. Sys., 1995—99; mem. N.C. Econ. Devel. Bd., Raleigh, 1984—91; bd. dirs. N.C. Citizens for Bus. and Industry, chmn., 1999—2000. Named Young Man of Yr., High Point Jaycees, 1971, High Point Citizen of Yr., 2000; named one of Five Outstanding Young Men, N.C. Jaycees, 1971; recipient Global Leadership award, Kenan-Flagler Bus. Sch., U. N.C., 2001, Disting. Alumnus award, U. N.C. Alumni Assn., 2002. Mem. Nat. Comml. Fin. Assn. (bd. dirs.), The Brook Club (N.Y.C.), Country Club of N.C. (Pinehurst), High Point C.C. Club, String and Splinter Club (High Point), Linville (N.C.) Golf Club, Gorgons Head Lodge. Office: Phillips Interests Box 830 101 S Main St High Point NC 27261

PHILLIPS, EDUARDO, surgeon, educator; b. Guadalajara, Mex., Oct. 25, 1943; m. Marion Paulette Khan; children: Mark, Anthony, Cynthia. MD with honors, Nat. U. Mexico City, 1967. Diplomate Am. Bd. Surgery. Rotating intern Hosp. Frances, Mexico City, 1966, resident in gen. surgery, 1967-69; rotating intern Sinai Hosp., Detroit, 1969, resident in gen. surgery, 1970-73, coord. surg. edn., 1974-76, chief surg. endoscopy, 1984-99, acting chmn. dept. surgery, 1991, chmn. dept. surgery, 1992-98; clin. asst. prof. surgery Wayne State U., 1992-97, clin. assoc. prof., 1997—; chief dept. surgery N.W. region Detroit Med. Ctr./Sinai-Grace Hosp., 1998—, dir. med. affairs Northwest Region, 1998-99. Contbr. articles to profl. jours. Fellow Internat. Coll. Surgeons (pres. Mich. divsn. 1995-99, vice regent Mich 1993-95, regent Mich. 1995—, Vice Regent of Yr. 1993), Am. Coll. Surgeons; mem. AMA, Am. Soc. Abdominal Surgeons, Am. Soc. Gastrointestinal Endoscopy, Am. Soc. Bariatric Surgery, Acad. Surgery Detroit (coun mem., chmn. membership com. 1995-97, pres.-elect 1997, pres. 1998-99), Detroit Gastroent. Soc. (pres. 1985-86), Detroit Surg. Assn., Mich. State Med. Soc., Soc. Laparoendoscopic Surgeons, Mich. Soc. Gen. Surgeons, Wayne County Med. Soc., Mich. Soc. Gastrointestinal Endoscopy, Frederick A. Coller Surg. Soc., Southeastern Mich. Surg. Soc. Jewish. Avocations: outdoor activities, classical music, reading classics. Office: Sinai-Grace Hosp 6071 W Outer Dr Detroit MI 48235-2624

PHILLIPS, EDWARD JOHN, consulting firm executive; b. Phila., Sept. 8, 1940; s. Harold E. and Mary C. P.; m. Kathleen A. Everett, July 23, 1960; children: Elizabeth J., Edward J. B of Mech. Engring., Villanova U., 1973; MBA, Widener U., 1975. Registered profl. engr., Ill., Kans., Mo., Pa., Ohio; chartered engr., U.K. Tech. ops. mgr. Motorola, Inc., Franklin Park, Ill., 1976-81; v.p. engring. Rival Mfg. Co., Kansas City, Mo., 1981-82; prin., sr. cons. Richard Muther & Assocs., 1982-85; chmn. KANDE, Inc., Overland Park, Kans., 1983-86; pres., CEO Sims Cons. Group Inc., Lancaster, Ohio, 1986—; chmn. bd. dirs., pres. Sims Consulting Group. Bd. dirs. KANDE, Inc., Wilmington, Del. Author: Manufacturing Plant Layout, 1997; contbr. articles to profl. jours. Mem. NSPE, ASME (chmn. material handling divsn. 1989-91, mem. internat. mgmt. com. 1977), MIMechE, Soc. Mfg. Engrs., Tau Beta Pi, Pi Tau Sigma. Office: Sims Cons Group Inc PO Box 968 314 N Columbus St Lancaster OH 43130-3009

PHILLIPS, EDWIN CHARLES, gas transmission company executive, retired; b. Saskatoon, Sask., Can., Oct. 19, 1917; s. Charles Henry and Beatrice Grace (Johnson) P.; m. Elizabeth Winnifred Johnston, June 27, 1942; children: Diane, Carol, Glen, Earl, Jane, Sue. Student, Lethbridge Collegiate Inst., 1931-35. Asst. buyer Loblaw Groceries Co. Ltd., Toronto, 1938-42; advt. mgr. Can. and Dominion Sugar Co., Chatham, Ont., 1945-47; asst. to gen. mgr. Consumers Gas Co., Toronto, 1947-52; with Trane Co. Can., Ltd., 1952-68, exec. v.p., gen. mgr., 1964-65, pres., 1966-68; group v.p. Westcoast Energy Inc., Vancouver, 1968-70, exec. v.p., 1971-72, pres., 1972-82, chief exec. officer, 1976-83, chmn. bd., 1980-83, also dir.; dir. emeritus, 1989. Bd. dirs. Belkin Enterprises Ltd., Weiser Inc. Served with RCAF, World War II. Home: 4458 W 2nd Ave Vancouver BC Canada V6R 1K5 also: 5125 C Renaissance Ave San Diego CA 92122-5575

PHILLIPS, ELAINE LEE, psychologist, educator; b. Atlanta; BA summa cum laude, Western Mich. U., 1973, MA, 1975, PhD, 1986. Lic. psychologist, Mich. Sch. psychologist Eastern Svc. Dist., Galesburg, Mich., 1975-77; coord. Family and Children's Svcs. Barry County Mental Health, Hastings, 1977-82; psychologist Pheasant Ridge Ctr., Kalamazoo, 1982-83, Kalamazoo Regional Psychiat. Hosp., 1983-87; assoc. prof. to prof. Western Mich. U., Kalamazoo, 1987—. Cons. in field; presenter on health beliefs and practices of Am. youth, physician psycho-social assessment adolescents. Contbr. articles to profl. jours. Bd. dirs. Hospice Greater Kalamazoo, 1987—, mem. clin. records evaluation and rev. com., 1987—, mem. program evaluation and adv. com., 1987—, chmn. bereavement evaluation com., 1989—; sec. Commn. on Status Women, 1989-90, pres., 1990-92. Kalamazoo Consortium Higher Edn. grantee, 1989. Mem. APA, Women in Psychology and Clin. Group Psychology. Avocations: sailing, swimming.

PHILLIPS, ELIZABETH VELLOM, social worker, educator; b. Visalia, Calif., Nov. 7, 1922; d. Ralph Cauble and Mary Amelia (Cole) Vellom; m. William Clayton Phillips, Sept. 10, 1950 (div. 1976); children: Peter Clayton, David Cole, Ann Harper. BA, UCLA, 1943; MSW, Columbia U., 1950; MPH, Yale U., 1970; PhD, Union Grad. Sch., 1980. Lic. clin. social worker; diplomate Am. Bd. Examiners Clin. Social Work. Psychiat. social worker Jewish Bd. Guardians, N.Y.C., 1950-51, Cmty. Svc. Soc. Family Camp, N.Y.C., 1955-57, Jewish Family Svc., New Haven, 1962-64, New Haven Family Counseling, 1964-68; ass. clin. prof. psychiatry Sch. Medicine Yale U., New Haven, 1973—; pvt. practice, 1981—. Sr. social work supr. mental health dept. Hill Health Ctr., New Haven, 1973-81; prof. Sch. Social Work Smith Coll., Northampton, 1981-84; initiator teen pregnancy program Hill Health Ctr., 1977-81, cons., 1975-79. Found. Women's Health Svcs., New Haven, 1985, Inner City Co-op Farm, New Haven, 1978; organizer Big Brother/Big Sister program Yale U., 1976. Named Disting. Practitioner Nat. Acads. Practice, 1996. Mem. NASW, Am. Group Psychotherapy Assn., Nat. Fedn. Socs. Clin. Social Work (sec. 1988, v.p. 1993, pres.-elect 1994-96, pres. 1996-98), Conn. Soc. Clin. Social Work (pres. 1987-88). Democrat. Jewish. Avocations: playing musical instruments, writing poetry, hiking, bridge, travel. Home: 13 Cooper Rd North Haven CT 06473-3001

PHILLIPS, ELLIOTT HUNTER, lawyer; b. Birmingham, Mich., Feb. 14, 1919; s. Frank Elliott and Gertrude (Zacharias) P.; m. Gail Carolyn Isbey, Apr. 22, 1950; children— Elliott Hunter, Alexandra. AB cum laude, Harvard U., 1940, JD, 1947. Bar: Mich. 1948. Since practiced in, Detroit; ptnr. Hill Lewis (formerly Hill, Lewis, Adams, Goodrich & Tait), 1953-89, of counsel, 1989-96, Clark Hill, 1996—. Chmn. bd. dirs. Detroit & Can. Tunnel Corp.; pres., dir. Detroit and Windsor Subway Co.; mem. Mich. Bd. Accountancy, 1965-73. Contbr. to legal and accounting jours. Chmn. bd. dirs. Southeastern Mich. chpt. ARC; pres., trustee McGregor Fund; trustee Boys Republic, Detroit Inst. for Children, United Way Southeastern Mich., Univ. Liggett Sch.; mem. nat. maj. gifts com. Harvard U., Harvard Pres.'s Assocs., 1974—99; Pres.'s Coun., 1990, mem. overseers com. to visit Law Sch., overseers com. univ. resouces, Mich. chmn. Harvard Coll. Fund; trustee, pres. Ch. Youth Svc.; mem. Detroit Area coun. Boy Scouts Am. Lt. comdr. USNR, 1946. Recipient Spitzley award Detroit Inst. for Children, 1986, Harvard Alumni Assn. Disting. Svc. award, 1991. Fellow Mich. State Bar Found. (life), Am. Bar Found. (life); mem. ABA, State Bar Mich., Detroit Bar Assn., Lincoln's Inn Soc., Soc. Colonial Wars in Mich. (gov. 1999—) and Fla., Country Club Detroit, Detroit Club (pres. 1988-89), Yondotega Club, Grosse Pointe Club, Harvard Ea. Mich. Club (pres. 1955-56, Disting. Alumnus award 1992), Harvard Club N.Y.C., John's Island Club. Episcopalian (vestryman, sr. warden). Home: 193 Ridge Rd Grosse Pointe Farms MI 48236-3554 E-mail: elliottphillips@earthlink.net.

PHILLIPS, ELVIN WILLIS, lawyer; b. Tampa, Fla., Feb. 27, 1949; s. Claude Everett and Elizabeth (Willis) P.; m. Sharon Gayle Alexander, June 20, 1970; children: Natasha Hope, Tanya Joy, Trey Alexander. BA, U. Fla., 1971; MA, Western Carolina U., 1974, EdS, 1975; JD, Stetson U., 1980. Bar: Fla. 1980, U.S. Dist. Ct. (mid. dist.) Fla. 1981, U.S. Dist. Ct. (so. dist.) Fla. 1982, U.S. Ct. Appeals (11th cir.) 1988. Tchr. Monroe County Schs., Key West, Fla., 1970-73; asst. prin. Habersham County Schs., Clarksville, Ga., 1973-77; assoc. Dixon, Lawson & Brown, Tampa, Fla., 1980-81, Yado, Keel, Nelson et al, Tampa, 1981; ptnr. Lawson, McWhirter, Grandoff & Reeves, 1981-88, Williams, Parker, Harrison, Dietz & Getzen, Sarasota, 1988—. Leadership Devel. Program fellow Southern Regional Coun., Atlanta, 1975. Mem. ABA (forum com. constrn. industry 1989-96), Assn. Legal Adminstrs., Fla. Bar (chmn. 1991-92, vice chmn. 1990-91, mem. benefits com.), Sarasota County Bar Assn., Phi Kappa Phi, Phi Alpha Delta, Phi Delta Kappa. Democrat. Baptist. Home: 3310 Del Prado Ct Tampa FL 33614-2721 Office: Williams Parker Harrison Dietz & Getzen 200 S Orange Ave Sarasota FL 34236-6802 E-mail: ephillips@williamsparker.com.

PHILLIPS, EUAN HYWEL, publishing executive; b. Chipstead, Surrey, Eng., Mar. 31, 1928; s. Edgar Aneurin and Elsie Llewella (Davies) P.; m. Margaret June Savage, June 12, 1954; children: David John, Janet Margaret. BA, Emmanuel Coll., Cambridge, Eng., 1949, MA, 1965. Cost acct. J. Lyons & Co. Ltd., London, 1950-53; dispatch mgr. Pickerings Produce Canners Ltd., Manchester, Eng., 1953-56; mgmt. cons. P.A. Mgmt. Cons. Ltd., London, 1956-65; mng. dir. Unwin Bros. Ltd., Old Woking, Eng., 1965-73; univ. printer designate Cambridge (Eng.) U. Press, 1973-74, univ. printer, 1974-76; dir. Cambridge (Eng.) U. Press (Am. br.), N.Y.C., 1977-82; owner New Canaan Bibles and Manx Knitwear, Stamford, Conn., 1982-87; exec. dir. Assn. Am. Univ. Presses, 1987-90. Gov. Guildford Sch. Art, 1966-69, Cambridge Coll. Arts and Tech., 1974-76; dir. East Asian History of Sci., Inc., 1978-81 Contbr. to scholarly pub. With Royal Navy, 1946-48. Mem. Brit. Printing Industries Fedn. (coun. 1966-73, pres. Home Counties Alliance 1970-71), Troupers Light Opera Co., Connestee Falls Golf Assn. (pres. 1996-97), Connestee Falls Property Owners Assn. (bd. dirs. 2001—). Home: 140 Connestee Trl Brevard NC 28712

PHILLIPS, FLORENCE TSU, lawyer, choreographer, dance educator; b. Taipei, Republic of China, May 2, 1949; came to U.S., 1957; d. Victor Z.M. and Dulcie (Ling) Tsu; m. Patrick J. Phillips; 1 child, Roderick James. Student, NYU, 1967-69; BA summa cum laude, UCLA, 1971, JD, 1974. Bar: Calif. 1974. Dancer Imperial Japanese Dancers, N.Y.C., 1965-70, Ballet de Paris, Paris and Montreal, Que., Can., 1967-68, Grands Ballets Canadiens, Montreal, 1968-69; atty. HUD, Washington, 1974, L.A. Pub. Defender's Office, 1975-77, Minami, Lew & Tamaki, LLP, San Francisco, 1997—. Choreographer, dir. Sinay Ballet, L.A., 1979—; owner, dir. Danceworks Studio, L.A., 1978-99. Choreographed over 30 ballets, 1979—; consulting editor Dance Teacher Mag. Mem. Bar Assn. San Francisco, Phi Beta Kappa, Pi Gamma Mu. Avocations: reading, needle crafts.

PHILLIPS, FRED RONALD, insurance company executive; b. Lewisburg, Pa., May 5, 1940; s. Fred Oscar and Luella Mae (Herold) P.; m. Dorothy Helen Hayes, Feb. 18, 1961; children: Christopher S., George J., Fred R. Jr. Student, U. Pa., 1962-67. CPCU. Underwriter Employers Mut. Casualty Co., Phila., 1958-60, Gen. Accident Ins. Co., Phila., 1960-62; sr. v.p., sec. Pa. Lumbermens Mut. Ins. Co., 1962—. Treas., dir. Phila. Fire Dept. Hist. Corp. Mem. Chartered Property and Casualty Underwriters Soc., Train Collectors Assn. Am., Pa. Assn. Mut. Ins. Cos. (bd. dirs.). Avocations: collecting antique toy trains, fishing, golf. Office: Pa Lumbermens Mut Ins Co Curtis Ctr Philadelphia PA 19106

PHILLIPS, FREDERICK FALLEY, architect; b. Evanston, Ill., June 18, 1946; s. David Cook and Katharine Edith (Falley) P.; m. Gay Fraker, 1983 (div. 1993). BA, Lake Forest Coll., 1969; MArch, U. Pa., 1973. Registered architect, Ill., Wis. Draftsman Harry Weese & Assocs., 1974, 75; architect pvt. practice, Chgo., 1976-81; pres. Frederick Phillips and Assocs., 1981—. Bd. dirs. Landmarks Preservation Coun., 1981-85, Chgo. Acad. Sci., 1988-97, Friends of Ceuros de Escazu, Costa Rica, 1992-95; mem. aux. bd. Chgo. Architecture Found., 1975-89. Recipient award Townhouse for Logan Sq. Competition, AIA and Econ. Redevel. Corp. Logan Sq., 1980, Gold medal award Willow St. Houses, Ill. Ind. Masonry Coun., 1981, Silver award for pvt. residence, 1989, Gold medal award pvt. residence, 1994, Three Record Houses awards Archtl. Record, 1990, 95, award 2d Compact House Design Competition, 1990, award of exellence for pvt. residence AIA/Nat. Concrete Masonry Assn., 1992, 98, award pvt. residence Am. Wood Coun., 1993, Honorable mention-Best in Am. Living award Profl. Builders Mag., 1995, Builder's Choice award pvt. residence, Builder Mag., 1996, Jury's Choice award pvt. residence Chgo. Athenaeum, 1996, 2001, Am. Architecture award Chgo. Athenaeum. Fellow AIA (Disting. Bldg. award for Willow St. Houses, Chgo. chpt. 1982, for Pinewood Farm 1983, for Pvt. Residences 1990, 92, 98, for Tower Ho., 2001, chmn. task group mfg. housing Nat. Com. Design 1994-96, mem. awards task group 1998—, chmn. 2000-2001); mem. Chgo. ARchtl. Club, Racquet Club (bd. govs. 1983-89), Arts Club, Cliff Dwellers Club (bd. govs. 1985-88). Office: Frederick F Phillips & Assocs 1456 N Dayton St Ste 200 Chicago IL 60622-2636

PHILLIPS, GENEVA FICKER, academic editor; b. Staunton, Ill., Aug. 1, 1920; d. Arthur Edwin and Lillian Agnes (Woods) Ficker; m. James Emerson Phillips, Jr., June 6, 1955 (dec. 1979). BS in Journalism, U. Ill., 1942; MA in English Lit., UCLA, 1953. Copy desk Chgo. Jour. Commerce, 1942-43; editl. asst. patents Radio Rsch. Lab. Harvard U., Cambridge, Mass., 1943-45; asst. editor adminstrv. publs. U. Ill., Urbana, 1946-47; editl. asst. Quar. of Film, Radio and TV UCLA, 1952-53; mng. editor The Works of John Dryden, Dept. English UCLA, 1964—2002. Bd. dirs. Univ. Religious Conf., L.A., 1979— . UCLA teaching fellow, 1950-53, grad. fellow 1954-55. Mem. Assn. Acad. Women UCLA, Friends of Huntington Libr., Friends of UCLA Libr., Friends of Ctr. for Medieval and Renaissance Studies, Samuel Johnson Soc. So. Calif., Assocs. U. Calif. Press, Conf. Christianity and Lit., Soc. Mayflower Descendants. Lutheran. Home: 213 First Anita Dr Los Angeles CA 90049-3815 Office: UCLA Dept English 2225 Rolfe Hall Los Angeles CA 90024

PHILLIPS, GERALD BAER, internal medicine scientist, educator; b. Bethlehem, Pa., Mar. 20, 1925; s. Abel H. and Cecilia (Blum) P.; m. Maria Bonzi Lewis, July 15, 1970; children: Abigail, Elizabeth. AB, Princeton U., 1948; MD, Harvard U., 1948. Diplomate Am. Bd. Internal Medicine. Intern Presbyn. Hosp., N.Y.C., 1948-50; rsch. fellow Thorndike Meml. Lab., Med. Sch. Harvard U., Boston, 1950-53; vis. fellow biochemistry Columbia U. Coll. Physicians and Surgeons, N.Y.C., 1954-56, from assoc. in medicine to assoc. prof., 1956-73, prof., 1973—. Sr. attending physician Roosevelt Hosp.; attending physician Presbyn. Hosp. Sr. asst. surgeon USPHS, 1952-54. Mem. Am. Fedn. for Clin. Rsch., Am. Soc. for Clin. Investigation, Am. Soc. for Biochemistry and Molecular Biology, Alpha Omega Alpha. Home: 196 E 75th St New York NY 10021-3257 Office: 1000 10th Ave New York NY 10019-1147 E-mail: gbpl@columbia.edu. *I attribute any success I may have had to heredity and luck.*

PHILLIPS, GLYNDA ANN, editor; b. Riverside, Calif. d. Henry Grady and Patricia (Loflin) P. BA in English, Millsaps Coll., 1977; MS in Comms., Miss. Coll., 1996; postgrad., Inst. Children's Lit., 1998—. News editor The Magee (Miss.) Courier, 1981-84; editor Miss. Farm Country mag., Jackson, 1984—. Contbr. articles to profl. jours. Recipient first place personal column Nat. Fedn. Press Women, 1984, first place personal column Miss. Press Women's Assn., 1984, first place feature articles Miss. Press Women's Assn., 1984, Best Media Campaign award AFBF Info. Contest, 1996. Mem. PRAM, Soc. Profl. Journalists.

PHILLIPS, GRETCHEN, clinical social worker; b. Erie, Pa., July 14, 1941; life ptnr. Beverly Campbell, June 10, 1989. BA, Mercyhurst Coll., 1966; MSW, Yeshiva U., 1972; postgrad., Advanced Ctr. Psychotherapy, 1972-73, Washington Sq. Inst., 1973-77. Diplomate clin. social work; cert. social worker, N.Y. Psychiat. social worker, forensic social worker Creedmoor Psychiat. Ctr., Queens Village, N.Y., 1972-80; Med. social worker Bellevue Hosp. Ctr., N.Y.C., 1980-83; intake probation officer N.Y.C. Probation, Family Court, Bklyn., 1983—. Mem. NASW, Internat. Soc. for Traumatic Stress Studies (N.Y. chpt.). Home: 125 Radford St Apt 3C Yonkers NY 10705-3014 Office: Probation Intake Kings Family Ct 283 Adams St Brooklyn NY 11201-2804

PHILLIPS, GWETHALYN, political organization administrator; Chair Maine Dem. Party, Augusta. Office: Maine Dem Party PO Box 5258 Augusta ME 04332*

PHILLIPS, HARVEY, musician, soloist, music educator, arts consultant; b. Aurora, Mo., Dec. 2, 1929; s. Jesse E. and Lottie A. (Chapman) P.; m. Carol A. Dorvel, Feb. 22, 1954; children: Jesse E., Harvey G., Thomas A. Student, U. Mo., 1947-48, Juilliard Sch. Music, 1950-54, Manhattan Sch. Music, 1956-58; MusD (hon.), New England Conservatory of Mu, 1971; HHD (hon.), U. Mo., Columbia, 1987. Founder, v.p. Mentor Music, Inc., N.Y.C., 1958-79; v.p. Wilder Music, Inc., 1964-77, Magellan Music, Inc., N.Y.C., 1971—, Peaslee Music Inc., 1971—; mem. faculty Aspen Sch. Music, summer 1962, U. Wis., summer 1963, Hartt Sch. Music, Hartford, Conn., 1962-64, Mannes Sch. Music, N.Y.C., 1964-65; exec. v.p. Orch. USA, 1962-65; exec. v.p., pers. mgr., tubist Symphony of the Air N.Y.C., 1957-66; v.p. Brass Artists, Inc., N.Y.C., 1964—; adminstrv. asst. to Julius Bloom, Rutgers U., New Brunswick, N.J., 1966-67; v.p. fin. affairs New Englandonservatory of Music, Boston, 1967-71; mem. faculty Sch. Music, Ind. U., Bloomington, 1971-94, disting. prof. music, trustee, 1979, disting. prof. emeritus, 1994. Adv. bd. Am. Brass Chamber Music, Inc., 1971—; chmn. bd. Summit Brass/Keystone Brass Inst., 1985—92, Rafael Mendez Brass Inst., 1993—; cons. Margun Music, Inc., 1977—; bd. dirs. Summit Brass. Brass coach Festival at Sandpoint, Idaho, 1986-94; mem. faculty Joven Orch., Spain, 1987-94, Festival Casal Orch., San Juan, P.R., 1964-76; dir. 1st Internat. Tuba Symposium Workshop, 1973, Brass-Wind Music Studios, Carnegie Hall, N.Y.C., 1961-67; tubist, King Bros. Circus Band, 1947, Ringling Bros. & Barnum & Bailey Circus Band, 1948-50, N.Y.C. Ballet Orch., 1951-71, N.Y.C. Opera Orch., 1951-62, Voice of Firestone Orch., 1951-53, Sauter-Finegan Orch., 1952-53, Band of Am., 1952-54, NBC Opera Orch., 1956-65, Bell Tel. Hour Orch., 1956-66, Goldman Band, 1957-62; founding mem., tubist N.Y. Brass Quintet, 1954-67; condr., co-prodr. Burke-Phillips All Star Concert Band, 1960-62; co-founder, tubist Matteson-Phillips Tubajazz Consort, 1976—; founding mem. TubaShop Quartet, 1996—; rec. artist Crest Records, 1958-78—; originator Octubafest, TubaChristmas, Tubasantas, Tubajazz, TubaEaster, Tubacompany, Summertubafest; exec. editor Instrumentalist mag., 1986-96, bd. advisors, 1996—. Founder, pres. Harvey Phillips Found., Inc., N.Y.C., 1977—; bd. dirs. Mid-Am. Festival of the Arts, 1982-90, Bloomington Area Arts Coun., 1983-90; judge 1st Internt. tuba competition of CIEM Internat. Competition for Musical Performers, Geneva, 1991. Served with U.S. Army Field Band,

1955-56. Recipient Disting. Svc. to Music award Kappa Kappa Psi, 1978, Cmty. Svc. award City of Bloomington, 1978, Nat. Assn. Jazz Educators award, 1977, 78, Nat. Music Conf. award, 1977, T.U.B.A. award, 1978, MI Hummel The Tuba Player award, 1990, Disting. Achievement award Ednl. Press Assn. Am., 1991, Mentor Ideal award Assn. Concert Bands, 1994, Lifetime Achievement award United Music Instruments, 1995, Sudler award medal of the Order of Merit Sousa Found., 1995, Summit Brass Outstanding Svc. and Support Internat. Brassfest, 1995, Orpheus award Phi Mu Alpha Sinfonia, 1997; elected to Acad. Wind and Percussion Arts Nat. Band Assn., 1995; recipient Edwin Franko Goldman citation Am. Bandmasters Assn., 1996, Devel. of Mus. Artistry and Opportunities for Future Generations award Colonial Euphonium Tuba Inst., 1998, Lifetime Achievement award Rafael Mendez Brass Inst., 1998, Platinum Piston Lifetime Achievement award, U. Ga., 1999; Harvey Phillips Day proclaimed New England Conservatory Music, 1971, Harvey Phillips Day proclaimed Marionville, Mo. Bicentennial, 1976, Harvey Phillips Weekend Gov. of Mo., 1982; named hon. mem. U.S. Army Band, 1984. Mem. Am. Fedn. Musicians, Tubists Universal Brotherhood Assn. (bd. advs. 1973—, pres. 1984-87, hon.), Hoagy Carmichael Jazz Soc. (founder, acting pres. 1983—), Tau Beta Sigma, Phi Mu Alpha Sinfonia (Orpheus award 1997), Kappa Gamma Psi. Home and Office: Tubaranch 4769 S Harrell Rd Bloomington IN 47401-9028 Office: Sch of Music Ind U Bloomington IN 47405 E-mail: philliph@indiana.edu. *The role of a performer and teacher is to give, to share skills and knowledge. My primary goal in life is to create new opportunities in the music profession, to develop, expand, and preserve the music arts.*

PHILLIPS, HOWARD WILLIAM, investment banker; b. N.Y.C., May 16, 1930; s. Louis and Helen (Klein) P.; children: Jan Davis, Richard Louis; m. Carol Napack, June 9, 1985. BA, Dartmouth Coll., 1951, MBA, 1952; JD, Harvard U., 1957. Bar: N.Y. 1957. Asso. Cahill, Gordon, Reindel & Ohl, N.Y.C., 1957-64; v.p., gen. counsel McCall Corp., 1964-68, sr. v.p., 1968-69; partner Oppenheimer & Co., N.Y.C., 1969-81; chmn. Holmes, Phillips & Co., 1981-83; dir. corp. fin. D.H. Blair Investment Banking Corp., 1983-95. Bd. dirs. Pioneer Behavioral Health, Boston, Asolo Theatre Co., Sarasota, Fla. Served to lt. (j.g.) USNR, 1952-54. Mem. Easthampton (N.Y.) Tennis Club, Longboat Key Club (Sarasota, Fla.), Sara Bay Country Club (Sarasota). Home: Box 2047 3 Cove Hollow Farm Rd East Hampton NY 11937 Office: 500 S Palm Ave Sarasota FL 34236

PHILLIPS, JAMES CHARLES, physicist, educator; b. New Orleans, Mar. 9, 1933; s. William D. and Juanita (Hahn) P.; m. Joanna Vandenberg, Mar. 1, 1996. BA, U. Chgo., 1952, BS, 1953, MS, 1955, PhD, 1956. Mem. tech. staff Bell Labs., 1956-58; NSF fellow U. Calif. at Berkeley, 1958-59, Cambridge (Eng.) U., 1959-60; faculty U. Chgo., 1960-68, prof. physics, 1965-68; mem. tech. staff Bell Labs., 1968-96; cons. Bell Labs., Lucent Tech., 1996—. Sloan fellow, 1962-66; Guggenheim fellow, 1967. Fellow Am. Phys. Soc. (Buckley prize 1972), Minerals, Metals and Materials Soc. (William Hume-Rothery award 1992); mem. NAS. Home: 204 Springfield Ave Summit NJ 07901-3909

PHILLIPS, JAMES D. retired diplomat; b. Peoria, Ill., Feb. 23, 1933; s. James D. and Ehila (Hardy) P.; m. Rosemary Leeds, Mar. 30, 1957 (div. Dec. 1981); children: Michael, Madolyn, Catherine; m. Lucie Gallistel, Jan. 7, 1984; stepchildren: Charles, David BA, Wichita State U., 1956, MA, 1957; cert., U. Vienna, Austria, 1956; postgrad., Cornell U., 1958-61. Joined fgn. svc. Dept. State, 1961; served at Am. embassy Paris, before 1975; Am. Consulate Zaire, before 1975; Dept. State Washington, before 1975; dep. chief of mission Am. Embassy, Luxembourg, 1975-78, charge d'affaires The Gambia, 1978-80; student Nat. War Coll., Washington, 1980-81; office dir. Dept. State, 1981-84; consul gen. Am. Consulate, Casablanca, Morocco, 1984-86; U.S. Amb. to Burundi, 1986-90; U.S. Amb. Republic of the Congo, 1990-93; diplomat in residence The Carter Ctr., Atlanta, 1993-94; ret., 1994; pres. Dan Phillips & Assocs., Arlington, Va., 1994—. Bd. dirs. Gulf Resources, H.M. Salaam Found. Contbr. articles to Fgn. Svc. Jour. Bd. dirs. Jane Goodall Inst., 1994—. Avocations: golf; tennis; skiing. Home: 3607 Military Rd Arlington VA 22207-4829 Office: 1101 30th St NW Ste 200 Washington DC 20007-3769

PHILLIPS, JAMES DIXON, mediator, consultant, educator; b. Richmond, Va., Jan. 21, 1952; s. Ralph Dixon P. and Frances L. Gibbs; m. Cherly Anne Campbell, May 19, 1979 (div. Mar. 1983); m. Nancy Ellen Brister, Mar. 16, 1997. BA, Hampden-Sydney Coll., 1974; JD, U. Richmond, 1979; PhD, U. Colo., 1997. Bar: Va. 1979, Colo. 1992. Staff atty. Ctrl. Va. Legal Aid Soc., Richmond, 1979-85; assoc. Burcin and Assocs., 1985-87; asst. atty. State of Va., 1987-93; assoc. Shuford, Rubin & Gibney, 1997-2000; dir. Conflict Resolution Inst., 2000—. Contbr. articles to profl. jours. Pres. Westhampton Place, Richmond, 1988-92. Mem.: Assn. for Conflict Resolution (pres. Va. chpt.), Richmond First Club (treas. 1999—). Avocations: running, golf, tennis. Home: 1006 Normandy Dr Richmond VA 23229 Office: Conflict Resolution Inst Va Commonwealth U 923 W Franklin St Richmond VA 23284 E-mail: jphillip@saturn.vcu.edu.

PHILLIPS, JAMES EDGAR, lawyer; b. N.Y.C., Aug. 30, 1947; s. Jack Louis Phillips and Jacqueline (Kasper) Ehrman; children: Zachary J., Mark H. BA, Boston U., 1971; JD, Case Western Reserve U., 1975. Bar: Ohio 1975, U.S. Supreme Ct. 1977, U.S. Dist. Ct. (so. dist.) 1978, U.S. Ct. Appeals (6th cir.) 1981, U.S. Dist. Ct. (no. dist.) 1982. Asst. prosecutor Franklin County Prosecutor Office, Columbus, Ohio, 1975-77, sr. asst. prosecutor, 1977-79; assoc. Vorys, Sater, Seymour & Pease, 1979-84, ptnr., 1984—; spl. prosecutor State of Ohio, 1993—. Gen. counsel Nat. Fraternal Order of Police, Washington, 1987—, Conrail Police #1, U.S. Postal Police #2; mem. Bd. Profl. Law Enforcement Certification; pres. Ohio Ctr. for Law-Related Edn., 1985-95; mem. Wong Sun Soc., 1997—. Author: Civil Recovery in Ohio, 1986, Collective Bargaining in the Pub. Sector, 1988; editor Bar Briefs; contbr. articles Jours., 1987-89. Fellow Ohio Bar Found., Columbus Bar Found., Ohio Bar Assn. (chmn. com. law-related edn. 1982-86), Columbus Bar Assn., Am. Judicature Soc., Sixth Cir. Jud. Conf. (life); bd. dirs. Ohio Assn. Criminal Defense Lawyers. Office: Vorys Sater Seymour & Pease PO Box 1008 52 E Gay St Columbus OH 43215-3161 E-mail: phillips@vssp.com.

PHILLIPS, JAMES W. music educator; b. Missoula, Mont., May 11, 1972; s. James (Bill) W and Joan A Phillips. BA in Music, Wash. State U., Pullman, 1995; MA, Wash. State U., Pullman, WA, 1996—98, MusB in Trumpet Performance, 1995. Instrumental music dir. Coeur d'Alene (Idaho) H.S., 1998—; comdr./condr. Air N.G. Band of the NW, Fairchild AFB, Wash., 1998—. Prin. cornet Spokane Brit. Brass Band, Wash., 2001—. Composer (arranger): (concerto) Concerto for Two Trumpets and Organ, Vivaldi, 1994, (trumpet quartet) Leyenda, Albinez, 1998, Sheep May Safely Graze, Bach, 1998, O Mio Babbino Caro, Puccini, 1998. 1lt Wash. Air N.G., 1998—, Fairchild AFB Wash. Avocations: my dog, reading, travel. Home: PO Box 3549 Hayden ID 83835 Office: Coeur d'Alene HS North 5530 Fourth St Coeur D Alene ID 83815 Office Fax: 208-664-5785. Personal E-mail: jwp3coug@hotmail.com. E-mail: jphillip@sd271.k12.id.us.

PHILLIPS, JANET COLLEEN, retired educational association executive, editor; b. Pittsfield, Ill., Apr. 29, 1933; d. Roy Lynn and Catherine Amelia (Wills) Barker; m. David Lee Phillips, Feb 7, 1954; children— Clay Cullen, Sean Vincent BS, U. Ill, 1954. Reporter Quincy (Ill.) Herald Whig, 1951, 52, soc. editor, 1953; editorial asst. Pub. Info. Office U. Ill.-Urbana, 1953-54, asst. editor libr., 1954-61; asst. editor Assn. for Libr. and Info. Sci. Edn., State College, Pa., 1960-61, mng. editor, 1961-89, exec. sec., 1970-89; adminstrv. dir. Interlibr. Delivery Svc. of Pa., 1990-99; ret. Mem. AAUW, Assn. for Libr. and Info. Sci. Edn., Embroiderer's Guild Am., Pa. State Blue Course Club, Pa. State U. Women's Club, Theta Sigma Phi, Delta Zeta. Presbyterian. Avocations: travel; golf; sewing; needlecraft. Address: 471 Park Ln State College PA 16803-3208 E-mail: janph2@aol.com.

PHILLIPS, JEANNE See VAN BUREN, ABIGAIL

PHILLIPS, JEANNETTE VERONICA, management consultant, gerontologist; b. Batesburg, S.C., Sept. 29, 1940; d. Katherine Louise (Ramey) Ray; s. William Alfred Phillips, June 23, 1962; children: Veronica Lynn, Marguerite Kathleen. BA in Sociology, Ohio Wesleyan U., 1962; MA in Pub. Adminstrn., William Paterson Coll., 1980. Cert. vocat. rehab. counselor. Asst. teen program dir. YWCA, Toledo, 1962-66; recreation therapist Mo. Inst. Psychiatry, St. Louis, 1967-70, rehab. specialist, 1970-72; counselor, mgr. Vocat. Bur. of Rehab., Toledo, 1972-74; skills ctr. dir. Passaic County Bd. Tech. & Vocat. Edn., Wayne, N.J., 1974-76, personnel dir., 1976-81; asst. personnel dir. City of Stamford, Conn., 1981-87; sec., treas. Phillips Packaging, Inc., Orange, 1985—; exec. dir. commn. aging City of Stamford, 1987-92; exec. dir. social svcs., 1992-96; dir. eldercare Team, Inc., Derby, Conn., 1996-98; dir. Elder Options Resource Ctr., Shelton, 1998—2002. Mgmt. cons. pvt. practice, Orange, Conn., 1986—. Sec. Stamford United Way, 1991-96; mem. Cystic Fibrosis Found., 1986-97; commr. Orange Conn. Cmty. Svcs. Commn., 1997—. Named Woman of Yr., Conn. Am. Assn. Univ. Women, 1990. Mem.: AAUW (state v.p. membership 1995—98, Conn. state pres. 1998—2000, nat. membership com.), S.W. Conn. Agy. on Aging (pres. 1990—92), Orange Conn. Lions Club (pres.), Lions Club Internat. Avocations: walking, swimming, knitting. Home: 520 Hundred Acre Rd Orange CT 06477-3705 Office: Hewitt Found 230 Coram Ave Shelton CT 06484-3332

PHILLIPS, JERRY JUAN, law educator; b. Charlotte, N.C., June 16, 1935; s. Vergil Ernest and Mary Blanche (Wade) P.; m. Anne Butler Colville, June 6, 1959; children: Sherman Wade, Dorothy Colville. BA, Yale U., 1956, JD, 1961; BA, Cambridge (Eng.) U., 1958, MA (hon.), 1964. Bar: Tenn. bar 1961. Assoc. firm Miller & Martin, Chattanooga, 1961-67; asst. prof. law U. Tenn., 1967-72, assoc. prof., 1972-73, prof., 1973—, W.P. Toms prof., 1980—. Advisor Tenn. Law Revision Commn., 1968-70; mem. Tenn. Jud. Council, 1970-74; adv. Fed. Interagy. Task Force on Products Liability, 1976-77; lectr. in field. Author: Products Liability in a Nutshell, 5th edit., 1998, Products Liability Cases and Materials on Torts and Related Law, 1980, Products Liability Treatise, 3 vols., 1986, Cases and Materials on Tort Law, 1992, 2d edit., 1997, Products Liability-Cases, Materials, Problems, 1994; advisor Tenn. U. Law Rev., 1977—. U. Tenn. grantee, 1978 Mem. ABA, Am. Law Inst., Knoxville Bar Assn., Am. Assn. Law Schs., Order of Coif, Phi Beta Kappa. Clubs: Knoxville Racquet. Democrat. Episcopalian. Office: 1505 Cumberland Ave Knoxville TN 37996-0001 E-mail: jphilli2@utr.edu.

PHILLIPS, JILL META, novelist, critic, astrologer; b. Detroit, Oct. 22, 1952; d. Leyson Kirk and Leona Anna (Rasmussen) P. Student pub. schs., Calif. Lit. counselor Book Builders, Charter Oak, Calif., 1966-77; pres. Moon Dance Astro Graphics, Covina, 1994—. Author: (with Leona Phillips) A Directory of American Film Scholars, 1975, The Good Morning Cookbook, 1976, G.B. Shaw: A Review of the Literature, 1976, T.E. Lawrence: Portrait of the Artist as Hero, 1977, The Archaeology of the Collective East, 1977, The Occult, 1977, D.H. Lawrence: A Review of the Literature and Biographies, 1978, Film Appreciation: A College Guide Book, 1979, Annus Mirabilis: Europe in the Dark and Middle Centuries, 1979, (with Leona Rasmussen Phillips) The Dark Frame: Occult Cinema, 1979, Misfit: The Films of Montgomery Clift, 1979, Butterflies in the Mind: A Précis of Dreams and Dreamers, 1980; The Rain Maiden: A Novel of History, 1987, Walford's Oak: A Novel, 1990, The Fate Weaver: A Novel in Two Centuries, 1991, Saturn Falls: A Novel of the Apocalypse, 1993, Birthday Secrets, 1998, Your Luck is in the Stars, 2000; columnist Horoscope Guide Monthly; contbr. book revs. to New Guard mag., 1974-76; contbr. numerous articles to profl. jours. including Dell Horoscope, Midnight Horoscope, Astrology-Your Daily Horoscope, Am. Astrology. Mem. Young Ams. for Freedom, Am. Conservative Union, Elmer Bernstein's Film Music Collection, Ghost Club London, Count Dracula Soc., Dracula Soc. London, Richard III Soc. Republican. Home: 2945 SE Steele St #109 Portland OR 97202 Office: Moon Dancer Astro Graphics 425 E Arrow Hwy Ste 252 Glendora CA 91740-5607

PHILLIPS, JOHN L. astronaut; b. Fort Belvoir, Va., Apr. 15, 1951; m. Laura Jean Doell; 2 children. BS in Math. and Russian, U.S. Naval Acad., Annapolis, Md., 1972; MS in Aero. Systems, U. W. Fla., 1974; MS in Geophysics and Space Physics, UCLA, 1984, PhD in Geophysics and Space Physics, 1987. Commd. ensign USN, Annapolis, 1972; advanced through grades to Capt. USNR; Navy Corsair pilot USN, Lemoor , Calif., 1975—76, resigned, 1982; postgrad studies UCLA, 1982—89; Oppenheimer fellow Los Alamos Nat. Lab. , N.Mex., 1987—89, rschr., 1989—93; prin. investigator Solar Wind Plasma Experiment aboard Ulysses Spacecraft, 1993—96; astronaut NASA, Houston, 1996—. Contbr. scientific papers on plasma environs. of sun, earth, other planets, comets etc. Recipient NASA Space medal, 2000, Disting. Performance award, Los Alamos Nat. Lab., 1996. Avocations: fitness, hiking, kayaking, skiing. Office: Astronauts Office Johnson Space Ctr Houston TX 77058

PHILLIPS, JOHN A(TLAS), III, geneticist, educator; b. Sanford, N.C., Jan. 24, 1944; s. John A. and Rachael (Sloan) P.; m. Gretchen Lynch, Aug. 1, 1965; children: Jennifer Allene, John Atlas IV, Charles Andrew, James William. Student, U. N.C., 1962-65; MD, Wake Forest U., 1969. Diplomate Am. Bd. Pediatrics, Am. Bd. Med. Genetics. Intern Children's Hosp. Med. Ctr., Boston, 1969-70, jr. resident, 1970-71, sr. resident, 1973-74, chief resident, 1974-75; asst. prof. Johns Hopkins U., Balt., 1978-82, assoc. prof., 1982-84; prof. pediatrics Vanderbilt U., Nashville, 1984—, prof. biochemistry, 1986—, David T. Karzon chair genetics, 1992—. Bd. sci. counselors Nat. Inst. Child Health, Washington, 1984-88; counsilor Ctr. Study Polymorphisme Humain, Paris, 1988—; mem. adv. com. Ctr. Reproductive Biology, Nashville, 1990-94; bd. dirs. March of Dimes Birth Defects Found., Nashville, 1986—; mem. adv. bd. Nat. Neurofibromatosis Found., Tenn., 1990—; mem. Tenn. Genetics Adv. Com., Nashville, 1984—. Contbr. to profl. publs. Lt. comdr. USNR, 1971-73. Recipient Sidney Farber award Children's Hosp., Boston, 1975, E Mead Johnson award Mead Johnson Co., 1984; Pediatric Postdoctoral fellow Johns Hopkins U. Sch. Medicine, 1975-77. Mem. Am. Soc. Clin. Investigation, Soc. Pediatric Rsch., Am. Coll. Med. Genetics (founding, bd. dirs. 1995—), Phi Beta Kappa, Alpha Omega Alpha. Achievements include discovery of cause of hemoglobin H disease in Black Americans; chromosomal location of multiple genes in humans; improved diagnoses of cystic fibrosis, hemophilia, inborn metabolic errors, familial neurodegenerative diseases, familial pulmonary hypertension, familial pulmonary fibrosis. Office: Vanderbilt U Sch Medicine Dept Genetics DD 2205 Nashville TN 37232-0001

PHILLIPS, JOHN BOMAR, lawyer; b. Murfreesboro, Tenn., Jan. 28, 1947; s. John Bomar Sr. and Betty Blanche (Primm) P.; m. Ellen Elizabeth Ellis, Aug. 9, 1969; children: John Bomar III, Anna Carroll, Ellis Elizabeth. BS, David Lipscomb Coll., 1969; JD, U. Tenn., 1974. Bar: Tenn. 1974, U.S. Dist. Ct. (ea. dist.) Tenn. 1975, U.S. Ct. Appeals (6th cir.) 1980. Assoc. Stophel, Caldwell & Heggie, Chattanooga, 1974-79; ptnr. Caldwell, Heggie & Helton, 1979-91, Miller & Martin, Chattanooga, 1991—97, mng. ptnr., 1997—2002; deputy gen. counsel labor and employment Coca-Cola Enterprises, Inc., 2002—. Author: Tennessee Employment Law, 1989, 3d edit., 2000, Employment Law Desk Book for Tennessee Employers, 1989; editor: The Tennessee Employment Law Letter, 1986—; host Danger Zones Video Tng. Series for Suprs., 1998—; mem. nat. moot ct. team U. Tenn. Law Rev. Pres. Chattanooga State coll. Found., 1992-94, Boys Club of Chattanooga, 1983-84; sec. Tenn. Aquarium, 1989—; chmn. Chattanooga Conv. and Visitors Bur., 1996-97; bd. dirs. Vol. Comty. Sch., Chattanooga, 1980-85, Coun. for Alcohol and Drug Abuse, Chattanooga, 1981-83, Creative Discovery Mus., 1994-99, Girls Prep. Sch., 1997-2002, Allied Arts of Gtr. Chattahooga, 1997-2002; mem. Hamilton County Juvenile Ct. Commn., 1995-99. Fellow Tenn. Bar Found., Chattanooga Bar Found.; mem. ABA (labor law sect.), Tenn. Bar Assn. (chair labor law sect. 1992-93, Justice Joseph W. Henry award 1986-87), Chattanooga Bar Assn. (bd. govs. 1978-79), Chattanooga C. of C. (bd. dirs. 1998-2001), Order of Coif, Fairyland Country Club (Lookout Mountain, Tenn.), Walden Club (bd. govs. 1992-95), Mountain City Club, Kiwanis (pres. Chattanooga 1986-87). Episcopal. Avocations, reading, writing. Home: 1107 E Brow Rd Lookout Mountain TN 37350-1015 Office: Miller & Martin 832 Georgia Ave Ste 1000 Chattanooga TN 37402-2289 E-mail: jphillips@millermartin.com.

PHILLIPS, JOHN C. lawyer; b. S.I., N.Y., June 6, 1948; s. John D. G. and Eleanor (Stier) P.; m. Karen Francis McKenna, June 5, 1971; children: James, Thomas, Robert. AB in Govt., Cornell U., 1970; MA in Polit. Sci., Rutgers U., 1972, JD, 1975. Bar: N.J. 1975, U.S. Dist. Ct. N.J. 1975, N.Y. 1982, U.S. Supreme Ct. 1985, U.S. Ct. Appeals (3d cir.) 1985, Fla. 1988. Assoc. Carpenter, Bennett & Morrisey, Newark, 1975-79, Buttermore, Mullen & Jeremiah, Westfield, N.J., 1979-80; mng. ptnr. Buttermore, Mullen, Jeremiah & Phillips, 1981-85, 87-2001; with DeVos, Phillips & Co. PC, 1986-87; of counsel Price, Meese, Shulman & D'Arminio, 2001—. Trustee, dir. Animal Care Fund Inc., East Smithfield, Pa., 1983-98. Author: (with others) New Jersey Transactins, Zoning and Planning, 1993. Dir., coach Police Athletic League, Berkeley Heights, N.J., 1967-99; mem. Kappa Alpha Literary Soc., 1967—, trustee Kappa Alpha Assn., 1974-90, v.p. Kappa Alpha Assn. Found., 1978-87, vice-chmn., 1983, chmn., 1984; dir. Youth Soccer Club, Berkeley Heights, 1983-94; mem. Berkeley Heights Twp. Com., 1985-87, dep. mayor, 1986, 87; Twp. atty., Berkeley Heights, 1989, 91, 94—; planning bd. atty. Twp. Warren, 1987-2001; mem. N.J. Hotel and Multiple Dwelling Safety Bd., 1988—, vice chmn., 1998—; mem. Rep. Mcpl. Com., 1985-2000, vice chmn., 1990-92, 98-2000, mem. dist. XII ethics com., 1993-97, dist. XII fee arbitration com., 1998—. Recipient award for Assistance and Dedication to youth, Police Athletic League, Berkeley Heights, 1975, Dedicated Svc. award Berkeley Heights Twp. Com., 1983. Mem.: ABA, Inst. of Mcpl. Attys., Fedn. of Planning Ofcls., Urban Land Inst., Union County Bar Assn., N.J. State Bar Assn., Canoe Brook Country Club, Jaycees (sec. New Providence-Berkeley Heights chpt. 1982, Jaycee of Yr. 1982). Republican. Methodist. Home: 56 Emerson Ln Berkeley Heights NJ 07922-2414 Office: Price Meese Shulman & D'Arminio 50 Tice Blvd Woodcliff Lake NJ 07677 E-mail: jphillips@pricemeese.com.

PHILLIPS, JOHN EDWARD, zoologist, educator; b. Montréal, Que., Can., Dec. 20, 1934; s. William Charles and Violet Mildred (Lewis) P.; m. Eleanor Mae Richardson, Sept. 8, 1956; children: Heather Anne, Jayne Elizabeth, Jonathan David, Catherine Melinda, Wendy Susannah. BSc with honors, Dalhousie U., Halifax, N.S., 1956, MSc, 1957; PhD, Cambridge U., Eng., 1961. Asst. prof. Dalhousie U., Halifax, N.S., 1960-64; assoc. prof. U. B.C., Vancouver, Can., 1964-71, prof. Can., 1971—, head dept. zoology Can., 1991-96. Vis. rschr. Cambridge (Eng.) U., 1972, 76, 81; chair grant selection com. Nat. Rsch. Coun. Can., Ottawa, Ont., 1969-71; mem. coun. Nat. Sci. and Engring. Rsch. Coun., Ottawa, 1983-87. Mem. editorial bd.: Can. Jour. Zoology, 1971-75, Am. Jour. Physiology, 1978-93, Jour. Experimental Biology, 1981-85, Am. Zool., 1996-01; contbr. articles to profl. jours. Mem. grant selection com. Can. Cystic Fibrosis Found., Toronto, 1989-91; active Vancouver Bach Choir. Named to James chair St. Francis Xavier U., Antigonish, N.S., 1993; recipient Killam Rsch. prize U. B.C. Fellow Royal Soc. Can.; mem. Can. Soc. Zoologists (sec. 1972-76, v.p. 1976-78, pres. 1979, Fry medal 2000), Am. Soc. Zoologists (exec. 1983-85, chair divsn. comp. physiol. biochemistry 1983-85). Avocations: music, choir. Home: 12908 22 B Ave White Rock BC Canada V4A 6Z3 Office: U BC Dept Zoology Vancouver BC Canada V6T 1Z4

PHILLIPS, JOHN GRANT (JACK PHILLIPS), theatre director; b. Chgo., May 17, 1941; s. Edward Grant and Mary Kathryn Phillips; m. Sharon Ferguson, June 29, 1964 (div. June 1976); 1 child, Brendan Grant; m. Deborah King Anderson, Apr. 22, 1978; 1 child, Kathryn Sarah. BA, Beloit Coll., 1963; MFA, Yale U., 1974. Actor, tech. dir. Ct. Theatre, Beloit, Wis., 1960-70; assoc. prodr. Westwood Playhouse, L.A., 1976-77; v.p. Garrett Co., 1977-81; prodn. stage mgr. Getting My Act Together..., L.A., Phila., 1980-81, Am. Repertory Theatre, Cambridge, Mass., 1982-88; co-chmn. Harvard Advanced Theatre Tng. Inst., 1988-89; exec. dir. Spokane (Wash.) Civic Theatre, 1991—. Guest artist Ithaca Coll., 1990; adj. faculty Lesley U. Grad. Sch. of Edn., Cambridge, 1988—. Dir over 200 live stage plays; actor various roles. Mem. Leadership Spokane, 1992; citizen's adv. com. Spokesman-Rev., 1993-2000. John Shubert Meml. scholar Yale Drama Sch., 1973-74; recipient Local Emmy, 1993. Mem. Am. Assn. Cmty. Theatre (pres. 1999-2001), Actors' Equity Assn., Screen Actors' Guild, Rotary Internat. Avocations: reading, hiking, camping. Office: Spokane Civic Theatre 1020 N Howard St Spokane WA 99201-2204 E-mail: civictheatre@mindspring.com.

PHILLIPS, JOHN ROBERT, political scientist, educator; b. Henderson, Ky., Dec. 16, 1942; s. Leander Armstead and Ann Reid (Brown) P. Diploma, Lang. Inst., Chateauroux, France, 1966; BA, Centre Coll., Danville, Ky., 1969; MA, Western Ky. U., Bowling Green, 1973. Instr. Drury Coll., Springfield, Mo., 1971-73, Western Ky. U., Bowling Green, 1975-79; asst. prof. Thiel Coll., Greenville, Pa., 1979-83, scholar-in-residence, 1983-85; pvt. cons., 1985—; adj. prof. Lockyear Coll., Evansville, Ind., 1987-88, prof. adminstrv. and social scis., 1988-91, acad. dean, 1988-90, v.p. acad. affairs, dean coll., 1990-91, Helen Hoffman disting. svc. prof., 1990-91; exec. dir. Henderson County Human Rels. Commn., 1991-93; dean acad. affairs, prof. political studies/govt. Springfield (Ill.) Coll., 1993-97, acting pres., 1996-97, provost, dean coll., 1997-98, prof. polit. and social scis., 1998—. Adj. prof. pub. adminstrn. Ind. State U., Terre Haute, 1991-92; field investigator on religion and culture in ancient city of Taxila, Pakistan, 1968, on indsl. pollution of hist. bldgs. and monuments, France, Italy, Austria, 1969; rschr. on nationalism, Scotland, 1972, on local Scottish govt. and urban deves., 1993; participant in internat. confs. on The Future of a United Germany, 1991; mem. adv. coun. St. John's Hosp. Sch. Respiratory Therapy, 1993-97, Ursuline Acad Sch. Bd., v.p., 1995-97, pres., 1997-99, Cen. Ill. Fgn. Lang. and Internat. Studies Consortium, 1993—, chmn., 1994-96; cons.-evaluator Commn. on Instns. of Higher Edn., North Ctrl. Assn. Colls. and Schs., 1999—. Mem. editl. bd. Jour. Urban Affairs, 1985-89; manuscript referee Pub. Adminstrn. Rev., 1985-87; contbr. chpts. to multi-vol. reference series The Small City and Regional Cmty. 1981, 85, 87, 95, 99; asst. editor Pub. Voices, 2001-; contbr. articles on urban affairs, ednl. policy and practice, the Am. Presidency, policy planning, and federalism/intergovtl. rels. to profl. jours. Policy advisor Lt. Gov.'s Office, Frankfort, Ky., 1985-86; cons. Commn. on Ky.'s Future, Frankfort, 1985-87; mem. Bd. Cath. Edn., Diocese of Springfield, 1994-97; trustee Springfield Coll., 1996-97, commn. on human sexuality Episcopal Diocese of Springfield, 1997-98; bd. dirs. Liturgical Arts Festival of Springfield, 1998-2001. With USAF, 1963-68. Mem. Am. Polit. Sci. Assn. (Leon Weaver Disting. Rsch. Award com. 1990-93), Am. Soc. Pub. Adminstrn. (publs. com. 1984-88, 92-95), Urban Affairs Assn. (publs. com. 1985-89, nominating com. 1984-85, 88-89), Pi Sigma Alpha, Alpha Sigma Lambda. Democrat. Episcopalian. Home: 2605 Delaware Dr Springfield IL 62702-1213 Office: Springfield College L-106 Becker Libr 1500 N 5th St Springfield IL 62702-2643 E-mail: phillips@sci.edu.

PHILLIPS, J(OHN) TAYLOR, judge; b. Greenville, S.C., Aug. 20, 1921; s. Walter Dixon and Mattie Sue (Taylor) P.; m. Mary Elizabeth Parrish, Dec. 18, 1954; children: John Allen, Susan, Linda-Lea, Julia. AA, Glenville State Coll., 1952; JD, Mercer U., 1955; LLD, Asbury Coll., 1992. Bar: Ga. 1954, U.S. Supreme Ct. 1969. Mem. Ho. of Reps. State of Ga., Atlanta, 1959-62, Senate, 1962-64. With USMC, 1942-51. Methodist. Home: 1735 Winston Dr Macon GA 31206-3241 Office: State Ct Bibb County PO Box 6242 Macon GA 31208

PHILLIPS, JOSEPH BRANTLEY, JR. lawyer; b. Greenville, S.C., Dec. 5, 1931; BS in Bus. Adminstrn., U. S.C., 1954, JD, 1955. Bar: S.C. 1955. Assoc. Leatherwood, Walker, Todd & Mann, Greenville, 1958-63, ptnr., 1963—. Chmn. bd. deacons Presbyterian Ch., 1970-71, pres. Men of Ch., 1968-69, chmn. Christian Service Ctr., 1972-73; bd. dirs. Greenville Urban Ministry, 1978. Mem. ABA, S.C. Bar Assn., Greenville Bar Assn., Greenville Young Lawyers Club (pres. 1961-62), Lawyers Pilot Bar Assn., Kiwanis (pres. 1973). Clubs: Greenville Country (pres. 1977). Home: 207 Butler Springs Rd Greenville SC 29615-2261 Office: PO Box 87 Greenville SC 29602-0087 E-mail: jbphillipsjr@aol.com.

PHILLIPS, JOSEPH DANIEL, geophysicist, oceanographer; b. Woodbury, N.J., Sept. 11, 1938; s. Joseph Francis and Katherine Cecelia (Browne) P.; m. Gwendolyn Williams, 1961; children: Julia Kear, Stephanie Morgan, Joseph Williams. BA, Rutgers U., 1961; MS in Engring., Princeton U., 1963, MA, 1964, PhD, 1966. Engr. trainee Mobil Oil Co., N.Y.C., 1957, N.Y. Shipbuilding Corp., Camden, N.J., 1958-60; engr. mgmt. trainee N.J. Bell Tel. Co., Newark/Camden, 1961; rsch. asst. Princeton (N.J.) U., 1962-65; asst. scientist Woods Hole (Mass.) Oceanographic Inst., 1965-68, assoc. scientist, 1968-77; staff rsch. scientist MIT, Cambridge, 1977-79; sr. rsch. scientist U. Tex., Austin, 1978-96; chief scientist World Geoscience Corp., Houston, 1996-1999; chief scientist, dir. tech. svcs. Fugro Airborne Surveys, 1999-2000, Integrated Geophysics Corp., Houston, 2000—. Cons. Mobil Oil Corp., Dallas, 1969, Exxon Corp., Houston, 1977, Bell Tel. Labs., Whippany/Murray Hill, N.J., 1976-78; vis. scholar U. Cambridge, Eng., 1974-75; adj. prof./instr. marine geophysics, seismics and geomagnetism, oceanography, acoustics and potential fields, faculty advisor MIT, Woods Hole Oceanographic Inst., U. Tex., 1968-96; cons. airborne/marine archeology Nat. Underwater and Marine Archeologic Agy., 1997-98. Contbr. articles to Jour. Geophys. Rsch. Sci., Geol. Soc. Am., Am. Petroleum Geologist, Ency. Brittanica. Fellow Explorers Club; mem. Am. Soc. Naval Engrs., Am. Geophys. Union, Soc. Exploration Geophysicists, AAAS, Marine Lodge, Phi Beta Kappa, Sigma Xi. Achievements include research in use/design of lock-in amplifiers for rock magnetometers, USN multi-beam sonar for seafloor geology, acoustically navigated vehicles for seafloor studies, vertical seismic profiling aboard deep ocean drilling project ships, aeromagnetic location of archeologic targets, pipeline and wellhead surveying. Home: 3805 Gaines Ranch Austin TX 78735 E-mail: joephillips@netscape.net.

PHILLIPS, JOSEPH MICHAEL, JR. economist, educator; b. Upper Darby, Pa., July 28, 1956; s. Joseph Michael and Bertha Anne (Hughes) P.; m. Mary Elizabeth Sebek, Sept. 6, 1986; children: Joseph Michael III, Elizabeth Anne, Gregory Steven. BA, LaSalle U., Phila., 1978; MA, U. Notre Dame, 1981, PhD, 1982. Asst. prof. econs. Creighton U., Omaha, 1982-88, assoc. prof., 1988—. Outside dir. Prodn. Credit Assn. of the Midlands, Omaha, 1989—; chmn. supervisory com. Creighton Fed. Credit Union, 1992—. Contbr. articles to profl. jours. Bd. dirs., treas, v.p., pres. Siena-Francis House, Inc., Omaha, 1983-90; mem. fin. adv. bd. Servants of Mary, Am. Province, Omaha, 1988—; mem. fin. com. Holy Family Ch., Omaha, 1983—. Mem. Am. Econs. Assn., Midwest Econs. Assn., Ea. Econ. Assn., Omaha Com. on Fgn. Rels., Omaha Assn. Bus. Economists. Office: Creighton U 2400 California St Omaha NE 68178-0001

PHILLIPS, JOSEPH ROBERT, museum director; b. Utica, N.Y., Mar. 14, 1950; m. Dixie Anne Stedman, 1988. BS in Marine Transp., SUNY Maritime Coll., 1972; MA in History Mus. Studies, SUNY, Cooperstown, 1981; MBA, N.H. Coll., 1990. Capt., exec. dir. Hudson River Sloop Clearwater, Poughkeepsie, N.Y., 1972-75; capt., assoc. project dir. N.Y. Bicentennial Barge, Albany, 1975-76; various project positions Maine Maritime Mus., Bath, 1978-81; various program mgmt. and mktg. positions Bath Iron Works Corp., Shipbuilders, 1982-92; mus. dir. Maine State Mus., Augusta, 1992—. Bd. dirs. Friends of Maine State Mus., 1992—, Maine Archives and Museums, 1996—; mem. Maine Cultural Affairs Coun., 1992—, State House and Capitol Park Commn., 1992—, Blaine House Commn., 1994—, Maine-Aomori Sister State Coun., 2001—. Office: Maine State Mus 83 State House Sta Augusta ME 04333-0083 E-mail: joseph.phillips@state.me.us.

PHILLIPS, JOY EUGENIA, counselor, consultant; b. Colon, Panama, Oct. 25, 1938; d. Ernesto Adolfo and Maria Luisa (Chin) Lee; m. R. Lee Phillips, May 19, 1962; children: Melinda, Lynam, Trevor. BA, U. Md., 1984; MEd, George Mason U., 1987; EdD, Va. Poly. Inst., 1993. Intern Cmty. Mental Health Ctr., Prince William County, Va., 1986; counselor Ctr. for Counseling and Devel., Fairfax, 1987; dir. of guidance Linton Hall Mil. Sch., Bristow, 1987-88; instr. George Mason U., Fairfax, 1987-88; presenter, speaker Benedictine Pastoral Ctr., Bristow, 1987-88; sch. counselor Prince William County Schs., Manassas, Va., 1989-95; adj. faculty mem. in psychology No. Va. Community Coll., 1990—; presenter, speaker Archdiocese of Arlington, Va., 1989—; counselor in pvt. practice Prince William County, 1994-98, Leesburg, 1998—. On-site supr. practicum students Va. Tech./Prince William County Schs., Manassas, 1989-95; cons. in field; trainer in-svc. Incoming Counselors, Manassas, 1989-95; univ. supr. practicum grad. studnets Virginia Tech., 1992—; dir. behavioral health Piedmont Behavioral Health Ctr., Leesburg, 2000. Nominated Agnes Meyer Outstanding Tchr. award, 1992, 93; Blue Cross-Blue Shield Va. grantee, 1991. Mem. ACA, Nat. Assn. Cognitive Behavioral Therapists (Va. state rep.). Roman Catholic. Avocations: painting, reading, gardening. E-mail: phillipshail@erols.com.

PHILLIPS, JUANITA M. maternal/women's health and neonatal nurse; b. Sylvania, Ga., Nov. 7, 1941; d. Robert and Mary (Jones) Parish; m. Nathaniel Phillips, Aug. 29, 1987; 1 child, Darryl L. Glenn. Diploma, Grady Meml. Hosp. Sch. Nursing, Atlanta, 1960; BSN, U. So. Colo., 1977. RN, Colo.; cert. childbirth educator, neonatal resuscitation, BCLS and pediatric advanced life support instr. Commd. 2d lt. U.S. Army, 1983, advanced though grades to lt. col., 1986; charge nurse, newborn nursery and pediatrics Ft. Carson (Colo.) Army Hosp., 1970-82; head nurse Evans Army Community Hosp., Ft. Carson, 1982-98, staff officer divsn. quality support, 1998—. Neonatal resuscitation regional trainer. Mem. NAACOG, Nat. Assn. Neonatal Nurses, Colo. Assn. Neonatal Nurses, Sigma Theta Tau, Iota Pi.

PHILLIPS, JUDITH PARKER, interior designer; b. Guantanamo Bay, Cuba, Sept. 16, 1954; d. John Adams and Frances Adeline (Zaino) Parker; B.S., U. Conn., 1976; m. Nicholas William Phillips, III, Apr. 14, 1978; 1 child, Kirsten Marie. Designer, Clark Contract Interiors, Hartford, Conn., 1976-78; project designer Contract Interiors, Detroit, 1978-79, Silvers, Inc., Detroit, 1980; sr. project designer Interiors Internat., Inc., Grand Rapids, Mich., 1980-81, design mgr., 1982-84, mgr. corporate showroom design, 1984-85; designer, Space planner Allied Office Interiors, 1985-86; corp. sales SteelCase Inc., Grand Rapids, Mich., 1986-87, product specialist, nat. accounts devel., 1987— ; works include: sports complexes, schs. and housing in Saudi Arabia, Gen. Motors; freelance designer pvt. residences. Worthy advisor Rainbow Girls, Order Eastern Star, 1976— , recipient Grand Cross of Color; organizer glass recycling center, 1972. Recipient lst prize student competition Inst. Bus. Designers, 1976. Mem. Inst. Bus. Designers (affiliate), Profl. Women's Network, Mgrs. and Suprs. Am. Seating Club, Blodgett Area Neighborhood Assn. Republican. Congregationalist. Home: 15 Grace Dr Medfield MA 02052-2819 Office: 155 Federal St Boston MA 02110-1727

PHILLIPS, JULIA MAE, physicist; b. Freeport, Ill., Aug. 17, 1954; d. Spencer Kleckner and Marjorie Ann (Figi) Phillips. BS, Coll. William and Mary, 1976; PhD, Yale U., 1981. Mem. tech. staff AT&T Bell Labs., Murray Hill, 1981-88, supr. thin film rsch. group, 1988-95; dept. mgr. materials process computation and modeling dept. Sandia Nat. Labs., Albuquerque, 1995-2000, dep. dir. materials and process scis. ctr., 2000-01, dir. phys. and chem. sci. ctr., 2001—. Program mgr. Consortium Superconducting Elecs., 1989-92; mem. com. on condensed matter and materials physics NRC, 1996-99, mem. solid state scis. com., 1998-2001, mem. nat. materials adv. bd., 1999—, chair, 2002—, mem. com. on materials rsch. for def.-after-next, 1999-2002; vice chair Solid State Scis. com., 1999-2001, mem. bd. on physics and astronomy, 2000—; mem. adv. com. math. and phys. scis. NSF, 2000-. Editor: Heteroepitaxy on Silicon Technology, 1987, Epitaxial Oxide Thin Films and Heterostructures, 1994; prin. editor Jour. Materials Rsch., 1990—; mem. editl. bd. Applied Physics Letters and Jour. Applied Physics, 1992-94, Applied Physics Revs., 1998—; contbr. articles to profl. jours. Fellow Am. Phys. Soc. (exec. com. divsn. materials physics 1997-2000); mem. AAAS, Materials Rsch. Soc. (sec. 1987-89, councillor 1991-93, 2d v.p. 1993, 1st v.p. 1994, pres. 1995), Fedn. Materials Soc. (exec. com. 1997), Sigma Xi, Phi Beta Kappa.

PHILLIPS, KAREN, secondary education educator; Physical edn. tchr., adminstr. Walter D. Johnson Jr. H.S., Las Vegas, 1993-97; asst. prin. Lied Mid. Sch., 1997-99; prin. Clifford J. Lawrence Jr. High Sch., 1999—. Recipient Middle Sch. Physical Edn. Tchr. of the Yr. Nat. Assn. for Sport and Physical Edn., 1993. Office: Clifford J Lawrence Jr High Sch 4410 S Juliano Rd Las Vegas NV 89147-8691

PHILLIPS, KAREN ANN, psychiatric-mental health nurse; b. Latrobe, Pa., July 6, 1944; d. G.W. and Verna W. (Cassidy) Lamproplos; m. Thomas D. Phillips, May 1, 1982; children: Jody Lynn Nikirk, Joseph D. Nikirk III. Student, Lake Erie Coll. for Women, 1962-63, Allegany C.C., 1970-76, U. Pitts., 1978-79; BSS, Ohio U., Lancaster, 2001; diploma, Meml. Hosp. Sch. Nursing, Cumberland, Md., 1967. RN Ohio. Staff nurse, pediatrics and vis. nurse home health care Meml. Hosp., 1967, 68-76; staff nurse med.-surg. unit Cape Fear Hosp., Fayetteville, N.C., 1967-68; asst. coord. home care dept. West Penn Hosp., Pitts., 1978-79; vis. nurse Westmoreland Home Health Care Agy., Greensburg, Pa., 1976-78; staff pool nurse, staff nurse neurosurg. ICU, Westmoreland Hosp., 1979-80, coord. utilization rev., 1980; staff nurse renal transplant unit and rehab. ctr. Ohio State U. Hosps., Columbus, 1980, 82-89; dir. nursing Logan (Ohio) Health Care Ctr., 1980-81; nursing supr. Oakfield Convalescent Ctr., Columbus, 1981-82; staff nurse IV Fairfield Med. Ctr., Lancaster, Ohio, 1989-93, patient rep. emergency dept., 1993—. Instr. geriatric nursing aid Tri-County Joint Vocat. Sch., Nelsonville, Ohio, 1981; clk. The Toy Store, Worthington, Ohio, 1984-86; sales rep. Irwin & Assocs., Bremen, Ohio, 1985-87. Recipient Circle of Excellence award Sigma Theta Tau, 1997. Mem.: Ohio Soc. Healthcare Consumer Advocacy (bd. dirs. 1997—98, 2000—01), Daus. Union Vets. Civil War. Avocations: reading, films, genealogy, collecting teddy bears, dolls, videos, movie-related books. Home: RR 1 Box 509 Sugar Grove OH 43155-9604 Office: Fairfield Medical Center Patient Rep Office 401 N Ewing St Lancaster OH 43130-3371 E-mail: ttomkar@cs.com.

PHILLIPS, KAREN BORLAUG, economist, railroad industry executive; b. Long Beach, Calif., Oct. 1, 1956; d. Paul Vincent and Wilma (Tish) Borlaug. Student, Cath. U. P.R., 1973-74; BA, BS, U. N.D., 1977; postgrad., George Washington U., 1978-80. Rsch. asst. rsch. and spl. programs adminstrn. U.S. Dept. Transp., Washington, 1977—78, economist, office of sec., 1978—82; profl. staff mem. (majority) Com. Commerce Sci., Transp. U.S. Senate, 1982—85, tax economist (majority) com. on fin., 1985—87, chief economist (majority) senate com. on fin., 1987—88; commr. Interstate Commerce Commn., 1988—94; v.p. legis. Assn. Am. Railroads, 1994—95, sr. v.p. policy, legis. and comm., 1995—98; pres. Policy & Advocacy Assocs., Alexandria, Va., 1998—2000; v.p. U.S. govt. affairs Can. Nat. Rlwy. Co., 2000—. Contbg. author studies, publs. in field. Recipient award for Meritorious Achievement, Sec. Transp., 1980, Spl. Achievement awards, 1978, 80, Outstanding Performance awards, 1978, 80, 81. Mem. Am. Econ. Assn., Women's Transp. Seminar (Woman of Yr. award 1994), Transp. Rsch. Forum, Assn. Transp. Law, Logistics and Policy, Tax Coalition, Blue Key, Phi Beta Kappa, Omicron Delta Epsilon. Republican. Lutheran. Office: Can Nat Rlwy Co Ste 500 601 Pennsylvania Ave NW Washington DC 20004 E-mail: karen.phillips@cn.ca.

PHILLIPS, KAY ELLEN, interior designer; b. Elkhart, Ind., Oct. 9, 1945; d. Charles Raymon and Bernetha (Threlkeld) Cook; m. Ronald Lee Phillips, Aug. 25, 1967; children: Eric Wayne, Dana Lynne. BA, Ariz. State U., 1967, MA, 1970; color analysis cert., Beauty for All Seasons, Orlando, Fla., 1983; postgrad. in interior design Seminole Community Coll., 1984—. Color analyst, ind. rep. Beauty for All Seasons, 1983—; interior designer Anne Spalla Interiors, Inc., Longwood, Fla., 1985—. Mem. assoc. bd. Fla. Symphony, Orlando, 1980—, sec., 1984; vol. Additions program Orange County Sch. System, Orlando, 1980—. Recipient Service award Orange County Sch. System, 1980-85. Mem. Pi Lambda Theta, Phi Theta Kappa. Republican. Presbyterian. Club: Semoran Jr. Woman's (treas. 1977-79). Avocations: travel, gourmet cooking, aerobics, reading. Home: 8755 Larwin Ln Orlando FL 32817-1342

PHILLIPS, KEITH WENDALL, minister; b. Portland, Oreg., Oct. 21, 1946; s. Frank Clark and Velma Georgina (Black) P.; m. Mary Katherine Garland, July 16, 1973; children: Joshua, Paul, David. BA, UCLA, 1968; MDiv, Fuller Theology Sem., 1971, D. of Ministries, 1972; LHD (hon.) , John Brown U., 1990; LHD (hon.) , Sterling Coll., 2002. Dir. Youth For Christ Clubs, L.A., 1965-71; pres. World Impact, 1971—. Commencement speaker Tabor Coll., 1969, 91, John Brown U., 1990, Sterling Coll., 2002. Author: Everybody's Afraid in the Ghetto, 1973, They Dare to Love the Ghetto, 1975, The Making of a Disciple, 1981, No Quick Fix, 1985, Out of Ashes, 1996. Chmn. L.A. Mayor's Prayer Breakfast Com., 1985—; bd. dirs. Christian Cmty. Devel. Assn., 1992—; founder/coord. Crowns of Beauty Confs.; spkr. Promise Keeper. Named Disting. Staley lectr., 1969. Mem. Evangelistic Com. of Newark (pres. 1976—), World Impact of Can. (pres. 1978—), The Oaks (pres. 1985—), Faith Works (pres. 1987—) Baptist. Office: World Impact 2001 S Vermont Ave Los Angeles CA 90007-1279 *Our knowledge of God's Word outruns our obedience. The challenge for Christians is to live what we know.*

PHILLIPS, LARRY EDWARD, lawyer; b. Pitts., July 5, 1942; s. Jack F. and Jean H. (Houghtelin) P.; m. Karla Ann Hennings, June 5, 1976; 1 son, Andrew H.; 1 stepson, John W. Dean IV. BA, Hamilton Coll., 1964; JD, U. Mich., 1967. Bar: Pa. 1967, U.S. Dist. Ct. (we. dist.) Pa. 1967, U.S. Tax Ct. 1969. Assoc. Buchanan, Ingersoll, Rodewald, Kyle & Buerger, P.C., Pitts., 1967-73, mem., 1973—. Mem. ABA (sect. taxation, com. on corp. tax and sect. real property, probate and trust law), Am. Coll. Tax Counsel, Pa. Bar Assn., Tax Mgmt. Inc. (adv. bd.), Pitts. Tax Club, Allegheny County Bar Assn., Duquesne Club. Republican. Presbyterian. Office: Buchanan Ingersoll PC One Oxford Ctr 301 Grant St Fl 20 Pittsburgh PA 15219-1410 E-mail: phillipsle@bipc.com.

PHILLIPS, LARRY ARTHUR, artist; b. Syracuse, N.Y., Mar. 6, 1951; s. Arthur Foster and Vivian Phillips. Home: 709 S West St Apt 4 Syracuse NY 13202

PHILLIPS, LARRY DUANE, gemologist, appraiser; b. Silver City, N.Mex., Nov. 19, 1948; s. Fredric Duane and Bernice Larry (Dannelley) P.; m. Ellen Catherine Keaveny, May 6, 1972; 1 child, Tamara Lynn. Student, N.Mex. State U., 1966-70, Ind. U., 1986—; grad. in gemology, Gemological Inst. Am. Cert. gemologist and appraiser. Jeweler, designer Larry Phillips Studios, Albuquerque, 1971-73; jewelry mfr. The Cloud Gatherer, 1973-78; custom jeweler, gemologist The Jewelry Works, 1978-82; gemologist, appraiser Butterfield Jewelers, 1982-90; owner Phillips & Assocs., 1990—. Musician, entertainer Larry Phillips Studios, Albuquerque, 1971—; entertainment dir. Four Hills Country Club, Albuquerque, 1984-85. Mem. Am. Soc. Appraisers (v.p. N.Mex. chpt. 1987-88, treas. 1990-91, pres. 1991-92, nat. gem. and jewelry com. 1991-95, chair internat. gems and jewelry com. 1993-95, profl. devel. com., regional gov. 1995-99, internat. issues task force 1996, internat. edn. com. 1999-2001, constitution and bylaws com. 1999-2001, chmn. uniform stds. profl. appraisal practice issues task force 1999—, internat. sec. 2001—), Internat. Soc. Appraisers (designated, Disting. Svc. award 1990), Nat. Jewelers Assn., N.Mex. Jewelers Assn. (arbitration bd., treas. 1984, bd. dirs. 1989-92), Appraisal Found. (personal property stds. task force, mem. jewelers vigilance com. appraisal task force, issues and resources panel, stds. chair), Accredited Gemologists Assn., Nat. Cert. Master Gemologist Com. (bd. govs. 1993-95, chmn. 1992-93), Albuquerque Musicians Co-op (publicity chair 1977-78). Avocations: musician, graphic artist, computer programmer. Home: 801 Marie Park Dr NE Albuquerque NM 87123-1718

PHILLIPS, LAUGHLIN, art museum chairman emeritus, former magazine editor; b. Washington, Oct. 20, 1924; s. Duncan and Marjorie Grant (Acker) P.; m. Elizabeth Hood, 1956 (div. 1975); children: Duncan Vance, Elizabeth Laughlin; m. Jennifer Stats Cafritz, 1975. Student, Yale U., 1942-43; MA, U. Chgo., 1949. Fgn. service officer, 1949-64, Hanoi, Vietnam, 1950-53, Tehran, Iran, 1957-59; co-founder Washingtonian mag., 1965, editor, 1965-74, editor-in-chief, 1974-79; pres. Washington Mag., Inc., 1965-79; dir. Phillips Collection, 1972-92, chmn. of bd., 1967—2002. Bd. dirs. Nat. Coun., UN Assn., Am. and Nat. Capital Area divsn. Trustee MacDowell Colony, 1977-79, Nat. Com. for an Effective Congress, 1966—. With AUS, 1943-46, PTO. Decorated Bronze Star; comendador Orden de Mayo al Mérito (Argentina); chevalier de l'Ordre de la Couronne (Belgium), knight's cross 1st class Order of Danebrog (Denmark); officier Arts et Lettres (France). Mem.: Cosmos (Washington), Metropolitan (Washington), Rolling Rock (Ligonier, Pa.). Office: Dubois 3031 Federal Hill Dr Falls Church VA 22044

PHILLIPS, LAWRENCE H., II, neurologist, educator; b. Clarksburg, W.Va., Dec. 30, 1947; m. Elayne K. Phillips, 1985; children: Joshua, Melanie. AB, Princeton U., 1970; MD, U. W.Va., 1974. Diplomate Am. Bd. Psychiatry and Neurology. Intern U. Wis. Hosps., Madison, 1974-75; resident in neurology Mayo Clinic, Rochester, Minn., 1975-78, rsch. fellow neurophysiology, 1978-79; instr. neurology Mayo Med. Sch./U. Minn., 1979-80; asst. prof. U. Va. Med. Ctr., Charlottesville, 1981-87, dir. electromyography lab., 1981—, assoc. prof., 1987-95; dir. neuromuscular ctr. Muscular Dystrophy Assn. Clinic, 1983—; prof. U. Va. Med. Ctr., 1995—, vice chair dept. neurology and T.R. Johns prof., 1995—. Mem. med. adv. com. Diabetes Rsch. and Tng. Ctr., U. Va., 1981-88; cons. neurologist Mayo Clinic, 1979-80, VA Hosp., Salem, 1983—; cons. panel AMA Diagnostic and Therapeutic Tech. Assessment, 1989—, arbitrator panel, 1990—; expert panel mem. NIH, 1991. Recipient Young Investigator Travel award Internat. Congress Electromyography, 1979. Mem. Am. Neurol. Assn., Am. Acad. Neurology, Am. Assn. Electrodiagnostic Medicine, Assn. Univ. Profs. Neurology, Sigma Xi. Office: U VA Neuromuscular Ctr Med Health Sys PO Box 800394 Charlottesville VA 22908-0001

PHILLIPS, LAYN R. lawyer; b. Oklahoma City, Jan. 2, 1952; s. James Arthur Cole and Eloise (Gulick) P.; m. Kathryn Hale, Aug. 17, 1986; children: Amanda, Parker, Graham. BS, U. Tulsa, 1974, JD, 1977; postgrad., Georgetown U., 1978-79. Bar: Okla. 1977, D.C. 1978, Calif. 1981, Tex. 1991. Asst. U.S. atty., Miami, 1980-81, L.A., 1980-83; trial atty. Bur. of Competition, Washington, 1977-80; U.S. atty. U.S. Dist. Ct. (no. dist.) Okla., Tulsa, 1983-87; judge U.S. Dist. Ct. (we. dist.) Okla., Oklahoma City, 1987-91; litigation ptnr. Irell & Manella, Newport Beach, Calif., 1991—. Tchr. trial practice U. Tulsa Coll. Law, Okla. City U. Law Sch.; lectr. Attys. Gen's. Adv. Inst., Washington. Pres. Am. Inn of Ct. XXIII, Sch. Law, Okla. U., 1989-90; pres. Am. Inn. of Ct. CVIII, Sch. Law., Okla. City U. 1990-91. Named one of Outstanding Young Ams., U.S. Jaycees, 1989. Fellow: ACTL; mem.: Fed. Bar Assn. (pres. Orange County chpt.). Office: Irell & Manella 840 Newport Center Dr Ste 400 Newport Beach CA 92660-6323

PHILLIPS, LEO HAROLD, JR. lawyer; b. Jan. 10, 1945; s. Leo Harold and Martha C. (Oberg) P.; m. Patricia Margaret Halcomb, Sept. 3, 1983. BA summa cum laude, Hillsdale Coll., 1967; MA, U. Mich., 1968, JD cum laude, 1973; LLM magna cum laude, Free U. of Brussels, 1974. Bar: Mich. 1974, N.Y. 1975, U.S. Supreme Ct. 1977, D.C. 1979. Fgn. lectr. Pusan Nat. U., Korea, 1969-70; assoc. Alexander & Green, N.Y.C., 1974-77; counsel Overseas Pvt. Investment Corp., Washington, 1977-80, sr. counsel, 1980-82, asst. gen. counsel, 1982-85, Manor Care, Inc., Gaithersburg, Md., 1985-91, asst. sec., 1988-99, assoc. gen. counsel, 1991-99, v.p., 1996-99. Vol. Peace Corps, Pusan, 1968-71; mem. program for sr. mgrs. in govt. Harvard U., Cambridge, Mass., 1982. Contbr. articles to legal jours. Chmn. legal affairs com. Essex Condominium Assn., Washington, 1979-81; mem. fin. com., cmty. leadership bd. Miami City Ballet, 2001—; deacon Chevy Chase Presbyn. Ch., Washington, 1984-87, moderator, 1985-87, supt. ch. sch., elder, trustee, 1987-90, pres., 1988-90, mem. nominating com., 1995-96. Recipient Alumni Achievement award Hillsdale Coll., 1980; Meritorious Honor award Overseas Pvt. Investment Corp., 1981, Superior Achievement award, 1984. Mem. ABA (internat. fin. transactions com., vice-chmn. com. internat. ins. Law), Am. Soc. Internat. Law (Jessup Internat. Law moot ct. judge semi-final rounds 1978-83, chair corp. counsel com. 1993-97), Internat. Law Assn. (Am. br.; com. sec. 1982), D.C. Bar, N.Y. State Bar Assn., Royal Asiatic Soc. (Korea br.), State Bar Mich., Washington Fgn. Law Soc. (sec.-treas. 1980-81, bd. dirs., program coord. 1981-82, v.p. 1982-83, pres.-elect 1983-84, pres. 1984-85, chmn. nominating com. 1986, 88), Washington Internat. Trade Assn. (bd. dirs. 1984-87), Assn. Bar City N.Y., Hillsdale Coll. Alumni Assn. (co-chmn. Washington area 1977-90), Univ. Club (N.Y.C.). Home: 4740 Connecticut Ave NW Apt 702 Washington DC 20008-5632

PHILLIPS, LINDA DARNELL ELAINE FREDRICKS, retired psychiatric and geriatrics nurse; b. Calgary, Alta., Can., July 23, 1940; came to U.S., 1964; d. Richard and Adeline Ruth (Kuch) Fredricks; m. Marion Rolley Phillips, June 25, 1960 (div. 1962). Cert. in nursing with honors, Broward C.C., Ft. Lauderdale, Fla., 1983. Exec. sec. Grandeur Motor Cars, Pompano Beach, Fla., 1975-80; charge nurse Las Olas Hosp., Ft. Lauderdale, 1983-85; nurse Med. Pers. Pool, 1984-85; pvt. duty nurse, 1985—2002; pres., v.p. L.P.R.N. Inc., 1992-93; ret., 2002. Cons. nurse Waterford Point Condo, Pompano Beach, Fla., 1980-90. Mem.: Fla. Nurses Assn. Avocations: travel, swimming, reading, languages. Address: 2910 NE 55th St Fort Lauderdale FL 33308-3452

PHILLIPS, LINDA LOU, pharmacist; b. Sept. 3, 1952; d. Reece Webster and Bettye Frances (Martin) P. BS in Pharmacy, U. Ark., 1976; MS in Pharmacy, U. Houston, 1980. Registered pharmacist, Tex. Intern Palace Drug Store, Forrest City, Ark., 1976-77; resident in pharmacy Hermann Hosp., Houston, 1978-79; dir. pharmacy Alvin Cmty. Hosp., 1979-80; relief pharmacist Twelve Oaks Hosp., Houston, 1980; cons. pharmacist Health Facilities, Inc., 1980-81; pharmacy supr. Meth. Hosp., 1981-99; pharmacist Walmart, Fayetteville, Ark., 1999—2001; ind. relief pharmacist, 2001—. Sec. spl. interest group, IBAX Pharmacy, 1990-93; chmn. HBO and Co., Series 4000, materials mgmt. spl. interest group, 1994-98. Mem. Am. Soc. Hosp. Pharmacists, So. Meth. U. Alumni Assn., Ark. Alumni Assn., Girls' Cotillion Club (bd. dirs. 1983-85), Rho Chi, Pi Sigma Alpha. Republican. Methocist. Home and Office: 1732 Lancaster Dr Springdale AR 72762-8298

PHILLIPS, MARGARET A. pharmacology educator; BS in Biochemistry, U. Calif., Davis, 1981; PhD in Pharm. Chemistry, U. Calif., San Francisco, 1988. Prof. dept. pharmacology U. Tex. Southwestern Med. Ctr., Dallas. Office: U Tex Southwestern Med Ctr Dept Pharmacology 5323 Harry Hines Blvd Dallas TX 75390-9041

PHILLIPS, MARION GRUMMAN, writer, civic worker; b. N.Y.C., Feb. 11, 1922; d. Leroy Randle and Rose Marion (Werther) Grumman; m. Ellis Laurimore Phillips, Jr., June 13, 1942; children: Valerie Rose (Mrs. Adrian Parsegian), Elise Marion (Mrs. Edward E. Watts III), Ellis Laurimore III, Kathryn Noel Phillips, Cynthia Louise (Mrs. Charles Prosser). Student, Mt. Holyoke Coll., 1940-42; BA, Adelphi U., 1981. Civic vol. Mary C. Wheeler Sch., 1964-68, Historic Ithaca, Inc., 1972-76, Ellis L. Phillips Found., 1960-91. Bd. dirs. North Shore Jr. League, 19660-61, 64-65, 68-69, Family Svc. Assn. Nassau County, 1963-69, Homemaker Svc. Assn. Nassau County, 1959, 61. Author: (light verse) A Foot in the Door, 1965, The Whale-Going, Going, Gone, 1977, Doctors Make Me Sick (So I Cured Myself of Arthritis), 1979; editor: (with Valerie Phillips Parsegian) Richard and Rhoda, Letters from the Civil War, 1982, Wooden Shoes the story of my Grandfather's Grandfather (F.M. Sisson), 1990, Irish Eyes, family hist. of McTarsneys and Sissons, 1990, The Log Chapel, A History of the Congregational Community Church, Rockwood, Maine, 1999; editor Jr. League Shore Lines, 1960-61, The Werthers in America-Four Generations and their Descendants, 1987; A B-Tour of Britain, 1986; contbr. articles on fund raising to mags. Mem. New Eng. Hist. Geneal. Soc., N.Y. Geneal. Biographical Soc., Moorings Club, Creek Club, Hannah Adams Womens Club, PEO Sisterhood. Congregationalist. Address: 279 North St Medfield MA 02052-1211

PHILLIPS, MARRISE MASON, clinical research coordinator; b. York, S.C., Sept. 28, 1946; d. George T.C. and Terether Ella Mae (Stowe) Mason; m. George Ray Phillips, Sept. 5, 1970; children: Adrian Masonray, Persephone Dionne. ADN, Ctrl. Piedmont C.C., 1969; BSN, Wingate Coll., 1988. RN, N.C.; cert. clin. rsch. coord.; cert. dermatology nurse. Staff nurse pediat. ICU, Carolinas Med. Ctr., Charlotte, N.C., 1969-70, staff nurse gen. pediat., 1970-73, nurse mgr. gen. pediat., 1973-82, nurse mgr. adolescent unit, 1982-85, nurse mgr. adult med. surg., 1985-91, diagnostics and therapeutics, 1985-91, clin. rsch. coord., 1991—, office mgr., 1999—. Dir. clin. trials, 2000—. Author: (manual) Diagnostics & Therapeutics Patient Education, 1990; co-author: (with others) DNA's Textbook Dermatologic Nursing Essentials: A Core Curriculum, 1998. Mem. Dermatology Nurses Assn. (pres. N.C. chpt. S.E. region 1995-97, chairperson nat. nominating com. 1998-99, dir. S.E. region 2000—, nat. bd. dirs., pres.-elect), Soc. for Clin. Trials, Rsch. Coords. Network, Assn. Clin. Pharmacology, HPV Support Group, Chi Eta Phi. Democrat. Baptist. Avocations: reading, walking, sewing, cross stitching, crocheting. E-mail: mphillrn@bellsouth.net.

PHILLIPS, MARTI, editor; b. Flora, Ill., Sept. 6, 1954; d. Leonard and Ethel M. Payne; m. Jim L. Phillips, Dec. 6, 1987; children: Jacqueline M., Steven D. Grad., Clay City H.S., 1972. Med. records clk. Olney (Ill.) Clinic, 1985—92; practical nursing provider Am. Med. Home Health, 1992—; editor, book compiler So. Star Pub., Ormond Beach, Fla. Author: The Road to Camelot, 1997, The Last Pirate, 2000; author, editor: Southern Nights, 2001, featured in Tenn. Writer:. Recipient Book of the Month award, Top 50 Rev., Paintedrock-.com, Top 15 Hist. Pirate Novels List award, Amazon.com. Mem.: Romance Writers Am., Book Star Revs. Authors Group (pres.), Hist. Romance Writers, So. Star Author's Group (book compiler). Office: So Star Pub 4 Timberline Trail Box D 32174 E-mail: SouthernPb@aol.com.

PHILLIPS, MARY ANN, artist, writer, retired legal secretary; b. Wolfe City, Tex., June 7, 1924; d. Lewis Jennings and Thelma Louise Grace Haywood; m. Delma Phillips, Nov. 3, 1941; children: Anita Sharon, Peggy Ann, James Ralph. Degree, Brantley Draughan Bus. Sch., 1943; MA in History and Govt., Tex. Woman's U., 1986; sculpture under Evaline Sellors, 1962-64; MFA, Tex. Woman's U., 1988. Legal sec. Zweifel, Floore & Hicks, Ft. Worth, 1943-47; sec. Western Hills Hotel, 1957-59; asst. to dist. supr. census dept. Dept. Commerce, 1959-60; sec. Rep. Party Tarrant County, 1960-65; legal sec. James Morgan Patent Atty., 1965, Morgan and Coffey, Ft. Worth, 1965-67. Sculptor Clay Portraits. Author: Fletcher Warren Reporting for Duty, Sir, 1995, (hist. column) Echoes From Yesteryear, 1979-82. Mem. AAUW, Nat. Assn. Scholars, Tex. Woman's U. Alumnae Assn., Phi Alpha Theta, Delphi Phi Delphi. Avocations: travel, plays, art and sculpture shows, reading, writing, poetry. Home: 6208 Abbott Ave Fort Worth TX 76180-6240

PHILLIPS, MARY LINDA, actress; b. Mpls., May 1, 1947; d. Elmer and Alice (Doherty) Johnson; children: William D. Jr., Henry W.; m. Bill Wiley, May 5, 1966. Student, Oxford U., Eng., 1992. Voice specialist for movies, TV shows and commls. including Pet Sematary (voice of the demon child), X-Files (voice of the demon doll), As The World Turns, Lonesome Dove, The Lion King, Babe, 1995, Mars Attacks, 1996, Stigmata, 1999; appeared on TV series L.A. Law, CHIPS, Hallmark's Ransom of Red Chief, and on stage, including A Woman's Voice, L.A.T.C., 1996, Chamber music, 1997, Blinders, Children of Shame, 1998, Same Time, Next Year, Palm Canyon Playhouse 2000, An Evening of Horton Foote, 2001, Spoon River Anthology, 2002. Recipient Robby award for best supporting actress in a comedy, 1982. Episcopalian. Avocations: gourmet cooking, gardening, tennis. Home: 3808 Los Amigos St La Crescenta CA 91214-1611 E-mail: philpong@webtv.net.

PHILLIPS, MICHAEL M. gastroenterologist; b. Bklyn., Aug. 20, 1940; s. Jacob and Ruth (Gordon) P.; m. Barbara Mary Posner, Dec. 25, 1966; children: Bradley Morse, Julie Anne. BA, Bklyn. Coll., 1962; MD, SUNY, Buffalo, 1967. Diplomate Am. Bd. Internal Medicine, Am. Bd. Gastroenterology. Intern San Francisco Gen. Hosp., 1967-68; resident in internal medicine Montefiore Hosp. & Med. Ctr., Bronx, N.Y., 1968-70; fellow in gastroenterology Johns Hopkins U., Balt., 1970-71; fellow in liver disease Yale U., New Haven, 1971-72; gastroenterologist Malcolm Grow Hosp. USAF, Washington, 1972-74; chief divsn. gastroenterology Malcolm Grow Hosp., 1973-74; pvt. practice Washington, 1974—; assoc. clin. prof. medicine George Washington U. Sch. Medicine, 1978-2001; clin. prof. of medicine George Washington U. Sch. of Medicine, 2001—. Cons. gastroenterologist Social Security Adminstrn., Washington, 1976—. Contbg. editor Oakstone Publs. Educational Reviews in Gastroenterology, 1989—. Maj. USAF, 1970-72. Fellow ACP; mem. Am. Gastroenterology Assn., Am. Assn. for Study of Liver Disease, Am. Soc. Internal Medicine. Avocations: oenology, travel. Office: Michael M Phillips MD PC 2021 K St NW # 412 Washington DC 20006-1003 E-mail: barmike@bellatlantic.net.

PHILLIPS, NICHOLAS GEOFFREY, physicist, researcher; b. London, Oct. 3, 1964; s. Geoffrey Keith Phillips, Christine Mary Phillips; m. Susan Katherine Gregurick; children: Andrew. BA, U. Va., 1990; PhD, U. Md., 1998. Rsch. scientist NASA, Greenbelt, Md., 1993—. Contbr. articles to profl. jours. Grantee Long Term Space Astrophysics, NASA, 2002—. Mem.: Am. Astron. Soc.

PHILLIPS, NORMAN EDGAR, chemistry educator; b. Detroit, Dec. 20, 1928; s. Norman Christopher and Margaret Elma (Watson) P.; m. Paula Mae McCreery, July 3, 1951; children: Norman Christopher, Susan Margaret. BA, U. B.C., Vancouver, Can., 1949; MS, U. B.C., 1950; Phd, U. Chgo., 1954. Postdoct. fellow Nat. Rsch. Coun. U. Calif., Berkeley, 1954-55, instr. dept. chemistry, 1955-56, asst. prof. dept. chemistry, 1956-60, assoc. prof. dept. chemistry, 1960-66, prof. dept. chemistry, 1966—, assoc. dean grad. divsn., 1966-70, dean Coll. Chemistry, 1975-81; prin. investigator, sr. scientist Lawrence Berkeley Lab, 1960—, assoc. dir., 1984-91, head materials and molecular rsch. divsn., materials and chems. scis. divsn., 1984-91. Invited prof. U. Joseph Fourier, Grenoble, 1985; invited lectr. in physics Nat. Sci. Coun. Rep. of China, 1992. Alfred B. Sloan rsch. fellow, 1961-64; Guggenheim fellow Clarendon Lab. Oxford U., 1963-64; sr. fellow NSF Technical U. Helsinki, 1970-71; recipient Alexander von Humboldt Rsch. award for sr. U.S. scientists Technische Hochschule, Darmstadt, Germany, 1991-92. Fellow APS, AAAS; mem. ACS, Materials Rsch. Soc., Sigma Xi. Achievements include research in specific heat measurements, under high pressures and in high magnetic fields at temperatures from 5mK to 300K; superfluids, superconductors, normal metals, spin glasses, heavy-fermion compounds, other magnetic materials; development of techniques and temperature scales. Office: U Calif Dept Chemistry Berkeley CA 94720-1460

PHILLIPS, OLIVER, topical forest ecologist; NERC Rsch. fellow U. Leeds, Eng., 1996-99, lectr. Eng., 1999—; rsch. assoc. Mo. Bot. Garden, 1997—. Recipient Edmund H. Fulling award Soc. Econ. Botany, 1992. Mem. Soc. for Econ. Botany (mem. coun. 1996-99), Assn. Trop. Biology, Brit. Ecol. Soc. Office: U Leeds Geography Sch Ctr Biodiver & Conservation Leeds LS2 9JT England E-mail: oliverp@geog.leeds.ac.uk.

PHILLIPS, OLIVERIO MICHELSEN, retired chemical engineer; b. Fusagasuga, Colombia, June 6, 1928; s. Oliverio M. and Yolanda V. (Villaveces) P.; m. Yolanda M. Villaveces, Mar. 25, 1950; children: Jorge, Gustavo, Yolanda, Roberto, Francis, Alberto, Jose, Carolina. BS, MIT, 1948, MS, 1950, DSc, 1957. Indsl. cons., Bogota, 1968-95; cons. UN OAS, N.Y.C., Washington, 1972-76; pres. Corp. Nal. Investigacion Forestal, Bogota, 1978-81; project mgr. Arinco S.A., 1982-87, gen. mgr., 1987-92; ret., 1997. Bd. dirs. Corp. Financ. Popular, Bogota, 1968-71, Colciencias, Bogota, 1969-77, Ingeominas, Bogota, 1976-82. Mem. Inst. Colombiano de Normas Tecnicas, Inst. Investigaciones Tecnologicas (bd. dirs. 1983-87), Fedesarrollo (bd. dirs. 1969-95), Cooperacion Tecnica Internat. (bd. dirs. 1992-95), MIT Club (pres. 1966-68), Soc. Colombiana de Ciencias Quimicas (pres. 1962), N.Y. Acad. Scis. Roman Catholic. Avocations: music, reading, walking. Home: 6804 Chesterbrook Ct Apt 304 Raleigh NC 27615-7815 E-mail: ophillm@earthlink.net.

PHILLIPS, PATRICIA JEANNE, retired school system administrator; b. Amarillo, Miss., Jan. 13, 1935; d. William Macon and Mary Ann (Cawthon) Patrick; m. William Henry Phillips, June 22, 1962; 1 child, Mary Jeanne. BA, Millsaps Coll., 1954; MA, Vanderbilt/Peabody U., 1957; EdD, U. So. Miss., 1978. Tchr. Jackson (Miss.) Pub. Schs., 1954-73, prin., 1973-75, asst. prin., 1975-77; dir. ednl. program Eden Prairie (Minn.) # 272, 1977-80; dir. elem. edn. Meridian (Miss.) Pub. Schs., 1980-91, asst. supt. curriculum, 1991; ret., 1991. Prof. Miss. Coll., Clinton, 1977, Miss. State U., Meridian, 1981-2000; cons. in field. Co-author: (testing practice) Test Taking Tactics, 1987; developer tng. materials Best Practices; contbr. articles to profl. jours. pres. Meridian Symphony Orch., 1987, 2000—; v.p. Meridian Coun. Arts, 1986; bd. dirs. Meridian Art Mus. Named Boss of Yr., Meridian Secretarial Assn., 1985, Arts Educator of Yr., Meridian Coun. Arts, 1991; recipient Excellence award Pub. Edn. Form, 1993. Mem. ASCD, Miss. ASCD, Miss. Assn. Women (pres.), Rotary, Phi Kappa Alpha, Phi Delta Kappa (pres. 1986-87), Alpha Delta Kappa Gamma (pres. 1962). Republican. Methodist. Avocations: grant writing, computers, heirloom sewing, golf. Home: 322 51st St Meridian MS 39305-2013 E-mail: bjphill@mississippi.net.

PHILLIPS, PATRICIA ALWOOD RICH, librarian; b. Richmond, Va., July 28, 1942; d. Arthur Melville and Mary Wilson (Bellinger) Rich; m. Stanley Josephus Phillips, July 28, 1963; children: Stanley Josephus Jr., Asha Marie. AB in English, U. N.C., 1965, MSLS, 1967; EdD in Gen. Adminstrv. Leadership, Vanderbilt U., 1995. Cataloger Tenn. Tech. U., Cookeville, 1966-75, head catalog dept., 1976-82, coord. bibliographic control, 1981-83; coord. tech. svc. U. of South, Sewanee, Tenn., 1983-1996; univ. libr. U. Tex. at El Paso, 1996—. Mem. ALA, AAUP (v.p. pub. instrn. 1978-82, v.p. pvt. instrn. 1984-86), Southeastern Libr. Assn., Tenn. Libr. Assn. Democrat. Episcopalian. Home: 345 Shadow Mountain Dr Apt 1610 El Paso TX 79912-4062 Office: Library Utep El Paso TX 79968-0001

PHILLIPS, PAUL EVERARD, physician, medical educator; b. London, Feb. 2, 1937; came to U.S., 1940; s. Ralph Francis and Barbara Alison (Reeves) P.; m. Charlotte Wood, 1962 (div. 1981); children: Christopher, Diane, Hugh; m. Sharon Patricia Sullivan, Mar. 10, 1984; 1 child, Margaret Helen. AB, Princeton U., 1958; MD, Albany Med. Coll., 1962. Diplomate Am. Bd. Internal Medicine, Am. Bd. Rheumatology. Resident in Medicine Roosevelt Hosp., N.Y.C., 1962-63; assoc. in Virology NIH, Bethesda, Md., 1963-65; resident in Medicine Bellevue Hosp., N.Y.C., 1965-67; fellow in rheumatology Columbia-Presbyn. Hosp., 1967-69, assoc. in medicine, 1969-70; from asst. to assoc. prof. medicine Cornell U. Med. Coll., 1970-81; prof. medicine SUNY Upstate Med. U., Syracuse, 1981—; also prof. pediatrics assoc. prof. rehab. medicine SUNY, 1981—, chief divsn. rheumatology, 1981-2001. Attending physician Univ. Hosp., Crouse-Irving Meml. Hosp., Syracuse, 1981—; cons. VA Med. Ctr., Syracuse, 1981—. Editor Clin. and Exptl. Rheumatology, 1982-2000; contbr. 70 articles to profl. jours. Trustee Everson Mus., 1998—. Recipient 40 rsch. grants various sources, N.Y.C., Syracuse, 1967—. Fellow Am. Coll. Physicians, Am. Coll. Rheumatology, Dewitt Fish and Game Club (pres. 1993-95). Avocation: shooting sports. Office: SUNY Upstate Med U 750 E Adams St Syracuse NY 13210-2306 Business E-Mail: phillipp@upstate.edu.

PHILLIPS, PEGGY V. science administrator; MS in Microbiology, U. Idaho. With Immunex Corp., Seattle, 1986—94, sr. v.p. pharm. devel., 1994—99, exec. v.p., COO, 1999—; sr. v.p., COO Immunex R & D Corp., 1991—95. Office: Immunex Corp 51 University St Seattle WA 98101*

PHILLIPS, PETER CHARLES BONEST, economist, educator, researcher; b. Weymouth, Dorset, Eng., Mar. 23, 1948; came to U.S., 1980; s. Charles Bonest and Gladys Eileen (Lade) P.; m. Emily Dowdell Birdling, Feb. 10, 1971 (div. 1980); 1 child, Daniel Lade; m. Deborah Jane Blood, June 13, 1981; children: Justin Bonest, Lara Kimberley. BA, Auckland (New Zealand) U., 1969, MA, 1971; PhD, London U., 1974; MA (hon.), Yale U., 1979. Teaching fellow U. Auckland, 1969-70, jr. lectr., 1970-71; lectr. in econs. U. Essex, Colchester, Eng., 1972-76; prof. econs. U. Birmingham, Eng., 1976-79, Yale U., New Haven, 1979-85, Stanley Resor prof. econs., 1985-89, Sterling prof. econs., 1989—; Alumni disting. prof. econs. U. Auckland, 1991—; pres. Predicta Software Inc., Madison, Conn., 1994—. Vis. scholar Ecole Polytechnique, Paris, 1977; univ. vis. prof. Monash U., Melbourne, Australia, 1986; vis. prof. Inst. Advanced Studes, Vienna, Austria, 1989; disting. visitor London Sch. Econs., 1989. Editor Econometric Theory jour., 1985; joint editor Asia Pacific Economic Review, 1995—; contbr. over 180 articles, book revs., notes to profl. jours. Recipient award for promotion of sci. Japan Soc., 1983, New Zealand medal Sci. and Tech., 1998, Plura Scripsit, 1997, Plurima Scripsit Econometric Theory award, 2000, Nzier Qantas Economist of Yr., 2000; Commonwealth Grants Com. scholar, Eng., 1971, Guggenheim fellow, N.Y., 1984-85. Fellow Am. Acad. Arts & Scis., Royal Soc. New Zealand (hon.), Econometric Soc., Jour. Econometrics, Am. Statis. Soc.; mem. Inst. Math. Stats. Avocations: building, poetry, reading. Home: 133 Concord Dr Madison CT 06443-1814 Office: Cowles Found PO Box 208281 New Haven CT 06520-8281 E-mail: peter.phillips@yale.edu.

PHILLIPS, PETER LAWRENCE, communications executive; b. Lynn, Mass., June 22, 1942; s. Raymond A. and Edna M. (Peterson) P.; m. Sybil Jean Lewis, Aug. 21, 1971; children: Benjamin James, Rebecca Lewis. BFA, U. Conn., 1964; MA, UCLA, 1966. Prof. Centenary Coll., Hackettstown, N.J., 1966-70; TV prodr./dir. Group W, Westinghouse Broadcasting Co., Boston, 1970-73; dir. promotional program devel. Stanmar, Inc., Sudbury, Mass., 1973-75; mgr. creative svcs. Gillette Co., Boston, 1975-79; pres., owner Creative Svcs. Group Ltd., Marblehead, Mass., 1979-80; cons. Newsome & Co., Inc., Boston, 1980-81; corp. creative dir. corp. comm. Digital Equipment Corp., 1982-87, mgr. corp. identity and design, 1987-89, dir. corp. identity, 1989-94; prin. Phillips Corp. Identity & Design Strategy, 1994—. Sec. bd. dirs. Design Mgmt. Inst., 1990—; mem. design mgmt. adv. coun. U. Westminster, London, 2000—. Author: An Iconography of American Scenic Design, 1966. Bd. dirs. Marblehead Cmty. Counseling Ctr.; chmn. bd. dirs. Salem Mission at Crombie St., 1998—. Mem. NATAS, Am. Inst. Graphic Arts, Corinthian Yacht Club, Masons. Episcopalian. Home and Office: 9 Upland Rd Marblehead MA 01945-1341

PHILLIPS, PETER MARTIN, sociologist, educator, media researcher; b. Sacramento, Dec. 9, 1947; s. Donald B. and Jeanne Marie (Perrin) P.; m. E. Susan Phillips,Nov. 19, 1967 (dec. Dec. 1979); 1 child, Jeff; m. Mary M. Lia, June 24, 2000. BA, Santa Clara (Calif.) U., 1970; MA, Calif. State U., Sacramento, 1975, U. Calif., Davis, 1992, PhD, 1994. Prof. sociology Sacramento City Coll., 1975-94; asst. prof. sociology Sonoma State U., Rohnert Park, Calif., 1994-98, assoc. prof. sociology, 1998—. Instr. U. Calif. Davis Extension, 1990—; social welfare cons. various social welfare agys., 1979-94; dir. Project Censored, Rohnert Park, 1996—. Author: Censored 1997: The News That Didn't Make the News, 1997, Censored 1998: The News That Didn't Make the News, 1998, Censored 1999: The News That Didn't Make the News, 1990, Censored 2000: The Year's Top 25 Censored Stories, Censored 2001: 25th Anniversary Edition. Mem. Am. Sociol. Assn., Pacific Sociol. Assn. Office: Sonoma State U 1801 E Cotati Ave Rohnert Park CA 94928 E-mail: peter.phillips@sonoma.edu.

PHILLIPS, PHIL E. lawyer, law administrator; b. Abilene, Tex., July 23, 1966; BS, Pepperdine U., 1988, JD, 1992. Bar: Calif. 1992, U.S. Dist. Ct. (ctrl. dist.) Calif. 1992. Dir. regulatory affairs Pepperdine U., Malibu, Calif., 1993—. Mem. L.A. County Bar Assn. Mem. Ch. of Christ. Avocations: reading, martial arts, fly fishing, family. Office: Pepperdine U 24255 PCH Malibu CA 90263

PHILLIPS, RENEÉ, editor-in-chief, author, public speaker; b. Freeport, N.Y. Student, Art Students League, 1979, Am. Art Sch., 1979, Fashion Inst. Tech., 1980, New Sch. for Social Rsch., 1980. Dir., founder Artopia, not-for-profit art orgn., N.Y.C., 1980-84; pub., editor-in-chief Manhattan Arts Internat., 1983—; editor-in-chief www.Manhattan Arts.com. Lectr. mus. and galleries, including Katonah Art Mus., N.Y. Artists Equity, Salmagundi Club, Learning Annex, Marymount Manhattan Coll., N.Y.C.; juror Excellence in Arts Awards, 1988, N.Y. Lung Assn. Ann. Exhbn., 1990, Manhattan Arts Internat. Ann. Internat. Art Competition, 1992-2002; juror, co-curator Redefining Visionary Art, Doma Gallery, N.Y.C., 1989; curator Synthesis of Painting and Sculpture exhbn., 1st Women's Bank, N.Y.C., 1984, Salute to Liberty internat. art exhbn., N.Y.C., 1986; organizer over 40 art and cultural events; spkr. in field; editor-in-chief www.ManhattanArts.com. Author: New York Contemporary Art Galleries Annual Guide, 1995-02, Presentation Power Tools for Fine Artists, 1998, 2d edit., 2000, 3rd edit., 2002, Success Now! for Artists: A Motivational Guide, 1998, 2nd edit., 2001, Creating Success: The Artist's Complete Guide, 2002; editor-in-chief Success Now!, 1991—. Recipient award of merit Muscular Dystrophy Assn., 1986, award for outstanding contbns. to arts Mayor of N.Y.C., 1987. Mem. Internat. Assn. Art Critics, N.Y. Artists Equity (former bd. dirs.). Office: Manhattan Arts Internat 200 E 72nd St New York NY 10021-4537 E-mail: manarts@aol.com.

PHILLIPS, RICHARD CAREY, real estate executive; b. Oklahoma City, Oct. 22, 1964; s. Carey R. and Margaret R. (Anderson) P.; m. Chalynn Lee Claunch. BBA in Fin., U. Okla., 1988. V.p. Womack Property Mgmt., Inc., Oklahoma City, 1988-93; owner, pres. Thomas Drayton & Co., 1993—; mem. Okla. Ho. of Reps., 1992—. Area coord. Inst. Real Estate Mgmt., Oklahoma City, 1992. Councilman, City of Warr Acres, Okla., 1989-92; vol. ARC, 1990. Mem. Warr Acres Putnam City C. of C., Putnam City Jaycees (dir. 1992—), Nat. Assn. Realtors, Met. Bd. Realtors. Republican. Baptist. Home: 5817 NW 40th St Warr Acres OK 73122-3101

PHILLIPS, ROBERT ALLAN, scientist, administrator; b. St. Louis, July 2, 1937; s. Allan B. and Mildred (Fandrich) P.; m. Corley F. Hamill, June 12, 1959; children: Kristin, Michael, Scott. BA, Carleton Coll., 1959; PhD, Washington U., St. Louis, 1965. Scientist Ont. Cancer Inst., 1967-86; prof. U. Toronto, 1967—, chair dept. med. biophysics, 1981-86; scientist Hosp. for Sick Children, Toronto, 1986-96, head divsn. cancer rsch., 1990-96; exec. dir. Nat. Cancer Inst. Can., 1996—2001; dir. Ont. Cancer Rsch. Network, 2001—. Author more than 200 sci. papers; editor meeting reports. Bd. dirs. nat. Cancer Inst. Can., 1991-96, Can. Cancer Soc., 1990-96. Named Citizen of Yr., Civitan, Can., 1973. Mem. Phi Beta Kappa, Sigma Xi. Home: 66 Collier St Toronto ON M4W 1L9 Canada Office: Ont Cancer Rsch Network 149 College St Ste 501 Toronto ON Canada M5T 1P5 E-mail: bob.phillips@ocrn.on.ca.

PHILLIPS, ROBERT BENBOW, financial planner; b. Winston-Salem, N.C., Aug. 20, 1959; s. Clifford Clayton and Roberta George (Stouch) P.; m. Christine Theresa Rudolf, Feb. 12, 1994; 2 children. BS in Biology, Va. Poly. Inst. and State U., 1981; MS in Fin. Planning, Hamilton U., 2001. Registered investment advisor; registered fin. cons.; cert. investment specialist. Pharm. salesman The Sporicidin Co., Washington, 1982-85; stockbroker Legg-Mason, Radford, Va., 1985-88; brokerage mgr. Golden Rule Ins. Co., Roanoke, 1988-91; fin. planner Fin. Planning Svcs.-Internat., Brazil, 1991-95; wholesaler mut. funds Calvert Group, Bethesda, Md., 1995-96; v.p. Schield Mgmt. Co., Denver, 1996-98; dir. mut. fund sales, v.p. sales Mainstay Funds, 1998-99; v.p. sales GE Fin. Assurance, 1999—2001; regional v.p. Ameritus/AVLCI, 2001—. Mem. Fin. Planning Assocs., Ducks Unlimited, Va. Wine Soc., Delta Kappa Epsilon (past officer). Lutheran. Avocations: golf, stained glass, wine and beer making, racquetball, hiking. Office: PO Box 312 Haymarket VA 20168-0312

PHILLIPS, ROBERT DERRICK, psychiatrist; b. Laurinburg, N.C., Dec. 2, 1925; s. James Dickson and Helen Shepherd Phillips; m. Frances Dana Fulcher Olson, July 28, 1951 Idiv. Dec. 1974); children: Robert, Stuart, Helen, Jane, Anna, Betsy, Frances; m. Dorothy Jean Andersen, Oct. 17, 1997. BS, Davidson Coll., 1948; MD, U. Pa., 1952. Diplomate Am. Bd. Psychiatry, Am. Bd. Surgery. Surg. resident Med. Coll. S.C., Charleston, 1952-56, chief surg. resident, 1956-57; staff surgeon Presbyn. Med. Ctr., Chonju, Korea, 1957-59; psychiat. resident U. N.C. Meml. Hosps., Chapel Hill, 1960-63; pvt. practice psychiatry, 1963-95; clin. asst. prof. psychiatry Duke U., Durham, N.C., 1972-95; clin. prof. psychiatry U. N.C. Sch. Medicine, Chapel Hill, 1974-95; ret., 1995. Exec. com. Com. of Responsibility to War-Injured and Burned Vietnamese Children, Boston, 1964-67. Author: The Recovery of the True Self, 1995, (monograph) Structural Symbiotic Systems, 1975. Trustee Union Theol. Sem., Richmond, Va., 1965-67; chmn. Human Rels. Commn., Chapel Hill, 1962-63; founder All Races Coalition with Native Am. People, Chapel Hill, 1991X. Ens. USNR, 1943-46, ATO. Recipient Martin Luther King award Orange County Black Caucus, 1987, Founders' Cir., Buffalo Trust, 1999. Mem. Am. Psychiat. Assn., Am. Coll. Surg.; mem. N.C. Psychiat. Soc. Democrat. Avocations: Native American network support, golf, hiking, workshop leading. Home: 1 Woodland Dr Black Mountain NC 28711-2597

PHILLIPS, ROBERT JAMES, JR. lawyer, corporate executive; b. Houston, Aug. 4, 1955; s. Robert James and Mary Josephine Phillips; m. Nancy Norris, Apr. 24, 1982; 1 child Mary Ashton. BBA, So. Meth. U., 1976, JD, 1980. Bar: Tex. 1980. Vp., gen. counsel Aegis Shipping Ltd., London, 1980-81; assoc. Bishop, Larrimore, Lamsens & Brown, 1981-82; pres. Phillips Devel. Corp., Ft. Worth, 1982-87; pvt. practice, 1982-87, 895; assoc. Haynes and Boone, 1988-89; sr. v.p. Am. Real Estate Group, 1989-93, Am. Savs. Bank, N.A., New West Fed. Savs. and Loan Assn., 1989-93, Am. Savs. Bank, Ft. Worth, 1991-92; chmn., CEO creative risk control Environ. Risk Mgmt. Inc., 1992-94; pres., CEO Pangburn Candy Co., 1996-99; exec. v.p. Ancor Holdings, 1999—; chmn., CEO Am. Staff Resources Corp., 1999—. Bd. dirs. Tex. Heritage, Inc.; chmn., CEO Am. Staff Resources Corp., 1999—. Bd. dirs., exec. com. Ft. Worth Ballet Assn., 1984-85, Van Cliburn Found.; v.p. planning, bd. dirs., exec. com. Ft. Worth Symphony Orch., 1984-85; bd. dirs. Mus. Modern Art, 19865; bd. dirs., exec. com., chmn. investment com. Tex. Boys Choir, 1983-85. Mem. ABA, Tex. Bar Assn., Ft. Worth Bd. Realtors, Crescent Club, Phi Delta Phi, Kappa Sigma, Beta Gamma Sigma. Clubs: River Crest Country, Ft. Worth. Avocations: hunting, fishing, photography. Home and Office: PO Box 470099 Fort Worth TX 76147-0099

PHILLIPS, ROGER, retired steel company executive; b. Ottawa, Ont., Can., Dec. 17, 1939; s. Norman William Frederick and Elizabeth (Marshall) P.; m. Katherine Ann Wilson, June 9, 1962; 1 child, Andrée Claire. B.Sc., McGill U., Montreal, 1960. Vice pres. mill products Alcan Can. Products Ltd., Toronto, Ont., Can., 1969-70, exec. v.p. Can., 1971-75; pres. Alcan Smelters and Chems. Ltd., Montreal, Que., Can., 1976-79; v.p. tech. Alcan Aluminium Ltd., Can., 1980-81; pres. Alcan Internat. Ltd., Can., 1980-81; pres., chief exec. officer IPSCO Inc., Regina, Canada, 1982—2001. Sr. mem. Conf. Bd, Inc., NY, 1987—; bd. dirs. Toronto Dominion Bank, Can. Pacific Rlwy., Fording Inc., Imperial Oil Ltd.; hon. dir. IPSCO Inc. Bd. dirs. Conf. Bd. of Can., 1984-87; chmn. Coun. for Can. Unity, 1987-88. Named Officer of Order of Can., 1999. Fellow Inst. of Physics U.K. (chartered physicist); mem. Can. Assn. Physicists, Am. Iron and Steel Inst. (bd. dirs. 1984—), Sask. C. of C. (bd. dirs. 1984-2001), Que. C. of C. (pres. 1981), Order of Can. (officer), Assiniboia Club (Regina), St. Denis Club, Univ. Club (Montreal). Home: 3220 Albert St Regina SK Canada S4S 3N9 Office: IPSCO Inc Armour Rd Regina SK Canada S4P 3C7 E-mail: rphillips@ipsco.com.

PHILLIPS, RONALD EDWARD, artist, sales executive; b. Clovis, N.Mex., Apr. 10, 1937; s. Rodney Vernon and Ethel Edna (Huff) Phillips; m. May Frances Willingham, Aug. 27, 1957; children: Rhonda Louise, Russell Kent, Teresa Gail; m. Janet Irene Johnsonbaugh Smith, July 4, 1972 (dec. Nov. 29, 1999); stepchildren: Steven, Gregg, Laura. Student, Ea. N.Mex. U., 1955-56, U. N.Mex., 1957, Famous Artist Schs., 1963-64, North Light Art Sch., 1989-90. Group merchandiser women's fashions J.C. Penney Inc., Albuquerque, 1957-64; chem. salesman Take Over Products, Clovis, 1964-65; with International Auto Leasing, Albuquerque, 1965; salesman Pennsalt Chems., N.Mex. div., 1965-67; N.Mex. sales rep. W.W. Grainger Inc., Chgo., 1967-72; nfounder Pueblo Arts, Inc., Albuquerque, 1972—; mgr. Dairy Queen, Santa Rosa and Lovington, 1982-85; owner, mgr. Western Pit n Grill & Food Gallery, Lovington, 1985-88; owner Pueblo Arts Inc./Trailwest Gallery, Albuquerque, 1988—. Tchr. quick draw, continuous line drawing, 1990; artist, guide Pueblo Arts Inc. Trailwest Paintouts, Guide for Artists, 1990—92; ind. sales cons. SWEPCO Bldg. Projects, 1993—. Sketchbooks, ; (movie extra): (films) Whitesands, 1991; Next Fire on Earth, 1992; Wyatt Earp, 1993; Desparate Trails, 1993; Buffalo Girls, 1995; East Meets West, 1995; Lazarus Man Premier, 1995—96. Pres. Albuquerque Wildlife and Conservation, 1963—64; active Albuquerque Conf. & Vis. Bur., 1988—, Albuquerque Arts Alliance, 1994—95, Tourism Assoc. N.Mex., Albuquerque Film Commn. Mem.: Guild Albuquerque Artist Models (advisor, bd. dirs. 1994—98), Albuquerque Arts Alliance, Indian Arts and Crafts Assn. (ethics com. 1973—74), N.Mex. Art League (hon.; pres. 1964—65, instr., bd. arts after sch. project 1995—96). Republican. Avocations: art, sales and marketing. E-mail: ronpuebloarts@juno.com.

PHILLIPS, RONALD FRANK, university administrator; b. Houston, Nov. 25, 1934; s. Franklin Jackson and Maudie Ethel (Merrill) P.; m. Jamie Jo Phillips, Apr. 5, 1957 (dec. Sept. 1996); children: Barbara Celeste Phillips Oliveira, Joel Jackson, Phil Edward. BS, Abilene Christian U., 1955; JD, U. Tex., 1965. Bar: Tex. 1965, Calif. 1972. Bldg. contractor Phillips Homes, Abilene, Tex., 1955-56; br. mgr. Phillips Weatherstripping Co., Midland and Austin, 1957-65; corp. staff atty. McWood Corp., Abilene, 1965-67; sole practice law, 1967-70; mem. adj. faculty Abilene Christian U., 1967-70; prof. law Pepperdine U., Malibu, Calif., 1970—, dean Sch. Law, 1970-97, dean emeritus, 1997—, vice chancellor, 1995—. Deacon North A and Tenn. Ch. of Christ, Midland, 1959-62; deacon Highland Ch. of Christ, Abilene, 1965-70; elder Malibu Ch. of Christ, 1978-95; mgr., coach Little League Baseball, Abilene, Huntington Beach and Malibu, 1968-78, 90-95; coach Youth Soccer, Huntington Beach, Westlake Village and Malibu, 1972-80, 85-86, 91. Recipient Alumni citation Abilene Christian U., 1974 Fellow Am. Bar Found. (life); mem. ABA, State Bar Tex., State Bar Calif., Christian Legal Soc., L.A. Bar Assn., Assn. Am. Law Schs. (chmn. sect. on adminstrn. law schs. 1982, com. on cts. 1985-87), Am. Law Inst., Nat. Conf. Commrs. on Uniform State Laws. Republican. Office: Pepperdine U 24255 Pacific Coast Hwy Malibu CA 90263-0002 E-mail: ronald.phillips@pepperdine.edu.

PHILLIPS, RONALD LEWIS, plant geneticist, educator; b. Huntington County, Ind., Jan. 1, 1940; s. Philemon Lewis and Louise Alpha (Walker) P.; m. Judith Lee Lind, Aug. 19, 1962; children: Brett, Angela. BS in Crop Sci., Purdue U., 1961, MS in Plant Breeding and Genetics, 1963, Doctorate (hon.) , 2000; PhD in Genetics, U. Minn., 1966; postgrad., Cornell U., 1966-67. Research and teaching asst. Purdue U., 1961-62; research and teaching asst. U. Minn., St. Paul, 1962-66, research assoc., 1967-68, asst. prof., 1968-72, assoc. prof., 1972-76, prof. genetics and plant breeding, 1976-93, Regents prof., 1993—, McKnight presdl. chair in Genomics, 2000—. Program dir. Competitive Rsch. Grants Office, USDA, Washington, 1979; mem. adv. grant panels NSF, USDA, AID; chmn. Gordon Conf. on Plant Cell and Tissue Culture, 1985; mem. sci. adv. coun. U. Calif. Plant Gene Expression Ctr., Berkeley, 1986-93, chair, 1992-93; vis. prof., Italy, 1981, Can., 1983, China, 1986, Japan, 1990, Morocco, 1996; dir. Plant Molecular Genetics Inst., 1991-94; chief scientist USDA, 1996-98; trustee Biol. Stain Commn.; mem. Nat. Plant Genetic Resources Bd.; mem. editl. bd. Proc. Nat. Acad. Sci., U.S., 1996-98; dir. Ctr. Microbial and Plant Genomics, 2000—. Co-editor: Cytogenetics, 1977, Molecular Genetic Modification of Eucaryotes, 1977, Molecular Biology of Plants, 1979, The Plant Seed: Development, Preservation and Germination, 1979, Genetic Improvement of Crops: Emergent Techniques, 1980, DNA-Based Markers in Plants, 1994, 2d edit., 2001; assoc. editor: Genetics, 1978-81, Can. Jour. Genetics and Cytology and Genome, 1985-90; mem. editl. bd. Maydica, 1978—, In Vitro Cellular and Devel. Biology, 1988-92, Cell Culture and Somatic Cell Genetics of Plants, 1983-91, Elaeis, 1994—, Proc. NAS; contbr. chpts. to Maize Breeding and Genetics, 1978, Staining Procedures, 1981, Chromosome Structure and Function, 1987, Corn and Corn Improvement, 1988, Plant Transposable Elements, 1988, Chromosome Engring. in Plants, 1991, Maize Handbook, 1994; contbr. sci. articles to profl. jours. Mem. chmn. coun. on ministries, lay leader United Meth. Ch., 1968, dir. Project AgGrad, 1983—; Cub Scout Pack co-chmn. Boy Scouts Am., 1976-77;

judge Minn. Regional and State Sci. Fair, 1970-80. Recipient Purdue Agrl. Alumni Achievement award, 1961, Purdue Disting. Agrl. Alumni award, 1993; NSF fellow, 1961; NIH fellow, 1966-67; recipient Northrup King Oustanding Faculty Performance award, 1985, Crop Sci. Rsch. award, 1988, DeKalb Genetics Crop Sci. Disting. Career award, 1997. Fellow AAAS (chair-elect sect. D), Am. Soc. Agronomy, Crop Sci. Soc. Am. (awards com., divsn. chmn., bd. rep. 1988-91, pres.-elect 1998-99, pres. 1999-2000, past pres. 2000-01); mem. NAS (chair sect. 62), Genetics Soc. Am., Am. Soc. Agronomy (award student sect., Caleb-Dorr award), Sigma Xi, Gamma Alpha (nat. treas.), Gamma Sigma Delta (award of merit 1994), Alpha Zeta. Office: U Minn Dpt Agronomy-Plant Genetics Saint Paul MN 55108 E-mail: phill005@umn.edu.

PHILLIPS, RUSSELL ALEXANDER, JR. retired foundation executive; b. Charlotte, N.C., Sept. 19, 1937; s. Russell Alexander and Robmae (Black) P. AB, Duke U., 1959; LLB (Edward John Noble fellow), Yale U., 1962. Bar: N.C. 1962, D.C. 1966. Clk. to Sr. Judge, U.S. Ct. Appeals, 4th Circuit, 1962-63; legal adv. Ministry of Fin., Govt. No. Nigeria, 1963-65; asst. commr. income tax (legal) East African Common Svcs. Orgn., Nairobi, Kenya, 1965-66; assoc. firm Wilmer, Cutler & Pickering, Washington, 1966-68; program officer Rockefeller Bros. Fund, N.Y.C., 1968-73, corp. sec., 1973-81, v.p., 1979-81, exec. v.p., 1982-98, acting pres., 1987-88. Trustee Asian Cultural Coun. Mem. N.C. Bar Assn., D.C. Bar, Phi Beta Kappa. Democrat. Presbyterian. Home: 40 E 88th St Apt 7D New York NY 10128-1176

PHILLIPS, RUSSELL S. physician, educator; b. Boston, Mar. 14, 1953; s. Martin Melvin and Janice Bernstein Phillips; m. Elise Tofias, June 27, 1982; children: Ezekiah, Jeremy, Adam. BS, MIT, 1975; MD, Stanford U., 1979. Diplomate Am. Bd. Internal Medicine. Intern Beth Israel Hosp., Boston, 1979-81, jr. asst. resident, 1981-82, sr. asst. resident, 1982-83; clin. fellow Harvard Med. Sch., 1983-85, instr. in medicine, 1985-89, asst. prof., 1989-98, assoc. prof., 1998—; chief divsn. gen. medicine and primary care Beth Israel Deaconess Med. Ctr., 2002—. Mem. editl. bd. Am. Jour. Medicine, San Francisco, 1997—; mem. com. clin. investigation Beth Israel Deaconess Med. Ctr., 1997—. Bd. dirs. Newton (Mass.) Soccer, 1997—. Recipient Clifford Barger award for Excellence in Mentoring. Fellow ACP; mem. Am. Fedn. Med. Rsch., Physicians for Nat. Health Program, Physicians for Social Responsibility, Phi Beta Kappa, Phi Lambda Upsilon. Avocations: biking, coaching soccer. Office: Beth Israel Deaconess Med Ctr 330 Brookline Ave Boston MA 02215-5400 E-mail: Phillips@caregroup.harvard.edu.

PHILLIPS, SANDRA, bank executive, educator; b. St. Louis, July 17, 1958; BS, N.W. Mo. State U., Maryville, 1980; MBA, St. Louis U., 1985, PhD, 1999. Lic. real estate broker. Mgmt. trainee Edward Jones & Co., St. Louis, 1981—81; grad. sch. advisor St. Louis U., 1982—85; bank examiner State of Mo., St. Louis, 1985—86; v.p. Bank of Am., 1986—2002. Panel mem., mem. fiscal subcom. United Way of Greater St. Louis, 1995—97; mem. Nat. Black M.B.A. Assn., St. Louis, 1987—97; Bd. dirs. Mo. Arts Coun. , 2001—02, Edn. Monitoring and Adv. Com., St. Louis, 1998—99, St. Louis Black Repertory Co., 1993—98.

PHILLIPS, SANDRA ALLEN, retired primary school educator; b. Newport News, Va., Mar. 10, 1943; d. Cecil Lamar and Mary (Schenk) Allen. BS, Appalachian State U., Boone, N.C., 1965; MEd, U. N.C., Charlotte, 1990. Tchr. Rockwell (N.C.) Elem. Sch., 1964-65, Granite Quarry (N.C.) Elem. Sch., 1965-68, Lillian Black Elem. Sch., Spring Lake, N.C., 1970, Berryhill Elem. Sch., Charlotte, 1970-71, 77-99, ret., 1999; tchr. J.C. Roe Sch., Wilmington, 1974-76. Elected to tchr.'s adv. coun. Charlotte-Mecklenburg Schs., 1995-96, 96-97, 97-98, 98-99; title I tchr., 1999. Named Tchr. of Yr., Berryhill Elem. Sch., 1989. Mem. Profl. Educators N.C., Classroom Tchrs. Assn. Office: Berryhill Elem Sch 10501 Walkers Ferry Rd Charlotte NC 28278-9721

PHILLIPS, SIAN, actress; b. Betws, Wales; d. D. and Sally P.; m. D.H. Roy, 1957 (div. 1960); m. Peter O'Toole, 1960 (div. 1979); 2 children: m. 2d, Robin Sachs, 1979 (div. 1992). Grad. with honors, U. Wales, 1955, DLitt (hon.), 1983. Newsreader, announcer, drama rep., mem. Repertory Co. BBC, 1953-55; toured for Welsh Arts Coun. with Nat. Theatre Co., 1953-55. Bd. govs. Welsh Coll. of Music and Drama, 1992, hon. fellow, 1992. (London stage appearances:): Hedda Gabler, 1959; Ondine and the Dutchess of Malf, 1960—61; The Lizard on the Rock, 1961; Gentle Jack, Maxibules and the Night of the Iguana, 1964 (nominated Best Actress); Ride a Cock Horse, 1965; Man and Superman (nominated Best Actress); Man of Destiny, 1966; The Burglar, 1967; Epitaph for George Dillon, 1972; A Nightingale in Bloomsburg Square, 1973; The Gay Lord Quex, 1975; Spinechiller, 1978; You Never Can Tell, Lyric Hammersmith, 1979; Pal Joey, 1980 (nominated Best Actress of Musical); Half Moon and Albery Theatres, 1980, 1981; Dear Liar, 1982; Major Barbara, 1983; Pey GiGi, 1985; Thursday's Ladies, 1987; Brel, 1988; Paris Match, 1989; Vanilla, 1990; The Manchurian Candidate, 1991; Painting Churches, 1992; Ghosts (nominated Welsh Artist of Yr.); An Inspector Calls, Broadway, 1995; A Little Night Music, 1996 (Olivier nomination , 1995); South Africa, Paris , 1997—98; (films include:): Becket, 1963; Goodbye Mr. Chips (Critics Circle award, N.Y. Critics award, Famous Seven Critics award , 1969); Laughter in the Dark, 1968; Murphy's War, 1970; Under Milk Wood, 1971; The Clash of the Titans, 1979; Dune, 1983; A Painful Case, 1984; Return to Endor, 1985; Valmont, 1988; The Age of Innocence, 1992; House of America, 1996 (BAFTA nomination); Alice Through the Looking Glass; (TV appearances include:): Shoulder to Shoulder, 1974; How Green Was My Valley , 1975 (BAFTA award); I, Claudius , 1976 (Royal TV Soc. award, BAFTA award , 1978); Heartbreak House, 1977; The Oresteia of Aeschylus, 1978; Crime and Punishment, 1979; Tinker, Tailor, Soldier, Spy, 1979; Sean O-Casey, 1980; Churchill: The Wilderness Years, 1981; How Many Miles To Babylon, 1982, 1982; Shadow of the Noose, 1988; Snow Spider, 1988 (Bafta nomination); Vanity Fair; (TV series) Emlyns Moon, 1991; The Chestnut Soldier, 1991 (Bafta nomination); Perfect Scoundrels, 1991; Tonight at 8:30, 1991; Royal TV Soc. Ann. Lectr., 1992; Intent to Kill (also Welsh lang.), 1994; (TV musical)) Nearest and Dearest (also Welsh lang. version), 1994; (TV series) The Borrowers; Ballykiss Angel, 1999; : (films) Heidi (Disney); (TV serial) The Vacillations of Poppy Carew , 1995; Scolds Bridle, 1997; Le Femme Nikita, 1998; The Aristocrats, 1998; Cabaret, I Wish You Love (Israel), (U.K.) , 1999; Cabaret Donmar (London), 2001; Marlene (Olivier nomination, nominated Best Actress in musical Drama Desk and Tony); Magicians House (Canada), 1999; (TV films) Cinderella, 1999; Nikita (Can.), 1999; author: Sian Phillips', Needlepoint, 1987, Private Faces, vol. I autobiography Pub Hodder, 1999, General Journalism; : albums Pal Joey, : albums GIGI, : albums Peg, : albums Single, : albums Bewitched, Bothered and Bewildered, : albums I Remember Mama, : albums A Little Night Music, : albums Marlene, 1997, : albums Middle East Tour in Concert, 1999, : , 1999, : T.V. Magician's House, Can., 2000, : Cabaret at the Firebird Cafe, N.Y.C., 2000, : Film Beckel-Festival, 2000, : Lettice and Lovage U.K Tour, 2001, : publs. Private Faces, 1999, : publs. Public Places, 2001, : autobiography Public Places, vol. II., 2001; (London state appearences): Divas at The Donmar; My Old Lady. Decorated comdr. Brit. Empire; hon. fellow Cardiff Coll., U. Wales, 1981, Poly. Wales, 1988, U. Swansea, 1998, Trinity Coll. Carmarthen, 1998. Fellow Welsh Coll. Music and Drama (v.p. 2001). Office: Lindy King c/o Peters Fraser & Dunlop London WC2 B5HA England

PHILLIPS, SIDNEY FREDERICK, gastroenterologist, educator; b. Melbourne, Australia, Sept. 4, 1933; s. Clifford and Eileen Frances (Fitch) P.; m. Decima Honora Jones, Mar. 29, 1957; children: Penelope Jane, Nichola Margaret, David Sidney. M.B.BS, U. Melbourne, 1956, MD, 1961. Resident med. officer Royal Melbourne Hosp., 1957-61, asst. sub-dean clin. sch., 1961-62; research asso. Central Middlesex Hosp., London, 1962-63; rsch. assoc. Mayo Clinic, Rochester, Minn., 1963-66, cons. in gastroenterology, 1966-2000; prof. medicine Mayo Med. Sch., 1976-2000, prof. medicine emeritus, 2000—, dir. gastroenterology rsch. unit, 1977-94; program dir. Mayo Gen. Clin. Rsch. Ctr., 1974-87; dir. Mayo Digestive Diseases Core Ctr., 1984-90; Karl F. and Marjory Hasselman prof. rsch., 1994-2000. Editor: Digestive Diseases and Sciences, 1977-82, Gastroenterology International, 1990-95; sr. assoc. editor: Gastroenterology, 1991-96; contbr. chpts. to books, articles to profl. jours. Fellow ACP, Royal Coll. Physicians, Royal Australian Coll. Physicians; mem. Am. Motility Soc. (pres. 1994-96), Am. Soc. Clin. Investigation (emeritus), Gastroenterology Soc. Australia (hon.), Am. Gastroenterology Assn. Assn. Am. Physicians, Brit. Soc. Gastroenterology (hon.). Home: 1207 19th Ave NE Rochester MN 55906-4317 Office: St Mary's Hosp Gastroenterology Unit 200 1st St SW Rochester MN 55905-0001 E-mail: phillips.sidney@mayo.edu.

PHILLIPS, SPENCER KLECKNER, retired surgeon; b. Freeport, Ill., Nov. 6, 1914; s. Nelson Chancellor and Bertha Diana (Kleckner) P.; m. Marjorie Ann Figi, July 19, 1948; children: Julia Mae, Spencer Frederick. BA, Colgate U., 1935; MB, Northwestern U., 1939, MD, 1940; MS in Surgery, U. of Minn., 1947. Diplomate Am. Bd. Gen. Surgery. Surg. fellow Mayo Found., Rochester, Minn., 1941, 46-47; 1st asst. surgery Mayo Clinic, 1947-48; practice medicine specializing in surgery Freeport, Ill., 1948-85; dir. of surgery Freeport Meml. Hosp., 1983-85; asst. sec., bd. dirs. Scientific Safety Tech., Inc., Wood Dale, Ill., 1987-88. Trustee, devel. coun. Freeport Health Network; bd. dirs. Cartel, Inc., Woodstock, Ill. Contbr. articles to profl. jours. Commr. Freeport Drug and Alcohol Commn., 1988-95; mem.trust bank and devel coun.of the Heart of Meml. of the Freeport Health Network; bd. dirs. Highland Coll. Found. Cmdr. USNR,, 1941-45 PTO. Decorated Legion of Merit. Fellow ACS; Phi Beta Kappa, Alpha Omega Alpha. Home: 1769 Highland Dr Freeport IL 61032-4605

PHILLIPS, STEPHEN S. lawyer; b. Phila., 1946; BA, Wesleyan U., 1968; JD, Dickinson U., 1971. Bar: Pa. 1971, U.S. Ct. Appeals (3d cir.) 1971, U.S. Supreme Ct. 1980, Tenn. 1998. Sr. ptnr. Pepper Hamilton LLP, Phila., 1979-97; exec. v.p., gen. counsel, sec. Sofamor Danek Group, Inc., Memphis, 1998-99; spl. counsel Medtronic, Inc., 1999—. Bd. dirs. Schindler Enterprises, Inc., Franke Holding USA, Inc., Rsch. Tech., Inc. Mem. ABA, Internat. Bar Assn., Pa. Bar Assn., Order of Barristers (pres. 1971-72), Phila. Country Club. Address: 976 Derring Ln Bryn Mawr PA 19010-1749

PHILLIPS, STONE, newscaster; b. Texas City, Tex. married; 1 child. BA in Philosophy with honors, Yale Univ. Past prodr., reporter WXIA-TV, Atlanta; formerly with documentary unit Close-Up ABC News, assignment editor, 1979-81, formerly gen. assignment corr., formerly corr. 20/20; prin. anchor Dateline NBC-TV, N.Y.C.; contbg. corr. MSNBC. Past remedial-reading tchr. Fulton County Juvenile Ct., Atlanta; substitute host Good Morning America, 1986; guest sports anchor World News Sunday, 1986; past substitute anchor NBC Nightly News, Today, Meet the Press. NCAA Post-Grad. scholar; named to Scholar Athlete Hall of Fame Nat. Football Found; recipient F. Gordon Brown award Yale Univ., 1976, 3 Nat. Headliner awards for Outstanding Journalism, Overseas Press Club award, Nat. Assn. Black Journalists award, AMA award, Am. Psychological Assn. award, B'nai B'rith award. Office: NBC News-Dateline Dateline 30 Rockefeller Plz Rm 408 New York NY 10112-0002*

PHILLIPS, STUART, retired composer, record producer; b. N.Y.C., Sept. 9, 1929; s. Tom and Minnie Phillips; m. Dori Fogel; children: Toni Phillips-Boim, Julie Stein. Grad., H.S. Music & Art, N.Y., 1947. A&R prodr. Colpix Records, N.Y.C., 1960—65, Capitol Records, Hollywood, Calif., 1964—66, Epic Records, Hollywood, 1967—69. Composer: (music TV) Man from the Diner's Club, 1963, Ride the Wild Surf, 1965, The Monkees, 1967, (book) Hells Angels on Wheels, 1967, Macon County Line, 1969, (music TV) Beyond the Valley of the Dolls, 1970, McCloud, 1974, Quincy, 1975, Battlestar Galactica, 1978, Knight Rider, 1981, Buck Rogers, 1980, The Fall Guy, 1981, The Donna Reed Show; author: (book) Stu Who? Forty years of Navagating the Minefields of the Music Business, 2002. Sgt. Band Infantry, 1953—55. Mem.: Nat. Acad. Rec. Arts & Sci., Acad. TV Arts & Sci., Acad. Motion Picture Arts & Sci. Home Fax: 818-985-8748. Personal E-mail: swp929@earthlink.net.

PHILLIPS, SUSAN MEREDITH, financial economist, university administrator; b. Richmond, Va., Dec. 23, 1944; d. William G. and Nancy (Meredith) Phillips. BA in Math., Agnes Scott Coll., 1967; MS in Fin. and Ins., La. State U., 1971, PhD in Fin. and Economics, 1973. Asst. prof. La. State U., 1973—74, U. Iowa, 1974—78; econ. fellow Directorate of Econ. and Policy Rsch., SEC, 1977—78; assoc. prof. fin. dept. U. Iowa, 1978—83, assoc. v.p. fin. and univ. svcs., 1979—81; commr. Commodity Futures Trading Commn., 1981—83, chmn., 1983—87; prof. fin. dept., v.p. fin. and univ. svcs. U. Iowa, Iowa City, 1987—91; bd. govs. Fed. Res. Bd., Washington, 1991—98; dean Sch. Bus. and Pub. Mgmt., prof. fin. dept. George Washington U., 1998—. Co-author (with J. Richard Zecher): The SEC and the Public Interest; contbr. articles to profl. jours. Fellow Brookings Econ. Policy fellow, 1976—77. Office: George Washington U Sch Bus and Pub Mgmt 710 21st St NW Ste 206 Washington DC 20052-0001

PHILLIPS, SUSAN DIANE, secondary school educator; b. Shelbyville, Ky., Aug. 28, 1955; d. James William and Catherine Elizabeth (Jones) P. B of Music Edn., Eastern Ky. U., 1977; postgrad., U. Ky., 1987. Ordained Christian minister, 2000. Tchr. music Breckinridge County Schs., Hardinsburg, Ky., 1978, Perry County Schs., Hazard, 1980-83, Music on the Move, Louisville, 1985-86, Cooter (Mo.) R-4 Sch., 1987-90, Lewis County Schs., Vanceburg, Ky., 1990—. Staff-cavalcade of bands Ky. Derby Festival, Louisville, 1984-86. Dir. Simpsonville (Ky.) United Meth. Ch. Handbell Choirs, 1985-86. Named Ky. Colonel Gov. Commonwealth of Ky., 1979. Mem. NEA, Ky. Educators Assn., Ky. Music Educators Assn., Music Educators Nat. Conf., Internat. Soc. Tech. in Edn. Office: Lewis County Mid Sch Lions Ln Vanceburg KY 41179 E-mail: sphillips@lewis.k12.ky.us.

PHILLIPS, T. STEPHEN, lawyer; b. Tennyson, Ind., Oct. 1, 1941; AB, DePauw U., 1963; LLB, Duke U., 1966. Bar: Ohio 1966, Ind. 1967. Assoc. Frost & Jacobs, Cin., 1966-72; ptnr. Frost & Jacobs (now Frost Brown Todd LLC), 1972—. Adj. prof. North Ky. U. Chase Coll. Law, Highland Hights, 1983—. Contbg. editor: Ohio Probate Practice (Addams and Hosford), Page on Wills. Trustee Spring Grove Cemetery, Cin.; chmn. Bethesda Found. Methodist. Office: Frost Brown Todd LLC 2500 PNC Ctr 201 E 5th St Ste 2500 Cincinnati OH 45202-4182

PHILLIPS, TEDDY STEVE, SR. conductor, saxophone player, production company executive; b. Chgo., June 15, 1917; s. Steve and Kaliope Phillips; children: Jody, Teddy. Saxophone player with big bands, across country, 1940-45; staff musician Radio Sta. CBS, Chgo., 1944-45; condr. Teddy Phillips Orch., across country, 1945-55, 57-62; prin. Teddy Phillips Show, Sta WBKB-TV-ABC, Chgo., 1956-57; condr. Tedd Phillips and Orch. Ambassador Hotel, L.A., 1962-80, Flamingo Hotel, Las Vegas, 1962-80, Statler Hotels, Aragon Ballroom, Hilton Hotels, Chgo.; dir. Guy Lombardo Orch. and Royal Conadians, 1980—. Pres. P&M Prodns., Woodland Hills, Calif., 1976—. Heads Hallmark Ltd.; pres. Encore Records, Encore Mgmt. Ltd.; sec./treas. Internat. Country Music Fanfest '94, L.A. TV prodr. Great Concert in the Sky; record prodr.; writer Do the Camel Hump?, Wishin; writer, arranger, condr. on tour Great Concert in the Sky, 1986—; prodr., condr., writer Lion and the Turtle; pres. Nostalgic Records. With U.S. Army, 1940-41. Recipient Gould Tech. Achievement award, Spl. award Rotary, Medal of Honor Heart Found., cert. Optimists Club, Musicians Union, Masons. Greek Orthodox. Home and Office: PO Box 8328 Calabasas CA 91372-8328

PHILLIPS, TERRY LEMOINE, investment advisor; b. Washington, July 27, 1938; s. Clifford LeMoin and Dorothy Louise (Schuman) P.; m. Lynne Ann Bruce, Aug. 12, 1962; children: Susan Rae, Stephen Kirk. BS, Purdue U., 1964, MS, 1966. CPA Ind., FPS, Ind. Assoc. program leader, data processing Purdue U. Lab. Applications of Remote Sensing, West Lafayette, Ind., 1966-71, program leader, 1971-74, dep. dir., 1974-85; mgr. personal computer svcs. Purdue U. Computing Ctr., 1986-92; adminstr. Continuing Edn. Ctr., 1992-2000; investment advisor rep. Diesslin & Assocs., 2000—. Cons. AID, Computer Scis. Corp. Scoutmaster, explorer advisor Boy Scouts Am., bd. dirs. Sagamore Coun.; sports coord. youth sports Battleground, Ind.; elder, deacon, trustee, treas. Presbyn. Ch.; bd. dirs. Tippecanoe chpt. Am. Diabetes Assn. With USN, 1956-59. Recipient Most Innovative Idea award Am. Diabetes Assn., 1987. Mem. IEEE (sr.), AICPA, Assn. Inst. for Certification of Computer Profls. (cert. in date processing), Assn. Computing Machinery, Data Processing Mgmt. Assn. (internat. dir., co-founder, v.p., pres., treas. Sagamore chpt., Individual Performance award 1983, 85, 88), Rotary (bd. dirs., treas.), Tau Beta Pi, Eta Kappa Nu. Home: 1522 E 600 N West Lafayette IN 47906-8625 Office: Diesslin & Assocs 2639 Yeager Rd West Lafayette IN 47906 E-mail: terry@diesslin.com., tlphilli@gts.net.

PHILLIPS, THEODORE LOCKE, radiation oncologist, educator; b. Phila., June 4, 1933; s. Harry Webster and Margaret Amy (Locke) Phillips; m. Joan Cappello, June 23, 1956; children: Margaret, John, Sally. BSc, Dickinson Coll., 1955; MD, U. Pa., 1959. Intern Western Res. U., Cleve., 1960; resident in therapeutic radiology U. Calif., San Francisco, 1963, clin. instr., 1963—65, asst. prof. radiation oncology, 1965—68, assoc. prof., 1968—70, prof., 1970—, chmn. dept. radiation oncology, 1973—98. Rsch. radiobiologist U.S. Naval Radiologic Def. Lab., San Francisco, 1963—65; rsch. physician Lawrence Berkeley Lab. Contbr. numerous articles to profl. publs. With USNR, 1963—65. Grantee, Nat. Cancer Inst., 1970—99. Mem.: Inst. Medicine, No. Calif. Radiation Oncology Assn., Radium Soc., Radiation Rsch. Soc. (pres. 1977), Am. Coll. Radiology, Calif. Med. Assn., Am. Assn. Cancer Rsch., N.Am. Hyperthermia Soc. (pres. 1994), Radiol. Soc. N.Am., Am. Soc. Clin. Oncology, Am. Soc. Therapeutic Radiologists (pres. 1984), Alpha Omega Alpha, Phi Beta Kappa. Democrat. Office: U Calif San Francisco Dept Radiation Oncology 1600 Divisidero St ste H1031 San Francisco CA 94143-1708

PHILLIPS, THOMAS EDWORTH, JR. financial advisor, investment mangement consultant; b. Danville, Va., July 7, 1944; s. Thomas Edworth Sr. and Jean (Worley) P.; m. Claudia Mitchell, July 23, 1966; children: Kelly Marie, Melissa Joyce. BS in Econs., Va. Tech., 1966; cert. in investments, N.Y. Inst. Fin., 1969; MS in Bus., Va. Commonwealth U., 1973; postgrad., U. Pa., 1989. Cert. investment mgmt. analyst; registered investment adviser. Edn. coord. Prince William County Schs., Manassas, Va., 1966-67; investment broker Conrad and Co., Richmond, 1967-68; investment exec. UBS Paine Webber, Inc., 1968—, divisional v.p., 1980-99; sr. v.p. and prime cons. Paine Webber, Inc., 2000—; registered prin. NYSE, NASD, 1987—. Access program nat. com. PaineWebber, N.Y.C., 1989-90, mem. dir.'s coun., 1987-88, managed accounts nat. adv. bd., 1991-93; mem. mut. fund Nat. Adv. Coun., 1996—, pres.' council, 1997—; bd. dirs. Madison Group, Inc., Richmond, Meadowbrook Assocs., Inc., Richmond; speaker in field. Bd. dirs. Va. Non-Profit Housing Coalition, pres., 1992—; chmn. bd. deacons. Mt. Olivet Ch., Hanover, Va., 1984-85; trustee Hanover Acad., Ashland, Va., 1980-84. Rotary Found. fellow, 1989. Mem. Investment Mgmt. Cons. Assn., Capital Soc., Melody Hills Property Owners Assn. (bd. dirs. 1980—), Va. Tech. Alumni Assn., VCU Alumni Assn., Rotary, Bull and Bear Club, Omicron Delta Epsilon. Baptist. Avocations: horses, tennis, golf. Home: 15058 Melody Hills Dr Doswell VA 23047-2075 Office: UBS Paine Webber Inc Prime Cons Grp 1021 E Cary St Ste 1800 Richmond VA 23219-4000

PHILLIPS, THOMAS EMBERT, artist; b. Chickasha, Okla., Apr. 7, 1927; s. William Ross and Bess Delia (Clark) P.; m. Marie Ellen McDivitt, Nov. 14, 1948 (div. Sept. 1981); children: Kathryn Marie, Thomas Richard, Stephen Ross, Donald Grayson. Student, Phillips U., 1939, Helen Lorenze Art Sch., 1936-38, 40-43, Kansas City Art Inst., 1975. Comml. artist Arnold-Chezem Advt., Oklahoma City, 1948, 49, M and H Advt., Oklahoma City, 1950; illustrator Murray Collens Studio, N.Y.C., 1952-56; art dir. William Barber & Co., Advt., Colorado Springs, 1956-64; staff artist, illustrator Am. Hereford Assn., Kansas City, Mo., 1964-69; artist Am. Hereford Jour., 1969-72; ptnr. Philan Aural, Visual Enterprises, San Francisco, 1976—. Art tchr. Army Spl. Svcs., Sapporo, Japan, 1951; demonstration painting Pikes Peak Art Assn., Colorado Springs, 1960-63, Assn. Fine Artists Greater Kansas City, Mo., 1972-74. Artist, author: (book) The Sketches of Tom Phillips, 1971, (paintings with essays) Dakota Mag., 1989; paintings for Am. Hereford Assn., 1967, 68, Western Horseman Mag., 1961-66, Am. Pork Prodr.'s Coun., 1970, Animal Science Textbook, 1990; cover design for 45th Divison History Book, 1951; painting of The Chase from Dances With Wolves for S.D. Hall of Fame, 1991, painting of Black Bear for ecology stamp, Mexico City, 1996; portraits included in Saddle and Sirloin Club Portrait Gallery, Louisville, 1971, 85, 88; mural included in Acta Lacota Mus., Chamberlain, 1991; represented in permanent collection Marion Eugene Ensminger and Audrey Helen Ensminger Internat. Rm., Iowa State U., Chickasaw Mus., Tishomingo, Okla., 1995-2000; sculptor bronze model for Statue of Equality, Chamberlain, 1995; contbr. essays on Native Am. History, Dakota Hist. Conf., Ctr. for Western Studies, Augustana Coll., Sioux Falls, S.D., 1990. Tchr. drawing Liberty (Mo.) Christian Ch. Day Care Ctr., 1973-75, Rocky Mountain Participation Nursery Sch. affiliated with City Coll. San Francisco, 1980—, video, edn. TV, Sacramento, 1998, CSU, Chico, 1998, Pub. Sch., Carmicael, Calif., 1998, Randall Mus., San Fran., 1998-99, 2000, water color, Sharon Studio, San Fran., 1999; trustee, CFO The Anstendig Inst., San Francisco, 1978—; voting mem. Chickasaw Nation, Ada, Okla. Sgt. U.S. Army, 1950-52, Korea; cadet midshipman U.S. Merchant Marine Cadet Corps, USNR, 1945. Inducted Chickasaw Hall of Fame, 1998. Home and Office: Philan Aural-Visual Enterprises 915 Fulton St San Francisco CA 94117-1701 also: 8209 E Rock Creek Rd Norman OK 73026-3170

PHILLIPS, THOMAS JOHN, lawyer; b. Mpls., Nov. 24, 1948; BA, U. Minn., 1970; JD, U. Utah, 1973; LLM in Taxation, NYU, 1974. Bar: Wis. 1974. Ptnr. Quarles & Brady, Milw.; law clk. Utah Supreme Ct., Salt Lake City, 1972-73. Co-author: Wisconsin Limited Liability Company Forms and Practice Manual, 1999. Mem. ABA (corp. tax com. tax sect.), Wis. Bar Assn., Profl. Inst. Taxation, Mil. Tax Club, North Shore Country Club, Order of Coif. Avocations: gardening, golf, hockey, jogging, racquetball. Office: 411 E Wisconsin Ave Ste 2550 Milwaukee WI 53202-4409

PHILLIPS, THOMAS ROYAL, state supreme court chief justice; b. Dallas, Oct. 23, 1949; s. George S. and Marguerite (Andrews) P.; m. Lyn Bracewell, June 26, 1982; 1 son, Daniel Austin Phillips; 1 stepson, Thomas R. Kirkham. BA, Baylor U., 1971; JD, Harvard U., 1974; LLD (hon.), Tex. Tech. U., 1997; DHL (hon.), St. Edwards U., 1998. Bar: Tex. 1974; cert. in civil trial law Tex. Bd. Legal Specialization. Briefing atty. Supreme Ct. Tex., Austin, 1974-75; assoc. Baker & Botts, Houston, 1975-81; judge 280th Dist. Ct., 1981-88; chief justice Supreme Ct. Tex., Austin, 1988—. Mem. com. on fed.-state rels. Jud. Conf. U.S., 1990-96; chair Tex. Jud. Dists. Bd., 1988—; mem. State Judges Mass Tort Litig. Com., 1991-96; bd. dirs. Elmo B. Hunter Citizens Ctr. for Jud. Selection, 1992-94, Southwestern Legal Found.; mem. Nat. Conf. Chief Justices, 1988—, pres., 1997-98; adv. dir. Rev. of Litig., U. Tex. Law Sch., 1990—; chair Nat. Mass Tort Conf. Planning Com., 1993-94. Bd. advisors Ctr. for Pub. Policy Dispute Resolution, U. Tex. Law Sch., 1993—; mem. planning com. South Tex. Coll. of Law Ctr. for Creative Legal Solutions, 1993—. Recipient Outstanding Young Lawyer award Houston Young Lawyers Assn., 1986, award of excellence in govt. Tex. C. of C., 1992, Disting. Svc. award Nat. Ctr. for State Cts., 1999; named Appellate Judge of Yr., Tex. Assn. Civil Trial and Appellate Specialists, 1992-93, Disting. Alumnus, Baylor U., 1998. Mem. ABA (task force lawyers polit. contbns. 1997-98), Am. Law Inst. (advisor Fed. Jud. Code Project 1996-2001), Nat. Ctr. for State Ctrs. (chair, bd. dirs. 1997-98), State Bar Tex. (chmn. pattern jury charges IV com. 1985-87, vice chmn. adminstrn. justice com. 1986-87), Am. Judicature Soc. (bd. dirs. 1989-95, 99—, exec. bd. 1995-96), Tex. Philol. Soc., Houston Philol. Soc., Houston Bar Assn., Travis County Bar Assn. Republican. Episcopalian. Office: Tex Supreme Ct PO Box 12248 Austin TX 78711-2248 E-mail: cj@tomphillips.com.

PHILLIPS, THOMAS WADE, judge, lawyer; b. Oneida, Tenn., July 6, 1943; s. W.T. and Lucille (Lewallen) P.; m. Dorothy Mills, Jan. 2, 1971; children: Lori Ann, Wade Thomas. BA, Berea (Ky.) Coll., 1965; JD, Vanderbilt U., 1969; LLM in Labor Law, George Washington U., 1973. Bar: Tenn. 1969, U.S. Supreme Ct. 1972, U.S. Ct. Appeals (6th cir.) 1980. Assoc., ptnr. Baker, Worthington, Crosley, Stansberry & Wolfe, Huntsville, Tenn., 1973-77; ptnr. Phillips & Williams, P.C., Oneida, 1977-91; U.S. magistrate judge ea. dist., 1991—. County atty. Scott County, Huntsville, 1976-91; city atty. Town of Oneida, 1978-91. Capt. JAGC, U.S. Army, 1969-73. Mem. ABA, Tenn. Bar Assn. (ho. of dels. 1989-91), Scott County Bar Assn. Office: US District Court Howard H Baker Jr Courtho 800 Market St Knoxville TN 37902-2327

PHILLIPS, VIRGINIA A. judge; BA magna cum laude, U. Calif., Riverside, 1979; JD, Boalt Hall, 1982. Ct. commr. Calif. Superior Ct., Riverside, 1991-95; magistrate judge U.S. Dist. Ct., L.A., 1995-99, dist. judge, 1999—. Office: US Courthouse 3470 Twelfth St Riverside CA 92501

PHILLIPS, WALTER MILLS, III, psychologist, educator; b. N.Y.C., Sept. 29, 1947; s. Walter Mills and Grace Mary (Mullen) P.; m. Anne Marie Boyle, July 3, 1971; children: Jonathan, Elizabeth. BS, Fordham U., 1970; MA, U.

S.D., 1973, PhD, 1975. Lic. clin. psychologist, Conn.; diplomate Am. Coll. Forensic Examiners, Am. Bd. Disability Evaluators, Am. Bd. Disability Analysts; cert. sr. disability analyst. Adolescent resident counselor Hawthorne (N.Y.) Cedar Knolls Sch., 1970—71; NIMH tng. fellow, 1971—75; clin. psychology intern Inst. of Living, Hartford, Conn., 1974—75, clin. staff psychologist, 1975—79, sr. staff psychologist, 1979—82, asst. dir. dept. clin. psychology, 1980—82, dir. clin. psychology tng., 1980—82; co-dir. outpatient psychiatry U. Conn., Farmington, 1982—88; asst. prof. psychiatry, dir. psychiatry evaluation svc. U. Conn. Health Ctr., 1982—88, dir. Anxiety Rsch. and Treatment Ctr., 1985—88; pvt. practice psychotherapy Hartford, 1976—; dir. adolescent/young adult svc. Grandview Psychiat. Resource Ctr., Waterbury, 1988—90; dir. psychology Waterbury Hosp., 1990—98; pvt. practice clin. psychology Waterbury and Middlebury, 1990—. Asst. clin. prof. psychiatry Sch. Medicine Yale U., New Haven, Conn., 1988—; mem. psychology exec. com. Sch. Medicine Yale U., New Haven, 1990-98. Contbr. articles to profl. jours. Mem. APA, Am. Psychotherapy Assn. (diplomate), Conn. Psychol. Assn., Soc. Psychotherapy Rsch., Soc. Personality Assessment, Conn. Hosp. Assn. (chmn., dir. psychology conf. 1992-96), N.Y. Acad. Scis., Sigma Xi. Office: 415 Middlebury Rd Middlebury CT 06762 E-mail: wphillips@attbi.com.

PHILLIPS, WALTER RAY, lawyer, educator; b. Democrat, N.C., Mar. 19, 1932; s. Walter Yancey and Bonnie (Wilson) P.; m. Patricia Ann Jones, Aug. 28, 1954; children: Bonnie Ann, Rebecca Lee. AB, U. N.C., 1954; LL.B., Emory U., 1957, LL.M., 1962, JD, 1970; postgrad., Yale U., 1965-66. Bar: Ga. 1957, Fla. 1958, Tex. 1969, Mo. 2001, U.S. Supreme Ct. 1962. With firm Jones, Adams, Paine & Foster, West Palm Beach, Fla., 1957-58; law clk. to chief judge U.S. Dist. Ct., Atlanta, 1958-59; with firm Powell, Goldstein, Frazer & Murphy, 1959-60; bankruptcy judge U.S. Cts., 1960-64; prof. law U. N.D., 1964-65; teaching fellow Yale U., 1965-66; prof. law Fla. State U., 1966-68, Tex. Tech. U., Lubbock, 1968-71; Disting. vis. prof. law Baylor U., 1971; atty. Commn. on Bankruptcy Laws of U.S., Washington, 1971-72; dep. dir., adminstrv. officer, 1972-73; prof. Sch. Law, U. Ga., 1973-2000, assoc. dean, 1975-83, acting dean, 1976, Joseph Henry Lumpkin prof., 1977-94, also dir. univ's self. study, 1978, Herman E. Talmadge prof., 1994-2000. Chapman disting. vis. prof. law U. Okla., 1985-86; vis. prof. law U. Okla., 1990, U. Mo., Columbia, 1993, 94, 2001—; reporter Gov.'s Legislation for Ga., 1973; v.p., dir. Killearn Estates, Inc.; mem. Conf. on Consumer Fin. Law; prof. London Law Consortium, 1999. Author: Florida Law and Practice, 1960, Encyclopedia of Georgia Law, 1962, Seminar for Newly Appointed Referees in Bankruptcy, 1964, Damages: Cases and Materials, 1967, (with James William Moore) Debtors' and Creditors' Rights, Cases and Material, 1966, 5th edit., 1979, The Law of Debtor Relief, 1969, 2d edit., 1972, supplement, 1975, (with James William Moore) Rule 6, Moore's Federal Practice, 1969, Adjustment of Debts for Individuals, 1979, 2d edit., 1981, supplement, 1982, 84, 85, Liquidation Under the Bankruptcy Code, 3d edit., 1988, supplement, 1989, 90, 91, 92, 93, 94, Cases and Materials on Corporate Reorganization, 1983, 3d edit., 1986, 4th edit., 1988, 5th edit., 1990, 7th edit., 1996, 8th edit., 1998, Family Farmer and Adjustment of Individual Debts, 1987, supplement, 1988, 89, 90, 91, 92, 93, 94, A Primer of Chapters 12 and 13 of the Bankruptcy Code, 1995. Bd. dirs. Lubbock Day Nurseries, 1969, pres., 1970-71. Served with USAF, 1950. Mem. ATLA, ABA (consumer bankruptcy com. 1973—, chmn. 1986-90), Fed. Bar Assn., Fla. Bar Assn., Tex. Bar Assn., Western Circuit Bar Assn., Ga. Bar Assn. (vice chmn. publs. com. 1977-89, com. on profl. responsibility 1983—2002), Mo. Bar Assn., Am. Judicature Soc., Phi Alpha Delta (chief tribune) Baptist. Home: 3800 Wakefield Dr Columbia MO 65203-5630 E-mail: wrppjp033209321@aol.com.

PHILLIPS, WARREN HENRY, publisher; b. June 28, 1926; s. Abraham and Juliette (Rosenberg) P.; m. Barbara Anne Thomas, June 16, 1951; children: Lisa, Leslie, Nina. AB, Queens Coll., 1947, LHD (hon.), 1987; JD (hon.), U. Portland, 1973; LHD (hon.), Pace U., 1982, L.I. U., 1987. Copyreader Wall St. Jour., 1947-48, fgn. corr. Germany, 1949-50, chief London bur., 1950-51, fgn. editor, 1951-53, news editor, 1953-54, mng. editor Midwest edit., 1954-57, mng. editor, 1957-65, pub., 1975-88; exec. editor Dow Jones & Co., 1965-70, v.p., gen. mgr., 1970-71, exec. v.p., 1972, editl. dir., 1971-88, pres., 1972-79, CEO, 1975-90, also bd. dirs., past chmn., 1972-97; co-pub. Bridge Works Pub. Co., 1992—. Copyreader European edit. Stars and Stripes, 1949; pres. Am. Coun. Edn. for Journalism, 1971-73; mem. Pulitzer Prize Bd., 1977-87; adj. faculty Grad. Sch. Journalism, Columbia U., 1992, John F. Kennedy Sch. Govt., Harvard Univ., 1992. Author: (with Robert Keatley) China: Behind the Mask, 1973. Trustee Columbia U., 1980-93, trustee emeritus, 1993—; mem. vis. com. John F. Kennedy Sch. Govt., Harvard U., 1984-90, 92-97; corp. adv. bd. Queens Coll., 1986-90, found. bd. trustees, 1990-97, trustee emeritus, 1997—. Named one of 10 Outstanding Young Men in U.S., U.S. Jaycees, 1958; inductee Info. Industry Assn.'s Hall of Fame, 1984. Mem. Am. Newspaper Pubs. Assn. (bd. dirs. 1976-84), Am. Soc. Newspaper Editors (pres. 1975-76), Bridgehampton Club, River Club. Office: Bridge Works Publ PO Box 1798 Bridgehampton NY 11932-1798

PHILLIPS, WILLIAM CHARLES, T'ai Chi instructor; b. N.Y.C., Jan. 28, 1947; s. Ned Richardson and Ruth Phillips. AA, S.I. C.C., 1966; BA, Bklyn. Coll., 1968; MS in Edn. Adminstrn., Supervision, St. Johns U., 1979; studied T'ai Chi under Grand Master, Ch'eng Man Ching, 1970-75. Chief instr., pres. Patience T'ai Chi Assn., Bklyn., 1982—. Instr. T'ai Chi and self def. Sheepshead Bay H.S. Adult Edn., 1975-77, Kingsborough C.C. divsn. continuing edn., 1977-80; adj. instr. T'ai Chi Kingsborough C.C. CUNY, 1987-92; lectr. Whole Life Expo, N.Y.C., 1983, 84, T'ai Chi Ch'uan Soc., Rutgers, N.J., 1983, Mind Devel. Assn., St. Louis, 1980, Festival of Yoga and Sci., Columbus, Ohio, 1980; demonstrator Oriental World of Martial Arts in Felt Forum, N.Y.C., 1977; designer T'ai Chi program for blind in conjunction with Kings Bay YMHA, Bklyn.; coord. ann. Holistic Weekends, Ellenville, N.Y., 1987—; presenter Chang San Feng Festival, Warwick, N.Y., 1989-99; judge T'ai Chi Nat. Tournament, Winchester, Va., 1991-93, U.S. Nat. Chinese Martial Arts Competitions, Houston, 1991; coach of competitors, 1997—. Author/narrator tape, video demonstrator T'ai Chi Meditative Exercise, 1984; columnist Natural Physique Mag., 1989. Mem. Manhattan Beach Cmty. Group, Bklyn., 1974-88; spl. advisor to pres. Am. Karate Coun., 1970-82, pres. coun., 1984-86; karate cons. 61st Precinct Youth Coun., 1984-86, Glenwood Houses recreation program, 1986; mem. N.Y. State Senator Donald Halperins Com. on Youth; mem. N.Y. Martial Arts Theater Group, 1985-87, Nat. T'ai Chi Referral Svc., 1990—; bd. dirs. Singles for Charities, 1991-95; organizer 100th Anniversary of birth of Prof. Cheng Man Ch'ing nat. event, 2000. Office: Patience T'ai Chi Assocs PO Box 350532 Brooklyn NY 11235-0532

PHILLIPS, WILLIAM DANIEL, physicist; b. Wilkes-Barre, Pa., Nov. 5, 1948; s. William Cornelius and Mary Catherine (Savine) Phillips; m. Jane Van Wynen, June 20, 1970; children: Catherine, Christine. BS, Juniata Coll., Huntingdon, Pa., 1970; PhD, MIT, 1976. Rsch. asst. MIT, Cambridge, 1970—76, Chaim Weizmann fellow, 1976—78; physicist Nat. Inst. Stds. and Tech., Gaithersburg, Md., 1978—90, group leader, 1990—95, fellow, 1995—. Vis. prof. Ecole Normale Sup+248rieure, Paris, 1989—90; disting. prof. physics U. Md., College Park, 1991—. Editor (author): Laser Manipulation of Atoms and Ions, 1992; contbr. articles to profl. jours. Co-recipient Nobel Prize for physics, 1997, Schawlow prize in laser sci., APS, 1998; named Outstanding Young Scientist, Md. Acad. Sci., 1982; recipient Gold medal, U.S. Dept. Commerce, 1993, Albert A. Michelson medal, Franklin Inst., 1996, Gold medal, Pa. Soc., 1999. Fellow: Am. Acad. Arts and Scis., Optical Soc. Am., Am. Phys. Soc.; mem.: NAS. Achievements include demonstrated laser cooling of atomic beams; electromagnetic trapping of neutral atoms; discovery of sub-doppler laser cooling; produced sub-microkelvin 3D kinetic temperatures. Office: Nat Inst Stds & Tech PHY A167 100 Bureau Dr Stop 8424 Gaithersburg MD 20899-0003

PHILLIPS, WILLIAM DAVID, history educator; b. Dallas, June 26, 1943; s. William David and Virginia (Mahan) P.; m. Carla Rahn, July 4, 1970. BA, U. Miss., 1964; MA, U. Tenn., 1966; PhD, NYU, 1971. Instr. R.I. Coll., Providence, 1969-70; asst. prof. history San Diego State U., 1970-75, assoc. prof., 1975-78, prof., 1978-88; prof. history U. Minn., Mpls., 1988—. Co-author: Spain's Golden Fleece, 1997 (Leo Gershoy award 1998), The Worlds of Christopher Columbus, 1992 (Spain in Am. prize 1993); author: Slavery From Roman Times to the Early Transatlantic Trade, 1985, Enrique IV and the Crisis of Fifteenth-Century Castile, 1978; editor: Testimonies from the Columbian Lawsuits, 2000; sect. reviewer Archiv fur Reformationsgeschichte-Literaturbericht, Tübingen, Germany, 1985-94. Recipient Founders' Day award NYU, N.Y.C., 1972, grants U. Minn. and San Diego State U., grant-in-aid Am. Philos. Soc., Phila., 1980, fellowship NEH, Washington, 1988-89. Mem. Am. Hist. Assn. (sect. editor Recently Pub. Articles 1987-90, mem. Premio del Rey com. 1998—, chair 2000-01), Soc. Spanish and Portuguese Hist. Studies (pres. 1994-96), Cnf. Latin Am. History (mem. Columbus quincentennial com. 1988-90), Medieval Acad. Am. (life), Forum on European Expansion and Global Interactions (founding mem.), Acad. Am. Rsch. Historians on Medieval Spain. Office: U Minn Dept History 267 19th Ave S Minneapolis MN 55455-0499 E-mail: phill004@tc.umn.edu.

PHILLIPS, WILLIAM E. advertising agency executive; b. Chgo., Jan. 7, 1930; s. William E. and Alice N. Phillips; children: Michael, Tom, Sarah; m. Barbara Smith, November 27, 1997. BS, Cornell U., 1951; MBA, Northwestern U., 1955. Brand mgr. Procter & Gamble, Cin., 1955-59; with Ogilvy & Mather, N.Y.C., 1959-90; CEO Ogilvy Group, 1981-88; exec. in residence, prof. Johnson Grad. Sch. Mgmt. Cornell U., 1989-90. Bd. dirs. Gen. Housewares, Sun Glass Hut, Inc., Alliance Nat. Office Ctrs. Chmn. emeritus Outward Bound Internat.; chair Outdoor Edn., Cornell U., 1990—; co-chair Cayuga Soc. for Planned Giving at Cornell U.; trustee emeritus Cornell U.; trustee Internat. Tennis Hall of Fame, Newport, R.I. Lt. (j.g.) USN, 1951-54, Korea/Pacific/Mediterranean. Mem. Old Lyme Country Club, Am. Alpine Club, Explorers Club, Cornell Club, Univ. Club, Naval Mil. Club (London), Achilles Club N.Y.C. (bd. dirs.). Home: 200 N Cove Rd Old Saybrook CT 06475-2537

PHILLIPS, WILLIAM ROBERT, physician; b. Wash., Apr. 26, 1950; BA, U. Wash., 1971, MD, MPH, U. Wash., 1975. Diplomate Nat. Bd. Med. Examiners, Am. Bd. Family Practice, Am. Bd. Preventive Medicine; lic. physician and surgeon, Wash. Resident family practice Providence Med. Ctr., Seattle, 1975-78; resident preventive medicine U. Wash. Sch. Pub. Health & Cmty. Medicine, 1976-79; vis. prof. U. Auckland, New Zealand, 1979, U. Tasmania, Hobart, Australia, 1979, U. Zimbabwe, Harare, 1993; clin. prof. family medicine U. Wash., Seattle, 1994—. Chief staff Ballard Cmty. Hosp., Seattle, 1985, chief family practice, 1984. Contbr. articles to profl. jours. Bd. trustees Ballard Cmty. Hosp., Seattle, 1985. Recipient USPHS primary care policy fellowship, 1995; named Family Physician of the Yr. Wash. Acad. Family Physicians, 1999. Fellow Am. Acad. Family Physicians (Mead Johnson award 1976, Warner-Chilcott award 1979), Wash. Acad. Family Physicians (Family Physician of Yr. 1999), Am. Coll. Preventive Medicine; mem. N.Am. Primary Care Rsch. Group (pres., rsch. awards), Soc. Tchrs. of Family Medicine. Office: Univ Washington Dept Family Medicine Box 356390 Seattle WA 98195-6390

PHILLIPS, WILLIAM RUSSELL, SR. lawyer; b. N.Y.C., June 4, 1948; s. Samuel Russell and Annie Laura (Galloway) P.; m. Dorothy Elizabeth Lowery, Apr. 10, 1976; 1 child, William Russell Jr. BS, Washington & Lee U., 1970; JD, Georgetown U., 1974. Bar: Va. 1975, Ga. 1977, U.S. Dist. Ct. (no. dist.) Ga. 1977, U.S. Ct. Appeals (11th cir.) 1979. Law clk., atty. advisor EPA, Washington, 1973-75, asst. regional counsel region IV Atlanta, 1976-85, assoc. regional counsel region IV, 1986-90; sr. assoc. Thompson, Mann & Hutson, 1990-91; of counsel Peterson, Dillard, Young, Asselin & Powell, 1992-97; chief dep. atty. gen. State of Ga., 1997—, sr. asst. atty. gen., 1998—. Editor: Environmental Desk Manual, 1992, 94. Apptd. by gov. to Legis. Wetlands Study Com., 1992; cubmaster Cub Scouts Am., Lilburn, Ga., 1989-92; pres. Wyndemere Neighborhood Assn., Stone Mountain, Ga., 1990-94; v.p. Meth. Men's Fellowship, Glenn Meml. United Meth. Ch., 1989, pres., 1990. 1st lt. U.S. Army, 1972. Mem. Ga. Bar Assn. (sec. environ. law sect. 1985, vice chmn. 1986, chmn. 1987), Va. Bar Assn., Lawyers Club Atlanta. Avocations: golf, tennis. Office: Ga Dept Law 40 Capital Sq Atlanta GA 30334

PHILLIPS, WINFRED MARSHALL, dean, academic administrator, biomedical researcher, mechanical engineer, educator, bank executive; b. Richmond, Va., Oct. 7, 1940; s. Claude Marshall and Gladys Marian (Barden) P.; children: Stephen, Sean. BSME, Va. Poly. Inst., 1963; MA in Engring., U. Va., 1966, DSc, 1968. Mech. engr. U.S. Naval Weapons Lab., Dahlgren, Va., 1963; NSF trainee, tchg., rsch. asst. dept. aerospace engring. U. Va., Charlottesville, 1963-67, rsch. scientist, 1966-67; asst. prof. dept. aerospace engring. Pa. State U., University Park, 1968-74, from assoc. prof. to prof., 1974-80, assoc. dean rsch. Coll. Engring., 1979-80; head Sch. Mech. Engring., Purdue U., West Lafayette, Ind., 1980-88; dean Coll. Engring., U. Fla., Gainesville, 1988-99, assoc. v.p. engring., 1989-99, v.p. rsch., dean Grad. Sch., Don & Ruth Eckis prof., 1999—. Bd. dirs. 1st Union Bank, Gainesville; bd. dirs., mem. exec. com. Enterprise North Fla. Corp., Gainesville; vis. prof. U. Paris, 1976—77; chmn. Fla. Tech. Devel. Bd., Southeastern Coalition for Minorities in Engring., vice-chmn., 1995—2000, chmn., 2001—; adv. com. Nimbus Corp., 1985—90, Hong Kong U. Sci. and Tech., 1990—93; co-founder, v.p. CEO Inc., 1990—; acad. adv. coun. Indsl. Rsch. Inst., 1990—93; sci. adv. com. Electric Power Rsch. Inst., 1994—99; adv. com. AvMed Inc.; exec. com. Accreditation Bd. on Engring. and Tech., 1991—96, internat. revs. for univs. in Saudi Arabia, USSR, The Netherlands, Kuwait, pres., 1995—96. Sect. editor Am. Soc. Artificial Internal Organs Jour., 1985-99; contbr. over 165 articles to profl. jours., chpts. to books. Bd. dirs. Ctrl. Pa. Heart Assn., 1974-80, U. Fla. Found., 1989-91, 95-01; mem. Ind. Boiler and Pressure Vessel Code Bd., 1981-88. Named Disting. Hoosier Ind., 1987, Sagamore of the Wabash, 1988, Am. Assn. Engr. Socs. Nat. Engring. award, 2000, Linton Grinter award, 2000; recipient Career Rsch. award NIH, 1974-78, NIH Surgery and Bioengring. Study sect., 1988-91, Fla. High Tech. and Industry Coun., 1990-94, So. Tech.Coun., 1991—. Fellow AAAS, AIAA, AAES (chair-elect 2000—, vice chair 2001-2002, chmn. bd. 2002-), ASME (sr. v.p. edn. 1986-88, bd. dirs. 1995-2000, pres. 1998-99, Dedicated Svc. award 2001), N.Y. Acad. Scis., Am. Astron. Soc., Am. Inst. Med. and Biol. Engring. (founding fellow, chair coll. fellows 1994-95, pres. 1996-97), Am. Soc. Engring. Edn. (past chmn. long range planning soc. awards 1990-92, vice chmn. engring. deans coun. 1991-93, chair 1993—, bd. dirs. 1994-98, 1st v.p. 1994-95, pres. 1996-97), Royal Soc. Arts; mem. Am. Soc. Artificial Internal Organs (trustee 1982-90, sec.-treas. 1986-87, pres. 1988-89, adv. bd. 1998—), Nat. Assn. State Univs. and Land-Grant Colls. (com. quality of engring. edn.), Univ. Programs in Computer-Aided Engring., Design and Mfg. (bd. dirs. 1989-91), Am. Phys. Soc., Biomed. Engring. Soc., Internat. Soc. Biorheology, Fla. Engring. Soc., Cosmos Club, Fla. Blue Key, Rotary (pres. Lafayette 1987-88), Sigma Xi, Phi Kappa Phi, Phi Tau Sigma, Sigma Gamma Tau, Tau Beta Pi (eminent engr.). Achievements include development of artificial heart pumps; research in reentry aerodynamics, on blood rheology, on modelling blood flow, on fluid dynamics of artificial hearts, on the use of smooth blood contacting surfaces, on prosthetic valve fluid dynamics and on laser Doppler studies of unsteady biofluid dynamics. Home: 4140 NW 44th Ave Gainesville FL 32606-4518 Office: U Fla Rsch and Grad Programs 223 Grinter Hall Gainesville FL 32611 E-mail: wphil@ufl.edu.

PHILLIPS, WINIFRED PATRICIA, radio producer, composer; b. Mobile, Ala., Apr. 13, 1972; d. Winifred Waldron Phillips. BA in Comms., Kean U., 1994. Composer, prodr., actress, writer Nat. Pub. Radio, Washington, 1996—. Composer, prodr., actress, writer: National Public Radio dramas Generations Radio Theater Presents: Radio Tales, 1996—2002. Recipient GRACIE award for best nat./network drama series, Am. Women in Radio and TV, 2001, N.Y. Festivals award, Internat. Radio Festivals, 1997, AUDIE Honors award, Audio Pubs. Assn., 1999, GOLDEN REEL Merit award, Nat. Fedn. Cmty. Broadcasters, 2001, GRACIE award for outstanding achievement by an actress, Am. Women in Radio and TV, 1998, N.Y. Festivals award, Internat. Radio Festivals, 2001; grantee Endowment grantee, Wallace - Reader's Digest Funds, 1996—2002, NEA, 1996—2002, Durkin Hayes Publ., 1998. Mem.: SAG, BMI, NARAS, Audio Pubs. Assn.n. Avocations: reading, Web design, computer art, travel.

PHILLIPS, ZAIGA ALKSNIS, pediatrician; b. Riga, Latvia, Sept. 13, 1934; came to U.S., 1949; d. Adolfs and Alma (Ozols) Alksnis; (div. 1972); children: Albert L., Lisa K., Sintija. BS, U. Wash., 1956, MD, 1959. Fellow Colo. Med. Ctr., Denver, 1961-62; sch. physician Bellevue and Issaquah (Wash.) Sch. Dists., 1970-77; pvt. practice Bellevue, 1977—; staff pediatrician Overlake Med. Ctr., 1977—, Childrens Hosp. and Med. Ctr., Seattle, 1977—, Evergreen Med. Ctr., 1977—. Attending physician Allergy Clinic, Childrens Hosp., Seattle, 1988—; cons. and contact to pediatricians in Latvia, 1988—; team mem. to Latvia, Healing the Children Contact with Latvia, 1993-97; bd. mem. Bellevue's Stay in Sch. Program, 1994-97. Mem. Am. Latvian Assn., 1972—, Wash. Latvian Assn., Seattle, 1972—; pres. Latvian Sorority Gundega, Seattle, 1990-93; bd. dirs. Sister Cities Assn., Bellevue, 1992-98, Wash. Asthma Allergy Found. Am., 1992-99. Fellow Am. Acad. Pediat.; mem. Am. Latvian Physicians Assn. (bd. dirs. 1998—), Wash. State and Puget Sound Pediatric Assn. Office: Pediatric Assn 2700 Northup Way Bellevue WA 98004-1463 E-mail: zap@u.washington.edu.

PHILLIS, JOHN WHITFIELD, physiologist, educator; b. Port of Spain, Trinidad, Apr. 1, 1936; came to U.S., 1981; s. Ernest and Sarah Anne (Glover) P.; m. Pamela Julie Popple, 1958 (div. 1968); children: David, Simon, Susan; m. Shane Beverly Wright, Jan. 24, 1969. B in Vet. Sci., Sydney (Australia) U., 1958, D in Vet. Sci., 1976; PhD, Australian Nat. U., Canberra, 1961; DSc, Monash U., Melbourne, Australia, 1970. Lectr./sr. Monash U., 1963-69; vis. prof. Ind. U., Indpls., 1969; prof. physiology, assoc. dean rsch. U. Man., Winnipeg, Can., 1970-73; prof., chmn. dept. physiology U. Sask., Saskatoon, Can., 1973-81, asst. dean rsch. Can., 1973-75; prof. physiology Wayne State U., Detroit, 1981—, chmn. dept. physiology, 1981-97. Mem. scholarship and grants com. Can. Med. Rsch. Coun., Ottawa, Ont., 1973-79; mem. sci. adv. bd. Dystonia Med. Rsch. Found., Beverly Hills, Calif., 1980-85, Curtis Rsch. Inst., Risingsun, Ohio, 1998-2000; mem. sci. adv. panel World Soc. for Protection of Animals, 1982-98; Wellcome vis. prof. Tulane U., 1986; mem. acad. scholars Wayne State U., 1995. Author: Pharmacology of Synapses, 1970; editor: Veterinary Physiology, 1976, Physiology and Pharmacology of Adenosine Derivatives, 1983, Adenosine and Adenine Nucleotides as Regulators of Cellular Function, 1991, The Regulation of Cerebral Blood Flow, 1993, Novel Therapies for CNS Injuries: Rationales and Results, 1996; editor Can. Jour. Physiology and Pharmacology, 1978-81, Progress in Neurobiology, 1973-97. Mem. grants com. Am. Heart Assn. of Mich., 1985-90, mem. rsch. coun., 1991-92, mem. rsch. forum com., 1991-96, chair, 1992-93; mem. Brain/Stroke Consortium Study Group, Am. Heart Assn., 1998. Wellcome fellow London, 1961-62; Can. Med. Rsch. Coun. grantee, 1970-81, rsch. prof., 1980; NIH grantee, 1983-2000. Mem. Brit. Pharmacol. Soc., Physiol. Soc., Am. Physiol. Soc., Soc. Neurosci., Internat. Brain Rsch. Orgn. Office: Wayne State U Dept Physiology 540 E Canfield St Detroit MI 48201-1928 E-mail: phillis@med.wayne.edu.

PHILLIS, MARILYN HUGHEY, artist; b. Kent, Ohio; d. Paul Jones and Helen Margaret (Miller) Hughey; m. Richard Waring Phillis, Mar. 19, 1949; children: Diane E., Hugh R., Randall W. Student, Kent State U., 1945; BS, Ohio State U., 1949. Chemist Battelle Meml. Inst., Columbus, Ohio, 1949-53; illustrator periodical Western Res. Hist. Mag., Garrettsville, 1974-78; illustrator book AAUW, Piqua, 1976; art instr. Edison State C.C., 1976; watermedia instr. Springfield (Ohio) Mus. Art, 1976-84. Juror art exhbns. state and nat. art groups, 1980—; painting instr. state and nat. orgns., 1980—; lectr. art healing Wheeling (W.Va.) Jesuit Coll., 1994—96; founder, coord. Nat. Creativity Seminar, Stretching Boundaries for Creative People, 1993, 1995, 1997, 1999, 2002. Author: Watermedia Techniques for Releasing the Creative Spirit, 1992, (chpt.) Bridging Space and Time, 1998; contbr. ; one-woman shows include Stifel Fine Art Ctr., Wheeling, Va., Springfield Art Mus., Zanesville (Ohio) Art Ctr., Ohio U., Lancaster, Ohio U. East. St. Clairsville, Cleve. Inst. Music, Columbus Mus. Art, Cheekwood Mus. of Art, Bot. Hall, Nashville, Idaho Falls Arts Coun., Monroe, exhibited in group shows, Flagstaff, 1993, exhibitions include , N.Y.C., Butler Mus. Am. Art, Youngstown, Ohio, Taiwan Art Edn. Inst., Taipei, 1994, Represented in permanent collections Ohio U., Lancaster and St. Clairsville, Springfield Mus. Art, Heritage Hall mus., Talladega, Ala., Ohio Watercolor Soc., also corp. collections. Co-chmn. Cmty. Health and Humor Program, Wheeling, 1992. Recipient First awards Watercolor West, Riverside, Calif., 1990, Hudson Soc. award Nat. Collage Soc., 1995, Art Masters award Am. Artist Mag., 1996; elected to Hall of Fame, Kent, Ohio, 2000, Hall of Fame, Wheeling, Va., 2000. Mem. Internat. Soc. Study of Subtle Energies and Energy Medicine (art cons. sci. jour. 1992—, art and healing workshop 1995), Am. Watercolor Soc. (dir. 1991-93, newsletter editor 1992—, Osborne award 1975), Soc. Layerists in Multi-Media (nat. v.p. 1988-93), Ohio Watercolor Soc. (sec. 1979-82, v.p. 1982-89, pres. 1990-96, dir. biennial creativity seminars 1993-95, 97, 99, 2002, Gold medal, Best of Show 1993), Nat. Watercolor Soc. (chmn. selection jury 2001), Int. Noetic Sci., West Ohio Watercolor Soc. (pres. 1979-80, 2nd award 1982), Allied Artists N.Y., W.Va. Watercolor Soc. (1st award 1993), Ky. Watercolor Soc., Ga. Watercolor Soc., So. Watercolor Soc. (pres. 1997-98, Silver award 1999). Avocations: hiking, reading, genealogy, music, travel. Home and Office: Phillis Studio 72 Stamm Cir Wheeling WV 26003-5549

PHILOGENE, BERNARD J. R. academic administrator, science educator; b. Beau-Bassin, Mauritius, May 4, 1940; came to Can., 1961; s. Raymond Pierre and Simone Marie (Ruffier) P.; m. Hélène Marie Lebreux, July 7, 1964; children: Simone, Catherine. BS, U. Montreal, 1964; MS, McGill U., 1966; PhD, U. Wis., 1970; DSc (hon.), Compiègne, 1995. Research officer Can. Forestry Service, Que., 1966-70, research scientist, 1970-71; asst. prof. U. B.C., Vancouver, 1971-74; asst. prof., assoc. prof., then prof. entomology U. Ottawa, Can., 1974—, vice dean sci. and engring. Can., 1982-85, acting dean Can., 1985-86, dean faculty of sci. Can., 1986-90, acad. vice rector Can., 1990-97; pres. Can. Consortium of Sci. Socs., 1992-94. Cons. OAS, Washington, 1979-80, Agence de Coop. Culture & Tech., Paris, 1982-83, Can. Internat. Devel. Agy., Ottawa, 1983-85, UN Environ. Program, Geneva, Switzerland, 1985-86, Internat. Devel. Research Ctr., Ottawa, 1985—. Mem. Ont. Pesticide Adv. Com., 1987-91. Decorated officier de l'Ordre des Palmes Académiques (France); knight of merit Order of St. John of Jerusalem. Fellow Entomol. Soc. Can. (bd. dirs. 1977-80); mem. Am. Inst. Biol. Scis., Entomol. Soc. Am., Can. Pest Mgmt. Soc., Assn. Can.-Française Advancement Sci. (bd. dirs. 1984-86), Internat. Soc. Chem. Ecology, Entomol. Soc. of Can. (Gold Medal 2000). Office: U Ottawa PO Box 450 30 Marie Curie St Ottawa ON Canada K1N 6N5 E-mail: bphilog@science.uottawa.ca.

PHILPOTT, HARRY MELVIN, former university president; b. Bassett, Va., May 6, 1917; s. Benjamin Cabell and Daisy (Hundley) P.; m. Pauline Breck Moran, Sept. 15, 1943; children: Harry Melvin, Jean Todd, Benjamin Cabell II, Virginia Lee. AB, Washington and Lee U., 1938, LL.D., 1966; PhD, Yale U., 1947; D.D., Stetson U., 1960; LL.D., U. Fla., 1969, U. Ala., 1970; H.H.D., Samford U., 1978, Montevallo U., 1980, Auburn U., 1981. Ordained to ministry Bapt. Ch., 1942; dir. religious activities Washington and Lee U., 1938-40; prof. religion U. Fla., 1947-52, v.p., 1957-65; dean, head dept. religion and philosophy Stephens Coll., 1952-57; pres. Auburn U., 1965-80. Mem. Regional Edn. Bd., 1966-82, vice chmn., 1973-75; chmn. Ala. Edn. Study Commn., 1967-69; pres. Southeastern Conf., 1972-74. Served to 1st lt. Chaplains Corps., USNR, 1943-46. Mem. Nat. Assn. State Univs. and Land-Grant Colls. (chmn. council presidents 1972-73, exec. com. 1973-78, pres. 1976-77), Fla. Blue Key, Kappa Alpha, Omicron Delta Kappa, Kappa Delta Pi, Phi Kappa Phi, Phi Beta Kappa. Home: PO Box 3037 Auburn AL 36831-3037

PHILPOTT, LARRY LA FAYETTE, horn player; b. Alma, Ark., Apr. 5, 1937; s. Lester and Rena (Owens) P.; m. Elise Robichaud, Nov. 24, 1962 (div. June 1975); children: Daniel, Stacy; m. Anne Sokol, Feb. 14, 1984. BS, Ga. So. Coll., 1962; Mus.M., Butler U., 1972. Instr. in horn Butler U., De Pauw U.; dir. music Cedarcrest Sch., Marysville, Wash., 1991—; instr. horn Western Wash. U., Dept Music, Bellingham, 1995-98. Mem., N.C. Symphony, 1960, Savannah (Ga.) Symphony, L'Orchestre Symphonique de Quebec, Que., Can., 1962-64, prin. horn player, Indpls. Symphony Orch., 1964-89, Flagstaff Summer Festival, 1968—; artist in-residence Ind.-Purdue Indpls.; appeared with, Am. Shakespeare Theatre, summer 1965, Charlottetown Festival, summers 1967-68, Flagstaff Summer Festival, 1968-85, Marrowstone Music Festival, 1985—. Served with USN, 1956-60. Mem. Music Educators Nat. Conf., Am. Fedn. Musicians, Internat. Conf. Symphony and Opera Musicians, Internat. Horn Soc., Coll. Music Soc., Phi Mu Alpha Sinfonia. Home: 14925 63d Ave SE Snohomish WA 98296-5277 also: Western Wash U Dept Music Bellingham WA 98225-9107

PHILPOTT, LINDSEY, civil engineer, researcher, educator; b. Bridestowe, Devonshire, Eng., Aug. 2, 1948; came to U.S., 1983; s. George Anthony and Joyce Thirza (Teeling) P.; m. Christine May Pembury, Aug. 20, 1974 (div.); children: David, Elizabeth; m. Kathleen Linda Matson, Feb. 17, 1982 (div.); children: Nicholas, Benjamin; m. Kim Elaine Moore, Nov. 24, 1991. Higher

Nat. Cert. in Civil Engring., Bristol (Eng.) Poly., 1973; BSCE, U. Ariz., 1986, MSCE, 1987. Registered profl. engr., Calif.; lic. water treatment plant operator, Calif.; USCG lic. operator 100 ton master. Area structural engr. Dept. Environment (Property Svcs. Agy.), Bristol, 1971-73; civil engr. Webco Civil Engring., Exeter, Eng., 1973-75; tech. mgr. Devon & Cornwall Housing Assn., Plymouth, Eng., 1975-79; prin., architect S.W. Design, 1979-81; archtl. engr. United Bldg. Factories, Bahrain, 1981-83; jr. engr. Cheyne Owen, Tucson, 1983-87; civil engr. Engring. Sci. Inc., Pasadena, Calif., 1987-89; project engr. Black & Veatch, Santa Ana, 1989-90; sr. engr. Brown & Caldwell, Irvine, 1990-91; environ. engr. Met. Water Dist. So. Calif., L.A., 1991—2002; instr. USCG and marlinespike seamanship Orange Coast Coll. Sailing Ctr., Newport Beach, 1999—; mgr. vol. support svcs. Ocean Inst., Dana Point, 2002—. Adj. prof. hydraulics and instrumentation, San Antonio Coll., Walnut, Calif., 1995—. Foster parent Foster Parents Plan, Tucson, 1985-87; vol. reader tech. books Recording for the Blind, Hollywood, Calif., 1988-89, South Bay, Calif., 1990-91, Pomona, Calif., 1991—; vol. sailor/tchr. L.A. Maritime Inst. Topsail Youth Program, 1994—, Ocean Inst., 1998—. Mem.: ASCE, Engrs. Soc. (pres. 1985—96), Water Environment Fedn., Am. Water Resources Assn. (water quality com. 1990—), Am. Water Works Assn., Santa Monica Bay Power Fleet (sec. Marina del Rey chpt. 2000—), Mensa, Internat. Guild of Knot Tyers (pres. Pacific Am. br. 2000), Marina Venice Yacht Club, South Bay Yacht Racing Club (Marina del Rey, Calif., commodore 1999), Internat. Order of Blue Gavel (treas. dist. 11 2002). Avocations: hiking, cycling, sailing, crosswords, knot-tying. Office: Met Water Dist Engring Svcs Sect PO Box 54153 Los Angeles CA 90054-0153 E-mail: lphilpott@mwdh2o.com., marlineman@aol.com.

PHINAZEE, HENRY CHARLES, systems analyst, educator; b. Birdnest, Va., Oct. 26, 1956; s. Charlie Phinazee and Johnnie Belle (Harris) Brice. BEd, Fort Hays State U., 1978, B of Psychology, 1979, M of Psychology, 1980; MEd, Wichita State U., 1985. Cert. tchr., Kans., Tex. Minority advisor Fort Hays State U., 1978-80; tchr. Wichita Pub. Schs., 1980-97, Wichita State U., 1988-92, dorm coord. coll. of health profession, 1986-92, work coord. coll. of health profession, 1988-91; computer analyst Beech Aircraft Corp., Wichita, 1992—; tchr. Denbigh H.S., Newport News, VA, 1997—. Author: (software) Dayreq, 1989. Mentor Grow Your Own Tchrs., Wichita Pub. Schs., 1990; liaison Com. on Polit. Edn., Wichita, 1988—. Recipient Svc. award Big Bros./Big Sisters, 1987. Mem. Am. Amature Racquetball, Wichita Assn. of Black Educators (treas. 1991-92), Wichita Fedn. of Tchrs. (2d v.p. 1988-92, Svc. award 1991), Kans. Assn. of Black Educators (com. head 1991-92), Phi Delta Kappa, Kappa Alpha Psi (polemark 1988-92, Svc. award). Democrat. Baptist. Avocations: racquetball, running, bicycling, reading, church. Home: 4326 Tindall Ct Newport News VA 23602-5257 Office: Denbigh HS 259 Denbigh Blvd Newport News VA 23608-3313

PHINIZY, ROBERT BURCHALL, electronics company executive; b. Ben Hill, Ga., June 30, 1926; children: Robert B., William, David. BS, U. Ariz., 1951; postgrad., U. So. Calif., 1952-55, UCLA, 1956-62. Pres. LB Products, Santa Monica, Calif., 1954—58, IMC Magnetics Western, South Gate, 1958—69, Am. Electronics, Fullerton, 1969-71; gen. mgr. electronics div. Eaton Co., Anaheim, 1971—72; pres., CEO Genisco Tech. Corp., Compton, 1972-83; chmn. bd., CEO Genisco Computers Corp., Costa Mesa, 1976—83, Trans Tech. Alliances, 1986—. Bd. dirs. Microsemi Corp., Santa Ana, Calif., Logisticsware, Inc.; bd. dirs., sec. Biosonics Inc., Seattle, 1989—. Contbr. articles to tech. jours.; patentee in field. Mem. Port Ludlow Yacht Club (commodore 1998).

PHINNEY, BERNARD O. research scientist, educator; b. July 29, 1917; s. Bernard Orrin and Frank Maude (Lawrence) P.; m. Sally Ball Bush; children: Scott, Katcha; m. Isabelle Jean Swift, Dec. 11, 1965; children: Peter, David. BA cum laude, U. Minn., 1940, PhD, 1946; DSc (hon.), U. Bristol, 1991. Teaching and rsch. asst. Dept. Botany U. Minn., Mpls., 1940-46; postdoctoral scholar Calif. Inst. Tech., Pasadena, 1946-48; from instr. to prof. U. Calif., L.A., 1947-88, prof. emeritus, 1988—. NSF sr. postdoctoral fellow Copenhagen U., 1959-60; NSF-U.S.-Japan rsch. sci. Internat. Christian U., Mitaka, Tokyo, 1966-67; vis. prof. Dept. Chem. U. Bristol, U.K., 1973, 83. Elected mem. Nat. Acad. Scis., Washington, 1985. Rsch. grantee NSF, Dept. Energy, 1956—. Mem. AAAS, Am. Soc. Plant Physiologists (pres. 1989-90), Am. Inst. Biol. Scis., Am. Chem. Soc., Botanical Soc. Am., Genetics Soc. Am., Japanese Soc. Plant Physiologists, Internat. Soc. Plant Molecular Biologists, Phytochem. Soc. Am. Democrat. Avocations: skiing, hiking, fishing, classical music. Home: 257 Beloit Ave Los Angeles CA 90049-3009 E-mail: bop@ucla.edu.

PHINNEY, FREDERICK WARREN, priest; b. Lawrence, Mass., May 15, 1922; s. Arthur Osgood and Lucile Snow (Flagg) P.; m. Eleanor Sanburn, May 31, 1947; children: Benjamin, Joanna, Frederick Jr., John, Martha, Harriet. AB, Harvard U., 1943; MDiv, Episc. Theol. Sch., Cambridge, Mass., 1948. Ordained priest Episcopal Ch., 1948. Rector Ch. of Our Saviour, Brookline, Mass., 1950-56, St. John's Ch., Beverly Farms, 1956-63, Ch. of the Holy Spirit, Lake Forest, Ill., 1963-81; warden St. Julian's Retreat & Tng. Ctr., Limuru, Kenya, 1981-83; asst. to bishop of Mass. Boston, 1984; priest in charge St. Paul's Within the Walls, Rome, 1985; interim priest Christ Ch., Cambridge, 1986-87, St. Andrew's, Wellesley, Mass., 1989-90; canon St. Luke's Cathedral, Butere, Kenya, 1987—. Dean Waukegan deanery Diocese of Chgo., 1971-81; chmn. Iran Diocesan Assn./USA, 1973-78; mem. standing com. Diocese of Chgo., 1969-72, pres., 1970-72; pres. trustees Episcopal Chaplaincy Harvard/Radcliffe, 1988-90. Assoc. editor The Living Ch. mag., 1984-89.

PHINNEY, LESLIE MARY, mechanical engineering educator; b. Princeton, N.J., Mar. 31, 1968; d. Hartley Keith Jr. and Mary Alice Phinney. BS in Aerospace Engring., U. Tex., 1990; postgrad. cert. in engring., Cambridge (Eng.) U., 91; MSME, U. Calif., Berkeley, 1994, PhD in Mech. Engring., 1997. Asst. prof. mech. engring. U. Ill., Urbana-Champaign, 1997—. Contbg. editor conf. procs.; contbr. articles to sci. jours., including Jour. Microelectromech. Sys. Recipient faculty early devel. award NSF, 2000; Churchill scholar Winston Churchill Found. U.S., 1990-91; NASA-Am. Soc. Engring. Edn. summer faculty fellow Jet Propulsion Lab., 2000. Mem. ASME (com. mem., editl. bd. Heat Transfer Recent Contents), Am. Soc. Engring. Edn., Optical Soc. Am., Soc. Women Engrs., Assn. for Women in Sci., Tau Beta Pi (life). Office: U Ill 1206 W Green St MC-244 Urbana IL 61801-2906

PHIPARD, NANCY MIDWOOD, retired educator, writer; b. Boston, Jan. 31, 1929; d. William Henry and Jean Estelle (Dubbs) McAdams; m. Kenneth E. Brown, June 17, 1949 (div.); children: Christopher M., Jennifer Prigodich, Michael H., Jeffrey D.; m. Arnold J. Midwood, Jr., July 2, 1980 (dec.); m. Harvey F. Phipard, Jan. 14, 1998. Student, Mt. Holyoke Coll., 1946-48; BA, Wellesley Coll., 1973; MEd, Boston Coll., 1975. Dir. confs. and insvc. tng., chmn. bd. Mass. Assn. for Children with Learning Disabilities, Waltham and Framingham, 1969-75; chmn. core edn. teams, cons. to spl. programs, grant writer Needham (Mass.) Pub. Schs., 1974-79, ret. Mass., 1979; pres., feature writer S.D. Assocs., Inc., 1980-81; dir. pub. rels., women's career conf. Babson Coll., 1982. Mem. program evaluation team Mass. Dept. Edn., Quincy, 1978. Co-author: (as Nancy Brown, with Louis Dickstein) Psychological Reports, 1974; contbr. poetry to Portraits of a Life, 1996, Fields of Gold, 1996, Ever-Flowing Stream, 1997, Best Poems of 1998, 1998, Colors of the Past, 2000, Echoes of Yesteryear, 2000, America at the Millennium, The Best Poems and Poets of the 20th Century, 2000, Memories of Tomorrow, 2000, Journey to Infinity, 2000, The Best Poems of 2002. Bd. dirs., chair cmty. rels. Lincoln Child Ctr., Oakland, Calif., 1983-85; docent Calif. Hist. Soc., San Francisco, 1982-87; bd. dirs., fund raiser Hospice of Palm Beach County South, Palm Beach, Fla., 1993-97; bd. dirs. La Coqueille Villas, Inc., Manalapan, Fla., 1994-98. Recipient 4 Editor's Choice awards Internat. Libr. of Poetry, 1996, 98, 2000. Mem. Internat. Soc. Poets (disting. mem.), Phi Beta Kappa. Avocations: tennis, travel, duplicate bridge. Home: 1630 Lands End Rd Lake Worth FL 33462-4762

PHIPPS, ALLEN MAYHEW, management consultant; b. Seattle, Oct. 3, 1938; s. Donald Mayhew and Virginia (McGinn) P.; m. Joyce Elisabeth Alberti, Aug. 21, 1971; children: Ramsey Mayhew, Justin Beckwith. BA in Econs., U. Calif., Berkeley, 1961; MBA with honors, Stanford U., 1969. Security analyst Morgan Guaranty Trust Co., 1968; with Boston Cons. Group, Inc., 1969—, mgr., 1971-74; mem. sr. team Calif., 1974-77; corp. v.p., dir., 1975—. Mgr. Boston Cons. Group, G.mb.H, Munich. W. Ger., 1978-82, partner-in-charge West Coast client devel., Menlo Park, Calif., 1982-84; pres. Techno Digital Systems, Inc., 1984-86; pres., chief exec. officer, Techno Digital System (Sellectek, Inc.), 1984-85; exec. v.p., Regis McKenna Inc., Palo Alto, Calif., 1985-87; pvt. practice mgmt. cons., Menlo Pk., 1987-95; chief exec. officer Bio Electro Systems, Palo Alto, 1989-92; mng. dir., Bus. Engring. Inc., Menlo Park, Calif., 1992-95; sr. v.p. bus. and policy group SRI Internat., Menlo Park, Calif., 1995-96; pres., CEO SRI Consulting, Menlo Park, 1996-2000, ret., 2000; cons. Allen M. Phipps Mgmt. Consulting, Atherton, Calif., 2000—. Served to capt. U.S. Army, 1961-67. Decorated Bronze Star, Army Commendation medal with 2 oak leaf clusters. Mem.: Menlo Country Club (Woodside), Bohemian CLub (San Francisco), Alpha Delta Phi. Republican. Presbyterian. Home: 33 Prado Secoya St Atherton CA 94027-4126 Office: Allen M Phipps Mgmt Consulting 33 Prado Secoya Atherton CA 94027 E-mail: allen@allenmphipps.com.

PHIPPS, BENJAMIN KIMBALL, II, lawyer; b. Boston, Jan. 16, 1933; s. Benjamin Kimball and Bertha Elizabeth (Forsyth) P.; m. Phyllis Jarrett Anderson, Jan. 10, 1962; children: Lisa Jarrett, Christina Caroline. BS in Commerce, U. Va., 1955, LLB, 1958. Bar: Fla. 1964, U.S. Dist. Ct. (no. dist.) Fla., U.S. Claims Ct., U.S. Ct. Appeals (5th and 11th cirs.), U.S. Tax Ct. Editor Mcpl. Code Corp., Tallahassee, 1964-65; pvt. practice, 1965—. Counsel tax com. Fla. Ho. of Reps., 1966-72, counsel to speaker, 1973-74, mem. adv. com. fin. & tax com., 1983-84; mem. Legis. Task Force Taxpayers' Bill Rights, 1989-91; cons. in field. Contbr. articles to profl. jours.; columnist Tallahassee Democrat. Chmn. Hist. Tallahassee Preservation Bd., 1970-91; trustee Maclay Sch.; mem. adv. coun., Sta. WFSU-TV, chmn., 1970-92; mem. Fla. Mus. History, 1990—, v.p., 1997-99, gen. counsel, 2000—; mem. Tallahassee Trust for Hist. Preservation, 1997—, treas., 1998—. Served to capt., U.S. Army, 1958-64. Listed in Am.'s Leading Lawyers. Mem. ABA (tax sect. state and local tax com.), Tallahassee Bar Assn., Fla. Bar (treas., vice chmn., chmn. tax sect. 1985-86, editl. bd. Fla. Bar News, chmn. 1975-76), Gov.'s Club, Univ. Ctr. Club, Cosmos Club, Exchange Club, Tiger Bay Club (dir.), Fla. Econ. Club, St. Andrews Soc. (pres. 1978-79), Sigma Alpha Epsilon, Phi Alpha Delta, Pi Delta Epsilon. Republican. Episcopalian. Office: PO Box 1351 Tallahassee FL 32302-1351

PHIPPS, CLAUDE RAYMOND, research scientist; b. Ponca City, Okla., Mar. 15, 1940; s. Claude Raymond Louis and Deva Pauline (DeWitt) P.; m. Lynn Malarney, Dec. 1, 1962 (div. Feb. 1989); 1 child, David Andrew; life ptnr. Shanti E. Bannwart. BS, MIT, 1961, MS, 1963; PhD, Stanford U., 1972. Rsch. staff Lawrence Livermore (Calif.) Nat. Lab., 1972-74, Los Alamos (N.Mex.) Nat. Lab., 1974-95, project leader engine support sys. tech. program, 1993; assoc. dir. Alliance for Photonic Tech., Albuquerque, 1992-95; pres. Photonic Assocs., Santa Fe, 1995—. Co-instr. "Paris" Relationship Tng., Sante Fe, N.Mex., 1990—; dir. Santa Fe Investment Conf., 1987; program com. MIT Workshop on High Temperature Superconductors, Cambridge, 1988; mem. Instl. R & D Com. Los Alamos Nat. Lab., 1990—92, project leader laser effects, 1982—87; mem. internat. rsch. troup Australia, Japan, Scotland, 1988—89; invited discussion leader Gordon Conf. on Laser Particle Interactions, NH, 1992; organizer, chmn. Santa Fe High Power Laser Ablation Conf., 1988, 2000, Osaka High Power Laser Ablation Conf., 1999, Taos High Power Laser Ablation Conf., 2002; spkr. in field; inventor in field. Co-author: Laser Ionization Mass Analysis, 1993; author internat. lecture series on laser surface interactions, Berlin, Antwerp, Marseilles, Xiamen, Cape Town, Durban, 1987—; contbr. articles to profl. jours.; inventor in field. Lt. USN, 1963-65. Grad. fellow W. Alton Jones Found., N.Y.C., 1962-63. Avocations: writing poetry, reading, travel, photography. Home and Office: Photonic Assocs 200A Ojo De La Vaca Rd Santa Fe NM 87508-8808 E-mail: crphipps@aol.com.

PHIPPS, DAVID LEE, lawyer; b. Fairfield, Iowa, Jan. 11, 1945; s. Sherman Richard and Dorothy Helen (Butterfield) P.; children: Rachelle, Martin, Robin, Kelly. BA, Drake U., 1967, JD with honors, 1969. Bar: Iowa 1969, U.S. Dist. Ct. (so. dist.) Iowa, 1969, U.S. Dist. Ct. (no. dist.) Iowa 1974, U.S. Ct. Appeals (8th cir.) 1975. Assoc. Whitfield & Eddy, Des Moines, 1969-74, ptnr., 1974—. Contbr. articles to profl. jours. Mem. ABA, Internat. Assn. Def. Counsel, Am. Coll. Trial Lawyers, Am. Bd. Trial Advocates, Iowa State Bar Assn., Iowa Def. Counsel Assn. (past pres.), Def. Rsch. Inst. (bd. dirs.), Iowa Acad. Trial Lawyers, Polk County Bar Assn. Mem. Cmty. Of Christ Ch. Avocations: reading, woodworking, collecting, biking. Office: Whitfield & Eddy PLC 317 6th Ave Ste 1200 Des Moines IA 50309-4195

PHIPPS, JOHN RANDOLPH, retired army officer; b. Kansas, Ill, May 16, 1919; s. Charles Winslow and Kelsey Ethel (Torrence) P.; m. Pauline M. Prunty, Feb. 8, 1946; children: Charles W., Kelsey J. Phipps-Selander. BS in Econs. with honors, U. Ill., 1941; M.P.A., Sangamon State U., 1976; assoc. course, Command and Gen. Staff Coll., 1959, nuclear weapons employment course, 1962; course, U.S. Army War Coll., 1973, U.S. Nat. Def. U., 1978. Owner, operator chain shoe stores in, Eastern Ill., 1946-70; commd. 2d lt. F.A. U.S. Army, 1941, advanced through grades to capt., 1943; service in Philippines and Japan; discharged as maj., 1946; organizer, comdr. Co. E, 130th Inf., Ill.; N.G., Mattoon, 1947, comdg. officer 2d Bn., 130th Inf., 1951, lt. col. 2d Bn., 130th Inf., 1951; called to fed. service, 1952; adv. (29th Regt., 9th Republic of Korea Div.), 1952-53; comdr. officer 1st Bn., 130th Inf., Ill. N.G., 1954, col., 1959; comdg. officer 2d Brigade, 33d Div., 1963-67; asst. div. comdr. 33d Inf. Div., 1967, brig. gen., 1967; comdr. 33d Inf. Brigade, Chgo., 1967-70, Ill. Emergency Ops. Hdqrs., 1970, asst. adj. gen. Ill., 1970-77, acting adj. gen., 1977-78, adj. gen., 1978, promoted to maj. gen., 1978, now maj. gen. ret. Decorated Silver Star, Bronze Star, Disting. Service medal, Combat Infantry Badge, Army Disting. Service medal Ill., various Philippine and Korean decorations; State of Ill. Long and Honorable Service medal. Mem. VFW, Adj. Gens. Assn. U.S., N.G. Assn. U.S., N.G. Assn. Ill., Am. Legion, Amvets. Home: 100 Wabash Ave Mattoon IL 61938-4524 Office: Phipps 100 Wabash Ave Mattoon IL 61938-4524

PHIPPS, LYNNE BRYAN, interior architect, educator, minister; b. Chapel Hill, N.C., Sept. 23, 1964; d. Floyd Talmadge and Sandra Patricia (McLester) Bryan. BFA, RISD, 1986, B in Interior Architecture, 1987; cert. in parent edn., Wheelock Coll., Boston, 1989; MDiv, Andover Newton Theol. Sem., 1997. Cert. interior arch. Apprentice Thompson Ventulett Stainback, Atlanta, 1983-85; jr. designer Flansberg & Assocs., Boston, 1986-87; sr. designer Andrew Samataro & Assocs., 1986-87; prin. Innovative Designs, Duxbury, 1987—97; prin. Design One Consortium LLC, 2001—. Parent educator Families First, Cambridge, Mass.; guest lectr., jurist Auburn (Ala.) U., 1988, RISD, Providence, 1990; guest jurist U. Memphis, 1995; assoc. prof. Mass. Bay C.C., Wellesley, 1997-2000; mem. adv. bd. U. R.I. Chamberlyne Sch. Design Alumni Coun., 1996—; guest lectr. Architectural and Family Issues; mem. adv. bd. Sch. Design IDA Coll., Newton, Mass. Designer furniture. Youth min. St. Andrew's Episcopal Ch., Hanover, Mass., 1992—95; youth and family min. St. Stephen's Episcopal Ch., Cohasset, 1993—96; pastor Kingston Congl. Ch. UCC, 1997—2000. Mem. AIA (assoc.), Internat. Interior Design Assn., Internat. Platform Assn. Avocations: sailing, tennis, antique boats. Office: Design One Consortium LLC 422D South Rd Wakefield RI 02879

PHIPPS, ROBERT MAURICE, lawyer; b. Detroit, Apr. 24, 1929; s. James Marion Phipps and Emma Holmes; m. Darleen Marie Rehbein, Aug. 23, 1952 (dec. Dec. 1999); children: David M., Robert Maurice II., Christina M. BS in Chemistry, U. Ala., 1954; JD, Akron U., 1959. Bar: Ohio 1960, U.S. Patent Office 1963, U.S. Supreme Ct. 1964, Mo. 1966, Can. Patent Office, 1967, U.S. Dist. Ct. (ea. dist.) Mo. 1968, D.C. 1969, Mich. 1971, U.S. Dist. Ct. (ea. dist.) Mich. 1974, Ill. 1977, U.S. Dist. Ct. (we. dist.) N.Y. 1981, N.Y. 1982. Patent atty. various cos., 1962-74; patent counsel, asst. sec. Velsicol Chem. Corp., Chgo., 1974-78; hearing officer dept. welfare State of Ill., 1979; sr. patent counsel Bausch and Lomb Inc., Rochester, N.Y., 1980-84; pvt. practice Mayfield, Ky., 1984—. Trustee Westbury Manor, Chesterfield, Mo., 1968-69; elder, trustee, deacon Presbyn. Ch., Penfield; trustee Hicks Cemetery Assn., Mayfield, 1975—. Sgt. U.S. Army, 1948-51. Mem. Am. INtellectual Property Law Assn., Rochester Intellectual Property Law Assn. (sec. 1983, v.p. 1989). Republican. Office: 106 Arbor Ridge Dr Mayfield KY 42066-1238

PHO, LONG AMBROSE BA, business educator, consultant; b. Hanoi, Vietnam, Apr. 25, 1922; arrived in U.S., 1975; s. Thuan Ba Pho and Ninh Thi Nguyen; m. Claire Trung-Nghia Dang, Oct. 15, 1940; children: Cyril Hong-Phong, Anne Le-Thu, Pacific Hong-Tam, Michael Hong-Quang, Helen Long-Chau, Edward Hong-Minh. Bachelor's degree 2e Partie, Lycee Albert Sarraut, Hanoi, 1944; Pharmacien d'Etat, U. Indochina, Hanoi, 1950; MBA, Harvard U., 1956. Advanced profl.c ert. Program dir. Georgetown U., Washington, 1983-95; seminar escort interpreter U.S. Dept. State, 1978—. Bus. edn. cons. Vietnam Found., McLean, Va., also in Laos, Cambodia, 1995—. Min. labor Govt. of Republic of Vietnam, Saigon, 1987-88. Capt., mil. pharmacist North Vietnamese mil., 1946-50. Recipient Congl. citation U.S. Senate, 1986. Mem. Vietnam Found. (hon. mem., founder, past pres. 1978-89). Office: Vietnam Foundation 6713 Lumsden St Mc Lean VA 22101

PHOCAS, GEORGE JOHN, international lawyer, business executive; b. N.Y.C., Dec. 1, 1927; m. Katrin Gorny, Feb. 26, 1966; 1 child, George Alexander. AB, U. Chgo., 1950, JD, 1953. Bar: N.Y. 1955, U.S. Supreme Ct. 1962. Assoc. Sullivan & Cromwell, N.Y.C., 1953-56; counsel Creole Petroleum Corp., Caracas, Venezuela, 1956-60; internat. negotiator Standard Oil Co. N.J. (Exxon), 1960-63; sr. ptnr. Casey, Lane & Mittendorf, London, 1963-72, counsel, 1972-76. Exec. v.p. Occidental Petroleum Corp., Los Angeles, 1972-74; adv., U.S. del. UN, ECAFE, Teheran, 1963 Trustee Assn. Naval Aviation, Washington, Owl's Head Aviation Mus., Maine; mem. vis. bd. U. Chgo. Law Sch.; bd. visitors U. Chgo. Law Sch. Capt. U.S. Army Mem. ABA, Law Soc. London, Brit. Inst. Comparative Law, Am. Soc. Internat. Law, Assn. Bar City N.Y.; Clubs: Boodles (London), Met. (N.Y.C.). Home: 29 Duchess of Bedford Walk London W87 QH England also: 1605 Middle Gulf Dr 102 Sanibel FL 33957-7601

PHOENIX, JOAQUIN, actor; b. San Juan, PR, Oct. 28, 1974; s. Bottom Amram John and Arlyn Dunetz Jochebed. Actor: (TV miniseries) Seven Brides for Seven Brothers; (TV films) Kids Don't Tell, 1985; (TV series) Morningstar/Eveningstar; (films) SpaceCamp, 1986, Parenthood, 1989, To Die For, 1995, Clay Pigeons, 1998, Return to Paradise, 1998, 8mm, 1999, Gladiator, 2000, Quills, 2000, Buffalo Soldiers, 2001, Signs, 2001. Office: 2603 NW 13th St Gainesville FL 32609 also: Iris Burton Agy 1450 Belfast Dr Los Angeles CA 90069

PHOON, COLIN KIT-LUN, pediatric cardiologist, medical educator; b. London, Dec. 7, 1963; came to U.S., 1968; s. Wai Wor and Alice Phoon; m. Janet Rose. BA in Biophysics, Johns Hopkins U., 1985; MPhil in Pharmacology, Cambridge (Eng.) U., 1986; MD, U. Pa., 1990. Diplomate in pediatrics and pediatric cardiology Am. Bd. Pediatrics. Intern, then resident in gen. pediatrics Johns Hopkins Hosp., Balt., 1990-93; fellow in pediatric cardiology U. Calif. Med. Ctr., San Francisco, 1993-96; asst. prof. pediatrics/pediatric cardiology NYU Sch. Medicine, N.Y.C., 1996—; attending physician NYU Med. Ctr./Bellevue Hosp. Ctr., 1996—, NYU Downtown Hosp., N.Y.C., 1998—2001, Hosp. for Joint Diseases, N.Y.C., 1999—; dir. pediatric echocard. lab. NYU Hosps. Ctr., 2002—. Cons. Chinatown Health Clinic, N.Y.C., 1998—. Author: Guide to Pediatric Cardiovascular Physical Examination or How to Survive an Outreach Clinic, 1998; contbr. Mem. Johns Hopkins Nat. Alumni Schs. Com. Recipient Dr. A.O.J. Kelly prize U. Pa., 1990, Francis Schwentker award Johns Hopkins Hosp.,1993, Clin Sci. Devel. award NIH/NHLBI, 2001—; Winston Churchill Found. scholar, 1985-86; Am. Heart Assn. fellow, 1995-96; rsch. career grantee NIH, 2001—. Fellow: Am. Acad. Pediatrics (Hon. Mention award resident rsch. competition 1993, 2d prize Young Investigator award competition 1998, Young Investigator Basic Sci. award sect. cardiology 1999), Am. Coll. Cardiology; mem.: Soc. Pediatric Rsch., N.Y. Pediatric Echocardiography Soc. (steering com. 1997, sec. 1999—), Am. Soc. Echocardiography, Am. Heart Assn. (mem. coun. basic cardiovascular scis. 1984—, mem. coun. in cardiovasc. disease in the young 1991—, Scientist Devel. grantee 2000—), Alpha Omega Alpha, Phi Beta Kappa, Churchill Scholars Soc. Avocations: reading, music, history of medicine, lacrosse, choral singing. Office: NYU Med Ctr Pediatric Echo Lab 540 First Ave TWR Ste 9U New York NY 10016-6402

PHOON, WAI WOR, physician; b. Hong Kong, Apr. 23, 1934; came to U.S., 1968; s. Seck Quai and Koon Sheung (Ng) P.; m. Alice Sukmen Tang, Oct. 20, 1962; children: Colin, Kelvin. MBBS, U. Hong Kong, 1958. Diplomate Am. Bd. Phys. Medicine Rehab., British Bd. Phys. Medicine. Intern in orthops. U. Hong Kong, 1959, intern in obstets. and medicine, 1959; med. officer Hong Kong Govt., 1960-66; pvt. practice Hong Kong, 1966-68; asst. prof. Case Western Res. U., Cleve., 1968-69, Temple U., Phila., 1969-70; assoc. prof. Hahnemann Med. Coll., 1970-71; pvt. practice Wilmington, Del., 1971—. Med. dir. Med. Rehab. Ctr., Hong Kong, 1966-68; cons. VA, Wilmington, 1987-2000. Am. Pres. Lines fellow NYU, 1962. Office: 314 E Main St Ste 402 Newark DE 19711-7182

PHUNG, NGUYEN DINH, medical educator; b. Ninh Binh, Vietnam, Sept. 25, 1950; came to U.S., 1975; s. Thu Dinh Nguyen and Minh Tuyet Le; m. Thuy Thanh Tran, Sept. 25, 1974; children: The-Ngoc, Khoi-Nguyen, Thien Huong. MD, Saigon Med. Sch., 1973. Diplomate Am. Bd. Internal Medicine, Am. Bd. Allergy and Immunology. Clin. instr. medicine, staff physician U. Okla. Health Scis. Ctr. & Vets. Hosp., Oklahoma City, 1982-84; clin. asst. prof. medicine U. Tex. Med. Sch., Houston, 1989—. Co-author: Practical Allergy & Immunology, 1983; contbr. articles to profl. jours. Mem. ACP, Am. Acad. Allergy and Immunology. Avocations: writing, music. Office: Allergy and Asthma Clinic 2905 Milam St Houston TX 77006-3609

PI, EDMOND HSIN-TUNG, psychiatry educator; b. China, June 1, 1948; MD, Cath. U. Coll. Medicine, 1972. Cert. Am. Bd. Psychiatry and Neurology. Chief resident U. Ky. Med. Ctr., Lexington, 1977-78; instr. psychiatry U. So. Calif. Sch. Medicine, L.A., 1978-80, asst. prof., 1980-83; assoc. prof. Med. Coll. Pa., Phila., 1983-85, U. So. Calif. Sch. Medicine, 1985-88, prof. clin. psychiatry, 1988—98; prof. Charles R. Drew U. Medicine and Sci., 1998—. Clin. prof. psychiatry, UCLA Sch. Medicine, 1999—; asst. dir. psychopharmacology U. So. Calif. Sch. Medicine, 1978-80; asst. dir. adult psychiat. clinic L.A. County and U. So. Calif. Med. Ctr., 1980-83; dir. adult psychiat. clinic Med. Coll. Pa., Phila., 1983-85; dir. Adult Psychiat. Inpatient Svcs., L.A. County and U. So. Calif. Med. Ctr., 1985-91, dir. Adult Psychiat. Outpatient Svcs., 1995-97; dir. transcultural psychiatry U. So. Calif. Sch. Medicine, 1991-98; med. dir. State of Calif. Dept. Mental Health, 1997-98; dir. Consultation and Liaison Svcs., L.A. County and U. So. Calif. Med. Ctr., 1998; exec. vice-chmn., assoc. ctr. dir. Augustus F. Hawkins Mental Health Ctr., Martin Luther King, Jr./Charles R. Drew U. Med. Ctr., 1998—. Author: Reactions to Psychotropic Medications, 1987, (book chpts.) Transcultural Psychiatry, Clinical Psychopharmacology, 1985—; contbr. articles to profl. jours. Mem. Calif. Gov.'s Com. Employment of Disabled Persons, Sacramento, 1993—; bd. dirs. Chinese Bus. Assn., L.A., 1990—92, Com. of 100, N.Y.C., 1993—98, San Gabriel chpt. ARC, Calif., 1994—97, Mental Health Assn., L.A. County, 1995—97, 1998—2001. Vis. scholar Com. on Scholarly Comm. with People's Republic of China U.S. Nat. Acad. Scis., Washington, 1987-88; Treval fellow Am. Coll. Neuropsychopharmacology, 1982. Fellow Am. Psychiat. Assn. (chair com. Asian-Am. psychiatrists 1998-2000), Am. Soc. Social Psychiatry, Pacific Rim Coll. Psychiatry (treas. 1991-97), Am. Coll. Psychiatrists; mem. Soc. Study Psychiatry and Culture, Pacific Rim Assn. Clin. Pharmogenetics, Assn. Chinese Am. Psychiatrists (pres. 1995—). Avocations: photography, writing, travel, tennis, media communications. Office: Charles R Drew U Medicine & Sci Dept Psychiatry & Human Beh 1720 E 120th St Ste 1021 Los Angeles CA 90059-3052 E-mail: edpi@cdrewu.edu.

PIACENTINI, NICHOLAS A., JR. military officer; b. Sacramento; AA, Sacramento City Coll.; BS, Sacramento State Coll. Commd. USAR, 1970, advanced through grades to sgt. maj.; from drill sgt. to 1st sgt. for cos. B and D 3d Bn., 360th Regiment, 1st Brigade, 91st Divsn., Sacramento, 1970; command sgt. mjr. hq. 5th Bn., Lathrop; command sgt. maj./commandant 91st Divsn. Leadership Drill Sgt. Sch., Dublin; command sgt. maj. hq. 1st Brigade, Sacramento; command sgt. maj. 351st Civil Affairs Command, Mountain View, Army Res. Pers. Ctr., St. Louis, 1994—98, 3d Med. Command, Atlanta, 1998—2000, USAR Command, Ft. McPherson, 2000—. Decorated Meritorious Svc. medal with 4 oak leaf clusters, Army Commendation medal, Army Res. Components Achievement medal with 4 oak leaf clusters, Armed Forces Res. medal with silver hourglass device, many others; recipient Mil. Outstanding Vol. Svc. medal. Office: Army Reserve Command Hq Fort McPherson Fort Mcpherson GA 30330-1069*

PIACITELLI, JOHN JOSEPH, county official, educator, pediatrician; b. Providence, Sept. 1, 1936; s. Joseph A. and Elsie (Mignacca) P.; m. Carol Ann Keirn, Aug. 19, 1961; 1 child, James. BS, U. R.I., 1958; MA, SUNY, Buffalo, 1963; MD, Creighton U., 1964. Diplomate Am. Bd. Pediatrics. Intern Buffalo Gen. Hosp., 1964-65; pediatric resident Children's Hosp. of Buffalo, 1965-67; pediatrician East Nassau Med. Group, North Babylon, N.Y., 1969-79; dir. Charlotte County Health Dept., Punta Gorda, Fla., 1980—. Asst. clin. instr. SUNY, Buffalo, 1965-67, instr. in clin. pediatrics, L.I., 1972-79, asst. prof. pediatrics, 1979. Contbr. articles to profl. jours. Mem. health adv. com. Charlotte County Sch., 1981-96; mem. local planning orgn. adv. com., Charlotte County, Fla., 1986-87; mem. Indigent Health Care Adv. Bd., Charlotte County, 1988—; chmn. Charlotte County AIDS Task Force, 1988-91; chmn. adv. com. Head Start Health Svcs., 1991-94. Maj. M.C., U.S. Army, 1967-69. Fellow Am. Acad Pediatrics (cert.); mem. Nat. Assn. County and City Health Ofcls., Fla. Pub. Health Assn., Fla. Assn. County Health Officers, Fla. Med. Assn., Charlotte County Med. Soc., Fla. Soc. for Preventive Medicine. Office: Charlotte County Health Dept 514 E Grace St Punta Gorda FL 33950-6121 E-mail: cjpiac@tnh.net.

PIAGET, GERALD WARREN, psychologist, educator; b. Paterson, N.J., Nov. 10, 1942; s. Warren Edward Piaget and Mary Grace Fitzgerald; m. Joan Emerson Gianatasio, Mar. 7, 1981; children: Ryan, Craig. BS with honors, Lehigh U., 1964; PhD with honors, U. Mass., 1968. Rsch. prof. Behavior Change, Inc., Los Altos, Calif., 1969-72; clin. assoc. prof. dept. behavioral scis. Stanford U. Sch. Medicine, Palo Alto, 1975—; pres., CEO IAHB, Inc., Portola Valley, 1977—. Author: Overcoming Your Barriers, 1985, Control Freaks, 1991. Tng. fellow NIMH, 1967-68. Mem. APA. Home: 624 Georgia Ave Palo Alto CA 94306 Office: IAHB Inc 4370 Alpine Rd Ste 209 Portola Valley CA 94028 Office Fax: (650) 851-0406. E-mail: gpiaget@aol.com.

PIAGGIO, JOANNE, peri-operative nurse; b. Bayonne, N.J., June 8, 1962; d. John Michael Sr. and Mary Ann (Stepanek) Valdora: m. Patrick A. Piaggio, Nov. 26, 1988; children: Patrick Jr., Christopher, Elizabeth. Diploma, St. Francis Sch. Nursing, Jersey City, 1986; BSN, Seton Hall U., 1995. RN, N.J.; CNOR. Staff nurse obstetrics, post partum, nursery, labor-delivery Community Med. Ctr., Toms River, N.J., 1986, staff nurse med.-surg. unit, 1987; staff nurse operating room Deborah Heart and Lung Ctr., Browns Mills, 1988-89; charge nurse oper. rm. Med. Ctr. Ocean County-Brick (N.J.) Div., 1989-96, staff RN, 1996—, perioperative nurse educator, 2001—. Mem. Assn. Oper. Rm. Nurses. Home: 54 Spruce St Beachwood NJ 08722

PIAKER, PHILIP MARTIN, accountant, educator; b. N.Y.C., Oct. 26, 1921; s. Jacob and Sarah (Schloss) P.; m. Pauline Strum, Sept. 22, 1946; children: Susan, Alan, Matthew. BA, CCNY, 1943, MBA, 1949. Lectr. CCNY, 1949-52; asst. prof. acctg. SUNY, Binghamton, 1952-57, assoc. prof., 1957-62, prof., 1962—, Disting. Svc. prof. acctg., 1980—, chmn. dept. acctg., 1970-76, 77-89; chmn. bd. Endicott Rsch. Group, Inc., Johnson City, N.Y., 1983—. Adv. dir. Endicott Bank N.Y.; mem. N.Y. State Bd. for Pub. Accountancy, 1973-83, chmn., 1982-83; v.p. Piaker, Lyons, P.C., CPA's; mem. Nat. Bd. to Evaluate CPA Exams., 1979-83; Danforth Seminar on Bus. Morality fellow Harvard U., 1959; Summer Study on Ethics in Bus. fellow U. So. Calif., 1982. Mem. editorial bd. Binghamton Reporter, 1975—. Bd. dirs. Broome chpt. Am. Cancer Soc., 1974-79, Tri-Cities Opera; trustee Temple Israel Binghamton, 1978—. With U.S. Army, 1943-46. SUNY SWANA fellow Jerusalem, 1966, Am. Profs. for Peace in Middle East fellow Jerusalem, 1974; recipient Chancellors award for teaching excellence, 1975, David Ben Gurion award State of Israel, 1979, Outstanding Contbn. to Acctg. award Found. for Acctg., 1979, Outstanding Educator award Found. for Acctg. Rsch., 1986 . Mem. AICPA, N.Y. State Soc. CPA's (pres. Binghamton chpt. 1963-65), Am. Acctg. Assn., Acctg. Rsch. Assn., Nat. Assn. Accts., Bus. Ethics Soc., SUNY Alumni Assn. (Disting. Svc. award 1989), CHABAD (pres. 1989-92). Home: 301 Manchester Rd Vestal NY 13850-3604 also: 7421 Hearth Stone Ave Boynton Beach FL 33437-2924

PIAN, CARLSON CHAO-PING, mechanical engineering educator, researcher; b. Beijing, China, Dec. 31, 1945; came to U.S., 1957; s. Charles H.C. and Juliette (Fan) P.; m. Sally Tseng, Aug. 23, 1969; children: Kevin, Phillip, Timothy. BS in Aerospace Engring., U. Mich., 1968, MS in Aerospace Engring., 1969, PhD in Aerospace Engring., 1974. Instr. dept. aerospace engring. U. Mich., Ann Arbor, 1965-74; vis. scientist dept. elec. engring. Eindhoven (Netherlands) Tech. U., 1974-75; rsch. engr. Lewis Rsch. Ctr. NASA, Cleve., 1975-79; prin. rsch. engr. Avco Everett (Mass.) Rsch. Lab., Inc., 1979-84, dir. magnetohydrodynamic power generation, 1987-94; with Miss. State U., 1994-95, prof., rschr., 1997-2000; sr. scientist Molten Metal Tech., Mass., 1995-97; prof. mech. engring. Alfred (N.Y.) U., 2000—. Assoc. editor, Jour. Propulsion and Power, 1993—; contbr. over 80 articles to symposiums and profl. jours. Fellow AIAA (assoc., terrestial energy systems tech. com. 1982-84, plasmadynamics and lasers tech. com. 1984-86, Space Shuttle Flag award 1984); mem. Am. Phys. Soc. Avocations: bicycling, sailing, photography. Office: Alfred U Mech Engring Divsn Alfred NY 14802 E-mail: pianccp@alfred.edu.

PIAN, RULAN CHAO, musicologist, scholar; b. Cambridge, Mass., Apr. 20, 1922; d. Yuen Ren and Buwei (Yang) Chao; m. Theodore Hsueh-huang Pian, Oct. 3, 1945; 1 child, Canta Chao-po. BA, Radcliffe Coll., 1944, MA, 1946, PhD, 1960. Teaching asst., instr. in modern Chinese Harvard U., 1947-60, lectr. Chinese and Chinese music, 1961-74, prof. Ea. Asian langs. and civilizations, prof. music, 1974-92; prof. emerita, 1992—; coordinator modern Chinese lang. instrn. Harvard U., 1962-68, mem. council E. Asian studies, 1975-92, faculty mem. Com. on Degrees in Folklore and Mythology, 1976-92, master of South House, 1975-78. Vis. prof. dept. music The Chinese U. Hong Kong, 1975, 78-79, 82, 94, inst. humanities Nat. Tsing Hua U., Taiwan, 1990, Sch. Humanities, Nat. Cen. U., Taiwan, 1992; hon. prof. Ctrl. China U. of Sci. and Tech., Wuhan, 1990, Ctrl. S. U. Tech., Changsha, China, 1991, S.W. Jiaoting U., Chengdu, 1994, Shah-shih U., Hupei, 1996; hon. rsch. fellow Shanghai Conservatory Music, China, 1991, Inst. Music Rsch., China Acad. of Arts, Beijing, 1997; academician Academia Sinica, Taiwan, 1990. Author: A Syllabus for the Mandarin Primer, 1961, Sonq Dynasty Musical Sources and Their Interpretation, 1967; compiler: Complete Musical Works of Yuen Ren Chao, 1987; contbr. articles to scholarly jours. Recipient Caroline Wilby dissertation prize Radcliffe Coll., 1960, Radcliffe Grad. Soc. medal, 1980; NDEA Fulbright-Hayes research grantee Chinese Music Taiwan, 1964; NEH grantee Hong Kong, 1978-79 Mem. Am. Musicological Soc. (coun. 1993-96, Otto Kinkeldey book award 1968), Internat. Musicological Soc., Soc. Ethnomusicology (coun. 1968-75, 87-90), Conf. Chinese Oral and Performing Lit. (co-founder, pres. 1983-90, permanent hon. pres. 1995—), Assn. for Chinese Mus. Rsch. (co-founder), Internat. Coun. for Traditional Music. Home: 14 Brattle Cir Cambridge MA 02138-4625 Office: 2 Divinity Ave Cambridge MA 02138-2020

PIAN, THEODORE HSUEH-HUANG, engineering educator, consultant; b. Shanghai, China, Jan. 18, 1919; came to U.S., 1943; s. Chao-Hsin Shu-Cheng and Chih-Chuan (Yen) P.; m. Rulan Chao, Oct. 3, 1945; 1 child, Canta Chao-Po. B in Engring., Tsing Hua U., Kunming, China, 1940; MS, MIT, 1944, DSc, 1948; DSc (hon.), Beijing U. Aeros. and Astronautics, 1990; PhD (hon.), Shanghai U., 1991. Engr. Cen. Aircraft Mfg. Co., Loiwing, China, 1940-42, Chengtu Glider Mfg. Factory, 1942-43; tchg. asst. MIT, Cambridge, 1946-47, rsch. assoc., 1947-52, asst. prof., 1952-59, assoc. prof., 1959-66, prof., 1966-89, prof. emeritus, 1989—. Vis. assoc. Calif. Inst. Tech., Pasadena, 1965-66; vis. prof. U. Tokyo, 1974, Tech. U., Berlin, 1975; vis. chair prof. Nat. Tsing Hua U., Hsin Chu, Taiwan, 1990, Nat. Ctrl. U., ChungLi, Taiwan, 1992; hon. prof. Beijing U. Aero. and Astronautics, Beijing Inst. Tech., Southwestern Jaiotong U., Dalian U. Tech., Huazhong U. Sci. and Tech., Changsha Rwy. U., Ctrl.-South U. Tech., Hohai U., Nanjing U. of Aero. and Astronautics, Dalian Rwy. U., Shashi U. of Sci. and Tech. of China. Recipient von Karman Meml. prize TRE Corp., Beverly Hills, Calif., 1974. Fellow AAAS, AIAA (assoc. editor jour. 1973-75, Structures, Structural Dynamics and Materials award 1975), U.S. Assn. Computational Mechanics (founding mem.); mem. ASME (hon.), NAE, Am. Soc. Engring. Edn., Internat. Assn. for Computational Mechanics (hon. mem. gen. coun.). Home: 14 Brattle Cir Cambridge MA 02138-4625 Office: MIT Dept Aeronautics and Astronautics 77 Massachusetts Ave Dept And Cambridge MA 02139-4307 E-mail: thhpian@aol.com., thhpian@mit.edu.

PIANKO, THEODORE A. lawyer; b. Dennville, N.J., Sept. 5, 1955; s. Theodore and Pasqualina (Liguori) P.; m. Beatriz Maria Olivera (div. Dec. 1985); m. Kathryn Anne Lindley, Feb. 18, 1990; children: Matthew James, Samuel Wahoo, Zoe Wahoo. BA, SUNY, 1975; JD, U. Mich., 1978. Bar: Mich. 1978, Ill. 1979, Calif. 1980. Atty. Ford Motor Co., Dearborn, Mich., 1978-80; assoc. Lillick McHose & Charles, L.A., 1980-83; ptnr. Sidley & Austin, 1983-94, Christie, Parker & Hale, Pasadena, Calif., 1994—. E-mail: ted@pianko.com.

PIASECKA JOHNSON, BARBARA, philanthropist, art historian and collector, business investor; b. Staniewicze, Poland; d. Pelagia and Wojciech Piasecki; m. J. Seward Johnson (dec.). Chair., dir. trustee Barbara Piasecka Johnson Found., 1974—. Owner extensive art collection, Barbara Piasecka Johnson Collection; mem. bd. mgrs. Wistar Inst., Phila., 1989-91; mem. chmn.'s coun. Met. Mus. Art, N.Y.C., 1986; mem. adv. com. Nat. Gallery Art, Washington, 1980-91; bd. dirs. Inst. for Polish-Jewish Studies, Oxford, Eng.; mem. fine arts com. U.S. Dept. State, 1978-85; mem. strategic adv. com. dept. molecular genetics and microbiology Robert Wood Johnson Med. Sch., U. Medicine and Dentistry N.J. Trustee, bd. dirs. Atlantic Found., 1972-85, Harbor Br. Found., 1972-85; trustee, chair Paderewski Ctr.; mem. coun. Found. for U. Wroclaw, 1991-92. Recipient Heritage award Polish Am. Congress, 1989, Nat. Citizen of Yr. award Am-Pol Eagle, 1989, Disting. Svc. award Am. Coun. for Polish Culture, 1990, Award St. Brother Albert Chmielowski, 1990, Hon. Citizen award State of Calif., 1990, Appreciation diploma Min. Fgn. Affairs Republic Poland, 1991, Gold medal U. Wroclaw, 1991, Sci. Devel. award Acad. Agriculture Wroclaw, 1991, Crystal Heart award Found. for Devel. Cardiac Surgery Zabrze, 1992, Merit cert. Pres. Coun. N.Y.C., 1993, Champion of Democracy award Coll. Democracy Washington, 1993, Waclaw Nizynski medal Polish Artists Agy, 1994, Living Legacy award Women's Internat. Ctr., 1994, The Order of Saint Charles Officer decoration conferred by H.S.H. Prince Rainier III in recognition of svcs. rendered to the Principality of Monaco, 1995. Mem. Am. Assn. for Polish-Jewish Studies (hon. chmn.), Rotary Internat. (Paul Harris fellow 1988).

PIASECKI, MARCELLA LOUISE, funeral science educator; b. Newark, Apr. 29, 1943; d. Frank Paul and Sally Katherine (Wodynski) P.; divorced; 1 child, Edward V. Francis. MA in Adminstrn., Seton Hall U., 1981. Cert. tchr., Fla. Owner, operator Piasecki Funeral Home, Harrison, N.J., 1965-82; sci. instr. Boca Raton (Fla.) Acad., 1983-88, Pope John Paul II H.S., Boca Raton, 1988-97; dir. funeral svc. edn. Lynn U., 1997—. Adj. instr. Mercer Coll., Trenton, N.J. Named Tchr. of Yr., Rotary, 1985, Bus. and Profl. Women, 1970. Mem. Nat. Funeral Dirs. Assn., Fla. Funeral Dirs. Assn., Broward County Funeral Dirs. Assn., Palm Beach County Funeral Dirs., Independent Funeral Dirs. Assn. Fla., Kappa Delta Pi. Roman Catholic. Avocations: reading, swimming. Home: 428 Ashwood Pl Boca Raton FL 33431 Office: Lynn U 3601 N Military Trl Boca Raton FL 33431 E-mail: mpiasecki@lynn.edu.

PIASECKI, PAUL JAMES, JR. accountant; b. Port Chester, N.Y., Mar. 31, 1958; s. Paul James and Lorraine G. (Swenning) P.; m. Katharine F. Dana, June 1, 1985; children: P. Christopher, Cammann S. BBA, Pace U., 1980. CPA, Conn. Staff Urbach, Kahn & Werlin, N.Y.C., 1979-82; sr. staff Bregman & Co., Stamford, Conn., 1982-85, ptnr., 1985-94; prin. Piasecki & Co., CPAs LLC, Darien, 1994—. Spl. investigator Conn. Superior Ct., Hartford, 1991—. Contbg. author: Financial Planning for Divorce in Connecticut, 1994. Mem. devel. com. Darien (Conn.) United Way, 1992-93; founding mem., bd. dirs. Fairfield Bus. Network, Stamford, 1992-94. Mem. AICPA, Conn. Soc. CPAs (1st v.p. 1995), Darien C. of C. (bd. dirs. 1994—, chair bus. edn. 1994—, pres. 1996—). Republican. Congregationalist. Avocation: tennis. Office: Piasecki & Co CPAs LLC 53 Old Kings Hwy N Darien CT 06820-4735

PIASSICK, JOEL BERNARD, lawyer; b. Atlanta, June 2, 1940; s. Louis S. and Sarah (Freeman) P.; m. Karen Pevow, Aug. 11, 1963; children: Joan, Louis. BA in Polit. Sci., Tulane U., 1962; LLB, U. Va., 1965. Bar: Va. 1965, Ga. 1966, Colo. 1999. Ptnr. Smith, Gambrell & Russell, Atlanta, 1967-90, Kilpatrick Stockton LLP, Atlanta, 1990—. Bd. dirs. Southeastern Bankruptcy Law Inst., Inc. Fellow Am. Coll. Bankruptcy. Office: Kilpatrick Stockton LLP 1100 Peachtree St NE Ste 2800 Atlanta GA 30309-4530 E-mail: jpiassick@kilstock.com.

PIATT, ALBERT EARL, educator, researcher, consultant; b. Bellaire, Ohio, Feb. 13, 1948; s. Albert Maxwell and Evelyn Lorena (St. John) P.; m. Linda Ruth Shirley, July 18, 1969; children: Ruth Lorraine, Bonita Nicole, Dorothy Elizabeth. BS, U. Tenn., Chattanooga, 1970; EdM, Wayne State U., 1973; MA in Edn., East Carolina U., 1976; EdD, U. Tenn., 1995. Cert. secondary tchr., Tenn. Commd. 2d lt. USAR, 1970; advanced through grades to lt. col. U.S. Army, 1987, ret., 1992; adminstrv. intern Challenger Ctr., Chattanooga, 1993-94, grad. asst., 1994-95; ednl. cons.; 7th grade math. tchr. Brown Mid. Sch., Harrison, 1997-2000; math. and sci. tchr. David Brainard Christian Sch., Chattanooga, 2000—. Deacon MacPherson Presbyn. Ch., Fayetteville, N.C., 1981-84; elder Clk. of Sessiion New Hope Presbyn. Ch., Chattanooga, 1995-98. Named Disting. grad. U.S. Army JFX Inst. for Mil. Assistance, Ft. Bragg, N.C., 1980. Mem. ASCD, ACA, Am. Evaluation Assn., Nat. Mid. Sch. Assn., Res. Officers Assn., Am. Legion, VFW, DAV, Nat. Coun. Tchrs. Math., Ret. Officers Assn., Pi Lambda Theta, Phi Kappa Phi. Avocations: photography, reading, music. Home: 1721 Julian Ridge Rd Chattanooga TN 37421-3321 Office: David Brainard Christian Sch 7553 Igou Gap Rd Chattanooga TN 37421 E-mail: apiatt@dbcsmiddle.org.

PIAZZA, DUANE EUGENE, biomedical researcher, college official; b. San Jose, Calif., June 5, 1954; s. Salvador Richard and Mary Bernice (Mirassou) P.; m. Sandra Patrignani, Sept. 19, 1992. BS in Biology, U. San Francisco, 1976; MA in Biology, San Francisco State U., 1986. Staff rsch. assoc. I U. Calif., San Francisco, 1975—81; sr. rsch. technician XOMA Corp., 1981—82; biologist II Syntex USA Inc., Palo Alto, 1982—85; pres., cons. Ryte For You, Oakland, 1985—; rsch. assoc. I Cetus Corp., Emeryville, 1986—90; rsch. assoc. II John Muir Cancer and Aging Rsch. Inst., Walnut Creek, 1991—92; rsch. assoc. Pharmagenesis, Palo Alto, 1993—96; asst. lab. mgr. DeAnza C.C., Cupertino, 1996—99; lab. mgr. San Jose City Coll., 1999—2000; content scientist Ingenuity, Alviso, Calif., 2000—01; sr. biologist ALZA Corp., Mountain View, 2000—, mem. emergency response team, 2001—. CPR & first aid instr. ARC, 1980-92, vol. 1st aid sta. instr., Santa Cruz, 1985-86, vol. 1st aid sta. disaster action team, Oakland, 1986-92, br. chmn. disaster action team, 1987-88; treas. Reganti Homeowner Assn., 1990-92. Mem. AAAS, Am. Soc. Microbiology, N.Y. Acad. Scis., Astron. Soc. Pacific, Planetary Soc., Mt. Diablo Astronomy Soc. Republican. Roman Catholic. Avocations: scuba diving, swimming, backpacking, photography, astronomy. Home: 1055 Rebecca Dr Boulder Creek CA 95006-9442 Office: 1058B Huff Ave Mountain View CA 94043 E-mail: duane.piazza@alza.com.

PIAZZA, MARGUERITE, opera singer, actress, entertainer; b. New Orleans, May 6, 1926; d. Albert William and Michaela (Piazza) Luft; m. William J. Condon, July 15, 1953 (dec. Mar. 1968); children: Gregory, James (dec.), Shirley, William J., Marguerite P., Anna Becky; m. Francis Harrison Bergtholdt, Nov. 8, 1970. MusB, Loyola U., New Orleans; MusM, La. State U.; MusD (hon.), Christian Bros. Coll., 1973; LHD (hon.), Loyola U., Chgo., 1975. Singer N.Y.C. Ctr. Opera, 1948, Met. Opera Co., 1950; TV artist, regular singing star Your Show of Shows NBC, 1950-54; entertainer various supper clubs Cotillion Room, Hotel Pierre, N.Y.C., 1954, Las Vegas, Los Angeles, New Orleans, San Francisco, 1956—; ptnr. Sound Express Music Pub. Co., Memphis, 1987—. Bd. dirs. Cemrel, Inc. Appeared as guest performer on numerous mus. TV shows. Nat. crusade chmn. Am. Cancer Soc., 1971; founder, bd. dirs. Marguerite Piazza Gala for the Benefit of St. Jude's Hosp., 1976; bd. dirs. Memphis Opera Co., World Literacy Found., NCCJ; v.p., life bd. dirs. Memphis Symphony Orch.; nat. chmn. Soc. for Cure Epilepsy. Decorated Mil. and Hospittaler Order of St. Lazarus of Jerusalem; recipient svc. award Chgo. Heart Assn., 1956, svc. award Fedn. Jewish Philanthropies of N.Y., 1956, Sesquicentennial medal Carnegie Hall, St. Martin De Porres award So. Dominicans, 1994, Lifetime Achievement award Germantown Arts Alliance, 1998; named Queen of Memphis, Memphis Cotton Carnival, 1973, Person of Yr., La. Coun. for Performing Arts, 1975, Woman of Yr., Nat. Am. Legion, Woman of Yr., Italian-Am. Soc. Mem. Nat. Speakers Assn., Woman's Exchange, Memphis Country Club, Memphis Hunt and Polo Club, New Orleans Country Club, Summit Club, Beta Sigma Omicron, Phi Beta. Roman Catholic. Home: 2813 Central Ave Memphis TN 38111-1822

PICARD, FREDERIC JEAN, orthopedic surgeon, consultant, researcher; b. Besancon, France, May 13, 1961; s. Guy and Marie-France (Drefuss) P.; children: Roxane, Guillaume, Mathis and Ludovic (twins); m. Lalao Hanitra Rakotoarivelo, July 18, 1998. MD, U. Besancon, 1987; Degree in Gen. Surgery, U. Grenoble, France, 1990; M in Biomechanics/Anatomy, U. Lyon and Grenoble, France, 1991; Degree in Hand and Upper Limb Surgery, U. Paris, 1993. Cert. hosp. practitioner. Resident Univ. Hosps., Grenoble/Lyon, 1987-93; hosp. asst. Univ. Hosp., Grenoble, 1993-96; lectr. anatomy U. Grenoble, 1993-96; responsible for application devel. computer assisted surgery Aesculap/B. Braun Co., France and Germany, 1997. Vis. scholar Northwestern U. and Northwestern Orthopedic Inst., Chgo., 1998; project engr./sys. developer Ctr. Orthopedic Rsch./Carnegie Mellon U., Pitts., 1999; mem. faculty Pitts. U., 1998, Berne (Switzerland) U., 1998. Contbr. articles to profl. jours; patentee in field. Mem. French Coll. Orthopedic and Trauma Surgeons. Avocations: swimming, reading, gathering, music listening. Office: Orthop Dept Polyclinique Fontainebleau 4 Rue Lagorsse 77300 Fontainebleau France

PICARD, M(EREDITH) DANE, geologist; b. Washburn, Mo., Aug. 7, 1927; s. Vincent Hayes and Velma Vestal Picard; m. Virginia Reitz Picard, July 5, 1958 (div.); children: Marion, Jacqueline, Dane, Bennet. Student, Swarthmore Coll., 1945; BS, U. Wyo., 1950; AM, Princeton U., 1962, PhD, 1963. Surveyor U.S. Soil Conservation Svc., Worland, Wyo., 1947; geologist Texaco Inc., Casper, 1950; geologist, dist. stratigrapher Shell Oil Co., Salt Lake City, 1950-56; geologist St. Helens Petroleum Corp., Casper, 1956-57; dist. mgr. Am. Stratigraphic Co., Durango, Colo., 1957-60; from assoc. prof. to prof. geology U. Nebr., Lincoln, 1963-68; prof. geology and geophysics U. Utah, Salt Lake City, 1968—. Vis. prof. U. Tex., Austin, 1967-68; cons. Utah Geol. Survey, Salt Lake City, 1969-74, Mountain Fuel Supply Co., Salt Lake City, 1972-75. Author: Grit and Clay, 1975, Mountains and Minerals, Rivers and Rocks, 1993; co-author: (with L.R. High Jr.) Sedimentary Structures of Ephemeral Streams, 1973, (with W.L. Stokes and Sheldon Judson) Introduction to Geology, 1978; editor: Henry Mountains Symposium, 1980, Geology and Energy Resources, Uinta Basin of Utah, 1985. With USN, 1945-46. Named Outstanding Alumnus, Coll. Arts and Scis., U. Wyo., 1994; recipient award for outstanding contbns. to pub. understanding of geology Am. Geol. Inst., 1998. Fellow AAAS, Geol. Soc. Am. (gen. chmn. nat. meeting 1975); mem. Am. Assn. Petroleum Geologists, Soc. Econ. Paleontologists and Mineralogists (pres. 1984-85), Nat. Assn. Geosci. Tchrs. (pres. 1988-89), Utah Geol. Assn. (hon.), Wyo. Geol. Assn. (hon.). Avocations: tennis, hiking. Home: 3520 Westwood Dr Salt Lake City UT 84109 Office: Dept Geol Scis U Utah Salt Lake City UT 84112

PICARDI, GERARD A. publisher; b. Boston, Apr. 24, 1949; s. Antonio Sabine and Jane Elizabeth Picardi. BA in English Lit., St. Michael's Coll., 1970. Office mgr. Love's Furniture Co., Stoneham, Mass., 1970-75; sec. Little, Brown & Co., Boston, 1975-76, prodn. asst., 1976-79, asst. prodn. mgr., 1979-84; prodn. coord. Harvard U. Press, Cambridge, Mass., 1984-92, prodn. supr., 1992-97, asst. prodn. mgr., 1997-2000, frontlist mgr., 2000—. Named Harvard U. Hero, 1999. Mem. Bookbuilders Boston (mem. fall roundtable com. 1988-90, co-chair 1990-91, mem. publicity com. 1990-91, chair 1991-93, mem. advanced seminar com. 1992-95, bd. dirs. 1991-94, sec. 1993-94, mem. nominations com. 1993-95, mem. edn. com. 1994-95, chair endowment fund com. 1994-95, 1st v.p. 1994-95, pres. 1995-96, chair Dwiggins award com. 1996-97, judge New Eng. book show 1998-99), Am. Assn. Univ. Presses, Am. Inst. Graphic Arts. Roman Catholic. E-mail: gerard. Home: 350 Sumner St East Boston MA 02128-2218 Office: Harvard U Press 79 Garden St Cambridge MA 02138-1423

PICARIELLO, PASQUALE, lawyer; b. Norristown, Pa., May 26, 1959; s. Pasquale J. and Helen Irene (Delpizzo) P.; m. Claudia Coulter. BA, Columbia U., 1981; JD, Rutgers U., 1984. Bar: N.J. 1984, U.S. Dist. Ct. N.J. 1984, N.Y. 1985, U.S. Ct. Appeals (3d cir. 1985), Pa. 1994, U.S. Dist. Ct. (ea. dist.) Pa. 1995. Assoc. Slimm, Dash & Goldberg, Westmont, N.J., 1984-89, Ballen and Gertel, Camden, 1989-93; pvt. practice, Hammonton, 1993-95; litigation atty. Jacoby & Meyers Law Offices, Phila., 1995-98; pvt. practice, Voorhees, N.J., 1999—. Mem. N.J. State Bar Assn., Camden County Bar Assn. (young lawyer com. 1987-90), Delta Phi. Home: 901 Central Ave Hammonton NJ 08037-1116 Office: PO Box 287 Hammonton NJ 08037-0287

PICCATO, PABLO, historian, educator; b. San Francisco, Argentina, Nov. 22, 1963; s. Miguel Angel Piccato and Ana Herminia Rodríguez; m. Xóchitl Medina; children: Catalina, Aida. Licenciatura, Universidad Nacional Autónoma de México, Mexico City, 1989; PhD, U. Tex., 1997. Assoc. dir. Museo de Arte Carrillo Gil, Mexico City, 1989—91; asst. prof. Columbia U., N.Y.C., 1997—. Author: (book) Congreso y Revolución: El Parlamentarismo en la XXVI Legislatura, 1991 (Instituto Nacional de Estudios Históricos de la Revolución Mexicana, "Salvador Azuela" prize for essays on the Mexican Revolution, 1990), City of Suspects: Crime in Mexico City, 1900-1931, 2001; mem. editl. bd.: Law and History Rev., 2000—. Recipient Beca Jovenes Creadores award for the category of lit. essay, Fondo Nacional para la Cultura y las Artes, México, 1992, Génesis, actualidad y perspectiva de la Constitución Política de 1917, Instituto Nacional de Estudios Históricos de la Revolución Mexicana, 1992. Mem.: Latin Am. Studies Assn., Am. Hist. Assn. Office: Columbia University, Dpt. of History 1180 Amsterdam Ave. New York NY 10027

PICCHIETTI, DANIEL LEIGH, neurologist; b. Chgo., Jan. 1953; s. Louis and Margaret Picchietti; m. Nanette Picchietti; 4 children. BS, No. Ill. U., 1975; MD, U. Chgo., 1979. Diplomate Am. Bd. Psychiatry and Neurology, Am. Bd. Pediatrics, Am. Bd. Sleep Disorders Medicine. Resident in pediatrics Children's Hosp./Washington U., St. Louis, 1979-81; fellow in neurology U. Chgo., 1981-84; med. dir. Carle Regional Sleep Disorders Ctr., Urbana, Ill., 1984—; asst. clin. prof. U. Ill., 1985-96, assoc. clin. prof., 1996—; head divsn. child neurology Carle Clinic Assn., 1988—. Bd. dirs. Am. Bd. Sleep Medicine, Rochester, Minn., 1997—, examiner, 1995—; mem. med. adv. bd. Resless Legs Syndrome Found., Rochester, 1994-99. Contbr. articles to profl. jours., chpt. to book. Fellow Am. Sleep Disorders Assn.; mem. Am. Acad. Neurology, Child Neurology Soc. Office: Carle Clinic Assn 602 W University Ave Urbana IL 61801-2594

PICCIANO, R.J. renal technician; b. Bronx, N.Y., Sept. 18, 1956; s. Robert and Josette LeBron. BA, Notre Dame Coll., 1978. Cert. nephrology technician, Ohio, hemodialysis technician, Ohio dialysis technician. Tech. patient care Ctr. Dialysis Care, Cleve., 1984—. Pres. Bd. Nephrology Examiners, Shawnee, Kans., 1999—. Office: Bd Nephrology Examiners PO Box 15945282 Shawnee Mission KS 66285 E-mail: rjpcht@aol.com.

PICCININO, ROCCO MICHAEL, librarian; b. Phila., Aug. 21, 1949; s. Rocco Anthony and Ida Marie (Minicozzi) P. BA in History magna cum laude, LaSalle Coll., 1971; postgrad., U. N.C., 1971-73; MSLS, Drexel U., 1981. Ednl. resources specialist C.C. of Phila., 1973-74; asst./assoc. libr. United Engrs. & Constructors Inc. (A Raytheon Co.) Libr., Phila., 1974-81, head libr. Boston, 1981-84; asst/assoc. dir. Wentworth Inst. of Tech. Libr., 1984-89; sci. libr. Smith Coll. Librs., Northampton, Mass., 1989-91, coord. br. libr. svcs., sci. libr., 1991—. Mem. ALA (Assn. Coll. Rsch. Librs. divsn., sci. and tech. sect., co-chair coll. libr. discussion group 1998-2002, forum for sci. and tech. libr. rsch. 2000-02); comparison of sci. and tech. com., 2002-; Libr. Adminstrn. and Mgmt. Assn.(bldg. and equipment sect., bldgs. for coll. and univ. librs. com., 2000-), Libr. and Info. Tech. Assn., Spl. Librs. Assn. (sci.-tech. divsn. Boston chpt., chair Western Outreach 1996—), Beta Phi Mu. Democrat. Roman Catholic. Avocations: travel, biking, reading, films. Home: 104 Woods Rd Northampton MA 01062-3507 Office: Smith Coll Young Sci Libr Northampton MA 01063-0001 E-mail: rpiccini@smith.edu.

PICCIONE, TAL P. insurance company executive; b. N.Y.C., Feb. 9, 1948; s. Patric Francis and Maria Rose (Scandariato) P.; m. Lena Marie Tamburello, Feb. 22, 1970; children: Michael John, Marc Patric. AAS, Pace Coll., 1971; BBA, Pace U., 1973. V.p. Guy Carpenter & Co., Inc., N.Y.C., 1972-87; chmn., CEO U.S. RE Cos., Inc., 1987—. Bd. dirs., mem. bus. adv. coun. Internat. Ins. Coun., Washington; chmn. CNSR Found., N.Y.C., Legatus; dir. Coun. Reins.

Brokers. Mem. NRA, Columbus Citizens Found., India House, Nippon Club, Safari Club Internat., Sloane Club (London). Avocations: fishing, hunting, boating, opera. Office: US Re Companies Inc 99 Park Ave New York NY 10016-1601

PICCO, STEVEN JOSEPH, lawyer; b. N.Y.C., Sept. 9, 1948; s. Carl and Constance (Speers) P.; m. Ada T. Ryan, July 15, 1972; children: Christopher, Timothy, Kaitlin. BS, Rider Coll., Lawrenceville, N.J., 1970; JD, Seton Hall U., 1975. Bar: N.J. 1975, U.S. Dist. Ct. N.J. 1975, U.S. Ct. Appeals (3d cir.) 1975. Data processing programmer-sys. engring. N.J. Dept. Labor and Industry, Trenton, 1970-75; project specialist N.J. Dept. Environ. Protection, 1975-76, dir. regulatory and govtl. affairs, 1976-78, acting dep. commr., 1979-80, asst. commr., 1979-81, N.J. Dept. Energy, Newark, 1978-79; ptnr. Greenstone & Sokol, Trenton, 1981-87, Picco Mack Herbert Kennedy Jaffe & Yoskin, Trenton, 1988-97, Reed Smith LLP, Princeton, N.J., 1997—. Chmn. bd. dirs. Northeast-Midwest Inst., Robert Wood Johnson Health Care Corp. at Hamilton; treas. N.J. Orgn. for a Better State; mem. N.J. Seed. Mem. Am. Credit Assn. (pres. 2001—). Avocations: golf, reading, community volunteer work. Office: Reed Smith LLP Princeton Forrestal Village 136 Main St Ste 250 Princeton NJ 08540 E-mail: spicco@reedsmith.com.

PICCOLI, MARTIN LINN, civil engineer; b. Elizabeth, N.J., Mar. 10, 1958; s. Martin L. and Nancy Catherine (Martin) P.; m. Susan Mary Horan, May 4, 1984 (div. 1986). BCE, Rutgers U., 1983, MBA, 1991. Registered profl. engr., N.J. Engr. Electric Boat Div., Groton, Conn., 1983-85; project engr. Crow Constrn. Co., N.Y.C., 1985—. 1st lt. U.S. Army, 1980-88. Mem. ASCE (assoc.). Republican. Roman Catholic. Home: 91 Edward Dr Franklin Park NJ 08823-1665 Office: Crow Constrn Co One Penn Pla New York NY 10119

PICCOLO, GERARD ANTHONY, lawyer; b. Omaha, Oct. 11, 1955; s. Salvatore and Maria Rose Piccolo. BSBA, Creighton U., 1977, JD, 1979. Bar: Nebr. 1979, U.S. Dist. Ct. Nebr. 1979, U.S. Supreme Ct. 1983. Pvt. practice, Omaha, 1984-88; dep. pub. defender Hall County Pub. Defender's Office, Grand Island, Nebr., 1988-90, pub. defender, 1990—. Judge advocate USAF, 1980-84. Republican. Roman Catholic. Avocations: chess, basketball, running. Home: 2020 N Sycamore St Grand Island NE 68801-2343 Office: Hall County Pub Defender 117 E 1st St Ste 2 Grand Island NE 68801-6022 E-mail: gerardp@hcgi.org.

PICCOLO, JOSEPH ANTHONY, hospital administrator; b. Phila., Aug. 1, 1953; s. Rudolph and Mary C. (Mellela) P.; m. Elizabeth J. Mullarkey, Mar. 24, 1984; children: Mary E., Sarah C., Theresa N. BA, U. Pa., 1975; MBA, LaSalle U., 1992. Cert. in healthcare compliance, Healthcare Compliance Bd. Mgr. health sci. store U. Pa., Phila., 1973-76; mgr. univ. store Hahnemann U., 1976-86, adminstr., clin. sr. instr. dept. pathology lab. medicine, 1986-94; assoc. adminstr., compliance officer, chief privacy officer Fox Chase Cancer Ctr., 1994—. V.p. Hahnemann Found. Pathology, Phila., 1986-94. Author: (with others): Health Science Store Manual, 1985; mem. editl. bd. Assn. Cancer Execs., 1999—. Mem. Med. Group Mgmt. Assn., Am. Mgmt. Assn., Healthcare Fin. Mgmt. Assn., Hahnemann Pathology Assocs., Inc. (v.p., treas. 1986-94), Big Sisters of Phila. Inc. (bd. dirs., 1996-98). Avocations: golf, music, reading. Office: Fox Chase Cancer Ctr 7701 Burholme Ave Philadelphia PA 19111-2497 E-mail: J_Piccolo@fccc.eou.

PICCONATTO, EVELYN CLARA, accountant; b. Milw., Mar. 22, 1974; d. John Arthur and Judy Marie Picconatto. BBA, Coll. William & Mary, 1996. CPA, Minn. Acct. Coopers & Lybrand LLP, Mpls., 1995, 96-97, Lurie, Besikof, Lapidus & Co. LLP, Mpls., 1998—2002. Mem. AICPA, Minn. Soc. CPAs. Roman Catholic. Avocations: outdoor activities, arts & crafts, photography.

PICHARD, AUGUSTO D. medical educator; b. Santiago, Chile, Sept. 26, 1945; came to U.S., 1971; s. Roberto M. Pichard and Eliana Merino Descalzi; m. Nancy L. Prendergast, June 29, 1973; children: Nicole, Dominique, Alicia. Robert. Grad., Cath. U. Chile, MD, 1969. Diplomate Am. Bd. Internal Medicine, Am. Bd. Cardiovascular Diseases. Assoc. mem. staff Cleve. Clinic, 1973-75; lab. dir. Mt. Sinai Hosp., N.Y.C., 1975-81; assoc. prof. medicine Mt. Sinai Med. Sch., 1978-81, Cath. U. Chile, 1981-82; lab. dir. Washington Hosp. Ctr., Washington, 1983—; prof. medicine George Washington U., 1983-89, clin. prof. medicine, 1990—. Mem. med. bd. Washington Hosp. Ctr., 1997, 99; chmn. bd. Medlantic Rsch. Inst., Washington, 1998—. Mem editl. bd. Am. Jour. Cardiology, 1992-98. Named Hon. Mem. Faculty Cath. U. Chile, 1994. Fellow ACP, Am. Coll. Cardiology, Am. Heart Assn., Soc. Cardiac Angio and Intervention. Roman Catholic. Avocations: tennis, ski, yoga. Office: Washington Cardiology Ctr 110 Irving St NW Washington DC 20010-2976 E-mail: adp1@mhg.edu.

PICHETTE, CLAUDE, former banking executive, university rector, research executive; b. Sherbrooke, Que., Can., June 13, 1936; s. Donat and Juliette (Morin) P.; m. Renée Provencher, Sept. 5, 1959 (dec. 1994); children: Anne-Marie, Martin, Philippe. BA, U. Sherbrooke, 1956; MScSoc (Econ.), U. Laval, 1960; Doct. d'Etat es Sc. Econ, U. D'Aix-Marseille, France, 1970. Prof. U. Sherbrooke, 1960-70; civil servant Govt. Que., 1970-75; vice rector adminstrn. and fins. U. Que., Montreal, 1975-77, rector, 1977-86; pres., chief exec. officer La Financière prêts-épargne, 1986-90, La Financière Entraide-Cooperants (holding co.), 1987-90; pres. Que. Found. Econ. Edn., 1979-81; CEO Institut Armand-Frappier Rsch. Inst., 1991-97; dir. gen. Fondation Armand-Frappier. Chmn. bd. La Financière Entraide-Cooperants (holding co.), 1987-90, Shermag, Hema-Quebec, Hydra-Fab Indsl. Inc.; pres. Que. Found. Econ. Edn., 1979-81; CEO Institut Armand-Frappier Rsch. Inst., 1991-97; chmn. bd. La Financière Credit-Bail, 1989-90; bd. dirs. Alternative Life Ins. Author: Analyse micro-economique et cooperative, 1972. Can. Council grantee, 1958; Federation nationale des cooperatives de consommation de France grantee, 1973 Mem. Que. Assn. Econs. (pres. 1977-78). Clubs: St.-Denis (Montreal). Home: 5123A Jeanne-Mance Montreal QC Canada H2V 4K2 Office: Fondation Armand-Frappier 531 Blvd des Prairies Laval QC Canada H7V 1B7 E-mail: fondation.armand-frappier@inrs-iaf.uquebec.ca.

PICHLER, JOSEPH ANTON, food products executive; b. St. Louis, Oct. 3, 1939; s. Anton Dominick and Anita Marie (Hughes) P.; m. Susan Ellen Eyerly, Dec. 27, 1962; children: Gretchen, Christopher, Rebecca, Josh. BBA, U. Notre Dame, 1961; MBA, U. Chgo., 1963, PhD, 1966. Asst. prof. bus. U. Kans., 1964-68, assoc. prof., 1968-73, prof., 1973-80; dean U. Kans. Sch. Bus., 1974-80; exec. v.p. Dillon Cos. Inc., 1980-82, pres., 1982-86; exec. v.p. Kroger Co., Cin., 1985-86, pres., COO, 1986-90, pres., CEO, 1990, chmn., CEO, 1990—, also bd. dirs. Spl. asst. to asst. sec. for manpower U.S. Dept. Labor, 1968-70; chmn. Kans. Manpower Svcs. Coun., 1974-78; bd. dirs. Cin. Milacron Inc., Federated Dept. Stores, Inc., Catalyst. Author: (with Joseph McGuire) Inequality: The Poor and the Rich in America, 1969; contbg. author: Creativity and Innovation in Manpower Research and Action Programs, 1970, Contemporary Management: Issues and Viewpoints, 1973, Institutional Issues in Public Accounting, 1974, Co-Creation and Capitalism: John Paul II's Laborem Exercens, 1983; co-editor, contbg. author: Ethics, Free Enterprise, and Public Policy, 1978; contbr. articles to profl. jours. Bd. dirs. Cin. Opera, 1987-96, adv. mem., 1996—; nat. bd. dirs. Boys Hope, 1983-96, Tougaloo Coll., 1986—; mem. Nat. Alliance of Bus. Bd., 1988-95, chmn., 1991-93; mem. fellow adv. com. Woodrow Wilson Found., 1990-93: mem. adv. bd. Salvation Army Sch. for Officers Tng., 1994-2000; mem. Cin. Bus. Com., 1991—, chmn., 1997-98. Recipient Disting. Svc. citation U. Kans., 1992, Disting. Svc. award Nat. Conf. Cmty. Justice, 2000; Woodrow Wilson fellow, Ford Found. fellow, Standard Oil Indsl. Rels. fellow, 1966; named Disting. Alumnus U. Chgo., 1994, William Booth award The Salvation Army, 1998, Horatio Alger award, 1999. Mem.: Greater Cin. C. of C. (trustee), Catalyst Bd., Bus. Roundtable, Comml. Club of Cin., Queen City Club. Office: Kroger Co 1014 Vine St Cincinnati OH 45202-1100

PICK, JAMES BLOCK, management and sociology educator; b. Chgo., July 29, 1943; s. Grant Julius and Helen (Block) P. BA, Northwestern U., 1966; MS in Edn., No. Ill. U., 1969; PhD, U. Calif., Irvine, 1974. Cert. computer profl. Asst. rsch. statistician, lectr. Grad. Sch. Mgmt., U. Calif., Riverside, 1975-91, dir. computing, 1984-91; co-dir. U.S.-Mex. Database Project, 1988-91; assoc. prof. mgmt. and bus., dir. info. mgmt. program U. Redlands, Calif., 1991-95, 99-01, prof. bus., 1995—, chair dept. mgmt. and bus., 1995-97, 98-99, chair faculty assembly Sch. Bus., 2001—. Vis. prof. U. Iberoam., Mexico City, 1997, Mexico City, 2001; cons. internat. divsn. US. Census Bur., 1978; mem. Univ. Commons. Bd., 1982—86; mem. nat. curriculum task force IS, 1997; mem. U. Commn. Future of Bus. Programs, 1998—2000; pres. Orange County chpt. Assn. Sys. Mgmt., 1978—79; mem. bd. govs. PCCLAS, Assn. Borderlands Studies, 1989—92, v.p., 2000—01, pres., 2002—. Author: Geothermal Energy Development, 1982, Computer Systems in Business, 1986, Atlas of Mexico, 1989, The Mexico Handbook, 1994, Mexico Megacity, 1997, Mexico and Mexico City in the World Economy, 2001; condr. rsch. in info. systems, population, environ. studies; contbr. sci. articles to publs. in field. Trustee Newport Harbor Art Mus., 1981-87, 88-96, chmn. permanent collection com., 1987-91, v.p., 1991-96; trustee Orange County Mus. Art, 1996—, chmn. collection com., 1996—; com. Block Mus., 1999-2001. Recipient Thunderbird award Bus. Assn. L.Am. Studies, 1993; Ford Found. grantee, 1998-99; sr. Fulbright scholar, 2001. Mem. AAAS, Assn. Computing Machinery, Assn. Info. Sys., Am. Sociol. Assn., Am. Statis. Assn., Population Assn. Am., Internat. Union for Sci. Study of Population, Sociedad de Demografia Mexicana, Standard Club (Chgo.). Office: U Redlands Sch Bus 1200 E Colton Ave Redlands CA 92374-3755

PICK, MICHAEL CLAUDE, international exploration consultant; b. Stuttgart, Fed. Republic Germany, Sept. 17, 1931; came to Can., 1963; s. Manfred and Berti (Baer) P.; m. Jeanette Patrucia Zaharko, Mar. 13, 1965; children—David, Christopher BA, U. New Zealand, Wellington, 1952, MA with honors, 1954; PhD, U. Bristol, Eng., 1963. Sr. geologist Todd Bros. Ltd., Wellington, 1954-58; research assoc. Stanford U., Calif., 1958-60; geologist Chevron Standard Ltd., Calgary, Alta., Can., 1963-68; regional geologist BP Oil & Gas Ltd., 1968-71; chief geologist, acting exploration mgr. Columbia Gas, 1971-80; sr. v.p. Asamera, Inc., 1980—86; pres. Torwood Assocs. Ltd., 1988-95, Terrenex Ventures Inc., Calgary, 1988-94. Contbr. articles to profl. jours. Mem. Am. Assn. Petroleum Geologists, Can. Soc. Petroleum Geologists. Avocations: music, reading, model railroading. Home and Office: 3359 Varna Crescent NW Calgary AB Canada T3A 0E4

PICK, RUTH, research scientist, physician, educator; b. Carlsbad, Bohemia, Czechoslovakia, Nov. 13, 1913; came to U.S., 1949; d. Arthur and Paula (Lenk) Holub; m. Alfred Pick, May 28, 1938 (dec. Jan. 1982). MD, German U., 1938. Resident in medicine Priessnitz Hosp., Graefenberg, Czechoslovakia, 1938; resident in psychiatry Hosp. Veleslavin, Prague, Czechoslovakia, 1945-47; extern in pathology State Hosp. Motol, 1948; research fellow cardiovascular dept. Michael Reese Hosp. & Med. Ctr., Chgo., 1949-50, research assoc., 1950-58, asst. dir., 1958-66, sr. investigator, 1966-71, chief exptl. atherosclerosis lab., 1971-83, attending physician div. cardiovascular diseases dept. medicine, 1964-98, chief cardiac morphology lab. Cardiovascular Inst., 1983-95; prof. emeritus medicine and pathology U. Chgo., 1973-98; part time rsch. assoc. Cardiovascular Inst., 1995-98, emeritus, 1998—. Mem. research council Chgo. Heart Assn., 1979-84, bd. govs., 1983, pres., 1985-86. Fellow Am. Heart Assn. (coun. on arteriosclerosis, coun. on circulation, established investigator), AAAS; mem. Am. Assn. Pathologists and Bacteriologists, Chgo. Heart Assn. (past pres. 1985-86), Am. Fedn. Clin. rsch., Am. Physiol. Soc., Ctrl. Soc. Clin. Rsch. Home: 400 E Randolph St Chicago IL 60601-7329 Office: Michael Reese Hosp and Med Ctr 2929 S Ellis Ave Chicago IL 60616-3395 E-mail: rpick2@compuserve.com.

PICKARD, AGNES LOUISE, small business executive; b. St. Albans, Maine, Feb. 25, 1933; d. Walter S. Stone and Louise Allen; m. James A. Pickard, Apr. 15, 1950 (dec. June 1971); children: Asa, Jamie, James. Grad., Milo High Sch., 1949. Mgr. Milo (Maine) Hotel, 1947-64; mgr., owner Milo Sport Shop, 1957-76; owner Pickard's Sport Shop, Brewer, Maine, 1976—. Owner Dakin Sporting Goods, Brown Tackle Co. Recipient Grand Cross of Color, Rainbow for Girls, 1973, numerous sales awards Johnson Motors, Starcraft Boats, 1969-91. Mem. Order of Eastern Star (sec. Rebakah Lodge 1972, award 1976). Republican. Avocations: hunting, fishing, reading, water sports, working with young people. Home and Office: 802 Wilson St Brewer ME 04412-1015

PICKARD, GEORGE LAWSON, physics educator; b. Cardiff, Wales, July 5, 1913; came to Can., 1947; s. Harry Lawson and Phoebe P.; m. Lilian May Perry; children— Rosemary Ann, Andrew Lawson BA, Oxford U., 1935, MA, 1947, D.Phil., 1937; D.MS (hon.), Royal Roads Mil. Coll., Victoria, B.C., Can., 1980. Sci. officer Royal Aircraft Establishment, Farnborough, Eng., 1937-42; sr. sci. officer ops. research sect. Coastal Command, RAF, 1942-46, prin. sci. officer ops. research sect., 1947; assoc. prof. dept. physics U. B.C., Vancouver, Can., 1947-54, prof. dept. physics Can., 1954-79, prof. emeritus Can., 1979—, dir. Inst. Oceanography Can., 1958-79; cons. Seaconsult Marine Research, Can., 1979—. Author: Descriptive Physical Oceanography, 1964, 5th edit., 1990; (with S. Pond) Introductory Dynamical Oceanography, 1978, 2d edit., 1983 Served with RAF, 1942-47 Decorated mem. Order Brit. Empire; recipient J.P. Tully medal Can. Meteorol. and Oceanographic Soc., 1987. Fellow AAAS, Royal Soc. Can. Avocations: aviation, diving, coral reef oceanography. Home: 4546 W 5th Ave Vancouver BC Canada V6R 1S7

PICKARD, JOHN BENEDICT, English language educator; b. Newton, Mass., Oct. 4, 1928; s. Greenleaf Whittier and Helen (Liston) P.; m. Margaret Suzanne Dederich, Nov. 24, 1956; children: Stephen, Ellen, Nathaniel, Thaddeus, John Samuel. BA, Holy Cross Coll., 1950; postgrad., Boston Coll., 1950-51; PhD, U. Wis., 1954. Instr. U. Calif. (Far East Extension), 1956; asst. prof. English Rice U., 1956-63; assoc. prof. U. Fla., Gainesville, 1963-68, prof., 1968—96; ret., 1996. Author: J.G. Whittier: an Introduction and Interpretation, 1961, Legends of New England by J.G. Whittier, 1965, Emily Dickinson, 1967, Memorabilia of J.G W., 1968, The Letters of John Greenleaf Whittier, 3 vols, 1975, Whittier and Whittierland, 1976, The Parkman Dexter Howe Library: Part IV, The John Greenleaf Whittier Collection, 1987; editor: Samuel Kipnis Film Collection, 1982, Historic Gainesville: A Tour Guide to the Past, 1990, rev., reprinted 1992, Florida's Eden: An Illustrated History of Alachua County, 1994, Historic Alachua County and Old Gainesville, 2002. V.p. Nat. Newman Orgn., 1962-63; bd. dirs. Hist. Gainesville, Inc., 1971-72, 86-90, v.p., 1987-88, editor newsletter, 1987-89, pres., 1988-89; bd. dirs. Matheson Hist. Ctr., 1989—, editor newsletter, 1991-98; bd. dirs. St. Augustine Sch. Religion, 1971-72; bd. dirs. Fla. Trail Assn., 1977-80, adv. bd., 1980-86; bd. dirs. Alachua County Hist. Soc., 1995-97, pres., 1997-99. Served with U.S. Army, 1954-56. Named Outstanding Tchr. Rice U., 1958; Am. Philos. Soc. grantee, 1962, 67, 69 Mem. MLA, South Cen. MLA, Fla. Coll. Tchrs., English, Am. Film Inst., Fla. Trail Assn., Fla. Trust for Hist. Preservation. Democrat. Roman Catholic.

PICKEN, HARRY BELFRAGE, aerospace engineer; b. Grimsby, Ont., Can., Jan. 8, 1916; s. John Belfrage and Leila Lucinda (Jarvis) P.; m. Florence Elizabeth Runciman, July 7, 1945 (dec. 1994); m. Marylyn Joan Beattie, 1997; children: Roger Belfrage, Donald William, Wendy Elizabeth, Brian John, Karen Evelyn. BSc in Aero. Engring., U. Mich., 1940. Lic. profl. engr., Ont., Can. Chief engr. White Can. Aircraft Ltd., Hamilton, Ont., 1940-45, Weston Aircraft Ltd., Oshawa, 1946-47, Field Aviation Ltd., Oshawa, 1947-51; pres., chief engr. Genaire Ltd. (Aerospace), St. Catharines, 1951-81; v.p., tech. dir. Ardrox Ltd. (Chems.), Niagara on the Lake, 1968-75, Avionics Ltd. (Electronics), Niagara on the Lake, 1953-67; v.p. Rotaire Ltd. (Helicopters), St. Catharines, Ont., 1958-63. Design approval rep. acting on behalf of Dept. of Transport Can., Ottawa, 1948-78; mem. bd. govs. Niagara Coll., Welland, Ont., 1974-80 Editor, pub.: Early Architecture Town and Township of Niagara, 1968, architecture student edit., 1991, Map of the Colonial Town of Niagara-on-the-Lake, 1981; composer (music book) Calgary Song Suite, 1983, Chacun a son Goût, 1991 Chmn. Planning Bd. of Niagara-on-the Lake, 1963-65; pres. Niagara-on-the-Lake C. of C., 1961-62; bd. dirs., v.p. Niagara Found., Niagara-on-the-Lake, 1963-80; mem. tech. adv. bd. Niagara Coll., 1966-74; vice chmn. bd. govs. Niagara Coll. Applied Arts and Tech., 1979-81; mem. Ont. Coun. of Regents, 1987-93. Named Citizen of Yr. Niagara-on-the-Lake C. of C., 1968; recipient Award of Merit, Mohawk Community Coll., Hamilton, Ont., 1990, Medal-Community Svc., Profl. Engrs. Ont., 1981, Citation for Outstanding and Meritorious Work, Transport Can. Civil Aviation Ont. Region, 1978, Caring and Sharing award Niagara Regional Govt., 1992, Citation from Premier Ont., 1993. Fellow Can. Aero. and Space Inst. (assoc.); mem. AIAA, Am. Helicopter Soc., Assn. Profl. Engrs. Ont. (lic. profl. engr.), Composers, Authors and Music Pubs. of Can. (assoc.), Am. Fedn. Musicians (bd. dirs. local 298 Niagara Falls, Ont.). Achievements include patent for developing an entirely new type of honeycomb primary structure and beams fabricated using staples and acrylic adhesives; research in thermal electric modules independently used in cooling and refrigeration techniques; also applied rsch. leading to the development of cold vulcanization techniques relative to rubber. Home: 68 Bertram Dr Dundas ON Canada L9H 4T3 Office: Genaire Ltd Niagara Dist Airport Box 84 Saint Catharines ON Canada L2R 6R4

PICKENPAUGH, THOMAS EDWARD, archaeologist, anthropologist; b. St. Clairsville, Ohio, Feb. 8, 1945; s. Douglas Giffin and Betty June (Brown) P. BA, Kent State U., 1970, MA, 1971; ABD, Cath. U., 1980. Anthropologist, instr. sociology and anthropology Wheeling (W.Va.) Coll., 1972-73; anthropologist, instr., asst. prof. anthropology Ohio U.-Eastern, 1972-74, 78, archaeologist, asst. prof. anthropology, 1986-95; mus. technician U.S. Dept. Interior, Nat. Pk. Svc., Washington, 1983; mus. technican Nat. Mus. Natural History, Smithsonian Instn., 1984-87; mus. specialist, loan officer USN, Naval Hist. Ctr., 1987—. Dir. archaeol. excavations Brokaw Village Site, St. Clairsville, Ohio, 1972-74, 76-78, 82, 86-96, 98, mem. archaeol. staff Thunderbird Site, Front Royal, Va., Savannah River, Ga., S.C., Richard B. Russell Dam Project, 1980, El Mirador Site, Guatemala, 1980, Louis Berger Internat. Project, Trenton, N.J., 1983-84, Sully Plantation, Loudon County, Va., 1984, Fells Point Project, Balt., 1984, exhibited rsch. on Symbols of Rank and Power, Ohio U. Eastern Art Gall., 1998, others. Contbr. articles to profl. publs. Rsch. grantee U.S. Dept. Interior, Nat. Pk. Svc., 1978-79, Nat. Geog. Soc., 1992-93. Mem. AAAS, Washington Assn. Profl. Anthropologists, Anthropol. Soc. Washington, Am. Assn. Museums, Internat. Platform Assn. Achievements include rsch. on prehistoric Am. Indians and the symbols of rank and power in traditional cultures. Home: # 201 12512 Village Square Ter Rockville MD 20852-1954 Office: Naval Hist Ctr Washington Navy Yard 805 Kidder Breeze SE Washington DC 20374-5138 E-mail: thomas.pickenpaugh@navy.mil.

PICKENS, ALEXANDER LEGRAND, education educator, retired; b. Waco, Tex., Aug. 31, 1921; s. Alex LeGrand and Elma L. (Johnson) P.; m. Frances M. Jenkins, Aug. 20, 1955. BA, So. Meth. U., 1950; MA, North Tex. U., Denton, 1952; EdD, Columbia U., 1959. Tchr. art public schs., Dallas, 1950-53, Elizabeth, N.J., 1953-54; instr. Coll. Architecture and Design U. Mich., 1954-59; assoc. prof. dept. art U. Ga., Athens, 1959-62; assoc. prof. Coll. Edn. U. Hawaii, Honolulu, 1962-68, prof. edn., 1968—, chmn. doctoral studies curriculum instrn. Coll. Edn. Honolulu, 1984-89, asst. to dean for coll. devel., 1989-01, ret., 2001, emeritus prof., 2002—. Dir. children's classes Ft. Worth Children's Mus., 1951-53; head art Nat. Music Camp, Interlochen, Mich., summers, 1957-58, U. Oreg., Portland, summers 1959-60, 62; cons. youth art activities Foremost Dairies, 1964-74; cons. art films United World Films, 1970-75; art edn. cons. Honolulu Paper Co., 1970-76, Kamehameha Sch., Bishop Estate, 1978-95. Exhibited ceramics, Wichita Internat. Exhbn., Syracuse (N.Y.) Nat. Exhbn., St. Louis Mus., Dallas Mus., San Antonio Mus., Detroit Art Inst., Hawaii Craftsmen, also others; editorial bd.: Arts and Activities mag, 1955-82; editor: U. Hawaii Ednl. Perspectives, 1964-99; contbr. articles to profl. jours. Memm. adult com. Dallas County chpt. Jr. ARC, 1951-53; exec. com. Dallas Crafts Guild, 1950-53; v.p., publicity chmn. U. Ga. Community Concert Assn., 1960-62, mem., program chmn. Gov.'s Commn. Observing 150 Yrs. Pub. Edn. in Hawaii, 1990-91; bd. dirs., dir. and mem. exec. bd. Honolulu Theatre for Youth, 1997—; dir., mem. bd. govs. Honolulu Symphony, 1998—. Served with USAAF. Recipient award merit, Tex. State Fair, 1957, All-Am. award, Ednl. Press Assn. Am., 1968, 70, 72, 75, 79, Regents' medal for excellence in teaching, U. Hawaii, 1989, Gov.'s Commn. Observance of 150 Yrs. Pub. Edn., 1990-91. Mem. AAUP, NEA, Internat. Soc. Edn., Nat. Art Edn. Assn., Coun. for Advancement and Support of Edn., Assn. Fundraising Profls., Nat. Planned Giving Coun., Hawaii Planned Giving Coun., Phi Delta Kappa, Kappa Delta Pi. Address: 1471 Kalaepohaku St Honolulu HI 96816-1804

PICKENS, FRANCES JENKINS, jewelry/metal artist, art educator; b. Dodd's, Tex., Feb. 26, 1927; d. John Morgan and Mary (Burton) Jenkins; m. Alexander Pickens, Aug. 20, 1955. BA, North Tex. U., 1947, MA, 1954; MEd, U. Hawaii, 1976. Tchr. art pub. schs., Dallas, 1948-55, Dearborn, Mich., 1955-58, White Plains, N.Y., 1958-59, Athens, Ga., 1960-62, Punahou Sch., Honolulu, 1963-65, The Kamehameha Schs., Honolulu, 1965-85; jewelry and metal artist, 1963—. Gallery lectr. Honolulu Acad. Arts, 1962-63, instr. jewelry U. Hawaii, Honolulu, 1967, 75, 77. Exhibited works in shows at Mus. of Contemporary Crafts, N.Y., Schmuckmuseum, Germany, Renwick Gallery, Wichita Nat., Women in Design Internat., 1981, Mich. Influence, Materials Hard and Soft, United States Metal, Hawaii Craftsmen Ann., Artists of Hawaii, 1965— (Disting. Artist 1991), retrospective Honolulu Acad. Arts, 2001; represented in permanent collection at Acad. of Arts, The Contemporary Mus., Honolulu, Hawaii State Art Mus., Renwick Gallery, Washington, Wichita Art Assn., Kans.; photographs of work included in Goldsmith's Jour., Jewelry, Contemporary Design and Technique, Jewelry/Metalwork Survey, The Metalsmith's Book of Boxes and Lockets; contbr. articles to Arts and Activities mag., Sch. Arts, Ornament mag. Chmn. state crafts State Fair Tex., Dallas, 1954; Crafts Symposium planning com. Hawaii State Found. Culture and Arts, Honolulu, 1968-69; workshop for instrs. U.S. Army Arts and Crafts, Ft. Shafter, 1975. Named Distinguished Artist of Hawaii, Honolulu Acad. Arts, 1991. Mem. Soc. N.Am. Goldsmiths, Dallas Craft Guild, Hawai Craftsmen (charter, v.p., pres.), Renwick Alliance. Avocations: travel, jewelry, metalwork. Home: 1471 Kalaepohaku St Honolulu HI 96816-1804

PICKENS, RANDI ELLEN, social worker; b. Tallahassee, Jan. 28, 1954; d. Andrew Lee and Anita Lee (Stone) P. BS, Fla. State U., 1976; MSW, Ohio State U., 1979. Diplomate Am. Bd. Social Workers. Clin. counselor I, partial hospitalization unit Spartanburg (S.C.) Area Mental Health Ctr., 1976-77; asst. health svc. officer, med. social worker Nat. Health Svc. Corps, USPHS, Johnson City, Tenn., 1979-82; sr. asst. health svcs. officer USPHS, 1979-82; casework cons. 1st Tenn. Regional Pub. Health Office, Johnson City, 1979-81; mental health counselor Santee-Wateree Mental Health Ctr., Camden, S.C., 1982-83, clin. social worker Columbia, 1983-89, 89-91; sr. social worker forensic svc. William S. Hall Psychiat. Inst., 1989-95, dir. social work I, forensic svc., 1995-99; accredited coord. behavioral disorders treatment program S.C. Dept. Mental Health, 1999—2001; human svc. coord. BDTP, S.C. Dept. of Mental Health, 2002—. Facilitator S.R.S. Self Help Group of Mental Health Assn., 1986-87, Anorexia Nervosa and Associated Disorders Group, 1984-85. Sec. Kershaw County Interagy. Coun., 1983; bd. dirs. Mus. Ptnrs., Columbia Art Mus., 1985-89; bd. dirs. Helpline, 1988-91. Recipient Pres. award Mid Carolina Mental Health Assn., Columbia, 1987. Mem. NASW, Am. Psychiat. Patient Edn. Assn., S.C. Assn. Social Workers, Columbia Art Mus., Columbia Ski Club. Avocations: sailing, downhill skiing, scuba diving, cooking. Office: SC Dept Mental Healthat BDTP 7901 Farrow Rd Bldg 17 Columbia SC 29203-3220

PICKER, WILLIAM A. retired computer engineer, consultant; b. Isenstedt, Westphalia, Germany, Aug. 4, 1933; m. Heide K., May 8, 1959; children: Robert, Ralph. MSEE, Kans. State U., 1966. Sr. engr. IBM, Boulder, 1966-92; ret., 1992. Pres. Schlaraffia Nordamerika, Princeton, N.J., 1999—. E5 U.S. Army, USAREUR, 1957-59. Mem. Schlaraffia Denvera (bd. dirs. 1990-2001). Office: Schlaraffia Nordamerika Jackson Cir Boulder CO 80303 E-mail: wapicker@prodigy.net.

PICKERELL, JAMES HOWARD, photojournalist; b. Dayton, Ohio, June 9, 1936; s. Howard and Frances (Harrison) P.; m. Mary Louise Fisher, June 26, 1965; children: Cheryl Elizabeth, Stacy Rae. Student, Ohio U., 1954-56; BA, UCLA, 1963. Comml. photographer, 1963—; ind. photographer Vietnam, 1963-67. Author: Vietnam in the Mud, 1966, Marketing Photography in the Digital Environment, 1994, Negotiating Stock Photo Prices, 5th edit., 2001; writer, pub. : newsletter Selling Stock. With USN, 1956-60. Mem. Nat. Press Photographers Assn. (1st Pl. Spot News award 1965), Am. Soc. Mag. Photographers (nat. bd. 1987-89), Profl. Photographers Assn., Beta Theta Pi. Address: 8104 Cindy Ln Bethesda MD 20817-6915 E-mail: jim@chd.com.

PICKERING, AVAJANE, specialized education facility executive; b. New Castle, Ind., Nov. 5, 1951; d. George Willard and Elsie Jean (Wicker) P. BA, Purdue U., 1974; MS in Spl. Edn., U. Utah, 1983, PhD, 1991. Cert. spl. edn. Co-dir. presch. for gifted students, 1970-74; tchr. Granite Community Edn., Salt Lake City, 1974-79; tchr. coordinator Salt Lake City Schs., 1975-85; adminstrv. dir., owner Specialized Ednl. Programming Svc., Inc., Salt Lake City, 1976—. Mem. Utah Profl. Adv. Bd.; adj. instr. U. Utah, Salt Lake City,

1985-97; instr. Brigham Young U., 1993-98; mediator/facilitator in field. Rep. del. Utah State Conv., also county conv.; vol. tour guide, hostess Temple Square, Ch. Jesus Christ of Latter-Day Saints, 1983-88. Mem. Coun. for Exceptional Children, Coun. for Learning Disabilities, Learning Disability Assn., Ednl. Therapy Assn. Profl., Learning Disabilities Assn. Utah (profl. adv. bd.), Attention Deficit Coalition Utah (treas.), Hadassah, Delta Kappa Gamma, Phi Kappa Phi. Home: 1595 S 2100 E Salt Lake City UT 84108-2750 Office: Specialized Ednl Programming Svcs 1924 S 1100 E Ste D Salt Lake City UT 84105

PICKERING, CHARLES W., JR. congressman; b. Laurel, Ms., Aug. 10, 1963; m. Leisha Jane Prather; children: Will, Ross, Jackson, Asher. BA in Bus. Adminstrn., U. Miss., 1986; MBA, Baylor U. Legis. asst. to U.S. Senator Trent Lott; apptd. to USDA; mem. U.S. Congress from 3d Mich. dist., 1997; co-chmn. congl. wireless com., congl. sportsmen's caucus. Mem. energy and commerce com., agriculture com., livestock, dairy and poultry subcom., forestry, resource conservation, rsch. subcom., Transp. and Infrastructure com., vice chair surface transp. subcom., aviation subcom., Sci. com., vice chair basic rsch. subcom., space subcom.; asst. minority whip; mem. House Rep. Policy com.; mem. exec. com. Nat. Rep. Congrl. com. Office: US House of Reps 427 Cannon House Office Bldg Washington DC 20515-0001*

PICKERING, GARRY MARLON, state official; b. Brookhaven, Miss., Sept. 27, 1949; s. Roy Lee and Minnie Marie (Davis) P.; m. Rosemary Moak, Nov. 24, 1971; children: Rebecca Geraé Pickering Fuller, Garry LaRon. Cert. in Programming, Jackson County Jr. Coll., Gautier, Miss. Profl. land surveyor, Miss. Svc. technician Lincoln Rural Water Assn., Brookhaven, Miss.; draftsman Litton Sys., Inc., Pascagoula, 1969-70, Toxie Craft, Civil Engr., Baton Rouge, 1970-72; design supr. McMullen Engring., Brookhaven, 1972-83; sr. engring. tech. Miss. Dept. Transp., 1983—. With Gerald Chatalain, Civil Engr., Baton Rouge, 1970-72; drafting, surveying, telecomm. design cons., Brookhaven, 1972—. Pres. Newell Cemetery Assn., Wesson, Miss., 1997—; sec. Pleasant Ridge Cemetery, Wesson, 1998—, Pleasant Ridge United Pentecostal Ch. Bldg. Fund, Wesson, 1971—. Mem. Am. Soc. Engring. Tech. (pres. S.W. chpt. 1997—), Miss. Assn. Profl. Land Surveyors, Brookhaven Light Arty. Sons of Confed. Vets. (2d lt. 2001). Avocations: music, history, woodwork. Home: 1590 Pleasant Ridge Rd NW Wesson MS 39191

PICKERING, JAMES HENRY, III, academic administrator, educator; b. N.Y.C., July 11, 1937; s. James H. and Anita (Felber) P.; m. Patricia Paterson, Aug. 18, 1962; children: David Scott, Susan Elizabeth. BA, Williams Coll., 1959; MA, Northwestern U., 1960, PhD, 1964. Instr. English Northwestern U., 1963-65; mem. faculty Mich. State U., East Lansing, 1965-81, prof. English, 1972-81, grad. and asso. chmn. dept., 1968-75, dir. Honors Coll., 1975-81; dean Coll. Humanities and Fine Arts U. Houston, 1981-90, sr. v.p., provost, 1990-92, pres., 1992-95. Author: Fiction 100, 1974, 78, 82, 85, 88, 92, 95, 98, 2001, The World Turned Upside Down: Prose and Poetry of the American Revolution, 1975, The Spy Unmasked, 1975, The City in American Literature, 1977, Concise Companion to Literature, 1981, Literature, 1982, 86, 90, 94, 97, Mountaineering in Colorado, 1987, Wild Life on the Rockies, 1988, A Mountain Boyhood, 1988, The Spell of the Rockies, 1989, Purpose and Process, 1989, Poetry, 1990, In Beaver World, 1990, Rocky Mountain Wonderland, 1991, A Summer Vacation in the Parks and Mountains of Colorado, 1992, Fiction 50, 1993, Knocking Round the Rockies, 1994, Drama, 1994, Frederick Chapin's Colorado, 1995; This Blue Hollow: Estes Park, The Early Years, 1859-1915, 1999, Mr. Stanley of Estes Park, 2000. Mem. Coll. English Assn. (pres. 1980-81), Phi Beta Kappa, Phi Kappa Phi, Omicron Delta Kappa. Office: U Houston Dept English Houston TX 77204-0001

PICKERING, JOHN HAROLD, lawyer; b. Harrisburg, Ill., Feb. 27, 1916; s. John Leslie and Virginia Lee (Morris) P.; m. Elsa Victoria Mueller, Aug. 23, 1941 (dec. Nov., 1988); children: Leslie Ann, Victoria Lee; m. Helen Patton Wright, Feb. 3, 1990. AB, U. Mich., 1938, JD, 1940, LLD, 1996, D.C. Sch. Law, 1995. Bar: N.Y. 1941, D.C. 1947. Practiced in N.Y.C., 1941; practiced in Washington, 1946—; assoc. Cravath, de Gersdorff, Swaine & Wood, 1941; law clk. to Justice Murphy, Supreme Ct. U.S., 1941-43; assoc. Wilmer & Broun, 1946-48, ptnr., 1949-62, Wilmer, Cutler & Pickering, 1962-79, Wilmer & Pickering, 1979-81, Wilmer, Cutler & Pickering, 1981-88, sr. counsel, 1989—. Vis. lectr. U. Va. Law Sch., 1958; mem. com. visitors U. Mich. Law Sch., 1962-68, chmn. devel. com., 1973-81; mem. com. on adminstrn. of justice U.S. Ct. Appeals (D.C. cir.), 1966-72, chmn. adv. com. on procedures, 1976-82, chmn. mediation project, 1988—; bd. govs. D.C. Bar, 1975-78, pres., 1979-80; dir. Nat. Ctr. for State Cts., 1987-93. Lt. comdr. USNR, 1943-46. Recipient Outstanding Achievement award U. Mich., 1978, Disting. Svc. award Nat. Ctr. for State Cts., 1985, 50 Yr. award from Fellows Am. Bar Found., 1993, Paul C. Reardon award Nat. Ctr. for State Cts., 1994, Pro Bono award NAACP Legal Def. Fund, 1990, Am. Bar Assn. medal, 1999, Justice William J. Brennan Jr. award, D.C. Bar, 1998, Justice Potter Stewart award, Coun. for Court Excellence, 1999, numerous other awards. Mem. ABA (state del. 1984-93, chmn. commn. on legal problems of elderly 1985-93, sr. advisor 1993-95, chmn. 1995-96, commr. emeritus 1996—, chmn. sr. lawyers divsn. 1996-97), D.C. Bar Assn. (Lawyer of the Yr. 1996), Am. Law Inst., Barristers Washington, Lawyers Club, Met. Club, Chevy Chase Club, Wianno Club, Order of Coif, Phi Beta Kappa, Phi Kappa Phi. Democrat. Mem. United Ch. Christ. Home: 8100 Connecticut Ave Chevy Chase MD 20815 Office: Wilmer Cutler & Pickering 2445 M St NW Ste 8 Washington DC 20037-1435 E-mail: jpickering@wilmer.com.

PICKERING, LARRY KENNETH, pediatrician, researcher; b. Pitts., Apr. 27, 1944; m. Margaret Jane Thompson, July 8, 1967; children: Margaret Anne, Andrew Michael. BS, W.Va. U., 1966, MD, 1970. Diplomate Am. Bd. Pediat., Am. Bd. Infectious Diseases, Nat. Bd. Med. Examiners. Intern pediat. svc. St. Louis Children's Hosp., 1970-71, resident pediat. svc., 1971-72; fellow pediat. infectious diseases St. Louis Children's Hosp. and Washington U. Sch. Medicine, 1972-74; asst. prof. pediat. U. Tex. Med. Sch., Houston, 1974-77, assoc. prof. pediat., 1977-82, prof. pediat. dept. pediat. divsn. infectious diseases, 1982-92, prof. program in immunology, 1982-92, David R. Park prof. pediat., 1989-92, dir. divsn. infectious diseases dept. pediat., 1975-89; prof., CHKD chair in pediatric rsch. Ea. Va. Med. Sch., Norfolk, 1992-2001; prof. pediats. dept. pediats. Emory U. Sch. Medicine, 2001—. Cons. M.D. Anderson Hosp. and Tumor Inst., Houston, 1974-78, St. Joseph Hosp., Houston, 1975-89, Meml. Hosp. Sys., Houston, 1977-92, AMA; assoc. prof. pediat. M.D. Anderson Hosp. and Tumor Inst., U. Tex. Cancer Ctr., 1978-83, prof. pediat., 1983-92; infection control med. advisor Speech and Hearing Inst., U. Tex. Health Sci. Ctr., Houston, 1978-87, prof. Grad. Sch. Biomed. Scis., 1982-89; adj. prof. pharmaceutics dept. pharmaceutics Coll. Pharmacy, U. Houston, 1983-92; vice chmn. for rsch., dir. Ctr. for Pediat. Rsch., Ea. Va. Med. Sch., Children's Hosp. of The King's Daus., Norfolk, 1992-2001; Ray A. Kroc vis. prof. Mich. State U., East Lansing, 1993; First Infectious Diseases vis. prof. Children's Hosp. L.A., U. So. Calif., 1993; Ben Kagan lectr. Cedars-Sinai Med. Ctr., L.A., 1994; Pfizer vis. prof. in infectious diseases SUNY, Stony Brook, 1996; Katherine White, M.D. Seventh Annual guest lectr. Miller Children's Hosp., Long Beach, Calif., 1996; external examiner and reviewer dept. pediat. U. Jordan, Amman, 1984; mem. subboard pediat. infectious diseases Am. Bd. Pediat., 1991-96; mem. planning com. First Internat. Pediat. Infectious Diseases Conf., Monterey, Calif., 1995; mem. sci. com. First World Congress of Pediat. Infectious Diseases, 1995; mem. steering com. E. Mead Johnson Award for Rsch. in Pediat., 1996-99; presenter in field; assoc. dir. spl. projects, nat immunization project, immunization program Ctrs. for Disease Control and Prevention, Atlanta, 2000-01, sr. advisor to dir., 2001—. Author: (with H.L. DuPont) Infections of the Gastrointestinal Tract, 1980, Infectious Diseases of Children and Adults; editor: (with R.R. Howell and F.H. Morriss) Human Milk in Infant Nutrition and Health, 1986, (with M.T. Osterholm, J.O. Klein and S.S. Aronson) Infectious Diseases in Child Day Care: Management and Prevention, 1987, Infections in Day Care Centers Seminars in Pediatric Infectious Diseases, 1990, Diarrheal Disease, 1994, (with S. Long and C. Prober) Principles and Practice of Pediatric Infectious Diseases, 1997, 2d edit., 2002; contbg. editor: Infectious Disease Clinics in North America, 1992; editor-in-chief Pediat. Infectious Diseases: Clin. Updates, Nat. Found. for Infectious Diseases, 1994-2000; mem. editl. bd. Infectious Diseases Newsletter, 1985-89, Infection, 1988, Pediat., 1990-93, Report on Pediat. Infectious Diseases, 1990-95, co-editor, 1993-95, Pediatric. Infectious Disease Jour., 1987-96, 2001--, Seminars in Pediat. Infectious Diseases, 1997—, Vaccine Bull., 1997-2001, Seminars in Infectious Diseases in Children, 1997—; contbr. articles to profl. jours. Med. adv. com. Met. Houston chpt. March of Dimes, 1974-76, bd. dirs., 1975-80, chmn. profl. adv. com., 1977-79; mem. rsch. com. March of Dimes, 1999—. Named Disting. Alumnus, W.Va. U. Sch. Medicine, Morgantown, 1995. Fellow Infectious Diseases Soc. Am. (exec. com. Emerging Infections Network 1997-200); mem. AAAS, Internat. Soc. for Rsch. in Human Milk and Lactation, Am. Soc. for Clin. Pharmacology and Therapeutics, Am. Soc. for Tropical Medicine and Hygiene, Am. Pediat. Soc., Am. Soc. Microbiology, Am. Acad. Pediat. (com. on infectious diseases 1990-96, assoc. editor RedBook 1990-97, editor 1997-03, exec. com. sect. breastfeeding 2001—), Am. Fedn. for Clin. Rsch., Nat. Found. of Infectious Diseases (bd. dirs. 1997—), Va. Pediat. Soc., Tex. Pediat. Soc., Tex. Med. Assn., Tex. Infectious Diseases Soc. (coun. mem. 1982-84), Harris County Pediat. Soc. (edn. com. 1975-79), Harris County Med. Soc., Houston Acad. Medicine, Houston Pediat. Soc. (constn. and by-laws com. 1978-82), So. Soc. for Pediat. Rsch. (coun. mem. 1981-83, Founder's award 1994), Soc. for Pediat. Rsch. (chair infectious diseases subspecialty sect. 1995, co-chair seminar Epidemiology 1995), Pediat. Infectious Diseases Soc. (editor 1987-96, pres. elect 1993-95, pres. 1995-97), The Milk Club (exec. com. 1995-99). Avocations: tennis, biking, canoeing. Office: CDC and Prevention Nat Immunization Program 1600 Clifton Rd NE # MsE05 Atlanta GA 30329-4018 Fax: 404-639-8626. E-mail: lpickering@cdc.gov.

PICKERING, POLLYANNA, artist; b. Leeds, Yorkshire, Eng., July 30, 1942; d. Johnathon and Mabel (Wells) Pollard; m. Kenneth Albert Pickering, Apr. 25, 1963 (dec. 1979); 1 child, Anna-Louise. Nat. diploma in design, Cen. Sch. of Arts, London, 1963. Cert. N.D.D. Head dept. Warwick County High Sch., Warwickshire, Eng., 1963-64; owner Pollyanna Pickering Gallery, Derbyshire, Eng., 1980—. Exec. producer Highbank Film Co., Surrey, Eng., 1986—. One-woman shows include Peter Simmonite Gallery, Sheffield, 1981, Pentameters Gallery, Hampstead, London, 1989, Derby Mus. and Art Gallery, 1999; exhibited in group shows including Tryon and Moorland Gallery, London, 1980, Royal Acad., London, 1983, Halcyon Gallery, Birmingham, 1989, Soc. Wildlife Artists, Mall Galleries, London, 1991; illustrator: (book) Giant Pandas and Sleeping Dragons, 1996; Author: (book) On top of the World, 2002. Prin. Brookvale Bird Rescue (Conservation), Derbyshire, 1980—; pres. (hon.) Hearing Dogs for Deaf, Derby, 1996—, Royal Soc. for Prevention of Cruelty to Animals, Derby, 1997—; amb. Hosp. Radio Link, 1999-2000; mem. ct. U. Derby; patron Raptor Rescue, 1999—, NatureWatch, 2000—, F.A.B.L.E., 2001—; trustee Irish African/Asian Conservation Trust, 2001—; founder Pollyanna Pickering Found., 2001. Recipient Silver Palette award Derby Mus. & Art Gallery, Derbyshire, 1983, Millenium trophy Wildlife Art Soc., 2000. Mem. Derbyshire Wildlife Trust (patron 1985—), World Wide Fund for Nature (commd. work 1991, 99), Royal Soc. for the Protection of Birds (commd. work 1983, 84, 98, 99), Zoocheck (exhbn. 1991), Royal Soc. for the Protection of Animals (Hong Kong, commd. work 1991-99). Avocations: conservation, theatre. Home and Office: Brookvale House Oaker DE4 2JJ England E-mail: pollyanna@pollyltd.freeserve.co.uk.

PICKERING, THOMAS REEVE, diplomat; b. Orange, N.J., Nov. 5, 1931; s. Hamilton R. and Sarah C. (Chasteney) P.; m. Alice J. Stover, Nov. 24, 1955; children: Timothy R., Margaret S. AB, Bowdoin Coll., 1953; MA, Fletcher Sch. Law and Diplomacy, 1954, U. Melbourne, Australia, 1956. Joined U.S. Fgn. Svc., 1959; fgn. affairs officer ACDA, 1961; polit. adviser U.S. del. 18 Nation Disarmament Conf., Geneva, 1962-64; consul Zanzibar, 1965-67; counselor of embassy, dep. chief mission Am. Embassy, Dar es Salaam, Tanzania, 1967-69; dep. dir. Bur. Politico-Mil. Affairs, State Dept., 1969-73; spl. asst. to Sec. of State, 1973-74; exec. sec. Dept. State, 1973-74; U.S. amb. to Jordan, 1974-78; asst. sec. for Bur. Oceans, Internat. Environ. and Sci. Affairs, Washington, 1978-81; U.S. amb. to Nigeria, 1981-83; U.S. amb. to El Salvador, 1983-85; U.S. amb. to Israel, 1985-88; U.S. permanent rep. to UN, 1989-92; U.S. amb. to India, 1992-93; U.S. amb. to Russia, 1993-96; pres. Eurasia Found., 1996-97; undersec. of state for polit. affairs Dept. of State, Washington, 1997—. Served to lt. comdr. USNR, 1956-59. Mem. Council Fgn. Relations, Internat. Inst. Strategic Studies, Phi Beta Kappa. Address: 2318 Kimbro St Alexandria VA 22307-1822 Office: Dept of State 2201 C St NW Washington DC 20520-0001 Fax: 703-465-3043.

PICKERING, WILLIAM HAYWARD, research scientist; b. Wellington, N.Z., Dec. 24, 1910; s. Albert William and Elizabeth (Hayward) Pickering; m. Muriel Bowler, Dec. 30, 1932 (dec. Mar. 1992); children: William B., Anne E.; m. Inez Chapman, July 28, 1994. BS, Calif. Inst. Tech., 1932, MS, 1933, PhD in Physics, 1936; degree (hon.) , Clark U., 1966, Occidental Coll., 1966, U. Bologna, 1974. Mem. Cosmic Ray Expdn. to India, 1939, Cosmic Ray Expdn. to Mex., 1941; faculty Calif. Inst. Tech., 1940—, prof. elec. engring., 1946—80, prof. emeritus, 1980—, dir. jet propulsion lab., 1954—76; mem. sci. adv. bd. USAF, 1945—48; chmn. panel on test range instrumentation (Research and Devel. Bd.), 1948—49; mem. U.S. nat. com. tech. panel Earth Satellite Program, 1955—60; mem. Army Sci. Adv. Panel, 1960—64. Dir. rsch. inst. U. Petroleum and Minerals, Dharan, Saudi Arabia, 1977—79; pres. Pickering Rsch. Corp., 1980—91, Lignetics, Inc., 1983—94, chmn., 1994—. Decorated Order of Merit Italy, Knight comdr. Order Brit. Empire; recipient James Wyld Meml. award, Am. Rocket Soc., 1957, Columbus medal, Genoa, 1964, Prix Galabert for Astronautics, Goddard trophy, Nat. Space Club, 1965, Disting. Svc. medal, NASA, 1965, Army Disting. Civilian Svc. award, 1959, Spirit of St. Louis medal, 1965, Crozier medal, Am. Ordnance Assn., 1965, Man of Yr. award, Indsl. Rsch. Inst., 1968, Interprofl. Coop. award, Soc. Mfg. Engrs., 1970, Marconi medal, Marconi Found., 1974, Nat. medal of Sci., 1976, Fahrney medal, Franklin Inst., 1976, award of merit, Am. Cons. Engrs. Coun., 1976, Francoix-Xavier Bagnoud Internat. award, 1993, Japan prize, Sci. and Tech. Found. Japan, 1994, Daniel Guggenheim medal for promotion of aeronautics, Guggenheim Fund, 2000. Fellow: IEEE (Edison medal 1972), NAE, AIAA (pres. 1963, Louis W. Hill Transp. award 1968, Aerospace Pioneer award 1986, AIAA Guggenheim medal 2001), AAAS; mem.: NAS, Internat. Astronautical Fedn. (pres. 1965—66), Am. Geophys. Union. Home: 294 Saint Katherine Dr Flintridge CA 91011-4109 E-mail: whpickering@aol.com.

PICKERSTEIN, HAROLD JAMES, lawyer; b. Bridgeport, Conn., July 9, 1946; s. Maurice L. and Sylvia (Kornblut) P.; m. Marjorie S. Feldman, Aug. 11, 1968; children: Andrew Louis, Michael Robert, Edward Jeffrey (dec. 1999). AB, U. Pa., 1967; JD, Boston U., 1970. Bar: Conn. 1970, D.C. 1992, U.S. Tax Ct. 1971, U.S. Ct. Appeals (2d, 8th, 9th and 10th cirs.) 1971, U.S. Ct. Appeals (D.C. cir.), 1992, U.S. Ct. Appeals (Fed. cir.) 1992, U.S. Dist. Ct. Conn. 1972, U.S. Supreme Ct. 1973, U.S. Dist. Ct. Ariz. 1997, U.S. Dist. Ct. (so. dist.) N.Y. 1998. Trial atty. U.S. Dept. Justice, Washington, 1970-72, asst. U.S. atty. for Conn. Bridgeport, 1972-74, U.S. atty. New Haven, 1974-75, chief asst. U.S. atty. Bridgeport, 1975-86; ptnr. Pepe & Hazard, L.L.P., Hartford, Southport, Conn., 1986-96. Fellow Am. Coll. Trial Lawyers. E-mila. Office: Pepe & Hazard LLP 30 Jelliff Ln Southport CT 06490-1482 E-mail: hpickerstein@pepehazard.com.

PICKETT, BETTY HORENSTEIN, psychologist; b. Providence, Feb. 15, 1926; d. Isadore Samuel and Etta Lillian (Morrison) Horenstein; m. James McPherson Pickett, Mar. 10, 1952. AB magna cum laude, Brown U., 1945, ScM, 1947, PhD, 1949. Asst. prof. psychology U. Minn., Duluth, 1949-51; asst. prof. U. Nebr., 1951; lectr. U. Conn., 1952; profl. assoc. psychol. scis. Bio-Scis. Info. Exch., Smithsonian Instn., Washington, 1953-58; exec. sec. behavioral scis. study sect. exptl. psychology study sect. div. research grants NIH, Bethesda, Md., 1958-61; rsch. cons. to mental health unit HEW, Boston, 1962-63; exec. sec. rsch. career program NIMH, 1963-66, chief cognition and learning sect. div. extramural research program, 1966-68, dep. dir., 1968-74, dir. div. spl. mental health programs, 1974-75, acting dir. div. extramural rsch. program, 1975-77; assoc. dir. extramural and collaborative rsch. program Nat. Inst. Aging, 1977-79; dep. dir. Nat. Inst. Child Health and Human Devel., Bethesda, Md., 1979-81, acting dir., 1981-82, dir. Div. Rsch. Resources, 1982-88. Mem. health scientist adminstr. panel CSC Bd. Examiners, 1970-76, 81-88; mem. coun. on grad. edn. Brown U. Grad. Sch., 1989-91. Contbr. articles to profl. jours. Mem. APA, Am. Psychol Soc., Psychonomic Soc., Assn. Women in Sci., AAAS, Phi Beta Kappa, Sigma Xi. Home: Morgan Bay Rd PO Box 198 Surry ME 04684-0198

PICKETT, CALDER MARCUS, retired journalism educator; b. Providence, July 26, 1921; s. Leland M. and Julia (Gessel) P.; m. Nola Agricola, Mar. 20, 1947; children: Carolyn Zeligman, Kathleen Jenson. BS, Utah State U., 1944; MS in Journalism, Northwestern U., 1948; PhD, U. Minn., 1959. Copy editor Salt Lake (City) Tribune, 1946, Deseret News, Salt Lake City, 1948-49; instr. Utah State U., Logan, 1946-48, U. Denver, 1949-51; prof. U. Kans., Lawrence, 1951—, Oscar Stauffer prof. Journalism, 1973-77, Clyde M. Reed prof. Journalism, 1985-88, ret., 1988. Author: Ed Howe: Country Town Philosopher, 1968; author, editor: Voices of the Past, 1977; writer, producer, narrator radio program The Am. Past; contbr. articles to profl. jours. Recipient Disting. Teaching award Standard Oil Found., 1967, Frank Luther Mott award, 1969, George Foster Peabody award, 1974, HOPE award U. Kans., 1975, Mortar Bd. award U. Kans., 1983, Armstrong Broadcasting award, 1983, Chancellor's Club Career Teaching award, 1987. Avocations: history, music. Home: 712 Lawrence Ave Lawrence KS 66049-4521

PICKETT, CHRISTA LANGFORD, elementary school counselor; b. Hoschton, Ga., Aug. 2, 1943; d. Grady and Ruth Geraldine Langford; children: Mark, Paige Pastor. BA Elem. Edn., Emory and Henry Coll., 1974; MEd Spl. Edn., U. Tenn., Chattanooga, 1981. Cert. sch. counselor (P-12), interrelated spl. edn., elem. edn. Teacher (grades 4/5 &1) Oak Hill Elem., Morganton, NC, 1975—79; tchr. spl. edn. Red Bank Jr. HS, Red Bank, Tenn., 1980—81; teacher (grade 4) Thrasher Elem. Sch., Signal Mountain, 1984; tchr. spl. edn. (gifted & handicapped) Lone Oak Elem., 1985—88; tchr. spl. edn. Berkeley Lake Elem., Duluth, Ga., 1989—99, counselor elem. sch., 1999—. Mem. curriculum and instrn. counsel Berkeley Lake Elem. Sch., Duluth, 1998—, mem. Berkeley Lake team planning com., 1999—, coord. Berkeley Lake Care team, 1999—; facilitator student support team i Berkeley Lake Elem. Sch. , Duluth, 1999—, member student support team ii, 2002—. Dir. mediation program Berkeley Lake; mem. Peachtree Presbyn. Ch., Atlanta, 1991—; mem., co-facilitator, facilitator Stephen's Ministry of Peachtree Presbyn. Ch., 1992—; relay for life team mem. of bles Am. Cancer Soc., Duluth, 1999—. Mem.: Am. Sch. Counselor Assn., Am. Counseling Assn., Pi Lambda Theta, Kappa Delta Pi. Protestant. Avocations: painting, reading, exercise. Office: Berkeley Lake Elem 4300 South Berkeley Lake Rd Duluth GA 30096 Office Fax: 770-582-7514. Business E-Mail: christa_pickett@gwinnett.k12.ga.us.*

PICKETT, DAVID FRANKLIN, JR. technology company executive; b. Littlefield, Tex., May 3, 1936; s. David Franklin and Dottie Ardell (Britton) P.; m. B. Christine Klop, Aug. 21, 1971. AA, Del Mar Coll., Corpus Christi, 1960; BS in Chem., U. Tex., 1962, MA, 1965, PhD, 1970. Rsch. chemist Am. Magnesium Co., Snyder, Tex., 1969-70; chemist, chem. engr. Air Force Aero Propulsion Lab., Dayton, Ohio, 1970-78; sect. head Hughes Aircraft Co., El Segundo, Calif., 1978-84, asst. dept. mgr., 1984-86, dept. mgr., 1986-89, product line mgr., 1990-91, program mgr., 1991-95; retired, 1995; sr. scientist Eagle-Richer Techs., Colorado Springs, Colo.; pres. AAAA Energy Enterprises, Inc. ECS coordinator ann. battery conf. Calif. State U., Long Beach, 1987-89; sr. scientist Eagle-Picher Techs., LLC. Author: Nickel Electrode and NiCd Cell Technology, 1984-88; inventor in field. With USN, 1955-57. Mem. AIAA, Southern Calif./Nev. Electrochem. Soc. (sec. 1980-81, vice chmn. 1981-82, chmn. 1982-83), Am. Chem. Soc., Phi Lambda Upsilon. Baptist. Avocations: travel, fishing. Home: PO Box 16146 Colorado Springs CO 80935-6146 Office: Eagle-Picher Techs LLC 3820 Hancock Expy Colorado Springs CO 80911-1263 also: AAAA Energy Enterprises Inc PO Box 16146 Colorado Springs CO 80935-6146 E-mail: AAAA_ENERGY_ENTERPRISES@msn.com.

PICKETT, DOYLE C. employment counselor; b. Greencastle, Ind., July 15, 1930; s. Joseph Virgil and Lora Clay (Phillips) P.; m. Judith Ann Marshall, 1956 (div. 1961); children: Brian Doyle, Marsha Ann; m. Dorothy Newgent McGinnis, 1964. AB, Wabash Coll., 1952; MBA, Ind. U., 1953. Exec. trainee, various staff and line exec. positions, asst. store mgr. L.S. Ayres & Co., Lafayette and Indpls., Ind., 1953-64; mgmt. analyst Cummins Engine Co., Columbus, 1964-67; adminstrv. asst. to pres., other exec. positions Baker & Taylor Co., 1967-80; v.p. mktg. Baker & Taylor Co. subs. W.R. Grace Co., N.Y.C., Somerville, N.J., 1980-82; pres. UNIPUB subs. Xerox Co., N.Y.C., 1982-86; mem. exec. com. R.R. Bowker Co., 1982-86; pres. D.C. Pickett Assocs., 1986-93; counselor Work Force Devel. Program N.J. Dept. Labor, Somerville, Perth Amboy, 1993-94, counselor Project Reemployment Opportunities Sys. Somerville, 1994-96; counselor, facilitator Career Transition Ctr., 1996-98, field office supr., 1998—. Mem. adv. bd. Fourth Internat. Conf. on Approval Plans/Collection Devel., 1979. Co-author: Approval Plans and Academic Libraries, 1977; mem. editorial adv. bd. Technicalities, 1980-81; contbr. articles to profl. jours. Chair membership com. Ctrl. Ind. Coun., Boy Scouts Am., 1961-62; mem. Dean's Assocs., Ind. U. Sch. of Bus., Bloomington, 1983-90, 97-99; mem. Friends of Somerset County/Bridgewater Libr.; mem. alumni admissions coun. Wabash Coll., 1996—. With U.S. Army, 1953-55. Mem. Assn. Coll. and Rsch. Librs. (publs. com. 1983-87), Soc. Logistics Engrs. (adv. bd. 1981-91), Nat. Assn. Wabash Men (bd. dirs. 1983-90), Am. Legion, Kiwanis (charter pres. N.W. Indpls. club 1958-59, dir. 1960-61, Ind. dist. zone chmn. membership and attendance, 1960-61, Ind. and N.J. clubs officer, chair com. 1962-68), Masons, Blue Key, Alpha Phi Omega, Delta Tau Delta (North Jersey coord. N.Y. area alumni chpt. 1986-88). Mem. Christian Ch. Home: 240 Great Hills Rd Bridgewater NJ 08807-1516

PICKETT, GEORGE BIBB, JR. retired military officer; b. Montgomery, Ala., Mar. 20, 1918; s. George B. and Marie (Dow) P.; BS, U.S. Mil. Acad., 1941; student Nat. War Coll., 1959-60; m. Beryl Arlene Robinson, Dec. 27, 1941; children: Barbara Pickett Harrell, James, Kathleen, Thomas; m. Rachel Copeland Peeples, July 1981. Commd. 2d lt. U.S. Army, 1941, advanced through grades to maj. gen., 1966; instr. Inf. Sch., Fort Benning, Ga., 1947-50, instr. Armed Forces Staff Coll., Norfolk, Va., 1956-59; comdg. officer 2d Armored Cav. Regt., 1961-63; chief of staff Combat Devel. Command, 1963-66; comdg. gen. 2d inf. divsn., Korea, 1966-67; ret., 1973; field rep. Nat. Rifle Assn., 1973-85. Decorated Purple Heart with oak leaf cluster, D.S.M. with two oak leaf clusters, Bronze Star with two oak leaf clusters and V device, Silver Star, Legion of Merit with two oak leaf clusters, Commendation medal with two oak leaf clusters. Mem. SAR (pres. Ala. Soc. 1984), Old South Hist. Assn. Episcopalian. Club: Kiwanis. Author: (with others) Joint and Combined Staff Officers Manual, 1959; contbr. articles on mil. affairs to profl. jours. Home: 3525 Flowers Dr Montgomery AL 36109-4719 Office: PO Box 4 Montgomery AL 36101-0004

PICKETT, OWEN B. lawyer, congressman; b. Richmond, Va., Aug. 31, 1930; BS, Va. Poly. Inst., 1952; LLB, U. Richmond, 1955. CPA Va.; bar: Va. 1955, D.C. 1962. Lawyer practice, Virginia Beach, Va., 1955—72; mem. Va. Ho. of Dels., Richmond, 1972—86, U.S. Congress from 2d Va. dist., Washington, 1987—2001; of counsel Troutman, Sanders, Mays & Valentine, Virginia Beach, Va., 2001—. Mem. resources com. Armed Svcs. Com.; chmn. Va. Dem. State Ctrl. Com., 1980—82. Mem.: D.C. Bar Assn., Va. Bar Assn. Office: Troutman Sanders Mays & Valentine 4425 Corporation Ln Virginia Beach VA 23462

PICKETT, STEPHEN WESLEY, university official, lecturer and consultant; b. Billings, Mont., May 27, 1956; s. Wesley William and Carol Ann (Bollum) P. BA, Houston Bapt. U., 1980; MS, U. North Tex., 1988. Cert. elem. tchr., rehab. counselor, Tex. Hosp. tchr. Houston Ind. Sch. Dist., 1981-85; asst. to assoc. dean of students U. North Tex., Denton, 1988-90, asst. coord. disabled student svcs., Office Student Devel., 1990-91, dir. Office Disability Accommodation, 1991—2001, univ. mentor/advisor, 1992—2001; dir. disability svcs. U. Oreg., Eugene, 2002—, assoc. dir. office of acd. advising, 2002—. Co-author: curriculum guide The Newspaper as a Student Communicator, 1982 (winner Exxon Found.'s Impact Two award for creative teaching). Chair Mayor's Com. on Employment of Persons with Disabilities, Denton, 1990; mem. coun.-at-large Sam Houston Area Coun. Boy Scouts Am., Houston, 1975—; grad. Denton C. of C. Leadership Program, 1992; pub. rels. chair leadership Denton Steering Com., 1993-94; mem. ad. bd. city of Denton Transit, 1990-2001; exec. bd. Svc. provision for Aging Needs, a United Way Agy., 1997-2001; mem. U. of North Tex. Adv. Bd. for ADA Access, 1992-2001, co-chair UNT ADA adv. com., 2000-01; mem. budget com. Denton County United Way, 1998-2001. Recipient Cmty. Svc. award U. North Tex., 1992, award for svcs. to persons with disabilities North Tex. Rehab. Assn., 1993, Disting. Alumnus award Houston Bapt. U., 1994, Outstanding Alumnus award Ctr. for Rehab. Studies, U. North Tex., 1995. Mem. Assn. Higher Edn. and Disability, Nat. Assn. Student Pers. Adminstrs., Tex. Assn. Coll. and Univ. Student Pers. Adminstrs. (chair multicultural com. 1994-95, v.p. 1995-96, co-chair endowment found. com. 1996-97), Tex. Assn. Higher

Edn. and Disabilities (sec. 1998-99, conf. co-chair 1999). Presbyterian. Avocations: reading, travel, stamp collecting. Office: U Oreg Disability Svc 164 Oregon Hall 5278 U Oreg Eugene OR 97403-5278 Office Fax: 541-346-6013. E-mail: stevewp@worldnet.att.net.

PICKETT, STEVEN HAROLD, elementary education educator; b. Danville, Ill., Sept. 15, 1946; s. Harold George and Mary Margaret (Watson) P.; m. Marlene Mae Brumleve, June 23, 1973; children: Vincent Steven, Ryan Stephen, Alexander Maurice (dec.). AS, Danville Jr. Coll., 1966; BS, U. Ill., 1968, MEd, 1970. Cert. secondary tchr., Ill. Self-contained 8th grade classroom tchr. Gifford (Ill.) Grade Sch., 1968-70; 8th grade tchr. lang. arts, reading Effingham (Ill.) Ctr. Sch., 1970-98, Effingham (Ill.) Jr. H.S., 1998—. Coach various basketball and track teams Effingham Cen. Sch., 1970-83. Mem. Effingham Pk. Dist. Bd., 1973—, v.p., 1978-88, 91, pres., 1979-80; basketball coach Effingham County Youth Commn., 1972-73; coach Small Fry Baseball Team, 1985-89, 93-96, Effingham Pony League, 1971-73, Effingham Bambino Little League, 1990-91, 99-2000, Effingham Babe Ruth Prep League, 1992, 2001, Effingham Park Dist. Khoury League Team, 1997-98; coach track team Effingham Flyers, AAU, 1977-78; coach Effingham Jr. Babe Ruth League, 2002. Mem. NEA, Nat. Assn. English Tchrs. (life), Ill. Edn. Assn., Effingham Classroom Tchrs. Assn., Elks. Avocations: traveling, swimming, biking, basketball, baseball. Home: 703 N Cardinal St Effingham IL 62401-3210 Office: Effingham Jr HS 600 S Henrietta St Effingham IL 62401-1951 Fax: 347-2429.

PICKETT, WILLIAM BEATTY, history educator; b. Crawfordsville, Ind., Mar. 12, 1940; s. Walter Nathan and Amy Beatty P.; m. Janet Elizabeth Hollingsworth, Aug. 29, 1963; children: Robert Matthew, Jeffrey Michael. BA, Carleton Coll., 1962; MA, Ind. U., 1968, PhD, 1974. Assoc. instr. Ind. U., Bloomington, 1968-69; asst. prof. Rose-Hulman Inst. Tech., Terre Haute, Ind., 1972-76, assoc. prof., 1976-82, prof. history, 1982—. Fulbright lectr. Nanzan U. and Nagoya U., Japan, 1989; vis. lectr. U. Md., Seoul, Republic of Korea, 1990. Author: Homer C. Capehart: A Senator's Life, 1990, Dwight David Eisenhower and American Power, 1995, To Be the Best: Rose-Hulman Institute of Technology, 1974-99, 1999, Eisenhower Decides to Run: Presidential Politics and Cold War Strategy, 2000; editor: Technology at the Turning Point, 1977. Mem. Am. Hist. Assn., Orgn. Am. Historians, Ind. Assn. Historians, Soc. Historians of Am. Fgn. Rels., Soc. Mil. History, Internat. House Japan. Methodist. Avocations: travel, photography, sailing. Home: 3224 Oak St Terre Haute IN 47803-2651 Office: Rose Hulman Inst Tech 5500 Wabash Ave Terre Haute IN 47803-3999

PICKETT-TRUDELL, CATHERINE, psychotherapist; b. Winslow, Ariz., May 30, 1953; d. Jack Roderick and Mary McLaws (Turley) Pickett; children: Rachael Kristy Grogan, Ericka Edan Grogan. BA in Mgmt. of Human Resources, George Fox Coll., Newberg, Oreg., 1992; MA in Counseling Psychology, Western Evang. Sem., Tigard, Oreg., 1996. Cert. profl. counselor; nat. cert. psychologist. Tchr./trainer Children's World Learning Ctr., Beaverton, Oreg., 1989-96; pvt. practice psychotherapist Portland, 1994—; outpatient therapist Cmty. Behavioral Health Svcs., Fredonia, Ariz., 1996—. Cons. Dept. Health and Human Svcs., 1996—. Democrat. Roman Catholic. Avocations: perennial floral gardening, dressmaking and design, hosting social gatherings. Home: 623 W Chamberlain Dr Kanab UT 84741-6189 Office: PO Box 522 Fredonia AZ 86022-0522

PICKHARDT, CARL EMILE, JR. artist; b. Westwood, Mass., May 28, 1908; s. Carl Emile and Louise (Fowler) P.; m. Marjorie Sachs, June 15, 1935 (div. 1952); children: Nancy Louise Arnold, Carl Emile III, Sally Anne Duncan; m. Rosamond Forbes Wyman, Mar. 28, 1953. BA, Harvard U., 1931; studied with Harold Zimmerman, 1931-37. Tchr. Fitchburg Art Mus., 1951-62, Worcester Mus. Sch., 1949-50, Sturbridge Art Sch., 1952-60. Author: Portfolio of Etchings, 1942; one-man shows, Berkshire Art Mus., 1941, Doris Meltzer Gallery, N.Y.C., 1961, 68, 70, 71, 72, Jacques Seligmann Gallery, N.Y.C., 1935, 51, 52, 54, Stuart Gallery, Boston, 1946, Margaret Brown Gallery, Boston, 1951, Fitchburg Art Mus., 1951, 91, 98, 99, 2000, 2001, 2002, Lawrence Gallery, Kansas City, Mo., 1955, Artek Gallery, Helsinki, Finland, 1959, Laguna Gloria Art Mus., Austin, Tex., 1966, Radcliffe Coll., 1983, Providence Art Club, 1986; exhibited in group shows at Carnegie Internat., 1951, Mus. Modern Art, N.Y.C., 1940, 63, 64, Whitney Mus., 1936, Nat. Acad., 1942, 49, Boston Inst. Contemporary Art, 1941, Internat. Exhbn., Japan., 1952, Exhbn. Am. Drawings, France, 1955, Art Inst. Chgo., Calif. Palace of Legion of Honor, 1953, Boston Arts Festival, 1950, Am. Drawing Biennial, Norfolk, 1964, Pa. Acad. Fine Arts, 1968, Laguna Gloria Art Mus., 1973, Fitchburg Art Mus., 1974, 91; represented in permanent collections, Mus. Modern Art, N.Y.C., Boston Mus. Fine Arts, Bklyn. Art Mus., Worcester Art Mus., Library of Congress, N.Y. Pub. Library, Newark Art Mus., Fogg Art Mus., Addison Gallery, Finch Coll. Art Mus., Pa. Acad. Fine Atrs, Boston Pub. Library, Fitchburg Art Mus., Wadsworth Athenaeum, De Cordova Mus. Served with USNR, 1942-45. Ford Found. and Am. Fedn. Arts artist-in-residence Laguna Gloria Art Mus. 1966; recipient Shope prize Nat. Acad. 1942. Address: 66 Forest St Sherborn MA 01770-1618 *My life-long purpose has been to create in visual images a new language and to express order in asymetrical terms.*

PICKHOLTZ, RAYMOND LEE, electrical engineering educator, consultant; b. N.Y.C., Apr. 12, 1932; s. Isidore and Rose (Turkish) P.; m. Eda Rebecca Mittler, June 30, 1957; children: Robin, Andrew, Julie. BEE, CUNY, 1954, MEE, 1958; PhD, Poly. U. N.Y., 1966. Research engr. RCA Labs., Princeton, N.J., 1954-57, ITT Labs., Nutley, 1957-61; assoc. prof. Poly. Inst. Bklyn., 1962-71; prof. elec. engring., chmn. dept. George Washington U., Washington, 1977-80, prof., 1971—; pres. Telecommunication Assocs., Fairfax, Va., 1963—; cons. Inst. Def. Analyses, 1971-90, IBM Research, Yorktown Heights, N.Y., 1968-72; del. Union Radio Scientifique, Geneva, 1979—, vice chmn., 1987; del. NRC, Washington, 1980-83; cons. Motorola, CBC, NAB, USADR, Lucent, Verizon, 1996—. Vis. prof. U. Que., 1977; vis. scholar U. Calif., 1983; chmn. U.S. Nat. Commn. C, Union Radio Sci. Internat., 1990-92; mem. sci. and indsl. adv. bd. Telecom. Inst. Ont., Can. and Inst. Nacionale de la Recherches Scientique; vice chair, wireless panel World Tech. Evaluation Ctr. Editor: book series Computer Science Press, 1979— ; IEEE Trans., 1975-80, Jour. of Comms. and Networks; author: Local Area and Multiple Access Networks, 1986; contbr. articles to profl. jours.; patentee in field. Recipient rsch. award RCA Labs., 1955; rsch. grantee Office of Naval Research, Washington, 1982, E-Systems, Falls Church, Va., 1983-96, MCI, Falls Church, Va., Instelsat, Washington, Nortel Networks, 1996—, DARPA, NSF, 1999—. Fellow IEEE (bd. govs. 1979-82, digital comm. com., Centennial medal 1984), AAAS, Washington Acad. Scis.; mem. IEEE Comm. Soc. (v.p. 1986-88, pres. 1990-92, Donald W. McLellan award, 1994, Erskine fellow New Zealand 1997, Third Millennium medal 2000, ACM MSWIN prize paper award, 1999, Best paper of 1999 in Jour. of Comms. and Networks, 2000, gen. chair, Infocom, Kobe, Japan 1997, gen. chair, ACM Mobicom Y2K, Boston, 2000), Math. Assn. Am., Cosmos Club, Sigma Xi, Eta Kappa Nu. Home: 3613 Glenbrook Rd Fairfax VA 22031-3210 Office: George Washington U Dept Elec Computer Engring Washington DC 20052-0001

PICKHOLZ, JASON R. lawyer; b. N.Y.C., Jan. 10, 1970; s. Marvin Gerald and Joyce (Merrick) P. BA, Colgate U., 1991; JD, NYU, 1994. Bar: N.Y. 1995, U.S. Dist. Ct. (so. dist.) N.Y. 1995. Law clk. Hon. Kevin Thomas Duffy, U.S. Dist. Ct., So. Dist., N.Y.C., 1994-95; assoc. Morvillo Abramowitz, Grand Iason & Silberberg, P.C., 1995-97, Paul, Weiss, Rifkind, Wharton & Garrison, N.Y.C., 1997—. Chair law fifth yr. reunion com. NYU, 1998-99. Mem. ABA (contbr. article to newsletter com. on pre-trial practice and discovery sect. litigation 1998, co-chair sect. litigation trail practice tech. subcom. 2001—), Assn. Bar City N.Y., NYU Law Alumni Assn. (dir. 1997—), N.Y. Athletic Club. Office: Paul Weiss Rifkind Wharton & Garrison Rm 3040 1285 Ave of the Americas New York NY 10019-6064

PICKINPAUGH, RICHARD NEAL, assistant principal, educator; b. Coranado, Calif., Jan. 20, 1954; s. Johnny Neal and Donita Corrine Pickinpaugh; m. Shawna Lynn Cargile-Pickinpaugh, June 17, 1990; children: Kallie, Matthew; m. Elizabeth Anne Rinaldo-Pickinpaugh, Aug. 1976 (div. 1986); children: Kaylee, Kristin. AA, Cen. Wyo. Coll., 1974; BS, U. Wyo., 1876, MEd, 1983. Tchr. Sweetwater County Sch. Dist. #1, Rock Springs, Wyo., 1977—86; adminstr. Park County Sch. Dist., Powell, 1986—87; tchr. Sweetwater County Sch. Dist. #2, Green River, 1988—98; adminstr. Fremont County Sch. Dist. # 25, Riverton, 1998—. Head deacon Wind River Cmty. Ch., 2002. Recipient Outstanding Citizen's award, 1996. Mem.: Nat. Assn. Secondary Sch. Prins., Wyo. Assn. Sci. Tchrs. (Outstanding Sci. Tchr. 1985), Wyo. H.S. Activities Assn. (bd. dirs. 1999—2001), N.W. Dist. Adminstrs. Assn. (pres., sec. 1994—2001), Wyo. Assn. Secondary Sch. Prins. (asst. prin. rep. 2000—, Asst. Prin. of Yr. 2001), Internat. Tae-Kwan-Do Fedn. (black belt). Avocations: hunting, camping, horseriding, carpentry, church activities. Home: 45 Ridge Rd Lander WY 82520 Office: Fremont County Sch Dist # 25 121 N 5th W Riverton WY 82501

PICKLE, JOSEPH WESLEY, JR. religious studies educator; b. Denver, Apr. 8, 1935; s. Joseph Wesley and Wilhelmina (Blacketor) P.; m. Judith Ann Siebert, June 28, 1958; children: David E., Kathryn E., Steven J. BA, Carleton Coll., 1957; B.D., Chgo. Theol. Sem., 1961; MA, U. Chgo., 1962, PhD, 1969. Ordained to ministry Am. Bapt. Conv., 1962. Asst. pastor Judson Meml. Ch., N.Y.C., 1959-60; acting dean summer session Colo. Coll., Colorado Springs, 1969-70, from asst. prof. to prof. religion, 1964—, faculty dir. internat. studies, 1994-98. Vis. prof. theology Iliff Sch. Theology, Denver, 1984; vis. prof. religious studies U. Zimbabwe, Harare, 1989; cons. Colo. Humanities Program, Denver, 1975-89; coord. Sheffer Meml. Fund, Colo. Coll., Colorado Springs, 1983—. Co-editor Papers of the 19th Century Theology Group, 1978, 88, 93. Pres. bd. dirs. Pikes Peak Mental Health Ctr., Colorado Springs, 1975; chmn. Colo. Health Facilities Rev. Coun., Denver, 1979-84; mem. Colo. Health Facilities Rev. Coun., Denver, 1976-84, Colo. Bd. Health, Denver, 1986-91; bd. dirs. Marson Found., Colorado Springs, 1994—. Am. Bapt. Conv. scholar, 1953-59; Fulbright Hays Grad. fellow U. Tübingen, Fed. Republic Germany, 1963-64, Danforth fellow, 1957-63, Joseph Malone fellow, 1987. Fellow Soc. for Values in Higher Edn.; mem. Am. Theol. Soc. (pres. 1996-97), Am. Acad. Religion (regional pres. 1983-84, 92-93), Cath. Theol. Soc. Am., Fulbright Assn., Phi Beta Kappa. Democrat. Home: 20 W Caramillo St Colorado Springs CO 80907-7314 Office: Colo Coll 14 E Cache La Poudre St Colorado Springs CO 80903-3298 E-mail: jpickle@ColoradoCollege.edu.

PICKLE, LINDA WILLIAMS, biostatistician; b. Hampton, Va., July 19, 1948; d. Howard Taft and Kathryn Lee (Riggin) Williams; 1 child from previous marriage, Diane Marie; m. James B. Pearson, Jr., Oct. 14, 1984. BA, Johns Hopkins U., 1974, PhD in Biostats., 1977; postgrad., George Washington U., 1986-87. Computer programmer Comml. Credit Computer Corp., Balt., 1966-69; systems analyst, computer programmer Greater Balt. Med. Ctr., 1969-72; grad. tchg. asst. biostats. Johns Hopkins U., 1974-77; adj. asst. prof. div. biostats. and epidemiology Georgetown U. Med. Sch., Washington, 1983—88, assoc. prof. div. biostats and epidemiology, 1988-91, dir. biostats. unit, V.T. Lombardi Cancer Rsch. Ctr., 1988-91; biostatistician Nat. Cancer Inst. NIH, Bethesda, Md., 1977-88; math. statistician office rsch. methodology Nat. Ctr. for Health Stats., Hyattsville, 1991-99; sr. math statistician divsn. cancer control/population scis. Nat. Cancer Inst. NIH, Bethesda, 1999—. Author: Atlas of U.S. Cancer Mortality Among Whites: 1950-80, 1987, Atlas of U.S. Cancer Mortality Among Nonwhites: 1950-1980, 1990, Atlas of United States Mortality, 1996; contbr. articles to profl. jours. Sr. troop leader Girl Scouts U.S., 1981-83; sci. fair judge, 1983-93. Recipient Hammer award, US Govt., 2000. Fellow Am. Statis. Assn.; mem. The Biometric Soc., Soc. Epidemiologic Research, Soc. Indsl. and Applied Math., Phi Beta Kappa, Sigma Xi. Achievements include research in statistical methods in epidemiology, mapping health statistics.

PICKLE, ROBERT DOUGLAS, lawyer, footwear industry executive; b. Knoxville, Tenn., May 22, 1937; s. Robert Lee and Beatrice Jewel (Douglas) P.; m. Rosemary Elaine Noser, May 9, 1964. AA summa cum laude, Schreiner Mil. Coll., Kerrville, Tex., 1957; BSBA magna cum laude, U. Tenn., 1959, JD, 1961; honor grad. seminar, Nat. Def. U., 1979; hon. grad., U.S. Army JAG Sch., U.S. Army Logistics Mgmt. Sch.; grad., U.S. Army Inf. Sch., Army Command-Gen. Staff Coll. Bar: Tenn. 1961, Mo. 1964, U.S. Ct. Mil. Appeals 1962, U.S. Supreme Ct. 1970. Atty. Brown Shoe Co., Inc., St. Louis, 1963-69, asst. sec., atty., 1969-74, sec., gen. counsel, 1974-85; v.p., gen. counsel, corp. sec. Brown Shoe Co., Inc. (formerly Brown Group, Inc.), 1985—. Indiv. mobilization augmentee, asst. army judge adv. gen. civil law The Pentagon, Washington, 1984-89. Provisional judge Municipal Ct., Clayton, Mo., summer 1972; chmn. Clayton Region attys. sect., profl. div. United Fund Greater St. Louis Campaign, 1972-73, team capt., 1974-78; chmn. City of Clayton Parks and Recreation Commn., 1985-87; liaison admissions officer, regional and state coordinator U.S. Mil. Acad., 1980—. Col. JAGC, U.S. Army, 1961-63. Decorated Meritorious Svc. medal; 1st U. Tenn. Law Coll. John W Green law scholar; recipient Cold War Recognition cert. Sec. Def. Fellow Harry S. Truman Meml. Library; mem. ABA, Tenn. Bar Assn., Mo. Bar Assn., St. Louis County Bar Assn., Bar Assn. Met. St. Louis, St. Louis Bar Found. (bd. dirs. 1979-81), Am. Corp. Counsel Assn., Am. Soc. Corp. Secs. (treas. St. Louis regional group 1976-77, sec. 1977-78, v.p. 1978-79, pres., mem. Quarter-Century Club 1979-80), U. Tenn. Gen. Alumni Assn. (pres., bd. dirs. St. Louis chpt. 1974-76, 80-84, bd. govs. 1982-89), U.S. Trademark Assn. (bd. dirs. 1978-82), Tenn. Soc. St. Louis (bd. dirs. 1980-88, treas., sec., v.p. 1984-87, pres. 1987-88), Smithsonian Nat. Assocs., World Affairs Coun. St. Louis, Inc., Am. Legion, University Club (v.p., sec. St. Louis chpt. 1976-81, bd. dirs. 1976-81), Stadium Club, West Point Soc. St. Louis (hon. mem., bd. dirs. 1992—), Conf. Bd. (coun. chief legal officers), Fontbonne Coll. Pres.'s Assocs. (O'Hara and Tower Socs), St. Louis U. Billiken Club, St. Louis U. DuBourg Soc. (hon. v.p.). Republican. Presbyterian. Avocations: reading, spectator sports. Home: 214 Topton Way Saint Louis MO 63105-3638 Office: Brown Shoe Co Inc 8300 Maryland Ave Saint Louis MO 63105-3645 E-mail: rpickle@brownshoe.com.

PICKOVER, BETTY ABRAVANEL, retired executive legal secretary, civic volunteer; b. N.Y.C., Apr. 20, 1920; d. Albert and Sultana (Rousso) Abravanel; m. Bernard Builder, Apr. 6, 1941 (div. 1962); children: Ronald, Stuart; m. William Pickover, Aug. 23, 1970 (dec. Nov. 1983). Student, Taft Evening Ctr., 1961-70. Sec. U.S. Treasury Dept., Washington, 1942-43; exec. legal sec. various attys., Bronx, N.Y., 1956-70, Yonkers, 1971-83, ret., 1983. Chair Uniongram Sisterhood of Temple Emanu-El, Yonkers, N.Y., 1975—, Honor Roll, 1975—, v.p. 1995-97, 98, 99; sr. citizen cmty. leader Yonkers Officer for Aging, 1984—, Westchester County Sr. Adv. Bd., White Plains, N.Y., 1989-96; v.p. Mayor's Cmty. Rels. Com. of Yonkers, 1985—, historian, photographer, 1988—; v.p. Mayor's Cmty. Rels. Com. Yonkers, 1995; mem. adv. coun. Westchester County Office Aging Srs., 1993—; mem. bd. Legislators Task Force for Sr. Citizens Westchester County, 1995-97, 98, 99; Mayor Silver City Coun. Yonkers, 1989; mem. Mayor's Adv. Coun. on Sr. Citizens, 1990. Named to Sr. Citizen Hall of Fame, 1992; recipient Cert. of Appreciation, Westchester County, 1992, Pres. Coun. City of Yonkers, 1992, Merit. cert., 1993, Comty. Svc., City Mayor Yonkers, 1995, 96, 97, 98, 99, John E. Andrus Meml. Vol., 1995, Cert. of Appreciation, Westchester County Office of County Exec., 1993, 94, Cert. of Disting. Svc., 1997, Merit cert., N.Y. State Senator, 1994, N.Y. State Senator, 1995, 97, 98, 99, 2000, Cert. of Congratulations, N.Y. State Senator, 2001, Merit cert., Proclamation Mayor of Yonkers, 1985, 89, 92, 2 awards, U.S. Ho. of Reps., 1992, Woman of Excellence, Yonkers C. of C., 1993, awards, Mayor of Yonkers, 1985-97, 98, 99, 2000, Cert. of Appreciation, Mayor of City of Yonkers, 2001, awards, N.Y. State Senator and Assemblyman, 1987—97, City of Yonkers, 1993, Cert. of Merit, N.Y. State Assembly, 2001, Cert. of Appreciation, Westchester County Bd. Legislators, 1996, 99, City Coun. Pres., Yonkers, N.Y., 1999, Cert. of Recognition, 2000. Democrat. Jewish. Avocations: writing, photography, entertaining at all nursing homes in Yonkers, history, public relations. Home: 200 Valentine Ln Yonkers NY 10705-3662

PICKREL, PAUL, English educator; b. Gilson, Ill., Feb. 2, 1917; s. Clayton and Inez (Murphy) P. AB, Knox Coll., 1938; MA, Yale U., 1942, PhD, 1944. Instr. English Lafayette Coll., 1941-42; instr. Yale U., 1943-45, asst. prof., 1945-50, lectr. English, 1954-66, chmn. Scholar of House Program, 1959-60, 61-66; fellow Morse Coll., 1962-66; adviser John Hay fellows, 1959-66; vis. prof. English Smith Coll., Northampton, Mass., 1966-67, prof., 1967-87, prof. emeritus, 1987—, chmn. dept., 1972-75, 81-82. Author: (novel) The Moving Stairs, 1948; also essays on fiction, numerous book revs.; mng. editor: Yale Rev., 1949-66; chief book critic: Harper's mag., 1954-65. Mem. Aurelian Honor Soc., Elizabethan Club (New Haven), Faculty Club (Northampton), Phi Beta Kappa. Clubs: Elizabethan (New Haven), Faculty (Northampton); Yale (N.Y.C.).

PICKRELL, THOMAS RICHARD, retired oil company executive; b. Jermyn, Tex., Dec. 30, 1926; s. Mont Bolt and Martha Alice (Dodson) P.; m. M. Earline Bowen, Sept. 9, 1950; children: Thomas Wayne, Michael Bowen, Kent Richard, Paul Keith BS, North Tex. State U., 1951, MBA, 1952; postgrad., Ohio State U., 1954-55; advanced mgmt. program, Harvard U., 1979. CPA, Tex. Auditor, acct. Conoco, Inc., Ponca City, Okla., 1955-62, mgr. acctg. Houston, 1965-67, asst. controller Ponca City, 1967-81, v.p., controller Stamford, Conn., 1982-83, Wilmington, Del., 1983-85; asst. prof. Okla. State U., Stillwater, Okla., 1962-63; controller Douglas Oil Co., Los Angeles, 1963-65. Mem. adv. bd. dept. acctg. North Tex. State U., Denton, 1978-85; mem. adv. bd. Coll. Bus., Kansas State U., Manhattan, 1979-81 Bd. dirs. YMCA, Ponca City, 1976-78, Kay Guidance Clinic, Ponca City, 1971-74, United Way, Ponca City, 1979-81; chmn. Charter Rev. Com., Ponca City, 1971-72. Served to sgt. U.S. Army, 1944-46; ETO Mem. AICPA, Fin. Execs. Inst. (pres. Okla. chpt. 1972), Am. Petroleum Inst. (acctg. com., gen. com.), Ponca City Country Club (pres. 1980-81), Rotary (pres. Ponca City club 1973-74), Beta Gamma Sigma, Beta Alpha Psi Republican. Presbyterian. Home: 10 San Juan Ranch Rd Santa Fe NM 87506-7539

PICOTT, JR. JERRY LEE, music educator; b. Philadelphia, Pa., June 24, 1968; s. Jerry and Deloris Picott; m. Tikija Picott; children: Jerry Picott, Jasmine Picott, Jordan Picott. BA Music Ed., Missing U. Info, Daytona Beach, FL, 1990; MS. Ed. Leadership, Missing Info, Fort Lauderdale, FL, 1997. Band dir. Campbell Mid. Sch., Daytona Beach, Fla., 1990—98, Mainland H.S., Daytona Beach, 1998. Recipient Outstanding Young Educator, Daytona Beach Jaycees, 1999. Mem.: MENC, VTO, Fla. Bandmasters Assn., Internat. Masons Daytona Beach, King Soloman (life), Phi Delta Honor Soc., Omega Psi Phi Frat. Baptist. Office: Mainland High School 125 South Clyde Morris Blvd Daytona Beach FL 32114-3954

PICOTTE, LEONARD FRANCIS, naval officer; b. Calumet, Mich., Dec. 8, 1939; s. Irving René and Maria (Tamborino) P.; m. Sandra Lees Whiteley, July 14, 1984; children from previous marriage: Mary Elizabeth, Lance, Michael. BS in Econs. cum laude, U. No. Mich., 1963; MA in Polit. Sci., San Diego State U., 1975; grad. with distinction, Armed Forces Staff Coll., Norfolk, Va., 1976; M in Strategic Studies, Naval War Coll., Newport, R.I., 1985. Commd. ensign USN, 1963, advanced through grades to rear adm., 1991; comdg. officer USS Marathon, Vietnam, 1971-73; exec. officer USS Point Defiance, San Diego, 1976-78; exec. officer, officer in charge Surface Warfare Officers' Sch., Coronado, Calif., 1978-80; exec. officer Naval Sta., San Diego, 1980; comdg. officer USS Alamo, 1980-82; surface warfare detailer Bur. Naval Pers., Washington, 1982-84; comdg. officer USS Duluth, San Diego, 1986-88; 1st comdg. officer USS Wasp, 1988-90; insp. gen. Comdr. in Chief, U.S. Atlantic Command, Comdr. in Chief, U.S. Atlantic Fleet, Norfolk, 1990-92; comdr. Amphibious Group Two, 1992-95; ret., 1995; v.p. expeditionary warfare programs Am. Systems Corp., Chesapeake, Va., 1995—. Decorated Legion of Merit (2); recipient Disting. Svc. medal. Mem. Surface Navy Assn., USS Wasp Assn. (hon.), Army and Navy Club, Town Point Club, Hampton Roads Coun. Navy League, Nat. Security Indsl. Assn. (exec. com. Naval Expeditionary Warfare). Republican. Roman Catholic. Avocations: jogging, hunting, reading, gardening, chess. Home: 119 Northgate Ln Suffolk VA 23434-4300 also: 213 Madawaska Rd Palmyra ME 04965-4064 Office: Am Sys Corp Greenbriar Circle Chesapeake VA 23320

PICOTTE, SUSAN GAYNEL, geriatrics nurse, nursing educator, rehabilitation nurse; b. Omaha, Nov. 15, 1948; d. Gordon Pierre and Gaynel Ruth (Voris) Picotte; m. Kurt C. Foley, May 25, 1978 (div. 1995); children: Alicia Kate, Betsy Lyn. AA in Respiratory Therapy, Wichita State U., 1971, BSN, 1976, MN, 1988. RN, Kans.; clin. nurse specialist, ARNP/clin. nurse specialist gerontology; therapeutic touch practioner. Staff devel. coord. Cherry Creek Village Nursing Home and Retirement, Wichita, 1987-88; pulmonary nurse specialist Pulmonary Clinic of Wichita, 1981-86; outpatient pulmonary coord. Wesley Med. Ctr., Wichita, 1988-2000; practice group RN-pulmonary Christi St. Francis Campus, 2000—. Adj. clin. instr. dept. nursing Wichita State U., 1991—; lectr. in field; stress mgmt. coord., 1994, smoking cessation coord., 1993.; pulmonart/med. attending nurse Med. Practice Group Via Christi St. Francis Med. Ctr. Mem. AACN (v.p. local chpt. 1980-81), Am. Assn. Cardiovascular and Pulmonary Rehab., Wichita State U. Nursing Alumni Assn. (pro-tem officer 1991, nominating com. 1992, chair nominating com. 1992-96, bd. dirs. 1997-99, 2000-2002), Sigma Theta Tau (chair by-laws com. 1987-89, treas. 1989-91, Upjohn adv. com. 1983-85, chair rsch. and awards 1998—), Nurse Healers Profl. Assocs. Internat. Home: 3410 S 231st St W Goddard KS 67052-9260 E-mail: sgprn@yahoo.com.

PICOTTE, TERRI ROSELLA, social services and chemical dependency counselor; b. Shakopee, Minn., Feb. 21, 1947; d. Peter Louis and Gertrude Margaret (Mueller) Zorn; m. Bernard Ramon Picotte Jr., Mar. 27, 1988; 1 child, Krystle Lee. BA, Mt. Mary Coll., Milw., 1976. Pastoral minister Holy Rosary Ch./Little Earth Housing Project, Mpls., 1976-80; sr. citizen advisor Mpls. Am. Indian Ctr., 1980-82, youth counselor, 1988-89; security officer Ctr. Cos. Southdale Mall, Edina, Minn., 1982-84; fin. worker Hennepin County Human Svcs., Mpls., 1984-85, Ramsey County Human Svcs., St. Paul, 1985-87; counselor St. Paul Urban Indian Health Bd., 1987-88; assessment specialist, chem. dependency counselor Minn. Indian Women's Resources, Mpls., 1989-91; program dir. New Vision Treatment Ctr., June-July, 1991; family advocate Minn. Indians Women's Resource Ctr., Sept. 1991; co-founder, exec. dir. North Stars Focal Point Ctr. for adolescents; exec. dir. Avocations: painting, reading, beading, camping, hiking. Address: North Star Focal Point 3010 Hennepin Ave # 189 Minneapolis MN 55408-2614

PICOWER, WARREN MICHAEL, editor; b. N.Y.C., Aug. 21, 1934; s. Abraham and Nell (Bloom) P.; divorced; children: Jenny Emelia, Eve Julie. BA, Queens Coll., 1956; MA, New Sch. for Social Rsch., 1978; PsyD in Psychology, Heed U., L.A., 1982. Editorial asst. Newsweek mag., N.Y.C., 1956-59; assoc. editor Zimmerman Pub. Co., 1961-63; assoc., mng. editor Fawcett Pubs., 1963, 64-65; mng. editor Tuesday Publs., 1965-67, exec. editor, v.p., 1967-73; sr. editor King Features Syndicate, 1974-78; mng. editor Food & Wine Mag., 1978-93; consulting editor Travel Holiday Mag., N.Y., 1993-94; mng. editor Zagat Survey restaurant and hotel guides, N.Y.C., 1994-97; sr. project editor Money Mag., 1997-98. Cons. in field; awards judge James Beard Found. Contbr. articles to profl. jours. Mem. Am. Soc. Mag. Editors, Assn. of Food Journalists.

PICOZZI, ANTHONY, dentist; b. Bklyn., Dec. 24, 1917; s. Louis and Ida (DeRosa) P.; m. Gloria Margaret Patinella, Feb. 9, 1952; children— Kathryn, Lori BS, Columbia U., 1939; DDS, NYU, 1944. Section chief Lever Bros. Rsch., Edgewater, N.J., 1955-68; prof. dentistry NYU, N.Y.C., 1968-74; adminstr., rschr. Fairleigh Dickinson U., Hackensack, N.J., 1974-89; rsch. cons. Warner Lambert Co., Morris Plains, 1989-97. Cons. Lever Research, Edgewater, 1968-74, W.R. Grace, Balt., 1979-81 Contbr. articles to profl. jours. Served to lt. col. USAR Mem. ADA (mem. coun. on dental rsch. 1987-91), Am. Assn. Dental Research (councillor 1981, bd. dirs. 1988-90), Am. Assn. Dental Schs. (sect. chmn. 1980-81) Home: 104 Cottage Pl Ridgewood NJ 07450

PICUS, JOEL, medical educator; b. Washington, Sept. 16, 1957; s. Charles and Judith Picus; m. Sue Picus, Aug. 13, 1988; children: Joshua, Samuel. BS, U. Ill., 1979, MD, 1984. Asst. prof. medicine Washington U., St. Louis, assoc. prof. medicine, 1998—. Office: Washington Univ Sch Medicine Box 8056 660 S Euclid Saint Louis MO 63110

PIDERIT, JOHN J. university educator; b. N.Y.C., Feb. 26, 1944; BA in Math. and Philosophy magna cum laude, Fordham U., 1967; Lic. in Sacred Theology cum laude, Philosophische und Theologische Hochschule Sankt Georgen, Frankfurt, West Germany, 1971; MPhil, Oxford U., 1974; MA, PhD in Econ., Princeton U., 1979. Ordained Jesuit priest Roman Cath. Ch., 1971. Tchr. math. Regis H.S., N.Y.C., 1967-68; asst. campus minister Fordham U., 1971-72, Princeton U., 1975-78, preceptor, 1976-77; asst. chairperson grad. studies Fordham U., 1984-88, dir. program internat. polit. econ. and devel., 1981-83, 87-88, asst. chairperson dept. econs., 1979-82, 88-89, asst. prof. econs., 1978-89, assoc. prof. econs., 1989-90; corp. v.p. Marquette U., 1990-93; pres. Loyola U. Chgo., 1993—. Vis. fellow Woodstock Theol. Ctr., Washington, summer 1982; sabbatical Santa Clara U., 1989-90; master Queen's Ct. Residential Coll., 1987-90; chmn. responsible investment com. N.Y. province SJ, 1986-88, mem. fin. com., 1986-88; mem. joint commn.

govtl. rels. of Am. Coun. Edn., 1994—; mem. exec. com. Nat. Planning Com. Jesuit Assembly '89, 1988-90. Contbr. articles to profl. jours. Founder, moderator Friends of Loyola, 1987-90; pres. Univ. Neighborhood Housing Corp., 1986-90, Maroon Enterprises, Inc., 1986-90; trustee Canisius Coll., Buffalo, 1983-88, 89-94, Loyola Marymount U., L.A., 1996—, John Carroll U., University Heights, Ohio, 1996—; bd. dirs. Corp. Cmty. Schs. of Am., 1993—; promoter PIVOT H.S. and Middle Sch. with Milw. Pub. Schs., 1990-93; mem. Greater Milw. Edn. Trust, 1990-93; mem. steering com., chair edn. task force Milw. Cmty. Traffic Safety Com., 1991-93; mem. steering com. Libr. Literacy Soc. Milw., 1991-93; mem. scholarship com. Knitworkers Union Local 155, N.Y.C., 1982-90; mem. Princeton Schs. Com. N.Y. Region, 1985-88, chmn. Federation of Indp. Colls. and Univs., 1999—. Mellon grantee Fordham U., summer 1983, summer grantee Fordham U., 1979, Princeton U. fellow, 1974-78. Office: Loyola U Chgo 820 N Michigan Ave Chicago IL 60611-2147

PIDGEON, JOHN ANDERSON, headmaster; b. Lawrence, Mass., Dec. 20, 1924; s. Alfred H. and Nora (Regan) P.; children: John Anderson, Regan S., Kelly; m. Barbara Hafer, May 1986. Grad., Phillips Acad., 1943; BA, Bowdoin Coll., 1949; Ed.D., Bethany Coll., 1973; D.Litt., Washington and Jefferson Coll., 1979. Instr. Latin, adminstrv. asst. to headmaster Deerfield Acad., 1949-57; headmaster Kiskiminetas Springs Sch., Saltsburg, Pa., 1957—. Dir. Saltburg Savs. & Trust. Trustee Winchester-Thurston Sch. Served as ensign USNR, 1943-46. Mem. New Eng. Swimming Coaches Assn. (pres. 1956-57), Cum Laude Soc., Delta Upsilon. Home and Office: Kiski Sch 1888 Brett Ln Saltsburg PA 15681-8951

PIDGEON, LESLEA SHARON, artist, writer; b. Dayton, Ohio, Jan. 5, 1940; d. Charles Henry and Lettie Kathleen (Myers) P. Student, Brenau Coll., 1958-59, Dayton Art Inst., 1959-63, George Washington U., 1970's, Wright State U., Dayton, 1977. Office worker, Dayton, 1958-69; clk.-typist U.S. Army, 1969-77; trainee signal U.S. Army Res., Wright-Patterson AFB, Ohio, 1977-78; clk.-typist VA, Dayton, 1977, Def. Electronics Supply Ctr., Kettering, Ohio, 1977-79; illustrator aero. sys. divsn. Wright-Patterson AFB, 1979-84; clk.-typist Smithsonian Instn., Washington, 1984-88. Exhibited in group show Nat. Capitol Ceramic Assn., 1998 (3d pl. award); contbr. poetry to books, jours. Democrat. Avocations: videos, books, tapes, jewelry, stuffed animals.

PIDGEON, STEVEN D. lawyer; b. Norwood, Mass., Mar. 28, 1957; s. Norman L. and Dorothy H. Pidgeon; m. Kathryn A. Pierson, Sept. 12, 1981; children: Tyler Steven, Gregory Michael, Austin Robert. BA, U. Miami, 1978, JD, 1981. Ptnr. Streich, Lang, P.A., Phoenix, 1981-94, Snell & Wilmer, LLP, Phoenix, 1994—. Bd. dirs. Enterprise Network, Phoenix, 1986—; mem. Ariz. Securities Coun., Phoenix, 1995—. Author articles. Mem. ABA, State Bar Ariz., Maricopa County Bar Assn. Avocation: golf. Office: Snell & Wilmer LLP 400 E Van Buren St Phoenix AZ 85004-2223 E-mail: spidgeon@swlaw.com.

PIECH, MARY LOU ROHLING, medical psychotherapist, consultant; b. Elgin, Ill., Jan. 20, 1927; d. Louis Bernard and Charlotte (Wylie) Rohling; m. Raymond C. Piech, Feb. 12, 1950 (dec. Feb. 1985); 1 child, Christine Piech. BA, U. Ill., 1948, MA, 1953; postgrad., Ill. Inst. Tech., 1966-68, Union Inst., 1991-98. Cert. clin. psychologist, Ill.; diplomate Am. Bd. Med. Psychotherapy. Instr. psychology Elmhurst (Ill.) Coll., 1955-61; asst. prof. psychology North Cen. Coll., Naperville, Ill., 1961-67, Elmhurst (Ill.) Coll., 1967-81; med. psychotherapist Shealy Pain & Health Rehab. Ctr., LaCrosse, Wis., 1977-82, Shealy Inst. Comprehensive Health Care, Springfield, Mo., 1982—. Author, editor: (video series) Mental Health, 1982, (audio tape series) Holistic Mental Health, 1983. Recipient award Lilly Found., Elmhurst Coll., Shealy Inst., 1977. Fellow Am. Bd. Med. Psychotherapy; mem. APA, N.Am. Soc. Adlerian Psychology, Assn. Psychol. Type (life), Phi Beta Kappa, Phi Kappa Phi, Mortar Bd. Office: Shealy Inst 1328 E Evergreen St Springfield MO 65803-6204

PIECUCH, PAMELA GAYLE, systems operator and coordinator; b. Chgo., Aug. 1, 1954; d. Leon Benjamin and Loretta Mae (Skronz) P. BA magna cum laude, Northeastern U., Chgo., 1987. From pension benefit processor to adminstrv. asst. Structural Ironworkers Pension Fund, Chgo., 1976-89; computer systems operator, coord. SIW, 1989—. Bd. dirs. Huntington Commons Assn., Mt. Prospect, Ill., 1989; outreach com. St. Michaels Orthodox Ch., Niles, Ill., 1993-96, trustee, 1997—, recording sec., 1998. Mem. Phi Alpha Theta (historian 1987-89), Pi Gamma Mu, Alpha Chi. Orthodox Christian. Avocations: skating, horseback riding, computers, hiking, historical research. Home: 50 Regent Cir Schaumburg IL 60193-1869

PIEDMONT, RICHARD STUART, lawyer; b. Niskayuna, N.Y., Mar. 28, 1948; s. Henry Stuart and Lucille (Gagnon) P.; m. Marcia J. Quick, Apr. 11, 1981; children: Denise Nicole Rochette, Michael Norman Rochette, Alexandria Q. BA, U. Notre Dame, 1971. Bar: N.Y. 1977, U.S. Dist. Ct. (no. dist.) N.Y. 1977. Pres. Phoenix Abstract Corp., Albany, N.Y., 1979-84, v.p., 1984-89; ptnr. Piedmont & Rutnik, 1980-85, Devine, Piedmont & Rutnik, Albany, 1985-89; 58482 Phoenix Abstract Corp., N.Y., 1979-84; pvt. practice Piedmont Law Firm, 1990-95; ptnr. Harris Beach, LLP (formerly Harris Beach & Wilcox LLP), Albany, 1995—2001, Piedmont Law Firm, Latham, NY, 2001—. Founding bd. dirs. Make-a-Wish Found. of Northeastern N.Y.; former trustee Empire State Aerosci. Mus.; mem. parish coun. St. John the Evangelist Ch. Mem. N.Y. State Bar Assn., N.Y. State Land Title Assn., Ea. N.Y. Land Surveyors Assn., Schenectady County Bar Assn., Albany County Bar Assn., Aircraft Owners and Pilots Assn., Notre Dame Club Northeastern N.Y. (bd. dirs.). Democrat. Roman Catholic. Home: 1016 N Country Club Dr Niskayuna NY 12309-5405 Office: Piedmont Law Firm 4 British American Blvd Latham NY 12110 E-mail: rich@piedmontlawfirm.com.

PIEHLER, WENDELL HOWARD, organist, choir director, fund raiser; b. Lyons, Kans., Sept. 21, 1936; s. Oscar Harold and Bessie Matilda (Colberg) P.; m. Nancy J. Nyren, Nov. 2, 1974. BM summa cum laude, Southwestern Coll., 1958; MusM, Yale U., 1961, MMA, 1970; PhD, U. Conn., 1985. Organist, asst. Yale U., New Haven, 1969-71; organist, choir dir. Whitneyville Congl. Ch., Hamden, Conn., 1969-72; music dir. United Ch. of Green, New Haven, 1973; choir dir. Salem Luth. Ch., Bridgeport, Conn., 1974; organist, choir dir. St. Peter's Episcopal Ch., Cheshire, 1976-86, Temple Mishkan Israel, Hemden, 1971—. Mem. vestry Trinity Episcopal Ch. on the Green, New Haven, 1994-97; sr. adminstrv. asst. Med. Devel. Yale U., 1980-90, office mgr., 1990-94, bus. mgr., 1994-2000; mem. faculty Colby Sawyer Coll., 1961-70, Conn. Coll., 1976; adminstrv. asst. Gordon Sci. Confs., 1961-72. Rec. artist Lyrichord Disc.; patentee in field. Lectr. Neighborhood Music Sch., New Haven, 1975-85; chmn. Lyons H.S. Scholarship Fund, 1983—; asst. registrar New Haven Dem. Com., 1984-89, moderator, 1989-92; mem. pres.'s coun. Southwestern Coll., 1987—. Recipient Service award Congregation Mishkan Israel, 1985; grantee Conn. Commn. Arts, 1976, U. Conn., 1984. Mem. Shubert Theatre Gold Club, Long Wharf Theatre, Met. Opera Guild, Mory's Assn., Order of Mound, Yale Club N.Y.C. Avocations: swimming, skiing, travel, cultural events. Home: Crown Towers 123 York St Apt 18G New Haven CT 06511-5640 E-mail: Piehler@gateway.net.

PIEKARZ, RICHARD LAWRENCE, oncologist; b. Silver Spring, Md., June 8, 1963; s. Rolf Rudolf and Dorothy Lylian Piekarz. BA, Yeshiva U., 1985, MS, 1989, MD, PhD, 1994. Resident Univ. Hosps. of Cleve., 1994-97; fellow NIH, Nat. Cancer Inst., Bethesda, Md., 1997—. Mem. AMA, ACP, AAAS, Am. Assn. for Cancer Rsch. Am. Soc. of Clin. Oncology. Avocation: swimming. Home: 8708 1st Ave Apt 309 Silver Spring MD 20910-3520 Office: Nat Cancer Inst NIH B10 R 12 N226 MSC 1906 9000 Rockville Pike Bethesda MD 20892-1906 E-mail: rpiekarz@nih.gov.

PIEL, EMIL J. retired science and engineering educator; b. Fairview, N.J., Apr. 17, 1918; s. Harry and Anna (Decker) P.; m. Elizabeth Mayer Lautenschlager, Apr. 7, 1945 (dec. July 1995); two children. BA, Montclair State U., 1940, MA, 1947; EdD, Rutgers U., 1960. Physics tchr. Ft. Lee (N.J.) H.S., 1940-41, 45-48; airway traffic controller FAA, Jacksonville, Fla., 1941-42; combat pilot USMC, South Pacific, 1942-45; physics tchr. Caldwell (N.J.) H.S., 1948-52; sci. dept. chair East Orange (N.J.) H.S., 1952-60; prin. West Essex H.S., North Caldwell, N.J., 1960-66; chair dept. sci. & technology SUNY, Stony Brook, 1966-87, prof. emeritus, 1987—. Co-author: The Man Made World, 1992, Technology: Handle with Care, 1978. Fellow AAAS; mem. Ret. Officers Assn. Home and Office: 3 Lockward Rd Caldwell NJ 07006 E-mail: JPIEL8402@aol.com.

PIEL, GERARD, science editor, publisher; b. Woodmere, L.I., N.Y., Mar. 1, 1915; s. William F.J. and Loretto (Scott) P.; m. Mary Tapp Bird, Feb. 4, 1938; children: Jonathan Bird, Samuel Bird (dec.); m. Eleanor Virden Jackson, June 24, 1955; child, Eleanor Jackson. AB magna cum laude, Harvard U., 1937; D.Sc., Lawrence Coll., 1956, Colby Coll., 1960; U. B.C., Brandeis U., 1965, Lebanon Valley Coll., 1977, L.I. U., 1978, Bard Coll., 1979, CUNY, 1979, U. Mo., 1985, Blackburn Coll., 1985; Litt.D., Rutgers U., 1961, Bates Coll., 1974; L.H.D., Columbia, 1962, Williams Coll., 1966, Rush U., 1979, Hahnemann Med. Coll., 1981, Mt. Sinai Med. Sch., 1985; LL.D., Tuskegee Inst., 1963, U. Bridgeport, 1964, Bklyn. Poly. Inst., 1965, Carnegie-Mellon U., 1968, Lowell U., 1986; Dr. (honoris causa), Moscow State (Lomonosov) U., 1985. Sci. editor Life mag., 1938-44; asst. to pres. Henry J. Kaiser Co. (and assoc. cos.), 1945-46; organizer (with Dennis Flanagan, Donald H. Miller, Jr.), pres.and pub. Sci. Am., Inc., 1946-84, chmn., 1984-87, chmn. emeritus, 1987-94. Translated edits.: Le Scienze, 1968, Saiensu, 1971, Investigacion y Ciencia, 1976, Pour la Science, 1977, Spektrum der Wissenschaft, 1978, KeXue, 1979, V Mire Nauki, 1983, Tudomany, 1985, Majallat Al Oloom, 1986; author: Science in the Cause of Man, 1961, The Acceleration of History, 1972, Only One World, 1992, Erde im Gleichgewicht, 1994, What Scientists Learned in the 20th Century, 2001. Chmn. Commn. Delivery Personal Health Services City N.Y., 1967-68; trustee emeritus N.Y. Bot. Garden, René Dubos Ctr.; trustee emeritus Am. Mus. Nat. History, Radcliffe Coll., Phillips Acad., Mayo Clinic, Henry J. Kaiser Family Found., Found. for Child Devel.; pub. mem. Am. Bd. Med. Specialities; bd. overseers Harvard U., 1966-68, 73-79. Recipient George Polk award, 1961, Kalinga prize, 1962, Bradford Washburn award, 1966, Arches of Sci. award, 1969; Rosenberger medal U. Chgo., 1973, In Praise of Reason award Com. Scientists for Investigation of Claims of Paranormal, 1987, A.I. Djavakhishvili medal U. Tbilisi, 1985; named Pub. of Yr. Mag. Pubs. Assn., 1980 Fellow Am. Acad. Arts and Scis., AAAS (pres. 1985, chmn. 1986); mem. Coun. Fgn. Rels., Am. Philos. Soc., Nat. Acad. Sci. Inst. Medicine, Harvard Club, Century Club, Met. Opera Club, Cosmos Club, Somerset Club, Phi Beta Kappa, Sigma Xi. Home: 1115 5th Ave New York NY 10128-0100

PIELE, PHILIP KERN, education infosystems educator; b. Portland, Oreg., May 14, 1935; s. Theodore R. (dec.) and Helen D. (Hanson) P.; m. Sandra Jean Wright, Aug. 10, 1963; children: Melissa, Kathryn. BA, Wash. State U., 1957; student, U. Wash., 1960, San Jose State U., 1964; MS, U. Oreg., 1963, PhD, 1968. From asst. prof. to prof. ednl. policy and mgmt. U. Oreg., Eugene, 1968—, mem. faculty applied info. mgmt. program, 1989-99, dir. numerous ednl. orgns. and coms. Coll. Edn., 1968—, dir. Edn. Resources Info. Ctr. (ERIC) clearinghouse on ednl. mgmt., 1969—, assoc. dir. Ctr. for Ednl. Policy and Mgmt., 1973-76, head dept. ednl. leadership, tech. and adminstrn., 1997-99. Vis. lectr. U. Western Australia, Monashe U., U. New S. Wales, and several other Australian Univs., 1973; vis. prof. Ontario Inst. for Studies in Edn., U. Toronto, 1974; vis. scholar Stanford U., 1984; exec. sec. Oreg. Sch. Study Coun., 1980-97; dir. Networks and Comms. Ctr. for Advanced Tech. in Edn., 1984-92. Author numerous books, chpts., monographs; editor numerous books; contbr. articles to profl. jours. Bd. dirs. Oreg. Bach Festival, Eugene, 1980-83, Oreg. Mozart Players, Eugene, 1995-97, Eugene Opera, 2001—. Mem.: Am. Ednl. Rsch. Assn. (sec. adminstrn. divsn. 1991—93), Nat. Sch. Devel. Coun. (pres. 1985—86), Nat. Orgn. on Legal Problems in Edn. (pres. 1977—78). Office: ERIC Clearinghouse on Ednl Mgmt 5207 Univ of Oreg Eugene OR 97403-5207 E-mail: ppiele@oregon.uoregon.edu.

PIELOU, EVELYN C. biologist; b. Eng. m. Patrick Pielou, June 22, 1944; 3 children. B.Sc., U. London, 1950, PhD, 1962, DSc, 1975; LLD (hon.), Dalhousie U., 1993; DSc (hon.), U. B.C., 2001. Research scientist Can. Govt., 1963-67; vis. prof. N.C. State U., 1968, Yale, New Haven, 1969; prof. biology Queen's U., Kingston, Ont., 1969-71, Dalhousie U., Halifax, N.S., 1971-84; vis. prof. U. Sydney, Australia, 1975; oil sands environ. vis. research prof. U. Lethbridge, Alta., 1981-86. Author: Introduction to Mathematical Ecology, 1969, Population and Community Ecology, 1974, Ecological Diversity, 1975, Mathematical Ecology, 1977, Biogeography, 1979, Interpretation of Ecological Data, 1984, World of Northern Evergreens, 1988, After the Ice Age, 1991, Naturalist's Guide to the Arctic, 1994, Fresh Water, 1998, The Energy of Nature, 2001; contbr. articles to profl. jours. Recipient Lawson medal Can. Bot. Assn., 1984, Eminent Ecologist award Ecol. Soc. Am., 1986, Disting. Statis. Ecologist award Internat. Congress Ecology, Commemorative medal for 125th Anniversary of Confedn. of Can., 1992. Mem. Brit. Ecol. Soc. (hon. life), Am. Acad. Arts and Scis. (fgn. hon. mem.), Ecol. Soc. Am. (hon. life).

PIELSTICK, CLAYTON DEAN, academic administrator; b. McMinnville, Oreg., Apr. 4, 1947; m. Carol J. Pielstick; children: Benjamin, Jana, Molly. BS, Oreg. State U., 1970, MBA, 1987, EdD, 1996. Rsch. instr. Oreg. State Sys. Higher Edn., Monmouth, 1972; sr. planning analyst State of Oreg., Salem, 1973-75; contr. White Oaks, 1979-86; instr. Western Oreg. State Coll., Monmouth, 1986-89; bus. office mgr. Chemeketa C.C., Salem, 1989-91, registrar, 1991-95; exec. dean Yavapai Coll., Prescott, Ariz., 1995—. Cons. in field, 1987-95. Contbr. articles, revs. to profl. publs. Fundraiser Big Bros./Big Sisters, Prescott, Ariz., 1996—; pres. bd. dirs. Salem Art Assn., 1983-91; mem. Leadership Salem, Salem C. of C., 1985-87. Recipient Toastmaster of Yr. award Toastmasters Club, 1984, Outstanding Mem. award Inst. Mgmt. Accts., 1994, Horizon award Phi Theta Kappa, 1994. Mem. Am. Assn. C.C.s, Nat. Assn. Coll. and Univ. Bus. Officers, Western Assn. Coll. and Univ. Bus. Officers., Rotary (chair com. 1995—), Phi Kappa Phi. Avocations: leadership research, golf, horseback riding. Office: Yavapai Coll 1100 E Sheldon St Prescott AZ 86301-3220

PIEMONTE, ROBERT VICTOR, association executive; b. N.Y.C., July 28, 1934; s. Rosario and Carmela (Santoro) P. BS, L.I. U., 1967; MA, Columbia U., 1968, MEd, 1970, EdD, 1976; DSc (hon.), L.I. U., Bklyn., 1993. Asst. dir. nursing svc. ANA, N.Y.C., 1968-69, dir. nursing svc., 1971-72, divsn. dir., 1983-85; asst. dir. nursing Univ. Hosp.-NYU, 1970-71; assoc. dir. ops. N.Y.C. Health and Hosps. Corp., 1972-76; assoc. prof. Tchr.'s Coll. Columbia U., 1976-78; exec. dir. N.J. State Nurses Assn., Montclair, 1978-80; dep. exec. dir. Nat. Student Nurses Assn., N.Y.C., 1980-83, exec. dir., 1985-96, cons., 1996—. Adj. prof. nursing Tchr.'s Coll. Columbia U., 1990-95; cons. Consensus Mgmt., N.Y.C., 1992-96. Contbr. articles to profl. publs.; mem. editl. adv. bd. Nursing and Health Care, 1985-95. Areawide chair nursing Greater N.Y. chpt. ARC, N.Y.C., 1990-93. Col. U.S. Army, 1987-94, ret. Recipient Disting. Alumni award L.I. U., 1984, Hon. Recognition award N.Y. State Nurses Assn., 1992. Fellow Am. Acad. Nursing (treas. 1993-97); mem. Am. Soc. Assn. Execs. (cert., bd. dirs. 1993-96), Am. Nurses Found. (trustee 1994-97), Nursing House, Inc. (pres. 1993-97), Nat. Adv. Coun. on Nurse Edn. and Practice, N.Y. Soc. Assn. Execs. (Outstanding Assn. Exec. 1991, pres. 1989-90), N.Y. State Nurses Assn. (pres. 2001-2003). Democrat. Roman Catholic. Avocations: theatre, reading, travel. Home: 76 W 86th St New York NY 10024-3607 E-mail: robertvpiemonte@aol.com.

PIEN, SHYH-JYE JOHN, mechanical engineer; b. Kaohsiung, Taiwan, Republic of China, July 14, 1956; came to U.S., 1980; s. Ke-Lee and Sue-Jean (Shen) P.; m. Fong-Ling Yang, July 15, 1982; children: Irene J., Jennifer M. BSME, Nat. Taiwan U., 1978; MSME, U. Ill., 1982, PhD, 1985. Asst. prof. U. Notre Dame, South Bend, Ind., 1985-89; sr. engr. Alcoa Tech. Ctr., Alcoa Ctr., Pa., 1989-91, staff engr., 1991-95, tech. specialist, 1995-99; chief engr. The Cheng Hsong Group, Hong Kong, 1999—. Sr. advisor UN Devel. Program for China, 1995; panelist on heat transfer in mfg. at profl. confs.; panel chmn. and panelist on spray forming tech. at profl. confs. Editor symposium procs.; contbr. articles to profl. publs. Co-chmn. Nat. Youth Day Assembly, Taiwan, 1977; pres. Chinese Inst. Engrs. in USA, U. Ill., Urbana, 1984; v.p. Orgn. Chinese Ams., Pitts., 1993-96; chmn. Pitts. Chinese Sch. Bd., C.C. Allegheny County, Pa., 1999—. Recipient Excellent Youth award Kashiung City Province, Taiwan, Nat. Coll. Excellent Youth award Govt. Taiwan, Rsch. Initiation award NSF, 1988, Alcoa Merit award, 1995, Alcoa Comty. Leadership award, 1996. Mem. ASME (materials processing and mng. com. heat transfer divsn. 1990—, planning and devel. com. 1993-96, chmn. indsl. liaison com. 1996). Roman Catholic. Achievements include 4 patents on continuous casting machine design, patents pending on spray casting device and twin-belt casting device; research on nuclear safety analysis, hysteresis effect in natural convection, thermal/fluid phenomena in continuous casting, electronic packaging, welding process control, extrusion flow modeling, die casting, spray forming. Office: Tai Po Indsl Estate 9-15 Dai Wang St Tai Po NT Hong Kong

PIEPER, DAROLD D. lawyer; b. Vallejo, Calif., Dec. 30, 1944; s. Walter A. H. and Vera Mae (Ellis) P.; m. Barbara Gillis, Dec. 20, 1969; 1 child, Christopher Radcliffe. AB, UCLA, 1967; JD, USC, 1970. Bar: Calif. 1971. Ops. rsch. analyst Naval Weapons Ctr., China Lake, Calif., 1966-69; assoc. Richards, Watson & Gershon, L.A., 1970-76, ptnr., 1976—; gen. counsel Foothill Transit, 2000—; spl. counsel L.A. Unified Sch. Dist., 2000—; gen. counsel Greater L.A. County Vector Control Dist., 2001—. Spl. counsel L.A. County Transp. Commn., 1984-93, L.A. County Met. Transp. Authority, 1993-94; commr. L.A. County Delinquency and Crime Commn., 1983-94, pres., 1987-94; chmn. L.A. County Delinquency Prevention Planning Coun., 1987-90. Contbr. articles to profl. jours. Peace officer Pasadena (Calif.) Police Res. Unit, 1972-87, dep. comdr., 1979-81, comdr., 1982-84; chmn. pub. safety commn. City of La Canada Flintridge, Calif., 1977-82, commr. 1977-88; bd. dirs. La Canada Flintridge Coordinating Council, 1975-82, pres. 1977-78; exec. dir. Cityhood Action Com., 1975-76; chmn. Youth Opportunities United, Inc., 1990-96, vice-chmn. 1988-89, bd. dirs. 1988-96; mem. L.A. County Justice Systems Adv. Group, 1987-92; trustee Lanterman Hist. Mus. Found., 1989-94, Calif. City Mgmt. Found., 1992—. Recipient commendation for Community Service, L.A. County Bd. Suprs., 1978, Commendation for Svc. to Youth, 1996. Mem. La Canada Flintridge C. of C. and Cmty. Assn. (pres. 1981, bd. dirs. 1976-83), Navy League U.S., Peace Officers Assn., L.A. County, UCLA Alumni Assn. (life), L.A. County Bar Assn., Calif. Bar Assn., ABA, U. So. Calif. Law Alumni Assn. Office: Richards Watson & Gershon 40th Fl 355 S Grand Ave Los Angeles CA 90071-3101

PIEPER, HEINZ PAUL, physiology educator; b. Wuppertal, Germany, Mar. 24, 1920; came to U.S., 1957, naturalized, 1963; s. Heinrich Ludwig and Agnes Marie (Koehler) P.; m. Rose Irmgard Hackl, Apr. 23, 1945. MD, U. Munich, Germany, 1948. Resident 2d Med. Clinic, U. Munich, 1948-50, asst. prof. dept. physiology, 1950-57, Coll. Medicine, Ohio State U., Columbus, 1957-60, assoc. prof., 1960-68, prof., 1968—, chmn. dept. physiology, 1974-85, prof. emeritus, 1985—. Established investigator Am. Heart Assn., 1962-67 Mem. editorial bd.: Am. Jour. Physiology, 1973-82; contbr. articles on cardiovascular physiology to profl. jours. Mem. Am. Physiol. Soc., Ohio Acad. Scis., Sigma Xi. Home: 2206 SE 36th St Cape Coral FL 33904-4434 Office: Ohio State U Coll Medicine 333 W 10th Ave Columbus OH 43210-1239

PIEPER, PATRICIA RITA, artist, photographer; b. Paterson, N.J., Jan. 28, 1923; d. Francis William and Barbara Margaret (Ludwig) Farabaugh; m. George F. Pieper, July 1, 1941 (dec. May 3, 1981); 1 child Patricia Lynn ; m. Russell W. Watson, Dec. 9, 1989. Student, Baron von Palm, 1937-39, Deal (N.J.) Conservatory, 1939, 40, Utah State U., 1950-52; student Baron von Palm, 1937—39, student Deal (N.J.) Conservatory, 1939—40, student Utah State U., 1950—52. One-woman shows include Charles Russell Mus., Great Falls, Mont., 1955, Fisher Gallery, Washington, 1966, Tampa City Libr., 1977-81, 83, 84, Ctr. Pl. Art Ctr., Brandon, Fla., 1985; exhibited in group shows Davidson Art Gallery, Middletown , Conn., 1968, Helena (Mont.) Hist. Mus., 1955, Dept. Commerce Alaska Statehood Show, 1959, Joslyn Mus., Omaha, 1961, Denver Mus. Natural History, 1955, St. Joseph's Hosp. Gallery, 1980, 82, 84-86; represented in pvt. collections. Pres. Bell Lake Assn., 1976-78, 79; mem. Pasco County (Fla.) Water Adv. Coun., 1978—, chmn., 1979-82, 83-84, 86-88, 92—; gov.'s appointee to S.W. Fla. Water Mgmt. Dist., Hillsborough River Basin Bd., 1981-82, 84-87, sec., 1988-91, vice chmn., 1992; active Save Our Rivers program, 1982-84, 85-86, 92—; ad hoc chmn., 1991-92; mem. adv. bd. Fla. Suncoast Expwy., 1988-90; pres. Bell Lake Assn., 1986, 87; mem. adv. bd. Tampa YMCA, 1979-80. Winner photog. competition Gen. Tel. Co. of Fla., 1979; recipient Outstanding Svc. award Bell Lake Assn., 1987, Meml. award Land O'Lake Bd. of Realtors, 1989, Appreciation award Southwest Fla. Water Mgmt. Dist., 1993, finalist, Awds. of Excellence, Photographers winner in top 100 out of 8,000 Nat. Wildlife Fedn. competition, 1986, 1st place photography MacDill AFB, 1991. Mem. VFW (life), Nat. League Am. Pen Women (v.p. Tampa 1976-78, Woman of Yr. award 1977-78), Tampa Art Mus., Ret. Officer's Wives Assn., Land O'Lakes C. of C. (bd. dirs. 1981-82, Outstanding Svc. award 1980), Fla. Geneal. Soc., West State Archaeol. Soc. (distaff mem.), Ret. Officer's Assn., Lutz Club, Land O'Lakes Women's Club, Moose. Home: 3304 E Derry Dr Sebastian FL 32958-8577 *I believe that those of us born with the gift of creativity are truly blessed. It is our duty to make the most of, and be worthy of that gift. And if we work hard and sincerely apply ourselves a chosen few will become immortal through the beauty we leave behind for others to enjoy. As an artist and photographer I am truly blessed.*

PIEPHO, LEE (EDWARD LEE PIEPHO), humanities educator; b. Detroit, Jan. 10, 1942; s. Edward Ernest and Dolores Faye (Dowis) P.; m. Susan Brand, June 13, 1964. AB, Kenyon Coll., 1964; MA, Columbia U., 1966; PhD, U. Va., 1972. Instr. Sweet Briar (Va.) Coll., 1969-72, asst. prof., 1972-78, assoc. prof., 1978-83, prof., 1983-94, Shallenberger Brown prof., 1994—, dept. chmn., 2000—01, coord. European civilization program, 1986-89. Author: Holofernes' Mantuan, 2001; translator, editor: Adulescentia: The Eclogues of Mantuan, 1989; contbr. articles to profl. jours. SIMRS fellow, 1979, Dulin fellow Folger Shakespeare Libr., 1989-90, Mednick fellow, 1996. Mem. Internat. Assn. for Neo-Latin Studies, Modern Lang. Assn. Am., Renaissance Soc. Am. Avocations: tennis, scuba diving. Home: 137 Woodland Rd Sweet Briar VA 24595-9999 Office: Sweet Briar Coll Dept English Sweet Briar VA 24595 E-mail: lpiepho@sbc.edu.

PIEPHO, ROBERT WALTER, pharmacy educator, researcher; b. Chgo., July 31, 1942; s. Walter August and Irene Elizabeth (Huybrecht) Apfel; m. Mary Lee Wilson, Dec. 10, 1981. BS in Pharmacy, U. Ill.-Chgo., 1965; PhD in Pharmacology, Loyola U., Maywood, Ill., 1972. Registered pharmacist, Ill., Colo. Assoc. prof. U. Nebr. Med. Ctr., Omaha, 1970-78; prof. pharmacy, assoc. dean Sch. Pharmacy U. Colo., Denver, 1978-86; prof. pharmacol., dean U. Mo. Sch. Pharmacy, Kansas City, 1987—. Contbr. articles to profl. jours., chpts. to books. Pres. Club Monaco Homeowners Assn., Denver, 1980-82. Named Outstanding Tchr. U. Nebr. Coll. Pharmacy, 1975; recipient Arthur Hassan Colo. Pharmacal Assn., 1983, Excellence in Teaching U. Colo. Med. Sch., 1983 Fellow Am. Coll. Clin. Pharmacology (regent 1983-88, 91-96, pres. 1998-2000); mem. Am. Soc. Hosp. Pharmacists, Am. Soc. Pharmacology and Exptl. Therapeutics, Rho Chi Roman Catholic. Office: U Mo Sch Pharmacy 5005 Rockhill Rd Kansas City MO 64110-2239

PIEPKE, WALTER J. art educator; b. Marienhof, Germany, Nov. 29, 1941; arrived in U.S., 1957, permanent resident; s. Emil and Martha Piepke; m. Susan Leedecke, June 21, 1975. BA, Hartwick Coll., Oneonta, N.Y., 1965; MA, U. N.H., 1978; MFA, Rochester Inst. Tech., 1984. Cert. Coll. Profl. Va. Tchr, of German Brockport (N. Y.)H.S., 1965—83; lang. instr. U. N.C., Greensboro, 1985—88, James Madison U., Harrisonburg, Va., 1988—91; art tchr. Prince William County Schs., Woodbridge, 1991—. One-man shows include Raleigh (N.C.) Contemporary Galleries, 1989, 1992, 1994, 1998, 2000, Bridgewater (Va.) Coll., 1990, Dario A. Covi Gallery U. Louisville, Ky., 1992, Fredricksburg (Va.) Art Ctr., 1993, Theater Gallery, Münster, Germany, 1993, The Frame Gallery, Staunton, Va., 1994, 1998, 2000, Bridgewater (Va.) Coll., 1995, Represented in permanent collections Musscarelle Mus. of Art Coll. Wm. and Mary, Allen R. Hite Art Inst. U. Louisville, Met. Mus. Art, N.Y.C., Yale U. Art Gallery, Boston Pub. Libr. Print Collection, Mint Mus., Charlotte, N.C., Montgomery Mus. of Art, New Orleans Mus. of Art. Recipient Print Publ. prize, N.C. Print and Drawing Soc., 1985, Juror's award, 1986. Avocations: music, opera. Home: 3085 Bridgeton Ct Woodbridge VA 22192 Office: Woodbridge Sr HS 2001 Old Bridge Rd Woodbridge VA 22192 E-mail: piepkewj@pwcs.edu.

PIERARD, RICHARD VICTOR, history educator; b. Chgo., May 29, 1934; s. John Perkins and Diana Florence (Russell) P.; m. Charlene Burdett, June 15, 1957; children: David, Cynthia. BA, Calif. State U., L.A., 1958, MA, 1959; PhD, U. Iowa, 1964. Prof. history Ind. State U., Terre Haute, 1964-2000, emeritus, 2000—. Vis. prof. Greenville (Ill.) Coll., 1972-73, Free Theol. Acad., Seeheim, Fed. Republic Germany, 1971, 78, Regent Coll., Vancouver, B.C., Can., 1975, Trinity Evang. Div. Sch., Deerfield, Ill., 1982, No. Bapt. Theol. Sem., Lombard, Ill., 1987, Fuller Theol. Sem., Pasadena, Calif., 1988,

91, Moscow Theol. Sem., 1997, 99, 2001, Gordon Coll., Wenham, Mass., 2000-2001; scholar-in-residence Gordon Coll., 2000—; Fulbright prof. U. Frankfurt, Fed. Republic Germany, 1984-85; Fulbright prof. U. Halle, German Dem. Republic, 1989-90, Gordon Coll., Wenham, Mass., 2000—; mem. nat. adv. coun. Ams. United for Separation of Ch. and State, 1985—; pres. Greater Terre Haute Ch. Fedn., 1987-88; del. Lausanne II Congress on World Evang., Manila, Philippines, 1989; mem. Bapt. Heritage Study Commn., Bapt. World Alliance, 1990—. Author: The Unequal Yoke: Evangelical Christianity and Political Conservatism, 1970, Bibliography on the Religious Right in America, 1986; co-author: Twilight of the Saints: Biblical Christianity and Civil Religion, 1978, Civil Religion and the Presidency, 1988, Two Kingdoms: The Church and Culture through the Ages, 1993, The Revolution of the Candles: Christians in the Revolution of the German Democratic Republic, 1996, The New Millennium Manual, 1999; contbr. articles to religious and hist. publs. Del. White House Conf. on Librs., Washington, 1979, Ind. Dem. Party Convention, Indpls., 1980, 88; precinct committeeman Dem. Party, Terre Haute, 1978-80, 90—; mem. Ind. Gov.'s Adv. Com. on Librs., 1980-81. With U.S. Army, 1954-56. Recipient Terre award for cmty. svc., Terre Haute, Ind., 1991; Fulbright scholar U. Hamburg (Fed. Republic Germany), 1962-63; rsch. fellow U. Aberdeen (Scotland), 1978; Chavanne scholar Baylor U., 1988. Mem. Conf. on Faith and History (sec.-treas. 1967—), Evang. Theol. Soc. (pres. 1985), Am. Hist. Assn., Am. Soc. Ch. History, Ind. Assn. Historians, Am. Soc. Missiology, Internat. Assn. Mission Studies, Soc. for Encouragement and Preservation of Barbershop Quartet Singing in Am., Am. Bapt. Hist. Soc. (bd. mgrs. 1993—). Democrat. Home: 11 Pine Rd Beverly MA 01915

PIERCE, ALLAN DALE, engineering educator, researcher; b. Clarinda, Iowa, Dec. 18, 1936; s. Franklin Dale and Ruth Pauline (Wright) P.; m. Penelope Claffey, Oct. 27, 1961; children: Jennifer Irene, Bradford Loren. BS, N.Mex. Coll. Agrl. and Mechanic Arts, 1957; PhD, MIT, 1962. Registered profl. engr., Mass. Staff rschr. Rand Corp., Santa Monica, Calif., 1961-63; sr. staff scientist Avco Corp., Wilmington, Mass., 1963-66; asst. prof. MIT, Cambridge, 1966-68, assoc. prof., 1968-73; prof. mech. engring. Ga. Inst. Tech., Atlanta, 1973-76, Regent's prof., 1976-88; Leonhard chair in engring. Pa. State U., University Park, 1988-93; chmn. dept aerospace and mech. engring. Boston U., 1993-99, prof., 1993—. Vis. prof. Max Planck Inst., Goettingen, Fed. Republic Germany, 1976-77; cons. in field. Author: Acoustics: An Introduction to Its Physical Principles and Applications, 1981; editor phys. acoustics monograph series, 1988-97; editor Jour. Computation Acoustics, 1992-99; contbr. articles to profl. jours. Recipient Sr. U.S. Scientist award Alexander von Humboldt Found., 1976, Cert. of Recognition Nat. Aeronautics and Space Adminstrn., 1984, Per Bruel Gold medal for noise control and acoustics ASME, 1995; NSF fellow, 1957-60, Shell Oil fellow, 1960-61, Faculty fellow U.S. Dept. Transp., 1979-80. Fellow Acoustical Soc. Am. (editor-in-chief 1999—, Silver medal 1991), ASME (Rayleigh lectr. 1992, Per Bruel Gold medal 1995, chair Noise Control and Acoustics Divsn. 1999-2000); mem. IEEE, AIAA. Home: PO Box 339 East Sandwich MA 02537-0339 Office: Boston U Dept Aerospace & Mech Engring 110 Cummington St Boston MA 02215-2407 E-mail: adp@bu.edu.

PIERCE, BENEDICT ENOL, social worker; b. Castries, St. Lucia, Mar. 23, 1942; came to U.S., 1955; d. Leon Joseph and Ionie (Mitchell) Williams; m. Allen Pierce, 1964; children: Gregory, Reginald. AAS, Bronx Community Coll., 1965; BA, CCNY, 1978; MSW, NYU, 1980. Cert. social worker, N.Y. Social worker St. Joseph Children Svc., Bklyn., 1980-82, social worker supr., 1982—, program dir., 1985-91. Counselor Enter Alcoholism Svcs., N.Y.C., 1988-89. Vol. Community Planning Bd., Bronx, N.Y., 1979; sec. Soc. for Advancement and Betterment of Children, 1966-78. Mem. Nat. Assn. Black Social Workers, Nat. Assn. Social Workers, N.Y. State Soc. Clin. Social Work (RSVCHO therapist), Network Orgn. Bronx Women. Democrat. Roman Catholic.

PIERCE, CHARLES EARL, software engineer, entrepreneur; b. Edenton, N.C., July 13, 1955; s. Charles William and Carrie (Rankins) P.; m. Jan Saunders, Nov. 16, 1991. BS in Math., L.I. U., 1977. Rsch. analyst Equitable Life, N.Y.C., 1977—80; systems analyst CTEK Software, 1980—83; asst. v.p. Bank N.Y., 1987—97, Chase Mellon Fin. Group, 1997—2001; sr. v.p. CEP Hatteras, Ridgefield, NJ, 2001—. Cons. Nibor Assocs., N.Y.C., 1983-85, Vital Cons., N.Y.C., 1985-87. Mem. IEEE, N.Y. Acad. Scis., Data Processing Mgmt. Assn., Assn. for Computing Machinery, Math. Assn. Am. Mem. Pentecostal Ch. Mem. Pentecostal Ch. Achievements include development of of English test interpreter/command processing for mainframe at CTEK Software; automated phased conversion of DMS system; intelligent training systems and customer systems.

PIERCE, CHARLES ELIOT, JR. library director, educator; b. Springfield, Mass., Dec. 25, 1941; s. C. Eliot and Dora Mason (Redway) P.; m. Barbara G. Hanson, Oct. 18, 1969; children: Sheila H., Charles Eliot III BA, Harvard U., 1964, MAT., 1966, PhD, 1970. Prof. English Vassar Coll., Poughkeepsie, N.Y., 1970-87; dir. Pierpont Morgan Library, N.Y.C., 1987—. Author: (literary criticism) The Religious Life of Samuel Johnson, 1983 Mem. vis. com. Harvard U. Libr., Vassar Coll. Art Gallery. Mem. Art Mus. Dirs., Johnsonians, Planned Parenthood N.Y.C., Century Assn., Grolier Club, Walpole Soc., Knickerbocker Club. Episcopalian. Home: 11 Clinton Corners Rd Salt Point NY 12578-2502 Office: Pierpont Morgan Libr 29 E 36th St New York NY 10016-3490

PIERCE, CHESTER MIDDLEBROOK, psychiatrist, educator; b. Glen Cove, N.Y., Mar. 4, 1927; s. Samuel Riley and Hettie Elenor (Armstrong) P.; m. Jocelyn Patricia Blanchet, June 15, 1949; children: Diane Blanchet, Deirdre Anona. AB, Harvard U., 1948, MD, 1952; ScD (hon.), Westfield Coll., 1977, Tufts U., 1984; D Engring. Tech. (hon.), Wentworth Inst. Tech., 1997. Instr. psychiatry U. Cin., 1957-60; asst. prof. psychiatry U. Okla., 1960-62, prof., 1965-69; prof. edn. and psychiatry Harvard U., 1969—; pres. Am. Bd. Psychiatry and Neurology, 1977-78; ret. Mem. Polar Research Bd.; cons. USAF. Author publs. on sleep disturbances, media, polar medicine, sports medicine, racism; mem. editorial bds. Advisor Children's TV Workshop; chmn. Child Devel. Assn. Consortium; bd. dirs. Action Children's TV. With M.C. USNR, 1953-55. Fellow Royal Australian and N.Z. Coll. Psychiatrists (hon.), Gt. Britain Royal Coll. Psychiatrists (hon.); mem. NAS, Inst. Medicine, Black Psychiatrists Am. (chmn.), Am. Orthopsychiat. Assn. (pres. 1983-84), Am. Acad. Arts and Scis. Democrat. Home: 17 Prince St Jamaica Plain MA 02130-2725

PIERCE, DANIEL THORNTON, physicist; b. L.A., July 16, 1940; s. Daniel Gordon Pierce and Celia Francis Thornton Thayer; m. Barbara Harrison, Nov. 19, 1988; children: Jed, Maia, Stephen. BS, Stanford U., 1962, PhD in Applied Physics, 1970; MA, Wesleyan U., Middletown, Conn., 1966. NSF rsch. asst. materials sci. dept. Stanford U., 1961; lectr in physics U.S. Peace Corps, Kathmandu, Nepal, 1962-64; rsch. asst. Wesleyan U., 1964-66, Stanford Electronics Lab., 1966-70, rsch. assoc., 1970-71; rsch. staff Solid State Physics Lab., Swiss Fed. Inst. Tech., 1971-75; physicist Nat. Inst. Standards and Tech. (formerly Nat. Bur Standards), Gaithersburg, Md., 1975—, fellow, 1994—. Contbr. chpts. to books, numerous articles to profl. jours. Trustee Unitarian Ch. of Rockville, Md., 1994-96 Recipient IR-100 award R&D Mag., 1980, 85, Gold medal Dept. Commerce, 1987, William P. Schlichter award Nat. Inst. Standards and Tech., 1992. Fellow Am. Phys. Soc. (exec. com. Materials Physics Divsn. 1998-2001), Am. Vacuum Soc. (surface sci. exec. com. 1984-88, Gaede-Langmuir prize 1994). Achievements include patents for source of spin polarized electrons, absorbed current and low energy spin polarization detectors; development of scanning electron microscopy with polarization analysis. Office: Nat Inst Standards and Tech Mail Stop 8412 Bldg 220 Rm B206 Gaithersburg MD 20899-8412 E-mail: daniel.pierce@nist.gov.

PIERCE, DANNY PARCEL, artist, educator; b. Woodlake, Calif., Sept. 10, 1920; s. Frank Lester and Letitia Frances (Parcel) P.; m. Julia Ann Rasmussen, July 19, 1943; children: Julia Ann, Mary L., Danny L., Duane Nels. Student, Art Ctr. Sch., L.A., 1939, Chouinards Art Inst., 1940-41, 46-47, Am. Art Sch., N.Y.C., 1947-48, Bklyn. Mus. Art Sch., 1950-53; BFA, U. Alaska, 1963. Instr. Hunter Coll., N.Y.C., 1952-53, Burnley Sch. Art, Seattle, 1954-58, Seattle U., 1956-59; publ. Red Door Studio Press, Kent, Wash., 1959—; artist-in-res. U. Alaska, College, 1959-63; asst. prof. U. Wisc., Milw., 1964; head art dept. Cornish Sch. Allied Arts, Seattle, 1964-65; prof. art U. Wisc., Milw., 1965-84, prof. emeritus, 1984—. One-man shows include Contemporaries Gallery, N.Y.C., 1953, Handforth Gallery, Tacoma, Washington, 1958, U. Alaska, College, 1959, 63, 73, 74, Gonzaga U., Bradley Galleries, Milw., 1966, 68, 70, 72, 74, 76, 78-80, 82, Martin-Zambito Gallery, Seattle, 1997, 2002, Apple Blossom Time, 2000; father/son exhbn. 2002 Desert Images, Martin-Zambito Gallery, 1999; represented in permanent collections Bibliothèque Nationale, Paris, Mus. Modern Art, N.Y.C., Libr. Congress, Washington, Smithsonian Instn., Washington, Seattle Art Mus., U. Washington Henry Art Gallery, Bklyn. Mus., Princeton U., U. Alaska, U. So. Calif., William and Mary Coll., Oostduinkerke (Belgium) Nat. Fishing Mus., Nat. Mus. Sweden, Stockholm, Johnson Wax Found., Racine, Wisc., Gen. Mills Collection Art, Mpls., Huntington Libr., San Marino, Calif., various pvt. collections; pub. 23 limited edition books, 1959-98. Recipient Best Oil Landscape award Conn. Acad. Fine Arts, Hartford, 1st Prize oil Kohler Gallery, Seattle, 1974, others; chosen one of twelve artists to represent State Wash. Expo 70, Osaka, Japan, rep. U.S. Internat. São Paulo Biannual Art Exhbn.; established archives at Golda Meier Libr., U. Wis.-Mils. Mem. Artist Equity Assn. (charter, pres. Seattle chpt. 1958), Am. Colorprint Soc., Internat. Arts and Letters (life). Office: Red Door Studio 404 Summit Ave N Kent WA 98030-4712

PIERCE, DAVID HYDE, actor; b. Albany, N.Y., Apr. 3, 1959; BA, Yale U., 1981. Appeared in plays Beyond Therapy, 1982, Holiday, 1982, Summer, 1983, That's It, Folks! 1983, Candida, 1984, The Seagull, 1984, The Grand Hysteric, 1984, The Three Zeks, 1984, Tartuffe, 1984, Donuts, 1985, Hamlet, 1986, The Author's Voice, 1987, The Maderati, 1987, Camille, 1987, The Cherry Orchard, 1988, Zero Positive, 1988, Much Ado About Nothing, 1988, The Heidi Chronicles, 1989, Elliot Loves, 1990, It's Only a Play, 1991; films include The Terminator, 1984, Moving Violations, 1985, Bright Lights, Big City, 1988, Crossing Delancey, 1988, Rocket Gibraltar, 1988, The Fisher King, 1991, Little Man Tate, 1991, Sleepless in Seattle, 1993, Addams Family Values, 1993, Wolf, 1994, Nixon, 1995, Hercules, 1998, A Bug's Life, 1998, Jackie's Back!, 1999, Mating Habits of the Earthbound Human, 1999, Isn't She Great, 2000, Chain of Fools, 2000, Osmosis Jones, 2001; TV series include The Powers That Be, 1993, Frasier, 1993— (seven Am. Comedy awards 1994-2000, Emmy award, 1995, 98, 99, Golden Globe award, SAG Award, 1996, 2000, Q Award 1994, 95, 96, 98, TV Guide award, 2000.); prodr. Wet, Hot, American Summer, 2001. Recipient Emmy award, 1995, 98, 99, SAG award, 1996, 2000, Q award, 1994, 95, 96, 98, TV Guide award, 2000*

PIERCE, DAVID R. educational administrator; AA in Math., Fullerton Coll., 1958; BA in Math., Long Beach State U., 1960, MA in Edn., 1961; MS in Math., Purdue U., 1965, PhD in Math. Edn., 1969. Math. instr. Orange Coast Coll., Costa Mesa, Calif., 1962-65; supr. math. student teaching Purdue U., Lafayette, Ind., 1965-66; chmn. natural scis. & math. divsn. Golden West Coll., Huntington Beach, Calif., 1966-67; dean instrn. Waubonsee C.C., Sugar Grove, Ill., 1967-70; supt., pres. North Iowa Area C.C., Mason City, 1970-80; exec. dir. Ill. C.C. Bd., Springfield, 1980-90; chancellor Va. C. C. Sys., Richmond, 1990-91; pres., chief exec. officer Am. Assn. C.C., Washington, 1991—; also joint Am. Assn. C.C./ACCT Commn. Fed. Rels. mem., 1984-86, 88-91; also bd. mem. Am. Assn. C.C., 1988-91, vice-chmn., 1990-91, chmn. task force on allied health, 1989-91, chmn. com. on fed. rels., 1990-91. Mem. Nat. Coun. State Dirs. Cmty. and Jr. Colls., 1981-91 (chmn. 1984-85), Ill. Employment & Edn. Subcabinet, 1980-90; cons., evaluator North Ctrl. Assn. Commn. Insts. Higher Edn. (commr.-at-large 1977-83). Mem. Ill. Econ. Devel. Subcabinet, 1980-90. Named Person of Yr. Nat. Coun. Cmty. Svcs. & Continuing Edn. Region 5, 1982, Nat. Person of Yr. Nat. Coun. Cmty. Svcs. & Continuing Edn., 1990; recipient Meritorious Svc. award Ill. C.C. Trustee Assn., 1988, Outstanding Ill. Citizen award Coll. Lake County, 1989, Outstanding Alumnus award Calif. C.C. League, 1991, Outstanding Alumnus award Fullerton Coll., 1992, B. Lamar Johnson Leadership award League for Innovation in the C.C., 1993. Mem. Nat. Policy Bd. Higher Edn. Instl. Accreditation, Washington Higher Edn. Secretariat, Nat. Alliance of Bus. Coun. on Workforce Excellence. Office: Am Assn Cmty Colls 1 Dupont Cir NW Ste 410 Washington DC 20036-1136

PIERCE, DEBORAH MARY, educational administrator; b. Charleston, W. Va. d. Edward Ernest and Elizabeth Anne (Trent) P.; m. Henry M. Armetta, Sept. 1, 1967 (div. 1981); children: Rosse Matthew Armetta, Stacey Elizabeth Pierce. Student, U. Tenn., 1956-59, Broward Jr. Coll., 1968-69; BA, San Francisco State U., 1977. Cert. elem. tchr., Calif. Pub. relations assoc. San Francisco Internat. Film Festival, 1965-66; account exec. Stover & Assocs., San Francisco, 1966-67; tchr. San Francisco Archdiocese Office of Cath. Schs., 1980-87; part-time tchr. The Calif. Study, Inc. (formerly Tchr's. Registry), Tiburon, Calif., 1988—; pvt. practice as paralegal San Francisco, 1989—; tchr. Jefferson Sch. Dist., Daly City, Calif., 1989-91. Author: (with Frances Spatz Leighton) I Prayed Myself Slim, 1960. Pres. Mothers Alone Working, San Francisco, 1966, PTA, San Francisco, 1979, Parent Tchr. Student Assn., San Francisco, 1984; apptd. Calif. State Bd. Welfare Cmty. Rels. Com., 1964-66; block organizer SAFE, 1996; active feminist movement. Named Model of the Yr. Modeling Assn. Am., 1962. Mem. People Med. Soc., Assn. for Rsch. and Enlightenment, A Course in Miracles, Commonwealth Club Calif, Angel Club San Francisco, San Diego Chat Club, Deepak Chopra 7 Spiritual Laws Group. Mem. Unity Christ Ch. Avocation: chess. Address: 3346 Taravel St San Francisco CA 94116 E-mail: deborahmpierce@hotmail.com. *Personal philosophy: We are living in the most exciting time on the planet. We must realize we are all one! As we achieve that one-to-one peace our planet will reflect a world peace. Planet Earth at peace.*

PIERCE, DIANE JEAN, artist; b. Evanston, Ill., Apr. 9, 1952; d. Kenneth William and Marjorie J. (Hansen) P.; m. William Carry Reuling, Sept. 8, 1991 (div. July 1992). BFA in Drawing and Painting, U. Utah, 1976. Illustrator Ensign Mag., Salt Lake City, 1977-79, Scott Foresman & Co. Pubs., Glenview, Ill., 1980, Children's Press, Chgo., 1981-82; mansion artist Adnan-Khoshagi's Devereaux Mansion, Salt Lake City, 1984-87; illustrator Friend Mag./Era Mag., 1978-80; artist-painter Lido Gallery, Park City, 1990-93, Thomas Charles Gallery, Las Vegas, Nev., 1994, Art Dimensions Gallery, Hollywood, Calif., 1994-96, Meyer Gallery, Park City, Utah, 1996-98; with Don Huntsman Gallery, Aspen, Colo., 1999—2001; artist Winter Olympics, Park City, Utah, 2002. Apprentice photographer Reynel Salgado Mirando, 1980 Elections, Acapulco, Mexico, 1980; juror exhbn. com. Alliance Gallery, Salt Lake Art Ctr., 1984, 85, invitational artist, fundraiser for Town and Country magazine: Women in Need, N.Y., 1998. Exhibited in group shows at New Genre, 1985, 5 Star Auction Invitational, 1985, Springville Nat. Salon, 1985, Utah Women Artists, 1985, Chase Mansion Guthrie Artists Show, 1986, Guthrie Artists, 1986, NAD, 1986, Eccles Art Ctr., 1986, 1987, Women's Show, 1987, 1989, 1991, 1993, Park City Open Painting Competition, 1989—90, 1993, Mus. Art, Alliance Gallery, Chase Mansion, Salt Lake Art Ctr., Tivoli Gallery, Cliff Lodge Gallery, U. Utah Mus. Art, Devereaux Mansion, 1984—87, Utah divsn. Assn. Women Artists traveling show, 1989—90, 100 Yrs.-100 Women traveling show, N.Y.C., 1989—91, Springville Mus. Art, 1992, Nat. Assn. Women ann. nat. competition, 1993, Janet Dumbar Interiors, Sun Valley, Idaho, 1991—93, Lido Gallery, 1990—93, Elouises' Interiors, Park City, Utah, 1993—98, Thomas Charles Gallery, 1994, Art Dimensions Gallery, 1994—96, Springville Mus. Art nat. competition, Art Space, 1995, Gallery Stroll, 1995, Nat. Assn. Women Artists ann., Soho, N.Y., 1995, Nat. Assn. Women Artists, Athens, Greece, 1996, NAWA NY Soho Show, 1999, Springville Mus. Natl. 75th April Salon, 1999—2000, Soho Nat. Assn. Women Artists, 1999, Represented in permanent collections Girl Scouts Hdqs., Salt Lake City, Profl. Figure Skaters Hdqs., Sun Valley, Springville Mus. Art, Moonie & O'Conner, Cin., Van Cott, Bagley, Cornwall & McCarthy, Salt Lake City, also pvt. collections; contbr. color plates , color plates in, articles to profl. jours. Recipient Art Dirs. award, Era Mag., 1979, Dirs. award, U. Utah Statewide Competition, Springville Mus. Fine Art, 1987, Best of Show, Eccles Statewide Competition, Ogden Utah, 1987, Best Traditional Painting, Nat. Assn. U. Women, Utah divsn., Ogden, 1989, Best of Show, Open Painting Exhbn., Kimball Art Ctr., Park City, Utah, 1989, 3rd pl. open painting competition, Kimball Art Ctr, 1990, Visual Merchandising & Design Mag. award, Designer Excellence, 1990, Best of Show open painting exhbn, Kimball Art Ctr., Park City, 1993, award of merit, Springville Mus. Fine Art, 1995; grantee, Artists Fellowship, Inc., N.Y.C., 1993. Mem. Nat. Assn. Women Artists (N.Y. chpt., Susan Kahn award 1987), Nat. Mus. Women in Arts.

PIERCE, DONALD SHELTON, retired orthopedic surgeon, educator; b. Castine, Maine, May 21, 1930; s. Frederick Ernest and Jeannie (Emmet) P.; m. Janet Ten Broeck, Dec. 29, 1956; children: Donald Shelton, Stanton ten Broeck, Frederick Ernest, Jennifer Emmet. AB cum laude, Harvard U., 1953, MD, 1957. Diplomate Am. Bd. Spine Surgery, Am. Bd. Orthop. Surgery. Intern U. Hosp., Cleve., 1957-58, resident, 1958-62; rsch. assoc. biomechanics lab. U. Calif., San Francisco, 1962-64; practice medicine specializing in orthopedic surgery, 1962-64; instr. orthopedic surgery U. Calif. Med. Sch., 1962-64, Harvard Med. Sch., 1964-66; clin. and rsch. assoc. J.P. Kennedy Jr. Meml. Hosp., Brighton, Mass., 1964-66; clin. assoc. in orthopedics Harvard Med. Sch., 1966-67, clin. asst. prof. orthopaedic surgery, 1979-87, clin. assoc. prof., 1987-2000; ret., 2000; sr. orthopedic surgeon Mass. Gen. Hosp., Boston. Chief dept. rehab. medicine Mass. Gen. Hosp., Boston, 1965-72, assoc. orthopedic surgeon, 1969—, vis. orthopedic surgeon, 1969—; lectr. dept. mech. engring. MIT, 1970-72. Co-author: Amputees and Their Porstheses, 1971; author: The Total Care of Spinal Cord Injuries, 1977; contbr. articles in field to profl. jours. Pres. Wellesley (Mass.) Friendly Aid Assn., 1965-67, dir., 1967-70; dir. Family Svc. Counseling Region West, Wellesley, 1965-67; exec. com., task force chmn., adv. bd. Mass. State Rehab. Planning Commn., 1966-68. With USAF, 1951-52. Fellow ACS, Am. Acad. Orthopedic Surgeons, Royal Soc. Health, Pan Am. Med. Assn., Soc. Internat. Chirurgerie, Ortopaedie et Traumatologie; mem. Othopedic Rsch. Soc., Am. Orthopaedic Assn., NRC (musculosbeletal com.), Cervical Spine Rsch. Soc. (pres. 1986), Fedn. Spine Assns. (pres. 1987), N.E. Med. Assn. (pres.). Home: 22 Lathrop Rd Wellesley MA 02482

PIERCE, ELIZABETH GAY, civic worker; b. N.Y.C., Mar. 26, 1907; d. Martin and Julia (Stone) Gay; AB, Barnard Coll., 1929; m. William Curtis Pierce, June 19, 1929; children: Martin Gay, Elizabeth Gay Pierce Fuchs, Josiah. Vol. worker Boston City Hosp., 1929-30, Community Service Soc., N.Y.C., 1931-32; mem. dependent children's sect. Welfare Council, N.Y.C., 1939-40; chmn. house com. North Shore Holiday House, Huntington, L.I., 1944, pres., 1945; co-chmn. thrift shop com. Knickerbocker Hosp., N.Y.C., 1957-64; mem. exec. com. of women's com. Legal Aid Soc., N.Y.C., 1958-59; mem. Women's Aux. Knickerbocker Hosp. (exec. com. 1960-64); adv. trustee Maine Citizens for Hist. Preservation, 1983-87; trustee Jones Mus. Ceramics and Glass, 1985-89. Mem. Soc. Colonial Dames in State N.Y. (bd. mgrs., 1962-67, corr. sec. N.Y. 1965-67, pres. 1967-70), Nat. Soc. Colonial Dames Am. (pres. 1972-76, nat. pres.), Soc. for Preservation New Eng. Antiquities (Maine council, former chmn. Marrett House, exec. com.), Mayflower Soc. N.Y. (sec. 1985-88), Daus. Founders and Patriots, Nat. Grange (mem. exec. com.). Episcopalian. Club: Colony, Ch. (N.Y.C.), Cumberland Club (Portland, Maine). Home: RR 1 Box 5140 West Baldwin ME 04091-9736

PIERCE, GORDON CARL, retired architect; b. Atlanta, Oct. 27, 1918; s. Carl Freeman and Leola May (Staebler) P. BArch, Carnegie Mellon U., 1941. Registered architect, Pa. Owner Gordon C. Pierce AIA, Greensburg, Pa., 1953-93; ret., 1993. Chmn. Greensburg City Planning commn., 1974-93. Mem. Greensburg City Redevel. Authority, 1975-90, G0-Greensburg C.D. Corp., 1970-90. Mem. AIA, Pa. Soc. Architects, Hist. Preservation Trust. Republican. Methodist. Avocations: art, gardening, writing poetry. Home: RR 6 Box 1479 Mount Pleasant PA 15666-8810

PIERCE, HARVEY R. insurance company executive; Chmn., CEO Am. Family Ins. Group, Madison, Wis. Office: Am Family Ins Group 6000 American Pky Madison WI 53783-0001

PIERCE, HILDA (HILDA HERTA HARMEL), painter; b. Vienna, Austria; arrived in U.S., 1940; m. Herman J. Slutzky; 1 child Diana Rubin Daly (dec.). Student, Art Inst. Chgo.; studied with Oskar Kokoschka, Salzburg, Austria. Art tchr. Highland Park (Ill.) Art Ctr., Sandburg Village Art Workshop, Chgo., Old Town Art Ctr., Chgo.; owner, operator Hilda Pierce Art Gallery, Laguna Beach, Calif., 1981-85. Guest lectr. major art mus. and Art Tours, France, Switzerland, Austria, Italy, Mex., San Diego, 1998—2002, Russian river cruise and major art mus., St. Petersburg, Moscow, 1994; organizer, tchr. art appreciation class, San Diego; lectr. , Mexico, 2002. One-woman shows include Fairweather Hardin Gallery, Chgo., Sherman Art Gallery, Marshall Field Gallery, exhibited in group shows at Old Orchard Art Festival, Skokie, Ill., Union League Club, North Shore Art League, ARS Gallery, Art Inst. Chgo., Represented in permanent collections numerous pvt. and corp. collections, commision, ; contbr. articles to profl. jours.; featured (video) Survivors of the Shoa, Stephen Spielberg Found., 1996. Recipient Outstanding Achievement award, Chgo. Immigrants Svc. League. *An artist's most precious quality is curiosity. It has kept me young for many years, kept me searching, experimenting and never being complacent, in my life and my work.*

PIERCE, ILONA LAMBSON, educational administrator; b. Blackfoot, Idaho, Dec. 3, 1941; d. Merlin A. Wright and Loa (Adams) Lambson; m. Sherman D. Pierce, Mar. 19, 1960. IBM cert., LDS Bus. Coll., Salt Lake City, 1960; BS, U. Utah, 1969, MEd, 1974, EdD, 1978. Cert. elem. tchr., adminstrv. endorsement, Utah; cert. tchr. ESL, Utah; lic. real estate agt., Utah. Key punch operator Mountain Bell Telephone Co., Salt Lake City, 1960-61; key punch supr. Hercules Powder Co., Bacchus, Utah, 1961-66; tchr. Cottonwood Heights Elem. Sch., Jordan Sch. Dist., Sandy, 1969-74; tchr. Willow Canyon Elem. Sch., Jordan Sch. Dist., 1974-76; postdoctoral fellow, grad. rsch. asst. U. Utah, Salt Lake City, 1976-78; tchr. Silver Mesa Elem. Sch. Jordan Sch. Dist., Sandy, Utah, 1978-79, tchr. specialist, 1979-80, asst. prin. Mt. Jordan Mid. Sch., 1980-84, prin. Union Mid. Sch., 1984-86, dir. instrnl. media and bilingual edn., 1986-97; retired. Mem. Utah Network Ednl. TV, 1986—; chmn. tech. adv. bd., chmn. bd. dirs. Math. Engring. Sci. Achievement, 1989, bd. dirs., 1987—; treas. State Film Depository Consortium, 1986—; mem. Utah Info. Tech. Consortium, 1987—; mem. prin. mentor program Brigham Young U., 1986. Sch. dist. co-chmn. United Way, 1986—. Recipient recognition award Math Engring. Sci. Achievement, 1991, Valuable Svc. award Emergency Preparedness Action Com., 1988, Disting. Svc. award Utah Ednl. Libr. Media Assn., 1988. Mem. ASCD, Utah ASCD (bd. dirs., editor 1986-89), NEA (life), Utah Edn. Assn., J'rdan Edn. Assn., Alpha Delta Kappa (state treas. 1980-84, state pres. 1984-86), Delta Kappa Gamma. Avocations: fossil hunting, travel, reading. Home: 8895 S 540 E Sandy UT 84070-1728

PIERCE, JAMES CLARENCE, surgeon, educator; b. Huron, S.D., Aug. 5, 1929; s. Henry Montraville and Carrie Bernice (Matson) P.; m. Carol Sue Wilson, 1967; children: Henry MacDonald, Richard Matson, Elizabeth Gail. BA, Carleton Coll., 1951; MD, Harvard U., 1955; MS, U. Minn., 1963, PhD in Surgery, 1966. Diplomate: Am. Bd. Surgery. Surg. intern Peter Bent Brigham Hosp., Boston, 1955-56; surg. fellow U. Minn., 1959-66; instr. surgery Med. Coll. Va., Richmond, 1966, prof. surgery and microbiology, 1972-75; dir. Tissue Typing Lab., 1969-75; attending surgeon, dir. surg. research, dir. transplantation service St. Luke's Hosp. Center, N.Y.C., 1975-78; prof. surgery Columbia U., 1976, Ailsa Mellon Bruce prof. surgery, 1977-78; clin. prof. surgery Pa. State U. and, 1979-88; chmn. dept. surgery Geisinger Med. Center, Danville, Pa., 1979-90, chmn. emeritus, 1990—. Clin. prof. surgery Jefferson U., 1990—. Contbr. articles to profl. jours. Elder Presbyn. Ch. With M.C., USAF, 1957-59. NIH fellow, 1963-65; Royal Soc. Medicine Found. travelling fellow, 1971; James IV Assn. Surg. traveller, 1978 Mem. ACS (pres. Ctrl. Pa. chpt. 1981-82), Transplant Soc., Am. Soc. Transplant Surgeons, Ea. Surg. Soc., N.Y. Clin. Soc., Soc. Univ. Surgeons, Sigma Xi. Republican. Home: 1906 Red Ln Danville PA 17821-8415

PIERCE, JEFFREY PAUL, engineer; b. Burbank, Calif., Aug. 27, 1963; AS in Indsl. Tech., L.A. Valley Coll., 1984; BS in Indsl. Tech., Calif. State U., 1988. Cert. mfg. technologist, Calif. Producibility engr. Douglas Aircraft Co., Long Beach, Calif., 1987; methods engr. TRW Space and Defense Div., Redondo Beach, 1988—. Instr. Nat. Handicapped Sports and Recreation Assn. Mem. Soc. Mfg. Engrs., TRW Bicycle Club, TRW Wilderness Club. Avocations: alpine and cross country skiing, bicycling. Office: TRW One Space Park Blvd # R9/1885 Redondo Beach CA 90278-1071

PIERCE, JERRY EARL, business executive; b. Hindsdale, Ill., Aug. 3, 1941; s. Earl and Adeline A. (Zaranski) P.; m. Carol Louise Martin, Aug. 15, 1964; children: Patricia, Barbara, Linda. Bradley. BS, U. Ill., 1964. With R.R. Donnelley & Sons, Chgo., 1964-70, Western Pub. Co., Racine, Wis., from 1970, nat. pubs. sales mgr., from 1975. Pres. Pierce Sale Co., Inc., Restaurant Equipment World, Inc., Heat Transfer Engring. Inc.; chmn. bd. Tech Industries & Millwork, Inc., 1989-93; pres. B.J. Installation Co., Inc., 1989-91, ROI World Equipment, 1993—; v.p., sec. Savers Clubs Am., Inc.; v.p. Pierce Aviation, 2000—; bd. dirs. Goldenrod Br., Bankfirst Bank, Winter Park, Fla. Mem. Leadership Trust of Nat. Fedn. Ind Bus. 1st lt. U.S. Army, 1968—70.

Mem. Printing Industry Am., Sales and Mktg. Execs., Fla. Restaurant Assn., Food Svc. Cons. Soc., Food Equipment Distbrs. Assn. (bd. dirs. 1997-98), Nat. Bus. Aviation Assn., Interlachen Country Club (Winter Park, Fla.), Cleve. Advt. Club. Republican. Episcopalian. Achievements include patents for refrigeration-to-water utility cost control system; invention of E-Commerce business model. Home: 2639 Ultra Vista Dr Maitland FL 32751 Office: 2413 N Forsyth Rd Orlando FL 32807-6455 E-mail: jerry@rewonline.com.

PIERCE, LAWRENCE WARREN, retired federal judge; b. Phila., Dec. 31, 1924; s. Harold Ernest and Leora (Bellinger) Pierce; m. Wilma Taylor (dec.); m. Cynthia Straker, July 8, 1979; children: Warren Wood, Michael Lawrence, Mark Taylor. BS, St. Joseph's U., Phila., 1948, DHL, 1967; JD, Fordham U., 1951, LLD, 1982, Fairfield U., 1972, Hamilton Coll., 1987, St. John's U., 1990. Bar: N.Y. 1951, U.S. Supreme Ct. 1968. Civil law practice, N.Y.C., 1951—61; asst. dist. atty. Kings County, N.Y., 1954—61; dep. police commr. N.Y.C., 1961—63; dir. N.Y. State Divsn. for Youth, Albany, 1963—66; chmn. N.Y. State Narcotic Addiction Control Commn., 1966—70; vis. prof. criminal justice SUNY, Albany, 1970—71; dist. judge So. dist. U.S. Dist. Ct. , NY, 1971—81; judge U.S. Fgn. Intelligence Surveillance Ct., 1979—81, U.S. Ct. Appeals 2d Cir., 1981—95; ret., 1995. Dir. Cambodian ct. tng. project Internat. Human Rights Law Group, 1995. Past bd. dirs. CARE, Havens Fund. Soc., Lincoln Hall for Boys, S-R , NY, Cath. Interracial Coun., Practising Law Inst. Mem.: ABA (site evaluation com., sec. legal edn. 1996—98, alt. observer U.S. Mission to UN 1988—90), Coun. Fgn. Rels. Home: PO Box 2234 Sag Harbor NY 11963-0111

PIERCE, LISA MARGARET, telecommunications executive, product and market development manager, lecturer; b. Nyack, N.Y., June 2, 1957; d. William and Elizabeth Pierce. BA with honors, Gordon Coll., Wenham, Mass., 1978; MBA, Atkinson Sch., Salem, Oreg., 1982. Campaign mgr. Carter/Mondale, Manchester, Mass., 1976; investigator Dept. Social Svcs., Nyack, 1977-78; paralegal Beverly, Mass., 1978-79; campaign mgr. Reagan Presdl. Primary, Rockland County, N.Y., 1980; cons. Sidereal, Portland, Oreg., 1981-82; performance analyst Dept. Social Svcs., Pomona, N.Y., 1982; market analyst Momentum Techs., Parsippany, N.J., 1983; cons. Booz Allen & Hamilton, Florham Park, 1984, Deloitte-Touche, Morristown, 1985; market researcher, forecaster AT&T, Bedminster, 1985-87, asst. pvt. line product mgr., 1987-89. Integrated Svcs. Digital Network product mgr., 1989-93; dir. Telecom. Rsch. Assocs., St. Marys, Kans., 1994-98; v.p., rsch. leader Giga Info. Group, Cambridge, Mass., 1998—. Panelist, contbr. TeleComms. Assn., San Diego, Internat. Comm. Assn., Atlanta, Ea. Comm. Forum, N.Y., Nat. Engrng. Consortium, Chgo.; contbr. N.Y. State ISDN/Internat User's Group; feature commentator Nat. Pub. Radio (All Things Considered), 1999, Pub. Broadcasting Svc. (Nightly Bus. Report), 1999, 2000, MSNBC and CNBC, 1999, Radio Wall Street, 2000. Grantee in field. Mem. IEEE, Am. Mktg. Assn. (profl.), Am. Mgmt. Assn.

PIERCE, MARGARET HUNTER, government official; b. Weedsport, N.Y., June 30, 1910; d. Thomas Murray and Ruby (Sanders) Hunter; m. John R. Pierce, Nov. 4, 1950 (div. May 1959); 1 dau., Barbara Hunter Churchill. BA, Mt. Holyoke Coll., 1932; JD, N.Y. U., 1939. Bar: N.Y. bar 1941, D.C. bar 1958. Atty. Office Alien Property Custodian, Washington, 1942-43, 45, Office Solicitor, Dept. Labor, 1943-45, NLRB, 1946, 47-48; atty.-adviser U.S. Ct. Claims, 1947-48, 48-59, reporter decisions, 1959-68; commr. U.S. Indian Claims Commn., 1968-78; pvt. practice Washington, 1978—. V.p. Monday Night Musicales, Inc., 1995—. Mem. D.C. Bar Assn. (ct. claims com. 1958—, mil. law com. 1967), Fed. Bar Assn. (Indian law com. 1955—), ABA (sec. adminstrv. law-vets. com., mil. law com., immigration and nationality com.), Women's Bar Assn., Nat. Assn. Women Lawyers, Exec. Women in Govt., Bus. and Profl. Women (Cosmopolitan br.), Am. Women Composers, Zonta (Washington pres. 1977-78), Harvard Club (D.C.), Nat. Press Club Washington. Home: 3829 Garfield St NW Washington DC 20007-1319

PIERCE, MARIAN MARIE, writer, educator; b. Cleve., Mar. 7, 1959; d. William Moses and Thelma Lee Pierce. MFA, U. Iowa, 1996. Creative writing instr. Marylhurst (Oreg.) U., 1999—, UCLA Ext. Writer's Program, 2000—. Author short stories. Named Frederick Exley Fiction Competition Winner, GQ mag., 1995; fellow Paul Engle fellow, The Iowa Writers' Workshop, 1996—97, MacDowell Colony fellow, The MacDowell Colony, 1997. Personal E-mail: marian.pierce@juno.com.

PIERCE, MELVIN ANDREW, engineer; b. Portsmouth, Va., July 28, 1957; s. George Nathaniel and Ruth Mae Pierce; m. Margaret Ann Davis, Jan. 16, 1982; children: Nacheshia, Nathaniel. BSEE, Howard U., 1979, MSEE, 1983. Elec. engr. Naval Rsch. Lab., Washington, 1981-84; communications engr. Sci. Applications Internat., Vienna, 1984-86; prin. engr. Fairchild Space & Def. Co., Germantown, Md., 1986—. Member Mt. Sinai Missionary Soc., Washington, 1976—. Nat. Consortium for Grad. Degrees for Minorities fellow, 1978. Mem. IEEE. Baptist. Achievements include demonstration that thin film techniques can be used to fabricate a millimeter wave antenna which operates over 75-110 GHZ. Home: 1918 Virginia Ave Hyattsville MD 20785-3930

PIERCE, MORTON ALLEN, lawyer; b. Liberec, Czechoslovakia, June 25, 1948; m. Nancy Washor, Dec. 14, 1975; children: Matthew J., Nicholas L. BA, Yale Coll., 1970; JD, U. Pa., 1974; postgrad., Oxford U., 1974-75. Bar: N.Y. 1975. Assoc. Reid & Priest, N.Y.C., 1975-83, ptnr., 1983-86, Dewey Ballantine, N.Y.C., 1986—, vice-chmn., 2002—. Mem. mgmt. com. 1988—, chmn. corp. dept., 1999—, chmn., mergers and acquisitions group, 1990—, mem. exec. com., 2001—. Contbr. articles to profl. jours. Mem. ABA (chmn. subcom. on internat. securities matters 1985-91, adv. com. to fed. regulation of securities com. 1991—, task force on rev. of the fed. securities law 1991—), Assn. of the Bar of the City of N.Y. (securities law com. 1988-91, chmn. subcom. on securities and exch. commn. enforcement matters 1990-91); Internat. Bar Assn. (com. on securities transactions). Home: 188 E 76th St New York NY 10021-2826 Office: Dewey Ballantine LLP 1301 Ave Of The Americas New York NY 10019-6022

PIERCE, NATHANIEL FIELD, medical researcher, educator; b. Rudyard, Mich., July 27, 1934; s. Warren David and Mabel Field Pierce; m. Diane June Baxter; children: Shanti, Christopher. MD, U. Mich., 1958. Staff physician Pu-Li (Taiwan) Christian Hosp., 1960—61; resident coord. Johns Hopkins Internat. Ctr. for Med. Rsch. and Tng., Calcutta, India, 1966—68; asst. prof. medicine Johns Hopkins U. Sch. Medicine, Balt., 1968—72, assoc. prof. medicine, 1972—79, prof. medicine, 1979—; prof. internat. health Johns Hopkins Bloomberg Sch. Pub. Health, 1996—. Dir. divsn. infectious diseases Balt. City Hosp., 1970—85; short term cons. multiple assignments WHO, Geneva, 1971—82, Geneva, 1996—, chairperson sci. working group on bacterial enteric infections, 1983—85, rsch. coord. program for control of diarrhoeal diseases, 1985—90, sr. tech. advisor divsn. diarrhoeal and acute respiratory disease control, 1990—96; mem. cholera adv. com. Nat. Inst. Allergy and Infectious Diseases, NIH, Bethesda, Md., 1971—73, mem. U.S. cholera panel U.S.-Japan Med. Sci. Program, Md., 1972—76, chmn. U.S. cholera panel, US-Japan Med. Sci. Program, Md., 1977—84; rsch. assoc. Sir William Dunn Sch. Pathology, Oxford (Eng.) U., 1973—74; mem. adv. com. on health, biomed. R&D commn. on internat. rels. NAS, Washington, 1981—83; chairperson steering com. for the trial of pneumococcal conjugate vaccine in The Gambia Med. Rsch. Coun. Labs., Fajara, 1998—; chairperson internat. adv. com. for trial of pneumococcal conjugate vaccine in South Africa South African Inst. Med. Rsch., Johannesburg, 1998—. Contbr. chapters to books, articles to profl. jours. Mem.: Am. Soc. for Clin. Investigation, Infectious Diseases Soc. Am. (life). Episcopalian. Avocations: cabinet making, gardening. Office: Johns Hopkins Sch Pub Health 615 N Wolfe St Baltimore MD 21205 Business E-mail: npierce@jhsph.edu.

PIERCE, PAUL, basketball player; b. Oct. 13, 1977; s. Lorraine Hosey. Degree in crime and deliquency studies, Kans. State U., 1999. Profl. basketball player Boston Celtics, 1998—. Avocation: music. Office: Boston Celtics 151 Merrimac St # 1 Boston MA 02114-4714*

PIERCE, PHILIP SARGENT, clinical psychologist; b. Medford, Mass., Aug. 25, 1941; s. Elmer Grandville and Pauline Dudley Pierce; m. Rae Foster, Oct. 10, 1967; children: Jennifer, Jessica, John, Jill. BA, U. Maine, 1963; MA, U. N.H., 1965; PhD, U. S.C., 1971. Lic. psychologist, Maine. Clin. psychologist Pineland Ctr., Pownal, Maine, 1965-77, Togus (Maine) Vets. Med. and Regional Office Ctr., 1977-83, sr. psychologist, 1983—. Vis. prof. psychology U. So. Maine, Portland, 1971-72; asst. prof. psychology St. Joseph's Coll., North Windham, Maine, 1972-78, U. Maine, Augusta, 1977-78; clin. assoc. psychology U. Maine, Orono, 1981—; lectr. on psychology grad. program in sch. and health psychology U. New Eng., Biddeford Pool, Maine; adj. clin. faculty mem. Antioch New Eng. Grad. Sch., 1996—; cons., spkr., presenter in field; northeastern regional exam. coord. Am. Bd. Clin. Psychology, 1993-95, nat. credential rev. officer, 1995-97; mem. Am. Bd. Profl. Psychology, Inc. Contbr. numerous articles to profl. jours. Trustee Falmouth Congl. Ch., 1981-84, chmn. bd. trustees, 1983-84, sec. mem. giving and investments subcom., 1982-84, mem. Christian enlistment com., 1985-88, chmn., 1987-88, mem. nominations com., 1989-92, chmn. ch. coun., 1990-93, mem. bylaws com., 1994-97; bd. dirs. Falmouth Little League, 1984-90, coach, 1983-85, treas., 1984-90, umpire, 1983-93; bd. dirs. Maine Running Hall of Fame, 1994—, vice chmn., 1995-96, chmn., 1996—; bd. dirs. Maine Sports Hall of Fame, 1994—, 1st v.p., 1995—, chmn. honors and selection com., 1996—. With U.S. Army, 1966. Fellow APA (divsn. newsletter editor 1981-84, exec. bd. 1981-82, pres. 1985-86, chmn. fellow com. 1990-96, coun. of reps. 1977-79, coun. liaison to Maine psychol. Assn. 1995-97, coun. reps. for Maine and Vt., 1998-2001, chmn. rural caucus), Maine Psychol. Assn. (newsletter editor 1971-74, mem. exec. bd. 1971-88, pres. 1975-77, chmn. ethics com. 1992-98, policy coun. 1992—), Am. Psychol. Soc., Acad. Clin. Psychology (bd. dirs. 1993—, v.p. 1998—); mem. AAAS, N.Y. Acad. Sci., Assn. VA Chief Psychologists (chmn. gero-psychology task force 1983-84, chmn. APA-VA interaction task force 1984-85), Soc. Maine Psychologists (chmn. continuing edn. com. 1990-92, 98-2000, pres. 1992-94, treas. 1994-98), Maine Soc. Forensic Psychologists, Maine Track Club (sec. 1985-86, v.p. 1986-87, pres. 1987-88, race dir. 1984-97). Democrat. Avocation: long distance running. Home: 79 Waites Landing Rd Falmouth ME 04105 E-mail: philip.pierce@med.va.gov.

PIERCE, PHYLIS MISE, lawyer; b. Middlesboro, Ky., Aug. 25, 1937; d. Clabe M. and Gladys (Orr) Mise; m. John T. Pierce, Dec. 20, 1959; children: John, Mary. BA, Berea (Ky.) Coll., 1960; MA, Ea. Tenn. State U., 1973; JD, U. Tenn., 1980. Bar: Tenn., 1980. Atty. advisor Social Security Adminstrn., Kingsport, Tenn., 1980-84, supervisory atty. advisor, 1984-86; solo practice, 1986-88; atty. Social Security Adminstrn., Tenn., 1990-98, supervisory atty. advisor, 1998-2000, sr. atty., 2000—. Home: PO Box 3762 Kingsport TN 37664-0762 E-mail: ppierce@preferred.com.

PIERCE, PONCHITTA ANN, TV host, producer, journalist, writer, consultant; b. Chgo., Aug. 5, 1942; d. Alfred Leonard and Nora (Vincent) P. Student, Cambridge (Eng.) U., summer 1962; BA in Journalism cum laude, U. So. Calif., 1964; DHL, Franklin Pierce Coll., 1986. Asst. editor Ebony mag., 1964-65, assoc. editor, 1965-67; editor Ebony mag. (N.Y.C. office), 1967-68; chief N.Y.C. editl. bur. Johnson Pub. Co., 1967-68; corr. news divsn. CBS, N.Y.C., 1968-71; contbg. editor McCall's mag., 1971-77; editl. cons. Philps Stokes Fund, 1971-78; staff writer Reader's Digest, 1976-77, roving editor, 1977-80; co-prodr., host Today in New York, Sta. WNBC-TV, N.Y.C., 1982-87; freelance writer, TV broadcaster, media cons. Co-host Sunday WNBC-TV, 1973—77, The Prime of Your Life, 1977—80; author: Status of American Women Journalists on Magazines, 1968, History of the Phelps Stokes Fund 1911-1972; contbg. editor: Parade mag., 1993, Earth Times Monthly, 2002. Del. to WHO Conf., Geneva, 1973; bd. dirs. Morris-Jumel Mansion, Hirshhorn Mus. and Sculpture Garden, Xavier U. of La., Housing Enterprise for the Less Privileged, Third St. Music Sch. Settlement, Inner-City Scholarship Fund, Josephson Inst. Ethics, Marina del Rey, Sta. WNET-TV; mem. women's bd. Madison Sq. Boys and Girls Club; mem. Columbia Presbyn. Health Scis. Adv. Coun. Recipient Penney-Mo. mag. award excellence women's journalism, 1967; John Russwurm award N.Y.C. Urban League, 1968; AMITA Nat. Achievement award in communications, 1974 Mem. NATAS, Women in Comm. (Woman Behind the News award 1969, Nat. Headliner award 1970), Fgn. Policy Assn. (mem. bd. govs., bd. dirs.), Coun. on Fgn. Rels., Calif. Scholarship Fedn. (life), Econs. Club N.Y., Lotos Club, Nat. Honor Soc., Mortar Bd.

PIERCE, RICHARD HARRY, oceanographer; PhD in Chem. Oceanography, U. R.I., 1973. Sr. scientist, dir. Ctr. for Eco-Toxicology, Mote Marine Lab., Sarasota, Fla. Office: Mote Marine Lab 1600 Ken Thompson Pkwy Sarasota FL 34236-1096

PIERCE, RICHARD WILLIAM, lawyer; b. Detroit, Sept. 30, 1941; s. Donald Allen and Sarah Elizabeth (Giffen) P. BA, Ohio Wesleyan U., 1963; JD, Northwestern U., 1966. Bar: Mich. 1971, U.S. Dist. Ct. (ea. dist.) Mich. 1971, U.S. Ct. Appeals (6th cir.) 1984. Assoc. Tinkham, Snyder & MacDonald, Wayne, Mich., 1967-68; asst. pros. atty Washtenaw County, Ann Arbor, 1968-70; ptnr. Ellis, Talcott & Ohlgren, 1971-82; sole practice, 1982—. Bd. dirs. Ann. Arbor Area Coun. Internat. Bus., 1984—87. Mem.: Am. Immigration Lawyers Assn. (chmn. I.N.S. liaison com. 1997—99), Washtenaw County Bar Assn. (pres. 1976—77), Mich. Bar Assn. (chmn. dist. H. subcom. character and fitness 1984—93). Presbyterian. Avocations: tennis, jogging. Office: 709 W Huron St Ste 200 Ann Arbor MI 48103-6705

PIERCE, ROBERT RAY, secondary education educator; b. Bryan, Tex., May 15, 1962; m. Gina Annette Sneed, Aug. 13, 1983; children: Taylor, Preston. BA, U. Tex., Arlington, 1983. Cert. tchr., Tex. Sci. tchr. Canyon Vista Mid. Sch., Austin, Tex., 1984-86; tchr. biology, anatomy and physiology Duncanville (Tex.) H.S., 1986-2000; tchr. biology and advanced placement biology Whitney (Tex.) H.S., 2000—. Cons. Ready For the World Edn., Duncanville, 1995—. Author motivational program Earning and Learning, Inc., 1994. Advisor Whitney H.S. Habitat for Humanity; youth sports coach, Whitney. Recipient Tchr. of Yr. award Tex. Med. Assn., 2001. Mem. Am. Physiology Soc., Human Anatomy and Physiology Soc., Tex. Assn. Biology Tchrs., Nat. PTA (Nat. Educator of Yr. 1995). Avocations: Motocross,travel, cmty. youth sports coach. E-mail: piercerr@whitney.isd.tenet.edu.

PIERCE, ROY, political science educator; b. N.Y.C., June 24, 1923; s. Roy Alexander and Elizabeth (Scott) P.; m. Winnifred Poland, July 19, 1947 PhD, Cornell U., 1950. Instr. govt. Smith Coll., Northampton, Mass., 1950-51, asst. prof., 1951-56; asst. prof. polit. sci. U. Mich., Ann Arbor, 1956-59, assoc. prof., 1959-64, prof., 1964-94, prof. emeritus, 1993—. Vis. prof. Columbia U., 1959, Stanford U., 1966, U. Oslo, 1976, Ecole des Hautes Etudes en Sciences Sociales, Paris, 1978 Author: Contemporary French Political Thought, 1966, French Politics and Political Institutions, 1968, 2d edit., 1973, (with Philip E. Converse) Political Representation in France, 1986, Choosing the Chief: Presidential Elections in France and the United States, 1995. Served with USAF, 1943-46 Mem. Am. Polit. Sci. Assn. (co-winner Woodrow Wilson Found. award 1987, George H. Hallett Book award 1996). Office: Inst for Social Rsch U Mich Ann Arbor MI 48106 E-mail: tetons@umich.edu.

PIERCE, SHAHEEDA LAURA, midwife, consultant; b. Jersey City, Apr. 13, 1959; d. Lawrence Everett Pierce and Mary Dean Applegate Swing; m. James Shuffield, May 28, 1994; children: Juniper, Rama, Jasmine, Elijah, Jamila, Tara. AAS, Pima Coll., 1984. Cert. paralegal, cmty. meditation svcs., dance leader Dances Universal Peace; cert. profl. midwife. Pvt. practice mediation and paralegal svcs., Tucson, 1991-95, 96-98, Maui, Hawaii, 1995-96, Silver City, N.Mex., 1998-99, Vashon Island, Wash., 1999—. Nat. coord. group Movement For A New Soc., Phila., 1982-83; bd. dirs. Food Conspiracy Cooperative, Tucson, 1993-95; steering com. S.W. Sufi Cmty., Silver City, 1994-95, bd. dirs., 1995-97; midwife, holistic health cons. Author: Recipes for the New Children, 1978; contbr. articles to profl. jours.; creator (bd. game) The Healing Game of Life, 1993; composer (musical album on cassette) Full Moon Woman, 1994; co-coord., disc jockey weekly women's radio program KXCI Cmty. Radio, Tucson, 1983. Active Georgians Against Nuc. Energy, Atlanta, 1980-81; organizer Nuc. Free State, Tucson, 1981-82; draft counselor Daring Disarmers, Phila., 1982. Recipient Ordinary Extraordinary Women's award, 1982. Mem. N.Mex. Midwives Assn., Ariz. Assn. Midwives (co-coord. AHCCCS reimbursement task force 1997-98), Midwives' Alliance Hawaii, Washington Alliance Rural Midwives. Avocations: art, music, dance, nature.

PIERCE, SHELBY CRAWFORD, management and oil industry consultant; b. May 26, 1932; s. William Shelby and Iris Mae (Smith) Pierce; m. Marguerite Ann Grado, Apr. 2, 1954; children: Cynthia Dawn, Melissa Carol. BSEE, Lamar U., Beaumont, Tex., 1956; grad. program for sr. execs., MIT, 1980. With Amoco Oil Co., Texas City Refinery, 1956—, elec. engr., elec. foreman, area foreman, 1956—60, zone supr., gen. foreman, maintenance, 1961—67, oper. supt., 1967—69, coord. results mgmt., 1969—72; dir. results mgmt. Amoco Oil Co. Corp. Hdqs., Chgo., 1972-75; mgr. ops. Amoco Oil Co., Whiting Refinery, Ind., 1975—76, asst. refinery mgr., 1977-79; dir. crude replacement program Amoco Oil Co. Corp. Hdqs., Chgo., 1979-81, mgr. corp. refining and transp. engrng., 1981-92, gen. mgr. engrng. and constrn., 1992, v.p. internat. bus. devel., 1993-94, ret., 1994. Pres., dir. Amoco Eurasia Oil Co., Amoco Mex. Oil Co., Amoco India, Inc., Amoco Tech. Assistance Co., Trinidad; chmn., dir. Amoco Orient Oil Co.; v.p. Amoco Corp. Devel. Co., Latin Am., 1994; pres. Pierce Cons. Svc., 1995—; CEO, pres. Environ. Constrn. Co., 1996—98; mem. steering com. contractor safety U.S. Dept. Labor, 1989. Trustee Lamar U. Found., 1994—. Mem.: AIChE (mem. exec. bd. 1985—89, chmn. engrng. constrn. contracting divsn. 1988, Divsn. Man of Yr. award 1995), N.W. Ind. Bus. Roundtable (organizer and user coun. chmn. 1986, chmn. exec. bd. 1986—87), The Bus. Roundtable (constrn. com., adv. bd., chmn. constrn. cost effectiveness task force 1992—94), Constrn. Industry Inst. (chmn. Bus. Roundtable coun., mem. strategic planning com. 1991—93), Flossmoor Country Club, Sigma Tau. Republican. Methodist. Home and Office: 1715 Brookwood Dr Flossmoor IL 60422-1823 Fax: (708) 957-4995. E-mail: ShelbyPierce@msn.com.

PIERCE, SIDNEY K., JR. biology educator, department chair; b. Holyoke, Mass., Sept. 19, 1944; s. Sidney K. and Mary Elizabeth Pierce; m. Christine Elizabeth Pierce, Aug. 5, 1974; children: Alisa, Michael. EdB, U. Miami, Fla., 1966; PhD, Fla. State U., 1970. Asst. prof. U. Md., College Park, 1970-73, assoc. prof., 1973-78, prof. dept. biology, 1978-99, prof., chmn. dept. biology, 1997-99; prof. emeritus, 1999—; prof., chmn. dept. biology U. South Fla., Tampa, 2000—. Program dir. NSF, Washington, 1987-89; assoc. dir. agrl. exptl. sta. U. Md., 1987-89. Co-author: Illustrated Invertebrate Anatomy, 1985; mem. editl. bd. Biol. Bull., Marine Biology, Jour. Exptl. Zoology, News in Physiologic Sci., Comparative Biochemistry and Physiology. Fellow AAAS; mem. Am. Physiol. Soc., Soc. Integrative and Comparative Biology. Office: Dept Biology SCA 110 U South Fla 4202 E Fowler Ave Tampa FL 33620-8000

PIERCE, THRESIA KORTE (TISH PIERCE), primary school educator; b. Maize, Kans. d. Herman and Marie Adeline (Lubbers) Korte; children: Judith, John, Mark. BS, Friends U., 1955; MS, U. Nev., Las Vegas, 1978. Cert. tchr., Nev., Nev. Life Ins. lic. Office worker Internat. Trust Co., Denver, 1951, Motor Equipment Co., Wichita, Kans., 1952-53; tchr. Wichita Pub. Schs., 1960-69, Clark County Sch. Dist., Las Vegas, Nev., 1970-2000. Author numerous short stories; contbr. acticles to profl. jours. Senator Clark County Edn. Assn., Clark County Classroom Tchrs. Mem. NEA, Epsilon Sigma Delta (v.p. 1962). bd. dirs. Kansas Newman U., Wichita, 1966-68. Home: 3105 Cardinal Dr Las Vegas NV 89121-2204

PIERCE, VERLON LANE, pharmacist, small business owner; b. Greensburg, Ky., July 13, 1949; s. Ogle Lee and Aleene (Hall) P.; m. Brenda Mildred Russell, May 20, 1973; children: Amanda Lee, Daniel Russell. BS in Math. and Chemistry, Western Ky. U., 1972; BS in Pharmacy, U. Ky., 1975. Relief pharmacist Shugart & Willis Drug Store, Franklin, Ky., 1975-78; staff pharmacist Franklin Simpson Meml. Hosp., Franklin, 1976-79; owner, pres. pharmacist Medicine Shoppe, Bowling Green, Ky., from 1978; now with ind. pharmacy Medicine Arts Pharmacy; pres. Westland Drug Inc., Bowling Green, 1984-89; pres. JP Solutions, Inc., DBA Option Care, 1988—; sec. 21st Investment Group, Bowling Green, 1984— . Bd. dirs. Bowling Green Mcpl. Utilities, 1998. Recipient Franny award Internat. Franchise Assn., 1980; Hall of Fame bust Medicine Shoppe, St. Louis, 1983. Mem. 4th Dist. Pharmacy Group (pres. 1983-84), Ky. Pharmacy Assn., Masons, Shriners. Democrat. Baptist. Avocations: golf, swimming. Home: 1414 Mount Ayr Circle Bowling Green KY 42103-4709 Office: Medicine Arts Pharmacy 818 US 31W Byp Bowling Green KY 42101-2314

PIERCE, WILLIAM RANDOLPH, secondary education educator; b. St. Louis, May 28, 1952; s. John Caldwell and Vincenza Friel Pierce; m. Rebecca Berry, July 22, 1978; children: Abigail, Caitlin. BS in Edn., U. Mo., 1974; MA in Speech, Bradley U., 1977. Tchr. Pattonville H.S., Maryland Heights, Mo., 1974—. Recipient Outstanding Tchr. award Speech Theatre Assn. Mo., 1996, E.A. Richter Citizenship Edn. award Mo. Bar Adv. Com., 1997, Loren Reid Svc. award Speech Theatre Assn. Mo., 1999; inductee Nat. Forensic League Hall of Fame, 2002. Mem. Nat. Forensic League (Disting. Svc. key 1989, Disting. Svc. plaque 1993, 96, 2000, 5-Diamond coach 2001), Nat. Comm. Assn., Nat. Debate Coaches Assn., Mo. State H.S. Activities Assn. (speech adv. com. 1984—), Greater St. Louis Speech Assn. (debate coord. 1983—). Avocations: traveling, running, military history. Home: 464 Redwood Forest Dr Manchester MO 63021 Office: Pattonville HS 2497 Creve Coeur Mill Rd Maryland Heights MO 63043 E-mail: randebate@aol.com.

PIERCE, WILLIAM SCHULER, cardiac surgeon; b. Wilkes-Barre, Pa., Jan. 12, 1937; s. William Harold and Doris Louis (Schuler) P.; m. Peggy Jayne Stone, June 12, 1965; children: William Stone, Jonathan Drew. BS, Lehigh U., 1958; MD, U. Pa., 1962. Intern U. Pa., 1962—63; resident in surgery Hosp. U. Pa., 1963—70; asst. prof. M.S. Hershey Med. Ctr., Pa. State U. Coll. Medicine, Hershey, 1970—73, assoc. prof., 1973—77, prof. surgery, 1977—, chief divsn. cardiothoracic surgery, 1991—95; assoc. chmn. dept. surgery, dir. rsch., dept. surgery, 1995—97. Contbr. With USPHS, 1965—67. Fellow: ACS; mem.: AAAS, AMA, Soc. Clin. Surgery., Am. Surg. Assn., Soc. Univ. Surgeons, So. Pa. Assn. Thoracic Surgery, Inst. Medicine, Assn. Acad. Surgery, Am. Heart Assn., Soc. Vascular Surgery, Am. Soc. Artificial Internal Organs, Internat. Cardiovascular Soc. Achievements include invention of inventor cardiac valve, blood pump. Office: Milton S Hershey Med Ctr PO Box 850 Hershey PA 17033-0850 E-mail: wpierce@psu.edu.

PIERCY, GORDON CLAYTON, bank executive; b. Takoma Park, Md., Nov. 23, 1944; s. Gordon Clayton and Dorothy Florence (Brummer) P.; m. Roberta Margaret Walton, 1985; children: Elizabeth Anne, Kenneth Charles, Virginia Walton, Zachary Taylor Walton. BS, Syracuse U., 1966; MBA, Pace U., 1973. Mgmt. trainee Suburban Bank, Bethesda, Md., 1962-66; mktg. planning assoc. Chem. Bank, N.Y.C., 1966-70; sr. market devel. officer Seattle-First Nat. Bank, 1970-74; product expansion adminstr., mktg. planning mgr. VISA, Inc., San Francisco, 1974-76; v.p., dir. mktg. Wash. Mut. Savs. Bank, Seattle, 1976-82; v.p., mktg. dir. First Interstate Bank of Wash. N.A., 1983-86; sr. v.p. mktg., dir. Puget Sound Nat. Bank, Tacoma, 1986-92; sr. v.p., dir. mktg. and sales Key Bank, 1993-94; dir. corp. sales KIRO-TV, Inc., 1994; sr. v.p., dir. mktg. and sales Pacific Northwest Bancorp, Oak Harbor, 1994—; pres. Whidbey Western Railroad, 1995—. Mem. Bank Mktg. Assn., Mktg. Comm. Exec. Internat., Pacific Railcar Operators (pres.), Ctrl. Whidbey Lions, Island County Econ. Devel. Assn., Wash. Bankers Assn. (mktg. com.), S.W. Railcar Ltd. (exec. com.), Motorcar Operators West, Sigma Nu, Alpha Kappa Psi, Delta Mu Delta. Episcopalian. Home: 750 N Snowberry Ln Coupeville WA 98239-3110 Office: Pacific Northwest Bancorp PO Box 1649 Oak Harbor WA 98277-1649

PIERCY, MARGE, poet, novelist, essayist; b. Detroit, Mar. 31, 1936; d. Robert Douglas and Bert Bernice (Bunnin) P.; m. Ira Wood, 1982. AB, U. Mich., 1957; MA, Northwestern U., 1958. Instr. Gary extension Ind. U., 1960-62; poet-in-residence U. Kans., 1971; disting. vis. lectr. Thomas Jefferson Coll., Grand Valley State Colls., fall 1975, 76, 78, 80; vis. faculty Women's Writers Conf., Cazenovia (N.Y.) Coll.; Elliston poetry fellow U. Cin., 1986. DeRoy Disting. vis. prof. U. Mich., 1992; adv. bd. mem. FEMSPEC; adv. bd. mem. Eastern Mass. Abortion Fund. Author: Breaking Camp, 1968, Hard Loving, 1969, Going Down Fast, 1969, Dance the Eagle to Sleep, 1970, Small Changes, 1973, To Be of Use, 1973, Living in the Open, 1976, Woman on the Edge of Time, 1976, The High Cost of Living, 1978, Vida, 1980, The Moon is Always Female, 1980, Braided Lives, 1982, Circles on the Water, 1982, Stone, Paper, Knife, 1983, My Mother's Body, 1985, Gone to Soldiers, 1988, Available Light, 1988 (May Sarton award 1991), Summer People, 1989, He, She and It, 1991, Body of Glass, 1991 (Arthur C. Clarke award 1993), Mars and Her Children, 1992, The Longings of Women, 1994, Eight Chambers of the Heart, 1995, City of Darkness, City of Light, 1996, What Are Big Girls Made Of?, 1997 (Notable Book award ALA 1997), Storm Tide, 1998, The Art of Blessing the Day, 1999, Early Grrrl, 1999, Three Women, 1999, (with Ira Wood) So You Want to Write: How to Master the

Craft of Writing Fiction and the Personal Narrative, 2001, Sleeping With Cats, A Memoir, 2002; editor Leapfrog Press, 1997—; poetry editor Lillith, 1999--; author of poetry. Cons. N.Y. State Coun. on Arts, 1971, Mass. Found. for Humanities and Coun. on Arts, 1974; mem. Writer Bd., 1985-86; bd. dirs. Transition House, Mass. Found. Humanities and Pub. Policy, 1978-85, Am. ha-Yam, 1988-98, v.p., 1995-96; gov.'s appointee to Mass. Cultural Coun., 1990-91, Mass. Coun. on Arts and Humanities, 1986-89; artistic adv. bd. ALEPH Alliance for Jewish Renewal, Am. Poetry Ctr., 1988—; lit. adv. panel poetry NEA, 1989. Recipient Borenstone Mountain Poetry award, 1968, 74, Lit. award Gov. Mass. Commn. on Status of Women, 1974, Nat. Endowment of Arts award, 1978, Carolyn Kizer Poetry prize, 1986, 90, Shaeffer-Eaton-PEN New Eng. award, 1989, Golden Rose Poetry prize, 1990, Brit ha-Dorot award The Shalom Ctr., 1992, Notable Book award, 1997, Paterson poetry prize, 2000. Mem.: NOW, PEN, Am. Poetry Soc., Writers Union, Authors League, Authors Guild, Citizens for the Preservation of Wellfleet, Mass. Audubon Soc., New Eng. Poetry Club. Address: PO Box 1473 Wellfleet MA 02667-1473

PIERIK, MARILYN ANNE, retired librarian, piano teacher; b. Bellingham, Wash., Nov. 12, 1939; d. Estell Leslie and Anna Margarethe (Onigkeit) Bowers; m. Robert Vincent Pierik, July 25, 1964; children: David Vincent, Donald Lesley. AA, Chaffey Jr. Coll., Ontario, Calif., 1959; BA, Upland (Calif.) Coll., 1962; cert. in teaching, Claremont (Calif.) Coll., 1963; MSLS, U. So. Calif., L.A., 1973. Tchr. elem. Christ Episcopal Day Sch., Ontario, 1959-60; tchr. Bonita High Sch., La Verne, Calif., 1962-63; tchr., libr. Kettle Valley Sch. Dist. 14, Greenwood, Can., 1963-64; libr. asst. Monrovia (Calif.) Pub. Libr., 1964-67; with Mt. Hood C.C., Gresham, Oreg., 1972-98, reference libr., 1983-98, chair faculty scholarship com., 1987-98, campus archivist, 1994-98; ret., 1998; pvt. piano tchr. Gresham, 1998—. Pvt. piano tchr., 1998; mem. site selection com. Multnomah County (Oreg.) Libr., New Gresham br., 1987, adv. com. Multnomah County Libr., Portland, Oreg., 1988-89; bd. dirs. Oreg. Episcopal Conf. of Deaf, 1985-92. Bd. dirs. East County Arts Alliance, Gresham, 1987-91; vestry person, jr. warden St. Luke's Episc. Ch., 1989-92; vestry person St. Aidan's Episcopal. Ch., 2000—; founding pres. Mt. Hood Pops, 1983-88, orch. mgr., 1983-91, 93—, bd. dirs., 1983-88, 91—. Recipient Jeanette Parkhill Meml. award Chaffey Jr. Coll., 1959, Svc. award St. Luke's Episcopal Ch., 1983, 87, Edn. Svc. award Soroptimists, 1989. Mem. AAUW, NEA, Oreg. Edn. Assn., Oreg. Libr. Assn., ALA, Gresham Hist. Soc. Avocations: music, reading. E-mail: pierikm@teleport.com.

PIERLUISI, PEDRO R. lawyer; b. San Juan, P.R., Apr. 26, 1959; s. Jorge A. and Doris (Urrutia) Pierluisi; children: Anthony, Michael, Jacqueline, Rafael. BA , Tulane U., 1981; JD, George Washington U., 1984. Bar: D.C. 1984, U.S. Dist. Ct. D.C. 1985, U.S. Ct. Appeals (D.C. cir.) 1985, P.R. 1990, U.S. Dist. Ct. P.R. 1990, U.S. Supreme Ct. 1990, U.S. Ct. Appeals (1st cir.) 1993. Assoc. Verner, Liipfert, Bernhard, McPherson & Hand, Washington, 1984—85, Cole, Corette & Abrutyn, Washington, 1985—90; ptnr. Pierluisi Pierluisi & Mayol-Bianchi, San Juan, 1990—93; atty. gen. Govt. of P.R., 1993—96; ptnr. O'Neill & Borges, San Juan, 1997—. Mem.: ABA (ho. of dels. 1995—96, standing com. on substance abuse 1995—98, coordinating com. on gun violence 1998—2001, state membership chair 2000—), Am. Arbitration Assn. (arbitrator), Nat. Assn. Securities Dealers (arbitrator), George Washington U. Internat. Law Soc. (pres. 1982—83), Nat. Assn. Attys. Gen. (chair ea. region 1996), Puerto Rico Homebuilders Assn. (bd. dirs. 1999—), N.Y. Stock Exch. (arbitrator), Phi Alpha Delta (hon.; Munoz chpt.). Avocation: jogging. Office: O'Neill & Borges 250 Ave Munoz Rivera Am Internat Plz San Juan PR 00918-1808

PIERONI, ROBERT EDWARD, internist, educator, military officer; b. Portland, Maine, June 20, 1937; s. Ansel Kirby and Agnes Mary (Dumais) P.; m. Dorothy Louise McDonnell, Oct. 3, 1970; children: Michelle Kirby, Robert Francis. BS, Boston Coll., 1959; MD, Pa. State U., 1971. Diplomate Am. Bd. Internal Medicine, Am. Bd. Family Practice, Am. Bd. Allergy and Immunology, Am. Bd. Quality Assurance, Am. Bd. Geriatric Medicine. Chemist Mass. Dept. Pub. Health, Boston, 1962-71, sr. bacteriologist, 1971-74; asst. prof. internal medicine U. Ala., Tuscaloosa, 1974-76, assoc. prof. dept. internal medicine and family practice, 1976-81, prof. internal medicine and family practice, 1981—; enlisted U.S. Army, 1961, advanced through grades to col., 1981. Prior cons. VA Hosp., Tuscaloosa, T. Hardin Med. Facility and Partlow State Hosp., Tuscaloosa, 1974—; cons. FDA, Dept. Def. Contbr. more than 250 textbooks, articles, chpts. and abstracts; mem. editl. bd. various jours. Decorated Bronze Star, 1991, Commendation for Valor; recipient Golden Stethoscope award, 1982, Faculty Recognition award, 1986, Ala. Golden Eagle Humanitarian award Ala. Sr. Citizens Hall of Fame, 1988 and Physicians award, 1998, Wright A. Garner scientist award Ala. Acad. Sci., 1997. Mem. AMA, ACP, Am. Coll. Allergy, Asthma and Immunology, Am. Geriatric Soc., Gerontol. Soc. Am., Am. Acad. Family Physicians, Physicians for Human Rights, VFW, Am. Legion. Democrat. Roman Catholic. Avocations: mountain trekking, scuba diving, studying medical and military history, reading. Home: 398 Riverdale Dr Tuscaloosa AL 35406-1814 Office: U Ala Dept Internal Medicine PO Box 870326 Tuscaloosa AL 35487-0001

PIERPOINT, KAREN ANN, marriage, family and child therapist; b. Puyallup, Wash., Sept. 1, 1944; d. Peyton Randolph Winn and Jessie Mae (Kenoyer) Kalmen; m. Randall Dean Pierpoint, Mar. 19, 1966; children: Janet, Wendy, Elizabeth, Nathan. BA, U. Oreg., 1966; MS in Counseling, San Diego State U., 1988. Lic. marriage, family and child counseling, Calif. Elem. tchr. Lane County Dist. 4, Eugene, Oreg., 1966-67, Umatilla County Dist. 19-R, Weston, 1967-70; internat. student ministry staff mem. Campus Crusade for Christ, Internat., San Bernardino, Calif., 1970-75; dir. Christian edn. Graeagle (Calif.) Community Ch., 1975-83; dir. women's ministries Pine Valley (Calif.) Community Ch., 1983-87; lectr. counselor edn. dept. San Diego State U., 1988-89; mental health cons. San Diego City Schs., 1988-89; staff therapist Heartland Bibl. Counseling, El Cajon, Calif., 1987-90, Shepperson Psychol. Assocs., Fullerton, 1990-91; pvt. practice family therapist Brea, 1992—. Ednl. cons. New Life Acad. Home Edn., San Diego, 1984-90; allied profl. Coastal Communities Hosp., Costa Mesa, 1991; allied health profl. Yorba Hills Hosp., Yorba Linda, Calif., 1991, Calif. Psychiat. Ctr., Santa Ana, 1992-95; profl. provider Ocean Hills Med. Group, 1996-97. Columnist Free Indeed Mag., 1976-78. 4-H club leader Mohawk Valley 4-H Club, Plumas County, Calif., 1976-83, Mt. Empire 4-H Club, San Diego County, Calif., 1984-87; 4-H club advisor Mohawk Valley 4-H Club, Plumas County, 1982-83. Named for 4-H Ten Yrs. of Leadership, Mt. Empire 4-H Club, 1986. Mem.: Am. Assn. Christian Counselors, Christian Assn. for Psychol. Studies (clin.), Am. Acad. Experts in Traumatic Stress (clin.), Am. Assn. Marriage and Family Therapy (clin.), Calif. Assn. Marriage and Family Therapists (clin.), Brea C. of C., Phi Kappa Phi. Republican. Avocations: reading, classical and folk music, writing, travel, sewing. Office: 749 S Brea Blvd Ste 43 Brea CA 92821-5388

PIERPONT, ROBERT, fund raising executive, consultant; b. Somers Point, N.J., Jan. 27, 1932; s. Robert E. and Elise D. (White) P.; m. Marion J. Welde, Oct. 11, 1958; children: Linda J. Staropoli, Nancy P. Oler, Robert W., Richard F. BS in Bus. Adminstrn, Pa. Mil. Coll., 1954; postgrad. Inst. Ednl. Mgmt, Harvard Grad. Sch. Bus. Adminstrn., 1970. Comml. sales rep. Atlantic City (N.J.) Electric Co., 1956-58; asst. dir. devel. Widener U. (formerly Pa. Mil. Coll.), Chester, 1958-61, asst. to pres., 1961-62, dir. devel., 1962-68, v.p. for devel., 1968-70; sr. cons. v.p. and dir. Brakeley, John Price Jones, Inc., N.Y.C., 1970-79; v.p. devel. Mt. Sinai Med. Center, 1979-85; ptnr. Pierpont & Wilkerson, 1986—. Guest faculty mem. Big 10 Fund Raisers Inst., Mackinac Island, Mich., 1971; mem. adv. com. on application of standards Philanthropic Adv. Service, Council of Better Bus. Burs., Washington, 1978-81; faculty The Fund Raising Sch., Ctr. on Philanthropy, Ind. U., 1989—. Mem. bishops adv. com. on stewardship Diocese of Pa., 1968-69; vestryman Trinity Episcopal Ch., Swarthmore, 1970-72; trustee Putnam Valley Free Libr., 1986-92; pres. Roaring Brook Lake Property Owners Assn., 1995—. Recipient Alumni Svc. award Widener U., 1989; named Disting. Alumnus in Econs., Widener U., 1986. Mem. Nat. Soc. Fund Raising Execs. (dir.-at-large 1970-78, pres. found. 1977-79, chmn. bd. 1979-82, chmn. cert. bd. 1982-87, presdl. search com. 1989, mem. ethics com. 1993-97, chmn. 1993-95). Office: The Stone House PO Box 179 1111 Route 9 Garrison NY 10524-3203

PIERPONT, ROSS Z. former surgeon; b. Woodlawn, Md., Sept. 7, 1917; s. Edwin Lowell and Ethel Celeste (Zimmerman) P.; m. Grace Schmidt, Feb. 5, 1942; 1 child, Christine Pierpont von Kiencke; m. Lippold von Kiencke. BS in Pharmacy, U. Md., 1937, MD, 1940. Diplomate Am. Bd. Surgery. Intern Md. Gen. Hosp., Balt., 1940-41; resident in surgery Balt. City Hosps., 1941-44, U. Iowa, Iowa City, 1944-45; asst. clin. prof. emeritus U. Md. Pres. PSCI Internat. Healthcare; cons. pres. Gempro Internat. Mfg. of Healthcare Supplements. Author: Indicted, 1982, Towson & The Tax Cap, 1991, Health Care System for USA "Its Not the Health Care it's the Health Care System Stupid", 1999, (autobiography) Never Never Ever Give Up, 2001. Bd. dirs. Heritage Found., Washington, 1995; mem. Empower Am., Washington, 1996; Rep. nominee U.S. Senate (Md.), 1998; chmn. adv. bd. Rep. Nat. Com.; active Rep. Senatorial Inner Cir.; candidate for Gov. of Md., 2002. Fellow ACS; mem. AMA, Soc. Am. Gastrointestinal and Endoscopic Surgeons, Kiwanis Internat. Republican. Methodist. Home: 215 Belmont Forest Ct Unit 408 Lutherville Timonium MD 21093-7792 E-mail: rzpierpont@aol.com.

PIERRE, CHRISTOPHE, mechanical engineer, educator, academic administrator; b. Lorient, France (incl. Monaco), Feb. 12, 1959; s. Gilbert Pierre, Madeleine Pierre; m. Myriam Simon; children: Hélène, Adrien. Diplôme d'Ingénieur, Ecole Centrale de Paris, Chatenay-Malabry, France, 1982; MS, Princeton U., 1983; PhD, Duke U., 1985. Assoch. chmn. mech. engring. U. Mich., Ann Arbor, Mich., 1996—99, prof. mech. engring., 1997—2002, Stephen P. Timoshenko Collegiate prof. mech. engring., 2002—02, assoc. dean Sch. Grad. Studies, 1999—2002. Assoc. dir. Automotive Rsch. Ctr., U. Mich., Ann Arbor, 1994—2002. Recipient Exxon Found. award, U. Mich., 1986. Fellow: ASME; mem.: AIAA, Am. Acad. Mechanics. Office: U Mich 3112 GG Brown Bldg Ann Arbor MI 48109-2125 Office Fax: 734-763-2447. Business E-Mail: pierre@umich.edu.

PIERRE, JOSEPH HORACE, JR. commercial artist; b. Salem, Oreg., Oct. 3, 1929; s. Joseph Horace and Miriam Elisabeth (Holder) Pierre; m. June Anne Rice, Dec. 20, 1952 (dec. June 2001); children: Joseph Horace III, Thomas E., Laurie E., Mark R., Ruth A.; m. Luverne Melba Starnes, Jan. 9, 2002. Grad., Advt. Art Sch., Portland, Oreg., 1954, Inst. Comml. Art, 1951-52. Lithographic printer Your Town Press, Inc., Salem, Oreg., 1955-58; correctional officer Oreg. State Correctional Instn., 1958-60; owner Illustrators Workshop, Inc., Salem, 1960-61; advt. mgr. North Pacific Lumber Co., Portland, 1961-63; vocat. instr. graphic arts Oreg. Correctional Instn., 1963-70; lithographic printer Lloyd's Printing, Monterey, Calif., 1971-72; illustrator McGraw Hill, 1972-73; owner Publishers Art Svc., Monterey, 1972-81; correctional officer Oreg. State Penitentiary, 1982-90; ret. Owner Northwest Syndicate, 1993—. Editor/publisher: The Pro Cartoonist & Gagwriter; author: The Road to Damascus, 1981, The Descendants of Thomas Pier, 1992, The Origin and History of the Callaway and Holder Families, 1992; author numerous OpEd cols. in Salem, Oreg. Statesman Jour., others; pub. cartoons nat. mags.; mural Mardi Gras Restaurant, Salem; cartoon strip Fabu, Oreg. Agr. mo. Mem. Rep. Nat. Com., Citizens Com. for Right to Keep and Bear Arms. Served with USN, 1946-51. Decorated victory medal WWII, China svc. medal, Korea medal, Navy occupation medal. Mem. U.S. Power Squadron, Nat. Rifle Assn., Acad. of Model Aeronautics, Oreg. Correctional Officers Assn. (co-founder, hon. mem.), Four Corners Rod and Gun Club. Republican. Avocations: sailing, flying, scuba, model aircraft building and flying. Home: 4822 Oak Park Dr NE Salem OR 97305-2931 E-mail: joe@joepierre.com.

PIERRE, NATASHA UNADA, accountant; b. San Fernando, Trinidad, June 14, 1973; d. Cleto Salazar Jamie and Leonora Shirley Pierre. BS, Jersey City State U., 1994; MBA, Seton Hall U., 1998. Acctg. specialist Prudential Ins. Co. Am., Newark, 1994—; sr. internat. analyst Nat. Starch & Chem. Co., Bridgewater. Roman Catholic. Avocations: travel, track and field.

PIERRE, PERCY ANTHONY, university president; b. nr. Donaldsville, La., Jan. 3, 1939; s. Percy John and Rosa (Villavaso) P.; m. Olga A. Markham, Aug. 8, 1965; children: Kristin Clare, Allison Celeste. BSEE, U. Notre Dame, 1961, MSEE, 1963, D of Engring. (hon.), 1977; PhD in Elec. Engring, Johns Hopkins U., 1967; postgrad., U. Mich., 1968; DSc (hon.), Rensselear Poly. Inst. Asst. prof. elec. engring. So. U., 1963; instr. Johns Hopkins U., Balt., 1963-64; instr. physics Morgan State Coll., 1964-66; instr. info. and control engring. U. Mich., Ann Arbor, 1967-68; instr. systems engring. UCLA, 1968-69; research engr. in communications RAND Corp., 1968-71; White House fellow, spl. asst. Office of Pres., 1969-70; dean Sch. Engring., Howard U., Washington, 1971-77; program officer for engring. edn. Alfred P. Sloan Found., 1973-75; asst. sec. for research, devel. and acquisition U.S. Dept. Army, 1977-81; engring. mgmt. cons., 1981-83; pres. Prairie View (Tex.) Agrl. and Mech. U. System, 1983-89, Honeywell prof. elec. engring., 1989-90; v.p. rsch. and grad. studies Mich. State U., East Lansing, 1990-95, prof. elec. enging., 1995—. Dir. engring. coll. council Am. Soc. for Engring. Edn., 1973-75; mem. sci. adv. group Def. Communications Agy., 1974-75; mem. adv. panel Office Exptl. Research and Devel. Incentives, NSF, 1973-74; mem. Commn. Scholars To Rev. Grad. Programs, Ill. Bd. Higher Edn., 1972-74; mem. panel on role U.S. engring. sch. in fgn. tech. assistance, 1972, co-chmn. symposium on minorities in engring., 1973; mem. rev. panel for Inst. for Applied Tech., Nat. Bur. Standards, 1973-77; chmn. com. on minorities Nat. Acad. Engring., 1976-77; cons. to dir. Energy Rsch. and Devel. Adminstrn., 1976-77; mem. Army Sci. Bd., 1984; mem. adv. bd. Sch. Engring., Johns Hopkins U., 1981-84; cons. Office Sec. Def., 1981-84; mem. adv. bd. Lincoln Labs., MIT. Contbr. articles on communications theory to profl. publs. Trustee U. Notre Dame, 1974-77, 81—; trustee, mem. exec. com. Nat. Fund for Minority Engring. Students, 1976-77; bd. dirs. The Hitachi Found., 1987, Ctr. for Naval Analysis, 1986, Assn. Tex. Colls. and Univs.; pres. Southwest Athletic Conf., 1985-87, bd. dirs. CMS Corp., 1990—, Defense Sci., 1992-94, Old Kent Fin. Corp., 1993—, bd. trustee Aerospace Corp., 1991—. Recipient Disting. Civilian Service award Dept. Army, 1981; award of merit from Senator Proxmire, 1979. Mem. IEEE (sr. mem.; Edison award com. 1978-80), Sigma Xi, Tau Beta Pi. Home: 2445 Emerald Lake Dr East Lansing MI 48823-7256 Office: Mich State U 357 Engineering East Lansing MI 48824-1226

PIERRE-BENOIST, JEAN (BARON DE VAUBUZIN), retired international trade specialist; b. N.Y.C., July 22, 1947; s. Yves Maurice and Madeleine (Maillet) P.; m. Matilde Eugenia Pefaur Fernández, Sept. 8, 1973; children: Angélique Madeleine, Jean-Louis Réginald, Paul-Michel Théodore. BA, Am. U., 1973, MA, 1982. Analyst C.W.W., Inc., Alexandria, Va., 1977-80; staff economist U.S. Dept. Agr., Washington, 1980-82; internat. trade analyst U.S. Internat. Trade Commn., 1982-99; retired, 1999. V.p., dir. mktg. intelligence Latin Am. Cons., Inc., 1984-85; with PBM Enterprises, Vienna, Va., 1970-92. Contbr. articles to profl. jours. Project leader and sec. 4-H, 1985-88; scoutmaster, mem. com. French Speaking Scouts of Washington, 1975-89, St. Dominic's Ch.; eucharistic minister 3d Order of Preachers, mem. coun. French-speaking Parish of Washington, 1984-87. With USAF, 1964-68, Vietnam. Mem. NRA (life), VFW (life), Thai-Laos-Cambodia Brotherhood, Am. Legion, Isaak Walton League. Republican. Roman Catholic. Avocations: fishing, hunting, archery, motorcycling. Home: 103 Elmar Dr SE Vienna VA 22180-5803 E-mail: j.pierrebenoist@verizon.net.

PIERRE-LOUIS, ROSAIRE, elementary school educator, educator; b. North Miami, Fla., U.S., Jan. 10, 1972; d. Brenord and Genevieve (Cantave) Duclona; m. Pierre-Louis, Jan. 28, 1999; children: Brittany, Kasidy. AA, Miami Dade CC; BA, St. Thomas U., Miami; MA, Novasoutheastern Univ. Tchr. Miami Skill Ctr., Fla., substitute tchr. Mailing: 14899 NE 18th Ave #4A North Miami FL 33181 E-mail: Rosairerоro@aol.com.*

PIERRI, MARY KATHRYN MADELINE, cardiologist, educator, emergency physician, educator; b. N.Y.C., Aug. 12, 1948; d. Charles Daniel and Margaret Loyola (Pesce) P. BA, Manhattanville Coll., 1969; MD, Med. Coll. Pa., 1974. Diplomate Am. Bd. Cardiology. Med. resident Med. Coll. Pa., Phila., 1974-77; fellow in cardiology N.Y. Hosp., N.Y.C., 1977-79; asst. physician Meml. Hosp., 1980-89, assoc. physician, 1989-97, chief cardiology svc., 1991—2002, attending physician, 1997—. Assoc. prof. medicine Cornell Med. Coll., 1989—97, prof. clin. medicine, 1997—. Fellow Am. Coll. Cardiology, N.Y. Cardiological Soc.; mem. ACP, Soc. Critical Care Medicine, Alpha Omega Alpha. Office: Meml Hosp Sloan Kettering Cancer Ctr 1275 York Ave New York NY 10021-6094

PIERRO, RICHARD SALVATORE, electrical engineer; b. N.Y.C., Nov. 17, 1944; s. Carmine and Elvira (Coccetti) Pierro; m. Diana Zannella, June 6, 1970; children: Richard C, Christopher T. BEE, NYU, 1965, MSEE, 1967. Radar rsch. engr. United Technologies Corp.-Norden Sys., Norwalk, Conn., 1967-72; sr. radar sys. engr. Sperry Rand Corp.-Def. Products Group, Great Neck, N.Y., 1972-86; owner, engring. cons. Rivere Radar Cons. Co., Bayville, 1986-97; sr. prin. sys. engr. Raytheon-Electronic Systems, Bedford, Mass., 1997-99; mem. corp. sr. staff Tech. Svc. Corp., Trumbull, Conn., 1999—. Mem.: IEEE (sr.), Eta Kappa Nu. Roman Catholic. Achievements include invention of Probability Density Function Gen; Low Angle, Air-Ground Ranging Radar. Avocations: health, fitness, sports, music, collectibles. E-mail: richard.s.pierro@ieee.org., rspierro@optonline.net.

PIERSKALLA, WILLIAM PETER, university dean, management-engineering educator; b. St. Cloud, Minn., Oct. 22, 1934; s. Aloys R. and Hilda A. Pierskalla; m. Carol Spargo, Children: Nicholas, William, Michael. AB in Econs., Harvard U., 1956, MBA, 1958; MS in Math., U. Pitts., 1962; PhD in Ops. Rsch., Stanford U., 1965; MA, U. Pa., 1978. Assoc. prof. Case Western Res. U., Cleve., 1965-68, So. Meth. U., Dallas, 1968-70; prof. dept. indsl. engrng. and mgmt. scis. Northwestern U., Evanston, Ill., 1970-78; exec. dir. Leonard Davis Inst., U. Pa., Phila., 1978-83; prof., chmn. health care sys. dept. U. Pa., 1982-90, prof. decision sci. and systems engring., dep. dean acad. affairs Wharton Sch., 1983-89, Ronald A. Rosenfield prof., 1986-93; dir. Huntsman Ctr. Global Competition and Leadership U. Pa. Wharton Sch., 1989-91; John E. Anderson prof. UCLA, 1993—, dean John E. Anderson Grad Sch. Mgmt., 1993-97. Cons. HHS, Bethesda, Md., 1974-87, MDAX, Chgo., 1985-91, MEDICUS, Evanston, 1970-75, Sisters of Charity, Dayton, Ohio, 1982-83, Project Hope, 1990—; bd. dirs., chmn. The Bush Found.;bd. dirs. No. Wilderness Adventures, Office Tenants Network, Informs. Contbr. articles to various publs. Mem. adv. bd. Lehigh U., 1986-93, U. So. Calif. Bus. Sch., 1987-93; regent St. Mary's Coll., 1998-2001, Hong Kong U. Sci. and Tech., 1992—. Recipient Harold Larnder Meml. prize Can. Oper. Rsch. Soc., 1993; grantee NSF, 1970-83, HHS, Washington, 1973-82, Office Naval Rsch., Arlington, Va., 1974-77. Mem. Ops. Rsch. Soc. Am. (pres. 1982-83, editor 1979-82, Kimball Disting. Svc. medal 1989), Inst. Mgmt. Scis. (assoc. editor 1970-77), Internat. Fedn. Operational Rsch. Socs. (pres. 1989-91), Inst. for Ops. Rsch. and Mgmt. Scis. (v.p. for publs. 2000—), Omega Rho. Office: UCLA Anderson Grad Sch Mgmt 110 Westwood Plz Box 951481 Los Angeles CA 90095-1481

PIERSOL, ALLAN GERALD, engineer; b. Pitts., June 2, 1930; s. Robert James and Irene Laticia (Dematty) P.; m. Gertrud Teresia Moller, June 8, 1958; children: Allan Gerald Jr., Marie Theresa, John Robert. BS in Engring. Physics, U. Ill., 1952; MS in Engring., U. Calif., 1961. Lic. profl. engr., Calif. Rsch. engr. Douglas Aircraft Co., Santa Monica, Calif., 1952-59; mem. tech. staff Ramo Wooldridge Corp., Canoga Park, 1959-63; v.p. Measurement Analysis Corp., Santa Monica, 1963-71; prin. scientist Bolt Beranek and Newman, Inc., Conoga Park, 1971-85; sr. scientist Astron Corp., Santa Monica, 1985-88; lectr. U. So. Calif., L.A., 1965—95; sole proprietor Piersol Engring., Woodland Hills, Calif., 1988--. Co-author: Measurement and Analysis of Random Data, 1966, Random Data: Analysis and Measurement Procedures, 1971, 86, 2000, Engineering Application of Correlation and Spectral Analysis, 1980, 93, Shock and Vibration Handbook, 2002. Mem. ASME, Inst. Environ. Scis. (Irwin Vigness meml. award 1991), Acoustical Soc. Am. Achievements include a patent for a method and apparatus for determining terrain surface profiles. Home: 23021 Brenford St Woodland Hills CA 91364-4830 Office: Piersol Engring Co 23021 Brenford St Woodland Hills CA 91364-4830

PIERSOL, LAWRENCE L. federal judge; b. Vermillion, S.D., Oct. 21, 1940; s. Ralph Nelson and Mildred Alice (Millette) P.; m. Catherine Anne Vogt, June 30, 1962; children: Leah C., William M., Elizabeth J. BA, U. S.D., 1962, JD summa cum laude, 1965. Bar: S.D. 1965, U.S. Ct. Mil. Appeals, 1965, U.S. Dist. Ct. S.D. 1968, U.S. Supreme Ct. 1972, U.S. Dist. Ct. Wyo. 1980, U.S. Dist. Ct. Nebr. 1986, U.S. Dist. Ct. Mont. 1988. Ptnr. Davenport, Evans, Hurwitz & Smith, Sioux Falls, S.D., 1968-93; judge U.S. Dist. Ct., 1993—; chief judge Dist. of S.D., 1999—. Mem. budget com. chair, economy sub com., Jud. Conf. U.S.; chmn. tribal ct. com., security com. 8th Cir. Jud. Coun.; editor-in-chief Law Review. Majority leader S.D. Ho. of Reps., Pierre, 1973-74, minority whip, 1971-72; del. Dem. Nat. Conv., 1972, 76, 80; S.D. mem. del. select commn. Dem. Nat. Com., 1971-75. Mem. ABA, State Bar S.D., Fed. Judges Assn. (bd. dirs., v.p.). Roman Catholic. Avocations: reading, running, painting, mountaineering. Office: US Dist Ct 400 S Phillips Ave Sioux Falls SD 57104-6824

PIERSON, ALBERT CHADWICK, business management educator; b. Pierson, Ill., Jan. 3, 1914; s. Charles Clevel and Gertrude Fannie (Gale) P.; 1 stepchild, Jay F. Lynch. BA in Liberal Arts and Scis, U. Ill., 1935; MBA with distinction, Harvard U., 1947; PhD, Columbia U., 1963. Merchandiser Montgomery Ward & Co., Chgo., 1935-41; mgmt. cons. N.Y.C., 1947-53; prof. mgmt. San Diego State U., San Diego State U., 1954—. Cons. in field; pub. accountant, Calif.; research editor Jour. Travel Research, 1967— Author: Trends in Lodging Enterprises, 1939-1963, 1963. Chmn. bd. Nat. Arts Found., N.Y.C.; mem. accreditation vis. teams Am. Assembly Collegiate Schs. Bus., 1977— . Served to col. AUS, 1941-46. Decorated Bronze Star. Fellow Soc. Applied Anthropology; mem. Acad. Mgmt. (pres. Western div. 1974-75), Western Council Travel Research (dir. 1965-67), Acad. Internat. Mgmt., Mil. Logistics Soc., James Joyce Soc., Beta Gamma Sigma, Sigma Iota Epsilon, Tau Sigma. Clubs: Harvard (Chgo.); Columbia (N.Y.C.); Marine Corps Officers (San Diego). Democrat. Methodist. Home: 1245 Park Row La Jolla CA 92037-3706 Office: San Diego State U Coll Bus San Diego CA 92182-0096

PIERSON, ANNE BINGHAM, physician; b. N.Y.C., June 9, 1929; d. Woodbridge and Ursula Wolcott (Griswold) Bingham; m. Richard N. Pierson Jr., July 10, 1954 (div. Aug. 1974); children: Richard N. III, Olivia Tiffany Jacobs, Alexandra deForest Griffin, Cordelia Stewart Comfort Smela; m. Richard Taliaferro Wright, Nov. 25, 1978 (div. Sept. 1997); m. Paul H. Altrocchi, May 9, 1998. Student, Katharine Branson Sch., Ross, Calif., 1943-47; BA, Vassar Coll., 1951; MD, Columbia U., 1955, MPH, 1972. Intern Lenox Hill Hosp., N.Y.C., 1955-56; substitute internship AUH, Beruit, Lebanon, 1955; mem. staff 7th Day Adventist Hosp., Taipei, Taiwan, 1957; clinic physician, med. dir. Planned Parenthood of Bergen County, Hackensack, N.J., 1960-74, also bd. dirs., 1966-69; asst. clin. prof. dept. ob-gyn. Columbia U. Coll. Physicians and Surgeons, Internat. Inst. Study of Human Reproduction, 1972-74; med. dir. Memphis Assn. for Planned Parenthood, Inc., 1974-75; staff physician N.Y. Telephone Co., 1976-87; med. dir. Planned Parenthood Assn. Hudson County, 1976-79; physician Sonalysts, Waterford, Conn., 1988—. Mem. nat. med. adv. com. Planned Parenthood-World Population, 1966-69. Pres. Vassar Class 1951, 1986-91; artist mem. Clinton Art Soc., 1989—, East Lyme Art League, 1991—; active Jr. League, 1964-69, sustainer, 1969—. Mem. AMA (Physicians Recognition award 1973—), Nat. Soc. Colonial Dames (life, asst. sec. 1991-94, 2d v.p. 1994-97), Cosmopolitan Club, Lyme Art Assn. (treas. 1998-99, pres. 1999—), Mystic Art Assn., Essex Art Assn. Office: Sonalysts 215 Parkway N Waterford CT 06385-1209

PIERSON, DOUGLAS H. special education educator; b. Newark, Jan. 24, 1951; s. John Henry and Isabella Davie (Ferguson) P. BE cum laude, Boston State Coll., 1975; MEd cum laude, Fitchburg (Mass.) State Coll., 1977, Keene (N.H.) State Coll., 1985; EdD, Clark U., 1993. Tchr. Concord State Prison, Boston, 1975-79; elem. prin. and tchr. Conval Sch. Dist., Peterborough, N.H., 1979-88; instr. spl. edn. Clark U., Worcester, Mass., 1987-89; tchr. emotionally disturbed Nazareth Home for Boys, Leicester, 1988-89; ednl. supr. Eagle Hill Sch., Hardwick, 1989-92; asst. prin. Ware (Mass.) Elem. Sch., 1992-93; prin. North Lincoln Elem. Sch. and St. James Elem. Sch., Lincoln, R.I., 1993-98, Hamilton Elem. Sch., North Kingston, 1998—. With USN, 1969-71. Named R.I. Elem. Prin. of Yr., 2001; named Nat. Disting. Prin., 2001. Mem. ASCD, NAESP, Coun. Exceptional Children, Nat. Assn. Edn. Young Children, R.I. Assn. Sch. Prins., Kappa Delta Pi. Home: 19 S River Dr Narragansett RI 02882-2700 E-mail: ride2223@ride.ri.net.

PIERSON, EDWARD JOSEPH, JR. business executive; b. Tarrytown, N.Y., Mar. 30, 1948; s. Edward J. and Louise P.; m. Martha Webster Ayers, Apr. 12, 1973; children: Mark Andrew, Eric James. BS in Fin., Boston Coll., 1970; MBA in Fin., Fordham U., 1977. Officer Nat. Bank of Westchester, White Plains, N.Y., 1971-76, Marine Midland Bank, N.Y.C., 1976-78; v.p. Mellon Bank, Pitts., 1979-86, Chase Manhattan Bank, N.Y.C., 1986-92; ptnr. Accord Group/JohnsonSmith & Knisely, Inc., 1992-98; pres., exec. resourcing divsn.

TMP Worldwide (formerly Accord Group/JohnsonSmith & Knisely), 1998—. Mem. bd. chmn. Chase Trade Inc., N.Y.C., 1988-92; bd. dirs. NCITD-Trade Facilitation Coun., N.Y.C., 1991-92. Vol. United Fund of Westfield, N.J., 1987-92. Mem. Coll. Men's Scholarship Club. Republican. Avocations: tennis, golf, carpentry. Home: 42 Sacramento St Cambridge MA 02138-1931 Office: TMP Worldwide Exec Resourcing Divsn 225 Franklin St Fl 17 Boston MA 02110-2804

PIERSON, EDWARD SAMUEL, engineering educator, consultant; b. Syracuse, N.Y., June 27, 1937; s. Theodore and Marjorie O. (Bronner) P.; m. Elaine M. Grauer, June 6, 1971; 1 child, Alan. BS in Elec. Engring., Syracuse U., 1958; SM, MIT, 1960, ScD, 1964. Asst. prof., fellow MIT, 1965-66; assoc. prof., assoc. dept. head U. Ill., Chgo., 1966-75; program mgr. Argonne Nat. Labs., Ill., 1975-82; head dept. engring. Purdue U. Calumet, Hammond, Ind., 1982-95, spl. asst. to chancellor for environ. programs, 1995—. Cons. Argonne Nat. Lab., 1972-75, 82-93, Solmecs Corp., 1982-88, HMJ Corp., Washington, 1983-88, LM Mfg., 1994—. Contbr. articles to profl. jours. NSF fellow, 1958-60 Mem. IEEE, ASME, Am. Soc. Engring. Edn. Office: Purdue U Calumet Hammond IN 46323 E-mail: pierson@calumet.purdue.edu.

PIERSON, JEFFREY LYNN, protective services officer; m. Sara A. Scorr, 1969; children: Christine, Jennifer, Jeffrey Jr. BS in Pub. Adminstrn., Roger Williams U., 1997; M in Adminstrv. Scis., Fairleigh Dickinson U., 2001; grad., Army War Coll., Command and Gen. Staff Coll., Field Artillery Basic and Advanced Officers Course. Staff, commd. U.S. Army Nat. Guard, 1961—85; asst. dep. chief of staff tng. Hdqs. Fourth U.S. Army, 1985—88; exec. officer Hdqs. 50th Armored Divsn. Art., 1988—89, G3, 1989—91; mobilization readiness officer, 1991—93; dir. Mil. Personnel Office, 1993; chief of staff, asst. adj. gen. N.J. Dept. Mil. Vet. Affairs, 1993—99; undersheriff correctional divsn. Cape May County (N.J.) Sheriff's Office, 1999—. Spkr. in field on leadership, mgmt. and weapons of mass destruction; adj. prof. Fairleigh Dickinson U. Dep. chief safety and tng. Marmora Vol. Fire Co.; past. pres. Marmora Vol. Fire Dept., v.p. Ret. brigadier gen. U.S. Army, NG, N.J. Mem. Am. Correctional Assn., Am. Jail Assn., NJ Jail Wardens Assn., Fairleigh Dickinson U. Alumni Assn., Army War Coll. Alumni, Roger Williams U. Alumni, Masons (Cannon Lodge # 104 F&AM, past master). Avocations: golf, jogging, basketball, softball. Office: Cape May County Correctional Ctr 4 Moore Rd Cape May Court House NJ 08210

PIERSON, JOHN THEODORE, JR. manufacturer; b. Kansas City, Mo., Oct. 13, 1931; s. John Theodore and Helen Marguerite (Sherman) P.; m. Susan K. Chadwick, Apr. 16, 1977; children by previous marriage— Merrill Sherman, Karen Louise, Kimberly Ann. BSE., Princeton U., 1953; MBA, Harvard U., 1958. With Vendo Co., Kansas City, Mo., 1960—, gen. automatic products salesman, 1960-61, mgr. new products, 1961-63; v.p. sales equipment for Coca-Cola, 1963-66; pres. Vendo Internat., 1966-69, exec. v.p., chief operating officer, 1969-71, pres., chief exec. officer, 1971-74; pres. Preco Industries, Inc., 1976-97, chmn., 1997—. Chmn. Internat. Trade and Exhbn. Ctr. Co-author: Linear Polyethylene and Polypropylene: Problems and Opportunities, 1958. Trustee Midwest Rsch. Inst.; bd. dirs. and chmn. MidAm. Mfg. Tech. Ctr.; bd. dirs. Johnson County Bus. Tech. Ctr., Youth Symphony Kansas City, 1965-69; past trustee Pembroke-Country Day Sch., Barstow Sch.; past mem. adv. coun. U.S.-Japan Econ. Rels. Coun.; mem. coun. chmn. for exploring Boy Scouts Am., mem. Nat. coun. Lt. M.I. USNR, 1953-56. Mem. Kansas City C. of C., U.S. C. of C. (dir. 1970-74), River Club (pres. 1994-96), Kansas City Country Club. Home: 2801 W 63rd St Shawnee Mission KS 66208-1866 Office: 9705 Commerce Pkwy Lenexa KS 66219-2403

PIERSON, JUANITA (NITA PIERSON), secondary school educator; b. Shreveport, La., Oct. 28, 1921; d. Henry and Rodessa (Scott) Thomas; m. Floyd Allen Pierson, Sept. 18, 1938; children: Annette Marilyn Pieson Poulard, Frederick Allen. Student, U. Md., 1965-66, Centennary Coll., 1967-68, So. U. Coll., 1967-69, Prairie View A&M U., 1969-70, Santa Clara U., 1974; BA, Wiley Coll., 1954; MS, La. Tech., 1975; postgrad., Northwestern U., 1972-74; D (hon.), Shreveport Bible Coll., 1987. Sec. Mooretown Sch., Shreveport, 1957-67; elem. music splst. Caddo Parish Schs., La., 1967-70; secondary edn. tchr., 1970-79. Ptnr. Pierson's Allendale Plz., Shreveport, 1979—; bookkeeper F & F Food Store, Shreveport, 1978—; artistic dir. Performing Arts Studio, 1983—; dir. music Antioch Baptist Ch., 1997—. Instr. Christian Edn., Shreveport, 1970—; organist Shiloh Bapt. Ch., Shreveport, 1975-78; mem. ways and means com. Greenwood Acres Civic Club, 1975-81, mem. econ. devel. and planning com., 1980-81; mem. Ctr. for Families, Shreveport, 1992-99; mem. music and art cultural awareness project, Jackson Heights Housing Cmty., Shreveport, 1998; mem. Shreveport Symphony Guild, Shreveport Little Theatre, Shreveport Opera Guild; min. music Antioch Bapt. Ch., music dir. Jackson Heights Housing Ctr., Avenue B.C. Shreveport. Grantee La. Divsn. Arts, 1995-99, Shreveport Regional Arts Coun., 1995-99; named Educator of Yr. Caddo Parish Sch. Bd., 1978; hon. state senator, La., 1980-81; recipient Cert. of Recognition of Svc. award, Antioch Bapt. Ch., Shreveport, La., 2000; honorarium during African-Am. History Month Celebration, 2002, Movers and Shakers award, Pan Hellinic Coun. of Greek Orgn., 2002 Mem. NEA, Nat. Coun. Tchrs. English, Shreveport Regional Area Coun., La. Coun. Tchrs. English, Music Tchrs. Nat. Assn., La. State Music Tchrs. Assn., Greater Shreveport Music Tchrs. Assn., Greater Shreveport C. of C. (Woman of the Century award, 2000), Univ. Club, Phi Delta Kappa, Basileus-Sigma Gamma Rho, Sorority Inc., Eta Psi Sigma Chpt. Baptist. Avocations: music, performing arts. Office: Performing Arts Studio 2332 Jewella Ave Shreveport LA 71109-2412

PIERSON, KATHLEEN MARY, child care center administrator, consultant; b. Detroit, Apr. 17, 1949; d. Peter and Elsa (Stanke) Kornberger; m. David Alan Pierson, Aug. 23, 1980 (div. Nov. 1981). AS, Macomb Coll., Mich., 1974; BS, Central U. Mich., 1976. Model, Detroit, 1970-74, also piano player, lounges; horse jockey, Detroit, 1974-78; recreation therapist Rehab. Inst., Detroit, 1978-81; exec. dir. Kreative Korners, Warren, Mich., 1981—, founder Kreative Korners Adult Day Care Ctr., 1987; cons. low income child care centers Mich., 1986—. Producer: children's ednl. video tapes Miss Kathy's Back to Basics, 1992. Bd. dirs. Macomb Coll., Warren, Mich., 1984—. Guest of Honor, Mich. Opportunity Soc., 1985, Easter Seal Soc., 1976; speaker United Found., 1987, 88. Mem. South Warren Cmty. Orgn., Nat. Exec. Female Assn., Internat. Platform Assn. (speech competition). Lutheran. Avocations: Doberman breeding; playing classical music; horseback riding. Home: 5487 Southlawn Dr Sterling Heights MI 48310-6565 Office: Kreative Korners Inc 5487 Southlawn Dr Sterling Heights MI 48310-6565

PIERSON, KENNETH LANTZ, motor carrier safety consultant; b. Akron, Ohio, May 29, 1932; s. Robert Arch and Grace Greer Pierson; m. Joy Roberta Burchett, June 8, 1952; children: Lavonne, Melinda, Lorrie, Paul, Mark. BS in Bus., U. Md., 1958. Investigator ICC, Balt., 1958-62, mem. staff Washington, 1962-67, Bur. Motor Carrier Safety, Washington, 1967-70, dep. dir., 1970-80, dir., 1980-86; motor carrier safety cons. Glenn Dale, Md., 1987—. Mem. Gov.'s Truck Safety Task Force, Annapolis, Md., 1988-99; mem. cert. commn. Profl. Truck Driver Inst., Alexandria, Va., 1989—. Mem. com. troop 1002 Boy Scouts Am., 1971-91. Sgt. U.S. Army, 1950-53, Korea and Germany. Recipient Bronze medal Fed. Hwy Adminstrn., 1968, Commendations Nat. Motor Carrier Adv. Com., Washington, 1987, Commercial Vehicle Safety Alliance, Washington, 1987. Mem. Am. Soc. Safety Engrs. (chpt. pres. 1978-79), Transp. Rsch. Bd., Sr. Execs. Assn., Am. Legion. Democrat. Methodist. Avocations: golf, travel. Home and Office: 3300 Glen Ave Glenn Dale MD 20769-9215

PIERSON, MARILYN EHLE, financial planner; b. Cleve., Feb. 27, 1931; d. Ernest John and Helen Irene (Steudel) Ehle; m. Edward G. Pierson, July 17, 1954; children: Melanie K., Edward G. III. BSBA, Miami U., 1953; grad., Coll. Fin. Planning, 1990, Inst. Cert. Divorce Planners, 1997. CFP. Sr. fin. advisor, advanced planner group Am. Express Fin. Advisors, Cleve., 1987—. Corp. presenter, fin. educator East Ohio Gas, AT&T, Cleve., Master Builders, Cleve., Preformed Line Products, Cleve., Parker Hannifin, Cleve.; guest lectr. Chagrin Valley C. of C., Chagrin Falls, Ohio; lectr. adult edn. Shaker Heights (Ohio). Fin. columnist Bainbridge Banter newspaper. Chair stewardship and resources Valley Presbyn. Ch., Bainbridge, Ohio, elder, 1991-93, planned giving chmn., 1991-95, 2000—. Mem. Fin. Planning Assn. (treas. exec. com. NE Ohio chpt. 1994-98), Exec. Women Internat. (advisor, bd. dirs. 1997, pres. 1996), Estate Planning Coun. Cleve. Avocation: travel. Home: 8178 Chagrin Mills Rd Chagrin Falls OH 44022-3807 Office: Am Express Fin Advisors 22901 Mill Creek Blvd #375 Cleveland OH 44122-4556 E-mail: marilyn.e.pierson@aefa.com.

PIERSON, ROBERT DAVID, banker; b. Orange, N.J., Mar. 5, 1935; s. Carleton Wellington and Muriel Browning (Potter) P.; m. Virginia Duncan Knight, Apr. 30, 1960; children: Lisa Boles, Alexandra Mead, Robert Wellington. BA, Lehigh U., 1957. Exec. asst. 1st Nat. City Bank N.Y., N.Y.C., 1958-61; asst. to pres. Cooper Labs. Inc., 1961-65; dir. mktg. svcs. Arbrook divsn. Johnson & Johnson, Somerville, N.J., 1965-69; v.p. Klemtner Advt. Inc., N.Y.C., 1969-71; sr. v.p. Bowery Savs. Bank, 1972-80; vice chmn., dir. Carteret Bancorp, Inc., Wilmington, Del., 1980-90; pres. No. Divsn. Collective Bank, 1990-96, Collective Fin. Svcs., Inc., Harbor Mortgage Co. (divsns. of Collective Bank), Montclair, N.J., 1997-98; pvt. investor, 1998—. Mayor Township of Mendham, N.J., 1995-96, mem. coun., 1992—, mem. planning bd., 1992-96. With USCG, 1958-59. Mem. Morris County Golf Club, Morristown Club. Republican. Presbyterian. Home: Green Hills Rd Mendham NJ 07945-3305

PIERSON, W. DEVIER, lawyer; b. Pawhuska, Okla., Aug. 12, 1931; s. Welcome D. and Frances (Ratliff) P.; m. Shirley Frost, Feb. 1, 1957; children: Jeffrey, Elizabeth, Stephen. AB, U. Okla., 1953, LLB, 1957. Bar: Okla. 1957, U.S. Dist. Ct. Okla. 1957, U.S. Supreme Ct. 1966, U.S. Ct. Appels D.C. 1969, U.S. Ct. Appeals (5th cir.) 1972, U.S. Ct. Appeals (10th cir.) 1975, U.S. Ct. Appeals (2d cir.) 1996. Assoc. Duval & Head, Oklahoma City, 1957-59; sole practice, 1959-65; chief counsel Joint Com. on Orgn. of Congress, 1965-67; assoc. spl. counsel to Pres. and Counselor White House Office, 1967-68; spl. counsel to Pres. of U.S., 1968-69; ptnr. Pierson Semmes and Bemis and predecessor firms, Washington, 1969-2000; spl. counsel Verner, Liipfert, Bernhard, McPherson and Hand Chartered, 2000—. Trustee U. Okla. Found., 1996—; chmn. bd. visitors U. Okla. Coll. of Law; mem. bd. visitors U. Okla. Internat. Programs Ctr.; dir. Atlantic Coun. of U.S., 1995—. Served to 1st lt. U.S. Army, 1953-54. Recipient Outstanding Alumnus award U. Okla., 1995. Mem. ABA, D.C. Bar Assn., Fed. Bar Assn., Okla. Bar Assn., Met. Club (Washington). Home: 5326 Chamberlin Ave Chevy Chase MD 20815-6661 Office: Verner, Liipfert, Bernhard, McPherson and Hand, Chartered 901 15th St NW Ste 700 Washington DC 20005

PIERSON, WILLARD JAMES, geophysics educator, researcher; b. Manhattan, N.Y., July 7, 1922; s. Willard James and Mary Abagail (Hand) P.; m. Joy Mary Kell, July 3, 1954 (dec. July 1999); children: Mary Jean, Arthur, Mark. BS, U. Chgo., 1944; PhD, NYU, 1949. From asst. prof. to assoc. prof. NYU, N.Y.C., 1949-61, prof., 1961-73, CUNY, N.Y.C., 1973-92, rsch. prof., 1992—. Co-author: HO Pub 603, 1957, Principles of Phyical Oceanography, 1966. Capt. USAF, ret. Recipient Exceptional Sci. Achievement medal NASA, 1980, cert. of appreciation Soc. Naval Arch. Marine Engrs., 1973. Fellow AAAS, IEEE (life), Am. Geophys. Union (Sverdrup Gold medal), Am. Meteorol. Soc. Methodist. Achievements include early research on remote sensing and ocean waves, radar scatterometry, radar altimetry, ship motions. Home: 103 Oakland Ave West Hempstead NY 11552-1924 Office: CCNY-CUNY Convent Ave at 138th St New York NY 10031 E-mail: bill@datatone.com.

PIERSON, WILLIAM GEORGE, lawyer; b. Pontiac, Mich., Oct. 13, 1951; s. Robert D. and Elizabeth C. (Brode) P.; m. Mary K. Grossa, Sept. 25, 1986; children: Megan Ewing, Robert John. BBA, Cen. Mich. U., 1973; JD, Detroit Coll. Law, 1980. Bar: Mich. 1980, U.S. Dist. Ct. (ea. dist.) Mich. 1982, U.S. Supreme Ct. 1985. Sr. assoc. Kohl, Secrest, Wardle, Lynch, Clark & Hampton, Farmington Hills, Mich., 1980-89, Schwartz & Jalkanen, Southfield, 1989-90; sole practice Howell, 1991-99; counsel Oakland County Corp., Pontiac, 1999—. Mem. ABA, Mich. Bar Assn. (negligence sect., elected to rep. assembly 1999—), Oakland County Bar Assn (dist. ct. com. 1983-84, cir. ct. com. 1984-85, negligence com. 1987—, chair negligence com. 2002, med.-legal com. 1989-96, pub. adv. com. on jud. candidates 2002—), Livingston County Bar Assn. Avocations: golf, skiing, boating, camping. Home: 2153 Ridge Rd White Lake MI 48383-1742 Office: Oakland County Dept Corp Counsel 1200 N Telegraph Rd Dept 419 Pontiac MI 48341-0419 E-mail: piersonw@co.oakland.mi.us., megrob1@msn.com.

PIES, RONALD E. retired city official; b. Rochester, N.Y., Mar. 21, 1940; s. Herman S. and Sylvia Pies; m. Bernita Orloff, Aug. 27, 1964; children: Cara Jean Tracy, David Paul. BS, Ariz. State U., 1963. Recreation leader City of Phoenix, Ariz., 1962-64; head recreation divsn. City of Scottsdale (Ariz.) Parks and Recreation Dept., 1964-69; dir. parks and recreation City of Tempe, Ariz., 1969-84, cmty. svcs. dir., 1984-98. Guest lectr. Ariz. State U.; spl. projects coord. Ariz. Lottery, 1999—. Mem., pres. Kyrene Sch. Dist. Governing Bd., 1979-82; chmn., bd. regents Pacific Revenue Sources Mgmt. Sch. NRPA; gen. chmn. Fiesta Bowl Soccer Classic, 1982-98; founding mem. Tempe YMCA bd. mgrs.; apptd. mem. Ariz. State Parks Bd., 1987-93, chair, 1991. Named Outstanding Young Man, Jaycees; recipient Superior Svc. Mgmt. award ASPA, Ariz. chpt., 1988; named to Hall of Fame, Ariz. State U. Alumni for Coll. Pub. Programs, 1996, Hall of Fame, Tempe Elem. Sch. Dist., 1996. Mem. Tempe C. of C., Ariz. Parks and Recreation Assn. (bd. dirs. 1986-98, pres. adminstrs., Disting. Fellow award 1983, Life Mem. award 1998, L.E.G.E.N.D. award 2000), Nat. Recreation and Parks Assn. (Outstanding Profl. 1991), Cactus League Baseball Assn. (pres. 1993-94, apptd. mem. Ariz. baseball commn. by Gov. Symington 1994—, chair 1995-2000), Tempe Diablos Club, Sigma Alpha Epsilon. E-mail: ronandbernita@earthlink.net.

PIESTER, DAVID L(EE), magistrate judge; b. Lincoln City, Nebr., Nov. 18, 1947; s. George Piester; married; children. BS, U. Nebr., 1969, JD, 1972. Bar: Nebr. 1972, U.S. Dist. Ct. Nebr. 1972, U.S. Ct. Appeals (8th cir.) 1976, U.S. Supreme Ct. 1979. Staff atty. Legal Svcs. S.E. Nebr., Lincoln, 1972-73, exec. dir., 1973-79; asst. U.S. atty. Dept. Justice, 1979-81; magistrate judge U.S. Dist. Ct. Nebr., 1981—. Cons. Legal Services Corp., Nat. Legal Aid and Defender Assn., 1974-77. Mem. Lincoln Human rights commn., 1978-79. Mem. ABA (jud. adminstrn. divsn., Nat. Conf. Fed. Trial Judges), Nebr. State Bar Assn., Fed. Magistrate Judges Assn., Lincoln Bar Assn., Eighth Cir. Jud. Coun. (ex officio 1993-96). Office: US Dist Ct 100 Centennial Mall North 566 Fed Bldg Lincoln NE 68508

PIETERS, CARLE MCGETCHIN, geology educator, planetary scientist, researcher; widow. BA, Antioch Coll., 1966; BS, MIT, 1971, MS, 1972, PhD, 1977. Tchr. math. Somerville (Mass.) H.S., 1966-67; tchr. sci. Peace Corps, Sarawak, Malaysia, 1967-69; staff scientist rschr. Planetary Astron. Lab. MIT, 1972-75; space scientist Johnson Space Ctr. NASA, 1977-80; asst. prof. Brown U., Providence, 1980-83, assoc. prof. geology, 1983-94, prof. geoscis., 1994—. Asteroid named in honor, Pieters. Mem. AAAS, Am. Geophys. Union, Am. Astron. Soc., Meteoritical Soc. Office: Brown Univ PO Box 1846 Providence RI 02912-1846

PIETERS, RICHARD SAWYER, JR. radiation oncologist, educator; b. Lawrence, Mass., June 1, 1948; s. Richard Sawyer and Norma Kenfield Pieters; m. Edith M. Jolin, May 22, 1982; 1 child, Jennifer R. AB, Princeton U., 1970; MEd, Boston U., 1974; MD, Brown U., 1982. Diplomate Am. Bd. Radiology. Intern Wayne State Affiliated Hosp., Detroit, 1982-83; resident in therapeutic radiology Tufts-New Eng. Med. Ctr., Boston, 1983-86, co-chief resident, 1985-86; dir. radiation oncology Jordan Hosp., Plymouth, Mass., 1994—. Asst. prof. clin. radiology Ohio State U. Coll. Medicine, James Cancer Hosp. and Rsch. Inst., Columbus, 1987-94; lectr. Harvard U. Med. Sch., Boston, 1994—; clin. asst. prof. radiology Boston U. Sch. Medicine, 1994-98, clin. assoc. prof. radiology, 1998—. Mem. AMA, Am. Coll. Radiology, Am. Soc. for Therapeutic Radiology and Oncology, Am. Soc. Clin. Oncology, Radiation Rsch. Soc., Gilbert H. Fletcher Soc., S.W. Oncology Group, Children's Oncology Group, Plymouth Dist. Med. Soc. (treas. 1997—, pres. 2000—). Office: Jordan Hosp Club Cancer Ctr 275 Sandwich St Plymouth MA 02360-2183 E-mail: rpieters@jordanhospital.org.

PIETON, RICHARD, anesthesiologist; b. Krakow, Poland, Feb. 6, 1946; s. Roman and Balbina Pieton. M of Psychology, Jagiellonian U., 1968; MD, Med. Acad., Krakow, Poland, 1973; PhD, Med. Acad., 1979. Diplomate Am. Bd. Anesthesiology, Am. Bd. Internal Medicine. Staff physician Med. Acad. Krakow, Poland, 1974-80; resident in internal medicine Shadyside Hosp., Pitts., 1982-84; resident in anesthesiology U. Nebr. Med. Ctr., Omaha, 1985-86; fellow in neuroanesthesiology Hosp. U. Pa., Phila., 1987-88; staff anesthesiologist VA Hosp., West L.A., 1988—; asst. clin. prof. UCLA. Mem. ACP, Am. Soc. Anesthesiologists. Home: 1253 11th St Unit 1 Santa Monica CA 90401-2050

PIETROFESA, JOHN JOSEPH, education educator; b. N.Y.C., Sept. 12, 1940; s. Louis John and Margaret P.; m. Cathy Marks, June 22, 1985; children: John, Paul, Maria, Dolores. EdB cum laude, U. Miami, 1961; MEd, 1963, Ed.D., 1967. Diplomate Am. Bd. Sexology; cert. cognitive behavior therapist, forensic counselor, sex therapist; lic. psychologist, social worker. Counselor Dade County (Fla.) pub. schs., 1965-67; prof. edn. Wayne State U., Detroit, 1967—; div. head theoret. and behavioral founds., 1977-83; dept. chair counselor edn., 1999—. Cons. to various schs., hosps. and univs. Author: The Authentic Counselor, 1971, 2nd edit., 1980, School Counselor as Professional, 1971, Counseling and Guidance in the Twentieth Century, 1971, Elementary School Guidance and Counseling, 1973, Career Development, 1975, Career Education, 1976, College Student Development, 1977, Counseling: Theory Research and Practice, 1978, Guidance: An Introduction, 1980, Counseling: An Introduction, 1984; mem. editl. bd. Counseling and Values, 1972-75. 1st lt. Mil. Police Corps, AUS, 1963-65. Mem. Am. Psychol. Assn., Am. Personnel and Guidance Assn., Mich. Personnel and Guidance Assn., Assn. Counselor Edn. and Supervision, Phi Delta Kappa. Home: PO Box 99 Bloomfield Hills MI 48303-0099 Office: Wayne State U 321 Education Detroit MI 48202

PIETRUSKA, ALEXANDER MICHAEL, investment banker; b. Passau, Germany, Mar. 19, 1959; m. Ann Shirley Hunter, June 7, 1986. MA in Econs., U. Colo., 1986; MBA, INSEAD, Fontainebleau, France, 1991. Fgn. exch. analyst Mfrs. Hannover Trust, N.Y.C., 1987-88; asst. v.p. Fgn. Exch. Concepts, 1988-90; sr. engagement mgr. McKinsey & Co. Inc., London and Zurich, 1992-97; exec. dir. UBS Warburg, London, 1997-2000; mng. dir. ABN Amro Corp. Fin. Ltd., 2000—. Fulbright scholar Fulbright Commn., 1984; Quadrille Ball scholar Germanistic Soc. of Am., 1985; scholar INSEAD, 1991. Avocation: skiing, yoga. Office: ABN Amro Corp Fin Ltd 250 Bishopsgate London EC2M 4AA England E-mail: apietruska@aol.com., alexander.pietruska@uk.abnamro.com.

PIETRUSKI, JOHN MICHAEL, JR. biotechnology company executive, pharmaceuticals executive; b. Sayreville, N.J., Mar. 12, 1933; m. Roberta Jeanne Talbot, July 3, 1954; children: Glenn David, Clifford John, Susan Jane. BS with honors, Rutgers U., 1954; LLD (hon.), Concordia Coll., 1993. With Proctor and Gamble Co., 1954-63; pres. med. products div. C.R. Bard, Inc., 1963-77; with Sterling Drug, Inc., N.Y.C., 1977-88; pres. Pharm. Group, 1977-81, corp. exec. v.p., 1981-83, pres., chief operating officer, 1983-85, chmn., chief exec. officer, 1985-88, ret., 1988; pres. Dansara Cons., 1988—; chmn. Tex. Biotech. Corp., 1990—. Bd. dirs. Hershey Foods Corp., First Energy Corp., Lincoln Nat. Corp., PDI, Inc., Xylos Corp. Regent Concordia Coll. 1st lt. U.S. Army, 1955-57. Mem. Phi Beta Kappa Clubs: Union League (N.Y.C.). Home: 27 Paddock Ln Colts Neck NJ 07722-1266 Office: One Penn Plaza Ste 3408 New York NY 10119

PIETRUSZKA, MICHAEL F. judge; b. Buffalo, Oct. 20, 1956; s. Walter J. and Dorothy (Lutomski) P.; m. Patricia Ann Joyce, July 19, 1986. BA magna cum laude, Canisius Coll., 1978; JD cum laude, Syracuse U., 1981. Bar: N.Y. 1982, U.S. Dist. Ct. (we. dist.) N.Y. 1982, U.S. Ct. Internat. Trade 1985, U.S. Supreme Ct. 1986. Pvt. practice law, Buffalo, 1982-87; asst. corp. counsel City of Buffalo, 1983-86, dir. parking enforcement div., 1986-87; gen. counsel Buffalo Mcpl. Housing Authority, 1987; judge City Ct. of Buffalo, 1988-98, Erie County Ct., Buffalo, 1999—. Competition judge N.E. Regional Jessup Internat. Moot Ct., 1996; mem. faculty N.Y. State Ann. Jud. Seminar; mem. exec. com. Nat. Conf. Spl. Ct. Judges, ABA jud. sect., 1997—. Exec. editor Syracuse Jour. Internat. Law and Commerce, 1980-81; legal columnist Am-Pol Eagle, 1982-83, Metro Cmty. News, 1990, Polish Am. Jour., 1993—; author: Polonia Connections, 1997. Active Buffalo Urban League; dir. Floss Ave. Men's Choir, East Buffalo Civic Assn., 1984-87, N.W. Buffalo Cmty. Ctr.; pres. Forest Dist. Civic Assn., Monsignor Healy Found. Scholarship Com.; pres. Western N.Y. chpt. Kosciuszko Found., mem. nat. adv. com.; bd. dirs. Buffalo-Rzeszow Sister City Com.; dir. Gen. Pulaski Assn. of Niagara Frontier; nat. dir. Polish Am. Congress; mem. Polish Am./Jewish Am. Coun. Western N.Y.; hon. dir. Polish Cadets Buffalo, 1998. Recipient Jurist Citation of Honor award Nat. Columbus Day Com., 1988, Martin Luther King Human Rels. award Erie County So. Christian Leadership Conf., 1990, N.W. Buffalo Cmty. Svc. award, 1991, Pres.'s award Buffalo-Rzeszow Sister Cities Inc., 1993, Cert. of Spl. Congl. Recognition, 1996, Civic Recognition award Forest Dist. Civic Assn., 1996, others; named Man of Yr., Pulaski Police Assn., 1989, Am.-Pol Citizen of Yr., 1991. Mem. NAACP, N.Y. State Bar Assn. (cert. of honor 1992, 93, 94), Erie County Bar Assn., Am. Judges Assn., Polish Cadets, Profl. and Businessmen's Assn., K.C., Advocates Club (sec. 1990, v.p. 1991, pres. 1992, Pres.'s award 1993), YMCA Greater Buffalo Century Club, 100 Club Buffalo, Buffalo Canoe Club, Polish Union Am., St. Joseph's Guild, Chopin Singing Soc. Democrat. Roman Catholic. Avocation: travel, computers, website. Office: Erie County Ct 92 Franklin St Buffalo NY 14202-3902 E-mail: pietruszka@aol.com.

PIETZ, LYNNE PEPI, lawyer; b. Rochester, N.Y., Mar. 1, 1952; d. Irvine Manne and Ethel Bernhardt (Jacobsen) Kriegsfeld; m. Jeffrey Thomas Pietz, June 29, 1975; children: Morgan Elliott, Brynna Michelle. AB cum laude, Washington U., St. Louis, 1973, JD, 1977. Bar: Mo. 1977, Calif. 1986, Ohio 1991, U.S. Dist. Ct. (so. dist.) Ohio 1991, U.S. Ct. Appeals (D.C. cir.) 1978. Congl. fellow U.S. Congl. Office of Tech. Assessment-Health Program, Washington, 1977-78; contracts specialist OTA-Adminstrv. Office, 1978-80; assoc. Rinos & Packer, Santa Ana, Calif., 1986-90, Louis & Froelich Co., LPA, Dayton, Ohio, 1990-92; pvt. practice, 1992—2001; exec. dir. The Disability Found., Inc., 1999—. Vol. instr. elder law U. Dayton-Inst. for Learning in Retirement, Dayton, 1995-99; spkr. elder law Sr. Network Alzheimers Assn., Dayton, 1993-99. Mem. City of Irvine (Calif.) Childcare Com., 1985-88; trustee Life Essentials, Inc., Dayton, 1993-99; vol. McGovern Presdl. Campaign, Cleve., 1967. Mem. Nat. Acad. Elder Law Attys., Ohio State Bar Assn., Calif. State Bar Assn., D.C. Bar Assn., Mo. Bar Assn., Phi Beta Kappa. Avocations: piano, walking, attending kids' sports events. Office: The Disability Found Inc 1530 Kettering Tower Kettering OH 45423-1395 E-mail: LynneP@daytonfoundation.org.

PIETZSCH, MICHAEL EDWARD, lawyer; b. Burlington, Iowa, Aug. 1, 1949; s. Walter E. and Leanna (Moore) P.; m. Ellen G. Hart; children: Christine E., Catherine M. AB, Stanford U., 1971; JD, U. Chgo., 1974. Bar: Ill. 1974, Ariz. 1976. Assoc. Schwartz & Freeman, Chgo., 1974-75; ptnr. McCabe & Pietzsch, Phoenix, 1975-90, Pietzsch & Williams, Phoenix, 1990-95, Polese, Pietzsch, Williams & Nolan, Phoenix, 1995—. Contbr. articles to profl. jours.; speaker at profl. confs. Del. White House Conf. Small Bus., Washington, 1986, White House Savs. Summit, 1998; chmn. bd. trustees Ariz. Sci. Ctr., 1994-98; pres. The Group, Inc., 1995-98. Fellow Am. Coll. Tax Counsel, Am. Coun. on Tax Policy; mem. ABA (chmn. personal svc. orgns. com. tax sect. 1986-90), Stanford Phoenix Club (pres. 1982-84). Office: 2702 N 3d St Ste 3000 Phoenix AZ 85004-4607

PIFER, ALAN (JAY PARRISH), former foundation executive; b. Boston, May 4, 1921; s. Claude Albert and Elizabeth (Parrish) P.; m. Erica Pringle, June 20, 1953 (div. 1994); children: Matthew, Nicholas, Daniel. AB, Harvard U., 1947; Lionel de Jersey Harvard student Emmanuel Coll., Cambridge (Eng.) U., 1947-48; LLD (hon.), Mich. State U., 1971, Hofstra U., 1974, Notre Dame U., 1975; DHL (hon.), Marymount Coll., 1983, Millsaps Coll., 1986; D of Univ. (hon.), Open U., Eng., 1974; JD (hon.), Atlanta U., 1980; DEd (hon.), U. Cape Town, South Africa, 1984. Exec. sec. U.S. Edni. Commn. in U.K., London, 1948-53; program officer Carnegie Corp. N.Y., 1953-63, v.p., 1963-65, acting pres., 1965-67, pres., 1967-82, pres. emeritus, sr. cons., 1982-87; chmn., pres. Southport Inst. for Policy Analysis, 1987-91, chmn., 1991-94; v.p. Carnegie Found. for Advancement of Teaching, 1963-65, acting pres., 1965-67, pres., 1967-79, trustee, 1979-87. Bd. dirs. Technoserve, Inc. Author: (with others) Our Aging Society, 1986, (with others) Women on the Front Lines: Meeting the Challenge of an Aging America, 1993; Government for the People, 1987. Mem. mgmt. com. U.S.-South Africa Leader Exch. Program, 1957—, pub. policy com. Advt. Coun., 1987-91, adv. coun. Columbia U. Sch. Social Work, 1963-69, R & D ctr. panel U.S. Office Edn., 1963-65, adv. com. higher edn. U.S. Dept. Health Edn. and Welfare, 1967-68, bd. of overseers Harvard U., 1969-75, Charles Stark Draper Lab. bd. MIT, 1970-76, Commn. Pvt. Philanthropy and Pub. Needs, 1973-75; chmn. Consortium Advancement Pvt. Higher Edn., 1983-92, mayor's adv. com. Bd. Higher Edn. N.Y.C., 1966-69, Pres.'s Task Force on Edn., 1968, Aging Soc. Project, 1982-87, Nat. Conf. on Social Welfare Project, 1983-87; co-chmn. N.Y. State Nutrition Watch com., 1982; trustee U. Bridgeport, Conn., 1973—, Assn. Governing Bds. Colls. and Univs., 1985-91, African Am. Inst., 1957-71, Found. Libr. Ctr., 1967-71, Am. Ditchley Found., 1973-81; bd. dirs. Bus. Coun. Effective Literacy Inc., 1984-93, N.Y. Urban Coalition, 1967-71, Nat. Assembly for Social Policy and Devel., 1967-71, Coun. on Founds., Inc., 1970-76, Fed. Reserve Bank N.Y., 1970-76, Harry Frank Guggenheim Found., 1989—. Capt. U.S. Army, 1942-46, ETO. Recipient Barnard Coll. medal of distinction, 1980, Cleveland E. Dodge medal of distinction Tchrs. Coll., Columbia U., 1982. Fellow Am. Acad. of Arts and Scis., African Studies Assn. (founding), Royal Soc. Arts (London); mem. Am. Assn. for Higher Edn. (bd. dirs. 1982-90), Century Assn. Clubs: Harvard (N.Y.C.). Democrat. Avocation: gardening.

PIGA, STEPHEN MULRY, retired lawyer; b. Bklyn., Apr. 9, 1929; s. Stephen Paul and Ella (Mulry) P.; married, Feb. 23, 1952 (div.); children: Maureen, Stephen, Susan, Elizabeth; m. Emilie Halliday, Aug. 1, 1975; 1 dau., Margaret. AB, Princeton U., 1950; LL.B., Columbia u., 1955. Bar: N.J. 1955, N.Y. 1956. Assoc. White & Case, N.Y.C., 1955-63, ptnr., 1964-92; ret., 1992. Lectr. Practicing Law Inst. N.Y. and various insts., bar assns. Served to capt. USMCR, 1951-53. Mem. ABA, N.Y. State Bar Assn. (exec. com. tax sect. 1981-89, chmn. employee benefits com.), Assn. of Bar of City N.Y., N.J. Bar Assn., Am. Contract Bridge League (life master), Profl. Bowlers' Assn. Am. Republican. Avocations: fishing, golf, bowling.

PIGFORD, THOMAS HARRINGTON, nuclear engineering educator; b. Meridian, Miss., Apr. 21, 1922; s. Lamar and Zula Vivian (Harrington) P.; m. Catherine Kennedy Cathey, Dec. 31, 1948 (dec. 1992); children: Cynthia Pigford Naylor, Julie Pigford Brink; m. Elizabeth Hood Weekes, Nov. 12, 1994. BS in Chem. Engring., Ga. Inst. Tech., 1943; S.M. in Chem. Engring., M.I.T., 1948, Sc.D. in Chem. Engring., 1952. Asst. prof. chem. engring., dir. Sch. Engring. Practice, M.I.T., 1950-52, asst. prof. nuclear and chem. engring., 1952-55, assoc. prof., 1955-57; head engring., dir. nuclear reactor projects and asst. dir. research lab. Gen. Atomic Co., La Jolla, Calif., 1957-59; prof. nuclear engring., chmn. dept. nuclear engring. U. Calif., Berkeley, 1959—; sr. rsch. scientist Lawrence Berkeley Lab., 1959—. Mem. panel Nat. Atomic Safety Licensing Bd. AEC-Nuclear Regulatory Commn., 1963-77; mem. Pres.'s Commn. on accident at 3-Mile Island, 1979; mem. bd. radioactive waste mgmt. and energy engring. bd., NAS-NAE, chmn. waste isolation systems panel, waste isolation pilot plant panel, fusion hybrid panel, separations and transmutations panel, transmutation of military plutonium panel, panel on health standard for radioactive waste disposal, chmn. adv. coun. Inst. Nuclear Power Op.; mem. Sec. of Energy's expert cons. group on Chernobyl accident; chmn. nuclear oversight com. Sacramento Mcpl. Utility Dist.; chmn. nuclear safety com. Gulf States Utilities Co.; mem. expert cons. group Swedish Nuclear Power Inspectorate; mem. peer rev. group for waste isolation pilot plant; mem. corp. rev. com. Oak Ridge Nat. Lab; lectr. Taiwan Nat. Sci. Found., 1990; vis. prof. Kyoto U., 1975, Kuwait U., 1976; cons. in field. Author: (with Manson Benedict) Nuclear Chemical Engineering, 1958, 2d edit., 1981; contbr. numerous articles to profl. jours.; patentee in field. Served with USNR, 1944-46. Recipient John Wesley Powell award U.S. Geol. Survey, 1981; named Outstanding Young Man of Greater Boston, Boston Jaycees, 1955; E. I. DuPont DeNemours rsch. fellow, 1948-50; Berkeley citation U. Calif., 1987; Japan Soc. for Promotion Sci. fellow, 1974-75; grantee NSF, 1960-75, EPA, 1973-78, Dept. Energy, 1979-92, Ford Found., 1974-75, Electric Power Rsch. Inst., 1974-75, Mitsubishi Metals Corp., 1989-90; named to Ga. Tech. Hall of Fame, 1995. Fellow Am. Nuclear Soc. (bd. dirs., Arthur H. Compton award 1971); mem. AIME, NAE, Am. Chem. Soc., Am. Inst. Chem. Engrs. (Robert E. Wilson award 1980, Service to Society award 1985), Atomic Indsl. Forum (dir.), Sigma Xi, Phi Kappa Phi, Tau Beta Pi. Home: 166 Alpine Ter Oakland CA 94618-1823 Office: U Calif Dept Nuclear Engring Berkeley CA 94720-0001 E-mail: pigford@nuc.berkeley.edu.

PIGNATARO, LOUIS JAMES, engineering educator; b. Bklyn., Nov. 30, 1923; s. Joseph and Rose (Capi) P.; m. Edith Hoffmann, Sept. 12, 1954; 1 child, Thea. B.C.E., Poly. Inst. Bklyn., 1951; MS, Columbia U., 1954; Dr. Tech. Sci., Tech. U. Graz, Austria, 1961. Registered profl. engr., N.Y., Calif., Fla. Faculty Poly. Inst. N.Y., 1951—85, prof. civil engring., 1965—, dir. divsn. transp. planning, 1967—, head dept. transp. planning and engring., 1970, dir. Transp. Tng. and Rsch. Ctr., 1975; Kayser prof. transp. engring. CCNY, N.Y.C., 1985—88, assoc. dir. Inst. for Transp., 1985—88; mem. faculty N.J. Inst. Tech., 1988—, disting. prof. transp. engring., 1988—, dir. ctr. transp. studies and research, 1988—93, exec. dir. Inst. for Transp., 1988—2000, dir. Transp. Info. and Decision Engring. Ctr., 1999—. Cons. govtl. agys., pvt. firms. Mem. Gov.'s Task Force Advisers on Transp. Problems, Gov.'s Task Force on Alcohol and Hwy. Safety; commr.'s council advisers N.Y. State Dept. Transp.; mem. adv. bd. freight services improvement conf. Port Authority N.Y. and N.J.; mem. adv. com. N.Y.C. Dept. Transp.; mem. rev. com. N.Y.C. Dept. City Planning; mem. Mayor's Transp. Commn., City of Newark; mem. N.J. Legislature's Coun. Acad. Policy Advisors; bd. dirs., treas., Com. for a Smart N.J. Sr. author: Traffic Engineering-Theory and Practice, 1973; contbr. over 80 papers to profl. jours. Bd. dirs., treas. Com. for a Smart N.J. Served with AUS, 1943—46. Recipient Distinguished Tchr. citation Poly. Inst. Bklyn., 1965, Dedicated Alumnus award, 1971, Distinguished Alumnus award, 1972; citation for distinguished research Poly. chpt. Sigma Xi, 1975; named Engr. of Year N.Y. State Soc. Profl. Engrs., 1974 Fellow ASCE (dir.), Inst. Transp. Engrs. (Transp. Engr. of Yr. Met. sect. N.Y. and N.J. 1982, Wilbur S. Smith Disting. Transp. Educator award 1999); mem. Am. Rd. and Transp. Builders Assn. (div. dir.), Transp. Resch. Bd. (univ. liaison rep., Outstanding Paper award 1980 ann. meeting), Sigma Xi, Chi Epsilon, Tau Beta Pi. Home: 230 Jay St Brooklyn NY 11201-1948 Office: NJ Inst Tech Inst for Transp 323 Martin Luther King Jr Blvd Newark NJ 07102-1824

PIGNATELLI, DEBORA BECKER, state legislator; b. Weehawken, N.J., Oct. 25, 1947; d. Edward and Frances (Fishman) Becker; m. Michael Albert Pignatelli, Aug. 22, 1971; children: Adam Becker, Benjamin Becker. AA, Vt. Coll., 1967; BA, U. Denver, 1969. Exec. dir. Girl's Club Greater Nashua, N.H., 1975-77; dir. tenant svcs. Nashua Housing Authority, 1979-80; vocat. counselor Comprehensive Rehab. Assocs., Bedford, N.H., 1982-85; specialist job placement Crawford & Co., 1985-87; mem N.H. Ho. of Reps., Concord, 1986-92, mem. appropriations com., 1986-91, asst. minority leader, 1989-92; mem. N.H. Senate, 1992—, dep. Dem. whip, vice chair judiciary com., mem. capital budget com., chair enrolled bills com., long range capital budget overview com. Del. Am. Coun. Young Polit. Leaders, Germany, 1987. Mem. Nashua Peace Ctr., 1980—; asst. coach Little League Baseball, Nashua, 1987-90; steering com. Gephardt for Pres. Campaign, N.H., 1987-88; del. Dem. Nat. Conv., 1988; Gore del. Dem. Nat. Conv., 2000. Named One of 10 Most Powerful Women in N.H., N.H. Editions mag., 1995; recipient Meritorious Svc. award N.H. Women's Lobby, 1997, John F. Kennedy award Hillsborough County Dems., 2001. Mem. N.H. Children's Lobby, Women's Lobby. Jewish. Avocations: skiing, children, swimming, boating. Home: 22 Appletree Grn Nashua NH 03062-2252 Office: NH Senate State House Rm 115 Concord NH 03301

PI-GONZÁLEZ, AMAURY FRANCISCO, announcer, journalist; b. Havana, Cuba, Oct. 4, 1944; arrived in U.S., 1961; s. Joaquin Pi and Olga Isabel González; m. Gail Ann Clardy; children: Jonathan Amaury, Geoffrey Walter Armando. Diploma, U.S. Army Audio Visual, Ft. Lewis, Wash., 1967. Spanish play-by-play broadcaster CBS Hispanic Network, San Francisco, 1986—89, Oakland (Calif.) Athletics, 1977—94, Golden State Warriors (NBA), Oakland, 1991—97; sports anchor, prodr. Telemundo Network, San Jose, 1991—95; Spanish play-by-play broadcaster San Francisco Giants baseball, 1995—; Spanish play-by-play broadcaster World Series Caracol Radio Network, 2000; Spanish play-by-play broadcaster Nat. League playoffs Latino Broadcasting Co., 2001; English play-by-play broadcaster Fox Sports Internat., L.A., 2001. Cons. APG Sports, Fremont, Calif., 1988—, Sports Byline USA, San Francisco, 1997—98; mem. adv. com. Oakland A's All Star Game, 1997. Author: (pamphlet) Candlestick Park Years, 1999; columnist: La Oferta News, columnist, feature writer: www.latinobaseball.com, writer: www.loveofthegame.com, writer, prodr., narrator: (audio cassette) Latin Baseball Legends, 1988. Bd. dirs., v.p. Hispanic Heritage Baseball Mus., San Francisco, 1999—. With U.S. Army, 1966—68. Named Announcer of Yr., Latin Am. Awards, 1987; recipient award of merit, San Francisco Mayor Dianne Feinstein, 1982. Mem.: CNP Profl. Assn. Cuban Journalists, Am. Sportscasters Assn. Republican. Roman Catholic. Achievements include being first Spanish play-by-play announcer in the USA to broadcast major league baseball and NBA games in concurrent seasons. Avocations: music, movies, collecting sports memorabilia. Fax: 510-770-9182. E-mail: scrmeagles@aol.com.

PIGOTT, JOHN DOWLING, geologist, geophysicist, geochemist, educator, consultant; b. Gorman, Tex., Feb. 2, 1951; s. Edwin Albert and Emma Jane (Poe) P.; m. Kulwadee Lawwongngam, May 28, 1994. BA in Zoology, BS in Geology, U. Tex., 1974, MA in Geology, 1977; PhD in Geology, Northwestern U., 1981. Geologist Amoco Internat., Chgo., 1978-80, sr. petroleum geologist Houston, 1980-81; asst., then assoc. prof. U. Okla., Norman, 1981—. Vis. prof. Mus. Natural History, Paris, 1988, Sun Yat Sen U., Kaohsiung, Taiwan, 1991; rsch. dir. 5 nation Red Sea-Gulf of Aden seismic stratigraphy and basis analysis industry consortium, 1992—; internat. energy cons., 1981—; instr. I.H.R.D.C., Boston, 1987-91, O.G.C.I., Tulsa, 1991—; energy advisor Ministry of Oil and Mineral Resources, Republic of Yemen, 1998—; advisor Prime Min. Rep. Yemen, 1998-2000; energy advisor Empresa Colombiana de Patroleos, Colombia, 2001, Petroleos de Venezuela, 2002—. Mem. editl. bd. Geotectonica et Metallogenin Jour., 1992—. Mem. Am. Assn. Petroleum Geologists, Soc. Exploration Geophysicists, Soc. Petroleum Engrs., Geol. Soc. Am., Indonesian Petroleum Assn., Sigma Xi. Roman Catholic; Theravada Buddhist. Achievements include discovering relationship between global CO2 and natural tectonic cycles on the scale of millions of years showing previous greenhouse times during the Phanerozoic, processing first three-dimensional amplitude variation with offset seismic survey to quantify rocks, fluids, and pressures in rocks, processing and displaying first ground penetrating radar survey as a seismic section for ultrahigh resolution sequence stratigraphy, developing tectonic subsidence analysis as a practical tool for investigating the comparative anatomy of a sedimentary basins, their tectonic history, and evolving hydrocarbon potential, and constructing first paleo-heatflow maps of the Red Sea for the past 25 ma. Office: U Okla Sch Geology & Geophysics 100 E Boyd St Norman OK 73019-1000

PIGOTT, MARK C. automotive executive; Chmn., CEO PACCAR, Bellevue, Wash., 1997—. Office: PACCAR PO Box 1518 777 106th Ave NE Bellevue WA 98004*

PIGOTT, MELISSA ANN, social psychologist; b. Ft. Myers, Fla., Jan. 28, 1958; d. Park Trammell and Leola Ann (Wright) P.; m. David H. Fauss, Jan. 1, 1988. BA in Psychology, Fla. Internat. U., Miami, 1979; MS in Social Psychology, Fla. State U., 1982, PhD in Social Psychology, 1984. Rsch. asst. Fla. Internat. U., 1978-79, Fla. State U., Tallahassee, 1980-84; dir. mktg. rsch. Bapt. Med. Ctr., Jacksonville, Fla., 1984-89; rsch. assoc. Litigation Scis., Inc., Atlanta, 1989-91; sr. litigation psychologist Trial Cons., Inc., Miami, 1991-93; dir. rsch. Magnus Rsch. Cons. Inc., Ft. Lauderdale, 1993—. Adj. prof. psychology U. North Fla., Jacksonville, 1985-89, Nova Southeastern U., Ft. Lauderdale, 1995—. Author: Social Psychology: Study Guide, 1990, Social Psychology: Instructors Manual, 1990; contbr. articles to profl. jours. Mem. ACLU, Am. Psychol. Assn., Am. Psychol. Law Soc., Amnesty Internat., Civitan Internat., Southeastern Psychol. Assn., Soc. for Psychol. Study of Social Issues, Soc. Personality and Social Psychology, Greenpeace, Psi Chi. Democrat. Avocations: concerts, playing piano, going to the beach. Office: Magnus Rsch Cons Inc 1305 NE 23rd Ave Ste 1 Pompano Beach FL 33062-3748

PIHL, JAMES MELVIN, electronic engineer; b. Seattle, May 29, 1943; s. Melvin Charles and Carrie Josephine (Cummings) P.; married; 1 child, Christopher James. AASEE, Seattle, 1971; BSA, City Univ., Bellevue, Wash., 1996. 1st class operators lic., FCC; lic. in real estate sales. Journeyman machinist Svc. Exch. Corp., Seattle, 1964-67; design engr. P.M. Electronics, 1970-73, Physio Control Corp., Redmond, Wash., 1973-79; project engr. SeaMed Corp., 1979-83; sr. design engr. Internat. Submarine Tech., 1983-85; engring. mgr. First Med. Devices, Bellevue, Wash., 1985-89; rsch. engr. Pentco Products, Woodinville, 1989—. Inventor, patentee protection system for preventing defibrillation with incorrect or improperly connected electrodes, impedance measurement circuit. With U.S. Army,, 1961-64. Mem. N.Y. Acad. Scis. Avocations: boating, target shooting, violin. Home: 13623 184th Ave NE Woodinville WA 98072-6337 Office: Traffic Count Cons 13623 184th Ave NE Woodinville WA 98072-6337 E-mail: tc2inc@aol.com.

PIIRMA, IRJA, chemist, educator; b. Tallinn, Estonia, Feb. 4, 1920; came to U.S., 1949; d. Voldemar Juri and Meta Wilhelmine (Lister) Tiits; m. Aleksander Piirma, Mar. 10, 1943; children: Margit Ene, Silvia Ann. Diploma in chemistry, Tech. U., Darmstadt, Fed. Republic of Germany, 1949; MS, U. Akron, 1957, PhD, 1960. Rsch. chemist U. Akron, Ohio, 1952-67, asst. prof., 1967-76, assoc. prof., 1976-81, prof., 1981-90, prof. emerita, 1990—, dept. head Ohio, 1982-85. Author: Polymeric Surfactants, 1992; editor: Emulsion Polymerization, 1982; contbr. articles to profl. jours. Recipient Extra Mural Rsch. award BP Am., Inc., 1989. Mem. Am. Chem. Soc. Avocations: swimming, skiing. Home: 3528 Adaline Dr Cuyahoga Falls OH 44224-3929 Office: U Akron Inst Polymer Sci Akron OH 44325-3909 E-mail: irja@uakron.edu.

PIIRTO, DOUGLAS DONALD, forester, educator; b. Reno, Sept. 25, 1948; s. Rueben Arvid and Martha Hilma (Giebel) P.; m. Mary Louise Cruz, Oct. 28, 1978. BS, U. Nev., 1970; MS, Colo. State U., 1971; PhD, U. Calif., Berkeley, 1977. Registered profl. forester, Calif.; cert. silviculturist USDA Forest Svc. Rsch. asst. Colo. State U., 1970-71, U. Calif., Berkeley, 1972-77; forester, silviculturist USDA, Forest Svc., Sierra Nat. Forest, Trimmer and Shaver Lake, Calif., 1977-85; assoc. prof. natural resources mgmt. dept. Calif. Poly. State U., San Luis Obispo, 1985-90, prof., 1990—, interim dept. head, 2001—. Rschr. in field; instr. part-time Kings River C.C., Reedley, Calif.; forestry cons., expert witness. Contbr. articles to sci. and forestry jours. Mem. State Forest Adv. Com.; mem. sci. adv. com. Sequoia Nat. Monument. Recipient Meritorious Performance and Profl. Promise awards CalPoly, 1989, 96-2001, CalPoly Coll. Agr. Outstanding Tchg. award Dole Food Co., 1995, Outstanding Contbn. to Coll. Agr. CalPoly award Plant Sci. Corp., 2000. Mem. Soc. Am. Foresters, Am. Forestry Assn., Forest Products Rsch. Soc., Soc. Wood Sci. and Tech., Alpha Zeta, Xi Sigma Pi, Sigma Xi, Beta Beta Beta, Phi Sigma Kappa. Lutheran. Home: 115 Eagle Creek Ct Atascadero CA 93422-5957 Office: Calif Poly State U Dept Nat Resources Mgmt San Luis Obispo CA 93407 E-mail: dpiirto@calpoly.edu.

PIIRTO, JANE MARIE, poet, novelist, educator; b. Negaunee, Mich., Dec. 19, 1941; d. George Isaac and Helmi Helena (Eskelinen) P.; m. Paul Edward Navarre, Aug. 29, 1963 (div. June 1980); children: Steven David, Denise Ruth. BA, No. Mich. U., 1963; MA, Kent State U., 1966; MEd, S.D. State U., 1974; PhD, Bowling Green State U., 1977. Tchr. Atwater (Ohio) H.S., 1965-66; instr. No. Mich. U., Marquette, 1966-71; tchr. Florence (S.D.) Schs., 1972-73; counselor Brookings (S.D.) H.S., 1973-74; cons. Hardin County (Ohio) Schs., 1977-79, Monroe County Interm. Sch. Dist., Monroe, Mich., 1979-83; prin. Hunter Coll. Campus Schs., N.Y.C., 1983-88; prof. Ashland (Ohio) U., 1988—. Vis. prof. U. Ga., Athens, 1996; cons. and spkr. in field, U.S. and Europe. Author: (novel) The Three-Week Trance Diet, 1985 (award 1985), (nonfiction) Understanding Those Who Create, 1992, (collected works) A Location in the Upper Peninsula, 1995, (textbook) Talented Children & Adults, 1994. Individual Artist fellow Ohio Arts Coun., 1982, 93, Fulbright fellow, 1990. Avocations: reading, walking, traveling. Home: 233 W Walnut St Ashland OH 44805-3148 Office: Ashland U Ashland OH 44805

PIKE, BURLYN, retired bank executive, lawyer; b. Brodhead, Ky., May 28, 1921; s. John Daniel Pike and Jewel Francisco; m. Edith Nell Sanders, 1942 (div. 1971); children: Burnell True, David Alford; m. Joan Thomason, 1983. Student, U. Louisville, 1939-43. Bar: Ky. 1944. Free lance writer The Courier Jour., Louisville, 1941-43; pub. various, 1946-51; ptnr. Taylor & Pike-Pike & Schmidt, Shepherdsville, Ky., 1952—2002. Bd. dirs. First Fed. Savings Bank, Etown, Ky. Author: Railroad Town, 2d edit., 1997. Sgt. U.S. Army, 1943-46. Mem.: Omicron Delta Kappa. Republican. Roman Cath. Avocation: historical research. Home: 2317 Woodford Pl Louisville KY 40205-1653 Office: Pike & Schmidt Law Offices 148 E 2d St Shepherdsville KY 40165 E-mail: bpike01@aol.com.

PIKE, GEORGE HAROLD, JR. religious organization executive, clergyman; b. Summit, N.J., Jan. 14, 1933; s. George Harold and Ann Aurelia (Brewer) P.; m. Pauline Elizabeth Blair, Aug. 27, 1955; children: Elizabeth, George 3d, James. BA, Trinity Coll., Hartford, Conn., 1954; MDiv, Dubuque (Iowa) Theolog. Sch., 1957; DDiv (hon.), U. Dubuque, 1998. Ordained to ministry Presbyn. Ch. USA., 1957. Pastor 1st PResbyn. Ch., Kasson, Minn., 1956-59, 3d Presbyn. Ch., Dubuque, 1959-64; sr. pastor Presbyn. Ch., Bettendorf, Iowa, 1964-68, 1st Presbyn. Ch., Vancouver, Wash., 1968-78, Cranford, N.J., 1978-88; exec. chair Presbyn. Ch. USA, Louisville, 1988-93; interim pastor 2d Presbyn. Ch., Kansas City, Mo., 1993-95; dir. sem. devel. U. Dubuque, Iowa, 1995-98; retired, 1998; interim pastor Valley Presbyn. Ch., Green Valley, Ariz., 2000. Mem. exec. com. Consultation on Ch. Union, Princeton, 1980-89, pres., 1984-88. Dir. Bettendorf Bd. Edn., 1964-68, pres. 1967-68; bd. dirs. Southwest Wash. Hosps., Vancouver, 1969-78. Named Citizen of Yr., Jaycees, Bettendorf, 1967, Citizen of Yr., B'nai B'rith, Cranford, 1988; named to Honorable Order of Ky. Cols., 1989 Avocations: golf, photography. Home: 928 W Union Bell Dr Green Valley AZ 85614-5928 E-mail: Ghpike@aol.com.

PIKE, JOHN NAZARIAN, optical engineering consultant; b. Boston, Feb. 13, 1929; s. Arthur Thorndike and Sarah Lucy (Nazarian) P.; m. Margaretta May Horner, Dec. 28, 1957; children: Sally Katharine, Susan Horner. AB, Princeton U., 1951; PhD in Physics and Optics, U. Rochester, 1958. Staff scientist Parma (Ohio) Rsch. Ctr., Union Carbide Corp., 1956-63; mem. physics faculty Baldwin-Wallace Coll., Berea, Ohio, 1961-63; sr. scientist Tarrytown (N.Y.) Tech. Ctr., Union Carbide Corp., 1963-85; pres. J.J. Pike & Co., Inc., Pleasantville, N.Y., 1986—. Patentee in applied indsl. optics; contbr. numerous articles to profl. jours. Bd. dirs. United Way of Westchester and Putnam, N.Y., 1979-85, 95—, chmn., 1996-98, 99-2000; bd. dirs. United Way of N.Y. State, 1999—; mem. nat. com. for planned giving United Way of Am., 1997—. Recipient Harold J. Marshall Citation for Cmty. Svc., United Way No. Westchester, 1976, Cmty. Svc. award Union Carbide Corp., 1982, Spirit of Westchester and Putnam Vol. Leadership award United Way Westchester and Putnam, 2001. Mem. Optical Soc. Am., SPIE-The Internat. Soc. for Optical Engring., Phi Beta Kappa, Sigma Xi. Home: 71 Cedar Ave Pleasantville NY 10570-1932 Office: JJ Pike & Co Inc PO Box 186 Pleasantville NY 10570-0186

PIKE, JONATHAN HAMILTON, writer; b. Cambridge, Mass., Aug. 2, 1960; s. Galen Woodsum and Irene Rose (Mugar) Pike. BA in Econs. and Mgmt., Beloit Coll., 1983; MS in Print Journalism, Boston U., 1993. Freelance writer, Lowell, Mass., 1985—. Home and Office: Three River Pl Apt A2109 Lowell MA 01852-1065 E-mail: theroundtable@attbi.com.

PIKE, KERMIT JEROME, library director; b. East Cleveland, June 19, 1941; s. Frank James and Pauline Frances (Prijatel) P.; m. Joyce Rita Massillo, June 27, 1964; children: Christopher James, Laura Elizabeth. BA, Case Western Res. U., 1963, MA, 1965. Rsch. asst. Western Res. Hist. Soc., Cleve., 1965-66, curator manuscripts, 1966-72, chief libr., 1969-75, dir. libr., 1976—, COO, 1997—. Adj. prof. history, libr. sci. Case Western Res. U., 1975-84. Author: Guide to the Manuscripts and Archives, 1972, Guide to Shaker Manuscripts, 1974; editor: Guide to Jewish History Sources, 1983; Compiler: Guide to Major Manuscript Collections, 1987. Mem. Super Sesquicentennial Com., Cleve., 1971, Cleve. Bicentennial History Com., 1992—96, Ohio Preservation Coun., 1997—, Ohio Hist. Records Adv. Bd., 2002—; chmn. Family Heritage Adv. Bd., Numa Corp., 1995—99; chmn. vis. com. on humanities and arts Cleve. State U., 1980—82; trustee Nationalities Svc. Ctr., Cleve., 1978—86. Recipient Achievement award No. Ohio Live, Cleve., 1987; Spl. Recognition award Gov. Richard F. Celeste of Ohio, 1990. Mem. Soc. Ohio Archivists (co-founder 1968, pres. 1971-72), Black History Archives (founder 1970), Orgn. Am. Historians, Soc. Am. Archivists, Manuscripts Soc., Midwest Archives Conf., Ohio Geneal. Soc., Early Settlers Assn. of the Western Res., Rowfant Club, Lake County Farmers' Conservation Club, Lambda Chi Alpha. Roman Catholic. Home: 3985 Orchard Rd Cleveland OH 44121-2411 Office: Western Res Hist Soc 10825 East Blvd Cleveland OH 44106-1777 E-mail: kermit@wrhs.org.

PIKE, LARRY SAMUEL, lawyer; b. Savannah, Ga., Feb. 23, 1939; s. Abram and Ida (Feinberg) P.; m. Bonnie Jo Haykin, June 21, 1959; children: Douglas, Stacey, Scott. BA, Emory U., 1960, LLB, 1963; postgrad., Leeds (Eng.) U., 1960-61. Assoc. L. Jack Swertfeger Jr. Atty., Decatur, Ga., 1963-65; ptnr. Swertfeger, Scott, Pike & Simmons, 1966-75, Simmons, Pike & Warren, Decatur, 1975-76, Lefkoff, Pike & Sims, Atlanta, 1976-85, Branch, Pike & Ganz, Atlanta, 1985-95, Holland & Knight LLP, Atlanta, 1995—. Pres. Ansley Park Civic Assn., Atlanta, 1977-79, Northshore Homeowners Assn., Tybee Island, Ga., 1992-95, The Temple, Atlanta, 1979-81, trustee, 1977—, Am. Cancer Soc., DeKalb County, Ga. unit, 1970-71, crusade chmn., 1969-70; trustee Ansley Park Beautification Found., Inc., Atlanta, 1984—, treas., 2000—; trustee The Temple Endowment Fund, Atlanta, 1979-87, Atlanta Jewish Cmty. Ctr., 1973-76; bd. overseers Hebrew Union Coll., Cin., 1987-93; alumni coun. Emory U., Atlanta, 1966-72; bd. trustees Union of Am. Hebrew Congregations, 1991-99; mem. Rabbinical Placement Commn., 1994-2000. Editor-in-chief law jour. and newspaper; contbr. articles to profl. jours. Fulbright fellow, 1960-61; named Outstanding Young Man of Yr. North DeKalb Jaycees, 1968. Mem. ABA, State Bar Ga. (exec. coun. Young Lawyers sect. 1968-72), Atlanta Bar Assn., Decatur-DeKalb Bar Assn. (sec. 1965-66), Atlanta Legal Aid Soc. (pres. 1974-75, past bd. dirs.), Atlanta Tax Forum, Lawyers Club Atlanta, B'nai B'rith (pres. Atlanta lodge 1970-71, Ga. pres. 1974-75, dist. 5 bd. govs. 1973-76, chair Youth Orgn. Bd. 1971-73), Phi Beta Kappa, Omicron Delta Kappa. Office: Holland & Knight LLP 2000 One Atlantic Ctr Atlanta GA 30309 E-mail: lpike@hklaw.com.

PIKE, NANCY M. librarian; b. Rockford, Ill., June 23, 1938; d. Hjalmar Magnusson and Violet Lucille Kirby; m. David E. Pike, Aug. 26, 1960; children: Christopher David Pike, Kimberly Ann Pike Greer. BA, Rockford Coll., 1960; MLS, U. Wis., 1984. Tchr. English Keith Country Day Sch., Rockford, 1963-66, 68-70; tchr. Romper Room Sch. Sta. WCEE-TV, WQAD-TV, Moline, 1966-67; libr. asst. L.D. Fargo Pub. Libr., Lake Mills, Wis., 1973-80; libr. technician U. Wis. and Wis. Inter Libr. Svcs., Madison, 1980-84; pub. svcs. libr. Venice (Fla.) Pub. Libr., 1985-87, head libr., 1987-2000; dir. Sarasota County Libr. Sys., 2000—. Bd. dirs. United Way So. Sarasota County, Venice, 1988—, pres., 1994; bd. dirs. Human Svcs. Planning Assn., Sarasota, 1994-2000, chair, 1997-99. Recipient Gerd Meuhsam award Art Librs. Soc. N. Am., 1983; named Woman of Impact, Sarasota County Commn. on Status of Women, 1995, Woman of Distinction, Women's Support and Enrichment Ctr., 1998. Mem. ALA, Fla. Libr. Assn. (writer column 1992—, Fla. Librs. award 1998), Pub. Libr. Assn., Libr. Adminstrn. and Mgmt. Assn. Home: 420 Baynard Dr Venice FL 34285-3301 Office: Twin Lakes Park Cmty Svcs Bus Ctr 6700 Clark Rd Sarasota FL 34241-2498 E-mail: nmpike@co.sarasota.fl.us.

PIKE, PATRICIA LOUISE, psychology educator; b. Mexico City, May 8, 1951; d. Howard Paul and Barbara Jean (Budroe) McKaughan; m. Stephen Bernard Pike, May 23, 1980; 1 child, Andrew Stephen Lee. BA, U. Hawaii, Honolulu, 1973, MA, 1975, PhD, 1979; postgrad., Calif. Sch. Profl. Psychology, L.A., 1986. Lic. psychologist, Calif. Lectr. U. Hawaii, 1978-79; mem. faculty Internat. Linguistics Ctr., Dallas, 1980-83; instr. Mountain View Coll., 1981-83; asst. prof. Rosemead Sch. of Psychology Biola U., La Mirada, Calif., 1983-92; assoc. prof., 1992—; dean Biola U., La Mirada, Calif., 1994—; psychologist Child Guidance Ctrs., Inc., Santa Ana, 1985-86; staff psychologist Biola Counseling Ctr., La Mirada, 1986—. Statis. cons. Wycliffe Bible Translators, Dallas, 1982; seminar speaker on parenting. Contbg. editor Jour. Psychology and Theology, 1987-90, editor elect, 1991-92, editor, 1992—; contbr. articles to profl. jours. Member Whittier (Calif.) Area Cmty. Ch., 1985. Mem. APA, Soc. for Rsch. in Child Devel., Phi Kappa Phi, Phi Beta Kappa. Office: Biola U Rosemead Sch Psychology 13800 Biola Ave La Mirada CA 90639-0002

PIKE, RALPH WEBSTER, chemical engineer, educator, university administrator; b. Tampa, Fla., Nov. 10, 1935; s. Ralph Webster and Macey (Adams) P.; m. Patricia Jennings, Aug. 23, 1958. B Chem. Engring., Ga. Inst. Tech., 1957, PhD, 1962. Rsch. chem. engr. Exxon R & D Co., Baytown, Tex., 1962-64; Paul M. Horton prof. chem. engring. and sys. sci. La. State U., Baton Rouge, 1964—, assoc. vice chancellor for rsch., 1975-96, dir. La. Mineral Inst.,

1979—, dean engring., 1999-2001. Cons. to chem. and petroleum refining industry, fed. govt. and State of La., 1964—. Author: Formulation and Optimization of Mathematical Models, 1970, Optimization for Engineering Systems, 1986, Optimizacion en Ingenieria, 1989. Active various civic, ch. and community orgns., Baton Rouge, 1964—. 2d lt. U.S. Army, 1958-60. Recipient over 80 rsch. grants, including NASA, NSF, Dept. Interior, EPA, NOAA, state agys. and pvt. industry, 1964—. Fellow Am. Inst. Chem. Engrs. (chmn. nat. program com. 1984, local sect. 1985); mem. Am. Chem. Soc. (Charles E. Coates Mem. Award, 1994, univ. and profl.), Sigma Xi. Democrat. Methodist. Avocation: skiing. Home: 6063 Hibiscus Dr Baton Rouge LA 70808-8844 Office: La State U 106 Ctr Energy Studies Baton Rouge LA 70803-0001 E-mail: pike@lsu.edu.

PIKE, ROBERT WILLIAM, insurance company executive, lawyer; b. Lorain, Ohio, July 25, 1941; s. Edward and Catherine (Stack) P.; m. Linda L. Feitz, Dec. 26, 1964; children: Catherine, Robert, Richard. BA, Bowling Green State U., 1963; JD, U. Toledo, 1966. Bar: Ohio 1966, Ill. 1973. Ptnr. Cubbon & Rice Law Firm, Toledo, 1968-72; asst. counsel Allstate Ins. Co., Northbrook, Ill., 1972-74, assoc. counsel, 1974-76, asst. sec., asst. gen. counsel, 1976-77, asst. v.p., asst. gen. counsel, 1977-78, v.p., asst. gen. counsel, 1978-86, sr. v.p., sec., gen. counsel, bd. dirs., 1987-99, exec. v.p., 1999—. Bd. dirs. Allstate subs. Bd. dirs., exec. com. Nat. Assn. Ind. Insurers; mem. bd. overseers Inst. for Civil Justice. Served to capt. inf. U.S. Army, 1966-68. Mem. ABA, Ill. Bar Assn., Ohio Bar Assn., Ivanhoe (Ill.) Club. Roman Catholic. Home: 1795 W North Pond Ln Lake Forest IL 60045- Office: Allstate Ins Co 2775 Sanders Rd Ste F8 Northbrook IL 60062-6127

PIKE, THOMAS HARRISON, plant chemist; b. West Palm Beach, Fla., Oct. 9, 1950; s. Rufus Draper and Dora Marie (Thomason) P.; m. Julie Lynn Simpson, Aug. 19, 1972; 1 child, Thomas Simpson. BS, Baylor U., 1972; MS, Calif. State U., 2001. Sci. instr. Valliant (Okla.) Pub. Sch., 1975-76; sch. adminstr. Swink (Okla.) Pub. Sch., 1976-81; plant chemist Western Farmers Electric Coop., Ft. Towson, Okla., 1981—. Instr. dept. sci. and engring., Eastern Okla. State Coll., 1997—; mem. adv. bd. Kiamichi Vo-Tech Sch., Idabel, Okla., 1985-87. Charter mem. Valliant Youth Assn., 1987-91. Mem. ASME (co-chmn. task force 1988-90), ASTM, Nat. Assn. Corrosion Engrs. Achievements include research in corrosion control of condensers, case history of turbine problems, improving boiler efficiency, preservation of turbines during extended outages, metal oxide transport, and water clarification; 2 patents in chemical process control technology. Home: RR 1 Box 299 Garvin OK 74736-9755 Office: Western Farmers Electric Coop PO Box 219 Fort Towson OK 74735-0219 E-mail: tpike@wfec.com.

PIKE, WILLIAM EDWARD, business executive; b. Ft. Collins, Colo., Jan. 25, 1929; s. Harry H. and Alice Francis (Swinscoe) P.; m. Catherine Broward Crawford, June 26, 1965; children: Elizabeth Catherine, Robert Crawford, Daniel William. Student, U. Colo., 1947-48; BS, U.S. Naval Acad., 1952; MBA, Harvard, 1960. Commd. ensign USN, 1952, advanced through grades to lt., 1958; ret., 1958; asst. treas. Morgan Guaranty Trust Co., N.Y.C., 1962-64, asst. v.p., 1964-66, v.p., 1966-71, sr. v.p., 1971-74, chmn. credit policy com., 1974-86; exec. v.p. J.P. Morgan & Co. Inc., 1986-89; corp. dir., trustee, pvt. investor. Bd. dirs. Global Lift Techs., Inc., Somat Corp. Mem. Harvard Club N.Y.C. Clubs: Country (New Canaan, Conn.). Episcopalian. Home: Indian Waters Dr New Canaan CT 06840 Office: 36 Grove St New Canaan CT 06840-5329

PIKLO, CHARLENE LORRAINE, retail management executive; b. Camden, N.J., Sept. 21, 1954; d. John Alfred and Loretta H. (Vogt) P. BS, U. Tampa, 1975. Mgr. trainee Roses Stores Inc., Macon, Ga., 1975-76, asst. mgr. Onley, Va., 1976, sr. asst. mgr. Burlington, N.C., 1976-77, merchandiser Henderson, 1977-78, asst. buyer N.Y.C., 1978-79, buyer Henderson, 1979-83, div. mgr. mdse., 1983-86; v.p., gen. mdse. mgr. Conston Corp., Phila., 1986-90; gen. mdse. mgr., v.p. Crystal Brands Retail, Reading, 1990-93; pres. Creative Giftworks, 1993-95; dir. retail merchandising Disney Direct Mktg. Svcs., Inc., Edison, N.J., 1994-95; v.p., gen. mgr. retail divsn. Totes Inc., Loveland, Ohio, 1995-97; COO Mktg. Concepts, Chalfont, Pa., 1997—; pres., CEO Party Ptnrs., Inc., Ardmore, 1998—2001, Kamikaze Kids Enterprises, Inc., Newtown, 2001—. Recipient Torch of Liberty, Anti-Defamation League, 1988—; Phi Gamma Nu scholar, 1975. Mem. NAFE, Profl. Bus. Sorority, Phi Gamma Nu. Office: 2 Virginia Ave # 513 Rehoboth Beach DE 19971-2813 E-mail: mconcept@bellatlantic.net.

PIKUL, FRANK JOHN, pathologist; b. E. St. Louis, Ill., July 23, 1951; s. Frank John and Frances Helen (Czosnyka) P.; m. Danuta Jadwiga Walczyk, Oct. 8, 1979; children: Frank John, Sarah Diane. BS, Bradley U., 1973; postgrad., Jagiellonian U., Krakow, Poland, 1976; MD, Acad. of Medicine, Wroclaw, Poland, 1981. Diplomate Am. Bd. Pathology. Grad. rsch. asst. So. Ill. U., Edwardsville, 1973-75; resident in pathology Barnes Hosp./Wash. U., St. Louis, 1981-84, chief resident, 1984-85, fellow in hematopathology, 1985-86, St. Jude Children's Hosp., Memphis, 1985-86; resident in lab. medicine Barnes Hosp./Wash. U., St. Louis, 1986-88; asst. prof. pathology, dir. blood bank, surg. pathologist Health Scis. Ctr. Okla. U. and VA Med. Ctr., 1988—. Contbr. articles to profl. jours. Soccer coach Our Lady of Assumption, Fairview Hgts., Ill., 1986, 87; baseball coach Fairview Hgts. Recreational Assn., 1986, 87; physician adult leader Christ the King Troop 120, Oklahoma City; reviewer sci. com. Am. Assn. Blood Banks; bd. dirs. Am. Red Cross, Tulsa. Recipient fellowship Am. Cancer Soc., St. Louis, 1985-86, Nat. Sci. Found. Undergrad. Rsch. Participation award, 1972; grantee NIH, St. Louis, 1982-83; scholarship Nat. Cancer Inst., Chgo., 1986. Mem. AMA, Okla. State Med. Soc., Okla. City Med. Soc., St. Clair County Med. Soc., Am. Ass. Blood Banks, Acad. Clinical Lab. Physicians and Scientists. Roman Catholic. Avocations: camping, fishing. Home: 42 Gamlin Dr Fairview Heights IL 62208-1718 Office: Okla Med Ctr PO Box 26307 Oklahoma City OK 73126-0307

PILAND, NEILL FINNES, health services economist, researcher; b. Pomona, Calif., Nov. 6, 1943; s. Finnes Elmer and Sylvia Beatrice (Renick) PiL.; m. Diane Lynn Fiedor, Aug. 12, 1977; children: Evan Neill, Spencer Lowell, Arden Geneva. BA, UCLA, 1965, MPH, 1970, DrPH, 1979; MA, U. Calif., Davis, 1966. Rsch. assoc. Sch. Pub. Health UCLA, 1971-73, sr. rsch. assoc., 1973; health economist Stanford Rsch. Inst., Menlo Pk., Calif., 1973-77, asst. mgr. health svcs. rsch., 1974-77; dir. health ctr. study Jicarilla Apache Tribe, Dulce, N.Mex., 1978-82; dir. health systems evaluation program Lovelace Med. Found., Albuquerque, 1982-83, dir. health svcs. rsch. and edn., 1983-91; dir. Ctr. Health & Population Rsch., 1991-94, Lovelace Inst. for Health and Population Rsch., Albuquerque, 1994-96; rsch. dir. Ctr. Rsch. Med. Group Mgmt. Assn., Englewood, Colo., 1996—2002; prof. and dir. Inst. Rural Health, Idaho State U., Pocatello, 2002—; clin. assoc. prof. U. Colo. Sch. Medicine; rsch. prof. U. Denver; 0. Clin. asst. prof. medicine U. N.Mex., Albuquerque, 1981, clin. assoc. prof., 1994—; vis. prof. U. N.H., Durham, 1989-90. Co-author: Strategic Nursing Management: Power and Responsibility in a New Era; mem. editorial bd. Jour. Managerial Issues, 1991—; co-editor: Physician Profiling: A Sourcebook for Adminstrators, Chart Accounts for Healthcare Organizations; contbr. over 90 articles to profl. jours. Mem. rsch. com. N.Mex. HealthNet, 1986-88; chair econ. issues N.Mex. Com. on Pub. Health Impact of Smoking, 1988; bd. dirs. Am. Geriatrics and Gerontology, 1984-87, Healthcare for Homeless, 1988-92; mem. exec. coun. N.Mex. ASSIST Com., 1992—, sci. adv. com. N.Mex. ASSIST Project, 1992—; mem. steering com. Group Practice Improvement Network, 1996—; mem. workgroup smoking control Colo. Dept. Health and Environment, 1999— Recipient traineeship, USPHS, 1968-70. Mem. APHA, Am. Econ. Assn., Soc. Rsch. Adminstrs., Assn. Health Svcs. Rsch. Avocations: tennis, hockey, hiking, biking. Office: IRH/ISV Gravely AP11 215 Idaho State U Pocatello ID 83209 Home: 132 Fairway Dr Pocatello ID 83201 E-mail: pilaneil@isu.edu.

PILARCZYK, DANIEL EDWARD, archbishop; b. Dayton, Ohio, Aug. 12, 1934; s. Daniel Joseph and Frieda S. (Hilgefort) P. Student, St. Gregory Sem., Cin., 1948-53; PhB, Pontifical Urban U., Rome, 1955, PhL, 1956, STB, 1958, STL, 1960, STD, 1961; MA, Xavier U., 1965; PhD, U. Cin., 1969; LLD (hon.), Xavier U., 1975, Calumet Coll., 1982, U. Dayton, 1990, Marquette U., 1990, Thomas More Coll., 1991, Coll. Mount St. Joseph, 1994, Hebrew Union Coll.- Jewish Inst. Religion, 1997. Ordained priest Roman Catholic Ch. , 1959; asst. chancellor Archdiocese of Cin., 1961-63; synodal judge Archdiocesan Tribunal, 1971-82; mem. faculty Athenaeum of Ohio, St. Gregory Sem., 1963-74; v.p. Athenaeum of Ohio, 1968-74, trustee, 1974—; also rector St. Gregory Sem., 1968-74; archdiocesan dir. ednl. services, 1974-82; aux. bishop of Cin., 1974-82; vicar gen., 1974-82; archbishop of Cin., 1982—. Bd. dirs. Pope John Ctr., 1978-85; trustee Cath. Health Assn., 1982-85, Cath. U. Am., 1983-91, 97—, Pontifical Coll. Josephinum, 1983-92; v.p. Nat. Conf. Cath. Bishops, 1986-89, pres., 1989-92, chmn. Com. on Doctrine, 1996-2000; U.S. rep. Episc. Bd. Internat. Commn. on English in Liturgy 1987-97; chmn., 1991-97; mem. jt. com. Orthodox and Cath. Bishops, 2002. Author: Praepositini Cancellarii de Sacramentis et de Novissimis, 1964—65, Twelve Tough Issues, 1988, We Believe, 1989, Living in the Lord, 1990, The Parish: Where God's People Live, 1991, Forgiveness, 1992, What Must I Do?, 1993, Our Priests: Who They Are and What They Do, 1994, Sacraments, 1994, Bringing Forth Justice, 1996, 1999, Thinking Catholic, 1998, Practicing Catholic, 1999, Believing Catholic, 2000, Live Letters, 2001, Twelve Tough Issues and More, 2002. Ohio Classical Conf. scholar to Athens, 1966 Mem. Am. Philol. Assn. Home and Office: 100 E 8th St Cincinnati OH 45202-2129

PILCHER, JAMES BROWNIE, lawyer; b. Shreveport, La., May 19, 1929; s. James Reece and Martha Mae (Brown) P.; m. Lorene Pilcher; children: Lydia, Martha, Bradley. BA, La. State U., 1952; JD summa cum laude, John Marshall Law Sch., 1955; postgrad., Emory U., 1957. Bar: Ga. 1955. Legal aide to Spkr. of Ho. of Reps., Ga., 1961-64; assoc. city atty. City of Atlanta, 1964-69; pvt. practice law Atlanta, 1969—. Exec. committeeman Dem. Exec. Com. of Fulton County, Ga., 1974-86; bd. dirs. Whitehead Boys Club, 1961-89; trustee Ga. Inst. Continuing Legal Edn., 1988-89. Fellow Lawyers Found. Ga., 1996—. Mem. ABA, State Bar Ga. (chmn. 1988-89, gen. practice and trial sect., chmn. criminal law sect. 1986-87), Ga. Assn. Criminal Def. Lawyers (pres. 1980-82), Ga. Trial Lawyers Assn. (life), Ga. Claimants Attys. Assn. (pres. 1983-84), NACDL (bd. dirs. 1980-85), Ga. Inst. Trial Advocacy (bd. dirs. 1986-89), South Fulton Bar Assn. (pres. 1987-88), Am. Bankruptcy Inst., Nat. Assn. Consumer Bankruptcy Attys., Trial Lawyers for Pub. Justice, Atlanta Consumer Bankruptcy Attys. Group (pres. 2001—), Kiwanis (Peachtree, Atlanta pres. 1983-84, gov. Ga. dist. 1992-93), Sierra Club of Am. (life). Presbyterian. Home: 1195 W Wesley Rd NW Atlanta GA 30327-1407 Office: One Northside 75 Atlanta GA 30318-7715 E-mail: pilcherj@bellsouth.net.

PILCHIK, ELY EMANUEL, rabbi, writer; b. Russia, June 12, 1913; came to U.S., 1920, naturalized, 1920; s. Abraham and Rebecca (Lipovitch) P.; m. Ruth Schuchat, Nov. 20, 1941 (dec. 1977); children: Susan Pilchik Rosenbaum, Judith Pilchik Zucker; m. Harriet Krichman Perlmutter, June, 1981. AB, U. Cin., 1935; M.Hebrew Lit., Hebrew Union Coll., 1936, D.D., 1964. Ordained rabbi, 1939; founder, dir. Hillel Found. at U. Md., 1939-40; asst. rabbi Har Sinai Temple, Balt., 1940-41; rabbi Temple Israel, Tulsa, 1942-47, Temple B'nai Jeshurun, Short Hills, N.J., 1947-81; prof. Jewish Thought Upsala Coll., 1969—. Pres. Jewish Book Council Am., 1957-58 Author: books, including Hillel, 1951, From the Beginning, 1956, Judaism Outside the Holy Land, 1964, Jeshurun Essays, 1967, A Psalm of David, 1967, Talmud Thought, 1983, Midrash Memoir, 1984, Touches of Einstein, 1987, Luzzatto on Loving Kindness, 1987, Prayer in History, 1989; author: play Toby, 1968; lyricist 6 cantatas; contbr. articles to profl. and gen. jours. Bd. dirs. Newark Mus.; mem. ethics com. N.J. Bar Assn. Served as chaplain USNR, 1944-46. Mem. N.J. Bd. Rabbis (pres. 1955-57), Central Conf. Am. Rabbis (pres. 1977-79) Office: 1025 S Orange Ave Short Hills NJ 07078-3135 *I have been influenced by the teaching of the 1st Century sage Hillel who said: "If I am not for myself, who will be for me? And if I am for myself only, what am I? And if not now, when?".*

PILCZ, MALETA, psychotherapist; b. Poland, June 5, 1945; came to U.S., 1949; s. Victor and Hana (Oks) P. BA in Psychology, Bklyn. Coll., 1967; MA in Social Work, U. Chgo., 1969. Diplomate Am. Bd. Examiners Clin. Social Work, diplomate in clin. social work; cert. social worker, N.Y. Psychotherapist Scholarship and Guidance Assn., Chgo., 1969-71; family therapist, supr. Northwestern Meml. Hosp., 1972-75; pvt. practice, psychotherapist, cons., 1974-80, N.Y.C., 1980—. Field work instr. U. Chgo. Sch. of Social Svcs., 1974-75; instr. dept. psychiatry Northwestern U. Med. Sch., 1973-75; cons. faculty Ctr. for Family Studies, Family Inst. Chgo., 1978-80; assoc. staff Ackerman Inst. Family Therapy, N.Y.C., 1983-88; part-time instr. Hunter Coll. Sch. of Social Work, N.Y.C., 1985-88; cons. N.Y.C. Bd. Edn., 1988—. Author: Understanding the Survivor Family; thematic cons. documentary film The Legacy, 1979 (Cigne Gold Eagle, Red Ribbon Am. Film Festival, 1980). Fellow Am. Orthopsychiat. Assn.; mem. NASW (diplomate clin. social work), Am. Group Psychotherapy Assn., Acad. Cert. Social Workers. Avocations: world travel, hiking, theater, the arts. Office: 330 E 46th St Apt 12D New York NY 10017-3076

PILETTE, PATRICIA CHEHY, healthcare organizational management consultant; b. Rutland, Vt., June 28, 1945; d. John Edward and Mary T. (McNamara) Chehy; m. Wilfrid Pilette, July 22, 1972; 1 child, Patrick John. Diploma, Jeanne Mance Sch. Nursing, 1966; BSN magna cum laude, St. Anselm Coll., 1971; MS summa cum laude, Boston U., 1974, EdD in Counseling and Human Svcs. Adminstrn. summa cum laude, 1984. RN, Mass. Clin. specialist adult psychiatry counseling practice, Natick, Mass.; employee assistance counselor St. Elizabeth's Med. Ctr., 1984—. Contbr. articles to profl. publs., chpts. to books. Mem.: Am. Mental Health Counselors Assn., N.Am. Soc. Employee Assistance, Assn. for Humanistic Psychologists, Am. Psychotherapy Assn. (diplomate), N.E. Soc. Group Psychotherapists, N.E. Assn. for Specialists in Group Work, Mass. Orgn. Nurse Execs., Sigma Theta Tau, Pi Lambda Theta.

PILGERAM, LAURENCE OSCAR, biochemist; b. Great Falls, Mont., June 23, 1924; s. John Rudolph and Bertha Roslyn (Phillips) P.; m. Cynthia Ann Moore, Apr. 16, 1971; children: Karl Erich, Kurt John. AA, U. Calif., Berkeley, 1948, BA, 1949, PhD, 1953. Instr. dept. physiology U. Ill. Profl. Coll., Chgo., 1954-55; asst. prof. dept. biochemistry Stanford (Calif.) U. Sch. Medicine, 1955-57; dir. arteriosclerosis research lab. U. Minn. Sch. Medicine, Mpls., 1957-65, Santa Barbara, Calif., 1965-71; dir. coagulation lab., assoc. dir. Cerebrovascular Research Ctr., Baylor Coll. Medicine, Tex. Med. Ctr., Houston, 1971-75; dir. Thrombosis Control Labs., Palo Alto, Calif., 1975-79, Santa Barbara, 1979—. Cons. NIH, Bio-Sci. Labs., FDA; del. Council on Thrombosis and Council on Strokes, Am. Heart Assn. Assembly. Co-editor: Nutrition and Thrombosis for the Nat. Dairy Council, 1973; contbr. sci. articles to profl. jours. Recipient CIBA award, London, 1958, Karl Thomae award, Germany, 1973; NIH grantee, 1954-75; LIfe Ins. Med. Research Fund fellow, 1952-54. Mem. Am. Soc. for Biochemistry and Molecular Biology. Office: PO Box 1583 Goleta PO Santa Barbara CA 93116

PILGRIM, DIANNE HAUSERMAN, retired museum director; b. Cleve., July 8, 1941; d. John Martin and Norma Hauserman; divorced. BA, Pa. State U., 1963; MA, Inst. Fine Arts, NYU, 1965; postgrad., CUNY, 1971-74; LHD (hon.), Amherst Coll., 1991, Pratt Inst., 1994. Chester Dale fellow Am. wing. Met. Mus. Art, N.Y.C., 1966-68, rsch. cons. Am. paintings and sculpture, 1971-73; asst. to dirs. Pyramid Galleries, Ltd., Washington, 1969-71, Finch Coll. Mus. Art, Washington, 1971; curator dept. decorative arts Bklyn. Mus., 1973-88, chmn. dept., 1988; dir. Cooper-Hewitt Nat. Design Mus., N.Y.C., 1988-2000, dir. emeritus, 2000—. Mem. adv. com. Gracie Mansion, N.Y.C., 1980; mem. design adv. com. Art Inst. Chgo., 1988; mem. Hist. House Trust N.Y.C., Mayor's Office, 1989-94. Co-author, curator: (book and exhbn. catalogue) Mr. and Mrs. Raymond Horowitz Collection of American Impressionist and Realist Paintings, 1973, The American Renaissance 1876-1917, 1979; (book) The Machine Age in America 1918-1941, 1986 (Charles F. Montgomery prize Decorative Arts Soc.). Bd. dirs. Nat. Multiple Sclerosis Soc., 1989. Recipient Disting. Alumni award Pa. State U., 1991. Mem. Decorative Arts Soc. (pres. 1977-79), Art Deco Soc., Victorian Soc., Art Table.*

PILGRIM, JAMES ROLLINS, retail furniture company executive; b. Atlanta, July 16, 1947; s. George Ezra and Lula May (Rollins) P.; children: Kelley P. Watkins, Amy M. Paul. AS, Gainesville Coll., 1970; BS in Edn., U. Ga., Athens, 1972. Div. mgr. Sears Roebuck & Co., Gainesville, 1965-72; mgr. Power Bldg. Products, Athens, 1972-78; salesman Pilgrim-Estes Furniture Co., Inc., Gainesville, 1978-88, v.p., 1988-90, Pilgrim Holding Co., Gainesville, 1990—; mgr. Loosier of Gainesville DBA Pilgrim-Estes Furniture Co., 1990-95; pres. 45th Trading Co., Inc., Gainesville, 1996—; mgr. Allen Waters, Inc. Furniture Gallery, 1997—; v.p. Allen Waters, Inc. Pres. Friends of Parks, 2000-01. Mem. Downtown Mchts. Assn. (pres. 1980-84), Chattahoochee Country Club (mem. com. 1992-94), Elks (exalted ruler Gainesville 1994-95, v.p. Ga. chpt. 1995-96, pres. Ga. assn. 2001—, dist. dep. grand exalted ruler 1996-97). Republican. Methodist. Avocations: golf, music, investments. Home: 4038 Oak Harbour Cir Gainesville GA 30506-3060 Office: 1001 Riverside Dr Gainesville GA 30501-1825

PILIAWSKY, MONTE EDDY, college program director; b. New Orleans, Feb. 6, 1944; s. Nathan and Sadye (Washofsky) P.; m. Joan Ellen Mahoney, Mar. 12, 1988; 1 child, Rachel Hannah. BA, U. New Orleans, 1965; MA, Tulane U., 1968, PhD, 1970. Asst. prof. polit. sci. U. So. Miss., Hattiesburg, 1970-72; prof. polit. sci., dir. instl. rsch. Dillard U., New Orleans, 1974-87; prof. polit. sci. Penn Valley C.C., Kansas City, Mo., 1988-94; dir. ednl. studies program Trinity Coll., Hartford, Conn., 1995-98; assoc. prof. edn. Wayne State U., Detroit, 1999—. Vis. prof. polit. sci. U. Mo., Kansas City, 1990-94; cons. Random House Pubs., N.Y.C., 1986, Ednl. Testing Svc., Princeton, N.J., 1976, U.S. Bur. of Census, New Orleans, 1973-74. Author: Exit 13: Oppression and Racism in Academia, 1982; contbr. articles to jours. in field; mem. editl. bd. So. Conf. on Afro-Am. Studies, Houston, 1992—. Mem. Mayor's Task Force revision of police acad. curriculum, New Orleans, 1981; mem. program com. Met. Area Com., New Orleans, 1982; mem. adv. coun. La. Sch. for Math., Sci. and Arts, New Orleans, 1983; mem. adv. com. Alliance for Affordable Energy, New Orleans, 1986. Strengthening the Humanities fellow United Negro Coll. Fund, 1987-88, Nat. Def. Edn. Act fellow U.S. Govt., 1965-68. Mem. Am. Polit. Sci. Assn., Nat. Conf. Black Polit. Scientists, Assn. for Study of Afro-Am. Life and History, Soc. Ednl. Reconstrn., So. Polit. Sci. Assn., So. Conf. on Afro-Am. Studies. Jewish. Avocations: jogging, travel. Home: 28173 Brentwood Southfield MI 48076 E-mail: AG1844@wayne.edu.

PILISUK, MARC, community psychology educator; b. N.Y.C., Jan. 19, 1934; s. Louis and Charlotte (Feferholtz) P.; m. Phyllis E. Kamen, June 16, 1956; children: Tammy, Jeff. BA, Queens Coll., 1955; MA, U. Mich., 1956, PhD, 1961. Asst. prof., assoc. rsch. psychologist U. Mich., Ann Arbor, 1961-65, founder teach-in, 1965; assoc. prof. Purdue U., West Lafayette, Ind., 1965-67; prof.-in-residence U. Calif., Berkeley, 1967-77, prof. cmty. psychology Davis, 1977—. Vis. prof. U. Calif., Wright Inst., 1991—93; cons. Ctr. for Self Help Rsch., Berkeley, Calif., 1991—93; prof. psychology Saybrook Inst. and Grad. Ctr., San Francisco, 1993—. Author: (novels) International Conflict and Social Policy, 1972, The Healing Web: Social Networks and Human Survival, 1986; editor The Triple Revolution , 1969, Poor Americans, 1970, Triple Revolution Emerging, 1972, How We Lost the War on Poverty, 1973. Fellow, NIMH, 1959—60; grantee, NSF, 1962—66, tng. grantee, Nat. Inst. Alcoholism and Drug Abuse, 1973—77. Fellow: ACLU, APA (pres. divsn. peace psychology 1996—97, cadre exports violence), Am. Orthopsychiat. Assn., Soc. for Psychol. Study Social Issues (coun.), Soc. for Cmty. Rsch. and Action; mem.: APHA, Faculty for Human Rights in C.Am., Psychologists for Social Responsibility (steering com., Disting. Svc. award 2001), Am. Soc. on Aging. E-mail: mpilisuk@saybrook.edu.

PILKERTON, ARTHUR RAYMOND, JR. surgeon, educator; b. Washington, Mar. 27, 1935; s. Arthur Raymond and Mary Rose (Ginechesi) P.; m. Sally Ann Madden, Aug. 6, 1966; children: A. Raymond III, Joseph A., Mary, Christopher, Jeanne Marie. BS in Biology, Georgetown U., 1952-56, MD, 1960. Diplomate Am. Bd. Opthalmology. Intern. U. Pitts., 1961; fellow retina surgery Wills Eye Hosp., Phila., 1964-65; resident ophthalmology Georgetown U. Med. Ctr., Washington, 1961-64, asst. prof., 1965-70, assoc. prof., 1971-78, clin. prof., 1978—; asst. clin. prof. George Washington U., 1985—. Chief ophthalmology Veteran's Adminstrn. Hosp., Washington, 1965-82; chmn. ophthalmology cons., Veterans Adminstrn., Washington, 1978-82. Served with U.S. Army, 1961-70. Named Knight of Malta, Knight Comdr. Holy Sepulchre. Fellow Am. Acad. Ophthalmology, Am. Coll. Surgeons; mem. Retina Soc. U.S., Uitreous Soc. Republican. Roman Catholic. Office: Retina Group Washington 5454 Wisconsin Ave Suite 1540 Chevy Chase MD 20815

PILKINGTON, MARY ELLEN, stockbroker, trader; b. N.Y.C., Feb. 16, 1955; d. Charles Arthur Bertrand and Mary (Lynch) Perez; m. Scott Douglas Ballin (div. 1986); m. John J. Pilkington, Aug. 19, 1994. BA in Polit. Sci., Mt. Vernon Coll., Washington, 1976. Dir. materials ctr. Gen. Fedn. of Women's Clubs, Washington, 1978-80; broker, asst. to the chmn. Folger Nolan Fleming Douglas, 1980-85; broker, account exec. Rose & Co., N.Y.C., 1985-86; trader Bear Stearns, 1986-88; trader, broker Robyns Capital, 1988-89; trader, v.p. trading Jessop Capital Corp., 1989-91, Kidder Peabody, 1992-94, Dean Witter, 1994-95, Gabelli & Co., 1996—. Trustee Mt. Vernon Coll., Washington, 1999. Roman Catholic. Avocations: golf, skiing, tennis, squash, photography.

PILL, CYNTHIA JOAN, social worker; b. N.Y.C., Mar. 30, 1939; d. Alfred and Edna (Strauss) Fruchtman; m. Robert Pill, July 29, 1961; children: Laura, Daniel, Karen. BS cum laude, Jackson Coll., Tufts U., 1961; MS in Social Work, Simmons Coll., 1963, PhD in Social Work, 1987. Lic. ind. clin. social worker. Clin. social worker Concord (Mass.) Family Sc., 1965-78; coord. family life edn. Family Counseling Svc., Newton, Mass., 1979-83; pvt. practice clin. social work, 1979—; adj. asst. prof., rsch. advisor Smith Coll. Sch. for Social Work, 1988—99. Adj. asst. prof. Simmons Coll. Sch. Social Work, Boston, 1989-93. Contbr. articles to profl. jours. Vol. coord. Hospice at Home, Sudbury, Mass., 1986-88. Mem. NASW, Mass. Soc. Clin. Social Work, Register Clin. Social Workers (bd. cert. diplomate). Address: 14 Mason Rd Newton Center MA 02459-1506

PILLANS, CHARLES PALMER, III, lawyer; b. Orlando, Fla., Feb. 22, 1940; s. Charles Palmer Jr. and Helen (Scarborough) P.; m. Judith Hart, July 6, 1963; children: Charles Palmer IV, Helen Hart. BA, U. Fla., 1962, JD, 1966. Bar: Fla. 1967, U.S. Dist. Ct. (mid. dist.) Fla. 1967, U.S. Ct. Appeals (2d cir.) 1968, U.S. Supreme Ct. 1971, U.S. Ct. Appeals (3d cir.) 1976, U.S. Ct. Appeals (5th and 11th cirs.) 1981. Assoc. Bedell, Bedell, Dittmar, Smith & Zehmer, Jacksonville, Fla., 1966-70; asst. state atty. 4th jud. cir., 1970-72; asst. gen. counsel City of Jacksonville, 1972; ptnr. Bedell, Dittmar, DeVault Pillans & Coxe, P.A., Jacksonville, 1972—. Mem. Fla. Bd. Bar Examiners, Tallahassee, 1979-84, chmn., 1983-84, Jud. Nominating Commn., 1988-92, chmn., 1990-91, 1st Dist. Ct. Appeal, Tallahassee, 1988-92, chmn., 1990-91, Supreme Ct. com. on standard jury instructions in civil cases, 1998—. Master Chester Bedell Inn of Ct.; fellow Am. Coll. Trial Lawyers, ABA; mem. Am. Bar Found., Fla. Bar Assn. (chmn. profl. ethics com. 1998—, chmn. 1998-99). Methodist. Home: 10 Buckthorne Dr Amelia Island FL 32034-6518 Office: Bedell Dittmar DeVault Pillans & Coxe PA Bedell Bldg 101 E Adams St Jacksonville FL 32202-3303 E-mail: cpillans@bedellfirm.com.

PILLARELLA, DEBORAH ANN, fitness program manager, elementary education educator, consultant; b. Chgo., Oct. 2, 1960; d. Richard J. and Josephine A. (Miceli) Ban; m. James J. Pillarella, Sept. 1, 1989; children: Joseph, Luke. BA in Edn., U. Ill., 1983, MEd in Ednl. Leadership, 1992. Tchr. elem. sch. Chgo. Bd. Edn., 1983-98; fitness program mgr., program developer Cmty. Hosp. Fitness Pointe, Munster, Ind., 2001—. Youth and adult cons. Bodyworks, Chgo., 1982-98; sec. Profl. PPAC, Chgo., 1990-94; cons. IDEA, San Diego, 1989-99; adv. bd. Am. Coun. on Exercise, 1995, youth fitness spokesperson, 2001—. Author: Healthy Choices for Kids, 1993, Step Fitness, 1995, Adventures in Fitness, 1995. Vol. activist City of Hope, Chgo., 1990-99; side coord. Cystic Fiborsis Found., Chgo., 1988; vol. Chgo. Heart Assn., 1989. Mem. AAHPERD, Am. Coll. Sports Medicine, Chgo. Tchrs. Union, Phi Kappa Phi. Avocations: biking, hiking, swimming, walking, reading. Home: 8409 Castle Dr Munster IN 46321-1933 Office: Cmty Hosp Fitness Pointe 9950 S Calumet Ave Munster IN 46321 E-mail: dpillarella@comhs.org.

PILLARI, VINCENT THOMAS, obstetrician-gynecologist, educator; b. N.Y.C., 1936; MD, Loyola U., 1962. Intern St. Vincents Hosp., N.Y.C., 1962-63; resident ob-gyn. Nassau Hosp., Mineola, N.Y., 1963-64, SUNY Upstate, Syracuse, 1964-66; chmn. dept. ob-gyn. St. Vincents Med. Ctr.-Richmond, S.I., N.Y. Clin. assoc. prof. ob-gyn. N.Y. Med. Coll., Valhalla. Fellow ACOG; mem. Bklyn. Gynecol. Soc., Martin L. Stone Ob-gyn Soc., N.Y. State Med. Soc. Office: 355 Bard Ave Staten Island NY 10310-1664

PILLINGER, MICHAEL H. physician; b. Queens, N.Y., July 13, 1959; s. James J. and Evelyn S. P.; m. Judy Goldman; 1 child, Kaley Pillinger. BA in Biochemistry cum laude, Harvard Coll., 1981; MD, NYU, 1987. Diplomate Nat. Bd. Med. Examiners, Am. Bd. Internal Medicine, Am. Bd. Rheumatology. Resident in internal medicine Albert Einstein Coll. Medicine, 1987-90; fellowship in rheumatology NYU Med. Ctr./Hosp. for Joint Diseases, 1990-93; tchg. asst. NYU Sch. Medicine, 1990-93, instr., 1993-96, asst. prof., 1996—, faculty Post-Grad. Med. Sch. Seminar, 1994—, dir. med. edn. divsn. rheumatology, 1999—; chmn. rheumatology Manhattan VA Hosp., 2000—. Guest lectr. in medicine SUNY Coll. of Optometry, 1990—; rschr. in field. Bd. dirs. Coyote Theatre Co., Chappaqua, NY, 1995—; chmn. med. and sci. com. Arthritis Found. N.Y., 2000—. Recipient Arthritis Investigator award (Hulda Irene Duggan award), 1995—; Skirball Clin. fellow, 1994; grantee N.Y. Arthritis Found., 1994, Am. Cancer Soc., 1996, others. Mem.: Am. Coll. Rheumatology (abstract selection com. 2000—). Democrat. Jewish. Avocations: writing fiction and poetry, theatre-set designer, marathon running. Office: Manhattan VA Hosp Dept Medicine 423 E 23rd St New York NY 10010-5099 E-mail: michael.pillinger@med.nyu.edu.

PILLOT, GENE MERRILL, retired school system administrator; b. Canton, Ohio, Apr. 13, 1930; s. John D. Pillot and Vera R. Granstaff; m. Beverly Ann Shaw, June 4, 1982; children: Vera Kathleen Martin, Michael Gene, Patrick Merrill. BS in Math., Ohio State U., 1952; MEd in Adminstrn. and Supvervision, Kent State U., 1957; EdD in Adminstrn. and Supervision, U. Fla., 1970. Asst. prin. North Royalton (Ohio) High Sch., 1959-61, prin., 1961-63; asst. prin. Sarasota (Fla.) Sr. High Sch., 1963-64, prin., 1964-68; dir. staff development Sarasota Dist. Schs., 1968-70, asst. supt., 1970-71, supt., 1971-80; dir. human resources Sarasota Meml Hosp., 1980-83; owner, broker Pillot Realty, Sarasota, 1986-90; commr. Sarasota City, 1989-2001, vice mayor, 1992-93, 96-97, 99-2000, mayor, 1993-94, 97-98, 2000-2001. Prof. Am. Assn. Sch. Adminstrn., Nat. Acad. Sch. Execs., 1969-73; adj. prof. U. South Fla., Tampa, 1978-81; pvt. cons. edn. orgns., 1969-76. Author (chpt.) Differentiated Staffing, Strategies for D.S., 1971; contbr. articles to profl. jours. Trustee Fla. Sch. Deaf/Blind, St. Augustine, 1980-89, chmn. bd. trustees, 1986-89; bd. dirs. Riverview Found., 1985-94, Girls Club, Sarasota, 1985-89, Hospice Found., Sarasota Opera Assn., Hispanic Am. Alliance; mem. Civil Svc. Bd. Sarasota, 1984-89; mem. adv. bd. Cath. Social Svcs., 1987-89. Mem.: Phi Delta Kappa (Educator of Yr. 1980). Republican. Roman Catholic. Avocations: genealogy, ballroom dancing. Home: 1212 Hillview Dr Sarasota FL 34239-2020 E-mail: gpillot@aol.com.

PILLOTE, BARBARA WIEGAND, volunteer; b. Washington, Jan. 31, 1930; d. Martin Tripp and Elizabeth Beryl (Wagner) Wiegand; m. Robert Lawrence Pillote, July 25, 1953; children: Margaret Lynn, Katherine Elizabeth, Robert Lawrence, Jr. BA, Conn. Coll., New London, 1951. Lab technician Hunter Labs., Washington, 1951-52; sec. Bur. Svc. Mil. Personnel, Luth. Ch. Am., 1953-54. Pres., bd. trustees Nat. Luth. Home for Aged, 1991-93; active St. Paul's Luth. Ch., Washington, Montgomery County Lung Assn. Recipient Achievement award Montgomery County Lung Assn., 1977-85. Mem. Woman's Club Chevy Chase Md. (pres. 1973-75), Montgomery County Fedn. Women's Clubs (pres. 1990-92), Md. Fedn. Women's Clubs (first v.p. 1996-98, pres. 1998-2000, Md. Clubwoman of Yr. 1980), Md. Assn. Parliamentarians, Conn. Coll. Alumni Assn. Republican. Avocations: knitting, golf, family activities.

PILLSBURY, GEORGE STURGIS, investment adviser; b. Crystal Bay, Minn., July 17, 1921; s. John S. and Eleanor (Lawler) P.; m. Sally Whitney, Jan. 4, 1947; children: Charles Alfred, George Sturgis, Sarah Kimball, Katharine Whitney. BA, Yale U., 1943. Dir. emeritus Sargent Mgmt. Co. Mem. Seminole Golf Club (Juno Beach, Fla.), Lafayette Club, Woodhill Club, Minnetonka Yacht Club, Mpls. Club, River Club (N.Y.C.). Home: 1300 Bracketts Point Rd Wayzata MN 55391-9393 Office: 901 Marquette Ave Ste 2630 Minneapolis MN 55402-3230 E-mail: gspbury@smcinv.com.

PILLSBURY, HAROLD CROCKETT, III, otolaryngologist; b. Balt., Dec. 5, 1947; m. Sally Adrienne Pillsbury; children: Matthew, Benjamin, Thomas. BA, George Washington U., Washington, 1970, MD, 1972. Diplomate Nat. Bd. Med. Examiners, Am. Bd. Otolaryngology; lic. Conn., N.C. Resident gen. surgery U. N.C., Chapel Hill, 1972-73, resident otolaryngology, 1973-76; fellow Kantonsspital, Zurich, Switzerland, 1977; asst. prof. otolaryngology Yale U., New Haven, 1977-81, assoc. prof. otolaryngology, 1981-82; assoc. prof. surgery, otolaryngology, head and neck surgery U. N.C. Sch. Medicine, Chapel Hill, 1982-86, prof. surgery, otolaryngology, head and neck surgery, 1986—, Thomas J. Dark Disting. Prof., 1991—. Civilian cons. USAF Surgeon Gen. for Otolaryngology-Head and Neck Surgery, 1993; hon. guest lectr. Alpha Omega Alpha Induction Ceremonies, U. N.C., Chapel Hill, 1990, 91, Sch. of Medicine Commencement Ceremony, U. N.C., 1990. Alpha Omega Alpha Induction Ceremonies, U. W. Va., 1991; Boies lectr. and prof. U. Minn. Dept. Otolaryngology, 1992, Whitehead lectr. Whitehead Med. Soc., U. N.C., 1994. Countbr. numerous articles to profl. jours. Recipient John A Kirchner Tchg. award, 1980, Harris Mosher award Am. Laryngological, Rhinological and Otological Soc., 1986. Mem. Am. Acad. Otolarygology-Head and Neck Surgery (pres. elect 1997, Honor award 1985, Disting. Svc. award 1994), Am. Bd. Otolaryngology (bd. dirs.), Alpha Omega Alpha. Office: U NC Divsn Otolaryngology Head & Neck Surgery 610 Burnett Womack Clb # 7070 Chapel Hill NC 27599-0001

PILLSBURY, PENELOPE DELAIRE, library director; b. Bristol, Conn., Jan. 5, 1949; d. Edward William and Ellen Caroline (Jewett) DeLaire; m. Keith Anthony Pillsbury, Aug. 3, 1973; children: Ellen Kathleen Elizabeth, Caleb Edward Marshall. BA in History, U. Vt., 1971; MALS, U. Mich., 1973. Reference libr. U. Vt. Bailey/Howe Libr., Burlington, 1973-80, Fletcher Free Libr., Burlington, 1980-83; dir. N.W. Regional Libr. Dept. of Librs., Georgia, Vt., 1983-86; dir. Brownell Libr., Essex Junction, 1986—. Author: Essex, Vermont, An Annotated Bibliography to Sources, 1992; author essays and articles. Youth leader Cathedral Ch. St. Paul, Burlington, 1998—, chmn. parish life com., 2001—. Mem. Vt. Libr. Assn. (pres. coll./spl. libr. sect. 1978-79, assn. pres.), New Eng. Libr. Assn. (bd. dirs.), Essex Rotary Club (pres. 1999-2000), Mortar Board, Phi Beta Kappa, Delta Delta Delta (scholar 1970). Democrat. Avocations: reading, bicycling, singing, cross country skiing, gardening. Home: 25 University Ter Burlington VT 05401-3527 Office: Brownell Libr/ Village of Essex Junction 6 Lincoln St Essex Junction VT 05452-3154 E-mail: jct@aol.state.vt.us.

PILSON, BARRY H. clinical social worker; b. L.A., May 21, 1951; s. Victor Morris and Barbara Phyllis (Berkowitz) P.; m. Barbara Ethel Pierre, Dec. 29, 1977. BA in Psychology with honors, U. Calif., Berkeley, 1973; MSW, Tulane U., 1975, DSW, 1996. Bd. cert. diplomate in social work. Social worker Family Svc. of Greater New Orleans, 1977-83; program coord. addictive disorders unit River Oaks Psychiat. Hosp., New Orleans, 1988—; adj. prof. Tulane U. Sch. of Social Work, 1990—; pvt. practice, 1983—. Bd. dirs. Bridge House, New Orleans, 1995-96. Recipient Cert. of Merit City of New Orleans, 1994. Mem. NASW (chairperson peer assistance com. 1992—, Social Worker of Yr. 1994, Pres. Citation 1992). Avocations: reading, music, biking. Office: 3535 Ridgelake Dr Ste B Metairie LA 70002-3612

PILSON, MICHAEL EDWARD QUINTON, oceanography educator; b. Ottawa, Ont., Can., Oct. 25, 1933; came to U.S., 1958; s. Edward Charles and Frances Amelia (Ferguson) P.; m. Joan Elaine Johnstone, July 6, 1957; children: Diana Jane, John Edward Quinton. BSc, Bishops U., Lennoxville, Que., Can.; MSc, McGill U., Montreal, Que., Can., 1958; PhD, U. Calif., San Diego, 1964. Chemist Windsor Mills (Can.) Paper Co., 1954-55; asst. chemist Macdonald Coll. of McGill U., 1955-58; biologist Zool. Soc. San Diego, 1963-66; asst. prof. U. R.I., Narragansett, 1966-71, assoc. prof., 1971-78, prof., 1978-2000, prof. emeritus, 2000—. Dir. Marine Ecosystems Rsch. Lab., Narragansett, 1976-97. Contbr. articles to profl. and popular jours.; author chpts. for 5 books, 1 textbook. Grantee NSF, NOAA, EPA, NIH. Mem. AAAS, AGU, ASLO, Oceanography Soc., Am. Soc. Mammalogists, Saunderstown Yacht Club (bd. govs. 1974-87, commodore 1985-87). Home: PO Box 27 Saunderstown RI 02874-0027 Office: U RI Grad Sch Oceanography Narragansett RI 02882 E-mail: pilson@gso.uri.edu.

PILZ, ALFRED NORMAN, manufacturing company executive; b. Evergreen Park, Ill., Oct. 12, 1931; s. Alfred and Erma Louise (Deane) P.; m. Constance Ney, Nov. 1957; children: Kerry, Kurt, Stephen, Matthew. BS, Ill. Inst. Tech., 1953; MBA, Harvard U., 1960. Registered profl. engr., Mass. Indsl. engr. Harnischfeger Corp., Milw., 1956-58; cons. Arthur D. Little Co., Cambridge, Mass., 1959-60; asst. to exec. v.p., mgr. prodn. engring. Nat. Forge Co., Irvine, Pa., 1960-62; mgmt. cons. McKinsey & Co., N.Y.C. and Cleve., 1962-67; pres., gen. mgr. Ajax Iron Works div. Cooper Industries, Corry, Pa., 1967-72; pres., chief exec. officer WDP, Inc., 1972-79, Swank Refractories Co., Johnstown, Pa., 1972-77, Hyde Park (Pa.) Foundry & Machine Co., 1974-79, Shepard-Niles Corp., Montour Falls, N.Y., 1979-82, Acco Babcock Materials Handling, Frederick, Md., 1982-85; ptnr. Fagan and Co., Ligonier, Pa. Bd. dirs. Acco Babcock, Inc., Babcock Internat., Chemung Foundry, Parnell Precision Products Co., Carre-Orban and Partners, Liberty Mut. Ins. Co., Ind. Steel and Engring. Corp., Bedford Crane Co., Shepard Niles Corp., Marine Bank, WDP, Inc.; chmn. Parnell Precision Products, 1980-82, Ind. Steeland Engring., Bedford Crane Co., 1981-82, pres., chmn., chief exec. officer, Greenway Products. Served with USN, 1948—56, Korea. Mem. Crane Mfrs. Assn., Hoist Mfrs. Assn., Conveyor Equipment Mfg. Assn., Nat. Trust Soc., Tin Can Sailors Assn., Navy League. Clubs: HYP (Pitts.). Auburn-Cord-Duesenberg. Home: 139 Ramsey Rd Ligonier PA 15658-2204 Office: 223 E Main St Ligonier PA 15658-1347 E-mail: alpliz@stargate.net.

PIMENTAL, PATRICIA ANN, neuropsychologist, consulting company executive, author; b. Warwick, R.I., Feb. 2, 1956; d. Thomas Robert and Veronica Madeleine (Costa) P.; m. John V. O'Hara, Dec. 16, 1989; children: John Bernard, Padraic James. BS in Pre-Med, Speech Pathology, Northwestern U., 1978, MA in Speech Pathology with honors, 1980; PsyD in Clin. Psychology with honors, Chgo. Sch. Profl. Psychology, 1987. Lic. psychologist, speech pathologist, Ill.; diplomate Am. Bd. Vocat. Neuropsychology, Am. Acad. Pain Mgmt., Am. Bd. Prof. Disability Cons., Am. Bd. Profl. Neuropsychology (mem. exec. bd.). Clin. psychology extern child psychology clinic U. Ill., Chgo., 1984-85, dir. psychol. svcs. dept. phys. medicine and rehab., 1987-91, asst. prof. dept. phys. medicine and rehab., 1987-91; clin. psychology extern Filmore Mental Health Ctr., Berwyn-Cicero (Ill.) Sr. Svcs., 1985-86; clin. psychology intern St. Elizabeth's Hosp., Chgo., 1986-87; mem. faculty Chgo. Sch. Profl. Psychology, 1991—; pres. Neurobehavioral Medicine Cons., Ltd., Oak Brook, Ill., 1991—. Author (sr.): Neuropsychological Aspects of Right Brain Injury, 1989, Mini Inventory of Right Brain Injury, 1989, Mini Inventory of Right Brain Injury 2, 2000; book reviewer: Contemporary Psychology, 1991; book reviewer: Jour. Applied Neuropsychology, 2001, manuscript reviewer: Archives of Clinical Neurpsychology, 2001—, mem. editl. bd.: The Professional Neuropsychologist, 2002—. Vol. trainer ARC Disaster Stress Relief Program, 1991—; leader U. Ill. Stroke Club, 1988-91; bd. dirs. Older Adult Rehab. Svcs., Cicero, 1987-90; active Chgo. Anti-Cruelty Soc.; mem. music ministry-vocal soloist, choir Oak Brook Cmty. Ch. Named one of Outstanding Young Women Am., 1984, 92; Am. Cancer Soc. scholar, 1979, Outstanding Spkr. of 21st Century, 2001; recipient Outstanding Manuscript of Yr. award Am. Jour. of Pain Mgmt., 1993, Black Belt 1st Degree Sch. of Chung Moo Quan, 1998. Fellow: Am. Acad. Learning Devel. Disabilities, Am. Coll. Profl. Neuropsychology, Nat. Acad. Neuropsychology, Ill. Psychol. Assn. (adv. bd. 1989—93, chair-elect, chair health and rehab. sect. 1991—92, 1992—93, chair prescription privilege task force 1992—95, continuing edn. chair/clin. practice sect. 1993—95, pres.-elect 1995—96, pres. 1996—97, immediate past pres. 1997—98, co-chair 1998—, Disting. Psychologist award 1997); mem.: APA, Am. Bd. Profl. Neuropsychology (mem.-at-large 2000, pres. elect 2001—), Am. Speech and Hearing Assn., Midwest Neuropsychology Group, Soc. Clin. and Exptl. Hypnosis, Am. Congress Rehab. Medicine, Nat. Acad. Neuropsychology, Internat. Neuropsychol. Soc., Nat. Brain Injury Rsch. Found. (med. adv. coun. 1992—96), Am. Pain Soc. Avocations: gourmet cooking, piano, voice, martial arts. Office: Glen Oaks Hosp Med Ctr Neurobehavioral Medicine 701 Winthrop Ave Glendale Heights IL 60139-1405

PIMENTEL, BENJAMIN IMPELIDO, journalist; b. Manila, Philippines, June 20, 1964; s. Benjamin C. and Isabel (Impelido) P.; m. Maria Teresita Torres, Dec. 23, 1992. BA in Polit. Sci., U. The Philippines, 1985; M.Journalism, U. Calif., Berkeley, 1993. Staff writer Nat. Midweek mag., Manila, 1986-89; gen. assignment, Asian Am. affairs and transp. reporter San Francisco Chronicle, 1993—. Author: Rebolusyon: A Generation of Struggle in the Philippines, 1991; writer, prodr. Toxic Sunset: On the Trail of Hazardous Waste from Subic and Clark, Philippine Ctr. for Investigative Journalism, Manila, 1993. Mem. Asian Am. Journalists Assn. Office: San Francisco Chronicle 901 Mission St San Francisco CA 94103-2905

PIMENTEL, DAVID, ecologist, educator; b. Fresno, Calif., May 24, 1925; s. Frank and Marion V. (Sylva) P.; m. Marcia R. Hutchins, July, 16, 1949; children: Christina, Susan, Mark David. Student, St. John's U., Collegeville, Minn., 1943, Clark U., summer 1946; BS, U. Mass., 1948; PhD, Cornell U., 1951. Chief tropical rsch. lab. USPHS, San Juan, chief tropical research lab. P.R., 1951-54, project leader tech. devel. lab Savannah, Ga., 1954-55; postdoctoral investigator U. Chgo., winters 1954-55; postdoctoral investigator, OEEC rsch. fellow Oxford (Eng.) U., 1961; postdoctoral investigator, NSF computer scholar MIT, Cambridge, summer 1961; mem. faculty Cornell U., 1955—, prof. insect ecology, 1963-76, head dept. entomology and limnology, 1963-69, prof. entomology, ecology and systematics, 1969-76, prof. insect ecology and agrl. scis., 1976—; prof., core faculty Center Environ. Quality Mgmt., 1973-74. Cons. Office Sci. and Tech., Exec. Office Pres., 1964-67, 69-70, EPA, 1971; co-chmn. Commn. on Mosquito Control for Developing Countries, Nat. Acad. Scis., 1972-73; mem. commn. on pesticides and pest mgmt. in Inter-Am., 1973-77; mem. Nat. Adv. Coun. on Environ. Edn., 1973-74; chmn. panel on environ. impact of herbicides EPA, 1972-74, pesticide adv. coun., 1975-78; nat. adv. coun. environ. edn. Office Edn., HEW, 1975-78, chmn., 1975; chmn. study team on interdependence of food, population, health, energy, and environment World Food and Nutrition Study, Nat. Acad. Scis., 1976-77, chmn. environ. studies bd., 1980-83, mem. Opportunities in Agrl. Rsch. com., 2001—; mem. energy rsch. adv. bd. Dept. Energy, 1979-85; mem. rsch. adv. com. USAID, 1979-82, chmn. panel on land productivity; mem. Office of Tech. Assessment, U.S. Congress, 1979-80; hon. prof. Inst. Applied Ecology, Shengang, China, 1995—. Assoc. editor: Am. Midland Naturalist; contbr. articles to profl. jours. Trustee Village of Cayuga Heights, 1974—; pres. Rachel Carson Coun., 2001—. Served to 2d lt., pilot USAAF, 1943-45. Recipient Disting. Svc. award Rural Sociol. Coun., 1992. Mem. AAAS (climate com. 1979-82, population, resource and environ. com. 1985-91, chmn. subcom. on food, population, and resources 1986-87), NAS (chmn. panel on biology and renewable resources, exec. bd. com. on life scis. 1966-68, com. on world food, health and population 1974-75, chmn. panel on econ. and environ. aspects of pest mgmt. in Ctrl. Am. 1974-76, chmn. bd. on sci. and tech. for internat. devel. 1975-79, com. on food and food prodn. 1974-76, alt. agr. com. 1985-89, com. on role of alt. farming methods in modern productive agr. 1985-89), Entomol. Soc. Am. (gov. bd., chmn. editl. bd., pres. Eastern br. 1974-75), Ecol. Soc. Am., Am. Soc. Naturalists, Soc. Study of Evolution, Entomol. Soc. Can., Am. Soc. Zoologists, Nat. Geog. Soc. (com. on rsch. and explorations 1993-2000), Internat. Union for Conservation of Nature and Natural Resources (commn. on ecology 1981-90), Royal Swedish Acad. Scis. (bd. dirs. Beijer Inst. 1994-2000), Chinese Acad. Scis. (hon. prof., acad. com. Inst. Applied Ecology 1994—), Nat. Audubon Soc. (bd. dirs. 2000—), Rachel Carson Coun. (pres. 2001—), Sigma Xi, Phi Kappa Phi, Gamma Alpha (nat. recorder 1960-62, AIBS bd. 1999—). Office: Cornell U Dept Entomology Comstock Hall Ithaca NY 14853

PIMENTEL, JULIO GUMERESINDO, lawyer, accountant; b. Chgo., Aug. 11, 1961; s. Julio Caesar and Jeannie Irene (Jakovac) P.; m. Margaret Mary O'Donnell, July 5, 1987 (div. Jan. 1995); children: Ashley Adel, Benjamin Maximillion. BS in Commerce, DePaul U., 1983, M of Accountancy, 1984; JD, John Marshall Law Sch., 1991. Bar: Ill. 1992; CPA, Ill.; cert. internal auditor. Deli clk. Jewel Food Stores, Chgo., 1978-84; field auditor Harris Bank, 1984-85; asset-based lending field auditor Chase Comml. Corp., 1985-86; acct. Allstate Ins., Northbrook, Ill., 1986-87; revenue agt. IRS, Chgo., 1987-91, estate tax atty., 1991—; pvt. practice, acct., 1992—. Ill. State scholar, 1979. Mem. ATLA, Inst. Internal Auditors, Chgo. Bar Assn., IRS Bowling League (Most Polite award 1994-95), Freemen. Avocations: weightlifting, martial arts, gun collecting, old cars, archery. Home and Office: PO Box A3761 Chicago IL 60690-3761

PIMLEY, KIM JENSEN, financial training consultant; b. Abington, Pa., Apr. 29, 1960; d. Alvin Christian Jensen and Helen Marie (Kairis) Meinken; m. Michael St. John Pimley, Nov. 10, 1988; 1 child, Oliver Jensen Pimley. BA, MA magna cum laude, Emory U., 1982; postgrad., U. Chgo., 1985—. Mgr. tng. ops. Continental Bank, Chgo., 1986-88, mgr. coll. rels., 1988-90; mgr. client svcs. The Globecon Group, N.Y.C., 1990-92; prin. Pimley & Pimley, Inc., Princeton, N.J., 1992-93; pres. P&P Tng. Resources, Inc., 1993—. Owner Jr. League Designer Showhouse, 1997. Contbr. poetry to various jours. 27012079en's leadership forum Dem. Nat. Com., 1997—; chmn. silent auction Princeton Friends Sch., 1997, 99, 2000; trustee Opera Festival N.J., 2000; bd. dirs. Jewish Ctr. of Princeton, 1999—. Scholarship U. Chgo., 1984. Mem. ACLU, NOW, Oxford and Cambridge Club, Poetry Soc. Am. Office: P&P Tng Resources Inc 117 Library Pl Princeton NJ 08540-3019

PIMPER, ELIZABETH MARIE, naval officer; b. Flint, Mich., Aug. 28, 1973; d. Arthur Bowers Reid; m. Gregory David Pimper, July 8, 1997. BA summa cum laude, U. Md., 1999. Advanced through grades to lt. (j.g.) USN, 2002; naval flight officer. Vol. St. Vincent de Paul's Dining Rm., San Antonio, 2000-01. Mem. MLA, Women Officer's Profl. Assn., Assn. Naval Aviators, Chinese Lang. Tchrs. Assn., U.S. Naval Inst., Golden Key, Phi Beta Kappa. Avocations: swimming, cooking, running, weight lifting. Office: VP-9 Kaneohe HI 96601 E-mail: empimper@hotmail.com.

PINAC, ANDRÉ LOUIS, III, obstetrician, gynecologist; b. New Orleans, Dec. 8, 1955; s. André Louis Jr. and Patricia Elaine (Ledet) P.; 1 child, Amy Elizabeth; 1 stepchild, Robby Nicholas LaFleur. BS, U. Southwestern La., 1977; MD, La. State U., New Orleans, 1981. Diplomate Am. Bd. Ob-Gyn. Resident ob-gyn La. State U. Affiliated Hosps., New Orleans, Lafayette, Lake Charles and Baton Rouge, 1981-85; practice medicine specializing in ob-gyn Opelousas, La., 1985—; chief of staff Doctor's Hosp. Opelousas, 1993-94. Participant Cmty. Health Fair, Opelousas, 1987—; bd. dirs. Drs. Hosp. of Opelousas. Safety officer St. Landry Parish; bd. dirs. Little League, 1992-94. Named Duke at Mardi Gras Festival, Opelousas Garden Club, 1994, King Mardi Gras Ball Masque King Orme, 1999. Fellow Am. Coll. Ob-Gyn; mem. AMA, So. Med. Assn., La. State Med. Soc., St. Landry Parish Med. Soc., Opelousas Cath. Soccer Assn. (pres. 1991-93), Alpha Phi Alpha (life), Sigma Alpha Epsilon. Roman Catholic. Avocations: golf, jogging, swimming, trivia, basketball. E-mail: alp3md.aol.com. Office: 816 Cresswell Ln Ste 1 Opelousas LA 70570-5881

PINALS, ROBERT STANTON, physician; b. Elizabeth, N.J., Aug. 23, 1931; s. Herman and Goldie (Kotler) P.; m. Emmanuella DiAssisi, June 20, 1953; children: Deborah, David, Stephen. BA, Cornell U., 1952; MD, U. Rochester, 1956. Diplomate in internal medicine and rheumatology Am. Bd. Internal Medicine. Fellow in rheumatology Mass. Gen. Hosp., Boston, 1961-63; chief rheumatology Lemuel Shattuck Hosp., 1961-63; from instr. to asst. prof. medicine Tufts U. Sch. Medicine, 1963-69; from assoc. prof. to prof. medicine SUNY, Syracuse, 1969-78; prof. medicine U. Tenn., Memphis, 1978-84, UMDNJ-Robert Wood Johnson Med. Sch., Piscataway, 1984—, vice chmn. dept. medicine, 1997—; chmn. dept. medicine Med. Ctr. at Princeton, N.J., 1984-97. Mem., cons. arthritis adv. com. FDA, Wasington, 1985-93, chmn., 1986-89; mem. rheumatology subsplty. com. Am. Bd. Internal Medicine, 1988-95. Contbr. numerous chpts. to books, more than 100 articles to profl. jours. Bd. dirs. Ctrl. N.Y. chpt. Arthritis Found., 1969-78, pres., 1976-77. Capt. USAF, 1957-59. Master: Am. Coll. Rheumatology; fellow: ACP. Office: UMDNJ-Robert Wood Johnson Med Sch Dept Medicine PO Box 19 New Brunswick NJ 08903-0019

PINATARO, JEAN ELEANOR, artist; b. L.A. d. Pasqual and Anna (Maresca) P. Student, UCLA, 1960-70; BA in Fine Arts, Calif. State U., Long Beach, 1988. Tech. artist, designer, illustrator N.Am. Aviation Inc. (now Boeing). Designer Apollo/Soyuz Patch NASA, 1974; artist in residence Villa Montalvo Ctr. Arts, Saratoga, Calif., 1984. Author, editor: Pinataro, 1976, Live From the Pyramids, 1979, Names Have Been Changed to Protect the Guilty, 1989; exhibitions include Calif. State U., Long Beach, 1987, System M Gallery, Long Beach, 1988, Palos Verdes Art Ctr. (Calif.), 1990, Graham Horstman Gallery, Denton, Tex., 1990, The Gate Gallery, San Pedro, Calif., 1991, Sasama Gallery, Chgo., 1992, The Bridge Gallery, L.A., 1992, Muckenthaler Cultural Ctr., Fullerton, Calif., 1992, Artspace Gallery, Woodland Hills, Calif., 1993, Downey Mus. Art, 1993, 94, 96, Gallery 57, Fullerton, 1995 (Gallery Choice), Borders Books, Long Beach, Calif., 1997, Center Gallery, Long Beach, 1997, Lincoln Heights Jail, L.A., 1998. Mem. Nat. Watercolor Soc., Artists Support Group. Avocations: singing, playing guitar.

PINCHUK, NICHOLAS THOMAS, manufacturing executive; b. Troy, N.Y., Oct. 11, 1946; s. Nicholas Thomas and Mildred Frances Pinchuk; m. Lee Joyce Pinchuk, Aug. 8, 1970; children: Madeline Pinchuk Boehning, Tanya, Thomas. BSEE, Rensselaer Poly. Inst., 1968, MEE, 1969; MBA, Harvard U., 1976. V.p., CFO Carrier Internat., Syracuse, N.Y., 1985-86; v.p. strategic planning Carrier Corp., 1986-87; pres. Carrier Asia Pacific Ops., Singapore, 1987-97. Mem. mgmt. adv. bd. Syracuse U., 1997—. Capt. U.S. Army, 1970-71, Vietnam. Mem. Am. Soc. Refrigeration and Air Conditioning Engrs. Office: Carrier Corp Carrier Pkwy PO Box 4805 Syracuse NY 13221-4805

PINCKNEY, CHARLES COTESWORTH, lawyer; b. Richmond, Va., Oct. 23, 1939; s. Thomas and Charlotte (Kent) P.; m. Helen Raney, Aug. 13, 1966; children: Sarah Whitley, Thomas. BA, Yale U., 1961; LLB, U. Va., 1967. Bar: Va. 1967. Assoc. Mays, Valentine, Davenport & Moore, Richmond, 1967-72; ptnr. Mays & Valentine, LLP, 1972-2000, Troutman Sanders LLP, Richmond, 2001—. Bd. dirs. Sweet Briar Coll., 1996-2000; pres. Sheltering Arms Hosp., Richmond, 1986-87, bd. dirs., 1970-99; trustee William H.-John G.-Emma Scott Found., 1974—, sec., 1994-99, v.p., 1999—; campaign chmn. United Way Svcs., 1998. Ensign lt. j.g. USNR, 1961-64. Mem. ABA, Va. Bar Assn., Phila. Quarry Club (pres. 1985-91), Country Club of Va., Commonwealth Club (bd. govs. 1986-92, pres. 1991-92), Richmond German (pres. 1996-98), Soc. of Cin. Republican. Episcopalian. Home: 2 Roslyn Rd Richmond VA 23226-1610 Office: Troutman Sanders LLP 1111 E Main St PO Box 1122 Richmond VA 23218-1122 E-mail: cotes.pinckney@troutmansanders.com.

PINCOCK, DOUGLAS GEORGE, electronics company executive; b. Vancouver, B.C., Can., Sept. 29, 1940; s. George Leyland and Sadie McElvenna (Boyle) P.; m. Gloria Dawn Werth, Sept. 5, 1964 (div. 1985); children: Barry, James, David, Lisa; m. Marilyn Marie Spearns, Oct. 28, 1990. BSEE, Man. (Winnipeg, Can.) U., 1963, MSEE, 1967; PhD, New Brunswick U., Fredericton, 1971. Registered profl. engr., N.S. Asst. prof. St. Francis Xavier U., Antigonish, N.S., 1969-70; from lectr. to asst. prof. to assoc. prof. U. N.B., 1970-75, 76-79; maitre de conf. U. Paris, 1975-76; prof. Tech. U. N.S., Halifax, 1979-82; chmn., founder Amirix Sys. Inc. (formerly Applied Microelectronics), 1982—. Bd. dirs. VEMCO, Shad Bay, N.S.; pres., bd. dirs. AMI Techs., Halifax, 1992-95; mem. adv. bd. Can. Intellectual Property Orgn. Contbr. 25 papers to profl. jours. Head coach basketball Tech. U. N.S., 1986-95. With Can. Air Force, 1963-66. Achievements include co-invention weatherstar 4000, electronic parking meter, other inventions in underwater telemetry products. Office: Amirix Sys Inc 77 Chain Lake Dr Halifax NS Canada B3S 1E1 E-mail: doug.pincock@amirix.com.

PINCOCK, GARRY LAMAR, association administrator; b. Phila., June 11, 1949; s. Lamar R. and Barbara (Henry) P.; children: Jacqueline Meredith, Amy Lauren. BS, West Chester (Pa.) U., 1975; postgrad., Ind. U., 1982. Tchr. Penn Delco Sch. Dist., Aston, Pa., 1975-77; v.p. Atlas Maintenance, Inc., Brookhaven, 1972-83; exec. dir. Pa. div. Am. Cancer Soc., Media, 1979-83, asst. v.p. field svcs. Ga. div. Macon, 1983-86, v.p. field svcs. Ga. div. Atlanta, 1986-89, sr. v.p. div. ops., 1989-91, exec. v.p., CEO Pa. divsn., 1991—, CEO Pa. divsn., 1996—, chair cmty. health campaign, 1998—. Instr., cons. S.E. Pa. Cmty. Health Assn., Bethlehem, 1980-81; founding mem. Cmty. Health Campaign, 1993, bd. dirs., 1996—. Mem. bldg. campaign com. Piedmont Baptist Ch., Marietta, Ga., 1987; mem. city com. Young Life, Media, 1982; v.p. Garage Youth Ctr., Brookhaven, Pa., 1970-74. Republican. Avocations: golf, tennis, jogging. Office: Am Cancer Soc Pa Divsn Rt 422 & Sipe Ave Hershey PA 17033

PINCOCK, HOLLIS BURT, JR. music educator; b. Huntington Park, Calif., Aug. 23, 1951; s. Hollis Burt and Suzanne Janet (Sanders) B.; m. Janette Booth Pincock; children: Alyson, Derek, Bryce, Heidi, Maryn. BEd, Brigham Young U., 1975; MEd, U. Idaho, 1992, cert. 6th yr. specialist, 1995. Music educator Boise (Idaho) H.S., 1979-83, 1990—; small bus. owner, 1981-90. Coach CYSA, Y-Ball, N.W. ADA Youth Baseball. Mem. ASCD, NEA, Idaho Edn. Assn., Boise Edn. Assn., Dist. III Music Educators (pres. 1994-96), Idaho Music Educators Assn. (bd. dirs. 1994—. pres.-elect 1996-98, dist. III bd.

control 1982-83). Republican. Mem. Lds Ch. Avocations: sports, tennis, philatelics, numismatics. Office: Boise High Sch 1010 W Washington St Boise ID 83702-5446 Home: 2703 Annett St Boise ID 83705-4412

PINCOCK, RICHARD EARL, chemistry educator; b. Ogden, Utah, Sept. 14, 1935; s. Earl Samuel and Virginia (Christenson) P.; m. Elke Gertrud Hermann, Aug. 20, 1960; children— Christina, Gordon, Jennifer. BS, U. Utah, 1956; A.M., Harvard U., 1957, PhD, 1960. Postdoctoral research fellow Calif. Inst. Tech., 1959-60; faculty U. B.C., Vancouver, Can., 1960—, prof., 1969—. Mem. Phi Beta Kappa, Sigma Pi. Office: U BC Chemistry Dept Vancouver BC Canada V6T 1Y6 E-mail: pincock@chem.ubc.ca.

PINCUS, HOWARD JONAH, geologist, engineer, educator; b. N.Y.C., June 24, 1922; s. Otto Max and Gertrude (Jankowsky) P.; m. Maud Lydia Roback, Sept. 6, 1953; children: Glenn David, Philip E. BS, CCNY, 1942; PhD, Columbia U., 1949. Faculty Ohio State U., 1949-67, from instr. to assoc. prof., 1949-59, prof., 1959-67, chmn. dept. geology, 1960-65; rsch. geologist U. S. Bur. Mines, summers 1963-67; geologist, rsch. supr. U.S. Bur. Mines, 1967-68; prof. geol. sci. and civil engring. U. Wis., Milw., 1968-87, prof. emeritus, 1987—, dean Coll. Letters and Sci., 1969-72; rsch. assoc. Lamont Geol. Obs., Columbia, 1949-51; geologist Ohio Dept. Natural Resources, summers 1950-61; cons. geology and rock mechanics, 1954-67, 68—. Sr. postdoctoral fellow NSF, 1962; U.S. nat. com. on tunnelling tech. NAE, 1972-74, U.S. nat. com. on rock mechanics NAS/NAE, 1975-78, 80-89, chmn., 1985-87; U.S. com. Internat. Assn. Engring. Geology/NAS, chmn., 1987-90. Tech. editor Geotech. Testing Jour., 1992-95, mem. edit. bd., 1996—. 1st lt. C.E. AUS, 1942-46. Recipient award for teaching excellence U. Wis.-Milw. Alumni Assn., 1978. Fellow ASTM (Reinhart award 1987, Award of Merit 1989), AAAS, Geol. Soc. Am.; mem. AAUP (pres. Ohio State U. chpt. 1955-56, mem. coun. 1965-67, pres. U. Wis.-Milw. chpt. 1976-77), Am. Geophys. Union, Geol. Soc. Am. (chmn. engring. geology divsn. 1973-74), Soc. Mining Engrs., Internat. Assn. Engring. Geology, Internat. Soc. Rock Mechanics, Am. Rock Mechanics Assn., Assn. Engring. Geologists, Am. Inst. Profl. Geologists (pres. Ohio sect. 1965-66), Phi Beta Kappa (pres. Ohio State U. chpt. 1959-60, pres. U. Wis.-Milw. chpt. 1976-77), Sigma Xi. Home: 17523 Plaza Marlena San Diego CA 92128-1807 Office: PO Box 27598 San Diego CA 92198-1598

PINCUS, JONATHAN HENRY, neurologist, educator; b. Bklyn., May 4, 1935; s. Joseph Bernhard and Hannah Martha (Palestine) P.; m. Cynthia Sterling Deery, Jan., 1961 (div. 1983); children: Daniel, Jeremy, Adam; m. Fortuna Mizrahi Fries, Nov. 1983 (div. 1995). AB, Amherst Coll., Mass., 1956; MD, Columbia U., 1960; MA, Yale U., 1973. Asst. prof. neurology Yale U., New Haven, 1965-69, assoc. prof. neurology, 1969-73, prof. neurology, 1973-86; prof., chmn. neurology Sch. Medicine Georgetown U., Washington, 1987-95, prof. neurology, chmn. emeritus, 1995—; chief neurology VA Med. Ctr., 2001—. Author: Behavioral Neurology, 1974, 2002, Base Instincts - What Makes Killers Kill, 2001. Fellow Am. Acad. Neurology (v.p. 1991-93); mem. Am. Neurol. Assn. (counselor 1984-86). Achievements include linkage of anticonvulsant properties of phenytoin to reduction of Ca influx; introduction of protein redistribution diet to restore 1-dopa responsiveness in end stage Parkinsonism; correlation of neurologic deficits, the experience of abuse and paranoia with episodic violence in delinquents and criminals; proposition of defect in thiamine triphosphate as cause of Leigh's encephalomyelopathy. Office: VA Med Ctr Washington Dept Neurology 50 Irving St NW Washington DC 20422 E-mail: johnathan.pincus@med.va.gov.

PINCUS, LIONEL I. private equity investor; b. Phila., Mar. 2, 1931; s. Henry and Theresa Celia (Levit) P.; m. Suzanne Storrs Poulton (dec.). BA, U. Pa., 1953; MBA, Columbia U., 1956. Assoc. gen. ptnr. Ladenburg, Thalmann & Co., N.Y.C., 1955-63; pres. Lionel I. Pincus & Co., Inc., 1964-66; pres., CEO E.M. Warburg & Co., Inc., 1966-70; chmn., CEO E.M. Warburg, Pincus & Co., LLC, 1970—. Trustee Montefiore Hosp., N.Y.C., N.Y. Presbyn. Hosp.; trustee Ittleson Found., Inc., Columbia U., chmn. emeritus; trustee Sch. Am. Ballet, Citizens Budget Commn., German Marshall Fund USA, 1982-88; mem. bd. overseers Columbia Grad. Sch. Bus.; bd. dirs. Am. Mus. Natural History, Nat. Park Found.; mem. N.Y.C. Investment Fund. Mem. Coun. Fgn. Rels., World Wildlife Fund (nat. coun.), Nat. Golf Links Am. Club, Meadow Club. Office: Warburg Pincus 466 Lexington Ave Fl 10 New York NY 10017-3147 E-mail: yoli2m@aol.com.

PINCUS, ROBERT LAWRENCE, art critic, cultural historian; b. Bridgeport, Conn., June 5, 1953; s. Jules Robert and Carol Sylvia (Rosen) P.; m. Georgianna Manly, June 20, 1981; 1 child, Matthew Manly. BA, U. Calif., Irvine, 1976; MA, U. So. Calif., 1980, PhD, 1987. Instr. U. So. Calif., L.A., 1978-83; art critic L.A. Times, 1981-85, San Diego Union, 1985-92, San Diego Union-Tribune, 1992—. Vis. prof. San Diego State U., 1985-86, 92. Author: On A Scale That Competes with the World: The Art of Edward and Nancy Reddin Kienholz, 1990, (with others) West Coast Duchamp, 1991, But Is It Art: The Spirit of Art as Activism, 1994, Paradise, 1994, Anne Mudge: Traces, 1996; author introduction to W.D.'s Midnight Carnival, 1988, Kitchen: Liza Lou, 1996, Manuel Neri: Early Work, 1953-78, 97, Gordas: Paintings and Installations by Tania Candiani, 2002. Recipient Chem. Bank award, 1994, Best Critical Writing award San Diego Press Club, 1994. Mem. Internat. Assn. Art Critics, Coll. Art Assn. Democrat. Office: San Diego Union Tribune PO Box 120191 350 Camino De La Reina San Diego CA 92108-3003

PINCUS, STEPHANIE HOYER, dermatologist, educator; b. Lakehurst, N.J., Feb. 28, 1944; d. Ernest Carl and Aviva (Silbert) Hoyer; m. David Frank Pincus, Aug. 22, 1965 (div. Dec. 1984); children: Matthew Jonah, Tamara Hope; m. Allan Roy Oseroff, Mar. 24, 1985; 1 child, Benjamin Henry Oseroff. BA, Reed Coll., 1964; MD cum laude, Harvard U., 1968; MM (MBA), Northwestern U., 1998. Diplomate Am. Bd. Dermatology, Am. Bd. Internal Medicine. Intern Boston City Hosp., 1968-69; rsch. fellow U. Wash., Seattle, 1969-71, resident internal medicine, 1971-72; resident-fellow dermatology U. Washington, 1972-74; fellow instr. dept. dermatology Harvard Med. Sch., Boston, 1974-75; asst. prof. medicine U. Wash., Seattle, 1975-77; lectr. Sch. Medicine Boston U., 1977-89; asst. prof. medicine Sch. Medicine Tufts U., Boston, 1977-82, mem. dept. immunology, 1977-89, asst. prof. dermatology, 1979-82, assoc. prof. dermatology and medicine, 1982-89; prof. medicine and dermatology, chairperson dermatology SUNY, Buffalo, 1989-2000; chief acad. affiliations officer Dept. Vets. Affairs, Washington, 2000—. Dermatology Found. fellow, Evanston, Ill., 1974-75, 77-78; Vets. Adminstrn. rsch. assoc., 1975-77; recipient Clin. Investigator award NIH, Bethesda, Md., 1979-81. Mem. Am. Contact Dermatitis Soc. (mem. liaison com. 1993—), Women's Dermatologic Soc. (bd. dirs. 1992—), Soc. Investigative Dermatology (chmn. com. on govt. and pub. rels. 1992-96), Profs. of Dermatology (mem. program com. 1993—), Internat. Soc. for Study of Vulvar Disease (mem. exec. com. 1993-95), Harvard Med. Alumni (pres. 1995-96), Phi Beta Kappa, Alpha Omega Alpha. Office: Dept Vets Affairs Office Acad Affilitation 810 Vermont Ave Washington DC 20420

PINCUS, THEODORE HENRY, public relations executive; b. Chgo., Sept. 15, 1933; s. Jacob T. and J. (Engel) P.; m. Sharon Barr, Jan. 16, 1988; children: Laura, Mark, Susan, Anne, Jennifer. BS in Journalism, Ind. U., 1955. Free-lance bus. writer, 1955-58; sr. exec. Harshe Rotman & Druck, Chgo., 1958-62; dir. comm. Theodore Pincus & Assocs., 1962-64; chmn., CEO, Fin. Rels. Bd., Inc. subs. BSMG Worldwide, 1998—; vice chmn. BSMG Worldwide divsn. Interpub. Group, N.Y.C., 1998—2001; sr. cons. Interpub. Group, 2001—. Adj. prof. mktg. Northwestern U. Kellogg Grad. Sch., 2002—; pub. affairs advisor to Nelson Rockefeller, N.Y.C., 1960, 68; advisor U.S. Info. Agy., 1993—; former mem. adv. bd. NASDAQ. Author: Giveaway Day, 1977; contbr. articles to profl. publs. including Wall St. Jour., Fortune, and N.Y. Times. Active presdl. nomination campaigns; vice-chmn. Midwest region Am. Jewish Com.; mem. adv. bd. Ind. U. Bus. Sch.; bd. dirs. The Ill. Coalition. With USAF, 1955-57. Recipient numerous nat. awards for profl. excellence in investor rels. and corp.pub. rels. including Silver Anvil award Pub. Rels. Soc. Am., 1966, Civic Achievement award Am. Jewish Com., 1993; named Entrepreneur of Yr., Ernst & Young Merrill Lynch, 1998, Pub. Rels. Profl. of Yr., Pub. Rels. Soc. Am., 2002. Mem. Young Pres.'s Orgn., Nat. Investor Relations Inst. (founding), Std. Club. Clubs: Union League. Office: Theodore Pincus & Assocs 444 N Michigan Ave Ste 3530 Chicago IL 60611

PINCUS, WALTER HASKELL, editor; b. Bklyn., Dec. 24, 1932; s. Jonas and Clare (Glassman) Pincus; m. Betty Meskin, Sept. 12, 1954; 1 child Andrew John ; m. Ann Witsell Terry, May 1, 1965; children: Ward Haskell, Adam Witsell, Cornelia Battle Terry. BA, Yale, 1954; JD, Georgetown U., 2001. Cons. Senate Fgn. Relations Com., 1962-63; spl. writer Washington Evening Star, 1963-66; editor, reporter Washington Post, 1966-69; chief cons. Symington subcom. Senate Fgn. Relations Com., 1969-70; asso. editor New Republic, 1972-74, exec. editor, 1974-75; spl. writer Washington Post, 1975—; Cons. NBC News, 1971-79, CBS News, 1979-86, NBC News, 1987-88, Washington Post Co., 1989—. Vis. lectr. Yale U, 1988, 2002. Trustee Shakespeare Theater, 1988—, co-chmn. edn. com., 1989—91, chmn. nominating com., 1992—96. Co-recipient Pulitzer prize, 2001; recipient Page One award, 1960, George Orwell award, 1977, George Polk award, 1978, Emmy award, 1981, Stewart Alsop award, 1999. Mem.: Coun. Fgn. Rels., Yale Club Washington, Federal City Club Washington. Home: 3202 Klingle Rd NW Washington DC 20008-3403 Office: Washington Post 1150 15th St NW Washington DC 20071-0001 E-mail: pincusw@washpost.com.

PINCUS-WITTEN, ROBERT, art history educator, art gallery director, critic; b. N.Y.C., Apr. 5, 1935; Diploma, The Cooper Union, N.Y.C., 1956; MA, U. Chgo., 1962, PhD, 1968. Prof. art history CUNY, 1964-90, prof. art history, doctoral faculty, 1970-90; sr. editor Artforum, N.Y.C., 1966-76; assoc. editor Arts Magazine, 1976-89; dir. The Gagosian Gallery, 1990-96; exhbn. dir. C&M Arts, NYC, 1996-. Author: Postminimalism into Maximalism: American Art 1966-1986, 1987, Eye to Eye: Twenty Years of Art Criticism, 1984; Occult Symbolism in France: Joséphin Peladan and the Salons de la Rose+Croix; catalogues for The Mus. of Modern Art, N.Y., The Whitney Mus. of Am. art, N.Y., The New Mus., N.Y., The Inst. of Contemporary Art, Phila., Mus. Contemporary Arts, Chgo., numerous others; contbr. numerous articles to profl. jours. E-mail: pincus-witten@c-m-arts.com.

PINCZOWER, KENNETH EPHRAIM, lawyer; b. N.Y.C., Aug. 24, 1964; s. Joachim and Dinah Pinczower; m. Julie Rieder; children: Devorah, David C., Chana. BA, Queens Coll., 1985; postgrad., Rabbinical Sem. of Am., N.Y.C., 1983-86; JD, Benjamin N. Cardozo Sch. Law, 1989. Bar: N.Y. 1990, N.J. 1990, D.C. 1991, Fla. 1993, U.S. Dist. Ct. (so. and ea. dist.) N.Y. 1990, U.S. Dist. Ct. N.J. 1990. Auditor Seidman & Seidman/B.D.O., N.Y.C., 1986-87; summer assoc. U.S. Attys. Office, So. Dist. N.Y., 1988; Alexander jud. fellow U.S. Dist. Judge, So. Dist. N.Y., 1987-88; asst. corp. counsel N.Y.C. Law Dept., 1989-95; atty. Barron, McDonald, Carroll & Cohen, N.Y.C., 1995—. Editor Cardozo Arts & Entertainment Law Jour., 1988-89. Vol. instr. Jewish Edn. Program, N.Y.C., 1983-86; instr. Aish Ha Torah, 1994-98; chmn. Torah Chesed Fund, Yeshiva U., 1995—; Talmud assoc. Artscroll Mesorah Heritage Found., 1993—; com. mem. Nat. Conf. Synagogue Youth, 1991—. Avocations: Talmudic law, tennis, basketball. Home: 3950 Blackstone Ave Bronx NY 10471-3703 Office: Barron McDonald et al 1 Whitehall St New York NY 10004-2109 E-mail: pinczok@nationwide.com.

PINCZUK, ARON, physicist; b. San Martin, Argentina, Feb. 15, 1939; s. Faiwel and Ester (Wejeman) P.; m. Gladys Norma Teitelman, June 14, 1962; children: Ana Gabriela, Guillermo Fabian. Licenciado, U. Buenos Aires, Argentina, 1962; PhD, U. Pa., 1969; D (hon.), U Autonoma, Madrid, 1997. Staff mem. Nat. Rsch. Coun., Argentina, 1971-76; head physics dept. Faculty of Scis., U. Buenos Aires, Argentina, 1974; vis. scientist Max Planck Inst., Stuttgart, Germany, 1976, IBM Rsch., Yorktown Heights, N.Y., 1976-77; staff mem. Bell Labs., Murray Hill, N.J., 1978—; prof. Columbia U., N.Y.C., 1998—. Sec. Argentina Phys. Soc., Buenos Aires, 1972-75; editor Solid State Communications, 1989-92, assoc. editor in chief, 1992—. Contbr. over 200 articles to profl. jours. and numerous chpts. to books. Recipient Oliver E. Buckley Condensed-Matter Physics prize Am. Physical Soc., 1994. Fellow: AAAS, Am. Phys. Soc. Achievements include use and devel. novel optical methods in studies of structural phase transitions, semiconductor interfaces and interactions of free electrons in semiconductors; discovered novel phenomena in studies of quantum electron fluids. Office: Columbia U Dept Physics and Applied Physics New York NY 10027 also: Bell Labs Lucent Techs 600 Mountain Ave Rm 1d-433 New Providence NJ 07974-2008

PINDELL, HOWARDENA DOREEN, artist; b. Phila., Apr. 14, 1943; d. Howard Douglas and Mildred Edith (Lewis) P. BFA, Boston U., 1965; MFA, Yale U., 1967; DFA (hon.), Mass. Coll. Art, 1997, New Sch./Parsons Sch. Design, 1999. Curatorial asst. Mus. Modern Art, N.Y.C., 1969-71, asst. curator, 1971-77, assoc. curator dept. prints and illus. books, 1977-79; asso. prof. art SUNY, Stony Brook, 1979-84, prof. art, 1984—. Contbr. articles to profl. jours.; exhbns. include, Mus. Modern Art, Stockholm and 5 European mus., 1973, Fogg Art Mus., Cambridge, Mass., 1973, Indpls. Mus., Taft Mus., Cin., 1974, Gerald Piltzer Gallery, Paris, 1975, 9th Paris Biennale, Mus. Modern Art, Paris, 1975, Vassar Coll. Art Gallery, 1977; represented in permanent collections, Mus. Modern Art, N.Y.C., Fogg Art Mus., Met. Mus., N.Y.C., Whitney Mus. Am. Art; represented in travelling exhbns. Brandeis U., U. Calif. at Riverside, Cleve. Inst. Arts, SUNY, Potsdam, New Paltz, Wesleyan U., Davison Art Ctr., others. Recipient Artist award Studio Mus. of Harlem, 1994, Joan Mitchell Painting award Joan Mitchell Found., 1994/95, Women's Caucus for Art award for Disting. Contbns. and Achievement in Arts, 1996, Cmty. Svc. award N.Y. State United Tchrs., 1998, Juneteenth award Heckscher Mus., 1999, IAM Pioneer award, 2000; Japan/U.S. Friendship fellow, 1981-82, Guggenheim fellow, 1987-88; Ariana Found. grantee, 1984-85. Mem. Arts Coun. African Studies Assn., Coll. Art Assn. (Best Exhbn./Performance award 1990), Internat. Assn. Art Critics, Internat. House of Japan (acad.). Office: SUNY/Stonybrook Art Dept Stony Brook NY 11794-0001 Fax: (631) 632-7261. E-mail: Howardena.Pindell@sunysb.edu.

PINDER, GEORGE FRANCIS, engineering educator, scientist; b. Windsor, Ont., Can., Feb. 6, 1942; s. Percy Samuel and Stella Marie P.; m. Phyllis Marie Charlton, Sept. 14, 1963; children— Wendy Marie, Justin George. B.Sc., U. Western Ont., 1965; PhD, U. Ill., 1968. Research hydrologist U.S. Geol. Survey, 1968-72; mem. faculty dept. civil engring. Princeton U., 1972-89, prof., 1972-89, chmn. dept., from 1980, dir. water resources program, 1972-80; dean Coll. Engring. and Math. U. Vt., Burlington, 1989-96, dir. Rsch. Ctr. for Groundwater Remediation Design, 1993—. Recipient O.E. Meinzer award Geol. Soc. Am., 1975, WUC medal, 1992; U. Vt. Univ. scholar, 1993. Fellow Am. Geophys. Union (Robert E. Horton award 1969); mem. ASCE (Julian Hinds medal 2002), Am. Geophys. Union. Home: 188 Bishop Rd Shelburne VT 05482-6933 Office: U Vt Coll Engring And Math Burlington VT 05405-0001

PINDER, RENEE MONIQUE, diplomat; b. Nassau, Bahamas, Nov. 21, 1967; arrived in U.S., 1999; d. Harcourt Maxwell and Hazel Mae Pinder. BSc, Ga. Coll., 1994; MBA, U. Miami, 1996; cert. in Spanish, Coll. of the Bahamas, 1997; diplomatic tng. cert., Santiago, Chile, 1999. Clk. Min. Fgn. Affairs, Nassau, The Bahamas; exec. officer Passport Office, The Bahamas, 1986—96, supr. The Bahamas; adminstrv. cadet Min. Fgn. Affairs, The Bahamas, 1996—99, asst. sec. The Bahamas, 1999—, vice counsul Miami, 1999—. Mem. Fgn. Affairs Investigative, Nassau, 1996—99, Diplomatic Corps. Com., Miami, 1999—. Active Bahamas Red Cross Soc., 1994—. Mem.: Delta Sigma Theta (pres. 1993—94). Home: 16135 NW 64th Ave Apt 223 Miami Lakes FL 33014 Office: Bahamas Consulate Gen 25 SE 2nd Ave Ste 818 Miami FL 33131-1540 Fax: 305-373-6312. E-mail: bcg@bellsouth.net.

PINDLE, ARTHUR JACKSON, JR. philosopher, researcher; b. Macon, Ga., May 26, 1942; s. Arthur Jackson Sr. and Beatrice Rosetta (Williams) P.; 1 child, Zhinga D. BS in Physics, Morehouse Coll., 1964; MA in Philosophy, Yale U., 1973, MPhil, 1974, PhD in Philosophy, 1978. Physicist IBM, Inc., Poughkeepsie, N.Y., 1964, Naval Ordinance Station, Indian Head, Md., 1966-69, Satellite Experiment Lab, Suitland, 1970-71; philosophy prof. Fayetteville (N.C.) State U., 1976-83; pres. HRG, Inc., New Orleans, 1983—; dir. rsch. NITRT, Inc., 1993—; prof. philosophy So. U., 1997—; pres. Grael Electronics, Inc., 1998. Mem. bd. advs. Inst. Philosoph. Rsch., Boulder, Colo., 1980-83. Contbr. articles to profl. jours.; patentee personal computer console. Mem. Dem. Nat. Com., 1993-98. Avocations: yoga, chess. Home: 5000 Good Dr New Orleans LA 70127-3814 Office: Grael Electronics Inc 5000 Good Dr New Orleans LA 70127-3814 E-mail: apindle@netscape.net.

PINDYCK, BRUCE EBEN, lawyer, corporate executive; b. N.Y.C., Sept. 21, 1945; s. Sylvester and Lillian (Breslow) P.; m. Mary Ellen Schwartz, Aug. 18, 1968; children: Ashley Beth, Eben Spencer, Blake Michael Lawrence. AB, Columbia U., 1967, JD, 1970, MBA, 1971. Bar: N.Y. 1971, Wis. 1987. Assoc. Olwine, Connelly, Chase, O'Donnell & Weyher, N.Y.C., 1971-80; asst. gen. counsel Peat, Marwick, Mitchell & Co., 1980-82; ptnr. Hollyer, Jones, Pindyck, Brady & Chira, 1983-87; pres., CEO Meridian Industries, Inc., Milw., 1985—, also chmn. bd. dirs.; CEO Majilite Corp., Dracut, Mass., 1987—, also chmn. bd. dirs. Mem. capital campaign com. Columbia U., 1984-87. Mem. bd. visitors Columbia Coll., 2001—; bd. dirs. Harambee Cmty. Sch., 1991—96, Milw. Ballet Co., 1993—97, Milw. Pub. Mus., 1994—98. Mem. Columbia Coll. Alumni Assn. (regional dir. 1988-94, v.p. 1994-98, exec. com., 1994-98), World Pres.'s Orgn. Address: 100 E Wisconsin Ave Milwaukee WI 53202-4107 E-mail: bpindyck@meridiancompanies.com.

PINE, BESSIE MIRIAM, social worker, editor, columnist; b. Toronto, Jan. 6, 1919; d. Moses and Annie (Rosenberg) Hadler; m. Kurt Pine, Mar 24, 1943 (dec. May 1962); children: Alfred Marc, Annie Laurie Reuveni. BA in Psychology, U. Toronto, 1939; M in Social Work, U. Pitts., 1944. Lic. social worker, N.Y. Br. dir. YM-YWHA, Toronto, 1940-42; case worker Family Svc. of Greater New Haven, Conn., 1944-47, Jewish Family Svc., Phila., 1947-49; divsn. unit supr. Edl. Alliance, N.Y.C., 1949-51; older adult supr. Kings Bay YM-YWHA, Bklyn., 1955-59; editor pers. reporter Jewish Comty Ctr. Program Aids, dir. part time pers. bur., N.Y.C., 1962-67; assoc. dir. pers. svcs. Jewish Comty. Ctrs. Assn., 1967-93. Editor: (booklet) Viewpoints on Social and Social Work Issues, 1965; author: (rsch. study) Making Retirement Count: Options and Opportunities, 1989; author: (publ.) Looking Back and Looking Forward: A 75 Year Retrospective on the Assn. of Jewish Center Workers, 1993. Recipient Florence G. Heller award Jewish Comty. Ctrs. Assn., N.Y.C., 1994. Mem. Com. to Strengthen Group Work in Jewish Comty. Ctrs. (co-chair 1992-99), Assn. of Jewish Ctr. Profls. (columnist Ask Bessie 1994—, Profl. of Yr., Phila. 1990, Tikkun Olam award Balt. 1993), Nat. Assn. Social Workers (cert. social worker). Home: 150 Beaumont St Brooklyn NY 11235-4119

PINE, CHARLES, retail executive; b. Tucson, June 3, 1943; s. Gale Oren and Evelyn Jeannette (Burnett) P.; m. Brenda Elaine Porterfield, Jan. 14, 1967; children: Kenneth Charles, Kevin Scott. Student, Old Dominion Coll., Norfolk, Va., 1961-63, U. N.C., 1987. Asst. mgr. Woolworth, Norfolk, 1963-67, mgr. High Point, N.C., 1967-68; asst. mgr. Belk, Orangeburg, S.C., 1968-72, div. mdse. mgr. Myrtle Beach, 1978-82; mdse. mgr. Belk of Asheville, N.C., 1982-83, store mgr., 1983-84, v.p., 1984-85, sr. v.p., 1985—; sales rep. Atlantic Boutique Jewelry, Charlotte, 1972-76; mgr. Collins Dept. Store, Myrtle Beach, 1976-78. Bd. dirs. 1st Citizens Bank, Asheville. Bd. dirs. Better Bus. Bur., Asheville, 1984—, Daniel Boone coun. Boy Scouts Am., 1984, Salvation Army, Asheville, 1984—; vol. United Way, Asheville, 1967—, mem. capital funds com., 1988—; bd. advisors Mars Hill Coll., 1994; chmn. Reynolds Vol. Fire Dept. Republican. Methodist. Mem. Asheville Mchts. Assn. (bd. dirs. 1983—), Asheville C. of C. (bd. dirs. 1987—), Mars Hill Coll. (bd. advisors 1994), Reynolds Vol. Fire Dept. (chmn.). Republican. Methodist. Avocations: fishing, hunting, swimming, skeet shooting. Office: Belk of Asheville 5 S Tunnel Rd Asheville NC 28805-2218

PINE, LOIS ANN HASENKAMP, nurse; b. Cheyenne, Wyo., Feb. 21, 1950; d. Clifford Norbert and Julie Adda (Younglund) Hasenkamp; m. Julius William Pine Jr., Feb. 16, 1974; children: Margaret Ann, Julius William Pine III, Lawrence Michael. BS, U. Wyo., 1976, MS in Parent-Child Nursing, 1989. Registered RN. From staff nurse to charge nurse Ivinson Meml. Hosp., Laramie, Wyo., 1976-86; maternal-child nurse cons. Perinatal and Prevention Program, Wyo. Dept. Health, Cheyenne, 1988-96; spl. infant care nurse Luthern Home Health Svcs./Banner Home Health Svcs., Laramie, 1996—2001; prepared childbirth educator Ivinson Meml. Hosp., 1997—; spl. infant care nurse Laramie Home Health Care, 2001—. CPR instr, neonatal resuscitation regional instr. Mem. Albany County PTA, Laramie, 1985—91; mem. health profl. adv. com. March of Dimes Wyo. chpt., 1988—99, chmn., 1998—99, mem. exec. bd., 1998—99, dir. Birth Defect Found., 1999—2001; mem. Laramie well aware com. Cmty. Healthy Youth & Children's Task Force; mem. St. Laurence Coun. of Cath. Women, Laramie, 1980—, St. Cecilia's Group, Laramie, 1980—. Mem.: ICCE, ICEA, Nat. Assn. Neonatal Nurses (charter), Am. Acad. Pediat. (perinatal pediat. dist. VIII sect.), Obstetric and Neonatal Nurses (sect. vice chmn. 1980—86), Assn. Women's Health, Internat. Cert. Childbirth Educator, Internat. Childbirth Edn. Assn., Sigma Theta Tau (Alpha Pi chpt. treas. 1990—94, corr. sec. 1983—84, sec. 1994—99, pres. 1999—2001). Democrat. Avocation: Avocations: reading, knitting, crocheting, basketball, football. Home: 1062 Empinado St Laramie WY 82072-5019 Office: Laramie Home Health Care 1268 N 7th St Laramie WY 82072-3132 also: Ivinson Meml Hosp 255 N 30th St Laramie WY 82072-5140

PINE, MARTIN E. management consultant, technology consultant; b. Washington, 1955; s. Irvin and Doris Pine. BS in Bus. and Mgmt. (Fin. and Mktg.), U. Md., 1978, BS in Computer Sci., 1981. Sys. analyst Advanced Sys. Tech., 1979-82; sr. con. Price Waterhouse, 1982-83; pres., chief tech. officer, prin. cons. Pine Sys., 1983-98; CEO, chmn. Methodplex, 1998—; mng. dir. Internat. Consortium Time-Oriented Cons., 1998—. Writer, presenter numerous info. sys. modeling courses, workshops, and seminars. Editor-in-chief, pub. (E-zine) The Eleventh Hour, 1998—; co-writer: (TV) Father's Day, Courtroom Instruction; creator: (computer aided software engring. tool) Demand Users Environment, (analytical modeling) Time-Oriented Technology, (requirements engring.) Time-Oriented Methodolgies, Computational Paradigm, SST (Strategy-Strategic Theory), SIMPLE (Strategic Info. Modeling and Process Logic for Enterprises), Hyperabstraction, Enterprise Evolution, Quality-Centric Modeling, Process Continuum Framework, Strategic Enterprise Model, TOTAL (Time-Oriented Technology for Accurate Logic), ALIVE (Autonomous Logic for Interactive Virtual Environments), EVOLVE (Engineering Volital Oporations and Logic for Virtual Enterprises), UTOPIA (Universal Time-Oriented Process for Intelligent Analysis), EDICT (Enterprise-wide Dynamic Information for Controlling a Transformation), PFM (Product Flow Model), ASM (Adaptive Strategic Modeling); writer numerous stories; voice-over work in TV. Campaign advisor Charles Janus 7th cir., Circuit Ct. Judge contender, Md., 1994. Mem. Software Maintenance Assn., Java Developer Connection, Netpreneur, Delta Sigma Pi, American Soc. for Quality (mem. Quality Mgmt. Divn., Cmty. Quality Coun., Product Safety and Liability Interest Group). Office: Methodplex PO Box 2452 Gaithersburg MD 20886-2452 E-mail: mpine@methodplex.com.

PINE, PATRICIA PALMER, aging services administrator; b. Portland, Maine, Mar. 14, 1940; d. Maurice George and Elizabeth Wadsworth (Syphers) Palmer; m. James Erlon Hannaford, Oct. 1, 1960 (div. June 1970); children: Paula L., Brenda J.; m. Vanderlyn Russell Pine, Aug. 9, 1974; stepchildren: Gordon K., Brian T., Daniel R. AB, Vassar Coll., 1972; MA, Columbia U., 1975; PhD, SUNY, Albany, 1993. Dir. Dutchess County Office for the Aging, Poughkeepsie, N.Y., 1976-80; assoc. dir. Hudson Valley Health Systems Agy., Tuxedo, 1980-83; exec. dir. Hospice Assn. of Ulster County, Kingston, 1983-84; assoc. exec. dir. WellCare N.Y., Kingston and Newburgh, 1984-86; dir. Ulster County Office Aging, Kingston, 1986-95; exec. dep. dir. N.Y. State Office For The Aging, Albany, 1995-2001; dir. N.Y. State Office Aging, 2001—. Adj. prof. SUNY, New Paltz, 1973-95, Marist Coll., Poughkeepsie, 1976-79, 95, Adelphi U., L.I. City, 1983; pres. CEO The Gerontol Inst., 1993—; mem. faculty Brookdale Ctr. Spig of Hunter Coll., 2000—. Pres. United Way of Ulster County, Kingston, 1989-90; mem. N.Y. State Adv. Commn. on Aging-In Initiative, 1991—; trustee The Kingston Hosp., 1993-96. Gerontol. Soc. Am. rsch. fellow, 1987, Paul Harris fellow Rotary Internat., 1989; named Vol. of the Yr., United Way of Ulster County, 1990. Mem. NASW, Nat. Coun. on Aging, Gerontol. Soc. Am., N.Y. State Assn. Area Agys. on Aging (rec. sec. 1978-80, chair statewide conf. 1980, chair tng. com. 1986-88, pres. 1995). Avocations: skiing, traveling, family, reading. Home: 18 Plattekill Ave New Paltz NY 12561-1917

PINE, WILLIAM CHARLES, foundation executive; b. Canton, Ill., Nov. 4, 1912; s. William Charles and Katherine Pauline (Prichard) P.; m. Virginia Rae Keeley, June 14, 1945; children: William Charles, Barry Scott, Nancy Katherine Pine McMahon. BS, Monmouth Coll., Ill., 1939; DHL (hon.), Southwestern at Memphis, 1961; Dr.Laws (hon.), Mercy Coll. Detroit, 1966. Asst. dir. admissions Monmouth Coll., 1939-42; spl. agt. FBI, 1942-45; assoc.

dir. Am. City Bur., N.Y.C. and Chgo., 1945-47; dir. pub. relations Lake Forest (Ill.) Coll., 1947-48, v.p., 1948-51; dir. scholarship prog. Ford Motor Co. Fund., Dearborn, Mich., 1951-72, asst. dir., 1972-75; prog. dir. The Collins Found., Portland, Oreg., 1976-79, exec. v.p., 1979-97; grant advisor Providence St. Vincent Med. Found., 1997—. Contbr. articles to profl. jours. Mem. Historic Records Adv. Bd., Salem, Oreg., 1984-87. Mem. Soc. Former Spl. Agts. of FBI. Avocations: reading, mail order bus. Office: Providence St Vincent Med Found 9205 SW Barnes Rd Portland OR 97225-6603

PINEDA, ALBERT ANTHONY, obstetrician, gynecologist, educator; b. N.Y.C., Feb. 15, 1937; MD, N.Y. Med. Coll., 1963. Diplomate Am. Bd. Ob-gyn. Intern St. Vincents Hosp., N.Y.C., 1963-64; resident in ob-gyn. Flower-Fifth Ave Hosp.-N.Y. Med. Coll., 1964-68; fellow in gynecol. oncology Met. Hosp., 1968-69; med. staff St. Joseph's Hosp. Med. Ctr., Paterson, N.J.; clin. assoc. prof. N.Y. Med. Coll., 1976, Seton Hall U. Grad. Sch. Med. Edn., 1991—; clin. prof. St. George's U. Sch. Medicine, 1995—; pvt. practice Clifton, N.J. Mem. ACOG, Soc. Gynecol. Oncology, N.J. Med. Soc., Passaic County Med. Soc. Office: 1035 Route 46 Clifton NJ 07013-2430

PINEDA, ROBERTO, II, ophthalmologist; b. Mpls., Nov. 30, 1962; s. Roberto and Anne Pineda. BS, U. Minn., 1984, MD, 1996. Diplomate Am. Bd. Ophthalmology. Intern Hennepin County Med. Ctr., Mpls., 1990-91; resident in ophthalmology Mass. Eye and Ear Infirmary, Boston, 1991-94, chief resident, 1994-95, cornea fellow, 1995-96; asst. prof. ophthalmology Harvard Med. Sch., 1999—. Heed Found. Ophthalmic fellow, 1995. Fellow Am. Acad. Ophthalmology. Office: Brigham & Womens Hosp Dept Ophthalmology 221 Longwood Ave Boston MA 02115-5804 Fax: 617-277-2085.

PINELESS, HAL STEVEN, neurologist; b. Chgo., Oct. 19, 1954; s. William and Sophie (Lubnicka) P.; m. Edy Dianne Rudnick, Mar. 10, 1985; children: Adam, Emily. BS in Zoology, U. Ill., 1976; DO, Chgo. Coll. Osteo. Medicine, 1981. Diplomate Am. Osteo. Bd. Neurology and Psychiatry. Intern Chgo. Osteo. Hosp., 1981-82; resident Loyola U. Med. Ctr./Hines (Ill.) VA Ctr., 1982-85; asst. prof. neurology Chgo. Coll. Osteo. Medicine, 1985-86; pvt. practice Winter Park, Fla., 1986—. Pres. med. staff Fla. Hosp. East Orlando, 1990-93, bd. trustees, 1990-94. Contbr. articles to profl. jours and newspapers. Mem. AMA, Am. Osteo. Assn., Am. Acad. Neurology, Am. Coll. Neuropsychiatrists, Nat. Headache Found., Chgo. Coll. of Osteopathic Alumni Assn. (pres. 2000—). Avocations: golf, racquetball, swimming, computers, photography. Office: 1890 Semoran Blvd Ste 255 Winter Park FL 32792-2285

PINES, BURTON YALE, media executive; b. Chgo., Apr. 6, 1940; s. Hyman and Mary Pines; m. Helene Brenner, May 21, 1972. BA, U. Wis., 1961, MA, 1963. Instr. U. Wis., Madison, 1962-65; corr., bur. chief Time mag., Bonn, Saigon and Vienna, 1966-73, editor N.Y.C., 1973-81; sr. v.p. Heritage Found., Washington, 1981-92; chmn. Nat. Ctr. for Pub. Policy Rsch., 1982-94; co-founder, exec. v.p. COO NET Polit. Newstalk Network (later known as America's Voice Cable TV Network), 1992-95; pres., CEO Booknet Cable TV Network, N.Y.C., 1995—; exec. editor Internet ops. GOP Nat. Conv., 2000—. Author: Back to Basics, 1982, Out of Focus, 1994; editor: Mandate for Leadership II, 1984, Mandate for Leadership III, 1988. Recipient Page One award N.Y. Newspaper Guild, 1976, 77, 78, Freedom's Found. award, 1983. Jewish. Office: BookNet 150 W 51st St Ste 1804 New York NY 10019-6848

PINES, MAYA, writer, editor; b. Berlin, Germany, May 13, 1928; came to U.S., 1940; d. Joseph and Rachela (Burawoy) P.; m. Joseph N. Froomkin, Dec. 12, 1959; children: A. Michael, Daniel P. BA, Barnard Coll., 1947; MS, Columbia U., 1949. Sci. dept. reporter Life mag., N.Y.C., 1952-60; ind. writer Life Sci. Libr., among others, N.Y.C. and Washington, 1960-87; contbg. editor Psychology Today, 1980-87; sci. times reporter N.Y. Times, N.Y.C., 1982; sr. sci. editor Howard Hughes Med. Inst., Chevy Chase, Md., 1987-98, editl. cons., 1998—; ind. writer, editor Bethesda, 1998—. Mem. task force on early childhood edn. HEW, Washington, 1966; mem. adv. bd. U.S. Commn. on Mental Health, Washington, 1975; cons. HHMI Study on the Need for Genome Mapping, Chevy Chase, Md., 1986. Author: (with Cornell Capa) Retarded Children Can Be Helped, 1957, (with Rene Dubos) Health and Disease, 1965, Revolution in Learning: The Years from Birth to Six, 1967 (Best Book of Yr., Delta Kappa Gamma Soc. 1968), The Brain Changers, 1973 (Nat. Media award, APA 1974), Inside the Cell, 1978, Medicines and You, 1981, The New Human Genetics, 1985, The Structures of Life, 1986, (with others) The Incredible Machine, 1986; editor, prin. writer: Exploring the Biomedical Revolution, Finding the Critical Shapes, Blazing a Genetic Trail, From Egg to Adult, Blood: Bearer of Life and Death, Seeing, Hearing, and Smelling the World, The Race Against Lethal Microbes, Arousing the Fury of the Immune System, 1999, The Genes We Share with Yeast, Flies, Worms, and Mice, 2000; contbr. articles to profl. jours. and mags. including N.Y. Times Mag., Harper's Mag., Smithsonian Mag., Sci., Psychology Today, Life mag., Saturday Rev., Am. Jour. Psychiatry, Washington Post Book World. Recipient Claude Bernard Sci. Journalism award Nat. Soc. for Med. Rsch., 1976, 1st award for Disting. Med. Writing Am. Med. Writers Assn., 1979, 1st prize Odyssey Inst. Annual Media awards, 1982, Significant Contbn. to Psychiatry award Washington Psychiat. Soc., 1983, Sustained Contbr. award APA, 1987. Mem. Am. Soc. Journalists and Authors, Nat. Assn. Sci. Writers, D.C. Sci. Writers Assn. (bd. dirs. 1996). Avocation: tennis. Home: 4701 Willard Ave Chevy Chase MD 20815 E-mail: pinesm@hhmi.org.

PINES, WAYNE LLOYD, public relations counselor; b. Washington, Dec. 31, 1943; s. Jerome Martin and Ethel (Schnall) P.; m. Nancy Freitag, Apr. 16, 1966; children: Noah Morris, Jesse Mireth. BA, Rutgers U., 1965; postgrad., George Washington U., 1969-71. Reporter, city editor Middletown (N.Y.) Times Herald-Record, 1965-68; copy editor Reuters News, 1968-69; assoc. editor FDC Reports, Washington, 1969-72; chief Consumer Edn. and Info., FDA; also editor FDA Consumer, 1972-74; exec. editor Product Safety Letter and Devices and Diagnostics Letter, Washington, 1974-75; dep. asst. commr. for pub. affairs, chief press rels. FDA, Rockville, Md., 1975-78, assoc. commr. pub. affairs, 1978-82; spl. asst. to dir. NIMH, 1982-83; sr. v.p., sr. counselor Burson-Marsteller, 1983-87, exec. v.p., dir. med. issues, 1987-93; pres. regulatory svcs. APCO Worldwide, Washington, 1993—; dir. crisis com. APCO Assocs.; sr. counselor Grey Healthcare Group, 1993—; mng. dir. Comms. Ptnrs. and Assocs., 1999—. Adj. prof. Washington Public Affairs Ctr., U. So. Calif., 1980-81; instr. N.Y.U. Sch. Continuing Edn., 1982-84; instr. Profl. Devel. Inst., 1983-85; mem. adv. bd. Nat. Orgn. Rare Disorders, Orphan Med.; mem. corp. adv. bd. ANA; chmn. Therametrix Inc., 1999-2001; columnist WebMD, 1999-2001, Med. Advt. News, 1985-90. Author: The Sermons of Jerome Martin Pines, FDA Advertising and Promotion Manual, When Lightning Strikes: A How-to Crisis Manual, A Practical Guide to Food and Drug Law and Regulation, How to Work with the FDA, Crisis Communications in Healthcare: A Delicate Balance; contbr. numerous articles in field to profl. jours. Home: 5821 Nevada Ave NW Washington DC 20015-2547 Office: APCO Assocs 1615 L St NW Washington DC 20036-5610 E-mail: wpines@apcoworldwide.com.

PING, CHARLES JACKSON, philosophy educator, retired university president; b. Phila., June 15, 1930; s. Cloudy J. and Mary M. (Marion) P.; m. Claire Oates, June 5, 1951; children: Andrew, Ann Shelton. BA, Rhodes Coll., 1951; B.D., Louisville Presbyn. Theol. Sem., 1954; PhD, Duke, 1961. Assoc. prof. philosophy Alma Coll., 1962-66; prof. philosophy Tusculum Coll., 1966-69, v.p., dean faculty, 1967-68, acting pres., 1968-69; provost Central Mich. U., Mt. Pleasant, 1969-75; pres. Ohio U., Athens, 1975-94, pres. emeritus, Trustee prof. philosophy and edn., 1994—, exec. dir. Manasseh Cutler Scholars Program, dir. Ping Inst. for Tchg. Humanities, 1994-99, dir. emeritus, 1999—. Bd. dirs. Wing Lung Bank Internat. Inst. for Bus. Devel., Hong Kong; trustee Louisville Presbyn. Theol. Sem., Muskingum Coll., Ohio; mem. adv. bd. Inst. Ednl. Mgmt. of Harvard U.; chair Commn. Planning for Future of Higher Edn., Kingdom of Swaziland; mem. Commn. on Higher Edn. Republic of Namibia. Author: Ohio University in Perspective, 1985, Meaningful Nonsense, 1966, also articles. Fulbright Sr. Rsch. scholar to So. Africa, 1995. Mem. Coun. on Internat. Ednl. Exch. (chair bd.), David C. Lam Inst. for East-West Studies (bd. dirs.), Coun. Internat. Exch. Scholars (bd. dirs., chair Africa com.). Office: Ohio U Office of Pres Emeritus Athens OH 45701 E-mail: ping@ohio.edu.

PINGREE, BRUCE DOUGLAS, lawyer; b. Salt Lake City, June 6, 1947; s. Howard W. and Lois (Ivie) P.; m. Lorraine Bertelli, Oct. 11, 1981; children: Christian James, Matthew David, Alexandra Elizabeth, Meredith Gillian, Lauren Ashley, Geoffrey Nicholas. BA in Philosophy, U. Utah, 1970, JD, 1973. Bar: Ariz. 1973, Tex. 1990. Ptnr. Snell & Wilmer, Phoenix, 1973-89; shareholder Johnson & Gibbs, Dallas, 1989-93; ptnr. Gardere & Wynne, 1993-95, Baker Botts, L.L.P., Dallas, 1995—. Lectr. in field of taxation. Contbr. articles to profl. jours. Served to capt. USAR. Fellow Am. Coll. Employee Benefit Counsel, Inc. (charter); mem. ABA (tax sect., past chair employee benefits com., past vice chair, past chmn. various sub-coms., 1993-94, chair joint com. on employee benefits 1994-95), Tex. State Bar Assn. (chair, tax sect. benefits and compensation com. 2000), Dallas Bar Assn. (chair employee benefits sect. 2001-2002), S.W. Benefits Conf., Nat. Assn. Stock Plan Profls., Order of Coif. Episcopalian. Home: 4065 Bryn Mawr Dr Dallas TX 75225-7032 Office: Baker & Botts LLP 2001 Ross Ave Ste 600 Dallas TX 75201-2900

PINGREE, DIANNE, psychotherapist; b. Dallas; BFA magna cum laude, So. Meth. U., 1976, MLA, 1989; PhD in Sociology, Tex. Woman's U., 1994. Lic. Marriage and Family Therapy Assn., cert. family life educator. Found., editor, pub. Tex. Woman Mag., 1977-80; pres. Tex. Woman Inc., 1980-85; owner, pres. Dianne Pingree & Assoc., 1985-88; pub. cons. Tex. Elite Publications, Dallas, 1988-89; mediator Ctr. for Dispute Resolution Denton County, 1991; grad. tchng. assoc. Tex. Woman's U., 1990-92; postgrad. clin. intern SW Family Inst., Dallas, 1993-94; therapist J&L Human Sys. Devel., 1994-95; psychotherapist Child and Family Svc. Inc., Austin, 1995-96; cons., 1996-98; dir. Liaison Assocs. Profl. Devel. Consultants, 1998—2001; psychotherapist, assoc. clin. staff mem. Austin Acad. for Individual and Relationship Therapy, 2002—. Spkr. in field. Vol., vice chmn. mental health com. United Way Capital Area, 1998—99; vol., legal adv. Safeplace; spkr. on cmty. edn.; mem. Leadership Austin, 2000—01. Recipient Matrix award for outstanding achievement, Women in Comms., Women Helping Women award, Women's Ctr. Dallas, Dallas Press Club award. Mem.: AAUW, Nat. Coun. on Family Rels., Am. Sociol. Assn., Tex. Assn. for Marriage and Family Therapy (assoc.), Am. Assn. for Marriage and Family Therapy (assoc.), Internat. Sociol. Honor Soc. (pres. chpt. 1992), Alpha Kappa Delta. Office: PO Box 160277 Austin TX 78716-0277

PINGS, ANTHONY CLAUDE, architect; b. Fresno, Calif., Dec. 16, 1951; s. Clarence Hubert and Mary (Murray) P.; m. Carole Clements, June 25, 1983; children, Adam Reed, Rebecca Mary. AA, Fresno City Coll., 1972; BArch, Calif. Poly. State U., San Luis Obispo, 1976. Lic. architect, Calif.; cert. Nat. Council Archtl. Registration Bds. Architect Aubrey Moore Jr., Fresno, 1976-81; architect, prin. Pings & Assocs., 1981-83, 86—, Pings-Taylor Assocs., Fresno, 1983-85. Prin. works include Gollaher Profl. Office (Masonry Merit award 1985, Best Office Bldg. award 1986), Fresno Imaging Ctr. (Best Instnl. Project award 1986, Nat. Healthcare award Modern Health Care mag. 1986), Orthopedic Facility (award of honor Masonry Inst. 1987, award of merit San Joaquin chpt. AIA 1987), Modesto Imaging Ctr. (award of merit San Joaquin chpt. AIA 1991), Peachwood Med. Ctr. (award of merit San Joaquin chpt. AIA). Mem. Calif. Indsl. Tech. Edn. Consortium Calif. State Dept. Edn., 1983, 84. Recipient Excellence in Bus. award Fresno, 1999. Mem. AIA (bd. dirs. Calif. chpt. 1983-84, v.p. San Joaquin chpt. 1982, pres. 1983, Calif. Coun. evaluation team 1983, team leader Coalinga Emergency Design Assistance team), Fresno Arts (bd. dirs., counsel 1989—, pres. 1990-93), Fig Gardens Home Owners Assn. (bd. dir. 1991—, pres. 1994—). Republican. Home: 4350 N Safford Ave Fresno CA 93704-3509 Office: Pings & Assocs 1640 W Shaw Ave Ste 107 Fresno CA 93711-3506

PINGS, CORNELIUS JOHN, educational consultant, director; b. Conrad, Mont., Mar. 15, 1929; s. Cornelius John and Marjorie (O'Loughlin) P.; m. Marjorie Anna Cheney, June 25, 1960; children: John, Anne, Mary. BS, Calif. Inst. Tech., 1951, MS, 1952, PhD, 1955. Inst. chem. engring. Stanford U., 1955-56, asst. prof., 1956-59; assoc. prof. chem. engring. Calif. Inst. Tech., 1959-64, prof., 1964-81, exec. officer chem. engring., 1969-73, vice-provost, dean grad. studies, 1970-81; provost, sr. v.p. acad. affairs U. So. Calif., 1981-93; pres. Assn. Am. Univs., Washington, 1993-98. Mem., dir. Nat. Commn. on Rsch., 1978—80; mem. bd. mgmt. Coun. on Govtl. Rels., 1980—83; bd. dirs. Nations Funds, Edelbrock, Inc., L.A.; pres. Assn. Grad. Schs., 1977—78, Western Coll. Assn., 1988—90; mem. sci. engring. and pub. policy com. NAS, 1987—92, chmn., 1988—92; bd. dirs. Amervest Inc. Contbr. articles to tech. jours. Mem., chmn. bd. trustees Mayfield Sr. Sch. Bd., 1979-85; mem. Pasadena Redevel. Agy., 1968-81, chmn., 1974-81; bd. dirs. Huntington Meml. Hosp., Pasadena, 1986-92; chmn. L.A. Ctrl. City Assn., 1992. Recipient Arthur Nobel medal, City of Pasadena, 1981, Disting. Alumni award Calif. Inst. Tech., 1989, Presdl. medallion U. So. Calif., 1993. Fellow AIChE, Am. Acad. Arts and Scis.; mem. NAE, Calif. Club, Twilight Club, Bohemian Club, Cosmos Club, Valley Hunt Club. Roman Catholic. Office: 480 S Orange Grove Blvd # 6 Pasadena CA 91105-1736 E-mail: cjpings@usc.edu.

PINHEY, FRANCES LOUISE, retired physical education educator; b. Canton, Ohio, Apr. 18, 1927; d. Frederick Otto and Rose June (Wolf) Sengleitner; m. Donald Charles Pinhey, June 13, 1952; children: Val Don, Shauna Rae, Kaye Dorrell, Lon Pernell. BA, Muskingum Coll., 1949; MS, U. R.I., 1977; postgrad., Ind. U., 1958. Cert. tchr., Ohio. Tchr. Canton Pub. Schs., 1949-50; instr. Muskingum Coll., New Concord, Ohio, 1950-52; tchr. New Concord Pub. Schs., 1950-52, Barberton (Ohio) High Sch., 1952-53, Ottawa (Ont., Can.) Pub. Schs., 1954-57, Ottawa YMCA, 1954-57; instr. Dakota Wesleyan U., Mitchell, S.D., 1959-63, Wilmington (Ohio) Coll., 1963-67; tchr. New London (Conn.) Pub. Schs., 1967-68; asst. prof. phys. edn., coach Mitchell Coll., New London, 1968-96; asst. instr. badminton, tennis Coast Guard Acad., 1996-99; asst. coach mens baseball USCG Acad., New London, Conn., 1999; ret., 1999. Chair, mem. Conn. Sports Officiating Rating Bd., 1968-78. Nat. ofcl. women's volleyball & basketball, 1958-80; pres. PTA, Wilmington, 1967, PTA mem., New London, Conn., 1968-77; vol. New London Recreation Dept., 1986, Little League, 1970-75; vol. condr. CBA Badminton Tournaments. Inducted into Mitchell Coll. Hall of Fame, 1993. Mem. AAHPERD, Nat. Jr. Coll. Field Hockey Coaches Assn. (pres. 1991—), Nat. Jr. Coll. Men's Tennis Assn., U.S. Badminton Assn., Nat. Assn. Sport and Phys. Edn., Nat. Dance Assn., Nat. Dance-Exercise Instrs. Tng. Assn., Nat. Jr. Coll. Athletic Assn. (chmn. New Eng. region XXI field hockey com. 1975-89, women's field hockey Coach of Yr. region XXI 1975, 78-84, 90, nat. championships and Nat. Coach of Yr. 1979, 81, 83, 84, 90, Men's Tennis Coach of Yr. Region XXI 1983, 87, 89, 90). Avocations: badminton (ranked player, singles and doubles Conn. Badminton Assn. Top 10, 1981, 83, 84, 85, 86 and 87), tennis, gardening, dance. Home: 43 Bellevue Pl New London CT 06320-4701

PINIAT, SHIRLEY ZINA, artist, educator; b. Bklyn., July 13, 1925; d. Max and Sadie Frances (Allweiss) Wohl; m. John Piniat, June 24, 1950. BSEd in Psychol. Svcs., CCNY, 1948, MSEd in Psychol. Svcs., 1949. Sch. sec. N.Y.C. Bd. Edn., 1945-54, substitute tchr., 1986-88. Exhibited in group shows Monique Mus. and Art Gallery, Queens, 1998, Jackson Heights Art Club, Queens, 1999, Europe Gallery, Jackson Heights, Queens, 1999, 2000, Salmagundi Club, N.Y.C., 1999, AQA Gallery, Queens, 2000, New Century Artists, N.Y.C., 2000, Good Monkeys Gallery, Eugene Oreg., 2000, Queens Mus. Art, 2001, Collage/Assemblage Soc., New Century Artists, N.Y.C., 2001, Times Square Lobby Gallery, N.Y.C., 2001, Women's Studio Ctr., L.I. City Art Frenzy, 2001; TV appearances include Queens Pub. TV, 2000, Manhattan Neighborhood Network, Manhattan Cable, Channel 67, 2000. Mem. Flushing coun. on Arts, 1998—, Queens Mus. Art, 2000—. Recipient 3d place award Stage Gallery, 2000, award of merit Manhattan Arts Internat., 2000. Mem. Flushing Art League, Collage/Assemblage Soc., New Century Artists, Jackson Heights Art Club (2d prize for oil 1999). Avocations: travel, museums, painting and sketching, cultural activities.

PINILLA, ANA RITA, neuropsychologist, researcher; b. N.Y.C., May 20, 1957; d. Louis and Luz Maria (Diaz) P.; children: Jorge Javier, Juan Carlos, Ana Mari. BS magna cum laude, U. P.R., Rio Piedras, 1978; MS, Caribbean Ctr., San Juan, P.R., 1980, PhD, 1988. Lic. psychologist, P.R. Prof. psychology Inter-Am. U., San Juan, 1980-91; neuropsychologist Neuropsychol. Svcs. to Developmental Deficiencies Children, Bayamon, P.R., 1987-88; asst. dir. Gov.'s Prevention Program, San Juan, 1988-90; exec. dir. Learning Disability Ctr., 1990-94; external evaluator prevention program Roberto Clemente Sports City, Carolina, P.R., 1990-95. Cons. ednl. programs Gov.'s Office; adviser, evaluator drug prevention programs, 1994-96; clin. dir. Options, P.R., 1996-97; med. subdir. Learning Ctr.-Hosp. Interamericano de Medicine Avanzada; cons. in field; pres. Alternative Psychol. Svcs., 2000-01; faculty Pontificia U. Cath. P.R., 2000—. Author: Analysis of Wisc-R, 1988, Managing the Divorce Crisis: An Integrated Model, 1999; contbr. articles to profl. publs. Mem. Internat. Neuropsychol. Soc., Nat. Acad. Neuropsychology. Achievements include development of program of services to learning disabled children using neuropsychological approach, development of tests for measurement character traits. E-mail: anap@prtc.net.

PINKARD, ANNE MERRICK, foundation administrator; b. Baltimore, Feb. 8, 1924; d. Robert Graff M.; m. Walter Devier Pinkard, Sept. 24, 1949 (dec. June, 1994); children: Walter D. Jr., Robert Merrick, Gregory Clyde, Peter McEvoy. BA, Goucher Coll., 1946; student, Cornell U., 1944-45; LLD (hon.), Johns Hopkins U., 1994. Bd. dirs. Citizens Planning and Housing, Balt., 1950-60; bd. dirs., sect. Soc. Md. Antiquities, 1955-63; pres. women's bd. Johns Hopkins Hosp., 1968-72, bd. dirs., 1976-92; pres. France Merrick Found., Balt., 1987—. Bd. dirs. Johns Hopkins U., Balt., 1972-94, trustee, 1972-94; trustee St. Mary's Sem. and U., 1974-80. Home: 613 Brightwood Club Dr Lutherville MD 21093-3632 Office: France Merrick Found 1122 Kenilworth Dr Baltimore MD 21204-2139

PINKEL, DONALD PAUL, pediatrician; b. Buffalo, Sept. 7, 1926; s. Lawrence William and Ann (Richardson) P.; m. Marita Donovan, Dec. 26, 1949 (div. 1981); children: Rebecca, Nancy, Christopher, Mary, Thomas, Anne, Sara, John, Ruth; m. Cathryn Barbara Howarth, May 16, 1981; 1 child, Michael. BS, Canisius Coll., 1947; MD, U. Buffalo, 1951. Diplomate Am. Bd. Pediatrics, Pediatric Hematology and Oncology, Nat. Bd. Med. Examiners. From intern to resident to chief resident Children's Hosp., Buffalo, 1951-54; research fellow Children's Hosp. Med. Ctr., Boston, 1955-56; chief. of pediatrics Roswell Park Meml. Inst., Buffalo, 1956-61; med. dir. St. Jude Children's Research Hosp., Memphis, 1961-73; chmn. pediatrics Med. Coll. Wis., Milw., 1974-78; pediatrician-in-chief Milw. Children's Hosp., 1974-78; founding dir. Midwest Children's Cancer Ctr., Milw., 1974; chief. of pediatrics City of Hope Med. Ctr., Duarte, Calif., 1978-82; chmn. pediatrics Temple U. Sch. Medicine, Phila., 1982-85; prof., Kana Rsch. chair, dir. pediatric leukemia program U. Tex. System Cancer Ctr., M.D. Anderson Hosp. and Tumor Inst., Houston, 1985-93; prof. pediat. U. Tex. Med. Sch., 1985-99; prof. emeritus U. Tex.-M.D. Anderson Cancer Ctr., 1994—. Clin. prof. pediats. U. So. Calif., L.A., 2002—; adj. prof. biol. scis. Calif. Polytechnic State U., San Luis Obispo, Calif., 2001—. Contbr. numerous articles to profl. jours. Bd. dirs. Lee County Coop. Clinic, Mariana, Ark., 1972-74. Served with USN, 1944-45, served to 1st lt. U.S. Army, 1954-55. Recipient Albert Lasker award for Med. Research Lasker Found., 1972, Windermere Lectureship Brit. Pediatric Assn., 1974, David Karnofsky award Am. Soc. Clin. Oncology, 1978, Zimmerman prize for Cancer Research Zimmerman Found., 1979, Charles Kettering prize Gen. Motors Cancer Research, 1986, Clin. Rsch. award Am. Cancer Soc., 1988, Return of the Child award Leukemia Soc. Am., 1992. Mem. Am. Soc. Clin. Oncology, Am. Pediat. Soc., Am. Assn. Cancer Rsch., Soc. Exptl. Biology and Medicine, Am. Soc. Hematology. Democrat. Roman Catholic. Avocations: swimming, sailing. Home: 275 Marlene Dr San Luis Obispo CA 93405 E-mail: donpinkel@yahoo.com.

PINKENBURG, RONALD JOSEPH, ophthalmologist; b. Nov. 25, 1940; s. William Joseph and Winnie Vale (Downs) P.; m. Patricia Anne Regan, Oct. 21, 1967; children: Lisa, Anne Marie, Steven, Renèe. BA cum laude, U. St. Thomas, 1963; MD, Baylor U., 1967. Intern U. Iowa, 1967-68; resident U. Okla., 1971-74, asst. clin. prof. ophthalmology, 1974-88; assoc. clin. prof. ophthalmology U. Tex. Health Sci. Ctr., Tyler, 1988-93; gen. practitioner So. Calif. Permanente Med. Group-Kaiser Found. Hosp., Fontana, 1970-71; pvt. practice medicine specializing in opthalmology Tyler, 1974—. Mem. staff Med. Center Hosp., Tyler, Mother Francis Hosp. Trustee Tex. Med. Assn. Ins. Trust, 1988-89, chmn. bd. trustees, 1989-97. With USAF, 1968-70. Fellow ACS, Royal Soc. Medicine, Tex. Soc. Ophthalmology and Otolaryngology; mem. AMA, Smith County Med. Soc. (pres.-elect 1991-92, pres. 1992-93), Tex. Med. Assn. (chmn. com. assn. ins. programs 1981-88), Tex. Med. Assn. Found. (bd. trustees 1997—), Tex. Ophthalmology Assn. (pres.-elect 1987-88, pres. 1988-89), Am. Acad. Ophthalmology, Am. Soc. Cataract Refractive Surgeons, Retina Found. S.W. (bd. med. advisors), Eye Care Consortium Tex. (bd. dirs., sec.-treas. 1996—). Roman Catholic. Home: 321 Cumberland Rd Tyler TX 75703-9321 Office: 2440 E 5th St Tyler TX 75701-3592

PINKER, STEVEN A. cognitive science educator; b. Montreal, Que., Can., Sept. 18, 1954; arrived in U.S., 1976; s. Harry and Roslyn (Wiesenfeld) P. BA, McGill U., Montreal, 1976; PhD, Harvard U., 1979; DSc (hon.), McGill U., 1999. Asst. prof. Harvard U., Cambridge, Mass., 1980-81, Stanford U., Palo Alto, Calif., 1981-82; prof. cognitive sci. MIT, Cambridge, 1982—, Peter de Florez prof., 2000—. Author: Language Learnability and Language Development, 1984, Learnability and Cognition, 1989, The Language Instinct, 1994, How the Mind Works, 1997, Words and Rules, 1999, The Blank Slate, 2002; mem. editl. bd. Cognition, 1984—. Recipient Troland Rsch. award NAS, 1993, Book prize L.A. Times, 1998. Fellow AAAS, APA (Disting. Early Career award 1984, Boyd McCandless award 1986, William James Book prize 1995, 99), Linguistics Soc. Am. (Linguistics, Lang. and Pub. Svcs. award 1997), Am. Psychol. Soc. Office: MIT Dept Brain Cognitive Scis NE20-413 77 Massachusetts Ave Cambridge MA 02139-4301

PINKERTON, ALBERT DUANE, II, lawyer; b. Portland, Oreg., Aug. 28, 1942; s. Albert Duane and Barbara Jean Pinkerton; 1 child, Albert Duane III. BA, Willamette U., 1964, JD, 1966. Bar: Oreg. 1966, U.S. Dist. Ct. Oreg. 1966, U.S. Ct. Appeals (9th cir.) 1966, Alaska 1985, Calif. 1986, U.S. Dist. Ct. Calif. 1987. Gen. practice, Springfield, Oreg., 1966-69, Burns, 1969-86, Concord, Calif., 1986-88; assoc. Sellar Hazard McNeely Alm & Manning, Walnut Creek, 1988—. Mem. Oreg. State Bar (com. Uniform Jury Instrns. sec. 1972-73, 82-83, chmn. 1973-74, 83-84; com. Procedure and Practice sec. 1985-86, chmn. 1986-87), Am. Judicature Soc., Masons (master 1980-81), Grand Lodge of Oreg. (dist. dep. 1983-86). Home: PO Box 21347 Concord CA 94521-0347 Office: 1111 Civic Dr Ste 300 Walnut Creek CA 94596-3894 E-mail: dpinkerton@sellarlaw.com.

PINKERTON, C(HARLES) FREDERICK, lawyer; b. Salt Lake City, Mar. 7, 1940; s. Charles Frederick II and Margaret L. (McDowell) P.; m. Joyce Montelione; children: Charles Frederick, John Dale. BA, Calif. Luth. Coll., 1964; JD, U. Oreg., 1967. Bar: Nev. 1968, U.S. Dist. Ct. Nev. 1968, U.S. Ct. Appeals (9th cir.) 1976. Dep. dist. atty Washoe County Dist. Atty.'s Office, Reno, 1968-71, chief crim. dep. dist. atty., 1971. Served as cpl. USMC, 1959-62. Fellow ATLA, Am. Coll. Criminal Lawyers; mem. ABA, Am. Coll. Trial Lawyers, Nat. Assn. Criminal Def. Lawyers, No. Nev. Trial Lawyers Assn., Am. Inns of Ct. (pres. Bruce R. Thompson chpt. 1995-96). Office: 203 S Arlington Ave Reno NV 89501-1702

PINKERTON, DANIEL WALTER, financial planner; b. Anchorage, Jan. 14, 1965; s. Frank W. and Carol J. (Moore) P.; m. Kathryn Elaine Ballard, Nov. 11, 1989; children: Daniel W. II, Sarah K., Rachael C., David M. BA, Stanford U., 1987. CFP. Regional coord. Cal Fed Bank, San Jose, Calif., 1988-91; pres. Pinkerton Retirement Specialists LLC, Anchorage, 1991—, Coeur d'Alene, Idaho, 1997—; br. mgr. Linsco/Pvt. Ledger. Author: Getting the Most Out of Your Mortgage, 1991. Nat. Honor Soc. grantee, 1983, Arco Alaska, 1983, Anchorage Rotary Club, 1983, Anchorage Elks, Anchorage Zonta, 1983; scholar Whitman Coll., 1983. Mem. NASD/SIPC, Internat. Assn. Fin. Planning, Inst. Cert. Fin. Planning, Top of Table, Stanford Alumni Assn, Million Dollar Roundtable, Estate Planning Coun., Nat. Assn. Life Underwriters, LPL's Patriots Club. Office: 2201 Ironwood Ste 100 Coeur D Alene ID 83814

PINKERTON, HELEN JEANETTE, health care executive; b. Chattanooga, Mar. 17, 1956; d. Jesse Robert and Irene Louise (Boyd) Pinkerton. BS, U. Tenn.-Knoxville, 1979, MPH, 1980. Dir. Hypertension/Diabetes Program Alton Park Health Ctr., Chattanooga, 1981—; bd. dirs. Bethlehem Cmty. Ctr., Hospice of Chattanooga, sec. 1998-99; Contbr. to Tenn. Hypertension Control Manual, 1984, 3rd Edit., 1996. Dir. Choirs, fin. officer First Bapt. Ch., Hixson; v.p. Cmty. Svcs. Club, 1986—, pres. 1998-99; mem. Chattanooga Hunger Coalition; sec. Bethlehem Cmty. Ctr., 1998-99; pres. Hospice Chattanooga, 1999—. Recipient Neighbors For Life award, 1995-96, Steven A. Ulin award, 1996-97; Doak scholar, 1977. Mem. NAFE, So. Health Assn., Tenn. Pub. Health Assn., Am. Diabetes Assn. (sec.-treas., v.p. 1998-99), Hypertension Coalition (chmn. 1984-90), Am. Cancer Soc. (bd. dirs.), Neighbors for Life (chairperson, Am. Cancer Soc.), Alton Park C. of C. (council mem. 1982-86), Alpha Kappa Alpha. Democrat. Avocations: walking, reading, singing, jogging. Home: 5419 Moody Sawyer Rd Hixson TN 37343-3646 Office: Alton Park Health Ctr 100 E 37th St Chattanooga TN 37410-1498

PINKERTON, RICHARD LADOYT, retired management educator; b. Huron, S.D., Mar. 5, 1933; s. Abner Pyle and Orral Claudine (Arneson) P.; m. Sandra Louise Lee, Aug. 28, 1965 (div. 1992); children— Elizabeth, Patricia. BA (La Verne Noyes scholar 1952-55), U. Mich., 1955; MBA, Case Western Res. U., 1962; PhD (Nat. Assn. Purchasing Mgmt. fellow 1967-68), U. Wis., 1969. Sr. market research analyst Harris-Intertype Corp., Cleve., 1957-61; mgr. sales devel. Triax Corp., 1962-64; coord. mktg. program Mgmt. Inst., U. Wis., 1964-67; dir. exec. programs Mgmt. Inst., U. Wis. (Grad. Sch. Bus.), also asst. prof. mktg., 1969-74; prof. mgmt., dean Grad. Sch. Adminstrn., Capital U., Columbus, Ohio, 1974-86; prof. mgmt., dir. Univ. Bus. Ctr., Craig Sch. Bus.. Calif. State U., Fresno, 1986-89, prof. mktg., 1989-2000, chmn. mktg. and logistics dept., 1996-2000, dir. London semester, prof. emeritus, mem. bd., 2000—. Trustee Ohio Coun. Econ. Edn., 1976-87; cons. to govt. and industry, 1960—. Co-author: The Purchasing Manager's Guide to Strategic Proactive Procurement, 1996; contbr. articles to profl. jours. Bd. govs. Hannah Neil Home for Children, Columbus, 1975—78; trustee Home Owners Assn., The Woods of Strongsville; mem. indsl. and cmty. devel. commn. City of Strongsville; bd. dirs. The Fresno Townhouse Assn., 1992—2001. Officer USAF, 1955—57, lt. col. USAF, 1957—78. Mem.: Am. Mktg. Assn. (chpt. pres. 1972—73), Nat. Assn. Purchasing Mgmt. (chmn. acad. planning 1979—84, rsch. symposium 1992), Nat. Assn. Contract Mgmt. (chmn. validation cert. com. 1990), Navy League, Air Force Assn., Res. Officers Assn., Marines Meml. Club, Columbia Hills Country Club, Phi Gamma Delta, Alpha Kappa Psi, Beta Gamma Sigma. Home: 18487 Woodside Crossing South Strongsville OH 44149-6891

PINKERTON, ROBERT BRUCE, mechanical engineer; b. Detroit, Feb. 10, 1941; s. George Fulwell and Janet Lois (Hedke) P.; m. Barbara Ann Bandfield, Aug. 13, 1966; 1 child, Robert Brent. BSME, Detroit Inst. Tech., 1965; MA in Engring., Chrysler Inst. Engring., 1967; JD, Wayne State U., 1976. From mech. engr. to emissions and fuel economy planning specialist Chrysler Engring. Office Chrysler Corp., Highland Park, Mich., 1967-80; dir. engring. Replacement div. TRW, Inc., Cleve., 1980-83; v.p. engring. TRW Automotive Aftermarket Group, 1983-86; v.p. engring. and rsch. Blackstone Corp., Jamestown, N.Y., 1986-89, pres., CEO, 1989-90, Athena Corp., Beaufort, S.C., 1990—, Cedar Crest Corp., Beaufort, 1990—, Value Built Homes, 1998—; chmn., CEO Beaufort Land Co., 1998—; pres., CEO Classic Custom Homes, Hilton Head, S.C., 1999—. Bd. dirs. VRI, LLC, Coastal Banking Co., Inc., Low Country Nat. Bank, Village Renaissance, Inc., Carpenters Hall, Coastal Banking Co., Inc., Beaufort-Hilton Head Econ. Devel. Partnership. Mem. exec. com. Beaufort Schs. Oversight Com., 1995-99, Pvt. Industry Coun., 1996-99. Mem. Gtr. Beaufort C. of C. (bd. dris. 1997—), Rotary (asst. dist. gov. 1997—) Beaufort Roundtable (pres. 2000—). Presbyterian. Home: PO Box 2417 Beaufort SC 29901-2417 Office: PO Box 2115 128 Castle Rock Rd Beaufort SC 29906-9047 E-mail: rbp@athenacorp.com.

PINKHAM, DANIEL, composer; b. Lynn, Mass., June 5, 1923; s. Daniel R. and Olive C. (White) P. AB, MA, Harvard, 1944; Litt.D. (hon.), Nebr. Wesleyan U., 1976; Mus.D. (hon.), Adrian Coll., 1977, Westminster Choir Coll., 1979, New Eng. Conservatory, 1993, Ithaca Coll., 1994, Boston Conservatory, 1998. Mem. faculty New Eng. Conservatory Music, 1959—; music dir. King's Chapel, Boston, 1958-2000; co-founder Cambridge Festival Orch., 1948; retired, 2001. Composer: Sonatas for Organ and Strings, 1943, 54, 86, Piano Concertino, 1950, Concerto for Celesta and Harpsichord, 1954, Wedding Cantata, 1956, Christmas Cantata, 1958, Easter Cantata, 1961, Symphonies, 1961, 64, 85, Signs of the Zodiac, 1964, St. Mark Passion, 1965, Jonah, 1966, In the Beginning of Creation, 1970, Ascension Cantata, 1970, Organ Concerto, 1970, When the Morning Stars Sang Together, 1971, the Other Voices of the Trumpet, 1971, Safe in Their Alabaster Chambers, 1972, To Troubled Friends, 1972, Daniel in the Lions' Den, 1973, The Seven Deadly Sins, 1974, Four Elegies, 1974, The Passion of Judas, 1975, Garden Party, 1976, Blessings, 1977, Company at the Creche, 1977, Miracles, 1978, Epiphanies, 1978, Serenades, 1979, Proverbs, 1979, Diversions for Organ and Harp, 1980, Descent Into Hell, 1980, Before the Dust Returns, 1981, The Death of the Witch of Endor, 1981, Prelude and Scherzo for Wind Quintet, 1981, The Dreadful Dining Car, 1982, Brass Quintet, 1983, In Heaven Soaring Up, 1985, The Left-Behind Beasts, 1985, A Biblical Book of Beasts, 1985, Versets, 1985, A Mast for the Unicorn, 1986, A Crimson Flourish, 1986, Winter Nights, 1986, De Profundis, 1986, In the Isles of the Sea, 1986, Antiphons, 1987, Getting To Heaven, 1987, Angels Are Everywhere, 1987, Heav'n Must Go Home, 1988, Four Marian Antiphons, 1988, Alleluias, 1988, Sonata da Chiesa, 1988, Sonata da Camera, 1988, Petitions, 1988, Pedals, 1988, The Seasons Pass, 1988, Reeds, 1988, Concerto Piccolo, 1989, The Small Passion, 1989, Requiem Collects, 1989, The Saints Preserve Us!, 1989, String Quartet, 1989, Stabat Mater, 1990, Symphony Number 4, 1990, The Book of Hours, 1990, Carols and Cries, 1990, The Dryden Te Deum, 1990, Pentecost Cantata, 1991, Three Canticles from Luke, 1991, For Solace in Solitude, 1991, Advent Cantata, 1991, Smart Set, 1991, First Organbook, 1991, The Small Requiem, 1991, Second Organbook, 1992, Christmas Symphonies, 1992, Overture Concertante, 1992, Nocturnes for Flute and Guitar, 1992, Vowels, 1993, Adagietto for Organ and Strings, 1993, Wondrous Love, 1993, When Love Was Gone, 1993, Missa Domestica, 1993, Miserere mei Deus, 1993, The Guiding Star, 1994, The Creation of the World, 1994, Reed Trio, 1994, Morning Music, 1994, Organ Concerto Number Two, 1995, Preludes for Piano, 1995, Passion Music, 1995, The Tenth Muse, 1995, The Inner Room of the Soul, 1995, Festive Processional, 1995, The White Raven, 1996, O Come, Emmanuel, 1996, Called Home, 1996, Organ Concerto Number Three, 1996, Tidings, 1996, Divertimento for Trumpet and Harp, 1997, Sagas, 1997, Music for an Indian Summer, 1997, The Four Winds, 1997, Celebrations, 1998, String Trio, 1998, Odes, 1998, Evening Music, 1998, Music for a Quiet Sunday, 1998, Saints' Days, 1999, Quarries, 1999, Weather Reports, 1999, Oration, 1999, The Green Wall, 1999, Shards, 2000, The Salutation of Gabriel, 2000, Picnic Music, 2000, The House of the Lord, 2000, January Music, 2000, Duo for Viola and Violoncello, 2000, Solemnities, 2001, September Music, 2001, Dragons and Deeps, 2001, Partita for Violoncello and Double bass, 2001, Triple Concerto, 2001, The Cask of Amontillado, 2001, others. Fellow Am. Acad. Arts and Scis.; mem. Am. Guild Organists (past dean Boston chpt.) Home: 150 Chilton St Cambridge MA 02138-1227

PINKHAM, FREDERICK OLIVER, foundation executive, consultant; b. Ann Arbor, Mich., June 16, 1920; s. Frederick Oliver and Leah Winifred (Hallett) P.; m. Helen Kostia, June 20, 1943; children: Peter James, Gail Louise, Steven Howard. AB, Kalamazoo Coll., 1942, LLD (hon.), 1958; MA, Stanford U., 1947, EdD, 1950; LLD (hon.), Lawrence Coll., 1957; DSc (hon.), Ripon Coll., 1990. Tchr., counselor Sequoia Union High Sch., Redwood City, Calif., 1947-49; researcher Stanford (Calif.) Consultation Service, 1949-50; asst. to pres. George Washington U., 1950-51; exec. sec. Nat. Commn. on Accrediting, 1951-55; pres. Ripon (Wis.) Coll., 1955-66; dir. The Yardstick Project, Cleve., 1966-67; v.p., dir. Western Pub. Co., 1967-70; founder, pres. Edn. Mgmt. Services, Inc., 1970-76; asst. adminstr. for population and humanitarian affairs AID, Dept. State, 1976-77; chmn., pres. Population Crisis Com., 1977-87; assoc. dir. Inst. for Population and Resource Studies, Stanford U., 1987-90; program officer David and Lucile Packard Found., 1988-92; cons. for population David and Lucile Packard Found., Los Altos, Calif., 1993-99; cons. True North Found., Portland, Oreg., 1993-97, Compton Found., Menlo Park, Calif., 1993-97, Mgmt. Scis. for Health, 1995-97, Poptech, Washington, 1995. V.p., dir. rsch. Ednl. Recs. Bur., Darien, Conn., 1970-72; founder, pres. Edn. Mgmt. Svcs., Inc., 1970-76; v.p., co-founder World Bus. Coun., 1970-77; pres. Capital Higher Edn. Svc., 1975-76; pres., dir. The Omni Group, 1977-83; treas., co-founder Monterey Peninsula coll. Found., 1994-00; cons. Program for the Topical Prevention of Conception and Disease Chgo. Rush U., 1999—. Chmn. Wis. adv. com. Nat. Commn. on Civil Rights; bd. visitors Air U.; pres. Wis. Found. of Ind. Colls.; chmn. Assn. colls. Midwest, Midwest Coll. Council; sec., trustee, mem. exec. com. Young Pres.'s Found.; chmn. task force on fgn. assistance Pres.'s Pvt. Sector Survey on cost Control (Grace Comm.); chmn. bd. Global Tomorrow Coalition, 1985-89; bd. dirs. Internat. Human Assistance Programs, N.Y.C., 1984-87, Mineral Fibre Internat. and Kings Mills Internat., 1986-90, Mgmt. Scis. for Health, 1997-2000; v.p. Big Sur Land Trust, 1990-00; founder, pres. Inst. Reproductive Health, Calif., 2000—. Served with AUS, 1942-45, ETO. Decorated Bronze Star, Purple Heart. Mem. Young Pres. Orgn. (nat. sec., dir., exec. com.), Soc. Internat. Devel., Nat. Heritage Soc. watchkeeper, bd. govs. Old Capital Club Monterey, Calif. (gov.). Home and Office: 8 Skyline Crst Monterey CA 93940-4111 Fax: 831-649-1828. E-mail: fpinkham@aol.com.

PINKNEY, D. TIMOTHY, investment company executive; b. Long Beach, Calif., June 6, 1948; s. Robert Patten and Mary (Chernus) P.; m. Nancy Dianne Fisher, Aug. 21, 1971; 1 child, Heather Anne. BA, Calif. Luth. U., 1970; MA, Pepperdine U., 1976. CFP. Membership mgr. Seattle C. of C., 1977-79; v.p. mktg. John L. Scott Investment, Bellevue, Wash., 1980-81, SRH Fin., Bellevue, 1981-82, Foster Investment Co., Bellevue, 1982-83; pres., CEO Footprint Fin. Planning, 1983-88, Sheppard & Assocs. Personal Fin. Advs., Bellevue, 1988-91; mgr. and v.p. asset mgmt. div. U.S. Bank, Tacoma, 1991-92; v.p., Calif. and Nev. mgr. trust and investment mgmt. U.S. Bank of Calif., Sacramento, 1992-96; prin. Savant/Russell, Inc., Citrus Heights, Calif., 1996—; founder, chief exec. officer Wealth Link Enterprises. Author: book, video and cassete series Pathways to Wealth, Yes IRA's Still Make Cent$?, 1988. Co-chmn. Fin. Independence Week, Western Wash., 1987; bd. dirs. Traveler's Aid Soc., A United Way Agy., Seattle, 1988, pacesetter United Way, 1988-91; alumni class steward Calif. Luth. U., 1992, 93; chmn. Friends Scouting, 1994, chmn. bd. 1999, v.p. finance, 1997-98, Golden Empire coun. Boy Scouts Am., 1999; chmn. investment com. Calif. State U. Sacramento Found., 1998-99; bd. dirs. McClennan Aviation Mus., 2000--; pres. Sacramento Rotary Found., 2000—. Lt. USN, 1970-77, comdr. USNR, ret., 1992. Selected as Jr. Officer of Yr., USNR, 1984, 85; Career Achievement award Calif. Luth. U., 2002. Mem. Nat. Spkrs. Assn. (bd. dirs. N.W. chpt. 1992), Internat. Assn. Fin. Planning (chmn. West Region 1987-90, pres. Western Wash. chpt. 1986-87), Seattle Soc. Fin. Planners (bd. dirs. 1985-86), Inst. CFPs, Real Estate Securities and Syndication Inst. (v.p. 1980-83), East King County and Pierce County Estate Planning Coun., Seattle Res. Officer Assn. (pres., v.p. 1983-85), Puget Sound Naval Res. Assn. (v.p. 1985-90), Sacramento Rotary (chmn. edn. com. 1994), Sacramento Rotary Found. (pres. 2000-2002, bd. dirs. 1996-2002), Seattle Rotary (bd. dirs., chmn. membership devel. com.). Avocations: flying gliders, giant pumpkin growing and sculpting, photography.

PINKSTON, ISABEL HAY, minister, writer, educator, therapist; b. Cambridge, Ohio, Oct. 30, 1922; d. Wilmer Martin and Mary Nola (Clark) Hay; m. Benedict George Dudley, Mar. 12, 1969 (dec. Feb. 1974); m. Robert Sherrill Pinkston, May 1, 1984 (dec. Dec. 1985). BA cum laude, Monmouth (Ill.) Coll., 1944; postgrad., Wheaton (Ill.) Coll., 1948-49; M of Therapeutic Counseling, Open Internat. U., Sri Lanka, 1994. Ordained to ministry Nat. Assn. Congl. Chs., 1985. Instrumental and vocal music tchr. United Presbyn. Mission Sch., Frenchburg, Ky., 1944-48; dir. Christian edn. United Presbyn. Ch., Zanesville, Ohio, 1949-51; Christian edn. dir. A.R. Presbyn. Ch., Augusta, Ga., 1952-55; staff Koinonia Found., Pikesville, Md., 1956-66; min., pres. bd. dirs. Ch. Religious Rsch., Inc., Grand Island, Fla., 1988-94; pres. Spiritual Devel. Internat., Inc., Eustis, from 1996. Del., participant Internat. Conf. Paranormal Rsch., Ft. Collins, Colo., 1988-89; tchr. psychography course Sancta Sophia Sem., 1991; spkr. Conf. of Internat. Inst. of Integral Human Scis. and Spiritual Scis. Fellowship, 1994-95, Ann. Conf., World U., 1994; founder, pres. Spiritual Devel. Internat., Inc., 1996. Author: (biography) Seed-Sower for God's Kingdom, 1987, Understanding Homosexuality, 1993, A Comprehensive Study of the Soul, 1999; co-editor: Psychography, 1990; editor: (newsletter) Koinonia Epistle, 1957-66, Religious Rsch. Jour., 1988-96, Religious Rsch. Press, 1988-96, The Good Newsletter, 1997—. Mem. Internat. Coun. Cmty. Chs. (del. 1988—), Assn. for Past-Life Rsch. and Therapy (workshop leader 1989). Died Dec. 17, 2000.

PINKUS, OSCAR, mechanical engineer, writer; b. Losice, Poland, June 10, 1927; came to U.S., 1947; s. Abraham and Chaja (Perelmuter) P.; m. Ilse Strasser, Nov. 24, 1956; children: Dena, Michael. BS, Iowa State U., 1950; MME, Rensselaer Polytech. Inst., 1951. Devel. engr. GE, Lynn, Mass., 1951-61; rsch. engr. Republic Aviation, Farmingdale, N.Y., 1961-70; assoc. prof. Israel Inst. Tech., Haifa, 1970-74; cons. engr. Mech. Tech. Inc., Latham, N.Y., 1974-89; dir. Sigma Tribology, Sandia Park, N.Mex., 1990—. Vis. prof. Tex. A&M U., College Station, 1989-90. Author: Theory of Hydrodynamic Lubrication, 1961, Thermal Aspects of Fluid Film Tribology, 1990, (novels) Victor, 2001, The Son of Zelman, 1980, A Choice of Masks, 1970, Friends and Lovers, 1964, The House of Ashes, 1964, (poetry) Embers, 1979. Recipient Nat. award Soc. Tribologists and Lubrication Engrs., 1996. Avocations: painting, book binding. Home and Office: 17 Del Sol Ct Sandia Park NM 87047

PINN, ANTHONY BERNARD, educator; b. Buffalo, May 2, 1964; married. BA, Columbia U., 1986; MDiv, Harvard Divinity Sch., 1989; MA, Harvard U., 1991, PhD, 1994. Asst. prof. religious studies Macalester Coll., St. Paul, 1994—99, assoc. prof. religious studies, 1999—2002, prof. religious studies, 2002—. Author: Why, Lord?: Suffering and Evil in Black Theology, 1995, Varieties of African American Religious Experience, 1998, Making the Gospel Plain: The Writings of Bishop Reverdy C. Ransom, 1999, Social Protest Thought in the AME Church, 2000, The Ties That Bind, 2001, By These Hands: A Documentary History of African American Humanism, 2001, Fortress Introduction to Black Church History, 2001, The Black Curch in the Post-Civil Rights Era, 2002, Moral Evil and Redemptive Suffering, 2002. Recipient The African Am. Humanist award, Coun. Secular Humanism, 1999. Mem.: Soc. Study of Black Religion (exec. dir. 2002, program chair 1999—2001), Am. Acad. Religion (co-chair black theology group 1999—2001). Avocation: travel. Office: Macalester Coll 1600 Grand Ave Saint Paul MN 55105

PINN, VIVIAN W. pathologist, federal agency administrator; b. Halifax, Va., 1941; BA, Wellesley Coll., 1963; MD, U. Va., 1967. Intern in pathology Mass. Gen. Hosp., Boston, 1967-68, rschr. in pathology, 1968-70; asst. pathologist Tufts U. New England Med. Ctr. Hosp., 1970-77, pathologist, 1977-82; from asst. to assoc. prof. pathology Tufts U., 1971-82, asst. dean student affairs, 1974-82; prof., dept. chair pathology Howard U., 1982-91; first dir. Office Rsch. on Women's Health, NIH, Bethesda, Md., 1991—, assoc. dir. women's health rsch., 1994—, dir. Office Women's Health Rsch. Office: NIH Office Rsch on Women's Health 9000 Rockville Pike Rm 201 Bethesda MD 20892*

PINNELL, SHELDON RICHARD, physician, medical educator, dermatologist; b. Dayton, Ohio, Feb. 3, 1937; s. Jacob and Nevella P.; m. Doren Madey, 1983; children: Kevin, Alden, Tyson. AB, Duke U., 1959; MD, Yale U., 1963. Intern in medicine U. Minn. Hosp., Mpls., 1963-65; resident in dermatology Harvard U., Boston, 1968-71; prof. medicine Duke U. Med. Ctr., Durham, N.C., 1978—, chief div. dermatology, 1982-97, asst. prof. biochemistry, 1988—, J. Lamar Callaway prof. dermatology, 1989—2002, prof. emeritus, 2002—. Founding scientist Fibrogen, 1994—. Contbr. over 100 articles to profl. jours.; five patents in field. Office: Duke U Med Ctr PO Box 3135 Durham NC 27710-0001 E-mail: pinne002@mc.duke.edu.

PINNER, STEPHEN JOHN, management consultant; b. Aug. 23, 1951; s. Ronald Wilfred and Pamela Ethel (Goodacre) P.; divorced; children: Simon Edward, Hayley Jane; m. Ivy Murphy, Mar. 22, 1997. Mgr. Centre-File, 1970—83; dir. Extel, London, 1983-87; assoc. dir. Hoare Govett, 1985-87; dir. Fin. Clearing and Svcs. U.K. Ltd., 1985-87; mng. dir. Soc. Gen. Security Settlements, 1987-90; dir. City Cons., 1991-95, 1998; mng. dir. City Deal Svcs., 1993-97; dir. Summerson Goodacre, 1998—. Dir. City Compass Ltd., 1998—. Fellow Securities Inst. Avocation: football. Office: Summerson Goodacre 48 Artillery Lane London E1 7LS England E-mail: pinner@sumgood.com.

PINNEY, FRANCES BAILEY, art therapist, artist, consultant; b. Newton, Mass., July 18, 1935; d. Gage and Ellen (Nealley) Bailey; m. Peter T. McKinney, June 7, 1957 (div. Nov. 1981); children: Peter, Karen, David; m. Edward Lowell Pinney, Nov. 24, 1988. A.B., Vassar Coll., 1957; M.A., U. Houston-Clear Lake, 1979. Social worker State Bd. Child Welfare, Elizabeth, N.J., 1957-58; art therapist Mental Health and Mental Retardation Authority, Houston, 1979-81; exec. dir. Creative Alternatives, Houston, 1982-87. Bd. dirs. Citizens Alliance for Mentally Ill, Houston, 1983, 84, 85; pres. Berkeley County League of Women Voters, 1993-94. Mem. Internat. Assn. Dynamic Psychotherapy (bd. dirs. 1996), Am. Art Therapy Assn., Nat. Art Edn. Assn., Am. Group Psychotherapy Assn., Am. Assn. Counseling and Devel., Artist's Equity. Episcopalian. Avocation: scuba diving. Home: Playa Azol III Apt 1301 Luquillo PR 00773 Office: 312 Calle Fernandez Garcia Luquillo PR 00773-2220

PINNEY, SIDNEY DILLINGHAM, JR. lawyer; b. Hartford, Conn., Nov. 17, 1924; s. Sydney Dillingham and Louisa (Griswold) Wells P.; m. Judith Munch, Sept. 30, 1990; children from previous marriage: William Griswold, David Rees. Student, Amherst Coll., 1941-43, Brown U., 1943; also, M.I.T., 1943-44; BA cum laude, Amherst Coll., 1947; LLB, Harvard U., 1950. Bar: Conn. 1950. Pvt. practice, Hartford, 1950; assoc. Shepherd, Murtha and Merritt, 1950-53; ptnr. Murtha, Cullina, Richter & Pinney (1967) (name changed to Murtha Cullina LLP 2000), 1953-92; of counsel Shepherd, Murtha and Merritt (name changed to Murtha Cullina LLP 2000), 1993—. Lectr. on estate planning. Contbr. to: Estate Planning mag. Bd. dirs. Greater Hartford Area TB and Respiratory Diseases Health Soc., 1956-69, pres., 1966-67; mem. Wethersfield (Conn.) Town Coun., 1958-62; trustee Hartford Conservatory Music, 1967-71, 75-81; trustee, pres. Historic Wethersfield Found., 1961-81; bd. dirs. Hartford Hosp., 1971-80, adv. bd., 1980—; mem. adv. com. Jefferson House, 1978-82; mem. Mortensen Libr. Bd. of Visitors U. Hartford, 1984—; corporator Hartford Pub. Libr., 1969—, Renbrook Sch., West Hartford, Conn., 1970-75. 1st lt. USAF, 1943-46. Fellow Am. Coll. Trust and Estate Counsel; mem. ABA, Nat. Acad. Elder Law Attys., Conn. Bar Assn. (com. elder law sect.), Hartford County Bar Assn. Republican. Congregationalist. Office: City Place 185 Asylum St Hartford CT 06103-3408

PINNEY, THOMAS CLIVE, retired English language educator; b. Ottawa, Kans., Apr. 23, 1932; s. John James and Lorene Maude (Owen) P.; m. Sherrill Marie Ohman, Sept. 1, 1956; children— Anne, Jane, Sarah. BA, Beloit Coll., Wis., 1954; PhD, Yale U., New Haven, 1960. Instr. Hamilton Coll., Clinton, N.Y., 1957-61; instr. English Yale U., New Haven, 1961-62; asst. prof. to prof., chmn. dept. English Pomona Coll., Claremont, Calif., 1962-97; ret., 1997. Editor: Essays of George Eliot, 1963, Selected Writings of Thomas Babington Macaulay, 1972, Letters of Macaulay, 1974-81, Kipling's India, 1986, A History of Wine in America, 1989, Kipling's Something of Myself, 1990, Letters of Rudyard Kipling, 1990, The Vineyards and Wine Cellars of California, 1994, The Wine of Santa Cruz Island, 1994. Guggenheim fellow, 1966, 84,Recipient Disting. Svc. citation Beloit Coll., 1984; fellow NEH, 1980; grantee Am. Coun. Learned Socs., 1974, 84, Am. Philos. Soc., 1968, 82, 94. Mem. MLA, Elizabethan Club (New Haven), Zamorano Club (L.A.), Phi Beta Kappa. Home: 228 W Harrison Ave Claremont CA 91711-4323 Office: Pomona Coll Dept English Claremont CA 91711

PINNISI, MICHAEL DONATO, lawyer, educator; b. Buffalo, Oct. 12, 1960; s. Frank Joseph and Dolores Ann Pinnisi; children: Kerry Lynn, Rose. AB cum laude, Cornell U., 1982, JD, 1985. Bar: N.Y. 1986, U.S. Dist. Ct. (so. dist.) N.Y. 1987, U.S. Ct. Appeals (2d cir.) 1988, U.S. Dist. Ct. (no. dist.) N.Y. 1991, U.S. Dist. Ct. (we. dist.) N.Y. 1993, U.S. Ct. Appeals (fed. cir.) 1998. Trial atty. honor program U.S. Dept. of Justice, Washington, 1985-87; assoc. atty. Shearman & Sterling, N.Y.C., 1987-88; asst. U.S. atty. U.S. Atty., So. Dist. N.Y., 1988-91; assoc. atty. Cleary, Gottlieb, Steen & Hamilton, Washington, 1991-92; prin. atty. Pinnisi, Wagner et al, Ithaca, N.Y., 1992-97, Brown, Pinnisi and Michaels, Ithaca, 1997-2000; gen. counsel Kionix Inc, 1999—. Bd. dirs. Evaporated Metal Films Corp., Ithaca; adj. prof. law Cornell law Sch., Ithaca, 1992—2000; cert. arbitrator U.S. Dist. Ct. (no. dist.) N.Y., 1993—2000; spkr. in field. Dir. Ithaca Cmty. Childcare, 1993—94, F.I.R.S.T., Phila., 1996—97. Mem.: Phi Delta Phi. Office: Kionix Inc 36 Thornwood Dr Ithaca NY 14850 E-mail: mpinnisi@kionix.com.

PINNIX, JOHN LAWRENCE, lawyer; b. Reidsville, N.C., Oct. 8, 1947; s. John Lawrence and Esther (Cobb) P.; m. Sally Auman, June 15, 1985; children: Jennifer Elizabeth Haigwood, William C. Haigwood. BA, U. N.C., Greensboro, 1969; JD, Wake Forest U., 1973; MA, U. N.C., Greensboro, 1975. Bar: N.C. 1973, D.C. 1981; U.S. Dist. Ct. (ea. dist.) N.C. 1977, U.S Dist. Ct. (mid. and we. dists.) N.C. 1981; U.S. Ct. Appeals (4th cir.) 1981; U.S. Supreme Ct. 1981. Assoc. Fagg, Fagg & Nooe, Eden, N.C., 1973-74; spl. counsel Adminstrv. Office of the Cts., Morganton, 1975-76; ptnr. Allen and Pinnix (formerly Barringer, Allen & Pinnix), Raleigh, 1977—. Adj. N.C. Ctrl. U. Sch. Law, 1997; sr. lecturing fellow Duke U. Sch. Law, 1999. Contbr. articles to profl. jours. Alt. del. Dem. Nat. Conv., Miami, 1972, mem. rules com., Washington and Atlanta, 1988; bd. dirs. Farmworkers Legal Svcs., Raleigh, 1990-92. Mem. Am. Immigration Lawyers Assn. (founding mem. Carolinas chpt. 1980, chpt. chair 1984-85, 87-88, nat. bd. govs. 1993-2001, sec. nat. exec. com. 1997-99, 2d v.p. 1999-2000, 1st v.p. 2000-2001, pres.-elect 2001—), Am. Immigration Law Found. (trustee 1992-97, vice chair 1994-97), N.C. Bar Assn. (chmn. immigration and nationality law com. 1989-91), N.C. State Bar (bd. cert. immigration specialist, immigration law specialty com. bd. legal specialization 1996—), U. N.C. Greensboro Alumni Assn. (bd. dirs. 1975-76, bd. dirs. Excellence Found. 1995-97), Internat. Focus Inc. (bd. dirs. 1998-99), N.C. Bar Assn. (internat. law sect. coun. 1999—). Baptist. Avocations: photography, film, reading. Home: 125 Ammons Dr Raleigh NC 27615-6501

PINO, ROBERT SALVATORE, radiologist; b. Bklyn., May 20, 1939; s. Carmine M. and Olga (Aversa) P. BA, NYU, 1960; MD, SUNY, 1964. Diplomate Am. Bd. Pediatrics, Am. Bd. Radiology. Intern N.Y. Hosp., N.Y.C., 1964-65, resident pediatrics, 1965-67; pvt. practice pediatrics Ft. Lee, N.J., 1969-74; resident radiology N.Y. Hosp./Cornell Med. Ctr., N.Y.C., 1974-76, chief resident radiology, 1976-77; radiologist St. Mary's Hosp., Passaic, N.J., 1977—, dir. radiology, 1986—. Maj. U.S. Army, 1967-69. Home: 2055 Center Ave Fort Lee NJ 07024-4948 Office: St Marys Hosp 211 Pennington Ave Passaic NJ 07055-4698

PINSDORF, MARION KATHRYN, business executive, educator, author; b. Teaneck, N.J., June 22, 1932; d. Charles W. and Katheryn S. (Green) P. BA cum laude, Drew U., 1954; MA, NYU, 1967, PhD, 1976; DSc in Bus. Adminstrn. (hon.), Nichols Coll., 1982. Polit. reporter, editor women's dept. The Record, Hackensack, NJ, 1954—61; assoc. copy editor Good Housekeeping mag., 1962-64; comms. specialist Borden, Inc., 1964-69; v.p. Hill and Knowlton, N.Y.C., 1970-77; v.p. corp. rels. Textron, Inc., Providence, 1977-80; v.p. corp. comms. INA Corp., Phila., 1980-82; ind. mgmt. cons. 1982—. Adj. asst. prof. Brazilian studies Brown U., 1979—; assoc. prof. grad. sch. bus. Fordham U., 1987-94, sr. fellow in comms., 1994—; lectr. in field. Author: Communicating When Your Company Is Under Siege, Surviving Public Crisis, 1987, 3d edit., 1998, German Speaking Entrepreneurs: Builders of Business in Brazil South, 1990; mem. editl. adv. bd. Pub. Rels. Quar.; author book revs.; contbr. articles to profl. jours. Trustee, Drew U., Madison, N.J., 1977-81; pres. Leonia (N.J.) Pub. Libr., 1973-76. Mem. Arthur W. Page Soc. Home: 114 Leonia Ave Leonia NJ 07605-1916

PINSKER, PENNY COLLIAS (PANGEOTA PINSKER), television producer; b. Miami, Fla., Aug. 22, 1942; d. Theodore Peter and Agatha Madge (Bridgeman) Collias; m. Raymond Robert Elman , Feb. 19, 1962 (dec. 1967); 1 child, Alan; m. Lewis Harry Pinsker, Oct. 22, 1968. Grad. high sch., Miami, Fla. Operator So. Bell Telephone Co., Miami, 1960-67; asst. dir. pub. affairs Sta. WCKT-TV, 1968-70; dir. pub. affairs Sta. WOR-AM, N.Y.C., 1971-78; reporter documentary and consumer affairs Sta. WTFM, 1978-81; dir. editorials and sta. svcs. Sta. WWOR-TV, N.Y.C. and Secaucus, N.J., 1981-87, mgr. community affairs and spl. projects Secaucus, 1987-91, dir. cmty. affairs and spl. projects, 1991-2000, exec. prodr., pub. affairs programming and spl. projects, 1994—, dir. pub. affairs, 2000—. Author, editor: (resource directory) Sta. WOR on Crime, 1982 (recipient George Washington Medal Honor Freedom Found., Emmy award for Outstanding Editorial, 1981), The Changing Family, 1982 (recipient Broadcast Media award San Francisco State U., Emmy nominated), A Child is Missing, 1983 (recipient Broadcast Media award San Francisco State U., Emmy nominated), Taking the High Out of High School, 1984 (recipient Broadcast Media award San Francisco State U, Angel award Religion Media, Bronze medal Internat. TV and Film Soc.); project mgr. A+ For Kids (Emmy award 1989, also Emmy nomination, named 12th nat. Point of Light, 1989), A+ For Kids: Project Director National, (Emmy nominations 1989-91; N.Y. Emmy award 1989, 1991; Nat. Edn. Assn. award 1991). Media advisor N.J. Crime Prevention Officers Assn.; mem. comm. com. N.J. affiliation Am. Heart Assn., Am. Cancer Soc.; bd. dirs. Queensboro Soc. Prevention Cruelty to Children, 1978-83, Hoboken Chamber

Orch., 1989-90, N.J. Edn. Found., 1991-92; pub. mem. N.J. Gov.'s Task Force on Child Abuse and Neglect, 1988-97; mem. N.J. Task Force on Cild Abuse and Neglect, 1990—; trustee Assn. for Children of N.J., 1990—; mem. AARP N.J. exec. coun. for comm., mem. N.J. Coun. on Adult Edn. and Literacy, 1992-93; mem. exec. com. Partnership for a Drug Free N.J., 1997—; mem. N.J. Bus.-Edn. Summit, 1997-99. Recipient Disting. Svc. award, N.J. Speech-Lang.-Hearing Assn., 1987, Cmty. Svc. award, Urban League Hudson County, 1986, Media award for achievement in preventing child abuse, N.J. Child Assault Prevention Project, 1993, Cmty. Svc. award, N.J. Gov.'s Conf. in Divesity, 1998, Seton Hall U., 2000, Triangle award for excellence in comms., March of Dimes, 2001. Mem.: NAFE, N.J. Broadcasters Assn. (bd. dirs. 1992—99, state legis. chair 1999—2001), Advt. Coun. N.J. (trustee 1986—2000), Nat. Broadcast Assn. Cmty. Affairs, Nat. Broadcast Editl. Assn. (bd. dirs. 1986—87), Meadowlands Regional C. of C. (bd. dirs. 1991—92), Leadership N.J. Grad. Orgn. Avocation: breeder thoroughbred horses. Home: Winterwood Farm 449 Kingwood-Locktown Rd Flemington NJ 08822 Office: 9 Broadcast Plz Secaucus NJ 07094-2913 E-mail: ppinsker@wwortv.com.

PINSKER, TILLENE GILLER, retired special education administrator; b. Omaha, Oct. 29, 1936; d. Hyman Herman and Rebecca (Winokur) Giller; m. Walter Pinsker, June 15, 1958; children: Neil, Andrew, Susann. BA, Roosevelt U., 1958; MS, Post U., 1977, PD, 1981. Cert. tchr., adminstr., supr., spl. edn. tchr., N.Y., tchr., Calif., Ill. Tchr. Massapequa (N.Y.) Sch. Dist., 1958-60, Westminster (Calif.) Sch. Dist., 1960-62; resource tchr. West Islip (N.Y.) Sch. Dist., 1975-77; coord. infant svcs. Boces 111, Deer Park, N.Y., 1977-83; dir. direction ctr. SCDC, Smithtown, 1983-85; dir. early intervention program Adults and Children with Learning Devel. Disabilities, Bay Shore, 1985—; ret. Lectr. C.W. Post Coll., Westbury, N.Y., Dowling Coll., Oakdale, N.Y.; mem. various panels in field; cons. Camp NYABIC, ACLD Kramer Learning Ctr., 1999; spkr. in field. Mem. Suffolk Network of Adolescent Pregnancy; bd. dirs. Office Mental Retardation; mem. subcom. Devel. Dist.; v.p. Good Samaritan Hosp. Aux., West Islip; active polit. orgns. Named Woman of Yr., NOW, 1975-76, Co-Humanitarian of Yr., Adults and Children with Learning and Devel. Disabilities, 1994. Avocations: tennis, golf. Address: 10150 Dover Carriage Ln Lake Worth FL 33467-8116 Office: ACLD Kramer Learning Ctr 1428 5th Ave Bay Shore NY 11706-4147

PINSKER, WALTER, retired allergist, immunologist; b. Bay Shore, N.Y., Mar. 27, 1933; s. Albert and Irene (Kuchlick) P.; m. Tillene Giller, June 15, 1958; children: Neil, Andrew, Susann. BA, U. Rochester, 1954; MD, Chgo. Med. Sch. U. Health Sci., 1958. Diplomate Am. Bd. Allergy and Immunology. Intern L.I. Jewish Hosp., New Hyde Park, N.Y., 1958-59; resident internal medicine Bklyn. VA Hosp., 1959-60, Long Beach (Calif.) VA Hosp., 1960-61, resident allergy and immunology, 1961-62; chief of allergy Letterman Army Hosp., San Francisco, 1962-64; pres. Bay Shore Allergy Group, 1964-94. Attending physician Mather Hosp., Port Jefferson, N.Y., St. Charles Hosp., Port Jefferson, 1981-95, Southside Hosp., Bay Shore, 1964—, Good Samaritan Hosp., West Islip, N.Y., 1964-95, asst. clin. prof. medicine SUNY, Stony Brook, 1968—; mem. physicians adv. com. Group Health, 1997—. Contbr. articles to profl. jours.; patentee in treatment of migraine headaches and formulations. Bd. visitors Pilgrim State Hosp., Brentwood, N.Y., 1974-77; pres. Suffolk Assn. Children with Learning Difficulties, N.Y., 1972-74; trustee Leeway Sch., Stony Brook, 1974-75, Bay Shore Jewish Ctr., 1974-84; com. for handicapped West Islip Schs., 1971—. Capt. U.S. Army, 1962-64. Named Co-Humanitarian of Yr. L.I. Adults and Children with Learning and Developmental Disabilities, 1994; recipient Physician's Recognition award AMA, 1969—. Fellow Am. Acad. Allergy and Immunology, Am. Coll. Allergy and Immunology, Am. Assn. Certified Allergists, Am. Coll. Chest Physicians, Am. Assn.- Study of Headaches, N.Y. Acad. Scis., Suffolk Acad. Medicine, Nassau-Suffolk Allergy Soc. (officer, bd. dirs. 1970-95, pres. 1980-82). Avocations: golf, boating, photography.

PINSKY, ELLEN DODGE, reading and language educator, education educator; b. St. Louis, June 1, 1946; d. Philip James and Noni Crown Dodge; m. Robert Alan Pinsky, Feb. 15, 1969. BA, U. Wis., 1972; MA, Concordia Coll., 1985; EdD, Nat.-Louis U., 1998. Cert. tchr., Ill. Tchr. River Fores (Ill.) Dist. # 90, 1983—; adj. faculty Nat.-Louis U., Evanston, Ill., 1988—; vis. lectr. reading and lang. arts instrn. Northeastern Ill. U., Chgo., 1999—. Mem. MAT/MSI program adv. com. Northeastern Ill. U., 2000—. Mem. ASCD, NEA, Internat. Reading Assn., Nat. Coun. Tchrs. English, Ill. Edn. Assn., River Forest Edn. Assn., Nat. Railway Hist. Soc. (asst. sec. 1998—), Delta Kappa Gamma. Avocations: horticulture, historic preservation. Home: 1040 Erie St Oak Park IL 60302 E-mail: epinsky@att.net.

PINSKY, STEVEN MICHAEL, radiologist, educator; b. Milw., Feb. 2, 1942; s. Leo Donald and Louise Miriam (Faldberg) P.; m. Sue Brona Rosenzweig, June 12, 1966; children: Mark Burton, Lisa Rachel. BS, U. Wis., 1964; MD, Loyola U., Chgo., 1967. Resident in radiology and nuclear medicine U. Chgo., 1968-70, chief resident in diagnostic radiology, 1970-71, asst. prof., 1973-77, assoc. prof. radiology and medicine, 1977-85, prof., 1985-89; prof., chmn. dept. radiology U. Ill., 1989-96, prof. radiology, 1996—. Dir. nuclear medicine Michael Reese Med. Ctr., Chgo., 1973-87, vice-chmn. radiology, 1984-87, chmn. radiology, 1987-93, v.p. med. staff, 1986-88, pres., 1988-90, trustee, 1984-86, 90-93; dir. nuclear medicine tech. program Triton Coll., River Grove, Ill., 1974-87. Contbr. chpts. to books, articles to med. jours. Maj., M.C., U.S. Army, 1971-73. Rsch. fellow Am. Cancer Soc., 1969-70. Fellow: Am. Coll. Nuclear Physicians (treas. 1982—84, Ill. del.), Am. Coll. Radiology; mem.: Ill. Radiologic Soc. (sec.-treas. 1992—94, pres.-elect 1994—95, pres. 1995—96, Chgo. chpt. Gold medal for disting. svc. 1999), Radiologic Soc. N.Am. (councilor 1994—99, chmn. tech. exhibits com. 1994—96, edn. coun. 1994—96), Soc. Nuclear Medicine (trustee 1979—87, pres. ctrl. chpt. 1980—81). Office: 1821 Lawrence Ln Highland Park IL 60035 E-mail: sspinsky1821@cs.com.

PINSON, ARTIE FRANCES, elementary school educator; b. Rusk, Tex., June 20, 1933; d. Tom and Minerva (McDuff) Neeley; m. Robert H. Pinson, Dec. 14, 1963 (div. Nov. 1967); 1 child, Deidre R. BA magna cum laude, Tex. Coll., 1953; postgrad., U. Tex., 1956, North Tex. U., 1958, 63, New Eng. Conservatory, 1955, 57, 59, 62, Tex. So. U., 1971-72; MEd, U. Houston, 1970. Music tchr. Bullock High Sch., LaRue, Tex., 1953-59; music tchr., 9th grade English tchr. Story High Sch., Palestine, 1959-64; 6th grade tchr. Turner Elem. Sch., Houston, 1964-66; 3d, 5th and 6th grade tchr. Kay Elem. Sch., 1966-70; 6th grade tchr. Pilgrim Elem. Sch., 1970-75; 3d to 6th grade gifted and talented math. tchr. Pleasantville Elem. Sch., 1975-79; kindergarten to 5th grade computer/math. tchr. Betsy Ross Elem. Sch., 1979—, coord., tchr. Instrnl. coord.; lead tchr. math./sci. program Shell/Houston Ind. Sch. Dist., 1986-87, Say "Yes" program, 1988-89; math. tchr. summer potpourri St. Francis Xavier Cath. Ch., 1991; math. tchr. sci. and engring. awareness and coll. prep. program Tex. So. U., 1993, 94, 95, 96, 97, 98, 99, 2000, 01, 02; participant Project Sail math. curriculum devel., Prairie View U., 1997-98, 99; presenter confs. in field; condr. tchr. tng. workshops. Author computer software in field; contbr. articles to mags. Musician New Hope Bapt. Ch., Houston, 1991—, Sunday sch. tchr.; pianist Buckner Bapt. Haven Nursing Home, Houston, 1990-91, inspirational spkr.; mem. N.E. Concerned Citizens Civic League. Recipient Excellence in Math. Teaching award Exxon Corp., 1990. Mem. Assn. African Am. Math. Educators (Salute to Math. Tchrs. award 1991, treas. 1991-93, sec. 1993-95), Nat. Coun. Tchrs. Math., Tex. Coun. Tchrs. Math. (Excellence in Math. Tchg. award 1988), Houston Coun. Tchrs. of Math. (Excellence in Math. Tchg. award 1993), Heoines of Jericho, Palestine Negro Bus. and Profl. Women (charter mem.). Avocations: needlework, number puzzles, piano, photography, gardening. Home: 5524 Makeig St Houston TX 77026-4021 Office: Betsy Ross Elem Sch 2819 Bay St Houston TX 77026-3203 E-mail: artpin@msn.com.

PINSON, CHARLES WRIGHT, transplant surgeon, educator; b. Albuquerque, May 29, 1952; s. Ernest Alexander and Jean Elizabeth (Farnsworth) P. Student, Miami U., Oxford, Ohio, 1970-72; BA, U. Colo., Boulder, 1974, MBA, 1976; MD, Vanderbilt U., 1980. Diplomate Am. Bd. Surgery, Am. Bd. Surg. Critical Care, Nat. Bd. Med. Examiners, Tenn., Mass., Oreg. Resident in gen. surgery Oreg. Health Scis. U., Portland, 1980-86; fellow gastrointestinal surgery Lahey Clinic, Burlington, Mass., 1986-87; fellow transplant surgery Harvard U., Boston, 1987-88; dir. liver transplant program VA Western region, Portland, 1989-90, Oreg. Health Scis. U., Portland, 1988-90; interim chmn. dept. surgery Vanderbilt U., Nashville, 1993-95, chief divsn. hepatobiliary surgery and liver transplantation, 1990—, vice-chmn. dept. surgery, 1995-2001; dir. Vanderbilt Transplant Ctr., 1993—; chmn. med. bd. Vanderbilt U. Med. Ctr., 1997-99; chief of staff Vanderbilt U. Hosp., 1997—; prof., chmn. dept. surgery Vanderbilt U., 2001—. Adv. bd. Pacific N.W. Transplant Bank, Portland, 1989-90, Tenn. Donor Svcs., Nashville, 1991—. Mem. editl. bd. Annals of Surgery, Jour. Gastrointestinal Surgery, 2001—; contbr. articles to profl. jours., chpts. to books. Bd. dirs. ARC, Nashville, 1992-94, Am. Liver Found., 1992-96, United Network for Organ Sharing, 2000—. Fellow, Am. Heart Assn., Oreg., 1983-84. Mem. Soc. Univ. Surgeons, Halsted Soc., Soc. Surg. Oncology, Am. Soc. Transplant Surgeons, Am. Soc. Study of Liver Diseases, Am. Gastroent. Assn., Am. Hepatopancreatobiliary Assn. (treas., exec. com. 1997—, pres. elect 2001—), Am. Physiologic Soc., So. Med. Assn. (chmn. sect. surgery 1997-2001), Am. Surg. Assn., So. Surg. Assn., Western Surg. Assn., North Pacific Surg. Assn. (sci. program 1990-92), Assn. Acad. Surgery, Soc. Surgery of Alimentary Tract, Internat. Liver Transplantation Soc., Sigma Xi, Phi Beta Kappa, Alpha Omega Alpha. Office: Vanderbilt Transplant Ctr 801 Oxford House Nashville TN 37232-0001

PINSON, JERRY D. lawyer; b. Harrison, Ark., Sept. 7, 1942; s. Robert L. and Cleta (Keeter) P.; m. Jane Ellis, Sept. 11, 1964; 1 child, Christopher Clifton. BA, U. Ark., 1964, JD, 1967. Bar: Ark. 1967, U.S. Ct. Appeals (8th cir.) 1967, U.S. Supreme Ct. 1967, U.S. Dist. Ct. (ea. and we. dists.) Ark. 1968. Dep. atty. gen. State of Ark., Little Rock, 1967-70; ptnr. Pinson & Reeves, Harrison, 1973-88; sole practice, 1970-73, 88—. Mem. Ark. Supreme Ct. com. on the unauthorized practice of law in Ark., 1979-91, chmn. 1990-91; spl. justice Ark. Supreme Ct., 1991, 94; active state bd. law examiners, 1997—. Pres. United Way Boone County, Harrison, 1974. Mem. ABA, Assn. Trial Lawyers Am., Ark. Bar Assn., Boone County Bar Assn., Harrison C. of C. (sec. bd. dirs. 1977). Lodges: Rotary (bd. dirs. 1975, v.p. 1976, pres. 1977). Office: Atty at Law PO Box 1111 Harrison AR 72602-1111

PINSON, JOHN DENNIS, real estate broker; b. Quansette Point, R.I., July 14, 1963; Student, U. Tampa, 1981-83, Palm Beach Atlantic Coll., 1983-84, 91, U. Surrey, Guildford, U.K., 1984-86, Johns Hopkins U.; grad., Realtors Inst. Cert. internat. property specialist, residential specialist, hist. property specialist. Broker Merrill Lynch Real Estate, Palm Beach, Fla., 1987-91, Prudential Fla. Real Estate, Palm Beach, 1991-95, mng. broker, 1995-99, Arvida, Palm Beach, 1999—. Pres. U.S. chpt. Fedn. Internat. Real Estate Scholarship Found., Washington, 1998-2000; v.p. Palm Beach Bd. Realtors, 1999-2000. Mem. Palm Beach Civic Assn., Palm Beach C. of C., Palm Beach Rep. Club (dir. 1999—). Home: PO Box 3386 Palm Beach FL 33480-1586 Office: Coldwell Banker NRT 340 Royal Poinciana Way Palm Beach FL 33480-4048 Fax: 561-366-1075. E-mail: john@pinson.com.

PINSON, LARRY LEE, pharmacist; b. Van Nuys, Calif., Dec. 5, 1947; s. Leland J. and Audrey M. (Frett) P.; m. Margaret K. Pinson, Mar. 18, 1972; children: Scott C., Kelly E. Student, U. Calif., Davis, 1967-69; AA, Am. River Coll., Sacramento, 1969; PharmD, U. Calif., San Francisco, 1973. Staff pharmacist/asst. dir. pharm. svcs. St. Mary's Hosp., Reno, 1973-77; chief pharmacist May Ang Base USAF, 1973-77; owner/chief pharmacist Silverada Pharmacy, Reno, 1979-2001; adj. prof. Idaho State U., Pocatello, 1989—; chief pharmacist Scolar's Food & Drug, Sak-N-Save Pharmacy, Reno, 2001—. Cons. pharmacist Physicians Hosp., 1974-93, Reno Med. Plaza, 1973—; pharmacist coordinator Intensive Pharm. Svcs., 1986-87; cons. Calif. Dept. Health & Corrections, Susanville, 1975-76, Nev. Med. Care Adv. Bd., Carson City, 1984-87; provider and reviewer Nev. State Bd. Pharmacy, Reno, 1975-84; instr. we. Nev. Cmty. Coll., 1974-76; cons. Rural Calif. Hosp. Assn., 1973-74. Co-author: Care of Hickman Catheter, 1984. Apptd. by Gov. Bob Miller, Nev. State Bd. Pharmacy, 1995-2000, pres., 1996—, re-apptd. by Gov. Kenny Guinn, 2001—; mem. Nev. Arthritis Found.; bd. dirs. Am. Cancer Soc., 1986—; softball coach Reno/Sparks Recreation Dept., 1973—; cubmaster Pack 153, Verdi, nev.; scoutmaster com. chmn. Reno troop 1, Boy Scouts Am., 1988-92. Recipient Bowl of Hygeia award (Pharmacist of the Year), Nev. Pharmacists Assn. and A.H. Robbins Co., 1984, named Pharmacist of the Year, Nevada Pharm. Alliance, 1999. Mem. Nat. Assn. Bds. of Pharmacy, Am. Pharm. Assn., Nev. Pharmacists Assn. (pres. 1981-82), Nev. Profl. Stds. Rev. Orgn., Greater Nev. Health Sys. Agy., Kappa Psi. Avocations: skiing, fishing, backpacking, softball, golf. Home: PO Box 478 Verdi NV 89439-0478 Office: Sak-N-Save Pharmacy 1901 Silverada Blvd Reno NV 89512-5032 E-mail: rx2005@aol.com.

PINSON, WILLIAM MEREDITH, JR. pastor, writer, administrator; b. Ft. Worth, Aug. 3, 1934; s. William Meredith and Ila Lee (Jones) P.; m. Bobbie Ruth Judd, June 4, 1955; children: Meredith Pinson Creasey, Allison Pinson Hopgood. *William M. Pinson, Jr's great grandfather Josiah F Pinson, was a pioneer settler in the Dallas area in the 1800s. He assisted in starting several Baptist churches in Texas as well as the Buckner Baptist Children's Home, now Buckner Baptist Benevolences. His great grandfather William G. Mulkey was a pioneer settler in West Texas, serving as an early mayor of Quanah named after the famous Indian Chief Quanah Parker and aiding in establishing Methodist churches in Texas.* BA, U. N. Tex., 1955; BD, Southwestern Bapt. Theol. Sem., Ft. Worth, 1959, ThD, 1963, MDiv, 1973; LittD (hon.), Calif. Bapt. Coll., Riverside, 1978; DD (hon.), U. Mary Hardin-Baylor, Belton, Tex., 1984; LHD (hon.), Howard Payne U., Brownwood, Tex., 1986; LittD (hon.), Dallas Bapt. U., 1990; LLD (hon.), Hardin Simmons U., 1999. Ordained to ministry Bapt. Ch., 1955. Assoc. sec. Christian Life Commn., Dallas, 1957-63; prof. Christian ethics Southwestern Bapt. Theol. Sem., Ft. Worth, 1963-75; pastor First Bapt. Ch., Wichita Falls, Tex., 1975-77; pres. Golden Gate Bapt. Theol. Sem., Mill Valley, Calif., 1977-82; dir. Tex. Bapt. Heritage Ctr., 2000—; disting. vis. prof. Dallas Bapt. U., 2001—, Baylor U., 2001—. Exec. dir. Bapt. Gen. Conv. Tex., 1982—2000, exec. dir. emeritus, 2000—; chmn. program com. Christian Life Commn. So. Bapt. Conv., spl. rschr. for home mission bd., mem. nat. task force planned growth in giving, 1984—94, mem. stewardship commn., 1986—96; bd. dirs. T.B. Maston Found., 1991—98, Assn. So. Bapt. Schs., 1997—; adj. prof. Southwestern Bapt. Theol. Sem., 1976—77; chmn. study commn. freedom, justice and peace Bapt. World Alliance, 1975—80, mem. study commn. on ethics, 1990—95, mem. commn. on racism, 1992—, mem. com. on polity an heritage, 2000—; v.p. Bapt. Gen. Conv. Tex., 1972—73, mem. state missions commn., 1976—77, vice chmn. urban strategy com., chmn. order of bus. com., 1976, chmn. steering com. Good News Tex., 1976—77, chmn. resolutions com.; author, spkr. in field. *In the field of education, William M. Pinson, Jr. was one of the youngest tenured full professors at Southwestern Seminary. In denominational service, he had the longest tenure of any Executive Director in the history of the Baptist General Convention of Texas. As Executive Director, he helped to coordinate eight universities, three seminaries, six medical centers with multiple hospitals, nine child and aging care institutions, a foundation and a weekly newspaper. He directed a staff responsible for encouraging and assisting 6,000 Baptist congregations in the state and 113 associations of churches with a special emphasis on starting thousands of new churches.* Contbr. articles to numerous theological publs. Named Lilly Found. scholar Southwestern Bapt. Theol. Sem., 1960-62; Recipient Disting. Alumni award Southwestern Bapt. Theol. Sem., 1979, U. North Tex., 1980, Mosaic Missions award Home Mission Bd., 1984. Mem. So. Bapt. Assn. Colls. and Schs., So. Bapt. Assn. of State Exec. Dirs. (pres. 1996-97). Avocations: travel, reading. Office: Bapt Gen Conv Tex 333 N Washington Ave Dallas TX 75246-1782 Fax: (214) 370-0228. E-mail: pinson@bgct.org.

PINSTRUP-ANDERSEN, PER, educational administrator; b. Bislev, Denmark, Apr. 7, 1939; came to U.S., 1965; s. Marinus and Alma (Pinstrup) Andersen; m. Birgit Lund, June 19, 1965; children: Charlotte, Tina. BS, Royal Vet. and Agrl. U., Copenhagen, 1965; MS, Okla. State U., 1967, PhD, 1969; Dr. Tech. Scis. (hon.), Swiss Fed. Inst. Tech., 1996; DSc (hon.), Tamil Nadu U., 1999, Animal Scis. U., 1999; LLD, U. Aberdeen, 1999; Dr. Agr. and Environment (hon.), Wageningen U., The Netherlands, 2000. Agrl. economist Centro Internacional de Agricultura Tropical, Cali, Colombia, 1969-72, head econ. unit Colombia, 1972-76; dir. agro.-econ. div. Internat. Fertilizer Devel. Ctr., Florence, Ala., 1976-77; sr. rsch. fellow, assoc. prof. Econ. Inst. Royal Vet. & Agr. U., 1977-80; rsch. fellow Internat. Food Policy Rsch. Inst., Washington, 1980, dir. food consumption and nutrition divsn., 1980-87, dir. gen., 1992—; dir. food and nutrition policy program, prof. food econs. Cornell U., Ithaca, N.Y., 1987-92; disting prof. Wageningen U., The Netherlands, 2000—. Cons. The World Bank, Washington, 1978-92, Can. Internat. Devel. Agy., 1982-83, 86, UNICEF, N.Y.C.; cons. subcom. on nutrition UN, Rome, 1980-87. Author: The World Food and Agricultural Situation, 1978, Agricultural Research and Economic Development, 1979, The Role of Fertilizer in World Food Supply, 1980, Agricultural Research and Technology in Economic Development, 1982; editor: (with Magaret Biswas) Nutrition and Development, 1985, Food Subsidies in Developing Countries: Costs, Benefits, and Policy Options, 1988, Macroeconomic Policy Reforms, Poverty, and Nutrition: Analytical Methodologies, 1990, The Political Economy of Food and Nutrition Policies, 1993, (with David Pelletier and Harold Alderman) Child Growth and Nutrition in Developing Countries: Priorities for Action, 1995, Seed of Contention, 2001; mem. editl. bd. coms. of several jours.; contbr. more than 200 articles to profl. jours. With Danish Army, 1958-59. Recipient cert. of appreciation People to People, 1967, competition prize Nordic Soc. agrl. Rschrs. and Norsk Hydro, 1979, cert. of merit Gamma Sigma Delta, 1991, Disting. Alumnus award U. Colo., 1993, Disting. Alumni award Okla. State U., 1998, World Food prize World Food Found., 2001; fellow Ford Found., 1965-66, Kellogg gravel fellow, 1979. Mem. Am. Assn. Agrl. Econs. (PhD Thesis award 1970, Outstanding Jour. Article award 1977, bd. dirs. 1996-99), Internat. Assn. Agrl. Econs., Columbian Nat. Orgn. Profls. in Agr. (hon., Charles Black award 1998, Agronomprisen 2000, World Food prize 2001). Home: 1451 Highwood Dr Mc Lean VA 22101-2516 Office: Internat Food Policy Rsch Inst 2033 K St NW Washington DC 20006-1002 E-mail: P.Pinstrup-Andersen@cgiar.org, Pinstrupa@hotmail.com.

PINTER, GABRIEL GEORGE, physiology educator; b. Bekes, Hungary, June 23, 1925; came to U.S., 1958; s. Lajos and Regina (Szilagyi-Farkas) Pinter; m. Berit Helgesen, Dec. 19, 1958 (dec. May 1980); children: Renee Astrid, Eva Ingelill; m. Vera Lederer Dallos, May 24, 1984. MD, U. Sch. Medicine, Budapest, Hungary, 1951. Asst. prof. U. Sch. Medicine, Budapest, Hungary, 1951-56; rsch. assoc. U. Inst. Med. Rsch., Oslo, Norway, 1957-58; asst. prof. U. Tenn., Memphis, 1958-61; from asst. prof. to prof. U. Md., Balt., 1961-92; retired. Vis. prof. King's Coll., London, 1990-94. Contbr. articles to profl. jours.; translator (with wife) philos. and lit. works into Hungarian. Recipient A.V. Humboldt prize, Germany, 1980; Swedish Royal Med. Soc. fellow, Uppsala, 1972. Mem. Am. Physiol. Soc., Physiol. Soc. Gt. Brit., Scandinavian Physiol. Soc., European Soc. Microcirculation. E-mail: ggvp@comcast.net.

PINTER, HAROLD, playwright; b. London, Oct. 10, 1930; s. Hyman and Frances (Mann) P.; m. Vivien Merchant, Sept. 14, 1956 (div. 1980); 1 son, Daniel; m. Antonia Fraser, Nov. 1980. Student, Brit. schs.; D.Litt. (hon.), U. Reading, 1970, U. Birmingham, 1971, U. Glasgow, 1974, U. East Anglia, 1974, U. Stirling, 1979, Brown U., 1982, U. Hull, 1986, U. Sussex, 1990, U. East London, London, 1994, U. Sofia, Bulgaria, 1995; hon. fellow, Queen Mary Coll., London, 1987, U. Aristotle, Thessaloniki, Greece, 2000, U. Florence, Italy, 2001. Actor in repertory theatres, 1949-57; dir. plays and films, 1970—; assoc. dir. Nat. Theatre, 1973-83; author (plays) The Dumb Waiter, 1957, A Slight Ache, 1958, The Hothouse, 1958, A Night Out, 1959, The Caretaker, 1959, Night School, 1960, The Dwarfs, 1960 (pub. 1990), The Collection, 1961, The Lover, 1962 (Italia prize 1963), Tea Party, 1964, The Homecoming, 1964, The Basement, 1966, Landscape, 1967, Silence, 1968, Night, 1969, Old Times, 1970, Monologue, 1972, No Man's Land, 1974, Betrayal, 1978 (screenplay 1981), Family Voices, 1980, A Kind of Alaska, 1982, Victoria Station, 1982, One for the Road, 1984, Mountain Language, 1988, The New World Order, 1991, Party Time, 1991, Moonlight, 1993, Ashes to Ashes, 1996, Celebration, 1999, others; (screenplays) The Caretaker, 1962, The Servant, 1962, The Pumpkin Eater, 1963, The Quiller Memorandum, 1965, Accident, 1966, The Birthday Party, 1967, The Go-Between, 1969, The Homecoming, 1969, Langrishe Go Down, 1970, A la Recherche du Temps Perdu, 1972, The Last Tycoon, 1974, The French Lieutenant's Woman, 1980, Betrayal, 1981, Victory, 1982, Turtle Diary, 1984, The Handmaid's Tale, 1987, Reunion, 1988, The Heat of the Day, 1988, The Comfort of Strangers, 1989, The Trial, 1989; (pub.); (novel) The Dwarfs, 1990, Various Voices, Prose, Poetry, Politics, 1948-1998, 1998. Decorated comdr. Order Brit. Empire; recipient Shakespeare prize Hamburg, Germany, 1970, Austrian prize lit., 1973, Pirandello prize, 1980, Commonwealth award, 1981, Donatello prize, 1982, Elmer H. Bobst award, 1984, David Cohen Brit. Lit. prize, 1995, Laurence Shivier Spl. award, 1996, Moliere D'Honneur, 1997, Sunday Times award, 1997, Critic's Circle award for Disting. Svcs. to Arts, 2000, Brianza Poetry prize, 2000, South Bank Show award for Outstanding Achievment in the Arts, 2001; BAFTA fellow, 1997, S.T. Dupont Golden Pen award, 2001, Premio Fiesole ai Maestri del Cinema, Italy, 2001, World Leaders award, Toronto, 2001, Hermann Kesten medallion German Pen, 2001; named Companion of Lit., RSL, 1998. Office: care Judy Daish Assocs Ltd 2 St Charles Pl London W10 6EG England

PINTO, EDWARD RALPH, internist, cardiologist; b. Mangalore, India, 1947; MD, Bangalore (India) U., 1970. Diplomate Am. Bd. Internal Medicine, Am. Bd. Cardiovascular Disease, Am. Bd. Geriatrics. Intern Bridgeport Hosp., 1971-72; resident internal medicine Bridgeport (Conn.) Hosp., 1972-75; fellow in cardiology Hosp. U. Pa., Phila., 1975-76; fellow cardiology Hershey Med. Ctr., 1976-77; sr. attending physician internal medicine and cardiology Bridgeport Hosp. Fellow Am. Coll. Cardiology. Office: 52 Beach Rd Fairfield CT 06430-6017

PINTO, LISA ELLMAN, congressional aide; b. Balt., Dec. 21, 1962; d. Alvin Franklin and Janice Lee (Steinberg) Ellman; m. Robert Peter Pinto, Oct. 7, 2000. BA, UCLA, 1985; JD, U. Calif., Davis, 1988. Assoc. Higgs, Fletcher & Mack, San Diego, 1988-91; staff atty. Dependency Ct. Legal Svcs., Monterey Park, Calif., 1991-96; dist. dir. to Congressman Henry Waxman L.A., 1996—. Democrat. Jewish. Avocations: travel, cooking, writing. Office: Congressman Henry A Waxman # 600 8436 W 3d St Los Angeles CA 90048 E-mail: lisa.pinto@mail.house.gov.

PINTO, MAXWELL SALUSTIANO, management consultant; b. Goa, India, Mar. 10, 1954; came to U.S., 1984; s. Maurice and Martha (Lopez) P.; m. Eusebia C. Fernandez, Jan. 25, 1987; children: Aaron Massimo, Esther Maxine. BA with honors, U. Leeds, Eng., 1978; PhD in Bus. Adminstrn., Pacific Southern U., 1987. Chartered acct., Eng. Auditor, acct. KPMG Peat Marwick Chartered Accts., London, 1978-82; dep. fin. and adminstrn. mgr. Elec. Bds. Mfg. Co., Kuwait, 1983-86; fin. cons. Tollafield & Assocs., Cyprus, 1986-87; dir. Brandon Planning & Corp. Analysis, Cyprus, 1987-88; mgmt. analyst Gurmeet, Inc., N.Y.C., 1989-93; bus. assoc. in ins. and investments N.Y. Life Ins. Co., 1993-96; trust acct. CI Mutual Funds, Inc., Toronto, Can., 1998—. Lectr. acctg. Plato Coll., 1987, Limassol, Cyprus, econs. Americanos Coll., Limassol, 1987, mgmt. and law, Intercollege, Limassol, 1988. Author: The Management Syndrome, 1998. Pacific Southern U. scholar, 1984. Mem. Inst. Profl. Mgrs. (life), Inst. Chartered Accts. (assoc.), Outdoor World, Coast to Coast. Avocations: tennis, swimming, pool, movies. Home and Office: 169 Morrison Ave Toronto ON Canada M6E 1M6 E-mail: crespin79@hotmail.com.

PINTO, ROSALIND, retired educator, civic volunteer; b. N.Y.C. d. Barney and Jenny Abrams; m. Jesse E. Pinto (dec.); children: Francine, Jerry, Evelyn. BA in Polit. Sci. cum laude, Hunter Coll.; MA in Polit. Sci., History, Columbia U.; postgrad., Queens Coll., LaGuardia C.C. Lic. social studies tchr. jr. H.S., N.Y., per diem lifetime substitute; cert. secondary sch. social studies grades 7-12, N.Y. Substitute tchr., 1966-69, 90, 91—; tchr. social studies I.S. 126Q, L.I., N.Y., 1969-88, Jr. H.S. 217 Briarwood, N.Y.C., 1988-89; ret., 1989; part-time cluster tchr. social studies and communication arts Pub. Sch. 140, Bronx, N.Y., 1990-92; substitute tchr. I.S. 227Q, 1992-93. Participant seminars and workshops. Author curriculum materials; contbr. study guide for regent's competency test, 1990; contbr. poems to anthologies, Nat. Libr. Poetry including Tears of Fire, 1994, Dance on the Horizon, 1994, Outstanding Poets of 1994, Best Poems of 1995, Seasons to Come, 1995, The Voice Within, 1996, Best Poems of 1996, Best Poems of 1997, 98; recorded poem for The Sound of Poetry, Nat. Libr. Poetry, 1992, 98 (Editor's Choice award 1993-94, 96, 2001), recorded poem for Sound of Poetry, 2001, American at the Millenium: The Best Poems and Poets of the 20th Century, Poetry Elite, 2001; contbr. poems on Internet; 2 poems and articles in 112th Police Precinct Newsletter, 2001, Poem in Newsletter, 2002. Enrollment asst. Insight Heart Team, 1989; vol. receptionist Whitney Mus., N.Y.C.; mem. com. on pub. transp. Cmty. Bd. 6, Queens, 1990—96, mem. com. on history, 1990—, chmn. beautification com., 1992—, mem. com. on planning and zoning, 1996—, mem. com. on environ. sanitation, 1999—; mem. Forest Hills Action League,

1999; advocate Census 2000 participation; active Gt. Smokies Song Chase Warren-Wilson Coll., NC, 1992; mem. Queens Hist. Soc., Forest Hills Van Ct. Homeowners Assn.; bd. dirs. Ctrl. Queens Hist. Soc.; mem. Rego Park Coalition Against Crime, Forest Hills Civic Assn., 1996—97; vol. local polit. campaigns. Recipient Cert. Appreciation for participation, Dept. Probate Cmty. Svc. Project, 1993, award for participation in Make a Difference Day, 1994—95, award for projects, Beautification Com., 1995, Rosemary Gunning award, Queens Borough Pres. for Women's History month, 2000, Editor's Choice award, Best Poems and Poets of 2001, 2001, Best Poems and Poets of 2002, 2002. Fellow Mcpl. Art Soc. (hon. mention design 2000 award); mem. NAFE, Internat. Soc. Poets (life mem. adv. panel, Internat. Poet of Merit award 1993, 2000, Editor's Choice award 2001), N.Y. Insight Alumni Assn., Columbia U. Grad. Sch. Arts and Scis. Alumni Assn., Hunter Coll. Alumni Assn., Robert F. Kennedy Dem. Assn. (bd. dirs.), Ctr. for Sci. in the Pub. Interest. Avocations: poetry, reading, long distance walking, art shows, plays. *Loving people and having faith in them and the possibility of happy outcomes is the greatest motivation toward achievement of goals.*

PINZON, BRIAN WILLIAM, inventor, consultant; b. Buffalo, May 27, 1965; s. Guillermo Arturo and Judith Ann (Tribunella) P. BA in Fin., N.Mex. State U., 1990; M in Healthcare Adminstrn., Webster U., 1993; postgrad., U. Phoenix, 1998—. CEO Am. Watchkey and Telekey Corp., El Paso, Tex., 1985—, Pindome Corp., El Paso, 1990—; COO El Paso Wireless, 1998; fin. advisor Dr. Pinzon, 1989—. Cons. Mexicali Rose, Inc., El Paso, 1998, Columbia/HCA Corp., El Paso, 1990-93. Achievements include first to xylotron spaced based transportation device to prove presence of antigravity (G=-n3) antigravity equation; research in in telekey-global range locking system and watchkey short-range infrafed/RF locking system. Home: PO Box 959 Santa Teresa NM 88008-0959 E-mail: bpinzon@elp.rr.com.

PINZUR, MICHAEL STEVEN, orthopaedic surgeon; b. Chgo., June 26, 1949; BS, U. Ill., 1971; MD, Rush Med. Sch., Chgo., 1974. Diplomate Am. Bd. Orthopaedic Surgery. Resident in orthop. surgery Northwestern U., 1974-79; orthop. surgeon, prof. Loyola Univ. Med. Ctr., Maywood, Ill. Office: Loyola U Med Ctr 2160 S 1st Ave Maywood IL 60153-3304 E-mail: mpinzu1@lumc.edu.

PIOMBINO, NICHOLAS, psychotherapist; b. N.Y.C., Oct. 5, 1942; s. Nicholas Bruce and Ruth Mary (Rothbart) P. BA with honors, CCNY, 1964; MSW, Fordham U., 1971; cert. in adult psychoanalysis and psychotherapy, Postgrad. Ctr. Mental Health, N.Y.C., 1982. Diplomate in clin. social work; cert. psychotherapist, social worker, N.Y. Social worker Manhattan State Hosp., N.Y.C., 1971-73; pvt. practice psychotherapy, 1976—; sch. social worker N.Y.C. Bd. Edn., 1974—2001; staff psychotherapist Postgrad. Ctr. Mental Health, 1978-86; supr., mem. faculty Psychoanalytic Inst. N.Y. Counseling and Guidance Svc., N.Y.C., 1987—. Author: Poems, 1988, Light Street, 1996, Theoretical Objects, 1999, (essays) The Boundary of Blur, 1993; contbr. articles and poems to numerous publs. Mem. Postgrad. Psychoanalytic Soc., Soc. Clin. Social Work Psychotherapists. Home: 119 W 95th St New York NY 10025-6636 Office: 680 W End Ave New York NY 10025-6815

PIONK, JEROME LEE, government official, association administrator; b. Watertown, S.D., Aug. 31, 1950; s. Jerome Ambrose and Helen Emeline Pionk; m. Song Yo Kim; childen: Jerome, Angela Pionk Curtis. BS, SUNY, Albany, 1981; MA, Liberty U., 1991; grad., Command and Gen. Staff Coll., Ft. Leavenworth, Kans., 1997. Cert. counselor. Enlisted man U.S. Army, 1970, advanced through grades to sgt. maj., 1989, recruiter Minn., Republic of Korea, 1970-84; retention and recruiting staff specialist Army Enlistment Eligibility Activity, St. Louis, 1984-87; dir. theater army retention 8th Army, Seoul, 1987-92; sr. retention policy advisor Hdqs. Dept. Army, Washington, 1992-2000; ret., 2000; sr. def. analyst, reschr. Dept. Def. (Resource Cons. Inc.)_, Washington, 2000—. Exec. dir. Nat. Assn. Recruiters and Career Counselors, Washington, 1983—; prof. Am. Mil. U., 2000—. Author: Prairie Vignettes, 1999 (MIdwest Lit. award 2000), History of Military Retention, 2001. Decorated Legion of Merit; recipient Olympic honor award Seoul Olympic Organizing Com., 1988, Order of Horatio Gates, Army Adj. Gen.'s Assn., 1992. Mem. VFW (life), Not Good Old Boys-Vets. Assn. (exec. dir. 1983—, Order of Merit 1994), Am. Vets. (life), Am. Legion. Republican. Avocations: travel, writing, fencing, automobile racing. Office: Army Office Human Resource Mgmt 300 Army Pentagon Washington DC 20310 Fax: 703-325-8987. E-mail: ngob1@aol.com.

PIONK, RICHARD CLETUS, artist, educator; b. Minn., Apr. 26, 1936; s. Franz E. Spielmann and Esther (Dufrane) Pionk. Cert. in fine arts painting, Art Students League, 1983. Tchr. Art Students League, N.Y.C., 1991—. Mem. bd. control Art Students League, 1983-90. Exhibited in one-man shows Moran Gallery, Tulsa, 1985, Connoisseur Gallery, Rhinebeck, N.Y., 1987, 88, 89, 90, Bklyn. Pub. Libr.; exhibited in group shows Queens Mus., N.Y.C., 1982, Hermitage Found., Norfolk, Va., 1985, Monmouth Mus., Lincroft, N.J., 1985, La Societe des Pastellistes de France, Lille, 1987, Canton (Ohio) Art Inst., 1987, Friends Art Mus., Naples, Fla., 1987, Mel Vin Gallery Southern Coll., Lakeland, Fla., 1987, Wind Borne Gallery, Southport, Conn., 1987, 89, Gregory Gallery, Darien, Conn., 1990, 91, 92, 93, 94, 95, 96, Geary Gallery, Darien, 1997, 98, 99, 2000, 01, 02, The Food Show at Grand Cen. Art Gallery, N.Y.C., 1989, Quincy (Ill.) Art Club, 1989, 90, Jordane Art Gallery, Ft. Myers, Fla., 1990, Pastel Soc., N.Y.C., 1991, Allied Artists, N.Y.C., 1991, Harman-Meek Gallery, Naples, 1992, Butler Inst. Art, 2000. Decorated more than 100 others; recipient Bernhardt Gold medal for pastel, 2002, Salzman award, 2001. Mem. Pastel Soc. Am. (1st v.p. 1978-91, exhbn. chmn. 1978—, master pastellist, Hall of Fame 1997), Allied Artists Am. (bd. dirs. 1986-91, asst. corr. sec. 1986—), Audubon Artists (juror 1989—), Artists Fellowship Inc. (bd. dirs. 1988—), Nat. Arts Club, Salmagundi Club (mem. curators com., chmn. art com. 1981—, pres. 1994—), Dutch Treat Club. Roman Catholic. Avocations: collecting 17th, 18th, and 19th century paintings and drawings. Home: 1349 Lexington Ave Apt 8B New York NY 10128-1511 Office: Studio 611 41 Union Sq W New York NY 10003-3208

PIORKOWSKI, JAMES PAUL, music educator, composer, guitarist; b. North Tonawanda, N.Y., July 23, 1956; s. Matthew Frank and Lottie (Jastrzemski) P.; m. Susan Elizabeth Marion, Oct. 10, 1980; children: Jacob, Benjamin. BA, SUNY, Buffalo, 1978; MMus in Theory and Composition, SUNY, Fredonia, 1987. Instr. SUNY, Buffalo, 1980-83, 1980-84, prof. Fredonia, N.Y., 1983—. Mem. Buffalo Guitar Quartet, 1982-2000; faculty advisor Fredonia Guitar Soc., 1987—. Composer (composition for guitar and flute) Freedom Flight, 1996, (CD), 1999, (composition for guitar and choir) The Greatest of These, 1999, (composition for four guitars) The Struggle of Jacob, 1984, (composition for two guitars) Leaping and Dancing for Joy, 2000, (composition for solo guitar) Who Do You Say I Am?. William T. Hagan young scholar/artist award SUNY, 1998; artist-in-residence grant Chamber Music Am., 1993-96. Office: Fredonia Sch Music Mason Hall SUNY Fredonia NY 14063 E-mail: james.piorkowski@fredonia.edu.

PIOTROWSKI, STEPHANIE DEANNE, special education educator; b. Oakland, Calif., June 17, 1971; d. Richard Paul and Teresa Ann (Magliocco) Triglia; m. Dominic Joseph Piotrowski, Dec. 17, 1994; 1 child Dominic Joseph. BA in Child Psychology, Humboldt State U., Arcata, Calif., 1992; M.Spl. Edn., Chapman U., Moreno Valley, Calif., 1999. Cert. tchr. spl. edn. With Nations Giant Hamburgers, San Pablo, Calif., 1988—89; waitress Uniontown Cafe, Arcata, 1989—91; apt. mgr. Campus Apts., 1991—92; substitute tchr. Murrietta and Temecula Sch. Dists., Calif., 1993—95; presch. tchr. Kindercare, Temecula, 1992—93; tchr. Crossroads Sch., Hemet, Calif., 1995—96; tutoring instr. Sulivan Tutoring Ctr., Moreno Valley, 2002—; spl. edn. tchr. Moreno Valley Unified Sch. Dist., 1996—. Contbr. Dir. Respect Life Ministry St. Patrick's Ch., Moreno Valley, 2001—. Recipient Bruin award, Box Springs Staff, 2000; grantee, Victor Bowers Assn., 1999; scholar Calif. Scholarship Fedn., Richmond Elks scholar, Diablo Valley scholar. Mem.: PTA, Moreno Valley Educators Assn., Turner Syndrom Soc. Roman Catholic. Office: Moreno Valley Unified Sch Dist 11900 Athens Dr Moreno Valley CA

PIPCHICK, MARGARET HOPKINS, clinical specialist psychiatric nursing, therapist, consultant; b. Bklyn., Dec. 14, 1942; m. Robert Pipchick, June 13, 1971; children: Christine, Kevin. BSN, Seton Hall U., 1968; MA, NYU, 1974; grad., Blanton Peale Grad. Inst., N.Y.C., 1981; PhD, The Union Inst., 2001. Cert. clin. specialist child-adolescent-adult. psychiat. nursing; lic. marriage and family therapist, N.J. Various staff positions hosps., N.Y./N.J.; teaching asst. Seton Hall U., South Orange, N.J., 1971-72; staff therapist, faculty Blanton-Peale Counseling Ctr., Cranford, 1974-90; pvt. practice individual, couple and family therapy, 1981—. Adj. faculty Fairleigh Dickenson U., Teaneck, N.J., 1989-93, Kean Coll., 1994, 95. Contbr. chpt. to Foundations of Psychiatric Mental Health Nursing. Mem. ANA, N.J. State Nurses Assn., Am. Assn. Marriage and Family Therapists, Soc. Cert. Clin. Specialists (treas.), Sigma Theta Tau.

PIPER, ANNETTE CLEONE, social services administrator, researcher; b. St. Paul, July 13, 1936; d. Frank Robert Zimmerman; m. Aaron Cleaves Piper, Apr. 17, 1958 (div. 1974); children: Michelle, Renee. BA, Wayne State U., 1960, MSW, 1965, postdoctoral, 1985—. Inst. rsch. Wayne State U., Detroit, 1965-69; program mgr. Ariz. Dept. Econ. Security, Bisbee, 1976-79; tng. and personnel coordinator Mich. Dept. Social Svcs., Detroit, 1971-73, mgr. svcs. sect., 1973-74, program mgr. Pontiac, 1974-76, dep. dir. Sta. WCCYS Detroit, 1979-88, dist. dir. Westland, 1988—; med. social worker Bariatric Treatment Ctrs., Ann Arbor, 1997-98. Instr., cons. Cochise Community Coll., Douglas, Ariz., 1979. Vol. Peace Corps, Dominican Republic, 1998. Mem. Nat. Assn. Child Welfare Adminstrs., Nat. Child Welfare Leadership Ctr., Am. Pub. Welfare Assn., Wayne State U. Alumni Assn, Psi Chi. Home: 23010 Webster Oak Park MI 48237-2119 E-mail: nettie7@juno.com.

PIPER, DON COURTNEY, political science educator; b. Washington, July 29, 1932; s. Don Carlos and Alice (Courtney) P.; m. Rowena Inez Wise, July 6, 1956; children: Sharon, Valarie. BA, U. Md., 1954, MA, 1958; PhD (James B. Duke fellow), Duke U., 1961. Research assoc. Duke U., 1961-62; exec. sec. Commonwealth-Studies Center, 1962-64; asst. prof. dept. govt. and politics U. Md., College Park, 1964-67, assoc. prof., 1967-69, prof., 1969-97, prof. emeritus, 1997—, head dept. govt. and politics, 1968-74, dir. grad. studies dept., 1982-95, mem. coun. of system faculty, 1989-90; chmn. faculty council College Park Faculty Assembly, 1974-75, chmn. campus senate, 1975-77, 89-90, univ. marshal, 1981-97, mem. Athletic Council, 1986-93, mem. senate ad hoc com. on undergrad. edn., 1986-88, chmn. chancellor's ad hoc com. on campus ceremonies, 1986-87, chmn. acad. com. of Athletic Council, 1986-89; chmn. campaign for College Park, 1988-89; chmn. retention review com. U. Md., 1990-91, chmn. budget and facilities com. athletic coun., 1991-93, chmn. senate com. on programs courses and curriculi, 1991-93, co-chair Mid. States self-study exec. com., 1995-97; teaching fellow Lilly Ctr. for Teaching Excellence, 1994-95. Rsch. asst. Am. Coun. on Edn., 1966-68; faculty adv. com., planning adv. com. Md. State Bd. Higher Edn., 1977-82; chmn. com. on dept. chairmen Am. Polit. Sci. Assn., 1973-75; mem. coun. So. Polit. Sci. Assn., 1970-72, chmn. Chastain award com., 1973-75. Author: International Law of Great Lakes, 1967; contbg. author: International Law Standard and Commonwealth Developments, 1966, De Lege Pactorum, 1970, Foreign Policy Analysis, 1975; editor: (with R. Taylor Cole) Post-primary Education and Political and Economic Development, 1964; co-editor, contbg. author: (with Ronald Terchek) Interaction: Foreign Policy and Public Policy, 1983; bd. editors: World Affairs, 1971-94; editl. adv. com.: Internat. Legal Materials, 1977-78. Served to 1st lt. USAF, 1955-58. Recipient U. Md. Regents award for excellence in teaching, 1966, Teaching Excellence award Div. Behavioral and Social Scis., 1982-83, Outstanding Tchr. award Greek System, U. Md., 1982, Pres.'s medal, U. Md., 1992. Mem. Am. Soc. Internat. Law, Internat. Law Assn., Internat. Studies Assn. (chmn. internat. law sect. 1981-83), Am. Peace Soc. (bd. dirs. 1972-94), UN Assn./USA, Phi Beta Kappa (pres. Gamma chpt. 1978-79), Phi Kappa Phi (chpt. pres. 1982-83), Omicron Delta Kappa (faculty adviser 1990-97), Pi Sigma Alpha. Methodist. Home: 4323 Woodberry St Hyattsville MD 20782-1174 Office: U Md Dept Govt & Politics College Park MD 20742-0001

PIPER, J. K. See GILES, KATHARINE EMILY

PIPER, JOHN RICHARD, political science educator; b. Sewickley, Pa., Oct. 2, 1946; s. John Hubert and Carol Elizabeth (Coleman) P.; m. Hoa Thuy Pham, June 6, 1970; 1 child, Carolyn Hoa. BA, Pa. State U., 1968; MA, Cornell U., 1971, PhD, 1972. Prof. polit. sci. Blackburn Coll., Carlinville, Ill., 1972-76; asst. prof. polit. sci. U. Tampa (Fla.), 1976-80, assoc. prof. polit. sci., 1980-83; prof. polit. sci. U. Tampa, Fla., 1983—, chmn. dept. history, polit. sci. and sociology, 1990-96; dir. honors program, 1996—. Author: Ideologies and Institutions: American Conservative and Liberal Governance Prescriptions Since 1933, 97; contbr. articles to profl. jours. Mem. Common Cause, 1990—; v.p. Fla. Collegiate Honors Coun., 1998-99, pres., 1999-2000. Recipient Outstanding Educator award Blackburn Coll., 1974, Louise Loy Hunter award U. Tampa, 1981, award for teaching excellence Sears Roebuck Found., 1990; Fulbright-Hays grantee, 1988. Mem. Am. Polit. Sci. Assn., AAUP, Omicron Delta Kappa, Phi Beta Kappa, Pi Kappa Phi. Democrat. Avocations: travel, swimming, reading. Office: Univ of Tampa 401 W Kennedy Blvd Tampa FL 33606-1490 E-mail: rpiper@ut.edu.

PIPER, LINDA AMMANN, personnel consulting firm executive; b. Nov. 29, 1949; d. Ernest D. and Marie (Liccese) Ammann; m. Stephen George Piper; 2 children. BA, W.Va. U., 1972. Cert. pers. cons. Mgr., asst. buyer Gilchrist Co., Boston, 1972-74; mgr. Harvard Coop. Soc., Cambridge, 1974-77; pers. cons. Wellesley Profl. Corp., 1977-82; pres. Career Connections, Inc., Nashua, N.H., 1982—; mem. regional adv. bd. BankBoston, 1998—2000. Mem. adv. bd. Women's Entrepreneur's Connection, BankBoston, 1998-2000. Mem.: N.H. Staffing Assn., Nat. Assn. Pers. Svcs., No. New Eng. Assn. Pers. Svcs. (bd. dirs. 1982—, treas. 1983—84, v.p. 1984—85, sec. 1986—88, 1996—, dir. 2001—), Nat. Human Resource Assn. N.H. (ways and means chair 1994—97, membership chair 1997—98, bd. dirs.), Greater Nashua C. of C. (mem. exec. bd.). Office: Career Connections Inc 74 Northeastern Blvd Ste 17 Nashua NH 03062-3192 E-mail: lpiper@careerconnectionsnh.com.

PIPER, LLOYD LLEWELLYN, II, engineer, government and service industry executive; b. Wareham, Mass., Apr. 28, 1944; s. Lloyd Llewellyn and Mary Elizabeth (Brown) P.; m. Jane Melonie Scruggs, Apr. 30, 1965; 1 child, Michael Wayne. BSEE, Tex. A&M U., 1966; MS in Indsl. Engring, U. Houston, 1973. Registered profl. engr., Tex.; diplomate hazardous waste mgmt. Am. Acad. Environ. Engrs. With Houston Lighting & Power Co., 1965-74; project mgr. Dow Chem. Engring. & Constrn Svcs., Houston, 1974-78, Ortloff Corp., Houston, 1978, mgr. engring., 1979-80, v.p., 1980-83; pres., chief exec. officer Plantech Engrs. & Constructors, Inc. subs. Dillingham Constrn. Corp., 1983-86; pres. The Delta Plantech Co., 1985-86; dir. on-site tech. devel. Chem. Waste Mgmt., Inc., Oak Brook, Ill., 1986-88, mgr. projects Houston, 1988-94, dir. facility devel., 1994-95; asst. mgr. Richland (Wa.) Ops. U.S. Dept. Energy, 1995-96, dep. mgr., 1996-99, adminstr., 1999—. Bd. dirs., pres. Harris County Water Control and Improvement Dist., 1973-83; bd. dirs. Environ. Sci. and Tech. Found., 1997-99; bd. dirs. United Way, 1998—, exec. com., 1998-2001, treas., 2000-2001; Ponderosa Joint Powers Agy. Harris County, 1977-83, pres., 1977-83; pres. bus. and industry adv. coun. North Harris Montgomery C. C. Dist., 1991-92. Contbr. articles to profl. jours. Recipient Disting. Svc. award Engrs. Coun. Houston, 1970, Outstanding Svc. award Houston sect. IEEE, 1974; named Tex. Young Engr. of Yr., 1976, Nat. Young Engr. of Yr., 1976. Mem. IEEE, Nat. Soc. Profl. Engrs. (chpt. pres. 1978, nat. chmn. engrs. in industry div. 1977, nat. v.p. 1977, chmn. nat. polit. action com. 1979-82, vice chmn. nat. engrs. week 1988-92, nat. trustee edn. found. 1988-90), Nat. Wildlife Fedn., Nature Conservancy, Audubon Soc., Project Mgmt. Inst., Phi Kappa Phi, Tau Beta Pi. Home: 129 Mountain View Ln Richland WA 99352-7652 Office: Dept Energy PO Box 550 Richland WA 99352-0550

PIPER, MARGARITA SHERERTZ, retired school administrator; b. Petersburg, Va., Dec. 20, 1926; d. Guy Lucas and Olga Doan (Akers) Sherertz; m. Glenn Clair Piper, Feb. 3, 1950; children: Mark Stephen, Susan Leslie Piper Weathersbee. BA in Edn., Mary Washington Coll U. Va., Fredericksburg, 1948; MEd, U. Va., 1973, EdS, 1976. Svc. rep. C&P Telephone, Washington, 1948-55, adminstrv. asst., 1955-56, svc. supr., 1956-62; tchr. Culpeper (Va.) County Pub. Schs., 1970-75, reading lab dir., 1975-80; asst. prin. Rappahannock (Va.) County Pub. Schs., 1980-81, prin., 1981-88, dir. pupil pers., spl. programs, 1988-95; ret., 1995. Chair PD 9 regional transition adv. bd. Culpeper, Fauquier, Madison, Orange and Rappahannock Counties, Va., 1991-94; vice chair Family Assessment and Planning Team, Washington, 1992-95. Recipient Va. Gov. Schs. Commendation cert. Commonwealth of Va., 1989-93. Mem. NEA, Va. Edn. Assn., Va. Coun. Adminstrs. Spl. Edn., Va. Assn. Edn. for Gifted, Rappahannock Edn. Assn. Democrat. Episcopalian. Avocations: creative writing, music, walking, crosstitch, knitting. E-mail: marglen@summit.net.

PIPER, MARK HARRY, retired banker; b. Flint, Mich., Apr. 17, 1931; s. James U. and Dorothy (Weed) P.; m. Wanda L. Hubbard, June 20, 1953; children: Mark T., Kathryn L. BS, St. John's Mil. Acad., 1949; AB with distinction and honors in Econs, U. Mich., 1953, JD cum laude, 1956. Bar: Mich. 1956. With Clark, Klein, Winter, Parsons & Prewitt, Detroit, 1956-57, Genesee Mchts. Bank & Trust Co., Flint, 1957-88, v.p., sr. trust officer, 1966-72, sr. v.p., 1972-88, NBD Genesee Bank (formerly United Mich. Corp.), 1985-88, cashier, sec. bd. dirs., 1985-88. Adj. instr. bus. adminstrn. U. Mich., Flint, 1976-80; interim co-pension officer Detroit Conf. United Meth. Ch, 1993-99; pres. Flint Estate Planning Coun., 1969-70; mem. Flint citizens adv. coun. U. Mich., 1974-82; vice chmn., 1975-82. Bd. dir. Retirement Homes of Detroit Ann. Conf. Meth. Ch., 1964-76, vice chmn. profl. ministry and support, 1975, mem. bd. support systems, 1975, coun. fin. and adminstrn., 1976-84, chmn. coun. fin. and adminstrn., 1980-84; bd. dirs. United Meth. Devel. Fund, 1986-90; gen. bd. pensions United Meth. Ch., 1988-96, mem. investment com., gen. bd. pensions, 1988-2000; mem. investment com. United Meth. Found. of Detroit. Conf. of United Meth. Ch., 1993—; trustee Flint YMCA Boysfarm Found., 1964-78, chmn., 1976-78; bd. mgmt. Flint YMCA Boysfarm, 1968-74; mem. Detroit Conf. Bd. P. United Meth. Ch., 1968-76, chmn., 1972-75, 88-2002, mem., 1986-2002; bd. dirs. U. Mich. Devel. Coun., 1980-82; bd. dirs., asst. treas., sec.-treas. Flint Area Young Life Found., 1979—, Mich. Area Young Life Com., 1980-88; bd. dirs., vice chmn. The Crim Road Race Inc., 1985-87; bd. mem. Stewardship Found. Mich., 2002—. Mem. Mich. Bar Assn., Genesee County Bar Assn., Inst. Continuing Legal Edn., U. Mich.-Flint Club (bd. dirs., pres. 1973-74), Rotary Club. Home: 1378 Ox Yoke Dr Flint MI 48532-2352 also: PO Box 3121 Estes Park CO 80517-3121 E-mail: MHPiper3@aol.com.

PIPER, ROBERT JOHNSTON, architect, urban planner; b. Byron, Ill., Feb. 2, 1926; s. Leo Edward and Helen Anna (Johnston) P.; m. Carol Jane White, June 23, 1951; children— Christopher White, Brian Douglas, Eric Johnston. BS in Archtl. Engring, U. Ill., 1951; M. City and Regional Planning, Cornell U., 1953. Architect, planner Orput & Assos., Rockford, Ill., 1953-61; dir. profl. services AIA, Washington, 1961-67; partner, v.p. Perkins & Will, Chgo., 1967-74; dep. dir. Northeastern Ill. Planning Commn., 1974-76; asso. Metz, Train, Olson & Youngren, Inc., 1976-79; dir. community devel. City of Highland Park, Ill., 1980-91; ret., 1991; coord. Chgo. '93 and Chgo. Design Consortium Chgo. Cultural Ctr., 1992—. Pres. Landmarks Preservation Council Ill., Chgo., 1976-80 Author: Careers in Architecture, vocat. guidance manuals, 1967, 71, 75, 80, 85, 93; author, editor: Architect's Handbook of Professional Practice, 7th edit., 1963; prin. works include Regional Open Space Plan, Northeastern Ill., Spring Valley Operations Breakthrough Housing Complex, Kalamazoo, CBD Streetscape and Skokie Corridor Master Plan, Highland Park. Trustee Village of Winnetka, Ill., 1978-83; mem. Potomac Planning Task Force Dept. Interior, 1967-68, Commn. on Fed. Procurement, Washington, 1970-71; mem. nat. advisory bd. community characteristics HEW, 1970-78. Served with USNR, 1944-46, PTO. Fellow AIA (mem. Task Force Future of Inst. 1974-75, various coms., pres. AIA Ill. coun. 1986, Disting. Achievement awards AIA Ill., AIA Chgo. 1993), Am. Inst. Cert. Planners; mem. Lambda Alpha (Chgo. Chpt. Mem. of Yr. award 1999). Episcopalian. Home: 1132 Oak St Winnetka IL 60093-2132

PIPER, SAMUEL O'DELL, engineer; b. Greenville, S.C., Feb. 13, 1951; s. Samuel Turrentine and Mary Ellen (O'Dell) P.; m. Betha Louise Roper, June 8, 1974; 1 child, Mark Samuel. BS in Physics with high honors, Ga. Inst. Tech., 1973, MS in Elec. Engring., 1976; postgrad., U. South Fla., 1980-85. Asst. rsch. scientist Ga. Tech. Engring. Exp. Sta., Atlanta, 1973-77, rsch. engr., 1977-78; sr. engr. Sperry Microwave Electronics, Clearwater, Fla., 1978-80, sr. staff engr., 1980-86; sr. rsch. engr. Ga. Tech. Rsch. Inst. Sensors and EM Applications Lab., Atlanta, 1986-2001, prin. rsch. engr., 2001—, assoc. lab. dir., 1989-93, branch head, 1993—2001, divsn. chief, 2002—. Cons. LTV, Dallas, 1987, Hercules Def. Electronics Systems, Inc., Clearwater, Fla., 1987, Cyber Engring. Svcs., Inc., Dover, N.J., 1997, Dragoon Techs., Inc., Gilbert, Ariz., 1998, SPARTA Inc., Billerica, Mass., 2001, Alliant Techsystems, Inc., Janesville, Wis., 2001, Clearwater, Fla., 2001. 1st Lt. U.S. Army Res., 1973-81. Mem. IEEE (sr., Atlanta sect. sec. 1991-92), Assn. Old Crows, Phi Kappa Phi, Omicron Delta Kappa, Phi Eta Sigma. Methodist. Avocations: sailing. Office: Ga Inst Tech Ga Tech Rsch Institute Atlanta GA 30332-0857 E-mail: sam.piper@gtri.gatech.edu.

PIPER, THOMAS LAURENCE, III, banker; b. Washington, June 20, 1941; s. Thomas Laurence and Edna (Milewski) P.; m. Ann Runnette, Apr. 8, 1967; children: Thomas Laurence IV, Andrew Kerr. Student, U. Va., 1959-61. Assoc. Hodgdon & Co., Inc., Washington, 1962-65; sr. v.p., dir. Hayden Stone Inc., N.Y.C., 1966-73; mng. dir. New Court Securities Corp., 1974-81, Dillon, Read & Co., Inc., N.Y.C., 1981—97, UBS Warburg LLC, 1997—2000, Citigroup Pvt. Bank. Chmn. fund dir. New Canaan chpt. ARC, 1978; bd. dirs. Manhattan coun. Boy Scouts Am., Waveny Care Ctr., New Canaan, Our Lady Queen of Angels, Manhattan; vice-chmn. adv. bd. U. Va. Art Mus., Charlottesville. Mem.: Bond Club NY, Investment Assn. NY (pres. 1974), Red Stick Golf Club, Blind Brook Club, Country Club of New Canaan, Brook Club (N.Y.C.), Racquet and Tennis Club (N.Y.C.). Home: Windrow Ln New Canaan CT 06840 Office: Citibank Pvt Bank 153 E 53rd St Fl 3 New York NY 10043 E-mail: thomas.l.piper@citicorp.com.

PIPER, THOMAS SAMUEL, minister, consultant; b. Racine, Wis., Feb. 26, 1932; s. Wallace William and Margaret Alice (Lahr) P.; m. Mary Alice Smith, Mar. 12, 1955; children: Daniel Thomas, David Michael, Grace Susan Piper Gonzales. BS, Lawrence U., 1954; ThM, Dallas Theol. Sem., 1969. Ordained to ministry Christian Ch., 1982. Mng. editor Good News Broadcaster mag., Lincoln, Nebr., 1969-82; pastor adminstrn. and edn. Faith Bible Ch., Sterling, Va., 1982-86; pres., cons. Ministries in Sync, 1986—. Mem. writers conf. faculty Mt. Hermon (Calif.) Christian Conf., 1978-80, Christian Writers Inst., Wheaton, Ill., 1980; mem. pres.'s coun. Loudon County, Good News Jail and Prison Ministry, Arlington, Va., 1984-86; pres. local chpt. Christian Ministries Mgmt. Assn., Washington, 1987-88; mem. Christian Mgmt. Assn., 1989-90, Nat. Assn. Ch. Bus. Adminstrs., 1986-90. Contbr. articles to profl. jours. Coord. studies on uncomprised living program Christ Cmty. Ch., Ashburn, Va., 2000-01, cons., 2000—; team leader, coach hosp./home visitation McLean (Va.) Bible Ch., 1996-99. With USN, 1956-58. Inductee Washington Park H.S. Hall of Fame, 2001. Mem. Voice of Bibl. Reconciliation (bd. dirs. 1991-93), Dallas Theol. Sem. Assn. (pres. local chpt. 1991-93), Internat. Assn. Bus. Communicators (life, pres. local chpt. 1977-79), Greater Washington Christian Edn. Assn. (cons. 1997—, program chmn., coord. 1997-2001, exec. editor 1998-2002, dir. conv. 1999-2002, bd. dirs. 1999-2002, chmn. planning com. 1999-2002, adminstrv. chmn., coord. 2001-02). Republican. Home and Office: Ministries in Sync 1307 E Holly Ave Sterling VA 20164-2614 *The strategic result of our calling today is helping churches in a me-centered high-tech age to synchronize their ministries to produce a pleasing and efficacious impact before a watching world.*

PIPES, DANIEL, writer, editor; b. Boston, Sept. 9, 1949; s. Richard and Irene (Roth) P.; married; three children Student, U. Tunis, Institut Bourguiba des Langues Vivantes, 1970; BA in History Sci., Harvard U., 1971; student, U. Cairo, 1971-72, Al-Azhâr U., Cairo, 1971-72, U. Calif. (Berkeley) Ctr. for Arabic Studies Abroad, 1971, 1972-73; reader, Orientalisches Sem., Freiburg U., 1976; PhD in Mid. Ea. Studies, Harvard U., 1978; hon. degree, Am. Coll. of Switzerland, 1988. Vis. fellow Princeton U., 1977-78; Harper instr., rsch. assoc. U. Chgo., 1978-82, mem. policy planning staff, 1982-83; lectr. history Harvard U., 1983-84; prof. U.S. Naval War Coll., 1984-86; dir. Fgn. Policy Rsch. Inst., Phila., 1986-93, Mid. East Forum, 1994—. Author: Slave Soldiers and Islam, 1981, In the Path of God, 1983, An Arabist's Guide to Egyptian Colloquial, 1983, The Long Shadow, 1988, Greater Syria, 1990, The Rushdie Affair, 1990, Damascus Courts the West, 1991, Syria Beyond the Peace Process, 1996, The Hidden Hand, 1996, Conspiracy, 1997, Militant Islam Reaches America, 2002; co-editor: Friendly Tyrants, 1991; editor: Sandstorm, 1993, Orbis: Jour. World Affairs, 1986-90, Mid. East Quar., 1994-2001. Vice chmn. J. William Fulbright Scholarship Bd., 1992-95; mem.spl. task force on terrorism and tech., Dept. Def. Woodrow Wilson nat. fellow, 1971-72, fellow

NDEA Title VI, 1974-76, Am. Rsch. Ctr. in Egypt, 1979, vis. fellow Heritage Found., 1984, Japan Soc., Nat. Inst. for Rsch. Advancement, Tokyo, 1985, Washington Inst. for Near East Policy, 1986, 91, 94-95; rsch. grantee Israel Inter-Univ., 1979, Smith Richardson Found., 1980-82, 95-96, Schumann Found., 1990-91, U.S. Inst. Peace, 1990-91, Ford Found., 1992-93, Scaife Found., 1995-96, Bradley Found., 1996—. Mem. Coun. on Fgn. Rels. (internat. affairs fellow 1982-83). Office: Middle East Forum 1500 Walnut Street, Suite 1050 Philadelphia PA 19102

PIPES, DORIS PERRY, secondary school educator, consultant; b. Tyrone, N.Y., Dec. 21, 1923; d. Raymond James and Mildred (Wood) Perry; m. Vernon Thomas Pipes, 1951 (div. 1965); 1 child, Vernon Thomas, Jr. AA, Cerritos Coll., 1962; BA, U. Calif., Fullerton, 1964; MA, U. Calif., L.A., 1972. Cert. secondary sch. tchr. Coord. spl. programs, dept. chair program Pioneer High Sch., Whittier, Calif., 1964-65, dir. reading program, coord. tchr. tng., dept. head, 1966-67; instr. grad. sch. Whittier Coll., 1967-71; tchg. cons., classroom materials cons. Scholastic Mag., N.Y.C., 1969-73; resource splst. Calif. High Sch., Whittier, 1973-90, cons. math dept., 1988-90; ret., 1990. Vis. guest lectr., dir. elem. reading clinic Loyola U., L.A., 1967-70; cons. Inglewood High Sch., 1971-72; adminstr. field testing parallel tests in Spanish and English, 1971, 77; reading tchr. Whittier Adult Sch., 1962-66. Contbr. article to jour. Mem. PTA Calif. High Sch., 1964-90 Recipient PTA award, 1989; named Outstanding Secondary Sch. Reading Program Nat. Assn. Secondary Sch. Prins., 1972, Outstanding Secondary Educator of Yr. Outstanding Secondary Educators, 1973. Mem. Internat. Reading Assn. (pres. Rio Hondo coun. 1967), Calif. Tchrs. Assn. (chair), Calif. High Sch. Tchrs. Assn., Alpah Gamma Sigma. Avocations: travel, reading, gardening. Home: 1005 Sugarloaf Blvd Big Bear City CA 92314-9350

PIPES, PAUL RAY, county commissioner; b. Truscott, Tex., Oct. 1, 1928; s. David and Maggie (Brown) Pipes; m. Linda Mullins, Dec. 17, 1961; children: Dana, Tricia. BBA, Sam Houston U., 1956, MEd, 1971. Acct. Pan Am. Petroleum Corp., Thibodaux, La., 1956-61; bus. tchr. Brenham (Tex.) H.S., 1962-90; county commr. Washington County, Brenham, 1991-98. With U.S. Army, 1951-53, Korea. Decorated Def. Disting. Svc. medal. Republican. Methodist. Avocations: gardening, nature study. Home: 2106 Jane Ln Brenham TX 77833-5331

PIPES, RICHARD, historian, educator; b. Cieszyn, Poland, July 11, 1923; came to U.S., 1940, naturalized, 1943; s. Mark and Sophia (Haskelberg) P.; m. Irene Eugenia Roth, Sept. 1, 1946; children— Daniel, Steven. Student, Muskingum (Ohio) Coll., 1940-43; AB, Cornell U., 1945; PhD, Harvard U., 1950; LLD (hon.), Muskingum Coll., 1988; LHD (hon.), Adelphi U., 1991; Doctor honoris causa, U. Silesia, Poland, 1994. Mem. faculty Harvard U., 1950—, prof. history, 1958-75, Frank B. Baird Jr. prof. history, 1975-96, Baird prof. emeritus, 1996-98, Baird Rsch. Prof., 1998-2001, Baird prof. emeritus, 2001—. Assoc. dir. Russian Rsch. Ctr., 1962-64, dir., 1968-73; sr. cons. Stanford Research Inst., 1973-78; expert Russian Constl. Ct., 1992; dir. East European and Soviet affairs NSC, 1981-82. Author: Formation of the Soviet Union, rev. edit., 1964, Karamzin's Memoir on Ancient and Modern Russia, 1959, Social Democracy and the St. Petersburg Labor Movement, 1963, Europe Since 1815, 1970, Struve: Liberal on the Left, 1870-1905, 1970, Russia Under the Old Regime, 1974, Struve: Liberal on the Right, 1905-1944, 1980, U.S.-Soviet Relations in the Era of Detente, 1981, Survival Is Not Enough, 1984, Russia Observed, 1989, The Russian Revolution, 1990, Communism: The Vanished Specter, 1993, Russia Under the Bolshevik Regime, 1994, A Concise History of the Russian Revolution, 1995, Three "Whys" of the Russian Revolution, 1996, Property and Freedom, 1999, Communism: A History, 2001; editor: Russian Intelligentsia, 1961; (with John Fine) Of the Russe Commonwealth (Giles Fletcher), 1966, Revolutionary Russia, 1968, Collected Works in Fifteen Volumes (P.B. Struve), 1970, Soviet Strategy in Europe, 1976, The Unknown Lenin, 1996; mem. editl. bd. Strategic Rev., Orbis, Comparative Strategy, Jour. Strategic Studies, Internat. Jour. Intelligence and Counterintelligence, Continuity, Nuova Storia Contemporanea. Mem. exec. com. Com. on Present Danger, 1977-92; chmn. Govt. Team B to Rev. Intelligence Estimates, 1976; mem. Reagan transition team Dept. State, 1980. Served with USAAF, 1943-46. Guggenheim fellow, 1956, 65, Walter Cabot Channing fellow Harvard U., 1990-91; fellow Am. Coun. Learned Socs., 1965; fellow Ctr. for Advanced Study in Behavioral Scis., Stanford, Calif., 1969-70; lectr. Spring lecture Norwegian Nobel Peace Inst., Oslo, 1993; recipient George Louis Beer prize Am. Historical Assn., 1955, Comdr.'s Cross of Merit, Republic of Poland, 1996; hon. consul Republic of Ga., 1997—; hon. citizen, 1997—. Fellow Am. Acad. Arts and Scis.; mem. Coun. Fgn. Rels., Polish Acad. (fgn. mem.). Home: 17 Berkeley St Cambridge MA 02138-3409 E-mail: rpipes23@aol.com.

PIPES, ROBERT BYRON, b. Shreveport, La., Aug. 14, 1941; s. Walter H. and Mattye Mae (Wilson) P.; m. Ruth Ellen Franz, June 27, 1964; children: Christopher Franz, Mark Robert. BS, La. Poly. Inst., 1964, MS, 1965; MSE, MA, Princeton U., 1969; PhD, U. Tex., 1972. Sr. structures engr. Gen. Dynamics Corp., 1969-72; asst. prof. mech. engrng. Drexel U., 1972-74; assoc. prof. mech. and aerospace engrng. U. Del., 1974-80, prof., 1980-91, also dir. Center Composite Materials, 1978-85, dean Coll. Engrng., 1985-91, provost, v.p. acad. affairs, 1991-93; pres. Rensselaer Polytech. Inst., N.Y., 1993-98; dir. Nat. Ctr. Composites Mfg. Sci. and Engrng., 1985; Goodyear Prof. Polymer Engrng. U. Akron, Ohio, 2001—. Disting. vis. scientist Coll. of William and Mary, 1998—2001; cons. in field; com. mem. NRC. Author: Experimental Mechanics of Fiber Reinforced Composite Materials, 1982, Characterization of Advanced Composite Materials, 1987; series editor 10 vols. Composite Materials; contbr. articles to profl. jours. Mem. ASME (Gustus Larson award 1983), Soc. Mfg. Engrs., Soc. Advancement of Material and Processing Engrng., Nat. Acad. Engrng. (elected 1987), Swedish Acad. Engrng., Am. Soc. Composites, ASTM, Sigma Xi, Tau Beta Pi, Pi Tau Sigma, Omicron Delta Kappa. Methodist. Home: 201 Moodys Run Williamsburg VA 23185-6566 E-mail: rbpipe@wm.edu.

PIPITONE, PHYLLIS L. psychologist, educator, author; b. Chgo. m. Joseph Pipitone, Aug. 28, 1948 (dec.); children: Guy, Daniel, Paul; m. Thomas A. Cox, Jan. 3, 1980. Student, Chgo. Conservatory Music, 1941-44, Peabody Conservatory Music, Balt., 1945, Chgo. Tchrs. Coll., 1946-47, So. Meth. U., 1951-52; MA, U. Akron, 1967; PhD, Kent State U., 1974. With B.S. and H. Advt. Agy., Chgo., 1974; instr. piano and theory Music Acad. Chgo.; psychologist, instr. U. Akron and Kent State U., 1970-79; pvt. practice psychology Akron, 1967—. Lectr. in field in U.S and abroad. With WAC, AUS, 1944-46. NIMH grantee, 1974, HEW Child Devel. fellow, 1974. Mem. APA, Nat. Assn. Sch. Psychologists, Mensa, Coun. Exceptional Children, Am. Hypnosis Soc., Study/Dreams, Am. Soc. Psychical Rsch., Akron Women's City Club, Wadsworth Women's Club, Phi Delta Kappa. Home: 224 Pheasant Run Wadsworth OH 44281-2344

PIPKIN, JAMES HAROLD, JR. lawyer; b. Houston, Jan. 3, 1939; s. James Harold and Zenda Marie (Lewis) P. BA, Princeton U., 1960; JD, Harvard U., 1963; Diploma in Law, Oxford (Eng.) U., 1965. Bar: D.C. 1964, U.S. Supreme Ct. 1969, D.C. Ct. Appeals, 1972. Law ck. to assoc. justice U.S. Supreme Ct., Washington, 1963-64; assoc. Steptoe and Johnson, 1965-70, ptnr., 1971-93; counselor to The Sec. of the Interior U.S. Dept. of the Interior, 1993-98; U.S. spl. negotiator for Pacific Salmon, Dept. of State, 1994-2001; rank of amb. Dept. of State, 1995-96; dir. office policy analysis U.S. Dept. Interior, 1998-2001; fgn. affairs officer U.S. State Dept., 2001—02. Counsel Friends of Music, Smithsonian Inst., Washington, 1984-88; mem. Nat. Arbitration Panel, 1983-94. Author or co-author: The English Country House: A Grand Tour, 1985, The Country House Garden: A Grand Tour, 1987, Places of Tranquility, 1990; contbr. photographs and articles to mags. including House & Garden, Smithsonian mag., The Mag. Antiques, Archtl. Digest. Grand officier Confrérie des Chevaliers du Tastevin, 1989—. Mem. ABA, D.C. Bar Assn., Met. Club. Home: 6109 Davenport Ter Bethesda MD 20817-5827

PIPKIN, MARVIN GRADY, lawyer; b. San Angelo, Tex., Nov. 15, 1949; s. Raymond Grady and Lillie Marie (Smith) P.; m. Dru Cheatham, July 24, 1971; children: Lacey Elizabeth, Matthew Todd. BBA, U. Tex., 1971, JD, 1974. Bar: Tex. 1974, U.S. Dist. Ct. (we. dist.) Tex. 1979, U.S. Ct. Appeals (5th cir.) 1983. Assoc. Green & Kaufman, San Antonio, 1974-79, ptnr., 1979-82, Kendrick & Pipkin, San Antonio, 1982-93, Drought & Pipkin L.L.P., San Antonio, 1993-98, Pipkin, Oliver & Bradley, LLP, San Antonio, 1998—. Mem. coms. on ethics and admissions Tex. Supreme Ct., admissions com.; adv. dir. Trinity Nat. Bank, San Antonio, 1983; bd. dirs. Allied Am. Bank, San Antonio, First Interstate Bank, San Antonio. Bd. dirs. Monte Vista Hist. Assn., San Antonio, 1975-78. Fellow Tex. Bar Found., San Antonio Bar Found.; mem. ABA, Tex. Assn. Def. Counsel, Tex. Bar Assn., San Antonio Bar Assn. Republican. Methodist. Avocations: sports, outdoor activities. Home: 2 Dorchester Pl San Antonio TX 78209-2203 Office: Pipkin Oliver & Bradley LLP 1020 NE 600 P 410 #810 San Antonio TX 78209 E-mail: mpipkin@texas.net.

PIPPEN, SCOTTIE, professional basketball player; b. Hamburg, Ark., Sept. 25, 1965; Student, U. Ctrl. Ark., 1983-87. With Seattle Super Sonics, 1987; guard/forward Chgo. Bulls, 1987-98, Houston Rockets, 1998-99, Portland Trailblazers, 1999—. Player NBA Championship Team, 1991, 92, 93, U.S. Olympic Basketball Team, 1992. Named to All-Star team, 1990, 92-93, NBA All-Defensive First team, 1992, 93, 94, All-Defensive second team, 1991, NBA All-Star Team, 1992-94, NBA All-Star MVP, 1994, All-NBA First Team, 1994; mem. NBA championship team, 1991-93, 96. Office: Portland Trailblazers One Ctr Ct Ste 200 Portland OR 97227*

PIPPENGER, JOHN JUNIOR, fluid power engineer; b. Huron, Ohio, July 26, 1917; s. John Curtis and Maude Olive (Haley) Pippenger; m. Ruth Agnes Gourd, Nov. 4, 1938 (dec. Oct. 2001); children: John Curtis, Louise Marie(dec.). Cert., Walsh Inst. Acct., 1937, Indsl. Tng. Inst., 1948; diploma, Ford Motor Co. Apprentice Sch., 1940. Registered profl. engr., Wis. Chief engr. Hydraulic HiSpeed Co., Detroit, 1942-47; v.p. Double A Products Co., Manchester, Mich., 1947-63; pres. Hydraulic Products, Inc., Sturtevant, Wis., 1963-72; asst. to pres. W.H. Nichols Co., Waltham, Mass., 1972-75, chief engr., 1975-79; mktg. cons. Nippon Oil Pump Co., Tokyo, 1979-82; pvt. practice various orgns., 1982—. Mng. dir. Nat. Conf. on Fluid Power, Ill., 1960-61; chmn. Am. Nat. Stds. Com. B-93, 1961-68. Author: Industrial Hydraulics, 1979, Fluid Power Basics, 1994, Fluid Power Maintenance, 1997, The Hidden Giant, 1992. Treas. Laurrium (Mich.) United Meth. Ch.; editor St. Anne's Preservation, Calumet, 1997. Mem. Fluid Power Soc. (cert. fluid power engr., dir.-at-large, pres. 1962-63), Nat. Fluid Power Assn. (pres. 1956-57, Ann. Achievement award 1965), Rotary (local treas.), Valley of Detroit Consistory (life), Manchester Lodge # 148 (life), Miscowaubik Club (pres. 1995-96). Methodist. Avocation: technical writing. Home: 124 Florida St Laurium MI 49913-2064 E-mail: pippen@pasty.com.

PIPPERT, JOHN MARVIN, sociology educator; b. Ft. Riley, Kans., Oct. 13, 1954; s. Donald Marvin and Doris Elizabeth Pippert; m. Katherine Sue Ellis, Feb. 10, 1996; children: Justin, Nathan, Anna, Eric, Richard, Anne, Cynthia. BS, James Madison U., 1977; MS, Va. Poly. Inst. and State U., 1979, PhD, 1985. Asst. prof. Longwood Coll., Farmville, Va., 1985-87, Roanoke Coll., Salem, 1987-93, assoc. prof., 1993-98; assoc. prof. sociology North Ga. Coll. and State U., Dahlonega, 1998—, dept. head psychology and sociology, 2001—, interim dept. head. Cons. Roanoke (Va.) Times and World News, 1990, Lewis Gale Hosp., Salem, 1990-91, Lavitch and Assocs., Atlanta, 1991, Yankolovich, Clancey Schulman, Salem, 1991; mem. Appalachian Regional Commn. Early Childhood Initiative. Contbr. articles to profl. jours., including Social Sci. Jour., African Am. Ency., Tchg. Sociology, Ency. of Appalachia. Vol. Roanoke Area Ministries, 1987-98, Food Pantry, Dahlonega, 1999—. Grantee NSF, 1995-96, 99, 2000, Roanoke Coll., 1997. Mem. Rural Sociol. Soc., Population Reference Bur., Assn. Christian Tchg. Sociology, So. Sociol. Soc., Ga. Sociol. Assn. Baptist. Avocations: camping, backpacking, fishing, family. Office: North Ga Coll and State U Dept Psychology Sociology Dahlonega GA 30597-0001 E-mail: jmpippert@ngcsu.edu.

PIPPI, MIKEL EUGENE, broadcast executive; b. Portland, Oreg., Apr. 20, 1947; BA, Lewis and Clark Coll., 1969. Exec. dir. Frohman Acad./Am. Musical Theatre Festival, Inc., Carmel, Calif., 1983-91; dir. internat. rels., co-founder Acad. Russian TV, Moscow, 1992-95; dir. spl. projects Turner Internat. Broadcasting, Atlanta and, Russia, 1993-95; global dir., artist recruitment and tng. Walt Disney Feature Animation, Burbank, Calif., 1996-99; exec. dir. Regional Arts and Culture Coun., Portland, Oreg., 1999—2000; dir. creative industries studies Portland (Oreg.) State U., 2000—. Mem. nat. policy bd. Americans for The Arts, Washington, 1999-2001; am. placement agent Russian Ministry of Culture, Moscow, 1987-92; vice chair cultural affairs com. St. Petersburg and LA Sister City Programs. Avocations: travel, metaphysics, internat. rels., event prodn., film and TV prodr. Home: 416 NW 13th Loft 402 Portland OR 97209 Office: Portland State Univ Sch Fine and Performing Arts PO Box 571 Portland OR 97207 Office Fax: (503)-725-3351.

PIPPIN, JOHN JOSEPH, cardiologist; b. Brookline, Mass., Jan. 7, 1950; s. Shirley Ann (Marson) P. AB in Internal History, Harvard U., 1971; MD, U. Mass., 1980. Diplomate Am. Bd. Internal Medicine, Am. Soc. Nuclear Cardiology. Police officer Harvard U., Cambridge, Mass., 1971-76, City of Cambridge, 1976; resident in medicine New Eng. Deaconess Hosp., Boston, 1980-83, chief resident, 1983-84, fellow in cardiology, 1984-86; fellow in nuclear cardiology U. Tex. Southwestern Med. Sch., Dallas, 1986-87; asst. prof. medicine Med. Coll. Va., Richmond, 1987-91; pvt. practice cardiology Okla. Heart Inst., Tulsa, 1991-97; assoc. prof. medicine U. Okla. Health Sci. Ctr., 1991-97; dir. cardiovasc. medicine Cooper Clinic, Dallas, 1998—. Dir. nuc. cardiology Hillcrest Med. Ctr., Tulsa, 1991-97, Cardiovasc. Assessment Ctr., 1991-97, dir. James D. Harvey Rsch. Ctr., 1991-97; chmn. Instl. Rev. Bd. Author 3 monographs; contbr. more than 50 abstracts, 15 articles to profl. jours. Recipient Clinician-Scientist award Am. Heart Assn., 1986-91. Fellow Am. Coll. Cardiology, Am. Soc. Nuclear Cardiology, Soc. Nuclear Medicine. Avocations: running, weightlifting, music, dogs. Office: Cooper Clinic 12200 Preston Rd Dallas TX 75230-2200 E-mail: jjpippin@cooper-clinic.com.

PIPPIN, KATHRYN ANN, state agency administrator; b. Wilmington, Del., July 12, 1947; d. Allen Davis and Mary T. (Thawley) P. BA, U. Del., 1968, MA, 1969, U. N.C., 1972, PhD, 1977. Cert. tchr., Del. Instr. U. Del., Newark, 1969; teaching asst. U. N.C., Chapel Hill, 1972-73; dir. rsch. and info. devel. SOICC-Dept. Labor, Wilmington, 1979-81; adminstrv. asst. to commr. Del. Dept. Correction, Smyrna, 1982-83, rsch. analyst Wilmington, 1983-98, Tunnell & Raysor, Georgetown, Del., 1998—. Chairperson Deljis Bd. Mgrs., Dover, Del., 1983-84; mem. adj. faculty Wesley Coll., Dover, 1985-86, Wilmington Coll., 1987—; exec. dir. Mother and Child Reading Program, New Castle, Del., 1993—. Author: Chesapeake Lore, 1980, Teachers: Guardians of our Hopes and Dreams, 1992, (play) Chains of Glory, 1983, The Devil's Crossroads, 1996; prodr.: (documentary film) A Secret Road North: Harriet Tubman & The Underground Railroad, 1993, Families in Transition: A Smyrna History, 1995, Living in Harmony with Nature, 1995, Wind in the Cane, 1999, Poor Little Butterflies, 2001. Del. Rep. State Conv., Lewes, Del., 1982; active Open Spaces Com., New Castle, 1982-83, Pacem in Terris, Wilmington, 1991—; bd. dirs. St. Patrick's Sr. Ctr., Wilmington, 1982-83; mediator Ctr. for Cmty. Justice, Georgetown, 1999—. Mem. Del. Correctional Assn. (sec. 1988-90, pres. 1990-92, historian 1993-95), Fort Del. Soc. (historian 1983—), Ea. Evaluation Rsch. Soc., Duck Creek Hist. Soc., Leadership Del., Rotary Internat., Phi Beta Kappa. Roman Catholic. Avocations: reading, writing, travel, hiking, photography. Home: 16 Fairway Vlg Lewes DE 19958-9669 Office: Tunnell & Raysor Pine and Race Sts Georgetown DE 19947 E-mail: kpippin88@hotmail.com.

PIPPIN, LINDA SUE, pediatrics nurse, educator; b. Abingdon, Va., Sept. 10, 1954; d. James Robert and Mary (Reedy) P. ADN, Midlands Tech. Coll., 1988; BSN, U. S.C., 1998. Registered pediatric nurse, S.C.; RNC, ANCC. RNC Lexington Med. Ctr., West Columbia, S.C., 1988—, mem. pediat. unit based practice com. SC. Adj. faculty Midlands Tech. Coll., 1990-95; PALS instr. Lexington Med. Ctr., 1994, 2002—, mem. various hosp. coms., 1992-98. Super sibling tchr. Lexington Med. Ctr., 1994, hosp. adventure instr., 1993-97; tchr. Sunday sch. Grace Chapel, West Columbia, 1982—, sponsor Pioneer Club, 1992-97; vol. Spl. Olympics, 1995-2000. Mem. Soc. Pediatric Nurses. Avocations: cross stitching, crocheting.

PIQUÉ, FERNANDO RAFAEL, international art dealer, artist; b. Havana, Cuba, Oct. 24, 1952; came to U.S., l961; s. Arturo Raimundo and Arthemis (Serru) P.; m. Joan Dee Bennett, July 23, 1985 (div. Apr. 1996); l child, Nicole Erin. Grad. high sch., Miami, Fla. Dist. mgr. EHP, Inc., Pompano Beach, Fla., l970-76; internat. account exec. to Africa, Europe, Mid. East, N.Am., South America Am. Beverage Machinery, Inc., Miami, 1976-78; salesman new car dealerships, l978-8l; account exec. Heath and Co., Dallas, l98l-83; founder, CEO Emporium Enterprises, Inc., 1982-97, You Name It-We Frame It, Dallas, 1984—97, Emporium Art and Frames, Dallas, 1986-97, Club Emporium, Dallas, 1988-97, The Enchanted Galleries, Dallas, 1998-2000, Mission Gallery, Dallas, 2000, Piqué Fernando R., 1997—, theunknownartist.com, Dallas, 2000—. Broker and cons. to collectors, galleries and frame shops. Mem. Profl. Picture Framers Assn. (adv. bd. North Tex. chpt. 1989), Profl. Assn. Divers Internat., Nat. Assn. Underwater Instrs. Republican. Roman Catholic. Avocations: movies, art, museums, collectables, painting. the. Office: theunknownartist.com 610 Stone Canyon Dr Valley Ranch TX 75063 E-mail: pique_@hotmail.com., theunknownartist@hotmail.com.

PIQUERO, ALEX R. criminology theory educator; b. Washington, May 6, 1970; s. Jorge Piquero, Nelly Piquero; m. Nicole L. Leeper, May 25, 1997. PhD, U. Md., 1996. Asst. prof. Temple U., Phila., 1996—2000; assoc. prof. Northeastern U., Boston, 2000—01, U. Fla., Gainesville, 2001—. Mem.: Acad. Criminal Justice Scis., Am. Soc. Criminology. Office: U Fla Ctr for Studies in Criminology & Law Gainesville FL 32606 Office Fax: 352-392-5065.

PIRAINO, BETH, medical educator; b. Gary, Ind., Mar. 3, 1949; d. Carl Albert and Dorothy Hans Holley; m. Paul M. Piraino; children: Matthew, Lisa. BS, U. Pitts., 1970; MD, Med. Coll. Pa., 1977. Bd. cert. medicine and nephrology. From asst. prof. to prof. U. Pitts. Sch. Medicine, 1982-95, prof. medicine, 1995—. Office: U Pitts 3504 5th Ave Ste 200 Pittsburgh PA 15213

PIRANI, CONRAD LEVI, pathologist, educator; b. Pisa, Italy, July 29, 1914; came to U.S., 1939, naturalized, 1945; s. Mario Giacomo Levi and Adriana P.; m. Luciana Nahmias, Mar. 12, 1955; children: Barbara, Sylvia, Robert. Diploma, Ginnasio-Liceo Beccaria, 1932; MD, U. Milano, Italy, 1938. Intern Columbus Meml. Hosp., Chgo., 1940-42; resident Michael Reese Hosp., 1942-45; instr. pathology U. Ill., 1945-48, asst. prof., 1948-52, asso. prof., 1952-55, prof., 1955-70; chmn. dept. pathology Michael Reese Hosp., Chgo., 1965-72; prof. pathology Coll. Physicians and Surgeons, Columbia U., N.Y.C., 1972-84, prof. emeritus, 1985—. Cons. Armed Forces Inst. Pathology; dir. Renal Pathology Lab., 1972-84; mem. sci. com. Kidney Found., N.Y., 1973-80; cons. and spl. lectr. Columbia U., 1985-95; mem. pathology study sect. NIH, 1973-78. Contbg. author various books.; assoc. editor Lab. Investigation, 1972-82, Nephron, 1975-92, Clin. Nephrology, 1989-92; contbr. numerous articles to profl. jours. USPHS, NIH grantee. Mem. Am. Assn. Pathologists, AAAS, Internat. Acad. Pathology (counselor 1966-69), Am. Soc. Nephrology (John P. Peters award 1987), Internat. Soc. Nephrology. Home: 235 Walker St Apt 233 Lenox MA 01240-2748 Office: 235 Walker St Apt 233 Lenox MA 01240-2748

PIRCHER, LEO JOSEPH, lawyer, director; b. Berkeley, Calif., Jan. 4, 1933; s. Leo Charles and Christine (Moore) P.; m. Phyllis McConnell, Aug. 4, 1956 (div. Apr. 1981); children: Christopher, David, Eric; m. Nina Silverman, June 14, 1987. BS, U. Calif., Berkeley, 1954, JD, 1957. Bar: Calif. 1958, (N.Y.) 1985, cert.: Calif. Bd. Legal Specialization (cert. specialist taxation law). Assoc. Lawler, Felix & Hall, L.A., 1957-62, ptnr., 1962-65, sr. ptnr., 1965-83, Pircher, Nichols & Meeks, L.A., 1983—. Adj. prof. Loyola U. Law Sch., L.A., 1959—61; corp. sec. Am. Metal Bearing Co., Gardena, Calif., 1975—; dir. Valco Internat., Inc., Orange, Calif.; spkr. various law schs. and bar assns. edn. programs. Author (with others): (novels) Definition and Utility of Leases, 1968. Chmn. pub. fin. and taxation sect. Calif. Town Hall, L.A., 1970—71. Mem.: ABA, Nat. Assn. Real Estate Investment Trusts Inc. (cert. specialist taxation law), L.A. County Bar Assn. (exec. com. comml. law sect.), N.Y. State Bar, Calif. State Bar, Regency (L.A.). Republican. Office: Pircher Nichols & Meeks Ste 1700 1925 Century Park E Los Angeles CA 90067-6022 E-mail: lpircher@pircher.com.

PIRCHNER, HERMAN, JR. foreign policy specialist; b. Cleve., June 26, 1946; s. Herman Sr. and Constance Pirchner; m. Elizabeth Scull Wood. BBA, U. Toledo, 1970. Dir. fin. Chuck Grassley for U.S. Senate, Des Moines, 1979-80; dir. legislation U.S. Senator Roger Jepsen, Washington, 1981-82; pres. Am. Fgn. Policy Coun., 1982—, also bd. dirs. Bd. dirs. Geoinformatic, Inc., Front Royal, Va.; cons. to polit. campaigns Roger Jepsen for U.S. Senate, Iowa, 1982-84, Bob Kasten for U.S. Senate, Wis., 1982-86, George Voinovich for U.S. Senate, Ohio, 1988. Bd. dirs. Herbert Hoover Presdl. Libr. Assn., 1998—. Mem. Univ. Club. Republican. Avocations: pocket billiards, chess, squash. Office: Am Fgn Policy Coun 1521 16th St NW Washington DC 20036-1463 E-mail: herpirch@aol.com.

PIREDDU, NICOLETTA, Italian and comparative literature educator; MA in Comparative Lit., UCLA, 1991, PhD in Comparative Lit., 1996; PhD in English Lit., U. Venice, Italy, 1997. Rsch. fellow Paris (France) Program UCLA, 1993-94; vis. asst. prof. Italian Duke U., Durham, N.C., 1996-97; asst. prof. French and Italian U. Houston, Tex., 1997-98; asst. prof. Italian Georgetown U., Washington, 1998—. Author: Antropologi alla corte della bellezza. Decadenza ed economia simbolica nell'Europa fin de siècle, 2002; contbr. articles to profl. jours. Office: Georgetown U Dept Italian Icc 307 Washington DC 20057-0001 E-mail: pireddun@georgetown.edu.

PIRET, MARGUERITE ALICE, investment banker; b. St. Paul; d. E.L. and Alice P.; children: Andrew, Anne. AB, Harvard U., 1969, MBA, 1974. Comml. loan officer Bank of New Eng. (now Fleet Bank), Boston, 1974-79; mng. dir. Kridel Securities, N.Y.C., 1979-81; pres., founder, dir. Newbury, Piret & Co., Inc., Boston, 1981—. Trustee, chmn. audit com. Pioneer Mutual Funds, Boston; gov. Investment Co. Inst., 1996—; bd. dirs. Organogenesis, Inc., 1995-2002. Vis. com. mem. Art of the Ams. Mus. Fine Arts, Boston, 1982—; mem. nominating com. for candidates for overseer of Harvard U. and for candidates for dir. of Harvard Alumni Assn.; adv. com. on shareholder responsibility Harvard U., 1986-87; trustee Boston Med. Ctr. and predecessor, 1979—, Mass. Hosp. Assn., 1983-86, Boston Ballet Ctr. for Dance Edn., 1989-93. Office: Newbury Piret & Co Inc One Boston Pl Boston MA 02108 E-mail: mpiret@newburypiret.com.

PIRIE, ROBERT BURNS, JR. defense analyst; b. San Diego, Sept. 10, 1933; s. Robert Burns and Gertrude May (Freeman) P.; m. Joan Adams, Dec. 23, 1960; children: John Winthrop, Carl Joseph Emil, Susan Gilman. Student, Princeton U., 1950-51; BS, U.S. Naval Acad., 1955; BA, Magdalen Coll., Oxford U., 1959, MA, 1963. Commd. ensign U.S. Navy, 1955, advanced through grades to comdr., 1969; comdg. officer (U.S.S. Skipjack), 1969-72; dep. asst. dir. Congl. Budget Office, 1975-77; prin. dep. asst. sec. for manpower, res. affairs and logistics Dept. Def., Washington, 1977-79, asst. sec., 1979-81; mgmt. cons., 1981—; def. analyst Ctr. for Naval Analyses, Alexandria, Va., 1981-83; asst. v.p. Inst. for Def. Analyses, 1983-86, v.p., 1986-87; exec. v.p. Essex Corp., 1987, pres., 1987-88; sr. economist Rand Corp., Washington, 1989; dir. strategic studies group U.S. Naval War Coll., 1989-92; v.p. Ctr. Naval Analyses, Alexandria, 1992-94; asst. sec. of Navy for Installations and Environ. USN, Washington, 1994-2000, undersec. of Navy, 2000—01; sr. fellow Ctr. for Naval Analysis, 2001—. Vestryman St. John's Episcopal Ch., Chevy Chase, Md., 1973-76, 81, jr. warden, 1982-84, sr. warden, 1984-87; trustee U.S. Naval Acad. Found., 1980-94. Rhodes scholar, 1956 Mem. U.S. Naval Inst., U.S. Naval Acad. Alumni Assn. (trustee 1967-70) Clubs: Vincent's. E-mail: rpirie@aol.com.

PIRKL, JAMES JOSEPH, industrial designer, educator, writer; b. Nyack, N.Y., Dec. 27, 1930; s. James and Ida Bertha (Gigrich) P.; m. Sarah B. W. Woolsey, June 8, 1974; children: Theo, James, Philip. Cert. advt. design, Pratt Inst., 1951, B of Indsl. Design cum laude, 1958. Design staff Gen. Motors Corp., Warren, Mich., 1958-65, sr. designer, 1961-64, asst. chief designer, 1964-65; instr. indsl. design Center for Creative Studies, Detroit, 1963-65; faculty dept. design Syracuse (N.Y.) U., 1965-92, assoc. prof., 1969-73, prof. indsl. design, 1974-92, prof. emeritus, 1992—, coord. indsl. design program, 1979-84, chmn. dept. design, 1985-91; exec. council chmn. Sch. Art, 1976-78, 80-81; sr. rsch. fellow All-U. Gerontology Ctr., 1990-92. Prin. James J. Pirkl/Design, 1965—; cons. Am. Soc. on Aging, 1995, Arthritis Found., 1993-96, GE Appliances, 1994, ProMatura Group, 1994—, Ford Motor Design Ctr., 1992, Loretto Geriatric Ctr., Pulos Design Assocs., 1972-80, Fed. Prison Industries, 1974, Gen. Electric Co., 1967-70, N.Y. State Council on Arts, 1968-69, Xerox Corp., 1975, Age Wave, Inc., 1993-96, universal kitchen product R.I. Sch. Design, 1996-98; chmn. accreditation council Design Found., 1982-84; interviewed on Nat. Pub. Radio, 1998; invited lectr. All Union Rsch. Inst., Moscow, 1974, The Bauhaus, Dessau, Germany, 1976,

Royal Coll. Art, London, 1993, 95, Netherlands Design Inst., Amsterdam, 1993, 95, Inst. for Gerontech., Eindhoven, 1995, Nat. Coll. Art and Design, Dublin, Ireland, 1995, U. Art and Design, Helsinki, 1995, China Instnl. Design Assn., Taiwan, 1990, Korea Indsl. Design Soc., Taijon, 1992, Internat. Design Internat. Symposium, Tokyo, 2001; project dir. The Transgenerational House, 2000—. Author: Transgenerational Design: Products for an Aging Population, 1994; co-author: Guidelines and Strategies for Designing Transgenerational Products, 1988; co-editor: State of Art and Science of Design, 1971; co-designer: Gen. Motors Futurama Exhbn., N.Y. World's Fair, 1964-65; contbr. articles to profl. jours. including Jour. Am. Soc. Aging, Design Mgmt. Jour., Jour. Indsl. Designers Soc. Am., Bus. Adminstrn. Jour., Design News, Design Perspectives, Indsl. Design. Mem. Everson Mus. Art, 1977-85; chmn. planning commn. Town of Cazenovia, N.Y., 1988-93; mem. senate Syracuse U., 1973-80; mem. adv. bd. SEARS Project, 1989-91; chmn. chancellor's citation com., 1988-92; mem. exhbns. com. Syracuse Cultural Resources Coun., 1992-93; coord. Tylenol/Arthritis Found. Student Design Awards Program, 1993-95. With SeaBees USN, 1951-55. Recipient Gold Indsl. Design Excellence award, Indsl. Designers Soc. Am. and Bus. Week Mag., 1994, Edn. award, Indsl. Designers Soc. Am., 2001. Fellow: Indsl. Designers Soc. Am. (nat. bd. dirs. 1977—81, chmn. Ctrl. N.Y. chpt. 1977—81, v.p. Mid-East region 1978—81, chmn. NASAD liaison com. 1984—88, archives com. 1988—92, U.S. rep., del. Internat. Congress Socs. Indsl. Design 1989, chmn. universal design com. 1991—94, Edn. award 2001); mem.: Author's Guild, Am. Soc. Aging (contbr. articles to jour.), Nat. Ctr. for a Barrier Free Environment (adv. task force 1981), Human Factors Soc. (life), Nat. Assn. Schs. Art and Design (accreditation evaluator 1985—95), The Design Found. (chmn. accreditation coun. 1982). Achievements include patent for 4-way handle. Home: 9739 Village Green Dr NE Albuquerque NM 87111-5854 E-mail: transgen@aol.com., jpirkl@transgenerational.com.

PIRKLE, ESTUS WASHINGTON, minister, writer; b. Vienna, Mar. 12, 1930; s. Grover Washington and Bessie Nora (Jones) P.; m. Annie Catherine Gregory, Aug. 18, 1955; children: Letha Dianne, Gregory Don. BA cum laude, Mercer U., 1951; BD, MRE, Southwestern Bapt. Sem., 1956, ThM, 1958; DD, Covington Theol. Sem., 1982. Ordained to ministry So. Bapt. Conv., 1949. Pastor Locust Grove Bapt. Ch., New Albany, Miss. Spkr. Camp Zion, Myrtle, Miss. Author: Wintertime, 1968, Preachers in Space, 1969, Sermon Outlines Book, 1969, Are Horoscopes All Right?, 1971, I Believe God, 1973, Who Will Build Your House?,1978, The 1611 King James Bible: A Study by Dr. Estus Pirkle, 1994; prodr. religious films: If Footmen Tire You, What Will Horses Do?, 1973, The Burning Hell, 1975, Believer's Heaven, 1977, Percy ray - A Ray for God, 1998. Home and Office: PO Box 80 Myrtle MS 38650-0080

PIRKLE, GEORGE EMORY, television and film actor, director; b. Sept. 3, 1947; s. George Washington and Glanna Adeline (Palmer) P.; m. Karen Leigh Horn, Oct. 20, 1973; 1 child, Charity Caroline. Student, North Ga. Coll., 1965-66; BA in Journalism, U. Ga., 1969, MA, 1971. Radio announcer, sportscaster various radio stations, North Ga. area, 1968-70; TV prodr., dir. Instructional Resources Ctr., Athens, Ga., 1969-70; info. officer Southeastern Signal Sch., U.S. Army, 1971; prodr., dir. DA MoPic Svc. Continental Army Command Network and Signal Corps TV Divsn., 1972-73; pub. info. officer Ga. Dept. Revenue, Atlanta, 1973-78; coord. TV prodn. svcs. So. Co. Svcs., Inc., Birmingham, Ala., 1978-88; exec. v.p. Mgmt. and Human Devel. Assocs., Inc., 1984-86; prodr. Prodn. Works, 1984-88. Actor for various radio and TV commercials, corp. TV programs, radio dramas, stage plays, 1968—; owner Talking Rock Prodns., Cumming, Ga., 1989—; instr. Cliff Osmond Acting Program, 1989-92 Editor monthly newsletter Ga. Revenews, 1973-78; editor, dir. Bankers TV Network, 1990-92; writer, prodr., dir., exec. prodr. more than 500 corp. and pub. svc. TV and film programs; exec. prodr. videotape for Birmingham Film Coun., 1985; prodr., dir. Highway in Crisis, 1986; writer, prodr., dir. campaign film Birmingham Area United Way, 1981, 86, 87; writer, prodr., narrator, 1987 campaign film; anchor This Week in Banking, 1990-92. Mem. Comms. com. Birmingham Area coun. Boy Scouts Am., 1983-85; Master of ceremonies gov.'s vet. awards presentation World Peace Luncheon, Birmingham, 1981, 82, 84; dir. campaign film Pensacola United Way, 1989; bd. dirs. Birmingham Internat. Ednl. Film Festival, 1987-91; chmn. Sadie award com., student video competition dir.; comml. acting instr. elan/Casablancas Modeling/Career Ctr., 1988-92; mem. tech. steering com. Forsyth Bd. Edn., 1995—; dir. City Parks Recreation Bd., 1996—; bd. dirs. United Way of Forsyth County, 1995—, permanent mem. allocations com., 2000—; mem. Forsyth County Bd. Ethics, 2002-; mem. bd. ethics, Forsyth County, 2002-; vol. Am. Cancer Soc. Relay for Life, 1996—. 1st lt. U.S. Army, 1971-73. Recipient So. Superlative Outstanding employee award, So. Co. Svcs., 1986, Battles award 1988, various others. Mem. Internat. TV Assn. (charter pres. Birmingham chpt. 1984-85, pres. pro tem 1984, editor newsletter Freeze Frame), So. Electric Sys. Visual Comms. Subcom. (founding), Ga. Hist. Soc., Hist. Soc. Forsyth County (pres. 1996), Cumming/Forsyth County C. of C., Rotary Club (Paul Harris fellow 2001). Avocations: photography, astronomy, genealogy, hist. rsch., archaeology. E-mail: trvideo@bellsouth.net.

PIRKLE, HUBERT CHAILLÉ, pathologist, educator; b. Indpls., Feb. 18, 1924; s. Hubert Beech and Freda (Chaillé) P.; m. Fern Hart, Nov. 28, 1951 (div. 1978); children: Joan, David Hart; m. Jacquelyn Cooper, Mar. 18, 1978. Student, DePauw U., 1942-45; MD, Ind. U., Indpls., 1949. Resident U. Chgo., 1952-55; asst. prof. pathology U. Louisville, 1955-61, assoc. prof., 1961-70, U. Calif., Irvine, 1970-86, prof., 1986-94, prof. emeritus, 1994—, acting chmn. dept. pathology, 1986-88. Mem. rev. com. NIH, Bethesda, Md., 1969-70. Editor: Hemostasis and Animal Venoms, 1988; editor Thrombosis Rsch., N.Y.C., 1989—; contbr. articles to Sci., Jour. Biol. Chemistry, Nature. Bd. dirs. Laguna Beach (Calif.) Chamber Music Soc., 1981-86, pres. 1982-83. Lt. USN, 1950-52, Korea. NIH spl. rsch. fellow/vis. investigator Karolinska Inst., Stockholm, 1964-65; rsch. grantee NIH, 1957-90; Markle Found. scholar, N.Y.C., 1960-65. Mem. Internat. Soc. on Thrombosis and Haemostasis (subcom. chmn. 1987-92), Am. Soc. Investigative Pathology (chmn. meeting Kinins 1975), Protein Soc., Internat. Fibrinogen Rsch. Soc. Democrat. Achievements include research in structure of desArg fibrinopeptide B, structural and functional properties of thrombin-like venom enzymes, amino terminal sequences of fibrinogen and prothrombin, and association of platelet pulmonary microembolism with unexpected sudden death; characterization of fibrinogen Seattle. Home: 122 Crystal Ave Newport Beach CA 92662-1312 Office: U Calif Med Sci I Dept Pathology Irvine CA 92697-0001 Fax: 949-824-2160. E-mail: hcpirkle@uci.edu.

PIRO, ANTHONY JOHN, radiologist; b. Boston, May 28, 1930; s. John Anthony and Josephine (Pepe) P.; m. Marian Giallombardo, Sept. 5, 1955; children— Anthony John, Janet, Jacquelyn. AB, Boston U., 1952, MD, 1956. Diplomate: Am. Bd. Internal Medicine, Am. Bd. Radiology. Intern Mass. Meml. Hosp., Boston, 1956-57; resident Boston VA Hosp., 1959-62; practice medicine specializing in internal medicine Framingham, Mass., 1962-63; staff physician Boston VA Hosp., 1963-66; sr. asso. Children's Cancer Research Found., 1966-70; radiotherapist Harvard Joint Center for Radiation Therapy, 1970-77; prof. therapeutic radiology, chmn. dept. therapeutic radiology Tufts-New Eng. Med. Center Hosp., 1977-79; radiation oncologist Salem (Mass.) Hosp., 1979-2000. Contbr. articles to profl. jours. Served with USAF, 1957-59. Nat. Cancer Inst. grantee, 1977-79 Fellow ACP, Am. Coll. Radiology; mem. Am. Soc. Clin. Oncologists, Am. Soc. Therapeutic Radiologists, Am. Assn. Cancer Rsch., Phi Beta Kappa, Alpha Omega Alpha. Unitarian Universalist. Home: 15 Vacation Ln Harwich MA 02645-2803 also: North Shore Cancer Ctr 17 Centennial Dr Peabody MA 01960-7923

PIROCH, JOSEPH GREGORY, internist, cardiologist; b. Pitts., Apr. 23, 1936; s. Joseph Anthony and Mary Elizabeth (Matasovsky) P.; m. Sigrid Kathleen Sample, Nov. 26, 1965; children: Deborah Mariel, Joseph Braden, Gregory Lawrence. BA magna cum laude, St. Vincent Coll., Latrobe, Pa., 1958; MD, U. Pitts., 1962. Intern Cleve. Clinic Found., 1962—63, fellow in internal medicine, 1963—65; resident in cardiology Cleve. Univ. Hosps., 1965—66; chief of medicine Spencer Hosp., Meadville, Pa., 1968—70; pvt. practice Meadville and Conneaut Lake, 1969—2001. Lectr. creative imagery. Contbr. articles to profl. publ. Bd. dirs., funding coord. Dance Theatre Erie, Pa., 1983-85. Lt. comdr. USN, 1966-68. Fellow Am. Coll. Chest Physicians, Fellowship of Cath. Scholars, coord. Trad. Latin Mass Apostolate of Erie Cath. Diocese; recipient Am. Heart Assn. (Outstanding Program Achievement award 1969-70, Disting. Svc. medallion 1971-72), Pa. Heart Assn. (v.p. 1973-74), N.W. Pa. Heart Assn. (pres. 1971-72), Franklin Club, Wanango Club. Republican. Roman Catholic. Avocations: gardening, mushroom picking, ethnic cooking, Lieder singing, historic research. Home: PO Box 308 261 Harvey Rd Foxburg PA 16036-0308 Office: Seven Lakeside Sq Conneaut Lake PA 16316

PIRODSKY, DONALD MAX, psychiatrist, educator; b. Freeport, N.Y., Feb. 2, 1945; s. Max and Doris Geilhard (Biedermann) P.; m. Gail Giufre Pallotta, Jan. 4, 1997; children: Laura Anne, Jason Donald. *Great-great-grandfather, August Julius Biedermann, a musician and composer, was profiled in the 1903-1905 edition of Who's Who in America. Mother, Doris Geilhard Biedermann, graduated cum laude with honors in biology from Hofstra University in 1940. Father, Max Pirodsky, retired from the United States Army Reserve as a Major. Wife, Gail Giufre Pirodsky, graduated with honors from Syracuse University with a Master of Social Work degree in 1983. She is an avid gardener and gourmet cook. Daughter, Laura Anne Pirodsky, graduated with honors from the University of Miami with a Master of Business Administration degree in 1995. She is employed by Burdine's and received the employee of the year award in 1996.* BA, Hofstra U., 1966; MD, SUNY, Syracuse, 1970. Diplomate Am. Bd. Psychiatry and Neurology, Nat. Bd. Med. Examiners. Intern Northwestern U. Med. Ctr., Chgo., 1970-71; resident in psychiatry Strong Meml. Hosp., Rochester, N.Y., 1973-74, U. Ariz. Med. Ctr., Tucson, 1974-76; instr. psychiatry SUNY Health Sci. Ctr., Syracuse, 1976-78, attending psychiatrist, 1976-91, asst. prof. psychiatry, 1978-85, mem. exec. com. of med. coll. assembly, 1979-82, clin. assoc. prof., 1985—, adj. attending psychiatrist, 1991—; pvt. practice Syracuse and Fayetteville, N.Y., 1976—; staff psychiatrist, dir. consultation/liaison svc. Syracuse VA Med. Ctr., 1976-87, chmn. pharmacy rev. and therapeutic agts. com., 1980-86. Psychiat. cons. Ariz. Sch. for Deaf and Blind, Tucson, 1975-76, Syracuse Devel. Ctr., 1977—, Rochester Sch. for Deaf, 1978-81; ex-officio mem. Family Counseling Agy., Tucson, 1975-76; adj. attending psychiatrist SUNY Health Sci. Ctr., Syracuse, 1991—. Author: Primer of Clinical Psychopharmacology: A Practical Guide, 1981, (with Jerry S. Cohn) Clinical Primer of Psychopharmacology: A Practical Guide, 2d edit., 1992; contbr. articles to profl. jours., chpts. to med. books. Lt. comdr. USPHS, 1971-73. Fellow Am. Psychiat. Assn. (mem. ctrl. N.Y. dist. br.); mem. Am. Psychosomatic Soc., Am. Assn. Mental Retardation, Med. Soc. State of N.Y., N.Y. State Psychiat. Assn., Onondaga County Med. Soc. Episcopalian. Avocations: sports, collecting baseball cards and other sports memorabilia. Office: 7000 E Genesee St Fayetteville NY 13066-1131 E-mail: dpirods1@twcny.rr.com.

PIROG, JAMES MICHAEL, writer; b. Keiserslaurtern, Germany, Sept. 25, 1953; s. Anthony Andrew and Helen Pirog. BSBA, Chapman U., 1994; MA in Managerial Orgn., U. Phoenix, 1996. Rschr. Bell Aerospace, Ft. Huachuca, Ariz., 1979—80; lectr. U. Ariz., 1991—92; CEO, chief scientist Pi Labs., Hereford, Ariz., 1992—. Author: Before the Storm, 1975, Prelude: Dream Sequence, 1975, Scientific Thoughts and revelations, 1994, Hills in the Mist, 1997, Until the Rising of the Dead, 2002. Mem. Aircraft Owners and Pilots Assn. Avocations: writing, music. Home: 120 N Patagonia # 18 Benson AZ 85602

PIRONTI, LAVONNE DE LAERE, developer, fundraiser; b. L.A., Jan. 11, 1946; d. Emil Joseph and Pearl Mary (Vilmur) De Laere; m. Aldo Pironti, May 21, 1977. BA in Internat. Rels., U. So. Calif., L.A., 1967; MA in Profl. Counseling, Argosy U., 2002. Commd. ensign USN, 1968-91, advanced through grades to comdr., 1979; pers. officer Lemoore (Calif.) Naval Air Sta., 1972-74; human rels. mgmt. specialist Human Resource Mgmt. Detachment, Naples, Italy, 1975-78; comms. staff officer Supreme Hdqrs. Allied Powers Europe, Shape, Belgium, 1979-83; dir. Navy Family Svc. Ctr. Sigonella Naval Air Sta., Sicily, 1983-85; exec. officer Naval Sta. Guam, Apra Harbor, 1985-87; comms. staff officer NATO Comm. and Info. Sys. Agy., Brussels, Belgium, 1987-89; polit. officer for Guam, trust Territories Pacific Islands Comdr. Naval Forces Marianas, Agana, Guam, 1989-91; store mgr. Sandal Tree, Lihue, Hawaii, 1991-92; CEO, exec. dir. YWCA of Kauai, 1992-2000; property mgr. Lihue Ct. Townhouses, 2000—. Chair adv. com. State Child Welfare Svcs., 1998-2000 Mem. Kauai Children's Justice com., Lihue, 1993—; bd. dirs. Hawaii Health and Human Svcs. Alliance, Lihue, 1993-99; chair Kauai County Family Self Sufficiency Program Adv. Bd., Lihue, 1993-2000. Decorated Navy Commendation medal, Meritorious Svc. Medal with 1 star, Def. Meritorious Svc. Medal with 2 stars, others; named Fed. Woman of the Yr. Comdr. Naval Forces Marianas, 1986-87. Roman Catholic. Avocations: racquetball, reading, aquacise.

PIROZZI, MILDRED JEAN, nursing administrator; b. Syracuse, N.Y., Jan. 22, 1943; d. Alfred George and Mildred Erma (Tripp) Farmer; m. Robert T. Pirozzi, Jan. 25, 1969; children: Matthew Robert, Michael Thomas. Diploma, Gen. Hosp. Syracuse, 1963; BS, SUNY, Utica, 1983. RN, N.Y. Med., surg. staff nurse Gen. Hosp. Syracuse, 1963-64; staff nurse ICU U. Rochester Strong Meml. Hosp., N.Y., 1964-65; nurse ICU Upstate Med. Ctr. U. Hosp., Syracuse, 1965-69, rschr. anesthesia Upstate Med. Ctr., 1969-70; nurse recovery room Highland Hosp., Rochester, 1970-71; nurse orthopedic unit Auburn (N.Y.) Meml. Hosp., 1978-80; home dialysis tng. unit nurse SUNY Health Sci. Ctr., Syracuse, 1980-88; with home dialysis tng. unit U. Dialysis Ctr., 1988-91, home program coord., 1991—. Chmn. com. profl. edn. Ctrl. N.Y. chpt. Nat. Kidney Found., Syracuse, 1986-91. Co-author: Hemodialysis Training Manual for Patients and Partners, 1981, CAPD Training Manual for Patients, 1982. Mem. folk ensemble St. Joseph's Ch., 1984—. Recipient Above and Beyond award Nat. Kidney Found., 1991. Mem. Am. Nephrology Nurses Assn. (pub. rels. com. 1988-91, sec., treas., pres. ctrl. N.Y. chpt. 1984-93, 96—, N.E. regional sec. 1987-89, legis. rep. 1991-95). Roman Catholic. Avocations: sewing, crafts, gardening, sports, music. Home: 4699 Howlett Hill Rd Marcellus NY 13108-9762 Office: U Dialysis Ctr/DCI 1127 E Genesee St Syracuse NY 13210-1911

PIROZZOLI, HEATHER JO, food company professional; b. Bridgeport, Conn., June 8, 1971; d. Charles Louis and Josephine Ann Pirozzoli. BS, U. Fla., 1992, MS, 1995. Lic. real estate salesperson, Fla. Instr., interim safety specialist U. Fla., Gainesville, 1993-95; safety and tng. supr. Tyson Foods, Jacksonville, Fla., 1995-97, complex safety mgr. Union City, Tenn., 1997-98, area safety mgr. Springdale, Ark., 1998-2000, team leader, 2000—. Cons. Nat. Ag Safety Database/Conceptual Arts, Gainesville, 1996. Author article and instructional videos. Bd. dirs. ARC, Union City, 1997-98; vol. Habitat for Humanity, Rogers, Ark., 1998-2000; instr. first aid and CPR, Fla., Tenn., Ark., 1994-2000. Workforce Tng. grantee, 1997. Mem. Am. Soc. Safety Engrs., Nat. Inst. for Farm Safety, Alpha Zeta. Avocation: antiques. Office: Tyson Foods PO Box 2020 Springdale AR 72765-2020 E-mail: heather.pirozzoli@tyson.com.

PIRRO, ALFRED ANTHONY, JR. physician; b. Stamford, Conn., May 17, 1961; s. Alfred Anthony Sr. and Frances (Battaglia) P. BA in Natural Scis., The Johns Hopkins U., 1983; MD, U. Conn., 1987. Diplomate in anesthesia and critical care medicine Am. Bd. Anesthesiology. Resident in surgery Hosp. of St. Raphael, New Haven, 1987-90; fellow in neurosurgery Hartford (Conn.) Hosp., 1991-92, resident in anesthesiology, 1992-95, critical care fellow, 1995-97, staff anesthesiologist, 1997-99; emergency medicine physician Windham Hosp., Willamantic, Conn., 1991—; instr. anesthesiology John Dempsey Hosp.-U. Conn. Sch. Medicine, Hartford, 1997-99; sr. hospitalist/intensivist Union Hosp.; founding ptnr. Hosp. Physician Specialists LLC, Elkton, Md.; pres. P&A Distbrs., Inc., Coram, NY. Founding ptnr. Hosp. Physician Specialists; pres. Alpeg Distbn., Inc., Sayville, NY. Advisor Lally for Congress campaign, Mineola, N.Y., 1994. Beneficial-Hodson scholarship Johns Hopkins U., 1979, Pitney Bowes scholarship, 1979. Mem. AMA, Md. State Med. Soc., Cecil County Med. Soc., Soc. Critical Care Medicine, NRA. Republican.

PIRRO, JEANINE FERRIS, lawyer; b. Elmira, N.Y., June 2, 1951; d. Leo and Esther Ferris; m. Albert J. Pirro, Aug. 23, 1975; children: Christi, Alexander. BA, U. Buffalo, 1972; JD, Albany Law Sch., 1975. Bar: N.Y. 1975. Legis. aide N.Y. State Senate, Albany, 1973-75; asst. dist. atty. Westchester County Dist. Atty. Office, White Plains, N.Y., 1975-78, chief Victim Witness Unit, 1978-79, chief domestic violence/child abuse bur., 1978-90, dist. atty., 1994—; county judge Westchester County, 1990-93. Contbr. articles to profl. jours. Chair Gov. Pataki's N.Y. State Commn. on Domestic Violence Fatalities Rev. Bd., 1996; bd. dirs. My Sister's Place, 1990—; bd. vis. Pace U. Sch. Law, 1994— Mem. N.Y. State Dist. Attys. Assn. (pres. 1999-2000), Nat. Mus. Women's History (bd. adv.). Republican. Roman Catholic. Office: Westchester County Dist Atty County Courthouse 111 Dr ML King Jr Blvd White Plains NY 10601-2507

PIRSCH, CAROL MCBRIDE, county official, former state senator, community relations manager; b. Omaha, Dec. 27, 1936; d. Lyle Erwin and Hilfrie Louise (Lebeck) McBride; m. Allen I. Pirsch, Mar. 28, 1954; children: Pennie Elizabeth, Pamela Elaine, Patrice Eileen, Phyllis Erika, Peter Allen, Perry Andrew. Student, U. Miami, Oxford, Ohio, U. Nebr., Omaha. Former mem. data processing staff Omaha Pub. Schs.; former mem. wage practices dept. Western Electric Co., Omaha; former legal sec.; former office mgr. Pirsch Food Brokerage Co., Inc.; former employment supr., mgr. pub. policy U.S. West Comm.; mem. Nebr. Senate, 1979-97; commr. Douglas County, 1997—, chair, 1999. Founder, 1st pres., bd. dirs. Nebr. Coalition for Victims of Crime (Lifetime award 2002); bd. dirs. Centris Fed. Credit Union. Mem. Omaha Douglas County Bldg. Commn., 1997—, sec., 2000—. Recipient Golden Elephant award, Kuhle award Nebr. Coalition for Victims of Crime, 1986, Outstanding Legis. Efforts award YWCA, 1989, Breaking the Rule of Thumb award Nebr. Domestic Violence Sexual Assault Coalition, 1989, Cert. of Appreciation award U.S. Dept. Justice, 1988, Partnership award N.E. Credit Union League, 1995, Wings award LWV Greater Omaha, 1995, N.E. VFW Spl. Recognition award for Exceptional Svc., 1995, Cert. Appreciation, Nebr. Atty. Gen., 1995. Mem. VASA, Nat. Orgn. Victim Assistance (Outstanding Legis. Leadership award 1981), Freedom Found., Tangier Women's Aux., Footprinters Internat. (bd. dirs., sec.), Douglas County Hist. Soc., Nebr. Taxpayers Assn., Keystone Citizen Patrol (Keystoner of the Month award 1987, Queen of Keystone 2002), Audubon Soc., N.W. Cmty. Club, Benson Rep. Women's Club, Bus. and Profl. Rep. Women Club. Office: Legis Chambers 2 Douglas County Civic Ctr Omaha NE 68102 E-mail: cpirsch@aol.com.

PIRSIG, ROBERT MAYNARD, author; b. Mpls., Sept. 6, 1928; s. Maynard Ernest and Harriet Marie (Sjobeck) P.; m. Nancy Ann James, May 10, 1954 (div. Aug. 1978); children— Christopher (dec. Nov. 17, 1979), Theodore; m. Wendy L. Kimball, Dec. 28, 1978; 1 dau., Nell. BA, U. Minn., 1950, MA, 1958. Author: Zen And The Art of Motorcycle Maintenance, 1974, Lila, 1991. Served with AUS, 1946-48. Recipient Award AAAL, 1979; Guggenheim fellow, 1974— Mem. Soc. Tech. Communicators (sec. Minn. chpt. 1970-71, treas. 1971-72) Office: care Bantam Books 1540 Broadway New York NY 10036-4039

PIRTLE, H(AROLD) EDWARD, lawyer; b. Detroit, Apr. 6, 1948; s. Edward Bensen Pirtle and Lorraine Virginia (La Pointe) Schwartz; m. Maxine Mary Stencel, June 10, 1971 (div. May 1981); children: Kimberly, Jeffrey, Michelle; m. Betsy Yvonne Mark, Sept. 1, 1984. AS, Macomb County Cmty. Coll., Warren, Mich., 1977; B in applied sci., Siena Heights Coll., 1983; JD, U. Toldeo, 1990. Bar: Mich. 1990, U.S. Dist. Ct. (ea. dist.) Mich. 1990, U.S. Ct. Appeals (6th cir.) 1997. Assoc. Beaman & Beaman, Jackson, Mich., 1990-91; pvt. practice, H. Edward Pirtle, Atty. at Law, Detroit, 1991-96; assoc. Calligaro & Meyering, PC, Taylor, Mich., 1996-97; mng. mem. H. Edward Pirtle, PLC, Detroit, 1997—. With U.S. Navy, 1967-72. Mem. ABA, Macomb County Bar Assn., Met. Detroit Bar Assn., Am. Mensa (gen. rep. 1984-85, legal counsel Mensa Edn. and Rsch. Found., trustee, found. sec.). Avocations: computers, financial markets. Office: 1805 Ford Bldg 615 Griswold Detroit MI 48226-3989 E-mail: epirtle@aol.com., detroitlaw1@aol.com.

PIRZADA, FAROUK AHMAD, cardiologist, educator; b. Srinagar, Kashmir, India, Aug. 11, 1945; came to U.S., 1968; s. G. Ahmad Pirzada and Sharifa Naquash Bandi; m. Natalie Frances STark, Feb. 22, 1975; 1 child, Ivan. Premed., U. Kashmir, 1961, MBBS, 1966. Diplomate Am. Bd. Cardiovasc. Disease, Am. Bd. Internal Medicine. Intern Malden Hosp., Boston, 1968-69; resident in interal medicine Boston VA Hosp., 1969-70; resident in internal medicine Tufts New Eng. Med. Ctr., Boston, 1970-71; fellow in cardiology Boston City Hosp., 1971-74, dir. heart sta., 1974-78; cardiologist Boston Med. Ctr., 1978—. Mem. staff dept. cardiology Mass. Gen. HOsp., Boston, Lahey Clinic, Burlington, Mass.; clin. prof. Boston U. Sch. Medicine, 1993, mem. admissions com., 1997; founder Pacemaker Bank, Kashmir, 1990—. Contbr. articles to profl. jours. Fellow: ACP, Am. Heart Assn., Am. Coll. Cardiology; mem.: Boston Pacemaker Club (co-founder). Moslem. Avocations: golfing, fishing. Office: 100 Hospital Rd Malden MA 02148-3573

PISANI, KRISTEN LYNN, foreign service officer; b. N.Y.C., June 8, 1971; d. Michael Joseph and Lynn Patricia Pisani. BS, Georgetown U., 1993; MPA, Princeton U., 1998. Corp. fin. legal asst. Sullivan and Cromwell, N.Y.C. and London, 1993-95; tchr. English World Teach, Chachoengsao, Thailand, 1995-96; def. plans officer intern U.S. Mission to NATO, Brussels, 1997; presdl. mgmt. intern Office of Sec. of Def. Dept. Def., Washington; fgn. svc. officer U.S. Dept. State, 2000—. Recipient Sinclair Lang. award Am. Fgn. Svc. Assn., 2001. Mem. Phi Beta Kappa.

PISANI, LAWRENCE FRANK, sociology educator; b. New Haven, Mar. 13, 1921; s. Anthony Vincent and Dora Pisani. BA, Yale U., 1942, PhD, 1951. Instr. sociology U. Mass., Amherst, Mass., 1946-48; asst. prof. sociology SUNY, Binghamton, 1948-55; assoc. prof. sociology Cedar Crest Coll., Allentown, Pa., 1955-61; prof., chair sociology So. Conn. State U., New Haven, 1961-89. Author: The Italian in America, 1955, History of a Boy Scout Camp, 1998; contbr. articles to profl. jours. Chair cath. com. Boy Scouts Am., 1962—, camp com.; dir. New Haven Boys and Girls Club Alumni. Recipient St. George award Boy Scouts Am., 1955, Silver Beaver award 1954, Gold Ring award New Haven Boys and Girls Club Alumni, 1991. Mem. Italian Am. Hist. Soc. (pres. 1991-99), New Haven Gridiron Club, Nat. Italian Am. Found., Am. Italian History Assn. Roman Catholic. Avocation: hiking. Home: 44 Belmont St Hamden CT 06517-2809

PISANKO, HENRY JONATHAN, command and control communications company executive; b. Trenton, N.J., Mar. 14, 1925; s. Isadore Stephen and Victoria (Gula) P.; m. Sophia Emily Zudnak, May 29, 1949 (dec. 1998); children: Barbara, Henry Jonathan, Jr., Michael. B in Naval Sci., U. Notre Dame, 1945, BA, 1947; cert. in Japanese, U. Colo. and Okla. State U., 1945; postgrad. Woodrow Wilson Sch., Princeton U., Columbia U., 1948-50. Constrn. reporter ea. div. F.W. Dodge div. McGraw-Hill, N.Y.C. and Phila., 1950-52; internat. affairs analyst Dept. Def., Washington, 1953-59, ops. officer Pacific Rim, Japan and Hong Kong, 1960-63; sr. intelligence officer Internat. Security Affairs, Dept. Def., Washington, 1964-70; overseas adminstr. diplomatic telecommunications Dept. State, Asia, Africa, 1971-73; spl. advisor Def. Intelligence Coll., Washington, 1974-75; ctr. dep. chief, adminstrn. dir. Intelligence Community, 1976-82; exec. officer USA-EIGO Svcs. Co., Rockville, Md., 1983-87, Princeton, N.J., 1983-87, now bd. dirs.; pres. P.K. Co. Ltd., Bethesda, 1987—, chmn. bd. dirs. emeritus Hong Kong; assoc. Dawson Sci. Corp., 1996—. Bd. dirs. Asia Mgmt. Internat., Princeton; assoc. Bi-Lingual U.S.A. Corp., Bethesda, Md., 1984, Mgmt. Logistics Internat., Arlington, Va., 1983-86; hon. dir. Pacific Rim Enterprises, Hong Kong, 1996. Editor, translator: Yoshio Kodama, 1952; author: (monographs) Items of Inquiry Far East, 1983, Japanese Technology-Ancient Culture, 1985, Augur, 1994 (pamphlet) Fiber Optics Across the Pacific, 1989; editor (handbook) Japanese-English Proprietary Business Lexicon for Command Control Communications Intelligence, 1990-93; author, producer handbook: Telecommunications Operations for Pacific Rim Enterprises, 1996. Sponsor, contbr. Pisanko-Kikan, 1982, Hotel Okura, Japan, 1983, Bungei Shunju, Japan, 1988. Lt. J.G., USN, 1942-46. Trenton Times scholar, 1942; recipient Moe Berg award Pub. Security Investigation Agy.-Japan, Tokyo, 1961, Order of Cariboe, Philippines, 1960-63, Telecommunications award Thai Gen. Staff, Bangkok, 1972, Shimoda Diplomatic award, Japan. Mem. Asian Rsch. Svc., Bus. Devel. Africa, Internat. Inst. Japan, Bus. Execs. for Internat. Security, Internat. Platform Assn., Info. Processing Soc. Japan, Naval Res. Officers Tng. Corps, Unit Alumni Club, Boulder (Colo.) Boys-Japanese Club, Shek-O Club (Hong Kong). Avocations: rare book collecting, cryptology, desert safaris. Office: PK Co Ltd Far East Hdqs Peninsula New Business Ctr Hong Kong Hong Kong *"I seek no other man's shoes. If I've misdirected my priorities, and I'm confident this is not so, I've had a fair time in lost country. There are no regrets."Moe Berg Pr #23.*

PISCANI, KATHLEEN FOLKERTS, clinical psychiatric nurse; b. Bklyn., Sept. 24, 1948; d. Henry A. and Catherine (Melusky) Bassler; m. Heiko Folkerts, 1968 (div. 1980); children: Shaun, Cort; m. Carl L. Piscani, July 22, 1988; children: Debra, Emil. AAS, diploma in nursing, SUNY, Farmingdale, 1968; BSN, SUNY, Stony Brook, 1981; MSEd, L.I. U., 1988. RN, N.Y.; cert. nurse adminstr. and clin. nurse specialist. Head nurse detox, psychiat. South Oaks Hosp., Amityville, N.Y.; head nurse rsch. unit VAMC, Northport, nurse rsch. coord. dept. psychiatry, clin. specialist, team mgr. acute psychiatry Bay Pines, Fla., 1996—, P.O.D. psychiatric triage and ER. Address: 920 Water Lily Ct NE Saint Petersburg FL 33703-3136 E-mail: piscani920@aol.com.

PISCHINGER, FRANZ FELIX, engineer, researcher; b. Waidhofen, Austria, July 18, 1930; s. Franz and Karoline (Bentz) P.; m. Elfriede Pischinger-Goessler, 1957; children: Gerhard, Martin, Stefan, Thomas, Alice. Diploma in Engring., Tech. U., Graz, Austria, 1952, DR in Internal Combustion Engines, 1954, Habilitation degree, 1958, Dr (hon.), 1994. Asst. Tech. U., Graz, 1953-58; head rsch. dept. Inst. Internal Combustion Engines (AVL), 1958-62; leading positions in rsch., devel. Kloeckner-Humboldt-Deutz AG, Cologne, Germany, 1962-70; dir. Inst. Applied Thermodynamics RWTH, Aachen, Germany, 1970-97; pres., CEO FEV Motorentechnik, 1978—; v.p. Deutsche Forschungsgemeinschaft, Bonn-Bad Godesberg, Germany, 1984-90. Contbr. articles to profl. jours. Decorated Ehrenring Sub asupiciis praesidentis republicae (Austria), 1954, Bundesverdienstkreuz 1st class (Germany), 1978; recipient Herbert Akroyd Stuard award Inst. Mech. Engrs., 1962, Carl-Engler-Medaille DGMK, Deutsche Wissenschaftliche Gesellschaft Erdöl, Erdgas Kohle, Hamburg, 1990, Austrian cross of Honor for Sci. and Art First Class, 1998. Fellow Soc. Automotive Engrs. U.S.A.; mem. ASME Internat. (Soichiro Honda medal 2000), NAE (USA) (fgn. assoc.), Verein Deutscher Ingenieure (medal of honor 1993, decoration of honor 1997), Deutsche Gesellschaft Mineralölwissenschaft U. Kohlechemie, Rheinisch-Westfälische Akademie Wissenschaften, Aachen-Frankenburg Club, Rotary. Office: FEV Motorentechnik Neuenhofstrasse 181 52078 Aachen Germany E-mail: pischinger_f@fev.de.

PISCHKE, VAIL W. lawyer, Judge; AB, LLB, JD, U. Notre Dame. Pres., chmn. bd., gen. counsel Met. Bank, Washington; developer, owner Nationally franchised hotels and motels, Shopping Ctr.; judge State of Va.; pvt. practice Falls Church, Va. Commr. chancery Cir. County Fairfax County, vol. judge pro tem; mem. Alcohol Safety Action Project Adv. Com. Va.; presenter, moderator state-wide Va. Jud. Seminars; legal advisor various ch. denominations in No. Va. and Washington; counsel, legal advisor Prison Fellowship; gen. counsel Christian Fellowship Ch. Past pres., v.p., chmn. bd. elders, gen. counsel, chmn. bd. trustees Our Savior Luth. Ch., Arlington, Va.; past pres., v.p., chmn. bd. elders, gen. counsel, trustee St. Paul's Luth. Ch., Falls Church; pres. Luth. Ch., Arlington, Va.; past pres. Fairfax chpt. Am. Cancer Soc., Va. Soc. Crippled Children and Adults; past dir. Salvation Army; past pres. Longfellow H.S. PTA, Fairfax County, Va.; past pres., v.p. McLean Sr. H.S. PTA, Fairfax County; past bd. dirs. Juvenile Detention Commn. No. Va., No. Va. Family Bd., No. Va. YMCA; bd. dirs. Washington United Givers Fund. Recipient Cert. Outstanding Svc., Va. Supreme Ct. Appeals. Mem. Assn. Dist. Ct. Judges in Va. (hon. life), Falls Church Bar Assn. (past pres., v.p., sec.), No. Va. Trial Lawyers Assn. (past parliamentarian, bd. dirs.), Va. Judges Assn. (life), Falls Church Rotary (past pres., v.p.), Nat. PTA (life). Office: 2043 Reynolds St Falls Church VA 22043-1634

PISCHL, ADOLPH JOHN, school administrator; b. East Orange, N.J., Mar. 28, 1920; s. Adolph and Anna (Ellerman) P.; m. Tennessee Wild, Sept. 9, 1947; 1 child, Sallyann. Certificate, Drake Coll., 1940. With Juilliard Sch. of Music, N.Y.C., 1962-86, asst. to concert mgr., 1962-66, dir. pub. relations, 1966-68, concert mgr., 1966-86; adminstr. The Sch. for Strings, 1987-88. With The Dance Mart, N.Y.C., 1950—, pub. dir. Am. Dance Festival, Conn. Coll., 1964-68; mgr. Betty Jones Dances I Dance, 1966-68, Ruth Currier Dance Co., 1966-68, Anna Sokolow Dance Co., 1966-68, Julliard Sch. Bookstore, 1971-86. Founder, editor: Dance Perspectives, 1958-64, Dance Data, 1977; editor: Juilliard News Bull. and Rev. Ann, 1964-85; pub.: Dance Horizons, 1965-86 (Dance mag. award 1999); Contbr. articles to dance mags. Bd. dirs. Dance Notation Bur.; sec. bd. dirs. Walter W. Naumburg Found., Inc. Served with AUS, 1940-46. Home: 878 Warren Pkwy Teaneck NJ 07666-5640

PISCIOTTA, SAMUEL JAMES, small business owner; b. Pueblo, Colo., Dec. 10, 1938; s. Sam Jr. and Eva May (Padula) P.; m. Cynthia Diane Garrett, Aug. 8, 1961; children: Samuel, Pamela, Richard, Michael. BA, Western State Coll., 1967. Pres., mgr. Pueblo (Colo.) Bus. Men's Club, Inc., DBA Capt. Sam's Family Athletic Club, Inc., 1961—. Composer symphonic music. Co-founder, v.p. Pueblo Performing Arts Guild, 1986—; founder, co-organizer Pueblo Office So. Colo. Better Bus. Bur., 1985—, chmn. bd. 1987-88). Recipient Order of Arrow, Boy Scouts Am., 1972, Small Bus. Ethics Merit award Better Bus. Bureau, 1999-2000; named Small Bus. of Yr., Pueblo and Colo. C. of C., 1988. Mem.: Order of Quetzalcoatl (charter camaxtli 1992), Royal Order Scotland, Dante Alighieri Soc., Pueblo Bus. Exch. (co-founder 1982, pres. 1984), Southern Colo. Consistory, Pueblo Jaycees (state bd. dirs. 1973—75), Nat. Swim and Recreation Assn. (pres. 1976—77), Greater Pueblo Sports Assn. and Hall of Fame (co-founder 1972), Kiwanis (bd. dirs. 1986), Shriners (potentate 1992), Royal Order of Jesters (dir. 2001), Masons, Elks, Knight Templar, Tau Kappa Epsilon. Republican. Avocations: golf, swimming, fishing, fast walking, tennis. Home: 27 Pedregal Ln Pueblo CO 81005-2917 Office: Capt Sams Family Athletic Club Inc 1500 W 4th St Pueblo CO 81004-1207 *Personal philosophy: Love is King.*

PISCIOTTA, VIVIAN VIRGINIA, psychotherapist; b. Chgo., Dec. 7, 1929; d. Vito and Mary Lamia; m. Vincent Diago Pisciotta, Apr. 1, 1951; children: E. Christopher, Vittorio, V. Charles, Mary A. Pisciotta Higley, Thomas Sansone. BA in Clin. Psychology, Antioch U., 1974; MSW, George Williams Coll., 1984; postgrad., Erickson Inst. of No. Ill., 1990. Lic. clin. social worker, Ill., Ariz.; diplomate in clin. social work; cert. ind. social worker, Ariz. Short-term therapist Woman Line, Dayton, Ohio, 1976-79; psychotherapist Cicero (Ill.) Family Svcs., 1982-83, Maywood (Ill.) - Proviso Family Svcs., 1983-84, Maple Ave. Med. Ctr., Brookfield, Ill., 1985-88, Met. Med. Clinic, Naperville, 1986-88; allied staff Riveredge Psychiat. Hosp., Forest Park, 1986-97; psychotherapist, pvt. practice Oakbrook, 1988-96; psychotherapist, co-founder Archer Austin Counseling Ctr., Chgo., 1988-89; founder Archer Counseling Ctr., 1989-97; psychotherapist Columbia Hospitals' Columbia Riveredge Hosp., Forest Park, 1997; allied staff Linden Oaks Psychiat. Hosp., Naperville, 1990-97; psychotherapist pvt. practice, 1988-01; founder Archer Ctr., Ariz., 1997-99. Substitute tchr. Chgo. Pub. High Sch., 1981. Author treatment prog., workshops in field. Co-founder Co-op Nursery Sch., Rockford, Ill., 1956; leader Great Books of the Western World series, Piqua, Ohio, 1977, Rockford, 1960-65; leader Girl Scouts U.S., St. Bridget Sch., Rockford, 1968-71. Mem. Assn. Labor-Mgmt. and Cons. on Alcoholism, Soc. Clin. Exptl. Hypnosis, Nat. Assn. Social Workers, Acad. Cert. Social Workers, Nat. Social Work Register (cert.), Antioch Univ. Alumnus Assn. Rockford Coll. Alumnae Orgn. (newsletter contbr. 1972-73), Soc. for Clin. and Exptl. Hypnosis (assoc. mem.), Internat. Soc. for Clin. and Exptl. Hypnosis (assoc. mem.). Republican. Roman Catholic. Avocations: reading, travel, study/research, music, religion. E-mail: arch3456@aol.com.

PISCITELLI, PETER A. lawyer; b. N.Y.C., Apr. 9, 1930; s. Antonio and Mary Domenica Piscitelli; m. Frances Marie Defina, Sept. 12, 1954; 1 child, Anthony. AB, CCNY, 1952; JD, St. John's U., 1958. Bar: N.Y. 1959, U.S. Dist. Ct. (so. and ea. dists.) N.Y. 1969, U.S. Supreme Ct. 1963. Atty. Dwyer & Lawler, Bklyn., 1959-61; chief investigator N.Y.C. Dept. Investigation, 1961-66; counsel to legis. rep. Mayor's Office, N.Y.C. and Albany, 1966-70; legis. rep. N.Y.C. Bd. of Edn., Bklyn., 1970-79, Mayor's Office, N.Y.C., 1978-79, dir. inter-govtl. rels., 1979-82; ptnr. Condello, Ryan & Piscitelli, N.Y.C. and Albany, 1982-90, Bower & Gardner, N.Y.C., 1990-94, Wilson, Elser, Moskowitz, Edelman & Dicker, N.Y.C., 1994—. Comdg. officer N.Y. Naval Militia, 1978-89; chmn. N.Y.C. Water Bd., 1985-88, Tchrs. Retirement Bd., N.Y.C., 1982-85; mem. Com. on Character & Fitness, 1992—. Del. Dem. Nat. Conv., Chgo., 1968; mem. Columbus Citizens Found., 1986—. Lt. USNR, 1952-55. Mem. Columbian Lawyers 1st Dept. Democrat. Roman Catholic. Avocations: reading, traveling, government. Office: Wilson Elser Moskowitz Edelman & Dicker LLP 150 E 42d St New York NY 10017 E-mail: piscitellip@wemed.com.

PISEGNA, JOSEPH ROCCO, gastroenterologist; b. Sharon, Pa., June 20, 1960; s. Rocco J. Pisegna and Rina M. Posada. BS, U. Miami, Coral Gables, Fla., 1982; MD, U. Miami, Fla., 1986. Staff physician W. L.A. VA Med. Ctr., 1996-99; divsn. chief gastroenterology VA Greater L.A. Health Care Sys., 1999—. Comdr. USPHS, 1990-96. Mem. AMA, Am. Gastroent. Assn. (Industry Rsch. Scholar award 1997-99), Am. Coll. Gastroenterology, Am. Soc. Gastrointestin Endoscopy, Baclus Soc. Roman Catholic. Home: 834 26th St Santa Monica CA 90403-2202 Office: VA Greater LA Health Care Sys 11301 Wilshire Blvd Bldg 115 Los Angeles CA 90073-1003 E-mail: jpisegna@ucla.edu.

PISKITEL, JOELLEN BONHAM, musician, educator; b. Paducah, Ky., July 21, 1938; d. Joseph E. and Thelma (Burnworth) Bonham; m. Milton Ray Blood, July 1963 (div. Feb. 1973); m. Leslie Edward Frank Piskitel, Mar. 21, 1975; children: Hiram Bonham, Margaret Ellen. BMusic, U. Mich., 1960, MMusic, 1961. Music instr. Centre Coll. Ky., Danville, 1961-64; choir dir. First Presby. Ch., Berkeley, Calif., 1974-75; pianist Talent Bank of San Francisco Opera, 1970-75; music dir. Opera Cameos, 1970-72; music. cons. Champaign (Ill.) Unit 4 Schs., 1966-69; accompanist coach San Francisco Boys Chorus, 1970-86; music specialist The Bentley Sch., Oakland, Calif., 1986—; freelance accompanist and organist San Francisco, Bay Area. Artistic advisor Young People's Symphony, Berkeley, Calif. Mem. parents' bd. dirs. Head Royce Sch., Oakland, Calif., 1984-87. Recipient award of merit San Francisco Suprs., 1980; Rsch. grantee Centre Coll. Ky., 1963. Mem.: Music Tchrs. Nat. Assn. (cert.), Berkeley Piano Club (bd. dirs., corr. sec. 1973—75), Mu Phi Epsilon (corr. sec. 1978—81, chair nominating com. 2001—02). Avocations: Tai Chi, cooking, travel, reading.

PISTER, KARL STARK, engineering educator; b. Stockton, Calif., June 27, 1925; s. Edwin LeRoy and Mary Kimball (Smith) P.; m. Rita Olsen, Nov. 18, 1950; children: Francis, Therese, Anita, Jacinta, Claire, Kristofer. BS with honors, U. Calif., Berkeley, 1945, MS, 1948; PhD, U. Ill., 1952. Instr. theoretical and applied mechanics U. Ill., 1949-52; faculty U. Calif., Berkeley, 1952-62, prof. engring. scis., 1962-96, Roy W. Carlson prof. engring., 1985-90, dean Coll. Engring., 1980-90, chancellor Santa Cruz, 1991-96, pres., chancellor emeritus, Roy W. Carlson prof. emeritus Berkeley, sr. assoc. to pres. Oakland, 1996-99, v.p. ednl. outreach, 1999-2000. Richard Merton guest prof. U. Stuttgart, W. Ger., 1978; cons. to govt. and industry; bd. dirs. Monterey Bay Aquarium Rsch. Inst.; trustee Monterey Inst. Internat. Studies, Am. U. of Armenia; chmn. bd. Calif. Coun. Sci. and Tech. Contbr. articles to profl. jours.; mem. editl. bd. Computer Methods in Applied Mechanics and Engring, 1972, Jour. Optimization Theory and Applications, 1982, Encyclopedia Phys. Sci. and Tech. With USNR, WWII. Fulbright scholar, Ireland, 1965, West Germany, 1973; recipient Wason Rsch. medal Am. Concrete Inst., 1960, Vincent Bendix Minorities in Engring. award Am. Soc. for Engring. Edn., 1988, Lamme medal, 1993, Alumni Honor award U. Ill. Coll. Engring., 1982, Disting. Engring. Alumnus award U. Calif. Berkeley Coll. Engring., 1992, Berkeley medal, 1996, U. Calif. Presdl. medal, 2000, World Tech. Network award for policy, 2002. Fellow: AAAS, ASME (Applied Mechanics award 1999, Internat. Pres.'s award 2000), Am. Acad. Arts & Sci., Am. Acad. Mechanics, Calif. Acad. Sci. (hon.); mem.: ASCE, NAE, Soc. Engring. Sci. Office: U Calif Dept Civil & Environ Engr Berkeley CA 94720 E-mail: pister@ce.berkeley.edu.

PISTOLAKIS, NICHOLAS STELIOS, advertising executive; b. Athens, Greece, Feb. 15, 1933; s. Stelios Nicholas and Aspasia (Stephano) P.; m. Susan Elizabeth Sell, Dec. 27, 1968; children: Christina, Nicholas Jr. Cert., U. Pa., 1955. Yellow Page rep. Reuben Donnelly Corp., Phila., 1953-54; gen. mgr. West Phila. Newspapers, Inc., 1954-64; Yellow Page rep. Athens, 1964-66; advt. rep. Internat. Herald Tribune, Paris, 1966-69; sales mgr. Dun and Bradstreet Internat., N.Y.C., 1969-79; owner Eclipse Advt. Assocs., Brick, N.J., 1979—. Developer tourism plan for Chania, Greece; mktg. cons., N.J., 1984—; cons. Young Marine Co., Asbury Park, N.J., 1984—, PAHCO Machine, Inc., Trenton, 1985—, Plastiglas Molded Products, Trenton, 1985—; chmn. bd. Alpha Omega Group, Inc. Internat. Pubs. Reps., 1993—. Assoc. pub. U.S. Mktg. Guide, 1978 (achievement award 1980), World Products, 1979 (achievement award 1980). Mem. World Trade Club of N.Y. (bd. dirs. 1979-80), Internat. Advt. Assn., Internat. Indsl. Mktg. Club, Nat. Assn. Pubs. Reps., Sales Exec. Club of N.Y., Am. Hellenic Prog. Assn., Am. Legion, Power Squadron Club, Metedeconk Yacht Club (Brick). Republican. Greek Orthodox. Avocation: yachting. Home: 1100B Argyll Cir Leizure Village E Lakewood NJ 08701 Office: Eclipse Industries Internat Eclipse Advt Assocs PO Box 4210 Brick NJ 08723-1410 Fax: (723) 920-0348.

PISTOLE, THOMAS GORDON, microbiology educator, researcher; b. Detroit, Sept. 17, 1942; s. Leotis Merton Pistole and Lillian Nell (Bosley) Besser; m. Donna Dulcie Straw, Sept. 11, 1965; children: James Alexander, Jennifer Katharine. PhB, Wayne State U., 1964, MS, 1966; PhD, U. Utah, 1969. Postdoctoral fellow U.S. Army, Frederick, Md., 1969-70; research assoc. U. Minn., Mpls., 1970-71; asst. prof. U. N.H., Durham, 1971-77, assoc. prof., 1977-83, prof., 1983—, chmn., 1983-92. Vis. scientist Weizmann Inst., Rehovot, Israel, 1979; vis. prof. U. Edinburgh, Scotland, 1986; faculty fellow Office of V.P. for Acad. Affairs U. N.H., 1996-99. Co-editor: Biomedical Application of the Horseshoe Crab, 1979; mem. editorial bd. Jour. Invertebrate Pathology, 1988-90. NRC fellow, 1969-70, NIH sr. internat. fellow, 1986; grantee NIH, 1975-77, 89-93, 96—, NSF, 1981-84. Mem. Am. Soc. for Microbiology, Am. Assn. Immunologists, Soc. for Leukocyte Biology. Avocations: singing, collecting old sheet music, walking, cooking. Office: U NH Rudman Hall Dept Microbiology Durham NH 03824-2617 E-mail: thomas.pistole@unh.edu.

PISTORIUS, ALVIN WILLIAM, JR. (BILL MILLER), communications educator; b. Carlinville, Ill., Aug. 25, 1923; s. Alvin William and Laura Amelia (Heitmeyer) P.; m. Stella Margaret Stapleton, Oct. 21, 1950; children: Nancy, Cynthia, Mary, William. BS, U. Ill., 1950. Dir. news WTAX Radio, Springfield, Ill., 1950-67; mgr. Capital Info. Bur., 1967-74; prof. journalism U. Ill. Springfield, 1974-93, prof. emeritus, 1993—. Mem., past chair Gov.'s Prayer Breakfast Com., Springfield, 1982-02. With U.S. Army, 1942-45, ETO. Recipient Edward R. Murrow award Radio/TV News Dir. Assn., 1966, Freedom of the Press award Ill. Press Assn., 1998. Mem. Soc. Profl. Journalists (First Amendment award 1982), Ill. News Broadcasters Assn. (pres. 1961-62, Illinoisan of Yr. 1989, Bill Miller Scholarship established 1978, Bill Miller Dist. Svce. award 1998). Roman Catholic. Avocations: tennis, racketball, golf. Home: 5055 W Panther Creek Dr #705 The Woodlands TX 77381-3535 E-mail: wp2500@aol.com.

PI-SUNYER, F. XAVIER, medical educator, medical investigator; b. Barcelona, Spain, Dec. 3, 1933; came to U.S., 1942; s. James and Mercedes (Diaz) Pi-S.; m. Penelope Wheeler; children: Andrea, Olivia, Joanna. BA, Oberlin (Ohio) Coll., 1955; MD, Columbia U., 1959; MPH, Harvard U., 1963. From instr. to asst. prof. Coll. of Physicians & Surgeons, Columbia U., N.Y.C., 1965-76, assoc. prof., 1976-85, prof. clin. medicine, 1985-91; prof. St. Luke's-Roosevelt Hosp. Ctr., 1991—; from asst. to assoc. attending physician St. Luke's Hosp., 1965-75; attending physician St. Luke's-Roosevelt Hosp. Ctr., 1975—, chief div. endocrinology, diabetes and nutrition, 1988—, dir. Obesity Rsch. Ctr., 1988—; dir. Joslin Diabetes Ctr. at St. Luke's Hosp., 1994—, Van Itallie Ctr. for Nutrition and Weight Mgmt., 1994—. Mem. adj. faculty Rockefeller U., 1984—; vis. physician Rockefeller U. Hosp., 1984—; attending physician Presbyn. Hosp., 1985—; sr. investigator N.Y. Heart Assn., 1968-73; Hsien Wu investigator St. Luke's-Roosevelt Hosp., 1982-90; Sigma Xi lectr. Pa. State U., 1989; Howard Heinz vis. prof. Med. Coll. Pa., 1987; Pfizer vis. prof. in diabetes Boston U./Tufts U./Harvard U., 1995, U. Md., 1997; mem. C study sect. NIDDKD, 1988-92, mem. task force on obesity, 1990—, mem. nutrition study sect., 1983-87; v.p. Am. Bd. Nutrition, 1987-88; chmn. task force obesity treatment and prevention Nat. Heart, Lung and Blood Inst., 1995—. Contbr. numerous articles to profl. jours. Fogarty Internat. fellow NIH, 1979-80. Mem. Am. Soc. for Clin. Nutrition (coun. 1987-90, pres. 1989-90), Am. Diabetes Assn. (exec. com. 1990-93, pres. 1992-93), N.Am. Assn. Study Obesity (v.p. 1992-93, pres. 1994-95), N.Y. State Health Rsch. Coun., N.Y. Acad. Medicine (com. on pub. health 1983-96). Avocations: tennis, skiing, hiking, theater. Home: 305 Riverside Dr New York NY 10025-5286 Office: St Luke's-Roosevelt Hosp Ctr Dept Medicine 1111 Amsterdam Ave New York NY 10025-1716

PITA, EDWARD GERALD, engineering educator; b. N.Y.C., Jan. 22, 1925; s. Edward and May Pita; m. Dorothy Greene, Apr. 2, 1955; children: Marianne, Henry. BSME, Purdue U., 1944; MSME, Columbia U., 1956; PhD, U. Md., 1969. Registered profl. engr., N.Y. Chief engr. Panero,Weidlinger and Salvadori, Rome, 1956—62; assoc. prof. Manhattan Coll., Bronx, NY, 1963—70, N.Y.C. Tech. College/CUNY, Bklyn., 1970—. Cons. engr. State City of the Vatican, Rome, 1960—62. Author: (book) Refrigeration Principles and Systems, 1984, Refrigeration, 1984, Air Conditioning Principles and Systems, 2002. Home: 1244 Sussex Rd Teaneck NJ 07666 Office: NYC Tech Coll/CUNY 300 Jay St Brooklyn NY 11201 Personal E-mail: egp@venice.com.

PITASI, JUDY, nurse; b. Oneida, Tenn., June 29, 1950; d. Roy Vernon and Hattie (Turner) Cadle; m. Joseph Anthony Pitasi, June 29, 1984; children: Lauren Leigh, Marc Andrew. Diploma, U. Tenn., 1970; grad., USAF Flight Nurse Course, 1979, USAF Nursing Mgmt. Sch., 1982, Aeromedical Ground Coord. Sch., 1983. Charge nurse Shepherd Spinal Ctr., Atlanta; supr. Met. Hosp. Mem. Nat. Rep. Senatorial com.; mem. Nicholas Gibbs Hist. Soc., High Mus. Art. Maj. USAF, 1974-87. Named Outstanding Jr. Officer Ga., 1984. Mem. Res. Officers Assn. (v.p. 1982, nat. com. 1980-84), Emergency Dept. Nurses Assn., Assn. Mil. Surgeons U.S. Baptist. Republican.

PITCHER, COLETTE BETH, artist; b. Greeley, Colo., June 30, 1960; BA, U. No. Colo., 1981; MBA, U. Long Island, Westpont N.Y., 1986. Owner The Art Dept., Greeley, Colo., 1986—; graphic artist Aurthur Anderson and Co., N.Y.C., 1984; designer Anglesoft Inc. Paperwing Press, White Plains, N.Y.; exec. dir. Greeley Town Ctr. Bus. Assn., 1996-98. Adj. prof. visual art U. No. Colo., 1996—. Exhbn. chair Nat. Greeley Art Mart, 1988-91; chair Arts Picnic, 1988; sec. Ch. and Arts Bd., 1988. Mem. AAUW (v.p. 1992, pres. 1993-94), Greeley Art Assn. (pres. 1990), Greeley C. of C., Madison and Main Gallery (sustaining mem.), Colo. Art Assn. (v.p. 1992), Rotary. Congregationalist. Office: Showcase 1335 8th Ave Greeley CO 80631-4601 E-mail: colette@artbycolette.com.

PITCHER, GRIFFITH FONTAINE, lawyer; b. Balt., Nov. 1, 1937; s. William Henry and Virginia Griffith (Stein) P.; m. Sandra E. Barnett, Dec. 16, 1994; children: Virginia T. Pitcher Ballinger, L. Brooke Pitcher Fick, William T.B., Margaret W. Pitcher Saylors. BA, Johns Hopkins U., 1960; JD, U. Va., 1963. Bar: Ala. 1963, Fla. 1971, Ga. 1996. Assoc. Bradley, Arant, Rose & White, Birmingham, Ala., 1963-71; mem. Van den Berg, Gay & Burke, Orlando, Fla., 1971-76, Mahoney, Hadlow & Adams, Jacksonville, 1976-82; ptnr. Squire, Sanders & Dempsey, Miami, 1982-93; of counsel Mershon, Sawyer, Johnston, Dunwoody & Cole, 1994-95, Chamberlain, Hrdlicka, White, Williams & Martin, Atlanta, 1996—2002, Seyfarth Shaw, 2002—. Contbr. articles to profl. jours. Vice chmn. Winter Park (Fla.) Planning & Zoning Bd., 1974-75. With Army N.G., 1961-64. Fellow: Am. Coll. Bond Counsel (founding fellow, dir.); mem.: ABA, Ala. State Bar Assn., Ga. State Bar, Fla. Bar Assn., Nat. Assn. Bond Lawyers, Order of Coif, Delta Phi. Republican.

PITCHER, HELEN IONE, advertising director; b. Colorado Springs, Colo., Aug. 6, 1931; d. William Forest Medlock and Frankie La Vone (Hamilton) Tweed; m. Richard Edwin Pitcher, Sept. 16, 1949; children: Dushka Myers, Suzanne, Marc. Student, U. Colo., 1962-64, Ariz. State U., 1966, Maricopa Tech. Coll., 1967, Scottsdale C.C., 1979-81. Design draftsman Sundstrand Aviation, Denver, 1962-65; tech. illustrator Sperry, Phoenix, 1966-68; art dir. Integrated Circuit Engring., Scottsdale, Ariz., 1968-71, dir. advt., 1981-92; advt. artist Motorola Inc., Phoenix, 1971-74; pres. Pitcher Tech. Pubs., Scottsdale, 1974-81; retired, 1996. Profl. advisor Paradise Valley Sch. Dist., Phoenix, 1984—; mem. bd. advisors graphic arts dept. Ariz. State U., Tempe. Mem. Nat. Audio Visual Assn., Bus. Profl. Advt. Assn. (treas. 1982-86), Direct Mktg. Club. Democrat. Mem. Ch. Christ. Avocations: raising and showing Arabian horses and Hackney ponies. Home: 13681 N 88th Pl Scottsdale AZ 85260-7655

PITCHER-MAURIÉR, KELLY JO, interior designer; b. Mpls., Apr. 2, 1959; d. Donald Eugene and Bettye Pitcher; m. Timothy Laurence Mauriér, Apr. 20, 1985. BS in Environ. and Interior Design, Colo. State U., 1981. Asst. designer Urban Design Group, Denver, 1982-83; designer Corona Pacific, Irvine, Calif., 1983-84; project designer Reel Grobman and Assocs., Santa Ana, 1984-86; project designer, planner Hill Pinckert Architects, Irvine, 1986—. Mem. Am. Soc. Interior Designers, Inst. Bus. Designers.

PITCHUMONI, CAPECOMORIN SANKAR, gastroenterologist, educator; b. Madura, India, Jan. 20, 1938; came to U.S., 1967; s. Sankara and Jaya (Lekshmi) Iyer; m. Prema Iyer, Nov. 11, 1964; children: Sheila, Shoba, Suresh. Student, St. Xavier Coll., India, 1953-55; MB BS, Trivandrum Med. Coll., India, 1959, MD, 1965. Intern Med. Coll., Trivandurm, India, 1961-63; resident in gastroenterology Yale U., 1967-69; N.Y. Med. Coll., 1969-72; practice medicine specializing in gastroenterology N.Y.C., 1972—; asst. prof. medicine Kottayam Med. Coll., India, 1967, N.Y. Med. Coll., 1972-75, assoc. prof., 1975-80, prof. clin. medicine, 1980-85, prof. medicine, 1985—; assoc. prof. preventive and social medicine, 1975-86, prof. community and preventive medicine, 1986—; chief sect. gastroenterology Our Lady of Mercy Med. Ctr., N.Y., 1980—, assoc. dir. medicine N.Y.C., 1985—, program dir. internal medicine, 1987—; dir. medicine, 1992. Contbg. author med. textbooks; contbr. articles to profl. jours. Recipient Om Prakash award Indian Soc. Gastroenterology, 1976, Outstanding Scientist of Yr. award MV Spltys., Madras, 1994, Oration award Thangavelu Endowment, 1994. Master Am. Coll. Gastroenterology (gov. 1996-2000); fellow Royal Coll. Physicians and Surgeons Can., Am. Coll. Nutrition; mem. Assn. Physicians India, Am. Coll. Nuitrition, Am. Gastroent. Assn., India Soc. Gastroenterology (life), Am. Inst. Nutrition, Gastrointestinal Endoscopy, Am. Soc. for Clin. Nutrition. Hindu. Home: 178 Fairmount Ave Glen Rock NJ 07452-3014 Office: Our Lady of Mercy Med Ctr 600 E 233rd St Bronx NY 10466-2697

PITCOCK, JAMES ALLISON, retired pathologist; b. Little Rock, Sept. 13, 1929; s. Radford Bolling and Anne (Whitelaw) P.; m. Cynthia Jean Dehaven, June 18, 1954; children: Allison P. Mays, James Dehaven. BS, MIT, 1951; MD, Washington U., 1955. Diplomate Am. Bd. Pathology. Intern Vanderbilt U., Nashville, 1955-56; resident Barnes Hosp., St. Louis, 1956-59, 61-62; asst. pathologist St. Vincents Hosp., Little Rock, 1963, Bapt. Meml. Hosp., Memphis, 1964-75, asst. dir. labs., 1975-87, dir. labs., 1987-95; ret. Vol. faculty U. Tenn. Med. Sch., Memphis, 1965-96, acting chair pathology, 1986-89; com. chair, mem. Am. Heart Assn., Memphis, 1976-84, exec. com., 1983-87, pres., 1985-86. Contbr. chpts. to books and articles to profl. jours. Capt. USAF, 1959-61. Mem. Alpha Omega Alpha, Sigma Xi. Episcopalian. Achievements include experimental and scholarly work in experimental hypertensi n and surgical pathology. E-mail: cpitcock@netten.net.

PITELKA, LOUIS FRANK, ecologist; b. Berkeley, Calif., Mar. 28, 1947; s. Frank Alois and Dorothy (Riggs) P.; m. Sandra Lea Sanders, Sept. 20, 1969; children: Erik Loren, Jessica Kristine. BS in Zoology, U. Calif., Davis, 1969; PhD in Biol. Scis., Stanford U., 1974. Asst. prof. biology Bates Coll., Lewiston, Maine, 1974-81, assoc. prof., 1981-84, chmn. dept. biology, 1982-84; program dir. NSF Population Biology & Physiol. Ecology Program, Washington, 1983-84; project mgr. Electric Power Research Inst., Palo Alto, Calif., 1984-96; prof., dir. Appalachian Lab., U. Md. Ctr. for Environ. Sci., Frostburg, Md., 1996—. Mem. various coms. NSF, DOE, Internat. Geosphere-Biosphere Program, other programs. Editor 2 books; mem. editorial bd. Ecol. Applications, 1991-95, editor-in-chief, 1995-2001; mem. editl. bd. Oecologia, 1997—; contbr. numerous articles to profl. jours. Predoctoral fellow NSF, 1969-72; research grantee NSF, 1980-85. Fellow AAAS; mem. Am. Inst. Biol. Scis. (bd. dirs. 1997-2000), Brit. Ecol. Soc., Am. Geophys. Union, Ecol. Soc. Am. (program chair 1989-90, treas. 1990-96), Bot. Soc. Am. (chmn., ecol. sect. 1982-83), Phi Kappa Phi, Phi Beta Kappa.

PITERNICK, ANNE BREARLEY, librarian, educator; b. Blackburn, Eng., Oct. 13, 1926; emigrated to Can., 1956, naturalized, 1965; d. Walter and Ellen (Harris) Clayton; m. Neil Brearley, 1956 (div. 1971); m. George Piternick, May 6, 1971. BA, U. Manchester (Eng.), 1948, F.L.A., 1983. Mem. library staff U. B.C., Vancouver, Can., 1956-66, head sci. div., 1960-61, head social scis. div., 1965-66, prof. Sch. Library, Archival and Info. Studies, 1966-91, prof. emerita, 1991—, assoc. dean Faculty of Arts, 1985-90. Mem. Nat. Com. Bibliog. Svcs. Can., 1975-80, chmn. com. on bibliography and info. services for social scis. and humanities, 1981-84; mem. adv. acad. panel Social Scis. and Humanities Research Council, 1981-84; mem. adv. bd. Nat. Libr. Can., 1978-84; mem. Nat. Adv. Com. Culture Stats., 1985-90; organizer Confs. on Can. Bibliography, 1974, 81; pres. Can. Assn. Spl. Librs. Info. Svcs., 1969-70, Can. Libr. Assn., 1976-77; bd. dirs. profs. emeriti, U.B.C., 1999—. Author articles on electronic info. svcs. and scholarly communication. Bd. dirs. Vancouver Friends of Chamber Music, 2001—. Recipient Queen's Silver Jubilee medal, 1977, award for Spl. Librarianship Can. Assn. Spl. Librs. and Info. Svcs., 1987, 75th Anniversary medal U.B.C., 1990, Can. 125 medal, 1993. Fellow Council on Library Resources (1980). Home: 1849 W 63rd Ave Vancouver BC Canada V6P 2H9 E-mail: annebp@interchange.ubc.ca.

PITINO, RICHARD, collegiate basketball coach, former professional basketball coach; b. N.Y.C., Sept. 18, 1952; Student, U. Mass. Asst. coach U. Hawaii, 1975-76, Syracuse U., 1976-78; coach Boston U., 1978-83; asst. coach N.Y. Knicks, 1983-85, coach, 1987-89, Providence U., 1986-87; basketball coach U. Ky., Lexington, 1989-97; head coach Boston Celtics, 1997—2001, Univ. of Louisville, 2001—. Author: (with Dick Weiss) Full Court Pressure: A Year in Kentucky Basketball, 1992. Named Coll. Coach of Yr., Sporting News, 1987. Office: Univ of Louisville Louisville KY 40292*

PITKIN, EDWARD THADDEUS, aerospace engineer, consultant; b. Putnam, Conn., Dec. 14, 1930; s. Thaddeus Eugene and Florence Mabel (Brown) P.; m. Clara Lucy Modliszewski, June 13, 1953; children— Gayle Linda, Dale Edward. BS, U. Conn., 1952; MS (Guggenheim fellow), Princeton, 1953; PhD (NASA fellow), UCLA, 1964. Project engr. Astro Div. Marquardt Co., Los Angeles, 1956-59, mgr. space propulsion, 1959-61; engring. cons. Los Angeles, 1961-64; asso. prof. aerospace engring. U. Conn., Storrs, 1964-70, prof. mech. and aerospace engring., 1970-90, prof. emeritus, 1990—; cons. engr., 1990—; asst. dean U. Conn., Storrs, 1977-87. Contbr. articles to tech. publs. Served as lt. USAF, 1953-55. Asso. fellow AIAA Mem. Solar Energy Soc. Home: 115 Brookside Ln Mansfield Center CT 06250-1001 Office: U Conn Dept Mech Engring U-139 191 Auditorium Rd Storrs Mansfield CT 06269-3139

PITKIN, ROY MACBETH, obstetrician, educator, retired; b. Anthon, Iowa, May 24, 1934; s. Roy and Pauline Allie (McBeath) Pitkin; m. Marcia Alice Jenkins, Aug. 17, 1957; children: Barbara, Robert Macbeth, Kathryn, William Charles. BA with highest distinction, U. Iowa, 1956, MD, 1959. Diplomate Am. Bd. Ob-Gyn. Intern King County Hosp., Seattle, 1959—60; resident in ob-gyn U. Iowa Hosps. and Clinics, Iowa City, 1960—63; asst. prof. ob-gyn U. Ill., 1965—68; assoc. prof. ob-gyn U. Iowa, Iowa City, 1968—72, prof., 1972—87, head dept. ob-gyn, 1977—87; prof. UCLA, 1987—97, head dept. ob-gyn., 1987—95, prof. emeritus, 1997—. Mem. residency rev. com. ob-gyn., 1981—87; chmn., 1985—87. Editor: Obstetrics and Gynecology, 1985—2001; contbr. Served to lt. comdr. M.C. USNR, 1963—65. Recipient NIH career awardee, 1972—77. Fellow: Royal Ob-Gyn. (ad eundem); mem.: Inst. Medicine, NAS, Soc. Perinatal Obstetricians (pres. 1978—79), Soc. Gynecol. Investigation (pres. 1985—86), German Soc. Gyn-Ob. (hon.), Ctrl. Asn. Ob-Gyn., Am. Ob-Gyn. Soc. (pres. 1994—95), Am. Coll. Ob-Gyns., AMA (Goldberger award in clin. nutrition 1982). Presbyterian. Home: 78900 Rancho La Quinta Dr La Quinta CA 92253-6252 E-mail: rpitkin@greenjournal.org.

PITLIK, CHRISTOPHER J. music educator; b. Evergreen Park, Ill., Dec. 21, 1966; s. Edward J. and Elaine J. Pitlik; m. Dana L. Pitlik, June 20, 1992; children: Kendal Payton, Cory James. BA, Western Ill. U., Macomb, IL, 1989; MA, Ill. State U., Normal, IL, 1991; Cert. Advanced Study, Lewis U., Romeoville, IL, 1999. Music educator Alan B. Shepard H.S., Palos Heights, Ill., 1991—. Recipient Disting. Allumni Award, Alan B. Shepard H.S., 2002. Mem.: Nat. Educators Assn., Ill. Music Educators Assn., Dist. 218 Credit Union Bd. (v.p. 2002).

PITMAN, LAVERN FRANK, retired librarian; b. Poynette, Wis., June 8, 1943; s. George and Carolyn (Hutchinson) P.; m. Rosa Papist, Sept. 8, 1973 (dec. Oct. 1996); 1 child, Christina. BA, Wis. State U., 1965; MSLS, Catholic U. Am., 1973; MA, Frostburg State U., 1985. Cataloger copyright office Libr. Congress, Washington, 1966-71, Spanish/Italian cataloger shared divsn., 1971-79; libr. Frostburg (Md.) State U., 1980-98. Author: The Family of John and Deborah Flick Meyers, 1989, The Robertsons: A Norwegian Family in America, 1993; co-author: A Century of Commitment: Frostburg State University, 1997; editor: Civil War Diary of Jesse Meyers, Co. I, 23d Regiment, Wisconsin Volumbeer Infantry, 2002. Historic Interpreter, Mt. Vernon, 1999—; curator Wayside Found., 1999-2000; libr. Md. Bur. Mines, 2000—. Mem. Geneal. Soc. Allegany County, Geneal. Soc. Wis., State Hist. Soc. Wis., Frostburg Mus. Assn., Sons of Norway, Vesterheim Norwegian-Am. Mus., Clan Rose Soc. Am.

PITMAN, SHARON GAIL, middle school counselor; b. Dayton, Ohio, June 13, 1946; d. Finley Andrew and Lena Kay (Wells) Jennings; m. Benjamin Pitman III, Jan. 19, 1980; children: Elizabeth Ann (dec.), Emily; stepchildren: Scott, Todd. BS in Edn., Miami U., Oxford, Ohio, 1968, MEd in Edn., 1970; sch. counseling cert., Ga. State U., 1979, MEd in Counseling, 1981, EdS in Guidance and Counseling, 1989. Tchr. pub. schs., Hamilton, Ohio, 1968-73, Gwinnett County, Ga., 1973-80; sch. counselor Buford (Ga.) Mid. Sch., 1981-89, Duluth (Ga.) Mid. Sch., 1989-96, Lanier (Ga.) Mid. Sch., 1998—. Conductor workshops in field. Mem. Am. Sch. Counseling Assn. (Nat. Mid. Sch. Counselor of Yr. 1989), Ga. Sch. Counselors Assn. (Mid. Sch. Counselor of Yr. 1988).

PITNEY, JOHN JOSEPH, JR. political science educator; b. Saratoga Springs, N.Y., June 18, 1955; s. John Joseph and Mary Katherine (Furey) P.; m. Lisa Michelle Minshew, May 27, 1989. BA, Union Coll., Schenectady, N.Y., 1977; MA, Yale U., 1978, MPhil, 1981, PhD, 1985. Legis. asst. N.Y. State Senate, Albany, 1978-80; Congl. fellow Am. Polit. Sci. Assn., Washington, 1983-84; sr. domestic policy analyst U.S. Ho. of Reps., 1984-86; dep. rsch. dir. Rep. Nat. Com., 1989-91; asst. prof. polit. sci. Claremont (Calif.) McKenna Coll., Calif., 1986-94, assoc. prof., 1994-2001, prof., 2001—. Co-author: Congress' Permanent Minority?, 1994; author: The Art of Political Warfare, 2000; contbr. articles to profl. jours. Dep. editor Rep. Nat. Conv. platform, Houston, 1992; rsch. advisor George Bush for Pres., Washington, 1988. Recipient rsch. grant Gould Humanities Ctr., Claremont, 1992, grad. fellowship Nat. Sci. Found., 1977, Danforth Found., St. Louis, 1977. Mem. Am. Polit. Sci. Assn. (rsch. grant 1987), Western Polit. Sci. Assn., Nat. Assn. Scholars, Phi Beta Kappa (chpt. pres. 2002—), Pi Sigma Alpha. Republican. Office: Claremont McKenna Coll Govt Dept 850 Columbia Ave Claremont CA 91711-3901 E-mail: Jpitney@mckenna.edu.

PITOFSKY, ROBERT, federal agency administrator, law educator; b. Paterson, N.J., Dec. 27, 1929; s. Morris and Sadye (Katz) P.; m. Sally Levy, June 4, 1961; children: Alexander, David, Elizabeth. BA, NYU, 1951; LLB, Columbia U., 1954; LLD (hon.), Georgetown U., 1989. Bar: N.Y. 1956, D.C. 1973, U.S. Supreme Ct. 1972. Atty. Dept. Justice, Washington, 1956-57; assoc. Dewey, Ballantine, Bushby, Palmer & Wood, N.Y.C., 1957-64; prof. law NYU, 1964-70; dir. Bur. Consumer Protection, FTC, 1970-73; prof. law Georgetown U. Law Ctr., Washington, 1973-83, 89-01, dean, exec. v.p. law ctr. affairs, 1983-89; commr. FTC, 1978-81, chmn., 1995-2001; of counsel Arnold & Porter, 1973-78, 81-95, 01—. Guest scholar Brookings Instn., Washington, 1989-90; vis. prof. law Harvard Law Sch., 1975-76; faculty mem. Salzburg (Austria) Seminar in Am. Studies, 1975; chmn. Def. Sci. Bd. task force on antitrust aspects of def. industry downsizing, 1994. Co-author: Cases on Antitrust Law, 1967, Cases on Trade Regulation, 4th edit. 1997; co-editor: Revitalizing Antitrust in Its Second Century, 1991; contbr. articles on consumer protection and antitrust to profl. publs. Served with U.S. Army, 1954-56. Recipient Disting. Service award FTC, 1972; named One of Ten Outstanding Mid-Career Law Profs. Time Mag., 1977. Mem. ABA (coun. antitrust sect. 1986-89), Am. Acad. Arts and Scis., Am. Law Inst., Assn. Am. Law Schs., Columbia U. Ctr. for Law Econ. Studies (adv. bd. 1975-95). Democrat. Jewish. Home: 3809 Blackthorn St Chevy Chase MD 20815-4905 Business E-Mail: Robert_Pitofsky@APorter.com.

PITONIAK, SCOTT MICHAEL, sportswriter; b. Rome, Apr. 10, 1955; s. Andrew Edward and Edna (Holloway) Pitoniak; m. Susan Ingison, June 9, 1984; children: Amy Leigh, Christopher Drew. BS in Pub. Comm. magna cum laude, Syracuse U., 1977. Baseball writer Evening Times, Little Falls, N.Y., 1977; sportswriter Daily Sentinel, Rome, 1977; sportswriter, columnist Observer-Dispatch, Utica, 1978-84; pro football writer Dem. & Chronicle, Rochester, 1985-90, sports projects writer, 1990—. Voter Heisman Trophy Award, 1981—; corr. Gannett News Svc., 1982—, Sporting News, 1982—; journalism prof. St. John Fisher Coll., 1995—. Author: (book) The Buffalo Bills Official Trivia Book, 1989, 1991; co-author: Silver Seasons: The Story of the Rochester Red Wings, 1996, Playing Write Field, 1997; contbr. articles to mags., newspapers, news svcs. including; co-host (TV series) Time Warner Comm., 1994—96. Vol. Alzheimer's Assn., Rochester, 1991—. Named one of Am.'s Top 10 Sports Columnist, APSE, 2000, torchbearer, Winter Olympics, 2002; named to Rochester Sports Walk of Fame, 1999, Syracuse U. Journalism Hall of Fame, 2000; recipient Disting. Health Journalism award Gold medal 1st Pl. newspaper divsn., 1991, 1st Pl. sports, N.Y. State AP Writing Contest, 1995, 2d Pl. features, 1993, 2d Pl. sports, 1991, 1997, 2d Pl. columns, 2001, Best of Gannett award, 1996—98, others; scholar Regents. Mem.: Basketball Writers Am., Coll. Football Writers Assn. Am. (bd. dirs.), Profl. Football Writers Am. (2d Pl. columns, 1st Pl. enterprise reporting 1999, 1st Pl. columns 2000), Phi Kappa Phi, Kappa Tau Alpha. Roman Catholic. Avocations: distance bicycle riding, reading, softball, sports memorabilia collecting. Home: 35 Western Pine Dr Rochester NY 14616-5014 Office: Gannett Rochester Newspapers 55 Exchange Blvd Rochester NY 14614-2001 E-mail: spitoniak@democratandchronicle.com.

PITONZO, BETH JESSIE, academic administrator, microbiologist; b. Hollywood, Calif., May 11, 1964; d. James Newton and Raquel Thormodsgard; m. David Gerard Pitonzo, April 8, 1989; children: Michael, Jesse. BS, U. Nev., 1988, PhD in Biol. Scis., 1996. Cert. med. technologist Am. Soc. Clin. Pathologists; cert. clin. lab. scientist Nat. Cert. Agy.; med. technologist Calif. Divsn. Health Svcs.; cert. clin. lab. technologist Nev. Divsn. Health Svcs. Dir., instr. Med. Lab. Technician Program C.C. Southern Nev., Las Vegas, 1996-2000, assoc. dean divsn. health scis., 2000—01; assoc. v.p. instrn. Mt. Hood C.C., Gresham, Oreg., 2001—. Adj. instr. dept. clin. lab. scis. U. Nev., Las Vegas, 1992-93, adj. instr. dept. biol. scis. U. Nev., Las Vegas, 1994-95; cons. Renal Diagnostic Labs., Las Vegas, 1997; accreditation evaluator N.W. Assn. of Schs. and Colls. and Univs., 2001-. Contbr. articles to profl. jours. Coll. rep. State Nev. Battelle High Tech. Com. Office Lt. Gov., Las Vegas, 2000-01; ex-officio mem. State of Nev. Sch. to Work Coun., Las Vegas, 2000-01; coll. rep. Nev. Health Ptnrs., Las Vegas, 2000-01; mem. tchg. scholar partnerships nat. mentor team Am. Assn. C.C./NSF, 2001-. Recipient Clin.Lab. Sci. Curriculum grant Nev. Sch. to Career Fund, 1998, Advanced Tech. Edn. Mentoring grant Am. Assn. C.C./NSF, 1999-2001, Biotechnology Curriculum grant Nev. Sch. to Career Fund, 2000. Mem. Am. Soc. Microbiology (alt. councilor 1997), Am. Soc. Clin. Pathologists (assoc., state advisor, legis. liaison 1998—, gen. exam com. 1998-), Am. Soc. Clin. Lab. Sci., Am. Assn. for Women in C.C., Sigma Xi (assoc.). Avocations: hiking, skiing, travel. Office: Mt Hood CC 26000 SE Stark St Gresham OR 97030 Fax: 503-491-7481. E-mail: pitonzob@mhcc.edu.

PITOT, HENRY CLEMENT, III, pathologist, educator; b. N.Y.C., May 12, 1930; s. Henry Clement and Bertha (Lowe) Pitot; m. Julie S. Schutten, July 29, 1954; children: Bertha, Anita, Jeanne, Catherine, Henry, Michelle, Lisa, Patrice. BS in Chemistry, Va. Mil. Inst., 1951; MD, Tulane U., 1955, PhD in Biochemistry, 1959, DSc (hon.) , 1995. Instr. pathology Med. Sch. Tulane U., New Orleans, 1955-59; postdoctoral fellow McArdle Lab. U. Wis., Madison, 1959-60, mem. faculty Med. Sch., 1960—, prof. pathology and oncology, 1966-99, prof. emeritus, 1999—, chmn. dept. pathology, 1968-71, acting dean Med. Sch., 1971-73, dir. McArdle Lab., 1973-91. Recipient Borden Undergrad. Rsch. award, 1955, Leaderle Faculty award, 1962, Career Devel. award, Nat. Cancer Inst., NIH, 1965, Parke-Davis award, 1968, Noble Found. Rsch. award, 1984, Esther Langer award, U. Chgo., 1984, Hilldale award, U. Wis., 1991, Founders award, Chem. Industry Inst. Toxicology, 1993, Midwest Regional chpt. Soc. Toxicology award, 1996, Emeritus Faculty award, U. Wis. Med. Sch., 2001. Fellow: AAAS, N.Y. Acad. Scis.; mem.: Soc. Toxicologic Pathologists, Soc. Toxicology, Soc. Surg. Oncology (Lucy J. Wortham award 1981), Soc. Exptl. Biology and Medicine (pres. 1991—93), Am. Soc. Investigative Pathology (pres. 1976—77), Am. Cancer Soc. (life), Japanese Cancer Soc. (hon.), Am. Chem. Soc., Am. Soc. Biochemistry and Molecular Biology, Am. Assn. Cancer Rsch., Am. Soc. Cell Biology. Roman Catholic. Home: 314 Robin Pkwy Madison WI 53705-4931 Office: U Wis McArdle Lab Cancer Rsch 1400 University Ave Madison WI 53706-1599 E-mail: pitot@oncology.wise.edu. *Where and who we are today is the result of those whom we have met and known and loved until now.*

PITOU, DAVID WALKER, consulting firm executive; b. N.Y.C., Mar. 6, 1930; s. Maurice Inslee and Eleanor Walker Pitou; m. Doris D. Pitou, Nov. 24, 1956 (div. Mar. 1992); children: Amy, Jeremy. BA, Wagner Coll., 1956; MBA, NYU, 1962. Mgr. IBM, N.Y.C., 1964-81, dir. stockholder svcs., 1981-87; pres. Stockholder Cons. Svcs., Inc., S.I., NY, 1987—2002, chmn., CEO, 2002—. 1st lt. AUS, 1952-53. Avocations: golf, opera, travel. Office: Stockholder Cons Svcs Inc PO Box 80260 Staten Island NY 10308-0260

PITT, BERTRAM, cardiologist, educator, consultant; b. Kew Gardens, N.Y., Apr. 27, 1932; s. David and Shirley (Blum) P., m. Elaine Liberstein, Aug. 10, 1962; children: Geoffrey, Jessica, Jillian BA, Cornell U., 1953; MD, U. Basel, Switzerland, 1959. Diplomate Am. Bd. Internal Medicine, Am. Bd. Cardiology. Intern Beth Israel Hosp., N.Y.C., 1959-60, resident Boston, 1960-63; fellow in cardiology Johns Hopkins U., Balt., 1966-67, from instr. to assoc. prof., 1967-77; prof. medicine, dir. div. cardiology U. Mich., Ann Arbor, 1977-91, prof. medicine Sch. Medicine, 1991—. Author: Atlas of Cardiovascular Nuclear Medicine, 1977; editor: Cardiovascular Nuclear Medicine, 1974; co-editor: Clinical Trials in Cardiology, 1997, Current Controlled Trials in Cardiovascular Medicine, 1999—. Served to capt. U.S. Army, 1963-65 Mem. ACP, Am. Coll. Cardiology, Am. Soc. Clin. Investigation, Assn. Am. Physicians, Am. Physiol. Soc., Am. Heart Assn., Assn. Univ. Cardiologists, Am. Coll. Chest Physicians, Royal Soc. Mich., Johns Hopkins U. Soc. Scholars. Home: 24 Ridgeway St Ann Arbor MI 48104-1739 Office: U Mich Divsn Cardiology 1500 E Medical Center Dr Ann Arbor MI 48109-0005 E-mail: bpitt@umich.edu.

PITT, BRAD, actor; b. Shawnee, Okla., Dec. 18, 1963; s. Bill and Jane P. Appearences include: (TV series) Dallas, Another World, Growing Pains, The Image(HBO), Glory Days, Two-Fisted Tales; (TV movie) Too Young To Die?, 1989; (films)Cutting Glass, Happy Together, 1989, Across the Tracks, 1990, Contact, Thelma and Louise, 1991, The Favor, 1992, Johnny Suede, 1992, Cool World, 1992, A River Runs Through It, 1992, Kalifornia, 1993, True Romance, 1993, Interview with the Vampire, 1994, Legends of the Fall, 1994, 12 Monkeys, 1995 (Golden Globe award for best supporting actor in film 1996, Acad. award nominee for best supporting actor 1996), Sleepers, 1996, Seven Years in Tibet, 1997, The Devil's Own, 1997, Dark Side of the Sun, 1997, Meet Joe Black, 1998, Fight Club, 1999, Snatch, 2000, The Mexican, 2001, Spy Game, 2001, Ocean's Eleven, 2001. Office: Creative Artists Agy care Kevin Huvane 9830 Wilshire Blvd Beverly Hills CA 90212-1825*

PITT, GEORGE, lawyer, investment banker; b. Chgo., July 21, 1938; s. Cornelius George and Anastasia (Geocaris) P.; m. Barbara Lynn Goodrich, Dec. 21, 1963 (div. Apr. 1990); children: Elizabeth Nanette, Margaret Leigh; m. Pamela Ann Pittsford, May 19, 1990. BA, Northwestern U., 1960, JD, 1963; hon. grad., U.S. Army Intelligence Sch., Ft. Holabird, Md., 1964; Leading Strategic Change course, U. Va., 1999. Bar: Ill. 1963. Assoc. Chapman and Cutler, Chgo., 1963-67; ptnr. Borge and Pitt, and predecessor, 1968-87, Katten Muchin & Zavis, Chgo., 1987-97; sr. mng. dir. Banc One Capital Markets, Inc. (formerly First Chgo. Capital Markets, Inc.), 1998-2000; mng. dir. UBS PaineWebber Inc., Chgo., 2000—. Conf. chmn. Bond Buyer's 3d Ann. Midwest Pub. Fin. Conf., 1994; conf. co-chmn. Bond Buyer's 8th Ann. Midwest Pub. Fin. Conf., 1999. Notes and comments editor Northwestern U. Law Rev., 1962-63. 1st lt. AUS, 1964. Fellow: Am. Coll. Bond Counsel; mem.: Ill. State Bar Assn., New Buffalo Yacht Club, Univ. Club. Chgo., Phi Gamma Delta, Phi Delta Phi, Eta Sigma Phi. Home: 600 N McClurg Ct Chicago IL 60611-3044 Office: UBS PaineWebber Inc One Wacker Dr 38th Fl Chicago IL 60606-2807 E-mail: gpitt@ubspw.com.

PITT, HARVEY LLOYD, federal agency administrator; b. Bklyn., Feb. 28, 1945; s. Morris Jacob and Sara (Sapir) P.; m. Saree Ruffin, Jan. 7, 1984; children: Robert Garrett, Sara Dillard; children from previous marriage: Emily Laura, Jonathan Bradley. BA, CUNY, 1965; JD with honors (Univ. scholar), St. John's U., N.Y.C., 1968. Bar: N.Y. 1969, U.S. Supreme Ct. 1972, D.C. 1979. With SEC, Washington, 1968-78, legal asst. to commr., 1969; editor Instl. Investor Study, 1970-71; spl. counsel Office Gen. Counsel, 1971-72, chief counsel div. market regulation, 1972-73, exec. asst. to chmn., 1973-75, gen. counsel, 1975-78; ptnr. Fried, Frank, Harris, Shriver & Jacobson, Washington, 1978—2001; chmn. SEC, 2001—. Adj. prof. law George Washington U. Nat. Law Ctr., 1974-82, U. Pa. Law Sch., 1983-84, vis. practitioner, 1984, Georgetown U. Law Ctr., 1976-84; comml. arbitrator Am. Arbitration Assn. Contbr. articles to profl. jours. V.p. Glen Haven Civic Assn., Silver Spring, Md., 1972-73, pres., 1974. Recipient Learned Hand award Inst. for Human Rels., 1988. Mem. ABA (past chmn. subcom. SEC practice and enforcement, past co-chmn. subcom. state takeover laws), Fed. Bar Assn. (Outstanding Young Lawyer award 1975), Adminstrv. Conf. U.S., Am. Law Inst. (project advisor on restatement law on corp. governance), Delta Sigma Rho, Tau Kappa Alpha, Phi Delta Phi. Office: Securities & Exch Commn 450 5th St NW Washington DC 20549 Office Fax: 202-942-9646.*

PITT, JANE, medical educator; b. Frankfurt, Fed. Republic Germany, Aug. 25, 1938; came to U.S., 1939. d. Ludwig Friederich and Vera (Aberle) Ries; m. Martin Irwin Pitt, Aug. 12, 1962 (dec. 1980); children: Jennifer, Eric Jonathan; m. Robert Harry Socolow, May 25, 1986; stepchildren: David, Seth. BA, Radcliffe Coll., 1960; MD, Harvard U., 1964. Diplomate Am. Bd. Pediatrics, Am. Bd. Pediat. Infectious Diseases. Resident Children's Hosp. Med. Ctr., Boston, 1964-66; fellow Tufts U. Med. Sch., 1966-67, Harvard U. Med. Sch., Boston, 1967-69; asst. prof. SUNY Downstate Sch. Medicine, N.Y.C., 1970-71; asst. prof. Coll. Physicians and Surgeons Columbia U., 1971-75, assoc. prof. Coll. Physicians and Surgeons, 1975-2000; prof. Coll. Physicians and Surgeons, 2000—. Mem. instl. rev. bd. Columbia Health Scis. Campus, N.Y.C., 1982—; mem. NIH study sect. Reviewer Jour. of Infectious Diseases, New Eng. Jour. Medicine, 1976—; contbr. articles to profl. jours. NIH grantee, 1974—. Fellow Infectious Disease Soc., Pediat. Infectious Disease Soc., Soc. Pediat. Rsch., Am. Pediatric Soc. Democrat. Jewish. Home: 34 Westcott Rd Princeton NJ 08540-3060 Office: Columbia U Coll Physicians Surgeons 630 W 168th St New York NY 10032-3702 E-mail: jp25@columbia.edu.

PITT, JUDSON HAMILTON, publisher, author; b. Glen Cove, N.Y., June 7, 1953; s. Gavin Alexander and Eleanore Gaehler (Whiting) P.; m. Elena U. Tokaeva, Dec. 16, 1995. BS in Communications, Ariz. State U., 1977. Resident advisor fraternity Ohio State U., Columbus, 1977-79; supr. student svcs. Loyola U., Chgo., 1979-81; asst. to CEO Flair Communications Agy., Inc., 1981—; v.p. Gavin Pitt Assocs., Inc., 1986—; pub. Water Tower Pub. House, 1989—. Dir. ops. Chgo. Marathon, 1984-93. Author: The Official Hard Rock Cafe Pin Collector's Guide, 1997. Mem. Am. Mktg. Assn., Newcomen Soc. U.S., Chgo. Soc. Assn. Execs., Saddle & Cycle Club, Pi Kappa Alpha. Republican. Presbyterian. Home: 5510 N Sheridan Rd Chicago IL 60640-1633 Office: 214 W Erie St Chicago IL 60610-3611

PITT, REDDING, political organization worker; b. Decatur, Ala., Mar. 29, 1944; s. Charles Kermit and Dorothea Rowena (Slaughter) P.; m. Jane Hanify, Sept. 20, 1969 (div. Dec. 1980); 1 child, William Rivers; m. Abigail P. van Alstyne, Aug. 24, 1985. Student, U. Ams., Mexico City, 1963; BA, U. Ala., 1967; JD, Boston Coll., 1977. Staff asst. to chmn. FDIC, Washington, 1977-79; staff asst. to comptr. of currency U.S. Treasury Dept., 1979-80; asst. atty. gen. State of Ala., Montgomery, 1981-94, counsel to sec. of state, 1981-84, asst. legal adviser to dir. fin., 1984-86, chief dep. atty. gen., 1987-91, counsel to atty. gen., 1991-94; U.S. Atty. middle dist., Ala., 1994—2001; Chair. Alabama Dem. Party, 2001—. Mem. Ala. Juvenile Justice Coordinating Coun. Supreme Ct. Ala., Montgomery, 1992-94. Editor: Powers and Duties of State Attorneys General, 1988. Mem. Ala. Gov. Drug Adv. Bd., Montgomery, 1994—; mem. adv. bd. Blackburn Inst. U. Ala., 1996—. Capt. U.S. Army, 1969-72. Recipient Pres. award Nat. Assn. Attys. Gen., 1988. Mem. ABA, ATLA, Fed. Bar Assn. (pres. 1995—), Ala. Law Inst. (mem. reform adv. com. 1982-93), Ala. Bar Assn. (mem. com. bench & bar rels. 1994-95). Democrat. Episcopalian. Avocations: history, golf. Office: Alabama Dem. Party PO Box 950 Montgomery AL 36104*

PITT, ROBERT ERVIN, environmental engineer, educator; b. San Francisco, Apr. 25, 1948; s. Wallace and Marjorie (Peterson) P.; m. Kathryn Jay, Mar. 18, 1967; children: Gwendolyn, Brady. BS in Engring. Sci., Humboldt State U., 1970; MSCE, San Jose State U., 1971; PhD in Civil and Environ. Engring., U. Wis., 1987. Registered profl. engr., Wis.; diplomate Am. Acad. Environ. Engrs. Environ. engr. URS Rsch. Co., San Mateo, Calif., 1971-74; sr. engr. Woodward-Clyde Cons., San Francisco, 1974-79; cons. environ. engr. Blue Mounds, Wis., 1979-84; environ. engr. Wis. Dept. Natural Resources, Madison, 1984-87; prof. depts. civil and environ. engring. and environ. health scis. U. Ala., Birmingham, 1987—2002, prof., dir. environ. engring. program Tuscaloosa, 2000—. Mem. Resource Conservation and Devel. Coun., Jefferson County, Ala., 1992-94; mem. com. on augmenting natural recharge of groundwater with reclaimed wastewater NRC, 1991-94; Ala. state dir. for energy and environment U.S. DOE EPSCOR, 1992-94; guest lectr. U. Gesamthochschule, Essen, Germany, 1994; mem. value engring. com. Combined Sewer Overflow, Cleve., 1993, mem. tech. adv. com., N.Y.C., 1997—. Author: Small Storm Urban Flow and Particulate Washoff Contributions to Outfall Discharges, 1987, Investigation of Inappropriate Pollutant Entries into Storm Drainage Systems, 1994, Potential Groundwater Contamination from Intentional and Non-Intentional Stormwater Infiltration, 1994, Groundwater Contamination from Stormwater Infiltration, 1996; co-author: Stormwater Effects Handbook: A Tool Box for Watershed Managers, Scientists, and Engineers, 2002; author software in field; mem. editl. bd. Ctr. Watershed Protection, 1994—. Asst. scoutmaster Boy Scouts Am., Birmingham, 1988-94. Recipient Disting. Svc. citation, U. Wis., 2002, 1st Pl. Nat. award U.S. Soil Conservation Svc. Earth Team, 1989, 94, award of recognition USDA, 1990, 1st Pl. Vol. award Take Pride in Am., 1991; Fed. Water Pollution Control Adminstrn. fellow, 1970-71, GE Engring. Edn. fellow, 1984-86. Mem. ASCE, Soc. for Environ. Toxicology and Chemistry, N.Am. Lake Mgmt. Soc. (Profl. Speakers award 1992), Water Environ. Fedn. (1st Pl. Nat. award 1992), Am. Water Resources Assn., Ala. Acad. Sci., Internat. Assn. Water Quality (mem. com. on solids in sewers 1996-96), Sigma Xi. Achievements include development of small storm urban hydrology prediction methods, toxicant control devices for stormwater source flows, methods to identify and correct inappropriate discharges to storm drain systems. Office: U Ala Dept Civil/Environ Engring Tuscaloosa AL 35487-2684

PITT, WILLIAM ALEXANDER, cardiologist; b. July 17, 1942; came to U.S., 1970; s. Reginald William and Una Sylvia (Alexander) P.; m. Judith Mae Wilson, May 21, 1965; children: William Matthew, Joanne Katharine. MD, U. B.C., Vancouver, 1967. Diplomate Royal Coll. Physicians Can. Intern Mercy Hosp., San Diego, 1967-68, resident, 1970-71, assoc. dir. cardiology, 1972-92; resident Vancouver Gen. Hosp., 1968-70, U. Calif., San Diego, 1971-72; with So. Calif. Cardiology Med. Group, 1984—; pvt. practice Clin. Cons. Cardiology. Bd. trustees San Diego Found. for Med. Care, 1983-89, 91—, pres., chmn. bd. trustees, 1986-88, med. dir., 1991-96; trustee Pacific Found. for Med. Care, 1996—, med. dir., 1996—; bd. dirs. Mut. Assn. for Profl. Services, Phila., 1984-92; pres. Alternet Med. Svcs., Inc., 1992-95; pres. and med. dir. San Diego IPA, 1995—. Fellow Royal Coll. Physicians Can., Am. Coll. Cardiology (assoc.); mem. AMA, Am. Heart Assn., Calif. Med. Assn., San Diego County Med. Soc., San Diego County Heart Assn. (bd. dirs. 1982-88). Episcopalian. Office: So Calif Cardiology Med Group 6386 Alvarado Ct Ste 101 San Diego CA 92120-4906 E-mail: wmapitt@aol.com.

PITT, WOODROW WILSON, JR. engineering educator, educator; b. Rocky Mount, N.C., Aug. 14, 1935; s. Woodrow Wilson Pitt and Stella Marie (Whitley) Wiggins; m. Katherine Ann Morton, Jan. 1, 1958; children: Deborah Ann, Abigail Marie, Katherine Elizabeth. BSChemE, U. S.C., 1957; MS, U. Tenn., 1966, PhD, 1969. Registered profl. engr., Tenn., Tex. Devel. engr. Oak Ridge (Tenn.) Nat. Lab., 1960-72, sr. devel. engr., 1972-81, sect. head, 1981-89; vis. prof. Tex. A&M U., College Station, 1989-90, prof. dept. nuclear engring., asst. dept. head, 1991-97, adj. prof., 1998—. Inventor multi-sample rotor assembly for blood function preparation, differential chromatography; contbr. articles to profl. jours. Councilman Oak Ridge City Coun., 1983-89. Lt. (j.g.) USN, 1957-60; comdr. USNR, Ret. Spl. fellow U.S. AEC, 1966-67;

recipient IR-100 awards, 1971, 80. Fellow AIChE; mem. ASTM, NSPE, Am. Nuclear Soc., N.Y. Acad. Scis., Sigma Xi, Tau Beta Pi. Methodist. Avocations: golf, tennis. Home: 12 Milnor Ter Fairfield Glade TN 38558-2770

PITTAWAY, DONALD EDWARD, endocrinology educator, gynecologist; b. Carbondale, Pa., May 8, 1947; s. Clifford Charles and Eleanor Ruth (Schwartztrauber) P.; m. Carmel Celine Imbalzano, June 27, 1970; children: Jennifer, Donald E. Jr. AB, Franklin and Marshall Coll., 1969; PhD, Tenn. U., 1974; MD, La. State U., Shreveport, 1977. Diplomate Am. Bd. Ob-Gyn, Am. Bd. Bioanalysis (high complexity lab. dir.); cert. reproductive endocrinologist. Clin. instr. Sch. Medicine La. State U., 1974-77; instr. Sch. Medicine Vanderbilt U., Nashville, 1981-83; from asst. to assoc. prof. reproductive endocrinology Wake Forest U., Winston-Salem, N.C., 1983-90, prof. endocrinology, sect. head, 1990-98, clin. prof., 1998—. Med. adv. bd. Smith Kline Beecham, Pitts., 1993—. Summer fellow NSF, 1971, Rsch. fellow March of Dimes Nat. Found., 1975-76, Ob-Gyn Clin. Rsch. fellow Mead Johnson Am. Coll., 1984-85. Mem. Soc. Gynecol. Investigation, Endocrine Soc., Am. Soc. Reproductive Medicine. Office: Brookview Women's Ctr Ste 105 3333 Brookview Hills Blvd Winston Salem NC 27103-5661

PITTELKO, ROGER DEAN, clergyman, religious educator; b. Elk Reno, Okla., Aug. 18, 1932; s. Elmer Henry and Lydia Caroline (Nieman) Pittelko. AA, Concordia Coll., 1952; BA, Concordia Sem., St. Louis, 1954, MDiv, 1957, STM, 1958; postgrad., Chgo. Luth. Theol. Sem., 1959-61; ThD, Am. Div. Sch., Pineland, Fla., 1968; DMin, Faith Evang. Luth. Sem., Tacoma, 1983. Ordained to ministry Luth. Ch., 1958. Vicar St. John Luth. Ch., S.I., NY, 1955—56, asst. pastor New Orleans, 1958-59; pastor Concordia Luth. Ch., Berwyn, Ill., 1959-63, Luth. Ch. of Holy Spirit, Elk Grove Village, 1963-67; chmn. Commn. on Worship, Luth. Ch.-Mo. Synod, 1982—92, chmn. Commn. on Worship, 1994—98, asst. bishop Midwest region English dist., 1983, pres. and bishop English dist., 1987-97, 3d v.p., 1997—; prof. pastoral theology Concordia Theol. Sem., Ft. Wayne, Ind., 1997—. Author: Guide to Introducing Lutheran Worship; contbr. articles. Mem.: Luth. Acad. for Scholarship, Concordia Hist. Inst., Itasca Country Club (Ill.), Maywood Sportsmans Club (Ill.). Republican. Office: Concordia Theol Seminary 6600 N Clinton St Fort Wayne IN 46825

PITTELKOW, MARK ROBERT, physician, dermatology educator, researcher; b. Milw., Dec. 16, 1952; s. Robert Bernard and Barbara Jean (Thomas) P.; m. Gail L. Gamble, Nov. 26, 1977; children: Thomas, Cameron, Robert. BA, Northwestern U., 1975; MD, Mayo Med. Sch., 1979. Intern then resident Mayo Grad. Sch., 1979-84, post-doctoral exptl. pathology, 1981-83; from asst. to assoc. prof. dermatology Mayo Med. Sch., Rochester, Minn., 1984-95, prof. dermatology, 1995—, assoc. prof. biochemistry and molecular biology, 1992—. Cons. Mayo Clinic/Found., Rochester, 1984— Fellow Am. Acad. Dermatology; mem. AAAS, Am. Dermatol. Assn., Soc. Investigative Dermatology, Am. Burn Assn., Am. Soc. Cell Biology, N.Y. Acad. Scis., Chi Psi. Home: 721 12th Ave SW Rochester MN 55902-2027 Office: Mayo Clinic 200 1st St SW Rochester MN 55905-0002

PITTENGER, DAVID J. psychologist, educator; b. Akron, Ohio, June 14, 1957; s. Tress E. and Aldah J. Pittenger; m. Denise M. Moore, June 21, 1980; children: Rebbecca, Alexander. PhD, U. Ga., Athens, 1984—89. Head and prof. psychology Marietta Coll., Marietta, Ohio, 1989—2000, U. of Tenn., Chattanooga, 2000—. Author: Fundamentals of Behavioral Statistics, 2000 (McCoy Teaching Fellow, 1997). Fellow: APA. Democrat. Avocations: gardening, reading. Office: U Tenn at Chattanooga 615 McCallie Ave Chattanooga TN 37403 Office Fax: 423-755-4284. Personal E-mail: david-pittenger@utc.edu.

PITTER, DONALD EDWIN, music educator; b. Alhambra, Calif., Jan. 23, 1951; s. Jack Francis and Eva Lou Pitter; m. Cindy Marie Ward, Nov. 18, 1978; children: Wesley, Christopher, Timothy. MusB, U. Redlands, 1974. Cert. tchr. Calif., 1974. Tchr. Pajaro Valley Unified Sch. Dist., Watsonville, Calif., 1974—. Composer: (band music) Ming Court, 2002. Conservative. Baptist. Avocation: walking, antique cars, family travel. Office: Rolling Hills Mid Sch 130 Herman Ave Watsonville CA 95076 Personal E-mail: creekside41@yahoo.com.

PITTMAN, EDWIN LLOYD, state supreme court chief justice; b. Hattiesburg, Miss., Jan. 2, 1935; s. Lloyd H. and Pauline P.; m. Virginia Lund, 1996; children: Melanie, Win, Jennifer. BS, U. So. Miss.; JD, U. Miss., 1960. Bar: Miss. Practiced law until, 1964; mem. Miss. Senate, 1964-72; treas. State of Miss., Jackson, 1976-80, sec. of state, 1980-84, atty. gen., 1984-88; justice Supreme Ct. Miss., 1990—; chief justice Miss. Supreme Ct., Miss., 2000—. Trustee William Carey Coll. 2nd lt., Inf. U.S. Army. Mem. U. Miss. Alumni Assn., U. So. Miss. Alumni Assn., Miss. Jaycees (past state dir.), ABA, South Central Miss. Bar Assn. Clubs: Lions, Masons. Democrat. Baptist. Office: Miss Supreme Ct Gartin Justice Bldg PO Box 249 Jackson MS 39205-0117*

PITTMAN, HAL WATSON, neurosurgeon; b. Orrum, N.C. s. Raymond Lee and Bertha Estelle (Newton) P.; m. Timona Miller, Mar. 23, 1952; children: Eric, Janet, Melissa, Arthur. BS, Wake Forest (N.C.) Coll., 1943; MD, Bowman Gray Sch. Medicine, 1945. Diplomate Am. Bd. Neurol. Surgeons. Intern Episcopal Hosp., Phila., 1945-46; resident in neurology/neuropathology Phila. Gen. Hosp., 1948-49; resident in gen. surgery James Walker Meml. Hosp., Wilmington, N.C., 1949-50; resident in neurol. surgery Ill. Neuropsychiat. Inst., Chgo., 1950-52; fgn. asst. neurosurgery Hopital de la Pitie, Paris, 1953-54; lab. fellow neurosurgery New Eng. Ctr. Hosp., Boston, 1955, neurosurgeon, 1955-57; clin. instr. neurosurgery Tufts U., 1955—57; neurosurgeon St. Josephs Hosp., Good Samaritan Hosp., Phoenix, 1957—99; vice chmn. neurosurgery Barrow Neurol. Inst., 1962—79, neurosurgeon, 1962—, Phoenix Children's Hosp., 1983—98, emeritus, 1998—; neurosurgeon Maricopa County Hosp., 1997—; clin. assoc. prof. surgery U. Ariz., Tucson, 1985—; chmn. neurosurgery Children's Rehabilitative Svcs. Contbr. articles to profl. jours. Pres. Ariz. Found. for Handicapped, 2000—02, Physicians for the Symphony, 1994—97; bd. dirs. Ariz. Found. for the Handicapped, Phoenix Symphony Assn., Ariz. Opera Assn., Phoenix Chamber Music Soc., Phoenix Bach Choir. Capt. MC AUS, 1946—48. Fellow ACS; mem. AMA, Am. Assn. Neurol. Surgeons, Congress of Neurol. Surgeons, Ariz. Neurosurg. Soc. (pres. 1977-78), Western Neurosurg. Soc. Baptist. Avocations: music, photography. Home: 44 E Palm Ln Phoenix AZ 85004-1529 Office: Maricopa County Hosp 2601 E Roosevelt St Phoenix AZ 85008-4956 Fax: (602) 254-8082. E-mail: phxpitt@aol.com.

PITTMAN, JACQUELYN, retired mental health nurse, nursing educator; b. Pensacola, Fla., Dec. 22, 1932; d. Edward Corry Sr. and Hettie Oean (Wilson) P. BS in Nursing Edn., Fla. State U., 1958; MA, Columbia U., 1959, EdD, 1974. Physician asst. Med. Ctr. Clinic, Pensacola, 1953-55; clin. instr., asst. dir. nursing svc. Sacred Heart Hosp., 1955-56; instr. psychiat. nurse Fla. State Hosp., Chattahoochee, 1958; instr. psychiat. nursing Pensacola Jr. Coll., 1959-60, 62-63; chmn. div. nursing Gulf Coast C.C., Panama City, Fla., 1963-66; asst. prof. U. Tex., Austin, 1970-72, assoc. prof., 1972-80; prof. nursing, coord. curriculum and tchg. grad. program La. State U. Med. Ctr., New Orleans, 1980-99, rep. faculty senate, 1997-99; pres.-elect faculty assembly Sch. Nursing La. State U. Med. Ctr. Sch. Nursing, 1997-98, pres., 1998-99; ret., 1999. Curriculum cons. Nicholls State U., Thibodaux, La., 1982, Our Lady of Lake Sch. Nursing, Baton Rouge, 1983; rsch. liaison So. Bapt. Hosp., New Orleans, 1987-89, Med. Ctr. La., 1992-99; mem. adv. bd. Sister Henrietta Guyot Professorship; mem. planning com. Nichols State U./La. State U. Med. Ctr. Partnership, 1996-99. Mem. ethics com., trustee Hotel Dieu Hosp., New Orleans, 1987—91; judge Internat. Sci. and Engring. Fair Assn., 1990, 1992; del. La. State Nurses' Assn. State Conv., 1992, 1994; assoc. Libr. of Congress, Smithonian Instn.; mem. Dem. Nat. Comm., Presdl. Task Force, 1992, Ctr. for Study of Presidency; tchr. Christian edn. program for mentally retarded St. Ignatius Martyr Ch., 1979—80; tchr. initiation team Rite of Christian Initiation of Adults, Our Lady of the Lake Cath. Ch., Mandeville, La., 1983—86; v.p., bd. dirs. St. Tammany Guidance Ctr., Inc., 1987—91; mem. parish outreach meals-on-wheels program St. Tammany, Covington, La., 2001—02. Mem. ANA, LWV, Am. Assn. Adv. Sci. Directory, N.Y. Acad. Scis., Acad. Polit. Sci., Libr. of Congress Assocs., Nat. Trust for Hist. Preservation, La. Endowment for Humanities, La. Nurses Assn. (archivist 1987-99, state task force com. to preserve hist. documents 1987-99), So. Nursing Rsch. Soc., Nat. League Nursing, Boston U. Nursing Archives, Women's Inner Cir. Achievement N.Am. Cmtys., Internat. Order of Merit, World Found. Successful Women, Wilson Ctr. Assocs., Kappa Delta Pi, Sigma Theta Tau. Democrat. Roman Catholic. Avocations: swimming, golf, travel, reading, Louisiana history. Address: 204 Woodridge Blvd Mandeville LA 70471-2604

PITTMAN, JAMES ALLEN, JR. physician, educator; b. Orlando, Fla., Apr. 12, 1927; s. James Allen and Jean C. (Garretson) Pittman; m. Constance Ming-Chung Shen, Feb. 19, 1955; children: James Clinton, John Merrill. BS, Davidson Coll., 1948; MD, Harvard, 1952; DSc (hon.) , Davidson Coll., 1980, U. Ala., Birmingham, 1984. Intern, asst. resident medicine Mass. Gen. Hosp., Boston, 1952—54; tchg. fellow medicine Harvard U., 1953—54; clin. assoc. NIH, Bethesda, Md., 1954—56; instr. medicine George Washington U., 1955—56; chief resident U. Ala. Med. Ctr., Birmingham, 1956—58, instr. medicine, 1956—59, asst. prof., 1959—62, assoc. prof., 1962—64, prof. medicine, 1964—92, dir. endocrinology and metabolism div., 1962—71, co-chmn. dept. medicine, 1969—71, also prof., physiology and biophysics, 1967—92, dean, 1973—92, U. Ala. Birmingham Disting. prof., 1992—. Mem. endocrinology study sect. NIH, 1963—67; mem. nat. adv. rsch. resources coun. NIH, 1991—95; asst. chief med. dir. rsch. and edn. in medicine U.S. VA, 1971—73; prof. medicine Georgetown U. Med. Sch., Washington, 1971—73; mem. grad. med. edn. nat. adv. com. HEW, 1976—78; mem. HHS Coun. on Grad. Med. Edn., 1986—90; hon. prof. Chung Shan Med. and Dental Coll., Taiwan, 1994; sr. advisor Internat. Coun. on Ctrl. of Iodine Deficiency Diseases, 1994—96. Author: Diagnosis and Treatment of Thyroid Diseases, 1963; contbr. articles in field to profl. jours. Master: Am. Coll. Endocrinology, ACP; fellow: AAAS; mem.: So. Soc. Clin. Investigation (Founder's medal 1993), Am. Fedn. Clin. Rsch. (pres. So. sect., nat. coun. 1962—66), Am. Chem. Soc., Am. Diabetes Assn., Soc. Nuclear Medicine, Endocrine Soc. Ecuador (hon.), N.Y. Acad. Scis. (life), Am. Ornithologists Union (life), Am. Thyroid Assn., Am. Assn. Clin. Endocrinologists, Endocrine Soc., Assn. Am. Physicians, NAS Inst. Medicine, Harvard U. Med. Alumni Assn. (pres. 1986—88), Wilson Ornithol. Club (life), Omicron Delta Kappa, Alpha Omega Alpha, Phi Beta Kappa. Office: U Ala Sch of Med Pittman CAMS 1924 7th Ave S Birmingham AL 35294-0001 *I hope that each time I meet a person, both of us leave the encounter the better for it.*

PITTMAN, JOEY JAY, music educator; s. James Paul and Betty Jo Pittman; m. Leah Ruth Adams, Mar. 13, 1993; children: Andrew Drew. Bachelor music edn., Ea. Ky. U., Richmond, Kentucky, 1986—90, master music edn., 1990; 1994. Grad. assistantt Ea. Ky. U., Richmond, Ky., 1990—91; elem. band asst. dir. Leslie county schools, Hyden, 1991—94; band dir. Georgetown county schools, Andrews, SC, 1994—98, Florence sch. dist., Johnsonville, 1998—2002, Georgetown county schools, Andrews, 2002—, Rosemary Mid. Sch., Andrews, 2002—02. Music dir. Trinity Uniter Meth. Ch., Andrews, SC, 1995—; interum program dir. Trinity United Meth. Ch., Andrews, SC, 2002—02. Advisor Andrews Gospel Music Storytelling Festival, Andrews, SC, 1995—97. Recipient Star Delta Omicron, Delta Omicron Music Frat., 1989. Mem.: SC Band Directors Assn., Music Educators Nat. Conv. Democrat-Npl. United Methodist. Avocations: baseball, boatinig, outdoor activities, arranging music. Home: 609 E Ashland Street Andrews SC 29510-4044 Office: Rosemary Middle School Andrews SC 29510 Home Fax: 843-264-3690. Personal E-mail: joeyandleah@aol.com.

PITTMAN, LISA, lawyer; b. Limestone, Maine, Jan. 4, 1959; d. William Franklin and Rowena Paradis (Umphrey) P.; 1 child, Graham Edward Paradis. BA, U. Fla., 1980, postgrad., 1981, JD, 1984; LLM, George Washington U., 1988. Bar: Fla. 1984, D.C. 1993, U.S Supreme Ct. 1993. Spl. asst. to gen. counsel Nat. Oceanic and Atmospheric Adminstrn., Washington, 1984-85, atty., advisor, 1985-87; minority counsel Com. on Mcht. Marine & Fisheries, Ho. of Reps., 1987-95; dep. chief counsel Com. on Resources U.S. Ho. of Reps., 1995-2001, chief counsel Com. on Resources, 2001—02, chief counsel, dep. chief of staff, 2002—. Home: 7325 Eldorado St Mc Lean VA 22102-2904 Office: US House of Reps 1324 Longworth HOB Washington DC 20515-0001

PITTMAN, PHILIP MCMILLAN, historian; b. Detroit, Apr. 6, 1941; s. Lansing Mizner and Sally Clotilde (Book) P.; m. Julie M. Ducharme, June 22, 1963 (div. 1975); children: Philip McMillan III, Mary Christine Steuart, Noel Ducharme; m. Adele Smith, June 26, 1976 (div. 1989); m. Margaret D. Schlueter, Aug. 26, 1990. AB, Kenyon Coll., 1963; MA, Vanderbilt U., 1964, PhD, 1967. Instr. Vanderbilt U., Nashville, 1966-67; asst. prof. U. Victoria, B.C., Can., 1967-68; assoc. prof. Marshall U., Huntington, W.Va., 1968-80; pres. W.Va. Assn. Coll. English Tchrs., 1978-79; author, historian Cedarville, Mich., 1980—; pub., salesman, v.p., sec., chmn. bd. Les Cheneaux Ventures Inc., 1985—. Adj. prof. W.Va. Coll. Grad. Studies, 1978-80. Author: The Les Cheneaux Chronicles: Anatomy of a Community, 1984, Ripples from the Breezes: A Les Cheneaux Anthology, 1988, North Shore Chinook: Lake Huron Salmon on Light Tackle, 1993, Don't Blame the Treaties: Native American Rights and the Michigan Indian Treaties, 1992; editor, compiler: The Portrayal of Life Stages in English Literature, 1500-1800, 1989, author various scholarly book reviews and articles. Active Les Cheaux Cmty. Action Com., 1985—, Mich. Nature Conservancy, 1994—; active Little Traverse Conservancy, 1990—, bd. dirs., 1994—; founding dir. Les Cheneaux Cmty. Found., 1997—; founding mem. Les Cheneaux Econ. Forum, 1997—. NEH fellow, 1971. Mem. Les Cheneaux Hist. Assn. (pres. 1987-89), Les Cheneaux Islands Assn. (pres. 1982-84, bd. dirs. 1996—), Les Cheneaux Club (sec. 1972-87, 97—), Delta Kappa Epsilon. Republican. Episcopalian. Avocations: sport fishing, boating, writing, walking in woods. Home: PO Box 187 Cedarville MI 49719-0187 Office: Les Cheneaux Ventures Inc RR 1 Box 15 Cedarville MI 49719-9706

PITTMAN, ROBERT TURNER, retired newspaper editor; b. Gates, N.C., Sept. 24, 1929; s. Thomas Everett and Lillian (Turner) P.; m. Ruth Fike, Aug. 25, 1956; children— Laura Emily, Mary Ann, Lillian Elizabeth BA, Washington and Lee U., 1951; MA, U. N.C., 1957. Reporter Times Dispatch, Richmond, Va., 1951; editor, pub. Daily Ranger, Glendive, Mont., 1957-58; writer editorials Times Union, Jacksonville, Fla., 1958-63; editorial editor Times, St. Petersburg, 1963-92; dir. Times Pub. Co., 1968-92. Trustee Poynter Inst. Media Studies, St. Petersburg, 1978-92. Editor: (jour.) Masthead, 1980—81. Active St. Petersburg Charter Revision Com., 1992-93; dir. Fla. Bar Found., 1994-96. Lt. (j.g.) USNR, 1951-55. Recipient Pinellas Civil Liberties award, 1993; U. N.C.-Chapel Hill scholarship established in honor, 1994, Liberty Bell award St. Petersburg Bar Assn., 1995. Mem. Am. Soc. Newspaper Editors, Nat. Conf. Editorial Writers (pres. 1978, life), Nat. Conf. Editorial Writers Found. Inc. (pres. 1984) Methodist. Home: 736 18th Ave NE Saint Petersburg FL 33704-4608

PITTMAN, ROBERT WARREN, former internet executive; b. Jackson, Miss., Dec. 28, 1953; s. Warren E. and Lanita (Hurdle) P.; m. Sandra Hill, July 27, 1979; 1 child, Robert Thomas; m. Veronique Choa, Nov. 28, 1997; 1 child, Andrew Forest. Student, Millsaps Coll., 1971-72, Oakland U., 1972-73, U. Pitts., 1973-74; AMP, Harvard U., 1984-85. Disc jockey Sta. WJDX-FM, Jackson, Miss., 1970-72, Sta. WRIT, Milw., 1972; research dir. Sta. WDRQ, Detroit, 1972-73; program dir. Sta. WPEZ, Pitts., 1973-74, Stas. WMAQ-WKQZ, NBC Radio, Chgo., 1974-77, Sta. WNBC, N.Y.C., 1977-79; exec. producer Album Tracks, NBC TV, 1977-78; dir., v.p., then sr. v.p. Warner Amex Satellite Entertainment Co. (now MTV Networks, Inc.), 1979-82; exec. v.p., chief oper. officer MTV Networks, 1983-85; pres., chief exec. officer Warner Amex Satellite Entertainment Co., 1985-86, Quantum Media, Inc., N.Y.C., 1987-89; exec. advisor Warner Communications, Inc., 1989-90; pres., chief exec. officer Time Warner Enterprises, 1990-95; CEO, Six Flags Entertainment, 1991-95; mng. ptnr., CEO, Century 21 Real Estate, 1995-96; pres., CEO Am. On-Line Networks, 1996-97; pres., COO Am. On-Line, Inc., 1997-2001; COO AOL Time Warner, 2001—02. Bd. dirs. Cendant Corp. Bd. dirs. N.Y.C. Ballet, N.Y. Shakespeare Festival, chmn., 1987—94. Recipient Program Mgr. of Yr. Billboard, 1977, Program Dir. of Yr. Hall Radio Report, 1978, Entrepreneur award White House SB Conf., 1986, Golden Plate award Am. Acad. Achievement, 1990, medal of Excellence Miss. U. Women, 1992, Vision award Retinitis Pigmentosa International, 1992, Lifetime Achievement Internat. Monitor award Internat. Teleproduction Soc., 1993; named Innovator of Yr. Performance Mag., 1981, Humanitarian of Yr., AMC, 1984, Time Mag. Man of Yr. runner-up, 1984, Esquire Mag. Under 40 Leadership, 1985; named one of Pioneers of New Am. Start-Up, Success mag., one of five Original Thinkers of 80s, Life mag, 1990, 8 of 50 Most Influential Baby Boomers, Life mag., 1996. Methodist. Office: 75 Rockefeller Plz 9th flr New York NY 10019

PITTMAN, ROY CLINTON, JR. neurosurgeon, lawyer, theologian, philospher; b. Florence, S.C., Oct. 12, 1931; s. Roy Clinton and Edna Hester (Altman) P.; m. Therese Huguette Lamarche Pittman, Apr. 1958 (div. May 1976); children: Charlotte Elisabeth, Clinton Christopher, Russell Roy; m. Jeanne Elmore Waters Pittman, Oct. 10, 1976. BS magna cum laude, Wofford Coll., Spartanburg, S.C., 1952; MD, Med. U. S.C., Charleston, 1956; JD, Washburn U. Coll. Law, Topeka, Kans., 1991; MDiv with honors, Emory U. Candler Sch. Theology, Atlanta, 1995; DSc (hon.), The London Inst., 1973. Diplomate Am. Bd. Neurol. Surgery, Am. Bd. Orthopedic Surgery; ordained to ministry Ea. Orthodox Ch., 2000; bar: Fla. 1992, U.S. Dist. Ct. (mid. dist.) Fla. 1992. Intern U.S. Naval Hosp., Newport, R.I., 1956-57; resident in neurology U.S. Naval Hosp.-Nat. Naval Med. Ctr., Bethesda, Md., 1957-58; neurologist East Coast Neuropsychiat. Ctr.-U.S. Naval Hosp., Phila., 1958-59, head neurology br., 1959; resident in neurosurgery Jefferson Med. Coll. Hosp., 1959-61, chief resident, 1961-62; resident in gen. surgery Hahnemann Med. Coll. Hosp., 1962-63; pvt. practice neurol. surgery Morton Plant and Mease Hosps., Clearwater-Dunedin, Fla., 1963-82, Cmty. Hosp. of New Port Richey, New Port Richey, 1978-88; pvt. practice legal medicine, med. jurisprudence & bioethics Pittman Profl. Assn., Clearwater, 1995-98, Tarpon Springs, 1995-98; pres., gen. counsel The Quintessential Corp., 1998-2000; founder, prior Trinity House Retreat, Greek Orthodox Monastery of the Holy Trinity, 2001—. Protestant chaplain Morton Plant/Mease Countryside Hosp., Clearwater, Fla., 1997-98. Contbr. articles to profl. jours. Pres. St. Petersburg (Fla.) Jr. Coll. Alumni Assn., 1975-77. Lt. MC, USN, 1956-59, lt. comdr., 1962. Recipient Top Paper Bioethics & The Law award Washburn U. Coll. Law, Topeka, Kans., 1990, Top paper Comparative Civil Law award Cumberland Sch. Law & U. Heidelberg Germany Faculty of Law, 1990. Fellow Internat. Coll. Angiology, Royal Soc. Health, Internat. Coll. Surgeons, Am. Coll. Legal Medicine; mem. AMA, Congress Neurol. Surgeons, Fla. Med. Assn., Fla. Bar, Phi Beta Kappa, Phi Delta Phi. Jeffersonian Democrat. Avocations: philately, anthropology, professional ethics, travel. E-mail address. Home: 90 S Highland Ave Apt 1201 Tarpon Springs FL 34689-5351 Fax: 727-934-6799. E-mail: pittmanrc@aol.com.

PITTMAN, SHEPARD CLIFTON, secondary principal; b. West Helena, Ark., Oct. 12, 1960; s. Amos and Palmer Lee P.; m. Yolander Marie Williams, Aug. 5, 1996; children: Latanya, Shepard Jr., Sean, Candice Williams. BS in Edn., U. Mo., 1984; MA in Tchg., Webster U., 1988. Cert. edn. adminstr., indsl. edn., instrnl. media tech. Indsl. tech. tchr. Ritenour H.S., Overland, Mo., 1984-97; assoc. prin. Kirkwood (Mo.) Sch. Dist., 1997—. Dir. media svcs. Kirkwood Sch. Dist., 1994-95. Recipient Bronze medal World Games, 1985. Mem. Nat. Assn. Secondary Sch. Prins. Office: Kirkwood HS 801 W Essex Kirkwood MO 63122 Home: 11929 Devonshire Ave Saint Louis MO 63131-4510

PITTMAN, STEUART LANSING, lawyer; b. Albany, N.Y., June 6, 1919; s. Ernest Wetmore and Estelle Young (Romeyn) P.; children by previous marriage— Andrew Pinchot, Nancy Steuart, Rosamond Pinchot, Tamara Pickering; m. Barbara Milburn White, Mar. 29, 1958; children— Patricia Milburn, Steuart Lansing, Anne Romeyn. Grad., St. Paul's Sch., Concord, N.H., 1937; BA, Yale U., 1941, LLB, 1948. Bar: N.Y. 1948, D.C. 1954. With Pan Am. Airways Africa Ltd., Cairo, 1941-42, China Nat. Aviation Co., Calcutta, India, 1942; with firm Cravath, Swaine & Moore, N.Y.C., 1948-50; with govt. agys. ECA, Mut. Security Agy. and FOA, 1950-54; founder Shaw Pittman (and predecessors), Washington, 1954-61, 64—; asst. sec. of def., 1961-64. Cons. 2d Hoover Commn., 1954-55, Dept. State, 1955, Devel. Loan Fund, 1958-59; sr. fellow Inst. Def. Analysis. Bd. dirs. Hudson Inst., Chesapeake Environ. Protection Assn.; mem. Atlantic Coun. 1st lt. USMCR, WWII, CBI. Decorated Silver Star. Mem. Met. Club (Washington). Office: Shaw Pittman 2300 N St NW Washington DC 20037-1172

PITTMAN, WILLIAM CLAUDE, electrical engineer; b. Pontotoc, Miss., Apr. 22, 1921; s. William Claude and Maude Ella (Bennett) P.; m. Eloise Savage, Apr. 20, 1952; children: Patricia A. Pittman Ready, William Claude III, Thomas Allen. BSEE, Miss. State Coll., 1951, MSEE, 1957. From electronic engr. to supr. elec. engring. dept. U.S. Army Labs., Redstone Arsenal, Ala., 1951-59; supr. electronic engr. to aero. engring. supr. NASA/Marshall Space Flight Ctr., 1960; electronic engr. Army Missile Labs., 1962-82; program mgr. Army Labs. and R&D Ctr., Redstone Arsenal, 1982-99; vol. cons. AMCOM, 1999—. Organizer numerous sci. and tech. confs. Author patents, reports, papers. Sgt. USMC, 1940-46, PTO. Recipient Medal of Honor, DAR, Meritorious Civilian Svc. award Dept. Army, 1993. Fellow AIAA (assoc.; chmn. Miss.-Ala. chpt. 1981-82, Martin Schilling award 1980); mem. IEEE (sr. life), First Marine Div. Assn., DAV, IRE (chmn. Huntsville sect. 1957-58), Madison Hist. Soc., SAR (pres. Tenn. Valley chpt. 1984-85, Ala. Soc. 1990-91, Cert. 1991, Patriot medal), Tau Beta Pi, Phi Kappa Phi, Kappa Mu Epsilon. Avocations: history, genealogy. Home: 704 Desoto Rd SE Huntsville AL 35801-2032 Office: US Army Aviation Missile Command Huntsville AL 35898-0001

PITTNER, STEFAN, engineering researcher; b. Vienna, Austria, June 1, 1968; came to U.S., 1995; s. Robert and Luise Pittner. MS, Vienna U. Tech., 1990, PhD, 1994. Computer engr. Siemens Austria, Vienna, 1991-95; vis. rsch. scholar Northeastern U., Boston, 1995-98, postdoctoral rsch. assoc., 1998—. Author: Wavelet Literature Survey, 1993. Erwin Schroedinger scholar Austrian Sci. Found., 1995. Office: Northeastern U 360 Huntington Ave Boston MA 02115-5000

PITTS, BARBARA TOWLE, accountant, painter; b. St. Paul, Nov. 8, 1944; d. James Francis and Helen (Gorman) Towle; m. E.R. Pitts, Oct. 19, 1965; 1 child, Paris Tucker Pitts. BSBA with honors, U. Ala., 1980. CPA, Wash., Tenn. Prin. Barbara M. Pitts Assocs., Fayetteville, Tenn., 1982-90, Barbara M. Pitts CPA, Seattle, 1990-98. Lectr. in the field; active numerous workshops and demonstrations. One-woman shows include: Wallenstien Gallery, Moses Lake, WA, 1998, Columbia Basin Allied Arts, 1998, Artstall Gallery, Seattle, 1998, Ballard Fetherston Gallery, Seattle, 1998, 2000, Arabella Gallery, Cannon Beach, OR, 1998, 2000; exhibited in group shows Frye Art Mus., Watercolor Art Soc., Houston, 1997, La. Watercolor Soc., 1997, 98, The Watercolor Soc. of Ala., 1997, Ga. Watercolor Soc., 1997, 98, Red River Watercolor Soc., 1997, Pacific Gallery Artists Ann. Open Show, 1997, Midwest Watercolor Soc., 1997, Aqueous 97', 1997, Nat. Watercolor Okla., 1997, Watercolor West, 1997, Ea. Wash. Watercolor Soc., 1997, N.W. Watecolor Soc., 1997, 99, 2000, Pacific Artists Gallery, 1997, Women Painters of Wash., Seattle, Mercer Island Gallery, Mercer Island, WA, 1998, Asian Art Mus. Kado Tea Garden, 1997, Janet Laurel: A Woman's Gallery, 1998, Midwest Watercolor Soc. 20th Ann. Nat. Open Show, 1996, Red River Watercolor Soc. 3d Ann. Nat. Juried Art Exhbn., 1996, Ea. Wash. Watercolor Soc. Ann. Nat. Competition, 1996 (Allied Arts award), Niagara Frontier Watercolor Soc. Nat. Exhbn., 1996, Ariz. Aqueous '97 Nat. Competition, Tubac (Ariz.) Ctr. of Arts, 1997, Tex. Watercolor Soc. 48th Ann. Mus. of S.W., 1997 (Best of Show award), Pacific Artists Gallery, 1997 (Best in show award 1997), Nat. Watercolor Okla., 1997 (third place award 1997), Ga. Watercolor Soc. 18th Nat. Exhbn., 1997 (Traveling show award 1997), Midwest Watercolor Soc. 21st Nat. Exhbn., 1997, Women Painters of Wash., 1997 (Dorothy Arntston award, Gold medal award, Nancy Moffet award 1998), Millennium Images internat. juried show, U.S. and Ireland, others; group exhbns. includ Everett (Wash.) Ctr. Arts, 1998, Brea (Calif.) Cultural Ctr., Tolles Gallery, Mercer Island, Wash., 1998, Western Colo. Ctr. Arts, Grand Junction, Colo., 1998, Journey Mus., Rapid City, S.D., 1998, Frye Art Mus., Seattle, 1999, Ahmed Al-Adwany Gallery, Kuwait City, Kuwait, 1999, Northwest Watercolor Soc. 59th Annual Open Show, 60th Annual Open Show, Northwest Watercolor Soc. Hist. Retrospective, Frye Art Mus., Seattle, Galway Arts Festival, Ireland, Waterfront Hall, Belfast, Northern Ireland, The Golden Thread Gallery, Belfast, others; pub. in Watercolor Magic, 1998, 2002, Best of Watercolor 2, 1997, Am. Artist, May 1999; Seacourt Print Wkshp., Bangor, County Down, Northern Ireland, commd. Pike Pl. Market Festival poster, 1998, Inn at the Market, Seattle; commn. include Sound Transit Rail Sta., Tukurla Pk. & Ride, Bellevue C.C./Costco Early Lng. & Family Ctr., Pike Place Mkt. Found., 2001, Lilac Lodge, S.E. Effective Development, Seattle, Wash., 2002; contbr. articles to profl. jours. Bd. dirs. United Way Lincoln County, Fayetteville, 1989, Lincoln County Bd. Edn., Fayetteville, 1988-90; mem. planning com. Tenn. Hist. Soc., Nashville, 1989. Recipient Cert. of Recognition Tenn. Main St. Program, 1989, Best of Show award Juried Arts Ocean Shores, Wash., 1996, Best of Show awards Tex. Watercolor Soc. 48th Ann., Traveling Show Tex. Watercolor Soc. 48th Ann., 1996, Best in Show Pacific Gallery Artists, 1997, Middle Ga. Art Assn. award Ga. Watercolor Soc., 1997, Traveling show, 1997, 3rd Pl. Okla. Watercolor Soc., 1997, Forstall award La. Watercolor Soc., 1998, Winsor and Newton award Watercolor West, 1996, ColorQ award Watercolor West, 1998; named Woman of Yr., Fayetteville Bus. and Profl. Women, 1988. Mem. AICPA, Nat. Watercolor Soc., Midwest Watercolor Soc., Am. Watercolor Soc., Wash. Soc. CPA, N.W. Watercolor Soc. (signature mem., treas., Past Pres. award 1997, Best of Show), Red River Watercolor Soc. (Gold medal of honor 1997), Group Health Coop. Puget Sound (cen. regional coun.), Women Painters Wash. (Gold medal award 1997, Dorothy Arntson award 1997, Nancy Mottet award 1998), Watercolor West (signature mem.). Home: 3515 E Marion St Seattle WA 98122-5258 Studio: 5840 Airport Way South Ste 216 Seattle WA 98108

PITTS, BRYAN, performing company executive; Artistic dir. Ballet Okla., Oklahoma City, 1986—. Office: Ballet Okla 7421 N Classen Blvd Oklahoma City OK 73116*

PITTS, CHARLES CAREY, music educator; b. Thomaston, Ga., June 8, 1944; s. Charles Milas and Addie Louise (Hunt) P.; m. Angela Jean Wheless, Aug. 4, 1968; children: Dana Caroline, Erin Elizabeth. AB, Mercer U., 1966; M of Ch. Music, So. Bapt. Theol. Sem., Louisville, 1969. Cert. music tchr., Ga. Minister of music, youth First Bapt. Ch., Forsyth, Ga., 1970-73, Rose Hill Bapt. Ch., Columbus, 1973-77, First Bapt. Ch., Cuthbert, 1977-85; minister of music Madison (Ga.) Bapt. Ch., 1985-87; sales assoc. Daniel's Men's Shop, Thomaston, 1987-89; tchr. Westwood Acad., 1989-90; tchr. music Upson-Lee South Elem. Sch., 1990—. Youth chairperson Kiwanis Club, Forsyth, 1981-82; minister of music Mt. Olive Bapt. Ch., Molena, Ga., 1988-2000. Named one of Outstanding Young Men of Am., 1979. Mem. Music Ministers Ga. Bapt. Conv. (regional dir. 1979-80). Baptist. Home: 300 Upson Ave Thomaston GA 30286-4518 Office: Upson Lee South Elem Sch 172 Knight Trl Thomaston GA 30286-3929

PITTS, DEBORAH KRUEGER, healthcare consultant; b. Jamestown, N.D., Mar. 11, 1956; d. Lester James and Phyllis Jean (Koenig) K.; B.A. in Biology, U. Calif.-Santa Barbara, 1978; M.H.A., Duke U., 1980. Cardiopulmonary clk. Cottage Hosp., Santa Barbara, 1978; patient account rep. Durham (N.C.) County Hosp., 1979-80; health adminstrn. fellow Duke U. Hosp., Durham, 1980-81; v.p. Amherst Assocs., Atlanta, 1981-84, Tampa, 1984-88; dir. cost analysis Daus. of Charity Nat. Health System-West, Los Altos Hills, Calif., 1988-89; dir. outpatient svcs. Seton Med. Ctr., 1989-91; exec. dir. Home Tech. Health Care, 1992-94; bus. advisor, 1994—. Vol. Imola State Hosp., Napa, Calif., 1973-74; big sister St. Vincents Sch. for Mentally Handicapped, Santa Barbara, 1974-78; fund raiser Duke U. Health Adminstrn. Dept., 1980-84; assoc. coordinator Catholic Young Adults, Durham, 1980-81; bd. dirs., vice chmn., chmn. fin., chmn. planning coms. Hospice of Pinellas County, St. Petersburg, Fla., 1984-88; v.p., Partners for Tampa Theatre, 1987-88; bd. dirs. Hospice of Tenn., 1995—; leader Girl Scouts Am., 1994—; pres. Overbrook Sch. Parent Club, 1994-96; active Jr. League, 1995—. Calif. State Scholar, 1974; scholar. Am. Bus. Women's Assn., Loyal Order of Moose, Napa, Calif. Mem. Am. Coll. Healthcare Execs., Nat. Assn. Home Health Care, Tenn. Assn. Home Health Care, Healthcare Fin. Mgmt. Assn., Am. Hosp. Soc. for Mktg. and Planning, Sun Coast Adminstrs. Group, Bay Area Healthcare Planners Assn., Alpha Delta Pi (v.p., pres. 1977; Violet award 1978), Phi Sigma Kappa (little sister). Roman Catholic.

PITTS, E. HAMPTON, business educator, dean; b. South Mont, N.C. s. Romaine W. and Winnie L. Pitts; m. Lawana Pitts, Mar. 21, 1970; 1 child, Katherine. BBA, Oglethorpe U., 1967; MA, West Ga. Coll., 1973; MBA, Pfeiffer Coll., 1988; PhD, U. Miss., 1975. Mgr. Lockheed Martin Aircraft, Atlanta, 1965-71; dean Palm Beach Atlantic U., West Palm Beach, Fla., 1975-79; CFO Chesterfield-Marlboro Coll., Cheraw, S.C., 1981-84; prof. mgmt., dean Bus. Sch. Wingate (N.C.) U., 1984—; CEO Walker County Health Dept., Lafayette, Ga., 1991-93. Trustee Union Regional Med. Ctr., Monroe, N.C., 2001; cons. HRM & Leadership; bus. sch. evaluator Assn. Collegiate Bus. Schs. and Programs Accrediting Agy. Contbr. articles to profl. jours. Vol. United Way, Monroe, 1996—; active County Econ. Devel. Task Force, 2000—, Wingate Bapt. Ch. Sgt. USMC, 1961. Mem. Rotary. Republican. Baptist. Office: Wingate Univ Wingate NC 28174

PITTS, FERRIS NEWCOMB, physician, psychiatry educator; b. St. Louis, Feb. 11, 1931; s. Ferris Newcomb and Florence A. (Morris) P.; m. Jocelyn Millner, May 14, 1955; children: Andrew Ferris, Jonathan Millner, Amy Pitts Buckner. BA, Washington U., St. Louis, 1952, MD, 1955. Diplomate Am. Bd. Pediats., Am. Bd. Psychology and Neurology. Intern Wash U., St Louis Children's Hosp, 1955-56; resident pediats. Washington U., St. Louis, 1955-56, resident psychiatry, 1959-62, assoc. prof. psychiatry, 1963-76; prof. psychiatry U. So. Calif., L.A., 1976—. Pres. med. staffs several hosps., 1970—, Am. Assn. Advancement Electrotherapy, 1986. Editor-in-chief Jour. Clin. Psychiatry, 1980-88; patentee in field of hyperimmunization therapy for AIDS and other viral disorders; contbr. over 100 articles to profl. jours. Lt. comdr. USN, 1957-62. Career Rsch. Devel. award, NIMH. Fellow Am. Psychiat. Assn. (life); mem. Psychiat. Rsch. Soc. (founding mem.), Internat. Soc. Neurochemistry (founding mem.), Am. Soc. Neurochemistry (founding mem.), West Coast Coll. Psychiat. Rsch. (founding mem.). Avocations: ice hockey, tennis. Home and Office: 3500 E California Blvd Pasadena CA 91107-5653

PITTS, GARY BENJAMIN, lawyer; b. Miss., Aug. 23, 1952; s. Dextar Derward Pitts and Eva Margaret Bush; m. Nicole Palmer; children: Andrew Ross, Caitlan Taylor, Austin Palmer. Student, U. Miss., Oxford, 1970-71, Coll. Charleston (S.C.), 1971-73; BA, McGill U., Montreal, Que., Can., 1973-74; JD, Tulane U., New Orleans, 1979. Bar: Tex. 1979, U.S. Ct. Appeals (5th cir.) 1980, U.S. Supreme Ct. 1983. Assoc. Julian & Seele, Houston, 1979-84, Ogletree, Pitts & Collard, Houston, 1984-85; ptnr. Pitts & Collard LLP, Houston and Dallas, 1985-96; owner Pitts & Assocs., Houston, 1996—. Organizer, legal counsel for Neighborhood Watch Coalition. Capt. USNG, 1975-87. Mem. ATLA, Maritime Law Assn. (Proctor in Admiralty 1980—). Office: Pitts & Assocs 8866 Gulf Fwy Ste 117 Houston TX 77017-6528

PITTS, JAMES ATWATER, financial executive; b. Greenwich, Conn., Apr. 8, 1940; s. Jeremiah Patrick and Mary Louise (McGregor) P.; m. Noreen Mary Kiggins, July 20, 1963; children: Paul, Andrew, Sarah. BBA with honors, Niagara U., 1962; MBA, U. Conn., 1971. CPA, N.Y. Staff acct. Price Waterhouse, Stamford, Conn., 1962; tax specialist Deloitte Haskins & Sells, Rochester, N.Y., 1965-68; div. contr. Xerox Corp., Stamford, 1968-76; asst. corp. contr. Digital Equipment Corp., Maynard, Mass., 1976-81; v.p., corp. contr. Data Gen. Corp., Westboro, 1981-86; exec. v.p. fin. adminstrn. and strategic planning Cullinet Software, Inc., Westwood, 1986-88; v.p., chief fin. officer Bain & Co. Inc., Boston, 1988-91; sr. v.p. fin. and adminstrn., treas., CFO Clean Harbors Inc., 1992-96; pres. The Pitts Group, Boston, 1996—; v.p. for fin. and adminstrn. The Boston Found., 1996—. Chmn. Sudbury (Mass.) Town Fin. Com., 1984; v.p., mem. exec. com. Children's Mus. Boston, 1984-96; bd. dirs. Mus. Wharf Inc., 1988-96, Lake Winniepesaukee Assn., Wolfeboro, N.H.; chmn. Sudbury Long Range Capital Expenditures Com., 1981; trustee Lake Regional Conservation Trust, Meridith, N.H. With U.S. Army, 1963-64, USAR, 1965-90, Desert Storm, 1991. Decorated Meritorious Svc. medal, 1991; recipient Internat. Exec. Mgmt. award Internat. Mgmt. Inst. U. Geneva, 1980. Mem. AICPAs, Conn. CPA Soc., N.Y. Soc. CPAs, Fin. Execs. Inst., Harvard Bus. Sch. Assn. Boston (bd. govs. 1992, pres. 1992-96), Res. Officers Assn. (life), Soc. Mil. Compts., Bald Peak Colony Club, Officers Club. Office: The Boston Foundation 75 Arlington St Boston MA 02116-3936 Home: 8 West Hill Pl Boston MA 02114-3265

PITTS, JOE W., III (CHIP PITTS), lawyer, law educator; b. Baton Rouge, Nov. 24, 1960; s. Joe Wise Pitts Jr. and Bobbie (Chachere) Edwards. Cert., Cambridge (Eng.) U., 1980; spl. diploma, Oxford (Eng.) U., 1981; BA, Tulane U., 1982; JD, Stanford U., 1985. Bar: Tex. 1986. Assoc. Legal Resources Ctr., Johannesburg, Republic South Africa, 1984, Carrington Coleman Sloman & Blumenthal, Dallas, 1985-88; vis. asst. prof. law So. Meth. U., 1988-89; ptnr. Baker and McKenzie, 1989-96; v.p., chief legal officer Nokia, Inc., 1996—. Del. UN Commn. on Human Rights, Geneva, 1989, 92-96; U.S. del. to internat. conf. on European security NATO, Rome, 1990. Author numerous articles in field. Bd. dirs. Shakespeare Festival Dallas, 1987-94, pres., 1990-91, chmn., 1991-93; bd. dirs. Proyecto Adelante, 1988—; bd. dirs. Dallas Dem. Forum, 1989-93, sec., 1991-92; chmn. pub. awareness effort Dallas Young Lawyers Constl. Bicentennial Program, 1985-87, bd. dirs., 1987-91; vol. Cath. Charities Dallas, 1987—, North Ctrl. Tex. Legal Svcs., 1985—. Recipient cert. of appreciation Lawyers Against Domestic Violence, Dallas, 1985-87, cert. of recognition North Cen. Tex. Legal Svcs., 1985-87. Fellow Tex. Bar Found.; mem. ABA (vice chmn. sect. of bus. law, young lawyers div. 1986-88, exec. com., internat. law com. 1990—, vice-chair 1991-92, chair 1993—, editor-in-chief law practice notes Barrister Mag. 1988-91, commn. on pub. understanding about law 1989-91), Dallas Bar Assn. (Disting. Pro Bono Svc. award, 1986, 87, 88, 91, coord. immigration amnesty appeals com. 1987-88, chair, minority participation com. 1988-89, Pro Bono Vol. of Yr. 1989, spl. recognition 1990, 92), Tex. Assn. Young Lawyers (internat. law, editorial coms. 1985-91, chair refugee com. 1988-90, co-chmn. internat. law com. 1991-93), Dallas Assn. Young Lawyers (co-chair internat. law com. 1990-92, chair membership com. 1987-88, chair bill of rights com. 1988-89, treas. 1989, v.p. 1989-90), Tex. Accts. and Lawyers for Arts, Dallas Com. Fgn. Rels. (gen. counsel 1987-96), Council on Fgn. Relations N.Y. (term mem.), Dallas Council on World Affairs, Dallas Assembly, Crescent Spa Club, Phi Beta Kappa, Pi Sigma Alpha, Omicron Delta Kappa. Democrat. Roman Catholic. Avocations: tennis, piano. Office: Nokia Inc 6000 Connection Dr Irving TX 75039-2600

PITTS, JOSEPH R. congressman; b. Lexington, Ky., Oct. 10, 1939; s. Joseph S. and Pearl Jackson P.; m. Virginia Pratt, 1961; children: Karen R., Carol J., Daniel J. AB, Asbury Coll., 1961; MEd, West Chester State Coll., 1973. Tchr. Great Valley (Pa.) H.S., 1969-73; rep. dist. 158 State of Pa., 1972-96; mem. U.S. Congress from 16th Pa. dist., 1997—, mem. energy and commerce com., internat rels. com. Transp. com. State of Pa., 1977-80, appropriations com., 1979-82, rep. policy com., chmn. labor rels. com., transp. and joint legis. budget and fin. coms., chmn. rep. appropriations com., 1989. Decorated Air medal with five oak leaf clusters; recipient Pub. Servant award Chester-Del. Pomona Grange, 1980, Cmty. Leadership award Pa. for Biblical Morality, 1984, Disting. Govt. Svc. award Am. Mushroom Inst., 1985, Defender of Life award Pro Life Coalition S.E. Pa., 1985, William Penn award Pa. FACTS, 1985. Mem. Brandywine Valley Assn., Rotary. Address: 905 Mitchell Farm Ln Kennett Square PA 19348-1319 Office: US Ho of Reps 204 Cannon Ho Office Bldg Washington DC 20515-0001*

PITTS, NEAL CHASE, rheumatologist; b. Jackson, Miss., Dec. 6, 1933; s. Guy Moselely and Nancy Salina (Chase) P.; m. Nelia Annette Gnuse; children: Erin Chase Scott, Heather Anne Pitts. BA, Culver-Stockton Coll., 1956; MD, U. Mo., 1960. Intern U. Miss., 1960-61, resident medicine, 1961-63, fellow, 1963-65; fellow rheumatology Mayo Clin., 1965-66; bd. dirs. Caylor Nickel Clinic, Bluffton, Ind., 1990—, pres., 1991-93, 95-97, treas., 1994-95. Pres. Ind. Arthritis Assn., Indpls., 1978; bd. dirs. Lupus Found., Ft. Wayne, Ind., 1990—. Maj. M.C., U.S. Army, 1966-69. Fellow Am. Coll. Rheumatology; mem. Ind. SAR (trustee 1997, Ind. Patriot medal 1997), Nat. Soc. Mil. Order Stars and Bars (surgeon gen. 1995-99), Huguenot Soc. Ind. (registrar 1994-98, pres. 1999), Ind. Soc. Colonial Wars (gov. 1993-95), Sons of Confederate Vets. (comdr. Ind. divsn. 1991-93, surgeon-in-chief 1998—), Masons (sr. steward 1996-97, sr. warden 1999—). Republican. Presbyterian. Avocation: genealogy. Home: 1020 Highland Park Cir Bluffton IN 46714-2807

PITTS, TERENCE RANDOLPH, museum director, consultant; b. St. Louis, Feb. 5, 1950; s. Benjamin Randolph and Barbara Avalon (Gilliam) P.; children: Jacob Richard, Rebecca Suzanne. BA, U. Ill., 1972, MLS, 1974; MA in Art History, U. Ariz., 1986. Registrar Ctr. for Creative Photography, Tucson, 1976-77, curator, 1978-88, dir., 1989-2000; exec. dir. Cedar Rapids (Iowa) Mus. Art, 2000—. Cons. Art and Architecture Thesaurus, Getty Mus., 1984—. Author: (with others) George Fiske: Yosemite Photographer, 1981, Edward Weston: Color Photography; author exhbn. catalogs Four Spanish Photographers, 100 Years of Photography in the American West, Photography in the American Grain, Reframing America. Fellow Nat. Endowment Arts, 1983; travel grantee Nat. Mus. Act, 1979, rsch. grantee U. Ariz., 1983. Office: Cedar Rapids Mus Art 410 3d Ave SE Cedar Rapids IA 52401 E-mail: pitts@crma.org.

PITTS, TYRONE S. reverend; Gen. sec. Progressive Nat. Bapt. Conv. Inc., Washington. Office: Prog Nat Baptist Conv 601 50th St NE Washington DC 20019-5498

PITTS, VIRGINIA M. human resources executive; b. Boston, Nov. 22, 1953; d. Harold Francis and Connie (Caico) Cummings; m. Daniel J. Pitts, Mar. 12, 1977. Student, Northeastern U., 1982-85, Harvard U., 1997—. Adminstrv. asst. J. Baker Inc., Hyde Park, Mass., 1980-82, fin. adminstr., 1982-84; dir. human resources Casual Male Corp., 1984—; 1st sr. v.p. J. Baker Inc., 1991—. Trustee New Eng. Joint Bd. AFL-CIO, Quincy, Mass., 1984-89; guest lectr. Aquinas Jr. Coll.; mem. bd. dirs. Boston Crusaders, Drum & Bugle Corps. Instr. Boston Crusaders Drum and Bugle Corps, 1973-85; regional v.p. 210 Charitable Assn., Watertown, Mass., 1989-90; bd. dirs. Handi-Kids, Boston Crusaders Drum and Bugle Corps. Mem. Am. Mgmt. Assn., Am. Compensation Assn. (cert. profl.), Soc. Human Resource Mgrs. Avocations: dressage, gardening. Office: Casual Male Corp 555 Turnpike St Canton MA 02021-2791 E-mail: gpitts@cmal.com.

PITTS, WILLIAM CLARENCE, physicist; b. Seattle, Apr. 19, 1929; s. Clarence H. and Emily B. (Kepp) P.; m. Joanne R. Lawson, May 18, 1952 (dec. Jan. 1978); children: Starr R., Nancy A.; m. Patricia A. (Kirkland) Adams, May 1, 1981. BS in Physics, U. Wash., 1951; postgrad., Stanford U., 1951-58. Rsch. scientist NACA/NASA, Moffett Field, Calif., 1951-86, Eloret Inst., Moffett Field, 1986-95; cons. Steve Miller and Assocs., Flagstaff, Ariz., 1995-99, Pitts Consulting, 1995—. Contbr. numerous articles to profl. publs.; inventor multilayer infrared radiation barrier for re-entry spacecraft; combined flexible blanket insulation for re-entry spacecraft; others. Avocations: golf, bridge, cosmology. Home and Office: 7753 Beltane Dr San Jose CA 95135-2138 E-mail: wcpitts@infi.net.

PITTSMAN, GEORGE, social worker, educator; b. Scranton, Pa., Aug. 26, 1971; s. George Joseph and Ruth Ann Pittsman; m. Jennifer Jo Henry, Nov. 3, 2001. BSW, Marywood Coll., 1993, MSW, 1994. LCSW Pa., 1997; cert. tchr. Pa., 01. Dir. social svcs. Carpenter Care Ctr., Tunkhannock, Pa., 1994—97; med. social worker Tyler Meml. Hosp., 1997—98; clin. therapist Stillmeadow, Inc., Jermyn, 1999—2000, residential svc. program mgr., 2000—. Coun. mem. Mayfield Bore, Mayfield, Pa., 2002—. Mem.: NASW, Coun. Exceptional Children. Democrat. Roman Catholic. Avocations: sports, travel, outdoors. Home: 606 Pine St Apt 15 Mayfield PA 18433 Office: Stillmeadow Inc PO Box 69 Jermyn PA 18433

PITYNSKI, ANDRZEJ PIOTR, sculptor; b. Ulanow, Poland, Mar. 15, 1947; naturalized citizen, 1987; s. Aleksander and Stefania (Krupa) P.; m. Christina Teresa Gacek, Aug. 6, 1976; 1 child, Alexander Mark. MFA in Sculpture, Acad. Fine Arts, Cracow, Poland, 1974; postgrad., Art Students League, N.Y., 1975. Cert. tchr., N.J.; supr. modeling, mold, enlarging, resin crafts. Supr. and instr. sculpture Tech. Inst. of Sculpture - Johnson Atelier, Mercerville, NJ, 1979—; instr. sculpture Rider U., Lawrenceville, 1992—97, Rutgers U., 1998—2002. Asst. to sculptor Alexander Ettl, Sculpture House, N.Y., 1975-79 Bronze/granite monumental sculptures include General Kosciuszko, St. Petersburg, Fla., 2002, Sarmatian - Spirit of Freedom, Hamilton, N.J., 2001, Flame of Freedom, Balt., 2000, Blue Army-1998, Warsaw, Poland, Katyn-1940, Jersey City, N.J., 1991-92, Pope John Paul II, Manhattan, N.Y., 1991, Ulanow, Poland, 1989, General Anders, Doylestown, Pa., 1995, Father J. Popieluszko, Trenton, N.J., 1987, Avenger, Doylestown, Pa., 1987, Portrait Bust M Curie, 1986, Bayonne, N.J.; aluminum sculpture Partisans II, Hamilton, N.J., 1999, Partisans, Boston, 1983, Ignacy Paderewski, Cracow, Poland, 1973; one-man show at Hamilton, N.J., 2000, N.Y., 2001; exhbn. Mus. of Polish Army, Warsaw, 1995, Contemporary Artists Guild, Lever House, N.Y., 1991, Zacheta Nat. Art Gallery, Warsaw, 1991, Fedn. Internat. De La Medaille/Brit. Mus., London, 1992, Cast Iron Gallery, Soho, N.Y., 1992, Alt. Ext. Gallery, Phila., 1992, Audubon Exhibits-54th Ann. Exhbn., Fed. Hall, N.Y.C., 1996, others. Recipient Polonia Restituta Cross, R.P. London, 1989, Gold Order of Merit, Rep. of Poland, 1990, Cultural award Am. Inst. Polish Culture, Washington, 1992; named Comdr. Order Merit of Republic of Poland, 1996, The Monuments Conservancy's Perennial Wisdom award-medal, N.Y.C., 1999, Honorary Citizen of Balt., 2001. Fellow Nat. Sculpture Soc.; mem. Allied Artists of Am. (Silver medal of honor 1985, Elliot Liskin Meml. award 1989, Mems. and Assocs. award 1994), Audubon Artists (Gold Medal of Honor 1996, Silver Medal of Honor 1997, 98), Contemporary Artists Guild, Am. Medallic Sculpture Assn. Republican. Roman Catholic. Avocations: horse jumping, hunting, judo. Office: PO Box 220380 Brooklyn NY 11222-0380

PITZER, MARTHA SEARES, nursing educator; b. Pasadena, Calif., June 29, 1938; d. Richard Urmy and Doris Ann (Dunton) Seares; m. Russell Mosher, Sept. 2, 1959; children: Susan Merle, Kenneth Richard, David Seares. RN, Bishop Johnson Coll. Nursing, L.A., 1959; BSN, Ohio State U., 1974, MS, 1976, PhD in Family Rels. and Human Devel., 1984. Asst. prof. Coll. Nursing Ohio State U., Columbus, 1985-90, adj. asst. prof., 1990—; perinatal clin. nurse specialist Ohio State U. Hosps., 1990-91, lactation cons., 1996-97; lactation educator specialist Riverside Meth. Hosp., 1993-95, 98—; educator Lamaze Childbirth Assn., 1991-96. Asst. prof. Otterbein Coll., Westerville, Ohio, 1978-79. Contbr. articles to profl. jours. NRSA predoctoral fellow; postdoctoral fellow U. Calif., San Francisco, 1988-89. Mem. Internat. Lactation Cons. Assn. (cert. lactation educator, cert. lactation cons.), Sigma Theta Tau. Home: 1308 Castleton Rd N Columbus OH 43220-3808 E-mail: pitzer.2@osu.edu.

PITZNER, RICHARD WILLIAM, lawyer; b. Fond du Lac, Wis., Sept. 19, 1946; s. Robert J. and Almira (Wurtz) P.; m. Georgene J. Thuerwachter, July 6, 1968 (div. 1991); children: Christie, Kyle; m. Ricki L. Mundstock, Jan. 4, 1998. BBA, U. Wis., 1968, MBA, 1969, JD, 1972. Bar: Wis. 1972, U.S. Dist. Ct. (we. dist.) Wis. 1972, U.S. Tax Ct. Ptnr. Murphy & Desmond, Madison, Wis., 1972—. Tchr. U. Wis., Madison, 1975-78. Mem. ABA, AICPA, Nat. Assn. Accts., Wis. Inst. CPAs, State Bar Wis., Wis. Inst. CPAs, Kensington Golf and Country Club, Nakoma Golf Club, Order of Coif, Beta Gamma Sigma. Avocations: golf, swimming. Home: 3123 Harlan Circle Madison WI 53711 Office: Murphy & Desmond 2 E Mifflin St Madison WI 53703-2889

PIVEN, FRANCES FOX, political scientist, educator; b. Calgary, Alta., Can., Oct. 10, 1932; came to U.S., 1933, naturalized, 1953; d. Albert and Rachel (Paperny) F.; 1 dau., Sarah. BA, U. Chgo., 1953, MA, 1956, PhD, 1962; L.H.D. (hon.), Adelphi U., 1985. Mem. faculty Columbia, 1966-72; prof. polit. sci. Boston U., 1972-82, Grad. Ctr., CUNY, 1982—. Co-author: Regulating the Poor: The Functions of Public Welfare, 1971, 2d edit., 1993, The Politics of Turmoil: Essays on Poverty, Race and the Urban Crisis, 1974, Poor People's Movements, 1977, New Class War, 1982, The Mean Season, 1987, Why Americans Don't Vote, 1988; editor: Labor Parties in Post Industrial Societies, 1992, The Breaking of the American Social Compact, 1997, Why Americans Still Don't Vote, 2000. Recipient C. Wright Mills award Soc. Study Social Problems, 1971, Fulbright Disting. Lectureship award U. Bologna, 1990, President's award APHA, 1993, Annual award Nat. Assn. Sec. of State, 1994, Lifetime Achievement award Pol. Sociology Am. Sociological Assn., 1995, Disting. Career award, 2000; Guggenheim fellow, 1973-74; Am. Council Learned Socs. awardee, 1982 Mem. Am. Polit. Sci. Assn. (v.p. 1981-82), Soc. Study Social Problems (pres. 1980-81, Lee founders award 1992), ACLU (dir.). Home: PO Box N Millerton NY 12546-0651 Office: CUNY Grad Sch 365 5th Ave New York NY 10016-4309

PIVEN, PETER ANTHONY, architect, management consultant; b. Bklyn., Jan. 3, 1939; s. William Meyer and Sylvia Lee (Greenberg) P.; m. Caroline Cooper, July 9, 1961; children: Leslie Ann, Joshua Lawrence. AB, Colgate U., 1960; MArch, U. Pa., 1963; MS, Columbia U., 1964. Diplomate: cert. Nat. Council Archtl. Registration Bds.; registered architect, N.Y., Pa., N.J. Architect Westermann-Miller Assocs., N.Y.C., 1964-66, Bernard Rothzeid, A.I.A., N.Y.C., 1967-68; v.p. Caudill Rowlett Scott, 1968-72; prin. Geddes Brecher Qualls Cunningham, Phila., 1972-87; pres. The Coxe Group, Inc., 1980-90, dir., prin. cons., 1980—. Adj. prof. U. Pa. Grad. Sch. Fine Arts, 1989—, Rensselaer Poly. Inst. Sch. Architecture, 1994—; vis. instr. Harvard U. Grad. Sch. Design. Author: Compensation Management: A Guideline for Small Firms, 1982, Architect's Essentials of Ownership Transition, 2002; co-author: Success Strategies for Design Professionals, 1987; contbg. editor: Archtl. Record and Design Intelligence; author (contbg.): Architects Handbook of Professional Practice, 1994, 2001. Mem. N.Y.C. Community Planning Bd., 1969-72. Fellow AIA (chmn. fin. mgmt. com. 1976-80, chmn. Fellows Jury 1998, mem. conv. task force 1998, mem. nat. ethics coun. 1999—, pres. Phila. chpt. 1980); mem. Phila. C. of C. (dir. 1980-81), The Carpenters Co. of City and County of Phila. (mng. com. 1989-91). Home: 112 N Lambert St Philadelphia PA 19103-1107 Office: The Coxe Group Inc 1218 3rd Ave Seattle WA 98101-3097

PIVER, M. STEVEN, gynecologic oncologist; b. Washington, Sept. 29, 1934; s. Harry Samuel and Sonia (Bard) P.; m. Susan Myers, June 25, 1958; children: Debra Ellen, Carolyn Jan, Kenneth Stuart. BS, Gettysburg Coll., 1957; MD, Temple U., 1961. Diplomate Am. Bd. Ob-Gyn, Am. Coll. Surgeons. Intern Nazareth Hosp., Phila., 1961-62; resident Johns Hopkins U. Hosp., Balt., 1962; resident ob-gyn. Pa. Hosp., U. Pa., Phila., 1965-68; fellow gynecologic oncology U. Tex., Hosp. and Tumor Inst., Houston, 1968-70; asst. prof. gynecologic oncology U. N.C. Sch. Medicine, 1970-71; assoc. chief gynecologic oncology Roswell Park Cancer Inst., Buffalo, 1972-83, founder, dir. Gilda Radner Familial Ovarian Cancer Registry, 1981—, chief gynecologic oncology, 1984-97; clin. prof., dir. div. gynecologic oncology SUNY, 1986-97, prof. gynecology, 1998—, chair emeritus gynecologic oncology, 1998—. Cons., editor Yearbook of Cancer, 1972-88; assoc. editor Nat. Cancer Inst., PDQ, 1984—; mem. editl. bd. The Female Patient, 1989—, Oncology Reports, 1993—; author: Ovarian Malignancies: Clinical Care of Adults and Adolescents, 1983, Gilda's Disease: Sharing Personal Experiences and a Medical Perspective on Ovarian Cancer, 1996, Myths and Facts About Ovarian Cancer, 1997; editor: Ovarian Malignancies: Diagnostic and Therapeutic Advances, 1987, Manual of Gynecologic Oncology/Gynecology, 1989, Conversations About Cancer, 1990, Handbook of Gynecologic Oncology, 1995; contbr. more than 300 articles to profl. jours. Bd. dirs. United Way of Buffalo and Erie County, 1986-91; chmn. bd. trustees D'Youville Coll., Buffalo, 1989—; pres. Friends of Night People, Buffalo, 1988-97. Capt. USAF, 1962-64. Hon. fellow Phi Beta Kappa, Gettysburg Coll., 1956, Tex. Assn. Obstetricians and Gynecologists, 1983, Alpha Omega Alpha, Temple U. Sch. Medicine, 1995; named Citizen of Yr., Buffalo News, 1989; recipient YMCA Leadership award Buffalo YMCA, 1990, Brotherhood/Sisterhood Award in Medicine (Western N.Y. Region), NCCJ, 1991, St. Marguerite D'Youville Coll. Community Svc. award, 1992. Fellow ACS, Am. Coll. Obstetricians and Gynecologists; mem. Am. Soc. Clin. Oncology, Soc. Gynecologic Oncologists, Soc. Surg. Oncology, Am. Radium Soc., Phi Beta Kappa, Alpha Omega Alpha. Achievements include documentation of hydroxyurea as a radiation sensitizer in cervix cancer that significantly improves cure rate and that ovarian cancer can be inherited; patent for method of enhancing the efficacy of anti-tumor agents. Home: 315 Lincoln Pky Buffalo NY 14216-3127 Office: Sisters Hosp 2157 Main St Buffalo NY 14214-2692 E-mail: mpiver@wnychs.org.

PIVERONUS, PETER JOHN, JR. education educator; b. Boston, Nov. 29, 1941; s. Peter John Sr. and Rose Camella (Pasciuto) P.; m. Bonnie Jean Kennedy, June 7, 1969 (div. 1981); children: Elizabeth Schaeffler, William Schaeffler, Michelle Montesano; m. Elibeth Doris Roth, Nov. 21, 1988; children: Shannon Roth, Sara Roth. BA, Boston U., 1964, MA, 1966; PhD, Mich. State U., 1972. Asst. prof. SUNY, Buffalo, 1967-69, Claflin Coll., Orangeburg, S.C., 1969-70; adj. prof. Lansing (Mich.) Community Coll., 1972—, Montcalm Community Coll., Sidney, Mich., 1973—, Jackson (Mich.) Community Coll., 1979—. Prof. humanities extended degree programs Cen. Mich. U., 1991—; vis. prof. Mich. State U., East Lansing, 1986, Alma (Mich.) Coll., 1987. Editor, contbr.: Conflict in Ireland, 1976; contbr. articles to profl. jours. Precinct del. Ingham County Dems., Lansing, 1980-81; trustee Southland Complex Condo Assn., Lansing, 1987-90; pres. Gaelic League of Lansing, 1981-82. HEW fellow Claflin Coll., 1969-70; postdoctoral rsch. grantee U. Mich. Ctr. for Russian and East European Studies, 1985. Mem. Am. Com. for Irish Studies, Nat. Ctr. for Employee Ownership, Irish-Am. Cultural Inst., Soc. for History of Discoveries, Mich. Assn. Higher Edn. (faculty senator 1978-79), Mich. Edn. Assn., Econ. and Bus. Hist. Soc. Unitarian Universalist. Avocations: reading, traveling, camping, boating. Home: PO Box 80452 Lansing MI 48908-0452 Office: Lansing Community Coll 419 N Capitol Ave Lansing MI 48933-1207

PIVIN, JEANETTE EVA, psychotherapist; b. Fall River, Mass., Feb. 24, 1932; d. Oscar and Ida Antoinette (Gauthier) P. B in Edn., Cath. Tchrs. Coll., 1956; MA in Theology, U. Notre Dame, 1967; cert. clin. pastoral edn., Worcester State Hosp., 1975; cert. interior design, Hall Inst. Tech., 1989; cert. divorce mediator, Roger Williams Univ, 1995. Tchr. St. Matthew Sch., Cranston, R.I., 1956-64; asst. prof. religious studies Salve Regina U., Newport, 1967-74; staff counselor La Salette Counseling Svcs., Attleboro, Mass., 1975-80; pastoral counselor Interfaith Counseling Ctr., Providence, 1975—; pvt. practice, 1980—. Mem.: Am. Assn. Pastoral Counselors. Home and Office: 139 Woodbine St Providence RI 02906-2543

PIXLEY, CARL PRESTON, mathematician; b. Omaha, Nov. 3, 1942; s. William Robert and Lillus Marie (Petty) P.; m. Cynthia Marie Nardone, Dec. 21, 1968; children: Laura Elizabeth, Margaret Marie. BS in Math., U. Omaha, 1966; MS in Math., Rutgers U., 1968; PhD in Math., SUNY, Binghamton, 1972. Instr. U. Tex., Austin, 1972-73, asst. prof., 1974-77; assoc. prof. S.W. Tex. State U., San Marcos, 1978-81; sr. rsch. scientist Burroughs Corp., Austin, 1981-82, mgr., 1986-88; sr. mem. tech. staff Microelectronics and Computer Tech. Corp., 1988-92; mgr. adv. design verification tech. Motorola Inc., Tex., 1992—2001; sr. dir. Synopsys Inc., 2001—. Lectr. in field; invited spkr. Schloss Dagstahl workshop on logic representations, Germany, 1996, DIMACS workshop, New Brunswick, N.J., 1996, Internat. Test Conf., Washington, 1996, Applied Math. Colloquium U. Ariz., 1996, formal verification in industry workshops, 1998, Concurrent Sys. Design Conf., Aizu, Japan, 1998, Internat. Test Conf. Roundtable on microprocessor verification, Washington, 1998; invited spkr. Internat. Symposium Quality Electronic Design, 2001, High Level Design Validation and Test, others; bd. dirs. Accellera. Contbr. articles to profl. publs. Mem. IEEE, Am. Math. Soc., Math. Assn. Am. Methodist. Achievements include co-invention of Pixley-Roy Space; selection theory on infinite dimensional spaces, symbolic model checking. Office: Synopsys 2025 NW Cornelius Pass Rd Hillsboro OR 97124 Home: 16670 NW Mission Oaks Dr Beaverton OR 97006-8410

PIZER, HOWARD CHARLES, sports and entertainment executive; b. Chgo., Oct. 23, 1941; s. Edwin and Estyr (Seeder) P.; m. Sheila Graff, June 14, 1964; children: Jacqueline, Rachel. BBA, U. Wis., 1963; JD magna cum laude, Northwestern U., 1966. Assoc. McDermott, Will & Emery, Chgo., 1966-72; ptnr. Katten, Muchin, Zavis, 1972-74; exec. v.p., gen. counsel Balcor Co., Skokie, Ill., 1975-80; exec. v.p. Chgo. White Sox, Chgo., 1981—. Exec. v.p. United Ctr. Joint Venture. Past pres. Chgo. Spl. Olympics; bd. dirs. Chgo. Conv. and Tourism Bur., Inc., 1983—, Spl. Children's Charities, 1984—, Chgo. Baseball Cancer Charities, 1983—, Near West Side Cmty. Devel. Corp. Mem. Chgo. Bar Assn., Standard Club Chgo., Briarwood County. Home: 300 Euclid Ave Winnetka IL 60093-3606 Office: Chgo White Sox 333 W 35th St Chicago IL 60616-3651

PIZITZ, RICHARD ALAN, retail and real estate group executive; b. Birmingham, Ala., Feb. 24, 1930; s. Isadore and Hortense (Hirsch) P.; m. Joan Black; children: Richard Alan Jr., Jill Carole, Susan Lyn. BA, Washington & Lee U., 1951; MBA, Harvard U., 1953. Mdse. mgr. Pizitz Dept. Stores, Birmingham, 1953-59, v.p., 1959-66, pres., 1966-86, chmn. bd., 1986-87; chmn. Pizitz Mgmt. Group, 1987—. Pres. United Way, Birmingham, 1988, Ala. Commn. on Higher Edn., 1987-95; pres. Better Bus. Bur., Birmingham, 1962; mem. Ala adv. commn. U.S. Commn. on Civil Rights, 1985. Recipient Erskine Ramsay award, 1974; named Mktg. Man of Yr., Am. Mktg. Assn., 1966, Man of Yr., Young Men's Bus. Club, 1970. Mem. Ala. Commn. on Higher Edn., Birmingham C. of C. (pres. 1970), Ala. Retail Assn. (pres. 1965). Avocations: pvt. pilot, skiing, tennis, scuba diving. Office: Pizitz Mgmt Group 2140 11th Ave S Ste 318 Birmingham AL 35205-2850 Address: 2936 Redmont Park Ln Birmingham AL 35205-2136

PIZZAGALLI, JAMES, construction executive; b. Burlington, Vt., Nov. 23, 1944; s. Angelo and Theresa (Moalli) P.; m. Judy Rock, June 21, 1969; 1 child, Michael. BS, U. Vt., 1966; JD, Boston U., 1969. Treas. Pizzagalli Constrn. Co., Burlington, Vt., 1969-76, v.p., 1976-91, chmn., CEO, 1991-98, co-chmn., 1998—. Dir. Chittenden Corp., Burlington, 1982—, AGC Edn. Found., Washington, 1992—, Shelburne (Vt.) Mus., 1983-92, 2000—; life dir. Assn. Gen. Contractors, Washington, 1976—, atty.-at law. Trustee U. Vt., 2000—. Mem. TheMoles, Ethan Allen Club. Republican. Roman Catholic. Home: 3393 Harbor Rd Shelburne VT 05482-7611 Office: Pizzagalli Constrn Co PO Box 2009 South Burlington VT 05407 E-mail: jpizzagalli@pizzagalli.com

PIZZAMIGLIO, NANCY ALICE, performing company executive; b. Oak Park, Ill., Aug. 22, 1936; d. Howard Joseph and Marian Louise (Henne) Gilman; m. Ernest George Lovas, May 17, 1957 (div. Nov. 1976); children: Lori Dianne, Randall Gilman; m. Albert Theodore Pizzamiglio, Mar. 27, 1978. Student, North Tex. State U., 1955-56. Stewardess North Cen. Airlines, Chgo., 1956-57; receptionist Leo Burnett Advt. Agy., 1957-59; office mgr. Judy Stallons Employment Agy., Oak Brook, Ill., 1973-75; mgr. and escort Prestige Vacations, Inc., 1975-76; corp. dir. Al Pierson Big Band U.S.A., Inc., Aubrey, Tex., 1976-2000, Al Pierson, Ltd., Aubrey, 1978—, corp. pres., 1997—, Gilman, Inc. Artists Mgmt., Aubrey, 1982-2000; owner Dancing Horse Ranch, Tex., 1983—; bus. mgr. Guy Lombardo's Royal Canadians, 1989—. Editor: (newsletter) Property Owners Assn., 1972-73; contbr. articles to profl. jours. Recipient expert award NRA, 1952. Mem. U.S. Lipizzan Registry (bd. dirs. 1986-89, 1996-98, treas. 1996, 97, 98), Dallas Dressage Club (bd. dirs. 1988-94), Am. Horse Shows Assn., U.S. Dressage Fedn. (qualified rider 1989, third/all breeds, first level 1989, first/all breeds, fourth level 1991, third Vintage Cup, fourth level 1991, third all-breeds first level 1992, third vintage cup first level 1992), Dallas-Ft. Worth Labrador Retriever Club Inc. (bd. dirs. 2000—). Republican. Episcopalian. Avocations: showing, breeding, and training Labrador Retrievers, world travel, Chinese history, gem stones. Address: Al Pierson Ltd 2469 Spring Hill Rd Aubrey TX 76227-3911 E-mail: dancehorse@aol.com.

PIZZELLA, PATRICK, federal agency administrator; BSBA, U. S.C., 1976. Adminstr. Dept. Edn., 1986—89; chief adminstrv. officer Fed. Housing Fin. Bd., 1990—95; govt. affairs counselor Preston Gates Ellis & Rouvelas Meeds LLP, 1996—2001; asst. sec. adminstrn. and mgmt. U.S. Dept. Labor, Washington, 2001—. Office: US Dept Labor 200 Constitution Ave NW Washington DC 20210*

PIZZI, ANTHONY C. real estate investor, consultant; b. Hancock, Mich., June 25, 1953; s. Antonio and Catherine Pizzi. Student, Mich. Technol. U., 1971-72; BA, Alma Coll., 1975. CPA, Mich. Officer, prin. Turnquist & Pizzi PC CPAs, Houghton, Mich., 1975-83; contr., CFO Copper Country Cmty. Mental Health Svcs. Authority, 1983-97; v.p., adminstr., CFO GRQ Properties Ltd., Hancock, 1993—. Active ARC, Hancock, 1979-99; chmn. Houghton County Republicans, 1980-82, 98—. Fellow Mich. Assn. CPAs; mem. AICPA, Beta Sigma Theta (treas. 1992—). Republican. Avocations: photography, music. Office: GRQ Properties Ltd PO Box 49 Hancock MI 49930-0049

PIZZINGRILLI, KIM, state official; B.Bus. Econs., U. Pitts., Johnstown, 1981; M.Govtl. Adminstrn., U. Pa., 1988. From auditor, acct. and asst. dir. Bur. of Audits Pa. Treasury Dept., 1981-87; sr. regulatory analyst Pa. Ind. Regulatory Rev. Commn., 1987-95; spl. asst. to sec. Dept. of State, Harrisburg, 1995-96, dep. sec. regulatory programs, 1996-98, acting sec., 1998-99, sec. of the commonwealth, 1999—2002; commr. Pa. Public Utility Comm., 2002—. Mem. Bd. of Property, Bd. of Fin. and Revenue, State of Pa.; mem. Pa. State Athletic Commn., Pa. State Navigation Commn. for the Delaware River and its Navigable Tributaries; mem. Pa. Mcpl. Retirement Bd.; keeper Great Seal of the Commonwealth. Mem. Nat. Assn. Secs. of State, Women Execs. in State Govt. Office: Pennsylvania Public Utility Commission P O Box 3265 Harrisburg PA 17105-3265*

PIZZITOLA, PATRICIA GALLMAN, music educator; b. Tuscaloosa, Ala., Sept. 10, 1938; d. Rawdon Lee and Gladys Odine (Thomas) Gallman; m. William Ferdinand Hunteman Jr., Oct. 4, 1958 (div. Feb. 1976); children: William Randolph, Jennifer Lee; m. Vito William Pizzitola, Feb. 21, 1976; 1 child, Joseph Michael. MusB, U. Montevallo, 1997, postgrad., 1997-2001. Legis. aide Titusville (Fla.) area, 1968-70; news editor WRMF AM-FM, Titusville, Fla., 1970-72; reporter, stringer Kennedy Space Ctr., 1972-76; reporter WBRC-TV, Birmingham, Ala., 1976-77; assignment editor WBMG-TV, 1986-87; substitute tchr. Vestavia Hills (Ala.) Sch. Bd., 1987-90; owner Round Tuit Needle Work, Montevallo, Ala., 1990-94; tchr. Sch. Performing Arts, Columbiana, 1997—. Mem. grad. student coun. U. Montevallo, 1997. Pres. Band Parents Assn., Vestavia Hills, Ala., 1984-86; chmn. Libr. Bd., Titusville, 1968-72; mem. Zoning Bd., Brevard County, Fla., 1969-72, Mchts. Assn., Montevallo, 1992-93; Ala. state chmn., coord. Nat. Barrier Awareness Day, 1987. Mem. Metro Music Forum, Am. Fedn. of Music Tchrs., Ala. Fedn. of Music Tchrs.,usic Tchrs. Nat. Assn., Ala. Music Tchrs. Assn., Birmingham Music Tchrs. Assn., Omicron Delta Kappa, Phi Alpha Mu. Democrat. Baptist. Avocations: needlework designing, writing, composing. Office: Sch Performing Arts 208 N Main St Columbiana AL 35051-5344

PIZZO, PHILIP A. pediatrics educator, university administrator; b. N.Y.C., Dec. 6, 1944; BA, Fordham U., 1966; MD, U. Rochester, 1970. Diplomate Am. Bd. Pediatrics, Am. Bd. Hematology/Oncology. Intern Children's Hosp. Med. Ctr., Boston, 1970-71, jr. asst. resident, 1971-72, sr. resident, 1972-73; tchg. fellow Harvard U. Sch. Medicine, 1972-73; clin. assoc. Pediatric Oncology Br. of Nat. Cancer Inst., 1973-75, investigator, 1975-76, sr. investigator, 1976-80; head infectious disease sect. Pediatric Br. of Nat. Cancer Inst., 1980-96, chief pediatrics, 1982-96; sci. dir. divsn. clin. scis. Nat. Cancer Inst., 1994-96; prof. pediatrics Sch. Medicine, Uniformed Svcs. U. Health Sci., 1987-96; Thomas Morgan Rotch prof., chmn. dept. pediatrics Harvard U. Sch. Medicine, Boston, 1996—2000; dean Stanford U. School of Med., Conn., 2000—. Mem. clin. rsch. subpanel of Nat. Cancer Inst., 1978-81, infectious disease clin. ctr., NIH, 1978-96, transfusion com., 1984-87, pediatric core com., pediatric AIDS clin. trials group, 1988-94, sec. HIV task force, 1988; mem. sci. adv. bd. Children's Hospice Internat., 1988-94, AIDS program Nat. Inst. Allergy and Infectious Diesases, 1988-89; mem. clin. rsch. subcom. AIDS Rsch. Adv. Com., 1990-94; physician-in-chief, chmn. dept. medicine Children's Hosp., Boston, 1996—, Myron Karon Meml. lectr., 1986, Melissa Anne Krinsky Meml. lectr., 1989. Mem. AAAS, NAS Inst. Medicine, Am. Soc. Hematology, Am. Fedn. for Clin. Rsch., Am. Soc. for Clin. Investigation, Am. Soc. Clin. Oncology (bd. dirs. 1996—), Elizabeth Glaser Pediatric AIDS Found. (bd. dirs. 1996—), Infectious Disease Soc. Am., Infectious Disease Soc. Am., Internat. Immunocompromised Host Soc. (pres.-elect), IDSA (bd. dirs. 1996—). Office: Stanford U, School of Med 300 Pasteur Dr, Ste M121 Palo Alto CA 94305*

PIZZO, SALVATORE VINCENT, pathologist; b. Phila., June 22, 1944; s. George J. P. and Aida (Alcaro) Lepore; m. Carol Ann Kurkowski, Dec. 28, 1968 (div. 1987); children: Steven, David, Susan. PhD, Duke U., 1972; BS, St. Joseph's Coll., 1966; MD, Duke U., 1973. Asst. prof. Duke U. Med. Ctr., Durham, N.C., 1976-80, assoc. prof., 1980-85, prof., 1985—, dir. med. scientist tng. program, 1987—, chmn., 1991—. Mem., chmn. program rev. com. NIH, Bethesda, Md., 1986-90; vice chmn. Gordon Conf. Proteases, Holderness, N.H., 1990, chmn., 1992-96; cons. in field, 1980—; mem. Cellular and Molecular Basis of Disease Rev. Com., 1990-96. Contbr. articles to profl. jours. Grantee NIH, 1976—, Am. Cancer Soc., 1976—. Fellow AAAS; mem. Am. Heart Assn. (exec. com. Thrombosis coun. 1990, 92), Am. Chem. Soc., Am. Assn. Pathologists (program com. 1985-88, long range planning com. 1990-92), Am. Soc. Biological Chemists, Alpha Sigma Nu, Phi Beta Kappa, Alpha Omega Alpha, Sigma Xi. Achievements include patents in field; research in lipoproteins in coagulation and fibronolysis, a link to atherosclerosis, anticoagulation drug development; identification of ATP synthase as the target for Angiostatin action. Office: Duke U Med Ctr PO Box 3712 Durham NC 27710-0001 E-mail: pizzo001@mc.duke.edu.

PIZZORNO, JOSEPH EGIDIO, JR. business executive; b. San Gabriel, Calif., Dec. 7, 1947; s. Joseph Egidio Sr. and Mary (Carmela) P.; 1 child, Raven Muir; m. Lara Elise Udell, Sept. 28, 1985; 1 child, Galen Udell. BS with Distinction, Harvey Mudd Coll., Claremont, Calif., 1969; Naturopathic Doctor with honors, Nat. Coll. Naturopathic Medicine, Portland, Oreg., 1975. Rsch. asst. Lockheed Aircraft, Ontario, Calif., 1968; rsch. technologist U. Wash., Seattle, 1970-75; practice naturopathic medicine, 1975-82; practice midwifery, 1978-82; pres. Bastyr U., 1978-2000, pres. emeritus, 2000—; pres. Salugenecists, Inc., 2001—. Pres. Coun. on Naturopathic Med. Edn., Portland, Oreg., 1985-87; apptd. adv. panel safety and efficacy of dietary supplements U.S. Office of Tech. Assessment, 1993-95; sr. med. advisor Alternative and Complementary Therapies, 1995-97; mem. White House Commn. Complementary and Alternative Medicine Policy, 2000-02. Author: Total Wellness, 1996; co-author: Handbook of Natural Medicine, 1985, 3d edit., 2001, Encyclopedia of Natural Medicine, 1990, 2d edit., 1998; contbg. editor: Let's Live mag., 1987—; contbr. Mem. Seattle/King County Bd. Health, 1996—; vice chair bd. dirs. Inst. for Functional Medicine. Mem.: Seattle Midwifery Sch. (edn. com. 1978—91), Wash. Assn. Naturopathic Physicians (edn. dir. 1976), Am. Assn. Naturopathic Physicians (bd. dirs. 1984—91). Libertarian. Avocations: microcomputers, basketball, ultimate frisbie. Home: 4220 NE 135th St Seattle WA 98125-3836 E-mail: president_emeritus@bstyr.edu., drpizzorno@salugenecists.com.

PIZZULLI, FRANCIS COSMO JOSEPH, lawyer, bioethicist; b. Bklyn., May 16, 1950; s. Dominick Lawrence and Rose Nancy (Ieracitano) P. BA in Math with high honors, U. Calif., Santa Barbara, 1971; JD, U. So. Calif., 1974. Bar: Calif. 1975. NEH fellow Inst. Soc., Ethics and Life Scis./Hastings Ctr., Hastings-on-Hudson, N.Y., 1974-75; law clk. U.S. Ct. Appeals (9th cir.), 1975-76; pvt. practice Santa Monica, Calif., 1981—. Cons. Nat. Commn. for Protection Human Subjects of Biomed. and Behavioral Rsch., Washington, 1976-77; spkr., lectr., panelist in bioethics field. Editor So. Calif. Law Rev., 1973-74; contbr. articles to profl. jours. Mem. Italian-Am. Lawyers Assn., Order of Coif, KC. Roman Catholic. Office: 718 Wilshire Blvd Santa Monica CA 90401-1708

PIZZURO, SALVATORE NICHOLAS, special education educator; b. Passaic, N.J., Jan. 25, 1945; s. John G. and Mary F. (Interdonato) P. BA, Jersey City State Coll., 1970, MA, 1973; profl. diploma, Fordham U., 1980; EdD, Columbia U., 1991. Tchr. spl. edn. Garfield (N.J.) Pub. Schs., 1970-71, Lodi (N.J.) Pub. Schs., 1971-75, 76-78; learning cons. Mt. Carmel Guild, Newark, 1976-76; instr. Columbia U., N.Y.C., 1988-91; asst. prof. spl. edn. Jersey City State Coll., 1990—; learning cons. Elmwood Park (N.J.) Dept. Special Svcs., 2000—. Post-doctoral fellow U. Ky., 1993-94; dir. Learning Consultation Svcs., N.Y.C., 1990—; coord. pre-svcs. program in mental retardation Tchrs. Coll., Columbia U., 1990-91; rsch. assoc. U. Ill., 1991-92; chmn. Early Childhood Inclusion Conf., Phila., 1993; dir. United Learning Consultants, 1994—; chmn. conf. "Assessment: Impact on Svc. Delivery", N.J., 1995; cons. Independent Child Study Teams, Inc., 1995—; mem. task force com. on econ. and ednl. opportunities U.S. Ho. of Reps., 1994-96, chair, cons. Com. Edn. & Workforce, 1997—; chmn. the Future of Edn. in N.J. Conf., 1996; adj. faculty mem. Kean Coll. of N.J., 1997—; cons. Ednl. Resource Ctr., N.J., 1998; learning cons. Elmwood Park Dept. Spl. Svcs., 2000-02, Rutherfod Dept. Spl. Svcs., 2002—; chmn. symposium on edn. funding Eagleton Inst. Politics Rutgers U., 1997; chmn. N.J. Com. on Pers. Stds. in Edn.; cons. U.S. Ho. of Reps. com. on edn. and workforce, 2002—; learning cons. Rutherford Pub. Schs., 2002—; chmn. symposium on sch. constrn. Kean U., 1998, chmn. symposium on urban edn., 1998, chmn. symposium on legis. initiatives in edn., 1998. Author: The Individuals with Disabilities Education Act and the Nature of American Politics, 1999; editor: Learning Consultant Journal, 1995, 96, Policy Statement on Education in New Jersey, N.J. Coalition for the Study for School Reform, 1998; cons. editor Diagnostique, 1997—. Chmn. Walk for Hunger, 1979, NE Regional Legis. Coalition, 1984-86, Nat. AD HOC Comm. on the Reauthorization of the Individuals with Disabilities Edn. Act, chmn. Nat. Forum on Reauthorization, 1996, Conf. on Future of Edn. in N.J., 1996—, N.J. Coalition on Study of Sch. Reform, 1996—; staff mem. for U.S. Congressman Major Owens, 1997—; chmn. press conf. with U.S. Congressman Robert Menendez on sch. constrn., 1998, with U.S. Congressman Donald Payne on urban edn., 1998; polit. cons. Dem. election orgn., 1999-2000; cons. Legis. Initiatives in Edn., 2000. Recipient award for dedication to mentally retarded Mt. Carmel Guild, 1972. Mem. Coun. for Exceptional Children, N.J. Coun. for Exceptional Children (pres. 1984-85), N.J. Divsn. on Mental Retardation (pres. 1986-87), Jersey City State Coll. Alumni Assn. (pres. 1974-75), Tchrs. Coll. Christian Fellowship (pres. 1988-90), Rehab. Engring. Soc. N.Am., Correctional Edn. Assn., Internat. Ctr. for Study of Psychiatry and Psychology. Roman Catholic. Avocations: writing nonfiction, jogging.

PIZZUTO, EMANUELINA MARIA, concert pianist, composer; b. Trenton, N.J. d. Paul Emile and Mildred (Corvine) P.; m. Robert Wayne Martin, Apr. 23, 1959. Student, Am. Conservatoire, Fontainebleau, France, 1938-47; studied with Robert Casadesus, Am. Conservatoire, 1947. Piano soloist Sta. WQXR, N.Y.C., 1947-52, Sta. WFIL, Phila., 1948-52; toured with Les Compagnons de la Chanson, U.S., 1954-55, CAMI, U.S., 1955-56. Piano soloist Sta. WEEI, Boston, 1948. Composer (songs) Le Chat Dans la Nuit, 1959, Crier de Journaux, 1959, (with Ricet Barrier) Material for Band and Strings; writer (with J. Mayes and R.W. Martin) numerous mus. shows; composer (with Robert Martin) numerous compositions for band and strings; composer (with Judith Mayes and Robert Martin) several musicals; author: (novel) Diamonds in the Sky, 2003. Mem. ASCAP, hon. mem. Sigma Alpha Iota.

PLACE, VIRGIL ALAN, physician, pharmaceutical researcher; b. Crown Point, Ind., Oct. 24, 1924; s. Virgil Alexander and Helen Rosetta (Scott) P.; m. Mary Jean Simpson, Aug. 2, 1952 (div. Jan. 1976); children: Tamara Ann Place Hutten, Andrea Marie Place Fournet, Nicola Jean; m. Ann Harrison, Aug. 31, 1982 (div. Mar. 1992); 1 child, Virgil Aristophanes K.A.H.; m. Irina Vlassova, Nov. 16, 1996. AB in Chemistry, Ind. U., 1944; MD, Johns Hopkins U., 1948. Diplomate Am. Bd. Internal Medicine. Pvt. practice internal medicine and endocrinology, Modesto, Calif., 1955-58; dir. clin. pharmacology Lederle Labs., Pearl River, N.Y., 1958-66, Syntex Rsch., Palo Alto, Calif., 1966-68; v.p. med. and regulatory affairs Alza Corp., 1969-91; founder, chmn. VIVAS, Inc., Mountain View, Calif., 1991—; founder, pres. ZZVAX LLC, Kawaihae, Hawaii, 1999—. Holder 25 patents. 1st lt. AUS, 1950-52. Mem. Phi Beta Kappa. Achievements include development of 45 acre botanical garden. Home and Office: ZZVAX LLC POB 44555 10 Ala Kahua Kawaihae HI 96743-4555

PLAČEK, ROMAN, cellist, music educator; b. Jesenik, Czech Republic, June 26, 1972; came to U.S., 1995; s. Bohumir and Marcela Plaček; m. Edita Blaskova, Apr. 15, 1976. Grad., Ostrava Conservatory, Czech Republic, 1993; grad. performing cert., Boston Conservatory, 1998; MusM, U. Mass., 2001. Ind. artist and educator, 1990—; founder, artist dir., composer Golden Mountain Chamber Ensemble and Golden Mountain Chamber Ensemble Music Acd., Czech Republic, 1993—. Mem. string trio in-residence U. Mass., Amherst, 1998-2001. Author project Art Instn. for Czech-Am. Cultural Exch., 1999—. Mem. Amateur Chamber Music Players (bd. advisors 1998-2000). Avocations: drawing, photography, home improvement. Home: Sokolská' 290 Zlaté Hory Czech Republic Office: 88 Federal St Millers Falls MA 01349-1223

PLACEK-ZIMMERMAN, ELLYN CLARE, school system administrator, educator, consultant; b. Chgo., Sept. 3, 1951; d. Clarence Joseph and Jerrine LaMarr (Ruhlow) Placek; m. Allan John Zimmerman, Aug. 10, 1974; 1 child, Alissa Jan. BS, No. Ill. U., 1973, MS, 1977, cert. in advanced study, 1978, EdD, 1982. Tchr. Arlington Heights (Ill.) Pub. Schs., 1973-75, 75-76, dir. libr. and learning ctr., 1976-81, tchr. lang. arts and reading jr. high sch., 1981-84, tchr. kindergarten, 1984-86; prin. Orchard Street Sch., Fox River Grove, Ill., 1988-89, Pritchett Sch., Buffalo Grove, 1989-90, Round Lake (Ill) Pub. Schs., 1992-93, asst. supt. curriculum and instrn., 1993-2001; asst. to supt. curriculum and instrn. Wood Dale (Ill) Pub. Schs., 2001—. Dir. Ill. State grant "At Risk Program" for pre-sch. children, Cary Pub. Schs., 1986-87; mem. part-time faculty Coll. Edn., Roosevelt U., Chgo., 1983-84, 88-89; tchr. jr. high social, reading and lang. arts studies, 1988; cons. in field; mem. steering com. Curriculum 2000 Conf., De Kalb, Ill., 1985; lectr. in field; supr. student tchrs. Ill. State U., Normal, 1986, Roosevelt U., Chgo., 1988-89, Elmhurst Coll., 1992; freelance writer Daily Herald newspaper. Contbg. author: Feeling Good About Food. Sec. Scarsdale Estates Homeowners Assn., Arlington Heights, 1983; bd. dirs. ABC/25 Found., 1991-92. Mem. Ill. ASCD (registration com. for fall conf. 1987, triple I arrangements com. 1988), Ill. Assn. Tchrs. English (cons., spkr. conf. 1984), Ill. Women Adminstrs. (publicty com. conf. 1985), PTA (hon. life). Avocations: playing guitar, calligraphy. Home: 402 E Orchard St Arlington Heights IL 60005-2660

PLACHNO, RONALD JOHN, electrical engineer; b. Chgo., June 1, 1945; s. Joseph John Plachno; m. Valerie Lynn Zahorak; children: Kenneth, Gregory. BSEE, Ill. Inst. of Tech., 1968. Electronics design engr. Magnavox Govt. Divsn., Urbana, Ill., 1968—71; ops. dir. Motorola Cellular Ops., Schaumburg, 1971—94; v.p. Motorola, Swindon, England, 1994—97, v.p. of mfg. Arlington Heights, Ill., 1997—2000; sr. v.p. of ops. Novatel Wireless Inc., San Diego, 2001—. Treas., team mgr. Itasca Athletic Assn., Itasca, 1988—93. Scholar, State of Ill., 1963—67. Mem.: IEEE. Roman Catholic. Achievements include invention of 8 software copyrights. Avocations: software, music, travel. Home: 6223 Paseo Colina Carlsbad CA 92009 Home Fax: 760-603-9314. Personal E-mail: plachnor@aol.com.

PLACKE, JAMES A(NTHONY), foreign service officer, international affairs consultant; b. Grand Island, Nebr., June 14, 1935; s. Gerhard F. and Florence E. (McCormick) P.; m. Mary Sabina Shea, July 25, 1959; children—Elizabeth, Stephen, Carolyn B.Sc., U. Nebr., 1957, MA, 1959. Commd. fgn. service officer Dept. State, 1958; econ. counselor Am. embassy, Tripoli, Libya, 1970-71; fgn. service insp. Dept. State, Washington, 1971-73, dir. office food policy, 1974-76; econ. counselor Am. embassy, Ottawa, Ont., Can., 1977-79, minister Jidda, Saudi Arabia, 1979-82; dep. asst. sec. Nr. Eastern and South Asian Affairs Bur., Dept. State, Washington, 1982-85, ret., 1986; internat. affairs cons., 1986-90; dir. Cambridge Energy Rsch. Assoc., 1991-2000, sr. assoc., 2001—; sr. fellow The Brookings Institution, 2002. Del. UN World Food Conf., 1974, non-resident sr. fellow The Brooking Inst., 2002—. Recipient Meritorious Honor award Dept. State, 1969, 71; Presdl. Meritorious Service award, 1985 Office: Ste 200 1150 Connecticut Ave NW Washington DC 20036-4104

PLADEL, JOHN GERALD, psychiatric nurse practitioner, psychologist, psychotherapist; b. Albany, N.Y., Nov. 7, 1959; s. John and Joan Margret (Peacock) P. ADN, Hudson Valley C.C., Troy, N.Y., 1979; BSN, Oreg. Health Scis. U., Portland, 1993, MS, 1995, postgrad., 1998—2002; PsyD, Calif. Coast U. Cert. specialist in adult mental health nursing, AACN. Staff nurse Park Royal Health Care, Portland, 1979-80, Good Samaritan Hosp., Portland, 1980-95, critical care credentialer, 1980-95, intern preceptor, 1980-95, assoc. charge Obstet. Post-Anesthesia Care Unit, 1987-89, charge nurse, 1989-91, staff nurse, 1991-95. Data mgr. Oreg. Hospice Assn., 1994-95; traineeship State of Oreg., 1993-94; presenter conf. in field, Australia, 1991. Author cross-tng. modules-in house teaching, 1990. Gen. mgr. Neighborhood Orgn., Portland, 1987, mem. exec. bd., 1987; organizer, coord. Local Crime Watch, Portland, 1986; cellist Columbia Symphony Orch., 1985-89, Marylhurst Symphony Orch., 1983-85, Sibelius String Quartet, 1985-88. Regent's scholar State of N.Y., 1977-79. Mem. ANA, Oreg. Nurses Assn., Sigma Theta Tau. Avocations: cello, piano, literature, comparative religions, languages.

PLAEGER, FREDERICK JOSEPH, II, lawyer; b. New Orleans, Sept. 10, 1953; s. Edgar Leonard and Bernice Virginia (Schiwetz) P.; m. Kathleen Helen Dickson, Nov. 19, 1977; children: Douglas A., Catherine E. BS, La. State U., 1976, JD, 1977. Bar: La. 1978, Tex. 1999, U.S. Dist. Ct. (ea. dist.) La. 1978, U.S. Ct. Appeals (5th cir.) 1981, U.S. Supreme Ct. 1989. Law clk. U.S. Dist. Ct. (ea. dist.) La., New Orleans, 1977-79; assoc. Milling, Benson, Woodward, Hillyer, Pierson & Miller, 1979-85, ptnr., 1985-89; v.p., gen. counsel, corp. sec. La. Land and Exploration Co., 1989-97; v.p., gen. counsel Burlington Resources Inc., Houston, 1997—. Selected mem. Met. Area Com. Leadership Forum, 1986; bd. dirs. Soc. Environ. Edn., La. Nature and Sci. Ctr., 1992—94; trustee Houston Ballet, 2001—; mem. adv. bd. Inst. for Energy Law, 2001—; bd. dirs. New Orleans Speech and Hearing Ctr., 1985—91, pres., 1988—90; bd. dirs. Children's Oncology Svcs. La. (Ronald McDonald Ho. of New Orleans), 1987—90. Recipient Service to Mankind award Sertoma, 1989. Mem. ABA, La. Bar Assn., Am. Corp. Counsel Assn. (bd. dirs. New Orleans chpt. 1995-98), Am. Petroleum Inst. (mem. gen. commn. law), Univ. Club, Lakeside Country Club. Republican. Avocations: computers, hunting, fishing. Home: 5105 Longmont Dr Houston TX 77056-2417 Office: Burlington Resources Inc 5051 Westheimer Rd Ste 1400 Houston TX 77056-5686

PLAGER, S. JAY, judge; b. Long Branch, N.J., May 16, 1931; s. A. L. and Clara L. Plager; children: Anna Katherine, David Alan, Daniel Tyler. AB, U. N.C., 1952; JD, U. Fla., 1958; LLM, Columbia U., 1961. Bar: Fla. 1958, Ill. 1964. Asst. prof. law U. Fla., 1958—62, assoc. prof., 1962—64; assoc. prof. law U. Ill., Champaign-Urbana, 1964—65, prof., 1965—77; dir. Office Environ. and Planning Studies, 1972—74, 1975—77; dean, prof. law Ind. U. Sch. Law, Bloomington, 1977—84, prof. law, 1984—90; counselor to undersec. U.S. Dept. Health and Human Svcs., 1986—87; assoc. dir. Office of

Mgmt. and Budget Office of Mgmt. and Budget, 1987—88; adminstr. info. and regulatory affairs Exec. Office of the Pres., 1988—89; cir. judge U.S. Ct. Appeals (fed. cir.), 1989—. Vis. rsch. prof. law U. Wis., 1967—68; vis. scholar Stanford U., 1984—85. Author (with others): Water Law and Administration, 1968; author: Social Justice Through Law-New Approaches in the Law of Property, 1970; author: (with others) Florida Water Law, 1980. Chmn. Gainesville (Fla.) Planning Commn., 1962—63; mem. Urbana Plan Commn., 1966—70; mem. nat. air pollution manpower devel. adv. com., 1971—75; cons. Ill. Inst. for Environ. Quality, U.S. EPA; chmn. Ill. Task Force on Noise, 1972—76; vice chmn. Nat. Commn. on Jud. Discipline and Removal, 1991—93. With USN, 1952—55. Office: US Ct Appeals for Fed Cir The National Courts Bldg 717 Madison Pl NW Washington DC 20439-0002

PLAINE, DANIEL J. lawyer; b. Washington, Aug. 23, 1943; s. Herzel H.E. and Norma (Stein) P.; m. Susan Ambrose, Oct. 5, 1985; children: Caroline, Meredith. BA magna cum laude, Williams Coll., 1965; LLB, Cambridge U., Eng., 1967; JD, Yale U., 1970. Bar: D.C. 1970, U.S. Dist. Ct. DC 1970, U.S. Ct. Appeals (D.C. cir.) 1970, U.S. Ct. Appeals (fed. cir.), 1985, U.S. Supreme Ct., 1974. Ptnr. Steptoe & Johnson, Washington, 1970-97, Gibson, Dunn & Crutcher, Washington, 1997—. Marshall scholar, 1967. Mem. ABA, Am. Soc. Internat. Law, Washington Inst. Internat. Law. Office: 1050 Connecticut Ave NW Ste 900 Washington DC 20036-5306 Fax: 202-467-0539. E-mail: dplaine@gibsondunn.com.

PLAINE, LLOYD LEVA, lawyer; b. Washington, Nov. 3, 1947; d. Marx Leva and Shirley P. Leva; m. James W. Hill. BA, U. Pa., 1969; postgrad., Harvard U.; JD, Georgetown U., 1975. Bar: DC 1975. Legis. asst. to U.S. Rep. Sidney Yates, 1971-72; with Sutherland, Asbill & Brennan, Washington, 1975-82, ptnr., 1982—. Fellow Am. Bar Found., Am. Coll. Trust and Estate Counsel (past regent), Am. Coll. Tax Counsel; mem. ABA (past chmn. real property, probate and trust law sect.). Office: Sutherland Asbill & Brennan Ste 6 1275 Pennsylvania Ave NW Washington DC 20004-2415

PLAISTED, CAROLE ANNE, elementary education educator; b. Meredith, N.H., Apr. 3, 1939; d. Morris Holman and Christina Martin (Dunn) Plaisted. BEd with honors, Plymouth (N.H.) Tchrs. Coll., 1960; MA, Columbia U., 1966; cert., N.Y. Inst. Photography, 1990. Cert. tchr., N.H. Tchr. Lang St. Sch., Meredith, 1960-61, Mechanic St. Sch., Laconia, N.H., 1961-62, Wheelock Lab. Sch., Keene, 1963-94; asst. prof. emeritus Keene State Coll. Summer tchr. Cheshire County Headstart, Hinsdale, N.H., 1965; tchr. children's lit. Keene State Coll., 1974, 75; classroom evaluator D.C. Heath Co., Lexington, Mass., 1985-86; dist. trainer for drug edn. supervisory unit, Keene, 1988-94. Author: The Graduates Speak, 1990; co-author curriculum materials; contbr. Kindergarten: A Sourcebook for School and Home, 1984. Trustee Reed Free Libr., Surry, N.H., 1988-2000; program chair Wheelock Sch. PTA, 1964-65. Named Outstanding Elem. Tchr. of Am., 1973. Mem. Cheshire County Ret. Tchrs. Assn., Delta Kappa Gamma (pres. Alpha chpt. 1996-98, 2000-02, corr. sec. Alpha chpt. 1972-76, state scholarship chmn. 1985—, Beta Alpha state scholarship 1989, Founders award, 2001). Avocations: reading, gardening, photography.

PLAISTED, JOAN M. diplomat; b. St. Peter, Minn., Aug. 29, 1945; d. Gerald A. and Lola May (Peters) Plaisted. Student, U. Grenoble, France, 1965-66, U. Calif., Berkeley, 1966; BA in Internat. Rels., Am. U., 1967, MA in Asian Studies, 1969; graduate, Nat. War Coll., 1988. Korea desk officer Commerce Dept., Washington, 1969-72, Japan desk officer, 1972-73; commercial officer Am. Embassy, Paris, 1973-78; internat. economist Orgn. Econ. Cooperation & Devel., 1978-80; econ. officer Am. Consulate Gen., Hong Kong, 1980-83; trade negotiator White House Office of Spl. Trade Rep., Geneva, 1983-85; deputy dir. China desk State Dept., Washington, 1985-87; acting dep. dir., chief econ./comml. sect. Am. Inst. in Taiwan, Taipei, 1988-91; chargé d'affaires, deputy chief of mission Am. Embassy, Rabat, Morocco, 1991-94; dir. Thai and Burma affairs Dept. of State, Washington, 1994-95; sr. advisor U.S. Mission to UN N.Y.C., 1995; 2000amb. to Republic of Marshall Islands and Republic of Kiribati, 1996—2000; sr. advisor U.S. Mission to the UN, N.Y.C., 2000—02. Recipient Lodestar award, Am. U., 1993, Disting. Civilian Svc. decoration, Sec. of the Army, 2000, Alumna of Yr. award, Am. U. Sch. Internat. Svc., 2001. Mem.: Am. Fgn. Svc. Assn., Asia Soc., Washington Inst. Fgn. Affairs, Hong Kong Wine Soc. (founding), Phillips Collection. Avocations: wine tasting, gastronomy, history, skiing, scuba diving. Address: 1310 33rd St NW Washington DC 20007-2717

PLAISTOWE, WILLIAM IAN DAVID, accountant; b. Oxhey, Eng., Nov. 18, 1942; s. David William and Julia (Ross Smith) P.; m. Carolyn Anne N. Wilson, June 1, 1968; children: Richard, Peter, Nicola. MA, Cambridge (Eng.) U., 1964. Ptnr. Arthur Andersen, London. Chmn. Auditing Practices Bd., London, 1994—. Contbr. articles to legal jours. Mem. Inst. Chartered Accts. in Eng. and Wales (pres. 1992-93). Avocations: golf, tennis, skiing, gardening. Home: Heybote, Ellesborough Aylesbury HP17 0XF England Office: Arthur Andersen 1 Surrey St London England

PLAKS, ALBERT I. electrical engineer, educator; b. Minsk, Russia, Apr. 17, 1941; came to U.S., 1990; s. Israel and Genia P.; children: Elena, Victoria, Giller; m. Anna Toporovsky. MSEE, Polytech. U., Minsk, 1963, PhD in Electrical Engring., 1973. Profl. engr., Israel. Designer, rschr. Inst. Autom. Industry, Minsk, 1963-67; asst. prof. Polytech. U., 1970-76; pres., owner Electromat, Inc., Tel-Aviv, Israel, 1977-81; sr. lectr. Singalovsky Tech. Coll., Israel, 1980-90; sr. project engr. Dept. Pub. Works, Rishon-le-Zion, Israel, 1981-90; control specialist Murray Corp., Hunt Valley, Md., 1990—; prof. Balt. Hebrew U., 1992—. Adviser Inst. Standards, Tel-Aviv, 1985-87, Ministry of Edn., Tel-Aviv, 1983-90; inspector edn. divsn. Min. of Labor, Jerusalem, Israel, 1985-90. Author: Electric Machines for Servo Systems, 1989, Power Electronics Basics, 2000; patentee in field. Program dir., host (radio show) Star of David, Washington-Balt., 1991—. Mem. Internat. Acad. Ecology Man and Nature Protection Scis. Avocations: swimming, theater, cinema, paper writer. Office: Murray Corp 260 Schilling Cir AP 1 Hunt Valley MD 21031-1109

PLAKS, LIVIA BASCH, foundation executive; b. Baia Mare, Romania, Apr. 29, 1947; came to U.S., 1964; naturalized, 1969; d. Kalman and Cecilia (Freund) Basch; m. Andrew H. Plaks, June 9, 1968; children: Jason, Eric. AB, Rutgers U., 1969; AM, NYU, 1971. Exec. assoc. Internat. Rsch. and Exch. Bd., Princeton, N.J., 1986-92; assoc. dir. Project on Ethnic Rels., 1992-94, exec. dir., 1994—. Rapporteur Orgn. Security Cooperation in Europe on Roma issues, Warsaw, Poland, 1994; mem. U.S. Task Force on Romania, 1990-92, Coun. Fgn. Rels.; mediation team between Romanian Govt. and Dem. Union of Hungarians in Romania, 1992—; mem. Coun. for Ethnic Accord, 1992—; mediation team between Slovak and ethnic Hungarian Parliamentary parties of Slovakia, 1995—; mediation team Serbs and Albanians of Kosovo, 1995—; testified to and for Commn. on Security and Cooperation in Europe on issues of Roma/Gypsies, 1994, 98. Recipient Certificate of Merit Pres. Romania, 1996, Govt. Hungary, 1996, Govt. Slovakia, 1998. Mem.: AAUW, Women in Internat. Security. Avocations: travel, reading, hiking. Office: Project on Ethnic Rels 15 Chambers St Princeton NJ 08542-3707 E-mail: livia.plaks@per-usa.org.

PLANE, DONALD RAY, management science educator; b. Evansville, Ind., July 17, 1938; s. Edward L. and Margaret I. (Downen) P.; m. Rosemary Bieber, Sept. 4, 1961; children: Brian Russell, Dennis Lowell, Margaret Diane. ME, U. Cin., 1961; MBA (NDEA fellow), Ind. U., 1963, D.BA (NDEA fellow), 1965. Instr. econs. U.S. Air Force Acad., 1965-67, asst. prof. econs., 1967-68; assoc. prof. mgmt. sci. U. Colo., Boulder, 1968-72, prof. mgmt. sci. and info. systems, 1972-84, head div. mgmt. sci., 1976-84; prof. mgmt. sci. Crummer Grad. Sch. Bus., Rollins Coll., Winter Park, Fla., 1984-2000, faculty pres. Crummer Grad. Sch. Bus., 1992-93, prof. emeritus, 2000—. Vis. Fulbright prof. mgmt. sci. U. Nairobi, 1978-79; cons. in field. Co-author: (with E.B. Oppermann) Business and Economic Statistics, 3d edit., 1986; (with J. Dinkel, G. Kochenberger) Management Science: Text and Applications, 1978, Quantitative Tools for Decision Support Using IFPS, 1986, Management Science: A Spreadsheet Approach for Windows, 1996. Served with USAF, 1965-68. Ford Found. fellow, 1965 Achievements include research, publs. in field. Home: 980 S Lake Sybelia Dr Maitland FL 32751-5403

PLANGERE, JULES LEON, JR. retired media company executive; b. Spring Lake, N.J., Dec. 30, 1920; s. Jules Leona nd Jesse Alene (Davidson) P.; m. Virginia Polhemus, 1942 (dec. 1977); 1 son, Jules L. III; m. Jane Wallhauser, Feb. 5, 1978; stepchildren: Mrs. John bickart, John C. Conover III, Jeffrey Conover. Student, Rutgers U., 1942. With Asbury Park (N.J.) Press, 1947-97, pub., 1977-91, CEO, 1980-91, chmn. bd., 1980-97. Former chmn. bd. trustees Monmouth U., West Long Branch, N.J.; past rpes. Welfare Coun. Monmouth County. Lt. U.S. Army, 1942-46. Mem. Asbury Park C. of C. (past pres.), N.J. Press Assn. (past pres.), Am. Newspaper Pubs. Assn., N.J. State C. of C. (bd. dirs.), Spring Lake Bath and Tennis Club, Nassau Club, Quail Ridge Country Club, Metedeconk Nat. Golf Club.

PLANINSIC, RAYMOND M. anesthesiologist, educator; b. Chgo., Sept. 13, 1959; s. Joseph and Claudia (Ressmann) P. BS with univ. honors, Carnegie-Mellon U., Pitts., 1981; MD, Mt. Sinai Sch. Medicine, N.Y.C., 1986. Diplomate Am. Bd. Anesthesiology, Am. Bd. Internal Medicine, Nat. Bd. Med. Examiners. Intern in internal medicine Beth Israel Med. Ctr./Mt. Sinai Sch. Medicine, N.Y.C., 1986-87; resident in internal medicine Allegheny Gen. Hosp./Med. Coll. of Pa., Pitts., 1988-90; resident in anesthesiology U. Pitts. Med. Ctr./U. Pitts. Sch. Medicine, 1990-92; anesthesiologist U. Pitts. Med. Ctr., 1993—, dir. hepatic transplantation anesthesiology, 1999—; asst. prof. anesthesiology and critical care medicine U. Pitts. Sch. Medicine, 1993—. Rschr. U. Pitts. Med. Ctr.; cons. numerous law practices in Pitts. Contbr. articles to profl. jours. Mem. Am. Soc. Anesthesiologists, Internat. Anesthesia Rsch. Soc., Internat. Liver Transplantation Soc., Pa. Soc. Anesthesiologists. Avocations: skiing, squash, travel, photography. Home: 110 Saint Andrews Dr Pittsburgh PA 15205-9797 Office: U Pitts Med Ctr 200 Lothrop St Pittsburgh PA 15213-2546

PLANK, BETSY (MRS. SHERMAN V. ROSENFIELD), public relations counsel; b. Tuscaloosa, Ala., Apr. 3, 1924; d. Richard Jeremiah and Bettye (Hood) P.; m. Sherman V. Rosenfield, Apr. 10, 1954. Student, Bethany (W.Va.) Coll., 1940-43; AB, U. Ala., 1944. Continuity dir. radio sta. KQV, Pitts., 1944-47; account exec. Mitchell McKeown Orgn., Chgo., 1947-54; pub. rels. counsel Chgo. chpt. A.R.C., 1954-57; dir. pub. rels. Chgo. Coun. on Fgn. Rels., 1957-58; v.p. Ronald Goodman Pub. Rels. Counsel, Chgo., 1958-61; exec. v.p., treas., dir. Daniel J. Edelman, Inc., 1961-73; dir. pub. rels. planning AT&T, N.Y.C., 1973-74; asst. v.p. corp. comm. Ill. Bell, Chgo., 1974-90; prin. Betsy Plank Pub. Rels., 1990—. Dep. chmn. VII World Congress on Pub. Rels., 1976; co-chmn. nat. commn. on Pub. Rels. Edn., 1984-86; mem. adv. bd. Ill. Issues, 1975—. Bd. dirs. United Way Chgo., 1986-90; chmn. Citizenship Coun. Met. Chgo., 1990-96, Betsy Plank chpt. Pub. Rels. Students Soc. Am., No. Ill. U.; trustee Found. for Pub. Rels. Rsch. and Edn., 1975-80; nat. bd. dirs. Girl Scouts U.S., 1975-85. Recipient Millennium award Coll. Journalism, U. Fla., 2000, Alexander Hamilton award, Inst. Pub. Rels., 2000; named one of World's 40 Leading Pub. Rels. Profls., Pub. Rels. News, 1984. Fellow Pub. Rels. Soc. Am. (accredited, nat. pres. 1973, Outstanding Profl. award 1977, Outstanding Cmty. Svc. award 1989, Disting. Svc. award 2001); mem. Publicity Club Chgo. (pres. 1963-64, Outstanding Profl. award 1961), Ill. Coun. on Econ. Edn. (past chmn. bd. trustees, Extraordinary Leadership award 2001), Internat. Pub. Rels. Assn., Chgo. Network (chmn. 1980-81), Arthur W. Page Soc. (lifetime achievement award 2000), Union League Club of Chgo., Econ. Club Chgo., Zeta Tau Alpha. Presbyterian. Home and Office: 421 W Melrose St Chicago IL 60657-3848

PLANK, EZRA LINCOLN, minister; b. Eugene, Oreg., Dec. 26, 1975; m. Emily Faye Schackmann, Dec. 15, 2001. BA in Religion, Pepperdine U., , 1999. Mem. Ch. Of Christ. Home: 24255 Pacific Coast Hwy #0140 Malibu CA 90263-0140

PLANO, JACK CHARLES, writer, retired educator; b. Merrill, Wis., Nov. 25, 1921; s. Victor James and Minna Ida (Hass) P.; m. Ellen Louise Ruehlow, June 25, 1954; children: Jay Charles, Gregory Victor, Vicki Lynn. BA, Ripon Coll., 1949; MA, U. Wis., 1950, PhD, 1954. Prof. Western Mich. U., Kalamazoo, 1952-87; ret., 1987. Author, editor: ABC-CLIO Political Dictionary series, 1982, New Issues Press, Western Michigan U., 1974-87; author: American Political Dictionary, 11th edit., 2001; co-author: The United Nations, 3d edit., 2000, Latin American Dictionary. Sgt. U.S. Army, 1942-45, ETO. Recipient Outstanding Emeritus Scholar award Western Mich. U., 1997; Ford Found. grantee Emory U., 1957; fellow U. Sussex, 1971-72.

PLANT, ALBIN MACDONOUGH, lawyer; b. Balt., July 30, 1937; s. Albin Joseph and Ruth E. (Frech) P.; m. Anne Warwick Brown, June 17, 1961; children: Katherine, Albin MacDonough Jr., Elizabeth Ashby. BA, Princeton U., 1959; LLB, U. Va., 1963; MLA, Johns Hopkins U., 1978. Bar: Md. 1963, U.S. Dist. Ct. Md. 1963, U.S. Ct. Appeals 1970. Assoc. Semmes, Bowen & Semmes, Balt., 1963-71, ptnr., 1971-91, Stewart, Plant & Blumenthal, Balt., 1991—. Adj. prof. law U. Balt., 1979, U. Md., 1979-83, 84-85. Bd. dirs. Ctr. Stage, Am. Horticulture Soc., Md. Club, T. Rowe Price Savings Bank, Balt. Choral Arts Soc. Mem. Am. Coll. Probate Counsel, Lawyers Roundtable, Md. Club, Wednesday Law Club. Democrat. amplant2spblaw.com. Office: 7 St Paul St Baltimore MD 21202-1626

PLANT, DAVID WILLIAM, lawyer; b. Ottawa, Ill., Apr. 22, 1931; s. Arthur Percival and Margery Elmina (Flick) P.; children: Susan W. BME, Cornell U., 1953, LLB, 1957. Bar: N.Y. 1957, U.S. Dist. Ct. (ea. and so. dists.) N.Y., U.S. Supreme Ct., 1968, U.S. Patent Office 1982; cert. CEDR mediator. Assoc. Fish & Neave, N.Y.C., 1957-70, ptnr., 1970-98, mng. ptnr., 1981-84. Domestic and internat. arbitrator, mediator, panel mem., arbitration cons. com. World Intellectual Property Orgn., 1994—; mem. panels of neutrals CPR, 1990—, AAA, 1982—, Internat. C. of C., 1992—, London Ct. Internat. Arbitration, 1992—, ea. dist. N.Y., so. dist. N.Y., dist. N.H.; adj. prof. Franklin Pierce Law Ctr., 1998—; sr. fellow U. Melbourne Law Sch., 2002; lectr. in field. Contbr. articles to profl. jours. Bd. dirs. Cornell Rsch. Found. Fellow Chartered Inst. Arbitrators, Coll. Comml. Arbitrators, Am. Coll. Civil Trial Mediators; mem. ABA, Assn. of Bar of City of N.Y. (com. on patents 1980-83, chmn. 1983-86, com. on arbitration and alternative dispute resolution 1987-90, 91-94, 97-99, chmn. 1994-97), Am. Arbitration Assn. (various coms. and panels of neutrals), N.Y. Intellectual Property Law Assn. (chmn. arbitration com. 1989-91, bd. dirs. 1994-96), Am. Intellectual Property Law Assn. (chmn. alternative dispute resolution com. 1993-95), Ctr. Pub. Resources (panels of neutrals, co-chmn. tech. com. 1995—), Cornell Law Assn. (exec. com., pres. 1994-96), Lic. Execs. Soc. (co-chmn. alternative dispute resolution com. 1995-97).13291786 Home: 215 Little Lake Sunapee Rd New London NH 03257-4211 E-mail: DPlantADR@aol.com.

PLANT, LINDA R. music educator; b. Eugene, Oreg., Mar. 25, 1949; d. Robert Ward and Ruth Adeline Johnston; m. Allan F. Plant, June 15, 1968; children: Glenn A., Jason R. Piano tchr. Linda Plant Piano Studio, Springfield, Oreg., 1973—; organist Emerald Baptist Ch., Eugene, 1989—. Vol. ARC, Oreg., 1983—, adminstr., 2001—; mem. bd., sec. Oreg. Camp Cherith, 1977—, pres., 1984-87, 89-94. Mem. Nat. Guild Piano Tchrs. (pres. 1981-84, chmn. 1985-97), Oreg. Music Tchrs. Assn. (state cert., event chmn. 1990-2000, libr. 2001—, dist. pres. 1995-97, state sec. 1996-98). Republican. Baptist. Avocation: lifeguard/canoe instructor for youth camps.

PLANTE, DAVID ROBERT, writer, educator; b. Providence, Mar. 4, 1940; s. Anaclet Joseph Adolph Plante and Albina Marie Bisson. BA in French, Boston Coll., 1961. Writer-in-residence U. East Anglia, Norwich, 1977—78, U. Tulsa, Okla., 1980—82, King's Coll., Cambridge, 1985—86, U. Quebec, Montreal, 1990, Gorky Inst. Lit., Moscow, 1990; prof. Columbia U., N.Y.C., 1998—. Author: The Ghost of Henry James, 1970, Slides, 1971, Relatives, 1972, The Darkness of the Body, 1974, paperback , 1977, Figures in Bright Air, 1976, The Family, 1978, The Country, 1981, 2nd edit., 1983, The Woods, 1982, The Francoeur Novels: The Family, The Woods, 1984, The Foreigner, 1984, 2nd edit., 1984, paperback, 1984, 2nd paperback edit., 1984, The Catholic, 1986, The Native, 1991, The Accident, 1991, Annunciation, 1994, The Age of Terror, 1999, paperback, 2000, (non fiction) Difficult Women: Portraits of Jean Rhys, Sonia Orwell, Germaine Greer, 1983, paperback, 1986. Office: Columbia U Dodge Hall New York NY 10027

PLANTE, PAUL JOSEPH, metallurgical engineer; b. Quincy, Mass., Oct. 26, 1957; s. Joseph J.M. and Teresa A. Plante; 1 child, Benjamin Plante. BS in Metallurgy, Colo. Sch. Mines, 1979, MS in Metallurgy, 1981. Registered profl. engr., Maine. Engr. Martin Marietta Corp., Denver, 1981-84; prin. engr. and project mgr. Maine Yankee Atomic Power Co., Wiscasset, 1984—. Instr. metallurgy Maine Tech. Colls., Bangor, 1992, 93, 94. Contbr. articles to profl. jours. Big bro. Big Bros. Big Sisters, Augusta, Maine, 1986-89. Recipient Technology Transfer award, Electric Power Rsch. inst., 1998. Mem. Nat. Assn. Corrosion Engrs. Republican. Avocations: gardening, numismatics, reading. Home: 37 Merritt Rd Harpswell ME 04079-4233 Office: Maine Atomic Power Co 321 Old Ferry Rd Wiscasset ME 04578-4922

PLANTE, ROBERT DONALD, management educator, university dean; b. Providence, Feb. 7, 1948; s. Robert Annaclet and Grace Joan Plante; m. Jean Karole Hostetler, May 29, 1982; children: Michael, Eric, Jason. BS in Physics, Worcester Poly. U., 1970; PhD in Mgmt., U. Ga., 1980. Electronic intelligence officer Army Security Agy., 1970-76; asst. prof. mgmt. Purdue U., West Lafayette, Ind., 1980-84, assoc. prof., 1985-89, prof., 1990—, assoc. dean, 1999-2000, sr. assoc. dean, 2000—. Area editor Prodn. and Ops., 1990—; mem. editl. bd. Strategic Mgmt., 1995—; contbr. over 50 articles to profl. jours. Mem. Elks. Roman Catholic. Office: Purdue U Krannert Grad Sch Mgmt 1310 Krannert Bldg West Lafayette IN 47907-1310

PLANTE, THOMAS GERARD, psychologist; b. Lincoln, R.I., Jan. 23, 1960; s. Bernard Rene and Marcia Carol (McCormick) P.; m. Lori Goldfarb, Nov. 6, 1988. BS magna cum laude, Brown U., 1982; MA, U. Kans., 1983, PhD, 1987. Diplomate Am. Bd. Profl. Psychology. Pvt. practice, Menlo Park, Calif., 1988—. Assoc. prof. psychology Santa Clara U., 1994-2002, prof. psychology, 2002—, chair, 1999-2002; clin. asst. prof. psychiatry Stanford U. Med. Sch., 1990-2000, clin. assoc. prof., 2000—; cons. assoc. prof. edn. Stanford U., 1997—; head psychology dept., dir. mental health svcs. Children's Health Coun., Palo Alto, Calif., 1990-94. Author: Contemporary Clinical Psychology, 1999, Bless Me Father For I Have Sinned: Perspective of Sexual Abuse Committed by Roman Catholic Priests, 1999, Getting Together and Staying Together: The Stanford University Course on Intimate Relationships, 2000, Faith and Health: Psychological Perspectives, 2001; contbr. articles to profl. jours. U. Kans. fellow, 1982-86, NIMH fellow Yale U., 1987-88, MacArthur/Ford Founds. fellow, 1988. Fellow: APA, Soc. Behavioral Medicine, Acad. Clin. Psychology. Roman Catholic. Avocation: running. Office: Santa Clara U Dept Psychology Santa Clara CA 95053-0333 E-mail: tplante@scu.edu.

PLANTS, WALTER DALE, elementary education educator, minister; b. Middlefield, Ohio, June 8, 1942; s. William E. and Hazel A. Plants; m. Sarah A. Gaddis, July 5, 1962; children: Dale Anthony, Jeanette Marie. BD, Azusa Pacific U., 1967; MEd, U. Nev., 1970. Cert. elem. tchr., elem. adminstr. Elem. tchr. Churchill County Sch. Dist., Fallon, Nev., 1967—69, 1970—72, elem tchr., 1988—2001; grad. asst. U. Nev., Reno, 1969-70; tchr. Kingman (Ariz.) Elem. Sch. Dist. #4, 1972-77; head sci. program E. C. Best Elem. Sch., Fallon, 1988—2001; ret., 2001. Adj. instr. Ariz. State U., Tempe, 1973-77; cons. sci. Ariz. State Dept. Edn., 1975-77. Bd. dirs. Solar Energy Commn. Mohave County, Ariz., 1974; coord. County Sci. Fair, 1988-93; active Western Regional Sci. Fair Com.; sci. fair coord. Churchill County, 1989-94; mem. com. Regional Sci. Fair, 1992-94. HEW fellow, 1969; NSF grantee, 1973; AIMS Found. scholar, 1988; recipient Ariz. State PTA award, 1977, Ruth Neldon award Ariz. State Dept., 1977, Conservation award Big Sandy Natural Resources Conservation Dist. Ariz., 1976, Community Builder Svc. award Masons, Fallon, 1991, Disting. Leadership award, 1991, 92, 93; named State Tchr. of Yr. Nev. PTA, 1991, Conservation Tchr. of Yr., 1991; named to Congl. Select Edn. panel U.S. Congress, 1993. Mem. NEA, AAAS, Nat. Sci. Tchrs. Assn., Nat. Coun. Tchrs. Math., Internat. Reading Assn., Churchill County Edn. Assn. (Tchr. of Yr. 1989), Internat. Platform Assn., Nat. Arbor Day Found., World Wildlife Fund, Nat. Parks and Conservation Assn., Nat. Audubon Soc., Nev. State Tchrs. of Yr. Assn. (pres. 1994-96, pres. 1996-97), Phi Delta Kappa.

PLANTZ, CHRISTINE MARIE, librarian, union officer; b. Moscow, July 28, 1946; d. John Albert and Marian Florence (Malm) Holmes; m. Charles Walter Plantz, May 19, 1973. BA, Shimer Coll., 1968; postgrad., U. Chgo. GLS, 1968-72; BS, Chadron State Coll., 1977. Children's libr. Chgo. Pub. Libr., 1969-73; libr. Rushville (Nebr.) Pub. Schs., 1974-77; tchr. Sheridan County Dist. 126, Rushville, 1979; libr. Bur. Indian Affairs, Pine Ridge, S.D., 1980-98; tchr. Oglala Lakota Coll., 1994—; libr. dir. Rushville (Nebr.) Pub. Libr., 1998—. Pres. local 150 Nat. Fedn. Fed. Employees, Pine Ridge, S.D., 1987-89, 91-92, 95-98, sec. BIA coun., 1988-96; owner LaserPress Desktop Pub., Rushville, 1992—; computer instr. Oglala Lakota Coll., Pine Ridge, S.D. Mem. Rushville City Coun., 1986-90, Rushville Pub. Libr. Bd., 1974-82; bd. dirs. Family Rescue Shelter, Gordon, Nebr., 1982-88, Black Hills Girl Scout Coun., Rapid City, S.D., bd. dirs. 1984-99, pres. 1995-99; mem. dept. congl. devel. Episcopal Diocese of Nebr., 1998—, exec. commn., 1999—. Episcopalian. Avocations: computers, reading. Home: PO Box 219 Rushville NE 69360-0219 Office: Laser Press PO Box 219 133 Main St Rushville NE 69360

PLAPP, BRYCE VERNON, biochemistry educator; b. DeKalb, Ill., Sept. 11, 1939; s. Vernon Edgar and Eleanor Barbara (Kautz) P.; m. Rosemary Kuhn, June 13, 1962; children— Brendan Bryce, Laurel Andrea BS, Mich. State U., East Lansing, 1961; PhD, U. Calif.-Berkeley, 1966. Research assoc. J.W. Goethe U., Frankfurt/Main, Germany, 1966-68; research assoc. Rockefeller U., N.Y.C., 1968-70; faculty U. Iowa, Iowa City, 1970—, prof. biochemistry, 1979—. Contbr. articles to profl. jours.; mem. editorial bd. Archives Biochemistry and Biophysics. Am. Cancer Soc. fellow, 1966-68 Mem. Am. Soc. for Biochemistry and Molecular Biology, Am. Chem. Soc., Sigma Xi Avocations: travel, sports. Office: U Iowa Dept Biochemistry 4-370 BSB Iowa City IA 52242 E-mail: bv-plapp@uiowa.edu.

PLASIL, FRANZ, physicist; b. Prague, Czechoslovakia, May 17, 1939; came to U.S., 1960; s. Frank and Eva (Wenger) P.; m. Catherine Logan, Feb. 15, 1964 (div. Sept. 1979); two children: Maia, David; m. Carol Baratz, Apr. 12, 1980. BS, Queen Mary Coll., U. London, 1960; PhD, U. Calif., Berkeley, 1964. Chemist Lawrence Berkeley (Calif.) Lab., 1964-65; rsch. assoc. Brookhaven Nat. Lab., Upton, N.Y., 1965-67; rsch. staff physics div. Oak Ridge (Tenn.) Nat. Lab., 1967-78, group leader physics div., 1978-86, sect. head physics div., 1986-99; fellow U. Tenn.-Battelle, 1999—2002; hon. rsch. prof. dept. physics and astronomy U. Tenn., Knoxville, 2002—. Contbr. articles to Annals of Physics, Phys. Rev., Phys. Rev. Letters, Nuc. Phys., Phys. Letters. Recipient Alexander von Humboldt award 1985, E. Mach medal of honor Acad. of Sci. of the Czech Republic, 1998. Fellow Am. Phys. Soc. Achievements include rsch. in fission-imposed limits on the stability of rotating nuclei and rsch. in nucleus-nucleus collisions at ultrarelativistic energies. Home: 964 W Outer Dr Oak Ridge TN 37830-8607 Office: Oak Ridge Nat Lab PO Box 2008 Oak Ridge TN 37831-2008 E-mail: plasilf@ornl.gov.

PLASKACZ, EDWARD JOHN, computational scientist, engineer; b. Chgo., Jan. 21, 1959; s. John T. and Pauline H. Plaskacz; m. Elizabeth Ellen Prindiville, July 14, 1990. BS, Ill. Inst. Tech., Chgo., 1981, MS, 1982; PhD, Northwestern U., 1990. Engr. in tng. City of Chgo. Dept. of Water, 1979-81; engrng. intern Sargent & Lundy Engrs., Chgo., 1981-82, engrng. analyst, 1982-85; rsch. asst. Northwestern U., Evanston, Ill., 1985-90; computational scientist Argonne (Ill.) Nat. Lab., 1990—. Contbr. numerous articles to profl. jours. Recipient Letter of Commendation Chgo. Dept. Water, 1980, Clinton Strycker award Ill. Inst. Tech., 1981, Atanasoff award Second Symposium on Parallel Computational Methods for Large-Scale Structural Analysis and Design, 1993, Exceptional Performance award Argonne Nat. Lab., 1995, 97. Mem. AAAS, Nat Geographic Soc., Nat. Trust Historic Preservation, Colonial Williamsburg Found., U.S. Assn. for Computational Mechanics, Sigma Xi, Tau Beta Pi, Chi Epsilon. Office: Argonne Nat Lab 9700 Cass Ave Argonne IL 60439-4803 E-mail: ejplaskacz@anl.gov.

PLASKETT, THOMAS GEORGE, transportation company executive; b. Raytown, Mo., Dec. 24, 1943; s. Warren E. and Frances S. P.; m. Linda Lee Maxey, June 8, 1968; children: Kimberly, Keith. B in Indsl. Engring., Kettering U.; MBA, Harvard U. Supr. indsl. engring. GM, Flint, Mich., 1968, supt. indsl. engring., 1969-73, sr. staff asst., treas. N.Y.C., 1973; asst. contr. Am. Airlines, 1974, v.p. mktg. adminstrn., 1975-76, sr. v.p. fin., 1976-80, sr. v.p. mktg. Dallas, from 1980; pres., CEO Continental Airlines Inc., Houston, until 1988; chmn., CEO, pres. Pan Am Corp., N.Y.C., 1988-91; mng. dir. Fox Run Capital Assocs., 1991—; dir., interim pres., CEO, acting CFO Greyhound Lines, Inc., Dallas, 1994-95; vice-chmn., exec. v.p. Legend Airlines, 1996-

2001. Bd. dirs. Radioshack Corp., Ft. Worth, Smart & Final, Inc., L.A.; chmn. Probex Corp., 1994-2000. Trustee Kettering U., Flint. Avocations: golf, skiing, squash. Office: 5215 N O Connor Blvd Ste 1070 Irving TX 75039-3738 E-mail: tom@foxruncapital.com.

PLASKITT, PIERS, sales and marketing executive; b. Penton Hook, Staines, Great Britain, Mar. 6, 1954; came to U.S., 1976; s. Peter Mallabey and Peggy Plaskitt; m. Pamela J. Rooff, July 7, 1989; children: Paige Nicole Mallabey, Courtney Paulina Mallabey. Student, Bloxham Coll., Oxford, England, 1967-72. Technician Apple Studios Ltd., London, 1972—74; engr. Trident Studios Ltd., 1974—76; studio mgr. Celebration Rec., 1976—80; dir. audio ops. Bullet Rec. Studios, Nashville, 1980—83; pres., CEO Solid State Logic Inc., Audio Processing Tech. Inc., N.Y.C., 1983—97, Solid State Logic Can., Inc., 1983—97; v.p. sales and mktg. worldwide Montage Group Ltd., N.Y.C., 1997-98; v.p., dir. sales and mktg. Post Perfect, 1998—99; pres. Euphonix, Inc., 1999—2001. Engr. for record album including Star Wars & Other Galactic Funk (Ampex Golden Reel award), 1977, Pointer Sisters Black and White, (Gold award), 1981, Fire, (Gold award), 1978, Slow Hand, (Gold award), 1981. Mem. Nat. Acad. Recording Arts & Scis., Country Music Assn., Acad. Country Music, Nashville Entertainment Assn., Fla. Motion Picture & TV Assn., Soc. Profl. Audio Recording Svcs., Audio Engring. Soc., Soc. Motion Picture & TV Engrs. Home: 521 31st St West Des Moines IA 50265-3103

PLASTARAS, THOMAS EDWARD, lawyer; BS in Hosp. Adminstrn., Ithaca Coll., 1979; JD cum laude, Calif. Western Sch. Law, 1982. Bar: Calif. 1982, U.S. Dist. Ct. (so. dist.) Calif. 1982, N.Y. State 1983, U.S. Dist. Ct. (ea. and so. dists.) N.Y. 1984, U.S. Tax Ct. 1984, Minn. 1984, D.C. 1989. Law clk. to presiding justice U.S. Dist. Ct. (so. dist.) Calif., San Diego, 1981-82; assoc. Kelly, Rode, Kelly & Burke, Westbury, N.Y., 1982-87; pvt. practice Smithtown, 1988-89; with Gallagher, Wadlker, Bianco & Plastaras, Mineola, 1995—. Appointed referee Suffolk County Supreme Ct., N.Y. Mem. N.Y. State Bar Assn., N.Y. State Trial Lawyers Assn., Nassau/Suffolk County Bar Assn. Lodges: Rotary (bd. dirs. Nesconset club). Office: Gallagher Walker Bianco & Plastaras 98 Willis Ave Mineola NY 11501-2611

PLASTER, DAVID ROY, college executive; b. Akron, Ohio, Nov. 6, 1949; s. William John and Jane Ann Plaster; m. Virginia Lynne Crees, Dec. 18, 1970; children: Andrew, Rachelle, Robert. Diploma, U. Lyon, France, 1970; BA, Grace Coll., 1971; MDiv, Grace Theol. Sem., 1974, ThM, 1984; ThD, Dallas Theol. Sem., 1989. Pastor Millwood Chapel, Etna Green, Ind., 1970-74, Valley Grace Brethren Ch., Armagh, Pa., 1974-79; sr. pastor Comty. Grace Brethren Ch., Warsaw, 1979-84; prof. Grace Theol. Sem., Winona Lake, 1984-90; v.p. for acad. affairs Grace Coll. and Sem., 1990—. Moderator Fellowship of Grace Brethren Chs., 1991-92. Author: (book) Ordinances, 1984; contbr. articles to profl. jours. Mem. Nat. Fellowship of Grace Brethren Ministries (chmn. 1988-89). Avocations: camping, gardening, reading. Home: 800 Arbor Ln Winona Lake IN 46590-5743 Office: Grace Coll & Sem 200 Seminary Dr Winona Lake IN 46590-1224 E-mail: drplaster@grace.edu.

PLASTER, GEORGE FRANCIS, Roman Catholic priest; b. Lafayette, Ind., Dec. 6, 1950; s. Robert Lee and Ann Elizabeth (Klinker) P. BS in Econs. and Fin., St. Joseph's Coll., Rensselaer, Ind., 1973; MDiv, Sacred Heart Sch. of Theology, Hales Corners, Wis., 1980. Ordained Roman Cath. Priest, 1980. Bank examiner dept. fin. instns. State of Ind., Indpls., 1973-76; deacon, assoc. pastor St. Patrick Ch., Kokomo, Ind., 1979-82; assoc. pastor Our Lady Mt. Carmel (Ind.), 1982-86, St. Charles Ch., Peru, Ind., 1986-88, St. Joan of Arc Ch., Kokomo, 1988-89; hosp. chaplain St. Vincent's Hosp., Indpls., 1989—. Spiritual counselor Jonah Ctr., Wabash, Ind., 1987-88; clin. pastoral educator Ctrl. State Hosp., Indpls., 1989-90, 91-92, 94-95. Mem. Nat. Right to Life, Washington, 1973—. Mem. Nat. Assn. Cath. Chaplains, KC (chaplain 1980-82, 84-85), Indpls. Cursillo (chaplain 1984, 89, 92, 96, 99). Avocation: playing organ and piano. Office: St Vincent Hosp 2001 W 86th St Indianapolis IN 46260-1991

PLASTINA, FRANK, communications executive; From pres. svc. provider and corp. networks to pres. metro and enterprise networks Nortel Networks, Brampton, Canada, 1987—. Bd. dirs. MicroElectronic Ctr. N.C., NC, S.E. Interactive, Research Triangle Park, NC. Bd. dirs. N.C. Govs. Bus. Coun., N.C. Symphony, Wake County Boys and Girls Clubs. Mem.: N.C. Electronics and Info. Tech. Assn. (bd. dirs.). Office: Nortel Metro and Enterprise Networks 8200 Dixie Rd Ste 100 Brampton L6T 5P6 Canada

PLASZCZAK, ROMAN THADDEUS, lawyer; b. San Diego, Oct. 3, 1943; s. Thaddeus Roman and Lorrine (Wiedenfeld) P. BA, Western Mich. U., 1965; JD, Detroit Coll., 1968. Bar: Mich. 1968, U.S. Supreme Ct, 1974, U.S. Dist. Ct. (we. dist.) 1979. Asst. pros. atty. Muskegon (Mich.) County, 1970-72; ptnr. Jerkins, Plaszczak, Hurley & Bauhof, Kalamazoo, 1972-79, Plaszczak & Bauhof P.C., Kalamazoo, 1979—. Leader Legal Explorer Scouts, Kalamazoo, 1975-77; vol. Cath. Family Services, Kalamazoo, 1982-83. Served as capt. U.S Army, 1968-70, Vietnam. Decorated Bronze Star; recipient Civil Rights Litigation award ACLU, 1986, Raymond W. Fox Advocacy Achievement award, 1990. Mem. ATLA, Mich. Bar Assn. (state trial cts. com. 1980-85, investigator Mich. atty. grievance com. 1980—), Mich. Trial Lawyers Assn., Greater Paw Paw C. of C. (pres. 1990-97). Republican. Avocations: offshore power boat racing, travel. Home: 729 Mapleview Dr Paw Paw MI 49079-1185 Office: Plaszczak & Bauhof PC 137 N Park St Ste 203 Kalamazoo MI 49007-3769

PLAT, FRANCIS RAYMOND, pharmaceutical company executive; b. Paris, Sept. 8, 1957; came to U.S., 1997; s. Edouard and Suzanne (Lipchitz) P.; m. Catherine Grandjean; children: Caroline, Emilie. Bachelor degree, Coll. Stanislas, Paris, 1976; MD, U. Paris VI, 1984; degree in cardiology, Hosp. Broussais, Brussels, 1990; degree in mgmt./comm., Eric Krauthamer SA, Paris, 1992. Cardio. dir. Bristol-Myers Squibb, Paris, 1989-91, exec. dir., 1994-96, Brussels, 1996-97, Princeton, N.J., 1997—. Home: 2 Seminole Rd Skillman NJ 08558-2325 Office: Bristol-Myers Squibb 206 Province Line Rd Princeton NJ 08543 E-mail: francis.plat@bms.com., francis.plat@gte.net.

PLAT, RICHARD VERTIN, corporate finance executive; b. San Jose, Calif., July 14, 1929; s. Gaston and Frances (Vertin) P.; children from previous marriage: Julie, Carl, Marsha; m. Janet Toll Davidson, Dec. 19, 1992. BEE, U. Santa Clara, 1951; MBA, Washington U., St. Louis, 1957. Sr. ind. econ. Stanford Rsch. Inst., Menlo Park, Calif., 1959-65; dir. planning Litton Industries, Inc., Beverly Hills, 1965-70; v.p. Waltham Industries, N.Y.C., 1970-71, Computer Machinery Corp., L.A., 1971-77; exec. v.p. Pacific Scientific Co., Newport Beach, Calif., 1978—. Bd. dirs. Powertec Indsl. Corp., Rock Hill, S.C., Automation Intelligence, Inc., Duluth, Ga., High Yield Tech., Inc., Sunnyvale, Calif., Pacific Sci. Ltd., Royce Thompson Ltd., Eng., Pacific Sci. S.A.R.L., France, Pacific Sci. GmbH, Eduard Bautz GmbH, Fed. Republic of Germany, Pacific Sci. Internat., Inc., U.S., V.I. 1st lt. U.S. Army, 1951-54. Mem. Fin. Execs. Inst. (bd. dirs., v.p. 1984—). Clubs: Jonathan (L.A.), Balboa Bay (Newport Beach, Calif.). Republican. Home: 2027 Bayside Dr Corona Del Mar CA 92625-1847 Office: Pacific Scientific Co 620 Newport Center Dr Newport Beach CA 92660-6420 E-mail: Richard-Plat@home.net.

PLATAU, GERARD OSCAR, chemist, consultant; b. Potsdam, Germany, June 29, 1926; s. Martin and Ottilie Platau; m. Caroline (Freeman) Platau, May 27, 1961; children: Steven. BA, Bklyn Coll., 1946; MS, Purdue U., 1948, PhD, 1950. From dept. mgr. to sr. adv. Chem. Abstracts Svc., Columbus, Ohio, 1961—79, sr. advisor, 1979—90; cons., 1990—. Conf. chmn. CODATA, Paris, 1987—90. Contbr. articles to profl. jours. Bd. dir. Upper Arlington Civic Orgn., Upper Arlington, Ohio, 1974—76. Fellow, Nat. Fedn. of Abstracting & Info. Svc., 1991. Mem.: Am. Soc. Info. Sci. & Tech. (dir. 1966—80, parliamentarian 1985—, Watson Davis award 1980), Am. Chem. Soc., The Ohio State U. Alumni Assn. Methodist. Avocations: travel, photography.

PLATE, THOMAS GORDON, newspaper columnist, educator; b. N.Y.C., May 17, 1944; s. John William and Irene (Henry) P.; m. Andrea I. Margolis, Sept. 22, 1979; 1 child, Ashley Alexandra. AB, Amherst Coll., 1966; MPA, Princeton U., 1968. Writer Newsweek, N.Y.C., 1968-70; editor Newsday, L.I., N.Y., 1970-72; sr. editor N.Y. Mag., N.Y.C., 1972-75; editor edit. page L.A. Herald Examiner, 1978-82; sr. editor Time Mag., N.Y.C., 1982-83; editor in chief Family Weekly, 1984-85; editor edit. pages N.Y. Newsday, 1986-89, L.A. Times, 1989-95, Times Op-Ed Page columnist, contbg. editor, 1995—. Adj. prof. UCLA Pub. Policy Sch. and Letters and Scis.; mem. founders bd. UCLA Sch. Pub. Policy; founder Asia Pacific Media Network; participant World Econ. Forum, Davos. Author: Understanding Doomsday, 1971, Crime Pays!, 1975, Secret Police, 1981; co-author: Commissioner, 1978. Recipient Best Deadline Writing award Am. Soc. Newspaper Editors, 1981, Best Edit. awards L.A. Press Club, 1979, 80, 81, Best Edit. award Calif. Newspaper Pubs. Assn., 1991, 92, 94; media fellow Stanford U. Mem. Pacific Coun. on Internat. Rels., Century Assn. (N.Y.C.), Phi Beta Kappa. Avocations: tennis, photography, travel to Asia. Office: LA Times 405 Hilgard Ave Los Angeles CA 90095-9000

PLATER, WILLIAM MARMADUKE, English language educator, academic administrator; b. East St. Louis, Ill., July 26, 1945; s. Everett Marmaduke and Marguerite (McBride) P.; m. Gail Maxwell, Oct. 16, 1971; children: Elizabeth Rachel, David Matthew. BA, U. Ill., 1967, MA in English, 1969, PhD in English, 1973. Asst. dir. Unit One, asst. to dean Coll. Liberal Arts and Scis. U. Ill., Urbana, 1971-72, acting dir. Unit One, 1972-73, asst. dean Coll. Arts and Scis., 1973-74, asst. dir. Sch. Humanities, 1974-77, assoc. dir., 1977-83, assoc. coordinator interdisciplinary programs, 1977-83; prof. English, dean Sch. Liberal Arts Ind. U., Indpls., 1983-87; dean of faculties Ind. U.-Purdue U., 1987—, exec. vice chancellor, 1988—. Bd. dirs. Met. Indpls. Pub. Broadcasting, Inc.; cons. in field. Author: The Grim Phoenix: Reconstructing Thomas Pynchon, 1978, also articles, revs., poetry. Trustee Coun. for Adult and Experiential Learning, 1995—; bd. dirs. Ind. Com. for Humanities, 1986—92, Ind. Repertory Theatre, 1987—93, Children's Mus., 1992—2001, U. Ill. YMCA, Urbana, 1982—83, Herron Gallery Contemporary Art, 1987—93; bd. govs. Ind. U. Ctr. on Philanthropy, 1997—; bd. dirs. Midwest Univs. Consortium for Internat. Activities, Inc., 1996—98. Recipient Program Innovation prize Am. Acad. Ednl. Devel., 1982. Home: 6477 Oxbow Way Indianapolis IN 46220- Office: IUPUI Adminstrn Bldg A0108 Indianapolis IN 46202 E-mail: wplater@iupui.edu.

PLATIS, CHRIS STEVEN, educator; b. East Chicago, Ind., May 21, 1926; s. Sam and Myra (Theodore) P.; m. Jeanette Brown. BS in Phys. Edn., Ind. U., 1955, MS in Edn., 1964, postgrad., 1965-68. Gen. foreman Cast Armor, Inc., East Chicago, 1951-53; tchr. East Chgo. and Ind. Pub. Schs., 1955—. Asst. sports editor East Chgo. Calumet News, 1973-78; asst. dir. No. Ind. State Sports Mus., 1984-95, 96, 97, 98, 00. Appearances include (films) A Bridge Too Far, The Longest Day, Bridge at Remagan, D-Day, The Battle of the Bulge; author: Teaching Kids of Tomorrow, 1978, Are Teachers Adequate for Today's Students?, 1997. Master Boy Scouts Am., East Chicago, 1965-87; asst. recreational dir. North Twp., Northern Ind., 1993; All-Pacific Army, Football, Basketball, Track, 1946. With U.S. Army, 1944-46. Named to East Chgo. Hall of Fame All Am. Amateur Baseball Congress, 1955, 56, 57, Ind. Amateur Baseball Hall of Fame, 1962, U.S. Masters Track and Field All Am., 1995-98 (ranked 8 times # 1 and 2 in the country in masters track and field, 8 times ranked # 1 and 2 in the world in masters track and field, 1996-98), 20 individual Indiana Hooster State Games Regional Medals, 20 individual Indiana Hooster State Games Final Medals, 1996, 97, 98, 2000; Nat. Sr. Olympic track and field qualifier, 1997-99; 90 Yr. Greatest Athletes in East Chgo.'s History; recipient 12 league batting titles, 11 MVP awards, 16 times Ind. All State in Baseball, 21 times League Mgr. of Yr., Nat./European Tchr. of Yr., 1984; mem. team won 53 league championships, 54 playoff championships, 40 Ind. State baseball championships, 7 world regional titles, 5 world finalists, 2 runner-up world championships, Nat. C.I.O. baseball championship, 1949 Big Ten Baseball Champions, Ind. U.; conf. baseball champions, 1942, 43, 44; all-conf. team, 1942, 43, 44, capt., 1942, 43, 44; Ind. State Jr. Legion champions, all-state, Midwest All-Star team, 1942, Ind.-Ill. Bi-State champions, 1950, Most Valuable, Batting Champion, Best Infielder award. Fellow VFW (charter mem. World War II Meml. 1998), Am. Legion, Normandy Invasion Club, Nat. Assn. of Basketball Coaches, Nat. Wildlife Assn. Republican. Avocations: reading, writing, baseball, tennis, golf. Home: 427 Fisher St Munster IN 46321-2330

PLATIS, JAMES GEORGE, secondary school educator; b. Detroit, Mar. 23, 1927; s. Sam and Myra (Theodore) P.; m. Mary Lou Campbell, Aug. 16, 1974. BS in Physical Edn., Ind. U., 1955, MS in Edn., 1965; postgrad., Ind. State U., 1967. Cert. physical edn. tchr., Ind. Foreman Cast Armor, Inc., East Chicago, Ind., 1951-53, Youngstown Sheet & Tube, East Chicago, 1953-54; dir., tchr. East Chicago Pub. Schs., 1955—. Sports editor East Chicago Globe/Calumet News, 1973-78, Herald Newspapers, Merrillville, Ind., 1973-78; asst. dir. No. Ind. State Sports Mus., 1984-99. Contbr. articles to newspapers, jours. Founder East Chicago Hall of Fame, 1975, Little Olympics, East Chicago, 1956; pres. Ind. Am. Amateur Baseball Congress, 1954-57, commr., 1984-98; dir. No. Ind. State Sports Mus., 1988-00. With AUS, 1945-47, ETO. Named to Ind. Amateur Baseball Hall of Fame, 1962, East Chicago Hall of Fame, 1976, All-Am. Amateur Baseball Congress, 1955, 56, The Athletic Congress Masters All-Am., 1986-98, 99, 2000; selected to 90 Yr. Greatest Athletes in East Chicago History, Nat. Athletic Congress, 1990; named Amateur Coach of Yr., U.S. Baseball Fedn. Ind., 1990, Amateur Runner-up Coach of Yr., 1988; recipient 47 World and 55 Nat. No. 1 track rankings, Athletic Congress Masters, 1989-98, 2000, 14 League Batting Titles, 12 MV League Players awards; Ind. Jr. Legion State Champions, All-State Batting Champions, MVP in tournament, Conf. Baseball Champions, 1943, 44, 45, All-Conf. Team, 1944-45, Conf. Batting Champion, 1944, Team Cptn., 1945, All-Midwest team, Best Outfielder, 1944; 18 times Ind. all-state team; Ind. Nat. Baseball State Champions; mem. team won 53 League Championships, 54 Playoff championships, 40 Ind. State Baseball Championships, 5 Ind. State Champions Runner Up, 7 World Regional Titles, 5 World Finalists, 2 runner-up World Champions, Big Ten baseball champions Ind. U., 1949, Best Outfielder Congress All-State team, Ill., Ind. Bi-State Champions, 1950; Nat. C.I.O. Baseball Championship, 1951, 12 Times League Mgr. Of The Year, 1982-96; Big Ten Baseball Champions, Ind. U., 1949; named Athlete of Yr. Ind. Masters Track and Field, 1992, World Sr. Olympic Masters Track & Field Champion, Spain, 6 gold medals, 3 Masters Track & Field World Records, 1992, Fla. Masters Track and Field Athlete of Yr., 1994-97; recipient 74 State Ind. Track and Field Individual medals, 1983-99, 2000, 74 Ind. state regional individual medals, 1983-98, 2000, 291 All Am. Masters Track and Field Certs., 1986-99, 2000, 39 Ill. Grand Prix individual titles, 1989-92, 45 Mid-West Track and Field individual titles, 1989-92, 5 gold medals, silver medal World Sr. Olympic Masters Track & Field, 1996, Ga., 5 Masters Track & Field World Records, 1997, 2 Masters Track & Field World Records, 1998, Nat. Senior Olympics Qualifer, 1991, 93, 95, 97, 99, 2001, 4 Gold medals, 2 World Records Nat. Sr. Olympics, 7 gold medals World Sr. Olympic Masters Track and Field, Sydney, Australia, 2000; named Internat. Man of the Yr. in Edn., 1991-92, 93, Professional of the Yr. in Edn., 1991, others. Fellow Nat. Assn. Basketball Coaches, Am. Assn. Health, Phys. Edn. and Recreation; mem. Athletic Dirs. Assn. Sportswriters Guild, VFW, Am. Legion, WWII Meml. (82nd Airborne Divsn., 1st Inf. Divsn. 1998), Mens Club Ind. U. Republican. Avocations: reading, running, baseball, writing. Office: East Chicago Pub Schs 2700 Cardinal Dr East Chicago IN 46312-3150

PLATIS, MARY LOU, media specialist; b. East Chicago, Ind., Jan. 21, 1946; d. Walter James and Mary Helen (Taus) Campbell; m. James George Platis, Aug. 16, 1974. BS, Ind. State U., 1972, MS, 1974. Tchr. 4th grade Holy Trinity Sch., East Chicago, Ind., 1968-72; tchr. phys. edn. Washington Elem. Sch., 1972-86; media specialist Ctrl. High Sch. Libr., 1986—. Recipient 47 Ind. track and field individual state medals, 1983-98, 99, 2000, 2001, 60 Ind. state regional individual medals, 1983-98, 99, 2000, 2001, 25 All Am. certs., 12 times Masters track and field All Am., 1989-98, 37 Ill. Grand Prix individual titles, 1989-93, 43 Midwest track and field individual titles, 1989-95, 3 times Nat. Masters track and field champion, 7 times Nat. runner-up; nat. sr. Olympics qualifier, 1997, 99, 2001; winner 6th pl. ribbons (2) Nat. Sr. Olympics, 1999; nat. and world ranked masters track and field, 1989-98; individual championship titles in racquetball; inducted into East Chicago Sports Hall of Fame, 1992. Mem. Nat. Assn. Basketball Coaches. Avocations: racquetball, tennis, working out. Home: 938 Troon Ct Schererville IN 46375 Office: Ctrl High Sch Libr 1100 W Columbus Dr East Chicago IN 46312-2582 E-mail: mlplatis@aol.com.

PLATNER, MICHAEL GARY, lawyer; b. Forest Hills, N.Y., June 18, 1957; s. Alan and Norma Platner; children: Marissa, Amanda, Carina. AB in Econs. cum laude, Washington U., St. Louis, 1979; JD, MBA, Emory U., 1982. Bar: Fla. 1983, Ga. 1983. Ptnr. Gunster, Yoakley, Valdes-Fauli & Stewart, P.A., Ft. Lauderdale, Fla., 1983—. Mem. legal affairs com. Internat. Franchise Assn. Mem. ABA, Fla. Bar Assn. (computer law subcom.), Computer Law Assn., Real Estate Securities and Syndication Inst. (pres. S.E. Fla. chpt. 1987). Office: 500 E Broward Blvd Ste 1400 Fort Lauderdale FL 33394-3076 Home: 1951 SE 19th St Pompano Beach FL 33062-7625

PLATNER, WARREN, architect; b. Balt., June 18, 1919; s. Warren Kelly and Alice Darling (Chapman) P.; m. Joan Payne, 1945; children: Bronson, Joan, Sharon, Madeleine. B.Arch., Cornell U., 1941. Assoc. Eero Saarinen and Assocs. (architects), 1950-65; propr. Warren Platner Assocs. (architects), New Haven, 1965—. Vis. lectr. archtl. schs. Prin. works include Kent Meml. Library, Suffield, Conn., 1972, Princeton U. Prospect Center, 1970, MGIC Hdqrs, Milw., 1973, Am. Restaurant, Kansas City, Mo., 1974; malls at Water Tower Pl., Chgo., 1975, Windows on the World, N.Y.C., 1976, Standard Brands Research Center, Wilton, Conn., 1979, Providence Athenaeum, 1980; Sea Containers Hdqrs., London, 1983, Wildflower Restaurant Lodge, Vail, Colo., 1985, Porter, Wright, Morris & Arthur Headqrs., Columbus, Ohio, 1986, Pan Am Bldg. additions, N.Y.C., 1987, ships Fantasia and Fiesta, 1990, Carlyle Hotel additions, 1990, Fair Residence, 1990, Friedman Residence, 1993. Recipient Rome prize architecture, 1955; advanced research Fulbright award architecture, 1955; Graham Found. award advanced studies fine arts, 1962; 1st ann. award Designers Lighting Forum, 1975; Pres.'s fellow R.I. Sch. Design, 1980; Interior Design Hall of Fame award, 1985; also several internat. design awards. Fellow AIA, Am. Acad. in Rome. Address: 18 Mitchell Dr New Haven CT 06511-2516

PLATNICK, NORMAN I. curator, entomologist; b. Bluefield, W.Va., Dec. 30, 1951; s. Philip and Fannie (Kascenewsky) P.; m. Nancy Stewart Price, June 14, 1970; 1 child, William Durin. BS in Biology, Concord Coll., 1968; MS in Zoology, Mich. State U., 1970; PhD in Biology, Harvard U., 1973. Asst. curator Am. Mus. Natural History, N.Y.C., 1973-77, assoc. curator, 1977-82, curator, 1982-98, chmn. dept. entomology, 1987-94, Peter J. Solomon Family curator, 1998—; program dir. biotic surveys and inventories NSF, 2002—. Sci. attaché Consulate of Gondwana, N.Y.C., 1976—. Author: Advances in Spider Taxonomy, 1989, 93, 98; co-author: Systematics and Biogeography, 1981; co-editor: Advances in Cladistics, 1983. V.p. Ctr. Internat. de Documentation Arachnologie, 1986-89 (pres. 1995-98). Fellow Willi Hennig Soc. (founder, pres. 1990-92); mem. Am. Arachnological Soc. (charter, membership sec. 1976—). Office: Am Mus Natural History Central Pk W At 79th St W New York NY 10024

PLATSOUCAS, CHRIS DIMITRIOS, immunologist; b. Athens, Greece, Apr. 17, 1951; came to U.S., 1973; s. Dimitrios Evagelos and Maria (Tsonidis) P.; m. Emilia L. Oleszak, Oct. 18, 1985. BS, U. Patras (Greece), 1973; postgrad., Purdue U., 1974; PhD, MIT, 1978. Rsch. fellow/assoc. Meml. Sloan-Kettering Cancer Ctr., N.Y.C., 1978-80, asst. mem., 1980-85, asst. prof., 1981-85, head lab. biol. response modifiers, 1981-85; assoc. prof. dept. immunology M.D. Anderson Cancer Ctr., Houston, 1985-89, prof., dep. chmn., 1989-93, Ashbel Smith professorship, 1991-92, H.L. and O. Stringer professorship in cancer rsch., 1992-93; L.H. Carnell prof. and chmn. dept. microbiology, immunology Temple U. Sch. Medicine, Phila., 1993—; acting dean Coll. Sci. & Tech. Temple U., 1998-2000, dean Coll. Sci. & Tech., 2000—. Biotech. cons., sci. reviewer study sects. NIH, Bethesda, 1982—. Contbr. numerous articles to profl. jours. Nat. Rsch. Svc. award NIH, 1978-79; grantee NIH, Am. Cancer Soc., State of Tex., many others. Mem. Am. Assn. Immunologists, Am. Soc. Hematology, Am. Assn. Biochem & Molecular Biology, Soc. Investigative Pathology, Am. Assn. Cancer Rsch. Greek Orthodox. Achievements include patents in field; research on human T cell immunology, on T-cell antigen receptors, on tumor-infiltrating lymphocytes in malignant melanoma and ovarian carcinoma, on organ transplantation, on chronic rejection, on AIDS, and on autoimmune diseases. Office: Temple U Sch Medicine Dept Microbiology and Immunology 3400 N Broad St Philadelphia PA 19140-5104 E-mail: cplatsoucas@vm.temple.edu.

PLATT, AUSTIN P. retired science educator; b. Evanston, Ill., Oct. 29, 1937; s. Sherwood Kellogg and Dorothy Platt; m. Pamela Jean Crooks; children: Stephen Sherwood Kellogg, Richard Austin. BA, Williams Coll., Williamstown, MA, 1959; MA, Univ. Mass., Amherst, MA, 1963, PhD, 1965. Zoology instr. Univ. RI, Kingston, RI, 1965—66; asst. prof. biology Wesleyan Univ., Middletown, 1966—69, UMBC, Baltimore, 1969—71, assoc. prof. biology, 1969—2001, assoc. prof. emeritus, biology, 2001—. Editor Jour. of the Lepidopterists' Soc., 1978—90; founder MD Entomol. Soc., Baltimore, Md., 1971—73, pres., Md., 1987—88. Fellow: Royal Entomol. Soc. Avocations: collecting insects, fossils, collecting indian artifacts, collecting indian artifacts. Home: 5401 Wilkens Ave Catonsville MD 21228-5334 Office: UMBC Dept Biol Scis 1000 Hilltop Circle Baltimore MD 21229 E-mail: platt@umbc.edu.

PLATT, FRANKLIN DEWITT, retired history educator; b. Marion, La., Nov. 15, 1932; s. Robert Baxter and Ethel Estelle (White) P.; m. Dixie Ferguson, Aug. 4, 1956; 1 dau. Dixie. BA, La. State U., 1955; Rockefeller Bros. Theol. fellow, Union Theol. Sem., 1955-56; A.M., Washington U., St. Louis, 1963, PhD, 1969. Instr. dept. humanities Mich. State U., East Lansing, 1964-69, asst. prof., 1969-72, assoc. prof., 1972-77, prof., 1977-89, asst. chmn. dept. humanities, 1971-78, chmn., 1978-80, prof. history, 1989-96, prof. emeritus, 1997—. Co-author: The Western Humanities, 1991 (named Best Coll. Textbook Bookbuilders West 1998), Readings in the Western Humanities, 1994. Served with USNR, 1956-60. Home: 1134 Southlawn Ave East Lansing MI 48823-3041 also: 5190 Far Oak Cir Sarasota FL 34238-3303 E-mail: plattf@msu.edu.

PLATT, GEORGE MILO, university administrator; b. Rapid City, S.D., Jan. 1, 1931; s. George Lee and Josephine M. (Paulson) P.; B.S., S.D. State U., 1953; M.A., Syracuse U., 1955, Ph.D., 1962. Asst. prof. U. S.D., 1962-65, U. Iowa, 1965-69; dir. planning and instl. research Wichita (Kans.) State U., 1969-79, assoc. v.p., 2nd assoc. prof. pub. adminstrn., 1979—97; Ford Found. adv. to secs. of local govt., East and West Pakistan, 1963, 65-66, 68. Served with AUS, 1955-57. Mem. Am. Soc. for Public Adminstrn., Am. Polit. Sci. Assn., Midwest Polit. Sci. Assn., Western History Assn., Soc. for Coll. and Univ. Planning. Author: (with Richard O. Niehoff) Local Government in East Pakistan, 1964; (with Alan L. Clem) A Bibliography of South Dakota Government and Politics, 1965, (with others) Administrative Problems in Pakistan, 1966. Office: Wichita State Univ Campus Box 155 Wichita KS 67260-0155 E-mail: george.platt@wichita.edu.

PLATT, JOSEPH BEAVEN, former college president; b. Portland, Oreg., Aug. 12, 1915; s. William Bradbury and Mary (Beaven) P.; m. Jean Ferguson Rusk, Feb. 9, 1946; children: Ann Ferguson Walker, Elizabeth Beaven Garrow. BA, U. Rochester, 1937; PhD, Cornell U., 1942; LLD, U. So. Calif., 1969, Claremont McKenna Coll., 1982; DSc, Harvey Mudd Coll., 1981. Instr. physics U. Rochester, N.Y., 1941-43, from asst. prof. to prof., 1946-56, assoc. chmn. dept. physics, 1954-56; staff mem. radiation lab. MIT, Cambridge, 1943-46; founding pres. Harvey Mudd Coll., Claremont, Calif., 1956-76, now part-time sr. prof. physics; pres. Claremont U. Ctr., 1976-81. Trustee Aerospace Corp., 1972-85, Consortium for Advancement of Pvt. Higher Edn., 1985-92; chief physics br. AEC, 1949-51; cons. U.S. Office Ordnance Rsch., NSF, 1953-56; mem. com. on sci. in UNESCO, NAS-NRC, 1960-62, mem. com. on internat. orgns. and programs, 1962-64, sci. advisor U.S. Del., UNESCO Gen. Conf., Paris, 1960, alt. del., 1962, chmn. Subcom. on Sino-Am. Sci. Cooperation, 1965-79; mem. panel on internat. sci. Pres.'s Sci. Adv. Com., 1961; trustee Analytic Svcs., Inc., 1958-89, chmn., 1961-89; mem. adv. com. on sci. edn. NSF, 1965-70, 72-76, chmn., 1969-70, 73-74, 74-75; bd. dirs. Lincoln Found., 1979-85, Bell & Howell Corp., 1978-88, Am. Mut. Fund, 1981-88, DeVry, Inc., 1984-87, Sigma Rsch., 1983-87, Jacobs Engring. Co., 1978-86. Author: Harvey Mudd College: The First Twenty YEars, 1994. Trustee China Found. for Promotion of Edn. and Culture, 1966—, Carnegie Found. for Advancement Tchg., 1970-78, Ancient Bibl. Manuscript Ctr., 1980—; chmn. select com. Master Plan for Higher Edn. Calif., 1971-73; mem. Carnegie Coun. for Policy Studies in Higher Edn., 1975-80. Fellow Am. Phys. Soc.; mem. IEEE, Automobile Club So. Calif. (bd. dirs. 1973-90, chmn. bd. dirs. 1986-87), Calif. Club, Sunset Club, Twilight Club, Cosmos Club, Bohemian Club, Phi Beta Kappa, Sigma Xi, Phi Kappa Phi. Home: 452 W 11th St Claremont CA 91711-3833 E-mail: joseph_platt@hmc.edu.

PLATT, LAURENCE ERIC, lawyer; b. Boston, May 6, 1954; s. Henry and Carolyn (Lindner) P; m. Elizabeth Clare Herington, Sept. 23, 1984; children: Benjamin, Timothy, Noah. BA cum laude, U. Pitts., 1976; JD with honors, George Washington U., 1982. Claims asst. Overseas Pvt. Investment Corp., Washington, 1978-81; ptnr. Brownstein Zeidman and Lore, 1982-95, Kirkpatrick & Lockhart LLP, Washington, 1995—. Co-author: Residential Mortgage Lending-State Regulation Manual, 1989, Practical Guide to Real Estate Settlement Procedures Act, 1995. Cubmaster Boy Scouts of Am., Potomac, Md., 1994-98; bd. dirs. Montgomery Housing Partnership, Wheaton, Md., 1990-97, Mortgage Bankers Assn. Met. Washington, 1991-92. Mem. ABA. Democrat. Office: Kirkpatrick & Lockhart LLP 1800 Massachusetts Ave NW Fl 2 Washington DC 20036-1806 E-mail: lplatt@kl.com.

PLATT, LESLIE A. lawyer; b. Bronx, N.Y., Aug. 7, 1944; s. Harold and Ann (Bienstock) P.; m. Marcia Ellin Berman, Aug., 1969; 1 son, Bill Lawrence. BA, George Washington U., 1966; JD, NYU, 1969. Bar: N.Y. 1970, U.S. Dist. Ct. D.C. 1972. Atty. advisor Office Gen. Counsel HUD, Washington, 1971-72, legis. atty., 1972-75, asst. gen. counsel for legis. svcs., 1975-78, assoc. gen. counsel for legis., 1978-80; dep. gen. counsel-legal counsel HEW (HHS 1980) Office Gen. Counsel, 1980-81, legal counsel and staff dir. White House Agent Orange group, 1980-81; pvt. practice, 1982-91; exec. asst. to dir. NIH, 1991-92; exec. v.p., COO, gen. counsel The Inst. for Genomic Rsch., Gaithersburg, Md., 1992-95; sr. v.p. strategic devel., gen. counsel Am. Type Culture Collection, Manassas, Va., 1996-98; prin., litig. adv. svcs., assurance and adv. bus. practice Ernst & Young LLP, McLean, 1999—. Pres, dir. Found. for Genetic Medicine, Inc., 1997—. Patentee in field. Chmn. cmty. adv. bd. Fairfax Hosp. Assn. Cameron Glen Facility; chair steering com. Reston/Herndon Bus.-H.S. partnership. Recipient Disting. Svc. award HUD, 1978. Mem. ABA, Fed. Bar Assn., Am. Jud. Soc., Fed. Sr. Exec. Svc. (charter), Internat. Bar Assn. Home: 11901 Triple Crown Rd Reston VA 20191-3015

PLATT, NICHOLAS, Asia specialist, retired ambassador; b. N.Y.C., Mar. 10, 1936; s. Geoffrey and Helen (Choate) P.; m. Sheila Maynard, June 28, 1957; children: Adam, Oliver, Nicholas. BA cum laude, Harvard U., 1957; MA, Johns Hopkins U., 1959. Commd. fgn. svc. officer Dept. State, 1959; vice consul Windsor, Ont., Can., 1959-61; Chinese lang. trainee, 1962-63; polit. officer consulate gen. Hong Kong, 1964-68; chief Asian Communist areas divsn. Bur. Intelligence and Rsch., Dept. State, Washington, 1969, chief North Asia div., 1970, dept. dir. Exec. Secretariat staff, 1971, dir. staff, 1972-73; chief polit. sect. U.S. Liaison Office, Peking, China, 1973-74; 1st sec. Am. embassy, Tokyo, 1974-77; dir. Office of Japanese Affairs, Dept. State, 1977-78; mem. staff Nat. Security Council, White House, 1978-79; dep. asst. sec. for internat. security affairs Dept. Def., 1980-81; dep. asst. sec. for internat. orgn. affairs Dept. State, 1981-82; amb. Lusaka, Zambia, 1982-84; exec. sec., spl. asst. to sec. state Dept. State, 1985-87; amb. to The Philippines Am. Embassy, Manila, 1987-91, amb. to Pakistan, 1991-92; pres. Asia Soc., N.Y.C., 1992—. Bd. dirs. Fiduciary Trust Internat. Recipient Meritorious award exemplary achievement pub. adminstrn. William A. Jump Found., 1973, Disting. Civilian Svc. medal Dept. Def., 1981, Presdl. Merit award, 1985, 87, Disting. Honor award U.S. Dept. State, 1987, 91, Wilbur Carr award, 1992. Mem. N.Y. Coun. Fgn. Rels., Met. Club (Washington), Century Club, Union Club. Home: 131 E 69th St New York NY 10021-5158

PLATT, ROGER, lawyer, lobbyist; b. N.Y.C., May 26, 1959; s. Frank Cheney and Judith (Van der Gracht) Platt; m. Christie Mercer, Aug. 17, 1985; children: Benjamin Cheney, Hilary. BA, Harvard U., 1982; JD, U. San Francisco, 1987. Bar: Calif. 1987, D.C. 1993. Assoc. atty. Bianchi, Paxton & Engel, San Rafael, Calif., 1987-89; sr. assoc. atty. Coblentz, Cahen, McCabe & Breyer, San Francisco, 1989-91; cons. White Ho. Office on Nat. Svc., 1992; sr. v.p., counsel The Real Estate Roundtable, Washington, 1992—. Editor: Environ. Law and Practice, 1998—99; contbr. articles to profl. jours. Fed. adv. bd. EPA, Washington, 1995—98; regioanl coord. Clinton for Pres., 1991; bd. dirs. Ctr. Watershed Planning, Silver Spring, Md., 1998—2000. Democrat. Roman Catholic. Avocations: foreign films, hiking, skiing, tennis. Office: The Real Estate Roundtable Ste 1100 1420 New York Ave NW Washington DC 20005 Business E-Mail: rplatt@rer.org.

PLATT, THOMAS COLLIER, JR. federal judge; b. N.Y.C., N.Y., May 29, 1925; s. Thomas Collier and Louise Platt; m. Ann Byrd Symington, June 25, 1948; children: Ann Byrd, Charles Collier, Thomas Collier, III, Elizabeth Louise. BA, Yale U., 1947, LL.B., 1950. Bar: N.Y. 1950. Assoc. Root, Ballantine, Harlan, Bushby & Palmer, N.Y.C., 1950-53; asst. U.S. atty. Bklyn., 1953-56; assoc. Bleakley, Platt, Schmidt, Hart & Fritz, N.Y.C., 1956-60, ptnr., 1960-74; judge U.S. Dist. Ct. (ea. dist.) N.Y., 1974—, chief judge, 1988-95. Former dir. Phoenix Mut. Life Ins. Co., RAC Corp., McIntyre Aviation, Inc.; atty. Village of Laurel Hollow, N.Y., 1958-74; acting police justice Village of Lloyd Harbor, N.Y., 1958-63 Alt. del. Republican Nat. Conv., 1964, 68, 72; del. N.Y. State Rep. Conv., 1966; trustee Brooks Sch., North Andover, Mass., 1968-82, pres., 1970-74. Served with USN, 1943-46 Mem. Fed. Judges Assn. (sec., bd. dirs. 1982-91). Clubs: Phelps Assn. (New Haven) (bd. govs. 1960-98); Cold Spring Harbor Beach (N.Y.) (bd. mgrs. 1964-70); Yale of N.Y.C. Episcopalian. Office: US Dist Ct 1044 Federal Plaza Central Islip NY 11722-4442

PLATT, WARREN E. lawyer; b. McNary, Ariz., Aug. 5, 1943; BA, Mich. State U., 1965; JD, U. Ariz., 1969. Bar: Ariz. 1969, Calif. 1991, Texas 1993. Atty. Snell & Wilmer, Phoenix. Mng. editor: Ariz. Law Rev., 1968-69. Fellow Am. Coll. Trial Lawyers; mem. Blue Key, Order of Coif, Phi Alpha Delta Office: Snell & Wilmer One Arizona Ctr Phoenix AZ 85004-0001

PLATT, WILLIAM HENRY, judge; b. Allentown, Pa., Jan. 25, 1940; s. Henry and Genevieve (McElroy) P.; m. Maureen Hart, Nov. 29, 1969; children: Meredith H., William H., James H. AB, Dickinson Coll., 1961; JD, U. Pa., 1964. Bar: Pa. 1967, U.S. Supreme Ct. 1971. Ptnr. Yarus and Platt, Allentown, 1967-77; asst. pub. defender Lehigh County (Pa.), 1972-75, chief pub. defender, 1975-76, dist. atty., 1976-91; ptnr. Eckert, Seamans, Cherin & Mellott, 1991-95; city solicitor City of Allentown, 1994-95; judge Ct. Common Pleas of Lehigh County, Allentown, 1996—, pres. judge, 2002—. Mem. criminal procedural rules com. Supreme Ct. Pa., 1982-92, chmn., 1986-92. Mem. Gov.'s Trial Ct. Nominating Commn. Lehigh County, 1984-87; mem. Pa. Commn. on Crime and Delinquency Victim Services Adv. Com., 1983-91. Served with M.P., U.S. Army, 1964-66. Mem.: ABA, Pa. Conf. of State Trial Judges (edn. com. 1997—), Pa. Assn. Dist. Attys. (exec. com. 1980—86, pres. 1983—84, chmn. 1986—87, tng. inst. mem. 1986—91), Nat. Assn. Dist. Attys. (state dir. 1982—84), Lehigh County Bar Assn., Pa. Bar Assn., Pa. Bar Inst. (hon.), Pa. Bar Inst. (life; bd. dirs. 1989—2000, exec. com. 1994—2000, pres. 1997—98). Office: Lehigh County Courthouse 455 W Hamilton St Allentown PA 18101-1614

PLATTHY, JENO, cultural association executive; b. Dunapataj, Hungary, Aug. 13, 1920; s. Joseph K. and Maria (Dobor) P.; m. Carol Louise Abell, Sept. 25, 1976 Diploma, Peter Pazmany U., Budapest, Hungary, 1942; PhD, Ferencz J. U., Kolozsvar, Hungary, 1944; MS, Cath. U., 1965; PhD (hon.), Yangmingshan U., Taiwan, 1975; DLitt (hon.), U. Libre Asie, Philippines, 1977. Lectr. various univs., 1956-59; sec. Internat. Inst. Boston, 1959-62; adminstrv. asst. Trustees of Harvard U., Washington, 1962-85; exec. dir. Fedn. Internat. Poetry Assns., 1976—. Pub. New Muses Quar., 1976— Author: Winter Tunes, 1974, Ch'u Yuan, His Life and Works, 1975, Springtide, 1976, Opera Bamboo, Collected Poems, 1981, The Poems of Jesus, 1982, Holiness in a Worldly Garment, 1984, Ut Pictures Poeta, 1984, European Odes, 1985, The Mythical Poets of Greece, 1985, Book of Dithyrambs, 1986, Asian Elegies, 1987, Space Ecologues, 1988, Cosmograms, 1988, Nova Comoedia, 1988, vols. II-III, 1992, Bartok: A Critical Biography, 1988, Plato: A Critical Biography, 1990, Near-Death Experiences in Antiquity, 1992, Celebration of Life, 1992, Idylls, 1992, Elegies Asiatiques, 1992, Paeans, 1993, Rhapsodies, 1994, Prosodia, 1994, Visions, 1994, Prophecies, 1994, Epyllia, 1994, Budapesttol Tokyoig, 1994, 2d edit., 1995, Walking Two Feet Above the Earth, 1995, Dictionarium Cumanico Hungaricum, 1996, Emblems, 1996, Epodes, 1996, Aeolian Lilts, 1996, Transformations, 1996, Inexpressions, 1996, Songs of the Soul, 1996, Sacrifices, 1996, Gifts with Poetic Horizons, 1997, Imperceptions, Hermeneutics of Poetry, 1997, From Silence to Silence, New Perspectives in Poetry, 1997, Lincoln the Poet, an Epic Poem, 1997, Looking Away, 1998, Commitments, 1998, The Duino Elegies of Rilke, 1999, Symmetries with Poetic Discoveries, Part I, 1999, Cosmos Flowers with Poetic Discoveries, Part II, 1999, Dreamtide with Principia Spiritualia I (Discoveries III), 2000, Demonstrations with Principia Spiritualia II-III (Discoveries IV-V), 2000, Pictorial Bio-Bibliography, 2000, also numerous others, also translations; editor-in-chief Monumenta Classica Perennia, 1967-84. Named Poet Laureate 2d World Congress of Poets, 1973; recipient Confucius award Chinese Poetry Soc., 1974, Yunus Emre award 12th Internat. Congress of Poets, Istanbul, Turkey, 1991, Jacques Raphael-Leygues prize Société des Poètes Français, 1992, French Ordre des Arts et des Lettres (officer), 1992. Mem. PEN, ASCAP, Internat. Soc. Lit., Die Literarische Union, Internat. Poetry Soc., Acad. Am. Poets, Assn. Lit. Scholars and Critics, 3d Internat. Congress Poets (pres. 1976, poet laureate 1976), Nat. Assn. of Scholars. Office: Fedn Internat Poetry Assns 961 W Sled Cir Santa Claus IN 47579-6251

PLATTI, RITA JANE, educator, draftsman, writer, inventor; b. Stockton, Calif., Aug. 29, 1925; d. Umbert Ferdinand and Concettina Maria (Natoli) Strangio; m. Elvin Carl Platti, July 27, 1955; 1 child, Kimberley Jane. Student, Dominican Coll., 1943-45; AB in Math, U. Pacific, 1947, postgrad., 1947-52, 68. Farmer, almond grower, Escalon, Calif., 1943—; tchr. math St. Mary's High Sch., Stockton, 1947-49, 52, 54; chem. analyst Petri Winery, Escalon, 1949; draftsman Kyle Steel Co., Stockton, 1950-52; pvt. practice as draftsman, 1952-66; tchr. math Montezuma Sch., 1956-57, Davis Elem. Sch., Stockton, 1957-58; with rental bus., 1958-81; tchr. math Amos Alonzo Stagg High Sch., 1961-80, Humphreys Coll., 1981-83, Hamilton Jr. High Sch., 1984-90. Owner, involved in prodn. and mktg. R.J. Creations, 1991—; farm realtor Century 21, Escalon, Calif., 1996-97; spkr. workshops Stanislaus State U., 1992, Calif. Math. Coun., Fresno State U., 1992, Nat. Sci. Found. Conf., 1993; spkr. math./sci. conf. Calif. State U., Bakerfield, 1994-96; evaluator Math. Framework (K-12) Calif. State Dept. Edn. Author: Math Proficiency Plateaus, 1979, Preparing Fundamentals of The Use of Sound in the Teaching of Mathematics, 1994, Book of Poems, 2002; author, pub. series, 1979-86; 3 patents in field. Mem. NEA, Calif. Tchrs. Assn. Democrat. Roman Catholic. Avocations: inventing, mathematics theoretical development, poetry, piano, environmental clean up.

PLATTNER, RICHARD SERBER, lawyer; b. N.Y.C., Aug. 10, 1952; s. Milton and Sallee Sarah (Serber) P.; m. Susan M. Madden, June 4, 1976 (div. June 1979); m. Susan K. Morris, Mar. 30, 1983; children: Samuel Morris, Katherine Elise. BA cum laude, Mich. State U., 1973; JD, Ariz. State U., 1977. Bar: Ariz. 1977, U.S. Dist. Ct. Ariz. 1977, U.S. Ct. Appeals (9th cir.) 1987; cert. specialist personal injury and wrongful death. Assoc. Wolfe & Harris, Pa., 1977-79, Monbleau, Vermeire & Turley, Phoenix, 1979-81, Phillips & Lyon, Phoenix, 1981; sole practice Phoenix, 1982-91; ptnr. Plattner Verderame, P.C., 1991—. Posse comdr. Maricopa County Sheriff Exec. Posse, 1986-87; judge pro tem Maricopa County Superior Ct., 1986—, Ariz. Ct. Appeals, 1993—. Editor: Trial Judges of Maricopa County, 1985; co-editor Jury Verdict Research newsletter, 1982-83. Mem. ATLA (sustaining mem.), Am. Bd. Trial Advs. (assoc. 1997—), Ariz. Trial Lawyers Assn. (sustaining mem., editor Ariz. Appellate Highlights, 1985—, bd. dirs., 1987—, pres. 1991), Ariz. Bar Assn. (mem. civil practice and procedure com. 1988-99, civil jury instrn. com. 1991), Maricopa County Bar Assn., Phoenix Trial Lawyers Assn. (bd. dirs. 1983-95, pres. 1986-87), Ariz. Bus. and Profl. Assn. (pres. 1984-86). Office: PO Box 36570 Phoenix AZ 85067-6570 E-mail: rplattner@plattner-verderame.com.

PLATTS, HOWARD GREGORY, scientific, educational organization executive; b. Aug. 14, 1947; s. Thayer Horton and Anne Elizabeth (Gregory) P.; m. Elizabeth Hertzler Murray, June 7, 1969; children: James Thayer, Christopher Wilke. AB, Harvard U., 1969; M. Pub. and Pvt. Mgmt., Yale U., 1980. Tchr. Potomac Sch., McLean, Va., 1969-72; investment officer First Am. Bank, Washington, 1972-78; fin. analyst Yale U., New Haven, 1979; fin. asst. to pres. Nat. Geog. Soc., Washington, 1980-82, asst. treas., 1982-91, v.p., treas., 1992—. Treas., bd. dirs. Edes Home Found., Washington, 1975-78; trustee Nat. Presbyn. Sch., Washington, 1988-91; chmn., trustee regional blood svcs. ARC, Balt., 1992-2000; treas., bd. dirs. Friends of Fort Dupont, Washington, 1995-2002; trustee Decatur House, Washington, 1994—; mem. governing bd. St. Albans Sch., Washington, 1997—; mem. bd. cons. Riggs Bank, N.A., Washington, 1997—. Trustee Westmoreland Congl. Ch., 1988-91. Mem. Washington Soc. Investment Analysts (pres., bd. dirs. 1985-91), Assn. Investment Mgmt. and Rsch., Alfalfa Club, Alibi Club, Metropolitan Club, Chevy Chase Club. Home: 5302 Portsmouth Rd Bethesda MD 20816-2929 Office: Nat Geog Soc 1145 17th St NW Washington DC 20036-4701 E-mail: platts@aya.yale.edu.

PLATTS, TODD RUSSELL, congressman, state legislator; b. Mar. 5, 1962; m. Leslie Platts. BS summa cum laude, Shippensburg U. Pa., 1984; JD cum laude, Pepperdine U., 1991. Atty. Barley, Snyder, Senft & Cohen; rep. dist. 196 State of Pa., 1993-2001; mem. U.S. Congress from 19th Pa. dist., 2001—; mem. transp. and infrastructure com., edn. and workforce com., govt. reform com. Aging & youth edn. com. State of Pa., 1993—. Office: 1032 Longworth Ho Office Bldg Washington DC 20515*

PLATTS-MILLS, THOMAS ALEXANDER E. immunologist, educator, researcher; b. Colchester, Essex, Eng., Nov. 22, 1941; came to U.S., 1982; s. John Faithful F. and Janet Katherine (Cree) P.-M.; m. Roberta Rosenstock, Apr. 9, 1970; children: Eliza, Timothy, James, Oliver. BA, Balliol Coll., Oxford (Eng.) U., 1963; MB, BChir, Oxford U., 1967; PhD, London U., 1982. Registrar in medicine Bury St. Edmunds, and New Market, Suffolk, Eng., 1968-71; fellow in medicine Johns Hopkins U., Balt., 1971-74; staff mem. Med. Rsch. Coun., U.K., 1976-82; hon. cons. physician Northwick Park Hosp., London, 1978-82; prof. medicine, head div. allergy and clin. immunology U. Va., Charlottesville, 1982—, dir. Asthma and Allergic Diseases Ctr., 1994. Mem. immunological scis. study sect. NIH, 1988. Editl. bd. Am. Jour. Respiratory Critical Care Medicine, Clin. and Exptl. Immunology, Clin. Allergy, Jour. Immunological Methods; contbr. articles to profl. jours. Grantee NIH. Fellow Royal Coll. Physicians, Am. Acad. Allergy; mem. Assn. Am. Physicians, Am. Acad. Allergy, Asthma and Immunology (bd. dirs. 1995-99), Southeastern Allergy Assn. (Hal Davidson award 1986, pres. 1987-88), Brit. Soc. Allergy and Clin. Immunology. Office: U Va Dept Medicine PO Box 225 Charlottesville VA 22908-0001

PLATUS, LIBBY, artist, sculptor, speaker; b. L.A., Aug. 18, 1939; d. Benjamin Lyon and Gertrude Goldman; children: Julie Linda, Diana Lisa. BA, UCLA, 1961. Lectr., condr. workshops numerous internat., nat., regional meetings and meetings in all 50 states, including World Craft Conf., Kyoto, Japan, 1978, Vienna, Austria, 1980, Glasgow (Scotland) Sch. Art, 1980, 84, Loughborough Coll. Art, Eng., 1980, 84, R.I. Sch. Design, 1982, Parsons Sch. Design, N.Y.C., 1982, Arrowmont, Gatlinburg, Tenn., 1978, 83, 87, Konstfackskolan, Sweden, 1984, Goldsmith's Coll., Eng., 1984, Taideteo Llinen Korkeakoulo, Finland, 1984, Savannah (Ga.) Coll. Art and Design, 1987, 89, 90, 92, 94, 99, East N.C. U., Greenville, 1989, 92, 97, 2000, Navajo C.C., Shiprock Reservation, N.Mex., 1992, World Wildfowl Carving Exhbn., Ward Found., Md., 1990, Kansas City Art Inst., 1990, 92, So. Ute Tribal Hdqrs., Ignacio, Colo., 1993, U. Western Sydney Design dept., 1993, Sydney Coll. Art, 1993, Victorian Coll. Art, Melbourne, Australia, 1993, U. South Australia, Underdale, 1993, Australian Nat. U., Canberra, 1993, Waiariki Polytech. Coll. Rotorua, New Zealand, 1993, Aotearoa Inst., mgr. South Auckland, New Zealand, 1993, Te Taumata Art Gallery, Auckland, New Zealand, 1993, Aotearoa Inst. Tertiary Sch., Te Awamutu, New Zealand, 1993, Small Bus. Devel. Ctr. Northland Pioneer Coll., Hollbrook, Ariz., 1994, N.Y. State Coll. Ceramics, Alfred U., 1994, 96, Bus. Dept., 2000, Tlingit-Gold Belt Corp., Juneau, 1993, Seneca Nation Econ. Devel. Corp., Jamestown, N.Y., 1996, Assiniboine/Sioux/Gros Ventre-Tribal Bus. Info. Ctr., Ft. Belknap Reservation, Harlam, Mont., 1996, Nat. Home Based Bus. Conf. U. Wis.-Whitewater, Milw., 1996, 10th nat. conf. U.S. Assn. Small Bus. Entrepreneurship, Atlanta, 1996, So. Meth. U., Dallas, 1996, 99, New Orleans Jazz and Heritage Festival, 1994, Small Bus. Devel. Ctr., Binghamton (N.Y.) U., 1996, Small Bus. Devel. Ctr. and N.Mex. Main St. Program, Carlsbad, 1997, So. Ill. U., Carbondale, 1999, Arts Coun. Northwest Fla., Pensacola, 1989, 95, 97, 99, 2001, Fla. Craftsmen and Pinellas County Art Coun., St. Petersburg, 1997, Oreg. Coll. Art and Craft, Portland, 1982, 99, Birmingham Mus. Art, Ala., 1995, 97, Montgomery Mus. Art, Ala., 1997, Huntsville Mus. Art, Ala., 1998, 2000, Syracuse (N.Y.) U., 1997, Va. Commonwealth Univ., Richmond, 1999, Towson Univ., Towson, MD, 1988, 99, Atlantic County Office of Cultural and Heritage Affairs, NJ, 1988, 91, 95, 98, 00, Bear Paw Devel. Corp., Havre, Mont., Ga. Appalachian Devel. Ctr. North Ga. Coll., Dahlonega, 2001, Riverbend Art Ctr., Dayton, Ohio, 1988, 90, 98, 99, 2001, Pride of Dakota, Dept. Agr., N.D., 1999, Keynote Utah Heritage Industry Conf. Utah Divsn. Bus. and Econ. Devel., Ephriam, 1999, Tenn. Comty. Econ. Devel., Nashville, 2000, Keynote Vt. Tech. Assistance Providers Assn., Montpelier, 1999, Wyo. Dept. Employment Vocat. Rehab., Casper, Sheyenne, Sheridan, Rock Springs, 2000, Native Am. Shoshone/Northern Arapahoe, Wind River Reservation, Wyo., 2000, Hand Made in Am., Asheville, N.C., 2000, numerous others; cons. Millstream Arts Festival Coll. St. Benedict, St. Joseph, Minn., 1992, Mountain State Art and Crafts Festival, Cedar Lakes, W.Va., 1992, Grand Junction area C. of C., Home Based Bus. Trade Fair, Colo., 1992, Yavapai Coll. Creative Comm. Convergence, Sedona, Ariz., 1995, culinary competition Western Food Svc. and Hospitality Expo, L.A., 2001, judge, Art Harvest Jr. League Clearwater-Dunedin, Fla., 2000, Mont. Food and Gift Show Made in Mont. Program Mont. Dept Commerce, Great Falls, Mont., 1999; juror regional exhbn. Fairbanks Art Assn., Alaska, 1984; juror, judge, Greater Gulf Coast Art Festival, Pensacola, Fla., 1999; judge Millstream Arts Festival, Coll. St. Benedict, St. Joseph, Minnesota, 1992; participant Charmin Care TV comml., 1989, Rotary Internat. Group Study Exchange, Bangalore, India, 1998. Group shows include Richmond (Calif.) Designer Craftsmen, 1971, E.B. Crocker Gallery, Sacramento, 1973, Comsky Gallery, Beverly Hills, Calif., 1973, Galeria del Sol, Santa Barbara, Calif., 1973, Laguna Beach (Calif.) Mus. Art, 1973, Riverside (Calif.) Art Ctr., 1974, Calif. State U. Northridge, L.A., 1974, Calif. State U., Fullerton, 1974, Calif. Design '76, L.A., 1976, Cleve. Mus. Art, 1977; represented in collections: Tex. Christian U., Faberge Hdqrs., N.Y.C., numerous other pub. and pvt. collections; commd. works: Big Canyon Country Club, Newport Beach, Calif., Carolando Hyatt Hotel, Orlando, Fla., McCulloch's Silver Lakes Resort Hotel, Victorville, Calif., Blue Cross So. Calif., L.A. Mem. L.A. Olympics 1984 Cultural and Fine Arts Commn., 1980-84, citizens adv. commn., 1980-84; adv. bd. Crafts Report Edn. Fund, 1985-88. Recipient Graphic Achievement award Fox River Paper Corp., 1974; winner Tex. Christian U. Nat. Invitational Fiberwork Competition, 1977. Mem. Artists Equity (adv. bd. L.A. chpt. 1981-87). Home and Office: PO Box 55026 Sherman Oaks CA 91413-0026 E-mail: libbyplatus@earthlink.net.

PLATZMAN, GEORGE WILLIAM, geophysicist, educator; b. Chgo., Apr. 19, 1920; s. Alfred and Rose I. K.; m. Harriet M. Herschberger, Feb. 19, 1945 (dec. 1985). BS, U. Chgo., 1940, PhD, 1948; MS, U. Ariz., 1941. Instr. U. Chgo., 1942-45, rsch. assoc., 1947-48, faculty, 1949—, head phys. scis. in coll., 1959-60, prof. geophys. scis., 1960-90, chmn. dept. geophys. scis., 1971-74, emeritus prof., 1990—. Cons. Inst. Advanced Study, Princeton, 1950-53 Author: A Catalogue of Early Printed Editions of the Works of Frédéric Chopin in the University of Chicago Library, 1997; contbr. articles to profl. jours. Hydrologic engr. C.E., U.S. Army, 1945-46. Guggenheim fellow, 1967-68 Fellow AAAS, Am. Geophys. Union, Am. Meteorol. Soc. (editor jour. 1948-49, chmn. publs. com. 1966-70, Meisinger award 1966). Office: U Chgo Dept Geophys Scis 5734 S Ellis Ave Chicago IL 60637-1434

PLATZNER, LINDA, publisher; Assoc. pub. Modern Bride PRIMEDIA, pub. Seventeen mag. Office: 850 3d Ave 9th New York NY 10022

PLAUD, JOSEPH JULIAN, psychology educator; b. Worcester, Mass., Mar. 25, 1965; s. Henry Emile and Barbara Ann (Perry) P.; m. Christine Marie Therlault, Mar. 14, 1987 (div. Mar. 1990); 1 child, Brianna Marie; m. Deborah Muench, Jan. 30, 1999. BA summa cum laude, Clark U., 1987; PhD in Psychology, U. Maine, 1993. Lic. clin. psychologist, Mass.; bd. cert. behavior analyst Behavior Analyst Certification Bd. Psychology resident U. Miss. Med. Ctr., Jackson, 1992-93; asst. prof. psychology U. N.D., Grand Forks, 1993-97; dir. rsch., webmaster Cambridge (Mass.) Ctr. for Behavioral Studies, 1999—. Cons. N.D. Devel. Ctr., Grafton, 1994—, State of N.H., 1999—; forensic cons., 1993—; vis. scholar Brown U., 1998—; COO New Sch. for Learning Scis.; forensic psychology cons. Applied Behavioral Cons., Inc. Author: From Behavior Theory to Behavior Therapy, 1997; editor-in-chief Jour. Behavioral Analysis and Therapy; contbr. articles to profl. jours. Lt. Med. Svc. Corps, USNR, 1997. Fellow APA, Behavior Therapy and Rsch. Soc. (clin.); mem. AAAS, Assn. for Advancement of Behavior Therapy, Am. Psychol. Soc., Am. Psychol. Assn., Phi Beta Kappa, Psi Chi. Democrat. Roman Catholic. Home: 44 Hickory Ln Whitinsville MA 01588-1356

PLAUT, ERIC ALFRED, retired psychiatrist, educator; b. N.Y.C., Nov. 16, 1927; s. Alfred and Margaret (Blumenfeld) P.; m. Eloine Raab, Sept. 5, 1976. BS, Columbia U., 1949, MD, 1953. Diplomate: Am. Bd. Psychiatry and Neurology. Intern Montefiore Hosp., Bronx, N.Y., 1953-54; psychiat. resident State Hosp., Worcester, Mass., 1954-55, Mass. Meml. Hosp., Boston, 1956-57; cons. psychiatrist Mass. Dept. Corrections, 1957; fellow student health psychiatry U. Calif., Berkeley, 1957-58; practice medicine specializing in psychiatry, 1958-74; staff psychiatrist Kaiser Hosp., Oakland, Calif., 1958-62, Cowell Meml. Hosp., U. Calif., Berkeley, 1958-62; cons. psychiatrist Bur. Indian Affairs, Dept. Interior, 1967-68; program chief Berkeley Mental Health Services, 1968-71; dep. commr. Ind. Dept. Mental Health, Indpls., 1974-76; commr. Conn. Dept. Mental Health, Hartford, 1976-81; prof. Northwestern U. Med. Sch., Chgo., 1981-93, prof. emeritus, 1994—; asst. clin. prof. psychiatry U. Calif. Med. Sch., San Francisco, 1958-74; asso. clin. prof. psychiatry U. Ind. Med. Sch., Indpls., 1975-76; clin. prof. psychiatry U. Conn. Med. Sch., Farmington, 1978-81, Yale U. Med. Sch., 1979-81. Cons. Assembly Sci. Adv. Coun., Calif. Legislature, 1970; chmn. Bay Area region Calif. Conf. Local Mental Health Dirs., 1970-71; gen. ptnr. Vanguard Investments, Berkeley, 1971-78. Author: Grand Opera: Mirror of the Western Mind, 1993; co-author (with K. Andersen) Marx on Suicide, 1999; mem. editl. bd. Yale Psychiat. Quar., 1976-81; sect. editor Northwestern Univ. Press, 1991-2000; contbr. articles to profl. jours. Bd. dirs. ACLU, Berkeley, 1960-65; mem. task force on access and barrier Pres.'s Commn. on Mental Health, 1977; mem. psychiatry panel Grad. Med. Edn. Nat. Adv. Com., 1979-81; bd. dirs. Nat. Assn. State Mental Health Program Dirs., 1978-81. With USN, 1944-46. Fellow Am. Psychiat. Assn. (chmn. com. task force on govt. rels. 1973-76, chmn. com. public info. 1975-76, mem. com. cert. in adminstrv. psychiatry 1979-82, chmn. task force on problems of Americans overseas 1984-88, chmn. task force on joint meeting with German Psychiat. Soc., 1989-90); mem. No. Calif. Psychiat. Soc. (chmn. com. law and legis. 1968-72, fed. legis. rep. 1972-74, councillor 1972-73, pres.-elect 1973-74, chmn. com. on internat. abuse of psychiatry 1997-98), Calif. Med. Assn. (alt. del. 1968-71), Alameda-Contra Costa Med. Assn. (chmn. mental health com. 1972), Chgo. Psychoanalysis Soc. Address: 9310 N Bennett Ave Evanston IL 60203-1401 E-mail: e-plaut@nwu.edu.

PLAUT, JONATHAN VICTOR, rabbi; b. Chgo., Oct. 7, 1942; s. W. Gunther and Elizabeth (Strauss) P.; m. Carol Ann Fainstein, July 5, 1965; children: Daniel Abraham, Deborah Maxine. BA, Macalester Coll., 1964; postgrad., Hebrew Union Coll., Jerusalem, 1967-68; BHL, Hebrew Union Coll., Cin., 1968, MA, 1970, DHL, 1977; DD (hon.), 1995. Ordained rabbi, 1970. Rabbi Congregation Beth-El, Windsor, Ont., Can., 1970-84; sr. rabbi Temple Emanu-El, San Jose, Calif., 1985-93; dir. comty. outreach and involvement Jewish Fed. of Met. Detroit, 1993-95; pres. JVP Fund Raising Cons., Inc., Farmington Hills, Mich., 1994—. Lectr. Assumption Coll. Sch., 1972-84, St. Clair Coll., 1982-84, U. Windsor, Ont., Can., 1984; adj. asst. prof. Santa Clara U., 1985-93; vis. Rabbinic scholar Temple Beth El, 1993—; pres. JVP Fund Raising Cons., 1994—; rabbi Congregation Beth El, Traverse City, Mich., 1999—, Temple Beth Israel, Jackson, Mich., 2000—. Contbg. author: Reform Judaism in America: A Biographical Dictionary and Sourcebook, 1993; editor: Through the Sound of Many Voices, 1982, Jour. Can. Jewish Hist. Soc., 1976-83; also articles; host weekly program Religious Scope, Sta. CBET-TV, Religion in News, Sta. CKWW, 1971-84. Pres. Jewish Nat. Fund Windsor, 1978-81, chmn. bd. dirs., 1981-84; chmn. United Jewish Appeal Windsor, 1981-83, State of Israel Bonds, Windsor, 1980; nat. bd. dirs. Jewish Nat. Fund Can., 1972-84; pres. Reform Rabbis of Can., 1982-84; bd. dirs. Can. Jewish Congress, 1978-84, Jewish Family Svc. Santa Clara County, 1987-90, Jewish Fedn. Greater San Jose, 1986-93; chaplain San Jose Fire Dept., 1987-93; mem. exec. cabinet United Jewish Appeal, Windsor, 1971-84, mem. nat. rabbinic cabinet, 1993-95; mem. exec. com. Windsor Jewish Community Coun., 1970-84, chmn. 1975-84; mem. adv. coun. Riverview unit Windsor Hosp. Ctr., 1972-81; pres. Credit Counselling Svc. Met. Windsor, 1977-79. Honoree Jewish Nat. Fund, 1985. Mem. NCCJ, Can. Jewish Congress (nat. exec. bd. 1978-84), Can. Jewish Hist. Soc. (nat. v.p. 1974-84), Calif. Bd. Rabbis,

Rabbinic Assn. Greater San Jose (chmn. 1986-87), Ctrl. Conf. Am. Rabbis, Nat. Assn. Temple Educators. Home and Office: 30208 Kingsway Dr Farmington Hills MI 48331-1648 Fax: (248) 788-4144. E-mail: jvplaut@earthlink.net.

PLAUT, THOMAS F.A. psychologist; b. N.Y.C., Dec. 29, 1925; s. Alfred and Margaret (Blumenfeld) P.; m. Evelyn Z. McPuroff, Dec. 26, 1950 (div. Sept. 15, 1976); children: Melanie, Anthony, Jeffrey, Daphne, Iris, Roger; m. Bonnie A. Cox, Nov. 27, 1976; stepchildren: Carole, Susan. BA, Swarthmore Coll., 1949; PhD, Harvard U., 1956, MPH, 1957. Dir. alcoholism program State Mass., Boston, 1961-62; rsch. assoc. Stanford (Calif.) Univ., 1963-67; asst. chief Ctr. for Alcoholism NIMH, Bethesda, Md., 1962-69, dir. tng. divsn. Rockville, 1969-71, dep. dir., 1974-79, dir. prevention, 1979-80, assoc. divsn. dir. biometry, 1987-92; pub. health advisor Ctr. Mental Health, 1993-95; cons. in field Bethesda, 1995—. Consumer advisor Giant Foods, Landover, Md., 1988-92. Author: Alcohol Problems, 1967; co-author: Personality In Communal Society, 1956, Treatment of Alcoholism, 1967. Served in U.S. Army, 1944-46. Fellow APA, Am. Sociol. Assn.; mem. APHA (life), Phi Beta Kappa, Delta Omega. Democrat. Home: 5809 Nicholson Ln # T25 Rockville MD 20852-5701 E-mail: tfaplaut@aol.com.

PLAUT, W. GUNTHER, minister, author; b. Muenster, Germany, Nov. 1, 1912; emigrated to U.S., 1935, arrived in Canada, 1961; s. Jonas and Selma (Gumprich) P.; m. Elizabeth Strauss, Nov. 10, 1938; children: Jonathan, Judith. LLB, U. Berlin, 1933, JD, 1934; MHL, Hebrew Union Coll., Cin., 1939, DD (hon.), 1964; LLD (hon.), U. Toronto, 1978; DLitt (hon.), Cleve. Coll. Jewish Studies, 1979; LLD (hon.), York U., 1987, McMaster U., 1998, Law Soc. Ont., 2000. Ordained rabbi, 1939. Rabbi B'nai Abraham Zion, Chgo., 1939-48, Mt. Zion Temple, St. Paul, 1948-61; sr. rabbi Holy Blossom Temple, Toronto, Ont., Can., 1961-77, sr. scholar, 1978—. Adj. prof. York U., 1991—. Author: Mount Zion, 1956, The Jews in Minnesota, 1959, The Book of Proverbs: A Commentary, 1961, Judaism and the Scientific Spirit, 1962, The Rise of Reform Judaism, 1963, The Growth of Reform Judaism, 1964, The Case for the chosen People, 1965, Your Neighbour Is a Jew, 1967, Page 2, 1971, Genesis: A Modern Commentary, 1974, Time to Think, 1977, Hanging Threads, 1978, (U.S. title) The Man in the Blue vest, 1980, Numbers: A Modern Commentary, 1979; editor, chief author: The Torah: A Modern Commentary, 1981, 12th edit., 1997, Unfinished Business (autobiography Vol. 1), 1981, Refugee Determination in Canada, 1985, The Letter, 1986, The Magen David: How the Six Pointed Star Became the Jewish Symbol, 1991, The Man Who Would be Messiah, 1988, 2d edit., 1990, Asylum--A Moral Dilemma, 1995, The Haftarah Commentary, 1996, More Unfinished Business, 1997 (autobiography Vol. 2), The Price and Privilege of Growing Old, 1999; co-author: The Rabbi's Manual, 1988, The Reform Judaism Reader, 2000; editor: Affirmation, 1981-87; co-editor: Teshuvot of the Nineties, 1997; editl. contbr. Toronto Globe and Mail, 1962-92, Can. Jewish News, 1980—; bibliography pub. in Through the Sound of Many Voices, 1982; contbr. to encys., anthologies, other books, articles to mags., newspapers. Chmn. Minn. Gov.'s Commn. on Ethics in Govt., 1958-61 ; pres. St. Paul Gallery and Sch. Art (name changed to Minn. Mus.), 1953-59, World Federalists Can., 1966-68; nat. pres. Can. Jewish Congress, 1977-80; vice chmn. Ont. Human Rights Commn., 1978-85; bd. govs. World Union for Progressive Judaism, 1970— pres. Central Conf. Am. Rabbis, 1983-85, bd. inquiry human rights cases, 1987-98. Capt. AUS, 1943-46. Decorated Bronze Star; decorated companion Order of Can., Order of Ont.; decorated Order of Merit (Germany); Plaut Chair for Project Mgmt. established in his honor at Ben-Gurion U., Israel, 1991, Plaut Manor (pub.-assisted housing project) named in his and his wife's honor, Toronto. Mem.: York Racquets, Oakdale Golf and Country. Office: 1950 Bathurst St Toronto ON Canada M5P 3K9

PLAVINSKAYA, ANNA DMITRIEVNA, artist; b. Moscow, Nov. 26, 1960; came to U.S., 1989, naturalized, 1995; d. Dmitri Petrovich and Nina Nicolaevna; m. Gennady Ioffe, Jan 9, 1988 (div. July 1993). Diploma in Costume Design, Theatrical Art Coll., Moscow, 1976-80. Costume designer Evgeny Vahtangov Theater, Moscow, 1980-82; artist freelance, 1983-89; art restorer pvt. studio, N.Y.C., 1990-93; artist freelance, 1993—. Exhibited in group shows at art colls., Moscow (hon. mention 1977), Gallery of Moscow Artists, 1983, Ctrl. Exhbn. Hall, Moscow, 1984, 88, Kuznetzky Most Gallery, Moscow, 1985, Tbilisi Acad. of Art, Georgia, 1986, Tallinna Moepaevad '87, Tallinn, Estonia, 1987 (hon. mention), Remizovo St. Gallery, Moscow, 1988, Pushkin Sq. Gallery, Moscow, 1988, The Textile Art Ctr., Chgo., 1991, The Russian Nobility Assn., N.Y.C., 1991, 11th Cleveland Internat. Drawing Biennale, Middlesbrough, Eng., 1993 (2nd prize award), BWA Gallery, Wroclaw, Poland, 1994, BWA Gallery, Lublin, Poland, 1994, Elblag (Poland) Gallery, 1994, Tatraniska Gallery, Poprad, Tatry, Slovakia, 1994, State Gallery, Ostrova, Czech Republic, 1994, Botanica '94, Port Royal Mus. Gallery, Naples, Fla., 1994, Art Addiction Gallery, Stockholm, 1996 (hon. mention), 97 (cert. of merit), 98, Art Addiction Gallery, Venice, Italy, 1998, Internat. Platform Assn., 1998, (first place award, best show, 1999) Le Salon, Paris, 2000 (Bronze medal), 45th Salon Internat. des Arts Plastiques, Beziers, France, 2001 (Bronze medal); 46th Salon Interat. des Arts Plastiques, Beziers, France, 2002, represented in permanent collections Cleveland Contemporary Art Collection, Middlesbrough, Eng., Zimmerli Art Mus., Norton and Nancy Dodge Collection, N.J. Mem. Nat. Fedn. French Culture. Russian Orthodox. Avocations: fashion design, antique textile restoration, tennis. Home: 815 W 181st St Apt 3E New York NY 10033-4530

PLAVSIC, BRANKO MILENKO, radiology educator; b. Zagreb, Yugoslavia, Croatia, Feb. 14, 1947; came to U.S., 1989; s. Milenko and Nevenka P.; m. Valerie H. Drnovsek, Aug. 26, 1991. MD, U. Zagreb, 1972, MS, 1974, PhD, 1975. Asst. prof. U. Zagreb, 1986, prof. radiology, chief abdominal radiology, 1988; prof. radiology, vice-chmn., dir. abdominal radiol./rsch. Tulane U., New Orleans, 1991—. Co-author: (with A.E. Robinson, R.B. Jeffrey) Gastrointestinal Radiology: A Concise Text, 1992; contbr. articles to profl. jours. Avocations: poetry, music. Home: 4460 Lennox Blvd New Orleans LA 70131-8348 Office: Tulane U Med Ctr Dept Radiology 1430 Tulane Ave New Orleans LA 70112-2699

PLAWSKY, BERNARD MORRIS, retired social work administrator; b. N.Y.C., Sept. 9, 1926; s. Abraham and Sarah (Lipman) P.; m. Jean Plotkin, May 25, 1952; children: Joel, Cheryl. B Social Sci., CCNY, 1949; MSW, U. Pa., 1961. Dir. Neighborhood Ctr., Phila., 1961-67, Health & Welfare Coun., Phila., 1967-72; exec. dir. Human Svcs. Planning Coun., Flint, Mich., 1972-76, NASW, Harrisburg, Pa., 1976-86; adult dir. Family & Children Svcs., 1987-90; exec. dir. Rutherford House, 1991—; ret., 2001. Instr., lectr. Harrisburg (Pa.) Area C.C., C.S. Mott C.C., Flint, Mich., Phila. C.C., Mich. U., Flint. Talk show host pub. radio, Flint, Mich., 1975. Bd. mem. Ctrl. Dauphin Sch. Dist., Harrisburg, 1992; chmn. Human Svcs. Adv. Coun., Harrisburg. Recipient Legion of Honor Chapel of Four Chaplains, Phila., 1971, Social Action award Reform Judaism, Harrisburg, 1990. Mem. NASW, Am. Soc. Pub. Adminstrn. Republican. Jewish. Avocations: writing, gardening. Home: 4480 Nantucket Rd Harrisburg PA 17112-1932

PLAX, KAREN ANN, lawyer; b. St. Louis, June 29, 1946; d. George J. and Evelyn G. Zell; m. Stephen E. Plax, Dec. 19, 1968; 1 child, Jonathan. BA magna cum laude, U. Mo., St. Louis, 1969; JD with distinction, U. Mo., Kansas City, 1976. Bar: Mo. 1976, U.S. Supreme Ct. 1980. Atty. Thayer, Gum & Wickert, Grandview, Mo., 1976-84, Plax & Cochet, Kansas City, 1984-87; pvt. practice, 1987—. Past chair divsn. 3, region IV Mo. Supreme Ct. Com. to review ethical conduct of attys., 1997-98. Author: Missouri Bar Practical Skills, 1998; asst. editor: Racial Integration in the Inner Suburb, 1970; contbr. articles to profl. jours. Recipient Pub. Svc. award U. Mo. Kansas City Law Found., 1998, Woman of Yr. award Assn. Women Lawyers of Greater Kansas City, 1999. Fellow: Am. Acad. Matrimonial Lawyers (pres. Mo. chpt. 1999—2001); mem.: ABA (family law sect. 1976—), Mo. Bar Family Law (legis. chair 1997—98, v.p. 1999—2000, Spl. Commendation for Legis. Role in Family Law 1998), Kansas City Met. Bar Assn. Office: Ste 300 1310 Carondelet Dr Kansas City MO 64114-4803 E-mail: kaplax@swbell.net.

PLAYER, THELMA B. librarian; b. Owosso, Mich. d. Walter B. and Grace (Willoughby) Player. BA, Western Mich. U., 1954. Reference asst. USAF Aero Chart and Info. Ctr., Washington, 1954-57; reference libr. USN Hydrographic Office, Suitland, Md., 1957-58, asst. libr., 1958-59; tech. libr.br. head USN Spl. Project Office, Washington, 1959-68, Strategic Sys. Project Office, Washington, 1969-76. Mem. ALA, AAUW, English Speaking Union, Spl. Librs. Assn. D.C. Libr. Assn., Nat. Geneal. Socl, Internat. Soc. Brit. Genealogy and Family History, Ohio Geneal. Soc. Royal Oak Found., Daus of Union Vets. of Civil War, David Ackerman Descs. Episcopalian. Home: 730 24th St NW Washington DC 20037-2546

PLAYFORD, NANCY JEAN, medical staff administrator; b. Lansing, Mich., May 23, 1960; d. Jack Frederick and Doris Jean Lillrose; children: Kimberley, Kristen. Med. staff coord. Valley Luth. Hosp., Mesa, Ariz., 1984-93, Scottsdale (Ariz.) Health Sys., 1993-95, credentials supr., 1995-97; dir. med. staff svcs. Tempe (Ariz.) St. Luke's Hosp., 1997—. Mem. adv. bd. Greater Ariz. Cen. Credentialing, Phoenix, 1995—; expert witness in ct. for credentialing issues. Mem. Nat. Assn. Med. Staff Svcs. (cert. med. staff coord. 1993, cert. provider credentialing specialist 1996), Ariz. Assn. Med. Staff Svc. (pres.-elect Superstition Mountain chpt. 1995-96, pres. Superstition Mountain chpt. 1996-97). Avocations: photography, hiking, playing piano, horses. Office: Tempe St Luke's Hosp 1500 S Mill Ave Tempe AZ 85281-6699 E-mail: nplayford@iasishealthcare.com.

PLAZEK, DONALD JOHN, materials science educator; b. Milw., Jan. 12, 1931; s. Stanley and Marian (Parker) P.; m. Patricia Lenore Filkins, Oct. 29, 1955; children: Mary, Joseph, Caroline, Daniel, John, David, Anne. BS in Chemistry, U. Wis., 1953, PhD in Phys. Chemistry, 1957. Postdoctoral rsch. fellow U. Wis., Madison, 1957-58; fellow Mellon Inst., Pitts., 1958-67; assoc. prof. materials engring. U. Pitts., 1967-74, prof., 1974-93, prof. emeritus, 1993—. Adj. prof. chemistry Carnegie-Mellon U., Pitts., 1987—; mem. adv. bd. Jour. Polymer Sci., 1991-98. Assoc. editor Rubber Chemistry and Tech., 1993-97; contbr. papers to profl. publs., chpts. to books. Brit. Rsch. Coun. sr. vis. fellow U. Glasgow, Scotland, 1976-77, Japan Soc. for Promotion of Sci. fellow, 1987-88, Bingham medal Soc. of Rheology, 1995. Fellow Am. Phys. Soc.; mem. Am. Chem. Soc. (George Stafford Whitby award for disting. tchg. & rsch. Rubber Divsn. 1993), Soc. Rheology. Avocations: tennis, tropical fish, mushrooms. Office: U Pitts Materials Sci Engring Dept Pittsburgh PA 15261-0001

PLEACHER, DAVID HENRY, secondary school educator; b. Reading, Pa., Dec. 29, 1946; s. John K. and Isabel Kathleen (Moyer) P.; m. Carol Elizabeth Jackson, June 8, 1968; children: Amy Elizabeth, Michael David, Sarah Catherine. BA in Math., Hartwick Coll., 1968; MS in Edn., James Madison U., 1971. Cert. tchr., Va. Tchr. Arlington (Va.) County Pub. Schs., 1968, Fairfax County Pub. Schs., Herndon, Va., 1968-73; tchr., dept. chair Winchester (Va.) City Schs., 1973—. Instr. James Madison U., Harrisonburg, Va., 1982-87; lectr., instr. Lord Fairfax C.C., Middletown, Va., 1986-89; project mem. Computer Software Devel. Project, 1985-90; participant Math. Inst. Woodrow Wilson Found., Princeton, 1986. Co-editor: (computer column) Va. Math. Tchr., 1982-84; author computer programs; contbr. articles to profl. jours. Recipient Presdl. award in excellence in math and sci. teaching NSF, Washington, 1985, Homer "Pete" Ice Svc. award Handley High Athletic Dept., 1991, Tandy Tech. Scholars award Tandy Corp./T.C.U., Washington, 1992. Mem. NEA (life), Va. Edn. Assn., Winchester Edn. Assn., Nat. Coun. Tchrs. Math. (presenter at confs.), Va. Coun. Tchrs. Math. (presenter at confs., William Lowry Outstanding Math Tchr. 1987), Valley Va. Coun. Tchrs. Math., Coun. Presdl. Awardees in Math. Presbyterian. Avocations: model railroading, sports, games, computer programming. Home: 304 Caroline Ave Stephens City VA 22655-5925 Office: John Handley High Sch PO Box 910 Winchester VA 22604-0910

PLEASANT, JAMES SCOTT, lawyer; b. Anniston, Ala., July 14, 1943; s. James C. and Barbara (Scott) P.; m. Susan M. Pleasant, May 17, 1966; children: Deborah Kaye, Carol Ann, Julie Ruth. BS, Oreg. State U., 1965; JD summa cum laude, Williamette U., 1972. Bar: Tex. 1972, U.S. Dist. Ct. (no. dist.) Tex. 1973, U.S. Ct. Appeals (5th cir.) 1975, U.S. Supreme Ct. 1977. Ptnr. Gardere Wynne Sewell, LLP, Dallas, 1972—. Mem. Smithsonian Assn., Washington, 1985—, Dallas Mus. of Art, 1987—. Capt. U.S. Army, 1966-69, Vietnam. Mem. ABA (partnership law sect. 1969—), Tex. Bar Assn. (partnership law sect. 1989—), Vietnam Pilots Assn., Dustoff Assn. Office: Gardere Wynne Sewell LLP 1601 Elm St Ste 3000 Dallas TX 75201-4761 E-mail: pleja@gardere.com.

PLEASANT, JUDITH, writer, lyricist; b. Stonega, Va., Sept. 10, 1945; married. Pub., author, songwriter BootSun Pub., Toledo, 1993—. Author: My Spirit Helpers- My Way of Coping With Cancer- Princess Shelia, 1998; songwriter: of over 80 songs (1999-2001). Mem.: ASCAP (several awards 1999—2001). Office: BootSun Pub PO Box 13139 Toledo OH 43613 Business E-Mail: BootSunP@aol.com.

PLEASANT-JACKSON, TONYA, therapist, consultant; b. Washington, Oct. 27, 1960; d. Oscar and Carolyn Estelle Pleasant; m. Anthony L. Jackson Sr., July 15, 1989; children: Anthony L. Jr., Amara N. V. BS in Family Therapy, U Md., 1984; D in Ministry, Friends Internat. Christian U., 1994; M in Rehab. Counseling, U. Md., 1996. Lic. mariage and family therapist, Va.; cert. rehab. counselor, Md., nat. cert. counselor, rehab. provider, Va., rehab. svc. provider, Md.; ordained to ministry Integrity Ch. Internat., 1993. Dir. counseling ministry Integrity Ch. Internat., 1990—; rehab. coord., vocat. evaluator, rehab. cons. St. Luke's Ho., Bethesda, Md., 1997-98; rehab. coord. CHI Ctrs., Silver Spring, 1998—; pvt. practice therapist Greenbelt, 1998—; therapist, cons. Residential Care Inc., 1999—. Outstanding Svc. award Regional Inst. Children and Adolescents, Md., 1986. Mem. Assn. Mental Health Counselors, Am. Assn. Christian Counelors. Avocations: singing, physical fitness. Office: 9841 Greenbelt Rd Ste 208 Lanham Seabrook MD 20706-6270

PLEASANTS, BEN, writer, poet, playwright, educator; b. Weehauken, N.J., Aug. 6, 1940; s. Ben and Mary Frances Pleasants; m. Pamela Walley, Dec. 23, 1961 (div. Nov. 1979); 1 child, Alexandra Pleasants Costa; m. Paula Gail Pleasants, Nov. 10, 1991. BA, Hofstra U., 1962; postgrad., UCLA, 1966. Cert. tchr., Calif. Spl. arts editor L.A. Free Press, 1975-76; arts editor L.A. Vanguard, 1976; book rev. editor Books West, L.A., 1977-78; contbg. editor L.A. Mag., 1994; book and theater reviewer L.A. Times, 1966-82; tchr. L.A. City Schs., 1968-98. Asst. to story editor TV Guide, Hollywood, Calif., 1976-80; poetry editor Calif. Quar., Eagle Rock, 1976-80. Author: (poetry) 53 Stations of the Tokaido, 1972, Airmail from Oblivion, 1977, A Streetcar named Clitoris, 2001; (drama) Winter in Mongolia, 1979, Hemingway/Dos Passos Wars, 1997, (plays) Lenin In Love, 1985, Contentious Minds: The Mary McCarty/Lillian Hellman Affair, 2002; prodr. (film) Making the Play, 2000. Recipient Best Plays of 1997 award Dramalogue, L.A. Mem. United Tchrs. L.A. (chpt. chair 1996-98), UCLA Alumni Assn., Sierra Club, Audubon Soc. Avocation: hiking in the Sierra. Home: 245 Tavistock Ave Los Angeles CA 90049-3228 E-mail: bpleasants@msn.com.

PLEASURE, ROBERT JONATHAN, association director, lawyer; b. Bayshore, N.Y., Nov. 17, 1942; s. Hyman and Edith Beatrice (Schlank) P.; children: Jennifer, Abigail, Benjamin, Jacob; m. Patricia A. Greenfield. BA, U. Pa., 1964; MSc, London Sch. Econs. and Polit. Sci., 1967; JD, U. Mich., 1967. Bar: N.Y. 1970, D.C. 1971, U.S. Ct. Appeals (D.C. cir.) 1971, U.S. Ct. Appeals (5th and 10th cirs.) 1975, U.S. Supreme Ct. 1974. Asst. to chmn. N.Y.C. Office of Collective Bargaining, 1968-69; atty. advisor NLRB, Washington, 1969-70; asst. gen. counsel Am. Fedn. State, County and Mcpl. Employees (AFL-CIO), 1970-72, United Brotherhood Carpenters and Joiners Am. (AFL-CIO), Washington, 1972-78, 79-84; gen. counsel Fed. Mine Safety and Health Rev. Commn., 1978; exec. dir. George Meany Ctr. for Labor Studies, Silver Spring, Md., 1984-96; asst. to pres. AFL-CIO, 1996-98; exec. dir. Ctr. to Protect Workers Rights, 1998-2001; pres., exec. dir. AFL-CIO Ctr. for Working Capital, 2001—. Mem. core faculty The McGregor Sch., Antioch U., chair labor studies, to 1996; vis. faculty grad. sch. U. Mass., Amherst, to 1997. Co-author: Organizing in the Construction Industry, 1978-84, 93-94, 2000; editor-in-chief: Manual on Collective Bargaining in Federal Sector of Federal Bar Association and American Arbitration Association, 1970. Vice-chmn. Village of North Chevy Chase, Md., 1983, 84; past mem. commn. on non-coll. ednl. credit and credentials Am. Coun. on Edn.; past AFL-CIO advisor on labor edn. Internat. Labor Orgn.; mem. FDA adv. com. on radiol. devices; panel mem. on residential constrn. Nat. Rsch. Coun.; environ. mgmt. adv. bd. subcom. on worker safety Dept. of Energy. Mem. ABA (mem. governing coun. sect. on labor and employment law 1984-88), Indsl. Rels. Rsch. Assn. (nat. bd. 1996-99), Fed. Bar Assn. (chmn. coun. on labor law and labor rels. 1970, Robert Rosenthal award 1969), Am. Coun. on Edn. (commr. commn. on acad. credit 1987-94). Democrat. Jewish. Home: 9350 Harvey Rd Silver Spring MD 20910-1639 Office: Ctr for Working Capital 888 16th St NW Washington DC 20006 E-mail: rpleasur@aflcio.org.

PLEBAN, SARAH SHELLEDY, lawyer; b. York, Nebr., June 13, 1956; d. James Edwin and Mary Patricia (Cornwall) Shelledy; m. C. John Pleban, Sept. 26, 1981; children: Jonathan Cornwall, Meredith Shelledy, Jacob Stevens. BA in Psychology, Quincy Coll., 1977; JD, St. Louis U., 1981. Bar: Mo. 1981, Ill. 1982, U.S. Dist. Ct. (we. dist.) Mo. 1981. Dir. placement St. Louis U. Law Sch., 1981-82; chief trial atty. St. Louis County Pub. Defenders Office, Clayton, Mo., 1982-89; pvt. practice St. Louis, 1989—. Planning and devel. bd. dirs. Franciscan Charities, St. Louis, 1988—; Affton Sch. Dist. Bd. Edn., 1996-99; pres. St. Michael's Sch. Bd., Shewsbury, Mo., 1991-94; exec. bd. Friends of Heritage House, 1999—. Mem. Ill. Bar Assn., Mo. Bar Assn. Office: 100 S 4th St Ste 600 Saint Louis MO 63102-1822

PLEMING-YOCUM, LAURA CHALKER, religion educator; b. Sheridan, Wyo., May 25, 1913; d. Sidney Thomas and Florence Theresa (Woodbury) Chalker; m. Edward Kibbler Pleming, Aug. 25, 1938 (dec. Nov. 1980); children: Edward Kibbler, Rowena Pleming Chamberlin, Sidney Thomas; m. William Lewis Yocum, Dec. 19, 1989 (dec. Apr. 1992). BA, Calif. State U., Long Beach, 1953, MA in Speech and Drama, 1954; postgrad., U. So. Calif., L.A., 1960-63; D Religion, Grad. Sch. Theology, Claremont, Calif., 1968. Internat. lectr. Bibl. studies, 1953—; adult seminar resource person, 1953—; Bibl. lectr. Principia Coll., Elsah, Ill., 1968—71; Bible scholar 1st Ch. of Christ, Scientist, Boston, 1970-75. Tchr. adult edn. Principia Coll., summers, 1969—91, tour lectr. to Mid. East, 1974—99; mem. archaeol. team, Negev, Israel. Author: Triumph of Job, 1979; editor (newsletter) Bibleletter, 1968-84. Mem. AAUP, Am. Acad. Religion, Soc. Bibl. Lit. and Exegesis, Am. Schs. Oriental Rsch., Inst. Mediterranean Studies, Religious Edn. Assn., Internat. Platform Assn., Congress Septuagint and Cognate Studies, Religious Edn. Assn., Zeta Tau Alpha (alumni pres. Long Beach chpt. 1960), Gamma Theta Upsilon (pres. Long Beach chpt. 1952).

PLENINGER, SUSAN ELAINE, women's health and pediatrics nurse; b. Charleston, W.Va., Aug. 27, 1963; d. James Lewis and Mary Kathryn (Rust) Fitch; m. Calvin Lee Pleninger, June 28, 1986; children: Daniel Ryan, Madeline Rose. BSN, Houston Bapt. U., 1986; MSN, Ind. U.Purdue U., Indpls., 1991. Cert. childbirth educator. Nurse technician, grad. nurse in obstetrics Women's Hosp. of Tex., Houston, 1985-86; staff nurse Eastland (Tex.) Meml. Hosp., 1986-87; staff nurse in adult oncology St. John's Health Care Corp., Anderson, Ind., 1987-89, staff nurse in newborn nursery and women's health, 1989—. Clin. instr. pediatrics ASN program Ind. U./Purdue U., Indpls., 1991-92, childbirth educator, 1994-2002. Mem. Assn. of Women's Health, Obstet. and Neonatal Nurses, Sigma Theta Tau. Home: 1305 Greenbriar Dr Anderson IN 46012-4531

PLEROU, VASILIKI, physicist; b. Halkida, Greece, Aug. 4, 1969; s. Ioannis Konstantinou and Ekaterini Christou (Triantafyllou) P. BS in physics, Univ. Athens, 1994; MA in physics, Boston Univ., 1996; PhD, Boston Coll., 2001. Rsch. asst. Ctr. for European Nuclear Rsch. CERN, Geneva, 1994-95; teaching fellow Boston Univ., Boston, 1994-96; rsch. asst. Boston Coll., Chestnut Hill, Mass., 1997-99, Boston Univ., 1999-2001, rsch. assoc., 2001—. Contbr. articles to profl. jours. Mem. Am. Physical Soc. Fax: 617 975 0342. E-mail: plerou@cgl.bu.edu.

PLESHETTE, SUZANNE, actress, writer; b. N.Y.C., Jan. 31; d. Eugene and Geraldine; m. Thomas Joseph Gallagher III, Mar. 16, 1968 (dec. Jan. 2000); m. Tom Poston, May 11, 2001. Student, Sch. Performing Arts, Syracuse U., Finch Coll., Neighborhood Playhouse Sch. of Theatre. Founder, prin. The Bedside Manor (later div. of J.P. Stevens). Theatre debut in Truckline Cafe; star in Broadway prodns. Compulsion, The Cold Wind and the Warm, The Golden Fleecing, The Miracle Worker, Special Occasions; star TV series Bob Newhart Show, 1972-78, Suzanne Pleshette is Maggie Briggs, 1984; starred in TV series Bridges to Cross, 1986-87, Nightingales, 1988-89, The Boys Are Back, 1994-95, The Single Guy, 1996-97; host (CBS spl.) Where Are They Now?, 1997, (TV series spl. appearance) Will & Grace, 2001, (TV series) Good Morning Miami, 2002—; star 30 feature films including The Birds, Forty Pounds of Trouble, If It's Tuesday This Must Be Belgium, Nevada Smith, Support Your Local Gunfighter, hot Stuff, Oh God! Book II, Lion King II Simba's Pride, Spirited Away; TV movies include Flesh and Blood, Starmaker, Fantasies, If Things Were Different, Help-Wanted Male, Dixie Changing Habits, One Cooks, The Other Doesn't, For Love or Money, Kojak, The Belarus file, A Stranger Waits, Alone in the Neon Jungle, Leona Helmsley: The Queen of Mean, 1990, Battling for Baby, 1991-92, A Twist of the Knife, 1993; writer, co-creator, producer two TV series; published author.

PLESS, LAURANCE DAVIDSON, lawyer; b. Jacksonville, Fla., Dec. 22, 1952; s. James William Pless III and Anne (Dodson) Martin; m. Dana Halberg, June 20, 1980; children: Anna Amesbury, William Davidson, Deane Ahlgren. AB cum laude with distinction, Duke U., 1975; JD, U. N.C., Chapel Hill, 1980. Assoc. Neely & Player, P.C., Atlanta, 1980-86, ptnr., 1986-92, Welch, Spell, Reemsnyder, Pless & Davis, P.C., Atlanta, 1992—. Contbr. articles to profl. jours.; mem. staff N.C. Law Rev. Vol. Saturday Vol. Lawyer's Found., Atlanta, 1980-92; mem. bd. visitors U. N.C., Chapel Hill, 2001—; bd. dirs. Christian Coun. Met. Atlanta, 1999—; trustee Asheville Sch., 2001–. Mem. ABA, Lawyer's Club of Atlanta, Atlanta Bar Assn. (bd. dirs. bus. and fin. law sect. 1999—), Capital City Club, Lake Rabun Assn. Democrat. Episcopalian. Avocations: hiking, tennis, coaching kid's sports, canoeing. Home: 25 Palisades Rd NE Atlanta GA 30309-1530 E-mail: ldp@welchspell.com.

PLĒSUMS, GUNTIS, architect, retired educator; b. Riga, Latvia, Dec. 17, 1933; came to U.S., 1950, naturalized 1954; s. Valdemārs and Velta Plēsums; m. Māra Mazutis, Aug. 28, 1965; children: Jāna, Kārla. BArch, U. Minn., 1961; MArch, MIT, 1964. Registered architect, N.Y., Oreg. Arch. Affleck, Desbarats, Dimakopoulos, Lebensold & Sise, Montreal, Que., Can., 1964-66; instr. RISD, Providence, 1967-69; prof. arch. U. Oreg., Eugene, 1969—95, prof. emeritus, 1995—; pvt. practice arch., 1980—. Vis. assoc. prof. Kans. State U., Manhattan, 1976; adj. assoc. prof. Oreg. Sch. Design, Portland, 1983; vis. prof., dir. MArch program Chinese U. Hong Kong, 1993-99; lectr. U.S., Eng., Japan, China, Latvia, Denmark, Tunisia. Author: Townframe: Environments for Adaptive Housing, 1978, (with Heino Engel, others) Structure Systems; contbr. articles to profl. publs., including Ency. of Vernacular Arch. of the World; prin. works include: theme pavilion Man the Producer for Expo 67, Montreal, 1964-66. Served as sgt. U.S. Army, 1953-56. Fulbright fellow, 1966-67, NEA fellow, 1982, 90; Graham Found. for Advanced Studies in Fine Arts grantee, 1974. Home: PO Box 1009 Lorane OR 97451-1009 E-mail: gplesums@darkwing.uoregon.edu.

PLETCHER, DAVID MITCHELL, history educator; b. Faribault, Minn., June 14, 1920; s. Nuba Mitchel and Jean (Hutchinson) P. BA, MA, U. Chgo., 1941, PhD, 1946. Asst. U. Chgo., 1943; instr. history U. Iowa, 1944-46; asso. prof. Knox Coll., Galesburg, Ill., 1946-56; asso. prof., then prof. Hamline U., St. Paul, 1956-65; prof. history Ind. U., 1965-90, prof. emeritus, 1990—. Author: Rails, Mines and Progress, Seven American Promoters in Mexico, 1867-1911, 1958, The Awkward Years, American Foreign Relations Under Garfield and Arthur, 1962, The Diplomacy of Annexation, Texas, Oregon and the Mexican War, 1973, The Diplomacy of Trade and Investment: American Economic Expansion in the Hemisphere, 1865-1900, 1998, The Diplomacy of Involvement: American Economic Expansion Across the Pacific, 1784-1900, 2001. Recipient McKnight Found. award, 1962; grantee Social Sci. Research Found., 1950-51, 62-63; grantee Nat. Archives, 1972; Fulbright sr. research fellow, 1953-54 Mem. Am. Historians, Am. Hist. Assn. (Albert J. Beveridge award 1957), Soc. Historians Am. Fgn. Relations (v.p. 1979, pres. 1980) Home: 509 N Fess Ave Bloomington IN 47408-3821 Office: Indiana Univ Dept History Ballantine Hall Bloomington IN 47405

PLETCHER, ELDON, editorial cartoonist; b. Goshen, Ind., Sept. 10, 1922; s. Arthur and Dora (Cripe) P.; m. Barbara Jeanne Jones, Jan. 29, 1948; children— Thomas Lee, Ellen Irene. Student, Chgo. Acad. Fine Arts, 1941-42, U. Aberdeen, Scotland, 1945, John Herron Art Sch., Indpls., 1946-47. Editorial cartoonist Sioux City (Iowa) Jour., 1949-66; editorial cartoonist The Times-Picayune, 1966-85; free-lance gag cartoonist Sat. Eve. Post, Rotarian, Nat. Enquirer, other publs. Rep. permanent exhbns., Syracuse U., U. South

Miss., U. Cin., Boston Mus. Art, Harry S. Truman Library, Lyndon B. Johnson Library, Wichita State U., John F. Kennedy Libr., Richard M. Nixon Libr., U. Mo.; cartoons appeared in The Continental Edit. of Yank (Army Weekly). Served with AUS, 1943-46. Recipient Christopher award, 1955, Freedoms Found. award, 12 years Mem. VFW, Assn. Am. Editorial Cartoonists. Democrat. Presbyterian. E-mail: epletch@aol.com.

PLETZ, THOMAS GREGORY, lawyer; b. Toledo, Oct. 3, 1943; s. Francis G. and Virginia (Connell) P.; m. Carol Elizabeth Connolly, June 27, 1969; children: Anne M., John F. BA, U. Notre Dame, 1965; JD, U. Toledo, 1971. Bar: Ohio 1971, U.S. Ct. Appeals (6th cir.) 1978, U.S. Supreme Ct. 1985. Ct. bailiff Lucas County Common Pleas Ct., Toledo, 1967-71; jud. clk. U.S. Dist. Ct. (no. dist.) Ohio, 1971-72; assoc. Shumaker, Loop & Kendrick, 1972-76, litigation ptnr., 1976—. Acting judge Sylvania (Ohio) Mcpl. Ct., 1990—; mem. Ohio Bar Bd. Examiners, 1993—, chmn., 1996-99. Active Toledo Parish Coun., 1987-2001; chmn., trustee Kiroff Trial Adv. Com., Toledo, 1982-91; mem. Nat. Conf. Bar Examiners Com., 1996-2001. With USNR, 1965-92; ret. CDR. Recipient Toledo Jr. Bar award, 1995. Mem. ABA, Ohio State Bar Assn., Toledo Bar Assn. (trustee 1981-93), Diocesan Attys. Bar Assn., 6th Cir. Jud. Conf. (life). Roman Catholic. Office: Shumaker Loop & Kendrick 1000 Jackson St Toledo OH 43624-1573 E-mail: tpletz@slk-law.com.

PLEVY, ARTHUR L. lawyer; b. N.Y.C., May 26, 1936; s. Louis and Sarah Plevy; children: Scott Eric, Robert Todd. Student, Bklyn. Coll., 1953-57; BEE, CCNY, 1959; LLB, JD, Bklyn. Law Sch., 1967. Bar: N.Y. 1965, N.J. 1970, Ct. Customs and Patent Appeals 1970, U.S. Supreme Ct. 1970. Design engr. IT&T Labs., Nutley, N.J., 1959-60; project engr. Westrex, N.Y.C., 1960-62; sr. mem. tech. staff RCA, 1962-65; patent counsel RCA Rsch. Ctr., Princeton, N.J., 1965-70; pvt. practice patent law Edison, 1970-98; sr. ptnr. Plevy & Assocs., 1991—. Cons. electronic firms; pres. New Ventures, Edison, N.J., 1970—; arbitrator Am. Arbitration Assn. Contbr. numerous articles on electronics, patent and trademark law to profl. jours.; patentee in field of electronics. Mem. ABA, IEEE, CCPA, N.J. Patent Law Sch., Fed. Bar Assn., N.Y. Bar Assn., N.J. Bar Assn., Masons. Home: 77 Colfax Rd Skillman NJ 08558-2310 Office: Buchanan Ingersoll 650 College Rd E Princeton NJ 08540-6603 E-mail: plevyal@bipc.com.

PLEVYAK, THOMAS JOSEPH, communications executive; b. Simpson, Pa., Feb. 11, 1938; s. Joseph Bernard and Anna Stasia (Klemak) P.; m. Maureen Naomi Hogan, June 25, 1960; children: Stephen, Laura, Sharon. BS in Nuclear Engring., U. Notre Dame, 1960; MS in Nuclear Engring., U. Conn., 1962; grad. Comm. Devel. Tng. Program, Bell Labs., 1964; MS in Advanced Mgmt., Pace U., 1978. MTS Bell Labs, 1962-70; mgr. gen. depts. AT&T, Holmdel, N.J., 1970-80; mgr. AT&T Network Sys., 1980-90; dir. internat. standards Verizon, Arlington, Va., 1990—. Vice chair Inter-Am. Telecomms. Commn., Washington, 1994-98. Co-author, co-editor: Telecommunications Network Management into the 21st Century, 1994, Telecommunications Network Management: Technologies and Implementations, 1997; contbr. articles to profl. jours.; holder patents in field. Fellow IEEE Comms. Soc. (bd. govs. 1995-97, pres. 1998-99, past pres. 2000—, Donald W. McLellan award 1995, 3d Millennium medal for outstanding achievements and contbns. 2000). Avocations: travel, reading. Office: Verizon 2107 Wilson Vlvd Arlington VA 22201-

PLIMPTON, CALVIN HASTINGS, physician, university president; b. Boston, Oct. 7, 1918; s. George Arthur and Fanny (Hastings) P.; m. Ruth Talbot, Sept. 6, 1941; children: David, Thomas, George (dec.), Anne, Edward. BA cum laude, Amherst Coll., 1939; MD cum laude, Harvard, 1943, MA, 1947; Med. Sci.D., Columbia, 1951; LL.D., Williams Coll., 1960, Wesleyan U., 1961, Doshisha U., Kyoto, Japan, 1962, St. Lawrence U., 1963, Amherst U., 1971; L.H.D., U. Mass., 1962; D.Sc., Rockford Coll., 1962, St. Mary's, 1963, Trinity Coll., 1966, Grinnell (Iowa) Coll., 1967; Litt.D., Am. Internat. Coll., 1965, Mich. State Coll., 1969; DSc, N.Y. Med. Coll., 1986. Diplomate: Nat. Bd. Med. Examiners, Am. Bd. Internal Medicine. Intern, asst. resident, resident medicine Presbyn. Hosp., N.Y.C., 1947-50; asst. attending physician Columbia-Presbyn. Med. Center, 1950-60; assoc. medicine (Coll. Phys. and Surg.), 1950-59, asst. prof. clin. medicine, 1959-60; prof. medicine, chmn. dept. Am. U. Beirut, Am. U. Hosp., Beirut, Lebanon, 1957-59; pres. Amherst Coll., 1960-71, Downstate Med. Center, SUNY, 1971-79, dean med. sch., 1971-74, 76-79, prof. medicine, 1971-82, prof. emeritus, 1982—; pres. Am. U., Beirut, 1984-87. Vis. prof. Columbia Presbyn. Med. Center, 1976-77. Trustee Am. U., Beirut, 1960-90, trustee emeritus, 1990—, chmn. bd., 1965-82; trustee World Peace Found., 1962-77, Phillips Exeter Acad., 1963-76, Commonwealth Fund, 1962-83, Hampshire Coll., 1963-71, U. Mass., 1962-70, L.I. U., 1972-82, N.Y. Law Sch., 1976-84; mem. Harvard Bd. Overseers, 1969-75. Capt. U.S. Army, 1944-46, ETO. Decorated comdr. Order of Cedars Lebanon; recipient award Nat. Geog. Soc., award New Eng. Soc., John Phillips award Phillip Exeter Acad., Battle Star Ctrl. Europe. Fellow ACP; mem. Am. Acad. Arts and Scis., Russian Fedn. Acad. Med. Tech. Scis., Coun. Fgn. Rels., Soc. Mayflower Descs., Harvey Soc., Alpha Omega Alpha, Sigma Xi. Clubs: Century, Univ. (N.Y.C.), Charaka (N.Y.C.), Riverdale Yacht (N.Y.C.), Pilgrims (N.Y.C.); Tavern Boston. also: 10 Longmont Dr Apt 411 Westwood MA 02090

PLIMPTON, GEORGE AMES, writer, editor, television host; b. N.Y.C., Mar. 18, 1927; s. Francis T.P. and Pauline (Ames) P.; m. Freddy Medora Espy, 1968 (div. 1988); children: Medora Ames, Taylor Ames; m. Sarah Whitehead Dudley, 1991; children: Olivia Hartley, Laura Dudley. Student, Phillips Exeter Acad., 1944; AB, Harvard U., 1948; MA, Cambridge (Eng.) U., 1952; L.H.D. (hon.), Franklin Pierce Coll., 1968; Litt.D. (hon.), Hobart Smith Coll., 1978, Stonehill Coll., 1982, L.I.U., 1984, U. S.C., 1986, Pine Manor Coll., 1988. Editor in chief Paris Rev., 1953—, Paris Rev. Edits. (subs. Doubleday and Co.), 1965-72; editor-in-chief Paris Rev. Edits. (subs. Brit. Am. Publs.), 1987—; instr. Barnard Coll., 1956-58; assoc. editor Horizon mag., 1959-61; dir. Am. Lit. Anthology program, 1967-71; assoc. editor Harper's mag., 1972-81; contbg. editor Food and Wine Mag., 1978; editorial adv. bd. Realities, 1978; TV host Dupont Plimpton Spls., 1967-69, Greatest Sports Legends, 1979-81, The Ultimate High, 1980, Survival Anglia, 1980—, Writers' Workshop, 1982, Mousterpiece Theater, 1983—, Challenge, 1987. Spl. contbr. Sports Illustrated, 1968— ; bd. dirs. Int. Film Investors, 1979-82, Leisure Dynamics, 1983-85; curator Tennis Week, 1990—. Author: Rabbit's Umbrella, 1956, Out of My League, 1961, Paper Lion, 1966, The Bogey Man, 1968, Mad Ducks and Bears, 1973, One for the Record, 1974, Shadow-Box, 1976, One More July, 1976, (with Neil Leifer) Sports!, 1978, (with Arnold Roth) A Sports Bestiary, 1982, Fireworks, 1984, Open Net, 1985, The Curious Case of Sidd Finch, 1987, The X-Factor, 1990, The Best of Plimpton, 1990, Truman Capote, In Which Various Friends, Enemies, Acquantances and Detractors Recall His Turbulent Career, 1998, Pet Peeves, 2000; also numerous articles.; editor; Writers at Work, Vol. 1, 1957, Vol. 11, 1963, Vol. 111, 1967, Vol. IV, 1976, Vol. V, 1981, Vol. VI, 1984, Vol. VII, 1987, Vol. VIII, 1989, Vol. IX, 1992, (with Jean Stein) American Journey: The Times of Robert Kennedy, 1970, Pierre's Book, 1971, The Fancy, 1973, (with Jean Stein) Edie, An American Biography, 1982, (with Christopher Hemphill) D.V., 1984; The Paris Review Anthology, 1989, The Writer's Chapbook, 1989, Women Writers at Work, 1989, Poets at Work, 1989, The Norton Book of Sports, 1992, (with Jean Kennedy Smith) Chronicles of Courage, 1992, Home Run, 2001; contbg. editor Gentlemen's Quar., 1983-85, Smart mag., 1988-90, Esquire mag., 1990; actor films including Lawrence of Arabia, 1962, The Detective, 1968, Reds, 1981, The Bonfire of the Vanities, 1990, Little Man Tate, 1991, Nixon, 1995, When We Were Kings, 1996, Good Will Hunting, 1997; actor TV mini-series The Civil War, 1990, Baseball, 1994, Nero Wolfe, 2000-2002. Commr. fireworks, N.Y.C., 1973— ; trustee WNET, 1973-81, Nat. Art Mus. Sport, 1967— , Police Athletic League, 1976-90, African Wildlife Leadership Found., 1980— , Guild Hall, East Hampton, 1980— , N.Y. Zool. Soc., 1985—; bd. dirs. Dynamite Mus., Nat. Tennis Found., 1979— , Squaw Valley Center for Written and Dramatic Arts, 1979— , Authors Trust Am., 1979, Friends of the Masai Mara, 1986, Friends of Conservation, 1988-2002, Roger Tory Peterson Inst., The Carnegie Cook Ctr. for the Arts; chmn. Books Across the Sea, English Speaking Union, 1988—; bd. dirs., pres. N.Y. Philomusica, Pen/Faulkner, 1995; mem. adv. bd. Coordinating Council Lit. Mags., 1979, Yoknapatawpha Press, Am. Chess Found., East Harlem Tutorial, Boy's Harbor. Served to 2d lt. AUS, 1945-48. Assoc. fellow Trumbull Coll., Yale, 1967; recipient Disting. Achievement award U. So. Calif., 1967, Blue Pencil award Columbia Spectator, 1981, Mark Twain award Internat. Platform Assn., 1982, Chancellor's award L.I. U., 1986, l'Ordre des Arts et des Lettres, France, 1994, Guild Hall Lifetime Achievement award, 2002, Chevelier Legin d'honeurs, 2002. Mem. NFL Alumni Assn., Am. Pyrotechnics Assn., Acad. Arts Letters, Pyrotechnics Guild Internat., Explorers Club., Linnean Soc., PEN, Mayflower Descendants Soc. Clubs: Century Assn, Racquet and Tennis, Brook, Piping Rock, Dutch Treat, River, Coffee House, Devon Yacht; Travellers (Paris). Address: Paris Review Inc 541 E 72nd St New York NY 10021-4075

PLIMPTON, PEGGY LUCAS, trustee; b. Nov. 3, 1931; d. David Nicholson and Margaret (MacMillan) Lucas; m. Hollis Winslow Plimpton, June 11, 1955; children: Victoria P. Babcock, Priscilla P. Morphy, Hollis Winslow Plimpton III. AB, Duke U., 1954. Trustee Cape Cod Conservatory of Music, 1989—. Bd. trustees Carleton Williard Retirement Home, Bedford, Mass., 1968—, Cape Cod Conservatory Music, 1990—; bd. dirs. Episcopal Ch. Women, 1968-78, Brigham & Women's Hosp., Boston, 1975—; pres. Boston Lying-In Hosp., 1970-72; chmn. Mass. Nat. Cathedral Assn., Boston, 1978-80, 1985-88; pres. bd. trustees Women's Ednl. and Indsl., Boston, 1980-83. Mem. New Eng. Farm and Garden Club (bd. dirs. 1965—, pres. 1995—), Chestnut Hill Garden Club (bd. dirs. 1970-74), Jr. League Garden Club (pres. 1981-83), Colonial Dames (bd. mgrs. 1983-89, v.p. 1993-98, pres. 1998—), Vincent Club, Chilton Club. Republican. Episcopalian. Avocations: gardening, golf, bridge, grandchildren.

PLISCHKE, LE MOYNE WILFRED, research chemist; b. Greensburg, Pa., Dec. 11, 1922; s. Fred and Ruth Naomi (Rumbaugh) P.; m. Joan Harper, Mar. 11, 1966. BS, Waynesburg Coll., 1948; MS, W.Va. U., 1952. Rsch. chemist U.S. Naval Ordinance Test Sta., China Lake, Calif., 1952-53; asst. prof. chemistry Commonwealth U., Richmond, Va., 1953-54; rsch. chemist E.I. du Pont, Gibbstown, N.J., 1955-57, Monsanto Chem. Co., Pensacola, Fla., 1957—. Mem. Am. Chem. Soc. Achievements include 18 U.S. patents and 50 foreign patents in field. Home: 2100 Club House Dr Lillian AL 36549-5402 Office: Monsanto Co The Chem Group PO Box 97 Gonzalez FL 32560-0097 E-mail: plis123@gulftel.com.

PLISKIN, WILLIAM AARON, physicist; b. Akron, Ohio, Aug. 9, 1920; s. Max and Lena (Slavin) P.; m. Miriam Jaffee, Mar. 15, 1944; children: Karen, Michael, Bina. BS, Kent State U., 1941; MS, Ohio U., 1943; PhD, Ohio State U., 1949. Rsch. physicist Texaco Rsch. Ctr., Beacon, N.Y., 1949-59; staff physicist IBM, Poughkeepsie, 1959-60, adv. physicist, 1960-63, sr. physicist, mgr. N.Y., 1964-79, sr. staff mem., 1979-82, mgr., sr. tech. staff mem., 1982-87, sr. tech. staff mem., 1987-90; cons. characterization and measurement of dielectric films, 1990—. Contbr. numerous articles to profl. jours., chpts. in books; patentee in field. Served to 1st lt. U.S. Army, 1943-46, PTO. Fellow IEEE, Electrochem Soc. (ann. award electronics div. 1973); mem. Am. Phys. Soc., Am. Chem. Soc. (ann. award Mid Hudson sect. 1964), Sigma Xi, Pi Mu Epsilon, Sigma Pi Sigma. Jewish. Home: 31 Greenvale Farms Rd Poughkeepsie NY 12603-4201 E-mail: WAPlisk@aol.com.

PLISKOW, VITA SARI, anesthesiologist; b. Tel Aviv, Israel, Sept. 13, 1942; arrived in Can., 1951; came to U.S., 1967; d. Henry Norman and Renee (Mushkatel) Stahl; m. Raymond Joel Pliskow, June 30, 1968; children: Tia, Kami. MD, U. B.C., Vancouver, 1967. Diplomate Am. Bd. Anesthesiology. Ptnr. Olympic Anesthesia, Bremerton, Wash., 1971-84, pres., anesthesiologist, 1974-84; co-founder Olympic Ambulatory Surgery Ctr., 1977-83; ptnr., anesthesiologist Allenmore Anesthesia Assocs., Tacoma, 1983—. Staff anesthesiologist Harrison Meml. Hosp., Bremerton, 1971-95, Allenmore Hosp., Tacoma, 1983—. Trustee Tacoma Youth Symphony Assn., 1994—; active Nat. Coun. Jewish Women, 1972—. Fellow Am. Coll. Anesthesiologists, Am. Coll. Chest Physicians; mem. Am. Soc. Anesthesiologists (del. Wash. State 1987—), Wash. State Med. Assn. (del. Pierce County 1993-94), Wash. State Soc. Anesthesiologists (pres. 1985-87), Pierce County Med. Soc. (sec.-treas. 1992). Avocations: classical music, opera, singing (mezzo soprano). Office: Ctrl Billing PO Box 640 Tracyton WA 98393-0640

PLODINEC, M. JOHN, physical chemist; b. Kansas City, Mo., Mar. 29, 1946; s. Matthew J. and Betty J. (White) P.; m. Louise N. Robinson, Sept. 7, 1968; children: Matthew J. III, Nicole L. BA, Franklin & Marshall Coll., 1968; PhD, U. Fla., 1974. Interrogator U.S. Army, Bien Hoa, Vietnam, 1971; from chemist to mgr., sr. rsch. assoc. DuPont, Aiken, S.C., 1974-89; mgr., sr. adv. scientist Westinghouse, 1989-97; dir. diagnostic instrumentation and analysis lab. Miss. State U., Starkville, 1997—. Fellow Am. Ceramic Soc.; mem. Am. Chem. Soc., Materials Rsch. Soc. Home: 116 Little John Ln Starkville MS 39759-3856 E-mail: plodinec@dial.msstate.edu.

PLOGER, ROBERT RIIS, retired military officer, engineer; b. Mackay, Idaho, Aug. 12, 1915; s. Robert and Elfrieda (Riis) P.; m. Marguerite Anne Fiehrer, June 13, 1939 (dec. Feb. 1982); children: Wayne David, Robert Riis III, Daniel Bruce, Marguerite Anne, Marianne Ploger Hill, Gregory Fiehrer; m. Jeanne Allys Pray, Nov. 20, 1982 (dec. Aug., 1998). BS, U.S. Mil. Acad., 1939; MS in Engring., Cornell U., 1947; MBA, George Washington U., 1963. Registered civil engr., D.C. Commd. 2d lt. U.S. Army, 1939, served in corps of engrs. ETO, Okinawa, 1939-65, advanced through grades to maj. gen., 1966, div. engr. New England div., 1965, comdg. gen. 18th engr. brigade, 1965-66, comdg. gen. engr. command, Vietnam, 1966-67, dir. topography and mil. engring., Office Chief Engrs., 1967-70; comdg. gen. Ft. Belvoir and commandant U.S. Army Engr. Sch. Va., 1970-73; ret. U.S. Army, 1973; engr. specialist Bechtel Power Corp., Ann Arbor, 1974-80, mgr. adminstrv. services, 1980-81; counselor SCORE, Mich., 1984—, ret., 2002—. Lectr. Indsl. Coll. Armed Forces, 1962-65. Author: Vietnam Studies, U.S. Army Engineers 1965-70; contbr. numerous articles on war and mil. engring. to profl. jours. Chmn. gift com. Class of 1939 50th Reunion of U.S. Mil. Acad., 1985-89; pres.-elect residents assn. Glacier Hills Retirement Ctr., Ann Arbor, Mich., 2001—, pres., 2002—. Decorated DSM with oak leaf cluster, Legion of Merit, Silver Star with oak leaf cluster, Bronze Star with oak leaf cluster, Air medal, Purple Heart, Korean Order Mil. Merit Chung Mu, Nat. Order 5th Class Republic of Vietnam; recipient George Washington medal ICAF, 1965, Wheeler medal Soc. Am. Mil. Engrs., 1966, Silver Beaver award Boy Scouts Am., 1973, Médaille du Jubilé, Vire, France, 1994. Fellow Soc. Am. Mil. Engrs.; mem. NSPE (priviliged; chpt. pres. 1979-80), 29th Inf. Divsn. Assn. (Phila. award 1985), West Point Soc. Mich. (pres. 1981-84), SCORE (at-large exec. com. 1991, counselor chpt. 18, chpt. 655 2000—, membership com. chmn. chpt. 655 2000—), Ann Arbor C. of C. (counselor svc. corps ret. execs.), Army Engr. Assn. (life, Silver Order de Fleury medal 1995), SHAPE Officers Assn. (life). Baptist. Avocations: tennis, skiing, sailboarding. Home: 1200 Earhart Rd # 414 Ann Arbor MI 48105-2768 Address: Major General US Army Ret 1200 Earhart Rd # 414 Ann Arbor MI 48105-2768 E-mail: robert_ploger@msn.com.

PLOMP, TEUNIS (TONY PLOMP), minister; b. Rotterdam, The Netherlands, Jan. 28, 1938; arrived in Can., 1951; s. Teunis and Cornelia (Pietersma) P.; m. Margaret Louise Bone, July 21, 1962; children: Jennifer Anne, Deborah Adele. BA, U. B.C. (Can.), Vancouver, 1960; BD, Knox Coll., Toronto, Ont., Can., 1963, DD (hon.), 1988. Ordained to ministry Presbyn. Ch., 1963. Minister Goforth Meml. Presbyn. Ch., Saskatoon, Sask., Can., 1963-68, Richmond (B.C.) Presbyn. Ch., 1968—. Clerk Presbytery of Westminster, Vancouver, 1969—; moderator 113th Gen. Assembly Presbyn. Ch. Can., 1987-88, dep. clk., 1988—; chaplain New Haven Correctional Centre, Burnaby, B.C., 1973-99 Contbr. mag. column You Were Asking, 1982-2002. Avocations: record collecting, audiophile, biking, swimming. Office: Richmond Presbyn Ch 7111 # 2 Rd Richmond BC Canada V7C 3L7 E-mail: tony_plomp@telus.net.

PLONK, WILLIAM MCGUIRE, retired minister; b. Franklin, N.C., Aug. 19, 1925; s. Thomas Motley and Mary Louise (McGuire) P.; m. Nancy Marie Moore, June 29, 1957; children: Mary Evelyn Plonk Lucas, William McGuire Plonk, Jr. *William Plonk's daughter, Mary Plonk Lucas, graduated from Westhampton College in 1980, BA. She married Richard D. Lucas, lawyer, Roanoke, Virginia. They have four children: Ben, Beth, John, and Scott. William's son, William M. Plonk Jr., graduated from Princeton University in 1983, BS and from University of Virginia Medical School in 1989, MD. He is a family Physician in Waynesboro, Virginia. He has also hiked the complete Appalachian Trail in 2002. He married Beth Hartman Plonk and they have three children: John Natalie, and Wilson.* BS, Davidson Coll., 1949; BD, Union Theol. Seminary, Richmond, Va., 1954. Ordained to ministry Presbyn. Ch., 1954. Pastor Lawrenceville (Va.) Presbyn. Ch., 1954-56, Rivermont Presbyn. Ch., Chester, Va., 1956-58; youth minister First Presbyn. Ch., Greensboro, N.C., 1958-61; pastor Westminster Presbyn. Ch., Columbia, S.C., 1961-66, Covenant Presbyn. Ch., Spartanburg, 1966-69, Bow Creek Presbyn. Ch., Virginia Beach, Va., 1969-72; spl. agt. Jefferson Standard Ins. Co., Norfolk, 1972-73; exchange pastor St. Stevens and West Church of Scotland, Broughty Ferry, Scotland, 1972; pastor Makemie/Naomi Makemie Presbyn. Chs., Accomac, Onancock, Va., 1974-90; interim pastor Manokin Presbyn. Ch., Princess Anne, Md., 1991, 92; stated supply Clark Presbyn. Ch., Daugherty, Va., 1993—2001. Dist. chmn. Boy Scouts Am. 1st lt. U.S. Army, 1944-46. Mem. Rotary (pres. Onancock Club, Paul Harris Fellow 1993), Drummondtown-Lee Ruritan Club (pres.). Avocations: singing, early Am. ch. history. Home: 107 Settlers Bend Martinsville VA 24112-6616

PLONSEY, ROBERT, electrical and biomedical engineer; b. N.Y.C., July 17, 1924; s. Louis B. and Betty (Vinograd) P.; m. Vivian V. Vucker, Oct. 1, 1948; 1 child, Daniel. BEE, Cooper Union, 1943; MSEE, NYU, 1948; PhD, U. Calif., Berkeley, 1955; postgrad. med. sch., Case Western Res. U., 1969-71; D of Technol. Scis., Slovak Acad. Scis., 1995. Registered profl. engr., Ohio. Asst. prof. elec. engring. U. Calif., Berkeley, 1955-57, Case Inst. Tech., Cleve., 1957-60, assoc. prof., 1960-66, prof., 1966-68, dir. bioengring. group, 1962-68; prof. biomed. engring. Sch. Engring. and Sch. Medicine Case Western Res. U., 1968-83, chmn. dept., 1976-80; vis. prof. biomed. engring. Duke U., Durham, N.C., 1980-81, prof., 1983-96, prof. biomed. engring., Hudson prof. engring., 1990-93, Pfizer-Inc.-Edmond T. Pratt Jr. Univ. prof. biomed. engring., 1993-96, Pfizer-Inc.-Edmond T. Pratt Jr. Univ. prof. emeritus, 1996—. Mem. biomed. fellowships rev. com. NIH, 1966-70; mem. tng. com. Engrs. in Medicine and Biology, 1972-73, cons., 1974-96; cons. NSF, 1973-93; mem. internat. sci. adv. com. Ragnar Granit Inst., Tampere (Finland) U. Tech., 1992—; ad hoc mem. sci. adv. com. Whitaker Found., 1989-91. Author: (with R. Collin) Principles and Applications of Electromagnetic Fields, 1961, Bioelectric Phenomena, 1969, (with J. Liebman and P. Gillette) Pediatric Electrocardiography, 1982, (with T. Pilkington) Engineering Contributions to Biophysical Electrocardiography, 1982, (with J. Liebman and Y. Rudy) Pediatric and Fundamental Electrocardiography, (with R.C. Barr) Bioelectricity: A Quantitative Approach, 1988, 2d edit., 2000, (with J. Malmivuo) Bioelectromagnetism, 1995; mem. editorial bd. Trans. IEEE, Biomed. Engring, 1965-70; assoc. editor, 1977-79, editorial bd. TIT Jour. 1971-81, Electrocardiology Jour., 1974—, Medical and Biological Engineering and Computing, 1987—; procs. editor Engring. in Medicine and Biology, 17th Ann., Conf., 1965. Mem. com. on electrocardiography Am. Heart Assn., 1976-82; v.p. Your Schs., Cleveland Heights, Ohio, 1968-69, 73-75; provisional trustee Am. Bd. Clin. Engrs., 1973-74, pres. 1975, trustee, 1976-85. With AUS, 1944-46. Recipient sr. postdoctoral award NIH, 1980-81, Merit award Internat. Union Phys. and Engring. Scis. in Medicine, 1997. Fellow AAAS, IEEE (chmn. Cleve. chpt. group on biomed. electronics 1962-63, chmn. publs. com. group on engring. in medicine and biology 1968-70, v.p. adminstrv. com. 1970-72, pres. 1973-74, chmn. fellows com. Engring. in Medicine and Biology Soc. 1986-88, 2000, v.p. tech. and conf. activities 1991, William S. Morlock award 1979, Centennial medal 1984, co-program chair ann. conf., Paris 1992, chmn. awards com. 1996, Millennium medal 2000); mem. AAUP, NAE (bioengring. peer com. 1988-91, 2001—, chair 1990-91, nominating com. 1991-92, mem. com. 1992-94, program adv. com. 1996-98, NRC postdoctoral rsch. associateships evaluation panel 1987-90, Russ prize com. 2000-01, 2002-), Internat. Acad. Med. and Biol. Engring. (founding mem. 1997), Am. Inst. Med. and Biol. Engring. (founding fellow 1992—), Alliance for Engring. in Medicine and Biology (treas. 1976-78), Biomed. Engring. Soc. (bd. dirs. 1975-78, 79-83, pres. 1981-82, chmn. affiliations com. 1987-89, ALZA Disting. lectr. 1988), Am. Physiol. Soc., Am. Soc. Engring. Edn. (bd. dirs. biomed. engring. divsn. 1978-83, chmn. 1982-83). Office: Duke U Box 90281 Dept Biomed Engring Durham NC 27708-0281 E-mail: robert.plonsey@duke.edu. *External recognition of success is not nearly so important as the inner awareness of coming to full grips with life, to be fully involved, bending all strengths to fulfill one's goals and philosophies. And of all involvements, those with people are most meaningful (to be aware of and share the feelings of colleagues, students, friends, and family—and to enrich these relationships)—and for me most difficult.*

PLONSKI, HALINA MARIA, pharmacist; b. Sejny, Poland, Aug. 1, 1923; came to U.S., 1962; d. Jozef and Wanda (Dlugoborska) Tarkowska; m. Witold Plonski, Jan. 6, 1944; children: Olgierd-Piotr, Ewa Maria Hyjek, Anne-Marie Kern. M in Pharmacy Sci., Sch. of Pharmacy, Warsaw, 1950; PhD in History of Pharmacy, Med. Sch., Lublin, Poland, 1991. Lic. clin. lab. supr.; registered pharmacist, Poland. Sr. rsch. asst. Coll. Agr. Rutgers U., New Brunswick, N.J., 1962-63; rsch. assoc. dept. biochemistry Flower and Fifth Ave. Med. Sch., N.Y.C., 1963-66; staff dept. rehab. medicine Columbia U., 1966-70; supr. clin. chemistry lab. N.Y. Infirmary, 1970-71, Bronx-Lebanon Hosp., 1971-72; rsch. assoc., lab. supr. dept. exptl. medicine NYU, N.Y.C., 1972-76. Sr. rsch. asst. dept. biochemistry Coll. Agr., Warsaw, 1961-62; rsch. project supr. Inst. Meat Industry, Warsaw, 1958-61; with rsch. lab. Inst. Hygiene Bromatology Dept., Warsaw, 1951-53. Mem. AAUW, Am. Inst. History of Pharmacy, Polish-Am. Med. Assn. (exec. sec., pres. charitable and ednl. fund 1976-91, Golden medal 1989), Polish-Am. Hist. Assn., Polish Nat. Alliance North Am., Oreg. Hist. Soc. Roman Catholic. Avocations: cultivation and use of medical plants and spices, travel, swimming. Home: 16525 SW Monterey Ln Portland OR 97224-2109 E-mail: halinaplon@aol.com.

PLORDE, JAMES JOSEPH, physician, educator; b. Brewster, Minn., Feb. 16, 1934; s. James Arthur and Mary Jeanette (Lutz) P.; m. Diane Sylvia Koenigs, Aug. 28, 1964 (div. July 1974); children: Lisa Marie, Michele Louise, James Joshua; m. Jo Ann Gates, Dec. 22, 1986. BA, U. Minn., 1956, BS, 1957, MD, 1959. Diplomate Am. Bd. Internal Medicine, Am. Bd. Pathology. Vol. leader Peace Corps, Gondar, Ethiopia, 1964-66; intern King County Hosp., Seattle, 1959-60; resident U. Wash., 1960-62, fellow infectious diseases, 1962-64; chief med. resident King County Hosp., 1966-67; asst. prof. medicine U. Wash., 1967-71, assoc. prof., 1971-78; fellow clin. microbiology, 1972-73; prof. medicine, lab. medicine U. Wash. Sch. Medicine, Seattle, 1978-98 (ret.), prof. emeritus, lab. medicine, 1998—; head clin. investigation U.S. Naval Med. Research, Addis Ababa, Ethiopia, 1968-71; chief infectious diseases VA Hosp., Seattle, 1973-89, chief clin. microbiology, 1973-98; ret., 1998. Instr. U. Wash., 1966-67; cons. WHO, 1975, Suez Canal U. Faculty of Medicine, Ismailia, Arab Republic of Egypt, 1981-85. Contbr. numerous articles to profl. jours., chpts. to books. Fellow Infectious Disease Soc., ACP; mem. AAAS, Am. Soc. Microbiology, Acad. Clin. Lab. Physicians and Scientists. Home: 3164 W Laurelhurst Dr NE Seattle WA 98105-5346 Fax: 206-523-3541. E-mail: jjplorde@u.washington.edu.

PLOSKER, HARVEY, anesthesiologist; b. Bronx, N.Y., July 16, 1954; MD, U. N.Y., Albany, 1984. Cert. in anesthesiology. Intern Queens Hosp. Ctr., Jamaica, N.Y., 1979-80; resident in gen. surgery Montefiore Hosp., Bronx, 1980-82; resident in anesthesiology Mt. Sinai Med. Ctr., N.Y.C., 1982-84; fellow in obstet. anesthesiology Columbia P&S, 1984-85; med. dir. Boca Raton (Fla.) Outpatient Surgery and Laser Ctr., 1992—. Mem. AMA, Am. Soc. Anesthesiologist, Am. Acad. Pain Mgmt., Am. Pain Soc., Internat. Anesthesia Rsch. Soc., Soc. Ambulatory Anesthesia, Fla. Med. Assn., Fla. Soc. Anesthesiology. Office: 501 Glades Rd Boca Raton FL 33432-1419

PLOSSER, CHARLES IRVING, university dean, economics educator; b. Birmingham, Ala., Sept. 19, 1948; s. George Gray and Dorothy (Irving) P.; m. Janet Schwert, June 26, 1976; children: Matthew, Kevin, Allison. B.E. cum laude, Vanderbilt U., 1970; MBA, U. Chgo., 1972, PhD, 1976. Cons. Citicorp Realty Cons., N.Y.C., 1972-73; lectr. Grad. Sch. Bus., U. Chgo., 1975-76; asst. prof. Grad. Sch. Bus. Stanford (Calif.) U., 1976-78; asst. prof. econs. W.E. Simon Grad. Sch. Bus., U. Rochester (N.Y.), 1978-82, assoc. prof., 1982-86, prof., 1986-89; Fred H. Gowen prof. econs. U. Rochester, N.Y., 1989-92, John M. Olin Disting. prof. econs. and pub. policy, 1992—, acting dean W.E. Simon Grad. Sch. Bus., 1990-91, 92-93; dean W.E. Simon Grad. Sch. Bus., 1993—. Chmn. bd. Consortium for Grad. Study in Mgmt., 1995-97; bd. dirs. ViaHealth, Inc., 1995-2000, Rochester Gas & Electric Corp., 1996—; bd. dirs. Grad. Mgmt. Admission Coun., 1997—, chmn. bd., 2002–. Editor, Jour. Monetary Econs., 1983—, Carnegie-Rochester Conference Series on Public Policy, 1989—; contbr. articles to profl. jours. 1st lt., U.S. Army, 1972-73.

NSF research grantee, 1982, 84. Mem. Am. Econs. Assn., Econometrics Soc., Am. Fin. Assn., Tau Beta Pi, Beta Gamma Sigma. Home: 95 Ambassador Dr Rochester NY 14610-3402 Office: U Rochester Dean Of Simon Grad Sch Rochester NY 14627

PLOTKIN, IRVING H(ERMAN), economist, consultant; b. Bklyn., July 19, 1941; s. Samuel H. and Dorothy (Falick) P.; m. Janet V. Bufe, July 26, 1969; children: Aaron Jacob, Joshua Benjamin. BS in Econs., U. Pa., 1963; PhD in Math. Econs., MIT, 1968. Corp. planning analyst Mobil Oil Co., N.Y.C., 1962-63, Mobil Oil Italiana, Genoa, Italy, 1965; ind. cons. econs. and ops. rsch. to banks, mut. funds, ins. cos., govt. agys. Cambridge, Mass., 1965-68; sr. economist Arthur D. Little, Inc., 1968—2002. Dir. regulation and econs., 1974-2002, v.p., 1979-2002; bd. dirs. Arthur D. Little Valuation, Inc.; trustee Arthur D. Little, Inc., ESOP, 1988-2002; mgr. dir. tax svc. Pricewaterhouse-Coopers LLP, Boston, 2002—; instr. fin. and computer scis. MIT, 1965-68; lectr. maj. univs. U.S. and abroad; expert witness U.S. Ho. of Reps. and Senate coms., U.S. Ct. Claims, U.S. Tax Ct. I.C.C., FTC, Fed. Martime Commn., Fed. Dist. Cts., Fed. Res. Bd., other fed. and state govt. agys., 1967—. NASA fellow, 1963-66, NSF fellow, 1967, Am. Bankers Assn. fellow, 1968. Mem. Am. Econ. Assn., Econometric Soc., Am. Fin. Assn., Beta Gamma Sigma, Pi Gamma Mu, Tau Delta Phi (chpt. pres. 1962-63). Home: 975 Memorial Dr Apt 910 Cambridge MA 02138-5754 Office: One Post Office Square Boston MA 02109-2301

PLOTKIN, LOREN H. lawyer; b. Bklyn., Feb. 8, 1943; s. Arthur and Betty Ann (Strugatz); m. Carol Baxter, Aug. 25, 1990; children: Lily, Kate. BA, Harpur Coll., SUNY, Binghamton, 1963; JD, St. John's U., N.Y.C., 1966. Bar: N.Y. 1966, U.S. Dist. Ct. (so. and ea. dists.) N.Y. 1972, U.S. Tax Ct. 1976. Law asst. appellate divsn., first dept. N.Y. State Supreme Ct.; ptnr. Lans Feinberg & Cohen, N.Y.C., 1969-81; mem. Levine & Thall, P.C., 1981-84, Levine Thall and Plotkin, N.Y.C., 1984-96, Levine Thall, Plotkin & Menin, L.L.P., N.Y.C., 1996-99, Levine, Plotkin & Menin, L.L.P., N.Y.C., 2000—. Lectr. on entertainment law. Notes and comments editor St. John's U. Law Rev., 1965-66. Home: 34 Lawrence Ln Palisades NY 10964-1604 Office: Levine Plotkin & Menin LLP 1740 Broadway Fl 22 New York NY 10019-4315

PLOTKIN, MANUEL D. management consultant, educator, former corporate executive and government official; s. Jacob and Bella (Katz) P.; m. Diane Fern Weiss, Dec. 17, 1967; 1 child, Lori Ann. BS with honors, Northwestern U., 1948; MBA, U. Chgo., 1949. Price economist, survey coordinator U.S. Bur. Labor Statistics, Washington, 1949-51, Chgo., 1951-53; sr. economist Sears Roebuck & Co., 1953-61, mgr. market research, 1961-66, chief economist, mgr. mktg. rsch., 1966-73, dir. corp. planning and research, 1973-77, exec. corp. planner, 1979-80; dir. U.S. Bur. Census, Washington, 1977-79; v.p., dir. group practice Divsn. Mgmt. Cons. Austin Co., Evanston, Ill., 1981-85; pres. M.D. Plotkin Research & Planning Co., Chgo., 1985—. Tchr. statistics Ind. U., 1953-54; tchr. econs. Wilson Jr. Coll., Chgo., 1954-55; tchr. quantitative methods and managerial econs. Northwestern U., 1955-63; tchr. mktg. rsch. and mktg. mgmt. DePaul U., Chgo., 1992-95; mem. Conf. Bd. Mktg. Rsch. Adv. Coun., 1966-77, chmn.-elect, 1977; chmn. adv. com. U.S. Census Bur., 1974-75; trustee Mktg. Sci. Inst., 1968-77; mem. Nat. Commn. Employment and Unemployment Stats., 1978-79, Adv. Coun. Edn. Stats., 1977-79, Interagy. Com. Population Rsch., 1977-79; mem. adv. coun. Kellstadt Ctr., DePaul U., 1987-92; trustee U.S. Travel Data Ctr., 1977-79. Contbr. articles to profl. jours. Served with AUS, 1943-46, ETO. Decorated Bronze Star medal with oak leaf cluster. Mem. Am. Mktg. Assn. (pres. Chgo. 1968-69, nat. dir. 1969-70, nat. v.p. mktg. rsch. 1970-72, nat. v.p. mktg. mgmt. 1981-83, pres., CEO 1985-86), Am. Statis. Assn. (pres. Chgo. 1966-67, Forecasting award 1963), Am. Econ. Assn., Nat. Assn. Bus. Economists, Planning Execs. Inst., World Future Soc., Midwest Planning Assn., U. Ill. Businessmen Rsch. Adv. Group, Chgo. Assn. Commerce and Industry, Beta Gamma Sigma, Alpha Sigma Lambda, Delta Mu Delta. Home and Office: 2650 N Lakeview Ste 3910 Chicago IL 60614-1831

PLOTKIN, STANLEY ALAN, medical virologist; b. N.Y.C., May 12, 1932; s. Joseph and Lee (Fishbein) P.; m. Susan Lannon, Nov. 24, 1979; children: Michael, Alec. BA, NYU, 1952; MD, SUNY, N.Y.C., 1956; MA (hon.), U. Pa., 1974. Diplomate Am. Bd. Pediat., Am. Acad. Pediat. Intern Cleve. Met. Gen. Hosp., 1956-57; resident pediat. Phila. Children's Hosp., 1961—62, dir. divsn. infectious diseases, sr. physician, 1969—90; registrar Hosp. for Sick Children, London, 1962-63; assoc. mem. Wistar Inst., Phila., 1963-74, prof. virology, 1974—; asst. prof. pediat. U. Pa., 1966-71, assoc. prof., 1971-74, prof., 1974-91; prof. emeritus, 1991—; assoc. chmn. dept. pediat. U. Pa., Phila., 1986-88; med. and sci. dir. Pasteur-Mérieux-Connaught Labs. (now Aventis-Pasteur), Marnes-la-Coquette, France, 1991-97; advisor to pres. Aventis Pasteur, Lyon, France, 1997—. Assoc. editor: Am. Jour. Epidemiology, 1967-87, Proc. Soc. Exptl. Biology and Medicine, 1968-85, Pediatric Infectious Disease jour., 1982-87, Vaccine jour., 1983—, Molecular and Cellular Probes jour., 1987—, Clin. Diagnostic Lab. Immunology, 1996—. Served as med. officer USPHS, 1957-60. Joseph P. Kennedy Found. grantee, 1964-66, Hartford Found. grantee, 1971-73, NIH grantee, 1973—; recipient Bruce medal ACP, 1987, Clin. Virology award Pan Am. Group Rapid Viral Diagnosis, 1995, Gold medal Sabin Found., 2002; named Disting. Physician Pediatric Infectious Diseases Soc., 1993, Disting. Alumnus, Children's Hosp. of Philadelphia, 2001; named to Legion of Honor, France, 1998. Mem. Soc. Pediatric Rsch., Am. Pediatric Soc., Infectious Diseases Soc. Am.,Am. Epidemiology Soc., Am. Soc. Microbiology, Am. Acad. Pediatrics (chmn. infectious diseases com. 1987-90). Achievements include pioneering work on vaccine strains for protection against polio, rubella and cytomegalovirus. E-mail: stanley.plotkin@aventis.com.

PLOTNICK, HARVEY BARRY, publishing executive; b. Detroit, Aug. 5, 1941; s. Isadore and Esther (Sher) P.; m. Susan Regnery, Aug. 16, 1964 (div. Apr. 1977); children: Andrew, Alice; m. Elizabeth Allen, May 2, 1982; children: Teresa, Samuel. BA, U. Chgo., 1963. Editor Contemporary Books, Inc., Chgo., 1964-66, pres., 1966-94; CEO Molecular Electronics Corp., Chgo., 2000—01, Paradigm Holdings, Inc., Chgo., 1994—. CEO Molecular Electronics Corp., 2000—. Trustee U. Chgo., 1994—, Chgo. Acad. Scis., Argonne Nat. Lab. Office: Paradigm Holdings Inc 2 Prudential Plz Ste 3150 Chicago IL 60601-6790 E-mail: harvey1844@aol.com.

PLOTNICK, PAUL WILLIAM, lawyer; b. Chgo., Mar. 16, 1947; s. Sam and Mary P.; m. Eleanor Levy, Jan. 18, 1970; 1 child, Sarah Jennie. BA, So. Ill. U., 1969; JD, DePaul U., 1974. Bar: Ill. 1974., U.S. Dist. Ct. (no. dist.) Ill. 1974, U.S. Ct. Appeals (7th cir.) 1974, U.S. Tax Ct. 1975, U.S. Supreme Ct. 1977. Tchr. Chgo. Pub. Schs., 1969-74; pvt. practice Chgo., 1974-75; pres. Paul W. Plotnick, Ltd., Skokie, Ill., 1979—; asst. pub. defender Cook County Pub. Defender's Office, Chgo., 1975-79. Felony asst. Cook County Pub. Defender's Office, Evanston, Ill., 1976-79. Contbr. articles, poem to profl. publs. Pres. Budlong Woods Civic Group, Chgo., 1982-83; candidate for judge Circuit Ct. Cook County, 1998-2000. Staff sgt. U.S. Army, 1969. Named Man of the Yr. Midwest Fedn. Men's Clubs, 1995; recipient Disting. Svc. award Chgo. Vol. Legal Svcs., 1995. Mem. ABA, ATLA, Ill. State Bar Assn., Chgo. Bar Assn., N.W. Suburban Bar Assn., N. Suburban Bar Assn., Kiwanis (pres. Skokie Valley chpt. 1989-90, Disting. Sec. award 1987, Disting. Pres. award 1991, Lay Person of the Yr. I.I. Dist. divsn. 7), Beth Hillel Men's Club (pres. 1991-93), Decalogue Soc., Phi Kappa Phi (DePaul U. chpt. Disting. Alumnus). Office: Paul W Plotnick Ltd 9933 Lawler Ave Ste 312 Skokie IL 60077-3706

PLOTNICK, ROBERT DAVID, educator, economic consultant; b. Washington, Aug. 3, 1949; s. Theodore and Jean (Hirshfeld) P.; m. Gay Lee Jensen, Dec. 22, 1972. BA, Princeton U., 1971; MA, U. Calif., Berkeley, 1973, PhD, 1976. Rsch. assoc. Inst. Rsch. on Poverty, Madison, Wis., 1973-75; asst. prof. Bates Coll., Lewiston, Maine, 1975-77, Dartmouth Coll., Hanover, N.H., 1977-84; assoc. prof. U. Wash., Seattle, 1984-90, prof., 1990—, assoc. dean, 1990-95; acting dean, 1994-95. Vis. scholar Russell Sage Found., 1990, U. New South Wales, 1997; rsch. affiliate Inst. for Rsch. on Poverty, 1989—; dir. Ctr. for Studies in Demography and Ecology, 1997—; adj. fellow Pub. Policy Inst. Calif., 1998-2000; cons. Wash. Dept. Social and Health Svcs., Olympia, 1984-86, 90-96, 2000; cons. in field. Author: Progress Against Poverty, 1975; contbr. articles to profl. jours. Recipient Teaching Excellence award U. Wash., 1985, 89. Mem. Am. Econ. Assn., Assn. Policy Analysis and Mgmt., Population Assn. Am. Avocations: tennis, hiking, bird watching, scuba. Office: U Wash Evans Sch Pub Affairs PO Box 353055 Seattle WA 98195-3055 E-mail: plotnick@u.washington.edu.

PLOTNIK, ARTHUR, author, columnist; b. White Plains, N.Y., Oct. 1, 1937; s. Michael and Annabelle (Taub) P.; m. Meta Von Borstel, Sept. 6, 1960 (div. 1979); children: Julia Nicole, Katya Michelle.; m. Mary Phelan, Dec. 2, 1983. BA, State U. N.Y., Binghamton, 1960; MA, U. Iowa, 1961; MS in L.S, Columbia U., 1966. Gen. reporter, reviewer Albany (N.Y.) Times Union, 1963-64; freelance writer, 1964-66; editor Librarians Office, Library of Congress, 1966-69; assoc. editor Wilson Library Bull., Bronx, N.Y., 1969-74; editor-in-chief Am. Libraries, Chgo., 1975-89; assoc. pub. ALA, 1989-97; editl. dir. ALA Editions, 1993-97; writer, 1997—. Adj. instr. journalism Columbia Coll., Chgo., 1988-89; speaker in field. Author: The Elements of Editing: A Modern Guide for Editors and Jouranlists, 1982, Jacob Shallus, Calligrapher of the Constitution, 1987, Honk If You're a Writer, 1992, The Elements of Expression, 1996, The Urban Tree Book, 2000; columnist: Editorial Eye, 1995—2001; contbg. editor: The Writer, 2000—; also fiction, articles, vide scripts, photographer: ; exec. prodr.: Libr. Video mag., 1986—91. Bd. dirs. Am. Book Awards, 1979-82; bd. advs. Univ. Press of Am., 1982— . Served with USAR, 1962-67. Fellow Iowa Writers Workshop Creative Writing, 1961; recipient award Ednl. Press Assn. Am., 1973 (3), 77, 82, 83; cert. of excellence Internat. Reading Assn., 1970, First Pl. award Verbatim essay competition, 1986, award Am. Soc. Bus. Press Editors, 1987. Mem. ALA, Am. Forests, Morton Arboretum, Treekeepers (Openlands Project). Home and Office: 2120 W Pensacola Ave Chicago IL 60618-1718 also: N E Pub Assocs Literary Agents PO Box 5 Chester CT 06412-0005 E-mail: baronplot@aol.com.

PLOTNIK, KATYA MICHELE, lawyer; b. N.Y.C. d. Arthur and Meta (Von Borstel) P.; 1 child, Sondra. BA, U. Wis., 1990; JD, CUNY, Queens, 1994. Bar: N.J. 1994, N.Y. 1995. Assoc. Law Office of Bruno Joseph Bembi, Hempstead, N.Y., 1994-96; founding ptnr. Rodriguez & Plotnik, N.Y.C., 1996—. Mem. Am. Immigrtion Lawyers Assn. Democrat. Avocation: martial arts. Office: Rodriguez & Plotnik Ste 502 39-15 Main St Flushing NY 11354 E-mail: plotrod@ix.netcom.com.

PLOTTEL, GLORIA SUSANNE STONE, marketing professional; b. N.Y.C., Feb. 16, 1966; d. Leroy Saul and Karen Lila Stone; m. Philip Benjamin Plottel, June 9, 1996. BA cum laude Univ. Profs. Program, Boston U., 1988; MS in Forest Resources Mgmt, SUNY, Syracuse, 1992; postgrad., NYU. Mgr. dept. geography Boston U., 1989-90; tchg. asst. coll. environ. sci. and forestry SUNY, Syracuse, 1990-92; asst. acct. exec. Lowe and Ptnrs./SMS, N.Y.C., 1993-95; asst. mgr. Champion Internat. Corp., Stamford, Conn., 1995-97; mktg. mgr. Bus. New Haven, 1997-98. Cons. Mass. Dept. Environ. Mgmt., Boston, 1993, No. Forest Lands Coun., Concord, N.H., 1993. Screenwriter: Seasoned Trails, 1989. Mem. exec. bd. U. Profs. Program, Boston U., 1997—; coun. mem. YMCA-YWCA Camping Svcs. of Greater N.Y., 1998—. SUNY internat. conf. grantee, 1991. Mem. Advt. Club N.Y., Soc. Am. Foresters, Women in Natural Resources. Avocations: hiking, camping, swimming, ballroom dancing.

PLOTTEL, JEANINE PARISIER, foreign language educator; b. Paris, Sept. 21, 1934; came to U.S., 1943; m. Roland Plottel, 1956; children: Claudia S., Michael E., Philip B. Baccalauréat lettres, Lycée Français de N.Y., 1952; BA with honors, Barnard Coll., 1954; MA, Columbia U., 1955, PhD with distinction, 1959. Lectr. dept. French and Romance philology Columbia U., N.Y.C., 1955-59; rsch. assoc. fgn. lang. program MLA of Am., 1959-60; lectr. dept. romance langs. CUNY, 1960; asst. prof. div. humanities Julliard Sch. Music, 1960-65; dir. lang. labs. Hunter Coll. CUNY, 1965-69; asst. prof. dept. romance langs. Hunter Coll. CUNY, 1965-69, assoc. prof. dept. romance langs., 1969-81, prof. dept. romance langs., 1981—, assoc. prof. French doctoral program grad. sch., univ. ctr., 1980-81, prof. French doctoral program grad. sch., univ. ctr., 1981—. Extensive adminstrv. experience in CUNY including chairperson Dept. Romance Langs. Author: Les Dialogues de Paul Valéry, 1960; pub., editor N.Y. Literary Forum, 1978-88; contbr. articles to profl. jours., chpts. to books. Pres. Maurice I. Parisier Found., Inc. Named Officer des Palmes Acad., 1999; recipient NEH fellowship, 1979; grantee N.Y. Coun. for the Humanities, 1986, Helena Rubenstein Found., 1986, Florence J. Gould Found., 1986, 88, N.Y. Times Found., 1986. Mem. Maison Française (bd. dirs. Columbia U.), Peyre Inst., CUNY, Soc. French Am. Cultural Svcs. & Ednl. Aid, Hunter Coll. Art Galleries. Home: 50 E 77th St Apt 14A New York NY 10021-1842 Office: Hunter Coll-CUNY 695 Park Ave New York NY 10021-5024 E-mail: plottel@worldnett.att.net.

PLOTTEL, ROLAND, lawyer; b. N.Y.C., Oct. 1, 1934; s. Charles and Frances (Banner) P.; m. Jeanine Parisier, June 3, 1956; children— Claudia, Michael, Philip. B.A., Columbia U., 1955, LL.B., 1958, M.S. in E.E., 1964. Bar: N.Y. 1958, U.S. Patent Office 1962, U.S. Ct. Appeals 1964, U.S. Supreme Ct. 1964. House counsel Radiotronix Communications Labs., N.Y.C., 1958-61; patent atty. Bendix Corp., Teterboro, N.J., 1961-64; internat. patent atty. Western Electric Co., N.Y.C., 1964-70; sole practice, N.Y.C., 1970—; of counsel Frishauf, Holtz, Goodman & Woodward, N.Y.C.; lectr. patent law Practising Law Inst.; arbitrator Civil Ct., 1964—. Harlan Fiske Stone fellow. Mem. ABA, N.Y. County Lawyers Assn., Am. Intellectual Property Law Assn., N.Y. Patent Trademark and Copyright Law Assn., IEEE, Internat. Soc. Hybrid Microelectronics, Am. Arbitration Assn. Club: City N.Y. Home: 50 E 77th St New York NY 10021-1842 Office: 45 Rockefeller Plz New York NY 10111-0100

PLOTZ, CHARLES MINDELL, physician, educator; b. N.Y.C., Dec. 6, 1921; s. Isaac and Rose (Bluestone) P.; m. Lucille Weckstein, Aug. 5, 1945; children: Richard, Thomas, Robert. BA, Columbia U., 1941, D.Sc., 1951; MD, L.I. Coll. Medicine, 1944. Diplomate: Am. Bd. Internal Medicine. Intern New Haven Hosp., 1944-45; resident internal medicine Kings County Hosp., 1945-46, Maimonides Hosp., 1948-49; postdoctoral research fellow USPHS, Columbia Coll. Phys. and Surgs., 1949-50; practice medicine, specializing in internal medicine Bklyn., 1950—; chief Arthritis Clinic, attending physician Kings County Hosp. Center, 1950-85; chief L.I. Coll. Hosp. (Arthritis Clinic), 1950-65; asst. attending physician Mt. Sinai Hosp., 1955—; chief Mt. Sinai Hosp. (Arthritis Clinic), 1955-65, Arthritis Clinic, State U., Hosp., 1967-85; asst. physician Columbia-Presbyn. Med. Center, 1949-71; attending physician Bklyn. State Hosp.; dir. ambulatory care Bklyn. Hosp.Ctr., 1991-93; emeritus prof. medicine SUNY, 1991—; professorial lectr. Mt. Sinai Sch. Medicine, 1992—; emeritus prof. in medicine SUNY, 1991—. Cons. physician Peninsula Gen. Hosp., Jamaica Hosp.; cons. on rheumatology VA Hosp., Bklyn., L.I. Coll. Hosp.; cons. family practice Luth. Med. Ctr.; vis. cons. internal medicine Jewish Gen. Hosp., Mont., Que., Can., 1965; cons. internal medicine Avicenna Hosp. and Wazir Akbar Hosp., Kabul, Afganistan, 1965; prof. medicine, dir. continuing edn., chmn. dept. family practice SUNY Downstate Med. Ctr., 1967-91, prof. emeritus medicine and family practice, 1991—; Fulbright lectr. U. Paris, 1984, 91; professorial lectr. Mt. Sinai Sch. Medicine, 1992—. Editorial adv. bd.: Pakistan Med. Forum; editor-in-chief: Clin. Rheumatology in Practice, 1981—; editor-in-chief: Advances in Rheumatology, 1986—, Rheuma21st.com, 1998—. Mem. nat. bd. govs. Arthritis Found., 1964-82, bd. govs. N.Y. chpt., 1965— , v.p., 1971-83, trustee, 1977-82, N.Y. chpt. sr. v.p., 1977-82, vice chmn. bd. trustees, 1983-85, 87—, pres., 1985-87; trustee Leo N. Levi Meml. Nat. Arthritis Hosp., Alumni Fund-Alumni Assn. SUNY Downstate Med. Center, Bklyn. Inst. Arts and Scis., Bklyn. Bot. Garden; mem. adv. bd. MEDICO, corp. mem., 1977— ; treas. Internat. League Against Rheumatism, 1981-89; trustee Internat. League Against Rheumatism Trust, 1981-89. Served to capt. AUS, 1946-48. WHO fellow U. Negev, 1974; master Am. Coll. Rheumatology, 1991—; recipient Gold medal Am. Coll. Rheumatology, 1992. Master Am. Coll. Rheumatology (Gold medal 1992), fellow ACP, Am. Acad. Family Physicians (charter), N.Y. Acad. Medicine (chmn. edn. com. 1976-78); mem. AMA, (N.Y. chpt.), AAUP, Internat. Soc. for Rheumatic Therapy (chmn. 1987-89), Am. Fedn. Clin. Rsch., Am. Rheumatism Assn. (past sec.-treas.), N.Y. Rheumatism Assn. (past pres., exec. com.), Harvey Soc., (N.Y. chpt.), Kings County med. socs., Bklyn. socs. internal medicine, Soc. Tchrs. Family Medicine, N.Y. State Acads. Family Physicians, Soc. Urban Physicians, Mystery Writers Am., Sigma Xi, Alpha Omega Alpha; hon. mem. Rheumatology Soc. France, Rheumatology Soc. Japan, Rheumatology Soc. Mex., Rheumatology Soc. Brazil, Rheumatology Soc. Yugoslavia, Rheumatology Soc. Norway, Rheumatology Soc. Egypt, Med. Soc. Czechoslovakia, Cosmos Club. Clubs: Heights Casino. Home: 184 Columbia Hts Brooklyn NY 11201-2105 also: 450 Clarkson Ave Brooklyn NY 11203-2056 E-mail: rheuma21st@aol.com.

PLOTZ, RICHARD DOUGLAS, pathologist; b. Bklyn., Aug. 15, 1948; s. Charles Mindell and Lucille (Weckstein) P.; m. Judith Anker, Mar. 28, 1971; children: Martha Anne, Michael David. AB cum laude, Harvard U., 1971; MD, U. Pitts., 1977; MPH, Boston U., 1992. Resident Brown U., Providence, 1977-81; staff pathologist Women & Infants Hosp., 1982-88; med. dir. Corning Metpath (formerly Damon Clin. Lab.), Westwood, Mass., 1988-95, CytoStat, Providence, 1996—; cytopathologist Harvard Vanguard Med. Associs., Boston, 1995—; mem. Fletcher Allen Health Care, Burlington, Vt., 1999. Del. White Ho. Conf. on Libr. & Info. Svcs., Washington, 1979. Fellow Coll. Am. Pathologists (inspector lab. accreditation program); mem. Am. Soc. Cytopathology, New Eng. Soc. Pathologists, R.I. Med. Soc., R.I. Soc. Pathologists. Democrat. Jewish. Avocation: genealogy. Home: 104 11th St Providence RI 02906-2912 E-mail: Dick@plotz.com.

PLOUGH, CHARLES TOBIAS, JR. retired electronics engineering executive; b. Oakland, Calif., Sept. 7, 1926; s. Charles Tobias Sr. and Miriam Lucille (Miller) P.; m. Jean Elizabeth Rose, June 13, 1950 (div. May 1969); children: Charles III, Cathleen, Mark, Barbara; m. Janet Mary Ansell Lumley, July 5, 1969; children: Mark Ansell Lumley, Simon John Lumley. AB with honors, Amherst Coll., 1950; BSEE with honors, U. Calif., Berkeley, 1953. Mgr. tech. devel. Fairchild Semiconductor, Palo Alto, Calif., 1958-71; v.p. Multi-State Devices, Montreal, Can., 1971-78; mgr. research and devel. Dale Electronics, Norfolk, Nebr., 1978-89, ret., 1989. Patentee in field. Treas. First Unitarian Ch., 1996-99. Mem. Lions (sec. Norfolk 1982-86; pres. Albuquerque chpt. 1999-2000); Leader Albuquerque Interfaith 1993—. Avocation: golf. Home: 2030 Quail Run Dr NE Albuquerque NM 87122-1100

PLOVANICH, PATRICIA ANN, theologian, educator; b. Charleston, W.Va., Mar. 5, 1938; d. John Paul and Roberta Patricia (Rynd) P. BA, Rosary Hill Coll., 1968; MA, Fordham U., 1972, PhD, 1990. Asst. to v.p. student affairs Rosary Hill Coll., Buffalo, 1968-70; lectr. Fordham U., Bronx, N.Y., 1974-78; adj. asst. prof. U. Va., Charlottesville, 1979-80; asst. prof. Loyola Coll., Balt., 1981-83, U. San Diego, 1990—; postdoctoral rschr. Karl Eberhard U., Tübingen, Germany, 1997—2002. Mem. bd. dirs. Theta Alpha Kappa Nat. Honor Soc., 1996-98, v.p., 1998—. Vol. Soujourners Family Homeless Shelter, Charleston, W. Va., 1989, 90. Recipient Faculty Rsch. grants U. San. Diego, 1992, 93, 2001; named Steber prof., 1994-95. Mem.: Coll. Theology Soc. (conv. presenter 1982, 1991, 1992, conv. sect. head 1992—95, conv. presenter 1993, 1994, 1995, 1996, 2001, 2002, 2002), Am. Acad. Religions (conv. presenter 1994). Roman Catholic. Office: U San Diego Dept Religious Studies 5998 Alcala Park San Diego CA 92110-2476 E-mail: pplov@sandiego.edu.

PLOVNICK, MARK STEPHEN, business educator; b. N.Y.C., June 8, 1946; s. Jacob and Dorothy Edith (Berger) Plovnick; m. Daisy Shulan Chan, Mar. 13, 1982. BSME, Union Coll., 1968; BA in Econs., Union Coll., 1968; MS in Mgmt., MIT, 1970, PhD in Mgmt., 1975. Instr., rschr. MIT, Cambridge, 1970—76; asst. prof. Clark Univ., Worcester, 1976—79, assoc. prof., 1979—89, chmn. dept. mgmt., 1979—82, assoc. dean Grad. Sch. Mgmt., 1982—89; prof., dean Sch. Eberhardt Sch. Bus. U. Pacific, Stockton, Calif., 1989—. Cons. to various orgns., 1970—; dir. Devel. Rsch. Assocs., Reston, Va., 1979—82; adj. assoc. prof. U. Mass. Med. Sch., Worcester, Mass., 1982—89; adj. asst. prof. Boston Univ. Sch. Medicine, 1974—75; clin. instr. Harvard Med. Sch., Boston, 1977—78. Author: 5 books; contbr. numerous articles to profl. jours. Mem. Civil Svc. Commn., San Joaquin County, 1989—94. Mem.: Greater Stockton C. of C. (bd. dirs. 1990—94). Office: U Pacific Eberhardt Sch Bus Stockton CA 95211-0001 E-mail: mplovnic@uop.edu.

PLOWDEN, DAVID, photographer; b. Boston, Oct. 9, 1932; s. Roger and Mary Russell (Butler) P.; m. Pleasance Coggeshall, June 20, 1962 (div. 1976); children: John, Daniel; m. Sandra Oakes Schoellkopf, July 8th, 1977; children: Philip, Karen. BA Econs., Yale U., 1955; pvt. study with Minor White, Rochester, N.Y., 1959-60. Asst. O. Winston Link Studio, N.Y.C., 1958-59, George Meluso Studio, N.Y.C., 1960-62; photographer, writer, 1962—. Assoc. prof. Inst. Design, Ill. Inst. Tech., Chgo., 1978-86; lectr. U. Iowa Sch. Journalism, 1985-88; vis. prof. Grand Valley State Univ., 1988-90, 91—; artist-in-residence U. Balt., 1990-91. Author and photographer: Farewell to Steam, 1968, Lincoln and His America, 1970 (Benjamin Barondess award 1971), The Hand of Man on America, 1971, 2d edit, 1974, The Floor of the Sky: the Great Plains, 1972, Bridges: the Spans of North America, 1974, 2d edit. 1984, 3d edit., 2002, Commonplace, 1974, Tugboat, 1976 (notable Children's books ALA 1976, Children's Book Showcase 1976), Steel, 1981, An American Chronology, 1982 (Notable Books ALA 1982, Booklist's Best of the 80s 1989), Industrial Landscape, 1985, A Time of Trains, 1987, A Sense of Place, 1988, End of an Era: The Last of the Great Lakes Steamboats, 1992, Small Town America, 1994, Imprints: The Photographs of David Plowden, 1997; co-author, photographer, Nantucket, 1970, Cape May to Montauk, 1973, Desert and Plains, the Mountains and the River, 1975, The Iron Road, 1978 (notable children's books 1978, Honor list Horn Books 1979), Wayne County: the Aesthetic Heritage of a Rural Area, 1979; introduction The Gallery of World Photography/the Country, 1983; commd. illustrator Gems, 1967, The Freeway in the City, 1968, America the Vanishing, 1969, New Jersey, 1977, North Dakota, 1977, Vermont, 1979, New York, 1981, A Place of Sense, 1988; contbr. articles to numerous jours. including Time, Newsweek, Life, Audubon, Fortune, Smithsonian, Camera Arts, Lenswork; one-man shows include Columbia U., 1965, Smithsonian Instn., 1970, 71, 75, 76, 81, 89, Internat. Ctr. Photography, N.Y., 1976, Witkin Gallery, N.Y.C., 1979, Cin. Art Acad., 1979, The Gilbert Gallery, Chgo., 1980, 81, Chgo. Ctr. Contemporary Photography, 1982, Fed. Hall Mus., N.Y.C., 1982, Calif. Mus. Photography, Riverside, 1982-83, Chgo. Hist. Soc., 1985, Martin Gallery, Washington, 1987, Kunstmuseum, Luzern, Switzerland, 1987, Burchfield Ctr., Buffalo, 1987-88, Iowa State Mus., Des Moines, 1988-89, Catherine Edelman Gallery, Chgo., 1990, Grand Valley State U., 1993, Ewing Gallery, Washington, 1994, Beinecke Rare Book and Manuscript Lib. Yale U., 1997, Albright-Knox Art Gallery, 1997, Mus. Contemporary Photography, Chgo., 1998, Albin O. Kuhn Libr. & Gallery, U. Md., Balt., 1998, Tatar/Alexander Photogallery, Toronto, Ont., 1999, Lawrence Miller Gallery, N.Y.C., 2000; exhibited in group shows at Met. Mus. Art, N.Y.C., 1967, Kodak Gallery, N.Y.C., 1976, Currier Gallery Art, Manchester, N.H., 1978, Whitney Mus., 1979, Art Inst. Chgo., 1983-86, 87, Witkin Gallery, N.Y.C., 1988, Davenport (Iowa) Mus. Art, 1992, Mus. Contemporary Photography, Chgo., Ill., 1996, 98, 99, City, 2000, Peter Fetterman Gallery Photographic Works of Art, Santa Monica, Calif., 2001; represented in permanent collections Albright-Knox Gallery, Art Inst. Chgo., Calif. Mus. Photography, Ctr. Creative Photography, Chgo. Hist. Soc., Libr. Congress, Smithsonian Instn., U. Md., J.B. Speed Mus., Iowa Humanities Bd., Iowa State Hist. Dept., Burchfield Art Ctr., Buffalo and Erie County Hist. Soc., Internat. Mus. Photography George Eastman House, Internat. Ctr. Photography, Ekstrom Libr. U. Louisville, Beinecke Rare Book and Mauscript Library, Yale U., 1995—, Mus. Contemporary Photography, Chicy, Bayly Mus. U. Va., Charlottesville. John Simon Guggenheim fellow, 1968; grantee N.Y. State Coun. Arts, 1966, 87, Smithsonian Inst., 1970-71, Dept. Transp. and Smithsonian Inst., 1975-76, H. E. Butt Found., 1977, United Bd. Homeland Ministries, 1976, Chgo. Hist. Soc., 1980-84, Seymour H. Knox Found., 1987, Baird Found., 1987, State Hist. Soc. Iowa, 1987-88, Iowa Humanities Bd., 1987-88; recipient Railroad History award, 1989; subjectof PBS documentary: David Plowden: Light, Shadow & Form, 2000. Mem. Am. Soc. Media Photographers. Home and Office: 609 Cherry St Winnetka IL 60093-2614 Fax: 847-446-2795. E-mail: dplowden@enteract.com.

PLOWMAN, JACK WESLEY, lawyer; b. Blairsville, Pa., Sept. 12, 1929; s. Ralph Waldo, Sr., and Ethel Beatrice (Nicely) P.; m. Barbara Ellen Brown, Apr. 5, 1952; children: Linda Ellen, Judith Lynn AB, U. Pitts., 1951, LL.B. with honors, 1956. Bar: Pa. 1956, U.S. Dist. Ct. (we. dist.) Pa. 1956, U.S. Ct. Appeals 1960, U.S. Supreme Ct. 1978. Assoc. Campbell, Houck & Thomas, Pitts., 1956-57; ptnr. Rose, Houston, Cooper & Schmidt, 1957-63, Plowman, Spiegel & Lewis, Pitts., 1963-2000; of counsel Bentz Law Firm, P.C., 2000—. Adj. prof. emeritus Duquesne U. Sch. Law, 1963—70, 1983—2002. Editor-in-chief Pitts. Legal Jour., 1971-81, U. Pitts. Law Rev., 1955-56 Bd. dirs. United Meth. Pub. House, 1984-96, Ward Home for Children, United Meth.

Ch. Union, 1977-83, Wesley Inst., 1977-81, Neighborhood Legal Svcs. Assn., 1969-74; chancellor emeritus Western Pa. Ann. Conf., United Meth. Ch. Capt. USAF, 1951-53. Fellow Am. Bar Found. (life mem.), Am. Coll. Trial Lawyers, Allegheny County Bar Found. (trustee, sec.); mem. ABA, Pa. Bar Assn., Allegheny County Bar Assn. (pres. 1982), Pa. Bar Inst. (bd. dirs. 1988-92), Am. Law Inst., Supreme Ct. Pa. Hist. Soc. (trustee, pres.). Republican. Home: 1025 Lakemont Dr Pittsburgh PA 15243-1817 Office: The Washington Ctr Bldg 680 Washington Rd Pittsburgh PA 15228

PLOWMAN, JOHN BRENT, small business owner; b. Owosso, Mich., Apr. 16, 1949; s. Thomas Hugh and Gene Lenore (Lewis) P.; m. Mary Cecil Bond, Sept. 7, 1974; children: David, Michael, Elizabeth. BA in Bus. Acctg., Alma (Mich.) Coll., 1971. Owner, pres. Plowman Ford Inc., Perry, Mich., 1971—, Plowman Gas & Oil Co., Perry, 1978—. Mem. Shiawassee County Rep. Party, Corunna, Mich., 1972—; trustee Perry Area Fire Dept. Bd., 1972—, Meml. Healthcare Ctr. of Owosso, 1984—, Found. Bd., 1994—; county commr. Shiawassee County, 1984-92; mayor City of Perry, 1976-80; past pres. Mich. Assn. Local Pub. Health, Lansing, 1985—; treas. Capitol Area Substance Abuse Commn., Lansing, 1989—. Recipient Past Pres. award Mich. Assn. Local Pub. Health, Lansing, 1992. Mem. Mich. Auto Dealers Assn. (pres. 1993-94), Mich. Petroleum Assn. Republican. Congregationalist. Avocations: golf, coaching, raising flowers. Home: 202 Meadowdale Ln Perry MI 48872-9708 Office: 108 W 3rd St Perry MI 48872

PLOWRIGHT, JOAN ANNE, actress; b. Brigg, Lincolnshire, Eng., Oct. 28, 1929; d. William and Daisy (Burton) P.; m. Roger Gage, 1953 (div.); m. Sir Laurence Olivier, 1961 (dec.); 3 children. Student, Old Vic Theatre Sch. Mem. Old Vic Co., toured S. Africa, 1952-53; 1st leading role in the Country Wife London, 1956; mem. English Stage Co., 1956, Nat. Theatre, 1963-74. Appearances include (plays) The Chairs, 1957, The Entertainer, 1958, Major Barbara and Roots, 1959, A Taste of Honey, 1960 (Tony Best Actress award 1960), Uncle Vanya, 1962-64, St. Joan, 1963 (London Evening Standard Best Actress award 1964), Hobson's Choice, 1964, The Master Builder, 1965, Much Ado About Nothing, 1967, Tartuffe, 1967, Three Sisters, 1967, 68, 69, The Advertisement, 1968, 69, Love's Labour's Lost, 1968, 69, The Merchant of Venice, 1970, 71-72, Rules of the Game, 1971-72, Woman Killed with Kindness, 1971-72, Taming of the Shrew, 1972, Doctor's Dilemma, 1972, Rosmersholm, 1973, Saturday Sunday Monday, 1973, Eden's End, 1974, The Sea Gull, 1975, The Bed Before Yesterday, 1975 (Variety award 1976), Filumena, 1977 (Soc. West End Theatres Best Actress award 1978), Enjoy, 1980, Who's Afraid of Virginia Woolf?, 1981, Cavell, 1982, The Cherry Orchard, 1983, The Way of the World, 1985, The House of Bernada Alba, 1986-87, Uncle Vanya, 1988, Time and The Conways, 1991, If We Are Women, 1995, (films) Much Ado About Nothing, 1969, Equus, 1976, Richard Wagner, 1982, Brimstone and Treacle, 1982, Brittania Hosp., 1983, Revolution, 1985, The Dressmaker, 1987, Drowning By Numbers, 1987, I Love You To Death, 1990, Avalon, 1990, Enchanted April, 1992 (Acad. award nominee Best Supporting Actress, Golden Globe award 1992), Dennis the Menace, 1993, A Pin for the Butterfly, 1993, Last Action Hero, 1993, The Summer House, 1993, Widows' Peak, 1994, The Scarlet Letter, 1994, Pyromaniacs: A Love Story, 1995, The Grass Harp, 1995, Hotel Sorrento, 1995, Jane Eyre, 1995, Surviving Picasso, 1996, 101 Dalmations, 1996, Mr. Wrong, 1996, The Assistant, 1997, Tea with Mussolini, 1998, The Last Spy, 1998, Bailey's Mistake, 2000, Global Heresy, 2000, Calas Forever, 2001, George and the Dragon, 2002; (tv films) Merchant of Venice, 1973, Daphne, Laureola, 1977, Saturday Sunday Monday, 1977, The Importance of Being Earnest, 1988, The Birthday Party, 1987, House of Bernarda Alba, A Nightingale Sang, 1989, Stalin, 1992 (Golden Globe Awd. 1992, Emmy nomination, supporting actress - miniseries, 1993), A Place for Annie, 1994, On Promised Land, 1994, Return of the Natives, This Could Be the Last Time, 1998, Encore, Encore, 1998, Back to the Secret Garden, 1999, Frankie and Hazel, 1999. Office: ICM care Harriet Robinson 76 Oxford St London WIN 0AX England

PLUFF, STEARNS CHARLES, III, investment banker; b. Biloxi, Miss., Jan. 30, 1953; s. Stearns Charles Jr. and Patricia Elizabeth (Diaz) P.; m. Joan Marie Jay Jones, May 28, 1987; children: Micleah Frances, Ashleigh Nicole. BA, U. Miss., 1975. Supr. Host Internat., New Orleans, 1975-77; contractor Greg Edwards & Co., Falls Church, Va., 1977-80; registered rep. Donald Sheldon & Co., Houston, 1982-85; sr. v.p. GMS Group Inc., 1985—. Dir., sr. v.p. MMP Investments, Inc., Cary, Ill., 1989—; pres. R.P. Telekom U.S.A., Warsaw, 1993—. Vol. Petrosky Elem. Sch., Alief, Tex., 1991—. Mem. Chi Psi. Avocations: world travel, hiking, camping, gardening. Office: 5075 Westheimer Rd Ste 1175 Houston TX 77056-5675 Home: 11506 Alberta Dr Austin TX 78739-1459

PLUHAR, GRACE ELIZABETH, veterinary orthopedic surgery educator; b. Chgo., Nov. 22, 1956; d. Russell A. and Grace S. Pluhar. BS, No. Ill. U., 1978, MS, 1979; DVM, Oreg. State U., 1989; MS, Wash. State U., 1995; PhD, U. Wis., 1999. Vet. intern Animal Med. Ctr., N.Y.C., 1989-90; resident in small animal surgery Wash. State U., Pullman, 1992-95; rsch. fellow U. Wis., Madison, 1995-99; asst. prof. vet. orthopedic surgery Colostate State U., Ft. Collins, 1999—. Contbr. articles to med. jours., including Jour. Orthopaedic Rsch., Am. Jour. Vet. Rsch., Am. Animal Hosp. Assn., Clin. Orthopaedics and Related Rsch., Vet. Surgery, Vet. Radiology and Ultrasound, Jour. AVMA. Recipient nat. svc. rsch. award NIH, 1996-99, 1st place pre-doctoral abstract award VA, 1998, William Harris Hip award, 2002; Dr. Lynn A. George Meml. scholar Wash. State U., 1993, 94, Drs. Pettit and Robinette surg. scholar, 1994, 95; travel grantee U. Wis., 1999. Fellow Am. Coll. Vet. Surgeons (diplomate); mem. AAAS, Vet. Orthopedic Soc., Orthopaedic Rsch. Soc., Internat. Soc. Limb Salvage. Office: Colostate State U 300 W Drake Rd Fort Collins CO 80523 Fax: 970-491-1275. E-mail: epluhar@vth.colostate.edu.

PLUIMER, EDWARD J. lawyer; b. Rapid City, S.D., 1949; BA cum laude, U. S.D., 1971; JD cum laude, NYU, 1974. Bar: Minn. 1975. Law clk. to Hon. Robert A. Ainsworth, Jr. U.S. Ct. Appeals (5th cir.), 1974-75; ptnr. Dorsey & Whitney, Mpls., 1975—. Mem. Minn. Supreme Ct. ADR Task Force, 1988-92. Editor N.Y. U. Law Rev. Mem. Order of the Coif. Office: Dorsey & Whitney LLP Ste 1500 50 S 6th St Minneapolis MN 55402-1498 E-mail: pluimer.ed@dorseylaw.com.

PLUM, CHARLES WALDEN, retired business executive and educator; b. Circleville, Ohio, Apr. 13, 1914; s. Horace Walden and Anna Frances (Eaton) P.; m. Margaret E. McCollister, Sept. 1939; children: David Walden, Donald Alan (dec.). BS, Ohio State U., 1936; MBA, Case Western Res. U., 1951; postgrad., Advanced Mgmt. Program, Harvard, 1954. CPA, N.Y., Ohio, Tex. Sr. accountant Coopers and Lybrand, N.Y.C., 1936-42; supr. acctg. Amertorp Corp., Naval Ordnance Plant, St. Louis, 1942-45; various positions including asst. contr., dep. contr., contr. to v.p. acctg. and mgmt. systems Standard Oil Co. (Ohio), Cleve., 1945-78; prof. bus. adminstrn. Tex. A&M U., College Station, 1978-89. Dir., chmn. audit com. Hospitality Motor Inns, Inc., Cleve., 1976-79; sec.-treas., dir., mem. mgmt. com. Am. Assembly Collegiate Schs. Bus., 1977-78; lectr. acctg. Western Res. U., 1946-54; bus. exec. in residence, disting. lectr. Tex. A. and M. U., 1976; Mem. bus. adv. council Kent State U., 1967-77 Mem. AICPA, Fin. Execs. Inst., Am. Petroleum Inst. (chmn. com. on cooperation with AICPA 1955-68), Tex. Soc. CPAs, Sigma Phi Epsilon, Beta Gamma Sigma, Beta Alpha Psi. Home: Apt 405 14645 Preston Rd Dallas TX 75254

PLUM, FRED, neurologist; b. Atlantic City, Jan. 10, 1924; s. Fred and Frances (Alexander) Plum; m. Susan Butler, Apr. 23, 1990; children from previous marriage: Michael, Christopher, Carol. BA, Dartmouth Coll., 1944, postgrad., 1944—45; MD, Cornell U., 1947, Karolinska Inst., Stockholm, 1982; DSc (hon.) , L.I. U., 1990. Resident N.Y. Hosp., 1947—50, fellow, 1950—53, neurologist-in-chief, 1963—98, attending neurologist, 1998—. Instr. neurology Sch. Medicine Cornell U., 1950—53, Anne Parrish Titzell prof. neurology, 1963—98, univ. prof., 1998—, chmn. dept. neurology, 1963—98; head neurology sect. U.S. Naval Hosp., St. Albans, NY, 1951—53; from asst. prof. to prof. neurology Sch. Medicine U. Wash., 1953—63; vis. scientist U. Lund, Sweden, 1970—71; vis. physician Rockefeller U. Hosp., 1975—85; assoc. neurosci. rsch. program MIT and Rockefeller U., 1977—87, mem. neurology study sect., 1964—68, grad. tng. com., 1959—63, 1971, nat. adv. coun., 1977—81, Nat. Inst. Neurol., Communicative Disorders and Stroke, 1984—86; founding mem. McKnight Endowment Fund for Neurosci., 1986, pres., 1986—90. Author (with J.B. Posner): Diagnosis of Stupor and Coma, 1966; author: 3d edit., 1982, Clinical Management of Seizures, 1976, 2d edit., 1983; author: (with others) Cecil Essentials of Medicine, 1986, 3d edit., 1995; editor, contbg. author: Cecil's Textbook of Medicine, 1968, chief editor neurology sect.: Contemporary Neurology series, founding editor: Vols. 1-40, 1966—93, founding editor: Brain Dysfunction in Metabolic Disorders, 1974, mem. editl. bd.: Archives Neurology, 1958—68, chief editor: , 1972—76; editor: Annals of Neurology, 1977—85; founding editor: , 1986—; editor: Neurology Alert, 1981—2002; contbr. articles to sci. and profl. jours. Mem.: NAS, Assn. Am. Physicians, Assn. Rsch. Nervous Mental Diseases (pres. 1973, 1987), Am. Soc. Clin. Investigation, Soc. Neurosci., Am. Acad. Neurology (past mem. coun.), Am. Neurol. Assn. (v.p. 1974—75, pres. 1976—77, Jacoby award 1984), Inst. of Medicine, Am. Acad. Arts and Scis., Can., Brit., French, Itatlian, Swiss neurol. socs. (hon.), Alpha Omega Alpha. Achievements include research in conciousness, coma and stroke. Office: Weill-Cornell U Med Coll 525 E 68th St # A565 New York NY 10021-4870 E-mail: frp2005@mail.cornell.edu.

PLUM, KENNETH RAY, state legislator; b. Shenandoah, Va., Nov. 3, 1941; m. Jane M. Meacham, Aug. 9, 1990; children: Timothy R., David W., Helen, Augusta Meacham. BA, Old Dominion U., 1965; MEd, U. Va., 1967. Mem. Va. Ho. of Dels., Richmond, 1978-80, 82—. Mem. Sci. and Tech. Com., Higher Edn. Subcom., Transp. Subcom., Natural Resources Subcom. Appropriations, Corps., Ins. and Banking Com. (co-chair), Conservation and Natural Resources Com., Joint Subcom. Study Restructuring and Potential Changes in the Electirc Utility Industry, Joint Subcom. Studying Needs of Certain Underserved Gifted Student, Joint Subcom. Studying Early Intervention Svcs. for Infants and Toddlers with Disabilities, Joint Subcom. to Study the Future of Va.'s Environment,; chmn. Joint Commn. on Tech. and Sci.. Mem. United Christian Parish of Reston (Va.); charter bd. dirs. Va. Literacy Found.; bd. dirs. Arts Coun. Fairfax County, Dem. Party Va., nat. capital area Coun. Boy Scouts Am. Recipient Human Rights award Fairfax County, 1982, Warren G. Stambaugh award forsupport of mental health programs, 1992, Good Guy award Nat. Women's Polit. Caucus, 1992, Outstanding Svc. award Va. Network for Victims and Witnesses of Crime, Inc., 1994, Outstanding Svc. to Children award No. Va. Assn. Edn. Young Children, 1995, Legislator of Yr. Chesapeake Bay Found., 1993, 95, Va. Assn. Soil and Water Conservation Dists., 1996, Pub. Citizen of Yr. award Va. chpt. Nat. Assn. Social Workers, 1995-96, Eco-Hero award Sierra Club, 1996, Legis. Leadership award Va. Ctr. Aging, 1996, Legis. award Va. Literacy Coun., 1996, Tech. Ten Legis. No. Va. Tech. Coun., 1996, 97, 98; named Adult Educator of Yr. Va., 1972, Drug Abuse Prevention Warrior of the Year, 1990, Champion of Children's Health Va. Coalition Children's Health, 1998; chosen to represent Gen. Assembly at Nat. Leadership Inst., 1997. Mem. NEA, Va. Edn. Assn., Fairfax Edn. Assns. Office: 2073 Cobblestone Ln Reston VA 20191-4039 E-mail: Kenplum@aol.com.

PLUMB, ROBERT THOMPSON, II, lawyer; b. San Diego, 1951; s. Robert T. and Elsie Jane (Burket) P.; m. Rita Robbins. BA, Coll. Idaho, 1973; JD, Thomas Jefferson Sch. Law, 1977. Bar: Calif. 1979; cert. legal specialist in family law. Pvt. practice Law Offices of Robert T. Plumb II, Coronado, Calif., 1979—. Mem. Rotary. Avocations: golf, bridge, travel. Office: PO Box 180734 Coronado CA 92178-0734

PLUMER, ALVIN H. (BUD), realtor; b. Phila., Sept. 10, 1925; s. Louis J. and Mary B. Plumer; m. Pearl Plumer, Dec. 24, 1950; 1 child, Mona Ann. BS, Temple U., 1947. Pres. Plumer & Assocs., Phila., 1947—. Pres. South Phila. Bd. Realtors, 1969-70; Hollywood Savs. Assn., Phila., 1980-90; v.p. Phila. Bd. Realtors, 1969-70. Vice-chmn. South St. Headhouse Dist., Phila., 1998, treas., 1999-2000; pres. Center City Coun. Realtors, 1985-87. Named to South St. Hall of Fame, South St. Headhouse Dist., 2000. Mem. Phila. Assn. Realtors (chmn. profl. stds. 1992—, Hall of Fame award 1999). Republican. Office: Plumer & Assocs 226 South St Philadelphia PA 19147-2310

PLUMERI, JOSEPH JAMES, II, financial executive; b. Trenton, N.J., July 7, 1943; s. Samuel J. and Josephine (Vaccaro) P.; m. Nancy Plumeri, June 18, 1966; children: Christian, Jay Michael, Leslie BA in History, Coll. of William and Mary, 1966; postgrad., N.Y. Law Sch., 1967-69. Trainee Carter Berlind & Weill, N.Y.C., 1968-69; stockbroker CBWL-Hayden Stone, 1968-73; br. mgr. Shearson Hayden Stone, Fort Lauderdale, Fla., 1973-74, exec. v.p. western region San Francisco, 1974-81; sr. exec. v.p. Shearson Lehman Hutton, N.Y.C., 1981—, dir. mktg. and nat. sales, 1981-89, dir. domestic br. div., 1990-94; vice chmn., group CEO Travelers Group, Inc., 1994-2000; chmn., CEO Willis Group, Ltd., Jacksonville, Fla., 2000—. Bd. dirs., trustee endowment assn. Coll. William and Mary Mem.: Columbus (N.Y.C.). Avocations: golf; reading. Home: 1461 Martine Ave Scotch Plains NJ 07076-2501

PLUMEZ, JEAN PAUL, advertising agency executive, consultant; b. N.Y.C., Oct. 31, 1939; s. Jean Paul and Marie Antoinette (Compagne) P.; m. Jacqueline Hornor, Feb. 20, 1965; children: Jean Paul, Nicole. BS in Chem. Engring., BA in Chemistry, Bucknell U., 1962; MBA, U. Pa., 1968. Product engr. Mobil Oil Co., Paulsboro, N.J., 1965-66; account mgr. Dancer Fitzgerald, Sample, Inc., N.Y.C., 1968-86, exec. v.p., 1979-86; pres. Leadership on Paper, Larchmont, N.Y., 1986—; founding ptnr. The Right Direction, 1987—. Served to capt. Signal Corps U.S. Army, 1962-64. Mem. Alpha Chi Sigma, Beta Gamma Sigma, Kappa Delta Rho Clubs: Larchmont Yacht, Wharton of N.Y., Princeton of N.Y. Home and Office: 90 Beechtree Dr Larchmont NY 10538-1202

PLUMLEY, DANIELLE L. social worker; b. Rochester, N.Y., Nov. 10, 1967; d. Michael Pratt and Barbara Janet (Sautter) LaGrange; m. James Donald Plumley, Aug. 22, 1992. BA magna cum laude, Hamilton Coll., 1990; MSW, Syracuse U., 1994. Cert. social worker, N.Y. Residence counselor Catholic Charities, Utica, NY, 1990—92, Ctrl. N.Y. Devel. Svcs. Office, Rome, 1994—98, social worker II, 1998—. Vol. adv. Ctrl. N.Y. D.S.O., Verona, 1992-96; mem. United Meth. Ch. of Camden, N.Y., 1997—; facilitator Nurturing Program for Parents and Children. Mem. NASW, Acad. Cert. Social Workers, Phi Beta Kappa. Republican. Avocations: flower gardening, karate, whitewater rafting. Home: 10045 Pennymix Rd Camden NY 13316-4604 Office: Ctrl NY DSO 287 Genesee St Utica NY 13501

PLUMMER, AMANDA, actress; b. N.Y.C., Mar. 23, 1957; d. Christopher and Tammy (Grimes) Plummer. Student, Middlebury Coll. Has appeared in theatre roles: A Taste of Honey, 1981; A Month in the Country, 1980; N.Y.C. debut: Artichoke, 1979; The Glass Menagarie, 1983-84; motion picture debut: Cattle Annie and Little Britches, 1981, The World According to Garp, 1982, Daniel, 1983, Hotel New Hampshire, 1984, Static, 1985, Made in Heaven, 1987, Prisoners of Inertia, 1989, Joe Versus the Volcano, 1990, The Fisher King, 1991, Freejack, 1992, The Lounge People, 1992, So I Married an Axe Murderer, 1993, Needful Things, 1993 (Saturn award, 1994), Pax, 1994, Nostradamus, 1994, Pulp Fiction, 1994, The Final Cut, 1995, The Prophecy, 1995, Search and Destroy, 1995, Butterfly Kiss, 1995, Hysteria, 1996, Freeway, 1996, Dead Girl, 1996, American Perfect, 1997, Drunks, 1997, A Simple Wish, 1997, You Can Thank Me Later, 1998, October 22, 1998, L.A. Without a Map, 1998, Elizabeth Jane, 1998, Great Sex, 1999, Eight and a Half Women, 1999, The Million Dollar Hotel, 2000, Seven Days to Live, 2000, Triggermen, 2002, Ken Park, 2002, TMA, 2002, Pulp Fiction: The Facts, 2002, My Life Without Me, 2002, The Last Angel, 2002; (TV movies) The Dollmaker, 1984, True Blue, 1989, Kojak: None So Blind, 1990, Sidney Sheldon's The Sands of Time, 1992, Last Light, 1993, Whose Child Is This? The War for Baby Jessica, 1993, Under the Piano, 1995, Don't Look Back, 1996, The Right to Remain Silent, 1996, (voice) Hercules, 1997, Shadow Realm, 2002, Get a Clue, 2002, Broadway: The Golden Age, by the Legends Who Were There, 2002; other theatre roles include: Agnes of God (Tony, Drama Desk award, Outer Circle Critics award), 1982, A Lie of the Mind, 1985; TV appearances include Hallmark Hall of Fame: Miss Rose White (Emmy award supporting actress, 1992), TV series L.A. Law, Moonlighting, The Equalizer, The Outer Limits, (Emmy award best guest actress, 1996). Office: Innovative Artists Ste 2850 1999 Avenue Of The Stars Los Angeles CA 90067-4612*

PLUMMER, CAROL ANN, social worker; b. Paulding, Ohio, May 25, 1952; d. Rex Eugene and Anna Marie (Stoller) P.; 1 child, Anthony Rene. BA in Psychology, Goshen (Ind.) Coll., 1976; MSW, ACSW, Western Mich. U., 1984, postgrad., U. Mich. Cert. social worker. Program dir. Elkhart County Juvenile Detention, Elkhart, Ind., 1972-74; dir. St. James Day Care Ctr., 1976-77; counselor Youth Svcs. Bur., 1977-80; project dir. Bridgework Theater, Goshen, Ind., 1980-83; therapist Van Buren Mental Health Ctr., Paw Paw, Mich., 1984-85; dir. Prevention Tng. Assocs., Kalamazoo, 1985-91; pvt. practice therapist Ann Arbor, 1991—; cons. U. Mich. Family Assessment Clinic, 1991—. Cons., trainer USAF, 1986; cons., grant writer Planned Parenthood, Kalamazoo, 1988-89; conf. presenter in field; mem. faculty APSAC Forensic Tng. Inst., 1997, 99; cons. Dept. Edn., Hawaii, 2000-01; mem. faculty Nat. Symposium on Child Sexual Abuse, 1997, 2000, 2001. Author: Preventing Sexual Abuse, 1984, 2d edit., 1998; playwright: Little Bear, playwright: Out of the Trap, playwright: Parental Guidance Suggested (Best Project Dir., 1982); contbr. . Bd. dirs. The Kazoo Sch., Kalamazoo, 1985, Bridgework Theater, Goshen, Ind., 1979-80; mem. Kalamazoo County Task Force on Violence, 1990; mem. adv. bd. Sexual Assault Info. Network, 1989-92; cons., trainer Soundings: A Women's Counseling Agy., 1992-97; expert witness on child sexual abuse various Mich. cts., 1988—; mem. planning com. Imagine: Internat. Conf. on Child Sexual Abuse Prevention, 1992-94; staff trainer Kalamazoo Valley Intermediate Sch. Dist., 1989-92; mem. County Wraparound Com., 1995-97, Washtenaw Family Svcs. Collaborative, 1995—. Mem. Assn. Sexual Abuse Prevention (co-founder, bd. mem. 1986-95, cert. of appreciation, statewide awards for contbn. to sexual assault awareness 1995-97). Avocations: walking, reading, camping, music, yoga, cooking. E-mail: plummerc@umich.edu.

PLUMMER, DIRK ARNOLD, chemical, electrical, and electronics engineer; b. Stamford, Conn., Apr. 18, 1930; s. Charles Arnold Plummer and Edwina Woodling Johnson; m. Janis Susan Lowery Stuart, Feb. 18, 1967 (div. 1973); 1 child, Julie. SB in Chem. Engring., MIT, 1952; BSEE, U. Calif., Berkeley, 1961; MSEE, Monmouth U., 1995. Registered profl. engr., Conn., N.J.; cert. nondestructive test examiner of inspectors for radiography, magnetic particle, liquid penetrant and ultrasonic testing methods; cert. comml. pilot. Chem. engr. Foster Wheeler Corp., N.Y.C., 1952; engr. The M.W. Kellogg Co., 1954; project engr. Am. Machine & Fdry. Co., Greenwich, Conn., 1955-56; devel. engr. Aerojet-Gen. Corp., Azusa, Sacramento, San Ramon, Calif., 1956-61; sr. mem. tech. staff Aerospace Comm. & Controls Divsn. RCA, Burlington, Mass., 1961-62; engr. Elec. Boat Div. Gen. Dynamics Corp., Groton, Conn., 1963; electronics engr. U.S. Civil Svc., various locations, 1963-88; pvt. practice profl. engring. Sea Bright, N.J., 1988-94; constrn. inspector Bd. Chosen Freeholders, Freehold, 1994; pvt. practice prof. engr. Sea Bright, 1994—. Contbr. articles to profl. jours. Archtl. control officer Sea Bright Village Assn., 1991. 1st lt. U.S. Army, 1952-54. Recipient Meritorious Svc. medal Pres. of U.S., 1982, Cert. for Commendable Svc. Def. Supply Agy., 1972. Mem. AAAS, NSPE, ASCE, Internat. Soc. of Logistics, Am. Chem. Soc., AIChE (profl. devel. officer 1990), IEEE (chmn. nuclear and plasma sci. chpt. 1990), Am. Phys. Soc., Am. Math. Soc., Math Assn. Am. Home and Office: 45 Village Rd Sea Bright NJ 07760-2233 E-mail: dap@alum.mit.edu.

PLUMMER, GAYTHER L(YNN), ecologist, climatologist, researcher; b. Indpls., Jan. 27, 1925; s. Conley L. and Rowena H. (Huber) P.; m. H. Eileen Barr, June 3, 1950. BS, Butler U., 1948; MS, Kans. State U., 1950; PhD, Purdue U., 1954. Instr. biology Knox Coll., Galesburg, Ill., 1950-51; naturalist Ind. Dept. Conservation, various locations, 1947-52; asst. prof. biology Antioch Coll., Yellow Springs, Ohio, 1954-55; prof. botany U. Ga., Athens, 1955-95, state climatologist, 1978-95. Rsch. fellow Oak Ridge (Tenn.) Inst. Nuclear Studies, 1958-62. Author: Georgia Weather Watchers, 1991, Georgia Temperatures, 1993; cartographer 160 vegetation maps of Ga., 1972-74; editor Ga. Jour. Sci., 1977-84; author over 200 rsch. reports. 2d lt. USAAF, 1943-46. Fellow AAAS; mem. Ecol. Soc. Am., Ind. Acad. Sci., Ga. Acad. Sci., Soil Sci. Soc. Am., Crop Sci. Soc., Agron. Soc. Am., Sigma Xi, Phi Kappa Phi. Achievements include research in droughts in S.E. U.S. relating to astrogeophysical processes via geomagnetics; lightning history in Piedmont for over 70 million years etched in Stone Mountain granite. Office: Ga Climatology Assoc Inc 995 Timothy Rd Athens GA 30606-3838

PLUMMER, JACK MOORE, psychologist; b. Galveston, Tex., Apr. 19, 1940; s. Jack Moore and Sarah Carroll (Cochran) P.; m. Rose Marie Taylor, July 22, 1960; children: Cynthia Marie, Edward Moore, Elizabeth Anne, Sarah Lorraine, Jack Moore. BA, St. Mary's U., 1962; MS, Trinity U., 1968; PhD, Tex. Tech. U., 1969; AAS in Criminal Justice, Garland County Community Coll., 1978. Psychologist Okla. rehab. div. Okla. State Reformatory, Granite, 1968-69; dir. tng. Ark. Rehab. Rsch. and Tng. Ctr., Hot Springs, 1970-71; pvt. practice psychology, Hot Springs, 1971—; exec. dir. Plummer Assocs. for Consultation and Tng., 1982—; dir. Ark. Behavioral Svcs. Clinic, 1983—; exec. officer Tng. Inst. for Edn. in Security, 1983—; clin. dir. Transpersonal Psychology Inst., Pine Bluff, Ark., 1989-91, behavioral medicine, 1995—, hosp. affliate allied health, diabetes mgmt. and edn., diabetes rsch.; psychol. cons. to Rehab. Svcs., Dept. Correction, Probation and Parole Div., 1971-98, also to physicians, attys., cts., law enforcement agys.; instr. Garland County C.C., Hot Springs, 1973—; continuing edn. instr. nursing degree program Coll. St. Francis, Joliet, Ill., 1979-86; cons. Parents Without Ptnrs. Mem. bd. L.P.N. nurse program Ouachita Vocat.-Tech. Sch., Hot Springs, 1979-85. Fellow Ark. Psychol. Assn.; mem. Nat. Rehab. Assn., Nat. Rehab. Counseling Assn., Am. Psychol. Assn., Ark. Psychol. Assn. (chmn. fellow status rev. com. 1980, 81, chmn. profl. standards rev. com. 1982, 83), Hot Springs Psychol. Assn. (pres. 1979, 80), Internat. Soc. for Study Symbols, Elks, Lions. Democrat. Roman Catholic. Contbr. articles to profl. jours., chpt. in Handbook of Measurement and Evaluation in Rehabilitation. Address: 614 Ridgeview Dr Hot Springs National Park AR 71901-7901 Office: 320 Ouachita Ave Hot Springs National Park AR 71901-5167

PLUMMER, JASON STEVEN (JAKE PLUMMER), professional football player; b. Boise, Idaho, Dec. 19, 1974; Student, Ariz. State U. Quarterback Ariz. Cardinals, Phoenix, 1997—; mem. NFC wildcard team, 1998-99. Named quarterback The Sporting News col. All-Am. 2d team, 1996. Holder regular-season record as starting NFL quarterback. Office: c/o Arizona Cardinals PO Box 888 Phoenix AZ 85001-0888 also: Arizona Cardinals 8701 S Hardy Dr Tempe AZ 85284 Office Fax: 602-379-1819.*

PLUMMER, JOHN MITCHELL, postal clerk; b. Waterbury, Conn., Nov. 18, 1950; s. John Frederick and Judith Ann (Mitchell) P. BA, New Eng. Coll., 1973; MA, Columbia U., 1998. Clk. U.S. Postal Svc., Waterbury, 1977—. Mem. Sheldon Family Assn., Conn. Profl. Genealogists Assn., N.Y. Geneal. and Biographical Soc., Conn. Soc. Genealogists, Maine Hist. Soc. Libertarian. Mem. Ch. Scientology. Avocations: walking, swimming, science fiction, paleontology, art. Home: 148 Grand St Apt 34 Waterbury CT 06702-1922 E-mail: john.plummer@snet.net.

PLUMMER, LEONE POINDEXTER, marriage and family therapist, nursing educator, nurse practitioner; b. Amarillo, Tex., Jan. 25, 1953; d. Hershel Clayton and Ellen Gertrude (Hadba) Poindexter; m. Dennis Patrick Plummer, May 20, 1978; 1 child, Cassandra Lanelle. RN diploma, NW Tex. Hosp. Sch. Nursing, Amarillo, 1975; BSN, West Tex. State U., 1978, M in Nursing, 1980; PhD, Tex. Tech U., 1985. Lic. profl. counselor; cert. respiratory therapist. From nurse critical care to nursing supr. NW Tex. Hosp., Amarillo, 1975-80; pvt. practice, 1985—; dir. grad. nursing, assoc. prof. West Tex. State U., Canyon, 1986-92; statis. cons. Amarillo Cardiovascular Surgeons, 1992-95; geriatric and family nurse practitioner Bapt. St. Anthony Health Sys., Amarillo, 1996—. Cons. Vets. Affairs Med. Ctr., Big Springs, Tex., 1988-92, Harrington Cancer Ctr., Amarillo, 1989-92. Contbr. articles to profl. jours. Mem. Assn. Marriage and Family Therapy (workshop presenter), Nat. Coun. Family Rels. (workshop presenter), Tex. Nursing Assn. (nominating com. 1987-89), Sigma Theta Tau (pres. elect 1990-92, treas. 1989-90, rec. sec. 1987-88). Avocations: restoring antiques, needlework, piano, reading, decorating.

PLUMMER, MARY ELIZABETH, cosmetologist; b. Topeka, Sept. 20, 1962; d. Robert Eugene Plummer and Nancy (Mett) Roseberry; m. Roger Eric Haubold, July 13, 1996 (div.). Grad., Hay's Sch. Hairdressing, Topeka, 1984; student, Washburn U. Cert. State Bd. Cosmetology. Cosmetologist Trade Secrets, Topeka, 1984-85, Hairitage Salon, Topeka, 1985-86, Jellybeans Hair Salon, Topeka, 1986-88, Silhouettes Hair Salon, Naples, Fla., 1988-89; cosmetologist, owner Salon Renaissance (formerly Silkey Expressions),

Topeka, 1990—. Avocations: sculpting clay figures, making paper and soap, recitating poetry. Home: 2514 SE Ohio Ave Topeka KS 66605-1320 Office: Salon Renaissance 2809 SW Fairlawn Rd Topeka KS 66614-1516 E-mail: ta_da@terraworld.net.

PLUMMER, MICHAEL KENNETH, financial consultant; b. Jacksonville, Fla., Apr. 24, 1954; s. Kenneth Albert and Edith Lorraine (O'Brien) P.; m. Amy Forté, 1992; children: Brian Michael, Daniel James. BBA in Econs., U. North Fla., 1976; MS in Real Estate, Ga. State U., 1993, postgrad., 1993—. Econ. analyst Barnett Banks of Fla., Jacksonville, 1976-78; exec. v.p. Home Owners Warranty Corp., 1978-80; market analyst Plantec Corp., 1980-81; assoc. Laventhol & Horwath, Miami and Denver, 1981-84; sr. mgr., nat. coord. corp. real estate consulting svcs. KPMG Peat Marwick (formerly Peat, Marwick, Main & Co.), Atlanta, 1984-91; sr. mng. dir. Instnl. Real Estate Advisors, Inc., 1991—. Mem. Gov.'s Econ. ADv. Com., Fla., 1982-84; econ. cons. Atlanta com. for 1996 Olympic Games; mem. steering com. Mt. Pisgah Charter Sch. Fla. Bankers Assn. scholar; named Eagle Scout Boy Scouts Am., 1972. Mem. Urban Land Inst., Country Club of the south (mem. fin. com.). Republican. Methodist. Avocations: sailing, skiing. Office: Ire Advisors Inc Ste 170 33 Technology Pkwy S Norcross GA 32097

PLUMMER, ORA BEATRICE, nursing educator, trainer; b. Mexia, Tex., May 25, 1940; d. Macie Idella (Echols); childeren: Kimberly, Kevin, Cheryl. BSN, U. N.Mex., 1961; MS in Nursing Edn., UCLA, 1966. Nurse's aide Bataan Meml. Meth. Hosp., Albuquerque, 1058-60, staff nurse, 1961-62, 67-68; staff nurse, charge nurse, relief supr. Hollywood (Calif.) Cmty. Hosp., 1962-64; instr. U. N.Mex. Coll. Nursing, Albuquerque, 1968-69; sr. instr. U. Colo. Sch. Nursing, Denver, 1971-74, asst. prof., 1974-76; staff assoc. III, Western Interstate Commn. for Highr Edn., Boulder, 1976-78; DON, Garden Manor Nursing Home, Lakewood, 1978-79, nurse surveyor, cons., 1979-87; ednl. coord. Colo. Dept. Health, Denver, 1987—96. Active in faculty devel. Colo. Cluster of Schs.; bd. dir. Domestic Violence Initiative, 2000—. Contbr. articles to profl. jours. Mem. adv. bd. Affiliated Children's and Family Svcs., 1977; mem. Colo. Instnl. Child Abuse and Neglect Adv. Com., 1984-92; trustee Colo. Acad., 1990-96; mem. planning com. State Wide Conf. on Black Health Concerns, 1977; mem. staff devel. com. Western Interstate Commn. for Higher Edn., 1978, mem. minority affairs com., 1978, mem. coordinating com. for baccalaureate program, 1971-76; active in minority affairs, U. Colo. Med. Ctr., 1971-72; mem. ednl. resources com., pub. rels. com., rev. com. for reappointment, promotion and tenure U. Colo. Sch. Nursing, 1971-76, mem. regulatory tng. com., 1989-93; mem. gerontol. adv. com. Met. State Coll., 1989-94; mem. expert panel long term care tng. manual Health Care Financing Adminstrn., Balt., 1989; mem. employee diversity com. Colo. Dept. Health, 1989-96. Mem. ANA, ASTD, NAFE, Colo. Nurses Assn. (affirmative action com. 1977-79, 93—), Phi Delta Kappa. Avocations: public speaking, training. Office: 4300 Cherry Creek South Dr Denver CO 80246-1523

PLUMMER, PAUL JAMES, consulting company executive, energy executive; b. Scottsbluff, Nebr., Aug. 3, 1946; s. Virgil Frank and Helen Louise (Hultberg) Plummer; m. Pamela Lee Purdom, June 26, 1976; 1 child Brittany Lane. BA, U. Nebr., 1968; postgrad., Platte Coll., 1974-75; MBA, U. Iowa, 1982. With Gen. Tel. Co. of the Midwest, 1968-82, divsn. traffic supr. Nebr., 1969-75, divsn. traffic mgr. Columbia, Mo., 1975-78, labor rels. adminstr. Grinnell, Iowa, 1978-79, labor rels. mgr., 1979-82, compensation and svcs. mgr., 1982; staff specialist customer svc. GTE Svc. Corp., Stamford, Conn., 1982-83, group specialist cusotmer svc., 1983-84, customer svcs. mgr., 1984-87, ops. support planning mgr., 1987-90, mgr. strategic planning telephone ops. Irving, Tex., 1989-95; mgr. bus. devel. GTE Intelligent Network Svcs., Inc., 1995-96, group product devel. mgr. Vertical Markets, 1996-97; pres., dir., CEO Cytware Corp., Bedford, Tex., 1997-99; v.p. A-Net Consulting, Inc., 1998-2000; pres., CEO I-Mgmt. Svcs. Ltd., Colleyville, Tex., 2000—01; product delivery mgr. TXU Energy, Dallas, 2001—. Vol. Nat. Marrow Donor Program; active Boy Scouts Am.; membership com. mem. North Tex. Tech. Coun.; vol. Tex. Scholar's Program; chmn. citizen's adv. com. Grapevine-Colleyville Ind. Sch. Dist., 1989—93; pres. parent-tchr. club St. Vincent Episcopal Sch. , 1993—95. Mem.: Pers. Mgmt. Assn. Columbia (exec. bd. dirs., 1st v.p. 1975—78), Ind. Telephone Pioneer Assn., Am. Assn. Pers. Adminstrn., Brookmeadows Homeowner's Assn. (pres.), Elks, Optimists Club (past. pres. Columbus, Nebr., lt. gov. Nebr. 1973—74). Episcopalian. Home: 2808 Meadowview Dr Colleyville TX 76034-4753 Office: 1601 Bryan St Dallas TX 75201 E-mail: pplummer@bigplanet.com.

PLUMMER, RISQUE WILSON, retired lawyer; b. Mobile, Ala., Oct. 13, 1910; s. Frederick Harvey and Caroline (Wilson) P.; m. Constance M. Burch, Feb. 21, 1939; children: Risque Wilson Jr., Richard Randolph. JD, U. Va., 1933. Bar: Va. 1932, Md. 1938. Atty. in charge of litigation Balt. Regional Office HOLC, 1933-38; pvt. practice law, 1938—; counsel U.S. Maritime Commn., 1942; partner firm Griffin & Plummer, 1951-73; counsel O'Connor, Preston, Glenn & Smith, Balt., 1979—. Prof. law Am. Inst. Banking, 1948—52; chmn. spkrs. com. ARC Blood Bank for Md. Contbr. articles to profl. jours. Exec. sec. Md. Commn. on Anti-Subversive Activities, 1949-50; co-founder, pres. Roland Park Baseball Leagues, Inc., 1956-57; co-founder, pres. Wyndhurst Improvement Assn., Inc., 1957-59; mem. Selective Service Adv. Bd., 1940-42. Served to lt. USNR, 1943-46, ATO, PTO, Philippines Area Ops.; gunnery officer, WWII. Fellow Internat. Acad. Law and Sci.; mem. ABA (council sect. of family law 1966-70), Md. Bar Assn. (council sect. of family and juvenile law 1968-70), Md. Assn. Trial Lawyers (gov. 1966-67), Bar Assn. Baltimore City (com. on grievances 1966-69, chmn. com. on profl. ethics 1969-70, exec. com. 1969-70), Am. Judicature Soc., Md. Health Claims Arbitration Commn. (chair arbitration panels), Am. Contract Bridge League (Silver life master, cert. dir., author The Small Club), Soc. Colonial Wars, Sons of the Revolution, Delta Tau Delta (pres. U. Va. chpt.), Phi Delta Phi. Episcopalian. Home: Highfield House Unit 512 4000 N Charles St Baltimore MD 21218-1760

PLUMMER, SAMUEL CRAIG, editor; b. Chgo., Dec. 12, 1934; s. Samuel Craig and Anne Elizabeth (Blanchard) P.; m. Vera Frances Maggia, May 6, 1967; children: Elizabeth Frances, William Middleton. BA, Knox Coll., 1956; MBA, Fordham U., 1980. Editor various publs., Chgo., 1959-63, N.Y.C., 1963-79, 87-92; freelance editor Croton on Hudson, N.Y., 1979-87, 92—. Trustee Croton-Harmon Sch. Dist., Croton on Hudson, 1982—91, Bennett Conservatory of Music, Croton on Hudson, 1981—2001, Croton Caring Com., Croton on Hudson, 1998—. Served with U.S. Army, 1957—58. Democrat. Home: 124 Young Ave Croton On Hudson NY 10520

PLUMSTEAD, WILLIAM CHARLES, quality engineer, consultant; b. Two Rivers, Wis., Nov. 2, 1938; m. Peggy Bass, July 19, 1959 (div. July 1968); children: William Jr., Jennifer, Kevin A., Keith M.; m. Vicki Newton, June 27, 1981. Student, U. Fla., 1956-58, Temple U., 1966-72, Albright Coll., 1973-75; BSBA, Calif. Coast U., 1985, MBA, 1989. Registered profl. engr., Calif. V.p. U.S. Testing Co., Inc., Hoboken, N.J., 1963-76; div. mgr. Daniel Internat., Inc., Greenville, S.C., 1976-83; group mgr. Bechtel Group, Inc., San Francisco, 1983-89; prin. engr. Fluor Daniel, Inc., Greenville, 1989-94; pres. PQT Svcs., Inc., S.C., 1994—. Author: (with others) Code/Specification Syndrome, 1976, NDT Laboratories Update, 1991, NDT in Construction, 1991, NDT-A Partner in Excellence, 1994; contbr. articles to profl. jours. Bd. dirs. Piedmont Food Bank, 1994-97. Fellow Am. Soc. Nondestructive Testing (coun. chmn. 1985-88, nat. sec., treas. 1992-93, nat. v.p. 1993-94, pres. 1994-95, chmn. bd. dirs. 1995-96), ASTM (sec. 1989-93, vice chmn. 1994-96, chmn. 1996-98, Charles Briggs award 1993, award of Merit 2000); mem. Toastmasters Internat. (pres. local chpt. 1990-91, Competent Toastmaster award 1986, Able Toastmaster award 1993). Avocations: sports, wine tasting. Home and Office: Plumstead Quality and Tng Svcs 806 Botany Rd Greenville SC 29615-1608

PLUNKET, DANIEL CLARK, retired pediatrician; b. Birmingham, Ala., May 7, 1929; s. Henry Clark and Carolyn Clark (Langford) P.; m. Lillian C. Barrington, Dec. 31, 1971; children: Dennis, Beth, Ann, Brenda, Scott. BS, Emory U., 1949, MD, 1952. Diplomate Am. Bd. Pediatrics. Intern Med. Coll. Va. Hosp., Richmond, 1952-53, resident in pediatrics, 1953-54, Tripler Army Med. Center, Honolulu, 1958-59, Walter Reed Army Inst., 1962-64; pediatrician, pediatric hematologist/oncologist acad. medicine, chief pediatric service William Beaumont Gen. Hosp., El Paso, Tex., 1959-62; commd. 1st lt. U.S. Army, 1955, advanced through grades to col., 1967; asst. chief dept. pediatrics Letterman Army Med. Center, San Francisco, 1964-65; chmn. dept. pediatrics Fitzsimons Army Med. Center, Denver, 1965-75; prof. pediat. U. Okla. Coll. Medicine, Tulsa, 1975-2000; sr. assoc. dean for clin. affairs U. Okla. Health Scis. Ctr., 1993-2000; chmn. dept. pediat. U. Okla. Coll. Medicine, 1975-96. Clin. prof. pediatrics U. Colo., Denver, 1974-75. Mem. adv. chmn. March of Dimes, Tulsa chpt., 1975-92; bd. dirs. ARC, Tulsa chpt., 1981—. Decorated Legion of Merit; Walter Reed Inst. Research fellow hematology and research, 1962-64 Mem. AMA, cad. Pediatrics, Am. Pediatric Soc., Am. Soc. Hematology. Episcopalian. Home: 2436 E 33rd St Tulsa OK 74105-2316 Fax: 918-742-2046. E-mail: dan5729@aol.com.

PLUNKET, DOLORES, art and archaeology educator; b. Chgo., Sept. 2, 1916; d. John Nagoda and Evangeline Kompare; m. John T. Plunket, July 15, 1944; children: Lucy Silver, Robert, John T. Jr., Patricia. BS, U. Ill., 1937; MA in Pre-Colombian Art, Nat. U. Mexico, Mexico City, 1975. V.p. Mexican-N.Am. Cultural Inst., Mexico City, 1985-88; dir. lecture series Selby Libr., Sarasota, Fla., 1992-96; lectr. in field. Co-author: (with A.R. L'huillier) Vision del Mundo Maya, 1978; editor Gardening in the Federal District, 1986; contbr. articles to profl. jours. V.p. Friends Selby Libr., 1992-95; pres. Mexico City Garden Club, 1985; bd. dirs. Am. Soc. Mexico, 1986-88. Home: 1301 N Tamiami Trail apt 406 Sarasota FL 34236-2423 E-mail: jplunket@aol.com.

PLUNKETT, JACK WILLIAM, writer, publisher; b. Dallas, May 17, 1950; s. Ivan Wayne and Waltina Lee (Roark) P.; m. Lynn Ann Richards (div.); 1 child, Jack W. Plunkett Jr.; m. Mary Lee Hartfelder, Dec. 8, 1972 (div.); children: Altus W., Robert L.; m. Martha Menefee Burgher, Oct. 7, 2000. Pres. Plunkett Properties Corp., Dallas, 1968-74; ind. mktg. cons., 1974-83; mgr. ptnr. Brown-Plunkett, Waxahachie, Tex., 1983—; CEO, pub. Plunkett Rsch. Ltd., Houston, 1986—. Cons. Houston Symphony, 1996-97, The Odyssey House, Houston, 1997—. Author: The Almanac of American Employers, 1985, 6th edit., 2002, Plunkett's Health Care Industry Almanac, 1995, 5th edit., 2002, Plunkett's InfoTech Industry Almanac, 1995, 3d edit., 2001, Plunkett's Financial Services Industry Almanac, 1996, 3d edit., 2002, Plunkett's Retail Industry Almanac, 1996, 3d edit., 2001, Plunkett's Entertainment and Media Industry Almanac, 1998, 2d edit., 2000, Plunkett's Energy Industry Almanac, 1999, 2d edit., 2001, Plunkett's Telecommunications Industry Almanac, 2000, 2d edit., 2002, Plunkett's E-Commerce and Internet Business Almanac, 2000, 2d edit., 2001, Plunkett's Engineering and Research Industry Almanac, 2000, Plunkett's Biotech and Genetics Industry Almanac, 2001. Chmn. Mayor's Libr. Fundraising Com., Boerne, Tex., 1988-89; founding pres. Greater Boerne Area Econ. Devel. Corp., 1986-87; dir. Boerne Area Cmty. Ctr., 1983-86; area chmn. Lamar Smith for Congress, Boerne, 1986; bd. dirs. Boerne Econ. Devel. Coun., 1992-94, Galveston Hist. Found., 1996--, Sch. of Nursing, U. Tex. Med. Br., 1996—, Sch. of Bus., U. of Houston Downtown Campus, 2001—, Strand Theater, 1996—; trustee Galveston County United Way, 1996-97; bd. dirs. Houston Symphony Orch., 1999-2000; mem. Dickens on the Strand 25th Ann. Com., 1997-98; v.p. Houston Symphony Ptnrs., 1997-98, pres.-elect, 1998-99, pres., 1999-2000; founding pres. Tex. Entrepreneurs Exch., 2000—. Recipient Houston's Singular Best award Cystic Fibrosis Found., 1997, Outstanding Acad. Book of the Yr. award Choice Mag. Editors, 1996; named outstanding chmn. Boy Scouts Am., 1983, Cmty. Vol. of Yr., Boerne Area C. of C., 1989; elected to Knights of Momus, 1998. Mem. Rotary (pres. Boerne chpt. 1988-89), The Centurions, Knights of Maximillian. Republican. Office: Plunkett Rsch Ltd PO Box 541737 Houston TX 77254-1737

PLUNKETT, JOSEPH CHARLES, electrical engineering educator; b. Centerville, Tenn., Dec. 3, 1933; s. Harold D. and Lorraine (Lewis) P. B.S., Middle Tenn. State U., 1964; B.S.E.E., U. Tenn., 1966; M.S.E.E., Ga. Inst. Tech., 1973; Ph.D., Tex. A&M U., 1978. Registered profl. engr., Mass. Devel. engr. Martin Marietta Co., Orlando, Fla., 1966-69; research engr. Raytheon Co., Wayland, Mass., 1969-71, IIT Research Inst., Annapolis, Md., 1971-72, Tex. A&M U., College Station, 1974-77; assoc. prof. elec. engring. Calif. State U.-Fresno, 1977-80, prof., 1980-93, chmn. dept., 1980-84, 89-92, prof. emeritus, 1993—; cons. Author numerous articles in field. Served to capt. Ordnance Corps, USAR, 1958-66. Mem. IEEE, Nat. Soc. Profl. Engrs., N.Y. Acad. Scis., Sigma Xi, Eta Kappa Nu. Republican. Mem. Ch. of Christ. Home: PO Box 410 Black Rock AR 72415-0410

PLUNKETT, MARVIN WAYNE, data processing company executive; b. Roseburg, Oreg., Mar. 16, 1952; s. Kenneth V. and Minnie E. (Bible) Plunkett. Student, Umpqua C.C., 1978-79. Founder, owner Profit Systems Software, Roseburg, 1979—; founder, exec. dir. 1st Hand History Found., 2001—. Mem.: Roseburg Optimist Club (bd. dirs. 1993—95). Office: Profit Sys Software 1641 NW Rutter Ln Roseburg OR 97470-1949

PLUSK, RONALD FRANK, manufacturing company executive; b. Chgo., Mar. 30, 1933; s. Frank and Ann (Petrauskas) P.; m. Rose Marie Pawlikowski, May 25, 1957; children— Frank A., Ronald S., Cynthia Marie. BSC., Loyola U., Chgo., 1954; postgrad., Northwestern U., 1957-59. Mgmt. cons. Peat, Marwick, Mitchell & Co., Chgo., 1963-66; corp. controller Varo, Inc., Garland, Tex., 1966-69; dir. planning and mgmt. systems Rucker Co., Oakland, Calif., 1969-72, dir. ops., audit and systems, 1972-76, v.p. ops., audit and systems, 1976-77; v.p. fin. adminstrn. Rucker Co. (merged with NL Petroleum Svcs. Co.), Houston, 1977-79; v.p. fin., treas. Cobe Labs., Inc., Lakewood, Colo., 1979-92; dir. Ctr. for Hearing Speech and Learning, Denver, 1996—. Contbr. articles to profl. jours. Served to 1st lt. AUS, 1954-56, ETO. Mem. Am. Mgmt. Assn., Planning Execs. Inst., Fin. Execs. Inst. Roman Catholic. Home: 6151 S Middlefield Rd Littleton CO 80123-6620

PLUSQUELLEC, HERVE LOUIS, irrigation and agricultural engineering consultant; b. France, Oct. 23, 1935; s. Andre Jules and Annick Germaine Plusquellec; m. Kyung-Hee Kim, Oct. 1997. Degree in hydraulics engring., Ecole Nat. Sup. d'Hydraulique, Grenoble, France, 1960; MS, U. Grenoble, 1960. Engr. Office Nat. des Irrigations, Rabat, Morocco, 1963-71; project mgr. ELC Electroconsult, Milan, 1971-76; adviser World Bank, Washington, 1976-97, cons., 1997—. Author: Water Control in Irrigation, 1990; Performance of Irrigation: Design Mgmt. and Policy, FAO book, 2002; contbr. articles to sci. and profl. jours. With French Navy, 1960-62. Recipient Best Response award ASCE, 2001. Mem. Assn. Française de l'Irrigation et du Drainage, Internat. Commn. on Irrigation and Drainage (observer). Avocations: overseas travel, hiking. Home: 3257 A Sutton Pl Washington DC 20016 E-mail: plusquel@earthlink.net.

PLUSQUELLIC, DONALD L. mayor; b. Akron, Ohio, July 3, 1949; m. Mary Plusquellic; children: Dave, Michelle. BS, Bowling Green State U., 1972; JD, U. Akron, 1981. Councilman Akron City Council, 1973-81, councilman-at-large, 1982-86, council pres., 1984-86; mayor City of Akron, 1987—. Trustee U.S. Conf. of Mayors. Home: 2785 Nesmith Lake Blvd Akron OH 44314-3427 Office: Office of the Mayor 200 Municipal Bldg 166 S High St Akron OH 44308-1626

PLUTA, RYSZARD, neuropathologist, educator; b. Biała Podlaska, Poland, Apr. 16, 1952; s. Marian and Antonina (Szarubko) P. Student, Humboldt U., Berlin, 1975, U. Cologne, Germany, 1976; MD, scientist, Med. Acad., Lublin, Poland, 1977; PhD, Polish Acad. Scis., Warsaw, 1983. Intern gynaecology unit State Hosp., Biała Podlaska, 1977; intern dept. pediatry Med. Acad., Warsaw, 1978; intern internal medicine and surgery units Czerniakowski Hosp., 1978; sci. visitor lab. of CNS Resuscitation Pathology, Inst. Gen. Reanimatology, USSR Acad. Med. Scis., Moscow, 1979; sr. rsch. asst. Polish Acad. Sci., Warsaw, 1981-87, asst. prof., 1987-94, assoc. prof., 1994—; postdoctoral fellow NIH, Bethesda, Md., 1986-88; prof. Acad. Phys. Edn., Warsaw, 1995—2002; resident neurology Med. Acad., 1997. Postdoctoral rsch. fellow, vis. prof. N.Y. State Inst. Basic Rsch., Staten Island, 1988—89, 1990—91, 1993—94, 1997; vice-chmn., bd. dirs. State Hosp., Biala Podlaska, 1999—2000; mem. sci. coun. Acad. Phys. Edn., Warsaw, 1995—2002, mem. senate, 1996—99; mem. sci. coun. Inst. Phys. Edn. and Sport, Biala Podlaska, 1996—2002; mem. Polish com. sci. rsch. SPUB, Warsaw, 2001—. Contbr. articles to profl. jours. Mem. Polish com. sci. rsch. SPUB, Warsaw, 2001—; chief Trade Union Solidarnosc Med. Rsch. Ctr., 1980—90, Dem. Union, Dist. Biala Podlaska, 1990—94; candidate Polish Parliament, 1991, 1993. 2nd lt. Polish mil., 1977. Mem.: U. Sports Assn. of Acad. Phys. Edn., Polish Acad. Sci., Polish Assn. Neuropathologists, N.Y. Acad. Sci., Internat. Soc. Neuropathology, Internat. Soc. Cerebral Blood Flow and Metabolism, Internat. Soc. Brain Edema Rsch., Polish Neurosci. Soc., European Soc. Clin. Respiratory Physiology. Roman Catholic. Avocations: politics, sports, good food, cooking. Office: Med Rsch Ctr Dept Neuropath Pawińskiego Str 5 02-106 Warsaw Poland

PLUTA, TOM, lawyer; b. Ludlow, Mass., Oct. 16, 1950; s. John J. and Stella M. (Gruszka) P. Cert., A. Mickiewicz U., Poznań, Poland, 1971, Gosudarstvenniy U., St. Petersburg, Russia, 1972; BA, Boston U., 1972; JD, Boston Coll., 1975; cert., Harvard U., 1975. Bar: Mass. 1975, D.C. 1977, U.S. Ct. Internat. Trade 1981, U.S. Supreme Ct. 1981. Fgn. svc. officer U.S. Dept. State, Washington and Helsinki, Finland, 1976-81; lawyer Arlington, Va., 1981-83; counsel, Bd. Vets. Appeals U.S. Dept. Vets. Affairs, Washington, 1983—. Editor Boston Coll. Jour. Internat. Law, 1974-75. Republican. Roman Catholic. Avocations: history, politics, foreign travel, beaching. Home: 5610 Durbin Rd Bethesda MD 20814-1014 Office: 810 Vermont Ave NW Washington DC 20420-0001

PLUTCHAK, NOEL BERNARD, meteorologist, consultant; b. Green Bay, Wis., Dec. 14, 1932; s. Bernard Edward and Violet Marie P.; m. Sandra Kolvig (div.); 1 child, Channin. BS in Geology, U. Wis., 1960; MS in Meteorology, Fla. State U., 1964; postgrad., Oreg. State U. Research asst. Columbia U., Lamont Geol. Inst., Nyack, N.Y., 1960-64; dir. theoretical studies Bendix Marine Advisors, La Jolla, Calif., 1965-69; research assoc. U. So. Calif., Los Angeles, 1972-75; chief scientist Interstate Electronics, Ocean Engring. Div., Anaheim, Calif., 1975-83, Raytheon Svcs., Ocean Engring. Div., Ventura, 1984-87; chief exec. officer, chief scientist Active Leak Testing, Inc., San Pedro, 1987—. Contbr. articles to profl. jours.; patentee in field. With USAF, 1952-56. Mem. Am. Geophys. Union, Marine Tech. Soc., Exptl. Aircraft Assn., Am. Chem. Soc. Republican. Avocations: soaring, wind surfing, tennis. Office: Active Leak Testing Inc 2500 via Cabrillo Marina Ste 200 San Pedro CA 90731-7224 E-mail: noel90007@yahoo.com.

PLYLER, JOHN LANEY, JR. retired healthcare management professional; b. Greenville, S.C., Jan. 31, 1934; s. John Laney and Beatrice Elizabeth (Dennis) P.; m. Caroline Raysor Williams, June 26, 1959; children: Sharon, John III, James (dec.). Student, U.S. Naval Acad., 1953-54; BA, Furman U., 1956; MHA, Duke U., 1970. Prodn. planner J. P. Stevens & Co., Greenville, 1958-65; mgmt. engr., outpatient mgr. Greenville Hosp. Sys., 1967-68; assoc. dir. Cleveland Meml. Hosp., Shelby, N.C., 1970-79; exec. v.p., COO Bapt. Med. Ctr., Oklahoma City, 1979-85; group v.p. SunHealth Alliance, Charlotte, N.C., 1985-86, sr. v.p., 1986-96, ret., 1996. 2d lt. U.S. Army, 1957, capt. USAR, 1957-65. Fellow Am. Coll. Healthcare Execs. (life fellow, ethics com. 1990-93, chmn. 1992-93), Okla. Hosp. Assn. (coun. on edn.), N.C. Hosp. Assn. (coun. on pers.). Avocations: travel, photography. Home: PO Box 909 Davidson NC 28036-0909 E-mail: plylerj@bellsouth.net.

PLYMALE, IDA RUTH DUFFEY, journalist, educator; b. Huntington, W.Va., Jan. 4, 1936; d. Joseph Ivanhoe and Ruth (Wilson) Duffey; m. John F. Plymale, Dec. 26, 1956 (div. Dec. 1973); children: Melinda Kay, John Alan. AB cum laude, Marshall U., 1957, MA in broadcasting, 1971; PhD in Journalism, U. N.C., 1978. Vis. prof. N.C. State U., Raleigh, 1974-77; coord. hosp. programs Duke U. Med. Ctr., Durham, N.C., 1978-81; dir. devel. pub. rels. N.C. Mus. Life Sci., 1981-84, Castle Heights Mil. Acad., Lebanon, Tenn., 1984-86; v.p. devel. pub. rels. Literacy Vols. Am., Syracuse, N.Y., 1986-88; exec. dir. La. Mus. Found., New Orleans, 1988-90; dir. devel.-corp. and found. rels. St. Mary's Coll. Minn., Winona, 1990-92; assoc. prof. pub. rels. Murray (Ky.) State U., 1992-94; assoc. prof. journalism Southern U., New Orleans, 1994—. Contbr. articles to profl. jours. Mem. ASCD, Nat. Coun. Tchrs. English, Journalism Edn. Assn., Pub. Rels. Soc. Am., Nat. Soc. Fund Raising Execs., Kappa Tau Alpha. Democrat. Avocation: southern cooking. Home: 1224 Lake Ave Apt 308 Metairie LA 70005-1928 Office: Southern U at New Orleans 6400 Press Dr New Orleans LA 70126-1009

PNIAKOWSKI, ANDREW FRANK, structural engineer; b. Grodno, Poland, Aug. 18, 1930; s. Josef Leon and Janina (Kodzynski) P.; Diploma Engr., Politechnika Warszawska, 1952; m. Margaret M. Czajkowski, Aug. 15, 1957; 1 dau., Mary. Bridge design and field engr. Govt. of Poland, Ministry of R.R., Warsaw, 1952-57; bridge design engr. Dept. Hwys., of Ont. (Can.), Toronto, 1958-66; sr. structural engr. Sverdrup & Parcel Assos. Inc., Boston, 1967-71; chief structural engr. Louis Berger & Assos. Inc., Needham, Mass., 1972-96; cons. engr. in transp., bridges, hwys., railroads, pub. bldgs., others. Registered profl. engr., Ont., Mass., Maine, N.H. Mem. Am. Inst. Steel Constrn., Am. Concrete Inst., Prestressed Concrete Inst., Assn. Profl. Engrs. of Province Ont. Roman Catholic.

POACELLI, DOLORES, fine artist, graphic designer; b. Phila., Oct. 3, 1945; d. Joseph John and Ida Rita (Quartapella) Esposito; m. Michael Angelo Poacelli, Nov. 12, 1966; children: Michele, Michael and Joseph (twins). Artist, painter, graphic designer, 1964—. Exhbited in numerous shows; included in many collections including Global Focus Collection, Beijing, China; designer Collingwood Centennial History Book and Calendar, 1988; designer-producer Collingswood Calendars, 1988, 89, 90, 91. Trustee Collingswood (N.J.) Pub. Libr., 1977—. Design awards include Artistic Designer award Print Mag., 1986, 87, Phila. Mus. Art Posters. Home: 306 Harrison Ave Collingswood NJ 08108-2919

POAD, FLORA VIRGINIA, retired librarian and educator; b. Roanoke, Va., Oct. 8, 1921; d. Thomas Franklin and Ethlind (Wertz) Huff; m. Stanley Theodore Benton, Dec. 24, 1942 (div. Oct. 1983); children: Peggy, Betty, Mary Jo, Lucy; m. James Joseph Poad, June 6, 1986. Student, Radford Coll., 1939-41, Ohio U., 1956-57; BS in Edn., Ohio No. U., 1960; MA in LS, U. Toledo, 1964; postgrad., Kent State U., 1964-66, 71. Reference asst. Roanoke Pub. Libr., 1939-42; catalog asst. Univ. Libr., Emory U., Atlanta, 1942; sec. ARC; catalog asst. Pickerington (Ohio) Pub. Libr., 1950-51; tchr. Celina (Ohio) Pub. Schs., 1957-62; tchr., libr. Toledo Pub. Schs., 1962-64; libr. supr. Oregon (Ohio) Pub. Schs., 1964-85; instr. U. Toledo, 1970, reference libr., 1971-86; tchr. Sylvan Learning Ctr., Toledo, 1985-92; ret., 1992. Mem. evaluation team Ohio Dept. Edn., Columbus, 1973; rep. Ohio Gov.'s Conf. on Librs., Columbus, 1974; chmn., mem. adv. bd. libr. sci. dept. Cmty.-Tech. Coll., 1965-69. Editor Ohio Assn. Sch. Librs. Bull., 1968-71. Vol. Am. Cancer Soc., Toledo, 1946-48, 86-87, Mobile Meals, Toledo, 1986-93, Helping Hands, Toledo, 1994—. Mem. Am. Assn. Ret. Persons, Delta Kappa Gamma, Pi Lambda Theta, Kappa Delta Pi, Phi Kappa Phi. Avocations: reading, walking, crafts.

POATS, LILLIAN BROWN, education educator; b. Gary, Ind., Dec. 4, 1951; d. Joe Freeman and Jimmye Marie (Jones) Brown; m. Greyling Byron Poats, June 30, 1973; 1 child, Greyling Byron II. BA, Purdue U., 1972; MEd, Tex. So. U., 1975, EdD, 1984. Tchr. Gary (Ind.) Cmty. Sch. Corp., 1972-74; univ. psychomotreist Tex. So. U., Houston, 1974-77, 81-84; coord. acad. advising Purdue U., Hammond, Ind., 1977-79; educator, counselor Planned Parenthood-Northwest Ind., Merrillville, 1979-81; dir. student support U. Tex. Health Sci. Ctr., Houston, 1984-89; prof. edn. Tex. So. U., 1989—. Chair black caucus exec. bd. Am. Assn. Higher Edn., Washington, 1995-97; faculty fellow U.S. Dept. Def., Pentagon, Washington, 1993. Contbr. articles to profl. jours., chpts. to books. Mem. Ft. Bend Edn. Found., Ft. Bend County CPS Bd. Named Woman of Excellence Suburban Sugarland (Tex.) Women's Assn., 1994. Mem. Purdue U. Alumni Assn., Phi Delta Kappa, Delta Sigma Theta (pres. suburban Houston-Ft. Bond chpt. 1991-92). Avocations: reading, sewing. E-mail: Poats. Home: 3702 Pin Oak Ct Missouri City TX 77459-7017 Office: Tex Southern U 3100 Cleburne St Houston TX 77004-4501 E-mail: lb@tsu.edw., Poats2@cs.com.

POBER, JORDAN STUART, pathology, immunobiology and dermatology educator; b. N.Y.C., May 13, 1949; s. Irving and Ruth Pober; m. Barbara R. Herzog, June 6, 1971; children: Jeremy, Jonathan. BA, Haverford Coll., 1971; MD, PhD, Yale U., 1977. Diplomate Am. Bd. Anatomic Pathology. Resident in pathology Yale-New Haven Hosp., 1977—78; postdoctoral fellow in biochemistry Harvard U., 1978—80; resident in pathology Brigham and Women's Hosp., Boston, 1980—81; asst. prof. pathology Harvard Med. Sch., 1981-86, assoc. prof. pathology, 1986-91; prof. pathology, immunobiology and biology Yale U., New Haven, 1991-98, prof. pathology, immunology and dermatology, 1998—. Dir. molecular cardiobiology program Yale Med. Sch., 1991-99, dir. vascular biology and transplantation, 1999—; cons. in field. Author: Cellular and Molecular Immunology, 1991, 4th edit., 2000; editor jour. Lab. Investigation, 1995—, Immunity, 2000—; contbr. over 200 articles to profl. jours. Recipient Merit award Nat. Heart, Lung and Blood Inst., 1992-2002, Established Investigator award Am. Heart Assn., 1985, 90, Warner Lambert/Parke Davis award Am. Assn. Pathologists, 1988; Searle scholar, 1982-85. Mem. Am. Soc. Investigative Pathology (councilor 1996-99), Am. Assn. Immunologists, U.S.-Can. Acad. Pathology, N.Am. Vascular Biology Orgn. (pres. 1997-98), Molecular Medicine Soc. Office: 295 Congress Ave New Haven CT 06536-0812 E-mail: jordan.pober@yale.edu.

POBEREZNY, TOM, federal agency administrator; m. Sharon Poberezny; 1 child Lesley. B in Indsl. Engring., Northwestern U. Pres., CEO Exptl. Aircraft Assn., Oshkosh, Wis., 1989—. Mem. Eagles Aerobatic Team; chmn. ann. AirVenture Fly-In Conv. Exptl. Aircraft Assn., 1972—; founder Project SchoolFlight, EAA Air Acad., Air Adventure Days, Vision of Eagles; mem. Centennial of Flight Commn.; bd. dirs. Competitive Wis.; founding mem. U.S. Aerobatic Found. Achievements include U.S. Nat. Aerobatic champion, 1972; mem. team World Aerobatic Championship, France, 1972. Office: EAA Aviation Ctr PO Box 3086 Oshkosh WI 54903-3086*

POCH, HERBERT EDWARD, retired pediatrician, educator; b. Elizabeth, N.J., Sept. 4, 1927; s. William and Min (Herman) P.; m. Leila Kosberg, Aug. 27, 1952; children: Bruce Jeffrey, Andrea Susan, Lesley Grace. AB, Columbia U., 1949, MD, 1953. Diplomate Am. Bd. Pediatrics. Intern Kings County Hosp. Ctr., Bklyn., 1953-54; resident Babies Hosp., Columbia-Presbyn. Med. Ctr., N.Y.C., 1954-56; pvt. practice medicine specializing in pediatrics Elizabeth, 1956-92. Pres. med. staff, 1989, attending pediatrician Elizabeth Gen. Med. Ctr., 1973, sr. attending pediatrician, 1990, hon. staff, 1993—; attending pediatrician St. Elizabeth Hosp., 1968, chmn. dept. pediatrics, 1971-81, attending pediatrician Monmouth Med. Ctr., 1991-99, emeritus, 1999—, assoc. program dir. pediatrics; instr. pediatrics Columbia U., 1956-72, asst. clin. prof. pediatrics, 1972-91; clin. assoc. prof. pediatrics MCP Hahnemann Sch. Medicine, 1997-99; ret. With AUS, 1945-46. Fellow Am. Acad. Pediatrics; mem. N.J. Med. Soc., Ambulatory Pediatric Assn. Address: 1175 Ocean Ave Long Branch NJ 07740-4518 E-mail: hpoch@comcast.net.

POCHAPIN, JAY FRANK, marketing executive; b. Pitts., Feb. 4, 1954; s. Sherman Wallace Pochapin and Freda Roberta (Kahn) Lindblom. BS in Radio-Television, Syracuse U., 1975. Newswriter, announcer WAER-FM, Syracuse, N.Y., 1972-73; announcer, engr. WMBA-Radio, Inc., Ambridge, Pa., 1973, WKEG Radio, Inc., Washington, 1974; newswriter, announcer WQED-FM, Pitts., 1975-76; dir. news & pub. affairs WFFM/WLOA Radio, Inc., 1977-79; prodr. pub. affairs WWSW, Inc., 1979-80; customer svc. rep. WRSMotion PictureLab., 1981-82; traffic reporter AAA West Pa./W.Va., 1983-94; dir. news & pub. affairs WLTJ-FM & WRRK-FM, 1995-98; media rels. mgr. St. Barnabas Health Sys., Gibsonia, 1998—2000; dir. comms. Pitts. Airport Area C. of C., 2001—. Mem.: AFTRA, Soc. Profl. Journalists (bd. dirs. Pitts. chpt.), Am. Mktg. Assn. (bd. dirs. Pitts. chpt.). Democrat. Jewish.

POCHI, PETER ERNEST, physician; b. Boston, Mar. 8, 1929; s. Anesti and Alice (Peterson) P.; m. Barbara Orlob, June 11, 1955; children: Alan, Rena. AB cum laude, Harvard Coll., 1950; MD, Boston U., 1955. Diplomate Am. Bd. Dermatology. Intern Boston City Hosp., 1955-56, vis. dermatologist, 1978-91, assoc. dir., 1967-74, 78-84, acting chief dermatology, 1984-85; resident in dermatology Boston U. Hosp., 1958-61, vis. dermatologist, 1977-91, acting chief dermatology, 1984-85; assoc. in medicine Peter Bent Brigham Hosp., Boston, 1972-78; sr. cons. in dermatology Lemuel Shattuck Hosp., 1975-91; Herbert Mescon prof. dermatology Sch. Medicine, Boston U., 1988-91, prof. emeritus, 1991—, interim chmn. dept. dermatology, 1984-85. Cons. med. service in dermatology Boston VA Hosp., 1978-82; lectr. dermatology Sch. Medicine, Tufts U., 1980-91; assoc. staff New Eng. Med. Ctr. Hosp., 1981-91. Assoc. editor: Jour. Investigative Dermatology, 1968-73; contbg. editor: Year Book of Dermatology, 1983-90; mem. editorial bd.: Archives of Dermatology, 1979-84, Jour. Am. Acad. Dermatology, 1981-90; contbr. articles to med. jours. Bd. dirs. Cmty. Music Ctr., 1973-77, 97—, corp. mem., 1994-97; governing bd. Boston Musical Theater, 2000—. With USN, 1956-58. USPHS fellow, 1960-62, 62-63; USPHS grantee, 1965-84 Fellow Am. Acad. Dermatology (bd. dirs. 1981-85); mem. Am. Fedn. Clin. Research, AMA, Boston Dermatological Club (sec.-treas. 1967-69), Boston U. Sch. Medicine Alumni Assn. (pres. 1979-80), Boston U. Nat. Alumni Council, Dermatology Found., Evans Med. Found. (dir., sec.), Internat. Soc. Dermatology, Mass. Acad. Dermatology, Mass. Med. Soc. (chmn. sect. dermatology 1977-78), New Eng. Dermatol. Soc., Soc. Investigative Dermatology (bd. dirs. 1976-81, v.p. 1986-87). Home: 333 Commonwealth Ave Boston MA 02115-1933 E-mail: pepderm@bu.edu.

POCHICK, FRANCIS EDWARD, financial consultant; b. Metuchen, N.J., May 28, 1931; s. Frank Stephen and Bertha Barbara Pochick; m. Shirley Ann Elliott, Feb. 16, 1957; children: Bonnie Lynn, Keith Francis. Student, Rutgers U., 1949-50, 54-55. Agt. New Eng. Mut. Life. Ins. Co., Newark and New Brunswick, N.J., 1958-61, Lambert M. Huppeler Co., Inc., N.Y.C., 1962-64, cons., 1964, sr. cons. employee benefits, 1967-87; fin. cons. Francis E. Pochick Assocs., 1987—. Mem. adv. bd. Mercer Fund, Cmty. Found. N.J., 1986—, Rec. for the Blind, Princeton, 1989, charitable devel. officer Nat. Found., Inc., 1992, Nat. Coun. on The Aging, Planned Giving Coun. 1994; mem. com. bd. dirs. health Princeton Coun. Planned Giving, 1993; v.p. The Benefits Planning Co., Ltd., Charlottesville, Va., 1995. With USMC, 1951-54. Mem. Am. Soc. Pension Actuaries, Nat. Assn. Life Underwriters, Fin. Planning Assn., Estate Planning Coun., Nat. Assn. Philanthropic Planners, Lions, Glenmore Country Club. Home: 1451 Bremerton Ln Keswick VA 22947-9147 Office: PO Box 518 Keswick VA 22947-0518 also: No Jersey Br 30 Two Bridges Rd Fairfield NJ 07004-1550

POCHINI, JUDY HAY, interior designer, writer, editor; b. Phoenix, Mar. 16, 1932; d. Cecil Clifford and Nadine Mary (Larimer) Cook; m. Gordon Eugene Hay, June 5, 1971 (dec. 1974); m. Robert Frank Pochini, Sept. 18, 1983 (dec. 1995). BA, U. Calif., Santa Barbara, 1953; MA in Journalism, U. Calif., Berkeley, 1965. Exec. sec. Mobil Oil Corp., Mpls., 1958-60, Kaiser Aluminum & Chem. Corp., Oakland, Calif., 1960-64; asst. trade publ. editor Sunset mag., Menlo Park, 1966-68, trade publ. editor, 1968-73; owner, home furnishings editor Lifestyle West, Walnut Creek, 1974-79; interior designer Berman's Drexel-Heritage, Oakland, 1979-85, Suburban House Drexel-Heritage, Concord, Calif., 1986-87; ptnr., interior designer Judy Hay Interiors, Lafayette and Santa Barbara, 1987-95, owner, 1995—. Mem. nat. consumer action panel Carpet & Rug Industry, Dalton, Ga., 1973-75; cons. in field. Contbr. articles to profl. jours. Mem. Internat. Furnishings & Design Assn., Women in Communications Inc., Am. Assn. of U. Women, Chi Omega. Democrat. Mem. Unity Ch. Office: Judy Hay Interiors 1324 State St # J173 Santa Barbara CA 93101-2620

POCKER, YESHAYAU, chemistry, biochemistry educator; b. Kishinev, Romania, Oct. 10, 1928; came to U.S., 1961; naturalized, 1967. s. Benzion Israel and Esther Sarah (Sudit) P.; m. Anna Goldenberg, Aug. 8, 1950; children: Rona, Elon I. MSc, Hebrew U., Jerusalem, 1949; PhD, Univ. Coll., London, Eng., 1953; DSc, U. London, 1960. Rsch. assoc. Weizmann Inst. Sci., Rehovot, Israel, 1949-50; humanitarian trust fellow Univ. Coll., 1951-52, asst. lectr., 1952-54, lectr., 1954-61; vis. assoc. prof. Ind. U., Bloomington, 1960-61; prof. U. Washington, Seattle, 1961—. Bicentennial lectr. Mont. State U., Bozeman, 1976; Horizons in Chemistry lectr. U. N.C., Chapel Hill, 1977, guest lectr. U. Kyoto, Japan, 1984; Edward A. Doisy vis. prof. biochemistry St. Louis U. Med. Sch., 1990; plenary lectr. N.Y. Acad. Sci., 1983, Fast Reactions in Biol. Systems, Kyoto, Japan, 1984, NATO, 1989, Consiglio nat. delle Richerche, U. Bari, Italy, 1989, Sigma Tau, Spoleto, Italy, 1990; Internat. lectr. Purdue U., 1990; cons. NIH, 1984, 86, 88; Spl. Topic lectr. on photosynthesis, Leibniz House, Hanover, Fed. Republic Germany, 1991; enzymology, molecular biology lectr., Dublin, Ireland, 1992; 3M lectr., St. Paul, 1996; enzymology, molecular biology, retinal metabolism lectr., Deadwood, S.D., 1996, fast reactions in solutions and Bronsted symposium lectr., Copenhagen, 1997, self assembly kinetics of Alzheimer beta-amyloid peptides, ultrafast studies of insulin-insulin and insulin-receptor interactions; 1st Bannan invited lectr. Seattle U., spring, 1999; invited Bannan lectr. Seattle U., 2000, Alzheimer and Prion Proteins; internat. conf. Port Townsend, Wash., 2000, lectr. water sensing mechanisms, internat. symposium, Taos, N. Mex., 2000, internat. lectr. enzymology, molecular biology. Mem. editorial adv. bd. Inorganica Chimica Acta-Bioinorganic Chemistry, 1981-89; bd. reviewing editors Sci., 1985-2000; contbr. numerous articles to profl. jours.; pub. over 220 papers and 12 revs. Numerous awards worldwide, 1983-97. Mem. Royal Soc. Chemistry, Am. Chem. Soc. (nat. spkr. 1970, 74, 84, chmn. Pauling award com. 1978, plaque awards 1970, 74, 84, Outstanding Svc. award 1979, chmn. selection com. Pauling award 1996), Soc. Exptl. Biology, Am. Soc. Biol. Chemists, N.Y. Acad. Scis., Sigma Xi (nat. lectr. 1971). Avocations: Aramaic, etymology, history, philology, poetry. Office: U Wash Dept Chemistry PO Box 351700 Seattle WA 98195-1700

POCOCK, FREDERICK JAMES, environmental scientist, engineer, consultant; b. Canton, Ohio, May 28, 1923; s. Frederick Stanley and Mary Elizabeth (Tinker) P.; m. Lois Jean Rice, Jan. 12, 1952; children— Kathleen Jean, David Walter. BS in Chemistry, Mt. Union Coll., 1950; grad., Lincoln Aero Inst., 1942; postgrad., Akron U., 1953. Aircraft insp. Bell Aircraft Corp., 1942; in tech. sales Republic Steel Corp., 1949-50; with Babcock & Wilcox Co., Alliance, Ohio, 1950-88; sr. scientist Alliance Research Center, 1974-88. Cons. water technology, 1989-99. Contbr. articles to profl jours. Served with USAAF, 1943-46. Recipient recognition for 30 yrs. rsch. Ohio Ho. of Reps., 1980, award of merit Internat. Water Conf., 1985; co-recipient Paul Cohen Meml. award, 1993, Engrs. award for disting. svc. Soc. Profl. Engrs., 1987; named to Minerva H.S. Hall of Fame; recognized by 122d Ohio Senate, 1997. Fellow ASME (co-recipient Prime Movers award 1962, Disting. Svc. award 1987, Dedicated Svc. award 1987); mem. Am. Chem. Soc. (Cert. of Merit 1967, emertius mem. award).

POCOSKI, DAVID JOHN, cardiologist; b. Waterbury, Conn., July 15, 1945; s. Edward J. and Stella E. (Kolpa) P.; m. Madelyn M. Pocoski, Sept. 25, 1971; 1 child, Sarah C. BS, U. Conn., 1967; MD magna cum laude, Upstate Med. Ctr., Syracuse, N.Y., 1971. From intern to fellow in cardiology U. Rochester, N.Y.; founder, pres. Osler Clin. of Medicine, Melbourne, Fla.; pres., chief of staff, dir. cardiac rehab. Sea Pines Rehab. Hosp. Commr. Holy Name Jesus Cath. Ch. Maj. USAF, 1974-76. Recipient Outstanding Scientist of the 20th Century award. Fellow Am. Coll. Cardiology; mem. AMA. Republican. Roman Catholic. Avocations: music, art, running, community service. Office: 930 S Harbor City Blvd Melbourne FL 32901-1963

POCRASS, RICHARD DALE, management consultant; b. Meadville, Pa., Mar. 7, 1940; s. Irving F. and Roslyn (Sperber) P.; m. Rena Levy, Feb. 3, 1968; children: Michael B., S. Douglas. BS in Math., U. Pitts., 1962, MBA in Fin., 1964. EDP sales mgr. NCR Corp., Pitts., 1962-67, retail mktg. mgr. L.A., 1972-74; v.p., dir. Nanoseconds Sys., Fairfield, Conn., 1967-69, dir., 1968-72; v.p. gen. mgr. Hart Jewelry Co., Warren, Ohio, 1969-71, dir., 1981-84; mktg. mgr. Data Source Corps subs. Hercules, Inc., El Segundo, 1974-75; pres. Webster-Pocrass & O'Neil (name changed to Pocrass Assocs. 1981), L.A., 1976—, Health Tech. Inc. Pub. CEO, chmn. bd. dirs. Chocolates a la Carte, Valencia, Calif. Author: The Recruitment Letter; author (with Maronde) Drug Abuse Study for Hoffman LaRoche, 1980. Bd. dirs. West Valley Little League, U.S. Pastry Alliance, Providence Holly Cross Med. Ctr. Found., L.A. Mission Coll. Found., Western Overseas, Inc., Long Beach, Calif. Mem. Am. Mktg. Assn. L.A. Spkrs. Bur., Soc. for Human Resource Mgmt., L.A. Area C. of C., Bank Mktg. Assn., Retail Controllers Assn., Calif. Exec. Recruiters Assn., Pers. and Indsl. Rels. Assn., Internat. Platform Assn., Rotary. Republican. Jewish. Home: 18815 Paseo Nuevo Dr Tarzana CA 91356-5136 Office: 28455 Livingston Ave Valencia CA 91355-4173 E-mail: rick@candymaker.com.

POCS, MARTIN M. executive search consultant; b. Rockford, Ill., Sept. 25, 1961; s. Eugene and Mara Pocs; m. Christine Ann Pocs, June 8, 1985; children: Erica, Lara. BSBA, No. Ill. U., 1983, MS in Mgmt., 1987. Human resources mgr. Sundstrand Corp., Rockford, 1983-94; dir. human resources Founders Funds, Denver, 1994-96; exec. v.p., vice chmn. DHR Internat., 1996—. Acct. exec. United Way, Rockford, Denver, 1986-91; treas., vice chmn., chmn. Goodwill Industries, Denver, 1990—. Named Forty under 40 Denver Bus. Jour., 1999; inductee Rock Valley Coll. Alumni Hall of Fame, 2000. Mem. LKSA Ozintars. Roman Catholic. Avocations: golfing, skiing, traveling, biking. Home: 10999 Meade Ct Westminster CO 80031-2128 Office: DHR Internat Inc 1200 17th St Denver CO 80202-5835 E-mail: mpocs@dhrintl.net.

PODBERESKY, SAMUEL, lawyer; b. Cremona, Italy, Mar. 16, 1946; came to U.S., 1947; s. Noah and Mina (Milikowsky) P.; m. Rosita Rubinstein, March 8, 1970; children: Daniel J., Michael J. BS in Aeronautical Engring., U. Md., 1967; JD, U. Md., Balt., 1971. Bar: Md. 1972. Flight test engr. Vertol div. Boeing Co., Phila., 1967-68; regulatory atty. FAA, Washington, 1971-78; dep. asst. gen. counsel U.S. Dept. Transp., 1978-86, asst. gen. counsel aviation enforcement and proceedings, 1986—. Office: US Dept Transp 400 7th St SW Washington DC 20590-0001

PODBOY, ALVIN MICHAEL, JR. law library director, lawyer; b. Cleve., Feb. 10, 1947; s. Alvin Michael and Josephine Esther (Nagode) P.; m. Mary Ann Gloria Esposito, Aug. 21, 1971; children: Allison Marie, Melissa Ann. AB cum laude, Ohio U., 1969; JD, Case Western Res. U., 1972, MLS, 1977. Bar: Ohio 1972, U.S. Dist. Ct. (no. dist.) Ohio 1973, U.S. Supreme Ct. 1992. Assoc. Joseph T. Svete Co. LPA, Chardon, Ohio, 1972-76; dir. pub. svcs. Case Western Res. Sch. Law Libr., Cleve., 1974-77, assoc. law libr., 1977-78; libr. Baker & Hostetler, LLP, 1978-88, dir. librs., 1988—. Instr. Notre Dame Coll. of Ohio, Cleve., 1991-2002, Am. Inst. Paralegal Studies, Cleve., 1991-96. Bd. overseers Case Western Res. U., 1981-87, mem. vis. com. sch. libr. sci., 1980-86, mem. Westlaw adv. bd., 1987-92, bd. govs. law sch. alumni assn., 1992-95, West's Legal Directory Ohio Adv. Panel, 1990-91; mem. adv. com. West's Info. Innovators Inst., 1995-97; chmn. Case Western Res. Libr. Sch. Alumni Fund, 1979-80; Rep. precinct committeeman Cuyahoga County, Cleve., 1981-95, mem. exec. com., 1984-87. 1st lt. USAF, 1972. Mem.: Am. Assn. Law Librs. (cert., chmn. pvt. law librs. spl. interest sect. 1994—95, mem. exec. bd. 2001—), ABA, Arnold Air Soc., Case Western Res. U. Libr. Sch. Alumni Assn., Ohio Regional Assn. Law Librs., Cleve. Bar Assn. (pres. 1981), Ohio State Bar Assn. (chmn. librs. com. 1989—91, pres. 1985), KC, Phi Alpha Theta, Pi Gamma Mu. Roman Catholic. Avocation: alpine skiing. Home: 417 East Parkway Blvd Aurora OH 44202 Office: Baker & Hostetler LLP 3200 National City Ctr Cleveland OH 44114-3485 E-mail: apodboy@bakerlaw.com.

PODBOY, JOHN WATTS, clinical, forensic psychologist; b. York, Pa., Sept. 27, 1943; s. August John and Harriett Virginia (Watts) P.; 1 son, Matthew John. B.A., Dickinson Coll., 1966; M.S., San Diego State Coll., 1971; Ph.D., U. Ariz., 1973. Dir., Vets. Counseling Center, U. Ariz., Tucson, 1972-73; project dir. San Mateo County (Calif.) Human Relations Dept., Redwood City, 1974; staff psychologist Sonoma State Hosp., Eldridge, Calif., 1975-81; cons. clin. psychologist Comprehensive Care Corp., Newport Beach, Calif., 1974-75, Sonoma County (Calif.) Probation Dept., 1976-88; pvt. practice, Kenwood, Calif., 1982—; cons. to No. Calif. Superior Cts., 1983-85; asst. prof. Sonoma State U., 1977-81; dir. Sonoma Diagnostic and Remedial Center, 1979-82. Chmn. San Mateo County Diabetes Assn., 1975. Served to lt. USNR, 1966-69. Fellow Am. Coll. Forensic Psychology, Am. Bd. Med. Psychotherapists (fellow); mem. APA, Western Psychol. Assn., Redwood Psychol. Assn. (pres. 1983), Nat. Council Alcoholism, Nat. Rehab. Assn. Home: PO Box 488 Kenwood CA 95452-0488

PODD, ANN, newspaper editor; b. Buffalo, Jan. 15, 1954; d. Edward and Florence (Bojan) P.; m. Timothy Murray, 1980; children: Laura, Gregory. AB, Syracuse U., 1976; MBA, SUNY, Buffalo, 1981. Reporter AP, 1977, Buffalo Courier-Express, 1977-80, bus. editor, 1980-82, Bergen (N.J.) Record, 1982-88, New York Daily News, 1988-90, assoc. editor, 1990-92, assoc. editor, dir. human resources, 1992-93; dep. spot news editor Wall St. Jour., N.Y.C., 1994, spot news editor, 1994—2000, nat. TV editor, 2000—. Office: Wall St Journal 200 Liberty St New York NY 10281-1003

PODELL, JEAN ELIZABETH MESBERG, artist; b. Eveluth, Minn., Feb. 19, 1917; d. George and Clara (Belond) Mesberg; m. William B. Podell, Nov. 30, 1941 (dec. 1973); 1 child, Penny E. Podell Ballantyne. Student, Layton Sch. Art, Milw., 1935-36. Mem. Wis. Designer Craftsman, Milw., 1957-71, pres., 1962-64, dir., 1965-68; profl. enamelist. One-woman shows Charles Dix Gallery, Delafield, Wis., Marian Studios Mt. Mary Coll., Milw., Alverno Coll. Floretti Gallery, Milw., Kenosha (Wis.) Mus., Chgo. Pub. Libr.; exhibited in group shows Smithsonian Inst., Rochester (Minn.) Art Ctr., Madison (Wis.) Art Ctr., others; represented in permanent collections Milw. Art Ctr., St. Mary and Alverno Colls., pvt. collections in no. Calif. and other locations. Mem. Wis. Designer-Craftsman (pres. 1962-64, dir. 1965-68), Am. Craftsman Coun., Lamorinda Arts Alliance. Avocation: watercolor painting. Home: 1375 Camino Peral Moraga CA 94556-2046

PODELL, ROBERT MANN, obstetrician-gynecologist; b. Elizabeth, N.J., Jan. 17, 1941; s. William S. and Ceil (Silverman) P.; m. Judy Rothenberg, Aug. 27, 1967; 1 child, Deborah P. Fishkind. BA, Columbia U., 1963; MD, Georgetown U., 1967. Diplomate Am. Bd. Ob-Gyn. Intern Jewish Hosp. Med. Ctr., Bklyn., 1967-68; resident in ob-gyn. Bellevue Hosp. Ctr.-NYU, N.Y.C., 1968-72; staff Beth Israel Hosp. Clin. asst. prof. NYU. Fellow ACOG. E-mail: robertpodell@msn.com.

PODESTA, ROBERT EDWARD, artist; b. Sept. 7, 1921; BCS, U. Santa Clara, 1943. Prin. R. Podesta & Assocs., San Jose, Calif., 1946-66; owner/mgr. Sta. KREP-FM, Santa Clara-San Jose, 1965-72; cartoonist Honolulu Advertiser, 1991—. Lectr. Coll. Bus. Adminstrn., U. Santa Clara, 1948-57. Cartoonist San Jose Bus. Jour., Denver Bus. Jour., Ft. Worth Bus. Jour., Pacific Bus. Rev. Home: # 3 Deer Path Rd Santa Cruz CA 95060 E-mail: topfish@cruzio.com.

PODESTO, GARY, mayor; b. 1941; Attended, Marquette U., Milw.; BS in Economics, BS in Corp. Fin., Santa Clara U. Mayor City of Stockton, Calif., 1997—. Founding dir. Crime Stoppers & New Directions; mem. City Coun. Intergovernmental Liaison Com. Office: Office Mayor & City Coun 425 N El Dorado St Stockton CA 95202-1951*

PODGORNY, GEORGE, emergency physician; b. Tehran, Iran, Mar. 17, 1934; s. Emanuel and Helen (Parsian) P.; came to U.S., 1954, naturalized, 1973. B.S., Maryville Coll., 1958; postgrad. Bowman Gray Sch. Medicine, 1958; M.D., Wake Forest U., 1962; m. Ernestine Koury, Oct. 20, 1962; children: Adele, Emanuel II, George, Gregory. Intern in surgery N.C. Bapt. Hosp., Winston-Salem, 1962-63, chief resident in gen. surgery, 1966-67, in cardiothoracic surgery, 1967-69; sr. med. examiner Forsyth County, N.C., 1972—; dir. dept. emergency medicine Forsyth Meml. Hosp., Winston-Salem, 1974-80; sec.-treas. Forsyth Emergency Services, Winston-Salem, 1970-80; clin. prof. emergency medicine East Carolina U. Sch. Medicine, Greenville, 1984—, chmn. residency rev. com. on emergency medicine, 1980-88; mem. Accreditation Coun. for Grad. Med. Edn. Dir. Emergency Med. Svcs. Project Region II of N.C., 1975—; chmn. bd. trustees Emergency Medicine Found.; chmn. residency rev. com. emergency medicine Accreditation Coun. Grad. Med. Edn.; founder Western Piedmont Emergency Med. Svcs. Coun., 1973; mem. N.C. Emergency Med. Svcs. Adv. Coun., 1976-81; assoc. prof. clin. surgery Bowman Gray Sch. Medicine, Wake Forest U., Winston-Salem, 1979—. Bd. dirs. Piedmont Health Systems Agy., 1975-84; trustee Forsyth County Hosp., Authority, 1974-75; bd. dirs. N.C. Health Coordinating Coun., 1975-82, Medic Alert Found. Internat. Fellow Internat. Coll. Surgeons, Internat. Coll. Angiology, Royal Soc. Health (Great Britain), Royal Soc. Medicine, Southeastern Surg. Congress; mem. Am. Coll. Emergency Physicians (charter, pres. 1978-79), AMA, (chmn. coun. of sect. emergency medicine 1978-90, alt. del. for Am. Coll. Emergency Physicians, 1990—), Am. Bd. Emergency Medicine (pres. 1976-81). Contbr. articles to profl. publs. on trauma, snake bite and history of medicine; editorial bd. Annals of Emergency Medicine, Med. Meetings. Home and Office: 2115 Georgia Ave Winston Salem NC 27104-1917

PODGORSAK, ERVIN B. medical physicist, educator, administrator; b. Vienna, Austria, Sept. 28, 1943; arrived in Slovenia, 1946, came to U.S., 1968, Can., 1973; s. Franc and Gabriella (Cukale) P.; m. Mariana Ambrozic, Oct. 23, 1965; children: Matthew, Gregor. Dipl.Ing. in Physics, U. Ljubljana, Slovenia, 1968; MSc in Physics, U. Wis., 1970, PhD in Physics, 1973. Diplomate Am. Bd. Med. Physics. Rsch. asst. U. Ljubljana, 1965-68, U. Wis., Madison, 1968-73; postdoctoral fellow U. Toronto, Ont., Can., 1973-74; asst. prof. McGill U., Montreal, Que., Can., 1975-79, assoc. prof. Can., 1980-84, prof. med. physics Can., 1985—, dir. med. physics unit Can., 1991—; dir. dept. med. physics Montreal Gen. Hosp., 1979—. Hon. vis. prof. U. Ljubljana, 1995—; presenter in field. Contbr. numerous articles to sci. jours., chpts. to books. Recipient (with C. Zankowski) of Sylvia Fedoruk prize in Med. Physics, 1997, Farrington Daniels award in Med. Physics, 1997. Fellow Can. Coll. Physicists in Medicine (bd. dirs. 1981-89, v.p. 1984-87, pres. 1987-89), Am. Assn. Physicists in Medicine (bd. dirs. 1990-93, assoc. editor Med. Physics Jour. 1989—, radiother. com. 1994-96); mem. Am. Coll. Med. Physics (bd. chancellors 1997-99), Am. Soc. Ther. Radiology and Oncology, Can. Assn. Physicists, Can. Orgn. Med. Physics, Can. Assn. Radiation Oncologists, Can. Radiation Protection Assn., Internat. Stereotactic Radiosurgery Soc. (bd. dirs. 1991-95). Home: 1540 croissant Seville Brossard QC Canada J4X 1J4 Office: Montreal Gen Hosp Dept Med Physics 1650 Cedar Ave Montreal QC Canada H3G 1A4 E-mail: epodgorsak@medphys.mcgill.ca.

PODGORSKI, MIRIAM CODER, volunteer; b. Calvin, Pa., Apr. 19, 1915; d. Jacob Coy and Sarah Odessa (Pheasant) Coder; m. Edward Marion Podgorski, Mar. 6, 1949; children: Cathy Mariam Pedgorski Pumphrey, Edward Marion Jr. AB, Juniata Coll., 1937; MEd, Pa. State U., 1949. Cert. tchr., Pa., N.J. Tchr. Lincoln Twp. Schs., Huntingdon County, Pa., 1937-41, Huntingdon Pub. Schs., 1941-49, Bonsall Sch., Camden, N.J., 1950-55. Author: (plays) Rachel's Colonial Belles, 1965 (1st Place award DAR 1968), 3 B's in Bicycleville, 1971 (Hon. Mention award DAR 1972). Sec., chair social svc. dept. com. Jefferson Hosp., 1963—. Mem. DAR (N.J. state chaplain 1989-92), U.S. Daus. of 1912 (N.J. state pres. 1988-91), N.J. Med. Soc. Auxiliary (N.J. state sec. 1975), Camden County Med. Soc. Auxiliary (pres. 1969), Ladies of Grand Army of Republic (pres. Hatch cir.) 1992). Republican. Methodist. Avocations: water colors, embroidery, historical writing. Home: 650 W Crystal Lake Ave Haddonfield NJ 08033-2751

PODGORSKI, ROBERT PAUL, human resources executive; b. Chgo., July 18, 1943; s. Joseph Paul and Lillian Violet (Zahara) P.; m. Constance Francis Moore, Sept. 4, 1965; children: Debra Lynn, Katherine Ann, David Joseph. Student, Wright C.C., Chgo., 1966-75, Roosevelt U., 1975-78. Personnel specialist Teletype Corp., Skokie, Ill., 1961-75; mgr. human res. North Am. Philips Corp. subs., 1975-79, Alliance, Ohio, 1975-79; dir. empl. and staffing Northrop Grumman Corp., Rolling Meadows, Ill., 1979-89, 90-99; v.p. human res. Gen. Datacom Ind., Inc., Middlebury, Conn., 1989-90, Benton Schneider & Assoc., Inc., Lisle, Ill., 1990; pres. R.P.P. Enterprises, 1999—. Pres. Corporate Relocation Coun., Chgo., 1986-88; cons. princ. RPP Ent., Chgo., 1982-91; chmn. Human Resources North Bus. and Ind. Coun., Chgo., 1975-76. Contbg. writer, Outdoor Notebook, Midwest Outdoors, Muskie Mag., 2000—; contbr. articles to profl. jours. Co-chmn., dir. Chicagoland Proj. with Ind., 1980—98; mem. Hoffman Estates (Ill.) Environ. Commn., 2001—; mem. adv. bd. Parks Coll. Tech. Program, 1969, Truman Coll. Tech. Program, 1971, Harper Coll. Transition Ctr., 1991—97, mem. bus. and mgmt. program adv. bd., 1999—, mem. supervisory program adv. bd., 2001; mem. adv. bd. Harper Coll. Mgmt. Program, 1999; bd. dirs., newsletter editor Fox River Valley chpt. Muskies, Inc., 2000—. Recipient Decade of Leadership award, Electronics Ind. Found., 1990. Mem. Electronics Pers.l Assn. (editor 1982-90, pres. 1984), Human Resource Assn. (editor 1990, bd. dirs. Oakbrook chpt.), Employment Mgmt. Assn. (regional dir. 1989-96, chair coll. rels. 2000, Nat. Pericles award 1987), Soc. Human Resources Mgmt., Chicagoland Human Resources Assn. (bd. dirs. 2001--). Republican. Roman Catholic. Avocations: lecturer, writing, fishing, magic.

PODHORETZ, NORMAN, magazine editor, writer; b. Bklyn., Jan. 16, 1930; s. Julius and Helen (Woliner) P.; m. Midge Rosenthal Decter, Oct. 21, 1956; children: Rachel, Naomi, Ruth, John. AB, Columbia, 1950; BHL, Jewish Theol. Sem., 1950, LLD (hon.), 1980; BA (Kellett fellow), Cambridge (Eng.) U., 1952, MA, 1957; LHD (hon.), Hamilton Coll., 1969, Yeshiva U., 1991, Boston U., 1995, Adelphi U., 1996. Assoc. editor Commentary, 1956-58, editor in chief, 1960-95, editor-at-large, 1995—; editor in chief Looking Glass Library, 1959-60; sr. fellow Hudson Inst., 1995—. Mem. U. Seminar Am. Civilization, Columbia, 1958. Author: Doings and Undoings, The Fifties and After in American Writing, 1964, Making It, 1968, Breaking Ranks, 1979, The Present Danger, 1980, Why We Were in Vietnam, 1982, The Bloody Crossroads, 1986, Ex-Friends, 1999, My Love Affair With America, 2000, The Prophets, 2002; editor: The Commentary Reader, 1966. Chmn. new directions adv. com. USIA, 1981-87. With AUS, 1953-55. Fulbright fellow, 1950-51. Mem. Coun. on Fgn. Rels. E-mail: NHP30@hotmail.com.

PODHURST, AARON SAMUEL, lawyer; b. N.Y.C., Apr. 29, 1936; s. Louis and rae (Pomerantz) P.; m. Dorothy Ellen Podhurst, Sept. 7, 1958; children: Karen Beth Dern, Laura Koffsky, Julie Weinberg. BBA, U. Mich., 1957; JD, Columbia U., 1960. Bar: Fla., 1961, N.Y., 1961. Assoc. Nichols, Gaither, Miami, Fla., 1962-67; founding ptnr. Podhurst, Orseck, Josefsberg, Eaton, Meadow, Olin & Perwin, P.A., 1967—. Vice pres. Miami Coalition for Safe Cmty., 1994—; mem. Orange Bowl Com., Miami, 1996—. Recipient Nat. Medallion award NCCJ, 1994; Harlan Fiske Stone scholar, 1960. Mem. ABA (aviation com.), Internat. Acad. Trial Lawyers (pres. 1990), Acad. Fla. Trial Lawyers (pres. 1978, aviation com.), Am. Coll. Trial Lawyers, Assn. Trial Lawyers Am. (bd. govs., aviation com.), Internat. Soc. Barristers, Inner Cir. of Advocates. Office: Podhurst Orseck Josefsberg Eaton Meadow Olin & Perwin PA 25 W Flagler St Miami FL 33130-1712

PODOLSKY, ARNOLD MARK, lawyer, physician; b. Detroit, Oct. 11, 1951; BA, Oakland U., 1972; MD, Wayne State U., 1977; JD, Detroit Coll. Law, 1986. Diplomate Am. Bd. Anesthesiology; Bar: Mich. 1986. Med. cons. Lopatin & Miller PC, Detroit, 1984-86, atty., 1986-91; ptnr. Ravid & Podolsky PC, Southfield, Mich., 1991-93; CEO Podolsky & Assocs. PC, Birmingham, 1993—. Faculty scholar Detroit Coll. Law, 1983-86. Fellow Am. Coll. Legal Medicine; mem. Am. Soc. Anesthesiologists, Mich. Soc. Anesthesiologists, Mich. Trial Lawyers Assn. (mem. exec. bd. 1991-95)., Mich. State Med. Soc., Assn. Trial Lawyers Am., State Bar Assn. Mich. Office: Podolsky and Assocs PC 999 Haynes St Ste 395 Birmingham MI 48009-6775 E-mail: medical-legal@consultant.com.

PODRATZ, KARL C. gynecologic surgeon, oncologist, educator; b. New Ulm, Minn., Feb. 7, 1943; s. Clarence F. and Elsa (Sievert) P.; m. Roxann Rochford; 1 child, Scott Karl. BA, U. Minn., 1966; MD in Medicine, PhD in Biochemistry, St. Louis U., 1974. Resident in ob-gyn. U. Chgo., 1974-77; gynecologic oncology fellow Mayo Clinic, Rochester, Minn., 1977-79, gynecologic surgeon/oncologist, 1979—, chmn. dept. ob-gyn., 1986-2000, Joseph and Barbara Ashkins prof. surgery, 1990—. Dir. gynecologic oncology tng. program Mayo Clinic, Rochester, 1985—. Assoc. editor Gynecologic Oncology; contbr. numerous articles to profl. jours. Fellow ACOG, ACS; mem. Soc. Gynecologic Oncology (pres. 1998-99), Cen. Assn. Ob-Gyn. (pres. 1997, past sec.-treas. 1987-95), Western Assn. Gynecologic Oncologists (past pres. 1991). Avocations: downhill skiing, golfing, gardening, cooking, traveling. Office: Mayo Clinic 200 1st St SW Rochester MN 55905-0002 E-mail: podratz.karl@mayo.edu.

PODREBARAC, ROSEMARY, lawyer; b. Kansas City, Mo., Sept. 15, 1961; d. Eugene George and Mary Josephine (Musick) Podrebarac. BA in Math. and French, U. Kans., 1983; JD, Washington U., St. Louis, 1986. Bar: Kans. 1986, U.S. Dist. Ct. Kans. 1986, Mo. 1987, U.S. Dist. Ct. (we. dist.) Mo. 1987. Assoc. McAnany, Van Cleave & Phillips, P.A., Kansas City, Kans., 1986-90, shareholder, 1991—. Contbr. chpts. to legal handbooks. Bd. dirs. Caritas Clinics, Inc., Kansas City, 1995-2001; bd. dirs. United Way Wyandotte County, Inc., 2000—. Mem. Mo. Bar, Kans. Bar Assn., Wyandotte County Bar Assn. (treas. 1990-92), Wyandotte County Bar Found. (bd. dirs., treas. 1993-2001), Kansas City, Kansas Rotary Club (bd. dirs. 1998-2001, 2002—). Office: McAnany Van Cleave & Phillips PA 707 Minnesota Ave 4th Fl PO Box 171300 Kansas City KS 66117-0300 E-mail: rpodrebarac@mvplaw.com.

PODUSKA, ELLEN MARIE, writer, paralegal; b. Ft. Dodge, Iowa, Aug. 14, 1954; d. Paul Joseph and Velma Darlene Poduska; children: Johanna Powell, Alexis. Paralegal, Des Moines Area C.C., Ankeny, Iowa; B of Gen. Studies, Drake U.; JD, fellow internat. law, Northwestern U. Paralegal Coppola, Trout, Taha & Gazzo, Des Moines, 1978—82; legal sec. Davis Law Firm, 1983—84; legal sec. II Atty. Gen., Phoenix, 1987—91; author, writer 1st Books Libr., Bloomington, Ind. Author: Traditional Bohemian Recipes, 1999, Democratic Perspectives, 2000. With U.S. Army, 1983—85. Roman Catholic. Home: Apt 6 205 4th Ave NE Pocahontas IA 50574-1737 E-mail: ellenmpoduska@hotmail.com.

PODUSKA, JOHN WILLIAM, SR. computer company executive; b. Memphis, Dec. 30, 1937; s. Ben F. and Lily Mae (Reid) Poduska; m. Susan McElaney, Oct. 1, 1983; 1 child Lily ;children from previous marriage: Alice Casey, Margaret Kay, John Jr., Mary Beth Pandiscio. BS, MS, MIT, 1960, ScD, 1962; LHD (hon.), U. Lowell, 1986. Dir. Honeywell Info. Systems, Cambridge, Mass., 1970-72; v.p. research and devel. Prime Computer, Framingham, 1972-79; chmn., chief exec. officer, pres. Apollo Computer, Chelmsford, 1980-85; chmn., chief exec. officer, founder Stellar Computer Inc., Newton, 1986-89; CEO Stardent Computer, Inc., 1989-92; chmn. bd. dirs., founder Advanced Visual Systems Inc., Waltham, Mass., 1992—2001. Bd. dirs. Safeguard Sci., Novell, Inc., Anadarko Petroleum Corp. Trustee Bentley Coll., Boston Ballet. Named Man of the Yr., Boy Scouts Am., 1983; recipient Ah Wang award, C. of C., North Middlesex, Mass., 1985. Fellow: IEEE; mem.: NAE. Office: 44 Silver St Lancaster MA 01523

PODWALL, KATHRYN STANLEY, biology educator; b. Chgo., Oct. 14; d. Frank and Marie C. Stanley. BS, U. Ill.; MA, NYU. Prof. biology Nassau C.C., Garden City, N.Y. Developmental reviewer West Ednl. Pub., Amesbury, Mass. and Highland Park, Ill., 1989, 91-92; reviewer AAAS, Washington, 1970—; exec. bd., advisor Women's Faculty Assn., Nassau C.C., 1990—, pres, 2000-2002; lectr. in field. Author: Tested Studies for Laboratory Teaching, vol. 5, 1993; editor: (books and cassettes) Rhyming Simon Books and Cassettes, 1990, Sight Reading Syncopation, 1998, Today's Way To Play the Standards, 2000, Today's Way To Play the Classics, 2000, (book and CD) Cartoones & Car Tunes, 2001. Recipient L.I. Alzheimer's Found. Svc. award, 2002. Mem. AAUW, Nat. Assn. Biology Tchrs. (life), Nat. Sci. Tchrs. Assn. (life), Soc. for Coll. Sci. Tchrs., Am. Women in Sci., Met. Assn. Coll. and Univ. Biologists, Nat. Cathedral Assn., N.Y. Acad. of Scis., Friends of Archives (charter), Xerces Soc., Southampton Colonial Soc., LaSalle County Hist. Soc. (life), Garden City Hist. Soc. (life), Soroptimists (bd. dirs. dist. 1 1994-96, club pres. 1992-94, Nassau County Pres. award 2001), L.I. Alzheimer's Found. (Svc. award 2002), U. Ill. Alumni Assn. (life). Avocations: travel, gardening, zoological pursuits. Office: Nassau Community College One Education Dr Garden City NY 11530 E-mail: podwalk@ncc.edu.

POE, BOB, political organization worker, communications company executive; Exec. v.p., dir. mktg. Magnetix Corp., Orlando, Fla. Chmn. Fla. Dem. Party, 2000.

POE, GERALD DEAN, music educator, consultant; b. Grandby, Colo., Sept. 18, 1942; s. Chester Harvey and Esther Jane Poe; m. Cheryl Toni Poe, Aug. 6, 1965 (div. July 1998); children: Lauren, Russell; m. Joan Benke Poe, June 17, 1999. BA, Western State Coll., 1964; M in Music Edn., Fla. State U., 1965; D in Musical Arts, U. Colo., 1973. Band dir. Pub. Sch., Colo., 1965—68, Calif., 1965—68; band dir., tchr. Minot (N.D.) State Coll., 1969—72; band dir. U. Colo., Boulder, 1973, U. Oreg., Eugene, 1974—81, U. Fla., Gainesville, 1982—86. Band dir., tchr.; profl. trumpet player, 1965—. Contbr. articles to profl. jours. Mem.: FMENC, NBA, CBDNA, MENC. Avocations: fishing, travel, gardening. Home: 9189 SE 70th Ave Trenton FL 32693 Office: Kanapaha Middle 5005 75th Ave Gainesville FL 32608

POE, GERTIE LAVERN, sales executive; b. Chgo., Feb. 7, 1949; d. L.C. and Gertrude (Winfrey) Poe. BSBA, Roosevelt U., 1978, MBA, 1984. Policy analyst Continental Bank, Chgo., 1971-87; fin. planner IDS/Am. Express, Merrillville, Ind., 1987-89; sales rep. Valic, Chgo., 1990-94, Invest Fin. Svcs., Bridgeview, IL, 1994-95; tng. cons. Dearborn Fin. Inst., Chgo., 1995-99; tax cons. HR Block, 1999—; customer svc. rep. ComEd, 1999—. Mem. Sigma Gamma Rho. Baptist. Home: PO Box 19201 Chicago IL 60619-0201

POE, JERRY B. financial educator; b. Springfield, Mo., Oct. 3, 1931; s. Carlyle and Eunice P.; m. Carol J. Mussler, Sept. 9, 1959; children: Cheryl Marie, Jennifer Brenna. AB, Drury Coll., 1953; MBA (Weinheimer fellow), Washington U., St. Louis, 1957; D.BA (Ford Found. fellow), Harvard U., 1963. Instr. U. Ark., spring 1957; indsl. engr. McDonnell Aircraft Corp., St. Louis, 1957; lectr. on fin. Boston U., 1959-61; asst. prof. bus. adminstrn. Drury Coll., 1961-64, assoc. prof., 1964-68, prof., 1968-74; dir. Breech Sch. Bus. Adminstrn., 1968-74; prof. fin. Ariz. State U., 1974—, chmn. dept. fin., 1974-82. Vis. prof. Fla. Tech. U., 1971; examiner, commr. North Central Assn. Colls. and Schs.; dir. NDEA Inst. Econs.; cons. in field Author: Essentials of Finance: An Integrated Approach, 1995, An Introduction to the American Business Enterprise, 1969, 7th rev. edit., 1989, Cases in Financial Management, 1977, 3d rev. edit., 1987. Mem. Regional Manpower Adv. Com.; mem. bus. and profl. adv. council Empire Bank. Served to lt. comdr. USNR, 1953-55. Mem. Fin. Mgmt. Assn., Kappa Alpha, Beta Gamma Sigma, Omicron Delta Kappa. Methodist. Office: Ariz State U Coll Bus Dept Fin Tempe AZ 85287-3906

POE, LUKE HARVEY, JR. lawyer; b. Richmond, Va., Jan. 29, 1916; s. Luke Harvey and Alice Morris (Reddy) P. BS in Math, U. Va., 1938, JD, 1941; postgrad. (Rhodes scholar), Oxford (Eng.) U., 1939; D.Phil., Christ Ch., 1957. Bar: Va. bar 1940, D.C. bar and D.C. Ct. Appeals bar 1967, U.S. Supreme Ct. bar 1969, Md. bar 1974. Asso. firm Cravath, Swaine & Moore, N.Y.C., 1941-42; tutor St. John's Coll., Annapolis, Md., 1946-50, asst. dean, 1947-49, tenure tutor, 1953-60, dir. physics and chemistry lab., 1959-60; asst. chmn. Nat. Citizens Com. for Kennedy and Johnson and chmn. Citizens Com., Pres.'s Inaugural Com., 1960-61; asst. to chmn. bd. Aerojet-Gen. Corp., El Monte, Calif., 1961-63; div. pres. Internat. Tech. Assistance and Devel. Co., Washington, 1963-66; ptnr. Howard, Poe & Bastian, 1966-83; pvt. practice law, 1983—. Bd. dirs. First Am. Bank of Md.; cons. Dept. Transp., Dept. State, NEH; lectr. War Coll. of USAF, Gen. Studies program U. Va.; seminar leader Aspen Inst. Humanistic Studies; guest panelist Panel on Sci. and Tech. of Com. on Sci. and Astronautics, U.S. Ho. of Reps., 1970; pres. bd. dirs. Watergate East, Inc., 1976-79, 90-92; organizer U. Va. Unified Liberal Arts Program, 1988—. Author: The Combat History of the Battleship U.S.S. Mississippi, 1947, The Transition From Natural Law to Natural Rights, 1957; (with others) lab. manuals Einstein's Theory of Relativity, 1957, Electro-Magnetic Theory, 1959; editor: (with others) Va. Mag., 1936-38, U. Va. Law Rev., 1940-41. Dean's adv. coun. Lehigh U., 1962-65, mem. Seminar on Sci., Tech. and Pub. Policy, Brookings Instn., 1964-66; coun. on trends and perspectives U.S. C. of C., 1966-69; chmn. bd. Bristol Property Mgmt. and Svcs., Inc., 1967-88; chmn. Annapolis Bd. Zoning Appeals, 1966-75; mem. Annapolis Mayor's Task Force, 1967-74, Md. Gov.'s Commn. on Capital City, 1970-76. Lt. comdr. USNR, 1942-46. Decorated Jhalavada Order of Durbargadh, Dhrangadhara. Mem. Am. Law Inst., AAUP, Raven Soc. (pres.), Soc. of Cincinnati, Sr. Common Room and High Table (Christ Church), Met. Club (Washington), Travellers Club (London), Brook Club (N.Y.C.), New Providence Club (Annapolis), Vincent's Club (Oxford), Phi Beta Kappa, Phi Delta Phi. Episcopalian. Home: 139 Market St Annapolis MD 21401-2628 also: 2500 Virginia Ave NW Washington DC 20037-1901 Office: 2600 Virginia Ave NW Washington DC 20037-1905

POE, MICHAEL KELLIE, financial executive; b. Raleigh, N.C., Feb. 15, 1955; s. William Curtis and Eileen H. Poe; m. Barbara H. Hochuli, Apr. 6, 1985; children: Robert C., Kelly M. BA in Acctg., N.C. State U., 1977. CPA, NC. V.p. fin. and info. sys. Insilco Techs. Group, Durham, N.C., 1995-97; v.p. fin., CFO Channel Master Holdings, Inc., Smithfield, 1998—. Mem. Fin. Execs. Internat., Morristown, N.J., 2000—. Recipient Nicholson award for Best in Industry, Nat. Assn. Investors Corp., 1995. Mem. AICPA. Avocations: water skiing, snow skiing, mountain biking. Home: 7721 Sandy Bottom Way Raleigh NC 27613 Office: Channel Master Holdings Inc 1315 Industrial Park Dr Smithfield NC 27577 E-mail: mpoe@cmnc.com., mpoe@starband.net.

POE, RANDALL ELLSWORTH, public relations executive, author; b. Colorado Springs, Colo., Nov. 2, 1935; s. Everett E. and Emilie (Hamburger) P.; m. M. Catherine Ferguson, June 12, 1959 (div. July 1988); 1 child, Andrea Catherine. BA in Journalism, U. Calif., San Jose, 1958. Exec. dir. pub. rels. The Conf. Bd., N.Y.C., 1961-68, news dir., 1968-74, news dir./media mgr., 1974-88, dir. comm., exec. dir., 1988—. Contbr. articles to maj. mags., chapters to books. Office: The Conf Bd 845 3rd Ave 2nd Fl New York NY 10022-6601

POE, ROBERT ALAN, lawyer; b. Bracken County, Ky., Apr. 25, 1951; Student, U. Ky.; BA, Centre Coll., 1973; JD, U. Va., 1976. Bar: Colo. 1976. Mem. Holland & Hart, Denver, 1976—. Adj. prof. taxation U. Denver, 1986-88. Articles editor Va. Law Review, 1974-76. Mem. ABA, Order Coif, Phi Beta Kappa. Office: Holland & Hart 8390 E Crescent Pkwy Ste 400 Greenwood Village CO 80111-2822

POE, SUZY CROWBAR, publisher, author; b. Kalamazoo, Apr. 3, 1950; married 1973 (div. 1980); children: Sarah Rachel, Caleb David. Social worker Kalamazoo Youth Ministry, 1973-81; pastor Calvary Grace Ch. of Faith, Kalamazoo, 1979-84; journalist Kalamazoo News, 1980-84; pub. Popular Reality, Lansing, Mich., 1984—. Bd. dirs. Albany Gender Project. Author: My Date with Henry Miller, 1997, Crooze Control, 1999; pub. Popular Reality periodical, 1984-87, 99—. Grantee (small press grants), 1993—. Mem. Nat. Gender Dysphoria Orgn. (founder Albany gender project). Avocation: videography. Office: Albany Gender Project PO Box 66016 Albany NY 12206

POEHLEIN, GARY WAYNE, retired chemical engineering educator; b. Tell City, Ind., Oct. 17, 1936; s. Oscar Raymond and Eva Lee (Dickman) P.; m. Sharon Eileen Wood., Jan. 1, 1958; children: Steven Ray, Timothy Wayne, Valorie Ann, Sandra Lee. BSChemE, Purdue U., 1958, MSChemE, 1961, PhD, 1966. Design engr. Proctor & Gamble, Cin., 1958-61; from asst. prof. to assoc. prof. Lehigh U., Bethlehem, Pa., 1965-75, prof. chem. engring., 1975-78, co-dir. emulsion polymers inst., 1973-78; dir. sch. chem. engring. Ga. Inst. Tech., Atlanta, 1978-86, assoc. v.p. rsch., dean grad. studies, 1986-91, v.p. interdisciplinary programs, prof. chem. engring., 1991-95; prof. chem. engring., 1978-96; dir. Chem. and Transport Systems Divsn. NSF, 1996-2000; ret., 2000. Bd. dirs. Flexible Products Co., Marietta, Ga.; interim chair chem. engring. dept., vis. prof. Lehigh U., 2001—02. Contbr. over 100 articles to tech. publs. Mem. sch. bd. Bethlehem Area Sch. Dist., 1969-75. Recipient Honor Scroll award Phila. br. Am. Inst. Chemists, 1977, Mac Pruitt award Coun. for Chem. Rsch., 1989. Fellow AIChE; mem. Am. Chem. Soc., Am. Soc. Engring. Edn., Sigma Xi. Avocations: woodworking, sailing. Home: 407 S Henry St Alexandria VA 22314-5901 E-mail: gspoehlein@aol.com.

POEHLMANN, CARL JOHN, agronomist, researcher; b. Jamestown, Mo., Jan. 29, 1950; s. Edwin William and Lucille Albina (Neu) P.; m. Linda Kay Garner, Dec. 29, 1973; children: Anthony, Kimberly. BS, U. Mo., 1972, MS, 1978. Farmer, Jamestown, Mo., 1972-73; vocat. agrl. tchr. Linn (Mo.) Pub. Schs., 1973-75, Columbia (Mo.) Pub. Schs., 1975-78; dir., mgr. agronomy rsch. ctr. U. Mo., Columbia, 1978-2000; dir. MOAES Field Ops., 2000—. Mem. Am. Soc. Agronomy (div. A-7 chair 1985-86, bd. mem. 1991-94, cert. crop advisor 1993—), Crop Sci. Soc. Am., Soil Sci. Soc. Am., Internat. Assn. Mechanization Field Experiments. Mem. Christian Ch. (Disciples Of Christ). Office: MU Field Ops 3600 New Haven Rd Columbia MO 65201 E-mail: poehlmannc@missouri.edu.

POEHNER, RAYMOND GLENN, retired bank executive; b. Cleve., Oct. 2, 1923; s. Raymond Frank and Winifred (Kirchbaum) P.; m. Frances E. Dunaway Gillespie, Jan. 4, 1958 (dec. 1993); children: R. David, Jacqueline Diane, Leslie Marie, Jon Anthony, Rebecca Glen; stepchildren: Bruce Gillespie, Tony Gillespie. Student, pub. schs., Chgo. and Cleve. Enlisted USN, 1941, advanced through grades to chief petty officer, 1957, ret., 1965; with Security Pacific Nat. Bank, San Diego, 1966-80, loan officer, 1971-74, credit card officer, 1975-80, asst. br. mgr., 1974-80, asst. mgr.; ret., 1980. Mem. VFW, U.S. Naval Inst. (assoc.), Sierra Club, Fla. Sheriff's Assn., Am. Biog. Soc. (nat. bd. advisors), R.I. Rsch. (cert. assoc.), Fleet Res. Assn., Rep. Legion of Merit, Nat. Geographic Soc., Am. Legion, Animal Protection Inst. Am., Nat. Assn. Civilian Conservation Corps Alumni, Optimist Club (dir. 1978), Fraternal Order Police (booster Fla. chpt.). Republican.

POEL, ROBERT WALTER, air force officer, physician; b. Muskegon, Mich., July 24, 1934; s. Abel John and Fannie M. (Vanderwall) P.; m. Carol Anne Noordeloos, June 24, 1960; children: Kathryn Anne Poel Engle, James Robert, Sharon Kay Poel Thompson. BS, Calvin Coll., 1957; MD, U. Mich., 1959. Diplomate Am. Bd. Surgery. Commd. capt. USAF, 1962, advanced through grades to brig. gen., 1988, ret., 1993; comdr. Hosp. Malmstrom AFB, Great Falls, Mont., 1971-73; dir. profl. svcs. Hdqrs. Tactical Air Command Command Surgeon's Office, Langley AFB, Va., 1973-74; div. chief, med. plans Office of Air Force Surgeon Gen., Wash., 1974-78; comdr. regional hosp. Sheppard AFB, Wichita Falls, Tex., 1978-83; dir. profl. svcs. Office of Air Force Logistics Command Surgeon, Wright-Patterson AFB, Ohio, 1983-85; vice-comdr. Wilford Hall USAF Med. Ctr., San Antonio, 1985-87; chief, quality assurance, dir. plans and resources Air Force Surgeon Gen., Bolling AFB, Washington, 1987-89; hosp. comdr. Malcolm Grow Med. Ctr., Andrews AFB, 1989-93; med. dir. near south office Meth. Occupational Healthctrs. Inc., Indpls., 1995—. Dir. Andrews Fed. Credit Union, 1991-95, vice chmn. bd. dirs., 1992-95. Advisor, bd. regents Uniformed Svcs. U. the Health Scis., Bethesda, Md., 1989-93; mem. pres. coun. Calvin Coll., 1990. Named Disting. alumnus, Calvin Coll., 1990; Paul Harris fellow Rotary Club of Wichita Falls, 1982. Mem. AMA, Am. Coll. Occupl. and Environ. Medicine, Assn. Mil. Surgeons of U.S. (life), Ret. Officers Assn. (life). Republican. Home: 12085 Waterford Ln Carmel IN 46033-5501 Office: 1101 Southeastern Ave Indianapolis IN 46202-3946 E-mail: poelrc@earthlink.net.

POELLOT, LUTHER, minister; b. Palatine, Ill., Oct. 23, 1913; s. Sigfried Daniel and Lisette (Brueggemann) P.; m. Esther Maaser, May 23, 1942; children: Sharon Ruth, Carolyn May Gluesenkamp, Marion Kay, Celia Louise (Mrs. Allen Thomas). Student, Concordia Coll., Milw., 1927-33, Concordia Sem., St. Louis, 1933-37, LittD, 1999. Ordained to ministry Luth. Ch.-Mo. Synod, 1942. Head clk. Concordia Sem. Libr., St. Louis, 1937-39; missionary Ft. Myers, Fla., 1940; pastor Dallas, 1940-50, Mercedes, Tex., 1950-52, Pitcairn, Pa., 1952-62, Waterloo, Ont., Can., 1962-64. Indexer, editor Concordia Pub. House, St. Louis, 1964-78. Author: Revelation, 1962, 76, reprinted in Concordia Classic Commentary Series, 1987; translator chpts.: (J. Quenstedt's Theologia) The Nature and Character of Theology, 1986, The Holy Ministry, 1991, The Church, 1999; (M. Chemnitz's Enchiridion) Ministry, Word, and Sacraments, 1981; contbr. articles to profl. jours.; composer, poet. Home: 753 Buckley Rd Saint Louis MO 63125-5347 *Hope fills the heart and drives all fear away of hell and of death that ends life's little day. Faith soars beyond the grave. We hasten home. Our Savior rose—we are not here to stay.*

POESCH, JESSIE JEAN, art historian; b. Postville, Iowa, May 19, 1922; parents: Edward H. and Vina (Meier) P. BA, Antioch Coll., 1944; MA, U. Del., 1956; PhD, U. Pa., 1966. Relief worker Am. Friends Svc. Com., Phila., also, France, Germany, 1946-54; curatorial asst. H.F. DuPont Winterthur (Del.) Mus., 1956-58; from asst. prof. to prof. art history Tulane U., New Orleans, 1963-92, Maxine and Ford Graham chair in fine arts, 1988-92. Guest curator "Painting in the South", Va. Mus. Fine Arts, Richmond, 1980-84; curator "Newcomb Pottery: An Enterprise for So. Women, 1895-1940", Newcomb Coll. Tulane U. and Smithsonian Instn. traveling exhbn. svc., 1980-87. Author: Titian Ramsay Peale, 1799-1885, and His Journals of the Wilkes Expedition, 1961, The Art of the Old South: Painting, Sculpture, Architecture and the Products of Craftsmen, 1560-1860, 1983, (with John Cuthbert) David Hunter Strother: "One of the Best Draughtsmen the Country Possesses", 1997; (book/exhbn. catalogue) The Early Furniture of Louisiana, 1972, Newcomb Pottery: An Enterprise for Southern Women 1895-1940, 1984, Will Henry Stevens, 1987; editor: (with Barbara Bacot) Louisiana Buildings 1720-1948, 1997, (with Nancy E. Green) Arthur Wesley Dow and American Arts and Crafts, 1999; also numerous articles and book revs. Fellow U. Del., 1954-56; Fulbright scholar U. London, 1960-62; NEH grantee, London, 1969-70. Mem. Soc. Archtl. Historians (bd. dirs. 1986-89), Coll. Art Assn., Am. Antiquarian Soc., La. Endowment for the Humanities (bd. dirs. 1984-90, La. Humanist of Yr. 1992), Victorian Soc. Am. (bd. dirs. 1988-92). Office: Tulane U Dept Newcomb Art New Orleans LA 70118 E-mail: jpoesch@tulane.edu.

POETTCKER, HENRY, retired seminary president; b. Rudnerweide, Russia, Mar. 27, 1925; s. John and Margaretha (Voth) P.; m. Aganetha Baergen, July 4, 1946; children: Victoria, Ronald, Martin. AB, Bethel Coll., North Newton, Kans., 1950; B.D., Mennonite Bibl. Sem., Chgo., 1953; Th.D., Princeton Theol. Sem., 1961, converted PhD, 1973. Ordained to ministry Mennonite Ch., 1948; instr. Can. Mennonite Bible Coll., Winnipeg, Man., 1954-59, pres., 1959-78, Mennonite Bibl. Sem., Elkhart, Ind., 1978-90, assoc. for devel., 1991-93;, 1993. Interim dean Bluffton (Ohio) Coll., 1965-66; vis. lectr. Taiwan Theol. Coll. and Tainan Theol. Coll., Taiwan, 1973-74 Editor: (with Rudy A. Regehr) Call to Faithfulness, 1972, Alumni Bull. Can. Mennonite Bible Coll, 1960-73. Pres. Gen. Conf. Mennonite Ch., Newton, Kans., 1968-74. Mem. Soc. Bibl. Lit. and Exegesis. Home: 475 Lindenwood Dr E Winnipeg MB Canada R3P2P3 E-mail: henr2502@mts.net. *The secret of happiness lies not in doing what one likes, but in liking what one does.*

POFF, FRANKLIN ALBRIGHT, JR. lawyer; b. Hot Springs, Ark., Sept. 27, 1956; s. Franklin Albright and Carolyn Virginia (Hanson) P.; m. Theresa Ann Wolf, Aug. 19, 1978; children: Franklin A. III, William Wolf, Christopher Curtis. BA in History and Polit. Sci., Hendrix Coll., 1979; JD, U. Ark., 1982. Bar: Ark. 1982, U.S. Dist. Ct. Ark. 1982, U.S. Ct. Appeals (8th cir.) 1982, U.S. Supreme Ct. 1988, Tex. 1990, U.S. Ct. Appeals (5th cir.) 1990, U.S. Dist. Ct. Tex. 1990. Atty. Walker & Poff, Little Rock, 1982-90; assoc. Gooding & Dodson, Texarkana, Tex., 1990-92; mem. exec. com. Gooding & Dodson, P.C., 1992-98; of counsel Crisp, Jordan & Boyd, 1998-99; ptnr. Crisp, Boyd & Poff, L.L.P., 2000—. Bd. dirs. Boys and Girls Club of Texarkana, Inc., 1996-98, Easter Seals of Texarkana, Inc., 1995—, chmn., 2000—, Texarkana Resources for Disabled, 1999—, treas., 2000—; adv. bd. Teen Ct. of Texarkana, 1999—; pres. Texarkana Repertory Co., 2000-02. Mem. Ark. Bar Assn. (Ho. of Dels. 1999—), Tex. Bar Assn., S.W. Ark. Bar Assn., N.W. Tex. Bar Assn., Texarkana Bar Assn. (treas. 2001-02, pres.-elect 2002—), Ark. Trial Lawyers Assn. Office: Crisp Boyd & Poff LLP PO Box 6297 Texarkana TX 75505-6297 Fax: 903-832-8489. E-mail: fpoff@cbplaw.com.

POFF, JAMES MICHAEL, secondary school educator, music educator; b. Berea, Ky., Dec. 22, 1974; s. James Thomas, Jr. and Sarah Lynn Poff. BA in Music Edn., BA in Math., Berea Coll., 1997. Tchg. cert. rank III Ky. Ct. dir. Berea Coll. Upward Bound, 1998—; choral dir., math. tchr. Madison So. HS, 1999—. Mem.: Ky. Edn. Assn. (bd. dirs. ctrl. dist. 2001—02), Ky. Music Educators Assn., Am. Choral Dirs. Assn. Home: 200 Courtland Ave Apt 5 Berea KY 40403 Office: Madison So HS 279 Glades Rd Berea KY 40403

POFF, RICHARD HARDING, state supreme court justice; b. Radford, Va., Oct. 19, 1923; s. Beecher David and Irene Louise (Nunley) P.; m. Jo Ann R. Topper, June 24, 1945 (dec. Jan. 1978); children: Rebecca, Thomas, Richard Harding; m. Jean Murphy, Oct. 26, 1980. Student, Roanoke Coll., 1941-43; LL.B., U. Va., 1948, LL.D., 1969. Bar: Va. 1947. Partner law firm Dalton, Poff, Turk & Stone, Radford, 1949-70; mem. 83d-92d congresses, 6th Dist. Va.; justice Supreme Ct. Va., 1972-89, sr. justice, 1989—. Vice chmn. Nat. Commn. on Reform Fed. Crime Laws; chmn. Republican Task Force on Crime; sec. Rep. Conf., House Rep. Leadership. Named Va.'s Outstanding Young Man of Year Jr. C. of C., 1954; recipient Nat. Collegiate Athletic Assn. award, 1966, Roanoke Coll. medal, 1967, Distinguished Virginian award Va. Dist. Exchange Clubs, 1970, Presdl. certificate of appreciation for legislative contbn., 1971, legislative citation Assn. Fed. Investigators, 1969, Thomas Jefferson Pub. Sesquicentennial award U. Va., 1969, Japanese Am. Citizens League award, 1972, Cario Professionalism award Va. State Bar Assn. Criminal Law Sect., 1998; named to Hall of Fame, Am. Legion Boys State, 1985; fellow Va. Law Found., 1997. Mem. Bar Assn., VFW, Am. Legion, Pi Kappa Phi, Sigma Nu Phi. Clubs: Mason, Moose, Lion. Office: Va Supreme Ct 100 N 9th St Richmond VA 23219-2335 *When you know you are right, fight. When you are in doubt, wait. When you know you are wrong, admit your mistake and correct it.*

POFSKY, NORMA LOUISE, interior designer, behavioral consultant; b. Bklyn., Mar. 21, 1945; d. Abraham and Bessie (Kammerman) Eiger; m. Leonard Harris Pofsky, Dec. 29, 1968 (div. Mar., 1994); children: Russell, Jonathan. BS in Edn., SUNY, Buffalo, 1965; MS in Edn., Queens Coll., 1968; cert., N.Y. Sch. Interior Design, 1987. Cert. neuro-linguistic programming master practitioner, advanced clin. hynotherapist. Tchr. Sachem Cen. Sch. Dist., Holtsville, N.Y., 1965-66, N.Y.C. Schs., 1966-70; asst. designer Quadric, Inc., N.Y.C., 1986-87; pres. Norma Pofsky, Inc., Marlboro, N.J., 1987-94; pvt. practice behavioral cons., 1993—; pres. Collaborative Design Group, Freehold, N.J., 1994—; ptnr. Fancy Fixtures, Inc., 1995—. Work appeared in Planning the Perfect Living Room, 1991, also in newspaper, 1992, 95; subject of articles in newspaper Night and Day, 1988, mag. Contrasting Statements, 1990; contbr. articles to profl. publs.; columnist Asbury Park Press Home Sect. Mem. Nat. Guild Hypnotherapists, Am. Soc. Interior Designers (Rene Baron Hennessy Meml. award for excellence N.J. chpt. 1999), N.J. Assn. Women Bus. Owners, Western Monmouth C. of C. (women in bus. com. 1988—), Allied Bd. Trade. Jewish. Office: 393 W Main St Freehold NJ 07728-2517

POGNONEC, YVES MAURICE, steel products executive; b. Rennes, Bretagne, France, Jan. 21, 1948; came to U.S., 1983; s. Jean P. and Simone J. (Boudot) P. M in Engring., Centrale Paris, 1970; MA in Bus., CPA, Paris, 1982. Cons. Office of Graham Parker, Paris, 1972-75; sales mgr. fittings dept. Vallourec S.A., 1975-79, mgr. engring. dept., 1980-82; v.p. mktg. and sales Vallourec Inc., Houston, 1983-88, exec. v.p., 1989-97, pres., 1998—; v.p. Vallourec & Mannesmann Tubes Corp., 1997—. Advisor French Fgn. Trade Counselors, Houston, 1987—. Bd. trustees Awty Internat. Sch., Houston, 1997—. Lt. French Air Force, 1970-71. Mem. Assn. Ecole Centrale, Nat. Assn. Steel Pipe Distbrs. (bd. dirs.). Avocations: pilot, scuba diving, tennis. Office: Vallourec Inc 1990 Post Oak Blvd Ste 1400 Houston TX 77056-3813

POGREBIN, BERTRAND B. lawyer; b. Bklyn., Apr. 10, 1934; s. Abraham and Esther Pogrebin; m. Letty Cottin; children: Abigail, Robin, David. AB, Rutgers U., 1955; LLB, Harvard U., 1958. Bar: N.Y. 1959, U.S. Dist. Ct. (ea. and so. dists.) N.Y. 1963, U.S. Ct. Appeals (2d cir.) 1965, U.S. Ct. Appeals (4th cir.) 1965, U.S. Ct. Appeals (6th cir.) 1970, U.S. Ct. Appeals (9th cir.) 1987, U.S. Supreme Ct. 1991. Pres. Rains & Pogrebin, P.C., N.Y.C., 1959—. Adj. prof. law NYU, 1975-90, Hofstra Law Sch., 1980-82, 86-91, 97-98; vis. lectr. Yale Law Sch., 1983. Co-author: Labor Relations: The Basic Process, Law and Practice, 1988, 2d edit., 1999. Mem. Am. Jewish Congress; v.p., bd. dirs. Appleseed Found. Mem. ABA, N.Y.C. Bar Assn., Nassau County Bar Assn., Suffolk County Bar Assn., Indsl. Rels. Rsch. Assn. Home: 33 W 67th St New York NY 10023-6224 Office: 210 Old Country Rd Mineola NY 11501-4218 also: 375 Park Ave New York NY 10152-0002 E-mail: BPogrebin@Rainslaw.com.

POGREBIN, LETTY COTTIN, writer, lecturer; b. N.Y.C., June 9, 1939; d. Jacob and Cyral (Halpern) Cottin; m. Bertrand B. Pogrebin, Dec. 8, 1963; children: Abigail and Robin (twins), David. AB cum laude with spl. distinction in English and Am. Lit, Brandeis U., 1959. V.p. Bernard Geis Assocs. (book pubs.), N.Y.C., 1960-70; columnist The Working Woman column Ladies Home Jour., 1971-81; founder, editor Ms mag., N.Y.C., 1971-87, columnist, editor at large, 1987-89, contbg. editor, 1990—; columnist The N.Y. Times, Newsday, Washington Post, Moment Mag., Washington, 1990—, Moment Mag., Washington, 1990—; contbg. editor Family Circle, Ms. mag., Tikkun mag. Cons. Free to Be, You and Me projects, 1972—; lectr. women's issues and family politics, changing roles of men and women, friendship in Am., non-sexist child rearing and edn., Judaism and feminism, Mid-East politics. Author: How to Make It in a Man's World, 1970, Getting Yours: How to Make the System Work for the Working Woman, 1975, Growing Up Free, 1980, Stories for Free Children, 1982, Family Politics, 1983, Among Friends, 1986, Deborah, Golda, and Me: Being Female and Jewish in America, 1991, Getting Over Getting Older: An Intimate Journey, 1996, Three Daughters: A Novel, 2002; mem. editl. bd. Tikkun Mag., Commonquest mag.; contbr. articles to N.Y. Times, Washington Post, Boston Globe, The Nation, TV Guide, Family Circle, Elle, Travel & Leisure, also other mags., newspapers. Pres. Author's Guild, 1998-2002; bd. dirs. Ms. Found. for Edn. and Comm., New Israel Fund, Jewish Fund for Justice, Commn. on Women's Equality, Am. Jewish Congress, PEN Am.; mem. Task Force on Women Fedn. Jewish Philanthropies, Women's Forum. Pointer fellow Yale U., 1982, MacDowell Colony fellow, 1979, 89, 94, 2000, Cummington Colony Arts fellow 1985, Edna St. Vincent Millay Colony fellow, 1985; recipient Matrix award Women in Comm., 1981, Gloria Steinem Women of Vision award Ms. Found. for Women, 1990, Abram L. Sachar medal Brandeis U., 1994, Woman of Valor award Jewish Fund for Justice, 1997, Woman of Achievement award N. Shore Child and Family Assn., 1997, Hannah G. Solomon award Nat. Coun. Jewish Women, 1997, Woman of Distinction award Kingsborough Coll., 1998, U.S./Israel Women-to-Women award, 1999, N.Y.C. Contr.'s Jewish Heritage award, 1999; named Woman of Yr. Fifty-Plus Expo, 1997, Outstanding Scholars 21st Century, 2000, Vet. Feminists of Am. Hon. Roll, 2002. Address: care Rosenstone/Wender 3 E 48th St New York NY 10017-1027

POGSON, STEPHEN WALTER, lawyer; b. N.Y.C., May 11, 1937; s. Percy Walter and Catherine (Hawbaker) P.; m. Linda Hammond, Aug. 20, 1966; children: Clyde Hammond, Catherine Anne. BA, U. Ariz., 1958, LLB, 1961. Bar: Ariz. 1961, U.S. Ct. Appeals (9th cir.) 1968, U.S. Supreme Ct. 1970. Assoc. Evans, Kitchel & Jenckes, Phoenix, 1962-67, ptnr., 1967-90; adminstrv. law judge Indrl. Commn. Ariz., 1990—, vice chief ALJ, 1997—. Served with U.S. Army, 1961-62. Mem. ABA. Democrat. Presbyterian. Office: 800 W Washington St Ste 400 Phoenix AZ 85007-2934

POGUE, DONALD CARL, federal judge; b. 1947; BA magna cum laude, Dartmouth Coll., 1969; student, U. Essex, 1969-70; MA, JD, Yale U., 1974. Bar: Conn. 1974. Pvt. practice, 1974-75; ptnr. Kestell, Pogue & Gould, 1976-89; commr. Conn. Commn. Hosps. and Health Care, 1989-94; judge Conn. Superior Ct., 1994-95, U.S. Ct. Internat. Trade, N.Y.C., 1995—. Mem. Phi Beta Kappa. Office: US Ct Internat Trade One Federal Plz New York NY 10278-0001

POGUE, JOHN MARSHALL, physician, editor, researcher; b. Washington, Sept. 21, 1945; s. L(loyd) Welch and Mary Ellen (Edgerton) P. *His father and mother are his guiding lights. Ancestor William Bradford "was the first American citizen of the English race who bore rule by the free choice of his brethren", the first American historian, and thus the Father of American History. Ancestor Hannah (Bradford) Ripley (Governor William Bradford's granddaughter) was America's first physician of her gender. His uncle, Massachusetts Institute of Technology Institute Professor Harold Eugene Edgerton, enhanced his interest in Science. He worked with Harold on ultra-high-speed photography in Harold's Stroboscopic Light Laboratory and on sonar probes. The difficult Harold did at once; the impossible took a little longer.* AB with honors, Princeton U.; MD, Georgetown U. Diplomate Nat. Bd. Med. Examiners. Intern/resident Georgetown U. Hosp., Washington; editor, author Bradford Jour., 1983—; historian Gov. Bradford Compact, 1996—, surgeon, 1999—. Spkr. in field of cardiology. *He is a Fellow of five Scientific and Learned Societies, and he is active in numerous Cardiology Societies. He received Honors in various Medical School courses, having ranked within the top 5% of the entire Medical School class in those courses. As a premedical student at Princeton University, he achieved high academic distinction climaxed by his ranking within the top 2% of his class of 789 students in the junior year-the year that is particularly important for premedical students. He also received a Letter of Individual Commendation for his scholarship from the Dean of the College at Princeton.* Designer ofcl. flag Gov. William Bradford Flag, 1987 (New Constellation award Nat. Flag Found., 1996); editor, contbr.: Pogue/Pollock/Polk Genealogy as Mirrored in History, From Scotland to Northern Ireland/Ulster, Ohio, and Westward, 1990 (recipient 7 awards, 5 first-place in genealogy and 2 meritorious in history); assoc. editor: Hereditary Soc. Blue Book, 1997—; author: Herbert Martin Giffin, M.D., A Role Model Physician and a Doctor's Doctor: From Princeton to Johns Hopkins, Mayo Clinic, USN, and Yater Clinic, 2000; contbr. articles on cardiology to med. jours. Fellow Royal Soc. Medicine, Royal Microscopical Soc. Oxford, Royal Statis. Soc., Royal Geog. Soc., Royal Soc. Arts; mem. AMA, Cardiothoracic Sect. Royal Soc. Medicine, Coun. Clin. Cardiology of Am. Heart Assn., Laennec Cardiovascular Sound Soc., European Soc. Cardiology, Am. Soc. Echocardiography (coun. on cardiac sonography, coun. on intraoperative echocardiography), Internat. Soc. Cardiovasc. Ultrasound, Internat. Cardiac Doppler Soc., Internat. Soc. Electrocardiology (Glasgow U.), Internat. Soc. for Holter and Noninvasive Electrocardiology, Soc. for Cardiovasc. Magnetic Resonance, Heart Failure Soc. Am., Capital area Heart Failure Soc. (founding mem) 2002, Internat. Soc. Cardiovascular Pharmacotherapy (Switzerland), Internat. Soc. Heart Rsch. (Can.), Cardiac Muscle Soc., World Heart Fedn. (Switzerland), Friends of Nat. Libr. Medicine (founding mem.), Friends of McGill U. Osler Med. Libr., Friends of Oxford U. Mus. of History of Sci., Ashmolean Natural History Soc. Oxford, Oxford Hist. Soc., Internat. Shakespeare Assn. Stratford-upon-Avon, Princeton U. Alumni Assn., Princeton Tigertones Alumni, Soc. of Mayflower Descs. D.C. (surgeon 1998—), Order Descs. of Colonial Physicians and Chirurgiens (surgeon gen. 1994-2000, chmn. hon. membership com. 1994—, v.p. 2000—), Provincial Families Maryland, Royal Soc. Medicine Book Club, RSM Music Soc./Royal Soc. Medicine Music Club, The Princeton Univ. Club (Washington), Oxford Bibliogr. Soc. of Oxford U. Bodleian Libr. Avocations: reading Shakespeare, classical music. Home and Office: 5204 Kenwood Ave Chevy Chase MD 20815-6604

POGUE, L(LOYD) WELCH, lawyer; b. Grant, Iowa, Oct. 21, 1899; s. Leander Welch and Myrtle Viola (Casey) P.; m. Mary Ellen Edgerton, Sept. 8, 1926; children: Richard Welch, William Lloyd, John Marshall. AB, U. Nebr., 1924; JD, U. Mich., 1926; SJD, Harvard U., 1927. Bar: Mass., N.Y., D.C., Ohio, U.S. Supreme Ct. Assoc. Ropes, Gray, Boyden and Perkins, 1927-33; ptnr. affiliated firm Searle, James and Crawford, N.Y.C., 1933-38; asst. gen. counsel CAB, 1938-39, gen. counsel, through 1941, chmn. bd., 1942-46; mem., mng. ptnr. Pogue & Neal, Washington, 1946-67; Washington mng. ptnr. Jones, Day, Reavis & Pogue, 1967-79, ret., 1981. Lindbergh Meml. lectr. Nat. Air and Space Mus., Smithsonian Inst., 1991; presenter essay 50th Ann. Internat. Civil Aviation Orgn., Montreal, 1994; Wright Bros. Meml. lectr., 1999; spkr. and lectr. in field. Author: International Civil Air Transport—Transition Following WW II, 1979, Pogue/Pollock/Polk Genealogy as Mirrored in History, 1990 (1st pl. in Anna Ford Family history book contest 1991, Nat. Genealogical Soc. award for excellence genealogy and family history 1992, William H. and Benjamin Harrison Book award Coun. Ohio Genealogists 1992, Outstanding Achievement award County and Regional History category Ohio Assn. Hist. Socs. and Mus. 1992, 1st pl. award Iowa Washington County Geneal. Soc. 1994, cert. commendation Am. Assn. State and Local History 1994, 1st place award Lake Havasu Geneal. Soc. 1996), Airline Deregulation, Before and After: What Next? (Lindbergh Meml. lectr. 1991), The International Civil Aviation Conference, and Its Sequel, The Anglo-American Bermuda Air Transport Agreement, 1946, 94; The Wright Brothers Memorial Lecture (Annually given) NASA Langley Research Center, 1999; contbr. articles to profl. publs. Mem. U.S. dels.: Chgo. Internat. Civil Aviation Conf., 1944; vice chmn. Bermuda United Kingdom-U.S. Conf., 1946; vice chmn. Provisional Internat. Civil Aviation Orgn. Assembly, 1946; active Internat. Civil Aviation Orgn. Assembly, 1947. With AUS, 1918. Recipient Elder Statesman of Aviation award Nat. Aeronautic Assn., Golden Eagle award Soc. Sr. Aerospace Execs., 1st annual recipient of L. Welch Pogue award for Aviation Achievement, McGraw-Hill Orgn.'s Aviation Week Group, 1994, Laurel Legend award and named to Laureate Hall of Fame; fellow Am. Helicopter Soc., Benjamin Franklin fellow Royal Soc. Arts. Fellow Royal Aero. Soc.; mem. AIAA (hon., Certificate of 60 yrs. continuous membership), Soc. of Sr. Aerospace Execs. (hon.), Helicopter Assn. Internat. (hon. mem.), Am. Air Mus. in Britain (founding mem.), Can. Aeronautics and Space Inst., Nat. Aeronautic Assn. (pres. 1947), Nat. Air and Space Soc. (founder), Nat. Geneal. Soc., Soc. Sr. Aerospace Execs., New Eng. Hist. Geneal. Soc. (life, former trustee), Ohio Geneal. Soc. (life), Md. Geneal. Soc. (life), Md. Hist. Soc. (life), Provincial Families of Md., First Families of Ohio, Met. Club, Univ. Club, Wings Club (hon., N.Y.C.), Bohemian Club (San Francisco), Cosmos Club, Masons, Order of the First World War (charter), Nat. Aviation Club, Aero Club of Washington (hon. mem., Donald D. Engen trophy for aviation excellence), Am. Legion (cert. of 80 years continuous membership, Life Membership, 2002). Home: 5204 Kenwood Ave Chevy Chase MD 20815-6604 Office: Jones Day Reavis & Pogue 51 Louisiana Ave NW Washington DC 20001-2113

POGUE, MARY ELLEN E. (MRS. L(LOYD) WELCH POGUE), youth and community worker; b. Fremont, Nebr., Oct. 27, 1904; d. Frank Eugene and Mary Nettie (Coe) Edgerton; m. L. Welch Pogue, Sept. 8, 1926; children: Richard Welch, William Lloyd, John Marshall. BFA in Edn. Music, U. Nebr., 1926; studied violin with Harrison Keller, Boston Conservatory of Music, 1926-28; studied violin with Kemp Stillings, Violin Master Class, 1935-37. Mem. Potomac String Ensemble, Washington, 1939-80. Compiler, editor: Favorite Menus and Recipes of Mary Edgerton of Aurora, Nebraska, 1963, Family History of Frank Eugene Edgerton and Mary Coe Edgerton of Aurora, Nebraska, 1965. Historian, Gov. William Bradford Compact, 1966—; vice chmn. Montgomery County (Md.) Victory Garden Ctr., 1946-47; pres. Bethesda Cmty. Garden Club, 1946-47; founder Montgomery County YWCA, bd. dirs., 1946-50, 52-55; founder Welcome to Washington Internat. Club Music Group, 1967—; co-founder Group Piano in Montgomery County, Md. schs., 1954. Recipient Gov. William Bradford Compact Cert. of Merit award, 1970, Outstanding Svc. award Bethesda United Meth. Ch., 1984, Bethesda Cmty. Garden Club award, 1985, 93, Devoted Svc. award Mayflower Descendants in D.C., 1985, 89, Welcome to Washington Internat. Club award, 1986, Mortar Board award, 1986. Mem. Gen. Soc. Mayflower Descs., Soc. Mayflower Descs. D.C. (dir. D.C. 1954—, elder 1974-92, elder emeritus 1992—), Nat. Soc. Daus. Founders and Patriots Am., PEO Sisterhood (pres. 1957-59, charter mem. chpt. R, 75 Year Mem. Tribute), Mortar Bd. Alumnae Club (pres. 1965-67, award 1986, 75 Year Member Honor.), Nat. Capitol Area Fedn. Garden Clubs, Nat. Coun. State Garden Clubs, Bethesda United Meth. Women, Nat. Geneal. Soc., New Eng. Historic Geneal. Soc. (life), Ohio Geneal. Soc. (life), Md. Geneal. Soc., Md. Hist. Soc., Conn. Soc. Genealogists, Pilgrim Soc. (life), Plimoth Plantation, Hereditary Order Descs. Colonial Govs., Nat. Soc. Magna Charta Dames, Colonial Order of Crown, Sovereign Colonial Soc. Ams. Royal Descent, Order of Descs. Colonial Physicians and Chirurgiens, Hereditary Soc. Blue Book (perpetual mem.), Nat. Soc. Women Descs. Ancient and Hon. Arty. Co., First Families Ohio, First Families Nebr., Century Families Nebr., Oreg. Trail Pioneers, Sons and Daus. Colonial and Antebellum Bench and Bar 1565-1861 (charter), Welcome to Washington Internat. Club, Ind. Agy. Women (assoc.), Capital Spkrs. Club (Washington), The Plantagenet Soc., Soc. Descs. Knights of Most Noble Order of Garter, DAR, Order Ams. Armorial Ancestry, Saybrook Colony Founders Assn., Soc. Founders Norwich Conn. (cert. desc. Richard Edgerton), Kenwood Country Club, Alpha Phi (75 yr. mem. cert.), Alpha Rho Tau, Delta Omicron Music (life). Methodist. Avocations: genealogy, gardening, music. Home: 5204 Kenwood Ave Chevy Chase MD 20815-6604

POGUE, RICHARD WELCH, lawyer; b. Cambridge, Mass., Apr. 26, 1928; s. Lloyd Welch and Mary Ellen (Edgarton) P.; m. Patricia Ruth Raney, July 10, 1954; children: Mark, Tracy, David. BA, Cornell U., 1950; JD, Mich. Law Sch., 1953. Bar: Mich. 1953, Ohio 1957, U.S. Dist. Ct. (no. dist.) Ohio 1960, U.S. Ct. Appeals (6th cir.) 1972, U.S. Ct. Appeals (D.C. and 9th cirs.) 1979. Assoc. Jones, Day, Reavis & Pogue, Cleve., 1957-60, ptnr., 1961—, mng. ptnr., 1984-92, sr. ptnr., 1993-94; sr. advisor Dix & Eaton, 1994—. Vis. prof. Mich. Law Sch., 1993-95; bd. dirs.Continental Airlines, Inc., Houston, Roten Inc., Aurora, Ohio, Viztek Inc., Twinsburg, Ohio. Chmn. Cleve. Found., 1985-89, Greater Cleve. Roundtable, 1986-89, Greater Cleve. Growth Assn., 1991-93, Univ. Hosps., 1994—, trustee 1975—, Cleve. Ballet, 1983-85, United Negro Coll. Fund., Cleve., 1979, United Way Cleve., 1989, Kulas Found., 1998-, Bus. Vol. United, 1998-2001, Nat. Inventors Hall of Fame, 1996-, Newcomen Soc. U.S., Phila., 2000-; mem. Adminstrv. Conf. U.S., 1974-80; vice chmn. Cleve. Tomorrow, 1988-93; trustee Case Western Res. U.; active Coun. Fgn. Rels., 1989—, Am./EC Assn. Bus. Adv. Coun., 1988-93; trustee Rock and Roll Hall of Fame and Mus., 1986—; co-chmn. 1996 Cleve. Bicentennial Commn., interim chmn. Cleve. Inst. Music, 1994. Capt. U.S. Army, 1954-57. Recipient Outstanding Alumnus award U. Mich. Club, Cleve., 1983, Torch of Liberty award Anti-Defamation League, 1989, Leadership Cleve. Vol. of Yr. award, 1990, 1st Econ. Devel. Workshop award Nat. Coun. on Urban Econ. Devel., 1992, Humanitarian award Nat. Conf. Christians and Jews, 1992; named Cleve. Bus. Exec. of Yr., 2000, Cleve. United Way Vol. of Yr., 2002. Mem. ABA (chmn. antitrust sect. 1983-84), Ohio State Bar Assn. (chmn. antitrust sect. 1969-73). Clubs: Bohemian (San Francisco), Soc., Union (Cleve.). Republican. Mem. United Ch. of Christ.

POGUE, THOMAS FRANKLIN, economics educator, consultant; b. Roswell, NMex., Dec. 28, 1935; s. Talmadge Franklin and Lela (Cox) P.; m. Colette Marie LaFortune, June 10, 1961; children: Michael Frederick, Robert Franklin. BS, N.Mex. State U., 1957; MS, Okla. State U., 1962; PhD, Yale U., 1968. Asst. prof. econs U. Iowa, Iowa City, 1965-69, assoc. prof., 1970-75, prof., 1975—, chmn dept., 1983-84. Vis. prof. Tex. Tech. U., Lubbock, 1975-76, U. Adelaide, Australia, 1985, 89. Author: Government and Economic Choice, 1978; editor: State Taxation of Business, 1992; contbr. articles to profl. jours.; cons. on tax policy, welfare reform, pub. sch. fin., bus. taxation, and econ. devel. Tax Studies for Iowa, 1992, Minn, 1984, Ariz., 1989. Commd. officer with USAF, 1957-60. Grantee Nat. Inst. Justice, Washington, 1979, U.S. Dept. Transp., 1994. Mem. Am. Econ. Assn., Nat. Tax. Assn. Office: U Iowa Dept Econs 108 Pappajohn Bus Adminstrn Bldg Iowa City IA 52242 Home: 24 Colwyn Ct Iowa City IA 52245-1578 E-mail: thomas-pogue@uiowa.edu.

POGUE, WILLIAM REID, former astronaut, foundation executive, business and aerospace consultant; b. Okemah, Okla., Jan. 23, 1930; s. Alex W. and Margaret (McDow) P.; m. Jean Ann Pogue; children: William Richard, Layna Sue, Thomas Reid. BS in Secondary Edn., Okla. Bapt. U., 1951, D.Sc. (hon.), 1974; MS in Math., Okla. State U., 1960. Commd. 2d lt. USAF, 1952, advanced through grades to col., 1973; combat fighter pilot Korea, 1953; gunnery instr. Luke AFB, Ariz., 1954; mem. acrobatic team USAF Thunderbirds, Luke AFB and Nellis AFB, Nev., 1955-57; asst. prof. math. USAF Acad., 1960-63; exchange test pilot Brit. Royal Aircraft Establishment, Ministry Aviation, Farnborough, Eng., 1964-65; instr. USAF Aerospace Research Pilots Sch., Edwards AFB, Calif., 1965-66; astronaut NASA Manned Spacecraft Center, Houston, 1966-75; pilot 3d manned visit to Skylab space sta.; ret. Decorated Air medal with oak leaf cluster, D.S.M.; named to Five Civilized Tribes Hall of Fame, Choctaw descent; recipient Distinguished Service medal NASA, Collier trophy Nat. Aero. Assn.; Robert H. Goddard medal Nat. Space Club; Gen. Thomas D. White USAF Space Trophy Nat. Geog. Soc.; Halley Astronautics award, 1975; de la Vaalx medal Fedn. Aeronautique Internat., 1974; V.M. Komarov diploma, 1974; inducted into Okla. Aviation and Space Hall of Fame, 1980, U.S. Astronaut Hall of Fame, 1997. Fellow Acad. Arts and Scis. of Okla. State U., Am. Astron. Soc.; mem. Soc. Exptl. Test Pilots, Explorers Club, Sigma Xi, Pi Mu Epsilon. Baptist (deacon). Home: 4 Cromer Dr Bella Vista AR 72715-5318

POH, CHURN K. chemical engineer, researcher; b. Labuan, Malaysia; s. Tiong Ho and Li Cheng (Chen) P. BSChemE, U. Ky., 1998, MSME, 2000. Rschr. U. Ky., Lexington, 1998—. Contbr. articles to sci. jours. including Advances in Heat and Mass Transfer in Biotech., Procs. AIChE, Procs. Am. Soc. Nephrology, Procs. Am. Soc. Artificial Internal Organs, Procs. Internat. Soc. Magnetic Resonance Medicine, Jour. Membrane Sci., Procs. N.Am. Membrane Soc., Procs. Soc. Cryobiology. Mem. AIChE (1st place award for Regional Reactor Design award 1997), ASME, Soc. Cryobiology, Am. Soc. Artificial Internal Organs (Fellowship award 2001), Order of Engr., Omega Chi Epsilon. Achievements include research on characterization of fluid flow in artificial kidneys using magnetic resonance imaging. Avocations: golf, tennis, skiing, hiking, travel. Office: U Ky UK Med Ctr 40 MRISC Bldg Lexington KY 40536-0098 E-mail: ckpoh01@engr.uky.edu.

POHAN, ARMAND, transportation executive, professional hockey club executive, lawyer; b. Langley Field, Va., Apr. 28, 1944; s. Armen and Helen (Turner) P.; m. Margaret A. Neigel, Dec. 18, 1976; children: Andrew Stephen, Alicia Margaret, Amanda Turner AB, Harvard U., 1964, JD, 1967. Bar: N.J. 1967. Assoc. McCarter & English, Newark, 1968-70; asst. prosecutor Hudson County, N.J., 1970-72; assoc. McCarter & English, 1973-76, ptnr., 1976-77; v.p. A-P-A Transport Corp., North Bergen, N.J., 1977-83, pres., 1983—, Colo. Rockies Hockey Club, Denver, 1978-81, chmn. bd. dirs., 2001—, NY Waterway, 2001—. Mem. Fort Lee Bd. Adjustment, N.J., 1977-78; mem. Fort Lee Planning Bd., 1979, 2002—, borough atty., Fort Lee, 1973-76; bd. govs. Nat. Hockey League, 1978-81; trustee Bede Sch., Englewood, N.J., 1984-90; trustee Dwight-Englewood Sch., 1984-92, pres., 1985-92. Mem. N.J. Bar Assn. Office: A-P-A Transport Corp 2100 88th St North Bergen NJ 07047-4721

POHL, ADOLF LEOPOLD, clinical chemist, quality assurance consultant; b. St. Poelten, Austria, Dec. 14, 1936; s. Adolf Theodor and Cornelia Maria Anna (Moerth) P.; m. Ingrid Maria Antonia Payer, Feb. 24, 1962 (div. Dec. 11, 1975); children: Martin, Ulrike; m. Nanako Tanaka, Mar. 14, 1989; 1 child, Anna Yumi. Grad. in classical studies, Stiftsgymnasium Melk, 1954; BSc, U. Vienna, 1957, MSc, 1965, DPhil, 1968. Rsch. asst. med. dept. I U. Vienna Med. Sch., 1967-69, asst. prof., 1969-85, head erythrocyte enzyme lab. med. dept. I, 1969-85, founder tumor marker lab., 1978, head tumor marker lab., 1984-85, assoc. prof. med. dept. I, dept. chemotherapy, 1985-87, assoc. prof. dept. clin. labs., 1987-97. Quality assurance cons. Med. Pharm. Rsch. Ctr., Vienna, 1993—. Mem. editl. bd. Cancer Molecular Biology Jour., 1994—; contbr. articles to profl. jours., chpts. to books. Recipient Austrian Med. Assn. award, 1969. Mem. Am. Assn. for Clin. Chemistry, N.Y. Acad. Scis., IEEE Computer Soc., Drug Info. Assn. Achievements include discovery in human blood serum of a new ADP-ribosyltransferase, implementation of advanced data analysis in clinical chemistry, detection by new micromethods of phospholipid metabolism in red blood cell membranes and study of its abnormalities in hemolytic anemia; research on serum glycosyltransferases as possible cancer markers and critical analysis of galactosyltransferase heterogeneity; leading of 1st foldboat expedition on Tenojoki, 1st behavioral studies of Thai ferret badger. Avocations: botany and wildlife research, humanitarianism, philosophy, poetry. Home: Lambrechtgasse 3/10 A-1040 Vienna Austria E-mail: adolf.pohl@chello.at.

POHL, FREDERIK, freelance/self-employed writer; b. N.Y.C., Nov. 26, 1919; s. Fred George and Anna Jane (Mason) P.; m. Carol Ulf, Sept. 15, 1953 (div. 1981); children— Ann, Karen, Frederik, Kathy; m. Elizabeth Anne Hull, July 27, 1984 Editor Popular Pubs., N.Y.C., 1939-43; editor Popular Sci., 1946-49; freelance writer, 1950-60, 80—; editor Galaxy Pubs., 1961-69, Bantam Books, N.Y.C., 1973-80. Author: Man Plus, 1977 (Nebula award), Gateway, 1978 (Nebula, Hugo, Campbell awards, Prix Apollo award), Jem, 1979 (Am. Book award), The Years of the City (Campbell award 1985), Chasing Science, 2000. Served to sgt. USAAF, 1943-45; Italy Recipient Popular Culture Assn. award, 1982 Fellow AAAS, Brit. Interplanetary Soc.; mem. Sci. Fiction Writers of Am. (pres. 1974-76, Grand Master award 1993), World Sci. Fiction (pres. 1980-82), Authors Guild, N.Y. Acad. Scis., Astron. Soc. Pacific. Democrat. Unitarian Universalist. Home: 855 Harvard Dr Palatine IL 60067-7026

POHL, GUNTHER ERICH, retired library administrator; b. Berlin, July 22, 1925; came to U.S., 1927; s. Erich Ernst and Martha (Seidel) P.; m. Dorothy Edna Beck, Aug. 21, 1949; children: Christine, Louise, Elizabeth, Ronald BA, NYU, 1947, MA, 1950; MLS., Columbia U., 1951. Librarian local history and genealogy divsn. N.Y. Pub. Libr., N.Y.C., 1948-69, chief local history and genealogy divsn., 1969-85, ret., 1985. Compiler: N.Y. State Biography and Portrait Index. Fellow N.Y. Geneal. and Biog. Soc.; mem. ALA (chmn. genealogy com. 1971-73, 76-78, History sect. award 1996), N.Y. Geneal. and Biog. Soc. (libr., trustee 1982-92), Sigma Phi Epsilon (trustee local chpt. 1978—). Republican. Avocations: stamps, opera, collecting New Yorkiana. Home: 24 Walden Pl Great Neck NY 11020-1065

POHL, JOHN MARTIN DELAND, archaeologist; b. Mpls., Aug. 16, 1952; s. John Florian Pohl and Alice Elizabeth Croze; m. Georganne Deen, Aug. 17, 1989. BA, Hampshire Coll., 1975; postgrad., Calif. Inst. of the Arts, 1975-76; MA, UCLA, 1978, PhD, 1984. Staff artist Tyrone Guthrie Theatre, Mpls., 1970-75; creative cons. Walt Disney Imagineering, L.A., 1980-98; series writer, prodr.-computer graphics CBS TV series 500 Nations, 1991-94; visual cons. Dreamworks SKG, 1996-2000; writer, designer The Mus. of the Cherokee Indian, Cherokee, N.C., 1996-98; prodr., writer, designer Moundville (Ala.) Archaeol. Mus., 2000—. Adv. bd. Found. for the Advancement of Mesoamerican Studies Inc., Crystal River, Fla., 1999—; dir. Mixtec studies Maya Meetings Found., U. Tex., Austin, 1992—; rsch. assoc. Fowler Mus. of Cultural History, UCLA, 1991—; vis. prof. dept. art history UCLA, 1995—, U. Calif., Irvine, 2000; vis. prof. dept. anthropology U. Calif., Riverside, 1996; spkr. in field. Author: Exploring Mesoamerica, 1999, Politics and Symbolism of the Mixtec Codices, 1994, In the Realm of Eight Deer, 1994, Aztec, Mixtec and Zapotec Armies, 1990, Aztec Warriors, 2001, Conquistador, 2001, The Epic of Eight Deer, 2001. Grantee Wenner Gren Found., 1989, CUNY, 1985, 87, 89, The Can. Coun., 1982; Alisa Mellon Bruce fellow Nat. Gallery of Art, 1994, Trustees for Harvard U. fellow Dumbarton Oaks, 1988, 90-91, CLIO award CLIO Enterprises, Inc., 1988. Mem. Coll. Art Assn., Nat. Broadcast Designers Assn., Am. Illustration. Achievements include discoverer The Arago skull 500,000 B.P. Avocations: painting, sculpture. Home: 3834 Aloha St Los Angeles CA 90027 E-mail: johnpohl@mac.com.

POHL, ROBERT OTTO, physics educator; b. Gottingen, Germany, Dec. 17, 1929; came to U.S., 1958; s. Robert Wichard and Auguste Eleonore (Madelung) P.; m. Karin Ursula Koehler, May 6, 1961; children: Helen M., Robert S., Otto C. Vordiplom, U. Freiburg, Fed. Rep. Germany, 1951; diploma, U. Erlangen, Fed. Rep. Germany, 1955, Dr. rer. nat., 1957. Asst. U. Erlangen, 1957-58; rsch. assoc. Cornell U., Ithaca, NY, 1958-60, asst. prof., 1960-63, assoc. prof., 1963-68, prof., 1968-2000, Goldwin Smith prof. physics emeritus, 2000—. Vis. prof. Tech. Hochschule Stuttgart, 1966-67, Tech. U. Munchen, 1973-74, Konstanz U., Regensburg U., 1987-88, all Fed. Republic Germany; vis. scientist Nuc. Research Ctr., Juelich, Fed. Rep. Germany, 1980-81, Hahn-Meitner Inst., Berlin, 1995. Contbr. articles on solid state physics to profl. jours. Recipient Sr. Scientist award Alexander von Humboldt Found., 1980; Guggenheim Found. fellow, 1973, Erskine fellow U. Canterbury, New Zealand, 1988. Fellow AAAS, Am. Inst. Physics (O.E. Buckley award 1985); mem. NAS, Internat. Thermal Conductivity Confs. Office: Cornell U Physics Dept Ithaca NY 14853-2501 E-mail: pohl@ccmr.cornell.edu.

POHLAND, FREDERICK GEORGE, environmental engineering educator, researcher; b. Oconomowoc, Wis., May 3, 1931; s. Arnold Ernest and Eda Karoline (Petermann) P.; m. Virginia Ruth Simmons, Sept. 10, 1966; 1 child, Elizabeth Eda. BS in Civil Engring., Valparaiso U., 1953; MS in Civil Engring., Purdue U., 1958, PhD, 1961; DSc (hon.), Valparaiso U., 1996. Profl. engr.; diplomate Am. Acad. Environ. Engrs. Civil engr. Erie Railroad Co., Huntington, Ind., 1953; preventive medicine specialist U.S. Army, Ft. Bragg, N.C., 1953-56; grad. rsch. asst. Purdue U., West Lafayette, Ind., 1956-61; asst. prof. Ga. Inst. Tech., Atlanta, 1961-64, assoc. prof., 1964-71, prof., 1971-88; Weidlein prof. U. Pitts., 1989—. Vis. scholar U. Mich., Ann Arbor, 1967-68; guest prof. Delft U. Tech., Netherlands, 1976-77; mem. sci. adv. bd. EPA, Washington, 1989—, Nat. Inst. for Environ. Renewal, 1995-99; mem. sci. adv. com. Gulf Coast Hazardous Substance Rsch. Ctr., Beaumont, Tex., 1989-92, EPRI, Palo Alto, Calif., 1990-94; mem. adv. commn. Purdue U., 1990-94; mem. com. on water rsch., adv. tech. human support in space and on innovative techs. NRC, 1993-96, mem. com. environ. mgmt. techs., 1997-99, mem. com. on toxicants and pathogenisn biosolids applied to soil, 2000—, mem. com. environ. remediation at Naval facilities, 2000—, mem. com. rev. and evaluation of Army chem. stockpile disposal program, 2000—; mem. indsl. adv. com. DOD Advanced Applied Tech. Demonstration Facility, 1994-99; co-dir. EPA Ctr. for Groundwater Remediation Tech. Analysis, 1995—; mem. engring. dean's coun. U. Buffalo, 2001-. Author: Emerging Technologies in Hazardous Waste Management, 1990, 91, 93, 94, 95, 96, 97, 2000, Design of Anaerobic Processes for the Treatment of Industrial and Municipal Waste, 1992; regional editor (jour.) Water Rsch., 1983—2002, hon. exec. editor Water Rsch., 1994-2000; author over 130 publs. in field. Served with U.S. Army, 1953-56. Recipient Harrison Prescott Eddy medal Water Pollution Control Fedn., 1964, Charles Alvin Emerson medal, 1983, Gordon Maskew Fair medal, 1989; recipient Rsch. award Water Pollution Control Assn. Pa., 1991. Fellow ASCE (Freese lectr 2001), Am. Acad. Microbiology; mem. AIChE, NSPE, Am. Acad. Environ. Engrs. (diplomate, pres. 1992-93, Stanley E. Kappe award 1995, Gordon Maskew Fair award 2000), Assn. Environ. Engring. Profs. (sec.-treas. 1970-71, disting. lectr. 1992), Solid Waste Assn. N.Am. (Lawrence lectr. 1992), Am. Water Works Assn. (life), Nat. Acad. Engring., Am. Chem. Soc., Am. Soc. Microbiology, Ga. Soc. Profl. Engrs., Internat. Water Assn. (hon.), Pa. Soc. Profl. Engrs., Pa. Water and Pollution Control Assn., Sigma Xi, Tau Beta Pi, Chi Epsilon, others. Achievements include major contributions to phase separation in anaerobic treatment processes; originated concept of leachate recirculation for accelerated stabilization in landfill bioreactors. Home: 118 Millstone Ln Pittsburgh PA 15238-1624 Office: U Pittsburgh Dept Civil And Environ Engri Pittsburgh PA 15261-0001

POHLHAUS, JOHN ERNEST, international marketing executive, consultant; b. Phila., June 9, 1966; s. Ernest George and Joan Elizabeth (Sailer) P. BA magna cum laude, Temple U., 1989; MBA magna cum laude, Monterey (Calif.) Inst., 1995. Cons. Mgmt. Internat., Phila., 1988-89; cons., instr. Yokohama (Japan) Bd. Edn., 1989-90; instr. Ministry Edn., Atsugi, Japan, 1991-93; mem. staff internat. ops. Wilderness Trail Bikes, Mill Valley, Calif., 1994-95; mktg. rschr. Nihon Schering KK, Osaka, Japan, 1995; internat. mktg. supr. ship sales dept. Mitsubishi Internat. Corp., N.Y.C. Cons. Wilderness Trail Bikes, 1994-95; mentor Monterey Inst., 1995—. Author: The Guide to Atsugi, 1993. Player U.S. Embassy soccer team, Tokyo, 1991-93, Monterey Inst. soccer team, 1993-95; v.p. Japan Forum, Monterey, 1993-95. Named Hon. Japanese Citizen, Mayor of Atsugi, 1993. Mem. JET Program Alumni. Republican. Lutheran. Avocations: soccer, karate, mountain biking, chess, surfing. Home: 8531 Town Court North Lawrenceville NJ 08648 Office: Mitsubishi Internat Corp 520 Madison Ave New York NY 10022-4213

POHLMANN, MARCUS D. political science educator; b. Davenport, Iowa, Sept. 18, 1950; s. Clement A. and Lois L. (Smith) P.; m. Barbara A. Heimann, May 27, 1972; 1 child, Justin. BA, Cornell Coll., 1972; MA, Columbia U., 1974, MPhil, 1975, PhD, 1976. Rsch. assoc. Met. Applied Rsch. Ctr., N.Y.C., 1975-76; instr. The Spence Sch., 1975-76; cons. Media and Soc., 1982; Fulbright sr. lectr. Yerevan St. U., Armenia, USSR, 1982; asst. prof. Coll. of Wooster, Ohio, 1977-83; assoc. prof. Ark. State U., Jonesboro, 1983-86; prof. Rhodes Coll., Memphis, 1986—. Vis. asst. prof. Bates Coll., Lewiston, Maine, 1976-77. Author: Political Power in the Postindustrial City, 1986, Black Politics in Conservative America, 1990, 2d edit., 1999, Governing the Postindustrial City, 1993, Racial Politics at the Crossroads, 1996. Recipient Lydia C. Roberts fellowship Columbia U., N.Y.C., 1972-76. Mem. Am. Polit. Sci. Assn., Acad. Polit. Sci., Am. Mock Trial Assn. (bd. dirs.), Authors Guild. Democrat. Avocations: basketball, bridge, golf, hiking, canoeing. Home: 367 Forest Hill Irene Cordova TN 38018-4628 Office: Rhodes Coll 2000 North Pky Memphis TN 38112-1624 E-mail: pohlmann@rhodes.edu.

POHLMANN, WILLIAM HOWARD, lawyer; b. N.Y.C., Dec. 16, 1944; m. Linda Marie Fata, Nov., 1973; children: Craig, Christopher, Darren. BBA, Bernard M. Baruch Sch. Bus. and Pub. Adminstrn., 1966; JD, St. John's U., 1968; postgrad., NYU, 1970. Bar: N.Y. 1968, U.S. Supreme Ct. 1972, U.S. Dist. Ct. (ea. and so. dists.) N.Y. 1975, U.S. Ct. Appeals (2d cir.) 1975. Pvt. practice, Bronx, N.Y., 1968-69; asst. to justices appellate divsn. N.Y. State Supreme Ct., 1969-74, sr. law asst., 1974-76, jud. asst. to justice, 1976-89; pvt. practice N.Y., 1998-2000; asst. dep. commr. N.Y. State Dept. Taxation and Fin. Office Tax Enforcement, 2000—. Pres. Ardsley Engine Co. No. 1; adj. prof. law Iona Coll. Sch. Bus., 1982-83; asst. to chmn. Westchester County Bd. Legislators, 1990-95, legis. counsel to county bd., 1995-96, asst. to county exec., 1996-97; lectr. in field. Acting Village Justice, 1983-91; chmn. Greenburgh Rep. Town Com., 1995-99. Lt. col. USAR, 1981—. Mem. N.Y. State Bar Assn., Westchester County Bar Assn., White Plains Bar Assn., N.Y. State Magistrates Assn., Westchester County Magistrates Assn.

POHORECKY-DOLINSKY, LARISSA ALEXANDRA, pharmacologist; b. Cholm, Ukraine, Jan. 16, 1942; came to U.S., 1959; d. Roman and Maria Pohorecky; m. Adrian A. Dolinsky. BS in Pharmacy, U. Ill., 1963; PhD in Pharmacology, U. Chgo., 1967. Postdoctoral fellow MIT, Cambridge, Mass., 1967-70, rsch. assoc., 1970-71; asst. prof. Rockefeller U., N.Y.C., 1971-79; assoc. prof. Rutgers U., Piscataway, N.J., 1979-86, prof., 1986—. Cons. Nat. Inst. Alcoholism and Alcohol Abuse, Bethesda, Md., 1976-81, VA, Washington, 1992-95. E-mail: larissa@rci.rutgers.edu.

POHORELSKY, VIKTOR VACLAV, federal magistrate judge; b. 1949; BS, Tulane U., 1971, JD, 1980. Bar: NY 1982. Clk. to Hon. John M. Wisdom, U.S. Ct. Appeals for 5th Circuit, N.Y.C., 1980-81; assoc. Debevoise & Plimpton, 1981-84; asst. U.S. atty. for so. dist. N.Y., U.S. Dept. Justice, 1984-91; ptnr. Gold & Wachtel, 1991-94; magistrate judge for ea. dist. N.Y. U.S. Dist. Ct., Bklyn., 1995. Office: US Courthouse 225 Cadman Plz E Brooklyn NY 11201-1818

POIAN, EDWARD LICIO, historian; b. Trieste, Friuli, Italy, June 10, 1946; came to U.S., 1954; s. Angelo Del Picollo and Zaira (de Bourbon-Comelli) P.; m. Maria Del Carmen Lopez Cintron, Nov. 22, 1969 (div. Mar. 1980); children: Jeanne Marie, Nicole Anna; m. Nancy FLynn, Sept. 18, 1982. AS, U.S. Govt. Inst., 1965; BS, Mercy Coll., 1988; MS, L.I. U., 1989; PhD, U. Ariz., 1992. Chief exec. Budget Fin. Inc., Pittsfield, Mass., 1968-70; acting postmaster U.S. Postal Svc., Chappaqua, 1971-80; pres. chief exec. Nat. Assn. Letter Carriers, Cappaqua, N.Y., 1973-78; v.p. Lehman Bros Khun Loeb, N.Y.C., 1980-83; chief exec. officer Cosmopolitan Armaments, 1983-90; intern The UN Univ., 1989-90; prof. history Mercy Coll., Dobbs Ferry, N.Y., 1991—, prof. history and polit. sci., 1991—. Cons. in field; trustee archaeology dept. U. Trieste, 1986—; rector, CEO The Internat. Ednl. Rsch. Found. Inc., Yonkers, N.Y., 1991—; intern UN Univ., 1990; dir. history and govt. assn. Mercy Coll., 1988. Author: On the Outside Looking In, 1972, Peace and Regional Security Through Education in Africa, 1992, Problems in Coordination Among Western Donor Governments in Relations to Multilateral and Social Programmes of the United Nations System, 1990; contbr. articles to profl. jours. Active Amnesty Internat. With USCG, 1963-67, USCG Res., 1968-98. Decorated Knight of Malta Cross of Gregory the Great Vatican City. Recipient UN award, 1988. Fellow World Assn. of Former United Nations Interns and Fellows, U.S. Naval Inst. (life); mem. VFW, Yonker Hist. Soc., Am. Soc. Polit. Sci., Am. Legion, Navy League (life N.Y. chpt.), Freedom Coalition, Ret. Officers Assn., Phi Alpha Theta, Phi Gamma Mu. Republican. Roman Catholic. Avocations: archeology, historical research, art collector, philanthropy. Home: 1930 Hone Ave Bronx NY 10461-1304 Office: Mercy Coll Dept History and Polit Sci 555 Broadway Dobbs Ferry NY 10522-1134

POIANI, EILEEN LOUISE, mathematics educator, college administrator, higher education planner; b. Newark, Dec. 17, 1943; d. Hugo Francis and Eileen Louise (Crecca) P. BA in Math., Douglass Coll., 1965; MS in Math., Rutgers U., 1967, PhD in Math., 1971. Tchg. asst., grad. preceptor Rutgers U., New Brunswick, N.J., 1966-67; asst. counselor Douglass Coll., 1967, 69-70; instr. math. St. Peter's Coll., Jersey City, 1967-70, asst. prof., 1970-74, dir. of self-study, 1974-76, assoc. prof., 1974-80, prof., 1980—, asst. to pres., 1976-80, asst. to pres. for planning, 1980-96, exec. asst. to pres., 1996-98, v.p. for student affairs, 1999—. Chair U.S. Commn. on Math. Instrn., NRC of NAS, Washington, 1983-90; founding nat. dir. Women and Math. Lectureship Program, Washington, 1975-81, adv. bd., 1981—; project dir. Consortium for Advancement of Pvt. Higher Edn., Washington, 1986-88; mem. N.J. Math. Coalition, 1991—, Nat. Seminar on Jesuit Higher Edn., 1990-94, strategic planning com. N.J. Assn. Ind. Colls. and Univs., 1990-92; charter trustee Rutgers U., 1992—; Nutley panelist Centennial Celebration, 2002. Author: (with others) Mathematics Tomorrow, 1981; contbr. articles to profl. jours. Mem. Newark Mus., Nutley (N.J.) Hist. Soc., Friends of Newark Libr.; trustee Nutley Free Pub. Libr., 1974-77, St. Peter's Prep. Sch., Jersey City, 1986-92; active fee arbitration commn. N.J. Supreme Ct., 1983-86, ct. ethics com., 1986-90; U.S. nat. rep. Internat. Congress Math. Edn., Budapest, Hungary, 1988; statewide planning com. NCCJ, 1988-92; chair evaluation teams Mid. States Assn. Coll. and Schs.; U.S. del. Internat. Congress on Math; trustee The Cath. Advocate, 1993—, Ency. of Math. Edn., 2001—. Recipient George F. Johnson, S.J. Alumni Faculty award, 1976, Douglass Soc. award Douglass Coll., 1982, Outstanding Cmty. Svc. award Christopher Columbus Found., N.J., 1994, Outstanding Svc. award Middle States Assn. Colls. and Schs., 1994, Cert. of Appreciation for outstanding contbns. as nat. dir. women and math. program, 1993, Varsity Letter plaque for leadership and svc. St. Peter's Prep, 1997; named Danforth Assoc., Danforth Found., 1972-86, SPC Legend, Students of St. Peters Coll., 2002. Mem. AAUP, Math. Assn. Am. (bd. dirs. lectureship program, gov. N.J. chpt. 1972-79, chair human resources coun. 1991—, Outstanding Coll. Tchg. award 1993), Am. Math. Soc., Nat. Coun. Tchrs. Math. (spkr. 1974—), Soc. Coll. and Univ. Planning (program com. 1989—, spkr. nat. conf. 1986, 88, 89, 90, judge grad. paper competition), Pi Mu Epsilon (1st woman pres. in 75 yrs. 1987-90, C.C. MacDuffee award for disting. svc. and to math. 1995), Phi Beta Kappa, Alpha Sigma Nu. Roman Catholic. Avocations: gourmet cook, traveling, golf. Office: St Peter's Coll 2641 Kennedy Blvd Jersey City NJ 07306-5997

POINDEXTER, ALAN, astronaut; b. Pasadena, Calif., Nov. 5, 1961; s. John M. and Linda A. Poindexter; m. Lisa A. Pfeiffer; 2 children. B of Aerospace Engring., Ga. Inst. Tech., 1986; MS in Aeronautical Engring., Naval Postgrad. Sch., 1995. Commd. 2d lt. USN, 1986, advanced through grades to comdr.; with Hypervelocity Wind Tunnel Facility, Naval Surface Weapons Ctr., White Oak, Md.; naval aviator Naval Air Sta., Miramar, Calif.; wing qualified landing signal officer Fighter Squadron 211, Arabian Gulf, Operation Desert Storm, Operation So. Watch; test pilot, project officer Naval Strike Aircraft Test Squadron, Naval Air Sta., Patuxent River, Md., lead test pilot; dept. head Astronaut Tng. Fighter Squadron 32, Naval Air Sta.; astronaut NASA, Houston, 1998—, tech. advisor Astronaut Office Shuttle Ops. Br. Mem.: Soc. Exptl. Test Pilots, Tau Beta Pi. Achievements include logged over 2,000 hours in 30 different aircraft; logged over 450 carrier landings. Office: Astronaut Office/CB NASA Johnson Space Ctr Houston TX 77058*

POINDEXTER, BARBARA GLENNON, secondary school educator; b. Dallas, Oct. 19, 1937; d. Victor and Ruth (Gaskins) Ward; m. Noble Turner Poindexter, Aug. 2, 1994; 1 child, Victoria Angela Glennon Betts. BS, Tex. Woman's U., 1958; postgrad., Kans. State U., 1969-70. Cert. tchr. S.C., Kans., N.Mex., Tex. Drama and English tchr. Linn (Kans.) H.S., 1968-69; tchr. Mosquero (N.Mex.) H.S., 1973-74, Sumter (S.C.) Sch. Dist., Maywood Sch., 1974-76, Harleyville (S.C.) H.S., 1976-78, Hampton (S.C.) H.S., 1978-79, Centerville Sch., Cottageville, S.C., 1979-80; tchr. English Scurry-Rosser Sch., Scurry, Tex., 1981-82; tchr. French and Spanish Christ the King, Dallas, 1982-83; tchr. French and English, chmn. fgn. lang. dept. Wilmer-Hutchins H.S., 1983-94; tchr. French and English Molina H.S., 1997—. Mem. Theta Alpha Phi. Democrat. Methodist. Home: 5315 Maple Springs Blvd Dallas TX 75235-8326 Office: Molina HS 2355 Duncanville Rd Dallas TX 75211-6532

POINDEXTER, BEVERLY KAY, media and communications professional; b. Noblesville, Ind., Nov. 12, 1949; d. Wayne Francis and Rosalie Christine (Nightenhelser) Hunter; m. Jerry Roger Poindexter, Dec. 7, 1969; children: Nick Ashley, Tracy Lynne, Wendy Dawn, Cory Matthew. Student, Purdue U., Bethany Seminary. Editor Tri Town Topics Newspaper, 1965-69; reporter, photographer Noblesville Daily Ledger, 1969-70; asst. mgr., sales mgr., sports dir. Sta. WHYT Radio, Noblesville, Ind., 1973-79; sales mgr., music dir., DJ, news Sta. WBMP Radio, Elwood, 1979-88; acct. exec. Stas. WAXT-WHBU Radio, Anderson, 1988-89; gen. mgr., sales mgr. Sta. WEWZ, Elwood, 1989-90; now news stringer Sta. WTHR TV-13, Indpls.; acct. exec. Sta. WLHN Radio, Elwood; real estate broker Booker Realty, Cicero, 1990-98; real estate broker, owner Poindexter Agy., Atlanta, 1998—. Area rep. Youth for Understanding, 1993-95; Am. Field Svc. liaison, ctrl. Ind. pres., Ind. team support coord. Hamilton County, Ind.; pres. bd. dirs. Hamilton Heights Elem. Football, Arcadia, Ind., 1981-83; founder, chmn. Hamilton Heights Elem. Cheerleaders, Arcadia, 1981-87; youth leader, counselor Ch. of the Brethren, Arcadia, 1991-94; active Ch. of Brethren Women's Fellowship. Mem. Nat. Assn. Realtors, Ind. Assn. Realtors, Met. Indpls. Bd. Realtors. Republican. Avocations: horseback riding, canoeing, swimming, singing, dancing. Home: 14645 E 281st St Atlanta IN 46031-9722 Office: Poindexter Agy 14645 E 281st St Atlanta IN 46031-9722 E-mail: motherabbitwo@yahoo.com.

POINDEXTER, GRAHAM S. chemist; b. Louisville, Dec. 18, 1948; s. Charles W. and Marguerite B. Poindexter; m. Sherry M Mayhall; children: Kristen, Sarah-Jane. BS, U. Louisville, 1971; PhD, U. N.C., 1975. Sr. prin. scientist Bristol-Myers Squibb Co., Wallingford, Conn., 1987—. Office: Bristol-Myers Squibb Co 5 Rsch Pkwy Wallingford CT 06492-7660

POINDEXTER, JOHN MICHAEL, language educator, writer; b. Terre Haute , Ind., Jan. 15, 1951; m. Paula Wright, May 8, 1970; children: Clayton, Patrick. BS in English/Sociology Tchg., Ind. State U., 1990. Tchg. lic. Ind. English tchg. Knox (Ind.) Cmty. H.S., 1990—. Author: (novels) Deadly Revenge. Spl. agt. USAF, 1972—86. Avocations: writing, fishing, travel, amateur radio.

POINDEXTER, WILLIAM MERSEREAU, lawyer; b. Los Angeles, June 16, 1925; s. Robert Wade and Irene M. Poindexter; m. Jani Jennifer Wohlgemuth, Feb. 14, 2000; children: James Wade, David Graham, Honour Hélenê, Timothy John, Cory Christenson, Greg Christenson. BA, Yale U., 1946; postgrad., U. Chgo., 1946-47; LL.B., U. Calif., Berkeley, 1949. Bar: Calif. 1952. Practiced in, San Francisco, 1952-54, Los Angeles, 1954—; mem. firm Poindexter & Doutre, Inc., 1964—. Pres. Consol. Brazing & Mfg. Co., Riverside, Calif., 1949-52. Pres. South Pasadena-San Marino (Calif.) YMCA, 1963; Mem. San Marino Sch. Bd., 1965-69, pres., 1967; pres. Conf. of Ins. Counsel, 1975. Served with USMCR, 1943. Fellow Am. Coll. Trust and Probate Counsel; mem. ABA, L.A. County Bar Assn., State Bar Calif., Yale Club (pres. So. Calif. chpt. 1961), Calif. Lincoln Clubs (L.A. downtown chpt. chmn. 1997—). Republican. Presbyterian. Office: 1 Wilshire Bldg Ste 2420 Los Angeles CA 90017

POINSETTE, DONALD EUGENE, business executive, value management consultant; b. Ft. Wayne, Ind., Aug. 17, 1914; s. Eugene Joseph and Julia Anna (Wyss) P.; m. Anne Katherine Farrell, Apr. 15, 1939; children: Donald J., Eugene J., Leo J., Sharon Poinsette Smith, Irene Poinsette Snyder, Cynthia Poinsette West, Maryanne Poinsette Stohler, Philip J. Student, Purdue U., 1934, Ind. U., 1935-37, 64. With GE Corp., RCA, Stewart Warner Corp., 1937-39; metall. rsch. and field sales cons. P.R. Mallory Corp., 1939-49; dist. sales mgr. Derringer Metall. Corp., Chgo., 1949-50; plant engr. Cornell-Dubilier Electric Corp., Indpls., 1950-53; with Jenn-Air Corp., 1953-74, purchasing dir., 1953-71, mgr. value engring. and quality control, 1969-74; bus. mgmt. cons. Mays and Assocs., 1974-76. Pres. Marian Coll. Parents Club, Indpls., 1969-70; com. mem. Boy Scouts Am.; nat. trustee Xavier U., 1972-73, Dad's Club, Cin.; mem. Triad choral groups. Recipient Testimonial Golden Anniversary award Purdue U., 1987; named to U.S. Finder's List, Nat. Engrs. Register, 1956, Army Navy E award for excellence in engring. and prodn., 1944. Mem. Nat. Assn. Purchasing Mgmt., Indpls. Purchasing Mgmt. Assn., Soc. Am. Value Engrs. (cert. value specialist, sec.-treas. Ctrl. Ind. chpt. 1972-73), Soc. Ret. Execs. Indpls., Ind. U. Alumni Assn., Purdue U. Alumni Assn., Columbian (pres. 1972-73), Internat. Platform Assn., Tau Kappa Epsilon, K.C. (4 deg.). Home: 5760 Susan Dr E Indianapolis IN 46250-1760

POINTER, MARK WAYNE, poet, computer technician, consultant; b. Morenci, AZ, July 29, 1956; s. Alvin Lee and Mary Jeanette Pointer; m. Rhonda Jane Thompson, June 8, 1999. Student, Brigham Young U., 1977—79; diploma in computer technician, Control Data Inst., Anaheim, Calif., 1987. Contbr. poetry anthology (Editor's Choice Award, 2000), (Editor's Choice Award, 2000), (Editor's Choice Award, 2000), (Editor's Choice Award, 2000), (Editor's Choice Award, 2000), (Editor's Choice Award, 2000), , (Selection as Poet of the Year Candidate, 2002), (Selection as Poet of the Year Candidate, 2001), (Selection as Poet of the Year Candidate, 2000). Rep. team leader Rep. Nat. Com., Muncie, Ind., 2001—02. Mem.: Nat. Hunting Club Am. Mem. Lds Ch. Avocations: computers, model building, hunting, fishing, woodworking. Home and Office: 3720 N Bennington Ct Apt C Muncie IN 47303-5923 Home Fax: 208-441-5704. Personal E-mail: mark_pointer@hotmail.com.

POINTER, PETER LEON, investment executive; b. Erie, Pa., Aug. 3, 1934; s. Leon Royce and Katherine (Hermen) P.; m. Linda Milla Jensen, Sept. 21, 1957; children: Philip Leon, David Andrew. BS in Econs., U. Pa., 1956; MBA, U. Mo., 1968. V.p. Roose-Wade & Co. Inc., Toledo, 1976-78; br. mgr. Wm. C. Roney & Co., Detroit, 1978-79; v.p. Lowe & Assocs., Columbus, Ohio, 1979-88; pres. Pointer Investment Co., 1988—. Arbitrator Nat. Assn. Security Dealers, Washington, 1987—; adv. com. mem. Dept. Commerce Div. of Securities, Columbus, 1988—. Trustee, sec.-treas. Univ. Urology Ednl. and Rsch. Found., 1993—. Lt. col. USAF, 1956-76. Mem. Brookside Golf and Country Club (treas., trustee 1991-94), Sigma Nu (treas. 1955-56). Republican. Methodist. Avocations: aviation, golf, gardening. Home: 2290 Haverford Rd Columbus OH 43220-4320 Office: Pointer Investment Co 1550 Old Henderson Rd Ste N 152 Columbus OH 43220-3626 E-mail: plpointer@ameritech.net.

POINTER, SAM CLYDE, JR. retired federal judge, lawyer; b. Birmingham, Ala., Nov. 15, 1934; s. Sam Clyde and Elizabeth Inzer (Brown) P.; m. Paula Purse, Oct. 18, 1958; children: Minge, Sam Clyde III. AB, Vanderbilt U., 1955; JD, U. Ala., 1957; LL.M., NYU, 1958. Bar: Ala. 1957. Ptnr. Brown, Pointer & Pointer, 1958-70; judge U.S. Dist. Ct. (no. dist.) Ala., Birmingham, 1970-2000, chief judge, 1982-99; judge Temp. Emergency Ct. Appeals, 1980-87; mem. Jud. Panel Multi-dist. Litigation, 1980-87; ptnr. Lightfoot, Franklin & White, 2000—. Mem. Jud. Conf. U.S., 1987-90; mem. Jud. Coun. 11th Cir., 1987-90, mem. standing com. on rules, 1988-90, chmn. adv. com. on civil rules, 1990-93. Bd. editors: Manual for Complex Litigation, 1979-91. Mem. ABA, Ala. Bar Assn., Birmingham Bar Assn., Am. Law Inst., Am. Judicature Soc., Farrah Order of Jurisprudence, Phi Beta Kappa. Episcopalian. Office: Lightfoot Franklin & White The Clark Bldg 400 N 20th St Birmingham AL 35203 E-mail: spointer@lfwlaw.com.

POINTON, MARY LOU, special education educator; b. Ft. Smith, Ark., Aug. 1, 1933; d. Clyde Morgan and Rilla Belle (Prater) Dollar; m. Vernie Rodney Pointon, Oct. 24, 1954; children: Pamela Kaye Pointon McDonald, Susan Gail Pointon Friberg. Assoc. BA, Ft. Smith Jr. Coll., 1953; BS Ed in Speech and English, Tex. Tech U., 1962; MEd in Spl. Edn., Tex. A&M U., 1989. Cert. real estate agt., appraiser Tex. Real Estate Commn. English and drama tchr. Wolforth (Tex.) H.S., 1962-63; drama tchr. Monterrey H.S., Lubbock, Tex., 1963-64; English and history tchr. Meml. Cath. H.S., Enid, Okla., 1964-66; reading and drama tchr., libr. Covington (Okla.) H.S., 1966-68; spl. edn. tchr. drug abuse unit Mercer Island (Wash.) H.S., 1968-69; English, bus. and drama tchr. LaConner (Wash.) H.S., 1969-72; English tchr. Tehran (Iran) Am. Sch., 1972; v.p., dir. tng. and devel. Mary Lou English Tng. Ctr., Tehran, 1972-78; spl. edn. tchr. Mills Elem. Sch., Midlothian, Tex., 1987-88; tchr. learning difference students Fairhill Sch., Dallas, 1988-93; tutor learning difference students Masterpiece Co., Plano, 1993—98. Owner, v.p. Masterpiece Real Estate Co., Duncanville, Tex., 1978-89. Author: Teacher Training Manual/Individual English Training, 1973, also lang. program, 1972-78. V.p. Duncanville C. of C., 1983-85; mem. polit. action com. Dallas Assn. Realtors, 1982-84. Named Outstanding Mem. of Yr. Duncanville C. of C., 1983. Mem. DAR (v.p., founding mem. Duncanville chpt. 1980-88), NAFE, Nat. Safety Assn. Dallas Coop. (outstanding sales team 1994), Nat. Chrysanthemum Soc., N.W. Ark. Chrysanthemum Club (v.p., founding mem. 1988—), Ft. Smith Garden Club (pres. 2001-, master gardner 1999). Avocations: plants, flowers, music, reading. Home and Office: 1400 N 52nd St Fort Smith AR 72904-7310

POINTS, ROY WILSON, municipal official; b. Quincy, Ill., Oct. 21, 1940; s. Jess C. and Gladys (Wilson) P.; m. Karen Lee Olsen, July 23, 1966; children: Eric, Holly. BBA, Culver Stockton Coll., 1968. Tchr., coach Lewis County C-1, Ewing, Mo., 1968-69, Community Unit 3, Camp Point, Ill., 1969-78; real estate salesman Landmark, Quincy, 1978-80; supr. of assessment County of Adams, 1980-90; assessor City Twp. of Quincy, 1990—. Mem., chmn. Adams County Bd. Rev., 1977-80. Bd. dirs., 1st v.p., sec. Quincy Jaycees, 1970-76, Quincy Rotary East, 1980. Mem. Cert. Ill. Assessing Officers, Internat. Assn. Assessing Officers (cert. ednl. recognition 1988), Ill. Assessors Assn. (bd. dirs. 1992—), Twp. Ofcls. Ill. (bd. dirs. 1995-2001), North Ctrl. Regional Assn. Assessing Officers (bd. dirs. 1997—). Democrat. Avocations: fishing, hunting, jogging, raising cattle. Office: Quincy Twp Assessor City Hall Annex 706 Maine St Quincy IL 62301-4013

POIRIER, HELEN VIRGINIA LEONARD, elementary education educator; b. Worcester, Mass., Oct. 2, 1954; d. Robert O'Donnell and Rose C. (Pepper) Leonard; m. Paul Nelson Poirier, Aug. 3, 1985; 1 child, Joseph Paul Robert. BS, Worcester State Coll., 1976. Cert. tchr. K-6, reading supr. K-12, adminstrn. K-8. Tchr. grade 5-6 reading and social studies Quabbin Regional Sch. Dist., Oakham, Mass., 1980—. Sec. Local Cable Access Com., Auburn, 1985-92. NEH grantee, 1986; town history grantee Oakham Hist. Soc., 1986, Oakham Hist. Commn., 1986. Mem. Cen. Mass. Coun. Social Studies (bd. dirs., sec. 1986-90, treas. 1990—), Hodges Village Environ. Edn. Assn., Tanheath Hunt Club (pres. 1995-96, sec./newsletter editor 1988-95). Avocations: horseback riding, fox hunting. Office: Oakham Center Sch Deacon Allen Dr Oakham MA 01068

POIRIER, LOUIS JOSEPH, neurology educator; b. Montreal, Que., Can., Dec. 30, 1918; s. Gustave Joseph and Calixta (Brault) P.; m. Liliane Archambault, June 11, 1947; children: Guy, Michel, Louise, Esther. BSc, U. Montreal, 1942, MD, 1947; PhD, U. Mich., 1950; D (hon.), U. Rennes, France, 1973. Asst. prof. U. Montreal, 1950-55, assoc. prof., 1955-58, prof. faculty of medicine, 1958-65; chmn. dept. anatomy Faculty of Medicine, Laval U., Cité Universitaire, Que., 1970-78, prof. exptl. neurology, 1970-83; dir. Centre de Research in Neurobiology, Laval U. and Hosp. de l'Enfant-Jesus, 1977-85, prof. emeritus, 1985—. Contbr. articles to profl. jours.; editor the extrapyramidal system and its disorders in: Advances in Neurology, vol. 24, 1979. Pres. Que. Health Scis. Research Council, 1978-81. Decorated officer Order of Can.; recipient Que. sci. award, 1975; Killam commemorative scholar, 1977. 78 Mem. Royal Soc. Belgium (hon.), Neurol. Soc. France (hon.), AAAS, Am. Assn. Anatomists, Am. Physiol. Soc., Soc. for Neuroscis., Internat. Brain Research Orgn. Address: 603 Chemin Caron Lac Simon Montpellier QC Canada J0V 1M0

POIRIER, RICHARD, literary critic, educator, editor; b. Gloucester, Mass., Sept. 9, 1925; s. Philip and Annie (Kiley) P. AB, Amherst Coll., 1949; MA, Yale U., 1951; PhD, Harvard U., 1959; student, U. Paris, France, 1944-45;

H.H.D., Amherst Coll., 1978. Mem. faculty Williams Coll., 1950-52, Harvard U., 1953-63; Disting. prof. English Rutgers U., 1963—. Bd. dirs., co-founder, chmn. bd. Libr. of Am.; Beckman prof. U. Calif., Berkeley, 1973; chmn. adv. English com. Harvard U., 1988-91; delivered Gauss Seminars, Princeton U., 1990, T.S. Eliot lectures, U. Kent, 1991, Henry James lectures, NYU, 1992. Editor: Partisan Rev, 1963-73, O Henry Prize Stories, 1961-65; editor/founder Raritan Quar., 1981—; author: The Comic Sense of Henry James, 1960, In Defense of Reading, 1962, A World Elsewhere, 1966, The Performing Self, 1971, Norman Mailer, 1973, Robert Frost: The Work of Knowing, 1977, The Renewal of Literature, 1987, Poetry and Pragmatism, 1992, Trying It Out In America, 1999; founder, editor: Raritan Quar., 1981—; contbr. author numerous articles, revs. to profl. jours. Served with AUS, 1943-46. Recipient achievement award AAAL, 1978, Jay B. Hubbell award, 1988, Lit. Lion award N.Y. Pub. Libr., 1992; Fulbright scholar, Cambridge, Eng., 1952-53; Bollinger fellow, 1962-63, Guggenheim fellow, 1974-75, fellow NEH, 1978-79. Mem. Am. Acad. Arts and Scis., Am. Acad. Arts and Letters, P.E.N. (exec. bd. 1986), PMLA (editorial bd. 1977-79), nominating com. Nat. Medal for Lit., 1986, 87, Nat. Book Critics Cir., 1977-85, Century Club. Clubs: Century. Home: 104 W 70th St Apt 9B New York NY 10023-4457 Office: Libr of Am 14 E 60th St New York NY 10022-1006

POIROT, JAMES WESLEY, engineering company executive; b. Douglas, Wyo., 1931; m. Raeda Poirot. BCE, Oreg. State U., 1953. With various constrn. firms, Alaska and Oreg., CH2M Hill Inc., 1955, v.p., Seattle and Atlanta, from 1967; chmn. bd. CH2M Hill Ltd., Englewood, Colo., 1983-93. Former chmn. Western Regional Coun., Design Profls. Coalition, Accreditation Bd. Engring. and Tech., Indsl. Adv. Coun.; former mem. Oreg. Joint Grad. Schs. Engring., Engring. Coun.; mem. U.S. delegation UN Gen. Assembly, 1997; mem. internat. adv. bd. NRC, 1998—, chmn. com. truck size and weight, 1998—. Founding dir. World Partnership for Sustainable Devel.; mem. U.S. Earth Charter Commn.; trustee Oreg. State U. Fedn., 1992—. Named ENR Constrn. Man of Yr., 1988. Fellow: ASCE (pres. 1993—94), Am. Assn. Engring. Socs. (vice chmn. 1995), Am. Acad. Environ. Engrs. (diplomate), Am. Cons. Engrs. Coun. (life; pres. 1989—90); mem.: World Fedn. Engring. Orgns. (v.p. 1997—2001, com. on tech. transfer, pres. 1995—2001, Disting. Achievement in the Svc. of Humanity medal 2001), Japan Soc. Civil Engrs. (hon.), Nat. Acad. Engring. (nat. chmn. engrs. week 1994). Office: CH2M Hill Inc PO Box 22508 Denver CO 80222-0508

POISSON, ERIC, science educator; b. Montreal, Can. BSc, Laval U.; PhD, U. Alberta, Edmonton, Can., 1991. Rschr. Calif. Inst. Tech., Pasadena, 1991—94, Wash. U., St. Louis, 1994; faculty U. Guelph, Canada, 1995—, assoc. prof. dept. physics Canada. Avocations: guitar, bicycling, movies. Office: Univ Guelph Dept Physics Guelph N1G 2W1 Canada*

POITEVENT, EDWARD BUTTS, II, lawyer; b. New Orleans, Oct. 19, 1949; s. Eads and Elizabeth (Schramm) P.; m. Julia Dunbar Baños, Dec. 29, 1972; children: Sarah Dunbar,Elizabeth Grehan, Edward Scott, Mary McCutchen. BA, Tulane U., 1971, JD, 1974. Assoc. Jones, Walker, Waechter, Poitevent, Carrere & Denegre, New Orleans, 1974-79, ptnr., 1979-91, Phelps Dunbar, New Orleans, 1991—2001, King & Spalding, Houston, 2002—. Mem. ad hoc com. Pipeline div. La. Office of Conservation; mem. adv. coun. La. Mineral Law Inst. Mem. editorial bd. Oil and Gas Law and Taxation Rev.; contbr. articles to profl. jours.; presenter in field. Pres. La. chpt. Leukemia Soc. Am., Inc., New Orleans, 1991; trustee Ea. Mineral Law Found., 1988-93; co-chmn. oil and gas sect. Rocky Mountain Mineral Law Found. 36th Ann. Inst., Santa Fe; trustee-at-large Rocky Mountain Mineral Law Found., 1995-97. Mem. ABA (sect. on natural resources, energy and environ. law natural gas and oil coms., litigation sect. energy litigation com., chair program com., editor energy litigation com. newsletter, chair energy litigation com. natural gas mktg. and trans. com., mem. coun. 1994-98, mem. nominating com. 1995-96, CLE officer 1995-96, mem. exec. com. 1996-97), La. State Bar Assn., Fed. Energy Bar Assn., Am. Assn. Petroleum Landmen (chair ad hoc com. on model form gas Balancing Agreement). Republican. Roman Catholic. Office: Phelps Dunbar 365 Canal St Ste 2000 New Orleans LA 70130-6534

POITIER, SIDNEY, actor, director; b. Miami, Fla., Feb. 20, 1927; s. Reginald and Evelyn (Outten) P.; m. Juanita Hardy (div.); children: Beverly, Pamela, Sherri, Gina; m. Joanna Shimkus; children: Anika, Sydney. Ed. pub. schs., The Bahamas. Ind. stage, screen, TV actor, 1948—. Bd. dirs. Walt Disney Co.; amb. to Japan from the Commonwealth of the Bahamas. Appeared at Am. Negro Theater in numerous prodns. including: Days of Our Youth, Strivers Road, You Can't Take It With You; various roles in Broadway prodns. including: Anna Lucasta, 1948, A Raisin in the Sun, 1959; films include: No Way Out, 1950, Cry, the Beloved Country, 1951, Red Ball Express, 1952, Blackboard Jungle, 1955, Something of Value, 1957, Edge of the City, Band of Angels, 1958, The Defiant Ones, 1958; film adaptation of Porgy and Bess, 1959, A Raisin in Sun, 1960, Paris Blues, 1960, Pressure Point, 1962, The Long Ships, 1964, Lilies of the Field, 1963 (Acad. award Best Actor), The Greatest Story Ever Told, 1965, Slender Thread, 1965, Duel of Diablo, To Sir With Love, 1967, In the Heat of the Night, 1967, Guess Who's Coming to Dinner, 1967, The Lost Man, 1968, For the Love of Ivy, 1968, They Call Me Mr. Tibbs, 1969, The Organization, 1971, Brother John, 1971, The Wilby Conspiracy, 1975, Little Nikita, 1987, Shoot to Kill, 1988, Sneakers, 1992, The Jackal, 1997; star, dir.: Buck and the Preacher, 1972, A Warm December, 1973, Uptown Saturday Night, 1974, Let's Do It Again, 1975, A Piece of the Action, 1977; dir.: Stir Crazy, 1980, Hanky Panky, 1982, Fast Forward 1984, Ghost Dad, 1990; TV mini series Separate But Equal, 1991, Children of the Dust, 1995; (tv movie) To Sir With Love II, 1996; (cable movie) Mandela and de Klerk, 1997; author: This Life, 1981. Served with 1267th Med. Detachment AUS, 1944-45. Decorated knight comdr. Order Brit. Empire; recipient Silver Bear award Berlin Film Festival, 1958, N.Y. Film Critics award and Acad. award nomination for The Defiant Ones, 1958, Best Actor award For Love of Ivy, San Sebastian Film Festival, 1968, Am. Film Inst. Lifetime Achievement award, 1992, Kennedy Ctr. Honors, 1995, Screen Actors Guild award for Lifetime Achievement, 1999, NAACP Hall of Fame Image Award, 2001, Honorary Oscar, 2002.*

POJETA, JOHN, JR. geologist, researcher; b. N.Y.C., Sept. 9, 1935; s. John and Emilie (Pilat) P.; m. Mary Louise Eberz, June 23, 1957; children: Kim Louise, John Martin. BS, Capital U., Columbus, Ohio, 1957; MS, U. Cin., 1961, PhD, 1963. Teaching fellow U. Cin., 1957-63; geologist U.S. Geol. Survey, 1963—, chief lower paleozoic studies unit, 1969-74, chief br. paleontology and stratigraphy, 1989-94. Assoc. prof., lectr. George Washington U., 1965-74; research assoc. Smithsonian Instn., 1969— ; U.S. Geol. Survey-Australian Bur. Mineral Resources exchange scientist, 1974-75 Author papers in field. Pres. Potomac Woods Citizens Assn.; mem. area 4 coun. Montgomery County (Md.) Bd. Edn.; mem. bd. Citizens for Good Govt.; trustee Paleontol. Rsch. Instn., 1976—85, 1999—, v.p., 1978—79, pres., 1980—82. Fellow: AAAS (coun.), Geol. Soc. Am.; mem.: Australasian Paleontologists, Paleontol. Soc. (sec. 1982—88, pres. 1989—, bus. mgr. spl. studies). Home: 1492 Dunster Ln Rockville MD 20854-6119 Office: US Geol Survey Smithsonian Instn Rm E-308 MRC137 Mus Natural History Washington DC 20560-0137 E-mail: pojeta.john@nmnh.si.edu.

POKEMPNER, JOSEPH KRES, lawyer; b. Monessen, Pa., June 11, 1936; s. Leonard and Ethel Lee (Kres) P.; m. Judith Montague Stephens, Aug. 23, 1970; children: Elizabeth, Jennifer, Amy. AB, Johns Hopkins U., 1957; LLB, U. Md., 1962. Bar: Md. 1962. Law clk. to judge Supreme Bench Balt., 1960-62; field atty. 5th region NLRB, 1962-64; pvt. practice labor law Balt., 1964—; ptnr. Wolf, Pokempner & Hillman, 1972-86, Whiteford, Taylor & Preston, Balt., 1986—. Contbr. articles to legal jours. Capt. AUS, 1969-74. Mem. ABA, Fed. Bar Assn. (pres. Balt. chpt. 1979-80), Md. Bar Assn., Balt. Bar Assn. (pres. 1984-85), Serjeant's Inn Law Club. Jewish. E-mial. Home: 1500 Willow Ave Baltimore MD 21204-3611 E-mail: jpokempner@wtplaw.com.

POKER, NATHAN, retired radiologist; b. N.Y.C., Sept. 13, 1921; MD, Columbia P&S, 1950. Diplomate Am. Bd. Radiology. Intern Bellevue Hosp. Ctr., N.Y.C., 1950-51; resident in radiology N.Y. Hosp., 1951-54; prof. emeritus Cornell U. Med. Coll., 1992—. Lt. USNR, 1942-46. Mem. Am. Coll. Radiology.

POKKY, ERIC JON, clinical pharmacist; b. Ft. Worth, Oct. 24, 1957; s. Arne Huntus and Helen Theodora Pokky; m. Pamela A. McQuillin; 1 child, Allison Christine. Student, U. Tex., Arlington, 1976-80; BS in Pharmacy, U. Houston, 1983; postgrad., Midland (Tex.) Coll., 1984; PharmD, U. Houston, 2001. Cert. anticoagulation therapist; cert. Parkinson's disease therapist, cert. long term care pharmacist. Rec. engr. Hallmark Prodns./Sundown Rec. Studios, Friendswood, Tex., 1980-83; salesman, cons. Future Sys., Midland, 1983-86; pharmacist Town and Country Drug, Odessa, Tex., 1983-92; outpatient pharmacy supr. Med. Ctr. Hosp., 1992-95, clin. pharmacy supr., 1995-98, clin. pharmacy coord., 1998—, chmn. continuum of care com., 1999-2000; clin. pharmacy clerkship preceptor Creighton U., Omaha, 1999—; clinical pharmacy clerkship preceptor Univ. Fla., 2000—, U. Houston, 2000—. Pres. ECF Cons. Svcs., 1989—; mem. steering com. Pub. Hosp. Pharmacy Coalition. Active Tex. Soc. for Prevention of Child Abuse, 1997—; bd. dirs. Am. Cancer Soc., 1998—, Juvenile Diabetes Found., 1999-2001. Fellow Am. Soc. Cons. Pharmacists, Tex. Pharmacy Assn. (sect. consulting pharmacists 1997—, del. to house 1994-2000); mem. Am. Coll. Clin. Pharmacists, Am. Soc. Consulting Pharmacists (cons. nat. meeting 1997), Permian Basin Pharm. Assn. (v.p. 1986-88, pres. 1988—), Permian Basin Immunization Coalition, Tex. Children's Health and Safety Initiative, Am. Soc. Health System Pharmacists, Tex. Soc. Hosp. Pharmacists, West Tex. Pharm. Assn., Kappa Psi (sec. 1982-83). Lutheran. Avocations: water and snow skiing, hunting, fishing, camping, scuba diving, computers. Home: 4420 Haner Dr Odessa TX 79762-4671 Office: Med Ctr Hosp PO Box 7239 Odessa TX 79760-7239

POKORNI, ORYSIA, musician, educator; b. Ternopil, Ukraine, Aug. 4, 1938; came to U.S., 1951; d. Gregory and Olha (Moroz) Danylkiw; m. Paul Pokorni, Jan. 25, 1958; children: Daniel, Mark. Student, Cosmopolitan Sch. Music, 1962; AA, Truman Coll., 1984; BA, Northeastern Ill. U., 1989. Mgr. Internat. Theatre of Chgo., 1963—; asst. office mgr. Ravenswood Hosp., Chgo., 1980-83. Radio announcer Sta. WEDC, Chgo., 1965-66; tchr. Sch. Ukrainian Studies, Chgo., 1966—, Chgo. Pub. Schs., 1990—; choir dir. Moloda Dumka Children's Choir, Chgo., 1981-85. Accompanist various choirs and soloists, 1960—. All City Youth Chorus of Chgo., 1992—; composer songs; music arranger for children's plays. Active Ukrainian Women's League, Chgo., 1985. Mem. Ukrainian Congress Com. (chmn. spl. events com. 1984—). Home and Office: 4520 N Richmond St Chicago IL 60625-3826

POKORNY, ALEX DANIEL, psychiatrist; b. Taylor, Tex., Oct. 18, 1918; s. John Robert and Olga Frances (Susen) P.; m. Jeanice Brooke Allen, Mar. 13, 1948; children: Martha, Ross, Ellen, Sally. BA, U. Tex., 1939; MD, U. Tex., Galveston, 1942. Diplomate Am. Bd. Psychiatry and Neurology. Psychiatrist VA Hosp., Houston, 1949-55, chief psychiatry and neurology svc., 1955-73; from instr. to prof. psychiatry Baylor Coll. Medicine, 1949-89, acting chmn. dept. psychiatry, 1968-72, vice chmn. dept. psychiatry, 1972-89; ret. Editor (with others) 7 books, including Phenomenology and Treatment of Anxiety, 1979, Phenomenology and Treatment of Alcoholism, 1980, Phenomenology and Treatment of Psychosexual Disorders, 1983, Phenomenology and Treatment of Psychiatric Emergencies, 1984; editor numerous publs.; contbr. 100 articles to profl. jours. Capt. U.S. Army, 1943-46. Recipient Amersa award for Excellence in Med. Edu. Assn. Med. Edn. & Rsch. Substance Abuse, 1989, Dublin award Am. Assn. Suicidology, 1992. Fellow AAAS, Am. Psychiat. Assn. (life), Am. Coll. Psychiatrists (life); mem. Soc. Psychophysiological Rsch. Home and Office: 813 Atwell St Bellaire TX 77401-4718

POKRAJAC, DRAGOLJUB MILOS, engineering educator; b. Sibenik, Croatia, Dec. 12, 1970; arrived in U.S., 1997; s. Milos Pokrajac and Cveta Cvetkovic; m. Dragana Jankovic. BSEE, U. of NIJ, Serbia, 1993, MS in Telecomms., 1997; PhD, Temple U., 2002. Rsch. asst. U. of Nis, Nis, 1994—97, Wash. State U., Pullman, Wash., 1998—2000; software engr. Advanced Biometrics, Inc., Puyallup, 2000; rsch. asst. Temple U., Phila., 2000—02; asst. prof. Del. State U., Dover, Del., 2002—. Author: Telecommunication Laboratory Manual, 1998. Treas. Serbian Orthodox Ch., 2002—. Orthodox. Office: Delaware State Univ 1200 N Dupont Hwy SC 305D Dover DE 19901

POLACHEK, SOLOMON WILLIAM, economics educator, consultant; b. Washington, Aug. 27, 1945; s. Harry and Blanche (Katz) P.; m. Dora Eisenberg, July 23, 1972; 1 child, Nathaniel. AB, George Washington U., 1967; PhD, Columbia U., 1973. Postdoctoral fellow U. Chgo., 1972-73; from asst. prof. to assoc. prof. U. N.C., Chapel Hill, 1973-83; prof. econs. SUNY-Binghamton, 1983-96; disting. prof. econs., 1996—, acting chair econs., 1987, chair econs., 1994-96, dean Harpur Coll. Arts and Scis., 1996—; referee numerous acad. jours., pubs., govt. orgns., 1973—; cons. to govt. agys., law firms, 1975—; expert witness U.S. Civil Rights Commn., Washington, 1984, U.S. Senate Subcom. Hearings, Washington, 1985; vis. research prof. Erasmus U., Netherlands, 1984; vis. prof. Cath. U., Leuven, 1987, Bar Ilan U., 1992, Tel Aviv U., 1992; speaker, presenter in field. Editor Rsch. in Labor Econs., 1994—; mem. editorial bd. Internat. Studies Quar., 1989-94, Conflict Mgmt. and Peace Sci., 1989—. Co-author The Economics of Earnings, 1993, co-editor Peace Economics, Peace Science and Public Policy, 1994; contbr. articles to profl. publs. Presdl. fellow Columbia U., N.Y.C., 1968-72; Ford Found. faculty fellow, 1974-75; nat. fellow Hoover Instn., Stanford U., Palo Alto, Calif., 1979-80; grantee various govt. agys., 1975-85. Mem. Am. Econ. Assn., Econometric Soc., Internat. Peace Sci. Soc. (exec. com. 1983), Ea. Econ. Assn. (program com. 1985), N.Am. Econ. and Fin. Assn. (program com. 1989), Avocations: travel, swimming, cross-country skiing. Office: SUNY Dept Econs Binghamton NY 13902

POLACHEK-LIPTAK, MICHELLE, agency executive; b. Cleve., Sept. 21, 1954; d. Mike and Amelia (Giuliano) Polachek; m. George Louis Liptak, Apr. 3, 1976. Grad., Television Workshop, 1984; student, Cuyahoga Community Coll., 1985-86. EMT Ohio, 1990. Co-founder Television Workshop, Beachwood, Ohio, 1982-84; exec. dir. Cleve. Ballet Coun., 1982-86; dir. instrn. John Casablancas, Beachwood, Ohio, 1984-85; pres., chief exec. officer Liptak, Oshaben & Assocs., Inc., Garfield Heights, 1986—; dir. devel. Cleve. Sports Legend Found., 1987-88; soc. editor The Leader Newspaper, Garfield Heights, Ohio, 1988-89; pres., CEO, chairperson of bd. Health Exams, Inc., 1993; co-founder, co-pres. Prime Life Care Ctr., Inc., Cleve., 1993. Dir. pub. rels. Providence House, Cleve., 1987-88, OASIS, Cleve., 1987-88; mem. adv. bd. Harper's Bazaar. Dir. pub. rels. City Club of Cleve., 1983-88 (Pub. Rels. Svc. award 1988); mem. Nat. Mus. Women in Arts; trustee Leukemia Soc. Am. Named One of Most Interested People in Ohio, No. Ohio Live Mag., 1987; proclaimed Michelle A. Liptak Day City of Garfield Heights, 1988. Mem. NAFE, Nordonia Hills C. of C. (dir. pub. rels. 1991-92), Garfield Heights C. of C., 1995, City Club of Cleveland, Am. Heart Assn. Duck Race (chairperson 1995). Avocations: singing, dancing, roller skating, organist. Home and Office: 10712 Wadsworth Ave Garfield Heights OH 44125-2255

POLAGE, DANIELLE CRISTI, psychology educator; b. Englewood, N.J., Dec. 28, 1972; d. Claudio GianCarlo and Margot Christine (Vold) Barbarini; m. Daniel Brian Polage, Aug. 17, 1997. BA in Math., Emory U., 1993; PhD in Psychology, U. Wash., 1999. Tchg. asst. U. Wash., Seattle, 1994-99; asst. prof. Pepperdine U., Malibu, Calif., 1999—. Contbr. articles to profl. jours. including Devel. and Psychopathology, Psychiat. Clinics N.Am., among others. Mem. APA, Am. Psychol. Soc., Soc. for Applied Rsch. in Memory and Cognition, Am. Psychology and Law Soc., Teaching of Psychology Soc., Delta Phi Epsilon. Avocations: tennis, scuba, diving, skiing, hiking. Home: # 208 28947 Thousand Oaks Blvd Agoura Hills CA 91301 E-mail: dpolage@pepperdine.edu.

POLAK, ELIJAH, engineering educator, computer scientist; b. Bialystok, Poland, Aug. 11, 1931; came to U.S., 1957, naturalized, 1977; s. Isaac and Fruma (Friedman) P.; m. Virginia Ann Gray, June 11, 1961; children: Oren, Sharon. BSE.E., U. Melbourne, Australia, 1957; MSE.E., U. Calif., Berkeley, 1959, PhD, 1961. Instrument engr. ICIANZ, Melbourne, Australia, 1956-57; summer student IBM Research Labs., San Jose, Calif., 1959-60; vis. asst. prof. M.I.T., fall 1964; asst. dept. elec. engring. and computer scis. U. Calif., Berkeley, 1958-61, asst. prof. elec. engring. and computer scis., 1961-66, asso. prof., 1966-69, prof., 1969-94, prof. Grad. Sch., 1994—. Author: (with L.A. Zadeh) System Theory, 1969, (with E. Wong) Notes for a First Course on Linear Systems, 1970, (with others) Theory of Optimal Control and Mathematical Programming, 1970, Computational Methods in Optimization, 1971, Optimization: Algorithms and Consistent Approximations, 1997. Guggenheim fellow, 1968; U.K. Sci. Research Council sr. fellow, 1972, 76, 79, 82 Fellow IEEE; mem. Soc. Indsl. and Applied Math. (asso. editor Jour. Theory and Applications Optimization 1972—), Soc. Math. Programming. Home: 38 Fairlawn Dr Berkeley CA 94708-2106 Office: U Calif Dept Elec Engring Cp S Berkeley CA 94720-0001 E-mail: polak@eecs.berkeley.edu.

POLAK, JOSEPH A. rabbi, judge; b. The Hague, The Netherlands, Oct. 16, 1942; came to U.S., 1948; s. Aaron and Ilonka (Hershenfield) P.; m. Reizel Polak, Dec. 15, 1979; children: Yaakov, Esther Zissel, Ilonka; children from previous marriage: Aaron, Rivka. BA, Sr. George Williams U., Montreal, 1964; MA, Rabbi, Rabbinical Coll. Can., Montreal, 1967; DHL, Boston U., 1995. Dir., rabbi, Hillel Ohio U., Athens, 1967-70, Boston U., 1970—; chief justice Rabbinical Ct. Mass., Boston, 1996—. Mem. Rabbinical Coun. Am., Campus Ministry Assn. Boston U. Office: Hillel Found 233 Bay State Rd Boston MA 02215

POLAK, WERNER L. lawyer; b. May 19, 1936; arrived in U.S., 1946, naturalized, 1955; s. Ludwig and Hilde (Schultz) Polak; m. Evelyn F. Ruthmann, June 21, 1959; children: Douglas H., Deborah L. BA, Columbia U., 1960, LLB, 1963. Bar: NY 63. Assoc. Shearman & Sterling, N.Y.C., 1963—72, ptnr., 1972—, ret. Mem.: Trustee Practicing Law Inst.

POLAKIEWICZ, LEONARD ANTHONY, foreign language and literature educator; b. Kiev, Ukraine, Mar. 30, 1938; came to the U.S., 1950; s. Wladyslaw and Aniela (Ossowska) P.; m. Marianne Helen Swanson, Sept. 7, 1963; children: Barbara, Kathryn, Janet. BS in Russian with distinction, BA in Internat. Rels., U. Minn., 1964; MA in Russian, U. Wis., 1968; cert. Russian area studies, 1969; PhD in Slavic Langs./Lit., U. Wis., 1978; diploma in Polish Curriculum and Instrn., Curie-Sklodowska U., Lublin, Poland, 1981. Instr. U. Minn., Mpls., 1970-78, asst. prof., 1978-90, assoc. prof., 1990—, Morse Alumni disting. teaching assoc. prof. Slavic langs. and literatures, dir. Inst. Langs., 1991-93, chair Slavic dept., 1993-97, 99-2000. Vis. asst. prof. U. London, Eng., fall 1984; dir. U. Minn. Polish Lang. Program, Curie-Sklodowska U., Lublin, Poland, summers 1984-89, dir. Russian Faculty Exch., Herzen Pedagogical U., St. Petersburg, Russia, 1993—; mem. selection com. Fulbright Tchr. Exch. Program, USIA, 1989, Title VI Dept. Edn., 1990, NEH Tchr.- Scholar Program, 1994; reviewer divn. ednl. programs NEH, 1990, translation program, 1993, 94; mem. rev. bd. Ctr. Applied Linguistics Polish Proficiency Test, 1990; mem. exec. com. Coun. on Internat. Edn., N.Y.C., 1991-94; mem. Russian Lang. Program Acad. Policy Com. CIEE, N.Y.C., 1994—; mem. nat. task force Polish Studies in Am., Ind. U., 1995-96; project dir. Nat. Coun. Orgns. of Less Commonly Taught Langs. Polish Lang. Learning Framework, 1995-2001; dir. U. Minn. Curie Sklodowska U. Faculty Exch., 1998—, U. Minn. Cath. U. of Lublin Faculty Exch., 1995-2001; coord. Def. Lang. Inst. Polish Proficiency Testing, 1998. *Leonard A. Polakiewicz has a distinguished record in scholarship, teaching and service. He is an authority on Anton Chekhov, a leading specialist in Slavic pedagogy, and the recipient of the University of Minnesota's most prestigious teaching awards: the College of Liberal Arts Distinguished Teacher Award (1978), the Continuing Education and Extension Distinguished Teacher Award (1995) and the All-University Horace T. Morse Award for Outstanding Contributions to Undergraduate Education in teaching, advising and programmatic development (1992). In 1994 he received national recognition through the American Association of Teachers of Slavic and East European Languages Award for Excellence in Teaching in the U.S.* Author: Supplemental Materials for First Year Polish, 1991, Supplemental Materials for Fifteen Modern Polish Short Stories, 1994, Directory of US Institutions of Higher Education and Faculty Offering Instruction in Polish Language, Literature and Culture, 1996-97, Intermediate Polish: A Cultural Reader with Exercises, 1999, (with Joanna Radwanska Williams and Waldemar Walczynski) Polish Language Learning Framework, 2001; assoc. editor Slavic and East European Jour., 1988-94; editl. bd. The Learning and Tchg. of Slavic Langs. and Cultures: Toward the 21st Century, 1996-2000; reviewer Choice Mag., Modern Lang. Jour., Canadian Slavonic Papers, Slavic and East European Jour. Bd. dirs. Immigration Hist. Rsch. Ctr., Mpls., 1984-89; co-founder Polish-Am. Cultural Inst., Mpls., 1986; vice-chair Polish Am. Congress' Commn. Edn., 1987; mem. gov.'s Commn. on Ea. Europe, St. Paul, 1991. With U.S. Army, 1961-63. Ford Found. fellow, 1964-65, Nat. Def. Edn. Act fellow, Title IV, 1966-68; grantee Kościuszko Found., 1981, Coun. for European Studies grantee Columbia U., 1981, 84, 86, Rsch. Assoc. grantee Russian and East European Ctr., U. Ill., 1982, 83, 84, Wasie Found. grantee, 1983, IREX Collaborative Activities and New Exchs. grantee, 1984, Ireland Travel grantee Trinity Coll., Dublin, 1984, Bush Found. Rsch. grantee, 1986-87, grantee U.S. Dept. Edn., 1988-91; Fulbright-Hays Group Projects Abroad grantee for Poland, 1989, USIA U. Linkage grantee for Poland, 1989-93, IREX Short Term Travel grantee, 1995, USIA Coll. & U. Affiliations grantee for Poland, 1995-2000; recipient Polanie Club of the Twin Cities Merit award, 1982, Curie-Sklodowska U. medal for acad. linkage devel., 1992, Cavalier's Cross of Order of Merit of Republic of Poland, 1999, Disting Svc. award Herzen Pedagogical U., St. Petersburg, Russia, 2002. Mem. AAUP, Am. Assn. for the Advancement Slavic Studies, Am. Assn. Tchrs. Slavic and East European Langs. and Lits. (com. on testing and profl. devel. 1997—, Excellence in Tchg. in U.S. award 1994), Internat. Czeslaw Milosz Soc. (pres. 1984-85), N.Am. Chekhov Soc., Am. Coun. Tchrs. of Russian, Polish Inst. Arts & Scis. Am. (N.Y.C., Waclaw Lednicki Humanities award com. 1996), Assn. Literary Scholars & Critics, Soc. of Lovers of the Russian Book, Irish Assn. of Russian and East European Studies, Polish Tchrs. Assn. of Am., Polish Studies Assn. (mem. biennual prize jury 1998), Bristol Group Internat. Assn. Tchrs. Polish, U. Minn. Acad. Disting. Tchrs. Roman Catholic. Avocations: reading, philatelics, genealogy, touring, gardening. Home: 466 Oak Creek Dr S Saint Paul MN 55127-7008 E-mail: polak001@tc.umn.edu.

POLAKOFF, ABE, baritone; b. Bucharest, Rumania; s. Sam and Mary P. Ousherenkova; children: David Fred, Mark Evan, Robert Ira; m. Judyth Kanner, Dec. 5, 1992. Civil engring. student, CCNY; profl. tng. program, Am. Theater Wing, 1952-54; student, N.Y. Coll. Music, 1955-57. Dir. Island Opera Players; opera lectr. Arts Couns. (municipalities and schs.); cantor Progressive Shaari Zedek synagogue, Bklyn., 1972-77, Temple Emanuel, Denver, 1984-94. Debuts include Marcello in La Boheme, Milan, Florence, 1960; leading baritone Zurich Opera, 1961-63, numerous appearances with N.Y. Met. Opera, City Opera N.Y., Phila. Lyric Opera, Pitts. Opera, Seattle Opera, Berlin Deutsche Opera, Frankfurt Opera, Cinn. Opera, Hamburg, Munich Staatsoper, Stuttgart Staatsoper, The Netherlands Opera, Cin. Opera, Kansas City Lyric Opera, Canadian Opera Co., others; soloist with Mex. State Symphony Orch., Kalamazoo Symphony Orch., Winston-Salem (N.C.) Symphony, numerous concert and recital appearances Sgt. U.S. Army, 1943-46. 1st prize winner Am. Theatre Wing Vocal Profl. Scholarship award, 1954, 1st prize winner Am. Opera Auditions, 1960, Silver medal Vercelli (Italy) Internat. singing contest, 1960; Rockefeller Found. grantee, 1961-62; Bayreuth Festival Masterclass scholar. Mem. Cen. Opera Service, Am. Guild Musical Artists, Actors Equity Assn. Address: 11132 76th Ave Apt 7H Forest Hills NY 11375-6409

POLAKOFF, MURRAY EMANUEL, university dean, economics and finance educator; b. N.Y.C., Dec. 18, 1922; s. Joseph and Elizabeth (Zimmerman) P.; m. Sheila Doreen Brazil, Dec. 23, 1951; children: Michael Anton, Toni. BA summa cum laude, NYU, 1946; MA, Columbia U., 1951, PhD, 1955. Asst. prof. econs. U. Tex., Austin, 1951-57, assoc. prof. econs., 1957-61; prof. econs. and fin. U. Rochester, N.Y., 1961-63; prof., chmn., vice dean Grad. Sch. Bus. Adminstrn. NYU, 1968-71; leading prof., dean Sch. Mgmt. SUNY, Binghamton, 1971-77; prof. econs. and fin., provost U. Md., College Park, 1977-86, dean, 1986-91, dir. internat. devel. and conflict mgmt., 1991-92, prof. emeritus, 1993—. Cons. U.S. House Com. on Banking and Currency, Washington, 1964; lectr. and cons. Brazilian Central Banking, Dept. State, São Paulo, 1966-68; chmn. bd. advisors of joint ventures Cen. Inst. Mathematical and Econ. Modelling of Soviet Acad. Scis., USSR and U. Md., College Park, 1989 Editor, contbg. author: Financial Institutions and Markets, 2d edit., 1981; contbr. articles to profl. jours. Scholar Sch. Law Columbia U., N.Y.C., 1946; Fund for Advancement Edn. faculty grantee, 1955-56; Found. Econ. Edn. fellow, summer 1956; Social Sci. Research Council fellow, 1957; Ford Found. faculty research grantee, 1961-62. Mem. Fin. Mgmt. Assn., Phi Beta Kappa. Jewish. Avocations: squash, theater. E-mail: murf121822@aol.com.

POLAN, ANNETTE LEWIS, artist, educator; b. Huntington, W.Va., Dec. 8, 1944; d. Lake and Dorothy (Lewis) P.; m. Arthur Lowell Fox Jr., Aug. 31, 1969 (div. 1994); children: Courtney Van Winkle Fox, Arthur Lowell Fox III. 1st degree, Inst. des Profs. de Francaise, Paris, 1965; BA, Hollins Coll., 1967; postgrad., Corcoran Sch. Art, 1968-69. Vis. artist Art Therapy Italia, Vignale, Italy, 1986; dir. summer program La Napoule Art Found., Chateau de la Napoule, France, 1987, 88, 90; guest lectr. China, Japan, 1989, Australia, 1996; prof. Corcoran Sch. Art, Washington, 1974—; chmn. painting dept. Corcoran Coll. Art and Design, 1991—. Dir. Washington Project for Arts/Corcoran Mus. Illustrator: Say What I Am, 1989, Relearning the Dark, 1991; cover designer Doers of the Word, 1995; portrait commns. include Sandra Day O'Connor, Va. Gov. Gaston Caperton, Edward Villela. Bd. dirs. Washington Project for the Arts/Corcoran, 1994-2000, v.p. 1995—; bd. dirs. Smith Farm. Mem. Internat. Women's Forum, Washington Women's Forum, Corcoran Faculty Assn. (pres. 1988-89). Avocations: equitation, skiing. Office: Corcoran Sch Art 1801 35th St NW Washington DC 20007-2211 E-mail: apolan@aol.com.

POLAN, JODIE LEA, physiologist researcher; b. Galliano, La., Sept. 4, 1963; d. John Lee and Janice Eleanor (Ferris) Polan; children: Johnna Lela, Jeanette Bevelry. BS in Biology, U. Tex., San Antonio, 1984, MS in Biology, 1989. Teaching asst. U. Tex., San Antonio, 1989, rsch. assoc. I, 1989-90, teaching assoc., 1990-93, rsch. assoc. II, 1990-93; sr. rsch. assoc. U. Tex. Health Sci. Ctr., 1994—. Contbr. articles to profl. jours. Mem. Soc. Neurosci. Address: 4302 Spiral Crk San Antonio TX 78238-3618

POLANCO, JACQUELINE JIMENEZ, political scientist, educator, political scientist, researcher, political scientist, consultant; b. Santiago, Dominican Republic, May 27, 1962; arrived in U.S., 1996; d. Teofilo Jimenez and Joana Maria Polanco. BS, JD, Cath. Madrey Maestra U., Santiago, 1985; JD, Complutense U., Madrid, 1988, PhD in Polit. Sci. and Sociology, 1992. Rschr. Spanish Agy. for Internat. Corp., Madrid, 1989—90, The Spanish Ctr. for L.Am. Studies, Madrid, 1991; immigration atty. Ctr for Hispanic-Am. Integration, 1993—95; rschr. Spanish Coun. for Sci. Rsch., 1993—95; instr. Complutense U., 1992—94; instr. U. Salamanca, Salamanca, Spain, 1994—96; asst. prof. John Jay Coll./CUNY, N.Y.C., 1996—. Bilingual guide Santiagos Villa Mus., Santiago, 1979—84; atty. at law Juridic Bur., Santiago, 1984—86. Author: Political Parties in the Dominican Republic, 1999. Treas. Everything for Health, Santiago, 1997—2001; exec. bd. Batey Relief Alliance, N.Y.C., 2001—02, Santo Domingo, 2001—02, Our People of Color Polit. Action Club, N.Y.C., NY, 2001—02. Mem.: L.Am. Studies Assn., Am. Polit. Sci. Assn., Internat. Polit. Sci. Assn., Caribbean Studies Assn., Spanish Polit. Sci. Assn. Avocations: snorkle, bicycling, skating, reading, movies. Office: John Jay Coll Criminal Justice/CUNY 445 W 59th St New York NY 10019

POLANCO, RODRIGO BUENO, scientist; b. Ibague, Tolima, Colombia, July 6, 1951; s. Ernesto Polanco and Beatriz Bueno P.; m. Virginia Lara, Aug. 31, 1984; children: Paula, Ernesto. BA, U. Los Andes, Bogota, 1976; MA, U. Chgo., 1982; PhD, Anahuac U., Mexico, 1996. Prof. Nat. Autonomous U. Mex., 1976-80, head of area, 1978-80, rschr., 1982-84; prof. U. Los Andes, Bogota, 1984-88; rschr. Instituto Tecnológico y de Estudios Superiores de Monterrey, Mexico, 1989-95, project head, 1995—. Psychotherapist Unidad de Psico-terapia y Sexua, Bogota, 1984-88, Clinica de Atencion Integral, Mexico, 1988-90, Psicologia Integral Mexico, 1990—. Author: (CD-ROM software) Kairos I - Communication and Effective Action, 1996, Kairos II - Teamwork, 1998, Educacion Media Interdisciplinanc, 2001; contbr. articles to profl. jours. and papers to internat. meetings; assoc. editor: Revista Intercontinental de Psicologia y Educacion, 1995. Mem. Am. Ednl. Rsch. Assn. Home: Presa Don Martin 132-PB 11500 Mexico Mexico Office: ITESM RZS Apartado Postal 10 52926 Atizapan/Mexico Mexico E-mail: rpolanco@rmx.itesm.mx .

POLAND, PHYLLIS ELAINE, secondary school educator, consultant; b. Norwood, Mass., May 10, 1941; d. Kenneth Gould Vale and Mildred Eloise (Fisk) Arnold; m. Thomas Charles Poland, June 6, 1968 (div. Nov. 1991); 1 child, Sherilyn Ann Poland Colon. AB in Math., Ea. Nazarene Coll., 1963; MS in Math., Nova U., 1986. Cert. secondary tchr., Fla. H.S. math. tchr., Burrillville, R.I., 1963-64; jr. H.S. math. tchr. Quincy, Mass., 1964-65; math. tchr. Seekonk (Mass.) H.S., 1965-68, Howard Jr. H.S., Orlando, Fla., 1968-74, Lake Highland Prep. Sch., Orlando, 1977-81, Lake Brantley H.S., Altamonte Springs, 1981—. Mem. coun. Joy Club Ctrl. Nazarene Ch., 1988—, adult edn. sec., 1990—, mem. choir, 1986—. Grantee NSF, 1969, 70, 71, 72. Mem. NEA. Home: 401 Navarre Way Altamonte Springs FL 32714-2224

POLAND, SYDNEY WADE, software designer; b. Heflin, La., June 18, 1933; s. Howard Brazil and Helen Lucille (Ryan) P.; m. Evelyn Lucille Miller, Nov. 30, 1956; children: Susan Elizabeth Poland Finch, Stanley Eugene. BS in Physics, La. Tech. U., Ruston, 1955; MS in Math., Tex. Christian U., 1962; MS in Computer Sci., So. Meth. U., 1972. Sci. programmer Temco Aircraft co., Dallas, 1955-58, Chance Vought Aircraft, Dallas, 1958-60; sys. programmer Tex. Instruments Geophys. Svcs., 1960-72; sys. designer Tex. Instruments Calculator Divsn., 1972-77, Tex. Instruments Equipment Group, Dallas, 1977-80, Tex. Instruments Corp. Engring. Ctr., Dallas, 1980-82; sr. cons. BP Exploration, Dallas and Houston, 1982-90; sys. designer Tex. Instruments DSP R&D, Stafford, Tex., 1990-95; sr. sys. software designer Tex. Instruments Tech. Tng., 1995-98. Author manual and applications notes. Mem. Am. Bonanza Soc., Aircraft Owners and Pilots Assn. Achievements include 29 patents for calculators, digital signal processors, others. Avocations: music, reading, travel. Home: 22307 Prince George Ln Katy TX 77449-2811

POLANSKY, LARRY PAUL, court administrator, consultant; b. Blkyn., July 24, 1932; s. Harry and Ida (Gershgom) P.; m. Eunice Kathryn Neun; children: Steven, Harriet, Bruce. BS in Acctg., Temple U., 1958, JD, 1973. Bar: Pa. 1973, U.S. Dist. Ct. (ea. dist.) Pa. 1973, U.S. Ct. Appeals (3d cir.) 1973, D.C. 1978, U.S. Supreme Ct. 1980. Acct., systems analyst City of Phila., 1956-63; data processing mgr. Jefferson Med. Coll. and Hosp., Phila., 1963-65; systems engr. IBM Corp., 1965-67; dep. ct. adminstr. Common Pleas Cts. of Phila., 1967-76; dep. state ct. adminstr. Pa. Supreme Ct., Phila., 1976-78; exec. officer D.C. Cts., Washington, 1979-90. Presdl. appt. to bd. dirs. State Justice Inst., 1985-89; bd. dirs. Search Group, Inc. Author: A Primer for the Technologically Challenged Judge, 1995; contbr. articles to profl. jours. Served as cpl. U.S. Army, 1951-53, Korea. Fellow Inst. for Ct. Mgmt., Denver, 1984; recipient Reardon award Nat. Ctr. for State Cts., 1982, Disting. Svc. award Nat. Ctr. for State Cts., 1986, Justice Tom C. Clark award Nat. Conf. of Metro. Cts., 1991, award of merit Nat. Assn. Ct. Mgmt., 1996. Mem. ABA (jud. adminstrn. divsn., chmn. tech. com. 1991-93, 95, exec. com. lawyers conf. 1985-98, chmn. 1991-92, JAD coun. 1994-97), Conf. State Ct. Adminstrn. (bd. dirs. 1980-86, pres. 1984-85). Republican. Jewish. Avocations: tennis, skiing, computers, golf. Home and Office: PO Box 752 Lake Harmony PA 18624-0752 E-mail: polanskyl@aol.com.

POLANSKY, MARK L. astronaut; b. Paterson, N.J., June 2, 1956; s. Irving and Edith Polansky. BS in aero. and astronautical engring., MS in aero. and astronautical engring., Purdue U., West Lafayette, Ind. , 1978. Commd. 2d lt. USAF, 1978, student pilot Okla., 1978—80, pilot F-15 Langley AFB, Va., 1980—83; pilot F-5E aggressor pilot for tng. Clark AFB, Philippines, 1983—86; trainee Test Pilot Sch. USAF, Edwards AFB, Calif., 1986—87; test pilot USAF , Eglin AFB, Fla., 1987—92; astronaut NASA Johnson Space Ctr., Houston, 1992—. Recipient Flying Tng. award, USAF, 1980. Achievements include 5000 flight hours in 3 different aircraft; 1 space mission, over 309 hours in space. Office: NASA Astronaut Office Johnson Space Ctr Houston TX 77058

POLANSKY, PATRICIA ANN, librarian; b. Billings, Mont., Apr. 6, 1944; d. Frank Wheeler and Anna Eleyne (Sexton) Bradley; m. Anthony Herbert Polansky, May 1971 (div. Aug. 1989). BA in Russian Lang., U. Hawaii, 1967, MLS, 1969. Cataloger NUS Corp., Washington, 1968; cataloger Hamilton Libr., U. Hawaii, Honolulu, 1969-70, Russian bibliographer, 1970—, dir. Ctr. for Russia in Asia, 1988-92. Contbr. articles to profl. jours. Fujio Matsuda fellow, 1986, fellow Coun. Libr. Resources, 1979; grantee IREX, 1977, 84, 86, 91, 95, 96. Mem. Am. Assn. Advancement Slavic Studies, Western Slavic Assn., Internat. Assn. Orientalist Librarians. Republican. Methodist. Office: U Hawaii Hamilton Libr 2550 The Mall Honolulu HI 96822-2233

POLANSKY, STEVEN JAY, lawyer; b. Phila., Nov. 21, 1956; s. Larry P. and Eunice K. (Neun) P.; m. Kathleen Diane Spofford; children: Michelle, Jeffrey, Scott. BBA magna cum laude, Temple U., 1978; JD magna cum laude, Syracuse U., 1981. Bar: Pa. 1981, N.J. 1981, D.C. 1983; cert. civil trial atty., N.J. Assoc. Cozen, Begier and O'Conner, Phila., 1981-85, LaBrum and Doak, Woodbury (N.J.) and Phila., 1985-88; ptnr. Ostrager, Fieldman & Zucker, Moorestown (N.J.), Bala Cynd (Pa.), 1988-92; shareholder Spector Gadon & Rosen P.C., Moorestown, 1992—2002, Marshall, Dennehey, Warner, Coleman & Goggin, Cherry Hill, NJ, 2002—. Elected mem. Cherry Hill Bd. of Edn., 1990-93; trustee Georgetowne Condo Assn., Lindenwold, N.J., 1982-83. Mem. ABA, N.J. Bar Assn., Pa. Bar Assn., Phila. Bar Assn., Pa. Def. Inst., Camden County Bar Assn., Def. Research Inst. Jewish. Avocations: skiing, carpentry. Office: Marshall Dennehey Warner et al 200 Lake Dr E Ste 300 Cherry Hill NJ 08002- E-mail: spolansky@mdwcg.com.

POLASCIK, MARY ANN, ophthalmologist; b. Elkhorn, W.Va., Dec. 28, 1940; d. Michael and Elizabeth (Halko) Polascik; m. Joseph Ellie, Oct. 2, 1973; 1 dau., Laura Elizabeth Polascik Jr. BA, Rutgers U., 1967; MD, Pritzker Sch. Medicine, 1971. Jr. pharmacologist Ciba Pharm Co., Summit, N.J., 1961-67; intern Billings Hosp., Chgo., 1971-72; resident in ophthalmology U. Chgo. Hosp., 1972-75; practice medicine specializing in ophthalmology Dixon, Ill., 1975—. Pres. McNichols Clinic, Ltd.; cons. ophthalmology, Jack Mabley Devel. Ctr., 1976-93; mem. staff Katherine Shaw Bethea Hosp. Bd. dirs. Sinnossippi Mental Health Ctr., 1977-82, Dixon Cmty. Trust Mental Health Ctr., 1989—. Mem. Am. Acad. Ophthalmology, Alpha Sigma Lambda, Galena Territory Club. Roman Catholic. Office: 1700 S Galena Ave Dixon IL 61021-9695

POLASEK, EDWARD JOHN, retired electrical engineer, consultant; b. Cudahy, Wis., Oct. 12, 1927; s. John Vincent and Mary Ann (Totka) P.; m. Alice S. Nee (Harnecki), Aug. 18, 1948. BSEE, Marquette U., 1948. Registered profl. engr., Wis., Fla. Cons. engr. Eau Claire, Wis., Gainesville, Fla., 1955-60, various countries, Korea, Vietnam, Nicaragua, 1960-72; v.p., dir. Finley Engring. Co., Eau Claire, 1972-78; pres. Chippewa Devel. Co., 1978-82; planning engr. Harza Engring. Co. in Cairo, Egypt and Dominican Rep., 1982-86; cons. engr. Gainesville, 1986-99; ret. Cons. Lake Altoona Rehab. Dist., Eau Claire, 1974. Author: Planning Methods, 1982, Feasibility Study, 1984; editor: Field Engineer's Handbook, 1982. Chmn. Eau Claire chpt. Am. Cancer Soc.; master gardner U. Fla. Ext. Svc., Gainesville, 1990. With USN, 1944-46, PTO. Mem. Nat. Soc. Profl. Engrs. (pres. 1956), IEEE, Audobon Soc., Tau Beta Pi, Eta Kappa Nu. Avocations: mycology, fishing, arts. Home: 8620 NW 13th St Lot 350 Gainesville FL 32653-7971

POLASKI, ANNE SPENCER, lawyer; b. Pittsfield, Mass., Nov. 13, 1952; d. John Harold and Marjorie Ruth (Hackett) Spencer; m. James Joseph Polaski, Sept. 14, 1985. BA in Psychology, Allegheny Coll., 1974; MSW, U. Pa., 1976; JD, George Washington U., 1979. Bar: D.C. 1979, U.S. Dist. Ct. (D.C. dist.) 1980, U.S. Ct. Appeals (D.C. cir.) 1980, Ill. 1982, U.S. Dist. Ct. (no. dist.) Ill. 1982, U.S. Ct. Appeals (7th cir.) 1982. Law clk. to assoc. judge D.C. Ct., Washington, 1979-80; trial atty. Commodity Futures Trading Commn., Chgo., 1980-84, sr. trial atty., 1984, dep. regional counsel, 1984-88; assoc. Gottlieb and Schwartz, 1988-91; staff atty. Chgo. Bd. of Trade, 1991-92, sr. atty., 1992-94, asst. gen. counsel, 1994—. Mem. ABA, Chgo. Bar Assn. Office: Chgo Bd of Trade 141 W Jackson Blvd Chicago IL 60604-2992

POLATNICK, LOIS ANN, neuro-ophthalmologist; b. N.Y.C., Sept. 11, 1952; d. Jerome Polatnick and Selma Amster; m. Fred Harden Geisler, Aug. 20, 1977; children: David Jason, Rachael Sarah. BA, Swarthmore (Pa.) Coll., 1974; MD, SUNY, Buffalo, 1978. Intern SUNY, Buffalo, 1978-79, resident, 1979-82; neuro-ophthalmologist Columbia Med. Plan, 1982-92, Columbus Hosp., Chgo., 1992—2001, Ravenswood Hosp., Chgo., 2002—. Fellow Am. Acad. Ophthalmology; mem. Orgn. of Women Physicians at Columbus Hosp. (pres. 1997—), Alpha Omega Alpha. Avocations: reading, skiing, traveling, gardening. Home: 3045 Normandy Pl Evanston IL 60201-1805 Office: 4550 N Winchester Ave 3rd Floor Chicago IL 60640-5205

POLCHINSKI, JOSEPH, physicist, science educator; Prof. physics U. Calif., Santa Barbara. Mem.: Inst. Theoretical Physics. Office: Univ Calif Inst for Theoretical Physics Santa Barbara CA 93106-4030*

POLEFKA, THOMAS GREGORY, biochemist; b. Passaic, N.J., Mar. 12, 1952; s. Emil Stanley and Stephanie (Kroczynski) P.; m. Maryann Brigida, Aug. 29, 1981; 1 child, Sara Jane. BS, Upsala Coll., 1974; PhD, U. Medicine/Dentistry N.J., 1979. Postdoctoral rsch. fellow Boston Biomed. Rsch. Inst./Harvard U. Med. Sch., 1979-80; rsch. assoc. Colgate-Palmolive Tech. Ctr., Piscataway, 1980—, dir. skin rsch. NJ, 1995—. *Thomas Polefka develops and manages the technical strategy for Colgate-Palmolive's $1.22BB skin care business. His recent accomplishments include the launch of Palmolive / Softsoap Vitamin Bodywash, Palmolive Moisture Retention bar soap, and Protex Germ Control bar soap with bacteria anti-attachment technology.* Patentee in field; contbr. chpts. to books, articles to profl. jours. Mem. AAAS, Soc. Investigative Dermatology, Am. Chem. Soc., U. Medicine/Dentistry N.J. Sch. Biomed. Scis. Alumni Assn. (exec. coun. 1990-95). Avocations: bicycling, fishing, gardening, outdoor activities. Home: 79 Ellison Rd Somerset NJ 08873-2257 Office: Colgate-Palmolive Tech Ctr 909 River Rd Piscataway NJ 08854-5596 E-mail: thomas_polefka@colpal.com.

POLEMITOU, OLGA ANDREA, accountant; b. Nicosia, Cyprus, June 28, 1950; d. Takis and Georgia (Nicolaou) Chrysanthou. BA with honors, U. London, 1971; PhD, Ind. U., Bloomington, 1981. CPA Ind. Asst. productivity officer Internat. Labor Office/Cyprus Productivity Ctr., Nicosia, 1971-74; cons. Arthur Young & Co., N.Y.C., 1981; mgr. Coopers & Lybrand, Newark, 1981-83; dir. Bell Atlantic, Reston, Va., 1983-97; v.p. corp. auditing Columbia Energy Group, Herndon, 1997—2000; pres., CEO Aristion, Inc. , Reston, 2000—. Chairperson adv. coun. Extended Day Care Cmty. Edn., West Windsor Plainsboro, NJ, 1987—88. Contbr. articles to profl. jours. Bus. cons. project bus. Jr. Achievement, Indpls., 1984—85. Mem.: AICPAs, NAFE, Princeton Network Profl. Women, Va. Soc. CPAs, N.J. Soc. CPAs (sec. mem. in industry com.), Ind. CPA Soc., Nat. Trust Hist. Preservation. Avocations: water-skiing, tennis. Home: PO Box 2744 Reston VA 20195-0744 Office: 11921 Freedom Dr Ste 550 Reston VA 20190

POLEN-DORN, LINDA FRANCES, communications executive; b. Cleve., Mar. 23, 1945; d. Stanley and Mildred (Kain) Neuger; m. Samuel O. Dorn; children: Lanelle, Brian, Adam, Dawn. BA cum laude, U. Miami, 1967; MBA, Nova Southeastern U., 1993. Reporter Miami (Fla.) News, 1966-67; writer Miamian Mag., 1967-68; dir. pub. rels. Muscular Dystrophy Assn., Miami, 1968-72; cons., adv. and pub. rels. Ft. Lauderdale, 1974-77; pub. rels. writer J. Cory and Assocs., Fla., 1978-79; account supr. Maizner & Franklin, 1979-86; v.p. mktg., communications mgr. Glendale Fed. Bank, 1986-95; prod. mktg. mgr. Ryder Sys., Inc., Miami, 1995—. Sustaining mem. Mus. Art., Ft. Lauderdale, 1986—, Philharmonic Soc., Ft. Lauderdale, 1987—. Mem. Internat. Assn. Bus. Communicators, Am. Mktg. Assn., Broward C. of C. (vice chmn. govt. affairs 1984-85). Avocation: traveling. Office: Ryder System Inc 3600 NW 82nd Ave Miami FL 33166-6623

POLENZ, JOANNA MAGDA, psychiatrist; b. Cracow, Poland, Oct. 20, 1936; came to U.S., 1961; d. Mieczyslaw and Nusia (Goldberger) Uberall; m. Daryl Louis Polenz, July 8, 1962 (div. 1991); children: Teresa Ann, Daryl Philip, Elizabeth Sophia. MD, U. Sydney, Australia, 1960; MPH, Columbia U., 1992. Diplomate Am. Bd. Psychiatry and Neurology. Intern Bklyn. Hosp., 1961-62; resident in psychiatry Mt. Sinai Med. Ctr., N.Y.C., 1962-65, ednl. fellow, 1965-66, rsch. assoc., 1966-67; med. dir. Tappan Zee clin. Phelps Meml. Hosp., Tarrytown, N.Y., 1968-71, dir. dept. psychiatry, 1972-77; sr. attending psychiatrist Meml. Hosp. Ctr., 1972-93; pvt. practice Briarcliff Manor, N.Y., 1971-91; physician Joint Commn. Accreditation of Healthcare Orgns., Oakbrook Terrace, Ill., 1993—; pres. Van Sant Healthcare Assoc. Inc., N.Y.C., 1998—. Lectr. in field. Author: In Defense of Marriage, 1981; (with other) Test Your Marriage IQ, 1984, Test Your Success IQ, 1985, The Last Sick Generation, 2000; contbr. articles to profl. jours.; numerous TV appearances including Phil Donahue, 1988, Oprah Winfrey 1984. Grant Found. grant, 1970. Fellow Am. Psychiat. Assn.; mem. AMA, Am. Coll. Physician Execs., N.Y. Acad. Scis., Pan Am. Med. Assn., Westchester Psychiat. Assn. (sec. 1982-85, chmn. fellowship com. 1989-98). Avocations: travel, international affairs. Home: 360 E 88th St Apt 37A New York NY 10128-4993 Office: Van Sant Healthcare Assocs 360 E 88th St Ste 37A New York NY 10128-4993 Fax: 212-828-2507. E-mail: vansanthc@aol.com.

POLESETSKY, HAROLD H. contractor; b. N.Y.C., Apr. 24, 1928; s. Solomon and Sara Rachel Polesetsky; m. Angela Anne Polesetsky; 1 child, Matthew Patric. BA, Columbia U., 1949, MA, 1950; postgrad., Stanford U., 1950-51, U. Iowa, 1950. Feature writer N.Y. Daily News, N.Y.C., 1951-53; reporter UP, Newark, 1954-55; tech. writer Electric Boat Divsn., Groton, Conn., 1956-58; acct. exec. Sid Wain Pub. Rels., N.Y.C., 1959-60; mgr. proposals Gen. Precision Inc., Little Falls, N.J., 1961-68; proposal mgr. TRW Aerospace, Redondo Beach, Calif., 1969-70; owner A/P Builders, Escondido, 1971—. Lectr. on Jewish novel and English and Am. poetry. Candidate state assembly Dem. Party, 76th Assembly Dist., 1984, state exec. com., 1982-86; bd. dirs. Utility Consumers Action Network, San Diego, 1990-98, UN Assn., San Diego, 1994-98. With U.S. Army, 1945-46. Jewish. Avocation: reading. Home: 2661 Groton Pl Escondido CA 92025

POLESKIE, STEPHEN FRANCIS, artist, retired educator, writer; b. Pringle, Pa., June 3, 1938; s. Stephen Francis and Antoinette Elizabeth (Chludzinski) P.; m. Jeanne Mackin, 1979. BS, Wilkes Coll., 1959; postgrad., New Sch. for Social Research, 1961. Owner Chiron Press, N.Y.C., 1961-68; instr. Sch. Visual Arts, 1968; prof. art Cornell U., Ithaca, N.Y., 1969-2001, prof. emeritus, 2001—. Vis. critic Pratt Graphic Arts Center, N.Y.C., 1965-68; vis. artist Colgate U., Hamilton, N.Y., 1973, USSR, 1979, Escuela de Bellas Artes, Honduras, 1980, Loughborough Coll. Art and Design, Eng., 1989; vis. prof. U. Calif., Berkeley, 1976 Contbr. short stories to mags. and book; one-man shows include Louis K. Meisel Gallery, N.Y.C., 1978-80, Galerie Kupinski, Stuttgart, Germany, 1979, Palace of Culture and Sci., Warsaw, Poland, 1979, Sky Art Presentation, MIT, 1981, Am. Ctr., Belgrade, 1981, William and Mary Coll., 1983, McPherson Art Gallery, Victoria, B.C., Can., 1984, Studio D'Ars, Milan, 1985, Gallery Flaviana, Locarno, Switzerland, 1985, Il Salatto Gallery, Como, Italy, 1985, Galleria Schneider, Rome, 1987, Mus. Sztuki Lodz, Poland, 1987, Alternative Mus., Lido di Spina, Italy, 1987, Galerie Klaus Lea, Munich, 1987, Patricia Carega Gallery, Washington, 1988, Nine Columns Gallery, Palermo, Italy, 1988, John Hansard Gallery, Southampton, Eng., 1989, Quai Art Gallery, Isle of Wight, Eng., 1989, Lee Art Gallery, Clemson (S.C.) U., 1990, Apogeeairway, N.Y.C., 1991, Nine Columns Gallery, Brescia, Italy, 1991, Glenn Curtiss Mus., Hammondsport, N.Y., 1993, Caproni Mus., Trento, Italy, 1995, Temple U., Rome, 1995, Gallery of Modern Art, Maribor, Slovenia, 1995, Palazzo Communale, Todi, Italy, 1995, Palazzo Della Pretura, Piacenza, Italy; works represented in collections at Met. Mus., N.Y.C., Mus. Modern Art, N.Y.C., Victoria and Albert Mus., London, Whitney Mus., N.Y.C., Walker Art Center, Mpls., Tate Gallery, London, Fort Worth Art Center, Nat. Collection, Washington, others. Am. Fedn. of Arts grantee, 1965; Carnegie Found. grantee, 1967; Nat. Endowment for Arts grantee, 1973; N.Y. State Council on Arts grantee, 1973; Creative Artists Public Service Program grantee, 1978; Best Found. grantee, 1985 Mem. Exptl. Aircraft Assn., Aircraft Owners and Pilots Assn., Polish Acad. Sci. and Art, Internat. Aerobatic Club. Home: PO Box 849 Ithaca NY 14851-0849 *I have taken my artwork out of the museums and galleries into the sky. I use an aerobatic bi-plane which I build and fly to make large works in space. The airplane is flown through a series of complex maneuvers while trailing smoke in order to make a four-dimensional piece visible to the spectators for only a few short moments. The work of art has no existence other than in the memory or in documentation.*

POLETO, MARY MARGARET, orthopedic nurse; b. Troy, N.Y., May 4, 1959; d. Vincent P. and Marianne (DiDomenicantonio) P. BSN, Russell Sage Coll., 1981. Cert. Orthopedic Nurse. Staff nurse Albany (N.Y.) Med. Ctr., 1981-84, asst. nurse mgr., 1984-91, staff nurse, 1991—. Vol. post anesthesia care nurse Albany Plasticare Internat., Dominican Republic. Mem. Nat. Assn. Orthopedic Nurses, Capital Dist. Nurses Assn., Am. Assn. Spinal Cord Injured Nurses, Sigma Theta Tau. Republican. Roman Catholic. Avocations: reading, decorative painting. Home: 11 Cooper Ave Troy NY 12180-2703 Office: Albany Med Ctr Hosp New Scotland Ave Albany NY 12208-3491

POLEVOY, NANCY TALLY, lawyer, social worker, genealogist; b. N.Y.C., May 27, 1944; d. Charles H. and Bernice M. (Gang) Tally; m. Martin D. Polevoy, Mar. 19, 1967; children: Jason Tally, John Gerald. Student, Mt. Holyoke Coll., 1962-64; BA, Barnard Coll., 1966; MS in Social Work, Columbia U., 1968, JD, 1986. Bar: N.Y. 1987. Caseworker unmarried mothers' svc. Louise Wise Svcs., N.Y.C., 1967, caseworker adoption dept., 1969-71; caseworker Youth Consultation Svc., 1968-69; asst. rsch. scientist, psychiat. social worker NYU Med. ctr., 1973-81; adv. ct. appted. spl. advs. Manhattan Family Ct., 1981-82; cons. social work, 1981-86; matrimonial assoc. Ballon, Stoll & Itzler, 1987, Herzfeld & Rubin, P.C., 1987-88; pvt. practice N.Y.C. Contbr. articles on early infantile autism and geneaology to profl. jours. Mem. parents' adv. bd. Riverdale Country Sch., 1988-93; mem. outreach bd. Manhattan divsn. United Jewish Appeal Fedn., 1990-94, exec. bd. Manhattan divsn., 1992-94, mem. met. campaign cabinet, 1994-95; mem. archives com. Ctrl. Synagogue, 1991—, chmn. 1994—; trustee Am. Jewish Hist. Soc., 1992—, asst. treas., 1995-98, v.p., 1998—; trustee Jewish Assn. for Svcs. for the Aged, 1996—, v.p., 1999—; bd. dirs. Ctr. for Jewish History, 1996—. Recipient French Govt. prize, 1963. Mem. Assn. of Bar of City of N.Y., N.Y. State Bar Assn., NASW, Acad. Cert. Social Workers, Barnard Coll. Alumni Assn. (v.p. 1966, class pres. of 1966, 1996—). Home and Office: 1155 Park Ave New York NY 10128-1209

POLEYEFF, ISRAEL, rabbi, educator; b. Bklyn., June 23, 1928; s. Morris Aaron and Rachel Poleyeff; m. Eugenie Poleyeff, Nov. 18, 1952 (dec. Feb. 1997); children: Jacob, Susan, Arthur; m. Alizah Poleyeff, June, 1999. BA, Yeshiva U., 1949. Ordained rabbi, 1951. Chaplain U.S. Army, Ft. Pickett, Va., 1954, Japan, 1954—56; rabbi Congregation Tifereth Israel, New Castle, Pa., 1956-63, Congregation Agudath Achim, Freehold, N.J., 1963-67, Congregation Ahavath Achim, Bklyn., 1967-97, rabbi emeritus, 1997—; tchr. Hebrew Acad. of Five Towns, Cedarhurst, N.Y., 1970-99. Asst. editor Jour. Contemporary Halacha, 1980—. Capt. U.S. Army, 1954-56. Mem. Rabbinic Alumni Yeshiva U. (regional v.p. 1964-65), Rabbinical Bd. of Flatbush (pres. 1979-81, 91-2001).

POLGAR, LESLIE GEORGE, venture executive; b. Budapest, Hungary, July 26, 1943; s. Laszlo Polgar and Antonia (Szilard) Polgar Zala; m. Susan Elisabeth Cook, May 8, 1965; children: DAvid Szilard, Sara Elisabeth. BS in Physics and Math., U. Mich., 1965; PhD in Physics, Carnegie-Mellon U., 1971; MBA, U. Conn., 1977. Mgr. environ. planning, rsch. scientist TRC Environ. Cons., East Hartford, Conn., 1972-77; sr. assoc. Am. Petroleum Inst., Washington, 1977-79; dir., elec. materials mgr., corp. planning Stauffer Chem. Co., Westport, Conn., 1979-86; v.p. Emcore Corp., Somerset, N.J., 1986-88, Bertram Labs., Inc., Somerville, 1988-92, pres., 1992-94; v.p. electronics Air Liquide Am., Walnut Creek, Calif., 1995—. Reviewer Conservation Found., Washington, 1979; invited speaker Nat. Petroleum Refiners Assn., 1977, World Congress on Small Bus., 1987; vis. physics scientist Tech. U. of Eindhoven, The Netherlands, 1971-72. Contbr. articles to profl. jours. Trustee First Unitarian Soc. of Plainfield (N.J.), 1991—; fund raiser Carnegie-Mellon U., Pitts., 1975-87, alumni recruiter, 1991-94. Mem. IEEE, Am. Phys. Soc., Sigma Xi, Phi Kappa Phi, Beta Gamma Sigma. Avocations: sailing, travel, old MG automobiles, sports. Home: 974 Oak Vista Ct Lafayette CA 94549-1731 Office: Air Liquide Electronics 2121 N California Blvd Walnut Creek CA 94596-3572

POLHAMUS, GARRETT DOUGLAS, biomedical engineer; b. Norfolk, Va., Jan. 28, 1950; s. Douglas Clinton and Loraine Edith (Garrett) P.; m. Hattie Tangman, Aug. 7, 1976; children: Daniel Garrett, Lauren Elizabeth. BSME, U. Tex., 1972, MS, 1974, PhD, 1976. Commd capt. USAF, 1976, advanced through grades to col., 1994; laser bioeffects scientist Sch. of Aerospace Medicine, Brooks AFB, Tex., 1976-81; liaison officer for R&D Army Med. Rsch. Inst. Chem. Def., Aberdeen Proving Ground, Md., 1981-85; exch. officer Chem. Def. Establishment, Porton Down, Eng., 1985-88; chief human systems divsn. Hdqr. Air Force Systems Command, Andrews AFB, Md., 1988-91; dep. human systems tech. sci. and tech. Sec. of the Air Force, Pentagon, 1991-94; dir. plans directorate Armstrong Lab., Brooks AFB, 1994-97; sr. prin. mem. tech. staff Northrop Grumman, 1997—. Author: (with others) Laser Applications in Medicine and Biology, vol. 5, 1981; contbr.

articles to profl. jours. including Invest. Ophthal., Jour. Heat Transfer, IEEE Trans on Biomed. Engr., others. Mem. IEEE (sr.), AAAS, Tex. Soc. Profl. Engrs. Presbyterian. Achievements include research on understanding mechanisms of laser injury to the eye; developing new antidotes for nerve agent chemical weapons. Office: Northrop Grumman 4241 Woodcock Dr Ste B-100 San Antonio TX 78228-1330 E-mail: gdpolhamus@tasc.com.

POLI, KENNETH JOSEPH, editor, writer, photographer; b. Bklyn., June 8, 1921; s. Joseph H. and Irene (Seeman) P.; m. Virginia Osk, Dec. 14, 1946; 1 child, Bruce. Student, Goddard Coll., 1938-40. Writer, photographer North Atlantic Area Office ARC, N.Y.C., 1946-49. Editorial cons., 1965— Author Critical Focus Column, 1972-83; editor: External House Mags., Internat. Nickel Co., N.Y.C., 1949-53, Leica Photography mag., E. Leitz, Inc., N.Y.C., 1953-65; assoc. editor Popular Photography mag., Ziff-Davis Pub. Co., N.Y.C., 1965-69, sr. editor, 1969-70, editor, 1970-83, cons. editor, 1983-87; cons. editor Photography Ann., 35-mm Photography, Photography Directory and Buying Guide, 1970-83; contbr. articles to photog. jours. and encys. With inf. U.S. Army, 1942-45, PTO. Decorated Purple Heart medal. Mem. Am. Photog. Hist. Soc., Photographic Adminstrs., Circle of Confusion, Mensa. Home and Office: Apt 6167 1 Jefferson Ferry Dr South Setauket NY 11720-4727 E-mail: heremi_2000@yahoo.com.

POLIAKOFF, GARY A. lawyer, educator; b. Greenville, S.C, Nov. 25, 1944; s. Herman and Dorothy (Ravitz) P.; m. Sherri D. Dublin, June 24, 1967; children: Ryan, Keith. BS, U. S.C., 1966; JD, U. Miami, 1969. Bar: Fla. 1969, D.C. 1971, Colo. 1999. Founding prin., pres. Becker & Poliakoff, P.A., Hollywood, Miami, Naples, Sarasota, West Palm Beach, founding prin., sr. ptnr., pres. Largo, Tampa, Jacksonville, Ft. Myers, Boca Raton, St Petersburg, Orlando, Ft. Walton Beach, Fla., Prague and Beijing, 1973—. Adj. prof. condominium law and practice Nova Southeastern U.; panelist Nat. Confs. Community Assns.; testified before coms. of the U.S. Senate on Condominiums; lectr. ann. condominium seminars Fla. Bar; participant Fla. Law Revision Council; cons. to State Legis. and the White House in drafting Condominium and Coop. Abuse Relief Act, 1980; mem. condominium study commn. State of Fla., 1990; chmn. State of Fla. Advisory Coun. on Condominiums, 1992, 93.; atty. Town of Southwest Ranches. Author: The Law of Condominium Operations, 1988; co-author: Florida Condominium Law and Practice, 1982, The Florida Bar Continuing Legal Education, 1982; contbr. articles to legal jours. Mem. pres.'s adv. group U. S.C., U.S.C. Ednl. Found., 1999—. Recipient Judge Learned Hand award Am. Jewish Com. for devel. of co-ownership housing law, 1999. Mem. Fla. Bar, Coll. Cmty. Assn. Lawyers (bd. govs.), Scribes.

POLICH, JOHN ELLIOTT, computer company executive, educator, writer; b. Ft. Bragg, Calif., May 18, 1946; s. Aloysius J. and Mildred I. (Johnson) P.; m. Ina Lee Selden, Apr. 23, 1982. BA in Journalism cum laude, Ariz. State U., 1968; MA in Comm., Stanford U., 1974, PhD in Comm., 1976. Reporter Evening Am., Phoenix, 1964-65, Ariz. Rep., Phoenix, 1965-67, KTAR-TV (now KPNX-TV), Phoenix, 1967-68, Express, San Antonio, 1968-72; staff writer Free Press, Detroit, 1975-76; mgr. Media Divsn. Market Opinion Rsch., 1976-77; mktg. rsch. mgr. N.Y. Times, N.Y.C., 1977-82, group mktg. dir. regional newspapers, 1982-84; pres. Simmons Scarborough, 1984-86; assoc. dir. freedom forum media studies ctr. Columbia U., 1986-88; pres. MOR/New York, 1988-90; global media and visual mktg. prof. Fordham Grad. Sch. Bus. at Lincoln Ctr., 1990-99; pres. Polich Media Mgmt., 1991-2000; mem. faculty New Sch. for Social Rsch., 1999-2000; v.p., R & D Engage, Inc., San Francisco, 2000—. Clients include Asia Found., Guangzhou (China) Daily Press Group, CBS TV Network; newspaper rsch. coun. Advt. Rsch. Found., N.Y., 1978-84; readership and mktg. com. Am. Newspaper Pub. Assn., 1979-82; editorial bd. Newspaper Rsch. Jour., 1981—; dean's adv. coun. Newhouse Sch. Pub. Communication Syracuse (N.Y.) U., 1984-89. Co-author: Newspaper Leadership, 1986; travel editl. and art photographer; contbr. articles to profl. jours. Inducted Hall of Fame Walter Cronkite Sch. of Journalism and Telecom. Coll. of Pub. Programs, Ariz. State U., 1998. Mem. Am. Soc. Media Photographers, Advt. Photographers of Am., Overseas Press Club (editor bull. 1990-93, gov. 1993-97, 98—, awards com. 1990—), N.Y. Friars Club.

POLICHINO, JOSEPH ANTHONY, JR. wholesale company executive; b. Oct. 17, 1948; s. Joseph Anthony and Josephine Adeline Polichino; m. Jean Elliott McDowell, Oct. 7, 1978; 2 children. Student, Spring Hill Coll., 1966-67; AA cum laude, South Tex. Jr. Coll., 1969; postgrad., U. Houston, 1969-71. Sales posting clk. Jax Beer Co., Houston, 1971-72, route salesman asst., 1972; sales supr. Nat. Beverage Co., 1972-74, pres., 1974-76; owner, pres. Coors N.E. Distbg. Co., 1976-84; founder, v.p. Alessandra Import Co., 1980-86; exec. v.p. Internat. Brands, 1984-92; founding ptnr., mktg. dir. Hillman Internat. Brands, Ltd., 1992—. Founder, mng. ptnr. The Mktg. Advisors Group, Houston, 1997; cons. to radio medium and small bus. orgnl. and personal devel.; ptnr. Mktg. Plus, Houston, 1999. Bd. dirs. Houston Livestock Show and Rodeo, 1978—, Houston Muscular Dystrophy Assn. Exec. Com., 1977-91, Bill Williams Capon Charity Dinner, 1977—, Strake Jesuit Coll. Prep. Sch., 1986-99, Houston Proud, 1989-91; mem. adv. bd. Houston and S.E. region Am. Lung Assn., 1996—; commr. City of West University Place, Tex., 1981-83, councilman, 1983-85. Mem. Sons of Bosses Internat. (regional v.p. 1974-75), Jesuit Coll. Prep. Alumni Assn. (pres. 1977-79), Houston Citizens C. of C. (dir. 1977—), Nat. Beer Wholesalers Assn., Wholesale Beer Distbrs. Tex., Harris County Wholesale Beer Distbrs. Assn., Toastmasters. Roman Catholic.

POLICINSKI, EUGENE FRANCIS, newspaper editor, foundation executive , radio producer; b. South Bend, Ind., Aug. 31, 1950; s. E.T. and Margaret C. (O'Neill) P.; m. Kathleen Beta O'Donnell Powell, Aug. 19, 1972; children: Ryan, David. Degree in journalism and polit. sci., Ball State U., 1972. Corr. Gannett News Svc., Washington, 1979-82; Washington editor USA Today, Arlington, Va., 1982-83, page one editor, 1983-85, mng. editor sports, 1985-96; spl. asst. to chmn./CEO The Freedom Forum, 1996-98; wash. editor Freedom Forum Website, 1998-99; dep. dir. First Amendment Ctr., Nashville, 1999—. Host, commentator USA Today Sky Radio, Arlington, 1992—95; host Newseum Radio, 1998—2001; adj. faculty Winthrop U., 1999—. Founding editor USA Today Baseball Weekly, 1991. Bd. advisors Ctr. Study Sport in Soc., 1995—; trustee U.S. Sports Acad., 1997—, Watkins Coll. of Art and Design, 2001—. Named one of 100 Most Important People in Sports Sporting News, 1992-93, 95, Sports Person of Yr., U.S. Sports Acad., 1996; named to Journalism Hall of Fame, Ball State U., 1989, Alumni of Yr., 1996. Mem. Am. Soc. Newspaper Editors, Soc. Profl. Journalists, Assn. Educators in Journalism and Mass Comms. Avocations: sailing, tennis, bicycling, golf. Office: First Amendment Center Deputy Director 1207 18th Ave S Nashville TN 37212-2807 E-mail: gpolicinski@fac.org.

POLICOFF, LEONARD DAVID, physician, educator; b. Wilmington, Del., Apr. 22, 1918; s. David and Rosalie (Rochkind) P.; m. Naomi Lewis, June 25, 1942; children: Susan, Stephen. BS, U. Richmond, 1938; MD, Med. Coll. Va., 1942. Diplomate Am. Bd. Internal Medicine, Am. Bd. Phys. Medicine and Rehab. (mem. 1968-80). Asst. prof. Med. Coll. Va., 1948-55; prof., chmn. dept. phys. medicine and rehab. Albany Med. Coll., Union U., 1955-67, Temple U., Phila., 1967-70; prof., chmn. Hahnemann Med. Coll., 1970-71; prof. clin. phys. medicine U. Pa.; chmn. dept. rehab. medicine Princeton (N.J.) Hosp., 1971-75, cons., 1975-78; dir. rehab. medicine Somerset Hosp., Somerville, N.J., 1975-78; acting chmn., prof. clin. phys. medicine Rutgers Med. Sch., 1976-78; clin. prof. phys. medicine and rehab. U. Calif.-Davis Sch. Medicine, 1980-86; chmn. dept. rehab. medicine Pacific Med. Center, San Francisco, 1978-81. Med. cons. Dept. Health Svcs., State of Calif., 1987-91; chief rehab. medicine svc. VA Med. Ctr., Martinez, Calif., 1983-85; med. dir. Rehab. Ctr., John Muir Meml. Hosp., Walnut Creek, Calif., 1985-87; mem. Bd. Med. Examiners, N.Y. State, 1962-67; chief of staff VA Hosp., Livermore, Calif., 1987-88. Contbr. articles to profl. jours., textbooks. Bd. dirs. Commn. on Edn. in Phys. Medicine and Rehab., 1968-80, com. for Handicapped People-to-People Program, 1967-75. Served to maj. M.C., AUS, 1943-46. Nat. Inst. Neurologic Diseases fellow, 1953-55 Fellow ACP, Am. Acad. Phys. Medicine and Rehab., Am. Acad. Cerebral Palsy; mem. Am. Congress Rehab. Medicine (pres. 1971), Assn. Acad. Physiatrists, AMA (chmn. phys. medicine sect. 1965-66), Phi Beta Kappa, Alpha Omega Alpha, Sigma Zeta. Home: 1304 Henry St Berkeley CA 94709-1929 E-mail: lennapol@aol.com.

POLICY, CARMEN A. professional sports team executive; b. Youngstown, Ohio, Jan. 26, 1943; s. Albert and Ruby (Tisone) P.; m. Aug. 8, 1964 (div. Mar. 1989); children: James, Daniel, Edward, Kerry, Kathy; m. Gail Marie Moretti, June 27, 1991. Grad., Youngstown State U., 1963; JD, Georgetown U., 1966. Bar: Ohio 1966, Va. 1966, D.C. 1966. Assoc. Nadler & Nadler, Youngstown, 1966-68; asst. prosecutor City of Youngstown, 1968-69; ptnr. Flask & Policy, Weimer & White, Youngstown, 1969-90; spl. counsel to atty. gen. State of Ohio, 1970-91; v.p., gen. counsel San Francisco 49ers, NFL, 1983-90, pres., 1990-99; pres., CEO & co-owner Cleve. Browns, 1998—. Mem. various coms. NFL, 1990—; bd. dirs. World League Am. Football, N.Y.C., 1991—. Com. mem. various charities, Youngstown, 1969-90, San Francisco, 1990—. Mem. Va. Bar Assn., Ohio Bar Assn., D.C. Bar Assn. Roman Catholic. Avocations: scuba diving, hiking. Office: Cleve Browns 76 Lou Groza Blvd. Berea OH 44017*

POLICY, VINCENT MARK, lawyer; b. Warren, Ohio, Mar. 29, 1948; s. Vincent James and Anna Marie (Berardi) P.; m. Katherine Anne Veazey; children: Nicholas, Katherine Nicole. BA, U. Md., 1970; JD, Georgetown U., 1973. Bar: N.Y. 1974, D.C. 1975, U.S. Supreme Ct. 1977. Assoc. Cahill Gordon & Reindel, Washington and N.Y.C., 1973-78, Hogan & Hartson, Washington, 1978-85; prin. Pohoryles & Greenstein PC, 1985-89, Greenstein, Delorme & Luchs, P.C., Washington, 1989—. Author: Speedy Trial, A Constitutional Right in Search of Definition, 1973. Mem. D.C. Bar Assn. (chmn. rental housing com. 1985-88), D.C. Assn. Realtors (speaker 1984—), Apt. and Office Bldg. Assn. (lectr. 1985—), Greater Washington Bd. Trade (subcom. on initiatives, econ. growth com.), D.C. Builders Assn. (legis. affairs com.), Phi Beta Kappa, Omicron Delta Kappa. Lodges: KC. Democrat. Roman Catholic. Avocation: sailing. Office: Greenstein DeLorme & Luchs 1620 L St NW Ste 900 Washington DC 20036-5613

POLIN, ALAN JAY, lawyer; b. N.Y.C., Sept. 5, 1953; s. Mortin and Eleanor (Clarke) P.; m. Sharon Lynn Hirschfeld, Oct. 10, 1976; children: Jay Michael, Meryl Beth. Student, Cornell U., 1971-74; BA cum laude, Seton Hall U., 1978; JD, Nova U., 1981. Bar: Fla. 1981, N.Y. 1990; lic. athlete agt., Fla. Assoc. Berryhill, Avery, Williams & Jordan, Esq., Ft. Lauderdale, Fla., 1981-82, Greenspoon & Marder, P.A., Miami, 1982-83; pvt. practice Ft. Lauderdale, 1983-86; ptnr. Mousaw, Vigdor, Reeves & Hess, 1986-90; pvt. practice Coral Springs, Fla., 1990—. Adj. faculty mem. Nova U.; mem. grievance com. Fla. Bar, 1989-92, vice chair, 1990-91, chair, 1991-92. Chmn. Broward County Crct. Ct. Handbook, 1988; contbr. chpt. to Bridge the Gap Attorney's Handbook, 1987. Mem. Anti-Defamation League Fla. Regional Bd., 1994—; chmn. Fla. Intergovtl. Fin. Commn., 2002—; mem. exec. com. Broward County Dem., 1989—96; vice mayor City of Coral Springs, 1994—96, commr., 1991—; vice chmn. Fla. Intergovtl. Fin. Commn., 2001; vice mayor City of Coral Springs, 2002—; dir. Temple Beth Am., Margate, Fla., 1991—93; bd. dirs. Fla. Regional Bd. of Anti-Defamation League, 1994—, Children's Cardiac Rsch. Found., Inc., 1996—, The Irving Fryer Found., Inc., 1995—96, Am. Heart Assn., 1997—, Jr. Achievement So. Fla., 2001—. Recipient Am. Jurisprudence award Nova U. Law Ctr., 1981, Disting. Pub. Svc. award, Anti-Defamation League, 2000. Mem. Fla. Bar Assn. (bd. govs. young lawyers divsn. 1987-89), Broward County Bar Assn. (exec. com. young lawyers sect. 1986-87), North Broward Assn. Realtors, Inc. (affiliate, std. contract forms com. 1989-95, atty./realtor rels. com. 1989-91), Kiwanis (Key Club advisor 1990-91). Office: 3300 University Dr Ste 601 Coral Springs FL 33065-4132 E-mail: alanpolin@polinlaw.com.

POLIN, JANE L. foundation official; b. N.Y.C., Sept. 30, 1958; d. Raymond and Constance F. (Caplan) P. BA, Wesleyan U., Middletown, Conn., 1980; MBA, Columbia U., 1988. Asst. dir. ann. giving Wesleyan U., 1980-82; centennial fund assoc. Met. Opera Assn., N.Y.C., 1982-84; devel. officer Columbia U., 1984-88; program mgr., compt. GE Fund, Fairfield, Conn., 1988-99; v.p. cmty. devel. and corp. affairs Sperry & Hutchinson, Inc., 1999—2000, philanthropic advisor, 2001—. Panelist arts-in-edn. Nat. Endowment for Arts, Washington, 1989—90, 1994—95, Nat. Endowment Humanities, 1997; adv. bd. mem. ARC, 1991—99, United Way Am., 1991—99, Inst. for Internat. Econs., 1995—99, Young Audiences, N.Y.C., 1991—2000; judge Frances Hesselbein Cmty. Innovation Fellows Program, 2001—, Peter F. Drucker Award for Nonprofit Innovation, 1996—2000. Mem.: Advt. Coun., Ams. for the Arts, Alpha Delta Phi. Home and Office: 67 Riverside Dr Apt 7D New York NY 10024-6136 Fax: 212-873-1568. E-mail: janepolin@aol.com.

POLING, JEROME PAUL, journalist; b. Eau Claire, Wis., July 20, 1958; s. John Craig and Edna Merle (Flanscha) P.; m. Lynn Marie Ripienski, Oct. 22, 1983; children: Jerad, Matthew. BS in Mktg., U. Wis., La Crosse, 1980; MA in English Lit., U. Wis., Eau Claire, 1990. Sect. editor Dunn County News, Menomonie, Wis., 1980-82, Leader-Telegram, Eau Claire, 1982-89, news editor, 1989—. Instr. English dept. Mount Senario Coll., Ladysmith, Wis., 1994; instr. journalism dept. U. Wis., Eau Claire, 1996, instr. English dept., 1998, 99, 2000; freelance writer, 1990—. Author: Downfield, 1996, A Summer Up North, 2002; columnist Leader-Telegram, Eau Claire, 1993—; author of short story; co-author: Wisconsin Golf Getaways, 2001. Chmn., founder Henry Aaron Tribute, Eau Claire, 1994. Recipient 1st place column writing Wis. Newspaper Assn., 1985, 97. Mem. Phi Kappa Phi. Lutheran.

POLINSKY, JANET NABOICHECK, retired state official, former state legislator; b. Hartford, Conn., Dec. 6, 1930; d. Louis H. and Lillian S. Naboicheck; m. Hubert N. Polinsky, Sept. 21, 1958 (div.); children: Gerald, David, Beth. BA, U. Conn., 1953; postgrad., Harvard Bus. Sch., 1954. Mem. Waterford 2d Charter Commn. (Conn.), 1967-68, Waterford Conservation Commn., 1968-69; Waterford rep. Town Meeting, 1969-71, S.E. Conn. Regional Planning Agy., 1971-73; mem. Waterford Planning and Zoning Commn., 1970-76, chmn., 1973-76; mem. Waterford Dem. Town Com., 1976-92. Del. State Dem. Conv., 1976, 78, 80, 82, 84, 86, 90, 92; mem. Conn. Ho. of Reps. from 38th Dist., 1977-82, asst. majority leader, 1981-83, chmn. appropriations com., 1983-85, 87-89, ranking mem., 1985-87, minority whip, 1985-86, dep. spkr., 1989-92; dep. commr. dept. adminstrv. svcs. State of Conn., 1993-94, chmn., 1994-95, asst. sec. of state, 1995, commr. utilities ctrl. auth., 1995-97. Trustee Eugene O'Neill Meml. Theatre Ctr., 1973-76, 81-92; corporator Lawrence and Meml. Hosps., 1987-88; mem. New Eng. Bd. Higher Edn., 1981-83; mem. fiscal affairs com. Eastern Conf. Coun. State Govts., 1983-88; bd. dirs. Cascades Limoge Village, 2000—, Cascades Master Bd., 2001—. Named Woman of Yr., Waterford Jr. Women's Club, 1977, Nehantic Women's Bus. and Profl. Club, 1979, Legislator of Yr., Conn. Libr. Assn., 1980. Mem. Order of Women Legislators, Delta Kappa Gamma (hon.). Home: 7141 Haviland Cir Boynton Beach FL 33437-6463 E-mail: janet126@adelphia.net.

POLINSKY, JOSEPH THOMAS, recruiting and training consultant; b. Kingston, Pa., Mar. 10, 1947; s. Joseph Patrick and Margaret Ceclia (Matej) P.; m. Donna Lee Miles, Dec. 28, 1968 (div. Nov. 1990); children: Jon Douglas, Jennifer Susan, Jeffrey David; m. Diane Walsh, Apr. 19, 1997. BSBA, King's Coll., 1968; MBA in Mgmt., Fairleigh Dickinson U., 1977. Fin. svcs. specialist Bell Labs., Murray Hill, N.J., 1968-74, adminstrv. asst. Whippany, 1974-76, supr. adminstrn. svcs., 1977, tech. employment rep. Holmdel, 1977-80, sr. systems analyst Short Hills, 1981-82; mgr. tech. employment Bellcore, Piscataway, 1983-85, mgr. logistics, 1986-92, mgr. purchasing, 1992-96; dir., tech. recruiting Youngtech, Inc., Edison, 1996; employment rep. Lucent Tech., Holmdel, 1996-97, coll. recruiting and tng. cons., 1997-98, mem. faculty, 1999-2000; dir. recruiting and talent devel. Cybertel, Inc., Middletown, N.J., 2000; cons., owner JTP Cons., Holmdel, 2000—; adj. prof. Sch. Bus. Adminstrn., Monmouth U., Long Branch, NJ, 2001—. Adj. prof. Sch. Bus. Adminstrn. Monmouth U., West Long Branch, NJ, 2001—. Mem. indsl. com. United Way, Morris County, N.J., 1977, allocation com., Monmouth County, N.J., 1985; cub master Boy Scouts Am., Raritan, N.J., 1983-86; mem. Bd. Adjustment, Raritan, 1988-89. With U.S. Army, 1969-70. Roman Catholic. Avocations: fishing, philately, cooking, baseball cards. Home and Office: 185 Escondido Ct Holmdel NJ 07733-2531 E-mail: joesonline@aol.com.

POLIOS, NANCY LOUISE, secondary school educator; b. Moline, Ill., Mar. 19, 1941; d. Everett Austin and Esther Laura (Anderson) Ross; m. George Michael Polios, April 21, 1963; children: Michelle, Stephanie. BA, Augustana Coll., 1963; MEd, Western Ill. U., 1983. Tchr. United Township High Sch., East Moline, Ill., 1963-64, 1979—, Glenview Jr. High Sch., East Moline, 1972, Moline Adult Edn., Moline, Ill., 1973-76. Tutor United Township High Sch., East Moline. Coord. Upward Bound, Davenport, Iowa, 1993-97. Recipient Quarterly Tchg. award John Deere Harvestor Works, East Moline, 1992. Mem. AAUW, Delta Kappa Gamma (chapt. pres. 1996-98, state literacy chair 1999-). Methodist. Avocations: sewing, physical fitness, crafts. Home: 1812 21st Ave East Moline IL 61244-2350 Office: United Township High School 1275 42nd Ave East Moline IL 61244-4145 E-mail: npolios@gconline.com.

POLIS, MICHAEL PHILIP, electrical and systems engineering educator; b. N.Y.C., Oct. 24, 1943; s. Max and Sylvia (Goldner) P.; m. Claudette Martin, May 28, 1966; children: Melanie Bobby, Martin Pascal, Karine Melissa. BSEE, U. Fla., 1966; MSEE, Purdue U., West Lafayette, Ind., 1968, PhD, 1972. Grad. instr. elec. engring. Purdue U., West Lafayette, 1966-71; post-doctoral fellow Ecole Polytechnique, Montreal, 1972-73, asst. prof. elec. engring., 1973-74, assoc. prof., 1974-82, prof., 1982-83; program dir. sys. theory NSF, Washington, 1983-87; chmn. dept. elec. and computer engring. Wayne State U., Detroit, 1987-93; dean Sch. Engring. and Computer Sci. Oakland U., Rochester, Mich., 1993-2001, prof. elec. and systems engring., 2001—. Expert witness various law firms, 1989—; cons. Mich. Bell-Ameritech, Detroit, 1989-95, ICAM Technologies, Inc., Montreal, 1981-83; vis. rsch. assoc. LAAS, Toulouse, France, 1978. Contbr. articles to profl. jours. Mem. IEEE (sr.), IEEE Control Sys. Soc. (bd. govs. 1993-95, 98-2000, Best Paper Trans. on Automatic Control 1974-75, Disting. Mem. 1993, v.p. mem. activities 1990-91, assoc. editor 1981-82). Office: Oakland Univ Sch Engring & Computer Sci Rochester MI 48309-4778

POLISAR, JOSEPH MICHAEL, protective services official; b. Bklyn., June 25, 1952; s. Ira Allen and Rose (Gimpelman) P.; m. Shirley Elizabeth Chavez, Nov. 1, 1986; children: Brooklyn Joseph, Savannah Janelle. BA in Mgmt., U. Phoenix, 1993; grad., FBI Acad., 1993; postgrad., FBI Nat. Exec. Inst., 1995; grad., JFK Sch. Govt., 1996. Officer, detective Albuquerque Police Dept., 1977-81, sgt., 1981-85, lt., 1985-92, capt., 1992-94, chief of police, 1994-97, Garden Grove (Calif.) Police Dept., 1998—. Staff instr. Northwestern U., Evanston, Ill., 1989—. Fund raiser Am. Cancer Soc., Muscular Dystrophy, Juvenile Diabetes, Crimestoppers, Cystic Fibrosis. Recipient 1995 Albuquerque Human Rights award, Martin Luther King "Keep the Dream Alive" award NAACP, Albuquerque, 1996. Mem. Internat. Police Assn., FOP, Internat. Assn. Chiefs of Police (1st v.p.), FBI Nat. Acad. Assn., Kiwanis (v.p.). Avocations: bowhunting, motorcycle touring, jogging.

POLISAR, LEONARD MYERS, lawyer; b. Bklyn., Oct. 25, 1929; s. Aaron and Anna (Myers) P.; m. Judith Sarah Weisstein, Aug. 16, 1959; children: Mark Joseph, Daniel Aaron. BA, Bklyn. Coll., 1950; LLB, Yale U., 1953; LLM in Taxation, NYU, 1959. Bar: N.Y. 1954. Assoc. Hays, Podell, Algase, Crum & Feuer, N.Y.C., 1955-63; asst. to gen. counsel CIT Fin. Corp., 1963-65; v.p. law and pub. affairs Mgmt. Assistance Inc., 1966-72; v.p., gen. counsel Internat. Controls Corp., Fairfield, N.J., 1972-73; v.p., sec., gen. counsel Baker Industries Inc., Parsippany, 1973-80; ptnr. Herzfeld & Rubin, P.C., N.Y.C., 1980—, co-chmn. corp. and securities law dept., 1988—, also bd. dirs. Arbitrator N.Y. Stock Exch., 1987—; speaker at computer, securities and corp. seminars. Editor Yale Law Jour., 1953. Bd. dirs. Mental Health Assn. of N.Y.C., 1960—, chmn., 1985—; trustee Union Temple Bklyn., 1988—, v.p. 1990-99; bd. dirs. Routes to Roots Found. Mem. ABA, Assn. of Bar of City of N.Y., Am. Soc. Corp. Secs. (chmn. audit com. 1989-92), Bus. Coun. for UNA (bus. adv. com.), Bus. Execs. for Nat. Security, Computer Law Assn., Citizens Union, Yale Club of N.Y., Yale Club of Montclair, Phi Beta Kappa. Jewish. Avocations: skiing, sailing, spectator sports, music, drama. Home: 63 Briarcliff Rd Mountain Lakes NJ 07046-1304 Office: Herzfeld & Rubin PC 40 Wall St Fl 54 New York NY 10005-2301

POLISHOOK, LEWIS A. lawyer; b. Englewood, N.J., Mar. 22, 1970; s. Irwin H. and Sheila S. Polishook. AB, Brown U., 1992; JD, Harvard U., 1995. Bar: N.J. 1995, N.Y. 1996, Mass. 1997. Law clk. to Judge Bruce Selya U.S Ct. Appeals (1st cir.), Providence, 1995-96; assoc. Winthrop, Stimson, Putnam & Roberts, N.Y.C., 1996-98, Kornstein, Veisz & Wexler, LLP, N.Y.C., 1998—. Contbr. articles to profl. jours. Mem. ABA, Assn. Bar City N.Y. Office: Kornstein Veisz & Wexler 757 3d Ave New York NY 10017

POLISI, JOSEPH W(ILLIAM), academic administrator; b. N.Y.C., Dec. 30, 1947; married. BA in Polit. Sci., U. Conn., 1969; MA in Internat. Relations, Tufts U., 1970, MusM, 1973, M of Mus. Arts, 1975; DMA, Yale U., 1980; DHL (hon.), Ursinus Coll., Collegetown, Pa., 1986; MusD (hon.), Curtis Inst. Music, 1990; DMA, New England Conservatory Music, 2001. Exec. officer Yale Sch. of Music, New Haven, 1976-80; dean of faculty Manhattan Sch. of Music, N.Y.C., 1980-83; dean Coll. Conservatory of Music U. Cin., 1983-84; pres. The Juilliard Sch., N.Y.C., 1984—. Performances as bassoonist throughout the U.S.; contbr. articles to various publs. in U.S. and France. Office: Juilliard Sch Office of the Pres 60 Lincoln Center Plz New York NY 10023-6588

POLISTUK, EUGENE V. electronics executive; B Applied Sci. in Elec. Engring., U. Toronto; D Engring. (hon.) , Ryerson U., 2001. Founder, chmn., CEO Celestica Inc., Toronto, Canada, 1994—, pres. Canada, 1994—2001; with IBM Can. Recipient Meritorious Svc. medal, U. Toronto Engring. Alumni Assn., Outstanding CEO award, Electronic Bus. Office: Celestica Inc 12 Concorde Pl Toronto ON Canada M3C 3R8

POLITE, CARLENE HATCHER, writer, educator; b. Detroit; d. John and Lillian Hatcher; divorced; children: Glynda Morton, Lila Ashaki. Student, Martha Graham Sch. Dance, N.Y.C., 1952-56; diploma, Acad. Leonardo da Vinci, Rome, 1980. Dancer, student Martha Graham Sch., N.Y.C., 1952-56; dancer Alvin Ailey Dance Co., 1957-58, Edith Stephen Co., N.Y.C., 1958; dancer, actress Vanguard Playhouse, Detroit, 1960-62; prof. English SUNY, Buffalo, 1971—, chair dept. Am. Studies, 1981, prof. emerita, 2000. Tchr. Golden Dragon Kung Fu Acad., 1974-75, Himalayan Inst. Yoga, 1980-82; panelist NEA, Washington, 1981, N.Y. State Coun. Arts, N.Y.C., 1982, N.Y. Found. Arts, 1983, Seattle Arts in Pub. Places, 1989. Author: The Flagellants, 1966 (Pulitzer Prize nominee 1967, NEA grant 1967, Rockefeller grant 1968), Sister X and The Victims of Foul Play, 1975. Coord. Walk to Freedom with Martin Luther King, Detroit, 1963; del., participant UN-Non-Govtl.Orgns. 4th World Conf. on Women, Beijing, 1995. Recipinet numerous nat. and internat. awards as artist and educator; invited 1st Ann. Conf. African Presence, Paris, 1991, Internat. Educators and Writers Oxford U., 1997. Avocations: T'ai Chi Ch'uan, Hatha Yoga.

POLITE, EDMONIA ALLEN, consultant; b. Washington, June 22, 1922; d. Thomas Samuel and Narcissus Bertha (Porter) Allen-Sylvester; m. George Frederick Polite, Jan. 5, 1947; 1 child, Frederick Gartrell. BA, Roosevelt U., 1958; MEd, Loyola U., Chgo., 1966; PhD in Adminstrn. and Supervision, Purdue U., 1973; DDiv, Ea. U., Tampa, Fla., 1971; DEd in Psychology, Ea. U., 1972. Dir. Media Ctr., Chgo., 1958-69, 73-81; instr. media scis. Purdue U., West Lafayette, Ind., 1969-73; pres. Cons. Inc., Chgo., Orlando, Fla., from 1974; dir. Community Tutoring Ctr., Chgo., 1974-80, EAP Enterprises, from 1984. Dir. workshop U. Cen. Fla., 1987; cons. Lake Region Conf., Detroit, 1966, Librarians, Inc., Chgo., 1970-71. Author: In Passing, 1970, People Who Help Us, 1982. Founder South End Parents Council, Chgo., 1960, Humanitarian Profls., Chgo., 1974, Orlando, 1983—; bd. dirs. Salem House, Chgo., 1980—. Recipient Outstanding Service award Lions Club, Chgo., 1975, Outstanding Educator award Fla. Agrl. and Mech. U. Alumni Assn. Mem. Nat. Assn. Club Women (dir. archives 1980-84), Ill. Audio Visual Assn., Phi Delta Kappa. Club: Successful Progressors (Orlando) (pres. 1983-95). Avocations: writing, community service, counseling. Deceased.

POLITES, MICHAEL EDWARD, aerospace engineer, researcher; b. Belleville, Ill., Mar. 19, 1944; s. Matthew Charles and Edith Louise (Schwarz) P. BS in Sys. and Automatic Controls, Washington U., St. Louis, 1967; MSEE, U. Ala., 1971; PhD in Elec. Engring., Vanderbilt U., 1986. Aerospace rsch. engr., guidance, navigation and control sys. NASA/Marshall Space Flt. Ctr. Structures & Dynamics Lab, Huntsville, Ala., 1967-95; supervisory chief, instrumentation and control divsn. Astrionics Lab. NASA/Marshall Space Flight Ctr., 1995-98, dep. dir. astronics lab., 1998-99, dep. mgr. avionics dept., 1999-2001—; assoc. prof. aerospace engring. and mechanics U. Ala., 2001—. 4 patents in field; contbr. numerous articles to profl. jours.; referee various jours. and confs. Mem. adv. bd. Coll. Engring. leadership bd. U. Ala. Recipient

71 NASA awards in the field including NASA-Marshall Co-Inventor of Yr., 1995; U. Ala. Coll. Engring. Disting. fellow, elec. engring. dept. outstanding fellow; named Outstanding Engr., Engrs. Coun., 2000. Fellow AIAA (assoc., guidance navigation and control tech. com. 1990-2002, digital avionics tech. com. 1996-2002); mem. IEEE (sr. Outstanding Engr. Huntsville sect. 1995), ASME, Am. Astronautical Soc. (session co-chmn. 1995, 97, 98, 99, 2000, 01, Guidance and Control Conf.), Mensa, Tau Beta Pi, Eta Kappa Nu, Pi Tau Sigma. Office: U Ala Dept Aerospace Engring and Mechanics Box 870280 Tuscaloosa AL 35847

POLITI, BETH KUKKONEN, publishing services company executive; b. Englewood, N.J., Sept. 18, 1949; d. Andrew and Beatrice G. (Druskin) Kukkonen; m. Joseph Politi, Oct. 21, 1982; children: Andrew, Joseph. BS in Mktg., Miami U., Oxford, Ohio, 1971. Media buyer Schwab, Beatty & Porter, Inc., 1971-72; media planner Adler, Schwartz & Connes, 1972-73; media buyer/planner Schwab Beatty divsn. Marstellar, 1973-74; dir. insert advt. Benjamin Co., Inc., Elmsford, N.Y., 1975-78, prodn. mgr., 1978-80, v.p. client svcs., 1980-83, editor supr., 1979-83; v.p. Bergen County Profl. Svcs., Ft. Lee, N.J., 1983—. Assoc. pub. various books Benjamin Co., Inc., 1981-83; freelance proofreader Montge Media, Montvale, N.J., 1999—; mem. dist. fee com. Office of Atty. Ethics of the Supreme Ct. of N.J., 2001--. Trustee bd. edn. Pascack Valley Regional H.S. Dist., 1999—; mem. dist. fee com. Office of Atty. Ethics of Supreme Ct. of NJ, 2001—. Home: 4 Smoke Rise Ct Montvale NJ 07645-1139

POLITI, JOHN J. other: association and organizations; b. Sedalia, Mo. m. Terri Hatch; children: Pam, Eileen, Jay, Stephanie, Chip. BA in Polit. Sci., U. Colo.; MS in Econs., S.D. State U. Commd. 2d lt. USAF, 1966, advanced through grades to col.; comdr. Air Divsn.; with Joint Staff and Air Staff; ret. USAF, 1992; nat. dir. Air Force Assn., Arlington, Va., nat. v.p. Midwest Region, Mo. state pres., chmn. audit com., membership com., ad hoc fin. com., nat. pres., 2001—. Pres. Excellence in Mo. Found. Decorated Legion of Merit. Office: c/o AFA Nat Hqrs 1501 Lee Hwy Arlington VA 22209-1198*

POLITI, STEPHEN MICHAEL, lawyer, educator; b. Mass., Mar. 30, 1948; s. Selvi J. and Anne (Gargiulo) P.; m. Joan Spignesi, June 29, 1985. AB in Econs. cum laude, U. Mass., 1970; JD, Boston U., 1973, LLM in Taxation, 1974. Bar: Mass. 1973, U.S. Tax Ct. 1977, U.S. Dist. Ct. Mass. 1977. Counsel Joint Legis. Com. on Taxation, Boston, 1973-74; staff atty. Mass. Dept. Revenue, 1974-79, chief counsel, 1979-83; pvt. practice, 1983-86; ptnr. Hennessy, Killgoar & Politi, 1986—2001; of counsel Engel & Schultz, P.C., 2001—. Prof. Bentley Coll. Grad. Sch. of Taxation, Waltham, Mass., 1977—. Contbr. articles to profl. jours. Former chmn. Lexington Mass. Bd. of Selectman; former pres. Lexington Hist. Soc.; chmn. Lexington Hist. Dists. Commn., 1990-2000. Mem. Mass. Bar Assn., Boston Bar Assn. Office: Engel & Schultz PC 125 High St Boston MA 02110

POLITZ, NYLE ANTHONY, lawyer; b. Lake Charles, La., May 7, 1953; s. Henry Anthony and Jane Marie (Simoneaux) P.; m. Catherine Bordelon, May 28, 1977; children: Brandon, Jared, Caroline. Student, La. State U., Shreveport, 1971-72, U. Guadalajara, 1972, La. State U., 1972-74, JD, 1977. Bar: La. 1978, U.S. Dist. Ct. (ea., mid. and we. dists.) La. 1978, U.S. Ct. Appeals (5th cir.) 1979. Assoc. Booth, Lockard, Jack, Pleasant & LeSage, Shreveport, La., 1978-79; ptnr. Booth, Lockard, Politz, LeSage & D'Anna, L.L.C., 1979-96; assoc. Pendley Law Firm, Plaquemine, La., 1996-98; ptnr. Jones, Odom, Davis & Politz, LLP, Shreveport, 1998—. Lectr. La. State U., Shreveport. Resolutions com. La. Dem. Party, 1980; bd. dirs. Liberty Bank & Trust, Greenwood, La., 1980-86. Mem.: ATLA, N.W. La. Trial Lawyers Assn. (treas. 1987—90), Shreveport Bar Assn. (exec. com. 1983—85, 1993—94, bd. dirs. pro bono project, chmn. 1993—94), La. Trial Lawyers Assn. (bd. govs. 1983—94), La. State Bar Assn. (ho. of dels. 1986—98, 2002—), ABA, KC. Democrat. Roman Catholic. Avocations: whitetail deer and wild turkey hunting, golf. Office: Jones Odom et al PO Box 1320 Shreveport LA 71164-1320 E-mail: nyle.politz@jodplaw.com.

POLITZER, HUGH DAVID, physicist, educator; b. N.Y.C., Aug. 31, 1949; s. Alan A. and Valerie T. (Diamant) P. BS, U. Mich., 1969; PhD, Harvard U., 1974. Jr. fellow Harvard U. Soc. Fellows, 1974-77; mem. faculty Calif. Inst. Tech., 1977—, prof. theoretical physics, 1979—, exec. officer for physics, 1986-88. Recipient J.J. Sakurai prize, 1986. Fellow NSF, 1969-74; Sloan Found., 1977-81; Woodrow Wilson grad. fellow, 1969-74, Guggenheim fellow, 1997-98. Mem. Phi Beta Kappa. Address: 452-48 Calif Inst Tech Pasadena CA 91125-0001 E-mail: politzer@theory.caltech.edu.

POLIVCHAK, PHILIP MICHAEL, retired home builders institute administrator; b. Mpls., 1933; s. Michael and Ilona (Berta) P. Various positions, Washington, 1967-83; founder, pres., CEO, Home Builders Inst. of Nat. Assn. Home Builders, 1983-2000, pres. emeritus, 2000—. Participant White House Conf. on Corrections, 1971; founder Am. Polish Home Builders Inst., Gdansk, Poland, 1992; mem. President's Jobs for Vets. Nat Com., 1972, President's Com. for Prisoners of War, 1973; co-chmn. Job Corps at Work Competition, Dept. Labor, 1981; sponsor Builders Examine the Many Faces of Homlessness Nat. Symposium, 1988; mem. U.S.-Russia Bus. Summit, 1982. Home: 1721 P St NW Washington DC 20036-1342

POLIVKA, JIŘI, physicist; b. Prague, Czech Republic, Apr. 8, 1943; s. Josef Polívka and Libuse Polívka; m. Helena Glaserová, Aug. 8, 1970; children: Jiří, Helena. MSc in Radio Engring., Czech Tech. U., Prague, 1966, PhD, 1975. Rsch. specialist A.S. Popov Rsch. Inst., Prague, 1966-73, Geophys. Inst., Prague, 1973-74; rsch. scientist PTT Rsch. Inst., 1975-91; dir. experiment # 6 Dubna (USSR)-Intercosmos, 1985-87; invited prof. CINVESTAV-IPN, Mexico City, 1989-90, Monterrey (Mex.) Tech. Inst., 1990; chief comm. lab. PTT Tng. Inst., Prague, 1991-92; invited rschr. Japan Key Technol. Ctr., Tokyo, 1992, UNAM-PUIDE-INAOE, Mexico City, 1993; chief scientist SPACEK Labs., Inc., Santa Barbara, Calif., 1994-96, 98—; rsch. scientist, dielectrics Inst. Physics, Prague, 1997-98. Invited lectr. Madrid (Spain) Tech. Inst., 1990. Author: (textbook) Satellite Communication, (in Spanish) 1990, Microwave Radiometry and Applications, (in Spanish) 1993; contbr. over 120 articles to profl. jours. and conf. procs.; patentee in field of microwave components, systems and test methods. Mem. Astron. Union. Office: Spacek Labs Inc 212 E Gutierrez St Santa Barbara CA 93101-1705 E-mail: spacek@silcom.com.

POLK, HIRAM CAREY, JR. surgeon, educator; b. Jackson, Miss., Mar. 23, 1936; s. Hiram Carey and Dorris (Hemby) P.; m. Susan Galandiuk; children: Susan Elizabeth, Hiram Cary. BS, Millsaps Coll., 1956; MD, Harvard U., 1960. Intern Barnes Hosp., St. Louis, 1960-61, resident, 1961-65; instr. in surgery Washington U., St. Louis, 1964-65; asst. prof. surgery U. Miami, Fla., 1965-69, assoc. prof., 1969-71; prof. chmn. dept. surgery U. Louisville, 1971—; pres., chmn. bd. Univ. Surg. Assocs., P.S.C., 1971—; chmn. bd. Clin. Services Assn., Inc. Mem. merit rev. bd. for surgery VA, 1983-85. Author: (with H.H. Stone) Contemporary Burn Management, 1971, Hospital-Acquired Infections in Surgery, 1977; (with B. Gardner, H.H. Stone and W.L. Sugg) Basic Surgery, 1978, 2d edit., (with H.H. Stone and B. Gardner) 2d edit., 1983, 3d edit., 1987, 4th edit., 1992, 5th edit., 1995; (with D.C. Carter) Trauma, 1982; (with J.E. Conte Jr. and L.S. Jacob) Antibiotic Prophylaxis in Surgery: A Comprehensive Review, 1984; (with J.D. Richardson and L.M. Flint Jr.) Trauma: Clinical Care and Pathophysiology, 1987; contbr. numerous articles to profl. publs.; mem. editl. bd. So. Med. Jour., 1970-72, Jour. Surg. Rsch., 1970-72, 75-77, 78-80, Current Problems in Surgery, 1973—, Surgery, 1975-85, Current Surgery, 1977—, Current Surg. Techniques, 1977—, Emergency Surgery: A Weekly Update, 1977—, Collected Letters in Surgery, 1978—, Brit. Jour. Surgery, 1981-94; chief editor Am. Jour. Surgery, 1986—. Bd. govs. Trover Clinic Found., Madisonville, Ky. Fellow Royal Coll. Surgeons Edinburgh (hon.); mem. ACS (gov. 1972-80, commn. on cancer 1975-80), AMA, Allen O. Whipple Soc. (exec. coun. 1977-80), Am. Assn. Cancer Edn. (exec. coun. 1968-72), Am. Assn. Surgery of Trauma, Am. Burn Assn., Am. Cancer Soc. (pres. Ky. div. 1989-90, nat. del. dir. 1989-92, 93-95), Am. Surg. Assn. (sec. 1984-89), Acad. Surgery (pres. 1975-76), Cen. Surg. Assn., Assn. Am. Med. Colls. (chmn. ad hoc com. on Medicare and Medicaid 1978-79), Collegium Internationale Chirurgiae Digestivae (sec.-treas. 1981-86, pres. 1986-87), Council on Public Higher Edn. (task group on health scis.), Halsted Soc., Jefferson County Med. Soc., Ky. Med. Assn., Ky. Surg. Soc. (pres. 1982-83), Louisville Surg. Soc. (pres. 1989-90), Residency Rev. Com. for Surgery (vice chmn. 1981-83, chmn. 1983-85), Société Internationale de Chirurgie, Soc. Surgery Alimentary Tract (treas. 1975-78, pres. 1985-86), Soc. Clin. Surgery, Soc. Surg. Chairmen, Soc. Surg. Oncology (pres. 1984-85), Soc. Univ. Surgeons (treas. 1971-74, pres. 1979-80), James IV Assn. Surgeons (v.p. 2002—), Southeastern Surg. Congress (exec. coun. for Ky. 1985-86, pres. 1994-95), So. Med. Assn. (vice chmn. sect. on surgery 1969-70, chmn. sect. 1972-73, sec. 1970-72, exec. coun. for Ky. 1971-77, 89-90), So. Surg. Assn. (pres. 1988-89), Alpha Omega Alpha. Home: 5609 River Knoll Dr Louisville KY 40222-5846 Office: U Louisville Dept Surgery Louisville KY 40292-0001 E-mail: hcpolk01@gwise.louisville.edu.

POLK, JAMES RAY, journalist; b. Oaktown, Ind., Sept. 12, 1937; s. Raymond S. and Oeta (Fleener) P.; m. Bonnie Becker, Nov. 4, 1962; children: Geoffrey, Amy; m. Cara Bryn Saylor, June 21, 1980; 1 child, Abigail. BA, Ind. U., 1962. With A.P., Indpls., 1962-65, Milw., 1965, Madison, Wis., 1966-67, Washington, 1967-71; investigative reporter Washington Star, 1971-75; correspondent NBC News, Washington, 1975-92; sr. producer CNN Spl. Assignment, 1992—. Pres. Investigative Reporters and Editors, Inc., 1978-80, chmn. bd., 1980-82, nat. coll. chmn., 1983-90. With U.S. Navy, 1955-58. Recipient Pub. Affairs Reporting award, Am. Polit. Sci. Assn., 1961, Raymond Clapper Meml. award, 1972, 74, Pulitzer prize for nat. reporting on Watergate, 1974, Sigma Delta Chi award, 1974, Nat. Headliner award 2d place, 1994, 96, Emmy award for coverage of Oklahoma City bombing, 1996, Ind. U. Disting. Alumni award; named to Ind. Journalism Hall of Fame, 1994. Mem. Phi Kappa Psi. Office: CNN Center Atlanta GA 30348

POLK, LEE THOMAS, lawyer; b. Chgo., Feb. 25, 1945; s. Lee Anthony and Mary Josephine (Lane) P.; m. Susan Luzader, Mar. 21, 1975; children: Adam, Angela. AB, Coe Coll., 1967; JD, U. Chgo., 1970. Bar: Ill. 1970, U.S. Dist. Ct. (no. dist.) Ill. 1970, U.S. Ct. Mil. Appeals 1972, U.S. Dist. Ct. (ea. dist.) Mich. 1983, U.S. Claims Ct. 1983, U.S. Ct. Appeals (7th cir.) 1984, U.S. Ct. Appeals (6th cir.) 1987, U.S. Tax Ct. 1987, U.S. Ct. Appeals (3rd cir.) 1989, U.S. Dist. Ct. (ea. dist.) Wis. 1998, U.S. Dist. Ct. (no. dist.) Ind. 2001. Assoc. firm Vedder, Price, Kaufman & Kammholz, Chgo., 1970-72, 75-77, ptnr., 1977-86, Murphy, Smith & Polk, 1986-98, Ogletree, Deakins, Murphy, Smith & Polk, 1999—2002; Barnes & Thronburgptnr., 2002—. Author: ERISA Practice & Litigation, 1993, updated annually; contbr. articles on employee benefits and health law to profl. jours. Served to capt. JAGC, U.S. Army, 1972-75. Fellow Am. Coll. Employee Benefits Counsel (charter), Am. Bar Found.; mem. ABA (sects. on real property, trust and probate, chair ESOP com. tax and bus.), ESOP Assn., Am. Soc. Writers on Legal Subjects, Ill. Bar Assn., Chgo. Bar Assn. (chmn. employee benefits com. 1987-88), Midwest Pension Conf. (chmn. Chgo. chpt. 1986), Am. Health Lawyers Assn., Phi Beta Kappa, Phi Kappa Phi, Union League Club. Roman Catholic. Home: 820 Sheridan Rd Evanston IL 60202-2513 Office: Ogletree Deakins Murphy Smith & Polk 2 1st Nat Plz Fl 25 Chicago IL 60603 E-mail: lee.polk@odnss.com.

POLK, MILBRY CATHERINE, media specialist; b. Oxford, Eng., Feb. 24, 1954; came to U.S., 1956; d. William Roe Polk and Joan Alison Cooledge; m. Phillip Allen Bauman, Sept. 29, 1984; children: Adelaide Elisabeth, Milbry Catherine, Mary Harding. Student, U. London, 1972; BA in Anthropology with honors, Harvard U., 1976. Edn. and spl. projects staff Am. Mus. Natural History, N.Y.C., 1977-79; expedition leader, photographer Nat. Geog. Soc. Exploration of Egyptian Western Desert, Egypt, 1979; staff writer 10964, Palisades, N.Y., 1990—; founder, dir. Virtual Xplorations Web Site, 1996—. Comml. photographer; lectr. in field. Founder, asst. dir. and programmer Margaret Mead Film Festival, 1977-79; asst. prodr. (film) Margaret Mead, Portrait of a Friend, 1979, dir. (film retrospective for Mus. of Am. Indian) The Ancestors, 1979; script cons. (feature film) Rollover, 1979; rschr. (TV series) Legacy, 1982; dir. Leathercraft Mus. Project, 1983; project dir., photographer, illustrations editor: The History of Arabian Transportation, 1984-87; founder, dir. Palisades Art Fair, 1989-93; founder, dir. Women Explorers: An Oral History Project, 1991-95; contbr. articles and photographs to mags.; author: Egyptian Mummies, 1997, New Mothers Book, 1987, The Egyptian Door, 1976, Women of Discovery, 2001; author (sch. curriculum) Sy Montgomery and Man Eating Tigers of Sundarbans, 1996; exhibited in group shows at Ceres Gallery, N.Y., 1990-95, Somerstown Gallery, 1991, Schoolhouse, 1991, Nat. Arts Club, 1988-91, Palisades Art Fair, 1989-93, Thomsen Gallery, 1989-91, The Cathedral of St. John the Divine, 1989, Rockland Ctr. for the Arts, 1988, Wadsworth Athenaeum, Hartford, Conn., 1983, Foto Gallery, N.Y., 1980; contbr. editor, Explorer's Jour. Founder, trustee Wings Trust; mem. journalism adv. com. George Polk Awards; mem. bd. visitors N.Y. Acad. Medicine, 1996—; founder, bd. dirs. InterCulture, Inc., Ft. Worth; exec. coun. N.Y. Hall of Sci. Named Outstanding Woman of Yr. 1986, Am. Film Festival; grantee N.Y. State Coun. on Arts, 1979; subject CBS News Documentary They Also Dared, 1996, Gracie Allen award. Fellow Royal Geog. Soc., Explorers Club; mem. Soc. Woman Geographers (spl. events com. 1990-93, nat. coun. 1993-96), Nat. Arts Club, S.Am. Explorers Club, Dutch Treat Club, Piermont Rowing Club (bd. dirs.), Masters Rowing Assoc., Radcliffe Club N.Y. Episcopalian. Home and Office: Virtual Xplorations PO Box 52 Palisades NY 10964-0052 E-mail: milbry@post.harvard.edu.

POLK, STEVEN R. military officer; BS in Aero. Engring., USAF Acad., 1968; MS in Engring., Ariz. State U., 1974; MA in Nat. Security & Strategic Studies, Naval War Coll., 1988; nat. security leadership course, Johns Hopkins U., 1998; joint flag officer warfare course, Maxwell AFB, 1998. Commd. 2d lt. USAF, 1968, advanced through grades to maj. gen., 1997; aircraft comdr., instr. pilot, flight comdr. 55th Tactical Fighter Squadron, RAF, Upper Heyford, Eng., 1978-81; F-16 pilot 613th Tactical Fighter Squadron, chief tng. 401st Tactical Fighter Wing, Torrejon Air Base, Spain, 1983-84; ops. officer, comdr. 612th Tactical Fighter Squadron 401st Combat Support Group, 1984-87; chief war and mobilization planning divsn. Hdqs. USAF, Washington, 1988-89, exec. officer to vice chief of staff, 1989-90; vice comdr., comdr. 58th Tactical Tng. Wing, Luke AFB, Ariz., 1990-91; comdr. 58th Ops. Group, 1991-92, 8th Fighter Wing, Kunsan Air Base, South Korea, 1992-93; chief quality divsn. Directorate of Programs and Evaluation Hdqs. USAF, Washington, 1993-94; asst. chief of staff for ops. Hdqs. Allied Air Forces Northwestern Europe, 1994-95; comdr. 51st Fighter Wing, Osan Air Base, South Korea, 1995-97; dir. of ops. Hdqs. Pacific Air Forces, Hickam AFB, Hawaii, 1997-98, dir. air and space ops., 1998-99; commdr. 19th Air Force, Randolph AFB, Tex., 1999—. Decorated Def. Superior Svc. medal, Legion of Merit with oak leaf cluster, Meritorious Svc. medal with 4 oak leaf clusters; recipient Disting. Svc. medal. Office: 73 Main Cir Randolph A F B TX 78150-4543

POLK, WILLIAM ALLEN, city planner, architect; b. Ft. Worth, Apr. 17, 1946; s. William Jesse and Mary Ardell (Cowdrey) P.; m. Carrol Dian Graves, June 16, 1973; children: William Scot, Amy Dian. BA in Arch., U. Ark., Fayetteville, 1969; BA in Polit. Sci., U. Ark., Little Rock, 1978, MPA, 1984. Registered arch., Ark. Job capt. Stowers & Snelson Archs., Little Rock, 1972-77; archtl. coord. Ark. dept. Energy, 1977-81; coord. arch. Winrock Internat., Morrilton, Ark., 1981-83, cons. arch., 1983-84; arch. A/E S.W., Little Rock, 1983-85; assoc. arch. Brueggeman & Caulder, Archs., 1983-84; arch. Environ. Tech. Cons., 1984-85; dir. planning City of Conway, Ark., 1985—. Part-time polit. sci. lectr. U. Ark., Little Rock, 1984-85; mem. exec. com. Commn. on Ark.'s Future, State of Ark., 1989-96; mem. tech. coord. com. Ctrl. Ark. Regional Transp. Study, 1993—; mem. adv. coun. Donaghey Project for Urban Studies and Design, Little Rock, 1993-98; faculty mem. Cmty. Devel. Inst., U. Ctrl. Ark., 1998—; mem. exec. com. on energy Nat. Conf. States on Bldg. Codes and Stds., 1980-81. Author: Rules and Regulations for Energy Efficiency in New Building Construction, 1979. Mem. design com. chmn. Mainstreet Conway Bd., 1989-91; vol. coach, boys and girls basketball and softball Conway City League, 1985-90; mem. Transp. Adv. Com., Conway, 1985-87, chmn., 1991-95. Capt. C.E., U.S. Army, 1969-72. Mem. AIA, Am. Inst. Cert. Planners (cert., nominations com. 1995), Am. Planning Assn. (exec. com. Ark. chpt. 1985-99, past pres.), Kiwanis. Avocations: reading, sports, art. Home: 718 Farris Rd Conway AR 72034-4907 Office: Conway Planning Dept 1201 Oak St Conway AR 72032-5316 E-mail: billpolk@conwaycorp.net.

POLK, WILLIAM ROE, historian; b. Ft. Worth, Mar. 7, 1929; m. Joan Alison Cooledge, Dec. 1950; children: Milbry Catherine Polk, Alison Elizabeth Polk; m. Ann Borders Cross, June 9, 1962 (div. Oct. 1979); children: George Washington, Eliza Polk; m. Baroness Elisabeth von Oppenheimer, Dec. 29, 1981. BA with honors, Harvard U., 1951, PhD, 1958; BA with honors, Oxford, Eng., 1955, MA, 1959; LLD (hon.), Lake Forest Coll., 1967. Asst. prof. Harvard Univ., 1956-62; fgn. svc. res. officer class 1, mem. policy planning coun. U.S. State Dept., 1961-65; prof. U. Chgo., 1965-73; pres. Adlai Stevenson Inst., Chgo., 1967-72; chmn. EP Systems, N.Y.C., 1990-93, Chaika Oil Co., London and Moscow, 1993-95. Bd. dirs. Hyde Park Bank, Chgo., Microform Data Systems, Arlington Books, Cambridge, Naftex Ltd., Harris & Harris, Chaika Corp., Morrison Internat. Ltd., The Salzburg Seminar; cons. Aetna Life and Casualty, Time Inc., TWA, Crocker Nat. Bank, Wheelabrator Frye Inc., Fuller Petroleum, GTE, Teledyne, J. Henry Schroder, U.K., Power Corp., Can., Allianz Versicherungs A.G., Germany, Volkswagen A.G., Germany, Flughafen Frankfurt Main A.G., Germany, Louis Féraud & Cie, France, UN Stockholm and Vancouver Confs. on the Environment; lectr. in field. Author: What the Arabs Think, 1952, Backdrop to Tragedy, 1957, The Opening of South Lebanon, 1963, The United States and the Arab World, 1965, The United States and the Arab World, 3rd edit., 1975, Passing Brave, 1973, 1974, The Golden Ode, 1974, 1977, 1993, The Elusive Peace, 1979, The Arab World, 1980, The Arab World Today, 1991, The Vence Partitas, 1992, Neighbors and Strangers: The Fundamentals of Foreign Affairs, 1997, Polk's Folly: An American Family History, 2000, 2001; editor: The Civilization of Islam, 1962, 1975, The Developmental Revolution, 1963, The Beginnings of Modernization in the Middle East, 1968; contbr. articles to books and profl. jours. including. Dir. The Salzburg Seminar, YMCA C.C., The Middle East Inst., The Adlai Stevenson Inst. Recipient Medal of Honor, Kingdom of Afghanistan, 1967; fellow Rockefeller Found., 1951-55, Ford Found., 1954, Guggenheim Found., 1961. Mem. The Century Assn., Coun. on Fgn. Rels., Middle East Studies Assn. (bd. dirs.), Soc. of the Cin. Democrat. Avocations: exploration, tennis, sailing, gardening. Home: 669 Chemin de la Sine F-06140 Vence France

POLL, HEINZ, choreographer, artistic director; b. Oberhausen, Germany, Mar. 18, 1926; came to U.S., 1964, naturalized, 1975; s. Heinrich and Anna Margarete (Winkels) P. Co-founder, dir. The Dance Inst., U. Akron, 1967-77; founder, artistic dir., choreographer Ohio Ballet, Akron, 1968-99. Tchr. Chilean Instituto de Extension Musical, 1951-61, N.Y. Nat. Acad., 1965-66 Dancer Göttingen Mcpl. Theatre, 1947-49, Deutsches Theatre Konstanz, 1949-50, East Berlin State Opera, 1950-51, Nat. Ballet Chile, 1951-62, Ballet de la Jeunesse Musicales de France, 1963-64; guest appearances with Nat. Ballet Chile, 1964, Am. Dance Festival, 1965; choreographer works for Nat. Ballet Chile, Paris Festival Ballet, Ballet de la Jeunnesses Musicales de France, Nat. Ballet Can., Pa. Ballet, Ohio Ballet, Limon Dance Co.; solo dancer Ellen Kogan. Recipient Ohio Dance award, 1983, 88-89, Achievement Dance award No. Ohio Live Mag., 1985-86, 88-89, 93-94, 94-95, 96-97, Cleve. Arts prize, 1995, Irma Lazarus Govs. award, 1999; Nat. Endowment for Arts grantee, 1974-75. Mem. NEA (dance panelist 1987-89, 92-93).

POLL, MARTIN HARVEY, film producer; b. N.Y.C. s. David and Fay (Tamber) P.; m. Lee Lindenberg, May 21, 1954 (div. Oct. 10, 1967); children: Mark, Jonathan; m. Gladys Peltz Jaffe, Oct. 31, 1976; 1 son, Anthony. BS, Wharton Sch. Bus. U. Pa., 1943. Pres. Inter-Continental TV Films Inc., N.Y.C., 1952; exec. producer Theatre Network TV Inc., 1953; pres. Gold Medal Studios, Bronx, N.Y., 1954-62; ind. producer, 1962—. (Named Hon. Commr. Motion Picture Arts N.Y.C. 1958, recipient David Di Donatello Best Film Producer award Pres. Italy 1968, N.Y. Film Critics award 1968, Hollywood Fgn. Press Assn. Golden Globe award 1968, Brit. Acad. award 1968); films include Love is a Ball, 1962, Sylvia, 1964, The Appointment, 1968, The Lion in Winter, 1968 (Best Picture award), The Magic Garden of Stanley Sweetheart, 1970, Night Watch, 1972, The Man Who Loved Cat Dancing, 1973, Love and Death, 1975, The Sailor Who Fell From Grace with The Sea, 1976, The Dain Curse, Somebody Killed Her Husband, 1978, Nighthawks, 1981, Arthur the King, 1984, Gimme An F, 1984, Haunted Summer, 1987, My Heroes Have Always Been Cowboys, 1991, (TV miniseries) Diana—Her True Story, 1993. Served with AUS, 1944-47. Mem. Producers Guild of Am., Acad. Motion Picture Arts and Scis., Cinema Circulus, Friends of Library U. So. Calif.

POLL, ROBERT EUGENE, JR. bank executive; b. Urbana, Ill., Apr. 16, 1948; s. Robert E. Sr. and Dorothy (Baker) P.; m. Leslie Tompkins, Aug. 8, 1970 (div. Mar. 1980); m. Virginia O'Donnell, July 17, 1982; children: Alexandra, Bianca, Paulo Felipe Kos. BA, Kenyon Coll., 1970; MBA, Ind. U., 1972. V.p. Chase Manhattan Bank, N.Y.C., 1972-78; assoc. Lazard Freres & Co., 1978-82, mng. dir., mgr. mcpl. divsn., 1985-98; gen. ptnr. William Blair & Co., Chgo., 1982-84; sr. mng. dir. Poll Financial, LLC, 1998—. Adv. bd. Pub. Fin. Inst., N.Y.C., 1976, Worldvest, Sorceron, Bernard Techs.; bd. dirs. Chief Consolidated Mining Co. Trustee Citizens Budget Commn. Mem. N.Y. Acad. Sci. Clubs: Tavern (Chgo.); N.Y. Athletic. Office: Poll Fin LLC 59 E 78th St New York NY 10021-0204 E-mail: rppollfin@att.net.

POLLACHEK, ELLIN RONEE, photographer, writer, educator; b. N.Y.C., Sept. 25, 1950; PhD, NYU, 1999. Instr. coll. English, ESL, creative and expository writing and healing workshops; photographer creative portraits; founder Catskill Writing Camp; tchr. Yale Exploratory Program, Hostos C.C., Pace U. Author: novel and non-fiction; photographer Duke University: Literacy Through Photography , 1988. Mem. Authors Guild Am. E-mail: getyourphd@aol.com.

POLLACK, BARBARA GRACE, writer; b. N.Y.C., May 17, 1927; m. Merrill S. Pollack, Nov. 27, 1947; children: Elise, Diana, Steven, Anne. Student, Am. Acad. Dramatic Art, 1946, Fordham U., 1978-79, Georgetown U., 1980-81. Rsch. asst. art and archaeology dept. Princeton (N.J.) U., 1964-67; with Social Security Adminstrn. Office Hearings and Appeals U.S. Govt., N.Y.C., 1987—. Co-author: (with Doris Humphrey) The Art of Making Dances, 1959, The Collectors, 1962, (with Charles H. Woodford) Dance is a Moment, 1993; contbr. articles to mags. Vol. Smithsonian Instn., The White House, Cooper-Hewitt Mus., N.Y.C., ARC; vol. mentor in English lang. and Am. history to students. Home: 29 E 29th St New York NY 10016-7902

POLLACK, DAVID L. lawyer; b. Madison, Wis., May 1, 1956; s. Sidney Solomon and Elta Elizabeth (Spaulding) P.; m. Avery Elizabeth Schneider, June 14, 1986; children: Elsbeth Rose, Mollie Brown, Samantha Louise. AB, Haverford (Pa.) Coll., 1978; JD, Yale U., 1989. Bar: Pa. 1989, U.S. Dist. Ct. (we. dist.) Pa. 1989. Atty. Kirkpatrick & Lockhart LLP, Pitts., 1989-98, Gefsky and Lehman, P.C., Pitts., 1998—. Office: Gefsky and Lehman PC 1 Ppg Pl Ste 2301 Pittsburgh PA 15222-5435 E-mail: dpollack@geflaw.com.

POLLACK, FLORENCE K.Z. management consultant; b. Washington; d. Charles and Ruth (Isaacson) Zaks; divorced; children: Melissa, Stephanie. BA, Flora Stone Mather Coll., Western Res. U., 1961. Chmn., CEO Exec. Arrangements, Inc., Cleve., 1978—. Lobbyist Ohio Citizens Com. for Arts, Columbus, 1975-83; mem. Leadership Cleve., 1978-79; trustee jr. com. Cleve. Orch., mem. pub. rels. adv. com.; trustee Great Lakes Theatre Festival, 1989-90; mem. pub. rels. adv. com., Cleve. Ballet, Dance Cleve., Jr. Com. of No. Ohio Opera Assn., Cleve. Opera, Shakers Lakes Regional Nature Ctr., Cleve. Music Sch. Settlement, Playhouse Sq. Cabinet, Cleve. Ctr. Econ. Edn., ARC, Cleve. Conv. and Visitors Bur., domed stadium adv. com.; bd. dirs. ARC, Great Lakes Theatre Festival, City Club of Cleve., Cleve. Ballet. Named Idea Woman of Yr., Cleve. Plain Dealer, 1975, to Au Courrant list Cleve. Mag., 1979, one of Cleve.'s 100 Most Influential Women, 1985, one of 1988 Trendsetters Cleve. Woman mag. Mem. Cleve. Area Meeting Planning, Skating Club, Univ. Club, Women's City Club, Playhouse Club, Shoreby Club. Avocations: arts, traveling, reading. Office: Exec Arrangements Inc 24800 Chagrin Blvd Cleveland OH 44122 E-mail: executivearrange@ameritech.net.

POLLACK, GERALD ALEXANDER, economist, government official; b. Vienna, Austria, Jan. 14, 1929; came to U.S. 1938; s. Stephen J. and Tini (Herschel) P.; m. Patricia E. Sisterson; children: Nora S., Carol A. BA, Swarthmore (Pa.) Coll., 1951; MA, MPA, Princeton U., 1953, PhD, 1958. Corp. economist Leeds & Northrup Co., Phila., 1958-62; officer in charge internat. payments U.S. Dept. State, Washington, 1962-63; internat. economist Joint Econ. Com. of Congress, 1963-65; chief economist Office Spl. Rep. for Trade Negotiations, 1964; dep. asst. sec. U.S. Dept. Commerce, Washington, 1965-68; v.p. Loeb, Rhoades & Co., N.Y.C., 1968-69, Bendix Corp., Southfield, Mich., 1969-70, Citibank, N.Y.C., 1970-71; internat. economist Exxon Corp., 1971-86; v.p., chief economist Overseas Shipholding Group, 1986-89; assoc. prof. fin. Pace U., 1990-94; assoc. dir. for internat. econs. Bur. Econ. Analysis, U.S. Dept. Commerce, 1994-99. Contbr. articles to profl. jours. Bd.

dirs. Jamaica Estates Assn., 1976-80, Oakwood Sch., Poughkeepsie, N.Y., 1979-89; trustee Lindley Murray Fund, 1990-94; mem. Greenwich Dem. Town Com., 1992-94, 2001—; clk. Flushing Monthly Meeting Soc. of Friends, 1990-94; mem. Greenwich Rep. Town Meeting, 1999—. With U.S. Army, 1953-55. Mem. Coun. on Fgn. Rels., Phi Beta Kappa. Mem. Soc. Of Friends. Avocations: cello, classical music, photography, hiking, bicycling. E-mail: gapollack@hotmail.com.

POLLACK, HENRY NATHAN, geophysics educator; b. Omaha, July 13, 1936; s. Harold Myron and Sylvia (Chait) P.; m. Lana Beth Schoenberger, Jan. 29, 1963; children: Sara Beth (dec.), John David. AB, Cornell U., 1958; MS, U. Nebr., 1960; PhD, U. Mich., 1963. Lectr. U. Mich., 1962, asst. prof., asso. prof., prof. geophysics, 1964—, assoc. dean for research, 1982-85, chmn. dept. geol. scis., 1988-91. Rsch. fellow Harvard U., 1963-64; sr. lectr. U. Zambia, 1970-71; vis. scientist U. Durham, U. Newcastle-on-Tyne, Eng., 1977-78, U. Western Ont., 1985-86; chmn. Internat. Heat Flow Commn., 1991-95. Fellow: AAAS, Geol. Soc. Am.; mem.: Am. Geophys. Union. Achievements include research on thermal evolution of the earth, recent climate change. Office: U Mich Dept Geol Scis Ann Arbor MI 48109

POLLACK, IRWIN WILLIAM, psychiatrist, educator; b. Phila., Aug. 14, 1927; s. Nathan and Rose (Bergman) P.; m. Barbara Jean Callaway, Oct. 9, 1988; children from previous marriage: Nathaniel Edward, Joshua Frank, Jonathan Daniel. AB, Temple U., 1950; MA, Columbia, 1951; student, U. Pa., 1951-52; MD, U. Vt., 1956. Diplomate: Am. Bd. Psychiatry and Neurology. Intern Grad. Hosp. U. Pa., 1956-57; asst. resident psychiatry Henry Phipps Psychiat. Clinic (John Hopkins Hosp.), 1957-60; chief resident psychiatry Johns Hopkins Hosp., 1960-61, adminstr. psychosomatic clinic, psychiat. liaison service, 1961-64; psychiatrist-in-chief Sinai Hosp., Balt., 1964-68; mem. faculty psychiatry Coll. Medicine and Dentistry N.J. (Rutgers Med. Sch.), 1968-87, 1987—, clin. prof. psychiatry, 1998, prof. emeritus, 1999—. Assoc. prof. psychiatry, 1968-70, prof. psychiatry, 1979-99, emeritus prof. psychiatry 1999-, chmn. dept. Univ. Medicine and Dentistry, prof. neurology, dir. Ctr. for Cognitive Rehab.; exec. dir. Coll. Medicine and Dentistry (Community Mental Health Ctr.), 1970-77. Served with USNR, 1945-46. Fellow Am. Psychiat. Assn. (life); mem. N.J. Psychiat. Assn., Am. Psychosomatic Soc., Am. Congress Rehab. Medicine, Alpha Omega Alpha. Achievements include spl. research or problems of time and space perception, psychology of phys. disability, doctor-patient relationships, cognitive retraining of brain-injured persons. Home: 36959 S Ridgeview Blvd Tucson AZ 85739 Office: 36959 S Ridgeview Blvd Tucson AZ 85739 E-mail: iwpollack@aol.com.

POLLACK, JEFFREY LEE, restaurateur; b. San Francisco, May 1, 1945; s. Albert and Loretta (Popper) P.; m. Patricia Bowdle Connell, Feb. 20, 1983; children: Lizabeth Ann, Hilary Margaret, Nicholas Albert. BA, San Jose State U. Owner, surety underwriter North Beach Bonding Co., San Francisco, 1968-75; proprietor Old Waldorf, 1974-80, Punchline, 1978-80, Julius' Castle, San Francisco, 1980—, New Joe's, San Francisco, 1984-99, Shadows, San Francisco, 1985-95, Iron Horse, 1986-92, Pollack Group, San Francisco, 1985—, Nick's Lighthouse Restaurant, San Francisco, 1991—, Original Joe's # 2, 1992-95, O'Connell's, 1994-96, Dalla Torre, 1996—. Mem. Downtown Assn. (bd. dirs. 1987—, v.p. 1992), Union Sq. Assn., North Beach C. of C. (bd. dirs. 1989, v.p. 1992), Port Tenants Assn., Fisherman Wharf Assn., Commonwealth Club. Democrat. Avocations: classic car collecting, movies. Home: 302 Greenwich St San Francisco CA 94133-3210 Office: Pollack Group Ltd 1541 Montgomery St San Francisco CA 94133-3232

POLLACK, JOE, retired newspaper critic and columnist, writer; b. Bklyn., Feb. 3, 1931; s. Samuel H. and Anna (Weisman) P.; m. Joan S., Mar. 6, 1952 (div. 1964); children: Wendy, Dara, Sharon; m. Carol Atchison, Dec. 1, 1964 (dec. 1993); m. Ann Lemons, Nov. 20, 1994. BJ, U. Mo., 1952. Sports writer St. Louis Globe-Democrat, 1955-61; dir. pub. rels. St. Louis Football Cardinals, 1961-72; critic, columnist St. Louis Post-Dispatch, 1972-95. Critic Sta. KSDK-TV, St. Louis, 1973-88, Sta. KMOV-TV, St. Louis, 1988-92; commentator Sta. KMOX, St. Louis, 1960-85, Sta. KWMU, St. Louis, 1994—. Author: Joe Pollack's Guide to St. Louis Restaurants, 1988, updated, 1992, (with Ann Lemons Pollack) Beyond Toasted Ravioli, 1998, Beyond Gooey Butter Cake, 2001; contbr. numerous articles to mags. Mem. Am. Theatre Critics Assn., Profl. Football Writers Assn., Am. Soc. Profl. Journalists. Home: 7417 Oxford Dr Saint Louis MO 63105-2915 E-mail: jpalfood@aol.com.

POLLACK, JORDAN ELLIS, pharmaceutical company executive; b. N.Y.C., June 16, 1934; s. Irving and Ann Pollack; m. Francine Hornstein, Aug. 23, 1959; children: Robert, Randi. BS in Pharmacy, Columbia U., 1956; MBA in Mktg., Iona Coll., 1971. Registered pharmacist, N.Y., N.J., Fla. Med. rep./market researcher Geigy Pharm., Ardsley, N.Y., 1959-69; account exec. William Douglas McAdams, N.Y.C., 1970-71; account supr. Grey Advt., 1971-75; account dir. Carrafiello-Diehl Advt., Irvington, N.Y., 1975-79; sr. product mgr. Knoll Pharms., Whippany, N.J., 1979-85, mgr. new product planning, 1985-88, dir. new bus. devel. NJ, 1988—2002. Chmn. Florham Park (N.J.) Airport Adv. Com., 1989-99; mem. Florham Park Zoning Bd. of Adjustment, Capital Improvements Com. With U.S. Army, 1957-59. Mem. Pharm. Advt. Coun., Am. Soc. Hosp. Pharmacists, Lic. Exec. Soc. Avocations: walking, softball, swimming. Home and Office: 4 Partridge Ln Florham Park NJ 07932-1728 E-mail: jandfpollack@aol.com.

POLLACK, MICHAEL, lawyer; b. N.Y.C., July 14, 1946; s. Irving and Bertha (Horowitz) P.; m. Barbara Linda Shore, Aug. 23, 1970; children: Matthew, Ilana. BEng, Cooper Union, 1967; MS, U. Pa., 1970; JD, Temple U., 1974. Bar: Pa. 1974, U.S. Dist. Ct. (ea. dist.) Pa. 1974. Rsch. scientist Pa. Rsch. Assocs., Phila., 1968-69; engr. GE Co., Valley Forge, Pa., 1969-70, Burroughs Corp., Great Valley, 1970-71; assoc. Blank, Rome, Comisky & McCauley, Phila., 1974-82, ptnr., 1982—. Ptnr. and mem. mgmt. com. dept. real estate Blank, Rome, Comisky & McCauley, 1997—; lectr., course planner Pa. Bar Inst., Phila. Mem. ABA, Pa. Bar Assn., Phila. Bar Assn., Internat. Assn. Attys. and Execs. in Corp. Real Estate (bd. dirs.), Eta Kappa Nu, Tau Beta Pi. Republican. Avocations: music, tennis. Office: Blank Rome Comisky & McCauley 1 Logan Sq Fl 3 Philadelphia PA 19103-6998 E-mail: pollack@blankrome.com.

POLLACK, MILTON, federal judge; b. N.Y.C., Sept. 29, 1906; s. Julius and Betty (Schwartz) P.; m. Lillian Klein, Dec. 18, 1932 (dec. July 1967); children: Stephanie Pollack Miller, Daniel A.; m. Moselle Baum Erlich, Oct. 24, 1971. AB, Columbia U., 1927, JD, 1929. Bar: N.Y. 1930. Assoc. Gilman & Unger, N.Y.C., 1929-38; ptnr. Unger & Pollack, 1938-44; propr. Milton Pollack, 1945-67; dist. judge U.S. Dist. Ct. (so. dist.) N.Y., 1967—, sr. status, 1983. Mem. com. on ct. adminstrn. Jud. Conf., 1968-87, mem. Jud. Panel on Multi-dist. Litigation, 1983-95. Mem. Prospect Park So. Assn., Bklyn., pres., 1948-50, counsel, 1950-60, bd. dirs., 1945-60; mem. local SSS, 1952-60; chmn. lawyers div. Fedn. Jewish Philanthropies, 1957-61, vice chmn., 1954-57; chmn. lawyers div. Am. Jewish Com., 1964-66, bd. dirs., from 1967; hon. dir. Beth Isreal Hosp.; trustee Temple Emanu-El, from 1977, v.p., from 1978. Decorated chevalier Legion of Honor (France); recipient Learned Hand award Am. Jewish Com., 1967, Proskauer medal lawyers divsn. Fedn. Jewish Philanthropies, 1968, Disting. Svc. medal N.Y. County Lawyers Assn., 1991, Fordham-Stein Prize award, 1994, Devitt award Disting. Svc. to Justice, 1995. Mem. ABA, N.Y. State Bar Assn., Assn. of Bar of City of N.Y., Columbia Law Sch. Alumni Assn. (pres. 1970-72), Harmonie Club (past bd. trustees). Office: US Dist Ct US Courthouse Foley Sq New York NY 10007-1501

POLLACK, MURRAY MICHAEL, physician, medical services administrator; b. Bklyn., Nov. 1, 1947; s. Louis R. and Shirley Pollack; m. Mona Michaels, Dec. 2, 1973; children: Seth, Haley. BA in Biology, U. Rochester, 1970; MD, Albert Einstein Sch. Medicine, 1974. Diplomate Am. Bd. Pediatrics, Am. Bd. Pediatric Critical Care. Intern, then resident in pediatrics Children's Nat. Med. Ctr., Washington, 1974-77, intensivist, 1978-96, dir. health svcs. and clin. rsch., 1990-96, sect. head crit. care medicine, 1995—; exec. dir. Ctr. for Hosp. Bases Svcs., 1999—. Chief, critical care medicine, prof. anesthesiology and pediatrics George Washington U. Med. Sch., 1988—; dir. Ctr. Health Svcs. Rsch., Children's Rsch. Inst.; dir. Pediatric Intensive Care Unit Evaluations, 1994—; exec. chair Hosp. Based Ctr. of Excellence, 1999—; exec. dir. Ctr. for Hosp.-Based Profls., 1999—. Mem. editorial bd. Critical Care Medicine; contbr. articles to profl. jours. Recipient Disting. Career award, Am. Acad. Pediatrics, 2001, Disting. Investigator award, Am. Coll. Critical Care Medicine, 2002; grantee, PHHS, 1989—, Robert Wood Johnson Found., 1986—89. Fellow Coll.Critical Care Medicine (faculty, reviewer, moderator 1987—), Nat. Assn. Children's Hosps. (quality com. 1991-95), Am. Bd. Pediatrics (sub-bd. critical care 1991-95). Achievements include research in quantifying the relationship between physiologic instability and mortality risk, reduced risk of death associated with pediatric intensive care, creation of pediatric risk of mortality score. Office: Childrens Nat Med Ctr 111 Michigan Ave NW Washington DC 20010-2916

POLLACK, PAUL ROBERT, airline service company executive; b. N.Y.C., Nov. 17, 1941; s. Harry and Hilda (Tepper) P.; m. Linda Weinstein, Aug. 14, 1965; children: Mark, Melissa. BBA, CCNY, 1962; MBA, L.I. U., Greenvale, N.Y., 1993. CPA, N.Y. Staff acct. Seidman & Seidman, N.Y.C., 1962-68; with GlobeGround N.Am., Great Neck, NY, 1968—, exec. v.p., chief oper. officer, 1990—, pres., 1996—, sr. adviser, 2001—. With U.S. Army, 1962. Mem. N.Y. State Soc. CPAs (Haskins award 1966). Office: GlobeGround NAm 111 Great Neck Rd Ste 600 Great Neck NY 11021-5401

POLLACK, PHYLLIS ADDISON, ballerina; b. Victoria, B.C., Can., Aug. 31, 1919; d. Horace Nowell and Claire Melanie (Morris) Addison; m. Robert Seymour Pollack, Sept. 6, 1941; children: Robert Addison, Gwenda Joyce, Victoria Jean, Phyllis Anne. Student, SUNY, 1941-42, San Mateo Tech. Coll., 1958-62, U. Calif., San Francisco, 1962. Owner, dir. Phyllis Addison Dance Studio, Victoria, 1936-38; ballerina Taynton Dancers/Marcus Show Ballet Troupe, 1939-41, Ballet Russe, 1941; x-ray therapy tech. Meml. Hosp., N.Y.C., 1943-45; corr. fgn. tellers dept. N.C.B., 1945-46; owner, designer The Dancing Branch Studio, Sonoma, Calif., 1988—. Floral designer J. Noblett Gallery, Sonoma, 1988-94. Pres. PTA, 1955-56, 62-63; mem. Assistance League San Mateo, Calif., 1960-70. Mem. Metro. Club, Bay Area Arrangers Guild, Ikebana Internat., San Francisco Garden Club. Democrat. Unitarian Universalist. Avocations: dancing, choreography, fashion modelling, photography, reading. Home: 384 Avenida Barbera Sonoma CA 95476-8069

POLLACK, ROBERT ELLIOT, biologist, educator, author; b. Bklyn., Sept. 2, 1940; s. Hyman Ephraim and Molly (Pollack) P.; m. Amy Louise Steinberg, Dec. 23, 1961; 1 child, Marya BA in Physics, Columbia U., 1961; PhD in Biology, Brandeis U., 1966. Asst. prof. pathology Med. Sch. NYU, N.Y.C., 1969-70; sr. scientist Cold Spring Harbor Lab., N.Y., 1971-75; prof. microbiology Med. Sch., SUNY-Stony Brook, 1975-78; prof. biol. sci. Columbia U., N.Y.C., 1978—; dean Columbia Coll., 1982-89. Bd. dirs., chmn. sci. adv. bd. AMBI, 1994—; instr. Pratt Archtl. Sch., Bklyn., 1970; lectr. psychiatry Ctr. for Psychoanalytic Tng., Columbia U., 1999—, dir. Ctr. for the Study of Sci. and Religion, 1999—; vis. prof. pharmacology Albert Einstein Coll. Medicine, Bronx, N.Y., 1977-92; dean's disting. lectr. in Humanities, Columbia Med. Sch., 2000; lectr. Rosenthal Colloquium, March of Dimes, 1989; McGregory lectr. Colgate U., 1979; du Vigneaud lectr. Med. Sch., Cornell U., 1983. Co-editor: Readings in Mammalian Cell Culture, 1973, 3d rev. edit., 1981, Signs of Life, 1984 (translations in 7 langs., Lionel Trilling award 1995), The Missing Moment, 1999, The Faith of Biology and the Biology of Faith, 2000; mng. editor BBA Revs. on Cancer, 1980-86; contbr. numerous rsch. articles on molecular cell biology to profl. jours. Trustee N.Y. Found., 1988-96, Brandeis U., 1989-94, Solomon Schechter Sch. of N.Y.C., 1996-98; fellow World Econ. Forum, 1995—; bd. overseers List Coll. of the Jewish theol. Sem. of Am., 1996-99; pres. Jewish Campus Life Fund, Columbia U., 1997-2001. Recipient Rsch. Career Devel. award NIH, 1974, Alexander Hamilton medal, 1989, Lionel Trilling award Columbia U., 1995; NIH spl. fellow Weizmann Inst., Rehovot, Israel, 1970-71; grantee Nat. Cancer Inst., NIH, 1968-92, Am. Cancer Soc., 1985-94; John Simon Guggenheim fellow, 1993. Fellow AAAS; mem. N.Y. Acad. Scis., Am. Soc. Microbiology. Office: Columbia U Fairchild Hall 1212 Amsterdam Ave # Mc2419 New York NY 10027-7003 E-mail: pollack@columbia.edu.

POLLACK, ROBERT WILLIAM, psychiatrist; b. N.Y.C., May 22, 1947; s. George and Esther P.; m. Pam Gregory, Sept. 15, 1984; 1 child, Jessie. BS in Biology, Yale U., 1969; MD, SUNY Downstate Med. Ctr., Bklyn., 1973. Diplomate Am. Bd. Psychiatry and Neurology. Tng. resident U. Fla., 1973-76, chief resident dept. psychiatry, 1975-76, asst. prof. dept. psychiatry, 1976-77; clin. asst. prof. dept. psychiatry Shands Hosp., 1977—; chief dept. psychiatry Fla. Hosp., Orlando, 1983, 84; clin. dir. assessment and evaluation team West Lake Hosp., Longwood, Fla., 1984-87, clin. dir. intensive evaluation unit, 1987-89; med. dir. Fla. Psychiat. Assocs., Winter Park, 1989-92, Fla. Psychiat. Mgmt., Winter Park, 1990-97; corp. med. dir. FPM Behavioral Health, 1993-97; co-founder Profl. Quality Analysts, Inc., Casselberry, Fla., 1997—. Med. dir. consultation, liaison svc. and spl. med. unit Winter Park Meml. Hosp., 1992; integrated surveyor Jt. Commn. for Accreditation of Healthcare Orgns., 1998—2000, sentinel event, 1999—2000; pres., CEO The Rondo Group, Longwood, Fla., 2000—; CEO, Cory Marvin Erving Found, 2001—. Contbr. 4 articles to profl. jours.; author sci. reports. Chmn. Retinitis Pigmentosa Casino Night, Orlando, 1988-92; vice-chmn. nat. championship com. U.S. Blind Golfers Assn., 1991-92, chair 48th ann. championship com., 1992-93; bd. dirs. Tennis with a Different Swing, Orlando, 1988-92; mem. Seminole County Assn. on Domestic Violence, 1998—. Mem. U.S. Blind Golfers Assn. (chairperson, nat. championships 1998, 99, 2000), Alaqua Country Club (bd. dirs.). Achievements include introduction of use of computerized topographical brain mapping as a diagnostic tool in central Florida; development of Data Portals, a palm pilot/internet based data acquisition and auto-aggregation and display system. Office: The Rondo Group Inc 3302 Tala Loop Longwood FL 32779 E-mail: therondogroup@earthlink.net.

POLLACK, SEYMOUR VICTOR, computer science educator; b. Bklyn., Aug. 3, 1933; s. Max and Sylvia (Harrison) P.; m. Sydell Altman, Jan. 23, 1955; children: Mark, Sherie. BChemE, Pratt Inst., 1954; MChemE, Bklyn. Poly. Inst., 1960. Lic. chem. engr., Ohio. Engr. Schwarz Labs., Mt. Vernon, N.Y., 1954-55; design engr. Curtiss-Wright, Wood-Ridge, N.J., 1955-57, Fairchild Engines, Deer Park, N.Y., 1957-59, GE, Evendale, Ohio, 1959-62; rsch. assoc. U. Cin., 1962-66; prof. computer sci. Washington U., St. Louis, 1966-95, prof. emeritus, 1995—. Cons. Mo. Auto Club, St. Louis, 1969-82, United Van Lines, Fenton, Mo., 1984-86, Computer Sci. Accreditation Bd., N.Y.C., 1985-93. Author: Structured Fortran, 1982, UCSD Pascal, 1984, Studies in Computer Science, 1983, The DOS Book, 1985, Turbo Pascal Programming, 1991; cons. editor Holt Rinehart & Winston, N.Y.C., 1979-86. Bd. dirs. Hillel orgn., Washington U., 1983-84. Recipient Alumni Achievement award Pratt Inst., 1966, Outstanding Teaching award Burlington Northern Found., 1987. Mem. Assn. for Computing Machinery, Am. Assn. for Engring. Edn. Jewish. Avocations: classical and jazz piano, jogging. Office: Washington U PO Box 1045 Saint Louis MO 63188-1045

POLLACK, STANLEY P. lawyer; b. N.Y.C., Apr. 23, 1928; s. Isidor and Anna (Shulman) P.; m. Susan Aronowitz, June 16, 1974; 1 child, Jane. BA, NYU, 1948; JD, Harvard U., 1951; LLM in Taxation, NYU, 1959. Bar: N.Y. 1951, U.S. Dist. Ct. (so. dist.) N.Y. 1955. Sole practice, N.Y.C., 1955-61; v.p., gen. counsel James Talcott, Inc., 1961-73; sr. exec. v.p. Rosenthal & Rosenthal Inc., 1973—. Served to j.g. lt. USNR, 1951-54. Mem. Bklyn. Bar Assn. (banking com., bankruptcy com.), Fed. Bar Council, Assn. Comml. Fin. Atty.'s (pres. 1968), Factors Chain Internat. Clubs: Harvard (N.Y.C.). Home: 6 Peter Cooper Rd New York NY 10010-6701 Office: Rosenthal & Rosenthal Inc 1370 Broadway # 2 New York NY 10018-7302

POLLACK, STEPHEN J. stockbroker; b. N.Y.C., Aug. 25, 1937; s. Harold S. and Gladys H. P. BS in Econs., U. Pa., 1960. V.p. retail sales Drexel Burnham Lambert, N.Y.C., 1960-77; 1st v.p. investments Dean Witter Reynolds Inc., 1978-98; 1st v.p., fin. advisor Morgan Stanley Dean Witter, 1998—, v.p., fin. advisor, 2001—. Pres. B'nai B'rith Gothem, N.Y.C.; exec. v.p. Cosmopolitan League of City of HOpe, v.p. circle mem. Whitney Mus., N.Y.C.; treas. Sutton Pl. Synagogue, pres. Havurah Group. With USAR, 1966. Recipient Double Chai Citation, State of Israel Bonds, 1984, Appreciation award City of Hope, 1984, Kiter Key Club award Franklin Funds, Million Dollar Club Svc. award, B'nai B'rith Internat. award. Mem. Internat. Assn. Fin. Planners, Assn. Investment Brokers (dir.), Youngmen's Philanthropic League (bd. dirs.), Internat. Study Rsch. Inst., Town Club, Atrium Club, Schuylkill Country Club, Wharton Sch. Club, U. Pa. Club, Yale Club, East River Tennis Club, Fresh Meadow Country Club, Matterhorn Sports Club, East Side Rep. Club, Knickerbokker Rep. Club, Berks County Tennis Club, Penn. Club (charter). Home: 245 E 40th St Apt 14E New York NY 10016-1714 Office: Morgan Stanley Dean Witter 885 3rd Ave Fl 14 New York NY 10022-4834

POLLACK, WILLIAM SHELLEY, psychologist, organizational consultant; b. Bklyn., Nov. 7, 1950; s. Emanuel and Pearl C. (Balcoff) P.; m. Marsha A. Padwa, Nov. 7, 1982; 1 child, Sarah Faye. AB, U. Chgo., 1972; MA, Brandeis U., 1976; postgrad., Boston Psychoanalytic Inst., 1993—; MA, Boston U., 1978, PhD in Clin. Psychology, 1981. Diplomate Am. Bd. Profl. Psychology, Clin. Psychology; nat. register health svc. provider in psychology; lic. psychologist, health provider, Mass.; Qualified Psychologist, Mass. Trainee Boston V.A. Outpatient Clinic, 1977-78; intern Boston U. Med. Ctr., 1978-79, McLean Hosp., Belmont, Mass., 1979-80, asst. in psychology, 1980-81, asst. psychologist, 1981-88, assoc. attending psychologist, 1988-90, assoc. psychologist, 1990—; clin. fellow in psychology dept. psychiatry Harvard Med. Sch., Boston, 1979-80, instr. psychology dept. psychiatry, 1981-93, asst. clin. prof. psychology dept. psychiatry, 1994—; clin. assoc. in psychiatry Boston U. Med. Sch., 1980-82; staff psychologist Univ. Hosp., 1980-82; clin. assoc. in psychiatry Mass. Gen. Hosp., Boston, 1992—; lectr. dept. psychology Boston U., 1994. Rsch. assoc. Boston U. Pregnancy and Parenthood Project, 1978-81, investigator, 1982—; staff psychologist Psychol. Test Ctr. Boston U. Med. Sch., 1980-81; psychologist in charge North Belknap I, McLean Hosp., 1980-81, Day Program Partial Hosp. Svc., 1981-82, Codman House III, 1982-88, mem. subcom. Patterns of Patient Care Utilization Rev. Com., 1982-88, dir. continuing edn. in psychology, 1982—, registrar APA program in continuing edn., 1982—, mem. edn. and tchg. com., 1983—, chair audio visual task force edn. and tchg. com., 1984, mem. psychiatrist in chief's task force on governance, 1984, interim dir. Inst. Ednl. and Orgnl. Consultation, 1985-86, chair subcom. on media edn. and tchg. com., 1985-87, mem. task force on long term/chronic care dept. psychiatry, 1987-88, chair subcom. on data base, 1987-88, mem. task force on aftercare dept. psychiatry, 1987-88, mem. clin. case conf. com. dept. psychiatry, 1987-88, sr. cons. Rehab. Outpatient Svc., 1987-94, chair continuing edn. com. psychology dept., 1987—, mem., rep. attending psychiatrist and psychologist com., 1989-94, dir. continuing psychology edn. Dept. Continuing Edn. and Postgrad. Edn., 1991—; mem. faculty steering com. psychology internship program McLean Hosp./Harvard Med. Sch, 1983—, mem. psychology internship com., 1983—, mem. com. on continuing med. edn., 1990—, coord. psychology fellowship program, 1991-94, mem. psychology dept. exec. adv. com., 1995—, dir. Ctr. for Men, McLean Hosp., 1994—; supr. med. students, interns and residents; spkr. numerous seminars in field, developer courses of study in field. Co-author: In A Time of Fallen Heroes, Atheneum, 1993, Guilford, 1995, A New Psychology of Men, 1995; mem. editl. bd. Psychotherapy, 1985-94, Jour. Clin. and Consulting Psychology, 1986, Direction in Clin. Psychology, 1990—, Psychotherapy Newsletter, 1994—, Psychoanalysis and Psychotherapy (guest editor 1995), Gender and Psychoanalysis, 1995—; contbr. numerous articles to profl. jours. Psychology rep. Gov.'s Task Force on Stigma, Mass., 1988-92, Mass. Statewide Mental Health Adv. Coun., 1993—; mem. Curriculum Adv. Com. Dept. Mental Health, Mass., 1990—; panel mem. Tech. Consulting Group Harvard Resource-Based Relative Values Scale for Clin. Psychology, 1992—; examiner Am. Bd. Profl. Psychology, 1994—; trustee Boston Psychoanalytic Soc. Inst., 1994—; v.p. McLean Profl. Staff Assn., 1995—. Crown fellow, 1974, NIMH fellow, 1978. Fellow Am. Orthopsychiat. Assn., Mass. Psychol. Assn. (mem. sci. program com., coord. continuing edn. programs 1983, mem. profl. practice com. 1984—, hosp. practice subcom., profl. practice com., mem. state-wide legis. network 1984—, treas. bd. dirs. 1986-88, mem. long-range planning com. 1987—, dir. 1988-95, pres. 1991-93); mem. AAAS, APA (divsn. 12 clin. psychology, divsn. 27 cmty. psychology, divsn. 39 psychoanalysis, divsn. 29 psychotherapy 1982—, assoc. program chair divsn. psychotherapy 1987-88, mem. com. continuing edn. sponsor approval 1987-90, chair 1989-90, chair program com. divsn. 29 psychotherapy 1988-90, mem. task force on men's roles and psychotherapy divsn. 29 psychotherapy 1988—, Karl Heiser award 1995—), Soc. Psychotherapy Rsch., Am. Psychoanalytic Assn. (affiliate), Am. Group Psychotherapy Assn., Soc. for Psychol. Study of Men and Masculinity (founder divsn. 51 1990—), Internat. Soc. for Psychoanalytic Study of Orgns., Northeastern Soc. Group Psychotherapy, Phi Beta Kappa. Office: McLean Hosp 115 Mill St Belmont MA 02478-1048

POLLAK, BARTH, mathematics educator; b. Chgo., Aug. 14, 1928; s. Samuel and Esther (Hirschberg) P.; m. Helen Charlotte Schiller, Aug. 22, 1954; children: Martin Russell, Eleanor Susan. BS, Ill. Inst. Tech., 1950, MS, 1951; PhD, Princeton U., 1957. Instr. math. Ill. Inst. Tech., Chgo., 1956-58; asst. prof. Syracuse (N.Y.) U., 1958-63; assoc. prof. U. Notre Dame, Ind., 1963-67, prof., 1967-2000, prof. emeritus, 2000—. Office: U Notre Dame Dept Math Notre Dame IN 46556

POLLAK, HENRY OTTO, retired utility research executive, educator; b. Vienna, Austria, Dec. 13, 1927; came to U.S., 1940, naturalized, 1945; s. Ludwig and Olga (Weil) P.; m. Ida Jeanne Tobias, May 7, 1949; children: Katherine, James. BA, Yale, 1947; MA, Harvard U., 1948, PhD, 1951; DSc, Rose Poly. Inst., 1964; DSc (hon.), Monmouth Coll., 1975, Bowdoin Coll., 1977, Technol. U., Eindhoven, 1981; LLD (hon.), Montclair State Coll., 1984; DSc (hon.), Laval U., Que., 1992. With Bell Telephone Labs., Murray Hill, N.J., 1951-83, mem. tech. staff, 1951-59, head dept. communications fundamentals II, 1959-61, acting dir. math. and mechanics research center, 1961-62, dir. math. and statistics research center, 1962-83; asst. v.p. math., communications, computer scis. research Bell Communications Research, Morristown, N.J., 1984-86. Mem. sch. math. study group, com. on undergrad. program in math. Internat. Commn. on Math. Instrn., 1970-74, 82-86, mem. adv. bd. Unified Sci. and Maths. for Elem. Schs., 1969-77; mem. adv. com. for sci. edn. NSF, 1977-80, 85-89, chmn., 1978-80; program chmn. 4th Internat. Congress Math. edn., 1980; bd. dirs. Math. Inst. Woodrow Wilson Found.; vis. prof. Tchrs. Coll., Columbia U., 1987—. Trustee N.C. Sch. for Sci. and Math, Durham, 1979-89; bd. dirs. COMAP, 1987-96. Mem. Am. Math. Soc., Math. Assn. Am. (pres. 1975-76, Yueh-Gin Gung & Dr. Charles Y. Hu award for Disting. Svc. to Math. 1993), Nat. Coun. Tchrs. Math., Phi Beta Kappa, Sigma Xi. Mem. Christ Ch. Home: 40 Edgewood Rd Summit NJ 07901-3988

POLLAK, JAY MITCHELL, lawyer; b. Chgo., Apr. 5, 1937; s. Bertram L. and Florence (Molner) P.; m. Patricia Pollak, May 11, 1963; children: Mitchell Emery, John Andrew. BS, Miami U., Oxford, Ohio, 1959; JD, Northwestern U., 1962. Bar: Ill. 1962, U.S. Dist. Ct. (no. dist.) Ill. 1971, U.S. Ct. Appeals (7th cir.) 1982, U.S. Supreme Ct. 1982. V.p. Pollak & Hoffman LTD, Northbrook, Ill., 1963—. Atty. Counsel to Northbrook (Ill.) Hist. Soc.; prosecutor Village of Northbrook; mem. Page Ctr. for Entrepreneurship at Miami U. Pres. Northbrook Hockey League, 1986-88; mem. bus. adv. coun. Miami U., mem. adv. bd. Mem. ABA (anti-trust law sect.), Ill. Bar Assn., Chgo. Bar Assn., Forum Com. on Franchising, Atty. Gen.'s Ill. Franchise Adv. Bd. Home: 846 Dundee Rd Northbrook IL 60062-2705 Office: Pollak and Hoffman Ltd 1200 Shermer Rd Ste 301 Northbrook IL 60062-4563 E-mail: jomi37@aol.com.

POLLAK, JOANNE E. lawyer; b. Cleve., July 16, 1944; m. Mark Pollak, Dec. 26, 1976; children: Elizabeth, Joshua, Rebecca, Benjamin, Jonathan. BA magna cum laude, Dickinson Coll., 1965; JD with honors, U. Md., 1976. Bar: Md. 1976. V.p., gen. counsel The Johns Hopkins Health System Corp./Johns Hopkins Medicine, Balt.; assoc., ptnr. and head of health care practice group Piper & Marbury Law Offices, 1976-93. Instr. bus. of medicine Sch. Medicine, Johns Hopkins U., Internat. Bus. Sch. Bd. dirs. Charlestown Cmty., Inc.; chair bd. dirs. Mid-Atlantic affiliate Am. Heart Assn., chair rsch. for life campaign. Named One of Md.'s Top Women, Daily Record, 1996, 98, 2000. Office: Johns Hopkins Health Sys Corp 600 N Wolfe St Baltimore MD 21287-1974

POLLAK, LOUIS HEILPRIN, judge, educator; b. N.Y.C., Dec. 7, 1922; s. Walter and Marion (Heilprin) P.; m. Katherine Weiss, July 25, 1952; children: Nancy, Elizabeth, Susan, Sarah, Deborah. AB, Harvard, 1943; LL.B., Yale, 1948. Bar: N.Y. bar 1949, Conn. bar 1956, Pa. bar 1976. Law clk. to Justice Rutledge U.S. Supreme Ct., 1948-49; with Paul, Weiss, Rifkind, Wharton & Garrison, N.Y.C., 1949-51; spl. asst. to Amb. Philip C. Jessup State Dept., 1951-53; asst. counsel Amlgmated Clothing Workers Am., 1954-55; mem. faculty Yale Law Sch., 1955-74, dean, 1965-70; Greenfield prof. U. Pa., 1974-78, dean Law Sch., 1975-78, lectr., 1980—; judge U.S. Dist Ct. (ea.

dist.) Pa., Phila., 1978—, now sr. judge. Vis. lectr. Howard U. Sch. Law, 1953; vis. prof. U. Mich. Law Sch., 1961, Columbia Law Sch., 1962 Author: The Constitution and the Supreme Court: A Documentary History, 1966. Mem. New Haven Bd. Edn., 1962-68; chmn. Conn. adv. com. U.S. Civil Rights Commn., 1962-63; mem. bd. NAACP Legal Def. Fund, 1960-78, v.p., 1971-78. Served with AUS, 1943-46. Mem. ABA (chmn. sec. individual rights 1970-71), Fed. Bar Assn., Phila. Bar Assn., Assn. Bar City N.Y., Am. Acad. Arts and Scis., Am. Philos. Soc., Am. Acad. Polit. and Social Sci. (bd. dirs. 2001—), Am. Law Inst. (coun. 1978—). Office: US Dist Ct 16613 US Courthouse 601 Market St Philadelphia PA 19106-1713

POLLAK, MARK, lawyer; b. Paris, July 16, 1947; came to U.S., 1955; s. Joseph and Zofia (Berkowitz) P.; m. Joanne Elizabeth Harris, Dec. 26, 1976; children: Joshua David, Jonathan Stephen, Benjamin Eric, Rebecca Lynn. BA, Bklyn. Coll., 1968; MA in City Planning, JD, U. Pa., 1972. Bar: Md. 1972. Assoc. Piper & Marbury, Balt., 1972-81, ptnr., 1981-99, Wilmer, Cutler & Pickering, Washington, 1999—. Bd. dirs. Jack Kent Cook Found. Author: Sports Leagues and Teams--An Encyclopedia 1871 to 1996, 1997. Bd. dirs. Balt. Children's Mus., Downtown Partnership of Balt., Inc. Mem. ABA, Md. Bar Assn., Am. Coll. Real Estate Lawyers, Am. Planning Assn., Nat. Assn. Bond Lawyers. Office: Wilmer, Cutler & Pickering 100 Light St Baltimore MD 21202-1036

POLLAK, MARTIN MARSHALL, lawyer, training company executive; b. N.Y.C., July 31, 1927; s. Edward and Jennie (Horowitz) P.; m. Ellen R. Spiegel, Sept. 16, 1929; children: David W., Richard M., Barbara S. AB, Syracuse U., 1950; LLB, St. John's U., Bklyn., 1953. Bar: N.Y. 1953, U.S. Dist. Ct. (ea. and so. dists.) N.Y. 1957, U.S. Supreme Ct. 1959. Ptnr. Feldman & Pollak, Attys., N.Y.C., 1953-59; atty. N.Y. State, 1953—; founder, exec. v.p., treas. G.P. Strategies Corp. (formerly Nat. Patent Devel. Corp.), N.Y.C., 1959-99. Trustee Worcester Found. for Exptl. Rsch., Shrewsbury, Mass., 1977—; cons. Allergan Optical Corp., Irvine, Calif., 1988-89; chmn. bd. Czechoslovak-U.S. Econ. Coun., Washington, 1987-96, vice-chmn., 1996—; pres. Internat. Hydron Corp., Woodbury, N.Y., 1981-88, NPO Trading USA, Inc., N.Y.C., Washington, Prague, Czechoslovakia, 1990-98, Am. Drug Co., Washington, N.Y.C., Moscow, 1993-98, Millennium Cell Corp., 1998-2000; bd. dirs. GSE Sys., Inc. Vice chmn. bd. Worcester Found., 2000—. With USN, 1945-47. Recipient gold medal Czechoslovakian Rep. C. of C., 1984. Office: GP Strategies Corp 9 W 57th St Ste 4170 New York NY 10019-2795 also: Gen Physics Corp 6700 Alexander Bell Dr Ste 300 Columbia MD 21046-2185

POLLAK, NORMAN LEE, accountant; b. Chgo., Aug. 16, 1931; s. Emery and Helen P.; m. Barbara Zeff, Aug. 21, 1955 (div. 1980); children: Martin Joel, Elise Susan McNeal, Rhonda Louise Wilder. BS, Northwestern U., 1955. CPA, Calif.; lic. real estate agt. Calif. Sr. acct., staff acct., 1952-58; pvt. practice, 1958-88; fin. and mgmt. adv. svcs. Westlake Village. Expert witness on domestic dissolution, 1984-87; lectr. profl. orgns.; bus. mgr. for Steven Martin, Nitty Gritty Dirt Band, 1967-77. Former pres. Ventura County Estate Planning Coun., 1975-78, 78-79); founder San Fernando Valley Estate Planning Coun., 1962, chpt. pres., 1964-65; founder Ventura Co. Estate Planning Coun.; chmn. Comm. Contest for Hearing Impaired Optimist Club, emergency com. Disaster Preparedness, Oak Forest Mobile Estates Assn.; vol. disaster preparedness plan; coach Braille Olympics for Blind; mem. Conejo Future Found.; bd. dirs. Oak Forest Homeowners Assn., Honokowai Palms Homeowners Assn.; bd. trustees Westlake Cultural Found.; sponsor Code 3 for Homeless Children, 1993. Mem. AICPA (apptd. CPA key person for legis.-polit. program Washington), Calif. Soc. CPAs (former chmn. San Fernando tech. discussion group 1960-61, former mem. com. on cooperation with credit grantors), Nat. Assn. Accts., Westlake Village C. of C., Northwestern U. Alumni Club, Kellogg Sch. Mgmt. Alumni Club, UCLA Alumni Club, Delta Mu Delta. Address: 1930 Village Center Cir #3-428 Las Vegas NV 89134

POLLAK, OLIVER BURT, lawyer, educator; b. London, Nov. 10, 1943; came to U.S., 1953; s. William and Ruth Pollak; m. Karen F. Goldstein; children: Noah, Aaron. BA, Calif. State U., L.A., 1965; PhD, UCLA, 1973; JD, Creighton U., 1982. Bar: Nebr., 1982, Iowa, 1992. Prof. U. Nebr., Omaha, 1974—; atty. Pollak & Hicks, P.C., 1983—. Author 4 books; contbr. articles to profl. jours. Mem. Nebr. Humanities Coun., Lincoln, 1981-85, Omaha Jewish Press, 1984-91. Recipient Sandoz award, 1996. Mem. ACLU, Am. Jewish Hist. Soc., Am. Hist. Assn., B'nai B'rith. Jewish. Avocations: cycling, reading. Office: U Nebr Omaha History Dept Omaha NE 68182-0001 E-mail: obpomni@aol.com.

POLLAK, RAYMOND, general and transplant surgeon; b. Johannesburg, South Africa, Nov. 12, 1950; came to U.S., 1977; MB BCh, U. Witwatersrand, Johannesburg, 1973. Diplomate Am. Bd. Surgery. Rotating intern Gen. Hosp., Johannesburg, 1974; intern in surgery U. Ill. Hosps. and Clinics, Chgo., 1977-78, resident in surgery; immunology and transplant fellow U. Ill., 1982-84, assoc. prof. surgery, chief divsn. transplant dept. surgery, 1988-98, prof. surgery dept., surgeon, 1995—, chief divsn. transplant Peoria, 2000—. Fellow ACS, Royal Coll. Surgeons Edinburgh. Office: U Ill Dept Surgery 624 NE Glen Oak Ave North Bldg 2d Floor Peoria IL 61603-3135 Fax: 309-655-3630. E-mail: rpollak@uic.edu.

POLLAK, STEPHEN JOHN, lawyer; b. Chgo., Mar. 22, 1928; s. Maurice August Pollak and Laura (Kramer) Fisher; m. Ruth Scheinfeld, June 22, 1951; children: Linda Jan, David Michael, Roger Lincoln, Eve Juliette. BA, Dartmouth Coll., 1950; LLB, Yale U., 1956. Bar: Ill. 1956, D.C. 1957. Assoc. Covington & Burling, Washington, 1956-61; asst. to solicitor gen. Dept. Justice, 1961-64; legal counsel to Pres.'s Task Force War Against Poverty, 1964; dep. gen. counsel Office Econ. Opportunity, 1964-65; 1st asst. to asst. atty. gen. Civil Rights Divsn. Dept. Justice, 1965-67; advisor to Pres. for Nat. Capital Affairs, 1967; spl. asst. to atty. gen. Dept. Justice, 1967, asst. atty. gen. Civil Rights Divsn., 1967-69; ptnr. Shea & Gardner, 1969—; counsel, assoc. ind. counsel to ind. counsel James C. McKay Franklyn C. Nofziger Matters, 1987-88, 89-90; mem. panel mediators U.S. Ct. Appeals and Dist. Ct., D.C. Cir., 1989—; spl. master Vitamins Antitrust Litigation, 1999—. Bd. dirs. Draper and Kramer, Inc., Chgo. Pres. Housing Devel. Corp., 1976—80; D.C. Cir. Jud. Conf. chair Com. on the Adminstrn. of Justice Under Emergency Conditions, 1971—73, chair com. on pro bono legal svcs., 1997—2001; bd. dirs. Hist. Soc. D.C. Cir., 1993—, chair oral history project, 1994—; bd. dirs. NAACP Legal Def. and Ednl. Fund, Inc., 1987—95; bd. dirs., chair Black Student Fund, Washington, 1976—80, trustee, 1969—; bd. dirs. Nat. Lawyers' Com. for Civil Rights, 1969—, mem. exec. com., 1987—, co-chair, 1975—77; mem. Hist. Soc. D.C. Cir. Recipient Wiley A. Branton award Washington Lawyers' Com. for Civil Rights Under the Law, 1992, Whitney North Seymour award, 1994, Svc. of Justice award D.C. Legal Aid Soc., 1994. Mem.: ABA, Am. Law Inst., D.C. Jud. Nomination Commn. (sec. 1986—88, acting chair 1988—89, chair 1989—90), D.C. Bar Assn. (bd. govs. 1972—73, sec. 1974—75, pres.-elect 1979—80, pres. 1980—81, bd. govs. 1981—82, chair pub. svcs. activities com. 1989—95, Frederick B. Abramson award 1994, Thurgood Marshall award for svc. in the pub. interest 2001), Phi Beta Kappa, Order of the Coif. Office: Shea & Gardner Ste 800 1800 Massachusetts Ave NW Washington DC 20036-1872

POLLARA, BERNARD, immunologist, educator, pediatrician; b. Chgo. s. Joseph and Mamie P. PhB, Northwestern U., 1951, MS, 1954; MD, U. Minn., 1960, PhD, 1963. Intern USPHS Hosp., Seattle, 1960; resident in pediatrics U. Minn. Hosps., 1968-69; rsch. assoc. pediatrics U. Minn., 1960-63, assoc. prof. biochemistry and pediatrics, 1969; prof. pediatrics Albany (N.Y.) Med. Coll., 1969-94, chmn. dept., 1979-93; pediatrician in chief Albany Med. Ctr. Hosp., 1979-93; sabbatical leave, pediatrician Yukon Kuskokwim Regional Hosp., 1992-93; John and Aliese Price prof. pediatrics & adolescent medicine U. South Fla., Tampa, 1994—, head divsn. gen. pediatrics, dept. pediatrics, 1994—, interim chmn. pediats., 1999-2001. V.p. for rsch. affairs Albany Med. Ctr., 1986-89. Dir. N.Y. State Kidney Disease Inst., 1969-79. With USN, 1945-46. Recipient Acad. Laureate award SUNY, Albany, 1991; Arthritis and Rheumatism Found. fellow, 1961-64. Fellow Am. Acad. Pediats.; mem. AAAS, Am. Assn. Immunologists, Am. Pediat. Soc., Am. Soc. Cell Biology, Clin. Immunology Soc., Ambulatory Pediat. Assn., Sigma Xi, Phi Lambda Upsilon, Alpha Omega Alpha. Office: U South Fla Sch Medicine Dept Pediatrics 17 Davis Blvd Ste 308 Tampa FL 33606-3475 E-mail: bpollara@hsc.usf.edu.

POLLARA, JOANNE, learning disabilities educator consultant; b. Hoboken, N.J., Apr. 18, 1954; d. Ralph Frank and Katharine Stark (Cunningham) Pollara; children: Angela, Joshua. BA, St. Joseph Coll., 1976; MA, Montclair State U., 1994. Cert. tchr. elem., spl. edn., L.D.T.C., N.J. 4th grade tchr. Holy Trinity Sch., Hackensack, N.J., 1976-77; tchr. of handicapped Kessler Inst., West Orange, 1978-86; bedside instructor West Orange Bd. of Edn., 1976-86, spl. edn. inst. aide, 1986-88; tchr. of handicapped Redwood Sch., West Orange, N.J., 1988-97; learning disabled tchr. cons. West Orange Pub. Schs., 1997—. Mem. spl. edn. curriculum com., W. Orange, N.J., 1989, bldg. mgmt. com., 1991-92; spl. edn. rep. reading curriculum com., W. Orange, 1990; PTA faculty rep. Redwood Sch., W. Orange, 1994-95. Religious educator Our Lady of Lourdes Ch., West Orange, N.J., 1984-85, Notre Dame Ch., North Caldwell, N.J., 1991-92; girl scout leader Girl Scouts of U.S., W. Orange, N.J., 1983-84, 86-87. Mem. Coun. for Exceptional Children (learning disabilities divsn.), Coun. for Ednl. Diagnostic Svcs., Assn. Learning Consultants, Phi Kappa Phi. Avocations: reading, music (piano, guitar), swimming. Home: 23 Espy Rd Apt B5 Caldwell NJ 07006-4855 Office: Dept Student Support Svcs 179 Eagle Rock Ave West Orange NJ 07052

POLLARD, CAROLINE PRAY, legal assistant; b. Wellesley, Mass., Oct. 14, 1957; d. W. Howard and Margaret Louise (Sasseville) P.; m. Joseph W. Cialini, Jr., May 12, 1979; 1 child, Laura Anne. BS in Journalism, Boston U., 1979; cert. completion in gen. practice, Inst. for Paralegal Tng., Phila., 1981. Prodn. coord. E. Bruce Harrison Co., Washington, 1979-80; legal asst. Ballard, Spahr, Andrews & Ingersoll, Phila., 1981-83, sr. legal asst. for asbestos, 1983-89, gen. sr. legal asst., 1989-96, litigation support coord., 1996—. Vol. Phila. Folk Festival, Schwenksville, Pa., 1981—; vol. info. booth Pa. Hort. Soc. Flower Show, Phila., 1996—. Mem. Legal Asst. Mgmt. Assn. (chmn. Phila. chpt. 1988—, conf. chmn. 1998-99). Office: Ballard Spahr Andrews Et Al 1735 Market St Fl 51 Philadelphia PA 19103-7599 E-mail: pollard@ballardspahr.com.

POLLARD, EDWARD ELLSBERG, banker; b. Plainfield, N.J., Apr. 22, 1945; s. Goldwin Smith and Mary (Ellsberg) P.; m. Marilyn Pfaff, June 27, 1970 (div. Dec. 1976); 1 child, Nicholas Cooke Ellsberg; m. Carolyn Jans, June 14, 1985. BS in Econs., U. Pa., 1968. Salesman Solo Realty, Phila., 1968-71, McClain Securities, Phila., 1971-73; pres. Pa. Indls. Realty, King of Prussia, 1973-78, Old MacDonald's Foods, Lewistown, Pa., 1979-82, Remington Press, Ltd., St. Davids, 1983—. Chmn. Heirs and Beneficiaries, Inc., Bryn Mawr, Pa., 1991—. Ind. Trust Co. Am., Wilmington, Del., 1994—; dir. Montgomery Sch., Chester Springs, Pa., 1987-93; pres. Newbury Naturals, St. Davids, Pa., 1999—; pres. Health 911.com., St. Davids,1999—. Bd. dirs. Radnor Hist. Soc., Wayne, Pa., 1989—, Neighborhood Health Agys., West Chester, Pa., 1995—; state pres. Fathers' and Children's Equality, Drexel, Pa., 1981-83; commr. Radnor Twp., Pa., 1992-95; pres. Friends of Fenimore Park, 2001—. Democrat. Methodist. Avocations: tall ship sailing, tennis, art, collecting antiques. Home: 11 Fairview Dr Saint Davids PA 19087-3618 E-mail: TPollard@health911.com.

POLLARD, FRANK EDWARD, retired lawyer; b. Framingham, Mass., Oct. 26, 1932; s. Frank E. and Marjorie G. (Bayer) P.; m. Joyce A. Angell, June 4, 1955; children: Gary R., Jeffrey F., Donald B., Edward D., Laurie J. AB, Northeastern U., 1954; JD, Boston U., 1956. Bar: Conn. 1956, Mass. 1956, Fla. 1959, U.S. Dist. Ct. Mass., U.S. Supreme Ct. 1969. Ptnr., atty. Lee & Pollard, Westfield, Mass., 1958-80; pvt. practice, 1980-96; pres. Pollard & Pollard P.C., 1997-2000, ret., 2000. Pres. Westfield 2000 Redevel. Corp., 1978, counsel, 1980-2000; atty. City of Westfield, 1970-71; parlimentarian Mass. Jr. C. of C., 1964; pres. Boys Club Greater Westfield, Inc., 1972-73. Recipient Distinguished Svc. award U.S. Jaycees, Westfield, 1966. Mem. Westfield C. of C. (pres. 1975, counsel 1975-2000), Westfield Boys and Girls Club (pres. 1972-73, Man and Boy award 1973), Kiwanis (life mem., lt. gov. 1977-78, Westfield pres. 1967-68). Avocations: golf, photography, carpentry. Home: 7 Country Club Dr Southwick MA 01077-9675

POLLARD, FRED DON, finance company executive, director; b. Proctorsville, Vt., Sept. 15, 1931; s. Bryant Frank and Millie Viola (Brobst) P.; m. Sandra Jean Norton, Oct. 19, 1957; children: Fred Don, Bruce Gardiner, Mark Bryant. BA, Dartmouth Coll., 1953, MBA, 1954. CPA, N.Y. Staff auditor Touche, Niven, Bailey & Smart, Chgo., 1954-55, 57-58; with Hertz Corp., 1958-60, London, 1960-62, Paris, 1962-64, N.Y.C., 1964-65; European controller Avis Rent A Car, London, 1965-69, internat. treas., 1969-71, asst. v.p., dir. fin. N.Y., 1971-72, asst. treas., 1972-75; treas. Garcia Corp., Teaneck, N.J., 1975-78; v.p. fin., treas. Augsbury Orgn., Inc., Ogdensburg, N.Y., 1978-79, sr. v.p. fin., treas., 1979-83, also dir.; pres. Corp. Fin. Assocs. No. N.Y., Canton, 1983—, Agrl. Processing Corp., Canton, 1983-98; pres. and treas. AG Pro Ltd., Massena, NY, 1998—. Dir. Augsbury Corp., Halco Inc., Montreal, Que., Can., 1978-83, Carlton Holding Co./N.Y. Casualty, Watertown, N.Y., 1978-82, Creg System Inc., Watertown, Whalen, Daley & Looney (CPAs), Ogdenburg, N.Y., 1989—; Mem. adv. bd. Clarkson Sch. Mgmt., Potsdam, N.Y., 1979-83; vis. lectr. sch. of mgmt. Clarkson U., Potsdam, 1986-87; vis. lectr. dept. econs. St. Lawrence U., Canton, N.Y., 1987-88. Exec. bd. Seaway Valley coun. Boy Scouts Am., 1980-86, adv. bd., 1986-95. Served with U.S. Army, 1955-57. Mem. N.Y. State Soc. CPAs, Am. Inst. CPAs., St. Lawrence county C. of C. (bd. dirs. 1997—). Lodges: Masons; Shriners. Presbyterian. Home: Old Stone House 1129 County Route 25 Canton NY 13617-6539 Office: 1129 County Rte. 25 Canton NY 13617 E-mail: stonhous@northnet.org.

POLLARD, HARVEY B. physician, neuroscientist; b. San Antonio, May 26, 1943; BA in Biology, Rice U., 1964; MS in Biochemistry, MD, U. Chgo., 1969, PhD, 1973. Rsch. assoc. NIH-Nat. Inst. Arthritis and Metabolic Diseases, Bethesda, Md., 1969-71, sr. investigator, 1972-74, 1977-79, sect. chief, 1979-81; lab. chief Nat. Inst. Diabetes, Digestive and Kidney Diseases, 1981-96; prof., chair dept. anatomy, physiology and genetics Uniformed Svcs. U. Sch. Medicine, 1997—. Contbr. over 250 articles to profl. jours. With USPHS, 1969-96. Recipient Commendation medal USPHS, 1982, Alumni award for Disting. Svc., U. Chgo. Alumni Assn., 1989, NIH Inventor's award, 1991. Mem. Biophys. Soc., Soc. for Neurosci., Am. Soc. for Pharmacology and Exptl. Therapeutics, Soc. for Cell Biology, Endocrine Soc., Am. Coll. Psychoneuropharmacology, Am. Soc. for Biochemistry and Molecular Biology, Am. Assn. Anatomists., Am. Physiol. Soc., Institute of Medicine of Washington, D.C. Office: USU Sch Med Dept Anatomy Physiology and Genetics Bethesda MD 20814-4712 E-mail: hpollard@usuhs.mil.

POLLARD, HENRY, mediator, arbitrator; b. N.Y.C., Jan. 10, 1931; s. Charles and Sarah (Lanster) P.; m. Adele Ruth Brodie, June 16, 1954; children: Paul A., Lydia S. AB, CCNY, 1953; JD, Columbia U., 1954. Bar: N.Y. 1954, Calif. 1962. Assoc. Sullivan & Cromwell, N.Y.C., 1954, 56-61; ptnr. Kaplan, LIvingston, Goodwin, Berkowitz & Selvin, Beverly Hills, 1962-81, Pollard, Bauman, Slome & McIntosh, Beverly Hills, Calif., 1981-87, Seyfarth, Shaw, L.A., 1987-95; of counsel Oberstein, Kibre & Horwitz, 1995-99. Judge pro tem L.A. County Mcpl. Ct.; arbitrator/mediator, mem. large complex case program Am. Arbitration Assn.; arbitrator/mediator Nat. Assn. Securities Dealers, N.Y. Stock Exch., Am. Stock Exch., Pacific Stick Exch., L.A. County Dispute Resolution Svcs.; settlement officer Beverly Hills Mcpl. Ct., L.A. County Superior Ct. Editor Columbia U. Law Rev., 1953-54. Served with U.S. Army, 1954-56. Harlan Fiske Stone scholar, 1953-54. Mem. ABA, Calif. Bar Assn., Beverly Hills Bar Assn Fax: 310-457-1713. E-mail: adrpolllard@aol.com.

POLLARD, JEFFREY WALLACE, college counseling, health services director; b. Bethesda, Md., July 8, 1946; s. Eric George Frederick and Eldred (Wallace) P. BS, Old Dominion U., 1970, MS, 1994; PhD, U. Va., 1978. Lic. psychologist, Ohio; diplomate Am. bd. Profl. Psychology, Internat. Acad. Behavioral Medicine, Counseling, Psychotherapy. Probation officer Juvenile, Domestic Rels. Court, Norfolk, Va., 1970-74; counselor Comprehensive Addictive Svcs. Program, 1974-75; practicum counselor U. Va. Counseling Ctr., Charlottesville, 1976-77; intern in clinical psychology Eastern Va. Graduate Sch. Med., Norfolk, 1977-78; psychologist Villanova (Pa.) U. Counseling Ctr., 1978-82; dir. counseling svcs. Denison U., Granville, Ohio, 1982-89, dir. health and counseling svcs., 1989—. Author: Treatment of Violence Perpetrators, 1991, Treatment for Perpetrators of Rape and Other Violence, 1994; co-editor: Campus Violence: Kinds Causes and Cures, 1994; mem. editl. bd. Jour. of Counseling and Devel., 1996-99, Jour. of Coll. Student Psychotherapy, 1994—; contbr. articles to profl. jours. Grantee U.S. Dept. Edn. Fund, 1989. Fellow Acad. Counseling Psychology (treas. 1997—, pres.-elect). Home: 5025 Blendon Ravine Ct Columbus OH 43230-4214 Office: Denison University Whisler Hall Granville OH 43023-1368 E-mail: pollard@denison.edu.

POLLARD, JOSEPH AUGUSTINE, advertising and public relations consultant; b. N.Y.C., June 22, 1924; s. Joseph Michael and Mary Theresa (Sheerin) P.; m. Helen Frances O'Neill, Jan. 18, 1947 (dec.); children: Christopher (dec.), Kenneth, Eugene, Daniel (dec.), Theresa, Michael; m. Lee Sharon Rivkins, Jan. 1, 1981. Student, Pratt Inst., 1946-50. Advt. mgr. Boston Store, Utica, N.Y., 1951-53; sales promotion dir. Interstate Stores, 1954-60, 67-70; v.p. sales Cmty. Discount Stores, Chgo., 1960-63; dir. sales S. Klein, N.Y.C., 1964-66; v.p. advt. and pub. rels. Peoples Drug Stores, Alexandria, Va., 1970-89; ret. Trustee D.C. divsn. Am. Cancer Soc., 1978-95, pres., 1985-86, nat. del., 1991-94; pres. Modern Retailers Ill., 1962; bd. dirs. Brunswick County Literacy Coun., 2001—. With USAF, 1943-46, 50-51, 2001. Recipient Am. ADvt. Fedn. Silver medal award, 1982, St. Georges medal Am. Cancer Soc., 1984. Mem. Advt. Club Washington (pres. 1975-76), Country Club Fairfax (pres. 1994, bd. dirs. 1992-95), Lockwood Folly Country Club (Holden Beach, N.C., bd. dirs. 1997). Home and Office: 173 Clubhouse Dr SW Supply NC 28462-2108

POLLARD, MARGARET LOUISE, association administrator; b. Leominster, Mass., Nov. 15, 1934; d. Edward Francis and AliceMary (Sosvielle) Sasseville; m. Walter Howard Pollard III, Mar. 10, 1957 (dec. Oct. 1974); children: Caroline Pray, Walter Howard IV, Margaret Peirce, Melissa Anne; m. James L. Baird Jr., Jan. 9, 1993. BS, Simmons Coll., 1956; MS, Boston U., 1983. Editor Hist. Soc. Western Pa., Pitts., 1971-75; mgr. advtr. and promotions F.W. Faxon Co., Westwood, Mass., 1976-80; owner, mgr. Peg Pollard Communications, Boston, 1981-84; dir. comms. Mass. Dental Soc., Natick, 1984-93; coord. vols. Lyman Allyn Art Mus., New London, Conn., 1993-96; exec. dir. Norwich (Conn.) Heritage Trrust, 1994-96. Editor LWV, Westwood, 1966, pres., Greensburg, Pa., 1968-71; bd. dirs. First Night, Inc., Boston, 1982-89, Friends Boston Ctr. for Arts, 1985-88; mem. Leu Botanical Gardens, Friends of Orlando Philharm. Mem. Am. Soc. Assn. Execs., Am. Soc. Med. Writers, New Eng. Soc. Assn. Execs., Publicity Club New Eng. (Bellringer award 1984), Morse Mus. of Am. Arts Assoc. (sec.), Friends of the Orlando Philharmonic Bd., Univ. Club Winter Park. Avocations: historical research, reading, walking, theater, golf. Home: PO Box 3407 Nantucket MA 02584-3407 Office: 54 Arkansas Ave Nantucket MA 02554-2502 also: 660-114 Post Oak Cir Altamonte Springs FL 32701

POLLARD, MICHAEL ROSS, lawyer, health policy researcher and consultant; b. Flint, Mich., Apr. 14, 1947; s. Gail Winton Pollard and Evelyn Georgeanna (LeMire) Goplen; m. Penelope Brigham, Aug. 22, 1970. AB in Polit. Sci., U. Mich., 1969; JD, Harvard U., 1972, MPH, 1974. Bar: Mass. 1972, D.C. 1975. Profl. assoc. for program devel. Nat. Acad. Scis. Inst. Medicine, Washington, 1974-77, dir. law and ethics div., 1977-78; atty. advisor Office of Policy Planning, FTC, 1978-81, asst. dir. Bur. Consumer Protection, 1981-83; dir. Office of Policy Analysis, Pharm. Mfrs. Assn., 1983-88; exec. dir. Am. Pharm. Inst., 1988-89; counsel Michaels, Wishner & Bonner, P.C. (now Michaels & Bonner PC), 1988-89, ptnr., 1989—. Cons. Nat. Ctr. for Health Svcs. Rsch., Rockville, Md., 1975-80, Office Tech. Assessment U.S. Congress, 1984-95; dir. Inst. for Health Policy Solutions, 1992—. Contbr. articles to profl. jours. Treas. Nat. Leadership Coalition on AIDS, 1988-93; treas. and dir.-at-large Nat. Commn. on Cert. of Physician Assts., 1991-97, James B. Angell scholar U. Mich., 1967, 68, 69. Mem. ABA, Phi Beta Kappa, Pi Sigma Alpha. Democrat. Avocations: running, cycling, gardening, architectural drawing. Home: 7300 Maple Ave Chevy Chase MD 20815-5108 also: 29 Paradise Lane West Southport ME 04576 Office: Michaels & Bonner 1140 Connecticut Ave NW Ste 900 Washington DC 20036-4009

POLLARD, MORRIS, microbiologist, educator; b. Hartford, Conn., May 24, 1916; s. Harry and Sarah (Hoffman) P.; m. Mildred Klein, Dec. 29, 1938; children: Harvey, Carol, Jonathan. D.V.M., Ohio State U., 1938; MS, Va. Poly. Inst., 1939; PhD (Nat. Found. Infantile Paralysis fellow), U. Calif.-Berkeley, 1950; D.Sc. (hon.) Miami U., Ohio, 1981. Mem. staff Animal Disease Sta., Nat. Agrl. Research Center, Beltsville, Md., 1939-42; asst. prof. preventive medicine Med. br. U. Tex., Galveston, 1946-48, assoc. prof., 1948-50, prof., 1950-61; prof. biology U. Notre Dame, Ind., 1961-66, prof., chmn. microbiology, 1966-81, prof. emeritus, 1981—, dir. Lobund Lab., 1961-85, Coleman dir. Lobund Lab., 1985—. Vis. prof. Fed. U. Rio de Janeiro, Brazil, 1977; vis. prof. Katholieke U., Leuven, Belgium, 1981; mem. tng. grant com. NIH, 1965-70; mem. adv. bd. Inst. Lab. Animal Resources NRC, 1965-68; mem. adv. com. microbiology Office Naval Research, 1966-68, chmn., 1968-70; mem. sci. adv. com. United Health Found., 1966-70; cons. U. Tex., M.D. Anderson Hosp. and Tumor Inst., 1958-66; mem. colon cancer com. Nat. Cancer Inst., 1972-76, chmn. tumor immunology com., 1976-79; mem. com. cancer cause and prevention NIH, 1979-81; program rev. com. Argonne Nat. Lab, 1979-85, chmn., 1983-85; lectr. Found. Microbiology, 1978 Editor: Perspectives in Virology Vol. I to XI, 1959-80; contbr. articles to profl. jours. Served from 1st lt. to lt. col. Vet. Corps, AUS, 1942-46. Recipient Disting. Alumnus award Ohio State U., 1979, Army Commendation medal, Presdl. citation, Hope award Am. Cancer Soc., 2000; named Hon. Alumnus U. Notre Dame, 1989; McLaughlin Faculty fellow Cambridge U., 1956; Raine Found. prof. U. Western Australia, 1975; vis. scientist Chinese Acad. Med. Scis., 1979, 81; hon. prof. Chinese Acad. Med. Scis., 1982. Mem. Am. Acad. Microbiology (charter), Brazilian Acad. Scis., Soc. Exptl. Biology and Medicine, Am. Soc. Microbiology (Acad. Sci. Achievement award 1990), Am. Soc. Investigative Pathology, Am. Assn. Cancer Rsch., Am. Soc. Lab. Animal Sci., Assn. Gnotobiotics (pres.), Internat. Commn. Lab. Animal Sci., AAAS, Internat. Assn. Gnotobiology (pres.), Internat. Assn. Gnotobiotics (hon. pres. 1987), Sigma Xi, Phi Delta Epsilon (hon.), Phi Zeta (hon.). Home: 3540 Hanover Ct South Bend IN 46614-2331 Office: Lobund Lab Univ of Notre Dame Notre Dame IN 46556

POLLARD, OVERTON PRICE, state agency executive, lawyer; b. Ashland, Va., Mar. 26, 1933; s. James Madison and Annie Elizabeth (Hutchinson) P.; m. Anne Aloysia Meyer, Oct. 1, 1960; children: Mary O., Price, John, Anne, Charles, Andrew, David AB in Econs., Washington and Lee U., 1954, JD, 1957. Bar: Va. Claims supr. Travelers Ins. Co., Richmond, Va., 1964-67; asst. atty. gen. State of Va., 1967, 70-72; spl. asst. Va. Supreme Ct., 1968-70; exec. dir. Pub. Defender Commn., 1972—; ptnr. Pollard & Boice and predecessor firms, 1972-87. Bd. govs. Va. Criminal Law Sect., Richmond, 1970-72, 91-93; chmn. prepaid legal svcs. com. Va. State Bar, Richmond, 1982-85, chair sr. lawyers sect., 1999; pres. Met. Legal Aid, Richmond, 1978 Del. to State Dem. Cong., Richmond, 1985; mem. Va. Commn. on Family Violence Prevention, 1995; bd. dirs. Henrico Cmty. Housing Corp., 1999. With USN, 1957-59. Recipient Svc. award, Criminal Law Bd. of Govs. for Pub. Defender Study, 1971, Outstanding Svc. award, Pub. Defender Commn., 1998. Mem. ABA, Va. Bar Assn. (chmn. criminal law sect. 1991-93), Richmond Bar Assn., Nat. Legal Aid and Defender Assn. (Reginald Heber Smith award 1991), Va. Bar Assn. (Pro Bono Publico award 1995). Democrat. Baptist. Avocation: fishing. Home: 7726 Sweetbriar Rd Richmond VA 23229-6622 Office: Pub Defender Commn 701 E Franklin St Ste 1416 Richmond VA 23219-2510 E-mail: opollard@pdcmail.state.va.us.

POLLARD, SHIRLEY, employment training director, consultant; b. Brunswick City, Va., July 8, 1939; 1 child, Darryl. Degree in bus. adminstrn., Upper Iowa U., 1978. Adminstr. East. Balt. Community Corp.; tng. coord. Balt. County Concentrated Employment Tng. Program; exec. dir. Park Heights Community Corp., Balt.; dir. Linkages, Inc. Contbr. articles to Afro Am. newspaper. Pres. Park Hts. Cmty. Devel. Corp., United Black Fund, Balt., 1989—, Presdl. Task Force, 1992; active Balt. Urban League, Balt. Welfare Rights Orgn.; founder, pres. Balt. County Polit. Action Coalition, 1982—; founder, dir. Linkages, Inc., 1980; founder, dir. Tng. and Placement Svcs., 1989; active United Svc. Orgn., Md. Minority Contractors Assn., U.S. Civil Rights Mus. and Hall of Fame, Smithsonian Instn.; founder African Am. Culture Ctr.; co-founder Project Lou, Inc.; founder The Afro Fund, Inc.; active Fund for a Free South Africa's Founding Assocs. Leadership Coun., Nat. Women's Hall of Fame, Nat. Abortion Rights Action League, Srs. Coalition, Md. Edn. Coalition, CORE, So. Christian Leadership Conf., Nat. Trust for Hist. Preservation; presdl. appointment Md. Selective Svc. Bd., 1993, Exec.

Com. of Am. Friends Svc. Com.; mem. women's adv. coun. Sinai Hosp., 1994—. Recipient Outstanding Achievement award Md. Minority Contractors Assn., Mayor's Citation, Martin Luther King Civil Rights award, 1987, Md. State Dept. Edn. award, 1987, congl. Achievement award, Kool Achiever awards, 1990, Nat. Black Caucus Spl. award, 1990, Congressional Achievement award, 1988, Svc. award The Writers Club, 1991, USO Meritorious Svc. award, 1991, Gov.'s Vol. award, 1992, Acad. of Excellence award, 1992, Signs of Hope award, 1995, Mayor's citation, 1984, Gov.'s citation, 1995, Senatorial award, 1995; recipient Bud Achiever award 1996. Mem. Am. Soc. Pers. Adminstrn., Am. Soc. Health/Manpower/Edn./Tng., Assn. for Providers Employment and Tng., NAACP (founder, pres. Randallstown chpt. 1988-95, Signs of Hope award), Balt. Coun. on Fgn. Affairs, Transafrica, USO, Md. Minority Contractors Assn. (Achievement award 1986, bd. dirs. 1984-89), Smithsonian Assoc., Md. C. of C. (greater Balt. com. 1985). Office: PO Box 32051 Baltimore MD 21282-2051

POLLARD, THOMAS DEAN, cell biologist, educator; b. Pasadena, Calif., July 7, 1942; s. Dean Randall and Florence Alma (Dierker) Pollard; m. Patricia Elizabeth Snowden, Feb. 7, 1964; children: Katherine Pollaed, Daniel. BA, Pomona Coll., Claremont, Calif., 1964; MD, Harvard U., 1968. Intern Mass. Gen. Hosp., Boston, 1968—69; staff assoc. NIH, Bethesda, Md., 1969—72; from asst. prof. to assoc. prof. Harvard Med. Sch., Boston, 1972—78; prof., dir. dept. cell biology and anatomy Johns Hopkins Sch. Medicine, Balt., 1977—96; pres. Salk Inst. for Biological Studies, LaJolla, Calif., 1996—2000, prof., 1996—, U. Calif., San Diego, 1996—2001; prof. molecular, cellular and devel. biology Yale U., 2001—. Mem. Commn. on Life Sci, NRC, 1990—97; chair Commn. on Life Sci., NRC, 1993—97; mem. coun. Nat. Inst. Gen. Med. Scis., NIH. Recipient Lewis S. Rosentiel Disting. Work in Basic Med. Rsch. award, Brandeis U., 1966; fellow, Guggenheim Found., 1984. Fellow: Am. Acad. Arts and Scis.; mem.: Marine Biol. Lab. (trustee 1991—97), Biophys. Soc. (pres. 1992—93), Am. Soc. Cell Biology (pres. 1987—88, K.R. Porter lectr., 1989, pres. 1987-88), Inst. Medicine, NAS. Office: Dept Molecular, Cellular and Developmental Biology Yale U PO Box 208103 New Haven CT 06520-8103 E-mail: thomas.pollard@yale.edu.

POLLARD, VINCENT KELLY, political science educator; b. Evergreen Park, Ill., Aug. 1, 1944; AB with honors, Maryknoll Coll., 1966; AM, U. Chgo., 1968; PhD, U. Hawaii-Manoa, 1998, cert. in Tagalog, 1995. Substitute tchr. Ill. Dist. 299, Chgo., 1988-89; rsch. asst. Hawaii Rsch. Ctr. for Futures Studies Social Sci. Rsch. Inst., U. Hawaii-Manoa, Honolulu, 1996-98; lectr. polit. sci. and Asian studies U. Hawaii-Manoa, 1998—. Vis. rsch. fellow dept. polit. sci. Coll. Social Scis. and Philosophy, U. Philippines-Diliman, 1995-96; adj. faculty Kansai Gaidai Hawaii Coll. (now TransPacific Hawaii Coll.), Honolulu, 1997-98; student interchanger Spl. English Program, Outreach Coll., U. Hawaii-Manoa, 1998, conf. coord. Ctr. for Japanese Studies, 1999-2000; vis. fellow program on edn. East-West Ctr., Honolulu, 1998-99; affiliate rsch. assoc. Yuchengo Ctr. for East Asia, De La Salle U., Manila, 1997—. Contbr. rsch. articles to profl. jours.; co-prodr., interviewer TV spls. Fulbright-Hays Study Abroad grantee, 1995-96, travel grantee U. Hawaii-Manoa, 1999, City of Chgo., Dept. Cultural Affairs, Cmty. Arts Assistance Program/Ill. Arts Coun. Access Program grantee, 1990; U.S. Dept. Edn. Fgn. Lang. and Area Studies fellow, 1994-96; Pacific Asian scholar U. Hawaii-Manoa, 1994-95. Mem. Internat. Studies Assn., Am. Polit. Sci. Assn., Assn. for Asian Studies, Fulbright Alumni Assn. (Hawaii. chpt.), Tau Pi chpt. Pi Sigma Alpha (charter mem., v.p., colloquium coord.). Avocations: hiking, music, cinema, learning languages. Office: U Hawaii-Manoa Dept Selected Studies & Honors Honolulu HI 96822-2223 E-mail: pollard@hawaii.edu.

POLLARD, WILLIAM BARLOW, III, university educator; b. Greenville, S.C., Nov. 24, 1946; s. William Barlow and Nellie Griffin (Martin) P.; m. Betty Kathryn Henley, Nov. 21, 1970; children: William Joseph, Jeremiah Martin. BA in English, Mars Hill Coll., 1969; MA, Appalachian State U., 1974; M in Accountancy, U. S.C., 1980, PhD, 1981. Pub. sch. tchr. Hendersonville (N.C.) City Sch., 1970-72; tchg. asst. Appalachian State U., Boone, N.C., 1973-75, instr. acctg., 1976-77, prof. of acctg., 1981—; tchg. asst. U. S.C., 1978-80. Contbr. articles to profl. jours. With USAR, 1968-75. Mem. Am. Acctg. Assn., Inst. of Mgmt. Accts. Office: Appalachian State U Dept Acctg Boone NC 28608-0001

POLLARD-GOTT, LUCY, writer; b. Endicott, NY, May 20, 1957; d. Frank Trich and Virginia (Claxton) Pollard; m. J. Richard Gott III, June 10, 1978; 1 child, Elizabeth Marjorie. BA summa cum laude, Princeton U., 1978, PhD in Psychology, 1981. Psychology jour. editor Lawrence Erlbaum Assocs., Inc., Mahwah, N.J., 1985-95; writer Carol Pub. Group, N.Y.C., 1995-98; website designer, mgr. pvt. practice, 1998—. Admissions cons. Princeton (N.J.) U., 1985-86; abstract preparation cons. ERIC Document Svc., Princeton, 1987. Mem. editl. bd. Discourse Processes, 1983-93; contbr. articles to profl. jours. Nat. Merit scholar, 1974; Pre-doctoral fellow NSF, 1978-81, Postdoctoral fellow USPHS, 1981-82. Mem.: Phi Beta Kappa. Avocations: mandolin, yoga. Home and Office: 63 Cartwright Dr Princeton Junction NJ 08550-1934 E-mail: lucy@fictional100.com.

POLLARO, PAUL PHILIP, artist; b. N.Y.C., Aug. 2, 1921; s. Charles and Maria (Aprile) P.; m. Jo Ann Stover, July 16, 1962 (div. Nov. 1979); children: Lauren, Paul Jr.; m. Laura Clayton, Apr. 2, 1985. Student, Art Students League, 1945-48, Pratt Graphic Ctr., 1972. Instr. painting The New Sch. of Social Rsch., N.Y.C., 1964-69; vis. artist Notre Dame U., South Bend, Ind., 1965-67; asst. prof. art, chmn. art dept. Wagner Coll., Staten Island, N.Y., 1970-73; asst. dir. The MacDowell Colony, Peterborough, N.H., 1973-76; pvt. practice Hancock, 1976—. One-man shows include Jersey City Mus., N.J., 1966 (second prize), S.I. Mus. Art, N.Y., 1973, Manchester Inst. Arts and Scis., Manchester, N.H., 1970-85, Chryser Mus., Norfolk, Va., 1991, numerous others. Sgt. U.S. Army, 1942-45, PTO. Tiffany Found. grantee, N.Y.C., 1967, N.H. State Coun. Arts grantee, 1985; The MacDowell Colony fellow, 1965-69. Roman Catholic. Home: Norway Hill Hancock NH 03449

POLLET, ELIZABETH, retired writer, educator; b. N.Y.C. d. Joseph Pollet and Emily Hannah Smith; m. Delmore Schwartz (div.). BA, U. Chgo., 1948; MA, NYU, 1965, PhD, 1978. Instr. Rutgers U., Newark, 1967-73; guest writing faculty Sarah Lawrence Coll., Bronxville, N.Y., 1973-75; adj. asst. prof. NYU, 1981-92. Author: A Family Romance, 1951; editor: Portrait of Delmore: Journals and Notes, 1939-59, 1986. Mem.: PEN.

POLLET, SUSAN L. lawyer; b. Manhasset, N.Y., Dec. 17, 1954; d. Myron J. and Barbara Audrey (Kananack) Feldman; m. Richard Pollet, June 30, 1985; children: Katharine Ann, Eve Whitney. BS in Consumer Econ. and Pub. Policy, Cornell U., 1976; JD, Emory U., 1979. Bar: Ga. 1979, N.Y. 1980. Legal asst. ICC Industries, Inc., N.Y.C., 1979; lawyer Dwyer, Peltz & Walker, 1980-82, Acito & Klein P.C., N.Y.C., 1982-84; supervising atty. litigation Long Island Lighting Co., Hicksville, N.Y., 1984-86; part-time county atty. Westchester County Family Ct., Putnam County Dept. of Social Svcs., 1994-97; sr. ct. atty. Westchester County Family Ct., N.Y., 1997—. Adj. prof. Mercy Coll., N.Y., 1991-97; pvt. practice, 1988-97; law guardian for children, 1988-97. Contbr. articles to profl. jours. Legal facilitator P.E.A.C.E. Program; active 9th Jud. Dist. Task Force; nominating com. Temple Bethel, 1999—2001; bd. dirs. Chappaqua Children's Workshop, 1991—92, Pleasantville Children's Ctr., 1988—89; amb. Cornell Alumni Admissions, 1991—. Mem.: Women's Bar Assn. of the State of N.Y. (state dir. 1997—2002, co-chair legis. com. 1999—2001, v.p. 2001—02, co-chair legal rights of children com. 2001—02), Westchester County Bar Assn. (family ct. com. 1991—92), Westchester Women's Bar Assn. (v.p. 1993—95, pres. 1995—97), Westchester Children's Assn. (bd. dirs. 2000—, Gagliardi award com. 2002). Avocations: reading, art, hiking, writing. Home: 67 Ludlow Dr Chappaqua NY 10514-1222 E-mail: richsue67@aol.com.

POLLEY, CLAUDIA ANNE, film and radio producer, preservation consultant; b. Indpls., Oct. 21, 1949; d. Sherman James Polley Jr. and Jean Elizabeth (Douglas) Spears; children: Amanda, Evan. MusM, Stanford U., 1967; diploma, Juilliard Sch., 1971. Profl. singer, N.Y.C., Paris, 1967-72, 76-80; reporter, host talk show Sta. WNBC, N.Y.C., 1968-70, 74-76, Sta. KLJU, L.A., 1980-81; mgmt. cons. Dance Kaleidoscope, Indpls., 1982-83; devel. dir. In State Dem. Party, 1983-84; pres. AmeriAccord Found., Paris, 1987-88; newscaster Nat. Pub. Radio, Washington, 1989-92; freelance film and radio prodr. Indpls., N.Y.C., 1992—. Exec. prod. Mapleshade Records, 1989-91 (Downbeat Best Sound award 1991), (films) What's Love Got to Do With It, 1992, From the Mind's Eye, 1992; prodr. (film) Portrait of M. Horszowski. Nat. staff mem. George McGovern for Pres., 1971-72; chair African-Am. Landmarks Com., Indpls., 1992—; bd. dirs. Phoenix Theater, Indpls., 1984-85, 93—, Chamber Music Am., N.Y.C., 1991—, Historic Landmarks Found. of Ind., 1993—; advisor Black Film Ctr. Archive Ind. U., 1993—. Mem. NARAS, Nat. Assn. Black Journalists (founding dir. 1975—), Black Filmmakers Found., Radio TV News Dirs. Assn., Chamber Music Am., Film Soc. Lincoln Soc. Presbyterian. Home: 849 Camp St Indianapolis IN 46202-3049

POLLEY, HARVEY LEE, retired missionary, math and science educator; b. Wapato, Wash., Aug. 14, 1924; s. Edward Prestley and Alda June Polley; m. Corinne Weber; children: Catherine, David, Corinne, Robert. BA, Whitworth Coll., Spokane, Wash., 1951; postgrad., East Wash. Coll., 1953, Berkeley Bapt. Div. Sch., 1958-59; MEd, Cen. Wash. Coll., 1958; postgrad., Ecole d'Adminstrn. des Affaires Africaines, Brussels, 1959-60. Tchr. Quincy (Wash.) Pub. Schs., 1953-57, N.W. Christian Schs., Spokane, 1958; missionary Am. Bapt. Fgn. Missionary Soc., Zaire, 1958-89; tchr. Evang. Pedagogical Inst., Kimpese, Zaire, 1961-69, asst. legal rep., dir., prin., supt. Zaire, 1969-72; dir. BIM Hostel, Kinshasa, Zaire, 1972-73; mem. staff Ctr. for Agrl. Devel. Lusekele, Zaire, 1975-85, dir. Zaire, 1976-79, 83-85, Plateau Bateke Devel. Program, Kinshasa, 1985-89; ret., 1989. Author: Mpila Kele, a rural development guide written in the Kituba lang., 1989. Mem. Coun. Elders, Kimpese, 1969-72; pres. bd. adminstrn. Vanga (Zaire) Hosp., 1981-83; mem. exec. com. Nat. Human Nutrition Planning Coun. Govt. Zaire-USAID, Kikwit, 1983-85. With U.S. Army, 1946-47, USAF, 51-53. Home: 2405 W Johansen Rd Spokane WA 99208-9616

POLLEY, TERRY LEE, lawyer; b. Long Beach, Calif., June 2, 1947; s. Frederick F. and Geraldine E. (Davis) P.; m. Patricia Yamanoha, Aug. 4, 1973; children: Todd, Matthew. AB, UCLA, 1970; JD, Coll. William and Mary, 1973. Bar: Calif. 1973, U.S. Tax Ct. 1974, U.S. Supreme Ct. 1987. Assoc. Loeb & Loeb, L.A., 1973-78; ptnr. Ajalat, Polley & Ayoob, 1978—. Lectr. taxation law U. So.Calif., 1978-94. Author (with Charles R. Ajalat) California's Water's Edge Legislation, 1987; contbr. articles to profl. jours, legal jours.; editorial bd. William and Mary Law Rev. Chmn. bd. dirs. Greater Long Beach Christian Schs., 1988-92, sec., 1994-99; elder Grace Brethren Ch., Long Beach, 1988—. Mem. ABA (state and local tax com. 1973-92), Calif. Bar Assn. (chmn. taxation sect. 1990-91, exec. com. 1987-92, state and local tax com. 1975—, taxation sect., recipient V. Judson Klein award 1993), L.A. County Bar Assn. (exec. com. 1980-87, chmn. exec. com. 1985-86, taxation sect.), Nat. Assn. State Bar Tax Sects. (exec. com. 1990—, chmn. 1995-96, treas. 1998—). Republican. Office: Ajalat Polley & Ayoob 643 S Olive St Ste 200 Los Angeles CA 90014-1651

POLLI, ROBERT PAUL, lawyer; b. Miami, Fla., Nov. 22, 1947; s. Silas Frederick and Ann Martha (Papada) P.; m. Carolyn Jane Albritton, June 13, 1974. BA, U. South Fla., 1969, MA, 1971, 78; JD, Stetson U., 1983. Bar: Fla. 1983. Tchr. Project Headstart, various locations, 1968-69; exceptional child educator Hillsborough County Schs., Tampa, Fla., 1974-76, guidance counselor, 1976-80; profl. photographer Tampa, 1972—; assoc. Bennie Lazzara, Jr., P.A., 1983-87; ptnr. Lazzara, Caskey, Polli and Paul, 1987-91, Law Firm Robert P. Polli, P.A., Tampa, 1991—. Contbr. articles to profl. jours. Mem. ABA, Fla. Bar Assn. (chmn. grievance com.), Fla. Assn. Criminal Def. Lawyers, Hillsborough County Assn. Criminal Def. Lawyers (pres.). Democrat. Roman Catholic. Office: PO Box 1427 Kilauea HI 96754

POLLICOVE, HARVEY MYLES, manufacturing executive; b. Utica, N.Y., May 28, 1944; s. Maxwell Hymen and Carolyn (Vogel) P.; m. Catherine Mary Keady, Aug. 3, 1968; children: Carolyn, Sarah. AAS, Monroe Community Coll., 1968; BS, U. Rochester, 1973. Sr. engr. supr. optics Eastman Kodak Co., Rochester, 1978-82, engrng. mgr. optics, 1982-84, mfg. mgr., 1984-86, mgr. tech. mkts. (internat.), 1986-89; dir. Ctr. for Optics Mfg. U. Rochester, 1989—. U.S. del. (optics) to Internat. Stds. Orgn., 1995—; chmn. Optics and Electro-Optics Standards Coun., 1999—; hon. advisor Hong Kong Photographic and Optics Mfrs. Assn., 2000; lectr. in field. Editorial adv. bd. (optics mag. for mfg.) Laser Focus World, 1990-2000; contbr. articles to profl. jours. Advisor High Tech. of Rochester, 1988-89; advisor tech. applications rev. bd. Strategic Def. Initiative Orgn., 1990-92, Ballistic Missile Def. Orgn., 1993-96; industry advisor Monroe C.C., 1986-97. Recipient Dept. of Def. Mfg. Tech. Achievement award, 1992, 2000. Mem. ASME/Optics Stds. (chmn.), Am. Precision Optics Mfrs. Assn. (exec. com. 1987—), Internat. Soc. for Optical Engring., Optical Soc. Am. (hon. mem. Rochester sect. 1996), Optics and Electro-Optics Stds. Coun. Home: 177 Georgian Court Rd Rochester NY 14610-3416 Office: U Rochester Ctr for Optics Mfg 240 E River Rd Rochester NY 14623-1212

POLLIHAN, THOMAS HENRY, lawyer; b. St. Louis, Nov. 15, 1949; s. C.H. and Patricia Ann (O'Brien) P.; m. Donna M. Bickhaus, Aug. 25, 1973; 1 child, Emily Christine. BA in Sociology, Quincy U., 1972; JD, U. Notre Dame, 1975; Exec. Masters in Internat. Bus., St. Louis U., 1992. Bar: Mo. 1975, Ill. 1976. Jud. law clk. to judge Mo. Ct. of Appeals, St. Louis, 1975-76; from assoc. to ptnr. Greenfield, Davidson, Mandelstamm & Voorhees, 1976-82; asst. gen. counsel Kellwood Co., 1982-89, gen. counsel, sec., 1989-93, v.p., sec., gen. counsel, 1993—2002, sr. v.p., 2002—. Trustee Quincy (Ill.) U., 1987-93, 97—, pres. alumni bd., 1986-87; pres. S.W. Neighborhood Improvement Assn., St. Louis, 1984, Quincy (Ill.) U. Found., 1993-94, 97—; dir., sec. New Piasa Chautauqua, Ill., 1996-97. Named Quincy U. Alumnus of Yr., 1997. Mem. Bar Assn. Met. St. Louis. Roman Catholic. Avocations: soccer, cycling. Home: 415 Spring Ave Saint Louis MO 63119-2634 Office: Kellwood Co 600 Kellwood Pkwy Ste 300 Chesterfield MO 63017-5897 E-mail: tom_pollihan@kellwood.com.

POLLIN, ABE, professional basketball team executive, builder; b. Phila., Dec. 3, 1923; s. Morris and Jennie (Sack) P.; m. Irene S. Kerchek, May 27, 1945; children: Robert Norman, James Edward. BA, George Washington U., 1945; student, U. Md., 1941-44. Engaged in home bldg. bus., 1945—; pres. Abe Pollin Inc., Balt., 1962—; chmn. Balt. Bullets Basketball Club, Inc. (now Washington Bullets), 1964-97, Washington Wizards, 1997—; chmn. bd., CEO Washington Sports & Entertainment, Washington. Dir. County Fed. Savs. & Loan Assn., Rockville, Md. Bd. dirs. United Jewish Appeal, Nat. Jewish Hosp., Jewish Community Center; bd. dirs., adv. com. John F. Kennedy Cultural Center. Mem. Nat. Assn. Home Builders, Asso. Builders and Contractors Md., Washington Bd. Trade. Jewish. Office: Washington Wizards 718 7th St NW Washington DC 20001-3716 also: Washington Capitals US Air Arena Landover MD 20785 also: Washington Sports & Entertainment MCI Ctr 601 F St NW Washington DC 20004-1605*

POLLIN, BURTON RALPH, English educator; b. Worcester, Mass. s. Louis and Rae (Cohen) P.; m. Alice Pollin, Jan. 30, 1944; children: Diana Claire, Myles Clement. BA, CCNY, 1936; PhD, Columbia U., 1962. Tchr. English N.Y.C. Bd. of Edn., 1936-62, chmn. dept. English, 1956-62; lectr. English CUNY, 1957-62, assoc. prof. to full prof., 1962-73, prof. emeritus, 1973—. Author: Education and Enlightenment in the Works of William Godwin, 1962, Godwin Criticism: A Synoptic Bibliography, 1967, Dictionary of Names and Titles in Poe's Collected Works, 1968, Discoveries in Poe, 1970, Benjamin Constant's Translation of Godwin's Political Justice, 1972, The Music for Shelley's Poems: An Annotated Bibliography of 1309 Compositions, 1974, Poe, Creator of Words, 1974, The Imaginary Voyages, vol. 1 of Collected Writings of...Poe, 1994, Word Index to Poe's Fiction, 1982, The Brevities of Poe, vol. 2 of Collected Writings of Poe, 1985, Poe's Writings in the Broadway Jour., 1986, Insights and Outlooks: Essays on Great Writers, 1986, Images of Poe's Works: A Comprehensive Descriptive Catalogue of Illustrations, 1989, The German Face of Poe (with Thomas Hansen), 1995, Poe's Writings in the Southern Literary Messenger, vol. 5 of Collected Writings of Poe, 1986; adv. bd. editors Poe Studies, 1980—, Poe Rev., 2000—; contbr. over 180 scholarly articles to profl. jours. Founder, mem. continuing bd. dirs. Bronxville Beautification Coun., 1980—; mem. Friends of N.Y. Pub. Libr., Carnegie Hall, Poe Mus., Richmond, Va., Libr. of Bronxville, Eastchester Arts Coun., Columbia U. Libr. Friends, Supporters of Guggenheim Found. Recipient Poe award of Lit. excellence, Bronx County Hist. Soc., 2001; Rotary Club award, Alice and Burton Pollin for effective beautification of Bronxville, 2002; John Hay Whitney fellow, 1947; grantee Am. Philos. Soc., London, 1963, 65, U.S., 1964-65, Am. Coun. Learned Socs., 1968, 75, 84, SUNY, 1968, 70-71, 72, 73, NEH, 1983-84, N.Y. State U. Rsch. Found., 1966, SUNY, 1967, 68, 69, 73, CUNY, 1973, 80, 86, Guggenheim Found., 1973-74; Carl and Lily Pforzheimer grantee, 1966, 69, . Mem. MLA (life), Poe Studies Assn., Am. Lit. Assn. Avocations: piano playing, travel, environmentalism. Home: 3 Stoneleigh Plz Apt 4D Bronxville NY 10708

POLLINGER, WILLIAM JOSHUA, lawyer; b. Passaic, N.J., Dec. 14, 1944; s. Irving R. and Ethel (Groudan) P.; m. Helen Rizzo, May 30, 1977; children: Samantha, Zachary. BA, Rutgers U., 1966; JD, Am. U., 1969. Bar: N.J. 1969, U.S. Dist. Ct. N.J. 1969, N.Y. 1981, U.S. Supreme Ct. 1982, U.S. Ct. Appeals (3d cir.) 1986; cert. Civil Trial Atty. N.J. Supreme Ct., 1983; masters level cert. U.S.A. Track and Field Ofcl. Assoc. Krieger & Klein, Passaic, 1969-75; ptnr. Delorenzo & Pollinger, Hackensack, N.J., 1975-84; pres. William J. Pollinger, P.A., 1984-88, Pollinger, Fearns & Kemezis, P.A., 1988-90, Pollinger & Fearns, P.A., Hackensack, 1990-92, William J. Pollinger P.A., Hackensack, N.J., 1992—. Mem. Bergen County Ethics Com., NJ, 1984—88; lectr. ins. N.J.-ICLE. Arbitrator Better Bus. Bur. of Bergen and Rockland Counties, Paramus, N.J., 1983-89, Am. Arbitration Assn., 1983—. Assoc. of Yr. award Builders Assn. No. N.J., Paramus, 1981. Master: Justice Robert L. Clifford Am. Inn of Ct.; mem.: ATLA, Def. Rsch. Inst., Am. Arbitration Assn., Trial Attys. N.J., Bergen County Bar Assn., N.J. State Bar Assn. (ins. law com.), Masons (past master), Masons (past master), Phi Delta Phi. Avocation: track and field officiating. Office: 302 Union St Hackensack NJ 07601-4303

POLLINI, FRANCIS, author; b. West Wyoming, Pa., Sept. 9, 1930; s. Sem and Assunta (Ciani) P.; m. Gloria Ann Swann, Sept. 12, 1959; children: Susanne, Lisa. BA in Psychology, Pa. State U., 1951. Author: Night, 1959, Glover, 1965, Excursion, 1966, The Crown, 1967, Three Plays, 1967, Pretty Maids All In a Row, 1968, Dubonnet, 1973, The Hall, 1975. 1st lt. USAF, 1952-57. Home: 14 Oak Ln Hingham NR9 4JY Norfolk England

POLLIO, RALPH THOMAS, editor, writer, magazine publishing consultant; b. Bronx, N.Y., Nov. 1, 1948; s. Thomas and Dolores (Miccioli) P.; m. Rita Lucia Napolitano, Sept. 29, 1974; 1 child, Christopher. BCE, Manhattan Coll., 1978; postgrad., Columbia U., 1988—. Founding pub., editor, owner Ea. Basketball Publs., Franklin Square, N.Y., 1975-88; cons., ptnr., founder Ea. Basketball Mag., Rochester, Mich., 1988—; founding pub., owner, editor High School News, 1984, EB News, 1981; editor Harmon Consumer Group, Woodbury, N.Y. Contbr. articles to mags. and profl. jours., 1985—. Sgt. U.S. Army N.G., 1969-74. Mem. U.S. Basketball Writers Assn. (1st Place award for best mag. feature 1984), ASCE, Soc. Profl. Journalists, Sigma Delta Chi, Internat. Soc. Philos. Enquiry, World Lit. Acad., Mag. Pubs. Assn., Am. Soc. Mag. Editors, Mensa, and numerous other high IQ socs. Roman Catholic. Clubs: N.Y. Road Runners (N.Y.C.), Dix Hills Runners. Avocations: running, listening to jazz, gourmet cooking, reading, film. Home: 1201 Hempstead Ave Malverne NY 11565-1213

POLLITT, JEROME JORDAN, art history educator; b. Fair Lawn, N.J., Nov. 26, 1934; s. John Kendall and Doris B. (Jordan) P.; m. Susan Baker Matheson, Feb. 10, 1977. BA, Yale U., 1957; PhD, Columbia U., 1963. Instr. history of art Yale U., New Haven, 1962-64, asst. prof., 1964-68, assoc. prof., 1969-73, prof., 1973-98, prof. emeritus, 1998—, chmn. dept. classics, 1975-77, chmn. dept. history of art, 1981-84, dean, 1986-91. Author: Art and Experience in Classical Greece, 1972, The Ancient View of Greek Art, 1975, Art in the Hellenistic Age, 1986, The Art of Greece: Sources and Documents, 1990, Personal Styles in Greek Sculpture, 1996; editor-in-chief: Am. Jour. Archaeology, 1973-77; contbr. articles to profl. jours. Mem. Archaeol. Inst. Am., Coll. Art Assn. Home: 48 Dillon Rd Woodbridge CT 06525-1219 Office: Dept History of Art Yale U PO Box 208272 New Haven CT 06520-8272 E-mail: Jerome.Pollitt@yale.edu.

POLLITT, PHOEBE ANN, school nurse; b. Washington, Mar. 29, 1954; d. Daniel Hubbard and Jean Ann (Rutledge) P.; m. David Randolph Paletta, July 1, 1977 (div. Dec. 1989); children: Douglas, Andrew. BS in Nursing, U. N.C., 1977; MA in Edn., Appalachian State U., 1989; PhD in Curriculum and Instrn., U. N.C., Greensboro, 1994. Pub. health nurse Durham County Health Dept., Durham, N.C., 1977-80; disability devel. specialist Appalachian Devel. Evaluation Ctr., Boone, 1980-81; home health nurse Watauga County Health Dept., 1981-82; nursing instr. Caldwell C.C., Lenoir, N.C., 1989-91; adj. prof. nursing Winston-Salem (N.C.) State U., 1990—; sch. nurse, health edn. coord. Watauga County Schs., Boone, 1991—. Sec. Watauga County Adolescent Pregnancy Coalition, Boone, 1991—; mem. exec. com. Watauga County Healthy Carolinas 2000, Boone, 1993—; mem. statewide exec. com. Smoke Free 2000, Raleigh, 1994; mem. exec. bd. Watauga County Alcohol and Other Drugs Coun., Boone, 1993. Contbr. articles to profl. jours. Alumni fellow Appalachian State U., 1988, 89; recipient Certs. of Appreciation, Am. Heart Assn., 1992, 93, Hospitality House, 1987, 88, 89, Outstanding Vol. award N.C. Gov. Jim Hunt, 1989, Plaque of Appreciation, OASIS, 1992, Hist. Article award N.C. Hist. Soc., 1994; grantee Arts Coun., 1982, Appalachian State U., 1989, U. N.C., Greensboro, 1991, Healthful Living Sect., Dept. Pub. Instrn., 1992, 93, Janirve Corp., Asheville, N.C., 1992, Project Assist, 1996, N.C. Dept. Pub. Instrn., 1996, Watauga Ednl. Found., 1996. Mem. ANA, N.C. Nurse Assn. (named Great 100 Nurses 1995), Sch. Nurse Assn. N.C. (mem. exec. com., membership chair 1994), Dist. 23 Nurse assn., Sigma Theta Tau. Democrat. Unitarian-Universalist. Avocations: cooking, gardening, knitting, hiking, camping. Home: 554 Dogwood Rd Boone NC 28607-4556 Office: Watauga County Bd Edn PO Box 1790 Boone NC 28607-1790

POLLITT, RAYMOND DANIEL JOHN, writer, consultant; b. Berwyn, Ill., July 9, 1958; s. Raymond Douglas and Jean Isabel Pollitt; m. Judy Marie Pollitt, Sept. 1, 1983; 1 child, Geoffrey Richard. Assocs. degree, Morton Coll., 1985. Owner, pres. Daniel John Pollitt Enterprises, Riverside, Ill., 1983—. Avocations: origami, woodworking. Office: DJPE PO Box 1383 Riverside IL 60546-1383

POLLITZER, WILLIAM SPROTT, anatomy educator; b. Charleston, S.C., May 6, 1923; s. Richard Morris and Cora (Sprott) P.; m. Margaret Buhlig, Aug. 29, 1955; children— Virginia, Patricia AB, Emory U., 1944, MA, 1947; PhD, Columbia U., 1957. Instr. anatomy U. N.C., Chapel Hill, 1957-59, asst. prof., 1959-67, assoc. prof., 1967-73, prof., 1973-87, emeritus prof., 1987-99; ret. Contbr. articles to profl. jours. Served with U.S. Army, 1944-47 Mem. Am. Assn. Phys. Anthropologists (v.p. 1978-79, pres. 1979-81, editor jour. 1970-77), Human Biology Council (pres. 1986-88) Democrat. Home: Chapel Hill, NC. Died Mar. 12, 2002.

POLLOCK, ALEXANDER JOHN, banker; b. Indpls., Jan. 28, 1943; s. Alex S. and Doris L. (VanHorn) P.; m. Anne M. Fryfogle, Jan. 27, 1968; children: Elizabeth, Alexander, Evelyn, James. BA, Williams Coll., 1965; MA, U. Chgo., 1966; M.P.A., Princeton U., 1969. Instr. philosophy Lake Forest Coll., (Ill.), 1967; with internat. banking dept. Continental Ill. Nat. Bank, Chgo., 1969-77, v.p., 1977-82, sr. v.p., 1982-85; prin. Nolan Norton & Co., 1985-86; chief fin. officer Marine Corp., Milw., 1986; pres. Marine Bank N.A., 1987; pres., CEO Cmty. Fed. Savs., St. Louis, 1988-90; vis. scholar Fed. Res. Bank of St. Louis, 1991; pres., CEO Fed. Home Loan Bank Chgo., 1991—. Life mem. Ctr. for Fin. Insts. and Mkts.; bd. dirs. Gt. Lakes Higher Edn. Corp.; past pres. Internat. Union for Housing Fin. Trustee Ill. Coun. on Econ. Edn.; Bd. dirs. Great Books Found. Mem.: Union League Club, Bankers Club of Chgo. (past pres.), Phi Beta Kappa. Office: Fed Home Loan Bank Chgo 8th Fl 111 E Wacker Dr Chicago IL 60601-4204 E-mail: alex_pollock@fhlbc.com. *Omnia superans vi rationis et arte loquendi.*

POLLOCK, BRADLEY NEIL, lawyer; b. St. Charles, Ill., Sept. 23, 1970; s. Neil Edward and Karen Irene Pollock; m. Tara Lynne Kozlowski, Aug. 23, 1997; 1 child, Kent Bradley. BA with distinction, U. Ill., 1992; JD, Loyola U., Chgo., 1995. Bar: Ill. 1995, U.S. Dist. Ct. (no. dist.) Ill. 1995. Assoc. Williams & Montgomery, Ltd., Chgo., 1995, Robert N. Wadington & Assocs., Chgo., 1995-2000, Walsh, Knippen, Knight & Diamond, Wheaton, Ill., 2000—. Recipient Am. Jurisprudence award in Appellate Practice Lawyers Coop. Pub., 1993. Mem. ATLA, Ill. Bar Assn., DuPage County Bar Assn., Ill. Trial Lawyers Assn. Avocations: fly fishing, backpacking, other outdoor activities. Home: IN281 Prairie Ave Glen Ellyn IL 60137 Office: Walsh Knippen Knight & Diamond 601 W Liberty Dr Wheaton IL 60187

POLLOCK, BRUCE GODFREY, psychiatrist, educator; b. Toronto, Ont., Can., Aug. 18, 1952; s. Ira Justus and Sheila Joy (Godfrey) P.; m. Judith Arluk, May 18, 1982; children: Debra, Ariel. BS, U. Toronto, 1975, MD, 1979; PhD, U. Pitts., 1987. Chief resident Clarke Inst. Psychiatry, Toronto, 1982-83; fellow U. Pitts., 1983-84, asst. prof. dept. psychiatry, 1984-90, assoc. dir. clin. pharmacology dept. psychiatry, 1987-95, assoc. prof. dept. psychiatry and pharmacology, 1990-96, dir. geriat. psychopharm. dept. psychiatry and pharmacology, 1995—, prof. dept. psychiatry and pharmacology, 1997—, chief acad. divsn. geriatrics and neuropsychiatry, 2001. Contbr. over 200 articles to profl. jours.; contbg. author books in field. Centennial fellow Med. Rsch. Coun. of Can., Ottawa, 1983, Merck fellow geriatric clin. pharmacology, Am. Fedn. for Aging Rsch., N.Y.C., 1988; recipient Geriat. Mental Health award NIMH, Bethesda, Md., 1992, Ind. Scientist award, 1997, Sr. Investigation Award, Am. Assoc. for Geniatric Psychiatry, Bethesda, Md., 2002. Fellow Royal Coll. Physicians Can. Home: 7032 Meade St Pittsburgh PA 15208-2429 Office: Western Psychiat Inst/Clin 3811 Ohara St Pittsburgh PA 15213-2593 E-mail: pollockbg@msx.upmc.edu.

POLLOCK, BRUCE GERALD, lawyer; b. Providence, Feb. 18, 1947; s. Reuben and Stella (Reitman) P.; m. Sheri Barbara Tepper, Dec. 21, 1969; children: Dawn, Meah. BA, U. R.I., 1968; JD, Suffolk U., 1974. Bar: R.I. 1974, U.S. Supreme Ct. 1978, U.S. Dist. Ct. R.I. 1980. Law clk. R.I. Superior Ct., Providence, 1974, adminstrv. asst. to chief justice, 1975; asst. pub. defender R.I. Dept. Pub. Defender, 1975-80; pvt. practice Warwick and West Warwick, R.I., 1980—. Adj. instr. So. N.E. Law Sch., New Bedford, Mass., 1990. Dist. chmn. Narragansett Coun. Shawomet Dist. Boy Scouts Am., 1996-98. Fellow R.I. Bar Found. (bd. dirs. 1990-2000; v.p. 2000—); mem. ABA, Nat. Conf. Bar Pres., New Eng. Bar Assn. (del. 1991-93), R.I. Bar Assn. (pres. 1992-93, award of merit 1995). Democrat. Avocations: golf, skiing, stained glass craftsman, bicycling, Tai Chi. Office: 45 Providence St West Warwick RI 02893-3714 E-mail: brucepollock@juno.com., bgpollock@yahoo.com.

POLLOCK, DALE MICHAEL, dean; b. Cleve., May 18, 1950; s. Henry and Leona Pollock; m. Susan Margaret O'Keeffe, Dec. 23, 1973; children: Owen, Leo, Zoe. BA, Brandeis U., 1972; MS, San Jose State U., 1976. Co-founder Orson Welles Cinema, Cambridge, Mass., 1969-71; reporter Santa Cruz (Calif.) Sentinel, 1975-77; reporter/critic Daily Variety, Hollywood, Calif., 1977-80; chief film writer L.A. Times, 1980-85; devel. exec. Geffen Films, Beverly Hills, Calif., 1985-86; pres. A&M Films, Hollywood, 1986-90, Peak Prodns., Santa Monica, Calif., 1990—; dean sch. of filmmaking N.C. Sch. of the Arts, Winston-Salem, 1999—. Author: (biography) Skywalking: The Life and Films of George Lucas, 1984; prodr. (films): Blaze, 1989, A Midnight Clear, 1991, House of Cards, 1992 (Best Picture Houston Worldfest 1992), Mrs. Winterbourne, 1996, Set It Off, 1997. Mem. Gov.'s Task Force on Film, Raleigh, 1999. Mem. N.C. Film Coun., Am. Film Inst. (co-chair producing program 1996-99), Acad. Motion Picture Arts and Scis. (prodrs. br.), Winston-Salem Downtown Rotary. Avocations: collecting film posters, hiking, travel. Office: Sch of Filmmaking NC Sch of the Arts 1533 S Main St Winston Salem NC 27127-2738 Fax: 336-770-1339. E-mail: pollockd@ncarts.edu.

POLLOCK, EARL EDWARD, lawyer; b. Decatur, Nebr., Feb. 24, 1928; s. Herman and Della (Rosenthal) P.; m. Betty Sokol, Sept. 8, 1951; children: Stephen, Della, Naomi. BA, U. Minn., 1948; JD, Northwestern U., 1953; LLD (hon.), Morningside Coll., 1995. Bar: D.C. 1955, Va. 1955, Ill. 1959, U.S. Supreme Ct. 1960. Law clk., chief justices Vinson and Warren, U.S. Supreme Ct. Washington, 1953-55; atty. antitrust div. Dept. Justice, Washington, 1955-56, asst. to solicitor gen., 1956-59; ptnr. Sonnenschein Nath & Rosenthal, Chgo., 1959—. Trustee Loyola U., Chgo., 1983-92; life trustee Northwestern Meml. Hosp.; dir. Fla. West Coast Symphony. Mem. Chgo. Bar Assn. (chmn. antitrust law com. 1967-68), ABA (chmn. antitrust law sect. 1979-80), Alumni Assn. Northwestern U. Sch. Law (pres. 1974-75, svc. award 1976). Office: Sonnenschein Nath 233 S Wacker Dr Ste 8000 Chicago IL 60606-6491

POLLOCK, GEORGE HOWARD, psychiatrist, psychoanalyst; b. Chgo., June 19, 1923; s. Harry J. and Belle (Lurie) P.; m. Beverly Yufit, July 3, 1946; children: Beth L. Pollock Ungar, Raphael E., Daniel A., Benjamin B., Naomi R. Pollock Sneider. BS, U. Ill., 1944, MD cum laude, 1945, MS, 1948, PhD, 1951. Diplomate Am. Bd. Psychiatry and Neurology. Intern Cook County Hosp., Chgo., 1945-46; resident Ill. Neuropsychiat. Inst., 1948-51; practice medicine, specializing in psychiatry, 1948-91. Clin. assoc. prof. dept. psychiatry Coll. Medicine, U. Ill., 1955-64, clin. prof., 1964-72; prof. psychiatry Northwestern U., 1972-93, Dunbar prof. psychiatry and behavioral scis. emeritus, 1993—, dir. rsch. dept. psychiatry/behavioral scis.m 1988-93, emeritus, 1993—; faculty Inst. for Psychoanalysis, Chgo., 1956-92, asst. dean edn., 1960-67, tng. analyst 1961-92, supervising analyst, 1962-92, dir. rsch., 1963-71, pres., 1971-89; exch. program participant Hampstead Child Therapy Clinic, 1962-63; pres. Ctr. Psychosocial Studies, 1972-90 Chmn. bd. editors Ann. of Psychoanalysis, 1971-89; mem. editorial bd. Jour. Am. Psychoanalytic Assn., 1971-74; mem. editorial bd. sect. psychoanalysis Psychiat. Jour. U. Ottawa Faculty Medicine, 1976—; corr. editor Jour. Geriatric Psychiatry, 1975—; Med. Problems of Performing Artists, Psychoanalytic Edn., Psychoanalytic Psychology, Internat. Forum for Psychoanalysis, Internat. Jour. Behavioral Scis. and the Law, Internat. Psychogeriatrics, Depression and Stress. Mem. med. adv. com. Planned Parenthood Assn., 1966-70; pres. governing bd. Parents Assn. Lab. Schs., U. Chgo., 1966-70; mem. med. adv. coun. Asthma and Allergy Found. for Greater Chgo. Capt. U.S. Army, 1946-48. Commonwealth fellow, 1951; research grantee Founds. Fund for Research in Psychiatry, 1960-65 Fellow Am. Coll. Psychiatrists, Am. Orthopsychiat. Assn., Am. Psychiat. Assn. (treas. 1980-86, pres. 1987-88), Am. Coll. Psychoanalysts (pres. 1985-86); mem. Internat. Psychogeriatrics (mem. editorial bds.), Am. Acad. Polit. and Social Sci., Am. Anthrop. Assn., Nat. Council on Family Relations, AAAS, AAUP, Profs., Am. Electroencephalographic Soc., Am. Heart Assn., Assn. for Research in Nervous and Mental Disease, Soc. for Exptl. Biology and Medicine, Ill., N.Y. acads. scis., Chgo. Psychoanalytic Soc. (pres. 1984-85), Soc. for Gen. Systems Research, AMA, World Med. Assn., Am. Name Soc., Am. Psychoanalytic Assn. (pres. 1974-75), Am. Psychol. Assn., Am. Psychosomatic Soc., Am. Pub. Health Assn., Am. Sociol. Assn., Assn. Am. Med. Colls., Ill. Psychiat. Soc. (pres. 1973-74), Sigma Xi, Alpha Omega Alpha, numerous others. Home: 5759 S Dorchester Ave Chicago IL 60637-1726 Office: 30 N Michigan Ave Chicago IL 60602-3402

POLLOCK, JEFFREY M. lawyer; b. Morristown, N.J., Sept. 23, 1961; s. Stewart G. and Penelope (Morrow) P.; m. Holly Ann Tinkham, Jan. 21, 1988; children: Jeffrey Wentworth, Ann Marie. BA, Hamilton Coll., 1984; JD, NYU, 1987. Bar: N.J. 1987, D.C. 1988, U.S. Dist. Ct. N.J. 1988, N.Y. 1995. Jud. law clk. to Hon. Donald P. Lay U.S. Ct. Appeals 8th Cir., St. Paul, 1987-88; assoc. Pitney, Hardin, Kipp & Szuch, Morristown, 1988-94; ptnr. Sills Cummis, Newark, 1994—. Mem. com. on character and fitness N.J. Supreme Ct., 1998—. Contbr. articles to profl. jours. Mem. ABA (vice-chair sonreel hazardous waste com.), N.J. State Bar Assn. (dir. and sec. environ. law sect., chmn.). Mem. Soc. Of Friends. Avocation: fly fishing, running. Home: 11 Liberty Hills Ct Long Valley NJ 07853-3087 Office: Sills Cummis One Riverfront Plz Newark NJ 07102 E-mail: jpollock@sillscummis.com.

POLLOCK, JEFFREY LAWRENCE, lawyer; b. Phila., June 12, 1962; s. Burton Harold and Marolee (Morrison) P. BA, U. Pa., 1984; JD, U. Pitts., 1987. Bar: Pa. 1987, U.S. Dist. Ct. (we. dist.) Pa. 1987. Assoc. Feldstein, Grinberg, Stein & McKee, Pitts., 1987-89; pvt. practice, 1989—. Bd. dirs. Leukemia Soc. Western Pa. 1992-94; chmn. Jewish Cmty. Ctr. Theatre, 1992-96. Mem. Pa. Bar Assn. (Michael K. Smith award 1999), Allegheny County Bar Assn. (bd. govs. 1994-99, judiciary com. 1999-2002, chmn. young lawyers sect. 1995, 97, chmn. lawyer referral svc. 1999—, chmn. found. charity golf tourney 2001—), Mediation Coun. of West Pa. Avocations: golf, theatre, softball, basketball, charity work. Office: 1320 Shady Ave Ste 100 Pittsburgh PA 15217-1340

POLLOCK, JOHN PHLEGER, lawyer; b. Sacramento, Apr. 28, 1920; s. George Gordon and Irma (Phleger) P.; m. Juanita Irene Gossman, Oct. 26, 1945; children: Linda Pollock Harrison, Madeline Pollock Chiotti, John, Gordon. AB, Stanford U., 1942; JD, Harvard U., 1948. Bar: Calif. 1949, U.S. Supreme Ct. 1954. Ptnr. Musick, Peeler & Garrett, L.A., 1953-60, Pollock, Williams & Berwanger, L.A., 1960-80, Rodi, Pollock, Pettker, Galbraith & Cahill, L.A., 1980-89, of counsel, 1989—. Contbr. articles to profl. publs. Active Boy Scouts Am.; trustee Pitzer Coll., Claremont, Calif., 1968-76, Pacific Legal Found., 1981-91, Fletcher Jones Found., 1969—, Good Hope Med. Found., 1980—. Fellow Am. Coll. Trial Lawyers; mem. ABA, Los Angeles County Bar Assn. (trustee 1964-66). Home: 30602 Paseo Del Valle Laguna Niguel CA 92677-2317 Office: 444 S Flower St Ste 1700 Los Angeles CA 90071-2918 E-mail: Phleger1@msn.com.

POLLOCK, KAREN ANNE, computer analyst; b. Elmhurst, Ill., Sept. 6, 1961; d. Michael Paul and Dorothy Rosella (Foskett) P. BS, Elmhurst Coll., 1984; MS, North Cen. Coll., 1993. Formatter Nat. Data Corp., Lombard, Ill., 1985; computer specialist Dept. VA, Hines, 1985—. Lutheran. Avocations: cross-stitch, mystery books, bowling, bicycling, softball.

POLLOCK, M. DUNCAN, advertising executive; m. Christen Houlahan, 1983; children: Michael, John. BA in Art History, Yale U.; MBA, NYU. Journalist Rock Mountain News, Denver; asst. account exec. Young & Rubican, v.p., mgmt. supr.; with Hal Riney & Ptnrs., San Francisco; sr. v.p. Ammirati & Puris, N.Y.C., 1985-94; mem. merger transition team Ammirati Puris Lintas (merger Ammirati & Puris, Lintas N.Y.), 1994-95, chmn., CEO, 1995-98, pres. N.Am., 1997-98; pres. Focus Vision Worldwide Inc., Stamford, Conn., 1998—. Bd. dirs. Upward, Inc., The Advt. Coun.; trustee Kent Sch. Ford Found. fellow Ctr. for Internat. Studies, NYU. Mem. Am. Assn. Advt. Agys. (mem. bd. govs. Ea. region, mem. large agy. mgmt. com.). Office: Focus Vision Worldwide Inc 1266 E Main St Stamford CT 06902-3546

POLLOCK, MARC, media fundraising exec., consultant; b. Pitts., Mar. 27, 1945; s. Hyman Sidney and Beatrice (Berman) P.; m. Marjorie Ann Ginsburg, Dec. 16, 1967; 1 child, Brian Seth Ginsburg-Pollock. ABD in Eng., U. Pitts., 1973; BA in Eng. and Chemistry, Washington & Jefferson, 1966; MA in Eng., U. Pitts., 1969. Teaching fellow Eng. U. Pitts., 1968-74; instr. Eng. Chatham Coll., Pitts., 1972-79; exec. asst. to pres. WQED/Pitts., 1979-81, mgr. ednl. project devel., 1981-86; dir. edn. Sta. WQED/Pitts., 1986-93; WQED/Pitts., cons. media and devel., 1993-95, dir. found. and govt. support, 1995—. Lectr., presenter in field. Vol. March of Dimes, Pitts., 1990-92; cons. Am. Heart Assn., 1992-96, Nat. Kidney Assn., 1996, Leukemia Soc., 1999—. Recipient Gold Screen award, 2 CINE Golden Eagle awards, 1994. Mem. Acad. of TV Arts and Scis. (Emmy award Info. Series 1986), Modern Lang. Assn., Am. Assn. for Tng. and Devel., Melville Soc., Phi Beta Kappa. Avocations: tennis, skiing. Office: WQED 4802 5th Ave Pittsburgh PA 15213-2957

POLLOCK, NEAL JAY, electronics executive; b. Phila., Feb. 4, 1947; s. Sol J. and Shirley (Buchsbaum) P. BA in Physics, U. Pa., 1968; MS in Engring. Sci., Pa. State U., 1972; MBA, Temple U., 1975; postgrad., George Washington U., 1978-82; cert. chief info. officer, Info. Resources Mgmt. Coll., 2000. Student trainee Naval Air Devel. Ctr., Warminster, Pa., 1964-68, physicist, 1968-69, electronics engr., 1969-75, plans and programs asst., 1975-76; asst. for interface Naval Air Systems Command, Washington, 1976-78, budget and fin. mgr., 1978-79, asst. program mgr. for acoustic sensors, 1979-84; project engr. Naval Sea Systems Command, 1984-87; br. head, supr. electronics engring. Space and Naval Warfare Systems Command, 1987-90, div. head, 1990-93, tech. assessment mgr., program exec. office, space comm. & sensors, 1993-96, exec. asst. engring. and program assessment, 1996-99; exec. sec. internat. steering com. Multifunctional Info. Distbn. System, 1994-99; internat. coop. opportunities coord. Office of Dep. Undersec. Def. for Internat. Comml. Programs, 1998; chief acquisition engr. program Exec. Office for Info. Tech., 1999—; chief knowledge engr. Dept. Navy Chief Info. Office (Don CIO), 2001—; EEO counselor Naval Sea Sys. Command, Washington, 1986, sexual harassment avoidance trainer, 1993-99, acquisition reform trainer, 1994-99; chmn. comms. Quality Mgmt. Bd., 1992-93; bd. dirs. Juliette's Macrobiotic Svcs., Inc., pres., 1996-2000; mem. Knowledge Mgmt. Cmty. Practice; mem. specifications and stds. improvement policy bd. SPAWAR; spkr. in field. Author: Ethics Morality and Civilization, 1999; co-author: Extended Radiometer Analysis-The Point Target; contbr.: Organizations in a Changing Society, 1977; contb. articles to profl. jours. Unit commr. Boy Scouts Am., 1975-76; vol. income tax asst. Ayuda and Spanish Catholico, Washington, 1976-77; active, life mem. Save the Redwoods League, San Francisco, 1987, Nat. Aquariam Soc., Nature Conservancy, Charlottesville, Va., 1988, Archaeol. Conservancy, Nat. Parks and Conservation Assn., 1990—, Suriname termites and Hawaii dolphins expdns. Earthwatch; active mem., patron sponsor Pearl Buck Found., Glaucoma Rsch. Fund, 1993—, Internat. Rescue Com., World Wildlife Fund, 1991—, Nat. Coalition Against Censorship, 1992—, Nat. Audubon Soc., 1994—, others; vol. Race for the Cure (for breast cancer), Washington, 1996, 97, 98, 99; officer of elections Arlington County, 1991—, chief, 1996—; del. Va. State Rep. Conv., 1993; spl. friend of Internat. Campaign for Tibet; supporter Tibetan Aid Project. Recipient Combined Fed. Campaign Eagle award, 1990-98, Double Eagle award 1999; Trod-the-24 award Internat. Travel News, 1999; USN Student Engring. Devel. scholar, 1964, NSF scholar Stevens Inst. Tech., 1963, Phila. Mayor's scholar. Mem. NRA (life), Nat. Space Soc., Assn. Scientists and Engrs. (life, keyman 1987), U.S. Holocaust Mus. (charter), Alaska Natural History Assn. (life), Pa. State Alumni Assn. (life), Clipper Club (life), Admirals Club (life), Ionosphere Club (life), Worldclub (life), Ambs. Club (life), Red Carpet Club (life), U.S. Air Club (life), Delta Crown Club (life), Arctic Circle Club, Internat. Travel News (life), Crossed-the-Line Club, Antarctic Pendulum Club, Antarctic Discoverer's Club, Antarctican Soc., C.G. Jung Inst. Chgo. (life), Northeast H.S. Alumni Assn. (life), Pa. State U. Alumni Assn. (Washington chpt.), U. Pa. Alumni Assn. (life, Washington chpt.), Nat. Birdfeeding Soc., Humane Soc. U.S. (Pres.'s Club), Nat. Found. Depressive Illness (ptnr. 1998—), Forum Grad. Assn. (charter, v.p. 1994-95, bd. dirs.), Friends of Garlic, Arlington Coop. Assn. (life), N.Am. Butterfly Assn. (charter), Thomas Jefferson Pronaos Ancient Mystical Order Rosae Crucis (master 1980-82, Atlantis Lodge sec. 1984-85, treas. 1985-88, chmn. conv. 1980, patron), Mensa (life, millenium), Masons (32 degree), Wine Taster's Assn., Planetary Soc., The Arlington Coop. (life mem.), Beer Drinkers Am. (life), President's Club of WETA Pub. TV, Xerces Soc. (life), Beta Gamma Sigma. Republican. Jewish. Avocations: world travel, Vajrayana Buddhism, Kabbalah, psychology. Home: 2500 S Fern St Arlington VA 22202-2538 Office: DON CIO Office Chief Info Officer 1000 Navy Pentagon Washington DC 20350-1000 E-mail: neal.pollock@usa.net., neal.pollock@hq.navy.mil.

POLLOCK, RICHARD EDWIN, former county official; b. Phila., Aug. 27, 1928; s. Ernest Edwin and Evelyn Marie (Scarlett) P. Student Armstrong Coll., 1947, U. Calif., Berkeley, 1949-51, 55; BA in Recreation, San Jose State U., 1961; postgrad. San Fernando Valley State U., 1969-70, U. Calif., Davis, 1963-77, UCLA, 1964, U. Calif., Santa Barbara, 1970, U. Redlands, 1979; m. Yvonne May Graves, Oct. 11, 1952 (div. Aug. 1989); children: Colleen May, Karen Marie, Richard Irvin, Annette Yvonne, Mary Ann. Swim pool mgr. and instr. Berkley Tennis Club, 1955-56; police officer City of Berkeley, 1956; recreation and aquatic supr. Pleasant Hill (Calif.) Recreation and Park Dist., 1956-62; gen. mgr. Pleasant Valley Recreation and Park Dist., Camarillo, Calif., 1962-68; bldg. insp. Ventura County (Calif.), 1969-71; adminstr. Sacramento County-Carmichael Recreation and Park Dist., 1971-73; dir. parks and recreation Imperial County (Calif.), 1973-81; ret.; mem. faculty Imperial Valley Jr. Coll., 1974-94, aquatic cons., 1957—; real estate investor, 1984-97; chmn. San Francisco Bay Area Conf. for Cooperation in Aquatics, 1958-59. Adviser/scoutmaster Desert Trails council Boy Scouts Am.; bd. dirs., instr. ARC; work with devel. disabled and handicapped children and adults; res. dep. Sheriff, 1981-97, Served from pvt. to lt. U.S. Army, 1951-55; Korea. Recipient recognition for 52 years vol. service ARC, 1989; registered recreator and park mgr.; cert. elem., secondary and community coll. tchr., Calif.; reg. hypnotherapist. Mem. Nat. Recreation and Park Assn., AAHPER, Calif. Park and Recreation Soc., Calif. County Dirs. Parks and Recreation Assn., Calif. Boating Safety Officers Assn., Aircraft Owners and Pilots Assn., Nat. Assn. Emergency Med. Technicians. Democrat. Mormon. Author: Bibliography: A Pool of Aquatic Sources, 1960. Home: 961 S Sunshine Ave Apt 5 El Cajon CA 92020-5947

POLLOCK, ROBERT ELWOOD, nuclear scientist; b. Regina, Sask., Can., Mar. 2, 1936; s. Elwood Thomas and Harriet Lillian (Rooney) Pollock; m. Jean Elizabeth Virtue, Sept. 12, 1959; children: Bryan Thomas, Heather Lynn, Jeffrey Parker, Jennifer Lee. BSc with honors, U. Man., Can., 1957; MA, Princeton U., 1959, PhD, 1963. Instr. Princeton (N.J.) U., 1961—63, asst. prof., 1964—69, rsch. physicist, 1969—70; Nat. Rsch. Coun. Can. postdoctoral fellow Harwell, England, 1963—64; assoc. prof. Ind. U., Bloomington, 1970—73, prof., 1973—84, disting. prof., 1984—2001, prof. emeritus, 2001—, dir. Cyclotron Facility, 1973—79, mem. nuc. sci. adv. com., 1977—80. Recipient Alexander von Humboldt Sr. U.S. Scientist award, 1985—88. Fellow: Am. Phys. Soc. (Bonner prize 1992). Home: 2811 Dale Ct Bloomington IN 47401-2414 Office: Ind U Swain Hall Dept Physics Bloomington IN 47405

POLLOCK, SAMUEL, diversified financial services company executive; b. Montreal, Que., Can., Dec. 15, 1925; m. Mary Mimi Kinsella, Dec. 27, 1962; children: Mary, Sam, Rachel. Grad., Westmount H.S. Chmn. John Labatt Ltd., Carena Bancorp Equities Ltd.; chief exec. ofcr., gov. Toronto Blue Jays, Toronto, 1994-. Bd. dirs. Carena Devels. Ltd., John Labatt Ltd., Trizen Corp., Toronto Blue Jays Club, Hockey Can. Chmn. Internat. and Olympic Com. Hockey Can., 1982-88; corporate chmn. Can. Cerebral Palsy, 1989; co-chmn. Miss Edgars and Miss Cramps Bldg. Campaign, 1987-89. Decorated officer Order of Can.; named to Can. Sports Hall of Fame, Hockey Hall of Fame. Mem. Gt. Montrealers. Office: John Labatt Ltd, PO Box 811 BCE Place, 181 Bay St Ste 200 Toronto ON Canada M5J 2T3*

POLLOCK, STEPHEN MICHAEL, operations research engineer, educator, consultant; b. N.Y.C., Feb. 15, 1936; s. Meyer and Frances R. Pollock; m. Bettina Dorn, Nov. 22, 1962; children: Joshua, Aaron, Ethan. B in Engring. Physics, Cornell U., 1958; SM, MIT, 1960, PhD in Physics and Ops. Research, 1964. Mem. tech. staff Arthur D. Little Inc., Cambridge, Mass., 1964-65; asst. prof. Naval Postgrad. Sch., Monterey, Calif., 1965-68, assoc. prof., 1968-69, U. Mich., Ann Arbor, 1969-73, prof., dept. indsl. and ops. engring., 1974—, chmn. dept., 1980-90. Cons. to over 40 orgns. Area editor Ops. Rsch. Jour., 1977-82; sr. editor Inst. Indsl. Engrs. Trans., 1985-89, Army Sci. Bd., 1994-99; contbr. more than 60 tech. papers to profl. jours. Fellow, Space Tech. Labs., 1960; sr. fellow NSF, 1975. Fellow: AAAS; mem.: Nat. Acad. Engring., Ops. Rsch. Soc. Am. (pres. 1986—87), Inst. Mgmt. Sci. Home: 2694 Wayside Dr Ann Arbor MI 48103-2251 Office: U of Mich Dept Indsl Ops Engring Ann Arbor MI 48109-2117

POLLOCK, STEWART GLASSON, lawyer, former state supreme court justice; b. East Orange, N.J., Dec. 21, 1932; BA, Hamilton Coll., 1954, LLD (hon.), 1995; LLB, NYU, 1957; LLM, U. Va., 1988. Bar: N.J. 1958. Asst. U.S. atty., Newark, 1958-60; ptnr. Schenck, Price, Smith & King, Morristown, N.J., 1960-74, 76-78; commr. N.J. Dept. Pub. Utilities; counsel to gov. State of N.J., Trenton, 1978-79; assoc. justice N.J. Supreme Ct., Morristown, 1979-99; of counsel Riker Danzig Hyland & Perretti, 1999—. Mem. N.J. Commn. on Investigation, 1976-78; chmn. coordinating coun. on life-sustaining med. treatment decision making Nat. Ctr. for State Cts., 1994-96; bd. dirs. NYU Law Ctr. Found., Inst. of Jud. Adminstrn., N.J. Conv. Found. Assoc. editor N.J. Law Jour.; contbr. articles to legal jours. Trustee Coll. Medicine and Dentistry, N.J., 1976. Mem. ABA (chmn. appellate judges conf. 1991-92), N.J. Bar Assn. (trustee 1973-78), Am. Judicature Soc. (dir. 1984-88), Morris County Bar Assn. (pres. 1973). Office: 1 Speedwell Ave Morristown NJ 07960-6838

POLLOCK, TONY JOE, graphic designer, writer; b. St. Mary's, Ohio, Apr. 10, 1961; s. Gary D. and Loretta J. (Lowe) P. BSN, U. Minn., 1983. CCRN, CEN. Staff nurse ICU VA Med. Ctr., Martinez, Calif., 1986-88; charge nurse emergency room Mad River Community Hosp., Arcata, 1988-90; staff emergency med. technician, paramedic Hupa Health Assn. EMS, Hoopa, 1989-91; charge nurse emergency svcs. Health One Unity Hosp., Fridley, Minn., 1991-93; mgr. NurseLine United Healthcare, Golden Valley, 1993-95; sr. ptnr. Midwest Legal Nurse Cons., Inc., Edina, 1995-97; staff nurse Park Nicollet Clinic Phone Care, Wayzata, 1995—; designer, writer Baypoint Design, Mound, 1997—2001; Leica specialist Nat. Camera Exchange, Golden Valley, 2000—; owner Thunderbolt Photography, Mound, 2002—. Capt. Nurse Corps, U.S. Army, 1983-86. Home and Office: 1700 Finch Ln Mound MN 55364-1224 E-mail: pollot@earthlink.net.

POLLOCOFF, MICHAEL R. village administrator; b. Aurora, Colo., Nov. 3, 1953; s. David and Mary Lou (Becker) P.; m. Dawn Louise Jahnke, Apr. 12, 1953; children: Erin Elizabeth, Kyle Daniel. BA in Polit. Sci. and History, Western State Coll., 1976, MA in Social Studies, 1978; MPA, U. Okla., 1981. Mcpl. cons. Western Rural Commodities Inc., Gunnison, Colo., 1976-77; graphic artist Mountain Bell Telephone, Denver, 1977-79; asst. dir. water City of Oklahoma City, 1979-85; village adminstr. Village of Pleasant Prairie, Pleasant Prairie, Wis., 1985—. Chmn. Am. Soc. Pub. Adminstrs., Oklahoma City, 1984; mem. bd. dirs. Kenosha (Wis.) Area Tourism Corp., 1989-94; vice chair Wis. Utility Tax Assn., Madison, 1992—; chmn., bd. dirs. Kenosha Area Conv. of Visitors, Kenosha, 1994—. Author: Pleasant Prairie Diversion Great Lakes Symposium, , 1993. Del. state conv. Colo. Dem. Party, Denver, 1978, County Conv. Jefferson County Dem. Party, Lakewood, Colo., 1978, Gunnison County Dem. Party. Mem. Wis. City Mgmt. Assn., Am. Water Works Assn. Democrat. Roman Catholic. Avocations: racquetball, fishing, photography, travel. Office: Village of Pleasant Prairie 9915 39th Ave Pleasant Prairie WI 53158-6501

POLLOK, BRIAN ANDREW, biotechnology company executive; b. Frederick, Md., Mar. 14, 1957; s. Nicholas Lewis Pollok and Virginia Anne Jewell; m. Amy Catherine Breitenbach, Oct. 10, 1981; children: Christopher James, Benjamin Graham. BA, U. Va., Charlottesville, 1979; PhD, U. Ala., Birmingham, 1983. Postdoctoral fellow Fox Chase Cancer Ctr., Phila., 1983-85; asst. scientist Guthrie Rsch. Inst., Sayre, 1985-87; asst. prof. Wake Forest U., Winston-Salem, N.C., 1987-93; sr. rsch. investigator Pfizer Inc., Groton, Conn., 1993-97; assoc. dir., dir., sr. dir., v.p. discovery biology Aurora Biosci. Corp., San Diego, 1997—2002; sr. v.p. rsch. Ansata Therapeutics, LaJolla, 2002—. Contbr. articles to profl. jours.; patents pending in field. Recipient Faculty Rsch. award, Am. Cancer Soc., 1989, Investigator award, Arthritis Found., 1986; fellow Postdoctoral fellow, Damon Runyon-Walter Winchell Cancer Fund, 1983. Mem. Am. Assn. Immunologists, Soc. for Biomolec. Screening. Democrat. Episcopalian. Avocations: flat water canoeing, bodyboarding, tennis. Office: Aurora Bioscis Corp 11010 Torreyana Rd San Diego CA 92121 E-mail: pollokb@aurorabio.com.

POLO, RICHARD JOSEPH, engineering executive; b. Barranquilla, Colombia, Oct. 14, 1936; s. Pedro Pastor and Clotilde (Verano) P.; m. Ana Isabel Cepeda, Feb. 1, 1958; children: Richard J. Jr., James Alan. BCE, NYU, 1957; MS in Structural Engring., Iowa State U., 1963, PhD in Structural and Nuc. Engring., 1971; disting. grad., Command and Gen. Staff Coll., Ft. Leavenworth, Kans., 1970; grad., Inter-Am. Def. Coll., Ft. McNair, Washington, 1977; MBA, Marymount U., 1986. Registered profl. engr., Md., Iowa, Fla., Ga., Pa., Conn., N.Y. Commd. 2d lt. U.S. Army, 1957, advanced through grades to col., 1979, various positions, 1957-79; asst. dir. civil works Pacific U.S. Army Office Chief of Engrs., 1979-80; corps engr., engr. brigade comdr. U.S. Army, Ludwigsburg, Fed. Republic Germany, 1980-83; dep. study dir. U.S. Army Office Chief of Staff, Washington, 1984-85; ret. U.S. Army, 1985; v.p. constrn. inspection Kidde Cons. Inc., Balt., 1985, sr. v.p. constrn. inspection, 1986, exec. v.p., 1986-89, corp. sec., 1988-89, also bd. dirs.; v.p. Fla. region CRSS, Miami, 1989-90; CEO, program dir. CRSS/WRJ joint venture, 1989-90; assoc. v.p., dep. divsn. dir. fed. programs Greiner, Inc., Miami, 1991-92; dir. engring. & project ops. CKC (OSC), 1993-94; dir. L.Am. ops., dir. engring. devel. GeoSyntec Cons., Boca Raton, 1994-96; dir. Miami ops. ICF Kaiser Engrs., Inc., 1996-98, group v.p., 1997-98; mgr. Fla. ops. Stone & Webster Engring., Inc., 1998-2000; sr. v.p. Stone & Webster Transp. Svcs., 1998-2000; pres. Amerint, Miami, 1994—, Am. Enterprises Internat., Inc., Polo Mortgage-Plus, Miami, 1993—. Bd. dirs. KCI Holdings, 1988-90. Contbr. articles on mil. and structural engring. to profl. jours. Inventor arcuate space frame. Cmty. comdr. and sr. U.S. rep. Ludwigsburg Mil. Cmty., 1980-83. Decorated Legion of Merit with bronze oak leaf cluster, Bronze Star, others; Fed. Exec. fellow Brookings Institution, 1983-84. Fellow Soc. Am. Mil. Engrs. (bd. dirs. El Paso chpt. 1967-68, pres. Stuttgart chpt. 1980-82); mem. ASCE, NSPE, Md. Soc. Profl. Engrs., Va. Soc. Profl. Engrs. (dir. no. Va. chpt. 1985-89, pres. elect 1988-89), Assn. U.S. Army (pres. Ludwigsburg chpt. 1980-83), Fla. Engring. Soc., Ret. Officers Assn. (life), Army-Navy Club Coral Gables (dir. 1994-98, sec. 1995-96, v.p. 1996-97, pres. 1997-98), Greater Miami C. of C. (trustee 1989-92, 97-2000), Country Club Coral Gables (dir. 1997-2000, sec. 1997-98, v.p. 1999-2000), Rotary, Elks, Sigma Xi, Phi Kappa

Phi, Tau Beta Pi, Chi Epsilon, Psi Upsilon (pres. Delta chpt. 1956-57). Republican. Roman Catholic. Avocations: model airplanes, racquetball. Home and Office: Amerint/Am Enterprises Int 2401 Anderson Rd Unit 9 Coral Gables FL 33134

POLODNA, DAVID LEE, library director; b. Prairie Du Chien, Wis., Jan. 17, 1951; s. John Adolph and Eva Marie Polodna; m. Lynne Helen Marshall, Jan. 22, 1973; children: Emelia Lynne, Leigh Danya. BA in History summa cum laude, U. Wis., La Crosse, 1978; MLS, U. Wis., Madison, 1979. Cert. librarian, Wis. Supr. tech. svc. La Crosse Pub. Libr., 1979-84, New Canaan (Conn.) Libr., 1984-85; asst. dir. East Ctrl. Regional Libr., Cambridge, Minn., 1985-89, Winding Rivers Libr. Sys., La Crosse, 1989-97, dir., 1998—. Mem. adv. com. LSCA, Wis., 1993-96; mem. adv. coun. Gen. Minn. Librs. Exch., St. Cloud, 1986-89; mem. Wis. Statewide Automation Study Com., 1980-82. Pres., bd. dirs. East Ctrl. Regional Concert Assn., Cambridge, 1986-87; chmn. Wis. Interlibr. Loan Task Force, Madison, 1994-96; sec., bd. dirs. LaCrosse Area Comm. Consortium, 1997—, Wis. Libr. Info. Tech. Adv. Com. 2000—; trustee handbook revision task force Wis. Pub. Libr., 2001, mem. legislation and funding task force, 2002-. Trowbridge scholar, 1977. Mem. Wis. Libr. Assn. (chmn. com. on orgn. 1999—), Sys. and Resource Libr. Adminstrs. Assn. Wis. (treas. 1992—), Beta Phi Mu. Avocations: music, performing, bicycling. Office: Winding Rivers Libr Sys 800 Main St La Crosse WI 54601-4122 E-mail: dlp@wrlsweb.org.

POLOGE, BENNETT, psychologist, actor; s. Irving and Grace Pologe. BA, Columbia U., 1983; PhD, Fordham U., 1988. Lic. psychologist N.Y. Pvt. practice, N.Y.C., 1990—. Singer: Phantom, 1999; actor: I Hate Hamlet, 2002; composer: Hamlet, 1999. Mem.: Am. Psychotherapy Assn. (Diplomat 1999), N.Y. State Psychol. Assn. Office: 27 W 72nd St Ste 308 New York NY 10023

POLOIAN, LYNDA GAMANS, retailing educator; b. Manchester, N.H., Nov. 7, 1943; d. Herbert V. and Rose A. (Hammarbeck) Rauding; children: Kristen Soterion, Erik. BA in Psychology, U. N.H., 1976; MEd, Notre Dame Coll., Manchester, N.H., 1979. Sales promotion dir. A. Machinist, Inc., Manchester, 1966-78; prin. R.G. Cons., 1977-89; prof. retailing So. N.H. U. (formerly N.H. Coll.), 1975—; pres. Silk Accent, Inc., 1991-97. Ptnr. Sylyn Enterprise Senderian Berhad, Alor Setar, Kedah, Malaysia, 1991-93; asst. prof. Lansdown Coll., London, 1985-86; presenter in field. Co-author: (textbooks) Fashion: A Marketing Approach, 1983, Retailing: New Perspectives, 1992, Retailing Principles: A Global Outlook, 2003; (jour.) Nat. Bus. Edn. Assn. Yearbook, 1994. Mem. Miss N.H. Scholarship Program State Com., 1982-89. Mem. Am. Collegiate Retailing Assn. (pres. 2000—). Avocations: art, watercolor and oil painting, designing silk scarves. Office: So NH Univ 2500 N River Rd Manchester NH 03106-1045 E-mail: l.poloian@snhu.edu.

POLONSKY, ARTHUR, artist, educator; b. Lynn, Mass., June 6, 1925; s. Benjamin and Celia (Hurwitz) P.; children: Eli, D.L., Gabriel. Diploma with highest honors, Sch. of Mus. Fine Arts, Boston, 1948. Instr. painting dept. Sch. Mus. Fine Arts, Boston, 1950-60; asst. prof. dept. fine arts Brandeis U., 1954-65; assoc. prof. Boston U., 1965-90, prof. emeritus, 1990—. One-man shows include Boris Mirski Gallery, Boston, 1950, 54, 56, 64, Boston Pub. Libr., 1969, 90, 93, 96, 99, Durlacher Gallery, N.Y.C., 1965, Mickelson Gallery, Washington, 1966, 74, Boston Ctr. for Arts, 1983, Starr Gallery, Boston, 1987, Fitchburg Art Mus., 1990, Kantar Fine Arts, Newton, Mass., 2002; exhibited in group shows including Met. Mus., N.Y.C., 1950, The Salon Des Jeunes Peintres, Paris, 1950, Stedelijk Mus., Amsterdam, The Netherlands, 1950, Carnegie Internat. Expn., 1951, Inst. Contemporary Art, Boston, 1960, Mus. Fine Arts, Boston, 1976, Boston Arts Festival, 1954, 55, 85, Expressionism in Boston, Decordova Mus., Lincoln, Mass., 1986, Decordova Mus., 1987, Palais Univ. de Strasbourg, France, 1992, Boston's Honored Artists, Danforth Mus., Framingham, Mass., 1995, Decordova Mus., Lincoln, Mass., 2002, Boston U. Art Gallery, 2002; represented in permanent collections Mus. Fine Arts, Boston, Fogg Mus., Harvard U., Addison Gallery of Am. Art, Andover, Mass., Stedelijk Mus., Amsterdam, Walker Art Ctr., Mpls., Zimmerli Art Mus., Rutgers U., New Brunswick, N.J., Honolulu Acad. Arts. Recipient Louis Comfort Tiffany award for painting, 1951, 1st prize Boston Arts Festival, 1954; European travelling fellow Sch. Mus. Fine Art, Boston, 1948-50 Mem. Artists Equity Assn., Inc. (founding, former dir. New Eng. chpt.). Address: 364 Cabot St Newtonville MA 02460-2252

POLOSUKHIN, VASILIY VLADIMIROVICH, anatomist; b. Tsvetnogorsk, Russia, Apr. 22, 1961; s. Vladimir Trofimovich and Tamara Vasiljevna (Kozhurenko) P.; m. Zhanna Anatoljevna Libenko, Oct. 20, 1981 (div. Apr. 1991); 1 child, Maxim; m. Dina Akhatovna Tuganbaeva, Jan. 13, 1994; 1 child, Igor. MD, Tomsk Med. Inst., 1984; PhD, Inst. Clin. Exptl. Medicine, 1991; ScD, Inst. Clin. Exptl. Lymphology, 1998. Rschr. Inst. Clin. and Exptl. Medicine, Novosibirsk, Russia, 1987-91, Inst. Physiology, Novosibirsk, 1991-95, Inst. Clin. and Exptl. Lymphology, Novosibirsk, 1995-99, U. Nebraska Med. Ctr., Omaha, 1999—. Author: Morphogenetic Effects of Laser Induced Treatment in Therapy of Chronic Inflammation of the Bronchi, 1993, Diagnostic Bronchoalveolar Lavage (Ultrastructural Study of the Cell Populations), 1995, Pathological Anatomy of Inflammatory Lung Diseases, 1997, Chronic Bronchitis: Pathogenesis, Diagnosis, Clinical and Anatomic Description, 1998. Grantee Thoracal Laser Ctr., 1991-95, Pub. Health Siberia, 1996, Bank Khanty-Mansiysk, 1997. Mem. Siberian Soc. Lymphologists, Soc. of Ultrastructural Pathology. Avocations: mushrooming, fishing. Office: Dept Int Med Pulmonary Crit Care Med Sect Univ Nebraska Med Ctr Omaha NE 68198-5300

POLOUKHINE, OLGA, artist, educator; b. Paris, Nov. 1, 1934; came to U.S., 1948; d. Nikita and Sophie (Schidlovsky) Koulomzin; m. Nicolas Poloukhine, Nov. 20, 1960; children: Olga, Michael, Elena. BA, Rutgers U., 1956; MA, Columbia U., 1960. Cert. art tchr. K-12, N.Y. Art tchr. Nyack (N.Y.) Schs., 1957-59, White Plains (N.Y.) Sch. System, 1959-60, Locust Valley (N.Y.) Pub. Schs., 1960-62; represented by Galeria Boriken, Rhinebeck, N.Y. Exhibited in group shows at Wunchs Art Gallery,Taller Galeria Forte, Barcelona, Spain, Richard Gallery, Northea. U., Boston Le Chateau Royal de Collioure, France, Hecksher Mus., N.Y., Nassau County Fine Arts Mus., N.Y., Fine Arts Mus. L.I., Long Beach Mus. Art, numerous others; represented in permanent collection at Zimmerli Art Mus., Rutgers U., other corp. and pvt. collections, including IBM, AT&T, N.Y. Tel. Co., NYNEX, O.C.A. Mem. L.I. Graphic Eye Gallery (founder, pres. 1989-91), Nat. Assn. Women Artists, Nat. Mus. of Women in the Arts (charter), N.Y. Soc. Women Artists. Eastern Orthodox. Home: 83 Skidmore Rd Lagrangeville NY 12540-5033

POLOZOLA, FRANK JOSEPH, federal judge; b. Baton Rouge, Jan. 15, 1942; s. Steve A. Sr. and Caroline C. (Lucito) P.; m. Linda Kay White, June 9, 1962; children: Gregory Dean, Sheri Elizabeth, Gordon Damian. Student bus. adminstrn., La. State U., 1959-62, JD, 1965. Bar: La. 1965. Law clk. to U.S. Dist. Ct. Judge E. Gordon West, 1965-66; assoc. Seale, Smith & Phelps, Baton Rouge, 1966-68, ptnr., 1968-73; part-time magistrate U.S. Dist. Ct. (mid. dist.) La., 1972-73, magistrate, 1973-80, judge, 1980—, chief judge, 1998—. Adj. prof. Law Ctr., La. State U., 1977-95. Bd. dirs. Cath. High Sch. Mem. La. Bar Assn., Baton Rouge Bar Assn., Fed. Judges Assn., 5th Cir. Dist. Judges Assn., La. State U. L Club, KC, Wex Malone Inns of Ct., Omicron Delta Kappa. Roman Catholic. Office: US Dist Ct Russell B Long Fed Bldg & US Courthouse 777 Florida St Ste 313 Baton Rouge LA 70801-1717

POLSBY, GAIL K. psychotherapist; b. Washington, Jan. 13, 1939; d. Thomas Edward and Elise Wildman (Hammer) Kissling; m. Allen I. Polsby, Aug. 30, 1963; children: Daniel, Abigail. BA, U. Md., 1960; MSW, Cath. U., 1963. Mem. faculty Washington Sch. Psychiatry, 1967—2001, chmn. bd. dirs., 2001—; pvt. practice psychotherapy, Chevy Chase, Md., 1969—; cons. doctoral program Clin. Social Work Inst., Washington, 1999—. Sec., bd. dirs. Washington Sch. Psychiatry, 1995—2001, chair faculty coun. Editor quar. newspaper Washington Sch. Psychiatry News, 1997. Mem. Am. Group Psychotherapy Assn., Nat. Fedn. Clin. Social Workers. Avocations: hiking, biking. Home: 5651 Bent Branch Rd Bethesda MD 20816-1049

POLSFUSS, CRAIG LYLE, executive coach and leadership specialist, psychologist, social worker; b. Mpls., Nov. 16, 1950; s. Lyle Henry and Ethel Geneva (Langert) P.; m. Mary Louise Davenport, June 10, 1972; children: Zachary Abel, Samuel David, Benjamin James. BA with honors, Macalester Coll., 1972; MA with honors, U.S.I.U., 1976; MSW, U. Minn., 1979. Lic. ind. clin. social worker, psychologist, Minn. Pvt. practice counselor, psychotherapist, Mpls., 1972—; pvt. practice mgmt. cons., 1983—. Instr. Augsburg Coll., U. Minn., Mpls. Cmty. Coll., Lakewood Cmty. Coll., Nat. Coll. Bus., 1976-86; dir. Heartland Health Realization Ctrs., Twin Cities met. area, 1991; adj. faculty Grad. Sch. Bus. U. St. Thomas; radio talk show host W.A.L.E., Providence, 1997-99. Avocations: writing, speaking, fishing. Office: Vantage Place Cons 6950 France Ave S Ste 14 Edina MN 55435-2016 E-mail: clpolsfuss@msn.com.

POLSKY, DONALD PERRY, architect; b. Milw., Sept. 30, 1928; s. Lew and Dorothy (Geisenfeld) P.; m. Corinne Shirley Neer, Aug. 25, 1957; children: Jeffrey David, Debra Lynn. BArch, U. Nebr., Lincoln, 1951; postgrad., U. So. Calif., 1956, U. Calif., Los Angeles, 1957, U. Nebr., Omaha, 1964, U. Ill., 1965. Project architect Richard Neutra, Architect, Los Angeles, 1953-56, Daniel Dworsky, Architect, Los Angeles, 1956; prin. Polsky, AIA & Assocs., 1956-62, Omaha, 1964—; dir. dept. architecture MCA, Inc., Universal City, Calif., 1962-64. Prin. works include Mills residence, 1958, apt. bldgs., 1960, Polsky residence, 1961, Milder residence, 1965. Chmn. Design Control I480 Study Mayor's Riverfront Devel., Omaha, 1969, 71; pres. Swanson Sch. Community Club, Omaha, 1972; mem. Mayor's Adv. Panel Design Services, Omaha, 1974; vice chmn. Omaha Zoning Bd. Appeals, 1976; dir. Siena/Francis House. Recipient archtl. awards Canyon Crier Newspaper, Los Angeles, 1960, House and Home Mag., Life Mag., AIA, Santa Barbara, Calif., 1962. Mem. AIA (pres. Omaha chpt. 1968), Nebr. Soc. Architects (pres. 1975, awards 1964, 68, 87, 91, 93, 94, 95, 97, Firm of Yr. 1997). Office: Donald P Polsky AIA & Assocs 8723 Oak St Omaha NE 68124-3051

POLSKY, HOWARD DAVID, lawyer; b. Phila., Sept. 10, 1951; s. Herman and Meriam (Ternoff) P. BA, Lehigh U., 1973; JD, Ind. U., 1976. Bar: Pa. 1976, N.J. 1977, D.C. 1978, U.S. Ct. Appeals (D.C. cir.) 1976. Atty. FCC, Washington, 1976-79; assoc. Kirkland & Ellis, 1979-83; ptnr. Wiley, Rein & Fielding, 1983-92; v.p. fed. policy and regulation COMSAT Corp., Bethesda, Md., 1992-2000; v.p., gen. counsel Lockheed Martin Global Telecomms., 2000—. Adj. prof. law Del. Law Sch. Widner U., 1981-84. Mem. ABA, Fed. Comm. Bar Assn.

POLSKY, MICHAEL PETER, mechanical engineer; b. Kiev, Ukraine, Aug. 5, 1949; s. Peter and Basheva P.; m. Maya, June 28, 1975; children: Alan, Gabriel. BSME, Kiev Poly. Inst., 1973; MBA, U. Chgo., 1987. Registered profl. engr., Ill., Mich. Sr. devel. engr. Indsl. Power Corp., Kiev, Ukraine, 1973-76; mech. engr. Bechtel Power Corp., Ann Arbor, Mich., 1976-78; sr. application engr. Brown Boveri Corp., St. Cloud, Minn., 1978-80; product mgr. congeneration Fluor/Daniel, Chgo., 1980-85; pres. Indeck Energy Svcs., Wheeling, 1985-90, Polsky Energy Corp./SkyGen Energy, LLC, Northbrook, 1991—2000; founder, pres., CEO, Invenergy LLC, Chgo., 2001—. Author: Public Utilities Fortnightly, 1985, Power, 1984, 83, Hydrocarbon Processing, 1981, 82; author: (book chpt.) Handbook of Power Plant Engineering, 1991. Mem. ASME, Soc. Energy Engrs. Home: 199 E Lake Shore Dr # 8W Chicago IL 60611 Office: Invenergy LLC 233 S Wacker Dr Ste 9450 Chicago IL 60606

POLSTER, DAN AARON, judge; b. Cleve., Dec. 6, 1951; s. Lewis H. and Elinor Ruth (Guren) P.; m. Deborah Ann Coleman, May 29, 1977; children: Joshua, Shira, Ilana. AB, Harvard U., 1972, JD, 1976; PhD (hon.), Cleve. Coll. Jewish Studies, 1988. Bar: Ohio 1976, U.S. Dist. Ct. (no. dist.) Ohio 1981, U.S. Ct. Appeals (6th cir.) 1982. Atty. Dept. Justice, Cleve., 1976-82, asst. U.S. atty., 1982-98; U.S. dist. judge U.S. Dist. Ct., Akron, Ohio, 1998—. Pres. bd. trustees Agnon Sch., Beachwood, Ohio, 1993-96; chmn. bd. govs. Cleve. Coll. Jewish Studies, Beachwood, 1984-88; bd. dirs. Jewish Comty. Fedn. Cleve., 1989-95, 96-2001. Recipient Special Achievement award U.S. Dept. Justice, 1980, 84, Special Commendation, 1988. Mem. Fed. Bar Assn., Cleve. Bar Assn. Jewish. Office: US Dist Ct 2 S Main St Akron OH 44308-1813 E-mail: dan_polster@ohnd.uscourts.gov.

POLSTER, LEONARD H. investment company executive; b. Columbus, Ohio, June 24, 1921; s. Max and Henrietta Polster; m. Constance L. Buderus, Mar. 20, 1948 (dec. Aug. 1967); children: Leonard M., Lance E., Lewis E.; m. Edith Motridge, Nov. 19, 1968. BA, Ohio State U., 1942. Pres. Polster, Inc., 1952-68, pres. real estate and investments co., 1968—; sr. v.p. PaineWebber Inc., L.A. and Rancho Santa Fe, Calif., 1971-91. Author: Pearls Before Swine, 1994. Pres. Polster Found., Rancho Santa Fe, 1988—; fin. officer, bd. dirs. San Dieguito Boys Club, Solana Beach, Calif., 1991—; bd. dirs. Fairbanks Ranch Cmty. Svcs. Dist., Rancho Santa Fe, 1987-92; pres. Fairbanks Ranch Assn., Rancho Santa Fe, 1985-86, bd. dirs., 1984-86. With USAF, 1942-46. Recipient Commitment to Youth award San Dieguito Boys and Girls Club, 1989; Olympic torch bearer, 1996, 2002; Boys Club br. named in his honor, Carmel Valley, Calif., 2000, Scripps breast care bldg. named in his honor, 2001. Mem. Scripps Heritage Circle, Fairbanks Ranch Country Club, Phi Alpha Theta. Republican. Presbyterian. Avocations: tennis, reading, music. Home and Office: PO Box 8291 Rancho Santa Fe CA 92067-8291

POLSTON, RONALD WAYNE, law educator; b. Raymond, Ill., Nov. 1, 1931; s. Joseph M. and Minnie V. (Wilson) P.; m. Mary Ann Campbell, Aug. 5, 1961; children: Anne Campbell, Joseph Harrison. BS, Eastern Ill. U., 1953; LLB, U. Ill., 1958. Bar: Ill. 1959, Ind. 1967, U.S. Supreme Ct. 1964. Assoc. Craig & Craig, Mt. Vernon, Ill., 1958-64, ptnr., 1964-65; asst. prof. Ind. U. Sch. Law, Indpls., 1965-68, assoc. prof., asst. dean, 1968-71, prof., 1971-95, prof. emeritus, 1995—. Vis. prof. Monash U., Melbourne, Australia, 1972-73. Founder, pres. Panhandle Ednl. Found., 1999—. With U.S. Army, 1953-55. Democrat. Methodist. Home: 311 S McGown Raymond Raymond IL 62560 Office: Indiana Univ Sch Law 735 W New York St Indianapolis IN 46202-5222

POLUGA, JUDITH, education educator; b. Budapest, Hungary, Jan. 1, 1952; came to U.S., 1959; d. Laszlo and Irene Takacs; m. Charles Poluga, Dec. 16, 1972; children: Adam Charles, Mia Kyung-Choi, Nathan Lee, Hope Kyung-Choi, David Jonathan, Krystal Kyung-Choi, Danielle Marie (dec.). BS in Edn., Kent State U., 1980, MEd, 1990, postgrad. Cert. tchr., prin. Ohio. Kindergarten tchr. Mother of Sorrows Sch., Ashtabula, Ohio, 1980-85; kindergarten, 4th grade tchr. Ashtabula City Schs., 1985-97; prof. early childhood edn. Kent State U., Ashtabula, 1995—; prin. Kingsville elem. Buckeye Local Schs., 1997—. Dir. of edn. Intercultural Student Exch., Ashtabula, 1997—. Bd. dirs. Cath. Svc. League, Ashtabula, 1996; mem. Garden Trails Garden Club, Ashtabula, 1987-93. Martha Holden Jennings scholar Martha Holden Jennings Found., 1993. Mem. ASCD, AAUW, Assn. for Childhood Edn. Internat., Comparative and Internat. Edn. Soc., Am. Ednl. Rsch. Assn., Nat. Assn. for the Edn. of Young Children, Phi Delta Kappa. Roman Catholic. Avocations: woodworking, crafts. Home: 4005 W 13th St Ashtabula OH 44004-2109 Office: Buckeye Local Schs Kingsville 5875 Rt 193 Kingsville OH 44048

POLUNOVSKY, VITALY ALEX, cell biologist; b. Moscow, Oct. 24, 1940; came to U.S., 1990; s. Alexander and Nina Polunovsky; m. Elena Polunovsky, June 14, 1964 (div. Sept. 1968); 1 child, Asya; m. Liza Bezenson, Feb. 12, 1989. MS, 2d Moscow Med. Sch., 1969; PhD in Biology, Moscow State U., 1986. Rschr. Moscow State U., 1969—76; assoc. prof. State Pedagogical U., Moscow, 1976—86, prof., 1986—89; postdoctoral rsch. assoc. U. Minn., Mpls., 1990—92, asst. rsch. prof., 1992—96, assoc. rsch. prof. cell biology, 1996—2002, prof. medicine, 2002—. Author: Resting Cells, 1983; contbr. over 80 articles to profl. jours. Avocations: poetry, fine art, theatre, music, skiing. Office: Univ of Minn MMC 276 420 Delaware St SE Minneapolis MN 55455 E-mail: polun@tc.umn.edu.

POLVERINI, PETER, dean; DDS Dental-Oral Pathology, Marquette U. , 1973. Dean U. Minn., 1999—. Office: Sch Dentistry UMN Twin Cities 15-209 Moos T 515 Delaware St SE Minneapolis MN 55455 Address: Sch Dentistry Rm 15-209 Moos T 1291 515 Delaware St SE Minneapolis MN 55455 also: 1011 N University Ave # 1340 Ann Arbor MI 48109-1078 Office Fax: 612-626-2654. Business E-Mail: neovas@umn.edu.*

POMA, PEDRO ALFONSO, obstetrician, gynecologist; b. Lima, Peru, Mar. 11, 1938; came to U.S., 1966; s. Cesar S. and Rosa E. (Herrera) P.; m. Lydia Maria Marca, Mar. 27, 1965; children: Ana Elizabeth, Alfonso Martin. Student, San Marcos U., Lima, 1957-59, MD, 1965. Diplomate Am. Bd. Ob-Gyn., 1974. Resident in ob-gyn Cook County Hosp., Chgo., 1968-71; resident in ob-gyn pathology Northwestern U., 1969; practice medicine specializing in ob-gyn, 1972—; chmn. dept. ob-gyn., dir. ob-gyn clerkship and residency programs Ravenswood Hosp. Med. Ctr., 1993—. Clin. prof. Loyola U., Chgo., 1993-96, U. Ill., 1996—. Host bi-weekly show Sta. WSNS-TV; contbr. articles to profl. jours. Recipient Community Service award Met. Chgo. Healthcare Coun., 1987, Hispanic Health Alliance award, 1985. Fellow ACS (pres. Met. Chgo. chpt. 1998—2001), ACOG (chair Ill. sect. 1996-99), APHA (Latino caucus, Leadership in Pub. Health award 1999), Am. Fertility Soc., Ctrl. Assn. Ob-Gyn; mem. Ill. State Med. Soc. (trustee 1983-87, 1st v.p. 1987-89), Inst. Medicine of Chgo. (gov. 1984-88, v.p. 1986-88), Chgo. Gynecol. Soc. (pres. 1996-97), Chgo. Med. Soc. (pres. 1986-87, John T. O'Connell award 1991, Dist. Achievement award 1994), Kennedy Inst. Ethics. Avocation: writing. Office: Apt 4312 505 N Lake Shore Dr Chicago IL 60611-6435

POMALAPALLY, SRIKANTH SHARMA, information technologist, chemistry researcher; b. Andhra Pradesh, India, Jan. 1, 1964; arrived in U.S., 1991; s. Raghunath Sharma and Anusuya Devi Pomalapally; m. Sunitha Devi Siddhanthi, Dec. 30, 1994; 1 child, Pranav. BSc, Osmania U., Hyderabad, AP, India, 1985; PhD, SUNY, Albany, 1998. Cert. Oracle database adminstr. Database adminstr. Prolific Tech., Rochester, N.Y., 1997-99; sr. database adminstr. Electronic Data Systems, 1999-2000; technologist Amgen Inc., Thousand Oaks, Calif., 2000—. Jr. rsch. fellow Univ. Grants Commn., 1988. Mem. Sigma Xi. Hindu. Avocations: travel reading. Office: Amgen Inc One Amgen Ctr Dr MS 17-1-C Thousand Oaks CA 91320 Fax: 805-499-9096. E-mail: pomalapally@yahoo.com., srikanth@amgen.com.

POMBO, RICHARD, congressman, rancher, farmer; b. Tracy, Calif., 1961; m. Annette, 1983; children: Richard Jr., Rena, Rachael. Student, Calif. State U., Pomona, 1981-83. Councilman City of Tracy, 1991-92; mayor pro-tem Tracy City Coun., 1992; mem. U.S. Congress from 11th Calif. dist., 1993—; mem. agrl. com., chmn. subcom. on livestock and horticulture; mem. resources com., transp. and infrastructure com. Chmn. Pvt. Property Rights Task Force, 1993-94, Endangered Species Act Task Force, 1995-96; co-chmn. Spkr.'s Environ. Task Force, 1996. Co-founder San Joaquin County Citizen's Land Alliance, Calif., 1986—; active San Joaquin County Econ. Devel. Assn., Tracy Bus. Improvement Dist., City Coun. (vice chmn. Cmty. Devel. Agy., Cmty. Parks Com., and Waste Mgmt. Com.), San Joaquin County Rep. Ctrl. Com. Mem. Rotary Club. Roman Catholic. Office: US Ho Reps 2411 Rayburn HOB Washington DC 20515*

POMERANCE, JEFFREY JOSEPH, medical administrator, medical educator, clinical neonatologist; b. N.Y.C., May 13, 1942; s. William and Marjorie Joseph Pomerance; m. Linda Jayne Pomerance, Mar. 5, 1969; children: Elise, Michele. BS, Bklyn. Coll., 1962; MD, U. Vt., 1966; MPH, U. Calif., Berkeley, 1972. Dir. neonatology Cedars-Sinai Med. Ctr., L.A., 1974-97; prof. pediats. UCLA Sch. Medicine, 1989-97; clin. prof. pediats. U. Md. Sch. Medicine, Balt., 1998—; assoc. prof. pediats. Johns Hopkins U. Sch. Medicine, 1998—; head divsn. newborn medicine Greater Balt. Med. Ctr., 1997—. Adj. prof. pub. health UCLA Sch. Pub. Health, 1986-97; pres. Calif. Perinatal Assn., 1983-84, 93-94, Perinatal Adv. Coun. of L.A. Cmtys., 1982-83; treas. Parent Care, 1994-97. Co-editor: (book) Neonatology for the Clinician, 1993; contbr. articles to profl. jours. Chairperson neonatal intensive care unit stds. com. State Adv. Com. for Calif. Children Svcs., Sacramento, Calif., 1985-97. Lt. comdr. USN, 1969-71. Mem. Soc. for Pediat. Rsch., Western Soc. for Pediat. Rsch. Office: Greater Balt Med Ctr 6701 N Charles St Baltimore MD 21204-6808 E-mail: jpomeran@gbmc.org.

POMERANTZ, CHARLOTTE, writer; b. Bklyn., July 24, 1930; d. Abraham L. and Phyllis (Cohen) P.; m. Carl Marzani, Nov. 12, 1966; children: Gabrielle Rose, Daniel Avram. BA, Sarah Lawrence Coll., 1953. Children's books include The Bear Who Couldn't Sleep, 1965, The Moon Pony, 1967, Ask the Windy Sea, 1968, Why You Look Like You Whereas I Look Like Me, 1968, The Day They Parachuted Cats on Borneo, 1971 (chosen for Internat. Year of the Child 1977-78), The Princess and the Admiral, 1974 (Jane Addams Children's Book award), The Piggy in the Puddle, 1974 (Featured on Reading Rainbow in Claymation, 1992, NYT Outstanding Picture Book of the Year award 1974), The Ballad of the Long Tailed Rat, 1975, Detective Poufy's First Case, 1976, The Mango Tooth, 1977 (Jr. Literary Guild Selection), The Downtown Fairy Godmother, 1978, The Tamarindo Puppy and Other Poems, 1980 (an ALA Notable Book), Noah's and Namah's Ark, 1980, If I Had a Paka, 1982 (Jane Addams Honor award 1983), Buffy and Albert, 1982, Posy, 1983 (1984 Christopher award), Whiff, Sniff, Nibble and Chew, 1984, Where's the Bear?, 1984, The Half-Birthday Party (Jr. Literary Guild Selection), 1984, All Asleep, 1984, One Duck, Another Duck, 1984, How Many Trucks Can a Tow Truck Tow? (Children's Book of the Year Libr. of Congress 1991) 1987, Timothy Tall Feather, 1987, The Chalk Doll (Top 10 Picture Books of 1989 Boston Globe, Parents Choice award, 1990) 1989, Flap Your Wings and Try, 1989, Serena Katz, 1992, The Outside Dog (One of 100 Books Recommended by the N.Y. Pub. Libr., 1993, ALA Notable) 1993, Halfway to Your House, 1993, Here Comes Henny, 1994, Mangaboom, 1997, You're Not My Best Friend Anymore, 1998 (Jr. Libr. Guild Selection 1998), Poncho's Older Brother, 1998, The Birthday Letters, 2000, The Mousery, 2000; co-author, lyricist play Eureka!, 1997; author radio play Whiff Sniff Nibble and Chew, 1997; contbr. stories to mags.; spl. editorial asst.: Einstein on Peace, 1960; editor: A Quarter Century of Un-Americana, 1963. Address: 260 W 21st St New York NY 10011-3447

POMERANTZ, JAMES ROBERT, psychology educator, academic administrator; b. N.Y.C., Aug. 21, 1946; s. Mihiel Charles and Elizabeth (Solheim) P.; divorced; children: Andrew Emil, William James; m. Mary B. McIntire, May 23, 1998. BA, U. Mich., 1968; PhD, Yale U., 1974. Prize teaching fellow Yale U., New Haven, 1973-74; asst. prof. psychology Johns Hopkins U., Balt., 1974-77; assoc. prof. SUNY, Buffalo, 1977-83, prof., 1983-88, chmn. dept. psychology, 1986-88, assoc. dean, 1983-86; dean social scis., Elma W. Schneider prof. psychology Rice U., Houston, 1988-95; provost, prof. cognitive and linguistic scis. Brown U., Providence, 1995-98, acting pres., 1997; adj. prof. psychology, dir. neurosci. Rice U., Houston, 1998-99, prof. psychology, 2000—. Adj. prof. Baylor Coll. Medicine, 1992—. Editor: Perceptual Organization, 1981, The Perception of Structure, 1991. Fellow APA, Am. Psychol. Soc.; mem. Psychonomic Soc., Soc. Exptl. Psychologists. E-mail: pomeran@rice.edu.

POMERANTZ, JERALD MICHAEL, lawyer; b. Springfield, Mass., July 9, 1954; s. Lawrence Louis Pomerantz and Dolores (Barez) Chaudoir. BA in Econs. cum laude, Brandeis U., 1976; JD, Vanderbilt U., 1979; student, Am. Inst. Banking, 1983-99. Atty., McAllen, Tex., 1979-80, Weslaco, 1980-85; gen. counsel, sec. Tex. Valley Bancshares, Inc., 1985-87; atty. for Hidalgo County Rural Fire Prevention Dist., Tex., 1982-88; atty. SBA, Harlingen, 1987; pvt. practice Weslaco, 1987-89; adv. dir. South Tex. Fed. Credit Union, 1995-98. Atty. Elsa (Tex.) Housing Authority, 1993—, Weslaco (Tex.) Housing Authority, 1995—, Econ. Devel. Corp. Weslaco, 2001—02. Mem. Weslaco Charter Review Com., 1981-82,; drafted S.B. 139 (amending Tex. bus. and commerce code sect. 9.402(g)) regular session Tex. Legislature), 1989, S.B. 140, 1989, enacted as H.B. 2005 (amending Tex. Credit Code sect. 1.06) regular session Tex. Legislature, 1993. Recipient continuing edn. award Banking Law Inst., 1992. Mem.: Rio Grande Valley Bankruptcy Bar Assn. (v.p. 2000—01), Hidalgo County Bar Assn. (law libr. com. 1999—), Coll. State Bar Tex. (bd.dirs. 1990—95), Conf. on Consumer Fin. Law, State Bar Tex., Tex. Assn. Bank Counsel (bd. dirs. 1990—95, 1997—2000, v.p. 2001—02, pres.-elect 2002—03). Home and Office: PO Box 10 Weslaco TX 78599-0010 E-mail: jmp@justice.com.

POMERANTZ, MARTIN, chemistry educator, researcher; b. N.Y.C., May 3, 1939; s. Harry and Pauline (Sietz) P.; m. Maxine Miller, June 4, 1961; children: Lee Allan, Wendy Jane, Heidi Lauren. BS, CCNY, 1959; MS, Yale U., 1961, PhD, 1964. NSF postdoctoral fellow U. Wis.-Madison, 1963-64; asst. prof. Case Western Res. U., Cleve., 1964-69; assoc. prof. chemistry Yeshiva U., N.Y.C., 1969-74, prof., 1974-76, chmn. dept., 1971-72, 73-76; prof. chemistry U. Tex.-Arlington, 1976—; co-dir. Ctr. for Advanced Polymer Rsch., 1988-91; dir. Ctr. for Advanced Polymer Rsch., 1991—; vis. assoc. prof. U. Wis.-Madison, 1972; vis. prof. Columbia U., N.Y.C., 1970-75, Ben Gurion U. of the Negev, Beer Sheva, Israel, summers 1981, 85. Contbr. articles to sci. jours. Fellow Alfred P. Sloan Found., 1971-76, NSF and Sterling, 1962-63, Leeds and Northrup Found., 1960-62, Woodrow Wilson fellow,

1959-60; grantee NSF, Robert A. Welch Found., Def. Adv. Rsch. Projects Agy., Air Force Office Sci. Rsch., Dept. Energy, Petroleum Rsch. Fund, Tex. Advanced Tech. program, Tex. Advanced Rsch. program, Disting. Record of Rsch. award U. Tex., Arlington, 1997, also others. Mem. Am. Chem. Soc. (Wilfred T. Doherty award Dallas-Fort Worth sect. 1997), Royal Soc. Chemistry, Phi Beta Kappa, Sigma Xi. Achievements include research in synthesis, reactions and properties of organo lambda-5-phosphazenes, reactions of carbenes with other molecules, with themselves and with diazo precursors; design, synthesis and study of electronically conducting polymers with enhanced properties, synthesis and study of electroluminescent (light emitting) polymers, preparation and study of polymeric ionic self-assembled monolayers (ISAMs). Home: 5521 Williamstown Rd Dallas TX 75230-2127 Office: U Tex Dept Chemistry-Biochemistry PO Box 19065 Arlington TX 76019-0065 E-mail: pomerantz@uta.edu.

POMERANTZ, MARTIN A. astronomer, educator; b. Bklyn., Dec. 17, 1916; AB, Syracuse U., 1937; MS, U. Pa., 1939; PhD, Temple U., 1951; D (hon.), U. Uppsala, Sweden, 1967; ScD (hon.), Swarthmore Coll., 1973; DSc (hon.), U. Del., 2001. Rsch. asst. Bartol Rsch. Found., 1938—41, rsch. fellow, 1941—43, physicist, 1943—59, dir., 1959—85, pres., 1985—87; v.p. The Franklin Inst., 1967—85, exec. v.p., 1985—87, Bartol prof., 1968—89; prof. emeritus Bartol Rsch. Inst. U. Del., 1990—. Fulbright scholar, vis. prof. Muslim U., Aligarh, India, 1952—53; leader Nat. Geog. Soc. expeditions, 1948—59; chmn. U.S. Com. for Internat. Yrs. of the Quiet Sun Nat. Acad. Scis., 1962—66, mem. Com. on Polar Rsch., 1959—71, mem. Space Sci. Bd., 1963—70, mem. Geophysics Rsch. Bd., 1959—73; v.p. Com for Internat. Yrs. of the Quiet Sun Internat. Coun. Sci. Unions, v.p. Com. Internat. Geophysique, 1962—66; mem. Com. on Solar-Terrestrial Rsch. Nat. Acad. Scis., 1981—86; vis. prof. astronomy Swarthmore Coll., 1961, 64, 67; vis. prof. U. Tokyo, 1983, Potchefstroom U., South Africa, 1987; Sigma Xi nat. lectr., 68; OAS vis. prof., 73. Editor: Jour. of the Franklin Inst.; mem. editl. bd.: Space Sci. Revs., : Antarctic Rsch. Series. Recipient Centennial Gold medal, Syracuse U., 1970, Prix de la Belgica, Acad. Royal des Scis., des Lettres et des Beaux Arts de Belgique, 1985, Disting. Pub. Svc. award, NSF, 1987, medal for disting. sci. achievement, NASA, 1990. Fellow: AAAS, Am. Geophys. Union, Am. Phys. Soc.; mem.: Am. Polar Soc. (hon.), Rotary Internat., Cosmos Club, Explorers Club, Sigma Pi Sigma (hon.). Home: 100 Deer Valley Rd San Rafael CA 94903

POMERANTZ, MARVIN, thoracic surgeon; b. Suffern, N.Y., June 16, 1934; s. Julius and Sophie (Luksin) Pomerantz; m. Margaret Twigg, Feb. 26, 1966; children: Ben, Julie. AB, Colgate U., 1955; MD, U. Rochester, 1959. Diplomate Nat. Bd. Med. Examiners, Am. Bd. Surgery, Am. Bd. Thoracic Surgery (bd. dirs. 1989-95). Intern Duke U. Med. Ctr., Durham, NC, 1959—60, resident, 1960—61, instr. surgery, 1966—67; asst. prof. surgery U. Colo. Med. Sch., Denver, 1967—71, assoc. prof. surgery, 1971—74, assoc. clin. prof. surgery, 1974—93, prof. surgery, chief gen. thoracic surgery, 1992—; chief thoracic and cardiovascular surgery Denver Gen. Hosp., 1967—73, asst. dir. surgery, 1967—70, assoc.dir. surgery, 1970—73; pvt. practice Arapahoe CV Assocs., Denver, 1974—92; prof., chief gen. thoracic surgery sect. U. Colo. Health Sci. Ctr., 1992—; resident Duke U. Med. Ctr., Durham, NC, 1963—67. Clin. assoc. surgery br. NCI, 1961—63; mem. staff Univ. Hosp., Denver, Denver Gen. Hosp., Rose Med. Ctr., Denver, Denver VA Med. Ctr., Children's Hosp., Denver, U. Coll. Health Sci. Ctr., 1992—, bd. dirs., 1990—96; vice chmn. Am. Bd. Thoracic Surgery, 1995—97, chmn., 1997—99. Guest editor Chest Surgery Clinics N.Am., 1993; contbr. , chapters to books. Master: AMA; fellow: ACS, Am. Coll. Chest Surgeons; mem.: Soc. Vascular Surgeons, Soc. Thoracic Surgeons (nomenclature/coding com. 1991—95, standards and ethics com., govt. rels. com., chmn. program com. 1994—95), Rocky Mtgn. Traumatologic Soc., rgery Soc., Internat. Cardiovascular Soc., Denver Acad. Surgery (pres. 1980), Colo. Med. Soc., Am. Heart Assn. (bd. dirs. Colo. chpt. 1993), Am. Assn. Thoracic Surgeons (program com. 1991), Western Thoracic Surg. Assn. (v.p. 1992, pres. 1993—94, counselor-at-large 1988—90). Office: UCHSC Divsn CTS 4200 E 9th Ave # C310 Denver CO 80262-0001*

POMERANTZ, MARVIN ALVIN, business executive; b. Des Moines, Aug. 6, 1930; s. Alex and Minnie (Landy) P.; m. Rose Lee Lipsey, Nov. 12, 1950; children: Sandy Pomerantz, Marcie Morrison, Vickie Ginsberg, Lori Long. BS in Commerce, U. Iowa, 1952. Exec. v.p. Midwest Bag Co., Des Moines, 1952-60; founder, pres., gen. mgr. Gt. Plains Bag Corp., 1961-75; v.p. Continental Can Co. Inc., Greenwich, Conn., 1971-75; v.p., gen. mgr. Forest Products Brown Systems Operation (div. Continental Can Co. Inc.), 1975-77; pres. Diversified Group Internat. Harvester, Chgo., 1980-81, ex. v.p., 1981-82; pres., chmn., chief exec. officer The Mid-Am. Group, Des Moines, 1981—; chmn., chief exec. officer Gaylord Container Corp., Deerfield, Ill., 1986—2002. Mem. Greater Des Moines Commn.; trustee Drake U., 1978—; pres. Iowa State Bd. Regents, 1987-93, 95-96; mem. U.S. Olympic Budget and Audit Commn., Colorado Springs., Colo., 1989-92. Republican. Office: The Mid-Am Group 4700 Westown Pkwy Ste 303 West Des Moines IA 50266-6718

POMERANTZ, SHERWIN BERNARD, economic development consultant; b. N.Y.C., Nov. 18, 1939; s. Sidney and Ann (Simons) P.; m. Barbara Sue Rashbaum (dec. 1989); children: Debi, Shari (dec.); m. Rishona Miner, July 8, 1990. BS in Indsl. Engring., NYU, 1960; MS, U. Ill., 1962; MBA, Northwestern U., 1966. Instr. U. Ill., Champaign, 1960-62; mech. engr. NASA, Cleve., 1962-64; dir. mktg. Masten Corp., Chgo., 1964-66; pres. Controls For Industry, Inc., 1966-82; v.p. Luz Industries Ltd., Jerusalem, 1984-90; pres. Atid E.D.I. Ltd., 1991—. Columnist Chgo. Jewish Post & Opinion, 1974-76. Pres. Maine Twp. Jewish Congregation, Des Plaines, Ill., 1974-76, United Synagogue of Am., Chgo., 1976-79, Bd. Jewish Edn., Chgo., 1979-82, Assn. Ams. & Canadians in Israel, Jerusalem, 1990-92. Capt. U.S. Army Signal Corps, 1962-64, Cleve. Recipient Nehemian Gitelson medallion Alpha Epsilon Pi, 1975. Mem.: ASME, Israel-Am. C. of C. (dir. 1998—), Com. for Econ. Growth of Israel (dir. 2000—), Visit USA Assn. (sec. 1999—), Am. State Offices Assn. (chair 1996—), Am. Citizens Abroad. Avocations: reading, travel. Home: Hagidud Haivri 6 92144 Jerusalem Israel Office: ATID ETI Ltd 5 Kiryat Madda St 91450 Jerusalem Israel E-mail: sherwin@atid-edi.com.

POMERANZ, FELIX, accounting educator; b. Vienna, Austria, Mar. 28, 1926; s. Joseph and Irene (Meninger) P.; m. Rita Lewin, June 14, 1953; children: Jeffrey Arthur, Andrew Joseph. BBA, CCNY, 1948; MS, Columbia U., 1949; PhD, U. Birmingham, Eng., 1992. Diplomate Am. Bd. Forensic Acctg.; CPA, N.Y., Va., La., N.C.; cert. computer profl., fraud examiner, govt. fin. mgr. Audit staff Coopers & Lybrand, CPAs, N.Y.C., 1949-56; mgr. Marks, Grey & Shron (now Ernst & Young, CPA's), 1956-58; asst. chief auditor Am.-Standard, 1958-62; mgr. systems Westvaco Corp., 1962-66; dir. operational auditing Coopers & Lybrand, CPAs, 1966-68, ptnr., 1968-85; disting. lectr./dir. Ctr. for Acctg., Auditing, Tax Studies Fla. Internat. U., Miami, 1985-93, prof. acctg., 1993—, assoc. dir. sch. acctg., 1993-99, affil. faculty dept. religious studies, 1996—. Author: Managing Capital Budget Projects, 1984; The Successful Audit: New Ways to Reduce Risk Exposure and Increase Efficiency, 1992; co-author: Pensions-An Accounting and Management Guide, 1976; Auditing in the Public Sector: Efficiency, Economy, and Program Results, 1976; Comparative International Auditing Standards, 1985; contbr. articles to profl. jours. Emeritus trustee Nat. Ctr. for Automated Info. Rsch.; founding mem. Ctr. for Study of Islam and Democracy; founder Afghan Inst. Accts. 1st lt. AUS, 1944-46, 51-52. Recipient Spear Safer Harmon faculty fellow Coll. Bus. Adminstrn., 1987, Coll. Bus. Adminstrn., award for outstanding svc., 1998, Matriculation Merit award, 2000. Mem. AICPAs, N.Y. State Soc. CPAs, Assn. Systems Mgmt., Acad. Acctg. Historians, Assn. Govt. Accts., N.Y. Acad. Scis., Am. Acctg. Assn., Inter-Am. Acctg. Assn., Assn. Cert. Fraud Examiners, Beta Gamma Sigma, Beta Alpha Psi (Most Disting. and Most Outstanding Prof. awards 1993, Most Supportive Prof. award 2002), Alpha Kappa Psi (Dr. Felix Pomeranz Faculty of Yr. award, Endless Work award). Home: 250 Jacaranda Dr Apt 406 Fort Lauderdale FL 33324-2532 Office: Fla Internat U Sch Acctg University Park Miami FL 33199-0001 E-mail: pomeranf@fiu.edu.

POMERANZ, JEROME RAPHAEL, dermatopathologist; b. Newark, Dec. 29, 1930; s. Raphael and Zina (Rubinow) P.; m. Jacqueline R. Goldenberg, June 15, 1953 (div. 1973); m. Barbara P. Barna, May 5, 1978; children: Russell Carl, William Eric, Emily Suzanne. BS, George Washington U., 1952; MD, Boston U., 1956. Diplomate Am. Bd. Dermatology, Am. Bd. Dermatopathology. Intern Johns Hopkins Hosp., Balt., 1957-58, resident in dermatology, 1960-63, fellow in allergy, 1963-65, mem. staff; assoc. prof. dermatology Case Western Res. U., Cleve., 1965—95, assoc. prof. pathology, 1967—95, assoc. prof. emeritus, 1995; dir. dermatology Metro Health Med. Ctr., 1965-92, mem. staff, 1992—95. Contbr. articles to profl. jours. Served to capt. M.C., U.S. Army, 1958-60. Fellow ACP, Am. Am. Acad. Dermatology; mem. AAAS, NAS (drug efficacy study panel 1967-69, com. to rev. use of ionizing radiation for treatment of benign diseases 1975-78), Am. Dermatol. Assn., FDA Bur. Drugs (dermatology adv. com. 1981-85, 92-94), Cleve. Dermatol. Soc. (pres. 1973-75), Am. Soc. Dermatopathology, Soc. Investigative Dermatology (membership com. 1975, 76, 77, chmn. 1977, audit com. 1993—), Assn. Profs. Dermatology, N.Y. Acad. Scis., Cleve. Acad. Medicine. Home: 450 Old Reservoir Rd Berea OH 44017-2561 Office: Cleve Skin Pathology Lab 2475 E 22nd St Ste 611 Cleveland OH 44115-3206 E-mail: mutchka@prodigy.net.

POMERANZ, MORTON, lawyer, educator; b. Bklyn., Jan. 11, 1922; s. Jacob S. and Mildred M. (Gover) P.; m. Janet Putnam Morrison, Dec. 18, 1960 (div. 1980); children: John Putnam, Matthew David, Harold Robert; m. Judith Ann Davis, Sept. 2, 1984. AB, Columbia U., 1943, JD, 1945. Bar: N.Y. 1948, U.S. Dist. Ct. D.C. 1955. Vice consul U.S. Fgn. Svc., La Paz, Bolivia, 1945-48; legal cons. U.S. Dept. Commerce, Washington, 1949-59; internat. activities asst. U.S. Dept. Interior, 1960-65; various positions and acting gen. counsel U.S. Trade Rep., 1965-80; of counsel Gage, Tucker & Von Baur, 1980-86, Gage & Tucker, Washington, 1986-92, Faegre and Benson, Washington, 1993—95. Adj. prof. Antioch Ctr. Legal Svcs., Washington, 1983-84; panelist dispute resolutions Can.-U.S. Free Trade Agreement, 1989—. Contbr. articles to profl. jours. Mem. adv. bd. on social studies, Arlington (Va. Sch. Bd., 1978-80. Mem. ABA (chmn. L.Am. law com. 1958-61), Am. Soc. Internat. Law. Home: 1300 Crystal Dr # 1409 Arlington VA 22202-3234

POMERENE, JAMES HERBERT, retired computer engineer; b. Yonkers, N.Y., June 22, 1920; s. Joel Pomerene and Elsie Bower; m. Edythe R. Schwenn, Dec. 1, 1944; children: James Bennett, Katherine Ellen, Andrew Thomas Stewart. BSEE, Northwestern U., 1942; postgrad., Princeton U., 1950. Elec. engr. Hazeltine Corp., Little Neck, N.Y., 1942-46; mem. staff electronic computer project Inst. for Advanced Study, Princeton, N.J., 1946-51, chief engr., 1951-56; sr. engr. IBM Corp., Poughkeepsie, N.Y., 1956-67, sr. staff mem. Armonk, 1967-76. Cons. in field. Patentee in field. IBM fellow T.J. Watson Rsch. Ctr., 1976—. Fellow IEEE (Computer Pioneer award Computer Soc. 1986, Edison medal 1993); mem. NAE, Sigma Xi, Tau Beta Pi. Episcopalian. Home: 403 Bedford Rd N Chappaqua NY 10514-2207 E-mail: jhpomerene@aol.com.

POMEROY, BENJAMIN SHERWOOD, veterinary medicine educator; b. St. Paul, Apr. 24, 1911; s. Benjamin A. and Florence A. (Sherwood) P.; m. L. Margaret Lyon, June 25, 1938; children: Benjamin A., Sherwood R., Catherine A., Margaret D. D.V.M., Iowa State U., 1933; MS, Cornell U., 1934; PhD, U. Minn., 1944, D. Sci. (hon.), 2001. Diagnostician U. Minn., 1934-38, faculty, 1938-81, prof., 1948-81, prof. emeritus, 1981—, head dept. vet. microbiology and pub. health, 1953-73, assoc. dean, 1970-74, acting dean, 1979-80. Mem. adv. com. FDA; cons. animal scis. divsn. and animal health divsn., meat insp. service, animal health service USDA. Co-author: Diseases and Parasites of Poultry, 1958; contbg. author: Diseases of Poultry, 1972, 78, 84, 91, 97. Republican precinct officer, 1958-60, chmn., 1960-61; chmn. Ramsey County (Minn.) Rep. Com., 1961-65, 4th Congl. Dist., 1961-63, 67-69; mem. Minn. Rep. Central Com., 1961-71; del. Minn. Rep. Conv., 1960-71, 92, 94, 96, Rep. Nat. Conv., 1964. Named Veterinarian of Year in Minn., 1970; recipient Eminent Citizen award St. Anthony Park Legion Post and Aux., 1955, Alumni Merit award, 1975, Stange award, 1977, Disting. Achievement citation, 1981 (all Iowa State U.), Centennial Merit award U. Pa., 1984, Animal Health award USDA, 1986, Siehl Prize for Excellence in Agriculture, U. Minn., 1999; named to Am. Poultry Hall of Fame, 1977, Minn. Livestock Hall of Fame, 1997. Fellow Poultry Sci. Assn.; mem. Nat. Turkey Fedn. (life, Research award 1950), Tex. Poultry Assn. (life), Minn. Turkey Growers Assn. (life), Soc. Exptl. Biology and Medicine, Am. Assn. Avian Pathologists (life), Am. Coll. Vet. Microbiologists, Am. Acad. Microbiology, AVMA (council research 1961-73, Pub. Service award 1980, AVMA award 1999), U.S. Animal Health Assn. (life), Nat. Acad. of Practice, Minn. Vet. Med. Assn. (sec.-treas. 1950-75, pres. 1978-79, Disting. Service award 1980, presdl. award 1992), Sigma Xi, Phi Kappa Phi, Alpha Gamma Rho, Phi Zeta, Gamma Sigma Delta. Presbyterian (elder). Home: 1443 Raymond Ave Saint Paul MN 55108-1430

POMEROY, CARL FREDRICK, petroleum engineer; b. Topeka, Aug. 11, 1953; s. Elwaine Franklin and Joanne Carolynne (Bunge) P.; m. Deborah Diane Hall, Dec. 26, 1981; children: Brandon, Matthew, Tyler, Tessa. BS in Chem. Engring., U. Okla., 1975, MS in Petroleum Engring., 1979. Engr. asst. Texaco, Kingfisher, Okla., 1974; petroleum engr. Cities Svc. Co., Okla. City, 1975-81; prodn. mgr. Plains Resources, Inc., Oklahoma City, 1981-82; sr. staff reservoir engr. Koch Exploration Co., Wichita, Kans., 1982-90, Koch Exploration Co. Can., Ltd., Calgary, Alberta, Can., 1990-95; chief econ. engr. Koch Capital Svcs. Producer Fin., Wichita, 1995-96; chief evaluation engr. Koch Producer Svcs., Houston, 1996-98; prin. Kirkpatric Energy Assocs., 1998-2000; consulting engr. Madison Energy Advisors, Inc., 2000; ind. cons., 2000—01; resevoir engring. mgr. KCS Energy, Inc., Tulsa, 2001—. Chmn. dean's student adv. com., U. Okla., Norman, 1974-75; vis. asst. prof. U. Okla., Norman, 1978-79. Co-author: (book) Biomass Conversion Processes, 1979. Rep. state del., Okla., 1975-80. Named Mr. Future Bus. Leader of Am., 1971. Mem. NSPE, Soc. Petroleum Engrs., Kans. Engring. Soc. (Young Engr. of Yr. 1988). Home: 3023 Fox Ledge Dr Stillwater OK 74074 Office: 7130 S Lewis Ave Ste 700 Tulsa OK 74136 E-mail: carlpomeroy@hotmail.com.

POMEROY, EARL R. congressman, former state insurance commissioner; b. Valley City, N.D., Sept. 2, 1952; s. Ralph and Myrtle Pomeroy; m. Laurie Kirby, Dec. 26, 1986. BA, U. N.D., 1974, JD, 1979. Atty. Sproul, Lenaburg, Fitzner and Walker, Valley City, 1979-84; commr. of ins. State of N.D., 1984-92; mem. U.S. Congress from N.D. (at large), Washington, 1993—; mem. ways and means com. State rep. N.D. Legis. Assembly, 1980-84. Recipient Found. award Rotary, 1975; named Outstanding Young North Dakotan N.D. Jaycees, 1982. Mem. Nat. Assn. of Ins. Commrs. (chmn. midwest zone 1987-88, exec. com. 1987-88), Phi Beta Kappa. Democrat. Presbyterian. Office: US Ho Rep 1110 Longworth Bldg Washington DC 20515-3401*

POMEROY, HARLAN, lawyer; b. Cleve., May 7, 1923; s. Lawrence Alson and Frances (Macdonald) P.; m. Barbara Lesser, Aug. 24, 1962; children: Robert Charles, Caroline Macdonald, Harlan III BS, Yale U., 1945; JD, Harvard U., 1948. Bar: Conn. 1949, U.S. Supreme Ct. 1954, U.S. Ct. Appeals (fed. cir.) 1954, Ohio 1958, U.S. Dist. Ct. (no. dist.) Ohio 1958, U.S. Claims Ct. 1958, U.S. Ct. Appeals (6th cir.) 1958, U.S. Tax Ct. 1958, D.C. 1975, Md. 1981, U.S. Dist. Ct. (D.C. dist.) 1984, U.S. Ct. Internat. Trade 1984, U.S. Ct. Appeals (D.C. cir.) 1986; cert. county ct. mediator, Fla. Atty. trial sect. tax div. Dept. Justice, Washington, 1952-58; assoc. Baker & Hostetler, Cleve., 1958-62, ptnr., 1962-75, Washington, 1975-92. Gen. chmn. Cleve. Tax Inst., 1971; fgn. legal advisor to Romanian Securities Mkts., 1997, Macedonia, 1998, UN Interim Adminstrn. Mission in Kosovo, 2000-2001; arbitrator Nat. Assn. Securities Dealers, 1992—, N.Y. Stock Exch., 1995—, Sarasota Better Bus. Coun., 1997—; arbitrator Multistate Tax Commn., 1996—, mem. neutral roster IRS mediation program; lectr. on tax and comml. law. Author: (monographs) The Privatization Process in Bulgaria; Bulgarian Government Structure and Operation-An Overview; contbr. articles to profl. jours. Treas. Shaker Heights (Ohio) Dem. Club, 1960-62; trustee, mem. exec. com. 1st Unitarian Ch. Cleve., 1965-68; trustee River Road Unitarian Ch., Bethesda, Md., 1988-90; gen. counsel, former asst. treas. John Glenn Presdl. Com., 1983-87; participant Vol. Lawyers Project, Legal Counsel for Elderly, Washington, 1983-92; vol. Guardian Ad Litem Program, Sarasota, Fla., 1990-92, GED-H.S. Equivalency Program, Sarasota, 1990-92; participant Guardianship Monitoring program 12th Jud. Cir., Fla., 1996-97; vol. exec. fgn. legal advisor Internat. Exec. Svc. Corps. with Privatization Ministry, Prague, Czech Republic, 1994-95; mem. spl. mission to Bulgarian Ministry of Fin., U.S. Dept. Treasury, 1995. Mem. ABA (resident liaison Bulgaria for Ctrl. and East European Law Initiative 1992-93), Am. Arbitration Assn. (arbitrator 1992-2000), D.C. Bar Assn., The Field Club (Sarasota, Fla.), Yale Club of the Suncoast, Ivy League Club of Sarasota. Home: 7336 Villa D Este Dr Sarasota FL 34238-5648 Office: Baker & Hostetler 1050 Connecticut Ave NW Ste 11 Washington DC 20036-5351

POMEROY, HORACE BURTON, III, accountant, corporate executive; b. Bronxville, N.Y., July 11, 1937; s. Horace Burton Jr. and Juhn P.; m. Margarita Maria Benavidez, July 14, 1973; children: Josephine, Emily. BS in Bus Adminstrn., U. Ariz., 1964; MBA, Boise State U., 1982. CPA 1984. Comml. bank officer Continental Bank, Chgo., 1964-67; cons. Morgan Olmstead Kennedy Gardner, L.A., 1967-74; mgr. cash and banking Morrison Knudsen Corp., Boise, Idaho, 1974-88. Rep. Idaho State Legislature Dist. 16, 1988—; mem. com. Transp. and Def., Joint Fin. and Appropriations. With U.S. Army, 1959-60. Mem. NRA, Nat. Corp. Cash Mgrs. Assn., Nat. Philat. Assn., Rotary. Republican. Episcopalian. Avocations: stamp collecting, fishing, golf, tennis. Home: 6822 Kingsdale Dr Boise ID 83704-7343 Office: Statehouse Boise ID 83720-0001 E-mail: hodp@aol.com.

POMEROY, KENT LYTLE, physical medicine and rehabilitation physician; b. Phoenix, Apr. 21, 1935; s. Benjamin Kent and Laverne (Hamblin) Pomeroy; m. Karen Jodelle Thomas (dec. Dec. 1962); 1 child Charlotte Ann ; m. Margo Delilah Tuttle, Mar. 27, 1964 (div. Jan. 1990); children: Benjamin Kent II, Janel Elise, Jonathan Barrett, Kimberly Eve, Kathryn M.; m. Brenda Pauline North, Sept. 1, 1990. BS in Phys. Sci., Ariz. State U., 1960; MD, U. Utah, 1963. Diplomate Am. Bd. Phys. Medicine and Rehab., Am. Bd. Pain Medicine, lic. homeopathic medicine Ariz., diploma Brit. Inst. Homeopathy. Rotating intern Good Samaritan Hosp., Phoenix, 1963-64, resident in phys. medicine and rehab., 1966-69, asst. tng. dir. Inst. Rehab. Medicine, 1970-74, dir. residency tng., 1974-76, asst. med. dir., 1973-76; dir. Phoenix Phys. Medicine Ctr., 1980-85, Ariz. Found. on Study Pain, Phoenix, 1980-85; pvt. practice, Phoenix and Scottsdale, Ariz., 1985—. Lectr. in field. Contbr. Leader Theodore Roosevelt coun. Boy Scouts Am.; mem. exec. posse Maricopa County Sheriff's Office, Phoenix, 1981—, posse comdr., 1992—94, qualified armed posseman; mem. med. adv. bd. Grand Canyon-Saguaro chpt. Nat. Found. March of Dimes, 1970—78, missionary, 1955—57. Recipient Scouter's Tng. award, Theodore Roosevelt coun. Boy Scouts Am., 1984, Scouter's Woodbadge, 1985. Fellow: Am. Coll. Pain Mgmt. & Sclerotherapy; mem.: AMA, Ariz. Homeopathic and Integrative Med. Assn. (pres. 2001—), Am. Assn. Orthopedic Medicine (co-founder, past pres., mem. emeritus), Ariz. Narcotic Officers Assn., Law Enforcement Alliance of Am., Nat. Sheriff's Assn., Ariz. Med. Assn., Ariz. Soc. Phys. Medicine (pres. 1977—78), Nat. Eagle Scout Assn., Am. Acad. Pain Medicine, Prolotheraphy Assn. (pres. 1981—83). Mem. Lds Ch. Avocations: camping, drawing, painting, writing, music.

POMEROY, LEE HARRIS, architect; b. N.Y.C., Nov. 19, 1932; s. Alfred and Florence Pomeroy; m. Sarah Pomeroy; children: Jordana, Jeremy, Alexandra BArch, Rensselaer Poly. Inst., 1955; MArch, Yale U., 1961. Registered architect, N.Y., Conn., Mass., Vt., N.J., Fla., Pa., Maine, Nat. Coun. of Registrators Bd. Architect William Tabler, N.Y.C., 1958-59, The Architects Collaborative, Cambridge, Mass., 1959-60; asst. prof. CCNY, 1962-64; pres. Lee Harris Pomeroy Assocs., N.Y.C., 1965-87. Adj. prof. Sch. Architecture, CUNY, 1964-87; prin. solar rsch. group ECOSOL, Conn., Eng., Spain, 1965-84; dir. Project for Pub. Spaces, Inc., N.Y.C., 1982-88; dean's adv. coun. Sch. Architecture, Resselaer Poly, Inst., 1991—, adv. to pres., 1994-98. Prin. works include Swiss Bank Tower and Saks Fifth Ave. extension, N.Y.C. (Arthur Ross award 1991), restoration of Plaza Hotel, N.Y., Sch. Art and Dance City Coll., N.Y.C., 1989, New Rochelle Pub. Libr., 1980 (AIA-ALA design award 1980, N.Y. State AIA and Urban Design awards 1980), Dutchess County Jail, Poughkeepsie, N.Y. (AIA-ACA design award 1981), HBO Satellite Comm. Ctr., 1983 (N.Y. State AIA design award 1984), Manitou Sta. planned cmty., 1973 (AIA and Progressive Architecture awards 1973), Henry St. studios artists housing (Progressive Architecture mag. design award 1963, AIA design award 1975), Bedford Mews housing (AIA, Owens Corning energy conservation and Record Homes design awards 1980), Fulton Mall, Bklyn., 1985 (City Club N.Y.C. Bard award for design 1985), Trinity Ch. Bridge (AIA design award 1991), Hotel Usixtu, Prague, Czech Republic, Lally Sch. of Mgmt. and Tech., Rensselaer Polytech. Inst., Troy, N.Y., Reconstruction of Union Square Subway, Reconstruction Lincoln Ctr. Subway Sta., N.Y.C., 2001, M.O.M.A. and Lincoln Center Stas., N.Y.; renovated St. James Ch., N.Y.C.; Teda Convention Center, Hotel and Theme Park in Tonjuin, China, Cosco Housting and Comml. Ctr., Shanghai, Jin Lin Hotel on Hynon Island. Mem. Cmty. Bd. 5, Midtown Manhattan, N.Y.C., 1980-91; bd. dirs. Bellview Assn., with Bellview Med. Ctr., N.Y.C., 1992—; trustee Putnam County Hist. Soc. and Foundry Mus. 1st lt. USA Signal Corp., 1955-57. Recipient Mcpl. Arts Soc. award, N.Y.C., 1982; Nat. Endowment for Arts grantee, N.Y.C., 1983 Fellow AIA (bd. dirs. 1979-81), Inst. of Urban Design; mem. Mcpl. Arts Soc., Regional Plan Assn., Yale Club, Century Club, City Club N.Y. (co-chmn. Bard award program for excellence in urban design 1988-90, 94). Avocations: tennis, photography, travel. Home: 285 Central Park W New York NY 10024-3006 Office: 462 Broadway Fl 3 New York NY 10013-2696 E-mail: leepom@lhparch.com.

POMEROY, ROBERT CORTTIS, lawyer; b. Syracuse, N.Y., Sept. 17, 1943; s. Stuart E. and Elizabeth (Corttis) P.; m. Sandra Campbell; children: Lisa, Robert Jr., Heather. AB, Hamilton Coll., 1965; LLB, Harvard U., 1968. Bar: Mass. 1968, Fla. 1981. Assoc. Goodwin Procter LLP (formerly Goodwin, Procter & Hoar LLP), Boston, 1968-76, ptnr., 1977—. Mem. Am. Coll. Trust & Estate Counsel. Avocations: skiing, golf, sailing. Home: 3 Pier 7 Charlestown MA 02129-4225 Office: Goodwin Procter LLP Exchange Pl Boston MA 02109-2881 E-mail: rpomeroy@goodwinprocter.com.

POMEROY, WYMAN BURDETTE, business owner, consultant; b. Flint, Mich., Feb. 5, 1932; s. Burdette Talmadge and Bernice (Caywood) P.; m. Anna Lee Farley, May 23, 1953; children: Brian Lee, David Michael. Student, Eastern Mich. Coll. Commerc, 1951; student, U. Mich., 1972-73, 75, Mott Community Coll., 1972-75, Oakland Community Coll., 1974. Commanding officer 5th Dist. fire marshal div. Mich. State Police, Paw Paw, 1955-79; fire investigator Fla. State Fire Marshall, Tampa, 1979-80; pres. W.B. Pomeroy & Assocs., Inc., Brandon, Fla., 1980—. Pvt. practice comml. property mgmt. Highland Properties of Gulfcoast, Ltd., Hillsborough and Pinellas Counties, Fla.; cons. hazardous materials code fire marshal divsn. Mich. State Police, Paw Paw, 1978, cons. pub. assn. code, 1978. With prodn. and lighting coms. Houghton Lake (Mich.) Playhouse, 1967-71. Staff sgt. USAF, 1951-55, ETO Recipient Citation, Justice Ct., 1966, Cert. of Appreciation, Flint Fire Dept., 1977, Letter of Appreciation, FBI, 1980. Mem. Am. Soc. Safety Engrs., Internat. Assn. Arson Investigators, Fla. Adv. Commn. on Arson Prevention, Nat. Fire Protection Assn., Arson Coop. of Fla., Lions. Avocations: golf, boating, fishing. Office: WB Pomeroy & Assocs Inc PO Box 2042 Brandon FL 33509-2042 E-mail: wpalp@aol.com.

POMFRET, DAVID B. medical educator, internist; b. Somerset, Mass., Nov. 22, 1937; s. David B. Pomfret and Rhea Chouinard; m. Anna Rafferty, Mar. 31, 1964; children: Mark, Bruce, Scott, Heidi. BS, Stonehill Coll., 1959; MD, Univ. Coll., Dublin, Ireland, 1964. Diplomate Am. Bd. Internal Medicine. Chief of medicine Leonard Morse Hosp., Natick, Mass., 1968—71, chief of staff, 1976—80; clin. prof. Tufts U., Boston, 1976—; prof. medicine Tumaini U., Moshi, Tanzania, 1996—2000. Author: Computer Science, 1998, Dispatches From Kilimanjaro, 2001. Fellow: ACP. Avocations: skiing, sailing, offshore racing. Home: 20 Grey Gull Rd Jamestown RI 02835-2808 Office: Kilimanjaro Christian Med Ctr Box 3010 Moshi Tanzania Home Fax: 401-423-0291. E-mail: pomfret1@cox.net.

POMORSKI, STANISLAW, lawyer, educator; b. Lwow, Poland, Nov. 23, 1934; arrived in U.S., 1972, naturalized, 1983; s. Juliusz and Maria (Ziemba) Pomorski; m. Patricia Smith; children: Lukasz, Christopher, Maria. M.Law, U. Warsaw, 1956, D.Law, 1968. Law clk., 1958-61; pvt. practice law Warsaw, 1961-64; vis. scholar Harvard U. Law Sch., Cambridge, Mass., 1964-66; rsch. assoc. Polish Acad. Scis., 1966-72; mem. faculty Rutgers U. Law Sch., Camden, N.J., 1973—, prof. law NJ, 1977-81, disting. prof. law, 1981—. Fellow Soviet law U. Leyden, Netherlands, 1980—81; trustee Nat. Coun. Soviet and East European Rsch., Washington, 1988—94. Author: (book) American Common Law and the Principle Nullum Crimen Sine Lege, 2d edit., 1975, Restructuring the System of Ownership in the USSR, 1991, On

Multiculturalism, Concepts of Crime and the De Minimis Defense, 1997, Justice in Siberia, 2001. Fellow, Ford Found., 1972—73. Office: Rutgers U Law Sch 5th And Penn St Camden NJ 08102 E-mail: pomorski@crab.rutgers.edu.

POMPADUR, I. MARTIN, communications executive; b. Bklyn., June 25, 1935; s. Jack and Florence (Raitbord) P.; m. Joan Lynn Krassner, Dec. 18, 1960 (div. 1986); children: F. Douglas (dec.), Jana Sue; m. Marian Hackett, Dec. 23, 1987; 1 child, Chelsea Rae. BA, Williams Coll., 1955; LLB, U. Mich., 1958. Bar: Conn. 1958, N.Y. 1961. Atty. ABC-TV Network, N.Y.C., 1960-61, 61-66, chief adminstrv. officer, 1966-68, gen. mgr., 1968-70, v.p. broadcast div., 1970-72, corp. v.p., 1972; pres. ABC Leisure Group I, 1973-75, asst. to pres. parent co., 1975-76; also dir. parent co.; sr. v.p. Ziff Corp., 1977-78, pres., 1978-82; chmn., chief exec. officer GP Sta. Ptnrs., 1982-96; mng. gen. ptnr. TV Sta. Ptnrs., 1982-96; chmn., CEO PBTV, Inc., 1984-96; mng. gen. ptnr. Northeastern TV Investors Ltd. Partnership, 1984-96; prin. owner, sec. Caribbean Internat. News Corp., 1985—, also bd. dirs.; CEO, COO RP Media Mgmt., Inc., 1986-93; CEO ML Media Ptnrs., L.P., 1986—; CEO, COO RP Opportunity Mgmt., 1998—; CEO ML Media Opportunity Ptnrs., L.P., 1988—; exec. v.p. News Corp.; pres. News Corp. Ea. Ctrl. Europe; chmn. News Corp. Europe, 2000—. Prin. shareholder Hispanic Media Inc., 1986-90; prin. shareholder, vice-chmn. Hunter Pub. L.P., 1986-94; co-trustee Lidan Trust, 1983—; atty. Young & Rubicam, Inc., advt. agy., N.Y.C., summer 1961. Mem. Stamford bd. reps., chmn. legis. and rules com., 1959-60. Office: News Corp 4th Fl 1211 Ave of the Americas New York NY 10036 also: News Corp Europe 1 Virginia St 6th Fl London England

POMPAN, JACK MAURICE, management consultant; b. N.Y.C., Jan. 23, 1926; s. Maurice A. and Helen (Schmidt) P. m. Esther Terri Scharaga, July 4, 1958; children: Neil Charles, Lori Beth. BS in Indsl. Mgmt., Ga. Inst. Tech., 1948; MBA with distinction, NYU, 1973, advanced profl. cert., 1978. Trainee to budget mgr. Redmond Co., Owosso, Mich., 1948-55; mgmt. cons. Coopers and Lybrand, N.Y.C., 1955-60; contr. Hazel Bishop Inc., 1960-61; treas. Floyds Stores Inc., Valley Stream, N.Y., 1961-66; pres. Farmers Pantry Inc., Mamaroneck, 1966-68; v.p. pub. div. Intext, Inc., N.Y.C., 1968-74; prin. Baxter, Pompan & Storr, Mgmt. Cons., and predecessors, Greenwich, Conn. and N.Y.C., 1974-83, Jack M. Pompan, Mgmt. Cons., Rockville Centre, N.Y., 1983-92, Pompan & Co., Rockville Centre, 1992—; v.p. Eisner Computer Solutions, LLC, N.Y.C., 1997-98. Adj. prof. Hofstra U., 1977, Roth Grad. Sch. Bus. Adminstrn., C.W. Post Ctr., L.I. U., 1974-79, NYU, 1982-89. Bus. and econs. editor Info. Please Almanac, 1978-82. Trustee edn. chmn., v.p. Cen. Synogogue, Rockville Centre, N.Y., 1983-86, pres. 1986-88; ;bd. dirs. Rosa Lee Young Childhood Ctr. Lt. USNR, 1943-46, 51-53. Mem. Exec. Forum at NYU (bd. dirs.), Inst. Mgmt. Accts. (cert. merit 1953), Turnaround Mgmt. Assn., L.I. Venture Group, Inst. Mgmt. Cons., Am. Jewish Com., Princeton Club N.Y. Office: 70-01 Maine Ave Rockville Centre NY 11570-3641

POMPA-PILLAI, DONNA ANN, social worker, educator, psychotherapist; b. Astoria, N.Y., Feb. 19, 1953; d. Charles Nicholas and Theresa (Caputo) P. BA, Oneonta State U., 1975; MSW, Rutgers U., 1984. Cert. clin. social worker. Prof. NYU, N.Y.C., 1995—; dir. social work Woodbridge Multi-Svc. Program Aging, 1984-85; sr. social worker Project H.O.P.E., N.Y.C., 1986-87; sr. social worker ages 16 and up Beth Abraham Health Svcs., 1987—. Instr. Woodbridge High Sch. Adult Edn., 1986; field instr. Hunter Coll., N.Y.C., 1989-89, NYU, 1990—. Mem. NASW, Acad. Cert. Social Workers, N.Y. Inst. Integral Human Devel. (sec., bd. dirs. 1986—), Assn. for Anthropology and Gerontology, Am. Anthrop. Assn. Avocations: piano, violin, guitar, poetry, travel, field study. Home: 541 W 239th St Bronx NY 10463-1205

POMPER, PHILIP, history educator; b. Chgo., Apr. 18, 1936; s. Solomon and Rebecca (Fenigstein) P.; m. Alice N. Epstein, Aug. 27, 1961 (div.); children: Erica, Stephen, Karen; m. Emily Meyer, June 26, 1994. BA, U. Chgo., 1959, MA, 1961, PhD, 1965. Instr. history Wesleyan U., Middletown, Conn., 1964-65, asst. prof., 1965-71, assoc. prof., 1971-76, prof., 1976—, chmn. dept. history, 1981-84; William F. Armstrong prof. history, 1992—. Author: The Russian Revolutionary Intelligentsia, 1970, 2nd edit., 1993, Peter Lavrov and the Russian Revolutionary Movement, 1972, Sergei Nechaev, 1979 (Choice award 1979), The Structure of Mind in History: Five Major Figures in Psychohistory, 1985, Trotsky's Notebooks, 1933-35: Writings on Lenin, Dialectics and Evolutionism, 1986, Lenin, Trotsky, and Stalin: The Intelligentsia and Power, 1990; assoc. editor History and Theory, 1991—; editor: World History: Ideologies, Structures, and Identities, 1998; co-editor: History and Theory, Contemporary Readings, 1998; The Return of Science: Evolution, History, and Theory, 2002; co-editor: The Return of Science: Evolution, History and Theory, 2002; contbr. articles on Russian history and theory of history to profl. jours. Fellow, Ford Found., 1963-64, Social Scis. Rsch. Coun., 1968, Hoover Instn., 1987, Wilson Ctr., 1988; Russian Rsch. Ctr. scholar, 1987—. Mem. Am. Assn. for Advancement Slavic Studies, Conn. Acad. Arts and Scis. Home: 13 Red Orange Rd Middletown CT 06457-4916 Office: History Dept Wesleyan U Middletown CT 06459-0001 E-mail: ppomper@wesleyan.edu.

POND, DALE C. company executive; Sr. v.p. mktg. and merchandising Payless Cashway; sr. v.p. mktg. Montgomery Ward & Co., Chgo., 1989—92, Lowe's Cos. Inc., 1993—, exec. v.p. merchandising and mktg., 1998—. Address: PO Box 1111 North Wilkesboro NC 28656-0001 also: 1605 Curtis Bridge Rd Wilkesboro NC 28697

POND, LINDA RAE, senior research scientist, administrator; b. Flint, Mich., Aug. 22, 1944; d. Frederick Lewis and Orle Darlene (Fairbanks) Smith; m. Joseph M. Wood, Aug. 31, 1964 (div. 1979); children: Timothy Joseph, Melissa Jill; m. Daniel James Pond, June 18, 1983; children: David Alan, Steven Douglas. BS in Orgnl. Comm., U. Ctrl. Fla., 1983; MS in Human Resource Mgmt., Fla. Inst. Tech., 1985. System engrng. specialist Harris Corp., Melbourne, Fla., 1984-90; sr. rsch. scientist Pacific N.W. Lab., Richland, Wash., 1990-94, mgr. operational effectiveness, 1994—. Mem. Acad. Mgmt., Phi Kappa Phi. Home: 426 Vera Dr Santa Fe NM 87501-1360

POND, MARGUERITE ELIZABETH, music educator; b. Chgo., Aug. 14, 1930; d. Carl Herbert and Ada Marie (Gressens) Scaer; m. James Burton Pond, Aug. 10, 1957; children: James, Jeanne Marie, Christopher Allen. BA, Northwestern U., 1952. Professional singer, soloist summer stock and chs., Oak Park and Wheaton, Ill., 1952-70; piano instr. Exton, Pa., 1975—. Jordan Kitts Piano Co. grantee, 2001; Tchg. scholarship in name AAUW, 1996. Mem. Music Tchrs. Nat. Assn. (cert.), Pa. Music Tchrs. Assn. (bd. dirs. 1986-90), Phila. Music Tchrs. Assn. (bd. mem. 1984-87), Guild Am. Musicians, Main Line Music Tchrs. (pres. 1980-82, 91-93), Mu Phi Epsilon. Avocation: singing in choir. Home and Office: 321 Huffman Dr Exton PA 19341-2127 E-mail: jpond@early.com.

POND, PATRICIA BROWN, library science educator, university administrator; b. Mankato, Minn., Jan. 17, 1930; d. Patrick H. and Florence M. (Ruehle) Brown; m. Judson S. Pond, Aug. 24, 1959. BA, Coll. St. Catherine, St. Paul, 1952; MA, U. Minn., 1955; PhD, U. Chgo., 1982. Sch. libr., Minn., N.Y., 1952-62; asst. prof. libr. sci. U. Minn., 1962-63; reference libr. U. Mont., 1963-65; asst. prof. U. Oreg., 1967-72, assoc. prof., 1972-77; prof., dept. chair, assoc. dean Sch. Libr. and Info. Sci. U. Pitts., 1977-85. Mem. ALA (life), Phi Beta Kappa, Beta Phi Mu, Delta Phi Lambda, Kappa Gamma Pi. Home: 15829 SW Village Cir Beaverton OR 97007-3532 E-mail: ppond@iopener.net.

POND, PEGGY ANN, librarian; b. Balt., Sept. 27, 1951; d. William Garland and Charlotte Jane (Zepp) Born; m. William Wright Pond, May 13, 1950; children: Stephany Erin, Averil Paij. BA, U. Md., 1973; MLA, We. Md. Coll., 1988. With Carroll County Gen. Hosp., Westminster, Md., 1969-86; tchr. English Carroll County Bd. Edn., 1973-76, 86-89; ptnr., mgr. Classic Lady Clothing, 1985-89; info. asst. Carroll County Pub. Libr., 1989-90, program asst., 1990-96; dir. youth and family ministry St. Paul's United Ch. of Christ, 1996-2000; libr. asst. Carroll County Pub. Libr., 2000—. Tutor Carroll County Bd. Edn., 1979-84 Fair judge Carroll County 4-H Assn., 1983—; lay dir. Md. Chrysalis, 1993-94; elections judge Carroll County Elections Bd., 1984—. Mem. NEA, Md. Libr. Assn., Md. Tchrs. Assn., Puppeteers Am., Order Ea. Star (worthy matron 1982-84). Republican. Methodist. Avocations: reading, needle crafts, writing poetry, clowning.

POND, PHYLLIS JOAN RUBLE, state legislator, educator; b. Warren, Ind., Oct. 25, 1930; d. Clifford E. and Rosa E. (Hunnicutt) Ruble; m. George W. Pond, June 10, 1951; children: William, Douglas, Jean Ann. BS, Ball State U., Muncie, Ind., 1951; MS, Ind. U., 1963. Tchr. home econs., 1951-54; kindergarten tchr., 1961-98; mem. Ind. Ho. of Reps., Inpdls., 1978—, majority asst. caucus chmn., vice chmn. ways and means com., 1995. Active Rep. Precinct Com., 1976—; del. Ind. Rep. Conv., 1976, 80, 84, 86, 88, 90, 92, 96, 2000; alt. del. Rep. Nat. Conv., 1980, del., 1996; alt. del. to Rep. Nat. conv., 2000. Mem. AAUW, Regional Red Cross Bio-Med. Bd., New Haven Am. Legion Aux., New Haven Woman's Club. Lutheran.

POND, THOMAS ALEXANDER, physics educator, university official; b. L.A., Dec. 4, 1924; s. Arthur Francis and Florence (Alexander) P.; m. Barbara Eileen Newman, Sept. 6, 1958; children: Arthur Phillip Ward, Florence Alexandra. AB, Princeton U., 1947, A.M., 1949, PhD, 1953; DSc, SUNY, Stony Brook, 1998. Instr. physics Princeton U., 1951-53; asst. prof., then assoc. prof. physics Washington U., St. Louis, 1953-62; prof. physics SUNY, Stony Brook, 1962-81, prof. emeritus, 1982—, chmn. dept., 1962-68, exec. v.p., 1967-79, acting pres., 1970, 75, 78; prof. physics Rutgers U., New Brunswick, N.J., exec. v.p., chief acad. officer, 1982-91, exec. v.p., chief acad. officer emeritus, 1991—, acting pres., 1990, prof., 1991-97, prof. emeritus, 1997—; acting sr. v.p. for acad. affairs U. Medicine and Dentistry N.J., 1998. Bd. dirs. Action Com. for L.I., 1978-80, Tri-State Regional Planning Commn., 1979-82; trustee Univs. Research Assn., 1985-87; bd. dirs. Fermilab, 1987-89. Served to ensign USNR, 1943-46. Fellow AAAS; mem. Am. Phys. Soc., Phi Beta Kappa, Sigma Xi. Home: 2569 Heathrow Ln Manasquan NJ 08736-2229 E-mail: aandbpond@aol.com.

PONDER, CATHERINE, clergywoman, author; b. Hartsville, S.C., Feb. 14, 1927; d. Roy Charles and Kathleen (Parrish) Cook; 1 child, Richard. Student, Worth Bus. Coll., 1948; BS in Edn., Unity Ministerial Sch., 1956; doctorate (hon.) , Unity Sch., 1976. Ordained to ministry Unity Sch. Christianity, 1958. Min. Unity Ch., Birmingham, Ala., 1958-61, founder, min. Austin, Tex., 1961-69, San Antonio, 1969-73, Palm Desert, Calif., 1973—. Author: The Dynamic Laws of Prosperity, 1962, The Prosperity Secret of the Ages, 1964, The Dynamic Laws of Healing, 1966, The Healing Secret of the Ages, 1967, Pray and Grow Rich, 1968, The Millionaires of Genesis, 1976, The Millionaire Moses, 1977, The Millionaire Joshua, 1978, The Millionaire from Nazareth, 1979, The Secret of Unlimited Prosperity, 1981, Open Your Mind To Receive, 1983, Dare To Prosper!: The Prospering Power of Prayer, 1983, The Prospering Power of Love, 1984, Open Your Mind to Prosperity, 1984, The Dynamic Laws of Prayer, 1987. Office: 73-669 US Hwy 111 Palm Desert CA 92260-4033

PONDER, DAN, public relations executive; MBA , BA, Mich. State U.; grad., Leadership Detroit X. Mem. pvt. co. adv. svc. Deloitte & Touche, Detroit; CFO Franco Pub. Rels. Group, 1985, CEO, 1985—93. Mem.: Henry Ford Estate Adv. Bd., Mich. Coun. Econ. Edn. (bd. trustees), Alliance for a Safer, Greater Detroit (mem. bd. dirs.), Mich. State Chamber (mem. bd. dirs.), Detroit Regional Chamber (mem. bd. dirs., past chmn. small bus. exec. com., Svc. award 1996—97). Office: Franco Pub Rels Group 400 Renaissance Ctr Ste 1050 Detroit MI 48243 Office Fax: 313-567-4486. Business E-Mail: ponder@franco.com.*

PONDER, HENRY, educational association administrator; m. Eunice Wilson; children: Cheryl, Anna. BS, Langston U.; MS, Okla. State U.; PhD, Ohio State U. Asst. prof. Va. State Coll., Petersburg, chmn. dept. agri-bus.; chmn. dept. bus. and econs. Ft. Valley (Ga.) State Coll.; v.p. acad. affairs Ala. A&M U., Normal, dean; pres. Benedict Coll., Columbia, S.C., Fisk U., Nashville, Nat. Assn. for Equal Opportunity in Higher Edn., Silver Spring, Md. Cons. Fed. Res. Bank, N.Y., Phila. Nat. Bank, Chase Manhattan Bank, Irving Trust Co., Omaha Nat. Bank; bd. dirs. Fed. Res. Bank of Richmond, Va., chmn. bd. dirs.; bd. dirs. J.P. Stevens & Co., Inc., Suntrust Bank of Nashville, Tenn., SCANA Corp. S.C., C.C. of the Air Force, ETV Endowment S.C. Mem. scholarship fund com. Bishop Desmond Tutu So. African Refugee Assn.; chmn. United Negro College Fund, Inc., Nat. Assn. for Equal Opportunity in Higher Edn.; mem. exec. coun. Commn. on Colls. Mem. Tenn. Coll. Assn. (pres. 1992), Alpha Phi Alpha (gen. pres.).

PONDER, HERMAN, geologist; b. Light, Ark., Jan. 31, 1928; s. Herman Cook and Sylvia Adell (Cameron) P.; m. Barbara Elaine Sando, May 10, 1947; children: Teresa Elaine, David Mark. BA, U. Mo., 1955, PhD, 1959. Rsch. engr. A.P. Green Refractories Co., Mexico, Mo., 1959-61, lab mgr., 1961-63; project engr., then mgr. mining div. Colo. Sch. Mines Rsch. Inst., Golden, 1963-67, dir. rsch., 1967-70, pres., 1970-85, ATI Exploration, Golden, Colo., 1985-90; chmn. bd. dirs. Analytica, Inc. V.p. Copper Range Co., White Pine, Mich., 1985-89. Served with USN, 1946-47. Recipient Disting. Alumnus award U. Mo., 1993. Home: 1165 W Indian Hills Dr Saint George UT 84770-

PONDER, MARIAN RUTH, retired mathematics educator; b. Waterloo, Iowa, July 12, 1932; d. Lee Roland and Leone Hyacinth (Holdiman) Ridgon; m. Joseph Glen Ponder, June 28, 1953; children: Dwight Lee, David Glen, Dean Joseph. BA (Purple and Gold math. scholar), U. No. Iowa, 1952; MSE, Drake U., 1960; postgrad., U. Wis., 1961-62, San Diego State U., 1980-81, Carleton Coll., 1980-81, U. No. Iowa, 1961-66, Drake U., 1971-75, Chico State U., 1985-86, U. Iowa, 1988, U. Tex., 1990. Tchr. math., sci., Anamosa, Iowa, 1952-53, Monroe, 1953-56, Newton, 1956-64, 66-92; head dept. math. Newton Schs., 1978-92. Ch. treas. Cmty. Heights Alliance Ch., 1980-82, 83-87, Sunday sch. secretariat, 1966-82, fin. sec., 1993-94, 97-98, women's ministries treas., 1997-2001. Maytag scholar, 1960; Maytag Corp. grantee, 1962; Delta Kappa Gamma scholar, 1960, 81, 95. Mem. NEA, Nat. Coun. Tchrs. Math., Iowa Ret. Sch. Pers. Assn., Iowa Edn. Assn., Newton Cmty. Edn. Assn. (chief negotiator 1985-87, pres. 1985-87), Iowa Coun. Tchrs. Math., Jasper County Hist. Soc., Jasper County Geneaol. Soc., Delta Kappa Gamma (state treas. 1978—, internat. fin. chmn. 1990-92, trustee ednl. found. 1992-98), Jasper County Ret. Sch. Pers. Assn. (treas. 1992-96, v.p. 1996-98, pres. 1998-2000), Kappa Mu Epsilon, Kappa Delta Pi, Lambda Delta Lambda, Delta Kappa Gamma. Republican. Mem. Christian and Missionary Alliance Ch. Home: 3791 Highway F36 W Newton IA 50208-8061

POND-KOENIG, DONALEE, artist; b. Rochester, N.Y., June 29, 1946; d. R.D. and Ethelynn (Brown) Pond; m. Peter A. Koenig; 1 child, Moya. BFA, Pratt Inst., 1970. Lectr. Art Found., Tallahassee, 1979, Brainbridge (Ga.) Jr. Coll., 1980; pvt. art tutor Tallahassee, 1980-91. Guest lectr. Bainbridge Jr. Coll., Ga., 1980, Fla. State U., Tallahassee, 1985, adj. prof., 1991; adj. prof. Tallahassee C.C., 1992; pvt. art tutor Koenig Studio, Tallahassee, 1989-91; bd. dirs. Mus. Art, Big Bend Hospice Art Coun. Exhbns. include Bainbridge Jr. Coll., 1985, Ctr. Profl. Devel. Fla. State U., 1986, 89, LeMoyne Art Found., Tallahassee, 1986-2002, Tallahassee City Hall, 1987, 91, 94-2002, Thomasville (Ga.) Art Ctr., 1990-2002, Tallahassee Regional Airport, 1991, 621 Gallery, Tallahassee, 1994, 98-2002, Vlance C.C., Orlando, 1995, Merger Gallery, Rochester, N.Y., 1995, Valdosta (Ga.) Cultural Art Ctr., 1996, Fla. Art Ctr. & Gallery, Havana, 1996-2002, Internat. Mail Art Exhbn., Raleigh, N.C., 1997, ARTemis Gallery, Tallahassee, 1997, Big Bend Hospice, Tallahassee, 1997-2002, Planters Exch. Tallahassee Watercolor Exhbn., Havana, Fla., 1998, others; one-woman shows at Thomasville Cultural Ctr., Ga., 1999. Chez Pierres, Tallahassee, 1999, Sun Trust Bank, Tallahassee, 2001, Om, Tallahassee, 2000; prodr. video collections; represented in pvt. and pub. collections; contbr. to art publs. and mags. including the Artists' Mag. (finalist in exptl. category 1997), Manhatten Arts Internat. mag. (winner competition 1997), others. Mem. Tallahassee Watercolor Soc. (pres. 1996-98), Artscape, Nat. Mus. Women in the Arts, Artist's Space N.Y., So. Artist League (Valdosta, Ga.), Fla. Watercolor Soc., Artist League of Tallahassee, others. Avocations: walking, reading, cooking, music. Home: 7605 Broadview Farms Ln Tallahassee FL 32309-6103

PONEMAN, DANIEL BRUCE, lawyer; b. Toledo, Mar. 12, 1956; s. Meyer and Delores Suzanne (Shapiro) P.; m. Susan Anne Danoff, Aug. 12, 1984; children: Claire Gillian, Michael Bruder, William Meyer. AB in Govt. and Econs. magna cum laude, Harvard Coll., 1978; MLitt in Politics, Lincoln Coll., Oxford, Eng., 1981; JD cum laude, Harvard U., 1984. Bar: D.C. 1985, N.Y., 1985. Vis. fellow Internat. Inst. Strategic Studies, London, 1980-81; rsch. fellow ctr. sci. and internat. affairs Kennedy sch. govt. Harvard U., 1981-84; assoc. Covington & Burling, 1985-89; White House fellow U.S. Dept. of Energy, 1989-90; dir. def. policy and arms control NSC, Washington, 1990-93, spl. asst. to the Pres., sr. dir. nonproliferation and export controls, 1993-96; counsel Hogan & Hartson L.L.P., 1996-97, ptnr., 1998-2001; prin. The Scowcroft Group, 2001—. Author: Nuclear Power in the Developing World, 1982, Argentina: Democracy on Trial, 1987; contbr. articles to profl. jours. and newspapers including N.Y. Times, Washington Post, L.A. Times, Boston Globe. Mem. Commn. to Asses the Orgn. of Govt. to Combat the Proliferation of Weapons of Mass Distruction, 1997-99; mem. Pres.' Export Coun. Subcom. on Export Adminstrn. Grantee Corp. Pub. Broadcasting; Lord Crewe scholar. Mem. D.C. Bar, N.Y. Bar, Coun. Fgn. Rels., Phi Beta Kappa. Home: 1541 Forest Ln Mc Lean VA 22101 Office: The Scowcroft Group 900 17th St NW Ste 500 Washington DC 20006 E-mail: poneman@scowcroft.com.

PONITZ, DAVID H. former academic administrator; b. Royal Oak, Mich., Jan. 21, 1931; s. Henry John and Jeanette (Bouwman) P.; m. Doris Jean Humes, Aug. 5, 1956; children: Catherine Anne, David Robinson. BA, U. Mich., 1952, MA, 1954; EdD, Harvard U., 1964; degree (hon.), U. Dayton, 1996. Prin. Waldron (Mich.) Area Schs., 1956-58, supt., 1958-60; cons. Harvard U., Boston Sch. Survey, 1961-63; supt. Freeport (Ill.) Pub. Schs., 1962-65; pres. Freeport C.C., 1962-65, Washtenaw C.C., 1965-75, Sinclair C.C., 1975-97, pres. emeritus, 1997—. Cons. to community colls.; chmn., pres. Ohi Advanced Tech. Ctr. Mem. editorial adv. bd. Nations Schs, 1963-70; chmn. adv. bd. Community Coll. Rev, 1978-89. Past chmn. Dayton Mayor's Coun. on Econ. Devel., 1977-85; mem. Nat. Adv. Coun. on Nursing; former co-chair Performing Arts Edn. Task Force; bd. dirs. Alliance for Edn.; former campaign chmn. Ann Arbor and Dayton United Way; past vice chmn. Dayton Citizens Adv. Coun. for Desegregation Implementation; v.p. Miami Valley Rsch. Park; mem., past chmn. Area Progress Coun., Dayton; bd. dirs. Dayton Devel. Coun.; mem. F.S.B. bd. Citizens Fed. Banks, Universal Energy Systems Bd.; past chmn. Miami Valley Joint Labor/Mgmt. Profls., Area Progress Coun.; chmn. bd. dirs Ctr. Occupational R & D; bd. chair Wright Tech. Network; bd. dirs. Dean Family Funds; trustee Thomas B. Fordham Found.; mem. Midwestern Higher Edn. Commn.; vice chair Miami Valley Rsch. Found.; past chmn. bd. dirs. League Innovation C.C.; bd. dirs. Miami Valley Regional Planning Commn. Served with U.S. Army, 1954-56. Named Outstanding Alumnus, U. Mich., One of Top 100 Pres. in U.S. Coun. for Advancement and Support of Edn., Exec. of Yr., Bd. Realtors; named to Hall of Fame, Nat. Mgmt. Assn., 2001; recipient Presdl. medallion, Patron emeritus Horry-Georgetown Tech. Coll., Bogie Buster Red Jacket award, 1987, Thomas J. Peters award for Excellence, Assn. Cmty. and Jr. Colls., 1988, Marie N. Martin Chief Exec. Officer award, ACCT, 1989, The Living Legend award, Martin Luther King Jr. Holiday Celebration Com., 1991, Hon. Alumnus award, Sinclair, 1991, honor, India Found., 1992, Disting. Eagle Scout award, Nat. Eagle Scout Assn., 1993, Smitty award, Anti-Defamation award, Anti-Defamation League, 1996, Citizen Legion of Honor award, 1997, hon. award, Citizen Legion, 1997, Edn. award, Gov., 1999. Mem. Am. Assn. Community and Jr. Colls. (nat. future commn., bd. dirs., chmn. 1988-89, Nat. Leadership award 2002), Ohio Tech. and Community Coll. Assn. (pres. 1979-80), Nat. Mgmt. Assn. (Hall of Fame award 2001), Rotary. Methodist. Office: Sinclair Community Coll Office of Pres Emeritus 444 W 3rd St Dayton OH 45402-1421 Fax: 937-512-2865. E-mail: dponitz@sinclair.edu.

PONITZ, DORIS HUMES, volunteer; b. Marlette, Mich., May 5, 1932; d. Frederic Jerome and Lilah Belle (Robinson) Humes; m. David Henry Ponitz, Aug. 5, 1956; children: Catherine Anne, David Robinson. MusB with honors, Mich. State U., 1954; MA, U. Mich., 1976; LHD (hon.), U. Dayton, 1996. Contbr. columns to Dayton Philharm. Footnotes, 1987-89, Buckeye Bull., 1983-86. Pres. bd. dirs. Dayton Philharm. Orch. Assn., 1987-89; mem. nat. bd. dirs. Girl Scouts U.S.A., 1988-94; mem. conf. bd. pension com. United Meth. Ch., 1988-94; active Dayton Area United Way, YWCA; bd. dirs., mem. exec. com. Dayton Performing Arts Fund Bd. and Culture Works; state bd. mem., chair Kids Voting Ohio, 1992—; bd. mem. Dayton Peace Accords, 1998-99, Centerville/Wash. Twp. Found., 1999-2000, Washington-Centerville Libr., 1999—,chmn 2001, bd. mem Heritage Diversity Coun., 1999— NCCJ, 1990-99; past pres., mem. exec. com. Dayton Philharm. Orch. Assn., named hon. life mem., 1991; chmn. bd. Greater Dayton Pub. TV Bd., 1987-89; mem. adv. com. Centerville-Washington Twp. Edn. Found., Meth. Theol. Sem. Ohio; advisor Miami Valley Acad. Music; bd. dirs. NCCJ, 1991-99; bd. dirs., v.p. for edn.. vol. coun. Am. Symphony Orch. League, 1990-96; speaker, lectr. to many orgns.; mem. Mortar Bd. Nat. Found. Bd., 1982-89; commr. Ohio Edn. Broadcasting Commn., 1988-94; bd. mem. Kettering Children's Choir (chair 1998-99), 1997—2000, Engr. Club of Dayton, 1996-99, Montgomery County Conv. & Visitors Bureau, 1992-96, Dayton Contemporary Dance Co., 1992-95; bd. mem., chair Buckeye Trails Girl Scout Coun., 1976-87; mem. adv. coun. Jr. League of Dayton, 1997-99; mem. cmty. adv. bd. League of Women Voters, 1995-98, bd. dirs. Friendship Force. Named to Top Ten Women Dayton, 1981; named Sch. Citizen of Yr., Centerville City Schs., 1988, Centerville Edn. Found. Hall of Fame, 1991; recipient Citizen Legion of Honor award Pres.'s Club, 1986, Ohio Gov.'s award for comty svc., 1991, Torch of Liberty award Anti-Defamation League, 1996, Comty. Svc. Top Flight award City of Dayton, 1996, Bob Evans Leadership award Kids Voting USA, 1997, Jean Harris award District Rotary Club, 1998, Friendship award Nat. Conf. Comty & Justice, 1999; Mortar Bd. Nat. Found. fellow, 1991; 304 Club honoree Big Brothers Big Sisters, 1996, Women of Influence award,Y-WCA of Dayton, 2002 Mem. Dayton Philharm. Women's Assn. (edn. docent Symphony Guides, Symphon-Ears), Mich. State U. Alumni Club, Delta Omicron, Tau Sigma, Phi Kappa Phi; state hon. mem. Delta Kappa Gamma Internat. Home: 5556 Viewpoint Dr Dayton OH 45459-1455

PONITZ, JOHN ALLAN, lawyer; b. Battle Creek, Mich., Sept. 7, 1949; m. Nancy J. Roberts, Aug. 14, 1971; children: Amy, Matthew, Julie. BA, Albion Coll., 1971; JD, Wayne State U., 1974. Bar: Mich. 1974, U.S. Dist. Ct. (ea. dist.) Mich. 1975, (we. dist.) Mich. 1986, U.S. Ct. Appeals (6th cir.) Mich. 1981, U.S. Supreme Ct. 1992. Assoc. McMachan & Kaichen, Birmingham, Mich., 1973-75; atty. Grand Trunk Western R.R., Detroit, 1975-80, sr. trial atty., 1980-89, gen. counsel, 1990-95; ptnr. Hopkins & Sutter, 1995-2000, Maxwell, Ponitz & Sclawy, Troy, 2000—01; of counsel Fabrizio & Brook, P.C., 2002—. V.p. Beverly Hills (Mich.) Jaycees, 1981. Served to capt. USAR, 1974-82. Mem. Mich. Bar Assn., Nat. Assn. R.R. Trial Counsel, Oakland County Bar Assn. Lutheran. Avocation: golf. Office: Fabrizio & Brook PC City Ctr Bldg 888 W Big Beaver Ste 1470 Troy MI 48084-4738 E-mail: japonitz@pbmaxwell.com.

PONKA, LAWRENCE JOHN, automotive executive; b. Detroit, Sept. 1, 1949; s. Maximillian John and Leona May (Knobloch) P.; m. Nancy Kathleen McNamara, Feb. 20, 1988. AA, Macomb County C. C., Mich., 1974; BS in Indsl. Mgmt., Lawrence Tech. U., 1978; MA in Indsl. Mgmt., Ctrl. Mich. U., 1983, postgrad. in Bus. Mgmt. Cert. internat. cons. Engr.'s asst. Army Tank Automotive Command, 1967-68; with Sperry and Hutchinson Co., Southfield, Mich., 1973, Chrysler Corp., Detroit, 1973, GM Corp., Warren, Mich., 1973-82, coord. engrng. staff engring. systems, 1976-82; mfg. engr. Buick-Oldsmobile, Cadillac Group GM Assembly Divsn., Orion Pontiac, Mich, 1982-84; sr. anayst advanced vehicle engrng. Chevrolet-Pontiac-Can. group Engrng. Ctr., Warren, 1985-86; mfg. planning adminstr. Allanté Detroit Hamtramck Assembly Ctr. Cadillac Luxury Car Divsn., 1986-92, mgr. Cadillac Alante Assembly Ops., 1992—. Plant planning adminstr. Cadillac luxury car divsn. Detroit/Hamtramck Assembly Ctr., Cadillac El Dorado, Seville, Deville, Concours, 1993—, sr. mfg. project engr. N. Am. Ops., 1994, Flint, Mich., 96; advanced mfg. engr. N.Am. ops. mfg. process liaison Cadillac luxury car divsn., 1996—97; total mfg. integration engr. Advanced Product Devel. Ctr., 1997—2001, mfg. integration mgr., 2001; full size trucks Global Portfolio Devel. Ctr., 1997—2002; mem. people strategy team on environ. Cadillac Motor Car till 1992; mem. adj. faculty U. Phoenix Grad. Sch. Bus., Mich. campus. ; mfg. program mgr. concurrent build, full size trucks Pontiac Product Ctr. Elected del Dem. County Conv. With USAF, 1968—72. Decorated Air Force Commendation medal. Mem. DAV (life), Vietnam Vets Assn. (life), Am. Diabetes Assn. Roman Catholic. Home: 35537 Oakdale St Livonia MI 48154-2237 Office: U Phoenix Mich Campus 26999 Central Park Blvd Southfield MI 48076-4174 also: GM Corp Engring Ctr M/C 480-111-P04 30200 Mound Rd 111 Box 9010 Warren MI 48090-9010 E-mail: ljponka@prodigy.net.

PONKO, WILLIAM REUBEN, architect; b. Wausau, Wis., Apr. 4, 1948; s. Reuben Harrison and Ora Marie (Ranke) P.; m. Kathleen Ann Hilt, May 5, 1973; children: William Benjamin, Sarah Elizabeth. BArch magna cum laude, U. Notre Dame, 1971. Cert. Nat. Coun. Archtl. Registration Bds. V.p., arch., dir. ednl., instl. specialty Le Roy Troyer & Assocs. (now the Troyer Group), Mishawaka, Ind., 1971—; design instr. dept. arch. U. Notre Dame, 1976. Mem. Ind. State Bd. Registration for Architects, 1990—; mem. registration exam com. Nat. Coun. Archtl. Registration Bds., 1992—, vice chair 1996, chair 1997. Prin. archtl. works include: St. Peter Luth. Ch., Mishawaka, Ind., 1979, 4 brs. for South Bend Pub. Libr., 1983, Edward J. Funk & Sons office bldg. Taylor U., Upland, Ind., 1982, Taylor U. Lbir., carillon tower, 1985, Early Childhood Devel. Ctr. U. Notre Dame, 1994, Convents for Sisters of Holy Cross St. Mary's, Notre Dame, Ind., 1995. Mem. AIA (gold medal for exellence in archtl. edn. 1971), Ind. Soc. Archs. (Design Excellence award 1978, chpt. pres. 1985, Juliet Peddle award 2000). Office: The Troyer Group Inc 550 Union St Mishawaka IN 46544-2346

PONNÉ, NANCI TERESA, entertainment promoter, writer; b. Chgo., May 10, 1958; d. Joseph Anthony and Irene Theresa (Nasadowski) P.; m. Lee Darrow, Oct. 26, 1996. BA, DePaul U., 1980. Performer, 1961—; dancer, choreographer, 1974—; actress, model Chgo., 1978—; pub. Chgo. Talent Directory, 1985—, Spotlight, 1989; pres./owner Chgo. Talent Enterprises Inc., 1991—; freelance writer, 1992—; graphic designer, 1993—; clairvoyant, 1996—; website designer, 1998—. Prodr. VIP Forums on Progress in Chgo. Talent Industry, 1990; speaker in field; mem. Loretta Rozek Dance Co., 1975-79. Prodr.: (radio talk show) The Strange World of Lee Darrow, Sta. WONX-AM, 1993. Dem. vol. to Re-elect Mayor Washington, 1987; Dem. vol. for Clinton/Gore, 1992; Dem. vol. to elect Patrick Quinn to Sec. State, Ill., 1990. Named Miss Chgo., recipient Spl. Judges award Miss America Scholarship Pageant, 1981-82; Goodman Sch. of Drama scholar, 1978. Mem. NATAS, HEREIU, Nat. Assn. Photoshop Profls., Chgo. Conv. and Tourism Bur., Ice Skating Inst. (3 Gold medals World Championships, 1994), Ind. Writers of Chgo., Goldfish Soc. Am. Celtic Catholic. Avocations: competitive figure skating, Star Trek, raising exotic goldfish, metaphysics. Address: 5250 N Broadway St Ste 204 Chicago IL 60640-2304

PONOROFF, LAWRENCE, law educator, legal consultant; b. Chgo., Sept. 10, 1953; s. Charles Melvin and Jean Eileen (Kramer) P.; m. Monica J. Moses, July 25, 1981; children: Christopher J., Devon E., Laura J., Scott C. AB, Loyola U., Chgo., 1975; JD, Stanford U., 1978. Bar: Colo. 1978, Ohio 1988, U.S. Dist. Ct. Colo., U.S. Dist. Ct. (no. dist.) Ohio, U.S. Ct. Appeals (10th cir.). Assoc. Holme Roberts & Owen, Denver, 1978-84, ptnr., 1984-86; asst. prof. law U. Toledo, 1986-88, assoc. prof. coll. of law, 1988-90, prof. law, assoc. dean academic affairs, 1990-92, prof., 1990-95, Tulane U. Sch. Law, New Orleans, 1995-00, Mitchell Franklin prof., 2000—, vice dean, 1998-2001, dean, 2001—. Vis. prof. Wayne State U. Law Sch., 1993, U. Mich. Law Sch., 1997, lectr. fed. juc. ctr.; cons. long range planning subcom. of com. on adminstrn. of bankruptcy system Jud. Conf. of the U.S.; dir. Am. Bd. Certification, 2000—; bd. adv. editors Am. Bankruptcy Inst. Law Rev., 2000—; bd. dirs. Am. Bs. Certification. Co-author: (with S.E. Snyder) Commerical Bankruptcy Litigation, 1989, (with J. Dolan) Basic Concepts in Commercial Law, 1998, (with Epstein and Markell) Making and Doing Deals: An Introduction to Contract and Related Laws, 2001. Mem. ABA, Am. Bar Ist., Am. Law Inst., La. State Bar Assn. (bd. govs.). Home: 6025 Pitt St New Orleans LA 70118-6010 Office: Tulane Law Sch Coll Law 6329 Freret St New Orleans LA 70118-6231 E-mail: lponoroff@law.tulane.edu.

PON-SALAZAR, FRANCISCO DEMETRIO, diplomat, educator, deacon, counselor; b. Ica, Peru, July 18, 1951; came to U.S., 1982; s. Alejandro Sen Tac and Demetria (Salazar) P. MPhil, Leopold Franzer U., Innsbruck, Austria, 1977; MA in Hispanic Lit. and Lang., St. Louis U., 1985; M of Mgmt., Fontbonne U., 2001. Cert. univ. and coll. tchr., Nat. Coun. Peruvian Univs.; cert. adult literacy tchr.; notary pub., State of Mo. Tchr. San Juan Bautista Sch., Puno, Peru, 1972, Jose Toribio Polo High Sch., Ica, 1979-82; prof. Catalina Buendia Pecho Coll., 1980-82; instr. St. Louis U., 1983-85; asst. of the Consul Fgn. Rels. Consulate of Mex., St. Louis, 1988-97. Counselor, tutor Christian Bros. Coll., St. Louis, 1984-85; tchr. St. Gabriel's Hall Reformatory, Audubon, Pa., 1985; mentor Youth Svc. Mo./Pub. and Pvt. Ventures, 1992-93. Participant Internat. Alpach (Tirol, Austria) Forum, 1977; asst. scoutmaster Boy Scouts Am. (Wood badge C-34, 1998), St. Louis, 1990—; vol. State of Mo. Divsn. Youth Svcs. Pub. Pvt. Ventures, 1992-93; mem. adv. bd. Immigration Law Project, Legal Svcs. of Ea. Mo., Inc., St. Louis, 1995-97. Mem. Internat. Progress Orgn. of Vienna (Austria), Latin-Am. Soc. of St. Louis U. (v.p. 1983-85), Campus Ministry of Spanish Speaking People, Legal Svcs. of Ea. Mo., Inc. (adv. bd. of the Immigration Project, 1995), Sigma Delta Pi, Alpha Sigma Nu. Avocations: jogging, gymnastics, reading, videos, poetry. Home: 10727 Roxanna Dr Saint Louis MO 63128-1600 E-mail: fcopon@hotmail.com.

PONSETI, IGNACIO VIVES, orthopaedic surgery educator; b. Cuidadela, Balearic Islands, Spain, June 3, 1914; s. Miguel and Margarita (Vives) P.; 1 child, William Edward; m. Helena Percas, 1961. BS, U. Barcelona, 1930, MD, 1936, D honoris causa, 1984. Instr. dept. orthopaedic surgery State U. Iowa, 1944-57, prof., 1957—. Author papers and a book on cogenital and developmental skeletal deformities. Capt. M.C. Spanish Army, 1936-39. Recipient Kappa Delta award for orthopaedic rsch., 1955. Mem. Assn. Bone and Joint Surgeons, Am. Acad. Cerebral Palsy, Soc. Exptl. Biology and Medicine, Internat. Coll. Surgeons, N.Y. Acad. Sci., AMA (Ketoen gold medal 1960), Am. Acad. Orthopedic Surgeons, ACS, Am. Orthopedic Assn., Pediatric Orthopaedic Soc. (hon.), Iowa Med. Soc., Orthopedic Rsch. Soc. (Shands award 1975), Sigma Xi, Asociacion Argentina de Cirugia (hon.), Asociacion Balear de Cirugia (hon.), Sociedad de Cirujanos de Chile (hon.), Sociedad Espanola de Cirugia Ortopedica (hon.), Sociedad Brasilera de Ortopedia e Traumatologia (hon.). Home: 110 Oakridge Ave Iowa City IA 52246-2935 Office: Carver Pavilion U Iowa Hosps Iowa City IA 52242 E-mail: Ignacio-Ponseti@uiowa.edu.

PONSOR, MICHAEL ADRIAN, federal judge; b. Chgo., Aug. 13, 1946; s. Frederick Ward and Helen Yvonne (Richardson) P.; children from previous marriage, Anne, Joseph; 1 stepchild, Christian Walker; m. Nancy L. Coiner, June 30, 1996. BA magna cum laude, Harvard Coll., 1969; BA , Oxford U., 1971, MA, 1979; JD, Yale U., 1975. Bar: Mass., U.S. Dist. Ct. Mass., U.S. Ct. Appeals (1st cir.), U.S. Supreme Ct. Tchr. Kenya Inst. Administrn., Nairobi, 1967-68; law clk. U.S. Dist. Ct., Boston, 1975-76; assoc. Homans, Hamilton, Dahmen & Lamson, 1976-78; ptnr. Brown, Hart & Ponsor, Amherst, Mass., 1978-83; U.S. magistrate judge U.S. Dist. Ct., Springfield, 1984-94, U.S. dist. judge, 1994—. Adj. prof. Western N.E. Coll. Sch. Law, Springfield, 1988—, U. Mass., 1999-2001, Yale Law Sch., New Haven, 1989-91; presenter in field. Rhodes scholar Oxford U., 1969. Mem. Mass. Bar Assn., Hampshire County Bar Assn., Boston Bar Assn. Office: US Dist Ct Rm 539 1550 Main St Springfield MA 01103-1422

PONT, JOHN, football coach, educator; b. Canton, Ohio, Nov. 13, 1927; s. Bautista and Susie (Sikurinec) P.; m. H. Sandra Stoutt, June 23, 1956; children: John W., Jennifer Ann, Jeffrey David. BS, Miami U., Oxford, Ohio, 1952, MS, 1956. Profl. football player, Can., 1952-53; instr., freshman football and basketball coach Miami U., 1953-55, asst. prof., head football coach, 1955-62; head football coach Yale U., 1963-65; prof., head football coach Ind. U., Bloomington, 1965-73; head coach Northwestern U., Evanston, Ill., 1973-77, athletic dir., 1974-79; head football coach, athletic dir. Hamilton, Ohio; head football coach, tennis coach, asst. athletic dir. Coll. Mt. St. Joseph, Cin.; now head football coach Gakusei-Engo-Kai Inc., Tokyo, Japan. Agt. Equitable Assurance Soc., U.S., 1981-82; v.p. Fin. Leasing Corp., 1983-85, Splty. Brush, Inc.; athletic dir. Jewish Community Center, Canton, 1953; v.p. NCAA Coun., 1979-80; mem. bd. dirs. Cin. chpt. Nat. Football Found. Hall Of Fame. Mem. Pres.'s Coun. on Phys. Fitness; chmn. Ind. Easter Seal, 1968-69, Ind. div. Cancer Crusade, 1969; bd. dirs. Multiple Sclerosis, N.E. Ill. counc. Boy Scouts Am., Boys Hope. Served with USN, 1945-47. Named Coach of Year Coaches Assn., 1967, Coach of Year Football Writers, 1967, Coach of Yr. Washington Touchdown Club, 1968, Coach of Yr. Walter Camp Found.; recipient Significant Sig award, 1968, Disting. Am. award Nat. Football Found., 1987, Lifetime Achievement award All Am. Football Found., 1997; charter mem. Miami U. Hall of Fame, 1968; elected Ind. Football Hall of Fame, 1984, Butler County Hall of Fame, 1986, Mid-Am. Conf. Hall of Fame, 1992, Ind. U. Sports Hall of Fame, 1992. Mem. Am. Football Coaches Assn. (chmn. ethics com.), Kusatsu City Football Assn. Japan (hon. chmn.), Am. Legion, Blue Key, Sigma Chi, Phi Epsilon Kappa, Omicron Delta Kappa. Republican. Home: 482 White Oak Dr Oxford OH 45056-9272

PONTAROLO, MICHAEL JOSEPH, lawyer; b. Walla Walla, Wash., Sept. 1, 1947; s. Albert and Alice Mary (Fazzari) P.; m. Elizabeth Louise Onley, July 18, 1970; children: Christie, Amy, Nick, Angela. BA, Gonzaga U., 1969, JD, 1973. Bar: Wash. 1973, U.S. Dist. Ct. (ea. dist.) Wash. 1974. Assoc. Mullin & Etter, Spokane, Wash., 1973-74, William Iunker, Spokane, 1974-75, Delay, Curran & Boling, Spokane, 1975-77; prin. Delay, Curran, Thompson & Pontarolo, P.S., 1977-97, Delay, Curran, Thompson, Pontarolo & Walker, Spokane, 1997—. Mem. Spokane County Med. Legal Com., 1987-88, 91; chmn. liaison com. Superior Ct., 1987-88, 94-97, chair, 1994-95, mem. arbitration bd., 1987-2002; mem. Bench Bar Com., 1987-88; bd. govs., nom. com., superior ct. judge adv. com. to Gov. Locke, Wa.; adj. prof. Gonzaga U. Sch. Law, 1987—, bd. advisors, 2000—. Bd. dirs. Community Ctrs. Found., Spokane, 1986-89; active Spokane C.C. Legal Secretary Adv. Com.; mem. adv. bd. Spokane C.C., 1992—. Recipient Cert. of Recognition, Superior Ct. Clk., Spokane, 1986. Mem.: ABA, ATLA, Spokane County Bar Assn. (v.p. 1986—89, sec.-treas. 1986—89, pres. 1989—90, trustee 1984—86, membership com. chair 1992—93), Wash. State Trial Lawyers Assn. (v.p. east 1979—80, CLE program chmn. 1984, mem. awards com. 1995—99, chair 1995—96, Cert. of Appreciation 1982, 1990, 1992, Leadership award 1984), Wash. State Bar Assn. (interprofl. com. 1987—90, character and fitness com. 1991—94, com. chair 1993—94, spl. dist. counsel 1984—, mem. jud. recommendation com. 1994—98, co-chair jud. recommendation com. 1996—, chair jud. recommendation com. 1997—98, consumer protection com. 2000—01, spl. disciplinary counsel 2001, rules of profl. conduct com. 2000—), Alpha Sigma Nu. Office: Delay Curran Thompson Pontarolo & Walker PS 601 W Main Ave Ste 1212 Spokane WA 99201-0684 E-mail: dctpw@msn.com.

PONTE-CASTAÑEDA, PEDRO, mechanical engineering educator; b. Santa Cruz, Tenerife, Spain, Jan. 5, 1961; came to U.S., 1977; s. Pedro Ponte-Pedreira and Glenda (Castañeda) De Ponte. BS, BA, Lehigh U., 1982; SM, Harvard U., 1983, PhD in Applied Math., 1986. Rsch. officer U. Bath (Eng.), 1986-87; asst. prof. Johns Hopkins U., Balt., 1987-90, U. Pa., Phila., 1990-94, assoc. prof., 1994—. Vis. prof. Ecole Polytechnique, Paris, 1994. Contbr. articles to profl. jours. Recipient Rsch. Initiation award NSF, 1988; grantee NSF, Air Force Office of Sci. Rsch.. Mem. ASME, Soc. for Indsl. Applied Math. Office: U Pa 220 S 33rd St Philadelphia PA 19104-6315

PONTES, MARCOS C. astronaut; b. Bauru, Sao Paulo, Brazil, Mar. 11, 1963; s. Vergilio and Zuleika Pontes; m. Francisca de Fatima Cavalcanti; 2 children. BS in Aeronautical Tech., Brazil Air Force Acad., Pirassununga, Sao Paulo, 1984; BS in Aeronautical Engring., Instituto Tecnologico de Aeronautica, Sao Jose dos Campos, Sao Paulo, 1993; MS in Systems Engring., Naval Postgrad. Sch., Monterey, Calif., 1998. Commd. 2d lt. Brazil Air Force, 1984, advanced through grades to maj.; jet pilot 2/5 Instrn. Aviation Group, Natal; pilot 3/10 Strike Aviation Advanced Air Controlling; flight safety officer; astronaut NASA, Houston, with Astronaut Office Space Sta. Ops. Br. Achievements include logged over 1,700 flight hours in over 20 different aircraft. Avocations: weightlifting, soccer, guitar, piano, sketching. Office: Astronaut Office/CB NASA Johnson Space Ctr Houston TX 77058*

PONTIFF, PAUL E. lawyer; b. Bklyn., June 6, 1930; s. Louis J. and Catherine A. (Menig) P.; m. Judy A. Dufour, June, 13, 1998; children: Paul L., Thomas M., Matthew J., Kathy Braley, Shawna Braley, Lynn Lafond. BBA in Acctg., St. Johns U., N.Y.C., 1954, JD, 1959. Bar: N.Y. 1959, U.S. Tax Ct. 1962, U.S. Dist. Ct. (no. dist.) N.Y. 1974. Acctg. tax mgr. Ball George & Co. CPAs, Glens Falls, N.Y., 1960-62; lawyer Bartlett, Pontiff Stewart & Rhodes PC, 1962—. Bd. dirs. World Awareness Children's Mus., 1986—, past pres. Served with U.S. Army, 1954-56. Mem. Warren County Bar Assn. (pres. 1977-78), Estate Planning Coun. Eastern N.Y. (pres. 2000-01), Glens Falls Elks, Glens Falls Rotary Club (past pres.). Avocations: mountain climbing, tennis, golf. Office: Bartlett Pontiff et al PO Box 2168 One Washington St Glens Falls NY 12801 E-mail: pep@bpsrlaw.com.

PÖNTINEN, PEKKA JUHANI, anesthesiologist, consultant; b. Tampere, Finland, Apr. 5, 1932; s. Otto Edvard and Ellen Margareta (Heiniö) P.; m. Anja Anita Kuukankorpi; children: Anna-Katriina, Juha-Pekka, Riikka-Leena, Hanna-Maaria; m. Irja Tuulikki Ketovuori, Jan. 8, 1976; 1 child, Mika Juhani. B in med., Helsinki U., Finland, 1953; MD, Turku U., Finland, 1957; PhD, Kuopio U., Finland, 1977. Diplomate Finnish Bd. Health Legitimation, Finnish Bd. Anesthesiology. Chief dept. anesthesiology Savonlinna Cen. Hosp., Finland, 1965-69, Kainuu Cen. Hosp., Finland, 1969-75; asst. prof. neurophysiology Kuopio U., Finland, 1974-75; med. dir. Kankaanpää Rehabilitation Ctr., Finland, 1989-92; assoc. prof. anesthesiology Kuopio U., 1978—, Tampere U., Finland, 1980—. Chief acupuncture rsch. project Kuopio U., 1976—; cons. dept. neurology Tampere U. Hosp., 1976-93, adv. Ministry of Health & Social Affairs, Helsinki,. 1975—, WHO Com. Standardisation Acupuncture Nomenclature, Geneva, Switzerland, 1989-95, European Coun. Subcom. Higher Edn., Strassbourg, France, 1990-95. Author: Acupuncture as a Medical Treatment Modality (in Finnish), 1983, Laser as a Medical Treatment Modality (in Finnish), 1988, Low Level Laser as a Medical Treatment Modality (in Swedish), 1991, Low Level Laser Therapy as a Medical Treatment Modality, 1992, Laseracupuncture (in German), 1993, 2d edit., 1998; co-author: TENS Transcutaneous Electrical Nerve Stimulation in Pain Treatment (in German), 1992, 2d edit., 1996, Triggerpoints and Triggermechanisms, 1997, 2d edit. (in German), 2001, Alternative and Complementary Therapies in Veterinary Medicine, 1997, Lasers in Medicine and Dentistry, 2000; editor-in-chief Scandinavian Jour. Acupuncture and Electrotherapy, 1987-92; editor Acupuncture & Electrotherapeutics Rsch. Internat. Jour., 1981—, AKU, Akupunktur, Theorie und Praxis, 1991-99, Nordisk Tidskrift for Biologisk Medisin, 2000—; mem. sci. com. Internat. Jour. Pain Therapy, 1991-95. Recipient German Promotion award Pain Rsch. and Therapy, 1988. Fellow: Am. Soc. Laser Medicine and Surgery, European Med. Laser Assn. (2d v.p. 2001—), Am. Coll. Acupuncture (charter), Internat. Coll. Acupuncture and Electro-Therapeutics Rsch. (vice chmn. coun. 1987—), Am. Acad. Acupuncture (hon.), Acupuncture Found. of India (hon.); mem.: Finnish Soc. Anesthesiologists (v.p. 1970—71, pres. 1972—73), Soc. Internat. de Laserterapia Medico Chirugica (v.p. for Finland 1989—), Finnish Med. Acupuncture Soc. (hon.), German Med. Acupuncture Soc. (hon.), Brit. Med. Acupuncture Soc. (hon.), Can. Acupuncture Assn. (hon.), N.Y. Acad. Scis., Phys.Medicine Rsch. Found. (interdisciplinary bd. dirs. 1995—), Internat. Assn. Study of Pain (founding), Nordic Acupuncture Soc. (pres. 1980—87, 1989—), Am. Pain Soc. Avocations: classical music, fishing, gardening, skiing, ice hockey. Home: Pikkusaarenkuja 4B 77 33410 Tampere Finland

PONZI, JAMES DOUGHLAS, police officer, computer specialist; b. Denver, May 7, 1947; s. Andrew Joseph and Susie Marie Ponzi; m. Dixie Jean Ponzi, Oct. 17, 1993; children: James, Joseph, Matthew; stepchild: Shelly. BA in English, U. Colo., 1972, BA in Psychology, 1990; MA in Comm., U. Denver, 1999. Produce clk. Del Farm Foods, Denver, 1962-68, 70-73; patrolman Denver Police Dept., 1973-81, sgt., 1981-92, lt., 1992—. Instr. project Prince Denver Police Dept., 1996-98. Author: (manual) Building the Pentium II, 1999. Vol. restoration closed recreation ctr. Denver Police Brotherhood, 1996, fundraiser 1990—; youth fitness instr. Denver Police Dept., 1974. Sgt. U.S. Army, 1968-70. Decorated Bronze star. Mem. U.S. Powerlifting Fedn., Footprinters. Republican. Roman Catholic. Avocations: powerlifting, computers, reading, writing. Office: Denver Police Dept 1331 Cherokee St Denver CO 80204-2720

PONZI KAY, MARYLOU, human resources specialist; b. N.Y.C., Oct. 14, 1950; d. Bruno and Constance Louise (DeLuca) P.; m. William J. Kay, Jr., Oct. 24, 1993. BA, SUNY, Geneseo, 1972; MA, U. Iowa, 1974, SUNY, Buffalo, 1979; cert. in advanced study in labor rels., N.Y. Inst. Tech., 1995. Cert. sr. profl. in human resources Soc. for Human Resources Mgmt. Cert. Inst., 2002. Pers. adminstr. Michelin Tire Corp., Lake Success, N.Y., 1978-83; tech. recruiter 1st Data Resources, 1983-84; mgr. human resources Chem. Bank, Jericho, 1984-87; pers. officer J.P. Morgan Inc., N.Y.C., 1987-89; mgr. employment Am. Express Inc., 1989-92; dir. human resources RockBottom Stores, Inc., 1992-95; asst. dir. human resources Canon U.S.A., Lake Success, N.Y., 1995-97, dir. human resources, 1997-2000, dir. corp. human resources and devel., 2000; dir. human resources Esselte Ams., Melville, NY, 2000—. Adj. prof. human resources N.Y. Inst. Tech., 2000—; instr. French and Spanish, Amityville H.S. Adult Edn., 1986-96. Editor: New England Guide, 1982, Canada Guide, 1982. Pres. LeBourget Alliance, Amityville, N.Y., 1995-97; pres. bus. adv. coun. Adults and Children with Learning Disabilities, 1994-97, trustee, 1997—. Mem. ASTD, Soc. Human Resources Mgmt., Human Resources Strategic Issues Coun. Roman Catholic. Avocations: languages, travel, cooking, sports. Office: 48 S Service Rd Melville NY 11747 E-mail: mponzi@esselte.com., mwk93@aol.com.

POOL, JOHN THOMAS, health services coordinator, consultant; b. Spokane, Wash., July 13, 1943; s. Dean Layton and Alice Gwendalyn (Rygg) P.; m. Elaine W. Wirkkunen, Mar. 25, 1972; children: Matthew, Erik. BA in Econs., U. Wash., 1966. Detective Univ. Police Dept., Seattle, 1970-74; spl. agt. Drug Enforcement Adminstrn., Seattle and El Paso, Tex., 1976-83, tng. coord. Dallas, 1983-88, demand reduction coord. Seattle, 1988-95; exec. dir. Wash. Drug Free Bus., Bellevue, 1995—. Bd. dirs. Alaskans for Drug Free Youth, Ketchikan, 1989—, Gov.'s Substance Abuse Coun., Olympia, Wash., 1991-93; mem. bd. advisors Wash. State Substance Abuse Coalition, Bellevue, 1989-95; advisor bd. dirs. Oreg. Partnership, 1994-96; mem. Internat. Drug Strategy Inst., 1994—, Nat. Demand Reduction Adv. Coun., 1991-95. Author: (book) Creating The Drug Free Business, 1990; editor newsletter Business Taking Action, 1993—. Intelligence officer USN, 1966-70. Mem. Alpha Sigma Phi. Avocations: skiing, boating, computers.

POOL, MARY JANE, writer, lecturer; d. Earl Lee and Dorothy (Matthews) P. Grad., St. de Chantal Acad., 1942; BA in Art with honors, Drury Coll., 1946; LHD (hon.), Drury U., 2002. Mem. staff Vogue mag., N.Y.C., 1946-68, assoc. merchandising editor, 1948-57, promotion dir., 1958-66, exec. editor, 1966-68; editor House and Garden mag., 1969, editor-in-chief, 1970-80. Cons. Baker Furniture Co., 1981-94, Aves Advt., Inc., 1981-94, bd. dirs.; mem. bd. govs. Decorative Arts Trust; past mem. bd. govs. Fashion Group, Inc., N.Y.C. Author: The Gardens of Venice, 1989, The Gardens of Florence, 1992, Gardens in the City-New York in Bloom, 1999; co-author: The Angel Tree, 1984, The Angel Tree—A Christmas Celebration, 1993, The Christmas Story, 2001; editor: 20th Century Decorating, Architecture, Gardens, Billy Baldwin Decorates, 26 Easy Little Gardens. Mem. bus. com. N.Y. Zool. Soc., 1979-86; trustee Drury Coll., 1971— ; bd. dirs. Isabel O'Neil Found., 1978— . Recipient award Nat. Soc. Interior Designers, Disting. Alumni award Drury Coll., 1961, Edith Wharton Women of Achievement award, 1999. Address: 1 E 66th St New York NY 10021-5854

POOL, NANCY ELLEN, school social worker; b. Jersey City, Oct. 16, 1942; d. Frederick John and Anna Catherine (Harbers) Backhaus; m. Michael Furst, Jan. 22, 1967 (div. June 1992); 1 child, Matthew Alan; m. James Lawrence Pool, Jr., Nov. 20, 1992. Grad. in nursing, Paterson (N.J.) Gen. Hosp., 1963; BS, Montclair State Coll., 1978, MA, 1982; postgrad., Rutgers U., 1986—. RN, N.J. Staff nurse Bergen Pines County Hosp., Paramus, N.J., 1963-65, Holy Name Hosp., Teaneck, 1965-67, Akademische Ziekenhuis, Ghent, Belgium, 1967-70; sch. nurse, tchr. health edn. Bernardsville (N.J.) Bd. Edn., 1978-89, Rockaway Twp. (N.J.) Bd. Edn., 1980-89, social worker, 1989—, curriculum writer, 1975-89. Mem. exec. bd. Parents Exceptional Children, Roxbury, Mass. Mem. Coun. for Exceptional Children, AAUW, Am. Mensa, Eta Sigma Gamma, Phi Kappa Phi. Home: 165 Casterline Rd Denville NJ 07834-3616 Office: Roxbury Twp Spl Svcs 1 Bryant Dr Succasunna NJ 07876-1632

POOLE, BRENDA LYNNE, clinical nurse administrator; b. Uniontown, Pa., Dec. 13, 1952; d. Lawrence Anderson Tomb and Oweda Jane (Furry) Osolin; m. Donald Kevin Poole, Aug. 20, 1977; children: Bryan Kevin, Chandra Janay. BA in Biology, Greenville Coll., 1975; BSN, Rush U., 1980. RN, Ill. Staff RN Ctrl. Dupage Hosp., Winfield, Ill., 1980-91; pre-admission testing, same day surgery unit mgr. Edward Hosp., Naperville, 1991-99, endoscopy, post-anesthesia care unit mgr., 1991-99, adminstrv. dir. med.-surg. divsn., 1999—. Mem.: Am. Orgn. Nurse Execs., Sigma Theta Tau, Beta Beta Beta. Lutheran. Avocations: golfing, antiquing, bowling, traveling. Home: 5707 Essex Rd Lisle IL 60532-2642 Office: Edward Hosp 801 S Washington St Naperville IL 60540-7499 E-mail: bpoole@edward.org., brendalpoole@hotmail.com.

POOLE, CLIFFORD GEORGE, retired priest; b. Worcester, Eng., Oct. 8, 1936; s. George Ernest and Margaret (Brant) P.; m. Jean Balfour, Jan. 5, 1980; children: Robert, Charlotte. Grad., Keble Coll.; degree in French and German with honours, diploma in Religious Studies, postgrad. cert. in Edn. Ordained priest, 1987. Chaplain to English speaking ch. cmty., Luxembourg, Luxembourg, 1991—2002; secondary sch. tchr. European Sch., Luxembourg, 1991—. Home and Office: English Speaking Ch Cmty 89 rue de Muhlenbach L-2168 Luxembourg Luxembourg E-mail: clifford.poole@ci.educ.lu.

POOLE, EDWARD G. attorney; b. Palo Alto, Calif., May 26, 1960; s. Gordon Leicester and Lois (Teasdale) P.; m. Lynn Anderson, Oct. 17, 1992; children: Sara Elizabeth, William Michael. BA in History cum laude, Bowdoin Coll., Brunswick, Maine, 1982; JD, U. of the Pacific, 1985. Assoc. Ropers, Majeski, Kohn & Bentley, Redwood City, Calif., 1985-87, Anderson & Poole, San Francisco, 1987-90, ptnr., 1990—. Legis. editor McGeorge Law Jour., 1984-85. Bd. dirs., pres., sec. San Francisco Boys Chorus, 1989-96; chair Citizens for a Better San Francisco, 1995—; active alumni coun. Bowdoin Coll., Brunswick, 1998—. Mem. Pacific Union Club. Republican. Presbyterian. Avocations: gardening, bird watching, swimming. Office: Anderson & Poole 601 California St 1300 San Francisco CA 94108

POOLE, EVA DURAINE, librarian; b. Farrell, Pa., Dec. 20, 1952; d. Leonard Milton and Polly Mae (Flint) Harris; m. Tommy Lynn Cole, May 15, 1970 (div. Sept. 1984); 1 child, Tommy Lynn Cole; m. Earnest Theodore Poole, Sept. 22, 1990; 1 child, Aleece Remelle Poole. BA in LS, Tex. Woman's U., 1974, MLS, 1976; postgrad., U. Houston, 1989. Libr. asst. Emily Fowler Pub. Libr., Denton, Tex., 1970-74; children's libr. Houston Pub. Libr., 1974-75, 1st asst. libr., 1976-77; children's libr. Ector County Libr., Odessa, Tex., 1977-80; head pub. svcs. Lee Davis Libr. San Jacinto Coll., Pasadena, 1980-84; libr. dir. San Jacinto Coll. South, Houston, 1984-90; libr. svcs. mgr. Emily Fowler Pub. Libr., Denton, 1990-93, interim dir., 1993; dir. librs. Denton Pub. Librs., 1993—. Mem. Libr. Svcs. Constrn. Act Advisory Coun., 1994-97, Libr. Svcs. Tech. Act Adv. Coun., 1997-2000; mem. TEXSHARE adv. bd. Tex. State Libr. and Archives Commn., 1999—. Bd. dirs. Amigos Libr. Svcs., 2000—. Named to Outstanding Young Women of Am., 1991. Mem. ALA (chair Loleta Fyan jury com. 1999-2000), Pub. Libr. Assn. (mem. budget and fin. com. 1999-2002, chair budget and fin. com. 2001-2002, nat. conf. com. 2002--), Libr. Adminstrn. and Mgmt. Assn. (program com. 1994-97, mem.-at-large bd. dirs. 2000-02, chair cultural diversity com. 2000—), Tex. Libr. Assn. (pub. libr. divsn. sec. 1995-96, chair 1997-98, leadership devel. com. 1995-97, leadership devel. com. chair 1996-97, alumnae 1st class Tex. Accelerated Libr. Leaders 1994, legis. com. 1997-99, Dist. 7 coun. 1996-99, exec. bd. 1998-2000, ad hoc comn. on pub. lib. stds. com. chair 1998-2000, 2002 conf. local arrangements com. 2001-02, chair 2000 conf. program com. 1998-2000, chair awards com. 2001—), Pub. Libr. Adminstrs. North Tex. (vice chair 1994-95, chair 1995-96), Tex. Mcpl. Libr. Dirs. Assn. (pres. 1995-96, grantee 1993, Libr. of Yr. 1998), Denton Rotary Club, Tex. Mcpl. League (bd. dirs. 1997-2000). Office: Denton Pub Libr 502 Oakland St Denton TX 76201-3102 E-mail: eva.poole@cityofdenton.com.

POOLE, GALEN VINCENT, surgeon, educator, researcher; b. Pewee Valley, Ky., Apr. 13, 1951; s. Galen Vincent and Audrey (Taylor) P.; m. Carol Ruth Shepherd, Aug. 11, 1974; children: Erin Ruth, Matthew Shepherd. AB, Hanover Coll., 1973; MD, U. Ky., 1978. Diplomate Am. Bd. Surgery; added qualifications in surg. critical care. Intern, resident in surgery Bowman Gray-Wake Forest U., Winston-Salem, N.C., 1978-85; asst. clin. prof. Sch. Medicine U. Ill., Urbana, 1986-89; assoc. prof. Med. Ctr. U. Miss., Jackson, 1989-93, prof. surgery, 1993—. Author: Abdominal Wound Dehiscence, 1987; contbr. more than 85 articles to profl. jours.: Chmn. Miss. State Com. on Trauma, Jackson, 1993—; dir. Trauma, Surg., and Critical Care, Jackson, 1989-2001; mem. adv. coun. Emergency Med. Svcs. Trauma Care Task Force, Jackson, 1993-2001; mem. Miss. Trauma Adv. Coun., 1998-2002. Lt. col. USAFR, 1985—. Fellow ACS (com. on trauma), Southeastern Surg. Congress; mem. Southern Surgical Assn., Am. Assn. for Surgery of Trauma, Soc.

of Univ. Surgeons, Soc. for Surgery of the Alimentary Tract, Soc. for Critical Care Medicine, Alpha Omega Alpha. Home: 145 Summerwood Dr Jackson MS 39208-9075 Office: U Miss Med Ctr Dept Surgery 2500 N State St Jackson MS 39216-4500

POOLE, GORDON LEICESTER, lawyer; b. Mpls., Dec. 25, 1926; s. Arthur Bensell and Mildred Loyal (Wood) P.; m. Lois Claire Teasdale, Oct. 30, 1954; children— David Wilson, Edward Gray, Elisabeth Claire AB, Harvard U., 1949, LL.B., 1952. Assoc. Treadwell & Laughlin, San Francisco, 1953-54, Lillick, McHose & Charles, San Francisco, 1955-63, ptnr., 1963-97, mem. exec. com., 1977-81, chmn. mgmt. com., 1981-84, chmn., 1984-86; of counsel Lillick & Charles LLP, 1997-2001, Nixon Peabody LLP, 2001—. Contbr. articles to profl. jours. Pres. Young Republicans, San Mateo County, Calif., 1958-59; vestryman Trinity Episcopal Parish, Menlo Park, Calif., 1968, 70, 76-78, sr. warden, 1970. Served as sgt. U.S. Army, 1944-47, Korea Mem. Calif. Bar Assn., San Francisco Bar Assn., Maritime Law Assn. (com. on marine financing), Maritime Adminstrv. Bar Assn., ABA, Mng. Ptnrs. Assn. Clubs: Bohemian, World Trade (San Francisco); Ladera Oaks (Menlo Park). Avocations: stamp collecting; marine paintings, prints and memorabilia. Home: 2280 Stockbridge Ave Woodside CA 94062-1130 Office: Nixon Peabody LLP 2 Embarcadero Ctr Ste 2700 San Francisco CA 94111-3996

POOLE, HENRY JOE, JR. business executive; b. Rocky Point, N.C., July 5, 1957; s. Henry Joe Sr. and Marjorie (Morse) P.; m. Loretta Lynn Scott, Sept. 12, 1981; children: Robert Howard, Amanda Lynn. AA, Cypress Coll., 1977; student, San Diego State U., 1978, Calif. State U., Fullerton, 1978-79. Pres. Poole Ventura Inc., Ventura, Calif., 1979-92; gen. mgr. W.I.C. PVI systems divsn., 1992-94; pres. PVI, Oxnard, 1995—. Inventor in field. Mem. ASME, Soc. Mfg. Engrs., Am. Vacuum Soc., Am. Welding Soc., Soc. Vacuum Coaters. Office: PVI PO Box 5023 Oxnard CA 93031-5023 E-mail: pvi@vcnet.com.

POOLE, LOIS A. writer; b. Alliance, Ohio, Nov. 24, 1929; d. Clyde Clarence Erisey, Loretto Elizabeth Webber; m. Robert Neil Poole, July 24, 1956; children: Christopher Lee, Loretto Ruth, Gwendolyn Suzanne. Student, Antelope Valley C.C., Lancaster, Calif., 1985—87, UCLA. Lic. animal health technician Calif. Animal health technician State of Calif., 1970—95; columnist The Antelope Valley Press; columnist numerous newspapers. Tchr. on writing memoirs and creative non-fiction, Palmdale, Calif., 1998—; lectr. in field; vocalist Radio WFAH, Alliance, Ohio, 1953—56. Author: Ring Around the Moon, 1996; contbr. ; author: God's Vitamin "C" Book. Mem.: Amargosa Writers Network. Republican. Roman Catholic. Avocations: gardening, music. Home: 2607 W M-8 Palmdale CA 93551-1742

POOLE, MARION RONALD, civil engineering executive; b. Thomasville, N.C., July 2, 1936; s. Everette Worth and Mabel Emma (Crotts) P.; m. Janice Rochelle Dickens, May 9, 1959; children: Anne Kathleen, Amy Kathryn, Marie Elizabeth. BCE, N.C. State U., 1958, MSCE in Transp., 1961, PhDCE in Transp., 1982. Registered profl. engr., N.C., registered land surveyor, N.C. Engr.-in-tng. N.C. State Hwy. Commn., Winston-Salem, 1958, hwy. planning engr. Raleigh, 1961-63; thoroughfare planning engr. N.C. State Hwy. Commn./N.C. Dept. Transp., 1963-84; asst. mgr. planning and environ. N.C. Dept. Transp., 1984-91, mgr. statewide planning br., 1991—99; ret., 1999. Chmn. com. AIDO5 Transp. Rsch. Bd., NAS, 1992-98, sec., 1986-92; mem. com. AIBO7 Transp. Rsch. Bd., NAS, 1988—, mem. com. AIDO4, Transp. Rsch. Bd., 1988—, mem. com. AIAO6, 2000—. Contbr. articles to Transp. Rsch. Record, Jour. Advanced Transp.; author reports. Club rep. to Tarheel Swim Assn., Glen Forest Swim Club, Raleigh, 1982-88, v.p., 1982-84, bd. dirs., 1975-78. 2nd lt. C.E., U.S. Army, 1958-59, capt. C.E., USAR, 1960-66. Mem. NSPE, Inst. Transp. Engrs. Baptist. Achievements include research on the benefits matrix model for transportation project evaluation, on procedure for synthesizing travel movements. Home: 4605 Woodridge Dr Raleigh NC 27612-3255

POOLE, NANCY GEDDES, art gallery curator; b. London, Can., May 10, 1930; d. John Hardy and Kathleen Edwards (Robinson) G.; m. William Robert Poole, Aug. 15, 1952; 1 child, Andrea Mary. BA, U. Western Ont., 1956, LLD, 1990. Owner, dir. Nancy Poole's Studio, Toronto, Ont., Can., 1969-78; acting dir. London Regional Art Gallery, Can., 1981—, exec. dir. Can., 1985-89; dir. London Regional Art and Hist. Museums, Can., 1989-95. Chair governing coun. Ont. Coll. Art, 1972-73; bd. dirs. Robarts Rsch. Inst., 1995. Author: The Art of London 1939-1980, 1984; editor Jack Chambers, 1978, The Collection, 1990. Bd. govs. U. Western Ont., 1974-85; bd. dirs. Western Area Youth Svcs., 1996. Fellow Ont. Coll. Art. Office: 420 Fanshawe Park Rd London ON Canada N5X 2S9

POOLE, PENNE, interior designer; b. Chgo., Oct. 7, 1943; d. Rawlings Stine and Frances (Childers) P.; m. John Glenn Rhodes, Mov. 26, 1967 (div. 1969); 1 child, Christopher Stanley Rhodes; m. Edward George Fuehrer, Dec. 29, 1970. AA, Colby-Sawyer Coll., New London, N.H., 1963; BFA, Am. U., 1966. Asst. designer Woodward & Lothrop, Washington, 1965-66, W & J Sloane's, Washington, 1966-67, Designers Guild, Washington, 1967-68; designer Bea Keller Interiors, Arlington, Va., 1968-74; ind. designer S.D. Jeffrey, Inc., Bethesda, Md., 1974-79; pres. Penne Poole Interior Design, Inc., Washington, 1979—. Mem. Licensing Council for Interior Design, Md., 1970, Design Ctr. Adv. Council, Washington, 1983, Nat. Council for Interior Design Qualification, N.Y., 1984-86, Nat. Future Direction Com., 1987; mem. adv. bd. Internat. Sch. Design, Washington, 1987—. Designs published in various mags. Bd. dirs. Aged Women's Home Georgetown, Washington, 1985-86. Named Outstanding Designer, Washingtonian Mag., Outstanding Designer, Dossier Mag., 1985, Outstanding Designer, House Beautiful, 1985-86; Nat. Home Fashion League scholar, 1965. Fellow Nat. Home Fashion League (pres. Wash. exec. bd. 1983-84, sec. nat. exec. bd. 1986). Republican. Roman Catholic. Office: 3426 Prospect St NW Washington DC 20007-3218

POOLE, RHONDA ANN, editor, reporter; b. Lewisburg, Tenn., Sept. 16, 1958; d. Jimmie Thomas Pruitt, Nannie Ruth Pruitt; m. Russell Dean Poole. Grad., Marshall County H.S., Lewisburg, Tenn., 1976. Graphic artist, reporter Lewisburg (Tenn.) Tribune, 1987—91, reporter, 1991—93, mng. editor, reporter, 1993—2001, editor, reporter, 2001—. Recipient Vol. of Yr., March of Dimes, 2001, Svc. award, Am. Heart Assn., 2000, Good Citizenship award, Cornersville Lions Club, 1999, Cmty. Svc. award, Ladies Aux., Vets. of Foreign Wars, 1999, Svc. award, United Givers Fund, 1996, 1998, Cmty. Svc. award, Marshall County Edn. Assn., 1993, 1995, 1996, 1997, Dedication award, Berlin Vol. Fire Dept., 1996, Ptnrs. In Edn., Spot Lowe Tech. Ctr., 1995, Outstanding Coverage award, Tenn. Gen. Assembly. Mem.: Rotary (hon.; Lewisburg chpt., Paul Harris fellow 2000). Avocations: gardening, travel, writing, counted cross stitch. Office: Lewisburg Tribune 121 First Ave S Lewisburg TN 37091 Business E-Mail: rpoole@ltrib-gaz.com.

POOLE, RICHARD WILLIAM, economics educator; b. Oklahoma City, Dec. 4, 1927; s. William Robert and Lois (Spicer) P.; m. Bertha Lynn Mehr, July 28, 1950; children: Richard William, Laura Lynne, Mark Stephen. BS, U. Okla., 1951, MBA, 1952; postgrad., George Washington U., 1957-58; PhD, Okla. State U., 1960. Rsch. analyst Okla. Gas & Electric Co., Oklahoma City, 1952- 54; mgr. sci. and mfg. devel. dept. Oklahoma City C. of C., 1954-57; mgr. Office of J.E. Webb, Washington, 1957-58; from instr. to prof. econs. Okla. State U., Stillwater, 1960-65, prof. econs., dean Coll. Bus. Adminstrn., 1965-72, v.p., prof. econs., 1972-88, Regents Disting. Svc. prof., prof. econs., 1988-93, emeritus v.p., dean, Regents Disting. Svc. prof./prof. econ., 1993—. Cons. to adminstr. NASA, Washington, 1961-69; adviser subcom. on govt. rsch. U.S. Senate, 1966-69; lectr. Intermediate Sch. Banking, Ops. Mgmt. Sch., Okla. Bankers Assn., 1968-89; lectr. internat. off-campus programs Okla. City U., 1994-96. Author: (with others) The Oklahoma Economy, 1963, County Building Block Data for Regional Analysis, 1965. Mem. Gov.' Com. on Devel. Ark.-Verdigris Waterway, 1970-71, Gov.'s Five-Yr. Econ. Devel. Plan, 1993; past v.p., bd. dirs., past chmn. Mid-Continent Rsch. and Devel. Coun. 2d lt., arty. U.S. Army, 1946-48. Recipient Delta Sigma Pi Gold Key award Coll. Bus. Adminstrn., U. Okla., 1951, Tchg. award on Am. free enterprise sys. Merrick Found., 1992, Disting. Alumni award Okla. State U., 1995, Henry G. Bennett Distinguished Service Award, 1999; named to Coll. Bus. Adminstrn. Hall of Fame, Okla. State U., 1993, Stillwater Hall of Fame, Payne County Hist. Soc. and Stillwater C. of C., 1996, Okla. Higher Edn. Hall of Fame, 1998. Mem. Southwestern Econ. Assn. (past pres.), Am. Assembly Collegiate Schs. Bus. (past bd. dirs.), Nat. Assn. State Univs. and Land Grant Colls. (past chmn. commn. on edn. for bus. professions), Southwestern Bus. Adminstrn. Assn. (past pres.), Okla. C. of C. (past bd. dirs.), Okla. Heritage Assn. (bd. dirs. 2000—), Santa Fe Trail Assn. (bd. dirs. 2001—), Stillwater C. of C. (past bd. dirs. and pres.), Beta Gamma Sigma (past bd. dirs.), Phi Kappa Phi, Phi Eta Sigma, Omicron Delta Kappa. Home: 815 S Shumard St Stillwater OK 74074-1136

POOLE, ROB R. management educator, consultant; b. Houston, Sept. 3, 1957; s. Grover Quinton and Ruth Mildred P. BS in Econs., Tex. A&M U., 1979; MS in Sys. Mgmt., U. So. Calif., 1986; PhD in Prodn. Ops., U. North Tex., 1996. Prof. U. North Tex., Denton, 1989-94, Ctrl. Mo. State U., Warrensburg, 1994-96, Bellarmine U., Louisville, 1996—. Faculty advisor Phi Beta Lambda, Louisville, 1996—, Delta Sigma Phi, Louisville, 1996—. Reviewer: Decision Sci. Inst. Proceedings Jour., 1995-97, Nat. Assn. Global Bus., 1995-96, Nat. Acad. Mgmt., 1995-96. Lt. USMC, 1979-86. Mem. Nat. Assn. Purchasing Mgrs., Am. Soc. Quality, Decision Sci. Inst., Masonic Lodge, Beta Gamma Sigma, Delta Sigma Pi. Episcopalian. Office: Bellarmine U Louisville KY 40205 Address: 2001 Newburg Rd Louisville KY 40205-1863

POOLE, ROBERT WILLIAM, JR. foundation executive; b. Englewood, N.J., July 4, 1944; s. Robert William and Frances Ann (Giese) P.; m. Lou Villadsen, May 28, 1983; m. Marilyn V. Kinsky, June 1968 (div. 1974). BS, MIT, 1966, MS, 1967. Systems analyst Sikorsky Aircraft, Stratford, Conn., 1967-70; criminal justice analyst Gen. Rsch. Co., Santa Barbara, Calif., 1970-74; cons. local govt. mgmt., 1974-76; pres. Local Govt. Ctr., 1976-78, Reason Found., Santa Monica, Calif., 1978—. Author: Cutting Back City Hall, 1980; editor: Instead of Regulation, 1982, Defending a Free Society, 1984, Unnatural Monopolies, 1985; editor, pub. mag. Reason, 1971-89. Bd. dirs. Mission Canyon Assn., Santa Barbara, 1984-85, Santa Barbara Futures Found., 1982-83, Reason Found., 1978—, State Policy Network, 1999—. Fellow NSF, 1966-67. Mem. AAAS, Sigma Xi. Libertarian. Office: Reason Found 3415 S Sepulveda Blvd Ste 400 Los Angeles CA 90034-6014

POOLE, SHARON ALEXANDRA, lawyer; b. Hollywood, Calif., Jan. 31, 1950; d. James Earl and Lolly L. (Solo) P.; m. Larry E. Greenberger, July 4, 1972 (div. 1983); m. John Oren, Feb. 2, 1996. BS in Comm., Fla. State U., 1977; JD, Stetson Coll., 1980; LLM in Admiralty, Tulane U., 1982; postgrad., Oxford (Eng.) U., 1980. Bar: Fla. 1981, U.S. Dist. Ct. (mid. dist.) Fla. 1982. Ptnr. Cushman & Poole, St. Augustine, Fla., 1982-83; pvt. practice law, 1983—. Bd. dirs., sec. St. Augustine Humane Soc., St. Augustine, 1988-2000. Mem.: Fla. Bar Assn. Office: 10 Mc Millan St # 1 Saint Augustine FL 32084-1618

POOLE, STAFFORD, historian, priest; b. Oxnard, Calif., Mar. 6, 1930; s. Joseph Outhwaite Poole and Beatrice Hessie Smith. BA, St. Mary's Sem., Perryville, Mo., 1952; MA, St. Louis U., 1958, PhD, 1961. Ordained priest Roman Cath. Ch., 1956. Vice rector, prof. history Cardinal Glennon Coll., St. Louis, 1956—64; vice rector, dean of studies St. Mary's Sem., Perryville, 1964—71; prof. history St. John's Sem. Coll., Camarillo, Calif., 1971—90, pres., rector, 1980—84; historian L.A., 1990—. Vis. lectr. Mt. St. Mary's Coll., L.A., 1970, 72. Author: Pedro Moya de Contreras, 1987, Our Lady of Guadalupe, 1995; editor: In Defense of the Indians, 1974, 1992; exec. editor: Vincentian Heritage, 1989—96. Mem. exec. com. Rocky Mountain Coun. on Latin Am. Studies, 1998—. Named Disting. Guest, City of San Cristobal, Chiapas, Mex., 1974; grantee, NEH, 1991. Mem.: Am. Soc. Ethnohistory, Conf. on Latin. Am. History (exec. com. 1989—), Am. Hist. Assn. Home: 641 W Adams Blvd Los Angeles CA 90007 Fax: 213-748-9829. E-mail: spoole8257@aol.com.

POOLE, THOMAS RICHARD, endowment capital campaign director, fund raising counsel; b. Newark, July 15, 1947; s. Frank Baldwin and Edna Laura (Harper) Poole. BA, Ohio Wesleyan U., 1969; MEd, Wright State U., 1975. Cert. fund-raising exec., 1985. Assoc. program dir. Brakeley, John Price Jones Inc., Stamford, Conn., Newport Beach, Calif., 1976-79, program dir., 1979-81, v.p., 1981-91, sr. v.p., 1991—. Assoc. campaign dir. Columbia-Presbyn. Med. Ctr., N.Y.C., 1976-79; campaign dir. Manhattan Eye, Ear and Throat Hosp., N.Y.C., 1979-82; endowment/capital campaign dir., cons. Albany (N.Y.) Med. Ctr., 1984-89; endowment/capital campaign dir. Long Beach (Calif.) Meml. Med. Ctr., 1989-95; campaign dir. Samaritan Health Sys., Phoenix, 1995-2000; cons., 2001—. Author various corporate reports and feasibility studies. Mem. Nat. Soc. Fund-Raising Execs., Assocs. Ohio Wesleyan U. Avocations: reading, sailing, hiking, swimming. Office: Brakeley John Price Jones Inc 2503 Eastbluff Dr Ste 203 Newport Beach CA 92660-3550 Fax: 949-721-1502. E-mail: brakeleynb@aol.com.

POOLE, WALTER BRUCE, artist, art educator; b. Chgo., Apr. 9, 1954; s. Jim and Doris (Underwood) P.; m. Regina Ann Earnest, Sept. 17, 1994. BFA, Huntingdon Coll., 1991; MFA, Auburn U., 1996. Freelance artist, Tuscaloosa, Ala., 1976—; grad. assistantship Auburn U., 1994. Adj. prof. U. West Ala., Livingston. One-man shows include Froshins Gallery, Alexander City, Ala., 1992, Exhbn. 1048, Montgomery, 1993, Auburn U., Montgomery, 1994, Cultural Arts Ctr., Gadsden, Ala., 1997; exhibited in group shows at Huntingdon Coll., Montgomery, 1991, First Ala. Bank Exhbn., Montgomery, 1991, Montgomery Mus. Fine Arts, 1992, Ala. State Fair Fine Arts Exhbn., Montgomery, 1995 (1st place award), Miss. State U. Invitational Exhbn., 1995, Auburn U. MFA Exhbn., 1996, Ft. Smith Art Ctr., Ark., 1996, Baum Gallery, Conway, Ark., 1996, West Memphis City Hall, Ark., 1996, Lyon Coll., Batesville, Ark., 1996, Harding U., Searcy, Ark., 1996, Arts Ctr. of the Ozarks, Springdale, Ark., 1996, Harrison (Ark.) Art Ctr., 1996, U. Ark., Little Rock, 1996, Hope (Ark.) Art Inst., Henderson State Coll., Helena, Ark., 1996, Arts & Scis. of Ark., Pine Bluff, 1996, Clemson (S.C.) Nat. Printmaking Exhbn., 1996, West Ala. Arts Assn. Exhbn., Tuscaloosa, 1996, Huntingdon Coll. Invitational Exhbn., Ala., 1996, S.C.A.A. Art Exhbn., Mableton, Ga., 1996 (2nd place award); represented in permanent collections First Ala. Bank, Montgomery, 1991, Jenkins Brick Corp., Montgomery, 1994. Cpl. U.S. Army, 1972-76, Vietnam. Decorated Gallentry Cross with palm device; merit scholar Huntingdon Coll., Montgomery, Ala., 1991. Mem. West Ala. Art Assn., South Cobb Art Assn., Nat. Art Exhbn., Coll. Art Assn., Kappa Pi. Home: 3001 Paddlecreek Ln Northport AL 35473-1956

POOLE, WILL, information technology executive; BS in Computer Sci., Brown U. Sr. mktg. & engring. mgmt. Sun Microsystems Inc., 1985—90; co-founder eShop Inc., 1991—96; corp. v.p. Microsoft, Redmond, Wash., 1996—. Avocations: bicycling, sailing, building furniture. Office: One Microsoft Way Redmond WA 98052-6399*

POOLE, WILLIAM, bank executive; b. Wilmington, Del., June 19, 1937; s. William and Louise (Hiller) P.; m. Mary Lynne Ahroon, June 26, 1960 (div. May 1997); children: William, Lester Allen, Jonathan Carl; m. Geraldine S. Stroud, July 12, 1997. AB, Swarthmore Coll., 1959, LLD (hon.), 1989; MBA, U. Chgo., 1963, PhD, 1966. Asst. prof. polit. economy Johns Hopkins U., Balt., 1963-69; professorial lectr. Am. U., Washington, 1970-71; assoc. professorial lectr. George Washington U., 1971-73; lectr. professorial lectr. Georgetown U., 1972, Harvard U., Cambridge, Mass., 1973; vis. lectr. MIT, 1974, 77; Bank Mees and Hope vis. prof. econs. Erasmus U. Rotterdam, 1991; prof. econs. Brown U., Providence, 1974-98, dir. ctr. for study fin. markets and insts., 1987-92, chmn. econs. dept., 1981-82, 85-86; economist Bd. Govs. of FRS, Washington, 1964, 69-70, sr. economist, 1970-74; pres., CEO Fed. Res. Bank, St. Louis, 1998—. Adviser Fed. Res. Bank, Boston, 1973-74, cons., 1974-81; vis. economist Res. Bank of Australia, 1980-81; mem. Coun. Econ. Advisers, 1982-85; adj. scholar Cato Inst., 1985-98. Mem. Am. Econ. Assn., Am. Fin. assn. (mem. nominating com. 1979), Western Econ. Assn. (mem. internat. exec. com. 1986-89, mem. nominating com. 1995). Office: Fed Res Bank St Louis 411 Locust St Saint Louis MO 63102-2005

POOLE, WILLIAM DANIEL, writer, editor; b. Statesville, N.C., Nov. 3, 1932; s. William Oscar and Edna (Brewer) P.; m. Sandra Ball, June 14, 1980. BA, Wake Forest U., 1955. Reporter Norfolk (Va.) Virginian-Pilot, 1955-57, Washington Star, 1957-61, real estate editor, 1961-71, features editor, asst. mng. editor, 1971-81; v.p. Ins. Info. Inst., N.Y.C., 1981-91; pub. Insurance Rev. mag., 1986-91. Contbr. articles to profl. jours. Mem. White House Corr. Assn., Nat. Assn. Real Estate Editors (pres. 1970-71), Newspaper Comics Coun. (chmn. 1975-77), Soc. Am. Travel Writers, Mystery Writers of Am., Ins. Mktg. Comms. Assn., Am. Assn. Sunday and Feature Editors, Amateur Comedy Club, Dutch Treat Club, The Players Club (1st v.p.), Nat. Press Club (D.C.), Omicron Delta Kappa, Sigma Phi Epsilon. Republican. Baptist. Home: 139 E 63rd St New York NY 10021-7408

POOLE, WILLIAM S. pharmaceutical executive; With Am. Cyanamid Co., 1972—94; pres. Fisons Pharm., 1995—96; corp. v.p., pres. N.Am., Novo Nordisk Pharm., Inc., 1997—2000; pres. Biovail Corp., Mississauga, Canada, 2001—. Office: Biovail Corp 2488 Dunwin Dr Mississauga L5L 1J9 Canada

POOLER, DAVID KENNETH, social worker; b. Durham, N.C., Jan. 16, 1968; s. John Preston and Karen (Bryant) Pooler; m. Cheryl Ann Sharp, June 6, 1992; 1 child Josianne Li. BA, Lee U., 1993; MSW, U. Louisville, 1999. Cert. social worker Ky. Therapeutic aid Hiwassee Mental Health Ctr., Cleve., 1991; client coord. Atlanta Union Mission, 1993—95; case mgr. Seven Counties Svcs., Inc., Louisville, 1996—99, therapist, 1999—. Pres. bd. Fern Creek Highview United Ministries, Louisville, 2001—; family enrichment dir. Solid Rock Ch. of God, 2001—. With U.S. Army, 1986—88. Mem.: NASW. Home: 3905 Bayonne Ct Louisville KY 40299

POOLER, ROSEMARY S. federal judge; b. 1938; BA, Brooklyn Coll., 1959; MA, Univ. of Conn., 1961; JD, Univ. of Mich. Law Sch., 1965. With Crystal, Manes & Rifken, Syracuse, 1966—69, Michaels and Michaels, Syracuse, 1969—72; asst. corp. counsel Dir. of Consumer Affairs Unit, 1972—73; common counsel City of Syracuse Pub. Interest Rsch. Group, 1974—75; chmn., exec. dir. Consumer Protection Bd., 1975—80; commr. N.Y. State Pub. Services Commn., 1981—86; staff dir. N.Y. State Assembly, Com. on Corps., Authorities and Commns., 1987—94; judge Supreme Ct., 5th Jud. Dist., 1991—94; dist. judge U.S. Dist. Ct. (no. dist.) N.Y., Syracuse, 1994—98; cir. judge U.S. Ct. Appeals, 2nd cir., 1998—. Vis. prof. Syracuse Univ. Coll. of Law, 1987—88; v.p. legal affairs Atlantic States Legal Found., 1989—90. Mem.: Assn. of Supreme Ct. Justices of the State of N.Y., Women's Bar Assn. of the State of N.Y., N.Y. State Bar Assn., Onondaga County Bar Assn. Office: 40 Foley Square New York NY 10007*

POON, PETER TIN-YAU, engineer, physicist; b. Hengyang, Hunan, China, May 31, 1944; came to U.S., 1967; s. Sam. Chak-Kwong and Lai (Yiu) P.; m. Mable Tsang, Apr. 13, 1974; children: Amy Wei-Ling, Brian Wing-Yan. BS, U. Hong Kong, 1965; MA, Calif. State U., Long Beach, 1969; PhD, U. So. Calif., L.A., 1974. Tech. mgr., sr. engr. Jet Propulsion Lab./Calif. Inst. Tech., Pasadena, 1974-83; advisor Space Sta. Ada Task, task leader software mgmt. and assurance program NASA, 1984-85, software mgmt. stds., element mgr. software info. sys., 1986-88; systems mgr. for missions to Mars, Comet/Asteroid/Saturn, flight projects interface office Jet Propulsion Lab./Calif. Inst. Tech., 1988-91, multimission ground systems office mgr. Mission to Mars, 1991-93, telecomm. and mission systems mgr. Cassini Mission to Saturn, 1993-98, radio astronomy, French, German and Italian missions, 1998—2001, U.S. Mar global surveyor, Mars Odyssey, European radio astronom,y French and Italian Mars missions, 2001—. U.S. chmn., program mgmt. com., panel chair Internat. Software Engring. Stds. Symposium, Eng., 1992-93, Can., 1994-95, U.S., 1995-97, 2000—, Brazil, 1998-99; 5th Internat. Software Engring. Stds. Symposium, US, 2000—; session chair, mem. program com. IEEE Internat. Conf. on Engring. of Complex Computer Systems, Montreal, 1995-96, Como, Italy, 1996-97, Monterey, 1997-98, Tokyo, 1999-2000, Skövde, Sweden, 2000-01, Greenbelt, Md., 2001-02; mem. Internat. Orgn. for Standardization in Info. Tech. Subcom. and U.S. Tech. Adv. Group, 1995—; U.S. del., Prague, Czech Republic, 1996, Paris, 1996, Walnut Creek, U.S., 1997, Brisbane, Australia, 1997, Melbourne, Fla., 1998, Curitiba, Brazil, 1998; program chmn. Software Engring. Stds. Symposium, 1998—; 2nd World Congress on Software Quality, Tokyo, 2000—; program co-chmn. 5th Internat. Software Engring. Stds. Symposium, 2000—. Mem. editl. bd. Software Quality Profl., Am. Soc. for Quality, 1998—; contbr. articles to profl. jours. Active steering com. United Way, Jet Propulsion Laboratory, 1998—. Recipient Group awards NASA, 1977-2001, Recognition cert., Inventions and Contbns. Bd. Mem. IEEE (exec. com. software engring. stds. 1993-2000), Arcadia Music Club (pres. 1994-95), Sigma Xi, Eta Kappa Nu, Phi Kappa Phi, Athenaeum. Avocations: music appreciation, hiking, theatre arts. Office: Jet Propulsion Lab Calif Inst Tech 4800 Oak Grove Dr Pasadena CA 91109-8001 E-mail: Petertpoon@yahoo.com.

POON, YAT SUN, mathematician; b. Hong Kong, Mar. 14, 1958; m. Sau King Chiu, July 12, 1987; 1 child, Jessica B. BSc, Chinese U. of Hong Kong, 1981; PhD, Oxford (Eng.) U., 1986. Rsch. asst. SUNY, Stony Brook, 1985-87; asst. prof. Rice U., Houston, 1987—. Croucher Found. scholar, 1981-85; NSF grantee, 1986—. Mem. Yale Club of New Haven. Office: Rice U Dept Mathematics PO Box 1892 Houston TX 77251-1892

POONJA, MOHAMED, business reorganization, financial and management consultant; b. Mombasa, Kenya, Nov. 8, 1948; came to U.S., 1984; s. Abdulrasul and Maleksultan (Dharsee) P.; m. Zaitun Virji, Feb. 24, 1979; children: Jamil Husayn, Karim Ali. Student, Inst. Chartered Accts., Eng., Wales; MS in Mgmt. and Organizational Behavior, U.S. Internat. U. CPA. Audit supr. Ernst & Young (formerly Ernst & Whinney), Dublin, Ireland, 1966-72, Coopers & Lybrand, Dublin, 1973-76; CFO Diamond Trust of Kenya, Nairobi, 1976-78; CEO Kenya Uniforms, Ltd., 1978-81; sr. mgr. Coopers & Lybrand, Calgary, Alta., Can., 1981-84, ptnr. San Jose, Calif., 1984-92; chpt. 7 panel bankruptcy trustee No. Dist. Calif., 1991—; with Poonja & Co., 1992—; ptnr. Manzanita Capital Ptnrs. Ltd., 1993—. Former pres. Bay Area Bankruptcy Forum; bd. dirs. Calif. Bankruptcy Forum, Los Altos Edn. Found. Am. Youth Soccer Orgn. Mem. ABA, Am. Bankruptcy Inst., Assn. Insolvency Accts., Inst. Bus. Appraisers, Cert. Fraud Examiners, Rotary. Avocations: music, art. Home: 630 Milverton Rd Los Altos CA 94022-3930 Office: Poonja & Co 150 Giffin Rd Los Altos CA 94022-3940

POONS, LARRY, artist; b. Tokyo, Oct. 1, 1937; came to U.S., 1938; Student, New Eng. Conservatory Music, 1955-57, Boston Mus. Fine Arts Sch., 1958. Mem. vis. faculty N.Y. Studio Sch., 1967. Guest lectr. Winchester Coll. Author: The Structure of Color, 1971;exhibitions include include Green Gallery, N.Y.C., 1963—65, exhibitions include Art Inst. Chgo., 1966, Corcoran Gallery Art, Carnegie Inst., 1967, Leo Castelli Gallery, 1967—68, Documenta IV, Kassel, W. Germany, 1968, Whitney Mus. Am. Art Ann., 1968, 1972, Lawrence Rubin Gallery, 1970—73, Whitney Biennial, 1973, Knoedler & Co., 1973—78, Knoedler Contemporary Art, N.Y.C., 1974—78, Andre Emmerlich Gallery, 1979—87, Albright-Knox Art Gallery, Buffalo, 1968, 1970, Pasadena Art Mus., 1969, Gallery 99, Bar Harbor Islands, Fla., 1981, Mus. Fine Arts, Boston, 1981—82, Galerie Montaigne, Paris, 1990, Helander Gallery, Palm Beach, Fla., 1990, Salander-O'Reilly Galleries, N.Y.C., 1991—96, 1998, solo and group shows, , , exhibited in group shows at Matthew Mark, Pat Hearn, 1998, Sideshow 195, Bklyn., 1998, Art and the Am. Experience, Kalamazoo Inst. of the Arts, 1998, Staatliche Kunsthalle, Baden-Baden, Germany, 1999, Ameringe Howard Fine Art, N.Y.C., 2000, Bernard Jacobson, 2002, one-man shows include Salander-O'Reilly Gallery, N.Y.C., 2001, Represented in permanent collections Mus. Modern Art, Allen Meml. Art Mus., Oberlin Coll., Cleve. Mus. Art, Hirschhorn Mus. and Sculpture Garden, Washington, Milw. Art Ctr., Solomon R. Guggenheim Mus., N.Y.C., Tate Gallery, London, Whitney Mus. Am. Art, Met. Mus. Art, Chgo. Art Inst., Denver Mus., Boston Mus. Fine Arts, Albright-Knox Art Gallery, Stedelijk Mus., Amsterdam, Woodward Found., Washington, David Mirvish Gallery, Toronto, Bernard Jacobson Gallery, London, one-man shows include Theo Waddington, Boca Raton, Fla., 2000, Galleria Metta, Madrid, 2000, Perrella Gallery, Johnstown, N.Y., 2000, Bernard Jacobson, 2002; lectr. Perrella Gallery, Artists Talk on Art Dialogue with Jason Andrew Mass. Coll. Art, 2000. Address: 831 Broadway New York NY 10003-4706

POOPATANAPONG, ANNE, wildlife biologist; b. Burbank, Calif., Feb. 22, 1975; d. Andrew A. and Nongluck N. (Promvira) P. BS, U. Calif., Davis, 1997; MS in Biology, U. Nev., 2000. Hostess Disneyland, Anaheim, Calif., 1993-94; asst. II U. Calif., Davis, 1993, vet. medicine asst. II, 1994-97, animal sci. asst. III, 1996-97, acad. peer advisor, 1996-97; wildlife biologist USDA Forest Svc., Fresno, Calif., 1997-2000, San Bernardino Nat. Forest, Idyllwild, CA, 2000—. Primary investigator U. Calif., Davis, 1996-97; tchrs. asst., U. Nev., Reno, 1997-2000. Lobbist intern Mt. Lion Found., Sacramento, 1996; rsch. intern Native Grass Found., Davis, 1996-97. Mathias Rsch. grantee U. Calif., Davis, Jepson Prairie, 1996, 97, Blakely Rsch. grantee U. Calif., Davis, Jepson Prairie, 1996, 97. Mem. Wildlife Soc., Sigma Xi. Democrat. Buddhist. Achievements include research in management of small animals in a native perennial grassland and the effect of prescribed fire, the effects of California Spotted Owl predation on Northern Flying Squirrel population, behavior and demography. Avocations: hiking, theater and arts, cooking, swimming, gardening, animal rights. Office: US Forest Svc San Bernardino Nat Forest PO Box 518 54270 Pinecrest Idyllwild CA 92549 E-mail: apoopatanapong@fs.fed.us.

POOR, ANDREW FORD, music educator; b. Tucson, Oct. 20, 1965; s. William Brown and Shirley Yvonne Poor; m. Marilyn Claire King; 1 child Kathryne 1 child Addison. BA Music Edn., U. Fla., 1988; MMus Trumpet Performance, U. Cin., 1993, D Music Edn., 1999. Lic. tchr. Ga., 1999, cert. Clin. Educator Fla., 1996. Dir. bands Beaumont Mid. Sch., Kissimmee, Fla., 1988—91; instr. trumpet Cin. Conservatory Prep. Dept., 1992—95; dir. bands Haines City H.S., Fla., 1995—99; brass caption head Drum Corps Internat., Addison, Ill., 2000—02; dir. bands Osborne H.S., Marietta, Ga., 1999—2002. Music adjudicator Bands of Am., Schaumburg, Ill., 1996—2002; music cons. Bibb County Sch. Bd., Macon, Ga., 2002—02; music adjudicator Drum Corps Internat., 1994—2002. Composer: (musical work for band) United We Stand, 2002, (musical work for brass choir) Declarations, 2001, (musical work for band) To Challenge the Spartans, 2001, Faith!, 1999; author: (book) Middle School Music Education, 1999. Festival chmn. Fla. Bandmasters Assn., Tallahassee, 1995—98. Recipient Jim Ott Meml. Scholarship, Sponsors of Musical Enrichment, 1988; fellow, U. Cin., 1993—95. Mem.: Internat. Assn. of Jazz Educators, ASCD, Ga. Music Edn. Assn., Phi Mu Alpha Sinfonia (life; edn. leader for local chpt. 1984—87). Conservative-R. Methodist. Avocation: composing, golf, reading, drawing. Home: 4557 Darrowby Drive Powder Springs GA 30127 Office: Robert L Osborne HS 2451 Favor Rd Marietta GA 30060 Office Fax: 770-319-3904. Personal E-mail: andrewfpoor@cobbk12.org. Business E-Mail: andrewfpoor@cobbk12.org.

POOR, CLARENCE ALEXANDER, retired physician; b. Ashland, Oreg., Oct. 29, 1911; s. Lester Clarence and Matilda Ellen (Doty) P. AB, Willamette U., 1932; MD, U. Oreg., 1936. Diplomate Am. Bd. Internal Med. Intern U. Wis., Madison, 1936-37, resident in internal med., 1937-40, instr. dept. pathology Med. Sch., 1940-41, clin. instr., clin. asst. dept. internal med., 1942-44; pvt. practice med. specializing in internal med. Oakland, Calif., 1944-97; mem. emeritus staff Highland Alameda County Hosp., 1949—; mem. staff Providence Hosp., 1947-97, pres. staff, 1968-69; staff mem. Samuel Merritt Hosp., Oakland, 1947-97, Summit Med. Ctr. (merger Providence Hosp. and Samuel Merritt Hosp.), 1991-97; ret., 1997. Mem. Nat. Coun. on Alcoholism, 1974—, bd. dirs. Bay Area, 1977—. Mem. Am., Calif., Alameda-Contra Costa med. assns., Alameda County Heart Assn. (trustee 1955-62, 72-82, pres. 1960-61), Calif. Heart Assn. (dir. 1962-72), Soc. for Clin. and Exptl. Hypnosis, Am. Soc. Clin. Hypnosis, San Francisco Acad. Hypnosis (dir. 1966—, pres. 1973), The Commonwealth Club Calif. Home: 1241 West View Dr Berkeley CA 94705-1650 *Personal philosophy: No matter how easy or how hard the task, the goal is that it be an enjoyment on final review.*

POOR, HAROLD VINCENT, electrical engineering educator; b. Columbus, Ga., Oct. 2, 1951; s. Harold Edgar and Virginia (Hardin) P.; m. Connie Irene Hazelwood, Sept. 1, 1973; children: Kristin Elizabeth, Lauren Alissa. BEE with highest honors, Auburn U., 1972; PhD, Princeton U., 1977. Asst. prof. U. Ill., Urbana, 1977-81, assoc. prof., 1981-84, prof., 1984-90; prof. dept. elec. engring. Princeton (N.J.) U., 1990—. Acad. visitor Imperial Coll. London U., 1985; vis. prof. Newcastle (Australia) U., 1987; sr. visiting fellow Imperial Coll., London U., 1993; cons. and bd. mem. numerous orgns., 1978—. Author: An Introduction to Signal Detection and Estimation, 1988, 2d edit., 1994; co-editor: Wireless Communications: Signal Processing Perspectives, 1998; contbr. numerous articles to profl. jours. Grantee NSF, Office of Naval Rsch., Army Rsch. Office, 1978—; recipient Terman award Am. Soc. Engring. Edn., 1992, Centennial certificate Am. Soc. for Engring. Edn., 1993, NSF Dir.'s award Disting. Teaching scholars. Fellow IEEE (bd. dirs. 1991-92, Third Millennium medal 2000, grad. tch. award 2001), AAAS, Acoustical Soc. Am., Inst. Math. Stats., Optical Soc. Am.; mem. NAE, Info. Theory Soc. of IEEE (pres. 1990, joint paper award with IEEE Comm. Soc., 2001), IEEE Control Sys. Soc. (Disting. Mem. award 1994), Cosmos Club (Washington). Office: Princeton Univ Dept Elec Engring Princeton NJ 08544-0001

POOR, PETER VARNUM, producer, director; b. N.Y.C., May 17, 1926; s. Henry Varnum and Bessie Breuer (Freedman) P.; m. Eloise Marcovicci Miller, Sept. 27, 1950; children: Candida Eustacia, Anna Maria, Graham Varnum. BA, Harvard U., 1947; postgrad., Centro Sperimentale di Cinematografia, Rome, 1951-52. Prodn. asst. New World Films, N.Y.C., 1948; editor, dir. Willard Pictures, 1948-51; film editor, dir. and producer CBS News-Airpower, 1954-57, 7 Lively Arts, 1957-58, Twentieth Century, 1958-66, 21st Century, 1966-69, 60 Minutes, 1970-71, CBS Reports, 1971-75; sr. producer NBC News, Monitor, First Camera, White Paper, 1977-87; freelance producer and dir. Crow House Prodns., N.Y.C., 1988—. Instr. in TV journalism Fordham U., 1976-78; mem. Screening Com. for Fulbright Grants in Film, TV and Radio, 1965-67, chmn., 1967, 70; adj. assoc. history of documentary Columbia U. Grad. Sch. Journalism, 1987; adj. asst. prof. visual arts NYU, 1991-92. Producer-dir.: (TV documentary films) What's New at School, 1972, The IQ Myth, 1975, The Biggest Lump of Money in the World, 1985, The Japan They Don't Talk About, 1986, Nuclear Power in France, 1987, The Cronkite Report, 1993. Served with USAF, 1944-45. Recipient Emmy award Acad. TV Arts and Sci., 1961, 62, 67, Lasker TV award Lasker Found., 1968, 69, U.S. CEA Forum award, 1967, 87; hon. mention Robert Kennedy Journalism Award in TV, 1976; Fulbright scholar, 1951-52. Mem. Dirs. Guild Am. (coun. 1980-90), Film Editors Union, Writers Guild Am. East. Clubs: Phoenix S-K (Cambridge, Mass.). Avocations: bicycling, reading, photography, gardening. Home and Office: 1150 5th Ave New York NY 10128-0724

POORE, SHANNON LEIGH, lawyer; b. Wurzberg, Germany, June 9, 1969; parents U.S. citizens; d. David Robert and Sandra L. (Guess) P. BA, U. Ark., 1991, JD, 1994. Bar: Ark. 1995, U.S. Dist. Ct. (we. dist.) Ark. 1995. Pvt. practice, Fayetteville, Ark., 1995-96; assoc. Nobles, Poore & Jones, PA, 1996, Nobles & Poore, Fayetteville, 1997-99, Ball & Mourton, Ltd., PLLC, Fayetteville, 1999—. Active Washington County Dem. Ctrl. Com., Fayetteville, 1996-98. Recipient Law Sch. award Bur. Nat. Affairs, 1994. Mem. Washington County Bar Assn. Democrat. Avocations: outdoor activities, reading. Office: Ball & Mourton Ltd PO Box 1948 Fayetteville AR 72702-1948 E-mail: spoore@ballardmourton.com.

POORE-CHRISTENSEN, JULIE MARLENE, pastor; b. Des Moines, Sept. 19, 1958; d. Donald Roy and Thelma Beatrice Poore; m. Kenneth Mark Alexander, Aug. 15, 1981 (div. Jan. 1983); m. Allen Mark Poore-Christensen, June 9, 1984; children: LIef Cuillen, Patrick Erin. BA, Westmar Coll., Le Mars, Iowa, 1981; MDiv, Iliff Sch. Theology, Denver, 1984. Social worker Cherry Park Health Care Ctr., Englewood, Colo., 1984-85; pastor Kirk and Idalia (Colo.) United Meth. Ch., Idalia, 1984-85, Randalia, Maynard and Murphy (Iowa) United Meth. Ch., Randalia, 1985-88, Graettinger (Iowa) United Meth. Ch., 1988-94; chaplain, dir. fine arts Forest Ridge Youth Svcs., Estherville, Iowa, 1990-94; pastor Shell Rock (Iowa) United Meth. Ch., 1994-2000, Hansell and West Fork United Meth. Ch., Sheffield, Iowa, 2000—. Bd dirs. Friends of New Parents, Fayette, Iowa, 1986-88, Palo Alto Pub. Health, Emmetsburg, Iowa, 1990-94, Larrabee Ctr., Wavery, Iowa, 2000—; sch. liaison sexual abuse Graettinger Cmty. Sch., 1989-94; trustee Clarksville Pub. Libr., 2001-. Mem. Internat. Assn. Women Ministers, Iowa Women in Profl. Ministry (treas. leadership team 1997-2001), Order of Ea. Star. Home: PO Box 177 311 W Superior Str Clarksville IA 50619 Office: 2200 Tulip Ave Sheffield IA 50475-8113

POORMAN, ROBERT LEWIS, education consultant, former college president; b. Germantown, Ohio, Dec. 9, 1926; s. Dale Lowell and Bernice Velma (Krick) P.; m. Lois May Romer, Dec. 26, 1949; children: Paula Beth, Janice Marie, Mark Leon, John Alex, Lisa Ann, Daniel Romer. Student, Ohio Wesleyan U., 1944-45, U. Va., 1945-46; BSEd., Ohio State U., 1948, MA, 1950; postgrad., U. So. Calif., 1951-53; Ed.D. (Kellogg fellow 1960-62, Disting. Scholar Tuition grantee 1960-62), UCLA, 1964. Tchr., counselor, adminstr., secondary schs., Colo., Mo., Ariz., 1948-57; registrar Phoenix Coll., 1957-60; intern Bakersfield Coll., 1960-63, asst. to pres., 1963-64, asso. dean instrn., 1964-65, dean students, 1965-67; founding pres. Lincoln Land Community Coll., 1967-88, pres. emeritus; edn. cons. MARA of Malaysia, 1983; higher edn. cons. Springfield, Ill., 1988—; interim pres. Parkland Coll., Champaign, 1989-90. Fulbright lectr., cons. to Lithuania, 1993, to Ukraine, 1996-97, to People's Rep. of China, 2000-01; vis. assoc. prof. Fla. Internat. U., 1994-95; cons. Citizens Dem. Corps., Ukraine, 1998, USIA, Lithuania, 1999, Hong Kong U., 2001. Contbr. articles to profl. jours. Bd. dirs. (past) United Way of Springfield, bd. dirs. Urban League of Springfield, Good Will Industries of Springfield, Springfield (Ill.) Symphony, Catholic Youth Orgn., Springfield, Gov.'s Prayer Breakfast, Springfield Mental Health, Griffin H.S. Bd., Diocesan Sem.; mem. adv. bd. Sacred Heart Acad., Springfield Commn. on Internat. Visitors, Sister Cities Assn. Served with USNR, 1944-46. Recipient Midwest region Chief Exec. Officer of Yr. Assn. Community Coll. Trustees, 1988, recognition Ill. Community Coll. Trustees Assn., 1988; named an Outstanding Chief Exec. Officer for Ill. Community Colls. U. Tex. Leadership Program, 1987; named a leader in shaping the century State Jour. Register, 1999; Phi Theta Kappa fellow, 1981. Mem. Am. Assn. Community and Jr. Colls., Ill. Council Public Community Coll. Pres. (sec. 1973-74, vice chmn. 1974-75, chmn. 1975-76), Council North Central Community and Jr. Colls. (exec. bd. 1979-81), North Central Assn. (cons., evaluator 1984-88) Republican. Roman Catholic. Home and Office: 2324 Willemoore Ave Springfield IL 62704-4362 Fax: 217-793-6939. E-mail: robert.poorman@llcc.edu.

POP, ANCA, physician; b. Bucharest, Romania, July 21, 1967; arrived in U.S., 1991; s. Ioan and Lucia Pop. MD, Carol Davilla Medical Univ., Bucharest, 1991. Diplomate Am. Bd. Internal Medicine. Internal medicine resident Sinai Hosp., Detroit, 1993-96; gastroenterology fellow Detroit Medical Ctr., 1996-99; hepatology fellow U. Tenn., Memphis, 1999-2000; staff gastrohepatology James H. Quillen VA Med. Ctr., Johnson City, Tenn. Mem. Am. Gastroent. Assn., Am. Soc. Gastroenterologic Endoscopy, Am. Coll Gastroenterology, Am. Assn. for Study of Liver Disease. Avocations: music, reading, socializing with friends, exercising. Office: James H Quinen VA Med Ctr G Lab (111 D) At Mountain Home Johnson City TN 37684 E-mail: ancapop@aol.com.

POP, EMIL, research chemist; b. Tirgu Mures, Romania, Aug. 12, 1939; came to U.S., 1983; s. Victor and Rosalia (Graf) P.; m. Elena Petrina Petri, Apr. 28, 1964; 1 child, Andreea Christina. BS, Babes- Bolyai U., Cluj., Romania, 1961; PhD, Inst. Chemistry, Cluj., and Supreme Coun. for Sci. Titles, Dept. of Edn. B, 1973. Chemist Chem.-Pharm. Rsch. Inst., Cluj, 1962-65, rsch. sci., group leader, 1965-78, prin. rsch. sci., group and compartment leader, 1978-83; rsch. assoc. Dept. Medicinal Chemistry Coll. Pharmacy, U. Fla., Gainesville, 1983-86; rsch. sci. Pharmatec, Inc., Alachua, Fla., 1986-87, group leader, 1987-89, assoc. dir. chem. devel., 1989-92, dir. chemistry, 1992, Pharmos Corp., Alachua, 1992-95, sr. dir. chemistry, 1995-98; founder, pres., CEO Alchem Labs Corp., Alachua, Fla., 1998—. Courtesy prof. Health Sci. Ctr., Ctr. for Drug Discovery, U. Fla., 1998. Contbr. articles to profl. jours.; inventor in field. Inaugural mem. adv. bd. Fla. Ctr. for Heterocyclic Compounds, U. Fla., 1999—. Recipient N. Teclu award Romanian Acad. Sci., 1980. Fellow Am. Inst. Chemists; mem. AAAS, Am. Chem. Soc., Am. Assn. Pharm. Sci., Internat. Union Pure and Applied Chemistry, N.Y. Acad. Scis., Internat. Soc. Quantum Biology and Pharmacology, Assn. de Pharmacie Galenique Industrielle. Greek Catholic. Achievements include design and synthesis of pharmaceutical compounds in particular prodrugs and brain specific chemical drug delivery systems; M.O. calculations. Home: 810 SW 51st Way Gainesville FL 32607-3856

POPADAK, GERALDINE L. organizational development consultant, educator; b. Warren, Ohio, Sept. 14, 1948; d. John Edward and Leona Margaret (Franko) P. BA, Hiram Coll., 1984; postgrad., The Am. U., 1990; PhD, Union Inst., Cin., 1995. Supr. mfg., gen. supr. mfg., ops. devel. cons. GM Packard Elec. Divsn., Warren, 1966-91; cons. and trainer UAW-GM Human Resource Ctr., Auburn Hills, Mich., 1991-93; cons. GM Vehicle Devel. & Tech. Ops. Group, Warren, 1993-95, GM Powertrain Group, Pontiac, 1995—. Vis. lectr. Oakland U. Grad. Sch. Psychology, Rochester, Mich., 1992-93; adj. faculty Hiram (Ohio) Coll., 1995—, U. Phoenix Mich. Campus, Southfield, 1996—; mem. bd. governance Grad. Sch. Mgmt., U. Phoenix, Southfield, 1997. Vol. mediator The Resolution Ctr., Mt. Clemens, Mich., 1995—; mediator U.S. Postal Svc. Mem. APA, AAUW, Assn. Psychol. Type, Nat. Psychology Adv. Bd., Internat. Soc. Gen. Semantics, ODNetwork, Assn. Mgmt. Orgn. Design (bd. dirs. 1995), Inst. Noetic Scis. Democrat. Roman Catholic. Avocations: reading, walking, gardening, spiritual journeys. Home: 303 Baker St Royal Oak MI 48067-2205 Office: General Motors 777 Joslyn Ave Pontiac MI 48340-2925

POPE, ALEXANDER H. former non-profit administrator and lawyer; b. N.Y.C., June 4, 1929; s. Clifford H. and and Sarah H. (Davis) P.; m. Katherine Mackinlay, Sept. 14, 1985; children by previous marriage: Stephen C., Virginia L., Daniel M. AB with honors, U. Chgo., 1948, JD, 1952. Bar: Ill. 1952, Republic of Korea 1953, Calif. 1955, U.S. Supreme Ct. 1970. Pvt. practice, L.A., 1955-77, 87-96; assoc. David Ziskind, 1955; ptnr. Shadle, Kennedy & Pope, 1956, Fine & Pope, L.A., 1957-59, 61-77; legis. sec. to gov. State of Calif., 1959-61; county assessor Los Angeles County, L.A., 1978-86; ptnr. Mayer, Brown & Platt, 1987-88, Barash & Hill, L.A., 1989-92; of counsel Seyforth, Shaw, Fairweather & Geraldson, 1993-96; exec. dir. Calif. citizens budget commn. Ctr. Govtl. Studies, Los Angeles, 1997-2000. Nat. bd. mem. Vols. for Stevenson, 1952; vice-chmn. L.A. County Dem. Cen. Com., 1958-59; pres. Westchester Mental Health Clinic, 1963; mem. Calif. Hwy. Commn., 1966-70; mem. L.A. Bd. Airport Commrs., 1973-77, v.p., 1973-75, pres., 1975-76; trustee, sec. L.A. Theatre Ctr., 1984-89; trustee Spring St. Found., 1990—. With U.S. Army, 1952-54, Korea. Mem. ACLU, U. Chgo. Alumni Club Greater L.A. (pres. 1970-71), Zero Population Growth, Ams. United, Sierra Club, Common Cause, Order of Coif, Phi Beta Kappa. Democrat. Unitarian Universalist. Home: 1155 Euclid Ave Berkeley CA 94708-1602 E-mail: kandap@juno.com.

POPE, ANDREW, medical organization administrator; Acting dir., sr. program officer health scis. policy program Inst. of Medicine, 1998-99, dir. health scis. policy, 1999—. Office: Inst of Medicine 500 5th St, NW Washington DC 20418-0007*

POPE, ANDREW JACKSON, JR. (JACK POPE), retired judge; b. Abilene, Tex., Apr. 18, 1913; s. Andrew Jackson and Ruth Adelia (Taylor) P.; m. Allene Esther Nichols, June 11, 1938; children: Andrew Jackson III, Walter Allen. BA, Abilene Christian U., 1934, LLD (hon.), 1980; LLB, U. Tex., 1937; LLD (hon.), Pepperdine U., 1981, St. Mary's U., San Antonio, 1982, Okla. Christian U., 1983. Bar: Tex. 1937. Practice law Corpus Christi, Corpus Christi, 1937-46; judge 94th Dist. Ct., 1946-50; justice Ct. Civil Appeals, San Antonio, 1950-65, Supreme Ct. of Tex., Austin, 1965-82, chief justice, 1982-85. Author: John Berry & His Children, 1988; chmn. bd. editors Appellate Procedure in Tex., 1974; author numerous articles in law revs. and profl. jours. Pres. Met. YMCA, San Antonio, 1956-57; chmn. Tex. State Law Libr. Bd., 1973-80; trustee Abilene Christian U., 1954—. Seaman USNR, 1944-46. Recipient Silver Beaver award Alamo council Boy Scouts Am., 1961, Distinguished Eagle award, 1983; Rosewood Gavel award, 1962, St. Thomas More award, St. Mary's U., San Antonio, 1982; Outstanding Alumnus award Abilene Christian U., 1965; Greenhill Jud. award Mcpl. Judges Assn., 1980; Houston Bar Found. citation, 1985; San Antonio Bar Found. award, 1985; Disting. Jurist award Jefferson County Bar, 1985; Outstanding Alumnus award U. Tex. Law Alumni Assn., 1988; George Washington Honor medal Freedom Found., 1988; Disting. Lawyer award Travis County, 1992. Fellow Tex. Bar Found. (Law Rev. award 1979, 80, 81); mem. ABA, State Bar Tex. (pres. jud. sect. 1962, Outstanding Alumnus U. Tex. Sch. of Law 1994, Outstanding Fifty Years Lawyer award 1994), Tex. Bar Found., Order of Coif, Nueces County Bar Assn. (pres. 1946), Travis County Bar Assn., Bexar County Bar Assn., Tex. Philos. Soc., Austin Knife and Fork (pres. 1980), Am. Judicature Soc., Tex. State Hist. Assn., Tex. Supreme Ct. Hist. Soc. (v.p.), Sons of Republic of Tex., Statesmanship award State Bar Tex., 1998, Christian Chronicle Coun. (chmn.), Masons, K.P. (grand chancellor 1946), Alpha Chi, Phi Delta Phi, Pi Sigma Alpha. Mem. Ch. of Christ. Home: 2803 Stratford Dr Austin TX 78746-4626

POPE, BISMARK, III, software development and engineering executive; b. Laredo, Tex., Dec. 14, 1954; s. Bismark Pope Jr. and Peggy (Hardy) Studenroth; m. Sharron M. Bogner, Dec. 10, 1977; children: Meredith, Bismark IV. BS in Geology, Baylor U., 1977; BBA, U. Tex., 1980. Mgr. Western Union Telegraph, Dallas; mgr. tech. No. Telecom/Nortel, Richardson, Tex.; telecomms. cons. GSM Design Engring., 1994—. Cons. Quest Tech., Richardson, 1992-93; telecomm. cons. regarding digital networks, switching and internet design, provisioning and deployment. Leader Boy Scouts Am., 1993—. With U.S. Army, 1975-78. Mem. Masons (lodge #1314). Achievements include patents pending for full motion video via computer through normal telephone lines/internet connection to host computer, in medical field to run remote camera in human body during surgical procedure, on cancer analysis using personal computer. Home: 2806 Enchanted Cir Garland TX 75044-3724

POPE, CORY RICHARD, interior designer; b. Abilene, Tex., Feb. 6, 1974; s. Kenneth Eugene and Janice Marie Baker. B in Interior Design, Dallas Art Inst. Designer, project mgr. Design Solutions, Dallas, 1992—; visual designer William Horton Design, 1992—99; lighting designer Cory Pope Consulting, 1998—; fixture designer Fossil Hdqs., 1999—2000. Designer Neiman Marcus Showcase Home, Dallas, 1999; lighting designer Luminex, Georgetown, Tex., 2001. Prin. works include Rockefeller Ctr., Trump Towers, Prudential Ctr. Home: 10407 Pagewood Dr Dallas TX 75230

POPE, DALE ALLEN, investment company executive; b. Racine, Wis., Apr. 11, 1953; s. Warren Edward and Ruth Ann (Adams) P.; m. Colleen Rene Esson, Aug. 6, 1976; children: Shayna Ranee, Justin Daniel, Evan Hunter. BBA, U. Wis., Eau Claire, 1975; postgrad., U. Wis., Madison, 1976-77. CLU. Estate and ins. planning cons., 1978-81; asst. v.p. Am. Bankers Life, Miami, Fla., 1981-82; pres., COO IFS Capital Corp., North Palm Beach, 1982-87; founder, pres., CEO Am. Capital Corp., Valley Forge, Pa., 1987—2001; dir. bus. devel. Pan-Am. Fin. Advisers, 2001—. Mem. Fin. Planning Assn., Soc.Fin. Svc. Profls., Nat. Assn. Securities Dealers, Inc. (dist. bus. conduct com. 1990-92, bd. arbitrators), Rotary Internat. (dist. gov.'s rep. 1994-95, asst. dist. gov. 1996—, bd. dirs. 1996-97, Paul Harris fellow 1989), Rotary Club of Wayne (past pres., dir.). Avocations: golf, tennis, hunting, fishing. Office: Pan-Am Financial Advisers 1260 Valley Forge Rd #104 Valley Forge PA 19482 E-mail: info@americancapitalcorp.com.

POPE, FRED WALLACE, JR. lawyer; b. Sanford, Fla., Feb. 9, 1941; s. Fred Wallace and Dorothy (Marshall) P.; m. Jane Laird Miller, Dec. 27, 1962 (div. Oct. 1986); children: Catherine W., Gregory W.; m. Christine R. Fredrick, Jan. 4, 1991. BA in Polit. Sci., U. Fla., 1962, JD with honors, 1969; AM in Internat. Rels., Boston U., 1965. Bar: Fla. 1970, U.S. Dist. Ct. (so., mid. and no. dists.) Fla., U.S. Supreme Ct. 1975, U.S. Ct. Appeals (11th cir.) 1983. Rsch. aide 2d Dist. Ct. Appeal, Lakeland, Fla., 1970; assoc. Trenam, Simmons, Kemker, Scharf & Barkin, Tampa, 1970-74; ptnr. Johnson, Blakely, Pope, Bokor, Ruppel & Burns, P.A., Clearwater, 1974—. Dir. Citizens Bank Clearwater, 1986-98, First Nat. Bank of Fla., 1998-01. Trustee The Fla. Orch., Tampa, 1984—, chmn. bd. trustees, 1991-93; bd. dirs. Pinellas County Arts Coun., Clearwater, 1988-93. Capt. U.S. Army, 1962-67. Mem. ABA (coun. mem. sect. litigation 1983-86, editor, chief Litigation 1979-80), The Fla. Bar (gov. 1982-86), Clearwater Bar Assn. (pres. 1980-81). Office: Johnson Blakely Pope Bokor Ruppel & Burns PA 911 Chestnut St Clearwater FL 33756-5643 E-mail: wallyp@jbpfirm.com.

POPE, HARRISON GRAHAM, JR. psychiatrist, educator; b. Lynn, Mass., Dec. 26, 1947; s. H. Graham and Alice (Rider) P.; m. Mary M. Quinn, June 7, 1974; children: Kimberly, Hilary, Courtney. AB summa cum laude, Harvard U., 1969, MPH, 1972, MD, 1974. Diplomate Am. Bd. Psychiatry and Neurology. Resident in psychiatry McLean Hosp., Belmont, Mass., 1974-77, clin. rsch. fellow Mailman Rsch. Ctr., 1977-79, asst. psychiatrist, 1979-84, assoc. psychiatrist, 1984-92, psychiatrist, 1992—, chief biol. psychiatry lab., 1984—; Dupont-Warren rsch. fellow Harvard Med. Sch., Boston, 1976-77. Instr. psychiatry Harvard Med. Sch., Boston, 1977-82, asst. prof., 1982-85, assoc. prof., 1985-99, prof. 1999—; staff psychiatrist Hampstead (N.H.) Hosp., 1976-80; vis. fellow The Maudsley Hosp., London, 1977, Hôp. Ste. Anne, Paris, 1977; mem. Am. Psychiat. Assn., 1976-80, adv. com. on schizophrenic, paranoid and affective disorders, 1979, adv. com. on preparation of DSM-III-R, 1984, task force on nomenclature and stats., 1979, 84. Author: Voices from the Drug Culture, 1971, The Road East, 1974, (with J.I. Hudson) New Hope for Binge Eaters: Advances in the Understanding and Treatment of Bulimia, 1984; co-editor: The Psychobiology of Bulimia, 1987, Use of Anticonvulsants in Psychiatry: Recent Advances, 1988, Psychology Astray: Fallacies in Studies of "Repressed Memory" and Childhood Trauma, 1997; The Adonis Complex: The Secret Crisis of Male Body Obsession, 2000; contbr. numerous papers on biol. psychiatry, with emphasis on diagnosis of psychotic disorders, treatment of mood disorders and eating disorders, marijuana abuse, drug abuse by athletes, and false memory syndrome; mem. editl. bd. European Psychiatry, Paris, 1984—, Internat. Jour. of Eating Disorders, 1984—, Jour. Clin. Psychiatry, 1993—. Named one of Outstanding Americans under 40 Esquire mag., 1984; fellow Scottish Rite Schizophrenia Program, No. Masonic Jurisdiction, 1977-81, Charles A. King Trust, Boston, 1977-79. Avocation: weightlifting. Office: McLean Hosp 115 Mill St Belmont MA 02478-1048

POPE, INGRID BLOOMQUIST, sculptor, poet; b. Arvika, Sweden; became U.S. citizen. d. Oscar Emanuel and Gerda (Henningson) Brostrom; m. Howard Richard Bloomquist, Feb. 14, 1941 (dec. Nov. 1982); children: Dennis Howard, Diane Cecile Connelly, Laurel Ann Shields; m. Marvin Hoyle Pope, Mar. 9, 1985 (dec. June 1997). BA cum laude, Manhattanville Coll., 1979, MA in Humanities, 1981; MA in Religion, Yale U., 1984. Exhbns. include Manhattanville Coll., Purchase, N.Y., Yale Div. Sch., Ch. of Sweden in N.Y.C., Greenwich Arts Coun., Greenwich Arts Soc., First Ch. of Round Hill; author: (books) Musings, 1994, Hosannah, Help Please, 1999. Past bd. dirs. N.Y.C. Mission Soc., Greenwich YWCA, Greenwich Chaplaincy, Greenwich Acad. Parents' Assn., past pres; past trustee First Ch. Round Hill, Greenwich; pres. Ch. Women United, Greenwich, 1989-91. Mem. AAUW, Nat. Assn. Pen Women, English Speaking Union, Nat. Wildflower Assn., Yale Club N.Y.C., Lakeview Club (Austin, Tex.), Acad. Am. Poets, Nat. Mus. of Women in the Arts, Yale Alumnae Club (Austin and Greenwich, Conn.). Home: 538 Round Hill Rd Greenwich CT 06831-2641 *I need to share my feelings deep inside be it in verse or prose or form or line. I need to say it, do it, show, or write and so creatively I try to do my best. I lift up brush and paint a scene, I struggle with a stone or mold in clay or write my verse just as I do today.*

POPE, JOHN EDWIN, III, newspaper sports editor, columnist; b. Athens, Ga., Apr. 11, 1928; s. Henry Louis and Rose (McAfee) P.; m. Eileen Pope. BA in Journalism, U. Ga., 1948. Sports editor Banner-Herald, Athens, Ga., 1943-48; So. sports editor UPI, Atlanta, 1948-50; sports writer Atlanta Constn., 1950-54; exec. sports editor Atlanta Jour., 1954-56; asst. sports editor Miami (Fla.) Herald, 1956-67, sports editor, 1967—2001. Author: Football's Greatest Coaches, 1956, Baseball's Greatest Managers, 1960, Encyclopedia of American Greyhound Racing, 1963, Ted Williams: The Golden Year, 1970, (with Norm Evans) On the Line, 1976, The Edwin Pope Collection, 1988; contbr. articles to popular mags. and Ency. Brittanica, World Book. Recipient Bill Corum Meml. award Thoroughbred Racing Assn., 1962, top sports column award Nat. Headliners Club, 1962, 79, 82, 86, Eclipse award Thoroughbred Racing Assn., 1976, 82, 86, Red Smith award AP Sports Editors, 1989; named to Internat. Churchmen's Sports Hall of Fame, 1976; recipient Knight-Ridder editl. excellence award, 1996, Nat. Sportswriters and Sportscasters Assn. Hall of Fame, 1995, Fla. Sports Hall of Fame, 1996, Bert McGrane award Coll. Football Hall of Fame, 2000, Dick McCann award NFL Pro Football Hall of Fame, 2002; named to Coll. Football Hall of Fame, 2001. Mem. Profl. Football Writers Am. (pres. 1968-69), Football Writers Assn. Am., Golf Writers Am., U.S. Basketball Writers, Nat. Turf Writers, U.S. Tennis Writers. Presbyterian. Office: Miami Herald 1 Herald Plz Miami FL 33132-1693 E-mail: epope@herald.com.

POPE, JOHN M. journalist; b. Hattiesburg, Miss., Nov. 5, 1948; s. Paul M. Jr. and Mary Lee (Scott) P.; m. Diana Pinckley, May 19, 1984. BA cum laude, U. Tex., 1970, MA, 1972. Copy editor The States-Item, New Orleans, 1972-73, reporter, 1973-80, The Times-Picayune, New Orleans, 1980-86, med.-health reporter, 1986—. Co-author: American First Ladies: Their Lives and Their Legacy, 1996. Recipient Frank Allen award, La.-Miss. AP, 1989, Med. Writing award, La. State Med. Soc., 1990, 1998; fellow Knight Ctr. for Specialized Journalism fellow, 1999, Ctrs. for Disease Control, 2001, Phi Beta Kappa Soc. fellow. Mem. Soc. Profl. Journalists, Nat. Assn. Sci. Writers,

Investigative Reporters and Editors, Press Club New Orleans (4 1st pl. awards 1978-87, Alex Waller award 1987), Phi Beta Kappa. Avocations: running, travel, aerobics. Office: The Times-Picayune 3800 Howard Ave New Orleans LA 70125-1429 E-mail: jpope@timespicayune.com.

POPE, KERIG RODGERS, magazine executive; b. Waukesha, Wis., Sept. 30, 1935; s. Kerig James Pope and Mildred (Offerman) Troemel; m. Claudia T. Koralewski, Nov. 1961 (div. 1975); children— Kerig William, Giles Thomas; m. Beth Leslie Kasik, May 24, 1980; children: Kolin Jared, Zoe Alissa. Grad., Art Inst. Chgo., 1958. Designer Jack Denst Wallpaper Designs, Chgo., 1958-60; designer Continental Casualty Ins. Co., 1960-62, Leo Burnett Advt. Agy., Chgo., 1962-63; art dir. Mercury Records Corp., 1963-66; mng. art dir. Playboy mag., 1966—. Exhibited in group shows Whitney Mus. Am. Art, N.Y.C., 1969, Mus. Contemporary Art, Chgo., 1972, Bienal de Sao Paulo, Brazil, 1973, Museo de Arte Moderno, Mexico City, 1974, Nat. Collection Fine Arts, Washington, 1979, Moderno, Mexico City, 1974, Mus. Contemporary Art, Chgo., 1996; represented in permanent collections Nat. Collection Fine Arts, Washington, Mus. Contemporary Art, Chgo., Smart Mus., U. Chgo. Recipient silver medal Communigraphics, N.Y.C., 1971, gold medal, 1971, 72; award of excellence Soc. Publ. Designers, 1979, 4 awards of excellence Design Ann., 1984, Silver medal Illustrators 29, 1986, Silver medal Soc. of Illustrators, 1988. Mem.: Soc. Publ. Arts (3 Silver awards 1987), Soc. Typog. Arts (Silver medal 1998, Gold medal 1999, 2001), Art Dirs. Club N.Y., Soc. Illustrators (Gold medal 1981, 1984, Silver medal 1988, Gold medal 1991, Silver medal 1998, Gold medal 1999), Arts (Chgo.), Arts Club (Chgo.). Office: Playboy Enterprises Inc 680 N Lake Shore Dr Fl 15 Chicago IL 60611-4455 E-mail: kengp@playboy.com.

POPE, LEAVITT JOSEPH, broadcast company executive; b. Boston, Apr. 2, 1924; s. Joseph and Charlotte (Leavitt) P.; m. Martha Pascale, Nov. 20, 1948; children— Joseph, Daniel, Patricia, Elizabeth, Nancy, Maria, Joan, Christopher, Virginia, Matthew, Charles. BS, Mass. Inst. Tech., 1947. Adminstrv. asst. N.Y. Daily News, N.Y.C., 1947-51; asst. to gen. mgr. Sta. WPIX-TV, 1951-56, v.p. ops., 1956-72, Sta. WPIX-FM, N.Y.C., 1956-72; sec. WPIX, Inc., 1958-75, exec. v.p., 1972-75, pres., chief exec. officer, 1975-92, also dir. Sec., exec. v.p. Conn. Broadcasting Co., Bridgeport, 1967-75, pres., chief exec. officer, dir., 1975-87; dir. N.Y. Daily News, 1975-78, Tribune Co., 1978-81; founder Ind. Network News, 1978-89; chair N.Y.C. TV all industry com., advanced TV sys. com. HDTV; chair copyright com. NAB, 1985—. Mem. N.Y. State Regents Ednl. TV Adv. Council, 1958; bd. govs. Daytop Village, 1972— ; trustee Catholic Communications Found., St. Thomas Aquinas Coll., 1968-75, Cardinal Cooke Hosp., 1979—, vice chair, 1998—; dir. Archdiocese N.Y. Instructional TV com. 1976—; trustee St. Patrick's Cathedral, N.Y.C., 1992—. Served with Signal Corps U.S. Army, 1942-46. Mem. Assn. Ind. TV Stats. (pres. 1976-78, bd. dirs.), ASME, Internat. Radio and TV Soc., Nat. Assn. Broadcasters (dir. 1982-86), N.Y. State Broadcasters (pres. 1976-78), Sigma Nu, Knight of Malta. Clubs: Univ. (N.Y.C.); Riverbend (Tequesta, Fla.). Home: 173 Dorchester Rd Scarsdale NY 10583-6052

POPE, LISTON, JR. writer, journalist; b. New Haven, Dec. 26, 1943; s. Liston and Bennie (Purvis) P. BA in English, Duke U., 1965; postgrad., Sorbonne, Paris, 1965-70, U. Vienna, 1966-67. Probation officer Bronx (N.Y.) Supreme Ct., 1972-73; freelance journalist N.Y.C., 1972—; war correspondent World Coun. of Chs., Beirut, 1978-79, Nat. Cath. News Svc., Managua, Nicaragua, 1983-84; radio prodr. Pacifica Radio, N.Y.C., 1983-90; critic art/lit. Pacifica News, 1984-89; sr. editor N.A. Gilbert & Sons Publs., 1993—; pub. Mantis Press, 1995—. Press agent Liston Pope & Assocs., N.Y.C., 1983-90; media dir. Casa Nicaragua, N.Y.C., 1983-90. Author: Redemption: A Novel of War in Lebanon, 1994, Living Like the Saints: A Novel of Nicaragua, 1996, Floriane: Stages of Love, 1998, (plays) Somoza's Niece, 1987, Oratorio, 1987, Canto Epico, 1989. Vis., supporting vol. Meml. Sloan-Kettering, 1972-78; recreation dir., tutor Cath. Guardian Group Home, 1975-90; life skills tchr. Harlem I Men's Shelter, N.Y.C., 1991-93; AIDS support worker St. Vincent's Supportive Care, Bellevue Visitation Program, Bellevue Pediatrics. Recipient Narrative Poetry award N.Y. Poetry Soc., 1972, Grand prize Am. Poetry Assn., 1986, Poetry award Nat. Libr. of Poetry, 1993. Home and Office: 126 W 73rd St Apt 11A New York NY 10023-3031

POPE, MARK L. counseling psychologist, educator; b. St. Louis, Apr. 23, 1952; s. Isom Lavern Pope and Ethyle R. (Ray) Enderle. AB, U. Mo., 1973, MEd, 1974; student, Northwestern U., 1977-78; EdD, U. San Francisco, 1988. Nat. cert. counselor; nat. cert. career counselor; lic. psychol., Ill., master addictions counselor, approved clin. supr.; lic. profl. counselor, Mo. Drug abuse counselor Brotherhood Clinic Ill. Drug Abuse Program, Chgo., 1974-75; mental health worker, career counselor adolescent unit Northwestern Inst. Psychiatry, 1975-76; career counselor, psychol. test cons. Meth. Youth Svcs., 1976-77; rsch. interviewer, drug abuse counselor Cook County Treatment Alternatives to Street Crimes, 1977-78; cons., pres. Data Psych Systems, N.Y.C. and San Francisco, 1978-90; computer ops. mgr. Pacific Am. Group, San Francisco, 1981-83; supr. info. systems Bechtel Engring. & Constrn. Cos., 1983-87; software devel. editor Cons. Psychologists Press, Palo Alto, Calif., 1987-89; pres. Career Decisions, San Francisco, 1989—; pres., pub. Cognito Press, 1995-97. Dir., founder Horizons Gay and Lesbian Profl. and Peer Counseling Svcs., Chgo., 1975-77; lectr. Cen. YMCA Community Coll. Dept. Psychology, Chgo., 1977-78, Northwestern U. Indsl. Engring. and Orgn. Devel. Dept., 1977-78, John F. Kennedy U. Career Devel. and Planning, Orinda, Calif., 1987-90; adj. prof. Golden Gate U. Grad. Sch. Mgmt. Human Resource Mgmt., San Francisco, 1984-96, psychology dept., 1994-96, U. San Francisco Info. Systems Mgmt., 1986-94, counseling and edn. psychology, 1988-96; counseling San Francisco State U., 1990-96; clin. supr. counseling and health psychology Stanford U., 1990-96; assoc. prof. counseling and family therapy U. Mo., St. Louis, 1997—; career devel. cons. Pacific Bell, San Francisco, 1988-93; human resources cons. Alpha Computer Svcs., San Rafael, Calif., 1988-91; founder West Coast Counselors With Computers Conf., 1989; program chair Calif. Career Conf., 1989, 95; psychologist Am. Indian AIDS Inst., 1990-94, Native Am. AIDS Project, 1994-96; dir. tng. St. Louis Challenge Metro Crisis Line, 1998—. Author: Experiential Activities for Teaching Career Counseling Classes, 2000; contbr. articles to profl. jours. and chpts. to books. Mem. collaborative planning com. U. San Francisco Sch. Edn., 1987-88, Mo. Gen. Assembly drug abuse adv. com., 1972; bd. dirs. Ill. Civil Liberties Union, Chgo., 1976-78; appointee Mo. Gov.'s Reorganization Commn., 1973. Mem. ACA (mem. couseling software rev. bd. 1987-89, chmn. task force on exhibits 1990-92, mem. com. on gay, lesbian bisexual issues, 1991-92, human rights com. 1995-98, chair 1997-98, gov. coun. parliamentarian 2000—, Kitty Cole Human Rights Award, 2001), AAAS, APA (mem. divs. 5, 8, 17, 21, 44, 45), APA (divsn. 17, mem. vocational psychology sec., treas., 1996-2000, Gay and Lesbian bisesexual issues sec., chair hospitality suite com. 1997-98, chair special task group on disting. srs. awards 1999-2000, mem. program com. 1999—), Soc. Indian Psychologists, Assn. for Counselor Edn. and Supervision (co-chair internat. network 1988-90, chair subcom. on internat. counselor edn. database 1986-88, mem. counseling and tech. network 1985—, counseling in bus. and industry network 1985—), Assn. for Assessment in Counseling (chmn. interorgnl. affairs com. 1989-90), Bay Area Career Devel. Assn. (co-chair 1987-91), Nat. Mus. Am. Indian (charter), Calif. Assn. for Counseling and Devel. (life mem., chair subcom. human rights com. 1986-88, exec. com. 1989-91, chair gay, lesbian, bisexual caucus 1991, conv. program com. 1989-90, chmn. convention program com. 1991-92, mem. exec. com. 1989-91, State Human Rights award, 1996), Calif. Assn. Measurement and Evaluation in Counseling and Devel. (sec., treas. 1988-89, pres. elect 1989-90, pres. 1990-91, past pres. 1991-92), Calif. Assn. Multi-Cultural Counseling, Calif. Career Devel. Assn. (profl. devel. chair 1988-91, no. Calif. regional coord. 1991-93, chair task force to devel. registered career counselor exam. 1991-92, pres.-elect 1993-94, pres. 1994-95, past pres. 1995-96), Am. Counseling Assn. of Mo. (State Human Rights award 2000), N.Y. Acad. Scis., Computers in Psychology, Nat. Career Devel. Assn. (nat. sec. 1992-94, chair pub. rels. com. 1991-92, nat. treas. 1994-97, pres.- elect 1997-98, pres. 1998-99, past pres. 1999-2000, internat. conf. program chair 1997-98, elections com. chair, 1999-2000, eminent career award com. chair 1999-2000, site com. 1994-95, nat. conf. 1994-95, bd. dirs. exec. com. 1994-2000). Home: 4579 Laclede Ave PMB 436 Saint Louis MO 63108-2103 Office: U Mo Divsn of Counseling 8001 Natural Bridge Rd Saint Louis MO 63121-4499 E-mail: pope@umsl.edu.

POPE, MICHAEL THOR, chemistry educator; b. Exeter, Devon, Eng., Apr. 14, 1933; came to U.S. 1962; naturalized, 1992; s. Hector Maurice and Edith Mary (Hewett) P.; m. Ann Mavis Potter, July 12, 1957; children: Gregory (dec.), Lucy. BA, Oxford U., 1954, DPhil, 1957; postdoctoral, Boston U., 1957-59. Rsch. chemist Laporte Chems., Luton, Eng., 1959-62; asst. prof. Georgetown U., Washington, 1962-67, assoc. prof., 1967-73, prof., 1973—, dept. chair, 1990-96. Vis. prof. Tech. U., Vienna, Austria, 1970-71, Free U. of Berlin, 1979, Northeast Normal U., Changchun, China, 1985, U. Umeå, U. Bielefeld, Germany, 1989; prof. associé U. Pierre et Marie Curie, Paris, 1979, U. de Versailles, 1997. Author: Heteropoly and Isopoly Oxometalates, 1983, Polyoxometalates: From Platonic Solids to Anti-Retroviral Activity, 1994, Polyoxometalate Chemistry: From Topology vis Self-Assembly to Applications, 2001; contbr. articles to profl. publs. Recipient Sr. U.S. Scientist award Alexander von Humboldt Found., 1989-90, Hillebrand prize Chem. Soc. Washington, 1999; Petroleum Rsch. Fund Internat. award fellow, 1970-71; Rsch. grantee Dept. Energy, NSF, NIH, Petroleum Rsch. Fund, Office Naval Rsch., Army Rsch. Office, Air Force Office of Sci. Rsch. Mem. Royal Soc. Chemistry (London), Am. Chem. Soc., Sigma Xi (chpt. pres. 1969-70). Episcopalian. Avocations: music, art. Office: Georgetown Univ Chemistry Dept Washington DC 20057-1227

POPE, ROBERT DANIEL, lawyer; b. Screven, Ga., Nov. 29, 1948; s. Robert Verlyn and Mae (McKey) P.; children: Robert Daniel Jr., Veronica Teres, Jonathan Chase, Byron Christopher, Jessica Victoria. BS in Criminal Justice magna cum laude, Valdosta (Ga.) State Coll., 1975; JD, John Marshall Law Sch., Savannah, Ga., 1980. Bar: Ga. 1981, U.S. Dist. Ct. (no., mid. and so. dist.) Ga. 1983, U.S. Ct. Appeals Ga. 1982. Pvt. practice, Cartersville, 1981—. Mem. Valdosta Indigent Def. Atty. Panel, 1981-83, Bartow County Indigent Def. Panel, Cartersville, 1987-91, So. Dist. of Ga. Indigent Def. Panel, Brunswick, 1982-84; mem. Cobb County Cir. Defender's Panel for Indigent Criminal Def., Marietta, Ga., 1986— Recognized as one of most successful criminal def. lawyers Cobb County Cir. Defenders Office, 1994. Mem. Ga. Assn. Criminal Def. Lawyers, Ga. Bar Assn. (criminal law sect.), Am. Criminal Justice Orgn. (Valdosta chpt. pres. 1974-75). Home: 74 Spruce Ln SE Cartersville GA 30121-7643 Office: PO Box 1043 Acworth GA 30101

POPE, ROBERT DEAN, lawyer; b. Memphis, Mar. 10, 1945; s. Ben Duncan and Phyllis (Drenner) P.; m. Elizabeth Dante Cohen, June 26, 1971; 1 child, Justin Nicholas Nathanson. AB, Princeton U., 1967; Diploma in Hist. Studies, Cambridge U., 1971; JD, Yale U., 1972, PhD, 1976. Bar: Va. 1974, D.C. 1980. Assoc. Hunton & Williams, Richmond, Va., 1974-80, ptnr., 1980—. Mem. steering com. Bond Attys. Workshop, 1994—98; lectr. in law U. Va. Law Sch., 2000—; advisor, com. on govtl. debt and fiscal policy Govt. Fin. Officers Assn., 1993—99. Author: Disclosure Rules of Counsel in State and Local Government Securities Offerings, 2d edit., 1994, Making Good Disclosure: The Role and Responsibilities of State and Local Officials Under the Federal Security Laws , 2001. Mem. adv. com. Va. Sec. of Health and Human Svcs. on Continuing Care Legislation, 1992-94; mem. Anthony Commn. on Pub. Fin.; adv. coun. dept. history Princeton U., 1987-91; mem. Mcpl. Securities Rulemaking Bd., 1996-99, vice chmn. 1998-99. Mem.: NCCJ (bd. dirs. Richmond), Yale Law Sch. Assn. (exec. com. 1985—88), Va. Bar Assn. (chmn. legal problems of elderly 1982—88), Am. Coll. Bond Counsel, Am. Acad. Hosp. Attys., Nat. Assn. Bond Lawyers (treas. 1984—85, sec. 1985—86, pres. 1987—88, bd. dirs. 1982—89, Bernard P. Friel medal for contbns. to pub.fin. 1994), Bond Club Va. (bd. dirs. 1990—98, v.p. 1993—94, pres. 1994—95), Phi Beta Kappa. Republican. Episcopalian. Avocations: history, golf, music, book reviews. Home: 8707 Ruggles Rd Richmond VA 23229-7918 Office: Hunton & Williams 951 E Byrd Richmond VA 23219-4074 E-mail: dpope@hunton.com.

POPE, ROBERT E(UGENE), fraternal organization administrator; b. Wellington, Kans., Sept. 10, 1931; s. Samuel E. and Opal Irene (Davis) P. BSChemE with honors, U. Kans., 1952, MS, 1958. Registered profl. engr., Kans. Asst. instr. U. Kans., Lawrence, 1952-56; lab. technician Monsanto Co., St. Louis, 1952; project engr. Mallinckrodt, Inc., 1953-59; traveling sec. Theta Tau, 1959-62, exec. sec., 1963-84, exec. dir., 1984-96, exec. dir. emeritus, 1996—. Carillonneur, Grace United Meth. Ch., St. Louis, 1985—, chmn. adminstrv. coun., 1991-95, trustee, 1997-99, comms. chmn. 2000—; trustee Theta Tau Ednl. Found., 1997—. Mem. Am. Soc. Assn. Execs. (life), Am. Soc. Engring. Edn., Profl. Fraternity Execs. Assn. (charter), Profl. Fraternity Assn. (exec. sec. 1977-86, Disting. Svc. award 1995), Creve Coeur Country Club, Theta Tau (Alumni Hall of Fame 1988, mem. bd. editors The Gear of Theta Tau 1993—, editor-in-chief 1996—), Tau Beta Pi, Phi Lambda Upsilon, Omicron Delta Kappa. Democrat. United Methodist. Avocations: physical fitness, sports, photography, stamp collecting, writing. Home: 13 Sona Ln Saint Louis MO 63141-7742 Office: Theta Tau 655 Craig Rd Ste 128 Saint Louis MO 63141-7168

POPE, SARAH ANN, retired elementary education educator; b. Granite City, Ill., Dec. 4, 1938; d. Vance Guy and Lily Lovinia (Fischer) Morgan; m. Thomas E. Pope; children: Robert, Susan, James, John, William. BS in Edn., So. Ill. U., Edwardsville, 1970, MS in Edn., 1976. Tchr. lang. arts, humanities, sci., English, reading, math. Madison (Ill.) Cmty. Sch. Dist., 1970-99; dist. math. chair K-5, head tchr. Harris Elem. Sch., Madison, 1998-99; ret., 1999. Co-founder libr. Harris Elem. Sch., 1990. Fellow Old Six Mile Hist. Soc.; mem. Am. Hemerocallis Soc. Avocations: reading, growing flowers, visiting historical sites, swimming.

POPE, STEPHANIE MARIE, classicist, educator; b. Abilene, Tex., Apr. 19, 1953; d. Walter Steele and Ida Nora (Vickery) P. BA, Randolph-Macon Woman's Coll., 1975; MA, U. Cin., 1976. Latin tchr. Norfolk (Va.) Acad., 1977—. Sec. North Am. Cambridge Classics Project, Virginia Beach, Va., 1987—98, dir., 1996—2002; cons. Cambridge Latin Course, Cambridge U. Press, N.Y.C., 1989—, About Learning, Inc., 1990—92. Co-author: (text book) North America Unit 1 Cambridge Latin Course 4th edit., 2000; author: (work sheets to accompany Cambridge Latin Course) Culture, 1994, Units 1 and 2 Machine Scored Stage Tests, Unit 3 Machine Scored Stage Tests; head revision team (North Am. Latin Course 4th edit.), 1998—2003. Sec., v.p., pres. P.E.O., Norfolk, 1977—. Mem. Am. Classical League, Classical Assn. Mid., West and South, Classical Assn. Va. (v.p. 1993-94). Avocations: reading, book collecting, walking, cats. Office: Norfolk Acad 1585 Wesleyan Dr Norfolk VA 23502-5591 E-mail: smpope@infi.net.

POPE, THEODORE CAMPBELL, JR. utilities executive, consultant; b. Sanford, Fla., Oct. 28, 1932; s. Theodore Campbell and Mary (Cook) P.; m. Edith L. Carlton; children: Theodore, Jeffrey, Laura; m. Jeris Julia Dawson, Nov. 21, 1973. BSME, U. Fla., 1954, MBA, 1959. Registered profl. engr., Fla.; diplomate Am. Acad. Environ. Engrs. Chief mech. engr. Orlando Utilities, 1959-64, plant supt., 1964-67, dir. elec. generation, 1967-70, asst. mgr. elec. ops., 1970-72, mgr water ops., 1972-84, asst. gen. mgr., 1984-86, gen. mgr., 1986-92; pres. Ted Pope Enterprises, Orlando, 1992—. Contbr. articles to profl. jours.; patentee water treatment process. Bd. dirs. United Fund Brevard County; bd. dirs. Econ. Devel. Commn. of Mid-Fla., Orlando; bd. dirs., pres. Ctrl. Fla. Fair; trustee United Arts of Ctrl. Fla. 1st lt. U.S. Army, 1955-57. Recipient Abel Waldman award InterAm. Assn. San. Engrs., 1982. Mem. Am. Water Works Assn. (hon.; Disting. Pub. Svc. award 1991, George Warren Fuller award, chair emeritus Rsch. Found.), Greater Orlando Area C. of C. (pres. 1990-91), Fla. Engring. Soc. (Engr. of Yr.), Fla. Conservation Assn., Rotary Club of Orlando, Smyrna Yacht Club, Country Club of Orlando, Univ. Club, Delta Sigma Pi. Democrat. Avocations: sailing, golfing, travel, hunting, fishing. Home and Office: 39605 Swift Rd Eustis FL 32736-9510 E-mail: tcpopejr@aol.com.

POPE, WILLIAM L. lawyer, judge; b. Brownsville, Tex., Nov. 5, 1960; s. William E. and Maria Antonieta P.; m. Sandra Solis, May 16, 1992; children: Ana Lauren, William E.H. AA, Tex. Southmost Coll., 1980; postgrad., U. Tex., 1980-81, Tex. Christian U., 1982, Tex. Coll. Osteo. Medicine, 1982-83; JD, Baylor U., 1986; MD (hon.), Cosmopolitan U. & Rsch. Inst., Vina del Mar, Chile, 1998. Bar: Tex. 1986, U.S. Dist. Ct. (so. dist.) Tex. 1988, U.S. Supreme Ct. 1990. Assoc. Adams & Graham, Harlingen, Tex., 1986-91, ptnr., 1991—; mcpl. ct. judge City of La Feria, 1987—. Bd. trustees Episcopal Day Sch., Brownsville, Tex., 1999-2000. Mem.: Am. Coll. Legal Medicine, Tex. State Bar Assn. Mem. Ch. of Christ. Office: Adams & Graham L L P PO Box 1429 Harlingen TX 78551-1429 E-mail: Pope@adamsgraham.com.

POPEJOY, MICHAEL WILLIAM, business educator, consultant; b. Orlando, Fla., Apr. 2, 1954; s. William Howard and Jean Ann (Greer) P.; m. Jean Marie Enser, May 25, 1996; children: Tracy, Robert, Kathleen, Patricia, Kevin, Keith, Daniel, Christina. MBA, Barry U., Miami, Fla., 1987; PhD, Fla. Atlantic U., Boca Raton, 1994. Cert. nursing home adminstr. Contbg. editor Fla. Banker, Orlando, 1979-82; prin. ptnr. Quality Healthcare Assocs., Lake Worth, Fla., 1984-92; dist. curriculum coord. Palm Beach C.C., 1992-94; assoc. prof. bus. and pub. adminstrn. Rinker Sch. Bus., Palm Beach Atlantic Coll., West Palm Beach, 1994—. Cons. rschr. Bus. Devel. Bd. Palm Beach County, West Palm Beach, 1996. Editor: Public Budgeting, 3d edit., 1991; contbr. chpt. to book, work to jours. Lt. col. CAP/USAF Aux., 1975-87. Recipient Gill Robb Wilson award CAP/USAF Aux., 1982, Meritorious Svc. medal, 1982, others. Mem. Am. Soc. for Pub. Adminstrn., Am. Coll. Health Care Adminstrs., N.Y. Acad. Scis., Nat. Assn. Acad. Affairs Adminstrs., Phi Delta Kappa, Pi Alpha Alpha. Republican. Baptist. Avocations: ham radio, flying. Office: Palm Beach Atlantic Coll Rinker Sch Bus PO Box 24708 West Palm Beach FL 33416-4708 Home: 249 Beverly Rd West Palm Beach FL 33405-4729

POPEK, GERALD JOHN, computer software company executive, educator; b. Passaic, N.J., Sept. 22, 1946; s. Joseph John Popek; m. Paulene Bunker; children: Sarah, Darren. BS, NYU, 1968; SM, Harvard U., 1970, PhD, 1972. V.p. Palyn Assocs., San Jose, Calif., 1978-83; dir. Ctr. for Exptl. Computer Sci., UCLA, 1981-84; prof. computer sci. UCLA, from 1973; chief exec. officer Locus Computing Corp., Santa Monica, Calif., 1982-87, chmn., 1982-95; chief tech. officer Platinum Tech. Inc., 1995-99, CarsDirect.com, 1999-2000, NetZero, 2000—. Bd. dirs. Palyn Assocs., San Jose. Author, editor: The Locus Distributed System Architecture, 1985. Served to capt. USAF, 1972-78. Republican. Roman Catholic. Home: 1716 Roscomare Rd Los Angeles CA 90077-2213 Office: NetZero Inc PO Box 3009 Westlake Village CA 91359-0009

POPELYUKHIN, ALEKSEY, mathematician, educator, actuary, researcher; b. Kalarash, Russia, May 16, 1964; came to U.S. 1991; s. Semen and Aleksandra (Stopchik) P.; m. Valentina Kotova, Dec. 3, 1991; children: Masha, Alexander. MS in Math., Moscow U., 1985, PhD in Math., 1989; Gold Medal (honor degree), Math. Sch. #2, Kiev, Ukraine, 1980; Red Diploma (honor degree), Moscow U., 1985. Tchr. and methodologist Moscow All-Union Math Sch., 1982-88; supporting profl. Moscow Med.-Biol. Inst., 1984-85; jr. scientist Moscow Lab. of Math. Statistics, 1986-87; jr. rsch. scientist div. math. Moscow State U., 1988-89; asst. prof. math. Kishinev Poly. U., 1989-90, adj. prof., 1990-91; asst. actuary Home Ins. Co., N.Y.C., N.Y., 1991-93, sr. actuarial asst. N.Y., 1993-94; actuarial analyst, 1994-96; project leader Price Waterhouse LLP, Hartford, Conn., 1995-96, product mgr., 1996-97; mgr. IS Comml. Risk Reins., Stamford, 1997-98, v.p. info. sys., 1998—; sr. v.p. tech. Sam Sebe LLC, 1997—. Math. olympiad supr. Russian Acad. Sci., Moscow, 1981-86; rschr. Courant Inst. Math. Sci., NYU, 1991-92; cons. Video Internat., Inc., N.Y., 1992-98, creative dir., Moscow, 1988-91; official developer, plug-in ptnr. Autodesk, Inc., Sausalito, 1994-99, pres. 2 Wings Internat. LLC, Stamford, 1998—; advisor to bd. MarketPerform.com, N.Y., 2000—; spkr. and presenter in field. Contbr. articles to profl. jours.; screenplay author TV shows on Russian State TV, 1988—; author profl. paper (named Best 1997 Paper by Casualty Actuarial Soc.); designer, developer: (actuarial software) Affinity, 1995-97, Triangle Maker, 1994-96, Triangle Maker Pro, 1997—. Fellow Moscow Math. Soc., Am. Math. Soc.; mem. ACM. Avocations: computer graphics, mathematics. Home: 379 Mill Rd Stamford CT 06903-1624 E-mail: aleksey@intelligencia.com.

POPENOE, HUGH LLYWELYN, soils educator; b. Tela, Honduras, Aug. 28, 1929; s. Frederick Wilson and Dorothy (Hughes) P. BS, U. Calif., Davis, 1951; PhD, U. Fla., 1960. Mem. faculty U. Fla., Gainesville, 1960—, dir. ctr. tropical agr., 1965—2002, dir. internat. programs, 1966—92, dir. Fla. Sea Grant Coll., 1971—81. Bd. dirs. Escuela Agricola Panamericana, Zamorano, Honduras, Orgn. Tropical Studies. Contbr. numerous articles to profl. jours. Chari Assn. U.S. Univ. Dirs. Internat. Agrl. Programs, 1969-70, Joint Rsch. Com. Bd. Internat. Food and Agrl. Devel., 1977-82, Joint Com. Agrl. Rsch. and Devel., 1982-86; chair numerous reports Bd. Sci. and Tech. in Devel., 1979-84; trustee Internat. Found. for Sci., Stockholm, 1984-87; mem. sci. liaison officer Internat. Inst. for Tropical Agr., Nigeria, 1983-88; mem. adv. com. internat. programs NSF, 1985-87; bd. dirs. League for Internat. Food Edn., 1976-87. With U.S. Army, 1952-54. Recipient Sci. Pioneer prize Egyptian Vet. Assn. for Buffalo Devel., 1985. Fellow AAAS, Am. Soc. Agronomy, Am. Geog. Soc., Internat. Soil Sci. Soc., Am. Water Buffalo Assn. (pres. 1988—), Cosmos Club. Office: U Fla PO Box 110286 Gainesville FL 32611-0286 E-mail: hlp@ufl.edu.

POPENOE, JOHN, horticultural consultant, retired botanical garden administrator; b. L.A., Jan. 24, 1929; s. Paul and Betty (Stankowitch) P.; m. Geraldine V. Mann, June 29, 1952; children: Deborah Irene, Natalie, Juanita, Jennifer. BS, UCLA, 1950; MS, U. Md., 1952, PhD, 1955. Asst. horticulturist U.S. Dept. Agr., Miami, 1955-58; asso. prof. horticulture Ala. Poly. Inst., 1958-59; assoc. horticulturist U. Fla. Subtropical Experiment Sta., 1960-63; dir. Fairchild Tropical Garden, Miami, 1963-91; horticultural cons., 1991—. Served with U.S. Army, 1952-54. Home: 113 Washington St Hancock MD 21750-1127

POPESCU, DANIEL, interior designer; b. Bucharest, Romania, July 22, 1943; arrived in U.S., 98; s. Eugen and Lucia Popescu; m. Luminita Serbanescu, May 7, 1975 (div. Aug. 1995); 1 child Dinu ; m. Nina Bouzanis, July 22, 2000; 1 child Jason Bouzanis. Diploma, Archtl. Coll., Bucharest, 1972. Rsch. and design team leader R.D.I.A.D., Bucharest, 1970—82; pres. Jetset Design Interior Inc., Toronto, Canada, 1984—; chief designer, cons. Madison Design Group, Troy, Mich., 1998—; sr. design cons. Richard M. Tumis Inc., Chevy Chase, Md., 1998—. Cons., chief designer Poggempohl, Toronto, 1996—98; cons. Artcraft Kitchen, Niagara Falls, Ont., 1994—, Mazar Keer Arch., Detroit, 1998—. Cpl. Romanian armed forces, 1966—68. Orthodox. Avocations: art, classical music, travel, skiing, dancing. Home: 1501 Crystal Dr Apt 1029 Arlington VA 22202 Office: Richard M Tunis Inc 7032 Wisconsin Ave Bethesda MD 20815 Home Fax: 301-951-0878. E-mail: ninapopescu@aol.com.

POPESCU, GABRIEL, medical researcher; b. Bucharest, Oct. 24, 1971; arrived in U.S., 1997; Lic. in physics, Bucharest U., 1995, MS Physics, 1996; MS Optics, Sch. Optics/CREOL, Fla., 1999. Rsch. asst. Bucharest U., 1995—96; jr. scientist Nat. Inst. Lasers, Plasma and Radiation Physics, Bucharest, 1996—97; rsch. asst. Sch. Optics/CREOL, Orlando, 1997—. Instr. for hs Sch. Optics, Orlando, 1999—. Contbr. articles to profl. jours.; patentee in field. Pres. CAOS-CREOL Assn. Optics Students, 1999—2000. Mem.: Romanian Soc. Lasers in Med. and Biology, Am. Phys. Soc., Optical Soc. Am. Achievements include developed new fiber optics based instruments for investigation with application in biomedicine and industry; invented a new optical instrument to investigate rheological properties of biological matter. Home: 12154 E D Solon dr Orlando FL 32826

POPKIN, ALICE BRANDEIS, lawyer; b. N.Y.C. d. Jacob H. and Susan Brandeis Gilbert; m. Jordan J. Popkin; children: Susan Cahn, Anne, Louisa. AB magna cum laude, Radcliffe Coll., 1949; JD, Yale U., 1953. Bar: N.Y. 1953, U.S. Dist. Ct. (so. dist.) N.Y. 1956, U.S. Ct. Appeals (2nd cir.) 1959, U.S. Supreme Ct. 1962, D.C. 1972, Mass. 1987. Assoc. Cahill Gordon & Reindel, 1953-61; dir. internat. programs Peace Corps, 1961-63; project co-dir. Georgetown Inst. Criminal Law and Procedure, 1967-72; spl. counsel Senate Sub-Com. to Investigate Juvenile Delinquency, 1972-74; atty., prof. Antioch Sch. Law, 1974-77; assoc. adminstr. EPA, 1977-79; pvt. practice cons. on internat. environ. issues, 1979-81; practicing atty., 1981-87; of counsel Toabe and Riley, Chatham, Mass., 1987—. Fellow Brandeis U.; bd. trustees Radcliffe Coll.; mem. Chatham Harbor Mgmt. Com.; trustee Eldredge Pub. Libr., 1994—. Mem. ABA, Mass. Bar Assn., Barnstable County Bar Assn., Estate Planning Coun. Cape Cod, Planned Giving Coun. Cape Cod. Office: Toabe & Riley Box 707 154 Crowell Rd Chatham MA 02633-2800

POPKIN, JOEL, economic consulting company executive; b. Trenton, N.J., July 6, 1932; s. Nathaniel Robert and Betty (Finkle) P.; BS in Econs., U. Pa., 1954, PhD, 1965; m. Elizabeth Rose Alk, Oct. 17, 1968; children: Neil Robert, Sara Rachel. Asst. economist Allied Chem. Co., N.Y.C., 1957-59; lectr., researcher U. Pa., Phila., Northwestern U., Evanston, Ill., George Washington,

U., Washington, 1960-64; econometrician Dept. Commerce, Washington, 1964-66; div. chief, asst. commr. U.S. Bur. Labor Stats., Washington, 1966-73; sr. staff economist President's Council of Econ. Advs., Washington, 1973-74; dir., mem. rsch. staff Nat. Bur. Econ. Rsch., Washington, 1974-78; pres. Joel Popkin And Co., Washington, 1978—. mem. visitors econs. dept. U. Pa., 1987-2001. Served as lt. USAR, 1955-57. Recipient Julius Shiskin award for contbns. to econ. stats., 1994. Fellow Am. Statis. Assn.; mem. Am. Econ. Assn., Conf. Bus. Economists (chmn. 1989), Nat. Assn. Bus. Economists, Internat. Assn. for Rsch. on Income and Wealth. Clubs: Nat. Economists (chmn. bd., pres. 1978-80); Cosmos. Home: 6706 Loring Ct Bethesda MD 20817-3148 Office: 1155 15th St Washington DC 20005-2706

POPLE, JOHN ANTHONY, chemistry educator; b. Burnham, Somerset, Eng., Oct. 31, 1925; s. Herbert Keith and Frances (Jones) Pople; m. Joy Cynthia Pople, Sept. 22, 1952; children: Hilary Jane, Adrian John, Mark Stephen, Andrew Keith. BA in Math., Cambridge U., Eng., 1946, MA in Math., 1950, PhD in Math., 1951. Rsch. fellow Trinity Coll., Cambridge U., England, 1951—54, lectr. in math. England, 1954—58; Ford vis. prof. chemistry Carnegie Inst. Tech., Pitts., 1961—62; Carnegie prof. chem. physics Carnegie-Mellon U., 1964—74, J.C. Warner prof., 1974—91; prof. Northwestern U., Evanston, Ill., 1986—. Recipient Chemistry prize, Wolf Found., 1992, Kirkwood medal, Am. Chem. Soc., 1994, J.O. Hirschfelder prize in theoretical chemistry, U. Wis., Theoretical Chemistry Inst., 1994, Nobel prize in chemistry, 1998. Fellow: AAAS, Royal Soc. London; mem.: NAS. Office: Northwestern U Dept Chemistry 2145 Sheridan Rd Evanston IL 60208-0834

POPLER, KENNETH, behavioral healthcare executive, psychologist; BA in Psychology, CUNY, 1967; MA in Psychology, New Sch. Social Rsch., N.Y.C., 1969, PhD in Psychology, 1974; MBA, Wagner Coll., 1994. Diplomate Am. Bd. Profl. Psychology. Case worker N.Y.C. Dept. Social Svcs., 1967-70; intern Bklyn. Psychiat. Ctrs., 1970-72; sch. psychologist N.Y.C. Bd. Edn., 1972-73; psychologist Mid Nassau Community Guidance Ctr., Hicksville, N.Y., 1973-77; dir. St. Mary Community Mental Health Ctr., Hoboken, N.J., 1978-81; pres. and CEO Staten Island (N.Y.) Mental Health Soc., Inc., 1981—. Psychometrician L.I. Hillside Jewish Med. Ctr., Queens, N.Y., 1972-73; sr. psychologist, dir. psychol. svcs. HHC Gouverneur Hosp., N.Y.C., 1973-78; asst. rsch. scientist N.Y. State Psychiat. Inst., N.Y.C., 1971; vol. rsch. Manhattan Sch. for Seriously Disturbed Children, N.Y.C., 1972-73; instr. CUNY Bklyn. Coll. grad. divsn., 1972-73; pvt. practice, N.Y.C., 1976-85; asst. clin. prof. psychiatry Mt. Sinai Med. Sch., N.Y.C., 1978-95. Apptd. by mayor N.Y.C. Cmty. Svcs. Bd., 1984—, alcoholism subcom., 1987-91; pres. Coalition of Voluntary Mental Health Agys., Inc., 1991-94; sec. Head Start Sponsoring Bd. Coun. N.Y.C., 1985-92; chmn. Mental Health Coun. S.I., 1987-89, S.I. United Way Execs. Com., 1985. Mem. Rotary Club of Staten Island, Inc. Office: SI Mental Health Soc Inc 669 Castleton Ave Staten Island NY 10301-2099

POPLIN, SUSAN ELOISE, city planner; b. Fairfax, Va., Aug. 20, 1966; d. Matthew John and Ruth Eloise (Patrick) Prisutti; m. Michael Glen Poplin; children: Trevor, Matthew. BS in Pub. Adminstrn., Va. Poly. Inst. & State U., 1988; MS in Planning, Fla. State U., 1995. Cert. city planner. Property mgmt. asst. Long & Foster Realtors/The Gables Corp., Reston, McLean, Va., 1988-91; self-employed housing mgr. Tallahassee, 1992—; cmty. assistance cons. Fla. Dept. Cmty. Affairs, 1992-96, planner, 1996—. Vol. Shots by 2 Found., Tallahassee, 1992. Recipient Fla. Disting. Svc. award, 1992. Mem. Am. Inst. Cert. Planners, Am. Planning Assn., Sigma Kappa. Roman Catholic. Avocations: parenting, reading, swimming, riding horses, traveling. Office: Fla Dept Cmty Affairs 2555 Shumard Oak Blvd Tallahassee FL 32399-7018

POPNIK, MARLENE ALITA, school librarian, retired; b. Paterson, N.J., Aug. 31, 1942; d. Clarence L. and Katherine M. Borst; m. Joseph R. Popnik, Aug. 5, 1972. BS, SUNY, Geneseo, 1964. With Fonda-Fultonville Ctrl. Sch., 1964-65; libr. Spencerport (N.Y.) Ctrl. Sch., 1965-68, 69-72, U.S. Dependant Sch., Wethersfield, Eng., 1968-69, Susquehanna Twp. Schs., Harrisburg, Pa., 1973-2000; retired, 2000. Mem. NEA, ALA, Pa. Sch. Edn. Assn., Pa. Sch. Librs. Assn., Susquehanna Twp. Edn. Assn., Delta Kappa Gamma (1st v.p.). Home: 6349 Mifflin Ave Harrisburg PA 17111-4266 E-mail: jomarlene@aol.com.

POPOFSKY, MELVIN LAURENCE, lawyer; b. Oskaloosa, Iowa, Feb. 16, 1936; s. Samuel and Fannye Charlotte (Rosenthal) P.; m. Linda Jane Seltzer, Nov. 25, 1962; children: Mark Samuel, Kaye Sylvia. BA in History summa cum laude, U. Iowa, 1958; BA in Jurisprudence (first class honors), Oxford U., Eng., 1960; LLB cum laude, Harvard U., 1962. Bar: Calif. 1962. Assoc. Heller, Ehrman, White & McAuliffe, San Francisco, 1962-69, ptnr., 1969—, mem. exec. com., 1980-93, co-chair, 1988-93. Contbr. articles to law jours. Bd. dirs. Mt. Zion Hosp., San Francisco, 1982-88, U.S. Dist. Ct. (no. dist.) Calif. Hist. Soc., 1988—, Jewish Home for Aged, San Francisco, 1989-96, Golden Gate U., 1997-2000, Jewish Cmty. Fedn., 1997-2001. Recipient Anti-Defamation League's Disting. Jurisprudence award, 2000; named State Bar of Calif. Antitrust Lawyer of the Yr., 2000; Rhodes scholar, 1958. Fellow Am. Bar Found., Am. Coll. Trial Lawyers; mem. ABA, Calif. Bar Assn., San Francisco Bar Assn., Bur. Nat. Affairs (adv. bd. antitrust sect.), Calif. Acad. Appellate Lawyers. Democrat. Jewish. Home: 1940 Broadway Apt 10 San Francisco CA 94109-2216 Office: Heller Ehrman 333 Bush St Ste 3000 San Francisco CA 94104-2834

POPOVA, NINA, dancer, choreographer, director; b. Novorossisk, USSR, 1922; ed. in Paris, studied ballet with Olga Preobrajenska, Lubov Egorova, Anatole Vilzak, Anatole Oboukhov, Igor Schwezoff. Ballet debut with Ballet de la Jeunesse, Paris, London, 1937-39; soloist Original Ballet Russe, 1939-41, Ballet Theatre (now Am. Ballet), 1941-42, Ballet Russe de Monte Carlo, 1943, 47, Ballet Alicia Alonso, Cuba; mem. faculty Sch. Performing Arts, N.Y.C., from 1954; later artistic dir. Houston Ballet, 1975; tchr. Nat. Acad. Arts, Champaign, Ill., also N.Y.C., 1975—, now Eglevsky Ballet Sch., L.I.; tchr. ballet Mexico City, Mex.; asst. choreographer mus. comedy Birmingham So. Coll., Ala., 1960; numerous appearances on Broadway stage, TV; former mem. regular cast Your Show of Shows; currently teaching N.Y.C. Address: 33 Adams St Sea Cliff NY 11579-1614

POPOVIC, BOZENA (BO POPOVIC), artist; b. Kostajnica, Croatia, Jan. 2, 1957; d. Milorad and Dragica Skvorc; life ptnr. John Richard Tomasello. AA in Mdse., Fashion Inst. of Design & Mdse., San Francisco and L.A., 1977; BFA in Painting, Calif. Coll. Arts & Crafts, 1980; MPA in Pub. Policy Devel., Calif. State U., Hayward, 1997. Adminstr. Claims Tech. Svcs., Oakland, Calif., 1990-93; co-pub., owner Weekender Mag., West Contra Costa Ed., 1993—95; office mgr. Wild Oats Market, San Francisco, 1996-97; cons. fed. funded project Workers to Bus. Owners, Alameda, 1997; membership cons. Better Bus. Bur., San Francisco, 1998-99; rschr. Dominican U. of Calif., San Rafael, 1999—2002; devel. assoc. Found. Osteoporosis Rsch. and Edn., Oakland, 2002—. Bd. dirs. Women's Refuge, Oakland, 1999; outreach coord. San Pablo Hotel, Oakland, 1995; asst. dir. Voter Registration Project, San Francisco, 1987; active Re-Elect Marge Gibson campaign, Oakland, 1987, Don Perata campaign, Alameda, 1986-87. Mem.: AAUW, San Francisco Bus. Arts Coun., Assn. Fundraising Execs., Calif. Assn. Rschrs. for Advancement, Assn. Profl. Rsch. for Advancement, Soroptimists Internat. (regional del.). Avocations: Reading, racewalking, hiking, sketching. Office: Found Osteoporosis Rsch and Ed 300 27th St Suite 103 Oakland CA 94612 E-mail: bo@fore.org.

POPOVICH, GREGG, professional basketball coach; b. Jan. 28, 1949; m. Erin; 2 children. Grad. in Soviet studies, Air Force Acad., 1970; MA, Univ. of Denver. Asst. coach Air Force Acad., 1975-81; head coach Pomona-Pitzer Coll., Claremont, Calif., assoc. prof.; asst. to head coach San Antonio Spurs, 1988-92, head coach, exec. v.p. basketball ops., gen. mgr., 1996—; top asst. Golden State Warriors, 1992-96. 2nd lt. USAF, 1970-75. Recipient Daily Point of Light award President George Bush, 1992. Office: 100 Montana St San Antonio TX 78203-1033*

POPOVICI, ADRIAN, law educator; b. Bucharest, Rumania, Sept. 6, 1942; came to Can., 1951; s. Adrian and Alice (Moruzi) P.; children— Adrian, Alexandra. BA, Stanislas Coll., Montreal, 1959; B.C.L., McGill U., 1962; D.E.S., U. Paris, 1965. Bar: Que. 1963. Prof. law U. Montreal, Que., Can., 1968—. Author: L'Outrage au Tribunal, 1977, La Couleur du Mandat, 1995; editor: Problèmes de Droit Contemporain, 1974 Roman Catholic. Home: 5589 Canterbury Montreal QC Canada H3T 1S8 Office: U Montreal Faculte de Droit CP 6128 Succursale A Montreal QC Canada H3C 3J7 E-mail: adrian.popovici@unmontreal.ca.

POPOVICI, ALEXANDER MIHAI, geophysicist, business executive; b. Brad, Hunedoara, Romania, Sept. 19, 1962; came to U.S., 1987; s. Mihai Pavel and Galina Popovici; m. Catherine Ann Popovici, July 13, 1996; children: Andy, Michael, Stefan. BS, U. Bucharest, Romania, 1986; MS, Stanford (Calif.) U., 1990, PhD, 1995. Software engr. Guzik Tech., San Jose, Calif., 1987-88; dir. 3DGeo, Mountain View, 1995-98, CEO, 1999—. Contbr. articles to profl. publs.; patentee in field. Pres. Casa Romana, Hayward, Calif., 1997-2001, Romanian Orthodox Ch., Hayward, 1997-98. Grantee NSF, 1995, 97, 99. Mem. Soc. of Exploration Geophysicists, European Assn. of Geoscientists and Engrs. Republican. Avocations: scuba diving instructor, climbing, flying, karate, skiing. Office: 3DGeo 465 Fairchild Dr Mountain View CA 94043-2250

POPOVICS, SANDOR, civil engineer, educator, researcher; b. Budapest, Hungary, Dec. 24, 1921; came to U.S., 1957; s. Milan and Erzsebet (Droppa) P.; m. Lea M. Virtanen, Aug. 29, 1960; children: John, Lisa. 1st Degree in Civil Engring., Poly. U., Budapest, Hungary, 1944; Advanced Degree in Civil Engring., Poly. U., 1956; PhD, Purdue U., 1961. Registered profl. engr. Ariz., Pa. Rsch. engr. Met. Lab., Budapest, 1944-48; adj. prof. Tech. Coll., 1949-52; rsch. engr., mgr. Inst. for Bldg. Scis., 1949-56; grad. asst. Purdue U., Lafayette, Ind., 1957-59; prof. engring. Auburn (Ala.) U., 1959-69; prof. civil engring. No. Ariz. U., Flagstaff, 1968-76; prof. engring. King Abdulazziz U., Jeddah, Saudi Arabia, 1977-78; Samuel S. Baxter prof. civil engring. Drexel U., Phila., 1979-92, rsch. prof., 1992—. Pres. Optimum Engring. Rsch. Author: Fundamentals of Pc Concrete, 1982, Concrete Materials, 1992, Strength and Related Properties of Concrete, 1998, others; author more than 200 tech. papers in various langs. Recipient numerous grants and awards. Fellow ASCE (life), Am. Concrete Inst.; mem. ASTM, Ala. Acad. Scis., Ariz. Acad. Scis., Sigma Xi, Chi Epsilon. Avocations: jogging, music, fine art. Home and Office: 283 Congress Ave Lansdowne PA 19050-1206 Office: Drexel U Dept Civil & Archtl Engring 32nd and Chestnut Philadelphia PA 19104 E-mail: popovics@coe.drexel.edu.

POPOVSKY, MARK ALAN, physician; b. Boston, Aug. 1, 1950; s. Samuel and Sally Lillian (Taitz) P.; m. Andrea Leigh Lavender, June 7, 1981; 1 child, Erica Yael. BA magna cum laude, U. Mass., 1972; MD with honors, U. Vt., 1977. Diplomate Am. Bd. Pathology. Intern and resident in anatomic and clin. pathology NIH, Bethesda, Md., 1977-81; fellow in blood banking and transfusion medicine Mayo Clinic, Rochester, Minn., 1981-82, staff physician, 1982-85; asst. prof. med. lab. Mayo Med. Sch., 1982-85; med. dir. N.E. region ARC, Dedham, Mass., 1985—, chief med. officer New Eng. region, 1995-2000, CEO New Eng. region, 1996—; asst. prof. pathology Harvard U., Boston, 1985-96; assoc. clin. prof. pathology, 1996—; staff physician Beth Israel Hosp., Boston, 1985-96; clin. prof. pathology and lab. medicine Boston U., 1993—; staff physician Beth Israel Deaconess Hosp., Boston, 1996—; pres. cell processing divsn. and corp. med. dir. Haemonetics Braintree, Mass., 2000—. Del. Interam. Com. of Red Cross on Orgn. of Blood Transfusion Svcs., Geneva, Switzerland, 1986-90; mem. adv. bd. New Eng. region Aplastic Anemia Found., 1988-89; mem. expert panel on autogous transfusion Nat. Heart, Lung, Blood Inst., 1993-95, mem. nat. blood resource edn. program coord. commn., 1992-93; chmn. biomed. tech. curriculum com. Drew Inst., ARC, 1995-96. Editor: Transfusion Reactions, 1996, 2001; mem. editl. bd. Nat. Intravenous Therapy Assn., 1984-95, Immunohematology, 1992—, Am. Jour. Clin. Pathology, 1993—, Transfusion Medicine Reviews, 2000—, Transfusion, 1997—; contbr. 83 articles to profl. jours., 37 chpts. and monographs to books. Mem. Mass. coalition for the prevention of med. errors transfusion consensus group, 2001—. Lt. comdr. USPHS, 1977-81. Recipient Herbert Martin Sr. Excellence award U. Vt., 1977, Donor Svcs. Recognition award ARC, 1993, Morton Grove-Rasmussen award Mass. Assn. Blood Banks, 1996, Richard Davey lectureship NIH, 1997. Mem. Am. Red Cross Biomedical Svcs. (sr. v.p. Bd. Excellence, 1998), Am. Assn. Blood Banks (chmn. biotech. work group, autologous transfusion com., 1985-90, transfusion practices com., 1995—, transfusion-transmitted diseases com., 1998—, sci. sect. coord. com. 1990-92, chmn. Latin Am. affairs work group 1991-93, chmn. transfusion practices com. 1995—), Am. Soc. Hematology, Coll. of Am. Bd. Pathologists (mem. testwriting com. 1996-2001, mem. blood bank 1995—), Minn. Assn. Blood Banks (v.p. 1984-85), Am. Soc. Clin. Pathologists (mem. resident-in-tng. examination testing com.), Phi Beta Kappa, Phi Kappa Phi. Achievements include identification of linkage of passively transfused histocompatibility and granulocyte antibodies and recipient HLA phenotype in the diagnosis and pathogenesis of transfusion-related acute lung injury, recognition of circulatory overload. Office: Haemonetics Corp 400 Wood Rd Braintree MA 02184

POPOVYCH IHOR, L'VOVYCH, physician, researcher; b. Berezhany, Ukraine, Jan. 17, 1957; s. Lev Lavrentiyovych and Hanna Steranivna Vas'kiv Popovych; m. Milentyna Volodymyrivna Tyshchuk; 1 child, Andriy. Candidate Med. Scis., Bogomolets-Inst. Physiology, Kyiv, Ukraine, 1987. Jr. sci. co-worker Bogomolets-Inst. Physiology, 1984-89, sci. co-worker, 1989-93, sr. sci. co-worker, 1993-2000, conducting sci. co-worker, 2000—. Co-author: The Psychological Basis of Curative Effect of Water Naftussya, 1989, The Adaptogenes and Radiation, 1996, The Cholagogic Effect of Water Naftussya, 1997, The Water Naftussya and Hydrominerale Exchange, 1997 (Bogomolets Premium award Ukrainian Acad. Scis. 1998), The Adrenaline Myocardiodystrophy and Reactivity of Body, 1997, The Origin of Balneofactors of Water Naftussya and Essence its Curative Effect, 1999, The Bioactive Water Naftussya and Stomach, 2000, The General Adaptive Reactions and Resistance of Body by Liquidators of Accident in ChNPS, 2000 (Torosiewicz Premium award 2001); (brochure) The Evaluation of Vitality (General Value of Health), 2000. Mem. N.Y. Acad. Scis. Mem. Ukrainian Greece-Cath. Ch. Avocation: jogging. Home: Danylyshynykh 47/56 82200 Truskavets Lviv Ukraine Office: Pomirets'ka 51 82200 Truskavets Ukraine

POPOWSKI, KAREN JOYCE, social worker; b. Chgo., Oct. 12, 1942; d. Leon Clarence and Emily Kathryn (Wojnar) P. (dec.). BA, St Xavier Coll., 1966; MSW, U. Ill., 1972. Dir. Cook County Sheriff's Youth Svcs., Chgo., 1972-88; exec. dir. Polish Am. Assn., 1988—. Mem. Mayor's Citizenship Assistance Coun., Chgo., 1995—; bd. dirs. Polish Am. Leadership Initiative, 2000—. Author: (monograph) Chicago Youth Poll on Volunteerism and Service Learning, 1985. Bd. dirs. Ill. Coalition of Immigrant and Refugee Rights, Chgo., 1991-97; mem. adv. coun. Human Rels. Found., Chgo., 1996—. Decorated Cavalier's Cross Order of Merit, Polish Govt., Chgo., 1996; recipient cert. of merit Mayor of Chgo., 1993, Commrs. Noncitizen Team award Social Security Adminstrn., Balt., 1997. Mem. Nat. Assn. Social Workers, Acad. Cert. Social Workers (cert.). Office: Polish Am Assn 3834 N Cicero Ave Chicago IL 60641-3622 E-mail: kp@polish.org.

POPP, CHARLOTTE LOUISE, health development center administrator, nurse; b. Vineland, N.J., July 26, 1946; d. William Henry and Elfriede Marie (Zickler) P. Diploma in Nursing, Luth. Hosp. of Md., Balt., 1967; BA in Health Edn., Rowan U., 1972; MA in Human Devel., Fairleigh-Dickinson U., 1981. Cert. Sch. Nurse, N.J., Health Educator, N.J. Charge nurse Newcomb Hosp., Vineland, N.J., 1967-71; supr. Vineland Rehab. Ctr., 1971-72; charge nurse Bridgeton (N.J.) Hosp., 1972-73; dir. insvc. edn. Millville (N.J.) Hosp., 1973-76; dir. hosp. insvc. edn. Vineland Devel. Ctr. State of N.J., 1976-78, program asst. Vineland Devel. Ctr., 1978-87; dir. habilitation planning services State of N.J., Vineland Devel. Ctr., 1987—, lead program coord. Vineland Devel. Ctr., 1981—2001. Exam proctor State of N.J. Bd. Nursing, Newark, 1973-91. Editorial rev. bd. (jour.) Nursing Update, 1973-77. Instr. basic life support, Am. Heart Assn., bd. dirs. Tri-county chpt., 1979-83, South Jersey chpt., 1983-90. Mem. ANA, N.J. State Nurses Assn., Am. Assn. Mental Retardation, South Jersey Insvc. Exch. (life), Smithsonian Assn., Luth. Hosp. of Md. Alumni Assn., Glassboro State Coll./Rowan U. Alumni Assn., Fairleigh-Dickinson U. Alumni Assn. Lutheran. Avocations: reading, travel, collectable plates, animals, horseracing. Office: Vineland Devel Ctr 1676 E Landis Ave Vineland NJ 08361-2943

POPP, JOSEPH BRUCE, manufacturing executive; b. Chgo., July 9, 1919; s. Peter Leon and Anna (Chomyz) P.; m. Mabel Lydia Szymanski, Oct. 23, 1941 (dec. Mar. 1993); m. Elinor A. Maves, Jan. 27, 1996; children: Dianne, Lydia, Bruce, Anita, Gregory. Founder, owner Poultry Farm, Westville, Ind., 1941-48, Gary (Ind.) Undercoating Co., 1948-51; survey analyst George S. May Co., Chgo., 1952-54; gen. sales mgr. Maurey Instrument Corp., 1958-64; founder, owner Joe Popp Sales Co., North Riverside, Ill., 1964-89, Chart Pool USA Inc., Portage, Ind., 1966—. Inventor hand held berry picker, worldwide bloodhound property security (patents pending). Bd. dirs. YMCA Camp Tecumseh, Brookston, Ind., 1973—. Sgt. U.S. Army, 1942-46. Mem. Nat. Fedn. of Ind. Bus., Greater Portage C. of C., Ind. C. of C., Better Bus. Bur., The Gideons Internat. Republican. Home: 1133 Lincoln St Hobart IN 46342-6039 Office: Chart Pool USA Inc 5695 Old Porter Rd Portage IN 46368-1194

POPP, LILIAN MUSTAKI, writer, educator; b. N.Y.C. d. Peter and Mae Claire (Cary) Mustaki; m. Robert J. Popp. BA, Notre Dame Coll.; postgrad., Columbia U.; MS in Edn., Hunter Coll. Tchr. English McKee Vocat. and Tech. H.S., S.I., N.Y., 1946-63, chmn. acad. studies, 1963-71; prin. William Howard Taft H.S., Bronx, 1971-79; adj. prof. Wagner Coll., S.I., 1960-85; instr. Richmond Coll., CUNY, 1968-70; prof. St. John's U., 1991-93. Mem. Cmty. Sch. Bd., 1980—93, chmn., 1989—90, chmn. legis. com., chmn. substance abuse and adolescent issues com., chmn. pupil pers. svcs. com.; chmn. curriculum com.; asst. examiner N.Y.C. Bd. Edn., 1960—85. Author, editor: Journeys in Science Fiction, 1961, Four Complete World Novels, 1961, Gertrude Lawrence as Mrs. A., 1961, Four Complete Modern Novels, 1962, Four Complete Heritage Novels, 1963, Four Complete Novels of Character and Courage, 1964; contbr. articles to profl. jours. Chmn. vols. N.Y.C. Child Abuse Prevention Program, 1984—86; regional dir., mem. exec. bd. March of Dimes; book discussion leader Snug Harbor Cultural Ctr., 1981—; pres. Com. for a Nuclear-Free Island, 1986—91; v.p. Staten Islanders Against Nuclear Weapons, 1991—95; pres. Staten Island chpt. Brandeis U. Nat. Women's Com., 1996—99, leader News and Shmews; founder, pres. Coalition of S.I. Women's Orgns., 1996—; mem. edn. com. Staten Island Cmty. TV; mem. Libr. com. Staten Island Hist. Richmond Town; pres. Staten Island Youth Coun.; mem. libr. com. Coll. Staten Island; cmty. outreach chair Women for Women of Sierra Leone, 2001; bd. dirs. Staten Island Mental Health Soc. Recipient Women Helping Women award Soroptimists, 1985, Thomas Wilson award for Substance Abuse Prevention, 1990, S.I. Advance Woman of Achievement award, 1994, Cmty. Hero award S.I. Register, 1996, Woman of Distinction award World of Women, 1998, Paul O'Dwyer Humanitarian award Staten Is. Dem. Assn., 1999; named Outstanding Woman by N.Y. State Sen. Vincent J. Gentile, 1998, Women's History Month award N.Y. City Coun. Spkr. Peter Vallone and Councilmen Jeremiah O'Donovan, Oddo and Fiala, 2001. Mem. AAUW, Belles Lettres Lit. Soc. (pres.), S.I. Hist. soc., N.Y.C. Assn. Tchrs. English (pres. 1967-71), Nat. Coun. Tchrs. English (bd. dirs. 1968-69), Acad. Pub. Edn., McKee Tchrs. Assn. (pres. 1969), H.S. Prins. Assn. (exec. bd.), Coun. Suprs. and Adminstrs., Arista Hon. Soc. (hon.), Delta Kappa Gamma (pres.), Phi Delta Kappa (v.p. 1990-92). Avocations: travel, reading, photography, jewelry making. Home: 40 Flagg Pl Staten Island NY 10304-1119

POPPE, BARBARA, social services administrator; b. Columbus, Ohio, Oct. 12, 1958; d. John Allen and Beverly Reed Poppe; m. Bill Faith, Oct. 5, 1991; children: Elise Poppe Faith, Benjamin Poppe Faith. BA magna cum laude in Chemistry, William Woods Coll., 1981; MS in Environ. Health, U. of Cin., 1987. Shelter adv. Bathany House, Cin., 1985—86, fin. and devel. mgr., 1985—88; safety and health officer dept. environ. health U. of Cin., 1988—90, asst. dir. dept. environ. health, 1988—90; exec. dir. Friends of the Homeless, Columbus, 1990—95, Cmty. Shelter Bd., Columbus, 1995—. Mem. adv. group Nat. Alliance to End Homelessness, Washington, 2000—; mem. profl. adv. coun. United Way , Columbus, 1999—; chmn. urban affairs com. Columbus Found. , Columbus, 1997—. Event chair Girl Scouts Seal of Ohio, Columbus, 1999—2002; active Columbus Montessori Edn. Ctr., 1992—2002. Recipient Extra Mile award, Friends of the Homeless, 1997, Housing and Urban Devel. Recognition for Excellence award, US HUD, 1995, Recognition award, Columbus Coalition for the Homeless, 1995; fellow Jefferson fellowship, Jefferson Ctr. for Learning and the Arts, 1996. Office: Community Shelter Board 115 West Main Street Lower Level Columbus OH 43215 Office Fax: 614-221-9199. E-mail: bjpoppe@csb.org.

POPPEL, HARVEY LEE, strategic management consultant, investment banker; b. Bklyn., Dec. 18, 1937; s. Frank M. and Fannie (Axenzow) P.; m. Emily A. Daigneault, Jan. 2, 1959; children: Marc F., Clinton S. BS, Rensselaer Poly. Inst., 1958, MS, 1959. Sr. info. systems analyst Westinghouse Electric Corp., Pitts., 1959-65; mgr. industry systems Western Union, Paramus, N.J., 1965-67; from assoc. to mem. operating coun. Booz, Allen & Hamilton, N.Y.C., 1967-84; pres. Poptech, Inc., Sarasota, Fla., 1984—. Bd. dirs. Larscom, Santa Clara, Calif., 1996-02; mng. dir. Broadview Assocs., Ft. Lee, 1984-96; mem. panel, lectr. on computers, comms. and info. industry; judge Entrepreneur of Yr., 1991, 93, 94, 95, 96; investor in start-ups. Co-author: Information Technology: The Trillion-Dollar Opportunity, 1987; contbr. articles to profl. jours. Mem. Aspen Inst. Fellows, Inst. Mgmt. Cons., Soc. Mgmt. Info. Systems (exec. council), Rep. Jewish Coalition, Zeta Psi. Clubs: Road Runners, Banyan Golf Club. Office: 1391 6th St Sarasota FL 34236-4906 E-mail: hpoppel@msn.com.

POPPEL, SETH RAPHAEL, entrepreneur; b. Bklyn., Mar. 17, 1944; s. Frank M. and Fritzi R. (Axenzow) P.; m. Danine Vokt, Jan. 5, 1974; children: Clarysa, Jared, Stacy. BS magna cum laude, L.I. U., 1965; MBA, Columbia U., 1967. Asst. prof. L.I. U., Greenvale, N.Y., 1967-68; v.p. Synergistic Sys. Corp., N.Y.C., 1968-77; v.p., dir. corp. planning Chase Manhattan Corp., 1977-90; owner, pres. Yearbook Libr., 1980—; chmn., pres. Am. Vision Ctrs., 1990-96. Owner harness horses Seth Poppel Stables, 1983—; founder, owner, operator Seth Poppel Yearbook Archives, 1986-2000. Recipient Claire F. Adler award in math., 1964-65, Mepham H.S. Hall of Fame award, 1993; E.I. DuPont fellow, 1965-67, Downie Muir fellow, 1965-66. Mem. Am. Statis. Assn., Ops. Rsch. Soc. Am., Inst. Mgmt. Sci., Nat. Assn. Bus. Economy, N.Am. Soc. Corp. Planning, U.S. Trotting Assn., Beta Gamma Sigma, Psi Chi, Omega Epsilon. Home and Office: 38 Range Dr Merrick NY 11566-3233 E-mail: sethpoppel@aol.com.

POPPEN, MARCELLA MAY, music educator; b. Aug. 20, 1924; MusM, Eastman Sch. Music, 1952, U. Oreg., 1971; D of Music Edn., Ind. U., 1976. Instr. music Balko Jo Gakuin, Shimonoseki, Japan, 1951-55, Union Free Sch. Dist. #12, Molverne, N.Y., 1956-68, SUNY, Brockport, 1969-71, North Ctrl. Coll., Mpls., 1984-86; min. of music Evang. Luth. Ch. in Am., Bloomsburg, Pa., Budd Lake, N.J., 1986-93; ind. piano instr. Orange City, 1993—. Assoc. in ministry Evang. Luth. Ch. in Am. Ind. U. rsch. grantee, 1976. Mem. Am. Guild of Organists, Music Tchrs. Nat. Assn., Iowa Music Tchrs. Assn., Assn. Luth. Ch. Musicians, Ind. U. Alumni Assn., Mu Phi Epsilon.

POPPENDIEK, HEINZ FRANK, engineering executive; b. Altona, Germany, Nov. 8, 1919; arrived in U.S., 1925; s. Franz Ludwig Poppendiek and Helena Bertha Bunsen; m. Sarah Elizabeth Secrest, Aug. 15, 1943; children: Niel, Carolyn, Mark. BS in Mech. Engring., U. Calif., Berkeley, 1942, MS in Mech. Engring., 1944, PhD in Engring., 1949. Asst. prof. engring. U. Calif., Berkeley, 1946—49; sect. chief Oak Ridge (Tenn.) Nat. Lab., 1950—56; staff scientist Gen. Atomic, San Diego, 1956—58, Convair, San Diego, 1958—60; dir. rsch. Geophysics Corp. Am., 1960—61; pres. Geosci., Ltd., 1961—. Cons. nuc. propulsion and heat and momentum transfer Inst. Def. Analyses; indsl. cons. reactor heat and momentum transfer; cons. nuc. and chem. power systems mem. spl. task force on innovation, rsch. and tech., SBA. Contbr. chapters to books, articles to profl. jours. (Outstanding Paper award, Am. Geophys. Union). Micrometeorol. technician USN, 1944—45, P.R. Recipient Enterprise award, Bank of Am., 1998, Honorarium for heat transfer symposium, U. Mich.; grantee numerous rsch. grants. Mem.: ASTM (C16 com.), Tau Beta Pi (writing award), Sigma Xi. Achievements include patents in field. Office: Geosci Ltd 6260 Marindustry Dr San Diego CA 92121

POPPENSIEK, GEORGE CHARLES, veterinary scientist, educator; b. N.Y.C., June 18, 1918; s. George Frederick and Emily Amelia (Miller) P.; m. Edith M. Wallace, July 3, 1943; children: Neil Allen, Leslie Marion. Student, Cornell U., 1936-37, MS, 1951; student, U. Pa., 1937-42, V.MD, 1942.

Diplomate Am. Bd. Microbiology, Am. Coll. Vet. Microbiology (charter), Am. Coll. Vet. Preventive Medicine (hon.). Asst. instr. medicine U. Pa. Sch. Vet. Medicine, 1943; asst. prof. vet. sci. U. Md., 1943-44; head dept. vet. virus vaccine prodn. Lederle Labs. div. Am. Cyanamid Co., 1944-49; dir. diagnostic lab. N.Y. State Coll. Vet. Medicine Cornell U., 1949-51, research assoc. Vet. Virus Research Inst., 1951-55; veterinarian Plum Island Animal Disease Ctr., animal disease and parasite research div. Agrl. Research Service, U.S. Dept. Agr., 1955-56, acting-in-charge diagnostic investigations, 1956-58, charge immunological investigations, 1958-59; dean and prof. microbiology N.Y. State Coll. Vet. Medicine, Cornell U., 1959-74, James Law prof. comparative medicine, 1974-88, dean emeritus, James Law prof. comparative medicine emeritus, 1988—; guest prof. U. Bern, Switzerland, 1975. Mem. exam. com. Nat. Bd. Vet. Med. Examiners, 1976-79; bd. dirs. Cornell Research Found., 1963-74; chmn. bd. dirs. Cornell Veterinarian, Inc., 1976-86 Recipient Certificate of Merit award U.S. Dept. Agr., 1958; citation Sch. Vet. Med., U. Pa., 1978, Centennial medals U. Pa., 1984, Ohio State U., 1985; others. Charter fellow Am. Acad. Microbiology; fellow AAAS; charter mem. Am. Soc. Virology; mem. AVMA, N.Y. State Vet. Med. Soc. (disting. life), Am. Bd. Microbiology, U.S. Animal Health Assn., Assn. Am. Vet. Med. Colls. (pres. 1970-71), So. Tier Vet. Med. Assn., Am. Vet. Radiology Soc., Am. Soc. for Microbiology, N.Y. Agrl. Soc. (life), Argentine Nat. Acad. Agronomy and Vet. Medicine (hon.), Societas Polona Medicinae Veterinariae (hon.), Sigma Xi, Phi Kappa Phi, Alpha Psi, Omega Tau Sigma, Phi Zeta. Congregationalist. Home: 32 Horizon Dr Ithaca NY 14850-9769 E-mail: poppensiek@clarityconnect.com.

POPPER, ROBERT, law educator, former dean; b. N.Y.C., May 22, 1932; s. Walter G. and Dorothy B. (Kluger) P.; m. Mary Ann Schaefer, July 12, 1963; children: Julianne, Robert Gregory. BS, U. Wis., 1953; LLB, Harvard U., 1956; LLM, NYU, 1963. Bar: N.Y. 1957, U.S. Dist. Ct. (so. dist.) N.Y. 1962, U.S. Ct. Appeals (2d cir.) 1962, U.S. Supreme Ct. 1962, U.S. Dist. Ct. (ea. dist.) N.Y. 1969, U.S. Ct. Appeals (7th cir.) 1970, U.S. Ct. Appeals (8th cir.) 1971, Mo. 1971, U.S. Dist. Ct. (we. dist.) Mo. 1973. Trial atty. criminal br. N.Y.C. Legal Aid Soc., 1960-61; asst. dist. atty. N.Y. County, 1961-64; assoc. Seligson & Morris, N.Y.C., 1964-69; mem. faculty School of Law U. Mo, Kansas City, 1969-96, prof., 1973-96, acting dean, 1983-84, dean, 1984-93, dean and prof. emeritus, 1996—. Cons. and lectr. in field. Author: Post Conviction Remedies in a Nutshell, 1978, De-Nationalizing the Bill of Rights, 1979; contbr. articles to profl. jours. Bd. dirs. Midwestern Innocence Project. Fellow ABA; mem. Mo. Bar, Kansas City Met. Bar Assn., Mo. Inst. of Justice. Home: 6229 Summit St Kansas City MO 64113-1556 Office: U Mo Kansas City Sch Law 1500 Rockhill Rd Kansas City MO 64110-2467 Fax: (816) 235-5276. E-mail: popperr@umkc.edu.

POPPLETON, JANET WATERS, legislative staff member; b. Camden, Ark., Dec. 5, 1950; d. William J. and Sybil (Butcher) Waters; m. Glenn A. Perry, May 20, 1972 (div. Jan. 1993); 1 child, Marcus Perry; m. Miller John Poppleton Jr., Mar. 20, 1999; stepchildren: Ashley, Aubrey. BA with highest honors, So. State Coll., Magnolia, Ark., 1972; MA, Stephen F. Austin State U., 1976. Press sec. Rep. Ralph Hall, Washington, 1993-96, chief staff, 1996—. Bd. dirs., fundraiser Habitat for Humanity, Am. Cancer Soc., Longview, 1985-91; bd. dirs. Jr. League, Longview, 1988-91; pres., bd. dirs. Gregg County Early Childhood Devel. Ctr., Longview, 1990-92; precinct chmn. Gregg County Dems., Longview, 1990-92; trustee Trinity Sch. Tex., Longview, 1991-92. Mem. U.S. Ho. Rep. Adminstrv. Asst. Assn. Lutheran. Avocations: travel, performing arts, skiing, writing. Office: Rep Ralph Hall 2221 Rayburn Washington DC 20515-0001

POPRÁDY, GÉZA, librarian; b. Tök, Hungary, Mar. 19, 1940; s. Géza and Ilona (Lugmayer) P.; m. Maria Wéber, July 13, 1963; children: Géza, Judit, Peter. Student, Eötvös Lorand U., Budapest, Hungary, 1958-63. Cert. librarian, tchr. Librarian Architectural Info. Ctr., Budapest, 1963-64, Ctrl. Rsch. and Design Inst. for Silicate Industry, Budapest, 1964—83; head dept. Nat. Széchényi Library, 1984-90, dep. dir.-gen., 1990-93, acting dir.-gen., 1993-94, dir.-gen., 1994-99, counsellor, 1999—. Author: (book) The Application of Technical Information, 1977, The Systematic Catalogue, 1981, Preservation of Library Materials, 2000; contbr. articles to profl. jours. Recipient Szabó Ervin medal Min. of Culture, 1989. Mem. Assn. Hungarian Librarians (sec.-gen. 1987-90, v.p. 1990-98, award 1988). Avocations: reading, gardening. Home: Buza u 16 H-1033 Budapest Hungary Office: Nat Széchényi Library Budavári Palota F-épület 1827 Budapest Hungary E-mail: geza.poprady@oszk.hu.

POPRAWA, ANDREW, financial services executive, accountant; b. Toronto, Ont., Can., Nov. 13, 1952; s. Mieczyslaw and Wanda (Wolak) P.; m. Rita Poprawa, Oct. 10, 1981; children: Alexandra, Jason. B.Commerce, U. Toronto, 1975. Chartered acct., Can. CEO St. Stanislaus Credit Union, Toronto, 1980-82; dir. Office of Supt. of Fin. Instns. (Can.), 1982-92, Ministry of Fin., Province of Ont., Toronto, 1992-93; pres., CEO Depost Ins. Corp. of Ont., 1993—. Mem. Inst. Chartered Accts. Ont. (cert. govt. fin. mgr.), Lakeshore Yacht Club, Toronto Bd. of Trade. Roman Catholic. Avocations: sailing, tennis, skiing, hockey. Office: Deposit Insurance Corp of Ontario 4711 Yonge St #700 Toronto ON Canada M2N 6K8

POPS, RICHARD F. pharmaceutical executive; CEO Alkermes, 1991—. Bd. dirs. Alkermes, Inc., Neurocrine Bioscis., Inc., Reliant Pharmaceuticals, LLC, Genomics Collaborative, Inc., CombinatoRx, Inc., Biotechnology Industry Orgn., Mass. Biotechnology Coun., Harvard Med. Sch. Bd. Fellows; chair Harvard Med. Sch. Adv. Coun. for Biol. Chemistry & Molecular Pharmacology. Office: Corp Hqtrs Alkermes Inc 64 Sidney St Cambridge MA 02139*

PORACKY, BERNARD FRANCIS, radiologist; b. Whiting, Ind., Jan. 29, 1924; MD, Ind. U., 1946. Diplomate Am. Bd. Radiology, 1950. Intern St. Margaret Hosp., Hammond, Ind., 1946-47, resident, 1947-48, U. Pa., Phila., 1949-49; fellow Cook County Hosp., Chgo., 1949-51; staff radiologist Porter Meml. Hosp., Valparaiso, Ind., 1951—. Mem. AMA, Am. Coll. Radiologists (bd. cert.), Radiol. Soc. N.Am. Home: 148 Shore Dr Portage IN 46368-1015 Office: Porter Meml Hosp Valparaiso IN 46383

PORAD, FRANCINE JOY, poet, painter; b. Seattle, Sept. 3, 1929; d. Morris H. and Gertrude (Volchok) Harvitz; m. Bernard L. Porad, June 12, 1949; children: Laurie, Bruce, Ken, Constance, Marci, Jeffrey. BFA, U. Wash., 1976. Founder, coord. Haiku NW Poets/Readers, Mercer Isle, Wash., 1988—; editor Brussels Sprout, 1988-95; co-editor Haiku Northwest Anthology, Seattle, 1996, Red Moon Press, Berryville, Va., 1996. Workshop presenter Haiku Can., Toronto and Alymer, Que., Can., 1992, 95, Haiku N.Am., Calif., Toronto, 1993, 95, Haiku N.Am., Oreg., 1997, Haiku Internat., Tokyo, 1997; judge Internat. Haiku Contest New Zealand Poetry Soc., 1995, People's Haiku & Senryu Contest, Canada, 1999, San Francisco Contest for Haiku Poets of North Calif., 1992, Hawaii Edn. Assn., Honolulu, 1995, 99, Haiku Soc. Am., 1997, PEN Women (Seattle) Internat. Poetry Contest, 2000. Author: Connections, 1986, Pen and Inklings, 1986, After Autumn Rain, 1987, Blues on the Run, 1988, Free of Clouds, 1989, Without Haste, 1989 (Cicada Chapbook award 1990), Hundreds of Wishes, 1990, A Mural of Leaves, 1991, Joy is My Middle Name, 1993, The Patchwork Quilt, 1994 (Haiku Soc. Am. Merit Book 1994), Waterways, 1995 (Haiku Can. Sheet Book series 1995), All Eyes, 1995, Ladies and Jellyspoons, 1996, Extended Wings, 1996, Moon, Moon, 1997, Fog Lifting, 1997, All the Games, 1997, Let's Count The Trees, 1998 (Haiku Can. Sheet Selection 1998), (with M. Mountain) Cur*rent, 1998, The Perfect Worry-Stone, 2000, (with K. Kondo and M. Mountain) Other Rens, 2000, Other Rens Book Two and Book Three, 2000, Trio of Wrens, 2000, Second Blooming, 2001. Recipient 1st prize Internat. Tanka competition Poetry Soc. Japan, Tokyo, 1993, Itoen Tea award Haiku Internat., Tokyo, 1996, 98, Cicada award for Haiku sequences by Amelia, 1999, award Mainichi Internat. Haiku Contest, Tokyo, 1999. Mem. Nat. League Am. Penwomen (treas. 1992-94, Owl award 1982, 92, 1st prize state art exhbn. Frye Mus. 1993, 1st pl. Haiku, 1995), Haiku Soc. Am. (pres. 1993, 94, Merit book 1994, judge 1997, Brady Senryu Contest H.M. award 1997), N.W. Watercolor Soc. (treas. 1980-85), Women Painters Wash. (v.p. 1987, bd. 1985-93). Avocations: computer fun, travel. Home: 6944 SE 33d St Mercer Island WA 98040-3324 E-mail: poradF@aol.com.

PORCARO, MICHAEL FRANCIS, advertising agency executive; b. N.Y.C., Apr. 3, 1948; s. Girolamo M. and Marianna (DePasquale) P.; m. Bonnie Kerr, Apr. 7, 1972; children: Sabrina, Jon. BA in English, Rockford (Ill.) Coll., 1969. Broadcaster Sta. KFQD-AM; KENI-AM/TV, Anchorage, 1970-71, Sta. KENI-AM/TV, Anchorage, 1972-73; v.p. ops. Cook Inlet Broadcasters, 1973-74; owner Audio Enterprises, 1974-75; asst. Alaska Pub. Broadcasting Commn., 1975-76, exec. dir., 1976-81; CEO, ptnr. Porcaro Blankenship Advt. Corp., Anchorage, 1981-97; CEO Porcaro Comms., 1997—; chmn. bd. Bernholz & Graham, Pub. Rels., 2001—. Cons. Arco Alaska TV sta., Anchorage, 1981; expert witness U.S. Senate Subcom. on Telecom., Washington, 1978; chmn. citizens adv. com. dept. journalism U. Alaska, 1995-96. Afternoon talk show host KENI, 2000—. Chmn. Municipality of Anchorage Urban Design Commn., 1990-93; mem. mayor's transition team Municipality of Anchorage, 1987-88; bd. dirs. Anchorage Glacier Pilots Baseball Club, 1987-88, Anchorage Mus. History and Art, Alaska Ctr. Internat. Bus., 1996, Commonwealth North, 1996-2000, Friends of Alaska Children's Trust, 1996-97, Anchorage Symphony Orch.; chmn. bd. dirs. Brother Francis Shelter for the Homeless, Anchorage, 1993-96; mem. mktg. com. gov.'s transition team, 1995; mem. United Way Anchorage Cabinet, 1996; bd. dirs. Alaska Spl. Olmpics, 2001, Anchorage Econ. Devel. Corp., 2001, Alaska Moving Image Preservation Assn., 2001. Recipient Silver Mike award Billboard mag., 1974, Bronze award N.Y. Film Critics, 1981, Best of North award Ad. Fedn. Alaska, 1982—, Addy award, 1985, 91, Grand Addy award 1990, Cable TV Mktg. award 1986; Paul Harris fellow. Mem. Advt. Fedn. Alaska, Anchorage C. of C. (bd. dirs.), Alaska Moving Image Preservation Assn. (bd. dirs. 2001). Republican. Roman Catholic. Avocations: softball, hockey, travel, fitness. Office: Porcaro Comm 433 W 9th Ave Anchorage AK 99501-3519

PORCELLO, LEONARD JOSEPH, engineering research and development executive; b. N.Y.C., Mar. 1, 1934; s. Savior James and Mary Josephine (Bacchi) P.; m. Patricia Lucille Berger, July 7, 1962 (dec. Sept. 1991); children—John Joseph, Thomas Gregory; m. Victoria Roberta Smith, June 21, 1996. BA in Physics, Cornell U., 1955; MS in Physics, U. Mich., 1957, MS in Elec. Engring, 1959, PhD in Elec. Engring, 1963. Research asst. U. Mich., Ann Arbor, 1955-58, instr. elec. engring., 1958-61; research engr. Radar & Optics Lab., 1968-72; asso. dir. Willow Run Labs., 1970-72, asso. prof., 1969-72, prof., 1972-73, adj. prof., 1973-75. Dir. radar and optics divsn. Environ. Rsch. Inst. of Mich., Ann Arbor, 1973-76, v.p., 1973-76, trustee, 1975; asst. v.p., mgr. sensor sys. operation Sci. Applications Internat. Corp., Tucson, 1976-79, v.p., 1979-85, corp. v.p., 1985-87, mgr. def. sys. group, 1986-95, sr. v.p., 1987—, dep. mgr. tech. and advanced sys. sector, 1993-97, mgr. applied sys. group, 1995-2000, dep. mgr. space and tech. solutions sector, 1997-99. Bd. dirs. Tucson Jr. Strings, 1977-79, chmn., 1978-79 Fellow IEEE; mem. Optical Soc. Am., AAAS, Sigma Xi, Eta Kappa Nu. Roman Catholic. Achievements include research on imaging radar, synthetic aperture radar systems and radar remote sensing. Home: 5072 Grandview Ave Yorba Linda CA 92886-4216 Office: Sci Applications Internat Corp Attn LJ Porcello PO Box 820 Yorba Linda CA 92885-0820 E-mail: Leonard.J.Porcello@saic.com.

POREMBA, DAVID LEE, librarian, writer; b. Detroit, Oct. 1, 1953; m. Kathleen B. Larsen, May 25, 1979; children: Harold, Theresa, Joseph, Brian. BA in History, Wayne State U., 1978, MLS, 1990. Cert. archives adminstrn. Wayne State U. Librarian I Detroit Pub. Libr., 1990—91, librarian II, 1991—95, librarian III, 1995—2001, librarian IV, 2001—. Author: Detroit: A Motor City History, 2001, Baseball in Detroit, 1886-1968, 1998; editor: Detroit in its World Setting: A 300-year Chronology, 2001, 4 other books. Sgt. U.S. Army, 1971—74, Germany. Mem.: Mich. Archival Assn., Soc. Am. Baseball Rsch. Office: Detroit Pub Libr Burton Hist Collection 5201 Woodward Detroit MI 48202

PORFILIO, JOHN CARBONE, federal judge; b. Denver, Oct. 14, 1934; s. Edward Alphonso Porfilio and Caroline (Carbone) Moore; m. Joan West, Aug. 1, 1959 (div. 1983); children: Edward Miles, Joseph Arthur, Jeanne Kathrine; m. Theresa Louise Berger, Dec. 28, 1983; 1 stepchild Katrina Ann Smith. Student, Stanford U., 1952—54; BA, U. Denver, 1956, LLB, 1959, LLD (hon.) , 2000. Bar: Colo. 1959, U.S. Supreme Ct. 1965. Asst. atty. gen. State of Colo., Denver, 1962—68, dep. atty. gen., 1968—72, atty. gen., 1972—74; U.S. bankruptcy judge Dist. of Colo., 1975—82; judge U.S. Dist. Ct. Colo., 1982—85, U.S. Ct. Appeals (10th cir.), Denver, 1985—99, sr. judge, 1999—. Instr. Colo. Law Enforcement Acad., Denver, 1965—70, State Patrol Acad., Denver, 1968—70; guest lectr. U. Denver Coll. Law, 1978. Committeeman Arapahoe County Rep. Com., Aurora, Colo., 1968; mgr. Dunbar for Atty. Gen., Denver, 1970. Mem.: ABA. Roman Catholic. Office: US Ct Appeals Byron White US Courthouse 1823 Stout St Denver CO 80257-1823*

PORIES, MURIEL H. business executive, loan consultant; b. Milw., Dec. 19, 1925; d. Jacob and Jean Aronson; m. Walter J. Pories, Aug. 1951 (div. Apr. 1977). BS, U. Wis., Milw., 1951; MA, John Carroll U., 1979; JD, Am. Coll. Law, Brea, Calif., 1984. Cert. prin. Tchr. Rochester (N.Y.) Bd. Edn., 1952-56, Irondequoit (N.Y.) Bd. Edn., 1956-59, Shaker Heights (Ohio) Pub. Schs., 1973—77; counselor Lawyers Referral Svc., Santa Ana, Calif., 1983; mng. ptnr. Pories and Klein, Fullerton, 1984; mktg. analyst Display Techniques Internat., Santa Ana, 1986; dir. mktg. Peninsula Shipyard, Newport Beach, 1987-89; pres., owner Mar-Bruc Inc., Laguna Beach, 1995—. Loan cons. CPM Fin., Ont., 1999; pioneered open edn. Shaker Heights Bd. Edn., 1974; adj. prof. Am. Coll. Law, Anaheim, Calif., 2002—. Author: "That's Because We Love You," 1976, A Program for Dropout Reduction, 1978. Mem.Am. Coll. Law Alumni (pres. 1999). Democrat. Avocations: swimming, table tennis. Home: 231 Cozumel Laguna Beach CA 92651-4447

PORIES, SUSAN ELAINE, medical educator; b. Rochester, N.Y., Jan. 25, 1953; d. Walter Julius and Muriel Helen (Aronson) P.; m. Christopher Kiley, June 26, 1982; 1 child: Louis Walter Pories Kiley. BS, U. Vt., 1975, MD, 1984. Diplomate Am. Bd. Surgery. Resident in surgery U. Vt., Burlington, 1984-89; rsch. fellow in surgery Harvard U. Med. Sch., Boston, 1989-91, clin. instr. surgery, 1991-92, instr. surgery, 1992-93, asst. prof. surgery, 1993—. Chair profl. adv. bd. Wellness Cmty., Newton, Mass., 2000—; Inst. Edn. scholar Shapiro Inst. for Edn. and Rsch., Harvard Med. Sch/Beth Israel Deaconess Med. Ctr. Book rev. editor Current Surgery, 1990-99; co-editor Resident Resource column Current Surgery, 2000—; contbr. articles to profl. jours. Active breast cancer adv. com. Dept. Pub. Health, State of Mass., 1994-96; ednl./outreach cons. State Breast Health Initiative, Cambridge Hosp., 1994-96. Maj. SAR. Recipient Best Resident Paper award New England Surg. Soc., 1987. Fellow ACS (Vt.- Resident Rsch. award Trauma Com. 1988); mem. Am. Soc. Clin. Oncology, Am. Soc. Breast Surgeons, Am. Assn. Cancer Rsch., Mass. Med. Soc., Soc. Surg. Oncology (Beauchamps Rsch. fellow 1992), Assn. Women Surgeons, Assn. Acad. Surgery, New Eng. Cancer Soc., Boston Surg. Soc. Office: 725 Concord Ave Ste 3300 Cambridge MA 02138-1091

PORIES, WALTER JULIUS, surgeon, educator; b. Munich, Germany, Jan. 18, 1930; came to U.S., 1940; s. Theodore Francis and Frances (Lowin) P.; m. Muriel Helen Aronson, Aug. 18, 1951; children: Susan E., Mary Jane, Carolyn A., Kathy G.; m. Mary Ann Rose McCarthy, June 4, 1977; children: Mary Lisa, Michael McCarthy. BA, Wesleyan U., Middletown, Conn., 1952; MD with honors, U. Rochester, 1955. Diplomate: Am. Bd. Surgery, Am. Bd. Thoracic Surgery. Intern Strong Meml. Hosp., Rochester, N.Y., 1955-56, resident, 1958-62; chmn. dept. surgery Wright-Patterson AFB, Ohio, 1952-67; asst. prof. surgery and oncology U. Rochester, 1967-69; prof. surgery and assoc. chmn. dept. surgery Case Western Res. U., 1969-77; prof. surgery and biochemistry East Carolina U., Greenville, N.C., 1977—, chmn. dept. surgery, 1977-96; chief surgery Pitt County Meml. Hosp., 1977-96; prof. surgery U. Health Scis. of Uniformed Svcs., 1982—; founder, assoc. dir. Rochester Cancer Ctr., 1967-69; founder, dir. Cleve. Cancer Ctr., 1972-77, Hospice of Cleve., 1975; founder, chmn. bd. Hospice of Greenville, 1981; med. dir. Home Health Care of Greenville, 1978-83. Founder, chmn. bd. Ctr. for Creative Living, 1985-91; pres., chmn. Eastern Carolina Health Orgn. and Echo Mgmt. Orgn., 1994—; vis. scholar NIH, 1996; sec. treas., pres. N.C. Med. Bd., 1998-. Author: Clinical Applications of Zinc Metabolism, 1974; editor: Operative Surgery series, vols. 1-4, 1979-83, Office Surgery for Family Physicians, 1985; editor in chief Current Surgery, 1990—; editor Nat. Curriculum for Residency in Surgery, 1988—, mem. residency rev. com., 1992—; contbr. articles to profl. jours. Bd. dirs. Boy Scouts Am., Cleve., 1974-77, Greenville Arts Mus., 1980-82; pres., CEO, chmn. bd. dirs. Ea. Carolina Health Orgn.; bd. dirs. East Carolina Found. Maj. USAF, 1955-67; col. USAR, 1979-91, comdr. USAF Hosp., Durham, N.C.; activated Desert Shield, 1990. Decorated Legion of Merit; Thorndyke scholar, 1948-51; recipient McLester award USAF, 1966, Miss. Magnolia Cross, 1989, Presdl. citation for Desert Shield, 1994, O. Max Gardner award U. N.C. Bd. Govs., 2001; named to Hon. Order of Ky. Cols., 1965. Fellow ACS, Am. Coll. Cardiology, Am. Coll. Chest Physicians; mem. Soc. for Vascular Surgery, Soc. Surg. Oncology, Soc. Univ. Surgeons, Am. Surg. Assn., Soc. Environ. Geochemistry (past pres.), Residency Rev. Com. for Surgery (vice-chair 1992-98), So. Surg. Assn., Soc. for Thoracic Surgery, Ea. Carolina Health Orgn. (pres., chmn. bd. 1994-99), Assn. Programs Dirs. in Surgery (pres. 1995-96), N.C. Surg. Assn. (pres. 1995-96), Am. Soc. Bariatic Surgery (pres. 2002),Sigma Xi (O. Max Gardner prize), Phi Kappa Phi. Republican. Roman Catholic. Home: Deep Sun Farm 7464 NC 43 N Macclesfield NC 27852 Office: East Carolina U Dept Surgery Greenville NC 27858 E-mail: pories@aol.com.

PORILE, NORBERT THOMAS, chemistry educator; b. Vienna, Austria, May 18, 1932; came to U.S., 1947, naturalized, 1952; s. Irving and Emma Porile; m. Miriam Eisen, June 16, 1957; 1 son, James. BA, U. Chgo., 1952, MS, 1954, PhD, 1957. Rsch. assoc. Brookhaven Nat. Lab., Upton, N.Y., 1957-59, assoc. chemist, 1959-63, chemist, 1963-64; vis. prof. chemistry McGill U., 1963-65; assoc. prof. chemistry Purdue U., West Lafayette, Ind., 1965-69, prof. chemistry, 1969—. Rsch. collaborator Brookhaven Nat. Lab., Argonne Nat. Lab., Los Alamos Sci. Lab., Lawrence Berkeley Lab.; vis. prof. Facultes des Scis., Orsay, France; fellow Soc. Promotion of Sci. in Japan, Inst. Nuclear Study, U. Kyoto, 1961. Editor: Radiochemistry of the Elements and Radiochemical Techniques, 1986-90. John Simon Guggenheim meml. fellow Institut de Physique Nucleaire Orsay, 1971-72; recipient F.D. Martin Undergrad. Teaching award, 1977; Von Humboldt Sr. U.S. Scientist award Philipps U., Marburg, W. Ger., 1982 Mem. Am. Chem. Soc., Am. Phys. Soc. Office: Purdue U Dept Chemistry Chemistry Bldg Lafayette IN 47907 E-mail: porile@purdue.edu.

PORITZ, DEBORAH T. state supreme court chief justice, former attorney general; Atty. gen. State of N.J., 1994—96; chief justice Supreme Ct. N.J., Trenton, 1996—. Office: Supreme Ct NJ Hughes Justice Complex PO Box 23 Trenton NJ 08625-0023*

POROSOFF, HAROLD, chemist, research and development director; b. Bklyn., Apr. 3, 1946; s. Solomon and Ruth (Goldberg) P.; m. Leslie Pamela Freiman, May 19, 1948; children: Lauren, Stephen, Marc. BS, MIT, 1966; PhD, Brown U., 1970. Various rsch. and mgmt. positions fibers div. Am. Cyanamid Co., Stamford, Conn. and Milton, Fla., 1970-78, various mgmt. positions Shulton Rsch. div. Clifton, N.J., 1978-83, dir., 1983-88, v.p. R & D chem. rsch. divsn. Stamford, 1989-93; v.p. R & D Cytec Industries Inc., 1993-95; v.p., chief tech. officer Cytec Industries, Inc., 1995-98, cons., 1998—. Patentee in field. Mem. AAAS. Office: 22 Olmsted Rd Scarsdale NY 10583-2324 E-mail: hporosoff@hotmail.com.

PORRATA, SAMUEL M. education director, foreign language educator; b. San Juan, P.R., May 11, 1968; came to the U.S., 1997; s. Samuel Luis and Angeles Josefina Porrata; m. Sandra Porrata, Dec. 8, 2000. BA, Hofstra U., 1991; MA, Villanova U., 1993; PhD, Temple U., 1997. Part-time instr. Villanova (Pa.) U., 1991-93; lectr. Ursinus Coll., Collegeville, Pa., spring 1993; tchg. asst. Temple U., Phila., 1993-95; adj. instr. St. Joseph's U., 1995-96; instr. Temple U. Center City, 1996-97; lectr. U. Pa., 1996-98; instr. West Chester (Pa.) U., 1997-99; asst. prof. Spanish, dir. internat. edn. Fairmont (W.Va.) State Coll., 1999-2001; asst. prof. Spanish Shenandoah U., Winchester, Va., 2001—. Presenter in field. Editor: TPR Storytelling, 2000; author of poems. Mem. Ednl. Testing Svc., MLA, N.E. MLA, Am. Assn. Tchrs. Spanish and Portuguese, Faculty and Course Devel. in Internat. Studies, Nat. Assn. Fgn. Students Advisors, Internat. Soc. for Luso-Hispanic Humor, Sigma Delta Pi. Roman Catholic.

PORRATA-DORIA, RAFAEL ALFONSO, law educator; m. Christie Huddleston, Oct. 28, 1988; children: Rafael Jaime, Clara Isabel. BA in Polit. Sci. magna cum laude, MA in Polit. Sci., U. Pa., 1974; JD, Yale U., 1977. Bar: Pa. 1977, P.R. 1977, Fla. 1982, N.Y. 1984. Assoc. Dilworth, Paxson, Kalish & Kauffman, Phila., 1977-82, Valdes-Fauli, Richardson & Cobb, Miami, Fla., 1982-83; prof. law Temple U., Phila., 1983—. Vis. prof. law Rutgers U. Law Sch., Camden, N.J., 1993; cons. project on internat. insolvency Am. Law Inst., Phila., 1993—; cons. law and justice com. Senate of Pa., Harrisburg, 1985-88; cons. World Bank, 1995-97. Contbr. articles to profl. publs. Bd. dirs. Phila. Coun. for Cmty. Devel., 1984-86, Cmty. Legal Svcs., 1985-88, Regional Housing Legal Svcs., 1987-88, Police Athletic League Phila., 1983-91, Phila. Vols. for Indigent Program, 1986-89, 91-92, Eagleville Hosp., 1988—, Somerset Villas, Inc., 1988—, Eagleville Found., 1997—; mem. Mayor's Housing Partnership Coun., Phila., 1992-96; counsel Phila. Puerto Rican Week Festival Com., 1988; trustee Phila. Bar Found., 1986-88. Maj. JAG, USAR, 1988—. Mem. ABA (mem. commn. on opportunities to minorities in legal profession 1992-95, mem. exec. com. civil and human rights com. 1988-91, mem. internat. law com. 1988-90, standing com. on mil. law 1989-91), Phila. Bar Assn. (parliamentarian bd. govs. 1989-90, jud. selection and retention commn. 1985, investigative divsn. jud. selection and retention commn. 1992, chair internat. law com. 1986-87, chair mil. law com. 1992-95), Hispanic Nat. Bar Assn. (chair internat. com. 1987-88, regional v.p. 1983-84), Hispanic Bar Assn. of Pa. (pres. 1983-86), Assn. of Yale Alumni (v.p. 1996-98, pres. 1998-2000, immediate past pres. 2000—), Hispanic Assn. of Contractors and Enterprises (chair 1987—). Office: Temple U Sch of Law 1719 N Broad St Philadelphia PA 19122-6002 E-mail: porrata@aya.yale.edu.

PORRAZ, MAURICIO JIMENEZ LABORA, civil engineer, researcher; b. Mexico City, Mar. 24, 1938; s. Manuel Guillen Porraz and Dolores Jimenez Labora; m. Margarita Lando Coindreau, Oct. 1, 1966; children: Margarita, Mauricio, Miguel. BA, La Salle U., Mexico City, 1954; degree in civil engring. with honors, Autonomous Nat. U. Mex., Mexico City, 1961; degree in ocean engring., Assn. Orgn. des Stages France, Paris, 1964; degree in petroleum offshore engring., Assn. Coop. Technique Internat. Maritime, Marseille, France, 1968; postgrad., Nat. Engring. Acad., Mex., 1977, Corpus Christi, Toledo, Spain, 1988. Pres. Orgn. Submarina Mexicana, Mexico City, 1965-2001, Equipos y Tecnicas, Mexico City, 1967-2001, Control de Erosion, Mexico City, 1971-2001, Conersa, Mexico City, 1973-91, Estructuras Marinas Concreto, Mexico City, 1979-91, Constrn., Cons. y Comercializadora, Mexico City, 1991-2001, Soluciones Ecoambientales, 2000—. Engr. in geosyntetics, interlocked interconnected concrete blocks for breakwaters; patentee in field. Bd. dirs. Panam. Fedn. on Oceanic Coastal Engring., Stevens Inst. Tech., 1989; corr. mem. Royal Acad. Nice Arts and Hist. Scis., Toledo, 1989; mem. Royal Inst. Geography, Madrid, 1970-91. Lt. Mexican Infantry, 1956-57. Recipient Best Thesis in Yr. award Engring. Found. (Mex.), 1963, rsch. and invention medal Soc. for Rsch. and Invention (Paris), 1977, Internat. Coastal Engring. award ASCE, 1977, 91; named Man of Yr., Group Expansion Economy and Fins. Bus. (Mex.), 1983-84, Hon. Armed Knight Toledo, Spain, Knight Mil. and Hospitaller Order of St. Lazarus of Jerusalem, 1998. Fellow Mexican Assn. Architects and Engrs. (centenary 1968); mem. Venezuela's Engrs. Soc. (dir. A, goco award 1972), Panam. Fedn. Engring. Assn. (oceanic engring. com. 1981), Ctr. Profl. Actualization (prof. 1981), Mex. Acad. Engrs. Roman Catholic. Office: Acad Scis Gen Sec Pla Villa de Madrid # 3 06700 Mexico City Roma Mexico E-mail: mauricio@porraz.com., mporraz@hotmail.com.

PORRETTA, EMANUELE PETER, retired bank executive, consultant; b. N.Y.C., Aug. 4, 1942; s. Joseph Edward and Italia (Sesti) P.; m. Mary Valanzano, Apr. 18, 1964; children: Denise, Robert, Janice. Student, N.Y. Tech. Coll., 1960-61. Transfer clk. Mfrs. Trust Co., N.Y.C., 1961; sr. v.p. U.S. Trust Co. N.Y., 1984—, sr. v.p., dir. adminstrv. svcs., instn. asst. svcs. divsn., ret., 1996; cons. master trust and master custody adminstrn. and ops., 1997—; pres. E. Porretta Cons. Inc., N.J. Mem. payment system com. N.Y. Clearing House, 1978-80, chmn. Bank Ops. Conf., 1981-82. Treas. Manalapan, N.J. Rep. campaign, 1980; mem. adv. com. Williams Coll. Exec. Program. Mem. Am. Mgmt. Assn., Am. Bankers Assn. Roman Catholic. Avocations: running, reading, golf. E-mail: epporretta@aol.com.

PORRETTA, LOUIS PAUL, education educator; b. Malvern, Ohio, Sept. 24, 1926; s. Peter A. and Rosa (Tersigne) P.; B.A., Eastern Mich. U., 1950; Ed.M., Wayne State U., 1959, Ed.D., 1967; m. Elizabeth M. Murphy, Oct. 13, 1951; children—Leslie Elizabeth, Paul Louis, Jeffrey Mark. Tchr. elem. sch. Mason Consol. Sch., Erie, Mich., 1952-53, tchr., prin., 1953-54; prin. Mason Jr. High Sch., Erie, Mich., 1954-59; asst. prof. edn. Eastern Mich. U., Ypsilanti, 1959-62, assoc. prof., 1962-66, prof. edn., 1967-71, prof. dept. curriculum and instruction, 1974-83, prof. emeritus, 1983— , dir. Office Internat. Projects, 1979-81; dir., owner Sylvan Learning Ctr., Ann Arbor, Mich., 1984—; chief-of-party Nat. Tchr. Edn. Center, Somalia, 1967-70; mem. edn. survey team AID, Botswana, Lesotho and Swaziland, 1970, sr. adv. U. Botswana, Lesotho and Swaziland, 1972-74; campus coordinator Swaziland Primary Curriculum Devel. Project, AID, 1978; chief-of-party projects AID, Swaziland, 1975-78, Yemen, 1981-83. Chmn. March of Dimes, Westenaw County, Mich., 1956. Mem. Assn. Tchr. Educators, Inst. Internat. Edn., AAUP, ASCD, Phi Delta Kappa, Pi Gamma Mu. Club: Ypsilanti Rotary. Home: 2259 Woodview Ln Ann Arbor MI 48108-8917 Office: Sylvan Learning Ctr 1601 Briarwood Cir Ann Arbor MI 48108-1667

PORT, ARTHUR TYLER, retired government administrator, lawyer; b. Chgo., Oct. 4, 1916; s. Arthur Christopher and Helen Elizabeth (Brown) P.; m. Aline Helen Gooding, Oct. 21, 1950; children: Cynthia Helen, Christopher Tyler. BA cum laude, Davidson Coll., 1937; JD, Yale U., 1940; LLD, Coll. Advanced Sci., 1962. Bar: N.C. 1940. Law practice, Winston-Salem, N.C., 1940-41; radio announcer Sta. WMRF, Lewistown, Pa., 1941-43; civil atty. Judge Adv. div. Hdqrs. European Command, U.S. Army, Frankfurt, Germany, 1946-47; chief policy sect. Mil. Justice Div., 1947-48; legal asst. to spl. advisor to comdr.-in-chief ETO and mil. govt. Germany, 1949; spl. counsel Sec. of Army, 1949-50, spl. asst., 1950-55; dep. dir. office NSC Affairs Office Sec. Def., 1955-56; exec. asst. to asst. sec. def. ISA, 1956-57; dir. office of security policy and dir. indsl. pers. access authorization Office Asst. Sec. Defense, 1957-61; dep. asst. sec. logistics/installatons and logistics Dept. of Army, 1961-67; fgn. ser. res. officer Dept. of State, 1967-73; asst. sec. gen. def. support NATO, Brussels, 1967-73; spl. asst. Asst. Sec. of Army for Energy Policy, 1973-74; dep. for supply, maintenance and transp. Office Asst. Sec. Army, 1974. Cons. NATO affairs Stanford Rsch. Inst., Gen. Rsch. Corp., Logistics Mgmt. Inst., 1975-81. With USAAC, 1942-45, USASIGC, 1945-46, ETO, lt. col. USAR, 1946-68. Recipient Meritorious Civilian Svc. award Dept. Army, 1953, decoration for exceptional civilian svc., 1967; Disting. Civilian Svc. award Dept. Def., 1961. Mem. Confrerie de Chevaliers du Tastevin (Cote d'Or, France), Kenwood Golf and Country Club (Bethesda, Md.), Scabbard and Blade, Omicron Delta Kappa, Sigma Upsilon, Eta Sigma Phi, Phi Gamma Delta, Alpha Phi Epsilon. Home: Falcons Landing 20504 Langley Dr Sterling VA 20165-3571 E-mail: atport@att.net.

PORT, SIDNEY CHARLES, mathematician, educator; b. Chgo., Nov. 27, 1935; s. Isadore and Sarah (Landy) P.; m. Idelle Jackson, Mar. 24, 1957; children— Ethan, Jonathan, Daniel. AB, Northwestern U., 1957, MS, 1958, PhD, 1962. Staff mathematician Rand Corp., 1962-66; asso. prof. math. U. Calif. at Los Angeles, 1966-69, prof., 1969—. Author: (with P. Hoel and C. Stone) Probability, Statistics and Stochastic Processes, 1971, (with C. Stone) Brownian Motion and Classical Potential Theory, 1978, Theoretical Probability for Applications, 1993; contbr. articles to profl. jours. Fellow Inst. Math. Statistics; mem. Am. Math. Soc. Home: 680 Kingman Ave Santa Monica CA 90402-1334 Office: UCLA Dept Math Los Angeles CA 90024 E-mail: sport@ucla.edu.

PORT, STANLEY ROBERT, civil engineer, data management engineer; b. Belfast, Northern Ireland, Aug. 27, 1938; s. Robert and Mary (Christie) P.; m. Elizabeth Beattie, July 8, 1961; children: Julia Anne, Rosemary Elizabeth, Karin Louise. BSc in Engring. with I honors, Queens U., Belfast, 1960, PhD, 1964. Asst. lectr. civil engring. Queens U., Belfast, 1960-64; from asst. design engr. to asst. resident engr. Scott Wilson Kirkpatrick & Ptnrs., Glasgow, Scotland, 1964-66; head R & D Sir Frederick Snow & Ptnrs., London, 1966-79; project chief engr. Arabian Coop. Co., Riyadh, Saudia Arabia, 1979-80; pvt. practice Surrey, Eng., 1980-94; sr. cons. product data mgmt. CIMdata, Eng., 1995-99; pvt. practice, 1999—. Vis. prof. civil engring. Queens U., Belfast, 1985-87, vis. prof. sch. built environment, 1998—. Author: Computer-Aided Design for Construction, 1984, The Management of CAD for Construction, 1989, Market for CAD Systems in Europe, 1988, Engineering Data Management: Implementation Strategies in Europe, 1990, Product Data Management Case Studies 1996, Business Appraisal Guide for Product Data Management, 1997. Fellow Inst. Civil Engrs. (Telford Premium award 1993), Inst. Structural Engrs., Royal Soc. Arts; mem. Brit. Computer Soc. (chartered info. systems engr.). Avocations: long-distance running, walking, travel, painting, golf. Office: Dr Stanley Port 44 Busbridge Ln GU7 1QD Godalming England E-mail: stanley@s-port.com.

PORT, STEVEN CHARLES, cardiologist, educator; b. N.Y.C., Nov. 23, 1947; m. Karen Port; children: Jesse, Michelle. MD, Mt. Sinai Sch. Medicine, 1972. Diplomate Am. Bd. Internal Medicine, Am. Bd. Cardiovascular Disease, Am. Bd. Nuclear Cardiology. Intern, resident Mt. Sinai Hosp., N.Y.C., 1973-75; fellow in cardiology Duke U. Med. Ctr., 1975-79, rsch. assoc. medicine, 1979-80; asst. prof. medicine U. N.C., Chapel Hill, 1980-82, Sinai Samaritan Med. Ctr.-U. Wis. Med. Sch., Milw., 1982-86, assoc. prof., 1986-92, prof., 1992-95, clin. prof., 1995—; pvt. practice cardiology, 1995—. Active staff St. Luke's Med. Ctr., Sinai Samaritan Med. Ctr.; courtesy staff St. Francis Hosp., Waukesha (Wis.) Meml. Hosp., St. Agnes Hosp., West Allis (Wis.) Meml. Hosp., St. Mary's Hosp., St. Michael Hosp.; mem. cardiovascular task force Prime Care, Inc., 1993—. Contbr. articles to profl. jours. and chpts. to books; spkr. in field. Grantee Mt. Sinai Med. Ctr. Found., 1985-86. Fellow Am. Coll. Cardiology; mem. Am. Heart Assn., Am. Soc. Nuc. Cardiology (bd. dirs., treas. 1996—). Avocation: aviation. Office: Cardiovascular Assoc Ltd 2901 W Kk River Pkwy Ste 300 Milwaukee WI 53215-3660 E-mail: sport@cva-ltd.com.

PORTA, EDUARDO ANGEL, pathology educator, researcher; b. Dec. 12, 1924; came to U.S., 1957; s. Carlos Angel and Pilar (Palo) P.; m. Marta Dominga Cerretini, Dec. 12, 1955; children: Eduardo Dante, Amiel Carlos, Lydia Carmen. MD, U. Buenos Aires, 1952. Intern Children's Hosp., Buenos Aires, 1952-56; resident Barnes Hosp., St. Louis, 1957-58; instr. pathology Washington U., 1958-60; chief pathology dept. Inst. Biol. Medicine, Buenos Aires, 1960-61; rsch. assoc. Union U., Albany, N.Y., 1960-63; assoc. scientist Hosp. for Sick Children, Toronto, Ont., Can., 1963-70; prof., chmn. U. Buenos Aires, 1970-71; prof. pathology Sch. Medicine, U. Hawaii, Honolulu, 1971—. Author chpts. and articles in sci. jours. and books. Recipient 30 rsch. awards including Life Ins. Med. Rsch. Fund, 1958-60, Med. Rsch. Coun., Toronto, 1963-70, USPHS-NIH, 1975—; Outstanding Cmty. Svc. award Govt. of Hawaii, 1983. Mem. U.S. and internat. sci and med. socs. Office: Dept Pathology Sch Medicine Univ Hawaii 1960 E West Rd Honolulu HI 96822-2319 E-mail: porta@hawaii.edu.

PORTA, SIENA GILLANN, sculptor, scenic artist; b. N.Y.C., Nov. 5, 1951; d. Vincent Anthony Porta and Barbara Ann Gill Porta Hutchinson; m. Robert Christopher Dell, May 30, 1986; 1 child, Malcolm Vincent Dell. BS in Studio Arts, Bklyn. Coll., CUNY, 1977; MFA in Sculpture, Pa. State U., 1979. Sci. illustrator Columbia U./Lamont-Doherty Geol. Obs., Palisades, NY, 1980-87; scenic artist Saturday Night Live, N.Y.C., 1986-89, Met. Opera, N.Y.C., 1987-92; master scenic artist numerous Broadway prodns., 1992—; adj. prof. contemporary arts Ramapo Coll., 2000—; adj. prof. of art St. Thomas Aquinas, Sparkill, NY, 2000—. Exhibited works in solo shows at Noho Gallery, NY, 2002, 14 Sculptors Gallery, N.Y.C., 1984, 85, 88, 90, Mid-Hudson Arts and Sci. Ctr., Poughkeepsie, N.Y., 1992, 93, Dominican Coll., Blauvelt, N.Y., 1980,; group shows at Terrain Gallery, N.Y.C., 1984, Am. Cultural Ctr., Reykiavik, Iceland, 1988, Notre Dame U., South Bend, Ind., 1990, Lehigh U., Phila., Blue Hill Cult. Ctr., Pearl River., N.Y., 1995, Eighth Floor Gallery, N.Y.C., 1996, New Jersey City U., Jersey City, N.J., Nassau Cmty. Coll., Garden City, N.Y., The Interchurch Ctr., Riverside Dr., N.Y., 1998, Galleri Ofeigur, 2001, Xloho Gallery, 2001, 2002, Snaefelsness Regl. Museum, 2002, Hafnarborg Museum, 2002, others; represented in collections at Fulbright Commn., Reykjavik, Bergen C.C., Paramus, N.J., 1988, St. Philip R. C. Ch., Norwalk, Conn.; represented by 14 Sculptors Gallery, N.Y., 1982-96, Art South, Phila., 1991—, Seraphim Gallery, N.J., 1988—, A.B. Condon Gallery, N.Y., 1980-83, 14 Sculptors Inc., N.Y., 1996—, others; author, "Spray Metal" Maquette Journal, 1992; subject of video Me and The Mirror, 1990. Pa. State Arts Coun./Hershey Med. Coll. grantee, 1978-79; N.Y. State Coun. on the Arts grantee, 1986; USIA-Ptnrs. of Ams. travel grant to St. Lucia, W.I., 1992, NY Fdn. for the Arts grantee, 2002. Mem. Zen Ctr. of San Diego. Home: PO Box 46 Palisades NY 10964-0046

PORTAL, GILBERT MARCEL ADRIEN, oil company executive; b. Paris, Aug. 2, 1930; came to U.S., 1982; s. Emmanuel Jules and Henriette Josephine (Bonnard) P.; m. Monique Janine Adam, July 12, 1951; children: Dominique, Veronique, Marc-Emmanuel. Baccalaureate, Lycee Charlemagne U., Paris, 1949; Ingenieur Civil des Mines, Sch. of Mines, St. Etienne, 1955; diplome du C.P.A., Ctr. Advanced Bus., Paris, 1969; auditeur 30 eme session IHEDN, Higher Studies Nat. Defense, Paris, 1978. Geophysicist Societe Nationale Elf Aquitaine, Sahara, Algeria, 1957-63, exploration mgr. north sea, 1963-65, dep. exec. v.p. Europe, 1965-68, dep. exec. v.p. North and South Am., 1968-70, chief exec. officer Iraq, 1970-72, dir., chief exec. officer Africa, 1972-76, dep. exec. v.p. hydrocarbons, 1976-78, exec. v.p. North Africa, Mid. East, Far East, 1978-82; pres. Elf Aquitaine Petroleum, Houston, 1982-89; chmn., chief exec. officer Elf Exploration, Inc., 1989-90; sec.-gen. European Petroleum Industry Assn., 1990-95; ptnr. G.M.H. Internat. Oil and Gas Consulting, Paris, 1995—; pres. internat. devel. Howard Energy Internat. LLC, 1999—2002. Served to lt. French Army, 1955-57. Decorated Legion of Honor (France), Nat. Merit Order (France); Equatorial Star (Gabon). Mem. Cercle Royal Gaulois Artistique et Littéraire. Roman Catholic. E-mail: gportalgmh@compuserve.com.

PORTE, JOEL MILES, English educator; b. Bklyn., Nov. 13, 1933; s. Jacob I. and Frances (Derison) P.; m. Ilana D'Ancona, June 17, 1962 (div. 1977); 1 child, Susanna Maria; m. Helene Sophrin, Oct. 18, 1985. AB magna cum laude, CCNY, 1957; A.M., Harvard U., 1958, PhD, 1962. Instr. English Harvard U., Cambridge, Mass., 1962-64, asst. prof., 1964-68, assoc. prof., 1968-69, prof., 1969-82, Bernbaum prof. of lit., 1982-87, chmn. English and Am. Lit. Dept., 1985-87; Frederic J. Whiton prof. of English Cornell U., Ithaca, N.Y., 1987-89, Ernest I. White prof. Am. Studies and Humane Letters, 1989—. Vis. lectr. Am. Studies Research Ctr., Hyderabad, India, spring 1976. Author: Emerson and Thoreau: Transcendentalists in Conflict, 1966, The Romance in America: Studies in Cooper, Poe, Hawthorne, Melville and James, 1969, Representative Man: Ralph Waldo Emerson in His Time, 1979, In Respect to Egotism: Studies in American Romantic Writing, 1991; editor: Emerson in His Journals, 1982, Emerson: Prospect and Retrospect, 1982, Emerson: Essays and Lectures, 1983, New Essays on Portrait of a Lady, 1990, A Cambridge Companion to Ralph Waldo Emerson (with Saundra Morris), 1999, Emerson's Prose and Poetry: A Norton Critical Edit. (with Saundra Morris), 2000. Scholar in Residence, Rockefeller Found., Bellagio, Italy, 1979; fellow John Simon Guggenheim Found., 1981-82. Mem. Am. Studies Assn., Am. Lit. Assn., Phi Beta Kappa. Home: 604 Mitchell St Ithaca NY 14850-4917 E-mail: jp26@cornell.edu.

PORTÉ, THIERRY GEORGES, investment banker; b. N.Y.C., June 28, 1957; s. Michel and Huguette (Barbot) P.; m. Yasko Tashiro, Dec. 28, 1985; children: Jun Olivier, Aya Catherine, Kiko Adeline. BA, Harvard U., 1978, MBA, 1982. Exec. asst. Chem. Bank, Paris, 1978-79; analyst Morgan Stanley & Co. Inc., N.Y.C., 1979-80, assoc., 1982-83, Morgan Stanley Internat., Tokyo, 1983-85, mng. dir. London, 1985-93, Morgan Stanley Japan, Tokyo, 1993-95, pres., 1995—. Baker scholar Harvard Bus. Sch., 1982. Mem. Phi Beta Kappa. Roman Catholic. Avocations: reading, opera. Office: Morgan Stanley Japan Yebisu Garden Place Tower Shibuya-ku Tokyo 150 Japan

PORTEOUS, SKIPP, private investigator, writer; b. Hartford, Conn., Feb. 7, 1944; s. Charles Robert and Marian Berle (Guy) P.; m. Linda Marie Silvernail, Mar. 25, 1965 (div. Feb. 1977) children: Angela Monique, Charles Mark, Marylisa; m. Barbara Ann Simon, May 1, 1983 (div. June 2002). Student, Life Bible Coll., L.A., 1966-67, East L.A. C.C., 1969, Columbia Green C.C., Greenport, N.Y., 1978. Ordained to ministry Elim Fellowship, 1968; cert. radio mktg. cons. Licensed private investigator, Mass., N.Y. Evangelist Chapel on the Strip, Hollywood, Calif., 1967-68; pastor Pasadena (Calif.) Christian Fellowship, 1968-74, West Copake (N.Y.) Reformed Ch., 1974-76, Agape House Christian Ctr., Hillsdale, N.Y., 1976-77; sales exec., promoter various radio stas. and newspapers, N.Y., Mass., 1977-84; pres. Inst. for First Amendment Studies, Inc., Gt. Barrington, Mass., 1984—; pvt. investigator, owner Sherlock Investigations, N.Y. and Mass., 1998—. Radio and TV talk show guest, nationwide, 1986—; rschr. TV news networks, mags. Author: Jesus Doesn't Live Here Anymore-From Fundamentalist to Freedom Writer, 1991; co-author: Challenging, The Christian Right - The Activist's Handbook; author mag. articles, columns. Elim fellow. Democrat. Jewish. Avocations: photography, oil painting. E-mail: skipp@sherlockinvestigations.com.

PORTER, ALAN LESLIE, industrial and systems engineering educator; b. Jersey City, June 22, 1945; s. Leslie Frank and Alice Mae (Kaufman) P.; m. Claudia Loy Ferrey, June 14, 1968; children: Brett, Doug, Lynn. BSChemE, Calif. Inst. Tech., 1967; MS, UCLA, 1968, PhD in Psychology, 1972. Rsch. assoc., asst. prof. program social mgmt. tech. U. Wash., Seattle, 1972-74; asst. prof. indsl. and systems engring. Ga. Inst. Tech., Atlanta, 1975-78, assoc. prof., 1979-85, prof., 1986—, dir. tech. policy and assessment ctr., 1989—2001, prof. pub. policy, 1990—2001, prof. emeritus, 2001—, co-dir. tech policy and assessment ctr., 2002—; dir. rsch. and devel. Search Tech., Inc., Norcross, 2002—. Cons. Search Tech., IBM, Coca Cola, Rexam, SAIC, SRI. Author, editor: (with others) A Guidebook for Technology Assessment and Impact Analysis, 1980, Interdisciplinarity, 1986, Impact of Office Automation on Clerical Employment, 1985, Forecasting and Management of Technology, 1991, (with Wm. Read) Information Revolution: Present and Future Consequences, 1998, Environmental Methods Review, 1998. NSF grantee, 1974-75, 78-86, 89—, Dept. Transp. grantee, 1977-79. Mem. Internat. Assn. Impact Assessment (co-founder, sec. 1981-87, exec. dir. 1987-90, pres. 1995-96), IEEE Systems Man and Cybernetics Soc. (chmn. tech. forecasting com., Bellcore adv. coun.). Home: 110 Lake Top Ct Roswell GA 30076-3017 Office: Sch Indsl and Systems Engring Ga Tech Atlanta GA 30332-0001 E-mail: alan.porter@isge.gatech.edu.

PORTER, ANDREW CALVIN, educational administrator, psychology educator; b. Huntington, Pa., July 10, 1942; s. Rutherford and Grace (Johnson) P.; m. Susan Porter, June 5, 1967; children: Matthew, Anna, John, Joe, Kate. BS, Ind. State U., 1963; MS, U. Wis., 1965, PhD, 1967. Prof., co-dir. inst. rsch. on teaching Mich. State U., East Lansing, 1967-88; assoc. dir. basic skills group Nat. Inst. Edn., Washington, 1975-76; Anderson-Bascom prof. edn., prof. ednl. psychology, dir. Wis. Ctr. Edn. Rsch. U. Wis., Madison, 1988—. Vis. asst. prof. Ind. State U., Terre Haute, 1967; mem. adv. bd. Am. Jour. Edn., 1988—; chair bd. Internat. Studies, Nat. Acad. Scis., Nat. Rsch. Coun., 1993-2001; chmn. U.S. Dept. Edn., adv. coun. on edn. stats., 1994-2001. Author: Brookings Papers on Education Policy, 1998. Bd. dirs. Madison Urban League, 1992-96. Recipient Disting. Alumni award, Ind. U., 1994, award, U.S. Dept. Edn. Mem. Am. Ednl. Rsch. Assn. (pres. 2001), Nat. Coun. Edn. Measurement, Nat. Coun. Tchrs. Math., Psychometric Soc., Nat. Acad. Edn., Phi Delta Kappa (life). Office: U Wis Madison Wis Ctr Edn Rsch 1025 W Johnson St Madison WI 53706-1706 E-mail: andyp@education.wisc.edu.

PORTER, ARTHUR T. oncologist, educator, medical administrator; b. June 11, 1956; m. Pamela Porter; 4 children. Student, U. Sierra Leone, 1974-75; BA in Anatomy, Cambridge U., 1978, MB, BChir, MD, 1980, MA, 1984; DMRT, Royal Coll. Radiologists, Eng., 1985; postgrad., U. Alta., 1984-86; FRCPC, Royal Coll. Physicians and Surgeons, Can., 1986; cert. for physicians mgr. program, U. Toronto, 1990; MBA, U. Tenn., 1998. Lic., bd. cert., Mich., Can., Eng.; diplomate Health Care Adminstrn. House physician gen. medicine Norfolk and Norwich Hosp., Eng., 1981; house surgeon gen. surgery New Addenbrookes Hosp., Cambridge, Eng., 1981-82; sr. house officer clin. hematology No. Gen. Hosp., Sheffield, Eng., 1982; sr. house officer gen. medicine Huntington County Hosp., Hinchingbrooke Hosp., Eng., 1982-83; sr. house officer radiotherapy and oncology Norfolk and Norwich Hosp., Norwich, 1983-84; chief resident radiation oncology Cross Cancer Inst., Edmonton, Alta., Can., 1984-86, from radiation oncologist to sr. radiation oncologist Can., 1986-87, sr. radiation oncologist Can., 1987; asst. prof. medicine U. Alta., 1987, assoc. clin. prof. dept. surgery faculty medicine, 1988; head divsn. radiation oncology U. Western Ont., London, Can., 1988; cons. radiation oncologist, chief dept. radiation oncology London Regional Cancer Ctr., 1988, program dir. radiation oncology, 1989-91; chmn. dept. oncology Victoria Hosp. Corp., London, 1990; assoc. prof. dept. oncology U. Western Ont., 1990; program dir. radiation oncology Wayne State U., Detroit, 1991-92; prof., chmn. dept. radiation oncology Wayne State U. Sch. Medicine, 1991-99; chief Gershenson Radiation Oncology Ctr. Harper Hosp., 1991-99; radiation oncologist-in-chief Detroit Med. Ctr., 1991-99; pres., CEO Radiation Oncology R & D Ctr., Detroit, 1991-99; dir. multidisciplinary svcs. Meyer L. Prentice Comprehensive Cancer Ctr., 1992-99; chmn. radiation oncology Grace Hosp., 1993-99; assoc. dean Wayne State U. Sch. Medicine, 1998—. Pres., CEO Detroit Med. Ctr.; sr. v.p. Detroit Med. Ctr. Author: (with others) Fundamental Problems in Breast Cancer, 1985, Therapeutic Progress in Urological Cancers, 1988, Proceedings of the Consensus Meeting of the Treatment of Bladder Cancer-1987, 1988, Brachytherapy, 1989, High and Low Dose Rate Brachytherapy, 1989, Brachytherapy of Prostate Cancer, 1991; co-editor Treatment of Cancer, 1991—; assoc. editor Can. Jour. Oncology, 1990—, Antibody and Radiopharmaceuticals, 1992—; contbr. articles to profl. jours. Recipient Nat. award Sierra Leone, 1975-80, Commonwealth Found. scholarship, 1980, Best Doctor in Am. award, 1992, 93, 94, 95, 96, 97, 98, Testimonial Resolution, City of Detroit, 1993, Wayne County, 1993, Mich., 1997. Fellow Am. Coll. Angiology, Detroit Acad. Medicine, Royal Soc. Medicine, Royal Coll. Radiology, Am. Coll. Radiation Oncology (chancellor 1994-97); mem. AMA (Physicians Recognition award 1986), Am. Soc. Therapeutic Radiation Oncology, Am. Radium Soc., Am. Soc. Clin. Oncology, Am. Coll. Oncol. Adminstrs. (pres. 1994-96), Am. Acad. Med Adminstrs., Am. Endocurietherapy Soc. (pres. 1994-95), Mich. State Med. Soc., Mich. Soc. Therapeutic Radiation Oncology, Mich. Radiol. Soc. Detroit Med. Soc. (Ann. award for Excellence 1993), Wayne County Med. Soc., European Soc. Therapeutic Radiation Oncology, Brit. Inst. Radiology, Can. Oncology Soc., Can. Assn. Radiation Oncology, Royal Coll. Radiologists, Sierra Leone Med. and Dental Assn., Greater Detroit C. of C., Sigma Xi. Achievements include patent in a perineal applicator; research in novel methods in delivery dose, brachytherapy, intraoperative therapy, unsealed source therapy, verification and dosimetry, real time portal imaging, three-dimensional and planning, unsealed source dosimetry, the design of perineal applicators. Office: Detroit Med Ctr 3663 Woodward Ave Ste 200 Detroit MI 48201-2400 E-mail: ceo@dmc.org.

PORTER, BERNARD HARDEN, consulting physicist, author, publisher; b. Porter Settlement, Maine, Feb. 14, 1911; s. Lewis Harden and Etta Flora (Rogers) P.; m. Helen Elaine Hendron, July 15, 1946 (div. Aug. 1947); m. Margaret Eudine Preston, Aug. 27, 1955 (dec. April 1975); m. Lula Mae Blom, Sept. 9, 1976 (div. Nov. 1986). BS, Colby Coll., 1932; MS, Brown U., 1933; DSc (hon.), Inst. Advanced Thinking, Calais, Maine, 1959. Physicist Acheson Colloids Corp., Port Huron, Mich., 1935-40; rsch. physicist Manhattan Dist. Engrs., Princeton, N.J., Berkeley, Calif. and Oak Ridge, 1940-45; cons. physicist San Francisco and Pasadena, Calif., Waldwick, N.J., Rockland, Belfast, Maine, 1945—; chmn. bd. Bern Porter Inc., Pasadena, Rockland, Belfast, 1945—; pres. Bern Porter Books, 1929—, Bern Porter Internat., Belfast, 1974—. Cons. Internat. Exec. Service Corps, 1968, SBA, 1968-88. Author: The 14th of February, 1971, I've Left, 1971, Founds, 1972, Hand Coated Chocolates, 1972, Contemporary Italian Painters, 1973, Trattoria Due Forni, 1973, The Book of Do's, 1974, The Manhattan Telephone Book, 1975, Run-On, 1975, Where, 1975, Selected Founds, 1975, Gee-Whizzles, 1976, Don't Book, 1981, Last Acts, 1985, My, My, 1985, Left Leg, 1988, Neverends, 1988, Numbers, 1989, Sweetend, 1989, Bern Porter and Fa Gaga, 1990, Sounds That Arouse Me, 1992, Less Than Overweight, 1992, Mothering Time, 1993; contbr. numerous articles to profl. jours. Rep. candidate for gov. Maine, 1969; bd. dirs. Inst. Advanced Thinking, Belfast, chmn. bd., 1959—. Recipient awards PEN, 1975, 76, 77, Authors League, 1977; Carnegie author, 1975; diploma merit Centro Studi E Scambi Internazionale, Rome, 1976; Nat. Endowment for Arts lit. award, 1979. Fellow Am. Astronautical Soc., Tech. Pub. Soc., Am. Rocket Soc. (assoc.), Soc. Tech. Writers and Pubs. (assoc.), Internat. Acad. Poets (London, founding); mem. Am. Phys. Soc., Soc. Internat. Devel., Nat. Soc. Programmed Instrn., Fenway Club (Boston), Algonquin Club, St. Andrews Club (N.B., Can.), Phi Beta Kappa, Sigma Xi, Kappa Phi Kappa, Chi Gamma Sigma. Roman Catholic. Address: 50 Salmond St Belfast ME 04915-6111

PORTER, BETH RUTHERFORD, social worker; b. Shreveport, La., June 30, 1950; d. Paul Joseph and Annabelle (Hall) Rutherford; m. Don L. Porter, Aug. 10, 1979; children: Cassidy, Shannon. BA, Northeast La. U., 1972; MSW, La. State U., 1975. Children's caseworker La. Dept. Family Svcs., Shreveport, 1972-73, 74-75; dir. social work Beverly Hills Psychiat. Hosp., Dallas, 1975-77; pvt. practice social work Human Devel. Ctr., 1977; med. and psychiat. social worker St. Paul Hosp., 1977-80; med. social worker Vis. Nurses Assn., Kaufman, Tex., 1980; social work cons. Nat. Living Ctrs., Houston, 1981; psychiat. social worker Terrell (Tex.) State Hosp., 1982; EAP The Allen Group-AT&T, Shreveport, 1986—; pvt. practice social work, 1987—. Employee assistance program cons., Shreveport and Marshall, Tex., 1986—. Explorer leader Shreveport area Boy Scouts Am., 1973; mem. sch. bd. St. Joseph Cath. Sch., Marshall, 1990. Mem. NASW, Employee Assistance Profls. Assn. Avocation: cattle ranch management. Home: RR 2 Box 526 Marshall TX 75672-9651 Office: 9300 Mansfield Rd Ste 109 Shreveport LA 71118-3137 Also: 9300 Mansfield Rd Ste 202 Shreveport LA 71118-3137

PORTER, BLAINE ROBERT MILTON, sociology and psychology educator; b. Morgan, Utah, Feb. 24, 1922; s. Brigham Ernest and Edna (Brough) P.; m. Elizabeth Taylor, Sept 27, 1943 (dec.); children: Claudia Black, Roger B., David T., Patricia A. Hintze, Corinna; m. Myrna Katherine Kennedy, Feb. 26, 1988. Student, Utah State U., 1940-41; BS, Brigham Young U., 1947, MA, 1949; PhD (Grant Found. fellow family life edn. 1951-52), Cornell U., 1952. Instr. sociology Iowa State Coll., 1949-51; asst. prof. sociology and child devel. Iowa State U., 1952-55; prof., chmn. dept. human devel. and family relationships Brigham Young U., 1955-65, dean Coll. Family Living, 1966-80, Univ. prof., 1980-87. Vis. prof. Fulbright rsch. scholar U. London, 1965-66; vis. prof. U Wurzberg, 1980, 81, 83; facilitator human rels. workshops for the Human Devel. Inst., Denver, 1988-90, pres./CEO Families for Children Internat., Inc., 2001—. Editor: The Latter-day Saint Family, 1963, rev. edit., 1966; editor quar. jour.: Family Perspective, 1966-82; contbr. articles to profl. jours. Pres. elect Iowa Coun. Family Rels., 1954-55; pres. Utah Coun. Family Rels., 1957-58; chmn. sect. marriage counseling Nat. Coun. Family Rels., 1958-59, bd. dirs., 1957-60, exec. com., 1958-72, pres., 1963-64; bd. dirs. Am. Family Soc., 1975-85. Pilot USAAF, 1942-45. Recipient Prof. of Yr. award Brigham Young U., 1964. Mem. Am. Home Econs. Assn. (vice chmn. sect. family relations and child devel. 1955-56), Am. Sociol. Assn. (sec. sect. on family 1964-67), Am. Assn. Marriage and Family Therapy, Am. Psychol. Assn., Soc. Research in Child Devel., Sigma Xi, Phi Kappa Phi (chpt. pres. 1969-71) Home: 1675 Pine Ln Provo UT 84604-2163 Office: 4505 HBLL Brigham Young U Provo UT 84602

PORTER, BONNIE, artist, photographer; b. Mar. 26, 1959; BA in English and Photojournalism, Boston U., 1981; postgrad., Mass. Coll. Art, Boston, 1987; student, Sch. Mus. Fine Art, 1986-87. Guest lectr. Sch. of Mus. Fine Arts, Boston, 1988—; guest instr., 1989. One women show Gallery 22P, Boston, 1994, Howard Yezerski Gallery, Boston, 2000; group shows include Simmons Coll., Boston, 1989, Attleboro Mus., Mass., 1992, Danforth Mus., Framingham, Mass., (purchase award), 1992, 88 Room, Boston, 1994, Mus. Fine Arts, Boston, 1995, Fuller Art Mus., 1996, Photog. Resource Ctr., 1996, DeCordova Mus., Lincoln, Mass., 1997, Inst. Contemporary Art, Boston, 1998, Bellevue (Wash.) Art Mus., 1999, Sotheby's Art Link 2000, Tel Aviv, Vienna, Chgo., Fogg Art Mus., Harvard U., 2000, Exit Art, N.Y.C., 2002. Recipient Finalist award The Artist Found., 1991, Maud Morgan Purchase prize, 1995; St. Botolph Artist fellow, 1996. Studio: 1551 Cliff Dr Los Angeles CA 90065-1803 E-mail: bpfoto@yahoo.com.

PORTER, BRIAN STANLEY, state legislator; b. May 2, 1938; s. Jack D. and Margaret I. (Tuter) P.; m. Bette K. WSchakohl, Apr. 26, 1958; children: Kelle, Kerry, Kory. Grad., U. Alaska, 1970, Northwestern U. Traffic Inst., 1970-71, FBI Nat. Exec. Inst., 1981. With Anchorage Police Dept., 1960-87, chief of police, 1980-87; mem. Alaska Ho. of Reps., 1987—. Chmn. Alaska Police Stds. Coun., 1978-80; chmn. Ho. Jud. com. Served with U.S. Army, 1957-58. Office: Alaska State Legis 716 W 4th Ave Ste 300 Anchorage AK 99501-2107*

PORTER, BRUCE JACKMAN, military engineer, computer software engineer, application developer, investment broker, civil engineer; b. El Paso, Tex., Aug. 7, 1954; s. Covington Baskin and Carolyn Fee (Bruce) P.; m. Jeanette Anne Brown, Oct. 19, 1985; children: Laura, Holly, Travis. BS, US Mil. Acad., 1976; MS in Computer Sci., MS in Civil Engring., Stanford U., 1985; grad., U.S. Army War Coll., 1997. Engr. in tng., Pa. Commd. 1st lt. U.S. Army, 1979-80, advanced through grades to lt. col., 1993, co-commdr. 17th armored engr. bn. Tex., 1977-80, constrn. engr. Misawa, Japan, 1981-83, orgnl. evaluator Ft. Leavenworth, Kans., 1989-90, ops. officer 5th engr. combat bn. Saudi Arabia and Iraq, 1990-91; assoc. prof. mathematics U.S. Mil. Acad., West Point, N.Y., 1985-88; chief concepts officer USA Engr. Sch., Ft. Leonard Wood, Mo., 1991-93; logistics assistance officer 1st Cavalry Divsn., Ft. Hood, Tex., 1993-94; comdg. officer 20th Engr. Bn., 1st Cavalry Divsn., 1994-96; sr. engr. trainer Nat. Tng. Ctr., Ft. Irwin, Calif., 1997-98; cmdr., engr. brigade 4th Infantry Divn., Ft. Hood, Tex., 1998—99; exec. officer Army chief of staff for ops. Pentagon, Washington, 1999—2001; investment rep. Edward Jones & Co., Buellton, Calif., 2001—. Pioneer new courses in computer theory and discrete math. U.S. Mil. Acad., 1987-88; proponent Army Engr. Restructive Initiative, 1991-92; panel mem. Army Study Team for Battle Dynamics, 1992; mem. Summer Study for Chief of Staff of Army, 1992. Co-author: Army Keystone Operations Field Manual, 1993; pub. papers on combat engr. reorgn., 1991-92, 98. Decorated DSM, Bronze Star, Legion of Merit. Home: 262 Meadow Rd Buellton CA 93427 Office: 175-H McMurray Rd 93427

PORTER, BURTON FREDERICK, philosophy educator, writer, dean; b. N.Y.C., June 22, 1936; s. John and Doris (Neloway) P.; m. Susan Jane Porter, May 10, 1966 (div. 1974); 1 child, Anastasia; m. Barbara Taylor Metcalf, Dec. 31, 1980; 1 child, Mark Graham. BA Philosophy cum laude, spl. lit. hons., U. Md., 1959; PhD, St. Andrews U., Scotland, 1968; postgrad., Oxford (Eng.) U. Asst. prof. philosophy U. Md., London, 1966-69; assoc. prof. philosophy King's Coll., Wilkes-Barre, Pa., 1969-71; prof. philosophy, chmn. dept. Russell Sage Coll., Troy, N.Y., 1971-87; prof. philosophy, head dept. humanities-comm. Drexel U., Phila., 1987-91; dean arts and scis. Western New England Coll., Springfield, Mass., 1991-99, prof. philosophy, 1999—. Author: Deity and Morality, 1968, Philosophy, A Literary and Conceptual Approach, 1974, 80, 95, Personal Philosophy: Perspectives on Living, 1976, The Good Life, Alternatives in Ethics, 1980, 91, 94, 2001, Reasons for Living: A Basic Ethics, 1988, Religion and Reason, 1993, The Voice of Reason, 2001, Philosophy Through Fiction and Film, 2003; also articles and book revs. Named Outstanding Educator of Am., NEA, 1975. Mem. Am. Philos. Assn., MLA. Home: 30 Fearing St Amherst MA 01002-1912 Office: Dept Comm/Humanities Western New Eng Coll Springfield MA 01119

PORTER, CHARLES HENRY, photographer; b. Buffalo, Mar. 1, 1947; s. Charles Hunt and Jean Grace (Hasler) P.; m. Nora Roxanne Belanger, Nov. 1, 1969; children: Katherine, Elizabeth. BA, Cornell U., 1970. Freelance photographer, Poughkeepsie, N.Y., 1973—; chmn. photography dept. Oakwood Sch., 1986-92; staff photographer Hudson River Sloop Clearwater, 1982—. Photograpy cons. Vassar Coll., Poughkeepsie, 1986—. Author: (filmstrip series) The Hudson River Series, 1977; contbr. A Sense of Occasion: A Day in the Life of Vassar, 1992. Avocations: playing basketball, collecting CD's and comic books. E-mail: cn.porter@verizon.net.

PORTER, CHARLES KING, advertising executive; b. Mpls., Oct. 10, 1945; s. King E. and Bernetta Porter Andrews; m. Margit Gammeltoft, Feb. 26, 1972; children: Kristin, Catherine, James. BS in Journalism, U. Minn., 1967. Ptnr. Breen & Porter Co., Miami, Fla., 1974-85; pres. Porter Creative Svcs., 1985-88, Crispin, Porter & Bogusky Advt., Miami, 1988-97, chmn., ptnr., 1997—. Dir. Miami Ad Sch. Trustee Beacon Coun., Miami, 1988—. Recipient Nat. Addy award Am. Advt. Fedn., 1991, 92, Andy award Advt. Club N.Y., 1993, 94. Mem. Am. Assn. Advt Agys. (forum, Nat. A Plus award 1991, 94, 95, 96). Presbyterian. Avocations: skiing, travel, history. Office: Crispin Porter & Bogusky Advt 2699 S Bayshore Dr Miami FL 33133-5408*

PORTER, CHARLES MICHAEL (MIKE PORTER), retail company executive; b. Danville, Ill., Jan. 11, 1957; s. Charles K. Jr. and Constance K. (Kinnaman) P.; m. Kathryn S. Klein, July 15, 1990; children: Eric J., Jerry D. AA, Danville Area C.C., 1986; BS in Accountancy, U. Ill., 1988, MS in Taxation, 1989. Owner C.M. Porter Realty, Danville, Ill., 1980-85; staff acct. Clifton Gunderson & Co., 1989; staff tax acct. McGladrey & Pullen, Peoria, 1989-91, Galesburg, 1991-95; dir. tax Dollar Gen. Corp., Goodlettsville, Tenn., 1995—. Co-owner Thunder Run Ranch. Mem. Friends of Rodeo; bd. dirs., treas. Dollar Gen. Lit. Found. Mem. Tax Execs. Inst., Internat. Mass Retailers Assn. (chmn. tax adv. com.), Am. Paint Horse Assn., Am. Quarter Horse Assn., Profl. Rodeo Cowboys Assn. (assoc.), Gen. Literacy Found. (treas.), U. Ill. Alumni Assn. Avocations: rodeo, stock and ranch horses, performance horses, rodeo bull breeding. Office: Dollar Gen Corp 100 Mission Rdg Goodlettsville TN 37072-2171

PORTER, CHARLES RALEIGH, JR. retired lawyer; b. Waco, Tex., Sept. 22, 1922; s. Charles Raleigh and Virginia Louise (Bowen) P.; m. Alice Mungall, Sept. 16, 1946; children: Charles Raleigh III, Melissa Ann, Alice Marguerite, Daniel Bowen. BBA, U. Tex., 1943, JD, 1949. Bar: Tex. 1948, U.S. Dist. Ct. (so. dist.) Tex. 1949, U.S. Ct. Appeals (5th cir.) 1955, U.S. Dist. Ct. (we. dist.) Tex. 1972, U.S. Dist. Ct. (no. dist.) Tex. 1977. Asst. Nueces County Attys. Office, Corpus Christi, Tex., 1949-50, Dist. Attys. Office, Corpus Christi, 1950-53; ptnr. Anderson & Porter, 1953-63, Sorrell, Anderson & Porter, 1964-68, Porter, Rogers, Dahlman & Gordon, 1969-92; ret., 1992. Mem. adv. bd. dirs. Frost Nat. Bank, San Antonio. Past mem. exec. bd. Perkins Sch. Theology, So. Meth. U.; past chairperson adminstrv. bd. First United Meth. Ch.; mem. chancellor's com. U. Tex.; past mem. adv. bd. U. Tex. Marine Sci. Inst.; active Dean's Roundtable, U. Tex. Sch. Law, 2001; Past mem. bd. dirs. Meth. Home, Waco. Master: Spanish Oaks Golf Club; mem.: Rockport Country Club, Scottish Rite. Home: 33 Blue Heron Dr Rockport TX 78382-3771 E-mail: crockport@aol.com.

PORTER, DANIEL REED, III, museum director; b. Northampton, Mass., July 2, 1930; s. Daniel Reed and Eleanor (Parsons) P.; m. Joan Joyce Dornfeld, Nov. 22, 1958; children: Leslie Marie, Andrew Gregory. BA, U. Mass., 1952; MA, U. Mich., 1956. Asst. to dir. State Hist. Soc. Wis., Madison, 1956-58; dir. Hist. Soc. York County, Pa., 1958-61; asst. dir., dir. Ohio Hist. Soc., Columbus, 1961-74; exec. dir. Preservation Soc. Newport County, R.I., 1974-78; dir., prof. Cooperstown (N.Y.) Grad. Programs, 1978-82; dir. N.Y. State Hist. Assn. Farmer's Mus. Cooperstown, 1982-92. Hist. preservation officer State of Ohio, Columbus, 1967-74. Editor: N.Y. Heritage, 1984-92; contbr. articles to publs. in field. With U.S. Army, 1952-54, Korea. Recipient Spl. award of Merit Ohio Assn. Hist. Socs., 1970. Mem. Am. Assn. Mus. (accreditation commn. 1982-88, councillor-at-large 1981-84), Am. Assn. State and Local History (coun., Nashville 1971-73, councillor 1985-87). Congregationalist.

PORTER, DARWIN FRED, writer; b. Greensboro, N.C., Sept. 13, 1937; s. Numie Rowan and Hazel Lee (Phillips) P. BA, U. Miami, 1959. Bur. chief Miami Herald, 1959-60; v.p. Haggart Assocs., N.Y.C., 1961-64; editor, author Arthur Frommer Inc., 1964-67, Frommer/Pasmantier Pub. Corp., N.Y.C., 1967-86, Prentice Hall Press, N.Y.C., 1987-90, Simon & Schuster, N.Y.C., 1991—. Author: Frommer Travel Guides to: England, 1964, Spain, 1966, Scandinavia, 1967, Los Angeles, 1969, London, 1970, Lisbon/Madrid, 1972, Paris, 1972, Morocco, 1974, Rome, 1974, Portugal, 1968, England, 1969, Italy, 1969, Germany, 1970, France, 1970, Caribbean, Bermuda, the Bahamas, 1980, Switzerland, 1984, Austria and Hungary, 1984, Bermuda and the Bahamas, 1985, Scotland and Wales, 1985, the Virgin Islands, 1991, Scotland, 1992, Jamaica/Barbados, 1992, Puerto Rico, 1992, the Caribbean, 1993, Bermuda, 1993, the Bahamas, 1993, Austria, 1993, Madrid & the Costa del Sol, 1993, San Francisco, 1996, California, 1996, Caribbean Cruises, 1996, Caribbean Ports of Call, 1996, Georgia and the Carolinas, 1996, Charleston and Savannah, 1996, Munich and The Bavarian Alps, 1996, Vienna & the Danube, 1996, Guide to Caribbean Cruises, 1997, Frommer's Europe, 1997, Frommer's Venice, 1997, Barcelona, Madrid & Seville, 1997, Frommer's Portable London, 1998, Frommer's Portable Bahamas, 1998, Frommer's Portable Paris, 1998, Frommer's Portable Berlin, 1999; author: (novels) Butterflies in Heat, 1976, Marika, 1977, Venus, 1982, Razzle-Dazzle, 1998, Blood Moon, 1998, Frommer's Sweden, 1999, Frommer's Denmark, 1999, Midnight in Savannah, 2000, Hollywood's Silent Closet, 2000, Frommer's Frankfurt, 2001, Frommer's Great Britain, 2001, Bahamas for Dummies, 2002, Caribbean for Dummies, 2002, Rhinestone Country, 2002. Recipient Silver award Internat. Film and TV Festival N.Y., 1977 Mem. Soc. Am. Travel Writers, Smithsonian Assocs., Nat. Trust for Historic Preservation, Sigma Delta Chi Home: 75 Saint Marks Pl Staten Island NY 10301-1606

PORTER, DAVID HUGH, pianist, classicist, academic administrator, liberal arts educator; b. N.Y.C., Oct. 29, 1935; s. Hugh B. and Ethel K. (Flentye) P.; m. Laudie Ernestine Dimmette, June 21, 1958 (dec. Nov., 1986); children: Hugh, Everett, Helen, David; m. Helen Louise Nelson, Aug. 24, 1987. BA with highest honors, Swarthmore Coll., 1958; PhD (Danforth Grad. fellow, Woodrow Wilson Grad. fellow), Princeton U., 1962; student, Phila. Conservatory Music, 1955-61. Instr. in classics and music Carleton Coll., Northfield, Minn., 1962-63, asst. prof., 1963-68, assoc. prof., 1968-73, prof., 1973-87, William H. Laird prof. liberal arts, 1974-87, pres. faculty, 1980-82, coll. pres., 1986-87; pres. Skidmore Coll., Saratoga Springs, N.Y., 1987-98, prof. classics, 1987-98. Phi Beta Kappa vis. lectr., 1979-92, vis. scholar, 1994-95; vis. prof. classics Princeton U., 1986; vis. prof. classics Williams Coll., Williamstown, Mass., 1999—; Harry C. Payne vis. prof. liberal arts Williams Coll., 2000—; recitalist, lectr., especially on contemporary music, at colls., univs. throughout U.S., U.K., on radio and TV; chmn. Hudson-Mohawk Assn., 1990-92. Author: Only Connect: Three Studies in Greek Tragedy, 1987, Horace's Poetic Journey: A Reading of Odes I-III, 1987, Virginia Woolf and Logan Pearsall Smith, 2002; editor: Carleton Remembered, 1909-86, 1987, The Not Quite Innocent Bystander: Writings of Edward Steuermann, 1989; contbr. articles on classics, music, twentieth-century lit. and edn. to profl. jours. NEH research fellow, 1969-70, 83-84; Am. Council Learned Socs. research fellow, 1976-77. Mem. Am. Philological Assn., Classical Assn. Atlantic States. Democrat. Mem. United Ch. Christ. Avocations: hiking, reading, collecting rugs and books. Home: 5 Birch Run Dr Saratoga Springs NY 12866-1023 E-mail: ddodger@skidmore.edu.

PORTER, DAVID LINDSEY, history and political science educator, author; b. Holyoke, Mass., Feb. 18, 1941; s. Willis Hubert and Lora Frances (Bowen) P.; m. Marilyn Esther Platt, Nov. 28, 1970; children: Kevin, Andrea. BA magna cum laude, Franklin Coll., 1963; MA, Ohio U., 1965; PhD, Pa. State U., 1970. Asst. prof. history Rensselaer Poly. Inst., Troy, N.Y., 1970-75, co-dir. Am. studies program, 1972-74; ednl. adminstrv. asst. Civil Svc. Office State of N.Y., 1975-76; asst. prof. history William Penn U., Oskaloosa, Iowa, 1976-77, assoc. prof. history, 1977-82, prof. history and polit. sci., 1982-86, Louis Tuttle Shangle prof. history and polit. sci., 1986—, chmn. Sperry & Hutchinson Found. lectureship series, 1980-82, acting chair social and behavioral scis. divsn., 2000—01. Supr. legis. internship program Iowa Gen. Assembly, 1978—, records inventory project Mahaska County, 1978-79, internship program Washington Ctr., 1985—; active Franklin D. Roosevelt Meml. Commn.; chpt. adviser Phi Alpha Theta, 1977—. Author: The Seventy-sixth Congress and World War II, 1939-40, 1979, Congress and the Waning of the New Deal, 1980; co-author: The San Diego Padres Encyclopedia, 2002; contbr. to Dictionary of American Biography, 1981, 88, 94, 95, Directory of Teaching Innovations in History, 1981, The Book of Lists #3, 1983, Biographical Dictionary of Internationalists, 1983, The Hero in Transition, 1983, Herbert Hoover and the Republican Era: A Reconsideration, 1984, The History of Mahaska County, Iowa, 1984, Franklin D. Roosevelt, His Life and Times: An Encyclopedic View, 1985, The Rating Game in American Politics: An Interdisciplinary Approach, 1987, Sport History, 1987, Book of Days, 1988, Sports Encyclopedia North America, 1988, The Harry S. Truman Encyclopedia, 1989, Encyclopedia of Major League Baseball Team Histories: The National League, 1991, Twentieth Century Sports Champions, 1992, Statesmen Who Changed the World, 1993, Ency. Modern Social Issues, 1996, Advanced Placement U.S. History 2, 1996, Encyclopedia of United States Popular Culture, 1997, Encyclopedia of Civil Rights, 1997, Encyclopedia of Propaganda, 1997, Total Padres, 1997, The Scribner Encyclopedia of American Lives, 1998, 99, 2001, 02, American National Biography, 1999, The Sixties in America, 1999, Racial and Ethnic Relations in America, 1999, History of Mahaska County, Iowa, 2000, Great Athletes, rev. edit., 2001, The Scribner Encyclopedia of American Lives, Sports Figures, 2002, Great Events: 1900-2001, rev. edit., 2002; editor, contbr.: Biographical Dictionary of American Sports: vols. Baseball, 1987, Football, 1987, Outdoor Sports, 1988, Basketball and Other Indoor Sports, 1989, 1989-92 Supplement for Baseball, Football, Basketball and Other Sports, 1992, 1992-95, Supplement for Baseball, Football, Basketball and Other Sports, 1995, African-American Sports Greats, 1995, Baseball, revised and expanded edit., 3 vols., 2000; compiler, A Cumulative Index to the Biographical Dictionary of American Sports, 1993; assoc. editor: (with others) American National Biography, 24 vols., 1999; contbr. weekly column to Oskaloosa Herald, 1994—, numerous articles to various dictionaries, directories, encys., jours., revs., newspapers, commentary to Nat. Pub. Radio. Mem. Franklin D. Roosevelt Meml. Commn.; participant Green Bay Packers Project, 1992; historian United Meth. Ch. Grantee NSF, 1967, NEH, 1974, Rensselaer Poly. Inst., 1974, Eleanor Roosevelt Inst., 1981, William Penn Univ., 1986, 89, 92; recipient Choice Outstanding Acad. Book awards, 1989. Mem. AAUP, Am. Hist. Assn., Orgn. Am. Historians, N.Am. Soc. for Sport History, Soc. History Am. Fgn. Rels., Ctr. for Study of the Presidency, Soc. Am. Baseball Rsch., Friends of the Nat. Baseball Hall of Fame, Popular Culture Assn., Profl. Football Rschrs. Assn., Coll. Football Rschrs. Assn., Coll. Football Hist. Soc., State Hist. Soc. Iowa, Mahaska County Hist. Soc. (v.p.), Iowa State UN Assn. (chmn. ann. assembly 1982, nat. soc. Disting. Svc. award 1981), Mahaska County UN Assn. (v.p.), Oskaloosa Babe Ruth League (bd. dirs.), Oskaloosa Cmty. Choir, Friends of Oskaloosa Pub. Libr. (mem. nominating com.), Friends of the Nat. Baseball Hall of Fame, Phi Alpha Theta, Kappa Delta Pi. Home: 2314 Ridgeway Ave Oskaloosa IA 52577-9109 Office: William Penn Univ Dept Social and Behavioral Scis Divsn Oskaloosa IA 52577-1757

PORTER, DIXIE LEE, insurance company executive, consultant; b. Bountiful, Utah, June 7, 1931; d. John Lloyd and Ida May (Robinson) Mathis. BS, U. Calif., Berkeley, 1956; MBA, U. Calif., 1957. CLU. Personnel aide City of Berkeley, 1957-59; employment supr. Kaiser Health Found., L.A., 1959-60; personnel analyst UCLA, 1961-63; personnel mgr. Reuben H. Donnelley, Santa Monica, Calif., 1963-64; personnel officer Good Samaritan Hosp., San Jose, 1965-67; fgn. svc. officer AID, Saigon, Vietnam, 1967-71; gen. agt. Charter Life Ins. Co., L.A., 1972-77, Kennesaw Life Ins. Co., Atlanta, 1978—, Phila. Life Ins. Co., San Francisco, 1978—; pres. Womens Ins. Enterprises, Ltd., 1976—. Cons. in field. Co-chair Comprehensive Health Planning Commn. Santa Clara County, Calif., 1973-76; bd. dirs. Family Care, 1978-80, Aegis Health Corp., 1977-92, U. Calif. Sch. Bus. Adminstrn., Berkeley, 1974-76; task force on equal access to econ. power U.S. Nat. Womens Agenda, 1977—, Lake County Transp. Coun., 2000—. With USMC, 1950-52. Mem. AAUW, CLU Soc., U. Calif. Alumni Assn., U. Calif. Sch. Bus. Adminstrn. Alumni Assn., Bus. and Profl. Women, Prytanean Alumni, The Animal Soc. Los Gatos/Saratoga (pres. 1987-90), Beta Gamma Sigma, Phi Chi Theta. Republican. Episcopalian.

PORTER, DONNA JUNE, interior designer; b. Alva, Okla., June 24, 1937; d. Floyd Robert and Elsie Martha (Schick) Paris; b. Max. E. Walters, Aug., 1959 (div. 1981); m. Jerry R. Porter, Sept. 21, 1983; children: Terri Sue, Bradford Paris. B.S., Okla. State U., 1959; postgrad., 1970; Kansas City Art Inst., 1979. Tchr., Jefferson County Schs., Denver, 1962-64, Shawnee Mission Schs., Kans., 1964-66; dir. restaurant design Frontier Foods, Stillwater, Okla., 1967-72; dir. design Great Am. Restaurant Co., Kansas City, Mo., 1972-80; owner, designer D.J. Interior Design, Kansas City, 1980— . Bd. dirs. Kansas City Conv. and Vis. Bur., 1975-78, Kansas City Met. Parents Anonymous, 1984— (pres. bd. dirs.), The Crittenton Ctr., 1988. Recipient Key to City Mayor Cin., 1976. Mem. Interior Design Excellence Com., Nat. Assn. Women Bus. Owners, Friends of Art, Profl. Sources Greater Kansas City, Historic Kansas City Soc., Chi Omega (Outstanding Chi Omega, Okla. 1974, Chi Omega of Yr., Kans. City, 1981) Nat. Dir. extension 1979-82, PEO (chaplain 1979-81). Democrat. Mem. Disciples of Christ Ch. Clubs: Carriage (exec. com.), Chi O Mothers (pres.) (Kansas City). Avocation: tennis. Home and Office: 812 W 59th Ter Kansas City MO 64113-1338

PORTER, DOUGLAS TAYLOR, retired athletic administrator; b. Fayetteville, Tenn., Aug. 15, 1928; s. Waudell Phillip and Sophia Mae (Taylor) P.; m. Jean Butcher, Apr. 18, 1953; children: Daria C., Blanche E., Douglas V. BS, Xavier U., 1952; MS, Ind. U., 1960. Asst. football coach St. Augustine High Sch., Memphis, 1955, Xavier U., New Orleans, 1956-60; dir. athletics, head football coach Miss. Vocat. Coll., Itta Bena, Miss., 1960-65; assoc. dir. athletics, coach Grambling (La.) State U., 1966-73; head football coach Howard U., Washington, 1974-78; dir. athletics, head football coach Ft. Valley (Ga.) State Coll., 1979-97; ret., 1997. Pres. Nat. Athletic Steering Com., Ft. Valley, 1990-97. Lt. U.S. Army, 1951-54. Recipient Disting. Am. award Mid. Ga. Chpt. Nat. Football Found., 1997, Citation of Honor for contbns. to football Football Writers Assn. Am., 2000; So. Intra Collegiate Athletic Conf. Hall of Fame, 1997. Mem. Am. Alliance of Health, Phys. Edn. and Dance, Nat. Assn. of Collegiate Dirs. of Athletics (inducted Hall of Fame, 1997), Sigma Pi Phi, Alpha Phi Alpha (pres. 1983-87), Phi Delta Kappa. Democrat. Roman Catholic. Avocations: reading, listening to jazz. Home: 1415 Martin Luther King Jr Grambling LA 71245-2318 E-mail: ddporter@aol.com.

PORTER, DUNCAN MACNAIR, editor, educator; b. Kelseyville, Calif., Apr. 20, 1937; s. James Duncan and Dorothy May P.; m. Sarah Holyoke, Sept. 10, 1966; children: Charles Holyoke, Dorothy Carr, Christina Margaret, Susannah Reaves. AB, Stanford U., 1959, AM, 1961; PhD, Harvard U., 1967. Asst. Calif. Acad. Scis., San Francisco, 1966-67; asst. prof. biology U. San Francisco, 1967-68; curator flora Panama Mo. Bot. Garden, St. Louis, 1968-72; editor-in-chief flora N.Am. project Smithsonian Inst., Washington, 1972-73; assoc. program dir. systematic biology NSF, 1973-75; assoc. prof. bot. Va. Polytech. Inst. & State U., Blacksburg, 1975-84, prof. bot., 1984—; dir. Darwin Corr. Project, Cambridge, England, 1991—, sr. editor England, 1997—. Rsch. assoc. biology Stanford U., 1966-68; asst. prof. bot. Washington U., 1968-70, adj. asst. prof. biology, 1970-73; sec., program chmn. Am. Soc. Plant Taxonomists, 1972-73. Author: Rare and Endangered Vascular Plant Species of Virginia, 1980; co-author: Flora of the Calapagos Islands, 1971, The Portable Darwin, 1993, Categorical Glossery for the Flora of North America Program, 2000; editor: The Correspondence of Charles Darwin, Vol. 8, 1993, Vol. 9, 1994, Vol. 10, 1997, Vol. 11, 1999, Vol. 12, 2001. Vis. fellow U. Cambridge, 1980-81, U. Canterbury, New Zealand, 1986. Fellow AAAS, Linnean Soc. London; mem. Calif. Bot. Soc. (bd. editors 1970-76, 78-83), History Sci. Soc., Soc. History Natural Hist., Sigma Xi. Democrat. Episcopalian. Avocations: reading, travel, walking. Home: 1002 E Roanoke St Blacksburg VA 24060 Office: Va Tech Dept Biology Blacksburg VA 24061 Fax: 540-231-9307. E-mail: duporter@vt.edu.

PORTER, ELSA ALLGOOD, writer, lecturer; b. Amoy, China, Dec. 19, 1928; d. Roy and Petra (Johnsen) Allgood; m. Raeford B. Liles, Mar. 19, 1949 (div. 1959); children: Barbara, Janet; m. G. Hinckley Porter, Nov. 22, 1962; children: David, Brian, Wendy. BA, Birmingham-So. Coll., 1949; MA, U. Ala., 1959; M in Pub. Adminstrn., Harvard U., 1971; LHD (hon.), U. Ala., 1986. With HEW, Washington, 1960-73; with U.S. CSC, 1973-77; asst. sec. Dept. Commerce, 1977-81; disting. practitioner in residence Washington Pub. Affairs Ctr., U. So. Calif., 1982-84; v.p. R & D The Maccoby Group, 1990-96; sr. fellow Meridian Internat. Inst., 1990—. Chair comml. adv. subcom. NASA, 1997—. Fellow World Acad. Art & Scis., Nat. Acad. Pub. Adminstrs.; mem. Women's Nat. Dem. Club. Home: 2309 SW 1st Ave Apt 742 Portland OR 97201-5008

PORTER, GERALD JOSEPH, mathematician, educator; b. Elizabeth, N.J., Feb. 27, 1937; s. Fred and Tillie Florence (Friedman) P.; m. Judith Deborah Revitch, June 26, 1960; children: Daniel, Rebecca, Michael. AB, Princeton U., 1958; PhD, Cornell U., 1963; MA (hon.), U. Pa., 1971. Instr. MIT, 1963-65; asst. prof. math. U. Pa., Phila., 1965-69, assoc. prof., 1969-75, prof., 1975—, chmn. undergrad. affairs dept. math., 1971-73, assoc. dean computing Sch. Arts and Scis., 1981-91, dir. Interactive Math. Text Project, 1991-96. Chair-elect faculty senate U. Pa., 1992-93, chair, 1993-94, past chair, 1994-95, 2001—2002; prin. investigator NSF MACMATC Grant, 1997-2001. Author: (with D.R. Hill) Interactive Linear Algebra, 1996. Mem. Dem. Com., Haverford Twp., Pa., 1976-82, ward leader, 1980-84, treas., 1984-87. Postdoctoral fellow Office Naval Rsch., 1965-66. Mem. AAUP, Am. Math. Soc., Math. Assn. Am. (chmn. com. computers in math. edn. 1983-86, chmn. investment com. 1986—, bd. govs. 1980-83, 86-2002, mem. fin. com. 1986-2000, exec. com. 1992-2002, chmn. audit and budget com. 1988-90, 92, treas. 1992-2002, chair com. on profl. devel. 1995-2001, AAAS, Nat. Assn. Mathematicians. Democrat. Jewish. Home: 161 Whitemarsh Rd Ardmore PA 19003-1698 Office: U Pa 4N69 DRL 209 S 33rd St Philadelphia PA 19104-6395 E-mail: gjporter@math.upenn.edu.

PORTER, HAYDEN SAMUEL, computer science educator; b. Cin., June 2, 1945; s. Hayden Samuel and Thelma (Wulfeck) P.; m. Patricia Maloney, Sept. 28, 1967; children: Hayden, Emily. BS, U. Cin., 1967, PhD, 1973. Postdoctoral fellow U. Fla., Gainesville, 1973-76; sr. mem. tech. staff Computer Sci. Corp., Silver Springs, Md., 1976-79; pres. A2D, Co., Inc., Greenville, S.C., 1981—; Daniel disting. prof. computer sci. Furman U., 1979—, chmn., 1986-92. Author: Exploring Macintosh, 1989, Exploring Macintosh Applications, 1989, Exploring Microsoft Works, 1991, Essentials of Lotus 1-2-3 for Macintosh, 1992; contbr. articles to profl. jours. Grantee in field. Mem. Am. Geophys. Union, Am. Phys. Soc., IEEE, Assn. for Computing Machinery (activity monitor 1983-93), Sigma Xi. Avocations: sailing, boating, fishing.

PORTER, HENRY HOMES, JR. investor; b. Chgo., Nov. 13, 1934; s. Henry H. and Mary (Kinney) P.; m. Louisa Catherine Perkins, June 10, 1961; children: Mary Porter Johnson, Catherine. AB, Yale U., 1956; MBA, Harvard U., 1962. With Gen. Mills, Inc., Mpls., 1962-76, asst. treas., 1964-67, treas., 1967-76, v.p. fin., treas., 1969-76; sr. v.p., chief fin. officer, dir. Brown & Williamson Industries, Inc., 1977-79, Batus, Inc., 1980; now ret. Chmn. bd. Active Ankle Systems, Inc.; bd. dirs. SEI Corp., Dame Inc., Caldwell & Orkin Funds, Inc. Lt. (j.g.) USNR, 1957-60. Home and Office: 5806 River Knoll Dr Louisville KY 40222-5863

PORTER, HENRY OLIN, neurologist; b. Valdosta, Ga., Feb. 7, 1954; m. Carmela Ann Rapillo, Oct. 22, 1983; 1 child, Alexandra Elizabeth. BS, U. Fla., 1976; MD, U. Miami, Fla., 1982. Diplomate Am. Acad. Neurology, Nat. Bd. Med. Examiners. Commd. USN; asst. head Naval Hosp., Corpus Christi, Tex., 1984-85; MMART leader USS Tarawa, 1985; wing flight surgeon USN, Corpus Christi, 1985-87; head dept. neurology Naval Hosp., Pensacola, Fla., 1990-97; head internal medicine and neurology Naval Operational Medicine Inst., 1997—. Pres. Panhandle Macintosh Users, Pensacola, 1993. Mem. AMA, Am. Acad. Neurology, Assn. Mil. Surgeons U.S., Assn. U.S. Navy Flight Surgeons, Aerospace Med. Assn., So. Med. Assn., Internat. Brotherhood of Magicians (treas. 1994-96). Avocations: computers, magic, family entertainment, travel. Home: 6209 Vicksburg Dr Pensacola FL 32503-7555

PORTER, HOWARD LEONARD, III, health and education policy consultant; b. July 12, 1945; s. Howard Leonard and Margaret (Johnson) P.; m. Mary Ellen Biciste, June 22, 1968; 1 child, Andrew James. BA, Monmouth (Ill.) Coll., 1967; MS, U. Ill., 1968; MBA, U. Fla., 1995; PhD, U. South Fla., 2001. Pres. The Porter Co., 1968—. Sr. v.p. HCI Preferred Car, Inc., Auburndale, Fla., 1992—2001; v.p. Roswell E. Johnson Inst. Comm. Rsch., 1992—. Contbr. articles to profl. publs. With Med. Svc. Corps, USAF, 1969-72. Mem. Phi Kappa Phi (hon.). Republican. Presbyterian. Home: 2068 Katie Ct SE Winter Haven FL 33884-3113 Office: 509 Avenue B NW Winter Haven FL 33881-4607 E-mail: roswell@msn.com.

PORTER, J. RIDGELY, III, lawyer; b. Va., Apr. 28, 1948; s. John R and Mary Manning (Barclay) P.; m. DeLane Williams, 1978; 1 child, Eleanor M. BA, U. Va., 1970; JD, Washington & Lee U., 1973. Law clerk to U.S. judge, 1973-74; ptnr. Carr & Porter, 1974—; pres. Va. Internat. Terminals, 1985-92; chmn. bd. Chesapeake Gen. Hosp., 1986-96; owner Cattle Farms. Mem.: ABA, Met. Club (D.C.), Va. Bar Assn. Episcopalian. Office: 355 Crawford Pkwy Portsmouth VA 23704

PORTER, JACK NUSAN, writer, sociologist, educator, political activist; b. Rovno, Ukraine, USSR, Dec. 2, 1944; came to U.S., 1946; s. Irving Puchtik and Faye (Merin) P.; m. Miriam Almuly, Sept. 18, 1977 (div. 2000); children: Gabriel, Danielle. Cert., Machon Inst., Jerusalem, 1963; BAS cum laude, U. Wis., Milw., 1967; MA, Northwestern U., 1969; PhD, Northestern U., 1971; Rabbinical tng., Acad. for Jewish Religion, 1998-99. Ordained rabbi Vaad HaRabbainim, N.Y., 2000. Rsch. assoc. Harvard U. Ukrainian Rsch. Inst., Cambridge, Mass., 1982-84; pres. The Spencer Group, Newton, 1984—; exec. dir. The Spencer Sch. Real Estate, 1986—; dir. The Spencer Inst. for Bus. and Soc., 1984—; asst. prof. Coll. of Basic Studies Boston U., 1989-90. Vis. lectr. Boston U. Met. Coll., 1987, 88, Bryant Coll., Smithfield, R.I., 1991; adj. prof. U. Mass., Lowell, 1976-79, 94—; adj. prof. sociology Stonehill Coll., Easton, Mass., 1996-97; presenter White House Conf. on Family, 1980; mem. Gov. Dukakis' Adv. Coun., 1982-84; panelist on Comparative Genocide, The Oxford (Eng.) Conf., 1988; Boston area coord. Seminars on Zionist Thought,

World Zionist Orgn., 1996—; cons. in non-fiction Nat. Book Critics Circle Awards, 1997-98. Author or editor 30 books and anthologies including Confronting History and Holocaust, 1983, Sexual Politics in Nazi Germany, 1991, Kids in Cults, 1977, 85, 94, Jews and the Cults, 1981, Genocide and Human Rights, 1982, Conflict and Conflict Resolution: A Sociological Introduction, 1987, Jewish Radicalism, 1973, Jewish Partisans (2 vols.), 1982, Conflict and Conflict Resolution: A Historical Bibliography, 1982, The Jew as Outsider, 1981, The Sociology of Jewry: A Curriculum Guide, 1992, 99, The Sociology of American Jews: A Critical Anthology, 1980, 98, The Sociology of Jewry: Collected Essays, 1998, Forclosed Property (with Gerry Glazer), 1990, The Sociology of the Holocaust: A Curriculum Guide, 1992, 99, The Sociology of Business: A Curriculum Guide, 1992, Holocaust and Genocide: Theories, Cases, Implications, 1998, Women in Chains: Sourcebook on the Agunah, 1996, Holocaustal Suicides: Essays on the Sociology of Genocide, The Death of Sociology, A Life of Mitzvah: Rabbi Joseph Mayer Jacobsen of Boston; The Genodical Mind: Toward a Sociology of the Holocaust: Anti-Semitism: From Deicide to Genocide, others; contbr. chpts. in books, more than 500 articles and revs. to jours. in field; founder, editor Jour. of the History of Sociology, 1977-85, The Sociology of Bus. Newsletter, 1977-79; mem. editl. bd. Contemporary Jewry, 1995—; dep. editor, dep. pub. Jewish Family and Life, 1997-98. Founder Holocaust Survival Video Project, Newton, Mass., 1992—; judge Nat. Jewish Book Awards, 1993-95; mem. Jewish Radical Edn. Project, 1994-99; spiritual leader Temple Emmanuel, Chelsea, Mass., 1999-2001. John Atherton fellow Breadloaf Writers Conf., Middlebury, Vt., 1976; recipient Spl. award Boston Police Dept., 1986. Mem. PEN (newsletter com. 1992-95), Am. Sociol. Assn., Ea. Sociol. Soc., New Eng. Soc., Internat. Assn. of Genocide Scholaras (v.p. 1996-98), Tikkun, Workman's Circle, PEN New Eng. Avocations: collecting Jewish baseball cards, reading, spiritual thinking. E-mail. Home and Office: 17 Cross St Newton MA 02465 Fax: 617-964-3971. E-mail: jacknusan@earthlink.net. *The older I get, the important things in life are my children, good health, a few good friends, my brother and sister and Mom, a good meal, and lastly - some money and a little fame. That's all I need. Oh, yes - love. One needs lots of love.*

PORTER, JAMES KENNETH, retired judge; b. Newport, Tenn., Apr. 6, 1934; s. John Calhoun and Bessie Betis (Crouch) P.; m. Evelyn Janet Rhodes, Sept. 17, 1955; children: Jane Caroline, James Kenneth Jr. BS, U. Tenn., 1955, JD, 1957. Bar: Tenn. 1957, U.S. Dist. Ct. (ea. dist.) Tenn. 1958, U.S. Ct. Appeals (6th cir.) 1971. Ptnr. Porter, Porter & Dunn, Porter & Porter, Newport, 1957-74; state rep. Tenn. Gen. Assembly, Nashville, 1961-65, minority fl. leader, 1963-65; county atty. Cocke County, Tenn., 1961-63, commr. County Election Commn., 1966-72, chmn., 1968-70; mem. Tenn. Senate, Nashville, 1972-74; state cir. judge 4th Jud. Cir., Newport, 1974-93; ret., 1993; state presiding judge 4th Jud. Cir., Newport, 1984-86, 88-90, 1992-93; judgeship nominee U.S. Dist. Ct. (ea. dist.), Tenn., 1986; Tenn. Ct. Appeals nominee, 1990. Del. S.E. Law Rev. Conf., Durham, N.C., 1957, Nat. Conf. State Legislator Leaders, Boston, 1963; discussion leader Nat. Jud. Coll., Reno, 1981, faculty adviser, 1982; mem. Gov.'s Correction Overcrowding Commn., Nashville, 1985-86. Contbr. articles to U. Tenn. Law Rev., 1956-57, editor in chief, 1957. Active Farm Bur., 1962-82; mem. adv. coun., trustee Walters State Community Coll., Morristown, Tenn., 1975-86. Mem. ABA (Tenn. jud. del. 1984), Tenn. Jud. Conf. (v.p. 1980-81), Tenn. Trial Judges Assn. (bd. dirs. 1976-86, pres. 1982-85), Tenn. Bar Assn. (spl. trial counsel 1973-76), Cocke County Bar Assn., Smoky Mountain Country Club (bd. dirs. 1964-67, v.p. 1966-67), Order of Coif, Sigma Alpha Epsilon (Highest Effort Law award 1986), Phi Delta Phi. Republican. Baptist. Avocations: golf, gardening, guitar. Home: 306 North St Newport TN 37821-2413 Office: 106 S Mims Ave Newport TN 37821-3125 E-mail: porterk@planetc.com.

PORTER, JAMES MORRIS, retired judge; b. Cleve., Sept. 14, 1931; s. Emmett Thomas and Mary (Connell) P.; m. Helen Marie Adams, May 31, 1952; children: James E., Thomas W., William M., Daniel J. AB, John Carroll U., 1953; JD, U. Mich., 1957. Bar: Ohio 1957. Assoc. firm M.B. & H.H. Johnson, Cleve., 1957-62, McAfee, Hanning, Newcomer, Hazlett & Wheeler, Cleve., 1962-67; ptnr. firm Squire, Sanders & Dempsey, 1967-92; judge Ohio Ct. Appeals, 8th Dist., 1993-2000, Cuyahoga County Common Pleas Ct., Cleve., 2001. 1st lt. U.S. Army, 1953-55. Fellow Am. Coll. Trial Lawyers; mem. The Country Club (Cleve.). Republican. Roman Catholic.

PORTER, JEANNE SMITH, civic worker; b. Hammond, Ind., Feb. 27, 1930; d. Cyril Augustus and Mary (Mabley) Smith; m. William Harry Porter, Apr. 1, 1953; children: Wendy Alice, David William, Mary Elizabeth, Audrey Jeanne. Student, Hanover Coll., 1948-50; BA in Lit. with honors, Ind. U., 1953. Developer, area leader Recovery, Inc., Mont., 1971-82; mem. adv. bd. Mont. House Day Treatment Ctr., Helena, 1980-93; bd. dirs., libr. chmn., Mont. Alliance for Mentally Ill, Helena, 1979—; organizer, planner Columbarium garden, Episcopal Ch., Helena, 1988—; organizer T-House project Mental Health Svcs., 1983-88; developer Social Club-Mentally Ill., 1968—. Recipient Disting. Svc. award Jaycees Helena, 1974, svc. to cmty. award Carroll Coll., 1986, Electrum award Helena Arts Coun., 1988, award for long term svc. Mont. Alliance for Mentally Ill., 1989, Vol. of Yr. award Mental Health Assn. Mont., 1989, Dignity award Golden Triangle Mental Health Ctr., 2001. Mem. P.E.O. (philanthropic com. chpt. O 1994—), S.W. Ariz. Watercolor Guild. Avocations: painting, drawing, gardening, travel, reading. Home: 1425 Winne Ave Helena MT 59601-5224 also: 5887 N Misty Ridge Dr Tucson AZ 85718-3434

PORTER, JEANNETTE UPTON, elementary education educator; b. Mpls., Mar. 5, 1938; d. Robert Livingston and Ruby Jeannette (Thomas) Upton; divorced; children: Steven, Fritz, Susan Porter Powell. BS, U. Minn., 1960, Mankato State U., 1968; postgrad., St. Thomas U., 1991. Camp dir. St. Paul's Epsicopal Ch., Mpls., 1956-66; tchr. elem. sch. Bloomington (Minn.) Pub. Schs., 1967—, dir. title I, 1975-82, tchr. spl. assignment of rsch. and devel., 1990-91; ednl. adminstrn. Conf. Ctr. Office, Lac du Flambeau, Wis., 1991—. Cons. in ednl. change and innovations The Inst.; team cons. Hillcrest Cmty. Sch., Bloomington, 1990—95; res. tchr. spl. assignment, 1996—; vol. music therapist The Pines Sr. Care, Pine City, Minn., 2001—; edn. cons., 1996—; vol. Nature Conservancy, Avon Park, Fla., 2001—. Tutor Telephone Hot Line Minn. Fedn. Tchrs., Mpls., 1988-92; crisis counselor Neighborhood Improvement Programs, Mpls., 1988-93; adult literacy counselor Right to Read, Mpls., 1987-89; vol. Abbott Northwestern Hosp.; bd. dirs. The Inst. (profl. ednl. think tank, Lac du Flambeau), 1997—. Recipient 1st Bank award Mpls., Red Apple award, Mpls., 1988; named Minn. Tchr. of Excellence, 1988, 89. Mem. Assn. Early Childhood Edn. (treas. 1990-94), Bloomington Edn. Found., Delta Kappa Gamma (1st v.p. 1992-93), PEO (past pres. A.C. chpt.). Avocations: fishing, photography, back packing, global volunteer, music. Home: 4400 W 44th St Minneapolis MN 55424-1064 E-mail: porterfl@strato.net.

PORTER, JENNIFER MADELEINE, producer, director; b. Milw., Oct. 3, 1962; d. John Hamlin and Helen Meak (Smith) P. BA in Comm., Bowling Green State U., 1984. Audio visual supr. Liberty Mutual Ins. Group, Berwyn, Pa., 1985-88; sr. prodr. audio visual Prudential Ins. Co., Mpls., 1988-93; proprietor Shoot The Moon Prodns., Mound, Minn., 1993-96, Shoot the Moon Prodns., Mpls., 1996—. Prodr., dir., writer: (audio visual programs) Phantom Lake... A Lifetime of Memories, 1991 (Best of Show 1991, Script award Assn. for Multi-Image Internat. 1991), Vision... The Gamma Phi Beta Foundation, 1992 (First Place award 1993), prodr., prodn. coord. Stadium Theatre Experience-College Football Hall of Fame (Silver award Assn. for Multi-Image Internat. 1996), the Making of Homo Heights, 1997 (Women in Dirs. Chair Walker Art Ctr.). Mentor U. Minn., Mpls., 1989-96; fundraiser Gamma Phi Beta Found. Philanthropy-Spl. Camping for Girls, Minn., Wis., 1991—; chairperson 100th Celebration, Phantom Lake YMCA Camp, Mukwonago, Wis., 1994-96. Mem. Assn. for Multi-Image Internat. (exec. bd. local 1986-88), Gamma Phi Beta (internat. officer, pub. rels. speaker/prodr. 1991—). Avocations: travel, music, sports, camping, canoeing. Home and Office: Shoot The Moon Prodns 5104 26th Ave S Minneapolis MN 55417-1317 E-mail: shoothemoon@usinternet.com.

PORTER, JENNY LIND, writer; b. Fort Worth, Tex., Sept. 3, 1927; d. Drue J. and Josephine Trammell Porter; m. Lawrence E. Scott. BA summa cum laude, Tex. Christian U., 1948; MA, Tex. Christian U., Ft. Worth, 1949; PhD, U. of Tex., Austin, 1955; Hon. Doctorate (hon.) , Pepperdine U., 1980. Asst. prof. The U. Tenn., Knoxville, Tenn., 1958—59, West Tex. A&M U., Canyon, Tex., 1959—61; assoc. prof. Southwest Tex. State U., San Marcos, 1961—64, Tex. Luth. U., Sequin, 1964—68; prof. Huston-Tillotson Coll., Austin, 1968—96; guest prof. Pepperdine U., Malibu, Calif., 1981. Vis. prof. Pepperdine U., Malibu, Calif., 1981. Author: (numerous works including) Three Dramatic Monologues, 1980, Verses on Death, Les Vers de la Mort, 1999 (Tex. Inst. Letters Translation award, 2000), El Sol Colorado, 2001, O. Henry, Witter Bynner, and A Fog in Santone, 2002. Named Jenny Lind Porter Day in Austin, Tex. named in her honor for contbns. to lit. and the O. Henry Mus., City Coun., Austin, 1996; named to Tex. Women's Hall of Fame, Austin, 1985; recipient Piper Prof. award, Piper Found., San Antonio, Tex., 1976. Home: 51 Summit View Place Austin TX 78703

PORTER, JOHN EDWARD, former congressman; b. Evanston, Ill., June 1, 1935; s. Harry H. and Beatrice V. P.; m. Kathryn Cameron; 5 children. Attended, MIT; BSBA, Northwestern U., 1958; JD with distinction, U. Mich., 1961; DHL, Barat Coll., 1988; LLD (hon.), Kendall Coll., 1992. Bar: Ill. 1961, U.S. Supreme Ct. 1968. Former honor law grad. atty., appellate div. Dept. Justice, Washington; mem. Ill. Ho. of Reps., 1973-79, 96-106th Congresses from 10th Ill. Dist., Ill., 1980-2001; mem. legis. select com. on aging, 1980-92; ptnr. Hogan & Hartson, Washington, 2001—. Founder, co-chmn. Congl. Human Rights Caucus; founder Congl. Coalition on Population and Devel. Past editor: Mich. Law Rev. Bd. dirs. PBS Recipient Best Legislator award League of Conservation Voters, 1973, Ind. Voters Ill., 1974, Chgo. Crime Commn., 1976, Lorax award Global Tomorrow Coalition, 1989, Spirit of Enterprise award U.S. C. of C., 1988, 89, 90, Golden Bulldog award Watchdogs of the Treasury, 12 times, Taxpayer's Friend award Nat. Taxpayers Union, Taxpayer Superhero award Grace Commn.'s Citizens Against Government Waste. Republican. Office: Hogan & Hartson 555 13th St NW Washington DC 20004*

PORTER, JOHN FRANCIS, III, banker; b. Wilmington, Del., Sept. 17, 1934; s. John Francis, Jr. and Eloise Wilhelmina (Berlinger) P.; m. Ann Mayfield, Sept. 8, 1956; children: Leslie Gibson, Nina Porter Winfield, Sophie Porter Rohrer. BA, U. Va., 1956; MBA, U. Del., 1965. With Del. Trust Co., Wilmington, 1958-97, asst. treas., 1960-66, sec., 1966-68, v.p., sec., 1968-72, sr. v.p., sec., 1972-75, exec. v.p., 1975-79, pres., 1979-88; chmn., chief exec. officer Del. Trust Co. (now First Union), 1988-97; vice chmn. BANKPAC, 1982-86, chmn., 1986-88, Del. Trust Capital Mgmt., 1988-97. Mem. Ct. on Judiciary Preliminary Investigatory Com., 1991-97. Mem. bank adv. bd. State of Del., 1969-71; mem. Council on Banking for State of Del., 1970—, chmn., 1976—; trustee Alfred I. duPont Testamentary Trust, 1995—; pres. Wilmington and Brandywine Cemetery, 1974—; bd. dirs., trustee, mem. fin. com. mem. exec. com., chmn. audit com. Christiana Care, 1985-99; bd. dirs. Penjerdel, 1989-97, state v.p., 1990-97; bd. gov. Winterthur Corp. Coun., 1989-95, chmn., 1993-95; bd. dirs. Winterthur Mus., 1993-95, Nemours Found., 1995—, The Glenmede Trust Co. N.A., 2000—. Capt. arty., U.S. Army, 1957. Mem. Am. Bankers Assn. (govt. rels. coun. 1984-88), Del. Bankers Assn. (pres. 1984-85, bd. dirs. 1981-87), Del. Bus. Roundtable (vice chmn. exec. coun. 1989-92, chmn. 1993-94), Wilmington Country Club (bd. dirs. 1970—, pres. 1973-74), Wilmington Club (bd. govs. 1980-89), Vicmead Hunt, Nassau Club (Princeton, N.J.). Clubs: Wilmington Country (bd. dir.), Wilmington (bd. govs. 1980-89), Vicmead Hunt; Nassau (Princeton, N.J.). Home: 4821 Kennett Pike Wilmington DE 19807-1813 Office: The Nemours Found 1600 Rockland Rd Wilmington DE 19803-3607

PORTER, JOHN G. educational consultant; b. Sandusky, Ohio, May 15, 1952; m. Linda M. Porter; children: Jeff, Matthew. PhD Counseling, LaSalle U., Montreal, Canada, 1996; MBd, Spl. Edn., Bowling Green State University, Bowling Green, OH, 1980; BA Philosophy, Capital U., Roseau, Dominica, British Commonwealth, 1974. Educator Young Men's Club of Am., Erie and Preble Counties, Pa., 1968—80, Bd. of Metal Retardation, Lucas, Shelby, and Hamilton Counties, Ohio, 1980—92; spl. edn. educator Middletown Pub. Schools, Middletown, 1992—96; ednl. cons. Quest Ctr. for Profl. Devel., West Chester, 1991—. Bd. mem. Hoshin Internat., Lake Charles, La., 2000—. Author: (book) Madness in Martial Arts. Mem. Big Bros./Big Sisters, Butler County, Ohio, 2002; foster care parent Dept. of Human Services, 2002. Mem.: Bujinkan, ACA, ASTD. Office: Quest Center - Professional Development 7409 Cinnamon Woods Drive West Chester OH 45069-1041

PORTER, JOHN PAUL, artist, educator; b. Alturas, Calif., Nov. 26, 1935; s. Carlton Lewis and Bernice (Smith-Schulz) P.; m. Carol Lynn Jones, Apr. 20, 1957 (div. Apr. 1978); children: Sean Michal, Sheryl Lynn. BA in Art, Calif. State U., Chico, 1958; MA in Art, UCLA, 1962; postgrad., Calif. State U., Chico, 1958, Calif. State U., Sacramento, 1959-67, Calif. State U., Northridge, 1958-63, Calif. State U., San Jose, 1978, Stanford U., 1986. Cert. secondary tchr., Calif. Prof. art, chair dept., coord. dist. Antelope County Unified Sch. Dist. & Jr. Coll., Lancaster, Calif., 1958-67; prof. art Gavilan Coll., 1967-2000, chair fine arts and humanities, 1969-75. Vis. prof. U. London, 1988. Exhbns. and one-man shows include Chico State Libr., 1958, Benny Bario Gallery, Carmichael, Calif., 1959,. Greenlee-Porter Show, Allied Arts Gallery, Lancaster, 1961, Aldous Huxley Show Porter Show Allied Arts, 1962, Charles Parker Estates, Quartz Hill, Calif., 1963, Chic Sale Art Competition, Lancaster, 1964, Tumbleweed Gallery, Pearblossom, Calif., 1964, 65, 66, Edwards AFB, 1965, Oldfield Studio, Lancaster, 1967, Hollister Art League, 1967, 70, Gilroy Mus., 1972, 78, 80, Faye Dixon's Mariposa House, 1973, El Cerrito Open Studio Show, Gilroy, Calif., 1975, De Saisset Gallery, 1978, Oaktree Allied Arts Gallery, 1978-80, Spring Art-Music Fesitval, 1970-78, San Jose Art League, 1980, Children's Home Soc. Benefit, 1981, Friendly Inn Art and Flower Show, Morgan Hill, 1979, 80, 82, Vacaville State Art Competition, 1982, Am. Greeting Card Print Nat. Convention, 1983, Union Street Gallery, 1984, Russian River STate Festival, Forestville, Calif., 1984-85, Bay Area Fine Arts Exhbn., San Francisco, 1985, Steinbeck Gallery, 1986, Glen Loma Estates, 1987, Thackery House, London, 1988, Santa Clara County Fair, 1989, Avina Gallery, Sao Paolo, Brazil, 1991, Carlton House, London, 1992, Skyline Coll, 1993, San Jose Art League, 1994, Beaux Artes Show, Reno, Nev., 1995, Willows Mansion, 1996, So. Valley Symphony Benefit, 1997, Growth and Opportunity Exec. Offices, Morgan Hill, Calif., 1997, 98; editorial Bd. Collegiate Press, 1990-94; contbr. articles to profl. jours., chpts. to books; represented in over 1200 pvt. collections. Co-founder Mushroom Fesival, Morgan Hill, 1990—. Recipient Nat. AVIP Tchr. of Yr. award, 1964, award Nat. Neighborhood Youth Corp., 1967, Mayoral Citation Svc. City of Gilroy, 1978, 96; named Man of Yr. Lancaster C. of C., 1967. Mem. Commonwealth Club, South Bay Scottish Soc. (acting chief, bd. govs.), Hearaldry Soc. Great Britain, Clan Cian Soc., Nat. Thespians (award 1965). Democrat. Congregationalist. Avocations: dancing, swimming, tennis, crafts. Home: 4002 San Ysidro Way San Jose CA 95111 E-mail: art-e-facts@webtv.net.

PORTER, JOHN ROBERT, JR. space technology company executive, geochemist; b. Oklahoma City, Feb. 27, 1935; s. John Robert and Margaret Florence (Nicholson) P.; m. Amelie Alexanderson Wallace, June 2, 1963; children: Jennifer A. Porter Dowling, Amelie M. BA, Dartmouth Coll., 1957; MS, Okla. U., 1964. Cert. petroleum geologist, Am. Assn. Petroleum Geologists. Analyst CIA, Washington, 1962-66; chief Earth Resources Program NASA, 1966-69; chmn. Earth Satellite Corp., Rockville, Md., 1969—. Mem. space applications bd. NRC, Washington, 1983-86, GEOSAT Com., Norman, Okla., 1972-96. Trustee Washington Gallery Modern Art, 1966-67. 1st lt. U.S. Army, 1960-62. Mem. Am. Assn. Petroleum Geologists., Chevy Chase Club. Republican. Presbyterian. Avocation: writing fiction. Home: 4000 Cathedral Ave NW Apt 813 B Washington DC 20016-5272 Office: Earth Satellite Corp 6011 Executive Blvd # 400 Rockville MD 20852-3804 E-mail: rporter@earthsat.com.

PORTER, JOHN STEPHEN, retired television executive; b. Avoca, N.Y., Sept. 2, 1932; s. Frank R. and Margaret H. (McGreel) P.; m. Marie C. Eiffert, Sept. 6, 1958; children: Stephen, David, Mark, Kevin, Matthew. BA in English, St. John Fisher U., 1958; MS in Radio/TV, Syracuse U., 1959; postgrad. in Edn, U. Rochester, 1960-61. Producer, broadcaster weekly news analysis N.Y. State Empire State FM Sch. of Air, 1962-64; producer, narrator weekly series sta. WROC-FM, Rochester, N.Y., 1964-65; pres., gen. mgr. sta. WXXI-TV, 1966-69; trustee Eastern Ednl. TV Network, Boston, 1966-68, mem. exec. com., 1967-68, exec. dir., 1969-89, pres., mem. exec. com., 1989-92, Am. Program Svc. (formerly Ea. Ednl. TV Network), Boston, 1992—. Served to 1st lt. AUS, 1952-56. Mem. N.Y. State Ednl. Radio/TV Assn. (treas. 1962-64), Pub. TV Sta. Mgrs. New York State (chmn. 1968-69), Nat. Assn. Ednl. Broadcasters (adv. com.) Home: PO Box 405 Sandwich MA 02563-0405

PORTER, JOHN WESTON, counselor, consultant, administrator; b. Fostoria, Ohio, Dec. 26, 1939; s. William Thomas and Ida Elizabeth (Carter) P. Student, U. Cin., 1958; BA, Heidelberg Coll., 1961; MA in Cmty. Psychology, U. D.C., 1973, MA in Counseling, 1975; postgrad., Antioch Coll., 1974, Frostburg (Md.) U., 1970, George Washington U., 1968. cert. Nat. Bd. Cert. Counselors, D.C. Bd. Edn. Claims rep. Social Security Adminstrn., Cleve. and Akron, Ohio, 1961-62; office mgr. Phoenix Cos., Washington and L.A., 1966-70; rschr. Frostburg U., U.D.C., 1970-73; edn. and career devel. specialist D.C. Pub. Schs., 1973-79, career edn. unit, 1979-83, Career Assessment Ctr., 1983-85, asst. dir. guidance and counseling, 1985-95; mem. cmty. adv. coun. Washington Hosp. Ctr., 1987—. Dir. Westport Consulting, 2001—. Contbr. articles to profl. jours. Vice chmn. adv. coun. Group Health Assn., Washington, 1977-79, 81-83; sec. Md.-D.C. Am. Coll. Testing Coun., 1987-88, vice chair, 1988-90, chair, 1990-91, exec. com., 1991—; pres. N.E. Hill Found., 1990-92; mem. com. D.C. Career and Tech. Edn. Task Force, 2000. Lt. USNR, 1962-66. Recipient awards Ohio Acad. Sci., 1954-57, Cleve. Plain Dealer Operation Demonstrate, 1956, svc. award Heidelberg Coll. Publs., 1961, recognition certs. D.C. Assn. Career Devel., 1975, 76, D.C. City Coun., 1982, Childrens Edn. Found., 1990, recognition award Outstanding Contbn. to Guidance and Counseling, 1987, Youth Svc. award Wash. Hosp. Ctr., 1992. Mem. ACA (counselor advocate-legislation), D.C. Assn. Counseling and Devel. (sec. 1977-78, treas. 1975-77, 91-92, exec. bd. 1975-80, pres. 1979-80, trustee 1989-92, counselor advocate-legis.ation, Mem. of Yr. 1980, Outstanding Leadership award 1980), Assn. Counseling and Devel. (chmn. govt. rels. North Atlantic region 1980-81, cert. outstanding contbn. in govt. rels. 1982, Recognition award 1987), Am. Sch. Counselors Assn. (career guidance com., leadership recognition cert. 1987, chair rsch. com. 1990-91), Nat. Assn. Career Devel. (assembly del. 1984), D.C. Sch. Counselors Assn. (Outstanding Leadership award 1994), D.C. Career Devel. Assn. (treas. 1983-86, exec. bd. 1983-90), Children's Edn. Found. (adv. com. 1989-93, fund raising com. 1989—, exec. bd. 1992—, asst. treas. 1992-93, treas. 1993-95), Assn. Counselor Edn. and Supervision, Phi Delta Kappa (edn. found. rep. 1993-95, v.p. membership 1995-96, pres. 1996-97, MACI project, adv. coun. Hosp. for Sick Children 1997-98, lic. profl. counselor D.C. 1995—, rev. panel D.C. vocat. edn. grants 1998), Coun. Accreditation Counseling and Related Ednl. Programs (site visit team 2000—). Home: 821 Taylor St NE Washington DC 20017-2009 E-mail: jw.wb.porter@erols.com.

PORTER, JOHN WILSON, education executive; b. Ft. Wayne, Ind., Aug. 13, 1931; BA, Albion Coll., 1953; MA, Mich. State U., 1957, PhD, 1962; D in Pub. Adminstrn. (hon.), Albion Coll., 1973; LLD (hon.), Mich. State U., 1977, Cleary Coll., 1987; LHD, Adrian Coll., 1970, U. Detroit, 1979; LLD, Western Mich. U., 1971, Eastern Mich. U., 1975; HHD, Kalamazoo Coll., 1973, Detroit Coll. Bus., 1975, Madonna Coll., Livonia, Mich., 1977; DEd, Detroit Inst. Tech., 1978; AA, Schoolcraft Coll., Livonia, Mich., 1979; DBA, Lawrence Inst. Tech., 1988; LLD, Cleary Coll., 1989. Counselor Lansing (Mich.) Pub. Schs., 1953-58; cons. Mich. Dept. Pub. Instrn., 1958-61; dir. Mich. Higher Edn. Assistance Authority, 1961-65; assoc. supt. for higher edn. Mich. Dept. Edn., 1966-69, state supt. schs., 1969-79; pres. Ea. Mich. U., Ypsilanti, 1979-89; v.p. Nat. Bd. for Profl. Teaching Standards, 1989; gen. supt. Detroit Pub. Schs., 1989-91; CEO Urban Edn. Alliance, Inc., Ypsilanti, Mich., 1991—. Mem. numerous profl. commns. and bds., 1959— , including Commn. on Financing Postsecondary Edn., 1972-74, Commn. for Reform Secondary Edn., Kettering Found., 1972-75, Edn. Commn. of States, 1973-79, Nat. Commn. on Performance-Based Edn., 1974-76, Nat. Commn. on Manpower Policy, 1974-79, Mich. Employment and Tng. Svcs. Coun., 1976-79, Nat. Adv. Coun. on Social Security, 1977-79, Commn. on Ednl. Credit, Am. Coun. on Edn., 1977-80; task panel on mental health of family Commn. on Mental Health, 1977-80; mem. Nat. Coun. for Career Edn. (HEW), 1974-76; pres. bd. dirs. Chief State Sch. Officers, 1974-79; pres. Coun. Chief State Sch. Officers, 1977-78; bd. dirs. Comerica Bank; former chmn. bd. Coll. Entrance Exam. Bd., 1984-86. Trustee Nat. Urban League, 1973-79, Charles Stewart Mott Found., 1981—, Albion Coll., 1989—; bd. dirs. Mich. Internat. Council, 1977—, Mich. Congress Parents and Tchrs.; mem. bd. overseers com. for Grad. Sch., Harvard U., 1980-88; mem. edn. com. NAACP; convener goal 6 Nat. Edn. Goals Panel, 1990—; mem. East Lansing Human Relations Commn.; chmn. Am. Assn. State Colls. and U.'s Task Force on Excellence in Edn.; mem. Mich. Martin Luther King, Jr. Holiday Commn., Gov.'s Blue Ribbon Commn. on Welfare Reform; trustee East Lansing Edgewood United Ch.; mem. Catherine McAuley Health Systems Bd., 1990—. Recipient numerous awards including Disting. Svc. award Mich. Congress Parents and Tchrs., 1963, Disting. Svc. award NAACP, Lansing, 1968; cert. of outstanding achievement Delta Kappa chpt. Phi Beta Sigma, 1970; award for disting. svc. Assn. Ind. Colls. and Univs. Mich., 1974; Disting. Alumni award Coll. Edn., Mich. State U., 1974; award for disting. svc. to edn Mich. State U., 1974; Disting. Alumni award, 1979; award for disting. svc. to edn. in Mich. Mich. Assn. Secondary Sch. Prins., 1974; President's award as disting. educator Nat. Alliance Black Sch. Educators, 1977; Marcus Foster Disting. Educator award, 1979; recognition award Mich. Ednl. Rsch. Assn., 1978; recognition award Mich. Assn. Secondary Sch. Prins., 1978; recognition award Mich. Assn. Intermediate Sch. Adminstrs., 1979; recognition award Mich. Assn. Sch. Adminstrs., 1979; Mich. Sch. Bus. Ofcls., 1979; resolution Mich. State Legislature, 1978; Anthony Wayne award Coll. Edn., Wayne State U., 1979; Educator of Decade award Mich. Assn. State and Fed. Program Specialists, 1979; Spirit of Detroit award Detroit City Coun., 1981; Disting. Svc. award Ypsilanti Area C. of C., 1988; Philip A. Hart award Mich. Women's Hall of Fame, 1988; Summit award Greater Detroit C. of C., 1991; Mich. State C. of C. award 1991; inducted Mich. Edn. Hall of Fame, 1992; John W. Porter Disting. Chair endowed at Eastern Mich. U., 1999; Coll. of Edn. bldg. at Eastern Mich. U. named for him, 1999; recipient Olivet Coll. award for Leadership and Social Responsibility, 2001. Mem. Am. Assn. Sch. Adminstrs., Am. Assn. State Colls. and Univs. (president's council, chmn. task force on excellence in edn.), Nat. Measurement Council, NAACP (life), Greater Detroit C. of C. (Summit award 1991), Mich. State C. of C. (Disting. Svc. and Leadership award 1991), Tuskeegee Airmen (Disting. Svc. award 1991), Mich. PTA (hon. life), Ea. Mich. U. Alumni Assn. (Disting. Svc. award 1997), Econ. Club (dir. 1979), Sigma Pi Phi, Phi Delta Kappa. Office: Urban Edn Alliance Inc 1547 Fall Creek Ln Ann Arbor MI 48108-9579

PORTER, JOSEPH A. (JOE ASHBY PORTER), English language educator, fiction writer; b. Madisonville, Ky., July 21, 1942; s. Lawrence E. and Margaret (Wise) P. BA, Harvard U., 1964; MA, U. Calif., Berkeley, 1966, PhD, 1970. Asst. prof. English U. Va., Charlottesville, 1970-73, Murray (Ky.) State U., 1978-80; instr. dept. English U. Balt., 1974-75, Shoreline C.C., Seattle, 1976-77; asst. prof. English Duke U., Durham, N.C., 1980-88, assoc. prof., 1988-95, prof., 1995—. Vis. writer in residence Brown U., Providence, 1988; vis. prof. U. François Rabelais, Tours, France, 1997-98. Author: (novels) Eelgrass, 1977, Resident Aliens, 2000, (short stories) The Kentucky Stories, 1983 (Pulitzer Prize nominee 1984), Lithuania, 1990, Touch Wood, 2002, (scholarly books) The Drama of Speech Acts, 1979, Shakespeare's Mercutio, 1988; editor: Critical Essays on Shakespeare's Romeo and Juliet, 1997; editor-in-chief: New Variorum Othello. Mem. MLA, AAUP, Associated Writing Programs, South Atlantic MLA, Southeastern Renaissance Conf. (pres. 1992-93). E-mail: japorter@duke.edu.

PORTER, JOYCE KLOWDEN, theatre educator and director; b. Chgo., Dec. 21, 1949; d. LeRoy and Esther (Siegel) Klowden; m. Paul Wayne Porter, June 8, 1980; l child, David Benjamin. BA in Speech Edn., U. Ill., 1971; MA in Theatre, Northwestern U., 1972; postgrad., Northeastern U., Chgo., 1980, 89, 98, Ill. State U., 1985-90. Prof. theatre, play dir. Moraine Valley C.C., Palos Hills, Ill., 1972—2002, acting theatre coord., 1986-87, theatre coord., 2001—02. Mem. acad. senate steering com., 1995—97; adj. faculty Columbia Coll., 1988—92; lectr. Uniworld Cruises, 2002; co-owner, tour organizer Chgo. Theatre Arts Tours, Calumet City, Ill., 1988—93, actress, 1972—; text reviewer Harcourt Brace Pub., 1997, Simon & Schuster, 1998, Mayfield, 1999, Martins, 2000—, Pearsons Ednl., 2001—02. Author: (textbook) Humanities on the Go, 1992, Experiencing the Arts, 2000. Mem. adv. bd. Oak Park (Ill.) Park Dist., 1983; co-chmn. Moraine chpt. Chgo. Area Faculty for nuclear

Freeze, Palos Hills, 1985-87; announcer for blind Chgo. Radio Info. Svc., 1982-83; bd. dirs. Festival Theatre, Oak Park, 1989—, sec. 1996-97, pres., 1997-99; mem. play selection com. Village Players of Oak Park, 1992; guest dir. Triton C.C., 2000. Mem. Assn. for Theatre in Higher Edn., U.S. Inst. for Theatre Tech., Ill. Theatre Assn., C.C. Humanities Assn (presenter midwest conf. 1993, presenter & planning com. nat. conf. 1999), Ill. Fedn. Tchrs., Nature Conservancy, Zeta Phi Eta. Avocations: acting, singing, foreign travel, antiquities and antiques. Office: Moraine Valley CC 10900 S 88th Ave Palos Hills IL 60465-2175 E-mail: porter@moraine.cc.il.us.

PORTER, JUDITH DEBORAH REVITCH, sociologist, educator; b. Phila., Mar. 26, 1940; d. Eugene and Esther (Tulchinsky) Revitch; m. Gerald Joseph Porter, June 26, 1960; children: Daniel, Rebecca, Michael. Student, Vassar Coll., 1958-60; BA, Cornell U., 1962, MA, 1963; PhD, Harvard U., 1967. Lectr. Bryn Mawr (Pa.) Coll., 1966-67, asst. prof., 1967-73, assoc. prof., 1973-79, prof. sociology, 1979—, chair dept. sociology, 1987-93. Author: Black Child, White Child: The Development of Racial Attitudes, 1971; contbr. articles to profl. jours. Committeeperson Haverford Twp. Dem. Party, 1976-96; bd. dirs. Phila. AIDS Fund, 1992-98; Congreso de Latinos Unidos, Inc.; vice-chair Mayor's Commn. on Drugs and Alcohol, City of Phila. Recipient Shannon award NIMH, 1992-94; Ford Found. fellow, 1973-74; NSF fellow, 1967; NIDA grant Co-PI, 1998-2001. Mem. APHA, Am. Sociol. Assn., Phi Beta Kappa, Phi Kappa Phi. Jewish. Address: 161 Whitemarsh Rd Ardmore PA 19003-1634 Office: Bryn Mawr Coll Dept Sociology Bryn Mawr PA 19010 E-mail: jporter@brynmawr.edu.

PORTER, KAREN ANN, anthropologist, educator; b. Seattle, July 14, 1960; d. George Arnold Porter and Carole Diane Mattson. BA cum laude with distinction, U. of Wash., 1986; MA, U. of Rochester, 1988, PhD, 1997. Program dir. & folklorist Arts and Cultural Coun. of Greater Rochester, Rochester, NY, 1997—98; asst. prof. U. of Puget Sound, Tacoma, 1998—. Cons. in field; mem. various adv. com. U. of Puget Sound, 1999—. Editor: Demele: Making It - Migration and Adapation Among Haitian Boat People in the U.S.A., 1988; author: (manual) Folk Music, Dance, and Choreographed Dance, 1998; contbr. articles to profl. jours. Vol. Food Connections, Tacoma, 2000—02, Habitat for Humanity, Rochester, 1996—97, St. Joseph's Ho. of Hospitality, Rochester, 1994—98; vol. St. Paul's Episcopal Ch., 1994—98, chmn. refugee resettlement task force, 1997—98. Recipient Faith In Action award, Greater Rochester Cmty. of Ch., 1997; fellow Lewis Henry Morgan fellowship in Anthropology, U. of Rochester, 1986—89, Lang. Fellowship, Cornell U. Africana Studies and Rsch. Ctr., 1988—89, Fulbright Hays fellow, 1989, Rsch. in Africa fellow, Joint Com. on African Studies of the Social Sci. Rsch. Coun. & Am. Coun. of Learned Societies, 1990, Coun. of Ind. Coll. Tchg. fellowship, U.S. Dept. of Edn., 1994—95, U. of Rochester, 1996—97; grantee Geneseo Found. Rsch. Travel grant, SUNY-Geneseo, 1997, Oct. Event grant, N.Y. Coun. for the Humanities, 1998, W.M. Keck Found. & Project Kaleidoscope, 2002. Mem.: Soc. for the Anthropology of Work (gen. editor 1997—2001), Fedn. of Small Anthropology Programs, Am. Ethnol. Soc., Am. Anthrop. Assn., African Studies Assn., Inst. for Devel. Anthropology (rsch. assoc. 2001), Soc. for Applied Anthropology, YMCA, City Club, Phi Beta Kappa Soc. Avocations: gardening, travel, calligraphy. Office: University of Puget Sound 1500 North Warner Tacoma WA 98416 Office Fax: 253-879-3550.

PORTER, KAREN COLLINS, non-profit administrator; b. Detroit, Dec. 3, 1953; d. Cecil Allen and Mary Louise (Grzena) Collins; m. Frederick James Porter, Aug. 16, 1975; children: Suzanne Catherine, Kirstin Maureen. Student, Albion Coll., 1971-74, U. Mich., 1975; BA, U. Colo., Boulder, 1976; MA, U. Colo., Denver, 1979. Co-dir. Loveland (Colo.) Resource Ctr., 1982-84; asst. dir. Interim House-YWCA, Detroit, 1985; assoc. dir. First Step, Canton, Mich., 1985-2000; with Mich. Domestic Violence Prevention and Treatment Bd., 2001—. Bd. dirs., sec. Loveland Childbirth Edn. Assn., 1980-82; bd. dirs., chairperson Thompson Valley Presch., Loveland, 1980-84; advocate Larimer County Sexual Assault Team, Loveland, 1982-84, 1st Step Assault Response Team, 2000—; bd. dirs. Samaritan Counseling Ctr., Farmington Hills, Mich., 1985-91, 97-2000, chmn., 2000. Leader Girl Scouts Am., Farmington Hills, 1985-90; ch. leader Sunday Sch., various ch. and soc. coms. Avocations: camping, hiking, cross-country skiing, photography. Home: 29113 Forest Hill Dr Farmington MI 48331-2445 Office: PO Box 30037 235 S Grand Ave Ste 506 Lansing MI 48933-3875 E-mail: porterkm@juno.com.

PORTER, KARL HAMPTON, orchestra musical director, conductor; b. Pitts., Apr. 25, 1939; s. Reginald and Naomi Arzetta (Mitchell) P. Student, Carnegie-Mellon U., 1957-60, Peabody Conservatory, 1960-62, Juilliard Sch. Music, 1962-63, Domaine Sch. Condrs., 1961-63, Am. Symphony Orch. League, Tanglewood, 1962-72; student Polit. Sci., Fordham U., 1978; student Bus. Computer Tng., SUNY, 1986; BA, John Hopkins U., 1987. Judge for Congress of Strings, BMI Composers Competition, 1970-74; instr. theory Mt. Morris Park, 1969-73; instr. woodwind L.I. Inst. Music, 1969-75, U. Denver, 1963-64, Coll. New Rochelle, 1980; tchr. bassoon Newark Community Arts Center, 1969-71; instr. music N.Y.C. Tech. Coll., 1972-90; pres. Finale Prodns. Mem. Denver Symphony Orch., 1963-64, Met. Opera Nat. Co., 1965-67, Gil Evans Band, 1967-69, formed, Harlem Youth Symphony, 1968, Harlem Philharmonic Orch., 1969—, New Breed Brass Ensemble, Harlem String Quartet, Harlem Woodwind Quintet, 1970, condr., Balt, Symphony, 1970, mus. dir., condr., Harlem Philharmonic Orch., 1970—, N.Y.C. Housing Authority Orch., 1972-86, Massapequa (N.Y.) Symphony Soc., 1974-80, condr., Park West Symphony, Northeastern Philharmonic of Pa., Scranton Philharmonic, Ridgefield Symphonette, 1971, mus. dir. for Josephine Baker, 1972-75, free lance bassoonist, Am. Symphony, Bklyn. Philharmonic, N.J. Symphony, 1967—; min. of music St. Thomas the Apostle, 1989—; dir. Independence Community Ctr., 1993—; dir. counselor Elmcor Youth Ctr., 1991-93. Mem. nat. adv. bd. Dance Theatre of Harlem, Air Force Assn., Mental Health Assn.; bd. dirs. Empire Trust; hon. bd. dirs. Sickle Cell, Baton Rouge, La.; performing arts coord. Afro-Acad. Cultural Tech. Sci. Olympics; cons. N.Y. State Coun. Arts; dir. Ind. Cmty. Ctr., 1993—; field ops. supr.; U.S. Bur. Census. Recipient Martha Baird Rockefeller Found. grant, 1969, Nat. Endowment grant, 1970 Mem. NAACP, Nat. Soc. Lit. and Arts, N.Y. State Assn. Jr. Colls., Am. Symphony Orch. League, Performing Arts Assn. N.Y., Soc. Black Composers, Nat. Soc. Symphony Condrs. Clubs: The Bohemians. Home: 425 Central Park W New York NY 10025-4381 Office: PO Box 445 New York NY 10025-0008 also: 114 Taylor St Brooklyn NY 11211-6806

PORTER, KENNETH WAYNE, actuary; b. Brush, Colo., Apr. 2, 1948; s. William Stanley and Enid Myrle (Serr) P.; m. Karen Annette Krauss, Sept. 6, 1969; children: Rebecca Lynne Kleinschuster, Tracy Marie Curran, Kenneth Joel. BA in Math., Drew U., 1970. Enrolled Actuary, 1978. Actuarial student Prudential Ins. Co., Newark, 1970-73; actuary The DuPont Co., Wilmington, Del., 1973-80, supr., 1980-81, mgr., 1981-82, chief actuary, 1982-2000, fin. dir., 2000—. Mem. pension com. Actuarial Stds. Bd., 1985-91, mem. retiree health com., 1989-94, chair, 1989-91; bd. dirs. ERISA Industry Com., 1989—, vice chair, 1992-98, chair, 1998-2000; mem. Actuarial Bd. for Counselling and Discipline, bd. dirs., 1995-2000, chair, 1999-2000 Nat. Summit Retirement Savs., 1998, Wharton Exec. Edn. Bd., 1998—, Nat. Policy Commn. on Wealth Accumulation, 2000-01. Mem. cost audit group for Clinton Adminstrn.'s Nat. Health Reform, 1993; advisor to Clinton Adminstrn.'s Task Force on Mental Health, 1993; church elder. Fellow Conf. Consulting Actuaries; mem. Am. Acad. Actuaries (bd. dirs. 1991-94, fin. and budget com. 1991, health practice coun. 1991-95), Assn. Pvt. Pensions and Welfare Plans (bd. dirs. 1989—, exec. com. 1992—, sec. 1995, vice chair membership 1996, chair 1997). Home: 2541 Deepwood Dr Wilmington DE 19810-3633 Office: The DuPont Co 1007 Market St Wilmington DE 19898-0001 E-mail: kenneth.w.porter@usa.dupont.com.

PORTER, KIMBERLY RENÉ, epidemiologist; b. Chgo., Oct. 22, 1968; d. Kenneth Allen and Eugenia Ann Porter. Student, N.C. A&T State U., 1986-88; BS in Biology, Chgo. State U., 1990; MPH in Epidemiology, U. Ill., Chgo., 1995. Maternal and child health data specialist Sch. Pub. Health U. Ill., Chgo., 1995-98; rsch. analyst Sch. Pub. Health Harvard U., 1995-97; epidemiologist Chgo. Dept. Pub. Health, 1997—. Mem. APHA. Democrat. Avocations: reading, writing, exercising. Office: Chgo Dept Pub Health Epi Program Rm 2136 333 S State St Chicago IL 60604-3900

PORTER, LAEL FRANCES, retired communication consultant, educator; b. N.Y.C., July 30, 1932; d. Ronald William Carpenter and Frances Veneranda Fernandez Carpenter; m. Ralph Emmett Porter, June 9, 1954; children: Paula Lee Porter Leggett, Sandra Lynn Porter. BA in Comm. and Theater, U. Colo., Denver, 1982, MA in Comm. and Theater, 1986. Speech instr., Moultrie, Ga., 1954-55; owner, distributor Lael's Cosmetics & Wigs, Alexandria, Va., 1966-69; sales dept. mgr. May D & F, Denver, 1974-80; instr. comm. U. Colo., 1987-89, Red Rocks C.C., Lakewood, Colo., 1989-97; ret. Mem. coord. com. Nat. Hispana Roundtable, Denver, 1985; mem. diversity coun. and internat. dimensions Red Rocks C.C., Lakewood, Colo., 1994-96. Del. People to People, 1998; mem. adv. bd. cmty. liberal arts and scis. U. Colo., Denver, 1988—93; mem. utility consumers adv. bd. State of Colo., 1989—91; mem. exec. bd. Friends of Aurora Libr., 1997, v.p.; bd. dirs. Girls Count, Denver, 1991—2001, Colo. Statewide Systemic Initiative, Denver, 1994—98. Recipient Founding Star award Girls Count, 1995, Cert. of Appreciation USAF, 1974, Mack Easton award U. Colo., Denver, 1990. Mem.: AAUW (pub. policy com. 1994—98, state pres. 1992—94, Named Gift award 1991, Br. Named Gift award 1988, Br. Continuing Svc. award 1994), Leadership Lakewood. Episcopalian. Avocations: swimming, writing. Home and Office: 2613 S Wadsworth Cir Lakewood CO 80227-3220

PORTER, LAURINDA WRIGHT, communication educator; b. N.Y.C., June 10, 1946; d. Thomas Archibald Jr. and Christine (Allen) W.; m. Charles A. Porter Jr., June 14, 1969 (div. Mar. 1986); children: Elizabeth, Sarah. BS, Northwestern U., 1968; MA, U. Minn., 1971, PhD, 1981. From instr. to asst. prof. Concordia Coll., St. Paul, 1976-80; asst. prof. St. Olaf Coll., Northfield, Minn., 1984; from asst. to prof. St. Cloud (Minn.) U., 1984—. Asst. prof., assoc. prof. St. Mary's Grad. Ctr., Mpls., 1984-87; bd. dirs. Ctrl. Minn. Ch., Minn. Land Trust. Contbr. articles to profl. jours. Active Colonial Ch. of Edina, Minn., 1976-92. Grantee St. Cloud State U., 1988, 92-96, 99, Nat. Endowment for the Humanities, Washington, 1991. Mem. Minn. Hist. Soc., S.D. Hist. Soc., Nebr. Hist. Soc., Buffalo Bill Hist. Ctr., Inter Faculty Orgn., Sierra Club. Democrat. Avocation: American Indian history. Office: St Cloud State Univ 720 4th Ave S Saint Cloud MN 56301-4442

PORTER, LAWRENCE DON, musician; b. Texarkana, Alaska, Feb. 28, 1952; s. Elbert Morris and Frances Reeves Porter; children: Nicole. BM, U. Ark., Fayetteville, AR, 1976—76; MM, U. No. Ariz., Flagstaff, AZ, 1989—89. Author: (book) What Every Pianist Should Know, (reference book) Solomon & Healing, (book) The Pianist - The Techinic The Spirit. Home: 3530 Zafaraao Dr Suite 6 Santa Fe NM 87505 Personal E-mail: pianospianos@hotmail.com.

PORTER, LEAH LEEARLE, biological researcher, industry executive; b. Remington, Va., Sept. 19, 1963; d. James Wallace and Earline Yvonne (Moore) P. BS, U. Md., 1985; MS, Cornell U., 1990, PhD, 1993. Biol. technician U.S. Dept. Agr., Beltsville, Md., 1981-85; agrl. cons. Md. Dept. Agr., College Park, 1985; cons., office mgr. Carpigraphics, Inc., Beltsville, 1985-86; grad. rsch. asst. Cornell U., Ithaca, N.Y., 1986-94; mgr. internat. project Glahe Cons. Group, Washington, 1994-95; rsch. mgr. Chem. Mfrs. Assn., 1995-97; sci. mgr. ILSI, 1997-98; exec. dir. CropLife Am., 1999—. Cons., mktg. asst. Le Earle Enterprises, Ithaca, 1988—93. Md. State Senate scholar, 1984-85; faculty grad. fellow Cornell U., 1986-87. Fellow N.Y. Acad. Scis.; mem. Am. Phytopathological Soc., Assn. Women in Sci., Alpha Chi Sigma, Zeta Phi Beta. Democrat. Baptist. Avocations; church volunteer, reading, music. Office: 1156 15th St NW Washington DC 20005-1704

PORTER, LILIANA ALICIA, artist, photographer, painter, print and filmmaker; b. Buenos Aires, Argentina, Oct. 6, 1941; came to U.S., 1964, naturalized, 1982; d. Julio and Margarita (Galetar) P.; m. Luis Camnitzer, 1965 (div. 1978); m. Alan B. Wiener, May 28, 1980 (div. 1991). Grad., Nat. Sch. Fine Arts, Argentina, 1963. Co-dir., instr. Studio Camnitzer-Porter summer workshops, Lucca, Italy, 1974, 75, 76, 77; prof. art Queens Coll., CUNY, N.Y.C., 1991—. Adj. lectr. SUNY Coll., Old Westbury, N.Y., 1974-76, Purchase br., 1987; co-dir. Studio Porter-Wiener, N.Y.C., 1979-87. One-woman shows of prints/paintings/photographs include Galeria Artemultiple, Buenos Aires, Argentina, 1977, 78, Galleria Arte Comunale, Adro, Brescia, Italy, 1977, Hundred Acres Gallery, N.Y.C., 1977, Mus. Modern Art, Cali, Colombia, 1978, Center for Interamerican Relations, N.Y.C., 1980, Galeria Arte Nuevo, Buenos Aires, 1980, Barbara Toll Fine Arts, N.Y.C., 1979, 81, 82, 84, Galerie Jolliet, Montreal, 1983, Museo de Arte Contemporaneo, Panama City, Panama, 1984, Dolan/Maxwell Gallery, Phila., 1985, U. Alta., Edmonton, 1985, Dolan/Maxwell Gallery, Phila., 1985, Galeria Luigi Marrozzini, San Juan, P.R., 1986, Galería-Taller, Museo de Arte Moderno, Cali, Colombia, 1987, The Space, Boston, 1988, Syracuse U., N.Y., 1990, Steinbaum-Krauss Gallery, N.Y.C., 1993, Galeria Ruth Benzacar, Buenos Aires, 1994, U. Art Gallery, N.Mex. State U., Las Cruces, 1995, Monique Knowlton Gallery, 1996, Ruth Benzacar Gallery, N.Y., 1997, Mus. de Bellas Artes Juan Manuel Blanes, Montevideo, Uruguay, 1997, Espacio Minimo, Murcia, Espana, 1998, Annina Nosei Gallery, N.Y., 1999, Artcore Gallery, Toronto, Can., 1999, Espacio Minimo, Murcia, Spain, 2000, Ruth Benzacar Gallery, Buenos Aires, 2000, Sicardi Gallery, Houston, 2000, Annina Nosei, N.Y., 2000, Ctr. Photography, Woodstock, N.Y., 2000, Phoenix Mus., 2000, Galeria Espacio/Mimimo, Madrid, 2000, Brito-Cimino, Sao Paulo, Brazil, 2001, Annina Nosei Gallery, N.Y., 2002 ; retrospective exhibits 1968-90 Fundacion San Telmo, Buenos Aires, 1990, Museo Nacional de Artes Plasticas, Montevideo, Uruguay, 1991, Centro de Recepciones del Gobierno, San Juan, P.R., 1991, Bronx Mus. Art, N.Y.C., 1992, retrospective exhibit Archer Huntington Art Gallery U. Tex. Austin, 1993, Staller Ctr. for the Art SUNY at Stony Brook, N.Y., 1998; exhibited in group shows at Bonino Gallery, N.Y.C., 1964, N.Y.U., 1968, Inst. Contemporary Art, London, 1969, Paula Cooper Gallery, N.Y.C., 1969, Mus. Modern Art, N.Y.C., 1970, Biblioteque Nat., Paris, 1973, U. Mus., Berkeley, Calif., 1973, Bklyn. Mus., 1974, 75, Paris Biennial, 1975, Whitney Mus. Am. Art, N.Y.C., 1976, Lousiana Mus., Copenhagen, 1976, Fredrick Gallery, Washington, 1976, Australian Nat. Gallery, Sydney, 1977, Center for Interamerican Relations, N.Y.C., 1978, Chateau de L'Hermitage, Belgium, 1978, Mus. Fine Arts, Buenos Aires, 1978, Alternative Center for Internat. Arts, N.Y.C., 1978, Ben Shahn Gallery, N.J., 1979, Everson Mus., Syracuse, N.Y., 1979, Alternative Mus., N.Y.C., 1980, Alt. Mus., N.Y.C., 1981, Bronx Mus. Fine Arts, 1982, Musee d'Art Contemporain, Montreal, 1983, Queens Coll., Flushing, N.Y., 1983, Mus. Modern Art, San Francisco, 1983, Klein Gallery, Chgo., 1983, Cayman Gallery, N.Y.C., 1984, Artist Space, N.Y.C., 1984, U. Park, L.A., 1984, Jersey City Mus., 1986, 93, Hostos C.C., N.Y., 1986, Galeria Epoca, Santiago, Chile, 1986, Centro Wilfredo Lam, Cuba, 1986, Mus. Contemporary Spanish Art, N.Y.C., 1987, U. Tex., Austin, 1987, 88, Bronx Mus. Art, N.Y., 1988, San Diego Mus. Art, 1991, Soho 20, N.Y.C., 1992, 94, MOMA, N.Y.C., 1993, Milw. Art Mus., 1995, Mus. de Art Contemporaneo, Monterrey, Mex., 1996, 8th Fl. Gallery, N.Y.C., 1996, Old State House, Hartford, Conn., 1996, Monique Knowlton Gallery, N.Y., 1996, 97, Ctr. Cultural Recoleta, Buenos Aires, 1996, Assoc. Am. Artists, N.Y., 1997, Ctr. Cultural Tijuana, Mex., 1997, Queens Mus. Art, 1997, Index Gallery, Osaka, Japan, 1997, Boras Kommun Konstmuseet, Sweden, 1997, UCLA Fowler Mus. Cultural History, L.A., 1997, Inst. Ctr. Colombo-Am., Bogota, Colombia, 1997, Mus. Nat. de Bellas Artes, Buenos Aires, 1997, Galeria Ruth Benzacar, Art Miami, Miami Beach, Fla., 1998, Kunstforeningen Gl. Strand, Copenhagen, 1998, Arco, Madrid, 1999, Queens Mus., 1999, U. de Salamanca, Spain, 1999, Centro de la Imagen, Mexico City, 1999, Katonah Mus. Art, N.Y., 1999, New Mus., N.Y., 1999, El Mus. del Barrio, N.Y.C., 2000, Casa de America, Madrid, 2000, Contemporary Mus., Balt., 2000; represented in permanent collections Mus.Phila., Mus. Modern Art, N.Y.C., RCA Corp., N.Y.C., N.Y. Public Library, N.Y.C., La Biblioteque Nationale, Paris, France, Museo del Grabado, Buenos Aires, Museo Universitario, Mexico City, Mexico, Museo de Art Moderno, Cali, Colombia, Museo de Bellas Artes, Caracas, Venezuela, Met. Mus. Art, N.Y.C. Recipient 1st prize Argentinian Art 78 Mus. Fine Arts, Buenos Aires, 1978, Grand Prix XI, Internat. Print Biennial, Cracow, Poland, 1986, 1st prize VII Latin Am. Print Biennial, San Juan, Puerto Rico, 1986; fellow Guggenheim Found., 1980-81, N.Y. Found. for the Arts, 1985, grantee, 1999. Address: 178 Franklin St 5th Floor New York NY 10013 E-mail: porti@ix.netcom.com.

PORTER, MICHAEL PELL, lawyer; b. Indpls., Mar. 31, 1940; s. Harold Troxel and Mildred Maxine (Pell) P.; m. Alliene Laura Jenkins, Sept. 23, 1967 (div.); 1 child, Genevieve Natalie Porter Eason; m. Janet Kay Smith Hayes, Feb. 13, 1983 (div.). Student, DePauw U., 1957-58; BA, Tulane U., 1961, LLB, 1963. Bar: La. 1963, U.S. Ct. Mil. Appeals 1964, N.Y. 1969, Hawaii 1971. Clk. U.S. Ct. Appeals (5th cir.), New Orleans, 1963; assoc. Sullivan & Cromwell, N.Y.C., 1968-71, Cades Schutte Fleming & Wright, Honolulu, 1971-74, ptnr., 1975-94; mem. faculty Addis Ababa (Ethiopia) U. Sch. Law, 1995-99; sr. regulatory advisor Egyptian Capital Market Authority, Cairo, 1999—. Legal advisor St. Matthews Anglican Ch. Addis Ababa, 1995-99; cons. Rep. of Yemen, 1997; mem. deans coun. Law Sch. Tulane U., 1981-88; dep. vice chancellor Episcopal Diocese Hawaii, 1980-88, chancellor, 1988-94; chancellor Episcopal Ch., Micronesia, 1988-95. Author: Hawaii Corporation Law & Practice, 1989; Hawaii reporter State Limited Partnership Laws, 1992-94. Bd. dirs. Jr. Achievement Hawaii, Inc., 1974-84, Inst. Human Svcs., Inc., 1980-88; donor Michael P. Porter Dean's Scholastic Award, U. Hawaii Law Sch., 1977—. With JAGC, U.S. Army, 1963-66, Vietnam. Fulbright scholar, 1997-99; Tulane U. fellow, 1981; lectorship named in his honor, Addis Abba, 1994-97; established Michael P. Porter Prizes on Ethnic Harmony and Religious Tolerance in a Dem. Soc. at Addis Ababa, 1995. Mem. ABA, Hawaii State Bar Assn. Republican. E-mail: porterconsultant@yahoo.com.

PORTER, NORA ROXANNE, freelance graphic designer; b. Waterville, Maine, June 28, 1949; d. Thomas Joseph and Cecilia Anne (Joseph) Belanger; m. Charles Henry Porter II, Nov. 1, 1969; children: Katherine, Elizabeth. BA, Cornell U., 1971. Free-lance graphic artist, Poughkeepsie, N.Y., 1978—; art dir. The Hastings Ctr., Garrison, 1999—. Art dir. Hudson River Sloop Clearwater, Poughkeepsie, 1989-99; graphics coord. Hudson River Revival, Poughkeepsie, 1981-99, mem. exec. com., 1985-2000; design coord. Challenge of the Hudson Regatta, 1990; art dir. Hudson Valley Film Festival, 1997-99; mng. editor Trail Walker, The Ofcl. Publ. of the N.Y. N.J. Trail Conf., 1999—, Clearwater Navigator, 1999—. Editor: Clearwater Navigator, 2000—02;prin. works include The Long Path Guide, 2002. Designer, writer, curator Mid-Hudson Arts and Scis. Ctr., 1986-87. Avocations: reading, gardening. E-mail: cn.porter@verizon.net.

PORTER, PHILIP DREW, lawyer; b. Buffalo, Jan. 31, 1947; s. Verne William and Eleanor Marie Porter. BA, Canisius Coll., Buffalo, 1969; MEd, U. S.C., 1974, JD, 1982. Bar: D.C., Va. Tchr., guidance counselor, curriculum coord. Barnwell (S.C.) County Schs., 1969-76; coord. sec. curriculum Horry County Schs., Conway, S.C., 1976-79; assoc. Shaw Pittman, Washington, 1982-86, Fenwick & West, LLP, Washington, 1986-96; ptnr. Hogan & Hartson, LLP, McLean, Va., 1996—. Mem. and chair steering com. D.C. Bar, Washington, 1994-97. Contbr. articles to profl. jours. Bd. advisors George Mason U. Internet Multimedia Ctr., Fairfax, Va., 1998-2000; mem. D.C. Computer Law Forum, 1992-96. Recipient Golden Achievement awards D.C. Bar, 1995, 96, Cert. of Appreciation, 1999, Appreciation award Century Club of George Mason U., 1998. Mem. Computer Law Assn. Office: Hogan and Hartson LLP 8300 Greensboro Dr #1100 Mc Lean VA 22102 E-mail: pdporter@hhlaw.com.

PORTER, PHILIP THOMAS, retired electrical engineer; b. Clinton, Ky., Mar. 18, 1930; s. Philip Henry and Ruth Frances (Pennebaker) P.; m. Louise Monroe Jett, July 3, 1957; children: Philip C., Sara Shelby Porter Taylor. BA in Physics, Vanderbilt U., 1952, MA in Physics, 1953. Mem. tech. staff Bell Telephone Labs., Murray Hill, N.J., 1953-62, Holmdel, 1962-70, supr., 1971-78, West Long Branch, 1979-83; dir. wireless and wireline network compatiblity studies Telcordia Tech., Red Bank, 1984-94; ret., 1994. U.S. del. Consultative Com. for Internat. Radio, Geneva, 1984-93. Contbg. author: Electronics Engineers' Handbook, 1982, History of Science and Technology in the Bell System, 1985, Digital Communications, 1986; patentee in field. Fellow IEEE. Unitarian Universalist. Avocations: group singing, bridge.

PORTER, PHILIP WAYLAND, geography educator; b. Hanover, N.H., July 9, 1928; s. Wayland Robinson and Bertha Maria (LaPlante) P.; m. Patricia Elizabeth Garrigus, Sept. 5, 1950; children: Janet Elizabeth, Sara Louise, Alice Catherine. AB, Middlebury Coll., 1950; MA, Syracuse U., 1955; PhD, U. London, 1957. Instr. geography U. Minn., Mpls., 1957-58, asst. prof., 1958-64, assoc. prof., 1964-66, prof., 1966-2000, prof. emeritus, 2000—; assoc. to v.p. acad. affairs, also dir. Office Internat. Programs, 1979-83. Geography panel Com. on Space Programs for Earth Observations Nat. Acad. Scis., 1967-71; liaison officer Midwest Univs. Consortium for Internat. Activities, 1979-83 Author: (with Eric S. Sheppard) A World of Difference: Society, Nature, Development, 1998; contbr. articles to profl. jours. With AUS, 1952-54. Grantee Ctrl. Rsch. Fund, 1955-56, NSF, 1961-62, 78-80, 92-93, Social Sci. Rsch. Coun., 1966-67, Rockfeller Found., 1969, 71-73, Gen. Svc. Found., 1981-83, Exxon Edn. Found., 1983-84, Fulbright, 1992-93; Bush Sabbatical fellow, 1985-86. Mem. Assn. Am. Geographers. Home: 10 Burkehaven Terr Sunapee NH 03782-2402 Office: U Minn Dept Geography Minneapolis MN 55455 E-mail: pwporter@tds.net., porter@atlas.socsci.umn.edu.

PORTER, PRISCILLA, elementary education educator; b. Newburgh, N.Y., Jan. 8, 1943; d. Abner M. and Dorothy E. (Hanson) Harper; m. Charles W. Porter, July 12, 1986. BS, SUNY, New Paltz, 1963, MA, 1967; EdD, U. So. Calif., 1990. Elem. sch. tchr. various, New Paltz, 1964-69; supr. curriculum, interns, media ctr. El Camino Real (Calif.) Irvine Sch. Dist., 1969-75; supr. tchr. edn. U. Calif., Irvine, 1973-80; supr. curriculum and staff devel. Venado (Calif.) Irvine Sch. Dist., 1975-76; resource tchr., staff development, intern tchrs. Deerfield Sch., Irvine, Calif., 1976-77, tchr., 1977-78; staff devel. coord. Irvine Sch. Dist., 1978-79, 84-87, tchr. grades 4, 5 and 6, Bonita Canyon Sch., 1979-89, 90-91; assoc. prof. tchr. edn. Calif. State U., Dominguez Hills, 1991-98, prof. emeritus, 1998—; co-dir. Ctr. for History Social Sci. Edn. Editor column Social Studies and the Young Learner; cons. Reagan Predl. Libr., 2001. Author: Harcourt Brace Social Studies, 2000. Named Orange County Tchr. of Yr., 1985. Mem. ASCD, Nat. Coun. Social Studies. Home: 78440 Sunrise Mountain Vw Palm Desert CA 92211-2400 E-mail: chsse@csudh.edu.

PORTER, ROBERT CARL, JR. lawyer; b. Cin., Sept. 21, 1927; s. Robert Carl and Lavinia (Otte) P.; m. Joanne Patterson, July 5, 1952; children: Robert Carl III, David M., John E. BA with distinction, U. Mich., 1949; JD, Harvard U., 1952. Bar: Ohio 1952, U.S. Dist. Ct. (so. dist.) Ohio 1954, U.S. Ct. Appeals (6th cir.) 1954, U.S. Ct. Mil. Appeals 1956, U.S. Tax Ct. 1980, U.S. Supreme Ct. 1956. Ptnr. Porter & Porter, Cin., 1953-54; sole practice, 1954-63; sr. ptnr. Porter & McKinney, 1963-88, Porter & Porter, Cin., 1989—. Dir. and officer numerous cos. Served with JAGC, USAF, 1952-53. Mem. ABA, Ohio State Bar Assn., Cin. Bar Assn., Cin. Country Club, Univ. Club, U. Mich. Club, Harvard Law Sch. Assn., Masons, Scottish Rite, Shriners, Phi Beta Kappa. Presbyterian. Home: 2365 Bedford Ave Cincinnati OH 45208-2656 Office: Porter & Porter 2100 4th and Vine Tower Cincinnati OH 45202

PORTER, ROBERTA ANN, counselor, educator, school system administrator; b. Oregon City, Oreg., May 28, 1949; d. Charles Paul and Verle Maxine (Zimmerman) Zacur; m. Vernon Louis Porter, Dec. 27, 1975 (div. Dec. 1998). B in Bus. Edn., So. Oreg. Univ., 1971, M in Bus. Edn., 1977; cert. in counseling, Western Oreg. U., 1986; postgrad., Lewis and Clark Coll., 1995. Cert. in leadership Nat. Seminars. Tchr. Klamath Union H.S., Klamath Falls, Oreg., 1971-73, Mazama Mid./H.S., Klamath Falls, 1973-83; instr. Oreg. Inst. Tech., Oreg., 1975-92; counselor Mazama H.S., 1983-93; vice prin. Bonanza (Oreg.) Schs., 1993-95; counselor Klamath County Sch. Dist., Oreg., 1995—; TAG coordinator Lost River Jr./Sr. H.S., 1995—2002, gender equity team, 1997—. Participant Clinton Cuban-USA Edn. Initiative, Oct. 2000; Blue/Gold Officer USN Acad., 2000—; mem. Klamath County Sch. Dist. sch. improvement com. 2000—; presenter Oreg. and Nat. Assn. Student Coun., 1989-92, Oreg. Sch. Bds. Assn., Sch. Counselor Assn., 1995, state mini workshops counselors/adminstrs., Western Region Br. leadership tng. ACA, 1999, Klamath Youth Summit, 1999; mem. task force for ednl. reform in Oreg., 1993-94; trainer asst. Leadership Devel. Am. Sch. Counselor Assn.; trainer ACA. Mem. editl. bd. Eldorado Wellness, 1996—. Trainer U.S. Army and Marines Recruiters, Portland and Medford, Oreg., 1988-89; master trainer Armed Svcs. Vocat. Aptitude Battery/Career Exploration Program, 1992—; candidate Klamath County Sch. Bd., Klamath Falls; interpreter AMTRAK svc. Klamath Dept. Tourism and Nat. Parks, 1998—; mem. Klamath County Crisis Team. Recipient Promising, Innovative Practices award Oreg. Sch. Counselors, 1990. Mem. NEA, ACA (western region parliamentarian 1999-2001), COSA, ASCD, ASCA, Oreg. Sch. Counseling Assn. (presenter, v.p. h.s. 1988-91, mem. com. 1991-93, pres. 1992-95, pres.'s award), Oreg. Edn. Assn.,

Oreg. Counseling Assn. (pres. award 1995, parliamentarian 1994-95, area 8 rep. 1995-97, pres.-elect 1997-98, pres. 1998-99, past pres. 1999-2000), Oreg. Assn. Student Couns. (bd. dirs. activity advisors 1989-91), Nat. Assn. Student Couns., Klamath Falls Edn. Assn. (bldg. rep. 1990-93, sec. 1991-92, negotiations team 1992-93), Delta Kappa Gamma (exec. bd. Alpha chpt. 1985-94, pres. 1990-92, state conv. chmn. 1992, state legis. com. 1991-93, chmn. 1993-95, state expansion com., World Fellowship chair Alpha chpt., scholarship chair 2002—). Avocations: snowmobiling, travel, reading, camping, waterskiing. Home: 3131 Derby St Klamath Falls OR 97603-7313 Office: Lost River Jr/Sr High Sch 23330 Highway 50 Merrill OR 97633-9706

PORTER, ROGER BLAINE, government official, educator; b. Provo, Utah, June 19, 1946; s. Blaine Robert and Elizabeth M. (Taylor) P.; m. Ann Robinson, Jan. 6, 1972; children: Robert Roger, Stacy Ann, David R., Rachel Elizabeth. BA in History and Polit. Sci., Brigham Young U., 1969; PhB, Oxford U., 1971; MA, PhD, Harvard U., 1978. Asst. dean, tutor in politics Queen's Coll., Oxford U., 1971-72; spl. asst. to pres. The White House, 1974-77; rsch. assoc. Kennedy Sch. Govt. and Grad. Sch. Bus., Harvard U., Cambridge, Mass., 1977-79, asst. prof. pub. policy, 1979-81, assoc. prof., 1981, prof. govt. and bus., 1985—; spl. asst. to Pres. of U.S., 1981-82; dep. asst. to Pres. of U.S., 1982-85; dir. White Ho. Office of Policy Devel., Washington, 1982-85; counselor to sec. U.S. Treasury, 1981-85; exec. sec. Nat. Productivity Adv. Com., 1981-85, Cabinet Coun. on Econ. Affairs, 1981-85, Econ. Policy Coun., 1985; asst. to U.S. Pres. for econ. and domestic policy, 1989-93. Exec. sec. Pres.'s Econ. Policy Bd., 1974—77; sr. scholar Woodrow Wilson Internat. Ctr. for Scholars, 1993—; dir. Ctr. for Bus. and Govt. Harvard U., 1995—2000, master Dunster House, 2001—; mem. Pres.'s Commn. on White House Fellowships, 1976—2001; bd. dirs. Zions Bancorp., Pactiv Corp., Nat. Life Ins. Co., Tenneco Automotive, Inc. Author: Presidential Decision Making, 1980, U.S.-USSR Grain Agreement, 1984, Efficiency, Equity, Legitimacy: The Multilateral Trading System at the Millenium, 2001; asst. editor: Public Policy, 1979—81. Mem. Utahns for Effective Govt., Salt Lake City, 1971-72; mem. Rep. Nat. Com. Econ. Adv. Com., 1977-81. Rhodes scholar, 1969; Woodrow Wilson fellow, 1969; White House fellow, 1974; recipient spl. citation U.S. Sec. Treasury, 1977, Rolex Intercollegiate Tennis Achievement award, 1996; named One of 10 Outstanding Young Men in Am., 1981 Fellow Nat. Acad. Pub. Adminstrn.; mem. White House Hist. Assn. (bd. dirs. 1995—), Phi Kappa Phi, Pi Sigma Alpha, Phi Eta Sigma, Phi Alpha Theta. Mem. Lds Ch. Avocations: classical music, basketball, tennis, travel. Home: 12 Clifton St Belmont MA 02478-3363 Office: Harvard U Kennedy Sch Govt 79 JFK St Cambridge MA 02138-5801

PORTER, ROGER JOHN, medical research administrator, neurologist, pharmacologist; b. Pitts., Apr. 4, 1942; s. John Keaggy and Margaret (Parker) P.; m. Candace Marie Leland, Feb. 17, 1968; children: David, Stacey. BS, Eckerd Coll., 1964; MD, Duke U., 1968. Diplomate Nat. Bd. Med. Examiners, Am. Bd. Neurology, Am. Bd. Electroencephalography. Intern U. Calif., San Diego, 1968-69, resident in neurology San Francisco, 1971-74; fellow rsch. tng. program Duke U., Durham, N.C., 1966-67; staff assoc. sect. epilepsy Nat. Inst. Neurol. Diseases and Stroke, NIH, Bethesda, Md., 1969-71; dep. dir. Nat. Inst. Neurol. Disorders and Stroke, NIH, 1987-92; investigator U. Calif., San Francisco, 1972-73; sr. rsch. assoc. epilepsy br. neurol. disorders program Nat. Inst. Neurol. and Communicative Disorders and Stroke, NIH, Bethesda, 1974-78, asst. chief epilepsy br., 1977-79, acting chief, 1979-80, acting chief clin. epilepsy sect., IRP, 1979-84, chief epilepsy br. neurol. disorders program, 1980-84, chief med. neurology br. and clin. epilepsy sect. IRP, 1984-87; dep. dir. Nat. Inst. Neurol. Disorders and Stroke, NIH, 1987-92; v.p., clin. pharmacology Wyeth-Ayerst Rsch., Radnor, Pa., 1992-97, v.p., clin. rsch., 1997—99, v.p. and developing head, clin. rssch., 1999—. Adj. prof. neurology U. Pa., 1993—; prof. neurology Uniformed Svcs. U. Health Scis., Bethesda, 1980-93, adj. prof. pharmacology, 1982—; cons.-lectr. neurology Nat. Naval Med. Ctr., Bethesda, 1978-93; chmn. White House Subcom. on Brain and Behavioral Scis., 1990-92; scholar-in-residence Assn. Am. Med. Colls., Washington, 1989-90; mem. NIMH/Nat. Inst. Neurol. Disorders and Stroke Coun. of Assembly of Scientists, 1983-86, pres., 1985-86; mem. pharmacy and therapeutics com. NIH, 1977-86, chmn., 1978; mem. instnl. rev. bd. human subjects Nat. Inst. Neurol. Disorders and Stroke, 1984-87, chmn., 1986-87. Author/editor 13 books; mem. editl. bd. Acta Neurologica Scandanavica, 1991-97, Annals of Neurology, 1987-92, Epilepsia, 1982-86, Clin. Neuropharmacology, 1999—; contbr. articles to profl. jours.; writer, contbr. 5 motion pictures, 1 exhibit. Bd. trustees Eckerd Coll., 1994-97. With USPHS, 1969-92. Recipient MacArthur Outstanding Alumnus award Eckerd Coll., 1977, Fulbright Disting. Prof. award, 1985, Disting. Alumnus award Duke Duke U. Med. Ctr., 1989, USPHS Dist. Svc. Medal, 1991, USUHS Commendable Svc. Award, 2001. Fellow Am. Acad. Neurology, Am. Neurol. Assn.; mem. Am. Electroencephalographic Soc., Am. Epilepsy Soc. (pres. 1989-90), Soc. Neurosci., Am. Soc. Clin. Pharmacology and Therapeutics, Am. Soc. Experimental Neurol. Therapeutics, Internat. League Against Epilepsy (sec.-gen. 1989-93), Am. Soc. Pharmacology and Exptl. Therapeutics. Home: 461 Timber Ln Devon PA 19333-1232 Office: Wyeth Rsch PO Box 8299 Philadelphia PA 19101-8299

PORTER, RONALD, artist, educator; b. Knoxville, Tenn., Apr. 1, 1942; s. Dennis Kyle and Mildred Porter; m. Victoria Hill (div.); 1 child, Stacy Burke; m. Pamela S. Porter. BFA, Middle Tenn. State U., Murfreesboro, 1987; MFA, Ohio U., Athens, 1989. Adj. prof. art Shawnee State U., Portsmouth, Ohio, 1989-90, Ohio U., Athens, 1989-90, vis. prof. art, 1994-95, U. Wyoming, Laramie, 1991; adj. prof. art Middle Tenn. State U., Murfreesboro, 1997; sr. lectr. Vanderbilt U., Nashville, 1997—. Designer mus. exhibits Greenville County (S.C.) Mus. Art, 1967-69; curator Leehall Gallery, Clemson (S.C.) U., 1970-71. Recipient Juror's award Washington & Jefferson Coll., Best Show Painting award Brenau Coll., 1994; individual fellow Ohio Arts Coun., 1990, 93. Office: Vanderbilt U Dept Fine Arts 2301 Vanderbilt Dr Nashville TN 37235 E-mail: ronald.r.porter@vanderbilt.edu.

PORTER, RUSSELL MARK, law enforcement executive, educator, trainer; b. Little Sioux, Iowa, Apr. 8, 1957; s. Harold Henry and Gwendolyn Ruby Mae (Beebe) P.; m. Carla Jean Cammack, Nov. 4, 1979; children: Benjamin, Brandon, Blake. BS in Criminal Justice, U. Nebr., Omaha, 1981; MPA, Drake U., 1993; grad., FBI Nat. Acad. 195th Session, 1998; postgrad., U. Nebr., 1994—. Police officer, investigator La Vista (Nebr.) Police Dept., 1978-81; police officer Council Bluffs (Iowa) Police Dept., 1981-82; dep. sheriff Douglas County Sheriff's Office, Omaha, 1982; spl. agt., spl. agt. in charge intelligence bur. Dept. Pub. Safety, divsn. criminal investigation, Des Moines, 1982—. Mem. Lt. Gov.'s Com. on Diversity, State of Iowa, Des Moines, 1992-94, chair exec. bd. Iowa Law Enforcement Intelligence Network, Des Moines, 1992-97, exec. bd. Law Enforcement Intelligence Unit, 1998—; adj. faculty Iowa State U., Ames, 1997; chair investigative support com. Midwest High Intensity Drug Trafficking Area, Kansas City, Mo., 1997—, criminal justice adv.com., Simpson Coll., Indianola, Iowa, 1997—. Co-developer, editor Tng. Materials Law Enforcement Intelligence Ops., also book revs., articles profl. jours. Mem. Men's Chorus West Des Moines United Meth. Ch., 1990—, Celebration Quartet, 1991—; asst. scoutmaster troop 78 Boy Scouts Am., West Des Moines, 1994—. Mem. Internat. Assn. for Study Organized Crime, Am. Soc. Criminology, Acad. Criminal Justice Scis., Internat. Assn. Law Enforcement Intelligence Analysts, (dir. law enforcement liaison and advisory 1998—). Office: Iowa Dept Pub Safety Wallace State Office Bldg Des Moines IA 50319-0001

PORTER, SPENCE, playwright; b. Scranton, Pa., Dec. 17, 1948; s. Arthur Porter and Carol (Reiss) Lebost. AB, Harvard U., 1970; MFA, Ohio U., 1974. Plays include: Hippolytus, Francesca, Sick Minds, The Mouse Prince, Arguments with Myself. Mem. Dramatists Guild, Creative Coalition, Harvard Club N.Y.C. Home and Office: 3435 Giles Pl Apt 5F Bronx NY 10463-4338 E-mail: SpencePorter@post.harvard.edu.

PORTER, STEPHEN CUMMINGS, geologist, educator; b. Santa Barbara, Calif., Apr. 18, 1934; s. Lawrence Johnson Porter Jr. and Frances (Cummings) Seger; m. Anne Mary Higgins, Apr. 2, 1959; children: John, Maria, Susannah. BS, Yale U., 1955, MS, 1958, PhD, 1962. Asst. prof. geology U. Wash., Seattle, 1962-66, assoc. prof., 1966-71, prof., 1971—2002, dir. Quaternary Research Ctr., 1982-98, prof. emeritus, 2001—. Mem. bd. earth scis. Nat. Acad. Sci., Washington, 1983-85; mem. adv. com. divsn. polar programs NSF, Washington, 1983-84; vis. fellow Clare Hall Cambridge (Eng.) U., 1980-81; guest prof. Academia Sinica, People's Republic of China, 1987—; v.p. Internat. Union Quaternary Rsch., 1992-95, pres., 1995-99. Co-author: Physical Geology, 1987, The Dynamic Earth, 1989, 92, 95, 99, The Blue Planet, 1995, 99, Environmental Geology, 1996, Dangerous Earth, 1997; editor: Late Quaternary Environments of the United States, 1983; editor Quaternary Rsch., 1976-2000; assoc. editor Radiocarbon, 1982-89, Am. Jour. Sci., 1997—; mem. editl. bd. Quaternary Sci. Revs., 1988—, Quaternary Internat., 1989—. Served to lt. USNR, 1955-57. Recipient Benjamin Silliman prize Yale U., 1962; Willis M. Tale lectr. So. Meth. U., 1984, S.F. Emmons lectr. Colo. Sci. Soc., 1996; Fulbright Hays sr. rsch. fellow, New Zealand, 1973-74. Fellow Geol. Soc. Am., Arctic Inst. N.Am. (bd. govs.), AAAS; mem. Am. Quaternary Assn. (coun., pres. 1992-94). Avocations: photography, mountaineering. Home: 18034 15th Ave NW Seattle WA 98177-3305 Office: U Wash Dept Earth and Space Scis PO Box 351360 Seattle WA 98195-1310

PORTER, STEPHEN WINTHROP, stage director; b. Ogdensburg, N.Y., July 24, 1925; s. Charles T. and Anna (Newton) P. BA, Yale U., 1945, M.F.A., 1948. Asst. prof. English in charge of drama McGill U., Montreal, 1949-56. Stage dir. plays on Broadway Right You Are, Wild Duck, 1966, The Show Off, 1967, The Misanthrope, 1968, 83, The Wrong Way Light Bulb, Private Lives, 1969, Harvey, 1970, The School for Wives, 1971, Captain Brassbound's Conversion, 1972, Don Juan, 1973, Chemin de Fer, 1974, Rules of the Game, 1975, They Knew What They Wanted, 1976, Days in the Trees, 1976, The Importance of Being Earnest, 1977, Tartuffe, 1977, Man and Superman, 1978, Major Barbara, The Man Who Came to Dinner, 1980, You Never Can Tell, 1986, The Devil's Disciple, 1988, The Miser, 1990, Getting Married, 1991. Address: 25 W 54th St New York NY 10019-5404

PORTER, STUART WILLIAMS, investment company executive; b. Detroit, Jan. 11, 1937; s. Stuart Perlee and Alma Bernice (Williams) P.; m. Myrna Marlene Denham, June 27, 1964; children: Stuart, Randall. BS, U. Mich., 1960; MBA, U. Chgo., 1967, postgrad., 1967-68. Investment mgr., prin. Weiss Peck & Greer, 1978-98; mng. ptnr. SPC Capital Mgmt., 1999—. Chmn. Crusade of Mercy, 1973; chmn. investment com. Presbytery of Chgo. Served with USAF, 1961-62. Recipient Excellence in Bus. and Acctg. award Fin. Exec. Inst., 1966; Am. Acctg. Assn. fellow, 1967. Mem. Midwest Pension Conf., Investment Analysts Soc., Assn. Investment Mgmt. Rsch., Inst. Quantitative Rsch. in Fin., Chgo. Quantitative Analysts Soc., Turnberry Country Club, Econ. Club, The Res. Golf Club, Avondale Country Club, Wynstone Golf Club, Beta Gamma Sigma. Home: 130 Wyngate Dr Barrington IL 60010-4839

PORTER, VERNA LOUISE, lawyer; b. May 31, 1941; BA, Calif. State U., 1963; JD, Southwestern U., 1977. Bar: Calif. 1977, U.S. Dist. Ct. (ctrl. dist.) Calif. 1978, U.S. Ct. Appeals (9th cir.) 1978. Ptnr. Eisler & Porter, L.A., 1978-79, mng. ptnr., 1979-86; pvt. practice, 1986—. Judge pro-tempore L.A. Mcpl. Ct., 1983—, L.A. Superior Ct., 1989—, Beverly HIlls Mcpl. Ct., 1992—; mem. subcom. landlord tenant law, State Calif., panelist conv.; mem. real property law sect. Calif. State Bar, 1983; mem. client rels. panel, vol. L.A. County Bar Dispute Resolution; ct. appointed arbitrator civil cases, fee arbitrator L.A. Superior Ct.; mem. Better Bus. Bur. Abitrator Automobile Lemon Laws, 2000—. Editl. asst., contbr. Apt. Bus. Outlook, Real Property News, Apt. Age. Mem. adv. coun. Freddie Mac Vendor, 1995—; mem. World Affairs Coun. Mem. ABA, L.A. County Bar Assn. (client-rels. vol. dispute resolution fee arbitration 1981—; arbitrator lemon law claims), L.A. Trial Lawyers Assn., Wilshire Bar Assn. Women Lawyers' Assn., Landlord Trial Lawyers Assn. (founding, pres.), Da Camera Soc. Republican. Office: 2500 Wilshire Blvd Ste 1226 Los Angeles CA 90057-4365

PORTER, WALTER ARTHUR, retired judge; b. Dayton, Ohio, June 6, 1924; s. Claude and Estella (Raymond) P.; m. Patricia Reeves Higdon, Dec. 3, 1947; children— Scott Paul, David Bryant. BS in Engring, U. Cin., 1948, LL.B., 1949. Bar: Ohio 1949. Legal dep. Montgomery County Probate Ct., 1949-51; asst. pros. atty. Montgomery County, 1951-56; with Albert H. Scharrer (atty.), Dayton, 1956-61; mem. firm Smith & Schnacke, 1962-85, pres., 1980-85; judge Montgomery County Common Pleas Ct., 1985-95; of counsel Thompson Hine & Flory, Dayton, 1996-2001. Served with inf. U.S. Army, 1943-45, ETO. Mem. ABA, Ohio Bar Assn. (pres. 1973-74), Dayton Bar Assn., Am. Coll. Trial Lawyers, Am. Coll. Probate Counsel, Phi Alpha Delta, Omicron Delta Kappa. Clubs: Mason. Democrat. Presbyterian. Home: 872 Timberlake Ct Kettering OH 45429-3494 E-mail: wapphp@aol.com.

PORTER, WALTER THOMAS, JR. former bank executive; b. Jan. 8, 1934; s. Walter Thomas and Mary Rebecca (Brookes) P.; m. Dixie Jo Thompson, Apr. 3, 1959; children: Kimberlee Paige, Douglas Thompson, Jane-Amy Elizabeth. BS, Rutgers U., 1954; MBA, U. Wash., 1959; PhD, Columbia U., 1964. CPA, Wash., N.Y. Staff cons. Touche Ross & Co., N.Y.C., 1959-61, dir. edn., 1964-66; NDEA fellow Columbia ., 1961-64; assoc. prof. U. Wash., 1966-70, prof., 1970-74; vis. prof. N. European Mgmt. Inst., Oslo, Norway, 1974-75; nat. dir. planning Touche Ross & Co., Seattle, 1975-78, dir. exec. fin. counseling, 1978-84; exec. v.p., mgr. pvt. banking Rainier Nat. Bank, 1984-87, exec. v.p., mgr. capital mgmt. and pvt. banking, 1987-88, vice-chmn., 1988-89, Security Pacific Bank Washington, 1989-92; exec. v.p., mgr. capital mgmt. group Bank of Am., Seattle, 1992-99; chmn. Porter Investments LLC, 1999—. Vis. lectr. taxation U. Wash., 1978-85; bd. dirs. Shugard Self-Storage, Coldstream Capital Mgmt., ClearMed., Flexcar. Author: 11 books, the most recent being The Bank of America Guide to Personal Financial Solutions, 2d edit., 1998, The Glory of Washington: The People and Events That Shaped the Husky Athletic Tradition, 2001. Mem. Seattle adv. bd. Salvation Army, 1975-83, 89-97, pres., 1993-95; trustee Ryther Child Ctr., 1975-85, pres., 1979-81; trustee Lakeside Sch., 1977-87, pres., 1984-86; trustee Va. Mason Med. Ctr., 1986-97, chair bd. govs., 1994-96; chair Nat. Campaign for Student Athlete U. of Wash., 1995-2000, Mus. History and Industry, 1982-83, Olympic Park Inst., 1996-2001. With U.S. Army, 1955-57. Mem. Sand Point Country Club. Congregationalist. E-mail: djoporter@email.msn.com.

PORTER, WAYNE RANDOLPH, dermatologist; b. Washington, Jan. 10, 1948; s. James Randolph and Betty Rose (Burgess) P. BS, MIT, 1970; MD, Duke U., 1973. Diplomate Am. Bd. Internal Medicine, Am. Bd. Dermatology. Intern U. Miami (Fla.) Affiliated Hosps., 1973-74; resident in internal medicine U. Miami Sch. Medicine, 1973-76, resident in dermatology, 1976-78, clin. instr., then asst. prof. dermatology, 1978-85, assoc. prof., 1985—. Adj. prof. Barry U. Sch. Grad. medicine, 2000—; practice medicine specializing in dermatology, North Miami Beach, 1978—; mem. staff U. Miami-Jackson Meml. Hosp., North Shore Med. Ctr., Parkway Regional Med. Ctr., Aventura Hosp. Mem. med. adv. bd. Dade-Broward chpt. Lupus Found. Am. Fellow Internat. Soc. for Dermatologic Surgery, Am. Acad. Dermatology, Am. Assn. Dermatologic Surgeons; mem. AMA, ACP, Internat. Soc. Pediat. Dermatology, Fla. Med. Assn., Fla. Dermatology Soc., Miami Dermatol. Soc. (pres.), Dade County Med. Assn., So. Med. Assn., Bath Club (Miami Beach), Coral Reef Yacht Club. Office: 909 N Miami Beach Blvd Miami FL 33162-3712 E-mail: wrpmd@bellsouth.net.

PORTER, WILLIAM L. electrical engineer, retired; b. Leeds, N.D., July 2, 1929; s. Ernest Cecil and Dena Grace (Thompson) P.; m. Mary Lynn Lindsey, Oct. 9, 1948; children: Belinda Joyce, William Harry, Terry Jane, Derek Lewis, Michael Ronald. AA, Springfield Coll., 1960; BSEE, U. Ill., 1963. Registered profl. engr., Ill., Ind., Minn., Wis., Mich., Ohio, Nebr., Iowa, N.D., S.D. Lineman City Water, Light and Power, Springfield, Ill., 1947-54, troubleshooter, 1954-62, gen. supt. elec. divsn., 1962-76; prin. engr. R.W. Beck and Assocs., Columbus, Nebr., 1976-77, engring. mgr. Mpls., 1977-80, ptnr., mgr., 1980-90, sr. cons., 1990-97; ret., 1997. Spkr. on engring. and utilities; cons. to electric utilities. Author numerous engring. reports and engring. and utilities papers. Street light com. chair City of Springfield, 1964, mem. CATV com., 1966; mem. Planning Commn. Spring Park (Minn.), 1978-79; chair environ. quality com. region IV Ill. Soc. Profl. Engrs., chair ethics and practices com. Capital chpt.; mem. tech. adv. com. Fed. Power Commn's Nat. Power Survey; chair engring. and ops. com. Am. Pub. Power Assn., 1967-70, chair power supply planning com., 1973-74. Named Engr. of Yr., Capital chpt. Ill. Soc. Profl. Engrs., 1975. Mem. IEEE (life mem., chmn. Ctrl. Ill. sect. 1974-75), NSPE (life), Eta Kappa Nu. Republican. Home: 6208 Mackenzie Pl Springfield IL 62707-6748 E-mail: Biliam729@aol.com.

PORTER, WILLIAM LYMAN, architect, educator; b. Poughkeepsie, N.Y., Feb. 19, 1934; s. William Quincy and Lois (Brown) P.; m. Lynn Rogers Porter; children: Quayny Lyman, Zoe Lynn, Eve Lyman. BA, Yale U., 1955, M.Arch., 1957; PhD, MIT, 1969. Designer, job capt. Louis I. Kahn (architect), Phila., 1960-62; urban designer, asst. chief of design Ciudad Guayana project Joint Center for Urban Studies of Harvard and MIT, Caracas, Venezuela, 1962-64; Mellon fellow dept. urban studies and planning MIT, 1964-65; Samuel Stouffer fellow Joint Center for Urban Studies, Harvard and MIT, 1966-67; asst. prof. urban design, depts. architecture and urban studies and planning MIT, 1968-70, assoc. prof. urban design, 1970-71, prof. architecture and planning, 1971—, Norman B. and Muriel Leventhal prof. architecture and planning, 1988—, head. dept. architecture, 1987-91, dean Sch. Architecture and Planning, 1971-81; co-dir. Aga Khan Program for Islamic Architecture Harvard U.-MIT, 1979-85. Cons. in field; mem. Nat. Archtl. Accrediting Bd., 1978-80, pres., 1979; mem. Mass. Designer Selection Bd., 1978-79, chmn., 1979; mem. steering com. Aga Khan Award for Architecture, 1977-86, mem. master jury, 1989; prin. Four Architecture Inc., Boston, 1994—. Co-author: Excellence by Design: Transforming Workplace and Work Practice, 1999; co-founder, co-editor Places: A Quarterly Jour. Environ. Design, 1982-88; co-editor: Facilities Engineering and Management Handbook: Commercial, Industrial and Institutional Buildings, 2000. Trustee Milton (Mass.) Acad., 1989-2001; mem. bd. overseers Coll. Fine Arts, U. Pa., 1984-90, Mus. Fine Arts, Boston, 1992-94. Fellow AIA; mem. Boston Soc. Architects (dir. 1969-73, 77-81) Clubs: Harvard Musical Assn. (Boston). Home: 17 Concord Ave Cambridge MA 02138-2321 Office: MIT Sch Architecture & Planning 77 Massachusetts Ave Cambridge MA 02139-4307

PORTER, WILMA JEAN, educational consultant; b. Sylacauga, Ala., May 30, 1931; d. Harrison Samuel and Blanche Leonard Butcher; m. Douglas Taylor Porter, Apr. 18, 1953; children: Daria Cecile, Blanche Evette, Douglas Vincent. BS, Tuskegee U., 1951; MS, Mich. State U., 1966; PhD, Iowa State U., 1980. Asst. dietitian Miss. State Tb Sanatorium, 1951-52; therapeutic dietitian dept. of hosp. City of N.Y., S.I., 1952-53; libr. asst. Mississippi Valley State Coll., Itta Bena, Miss., 1963-65; asst. prof. Grambling (La.) State U., 1966-75, Howard U., Washington, 1976-80; country dir. U.S. Peace Corps, Tonga, 1980-82; asst. dir. internat. programs Ft. Valley (Ga.) Coll., 1983-84, dir. Inst. Advancement, 1984-88; dir. Sch. Home Econs., Tenn. Technol. U., Cookeville, 1989-96; pvt. ednl. cons., 1996-98. Project dir. Capitol Hill Health and Homemaker, Washington, 1982-83; interim dir. Inst. Advancement Alcorn State U., Lorman, Miss., 1988-89. Author lab. manual for quantity foods, 1977; editor: (cookbook) Some Christmas Foods and Their Origins from Around the World, 1983. Convenor Nat. Issues Forums, Ga. and Tenn., 1985-90; citizen participant Nat. Issues Forums Soviet Dialogue, Newport Beach, Calif., 1988; bd. dirs. Leadership Putnam, Cookeville, 1990-94; chmn. Tenn. Technol. U. campaign United Way, 1989; mem. devel. and planning com. Peach County Ft. Valley, 1985-87; mem. Peach County Heart Fund Dr., 1986-88; participant People to People Citizens Amb. program U.S./China Women's Issues Program, 1995. Title III grantee U.S. Dept. Edn., 1986, 87; Tenn. Dept. Human Svcs. grantee, 1993, 94. Mem. AAUW (program chair 1991-92, pres. Cookeville br. 1993-94), Am. Family and Consumer Scis. Assn., Am. Dietetic Assn., Nat. Coun. Adminstrs. Home Econs., La. Assn. Family and Consumer Scis., La. Dietetic Assn. Democrat. Roman Catholic. Avocations: writing, vegetable and flower gardening. Home: 1415 ML King Jr Ave Grambling LA 71245

PORTERA, ALAN A. educator; b. Buffalo, Jan. 29, 1951; s. Albert Andrew and Adele Beatrice (Pecorella) P.; m. Marcia Jean Urbaniak, May 16, 1975; 1 child, Alanna Jachelene. BS, State U. Coll. N.Y., Buffalo, 1974; MS in Edn., Niagara U., 1981; doctoral candidate, SUNY Coll. at Buffalo, 1984. Cert. nursery sch., kindergarten, grades 1-6, and art grades K-12, N.Y. Tchr. St. Gregory's, Williamsville, N.Y., 1974-75, St. Mark's, Buffalo, 1975—77, St. James, Depew, N.Y., 1977-79, St. Teresa's, Niagara Falls, 1979-89; dir. religious edn. St. Joseph's, North Tonawanda, 1978-92, Saint Joseph's, Niagara Falls, 1990-92; ednl. sales cons. Knowledge Nest, Chgo., 1989-90; elem. tchr. Niagara Falls Bd. Edn., 1992-93; religious edn. dept. chair St. John's Acad., Plattsburgh, N.Y., 1994-96; tchr. North Palm Beach (Fla.) Elem. Sch., 1997-98; ednl. sales cons. Stop, Look and Learn, Palm Beach Gardens, Fla., 1996-97, Get Smart, Palm Beach Gardens, 1998; dir. religious edn. St. Thomas More, Boynton Beach, 1998—. Religious edn. moderator Region 26, 29, 30, Diocese of Buffalo, 1981-83. Author: Concern for Peace and Justice, 1981, Foundations for Faith Formation, 1989, Fundamental Building Blocks of Faith, 1991. Mem. Nat. Conf. for Catechetical Leadership, 2002—, Palm Beach Diocesan Youth Adv. Bd., 1999—2000; mem. pastoral formation bd. St. Vincent de Paul Regional Sem., Boynton Beach, Fla., 2001—. Named Religious Educator of the Year Diocese of Buffalo, 1979. Mem. Nat. Cath. Educators Assn., Western N.Y. Assn. Dirs. and Coords. of Religious Educators (v.p. 1985-87). Democrat. Home: PO Box 14981 North Palm Beach FL 33408-0981 E-mail: STM2000@webmail.catholic.org. *Learning is a womb to tomb experience. I believe it truly is a lifelong process of change that permits the learners to apply the knowledge that they have acquired to their own life experience.*

PORTERFIELD, CHRISTOPHER, magazine editor, writer; b. Weston, W.Va., Apr. 3, 1937; s. James Herman and Irene (Smith) P.; m. Stephanie Brown, Jan. 20, 1962; children: Christopher Brown, Tessa Louise, Kevin Stephenson. BA, Yale U., 1958; MA, Columbia U., 1965. Music critic Time mag., N.Y.C., 1967-69, cultural correspondent London, 1969-72; exec. producer Daphne Prodns., N.Y.C., 1974-79; sr. editor Time mag., 1980-93, asst. mng. editor, 1993-96; exec. editor, 1996—. Co-Author: (with Dick Cavett) (books) Cavett, 1973, Eye on Cavett, 1983; contbr. articles to popular mags. and periodicals, 1975—. Mem. Writer's Guild of Am. Avocations: reading, music, tennis. Home: 315 Central Park W New York NY 10025-7664 Office: Time Mag 1271 Avenue Of The Americas New York NY 10020-1300

PORTERFIELD, CRAIG ALLEN, b. Geneva, May 11, 1955; s. Paul Laverne and Elizabeth Louise (Mearns) Porterfield; m. Alta Marie Herring, Aug. 1, 1977; children: Aleine Michelle, Brian Matthew. Student, Sorbonne U., Paris, 1975-76; BA, St. John Fisher Coll., 1977; MA, U. Tex., Austin, 1982, PhD, 1985. Lic. psychologist N.Y., Del., cert. sch. psychologist N.Y. Program evaluation intern Austin Ind. Sch. Dist., 1980, psychol. intern, 1982—83; program evaluator Austin Child Guidance Ctr., 1981—82; evaluation mgr. Child, Inc., Austin, 1981—82; staff therapist Psychotherapy Inst., 1984—85; consulting psychologist Albany (N.Y.) Psychol. Assocs., 1987—90; staff psychologist Berkshire Farm Ctr. and Svcs. for Youth, Canaan, NY, 1985—87, dir. rsch., 1987—90; psychologist Del. Psychiatry Svcs., Dover, 1990—94, sr. psychologist Del., 1994—95; pvt. practice psychology Camden, 1995—; owner Craig Porterfield Consulting Group, 2000—, Charter Prin., 2000—, The Global Consulting Partnership, 2000—. Adj. asst. prof. SUNY, Albany, 1986—87, Albany, 1989—91; psychologist privileges dept. psychiatry Kent Gen. Hosp., Dover, 1990—2000, Milford Meml. Hosp., Dover, 1995—2000; mem. com. life skills curriculum Lake Forest Sch. Dist., Harrington, Del., 1991; co-founder, advisor Children with Attention Deficit Disorders Kent County, Del., 1991—; active Children with Attention Deficit Disorders State Coun., Del., 1993—. Recipient Presenter of Yr., Del. Coun. on Exceptional Children, 1996; grantee, N.Y. State Integrated Task Force on Substance Abuse Programs for Youth, 1988. Mem.: APA, Soc. Human Resource Mgrs., Assn. Advancement Psychology, Preservation Del., Nat. Trust Hist. Preservation. Avocation: Victorian house restoration, exercise, Zen meditation. Office: 219 Old Camden Rd Camden Wyoming DE 19934-5524 E-mail: c_porterfield@tgpcinc.com.

PORTERFIELD, JAMES TEMPLE STARKE, business administration educator; b. Annapolis, Md., July 7, 1920; s. Lewis Broughton and Maud Paxton (Starke) P.; m. Betty Gold, Apr. 23, 1949 (dec. 1985); m. Janet Patricia Gardiner Roggeveen, Oct. 5, 1986. AB, U. Calif., Berkeley, 1942; MBA, Stanford U., 1948, PhD, 1955. From asst. to assoc. prof. Harvard U. Bus. Sch., Boston, 1955-59; prof. fin. Stanford (Calif.) U. Grad. Sch. Bus., 1959-79, James Irvin Miller Prof. fin., 1979-90, prof. emeritus, 1990—; prof. IMEDE Mgmt. Devel. Inst., Lausanne, Switzerland, 1962-63. Author: Life Insurance Stocks as Investments, 1955, Investment Decisions and Capital Costs, 1965; co-author: Case Problems in Finance, 1959. Served as lt. USNR, 1941-46. Recipient Salgo Noren award Stanford U., 1966, Richard W. Lyman award Stanford U. Alumni Assn., 1995. Home: 295 Golden Oak Dr Portola Valley CA 94028-7730 Office: Stanford U Grad Sch Bus Stanford CA 94305

PORTERFIELD, NEIL HARRY, landscape architect, educator; b. Murrysville, Pa., Aug. 15, 1936; s. Phil Frank and Alvira Clare (Rea) P.; m. Sandra Jean Beswarick, Aug. 9, 1958; children: Eric Jon, Jennifer Jane, Garrett Andrew. BS in Landscape Architecture, Pa. State U., 1958; M in Landscape Architecture, U. Pa., 1964. Landscape architect Pitts. Dept. Parks and Recreation, 1958-59; land planner Neil H. Porterfield & Assocs., Murrysville, 1961-64; dir. landscape architecture and planning Hellmuth, Obata & Kassabaum, Inc., St. Louis, 1964-70; exec. v.p. HOK Assocs., 1970-72, pres., 1972-85; prin., v.p., dir. Hellmuth, Obata & Kassabaum, Inc., 1977-80, corp. dir. planning, sr. v.p., dir., 1980-85; prof., head dept. landscape architecture Pa. State U., University Park, 1985-93, dean Coll. Arts and Architecture, 1993-2000, dean emeritus, 2000—. Lectr. in field; prof. Washington U., 1979; chmn. Landscape Archtl. Accreditation Bd.; co-founder The Porterfield Group, 2000—. Contbr. articles to profl. orgns., anthologies. Bd. dirs. Landscape Architecture Found., 1983-85; adv. coun. Coll. Architecture and Urban Studies, Va. Poly. Inst. and State U., Blacksburg, 1984-86; vice-chmn. The Commn. Fine Arts, Washington, 1985-93. Recipient honor award Married Student Housing, U. Mich., honor award Am. Soc. Landscape Architects, 1969, Merit award Parkside Campus Study U. Wis. at Kenosha, Merit award Am. Soc. Landscape Architects, 1969, Outstanding Alumnus award Coll. Arts and Architecture, Pa. State U., 1983, Outstanding Educator award Coun. Educators in Landscape Architecture, 2000. Fellow Am. Soc. Landscape Architects (v.p. 1985-87); mem. Coun. of Fellows (chmn. 2000-01). Presbyterian. Home: 311 Cedar Run Rd Centre Hall PA 16828-9801 E-mail: nporterfield@tpgpcan.com.

PORTES, RICHARD DAVID, economics educator; b. Chgo., Dec. 10, 1941; s. Herbert and Abra (Halperin) P.; m. Barbara Diana Frank, 1963; children: Jonathan, Alison. BA summa cum laude, Yale U., 1962; MA, Balliol and Nuffield Colls., Oxford, 1965, DPhil, 1969; DSc honoris causa, U. Libre de Bruxelles, 2000, London Guildhall U., 2000. Asst. prof. econs. and internat. affairs Princeton U., 1969-72; prof. econs. U. London, 1972-94; head dept. econs. Birkbeck Coll., 1975-77, 80-83; pres. Ctr. for Econ. Policy Rsch., 1983—; dir. Ecole des Hautes Etudes, Paris, 1978—; prof. econs. London Bus. Sch., 1995—. Disting. Global vis. prof. U. Calif., Berkeley, 1999—2000; assoc. Nat. Bur. Econ. Rsch., Cambridge, Mass., 1980—; vis. prof. Harvard U., Cambridge, 1977—78; dir. European Corp. Governance Inst. Editor, author: Planning and Market Relations, 1971, The Polish Crisis, 1981, Deficits and Detente, 1983, Threats to International Financial Stability, 1987, Global Macroeconomics, 1987, Blueprints for Exchange Rate Stability, 1989, Macroeconomic Policies in an Interdependent World, 1989, External Constraints on Macroeconomic Policy, 1991, The Path of Reform in Central and Eastern Europe, 1991, Economic Transformation in Central Europe, 1993, European Union Trade with Eastern Europe, 1995, Crisis? What Crisis? Orderly Workouts for Sovereign Debtors, 1995; contbr. numerous articles to profl. jours. Rhodes scholar; fellow Balliol Coll., 1965-69; Guggenheim fellow, 1977-78.. Fellow Econometric Soc.; mem. Coun. Royal Econ. Soc. (exec. com. 1987-92, sec.-gen. 1992—), Econ. Policy (bd. govs., sr. editor 1985—), Coun. on Fgn. Rels., Royal Inst. Internat. Affairs, Franco-Brit. Coun., Commn. Econ. de la Nation (France). Avocation: living beyond my means. Office: London Bus Sch Regents Park London NW1 4SA England E-mail: rportes@london.edu.

PORTIS, ALAN MARK, physicist, educator; b. Chgo., July 17, 1926; s. Lyon and Ruth (Libman) P.; m. Beverly Portis, Sept. 5, 1948; children: Jonathan, Stephen, Sara, Eliyahu. Ph.B., U. Chgo., 1948; AB, U. Calif., Berkeley, 1949, PhD, 1953. Mem. faculty U. Pitts., 1953-56, U. Calif.-Berkeley, 1956—, prof. physics, 1964-95, prof. emeritus, 1995—, asst. to chancellor for research, 1966-67, asso. dean grad. div., 1967-68, dir. Lawrence Hall Sci., 1969-72, univ. ombudsman, 1981-83, 92-94, assoc. dean Coll. Engring., 1983-87, 94-95. Author: Electromagnetic Fields/Sources and Media, 1978, Electrodynamics of High-Temperature Superconductors, 1993; contbg. author: Berkeley Physics Laboratory, 1964, 65, 66, 71. Fulbright fellow, 1961, 67, Guggenheim fellow, 1965, SERC sr. fellow, U.K., 1991-92. Fellow Am. Phys. Soc.; mem. Am. Assn. Physics Tchrs. (Robert Andrews Millikan award 1966). E-mail: portis@socrates.berkeley.edu.

PORTIS, CHARLES MCCOLL, reporter, writer; b. El Dorado, Ark., Dec. 28, 1933; s. Samuel Palmer and Alice (Waddell) P. BA, U. Ark., 1958. Reporter The Comml. Appeal, Memphis, 1958, Ark. Gazette, Little Rock, 1959-60, N.Y. Herald Tribune, N.Y.C., 1960-64. Author: Norwood, 1966, True Grit, 1968, The Dog of the South, 1979, Masters of Atlantis, 1985, Gringos, 1991. Sgt. USMC, 1952-55, Korea. Presbyterian. Home: 7417 Kingwood Rd Little Rock AR 72207-1734

PORTLAND, CHARLES DENIS, publishing executive; b. N.Y.C., July 11, 1952; s. William and Berta Portela. AAS, CUNY, N.Y.C., 1974; AA, U. Md., 1978, BS, 1979; M in Accounting, U. Okla., 1982; postgrad., Nova U. CPA, Fla. Sr. auditor Arthur Anderson & Co., Oklahoma City, 1982-86; sr. fin. analyst Knight Ridder, Inc., Miami, Fla., 1986-88; special project Miami Herald, 1988-89; prin. Denis Portela, CPA, Miami Beach, 1989-93; founder, pres. Grove Mktg. (dba Charlden Consulting), 1990-95; pub. Portland Pub., Miami, FL, 1997—. Cons. Carlson Travel Network, MGM Grand Hotel & Casino, City of Miami, Fla., Microsoft; owner, operator Miami Cruise, 1999—. Author: Portland's Computer Guide, 1996, Personal Computer Reference and Training, 1997, Mighty Good Stuff, 2001, The Crucial Concordance, 2001, The Sanctuary, 2002. With U.S. Army, 1974-80, Germany, Korea. Mem. AICPA's, Fla. Inst. CPA's, Am. Mgmt. Assn., Governor's Indsl. Dev. Bds. Subcomm. on Computing and Data Communications. Lutheran. Fax: 305-519-5789.

PORTMAN, GLENN ARTHUR, lawyer; b. Cleve., Dec. 26, 1949; s. Alvin B. and Lenore (Marsh) P.; m. Katherine Seaborn, Aug. 3, 1974 (div. 1984); m. Susan Newell, Jan. 3, 1987. BA in History, Case Western Res. U., 1968; JD, So. Meth. U., 1975. Bar: Tex. 1975, U.S. Dist. Ct. (no. dist.) Tex. 1975, U.S. Dist. Ct. (so. dist.) Tex. 1983, U.S. Dist. Ct. (we. and ea. dists.) Tex. 1988. Assoc. Johnson, Bromberg & Leeds, Dallas, 1975-80, ptnr., 1980-92, Arter, Hadden, Johnson & Bromberg, Dallas, 1992-95, Arter & Hadden LLP, Dallas, 1996—. Chmn. bd. dirs. Physicians Regional Hosp., 1994-96; mem. exec. bd. So. Meth. U. Sch. Law, 1994—; lectr. bankruptcy topics South Tex. Coll. Law, State Bar Tex.; mem. vis. com. Coll. Arts and Scis., Case Western Res. U., 1999—. Asst. editor-in-chief Southwestern Law Jour., 1974-75; contbr. articles to profl. jours. Firm rep. United Way Met. Dallas, 1982-92; treas. Lake Highlands Square Homeowners Assn., 1990-93. Mem. ABA, Am. Bankruptcy Inst., State Bar Tex. Assn., Dallas Bar Assn., So. Meth. U. Law Alumni Assn. (council bd. dirs., v.p. 1980-86, chmn. admissions com., chmn. class agt. program 1986-89, chmn. fund raising 1989-91), 500 Club Inc., Assemblage Club. Republican. Methodist. Home: 9503 Winding Ridge Dr Dallas TX 75238-1451 Office: Arter & Hadden LLP 1717 Main St Ste 4100 Dallas TX 75201-7389 E-mail: g.portman@att.net., gportman@anterhadden.com.

PORTMAN, NATALIE, actress; b. Jerusalem, June 9, 1981; BS in Psychology, Harvard U. Motion Pictures: The Professional, 1994, Developing, 1995, Heat, 1995, Everyone Says I Love You, 1996, Beautiful Girls, 1996, Mars Attacks!, 1996, Star Wars: Episode I-The Phantom Menace, 1999, Anywhere But Here, 1999, Where the Heart Is, 1999, Zoolander, 2001, Star Wars Episode II-Attack of the Clones, 2002; Stage prodns: Diary of Anne Frank, 1997, The Seagull, 2001. Office: Internat Creative Mgmt 8942 Wilshire Blvd Beverly Hills CA 90211-1934*

PORTMAN, ROB, congressman; b. Cin., Dec. 19, 1955; m. Jane Portman; children: Jed, Will. BA, Dartmouth Coll., 1979; JD, U. Mich., 1984. Ptnr. Head & Ritchey, Cin., 1986-89; assoc. counsel to President of U.S., then dep. asst. to President, dir. Office Legis. Affairs White House, Washington, 1989-92; mem. U.S. Del. to UN Subcom. on Human Rights, 1992, U.S. Congress from 2nd Ohio dist., 1993—, Ways & Means Com., Budget Com., Ethics Com.; mem. select com. Homeland Security; chmn. Rep. leadership. Bd. trustees Springer Sch., The United Way, Hyde Park Community United Meth. Ch.; founding trustee Cin.-China Sister City Com.; former bd. dirs. United Home Care; vice chmn. Hamilton County George Bush for Pres. Campaign, 1988, 92; chmn. Rep. Early Bird Campaign com., 1992; del. Rep. Nat. Conv., 1988, 92; active Hamilton County Rep. Party Exec. com., Hamilton County Rep. Party Fin. Com. Mem. Cin. World Trade Assn. Office: US Ho of Reps 238 Cannon Hob Washington DC 20515-3502 also: Dist Office 8044 Montgomery Rd Rm 540 Cincinnati OH 45236*

PORTMAN, RONALD JAY, pediatric nephrologist, researcher; b. Portsmouth, N.H., June 8, 1950; s. Harry and Sylvia Rosa (Applebaum) P.; m. Joan Marie Welch, June 29, 1974; children: Wendi Alana, Shayna Matana, Solomon Zachary. BS, Northeastern U., 1973; MD, Dartmouth Coll., 1976. Diplomate Am. Bd. Pediat., Am. Bd. Pediatric Nephrology. Commd. 2d lt. U.S. Army, 1976, advanced through grades to maj., 1981; pediatric house officer Fitzsimons Army Med. Ctr., Denver, 1976-79, pediatric nephrologist, 1983-86; chief dept. pediat. Würzburg (Germany) Army Hosp., 1979-81; fellow in pediatric nephrology Washington U., St. Louis, 1981-83; resigned, Fitzsimmons Army Med. Ctr., U. Colo., 1986; pediatric nepnrologist, assoc. prof. U. Tex. Med. Sch., Houston, 1986-92, dir. divsn. pediatric nephrology and hypertension, 1992—; dir. pediat. spl. care unit and Hermann Chronobiology Ctr., Hermann Hosp., 1992—; pediatric nephrologist Fitzsimmons AMC, Univ. Colo., 1983-86; prof. U. Tex. Med. Sch., 1997—. Mem. med. adv. bd. Nat. Kidney Found. S.E. Tex., Houston, 1986—; cons. M.D. Anderson Hosp., Houston, 1986—, Chronobiology Ctr. Tel Hashomer, Tel Aviv, 1995—; mem. med. rev. bd. End Stage Renal for Disease Network 14, Dallas, 1992-2000; mem. Kidney Disease Outcome Quality Initiative work group, 2000—. Contbr. numerous articles to med. jours., chpts. to books. Bd. dirs. Congregation Brith Shalom, Bellaire, Tex., 1990-94. Recipient svc. award Nat. Kidney Found., 1995; numerous rsch. grants. Mem. Am. Soc. Transplant Physicians, Am. Soc. Pediatric Nephrology, Am. Soc. Nephrology, Am. Soc. Hpertension, Am. Assn. Medical Chronobiology and Chronotherapeutics (sec., treas.), N.Am. Pediatric Renal Transplant Study Group, S.W. Pediatric Nephrology Study Group, Internat. Pediatric Hypertension Assn. (chmn. exec. com.). Jewish. Avocations: choir, baseball umpire, tennis, golf. Office: U Tex Med Sch 7431 Fannin St Houston TX 77054-1901

PORTNEY, JOSEPH NATHANIEL, retired aerospace executive, navigation consultant; b. L.A., Aug. 15, 1927; s. Marcus and Sarah (Pilson) P.; m. Ina Mae Leibson, June 20, 1959; children: Philip, Jeffrey. BS, U.S. Naval Acad., 1952. Commd. 2d lt. USAF, 1952, advanced through grades to maj., 1960; with Litton Systems, Inc., Woodland Hills, Calif., 1960—; project engr. Litton Aero Products, 1967-68; program mgr. Litton Aero Products Litton Systems, Inc., Woodland Hills, 1968-72, advanced program mgr. Guidance and Control Sys., 1972-85, mgr. advanced programs Guidance and Control Sys., 1985-98, ret., 1998; pres. NAVSENSE cons., 1998—. Navigator engr. on 3 historic inertial crossings of the North Pole. Author: Portney's Ponderables; creator: Earthshapes solar compass pilot and navigator's calendar. Mem. Inst. of Navigation (v.p. 1988-89, pres. 1989-90, Weems award 1994), U.S. Naval Acad. Alumni Assn. (trustee 1980-83). Jewish. Avocation: classical piano. Office: NAVSENSE 4981 Amigo Ave Tarzana CA 91356-4505 E-mail: navsense@earthlink.net.

PORTNEY, LESLIE GROSS, physical therapist; b. N.Y.C., Feb. 17, 1948; d. Harold and Ida (Stein) Gross; m. Merrill B. Portney, May 13, 1979; children: Devon, Lindsay. BA, Queens Coll., N.Y.C., 1968; Cert. in Phys. Therapy, U. Pa., 1969; MS, Med. Coll. Va., 1974; PhD, Lowy cert. in gerontol. studies, Boston U., 1993; DPT, MGH Inst. Health Professions, 2002. Lic. phys. therapist Mass., N.Y. Phys. therapist Rusk Inst. Rehab. Medicine, N.Y.C., 1969-72; lectr. NYU, 1971-72; asst. prof. Sargent Coll., Boston U., 1974-88, assoc. dean ad interim, 1982-83; rsch. therapist New Eng. Med. Ctr., Boston, 1987-89; assoc. prof. MGH Inst. Health Professions, 1990—, assoc. dir. grad programs in phys. therapy, 1994—2002, dir., prof. program in phys. therapy, 1994—2002, dir. grad. programs in phys. therapy, 2002—. Rsch. cons. Spaulding Rehab. Hosp., Boston, 1993-95; statis. cons. New Eng. Med. Ctr., Boston, 1985-90. Author: Foundations of Clinical Research, 1993 (Hawkins award 1993), 2d edit., 2000; contbr. articles to profl. jours., chpts. to books. Recipient doctoral edn. award Found. Phys. Therapy, 1988. Mem. Am. Phys. Therapy Assn. (sect. on rsch., sect. on edn., sect. on ortho, sect. on geriatrics, Outstanding Rschr. award Mass. chpt. 1986, Catherine Worthingham fellow 2002), Am. Soc. on Aging, Gerontol. Soc. Am., Internat. Soc. Electrophysiol. Kinesiology. Jewish. Office: MGH Inst of Health Prof Charlestown Navy Yard 36 1st Ave Boston MA 02129 E-mail: lportney@mghihp.edu.

PORTNOY, LYNN ANN, fashion retailer; b. Detroit, June 13, 1938; d. Morris and Betty (Diamond) P. Student, U. Wis., 1956-57, Harvard U., 1957; BA, U. Mich., 1960. Buyer trainee Joseph Magnin, San Francisco, 1960-65; buyer, pub. rels. Claire Pearone, Troy, Mich., 1968-80; owner, pres. Lynn Portnoy Inc., Detroit, 1980-97, Southfield, Mich., 1997—. Author: (book) Going Like Lynn, Paris (A Series of Liberating Travel Primers for Women), 1999, Going Like Lynn, New York, 2000, Going Like Lynn, Florence, 2001. Vol. Internat. Vis. Council, South Oakland Shelter, Alzheimers Assn., Mich. Abortion Rights Action League. Mem. Nat. Assn. Women Bus. Owners, Womens Economic Club, U. Mich. Alumni. Avocations: travel, reading, writing, cooking, walking. Office: 29260 Franklin Rd Southfield MI 48034-1161 E-mail: info@goinglikelynn.com.

PORTNOY, SARA S. lawyer; b. N.Y.C., Jan. 11, 1926; d. Marcus and Gussie (Raphael) Spiro; m. Alexander Portnoy, Dec. 13, 1959 (dec. 1976); children: William, Lawrence. BA, Radcliffe Coll., 1946; LLB, Columbia U., 1949. Bar: N.Y. 1949, U.S. Dist. Ct. (so. dist.) N.Y. 1952, U.S. Dist. Ct. (eas. dist.) N.Y. 1975, U.S. Ct. Appeals (2d cir.) 1975, U.S. Supreme Ct. 1975. Assoc. Seligsberg, Friedman & Berliner, N.Y.C., 1949-51; atty. AT&T, 1951-61; vol. atty. Legal Aid Soc. of Westchester, N.Y., 1966-74; assoc. Proskauer Rose Goetz & Mendelsohn, N.Y.C., 1974-78, ptnr., 1978-94; ret., 1994. Mem. Commn. on Human Rights, White Plains, N.Y., 1973-78; mem. bd. visitors Columbia Law Sch., 1996—; bd. dirs. Legal Aid Soc. of Westchester County, N.Y., 1975-83, Columbia Law Sch. Assn., 1990-94, Mosholu Montifiore Cmty. Ctr., 1998—; mem. Pres.'s Coun. Yaddo; dir. Muscular Dystrophy Assn., 2000—. Mem. Assn. Bar City of N.Y. (chair com. legal support staff 1994, mem. Com. on Homeless, Sr. Lawyer's Com. and Pub. Svc. Network), South Fork Country Club (dir. 1997—), The Children's Storefront (dir. 1998—).

PORTOGHESE, PHILIP SALVATORE, medicinal chemist, educator; b. N.Y.C., June 4, 1931; s. Philip A. and Constance (Antonelli) P.; m. Christine L. Phillips, June 11, 1960; children— Stephen, Stuart, Philip. BS, Columbia U., 1953, MS, 1958; PhD, U. Wis., 1961; Dr. honoris causa, U. Catania, Italy, 1986, Royal Danish Sch. Pharmacy, Copenhagen, 1992. Asst. prof. Coll. Pharmacy, U. Minn., Mpls., 1961-64, assoc. prof., 1964-69, prof. medicinal chemistry, 1969—, prof. pharmacology, 1987—, dir. grad. study in medicinal chemistry, 1974-86, head dept., 1974-83; disting. prof. medicinal chemistry —, 2000. Cons. NIMH., 1971-72; mem. med. chemistry B sect. NIH, 1972-76; mem. pharmacology, substance abuse and environ. toxicology interdisciplinary cluster President's Biomed. Research Panel, 1975; mem. expert panel of Flavor and Extract Mfrs. Assn. of U.S., 1984—. Mem. editorial adv. bd. Jour. Med. Chemistry, 1969-71; editor-in-chief, 1972— ; mem. editorial adv. bd. Med. Chem. series, 1972-77. U.S. Army, 1954—56. Named Highly Cited Rschr., Inst. for Sci. Info., 2001; recipient Ernest H. Volwiler award (outstanding contbns. to pharm. scis., Am. Assn. Colls. Pharmacy, 1984, N.B. Eddy Meml. award, Coll. on Problems of Drug Dependency-NAS NRC, 1991, Merit award, NIH, 1997, Oak and the Tulip award, European Fedn. Medicinal Chemistry, 1999. Fellow AAAS, Acad. Pharm. Scis., Am. Assn. Pharm. Scientists (Rsch. Achievement award 1990); mem. Am. Chem. Soc. (Medicinal Chemistry award 1990, E.E. Smissman-Bristol-Meyers-Squibb award 1991, Alfred Burger award in medicinal chemistry 2000), Am. Soc. Pharm. Exptl. Therapeutics, Internat. Union Pure and Applied Chemistry (commn. on medicinal chemistry 1978-82, internat. com. med. chemistry 1982-85), Soc. Neurosci., Sigma Xi, Rho Chi (lecture award 1999), Phi Lambda Upsilon. Home: 17 Oriole Ln Saint Paul MN 55127-6334 Office: U Minn Coll of Pharmacy 308 Harvard St SE Minneapolis MN 55455-0353

PORTOLANO, CHARLES JOSEPH, physical education educator, poet; b. Bklyn., Nov. 16, 1952; s. Charles A. and Rosemary Portolano; m. Elvira Pisano Portolano; 1 child Valerie Marie. A in Phys. Edn., Nassau C.C., 1972; B in Phys. Edn., Cortland (N.Y.) State U., 1974; M in Health Edn., Adelphi U., 1982. Cert. tchr. phys. edn., health edn., English, biology, earth sci., gen. sci. N.Y. Supervisor delivery U.S. Postal Svc., Babylon, NY, 1986—88; project mgr., expeditor Gray Constrn. Co., Southhold, 1988—92; tchr. phys. edn., health edn. Island Trees Sch. Dist., Levittown, 1992—; poet, pub. spkr. Wyndham Hall Press, 1996—; adj. prof. Adelphi U., Garden City, NY, 2001—; drama dir. Island Trees H.S., 1994—96; head coach tennis Jericho (N.Y.) Sch. Dist., 1996—2001. Translator (poet): Inspired By Their Spirit, 2000; poet: The Nature of Darkness, 2001. Avocations: tennis, reading.

PORTUONDO, JOSE FRANCISCO, management consultant; b. Havana, Cuba, Mar. 21, 1953; s. Jose Maria and Odette Maria (Diaz) P.; m. Maria Luisa Wilson, Sept. 4, 1977; children: Maria Cristina, Jose Francisco. B of Civil Engring., MIT, 1975, M of Civil Engring., 1976; MBA, Harvard U., 1980. Ops. rsch. analyst U.S. Dept. Transp., Washington, 1975-78; mgr. McKinsey & Co., Inc., N.Y.C., 1980-86; v.p. mktg. Glasrock Home Health Care, Atlanta, 1986-87; dir. Arthur D. Little, Inc., Cambridge, Mass., 1995-96; pres. Decision Analytics, Inc., Newton, 1987-94, 96—. Coach Newton Girls Soccer, 1987-93. Mem. Harvard Club Boston, MIT Club Boston. Roman Catholic. Avocations: marathon/long distance running, travel, stamp collecting, reading. Office: Decision Analytics Inc PO Box 182 Waban MA 02468-0002

PORTWAY, PATRICK STEPHEN, telecommunications consulting company executive, telecommunications educator; b. June 18, 1939; s. Christopher Leo and Ceciala (King) P.; m. Malle M. Portway: children by previous marriage: Shawn, Pam, Vicki. BA, U. Cin., 1963; MA, U. Md., 1973; postgrad., Columbia U. Regional ADP coord. GSA, Washington, 1963-68; mgr. strategic mkt. planning Xerox Corp., 1969-74; mgr. plans and programs System Devel. Corp., 1974-78; fin. indsl. mktg. exec. Satellite Bus. Sys., 1978-80; western regional mgr. Am. Satellite Co., 1980-81; CEO Applied Bus. Telecomm., Livermore, Calif., 1981-98; prof., lectr. Golden Gate U. Grad. Sch., San Francisco, 1983—. Pub. mag. Teleconference, 1981-98; pub. (newspapers) Discovery Bay, Delta Clippers; prodr. Telecon & Ioccon Confs., 1981-98, CEO ET3 Internet Edn. Co., 1998—. Author: (with others) Teleconferncing and Distance Learning, 1992, 3rd edit., 1997. Presdl. elector Electoral Coll., Va., 1976; candidate Va. State Legislature from 19th Dist., 1971; mem. Discovery Bay Mcpl. Adv. Coun., 1992-96, chmn., 1992; mem. adv. com. Congl. Internet Caucus. 1st lt. U.S. Army, 1963-65. Recipient Internat. Rotary award for Higher Edn., Bombay, India, 1999. Mem. Internat. Teleconferencing Assn. (founder, bd. dirs. 1983-88), Nat. Univ. Tleconferencing Network (mem. adv. bd., bd. dirs. 1986-89), U.S. Distance Learning Assn. (founder, exec. dir. 1987-99), Electronic Funds Transfer Assn. (founder, bd. dirs. 1980), Satellite Profls., Internat. Internet Assn. (pres. 2001—), Internat. Higher Edn. Acad. of Sci., Global Distance Learning Assn. (founder, exec. dir., COO 1998-99), Jaycees (charter pres. Chantilly, Va., Disting. Svc. award Dale City, Va.), Commonwealth. E-mail: portwayinva@aol.com.

PORTZ, BERNARD J. priest, educator; b. Sioux Falls, S.D., May 23, 1920; s. Joseph Nicolas and Caroline Elizabeth (Noll) Portz. AB, St. Louis U., 1943. Ordained Roman Catholic priest mem. Soc. Jesus. Math. tchr. Creighton Prep. Sch., Omaha, 1946—49; tchr. physics and math. Marquette U., Milw., 1955—60; tchr. math. and music Jesuit Coll., St. Bonifacius, Minn., 1960—70; asst. prof. math. Creighton U., Omaha, 1970—98, choir dir., 1971—98; retired, 1998—. Treas., mem. bd. dirs. Omaha Symphony Chorus, 1971—83; sec. acad. coun. Creighton U., Omaha, 1971—78. Composer: (choral) Day is Dying in the West, 1994; contbr. articles in profl. jours. Recipient Tchg. for Tomorrow award, Omicron Delta Kappa and Alpha Epsilon Nu, 1995. Roman Catholic. Home: 10101 W Wisconsin Ave Wauwatosa WI 53226

PORTZ, CHRISTOBALINA, medical/surgical nurse; b. Yauco, Puerto Rico, Dec. 25, 1949; arrived in U.S., 1962; d. Neidel Pacheco, Anthonia Pacheco; m. Ronald J. Portz; children: Maria, Brenda, Michael, Michelle. Diploma LPN Nursing, Monmouth County Sch. Pvt. duty nurse, Oakhurst, NJ, 1989—. Treas. Food Pantry, 2002—. Mem.: N.J. LPN Orgn. Avocations: writing, crafts, reading, gardening, singing. Home: 15 Corey Dr Oakhurst NJ 07755

PORZAK, GLENN E. lawyer; b. Ill., Aug. 22, 1948; m. Judy Lea McGinnis, Dec. 19, 1970; children: Lindsay and Austin. BA with distinction, U. Colo., 1970, JD, 1973. Bar: Colo. 1973. Assoc. Holme Roberts & Owen, Denver, 1973-80, ptnr., 1980-85, mng. ptnr. Boulder office, 1985-95; mng. ptnr. Porzak Browning & Bushong LLP, Boulder, 1996—. Bd. dirs. Wells Fargo Bank Boulder, 1993—. Contbr. articles to profl. jours. Bd. dirs. U. Colo. Found., 2002—. Named Disting. Alumnus U. Colo., 1991. Fellow Explorers Club (bd. dirs. 1995-96, Citation of Merit 1998); mem. Am. Alpine Club (pres. 1988-91), Colo. Mtn. Club (pres. 1983, hon. mem. 1983—), Colo. Outward Bound (trustee 1992-2002, vice chmn. 1997-99, chmn. 1999-2001), Phi Beta Kappa. Achievements include reaching summit of Mt. Everest, climbing highest peak on all seven continents. Home: 771 7th St Boulder CO 80302-7402 Office: Porzak Browning & Bushong 929 Pearl St Ste 300 Boulder CO 80302-5108

POSADA, JORGE RAFAEL, baseball player; b. Santurce, P.R. , Aug. 17, 1971; s. Jorge Posada Sr.. Assoc., Calhoon C.C., 1991. Profl. baseball player N.Y. Yankees, 1995—. Office: NY Yankees Yankee Stadium 161st St and River Ave Bronx NY 10451*

POSAMENTIER, ALFRED STEVEN, mathematics educator, university administrator; b. N.Y.C., Oct. 18, 1942; s. Ernest and Alice (Pisk) P.; children: Lisa Joan, David Richard. AB, Hunter Coll., 1964; MA, CCNY, 1966; postgrad., Yeshiva U., N.Y.C., 1967-69; PhD, Fordham U., 1973; Nostrifizierung of Doctorate, U. Vienna, Austria, 1992. Tchr. math Theodore Roosevelt H.S., Bronx, N.Y., 1964-70; asst. prof. math. edn. CCNY, N.Y.C., 1970-76, assoc. prof., 1977-80, prof., 1981—, dept. chmn. dept. secondary and continuing edn., 1974-80, chmn., 1980-86; assoc. dean Sch. Edn., CCNY, 1986-95, dep. dean, 1995-99, dean, 1999—; dir. select program in sci. and engring. CCNY, 1978—; dir. initiatives program City Coll. U.K., 1983—; dir. Germany/CCNY Exch. Program CCNY, 1985—, dir. Austria/CCNY Exch. Program, 1987—, dir. Czech Republic/CCNY Exch. Program, 1989—, dir. sci. lectr. program, 1981-94, dir. Ctr. for Sci. and Maths. Edn., 1986—. Chmn. bd. dirs. Salvadori Ednl. Ctr. on Built Environ., 1988—; dir. Exxon sponsored early childhood math. specialist tng. program at City Coll., 1988-92; supr. math. and sci. Mamaroneck H.S., N.Y., 1976-79; project dir. Math Proficiency Workshop, Ossining, N.Y., 1976-79, NSF math. devel. program for secondary sch. tchrs. math., 1978-82, N.Y.C., Profl. Preparation of Math. and Sci. Tchrs., 1978-79; project dir. numerous NSF sponsored math./sci. tchr. devel. insts., 1976—; cons. Croft Ednl. Svcs., New London, 1971, N.Y.C. Bd. Edn., 1973-75, N.Y.C. Bd. Edn. Office of Evaluation, 1974-80, N.Y.C. Bd. Edn. Examiners, 1979-92, Ossining Bd. Edn., 1975-83, numerous others; coord. NSF N.E. Resource Ctr. Sci. and Engring., 1980-90; lectr. various convs. and meetings; vis. prof. U. Vienna, Austria, 1985, 87, 88, 90, Tech. U., Berlin, 1989, 95, Tech. U., Vienna, 1993-98, Pedgogical Inst., Vienna, 1993—, Humboldt U., Berlin, 1996; dir. N.Y.C. Maths. Project, 1994—, Math for the New Millennium Project, 1995-2000. Author: (novels) Geometric Constructions, 1973, Geometry, Its Elements and Structure, 1972, 1977, Challenging Problems in Geometry, 1970, Challenging Problems in Algebra, 1970, A Study Guide for the Scholastic Aptitude Test in Math., 1969, 1983, Excursions in Advanced Euclidean Geometry, 1980, 1984, Teaching Secondary School Mathematics: Techniques and Enrichment Units, 1981, 1990, 1995, 1999, 2002, Uncommon Problems for Common Topics in Algebra, 1981, Unusual Problems for Usual Topics in Algebra, 1981, Using Computers in Mathematics, 1983, 1986, Math Motivators: Investigations in Pre-Algebra, 1982, Math Motivators: Investigations in Algebra, 1983, Using Computers: Programming and Problem Solving, 1984, 1989, Advanced Geometric Constructions, 1988, Challenging Problems in Algebra, 1988, 1996, Challenging Problems in Geometry, 1988, 1996, Arbeitsmaterialien: Mathematik, 1994, The Art of Problem Solving: A Resource for the Mathematics Teacher, 1996, Students! Get Ready for Mathematics for SAT-I: Problem Solving Strategies and Practice Tests, 1996, Teachers! Prepare Your Students for Mathematics for SAT-I: Methods and Problem-Solving Strategies, 1996, Deutsch-English Mathematik Worterbuch, 1996, 2000, Tips for the Mathematics Teacher: Research-Based Strategies to help Students Learn, 1998, Problem-Solving Strategies for More Effective and Elegant Solutions: A Resource for the Mathematics Teacher, 1998, Making Pre-Algebra Come Alive, 2000, Making Algebra Come Alive, 2000, Making Geometry Come Alive, 2000; author: (with Dr. H.A. Hauptman Nobel Laureate) 101 Great Ideas for Introducing Key Concepts in Mathematics, 2001; author: Advanced Euclidean Geometry: Excursions for Secondary Teachers and Students, 2002, others; contbr.

articles. Trustee Demarest Bd. Edn., 1977-80 Decorated Grand Medal of Honor, Austria, 1994; named Tchr. of Yr. CCNY Alumni Assn., 1993; hon. fellow U. South Bank, London, 1988; Fulbright scholar U. Vienna, 1990; recipient Medal of Distinction, City of Vienna, 1996, Medal of Honor, Technische Fachhochschule Berlin, 1996, 1000 Years Austria commemorative medal, Govt. of Austria, 1997, Hon. Prof. of Austria, 1999. Mem. Math. Assn. Am., Sch. Sci. and Math. Assn., Nat. Coun. Tchrs. Math., (reviewer new publs., referee articles Math. Tchr. Jour.), Assn. Tchrs. Math. N.Y.C. (exec. bd. 1966-67, referee articles assn. jour.), Assn. Tchrs. of Math. of N.Y. State, Assn. Tchrs. Math. N.J. (mem. editl. bd. N.J. Math. Tchr. Jour. 1981-84), Nat. Coun. of Suprs. of Math. Home: 634 Caruso Ln River Vale NJ 07675-6210 E-mail: asp2@juno.com.

POSCH, MARGARET A. education educator, researcher; b. Detroit, Nov. 21, 1944; d. James Adam and Gertrude E. (Brown) Kollar; m. Joseph L. Posch, June 15, 1968; 1 child Joseph Posch, III 1 child J. David 1 child Jean Posch Shore 1 child Michael 1 child Christina. PhD, Wayne State U., 1996. Dir., post-award rsch. dept., coll. of edn. Wayne State U., Detroit, 1999—2001, prin. investigator, 1999—. Dir. career devel. program Project R.E.A.C.H., 2000. Contbr. articles to profl. jours. Adv. bd. mem. Detroit Pub. Schs., Office Spl. Svcs./Transition, Detroit, 2000—02; LCCE adv. bd. mem. Coun. for Exceptional Children, Divsn. for Career Devel. and Transition, Reston, Va., 2000—02; pack 39 leader/administr. Boy Scouts Am., Grosse Pointe, Mich., 1978—80; bd. dirs. Grosse Pointe Shores (Mich.) Improvement Found., 1993—2002; exec. bd. Friends of Child Abuse Prevention, 1994—2002. Named Outstanding Young Woman of Am., Congl. Nomination, 1981; recipient Vol. award, Boy Scouts Am., 1979, State of NH Senate Resolution, City of Detroit Implementation Award, 2000. Mem.: ASCD, Am. Bus. Women's Assn., Am. Ednl. Rsch. Assn., Coun. for Exceptional Children, Am. Statis. Assn. (past pres., pres., v.p., sec. 1997—2002), Gtr Detroit Regional C. of C. (Leadership Detroit mem. 1994—), Jr. League Detroit (com. chair 1983—87, chair cmty. rsch. 1987—88, chair pub. affairs com. 1985—87). Avocations: performing arts, travel.

POSCHEL, JAMES EDWARD, mental health services administrator, psychotherapist; b. Springfield, Mo., July 25, 1944; s. Ralph Joseph and Verna Mary (Birchler) P.; m. Mary Margaret Key, Dec. 20, 1975 (dec. Oct. 1998); children: Derrick, Jessica, Marissa, Brandan; m. Lynette Dorothy Crouch, Aug. 10, 2002. BA, Cardinel Glennon Coll., 1966; MDiv, St. Louis U., 1971; MSW, Washington U., St. Louis, 1972. Cert. social worker, Mo., Ill. Psychiat. social worker Mo. Div. Mental Health, St. Louis, 1972; satellite coord. Belleville (Ill.) Mental Health Outpatient Ctr., 1972-73; exec. dir. Human Support Svcs., Waterloo, Ill., 1973—. Pres. bd. dirs. New Hope Living to Learn Ctr., Waterloo, 1982-91. Mem. Regional Adminsts. Assn. (pres. 1990, 93). Office: Human Support Svcs 988 N Illinois Route 3 Waterloo IL 62298-1000

POSCHMANN, ANDREW WILLIAM, information systems and management consultant; b. N.Y.C., June 24, 1939; m. Anne Florence Fugarini, July 14, 1962; children: Stephen, Robert. BBA in Mgmt. and fin., Baruch Coll., N.Y.C., 1968; MBA in Fin., Marist Coll., Poughkeepsie, N.Y., 1981. Cert. info. systems auditor, mgmt. cons., systems profl. EDP applications engr. GE, N.Y.C., 1964-66; software cons. Western Union, Mahwah, N.J., 1966-69; cons. A.T. Kearney & Co., N.Y.C., 1969-73; systems mgr. Curtiss-Wright Corp., Wood-Ridge, N.J., 1973-77; cons. Ernst & Whinney, N.Y.C., 1977-83; applications mgr. NYU Med. Ctr., 1983-86; info. systems mgr. McKinsey & Co., N.Y.C., 1986-93; v.p. Advanced Mgmt. Inc., East Fishkill, N.Y., 1993—. Mem. adv. bd. Advanced Mgmt., Inc., East Fishkill, N.Y., 1975—. Author: Standards and Procedures For Systems Documentation, 1984, Score-Company Review and Evaluation, 1985. Mem. Am. Arbitration Assn. (arbitrator), Nat. Railway Hist. Soc. Office: Advanced Mgmt Inc 49 Lynne Rd East Fishkill NY 12533-5859

POSCOVER, MAURY B. lawyer; b. St. Louis, Jan. 13, 1944; s. Edward and Ann (Chapnick) P.; m. Lorraine Wexler, Aug. 14, 1966; children: Michael, Daniel, Joanna. BA, Lehigh U., 1966; JD, Washington U., 1969. Bar: Mo. 1969. Assoc. Husch & Eppenberger LLC, St. Louis, 1969-75, ptnr., mem., 1975—. Lectr. Washington U., St. Louis, 1972—79. Editor-in-chief: The Business Lawyer, 1995-96; contbr. articles to profl. jours. Bd. dirs. Childhaven, St. Louis, 1978-92, pres. 1986; pres. Jewish Community Rels. Coun., 1990-92. Mem.: Am.-Israel C. of C. (pres. 2000—), Wash. U. Alumni Law Assn. (pres. 1980—81), Am. Judicature Soc. (dir. 1981—87), Mo. Bar Assn. (bd. govs. 1979—81), Bar Assn. Met. St. Louis (pres. 1983—84), ABA (chair bus. law sect. 1997—98, bd. govs. 1999—2002, mem. exec. com. bd. govs. 2001—, chair ops. and comms. com. 2001—, chmn. comml. fin. svcs. com. bus. law sect. coun., editor-in-chief jour.). Jewish. Office: Husch & Eppenberger LLC 190 Carondelet Plz Ste 600 Saint Louis MO 63105-3441 E-mail: maury.poscover@husch.com.

POSEN, ADAM SIMON, economist; AB in Govt. magna cum laude, Harvard Coll., 1988; PhD in Polit. Economy and Govt., Harvard U., 1997. Economist Internat. Rsch. Function Fed. Res. Bank N.Y., 1994-97; sr. fellow Inst. Internat. Econs., 1997—. Author: Disciplined Discretion: The German and Swiss Monetary Frameworks in Operation, 1997, Inflation Targeting: Lessons from the International Experience, 1999, Restoring Japan's Economic Growth, 1998. NSF Grad. fellow, 1989-92, Bosch Found. fellow, 1992-93, Okun Meml. fellow Brookings Inst, 1993-94, Short-term Policy fellow Am. Acad. in Berlin, 2000. Mem. Am. Coun. on Germany, Am. Econ. Assn., Brit.-Am. Project, Coun. on Fgn. Rels. (Internat. Affairs fellow 2000-2001), Phi Beta Kappa. Office: Inst Internat Econs 1750 Massachussets Ave NW Washington DC 20036-1903 E-mail: aposen@iie.com.

POSEN, SUSAN ORZACK, lawyer; b. N.Y.C., Nov. 5, 1945; BA, Sarah Lawrence Coll., 1967; JD, Bklyn. Law Sch., 1978. Bar: N.Y. 1979. Assoc. Stroock & Stroock & Lavan, N.Y.C., 1978-83, 84-86; ptnr. Stroock, Stroock & Lavan, LLP, 1987-2000; asst. gen. counsel Cablevision Systems Corp., Woodbury, N.Y., 1983-84; co-founder, ptnr. DIVA Capital LLC, N.Y.C., 2000—01. Office: Outspoke LLC 115 Spring St New York NY 10012-3817

POSER, CHARLES MARCEL, neurology educator; b. Antwerp, Belgium, Dec. 30, 1923; s. Maurice and Sadye (Gleitsman) P.; m. Joan Doris Crawford, Sept. 3, 1950; children: William John, Nicholas Charles. BS, CCNY, 1947; MD, Columbia U., 1951; DMS (hon.) , U. Sassari, Italy, 2000. Diplomate Am. Bd. Psychiatry and Neurology. Resident in neurology Neurol. Inst. Columbia-Presbyn. Med. Center, N.Y., 1952-55; Fulbright scholar Neuropathology Inst. Bunge, Antwerp, Belgium, 1955-56; instr. through assoc. prof. neurology U. Kans. Sch. Medicine, 1955-64; prof., head div. neurology U. Mo. Sch. Medicine, Kansas City, 1964-68; prof., chmn. dept. neurology U. Vt. Coll. Medicine, 1968-81; prof. neurology Boston U. Sch. Medicine, 1981-84, lectr., 1984—; sr. neurologist Beth Israel Hosp. Cons. prof. Tex. Tech. U. Sch. Medicine, Lubbock, 1981-90; neurology lectr. Harvard Med. Sch., 1981-96, vis. prof. neurology, 1996—; neurology lectr. Tufts U. Sch. Medicine, 1982-90; cons. in neurology U.S. Army and U.S. Navy, 1963—; Cross lectr. U. Witwatersrand, Johannesburg, Republic of South Africa, 1990; Oscar Trelles meml. lectr., Lima, Peru, 1997. Editor-in-chief Jour. Tropical and Geog. Neurology, 1989-92, Neurol. Infections and Epidemiology, 1995-97; contbr. numerous articles to med. jours. Served with U.S. Army, 1943-46. Decorated officer Order of Leopold II Belgium; recipient Silver Bicentennial medal Coll. of Physicians and Surgeons, 1967; named Luis Guerrero Meml. lectr. U. Santo Tomás, Manila, 1979, Wilder Penfield lectr. Am. U., Beirut, 1983, Salmon James lectr. London Med. Soc., 1987, Kroc lectr. Rush Med. Coll., Chgo., 1987; Wu Ho-Su Meml. Lectr., Taipei, Taiwan, 1994. Fellow ACP, Am. Acad. Neurology, Am. Acad. Pediat., Royal Soc. Medicine (London), Royal Soc. Tropical Medicine and Hygiene (London), Royal Coll. Physicians (Glasgow), Royal Coll. Physicians (Eng.), Royal Coll. of Physicians (Edinburgh); hon. fellow Japanese, Belgian, Cuban, French, Icelandic, Filipino, Dutch and Colombian socs. neurology, All-Russian Soc. Neurol. Sci., Neurol. Soc. India, Assn. Brit. Neurologists; mem. Am. Neurol. Assn. (sr.), Am. Assn. Neuropathologists, Assn. for Rsch. in Nervous and Mental Diseases, Nat. Acad. Medicine Colombia (hon.). Home: 11 Rutland Sq Boston MA 02118-3105 Office: Beth Israel Deaconess Med Ctr East Campus Dept Neurology Harvard Med Sch 330 Brookline Ave Boston MA 02215-5400 E-mail: cposer@caregroup.harvard.edu.

POSES, FREDERIC M. engineering company executive; b. 1942; BBA in Fin., NYU, 1965. Vol. Peace Corps, 1967-69; various positions Allied Corp., 1969-85; pres. plastics and engineered materials divsn. AlliedSignal Inc., Morristown, N.J., 1985-86, pres. fibers divsn., 1986-88, exec. v.p., pres. engineered materials, 1988-98, pres. & COO, 1998-99; chmn. & CEO Am. Standard Cos., Piscataway, NJ, 1999—. Office: 1 Centennial Ave Piscataway NJ 08854-3921*

POSES, ROY MAURICE, physician, educator; b. Bklyn., Apr. 13, 1952; m. June Axelrod, 1978. AB in English magna cum laude, ScB in Engring. magna cum laude, Brown U., 1974, MD, 1978. Diplomate Am. Bd. Internal MEdicine, Nat. Bd. MEd. Examiners; lic. physician N.J., Va., R.I. Intern in medicine Univ. Hosp-Boston U., 1978-79, resident in medicine, 1979-81; Henry J. Kaiser Family Found. fellow in gen. medicine U. Pa., Phila., 1981-83; asst. prof. medicine U. Medicine and Dentistry of N.J., Rutgers Med. Sch., Camden, 1983-87, Med. Coll. Va.-Va. Commonwealth U., Richmond, 1987-92, dir. rsch. activities divsn. gen. medicine and primary care, 1987-93, assoc. prof. medicine, 1992-94, vice chmn. for rsch. divsn. gen. medicine and primary care, 1993-94; assoc. prof. medicine and cmty. health Brown U. Sch. Medicine, 1994—; dir. rsch. divsn. gen., internal medicine Meml. Hosp. R.I., Pawtucket, 1994-99; dir. gen. internal medicine rsch. Brown U. Ctr. Primary Care and Prevention, 1999—. Dir. med. consultation svc. dept. medicine Cooper Hosp./Univ. Med. Ctr., Camden, 1983-87; adj. asst. prof. medicine U. Pa., Phila., 1985-87; test site coord. Ednl. Commn. for Fgn. Med. Grads., 1987; temp. advisor WHO, Geneva, Switzerland, 1988; cons. Nat. Libr. Medicine, U. Ill., Chgo., 1988, Nat. Heart, Lung and Blood Inst., New Brunswick, N.J., 1990, 92, Ctr. for Clin. Effectiveness, Henry Ford Health System, Detroit, 1992; cons. Nat. Bd. Med. Examiners, 1996; invited participant Forums 2 and 3 Global Forum for Health Rsch., 1998-99; cons. Agy. for Health Care Rsch. and Quality, 2001; presenter in field. Mem. health care tech. study sect. Agy. Health Care Policy and Rsch., 1990-94. Recipient Lange Med. Publs. awards, 1978; Dr. A. Blaine Brower traveling scholar ACP, 1991-92, alternate traveling scholar ACP, 1989. Mem. IEEE, ACP, Soc. Gen. Internal Medicine (ex officio coun. 1990-93, co-chmn. sci. program com. 1999, rsch. subcom. 1990, mem. sci. program 1993), Soc. Med. Decision Making (sec., treas. 1997-99, bd. trustees 1992-94, dir. advanced short courses 1988, sci. program com. 1987, 88, 93, awards com. 1991, chair mem. com. 1994-96, chair annual meeting short courses 1995, chair devel. com. 1999—, Eutene Saenger awrad for disting. svc. 2001), Soc. Judgement and Decision Making, Assn. for Health Svcs. Rsch., Internat. Soc. Pharmacoepidemiology, Brunswik Soc. (meeting co-chmn. 1991), Sydenham Soc., Tau Beta Phi, Phi Beta Kappa, Sigma Xi. E-mail: roy-poses@brown.edu.

POSEY, ADA LOUISE, management consultant; BA, Carleton Coll. Expense mgmt. and pension operation staff Prudential Ins. Co., 1978—85, internal auditing staff, 1985—89; corp. budgeting staff Minn. Mut., 1989—93; assoc. dir. for gen. svcs. Office Adminstrn., The White House, Washington, 1993-96, dep. dir., 1996-97, dir., 1997-99; spl. advisor Office of Nat. Drug Control Policy, 1999—; sr. policy advisor Dept. of Energy, 1999-2001; pres. Posey Cons. Group, 2001—. Trustee Carleton Coll.; mem. Capital City Links chpt., Washington. Office: Office Nat Drug Ctrl Policy 725 17th St NW Washington DC 20503 E-mail: noahsaunt@hotmail.com., poseyconsulting@aol.com.

POSEY, CLYDE LEE, business administration and accounting educator; b. Tucumcari, New Mex., Dec. 27, 1940; s. Rollah P. and Opal (Patterson) P.; m. Dora Diane Vassar; children: Amanda Bennett, Julia Forsyth, Rebecca; m. Judith James Jerry, July 31, 1991; stepchildren: David Jerry, Georgia Kenyan. BBA, U. Tex., El Paso, 1963; MBA, U. Tex., 1965; postgrad., U. So. Calif., 1968; PhD, Okla. State U., 1978. CPA, Calif. (ret.), La., Tex. (ret.). Lab. aide FBI, Washington, 1959-60; acct. Lipson, Cox & Colton (now Deloitte & Touche), El Paso, Tex., 1962; auditor Main & Co. (now KPMG), 1963; teaching asst. U. Tex., Austin, 1963-65; tax cons. Peat, Marwick, Mitchell & Co., Dallas, 1965-66; cons. Roberson, Martin, Horg and Ryckman, Fresno, Calif., 1967; pvt. practice acctg., 1966—, Ruston, La., 1966—; asst. prof. Calif. State U., Fresno, 1966-76; assoc. prof. La. Tech. U., Ruston, 1978-84, prof., 1984—. Vis. asst. prof. Ctrl. State U., Edmond, Okla., 1971-72, U. Okla., Norman, 1976-78; cons. J. David Spence Accountancy Corp., Fresno, 1974-76; many coms. at La. Tech. U. including acad. senator, new faculty welcoming com., acctg. scholarship chmn.; faculty senate rep.; Faculty Consortium, St. Charles, Ill., 1993; expert witness Superior Ct. Calif. and Dist. Ct., LA. Contbr. numerous articles to profl. jours., bus. mags., newspapers, also book reviews; presentations to profl. meetings. Past bd. dirs. Goodwill, Inc., Ctrl. Calif.; ch. deacon and mem. many coms.; pres., treas., state scripture coord. Gideons Internat. Ruston Camp; rep. United Way La. Tech. U., Ruston; deacon 1st Bapt. Ch., Ruston With USCG, 1965. Recipient El Paso CPA's Outstanding Jr. scholarship, Standard Oil scholarship, Price Waterhouse scholarship, Outstanding Educator award Gamma Beta Phi, 1986. Mem. AICPA, Am. Acctg. Assn. (La. membership com. chmn.), Am. Inst. for Decision Scis. (program com. chmn. acctg. track), La. Soc. CPAs, Am. Tax Assn. (internat. tax policy subcom.), Beta Gamma Sigma (pres.), Beta Alpha Psi, Delta Sigma Pi. Baptist. Avocations: triathlons, bicycle racing, golf, tennis, gardening. Home: 2700 Foxxwood Dr Ruston LA 71270-2509 Office: La Tech U Cab 129A Ruston LA 71272-0001 E-mail: posey@cab.latech.edu.

POSEY, DANIEL EARL, analytical chemist; b. Corpus Christi, Tex., Apr. 9, 1947; s. Earl Lloyd and Mary Lucille (Williams) P.; m. Mary Jewell King, Dec. 7, 1968; children: Amanda America, Matthew Daniel. BS in Chemistry, U. Houston, 1970. Rsch. technician Getty Oil Co. Exploration & Prodn. Rsch. Labs., Houston, 1968-69; lab. mgr. Inst. for Rsch., Inc., 1969-79, Am. Convertors, El Paso, Tex., 1979-84; tech. dir. Inst. for Rsch.-Austin, 1984-86; cons. chemist Spectro Chem Inc., Austin, 1986-88; quality engring. supr. Advanced Micro Devices, 1988—, sect. mgr. Tex., 1994—, mem. tech. staff, 1997—, sr. mem. tech. staff, 2000. Mem. Internat. Nonwoven & Disposables Assn., N.Y.C., 1981-83. Contbr. tech. papers to scholarly jours. Recipient Tech. Svc. award Am. Convertors R&D, 1981, Tech. Mgmt. award, 1982; recipient Cert. of Achievement, Am. Men and Women of Sci., 1986. Fellow Am. Inst. Chemists; mem. Am. Chem. Soc., Am. Soc. for Quality Control, Phi Eta Sigma. Republican. Achievements include patent for cleaning product for removal of mold and mildew composition and method of manufacture; invention of first lint particle generation test method for nonwoven fabrics; development of first antimicrobial surgical fabric. Office: Advanced Micro Devices Mail Stop 551 5204 E Ben White Blvd Austin TX 78741-7306 E-mail: dan.posey@amd.com.

POSEY, LORAN MICHAEL, pharmacist, editor; b. Albany, Ga., Aug. 22, 1955; s. Loran Willis and Rubye Jane (Lumpkin) P.; m. Teresa Maria McCoy, June 27, 1975 (div. Mar. 1983); m. Cheryl Ann Emerling, Jan. 31, 1989 (div. Mar. 1997); children: Evan Michael, Alan Michael, Loran Michael. BS in Pharmacy, BS in Microbiology, U. Ga., 1979, postgrad., 1992-96. Registered pharmacist, Ga. Sr. editor Am. Soc. Hosp. Pharmacists, Bethesda, Md., 1980-85; pres. PAS Pharmacy/Assn. Svcs., Athens, Ga., 1985-96, PNN Pharmacotherapy News Network, Athens, 1994-97, Pharmacy Editl. and News Svcs., Inc., Athens, 1996—. Dir. adminstrv. svcs. Ill. Soc. Hosp. Pharmacists, 1986-92, Va. Soc. Hosp. Pharmacists, 1990-98; exec. dir. Phi Delta Chi Pharmacy Frat., 1983-96, Ga. Soc. Hosp. Pharmacists, 1993-95. Author: Pharmacy Cadence, 1992—; editor: Pharmacotherapy: A Pathophysiologic Approach, 1989, Pharmacotherapy: A Pathophysiologic Approach, 5th edit., 2002, The Cons. Pharmacist, 1986—97, Jour. Managed Care Pharmacy, 1995—96, Jour. of Am. Pharm. Assn., 1997—, Pharmacy Today, 1998—, APhA DrugInfoLine, 2000—. Recipient George F. Archambault award Am. Soc. Cons. Pharmacists, 2000. Mem. Am. Med. Writers Assn. (chpt. pres. 1988-89, Pres.'s award 1988), Profl. Frat. Assn. (com. chair 1986-90), Am. Soc. Assn. Execs., Ill. Coun. Hosp. Pharmacists (hon.), Phi Delta Chi. Avocations: photography, swimming, reading. Office: PENS Pharmacy Editl and News Svcs Inc PO Box 6565 Athens GA 30604-6565

POSEY, TERRY WAYNE, lawyer; b. Springfield, Ohio, Nov. 9, 1950; s. William Eugene and Nancy Lougene (Lakins) P.; m. Deborah Lynn Henson, Oct. 4, 1977; children: Terry Wayne Jr., Ryan Christopher. BS, U. Dayton, 1983; JD, Capital U. Sch. Law, 1988. Bar: Ohio 1988, U.S. Dist. Ct. (so. dist.) Ohio 1988, U.S. Supreme Ct. 1992. Police officer Dayton (Ohio) Police Dept., 1968-87; pvt. practice law Dayton, 1987—. Recipient Mem. of Yr. award Fraternal Order of Police of Ohio, 1987. Mem. ABA, Ohio State Bar Assn., Dayton Bar Assn., Scottish Rite (trustee), Masons (Dayton pres. bd. dirs., 33 degree), Shriners. Home: 7842 Winding Way N Tipp City OH 45371-9243 Office: 7460 Brandt Pike Dayton OH 45424-3240

POSGAY, BETTY MARIE, medical equipment company executive, artist; b. Frankenstein, Mo., Dec. 15, 1933; d. August Peter and Gertrude Johanna (Koenigsfeld) Stiefermann; m. John George Posgay, Jr., June 12, 1954; children: Elaine Marie, Laura Elizabeth, Martin John. Student, U. Mo., 1952-54. Receptionist St. Mary's Hosp., Jefferson City, Mo., 1951; sec. March of Dimes, St. Louis, 1954-57; demonstrator CDI, 1983-86; sec. Archway Med. Supply, Inc., Clayton, Mo., 1988-96; pres. Crown Med. Equipment, Inc. (Southtown), St. Louis, 1996—. Exhibited in group shows at St. Louis Artists Guild/Two Oak Knoll Park, Clayton, Mo., 1998, Am. Art Alliance, St. Louis, 1997. Chmn. Am. Cancer Soc., Affton, Mo., 1984-85; former crusader Heart Fund, and March of Dimes, Affton. Mem. Am. Art Alliance (sec. 1997), Mo. Bot. Garden, Friends of Art Mus. Roman Catholic. Avocations: playing piano, sketching, writing in diary, painting, walking. Office: Crown Med Equipment Inc 5639 S Kingshighway Blvd Saint Louis MO 63109-3508

POSGAY, MATTHEW NICHOLS, lawyer; b. Ft. Lauderdale, Fla., Sept. 23, 1970; s. Raymond Joseph and Mary Lynn P. BA in Polit. Sci., U. Fla., 1991, JD, 1994. Bar: Fla. 1995, U.S. Dist. Ct. (mid. dist.) Fla. Shareholder Kubicki Draper, Jacksonville, Fla., 1995—. Mem. Fla. Bar Spkrs. Bur., 1997—. Mem. ABA, Fla. Bar Assn., Fla. Defense Lawyers Assn., Defense Rsch. Inst., U. Fla. Coll. Law Alumni Assn., Phi Alpha Delta, Phi Kappa Phi, Sigma Phi Epsilon, Fla. Blue Key. Democrat. Methodist. Avocations: scuba diving, golf, rowing. Office: 1650 Prudential Dr Ste 110 Jacksonville FL 32207 E-mail: mp@kubicfidraper.com.

POSIN, KATHRYN OLIVE, choreographer; b. Butte, Mont., Mar. 23, 1943; d. Daniel Q. and Frances (Schweitzer) P. BA in Dance, Bennington Coll., 1965; MFA in Interdisciplinary and World Dance, NYU, 1994; studies in composition, 1965-78, studies in ballet, 1965-90, studies in modern dance, 1967-80. Mem. dance co. Am. Dance Theater at Lincoln Ctr., 1965; dancer Anna Sokolow Dance Co., 1965-73; artistic dir. Kathryn Posin Dance Co., N.Y.C., 1972-91; choreographer Eliot Feld Ballet, 1978, Netherlands Dance Theater, Den Hague, Switzerland, 1980, Alvin Ailey Am. Dance Theater, N.Y.C., 1980; mem. dance faculty U. Wis., Milw., 1984-86, choreographer, 1984-88; tchr., choreographer UCLA, 1988-90, Trinity Coll., Hartford, Conn., 1990-91. Mem. dance faculty, choreographer U. Calif., Santa Barbara, 1986; tchr. dance technique and performance Tchr.'s Coll. Columbia U., spring 1990; tchr. composition and technique Nat. Inst. of Arts, Taiwan, 1991; founding chair Joffrey Ballet Sch., New Sch. U. BFA in Dance, 1998. Choreographer (performing cos./orgns.) Cherry Orchard, Lincoln Ctr., N.Y.C., 1978, Ballet West, Salt Lake City, 1981, Ohio Ballet, Akron, 1982, Ballet Pacifica, Laguna Beach, Calif., 1993, also Ohio Ballet, Repertory Dance Theater Utah, Extemporary Dance Co. London, Balletmet, Columbus, Ohio, Milw. Ballet, 1991, 93, 95, 96, Cin. Ballet, 1997; (prin. works) Salvation, Off-Broadway, N.Y.C., 1969, Waves, 1975 (Am. Dance Festival commn.), The Cherry Orchard, N.Y. Shakespeare Festival, 1979, Mary Stuart, Acting Co., 1980, Shady Grove (grantee joint program of Ohio Arts and Humanities Couns. 1991), The Tempest, Am. Shakespeare Festival, Stratford, Conn., 1982, Midsummer Night's Dream, Arena Stage, Washington, 1982, Boys From Syracuse, Am. Repertory Theater, Harvard U., 1983, The Paper Gramophone, Hartford Stage, 1989, Of Rage and Remembrance, 1990 (Premiere of Yr. in Music and Dance, Milw. Jour.), Stepping Stones, 1993 (co-recipient Meet the Composer/Choreographer award Milw. Ballet 1993), many others; subject of documentary Kathy's Dance. Grantee Guggenheim Found., 1978, N.Y. State Coun. on Arts, 1977, 79, 80, Jerome Robbins Found., 1972; grantee Nat. Endowment for Arts 1981, 82, 85-87, choreography fellow, 1995-96; Doris Humphrey fellow Am. Dance Festival, New London, Conn., 1968. Office: Kathryn Posin Dance Co 20 Bond St New York NY 10012-2406 E-mail: Pozndance@aol.com.

POSLER, GERRY LYNN, agronomist, educator; b. Cainsville, Mo., July 24, 1942; s. Glen L. and Helen R. Posler; m. O. Shirley Weeda, June 23, 1963; children: Mark L., Steven C., Brian D. BS, U. Mo., 1964, MS, 1966; PhD, Iowa State U., 1969. Asst. prof. Western (Macomb) Ill. U., 1969-74; assoc. prof. Kans. State U., Manhattan, 1974-80, prof., 1980—, asst. dept. head, 1982-90, dept. head, 1990-98. Contbr. articles to profl. jours. and popular publs., abstracts, book reviews. Fellow Am. Soc. Agronomy, Crop Sci. Soc. Am.; mem. Am. Forage Grassland Coun., Crop Science Soc. Am. (C-3 div. chmn. 1991), Coun. Agrl. Science Tech. (Cornerstone club), Nat. Assn. Colls. Tchrs. Agr. (tchr. fellow award 1978, ensminger interstate dist. teaching award, 1987, north cen. region dir. 1989, v.p. 1990, pres. 1991; life mem.), Kans. Assn. Colls. Tchrs. Agr. (pres. 1983-85), Kans. Forage Grassland Coun. (bd. dirs. 1989-92), Gamma Sigma Delta (Outstanding Faculty award 1991, pres. 1987). Home: 3001 Montana Ct Manhattan KS 66502-2300 Office: Kans State U Dept Agronomy Throckmorton Plant Sci Ctr Manhattan KS 66506 E-mail: gposler@oznet.ksu.edu.

POSNER, BARRY ZANE, management educator; b. Hollywood, Calif., Mar. 11, 1949; s. Henry and Delores Ann (Ginsberg) P.; m. Jacqueline Ann Schmidt, July 23, 1972; 1 child, Amanda Delores. BA, U. Calif., Santa Barbara, 1970; MA, Ohio State U., 1972; PhD, U. Mass., 1976. Prof. mgmt. Santa Clara (Calif.) U., 1976—, dir. grad. edn., 1987-90, assoc. dean, 1990-92. Mng. dir. Kouzes Posner Internat., Inc., Santa Clara, 1987—; chmn. MTP, Inc., Sepulveda, Calif., 1987-93; mng. ptnr. Exec. Devel. Ctr., 1993—. Author: (with others) The Leadership Challenge, 1987, 2d edit., 1995 (Book of Yr. award Am. Coun. Health Care Execs. 1989), Effective Project Planning and Management, 1988, Getting the Job Done, 1992, Credibility, 1994; contbr. articles to profl. publs. Bd. dirs. Big Bros./Big Sisters, 1994—, Ctr. for Excellence in Non-Profits. Mem. APA, Acad. Mgmt. (pres. western divsn. 1988), Orgn. Behavior Tchg. Soc. (bd. dirs. 1982-86), Sigma Phi Epsilon (bd. dirs. 1972-82), Beta Gamma Sigma. Democrat. Jewish. Avocations: tennis, theatre. Office: Leavey Sch Bus Adminstrn Santa Clara University Santa Clara CA 95053-0001

POSNER, DAVID S. lawyer; b. Pitts., Dec. 27, 1945; s. Mortimer B. and Lillian P.; m. Marilyn Hope Ackerman, Aug. 14, 1966; children: Morton J., Jennifer L. BS, Carnegie Mellon U., 1969; JD, U. Pitts., 1972. Bar: Pa. 1972, U.S. Supreme Ct. 1981. Ct. adminstr. Washington County, Pa., 1972-76, asst. dist. atty., 1976-79; ptnr. Goldfarb & Posner, Washington, 1979-97, Goldfarb, Posner, Beck, DeHaven & Drewitz, Washington, 1997—. Pres. Pa. Council of Trial Ct. Adminstrs., 1972-76; solicitor Clk. of Cts., Washington, 1983—. Mem. sect. 85 YMCA, Washington, 1980-85; chmn. East Washington Zoning Hearing Bd., 1992—; bd. dirs. Washington County Redevel. Authority, 2002—, United Way, Washington, 1979-85; pres. Beth Israel Congregation, 1992-94. With USAR, 1966-72. Mem. ABA, Pa. Bar Assn. (ho. of dels. 1995-97), Washington County Bar Assn. (treas. 1982-83, pres. 1995), B'nai B'rith (past pres.). Home: 149 S Wade Ave Washington PA 15301-4926 Office: Goldfarb Posner Beck DeHaven & Drewitz 26 S Main St Ste 200 Washington PA 15301-6812 E-mail: dsp@gpbdd.com.

POSNER, DONALD, art historian, educator; b. N.Y.C., Aug. 30, 1931; s. Murray and Frances (Teitel) P.; 1 dau., Anne Tyre. AB, Queens Coll., 1956; MA, Harvard U., 1957; PhD, NYU, 1962. Lectr. Queens Coll., 1957; asst. prof. art history Columbia U., 1961-62; mem. faculty Inst. Fine Arts, NYU, 1962—, Ailsa Mellon Bruce prof. fine arts, 1975—, acting dir. Inst. Fine Arts, 1978-79, now dep. dir.; Robert Sterling Clark prof. Williams Coll., 1973; William R. Kenan, Jr. prof. U. Va., 1976-77. Vis. prof. U. Wash., 1991. Author: Annibale Carracci, 1971, Watteau: A Lady at Her Toilet, 1973, Seventeenth and Eighteenth Century Art, 1971, Antoine Watteau, 1984; editor-in-chief: The Art Bull, 1968-71. Served with USAF, 1951-55. Am. Acad. in Rome fellow, 1959-61; Inst. for Advanced Study fellow, 1976; recipient Charles Rufus Morey award, 1972 Mem. Coll. Art Assn. Am. (dir. 1970-74), Am. Soc. 18th Century Studies. Office: Inst Fine Arts 1 E 78th St New York NY 10021-0178

POSNER, EDWARD MARTIN, lawyer; b. Phila., Oct. 20, 1946; BA, Amherst Coll., 1968; JD, Harvard U., 1974. Bar: Pa. 1974. Exec. asst. to sec. of pub. welfare Commonwealth of Pa., Harrisburg, 1971-72; assoc. Drinker Biddle & Reath, Phila., 1974-80, ptnr., 1980—. Democrat. Avocation: fly fishing. Office: Drinker Biddle & Reath LLP One Logan Sq 18th & Cherry Sts Philadelphia PA 19103-6996 E-mail: posnerem@dbr.com.

POSNER, GARY HERBERT, chemist, educator; b. N.Y.C., June 2, 1943; s. Joseph M. and Rose (Klein) P.; children: Joseph, Michael. BA, Brandeis U., 1965; MA, Harvard U., 1965, PhD, 1968. Asst. prof. Johns Hopkins U., Balt., 1969-74, assoc. prof., 1974-79, prof. dept. chemistry, 1979—, Scowe prof. chemistry, 1989—, prof. dept. environ. chemistry, 1982—, chmn. dept. of chemistry, 1987-90. Cons. Batelle Meml. Inst., Columbus, Ohio, 1983, S.W. Rsch. Inst., San Antonio, Nova Pharm. Co., Balt.; mem. Fulbright-Hays Adv. Screening Com. in Chemistry, 1978-81; Fulbright lectr. U. Paris, 1976; Michael vis. prof. Weizmann Inst. Sci., Rehovot, Israel, 1983; leader Round Table discussion Welch Found. Conf. Chem. Rsch., Houston, 1973, 83; Plenary lectr. Nobel Symposium on Asymmetric Synthesis, Sweden, 1984. Author: Introduction to Organic Synthesis Using Organocopper Reagents, 1980; mem. editl. bd. Organic Reactions, 1976-89; exec. editor Tetrahedron Reports, 1996—. Named Chemist of Yr., State of Md., 1987; fellow Japan Soc. for Promotion Sci., 1991; recipient Johns Hopkins U. Disting. Tchng. award, 1994. Mem. AAAS, Am. Chem. Soc., AAUP, NIH (medicinal chemistry study sect. 1986-89), Phi Beta Kappa Office: Johns Hopkins U Dept Chemistry 3300 N Charles St Baltimore MD 21218 E-mail: ghp@jhu.edu.

POSNER, JEROME BEEBE, neurologist, educator; b. Cin., Mar. 20, 1932; s. Philip and Rose (Goldberg) Posner; m. Gerta Grunen, Aug. 29, 1954; children: Roslyn, Joel, P.J. BS, U. Wash., 1951, MD, 1955. Intern King County Hosp., Seattle, 1955—56; asst. resident in neurology U. Wash. Affiliated Hosps., 1956—59, fellow in neurology, 1958—59; spl. fellow NIH, U. Wash., 1961—63; instr. medicine U. Louisville Sch. Medicine, 1959—61; attending neurologist King County Hosp., 1962—63; asst. prof. neurology Cornell U. Med. Coll., N.Y.C., 1963—67, assoc. prof., 1967—70, prof., 1970—, vice chmn. dept. neurology, 1978—87; asst. attending neurologist N.Y. Hosp., 1963—67, assoc. attending neurologist, 1967—70, attending neurologist, 1970—; assoc. Cotzias Lab. of Neuro-Oncology, Sloan Kettering Inst. Cancer Research, N.Y.C., 1967—76, mem., 1976—; chief neuropsychiat. service, attending physician dept. medicine Meml. Hosp. for Cancer and Allied Diseases, 1967—75, attending physician, 1975—, chmn. dept. neurology, 1975—87, 1989—97, Cotzias chair neuro-oncology, 1986—; Evelyn Frew clin. rsch. prof. Am. Cancer Soc., 1996—. Mem. med. adv. bd. Burke Rehab. Ctr., White Plains, NY, 1973—; adj. prof., vis. physician Rockefeller U. and Hosp., N.Y.C., 1973—75; mem. neurology B study sect. NIH, 1972—76; coun. mem. NINDS, 1998—2001. Author (with F. Plum): Diagnosis of Stupor and Coma, 3d edit., 1980; author: (with H. Gilbert and L. Weiss) Brain Metastasis, 1980, Neurologic Complications of Cancer, 1995; mem. editl. bd.: Archives of Neurology, 1971—76, mem. editl. bd.: Annals of Neurology, 1976—80, mem. editl. bd.: Am. Jour. Medicine, 1978—93, mem. editl. bd.: Neurology, 1992—96; contbr. articles to med. jours.; author (with L. DeAngeles, P. Gutin, S. Leibel): Intracranial Tumors, 2002; author: Intracranial Tumor (with DeAngeles), 2002. Served with M.C. U.S. Army, 1959—61. Fellow: AAAS; mem.: AMA, Soc. Neurosci., Inst. Medicine N.Y. Acad. Scis., Harvey Soc., Assn. Am. Physicians, Am. Physiol. Soc., Am. Neurol. Assn. (pres. 1997—99), Am. Fedn. Clin. Rsch., Am. Assn. Cancer Rsch., Am. Acad. Neurology (Farber Brain Tumor award 1988), Can. Neurol. Soc. (hon.), Alpha Omega Alpha. Office: Meml Sloan-Kettering Cancer 1275 York Ave New York NY 10021-6094

POSNER, LINDA IRENE, retired government official, marketing consultant; b. Balt., Feb. 6, 1939; d. Morris and Rosabelle (Hankin) Rosen; m. Allan Bernard Posner, Dec. 29, 1957; children: Larry Gregg, Michael Glenn, Robert Ira. BA summa cum laude, Coll. of Notre Dame, 1989. Dir., lectr. Montgomery Ward's Fashion, Modeling and Charm Sch., Md., 1962-66; fashion and pub. rels. dir. Montgomery Ward, 1966-75; freelance writer Balt., 1975-76; pres., co-owner Designer's Circle Ltd., 1976-78; TV writer, producer Dept. of Def., Ft. Meade, Md., 1979-87; TV mgr. Dept. Def., 1980-87, sr. edn. and tng. mgr., 1987-91, performance technologist, 1991-94, multi-media ops. mgr., 1994-96, sr. corp. mktg. strategist, 1996-98; mktg. and multimedia cons., 1999—. Regional dir. The Fashion Group, Balt., 1972-74. Mem. com. March of Dimes, Balt., 1976-78; chairperson Combined Fed. Campaign Com., 1987, U.S. Savs. Bonds, 1989. Dept. of Def. scholar, 1987-88. Mem. Women in Communications, Human Resources Mgmt. Assn., AFTRA. Jewish. Avocations: travel, writing. Home: 640 Grove Ave SW Cleveland TN 37311 E-mail: travelers_pos@msn.com.

POSNER, LOUIS JOSEPH, lawyer, accountant; b. N.Y.C., May 29, 1956; s. Alex Pozner and Hilda G. (Gottlieb) Weinberg; m. Betty F. Osin, June 21, 1986; 1 child, Daniel. BS in Acctg., Drexel U., 1979; MS in Taxation, Pace U., 1985; JD, N.Y. Law Sch., 1989. Bar: N.Y. 1990, N.J. 1990, U.S. Dist. Ct. (so. and ea. dists.) N.Y., 1990, D.C. 1991, U.S. Ct. Appeals (2d cir.) 1993, U.S. Supreme Ct. 1994. Auditor Arthur Andersen & Co., CPAs, Phila., 1979-81; tax sr. Kenneth Leventhal & Co., CPAs, N.Y.C., 1981-82; tax mgr. Mann Judd Landau, CPAs, 1983-86; tax dir. Integrated Resources, Inc., 1986-89; pvt. practice, 1989—. Spkr. in field. Producer, dir. TV show Your Legal Rights. Founder, exec. dir. Voter March, 2000—. Mem.: AICPA, ABA, N.Y. State Bar Assn. (trusts and estates sect.), Assn. Atty CPA's, N.Y. County Lawyers Assn. (trusts and estates sect.), N.Y. State Soc. CPA's (tax. com. 1985—90, mem. faculty N.Y.C. chpt. Found. for Acctg. Edn. 1989—90), Assn. Bar. City of N.Y., Mensa (coord. spl. interest group N.Y.C. chpt. 1978—99). Home: 160 E 48th St Apt 12T New York NY 10017-1225 Office: 39th Fl 245 Park Ave New York NY 10167 E-mail: lawline@nyc.rr.com.

POSNER, MARSHALL ROY, medical oncologist, internist, educator; b. N.Y.C., Apr. 16, 1949; s. Alan H. and Lillian J. Posner. BA, Yale U., 1971; MD, Tufts U., 1975. Resident Boston City Hosp., 1975-78; fellowship/staff Dana-Farber Cancer Inst., Boston, 1978-83; asst. prof. Roger Williams Med. Ctr., Brown U., Providence, 1983-91; from asst. to assoc. prof. NEDH, Harvard Med. Sch., Boston, 1991—; assoc. prof. Dana Farber Cancer Inst., Beth Israel Deaconess Med. Ctr., Mass. Gen. Hosp. Harvard Med. Sch., 1994—. Med. dir. head and neck oncology Dana-Farber Cancer Inst., Boston, 1994—. Author book chpts. and articles to profl. jours. Mem. Am. Soc. Clin. Oncology, Am. Soc. Hematology, Am. Assn. Immunology, Mass. Med. Soc. Home: 6 Birch Ln Medfield MA 02052-2234 Office: Dana Farber Cancer Inst 44 Binney St Rm SW430 Boston MA 02115-6084

POSNER, MICHAEL HOFFMAN, lawyer; b. Chgo., Nov. 19, 1950; s. Harry Randolph and Elizabeth (Hoffman) P.; m. Deborah Korzenik, Dec. 12, 1986. Children: Alexander Korzenik Posner, Hannah Korzenik Posner. BA with honors, U. Mich., 1972; JD, U. Calif., Berkeley, 1975. Bar: Calif. 1975, Ill. 1976, U.S. Dist Ct. (no. dist.) Ill. 1976. Research asst. Internat. Commn. Jurists, Geneva, 1974; assoc. Sonnenschein, Carlin, Nath & Rosenthal, Chgo., 1975-78; exec. dir. Lawyers Com. for Human Rights, N.Y.C., 1978—. Bd. dirs. Amnesty Internat., 1982-84; vis. lectr. Yale Law Sch., New Haven, 1981-84, Columbia Law Sch., N.Y.C., 1984—. Contbr. articles to profl. jours. Mem. Council Fgn. Relations, N.Y.C. Mem. ABA. Democratic. Jewish. Avocations: tennis, skiing, hiking. Office: Lawyers Com for Human Rights 333 7th Ave New York NY 10001-5004

POSNER, PAUL LEONARD, government official; b. Washington, Nov. 16, 1946; s. Bernard and Bess Posner; m. Arlene S. Posner; 1 child, Jennifer M. BA, Miami U. Ohio, 1968; MA, Columbia U., 1972, MPhil, 1989, PhD, 1995. Dir. fed. program review N.Y.C. Office Mgmt. and Budget, 1973-76; evaluator intergovtl. rels. GAO, Washington, 1976-84, asst. dir. intergovtl. rels., 1984-89, assoc. dir. tax policy, 1989-92, mng. dir. budget issues, 1992—. Adj. prof. Georgetown U., Johns Hopkins U. Author: The Politics of Unfunded Federal Mandates, 1998; contbr. articles to profl. jours. Fellow Nat. Acad. Pub. Adminstrn.; mem. ASPA (chmn. intergovtl. mgmt. sect. 1985), Am. Polit. Sci. Assn. (chmn. federalism sect.), Assn. for Budgeting and Fin. Mgmt. (pres. 2000). Avocations: biking, photography. Office: GAO 441 G St NW Washington DC 20548-0001 E-mail: posnerp@gao.gov.

POSNER, RICHARD ALLEN, federal judge; b. N.Y.C., Jan. 11, 1939; s. Max and Blanche Posner; m. Charlene Ruth Horn, Aug. 13, 1962; children: Kenneth A., Eric A. AB, Yale U., 1959, LLD (hon.) , 1996; LLB, Harvard U., 1962; LLD (hon.) , Syracuse U., 1986; LLD (hon.) , Duquesne U., 1987, Georgetown U., 1992, U. Pa., 1997; PhD (hon.) , U. Ghent, 1995. Bar: N.Y. 1963, U.S. Supreme Ct. 1966. Law clk. to Hon. William J. Brennan Jr. U.S. Supreme Ct., Washington, 1962—63; asst. to commr. FTC, 1963—65; asst. to solicitor gen. U.S. Dept. Justice, 1965—67; gen. counsel Pres.'s Task Force on Comm. Policy, 1967—68; assoc. prof. Stanford U. Law Sch., Calif., 1968—69; prof. U. Chgo. Law Sch., 1969—78, Lee and Brena Freeman prof., 1978—81, sr. lectr., 1981—; circuit judge U.S. Ct. Appeals (7th cir.), Chgo., 1981—, chief judge, 1993—2000. Rsch. assoc. Nat. Bur. Econ. Rsch., cambridge, Mass., 1971—81; pres. Lexecon Inc., Chgo., 1977—81. Author: Antitrust Law: An Economic Perspective, 1976, Economic Analysis of Law, 5th edit., 1998, The Economics of Justice, 1981; author: (with William M. Landes) The Economic Structure of Tort Law, 1987; author: The Problems of Jurisprudence, 1990, Cardozo: A Study in Reputation, 1990, Sex and Reason, 1990, Sex and Reason, 1992; author: (with Tomas J. Philipson) Private Choices and Public Health: The AIDS Epidemic in an Economic Perspective, 1993; author: Overcoming Law, 1995, Aging and Old Age, 1995, The Federal Courts: Challenge and Reform, 1996, Law and Legal Theory in England and America, 1996, The Federal Courts: Challenge and Reform, 1997, Law and Literature, revised and enlarged edit., 1998, The Problematics of Moral and Legal Theory, 1999, An Affair of State: An Investigation, Impeachment, and Trial of President Clinton, 1999, Frontiers of Legal Theory, 2001, Breaking the Deadlock: The 2000 Election, The Constitution, and the Courts, 2001, Antitrust Law, 2d edit., 2001, Public Intellectuals, 2001; pres. Harvard Law Rev., 1961—62, editor Jour. Legal Studies, 1972—81, Am. Law and Econs. Rev., 1999—; author (with William M. Landes): The Essential Holmes, 1992. Fellow: AAAS, Brit. Acad., Am. Law Inst. (pres. 1995—96); mem.: Am. Law and Econ. Assn., Am. Econ. Assn., Century Assn. Office: US Ct Appeals 7th Cir 219 S Dearborn St Chicago IL 60604-1702

POSNER, ROY EDWARD, retired finance executive; b. Chgo., Aug. 24, 1933; s. Lew and Julia (Cvetan) P.; m. Donna Lea Williams, June 9, 1956 (div. May 1991); children: Karen Lee, Sheryl Lynn. Student, U. Ill., 1951-53, Internat. Accountants Soc., 1956-59, Loyola U., Chgo., 1959; grad., Advanced Mgmt. Program, Harvard U., 1976. CPA, Ill. Pub. acct. Frank W. Dibble Co., Chgo., 1956-61; supr. Harris, Kerr, Forster & Co. (C.P.A.s), 1961-66; with Loews Corp., N.Y.C., 1966-98, v.p. fin. svcs., chief fin. officer, 1973-86, sr. v.p., chief fin. officer, 1986-98, ret. Fin. cons. N.Y. Football Giants, Inc., Rutherford, N.J.; bd. dirs. Bulova Italy S.P.A., Milan, Bulova Systems and Instruments Corp., N.Y.C., Loews Hotels Monaco S.A.M., Monte Carlo, Monaco, Loews Internat. Svcs. S.A., Switzerland, G F Corp., Youngstown, Ohio, Taj Mahal Holding Corp., Atlantic City, CNA Surety Corp., Chgo. Mem. editorial com.: Uniform System of Accounting for Hotels, 7th edit. Pres. No. Regional Valley High Sch. Music Parents Assn., 1978-79; trustee Loews Found., N.Y.C. With U.S. Army, 1953-55. Mem. AICPA, Fin. Execs. Inst., Ins. Acctg. and Stats. Assn., Internat. Hospitality Accts. Assn., Am. Hotel and Motel Assn., Ill. Soc. CPAs, N.Y. State CPAs (chmn. com. on hotel restaurant and club acctg. 1980-82), Tri-County Golf Assn. (treas. 1985-88, v.p. 1988-89), Alpine Country Club (bd. govs. 1982-94, exec. com. 1982-90, pres. 1988-90), Delta Tau Delta. Home: 273 Whitman St Haworth NJ 07641-1315 E-mail: sherylroy@aol.com.

POSNER, SIDNEY, advertising executive; b. Syracuse, N.Y., Jan. 14, 1924; s. Harry and Fannie (Hoffman) P.; m. Miriam Frances Kapfer, June 8, 1952; children: Steven Charles, Peter Scott, Robert Keith. BS, Syracuse U., 1947. Asst. advt. mgr. Rudolph Bros., Syracuse, 1947-48; copy chief Kaletski Advt. Agy., 1948-50; promotion mgr. Photo Trade News, N.Y.C., 1950-53; asst. to pres. Dobin Advt. Agy.; pres. S. Posner & Co. Advt. Agy., 1955-59, Constellation Art Corp., 1959-76, Communicorp, N.Y.C., 1959-76, Bus. Counselors Corp., N.Y.C., 1959-76, Newmark, Posner & Mitchell Inc., N.Y.C., 1959-92, Posner Comm. Inc., Boca Raton, Fla., 1993-94. E-mail: sidandmimi@aol.com.

POSNICK, JEFFREY CRAIG, plastic surgeon; b. Mpls., Mar. 1, 1952; s. Irving H. and Nan (Fine) P.; m. Patricia Joan Grundlegar, Jan. 7, 1989; children: Joshua, David. BA, U. Minn., 1973; DMD, Harvard U., 1977; MD, Vanderbilt U., 1979. Diplomate Am. Bd. Oral/Maxillofacial Surgery, Am. Bd. Plastic Surgery. Resident oral/maxillofacial surgery Vanderbilt U. Hosp., Nashville, 1977-79, resident gen. surgery, 1979-80, chief resident oral and maxillofacial surgery, 1980-81; resident gen. surgery Mass. Gen. Hosp., Boston, 1981-83; fellow pediatric craniofacial surgery U. Pa., Phila., 1983; resident plastic surgery Ea. Va. Sch. Medicine, Norfolk, 1984-86; dir. craniofacial surgery Hosp. for Sick Children, U. Toronto, Ont., Can., 1986-92; dir. Craniofacial Ctr. Georgetown Children's Med. Ctr., Georgetown U. Med. Ctr., Washington, 1992-98; dir. Posnick Ctr. for Facial Plastic Surgery, Chevy Chase, Md., 1998—. Clin. prof. plastic surgery, pediats., otolaryngology/head and neck surgery, oral and maxillofacial surgery Georgetown U., 1998—. Author, editor: Craniofacial and Maxillofacial Surgery in Children and Young Adults, 2000; contbr. articles to profl. jours. Rsch. grantee Med. Rsch. Coun. Can., 1990, Plastic Surg. Edn. Found., 1990, Saudi Arabia Edn. Found., 1992, Cleft Palate Found., 1995. Fellow ACS, Royal Coll. Surgeons (Can.); mem. Internat. Soc. Craniofacial Surgeons, Am. Cleft Palate/Craniofacial Assn., Am. Assn. Plastic Surgery, Am. Assn. Asthetic Plastic Surgeons, Am. Soc. Plastic Surgery, Am. Soc. Oral and Maxillofaciail Surgery. Avocations: collecting antiques, American history. Home: 10100 Counselman Rd Potomac MD 20854-5020 Office: Posnick Ctr Facial Plastic Surgery 5530 Wisconsin Ave Ste 1250 Chevy Chase MD 20815-4314 Fax: 301-986-1974. E-mail: jposnick@drposnick.com.

POSPISIL, GEORGE CURTIS, human research educator; b. Thomas, Okla., Aug. 8, 1945; s. George Frank and Zelpha Earline (Hensley) P.; children: Heather Elizabeth, Derek Curtis. Student, Wheaton Coll., 1963-64; BA, U. Okla., 1968; MA, 1971. Tchr. Peace Corps, Maseru, Lesotho, 1973-74; dir. health svcs. fin. project State of Wis., Madison, 1975-76; pub. health advisor USPHS, Rockville, Md., 1972-73, program/policy analyst, 1977—81, 1984—86, congl. liaison, 1989—99, clin. trials policy adv. Md., 1998-2001, contract mgr., 1982-84; dir. Svcs. Crime Victims/Witnesses Project, Tioga County, N.Y., 1986—; pub. health educator Office of the Sec., OHRP, HHS, 2001—. Guest lectr. U. Wis., Summer Inst., Carthage Coll.; analyst biomed. rsch. program NIH, 1989—; sci. editor The Johns Hopkins U. Krieger Mind/Brain Inst., 1993—95; pub. health analyst U.S. Dept. Health and Human Svcs., Office of Sec. Editor: Decde of the Brain, 1990, Maximizing Human Potential: Decade of the Brain, 1991. Mem. Rockville Humanities Commn., 1981-83; spokesperson Neighborhood Planning Com., 1980-82; coordinator mental health svcs. Cuban Refugee Project, Ft. McCoy, Wis., 1980; sec. cmty. adv. com. mental health program Montgomery House, 1982-86; rsch. and tng. adminstr. Cornell U., Ithaca, N.Y., 1986-89; bd. dirs. Family Svc. Mongomery County, 1984-86; legis fellow U.S. Senate Labor and Human Resources Com./Health Office, 1991; mem. county Spl. Olympics Com., 1982-86; mem. Citizens' Planning Subcom. Carroll County Md.; insp. gen. Civil Air Patrol; mem. adv. com. troop 321 Boy Scouts Am.; bd. dirs. Shepherd's Staff Cmty. Svc. program. Mem. Soc. Rsch. Adminstrs. Office: OHRP US Dept Health and Human Svcs Office of Sec Tower Bldg Rockville MD 20852-3802 E-mail: gpospisil@os.osphs.dhhs.gov.

POSPISIL, LEOPOLD JAROSLAV, anthropology and law educator; b. Olomouc, Czechoslovakia, Apr. 26, 1923; came to U.S., 1949, naturalized, 1954; s. Leopold and Ludmila (Petrlak) P.; m. Zdenka Smyd, Jan. 31, 1945; children: Zdenka, Mira. Juris Universae Candidatus, Charles U., Prague, Czechoslovakia, 1947, JD, 1991; BA in Sociology, Willamette U., Salem, Oreg., 1950; MA in Anthropology, U. Oreg., 1952; PhD, Yale U., 1956; ScD (hon.), Willamette U., 1969; PhD (hon.), Charles U., Prague, Czech Rep., 1994. Instr. Yale U., New Haven, 1956-57, asst. prof., 1957-60; asst. curator Peabody Mus., 1956-65, assoc. prof., 1960-65, prof., curator, 1965-93, dir. divsn. anthropology, 1966-93; prof. anthropology, 1965-93; prof. and curator emeritus, 1993—. Author: Kapauku Papuans and Their Law, 1958, Kapauku Papuan Economy, 1963, Kapauku Papuans of West New Guinea, 1963, Anthropology of Law, 1971, Ethnology of Law, 1972, Anthropologie des Rechts, 1981, Sprache, Symbole und Symbolverwendungen in Ethnologie, Kulturanthropologie, Politik, Religion und Recht, 1993, Obernberg: Quantitative Analysis of a Tyrolean Economy, 1996, Etnologie Prava, 1997; contbr. articles to profl. jours. Guggenheim fellow, 1962, NSF fellow, 1962, 64-65, 67-71, NIMH fellow, 1973-79; Social Sci. Rsch. Coun. grantee, 1966. Fellow AAAS, N.Y. Acad. Scis., Am. Anthrop. Assn.; mem. NAS, Conn. Acad. Arts and Scis., Explorers Club, Czechoslovakian Acad. Arts and Scis. (past pres.), Coun. Free Czechoslovakia, Assn. for Polit. and Legal Anthropology (pres.-at-large), Assn. for Social Anthropology in Oceania, Soc. for Econ. Anthropology, Sigma Xi. Home: 554 Orange St New Haven CT 06511-3819 Office: 51 Hillhouse Ave New Haven CT 06511-3703 E-mail: anthropology@yale.edu.

POSS, JEFFERY SCOTT, architect, educator; b. Harvey, Ill., May 20, 1956; m. Barbara Young Cook, May 1, 1999. BAS, U. Ill., 1978, MArch, 1980. Intern architect Charles Kober Assocs., Chgo., 1980-81, Skidmore, Owings and Merrill, Chgo., 1981; designer Newman/Lustig and Assocs., 1983-84; design assoc. Kevin Roche John Dinkeloo and Assocs., Hamden, Conn., 1985-87; project architect and designer Tai Soo Kim Assocs., Hartford, 1987-89; pvt. practice Urbana, Ill., 1989—; assoc. prof. U. Ill., Champaign-Urbana, 1989—; prof. U. Ill. Sch. Arch., 1991—. Vis. prof. Glasgow Sch. Art, 1999, 2001; invited juror, lectr. in field. Contbr. articles to profl. jours. Recipient 1st Alt. prize Nat. Inst. for Archtl. Edn., 1981, 1sr pl. Champaign Park Dist./AIA, 1989, Nat. Design award Concrete Steel Reinforcing Inst./AIA, 1992, 2d pl. WWII Meml., State of Md., 1996, Merit award Saluda Shoals Amphitheater, State of N.C. Mem. AIA (Excellence in Edn. Honors award 1993, Ctrl. Ill. award for design excellence, 1993, 97, 2000), Am. Soc. Archtl. Perspectives (Excellence in Graphic Representation Architecture award 1990, 93). Business E-Mail: j-poss@uiuc.edu.

POSS, STEPHEN DANIEL, lawyer; b. Buffalo, Jan. 13, 1955; s. Gilbert H. and Bernice L. (Lippman) Poss; m. Jane Fitz Simon, 1990. BA magna cum laude, Amherst Coll., 1978; JD, U. Chgo., 1981. Bar: N.Y. 1982, Mass. 1988; U.S. Dist. Ct. (so. dist.) N.Y. 1984, U.S. Dist. Ct. Mass. 1988; U.S. Tax Ct. 1983; U.S. Supreme Ct. 1986; U.S. Ct. Appeals (1st cir.) 1989, U.S. Ct. Appeals (fed. cir.) 1992. Assoc. Cravath, Swaine & Moore, N.Y.C., 1981-87, Goodwin Procter LLP, Boston, 1988-89, ptnr., 1989—. Teaching asst. to prof. Henry Steele Commager, 1977; lectr. Mass. Continuing Legal Edn., 1987—, Mass. Bar Assn. Ednl. Seminars, 1992-94; seminar chmn. SEC Inst. II, 1998; lectr. Nasdaq Exec. Forum, 1998, 2001; mem. civil litigation curriculum com. Mass. Continuing Legal Edn., 1997—; lectr. SEC Inst., 1999-2001, mem. nat. adv. bd., 2001--; mem. Nasdaq Investor Rels. Forum, 2000. Advisor campaign Bill Guy for U.S. Senate from N.D., 1974, Quentick Burdick for U.S. Senate, N.D., 1976, Bill Bradley for U.S. Senate, N.J., 1978, Gary Hart for U.S. Senate, Colo., 1980, Jeff Bingaman for U.S. Senate, N.Mex., 1982; pro bono counsel to Dem. Nat. Com., 1986-87; bd. dirs. Internat. Forum, N.Y.C., 1984; counsel of N.Y. Law Assocs., N.Y.C., 1985; mem. fin. com. Campaign to re-elect U.S. Senator John Kerry, 1990; assoc. dir., bd. dirs. Mass. Audubon Soc., 1997-2000, adv. counsel, 2001—. John Woodruff Simpson fellow, 1978. Mem.: ABA (vice chair securities litigation subcom. bus. law sect. 2000—), Boston Bar Assn., Mass. Bar Assn. (vice chair bus. litigation com. 1992—94), Internat. Churchill Soc. Office: Goodwin Procter LLP Exchange Pl Boston MA 02109-2803 E-mail: sposs@goodwinprocter.com.

POSSE, STEFAN, biomedical physicist, educator; b. Bonn, Germany, July 7, 1961; s. Günther and Renate (Naaf) P.; m. Mary Anthony Jacintha, Oct. 19, 1994; 1 child, Richard Kevin. Diploma in physics, U. Cologne, Germany, 1986; D Natural Scis., U. Berne, Switzerland, 1990; Habilitation, U. Düsseldorf, Germany, 1999. Postdoctoral fellow U. Berne, 1990-91; vis. fellow NIH, Bethesda, Md., 1991-94; head magnetic resonance group Rsch. Ctr. Jülich (Germany) GmbH, 1994-99; asst. prof. dept. psychiatry and behavioral neurosciences. Wayne State U. Sch. Medicine, Detroit, 2000—. Affiliate asst. prof. U. Wash., Seattle, 1995—; jour. reviewer Magnetic Resonance in Medicine, 1991—. Contbg. author: Diffusion and Perfusion: MRI, 1995; contbr. articles to Jour. Magnetic Resonance, Radiology, Magnetic Resonance in Medicine, Jour. Computer Assisted Tomography, Jour. Magnetism and Magnetic Materials. Richard Winter Found. scholar U. Fla., 1986-87, Swiss Nat. Sci. Found. scholar, 1987-92; fellow Fogarty Internat. Ctr., 1991-94. Mem. Soc. Magnetic Resonance (reviewer for meetings 1994—), Phi Beta Delta. Achievements include patents and patents pending for quantitative functional MRI, for real time functional MRI, and for PEPSI (proton echoplanar spectroscopic imaging), one of fastest spectroscopic imaging method known for whole body clinical magnetic resonance scanners; introduced functional MR spectroscopic imaging in human brain; research on real time functional magnetic resonance imaging and on advanced short echo time proton magnetic resonance spectroscopic imaging. Avocations: flying, gymnastics, tennis. Office: Wayne State U Sch Medicine Dept Psychiatry-Behav Neuro Univ Health Ctr 9B 18 Detroit MI 48201 E-mail: s.posse@wayne.edu.

POST, AUGUST ALAN, economist, artist; b. Alhambra, Calif., Sept. 17, 1914; s. Edwin R. and Edna (Stickney) P.; m. Helen E. Wills, Nov. 21, 1940; 1 child, David Wills. AB, Occidental Coll., 1938; student, Chouinard Inst. Art, 1938; MA, Princeton U., 1940; LLD, Golden Gate U., 1972, Occidental Coll., 1974, Claremont Grad. Sch., 1978. In banking bus., 1933-36; instr. econs. Occidental Coll., 1940-42; asst. prof. Am. U., 1943; economist Dept. State, 1944-45; rsch. dir. Utah Found., 1945-46; chief economist, adminstrv. analyst State of Calif., 1946-50, state legis. analyst, 1950-77. Cons. Com. Higher Edn. and State, 1964; mem. Nat. Com. Support of Pub. Schs., 1967;; mem. nat. adv. panel Nat. Ctr. Higher Edn. Mgmt. Systems, 1971-72; chmn. Calif. Gov.'s Commn. on Govt. Reform, 1978; mem. faculty U. So. Calif. Grad. Sch. Pub. Adminstrn., 1978-80; Regents' prof. U. Calif., Davis, 1983, vis. prof., 1984-85; spl. cons. Touche Ross and Co., 1977-87; cons., interim exec. dir. Calif. Commn. for Rev. of Master Plan for Higher Edn., 1985; mem. adv. bd. Calif. Tomorrow nat. shows and one-man shows; dir. Crocker Art Gallery Assn., pres., 1966-67. Trustee U. Calif., Berkeley Art Mus., 1986-91; mem. adv. com. on future ops. Coun. State Govts., 1965; bd. mgrs., pres. YMCA; bd. dirs. Sacramento Civic Ballet Assn.; trustee Calif. Coll. Arts and Crafts, 1982-86; chmn. Calif. State Task Force on Water Future, 1981-82, Sacramento Regional Found., bd. dirs., 1983-91; bd. dirs. Calif. Mus. Assn., pres., 1976-77, Policy Analysis for Calif. Edn., 1985—, Senate Adv. Commn. on Control of Cost of State Govt., 1986—, Pub. Policy Inst. Calif., 1994—; co-chmn. Calif. Citizen's Budget Commn., 1992-99, chmn., 1999—; chmn. Citizen's Commn. on Ballot Initiatives, 1992—, Catalonia Sister State Task Force, 1988—, Commn. on Innovation, Calif. Cmty. Colls., 1992; chair Judicial Coun. Select Com. on Judicial Retirement, 1993—; mem. Supreme Ct. Select Com. Judicial Ethics, 1995-96; bd. dirs. Ctrl. Valley Found., 1994-99. With USNR, 1943-44. Mem. Nat. Acad. Pub. Adminstrn., Phi Beta Kappa, Kappa Sigma. Home: 1900 Rockwood Dr Sacramento CA 95864-1527 E-mail: aphp@wnet.com.

POST, AVERY DENISON, retired church official; b. Norwich, Conn., July 29, 1924; s. John Palmer and Dorothy (Church) P.; m. Margaret Jane Rowland, June 8, 1946; children: Susan Post Ross, Jennifer C., Elizabeth Post Elliott, Anne Post Roy. BA, Ohio Wesleyan U., 1946; B.D., Yale U., 1949, S.T.M., 1952; L.H.D. (hon.), Lakeland Coll., Sheboygan, Wis., 1977; D.D. (hon.), Chgo. Theol. Sem., 1978, Middlebury Coll. (Vt.), 1978, Defiance Coll. (Ohio), 1979; LL.D. (hon.), Heidelberg Coll. (Ohio), 1982, Chapman Coll.; Litt.D. (hon.), Elmhurst Coll. Ordained to ministry, 1949; pastor chs. in Vt., Ohio, Conn. and N.Y., 1946-63; sr. minister Scarsdale (N.Y.) Congl. Ch., 1963-70; minister, pres. Mass. conf. United Ch. Christ, 1970-77; pres. United Ch. Christ, N.Y.C., 1977-89; mem. central com. World Council Chs., 1978-91; exec. com., bd. govs. Nat. Council Chs., 1977-89. Moderator, planning com. 7th Gen. Assembly World Coun. Chs.; lectr. Bible Adelphi Coll., Garden City, N.Y., 1958-59; Luccock lectr. Yale U. Div. Sch., 1961; lectr. homiletics Union Sem., N.Y.C., 1967-69, bd. dirs., 1967-77; trustee Andover Newton Theol. Sem., 1970-80; del. numerous internat. ch. meetings; sr. fellow Hartford Sem., 1989-93. Bd. dirs. Bridges for Peace, 1990-94; exec. dir. Bangor Theol. Sem., Hanover, N.H., 1991-93. With USNR, 1943-45. Decorated Comdr.'s Cross (Federal Republic Germany), 1990; recipient 1st Ecumenical award Mass. Coun. Chs., 1976; Disting. Achievement award Ohio Wesleyan U., 1983 Mem. PTA (life), Randolph Mountain Club (N.H.), Phi Beta Kappa, Omicron Delta Kappa. Democrat.

POST, BARBARA JOAN, elementary education educator; b. Passaic, N.J., June 29, 1930; d. John Ward and Florence Barbara (Barnum) Post; m. Edward Wayne Poppele, Apr. 10, 1954 (dec. Mar. 1978); children: E. Scott Poppele, Sara Elizabeth Poppele, Andrew John Poppele. BSE, William Paterson Coll., 1953; cert. in counseling, Rutgers U., 1981; postgrad., Columbia U., 1983, Northeastern U., 1983. Cert. tchr., N.J. Elem. tchr. Cen. Sch., Glen Ridge, N.J., 1953-55, Middletown (N.J.) Village Sch., 1956, Our Lady of Perpetual Help, Highlands, N.J., 1981-85; reading tchr. Monmouth Reading Ctr., Long Branch, 1985; tchr. gifted/talented Harmony Sch., Middletown, 1987-88; edn. coord. for Monmouth County Nat. Coun. on Alcoholism, Freehold, N.J., 1988-89; coord. math./sci. consortium Brookdale Community Coll., Lincroft, 1989-90; tchr., owner Learning Post and Creative Garden of Art for Children, Middletown, 1991—; dir. art Hillel Sch., Ocean, N.J., 1991—. Dir.-owner Learning Post, Middletown, 1986—; art tchr. Art Alliance of Monmouth County, Red

Bank, N.J., 1986-88; vol. case mgmt. worker St. Matthews House, Naples, Fla., 1997, 98. Author: (poem) The Lift, 1988 (short story) Sarah-Grand, 1984, Hooked on the Classics, 1988; artist (program cover) Country Christmas, 1990, 91. Demonstrator Family Reading Fair, Lincroft, 1989; participant Muscular Dystrophy Telethon, Eatontown, N.J., 1986; tchr. Tower Hill Vacation Bible Sch., Presbyn. ch., Red Bank, N.J., 1998. Mem. AAUW (tchr., mentor for teen women 1989-92, Appreciation award 1989-90), Nat. Soc. DAR (chairperson 1961-62), N.J. Shore Rose Soc. (exhibitor, 2d and 3d prize for roses 1986). Republican. Presbyterian. Avocations: art, swimming, choir, roses, golf. Home: 14 Oakland St Red Bank NJ 07701-1102 also: 167 Crown Dr Naples FL 34110 E-mail: post@mymailstation.com.

POST, DAVID ALAN, media and internet technology executive; b. N.Y.C., Oct. 20, 1941; s. Emil R. and Ruth (Rosen) P.; m. Arline Goldbrum, June 10, 1962 (div. 1981); children: Randee, Lori, Jill; m. Katlean de Monchy, Dec. 13, 1984. Student, CCNY, 1959-61; grad., Fleigenheimer Ins. Inst., 1961, N.Y. Inst. Fin., 1968. Sales rep. Aetna Life Ins. Casualty, Hartford, Conn., 1961-63; sales mgr. Globe Rubber Products, Phila., 1963-67; ptnr. Zuckerman Smith and Co., N.Y.C., 1968-71; dir. corp. fin. Andersen and Co., 1971-72; exec. v.p., dir. R.K. Pace Post Investment Bankers, 1973-76; chmn., chief exec. officer, founder Page Am. Group, Inc., Hackensack, N.J., 1976-86; co-founder, bd. dirs. Cellular Sys. Inc., 1991-92; chmn., founder Channel Am. TV Network, N.Y.C., 1987-96; chmn., co-founder Can Do Woman TV & Other Media, 1996-2000; chmn., CEO UMagic Systems, Inc., an Internet Tech. Co., 2000—; chmn., exec. prodr. Can do Woman Media Networks, 2000—; exec. prodr. Nextpert News Network, 2002—. Contbr. articles to INC. mag.; creator several TV series. Mem. Nat. Assn. TV Programming Execs. Republican. Jewish. Avocation: writing. Home: 400 E 57th St New York NY 10022-3019 Office: Can do Woman 213 W 35th St Ste 303 New York NY 10001 E-mail: david@candowoman.com.

POST, DIANA CONSTANCE, retired librarian; b. Anoka, Minn., Oct. 17, 1929; d. Kenneth Fred and Emma Constance (Fredrickson) Davis; husband dec., June 1996; children: Leslie Post, Paul Post, Tom Post. BS, U. Minn., 1970, MLS, 1976. Cert. libr., media specialist, Minn. Libr., media specialist Lake City (Minn.) H.S., 1970-94. Bd. dirs. Zumbrota (Minn.) Pub. Libr.; mem. SELCO governing bd. regional libr. sys., Rochester, Minn., 1980-86; pres. SELCO exec. com., 1984-86; SELS adv. com., 1990-94. Editor Lake City Sch. Dist. News, 1988-89. Scholar LaVerne Noyes Found., 1947-48, Delta Delta Delta, 1949. Mem. Beta Phi Mu. Avocations: golf, swimming, volunteering. Home: 695 Jefferson Dr Zumbrota MN 55992-1103 E-mail: DPost3@aol.com.

POST, EDWARD PATRICK, medical educator, researcher; b. North Tarrytown, N.Y., Mar. 17, 1965; BA with distinction, U. Va., 1987; MD, Med. Coll. Va., 1991; PhD, UCLA, 1998. Diplomate Am. Bd. Internal Medicine. House officer internal medicine U. Mich., Ann Arbor, 1991-94; primary care rsch. fellow, clin. instr. medicine UCLA, 1994-97; asst. prof. medicine U. Pitts., 1998—, core faculty mem. Ctr. for Rsch. on Health Care, 1998—. Reviewer: Jours. Am. Med. Assn., 1997, Med. Care, 1998—. Active Diocese of Richmond Haitian Ministry Commn., Va., 1988-91, chmn., 1990-91. Mem. ACP, Assn. for Health Svcs. Rsch., Soc. Gen. Internal Medicine. Avocations: hiking, golf. Office: U Pitts 200 Lothrop St Pittsburgh PA 15213-2546 Fax: 412-692-4838. E-mail: postep@msx.upmc.edu.

POST, GERALD JOSEPH, retired banker, retired air force officer; b. Braintree, Mass., Sept. 27, 1925; s. Robert Z. and Marjorie F. (Dunn) P.; m. Jane Stewart Curry, May 4, 1945; children: Sharyn, Gerald, J., Steven M., Richard J., Sean C., David D., Tracy Post Krupa. MBA, U. Chgo., 1958. Commd. 2d lt. U.S. Air Force, 1945, advanced through grades to lt. gen., 1978; comptroller, dir. materiel mgmt. San Antonio Air Materiel Area, 1970-73; dep. chief of Staff for Materiel Mgmt., Wright-Patterson AFB, Ohio, 1973-75; chief of staff Air Force Logistics Command, 1975-77; asst. dep. chief of staff for systems and logistics Hdqrs. USAF, 1977-78, dir. Def. Logistics Agy., 1978-81; ret., 1981; pres. Lackland Nat. Bank, 1981-82. Decorated Def. Disting. Service medal, Legion of Merit with oak leaf cluster, D.F.C., Air medal with 2 oak leaf clusters, others. Mem. Am. Soc. Mil. Comptrollers, Air Force Assn., Am. Inst. Aeros. and Astronautics, Am. Def. Preparedness Assn., Phi Beta Kappa, Beta Gamma Sigma. Home: 12534 Misty Crk San Antonio TX 78232-4629

POST, GERALD V. business educator; b. Chippewa Falls, Wis., Nov. 27, 1955; s. Vernon Otto and Doris Post; m. Sarah S. Post, Aug. 14, 1982. BA, U. Wis., Eau Claire, 1978; PhD, Iowa State U., 1983. Asst. prof. Oakland U., Rochester Hills, Mich., 1982-89; prof. Western Ky. U., Bowling Green, 1989-99; prof. dept. bus. U. of the Pacific, Stockton, Calif., 1999—. Cons. analyst/programmer The Wala Group, Arden Hills, Minn., 1985-99. Author: Database Management Systems, 2002; contbr. articles to profl. jours. Office: Univ of the Pacific 3601 Pacific Ave Stockton CA 95211-0197

POST, JAMES CHRISTOPHER, pediatric otolaryngologist, molecular geneticist; b. Miami, Fla., Aug. 27, 1953; s. James Marshall Post and Alice (Canton) Raum; children: Amanda, Margaret, James Carter. BS, U. Fla., 1980, MD, 1983; PhD in Human Genetics, U. Pitts., 1999. Diplomate Am. Bd. Otolaryngology. Resident in pediats. Mass. Gen. Hosp., Boston, 1983-85; intern in surgery, resident in ENT U. Fla., 1985-90; fellow in pediats. ENT Children's Hosp. of Pitts., 1990-92; asst. prof. U. Pitts. Sch. Medicine, 1992-97; prof. otolaryngology Med. Coll. of Pa./Hahnemann, Pitts., 1997—; med. dir. Ctr. for Genomic Scis. Alleghany Gen. Hosp., 1997—. Mem. study sect. NIH, Washington, 1994—; reviewer Deafness Rsch. Found., Washington, 1998—; hon. prof. West China Sch. of Medicine, Chengda, Sichuan, China, 1999. Contbr. articles to profl. publs. Lt. col. U.S. Army, 1986—. Recipient Fowler award Triologic Soc., 2001. Mem. Am. Acad. of Otolaryngology-Head and Neck Surgery (chair infectious disease com. 2000—, chair rsch. grants and prizes subcom. 1998—). Office: Allegheny Gen Hosp 320 E North Ave Pittsburgh PA 15212

POST, RICHARD BENNETT, retired human resources executive; b. Clyde, Ohio, July 5, 1936; s. Robert Irving and Elinor May (Bennett) P.; m. Nancy Jane Wardlow, Aug. 31, 1956; children: David Bennett, Todd McKinley, Amy Ellen, Brett Richard, Brina Marie. BS in Psychology, Iowa State U., 1958; student, Ohio U., Athens, 1954-56; postgrad., George Washington U., 1959-60, So. Ill. U., Edwardsville, 1972-74. With U.S. Civil Svc. Commn., 1958-79, chief evaluation div., 1967-71, chief staffing div., 1971-74, dep. reg. dir., 1974-79; dep. assoc. dir. staffing U.S. Office Pers. Mgmt., Washington, 1979-81, assoc. dir. staffing, 1982-86, dir. Washington area svc. ctr., 1986-94; retired, 1994. Cert. lay spkr. United Meth. Ch., 1973—. Recipient Dirs.' Disting. Svc. award U.S. Office Pers. Mgmt., 1986, Dirs.' citation for Exemplary Pub. Svc., 1994. Mem. Sr. Execs. Assn. (life), Fed. Exec. Inst. Alumni Assn., Vienna Choral Soc. (pres. 1987-89), Masterworks Chorus, King George, Va. Avocations: woodworking, singing, gardening, photography, stamp collecting. E-mail: Postrn@Worldskyline.com.

POST, RICHARD HENRY, pharmaceuticals executive; b. Glendale, Calif., May 3, 1956; s. Henry A. and Doris J. P. BA, Simpson Coll., 1978; M in Edn., Rutgers U., 1989. Tchr. Matawan Regional H.S., Aberdeen, NJ, 1980—89; guidance counselor Plainfield (N.J.) H.S., 1990, Bound Brook (N.J.) H.S., 1990—92; regional dir. Solvay Pharm., Inc., Flemington, NJ, 1998—. Home and Office: Solvay Pharm 32 Windham Ct Flemington NJ 08822

POST, ROBERT CHARLES, law educator; b. Bklyn., Oct. 17, 1947; s. Ted and Thelma (Feifel) P.; m. Fran Layton, Jan. 22, 1981; children: Alexander, Amelia. AB, Harvard U., 1969, PhD, 1980; JD, Yale U., 1977. Bar: D.C. 1979, Calif. 1983. Law clk. to chief judge U.S. Ct. Appeals (D.C. cir.), 1977-78; law clk. to justice William Brennen Jr. U.S. Supreme Ct. D.C., 1978-79; assoc. Williams & Connelly, Washington, 1980-82; acting prof. law U. Calif., Berkeley, 1983-87, prof. law, 1987-94, Alexander F. and May T. Morrison prof. law, 1994—. Author: Constitutional Domains, 1995; editor: Law and the Order of Culture, 1991, Censorship and Silencing: Practices of Cultural Regulation, 1998; co-editor: Race and Representation: Affirmative Action, 1998, Human Rights in Political Transistions: Gettysburg to Bosnia, 1999, Civil Society and Government, 2001; co-author: Prejudicial Appearances: the Logic of America Antidisaimation Law, 2001. Gen. counsel AAUP, 1992-94. Fellow Guggenheim Found., 1990-91, Am. Coun. Gen. Socs., 1990-91. Mem. AAUP, Am. Acad. Arts and Scis. Office: U Calif Sch Law Boalt Hall Berkeley CA 94720

POST, ROSE ZIMMERMAN, newspaper columnist; b. Morganton, N.C., Oct. 2, 1926; d. Samuel Sinai and Anna (Pliskin) Zimmerman; m. Edward Martin Post, July 8, 1947; children: David Bruce, Phyllis Post Lebowitz, Samuel Michael, Jonathan Alan, Anna Susan. BA, U. N.C., Greensboro, 1948; postgrad., U. N.C., 1972-74; LittD (hon.), Catawba Coll., 1981. Reporter Salisbury (N.C.) Post, 1951-83, columnist, 1983—. Adj. prof. journalism Catawba Coll., Salisbury, 1988-89. Mem. Temple Israel PTA, Salisbury, 1950-80s; bd. dirs. Nat. Coun. Jewish Women; various offices numerous orgns. Recipient Ernie Pyle award Scripps Howard News, 1989, O Henry award N.C. AP News Coun., 1991, 92, 95, N.C. Working Press Excellence in Writing award, 1988, 89, 90, 93, 98, 99; named Citizen of Yr. Salisbury Civitan Club, 1976, Woman of Achievement Salisbury B&PW, 1971; named to N.C. Journalism Hall of Fame, 1996. Mem. NCCJ, DAR (Excellence in Cmty. Svc. award 1996), Nat. Assn. Newspaper Columnists (1st pl. for gen. columns 1994), N.C. Press Assn. (awards 1990-2001), N.C. Press Women (sec. 1983, 2d v.p. 1984, 1st v.p. 1985, pres. 1986), N.C. Press Club. Democrat. Jewish. Avocations: reading, theatre-going, travel, knitting, skiing. Home: 125 E Corriher Ave Salisbury NC 28144-2427 Office: Salisbury Post 131 W Innes St Salisbury NC 28144-4338

POST, RUTH-ELLEN, lawyer, educator; b. Audubon, N.J., Mar. 6, 1946; d. Theodore J. and Margaret E. Post; m. D.R. Karklin (div. 1981); 1 child, Kenneth D. Karklin; m. Dale H. Corliss, May 23, 1984; 1 child, Rebecca Post Corliss. BA, Montclair State U., 1967; JD, Rutgers U., Camden, N.J., 1975. Bar: N.J. 1976, Mass. 1979, N.H. 1987. Gen. practice law William V. Eisenberg, Esq., Haddonfield, N.J., 1975-76; sole practitioner Medford, 1976-78, Pittsfield, Mass., 1983-84, Pelham, N.H., 1987-88; prof., chmn. dept. Rivier Coll., Nashua, NH, 1988—2001; prof. legal skills Franklin Pierce Law Ctr., Concord, 2001—. Mem. certifying bd. Nat. Assn. Legal Assts., Tulsa, 1994-98; bd. dirs. Am. Assn. for Paralegal Edn., Overland Park, Kans., 1970-91. Author: (textbook) Paralegal Internships: Finding, Managing, and Transitioning Your Career, 1999; co-author: (manual) Preventing Unauthorized Practice of Law: For the Paralegal in New Hampshire, 1998. Mem. Pelham Planning Bd., 1986-88. Named Atty. of Yr., Paralegal Assn. N.H., 1996. Mem. N.H. Bar Assn. (chair paralegal task force 1994, mem. com. on unauthorized practice of law 1996—). Office: Franklin Pierce Law Ctr Two White St Concord NH 03301

POST, STEPHEN LIGHTNER, psychiatrist, psychoanalyst, educator; b. St. Louis, May 4, 1927; s. Lawrence Tyler Post and Bernice Dorothy Clute Lightner; m. Ann Whelan, Aug. 31, 1953 (dec. Dec. 1958); m. Jane Conant, June 1960 (div. Oct. 1975); children: Nancy Whelan Post Hunter, Kenneth Conant, Louise Lightner, Eric Stephen; m. Ellen Eisendrath, Nov. 8, 1975; stepchildren: William C. Steinert, Sylvia C. Steinert, Eric C. Steinert. AB cum laude, Princeton U., 1950; MD, Columbia U., 1957; grad., Chgo. Inst. for Psychoanalysis, 1974. Diplomate Nat. Bd. Med. Examiners, Am. Psychoanalytic Assn. Intern Montefiore Hosp., N.Y.C., 1957-58; resident in psychiatry Strong Meml. Hosp., Rochester, NY, 1958, Wash. U., St. Louis, 1959-61, fellow in child psychiatry, 1960-62; faculty dept. psychiatry St. Louis U. Med. Sch., 1965—. Mem. adv. bd. Pastoral Counseling Inst., St. Louis, 1964-74; med. dir. St. Louis Clin. Assn. for Religious and Ednl. Counseling, 1979-81; mem. faculty St. Louis Psychoanalytic Inst., St. Louis, 1973—, chmn. cmty. edn. com., 1980-83, chmn. inst. edn. com., 1987-91, tng. and supervising analyst, 1982—, inst. assoc. dir., 2001—; clin. prof. psychiatry St. Louis U. Med. Sch., 1996—. Contbg. editor Psychoanalytic Inquiry, 1984—, issue co-editor, 1985, 94; contbr. chpts. to books and articles to profl. jours. Fellow Am. Coll. Psychoanalysts; mem. AMA, Am. Psychoanalytic Assn. (del. to exec. coun. 1982-85, fellow bd. profl. stds. 1987-91, mem. com. on founds. 1993—), Mo. State Med. Assn., Ea. Mo. Psychiat. Soc. (sec.-treas. 1967-69), Greater St. Louis Med. Soc., St. Louis Psychoanalytic Soc. (membership com. chmn. 1977-78, 87-88, program chmn. 1977-79, pres. 1980-82), Sigma Xi. Avocations: tennis, sailing, music, bicycling, snorkeling. Home: 9 Southmoor Dr Clayton MO 63105-3016 Office: 8820 Ladue Rd 3d Fl Saint Louis MO 63124-2079

POSTER, CAROL, writer, photographer; b. N.Y.C., Aug. 5, 1956; d. William Shakespeare and Constance (Hammett) P.; m. David Chris Allen, July 1987. BA summa cum laude, Hollins Coll., 1977; MFA, Ea. Washington U., 1992; PhD, U. Mo., 1994. Founder, dir. Necessary Repertory, Roanoke, Va., 1976-77; dir. Almost Street Theatre, Salt Lake City, 1985-86, Off Broadway theatres, N.Y.C., 1977-78; software writer Cen. Data Corp., Rockville, Md., 1980-81; assoc. programmer Sperry Corp., Salt Lake City, 1981-83, sci. programmmer, 1983-84; owner Amaryllis Software, 1984-89; grad. instr. dept. English U. Mo., 1992-94; asst. prof. dept. English U. No. Iowa, Cedar Falls, 1994-97; assoc. prof. dept. English Mont. State U., Bozman, 1997—. Judge Ariz. Authors Assn. poetry contest, 1987; lectr. various colls., univs., workshops, confs.; freelance writer, photographer, 1977—. Exec. editor: The Sports Guide, 1988-92; author: Selected Poems of Jacques Prevert, (trans.), 1987, Deceiving the Worms, 1984, Blackbird, 1979, Unnatural Fauna, 1992, Surrounded by Dangerous Things, 1995, Skiing!, 1995, and numerous others; contbr. photographs to profl. jours. Mem. Computer Profls. for Social Responsibility, 1986-88, Greenpeace, 1984—, Zero Population Growth (officer), 1982—. Recipient 2d prize Utah Original Writing Competition, 1986, Excellence award Ctrl. Data Corp., 1981. Mem. MLA, Speech Comm. Assn., Assn. Am. Soc. History of Rhetoric (mem. steering com.). Avocations: skiing, canoeing, backcountry hiking, ballet. Office: Mont State U Dept English 2-176 Wilson Bozeman MT 59717-0001

POSTER, DON STEVEN, internist, hematologist, oncologist; b. N.Y.C., Nov. 19, 1950; BS, Pace U., N.Y.C., 1970; DO, U. Des Moines, 1973. Diplomate Am. Bd. Internal Medicine, Am. Bd. Med. Oncology. Intern USPHS Hosp., S.I., 1973-74; resident in medicine SUNY and Northport VA Hosp., 1975-77; fellow hematologic oncology Roswell Park Meml. Inst., Buffalo, 1977-79; investigator NCI/NIH, Bethesda, Md., 1979-81; med. oncologist North Miami Beach, Fla., 1983—. Editor: Treatment of Nausea and Vomiting, 1981; contbr. articles to profl. jours. Bd. dirs. United Charities, Hollywood, Fla., 1989. With USPHS, 1978-81. Am. Cancer Soc. fellow, 1977-79. Fellow Am. Coll. Clin. Pharmacology, Am. Coll. Medicine.

POSTER, STEVEN BARRY, cinematographer, photographer, publisher, digital imaging consultant; b. Chgo., Mar. 1, 1944; s. David and Lillian Violet (Diamondstone) P. Student, So. Ill. U., 1962-64, L.A. Art Ctr. Coll. Design, 1964-66; BS, Ill. Inst. Tech., 1967. Pres. Posters Internat. Ltd., L.A., 1980. Dir. photography (films) Strange Brew, 1983, Testament, 1984, Heavenly Kid, 1985, Blue City, 1986, The Boy Who Could Fly, 1986, Someone to Watch Over Me, 1986, (Am. Soc. Cinematographers nomination 1987), Big Top Pee Wee, 1987, Next of Kin, 1988, Opportunity Knocks, 1989, Rocky V, 1990, Life Stinks, 1991, Cemetery Club, 1993, Roswell, 1994, Strangers on a Train, 1996, The Color of Justice, 1996, Rocket Man, 1997, Une Chance Sur Deux, 1997, Donnie Darko, 2000, Stuart Little II, 2001, Daddy Day Care, 2002. Mem.: Internat. Alliance of Theatrical & Stage Employees (bd. dir.), Can. Soc. Cinematographers, Acad. Motion Picture Arst & Sci., Am. Soc. Cinematographers (pres.). Democrat. Jewish. Avocations: still photography, computers.

POSTERARO, CATHERINE HAMMOND, librarian, gerontology educator; b. Hartford, Conn., Nov. 13, 1946; d. Joseph Francis and Elizabeth Claire (Desmond) Hammond; m. Anthony Francis Posteraro, Jr., June 20, 1970; children: Anthony Francis III, Christopher Clarke. AB, Emmanuel Coll., Boston, 1968; MS, Simmons Coll., 1970; MA, St. Joseph Coll., West Hartford, Conn., 1992. Lectr. gerontology St. Joseph Coll., 1991—; exec. dir. Wood Meml. Libr., South Windsor, Conn. Sec., treas. St. Joseph Coll. Faculty Com. of the Whole. Recipient Sister Mary Elizabeth Delice award Inst. Gerontology, St. Joseph Coll., 1992. Mem. ALA, Assn. Coll. and Rsch. Librs., Conn. Libr. Assn., Gerontol. Soc. Am., Sigma Phi Omega (nat. acad. hon. soc. gerontology). Home: 24 Mcdivitt Dr Manchester CT 06040-2240 Office: Wood Meml Libr Health Learning Ctr 783 Main St South Windsor CT 06074 E-mail: cposteraro@cox.net.

POSTHUMUS, RICHARD EARL, state offical, farmer; b. Hastings, Mich., July 19, 1950; s. Earl Martin and Lola Marie (Wieland) P.; m. Pamela Ann Bartz, June 23, 1972; children: Krista, Lisa, Heather, Bryan. BS in Agrl. Econs. and Pub. Affairs Mgmt., Mich. State U., 1972. Exec. v.p. Farmers and Mfrs. Beet Sugar Assn., Saginaw, Mich., 1972-74, Mich. Beef Commn., Lansing, 1974-78; dir. constituent relations Republican Caucus, Mich. Ho. of Reps., 1979-82, majority leader, 1991—; self-employed farmer, 1974—. Third vice-chmn. Mich. Republican Com., 1971-73; Lt. Governor, Michigan, 1998-; mem. Hope Ch. of the Brethren. Mem. Alpha Gamma Rho. Office: Office of Lt Gov PO Box 30026 State Capitol Bldg Lansing MI 48909*

POSTMA, HERMAN, physicist, consultant; b. Wilmington, N.C., Mar. 29, 1933; s. Gilbert and Sophia Postma; m. Patricia Dunigan, Nov. 25, 1960; children: Peter, Pamela. BS summa cum laude, Duke U., 1955; MS, Harvard U., 1957, PhD, 1959. Registered profl. engr., Calif. Summer staff Oak Ridge Nat. Lab., 1954-57, physicist thermonuclear div., 1959-62, co-leader DCX-1 group, 1962-66, asst. dir. thermonuclear div., 1966, asso. dir. div., 1967, dir. div., 1967-73, dir. nat. lab., 1974-88; v.p. Martin Marietta, 1984-88, sr. v.p., 1988-91. Vis. scientist FOM-Inst. for Plasma Physics, The Netherlands, 1963; cons. Lab. Laser Energetics, U. Rochester; arbitrator AAA 2002, mem. energy rsch. adv. bd. spl. panel Dept. Energy; bd. dirs. Nashville br. Fed. Res. Bank Atlanta, ICS Corp., PAI Corp., ORAS, Inc., Allmeds, M4 Corp., ASIC Corp., Studio212.com Corp. Contbr. numerous articles to profl. jours. Bd. dirs. The Nucleus; chmn. bd. trustees Hosp. of Meth. Ch.; mem. adv. bd. Coll. Bus. Adminstrn., U. Tenn., 1976-2000, Energy Inst., State of N.C.; bd. dirs., exec. com. Tenn. Tech. Found., 1982-88, Venture Capital Fund; vice chmn., commr. Tenn. Higher Edn. Commn., 1984-92; trustee Duke U., 1987-99, Pellissippi State Coll., 1991-98; chmn. Meth. Hosp. Found., 1990; pres. East Tenn. Econ. Coun., 1998; mem. adv. bd. Inst. Pub. Policy Vanderbilt U., 1986-88, conf. chmn. 1987. Fellow Am. Phys. Soc. (exec. com. div. plasma physics), AAAS, Am. Nuclear Soc. (dir., chair East Tenn. econ. coun. 1997—); mem. C. of C. (v.p. 1981-83, chmn. 1987), Indsl. Rsch. Inst., Gas Rsch. Inst. (adv. bd. 1986-88), Oak Ridge Rotary (pres. 1996-97), Phi Beta Kappa, Beta Gamma Sigma, Sigma Pi Sigma, Omicron Delta Kappa, Sigma Xi, Pi Mu Epsilon, Phi Eta Sigma. Home and Office: 104 Berea Rd Oak Ridge TN 37830-7829

POSTMA, STEVEN J. owner distribution business; b. Logan, Utah, Dec. 17, 1947; s. S.J. and Stella (Carlson) P.; m. Kathy Blair, Aug. 26, 1970; children: Tamara, Blair, Trish, Lisa, Mandy. BSME, Utah State U., 1972; postgrad, Ariz. State, 1973-74; MBA, U. Utah, 1978. Cert. profl. engr., Utah, nat. fluid power specialist, fluid power engr. Design engr. Caterpillar Tractor, Peoria, Ill., 1970-71, Garrett Airesearch, Phoenix, 1972-75; aerospace engr. E. System, Salt Lake City, 1975-76; product mgr. Elmco PEC, 1976-80; owner Interstate Hyrdaulics Inc., 1980 --. Cons. Postma and Assocs., Salt Lake City, 1986 --. Inventor: Compressor CNG, 1985, Wire Line Winch Control, 1982. Com. mem. Sandy City Dist. Coun., 1984-86; delegate Utah Rep. Convention, 1988; pres. LDS Stake, Sandy, 1985-90. Mem. Fluid Power Distbrs. Assn., Reroth Nat. Distbr. Coun. (Disting. Svc. award), Ad Hoc Distbr. Coun. (nad. chmn. 1989, 93), Parker/Ross Distbr. Coun., Phi Kappa Phi, Sigma Tau. Avocations: sports, skiing, boating. Office: Interstate Hydraulics Inc PO Box 827 Sandy UT 84091-0827

POSTOL, LAWRENCE PHILIP, lawyer; b. Bridgeport, Conn., Oct. 18, 1951; s. Sidney Samuel and Eunice Ruth (Schine) P.; m. Ellen Margaret Russell, Mar. 22, 1975; children: Raymond Russell, Stephan Russell, Carolyn Russell. BS, Cornell U., 1973, JD, 1976. Bar: Conn. 1976, D.C. 1977, U.S. Dist. Ct. D.C. 1977, U.S. Ct. Appeals (D.C. cir.) 1977, U.S. Supreme Ct. 1980, Va. 1982, U.S. Ct. Appeals (4th cir.) 1982, U.S. Dist. Ct. (ea. dist.) Va. 1985, U.S. Dist. Ct. Md. 1989, U.S. Dist. Ct. Conn. 1990. Assoc. Arent, Fox, Kintner & Plotkin, Washington, 1976-80, Seyfarth, Shaw, Washington, 1980-83, ptnr., 1985—; assoc. Jones, Day, Reavis and Pogue, 1983-85. Lectr. Loyola U., New Orleans, 1983—, U. Cin., 1987-93; bd. advisers The Environ. Counselor Jour.; spl. counsel Greater Washington Bd. Trade, 1991-93. Author: Legal Guide to Handling Toxic Substances in the Workplace, 1990, Americans with Disabilities Act - A Compliance Manual for Employers, 1993. Jewish. Avocation: sports. Home: 6340 Chowning Pl Mc Lean VA 22101-4129 Office: Seyfarth Shaw 815 Connecticut Ave NW Washington DC 20006-4004 Fax: 202-828-5393. E-mail: lpostol@dc.seyfarth.com.

POSTON, BEVERLY PASCHAL, lawyer; b. Birmingham, Ala., Aug. 21, 1955; d. Arthur Buel and Nellie Jo (Weaver) P.; m. Richard F. Poston, Aug., 1992. BA with honor, U. North Ala., 1976; JD, Birmingham Sch. Law, 1982. Bar: Ala. 1982, U.S. Dist. Ct. (no. dist.) Ala. 1982, U.S. Ct. Appeals (11th cir.) 1983. Assoc. St. John & St. John, Cullman, Ala., 1982-84; pvt. practice, 1984-85, 92-96; ptnr. Paschal & Collins, 1986-92. Pres. Cullman County Hist. Soc., 1986-87, bd. dirs., 1996—. Named one of Outstanding Young Women Am., 1984; recipient Citiation of Honor, Young Career Women Program, 1989. Mem. ABA, ATLA, Ala. Trial Lawyers Assn., Cullman County Bar Assn. (sec. tres. 1997-98, v.p. 1998-99, pres. 1999-2000), Pilot Club Internat. (Sweetheart award Cullman 1985), Cullman Bus. and Profl. Women's Assn. (young careerist award), Cullman Home Builder Assn. Avocations: horseback riding, rodeos, farming, writing. Home: 1797 County Road 972 Cullman AL 35057-5861 Office: 200 1st Ave SE Cullman AL 35055-3402

POSTON, JANICE LYNN, librarian; b. Louisville, Mar. 30, 1965; d. William Kenneth and Loretta Frances (Reece) Ferguson; m. Boyce Day Poston, Jan. 9, 1988. BS in Elem. Edn. with high honors, U. Louisville, 1987; MA in Sch. Media Librarianship, Spalding U., 1992. Part-time libr. page Louisville Free Pub. Libr., 1981-91; elem. sch. tchr. Jefferson County Pub. Schs., Louisville, 1988-91; cataloging svcs. libr. Spalding U. Libr., 1991—. Active Christian edn. bd. River City Ch. of God. Mem. Ky. Libr. Assn. Republican. Pentecostal. Avocations: teaching Sunday School, crafts. Office: Spalding U Libr 853 Library Ln Louisville KY 40203-2170

POSTON, LARRY ALLAN, religious studies educator; b. Leesburg, Va., Sept. 25, 1952; s. Leslie Aldridge and Joanne (Flynn) P.; m. Linda Kay Poston, May 24, 1975; 1 child, Helena Marie. Student, Bridgewater Coll., 1970-72; BA, Grace Coll. of the Bible, 1977; MA, Trinity Evang. Div. Sch., Deerfield, Ill., 1978; postgrad., Goteborgs U., Gothenburg, Sweden, 1980-81; MA, Northwestern U., 1986, PhD, 1988. Instr. Nordiska Bibelinstitutet, Saffle, Sweden, 1980-84; assoc. prof. Nyack (N.Y.) Coll., 1989-95; assoc. prof., dir. Inst. for Mus. Studies Wheaton (Ill.) Coll., 1995-96; prof. Nyack Coll., 1996—. Rep. Eastern region Rhodes Regional Consultations, Rhodes Coll., Memphis, 1998—. Author: Islamic Da'wah in the West, 1992, The Changing Face of Islam in America, 2000. Bd. dirs. North Jersey Christian-Muslim Project, Paterson, N.J., 1994-2000; mem. Mid. East studies program task force Coun. for Christian Colls. and Univs., Washington, 1991-93. Mem. Am. Acad. Religion, Evang. Missiological Soc. Avocations: running, backpacking, foreign travel. Home: PO Box 331 Valley Cottage NY 10989 Office: Nyack Coll 1 South Blvd Nyack NY 10960 E-mail: postonla@nyack.edu.

POSTON, REBEKAH JANE, lawyer; b. Wabash, Ind., Apr. 20, 1948; d. Bob E. and April (Ogle) P. BS, U. Miami, 1970, JD, 1974. Bar: Fla. 1974, Ohio 1977, U.S. Dist. Ct. (so. and mid. dists.) Fla., U.S. Ct. Appeals (11th cir.). Asst. U.S. atty. U.S. Atty.'s Office, Miami, Fla., 1974-76; spl. atty. organized crime and racketeering sect. Strike Force, Cleve., 1976-78; ptnr. Fine, Jacobson, Schwartz, Nash & Block, Miami, 1978-94, Steel Hector & Davis, Miami, 1994—. Adj. prof. U. Miami Law Sch., Coral Gables, 1986; mem. U.S. sentencing guidelines com. So. Dist. of Fla., Miami, 1987-88. Mem. Fla. Bar Assn., Nat. Assn. Criminal Def. Attys., Nat. Directory Criminal Lawyers, Am. Immigration Lawyers Assn., Dade County Bar Assn. Democrat. Lutheran. Avocations: power boat racing, swimming. Home: 1541 Brickell Ave Apt 3706 Miami FL 33129-1229 Office: 200 SE 2nd St Miami FL 33131 E-mail: RJP@steelhector.com.

POSTON, TOM, actor; b. Columbus, Ohio, Oct. 17, 1927; s. George and Margaret P.; m. Jean Sullivan, 1955; m. Kay Hudson, June 8, 1968; children: Francesca, Hudson, Jason. Student, Bethany Coll., 1938-40. First appeared on stage as a tumbler with The Flying Zebleys; acting and Broadway debuts in Cyrano de Bergerac, 1947; appeared on Broadway, regional theaters, and summer stock; stage appearances include: The Insect Comedy, King Lear, Will Success Spoil Rock Hunter?, Goodbye Again, Best of Burlesque, Romanoff and Juliet, Drink to Me Only, Golden Fleecing, The Conquering Hero, Come Blow Your Horn, Mary, Mary, Forty Carats, But Seriously..., A Funny Thing Happened on the Way to the Forum, The Odd Couple, Bye Bye Birdie, Mother Courage, host WABC-TV series Entertainment, 1955; regular on TV show The Steve Allen Show, 1956-58 (Emmy award for best supporting actor in comedy series 1959); host TV show Split Personality, 1959-60; panelist TV show To Tell the Truth; appeared in TV series On the Rocks, 1975-76, We've Got Each Other, 1977, Mork and Mindy, 1978-82, Newhart, 1982-90, Grace Under Fire, 1995-98; numerous TV appearances include The Bob Newhart Show; film appearances include: The Tempest, The City That Never Sleeps, 1953, Zotz, 1962, Soldier in the Rain, 1963, The Old Dark House, 1963, Cold Turkey, 1970, The Happy Hooker, 1975, Rabbit Test, 1978, Up the Academy, 1980, Carbon Copy, 1981, Krippendorf's Tribe, 1998, The Story of Us, 1999. Served with USAAF, World War II.*

POSTON, WALKER SEWARD, II, medical educator, researcher; BA in Biol. Scis., U. Calif., Davis, 1983; PhD in Psychology, U. Calif., Santa Barbara, 1990. Clin. psychology resident USAF Med. Ctr., Wright-PAtterson AFB, Ohio, 1989-90; dir. psychology svcs., asst. chief mental health svcs. 9th Med. Group, Beale AFB, 1990-92; fellow in behavioral medicine Wilford Hall Med. Ctr., 1992-93; chief health and rehab. psychology svc. Malcolm Grow Med. Ctr., 1993-95, faculty, 1993-95; clin. asst. prof. dept. med. and clin. psychology F. Edward Herbert Sch. Medicine, Bethesda, Md., 1993-95; asst. prof. medicine Baylor Coll. Medicine, Houston, 1995-99; asst. prof. U. Mo., Kansas City, 1999—. Rsch. exch. scientist Karolinska Inst., Stockholm, Sweden, 1997, 98. Contbr. articles to profl. jours. Recipient Minority Scientist Devel. award Am. Heart Assn., 1995; U. Calif. Doctoral scholars fellow, 1984-85, 85-86, 86-87, 88-89, Clin. fellow Wilford Hall Med. Ctr., Lackland AFB, 1992-93; Nat. Merit scholar, 1979-80. Office: Univ Mo 5319 Holmes St Kansas City MO 64110-2437

POSUNKO, BARBARA, retired elementary education educator; b. Newark, July 17, 1938; d. Joseph and Mary (Prystauk) P. BA, Rutgers U., Newark, 1960; MA, Kean U., Union, N.J., 1973; teaching cert., Seton Hall U., Newark, 1966. Cert. elem. tchr., reading specialist, N.J. Social case worker Newark City Hosp., 1960-65; elem. tchr. Plainfield (N.J.) Bd. Edn., 1966; elem., jr. and sr. high sch. tchr. minimum basic skills and reading Sayreville (N.J.) Bd. Edn., 1966-82, tchr. Chpt. I and minimum basic skills, 1982-95, cooperating tchr. to student tchrs., 1983-95, coord. testing, 1984-95; ret., 1995. Sch. coord. for congressionally mandated study of ednl. growth and opportunity, 1991-95; mem. numerous reading coms. Recipient Outstanding Tchr. award N.J. Gov.'s Tchr. Recognition Program, 1988. Mem. NEA, Internat. Reading Assn., N.J. Reading Assn., N.J. Edn. Assn. Home: 17 Drake Rd Mendham NJ 07945-1805

POSUNKO, LINDA MARY, retired elementary education educator; b. Newark, Dec. 24, 1942; d. Joseph and Mary (Prystauk) P. BA, Newark State Coll., Union, N.J., 1964; MA, Kean U., Union, 1974. Cert. permanent elem. tchr., supr., prin., N.J. Elem. tchr. Roselle (N.J.) Bd. Edn., 1964-65, Garwood (N.J.) Bd. Edn., 1965—95, head tchr., 1974-76, 79-81, head tchr. elem. and early childhood edn., tchr. 1st grade, 1992-95; ret., 1995. Cooperating tchr. to student tchrs.; instr. non-English speaking students and children with learning problems; mem. affirmative action, sch. resource coms.; conductor in-svc. workshops on early childhood devel. practices, 1993. Recipient honor cert. Union County Conf. Tchrs. Assn., 1972-73, The Garwood award N.J. Gov.'s Tchr. Recognition Program, 1983, 88, Outstanding Tchr. award N.J. Gov.'s Tchr. Recognition Program, 1988, Tchr. Recognition award Spanish Nat. Honor Soc., 1999, Most Memorable Tchr. Recognition award Spanish Nat. Honor Soc., 1999; nominee N.J. Gov.'s Tchr. Recognition award, 1993-94. Mem. ASCD, NEA, Internat. Reading Assn. (bd. dirs. suburban coun.), N.J. Edn. Assn., Garwood Tchrs. Assn. (sec., v.p., pres.), High/Scope Ednl. Found. Home: 17 Drake Rd Mendham NJ 07945-1805

POSVAR, MILDRED MILLER, opera singer; b. Cleve. d. William and Elsa (Friedhofer) Mueller; m. Wesley W. Posvar, Apr. 30, 1950; children: Wesley, Margot Marina, Lisa Christina. MusB, Cleve. Inst. Music, 1946; hon. doctorate, Cleve. Ins. Music, 1983; artists' diploma, New England Conservatory Music, 1948, hon. doctorate, 1966; MusD (hon.), Bowling Green State U., 1960; hon. doctorate, Washington and Jefferson U., 1988. Founder Opera Theater of Pitts., 1978—; mem. music faculty Carnegie-Mellon U., 1996—. Operatic debut in Peter Grimes, Tanglewood, 1946; appeared N.E. Opera Theater, Stuttgart State Theater, Germany, 1949-50, Glyndebourne Opera, Edinburgh Festival; debut as Cherubino in Figaro, Met. Opera, 1951; 23 consecutive seasons Met. Opera; radio debut Bell Telephone Hour; TV debut Voice of Firestone, 1952; appeared in films including Merry Wives of Windsor (filmed in Vienna), 1964; Vienna State Opera debut, 1963, appearances with San Francisco, Chgo. Lyric, Cin. Zoo, San Antonio, Berlin, Munich, Frankfurt, Pasadena, Ft. Worth, Kansas City, Pitts., Tulsa and St. Paul operas. Bd. dirs. Gateway to Music. Recipient Frank Huntington Beebe award for study abroad, 1949, 50, Grand Prix du Disque, 1965, Outstanding Achievements in Music award Boston C. of C., 1959, Ohioana Career medal, 1985, Outstanding Achievement in Opera award, Slippery Rock U., 1985, YWCA Ann. Tribute to Women award, 1989, Keystone Salute award Pa. Fedn. Music Clubs, 1994; named one of outstanding women of Pitts., Pitts. Press-Pitts. Post-Gazette, 1968, Person of Yr. in Music, Pitts. Jaycees, 1980. Mem. Nat. Soc. Arts and Letters (pres. 1989-90, Gold medal 1984), Disting. Daus. Pa. (pres. 1991-93), Tuesday Mus. Club, Phi Beta Kappa, Phi Delta Gamma, Sigma Alpha Iota. Office: Opera Theater of Pittsburgh PO Box 110108 Pittsburgh PA 15232-0608

POTASEK, MARY JOYCE, physicist, researcher; b. Mpls., Oct. 27, 1945; d. Chester and Millie Potasek. BA in Math., Coll. St. Catherine, 1967; MS in Physics, U. Ill., 1970, PhD, 1974. Research asst. U. Ill., Urbana, 1970-74; research scientist Internat. Bus. Machines, Watson Research Ctr., Yorktown Heights, N.Y., 1974-75; NSF, AAUW postdoctoral fellow Princeton (N.J.) U., 1975-78; NATO postdoctoral fellow Max Planck Inst., Gottingen, West Germany, 1978-80; mem. tech. staff AT&T, Princeton, 1980-86, AT&T Bell Labs., Murray Hill, N.J., 1986-90, Columbia U., N.Y.C., 1990-99; mem. tech. staff Brooks AFB USAF, San Antonio, 1994-2001; physicist NYU, N.Y.C., 2001—. Contbr. articles to profl. jours. Mem. Optical Soc. of Am., Am. Phys. Soc., Phi Beta Kappa, Pi Mu Epsilon. Avocation: horseback riding. Home: 269 Christopher Dr Princeton NJ 08540-2323

POTASH, JEREMY WARNER, public relations executive; b. Monrovia, Calif., June 30, 1946; d. Fenwick Bryson and Joan Antony (Blair) Warner; m. Stephen Jon Potash; 1 son, Aaron Warner. AA, Citrus Coll., 1965; BA, Pomona Coll., 1967. With Forbes Mag., N.Y.C., 1967-69, Japan External Trade Orgn., San Francisco, 1970-75; v.p., co-founder Potash & Co. Pub. Rels., Oakland, Calif., 1980-87. Founding exec. dir. Calif.-Asia Bus. Coun., Oakland, 1991—; exec. dir. Customs Brokers and Forwarders Assn., San Francisco, 1990—; adv. bd. Asia Pacific Econ. Rev., 1996—; mem. No. Calif. Dist. Export Coun., 2000—, Pacific Coun. Internat. Policy, 2000—. Editor: Southeast Asia Environmental Directory, 1994; editor: Southeast Asia Infrastructure Directory, 1995-96. Bd. dirs. Judah L. Magnes Mus., Berkeley, 1981-94, co-founder docent program, 1980, pres. Women's Guild, 1980-81; bd. dirs. Temple Sinai, Oakland, 1984-86; pres. East Bay region Women's Am. Orgn. for Rehab. Through Tng., 1985-86. Recipient Export Citizen of Yr. award No. Calif. Export Coun., U.S. Dept. Commerce, 1998. Mem. World Trade Club San Francisco, Oakland Women's Lit. Soc., Book Club Calif. Office: Potash & Co Pub Rels 1946 Embarcadero Oakland CA 94606-5213

POTASH, VELLA ROSENTHAL, lawyer, educator; b. Balt., Oct. 3, 1937; d. Joseph and Rona (Glasner) Rosenthal; m. Michael Donald Potash, June 20, 1957 (div. Aug., 1982); children: James Bennet, John Lawrence. BA in Edn., Goucher Coll., 1959; JD, U. Balt., 1974. Bar: Md. 1975, Pa. 1975, Family Mediation Fla., 1992. Tchr. Balt. Sch. System, 1959-62; pub. rels. dir. Citizens Planning & Housing Assn., Balt., 1968-69; asst. pub. defender Pub. Defender's Office, 1975-78; lawyer pvt. practice, 1978-82, Guardian Ad Litem Program Family Law Sect., Broward County, Fla., 1987—; family mediator pvt. practice, 1992—. Pres., lectr. The Changing Am. Family. Rev. bd. Palm Beach County Foster Care, 1999—. Mem. NOW (bd. dirs., chair women's ctr. Boca Raton), Md. Bar, Pa. Bar, Broward County Bar Assn. (assoc.), So. Fla. Goucher Alumnae Assn. (pres.), Broward County Mediation Assn. (bd. dirs.). Avocations: bus. investment, golf, reading. Home: 2900 N Palm Aire Dr Apt 301 Pompano Beach FL 33069-3445

POTEAT, JAMES DONALD, diaconal minister, retired military officer; b. Spindale, N.C., Feb. 27, 1935; s. Albert Carl and Daliah Elizabeth (Freeman) P.; m. Clara Walker Yelton, Oct. 12, 1957; children: Deborah Poteat Emmons, Clara Poteat Frederick, James Donald Jr., Teresa Poteat Morris. BA disting. mil. graduate, The Citadel, Charleston, S.C., 1957; MA, Kans. State U., 1973; graduate, U.S. Army War Coll., 1980. Ordained to ministry United Meth. Ch. Commd. 2nd lt. U.S. Army, 1957, advanced through grades to col., 1979, ret., 1983; mgmt. cons., 1983-88; pastor's adminstrv. asst. Prospect United Meth. Ch., Covington, Ga., 1988-95. Author: Long Range Planning, Prospect United Methodist Church, 1990, Presidential Decision-Making: Presidents Lincoln and Polk, 1973, others. Decorated Bronze Star medal, three Air medals, Vietnam Cross of Gallantry, three Army Commendation medals with v., Viet Nam Svc. Medal with 3 Campaign Battle Stars. Mem. Ret. Officers Assn., United Meth. Ch. Bus. Adminstrs. Assn. (cert.).

POTEMPA, KATHLEEN, dean, nursing educator; Diploma in nursing, Providence Hosp. Sch. Nursing, Southfield, Mich., 1970; BA in Psychology summa cum laude, U. Detroit, 1974; MS in Nursing, Rush U., 1978, D of Nursing Sci., 1986. Charge nurse coronary ICU Holy Cross Hosp., Ft. Lauderdale, Fla., 1970-71; staff nurse, charge nurse cardiovasc. ICU Henry Ford Hosp., Detroit, 1971-74; nurse practitioner Rush-Presbyn.-St. Luke's Med. Ctr., Chgo., 1974-75; nursing edn. coord. dept. nursing Michael Reese Hosp. and Med. Ctr., 1975-77, nursing supr., 1977-78; asst. unit leader dept. gerontol. nursing Rush U. Coll. Nursing, 1978-79, asst. chmn., 1979-80, assoc. chmn., asst. prof. gerontol. nursing, 1980-85, asst. prof. gerontol. nursing, 1985-86; asst. prof. nursing, dept. internal medicine, practitioner Rush Med. Coll., Rush U., 1987-88; asst. then assoc. prof. dept. med.-surg. nursing Coll. Nursing, U. Ill., Chgo., 1988—, dir. tng., pre and postdoctoral fellowship instnl. rsch., 1992—, exec. assoc. dean Coll. Nursing, 1994-95, interim dean Coll. Nursing, 1995-96; prof., dean Sch. Nursing Oreg. Health Scis. U., Portland, 1996—. Rsch. assoc. Robert Wood Johnson Tchg. Nursing Home Project, VA Edward Hines Jr. Hosp., Hines, Ill., 1985-86, co-dir. Exercise Rsch. Lab., 1985-86; dir. nursing Johnston R. Bowman Health Ctr. for Elderly, Rush Presbyn. St. Luke's Med. Ctr., Chgo., 1980-85. Contbr. articles to profl. jours. Fellow Am. Acad. Nursing; mem. ANA (coun. nurse rschrs.), Am. Soc. Hypertension, Gerontol. Soc. Am., Midwest Nursing Rsch. Soc., Heart Assn. Met. Chgo., Am. Heart Assn. Oreg., Ill. Coun. Nurse Rschrs., Am. Heart Assn. (coun. cardiovasc. nursing, coun. hypertension, coun. on strokes), Sigma Theta Tau. Office: SN ADM Oreg Health Scis U Sch Nursing 3181 SW Sam Jackson Park Rd Portland OR 97201-3011*

POTEMPA, PHILIP MATTHEW, entertainment journalist, columnist, communications educator; b. San Pierre, Ind., Aug. 13, 1970; s. Chester John and Peggy Louise Potempa. BA, Valparaiso U., 1992. Arts and entertainment reporter Vidette-Messenger Newspaper, Valparaiso, 1991-95, Times Newspaper of N.W. Ind., Munster, 1995—; adj. prof. comms. Valparaiso (Ind.) U., 1997—. Arts and entertainment corr. South Bend (Ind.) Tribune, 1993—; part-time prof. comms. Purdue U., Westville, Ind., 1998—. Bd. dirs. Ind. Journalism Hall of Fame. Recipient Reporting award Hoosier State Press Assn., 1995, AP Mng. Editors, 1997. Mem. Soc. Profl. Journalists (award 1996), Ind. Hist. Soc., Chgo. Headline Club (bd. dirs.). Republican. Roman Catholic. Avocations: collecting historical autographs. Home: PO Box 68 San Pierre IN 46374-0068 Office: Times Newspaper 601 W 45th St Munster IN 46321 E-mail: potempa@howPubs.com.

POTENTE, EUGENE, JR. interior designer; b. Kenosha, Wis., July 24, 1921; s. Eugene and Suzanne Marie (Schmit) P.; m. Joan Cioffe, Jan. 29, 1946; children: Eugene J., Peter Michael, John Francis, Suzanne Marie. PhB, Marquette U., 1943; postgrad., Stanford U., 1943, N.Y. Sch. Interior Design, 1947; DFA, Carthage Coll., 1997; DLitt (hon.), Concordia U., 1997. Cert. lighting Nat. Coun. on Lighting Qualification. With U.S. Army Mil. Govt., 1943—46; founder, chmn. Studios of Potente, Inc., Kenosha, Wis., 1949—; pres., founder Archtl. Svcs. Assocs., 1978—, Bus. Leasing Svcs. of Wis. Inc., 1978—. Past nat. pres. Inter-Faith Forum on Religion, Art and Architecture; vice chm. Wis. State Capitol and Exec. Residence Bd., 1981—. Sec. Kenosha Symphony Assn., 1968-74; bd. dirs. Ctr. for Religion and the Arts, Wesley Theol. Sem., Washington, 1983-84. With AUS, 1943-46. With AUS, 1943—46, WWII, with European campaign, 1944—45. Recipient Disting. Alumni award Marquette U., 1999. Mem. Am. Soc. Interior Designers (treas., pres. Wis. chpt. 1985-86, 94-95, chmn. nat. pub. svc. 1986), Illuminating Engrng. Soc. N.Am. Internat. Interior Design Assn., Elks, Am. Legion (life), Sigma Delta Chi. Roman Catholic. Home: 8609 2nd Ave Pleasant Prairie WI 53158-4720 Office: 914 60th St Kenosha WI 53140-4041 E-mail: sopi@sopi.com.

POTERBA, JAMES MICHAEL, economist, educator; b. Flushing, N.Y., July 13, 1958; s. William Samuel and Margaret Mary (Toale) P.; m. Nancy Lin Rose, June 23, 1984; children: Matthew Robert, Timothy James, Margaret Rose. AB, Harvard U., 1980; MPhil, Oxford U., Eng., 1982, DPhil, 1983. From asst. to assoc. prof. MIT, Cambridge, Mass., 1983-88, prof., 1988—, Mitsui prof., 1996—. Dir. pub. econs. rsch. program Nat. Bur. Econ. Rsch., Cambridge, 1990—; fellow Ctr. Advanced Study in Behavioral Scis., 1993-94, Hoover Instn. Stanford U., 2000-01. Editor: Economic Policy Responses to Global Warning, 1991, International Comparisons of Household Saving, 1994, Housing Markets in the United States and Japan, 1994, Empirical Foundations of Household Taxation, 1996, Fiscal Institutions and Fiscal Performance, 1999, Jour. Pub. Econs.; contbr. articles to profl. jours. Recipient award for Excellence in Sci. Reviewing NAS, 1999; Marshall scholar, 1980-83, Batterymarch fellow, 1986. Fellow: Ctr. Advanced Study in Behavioral Scis., Econometric Soc., Am. Acad. Arts and Scis.; mem.: Am. Econ. Assn. (exec. com. 2001—), Phi Beta Kappa. Office: MIT 50 Memorial Dr Rm E52-350 Cambridge MA 02142-1347 E-mail: poterba@mit.edu.

POTH, JODIE MEGAN, legislative staff member; b. Media, Pa., Nov. 7, 1977; d. John Paul Jr. and Janet Marion W. BA in Politics, Ursinus Coll., 1999. Campaign asst. Susan Burt-Collins for Dist. Atty., Merion, Pa., 1999; asst. exec. dir. Montgomery County Dem. Com., Norristown, 1999-2000; vol. coord. Hoeffel for Congress, 2000; dist. rep. Congressman Joe Hoeffel, 2000—01; vol. coord., fin. asst. Hoeffel for Congress, 2001—. Editor Jour. Am. Politics, 1999. Mem. Five County Women, Bryn Mawr, Pa., 1999—, Warrior Women, Norristown, 1999—; pres. Politics Assn. Ursinus Coll., Collegeville, Pa., 1998-99. Mem. Animal Legal Def. Fund, North Shore Animal League, World Wildlife Fund, Women's Humane Soc., Pi Sigma Alpha, Pi Nu Epsilon. Democrat. Avocations: reading, music. Home: 549 Willow Way West Chester PA 19380 Office: Hoeffel for Congress 1746 Old York Rd Abington PA 19001 E-mail: jodiepoth@yahoo.com.

POTH, STEFAN MICHAEL, retired sales financing company executive; b. Detroit, Dec. 9, 1933; s. Stefan and Anna (Mayer) P.; m. Eileen T. McClimon, May 28, 1966; 1 child, Stefan Michael Jr. Cert. in acctg., Walsh Inst., Detroit, 1954. CPA, Mich.; cert. consumer credit exec. Sr. acct. Lybrand, Ross Bros. & Montgomery, Detroit, 1953-56, 58-61; with Ford Motor Credit Co., Dearborn, Mich., 1961-91, v.p. leasing truck and recreational products and tractor financing, 1973-77; v.p. cen. and western U.S. ops. Ford Motor Credit Co., 1977-79; v.p. mktg. and ops. svcs. Ford Motor Credit Co., 1979-85, v.p. bus. planning, 1985-90, v.p. credit policy, 1990-91. Bd. dirs. GE Credit Auto Resale Svcs., Inc.; adv. coun. Credit Rsch. Ctr., Krannert Grad. Sch. Mgmt., Purdue U., 1984-91. Chmn. adv. coun. Credit Rsch. Ctr. Krannert Grad. Sch. Mgmt., Purdue U., 1989-90; mem. bd. dirs. Internat. Credit Assoc., 1989-91. With AUS, 1956-58. Roman Catholic. Home: 7230 Mohansic Dr Bloomfield Hills MI 48301-3550

POTHURI, REDDEPPA NAIDU, electrical engineer; b. Namboorivari Palle, India, July 1, 1942; came to U.S., 1978; s. Papaiah Naidu and Vengamma Pothuri; m. Kora Ranjani, Nov. 1, 1969; children: Bhavana, Bharat. BSEE, Sri Venkateswara U., India, 1963; MSEE, Jadavpur U., India, 1966; PhDEE, U. Wales, Cardiff, 1977. Engr., lectr. various cos., India, 1964-73; rsch. scholar U. Wales, Cardiff, 1974-77; sr. systems analyst Electronics Assocs. Inc., West Long Branch, N.J., 1978; from sr. mem. tech. staff to staff scientist ITT Advanced Tech. Ctr., Shelton, Conn., 1978-86; mem. tech. staff AT&T Bell Labs, Holmdel, N.J., 1986-91, disting. mem. tech. staff, 1991—. Patentee in field; contbr. articles to profl. jours. Chmn. fundraising Hindu Temple & Cultural Soc. of U.S.A. Inc., Bridgewater, N.J., 1991-92. Rsch. scholar U.K. Ministry of Def., 1974-77; Kellog Found. fellow, 1993-94. Mem. IEEE (sr.; chmn. 1989-92, chmn. cirs. and stds. com. 1992—). Avocations: bridge, chess, gardening. Home: 30 Marigold Ln Marlboro NJ 07746-2404 E-mail: naidu@att.com.

POTLURI, VENKATESWARA RAO, medical facility administrator; b. Krishna Dist., India, Jan. 1, 1955; came to U.S., 1983; s. Venkata Krishnaiah and Bulli Ademma (Koduru) P.; m. Padma Sree Peddu, Dec. 4, 1986; children: Vani, Vamsee Krishna, Varun. BSc, ANR Coll., Gudivada, India, 1975; MSc, AU Coll. Sci. and Tech., Waltair, India, 1977; MPhil, Delhi (India) U., 1979, PhD, 1982. Diplomate Am. Bd. Med. Genetics. Postdoctoral fellow Mt. Sinai Med. Ctr., N.Y.C., 1983-85, vis. asst. prof., 1985-87; lab. dir., adj. mem. med. staff Norwalk (Conn.) Hosp., 1987-98; lab. dir. Lab. Diagnostics (divsn. Cytogenetics), Norwalk, 1998—2001; lab dir. Ctr. for Genetic Svcs. Inc. (divsn. Lab. Corp. of Am.), Corpus Christi, Tex., 2001—. Fellow: Am. Coll. Med. Genetics (founding); mem.: Am. Soc. Human Genetics. Avocations: classical music, Telugu literature, home improvement. Home: 7033 Buttermilk Dr Corpus Christi TX 78413-4302 Office: Center for Genetic Services, Inc. Division of Laboratory Corp. of America 7121 SPID, Suite 202 Corpus Christi TX 78412

POTOCKY-TRIPODI, MIRIAM, social worker, educator; b. Prague, Czech Republic, Feb. 28, 1962; d. Pavel Potocky and Vlastimila Potocka; m. Tony Tripodi. BA, U. of Colo., 1984; MSW, U. of Kans., 1989, PhD, 1993. LCSW. Assoc. prof. Fla. Internat. U., Miami, Fla., 1993—. Author: Best Practices for Social Work with Refugees and Immigrants, 2002; contbr. articles 25 to profl. jours. Office: Florida International University University Park ECS 460 Miami FL 33199 Business E-Mail: potockym@fiu.edu.

POTOK, JULIAN WALTER, pathologist; b. Phila., Jan. 4, 1936; married; children: John, Mark, Paul. BS in Biology, St. Joseph's U., 1957; DO, Phila. Coll. Osteo. Medicine, 1961; postgrad., Thomas Jefferson U. Hosp., 1974. Diplomate Am. Bd. Pathology. Family practice, Phila., 1962-70; resident in pathology Thomas Jefferson U., 1970-74; pathologist Polyclinic Med. Ctr., Harrisburg, Pa., 1974-80, dir. of lab., 1980-91, assoc. dir. of lab., 1991-98, assoc. pathologist, 1998—. Office: Pinnacle Hlth Sys at Polyclinic Med Ctr Harrisburg PA 17110

POTOK, NANCY ANN FAGENSON, federal agency administrator; b. Detroit, May 20, 1955; d. William and Harriet Fagenson; m. Barry Potok, May 16, 1976; children: Benjamin, Leah. BA, Sonoma State U., 1978; MAS, U. Ala., 1980. Cert. govt. fin. mgr. Presdl. mgmt. intern U.S. Dept. Transp., Washington, 1980-82; budget examiner U.S. Office Mgmt. & Budget, 1982-89; deputy asst. adminstr. fin. and budget Adminstrv. Office U.S. Cts., 1989-95; controller U.S. Census Bur., 1995-97, prin. assoc. dir., CFO, 1997—. Pres., treas. Women's Transp. Sem., Washington, 1983-84; advisor Presdl. Mgmt. Intern Career Devel. Group, Washington; co-chmn. Census Bur. Labor-Mgmt. Partnership coun., 1997—; assoc. mem. exec. orgn./mgmt. panel, Nat. Acad. Pub. Adminstrn., 2000—. Contbr. articles to profl. jours. Chmn. Citizens Adv. Com., Crofton, Md., 1996-98; mem. exec. bd. PTA, Crofton, 1990-95; judge Odyssey of the Mind Creative Problem Solving Competition, Md., 1995; coach Destination Imagination, Creative Problem Solving 1st Pl. Team, 1999. Recipient Arthur S. Flemming award Creative Problem Solving 1st Pl. Team, 1991, Silver medal Sec. Commerce, 1998. Mem. Am. Asn. Budget & Program Analysts, Am. Soc. Pub. Adminstrn., Assn. Govt. Accts. Avocations: writing, music. Office: US Census Bur Fob 3 Washington DC 20233-0001 E-mail: Nancy.A.Potok@census.gov.

POTRA, FLORIAN ALEXANDER, mathematics educator; b. Cluj, Romania, Dec. 7, 1950; came to the U.S., 1982; s. Ioan and Ana (Popa) P.; m. ELena Lavric, Nov. 15, 1973; 1 child, Valentin. MS, Babes-Bolyai U., Cluj, 1973; PhD, U. Bucharest, 1980. Analyst IPGGH, Bucharest, Romania, 1974-78; researcher INCREST, 1978-82; postdoctoral researcher U. Pitts., 1982-83, asst. prof., 1983-84; assoc. prof. U. Iowa, Iowa City, 1984-90, prof., 1990-98, U. Md. Baltimore County, 1998—. Vis. rschr. Lawrence Livermore Nat. Lab., Rice U., U. Catania, Italy, Konrad Zuse Zentrum, Berlin, U. Darmstadt, Germany, 1990, U. Karlsruhe, Germany, 1987-91, Argonne Nat. Lab., 1991, U. Geneva, 1993, U. NSW, Sydney, 1995, U. Rome, 1996, INRIA, France, 1996, City U. Hong Kong, 1999; program dir. NSF, 1997-98; prof. U. Md., 1998—. Assoc. editor: SIAM Jour. on Optimization, 1991-99, Jour. Optimization Theory and Applications, 1991—, Jour. Optimization Methods and Software, 1997—, Numerical Functional Analysis and Optimization, 1999—, Optimization and Engineering, 1999—; co-author: Research Notes in Mathematics 103, 1984; contbr. articles to profl. jours. Andrew Mellon fellow, 1982, Old Gold fellow, 1984, James Van Allen fellow in natural scis., 1991; NSF grantee, 1985-87., 94-96, 97—. Mem.: Math. Programming Soc., Inst. Ops. Rsch. and Mgmt. Scis., Soc. Indsl. and Applied Math., NY Acad. Scis. Home: 13 Brian Daniel Ct Reisterstown MD 21136 Office: U Md Baltimore County Dept Math 1000 Hilltop Cir Baltimore MD 21250-0001

POTSIC, WILLIAM PAUL, physician, educator; b. Berwyn, Ill., May 22, 1943; s. Andrew M. and Estella (Buschak) P.; m. Roberta I. Kite; children: Amie, Jordan. BS, U. Ill., 1965; MD cum laude, Emory U., 1969; postgrad., U. Pa.; M in Med. Mgmt., Tulane U., 1998. Intern, resident U. Chgo., 1969-74; practice medicine specializing in pediatric otolaryngology Phila., 1974—; staff Presbyn. Hosp., U. Pa. Hosp., Phila., Children's Seashore House, Phila.; prof. otorhinolaryngology and human comm. U. Pa., 1974-93, E. Mortimer Newlin prof., 1993—; dir. div. otorhinolaryngology and human comm. Children's Hosp., 1975—, pres. med. staff, 1982-84, vice-chmn. clin. affairs dept. surgery, 1995—, dir. ambulatory surg. svcs., 1997—, dir. ctr. for childhood comm., 1999. Author: Surgical Pediatric Otolaryngology, 1997; contbr. articles to profl. jours. Recipient 1st prize for clin. rsch. Am. Acad. Ophthalmology and Otolaryngology, 1977, Sylvan E. Stool award for outstanding lifetime contbns. in ear nose and throat advances in children; NIH grantee. Mem. AMA, Am. Acad. Otolaryngology Head and Neck Surgery, Am. Laryngology, Otolgy and Rhinology Soc., Am. Coll. Physician Execs., Internat. Acad. Cosmetic Surgery, Pa. Med. Soc., Phila. Coll. Physicians, Phila. County Med. Soc., Phila. Laryngol. Soc. (treas. 1983), Phila. Pediatric Soc., Phila Laryngol. Soc. (pres. 1984), Phila. Soc. Facial Plastic Surgeons, Politzer Soc., Soc. Ear, Nose and Throat Advances in Children (pres. 1983), Am. Soc. Pediatric Otolaryngology (pres. 1991), Soc. Univ. Otolaryngologists, Am. Acad. Pediat., Alpha Omega Alpha, Phi Chi. Home: 1057 Beaumont Rd Berwyn PA 19312-2007 Office: Children's Hosp Phila 34th And Civic Center Blvd Philadelphia PA 19104 E-mail: potsic@email.chop.edu.

POTT, JAMES THOMAS, civil engineer, consultant; b. Shanghai, Feb. 28, 1927; (father Am. citizen); s. James Hawks and Nancy (Yang) P.; m. Lois Jane Donaldson, July 16, 1955; children: Nancy, Catherine, Margaret. BSCE, Stanford U., 1949, MSCE, 1950. Registered profl. engr., Calif., Colo. Civil engr. Kennedy/Jenks/Chilton, San Francisco, 1950-60; county engr. County of Santa Clara, San Jose, 1960-77, dir. pub. works, 1963-73, dir. transp., 1973-77, asst. county exec., 1977-78; city engr., dir. pub. works City of Long Beach, 1978-84; v.p. O'Brien-Kreitzberg & Assocs., Encino, 1984-87; propr., engring. cons. James Pott & Co., Long Beach, 1987—94. Patentee transit wheelchair lift. Bd. dirs. Rail Constrn. Corp. of L.A. County Transp. Commn. 1st lt. U.S. Army, 1944-46, 52-53. Recipient S.I.R. award Assoc. Gen. Contractors Calif., 1976; Disting. Service award Calif. Council Civil Engrs. and Land Surveyors, 1967. Fellow ASCE (life); mem. Am. Pub. Wks. Assn. (life, mem. rsch. found. 1982-84, Top Ten Pub. Wks. award 1976), County Engrs. Assn. Calif. (pres. 1971-72, life mem.), Nat. Assn. County Engrs. (1st v.p. 1976-77, Urban County Engr. of Yr. 1973), Pub. Wks. Officers League Calif. Cities (v.p. 1983-84), Long Beach Area C. of C. (vice chmn. 1986-90, chmn. strategic plan task force 1988), Tau Beta Pi. Rotary. Republican. Episcopalian.

POTTASH, A. CARTER, psychiatrist, hospital executive; b. Phila., Nov. 30, 1948; s. R. Robert and Elizabeth (Braunschweig) P. BS with high honors, Trinity Coll., Hartford, Conn., 1970; MD, Yale U., 1974. Intern Tufts U. Sch. Medicine, Springfield, Mass., 1974-75; clin. fellow Yale-New Haven Hosp., 1977-78; fellow Yale U., New Haven, 1975-78; med. dir. Psychiatric Diagnostic Labs. Am., Summit, N.J., 1979-83. Lectr., cons. in field; vis. prof. St. Elizabeth Med. Ctr., Northeastern Ohio U. Coll Medicine, 1979; clin. prof. NYU, 1989—; pres. Fla. Consultation Svcs., P.A., West Palm Beach, 1992—, Psychiatric Assocs. N.J., P.A., Summit, N.J., 1978-93, Met. Med. Group P.C., N.Y.C., 1981-92, So. Fla. Med. Group P.A., Delray Beach, 1984-93, Stony Lodge Hosp., Inc. and Stony Lodge Med. Group P.C., Briarcliff Manor, N.Y., 1985—, Hampton Med. Group, P.A., Rancocas, N.J., 1986—; exec. med. dir. Fair Oaks Hosp., Summit, 1978-92, The Regent Hosp., N.Y.C., 1981-92, Lake Hosp of the Palm Beaches, Lake Worth, Fla., 1984-92, Fair Oaks Hosp. at Boca/Delray, Fla., 1984-92, Hampton Hosp., Rancocas, N.J., 1986-95—; chmn. Stony Lodge Hosp., Briarcliff Manor, N.Y., 1985—. Editor Psychiatry Letter, 1980-91; mem. editl. bd. Internat. Jour. Psychiatry in Medicine, 1978-87, The Psychiatric Hosp., 1982—, Jour. Nat. Assn. Pvt. Psychiatric Hosps., 1980-81, Fla. Psychiatry Newsletter, 1992—; reviewer Jour. Nervous and Mental Disorders, Alcoholism, Clin. and Exptl. Rsch., JAMA, Hosp. and Cmty. Psychiatry; contbr. articles to profl. jours. Mem. adv. bd. Mothers for

More Halfway Houses, N.Y.C., 1986—; cons. com. on women and alcoholism Jr. League of N.Y.C., 1987; bd. dirs. Met. Soc. Arts, N.Y.C., 1984-87. Fellow Am. Coll. Clin. Pharmacology, Assn. Clin. Scientists, Nat. Acad. Clin. Biochemistry, Am. Psychiat. Assn., The Acad. Medicine N.J.; mem. AMA, Soc. Neurosci., Nat. Acad. Clin. Biochemistry, Palm Beach County Med. Soc., Am. Acad. Clin. Psychiatrists, British Brain Research Assn. (hon.), European Brain and Behavioral Soc. (hon.), Am. Soc. of Addiction Medicine, Am. Academy of Addiction Psychiatry (founding mem. 1987), Am. Psychiatricic Assn., Fla. Med. Soc., Palm Beach County Psychiatric Soc., Med. Soc. State N.Y., Med. Soc. N.J., Union County Med. Soc., N.Y. Athletic Club, Canoe Brook Country Club, Beacon Hill Club, Phi Beta Kappa, Delta Phi Alpha. Office: PO Box 511 West Palm Beach FL 33402-0511

POTTENGER, MARK MCCLELLAND, computer programmer; b. Tucson, Feb. 9, 1955; s. Henry Farmer and Zipporah Herrick (Pottenger) Dobyns. BA, UCLA, 1976, DDiv (hon.), 1998. Data entry operator Astro Computing, Pelham, N.Y., 1976-77; programmer/analyst LA-CCRS, L.A., 1977-80; programmer/analyst cons. L.A. and San Diego, 1977—, R. Gonzalez Mgmt., L.A., 1980—. Rsch. dir. Internat. Soc. for Astrol. Rsch., L.A., 1985-95. Editor: Astrological Research Methods, 1995; co-author: Tables for Aspect Research, 1986; editor The Mutable Dilemma, 1977-99; author: (computer programs) CCRS Horoscope program, 1977-92, Frequencies for Aspect Rsch., 1986-92. Recipient Jansky award Aquarius Workshops, L.A., 1989. Mem. Internat. Soc. for Astrol. Rsch., Nat. Coun. for Geocosmic Rsch. Democrat. Mem. Religious Sci. Ch. Avocations: reading science fiction and regencies. Home and Office: 3808 49th St San Diego CA 92105-2101 E-mail: markpott@pacbell.net.

POTTER, ALICE CATHERINE, clinical laboratory scientist; b. Oil City, Pa., June 24, 1928; d. Howard Taylor and Hilda Marian (Lewis) P. BA, U. Findlay, 1949; postgrad., Springfield (Ohio) City Hosp., 1949-50. Registerd med. technologist Am. Soc. Clin. Pathologists; cert. clin. lab. scientist. Med. technologist Mercy Hosp., Springfield, 1950-54, Oil City Hosp., 1954-67; staff med. technologist Thomas Jefferson U. Hosp., Phila., 1968-83, sr. med. technologist, 1983—97, retired, 1997. Vol. Acad. Natural Scis., Phila., 1995—. Mem. Am. Soc. Clin. Lab. Scientists, Pa. Soc. Clin. Lab. Scientists (membership chmn. Delaware Valley chpt. 1977-78, chmn. pub. rels. 1982-94, 96-97, bd. dirs. 1989-91, 97-98, 98-99, 99—, pres.-elect 1991-92, pres. 1992-93, Scrimshaw award 1992). Republican. Avocations: travel, needlework. Home: 1701 Wallace St Philadelphia PA 19130-4300

POTTER, BARRY M. radiologist, medical educator; b. Bklyn., Dec. 11, 1942; s. Irving and Laura Potter; m. Beverly R. Schreiber, June 12, 1966; children: Michelle, Stuart. BA, Bklyn. Coll., 1963; MD, SUNY, Bklyn., 1967. Diplomate Am. Bd. Radiology. Intern Sinai Hosp. of Balt., 1967-68; resident in diagnostic radiology U. Cin., 1968-71; fellow in pediatric radiology Children's Hosp. of Cin., 1971-72; assoc., acting and asst. chair radiology Children's Nat. Med. Ctr., Washington, 1974-92; prof. radiology and pediats. George Washington U., 1987—; assoc. chair radiology George Washington U. Med. Ctr., 1992, residency program dir., 1992—, dir. diagnostic radiology, 1992—, interim chair radiology, 1996—. Contbr. articles to profl. jours. Bd. dirs. Amcha for Tzedakah, Chevy Chase, Md., 1995—. Maj. USAF, 1972-74. Fellow Am. Coll. Radiology; mem. Am. Roentgen Ray Soc. (editl. and pub. com. 1991—), Radiol. Soc. N.Am., Soc. for Pediat. Radiologists, Soc. of Chmn. of Acad. Radiology Depts., Soc. of Program Dirs. in Radiology (membership chmn. 1997-99), Alpha Omega Alpha. Office: George Washington U Hosp 901 23d St NW Washington DC 20037 E-mail: radbmp@gwumc.edu.

POTTER, BEVERLY ANN, management psychologist, consultant, publisher; b. Summit, N.J., Mar. 3, 1944; d. Campbell McCloud and Alice Ceres (Modersohn) P. BA in Psychology, San Fracisco State U., 1965, MS in Rehab. Coun., 1968; PhD in Counseling Psychology, Stanford U., 1974. Pub. Ronin Publ. Inc., Berkeley, Calif., 1984—, Profl. Workshops, Oakland, 1976—, Books-By-Phone, Berkeley, 1984-95. Author: Turning Around: Keys to Motivation and Productivity, 1980, Overcoming Job Burnout, 1980, 2d edit., 1993, Preventing Job Burnout: A Workbook, 2d edit., 1995, Brain Boosters: Foods and Drugs That Make You Smarter, 1993, Finding a Path With A Heart, 1995, Conflict to Cooperation: How to Mediate a Dispute, 1996, The Worrywart's Companion: 21 Ways to Soothe Yourself and Worry Smart, 1997, The Healing Magic of Cannabis, 1998, Drug Testing at Work: A Guide for Employers, 1998, Pass The Test: An Employee's Guide To Drug Testing, 1999, High Performance Goal Setting: Using Intuition to Achieve Your Dreams, 2000, The Way of the Ronin, 2001. Ford Found. dissertation fellow, 1973. Mem. No. Calif. Book Publ. Assn., Bay Area OD Network. Avocations: pottery, crafts. Office: PO Box 3008 Oakland CA 94609 E-mail: beverly@docpotter.com.

POTTER, BLAIR BURNS, editor; b. Spartanburg, S.C., Mar. 11, 1946; d. Leonard Hill and Nancy Milner (Vaughan) Burns; m. Robert Arthur Potter, May 24, 1974; children: Lillian Howard, Gordon Leonard. BA, Hollins Coll., Roanoke, Va., 1968; MA, U. N.C., Chapel Hill, 1971. Editl. asst. Profl. Engr., Washington, 1968—69; manuscript editor Science, 1970—74; freelance editor, 1974—85; assoc. editor Health Adminstrn. Press/U. Mich., Ann Arbor, 1985—87; freelance editor NAS, Inst. Medicine, Office Tech. Assessment, Washington, 1987—92; assoc. editor Science News, 1992, mng. editor, 1992—98; dir. Urban Inst. Press, 1998—2000, dir. acquisitions, 2000—01; freelance editor, 2000—. Editl. cons. Surgeon Gen.'s Report on Youth Violence, Washington, 2000-2001, White House Task Force on Infant Mortality, Washington, 1990, Nat. Commn. on Orphan Diseases, Washington, 1988-89, Nat. Comm. on Children, Washington, 1992-93; lay mem. protocol com. Nat. Heart, Lung and Blood Inst., Bethesda, Md., 1973. Whittaker fellow, 1969-70; Hollins Coll. scholar, 1964-68, English-Speaking Union scholar, 1967. Mem. Nat. Press Club, Am. Soc. Mag. Editors. Avocations: gardening, historic preservation, antique American furniture, sailing. Address: 8607 North Bend Circle Easton MD 21601-7327 Home and Office: 8607 Northbend Cir Easton MD 21601-7327 E-mail: bpotter@ui.urban.org.

POTTER, BRAD J. dean, researcher, educator; BS, Colo. State U., 1975; DDS, Northwestern U. , 1979; MS, U. Tex., San Antonio, 1991. Prof. oral diagnosis and patient svcs. Med. Coll. Ga., prof. oral biology and maxillofacial pathology, prof. grad. studies, dean dentistry, 1997—. Office: 1459 Loney Walker Blvd Augusta GA 30912 Business E-Mail: bpotter@mail.mcg.edu.*

POTTER, CHARLOTTE ANN, health education educator, physical education educator; b. Sept. 21, 1943; d. Charles Douglas and Jessie (Lewallen) Faulkner; m. Gary D. Potter, Dec. 24, 1962; 1 child, Bill Douglas. BS in Health and Phys. Edn., Tex. A&M U., 1972, MS in Health and Phys. Edn., 1975. With Westinghouse Corp., 1965; sec. dept. microbiology U. Ky., 1966-67; sec. dept. poultry sci. Tex. A&M U., 1968-69, tchr. dept. phys. edn., 1973; tchr. health and phys. edn. dept. College Station Ind. Schs., A&M Consolidated High Sch., 1973—, dept. head health and phys. edn., coord. intramurals, 1973—, student tchr. supr., 1974—. Guest lectr. Tex. A&M U., College Station, 1993—. Adult leader Equestrian 4-H Club, 1971-83; vol. College Station Little League Baseball, 1971-81; vol. sch. health College Station Ind. Sch. Dist., 1972, com. chmn. PTO South Knoll, 1972-76; cardiopulmonary resuscitation instr. vol., 1972—; vol. Tex. A&M U. Horseman's Assn., 1982—; vol. Phoebe's Home Toy, 1989—. Mem. AAHPER, NEA, Nat. Assn. Secondary Sch. Prins., Am. Heart Assn., Assn. for Advancement Health Edn., Tex. AHPERD, Tex. Edn. Assn., College Station Edn. Assn., Ctrl. Tex. Assn. Student Coun. Sponsors, Tex. Assn. Student Coun. Sponsors, Tex. A&M Assn. Former Students, Am. Sch. Health Assn., Tex. Sch. Health Assn., Ctrl. Tex. Long Ears Assn., Am. Donkey and Mule Assn., S.W. Donkey and Mule Assn., Gulf Coast Donkey and Mule Assn., Delta Psi Kappa, Delta Kappa Gamma. Avocation: training and showing mules in driving events. Home: 5609 Straub Rd College Station TX 77845-6966

POTTER, CLEMENT DALE, district attorney general; b. McMinnville, Tenn., Dec. 22, 1955; s. Johnnie H. and Elnora (Harvey) P.; children: Cory, Sarah, John Warren. BS, Middle Tenn. State U., 1984; JD, U. Tenn., 1987; cert., Tenn. Law Enforcement Acad., 1980. Bar: Tenn. 1987, U.S. Dist. Ct. (ea. dist.) Tenn. 1989. Pvt. practice law, McMinnville, 1987-89; city judge City of McMinnville, Tenn., 1988-89; pub. defender 31st Dist. State Tenn., McMinnville, 1989-98, dist. atty. gen., 1999—. Asst. to gen. editor Tools for the Ultimate Trial, 1st edit., 1985. Mem. Leadership McMinnville, 1989, chmn., 1995, 96. Staff sgt. USAF, 1974-80. Named McMinnville Warren County C. of C. Vol. of Yr., 1995; recipient D. Porter Henegar & Fred L. Hoover Sr. Bell Ringer award, 1995, Upper Cumberland award of merit 2000. Mem. ABA, Cheer Mental Health Assn. (dir. 1988—, pres. 1991-96), Harmony House Inc. (dir. 1993-95), Noon Exch. Club McMinnville (dir. 1992-94, sec. 1994, pres.-elect 1995, pres. 1996-97), Kiwanis Club of Warren County (pres. 1986-87), Tenn. Secondary Schs. Athletic Assn. (h.s. football referee 1988—), Am. Legion. Avocations: computers, gardening, coaching youth softball. Office: Dist Atty Gen 31st Dist PO Box 510 455 N Chancery Mc Minnville TN 37111

POTTER, DAVID SAMUEL, former automotive company executive; b. Seattle, Jan. 16, 1925; children: Diana (Mrs. Paul Bankston), Janice (Mrs. Robert Meadows), Tom, Bill; m. Nancy Shaar, Dec. 1979. BS, Yale U., 1945; PhD, U. Wash., 1951. Mem. staff Applied Physics Lab., U. Wash., 1946-60, asst. dir., 1955-60; with Gen. Motors Corp., 1960-73; chief engr. Milw. ops. GM Delco Electronics div., 1970-73; dir. research and devel. Detroit Diesel Allison div., 1973; asst. sec. for research and devel. Dept. Navy, 1973-74, under sec., 1974-76; v.p. environ. activities staff Gen. Motors Corp., Detroit, 1976-78, v.p. and group exec. public affairs group, 1978-83, v.p. in charge power products and def. ops. group, 1983-85; ret., 1985. Mem. Gov. Calif. Adv. Commn. Ocean Resources, 1964-68; mem. adv. panel Nat. Sea Grant Program, 1966; adv. bd. Naval Postgrad. Sch., Dept. Energy; bd. dirs. Sanders Assocs. Inc., Sci. Applications Internat. Co., John Fluke Mfg. Co., Lockheed Martin Corp. Served to ensign USNR, 1943-46. Mem. Nat. Acad. Engring., NSF, Marine Tech. Soc., Am. Phys. Soc., AIAA, Am. Acoustical Soc., Nat. Oceanographic Assn. (v.p. 1966), Soc. Automotive Engrs. (chmn. tech. bd. 1978-79, dir. 1981-83), Cosmos Club (Washington), Detroit Club, Birmingham Athletic Club (Mich.), Birnam Wood Country Club (Montecito, Calif.), Santa Barbara Club. Achievements include research on cosmic rays, magnetics, underwater acoustics. Home: 877 Lilac Dr Santa Barbara CA 93108-1449

POTTER, DAVID STONE, Greek and Latin educator; b. Cambridge, Mass., Mar. 15, 1957; s. Harold David and Elizabeth Fleming (Stone) P.; m. Ellen Ann Bauerle, Aug. 18, 1990; children: Claire Penelope, Natalie Sarah Ni Qing. BA, Harvard U., 1979; PhD, Oxford U., 1984. Vis. asst. prof. Greek and Latin Bryn Mawr (Pa.) Coll., 1984-86; asst. prof. Greek and Latin U. Mich., Ann Arbor, 1986-91, from assoc. to prof. Greek and Latin, 1991-96—, dir. Lloyd Hall Scholars program, 1999—. Author: Prophecy and History in the Crisis of the Roman Empire, 1990, Prophets and Emperors: Human and Divine Authority from Augustus to Theodosius, 1994, Literary Texts and the Roman Historian, 1999, Life Death and Entertainment in the Roman Empire, 1999. Recipient Phi Beta Kappa award Harvard U., 1979, Conington prize Oxford U., 1988. Episc. Home: 2377 Timbercrest Ct Ann Arbor MI 48105-9269 Office: Univ Mich Dept Classical Studies Ann Arbor MI 48109-1003

POTTER, DEBORAH ANN, news correspondent, educator; b. Hagerstown, Md., June 10, 1951; d. Peter R. and H. Louise (McDevitt) P.; m. Robert H. Witten; children: Cameron, Evan. BA, U. N.C., 1972; MA, Am. U., 1977. Assignment editor Sta. WMAL-TV, Washington, 1972-73, prodr., 1973-74; reporter Voice of Am., 1974-77; anchor Sta. KYW, Phila., 1977-78, CBS Radio, N.Y.C., 1978-81; White House corr. CBS News, Washington, 1981-85, state dept. corr., 1985-87, congl. corr., 1987-89, environ. corr., 1989-91; contbg. corr. 48 Hours, 1989-90; host Nightwatch CBS News, Washington, 1991; Washington corr. Cable News Network, 1991-94; asst. prof. Sch. Comm. Am. U., 1994-95. Mem. faculty Poynter Inst. Media Studies, St. Petersburg, Fla., 1995-98; exec. dir. NewsLab, Washington, 1998—. Co-author: Poynter Election Handbook; host (video prodns.) Beyond the Spotted Owl, 1993, Health Beat, 1994, Risk Reporting, 1995, Kids at Risk, 1997, (PBS series) In the Prime, 1996-97. Mem. adv. coun. Environ. Journalism Ctr., Radio and TV News Dirs. Found., Washington, 1994—; lay reader St. Alban's Episc. Ch., Washington, 1988-89, vestry, 1998-01. Mem. Radio TV News Dirs. Assn., Investigative Reporters and Editors, Assn. for Edn. in Journalism and Mass Comm., Nat. Press Photographers Assn., U. N.C. Alumni Assn. (bd. dirs. 1990-93, Disting. Young Alumna award 1990). Office: NewsLab 1900 M St NW Ste 210 Washington DC 20036-3530 E-mail: potter@newslab.org.

POTTER, DONALD JOSEPH, JR. pension and investment consultant; b. Chgo., July 19, 1949; s. Donald Joseph and Mary Evelyn (MacDougall) P.; children: Jonathan Cobey, Erin Elizabeth; m. Gwendolyn H. Potter, May 28, 1994. BA in Econs., Roanoke Coll., 1971. Chartered life underwriter. Agt. John Hancock Life Ins. Co., Wilmington, Del., 1971-72, N.Y. Life Ins. Co., Roanoke, Va., 1972-74; brokerage rep. Hartford Ins. Group, 1974-75; mgr. Securities Ins. Corp., 1975-79; pres. Benefit Strategies Corp., 1979—. CLU. Pres. Young Reps., Roanoke, 1976. Mem. Am. Soc. Pension Actuaries (assoc.), Investment Mgmt. Cons. Assn., Chartered Life Underwriters (bd. dirs. 1980-81), Estate Planning Coun. Avocations: golf, skiing, guitar, oil painting. Home: 4710 Whipplewood Dr Roanoke VA 24014-5588 Office: Fin Strategies 2766 Electric Rd Ste B Roanoke VA 24018

POTTER, ELIZABETH STONE, academic administrator; b. Mount Kisco, N.Y., Oct. 18, 1931; d. Ralph Emerson and Elizabeth (Fleming) Stone; m. Harold David Potter, Aug. 1, 1953; children: David Stone, Nicholas Fleming. BA, Wellesley Coll., 1953. Tchr. Spence Sch., N.Y.C., 1960-62; from audiovisual head to asst. to the mid. sch. head Chapin Sch., 1970-94, sci. tchr., sci. coord., 1970-2000, ret., 2000. Evaluator NYSAIS, N.Y.C., 1994-95. Trustee Leopold Schepp Found., 2000—. Mem. NSTA, ATIS. Avocations: reading, skiing, tennis, swimming, gardening. Home: 220 Mountain Rd Norfolk CT 06058 E-mail: esp1034@cs.com.

POTTER, EMMA JOSEPHINE HILL, language educator; b. Hackensack, N.J., July 18, 1921; d. James Silas and Martha Loretta (Pyle) Hill; m. James H. Potter, Mar. 26, 1949. AB cum laude with honors in classics, Alfred U., 1943; AM, Johns Hopkins U., 1946. Tchr. Latin, Balt. County Pub. Schs., 1943-44; instr. French and Spanish, Balt. Poly. Inst., 1950-83, instr. Spanish adult edn. classes, 1946-48; treas. Bruno-Potter, Inc. Trustee James Harry Potter Gold Medal award of ASME. Donor commemorative plaque in honor of Martha Pyle Hill to Chenango County Coun. Arts, 1996. Mem. Internat. Platform Assn., Clan Hay Soc. Scotland (Am. br.), John Hopkins U. Faculty Club. Democrat. Home: 419 3d Ave Avon By The Sea NJ 07717-1244

POTTER, GARY THOMAS, lawyer; b. Boulder, Colo., Nov. 12, 1941; s. Ralph Boyce Potter and Patricia Jamie O'Rourke; m. Pamela Closson, Aug. 3, 1963 (dec. Jan. 1992); children: Matthew, Michael, Andrew, Katie. BA, Regis Coll., 1963; JD, U. Colo., 1966. Atty. Kayne Watson Potter, Boulder, 1966-67, State of Colo. Dept. of Law, Denver, 1967-68; trust atty. First Nat. Bank of Denver, 1968-77; mktg. v.p. Integrated Resource, Denver, 1977-78; pvt. practice, 1978—. Pres. Lakewood Jr. Basketball, 1977-78; athletic dir. St. Bernadettes, Lakewood, 1992-93; bd. dirs., pres. Tchrs. Award Found., Denver, 1974-75; bd. dirs. Craig Hosp., Denver, 1977-80. Mem. U.S. Golf Assn. (sectional affairs com. 1980-98), Colo. Golf Assn. (bd. govs. 1974-88), Trans-Miss. Golf Assn. (trustee 1980—), Pacific Coast Golf Assn. (past pres. 1977, 88), Denver. C. of C. (pres. 1994-95). Roman Catholic. Office: 1700 Broadway Ste 1217 Denver CO 80290-1201 E-mail: gpotter@mho.com.

POTTER, GEORGE WILLIAM, JR. mining executive; b. St. Louis, Aug. 5, 1930; s. George William and Fay Marguerite (Finch) P.; m. Emily Louise Withers, Feb. 11, 1956; 1 child, Anne Finch Russ. BA, U. Mo., Kansas City, 1952. Pres. Oritz Mines, Inc., Joplin, Mo., 1962-64, chmn. bd. dirs., 1964-87, Nancy Oil & Royalty Co., Joplin, 1981-86; pres., chmn. bd. dirs. Potter Industries, Inc., 1981-90; chmn. bd. dirs. Cresset Corp., 1986. Art exhibited in one-man shows at Barn Gallery, Kansas City, Mo., 1974, Fountain Valley Sch., Colorado Springs, Colo., 1974, U. Leyden, The Netherlands, 1977, others; author books (under pseudonym E.L. Withers): The House on the Beach, 1957, The Salazar Grant, 1959, Diminishing Returns, 1960, Heir Apparent, 1961, The Birthday, 1962, Royal Blood, 1964; fgn. edits. include Brit., French, Italian, German, Scandinavian, Japanese. Bd. dirs. Winfred L. and Elizabeth C. Post Meml. Art Reference Libr., 1977-82, Kansas City Ballet, 1976-79; trustee Conservatory of Music, Kansas City, 1988-2001. Recipient Mo. Writers award, 1967. Mem. Authors Guild, Nat. Trust for Hist. Preservation, Soc. Fellows Nelson Gallery Found. (coun. 1988-91), Kansas City Country Club. Home: 1239 W 61st Ter Kansas City MO 64113-1327

POTTER, JAMES DOUGLAS, pharmacology educator; b. Waterbury, Conn., Sept. 26, 1944; s. Herbert Eugene and Jean Gladys (Troske) P.; m. Priscilla F. Strang, Aug. 9, 1985; children: Liesse, Andrew, Ian Brown. BS, George Washington U., 1965; PhD, U. Conn., 1970; postgrad. (fellow), Boston Biomed. Rsch. Inst., 1970-74. Staff scientist Boston Biomed. Rsch. Inst., 1974-75; assoc. in neurology Harvard U. Med. Sch., 1974-75; asst. prof. cell biophysics Baylor Coll. Medicine, 1975-77; assoc. prof. pharmacology U. Cin., 1977-81, prof., 1981-83; chmn., prof. dept. molecular and cellular pharmacology U. Miami, 1983—; co-dir. Exec. Office of Rsch. Leadership, Sch. Medicine U. Miami , 2001—; external examiner U. West Indies, 1998-99. Grant reviewer in field. Contbr. articles to profl. jours. Grantee NIH, 1978-81, 83—, Nat. Heart Lung and Blood Inst., 1978— (Merit award 1989—), Muscular Dystrophy Assn., 1983-94. Fellow Muscular Dystrophy Assn.; mem. AAAS, Am. Chem. Soc., Am. Soc. Pharmacology and Exptl. Therapeutics, Assn. for Med. Sch. Pharmacology (chmn.), Internat. Soc. Heart Rsch., Am. Heart Assn. (established investigator 1974-79), Am. Soc. Biochem. and Molecular Biologists, Cardiac Muscle Soc. (sec.-treas. 1992-94, pres. 1994-96), Biophys. Soc., Sigma Xi. Home: 7240 SW 127th St Miami FL 33156-5336 Office: U Miami Sch Medicine Dept of Molecular & Cellular Pharm 1600 NW 10th Ave Miami FL 33136-1090

POTTER, JAMES EARL, retired international hotel management company executive; b. Utica, N.Y., July 25, 1933; s. Earl Moses and Helen May P. BS in Hotel Mgmt. with distinction, Cornell U., 1954, postgrad., 1955-56. Owner, propr. Old Drovers Inn, Dover Plains, N.Y., 1956-89; various acctg. positions Inter-Continental Hotels Corp., N.Y.C., 1960-62, fin. dir. for Asia and Pacific, 1963-69; v.p. Overseas Nat. Airways Hotels, 1969-71; sr. v.p. Inter-Continental Hotels Corp., 1972-89, London, 1990-92. Instr. acctg. Cornell U., Ithaca, N.Y., 1957-59. Author: A Room with a World View, 1996. Trustee Opera Co. Boston, 1978-85; mem. Cornell U. Coun., 1988-91; mem. patron com. Met. Opera, N.Y.C.; bd. dirs.and treas. Santa Fe (N.Mex.) Opera. Mem. Culinary Inst. Am. (trustees com. on acad. policy 1980-90), Met. Opera Club, Cornell Hotel Soc., Cornell Club (N.Y.C.),Santa Fe Opera Found. (exec. com.). Presbyterian. Avocation: opera.

POTTER, JAMES MILTON, city planner, consultant; b. Balt., Oct. 13, 1961; s. Milton James and Anna (Vidi) P.; m. Sharon Matlick. BS in Geography and Environ. Planning, Towson (Md.) State U., 1996; M City and Regional Planning, Morgan State U., Balt., 1998. Cert. Am. Inst. Cert. Planners; lic. profl. planner, N.J.. Site designer Century Engring., Balt., 1985-90; site designer, project planner Whitney, Bailey, Cox, and Magnani, 1990-97; project coord. Neighborhood Design Ctr., 1997-98; planner and project mgr. STV Inc., 1998—. Cons. and seminar presenter in field. Candidate from 1st dist. Balt. City Coun., 1992; pres. Waltherson Improvement Assn., Balt., 1993-94; mem. exec. com. Harbel Cmty. Assn., Balt., 1994-98, pres., chmn. bd., 1995-97, chmn. bylaws com., 1998. Scholar Md. Ho. of Dels., 1996. Mem. Am. Planning Assn. (planning awards com. Md. chpt. 2000), KC (cmty. activities dir. Balt. 1998-99), Golden Key. Avocations: travel, writing, reading, jewelry design.

POTTER, JAMES VINCENT, association executive; b. Walla Walla, Wash., July 17, 1936; s. James Floyd and Dorothy May (Turner) P.; m. Margaret Mae Fogerson, July 4, 1954 (div. Apr. 1970); children: Deborah Ann, David Allan, Rebecca Lynn, Mary Michelle, Randy J., Jonathan James; m. Paula Maureen Brutsman, Feb. 28, 1986; stepchildren: Carolyn June, Catherine Doreen, Paul Clayton, Connie Lynn. BA in Bibl. Studies, Logos Bible Coll., 1989; MA in Theology, Logos Grad. Sch., 1989; PhD, Vision Christian U., 1990, postgrad., 1991-95. Diplomate Nat. Bd. Addiction Examiners, Am. Coll. Profl. Mental Health Practitioners; lic. clin. pastoral counselor; cert. temperament therapist, doctoral addictions counselor, domestic violence counselor, diplomat clin. hypnotherapist; cert. clin. psychopathologist; cert. Christian marraige and family therapist. Lectr., nat. presenter, lit. evang. Seventh-day Adventist Ch., Idaho, 1956-60, Oreg., 1960-61; staff mem. U. of the Nations Family Ministries, Kailua-Kona, Hawaii, 1989; pastor Gospel of Salvation Ministries, 1989-93; dean Coll. Christian Counseling, Vision Christian U., Hilo, Hawaii, 1990-93; pres. Family Care Svcs. Internat., 1990-93; v.p., mem. faculty Vision Christian U., Ramona, Calif., 1991-92, 1998—; adminstr., clinician Hawaii Family Care Ctrs., Hilo, 1989-93; exec. dir. Agape Family Svcs., Inc. and Alliance Recovery Svcs., 1995—, Agape Family Svcs. Family Skills Inst. Vice chmn. Teen Challenge of Hawaii, 1991-93, govtl. apptd. mem. Hawaii Area Commn. on Mental Health and Substance Abuse, 1991-94; pres. Profl. Assn. Christian Therapists, 1989-94, Internat. Christian Counselors Assn., 1988—, Calif. Bd. Addiction Examiners, 2000—; lectr. western states, 1989—; nat. presenter on addictions and domestic violence and addictions prevention and treatment. Author: Soul Care, 1989, Untwisting Twisted Temperaments, 1991, (book and curriculum), Save Our Families, Pulling Down Strongholds, 1998, Breaking Free, 1998, Discovering Our True Selves, 1999, Mastery Over Anger, 2000, Assertiveness Training, 2000, Beyond Codependency, 2000, Man's Magnificent Mind, 2000, Healing Developmental Wounds, 2000, Reparenting the Self, 2000, Growing Beyond Our Genetcis, 2000, Toxic Shame and the Journey Out, 2000, Relapse Prevention and Rage, 2001; co-author: Family Care Center Manual, 1991, Christian Character Alignment, 1991; (newsletter) Gem-State Surveyor, 1976. Dem. nominee Idaho State Legis., House Rep., Boise, 1976, 78; vice chmn. Idaho Tech. Adv. Coun., Boise, 1976-83; pres. Idaho Assn. Land Surveyors, Boise, 1976-77; chmn. Western Fedn. Profl. Land Surveyors, 12 western states, 1979-80; nat. dir. Am. Congress Surveying Mapping, Washington, 1981-83; gov. Nat. Soc. Profl. Land Surveyors; state del. Mont./Hawaii State Rep. Conv., Turtle Bay, 1988. With USN, 1953. Am. Congress Surveying Mapping fellow, Washington, 1980. Fellow: Nat. Assn. Forensic Counselors (diplomate, cert. edn. provider); mem.: Am. Coll. Cert. Forensic Counselors (bd. govs.), Am. Assn. Christian Therapists, Christian Assn. Psychol. Studies, Am. Assn. Christian Counselors, Nat. Christian Counselors Assn. (bd. dirs. 1988), Nat. Assn. Family Counselors, Nat. Bd. Cert. Hypnotherapists, Nat. Bd. Addiction Examiners, Nat. Bd. Addiction Examiners. Office: PO Box 992168 1501 Market Redding CA 96099 E-mail: docpotter@digital-star.com., agapefs@digital-star.com. *Sin, which separated man from God, is the "distortion" from all that which God intended man to be. It is our "missing the mark" of being a fully realized child of God (Romans 8:18 27). Jesus Christ "became sin" (2 Corinthians 5:21), assuming in His flesh the distortion of humanity, that we might in Him have "the right to become children of God." (John 1:12). Christian ministries are called to minister this healing of personhood to a sin sick world. (Isaiah 61: 1,2). The "new-birth" experience enables an individual to reclaim his/her heritage as a child of God, and to begin to "grow-up" in the wisdom and stature thereof. A process that the entire universe-antimate and inantimate is waiting for with eager anticipation (Romans 8:18-27).*

POTTER, JANICE BABER, school superintendent, educator; b. Roann, Ind., May 15, 1938; d. Matthew and Emma E. (Shillinger) Baber; m. Marcus L. Potter III, Aug. 17, 1957; children: Susan, Julie. MS, No. Ill. U., 1972, CAS, 1976, EdD in Ednl. Adminstrn., 1979. Cert. spl. edn. tchr., chief sch. bus. ofcl., supt., Ill. Tchr. Winfield (Ill.) Pub. Schs., 1969-76; owner, operator Formative Yrs. presch., Wheaton, Ill., 1976-79; asst. supr. Bloomingdale (Ill.) Pub. Schs., 1979-81; asst. dir./bus. mgr. So. Met. Assn., Harvey, Ill., 1981-84; supt. Lisbon Grade Sch., 1984-87, 93—, So. Holland Sch. dist., 1987-89; mem. faculty Nat. Coll. Edn., 1970-90, Coll. Du Page, 1972-90. Mem. ASCD, Am. Assn. Sch. Adminstrs., Ill. Assn. Sch. Bus. Officers, Assn. Children Learning Disabilities, Ill. Women Adminstrs. Presbyterian. Home: 28W070 Mack Rd Wheaton IL 60187-6073

POTTER, J(EFFREY) STEWART, property manager; b. Ft. Worth, July 8, 1943; s. Gerald Robert Potter and Marion June (Mustain) Tombler; m. Dianne Eileen Roberb, Dec. 31, 1970 (div. Aug. 1983); 1 child, Christopher Stewart; m. Deborah Ann Blevins, Oct. 20, 1991. AA, San Diego Mesa Coll., 1967. Cert. apt. mgr., apt. property supr., housing adminstr. Sales mgr. Sta. KJLM, La Jolla, Calif., 1964-67; mgr. inflight catering Host Internat., San Diego, 1967-69; lead aircraft refueler Lockheed Co., 1969-70; property mgr. Internat. Devel. and Fin Corp., La Jolla, 1970-72; mgr. bus. property BWY Constn. Co., San Diego, 1972-73; mgr. residents Coldwell Banker, 1973-74; mgr. Grove Investments, Carlsbad, Calif., 1974-76, Villa Granada, Villa Seville Properties Ltd., Don Cohn, Chula Vista, 1976-83; gen. mgr. AFL-CIO Bldg. Trades Corp., National City, 1983—; instr., Cert. Apt. Mgmt. San Diego Apt. Assn., 1995-98. Bd. dirs. San Diego County Apt. Assn., 1995-97, San Diego County Policy Panel Youth Access to Alcohol; mem. com. San Diego Crime Victims Fund. Fellow Nat. City C. of C., Founding Families San Diego Hist. Soc., Am. Assn. Retired Persons, San Diego County Apt. Assn. (bd. dirs.), La Jolla

Monday Night Club (treas. 1984-89), La Jolla Hist. Soc. Roman Catholic. Avocations: golf, tennis, snow skiing. Office: AFL-CIO Bldg Trades Corp 2323 D Ave National City CA 91950-6730 E-mail: jspotter@san.rr.com.

POTTER, JOHN BUCHANAN, education consultant; b. Salisbury, Eng., Jan. 28, 1938; s. Robert James and Geraldine Elizabeth (Buchanan) P.; m. Celia Rubery, Apr. 18, 1964 (div. 1989); children: Andrew, Alasdair, Tanya; m. Valerie Oliver, Feb. 17, 1990. BA with honors, Politics Philosophy Econ., Oxford, Eng., 1961. Asst. curate Ch. of Eng., Coventry, 1963-66, vicar Writtle, 1970-78; sr. lectr. Warden Hall of Residence, Lanchester Poly., Coventry, 1966-70; canon Derby (Eng.) Cathedral, 1978-85; devel. officer Cmty. Svc. Vols., London, 1985-90, dir., 1990-2001. Dir. Writtle Pastoral Found., Chelmford, Eng., 1974-78; trainer Westminster Pastoral Found., London, 1985-90, 90—; dir. CSV Edn. for Citizenship. Contbr. articles to profl. jours. Gov. Bemrose Sch., Derby, 1979-84; chmn. Assn. Pastoral Care and Counseling, 1993-94. 2d lt. British mil., 1956-58. Fellow Royal Soc. Arts. Avocations: travel, photography, walking. Office: CSV 237 Pentonville Rd N19NJ London England

POTTER, JOHN FRANCIS, surgical oncologist, educator; b. N.Y.C., July 26, 1925; s. John Albert and Isabelle Cecelia (Sullivan) P.; m. Tanya Agnes Kristof, Nov. 19, 1955; children: Tanya Jean, Miriam Isabelle, John Mark. Student, Holy Cross Coll., 1943-45; MD, Georgetown Med. Sch., 1949. Intern Grasslands Hosp., Valhalla, N.Y., 1949-50, resident in surgery, 1949-50, Georgetown U. Hosp., Washington, 1953-56; sr. investigator Nat. Cancer Inst., Bethesda, Md., 1957-60; chief divsn. surg. oncology Georgetown Med. Ctr., Washington, 1960-85; instr, asst.prof., then assoc. prof. surgery Georgetown U. Sch. Medicine, 1957-64, prof., 1969—; dir. Vincent T. Lombardi Cancer Rsch. Ctr., Washington, 1967-87, U.S. Mil. Cancer Inst., Bethesda, Md., 2000—. Mem. U.S. Mil. Health Adv. Com.; presdl. apptd. mem. bd. regents Uniformed Svcs. U. of the Health Scis., 1999. Hon. prof. Universidad Cayetano Heredia, Lima, Peru, 1980. Lt. (j.g.) USNR, 1951-53. Recipient Pres.'s medal Georgetown U., 1991. Mem. Soc. Surg. Oncology (rep. adv. bd.), ACS, Assn. Am. Cancer Insts. (v.p. 1985-86, pres. 1986-87, bd. dirs. 1982, chmn. bd. dirs. 1987-88), So. Surg. Assn., Peruvian Cancer Soc. (hon.), Knights of Malta. Office: US Mil Cancer Inst 4301 Jones Bridge Rd Bethesda MD 20814 E-mail: john.potter.1@na.amedd.army.mil.

POTTER, JOHN LEITH, mechanical and aerospace engineer, educator, consultant; b. Metz, Mo., Feb. 5, 1923; s. Jay Francis Lee and Pearl Delores (Leeth) P.; m. Dorothy Jean Williams, Dec. 15, 1957; children: Stephen, Anne, Carol. BS in Aerospace Engring., U. Ala., Tuscaloosa, 1944, MS in Engring., 1949; MS in Engring. Mgmt., Vanderbilt U., 1976, PhD in Mech. Engring., 1974. Engr., educator various indsl., ednl. and govt. orgns., 1944-52; chief, flight and aerodyns. lab. Redstone Arsenal, Ala., 1952-56; mgr., div. chief, dep. tech. dir., sr. staff scientist Sverdrup Tech., Inc., Tullahoma, Tenn., 1956-83; research prof. Vanderbilt U., Nashville, 1983-92, prof. emeritus, 1992—; cons. engr., 1983—. Convener NATO-AGARD, U.S. and Eng., 1980-82, mem. working group, 1984-88; mem. adv. com. Internat. Symposium on Rarefied Gasdynamics, 1970—; invited lectr. USSR Acad. Scis., 1967; mem. NRC com. on assessment nat. aeronautical wind tunnel facilities, 1987-88; mem. NASA working groups, 1987—; mem. Engring. Accreditation Commn., 1985-90. Editor: Rarefied Gas Dynamics, 1977. Contbr. articles to profl. publs., chpts. to books Chmn. bd. dirs. Coffee County Hist. Soc., Tenn., 1971-72; bd. dirs. Southeastern Amateur Athletic Union, 1972-73; pres. Tullahoma Swim Club, 1972-73. Recipient Outstanding Fellow award U. Ala. Aerospace Engring. Dept., 1987; elected 150th Anniversary Disting. Engring. Fellow U. Ala. Coll. Engring., 1988; USAF Arnold Engring. Devel. Ctr. fellow, 1993. Fellow AIAA (assoc. editor jour. 1970-73, publs. com. 1973-78, assoc. editor Progress in Astronautics and Aeronautics 1981-85, Gen. H.H. Arnold award Tenn. chpt. 1964); mem. Capstone Engring. Soc. (regional bd. dirs. 1972-77), Sigma Xi, Tau Beta Pi, Theta Tau, Pi Tau Sigma, Sigma Gamma Tau. Home: 400 University Park Dr Apt 394 Birmingham AL 35209

POTTER, JOHN WILLIAM, federal judge; b. Toledo, Oct. 25, 1918; s. Charles and Mary Elizabeth (Baker) P.; m. Phyllis May Bihn, Apr. 14, 1944; children: John William, Carolyn Diane, Kathryn Susan. PhB cum laude, U. Toledo, 1940; JD, U. Mich., 1946. Bar: Ohio 1947. Assoc. Zachman, Boxell, Schroeder & Torbet, Toledo, 1946-51; ptnr. Boxell, Bebout, Torbet & Potter, 1951-69; mayor City of Toledo, 1961-67; asst. atty. gen. State of Ohio, 1968-69; judge 6th Dist. Ct. Appeals, 1969-82, U.S. Dist. Ct., Toledo, 1982—, sr. judge, 1992—. Presenter in field. Sr. editor U. Mich. Law Rev., 1946. Pres. Ohio Mcpl. League, 1965; past assoc. pub. mem. Toledo Labor Mgmt. Commn.; past pres., bd. dirs. Commn. on Rels. with Toledo (Spain); past bd. dirs. Cummings Sch. Toledo Opera Assn., Conlon Ctr.; past trustee Epworth United Meth. Ch.; hon. chmn. Toledo Festival Arts, 1980. Capt. F.A., U.S. Army, 1942-46. Decorated Bronze Star; recipient Leadership award Toledo Bldg. Congress, 1965, Merit award Toledo Bd. Realtors, 1967, Resolution of Recognition award Ohio Ho. of Reps., 1982, Outstanding Alumnus award U. Toledo, 1966, conf. rm. named in his honor, U.S. Courthouse, Toledo, 1998; named to Field Arty. Officer Candidate Sch. Hall of Fame, 1999. Fellow Am. Bar Found., Am. Judicature Soc., 6th Jud. Cir. Dist. Judges Assn., Fed. Judges Assn.; mem. ABA, Ohio Bar Assn. (Found. Outstanding Rsch. award 1995), Toledo Bar Assn. (exec. com. 1962-64, award 1992), Lucas County Bar Assn., U. Toledo Alumni Assn. (past pres.), Toledo Zool. Soc. (past bd. dirs.), Old Newsboys Club, Toledo Club, Kiwanis (past pres.), Phi Kappa Phi. Home: 2418 Middlesex Dr Toledo OH 43606-3114 Office: US Dist Ct 307 US Courthouse 1716 Spielbusch Ave Toledo OH 43624-1363

POTTER, JUNE ANITA, small business owner; b. La Crosse, Wis., Jan. 22, 1938; d. Christian John and Ethel Marie (Stafslien) Stefferud; m. James Oscar Potter, June 18, 1961; children: Jill Potter Rutlin, Todd. BA in Home Econs., St. Olaf Coll., Northfield, Minn., 1960; postgrad., N.Y. Sch. Interior Design, 1964; MS in Edn., U. Wis., Menomonie, 1977. Sr. high home econs. tchr., FHA advisor Tomah (Wis.) H.S., 1960-64, Black River Falls (Wis.) H.S., 1971-83; freelance interior designer Warrens, Wis., 1964-97; ptnr., mgr. James Potter Cranberry Marsh, Inc., 1968—; substitute tchr. Tomah Schs., 2001—. Co-pubr.: Warrens Centennial Book, 1968, Wisconsin Cranberry Centennial Book, 1989. Active various charitable and church orgns.; bd. dirs. Warrens Cranberry Festival, 1984—, chair 25th Anniversary Book, 1997; mem. Warrens Area Bus. Assn., 1990-98; sec. Wis. Cranberry Bd., Inc., 1990—; sec. Warren Mills Cemetery Assn., 1993-2000; mem. com. Wis. Alice in Dairyland Finale, 1993 (state Alice award, 2000); mem. Jellystone Campground and Ministry, Warrens Wis. 1970s Millennium Tree Com., Washington, 1999; found. bd. Wis. Exec. Residence, 1994—; pres. Gloria Dei Luth. Ch. Women, 1997-2000. Mem.: AAUW (v.p. 1983—2001), Wis. State Cranberry Growers Assn. (pub. rels. com. 1994—2000, mem. centennial com. 1988—, State Pres.'s award 2000), Tomah Pkwy. Garden Club, Beta Sigma Phi (officer, com. mem. 1961—, Nat. Order of Rose 1983, Silver Cir. award 1985, Girl of Yr.). Lutheran. Avocations: flowers, photography, travel, collecting foreign country items. Home and Office: 28353 County Hwy EW Warrens WI 54666-7513 E-mail: jpotter@tomah.com.

POTTER, LILLIAN FLORENCE, business executive secretary; b. Montreal, Que., Can., Oct. 19, 1912; came to U.S., 1934; naturalized citizen. d. Thomas Joseph and Lily Rose (Robertson) Quirk; m. Theodore Edward Potter, July 20, 1932 (dec. Apr. 1980); children: Peter Edward, Stephen Thomas. Grad. high sch., Montreal, 1929, grad., 1931. Sr. sec. S.D. Warren div. Scott Paper Co., Westbrook, Maine, 1955-69, editor indsl. publ. S.D. Warren div., 1969-72; editor Nat. Antiques Rev. mag., Portland, 1972-77; exec. sec. Humboldt Portland Litho div. Humboldt Nat. Graphics, Inc., Fortuna, Calif., 1977—. Free lance writer Guy Gannett Pub. Co., Portland, 1960-64. Author: (children's book) Once Upon an Autumn, 1984 (state 1st pl. award, nat. 3d pl. award), (antiques and collectibles) A Re-Introduction to Silver Overlay on Glass and Ceramics, 1992; co-author: (textbook, tchrs. manual) Foundations of Patient Care, 1981; asst. editor, N.E. dist. The Secretary mag., Profl. Secs. Internat., 1960-62; editor Maine Chpt. Bull., 1963-64. Recipient George Washington Honors medal Freedoms Found., Valley Forge, Pa., 1964, Sec. of Yr. award Portland chpt. Profl. Secs. Internat., 1967, Outstanding Svc. award State of Maine Sesquicentennial, 1970, Outstanding Svc. award Island Pond (Vt.) Hist. Soc. 1978. Mem. Maine Media Women (pres. 1970-71, Woman of Yr. 1973, Communicator of Achievement plaque and prize 1991), Maine Writers and Pubs. Alliance, Woman's Lit. Union, Portland Lyric Theater, Island Pond Hist. Soc., Jones Mus. Glass and Ceramics, Westbrook Woman's Club, OES (past matron, past pres.). Republican. Episcopalian. Avocations: reading, researching, antiques, swimming, gardening. Home: 80 Payson St Portland ME 04102-2851

POTTER, NED, science journalist, writer; b. N.Y.C., Sept. 23, 1956; s. Gene and Marlies Potter; m. Beth Thomas; children: David, Katherine. AB, Princeton U., 1977. Corr. CBS News, Chgo., Boston, 1980-87; environ. corr. ABC News, N.Y.C., 1987-95, chief sci. corr., 1995—. Contbr. articles to mags. Recipient Emmy award, NATAS, 1985, 97, World medal, N.Y. Festivals, N.Y.C., 1999, 2000, Golden Eagle award, CINE, Washington, 1997, duPont-Columbia award, Columbia U. Grad. Sch. Journalism, 1996. Office: ABC News 47 W 66th St New York NY 10023

POTTER, ROBERT JOSEPH, technical and business executive; b. N.Y.C., Oct. 29, 1932; s Mack and Ida (Bernstein) P.; married; children: Diane Gail, Suzanne Lee, David Craig. BS cum laude, Lafayette Coll., 1954; MA in Physics, U. Rochester, 1957, PhD in Optics, 1960. Cons. ANPA Research Inst., AEC Brookhaven Nat. Lab., RCA Labs., U.S. Naval Research Labs., 1952-60; mgr. optical physics and optical pattern recognition IBM Thomas J. Watson Research Center, Yorktown Heights, N.Y., 1960-65; assoc. dir. Applied Research Lab., Xerox Corp., Rochester, 1965-67; v.p. advanced engring. Xerox Corp., 1967-68, v.p. devel. and engring., 1968-69; v.p., gen. mgr. Spl. Products and Systems div. Spl. Products and Sys. divsn. Xerox Corp., Stamford, Conn. and Pasadena, Calif., 1969-71; v.p. info. tech. group Xerox Corp., Rochester, 1971-73, Dallas, 1973-75, pres. Office Sys. divsn., 1975-78; sr. v.p., chief tech. officer Internat. Harvester Co., Chgo., 1978-82; with R.J. Potter & Co., 1983-84; group v.p. integrated office sys. Nortel Networks, Richardson, Tex., 1985-87; pres. and CEO Datapoint Corp., San Antonio, 1987—90; pres., CEO R.J. Potter Co., Dallas, 1990—. Dir. Molex, Inc., Bradshaw Group, Speed FC; bd. govs., vice chmn. IIT Rsch. Inst.; chmn. Tatum CIO Ptnrs., LLP. Contbr. articles to profl. jours. Trustee Ill. Inst. Tech., Alliance for Higher Edn. Recipient IBM Outstanding Tech. Contbn. award, 1964, Disting. Achievement award Soc. Mfg. Engrs., 1981; Kroner scholar Lafayette Coll., 1954; Disting. Rochester scholar U. Rochester, 1995. Fellow Optical Soc. Am., Am. Phys. Soc.; mem. Phi Beta Kappa, Sigma Xi. Office: R J Potter Co 5215 N O Connor Blvd Ste 1110 Irving TX 75039-3739 E-mail: RJPotter@RJPotter.com.

POTTER, ROBERT WALLACE, JR. educator; b. Springfield, Mass., Aug. 15, 1947; s. Robert Wallace and Mary Louise (Tilli) P.; m. Betsy Rachael Coleman, Sept. 12, 1981; children: Christopher Coleman, Mary Elizabeth. BA cum laude, St. Anselm Coll., 1969; MEd, Keene State Coll., 1978. Tchr. St. Catherine Sch., Manchester, N.H., 1969-70, St. Patrick Sch., Jaffrey, 1970-74; tchr. social studies Antrim (N.H.) Mid. Sch., 1974-89, prin., 1978-89, Jaffrey-Rindge Mid. Sch., 1989-92, Athol (Mass.) Mid. Sch., 1992-94, Belmont Mid. Sch., 1994-96; asst. prin. Hawthorne Brook Mid. Sch., Townsend, Mass., 1996-98, Wilton (N.H.)-Lyndeborough Jr.-Sr. H.S., 1998—. Sec.-treas. Jaffrey War Meml. Com., 1983—; vice chmn. Jaffrey Planning Bd., 1983-84, chmn., 1984-86, vice chmn., 1986-91; mem. bandstand restoration com., Jaffrey, 1986-87, Jaffrey Hist. Dist. Commn., 1986-88; dir. Jaffrey-Gilmore Found., 1985—; incorporator Cathedral of Pines, Rindge, N.H., 1992-96. Mem. NEA, ASCD, New Eng. League Mid. Schs., Mass. Tchrs. Assn., N.H. Adminstrs. Assn., N.H. Assn. Secondary Sch. Prins., N.H. Assn. Curriculum and Devel., Contoocook Valley Adminstrs. Orgn. (pres. 1983-86), Jaffrey C. of C. (corr. sec. 1983-85, pres. 1985-86, dir. 1986-88, chmn. edn. com. 1989-92), Jaffrey Tree Farm Com. (sec. 1987-90), Rotary, Thorndike Club (bd. dirs.), Pi Gamma Mu. Republican. Roman Catholic. Home: 10 Wheeler St Jaffrey NH 03452-6566 Office: Wilton-Lyndeborough Jr-Sr H S 56 School Rd Wilton NH 03086 E-mail: pottercole@prodigy.net.

POTTER, TANYA JEAN, lawyer; b. Washington, Oct. 30, 1956; d. John Francis and Tanya Agnes (Kristof) P.; m. Howard Bruce Adler; 1 child, Alexandra Potter Adler. BA, Georgetown U., 1978, JD, 1981. Bar: D.C. 1982, U.S. Ct. Appeals (D.C. cir.), U.S. Ct. Appeals (fed. cir.), U.S. Dist. Ct. (D.C. dist.), U.S. Ct. Internat. Trade. Assoc. Ragan and Mason, Washington, 1981-88; atty.-adviser Office of Chief Counsel for Import Adminstrn., U.S. Dept. Commerce, 1989-92. Mediator D.C. Superior Ct., 1982-84. Author: Practicing Before the Federal Maritime Commission, 1986, supplement, 1988, Preferentiality Under the Proposed Commerce Department Regulations, 1990, Oil Refining in U.S. Foreign-Trade Zones, 1990. Rep. Avenel Homeowners Adv. Coun., 1994-97; dir. Avenel Bd. Dirs., 1997, 98, 99-2001. Recipient Cmty. Svc. Recognition award ARC, Washington, 1986. Mem. ABA, Bar Assn. of D.C. (exec. coun. ad law sect. 1985-89). Avocations: sports, travel, visiting museums and art galleries.

POTTER, TREVOR ALEXANDER MCCLURG, lawyer; b. Chgo., Oct. 24, 1955; s. Charles Steele and Barbara (McClurg) P. AB, Harvard Coll., 1978; JD, U. Va., 1982. Bar: Ill. 1983, D.C. 1988, U.S. Supreme Ct. 1997. Counsel office of legal policy U.S. Dept. Justice, Washington, 1982-84; asst. gen. counsel FCC, 1984-85; atty. Wiley, Rein & Fielding, 1985-88, ptnr., 1988-91,96-2001; commr. Fed. Election Commn., 1991—, vice chmn., 1993, chmn., 1994-95; ptnr. Caplin & Drysdale, 2001—. Merrill lectr. Sch. Law U. Va., 1996-97. Republican. Episcopalian. Fellow Brookings Instn. (sr.); mem. ABA (chmn. com. on election law, adminstrv. law sect. 1993-95, 99—, mem. standing com. on election law 2000—). Office: Caplin & Drysdale One Thomas Cir NW Washington DC 20005 E-mail: tp.@capdale.com.

POTTER, WILLIAM BARTLETT, business executive; b. Washington, Jan. 4, 1938; s. George Holland and Virginia (Bartlett) P.; m. Simone Robert, June 6, 1964; children: Eva Simone, William Bartlett. AB, Princeton U., 1960; MBA, Emory U., 1962. With Merc.-Safe Deposit & Trust Co., Balt., 1962—, asst. sec., asst. treas., 1964-66, asst. v.p., 1966-68, v.p., 1968-69, sr. v.p., 1969-76, exec. v.p., 1976, Preston Trucking Co., 1976-77, pres., 1977-86; chmn., pres. Preston Trucking, 1986-92; Preston Corp., 1986-93, chmn., 1994—. Home: 3215 Owen Baldwin Pkwy Trinidad CO 81082-9004

POTTER, WILLIAM GRAY, JR. library director; b. Duluth, Minn., Feb. 18, 1950; s. William Gray and Kathryn Martha (Scheuer) P.; m. Marsha Ann Munie, Sept. 23, 1982. BA, So. Ill. U., Edwardsville, 1973; MLS, MA, U. Ill., 1975, PhD, 1984; PhD (hon.), So. Ill. U., Edwardsville, 2001. Libr. U. Wis.-Whitewater, 1975-78; asst. dir. gen. svcs. U. Ill.-Urbana, 1978-85; assoc. dean librs. for tech. svcs., automation and systems Ariz. State U., Tempe, 1985-89; Univ. libr. U. Ga., Athens, 1989—. Editor: Serials Automation, 1980, Libr. Trends, 1981, Info. Tech. and Librs., 1984-89; mem. editl. bd. Multi-Media Rev., 1989-92, OCLC Micro., 1990-93, Libr. Hi-Tech., 1992—, Coll. and Rsch. Libr., 1996-2002. Contbr. articles to profl. jours. Bd. dirs. Richard B. Russell Found., 1989—, sec., 1990—, Southeastern Libr. Network, 2001—; trustee OCLC, 1994-2000; mem. adv. bd. Wiley Libr., 2000-. Recipient Disting. Alumnus of Yr. award So. Ill. U., Edwardsville, 2001. Mem. ALA (Hugh Atkinson Meml. award 1997, Blackwell scholarship award 1998, LITA/Gaylord award 2000), Libr. and Info. Tech. Assn. (pres. 1987-88), OCLC Users Coun. (del. 1990-94, pres. 1991-92), IBM (info. steering com. 1994-95, higher edn. adv. coun. 1995-96), Assn. Rsch. Librs. (bd. dirs. 1996-99), Ga. Libr. Assn. (mem. exec. com. 1994-2000, Nix-Jones award 1998), Beta Phi Mu. Home: 285 Blue Heron Dr Athens GA 30605-4961 E-mail: wpotter@arches.uga.edu.

POTTER, WILLIAM JAMES, investment banker; b. Toronto, Aug. 11, 1948; s. William Wakely and Ruby Loretta (Skidmore) P.; m. Linda Lee, Nov. 25, 1972; children: Lisa Michelle, Meredith Lee, Andrew David. AB, Colgate U., 1970; MBA, Harvard U., 1974. With White Weld & Co., Inc., N.Y.C., 1974-75, Toronto Dominion Bank, Toronto (Can.) and N.Y., 1975-78, group mgr. Toronto, 1979-82; 1st v.p. Barclays Bank PLC, N.Y.C., 1982-84; mng. dir. Prudential-Bache Securities, Inc., 1984-89; pres. Ridgewood Capital Funding Inc., 1989—, Ridgewood Group Internat. Ltd., N.Y.C., 1989—. Advisor Ladenberg Thalman Internat., 1990—92, Laidlaw Holdings, Inc., 1992—93; bd. dirs. Aberdeen Australian Equity Fund Inc., Md., Aberdeen Asia Pacific Income Fund Inc., Md., Aberdeen Asia Pacific Income Fund Ltd., New Zealand, Impulsora del Fondo Mex., Mexico City, Alexandria Bancorp, Canada, Columbus Mills Ltd., Ghana, E.C. Power Inc., First Commonwealth FUnd Inc., Md. Author: Finance for the Minerals Industry, 1985. Trustee Glen Ridge Ednl. Found, 1994—; fin. mem. Glen Ridge Congl. Ch., 1985—; bd. dirs. Glen Ridge (N.J.) Cmty. Fund, 1985—94. Mem.: Nat. Fgn. Trade Coun. (Washington, bd. dirs., chmn. fin. com., exec. com.), Internat. Platform Assn., Econ. Club N.Y., Buck Hill Country Club (Pa.), Glen Ridge Country Club (NJ), Nat. Club (Toronto), Williams Club (N.Y.C.), Harvard Club. Congregationalist. Avocations: golf, tennis. Office: Ridgewood Group Internat Inc 236 W 27th St Fl 3 New York NY 10001-5906

POTTER, WYLIE SHATTUCK, marketing professional; b. Albuquerque, July 31, 1970; s. Earl Wylie Potter, Beverly Baer. Degree in Classical Civilization, Boston U., 1992. Mkt. rschr. Johnson Mktg. Rsch., Oklahoma City, 1995—98; CEO Ecool Corp., El Paso, Tex., 1998—. Author: (book) Ecool, 2001. With U.S. Army, 1992—93. Republican. Roman Catholic. Avocations: Biblical Hebrew, ancient Greek, Arabic. Office: Ecool Corp 1606 E Yandell #4 El Paso TX 79902-5650

POTTERTON, BARBARA ALICE, artist, educator, illustrator; b. San Francisco, Feb. 17, 1930; d. Dale Howard and Marjorie Louise (Wilson) Drullinger; m. Kenneth Eugene Potterton, May 30, 1948; children: Kathleen Dale Millen, Kenneth Leon. Student, San Francisco Jr. Coll., 1947-48. Exclusive Seascape artist for the following galleries: Mendocino (Calif.) Art Ctr., 1965-73, Gallery Mendocino, 1973-90, Jack London Sq. Gallery, Oakland, Calif., 1978-80, Village Artistry, Carmel, Calif., 1979, Winters Gallery, 1980-83, Calico Whale Gallery, Mendocino, 1991-95, Franki Waters Gallery, Bodega Bay, Calif., 1995-96, Color and Light, Mendocino, 1996-97, Gallery One, Mendocino, 1997-2000; tchr. Gallery Mendocino, Plein Air Class, 1975-85, pvt. studio classes, Rancho Cordova, Calif., 1989—; workshop lectr., demonstrator Lincoln City (Oreg.) Art Ctr., 1979, Golden Valley Art Ctr. Yuba City, Calif., 1983-85. Artist specializing in seascape paintings: over 1500 of her paintings are in private collections throughout the world; illustrator: (childrens' books) Song of the Calico Whale, 1995, Watch Out for Tule Petunia, 1997; (interdisciplinary study unit) Journey to Africa, 1996. Recipient Best of Show awards, Roseville, Calif. Art Ctr. 1970, Stanford Ctr., Palo Alto, Calif., 1975; one-woman show Calif. State U., Sacramento, 1978. Mem. Crocker Art Mus., Soc. Marine Painters (Merit award 1970), Nat. Mus. Women in Arts, N.Y. Met. Mus. of Art (assoc.). Avocations: writing, reading, music, gardening, bird watching. Home: 11150 Trinity River Dr #53 Rancho Cordova CA 95670

POTTHOFF, TINA LOUISE, television anchorperson; b. St. Louis, Feb. 4, 1977; d. Ronald Lee and Diane Marie potthoff. BSBA in Mktg. and TV, U. Notre Dame, 1999. Prodr. Sta. WNDU-TV, Notre Dame, Ind., 1997-99; reporter Sta. KTVE-TV, Monroe, La., 1999-2000; TV anchorperson Sta. KOAM-TV, Joplin, Mo., 2000—, host Spotlight on Branson series, 2000—. Pub. speaker, various schs., Joplin, 2000—; mem. media panel Hoby found., Monroe, la., 2000. Vol. Hospice, Joplin, Race for the Cure, Susan B. Komen Found., Monroe, La., 2000; team capt. Walk Am., March of Dimes, Monroe, 2000. Mem. Am. Bus. Women's Assn., Soc. Profl. Journalists (Taishoff fellow 2000), Notre Dame Alumni Assn. Avocations: dancing, reading, yoga, travel. Office: Sta KOAM-TV PO Box 659 Pittsburg KS 66762 E-mail: tinapotthoff@yahoo.com.

POTTIE, ROSWELL FRANCIS, Canadian federal science and technology consultant; b. St. Peter's, N.S., Can., Oct. 28, 1933; s. John Henry and Margaret Mary (Landry) P.; m. Huguette Lacoste, Aug. 18, 1989; children: Michael F., Gregory J., Lisa M., David S. BS in Chemistry summa cum laude, St. Francis Xavier Univ., 1954; PhD in Chemistry, Notre Dame U., 1958. Postdoctoral fellow Notre Dame (Ind.) U., 1957-58, E.I. Du Pont de Nemours, Inc., Wilmington, Del., 1960-64, NRC Can., Ottawa, 1958-60, research officer, 1964-74, asst. to sr. v.p., 1976-80, Atlantic regional dir. Halifax, N.S., 1980-83, v.p. regional labs. Ottawa, 1983-84, v.p. physical scis. and engring., 1984-86, sr. v.p. labs., 1986-87, exec. v.p., 1987-91; pvt. cons., 1991—; program officer Ministry of State for Sci. and Tech. (secondment), Ottawa, 1974-75; program analyst Treasury Bd. Can. (secondment), 1975-76. Bd. govs. Ctr. for Cold Regions Resources Engring., St. John's; mem. N.B. (Can.) Research and Productivity Council, Fredericton, 1981—. Contbr. articles to profl. jours. Coach, exec. baseball, swimming and soccer clubs, Gloucester, Ont., 1970-76; pres. Gloucester Swim Club, 1973-75; exec. North Gloucester Recreation Assn., 1971-74. Recipient Gov. Gen.'s medal, St. Francis Xavier U., 1954. Mem. Can. Research Mgmt. Assn., St. Francis Xavier Alumni Assn. (Ottawa pres. 1970-73), Sigma Xi. Roman Catholic. Avocations: swimming, badminton, carpentry, ancient history. Home: 28 Bellefontaine Ct Lawrencetown NS Canada B2Z 1L3

POTTIER, GERALD J., JR. management consultant; b. Springfield, Mass., July 10, 1946; s. Gerald J. and Florence Lee (Flagg) P.; m. Sharon Lee Weatherby; children— Gerald J., Kelley Scott, Erica. Student Holyoke Community Coll. Mgmt. trainee Friendly's Ice Cream, Wilbraham, Mass., 1969-71; owner restaurant, Cromwell, Conn., 1971-76; state dir. Leisure Life, Inc., Erie, Pa., 1976-80; gen. mgr. Mgmt. Recruiters, Springfield, 1980-83; pres. Consignment Resources, Springfield, 1983—; pres. Gerald J. Pottier Jr. Mgmt. Cons., Pearce, Ariz., 1991—. Served with USMC, 1964-68, Vietnam. Mem. Am. Defense Prepardness Assn., Nat. Security Intelligence Assn., U.S. Defense Com., Old Crows. Mem. Christian Ch. Avocations: bridge; remodeling.

POTTORFF, JO ANN, state legislator; b. Wichita, Kans., Mar. 7, 1936; d. John Edward McCluggage and Helen Elizabeth (Alexander) Ryan; m. Gary Nial Pottorff; children: Michael Lee, Gregory Nial. BA, Kansas State U., 1957; MA, St. Louis U., 1969. Elem. tchr. Pub. Sch., Keats and St. George, 1957-59; cons., elem. specialist Mid Continent Regional Edn. Lab., Kansas City, Mo., 1971-73; cons. Poindexter Assocs., Wichita, 1975; campaign mgr. Garner Shriver Congl. Camp. 1976; interim dir. Wichita Area Rape Ctr., 1977; conf. coord. Biomedical Synergistics Inst., Wichita, 1977-79; real estate sales asst. Chester Kappelman Group, 1979-98, J.P. Weigard & Sons, Wichita, 1998—; state rep. State of Kans., Topeka, 1985—. Mem. exec. com. Nat. Conf. State Legis. Com. Mem. sch. bd. Wichita Pub. Schs., 1977-85; bd. dirs. Edn. Consol. and Improvement Act Adv. com., Kans. Found. for the Handicapped; mem. Children and Youth Adv. com. (bd. dirs.); active Leadership Kans.; chairperson women's network Nat. Conf., State Legislators; mem. Wichita Children's Home Bd.; bd. dirs. Nat. Assessment Governing Bd.; chair edn. com. assembly on state issues Nat. Conf. State legislators. Recipient Disting. Svc. award Kans. Assn. Sch. Bds., 1983, Outstanding Svc. to Sch. Children of Nation award Coun. Urban Bds., 1984, awards Gov.'s Conf. for Prevention of Child Abuse and Neglect, Kans. Assn. Reading. Mem. Leadership Am. Alumnae (bd. dirs., sec) Found. for Agr. in Classroom (bd. dirs.), Jr. League, Vet. Aux. (pres.), Bd. Nat. State Art Agys., Rotary, Ky. Assn. Rehab. Facilities (Ann. award), Nat. Order Women in Legislature (past bd. dirs.), Nat. Conf. State Legislatures (chmn. edn. assembly state issues, exec. com.), Rotary, Chi Omega (pres.). Avocations: politics, traveling. Office: Weigard 6530 E 13th St N Wichita KS 67206-1247

POTTRUCK, DAVID STEVEN, brokerage house executive; b. 1948; BA, U. Pa., 1970, MBA, 1972. Now pres., CEO U.S. Govt., 1972-74; with Arthur Young & Co., 1974-76, sr. cons.; with Citibank N.Am., 1976-81, v.p.; with Shearson/Am. Express, 1981-84, sr. v.p. consumer mktg. and advt.; with Charles Schwab & Co., San Francisco, 1984—; exec. v.p. mktg., br. adminstr. Charles Schwab & Co., Inc.; pres., co-CEO The Charles Schwab and Co., Inc; pres., CEO Charles Schwab & Co. Inc; pres., COO The Charles Schwab Corp., pres., co-CEO. Office: Charles Schwab & Co Inc 101 Montgomery St Ste 200 San Francisco CA 94104-4175*

POTTS, BARBARA ANN, health facility director; b. Poteet, Tex., Apr. 2, 1951; d. William Ira and Margaret Sophia (Lozano) Potts; (divorced); 1 child, Jennifer. BSN, U. Tex., 1975. RN, Tex.; cert. nursing adminstr. Am. Nurses Credentialing Ctr. Nursing house supr. Brackenridge Hosp., Austin, Tex., 1980-84, clin. coord., 1984-87, dir. med./surg. nursing, 1987-93, acting asst. adminstr., 1989-90, dir. nursing adminstrn., 1993-95; dir. nursing practice Seton Healthcare Orgn., 1996—. Mem. ANA, Tex. Nurses Assn. (dist. V, Nurse of Yr. 1990-91), U. Tex.-Austin Sch. Nursing Alumni Assn. (pres. 1990), Tex. Orgn. of Nurse Execs., Sigma Theta Tau (Epsilon chpt.). Home: 5904 Charles Schreiner Trl Austin TX 78749-1931 Office: Brackenridge Hosp Seton Healthcare Network 601 E 15th St Austin TX 78701-1996 E-mail: bapaustin@aol.com.

POTTS, BARBARA JOYCE, retired historical society executive; b. L.A., Feb. 18, 1932; d. Theodore Thomas and Helen Mae (Kelley) Elledge; m. Donald A. Potts, Dec. 27, 1953; children: Tedd, Douglas, Dwight, Laura. AA,

Graceland Coll., 1951; grad., Radiol. Tech. Sch., 1953; grad. program for sr. execs. in state and local govt., Harvard U., 1989. Radiol. technician Independence (Mo.) Sanitarium and Hosp., 1953, 58-59, Mercy Hosp., Balt., 1954-55; city coun. mem.-at-large City of Independence, 1978-82, mayor, 1982-90; exec. dir. Jackson County Hist. Soc., 1991-97; ret., 1997. Chmn. Mid-Am. Regional Coun., Kansas City, Mo., 1984-85; bd. dirs. Mo. Mcpl. League, Jefferson City, 1982-90, v.p., 1986-87, pres., 1987, 88; chmn. Mo. Commn. on Local Govt. Cooperation, 1985-90; chair ind. adv. bd. Mercantile Bank, 1997-99; bd. dirs. Women's Found. of Greater Kansas City, 1997—; mem. chancellor's adv. bd. UMKC Women's Ctr., 1996—; mem. adv. bd. Comprehensive Mental Health Svcs., 1997—. Author: Independence, 1985. Mem. Mo. Gov.'s Conf. Edn., 1976, Independence Charter Rev. Bd., 1977; bd. dirs. Hope House Shelter Abused Women, Independence, 1982—, Vis. Nurses Assn., 1990-93, Mid-Continent coun. U.S. Girl Scouts, 1991-95, adv. bd. Ewing M. Kauffman Fund, 2002—, Greater Kansas City Cmty. Found., 1999—, Salvation Army, 1999—; pres. Child Placement Svcs., Independence, 1972-89, Greater Kansas City region NCCJ, 1990—; bd. dirs. Harry S. Truman Libr. Inst., 1995—, Truman Med. Ctr., 2001—, Coun. on Philanthropy, 2001—; bd. vis. UMKC Sch. Medicine, 2002—; trustee Independence Regional Health Ctr., 1982-90, 94-2001; trustee Park Coll., 1989-99, chmn. bd. trustees, 1995-99; mem. Nat. Women's Polit. Caucus, 1978—; mem. adv. bd. Greater Mo. Focus on Leadership, mem. steering com., 1989—; bd. dirs. Truman Heartland Cmty. Found., 1990—, bd. chmn., 1997-99; trustee Eye Found. Kansas City, 1997-99. Recipient George Lehr Meml. award for cmty. svc., 1989, Woman of Achievement award Mid-Continent coun. Girl Scouts U.S.A., 1983, 75th Anniversary Women of Achievement award Mid-Continent coun. Girl Scouts, 1987, Jane Adams award Hope House, 1984, Cmty. Leadership award Comprehensive Mental Health Svcs., Inc., 1984, 90, Graceland Coll. Alumni Disting. Svc. award 1991, Disting. Citizen award Independence C. of C., 1993, Outstanding Cmty. Svc. award Jackson County Inter-Agy. Coun., 1994, Outstanding Cmty. Svc. award Cmty. Svcs. League, 1996, Jackson County Humanitarian of Yr. award, 1997, Disting. Citizen award, 1997, Paul Harris award Ind. Rotary Club, 1997, Outstanding Svc. award City of Independence Human Rels. Commn., 1999, Greater Kans. City Coun. Philanthropy Vol. of Yr. award, 2000; named Friend of Edn. Indpendence NEA, 1990. Mem. LWV (Community Svc. award 1990), Central Exchange, Jackson County Historical Soc., Nat. Trust for Hist. Preservation. Mem. Reorganized Lds Ch. Home: 18508 E 30th Ter S Independence MO 64057-1904

POTTS, BILLIE LUISI, college administrator; b. N.Y.C., Mar. 5, 1940; d. Harold and Esther Malka (Ulano) Meisner; m. Carmen John Luisi, May 18, 1962 (div. Jan. 1972); 1 child, Thecla Luisi. AB, Hunter Coll., N.Y.C., 1962; AM, Fordham U., Bronx, N.Y., 1964. Dir. tng. and tech. assistance Ctr. for Women in Govt., U. Albany, N.Y., 1986-91; dir. devel. Catskill Area Hospice, Oneonta, 1994-98, Regents Coll., Albany, 1999—2001; exec. dir. Nat. Women's Hall of Fame, Seneca Falls, NY, 2001—. Cons. human resources Developmental Dynamics, Summit, N.Y., 1979—. Author: A First Book of Clay, 1973, Small Scale Goatkeeping, 1979, 84, Ergonomics: A Problem Solver's Handbook. Mem. bd. Rotary of Seneca Falls. Winifred Found. grantee, Wainscott, N.Y., 1998. Mem. Kingston Sunrise Rotary (newsletter editor 1997—). Jewish. Avocations: gardening, hiking, sculpture, painting. Home: PO Box 293 Summit NY 12175-0293 Office: Nat. Womens Hall of Fame 76 Fall St Seneca Falls NY 13148

POTTS, CAROL JEAN FOX, geriatrics nurse, quality assurance coordinator; b. Plainwell, Mich., Jan. 26, 1954; d. Edward Iman and Grace (Dendel) Fox.; m. Stephen Potts, Dec. 1, 1978; children: Michael, Jonathan. BSN, U. N.Mex. Coll. Nursing, 1983. Clin. specialist, substance abuse instr. Pine Rest Christian Hosp., 1983-85; nursing quality assurance coord. Mich. Vets. Facility, Grand Rapids, 1985-91. Innovations panel presenter Nat. Quality Assurance Forum, Milw., 1990. Contbr. articles to profl. jours. Mem. APHA, Am. Soc. on Aging. Home: 1711 Kentucky Ave Saint Cloud FL 34769-5109

POTTS, CHARLES AARON, management executive, writer, publishing executive; b. Idaho Falls, Idaho, Aug. 28, 1943; s. Verl S. and Sarah (Gray) Potts; m. Judith Samimi, 1977 (div. 1986); children: Emily Karen, Natalie Larise; m. Ann Weatherill, June 19, 1988. BA in English, Idaho State U., 1965. Lic. real estate broker Wash. Owner Palouse Mgmt., Inc., Walla Walla, Wash., 1979—; pres. Walla Walla Rental Properties, 1984-86; dir. Washington Apt. Assocs., 1984-88. Founder, dir. Litmus Inc., 1967—77; founding editor COSMEP, Berkeley, Calif., 1968; host poetry radio program Oasis NPR-KUER, Salt Lake City, 1976—77; N.W. rep. Chinese Computer Comm., Inc., Lansing, Mich., 1988—94; pres. Tsunami Inc. Author: Blues from Thurston County, 1966, Burning Snake, 1967, The Litmus Papers, 1969, Little Lord Shiva, 1969, Blue Up the Nile, 1972, Waiting in Blood, 1973, The Trancermigracion of Menzu, 1973, The Golden Calf, 1975, Charlie Kiot, 1976, The Opium Must Go Thru, 1976, Valga Krusa, 1977, Rocky Mountain Man, 1978, A Rite to the Body, 1989, The Dictatorship of the Environment, 1991, Loading Las Vegas, 1991, How the South Finally Won the Civil War, 1995, 100 Years in Idaho, 1996, Lost River Mountain, 1999, Facist Haikus, 1999, Little Lord Shiva: The Berkeley Poems, 1968, 1999, Angio Gram, 2000, Nature Lovers, 2000, prophet/profit, 2001, Slash and Burn, 2001, Across the Pacific, 2002, Lucintite, 2002; editor: Pacific Northwestern Spiritual Poetry, 1998, The Temple, 1997—2002; columnist (with Kyushu Gleaner): Japan's Polit. Choices, 1995—. Rep. to exec. com. 5th Congl. Dist., Wash. State Dems., 1993—95. Recipient Profl. Achievement award, Idaho State U., 1994. Mem.: Soc. Neurolinguistic Programming (master practitioner), Chinese Lang. Computer Soc., Pacific N.W. Booksellers Assn., Toastmasters, Fukuoka Internat. Forum, Blue Mountain Arts Alliance, Downtown W2 Found., Walla Walla Area C. of C., Italian Heritage Assn. (ice cream chair 1990, award 1993). Avocations: tennis, raspberries. Office: Palouse Mgmt Inc 129 E Alder St PO Box 1773 Walla Walla WA 99362-1962 E-mail: tsunami@innw.net.

POTTS, DENNIS WALKER, lawyer; b. Santa Monica, Calif., Dec. 17, 1945; s. James Longworth and Donna (Neely) P.; m. Chung Wan; children: Brandon Earl Woodward, Trevor Shipley. BA, U. Calif., Santa Barbara, 1967; JD, U. Calif., San Francisco, 1970. Bar: Hawaii 1971, Calif. 1971, U.S. Dist. Ct. Hawaii 1971, U.S. Ct. Appeals (9th cir.) 1973, U.S. Supreme Ct. 1978, U.S. Dist. Ct. (cen. dist.) Calif. 1983. Assoc. Chuck Mau, Honolulu, 1971-74; sole practice, 1974—. Mem. litigation com. ACLU Hawaii, 1977-82; former mem. Hawaii Acad. Plaintiff's Attys. Disting. Svc. Cert. ACLU Hawaii. Fellow Internat. Napoleonic Soc.; mem. ATLA (sustaining), Consumer Lawyers Hawaii, Honolulu Club. Office: 2755 Pacific Tower 1001 Bishop St Honolulu HI 96813-3429

POTTS, GERALD NEAL, manufacturing company executive; b. Franklin, N.C., Apr. 10, 1933; s. Joseph Thomas and Virgie (Bryant) P.; m. Ann Eliza Underwood, Dec. 21, 1956 (div. 1991); children: Catherine, Thomas, Alice. BS, U. N.C., 1954; grad., Advanced Mgmt. Program, Harvard, 1973. With Vulcan Mold & Iron Co., Chgo., 1957-59, sales engr., 1959-62, gen. sales mgr. Pa., 1963-65, v.p. sales, 1965-68; v.p. Vulcan, Inc., Latrobe, 1968-72, exec. v.p., 1972-73, pres., 1973-85, chief exec. officer, 1977-85, chmn., 1981-85; group exec. Teledyne Inc., 1985-92; pres. Woodings Verona Tool Works Inc., 1993-97. Bd. dirs. Latrobe Area Hosp., 1967—, chmn., 1985-88; trustee Greater Latrobe Community Chest, 1970-87, pres., 1978-79; adv. bd. U. Pitts. at Greensburg, 1974-80; trustee Seton Hill Coll., Greensburg, 1978-80. Served with AUS, 1954-56. Mem.: Duquesne Club (Pa.), Rolling Rock Club, Chi Phi.

POTTS, GLENDA RUE, music educator; b. Butler, Ala., Nov. 26; d. Jennings Herschel and Erma Rue (Holdridge) Moseley; m. Billy Wayne Blackwell, June 23, 1963 (div. Aug. 1977); children: William Stephen, Melton Jennings; m. Willis Jones Potts, Jr., July 13, 1985; 1 stepchild, Timothy Brendon. BM in Music, Auburn U., 1963. Organist Beverly Meth. Ch., Birmingham, 1964-65; music tchr. grades 3-8 Birmingham Pub. Schs., 1964-65; music tchr. grades 7-9 Chattanooga Pub. Schs., 1965-66; tchr., owner piano/pipe organ studio Kreative Keyboards, Prattville, Ala., 1967-93, Savannah, 1993-99, Rome, 1999—. Owner piano/organ studio, Prattville, 1967-93. Pipe organist 1st Bapt. Ch., Prattville, 1969-85, 87-93, music asst. dir., 1980-85; pianist, dir. children's choirs, asst. organist Bull St. Bapt. Ch., Savannah, 1995-99; sec., mem. chair Savannah Symphony Women's Guild, 1993-99; soprano Savannah Symphony Chorale, 1993-94; mem. chair Savannah Newcomer's, 1994-95; substitute organist and pianist First Baptist Ch., Rome, Ga., 2000-. Honored as one of Top 400 Women Grads. of Centennial of Admission of Women Students, Auburn U., 1992. Mem. Ga. Music Tchrs. Assn. (pres. Savannah chpt. 1997-99, pres. Rome chpt. 2001—), Music Tchrs. Nat. Assn. (nat. and state cert. tchr. and adjudicator), Nat. Guild of Piano Tchrs. (nat. and state cert. tchr. and adjudicator, established audition ctrs., chmn. Prattville 1967-93, Rome area fall 2001—, Hall of Fame 1990), Am. Coll. Musicians. Republican. Baptist. Home: 2614 Horseleg Creek Rd SW Rome GA 30165-8583

POTTS, GLENN THOMAS, economics educator; b. Hoopeston, Ill., Jan. 11, 1950; s. Edgar Walter and Maxine (Menogh) P.; m. Jennette Kay Ramsey, Jan. 16, 1971; children: Edward, Mary. BA, MacMurray Coll., Jacksonville, Ill., 1972; MS, Iowa State U., 1974, PhD, 1976. Prof. econs. U. Wis., River Falls, 1976—. Dir. Investment Workshop, River Falls, 1987-90; assoc. dir. Ctr. for Pacific Rim Studios, River Falls, 1990—. Contbr. articles to profl. jours. Named Disting. Tchr. of Yr., U. Wis.-River Falls, 1982, Outstanding Tchr., 1989. Mem. Am. Econs. Assn. Office: U Wis River Falls Econs Dept River Falls WI 54022

POTTS, HAROLD FRANCIS, JR. elevator company executive; b. Pittsfield, Mass., July 25, 1955; s. Harold Francis and Dorothy (Anderson) P.; m. Annie Laura Towle, May 14, 1977; children: David Francis, Douglas Norman, Joseph Harold. AA, Holyoke (Mass.) Community Coll, 1975; BS in BA, We. New Eng. Coll., Springfield, Mass., 1977; MBA, We. New Eng. Coll., 1989. Sales rep. Bay State Elevator Co., Springfield, Mass., 1977-81, customer svc. mgr., 1981-84, v.p., treas., 1984-91; pres., 1991—; bd. dirs. Bay State Elevator Co., 1986—; treas., bd. dirs. Air Flyte, Inc., Westfield, Mass., 1989—. Bd. dirs. Nat. Elevator Industry, Inc. Sec. sch. bldg. com. Town of Granville, Mass., 1987-90, mem. fin. bd., 1988-89, moderator, 1990-91; mem. ops. com. Mt. Washington Obs., 1992-93, trustee, 1993-94; mem. devel. com. The Master's Sch., 1991-93, trustee, 1993-99, treas., 1994-99. Mem. Assn. Am. Weather Observers (v.p. 1988-89, 92-93, sec. 1991-92), Internat. Weather Watchers. Republican. Avocations: hiking, camping, computers, weather observation. Home: PO Box 6 West Suffield CT 06093-0006 Office: Bay State Elevator Co PO Box 910 Agawam MA 01001-0910

POTTS, RAMSAY DOUGLAS, lawyer, aviator; b. Memphis, Oct. 24, 1916; s. Ramsay Douglas and Ann Clifton (VanDyke) P.; m. Veronica Hamilton Raynor, Dec. 22, 1945 (dec. May 1993); children: Ramsay Douglas, David Hamilton, Lesley Ann, Lindsay Veronica. BS, U. N.C., 1941; LL.B., Harvard U., 1948. Bar: Tenn. 1948, D.C. 1954, U.S. Supreme Ct. 1957. Commd. 2d lt. USAAF, 1941, advanced through grades to maj. gen. Res., 1961; various combat and operational assignments (8th Air Force and Air Force Res.), 1942-60; chmn. Air Force Res. Policy Com., 1967-68; practice law, Washington, 1955—; spl. asst. to chmn. Nat. Security Resources Bd., 1951; pres. Ind. Mil. Air Transport Assn., 1952-55; ptnr. Shaw, Pittman, Potts & Trowbridge, 1956-86, sr. counsel, 1986—. Publisher: Air Power History, 1989-93; contbr. articles to profl. jours. Mem. State Council Higher Edn. for Va., 1968-71; Trustee Air Force Hist. Found., pres., 1971-75; pres. Washington Area Tennis Patrons Found., 1984-87; trustee emeritus. Physicians for Peace, 199789—. Decorated D.S.C., other combat decorations Mem. ABA, D.C. Bar Assn., Met. Club (Washington), Army Navy Country Club (Arlington, Va.), Internat. Lawn Tennis Club (U.S., Gt. Brit., India), Phi Beta Kappa. Home: 2818 27th St N Arlington VA 22207-4921 Office: Shaw Pittman Potts & Trowbridge 2300 N St NW Washington DC 20037-1172

POTTS, ROBERT LESLIE, academic administrator; b. Huntsville, Ala., Jan. 30, 1944; s. Frank Vines and Helen Ruth (Butler) P.; m. Irene Elisabeth Johansson, Aug. 22, 1965; children: Julie Anna, Robert Leslie. Student Newbold Coll., Eng., 1963-64; BA, So. Coll., 1966; JD, U. Ala., 1969; LLM, Harvard U., 1971. Law clk. to chief judge U.S. Dist. Ct. (no. dist.) Ala., 1969-70; researcher Herrick, Smith, Donald, Farley & Ketchum, Boston, 1970-71; lectr. Boston U., 1971, U. Ala., 1973-75, 88; ptnr. Potts & Young , Florence, Ala., 1971-84; gen. counsel U. Ala. System, 1984-89, pres. U. North Ala., 1990—; mem. Nat. Adv. Com. on Instnl. Quality and Integrity, 1994-2001; mem. commn. on colls. So. Assn. Colls. and Schs., 2001--; chair Nat. ROTC subcom. for Sec. of Army, 1999-2001; bd. dirs. Bank Ind., Florence, 1975-85; adv. com. Rules Civil Procedure, Ala. Supreme Ct., 1973-88; mem. Ala. Bd. Bar Examiners, 1973-79, chmn., 1983-86; trustee Nat. Conf. Bar Examiners, 1986-96, chmn., 1994-95; trustee Ala. State U., 1976-79, Oakwood Coll., 1978-81; pres. Ala. Higher Edn. Loan Corp., 1988-93. Mem. ABA (ho. of dels. 2001--), Ala. Bar Assn. (pres. young lawyers sect. 1979-80). Contbr. numerous articles to profl. jours., edn. and schs. Office: U North Ala PO Box 5004 Florence AL 35632-0001 E-mail: rpotts@unanov.una.edu.

POTTS, RONALD CLYDE, computer programmer, analyst; b. Macon, Ga., Apr. 27, 1952; s. James Herbert and Dorothy June (Brown) P.; m. Gloria Ann Lewis Simpson, July 7, 1990 (div. Sept. 2001); 1 former stepchild, Rebekah Andromeche Simpson. BS in Orgnl. Mgmt., Columbia Union Coll., Takoma Park, Md., 1992. Computer operator and programmer Clemson (S.C.) U., 1972-78; computer programmer, analyst project mgr. SMC-Fed. Sys., New Carrollton, Md., 1978-82; computer programmer, analyst p project mgr. DDD Co., 1982-86; computer programmer, analyst cons., Washington, 1986-87; computer programmer, analyst task leader Lamarian Sys., 1987-90; computer programmer, analyst Washington Post, 1990-95. Anti-racism lectr., 1995; laborer for day Christmas in April, Columbia, Md., 1995, 96. Democrat. Avocations: anti-discrimination activism, peace and justice advocacy, psychology, theology, writing.

POTTS, STEPHEN DEADERICK, lawyer; b. Memphis, Nov. 20, 1930; s. Ramsay Douglas and Anne (Van Dyke) P.; m. Irene Potter, Mar. 14, 1953; children: Lori Potts-Dupre, Stephen Deaderick Jr., Stacy Potts Krogh. AB, Vanderbilt U., 1952, LLB, 1954. Bar: Tenn. 1954, D.C. 1961. Assoc. Farris, Evans & Evans, Nashville, 1957-61; ptnr. Shaw, Pittman, Potts & Trowbridge, Washington, 1961-90; dir. U.S. Office Gov. Ethics, 1990-2000; chmn. fellows program, sr. ethics counselor Ethics Resource Ctr., 2001—. Past mem. Pres.'s Coun. on Integrity and Efficiency, Pres.'s Commn. on the Fed. Appt. Process. Past pres. Washington Tennis Patrons Found., 1970-72; mem. ethics oversight com. U.S. Olympic Com. 1st lt. U.S. Army, 1954-57. Mem. ABA, U.S. Supreme Ct. Bar Assn., D.C. Bar Assn., Chevy Chase Club (bd. govs. 1982-86), Met. Club (bd. govs. 2000), Alibi Club, U.S. Tennis Assn. (bd. dirs., won 5 nat., 1 internat. father/son championships, twice ranked 1st in U.S.). Methodist. Office: Ethics Resource Ctr Ste 400 1747 Pennsylvania Ave Washington DC 20006 E-mail: steve@ethics.org., sdpotts@attglobal.net.

POTUZNIK, CHARLES LADDY, lawyer; b. Chgo., Feb. 11, 1947; s. Charles William and Laverne Frances (Zdenek) P.; m. Mary Margaret Quady, Jan. 2, 1988; children: Kylie Brommell, Kathryn Mary. BA with high honors, U. Ill., 1969; JD cum laude, Harvard U., 1973. Bar: Minn. 1973. Assoc. Dorsey & Whitney LLP, Mpls., 1973-78, ptnr., 1979—. Co-head Broker-Dealer and Investment Markets Regulation Practice Group. Mem. Minn. State Bar Assn. (chmn. state securities law subcom. 1987-2000), Hennepin County Bar Assn., Minn. Securities Adv. Com., Phi Beta Kappa. Mem. Evang. Free Ch. Avocations: hunting, fishing, camping, canoeing, foreign travel. Office: Dorsey & Whitney LLP 50 South Sixth St Minneapolis MN 55402-1498 E-mail: potuznik.charles@dorseylaw.com.

POTVIN, ALFRED RAOUL, engineering executive; m. Janet Holm, Mar. 20, 1965 BEE, Worcester Poly. Inst., 1964; MEE, Stanford U., 1965, Engr. in EE, 1967; MS in Bioengring., MS in Psychology, U. Mich., 1970, PhD in Bioengring., 1971. Registered profl. engr., Tex. Asst. prof. elec. engring. U. Tex., Arlington, 1966-68, assoc. prof. biomed. engring. and elec. engring., 1971-76, prof., 1976-84, chmn. biomed. engring., 1972-84; dir. med. instrumentation systems research div. Eli Lilly & Co., Indpls., 1984-90, dir. tech. assessment and project mgmt., 1990-92; dir. engring., med. devices and diagnostics divsn., 1992-93; prof. elec. engring. Purdue Sch. Engring. and Tech., Ind. U.-Purdue U., Indpls., 1993-96; dean Ind. U.-Purdue U., 1993-96; pres. MEECO, Sarasota, Fla., 1996—. Faculty fellow, life scientist, cons. NASA, Houston, 1972-76, NASA and Moffett Field, 1974-76; clin. prof. biophysics U. Tex. Health Sci. Ctr., Dallas, 1967-84; mem. phys. med. device panel FDA, Washington, 1978-84; mem. adv. bd., reviewer Biomed. Engring. NSF, Washington, 1983-89, 92-97; founding dir. Ctr. Advanced Rehab. Engring., 1983-84, mem. adv. bd., 1984-88; mem. adv. bd. Engring. Rsch. Ctrs. NSF, Washington, 1988-92, Biomed. Engr. Worcester Polytech. Inst., Mass., 1987—, Coll. Engrs. Duke U., Durham, N.C., 1987-94, U. Calif., Berkeley, 1989-92, Coll. Engrs. U. Denver, 1990-93, Sch. Engr. and Tech. Ind. U.-Purdue U., Indpls, 1992-93, med. engring. Jet Propulsion Lab., Pasadena, Calif., 1989; chmn. NIH Resource Ctr. Case Western Res. U., Cleve., 1988-96; bd. advisors Sch. of Health and Rehab. Sci., U. Pitts., 1993-97; mem. adv. com. NIH, 1993, 95; bd. dirs. Biomed. Engring. Alliance for Conn., 2000—. Author: (with W.W. Tourtellotte) Quantitative Examination of Neurologic Functions, 1985; editl. bd. IEEE Spectrum, 1987-90, 92-95, Biomed. Sci. and Tech., 1990-93; co-editor spl. issue on biosensors IEEE Trans. on Biomed. Engring., 1986, spl. issue on status and future directions in biomed. engring. Medicine and Biol. Mag., 1989; mem. editl. bd. Biomed. Sci. and Tech., 1990-92; mem. adv. bd. The Biomed. Engring. Handbook, 1995, 2000. Mem. Masthead Property Owners Assn., Indpls., 1984-96, Manasota Key Property Owners Assn., Englewood, Fla., 1985-98. Recipient Life Scientist award NASA, 1974; spl. fellow NIH, 1968. Fellow IEEE (pres. Engring. in Medicine and Biology Soc. 1983, re-elected 1984, gen. chmn. annual conf. 1982, chmn. health care engring. com. 1986, mem. editorial bd. spectrum 1987-89, 92-94, founding mem. steering com. symposium on computer based med. systems 1988-94, Centennial award 1984, co-editor spl. issue Medicine and Biology, 1989, mem. internat. conf. com. 1993—), Am. Inst. Med. and Biol. Engring. (bd. dirs. 1991-94, v.p. pub. awareness 1993-94, elected founding fellow 1992, co-pres. world congress on med. biological engring. in Chgo in the yr. 2000, 1993-1999, devel. com. 1996-99), Houston Soc. Engrs. in Medicine and Biology (Career Achievement award 1993), Assn. Advancement of Med. Instrumentation; mem. Am. Soc. Engring. Edn. (chmn. biomed. engring. div. 1979-80), Biomed. Engring. Soc. (sr. mem. 1972-88, chmn. edn. and pub. affairs com. 1979-83), Alliance Engrs. in Medicine and Biology (v.p. nat. affairs 1987-89, pres. 1989-92), Assn. Advancement of Med. Instrumentation, Ind. Elec. Mfg. Assn. (bd. dirs. 1993-96, Svc. to Industry award 1996), Presdl. Founders Worcester Poly. Inst., Appalachian Trail Club, Freedom Boat Club, Ski Club Sarasota. Avocations: boating, travel, gourmet dining, skiing.

POTVIN, FELIX, professional hockey player; b. Anjou, Que., Canada, July 23, 1971; Goalie Chicoutimi, QMJHL, 1988-91, St. John's, AHL, 1991-92, Toronto Maple Leafs, 1991-99, N.Y. Islanders, 1999, Vancouver Canucks, 1999—2001, L.A. Kings, 2001—. Recipient Goaltender of the Year Award, Can. Hockey League, 1990-91, Hap Emms Mem. Trophy, 1990-91, Jacques Plante Trophy, 1990-91, Shell Cup, 1990-91, Guy Lafleur Trophy, 1990-91, Baz Bastien Trophy, 1991-92, Dudley Garrett Mem. Trophy, 1991-92. Achievements include All-Star first team goalie, QMJHL, 1990-91, All-Star first team goalie, AHL, 1991-92, All-Rookie Team, NHL, 1992-93. Office: LA Kings Staples Center 1111 S. Figueroa St. Los Angeles CA 90015*

POTVIN, PIERRE, physiologist, educator; b. Quebec City, Que., Can., Jan. 5, 1932; s. Rosario and Eva (Montreuil) P.; m. Louise Dube, Aug. 31, 1963; children: Aline, Bernard. BA, Laval U., 1950, MD, 1955; PhD, U. Toronto, 1962. Asst. prof. Faculty of Medicine Laval U., Quebec City, 1956-63, assoc. prof., 1963-68, prof., 1968-98, prof. emeritus, 1998—, vice dean exec., 1977-86, dean, 1986-94. V.p. Internat. Conf. of Deans of French-Speaking Faculties of Medicine, 1990-96, pres. evaluation coun., 1994—; hon. prof. Norman Bethune U. Med. Sci., Changchun, China, 1992. Assoc. editor Modern Medicine Can., 1958-61, Laval Med., 1962-70. Decorated comdr. Ordre Nat. des Palmes académiques (France), officer Ordre Nat. du Lion (Senegal). Fellow Royal Coll. Physicians and Surgeons Can.; mem. Order of Can. Roman Catholic. Avocation: painting. Home: 1915 Bourbonniere Sillery QC Canada G1S 1N3 Office: Laval U Faculty of Medicine Dept Anat & Physiology Quebec QC Canada G1K 7P4

POTVIN, WILLIAM TRACEY, management consultant; b. Milw., June 20, 1951; s. William John and Joan (Wach) P.; m. Louisa I. Vorosmarty, July 23, 1983. BS in Internat. Econs., Georgetown U., 1973; MBA, Am. U., 1975. Investment mgr. GEICO, Washington, 1973-78; mgmt. cons. Touche Ross & Co. (now Deloitte & Touch LLP), N.Y.C., 1978-85, ptnr., 1985-2000; nat. dir. Fin. Inst. Cons., 1987-90; mng. ptnr., CEO Deloitte & Touche CIS, Moscow, 1990-96; nat. dir. Deloitte & Touche Actuarial and Ins. Cons. Group, N.Y.C., 1996-99; ret. ptnr. Deloitte & Touche, 2000—; pres., CEO The ESP Group LLC, Arlington, Va., 1999—. Chmn. adv. group to Russian govt. on mass privatization World Bank, 1992-94, acting CFO Russian Privitization Ctr., 1996; speaker to ins. groups, N.Y.C., 1985—. Contbr. articles to profl. jours. Bd. dirs. Am. Russian Youth Orch., 1996—. Mem. Coll. of Ins. (mem. fin. industries task force 1985-90, lectr. 1985-90). Roman Catholic. Office: The ESP Group LLC Ste 1103 1225 Jeff Davis Hwy Arlington VA 22202 also: The ESP Group LLC 76 Chestnut Ridge Rd Armonk NY 10504-3001 E-mail: wpotvin@espgroup.net., potvin@msn.com.

POU, LINDA G. interior designer, architectural designer; b. Huntsville, Ala., Oct. 26, 1942; d. Louis and Lillian Maurice (Garvin) Grabensteder; m. Robert LeRoy Pou, Aug. 27, 1965; children: Susan Caroline, Stephanie Lynn. B of Interior Design, Auburn U., 1964; postgrad., Ecoles D'Art Americaines, 1964. Interior designer Martin Interiors, Huntsville, 1963, Blance Reeves Interiors, Atlanta, 1964-65, Militare, Atlanta, 1965, Loveman's Dept. Store, Huntsville, 1966, Southea. Galleries, Charleston, S.C., 1967; draftsman Brown Engring., Huntsville, 1967-68, Naval Electronics Systems Command, S.C., 1968, Leland Engrs., Charleston, 1968-69; owner Drafting Svc., Mobile, Ala., 1977-78, The Design Svc., Prattville, 1980-92, Savannah, Ga., 1992—. Composer songs including (adult anthems), Sing for Joy, 1983, Sing Hallelujah to the Lord, He's the Rainbow in My Life, 1984, (children's)_Lord of Harvest, 1984, Sing a Song to the Lord of Earth, 1985, (children's musical) Six Myths of Christmas, 1986; compiler and editor book of poetry, Nana's Legacy. Mem. jr. bd. Florence Crittendon Home for Unwed Mothers, Mobile, Ala., 1977-79, Prattville Planning Commn., 1980-92, chmn., 1985-88, vice-chmn., 1988-92; mem. Prattville Hist. Re-devel. Authority, 1988-89; children's choir dir. 1st United MEth. Ch., 1979-83, 87-89, adminstrv. bd., 1987-89, bldg. commn., 1987-89, trustee, 1990-92; mem. Savannah Symphony Women's Guild, 1993-95. Mem. ASCAP, Spinners (treas. 1982-83), Prattville C. of C., Garden Club of Savannah (2nd v.p. 1995-97, pres. 1997-99), Charlton Forge Garden Club (1st v.p. 2000, pres. 2000—), Alpha Gamma Delta. Avocations: reading, gardening, playing the piano, singing. Home and Office: 980 Marbury Ct SW Marietta GA 30064-2991

POUCHER, JOHN SCOTT, systems engineer, physicist; b. Evanston, Ill., Apr. 10, 1945; s. George Edward and Marcia Irene (Smith) P.; m. Lois Miriam Gross, Aug. 2, 1969; children: Gregory Evan, Brian Eric. BS, MIT, 1967, PhD, 1971. Instr. in physics MIT, Cambridge, Mass., 1971-74; asst. prof. physics Vanderbilt U., Nashville, 1974-80; mem. tech. staff AT&T Bell Labs., Holmdel, N.J., 1981-86, disting. mem. tech. staff, 1986-96, technology cons., 1996-98; network svcs. arch. Cisco Sys., Freehold, NJ, 1998—2002, team leader, 2002—. Vis. fellow Cornell U., Ithaca, N.Y., 1978-79. Contbr. articles to Phys. Rev. Letters, Phys. Letters, Phys. Rev., other jours. and confs. Mem. IEEE, AIAA, AAAS, Am. Phys. Soc., Union Concerned Scientists, Fedn. Am. Scientists, Common Cause, Sigma Xi. Achievements include architect for high speed data network services, strategic planning for high tech government projects, operations systems planning; research in electron-positron annihilation, deep-inelastic electron-nucleon scattering and nucleic acid structure. E-mail: poucher@alum.mit.edu.

POUL, FRANKLIN, lawyer; b. Phila., Nov. 6, 1924; s. Boris and Anna P.; m. Shirley Weissman, June 26, 1949; children— Leslie Poul Melman, Alan M., Laurie. Student, U. Pa., 1942-43, Haverford Coll., 1943-44; LL.B. cum laude, U. Pa., 1946. Bar: Pa. 1949, U.S. Supreme Ct. 1955. Asso. firm Gray, Anderson, Schaffer & Rome, Phila., 1948-56, Wolf, Block, Schorr and Solis-Cohen, Phila., 1956-60, partner, 1960-93. Bd. dirs. ACLU, Phila., 1955-80, pres., 1975-76. Served with AUS, 1943-46. Mem. ABA, Am. Law Inst., Order of Coif. Office: Wolf Block Shorr & Solis-Cohen 1650 Arch St Philadelphia PA 19103-2097

POULEUR, HUBERT GUSTAVE, cardiologist, consultant; b. Bouffioulx, Belgium, June 6, 1948; m. Michelle Leonet, July 7, 1973; children: Anne-Catherine, Jean-Hubert. MD, U. Louvain, Belgium, 1973, PhD, 1980. Intern, resident, then fellow in internal medicine U. Louvain, Belgium, 1973-77; Pub. Health Service internat. research fellow U. Calif, San Diego, 1977-79; asst. prof. U. Louvain, Brussels, 1979-83, assoc. prof., 1983-91, prof., 1991-94; assoc. dir. clin. rsch. Pfizer Inc., Groton, Conn., 1993-95; v.p. cardiovascular clin. R&D Bristol-Myers Squibb, Princeton, N.J., 1996-2000; sr. med. dir. cardiovasc. and metabolic group Pfizer Inc., N.Y.C., 2001—. Disting. clin. scientist Syntex Clin. Rsch., Palo Alto, Calif., Maidenhead, U.K., 1988-93.

Contbr. numerous sci. articles to profl. jours. Recipient Damman prize Damman Found., 1977, Bekales prize Bekales Found., 1986; Squibb Cardiovascular fellow Belgian Soc. Cardiology, 1982. Fellow Am. Coll. Cardiology; mem. Am. Heart Assn. (fellow Coun. of Circulation, fellow Coun. Clin. Cardiology), Atlantic Salmon Fedn., Trout Unltd. Avocation: fly fishing. Home: 43 Woodlane Rd Lawrenceville NJ 08648-5544 E-mail: hubert.pouleur@pfizer.com.

POULIN, MARIE-PAULE, Canadian government official; b. Sudbury, Ont., Can., June 21, 1945; d. Alphonse-Emile and Lucille (Ménard) Charette; m. Bernard A. Poulin, May 21, 1977; children: Elaine, Valérie. BA magna cum laude, Laurentian U., Sudbury, 1966; MSW, U. Montréal, Que., Can., 1969; PhD (hon.), Laurentian U., Sudbury, 1995. Lectr. U. Montreal, 1969-70, Coll. of Gen. and Profl. Instrn., Hull, Que., 1972-73; rschr. Ctr. Social Svcs., 1972-73; interviewer, rschr. French Radio and TV, Ottawa, Ont., 1973-74; prodr. Sta. CBOF-CBC, 1974-78; founder and dir. svcs. in N.E. and N.W. Ont. Sta. CBON (French Network-CBC), Sudbury, 1978-83; exec. dir. regional programming CBC, Ottawa, 1983-84, assoc. v.p. regional broadcasting, 1984-88, sec. gen., 1988-90, v.p. human resources, 1990-92; dep. sec. for comm. and consultation The Privy Coun. Govt. of Can., 1992-93; chmn., CEO Can. Artists and Prodrs. Profl. Rels. Tribunal, 1993-95; senator Can. Govt., 1995—. Mem. Senate Standing com. Internal Economy, Budgets and Adminstrn., Banking, Trade and Commerce, Rules, Procedures and the Rights of Parliament; former chair Senate Standing Com. on Transport and Comms., Can.'s Competitive Position in Comms.; bd. dirs. Cité Collégiale, Ottawa, 1988-91; mem. Fedn. Can.-France; hon. co-chair Heart & Soul Campaign. Commr. for French lang. svcs. Province of Ont., 1986-89; regent U. Sudbury, 1981-83; bd. dirs. Laurentian Hosp., Sudbury, 1980-88, Cambrian Coll-.Found., Sudbury, 1983-88; v.p. Art Ctr., Ottawa, 1988-90; pres. Regroupement gens d'affaires, Ottawa, 1991-92. Recipient medal for contbn. to Can. Culture, Coun. of French-Am. Life, 1987, Prix Marcel-Blouin for best morning program in Can., 1983, Profl. Woman of Yr. award Réseau des femmes d'affaires professionnelles, 1990; named Chevalier Ordre de la Pléiade, 1995, CEO of Yr., Bell Globemedia, ACTRA Fraternal. Mem. various parliamentary assns. and friendship groups. Avocations: running, reading, swimming. Home: 2094 Chalmers Ottawa ON Canada K1H 6K6 Office: Senate Can Ottawa ON Canada K1A 0A4

POULIOT, ASSUNTA GALLUCCI, retired business school owner and director, consultant; b. West Warwick, R.I., Aug. 14, 1937; d. Michael and Angelina (DeCesare) Gallucci; m. Joseph F. Pouliot Jr., July 4, 1961; children: Brenda, Mark, Jill, Michele. BS, U. R.I., 1959; MS, U. R.I., 1971. Bus. tchr. Cranston High Sch., R.I., 1959-61; bus. dept. chmn. Chariho Regional High Sch., Wood River Junction, 1961-73; instr. U. R.I., Kingston, 1973-78; founder, dir. Ocean State Bus. Inst., Wakefield, R.I., 1977-95, fin. aid cons., 1995—, ednl. cons., 1996—. Dir. Fleet Nat. Bank, 1985-91; bd. mgrs. Bank of New Eng., 1984-85; commr. Accrediting Coun. Ind. Colls. and Schs., 1995-98, chair accreditation com. team visits, 1998—, intermediate rev. com., 2000—, rev. bd., 2000—; spkr. in field including Glencoe/McGraw-Hill Pub. Co., 1995—. Ednl. author, Glencoe McGraw Hill Pub. Co., 1999—. Pres. St. Francis Women's Club, Wakefield, 1975; sec. St. Francis Parish Coun., Wakefield, 1980; mem. Econ. Devel. Commn., Wakefield, 1981-85; mem. South County Hosp. Corp., Wakefield, 1978-97; fin. dir. Bus. and Profl. Women's Club, Wakefield, 1982-84; chmn. Ladies Golf Charity, 1985-91; mem. Computer Info. Systems Com., Chariho Regional Career and Tech. Ctr. Mem. R.I. Bus. Edn. Assn. (newsletter editor 1979-81), New Eng. Bus. Coll. Assn. (sec. 1984-86, pres. 1985-87), R.I. Assn. Career and Tech. Schs. (treas., bd. dirs. 1979-95), Eastern Bus. Edn. Assn. (conf. leader), Nat. Bus. Edn. Assn. (conf. leader), Career Coll. Assn. (conv. speaker, pub. rels. com., govt. rels. com., membership com., key mem., nominating com., evaluator), Assn. Colls. and Schs. (commr. commn. on postsecondary schs. accreditation 1994-98), R.I. Women's Golf Assn., Am. Cancer Soc., U. R.I. Alumni Assn. (Excellence Bus. award 1992), Phi Kappa Phi, Delta Pi Epsilon (pres., newsletter editor). Clubs: Point Judith Country (past ladies golf chmn., R.I. Women's PGA rep.). Roman Catholic. Avocations: golfing, gardening. Home and Office: 137 Kenyon Ave Wakefield RI 02879-4242 Office: 15835 Sandy Point Dr Fort Myers FL 33917-5464 E-mail: sjpoulist@aol.com.

POULOS, JAMES THOMAS, endocrinologist, educator; b. Lynn, Mass., Apr. 11, 1938; s. Thomas Dimitrios and Christine Julia (Zorzy) Poulos; m. Mary Margaret White, June 22, 1963; 1 child Christopher Kreag. BS, Tufts U., 1959, MD, 1963. Diplomate Am. Bd. Internal Medicine, Am. Bd. Endocrinology and Metabolism. Intern New Eng. Med. Ctr., Boston, 1963-64, resident, 1964-65; resident and fellow in endocrinology U. Chgo., 1967-70; práctice medicine specializing in endocrinology Arnett Clinic, Lafayette, Ind., 1970—, v.p., bd. dirs., 1979-95. Adj. prof. clin. pharmacology Purdue U., West Lafayette, Ind., 1976—; clin. faculty Ind. U. Sch. Medicine; bd. dirs. Lafayette Home Hosp., 1980-85, dir., pres. med. staff, 1978-79; pres. Arnett HMO, 1986-97; dir. N. Cemn Health Svcs., 1985—. Co-author: The Metabolic Influence of Progestins Advances in Metabolis Disorders, 1971; contbr. articles to profl. publs. Active Nat. Rep. Senatorial Com., Nat. Rep. Congrl. Com. With M.C., U.S. Army, 1965-67. Fellow ACP, Am. Coll. Endocrinology, Am. Assn. Clin. Endocrinologists; mem. AMA, Am. Diabetes Assn. (dir. Ind. chpt. 1980—, pres. 1986-88, 96-98, bd. dirs. 1986—, com. profl. practice 1987-88, pres. 1994—), Internat. Diabetes Fedn., Am. Lung Assn. (pres. West Cen. Ind. 1982-83), Lafayette C. of C. Home: 1000 Windwood Ln West Lafayette IN 47906-4737 Office: 2600 Greenbush St Lafayette IN 47904-2477 Personal E-mail: jpoulos@insightbb.com. Business E-Mail: poulosj@arnett.com.

POULOS, JOAN GRAHAM, lawyer; b. Almena, Kans., June 7, 1936; d. Gilbert W. and Opal Z. Graham; m. John W. Poulos (div. 1978); children: John S., Alexandra J. Poulos Fullerton; m. David C. Lewis. BS, U. Kans., 1958; JD, U. Calif. Hastings Coll. of Law, 1962; MA, U. Calif., Riverside, 1978. Bar: Calif. 1963, U.S. Supreme Ct., U.S. Ct. Appeals (9th cir.), U.S. Dist. Ct. (so., ea. and no. dists.) Calif. Pvt. practice, Davis, Calif., 1978—. Dir. People Resources Inc., Yolo County, Calif., 1994-96. City coun. mem. City Davis, 1972-74, mayor, 1974-76; chmn. juvenile justice com. Mendo County, Ukiah, Calif.; commr. Nat. Commn. Uniform State Law, 1978-86; mem. Davis Chorale; pres. Mental Health Assn. Yolo County. Mem. ABA, Am. Women for Internat. Understanding, Yolo County Bar Assn. Democrat. Office: Poulos & Fullerton 1723 Oak Ave Davis CA 95616-1004 also: PO Box 1241 Bodega Bay CA 94923-1241 Fax: (530) 753-9457.

POULOS, MICHAEL JAMES, insurance company executive; b. Glens Falls, N.Y., Feb. 13, 1931; s. James A. and Mary Poulos; m. Mary Kay Leslie; children: Denise, Peter. BA, Colgate U., 1953; MBA, NYU, 1963. CLU, 1970. With sales and mgmt. U.S. Life Ins. Co., N.Y.C., 1958-70, dir., 1968, mem. exec. com., 1970; with Calif.-Western States Life Ins. Co., Sacramento, 1970-79, pres., chief exec. officer, 1975-79, dir., 1975; with Am. Gen. Corp., Houston, 1979-93, pres., 1981-91, mem. exec. com., dir., 1981-93, vice chmn., 1991-93; chmn., CEO, pres. Western Nat. Corp., Houston, 1993-98, now bd. dirs., 1998; ret., 1998. Mem. Sam Houston Area coun. Boy Scouts Am. Mem. Am. Soc. CLU's, Nat. Assn. Life Underwriters, Houston Assn. Life Underwriters, Am. Mgmt. Assn., River Oaks Country Club, Univ. Club of N.Y.C. Greek Orthodox. Home: 2121 Kirby Dr Unit 73 Houston TX 77019-6066 Office: 3 River Cir Ste 1310 Houston TX 77063-1502 Fax: 713-892-5553.

POULOS, STEPHEN PAUL, information systems specialist; b. Bklyn., Mar. 15, 1946; s. George Poulos and Dorothene C. Cooper; m. Carol Jean Thomas, Dec. 9, 1972; 1 child, Candace Annette Yant. BA in Russian, CCNY, 1968; MA in Russian Area Studies, Georgetown U., 1976; MBA, Loyola Coll., Balt., 1989. Mgr. govt. liaison Morrison-Knudsen Saudi Arabia Consortium, Saudi Arabia, 1977-79; dir. corp. planning and budgeting Sun Life Ins. Co. Am., Balt., 1979-82; dir. budgeting Md. Casualty Group, 1982-88, asst. v.p. support svcs., 1989-92, dir. disaster recovery, 1991-93; program mgr. JIL Info. Sys., Inc., Vienna, 1994-99; sr. project mgr. IBM, Inc., Bethesda, Md., 1999—. Cons., treas., bus. mgr. Glory Tabernacle, Inc., Washington, 1996-99. Treas. Vandenberge for Congress Com. 6th Dist. Campaign, Balt., 1986. Served with U.S. Army, 1968—76, col. USAR, 1976—2002. Mem. Fgn. Area Officers Assn. (bd. dirs. 1999—). Republican. Avocation: jogging. Office: IBM 6710 Rockledge Dr Bethesda MD 20817-1827 E-mail: spoulos@us.ibm.com.

POULOSE, KUTTIKATT PAUL, neurologist; b. Cochin, Kerala, India, Sept. 2, 1935; s. Paul Joseph Kuttikat and Mariamkutty (Paily) Maliakal; m. Queeny Poulose; children: Anil, Abraham, Benjamin. Interscience student, Univ. Coll., Kerala, 1951-53; MB, BS, Med. Coll., Trivandrum, Kerala, 1958, MD, 1964. Diplomate Am. Bd. Psychiatry and Neurology. Tutor in medicine Med. Coll., Kerala, 1965-66, asst. prof., 1970-72; chief of neurology VA Med. Ctr., Leavenworth, Kans., 1975, chief of medicine, 1975-80, chief of staff, 1980—; asst. prof. neurology Kans. U. Med. Ctr., Kansas City, 1975-80, assoc. prof., 1981-87, prof., 1987—, assoc. dean, 1989—; chief of staff VA Ea. Kans. Health Care Sys., 1999. Dir. continuing med. edn. VA Med. Ctr., Leavenworth, 1976-81; cons. Munson Army Hosp., Ft. Leavenworth, Kans. 1983-86. Contbr. numerous articles to profl. jours. Mem. planning com. for city recreational facility, Leavenworth, 1983. Served to maj. M.C. Indian Army, 1966-70. Recipient Superior Performance award, Administr. of Vets. Affairs, Washington, 1979. Fellow Am. Coll. Physicians, Am. Acad. Neurology, Royal Coll. Physicians, Can. Clubs: Officers (Ft. Leavenworth). Roman Catholic. Avocations: reading, walking, tennis. Home: 1216 Santa Fe St Leavenworth KS 66048-4200 Office: VA Med Ctr 4 South Leavenworth KS 66048 E-mail: Poulose.kpaul@topeka.va.gov.

POULSEN, FERN SUE, special events and public relations consultant; b. Chgo., Sept. 29, 1959; d. Herman and Renee (Greenberg) Bass; m. Gregory Carl Poulsen, June 13, 1987; children: Michael Carl, Michelle Jennifer. Ba, N. Ill. U., 1981. Corporate communications staff coordinator Centel Corp., Chgo., 1981-86; mgr. special events Network Mktg. Group, Oak Brook, Ill., 1986-88; pres. Poulsen Promotions, Chgo., 1988—. Cons. spl. events and pub. rels. Vol. Easter Seal Soc. and March of Dimes, Chgo., 1987-88, Penny Pullen Campaign Com., Park Ridge, Ill., 1981-83, Am. Cancer Soc., Des Plaines, Ill., 1983, Loaves and Fishes Food Pantry, Naperville, Ill.; exec. advisor Jr. Achievement, Chgo., 1982-83; active Lincoln Park Cen. Assn., Chgo., 1988; nominating com. exec. bd. dirs. Patterson Elem. Sch. PTA, 1987, mem., 1986—; vol. Dist. 204 Referendum Com.; coord. summer soccer camp MLS, Naperville, Ill.; vol. PTA, 1995—; team adminstr. Chgo. Magic Resolution soccer team, 2001-. Named Outstanding Woman Student Leader N. Ill. U. Women's Faculty, 1980. Mem. Internat. Assn. Bus. Communicators, Women's Am., ORT, Ad-Net Chgo., Parents and Child Edn. Soc., Nat. Coun. Jewish Women, Omicron Delta Kappa, Phi Kappa Phi. Avocations: travel, yoga, gardening, soccer mom. E-mail: fernapoulsen@msn.com.

POULSEN, IB, mass communications educator, researcher; b. Ringkobing, Denmark, Jan. 8, 1949; s. Johannes and Grethe (Rydstrom) P.; m. Gudrun Bodin, Mar. 30, 1982; 1 child, Christian. MA, U. Copenhagen, 1975, PhD, 1982. From asst. prof. to assoc. prof. U. Copenhagen, Denmark, 1976-99; prof. Royal Danish Sch. Ednl. Studies, 1999-2000, Danish Ednl. Univ., 2000—02, U.Roskilde, 2002—. External examiner Min. Edn., Denmark, 1980; ednl. cons. Danish Broadcasting Corp., 1983-91; mem. Danish Media Commn., 1994-95. Mem. Internat. Assn. Mass Comm. Rsch., Assn. Internat. Linguistique Appliqué. Avocations: traveling, jogging, art. Office: Univ of Roskilde Dept of Language and Culture PO Box 260 Dk-4000 Roskilde Denmark E-mail: ibpo@ruc.dk.

POULSEN, JENS KRISTIAN, ultrasonics researcher; b. Thisted, Denmark, Jan. 30, 1966; arrived in Can., 1998; s. Kjeld and Else Marianne Westergaard P. MSEE, Tech. U. Denmark, Lyngby, 1992. Rsch. asst. Radiometer, Copenhagen, 1988; instr. Tech. U. Denmark, 1988-89; rsch. asst. Jydsk Telefon, Aarhus, 1989, Skejby Sygehus, Aarhus, 1992-98; ultrasonics rschr. Toronto U., Ont., Can., 1998—. Computer cons. Medistim, Oslo, 1994-97. Inventor in field; contbr. articles to profl. jours. Mem. IEEE/Ultrasonics Ferroelectrics and Frequency Control (student mem.), IEEE/Engring. in Medicine and Biology Soc. (student mem.). Avocations: running, salsa dancing. Office: U Toronto Dept Med Biophys 2075 Bayview Ave Toronto ON Canada M4N 346

POULSON, RICHARD JASPER METCALFE, lawyer; b. Elizabeth City, N.C., Sept. 4, 1938; s. Richard Jasper and Dorothy (Morse) P.; m. Anne Keenan, Dec. 21, 1963 (div. 1976); m. Anne Dare Wrenn, Sept. 25, 1993; children: Richard Hugh Hundley, Anna Blair Masters. BA, U. Va., 1960; JD, Am. U., 1968; ML in Taxation, Georgetown U., 1970. Bar: Va. 1968, D.C. 1969, U.S. Supreme Ct. 1976. V.p. Am. Security & Trust Co., Washington, 1968-70; assoc. Hogan & Hartson, 1970-73, ptnr., 1973-94, sr. ptnr. London, 1990-93; chmn. Rapidan Capital Ptnrs., 1994—; CEO, sr. mng. dir. The Appian Group, Washington, 1995-98; chmn., CEO The Animex Capital Group, Warsaw, Poland, 1998—. Adj. prof. Georgetown U. Law Ctr., 1971-78; lectr. Law and Fgn. Svc. Schs. Georgetown U.; internat. advisor in field; active Euro-Arab Conciliation and Arbitration System. Trustee, bd. mgrs., U. Va., Charlottesville, 1992-98, v.p., 1994-95, pres., 1995-97; dir., chmn. exec. com. Mary & Daniel Loughran Found., Washington, 1976—; chmn., dir. Montpelier Steeplechase Found., Orange, Va., 1991-98; chmn., trustee U.S. Rugby Football Found., Boston, 1988-2001. 1st lt. USAR, 1961-63. Mem. Law Society of England and Wales, Metro. Club, Norfolk Yacht Club, Keswick Country Club, Commonwealth Club. Republican. Episcopalian. Avocations: horseback riding, hunting, steeplechase racing, thoroughbred breeding. Home and Office: Animex Group 499 Park Ave 5th Fl New York NY 10022

POULSON, RICHARD J.M. lawyer; JD, Am. U. Law Sch., 1968; MD in Taxation, Georgetown U. Law, 1970. Lawyer Hogan & Hartson, 1970—; bd. dirs. Stimsonite Corp., 1994—. Cons. in field. Office: Smithfield Foods Inc 200 Commerce St Smithfield VA 23430-1204

POULTON, ROBERTA DORIS, nurse, consultant; b. Balt., Oct. 19, 1943; d. Charles Robert and Mary Doris (Guercio) P. Nursing diploma, Md. Gen. Hosp., 1964. Staff nurse Md. Gen. Hosp., 1964-67, Project Hope, Colombia, 1967, Tunisia, 1969-70, St. Agnes Hosp., Balt., 1968-69, team leader, 1972-83, staff nurse-preceptor, 1983-88, nurse mgr. pediatric emergency rm./ambulatory svcs., 1988-93, pediat. hemophilia coord., 1994—. Pediat. ambulatory specialty clin. nurse; hemophilia nurse Johns Hopkins Med. I stn., Balt.; cons. Girl Scouts U.S.A., Balt., 1972—, Bapt. Conv. Md., 1963—. Mem.: ANA, Md. Nurses Assn. Democrat. Baptist. E-mail: rpoulton@stagnes.org.

POUND, RICHARD WILLIAM DUNCAN, lawyer, accountant; b. St. Catharines, Ont., Can., Mar. 22, 1942; s. William Thomas and Jessie Edith Duncan (Thom) P.; m. Julie Houghton Keith, Nov. 4, 1977. B.Commerce, McGill U., Montreal, 1962, B.C.L., 1967; BA, Sir George Williams U. (now Concordia U.), Montreal, 1963; B. in Civil Law, McGill U., 1967; PhD (hon.), U.S. Sports Acad., 1989; LLD (hon.), U. Windsor, Can., 1997. Bar: called to Que. bar 1968, Ont. bar, 1980; chartered accountant, 1964, F.C.A, 2001. Auditor Riddell, Stead, Graham & Hutchinson, Montreal, 1963-65; law clk., then atty. firm Laing, Weldon, Courtois, Clarkson, Parsons & Tétrault, 1965-71; mem. firm Stikeman, Elliott, Montreal, Toronto, Ottawa, Calgary, Vancouver, London, N.Y.C., Hong Kong, Sydney, 1972—. Lectr. taxation McGill U. Faculty Law; lectr. Que. Real Estate Assn.; mem. Ct. of Arbitration of Sport, Lausanne, 1991—; officer Order of Can., officer Ordre nat. du Quebec, Order of St. John of Jerusalem, Queen's Coun., 1992 Author: Five Rings Over Korea, 1994, Chief Justice W.R. Jackett: By the Law of the Land, 1999; editor-in-chief: Doing Business in Canada, 1987—, Canada Tax Cases, 1993—, Stikeman Income Tax Act (annotated); author: Pound's Tax Case Notes, 1988—, Legal Notes, CGA mag., 1986—; mem. editl. bd. Can. Tax Svc., 1972-82. Pres. Canadian Olympic Assn., 1977-82, sec., 1968-76, dir., 1968—; mem. Internat. Olympic Com., 1978—, exec. bd., 1983-87, 92-2000, v.p., 1987-91, 1996-2000; bd. govs. McGill U., 1986—, chmn., 1994-99, chancellor, 1999—; gov. Martlet Found.; former trustee Stanstead Wesleyan Coll.; chmn. McGill U. Athletic Bd.; chmn. McGill U. Fund Coun.; founding chmn., pres. World Anti-Doping Agy., 1999—. Named to Canadian Swimming Hall of Fame, 1969, Sports Fedn. Can. Hall of Fame, 1976, Can. Olympic Order, 1995, Quebec Sports Hall of Fame, 2001. Mem. Can. Bar Assn., Can. Tax Found., Internat. Fiscal Assn., Internat. Assn. Practicing Lawyers, Can. Squash Racquets Assn., Royal Life Savs. Soc., Alumni Assn. McGill U. (former pres.). Clubs: Montreal Amateur Athletic Assn. (pres. 1987-88), Badminton and Squash (Montreal); Jesters, Mt. Bruno Country. Home: 87 Arlington Ave Westmount QC Canada H3Y 2W5 Office: Ste 4000 1155 Rene Levesque Blvd W Montreal QC Canada H3B 3V2 E-mail: richardpound@ioc.olympic.org.

POUND, ROBERT VIVIAN, physics educator; b. Ridgeway, Ont., Can., May 16, 1919; arrived in U.S., 1923, naturalized, 1932; s. Vivian Ellsworth and Gertrude C. (Prout) Pound; m. Betty Yde Andersen, June 20, 1941; 1 child John Andrew. BA, U. Buffalo, 1941; AM (hon.) , Harvard Coll., 1950; DSc (hon.) , SUNY, Buffalo, 1994. Rsch. physicist Submarine Signal Co., 1941—42; staff mem. Radiation Lab. MIT, Cambridge, 1942—46; Soc. Fellows jr. fellow Harvard U., 1945—48; asst. prof. physics Harvard Coll., 1948—50, assoc. prof., 1950—56, prof., 1956—68; chmn. dept. physics, 1968—72; Mallinckrodt prof. physics, 1968—89; emeritus, 1989—; dir. Physics Lab. Harvard U., Cambridge, 1975—83. Fulbright rsch. scholar Oxford (Eng.) U., 1951; vis. rsch. fellow Merton Coll., 1980; Fulbright lectr., Paris, 58; vis. prof. Coll. de France, 1973; vis. fellow Joint Inst. Lab. Astrophysics, U. Colo., 1979—80; Zernike vis. prof. U. Groningen, The Netherlands, 1982; vis. sr. scientist Brookhaven Nat. Lab., 1986—87; vis. prof. U. Fla., 1987; W.G. Brickwedde lectr. Johns Hopkins U., Balt., 1992; Julian Mack lectr. U. Wis., 1992. Author, editor Mmicrowave Mixers, 1948; contbr. articles to profl. jours. Associated Univs., Inc., 1976—. Recipient B.J. Thompson Meml. award, Inst. Radio Engrs., 1948, Eddington medal, Royal Astron. Soc., 1965, Nat. medal Sci., Pres. U.S., 1990; fellow John Simon Guggenheim, 1957—58, 1972—73. Fellow: AAAS, Am. Acad. Arts and Scis., Am. Phys. Soc.; mem.: NAS, French Phys. Soc. (mem. coun . 1958—61), French Acad. Scis. (assoc.; fgn.), Sigma Xi, Phi Beta Kappa. E-mail: pound@fas.harvard.edu.

POUNDS, BUZZ R. educator; b. Grants Pass, Oreg., Sept. 26, 1960; s. Marvin D. P. and Sharen Lee (Plantz) Orwig; m. Kathy Sue Dircks, June 22, 1984; children: Robert Bruce, William Henry. BA in Philosophy, Westmont Coll., 1982; MA in Biblical Lit., Asbury Theol. Sem., 1984; BA in English Edn., U. No. Iowa, 1989, MA in English, 1997; PhD in Rhetoric and Composition, U. Louisville, 2001. Tchr. Houston Ind. Sch. Dist., 1990-93; profl. test scorer Am. Coll. Testing, Iowa City, 1994-95, Nat. Computer Systems, Iowa City, 1994-95; substitute tchr. Cedar Rapids (Iowa) Cmty. Schs., 1993—2001; tchg. asst. U. No. Iowa, Cedar Falls, 1995-97; asst. prof. Lewis U., Romeoville, Ill., 2002—. Part-time lectr., fellow U. Louisville, 1997-2001. Computer cons. Hopkinton (Iowa) Pub. Libr., 1990—; del. ctrl. com. Iowa Dem. Party, Delaware County, 1997-2002. Mem. Nat. Coun. Tchrs. English, Soc. Christian Philosophers. Democrat. Avocations: games, ancient history. Home: PO Box 214 Hopkinton IA 52237-0214 E-mail: brpounds@yahoo.com.

POUNDS, WILLIAM FRANK, management educator; b. Fayette County, Pa., Apr. 9, 1928; s. Joseph Frank and Helen (Fry) P.; m. Helen Anne Means, Mar. 6, 1954; children: Thomas Mcclure, Julia Elizabeth. BSChemE, Carnegie Inst. Tech., 1950, MS in Math. Econs., 1959, PhD in Indsl. Adminstrn., 1964. Indsl. engr. Eastman Kodak Co., 1950-51, 55-57; cons. Pitts. Plate Glass Co., 1958-59, asst. to gen. mgr. Forbes finishes divsn., 1960—61; faculty Sloan Sch. Mgmt., MIT, 1966-98, prof. mgmt., 1966-98, dean, 1966-80; sr. adv. Rockefeller Family and Assocs., 1981-91. Bd. dirs. Idexx Labs., Inc., Mgmt. Scis. for Health, Inc. Chmn. bd. trustees Boston Mus. Fine Arts, 2000—; trustee WGBH Edni. Found., 2002—. Served as aviator lt. (j.g.) USNR, 1951-55. Fellow Am. Acad. Arts and Scis. Home: 83 Cambridge Pkwy # W1205 Cambridge MA 02142-1241

POUNDSTONE, JOHN WALKER, preventive medicine physician; b. Lexington, Ky., May 1, 1940; s. Albert Bruce and Myra Walker (Shipp) P.; m. Ann Von Isakovics, May 16, 1963 (div. June 20, 1980); children: Katharine, Virginia; m. Mary Lucas Powell, Mar. 1, 1991. BA, St. John's Coll., 1962; MD, U. of Ky., 1966; MPH, Harvard U., 1968. Diplomate Am. Bd. Preventive Medicine. Intern Newton-Wellesley Hosp., Newtown Lower Falls, Mass., 1966-67; resident in epidemiology Harvard U. Sch. Pub. Health, Boston, 1967-70; commd. USN, 1970; head TB and VD control Bur. Medicine Surgery, U.S. Navy, Washington, 1970-73; advanced through grades to capt. USN, 1970-1980; chief, epidemiology and biometics Navy Med. Rsch. Unit #4, Great Lakes, Ill., 1973-74; chief, dept. occupational and preventive medicine Navy Reg. Med. Ctr., 1974-77; asst. officer in charge Navy environmental and preventive medicine unit #7, Naples, Italy, 1977-78, officer in charge Italy, 1978-80; commr. health Lexington-Fayette County health dept., Lexington, 1980—; ret. USNR, 1997; asst. prof. preventive medicine and environ. health U. Ky. Coll. Medicine, 1985—. Editor Bulletin, 1987-91, Am. Assn. Pub. Health Physicians Jour.; contbr. articles to profl. jours. Chmn. Emergency Med. Adv. Bd. for Lexington, Ky.; mem. Com. to Study Emergency Med. Needs of North Lexington, 1981-82, Commn. on Svcs. for Sr. Citizens of Fayette County, chmn. com. on health needs, Tobacco-Free Young Kentuckians, Water Mgmt. Task Force for Ky.; deacon Ctrl. Christian Ch., Lexington; exec. com. Bluegrass Coun. Boy Scouts Am., Lexington, 1989—; mem. planning devel. com. Ea. Ky. Health Sys. Agy., 1981-82; mem. health devel. com. and rsch and devel. com. United Way of Lexington; mem. adv. coun. Youth Svc. Ctr. Bryan Sta. Schs., Operation Family, Lexington; sec. AIDS Crisis Task Force of Lexington; bd. dirs. Ky. Health Care Access Found. Inc., 1984-90, 91—. Named Pub. Health Leadership Inst. scholar; USPHS Primary Care policy fellow 1995. Fellow Am. Coll. Preventive Medicine; mem. AAAS, AMA, APHA, Nat. Assn. County Health Officers (bd. trustees 1984-99), U.S. Conf. Local Health Officials (bd. trustees 1982-90, 92-95), Am. Coll. Epidemiology (assoc.), Am. Assn. Pub. Health Physicians (pres. 1988-90, treas. 1998—), Soc. Epidemiology Rsch., Ky. Pub. Health Assn. (pres. 1989-90, bd. dirs. 1998—), Ky. Primary Care Assn. (bd. dirs. 1981-89, 91—), Ky. Health Dept. Assn. (pres. 1985-86), Ky. Med. Assn. (cmty. and rural health com., del. 1987-90, 97—), Ky. Assn. Pub. Health Physicians (former pres., sec., treas.), Fayette County Med. Soc. (former v.p., bd. dirs, aging sub-com.), U. Ky. Coll. Medicine Alumni Assn. (former pres.), Rotary (co-chair cmty. needs com.). Democrat. Christian Ch. Avocations: photography, gardening, hiking. Home: 1660 Traveller Rd Lexington KY 40504-2002 Office: Lexington-Fayette County Dept Health 650 Newtown Pike Lexington KY 40508-1113 E-mail: johnw.poundstone@mail.state.ky.us.

POUNDSTONE, SALLY, library director; m. Robert Bruce Poundstone; children: Nancy Katrina, Holly Megan, Angus Bruce, Alice Heather. BA, U. Ky., 1954, MA in Libr. Sci., 1955. Asst. head ref. dept. Louisville (Ky.) Free Pub. Libr., 1955-59; libr. Folger Shakespeare Libr., Washington, 1959-60; chief acquisition dept. White Plains (N.Y.) Pub. Libr., 1960-62; libr. Bedford Hills (N.Y.) Pub. Elem. Sch., 1965-66; dir. Mamaroneck (N.Y.) Free Libr. and Emelin Theatre, 1966-87, Westport (Conn.) Pub. Libr., 1987-98; prin. SHP Libr. Consultants, 1998—. Instr. libr. sci. N.Y. U., 1968-69, Coll. of New Rochelle (N.Y.), 1970-71; adv. coun. mem. Pratt Inst. Grad Sch. of Libr. and Info. Sci., 1978-87; adminstrv. svcs. chmn. N.Y. Met. Ref. and Res. Libr. Agy., 1977-79, bd. trustees, 1979-88, 2d b.p. and chair, 1984-85, pres., 1985-88; planning and devel. com. mem. Bibliomation, Inc., 1988-90; chair Conn. State Adv. Coun. for Libr. Planning and Devel., 1988-90. Pres. Garden Club of Mamaroneck, 1969-70, Larchmont-Mamaroneck Film Coun., 1971-72, Mamaroneck Hist. soc., 1976-77, bd. mem., 1976-87; vice chmn. Village of Upper Nyack Planning Bd., 1988-89; leadership com. and task force mem. Westchester 2,000, 1984-87; com. mem. Rotary Club of Westport, 1987—; active Downtown Westport Adv. Com., 1989-90, Rep. Town. Com., Weston, Conn., 1990-93, Westport Bridge & Traffic Com., 1990-97, Honorable Order of Ky. Cols., 1995—, United Way Profl. Adv. Com., 1994-97, Westport Telecomm. Com., 1994-96, and others; v.p., dir. Woodcock Nature Ctr., 1998—, pres., 2001—; mem. Wilton Rep. Town Com., 2000—, Planning & Zoning Bd. Commns., 2000—. Mem. ALA, Conn. Libr. Assn., Fairfield Libr. Adminstrs. Group, Archons of Colophon, Pub. Libr. Dirs. Assn. Westchester County (various offices and chairs), N.Y. Libr. Assn. (sec. treas. adult librs. assn. 1970-72, pres. pub. librs. sect. 1981-82, chair planning com. 1984-85). Home and Office: 48 Sharp Hill Rd Wilton CT 06897-3531

POURARYAN, SIAMAK MICHAEL, management consultant; b. L.A., Oct. 27, 1964; s. Siroos Pouraryan and Mindo Mozaffari; m. Maryam Haeri, Oct. 14, 1998; 1 child, Arshia. AA, Pasadena City Coll., Calif., 1985; BA, Calif. State. U., L.A., 1987. Opers. mgr. Advanced Enterprise Solution, Santa Ana, Calif., 1992—2001; sr. mgr. order fulfillment MSC Software Corp., 2001—02, enterprise bus. uni mgr., 2002—. Founder, Aryan Ptnrs., 2001—. Democrat. Avocations: stamp collecting, writing, swimming. E-mail: spouraryan@hotmail.com.

POURBAIX, ALEXANDER, energy executive; Assoc. gen. counsel TransCanada, Calgary, 1994—97; exec. v.p., power devel. TransCanada PipeLines Ltd., 1997—; pres. TransCanada Power LP, 1997—. Office: TransCanada Power 450 1st St SW Calgary AT Canada T2P 5H1*

POURBEIK, POUYAN, power engineering consultant; b. Apr. 17, 1972; B of Engring. with honors, U. Adelaide, Australia, 1992, PhD in Elec. Engring., 1997. Application engr. GE Co., Schenectady, N.Y., 1997-2000; cons. engr. ABB Inc., Raleigh, NC, 2000—01, prin. cons., 2001—. Convenor CIGRE task force on modeling of gas turbines and steam turbines in combined-cycle power plants, 2001—. Office: ABB Inc 940 Main Campus Dr Ste 300 Raleigh NC 27606 Fax: 919-807-5060. E-mail: pouyan.pourbeik@us.abb.com.

POURCIAU, LESTER JOHN, JR. retired librarian; b. Baton Rouge, Sept. 6, 1936; s. Lester John and Pearlie M. (Hogan) P.; m. Rebecca Anne Thomas, 1975; 1 son, Lester John III. BA, La. State U., 1962, MS, 1964; PhD, Ind. U., 1975. Asst. ref. libr. U. S.C., Columbia, 1963-64; ref. libr. Florence (S.C.) County Pub. Libr., 1964-65; ref. svcs. coord. U. Fla., Gainesville, 1966-67; dir. librs. U. Memphis, 1970-99, assoc. v.p. for acad. affairs, dir. librs., 1987-91. Chmn. coun. of head librarians State Univ. and C.C. System Tenn., 1980, 87, 97; acad. assoc. Atlantic Coun. of U.S., U. Memphis; fgn. expert, vis. lectr. Beijing U. of Posts & Telecomms., Beijing Normal U., Peking U., Renmen U., Qinghua U., Chingqing Inst. Posts & Telcomms., Guizhou Normal U., Republic of China, 1993; fgn. expert/vis. lectr. Beijing U. Posts and Telecom, 1993; fgn. expert, vis. lectr. Nanjing U. Posts and Telecom., Anhui Normal U., Beijing U. Posts and Telecom., 1994, People's Republic of China, 1994; cons. prof. Beijing U. of Posts and Telecom., 1996—; participant 2d Internat. Conf. Crimea 95, Librs. and Assn. in the Transient World, Republic of Crimea; participant, mem. orgn. com. Crimea 1996-2001, Peking U. Internat. Conf., Beijing, 1998. Contbr. articles to profl. jours. With USAF, 1955-59. Recipient Adminstrv. Staff award Memphis State U., 1981, Commendation Boy Scouts Am., 1985, Commendation Tenn. Sec. State, 1989, Honor award Tenn. Libr. Assn., 1990, Allen J. Hammond award for Disting. Svc. U. Memphis, 1999, SLIS Disting. Alumni award Ind. U., 1999; named Outstanding Alumnus, La. State U., 1988; named Libr. of Yr., Memphis Libr. Coun., 1989; fellow Higher Edn. Act Ind. U.; named to 30th Ann. Honor Roll. ALA Office Intellectual Freedom and Freedom to Read Found. U. Memphis, 1999. Mem.: ALA, Memphis Old Time Car Club (sec. 1981, pres. 1982, 1989), Mid-Am. Old Time Automobile Assn., Antique Automobile Club Am., Nat. Assn. Watch and Clock Collectors (chpt. pres. 1983, sec.-treas. 1988—89). Office: Memphis State U U Libr Memphis TN 38152-0001

POUR-EL, MARIAN BOYKAN, mathematician, educator; b. N.Y.C. d. Joseph and Mattie (Caspe) Boykan; m. Akiva Pour-El; 1 dau., Ina. AB, Hunter Coll.; A.M., Harvard U., 1951, PhD, 1958. Prof. math. U. Minn., 1968—. Mem. Inst. Advanced Study, Princeton, N.J., 1962-64; mem. coun. Conf. Bd. Math. Scis., 1977-82, lectr. internat. congresses in logic and computer sci., Eng., 1971, Hungary, 1967, Czechoslovakia, 1973, 1998, Germany, 1983, 96, 97, Japan, 1985, 88, China, 1987; lectr. Polish Acad. Sci., 1974; lecture series throughout Fed. Republic of Germany, 1980, 1983 87, 89, 91,1996 Japan, 1985, 87, 90, 93, China, 1987, Sweden, 1983, 94, Finland, 1991, Estonia, 1991, Moscow, 1992, Amsterdam, 1992; mem. Fulbright Com. on Maths., 1986-89; invited spkr. Internat. Congress on Computability and Complexity Theory, Kazan U., Russia, 1997, Workshop on Computability and Complexity in Analysis, held in conjunction with 23rd Internat. Symposium on Math. Founds. of Computer Sci. and Computer Sci. Logic, Brno, Czech Republic, 1998, IEEE Workshop on Real Number Computation, 1998 Author: (with I. Richards) Computability in Analysis and Physics, 1989; author numerous articles on mathematical logic (theoretical computer sci.) and applications to mathematical and physical theory. Named to Hunter Coll. Hall of Fame, 1975; NAS grantee, 1966. Fellow AAAS, Japan Soc. for Promotion of Sci.; mem. Am. Math. Soc. (coun. 1980-88, numerous coms., spkr., orgn. spl. sessions on math. logic), Assn. Symbolic Logic, Math. Assn. Am. (nat. panel vis. lectrs.), Phi Beta Kappa, Sigma Xi, Pi Mu Epsilon, Sigma Pi Sigma. Achievements include research in mathematical logic (theoretical computer science) and in computability and noncomputability in physical theory—wave, heat, potential equations, eigenvalues, eigenvectors. Office: U Minn Sch Math Vincent Hall Minneapolis MN 55455-0488 E-mail: pour-el@math.umn.edu. *In order to practice our careers our family has evolved a pattern of life at variance with the norm. For more than twenty years we have lived apart most of the time. Our strong emotional and personal ties were intensified by this absence of continuous physical nearness. It is my belief that one can succeed personally, socially and professionally without having to accept the constraints of an existing social order.*

POURFAR, MOHAMAD, pediatrician, hematologist, oncologist; b. Tehran, Iran, Mar. 21, 1933; came to U.S., 1958; s. Abdoulfazl and Robabeh Pourfar; widowed; children: Michael, Susan. MD, Teheran U., 1958. Diplomate Am. Bd. Pediatrics. Rotating intern Jersey City Med. Ctr., 1958-59; resident in pediatrics Maimonides Med. Ctr., Bklyn., 1959-61; fellow in hematology, 1961-62; fellow inpediatric hematology SUNY, 1962-63, instr., 1963-64; attending Kings County Hosp., 1963-64; pediatrician Iranian Army Dispensary, 1964-66; chief attending Shahrazad Children's Hosp., 1964-66; chief divsn. pediatric hematology Coney Island Hosp., Bklyn., 1966-67; asst. dir. dept. pediatrics, attending Jewish Chronic Disease Hosp., 1967-70; pvt. practice Monroe, N.Y., 1970—. Contbr. articles to profl. jours. Fellow Am. Acad. Pediatrics, Am. Soc. Hematology. Address: 1530 Palisade Ave Fort Lee NJ 07024-5470

POUSADA, LIDIA, physician; b. Mt. Kisco, N.Y., July 21, 1957; d. Manuel and Maria Nieves (Mejuto) P.; m. Andrew Kemper Goodman, June 26, 1983 (div. Sept. 1986); 1 child, Sara Pousada Goodman; m. Wayne William Maibaum, Apr. 11, 1987 (div. July 1993); 1 child, Anna Pousada Maibaum; m. James Paul Kreindler, Mar. 2, 1996; 1 child, Victoria Pousada Kreindler. BS, CUNY, N.Y.C., 1978; MD, N.Y. Med. Coll., 1980. Diplomate Am. Bd. Internal Medicine, Am. Bd. Geriatric Medicine. Student geriatric fellowship NYU Med. Sch., N.Y.C., 1978-80; resident in internal medicine Montefiore Med. Ctr., Bronx, N.Y., 1980-83, dir. geriatric unit, 1986-89; with nat. health svc. North Cent. Bronx Hosp., 1983-84, Morris Heights Health Ctr., Bronx, 1985; instr. City Coll. Med. Sch., N.Y.C., 1982-85, Albert Einstein Coll. Medicine, Bronx, 1983-84, 86-89, asst. prof. medicine, 1988-89; assoc. prof. clin. medicine N.Y. Med. Coll., 1993—; pvt. practice geriatric medicine, 2002—. Dir. geriatric cons. svc. Montefiore Med. Ctr., 1987—89, assoc. chief divsn. geriatrics, 1988—92; chief divsn. geriatrics and gerontology Sound Shore Med. Ctr., 1992—2002. Author: Geriatric Diagnostics, 1983, Emergency Medicine for the House Officer, 1986, 2d edit., 1995, Emergency Medicine for Nurses, 1989, Perioperative Medical Care of the Geriatric Patient, 1989, Case Studies in Emergency Medicine for the House Officer, 1993. Physician scholar Nat. Health Svc., 1978-80. Fellow ACP, Gerontol. Soc. Am., Am. Geriatric Soc.; mem. Physicians for Social Responsibility. Office: 141 North State Rd Briarcliff Manor NY 10510

POUSCHINE, JOHN LAURENCE, private equity investment executive; b. Glen Cove, N.Y., Jan. 28, 1957; s. Ivan and Helen (Carlson) P.; m. Catherine Dana, Nov. 16, 1991; children: Alexander, Anna. BA, Princeton U., 1979; MBA, Harvard U., 1983. Officer's asst. JP Morgan, N.Y.C., 1979-81; assoc. Prudential Securities, Inc., 1983-85; v.p. Bradford Ventures Ltd., 1985-88; sr. v.p. Electra Inc., 1989-96; mng. dir. Pouschine Cook Capital Mgmt., LLC, 1997—. Bd. dirs. MasterCraft Boat Co., Inc., Vonore, Tenn., MedPay Corp., Memphis, Latex Form Internat., Shelton, Conn., Spring Air Ptnrs.-N.Am., N.Y.C. Bd. dirs. Russian Children's Welfare Soc., N.Y.C. Mem. Bridgehampton Club, Nassau Club, Princeton Club of N.Y., Union Club. Avocation: sports. Office: Pouschine Cook Capital Mgmt 410 Park Ave Ste 810 New York NY 10022-4407 E-mail: jpouschine@pouschinecook.com.

POUSSOT, DELPHINE CECILE, artist; b. Masevaux, France, Apr. 13, 1952; came to U.S., 1970; d. Jean Daniel and Jacqueline (Andre) Evette; m. Bernard Jean Poussot, May 15, 1976; children: Rodolphe, Eve, Juliette. BFA, U. N.C., 1972. Sculptor, 1972-73; freelance designer, 1974-75; designer Havas Advt., Morocco, 1976, Boucheron, Paris, 1978. Exhbn. chmn. Art League of Delaware County. Mem. Am. Watercolor Soc., Phila. Watercolor Club. Avocations: tennis, skiing. Home: 675 Church Rd Villanova PA 19085-1108

POUTSMA, MARVIN L. chemical research administrator; b. Grand Rapids, Mich., Aug. 7, 1937; m. Yolanda Arco, July 20, 1968; children: John C., Julie A. BS, Calvin Coll., 1958; PhD, U. Ill., 1962. Staff scientist corp. rsch. Union Carbide, Tarrytown, N.Y., 1961-65, group leader corp. rsch., 1965-68, sr. scientist corp. rsch., 1968-73, sr. group leader corp. rsch., 1972-78; group leader chemistry divsn. Oak Ridge (Tenn.) Nat. Lab., 1978-80, sect. head chemistry divsn., 1980-83, dir. chemistry divsn., 1984-93, dir. chem. & analytical scis. divsn., 1994-2000, ret., 2000. Contbr. chpts. to books and articles to profl. jours. Fellow AAAS; mem. Am. Chem. Soc. Office: Oak Ridge Nat Lab PO Box 2008 Oak Ridge TN 37831-6197

POUZYREV, ANATOLI TIMOFEYEVICH, molecular biologist, educator; b. Bergul, Novosibirsk , Russia, Jan. 4, 1948; s. Polina Ivanovna Pouzyreva, Timofey Ivanovich Spiridonov. PhD, Endelgard Inst. Molecular Biology, Moscow, 1982—82. Rsch. asst. prof. U. Mo., Columbia, 2000—, sr. postdoctoral assoc., 1997—2000. Author: (Article in "Genome Research") Changes in gene expression associated with developmental arrest and longevity in C. elegans, 2001. Grantee Grant, State Program "Human Genome", 1990-1991. Home: 311 N William Columbia MO 65201-7811 Office: University Missouri Tucker Columbia MO 65211-7400 Office Fax: (573)-884-9676. Business E-Mail: pouzyreva@missouri.edu.

POVICH, DAVID, lawyer; b. Washington, June 8, 1935; s. Shirley Lewis and Ethyl (Friedman) Povich; m. Constance Enid Tobriner, June 14, 1959; children: Douglas, Johanna, Judtih, Andrew. BA, Yale U., 1958; LLB, Columbia U., 1962. Bar: D.C. 1962, U.S. Ct. Appeals (4th cir.) 1980, U.S. Tax Ct. 1981, U.S. Ct. Appeals (5th and 11th cirs.) 1984, U.S. Dist. Ct. Md., U.S. Ct. Appeals (3d cir.) 1997. Law clk. to assoc. judge D.C. Ct. Appeals, Washington, 1962-63; ptnr. Williams & Connolly, 1963—, exec. com., 1986-87. Bd. dirs., officer Lisner Home for Aged. Mem.: ABA, Barristers (exec. com. 1992—93), Bar Assn. D.C., D.C. Bar Assn. Office: Williams & Connolly 725 12th St NW Washington DC 20005-5901 E-mail: dpovich@wc.com.

POVICH, LYNN, journalist, magazine editor, internet executive; b. Washington, June 4, 1943; d. Shirley and Ethyl (Friedman) P.; m. Stephen B. Shepard, Sept. 16, 1979; children: Sarah, Ned. AB, Vassar Coll., 1965. Rschr., reporter, writer, editor, sr. editor Newsweek mag., N.Y.C., 1965-91; editor-in-chief Working Woman mag., 1991-96; mng. editor, sr. exec. prodr. East coast programming MSNBC Interactive, Secaucus, N.J., 1996-2001. Co-chair Internat. Women's Media Found. Recipient Matrix award N.Y. Women in Comms., 1976; named to Acad. of Women Achievers YWCA, 1993. Office: 322 Central Park West New York NY 10025

POVISH, KENNETH JOSEPH, retired bishop; b. Alpena, Mich., Apr. 19, 1924; s. Joseph Francis and Elizabeth (Jachcik) P. AB, Sacred Heart Sem., Detroit, 1946; MA, Cath. U. Am., 1950; postgrad., No. Mich. U., 1961, 63. Ordained priest Roman Catholic Ch., 1950; asst. pastorships, 1950-56; pastor in Port Sanilac Mich., 1956-57, Munger, 1957-60, Bay City, 1966-70; dean St. Paul Sem., Saginaw, 1960-66, vice rector, 1962-66; bishop of Crookston Minn., 1970-75; bishop of Lansing Mich., 1975-95. Bd. consulators Diocese of Saginaw, 1966-70; instr. Latin and U.S. history St. Paul Sem., 1960-66 Weekly columnist Saginaw and Lansing diocesan newspapers. Bd. dirs. Cath. Charities Diocese Saginaw, 1969-70. Mem. Mich. Hist. Soc., Bay County Hist. Soc., Lions Club, KC (pres. Mich. Cath. Conf. 1985-95), Kiwanis.

POWDERLY, WILLIAM H., III, lawyer; b. Pitts., Feb. 23, 1930; BS, Georgetown U., 1953; LLB, U. Pitts., 1956. Bar: Pa. 1956. Ptnr. Metz Schermer & Lewis, LLC, Pitts. Office: Tucker Arensberg PC 1500 One PPG Pl Pittsburgh PA 15222

POWDRILL, GARY LEO, production operations manager; b. Butte, Mont., Nov. 26, 1945; s. Harold Holmes and Genevieve Marie (Tansey) P.; m. Marsha A. McKeon, Oct. 6, 1979 (div.); 1 child, Amy Marie. BS, Gonzaga U., 1969; MBA, U. Detroit, 1973; MPA in Environ. Policy, Ind. U., 1984. Lic. profl. engr., Ind.; cert. plant engr. Plant design engr. Ford Motor Co., Sterling Heights, Mich., 1969-73, divsn. plant engr. Chassis divsn., 1973-74, supr. plant engring. sect. Indpls. plant, 1974-78, mgr. plant engring., 1978-80, mgr. engring. and facilities, 1980-87, mgr. mfg., plant engring. dept., 1987-88, pres., mgr. prodn. ops. area A, 1988-95, mgr. plant engring. and tech. svcs., 1996-97, mgr. power steering pump product line, 1997-98, mgr. power steering gear product line, 1998-2000, mgr. facilities and indsl. engring., 2000-01, ret., 2001. Chmn. Ind. State Water Pollution Control Bd., 1986-91; mem. Indpls. Mayor's Tech. Adv. Com., 1975—; mem. labor and mgmt. del. to U.S.-USSR Emerging Leaders Summit Conf., USSR, 1990; bd. dirs., chmn. Ruth Lilly Health Edn. Ctr.,; chmn. environ. com. Ind. State C. of C. Mem. Ind. Soc. Profl. Engrs., Elks. Roman Catholic. Home: 6 Forest Ct Greenfield IN 46140-8739

POWE, LARRY KENNETH, clinical researcher; b. Mobile, Ala., Dec. 14, 1944; s. Prince and Lucille Delores Powe; m. Lynn Ann Newberry, Oct. 9, 1975; children: Kimberly, Jennifer, Lauren, Joshua. BS, Loyola U., 1967; MD, Meharry Med. Coll., 1972. Diplomate Am. Bd. Pediatrics, Am. Bd. Psychiatry and Neurology. Intern in pediatrics Cook County Children's Hosp., Chgo., 1972, resident in pediatrics, 1973; pediat. neurology fellow Hines VA Cook County Children's Hosp., Mt. Sinai Hosp. and Med. Ctr., 1974; neurology resident Hines VA Cook County Hosp., Mt. Sinai Hosp. and Med. Ctr., 1975-76; pediatric neurologist Cook County Hosp., 1977-78; med. officer neurology FDA, Rockville, Md., 1978-80; spl. asst. to dep. dir. Bur. of Health Professions, Hyattsville, 1980-81; assoc. CNS dir. Wyeth-Ayerst Rsch., Radnor, Pa., 1988-91; assoc. CNS dir./dir. Rhone-Poulenc Rorer R&D, Collegeville, 1991-96; dept. dir. Rhone-Poulenc Rorer Corp., 1996-99, Amgen Inc., Thousand Oaks, Calif., 1999—. Cons. Children's Haven Pediatric Nursing Home, Harvey, Ill., 1974-78, Mercy Hosp., U. of Ill. Affiliation, Chgo., 1978-98, NIH Developmental Neurology Br., Bethesda, 1979-81. Author: (with others) Pathogenesis and Therapy of Amyotrophic Lateral Sclerosis, 1995. Steering group mem. United Way, 1997; trustee Huntington's Disease Soc. Am., Ctr. for ALS Rsch. at Johns Hopkins U. Col. USAR, 1981—. Mem. AMA, Nat. Med. Assn. (chair neurology sect.), Am. Acad. Neurology, Am. Acad. of Pharm. Physicians. Roman Catholic. Avocations: playing Alto saxophone, golfing, drawing. Office: Amgen 1 Amgen Center Dr Thousand Oaks CA 91320-1799 E-mail: Lpowe@Amgen.com.

POWELL, ALAN, scientist, engineer; b. Buxton, Derbyshire, Eng., Feb. 17, 1928; arrived in U.S., 1956; s. Frank and Gwendolen Marie (Walker) P.; m. June Sinclair, Mar. 28, 1956. Student, Buxton Coll., 1939-45; diploma in aeros., Loughborough Coll., 1948; BSc in Engring. with 1st class honors, London U., 1949; honours diploma 1st class, Loughborough Coll., 1949; D.Tech. (hon.), Loughborough U. Tech., 1980; PhD, U. Southampton, 1953. Chartered engr. Engr. Percival Aircraft Co., Luton, Eng., 1949-51; from rsch. asst. to lectr. U. Southampton, Eng., 1951-56; rsch. fellow Calif. Inst. Tech., Pasadena, 1956-57; engr. Douglas Aircraft Co., 1956; assoc. prof. UCLA, 1957-62, prof. engring., 1962-65, head Aerosonics lab., 1957-65; assoc. tech. dir., head acoustics and vibration lab. David Taylor Model Basin, Dept. Navy, Washington, 1965-66, tech. dir., 1966-67, David Taylor Naval Ship Research & Devel. Center, Bethesda, Md., 1967-85; mem. Undersea Warfare Research & Devel. Council, 1966-76, chmn., 1971-72; mem. council on Fed. Labs., 1972-85; prof. mech. engring. U. Houston, 1985-2000, chmn., 1985-87, prof. emeritus, 2000—. Com. on hearing bioacoustics and biomechs. NAS-NRC, 1961-85, exec. coun., 1963-65, chmn., 1965-66, advisor, 1985-95, mem. naval studies bd. 1990-95; mem. various coms. Naval Studies Bd. and Marine Bd., 1990-96; advisor Chinese U. Devel. Project, 1989-91; cons. Douglas Aircraft Co., 1956-65, others; adv. coun. Internat. Towing Tank Conf., 1981-85; mem. advisor U.S.-Japan Program Natural Resources, 1987-90, mem. Marine Facilities Panel; gen. chmn. 3d advanced vehicles conf. AIAA and Soc. Naval Archs. and Marine Engrs., 1976; chmn. internat. conf. Computer Aided Design, Manufacture and Ops. in Marine and Offshore Industries, 1987-88; cons. Sci. Applications Internat., Inc., 1987-90; governing bd. Am. Inst. Physics, 1995-97. Contbr. articles to profl. jours. Recipient Navy Meritorious Civilian Service award, 1970; Brit. Empire scholar, 1945; named Meritorious Exec. Pres. of U.S., 1982; Capt. Robert Dexter Conrad gold medal for sci. achievement Sec. Navy, 1984. Fellow Royal Aero. Soc. London (Baden-Powell prize 1948, Wilbur Wright prize 1953), Acoustical Soc. Am. (biennial award 1962, assoc. editor Jour. 1962-67, chmn. edn. com. 1964-66, exec. coun. 1966-69, chmn. medals and awards com. 1978-81, v.p. elect 1981-82, v.p. 1982-83, pres. elect 1989-90, pres. 1990-91, past pres. 1991-92, Silver medal in engring. acoustics 1992, designated Nat. Spkr. in Engring. Acoustics 1994-98), Inst. Mech. Engrs., Inst. Acoustics (U.K.); mem. AIAA (assoc. fellow, Aeroacoustics award 1980), ASME (Rayleigh lectr. 1988, Per Brüel Gold medal 1991), Inst. Noise Control Engrs. (initial mem., dir. 1974-77, Disting. lectr. 1975, 83, v.p. 1981-84, bd. cert. 1993), Acoustics, Speech and Signal Processing Soc. (exec. com. 1969-72, awards com. 1971-73, bylaws com. chmn. 1973-75), Am. Soc. Naval Engrs. (life), Am. Acad. Mechanics, Tau Beta Pi (hon. life). Office: U Houston Dept Mech Engring Houston TX 77204-4006

POWELL, ALFRED MERRILL, JR. environmental services administrator, educator; b. Richmond, Va., Apr. 12, 1951; s. Alfred Merrill Powell, Sr and Helen Bedner Powell; m. Jennifer Lynn Powell; children: Jessica Parsons, Jeffrey Parsons. B in Physics, USAF Acad., 1974; B in Meteorology, U.Utah, 1975; M in Astronomy, U. M in Astronomy, M in Atmospheric Sci., U. Mich., 1979, D in Atmospheric Sci., grad. cert., U. Mich., 1986; M in Computer Sci., U. Santa Clara, 1983. Commd. officer USAF, 1974, advanced through grades to lt. col., detachment weather officer Nev., 1975—76, Osan Air Base, Republic of Korea, 1976—78, staff weather officer Sunnyvale, Calif., 1979—83, chief space environ. support br. Omaha, 1986—89, weather detachment comdr. Grand Forks, ND, 1989—92, staff officer Office of the Asst. Sec. of the Air Force Pentagon, Va., 1992—94, ret., 1994; environ. applications divsn. mgr. Boeing Autometric, Springfield, Va., 1994—. Adj. prof. Creighton U., Omaha, 1987—89, U. N.D. Lake Region, Grand Forks, 1990—92, U. N.D., Grand Forks, 1991—91, Embry Riddle U., Grand Forks. Mem.: IEEE, Air and Waste Mgmt. Assn., Am. Meteorol. Soc., The Ret. Officer's Assn. (life), The Sierra Club, The Nature Conservancy, Nat. Wildlife Fedn. Home: 20922 Gardengate Cir Ashburn VA 20147-4024 Office: Boeing Autometric 7700 Boston Blvd Springfield VA 22153 Personal E-mail: ampowelljr@erols.com. Business E-Mail: apowell@autometric.com.

POWELL, ANICE CARPENTER, retired librarian; b. Moorhead, Miss., Dec. 2, 1928; d. Horace Aubrey and Celeste (Brian) Carpenter; m. Robert Wainwright Powell, July 19, 1948 (dec. 1979); children: Penelope Elizabeth, Deborah Alma. BS, Delta State U., 1961, MLS, 1974. Libr. Sunflower (Miss.) Pub. Libr., 1958-61; tchr. English Isola (Miss.) H.S., 1961-62; dir. Sunflower County Libr., Indianola, Miss., 1962-97, ret., 1997. Mem. adv. bd. libr. svcs. and constrn. act com. Miss. Libr. Commn., 1978-80; mem. state adv. coun. adult edn., 1988-92 mem. steering com. NASA cmty. involvement program Miss. Delta C.C., 1990, mem. adult edn. adv. com., mem. dist. workforce coun., 1994—; commn. mem. Mid Delta Empowerment Zone Alliance, 1995—, exec. com. Sunflower County Alliance for Youth, 1998-99. Mem. AAUW, NOW, ALA (spkr. senate subcom. on illiteracy 1989, honoree ALA 50th Ann. 1996), Miss. Libr. Assn. (exec. dir. Nat. Libr. Week 1975, steering com. 1976, chmn. Right to Read com. 1976, co-chmn. 1987, chmn. legis. com. 1979, chmn. intellectual freedom com. 1975, 80, legis. com. 1973-86, 96, 98, chmn. membership com. 1982, 98, pres. 1984, chmn. nominating com. 1986, chmn. election com. 1989, co-chmn. awards com. 1998, legis. com. 1998, Peggy May award 1981), Sunflower County Hist. Soc. (pres. 1983-87), Sierra Club. Methodist. Home: PO Box 310 Sunflower MS 38778-0310

POWELL, ANNE ELIZABETH, editor; b. Cheverly, Md., Nov. 11, 1951; d. Arthur Gorman and Barbara Anne (MacAran) P.; m. John Alan Ebeling Jr., 1972 (div. 1983). BS, U. Md., 1972. Reporter Fayetteville (N.C.) Times, 1973-75; home editor Columbus (Ga.) Ledger-Enquirer, 1976; assoc. editor Builder mag., Washington, 1977-78; architecture editor House Beautiful's Spl. Publs., N.Y.C., 1979-81; editor Traditional Home mag., Des Moines, 1982-87, Mid-Atlantic Country mag., Alexandria, Va., 1987-89; editor in chief publs. Nat. Trust for Hist. Preservation, Washington, 1989-95; editor-in-chief Landscape Architecture Mag., 1995-98, Civil Engring. Mag., Washington, 1998—. Author: The New England Colonial, 1988. Mem. Nat. Press Club, Am. Soc. Mag. Editors. Home: 1105 Park St NE Washington DC 20002-6317 Office: American Society of Civil Engrs Civil Engring Mag 1801 Alexander Bell Dr Reston VA 20191-4344 E-mail: apowell@asce.org.

POWELL, BARRY BRUCE, classicist, educator; b. Sacramento, Apr. 30, 1942; s. Barrett Robert and Anita Louise (Burns) P.; m. Patricia Ann Cox; children: Elena Melissa, Adam Vincent. BA in Classics, U. Calif., Berkeley, 1963, PhD, 1971; MA, Harvard U., 1965. Asst. prof. Northern Ariz. U., Flagstaff, 1970-73; from asst. prof. to prof. U. Wis., Madison, 1973—, chmn. dept. classics, 1985-92, chmn. program integrated liberal studies. Author: Composition by Theme in the Odyssey, 1973, Homer and the Origin of the Greek Alphabet, 1991, Classical Myth, 1995, 2d edit., 1997, 3d edit., 2000, New Companion to Homer, 1997, A Short Introduction to Classical Myth, 2001, Writing and the Origin of Greek Literature, 2002; writer screenplays; contbr. articles to profl. jours. Woodrow Wilson fellow, 1965. Mem. Am. Philol. Assn., Am. Sch. Classical Studies at Athens (mng. com), Archeol. Inst. of Am., Classical Assn. of Midwest and South, Am. Academy in Rome, Phi Beta Kappa (former pres. Madison chpt.). Home: 1210 Sweetbriar Rd Madison WI 53705-2228 Office: Univ Wis Dept Classics Madison WI 53707 E-mail: bbpowell@facstaff.wisc.edu.

POWELL, BENJAMIN L. government management analyst; b. Boston, Sept. 26, 1970; s. Arthur George and Barbara Schieffelin Powell. AB, Haverford Coll., 1993; MS in Internat. Affairs, Georgetown U., 2000. Journalist The Mexico City News, 1993-94; dist. aide N.Y. State Senator Catherine Abate, N.Y.C., 1994-96; pres., founder City Golf Entretenimiento SA de CV, Puebla, Mexico, 1997—; state dept. program examiner White House Office of Mgmt. and Budget, Washington, 2000—. Editor-in-chief Georgetown Jour. Internat. Affairs, 1999-2000. Del. Trilateral Conf. on NAFTA, Ottawa, Can., 1999. Mem. Am. Acad. Achievement, Groton Sch. Alumnae Assn. Democrat. Avocations: tennis, travel, writing. Home: 1756 Columbia Rd Apt 401 Washington DC 20009 Office: City Golf Entretenimiento 45 Poniente 1908 La Noria Puebla Mexico E-mail: belopo@hotmail.com.

POWELL, BETTY CROWDER, artist, educator; b. Madison, N.C., Sept. 13, 1934; d. Roy Pleasant and Virginia (Dean) Crowder; m. George Robert Powell Sr., May 13, 1953; children: George Robert, Stephen Reed, Susan Diane, David Dean. Student, Elon (N.C.) Coll., 1952-53; AA, Wilkes C.C., Wilkesboro, N.C., 1971; BS, Appalachian State U., Boone, N.C., 1973, MA, 1985. Lic. art educator. Asst. gallery dir. Wilkes Art Gallery, North Wilkesboro, N.C., 1973; art tchr. Mulberry Elem. Sch., Traphill Elem. Boomer Ferguson Elem., Millers Creek Primary, 1981-84; art tchr. Wilkes Ctrl. H.S., 1984-85; profl. artist, 1985—. Dir. Wilke County Arts Coun., North Wilkesboro, 1985-86, 90-91. Dir. S.A.F.E., North Wilkesboro, 1996-98. Mem. Northwest Arts League (pres. 1994-95), Nat. Collage Soc., Greensboro Artist League, Nat. Mus. Women in Arts, Blue Ridge Art Clan, Winston Salem Associated Artists, The Depot Artists Assn., North Wilkesboro Rotary (bd. dirs. 1992-96, Paul Harris fellow 1995). Democrat. Presbyterian. Home: 530 Forest Dr Wilkesboro NC 28697-8730

POWELL, CAROL ANN, accountant; b. Bklyn., Dec. 5, 1954; d. William Preston and Adelaide Hertha (Sohl) Batty; m. Michael Robert Powell, Jan. 17, 1976; children: Michael David, David Jason. AAS, Delhi Agrl. and Tech. Coll., 1974; BS, Syracuse U., 1975. CPA, N.Y. Sr. acct. Hall & Yann, CPAs, Fayetteville, N.Y., 1975-78; pvt. practice acct. Cold Spring, 1979—. Adj. tchr. acctg. Onondaga C.C., Syracuse, N.Y., 1977, Dutchess C.C., Poughkeepsie, N.Y., 1982; vol. mem. faculty Am. Women's Econ. Devel. Corp. Den leader Philipstown Pack 137 Boy Scouts Am., Cold Spring, N.Y., 1987-95; treas. Philipstown Little League, Cold Spring, 1990—, Philipstown Babe Ruth League, Cold Spring, 1994, Haldane Sch. Found., Inc., 1999—. Mem. AICPA, N.Y. State Soc. CPAs. Methodist. Avocations: piano, quilting. Home: PO Box 312 Cold Spring NY 10516-0312 Office: 44 Chestnut St Cold Spring NY 10516-2510 E-mail: cpowell@nysscpa.org.

POWELL, CAROL SUE, pediatric special education educator, nursing consultant; b. Phoenix, Nov. 15, 1944; d. Leonard Newson and Rebecca Jane (Housh) Stephens; m. Howard Powell Jr., Aug. 26, 1967; children: Jim, Howard III, Nicole. LPN, Champaign (Ill.) Sch. Practical Nursing, 1965; BA, Ea. Ill. U., 1975, MS in Edn., 1979; ADN, Lincolnand C.C., 1986. RN, Ill.; cert. elem. and spl. edn. tchr., TMH, EMH, SED, LD, PH, early childhood approval, Ill.; qualified mental retardation profl., Ill. Nurse Pattie A. Clay Infirmary, Richmond, Ky., 1966-68, Clark County Hosp., Winchester, 1968-

69, Mattoon (Ill.) Hosp., 1970-77; substitute tchr. Mattoon, Charleston, Findlay, Arcola (Ill.) Schs., 1978-79; part-time kindergarten and learning disabilities tchr. Buda (Ill.) Sch. Dist., 1979-81; staff nurse St. John's Hosp., Springfield, Ill., 1981-87; health svc. supr. Springfield Area ARC, 1987-88; staff nurse St. Vincent's Hosp., Taylorville, Ill., 1988-89; spl. edn. tchr., asst. dir. edn., mental retardation profl. Luth. Social Svcs., Beardstown, 1989-97; early intervention coord., nurse cons. Jacksonville (Ill.) Area ARC, 1997-99; child devel. specialist, RN State of Ill. Early Intervention Sys., 1999—. Nurse Shrine Clinics, Springfield, 1989—96; nurse EMT first aid meets Boy Scouts Am., Springfield, 1988—. Mem. Ill. Tchrs. Physically Handicapped. Methodist. Home and Office: 834 Evergreen Dr Chatham IL 62629-1118

POWELL, CAROLYN WILKERSON, music educator; b. Hamburg, Ark., Oct. 9, 1920; d. Claude Kelly and Mildred (Hall) Wilkerson; m. Charles Luke Powell, Dec. 12, 1923; children: Charles Luke Jr., James Davis, Mark Wilkerson, Robert Hall. AB, Ctrl. Meth. Coll., Fayette, Mo., 1942; MA in Tchg., U. N.C., 1970. Life tchg. cert., Mo.; cert. tchr., N.C. Choral dir. Maplewood-Richmond Heights Sch., St. Louis, 1943-45; pvt. piano tchr., Greensboro, N.C., 1951-63; organist Presbyn. and Meth. chs., 1950-61; dir. ch. youth choirs, 1958-61; choral and humanities tchr. Page H.S., 1963-67; choral dir. Githens Jr. H.S., Durham, N.C., 1967-80; organist St. Peter's Episcopal Ch., Altavista, Va., 1981-83. Chmn. Dist. Choral Festival N.C. Dist., 1968-78; accompanist and music dir. Altavista Little Theatre Altavista, Va., 1981-83. Sunday and vacation schs. tchr., organist Grace Meth. Ch., Greensboro; den mother Boy Scouts Am., Greensboro, 1951-57; mem. Chapel Hill Preservation Soc., 1985—; vol., chapel organist, pediat. tutor U. N.C. Hosps., Chapel Hill, 1984-89; mem. Chapel Hill Hist. Soc. Mem. NEA, AAUW, Music Educators Nat. Conf., Am. Organists Guild, Classroom Tchrs. Assn., Ackland Art Mus. Assn., Chapel Hill Hist. Soc., Nat. Federated Music Club Euterpe, Chapel Hill Country Club, U. Woman's Club, The Carolina Club, Delta Kappa Gamma. Avocations: reading, golf, needlework, gardening, travel and antiques. Home: 750 Weaver Dairy Rd Apt 142 Chapel Hill NC 27514-1440

POWELL, CHARLES WILLIAM, former minister, personal and professional development coach; b. Gilman, Colo., May 9, 1937; s. Harold Hayes and Rosella Charlotte (Collins) B.; m. Myrna Beth, June 11, 1995. BS Colo. State U., 1970; postgrad., Western Sem., 1982; grad., Coach U., 1998. Ordained to ministry Evang. Ch. Alliance, 1976; cert. sec. tchr., Wash.; master cert. coach; cert. teleclass leader: distinctionist. Team leader The Navigators, Colorado Springs, 1966-72; sr. pastor Albion (Wash.) Community Ch., 1972-76; hon. v.p. Am. Missionary Fellowship Portland, Oreg., 1979-81; itinerant preacher Oreg., 1976-90; personal and profl. devel. coach, 1994—; security officer Port of Portland Security Dept., 1977-97. Field rep. Internat. Messengers, 1989-91. Contbr. articles to religious jours.; publisher Sundry Bits and Pieces, In Business for You, East County Coaching. Res. policeman Whitman County Sheriff's Office, Colfax, Wash., 1975-76. With USN, 1956-62. Mem. Internat. Coach Fedn., Am. Legion, Gresham Area C. of C., Mensa, Toastmasters, Top One Percent Soc., East Portland C. of C. (pub. adv. com.). Avocations: reading, computer science. E-mial. E-mail: coach@best-services.com. *Nothing is all of anything. We never have all the story, sometimes just enough to bother us, to tangle our mind and leave us chewing on it.*

POWELL, CHRISTA RUTH, educational training executive; b. Dodgeville, Wis., Mar. 3, 1957; d. Robert Franklin and Rachel Jean (Edge) P.; m. Fred L. Neff, Sept. 10, 1989; 1 child, Resalena Pauline Neff. BSN, Viterbo Coll., 1979. RN, Minn. Staff nurse Abbott Northwestern Hosp., Mpls., 1979-81, 83-87, asst. head nurse, 1981-83; legal asst. Hyatt Legal Asst., St. Paul, 1981-83, comms. dir. Minn. region, 1983-86; office coord. Neff Law Firm, P.A., Mpls., 1986—; pres., bd. dirs. Profl. Devel. Inst., Bloomington, Minn., 1994—. Cons. A Basic Legal Svc., Bloomington, 1990-94. Editor: Mysterious Persons, 1990, Great Puzzles in History, 1990; co-host TV program Great Puzzles in History, 1989-91. Investigator ethics com. Hennepin County Bar, Mpls., 1989-90; v.p. Endless Fist Soc., Inc. Scholar Gerry Graber Scholarship Com., 1975; State of Wis. honors grantee, 1975. Mem. Edina C. of C. Avocations: reading, sewing, walking, knitting, gardening. Home: 4515 Andover Rd Edina MN 55435-4031 Office: Neff Law Firm PA 7760 France Ave S Bloomington MN 55435-5800

POWELL, CHRISTOPHER ROBERT, systems engineering and management consultant; b. Summit, N.J., Feb. 2, 1963; s. Robin Powell and Nancy Mae (Spurling) Gould; m. Bonnie Jean Manning, June 10, 1989; 1 child, Emilie Alyson Grace. BS in Math. and Computer Sci., Clarkson U., 1984; postgrad., Syracuse U., 1984-88, Binghamton U., Binghamton, 1988-90; MBA summa cum laude, U. Wis., Eau Claire, 2001. Sr. assoc. program IBM Corp., Endicott, NY, 1984-90; sr. systems analyst/programmer Supercomputer Systems, Inc., Eau Claire, Wis., 1990-93; systems programmer prin. Network Systems Corp./Channel Networking Strategic Bus. Unit, Brooklyn Park, Minn., 1993-96; sys. engring. mgr. II Sequent Computer Sys., Eau Claire, Wis., 1996-99, IBM Corp., Eau Claire, 1999-2000; v.p. program mgmt. Tonbu, Inc., 2000; dir. integration High Performance Techs., Inc., Arlington, Va., 2001—. Exhibitor forum Supercomputing Conf., Boulder, Colo., 2001. Appt. City of Spring Lake Park Energy Commn., 1995; vice chmn. Energy Commn., 1996; treas. First Baptist Ch., Eau Claire, 2000—. Grad. fellow U. Wis., Eau Claire, 2001. Mem. IEEE, AAAS, Assn. for Computing Machinery, Nat. Systems Programmers Assn., NSC Leadership Forum, Alpha Phi Omega (torchbearer 1987-2001), Pi Mu Epsilon, Pi Delta Epsilon, Phi Kappa Phi. Democrat. Mem. Am. Baptist Ch. Achievements include assisting in Network Systems and Sequent computer systems registrations for ISO 9000; architect, developer NUMACenter Unix and Windows NT server system, including Advanced Detection and Availability Manager systems management solution. Home: 3311 W Country Club Ln Altoona WI 54720-1013

POWELL, COLIN LUTHER, secretary of state, retired military officer, author, public speaker; b. N.Y.C., Apr. 5, 1937; s. Luther and Maud Ariel (McKoy) P.; m. Alma V. Johnson, Aug. 25, 1962; children: Michael, Linda, Annemarie. BS, CUNY, 1958; MBA, George Washington U., 1971. Commd. 2d lt. U.S. Army, 1958; advanced through grades to gen., 1989; comdr. 2d Brigade, 101st Airborne Div., 1976-77; exec. asst. to sec. Dept. Energy, 1979; sr. mil. asst. to Dep. Sec. Def. Dept. Def., 1979-81, asst. div. comdr. 4th Inf. Div. Colo., 1981-83, mil. asst. to Sec. of Def. Washington, 1983-86; assigned to U.S. V Corps, Europe, 1986-87; dep. asst. to the pres. for nat. security affairs The White House, Washington, 1987; asst. to Pres. for nat. security affairs, 1987-89; comdr.-in-chief Forces Command, Ft. McPherson, Ga., 1989-94; chmn. Joint Chiefs of Staff The Pentagon, Washington, 1989-93; ret., 1993; sec. of state, 2001—. Founding chair Am.'s Promise. Author: My American Journey, 1995. Decorated Legion of Merit, Bronze Star, Air medal, Purple Heart; The White House fellow, 1972-73; recipient Medal of Freedom (2); named hon. knight comdr. Most Honorable Order of the Bath Queen Elizabeth II, 1993. Mem. Assn. U.S. Army. Episcopalian. Office: Dept State 2201 C St NW Washington DC 20520*

POWELL, CURTIS EVERETT, music educator, college official; b. Birmingham, Ala., Oct. 29, 1961; s. Henry Frank and Susie (Pen) P. Student, U. Rochester Eastman Sch. Music, 1982; BA, Talladega Coll., 1983; MA, Ala. State U., 1987; postgrad., Howard U., 1983-85, Westminster Choir Coll., 1989, U. N.C., Greensboro, U. Okla., 1992—. Vis. lectr. in music, coll. organist Talladega (Ala.) Coll., 1985-98, mem. faculty, 1996-97; dir. univ. choir, organist Selma (Ala.) U., 1986-91; dir. choral studies N.C. A&T State U., Greensboro, 1987-91; dir. choirs Prairie View (Tex.) A&M U., 1991-98; piano accompanist Howard U. Chorale, Washington, 1983-85; opera workshop personnel Duke Ellington Sch. Arts, 1983-84; organist, choir master Met. United Meth. Ch., Greensboro, 1989-91; dir. choirs Prairie View Tex. A&M U., 1991—; min. of music, activities coord. Big Bethel AME Ch., Atlanta, 1996-97; min. of music, sr. adminstrv. officer Morehouse Coll./Martin Luther King Jr. Internat. Chapel, 1997-98; coord. music ministry 6th Ave. Bapt. Ch., Birmingham, Ala., 1998—. Facilitator Arts D.C., Washington, 1987; participant Spl. Dirs. tour Italy, 1989-90; choral music clinician in field; hon. mem. rsch. bd. advisors Am. Biog. Inst., 1987. Recipient Bodman Scholarship United Negro Coll. Fund, 1983. Mem. Am. Choral Dirs. Assn., Nat. Assn. Negro Musicians, N.C. Music Educators Assn., Phi Mu Alpha, Alpha Phi Apha, Alpha Chi. Home: PO Box 19841 Birmingham AL 35219-0841 E-mail: CPowell920@aol.com.

POWELL, DAN CLAYTON, physician; b. Amarillo, Tex., July 23, 1965; s. Robert Luther and Merrilyn Kay (Gober) P.; m. Lisa Marie Gomez, June 10, 1989; children: Gabrielle Marie, Landon Wren. BS in Biology, Abilene Christin U., 1987; MD, U. Tex., 1991. Diplomate Am. Bd. Family Practice. Resident in family practice St. Joseph Hosp., Denver, 1991-94; family physician Family Medicine Ctr., Pampa, Tex., 1994-97. Chief dept. medicine Columbia Med. Ctr., Pampa, 1996, chmn. emergency com. 1997, med. dir. Columbia Home Health, Pampa, 1995-97; sec. staff Pampa Regional Med. Ctr., 2000. Author/co-editor: The Pickwicker, 1990, 91; author: (poetry) Of Time and Tide, 1998. Bd. dirs. ARC, Gray County, Tex., 1995-97; deacon and mem. Mary Ellen and Harvester Ch. of Christ, Pampa, 1997-2000; cmty. sponsor, spkr. Tar Wars, Pampa, 1996—; curriculum instr. Worth the Wait, 1997—, bd. dirs., 2001—; elder Body of Christ Ch., Pampa, 2001—. Recipient dean's scholarship U. Tex. Med. Sch., San Antonio, 1988; named Outstaning Young Man of Am., 1998. Mem. AMA, Tex. Med. Assn., Am. Acad. Family Practice, Tex. Acad. Family Practice, Internat. Soc. Poets. Avocations: reading, writing, music, church, running. Office: Family Medicine Ctr 3023 Perryton Pkwy Ste 101 Pampa TX 79065 E-mail: dpowmd@hotmail.com.

POWELL, DANNYE ROMINE, news columnist; b. Miami, Jan. 4, 1941; d. Daniel Webster Gibson and Elma Evans Cowan Gibson; m. Benjamin Houston Romine Jr., Aug. 11, 1962 (div. Mar. 1978); children: Benjamin Houston Romine III, Daniel Patrick Romine; m. Lewis Eddins Powell, Mar. 3, 1979. BA in English, Fla. State U., 1962. English tchr. Brooks County H.S., Quitman, Ga., 1962-63; reporter Durham (N.C.) Sun Newspaper, 1965-68; book rev. editor The Charlotte Observer, N.C., 1975-92, local news columnist, 1992—. Author: The New Republic, 1998, Paris Review, 1975, Poetry, 1995, (poetry) At Every Wedding Someone Stays Home, 1994, Parting the Curtains: Interviews with Southern Writers, 1994, The Ecstasy of Regret, 2002. Bd. dirs. Hezekiah Alexander Hist. Mus., Charlotte, 1995, Arts and Sci. Coun., Charlotte, 1975. Poetry fellowship Nat. Endowment for the Arts, 1993-94; N.C. Arts Coun. fellow in poetry, 1999; recipient ACE award Women in Comm., 1998, Sam Ragan award contbn. in arts, N.C., 2001. Mem. N.C. Press Assn., Nat. Book Critics, N.C. Writers Network (bd. dirs. 1997), Charlotte Writers Club, Caroliniana Soc.. Democrat. Baptist. Home: 700 E Park Ave Charlotte NC 28203-5146 Office: The Charlotte Observer 600 S Tryon St Charlotte NC 28202-1842 E-mail: Dannyc700@aol.com.

POWELL, DAVID THOMAS, JR. retired association administrator; b. Nashville, Dec. 29, 1941; s. David Thomas and Georgia Juanita (Pennington) P.; divorced; children: David Thomas III, Sheryl Renae, Natalie Sue, Joel Brian. Student, St. Leo's Coll., St. Leo, Fla., 1975. Enlisted USAF, 1959, advanced through grades to master sgt., 1976, ret., 1979; meteorologist Sta. KVET-CASE Radio, Austin, Tex., 1979-80; weather technician Nat. Weather Svc., Huron, S.D., 1980-82, Chattanooga, 1982—; regional councilman Nat. Weather Svc. Employees Orgn., Tenn., Ga. and Ala., 1982-84, exec. v.p., 1984-89, nat. pres., 1989-95, chief labor negotiator, 1985-89. Interface and coord. with various legislators; participant in drafting legis., coord. legis. betwen Ho. of Reps. and Senate coms. or subcoms.; cons. meteorology and labor/mgmt. matters; charter mem. Dept. Commerce Labor/Mgmt. Coun.; presenter in field. Judge Regional Sci. Fair, Chattanooga, 1983, 87. Named Mil. Airlift Command Tech. Advisor of Yr., 1977. Mem. Internat. Platform Assn., Dept. of Commerce Nat. Oceanic and Atmospheric Adminstrn. and Nat. Weather Svc. Labor/Mgmt. Partnership Couns. (charter), Nat. Weather Svc. Employees Orgn. (life). Democrat. Baptist. Avocations: shooting, bowling. Home: # K8 4639 Goldfinch Dr Zephyrhills FL 33541-7101

POWELL, DONALD ASHMORE, clinical research psychologist; b. Spartanburg, S.C., Oct. 29, 1938; s. Russell Kermit Powell and Mignon Kathlene Cox; m. Shirley L. Buchanan, Aug. 17, 1992 (dec. June 1998); children: Donald Langston, Donetta Plamyra, Ashley Preston, Stephanie Anne, Trisha Pope. BS, U. S.C., 1960, MA, 1962; PhD, Fla. State U., 1967. Rsch. pychologist Dorn VA Med. Ctr., Columbia, S.C., 1969—, acting dir. R&D, 1996-2000; assoc. prof. U. S.C. Sch. Medicine, 1979—. Adj. prof. U. S.C., Columbia, 1969—; cons. U.S. Heart, Lung and Blood Inst., Bethesda, 1986—; program specialist VA Mental Health and Behavioral Scis., Washington, 1984-88. Author: (with others) Eyeblink Conditioning, 1999. Rsch. fellowship NIH, 1967-69; vis. scholar NIH, 1974; recipient Merit Rsch. award Dept. of Vet. Affairs, 1996—. Mem. Soc. for Neurosci., Am. Psychol. Soc., Pavlovian Soc. (Pavlovian Rsch. award 1991), Soc. for Neurosci. (pres. S.C. chpt. 1980-81, councilor 1982-85). Democrat. Avocations: running, reading. Home: 405 Hunt Cliff Dr Columbia SC 29229 Office: Dorn VA Med Ctr 6439 Garners Ferry Rd Columbia SC 29209-1638

POWELL, DONALD E. federal agency administrator; b. Tex. m. Twanna Powell; 2 children. BS Econs., West Tex. StateU.; grad., So. Meth. U. CEO First Nat. Bank Amarillo, Tex.; chmn. FDIC, Washington, 2001—. Active City of Amarillo Housing Bd., Lindsay Student Aid Fund, Cal Farley's Boys Ranch; past bd. dirs. High Plains Bapt. Hosp., Harrington Regional Med. Ctr. Office: FDIC 550 17th St NW Washington DC 20429-0001*

POWELL, DURWOOD ROYCE, lawyer; b. Raleigh, N.C., Nov. 21, 1951; s. Albert Royce and Powell; m. Leej Ida Copperfield, Mar. 1, 1980. BS, U. N.C., 1974, JD, 1979; LLM in Taxation, Emory U., 1985. Bar: N.C. 1979, U.S. Dist. Ct. (ea., mid. and we. dists.) N.C. 1981, U.S. Tax Ct. 1981, U.S. Ct. Appeals (4th cir.) 1984, U.S. Ct. Claims 1984, U.S. Supreme Ct. 1984, D.C. 1988, U.S. Ct. Appeals (D.C. cir.) 1988, N.Y. 1989. Mgmt. analyst GAO, Norfolk, Va., 1974-76; tax staff Arthur Andersen & Co., Washington, 1979-80; assoc. Biggs, Meadows, Etheridge & Johnson, Rocky Mount, N.C., 1980-82, Biggs Law Firm, Rocky Mount, 1982-83; ptnr. Maupin, Taylor, Ellis & Adams, Raleigh, N.C., 1985—, also bd. dirs., 1985—. Adj. prof. corp. taxation Grad. Sch. Bus., U. N.C., Chapel Hill, 1989-92; faculty Duke U. Tax and Estate Planning Conf., 1991; mem. negotiation project Harvard U., Cambridge, Mass., 1992. Contbr. articles to profl. jours. Tax reform com. Duke U., Washington, 1988. Mem. ABA (tax, corp., banking and securities sects.), N.C. Bar Assn. (tax and corp. sects.), Phi Beta Kappa, Phi Eta Sigma. Home: 7616 Wingfoot Dr Raleigh NC 27615-5485 Office: Maupin Taylor Ellis & Adams 3200 Beech Leaf Ct Ste 500 Raleigh NC 27604-1064

POWELL, EARL ALEXANDER, III, art museum director; b. Spartanburg, S.C., Oct. 24, 1943; s. Earl Alexander and Elizabeth (Duckworth) P.; m. Nancy Landry Powell, July 17, 1971; children: Cortney, Channing, Sumner. AB with honors, Williams Coll., 1966; AM, Harvard U., 1970, PhD, 1974; DFA (hon.), Williams Coll., 1993. Tchg. fellow in fine arts Harvard U., 1970-74; curator Michener Collection U. Tex., Austin, 1974-76, asst. prof. art history, 1974-76; mus. curator, sr. staff asst. to asst. dir. and chief curator Nat. Gallery Art, Washington, 1976-78, exec. curator, 1979-80; dir. L.A. County Mus. Art, 1980-92, Nat. Gallery Art, Washington, 1992—. Trustee Am. Fedn. Arts, White House Hist. Assn., Nat. Trust Hist. Preservation; Georgia O'Keeffe Found.; mem. fine arts com. Friends of Art and Preservation in Embassies; nat. adv. bd. O'Keeffe Mus.; mem. com. for preservation The White House; fed. coun. Arts and Humanities; fine arts adv. panel Fed. Res. Bd.; mem. overseer's com. Visit the Art Mus., Harvard; mem. Fogg fellows coun. Harvard U. Art Mus.; mem. Nat. Portrait Gallery Com., Nat. Coun. on Arts; adv. com. Newport Art Mus. Author: American Art at Harvard, 1973, Selections from the James Michener Collection, 1975, Abstract Expressionists and Imagists: A Retrospective View, 1976, Milton Avery, 1976, The James A. Michener Collection: Twentieth Century American Painting, catalogue raisonne, 1978, Thomas Cole monograph, 1990. With U.S. Navy, 1966-69, comdr. Res., 1976-80. Decorated chevalier of Arts and Letters, 1985, Chevalier of the Legion of Honor, 2000; grand ofcl. Order of the Infante D. Henrique medal, 1995; recipient King Olav medal, 1978, Bicentennial medal Williams Coll., 1995; Harvard U. travelling fellow, 1973-74, Mexican Cultural award, 1996, Commendatore dell'Ordine al Merito della Republica Italiana, 1998. Mem. Walpole Soc., Assn. Art Mus. Dirs.

POWELL, EDMUND WILLIAM, lawyer; b. St. Paul, Dec. 23, 1922; s. George L. and Mary (Sexton) P.; m. Ellen M. Williams, May 7, 1949; children— Susan Marie, Sarah Ann, Daniel. Student, St. Thomas Coll., St. Paul, 1941-43, U. Minn., 1943, 46; LL.B., Marquette U., 1948. Bar: Wis. bar 1948. Pvt. practice, Milw., 1948-97; pres. firm Borgelt, Powell, Peterson & Frauen and predecessors, 1948-90. Served with USNR, 1943-45; to capt. USMCR, 1945-46, 52-53. Fellow Am. Coll. Trial Lawyers; mem. State Bar Wis. (sec. 1964-65, bd. govs. 1961-63, 65-67, sec., dir. ins. sect. 1962-69), Marquette Law Alumni Assn. (pres., dir. 1957-60), Town Club (Milw.), Country Club of Hilton Head. Home: 3113 E Hampshire Ave Milwaukee WI 53211-3117

POWELL, EDWARD LEE, broadcasting company executive; b. Columbus, Ohio, July 3, 1958; s. Louis Andrew and Margaret Letitia (Steen) P.; m. Denise Noel Harlow, July 11, 1981; children: Edward Lee II, Sarah Elizabeth. BS in Bus. Mgmt. and Mktg., Franklin U., 1988. Freelance square dance caller, rec. artist, Reynoldsburg, Ohio, 1976—; columnist Columbus Dispatch Newspaper, 1976-79; disc jockey, salesperson Sta. WWWJ, Johnstown, Ohio, 1978-79; disc jockey, ops. dir. Sta. WLGN-AM-FM, Logan, 1980-81; disc jockey Sta. WMNI, Columbus, 1980-89, creative dir., disc jockey, 1987-89; disc jockey Sta. WMGG-FM, 1987—; gen. mgr. Radio Sound Network, Ohio, 1989-90; prin. Group X, Reynoldsburg, 1990—, Radio Cafe Hour/Cafe Prodns. Inc., Branson, Mo., 1993-95. Cons. mktg. and advt. programs, 1984-95, Central Ohio Corp. of Dance Clubs, Columbus, 1982—, direct mail; spokeman, guest on TV; bd. dirs. Y.E.S. (wheelchair) Dancers, Inc., 1986-89, nat. and state square dance conventions, 1976—. Creative dir. advt. campaigns: Levi's, Cavalier; producer, talent advt. campaign Suzuki Motorcycles, 1981 (award of excellence), (record) Phoenix on Her Mind, 1978; author, pub.: So You Want to Be a Caller, 1979; songwriter BMI. Active Ctrl. Ohio Muscular Dystrophy Assn., 1990-92; co-host, organizer Muscular Dystrophy Local Telethon, Beulah Park, Grove City, 1987-89, Reynoldsburg, 1977-80; asst. scoutmaster Boy Scouts Am., 1975-80, den leader Cub Scouts; hon. dep. sheriff Franklin County, 1988-92. Recipient Eagle Scout award, 1971; Ohio State Life Ins. scholar, 1987, Farmer's Ins. Group scholar, 1986, Honda of Am. Found. scholar, 1986; named one of nation's Top 10 Square Dance Callers, 1979. Mem. Franklin U. Alumni Assn., Columbus Bd. Realtors, Ohio Bd. Realtors, Nat. Bd. Realtors, Cen. Ohio Sq. Dancers, Reynoldsburg Promenaders, Muscular Dystrophy Assn.-Cen. Ohio (past bd. dirs.) Franklin U. Top Execs. Club. Avocations: songwriting, entertainment and consumer marketing, recording and production, square dancing. Home: PO Box 40 Reynoldsburg OH 43068-0040 Office: Group X Inc Radiowriters PO Box 65 Reynoldsburg OH 43068-0065 E-mail: SignsByFastEddie@aol.com.

POWELL, EDWIN CHARLES, music educator, conductor, musician; b. Healdsburg, Calif., May 27, 1962; s. Martin Clark and Susan Chaffey Powell; m. Kristin Marie Wingard, June 17, 1989; children: Emily Rose. MusB Edn., U. Pacific, 1989; MusM Edn., U. of Cin., 1995; D Mus. Arts, U. North Tex., 1997. Dir. of bands McLennan C.C., Waco, Tex., 1997—2000; asst. prof. of music/asst. dir. of bands U. of Tenn., Knoxville, 2000—. Musician: (trumpet player) Opera, 2000; contbr. articles to profl. publs. Named Guest Artist, All-Kingdom Music Festival, Saudi Arabia, 2002. Mem.: Music Educators Nat. Conf., World Assn. for Symphonic Bands and Ensembles, Coll. Band Dir. Nat. Assn. (Tenn. state chair 2000—02), Pi Kappa Pi, Pi Kappa Lambda. Avocations: skiing, golf. Home: 1217 Raintree Rd Knoxville TN 37923 Office: U Tenn Bands 149 Music Building Knoxville TN 37996 Personal E-mail: edpowell@utk.edu.

POWELL, ERIC KARLTON, lawyer, researcher; b. Parkersburg, W.Va., July 23, 1958; s. James Milton and Sarah Elizabeth (Gates) P. BA in History, W.Va. U., 1980, BSBA, 1981; JD, Western State U., Fullerton, Calif., 1987. Bar: Ga. 1992, W.Va. 1993, U.S. Dist. Ct. (we. dist.) W.Va. 1993. Reference libr. Western State U., 1984; tchr. acctg. Rosary H.S., Fullerton, 1984-85; law clk. Zonni, Ginnochio Taylor, Santa Ana, Calif., 1986-93; temp. law sch. Gibson, Dunn & Crutcher, Irvine, 1993; pvt. practice, Parkersburg, 1993—. Asst. scoutmaster Boy Scouts Am., Parkersburg, 1981-83. Mem. ABA, ATLA, W.Va. Trial Lawyers Assn., Nat. Eagle Scout Assn., Elks, Delta Theta Phi. Republican. Presbyterian. Avocations: hiking, reading, canoeing, chess, astronomy. Home: 2002 20th St Parkersburg WV 26101-3606 Office: 500 Green St Parkersburg WV 26101-5131

POWELL, FREDRICK CHARLES, business executive; b. Meadville, Pa., Aug. 27, 1940; s. Robert Edward and Mary Orpha (Byham) P.; m. Rebecca Sue Hill, June 16, 1962; children: Kelly Powell Logan, Jeffrey S., Donald F., Sharon Powell Weidner. BA in Econs. and Bus., Alfred U., 1962; MPA, Cornell U., 1970. COO Arnot-Ogden Meml. Hosp., Elmira, N.Y., 1970-72; adminstr., faculty Cornell U. Health Svcs., Ithaca, 1972-74; pres., CEO Bradford (Pa.) Hosp., 1974-82; exec. v.p. Rehab. Hosp. Svcs. Corp., Camp Hill, Pa., 1982-87; pres., chair, founder Rehab. Systems Co., 1987-93; pres., CEO Interactive Health Co., 1995—; pres., founder OMNI Interactive Systems, 1993—. Bd. dirs. CORA Health Svcs., Inc., Lima, Ohio, Campania Ins.Co., Vienna, Va., Generations Mgmt. Svcs., Elderport Inc., Cascade Inst. Co.; cons. AlphaCare, Berks, Eng., 1996—. Bd. trustees Alfred U., 1992—, Wesley Theol. Seminary, Washington, 1992—, United Meth. Ch., Camp Hill, 1995--. Capt. U.S. Army, 1962-67. Mem. Sloan Alumni Assn., Delta Sigma Phi. Avocations: ecology, bridge, tennis, travel, gardening. Office: OMNI Interactive Systems 861 Market St Lemoyne PA 17043-1519 E-mail: moores690@aol.com.

POWELL, JAMES BOBBITT, biomedical laboratories executive, pathologist; b. Burlington, N.C., Aug. 28, 1938; s. Thomas Edward and Sophia (Sharpe) P.; m. Pamela Oughton, Sept. 12, 1969 (div. Sept. 1979); 1 child, Daphne P. Markcrow; m. Anne Ellington, Oct. 20, 1984; children: James Bobbitt (dec.), John Banks, James Rosser, Helen Bobbitt. BA, Va. Mil. Inst., 1960; MD, Duke U., 1964. Diplomate Am. Bd. Pathology. Intern Duke U. Med. Ctr., Durham, N.C., 1964-65; resident Cornell Med. Ctr., N.Y.C., 1965-67, Englewood (N.J.) Hosp., 1967-69; founder Biomed Labs, Burlington, N.C., 1969—; pres. Roche Biomed. Labs., 1982-95; pres., CEO Lab. Corp. Am. Holdings, 1995-97; CEO Tripath Imaging, Burlington, NC, 1997—2000; pres. Palatin Devel. Corp., 2000—. Bd. dirs. Mid-Carolina Bank, U.S. Trust N.C., Pathology Ptnrs., Inc., Lab. Corp., Inc., Warren Land Co., Carolina Drs. Care, Mercury, Md., Green Capital Fin. Contbr. articles to sci. publs. Trustee Elon (N.C.) U., 1979—; bd. overseers Duke U. Comprehensive Cancer Ctr.; chmn. bd. dirs. Alamance Found.; bd. dirs. Alamance Regional Med. Ctr. Maj. Med. Corps U.S. Army, 1969—72. Fellow Am. Soc. Clin Pathologists, Coll. Am. Pathologists; mem. Alamance Country Club. Republican. Methodist. Avocations: tennis, U.S. military history. Home: 1573 York Pl Burlington NC 27215-3360 Office: Palatin Devel Corp 1573 York Pl Burlington NC 27215 E-mail: jpowellyorkplace@aol.com.

POWELL, JAMES HENRY, lawyer; b. N.Y.C., May 1, 1928; s. Milton Jerome and Doris (Unterberg) P.; m. Connie Lu Egger, Oct. 5, 1958; children: David E., Andrew J., Jeffrey K. AB, Harvard U., 1949; LLB, Yale U., 1952. Bar: N.Y. 1952. Assoc. McLaughlin and Stern, N.Y.C., 1955-69; atty. ABC, 1969-72; assoc. Fried Frank Harris Shriver & Jacobson, 1972-76, Patterson Belknap Webb & Tyler, N.Y.C., 1976-80, ptnr., 1980-95; pvt. practice, 1996—. Mem. exec. com. Lexington Dem. Club, 1961-63. With U.S. Army, 1953-55. Mem. Assn. of Bar of City of N.Y., City Athletic Club N.Y.C. (mem. bd. govs. 1973-81), Phi Beta Kappa. Office: 477 Madison Ave New York NY 10022-5802

POWELL, JAMES LAWRENCE, museum director; b. Berea, Ky., July 17, 1936; s. Robert Lain and Lizena (Davis) P.; m. Joan Hartmann; children: Marla, Dirk, Joanna. AB, Berea Coll., 1958; PhD, MIT, 1962; DSc (hon.), Oberlin Coll., 1983; LHD (hon.), Tohoku Gakuin U., 1986; DSc (hon.), Beaver Coll., 1992. Mem. faculty Oberlin Coll., Ohio, 1962-83, also prof. geology, asso. dean, 1973-75, v.p., provost, 1976-83; pres. Franklin and Marshall Coll., Lancaster, Pa., 1983-88, Reed Coll., Portland, Oreg., 1988-91; pres., chief exec. officer The Franklin Inst., Phila., 1991-94; pres., dir. Los Angeles County Mus. Natural History, L.A., 1994—. Mem. Nat. Sci. Bd., 1986-98. Author: Strontium Isotope Geology, 1972, Pathways to Leadership: Achieving and Sustaining Success: A Guide for Nonprofit Executives, 1995, Night Comes to the Coctzcems; Dinosaur Extinction and the Transformation of Modern Geology, 1998. Fellow Geol. Soc. Am. Office: LA County Mus Nat Hist 900 Exposition Blvd Los Angeles CA 90007-4057*

POWELL, JAMES MATTHEW, history educator; b. Cin., June 9, 1930; s. Matthew James and Mary Loretta (Weaver) P.; m. Judith Catherine Davidorf, May 29, 1954 (dec. 1992); children: James, Michael, Mark, Mary Helen, Miriam, John BA, Xavier U., Cin., 1953, MA, 1955; postgrad., U. Cin., 1955-57; PhD, Ind. U., 1960. Instr. Kent State U., Ohio, 1959-61; asst. prof. U. Ill., Urbana, 1961-65, Syracuse U., N.Y., 1965-67, assoc. prof., 1967-72, prof. history, 1972—, dir. Ranke Cataloging Project, 1977—. Disting. vis.

prof. medieval history Rutgers U., New Brunswick, 1996—. Author: Medieval Monarchy and Trade, 1962, Civilization of the West, 1967, Anatomy of a Crusade, 1213-1221, 1986, 2d edit., 1990, Albertanus of Brescia: The Pursuit of Happiness in the Early Thirteenth Century, 1992; translator: Liber Augustalis, 1971; editor: Innocent III: Vicar of Christ or Lord of the World, 1963, revised and enlarged 2d edit., 1994, Medieval Studies, 1976, 2d edit., 1992; (with George G. Iggers) Leopold von Ranke and the Shaping of the Historical Discipline, 1989, Muslims Under Latin Rule, 1100-1300, 1990, (with Michael Gervers) Tolerance and Intolerance: Social Conflict in the Age of the Crusades, 2001; contbg. editor: New Catholic Encyclopedia, 2000—; cons. Ency. of the Crusades, 2000-; contbr. articles to profl. jours. Grantee NEH, 1977-84, 84, Inst. for Advanced Study, Princeton, N.J., 1989-90, Progetto Radici, Brescia, Italy, 1994-95; Fritz Thyssen Stiftung, 1986, 89; recipient John Gilmary Shea prize Am. Cath. Hist. Assn., 1987, Fellow Royal Hist. Soc. (corr.); mem. Am. Hist. Assn., Am. Cath. Hist. Assn., Medieval Acad. Am., Soc. for Italian Hist. Studies (coun. 1976-79, v.p. 1991-92, pres. 1993-95), Midwest Medieval Conf. (pres. 1965-66), Soc. for Study of the Crusades and the Latin East (sec. 1989-95), Haskins Soc. Democrat. Roman Catholic. Office: Syracuse U Maxwell School Syracuse NY 13244-0001

POWELL, JAMES MONROE, lawyer, singer; b. Ashtabula, Ohio, May 27, 1939; s. Gerald and Lois Powell; m. Judith M. Weir, Aug. 12, 1961; children: Janai Lane, Jennifer Ernst, Julene Zizza. BS, U.S. Mcht. Marine Acad., 1961; JD, U. Mich., 1964. Bar: Alaska 1965, U.S. Dist. Ct. Alaska 1965, U.S. Ct. Appeals (9th cir.) 1965. Law clk. Alaska Supreme Ct., Fairbanks, 1964-65; ptnr. Hughes Thorsness Powell Huddleston & Bauman, Anchorage, 1965—. Mem. Alaska Bd. Govs., Anchorage, 1970—74; trustee Sheldon Jackson Coll., 2001—. Capt. CAP U.S. Army, 1997—. Presbyterian. Avocations: flying (pilot), singing. Home: 2143 Churchill Dr Anchorage AK 99517-1311 Office: Hughes Thorsness Et Al 550 W 7th Ave Ste 1100 Anchorage AK 99501-3563 E-mail: JMP@htlaw.com.

POWELL, J(OHN) KEY, estate planner, consultant; b. Dallas, Dec. 14, 1925; s. Floyd Berkeley and Eloise (Sadler) P.; m. Ann Penniman, July 14, 1950; children: Nena Ann, Scott Key, Elliott Edward. , U. Ala., Tuscaloosa, 1946-47, , 1949-50, So. Meth. U., Dallas, 1947-48, Am. Coll., Bryn Mawr, Pa., 1973. CLU. Agt. Life Ins. Sales, Tuscaloosa, 1950-54; agt., sales mgr. John Hancock, Lubbock, Tex., 1954-57, asst. supt. gen. agys. Boston, 1957-59, gen. agt. S.C. Columbia, 1959-85; cons. Creative Giving Concepts, 1989—. Vice chmn. First Sun South Corp., Columbia, 1990—. Pres. John Hancock Gen. Agents Assn., Boston, 1969-70, Columbia Rotary Club, 1985-86; pres. Gen. Agts. and Mgrs. Assn., Columbia, 1974-75, nat. bd. dirs., Washington, 1975-77; chmn. Ctrl. Carolina Cmty. Found., Columbia, 1987-89, Richland Mem. Hosp. Ctr. Cancer Rsch., Columbia, 1988-89; immediate past chmn. Salvation Army. With USAAC, 1943-45. Mem. Nat. Assn. Life Underwriters, Citizens Advocating Decency and Revival of Ethics (past chmn.), U. S.C. Med. Sch. Ptnrs. Found. Republican. Presbyterian. Avocations: fishing, golf, reading, traveling, hunting. Office: Creative Giving Concepts 212 Holliday Rd Columbia SC 29223-3124

POWELL, JOUETT LYNN, college dean, philosophy and religious studies educator; b. Dallas, Dec. 2, 1941; s. Hiram Wheeler and Evelyn Ruth (Foster) P.; m. Mary Ellen Beall, Aug. 15, 1964; 1 child, Kristen Lynn. BA, Baylor U., 1964; BD, So. Bapt. Theol. Sem., 1967; MPhil, Yale U., 1970, PhD, 1972. Instr. relgion U. N.C., Chapel Hill, 1971-72, asst. prof. religion, 1972-78; asst. prof. philosophy and religious studies Christopher Newport U., Newport News, Va., 1978-80, assoc. prof., 1980-89, prof., 1989, dean Sch. Letters and Natural Sci., 1983-92, dean Coll. Arts and Humanities, 1992-95, dir. grad. studies, 1992-95, acting provost, 1995-96, dean Coll. Liberal Arts, 1996-2000. Vis. assoc. prof. religion Coll. William and Mary, 1984-85, 87-90. Contbr. articles to scholarly and profl. jours. Recipient summer seminar stipend NEH, 1981, summer rsch. stipend, 1982; Rockefeller doctoral fellow Yale U., 1969-70; Smith-Reynolds Found. grantee, 1974. Mem. AAUP, Am. Acad. Religion, Am. Philos. Assn., Am. Assn. Higher Edn. Democrat. Episcopalian. Avocations: classical music, carpentry. Home: 65 Rivermont Dr Newport News VA 23601-4232 Office: Christopher Newport U Newport News VA 23606-2998 E-mail: jouettpowell@netscape.net.

POWELL, KATHLEEN LYNCH, lawyer, real estate executive; b. N.Y.C., Dec. 30, 1949; d. Daniel Francis and Mary Margaret (Flynn) L.; m. P. Douglas Powell. BA in Math. cum laude, Coll. of Mt. St. Vincent, 1970; postgrad., U. Pa., 1976-77; JD cum laude, U. Md., 1977; LL.M. in Taxation, NYU, 1991. Bar: Pa. 1977, N.J. 1978, N.Y. 1984, D.C. 1985, Conn. 1995, U.S. Ct. Appeals (3d cir.) 1980, U.S. Supreme Ct. 1981. Research analyst, claims rep. Social Security Adminstrn., Balt., 1973-76; assoc. Drinker, Biddle & Reath, Phila., 1977-84, ptnr., 1984-86; v.p., gen. counsel M. Alfieri Co., Inc., Edison, N.J., 1987-89; v.p., counsel Berwind Property Group, Phila., 1992—. Instr. Inst. for Paralegal Tng., Phila. 1984—. Vol. atty. Support Ctr. for Child Advocates, Phila., 1979-86, Queen Village Neighbors Assn., Phila., 1984-86; pres. Soc. Hill Towers Buyers Assn., Phila., 1979-80; bd. dirs. Soc. Hill Civic Assn., 1980. Mem. ABA, Pa. Bar Assn., Phila. Bar Assn. (chair zoning and land use com. 1985-86), Conn. Bar Assn.

POWELL, KEITH RICHARDSON, pediatrician, administrator; b. Detroit, Jan. 28, 1946; s. Mary Elizabeth (Richardson) Dittman; m. Michele M. Hooper, Feb. 20, 1979; children: Lindsey Erin, Thomas Owen. AB, Washington U., St. Louis, 1967; MD, St. Louis U., 1971. Cert. physician exec. Pediatric resident Cardinal Glennon Hosp., St. Louis, 1971-73; infectious diseases fellow UCLA, 1973-75; spl. epidemiologist WHO, India, 1975; infectious disease fellow U. Va., Charlottesville, 1975-77; asst. prof. pediat. McGill U., Montreal, Que., Can., 1977-79; asst. prof. to prof. pediat. U. Rochester, N.Y., 1979-98, George Washington Coler prof. pediat., 1989; prof. pediat., chmn. dept. Northeastern Ohio Univs. Coll. Medicine, Rootstown, 1998—. Cons. on newly ind. states U.S. AID, 1993-97; Noah Miller chmn. pediat. Children's Hosp. Med. Ctr. Akron, 1998—, v.p., 1999—; trustee Children's Hosp. Physician Assocs., Ohio Children's Health Network, Inc., Child Dimension Ins. Co. Contbr. over 20 chpts. to books, over 100 articles to profl. jours. RWJ Found. Health Policy fellow, Washington, 1992. Fellow: Infectious Diseases Soc. Am. (pub. policy com. 2001—), Am. Acad. Pediat. (infectious disease com. 2001—); mem.: European Soc. Pediatric Infectious Diseases, Am. Coll. Physician Execs., Am. Pediatric Soc., Soc. Pediatric Rsch., Pediatric Infectious Diseases Soc. Am. (coun. mem. 1989—93). Democrat. Lutheran. Avocations: gardening, martial arts, basketball, making jam. Office: Childrens Hosp Med Ctr of Akron Exec Sec Terry L Cheronis One Perkins Sq Akron OH 44308-1062 E-mail: kpowell@chmca.org.

POWELL, KENNETH EDWARD, investment banker; b. Danville, Va., Oct. 5, 1952; s. Terry Edward and C. Anne (Wooten) P.; m. Cicely Grandin Moorman, Jan. 3, 1976; children: Tanner, Priscilla. Student, Hampden-Sydney Coll., 1971-73; BA in Polit. Sci., U. Colo., 1975; JD, U. Richmond, 1978; LLM in Taxation, Coll. of William and Mary, 1982. Bar: Va. 1978, U.S. Dist. Ct. (ea. dist.) Va. 1979, U.S. Tax Ct. 1980. Ptnr. Maloney, Yeatts & Barr, Richmond, Va., 1978-87; ptnr., owner Hazel & Thomas, P.C., 1987-94, mem. bus./tax team, internat. bus. team; v.p. Legg Mason, Va., 1994—. Vice chmn. Sci. Mus. Va., Richmond, 1984-91; chmn. Va. Police Found., Inc., 1987; bd. dirs. State Edn. Assistance Authority, 1991—; mem. adv. bd. Va. Opera, 1991—; candidate U.S. Congress, Va., 1986. Recipient Disting. Svc. award Fraternal Order of Police, 1986; named Outstanding Young Man of the Yr., Jaycees, 1981, Outstanding Young Alumni, U. Colo., 1982. Mem. ABA, Va. Bar Assn. (chmn. profl. responsibility com. 1989-92, chmn. com. on legal edn. and admission to the Bar 1991—), Richmond Bar Assn., Richmond C. of C. (bd. dirs. 1988), Va. Econ. Developers Assn. (gen. counsel), Va. Econ. Bridge Initiative. Episcopal. Office: Legg Mason Wood Walker Inc 2234 Monument Ave Richmond VA 23220

POWELL, LAUREL ANN, social worker; b. Portland, Oreg., May 14, 1947; d. Edmund Rust and Dorothy (Reed) Call; m. Richard A. Nevitt, Feb. 10, 1968 (div. Aug. 1981); 1 child, Corrie Ann; m. Dale Arthur Powell, Jan. 1, 1982; children: Michael Warren, Ryan Gary. BA with honors in Sociology, U. Puget Sound, 1969; MSW, U. Wash., 1971. Lic. social worker, Wash. Caseworker Dept. Social and Health Svcs., Tacoma, 1969, social worker, 1971-72; sch. social worker Tacoma Pub. Schs., 1972—. 2d v.p. Birney Sch. PTA, Tacoma, 1987-89; mem. Tacoma Sch. Dist. Crisis/Trauma team, 1992—. Recipient Golden Acorn award Birney Sch. PTA, 1990. Mem. NEA, NASW, Wash. Edn. Assn., Tacoma Edn. Assn., Wash. Assn. Sch. Social Workers, Acad. Cert. Social Workers, Gamma Zeta chpt. Alpha Phi (treas. 1988—, corp. bd.), Day Island Yacht Club. Methodist. Avocations: travel, day-hiking, visiting museums and art galleries, reading. Office: Tacoma Pub Schs PO Box 1357 Tacoma WA 98401-1357

POWELL, LESLIE, poet; b. N.Y.C., May 20, 1940; d. Morris Sorkin and Sylvia Sterne; m. John L. Gropper, Apr. 10, 1960 (div.); m. Ted Powell, July 4, 1981 (div.); 1 child Joanne Watson. BA in Psychology, UCLA, 1964. Owner www.poetrypower.net , L.A., 2001—, www.PeacePoem.net, L.A., 2002—. Author: (CD) Visions, 2001. Recipient Editors Choice award, Internat. Libr. Poetry, 2001, 2002. Mem.: Internat. Soc. of Poets. Avocations: cats, wildlife, animal rescue, swimming, walking. Personal E-mail: lesliep5@cs.com.

POWELL, LEWIS FRANKLIN, III, lawyer; b. Richmond, Va., Sept. 14, 1952; s. Lewis F. Jr. and Josephine (Rucker) P.; m. Lisa T. LaFata; children: Emily, Hannah, Luke. BA, Washington & Lee U., 1974; JD, U. Va., 1978. Bar: Va. 1978, U.S. Dist. Ct. (ea. and we. dists.) Va. 1979, U.S. Ct. Appeals (4th cir.) 1979, U.S. Ct. Appeals (2d cir.) 1983, U.S. Ct. Appeals (11th cir.) 1992, U.S. Supreme Ct. 1985. Law clk. to judge U.S. Dist. Ct. (ea. dist.), Richmond, 1978-79; assoc. Hunton & Williams, 1979-85, ptnr., 1985—. Pres. young lawyers conf. Va. State Bar, 1986-87. Bd. dirs. William Byrd Cmty. Ho., Richmond, 1982-87, Boys Club of Richmond, 1984-90, Maymont Found., Richmond, 1987-92, St. Christopher's Sch., Richmond, 1989-96. Mem. Richmond Bar Assn. (chmn. improvement justice com. 1982-83), 4th Cir. Jud. Conf., Am. Law Inst. Avocations: skiing, mountaineering, backpacking, fishing, duck hunting. Office: Hunton & Williams Riverfront Plz East Tower 951 E Bird St Richmond VA 23219

POWELL, LILLIAN MARIE, retired music educator; b. DeLand, Fla., June 1, 1927; d. Francis Charles and Jessie Agnes (Niven) P.; m. James Armbruster, May 1950 (div. 1957); children: Jeffrey L. Armbruster, Leslie J. Armbruster; m. Dwight M. Liller, Dec. 8, 1957 (div. June 1972). B. Pub. Sch. Music, Capital U., 1950; MA, Ohio State U., 1957. Lic. tchr., N.Y., N.J., Va., Ohio. Vocal and instrumental music tchr. Community Sch., Stoutsville, Ohio, 1949-50, Roosevelt Jr. High Sch., Newark, 1950-51; elem. music tchr. at several schs. Norfolk, Va., 1951-53; music tchr. Naval Base Sch., Guantanomo Bay, Cuba, 1953-55; instr. voice Otterbein Coll., Ohio, 1955-56; music tchr. several elem. and jr. high schs. Lorain, 1956-60; music cons. elem. schs. South Orange, N.J., 1960-61; music tchr. elem. schs. Livingston, 1963-66; music tchr. Roosevelt Jr. high Sch., West Orange, 1965-72; instr. music lit. County Coll. Morris County, Dover, 1970-72; elem. sch. tchr. music Pub. Sch. 86, Jamaica Heights, N.Y., 1973-75; tchr. Satellite East Jr. High Sch. for Gifted, Bklyn., 1977-89, Stephen Halsey Jr. High Sch., N.Y.C., 1989-96, ret., 1996. Music theater dir. Children's Theater, Guantanamo Bay, 1953-55; ch. choir dir. Naval Base Chapel, Guantanamo Bay, 1953-55; ch. choir dir., soloist Congregational Ch., Lorain, Ohio, 1956-60; ch. soloist, organist Religious Sci. Ch., Morristown, Ohio. CORO assoc. orgn. activities CORO Leadership Found., Manhattan, N.Y., 1985—; vol. vocal/drama coaching Vocal Students for Profl. Goals and Producing Major Musical Prodn., Bklyn., 1977-85. Named Outstanding Woman of State of N.Y., N.Y. State Senate, 1984. Eckankar. Avocations: equestrian activities, astrology, writing, musical composition. Home: 4551 College Ave Ellicott City MD 21043-6817 E-mail: LeeMPowell@aol.com.

POWELL, LOUISE FOX, real estate developer; b. Hickory, N.C., June 14, 1925; d. Lester Lee and Vesta Boliek Fox; m. Nelson Sherril Powell, May 23, 1953 (dec.); children: Cynthia Louise, Joan Marie, Suzanne Jayne. Grad. in Bus., King's Coll., Charlotte, N.C., 1942. Time study engr. Glenn L. Martin Co., Balt., 1942-44; owner, mgr. Isenhour Fabric Co., Lenoir, N.C., 1949-53; rsch. mgr. Alfred Politz Rsch., Tampa, Fla., 1957-63; cemetary sales mgr. Southea. Advt. and Sales, Hickory and Atlanta, 1954-56; owner, mgr. Louise Powell Realty, Hickory, 1964—; pres., owner Benson-Fox Assocs., Ltd., 1986—; owner, mgr. Fairway Shopping Ctrs., Inc., 1989—. Leader Girl Scouts U.S., Hickory and Tampa, 1967—; active First United Meth. Ch., Hickory; mem. Hickory Mus. Arts, 1983—, Am. Legion Aux., Hickory, 1973—, Hickory Cmty. Theatre. Avocations: helping others, dolls, quilting, dancing, music. Home: 1235 10th Street Blvd NW Hickory NC 28601-2367

POWELL, MARLYS KAYE, artist; b. L.A., May 17, 1942; d. Willys Gerald Stennes and Nanne Gloria Entner; m. Russell Lloyd Mallett, Nov. 24, 1961; children: Jeffrey Russell Mallett, Erik Lloyd Mallett; m. Allen Edward Powell, Aug. 19, 1984. Student, Cornish Sch. Allied Arts and, Burnley Sch. Profl. Art, 1962, John McCrady Art Sch., 1964. Freelance muralist, New Orleans, 1964-65; tchr. fine art Westgate, MIT, 1968; gallery dir. Pacific Art League, Palo Alto, Calif., 1975-80, tchr. calligraphy, 1982. Illustrator (book) Fun and Magic of Inventing, 1982; represented in various corp. collections including Del Webb Corp., Scottsdale Ins. Co., Hewlett-Packard, Oracle Corp., Catalytica Asso, Inc., MIT; pvt. collections include: Iris Litt, M.D., Stanford Med. Ctr., A.L. Zeigler, Bechtel Internat. Ctr., Stanford, Burton Reiss, Newport Beach, Calif., Donald Horowitz, Arts Coun., Seattle; numerous other exhibits include: Monterey (Calif.) Mus., 1983, NAU Art Mus., Flagstaff, Ariz., 1993, Casa Grande (N.Mex.) Mus., 1995, Lanning Gallery, Sedona, Ariz., 1997—, Sun City Mus., Ariz., 1998, D'Adamo/Hill Gallery, Seattle, 1999—. Graphic artist Cancer Soc., New Orleans, 1964; chmn. art exhibit Stanford (Calif.) Hosp., 1975-78; pres. San Francisco Artist' Coop., 1979-80; participant Sedona (Ariz.) Forum, 1995. Recipient Painting award Casa Grande Mus., 1995, award Ariz. Mural Competition for Sedona Arts Ctr., 1999. Mem. Assn. Pour La Promotion du Patrimoine Artistique Francais, Nat. Mus. Women in the Arts, Sedona Arts Ctr. (juror 1996-97, featured artist 1997). Avocations: climbing, scuba diving, aerobics, adventure travels, wine-tasting.

POWELL, MARY RUDD, interior design firm executive; b. Berkeley, S.C., Oct. 5, 1933; d. Hiram Eugene and Estee (Hilton) Rudd; m. Dennis T. Powell, Oct. 1, 1955; children: Dennis T. Jr., H. Keith, Candice E., Kristi Leigh. AA, Campell U., Buies Creek, N.C., 1952; BA, Furman U., 1954; postgrad., Parson's Sch. of Design, 1985, East Tenn. State U., 1975-87. 7th grade tchr. Denton (N.C.) Sch., 1954-55; substitute tchr. Spartanburg (S.C.) High Sch., 1957-60; tchr. Robinson Bus. Coll., Spartanburg, 1960-61; sales Jean Frick of Spartanburg, 1966-69; substitute tchr. Johnson City (Tenn.) Sch. System, 1970-72; design cons. Sears, Roebuck & Co., Johnson City, 1972-77; owner MRP Interiors, 1977—; studied Palladian Arch. Fla. State U., Italy, 1999. Owner Powell & Powell, Johnson City, 1981—; co-owner Markee Properties, Isle of Palms, S.C., 1989—. Past officer Johnson City Monday Club; mem. Haynes Hist. Assn.; mem. PEO, Community Theatre, Friends of Libr.; past bd. dirs. Cen. Bapt. Ch. Mem. Shady Oaks Garden Club (past pres.), Johnson City Coun. Garden Clubs (past pres.), Tenn. Fedn. Garden Clubs (past state officer 1975-81). Baptist. Avocations: cooking, reading, photography, travel, computer. E-mail: mrprudd@aol.com.

POWELL, MICHAEL VANCE, lawyer; b. San Diego, Sept. 30, 1946; s. Jesse Vance and Mable Louise (Cagle) P.; m. Sarada Marie Hughes, Dec. 23, 1967; children: Marilyn Jean, Michael Benjamin. AB, Davidson Coll., N.C., 1968; MA, U. Tex., 1972, JD with honors, 1974. Bd. cert. civil appellate law Tex. Bd. Legal Specialization. Law clk. to judge U.S. Ct. Appeals (9th cir.), 1974-75; assoc. Rain Harrell Emery Young & Doke, Dallas, 1975-80, ptnr., 1980-87; mem. Locke Purnell Rain Harrell, 1987-98; ptnr. Locke Liddell & Sapp, 1999—. Elder St. Barnabas Presbyn. Ch., Richardson, Tex. Avocations: music, travel. Home: 7312 Tophill Ln Dallas TX 75248-5642 Office: Locke Liddell & Sapp 2200 Ross Ave Ste 2200 Dallas TX 75201-6776 E-mail: mpowell@lockeliddell.com.

POWELL, RANDALL W. surgeon; b. Richmond, Va., Oct. 3, 1945; MD, Med. Coll. Va., 1971. Diplomate Am. Bd. Surgery with subspecialties in surg. critical care and pediat. surgery. Intern Naval Hosp., San Diego, 1971-72, resident in gen. surgery, 1972-76; resident in pediat. surgery Children's Meml. Hosp., Chgo., 1976-78; staff surgeon Naval Hosp., San Diego, 1978-84; prof. U. South Ala., Mobile; attending surgeon U. South Ala. Med. Ctr., 1984—. Mem. ACS, Am. Acad. Pediatrics, Am. Pediat. Surg. Assn., Am. Assn. for Surgery of Trauma, Assn. for Acad. Surgery. Office: Univ of South Ala Coll Med-Ped Su 1700 Center St Mobile AL 36604-3301 Fax: (251) 334-1038.

POWELL, RAYMOND WILLIAM, financial planner, school administrator; b. Waterbury, Conn., June 17, 1944; s. Don C. and Kathryn (Linhard) P.; m. Janet Yasinski, June 24, 1967; 1 child, Raymond Joseph. BS, So. Conn. State Coll., New Haven, 1966, MS, 1969; postgrad., U. Bridgeport, Conn. CRP; enrolled agt. CEO R.W. Powell Enterprises, Inc., fin. and tax cons., Prospect, Conn., 1972—; dir.-owner Educators Tax Svc., Watertown, 1972—, Powell's Acctg. Svc., 1975—, Powell's Fin. Planning Svc., 1977—; supt. of schs. Winchester, Conn., 1995—. Contbr. articles to profl. jours. Vice chmn. Watertown Town Coun., 1975-76. Mem. Nat. Assn. Enrolled Agts., Internat. Assn. Fin. Planners, Am. Soc. Tax Cons., Conn. Assn. Enrolled Agts. Democrat. Office: PO Box 7077 42 Waterbury Rd Prospect CT 06712-1238 E-mail: powells.financial@snet.net.

POWELL, ROBERT DOMINICK, lawyer; b. Bklyn., Mar. 30, 1942; s. Ralph and Dorothy Piccola; m. Pamela Van Horn, Aug. 19, 1978; 8 children. BA, U. Pa., 1963; LLB, St. John's Sch. Law, 1966; LLM, Georgetown U., 1978. Bar: N.Y. 1967, D.C. 1968, U.S. Supreme Ct. 1972, Md. 1974, U.S. Ct. Appeals (1st, 2d, 3d, 4th, 5th, 9th and 11th cirs.). Trial atty. FAA, 1966-68; assoc. Welch & Morgan, 1968-69; ptnr. Smith & Pepper, Washington, 1969-72, Powell & Becker, Washington, 1972-73, Sanders, Schnabel, Joseph & Powell, Washington, 1976-82, Joseph, Powell, McDermott & Reiner, Washington, 1982-86; prin. Law Office Robert D. Powell, 1986—; atty. pvt. practice, 1973-76. Gen. counsel Nat. Bus. Aircraft Assn., 1970-87. Author: (poetry) Faint and Low, Soft and Sweet, 1968. Mem. instnl. com. working group Ctr. High Speed Comml. Transp. Mem. ABA (forum com. on air and space law), Assn. Trial Lawyers Am., Am. Judicature Soc., InterAm. Bar Assn., Fed. Bar Assn., N.Y. State Bar Assn., D.C. Bar Assn., Internat. Law Soc., Civil Aviation Med. Assn., Internat. Aviation Med. Assn., Batelle Inst. High Speed Comml. Flight Working Group, Izaak Walton League Am. (sec. Bethesda-Chevy Chase chpt. 1990), Aero Club Washington, Wings Club, Rotary. Republican. Episcopalian. Home and Office: 8817 Tuckerman Ln Potomac MD 20854 E-mail: powellpc@bellatlantic.net.

POWELL, ROBERT ELLIS, mathematics educator, college dean; b. Lansing, Mich., Mar. 16, 1936; s. James Ellis and Mary Frances (Deming) P.; children: Carl Robert, Glenn Arthur, Charles Addison; m. Lisbeth Nilsen, Nov. 21, 1992. BA, Mich. State U., 1958, MA, 1959; PhD, Lehigh U., 1966. Instr. math. Lehigh U., 1964-66; asst. prof. math. U. Kans., Lawrence, 1966-69; vis. asst. research prof. U. Ky., Lexington, 1967-68; vis. asst. prof. math. Ind. U., Bloomington, summer 1969; assoc. prof. math. Kent State U., Ohio, 1969-74, prof. math., 1974-95, dean grad. coll., 1980-92, prof. math emeritus, dean emeritus grad. coll., 1995—; prof. math., dean grad. sch., dir. rsch. U. Scranton, Pa., 1995-2000. Mem. Ohio Bd. Regents' Adv. Com. on Grad. Study, 1980-92, chmn., 1983-84. Co-author: Summability Theory, 1973, rev. edit., 1988, Intuitive Calculus, 1973; contbr. numerous articles to profl. jours. Bd. dirs. Kent State U. Found., 1981-91. NSF summer grantee, 1964, 65, Fulbright award, 1988. Mem. Midwestern Assn. Grad. Schs. (bd. dirs. 1988-92, chmn. 1990-91), Coun. Grad. Schs. (bd. dirs. 1990-91), Northea. Assn. Grad. Schs. (bd. dirs. 1998-2000). Home: 3490 Wild Indigo Ln Bonita Springs FL 34134

POWELL, ROBERT EUGENE, computer operator; b. Fairmont, W.Va., Mar. 31, 1955; s. Grover E. and Mary Jo (Hart) P. BS, Kent State U., 1980. Clk. Premier Screening, 1987-89; computer operator Sage Computer Svcs., 1989-95, Greater Akron Right to Life, 1997-2000. Found mem., treas. Alliance for Mentally Ill; active Pres.'s Com. on Employment People with Disabilities Pres.'s Trophy Candidate for Ohio, 1992. Recipient award of Excellence Ohio Rehab. Assn., 1989, 90, named Internat. Man of Yr., 1992-93. Mem. KC. Democrat. Roman Catholic. Home: 1052 Welton Ave Apt 2 Akron OH 44306-2818 E-mail: bobpowell4@cs.com.

POWELL, ROBERTA A. medical social worker; b. Eugene, Oreg., Aug. 9, 1952; d. Robert A. and Ruthann B. (Cartier) Saul; m. Robert B. Powell, Apr. 12, 1980; adopted children: Dominic Michael, Catherine Rose.. BA, U. Oreg., 1974; MSW, Portland State U., 1978. Lic. clin. social worker, Oreg. Psychiat. technician St. John's Hosp., Longview, Wash., 1974-76; vets. counselor Portland (Oreg.) Military and Vets. Counseling Ctr., 1976-79; mental health counselor Adult Rehab. Svcs./Ind. Living Svc., Portland, 1979-84; social worker Rehab. Inst. Oreg. Outpatient Porgram, 1983-89; lead social worker Rehab. Inst. Oreg., 1989-91; social worker Legacy Rehab. Svcs., 1991—. Mem. Region I Adv. Bd. Vocat. Rehab. Div., Portland, 1983-89, NW Med. Case Mgmt. Group, Portland, 1992—. Vol. Bklyn. Action Corps., Portland, 1984-86; mem., lector Holy Trinity Parish, Beaverton, Oreg., 1986-92; mem. St. Cecilia Parish, Beaverton, 1993—, Holy Rosary Parish, Portland, 1993—. Mem. N.W. Med. Case Mgmt. Group, Am. Assn. Spinal Cord Injury Psychologists and Social Workers, Good Samaritan Hosp. Employee Activities Assn. Avocations: walking, weight training, hiking, swimming. Office: Rehab Inst Oreg 1040 NW 22nd Ave Ste 550 Portland OR 97210-3057

POWELL, ROGER NORMAN, lawyer; b. Balt., Sept. 26, 1942; s. Philip C. and Roslyn (Goldberger) P.; m. Michele Rae Cohen, Aug. 10, 1965 (div. 1978); children: Alan, Tamara; m. Iris Sandra Quirmbach, Oct. 15, 1978. BA, U. Md., 1965; JD, U. Balt., 1970. Bar: Md. 1971. Pvt. practice, Pikesville, Md., 1971—; atty. Md. State Fireman's Assn., Annapolis, 1974—. Editor: Fire Laws of Maryland, 1982-00, 9th edit. Bd. dirs. Md. affiliate Am. Diabetes Assn., 1988-90, Sugar Ball com., 1999—; founder, dir. Reister's Towne Festival. Named Vol. of Yr. Pikesville Vol. Fire Co., 1974. Mem. Md. Bar Assn., Md. State Fireman's Assn., Balt. County Bar Assn. Democrat. Jewish. Office: 107 Old Court Rd Baltimore MD 21208-4011

POWELL, RUTH AREGOOD, music educator; b. Rising City, Nebr. d. August Walter and Gussie Hobson (Bray) Aregood; m. Jack William Powell, June 27, 1953; children: Stephen Mark, Linda Lou, Timothy Vaughn. BA, Nebr. Wesleyan, Lincoln, 1949; MA, Northwestern U., Evanston, Ill., 1952. Dir. edn. Wauwotosa (Wis.) Meth., 1952-54; self-employed piano tchr. Wis., Hawaii, Ohio, 1955—. Mem. Music Tchrs. Nat. Assn. (pres. East Ctrl. Divsn. 1990-92), Nat. Guild Piano Tchrs., Ohio Music Tchrs. Assn. (pres. 1984-88, pres. ctrl. east dist. 1992-96, named Cert. Tchr. of Yr. 2000-01), Westerville Womens Music Club. Methodist. Avocations: reading, sewing.

POWELL, SANDRA THERESA, timber company executive; b. Orofino, Idaho, Jan. 9, 1944; d. Harold L. and Margaret E. Powell. BS in Bus. and Acctg., U. Idaho, 1966. CPA, idaho. Acct. Weyerhaeuser Co., Tacoma, 1966-67; with Potlatch Corp., 1967-2000, asst. sec. San Francisco, 1981, sec., asst. treas., 1981-89, treas., 1989-92, v.p. fin. svcs., 1993-98, sec., 1993-95, sr. v.p. fin., chief fin. officer, 1998-2000; retired, 2000. Mem. AICPA, Idaho State Bd. Accountancy, Idaho Soc. CPAs.

POWELL, STEPHEN KENNETH, financial planner; b. Atlanta, Dec. 4, 1964; s. James C. Powell and Kathy (Clarke) Martin; m. Paula Sue Grimes, May 16, 1992; children: Maegan Noelle, Kendal Marie, Caitlin Ann. BS in Biochemistry, George Washington U., 1988; student, Tidewater C.C., Virginia Beach, 1988-90. Cert. fin. planner; registered fin. planner; registered fin. cons. Area mgr. EMSI, Virginia Beach, 1989-91; field underwriter, agent Mony Fin. Svcs. Mutual of N.Y., Norfolk, Va., 1991-93; fin. planner assoc. Spence Fin. Group, 1993-95; prin. fin. planner Capital Planning Group, 1991—; asst. mng. dir. The MONY Group, 2001—. Prin. fin. planner Capital Fin. Group LLC, Norfolk, 1995—. Sponsor, Engaged Encounter, Richmond, Va., 1993-99; vol. Muscular Dystrophy Assn., Norfolk, 1995-97, 2000, Rescue Squad, Washington, 1984-87, Search and Rescue Team, Tidewater, Va., 1987-89, Cath. Charities of Hampton Rds., 1996—. Recipient New Agt. of Yr. award Tidewater, 1992, New Eng. Registered Rep. and Agt. of Yr., 1994. Mem.: Nat. Assn. Life Underwriters (Nat. Quality award 1993, 1995—, Nat. Sales Achievement award 1993, 1995—2000, Million Dollar Round Table 1996—2002), Internat. Assn. Fin. Planning, Little Bay Beach and Boat Club (pres. 1995—98). Republican. Roman Catholic. Avocations: golf, running, diving, family activities. Office: Capital Fin Group LLC 701 Town Point Ctr 150 Boush St Norfolk VA 23510 E-mail: capfingroup@aol.com.

POWELL, STEPHEN WALTER, judge; b. Hamilton, Ohio, Jan. 25, 1955; s. Walter E. and Bobbi M. (Powell) P.; m. Kathryn Powell; children: Eric R.W., S. Michael; stepchildren: Greggory A., Garrett A. BA, Heidelberg Coll., 1977; JD, U. Dayton, 1981. Bar: Ohio 1981, U.S. Dist. Ct. (so. dist.) Ohio 1982. Referee Common Pleas Ct., Juvenile, Domestic and Probate, Hamilton, 1984-88; ptnr. Powell, Napier, Carmella and Allen, 1986-91; judge Area II Ct.,

Butler County, Ohio, 1989-91; judge probate div. Butler County Common Pleas Ct., Hamilton, 1991-95; presiding judge Ohio Ct. Appeals, 12th Appellate Dist., Middletown, 1995-97, adminstrv. judge, 1997-98, presiding judge, 1999—. Agt. Commonwealth Land Title, Louisville, 1988-90; parliamentarian Judges Assn. Ohio Ct. Appeals, 1995—. Sec. Butler County Rep. Cen. Com., 1982-88; trustee Union Twp., Butler County, West Chester, 1979-88; bd. dirs. United Way Hamilton Area, 1986-90. Named Man of the Day Sta. WMOH, Hamilton, 1986; recipient Meritorious Svc. award Ohio Assn. Probate Judges, 1992, 93, 94. Mem. ABA, Ohio Bar Assn., Butler County Bar Assn. Presbyterian. Office: Ohio Ct Appeals 12th Appellate Dist 1 City Centre Plz # 1009 Middletown OH 45042-1901

POWELL, SUZANNE K. nurse, consultant; b. Chgo., Jan. 12, 1951; d. Harry and Leah Lillian (Reitman) Kotlicky; m. James Howard Powell, June 18, 1978. ADN, Phoenix Coll., 1987; BSN, U. Phoenix, 1991, MBA, 2002. Cardiovasc. ICU nurse St. Joseph's Hosp. and Med. Ctr., Phoenix, 1987-88; case mgr. utilization mgmt.-medicaid HMO plan Mercy Care Plan, 1988-92; primary care case mgr. St. Joseph's Hosp. and Med. Ctr., 1992-95; dir. case mgr., interventions mgr. Health Svcs. Adv. Gropu, Inc., 1995—. Spkr. Case Mgmt. Soc. Am., 1995—2000. Author: Nursing Case Management: A Practical Guide to Success in Managed Care, 1996, Case Management: A Practical Guide to Success in Managed Care, 2000, Advanced Case Management: Outcomes and Beyond, 2000; sr. editor Case Mgmt. Soc. Am.: Case Mgmt. Core Curriculum. Mem. Case Mgmt. Soc. Am. Avocations: composing music for harp, piano and keyboard, owning and breeding horses. Office: Health Svcs Adv Group Inc 301 E Bethany Home Rd Ste B157 Phoenix AZ 85012-1265

POWELL, THOMAS EDWARD, III, biological supply company executive, physician; b. Elon College, N.C., Aug. 1, 1936; s. Thomas Edward, Jr., and Sophia Maude (Sharpe) P.; m. Betty Durham Yeager, June 19, 1965; children: Frances Powell Barnes, Thomas Edward IV, Caroline Powell Rogers. AB in Biology, Va. Mil. Inst., 1957; MD, Duke U., 1961; MA, Harvard U., 1966. Surgeon USPHS, 1966-68; co-founder Biomed. Reference Labs., Inc., Burlington, N.C., 1969, exec. v.p., 1969-75, chmn. exec. com., 1979-82, also dir.; exec. v.p. Carolina Biol. Supply Co., Burlington, N.C., 1968-80, chmn., 1977-80, 94—, pres., 1980-94; pres. Wolfe Sales Corp., Burlington, 1980-84, Waubun Labs. Inc., Schriever, La., 1980—, Bobbitt Labs., Inc., Burlington, 1983-94; bd. mgrs. Wachovia Bank and Trust Co. N.A., Burlington. Contbr. articles to profl. jours. Bd. dirs. United Way Alamance County, Burlington, 1968—; bd. dirs. Elon Coll., N.C., 1968—, sec., 1975—; bd. dirs. Am. Cancer Soc., Burlington, 1971-81; bd. dirs. Burlington Day Sch., 1973—, pres., 1974-78, 80-84; bd. dirs. N.C. Citizens for Bus. and Industry, Raleigh, 1983-87, Nat. Found. for Study of Religion and Econs., Greensboro, 1984-88, Blue Ridge Sch., Dyke, Va., 1985-90. Served to capt. USAR, 1957-66. Recipient Citizens Service award Elon Coll. Alumni Assn., 1980. Mem. Assn. Biology Lab. Edn., N.C. Acad. Sci., Alamance-Caswell Med. Soc., N.C. Med. Soc., Assn. Venture Founders, Newcomen Soc. Democrat. Mem. United Ch. of Christ. Clubs: Alamance Country (Burlington); Capital City (Raleigh, N.C.); Congl. Country (Washington); N.C. Country (Pinehurst); Hope Valley Country (Durham, N.C.); Greensboro City.

POWELL, THOMAS ERVIN, financial consultant, small business owner; b. Trion, Ga., Mar. 19, 1947; s. Ervin and Myrtice (Wike) P.; m. Lana Lois Lang, June 20, 1976; children: Thomas Christopher, Alissa Lynne, Ashley Beth. BS, U. Ctrl. Fla., 1974, MS, 1977; postgrad. studies, U. Fla., 1979. CPA, Fla.; cert. internal auditor. Pub. acct. KPMG Peat Marwick, Orlando, Fla., 1974-75, Arthur Andersen & Co., Orlando, 1975-77; instr. acctg. U. Ctrl. Fla., 1977-81; dir. Inst. Internal Auditors, Altamonte Springs, Fla., 1981-95; pres. The Powell Group, Inc., Windermere, 1996—; dir. of consulting Graham & Cottrill, PA, 1998-2000; COO, treas., exec. v.p. fin. and trust svcs. Investment Trust Co. Fla., Inc., Ocoee, 2000—. Mem. accreditation com. Am. Assembly Collegiate Schs. Bus., 1992-93; adj. prof. Rollins Coll., Winter Park, Fla., 1999—. Author: Examination Writer's Guide, 1978, rev. edit., 1991, 96; mem. editl. bd. Issues in Acctg. Edn. Jour., 1995—. Vice chmn. audit bd. City of Orlando, 1990-95; treas. Christian Endowment Found., 1996—; chmn. Practice Advising Coun.; mem. Orlando/Orange County Airport Zoning Bd., 1997—; chmn. adv. coun. West Orange H.S., 1997-98; mem. West Orange H.S. Found.; mem. strategic dir. com. Orange County Pub. Schs, 1997-98. With USAF, 1967-71. Mem. AICPA, Am. Acctg. Assn. (profl. exam. com. 1986-89, 93-98, audit edn. conf. com. 1990-93, mem. profl. rels. com. 1997-98, v.p. profl. practices 1994-96, chmn. practice adv. coun. 1996-2000), Inst. Internal Auditors, Fla. Soc. CPAs (edn. com. 1990-93, legis. com. 1991), Beta Alpha Psi (adv. coun. 1993-95, Alumnus of Yr. U. Ctrl. Fla. 1992), Beta Gamma Sigma. Republican. Avocations: guitar, skiing, photography. Home: 1938 Maple Leaf Dr Windermere FL 34786-8003 Office: Investment Trust Co Fla Inc 2731 S Maguire Rd Ocoee FL 34761 E-mail: tpowell@investmenttrustco.com.

POWELL, TIMOTHY WOOD, information executive, consultant; b. Phila., June 22, 1949; s. James Rennie and Elizabeth Clay (Thurman) P.; children: Michael Ross, David Alexander. BA, Yale U., 1971, MBA, 1979. Field psychologist LEAP, Inc., 1971-73; outreach mgr. State of Conn., 1973-74; contracts analyst State of N.J., Trenton, 1975-76; sr. fin. analyst State of N.Y., N.Y.C., 1976-77; sr. cons. Peat, Marwick, Mitchell, 1979-83; mgr. nat. mktg. Coopers & Lybrand, 1983-89; tech. dir. FIND/SVP, 1989-95; mng. dir. TW Powell Co., 1995—; sec.-treas. Ambient Media, Inc., 1999—. Author: The High Tech Marketing Machine, 1993, Analyzing Your Competition, 1993; contbr. numerous articles to profl. jours. Fellow Soc. Competitive Intelligence Profls. (bd. dirs. 1994-97, Catalyst award 1994); mem. ASCAP, Am. Mktg. Assn. Avocation: music. Office: 315 Park Ave S New York NY 10010-3607 E-mail: tim.powell@knowledgeagency.com.

POWELL, TREVOR JOHN DAVID, archivist; b. Hamilton, Ont., Can., Feb. 3, 1948; s. David Albert and Morvydd Ann May (Williams) P.; m. Marian Jean McKillop, May 1, 1976. BA, U. Sask., Regina, 1971; MA, U. Regina, Sask., Can., 1980. Staff archivist Sask. Archives Bd., Regina, Sask., 1973-80, dir., 1980-86, acting provincial archivist, 1986-87, provincial archivist, 1988—. Co-author: Living Faith: A Pictorial History of Diocese of Qu'Appelle; author: From Tent to Cathedral: A History of St. Paul's Cathedral, Regina. Archivist Diocese of Qu'Appelle, Regina, Sask., 1971—, registrar, 1979—; archivist, eccles. Province of Rupert's Land, Winnipeg, Man., 1988—; mem. adv. coun. Sask. Order of Merit, 1988-95, Sask Honours, 1995—; chair selection com. Sask Vol. medal, 1995-96, Can. 125 medal, 1992. Mem. Soc. Am. Archivists, Can. Hist. Assn., Commonwealth Archivists Assn., Sask. Coun. Archives (sec.-treas. 1987-88, 90-92, pres. 1994-96, Can. Coun. Archives rep. 1994-96), Assn. Can. Archivists (bd. dirs. 1979-81). Anglican. Avocations: gardening, walking, reading, music, bird watching. Home: 241 Orchard Cres Regina SK Canada S4S 5B9 Office: Sask Archives Bd 3303 Hillsdale St Univ Regina Regina SK Canada S4S 0A2 E-mail: tpowell@archives.gov.sk.ca.

POWELL, WALTER HECHT, labor arbitrator; b. N.Y.C., Apr. 13, 1915; s. Arthur Lee and Stella (Hecht) P.; m. Dorothy Meyer, Mar. 15, 1945; children: Lawrence L., Alan W., Lesley A., Steven H. BS, NYU, 1938, JD, 1940; MA, U. Pa., 1948. Bar: N.Y. 1940, Pa. 1956. Asst. prof. Temple U., Phila., 1946-51, v.p. for pers. resources, 1973-78; asst. dir. pers. Am. Safety Razor, Kingsbury, Ind., 1951-53; v.p., dir. ops. Internat. Resistance Co., Phila., 1953-69, v.p., dir. indsl. rels., 1956-69; sr. v.p. 1st Pa. Banking & Trust Co., 1969-73; v.p. human resources Temple U., 1973-77; ind. labor arbitrator Phila., 1978—. Mem. panel Am. Arbitration Assn., Fed. Mediation and Conciliation Svc., Pa., N.J. labor rels. bds.; lectr. U. Pitts., Temple U., U. Richmond, Vanderbilt U., Am. U., others.; bd. dirs. Auerbach Corp., Phila. Contbr. book chpts., articles to profl. jours. Commr. Phila. Commn. on Human Rels., 1969—; bd. dirs. Opportunities Industrialization Ctr. Capt. AUS, 1942-46. Recipient award Phila. C. of C., 1968, Distinguised Svc. award Am. Arbitration Assn., 1997, citation City of Phila., 1997. Mem. Am. Mgmt. Assn. (adv. coun. 1963—), Indsl. Rels. Assn., Indsl. Rels. Rsch. Assn. (pres. local chpt. 1966), Nat. Acad. Arbitrators. Home and Office: 2401 Pennsylvania Ave Ste 9a7 Philadelphia PA 19130-3002

POWELL, WILLIAM ARNOLD, JR. retired banker; b. Verbena, Ala., July 7, 1929; s. William Arnold and Sarah Frances (Baxter) P.; m. Barbara Ann O'Donnell, June 16, 1956; children: William Arnold III, Barbara Calhoun, Susan Thomas, Patricia Crain. BSBA, U. Ala., 1953; grad., La. State U. Sch. Banking of South, 1966. With Am. South Bank, N.A., Birmingham, Ala., 1953—, asst. v.p., 1966, v.p., 1967, v.p., br. supr., 1968-72, sr. v.p., br. supr., 1972-73, exec. v.p., 1973-79, pres., 1979-83, vice chmn. bd., 1983-93, also bd. dirs.; pres. AmSouth Bancorp., 1979—. Bd. dirs. AmSouth Bank Fla., AmSouth Bancorp. Bd. dirs. United Way Found., Warrior-Tombigbee Devel. Assn.; life trustee Ala. Ind. Colls., trustee Ala. Hist. Soc., Birmingham Hist. Soc.; past pres. United Way, campaign chmn., 1987; mem. pres.'s coun. U. Ala., Birmingham; life mem. bd. visitors U. Ala.; life mem. Birmingham Met. Devel. Bd. Lt. AUS, 1954-56. Mem. The Club, Mountain Brook, Birmingham Country Club, Birmingham Area C. of C. (life mem. bd. dirs.), Metropolitan Development Assn. (life mem. bd. dirs.). Home: 2114 Hickory Ridge Cir Birmingham AL 35243-2925

POWELL, WILLIAM CLAYTON, music educator; b. Americus, Ga., Apr. 12, 1962; s. William and Emma Powell; m. Rosephanye T. Dunn; children: Camille. B in Music. Edn., Ala. State U., 1984; MusM in Music Edn., Westminster Choir Coll., 1987; PhD in Music Edn., Fla. State U., 1993. Instr. music Selma (Ala.) U., 1987—88; music tchr. Savannah (Ga.)-Chatham Co. Pub. Schs., 1988—90; grad. tchg. asst. Fla. State U., Tallahassee, 1990—93; assoc. prof. Philander Smith Coll., Little Rock, 1993—2001; asst. dir. choral activities Auburn (Ala.) U., 2001—. Composer: (Choral arrangement) Gabi, Gabi, 1999, Ning Wendete, 2000. Mem.: Coll. Music Soc., Am. Choral Dirs. Assn. (southwestern divsn. R&S chair on ethnic/multicultural perspectives 1997—2000), Ark. Choral Dirs. Assn. (state R&S chair on ethnic/multicultural perspectives 1995—97), Music Educators Nat. Conf. Office: Auburn Univ Music Dept 101 Goodwin Hall Auburn AL 36849 Office Fax: 334-844-3168. Business E-Mail: powelwc@auburn.edu.

POWELL, WILLIAM COUNCIL, SR. service company executive; b. Burlington, N.C., Nov. 5, 1948; s. Thomas Edward Jr. and Annabelle (Council) P.; m. Jacqueline Garrison, July 3, 1976; children: William C. Jr., Ashley C. Student, U. S.C., 1968-69; BS, Va. Mil. Inst., 1971; MBA, Wake Forest U., 1974; postgrad., Elon Coll., 1972. Lic. pilot. Lic. real estate broker, N.C. Adminstrv. assoc. Carolina Biol. Supply Co., Inc., Burlington, 1971-91; also bd. dirs.; v.p. Bobbitt Labs., Burlington, 1974-77; pres., 1977-82; owner HEADS, Inc., 1978—, pres., 1984—; owner Ashwil Acres Farm, Mebane, N.C., 1981—. Pres. Granite Diagnostics, Inc., Burlington, 1981-84, UST Specialists Inc., 1991-2000, Merrymount Property Owners Assn., Inc., 1996-2000, Merrymount Boat Slip Assn., Inc., 1996—, Stratonet Inc., 1996-2001, Forest Realm, Inc., 2001—, Goat Island Maritime Inc., 2001—, Powell Realm Inc., 2001—, Poignard Compact Inc., 2001—; owner Powell Real Estate, Burlington, 1979—; bd. dirs. Excalibur Lock Co., Inc., Waubun Labs., Inc., Schriever, La., Burlington, Warren Land Co., 1990-94, pres., 1994—; v.p. fin., bd. dirs. Environ. Responsible Bus. Inc., 1992-97; mem. Babcock Sch. Alumni Coun. Wake Forest U., 1981-85; mgr. Macon Farm, 1992-95; chmn. bd. Ensci Corp., Inc., 1991-95, ptnr. Port Assocs., 1987-2002, Port Assocs. II, 1992-2002; chmn. bd. Netpath Inc., 1995-96, bd., 2001—; filed for election N.C. Senate, 2000. Bd. advisors Elon Coll. (N.C.), 1984-86, bd. visitors, 1987-92; bd. advisors Duke U. Marine Lab., Beaufort, N.C., 1985-92; nat. adv. coun. Baruch Marine Inst., 1998—; mem. adv. panel Air Quality Compliance Panel State of N.C. Dept. Environ. Health and Natural Resources, 1994—; guardian mem. Boy Scouts Am., Burlington, 1985; trustee Dr. T.E. Powell Jr. Trust, 1989-95; v.p. fin. Cherokee Coun. Boy Scouts of Am., 1990-92, exec. bd., 1990-94, exec. bd. Old N. State Coun., 1994-95; mem. Front St. United Meth. Ch., Burlington, N.C. Capt. USAR, 1971-79. Recipient Bill Fish Cert. State of S.C., 1983, 2 Bill Fish Certs. State of N.C., 1990, Sower's award Duke U., 1985, N.C. Gov.'s Cup for Billfishing, 1991, 3rd Pl., Big Rock Blue Marlin Tourn, 1998. Mem. NRA (life), Newcomen Soc. N.Am. (life mem.), Billiard Congress Am., Am. Angus Assn., Billiard and Bowling Inst. Assn., N.C. Forestry Assn. (legis. affairs com. 1994—), N.C. Wildlife Habitat Found. (life), Ducks Unltd. (life sponsor, area chmn. 1985-87, 97—), N.C. Chpt. Safari Club Internat. (state pres. 1985-88, life mem.), Aircraft Owners and Pilots Assn., Cessna Owner Orgn., Atlantic Coast Conservation Assn. (life), Nat. Soc. of SAR, Alamance Wildlife Club (bd. dirs. 1992-95, 2000—, pres. 1999-2000), Rolls Royce Owners Club (life), N.Am. Hunting Club (life), Found. N.Am. Wild Sheep (life), Chaine des Rotisseurs (chevalier 1991), Brotherhood of the Knights of the Vine (master knight 1991), 10 Point Hunt Club, Am. Angus Assn., Nat. Wild Turkey Fedn., Quail Unltd. (life), N.C. Cattlemans Assn. (life), Nat. Cattlemans Assn., Inc., Internet Users Group Alamance, Debordieu Club, Nat. Soc. SAR, Sons Confederate Vets., Alamance County Cattleman's Assn., Citation Fishing Team (capt. 1979—), Alamance Country Club, Debordieu Beach Club, Litchfield Carriage House Club. Home: 1109 W Front St Burlington NC 27215-3610 Office: HEADS Inc 2608 NC Hwy 100 Elon College NC 27244-8539 also: Stratonet Inc 2260 S Church St Ste 601 Burlington NC 27215-5380 E-mail: wcp@netpath.net.

POWER, DAVID M. advertising executive; BA, Univ. of Louisville, 1993. Pres., COO Power Creative, Louisville. Office: 11701 Commonwealth Dr Louisville KY 40299-2358*

POWER, DENNIS MICHAEL, museum director; b. Pasadena, Calif., Feb. 18, 1941; s. John Dennis and Ruth Augusta (Mott) P.; m. Kristine Moneva Fisher, Feb. 14, 1965 (div. Aug. 1984); children: Michael Lawrence, Matthew David; m. Leslie Gabrielle Baldwin, July 6, 1985; 1 stepchild, Katherine G. Petrosky. BA, Occidental Coll., 1962, MA, 1964; PhD, U. Kans., 1967. Asst. curator ornithology Royal Ont. Mus., Toronto, Can., assoc. curator Can., 1971-72; asst. prof. zoology U. Toronto, 1967-72; exec. dir. Santa Barbara (Calif.) Mus. Natural History, 1972-94, Oakland Mus. of Calif., 1994—. Biol. rschr.; cons. ecology. Editor: The California Islands: Proceedings of a Multidisciplinary Symposium, 1980, Current Ornithology, vol. 6, 1989, vol. 7, 1990, vol. 8, 1991, vol. 9, 1992, vol. 10, 1993, vol. 11, 1993, vol. 12, 1995; contbr. articles to sci. jours. Bd. dirs. Univ. Club Santa Barbara, 1989-92, v.p., 1991-92; bd. dirs. Santa Barbara Chamber Orch., 1990-94, v.p., 1991-94; mem. adv. coun. Santa Cruz Island Found., 1989—; mem. discipline adv. com. for museology Coun. for Internat. Exch. of Scholars, 1991-95; mem. Cultural Affairs Commn., City of Oakland, 1999—. NSF fellow U. Kans., 1967; NRC grantee, 1968-72, 74-78. Fellow Am. Ornithologists Union (life, sec. 1981-83, v.p. 1988-89), Am. Assn. Mus. (mem. coun. 1980-83), Calif. Acad. Scis.; mem. AAAS, Cooper Ornithol. Soc. (bd. dirs. 1976-79, pres. 1978-81, hon. mem. 1993), Calif. Assn. Mus. (bd. dirs. 1981-92, chmn. 1987-89), Western Mus. Conf. (bd. dirs. 1977-83, pres. 1981-83), Am. Soc. Naturalists, Assn. Sci. Mus. Dirs., Ecol. Soc., Am. Soc. Study of Evolution, Soc. Systematic Zoology, Bohemian Club, Sigma Xi. Office: Oakland Mus Calif 1000 Oak St Oakland CA 94607-4820

POWER, ELIZABETH HENRY, consultant; b. Hickory, N.C., Sept. 28, 1953; d. William Henry Power and Katheryn Otis (Smith) Nelson. Cert. in creative writing, N.C. Sch. Arts, 1971; BA in Sociology, U. N.C., Greensboro, 1977; MEd in Human Resources Devel., Vanderbilt U., 1997. With adoption and foster home recruitment Davidson County Dept. Human Svcs., Nashville, 1980-81; behavioral cons. Nutri-System Weight Loss Ctr., 1982-84; corp. sec., cons. Quantum Leap Cons., Inc., 1984-86; owner EPower & Assocs., Granite Falls, N.C., 1980—, MPD/DD Resource & Edn. Ctr., Nashville, 1991-93; dir. instrnl. design Call Ctr. U., 1997-98. Cons. GM/Saturn, 1988-98; dir. instrnl. design Call Ctr. U., 1998; sr. cons. J.D. Power and Assocs., 1998-2000; sr. cons. cars.com, 2000; tng. mgr. Exult, 2001--. Author: If Change Is All There Is, Choice Is All You've Got, 1990, Managing Our Selves: Building a Community of Caring, 1992; contbg. author: Nonprofit Policies and Procedures, 1992, 98, 2000, 01, More than Survivors: Conversations with Multiple Personality Clients, 1992, 1998, also articles. Vol. West Chester (Pa.) Women's Resource Ctr., 1977; vol. instr. theology Lay Acad. Episc. Diocese Western N.C., Asheville, 1976-77; mem. Burke County Coun. Status Women, Morganton, N.C., 1977-79, sec., 1978; vol. Western N.C. Flood Com., 1977-78; exec. dir. N.C. Rape Crisis Assn., Raleigh, 1979, Foothills Mental Health Ctr., Morganton, 1978-79; mem. task force, writer, convener, facilitator N.C. Gov.'s Conf. Mental Health, 1979; trainer, vol. Rape House Crisis Ctr., Nashville, 1979-81; vol., trainer Rape and Sexual Abuse Ctr., Nashville, 1981-82, bd. dirs., 1981-82; mem. quality circles steering com. Tenn. Dept. Human Svcs., 1980-81; program cons. Women's Resource and Assistance Program, Jackson, Tenn., 1988-92. Recipient numerous awards N.C. Dept. Mental Health/Mental Retardation, 1979, State of N.C., 1979, Central Nashville Optimist Club, 1982, Waco YWCA, Waco, Tex., 1985. Mem. Internat. Soc. for Traumatic Stress Studies, Am. Soc. Tng. and Devel., Orgn. Devel. Network. Democrat. Home and Office: 1343 Saviour Ln Granite Falls NC 28630-9226 E-mail: powere@mindspring.com.

POWER, FRANCIS WILLIAM, newspaper publisher; b. Webster, S.D., Aug. 12, 1925; s. Frank B. and Esther C. (Fowler) P.; m. Margaret Jean Atkinson, Mar. 24, 1951; children: Patricia Ann, John Michael, Kerry Jean. BBA, U. N.Mex., 1948. Display advt. sales rep. The Register, Santa Ana, Calif., 1948-51; advt. mgr. Valley Morning Star, Harlingen, Tex., 1951-62; gen. mgr. Pampa (Tex.) Daily News, 1962-69; bus. mgr. Brownsville (Tex.) Herald, 1969-75; pub. The Lima (Ohio) News, 1975-91; v.p. Freedom Comm., Inc., until 1991; ret., 1991. Served with USNR, 1943-46. Mem.: Shawnee Country, Rotary, Elks. Roman Catholic. Office: Freedom Comm Inc 17666 Fitch Irvine CA 92614-6022

POWER, JOHN BRUCE, lawyer; b. Glendale, Calif., Nov. 11, 1936; m. Sandra Garfield, Apr. 27, 1998; children by previous marriage: Grant, Mark, Boyd. AB magna cum laude, Occidental Coll., 1958; JD, NYU, 1961; postdoctoral, Columbia U., 1972. Bar: Calif. 1962. Assoc. O'Melveny & Myers, L.A., 1961-70, ptnr., 1970-97, resident ptnr. Paris, 1973-75; Sheffelman disting. lectr. Sch. Law, U. Wash., Seattle, 1997. Mem. Social Svcs. Commn. City of L.A., 1993, pres., 1993; pres. circle, exec. com. Occidental Coll., 1979-82, 91-94, chair, 1993-94. Contbr. articles to jours. Bd. dirs. Met. L.A. YMCA, 1988—, treas., 1998-2001; mem. bd. mgrs. Stuart Ketchum Downtown YMCA, 1985-92, pres., 1989-90; mem. Los Angeles County Rep. Ctrl. Com., 1962-63; trustee Occidental Coll., 1992—, vice-chmn., 1998-2001, chmn., 2001—. Root Tilden scholar. Fellow Am. Coll. Comml. Fin. Lawyers (bd. regents 1999—); mem. ABA (comml. fin. svcs. com., com. 3d party legal opinions, UCC com., bus. law sect.), Am. Bar Found. (life), Calif. Bar Assn. (chmn. partnerships and unincorporated assns. com. 1982-83, chmn. uniform commn. code com. 1984-85, exec. com. 1987-91, chmn. bus. law sect. 1990-91, chmn. coun. sect. chairs 1992-93, liaison to state bar commn. on future of legal profession and state bar 1993-95), L.A. County Bar Assn. (exec. com. comml. law and bankruptcy sect. 1970-73, 86-89), Internat. Bar Assn., Fin. Lawyers Conf. (bd. govs. 1982—, pres. 1984-85), Exec. Svc. Corps (sec. 1985-2000, vice-chmn. 2000—, dir. 1994—), Occidental Coll. Alumni Assn. (pres. 1967-68), Phi Beta Kappa (councilor So. Calif. 1982—, pres. 1990-92). Office: O Melveny & Myers 400 S Hope St Los Angeles CA 90071-2899

POWER, JOSEPH EDWARD, lawyer; b. Peoria, Ill., Dec. 2, 1938; s. Joseph Edward and Margaret Elizabeth (Birkett) P.; m. Camille June Repass, Aug. 1, 1964; children— Joseph Edward, David William, James Repass Student, Knox Coll., Galesburg, Ill., 1956-58; BA, U. Iowa, 1960, JD, 1964. Bar: Iowa 1964. Law clk. to judge U.S. Dist. Ct., 1964-65; mem. Bradshaw, Fowler, Proctor & Fairgrave, P.C., Des Moines, 1965—. Bd. dirs. Moingona coun. Girl Scouts U.S.A., 1968-77, pres., 1971-74; bd. dirs. Des Moines United Way, 1976-82, v.p., 1979-81; trustee Am. Inst. Bus., 1987-2002, chmn., 1992-2002; bd. dirs. Iowa Law Sch. Found., 1992—, Plymouth Ch. Found., 1991-99; bd. dirs. Des Moines Found, 1996—, sec.-treas., 2001-; bd. dirs. Iowa Natural Heritage Found., 1995—, vice chmn., 2001-; mem. Des Moines Civil War Roundtable. Fellow Am. Coll. Trust and Estate Counsel (state chair 1994-2000), Am. Coll. Real Estate Lawyers; mem. ABA, Iowa Bar Assn. (chmn. probate, property and trust law com. 1983-87), Polk County Bar Assn., Des Moines Estate Planners Forum (pres. 1982-83) Republican. Mem. United Ch. of Christ. Clubs: Des Moines, Rotary. Home: 4244 Foster Dr Des Moines IA 50312-2542 Office: Bradshaw Fowler Proctor & Fairgrave 801 Grand Ave Ste 3700 Des Moines IA 50309-2727 E-mail: www.power.edward@bradshawlaw.com.

POWER, MARY SUSAN, political science educator; b. Hazleton, Pa., July 5, 1935; d. Younger L. and Cleo (Boock) P.; 1 dau., Catherine Laverne. BA, Wells Coll., 1957; postgrad., Exeter (Eng.) U., 1955-56, Yale U., 1958-59; MA, Stanford U., 1960; PhD, U. Ill., 1961. Asst. prof. Susquehanna (Pa.) U., 1961-64; assoc. prof. U. Ark., Fayetteville, 1965-68; assoc. prof. polit. sci. Ark. State U., State University, 1968-79, prof., 1979—2000. Author: Before the Convention, Religion and the Founding Fathers, 1984, Jacques Maritaln and the Quest for a New Commonwealth, 1992, Political Philosophy & Cultural Renewal: Collected Essays of Francis Wilson, 2001; contbr. articles to profl. jours. Mem. Fed. Edn. Commn. of States, 1982—84, Craighead County Election Commn., 1986—88; N.E. chair Arkansans for Progress, 1990—96; mem. State com. Ark. Rep. Com., 1968—96, sec., 1978—80; alt. del. Rep. Nat. Conv., 1972, 1976, 1988, del., 1992; chmn. Craighead County GOP, 1986—88, vice chmn., 1990—96, N.E. regional chmn., 1988—96; chmn. Craighead County Sheffield for Gov., 1990; mem. exec. com. Ark. Rep. Party, 1990—96, N.E. regional chair, 1988—96; treas. Women's Soc. Blessed Sacrament Ch., Jonesboro, 1996—, jubilee 2000 chair. Relm Found. fellow, 1960, NSF-Am. Polit. Sci. Assn. fellow, 1963, Nat. Def. Seminar, Nat. War Coll. fellow, 1973, NEH fellow, 1978, Pres.'s fellow Ark. State U., 1988-89. Mem. AAUP (pres. 1983-90, state sec. 1978-80), Ark. Polit. Sci. Assn. (bd. dirs., v.p. 1992-93, pres. 1993-94), Am. Polit. Sci. Assn., So. Polit. Sci. Assn., Phi Sigma Alpha, Phi Gamma Mu (sec.-treas. 1990-2000), Phi Kappa Phi (pres. 1991). Republican. Roman Catholic. Office: Ark State U Dept Polit Sci State University AR 72467 E-mail: spower@fastdata.net.

POWER, MICHAEL L. advertising executive; BA, Univ. of Louisville, 1965. CEO, founder Power Creative (formerly Power Graphics), Louisville, 1976—. Office: 11701 Commonwealth Dr Louisville KY 40299-2358*

POWER, THOMAS MICHAEL, economist, educator; b. Milw., May 12, 1940; s. Paul C. and Edith (Thomas) P.; m. Pamela Shore, June 13, 1977; children: Donovan, Kate. BA, Lehigh U., 1962; MA, Princeton U., 1965, PhD, 1971. Instr. Lehigh U., Bethlehem, Pa., 1966-67, Princeton (N.J.) U., 1967-68; from asst. to assoc. prof. U. Mont., Missoula, 1968-78, prof. econ., chmn., 1978—. Author: Economic Value of Quality of Life, 1980, The Economic Pursuit of Quality, 1987, Lost Landscapes and Failed Economies: The Search for an Economic Value of Place, 1996, Environmental Protection and Local Economic Well-Being: The Economic Pursuit of Quality, 1996, Post-Cowboy Economics: Pay and Prosperity in the New American West, 2001. Chmn. bd. dirs. Sussex Sch. Bd., Missoula, 1984-93. Woodrow Wilson Nat. fellow, 1963. Mem. Phi Beta Kappa. Avocations: mountaineering, mountain biking, skiing. Office: U Montana Dept Econs Missoula MT 59812-0001 E-mail: tom.power@mso.umt.edu.

POWERS, ALAN WILLIAM, literature educator; b. Springfield, Mass., Nov. 15, 1944; s. Roger Milton and Ida Maxine (Richardson) P.; m. Susan Elizabeth Mohl, June 1, 1944; children: Emily A. Lori, Tess Powers Brau. AB, Amherst Coll., 1966; MA, U. Minn., 1970, PhD, 1976. Tchg. assoc. U. Minn., Mpls., 1966-71; instr. English, Berkshire C.C., Pittsfield, Mass., 1971-73; asst. prof. Bristol C.C., Fall River, 1974-79, assoc. prof., 1980-86, prof., 1986—, chair dept. English, 1988—. Author: Birdtalk, 2002, Westport Soundings, 1995, co-author: Acting Funny in Shakespeare, 1994; composer (choral music) Settings to Yeats & Dylan Thomas, 1996; co-scriptwriter: A Loaded Gun, Keats and His Nightingale, 1986; trans. Candelaio, by Giordano Bruno; contbr. articles to profl. jours. Bd. dirs. New Bedford Unitarian Ch., 1992-97, Mass. Found. for Humanities, 1989-95, N.E. Modern Lang. Assn., 1992-95, Creative TV R.I., 1994-96, New Bedford Unitarian Ch., 1991-96. Rsch. fellow Brown U., Providence, 1979-80, Whiting Found. fellow, Milan & London, 1996, NEH fellow, Naples, Italy, 2000; Nat. Merit scholar, 1962-66. Mem. ASCAP, N.E. MLA (bd. dirs. 1993-95, del.), Assn. Lit. Scholars and Critics, Shakespeare Assn. Am., Renaissance Soc. Am., Acad. Am. Poets. Avocations: jazz trombone, translating. Office: Bristol C C 777 Elsbree St Fall River MA 02720-7307

POWERS, ANTHONY RICHARD, JR. educational sales professional; b. Chgo., June 14, 1942; s. Anthony Richard and Bernadine Rene (Schwenke) P.; m. Marianne Fugiel, Mar. 15, 1980; children: Kathleen Mary, Anthony Richard III. BA, Quincy Coll., 1964; MS, U. Notre Dame, 1974. Cert. tchr., Ill. Sci. tchr. St. Rene Sch., Chgo., 1964-70; sci. coord. Queen of All Saints Sch., 1970-76; sci. and math. product mgr. Ideal Sch. Supply Co., Oak Lawn, 1976-79, customer svc. mgr., 1980-83, Midwest sales mgr., 1983-85; nat. sales mgr. Ednl. Teaching Aids, Vernon Hills, 1985-89, v.p., 1989-97; accounts mgr. Numerical Algorithms Group, Downers Grove, 1997-2001; midwest acct. mgr. Freedom Sci., Vernon Hills, 2001—, midwest regional mgr., 2001—. Lectr., De Lourdes Coll., Des Plaines, Ill., 1970-78; sci. adviser, Archdiocese of Chgo., 1969-76. Author sci. edn. materials. Pres. Orchard Estates Condominium Assn., 1986-87; chmn. Vernon Hills Fire and Police Commn., 1995—. Mem. Northeastern Ill. Sci. Assn. (pres. 1970-75), U.S. Golf Assn., Internat. Brotherhood Magicians, K.C. Roman Catholic. Avocations: magic, music, golf. Home: 241 Tally Ho Dr Vernon Hills IL 60061-2900 Office: Freedom Sci 241 Tally Ho Dr Vernon Hills IL 60061

POWERS, ARLENE JORDON, lawyer; b. Plainfield, N.J., Jan. 23, 1963; d. Walter Matthew and Dorothy Jordon; m. James Francis Powers, Jan. 12, 1961; children: Rachael, Sarah, Olivia. BS ChE, Tufts U., 1985; JD, Suffolk U., 1991. Bar: Mass. 1991, U.S. Dist. Ct. Mass. 1992. Assoc. Samuels, Gauthier & Stevens, Boston, 1991—. Mem. Boston Patent Law Assn. Home: 3 Winnecunnet Way South Easton MA 02375-1464 Office: 225 Franklin St Ste 3300 Boston MA 02110-2898

POWERS, BRENDA AURETTA, social worker; b. Memphis, Dec. 15, 1949; d. George Ellis and Mattie Joe (Boyd) Harris; m. William Lawrence Powers, Sept. 29, 1978 (dec.); children: Brandy Allison, Brittany Jo. BA, Memphis State U., 1971, MEd, 1976. Cert. secondary sch. guidance counselor. Welfare worker State of Tenn., 1971-73; cirriculum coord. Fayette County Schs., Somerville, Tenn., 1973-74; career edn. counselor Tipton County Schs., Covington, 1974-75; human svcs. supr. State Tenn., Memphis, 1975-76, elibility supr., 1976-77, cmty. svcs. rep., 1977-91, program evaluator, 1991—. Bd. dirs. com. adminstrn. YWCA, 1981-83; nominating com. Mertie Buckman YWCA, 1989-92; chmn. com. ch. and soc. United Meth. Memphis Asbury Dist., 1987-94. Democrat. Avocations: music, going to plays and movies, walking. Home: 7541 Olivia Hill Dr Memphis TN 38133-2652 Office: Dept Fin & Adminstrn 3230 Jackson Ave Memphis TN 38122-1009

POWERS, BRUCE RAYMOND, writer, English language educator, consultant; b. Bklyn., Dec. 10, 1927; s. George Osborne and Gertrude Joan (Bangs) P.; m. Dolores Anne Dawson, July 25, 1969; children: Christopher, Patricia. Student, U. Conn., 1947-49; AB, Brown U., 1951, MA (tuition scholar 1961-62), 1965; postgrad., U. Pa., 1961. Announcer, engr. Sta. WNLC, New London, Conn., 1946-47; tng. officer CIA, Dept. Def., 1951-55; TV sales/svc. rep. NBC, 1955; TV news writer and reporter Movietone News, United Press Assns., Inc., 1955-56; asst. to pres. Gotham-Vladimir Advt., Inc., 1956-57; asst. account exec. D'Arcy Advt. Co., 1957-58; asst. campaign dir. Cmty. Counseling Svcs., Inc., 1958-59; fund-raising campaign dir. Tamblyn & Brown, Inc., 1959-60; instr. Brown U., Providence, 1963-65, Ryerson Poly. Inst., Toronto, 1966, Nazareth Coll., Rochester, N.Y., 1966-67; asst. prof. English and comm. studies Niagara U., Lewiston, 1967-86, assoc. prof., 1986-92, prof., 1986-92, chmn. permanent curriculum com. English dept., 1970-71; dir. Film Repertory Ctr., 1971-92, dir. comm. studies program, 1973-87. Prodr., mng. dir. Exptl. Film Retrospective, N.Y. State Coun. of the Arts, Buffalo, 1972; narrator (documentary) Niagara: Fading in the Mist, 1996; panelist, judge Artists Com. 2d World Festival of Animated Films, Zagreb, Yugoslavia, 1974; lectr., vis. artist ARTPARK, Lewiston, N.Y., 1975; project dir. Bicentennial Symposium, N.Y. State Am. Revolution Bicentennial Commn., Buffalo, 1975-76; rsch. assoc. Ctr. Culture and Tech., U. Toronto, 1977-81; keynote spkr. Dupont de Nemours & Co. Health and Safety Conf., Buffalo, 1990; ptnr. Moon Island Documentary Group, 1997—. Co-author: (with Marshall McLuhan) The Global Village, Oxford, 1989; editor The Film and Study Guide, 1973-74. Served with Underwater Demolition Teams, USNR, PTO, 1945-46. Recipient Carpenter prize in elocution Brown U., 1951. Mem. MLA, Underwater Demolitions Teams/Seal Assn. Va. Beach, Broadcast Edn. Assn., Soc. Cinema Studies, Am. Soc. Journalism Sch. Adminstrs., Assn. for Edn. in Journalism and Mass. Comm., Internat. Exptl. Film Soc. (founding pres. 1971-73), Ariz. Sr. Acad. U. Ariz. (Tucson), Western N.Y. Audio-Visual Assn., N.Y. Coll. English Assn., Phi Beta Kappa. Roman Catholic. Home: 915 Sun Valley St North Tonawanda NY 14120-1952 Office: 105 Main St Niagara Falls NY 14303-1111

POWERS, CLAUDIA MCKENNA, state legislator; b. Key West, Fla., May 28, 1950; d. James Edward and Claudia (Antrim) McKenna; children: Gregory, Theodore, Matthew, Thurston. BA in Edn., U. Hawaii, 1972; MA, Columbia U., 1975. Cert. tchr., N.Y. Mem. Greenwich (Conn.) Rep. Town Meeting, 1979-93, sec. bldg. com., 1982-84, sec. legis. com., 1986-88, 90-93; mem. Conn. Ho. of Reps., Hartford, 1993—, ranking mem. govt. adminstrn. and elections com., 1995-96, asst. minority leader, 1997-98, vice chmn. Rep. bill rev. com., 1997—, house minority whip, 1999—. Mem. editl. bd. Greenwich Mag., 1995-98. Conn. commr. Edn. Commn. of the States, 2000—; campaign chmn. Greenwich Rep. Town Com., 1984, 85, chmn., 1986-90; sec. Rep. Round Table, Greenwich, 1988-90; bd. govs. Riverside Assn., Greenwich, 1987-91, sec., 1991-92; class mother Riverside Sch., Greenwich, 1984-90; mem. altar guild Christ Ch., Greenwich, 1990—; adminstrv. coord. Greenwich Teen Ctr., 1990-91; alt. del. Rep. Nat. Conv., New Orleans, 1984—, San Diego, 1996; v.p. LWV of Greenwich, 1990-91. Episcopalian. Home and Office: 15 Hendrie Ave Riverside CT 06878-1808

POWERS, DAVID MURPHY, consumer products company executive; b. Lumberton, N.C., Oct. 27, 1959; s. Russell Hall Powers and Elizabeth Gwyne Atkins; m. Shreita Taylor, June 11, 1988. BA in Econs., BA in Bus. Mgmt., N.C. State U., 1983; MBA, Campbell U., 1988. Field rep. Helms for Senate Com., Raleigh, N.C., 1983-85; real estate rep. Franchise Enterprises, Inc., Rocky Mount, 1986-88; asst. v.p. facilities So. Nat. Bank, Lumberton, 1988-89; exec. dir. Internat. Shooting and Hunting Alliance, Washington, 1989-91; intergovernmental rels. officer U.S. Dept. Housing and Urban Devel., 1991-92; dir. state govt. rels. Smokeless Tobacco Coun., 1993-95, R.J. Reynolds Tobacco Co., Winston-Salem, N.C., 1995—. Mem. White House Initiative on Rural Econ. Devel., U.S. Dept. Housing and Urban Devel., Washington, 1991-92. Nat. Conv. alt. Rep. Nat. Com., Rep. Conv., New Orleans, 1988; conv. staff Dole/Kemp 1996, San Diego, 1996; fund raising com. Bush for Pres. 2000, N.C., 1999-2000. Mem. Nat. Rep. Legislators Assn. (policy com. 1999—), Washington Area State Rels. Group. Methodist. Avocations: jogging, reading, hunting, classical and jazz music. Office: RJ Reynolds Tobacco Co PO Box 2959 Winston Salem NC 27102-2959 E-mail: powersd@rjrt.com.

POWERS, DORIS HURT, retired engineering company executive; b. Indpls., Jan. 17, 1927; d. James Wallace Hurt Sr. and Mildred (Johnson) Devine; m. Patrick W. Powers, Nov. 12, 1950 (dec. 1989); children: Robert W. Powers, Jaye P., Laura S. Powers. Student, So. Meth. U., 1944-45; BS in Engring., Purdue U., 1949; postgrad., U. Tex., W. Tex., 1952-53, Ecole Normale Du Musique, Paris, 1965-68; grad., Harford County Leadership Acad., 1991. Flight instr. Red Leg Flying Club, El Paso, Lawton, Okla., 1951-57; check pilot Civil Air Patrol, 1952-57, ground instr. Washington, 1957-61; exec. v.p. T&E Internat., Inc., Bel Air, Md., 1979-88, pres., 1989-91; exec. v.p. T.E.I.S., Inc., 1979-88, pres., 1989-91, Shielding Technologies, Inc., Bel Air, 1987-95; retired, 1995. Mem. Purdue U. Engring. Vis. Com., 1999—2002. Mem. Northeastern Md. Tech. Coun., 1991—; bd. dirs. Leadership Acad., 1991-94; mem. vis. com. dept. engring. Purdue U., 1998--. Recipient Svc. award U.S. Army, 1978, Cert. of Appreciation U.S. Army Test and Evaluation Command, 1988, Woman of Distinction award Soroptimist Club, 1996; selected as Old Master Purdue U., 1995. Mem. CAP (lt. maj. 1951-58), Soc. of Women Engrs. (sr., v.p. 1977, treas. 1979, sec. rep. 1986-88, 98-00, mentor 1986—, speaker 1978—, selected to Coll. of Fellows 1993), Engring. Soc. Balt. (speaker 1980—), 99's (pres. 1951-53), Am. Soc. Indsl. Security, Am. Def. Preparedness Assn., Hartford County Econ. Devel. Coun., Assn. of U.S. Army, Northeastern Md. Tech. Coun. Avocations: ice dancing, music. Home: 11 Glen Gate Ct Bel Air MD 21014-5682

POWERS, EDWARD ALTON, minister, educator; b. Jamestown, N.Y., Oct. 26, 1927; s. Leslie Edgar and Mabelle Florence (Alton) P.; children: Randall Edward, Christopher Alan, Ann Lynn. BA, Coll. of Wooster, 1948; MDiv, Yale U., 1952; EdD, Columbia U., 1973. Ordained to ministry Congregational Ch., 1951; pastor Hamden, Conn., 1949-53, Pleasant Hill, Ohio, 1953-56; sec. dept. youth work Congl. Christian Ch. Bd. Home Missions, 1956-60; gen. sec. div. Christian edn., bd. home missions Congl. and Christian Chs., 1960-61; div. Christian edn., bd. homeland ministries United Ch. of Christ, 1962-73; gen. sec., div. evangelism, edn., ch. extension United Ch. Bd. Homeland Ministries, 1973-79; mem. faculty Inst. Mgmt. Competency, Am. Mgmt. Assn., N.Y.C., 1980-87. Affiliated faculty, Milano Grad. Sch., New Sch. University 1981—; mem. program bd. div. edn. and ministry Nat. Council Chs., 1963-80; mem. edn. working group World Council Chs.; chmn. Peace Priority Team, United Ch. of Christ, 1970-75, adminstr., editor sexuality study, 1977; ptnr. Cane Powers Cons., and Powers, Wayno & Assocs. Author: Journey Into Faith, 1964, Signs of Shalom, 1973, (with Rey O'Day) Theatre of the Spirit, 1980, In Essentials Unity, 1982, Youth in the Global Village, 1982; also articles. Home: 7 Gramercy Park W Apt 5B New York NY 10003-1759 Office: Graybar Bldg 420 Lexington Ave Rm 300 New York NY 10170-0399 E-mail: PowersEA@aol.com.

POWERS, EDWARD HERBERT, lawyer; b. Jersey City, N.J., June 21, 1942; s. Samuel and Ruth (Handman) P.; m. Phyllis Elinor Alpern, May 29, 1966; children: Alexander, Jill, Annette. BA, U. Mich., 1964, JD, 1967. Bar: Mich. 1968, U.S. Dist. Ct. (ea. dist.) Mich. 1968, U.S. Ct. Appeals (6th cir.) 1989, U.S. Supreme Ct. 1990. Owner, mem. Pelavin, Powers & Behm PC., Flint, Mich., 1968-2001; instr. Mott Adult Edn., Flint, 1970-74 Chmn. region XI U. Mich. Law Sch. Fund, 1980-81; v.p. Flint Jewish Fedn., 1978-82; chmn. Flint United Jewish Appeal, 1978; v.p. Congregation Beth Israel, 1979-82. Mem. Assn. Trial Lawyers Am., Mich. Trial Lawyers Assn., State Bar Mich., ABA (forum on constrn. industry), Genesee County Bar Assn., Am. Mensa Soc., Univ. Club (Flint). Home: 1071 Briarcliffe Dr Flint MI 48532-2102 Office: 300 Phoenix Bldg 801 S Saginaw St Flint MI 48502

POWERS, ELIZABETH WHITMEL, lawyer; b. Charleston, S.C., Dec. 16, 1949; d. Francis Persse and Jane Coleman Cotten (Wham) P.; m. John Campbell Henry, June 11, 1994 (dec. Jan. 1997); m. Henry C. B. Lindh, June 16, 2000. AB, Mt. Holyoke Coll., 1971; JD, U. S.C., 1978. Bar: S.C. 1978, N.Y. 1979. Law clk. to justice S.C. Cir. Ct., Columbia; assoc. Reid & Priest, N.Y.C., 1978-86, ptnr., 1986-97; of counsel LeBoeuf, Lamb, Greene & MacRae, 1997—. Exec. editor S.C. Law Rev., Columbia, 1977-78. Vol. N.Y. Jr. League, N.Y.C., 1983—; bd. dirs. The Seamen's Ch. Inst., 1996—; bd. trustees Ch. Club, 1991—94, 1997—2001, v.p., 1992—94. Mem.: Nat. Soc. Colonial Dames in State of N.Y. (pres. 1992—95), Nat. Soc. Colonial Dames of Am. (parliamentarian 1994—2000, regent Gunston Hall 2001—), S.C. Bar Assn., ABA. Avocations: bridge, tennis.

POWERS, EVELYN MAE, education educator; b. Norfolk, Va., Aug. 4, 1946; d. Albert Earl and Dorothy Mae (Weller) P.; m. Curtis Grubb Fitzhugh, June 21, 1969 (div. 1981). BA in Spanish, James Madison U., 1968; MEd in Curriculum & Instrn., Fgn. Langs., U. Va., 1976, PhD in Social Founds. of Edn., 1985. Spanish teacher pub. high schs., Va., 1969-77; grad. instr., instr. U. Va., Charlottesville, 1977-85; adj. and part-time faculty Va. Commonwealth U., Richmond, 1985-88; asst. prof. edn. Lycoming Coll., Williamsport, Pa., 1988-91; asst. prof. social founds. of edn. E. Carolina U., Greenville, N.C., 1991-98. Mem. Am. Ednl. Studies Assn., N.C. Founds. of Edn. Profs., So. Atlantic Philosophy of Edn. Soc. (yearbook editor 1994-98, archivist 1993-96), Phi Delta Kappa. Home: 19085 Sedley Lodge Rd Rapidan VA 22733-9512

POWERS, G. KAY, lawyer, mathematics educator; b. Durant, Okla. d. Horace M. and Georgia Hasting; m. Don M. Powers, Sept. 10, 1993. BS, Southeastern Okla. State U., 1963; MS, Okla. State U., 1965, PhD, 1970; JD, Oklahoma City U., 2000. Prof. math. U. Ctrl. Okla., Edmond, 1967-83, chair dept. math. and stats., 1983-88, dean Coll. Math. and Sci., 1988-2000; law practitioner, 2000—. Cons., evaluator North Ctrl. Assn. Schs. and Colls., 1994—. Mem. Math. Assn. Am., Rotary, Edmond Area C. of C. Avocations: ballroom dancing, auctioneering, fashion modeling. Office: Powers at Law LLC 325 French Park Dr Edmond OK 73034

POWERS, HENRY MARTIN, JR. oil company executive; b. Bath, Maine, July 18, 1932; s. Henry Martin and Eva (Saunders) P.; m. Hepzibah Hinchey Reed, June 20, 1959; children— Henry Martin III, Carlton Reed. BS, Maine Maritime Acad., 1954. Marine engr. Am. Export Lines, N.Y.C., 1954-58; staff engr. Bull & Roberts Inc., 1958-59; gen. sales mgr. Williams Bros., Inc., Portland, Maine, 1959-61; v.p. C.H. Sprague & Son Co., Boston, 1961-72, pres., 1972—, chmn. bd., 1987-99—, also bd. dirs.; chmn. bd. Sprague, Inc., Portsmouth, N.H., 1999—. Chmn. Pease Devel. Authority, 1990-93; bd. dirs. Shanley Corp., Strawbery Banke Inc., First N.H. Banks, Seaward Constrn. Co., Santa Holding Co., Intelligent Controls, Environ. Resource Return. Vice pres. Seacoast United Fund, 1967-69; chmn. fuels, energy com. New England Council, 1974-75; pres. Portsmouth Council, 1966-67; bd. visitors Maine Maritime Acad. Served to lt. USNR, 1956-58. Mem. Navy League, Mechanic Fire Soc., Algonquin Club (Boston), Cumberland Club (Portland), Masons. Home: 7 Boatclub Dr Stratham NH 03885-2356 Office: Sprague Inc. 2 International Dr Ste 1 Portsmouth NH 03801-6810

POWERS, HUGH WILLIAM, newspaper executive; b. Slaton, Tex., Dec. 20, 1926; s. James Jerome and Myrtle (Black) P.; m. Constance Margaret Cornwall, Aug. 30, 1952; children: Nan Margaret, Sarah Ann. Student, W.Va. U., 1943-47. Mng. editor AGC News Svc., Houston, 1949-56; city editor Houston Press, 1956-64; asst. city editor Houston Chronicle, 1964-65, bus. editor, 1965-67, feature editor, 1967-73, assoc. editor, 1973-95; dir. Taping for the Blind, 1995-98, v.p., 1997. Mem. Press Club of Houston (pres., dir. 1968-72), Ducks Unltd. (dir. Houston chpt. 1989—, chmn. 1995, Tex. State trustee Nat. Del., 1996—, zone chmn. 1997-2001), Phi Kappa Psi. Home: 10818 Hillcroft St Houston TX 77096-6031 E-mail: hpowers1@email.msn.com.

POWERS, JAMES MATTHEW, neuropathologist; b. Cleve., Sept. 15, 1943; s. Alfred Patrick and Margaret Anne (Gunther) P.; m. Karen P. Smith, 1983; children: Kristin, Scott, Conor. BS in Biology, Manhattan Coll., 1965; MD, Med. U. S.C., Charleston, 1969. Diplomate in anatomic pathology and neuropathology Am. Bd. Pathology. Asst. prof. pathology Med. U. S.C., Charleston, 1973-76; dir. electron micros. lab. VA Hosp., 1973-76; assoc. prof. pathology Med. U. S.C., 1976-80, prof. pathology, 1980-88; vice chmn. dept. pathology Columbia Coll. Physicians and Surgeons, N.Y.C., 1989-92; assoc. chair of edn. U. Rochester, N.Y., 1994-97, dir. residency tng. program, 1994—, prof., dir. neuropathology, 1992—. Sec. Biol. Stain Commn., 1994—. Author: (practice guidelines) Archives Pathology and Laboratory Medicine, 1995, (book chpt.) Anderson's Pathology, 10th edit., 1996, Greenfield's Neuropathology, 2002; mem. editl. bd.: Human Pathology, 1991—, mem. editl. bd.: Brain Pathology, 1995—2000, mem. editl. bd.: Acta Neuropathologica, 1995—, mem. editl. bd.: Biotech. and Histochemistry, 1994—2001, mem. editl. bd.: Modern Pathology, 1996—, mem. editl. bd.: Neurology, 1999—, mem. editl. bd.: Am. Jour. Surg. Pathology, 1999—, mem. editl. bd.: Jour. Neuropath. Exptl. Neurology, 2000—. Mem. Internat. Soc. Neuropathology (v.p. 1994-97), Am. Assn. Neuropathologists (pres. 1993, Moore award 1975, 76, 77, 81), U.S.-Can. Acad. Pathology, Am. Assn. Pathologists. Office: U Rochester Box 626 601 Elmwood Ave Rochester NY 14642-0001

POWERS, JANET F. special education educator; b. Wailuku, Hawaii, Aug. 3, 1948; d. Edward Chokin and Jane Fujiko (Arakaki) Sakugawa; 1 child, Lisa Ann Porter. BA, Calif. State U., Long Beach, 1979; MA, Calif. State Poly. U., Pomona, 1988. Cert. tchr., severely and learning handicapped edn. tchr., Calif. Rehab. therapist State of Calif., Costa Mesa, 1979-88, tchr. elem. spl. edn., 1988—. Contbr. article to profl. jour. Coach Spl. Olympics; producer, stage mgr., mem. stage crew La Habra Depot Playhouse, Laguna Playhouse, Cabrillo Playhouse. Mem. Niguel Art Assn., Hawaiian Surf Club San Onofre, Golden Key. Office: Fairview Devel Ctr 2501 Harbor Blvd Costa Mesa CA 92626-6143

POWERS, JOHN HENRY, industry executive; BSEE, Stevens Inst. Tech.; MS, Union Coll. Various positions including mgr. mfg. tech. & bus. ops. IBM, East Fishkill, N.Y., 1964-90; assoc. gen. mgr. for vol. svcs. IEEE, Inc., 1990-92, gen. mgr., 1992—, exec. dir., 1992-94; CEO, pres. Integrated Solutions and Svcs. Inc., 1995—. Founding mem. IBM Acad. Tech.; gen. chmn. Electronic Components Conf.; mem. steering com. Internat. Electronics Mfg. Tech. Symposium, Electronics Mfg. Tech. and Systems Conf., Internat. Semiconductor Mfg. Scis. Symposium, Mfg. Tech. Forum. Chmn. editorial bd.: IEEE Transactions on Semiconductor Manufacturing. Recipient Outstanding Contbn. award and Mfg. Tech. award Components, Hybrids and Mfg. Tech. Fellow IEEE (bd. dirs., exec. dir., exec. com., found. bd., facilities com., fin. com., employee benefits com., strategic planning com., compensation com., budget devel. com. all 1993), Coun. Engring. and Sci. Soc. Execs., Electronic Convs. Mgmt. (bd. dirs. 1993), Am. Assn. Engring. Socs. (bd. dirs. 1993, tech. activities bd. 1980-81), Soc. Components, Hybrids and Mfg. Tech. (pres. 1980-81, jr. past pres. 1982, sr. past pres. 1983, long range planning chmn. 1983, mfg. tech. chmn. 1983, chmn. joint com. on semiconductor mfg.).

POWERS, JOHN KIERAN, lawyer; b. Schenectady, Aug. 2, 1947; s. Paul Joseph and Anne Marie (Leahy) P.; children: Erin Kelly, Megan Kerry. BS, U. Notre Dame, 1969; JD, Union U., 1972. Bar: N.Y. 1973, U.S. Dist. Ct. (no. dist.) N.Y. 1973, U.S. Dist. Ct. (so., ea. and we. dists.) N.Y. 1982, U.S. Ct. Appeals (2d cir.) 1984, U.S. Supreme Ct. 1985, U.S. Dist. Ct. Vt. 1988. Assoc. Medwin and McMahon, Albany, 1973-77; pvt. practice law, 1973-80; pres. John K. Powers, P.C., 1980-87; ptnr. Powers and Santola, 1987—. Contbr. articles to profl. publs. Trustee N.Y. State Lawyers Polit. Action Com., 1983-88, treas., 1989-93, chair, 1993—; trustee ATLA Polit. Action Com., 1995-98. Fellow Roscoe Pound Found. Mem. ABA (sustaining vice-chair, legis. subcom., automobile law com., trial and ins. practice sect., state leader com. on state legis. sect.), Nat. Coll. Adv. (co-founder), ATLA (life, state del. 1990, bd. govs. 1990—, exec. com. 1995—), Am. Bd. Trial Advocates (advocate), N.Y. State Bar Assn. (sustaining, lectr., exec. com. and chmn. legis. com. trial lawyers sect.), N.Y. State Trial Lawyers Assn. (sustaining, bd. dirs. 1983-88, chmn. key person legis. com., chmn. pubs. com., chmn. atty. referral com., exec. com. 1986—, treas. 1988-89, v.p. 1989-91, 1st v.p. 1990-91, pres.-elect 1991-92, pres. 1992-93, award of merit 1990, 94, award of excellence 1991, Pres. award 1995, 96, 98, 99, 2000, dist. svc. award 1997), N.Y. Trial Lawyers Inst. (lectr. and program chmn. 1981—, treas. 1988-89, pres. 1992-93), (life) N.Y. State Head Injury Assn. (co-counsel 1983-85, bd. dirs. 1992-93, 1st v.p. 1993—), Capitol Dist. Trial Lawyers Assn. (bd. dirs. 1979-81, v.p. 1983-85, pres. 1985-86), Pa. Trial Lawyers Assn., Alban County Bar Assn. (lectr.), Chief Judge's Com. to Improve Availability of Legal Svcs., Chief Judge's Pro-Bono Monitoring Com., Civil Justice Found. (guest lectr. Law Sch. NYU, Albany Law Sch., U. Syracuse Law Sch., Albany Med. Coll.), Trial Lawyers for Pub. Justice, Lions (pres. Scotia, N.Y. chpt. 1979-80). Democrat. Roman Catholic. Home and Office: 39 N Pearl St Albany NY 12207-2785

POWERS, JOHN T., JR. mayor; Mayor City of Spokane, Wash., 2001—. Bd. dirs. Assn. Wash. Cities, Inland Northwest Tech. Edn. Ctr., Spokane Regional Econ. Devel. Coun.; co-chair Spokane Task Force on Race Rels.; mem. U.S. Conf. Mayors, Gas & Elec. Utility Restruction Task Force, Wash. State Competitiveness Coun., Assn. Northeast Wash. Mayors. Office: Spokane City Hall 808 W Spokane Falls Blvd Spokane WA 99201 E-mail: jpowers@spokanecity.org.*

POWERS, JOHN Y. federal judge; b. Lake Orion, Mich., Aug. 1, 1929; s. Henry Stephen and Bertha Mae (Youngerman) P.; m. Barbara Mathilda Levero, Aug. 25, 1958; children: Joshua A., Lucas A., John Matthew, Samuel David. Student, Union U., 1947-48; BA, Vanderbilt U., 1951, LLB, 1953. Bar: Tenn. 1954. Enlisted man U.S. Army, Ft. Holabird, Md., 1954; 1st Lt. Judge Adv. Gen. Corps, Charlottesville, Va., 1955; with Claims Divsn. Office of the Judge Advocate General, Ft. Holabird, Md., 1955-57; with Adminstrv. divsn. U.S. Dept. Justice, 1957-58; claims rep. State Farm Ins. Co., Miami, Fla., 1958-59; atty. Spears, Moore, Rebman & Wms, Chattanooga, 1959-70; ptnr. Hargraves, Curtis & Powers, 1970-74, Noone, Stringer & Powers, Chattanooga, 1974-78, Reingold, Powers & Schulman, Chattanooga, 1978-84; U.S. magistrate judge ea. dist. Tenn. U.S. Dist. Ct., 1984—. Office: US District Court US Courthouse 900 Georgia Ave Rm 401 Chattanooga TN 37402-2216

POWERS, MICHAEL J. retired financial company executive; Vice chmn. Ernst & Young LLP, N.Y.C.; chmn., CEO Intellinex LLC.

POWERS, MICHAEL KEVIN, architectural and engineering executive; b. Boston, Feb. 3, 1948; s. Albert Thomas and Claire Marie (Sullivan) P.; m. Patricia Marie Collins, July 10, 1971; children: Kristin Powers Goppel, Jennifer Anne. BSCE, Northeastern U., 1971; Grad., ACEC Sr. Execs. Inst., 1998. Registered profl. engr. N.Y., Vt., Minn., Maine, Mass., N.H., D.C., Pa., R.I., Ohio. Staff engr. Edwards and Kelcey, Boston, 1967-70; project mgr. DeLeuw Cather & Co., 1971-80; CEO, pres. Symmes Maini & McKee Assocs., Inc., Cambridge, Mass., 1980—, also chmn. bd. dirs. Guest spkr. Tradeline Forum on Bus. and Tech., Boston, 1986-88, Microcontamination Conf. and Expn., Santa Clara, Calif., 1987, Clean Rooms Conf., Balt., 1995, Santa Clara, 1995, 96, Boston, 1996, Clean Rooms East, Boston, 1996, Build Boston, 1999; lectr. facility design MIT, 1989, 92, 93, 97, 98, 2000, Wentworth Inst., 1993, 94, 97, 99, Pa. State U., 1995; lectr. engring. program MIT, 1997, 98, 99; bd. dirs. Mass. Alliance for Econ. Devel.; chmn. Mass. Bldg. Congress; chmn. ACEC Mass., mem. A/E com. Contbr. articles to profl. jours. Mem. ASCE, NSPE, Mt. River East Condominium Assn. (pres.). Roman Catholic. Avocations: Alpine skiing, tennis, golf, music. Office: Symmes Maini & McKee Assocs Inc 1000 Massachusetts Ave Cambridge MA 02138-5316 E-mail: m_powers@smma.com.

POWERS, MICHAEL ROLAND, educator, insurance consultant; b. Wilkinsburg, Pa., Nov. 19, 1959; s. John Nolan and Dorothy Ann (Hladio) P.; m. Imelda Wan-Har Yeung, June 9, 1984; children: Thomas Yang, Andrew Yang. BS, MA, Yale U., 1982; PhD, Harvard U., 1987. Ins. cons. Chang and Co., Boston, 1981-87; dep. ins. commr. Pa. Ins. Dept., Harrisburg, 1987-90; prof. risk mgmt. and ins. Temple U., Phila., 1990—. Contbr. articles to profl. jours. Active Pa. Health Care Cost Containment Coun., Harrisburg, 1989-90. Mem. Phi Beta Kappa. Office: Temple Univ 479 Ritter Anx Philadelphia PA 19122

POWERS, PATRICIA KENNETT, piano and organ educator; b. Detroit, Feb. 25, 1925; d. Frank and Dorothy (Hurley) Kennett; m. Jack Powers, Jr., June 4, 1948; 1 child, Brian K. BA in Music, Kalamazoo Coll., 1946; MA in Music History, U. Mich., 1947. Instr. music U. Ark., Fayetteville, 1947-49; pvt. tchr. music, Corpus Christi, Tex., 1953-62, 68-72, Beeville, 1972-99. Adj. instr. group piano, theory, applied piano and organ music Bee County Coll., Beeville, 1974-89. Pres. Beeville Concert Assn., 1992-94. Mem. Music Tchrs. Nat. Assn. (nat. cert. music tchr., pres. South Ctrl. divsn. 1992-94, bd. dirs. 1994-96, South Ctrl. divsn. rep. to ho. of dels. 1996-98), Tex. Music Tchrs. Assn. (past sec. and pres.-elect, pres. 1986-88, former cert. chmn., and South Ctrl. divsn. rep. on nat. cert. bd.), Am. Guild Organists, Music Educators Nat. Conf., Tex. Music Educators Conf., Midland Music Tchrs. Assn. Episcopalian. Avocation: music and computers. Home: 2401 Apperson Dr Midland TX 79705-6304 E-mail: ppow@swbell.net.

POWERS, PAULINE SMITH, psychiatrist, educator, researcher; b. Sept. 23, 1941; m. Henry P. Powers; children: Jessica, Samantha. AB in Math., Washington U., 1963; MD, U. Iowa, 1971. Med. intern Emanuel Hosp., Portland, Oreg., 1971-72; psychiatry resident U. Iowa, Iowa City, 1972-74, U. Calif., Santa Barbara, 1974-75; from asst. prof. to assoc. prof. psychiatry Coll. Medicine U. So. Fla., Tampa, 1975-85, prof., 1985—, dir. eating disorder program, 1979—, dir. psychosomatic medicine divsn., 1979—. Author: Obesity: The Regulation of Weight, 1980; editor: The Current Treatment of Anorexia Nervosa and Bulimia, 1984. Fellow: Am. Psychiat. Assn. (Rush Gold Outstanding Exhibit medal 1976, Dorfman Jour. Paper award 1987); mem.: Acad. Eating Disorders (founding pres., Women Helping Women award 1995, Profl. Excellence award 1997, Outstanding Clinician award 2000). Office: U So Fla Coll Medicine Dept Psychiatry 3515 E Fletcher Ave Tampa FL 33613-4706 E-mail: ppowers@hsc.usf.edu.

POWERS, RAY LLOYD, former state senator, dairy farmer, rancher; b. Colorado Springs, June 27, 1929; s. Guy and Cora (Hill) P.; m. Dorothy Parrish, Dec. 14, 1975; 1 child, Janet. Student, Pub. Schs. Dairy farmer, Colo. Springs, 1947—; v.p. bus. devel., dir. The Capitol Pulse Inc. , Washington, 2000—. Mem. Colo. Ho. of Reps., 1978-80; mem. Colo. Senate, 1981-2000, senate pres., 1998-2000; bd. dirs. Mountain Empire Dairyments Coop., Denver, 1967-81. Mem. Colo. Cattlemen, Republican Men's Club, Lions.*

POWERS, RICHARD DANIEL, banker; b. Albuquerque, July 11, 1956; s. Richard James and Laura Love (Daniel) P.; m. Savanna Lee Anderson, Aug. 26, 1988; 1 child, Sara Elizabeth. BA, SUNY, Albany, 1993; MBA, U. Chgo., 1995. Account rep. Covington Knox, Inc., Houston, 1976-78; sales mgr. Morse Realty, Inc., 1979-86; asst. v.p. Dollar Dry Dock Savs. Bank, White Plains, N.Y., 1986-87; cons. Deloitte & Touche, N.Y.C., 1987; sr. v.p. Gt. Western Mortgage Co., Chatsworth, Calif., 1987-94, Charter One Bank, Cleve., 1994—; pres., CEO Charter One Mortgage Corp., Richmond, Va.,

1997—. Bd. dirs. First Derivative Systems, Inc. Trustee Ohio Mortgage Bankers Assn. With USAF, 1973-75. Mem.: Bank Adminstrn. Inst., Mortgage Bankers Assn., Am.'s Cmty. Bankers (residential bd. govs.), Pine Lake Trout Club, Cleve. Athletic Club. Office: Charter One Bank 1215 Superior Ave E Cleveland OH 44114-3299 Home: 2068 W 10th St Cleveland OH 44113 E-mail: rpowers@att.net.

POWERS, RICHARD EDWARD, JR. lawyer; b. Evanston, Ill., July 20, 1952; s. Richard Edward and Helen Lufen Powers; m. Diane Wojda, Aug. 12, 1978. BS, Gonzaga U., 1974; JD, U. Notre Dame, 1977. Ptnr. Butler & Binion LLP, Washington, 1977-99, Dorsey & Whitney LLP, Washington, 1999—. Mem. ABA, Tex. Bar Assn., D.C. Bar, Energy Bar Assn. Home: 5233 Elliott Rd Bethesda MD 20816-2910 Office: Dorsey & Whitney 1001 Penn Ave NW Ste 300S Washington DC 20004-2505

POWERS, ROBERT DAVID, physician; b. Plainfield, N.J., Nov. 6, 1953; s. John B. and Marian E. (Kuhn) P.; m. Sally Ann Harmet, 1977; children: Alison, Elizabeth, Carolyn. BA, Amherst Coll., 1975; MD, U. Va., 1979; MPH, Yale U., 1999. Intern U. Minn., Mpls., 1979-81; resident U. Va., Charlottesville, 1981-83, from asst. to assoc. prof., 1983-94; assoc. prof. U. Conn. Sch. Medicine, Farmington, 1994—, chief emergency medicine, 1997—, vice chmn. dept. trauma and emergency medicine, 1997—, assoc. prof., 1994-99, prof., 1999—. Fellow ACP, Am. Coll. Emergency Physicians. Office: Hartford Hosp Dept Emergency Medicine Hartford CT 06115 E-mail: RPowers@Harthosp.org.

POWERS, ROBERT LAWRENCE, civilian military employee; b. Bklyn., Apr. 3, 1942; s. Lawrence Robert and Audrey Buchanan Powers; m. Susan McCormick, June 13, 1964; children: Jennifer Powers Kane, Megan Powers Dosher. BS in Chemistry, Math., U.S. Naval Acad., 1964; MS in Ops. Rsch., Naval Postgrad. Sch., Monterey, Calif., 1972. Commd. officer USN, 1964, officer, 1964-81; commdg. officer USS Fairfax County, Norfolk, Va., 1981-83; chief staff officer Amphibious Squadron 10, 1983-85; sr. analyst Sonalysts, Inc., 1985-92; tng. coord. Fleet Tactical Readings Group, 1992-98; sr. doctrine writer Fleet Info. Warfare Ctr., 1998—2000, with experimentation divsn., 2001—. Adj. prof. U.S. Naval War Coll., Norfolk, 1985—. Co-founder Children's Coun. S. Hampton Rds., Norfolk, 1998; mem. Naval War Coll. Found. Mem. U.S. Naval Inst., Retired Officers Assn., Kiwanis (Hixson fellow 1993, webmaster capital dist. 1998—, editor Great Bridge Kiwanis Newsletter 1998—, gov. 1998-99, Circle K internat. circle of svc.), Sigma Xi. Episcopalian. Avocations: computers, naval history, war games. Home: 1100 West Rd Chesapeake VA 23323 E-mail: bpowers100@aol.com.

POWERS, RONALD GEORGE, management consultant; b. N.Y.C., July 9, 1934; s. Lee Whitney and R. Anne Powers; m. Elizabeth Braislin McClellan, July 24, 1980. Chmn. Boardroom Advisors, Inc., Winter Park and Tampa, Fla., The Strategic Mgmt. Adv. Group, Inc., Winter Park and Tampa. Adviser to chief execs. of banks, corps. and govts. on strategic mgmt. issues, 1971—. Trustee Trinity Sch., Fla. Symphony Orch. Mem. Interlachen C. of C. Republican. Episcopalian. Home: PO Box 2174 Winter Park FL 32790-2174 Office: PO Box 1922 Winter Park FL 32790-1922 E-mail: boardroomadvisor@mindspring.com.

POWERS, RUNA SKÖTTE, artist; b. Anderstorp, Sweden, Oct. 29, 1940; d. Gösta Nils Folke and Kristina Torborg (Andersson) S.; m. David Britton Powers, Mar. 13, 1965; children: Kristina, Davis. Student, Art Inst. So. Calif., 1976-83; BMA, U. So. Calif., 1986. Exhbns. include Newport Festival Arts, Newport Beach, 1980, Costa Mesa Art League, 1980, Orange County Fair, Costa Mesa, 1980, Art Inst. So. Calif., Laguna Beach, 1976-83, Studio Sem Ghelardini, Pietrasanta, Italy, 1983, Design House, Laguna, 1984, Vorpal Gallery, 1983-84, Laguna Beach Mus. Art, 1984, Gallery Sokolov, Laguna Beach, 1985-93, Margareta Sjödin Gallery, Malibu, 1988, Ana Izax Gallery, Beverly Hills, 1988, Envision Art, 1991, Gallery Slottet, Hörle, Sweden, 1990-92, J.F. Kennedy Performing Arts Ctr., Washington, 1991, Internat. Art Expn., L.A., 1985, N.Y., 1986-87, San Bernardino County Mus., 1993. Founder Found. Hörle Manor House, Värnamo, Sweden, 1987—. Avocations: music, reading, cooking, swimming. Home: 1831 Ocean Way Laguna Beach CA 92651-3235

POWERS, SCOTT, producer, actor; b. Chgo., Aug. 23, 1948; s. Raymond Alford and Ruby Marilyn (Ivacko) P. BS, Ithaca Coll., 1970; MBA, Fairleigh Dickinson U., 1971. Producer Young & Rubicam, Inc., N.Y.C.; account exec. Kelly, Nason, Inc.; sr. account exec. Bozell & Jacobs, Inc.; account supr. Foote, Cone & Belding, Inc.; actor N.Y.C., L.A., 1982—; pres. Scott Powers Prodns., Inc., N.Y.C., 1988—. Pres. CaribCom, Inc., N.Y.C., 1996—. Author: Here's Looking At You!, 1997; contbr. articles to publs.; cartoonist Thankyounext, 1990—. Mem. Better Bus. Bur. N.Y.C., 1991—, Knickerbocker Rep. Club, N.Y.C., 1971—; bd. dirs. Profl. Comedians Assn., N.Y.C., 1988-91, v.p., 1989-91; bd. dirs. One World Arts Found., 1992—; judge Internat. Film and TV Festivals, N.Y.C., 1991—. Mem. AFTRA (bd. dirs. 1989-91), SAG, Actor's Equity Assn., NATAS (judge Emmys 1985—), N.Y.C. C. of C., Met. Club, N.Y. Athletic Club, Players Club, Mensa, Intertel. Republican. Congregationalist. Avocations: skiing, sailing, tennis, squash, international river running. Home: 180 Central Park S New York NY 10019-1562 Office: Scott Powers Prodns Inc Ste 405 22 W 21st St New York NY 10010-6904

POWERS, STEVEN EUGENE, procurement engineer; b. Milw., May 25, 1962; s. Walter Eugene and Dorothy Elaine (Nevenfeldt) P.; m. Tamar Alane Sholtes, June 6, 1992; children: Kyle Alexander, Brian Reed, Cory Robert. BS in Mech. Engring., U. Wis., 1984. Engr. IBM Corp, Endicott, N.Y., 1981-85, assoc. engr., 1985-87, sr. assoc. engr., 1987-92, staff engr., 1992—. Mem. ASME (chmn. local chpt. 1989-90), Odyssey of the Mind (judge 1989-97, head judge 1993). Home: 509 African Rd Vestal NY 13850-5333 Office: IBM Corp 1701 N St Dept FNB Endicott NY 13760 E-mail: spowers@us.ibm.com.

POWERS, THOMAS MOORE, writer; b. N.Y.C., Dec. 12, 1940; s. Joshua Bryant and Susan (Moore) P.; m. Candace Molloy, Aug. 21, 1965; children: Amanda, Susan, Cassandra. BA, Yale U., 1964. Reporter Rome (Italy) Daily American, 1965-67, U.P.I., N.Y.C., 1967-70; freelance writer, 1970—; contbg. editor The Atlantic mag.; editor, founding ptnr. Steerforth Press, So. Royalton, Vt., 1993—. Author: Diana: The Making of a Terrorist, 1971, The War at Home, 1973, The Man Who Kept the Secrets: Richard Helms and the CIA, 1979, Thinking About the Next War, 1982, Total War: What It Is, How It Got That Way, 1988, Heisenberg's War: The Secret History of the German Bomb, 1993, The Confirmation, 2000, Intelligence Wars: American Secret History from Hitler to Al Qaeda, 2002. Recipient Pulitzer prize for nat. reporting, 1971 Mem. PEN Am. Center, Council on Fgn. Relations. Address: 106 Chelsea St South Royalton VT 05068-9800 also: Lit Rep Lynn Nesbit 445 Park Ave New York NY 10022-2606 E-mail: tom@steerforth.com.

POWERS, WILLIAM EDWARD, emergency physician, educator; b. Atlanta, Sept. 16, 1957; s. Richard Candler and Olive Carol Osburn Powers; m. Nancy Carolyn Freeman, May 17, 1986; children: Nicole, Will. *Great grandfather William Alexander McCallum elected to Florida State Legislature. Grandfather Wilbur F. Osburn was elected Okaloosa County Judge in Florida. His term lasted thirty years. Father Richard C. Powers, Sr., was industrial and chemical engineer in Chicago and later worked for the Department of Defense. Brother Richard C. Powers was a police officer in the Chicago area, completed law school and is now employed in government service.* MS in Biomed. Engring., U. Ill., Chgo., 1981; MS in Aerospace Medicine, Wright State U., 1991; MD, Rush U., 1985; postgrad., U. Houston, 2001—. Diplomate Am. Bd. Emergency Medicine, Am. Bd. Preventive Medicine. Intern in gen. surgery Orlando (Fla.) Regional Med. Ctr., 1985-86, resident in emergency medicine, 1986-88; resident in aerospace medicine Wright State U., Dayton, Ohio, 1989-91; biomed. engr., rsch. asst. U. Ill., Chgo., 1980-81; chief resident emergency medicine Orlando (Fla.) Regional Med. Ctr., 1987; assoc. dir. emergency medicine Kissimmee (Fla.) Meml. Hosp., 1988-89; asst. med. dir. Martin-Marietta Aerospace, Orlando, Fla., 1988-89; emergency med. physician, clin. instr. Wright State U. Med. Sch., Dayton, Ohio, 1989-91; med. officer, flight surgeon NASA Johnson Space Ctr., Houston, 1991-92; asst. med. dir. Cape Canaveral Hosp., Cocoa Beach, Fla., 1991-93; Twin Cities Hosp., Niceville, 1991-93; asst. prof. emergency medicine, rsch. dir. U. Tex. Med. Sch., Houston, 1993-95; asst. prof. family medicine, dir. urgent care U. Tex. Med. Br., Galveston, 1995-96; asst. prof. medicine Baylor Coll. Medicine, Houston, 1996—2001; med. dir. emergency dept. Meml. Hermann Hosp. S.E. , 2002—. *Co-developed an artificial leg for amputees in running, developed a capillary rheometer to assess respiratory diseases, performed analysis of bone density changes in astronauts, and the toxic effects of carbon monoxide. Lectured in the areas of Emergency Medicine and Space Medicine in Cambridge, Vienna, Ontario, and Honduras. Began flying at age 15, and first soloed on 16th birthday. Continues to be active pilot with instrument rating and aerobatic experience. Formerly President of Powers Flight Inorperted,an aircraft leasing business.Currently a PhD student in physics at the University of Houston. Was named a Finalist for astronaut selection in 1996.* Contbr. articles to profl. publs. Med. missionary Missionary Ventures, Honduras, 1995, 98. Fulbright Found. grantee U. Vienna, Austria, 1996. Fellow Am. Coll. Emergency Physicians, Aerospace Med. Assn. (assoc. fellow); mem. AIAA, Am. Phys. Soc., Exptl. Aircraft Assn. Avocations: flying, soccer, basketball, photography, piano. Office: 2437 Bay Area Blvd #112 Houston TX 77058 E-mail: WEPowers@aol.com.

POWLEDGE, FRED ARLIUS, freelance writer; b. N.C., Feb. 23, 1935; s. Arlius Raymond and Pauline (Stearns) P.; m. Tabitha Morrison, Dec. 21, 1957; 1 child, Pauline Stearns. AB in English, U. N.C., 1957. Writer, editor AP, New Haven, 1958-60; reporter Atlanta Jour., 1960-63, N.Y. Times, N.Y.C., 1963-66; freelance journalist, 1966—. Lectr. New Sch., N.Y.C., 1967-69, 80-82; narrator, co-producer, writer WNET-TV/13, N.Y.C., 1972. Author: Black Power/White Resistance: Notes on the New Civil War, 1967, To Change a Child: A Report on the Institute for Developmental Studies, 1967, Model City: A Test of American Liberalism: One Town's Efforts to Rebuild Itself, 1970, Mud Show: A Circus Season, 1976, Born on the Circus, 1976, The Backpacker's Budget Food Book, 1977, Journeys Through the South, 1979, So You're Adopted: A Book About the Experience of Being Adopted, 1982, Water: The Nature, Uses and Future of Our Most Precious and Abused Resource, 1982, A Forgiving Wind: On Becoming a Sailor, 1983, Fat of the Land, 1984, The New Adoption Maze: And How to Get Through It, 1985, You'll Survive, 1986, Free at Last? The Civil Rights Movement and the People Who Made It, 1991, We Shall Overcome: The Heroes of the Civil Rights Movement, 1993, Working River, 1995, Pharmacy in the Forest, 1998. Mem. Bd. Library Trustees, St. Mary's County, Md. With USAR, 1957. Russell Sage fellow Russell Sage Found., 1966-67; travel and study grantee Ford Found., 1971, 93-94. Mem. Nat. Assn. Sci. Writers. Home and Office: 25040 Old Brick Way Hollywood MD 20636-2939 E-mail: fredpowledge@nasw.org.

POWLEN, DAVID MICHAEL, investment company executive; b. Logansport, Ind., May 28, 1953; s. Daniel Thomas and Bertha Frances (Cappa) P.; m. Karen Lamb Gentleman, Aug. 5, 1978 (div. Jan. 1984); 1 child, Brooks Ryan. AB, Harvard U., 1975, JD, 1978. Bar: Ind. 1978, U.S. Dist. Ct. (so. dist.) Ind. 1978, U.S. Ct. Appeals (7th cir.) 1985. Assoc. Barnes & Thornburg, Indpls., 1978-84, ptnr., 1985-01, chmn., adminstr. creditors rights dept.; mng. dir., co-mgr. restructuring group McDonald Investments Inc., Cleve., 2001—. Contbr. articles to profl. jours. Mem. ABA (bus. bankruptcy com., secured creditors and chpt. 11 subcom., comml. fin. svcs. com., creditors rights subcom.), Seventh Cir. Bar Assn., Ind. Bar Assn. (chmn. bankruptcy and creditors rights sect. 1990-91), Indpls. Bar Assn. (chmn. edn. com. 1984, chmn. ct. liaison com. 1985, bankruptcy and comml. law sect.), Am. Bankruptcy Inst., Turnaround Mgmt. Assn., Comml. Law League Am. (bankruptcy and insolvency sect.), Harvard Club, Phi Beta Kappa. Office: mail code OH-01-02-1645 McDonald Investments Inc 800 Superior Ave Ste 1600 Cleveland OH 44114 E-mail: dpowlen@mcdinvest.com.

POWLESS, DAVID GRIFFIN, accountant; b. Marion, Ill., June 16, 1953; s. Kenneth Barnett and Emily Mary (Cygnar) P.; m. Patricia Kay Walker, Aug. 23, 1975; children: Nathaniel Ryan, Nicholas Andrew. BS in Accountancy, U. Ill., 1975. CPA, Ill. Mgr. Gray Hunter Stenn, CPA's, Marion, 1974-81; pvt. practice acctg., 1981-87; ptnr. Powless & Hudgens (and predecessor firm), 1988—. Bd. dirs. John A. Logan Coll. Found., 1993-2002, Marion Cultural and Civic Ctr. Found., 1996-2001, treas., 1997-2001; bd. dirs. City of Marion Carnegie Libr., 1998—, treas. 2001—. Mem. AICPA, Ill. CPA Soc., Marion C. of C. (mem. com. 1992-94), U. Ill. Alumni Assn. (bd. dirs. 1985-91, Loyalty award 1992), Champaign-Urbana Alumni Coun. (bd. dirs. 1983-89), Egyptian Illini (pres. 1981-87, 89), Elks, Phi Sigma Kappa (alumni bd. dirs., treas. 1980-87, Outstanding Alumnus award 1984). Republican. Roman Catholic.

POWLEY, ELIZABETH ANN, health facility administrator; b. Massillon, Ohio, June 26, 1950; d. William Julius and Marilyn Helen Maier; m. Donald S. Powley Jr., June 16, 1984. Diploma, Mercy Hosp. Sch. Nursing, 1971; BS, U. Cin., 1988; postgrad., Kennedy-Western U., Cheyenne, Wyo. RN, Ohio. Staff nurse ICU Good Samaritan Hosp., Cin., 1977-80, critical care pool, 1980-81, asst. head nurse intermediate coronary care unit, 1981-82, nurse mgr. intermediate critical care unit, 1982-89, dir. diagnostic studies, 1989-93, adminstrv. dir. diagnostic and radiology svcs., 1993-95; dir. diagnostic imaging svcs. Tri Health, Cin., 1995—. Adv. bd. Xavier U. Sch. Radiology. Bd. dirs. Mental Health Svcs. Agy. Mem. Am. Healthcare Radiology Adminstrs., Ohio Breast and Cervical Cancer Coalition, Breast Health Network Con., Delta Tau Kappa, Sigma Theta Tau (Omicron Omicron chpt.). Office: Bethesda North Hosp 10500 Montgomery Rd Cincinnati OH 45242-4415

POWNALL, JAMES RICHARD, electronics executive; b. Buffalo, Oct. 18, 1951; s. Raymond Carroll and Mary Frances (McKenzie) P.; m. Jean Aitchison Robinson, Aug. 9, 1980; children: Jennifer Robinson Pownall, Jameson Robinson Pownall. AAS in Elec. Engring. Tech. summa cum laude, Alfred (N.Y.) State Coll., 1975; BS in Computer Engring. magna cum laude, Syracuse U., 1977. Mgr. computer systems Syracuse U., 1977-80; computer engr. GE, Syracuse, N.Y., 1980-86, unit mgr., 1986-87, sub-section mgr., 1987-89, sr. systems engr., 1989-91; prin. scientific analsyt Smith Kline Beecham, King of Prussia, Pa., 1991-93, mgr. sys. and svcs. engring., 1993—. Cons. VA Hosp., Syracuse, 1980-91. Home: 2204 Strawberry Ln Coatesville PA 19320-4746 Office: Smith Kline Beecham R&D 709 Swedeland Rd King Of Prussia PA 19406 E-mail: jim_pownall@sbphrd.com.

POWSNER, EDWARD RAPHAEL, physician; b. N.Y.C., Mar. 17, 1926; m. Rhoda Lee Moscovitz , June 8, 1950; children: Seth, Rachel, Ethan, David. SB in Elec. Engring., MIT, 1948, SM in Biology, 1949; MD, Yale U., 1953; MS in Internal Medicine, Wayne State U., 1957; MHSA, U. Mich. Diplomate Am. Bd. Nuclear Medicine, Am. Bd. Pathology in clin. pathology and anatomic pathology, Am. Bd. Internal Medicine; lic. physician, Mich., Calif., N.Y. Intern Wayne County Gen. Hosp., Eloise, Mich., 1953-54, resident internal medicine, 1954-55, Detroit Receiving Hosp., 1955-56; fellow in hematology Wayne State U. and Detroit Receiving Hosp., 1957-58; clin. investigator VA Hosp., Allen Park, Mich., 1958-61, chief nuclear medicine svc., 1961-78; dir. clin. labs. Mich. State U., East Lansing, 1978-81; staff pathologist Ingham Med. Ctr., Lansing, Mich., 1978-81; dir. nuclear medicine St. John Hosp., Detroit, 1982-95. Rsch. asst. biology MIT, 1948-49, 50; asst. instr. medicine Wayne State U. Coll. Medicine, 1954-56, instr., 1959-61; assoc. prof. pathology Wayne State U. Sch. Medicine, 1961-68, assoc. medicine, 1961, prof. pathology, 1968-78; prof. pathology Mich. State U., 1978-81, assoc. chairperson, 1980-81, clin. prof., 1981-82; chief clin. labs. Detroit Gen. Hosp., 1969-73; chief lab. svcs. Health Care Inst., Wayne State U., 1976-78; mem. adv. coun. Nuclear Medicine Tech. Cert. Bd., 1990-91. Bd. editors Am. Jour. Clin. Pathology, 1963-76, 83-88; author 2 textbooks, 11 chpts., 50 peer reviewed papers, 17 abstracts and other publs. With U.S. Army, 1944-47. Mem. AMA (sect. coun. on pathology), Am. Soc. Clin. Pathologists (rep. 1987-89, 93-2000, govt. rels. com. 1993-95, mem. coun. nuclear medicine 1978-82, chmn. 1982-84), Am. Coll. Nuclear Physicians, Am. Soc. Nuclear Cardiology, Coll. Am. Pathologists, Detroit Acad. Medicine, Mich. Soc. Pathologists, Mich. State Med. Soc., Soc. Nuclear Medicine, Washtenaw County Med. Soc., Sigma Xi, Tau Beta Pi. Office: Eastside Nuclear Medicine 2363 E Stadium Blvd Ann Arbor MI 48104-4810 also: St John Hosp & Med Ctr 22101 Moross Rd Detroit MI 48236-2148

POYDASHEFF, ROBERT STEPHEN, lawyer; b. N.Y.C., Feb. 13, 1930; s. Stephen Alexander Poydasheff and Pauline M. Miller; m. Anastasia Catherine Latto, Aug. 29, 1954; children: Catherine Alexandra, Robert Stephen Jr. BA in Polit. Sci., The Citadel, 1954; JD, Tulane U., 1957; MA, Boston U., 1966; diploma, Command and Gen. Staff Coll., 1969, Army War Coll., 1976. Bar: S.C. 1958, Ga. 1979, U.S. Supreme Ct. 1964, U.S. Ct. Mil. Appeals, U.S. Ct. Mil. Rev., U.S. Dist. Ct. (fed. dist.) S.C., U.S. Dist. Ct. (fed. and mid. dists.) Ga. Commd. 2d lt. U.S. Army, 1955, advanced through grades to col., 1975, ret., 1979; sr. v.p. SunTrust Bank of West Ga., Columbus, 1979-95; pvt. practice, 1995—. Instr. bus. law Am. U. Ext. Divsn., Ft. Benning, 1961-63; adj. prof. internat. law, Am. govt., and bus. law U. Md. Ext. Divsn., Berlin, 1964-67, Vietnam, 1967-68; adj. prof. Troy State U., Ft. Benning, Ga., 1976—; cons., exec. v.p. ATI-Allied Tech. Internat. Inc., Columbus, 1995—; past legal advisor to Sec. of Army and Sec. of Def. on mil. dependent schs. and labor rels. Contbr. commentaries, papers, and analyses to profl. jours. City councilor City of Columbus, 1996—; bd. dirs. Springer Opera House Assn., 1998—; trustee Ga. Coun. of Humanities, exec. com., 1998—; past mem. Bd. Edn., Ft. Benning Schs., 1976-79, chmn. pers. actions com., 1976-79; trustee Drs. Hosp., Columbia; bd. dirs. Columbus United Way; past pres. Chattahoochee coun. Boy Scouts Am., Columbus; past pres. Chattahoochee Valley, Assn. of U.S. Army, Anne Elizabeth Shepherd Home, Columbus Symphony; chmn. bd. dirs. Leadership Morality Inst.; chair Civilian Mil. Coun. Decorated Legion of Merit with 2 oak leaf clusters, Bronze Star; recipient Order of St. George, Episcopal Ch., 1997, Infantry Order of St. Maurice. Fellow Leadership Morality Inst. (chair of bd.); mem. Columbus Bar Assn., C. of C. (mil. affairs com.), Kiwanis, Masons (32 deg.), Phi Delta Phi, Pi Sigma Alpha. Republican. Episcopalian. Avocations: jogging, reading, gymnastics. Home: 6349 Mountainview Dr Columbus GA 31904-2213 Office: 3575 Macon Rd Ste 12 Columbus GA 31907-8229 E-mail: alliedtech@mindspring.com.

POYER, DAVID CHARLES, writer, retired military officer; b. DuBois, Pa., Nov. 26, 1949; s. Charles L. Poyer and Margeret M. Onuffer; m. Lenore Elizabeth Hart, Nov. 30, 1991; 1 child Naia Elizabeth Hart Poyer. BS, U.S. Naval Acad., 1971; MA, George Washington U., 1976. Capt. USN and USNR, 1971—2001. Co-author: The Insider's Guide to Southeastern Virginia, 1978, The Insiders Guide to the Outer Banks of North Carolina, 1979; author: White Continent, 1980, The Shiloh Project, 1981, Star Seed, The Return of Philo T. McGiffin, 1983, Stepfather Bank, 1987, The Dead of Winter, 1988, The Med, 1988, Hatteras Blue, 1989, The Gulf, 1990, Bahamas Blue, 1991, The Circle, 1992, Winter in the Heart, 1993, Louisiana Blue, 1994, The Passage, 1995, The Only Thing to Fear, 1995, As the Wolf Loves Winter, 1996, Down to a Sunless Sea, 1996, Tomahawk, 1998, Thunder on the Mountain, 1999, China Sea, 2000, Winter Light, 2001, Fire On the Waters, 2001, Black Storm, 2002. Office: c/o ICM 40 W 57th St New York NY 10019

POYER, JOSEPH JOHN, writer, publisher; b. Battle Creek, Mich., Nov. 30, 1939; s. Joseph John and Eileen Poyer; m. Bonnie Poyer, Nov. 1, 1987; children: Joseph John III, Geoffrey Robert. BA, Mich. State U., 1961. Asst. dir. pub. info. Mich. Tuberculosis Assn., Lansing, 1961-63; tech. writer Pratt & Whitney Aircraft, East Hartford, Conn., 1963-65; proposal writer Beckman Instruments, Fullerton, Calif., 1965-68; rsch. adminstr. Allergan Pharms., Irvine, 1968-77; pub. North Cape Publs., Inc., Tustin, 1991—. Author: (novels) Operation Malacca, 1969, North Cape, 1969, The Balkan Assignment, 1970, The Chinese Agenda, 1972, Shooting of the Green, 1974, Day of Reckoning, 1976, The Contract, 1977, Tunnel War, 1978, Vengeance 10, 1979, Devoted Friends, 1980, A Time of War, 1983, Come Evil Days, 1985, (non-fiction) (with A. Lightbody) The Complete Book of U.S. Fighting Power, 1989, Helicopter Fighters, 1989, U.S. Combat-Land-Based Forces, 1989, Illustrated History of Tanks, 1989, Illustrated History of Helicopters, 1989, The Complete Book of U.S. Naval Power, Submarines: Hunter/Killers and Boomers, 1990, The Complete Book of Top Gun, 1990; also author numerous books on antique and modern firearms, more than 400 mag. articles on mil. subjects. Avocations: reading, photography, travel, target shooting. Office: North Cape Publs PO Box 1027 Tustin CA 92781-1027

POYNOR, ROBERT ALLEN, JR. retired guidance counselor; b. Franklin, Tenn., Aug. 2, 1939; s. Robert Allen and Agnes Elizabeth (Gillespie) P.; m. Martha Bellah Stark, July 12, 1996; 1 child, Melissa Dawn Hay. BA, Belmont Coll., Nashville, 1967; MEd, Mid. Tenn. State U., 1972, EdS, 1975; postgrad., Tenn. State U. Cert. elem. tchr., elem. sch. counselor, elem. prin.-advanced, Tenn. Teller, mgmt. trainee Third Nat. Bank, Nashville, 1962-67; employment rep. S.S. Bd. of the S.B.C., 1967-68; tchr. Sumner County Bd. Edn., Gallatin, Tenn., 1968-69; asst. sec.-treas., br. mgr. Security Fed. Savs. and Loan Assn., Nashville, 1969-71; tchr. Sumner County Bd. Edn., Gallatin, 1971-79, 83-85, prin., 1979-83, guidance counselor, 1985-2000; ret. Mem. textbook adoption com. Sumner County bd. Edn., 1968-69, mem. gifted com., 1980-82. Charter sec. 100 Oaks Sertoma Club, Nashville, 1970; treas. Am. Savs. and Loan Inst., Nashville, 1970. With U.S. Army, 1957-59, France. Mem. Tenn. ACA, Tenn. Assn. Counselor Devel., Mid. Tenn. Assn. for Counselor Devel., United Tchg. Profession, Sumner County Elem. Prins. (past pres. 1982-83), Sumner County Edn. Assn. (past pres. 1978-79), Phi Delta Kappa. United Methodist. Avocations: jogging, reading, yard work, spectator sports, art. Home: 288 Indian Lake Rd Hendersonville TN 37075-4344

POYNTER, DAN, author, publisher, speaker; b. N.Y.C., Sept. 17, 1938; s. William Frank and Josephine E. (Thompson) P. BA, Calif. State U., Chico, 1960; postgrad., San Francisco Law Sch., 1961-63. federally lic. master parachute rigger; lic. pilot. Pub., prin. Para Pub., Santa Barbara, Calif., 1969—. Listed as expert witness Nat. Forensic Ctr., Tech. Adv. Service for Attys., Consultants and Consulting Organizations Directory, Lawyer's Guide to Legal Consultants, Expert Witnesses, Services, Books and Products. Author: The Parachute Manual, Parachuting, The Skydiver's Handbook, Parachuting Manual with Log, Hang Gliding, Manned Kiting, The Self-Publishing Manual, How to Write, Print & Sell Your Own Book, Publishing Short Run Books, Business Letters For Publishers, Computer Selection Guide, Word Processing and Information Processing, Publishing Forms, Parachuting Manual for Square/Piggyback Equipment, Frisbee Players' Handbook, Toobee Players' Handbook, Writing Nonfiction, Successful Nonfiction, 100 others, some translated in fgn. languages; past editor news mag. Spotter; monthly columnist Parachute mag., 1963—; contbr. over 500 tech. and popular articles and photographs to mags; patentee parachute pack, POP TOP. Recipient numerous certs. of appreciation for directing parachuting competitions. Mem. U.S. Parachute Assn. (life, chmn. bd., exec. com. 12 yrs., nat. and internat. del., achievement award, 1981, cert. 35 yr. mem., awarded Gold Parachute Wings, 1972), Parachute Industry Assn. (pres. 1985, 86), AIAA, Soc. Automotive Engrs., Nat. Aeronautic Assn., Aviation Space Writers Assn. (internat. conf. mem. 1978, 79, 82), Calistoga Skydivers (past sec.), No. Calif. Parachute Coun. (past sec.), U.S. Hang Gliding Assn. (life, past dir., del.), Internat. Assn. Ind. Pubs. (past bd. dirs., pres. Santa Barbara chpt. 1979-82), Assn. Am. Pubs., Pub. Mktg. Assn. (bd. dirs., v.p.), Book Pubs. So. Calif., Am. Booksellers Assn., Commn. Internat. de Vol Libre of Fedn. Aero. Internat. in Paris (U.S. del., past pres., lifetime Pres. d'Honneur award 1979, recipient Paul Tissander diploma, 1984), Nat. Spkrs. Assn. E-mail: Dan. Home: RR 1 Santa Barbara CA 93117-1047 Office: Para Publishing PO Box 8206 Santa Barbara CA 93118-8206 E-mail: danpoynter@ParaPublishing.com.

POZA, ERNESTO, business consultant, educator; b. Havana, Cuba, Mar. 27, 1950; came to U.S., 1961; s. Hugo Ernesto and Carmen (Valle) P.; m. Karen Elizabeth Saum, Oct. 14, 1978; 1 child, Kali Jennette. BS in Adminstrv. Sci., Yale U., 1972; MS in Mgmt., MIT, 1974. Personnel mgr. rsch. Sherwin Williams Co., Chgo., 1974-75, orgn. specialist Cleve., 1975-77, dir. orgn. planning, 1977-79; pres., sr. mgmt. cons. E.J. Poza Assoc., 1979—; prof. Weatherhead Sch. Mgmt. Case Western Res. U., 1996—. Advisor Family Firm Inst., 1986; bd. dirs. several privately held firms; vis. lectr. Yale U., U. Chile, MIT, Sloan Sch. Mgmt. *Ernesto J. Poza is an internationally recognized, top rated speaker and consultant to family-owned businesses. He is president of E.J. Poza Associates, Inc. and professor of Family Business at the Weatherhood School of Management, Case Western Reserve University. Poza challenges business owners to revitalize mature businesses through strategic thinking and succession planning without conflict. His work has been featured by CNN, NBC, NPR, Business Week, Fortune Magazine, Family Business Magazine, Inc., Industry Week, Nation's Business, and Family Business Review. He serves on the advisory boards of family-controlled corporations and helps private companies plan for continuity from generation to generation.* Author: Smart Growth: Critical Choices for Business Continuity and Prosperity, 1997, A la Sombra del Roble: La Empresa Privada Familiar y Su Continuidad, 1995, La Empresa Familiar Por Dentro, 1998; contbg. editor Family Bus. Mag.; mem. editl. bd. Family Bus. Rev., 1997—; contbr. articles to profl. jours. Bd. dirs. Neighborhood Health Care, 1980, Family Firm Inst., 1990; program com. United Way, Cleve., 1985, Hispanic Leadership, 1986; founding mem. Family Firm Inst., 1985. Recipient Richard Beckhard Practice award Family Firm Inst., 1996. Mem. Acad. Mgmt. (entrepreneurship div., 1980—, orgn. devel. network, 1975—). Office: EJ Poza Assocs 37300 Jackson Rd Chagrin Falls OH 44022-1922 E-mail: poza@family-business.com.

POZDRO, JOHN WALTER, music educator, composer; b. Chgo., Aug. 14, 1923; s. John and Rose Anna (Mossman) P.; m. Shirley Allison Winans, June 12, 1954; children— John Winans, Nancy Allison Thellman. Student, Am. Conservatory Music, Chgo., 1941-42; B.M. in Music, Northwestern U.-Evanston, Ill., 1948, M.M. in Music, 1949; PhD in Music, Eastman Sch. Music, 1958. Instr. Iowa State Tchrs. Coll., Cedar Falls, 1949-50; instr. to assoc. prof. U. Kans., Lawrence, 1950-64, prof. music, 1964-93, dir. theory and composition, 1961-88; ret., 1993; teaching fellow Eastman Sch. Music, Rochester, NY, 1956-57. Chmn. symposium com. U. Kans., Lawrence, 1958-69 Representative works include Third Symphony, 1960, Piano Sonata No. 4, 1976, Malooley & Fear Monster, 1977, Impressions, Winds, Piano, 1984, Tryptich for Carillon, 1996, the Spirit of Mt. Oread, 1989. Winds of Autumn, 1996. Served with U.S. Army, 1943-46. Recipient U. Calif. Berkeley medal for Disting. Svc., 1993; grantee Ford Found., 1960, Nat. Endowment Arts, 1976; nominated for Pulitzer prize in Music, 1962. Mem. ASCAP (award 1965-2002), Pi Kappa Lambda. Presbyterian. Avocations: golf, photography, writing. Home: 4700 Muirfield Dr Lawrence KS 66047-1820

POZEK, KATHLEEN DIANNE, nurse; b. Edina, Mo., Oct. 18, 1950; d. Paul and Mary (Shahan) Kriegshauser; m. Richard Eugene Pozek, June 24, 1978; two children. Nursing diploma, Jewish Hosp. Sch. of Nursing, St. Louis, 1971; BSN, St. Louis U., 1977; MSN, Kansas U., 1981. Diabetes clin. nurse Midwest Diabetes Ctr., Kansas City, Mo., 1981-83; instr. nursing Rsch. Coll. Nursing, 1983-85, So. Ill. Univ., Edwardsville, 1985-86; staff float nurse Barnes Hosp., St. Louis, 1986-91; clin. nurse specialist Kaiser Permanente, Kansas City, Mo., 1991-95; nurse cons. Health Care Financing Adminstrn., 1995—. Mem. Am. Diabetes Assn., Am. Assn. Diabetes Educators, Sigma Theta Tau. E-mail: klozek@hefa.gov.

POZNANSKI, ANDREW KAROL, pediatric radiologist; b. Czestochowa, Poland, Oct. 11, 1931; came to U.S., 1957, naturalized, 1964; s. Edmund Maurycy and Hanna Maria (Ceranka) P.; children: Diana Jean, Suzanne Christine. BSc, McGill U., 1952, MD CM, 1956. Diplomate: Am. Bd. Radiology, Royal Coll. Physicians and Surgeons Can. Intern Montreal (Que., Can.) Hosp., 1956-57; resident Henry Ford Hosp., Detroit, 1957-60, staff radiologist, 1960-68, U. Mich. Med. Center, Ann Arbor, 1968-79; co.-dir. pediatric radiology C.S. Mott Children's Hosp., 1971-79; radiologist-in-chief Children's Meml. Hosp., Chgo., 1979-99; prof. radiology U. Mich., 1971-79, Northwestern U. Med. Sch., 1979—. Bd. dirs. Nat. Coun. on Radiation Protection, 1983-90; mem. Internat. Commn. on Radiologic Protection, 1981-89; mem. adv. panel on radiologic devices FDA, 1975-77, chmn., 1976-77; trustee Am. Bd. Radiology, 1993—. Author: The Hand in Radiologic Diagnosis, 1974, 2d edit., 1983, Practical Approaches to Pediatric Radiology, 1976; bd. editors: Skeletal Radiology, 1975-95, Radiographics, 1980-84, Pediatric Radiology, 1986-91. Fellow: Am. Coll. Radiology; mem.: AMA, Internat. Skeletal Soc. (founder, pres. 1992—94), John Caffey Soc., Radiol. Soc. N.Am., Can. Assn. Radiologists (hon.), European Soc. Radiology (hon.), Polish Radiol. Soc. (hon.), Soc. Pediatric Radiology (pres. 1980—81), Am. Roentgen Ray Soc. (pres. 1993—94), Alpha Omega Alpha. Home: 2400 N Lakeview Ave Chicago IL 60614-2747 Office: Childrens Meml Hosp 2300 N Childrens Plz Chicago IL 60614-3394 E-mail: apoznanski@ameritech.net.

POZNER, LOUIS-JACK, lawyer; b. N.Y.C., Dec. 12, 1946; s. Harry Bear and Regina (Lindsey) P.; m. Rona Judkowitz, June 9, 1968; children: Samantha Brooke, Jo-Ellen, Zachary Blair. BA with honors in History, U. Rochester, 1968; JD, Bklyn. Law Sch., 1971. Bar: N.Y. 1972, U.S. Dist Ct. (no. dist.) N.Y. 1972, U.S. Dist. Ct. (so. and ea. dists.) N.Y. 1991, U.S. Supreme Ct. 1983. Law clk. N.Y. State Supreme Ct. Appellate Divsn. 3rd Dept., Albany, 1971-72; law clk. to Judge James Gibson N.Y. State Ct. Appeals, 1972; assoc. DeGraff Foy Conway Holt-Harris & Meeley, N.Y., 1973-74; pvt. practice, 1974—; pres. Louis-Jack Pozner, P.C., 1993—. Judge Albany Law Sch. Moot Ct. Competition, 1979, 80, 84, 86, 89-2001; advisor in 1982 State Mock Trial Tournament. Pres. Electronic Body Art Inc., 1979-80, bd. dirs., 1976-79; trustee Temple Israel Albany, 1976-82, 98—, v.p., 1980-82, exec. v.p., 1995-96, pres., 1996-98; bd. dirs. Friends of Albany Pub. Libr., 1982-84, Greater Albany Jewish Fedn., 1979-85, Horizon House, 1982-83, Bet Shraga Hebrew Acad. the Capital Dist., 1978-88, v.p., 1980-85, pres., 1985-88; co-chmn. cmty. rels. com. Greater Albany Jewish Fedn., 1980-82; trustee Daus. of Sarah Found., 1983-2002, v.p., 1988-90, pres., 1990-93; bd. trustees Greater Jewish Fedn. Northeastern N.Y., 1999—, bd. govs. endowment fund, 1999—. Recipient of Greater Albany Jewish Fedn. Samuel E. Aronowitz Young Leadership award, 1981. Mem. ABA (mem. character and fitness coms. 3d dist. 1990-99, mem. com. on profl. stds. 1999—), Albany County Bankruptcy Bar Assn., Albany County Bar Assn., Assn. Trial Lawyers Am., N.Y. State Bar Assn., N.Y. State Trial Lawyers Assn. (family law sect.). Home: 258 Lenox Ave Albany NY 12208-1408 Office: 11 N Pearl St Ste 1405 Albany NY 12207-2771

POZO-DIAZ, MARTHA DEL CARMEN, lawyer; b. Miami, Fla., May 24, 1965; d. Eduardo Esteban and Martha Josefina (Coll) Pozo; m. Ramon Jorge Diaz, Jan. 7, 1989; children: Ramon Eduardo, Martha del Carmen, Eduardo Manuel, Francisco Javier. BBA, U. Miami, 1986, JD, 1990. Bar: Fla. 1991. Owner, pres. Martha Pozo-Diaz, P.A., Miami, 1990—. Mem. ABA, Dade County Bar Assn., Cuban Am. Bar Assn. Republican. Roman Catholic. Office: 8000 W Flagler St Ste 203 Miami FL 33144-2153

POZZATTI, RUDY OTTO, artist; b. Telluride, Colo., Jan. 14, 1925; s. Innocente and Mary L. (Mimiolla) P.; m. Dorothy I. Pozzatti, May 20, 1946; children— Valri Marie, Rudy Otto, Gina Maria, Mia Ines, Illica Lara. B.F.A., U. Colo., 1948, M.F.A., 1950, D.H.L., 1973. Mem. faculty dept. art U. Nebr., Lincoln, 1950-52, 53-56, Ind. U., Bloomington, 1956-91, prof. fine arts, 1964-91, disting. prof., 1975-91; ret., 1991; artist-in-residence Roswell Mus. and Art Ctr. One-man exhbns. include Cleve. Mus. Art, 1955, Whitney Mus. Am. Arts, N.Y.C., 1961, Tyler Sch. Art, Rome, 1969, Sheldon Meml. Art Gallery U. Nebr., 1969, Mitchell Mus. Art, Mt. Vernon, Ill., 4 other sites, 1992-93, Ind. U. Art Mus., Bloomington, 2002, Evansville Mus. ARt, 2002; represented in permanent collections, Mus. Modern Art, N.Y.C., Libr. Congress, Washington, Art Inst. Chgo., Cleve. Mus. Art. Served with AUS, 1943-46. Recipient George Norlin silver medal U. Colo., 1974; Fulbright grantee, 1952-53, 63-64, grantee U.S. Dept. State, USSR, 1961, Yugoslavia, 1965, Brazil, 1974, Hungary, 1986; grantee Rockefeller Found., Bellagio, Italy, 1995; Guggenheim fellow, 1963-64; Fellow Ford Found., 1963, grantee, Japan, 1981. Mem. Soc. Am. Graphic Artists, Am. Color Print Soc., Coll. Art Assn. (bd. dirs.), Artists Equity Assn., Ind. Acad. (elected). Roman Catholic. E-mail: rpozzatt@indiana.edu., Pozzatti@kiva.net.

POZZO, RICCARDO, philosophy educator; b. Milan, June 7, 1959; came to U.S., 1996; s. Giancarlo and Carla (Rizzani) P.; m. Annette Popel, Sept. 4, 1992; 1 child, Carlo. Laurea in Philosophy, U. Milan, 1983; Promotion in Philosophy, U. Saarland, Saarbrücken, 1988; Habilitation in Philosophy, U. Trier, 1995. Rsch. assoc. U. Saarland, 1984-85; fellow Deutscher Akademischer Austauschdienst, 1985-97, Herzog August Bibliothek Wolfenbüttel, 1988-90, Alexander von Humboldt-Stiftung, 1990-98; h.s. tchr. Sch. Superintendency Lombardy, Milan, 1994-96; univ. tchr. Cath. U. Am., Washington, 1996—. Lectr. U. Trier, 1991-96. Author: Hegel: Introductio in Philosophiam, 1989, Kant und das Problem einer Einleitung, 1989, El giro kantiano, 1998, Georg Friedrich Meiers Vernunftlehre, 2000; co-editor: (with Karl-Otto Apel) Zur Rekonstruktion der praktischen Philosophie, 1990; (with Michael Oberhausen) Vorlesungsverzeichnisse der Universität Königsberg 1720-1804, 1999; (with Michael Oberhausen and Heinrich P. Delfosse) Vernunftkritik und Aufklärung, 2001; cons. editor: Longanesi Editore, 1988-89, Feltrinelli Editore, 1988-96. Recipient 6th Study Tour of Japan, Japanese Ministry of Fgn. Affairs, 1984. Mem. Am. Cath. Philos. Assn., N.Am. Kant Soc., Humboldt Assn. of Am., Società Italiana di Studi Kantiani, Deutscher Hochschulverband, Hegel Soc. N.Am. Roman Catholic. Avocations: golf, reading contemporary literature. Office: 112A Mcmahon Hl Washington DC 20064-0001 E-mail: pozzo@cua.edu.

PRABAKARAN, DANIEL, biochemist, researcher; b. Mel Siviri, Tamil Nadu, India, June 25, 1959; came to U.S., 1989; s. Daniel Chinathambi and Kamala Serkad (Mani) P.; m. Crenie Sarah Paul, Feb. 14, 1992; 1 child, Elizabeth Jane. BSc, U. Madras, India, 1979, MSc, 1982; PhD, All India Inst. Med. Scis., 1989. Asst. rsch. officer All India Inst. Med. Sci., New Delhi, 1984-85, rsch. officer, 1985-88, postdoctoral fellow, 1988-89, Beth Israel Deaconess Med. Ctr./Harvard Med. Sch., Boston, 1989-97, instr., 1998—. Contbr. numerous articles to profl. jours. Indian Coun. Med. Rsch. Jr. Rsch. fellow, 1983; Dept. Sci. and Tech. Travel grantee, 1988. Mem. AAAS, Am. Soc. Cell Biology, Endocrine Soc., N.Y. Acad. Scis. Home: 1 Trudeau Ter Wayland MA 01778-5122 E-mail: dprabakaran@rics.bwh.harvard.edu.

PRABHUDESAI, MUKUND M. pathology educator, laboratory director, researcher, administrator; b. Lolyem, Goa, India, Mar. 17, 1942; came to U.S., 1967; s. Madhav R. and Kusum M. Prabhudesai; m. Sarita Mukund Usha, Feb. 1, 1972; 1 child, Nitin M. MB, BS (MD), G.S. Med., Bombay, 1967, postgrad., 1973-75. Diplomate Am. Bd. Pathology. Asst. pathologist Fordham Hosp., Bronx, N.Y., 1973-74, assoc. pathologist, 1974-76; assoc. dir. clin. pathology Lincoln Med., 1976, dep. dir. pathology, 1977-79; chief pathology and lab. medicine svc., coord. R&D VA Med. Ctr., Danville, Ill., 1979—, dir. electron microscopy lab., 1987—. Senator U. Ill. Chgo.; co-investigator U. Ill. Coll. Medicine, Urbana-Champaign, clin. prof. pathology and internal medicine, 1982—. Contbr. articles to Am. Jour. Clin. Nutrition, Jour. AMA, Am. Jour. Clin. Pathology. Member Gifted Student Adv. Bd., Danville, 1984-86; v.p. Am. Cancer Soc. Vermilion County chpt., 1982, pres., 1986-88. VA rsch. grantee, 1980-82, 82-85, 83. Fellow Coll. Am. Pathology (inspector 1981—, Ill. state del. to C.A.P. Ho. Dels. 1992—, mem. reference com. 1993); mem. AAAS, Am. Coll. Physician Execs., Ill. State Soc. Pathologists (bd. dirs. 1990—, chmn. membership com. 1990—). Achievements include development of cancer of bladder following portocarval shunting; research in adverse effects of alcohol on lung structure and metabolism; on effects of soy and bran on cholesterol, endocrine response to soy protein, in induction and reversibility of atherosclerosis in trout, effects of ethanol on Vitamin A, lymphatics in atherosclerosis, iron in atherosclerosis, development of dermofluorometer for detection of P.V.D. Office: VA Med Ctr Pathology and Lab Med Svcs 1900 E Main St Danville IL 61832-5100 E-mail: mukund.prabhudesai@med.va.gov.

PRADERE, SONIA, accounting administrator; b. Bklyn., Sept. 22, 1965; d. Miguel Mercado and Candita P.; m. Mario Pradere, July 18, 1986; children: Michael, Stephanie. BS in Human Resource Mgmt., Palm Beach Atlantic Coll., 1995; M Acctg., Nova Southeastern U., 1998. Asst. controller Diversified Comms., Inc., West Palm Beach, Fla., 1990-95; sr. acct. Oxbow Corp., 1995-99; acctg. mgr. Sara Lee Branded Apparel, 1999—. Office: Sara Lee Branded Apparel 5100 Town Center Cir Boca Raton FL 33486-1049

PRADHAN, RAJENDRA PRASAD, physician, nephrologist; b. Kathmandu, Nepal, June 1, 1938; came to U.S., 1968; s. Indra Prasad and Matina (Shrestra) P.; m. Mary Baba Rajhhandari; 1 child, Manju. MBBS, Trivandrum Med. Coll., Kerala, India, 1963. Diplomate in internal medicine and nephrology Am. Bd. Internal Medicine. Chief of nephrology Cabrini Med. Ctr., N.Y.C., 1974-95; chief nephrology Saint Clares Hosp., 2000; assoc. attending physician Beth Israel Hosp., N.Y.C., 1996—. Colombo-Plan scholar, India, 1958-63. Avocations: chess, computer programing. Office: 237 E 20th St New York NY 10003-1805

PRADO, GERALD M. investment banker; b. Langeloth, Pa., Jan. 19, 1946; s. Caesar S. and Anita A. P.; m. Judith A. Pompe, May 20, 1967; children— Dennis, Eric, Lynn, Christopher. BA, Washington and Jefferson Coll., 1963-67; MBA, U. Pitts., 1983. Sr. acct. Haskins and Sells, Pitts., 1967-72; auditor G.C. Murphy Co., McKeesport, Pa., 1972-76, asst. controller, 1976-78, treas., 1979-80, asst. v.p., treas., 1980-82, v.p., treas., 1982-85, Russell, Rea & Zappala, Pitts., 1986-87, sr. v.p., 1987-90; pres. Westinghouse Mcht. Banking, Inc., 1990-94; prin., co-mgr. Main St. Capital Holdings L.L.C., 1994—. Roman Catholic. Home: 205 Overlook Dr Mc Murray PA 15317-2657 Office: Main St Capital Holdings LLC 135 Technology Dr Ste 501 Canonsburg PA 15317-9529

PRADZYNSKI, ANDRZEJ HENRYK, chemist; b. Plock, Poland, Jan. 1, 1924; came to U.S., 1969; s. Maurycy and Frania (Goldkind) Nejman; m. Halina Romana Bromberger, Apr. 1, 1946; children: Richard E. Neuman, Zgibniew Jacek. BS, U. Wroclaw, Poland, 1949, MS, 1951. Asst. prof. crystallography, chmn. dept. U. Wroclaw, 1948-51; sect. mgr. materials testing Inst. Aviation, Warsaw, Poland, 1951-57; adj. prof. Polish Acad. Scis., 1957-68; dept. dir. Atomic Energy Commn. Poland, 1959-68; rsch. assoc. IV nuclear reactor U. Tex., Austin, 1969-80; exec. v.p. Halinco Skin Care Products, Inc., 1980-2000. Cons. IAEA, Vienna, Austria, 1968-69. Author: Industrial Radiography (in Polish), 1957; also over 3o articles in IAEA Conf. Procs., Nukleonika, ISA Trans., also others. Mem. Am. Chem. Soc., Soc. Cosmetic Chemists, N.Y. Acad. Scis. Achievements include patent for method and apparatus for collection and analysis of mercury in the atmosphere; developer method of photo-nuclear activation analysis of copper in ores and concentrates, synthetic standards for EDX-ray analysis, method of collection and analysis of mercury in air, method of nondestructive X-ray analysis of heavy metals in toys. Developed pre-concentration methods of trace elements in water for EDX-ray analysis. E-mail: apradzynski@austin.vv.com.

PRAGER, ALICE HEINECKE, music company executive; b. N.Y.C., Aug. 2, 1930; d. Paul and Ruth (Collin) Heinecke; m. George L. Drescher, 1963. BA, Russell Sage Coll., 1951; postgrad., NYU, 1952-55. V.p. SESAC Inc., N.Y.C., 1956-73, pres., 1973-78, pres., chmn. bd., 1978-92. Chmn. bd. Personal Touch, Inc. Mem. Internat. Radio and TV Soc., Am. Inst. of Mgmt., NARAS, Country Music Assn. (bd. dirs., 1986, life), Gospel Music Assn. (life). Office: The Personal Touch Inc 68-34 Fleet St Forest Hills NY 11375-5051 E-mail: apd3700@aol.com.

PRAGER, BETTY RUTH, lawyer, medical scientist; b. Phila., July 11, 1932; d. Marcus and Lydia (Nickelspark) Tecker. AB, Temple U., 1954; JD, U. West L.A., 1980. Bar: Calif. 1989; lic. med. scientist Calif. Med.scientist, L.A., 1955—; pvt. practice, 1989—. Office: 12304 Santa Monica Blvd Los Angeles CA 90025-2551 Fax: 310-571-0515. E-mail: ruthjecker@aol.com.

PRAGER, DAVID, retired state supreme court chief justice; b. Ft. Scott, Kans., Oct. 30, 1918; s. Walter and Helen (Kishler) P.; m. Dorothy Schroeter, Sept. 8, 1945; children: Diane, David III. AB, U. Kans., 1939, JD, 1942. Bar: Kans. 1942. Practiced in, Topeka, 1946-59; dist. judge Shawnee County (Kans.) Dist. Ct., 1959-71; assoc. justice Kans. Supreme Ct., Topeka, 1971-87, chief justice, 1987-88; ret., 1988. Lectr. Washburn Law Sch., 1948-68. Served to lt. USNR, 1942-46, ETO, PTO. Mem. Kans. Dist. Judges Assn. (past pres.), Order of Coif, Phi Beta Kappa, Phi Delta Theta, Lions Lodge, Arab Shrine Lodge.

PRAGER, JONAS, economics educator, consultant; b. N.Y.C., Nov. 5, 1938; s. Julius and Bella (Tannenberg)P.; m. Helen May, June 9, 1963; children: Joel B., Sharon. AB magna cum laude, Yeshiva Coll., N.Y.C., 1959; PhD, Columbia U., 1964. Asst. prof. NYU, N.Y.C., 1964-69, assoc. prof. econs., 1969—, dir. grad. studies, 1977-81, 86-89. Vis. sr. economist Bank of Israel, Jerusalem, 1965-67; lectr. USIA, India, Yugoslavia, West Germany, 1983, 84, France, Hungary, 1989; Fulbright Hays faculty rsch. fellow U.S. Dept. Edn., Israel, 1971, 82-83; assoc. UN Devel. Programme, Interregional Network on Privatization; mem. Ctr. for Study of Ctrl. Banks. Author: Fundamentals of Money, Banking and Financial Institutions, 1982, 2d edit., 1987, Applied Microeconomics: An Intermediate Text, 1993; editor: Monetary Economics: Controversies in Theory and Policy, 1971; contbr. articles to profl. jours. Am. Philos. Soc. rsch. grantee, 1974-76. Mem. Am. Econ. Assn., Hagop Kevorkian Ctr. for Near Eastern Studies, C.V. Starr Ctr. for Applied Econs. Office: NYU Dept Econs 269 Mercer St New York NY 10003-6633

PRAGER, LESLIE BETH, career counselor; b. N.Y.C., May 9, 1953; d. Irving Prager and Ruth Rotenberg; m. Barry S. Bernstein, June 5, 1988; 1 child, Jared D. Bernstein. BA in Psychology, SUNY, Binghamton, 1974; MA in Art Therapy, U. Louisville, 1975. Cert. career mgmt. practitioner. Art therapist Houston Internat. Hosp., 1976-77; exec. trainee, asst. buyer Lord & Taylor, N.Y.C., 1977-80; corp. recruiter Chem. Bank, 1980-82; employment mgr. R.H. Macy & Co., 1982-84; asst. personnel mgr. Garan, Inc., 1984-85; v.p., human resources dir. Std. Security Life Ins. Co., 1986-90; sr. ptnr., career counselor The Prager Bernstein Group, 1991—. Spkr. in field. Contbr. articles to profl. jours. Mem. Internat. Assn. Career Mgmt. Profls. (pres. NY Chptr.), Am. Counseling Assn., N.Y. Assn. Career Mgmt. Profls. (treas. 1993-98), Soc. Human Resource Mgmt. Human Resources Assocs. N.Y. (jour. editor, dir., exec. bd. mem.), Exec. Women Internat. (treas., bd. dirs.). Jewish. Avocations: travel, hiking, reading, photography, antiquing. Home: 2 Bay Club Dr # 14G Bayside NY 11360 Office: The Prager-Bernstein Group 441 Lexington Ave Ste 1404 New York NY 10017 E-mail: Leslie-PBG@msn.com.

PRAGER, STEPHEN, chemistry educator; b. Darmstadt, Germany, July 20, 1928; came to U.S., 1941, naturalized, 1950; s. William and Gertrude Ann (Heyer) P.; m. Julianne Heller, June 7, 1948. B.Sc., Brown, 1947; PhD, Cornell, 1951. Mem. faculty U. Minn., Mpls., 1952—, assoc. prof. chemistry, 1956-62, prof., 1962-90, prof. emeritus, 1990—. Cons. Union Carbide Corp., Oak Ridge, 1954-74 Asso. editor: Jour. Phys. Chemistry, 1970-79. Fulbright scholar and Guggenheim fellow, 1958, 59; Fulbright lectr. and Guggenheim fellow, 1966-67 Mem. Am. Chem. Soc., Am. Phys. Soc. Home: 3320 Dunlap St N Saint Paul MN 55112-3709 E-mail: psprager@cs.com.

PRAGUE, RONALD JAY, lawyer; b. N.Y.C., May 1, 1963; s. Martin Malcolm Prague and Betty Mae Sorrin; m. Jerilyn Semon, Sept. 10, 1994; children: Haley Sara, Jessica Nikki. BS, Cornell U., 1985; JD, Northwestern U., Chgo., 1988. Bar: N.Y. 1988, U.S. Dist. Ct. (so. and ea. dists.) N.Y. Assoc. Richards & O'Neil, N.Y.C., 1988-92, Haythe & Curley, N.Y.C., 1992-98; sr. atty. Intel Corp., Parsippany, N.J., 1998—. Mem. N.Y. State Bar Assn., N.J. Corp. Counsel Assn. Home: 64 Davey Dr West Orange NJ 07052 Office: Intel Corp 1515 Route 10 Parsippany NJ 07054-4538 E-mail: ronald.prague@intel.com.

PRAHL, HELEN, primary school educator; b. Hishawaka, Ind., Oct. 10, 1910; d. Oscar and Maud Prahl. BE, ME, Northeastern Ill. U., Chicago, IL. Educator Hans Christian Anderson Sch., Chicago, Ill., 1956—66, Joseph Brennemann Sch., Chicago, 1966—76; first grade educator; educator EMITT Mobile; remedial reading educator; summer sch. educator Louis Nettlehorst, Chicago, Ill., 2000—. Author: (book) How to do Substitute Teaching in Chicago. Active Second Ch. of Christ, Scientist, Chicago, Ill. Home: 440 West Barry Chicago IL 60657

PRAIRIE, CELIA ESTHER FREDA, biochemistry educator; b. Buenos Aires, Sept. 30, 1940; came to U.S., 1963; d. Rafael Emilio A. and Celia Esther (Seijo) Freda; m. James Roland Prairie, Sept. 19, 1970; children: James Roger, Caryn Elizabeth. BS, U. Buenos Aires, 1961, MS, 1963; PhD, U. Pa., 1967. Fellow Nat. Rsch. Inst., Buenos Aires, 1961-63; rsch. assoc. dept. therapeutic rsch. U. Pa., Phila., 1967-70; postdoctoral rsch. assoc. Lab. Molecular Embryology, Arco Felice, Naples, Italy, 1970; lectr. biology and chemistry depts. Holy Family Coll., Phila., 1974-75, asst. prof. biology dept., 1975-80, assoc. prof., 1980-85, prof. biochemistry, 1985—, chmn. dept. natural scis. and math., 1986-88, acting chmn. biology dept., 1982-86. Sr. teaching staff assoc. Marine Biol. Lab., Woods Hole, Mass., 1968-69. Contbr. articles to profl. jours. Bd. dirs. Lower Bucks County Community Ctr., 1970—. Fellow USPHS, 1963-65, U. Pa., 1965-66, Am. Coun. Edn. and Fund for the Improvement of Post Sec. Edn., 1983-84. Mem. AAAS, Nat. Sci. Tchrs. Assn., Am. Inst. Biol. Scis., N.Y. Acad. Scis., Sigma Xi, World Federalist Assn. Democrat. Mem. Religious Soc. of Friends. Avocations: Tai Chi, yoga, swimming. Home: 31 Full Turn Rd Levittown PA 19056-1924 Office: Holy Family Coll Frankford and Grant Ave Philadelphia PA 19114-2094

PRAISNER, WANDA S. poet, educator; b. Staten Island, Ny, Dec. 15, 1933; d. Richard Gustav Schweizer and Wanda Bertha Knapp; m. Dr. Robert John Praisner, July 8, 1961; children: Dr. Robert Paul, Stephen John, Dr. Thomas James. BS, Wagner Coll., Staten Island, NY, 1951—54, MS, 1955—56. Kindergarten educator P.s. 35, Staten Island, New York City, NY, 1954—59; second grade educator John Muir Sch., Santa Monica, Calif., 1959—60; kindergarten educator P.s. 35, Staten Island, New York City, NY, 1960—62; first grade educator Gould Ave. Sch., North Caldwell, NJ, 1962—63; third grade tchr. Sch. St. Elizabeth, Bernardsville, 1981—2001; poet-in-resident NJ State Coun. Arts, 2002—. Vice-president NYC Kindergarten Teachers' Assn., Richmond, NY, 1957—59; student tchr. educator P.s. 30, Staten Island, NY, 1954—59, P.s. 35, Staten Island, NY, 1960—62, Sch. St. Elizabeth, Bernardsville, NJ, 1988—2000, poetry workshop educator, NJ, 1988—; writing workshop educator Chapters Women Who Write, Chatham Library, NY, 2001—01. Contbr. poetry to profl. jours. Pto pres. Bedminster Sch., Bedminster, NJ, 1973—77; corr. sec. Wagner Coll. Nat. Alumni Assn. Bd. of Directors, Staten Island, NY, 1999—2002; writing panel Wagner Coll., 2002—02. Recipient First Pl., Devil's Millhopper Contest, 1994, Egan Award, Md. Poetry Rev., 1995; fellow Poetry Fellowship, NJ State Coun. Arts, 1995-1996, Geraldine R. Dodge Found., Provincetown Fine Arts Workcenter. Mem.: NJ Audubon Soc., Nat. Audubon Soc., South Mountain Poets (treas. 1989—2002), U.S. Poets' Coop., Acad. Am. Poets, Poetry Soc. Am., NEA. R-Consevative. Lutheran And Catholic. Achievements include Read at Princeton's Institute Advanced study, Geraldine R. Dodge Foundation, Waterloo Poetry Festival. Avocations: tennis, travel, birding, birding, birding. Home: 34 Ski Hill Drive Bedminster NJ 07921-2529 Home Fax: 908-234-0923. Personal E-mail: praisner@webspan.net.

PRAKAPAS, EUGENE JOSEPH, art gallery director; b. Lowell, Mass., July 29, 1932; s. Joseph S. Prakapas and Viola Schensnol; m. Dorothy A. Seitner, Dec. 1, 1971. BA, Yale U., 1953; MA, Oxford U., Balliol, 1959. Editor-in-chief, v.p. Trident Press and Pocket Books divsn. Simon & Schuster, Inc., N.Y.C., 1960-70; co-dir. Carus Gallery, 1973-75; dir. Prakapas Gallery, 1976—. Vis. curator San Francisco Mus. Modern Art, 1986. Author: Bauhaus Photography, 1985. Lt. (s.g.) USNR, 1953-57. Fulbright fellow, 1957-59; Yale U. scholar, 1949-53. Mem. Art Dealers Assn. Am., Assn. Internat. Photography Art Dealers. E-mail: eugeneprakapas@earthlink.net.

PRAKASH, ARUN JAI, finance educator, consultant, researcher; b. Gaya, Bihar, India, Oct. 15, 1943; came to US, 1969; s. Aran Haran and Premlata Prasad; m. Nirmala Srivastava, Nov. 21, 1971; children: Rahul, Rohit. MA, U. Calif., Berkeley, 1970, MBA, 1977; PhD, U. Oreg., 1981. Asst. prof. fin. Fla. Internat. U., Miami, 1978-81, assoc. prof. fin., 1982-86, prof. fin., 1987—, chmn. dept. fin., 1988-96. Cons. Miami-Dade County, Fla. Author: Market Model, 1998; mem. edit. bd. Fin. India, Jour. of Bus. Fin. and Acctg. Fellow Royal Statis. Soc.(London, chartered statistician). Avocation: gardening. Home: 16280 SW 79th Ter Miami FL 33193-3429 Office: Fla Internat U Coll Bus Adminstrn Miami FL 33193 E-mail: prakasha@fiu.edu., prakashaj@cs.com.

PRAKASH, SATYA, biology educator; b. Pilkhuwa, U.P., India, July 8, 1938; came to U.S., 1962; s. Suraj Bali and Atar Kali; m. Louise Burlant; children: Ulka, Ravi, Anita, Sarita. PhD, Washington U., St. Louis, 1966. Asst. prof. biology U. Rochester, N.Y., 1969-74, assoc. prof., 1974-80, prof., 1980-93, U. Tex. Med. Branch, Galveston, 1993—. NIH grantee, 1972— Mem. Genetics Soc. Am., Am. Soc. Biochemistry and Molecular Biology. Hindu. Office: U Tex Med Branch Sealy Ctr Molecular Sci Galveston TX 77555-0001

PRAKASH, SHAMSHER, civil engineering educator, consultant; b. Panjab, India, Jan. 3, 1933; came to U.S., 1978; s. Rishi Ram and Kala Wati; m. Sally, Jan. 3, 1984. BE in Civil Engring., U. Roorkee (India), 1954, postgrad. diploma, 1959; MS, U. Ill., 1961, PhD, 1962. Registered profl. engr., Mo.; chartered engr., U.K., India. Asst. engr. Panjab PWD, India, 1954-57; lectr. U. Roorkee, 1957-62, reader, 1962-66, prof., 1966-78, prof., head civil egring. dept., 1982-83; assoc. prof. U. Mo., Rolla, 1978-80, prof., 1980—; dir. Ctrl. Bldg. Rsch. Inst., Roorkee, 1983-85. Pres. Shamsher Prakash Found., Rolla, 1991—, Shamsher Proaksh Assocs., Rolla, 1988—; yoga tchr., Rolla, 1979—; PhD and MS rsch. supr.; speaker and rschr. in field. Editl. bd. mem. Internat. Jour. of Soil Dynamics and Earthquake Engring.; author: Foundations for machines, Analysis and Design, 1988, Soil Dynamics, 1981, Pile Foundations in Engineering Practice, 1990, Fundamentals of Soil Mechanics, 1994; author numerous papers in field; spkr., rschr. in field. Fellow ASCE (soil dynamics com. 1980-84, 89—), Inst. Engrs., Inst. Civil Engrs., Indian Geotech. Soc.; mem. Am. Soc. Testing and MAterials, Earthquake Engring Rsch. Inst., Indian Soc. Earthquake Tech., Indian Soc. Tech. Edn., Indian Soc. Engr. Geology, Indian Road Congress, Indian Soc. Desert Tech., Phi Kappa Phi, Sigma Xi. Hindu. Avocation: yoga. Home: Anand Kutir 1111 Duane Ave Rolla MO 65401-2128 Office: U Mo Rolla Civil Engring Pine St Rolla MO 65401

PRALL, BARBARA JONES, artist; b. Cedar Rapids, IA, July 4, 1932; d. Paul Lester and Annie Shelor (Dyer) Jones; m. Bradley Joseph Schnittjer, June 24, 1951 (div. Aug. 1970); children: Kathy, Nancy, Candee, Jim; m. N. Clifford Prall, Feb. 7, 1976. BA, Upper Iowa U., Fayette, 1975; postgrad., Iowa U., 1978-86; student various world famous artists. Owner Barb's Art Barn, Delhi, Iowa, 1970-76, Pinicon Acres Fine Art Farm, Central City, 1976-89, Barb's Fine Art, Marion, 1989—. Tchr. Central City Cmty. Sch., 1976-80. Numerous one-person shows; exhibited in group shows including Outdoor Wild Life Art Show, Kansas City, Mo., 1996 (Best of Show). Recipient Toastmasters Internat. Gold award. Mem. Portrait Soc. Am., Am. Soc. Portrait Artists, N.Y. Soc. Portrait Artists.. Avocations: church, music, art, family. Home: 788 6th St Marion IA 52302-5770 E-mail: barbsfineart@hotmail.com.

PRAMANIK, BIRENDRA NATH, research executive; b. Santahar, Bogra, Bangladesh, Jan. 23, 1944; came to U.S., 1970; s. Kanai Lal and Charu Bala Pramanik; m. Nandita Pramanik, Aug. 16, 1964; children: Barnali, Bidyut. MSc, Rajshahi (Bangladesh) U., 1965; MS, Stevens Inst. of Tech., 1973, PhD, 1977. Sr. analytical chemist Richarson-Vicks, Inc., Mount Vernon, N.Y., 1978-80; sr. scientist Schering-Plough Corp., Bloomfield, N.J., 1980-83, prin. scientist, 1984-87; sr. prin. scientist Schering-Plough Rsch. Inst., 1987-90, devel. fellow Kenilworth, 1990-95, sr. devel. fellow, 1996, sr. rsch. fellow, 1996-2000, sr. disting. fellow, 2000—. Course dir. Ea. Analytical Symposium, 1996—; vis. scientist Stevens Inst. Tech., N.J., 1975-77, 96—; vis. spkr. mass spectrometry Columbia U., N.Y.C., 1990—; spkr. in field. Editor Applied Electrospray Mass Spectrometry, 2002; contbr. chpts. to books and over 100 articles to profl. publs. Recipient N.J. regional award in mass spectrometry Am. Chem. Soc., 2000. Mem. N.J. Mass Spectrometry Assn., (chmn.-elect 1989, chmn. 1990), Am. Soc. Mass Spetrometry (oral co-chair 1999). Avocations: gardening, tennis. Home: 3 Tara Dr Parsippany NJ 07054-3312 Office: Schering-Plough Rsch Inst 2015 Galloping Hill Rd Kenilworth NJ 07033-1300 E-mail: birendra.pramanik@spcorp.com.

PRAMANN, ROBERT FREDERICK, JR. psychologist; b. Panama City, Fla., July 24, 1954; s. Robert Frederick and Jane Carolyn P.; m. Pebble Lyn Messamore, June 2, 1979; children: Emery Alan, Amber Janene. BA in Psychology, Westmont Coll., 1977; MA in Clin./Counseling Psychology, Western Conservative Bapt.Sem., Portland, 1983; PhD in Clin. Psychology, Western Conservative Bapt.Sem., 1986. Lic. psychologist, Utah; cert. group psychotherapist, Nat. Register Cert. Group Psychotherapists; cert. trainer, educator and practitioner of psychodrama, Am. Bd. Examiners in Psychodrama, Sociometry, and group psychotherapy; nat. register for H.S.P. Clin. psychology intern Philhaven Hosp., Mt. Gretna, Pa., 1985-86; postdoctoral intern in psychol. assessment State of Utah, Salt Lake City, 1986-87; psychology resident Mt. Olympus Christian Counseling Ctr., 1986-87; psychologist Shepherd's Staff Christian Couns. Ctr., Sandy, Utah, 1989—, clin. dir., 1998—, psychodrama workshop trainer, 1997—. Presentor conferences in field. Author publs. in field. Mem. Internat Soc. Study Dissociation (founder Wasatch chap.), Christian Assn. Psychol. Studies. Avocations: running, skiing, camping, fishing. Office: Shepherds Staff Christian Couns Ctr 731 E 8600 S Sandy UT 84094-6312 E-mail: utpramann@aol.com.

PRAMER, DAVID, microbiologist, educator, research administrator; b. Mt. Vernon, N.Y., Mar. 25, 1923; s. Coleman and Ethel (Toback) P.; m. Rhoda Lifschutz, Sept. 6, 1950; children— Andrew, Stacey Student, St. John's U., 1940, Tex. A&M Coll., 1941; BS cum laude, Rutgers U., 1948, PhD, 1952. Vis. investigator Butterwich Research Labs., Welwyn, Eng., 1952-54; from asst. to assoc. prof. microbiology Rutgers U., New Brunswick, N.J., 1954-60, prof., 1960-67, disting. prof., 1967—, dir. biological scis., 1969-73, dir. univ. research, 1973-75, assoc. v.p. research, 1973-80; dir. Waksman Inst. Microbiology, 1980-88, assoc. v.p. corp. liaison, 1988-93; exec. asst. and disting. prof. emeritus, exec. asst. Rutgers U., New Brunswick, N.J., 1993—. Cons. various fed. agys., 1965—; dir. New Brunswick Sci. Co., Edison, R&D Coun. of N.J., Nanodyne, Inc., New Brunswick, Organica, Inc., Great Neck, N.Y.; served on numerous chmn., com. and adv. posts. Author: Life in the Soil, 1964, Experimental Soil Microbiology, 1965, The Microbes, 1971, Engineered Organisms in the Environment, 1985; also over 250 articles in profl. jours.; regional editor World Jour. Soil and Biology and Biochemistry; mem. editl. bd. Soil Sci., BioSci., Applied Microbiology and Biotech. Bd. dirs. Library, Highland Park, N.J., 1966-75, chmn., 1976-78; committeeman Democratic Party, Highland Park, 1958-66. Served to cpl. USAF, 1943-46 Fulbright-Hays Sr. Research fellow, 1969; recipient Waksman award, Theobald Smith Soc., 2000. Fellow Am. Acad. Microbiology; mem. Am. Soc. Microbiology, Internat. Commn. Microbial Ecology (chmn.), Internat. Cell Rsch. Orgn., Nat. Acad. Scis. India (hon.), Am. Soc. Microbiology (hon., founders award, 2001), Phi Beta Kappa, Alpha Zeta, Sigma Xi Jewish. Avocations: jogging, travel. Home: 407 Rhoads Dr Belle Mead NJ 08502-4113 Office: Rutgers Univ Office Rsch & Sponsord Programs 3 Rutgers Plaza New Brunswick NJ 08901 E-mail: pramer@orsp.rutgers.edu.

PRANG, JEFFREY, city councilman; b. Detroit, June 15, 1962; s. Donald John and Rita Imogene Prang. BA, Mich. State U., 1984. Mayor, mem. coun. City of West Hollywood, Calif., 1997—; spl. asst. to sheriff L.A. County Sheriff's Dept., Monterey Park, 1999—. Mem. Calif. Coun. on Criminal Justice, Sacramento, 2000—. Del. Dem. Nat. Conv., L.A., 2000. Home: 1230 N Sweetzer Ave # 107 West Hollywood CA 90069 Office: City of West Hollywood 8300 Santa Monica Blvd West Hollywood CA 90069 Fax: (323) 848-6562. E-mail: jprang@weho.org.

PRANGE, ARTHUR JERGEN, JR. psychiatrist, neurobiologist, educator; b. Grand Rapids, Mich., Sept. 19, 1926; s. Arthur Jergen and Martha Frances (Elliott) P.; m. Sarah Elizabeth Bowen, Feb. 4, 1950; children— Christine Anne, Martha Louise, Laura Beth, David Elliott. BS, U. Mich., 1947, MD, 1950. Intern Wayne County Gen. Hosp., Eloise, Mich., 1950-51; resident in psychiatry U. N.C., Chapel Hill, 1954-57, instr., 1957-60, asst. prof., 1960-64, asso. prof., 1964-68, prof. psychiatry, 1968-83, Boshamer prof. psychiatry, 1983—, acting chmn. dept. psychiatry, 1983-85, dir. NIMH Clin. Rsch. Ctr., 1979—. Vis. scientist Med. Rsch. Coun. Unit, Epson, Surrey, Eng., 1968-69; chmn. clin. projects rsch. rev. com. HEW, NIMH, 1975-76, chmn. bd. sci. counselors, 1986-87; mem. psychopharmacologic drugs adv. com. HEW, FDA, 1979-82. Editor: The Thyroid Axis, Drugs and Behavior, 74; Contbr. articles to med. jours. Recipient NIMH Career Devel. award 1961-69, Career Scientist award, 1969-95, Gold Medal award Soc. of Biol. Psychiatry, 1992, Exemplary Psychiatrist award Nat. Alliance for the Mentally Ill, 1997, Selo prize Nat. Alliance for Rsch. in Schizophrenia and Affective Disorders, 1997. Fellow Am. Psychiat. Assn. (life, Rsch. in Psychiatry award 1996), Am. Coll. Neuropsychopharmacology (life, pres. 1987, Hoch award 1995); mem. Internat. Soc. Psychoneuroendocrinology (founding mem.), N.C. Neuropsychiat. Assn., Collegium Internationale Neuropsychopharmacologicum, Royal Coll. Psychiatrists (London). Home: 6503 Meadowview Rd Hillsborough NC 27278-8314 Office: Univ NC Sch Medicine Dept Psychiatry Chapel Hill NC 27599-0001

PRANGE, HILMAR WALTER, neurology educator; b. Reichenbach/Eule, Silesia, Germany, Aug. 4, 1944; s. Georg Friedrich Reinhold and Gertrud Wilhelmine (Mueller) P.; m. Carin Juliane Schroeter, Mar. 14, 1970; children: Klaus Richard, Juliane. MD, U. Rostock, Germany, 1969, lic. specialist neurology and psychiatry, 1974; Habilitation, Georg-August U., Goettingen, Germany, 1982. Medical diplomate. Med. resident Regional Hosp., Stralsund, Germany, 1969-71; med. asst. then psychiatrist Univ. Hosp., Rostock, 1971-75; asst. med. dir. Ev. Johannes Hosp., Bielefeld, Germany, 1975-76; head neurologic out-patient clinic Univ. Hosp., Goettingen, Germany, 1976-78, asst. med. dir. dept. neurology Germany, 1979-87, dir. neurological intensive care unit Germany, 1987—. Author: Neurosyphilis, 1987, Infectious Diseases of the Central Nervous System, 1995, Emergencies in Neurology, 2002; editor: CNS Barriers and Modern CSF Diagnostics, 1993, Systemic Infections Causing Bacterial CNS Diseases, 1997; : Infectious Diseases of the Central Nervous System, 2001, Neurological Emergencia, 2002; contbr. articles to profl. jours. Grantee Deutsche Forschungsgemeinschaft, German Tech. Cooperation, German MS Soc. Mem. European Neurological Soc., German Med. Assn. (mem. commn. drug security). Lutheran. Avocation: Cultural history, sports, jogging (marathons), swimming..

PRANGE, ROY LEONARD, JR. lawyer; b. Chgo., Sept. 12, 1945; s. Roy Leonard and Marjorie Rose (Kauppi) P.; m. Carol Lynn Poels, June 5, 1971; children: David, Ellen, Susan. BA, U. Iowa, 1967; MA, Ohio State U., 1968; JD, U. Wis.-Madison, 1975. Bar: Wis. 1975, U.S. Dist. Ct. (we. and ea. dists.) Wis. 1975, U.S. Ct. Appeals (7th cir.) 1978, U.S. Supreme Ct. 1978. Assoc. Ross & Stevens, Svc. Corp., Madison, Wis., 1975-79, ptnr., 1979-90, Quarles & Brady, Madison, 1990—. Lectr. bankruptcy, debtor-creditor rights, U. Wis., Madison, 1982--. Contbr. Wis. Lawyer's Desk Reference Manual, 1987, Comml. Litigation in Wis. Practice Handbook, 1995, West's Bankruptcy Exemption Manual, 1997—. 1st lt. U.S. Army, 1969-72. Fellow Am. Coll. Bankruptcy; mem. ABA, Wis. State Bar (dir. bankruptcy, insolvency, creditors rights sect. 1985-91, chair 1990-92, mem. continuing legal edn. com. 1990-95), Am. Bankruptcy Inst., Dickens Fellowship (v.p. 1980-84). Avocations: swimming, bicycling, scuba diving. Office: Quarles & Brady PO Box 2113 1 S Pinckney St Madison WI 53703-2892

PRANSES, ANTHONY LOUIS, retired electric company executive, organization executive; b. Claracq, France, May 3, 1920; s. Anthony Kasimer and Georgette (Pilon) F.; m. Margaret Louise Hamill, July 24, 1943; children— Anthony Randolph, Terry Jay, Renee Louise. Student, Sorbonne, Paris, France, 1937-39; BS in Metall. Engring, Carnegie Inst. Tech., 1942, grad. student, 1946-48. With Westinghouse Electric Corp., 1945-86, mgr. mfg. planning Ohio, 1954-57, plant mgr., 1958-59, mgr. mfg. services, 1959-72, mgr. mfg., 1972-80, cons., 1980-86. Joined Am. Youth Hostels, 1935, founder Pitts. council, 1947, pres. council, 1947-50, mem. nat. bd. dirs., 1954-72, Midwest regional v.p., 1957-59, nat. pres., 1959-62, pres. Lima council, 1962-75, 87-91, chmn. nat. bd. dirs., 1963-67. Served to capt., C.E. AUS, 1942- 45. Home: 6005 Poling Rd Lima OH 45807-9492 E-mail: pranses@wcoil.com.

PRANSKY, JOAN E. lawyer, community organizer; b. N.Y.C., Apr. 26, 1946; d. John and Sharon (Harris) P.; 1 child, Leah. BS, Syracuse U., 1967; JD, Seton Hall U., 1974. Bar: N.J. 1974, U.S. Dist. Ct. N.J. 1974. Social worker Dept. Social Svcs., N.Y.C., 1967; elem. sch. tchr. V.I. Bd. Edn., St. Thomas, 1968; lawyer Essex-Newark Legal Svcs., 1974-83; supervising trial atty. Urban Legal Clinic, prof. Rutgers U. Sch. Law, Newark, 1983-86; atty. in pvt. practice Montclair, N.J., 1986—; atty., N.J. State Bar fellow Seton Hall Law Sch. Ctr. for Social Justice, Newark, 1992-94. Legal counsel N.J. Tenant Orgn., 1984—; legal counsel, advisor City-wide Tenant Orgns., East Orange, Newark, Paterson, Elizabeth, Orange, Jersey City, 1976-90; adv. mem. N.J. State Com. on Rent Control, , N.J. State Com. on Multifamily Dwellings, 1983-85. Editor, co-founder Shelterforce, 1976-85; contbr. articles to N.Y. Times, others. Bd. dirs. N.J. Citizen Action, 1990-94; mem. budget adv. com. Montclair Bd. Edn., 1996; co-founder Support Integrated Pub. Edn., Montclair, 1996; co-founder, mem. steering com. Montclair Civil Rights Coalition, 1997. Recipient Equal Justice medal Legal Svcs. N.J., 1989, Ronald B. Atlas Meml. award N.J. Tenant Assn., 1988, Cmty. Svc. award N.J. Citizen Action, 2002. Mem. N.J. State Bar, N.J. Nat. Lawyers Guild, N.J. Rainbow Coalition (Fannie Lou Hamer br.). Avocations: singing in chorus, hiking, whitewater rafting, jogging. Home: 11 Stephen St Montclair NJ 07042-5031 Office: 460 Bloomfield Ave Montclair NJ 07042-3552

PRASAD, ANANDA SHIVA, medical educator; b. Buxar, Bihar, India, Jan. 1, 1928; came to U.S., 1952, naturalized, 1968; s. Radha Krishna and Mahesha (Kaur) Lall; m. Aryabala Ray, Jan. 6, 1952; children: Rita, Sheila, Ashok, Audrey. BSc, Patna (India) Sci. Coll., 1946, MB, BChir, 1951; PhD, U. Minn., 1957; doctorate honoris causa, U. Claude Bernard of Lyon, 1999. Intern Patna Med. Coll. Hosp., 1951-52; resident St. Paul's Hosp., Dallas, 1952-53, U. Minn., 1953-56, VA Hosp., Mpls., 1956; instr. dept. medicine Univ. Hosp., U. Minn., 1957-58; vis. assoc. prof. medicine Shiraz Med. Faculty, Nemazee Hosp., Shiraz, Iran, 1960; asst. prof. medicine and nutrition Vanderbilt U., 1961-63; mem. faculty, dir. div. hematology dept. medicine Wayne State U., Detroit, 1963-84, assoc. prof., 1964-68, prof., 1968-2000, dir. research dept. medicine, 1984-97, disting. prof., 2000—. Mem. staff Harper-Grace Hosp., VA Hosp., Allen Park, Mich.; mem. trace elements subcom. Food and Nutrition Bd., NRC-Nat. Acad. Scis., 1965-68, NIH Coun.; chmn. trace elements com. Internat. Union Nutritional Scis.; mem. Am. Bd. Nutrition; pres. Am. Coll. Nutrition, 1991-93. Author: Zinc Metabolism, 1966, Trace Elements in Human Health and Disease, 1976, Trace Elements and Iron in Human Metabolism, 1978, Zinc in Human Nutrition, 1979, Biochemistry of Zinc, 1993; editor: Clinical, Biochemical and Nutritional Aspects of Trace Elements, 1982, Am. Jour. Hematology, Jour. Trace Elements in Exptl. Medicine; editor: Zinc Metabolism, Current Aspects in Health and Disease, 1977; co-editor: Clinical Applications of Recent Advances in Zinc Metabolism, 1982, Zinc Deficiency in Human Subjects, 1983, Essential and Toxic Trace Elements in Human Health and Disease, 1988, Essential and Toxic Trace Elements in Human Health and Disease: An Update, 1993; Jour. Am. Coll. Nutrition; contbr. articles to profl. jours., also reviewer. Trustee Detroit Internat. Inst., Detroit Gen. Hosp. Research Corp., 1969-72. Recipient Rsch. Recognition award Wayne State U., 1964, award Am. Coll. Nutrition, 1976, Disting. Faculty Fellowship award Wayne State U., 1986, Medal of Honor, City of Lyon, France, 1989, Pioneer in Sickle Cell Disease Rsch. award Nat. Heart Lung Blood Inst./NIH, 1997; Pfizer scholar, 1955-56, WCMS Spl. Recognition award for Profl. Ach., 1998, Klaus Schwartz medal Internat. Assn. Bioinorganic Scientists, 2001, Spl. Recognition awrd Am. Assn. Physicists India, 2001. Master ACP (recipient Mich. Laureate award), Am. Coll. Nutrition; fellow AAAS, Am. Inst. Nutrition (trace elements panel), Internat. Soc. Hematology; mem. AMA (Goldberger award 1975), Internat. Soc. Trace Element Rsch. in Humans (pres. 1986-92, chmn. steering com. 1985-86, Raulin award 1989), Am. Soc. Clin. Nutrition (awards com. 1969-70), Am. Fedn. Clin. Rsch. (pres. Mich. 1969-70), Am. Physiol. Soc., Am. Soc. Clin. Investigation, Am. Soc. Hematology, Assn. Am. Physicians, European Acad. Scis., Arts and Humanities (corr.), Ctrl. Soc. Clin. Rsch., Soc. Exptl. Biology and Medicine (Councillor Mich. 1967-71), Wayne State U. Acad. Scholars (pres.-elect 1997-98, pres. 1998-99), Wayne County Med. Soc., Internat. Soc. Internal Medicine, Am. Soc. Clin. Nutrition (Robert H. Herman award 1984), Nutrition Soc. India (Gopalan oration award 1988), Nat. Heart, Lung, Blood Inst. NIH (mem. coun. 82-), Assn. of Am. Physicists of Indian Origin (Resch. award 2001), Cosmos Club (Washington), Sigma Xi. Home: 4710 Cove Rd Orchard Lake MI 48323-3604 Office: Univ Health Ctr 5-C 4201 Saintt Antoine St Detroit MI 48201-2153

PRASAD, BIRENDRA BRIAN, mechanical engineer; b. Patna, Bihar, India, June 30, 1949; came to U.S., 1973; s. Baidyanath Prasad Gupta and Ramrati Devi; m. Pushpa Gupta, May 13, 1973; children: Rosalie, Gunjan, Palak. BSME, Bihar Coll. Engring., Patna, 1969; MSME, Indian Inst. Tech., Kanpur, 1971; DEng, Stanford U., 1975; PhD in Mech. and Aerospace Engring., Ill. Inst. Tech., 1977. Rsch. asst. Ill. Inst. Tech., Chgo., 1976-77, lectr., 1978-79; prin. rsch. scientist Sci. Rsch. Lab., Ford Motor Co., Dearborn, Mich., 1982-85; sr. cons. engr. Electronic Data Sys. Corp., West Bloomfield, 1985-98; dir. Unigraphics Solutions, Inc. Knowledge based Engring. (KBE) B, Cypress, Calif., 1998—, U. Calif. Continuing Edn., Irvine, 2001—. Author: 12 books; contbr. more than 100 articles to profl. jours. Recipient award NASA, 1981. Fellow AIAA (chmn. structural dynamics and materials conf. organizing com., treas. Mich. chpt. 1986—), ASME, ASCE (chmn., mem. control group aerospace div. conf. com.); mem. Soc. Automotive Engring. Home: 2966 Penman Tustin CA 92782-3313 Office: Speczmarker Solutions Mng Dir Knowledge Based Engring PO Box 3882 Tustin CA 92781-3882 E-mail: prasadb1@cox.net.

PRASAD, KRISHNA NANDAN, economist; MA in Econs., Delhi Sch. Econs., 1960; PhD in Econs., Gokhale Inst., Poona, India, 1969. Prof. planning devel. U. Mumbai, India, 1982—. Adv. bd. Varta; cons. Planning Commn., 1980-82; mem. internat. adv. bd. STD Forum, Internat. Conf., Karachi, 2000; vis. fellow Econ. Growth Ctr. Yale U., 1998; vis. prof. U. Hyderabad, India, 2001-2002; session chair Internat. Conf. on Input-Output Techniques, Macerata, Italy, 2000. Co-editor: Input-Output Analysis; mem. editl. bd. Internat. Jour. Devel. Lit.; contbr. articles to profl. jours. A.N. Sinha Inst. fellow, 1970, U. Bombay fellow, 1970-80. Mem. Internat. Input-Output Assn., Internat. Soc. Inventory Rsch., Inter-Univ. Consortium for Inter-Social Devel., Input-Output Rsch. Assn. India (sec.). Address: A-402 Shanti Complex Tunga Village L8T # 7 Powai Mumbai 400 072 India Fax: 91 022 857 4415. E-mail: drknprasad@hotmail.com.

PRASAD, NIRU, physician, television personality; b. Feb. 10, 1940; s. Sadashiu and Saraswati Prasad; m. Bala Prasad, Mar. 9, 1962; children: Abhilasha, Ashish, Anjali, Ashoke. PhD, PW Med. Coll., Bihar, India, 1962. Emergency rm. physician Henry Ford Hosp., Detroit, 2002; pediatric urgent care St. Joseph Mercy Hosp., Pontiac, 2002; occupl. physician Med. Plant Physician, Auhum Hills, 2002. Contbr. (book) How to Keep Your Child Safe and Healthy; contbr. articles to profl. jours.; host (television program) Health Talk. Recipient AMA Physician Recognition Award, 1992, Svc. of Justice and Mercy Recognition Award, 1993, America's Registry of Outstanding Professionals, 2001. Home: 264 Pine Ridge Drive Bloomfield Hills MI 48304 Home Fax: 248-540-1092. Personal E-mail: niruprasad@aol.com.

PRASAD, POTTUMARTHI VARA, health facility administrator; b. Guntur, India, Apr. 3, 1962; came to U.S., 1985; d. Rama Rao and Sarojini Pottumarthi; m. Raji Prasad, Feb. 12, 1992; children: Supritha, Omkar. MS in Med. Physics, Anna U., Madras, India, 1985; MS in Physics, E. Tex. State U., 1987; PhD in Radiol. Scis., U. Calif., Irvine, 1992. Diplomate Am. Bd. Med. Physics. Rsch. asst. in physics E. Tex. State U., Commerce, 1985-87; rsch. asst. in MRI U. Calif., Irvine, 1988-92; rsch. fellow in MRI Beth Israel Hosp., Boston, 1992-93, rsch. assoc. in MRI, 1993-98; dir. MRI rsch. Beth Israel Deaconess Med. Ctr., 1998-2000; asst. prof. Harvard Med. Sch., 1998—2000; assoc. prof. Northwestern U. Med. Sch., 2000—. Biomedical Engring. Rsch. grantee Whitaker Found., 1994; grantee Am. Heart Assn., 1997, NIH, 1998. Mem. Internat. Soc. Magnetic Resonance Medicine (Student Stipend award 1991), Am. Assn. Physicists Medicine (Norman A. Bailey award 1990), Harvard Faculty Club. Hindu. Avocation: classic rock. Office: Evanston Northwestern Healthcare 2650 Ridge Ave Evanston IL 60201 Fax: 617-667-7917. E-mail: pprasad@enh.org.

PRASANNA, PATAJE G.S. radiobiologist, researcher; came to U.S., 1993; s. Govindayya and Parameshwari Pataje; m. Sudha S. Rao, Jan. 27, 1993; 1 child, Anish. PhD, Mangalore (India) U., 1991. Postdoctoral assoc. NAS-NRC, Bethesda, Md., 1993-95; radiobiologist, molecular cytogeneticist Armed Forces Radiobiology Rsch. Inst., 1996—. Contbr. articles to profl. jours. Fellow Acad. Gen. Edn. (Manipal, India); mem. Radiation Rsch. Soc. (Young Scientist Travel grantee 1998. Office: AFRRI 8901 Wisconsin Ave Bethesda MD 20889-5603

PRASHER, RAVI SHANKAR, thermal engineer; b. Patna, Bihar, India, Sept. 14, 1973; s. Ramashray and Vasundhara Sharma. B of Tech., IIT Delhi, 1995; PhD, Ariz. State U., 1999. Grad. rsch. asst. Ariz. State U., Tempe, 1996—99; sr. thermal design engr. Intel Corp., Chandler, Ariz., 1999—. Mentor Semicondr. Rsch. Corp., Tempe, 2000—; reviewer Jour. Thermophysics and Heat Transfer, Tempe, 2002—, Jour. Enhanced Heat Transfer, Tempe, 2001—02; external rschr. Ariz. State U., Tempe, 1999—; indsl. advisor to Ph.D. students Stanford U., Palo Alto. Author: (book chpt.) Handbook of Heat Transfer; contbr. articles to profl. jours. Welfare sec. India Inst. Tech., Delhi, India, 1992—93. Mem.: Americal Society of Mechanical engineers, [00b7]Reagents’ graduate scholarship, ASU, Institute of Electrical and Electrnics Engineer (assoc.; chair CPMT-Phoenix chpt. 1999, 2000—01, reviewer CPMT transactions on packaging 2001—02), American Society of Mechanical Engineers (assoc.). Achievements include invention of novel system and method of heat extraction; patents pending for. Home: 17 sriniketen ndse appt New Delhi 110096 India Home Fax: 480-554-7615. Personal E-mail: ravi_prasher@intel.com.

PRATAP, SIDDHARTH, electromechanics researcher, educator; b. Bombay, Dec. 21, 1955; came to U.S., 1981; s. Bharatkumar m Dhirajlal and Snehlata Bharatkumar Pratap; m. Swati Siddharth Pratap, Oct. 17, 1985. B in Engring., U. Bombay, 1979; MS, U. Tex., 1982, PhD in Engring., 1996. Grad. engr. Tata Engring. and Locomotive Inc., Bombay, 1979-81; grad. rsch. asst. Ctr. for Electromechanics U. Tex., Austin, 1982-83, rsch. engr. assoc. II, 1983-84, rsch. engr. assoc. III, 1984-86, rsch. engr. assoc. IV, 1986-87, rsch. engr. assoc. V, 1987-90, spl. rsch. assoc., 1990-91, rsch. assoc., 1991-97, rsch. scientist, 1997, chief scientist, 1997—, sr. adj. prof., 1997—, co-prin. investigator, 1998—. Contbr. articles to profl. jours., chpt. to book; patentee in field. Mem. IEEE. Avocations: reading, flying kites, nature trekking. Office: Ctr for Electromechanics U Tex Austin PRC-EME Mail Code R7000 Austin TX 78712

PRATER, MICHAEL ALBERT, computer security executive; b. Lake Charles, La., June 29, 1973; s. Albert Ferdinand and Carole Marie Prater; m. Amy Denise Inman, Apr. 24, 1993; children: Denise Michelle, Matthew Ryan. Student, McNese State U., 1991-93. Mgr. sporting goods Kmart, Ruston, La., 1993-94; mgr. customer svc. Credit Bur. Lake Charles, 1994-96; Internet sys. adminstr. US Unwired, Lake Charles, 1996-97, competitive local exch./ISP data network engr., 1997-98, mgr. network security, 1998—. Mem. Pi Kappa Phi. Avocations: computer consulting, network consulting. Office: 1 Lakeshore Dr Ste 1900 Lake Charles LA 70629-0114 Home: 23623 Prairie Bird Dr Spring TX 77373-9251 E-mail: michael.prater@usunwired.com., mprater@usunwired.com.

PRATER, ROBERT STANLEY, JR. broker; b. Atlanta, Feb. 15, 1965; s. Robert Stanley and Linda Lynne (Haney) P.; m. Mary Jo Grippo, Oct. 5, 1996; children: Alison Christine, Robert III. BBA in Fin., U. Ga., 1987; MBA in Fin., Wake Forest U., 1990. Sr. analyst Pepsico, N.Y.C., 1990-92; 1st v.p. Interstate/Johnson Lane, Atlanta, 1992-97; investment ptnr. J.C. Bradford, 1997—. Baptist. Office: J C Bradford & Co 3060 Peachtree Rd NW Atlanta GA 30305-2234

PRATHER, DENNIS WARREN, electrical engineer, educator; b. Takoma Park, MD, Aug. 14, 1964; s. Geraldine Lee Prather; m. Christine Calomeris, May 9, 1964; children: Lindsay, Thomas. PhD in Elec. Engring., U. Md., 1997. Commd. officer USN, 1982, advanced through grades to lt. comdr., engring. duty officer Naval Res. DC, 1982—, rsch. engr. U.S. Army Rsch. Lab. Adelphi, Md., 1990—97. Recipient Career award, NSF, 1999. Office: U Del Dept Elec Engring Newark DE 19716

PRATHER, GERALD LUTHER, management consultant, retired air force officer, judge; b. LaGrange, Ga., Apr. 7, 1935; s. Luther Pate and Hazel Belle (McCullough) P.; m. Carolyn Pearson, Nov. 22, 1956; children— Dean Allen, Bryan Pate, Jeri Lynn, Angela BSE.E., Auburn U., 1966; MS in Mgmt., Air Force Inst. Tech., 1972; postgrad. advanced mgmt., U. Houston, 1978; grad., SQ Officer Sch., Maxwell AFB, 1963, ICAF, Washington, 1974. Enlisted USAF, 1954-56, commd. 2d lt., 1956, advanced through grades to maj. gen., 1981, various assignments as pilot, 1956-68, served in Vietnam, 1967-68, commdr. 1963d Comm. Squadron Ill., 1968-69, comdr. 1918th Comm. Squadron Scott AFB, 1969-70, dep. dir. comm.-electronics for 15th Air Force March AFB, Calif., 1970-72, chief comm. ops. div. hdqrs. Washington, 1972-75, comdr. strategic comm. div. Offutt AFB, Nebr., 1975-77, comdr. European Comm. Div. Ramstein AFB, W. Ger., 1977-80; dir. Command Control, Comm. & Computer Systems, Hdqrs. U.S. Readiness Command MacDill AFB, Fla., 1980-81; asst. chief of staff of Info. Systems Hdqrs. USAF, Washington, 1981-84, comdr. Air Force Comm. Command Scott AFB, Ill., 1984-86, ret., 1986; pvt. practice mgmt. cons. Del Rio, Tex., 1986-1997; Justice of the Peace Val Verde County, 1987-97. Lectr. in field; also air traffic controller, parachutist. Speech writer Team America 1983 (Freedom Found. nat. award 1984). Scoutmaster Boy Scouts Am., Sacramento, 1963, chmn. com., 1964, cub master Auburn, Ala.; sponsor Explorer Troop, Boy Scouts Am., Scott AFB, Ill., 1969; chmn. Amistad Dist. Boy Scouts Am., 1988; chmn. Eagle Scout advancement, 1994—2002, Val Verde County United Way campaign, 1989, pres., bd. dirs., 1990; pastoral counselor St. James Ch., 2002. Decorated DSM with oak leaf cluster, Legion of Merit with one oak leaf cluster, DFC, Bronze Star with V device, Air medal with two oak leaf clusters, Republic of Vietnam Gallantry Cross with Palm; recipient Gen. Edwin W. Rawlings award Air Force Inst. Tech., 1972, Comdt.'s award, 1972, also numerous other decorations and awards. Mem.: VFW (life), Del Rio C. of C. (v.p. 1989—90, bd. dirs. 1990—99, v.p. 1991—92, pres. 1995—96, v.p. 1995—96, 1995—96, bd. dirs. 1999—2000), Ret. Officers Assn., Air Force Assn. (Jimmy Doolittle award 1984), Telephone Pioneers of Am., Soc. Logistics Engrs., Justice of the Peace and Constables Assn., Soc. Am. Mil. Engrs., Air Traffic Control Assn., Armed Forces Comm.-Electronics Assn. (mem. com. 1981—82, chmn. ethics com. 1982—83, internat. v.p. 1982—84, assoc. dir. 1984—, Meritorious Gold medal 1976, 1983), Non-Commd. Officers Assn. (hon.), Air Force Sgts. Assn. (hon.), Disabled Am. Vets. (life),

Vietnam Vets. Am. (life), Del Rio Club, Lions (dir. 1989—94, v.p. 1994, Svc. award 1992—93), Civitan, Am. Legion, Order of Daedalians. Avocations: gardening, racquetball, sketching, automotive mechanics, private pilot. Address: HC 1 Box 7 Del Rio TX 78840-9720 E-mail: prather@delrio.com.

PRATHER, JOHN GIDEON, JR. lawyer; b. Lexington, Ky., Sept. 10, 1946; s. John Gideon Sr. and Marie Jeanette (Moore) P.; m. Hilma Elizabeth Skonberg, Aug. 4, 1973; children: John Hunt, Anna Russell. BS in Acctg., U. Ky., 1968, JD, 1970. Bar: Ky. 1971, U.S. Dist. Ct. (ea. dist.) Ky. 1978, U.S. Dist. Ct. (we. dist.) Ky. 1984, U.S. Ct. Appeals (6th cir.) 1988, U.S. Supreme Ct. 1988. Ptnr., prin. Law Offices John G. Prather, Somerset, Ky., 1972—; dir. Ky. Higher Edn. Assistance Authority, 2002—. Bd. dirs. Lawyers Mutual Ins. Co. Ky., 1989—, treas., 1995-2002, chmn. bd., 2002—. Bd. dirs. United Way, 1978—; mem. state cen. com. Ky. Young. Dems., Frankfort, 1972. Served to 1st lt. USAF, 1971-72, JAG, 1972. Fellow U. Ky., 1998—. Mem. ABA (house dels.), ATLA, Am. Bd. Trial Advs., Am. Coll. Trial Lawyers, Am. Bd. Trial Attys., Ky. Bar Assn. (ho. of dels. 1984-85, bd. govs. 1985-91, v.p. 1991-92, pres.-elect 1992-93, pres. 1993-94, lectr.), Coun. Sch. Bd. Attys. (state pres., bd. dirs. 1986—, lectr.), Ky. Def. Coun. (bd. dirs. 1987-91), Pulaski County Indsl. Found. (bd. dirs. 1982-95), Phi Delta Phi. Mem. Christian Ch. Avocations: boating, flying. Home: 510 N Main St Somerset KY 42501-1434 Office: PO Box 616 Somerset KY 42502-0616 E-mail: pratherlaw@msn.com.

PRATHER, LENORE LOVING, former state supreme court chief justice; b. West Point, Miss., Sept. 17, 1931; d. Byron Herald and Hattie Hearn (Morris) Loving; m. Robert Brooks Prather, May 30, 1957; children: Pamela, Valerie Jo, Malinda Wayne. BS, Miss. Univ. Women, 1953; JD, U. Miss., 1955. Bar: Miss. 1955. Practice with B. H. Loving, West Point, 1955-60; sole practice, 1960-62, 65-71; assoc. practice, 1962-65; mcpl. judge City of West Point, 1965-71; chancery ct. judge 14th dist. State of Miss., Columbus, 1971-82, supreme ct. justice Jackson, 1982-92, presiding justice, 1993-97, chief justice, 1998-2001; interim pres. Miss. U. for Women, Columbus, Miss., 2001—02. V.p. Conf. Local Bar Assn., 1956-58; sec. Clay County Bar Assn., 1956-71 1st woman in Miss. to become chancery judge, 1971, and supreme ct. justice, 1982, and chief justice, 1998-2001. Mem. ABA, Miss. State Bar Assn., Miss. Conf. Judges, DAR, Rotary, Pilot Club, Jr. Aux. Columbus Club. Episcopalian. Office: Miss U for Women 1100 College St Columbus MS 39701 Fax: 662-328-7119.

PRATHER, RICHARD SCOTT, author; b. Santa Ana, Calif., Sept. 9, 1921; s. Sydney Scott Prather and Effie Alberta Kuykendall Middleton; m. Alma Tina Hager, July 31, 1945. Student, Riverside (Calif.) Poly., 1936-39, Riverside Jr. Coll., 1940. Civilian clk. March AFB, Riverside, 1941, chief clk., surplus property disposal office, 1946-49; fireman, 2d engr. U.S. Merchant Marine, 1942-45. Author: Case of the Vanishing Beauty, 1950, Bodies in Bedlam, 1951, Everybody Had a Gun, 1951, Find This Woman, 1951, Way of a Wanton, 1952, Lie Down, Killer, 1952, Dagger of Flesh, 1952, Darling, It's Death, 1952, Too Many Crooks (originally, Ride a High Horse), 1953, Always Leave 'Em Dying, 1954, Pattern for Panic, 1954, Strip for Murder, 1955, Dragnet: Case #561, 1956, The Wailing Frail, 1956, Have Gat - Will Travel, 1957, Three's a Shroud, 1957, Slab Happy, 1958, Take a Murder, Darling, 1958, The Scrambled Yeggs, 1958 (originally Pattern for Murder by David Knight, 1952), The Peddler, 1958 (originally by Douglas Ring, 1952), Over Her Dear Body, 1959, Double in Trouble (with Stephen Marlowe), 1959, Dance With the Dead, 1960, Shell Scott's Seven Slaughters, 1961, Dig That Crazy Grave, 1961, Kill the Clown, 1962, Joker in the Deck, 1964, The Cockeyed Corpse, 1964, Dead Heat, 1964, The Trojan Hearse, 1964, Kill Him Twice, 1965, Dead Man's Walk, 1965, The Meandering Corpse, 1965, The Kubla Khan Caper, 1966, Gat Heat, 1967, The Cheim Manuscript, 1969, The Shell Scott Sampler, 1969, Kill Me Tomorrow, 1969, Shell Scott's Murder Mix, 1970, Dead Bang, 1971, The Sweet Ride, 1972, The Sure Thing, 1975, The Amber Effect, 1986, Shellshock, 1987, Hot Rock Rumble and the Double Take, 1994; editor: The Comfortable Coffin, 1960; stories in Manhunt, Cavalier, Thrilling Detective, Menace, Justice, Accused, Suspect, Murder!, Ed McBain's Mystery Book, Adam, Escapade, Man's World, Swank, For Men Only, Tiger, Shell Scott's Mystery Mag., several anthologiees. Recipient Life Achievement award Pvt. Eye Writers of Am., 1986. Avocations: organic gardening, books. Home: 810 E Saddlehorn Rd Sedona AZ 86351-7419

PRATHER, ROBERT FRANKLIN, fund administrator; b. N.Y.C., Aug. 20, 1935; s. Theodore Roosevelt and Evelyn Trimarco P.; m. Jessie Holtby Prather, Nov. 14, 1959 (dec. Jan. 1989); children: Craig, Keith, Debra Jo, Todd, Adam, Jennifer; m. Monica Marshall Prather, Feb. 10, 1990; children: Kathy, Natalie. BS in Journalism, Ohio U., 1957; MA, Columbia U., 1964, EdD, 1981. Mng. editor Corning (N.Y.) Glass Works, 1964-66; dir. devel. The Coll. of Ins., N.Y.C., 1966-73; v.p. for devel. Mercyhurst Coll., Erie, Pa., 1973-80, Olivet (Mich.) Coll., 1980-82; v.p. univ. rels. Tiffin (Ohio) U., 1984-86; pres. W.Va. Found. for Ind. Colls., Charleston, 1986-93, Tex. Ind. Coll. Fund, Fort Worth, 1993—. Presiding officer Found. for Ind. Higher Edn., Washington, 1998-2001, southwestern regional rep., 1995-98, midwestern regional rep., 1990-93, dir., 1995—. Edn. com. State of W.Va., Charleston, 1990-93, advanced placement adv. com., 1990-93; pres. Erie (Pa.) Playhouse, 1973-80; co-pres. Coun. on Adoptable Children, Erie, 1973-80. Capt. U.S. Army, 1957-59, 61-62. Mem. Fort Worth Rotary, Found. for Ind. Higher Edn. (dir 1995—). Democrat. Avocations: reading, thinking. Office: Tex Ind Coll Fund 4200 S Hulen St Ste 314 Fort Worth TX 76109 E-mail: rfprather@texasindecollegefund.org.

PRATHER, WILLIAM C., III, lawyer, writer; b. Toledo, Feb. 20, 1921; s. Hollie Cartmill and Effie Fern (Deppen) P. BA, U. Ill., 1942, JD, 1947. Bar: Ill. 1947, U.S. Supreme Ct. 1978. Co-pres. student govt. U. Ill., 1942, asst. dean, 1942-43; atty. First Nat. Bank Chgo., 1947-51; asst. gen. counsel U.S. Savs. and Loan League, Chgo., 1951-59; gen. counsel U.S. League of Savs. Instns., 1959-82, gen. counsel emeritus, 1982—; sole practice Cumberland County, Ill., 1981—. Sem. lectr. in law, banking. Editor: The Legal Bulletin, 1951-81, The Federal Guide, 1954-81; author: Savings Accounts, 8th edit., 1981; contbr. articles to publs. Lt. U.S. Armed Forces, 1943-45. Decorated Bronze Star. Mem. ABA, FBA, Internat. Bar Assn., Ill. Bar Assn., Chgo. Bar Assn., Union Internat. des Avocats, Nat. Lawyers Club Washington, Cosmos Club, Univ. Club Chgo., Kiwanis, Mattoon Golf and Country Club, Exeter and County Club (Eng.), Club de Bonmont Melisande (France), Tennis Club de Beaulieu (France), Soc. Colonial Wars, St. Andrew's Soc., Am. Legion, Phi Delta Phi, Phi Gamma Delta, Phi Eta Sigma, Phi Alpha Chi. Home: Applewood Farm PO Box 157 Toledo IL 62468-0157 Office: 142 Courthouse Sq Toledo IL 62468 also: L'Orangeraie 42 Av General Leclerc Villefranche-sur-Mer 06230 France

PRATO, KIMBERLY, public affairs officer; b. Waterbury, Conn., June 13, 1967; d. Thomas Elia Dimo and Gayla Belle Owens; m. Anthony Wayne Prto, June 8, 1991; children: Anthony, Nicholas. BA, Cen. Conn. State U., 1990; MA, U. Okla., 1998; cert. in pub. affairs, Def. Info. Sch., Ft. George Meade, Md., 1998. Anchorperson, promotional dir. Sta. WTLV, Jacksonville, 1990-93; newsrier Sta. KUSI-TV, San Diego, 1995-96; pub. affairs officer U.S. Dept. Army, Torii Sta., Japan, 1996-99, U.S. Dept. of Navy, Camp Pendleton, Calif., 1999—. Editor (manual) for Am. Assn. for Critical Care Nurses, (story) for Am. Chiropractic Assn., 2000. Mem. Oceanside (Calif.) Editl. Adv. Com., 1999—. Mem. Am. Soc. for Pub. Adminstrn., Healthcare Consumer Coun. Republican. Roman Catholic. Avocations: SCUBA diving, horseback riding, golf, running. Home: 3785 Carnegie Dr Oceanside CA 92056 Office: US Dept Navy Box 555191 Camp Pendleton CA 92055

PRATS, MICHAEL, petroleum engineer, educator; b. Tampa, Fla., Dec. 18, 1925; s. Miguel and Maria (Carbó) P.; m. Mary Blanche Flaherty, Apr. 7, 1951; children: Delicia Anne, Barbara Eileen, Teresa Kaye, Steven Michael. BS in Physics, U. Tex., 1949, MA in Physics, 1951. With Shell Devel. Co., Houston, 1950—, cons. research engr., then sr. research assoc., 1972-89; pres. Michael Prats & Assocs., 1989—. Cons. prof. petroleum engring. dept. Stanford U., 1997—; adj. prof. dept. geosystems petroleum engring. U. Tex., Austin, 1991—; participant scientist exchange Royal/Dutch Shell Lab., Amsterdam, The Netherlands, 1954, 55, Shell Internat. Petroleum, The Hague, The Netherlands, 1981, Maraven, S.A., Caracas, Venezuela, 1981-83. Author: Thermal Recovery, 1982, Spanish transl., 1987; contbr. articles to profl. jours.; 23 patents in field. Served to staff sgt. USAAF, 1944-46, PTO. Recipient Diploma of Honor Pi Epsilon Tau, 1986, Disting. Svc. award Rep. Honduras, 1989, Thermal Recovery Disting. Achievement award SPE Thermal Ops. Symposium, 1991, KAPITSA medal Acad. Natural Scis. (Moscow), 1995; named to Internat. Hall of Fame, 1989. Mem. AIME (hon.), NAE, Soc. Petroleum Engrs. (hon., bd. dirs. 1976-79, sr. tech. editor 1987-90, Enhanced Oil Recovery Pioneer 1986, Uren award 1974, Disting. Mem. award 1983, Anthony F. Lucas Gold medal 1993), Can. Inst. Mining, Asociacion De Ingenieros Petroleros De Mexico, Mex. Nat. Acad. Engring. (corr.), Acad. Engring. Armenia (fgn. mem.), Russian Acad. Nat. Scis. (fgn.), Pi Epsilon Tau (hon.). Avocation: travel. Address: 2834 Bellefontaine St Houston TX 77025-1610 E-mail: mikep@mprats.com.

PRATSCH, LLOYD WILMER, government official; b. Green Bay, Wis., Dec. 28, 1941; s. Lloyd Anthony and Blanche (Goffard) P.; m. Rita Noel Wormley, Feb. 16, 1974; children: Candice, Laurie. BA, U. Wis., 1964, postgrad., 1964-66. With Dept. Army, 1966-71, Dept. Interior, 1971-86, Dept. Commerce, 1986-87; dir. procurement svcs. divsn. Dept. Treasury, Washington, 1987-92; procurement exec. Dept. State, 1992—. Pres. Fox Lake Property Owners Assn., Oakton, Va., 1990-92. With USMCR, 1966-72. Avocations: swimming, snow skiing. Home: 11217 Sweetwood Ln Oakton VA 22124-1327 E-mail: pratschlw@state.gov.

PRATT, ALICE FORD, small business owner, music educator; b. Fairmont, W.Va., June 15, 1926; d. Dorsey Mackin and Gladys Sabina (Clem) Ford; m. William Spach Pratt, Mar. 28, 1953; children: Nancy, Sallie, Anna Laurie, James. Diploma in nursing, Duke U., 1948; diploma in pub. health, U. Pitts., 1950; diploma in pub. health edn., U. N.C., 1952; postgrad., Montgomery Coll., 1968-70. Pub. health nurse Marion County Health Dept., Fairmont, 1948-51; head nurse out patient Meml. Hosp., Chapel Hill, N.C., 1952-53; pvt. piano instr. Potomac, Md., 1969-91; owner Pratt Market Svc., 1984—92. Sec. Potomac Area Music Tchr. Assn., 1975-90. Mem. Montgomery County Music Assn. (judge, monitor 1989—). Republican. Lutheran. Avocations: gardening, crafts, reading, collecting. Home: 100 Mill Point Rd Kitty Hawk NC 27949-3805

PRATT, ALICE REYNOLDS, retired educational administrator; b. Marietta, Ohio, Mar. 5, 1922; d. Thurman J. and Vera L. (Holdren) Reynolds. BA, U. Okla., 1943. Reporter, high sch. tchr., 1944-50; asst. dir. Houston Office, Inst. Internat. Edn., 1952-58, v.p., 1975-87; ret., 1987. Founding mem. Houston-Galveston/Stavanger Sister City Assn.; past mem. nat. bd. dirs. Sister Cities Internat., Nat. Coun. Internat. Visitors; bd. dirs. Pan Am. Roundtable; bd. dirs. so. regional office Inst. Internat. Edn.; past mem. bd, govs. Houston Forum. Decorated Palmes Academiques (France), Order of Merit (Germany), knight Order of Leopold II (Belgium); named Woman of Yr., Houston Bus. and Profl. Women, 1958; recipient Matrix award Theta Sigma Phi, 1961, Nat. Carnation award Gamma Phi Beta, 1976. Mem. Houston Com. on Fgn. Rels., Japan Am. Soc., Houston Philos. Soc., Houston=Taipei Soc. (founding, pres. 1968-92). Republican. Episcopalian. E-mail: apratt7164@aol.com.

PRATT, BARBARA DAHL, nurse; b. Salt Lake City, July 27, 1939; d. Lester and Susie Mae (Peffer) Owens; m. Kenneth Warner Bloomquist (div.); children: DeLyle, Renel, Virgil, Cherie, Jodi, Denise, Shannan; stepchildren: Sheryl, Brenda; m. Ernest Elmer Pratt, Dec. 28, 1990. AS, No. Va. C.C., Annandale, 1980. RN, Va.; cert. CPR instr., first aide instr. Staff nurse Rockingham Hosp., Harrisonburg, Va., 1980-82, Washington Hosp. Ctr., 1982-84, Potomac Job Corps, Washington, 1984-86, Reston (Va.) Hosp. Ctr., 1986-89; supr. Cameron Glen Care Ctr., Reston, 1988-89, insvc. nursing instr., 1989, nursing instr. and insvc., asst. dir. nursing, 1989-90. Author children's books. Pres. Women's Ch. Orgn. Relief Soc., 1993-98. Mem. Va. Nurses ASsn. Mem. Ch. of Jesus Christ of Latter Day Saints.

PRATT, BILLY KENTON, police officer; b. Tampa, Fla., Nov. 27, 1948; s. Billy Paul and Vera (Parnell) P.; m. Vicki Lynn Throckmorton, Jan. 1, 1977; children: Angela Kristina, Billy Paul II. BS in Bus., Oklahoma City U., 1978; grad., FBI Computer Crime Investigation Sch., IRS Fin. Investigation Sch.; MPA, U. Okla., 1991. Office mgr. Lee Optical Co., Oklahoma City, 1968-72; police officer Police Dept. Oklahoma City, 1972-80, sr. police officer, 1980-82, detective, 1982-86, sgt., 1986-89, lt., 1989, capt., 1989—. Microcomputer cons. City of Oklahoma City, 1984—; computer security cons. Control Data Corp., Mpls., 1986; cert. govt. fin. mgr., 1993. Adviser police explorer post Boy Scouts Am., 1978; bd. dirs. Big Bros.-Big Sisters, 1989—. Mem. Internat. Assn. Chiefs of Police, Fraternal Order Police, Internat. City-County Mgrs. Assn., Govt. Fin. Officers Assn. Republican. Mem. Ch. of Christ. Avocations: music, golf, ice hockey. Office: Oklahoma City Police Dept 701 Colcord Dr Oklahoma City OK 73102-2205 E-mail: billy.pratt@ci.okc.ok.us.

PRATT, CHRISTINA CARVER, social work and women's studies educator; b. N.Y.C., Dec. 5, 1951; d. Harry S. and Frances Carver (Shaw) P.; 1 child, Cherish Marie. AAS, Rockland U., 1973; BA, Fairleigh Dickinson, 1975; MSW, Columbia U., 1976. Cons., educator Orange County Cmty. Mental Health, Gloshen, N.Y., 1976-80; prof. social work and gender studies Dominican Coll., Orangeburg, 1980—; prof. social work and women's studies NYU, N.Y.C., 1985—98. Exec. dir. Ptnrs. of Ams., Rockland, NY, 1987—97; tng. cons. Govt. of St. Lucia, 1987—93; commr. Coun. on Social Work Edn., Washington, 1990—93; del. NGO Forum-4th World Conf. on Women, 1995; trustee Green Meadow Waldorf Sch., NY, 1996—2000; bd. dirs. Hopf Enterprises, Englewood, NJ. Film maker (video documentaries) India: The Cultural Past, 1985, India: Rural Villages and Urban Villagers, 1986, Tunisia, 1990; editor Jour. Social Devel., 1987—; contbr. articles to profl. jours. Bd. dirs. Rockland Coalition for Freedom and Democracy, NY, 1995—97, Palisades Inst.; mem. com., del. N.Y.S. Liberal Party. Fulbright scholar, India, 1981, Pakistan, 1983; Malone Faculty fellow Nat. Coun. U.S./Arab Rels., Tunisia, 1989, Israel, Syria, Jordan and Palestine, 1991. Mem. NASW, NOW, AAUW, Amnesty Internat., Am. Adoption Congress. Buddhist. Avocations: jazz, opera, hiking, photography, cooking. Office: Dominican Coll 470 Western Hwy Orangeburg NY 10962-1210

PRATT, DANA JOSEPH, publishing consultant; b. Cambridge, Mass., Dec. 9, 1926; s. Carroll Cornelius and Marjory (Bates) P.; m. Therese Louis, July 14, 1957; children: Joseph Caldwell, Michael Louis, Benjamin Lyon B.Naval Sci., Tufts U., 1946, BA, 1948. Mgmt. trainee N.J. Bell Telephone Co., Newark, 1948-50; sales asst. Princeton U. Press, N.J., 1950-53; sales mgr. U. Ill. Press, Urbana, 1953-55; field cons. Franklin Book Programs, N.Y.C., 1955-59; staff assoc. Am. Book Pubs. Council, 1959-62; exec. sec. Assn. Am. Univ. Presses, 1962-66; asst. dir. Yale U. Press, New Haven, 1966-78; dir. pub. Library of Congress, Washington, 1978-93. Contbr. articles to profl. jours. Served as ensign USNR, comdg. officer PC 566, 1946-47 Recipient Award for Superior Svc. Libr. of Congress, 1993. Mem. Washington Book Pubs. (pres. 1984-85), Soc. for Scholarly Pub. (bd. dirs. 1982-86), Washington Map Soc., Washington Rare Book Group. Home and Office: 7514 Old Chester Rd Bethesda MD 20817-6163 E-mail: danajpratt@aol.com.

PRATT, DAVID TERRY, engineering consultant; b. Shelley, Idaho, Sept. 14, 1934; s. Eugene Francis and Bernice (Montague) P.; m. Marilyn Jean Thackston, Dec. 22, 1956; children: Douglas Montague, Elizabeth Joann, Brian Stephens. BSc in Mech. Engring., U. Wash., 1956; MSc, U. Calif., Berkeley, 1962, PhD, 1968. Asst. prof. marine engring. U.S. Naval Acad., Annapolis, Md., 1961-64; prof. mech. engring., asst. dean Wash. State U., Pullman, 1968-76; prof. mech. engring. U. Utah, Salt Lake City, 1976-78; prof., chmn. mech. engring. and applied mechanics U. Mich., Ann Arbor, 1978-81; prof., chmn. mech. engring. U. Wash., Seattle, 1981-86, prof. mech. engring., 1987-96, prof. emeritus; engring. cons. Rsch. dir. supercomputing Aerojet Propulsion Rsch. Inst., Sacramento, 1986-87. Author (with W.H. Heiser) Hypersonic Airbreathing Propulsion, 1994; editor (with L.D. Smoot) Combustion and Gasification of Pulverized Coal, 1976; contbr. articles to profl. jours. Served to 1st lt. USMC, 1956-60. NSF sci. faculty fellow, 1965-66; Fulbright-Hays sr. research fellow Imperial Coll., 1974-75; David Pierpont Gardner faculty fellow U. Utah, 1976 Fellow AIAA (assoc.; Summerfield award 1999); mem. ASME, Combustion Inst. Lutheran. E-mail: pratt@combustion.com.

PRATT, DIANE ADELE, talented and gifted education educator; b. Battle Creek, Mich., Oct. 24, 1951; d. John Robert and Kathleen Adele (Cooper) Dickert; m. Stephen Howard Pratt, Apr. 29, 1972; children: Eric Stephen, Elizabeth Adele. BS, Western Mich. U., 1972; MS in Edn., Buenta Vista U., 2000. Cert. elem. tchr., Ohio, Iowa, Mich., talented and gifted, Iowa. Elem. tchr. Berea (Ohio) Cmty. Schs., 1973-76; ednl. cons. Kolbe Products, Inc., Phoenix and Scottsdale, Ariz., 1982-84; tchr. Lemon Tree Nursery Sch., Battle Creek, 1985-88; elem. tchr. Ft. Dodge (Iowa) Cmty. Schs., 1976-78, middle sch. tchr., 1990—, team leader, 1994-97, tchr. talented and gifted, 1997—. Chearleading coach Ft. Dodge Sr. H.S., 1997-99, 2000-01, Pep Club advisor, 1997-99; exc. sec. Born Free Safari Club, Dodgen Industries, Humboldt, Iowa, 1988; advt. exec. Ft. Dodge Today mag., 1989-92; ednl. tutor, Battle Creek, Ft. Dodge, 1986-96; mem. adv. bd. Inst. for Instrn. Svcs., Battle Creek, 1984-88; dir., instr. Battle Creek Presch. Enrichment Program, 1984; chmn. Ft. Dodge Supr.'s Comty. Com. to Study K-8 Curriculum, 1988-89, facilitator K-3 human growth and devel. curriculum, 1989-92; mem. standing com. early childhood needs assessment com. Ft. Dodge Comty. Schs., 1989-95; mem. adv. bd., instr. Kids on Kampus Iowa Ctrl. C.C., Ft. Dodge, 1990-95; speaker State Conv. Childbirth Educators, Lansing, Mich., 1982; trustee Ft. Dodge Comty. Sch. Found. Bd., 1992-97, mem. talented and gifted selection com. Ft. Dodge Comty. Schs., 1993—, mem. promotion taskforce, 1998-99; mem. pub. rels. com. Ft. Dodge Comty. Sch. Dist., 1992-94, mem. ednl. outcomes standing com., 1993-94. Author, editor Headcase and various newsletters. Mem., past chmn. bd. Christian edn. 1st Bapt. Ch., Ft. Dodge, 1978-79, 89-96, music com., 1992-94, dir. children's choirs, 1988-90, mem. bell choir, 1990-91, ch. sch. supt. 1993-96, pastoral rels. com., 1997-99; membership chmn. Battle Creek Parents, 1981-83; neighborhood coord. mothers' march March of Dimes, Battle Creek, 1981-83; troop leader Lakota coun. Girl Scouts U.S., 1988-90; pres. La Mora Park PTA, 1985-87, Phillips Mid Sch. PTA, Ft. Dodge, 1990-91; bd. dirs. Main Stage Players, jr. theater, Ft. Dodge, 1990-91; sec., pres. Jr. Women's Club, Ft. Dodge, 1977-80; mem. kickoff com. United Way, 1991, Curriculum Instn. Adv. Coun., 2001-, Insvc. Adv. Com.; active Ft. Dodge Athletic Booster Club, 1994-98; tchr. mentor, 2001-. Recipient Mem. of Yr. award La Mora Park PTA, 1987, Iowa Talented and Gifted Rsch. award, 2000, David Belin Excellence in Tchg. award, 2000. Mem. NEA, ASCD, AAUW (sec., pres. Battle Creek br. 1986-88), PEO (N.J. chpt., Ft. Dodge chpt. 1990-94), Iowa Edn. Assn., Ft. Dodge Edn. Assn., Iowa Assn. Middle Level Educators, Iowa Assn. for Talented and Gifted, Study Club (treas. 1999—, pres. 2000—), Nat. Assn. Gifted Children Presbyterian. Avocations: educational research, cross-country skiing. Home: 1851 9th Ave N Fort Dodge IA 50501

PRATT, DONALD GEORGE, physician; b. Higgins, Tex., Oct. 19, 1946; s. George Horace and Esta Vici (Barker) P. BS in Biomed. Sci., West Tex. State U., 1970; MD, U. Tex., Galveston, 1974. Diplomate Am. Bd. Family Practice, Am. Bd. Radiology (Radiation Oncology). Intern Scott & White Meml. Hosp., Temple, Tex., 1974-75, resident in gen. surgery and pathology, 1975-77, physician, 1979-83; resident in family practice McLennan County Med. Edn. and Rsch. Found., Waco, 1977-79; physician Family Practice Assocs., El Paso, 1983; owner, pvt. contractor Minor Emergency Ctrs., Amarillo, 1983-85; resident in radiation therapy U. Tex., Galveston, 1985-88; ptnr. Cons. in Radiation Oncology, P.A., Amarillo, 1988—, pres., 1994—; dir. dept. radiation oncology Harrington Cancer Ctr., 1994—; pres. Cons. in Radiation Oncology, 1994—; pres. staff, bd. dirs. Harrington Cancer Ctr., 1995-99; prin. investigator Radiation Oncology Group, 1988-95; pres. of staff Harrington Cancer Ctr., 1995-99—. Mem. AMA, Am. Soc. Therapeutic Radiology and Oncology, Am. Acad. Family Physicians, Tex. Med. Assn., Potter/Randall County Med. Soc., Tex. Radiol. Soc. Home: 261 S Timbercreek Dr Amarillo TX 79118-3751 Office: Cons Radiation Oncology PA 1600 Coulter Dr Ste 402 Amarillo TX 79106-1721

PRATT, DREXDAL RAY, medical services administrator; b. King, N.C., June 12, 1954; s. Dilmer Ray and Ineida Fulk Pratt; m. Sheree Speas, June 2, 2000; children: Tracy Mikels, Dwayne. Cert. pub. mgr., N.C. State U., 2001. Cert. paramedic. Emergency med. svcs. mgr. N.C. Office of Emergency Med. Svcs., Raleigh, 1994-99, chief, 1999—. Dir. Stokes County Emergency Med. Svcs., Danbury, N.C., 1983-87. Contbr.: (computer-aided dispatch sys.) Stokes County CAD System, 1986 (Innovative award Nat. Assn. County Commrs. 1987). Mem. N.C. Jayees, King, N.C., 1974-78. Baptist. Avocations: travel, fishing. Home: 208 Deep Pool Ct Benson NC 27504 Office: NC Office Emergency Med Svcs 2707 Mail Service Ctr Raleigh NC 27699-2707 Office Fax: 919-733-7021. E-mail: drexdalpratt@msn.com.

PRATT, ELIZABETH HAYES, artist, art educator; b. Dayton, Ohio, Sept. 13, 1927; d. Charles Stevens and Florence Wayne Hayes; m. Abner Kingman Pratt, June 20, 1949; children: Sarah Lyon, George S.W., David Wayne. Student, Dayton Art Inst., 1944-45; BA in Fine Arts, Coll. of William and Mary, Williamsburg, Va., 1949. Instr. art U.S. Air Base, Kenitra, Morocco, 1957-59; contbg. painter Spectrum Gallery, Georgetown, D.C., 1966-78, gallery dir., 1975-76; instr. watercolor Creative Arts Ctr., Chatham, Mass., 1981-88, 90-94, Cape Mus. Fine Arts, Den, 1990-92, Truro (Mass.) Ctr. for Arts, 1983—. Advisor art curriculum for Montgomery County Schs., Bethesda, Md., 1969—; judge 15 regional exhbns., 1980-99. Illustrator: What Should I Do?, 1997; 50 one-man shows in various galleries and museums throughout U.S., 1951-99, including Spectrum Gallery, Georgetown, 1966-78, Copley Soc. Boston, 1978, 86, The Art Complex Mus., Duxbury, Mass., 1979, The Conservatory of Art and Music, Cape Cod, 1986, Stonehill Coll., Easton, Mass., 1986, Radford Coll., Roanoke, Va., 1988, The Ethel Putterman Gallery, Cape Cod, 1981-82, New Horisons Gallery, Cape Cod, 1990-92, Cummaquid Fine Arts, 1994-99, Addison Gallery, Cape Cod, 1998; group shows include North Am. Open, Boston, 1994, 96, Audubon Artists Ann., N.Y.C., 1994-99, numerous nat. watercolor exhbns., others; work collected in permanents exhbns. at Internat. Monetary Fund, Washington, U.S. Cath. Conf., Dir. of the CIA/D.C., Sperry Univac, D.C., Superior Ct. of D.C., Nat. Assn. of Mfrs., D.C., Citibank, N.Y., First Nat. Bank of Boston, Stonehill Coll., The Cape Mus. of Fine Arts; works pub. in The Art of Watercolor, 1994, rev. edit. 1999, The Best of Watercolor, 1995, Vol. 3, 1999, Painting Composition, 1997, People-Places-Flowers, 1996, Watercolor Expressions, 1999, others. Mem. Audubon Artists, Copley Soc. (6 awards 1979-99, Copley Master status 1990), Acad. Artists, Cape Cod Art Assn. (25 awards 1979-99), New Eng. Watercolor Soc. Episcopalian. Avocations: swimming, canoeing, world travel. Home: PO Box 238 180 Mill Rd Eastham MA 02642-2471

PRATT, GEORGE BYINGTON, III, pediatric radiologist; b. Goshen, Ind., Sept. 6, 1936; s. George Byington and Estelle (Hudson) P.; m. Patricia Mae Hammer, June 22, 1957 (div. 1970); children: George B. IV, Pamela; m. Susan Pettijohn, June 23, 1972; 1 child, Lisa Susan. BA, DePauw U., 1958; MD, Northwestern U., 1962; JD, Ind. U., 1978. Diplomate Am. Bd. Radiology. Pediatric radiologist Radiologic Specialists of Ind., Indpls., 1968-93; pvt. practice radiologist, 1993—. Med. adv. Cook Imaging, Bloomington, Ind., 1996—2002. Contbr. articles to profl. jours. Pres. Marion City Child Abuse and Neglect Coun., Indpls., 1984—86; bd. dirs. Family Support Ct., 1984—93, adv. com., 1993—2000; bd. dirs. Cmty. Found. Boone County, 1991—2001, v.p., 1995—2001, Zionsville (Ind.) Pk. and Recreation Bd., 1978—93, pres., 1994—95, Zionsville Little League, 1985—93; bd. dirs. ULEN C.C., 1991—, Wawasee Area Conservancy, 1999—. Capt. USAF, 1963—65. Fellow Am. Coll. Legal Medicine; mem. AMA, Am. Coll. Radiology, Radiol. Soc. N.Am., Ind. State Med. Assn. (3d place award Med. Exhibit 1970), Am. Acad. Pediatrics (3d place 1984), Ind. U. Alumni Club Boone County (bd. dirs.), Masons, Rotary, (treas. Zionsville chpt. 1994-95, sec. 1995-96, pres. 1997-98, dist. chair gift of life 1998—, asst. dist. gov. 2002-). Avocations: snow and water skiing, sailing. Home: 9015 Crystal Lake Dr Indianapolis IN 46240-6414 E-mail: pratts@qserve.net.

PRATT, GEORGE CHENEY, law educator, retired federal judge; b. Corning, N.Y., May 22, 1928; s. George Wollage and Muriel (Cheney) Pratt; m. Carol June Hoffman, Aug. 16, 1952; children: George W., Lise M., Marcia Pratt Burke, William T. BA, Yale U., 1950, JD, 1953. Bar: N.Y. 1953, U.S. Supreme Ct. 1964, U.S. Ct. Appeals 1974. Law clk. to Charles W. Froessel (Judge of N.Y. Ct. Appeals), 1953—55; assoc. then ptnr. Sprague & Stern, Mineola, NY, 1956—60; ptnr. Andromidas, Pratt & Pitcher, 1960—65, Pratt, Caemmerer & Cleary, Mineola, 1965—75; partner Farrell, Fritz, Pratt, Caemmerer & Cleary, 1975—76; judge U.S. Dist. Ct. (Ea. Dist. of N.Y.), 1976—82, U.S. Cir. Ct. Appeals for 2d cir. (Uniondale), NY, 1982—93; sr. circ. judge U.S. Cir. of Appeals for 2d Cir., 1993—95; counsel Parnon & Pratt L.L.P., N.Y.C., 1995—2000, Farrell Fritz PC, 2001—. Prof. Touro Law Sch.,

Huntington, NY, 1993—. Mem.: ATLA, ABA, Soc. Am. Law Tchrs., Nassau County Bar Assn., N.Y. State Bar Assn. United Ch. Of Christ. Office: Touro Law Ctr 300 Nassau Rd Huntington NY 11743-4342 E-mail: gpratt@farrellfritz.com.

PRATT, GEORGE JANES, JR. psychologist, author; b. Mpls., May 3, 1948; s. George Janes and Sally Elvina (Hanson) P.; m. Vonda Pratt; 1 child, Whitney Beth. BA cum laude, U. Minn., 1970, MA, 1973; PhD with spl. commendation, Calif. Sch. Profl. Psychology, San Diego, 1976. Diplomate Am. Bd. Med. Psychotherapists, Am. Acad. Pain Mgmt., Am. Coll. Forensic Examiners; lic. psychologist, Calif., 1976. Psychology trainee Ctr. for Behavior Modification, Mpls., 1971-72, U.Minn. Student Counseling Bur., 1972-73; predoctoral clin. psychology intern San Bernardino County (Calif.) Mental Health Svcs., 1973-74, San Diego County Mental Health Services, 1974-76; mem. staff San Louis Rey Hosp., 1977-78; postdoctoral clin. psychology intern Mesa Vista Hosp., San Diego, 1976; clin psychologist, dir. Psychology and Cons. Assocs. of San Diego, 1976-90; chmn. Psychology and Cons. Assocs. Press, 1977-94. Bd. dirs. Optimax, Inc., 1985-94; pres. George Pratt Ph.D., Psychol. Corp., 1979—; chmn. Pratt, Korn & Assocs., Inc., 1984-94; mem. staff Scripps Meml. Hosp., La Jolla, Calif., 1986—, chmn. psychology, 1993-95, 2000—; founder La Jolla Profl. Workshops, 1977-81; clin. psychologist El Camino Psychology Ctr., San Clemente, Calif., 1977-78; grad. teaching asst. U. Minn. Psychology and Family Studies divsn., 1971; teaching assoc. U. Minn. Psychology and Family Studies divsn., Mpls., 1972-73; instr. U. Minn. Extension divsn., Mpls., 1971-73; faculty Calif. Sch. Profl. Psychology, 1974-83, San Diego Evening Coll., 1975-77, Nat. U., 1978-79, Chapman Coll., 1978, San Diego State U., 1979-80; vis. prof. Pepperdine U., L.A., 1976-78; cons. U. Calif. at San Diego Med. Sch., 1976-78, also instr. univ., 1978—; psychology chmn. Workshops in Clin. Hypnosis, 1980-84; cons. Calif. Health Dept., 1974, Naval Regional Med. Ctr., 1978-82, ABC-TV; also speaker. Author: Sensory/Progressive Relaxation, 1979, Effective Stress Management, 1979, A Clinical Hypnosis Primer, 1984, 88, Clinical Hypnosis: Techniques and Applications, 1985, Rx for Stress, 1994; co-author: Hyper-Performance, 1987, Release Your Business Potential, 1988, Instant Emotional Healing, 2000, Emotional Self-Management, 2000; contbr.: Hypnosis: Questions and Answers, 1986, Handbook for Hypnotic Suggestions and Metaphors, 1990, Imagery in Sports and Physical Performance, 1994. With USAR, 1970-76. Fellow Am. Soc. Clin. Hypnosis (cert., approved cons.); mem. Am. Psychological Assn., Nat. Register of Health Svc. Providers in Psychology, Internat. Soc. Hypnosis, Am. Assn. Sex Educators, Counselors and Therapists (cert.), San Diego Soc. Sex. Therapy and Edn. (past pres.), San Diego Soc. Clin. Hypnosis (past pres.), San Diego Psychol. Assn., Soc. Clin. and Exptl. Hypnosis, U. Minn. Alumni Assn., Beta Theta Pi. Office: Scripps Meml Hosp Campus 9834 Genesee Ave Ste 321 La Jolla CA 92037-1216

PRATT, HARRY DAVIS, retired entomologist; b. North Adams, Mass., Apr. 13, 1915; s. Harry Edward and Ethel Mae (Davis) P.; m. Caroline Georgine Kreiss, Apr. 13, 1944 (dec. May 1951); children: Harry Davis Jr., Katherine Maria Pratt Garrison, George Kreiss; m. Dora Belle Ford, Nov. 29, 1952 (dec. July 1998). BS, Mass. State Coll., 1936, MS, 1938; PhD, U. Minn., St. Paul, 1941. Registered profl. entomologist. Asst. entomologist USPHS Malaria Control War Areas, San Juan, P.R., 1942-46; chief med. entomol. lab. USPHS Communicable Disease Ctr., Atlanta, 1946-53, chief insect rodent tr., 1953-63, chief Aedes aegypti control tng., 1964-68; chief insect rodent control tng. Environ. Control Agy., 1968-72; cons., tchr., writer, 1972—. Spl. cons. Econ. Coop. Administrn., Saigon, Vietnam, 1950, WHO, Geneva, 1966, Kuala Lumpur, Malaysia, 1969. Fellow Entomol. Soc. Am. (life); mem. Am. Mosquito Control Assn. (pres. 1967), Entol. Soc. Washington, Ga. Entomol. Soc. Mem. Christian Ch. (Disciples Of Christ). Home: 879 Glen Arden Way NE Atlanta GA 30306-3407 E-mail: hdpsr@juno.com.

PRATT, JAMES NORWOOD, scholarly writer; b. Winston Salem, N.C., Mar. 27, 1942; s. Eugene Roberdeaux Pratt and Helen Davis; m. Charlotte Aleta Saunders, May 1, 1979 (div. Jan. 1992); children: John Norwood Davis, Rowell Aleister Sterling, Amanda deStefano. BA, U. N.C., 1965. Expert on tea and its role in economic and cultural history in U.S., Asia, and Europe. Author: The Wine Bibber's Bible, 1972, The Tea Lover's Treasury, 1982, JNP's New Tea Lover's Treasury, 2000, Art of Tea, 2001. Pres. North Beach Neighbors Assn., San Francisco, 1997-99. Mem. Am. Premium Tea Inst. (founder), Darjeeling Planters Assn., Imperial Tea Court (hon. dir. 1993—), Tea Soc. (founder). Episcopalian. Avocation: travel. Home and Office: 828 Green St San Francisco CA 94133 E-mail: norwood@ossesso.com.

PRATT, JOHN EDWARD, law educator; b. Key West, Fla., June 29, 1945; s. Lloyd Edward and Marilyn June (Havercamp) P.; m. Sharon Louise Brown, Aug. 31, 1968; 1 child, Randolph Winfield. BA, So. Meth. U., 1967, JD, 1974. Bar: Tex. 1974, U.S. Dist. Ct. (no. dist.) Tex. 1975. Ptnr. Schuerenberg, Grimes & Pratt, Mesquite, Tex., 1974-77; asst. city atty. City of Dallas, 1978-80; mem. faculty Cedar Valley Coll., Lancaster, Tex., 1981—. Pres. Friends of Mesquite Pub. Libr., Tex., 1975-77; del. Dem. State Conv., Houston, 1988, 98; pres. Ponderosa Estates Homeowners Assn., 1986-96. Served to lt. USNR, 1967-71. Mem. State Bar Tex., Acad. Legal Studies in Bus., Tex. Jr. Coll. Tchrs. Assn., Cedar Valley Coll. Faculty Assn. (pres. 1983-85, 93-95, 97-99), ACLU, Mensa Internat., NAACP. Democrat. Home: 1032 Majors Dr Mesquite TX 75149-5817 Office: Cedar Valley Coll 3030 N Dallas Ave Lancaster TX 75134-3705

PRATT, JOHN JACKSON, property manager, retired telephone installer; b. Benton Harbor, Mich., July 25, 1946; s. Harry Adelbert Pratt and Edith Jane Monteverde; m. Binh-An Thi Pham; children: Joseph, Harold. AA, N.Mex. Mil. Inst., 1966. Lic. real estate salesperson, Calif. Assn. Realtors. Lineman, cable splicer installer, repairman Pacific Bell, Riverside, Calif., 1973-2000; property mgr. John J. Pratt Properties, 1978—; mem. grower Sunkist Coop. Growers, 1984—. With USAF, 1967-71, res. ret., 1994. Mem. Apt. Assn. of Greater Inland Empire, Comms. Workers of Am. (local 9400), Am. Legion (post 289). Avocation: history studies especially World War II and general world history. Home: PO Box 70122 Riverside CA 92513-0122 Office: JJP Properties 7929 Bolton Ave Riverside CA 92503-3125 E-mail: johnj.pratt@yahoo.com.

PRATT, JOHN PATRICK, lawyer; b. Managua, Nicaragua, Nov. 19, 1967; s. Alfred Sidney Pratt and Thelma Reyes; 1 child, Patrick Alexander. BA in Philosophy, Fla. State U., 1994; JD, Tulane U., 1997. Bar: Fla. 1998, D.C. 1999, U.S. Dist. Ct. (so. dist.) Fla. 1998, U.S. Ct. Appeals (11th cir.) 1998, U.S. Supreme Ct. 2001, U.S. Ct. Appeals (9th cir.) 2002. Law clk. Office of Dist. Counsel IRS, St. Paul, 1995; law clk. Office of Asst. Chief Counsel U.S. Customs Svc., New Orleans, 1996-97; assoc. Zyne, Saleeby & Saleh, P.A., Miami, 1997-98, Montiel Davis & Woodward Kimber, P.A., Miami, 1998-2000, Leaf & Assocs., P.A., Miami, 2000-01, Kurzban, Kurzban, Weinger & Tetzeli, P.A., 2001—. Cons. Greater Miami Chamber, Beacon Coun., Miami, Univision. Mem. ABA, ATLA, Am. Immigration Lawyers Assn., Hispanic Nat. Bar Assn., Dade County Bar Assn., Greater Miami C. of C., Beacon Coun. Roman Catholic. Avocations: reading, tennis. E-mail: jpatrickpratt@aol.com.

PRATT, JOHN WINSOR, statistics educator; b. Boston, Sept. 11, 1931; s. Frederic Wolsey and Theresa (Winsor) P.; m. Joy A. Wilmunen, Nov. 15, 1958; children: Maria Theresa Winsor Wright, Samuel Frederick Wolsey. AB, Princeton U., 1952; PhD, Stanford U., 1956; MA (hon.), Harvard U., 1966. Rsch. assoc. U. Chgo., 1955-57; mem. faculty Harvard U., Cambridge, Mass., 1957-98, prof. bus. adminstrn., 1966-98, prof. emeritus, 1998—. Dir. Social Sci. Rsch. Coun., 1971-76; vis. rsch. prof. Kyoto U., Japan, 1972-73; vis. lectr. Keio U. Bus. Sch., Japan, 1982; Yamaichi vis. prof. fin. Tokyo U., 1989-90; chmn. study group on environment. monitoring NRC, 1975-77, chmn. panel on decennial census methodology NRC, 1983-87, mem. com. nat. stats., 1982-88. Co-author: Introduction to Statistical Decision Theory, 1965, rev. edit., 1995, Social Experimentation: A Method for Planning and Evaluating Social Intervention, 1974, Concepts of Nonparametric Theory, 1981; editor: Statistical and Mathematical Aspects of Pollution Problems, 1974; co-editor: Principals and Agents: The Structure of Business, 1985. Trustee Middlesex Sch., Concord, Mass., 1964-67. Recipient Frank P. Ramsey medal, 1999, Internat. prize for ins. scis. INA-Acad. Nat. dei Lincei, 2000; Guggenheim fellow, 1971. Fellow AAAS (chmn. sect. U. 1977), Am. Statis. Assn. (editor jour. 1965-69, chmn. bus. and econs. sect. 1983), Inst. Math. Stats., Econometric Soc., Am. Acad. Arts and Scis.; mem. Internat. Statis. Inst., Bernoulli Soc. Math. Stats. and Probability, Math. Assn. Am. Home: 2 Gray Gdns E Cambridge MA 02138-1402 E-mail: jpratt@hbs.edu.

PRATT, JOSEPH HYDE, JR. surgeon; b. Chapel Hill, N.C., Mar. 9, 1911; s. Joseph Hyde and Mary (Bayley) P.; m. Hazel Housman, Dec. 11, 1943; children: Judith Housman, Lisa Mary, Joseph Hyde. AB, U. N.C., 1933; MD, Harvrad U., 1937; MS, U. Minn., 1947. Diplomate Am. Bd. Surgery, Am. Bd. Ob-gyn. Intern Boston City Hosp., 1938-39; fellow surgery Mayo Found., Rochester, Minn., 1940-43; mem. staff Mayo Clinic, 1943—, head sect. in surgery, 1945-77, sr. gynecol. surgeon, 1958—. Prof. clin. surgery Mayo Grad. Sch. Medicine U. Minn., 1963—; prof. surgery Mayo Med. Sch., 1973—. Contbr. articles to med. jours. Mem. ACS (bd. govs. 1966-71, bd. regents 1971-80), AMA, ACOG, Ctrl. Assn. Ob-Gyn., Minn. Ob-Gyn. Soc., Western Surg. Assn., soc. Vaginal Surgeons (pres. 1979-80), Soc. Pelvic Surgeons (pres. 1968), So. Surg. Assn., Ob-Gyn. Travel Club (pres. 1993—), Sigma Xi, Nu Sigma Nu. Republican. Episcopalian. Home: 1159 Plummer Cir SW Rochester MN 55902-2035 Office: 200 1st St SW Rochester MN 55905-0001

PRATT, KATHERINE MERRICK, environmental consulting company executive; b. Alexandria, Egypt, July 4, 1951; d. Theodore and Bettie (Curland) R.; m. Harry Kenneth Todd (div.); 1 child, Kirsten Todd Pratt. BBA in Mgmt. Systems, U. Iowa, 1980; postgrad., U. Tex., 1985-87. Program data mgr. Rockwell Internat., Dallas, 1981-85; support coord. GTE Govt. Systems, Taunton, Mass., 1987-89, support engr., 1989-93; pres. Enviro-Logistics Inc., Harwood, Md., 1993—; sole Internat. Soc. Logistics. Recipient Rear Admiral Bernard Eccles award, 1997, Cert. Commendation for Superior Performance as Dist. Dir., 1997. Mem. Soc. Logistics Engrs. (officer, mem. standing com. environ. applications, bd. dirs. New Eng. dist. 1996, dir. New Eng. dist., nat. chpt. newsletter judge), U.S. Pony Club (Ctrl. New Eng. championship chmn., nat. recognition for outstanding contbn. 1997). Avocations: sailing, reading, equitation. Office: Enviro-Logistics Inc PO Box 723 West River MD 20778-0723 E-mail: envirolog@earthlink.net.

PRATT, LAWRENCE ARTHUR, thoracic surgeon, foreign service officer; b. Paris, Dec. 20, 1907; s. Luther F. and Katherine (Kaufman) P.; m. Mai Thi NgocSuong, May 7, 1974; children: Elizabeth, Lawrie Porter, D. Jane. BS, Wayne State U., 1930, MB, MA, MD, 1934, MEd, 1960; LL.B., Woodrow Wilson Coll. Law, Atlanta, 1943. Diplomate Am. Bd. Surgery, Am. Bd. Thoracic Surgery. Intern Grace Hosp., 1934-35; practice thoracic surgery Detroit, 1935-41, 46-63; attending thoracic surgeon Grace, Detroit Meml. hosps.; courtesy staff St. John's Hosp.; cons. thoracic surgeon Holy Cross, Highland Park Gen. hosps., Detroit; U.S. fgn. svc. officer, 1963—; vis. prof. medicine U. Saigon, Vietnam, 1963-75; med. dir. Urban Health Clinic of Orange County, Calif., 1981—; pres., CEO, chmn. Seven Seas Devel. Corp., 1995—. Exec. v.p. Am. Fedn. Med. Ctrs., Inc., 1953-54; chief med. dental edn. divsn. AID/PH, Vietnam; cons. Vietnam Min. Edn., 1974-75; assoc. dean Minh Duc. Med. Sch., Saigon, 1974-75; cons. HEW, 1975-77; spl. asst. HEW (Divsn. Medicine Bur. Health Manpower), 1976; cons., mem. White House Task Force Internat. Health Policy, 1977; mem. World Bank Task Force Internat. Health Policy and Manpower, 1977, U.S. Pub. Health Assn.; leader design team Health Care Program, Mauritania, West Africa, 1978; physician in charge Refugee Transit Camps, Malaysia, 1980; med. dir. Urban Health Clinic, Orange County, Calif., 1981-84, Spl. Disease Specialist 1981—; cons. physician overseas ops. World Cons., Irvine, Calif., 1984-85; cons. to min. health, Rabat, Morocco, 1986; sr. cons. World Care Inc., 1988—; mem. Nat. Coun. for Internat. Health, 1988—. Author: Total Development for Survival, 1986. Bd. dirs. Sun Yet Middle Sch., Zhongshan, Quandong Province, People's Republic of China, 1986-92; chmn. bd. 100 For 1 Systems Corp., 1986-92. Lt. col., M.C. AUS, 1937-46. Active U.S-Mexican Border Health Assn., 1986—. Recipient Unit citation; medal of Culture and Edn.; medal of Merit Vietnam). Fellow ACS (life), Am. Coll. Chest Physicians; mem. AMA, Mich. Med. Soc., Wayne County Med. Soc., Internat. Bronchoesophagol. Assn. (founder), Am. Bronchoesophagol. Assn., 4th Aux. Surg. Group Assn. (pres. 1955-56), Nat. Coun. on Internat. Health, U.S. Pub. Health Assn., Wayne State U. Med. Alumni Assn. (pres. 1956-57), Ga. Bar Assn., Ret. Officers Assn. Clubs: Essex Cricket (Eng.); Lambs (N.Y.C.); Scarab (Detroit), Detroit Skating (Detroit); Grosse Pointe Yacht, Grosse Pointe Hunt, Am. Radio Relay League, El Cajon (Calif.) Radio. Office: Seven Seas Devel Corp 2302 N Lowell Ln Santa Ana CA 92706-1932 Office Fax: 714-541-1717. E-mail: lpratt_2001@yahoo.com.

PRATT, LEIGHTON CALVIN, state legislator; b. Hartford, Conn., Apr. 23, 1923; s. Calvin and Jessie (White) P.; m. Sally Burgess, Oct. 21, 1961; children: Randall Leighton, Bruce Charles. BS, U. Vt., 1951; MS, U. R.I., 1953. Plant pathologist Vt. Dept. Agr., Montpelier, 1952-62; tchr. sci. Cabot (Vt.) H.S. and J. H.S., 1962-65; tchr. biology, asst. prin. Newport (Vt.) H.S., 1965-67; tchr. biology North Country Union H.S., Newport, 1967-79; Coos agrl. ext. agt. U. N.H., Durham, 1969-88, prof. emeritus ext. edn., 1988—; mem. N.H. Ho. of Reps., Concord, 1991—. Named hon. state farmer Future Farmers Am., 1986. Mem. Rotary (dir. exch. to Brazil dist. 1986, pres. Lancaster, N.H.), Epsilon Sigma Phi. Republican. Congregationalist. Avocations: travel, gardening. Home: 63 Water St Lancaster NH 03584-3129

PRATT, LINDA, reading educator; b. Mass., May 28, 1948; BA, U. Mass., 1970, MEd, 1975, EDd, 1978. Cert. elem. edn., reading specialist, reading supr. Prof., exec. dir. edn. dept. Elmira (N.Y.) Coll.; prof. Gonzaga U., Spokane, Wash.; insvc. tchr. U. Mass., Amherst; reading specialist Southwick (Mass.) Pub. Sch. System. Author: (with J. Beaty) Transcultural Children's Literature, 1999, Early Literacy in Preschools- 2nd Kindergarten, 2003. Mem. IRA, NCTE, Nat. Reading Conf., Kappa Delta Pi, Phi Delta Kappa, Kappa Delta Gamma. Office: Elmira Coll Elmira NY 14901

PRATT, MARK ERNEST, retired mechanical engineer; b. Jackhorn, Ky., Nov. 22, 1939; s. James Corbit and Anna Marie (Johnson) P.; m. Yvonne Rose, Sept. 13, 1958; children: Mark Ernest Jr., Mary Yvonne, Bobby Lee, James Paul. Student, I.C.S. Ctr., Scranton, Pa., 1983. Registered profl. engr., Fla. Engr. Mercy Hosp., Miami, Fla., 1965-70; chief engr. Palmetto Gen. Hosp., Hialeah, 1970-72, Osteo. Gen. Hosp., North Miami Beach, 1972-77; owner, operator N. Am. Van Lines, Ft. Wayne, Ind., 1977-78; dir. plant ops. Internat. Hosp., Miami, 1978-79, Cypress Hosp., Pompano Beach, Fla., 1979-81, Johnston Meml. Hosp., Abingdon, Va., 1981-87, North Ridge Med. Ctr., Ft. Lauderdale, Fla., 1988-90; adminstrv. dir. plant ops. St. Jude Med. Ctr., Kenner, La., 1990-91; mechanic Bristol (Va.) Compressors, 1991-94; bldg. and grounds supt., dept. corrections, divsn. instl. svcs. Marion (Va.) Correctional Treatment Ctr., 1994-2001. With U.S. Army, 1955-56. Mem. Am. Soc. Hosp. Engrs., Nat. Fire Protection Assn., Fla. Hosp. Engrs. Assn., Nat. Assn. Power Engrs. (instr. 1980-81, chpt. pres. 1980-81). Baptist. Avocations: restoring classic cars, fishing, hunting, playing bass guitar in gospel quartet, playing stand up bass with a Bluegrass group. Home: 9613 Pratt Ln Abingdon VA 24210-2357

PRATT, MICHAEL FRANCIS, physician and surgeon, otolaryngologist; b. Washington, Dec. 14, 1950; s. James William and Eleanor Mary (LeVangie) P.; 1 child, James Michael. BS, U. Md., 1972; MD, U. Md., Balt., 1980. Diplomate Am. Bd. Otolaryngology. Intern Naval Hosp., San Diego, 1980-81, resident in otolaryngology, 1982-86; instr. George Washington U., Washington, 1974-76; from clin. instr. to asst. prof. Med. U. S.C., 1987-89; asst. prof. Ea. Va. Med. Sch., Norfolk, 1989-94, assoc. prof., 1994-96, dir. residency tng., 1989-96, vice chair dept. otolaryngology/head and neck surgery, 1994-95. Editl. reviewer The Laryngoscope Jour., 1994—, Head and Neck Jour., 1994—; contbr. numerous articles to profl. jours.; lyricist In Memorium, 1992; poet: Through the Hourglass, 1996. Bd. dirs. Va. ProMusica, Norfolk, 1991-93; mem. planning com. DePaul Charity Golf Com., Norfolk, 1990-95. Decorated Navy Commendation medal with gold star, Navy Achievement medal with gold star. Fellow ACS, Am. Acad. Facial Plastic and Reconstructive Surgery (Shuster award 1986), Am. Laryngol., Rhinol. and Otol. Soc. (Fowler award 1995), Am. Soc. Head and Neck Surgery, Am. Acad. Otolaryngology/Head and Neck Surgery; mem. Soc. Univ. Otolaryngoly/Head and Neck Surgery, Va. Soc. Otolarynology (bd. dirs. 1994-96). Avocations: golf, running, skiing, tennis, composing poetry and music. Office: Woodstock Ear Nose and Throat Ste 235 203 Woodpark Pl Woodstock GA 30188

PRATT, MICHAEL GERARD, finance educator; b. Erie, Pa., Oct. 8, 1965; s. David Arthur Pratt, Judith Ann Nedresky; m. Trudy Lynette Good; children: Lucas. BA, U. Dayton, 1988; MA, U. Mich., 1990, PhD, 1994. Asst. prof. U. Ill., Champaign, Ill., 1994—2001, assoc. prof., 2001—. Bd. pres. Ten Thousand Villages Champaign, Ill., 2000—. Contbr. author Media Selection and Identification in Distributed Groups, 2000, Owning Up or Opting Out: The Role of Identities and Emotions in Issue Ownership, 2000, Ambivalent Feelings in Organizational Relationships, 2000, Social Identity Dynamics in Modern Organizations, 2001, Symbols as a Language of Organizational Relationships , 2001; contbr. articles. Big Brother, sr. ptnr. CHASI, Champaign, 1995—2002. Mem.: Am. Psychol. Soc., Acad. Mgmt.

PRATT, MINNIE BRUCE, writer, educator; b. Selma, Ala., Sept. 12, 1946; d. William Luther Jr. and Virginia Earl (Brown) P.; m. Marvin Eugene Weaver II, Dec. 19, 1966 (div. Nov. 1976); children: Ransom Jones Weaver, Benjamin Carr Weaver; life ptnr.: Leslie Feinberg, July 31, 1992. BA with honors, U. Ala., 1968; PhD in English Lit., U. N.C., 1979. Lectr. Fayetteville (N.C.) State U., 1975-80; asst. prof. Shaw U., Raleigh, N.C., 1980-82; adj. lectr. Women's Studies Program, George Washington U., Washington, 1984-88; adj. lectr., vis. asst. prof. Women's Studies Program, U. Md., College Park, 1984-93; grad. faculty The Union Inst., Cin., 1990—; Jane Watson Irwin chair in women's studies Hamilton Coll. Writer-in-residence The Cmty. Writers' Project, Syracuse, N.Y., 1988, The Lit. Festival at St. Mary's Coll., St. Mary's City, Md., 1999, Nat. YMCA Writers Voice Program, N.Y.C., 2000. Author: The Sound of One Fork, 1981, Yours In Struggle: Three Feminist Perspectives on Anti-Semitism and Racism, 1984, We Say We Love Each Other, 1985, Crime Against Nature, 1990 (Lamont Poetry selection of Acad. Am. Poets 1990, ALA Gay and Lesbian Book award for lit. 1991), Rebellion: Essays 1980-1991, 1992 (Outstanding Book award Gustavus Myers Ctr. for Study of Human Rights in US 1992), S/HE, 1995, Walking Back Up Depot Street, 1999 (Best Gay and Lesbian Book of Yr., ForeWord: Mag. of Ind. Bookstores and Booksellers 1999); mem. editl. collective Feminary: A Feminist Jour. for the South, Emphasizing Lesbian Visions, 1978-83. Fulbright fellow, 1968, Woodrow Wilson fellow, 1968, NDEA fellow, 1968; recipient Creative Writing fellowship in poetry Nat. Endowment for Arts, 1990, Lillian Hellman-Dashiell Hammett award The Fund for Free Expression, 1991 Ind. grant for lit. DC. Commn. on Arts, 1992, Ind. Artist grant Puffin Found., 1994, Larry Levis award for poetry Prairie Schooner mag., 1999, Ind. Artist award Ludwig Vogelstein Found., 2000; named one of Top 31 Alumnae, 1892-1992, XXXI Women's Leadership Hon., U. Ala., 1992. Mem. Poetry Soc. Am. (judge Celia B. Wagner Award 1992), Nat. Writers Union, Southerners on New Ground, Phi Beta Kappa. Office: PO Box 8212 Jersey City NJ 07308 Fax: 201-795-3208. E-mail: mbpratt@earthlink.net.

PRATT, MURRAY LESTER, collaborative commerce specialist; b. Mt. Holly, N.J., Mar. 11, 1956; 8. John N. and Mildred E. P.; m. Sharon Louise Busby, Aug. 13, 1988; children: Kevin Harrison, Brian Gavel, Melissa Anne, Heather Marie. BS in Indsl. Engring., Northwestern U., 1976; MS in Computer Sci., Ill. Inst. Tech., Chgo., 1983. Systems analyst Gen. Foods USA, Chgo., 1981-84, systems specialist, 1984-87, computer integrated mfg. mgr., 1987-91; KF logistics systems mgr. Kraft Foods, Northfield, Ill., 1991-99, supply chain optimization mgr., 1999—. Presbyterian. Avocations: current affairs, tennis, volleyball, hiking. Home: 1241 Swainwood Dr Glenview IL 60025-2839 Office: Kraft Foods Three Lakes Dr NF168 Northfield IL 60093-2753 E-mail: mpratt@kraft.com.

PRATT, RAYMOND BURL, educator, researcher; b. Detroit, Aug. 5, 1940; s. Raymond Wilson Pratt and Mildred Elizabeth Cross. BA, Mich. State U., 1963, MA, 1965; PhD, U. Oreg., 1968. Asst. prof. Washington U., St. Louis, 1968-71; from asst. prof. to prof. Mont. State U., Bozeman, 1971-91, prof. polit. sci., 1991—. Author: Rhythm and Resistance, 1990, 2d edit. 1994, Projecting Paranoia, 2001. Nat. Endowment for the Humanities fellow U. Calif., Santa Barbara, 1978-79. Avocations: music lecturer, disk jockey. Office: Dept Polit Sci Montana State U Bozeman MT 59717-0001 E-mail: rpratt@montana.edu.

PRATT, ROBERT CRANFORD, political scientist, educator; b. Montreal, Que., Can., Oct. 8, 1926; s. Robert Goodwin and Henrietta (Freeman) P.; m. Renate Hecht, July 15, 1956; children: Gerhard, Marcus, Anna. BA, McGill U., Montreal, 1947; postgrad., Inst. Science Politique, Paris, 1948; MPhil, Oxford U., Eng., 1952. Lectr. McGill U., 1952-54, 56-58, Makerere U., Uganda, 1954-56; rsch. officer Oxford Inst. Commonwealth Studies, 1958-60; prin. Univ. Coll., Dar-es-Salaam, Tanzania, 1961-65; chmn. internat. studies program U. Toronto, Ont., Can., 1966-71, prof. polit. sci., 1966—. Spl. asst. to pres., Tanzania, 1965, 69; rsch. fellow Internat. Devel. Rsch. Ctr., 1978; commonwealth vis. prof. U. London, 1979-80; dir. Rsch. Project on Western Mid. Powers and Global Poverty, 1985-89; vis. fellow Devel. Ctr. Orgn. for Econ. Cooperation and Devel., Paris, 1986-87. Author: (with Anthony Low) Buganda and British Overrule, 1960, The Critical Phase in Tanzania, Nyerere and the Emergence of a Socialist Strategy, 1976, Towards Socialism in Tanzania, 1979, (with Robert Matthews) Human Rights in Canadian Foreign Policy, 1988, Internationalism Under Strain: The North-South Policies of Canada, The Netherlands, Norway and Sweden, 1989; (with Roger Hutchinson) Christian Faith and Economic Justice: A Canadian Perspective, 1989); Middle Power Internationalism: The North-South Dimension, 1990, Canadian International Development Assistance Policies: An Appraisal, 1994, 2nd edit., 1996. Rhodes scholar Oxford U., 1950; recipient Killam award Can. Coun., 1968 Fellow Royal Soc. Can.; mem. Can. Polit. Sci. Assn., Can. African Studies Assn. (past pres.), Can. Assn. for Study of Internat. Devel. (mem. exec. coun.), Ecumenical Forum Can. (past chmn.). Mem. New Democratic Party. Home: 205 Cottingham St Toronto ON Canada M4V 1C4 Office: U Toronto Dept Polit Sci Toronto ON Canada M5S 1A1 E-mail: cranford.pratt@utoronto.ca.

PRATT, ROBERT WINDSOR, lawyer; b. Findlay, Ohio, Mar. 6, 1950; s. John Windsor and Isabelle (Vance) P.; m. Catherine Camak Baker, Sept. 3, 1977; children: Andrew Windsor, David Camak, James Robert. AB, Wittenberg U., Springfield, Ohio, 1972; JD, Yale U., 1975. Bar: Ill. 1975, U.S. Dist. Ct. (no. dist.) Ill. 1976, U.S. Dist. Ct. (we. dist.) Mich. 1995, U.S. Ct. Appeals (fed. cir.) 1984, U.S. Ct. Appeals (7th cir.) 1996. Assoc. Keck, Mahin & Cate, Chgo., 1975—81, ptnr., 1981—97; pvt. practice Wilmette, 1998—99; sr. asst. atty. gen. Office Ill. Atty. Gen., 1999—2001, chief antitrust bur., 2001—. Bd. dirs. Chgo. region ARC, 1985-96, vice chmn., 1988-92, chmn., 1992-96, bd. dirs. Mid-Am. chpt., 1992-96. Mem. ABA, Chgo. Bar Assn., Yale Club (Chgo.).

PRATT, SHARON L. retired secondary and elementary education educator; b. Terrell, Tex., Dec. 5, 1946; d. Cecil and Bobbie Lou (Hodge) Brown; m. John E. Pratt, Aug. 31, 1968; 1 child, Randolph W. BS in Edn., U. North Tex., 1969, MS, 1980; ESL cert., East Tex. U., 1987. Cert. elem., English tchr., reading specialist, ESL tchr., Tex. Tchr. Mesquite (Tex.) Ind. Sch. Dist.; elem. tchr. sci. U.S. Govt., Manama, Bahrain; secondary tchr. McDonald Mid. Sch., Mesquite; tchr. ESL and reading improvement North Mesquite H.S., 1991—92, 1996—2001; adj. faculty devel. reading Cedar Valley C.C., Lancaster, Tex., 1992-95; secondary tchr. Robert T. Hill Mid. Sch. Dallas Ind. Sch. Dist., 1995-96; ESL and reading tchr. North Mesquite H.S., 1996—2001; ret., 2001. Tchr. ESL and adult edn. classes Dallas Ind. Sch. Dist.; instr. ESL class Eastfield Community Coll., Mesquite. Author poems. Mem. TESOL, Internat. Reading Assn., Tex. State Reading Assn. Home: 1032 Majors Dr Mesquite TX 75149

PRATT, STEPHEN W. music educator, conductor; b. Columbia, Sc, Apr. 26, 1953; s. Kenneth Le Roy and Helen Irene Pratt; m. Darlene Jean Yorke, July 7, 1984; children: Abigail, Nathan. BME, Ind. U., Bloomington, IN, 1975; MM, U. of Mich., Ann Arbor, MI, 1983. Dir. music Sturgis Pub. Schools, Sturgis, Mich., 1975—84; prof. music Ind. U., Bloomington, Ind., 1984—2002. Music dir., condr. Bloomington Symphony Orch., Bloomington, Ind., 1995—2000; dir. Ind. U. Summer Music Clinic, Bloomington, Ind., 1993—. Recipient Disting. Svc. to Music, Kappa Kappa Pui Nat., 1993, Outstanding U. Music Educator, Ind. Music Educators Assn., 2000-2001, Outstanding Band Master Award, Phi Beta Mu - Gamma Chpt., 1998. Mem.:

Phi Beta Mu, Coll. Band Directors Nat. Assn. (pres., north divsn. 2002), Am. Bandmasters Assn. Free Methodist. Office: Indiana University School of Music Merrill Hall Bloomington IN 47405 Office Fax: 812-856-4207. E-mail: pratts@indiana.edu.

PRATT, WILLIAM CROUCH, JR. English language educator, writer; b. Shawnee, Okla., Oct. 5, 1927; s. William Crouch and Irene (Johnston) P.; m. Anne Cullen Rich, Oct. 2, 1954; children: Catherine Cullen, William Stuart, Randall Johnston. BA, U. Okla., 1949; MA, Vanderbilt U., 1951, PhD, 1957. Rotary Internat. fellow U. Glasgow, Scotland, 1951-52; instr. English Vanderbilt U., 1955-57, Miami U., Oxford, Ohio, 1957-59, asst. prof., 1959-64, assoc. prof., dir. Freshman English, 1964-68, prof., 1968—98; prof. emeritus Mami U., 1998—. Fulbright-Hays lectr. Am. lit., prof. Am. lit. Univ. Coll., Dublin, Eire, 1975-76; resident scholar Miami U. European Ctr., Luxembourg, fall 1976; lectr. Yeats Internat. Summer Sch., Sligo, Eire, 1979, 81, 82, 83, James Joyce Summer Sch., Dublin, Ireland, 1996; writer-in-residence Tyrone Guthrie Ctr., County Monaghan, Ireland, summer 1992, 96. Author: The Imagist Poem, 1963, rev. edit., 2001, The Fugitive Poets, 1965, rev. edit., 1991, The College Writer, 1969, College Days at Old Miami, 1984, The Influence of French Symbolism on Modern American Poetry, 1985, Miami Poets, 1988, Homage to Imagism, 1992, The Big Ballad Jamboree, 1996, Singing the Chaos: Madness and Wisdom in Modern Poetry, 1996, Miami University: A Personal History, 1998, Ezra Pound, Nature and Myth, 2002; contbr. essays, translations, poems, revs. to lit. jours., books. Served to lt. USNR, 1953-55. Mem.: MLA, Soc. for Values in Higher Edn., St. George Tucker Soc., Soc. Study So. Lit., Coll. Conf. on Composition, Communication, Internat. Contemporary Lit. and Theatre Soc., Nat. Coun. Tchrs. English, Omicron Delta Kappa, Sigma Alpha Epsilon, Phi Beta Kappa. Republican. Home: 212 Oakhill Dr Oxford OH 45056-2710 *True happiness is to live in the understanding of what we love, the pursuit of what we believe in.*

PRATTE, ROBERT JOHN, lawyer; b. Victoria, B.C., Can., Feb. 14, 1948; s. Arthur Louis Jr. and Marie Bertha (Latremouille) P.; children from previous marriage: Merie Elise, Jessica Louise, Allison Adele; m. Erica Catherine Street, Oct. 20, 1984; 1 child, Chelsea Nicole. BA, Northwestern U., 1970; JD, Tulane U., 1976. Bar: Minn. 1976, Ariz. 1997. Ptnr. Best & Flanagan, Mpls., 1976-84, Briggs & Morgan, Mpls., 1985—, head mortgage banking group. Editor: Mortgage Lending in Minnesota—A Desktop Reference Guide, 1990. Ex-officio mem. Wilderness Inquiry, Minn.; pres. Twin Cities Northwestern U. Alumni Assn., 1978; active Wayzata Cmty. Ch., Mpls. Fellow Am. Coll. Mortgage Attys. (regent) Home: 19900 Manor Rd Excelsior MN 55331-9256 Office: Briggs & Morgan 2400 IDS Ctr 80 S 8th St Ste 2400 Minneapolis MN 55402-2157 E-mail: rpratte@briggs.com. *Undertake with enthusiasm and pursue to completion the tasks that others are unwilling or unable to do. Never be satisfied with mediocrity. Surround yourself with those who are smarter than you; have the patience and judgement to let them succeed. Success can be measured by the hours you spend with your children--reading, fishing, and playing.*

PRAUSNITZ, FREDERIK WILLIAM, conductor; b. Cologne, Germany, Aug. 26, 1920; came to U.S., 1937; s. Friedrich Julius and Maja Eleanor (Moritz) P.; m. Margaret Violet Prausnitz; children: Sebastian, Maja. Grad. diploma in conducting, Juilliard Grad. Sch., 1946. Condr., adminstr. Juilliard, N.Y.C., 1946-61; condr. of recs. for Angel Argo Columbia, EMI, Philips, 1947—; condr. New Eng. Conservatory, Boston, 1961-69; music dir. Syracuse (N.Y.) Symphony Orch., 1971-74; music dir. to dir. of conducting programs Peabody Conservatory of Johns Hopkins U., Balt., 1976-97. Cons. The Lincoln Ctr., N.Y.C., 1963, Oakland U., Sussex (Eng.) U., 1969-71, Libr. of Congress, 2000. Author: Score and Podium, 1983, Roger Pekious, How a Difficult Composer Got That Way, 2002. Recipient 1st prize for young condrs. Detroit Symphony, 1944, Mahler Medal of Honor Am. Bruckner Soc., 1974; Hon. Fellow Sussex U., 1969; Condr. Laureate Peabody Orch., Balt., 1982; Rockefeller Found. writing grantee. Mem. Savage Club (London). E-mail: frederik@peabody.jhu.edu.

PRAUSNITZ, JOHN MICHAEL, chemical engineer, educator; b. Berlin, Jan. 7, 1928; came to U.S., 1937, naturalized, 1944; s. Paul Georg and Susi Prausnitz; m. Susan Prausnitz, June 10, 1956; children: Stephanie, Mark Robert. B Chem. Engring., Cornell U., 1950; MS, U. Rochester, 1951; PhD, Princeton, 1955; Dr. Ing., U. L'Aquila, 1983, Tech. U. Berlin, 1989; DSc, Princeton U., 1995. Mem. faculty U. Calif., Berkeley, 1955—, prof. chem. engring., 1963—. Cons. to cyrogenic, polymer, petroleum and petrochem. industries. Author: (with others) Computer Calculations for Multicomponent Vapor-Liquid Equilibria, 1967, (with P.L. Chueh) Computer Calculations for High-Pressure Vapor-Liquid Equilibria, 1968, Molecular Thermodynamics of Fluid-Phase Equilibria, 1969, 2d edit., 1986, 3rd edit., 1999, (with others) Regular and Related Solutions, 1970, Properties of Gases and Liquids, 3d edit., 1977, 4th edit., 1987, 5th edit., 2000, Computer Calculations for Multicomponent Vapor-Liquid and Liquid-Liquid Equilibria, 1980; contbr. to profl. jours. Named W.K. Lewis lectr., MIT, 1993, Edward Mason lectr., Brown U., 1999, Danckwerts lectr., Royal Acad. Engring., London, 2000, hon. prof., Tech. U. Shanghai, 2001, Miller Rsch. Prof., 1966, 1978; recipient Alexander von Humboldt Sr. Scientist award, 1976, Carl von Linde Gold Meml. medal, German Inst. for Cryogenics, 1987, Solvay prize, Solvay Found. for Chem. Scis., 1990, Corcoran award, Am. Soc. for Engring. Edn., 1991, 1999, D.L. Katz award, Gas Processors Assn., 1992, Waterman award, Tech. U. Delft, 1998, Rossini award, Internat. Union of Pure and Applied Chemistry, 2002, Guggenheim fellow, 1973; fellow, 1962, fellow, Inst. Advanced Study, Berlin, 1985, Christensen fellow, St. Catherine's Coll. Oxford U., 1994, Erskine fellow, U. Canterbury, Christchurch, New Zealand, 1996. Mem. AIChE (Colburn award 1962, Walker award 1967, Inst. Lectr. award 1994), Am. Chem. Soc. (E.V. Murphree award 1979, Petroleum Chemistry Rsch. award 1995), NAE, NAS, Am. Acad. Arts and Scis. Office: U Calif 308 Gilman Hl Berkeley CA 94720-1462 E-mail: prausnit@socrates.berkeley.edu.

PRAVEL, BERNARR ROE, lawyer; b. Feb. 10, 1924; BSChemE, Rice U., 1947; JD, George Washington U., 1951. Bar: D.C. 1951, Tex. 1951, U.S. Supreme Ct. 1951. Sr. counsel Akin, Gump, Houston, 1999—2001. Patent editor George Washington U. Law Rev., 1950. Precinct chmn. Houston Rep. Com., 1972-74. Served to lt. (j.g.) USNR. Fellow Am. Bar Found., Tex. Bar Found.; mem. ABA (chair intellectual property sect. 1991-92), Tex. Bar Assn. (chmn. patent, trademark sect. 1968-69, bd. dirs. 1976-79, Outstanding Contbn. 1982), Nat. Coun. Patent Law (chmn. 1970-71), Am. Intellectual Property Law Assn. (pres. 1983-84), Houston Intellectual Property Law Assn. (pres. 1983-84, Outstanding Svc. award 1986), Order of Coif, Kiwanis, Tau Beta Pi. Home: 10806 Oak Hollow St Houston TX 77024-3017 E-mail: bpravel@wt.net.

PRAY, DONALD GEORGE, retired aerospace engineer; b. Troy, N.Y., Jan. 19, 1928; s. George Emerson and Jansje Cornelia (Ouwejan) P.; m. Betty Ann Williams, Oct. 1, 1950; children: Jennifer Loie, Jonathan Cornelius, Judy Karen, Jeffrey Donald. BA in Physics, Tex. Christian U., 1955; MSME, So. Meth. U., 1979. Sr. structures engr. Gen. Dynamics Corp., Ft. Worth, 1955-62, 67-84; engring. specialist LTV Astronautics Corp., Dallas, 1962-65, sr. engring. specialist, 1989-91; aero. group engr. space divsn. Chrysler Corp., New Orleans, 1965-67; V-22 group engr. Bell Helicopter Textron, Ft. Worth, 1984-89; E-3 structural integrity program mgr. Tinker AFB, 1991-95; sr. stress engr. Northrop Grumman Corp., Dallas, 1997; ret., 1997. Prin. Donald G. Pray, Cons., Ft. Worth, 1959-61. Contbr. articles to profl. jours. Chmn. bd. trustees Cope Cemetery Assn., Johnson County, Tex., 1987—; corps comdr., v.p. bd. dirs. Masqueraders Drum and Bugle Corps, New Orleans, 1965-67; scoutmaster, cubmaster, explorer advisor, dist. com. chmn. Longhorn coun. Boy Scouts Am., Ft. Worth, 1967-75. With USAF, post WWII. Recipient Grand Championship Mardi Gras award, 1966. Mem.: SAR (pres. Van Zandt chpt. Ft. Worth 1996—97, treas. 1997—, N.W. Tex. dist. v.p. 1999—, Patriot medal 2001), NRA (marksman award 1980), ASME, Acoustical Soc. Am. (emeritus 1997—), Internat. Pray Family Assn. (trustee 1996—), Ft. Worth Geneal. Soc. (bd. dirs. 1983—84), Train Collectors Assn., Soc. Mayflower Descendants Tex. (sec. 1983—85, 1988—91, chmn. Dallas colony scholarship com. 1988—2001, gen. soc. edn. com. 1990—99, gov. 1991—93, dep. gov. gen. 1993—98, gov. Dallas/Ft. Worth colony 1995—97, treas. 1999—2001), Shriners, Masons, Scottish Rite, Legion of Honor (adjutant/fin. officer 2000—01, comdr. 2002—), Pi Mu Epsilon, Sigma Pi Sigma. Baptist. Achievements include analytical engineering contributions to numerous aircraft and spacecraft programs including B-36, B-58, NX-2, Robot, Dynasoar, Scout, Apollo, F/FB-111, F-16, V-22 Osprey, C-17, E-3 AWACS. Home and Office: 3628 Wedgway Dr Fort Worth TX 76133-2135 also: Lazy Acres Farm 5750 Lazy Bend Rd Millsap TX 76066-3732 E-mail: dgpray1@swbell.net. *Learn what talents you have been blessed with; then exercise them for the betterment of humanity.*

PRAY, LLOYD CHARLES, geologist, educator; b. Chgo., June 25, 1919; s. Allan Theron and Helen (Palmer) P.; m. Carrel Myers, Sept. 14, 1946; children: Lawrence Myers, John Allan, Kenneth Palmer, Douglas Carrel. BA magna cum laude, Carleton Coll., 1941; MS, Calif. Inst. Tech., 1943, PhD (NRC fellow 1946-49), 1952. Geologist Magnolia Petroleum Co., summer 1942, U.S. Geol. Survey, 1943-44; hydrographic officer USN, 1944-46; Geologist U.S. Geol. Survey, 1946-56 part time; instr. to assoc. prof. geology Calif. Inst. Tech., 1949-56; sr. research geologist Denver Research Ctr., Marathon Oil Co., 1956-62, research assoc., 1962-68; prof. geology U. Wis., Madison, 1968-88; emeritus prof. geology, 1989—. Short course vis. prof. U. Tex., 1964, U. Colo., 1967, U. Miami, 1971, U. Alta., 1969, Colo. Sch. Mines, 1985; vis. scientist Imperial Coll. Sci. and Tech., London, 1977, U. Calif. Santa Cruz, 1987, Nat. Park Svc. Geology panel, 1993. Author articles sedimentary carbonates, the Permian Reef complex, stratigraphy and structural geology So. N.M. and W. Tex., porosity of carbonate facies, Calif. rare earth mineral deposits. Pres. Colo. Diabetes Assn., 1963-67, v.p., 1968; mem. adv. panel earth scis. NSF, 1973-76. Served as hydrographic officer USNR, 1944-46. Named Layman of Year Am. Diabetes Assn., 1968; recipient Disting. Teaching award U. Wis. Madison, 1988, Disting. Achievement citation Carleton Coll., 1991, Wallace Pratt Resources Stewardship award Guadalupe Mountains Nat. Pk., 1998. Fellow Geol. Soc. Am. (rsch. grants com. 1965-67, com. on nominations 1973, com.Penrose medal 1979-81); mem. Am. Assn. Petroleum Geologists (rsch. com. 1958-61, lectr. continuing edn. program 1966-69, continuing edn. com. 1978-80, Levorsen award 1966, Matson trophy 1967, Disting. lectr. 1986-87, 87-88, Disting. Educator award 1998), Soc. Sedimentary Geologists (hon. life mem. Permian Basin sect. 1977, hon. mem. internat. soc. 1982, sec.-treas. 1961-63, v.p. 1966-67, pres. 1969-70, Twenhofel award 1999), Am. Geol. Inst. (edn. com. 1966-68, ho. bd. dels. 1970-72), Phi Beta Kappa. Office: Univ Wis Dept Geology Madison WI 53706

PRAY, RALPH EMERSON, metallurgical engineer; b. Troy, N.Y., May 12, 1926; s. George Emerson and Jansje Cornelius (Owejan) P.; m. Beverley Margaret Ramsey, May 10, 1959; children: Maxwell, Ross, Leslie, Marlene. Student, N.Mex. Inst. Mining & Tech., 1953-56, U. N.Mex., 1956; BS, U. Alaska, 1961; DSc, Colo. Sch. Mines, 1966. Electrician, miner, 1944-57; engr.-in-charge Dept. Mines and Minerals, Ketchikan, Alaska, 1957-61; asst. mgr. mfg. rsch. Universal Atlas Cement div. U.S. Steel Corp., Gary, Ind., 1965-66; rsch. metallurgist Inland Steel Co., Hammond, 1966-67; owner, dir. Mineral Rsch. Lab., Monrovia, Calif., 1968—. Pres., Keystone Canyon Mining Co., Inc., Pasadena, Calif., 1972-79, U.S. Western Mines, 1973—, Silveroil Rsch. Inc., 1980-85, v.p. Mineral Drill Inc., 1981-90; pres., CEO Copper de Mex. S.A. de C.V.; prime contractor def. logistics agy. U.S. Dept. def., 1989-92; designer Vanavara Electrolytic Gold Refinery, Krasnoyarsk, Russia, 1995; owner Precision Plastics, 1973-82; bd. dirs. Bagdad-Chase Inc., 1972-75; ptnr. Mineral R&D Co., 1981-86; lectr. Purdue U., Hammond, Ind., 1966-67, Nat. Mining Seminar, Barstow (Calif.) Coll., 1969-70; guest lectr. Calif. State Poly. U., 1977-81, Western Placer Mining Conf., Reno, Nev., 1983, Dredging and Miner Conf., Reno, 1985, others; v.p. dir. Wilbur Foote Plastics, Pasadena, 1968-72; strategic minerals del. People to People, Rep. South Africa, 1983; expert witness, cons. Bur. Land Mgmt., U.S. Dept. of Interior, 2000-2002; hist. cons. gold mining History TV Channel, 1999; guest spkr. Greater L.A. County Svc. Clubs, 1980-81. Author: Jingu, The Hidden Princess, 2002; guest editor Calif. Mining Jour., 1978—; contbr. articles to profl. jours.; contbr. author Bre-x Gold Today, Gone Tomorrow, 1997. Vol. Monrovia Police Dept.; city coord. Neighborhood Watch., 1990-99, Monrovia Police Dept., 1997-99. With U.S. Army, 1950-52. Recipient Disting. Svc. medal Monrovia Police Dept. Citizen Patrol, 1998. Fellow Geol. Mining and Metall. Soc. India (life), Am. Inst. Chemists, South African Inst. Mining and Metallurgy; mem. Soc. Mining Engrs., Am. Chem. Soc., Am. Inst. Mining, Metall. and Petroleum Engrs., NSPE, Can. Inst. Mining and Metallurgy, Geol. Soc. South Africa, Sigma Xi, Sigma Mu. Achievements include research on recovery of metals from refractory ores, benefication plant design, construction and operation, underground and surface mine development and operation, mine and process plant management; syndication of natural resource assets with finance sources; freelance fiction and nonfiction writer; patents for chemical processing and steel manufacture. Office: 805 S Shamrock Ave Monrovia CA 91016-3651

PRAY, RALPH MARBLE, III, lawyer; b. San Diego, June 7, 1938; s. Ralph Marble Jr. and Doris (Thomson) P.; m. Karen L. Pray (div. May 1988); children: Matthew Thomson, Kristen Leigh; m. Sandra Anne Shaw, June 7, 1988. BS, U. Redlands, 1960; JD, U. Calif., San Francisco, 1967. Bar: Calif. 1967, U.S. Dist. Ct. (so. dist.) Calif. 1968, U.S. Supreme Ct. 1972, U.S. Dist. Ct. (ea. dist.) Calif. 1985, U.S. Dist. Ct. (ctrl. dist.) Calif. 1989, U.S. Dist. Ct. (no. dist.) Calif. 1992. Assoc. Gray, Cary, Ware & Friedenrich and predecessor, San Diego, 1967-73, ptnr., 1973—; mem. mgmt. com. Gary, Cary, Ames & Frye, 1975-80. Arbiter Superior Ct., San. Diego, 1984—. Lt. USN, 1960-64. Mem. ABA, SAR, NRA, Calif. Bar Assn., Am. Arbitration Soc. (arbiter), San Diego Zool. Soc., Ducks Unltd., Thurston Soc., Rotary Club of Coronado, Calif., Order of Coif. Republican. Episcopalian. Home: 535 C Ave Coronado CA 92118-1824 Office: Gray Cary Ware & Friedenrich 2000 Wells Fargo Plz 401 B St San Diego CA 92101-4240

PRAY, RALPH RUSTIN, internist; b. Fargo, N.D., Feb. 2, 1943; s. Laurence Gesner and Helen Louise (Van Atta) Pray; m. Sandra Kay Koch Portlock, May 5, 2001; children: Sarah Elaine, Gregory David. BA, Grinnell Coll., 1965; MD, U. Iowa, 1969. Diplomate Am. Bd. Internal Medicine. Pvt. practice internal medicine, Des Moines, 1973—. Fellow ACP; mem. AMA, Iowa Med. Soc., Polk County Med. Soc., Med. Libr. Club Des Moines. Office: 1221 Center St Ste 15 Des Moines IA 50309-1091

PRAY, RONALD WAYNE, protective services official; b. Kingsville, Tex., Dec. 20, 1971; s. Darrell Lynn Pray and Ronald Wayne Lawhorn; m. Elizabeth Hernandez, Mar. 25, 1979; children: Ronald. Lic. paramedic Tex. Dept. Health, cert. intermediate structural fire suppression Tex. Commn. on Fire Protection, driver/operator-pumper Tex. Commn. on Fire Protection, 2001, intermediate instr. Tex. Commn. on Fire Protection, arson investigator Tex. Commn. on Fire Protection, hazardous materials instr. 1999, nuc., biol. and chem. weapons of terrorism instr., lic. peace officer Tex. Commn. on Law Enforcement, cert. basic county jailer Tex. Commn. on Law Enforcement. Fire chief Ricardo Vol. Fire Rescue, Kingsville, Tex., 1993—98; tng. officer, engr., lic. paramedic, fire arson investigator Kingsville Fire Dept., 1993—. Scout leader Boy Scouts Am. Venado Dist. Troop 351, Kingsville; asst. supt. beef cattle divsn. Kleberg County Jr. Livestock Assn., Kingsville, 1990—2001; active Kleberg County Farm Bur., 1989—. Named Pub. Safety Officer of Yr., KC, 1997; recipient Lone Star Farmer Degree, Tex. Future Farmers Am., 1989, U.S. Nat. Agr. award, Nat. Future Farmers Am., 1990; scholar Congl. scholar, Nat. Young Leaders Conf., Congl. Youth Leadership Coun., 1990. Mem.: Lower Rio Grande Valley Fire Acad. Bd. Dirs. (bd. mem. 1998—), Tex. Assn. Fire Educators, Pi Sigma Alpha. Avocations: hunting, fishing, woodworking, reading, gunsmithing. Office: Kingsville Fire Dept 119 N Tenth Kingsville TX 78363 Business E-Mail: ronaldpray@hotmail.com.

PRAY, WALTER STEVEN, pharmacy educator; b. Holdenville, Okla., Sept. 21, 1949; s. Walter Leroy Pray and Flossie (Withrow) Wynema; m. Carole Lynn Grayson, Dec. 20, 1975; children: Joshua Jameson, Gabriel Elijah. BS, Southwestern State Coll., 1972; MPH, U. Okla., 1976; PhD in Clin. Pharmacy, Purdue U., 1983. Registered pharmacist, Okla. Extern pharmacist Jones' Drug, Broken Arrow, Okla., 1970, Oertle's Pharmacy, Tulsa, 1971, intern pharmacist, 1972-73; staff pharmacist Ross Drug, Broken Arrow, 1973, Getman Drug #3, Tulsa, 1973, St. Francis Hosp., Tulsa, 1973-74; pharmacy resident, staff pharmacist St. Anthony Hosp., Oklahoma City, 1974-75; prof. nonprescription products and devices Southwestern Okla. State U., Weatherford, 1976—. Cons. in pvt. practice, Weatherford, Okla., 1988—; author monthly column Consult Your Pharmacist in jour. U.S. Pharmacist, 1988—; mem. rev. com. N.Am. Pharmacy Licensure Exam., 1988—. Author (textbook) Nonprescription Product Therapeutics, 1999, (book chpt.) SelfCare/Diagnostic Products, 2000, Remington, 2000. Pres. agape Sunday Sch. Class United Meth. Ch., Weatherford, 1976-79, 99-2000, pres. Wesley Found. Bd. Dirs., 1987, 97-2000; vol. pharmacist Agape Free Clinic, Weatherford, 1999—. Mem. Nat. Assn. Bds. of Pharmacy (mem. NAPLEX rev. com. 1987—), Nat. Pediculosis Assn. (sci. adv. bd. dirs. 1990—), Am. Assn. Colls. of Pharmacy (Tchr. of Yr. 1995, 98, 99). Republican. United Methodist. Avocations: gardening, service work, reading, family recreation. Home: 1420 Steiner Rd Weatherford OK 73096-2334 Office: Sch Pharmacy Southwestern Okla State U 100 Campus Dr Weatherford OK 73096-3001

PRAYSON, ALEX STEPHEN, design engineering educator; b. Tulsa, Okla., June 24, 1939; s. Stephen Alexander and Frances Prayson; m. Jacqueline Ann Prayson; children: Stephen, David, Timothy, Anthony. AS, Edison Tech., 1967; DC, Cleveland Coll., 1972; AA, Summit U., 1996. Diplomate Am. Bd. Chiropractic Examiners. Owner Prayson Candies Co., Tulsa, 1963-68; cartographer Howard Needles Tammen and Bergendoff, Kansas City, Mo., 1968-71; supr. M. J. Harden Assocs., 1971-81; asst. prof. Tulsa C.C., 1981—. Advisor Phi Theta Kappa, Tulsa, 1991—. Author: A Love-Hate Anthology, 1993, Cad Systems Operation, 1996; inventor Taffy-Pull. Mem. selection com. Ahepa Civic Youth Svc. Award, Tulsa, 1992—. Named Most Disting. Regional Advisor, Phi Theta Kappa, Tulsa, 1994-95; recipient Robert Giles Disting. Advisor Internat. award, 1995-96, Continued Excellence award for advisors, 1996-97, 99-2000, Tchr. of Yr. award Tulsa C.C., 1997, Mosal Leader award Phi Theta Kappa, 2000. Mem. Am. Design and Drafting Assn., Okla. Tech. Soc., Tulsa C.C. Faculty Assn., Jaquar Club of Tulsa. Avocations: croquet, bridge, travel. Home: 204 E 27th St Tulsa OK 74114-3912 E-mail: aprayson@tulsa.cc.ok.us.

PRAYSON, STEPHEN ALEXANDER, pharmacist; b. Tulsa, June 27, 1961; s. Alexander Stephen Prayson and Sonja Sue (Drinkwater) Anderson; Mary Jane Williams, May 31, 1985; children: Jamie, Jason, Jacqueline. BS in Biology, Ctrl. Mo. State U., 1986; PharmD, U. Mo., Kansas City, 1991. Registered profl. pharmacist, Mo., Kans. Pharmacy adminstrn. resident U. Kans. Med. Ctr., Kansas City, 1991-92; hosp. pharmacist Trinity Luth. Hosp., 1992-93, Cox Health Sys., Springfield, Mo., 1993-94; clin. pharamcy resident St. John's Health Sys., 1994-95; project mgr. Pharmacotherapy Mgmt., 1995-96; staff pharmacist Dillons Pharmacy, 1996-99; cons. pharmacist, geriatric specialist St. John's Health Sys., 1999—. Instr. So. Mo. State U., Springfield, 1995-96, 2001. Contbr. articles to profl. jours. Mem. Am. Coll. Clin. Pharmacist, Am. Soc. Health-Sys. Pharmacists, Mo. Pharm. Assn., Ozark Soc. Hosp. Pharmacists. Avocations: computers, music. Office: St Johns Health System 1235 E Cherokee St Springfield MO 65804-2203 Home: 1634 S Raford Dr Springfield MO 65809-2336

PRAZAK, BESSMARIE LILLIAN, science educator; b. Chgo., June 6, 1941; d. William Felix and Bess Blanch (Kostka) Kolar; m. Charles J. Prazak III, June 15, 1963; 1 child Robin Marie. BS, Rosary U., 1963; MS, Northwestern U., 1965. Rsch. asst. Argonne Nat. Lab., Lemont, Ill., 1965-68; tchr. Morton Coll., Cicero, 1968-2000, tchr. emeritus, 2000—. Chair curriculum com. Morton Coll., 1984-2000. Author: Laboratory Manual of Anatomy and Physiology, 1997, Laboratory Manual of Microbiology, 1997. Mem. AAAS, Nat. Assn. Biology Tchrs., Ill. Assn. C.C. Biologists (sec.-treas. 1978), Human Anatomy and Physiology Soc. Avocations: painting, photography. E-mail: cp3@enteract.com.

PRCHALOVÁ, LEA, library director; b. Ostrava, Moravia, Czechoslovakia, July 17, 1957; d. Lubomír and Anna (Blažková) Šmrha; m. Miloslav Prchal, Apr. 19, 1980; 1 child, Luboš. Degree in Engring., U. Ednl. Tech. U., Ostrava, Czech Republic, 1981. Cert. sys. engring. Cons. for regional librs. State Rsch. Libr. in Ostrava, 1982-86, head rsch. dept., 1986-95, directress of libr., 1995—. Mem. of head libr. coun. Minitry of Culture, Prague, Czech Republic, 1997—. Mem. Czech Republic Libr. Assn. (mem. of the head 1995—). E-mial. Home: Krestova 1 CZ-70030 Ostrava Czech Republic Office: Moravian-Silesian Rsch Libr Ostrava Prokešovo Námesti 9 CZ-72800 Ostrava Czech Republic E-mail: prchalova@svkos.cz.

PREBLE, DARRELL WAYNE, systems analyst; b. Portsmouth, N.H., Dec. 8, 1946; s. Carlton Burt and Ellen (Plummer) P.; m. Deborah Young, Dec. 19, 1970; children: Jennifer, Megan. BA in Physics, Vanderbilt U., 1969; MS in Adminstrn. Systems Mgmt., George Wash. U., 1973; MS in Physics, Ga. State U., 1980. Field engr. Sperry Systems Mgmt., Great Neck, N.Y., 1969-73; systems analyst Ga. State U., Atlanta, 1973-85; sr. systems analyst So. Co. Svcs., 1985—. Fellow Space Studies Inst., Princeton, N.J., 1982—; participant NASA Space Exploration Outreach Study, 1991. Elder Riverdale (Ga.) Presbyn. Ch., 1984; pres. Atlanta L5 Soc., 1980-85. Fellow Space Studies Inst.; mem. IEEE, Nat. Space Soc., Am. Assn. for Artificial Intelligence. Avocations: soaring, scuba diving. Home: 2557 Betty Jean Dr Jonesboro GA 30236-4082 Office: So Co Svcs PO Box 192 Atlanta GA 30301-0192

PREBLE, LAURENCE GEORGE, lawyer; b. Denver, Apr. 24, 1939; s. George Enos and Ruth (Jewett) Preble; m. Deborah Joan Horton, Aug. 24, 1963; children: Robin Lee, Randall Laurence. B in Petroleum Refining Engring., Colo. Sch. Mines, 1961; JD cum laude, Loyola U., Los Angeles, 1968. Bar: Calif. 1969, D.C. 1983, N.Y. 1987, U.S. Dist. Ct. (cen. dist.) Calif. 1969. Assoc. firm O'Melveny & Myers, Los Angeles, 1968-76, ptnr. L.A., 1976—2000; dir. devel. KUD Internat. LLC, 2001—. Adj. prof. law Southwestern U., 1970-75, Loyola U. of L.A. Sch. Law, 1984-92, 99-2000, Fordham U. Sch. Law, 1992-98, Calif. Continuing Edn. of the Bar; lectr., author Practicing Law Inst. Trustee Harvey Mudd Coll., 1991-94, Citizens Bidget Commn. N.Y.C., 1994-98, Ho. Ear Inst., 1998—, vice-chmn., 2001—. Recipient Disting. Achievement medal, Colo. Sch. Mines, 1998. Mem. Los Angeles County Bar Assn. (chmn. real property sect. 1979-80, Outstanding Leadership award 1999), Assn. Bar City of N.Y. (real property sect. exec. com. 1993-96), N.Y. State Bar Assn. (exec. com. real property sect. 1996—), Calif. Bar Assn. (mem. exec. com. real property sect.), ABA, Am. Coll. Real Estate Lawyers (bd. govs. 1986—), Anglo-Am. Real Property Inst., La Canada-Flintridge C. of C. (pres. 1974-75), Loyola Law Sch. Alumni Assn. (pres. 1978). Office: KUD Internat LLC 100 Wilshire Blvd Ste 1800 Santa Monica CA 90401

PREBLE, ROBERT CURTIS, JR. insurance executive; b. Oak Park, Ill., Dec. 19, 1922; s. Robert Curtis and Dorothy (Seidel) P.; m. Lidia Blazik, May 29, 1963. BA, Amherst Coll., 1947; MBA, Harvard U., 1949, postgrad., 1971. CLU, Chartered Fin. Cons. Commd. 1st lt. U.S. Army, 1943—46; 33rd divsn. capt. Nat. Guard, Ill., 1950—53; asst. to gen. supt., asst. buyer Carson Pirie Scott & Co., Chgo., 1949-52; with sales dept. Northwestern Mut. Life Ins. Co., 1952-53, Nat. Life Ins. Co., Chgo., 1953-59; prin. Preble Assocs., 1959—; pres., treas. Savs. Plans Inc., 1980—. Cons. Iowa Savs. & Loan League, 1959-82; consul of Colombia, 1981-86, Bolivia, 1965-70; bd. dirs., chmn. fin. com. Guardsman Life Ins. Co., 1962-74; chmn. exec. com. World Book Life Ins. Co., 1974-83; gov.'s adv. bd. Ill. Dept. Ins., 1965-70; dir. Scandia Savs. & Loan Assn., 1968-83, Chgo. Coun. on Fgn. Rels., 1971-77, Chgo. Estate Planning Coun., 1977-80. Dept. regional chmn. Dem. Nat. Fin. Com., 1952; bd. dirs. Sr. Ctrs. Met. Chgo., 1974—77, McCormick Theol. Sem., 1977—83; deacon 4th Presbyn. Ch. of Chgo., 1967—70. Recipient Svc. award Chgo. coun. Boy Scouts Am., 1962. Mem. Soc. Fin. Svc. Profls. (past pres. Chgo. chpt., Huebner scholar 1991, Grauer award 1998), Million Dollar Roundtable (life), Nat. Assn. of Insurance and Fin. Advisors, Assn. for Advanced Life Underwriting (founding pres. 1957), Harvard Bus. Sch. Assn. (alumni coun. 1977-82), Harvard Alumni Assn. (dir. 1980-82), Inst. Internat. Edn. (midwest adv. bd., 1979-99), Found. Study Cycles (internat. adv. bd.), Soc. Colonial Wars (coun.), Mil. Order World Wars, Univ. Club, Chgo. Club, Harvard Bus. Sch. Club (past pres.), Amherst Club (past pres.), Oak Park Country Club, Spanish Wells Country Club, Econ. Club Chgo., Chi Psi (past chmn. ednl. trust, pres. 1992-95, Svc. award 1986). Home: 300 N State St Apt 5406 Chicago IL 60610-4870

PRECOURT, CHARLES J. astronaut, retired military officer; b. Waltham, Mass., June 29, 1955; s. Charles and Helen Precourt; m. Lynne Denise Mungle; 3 children. BS in Aeronautical Engring., USAF Acad., Colo. Springs, 0977; MS in Engring. Mgmt., Golden Gate U., 1988; MA in Nat. Security Affairs, Strategic Studies, US Naval War Coll., 1990. Commd. 2d lt. USAF, 1977; advanced through grades to Col. USAF (ret.); student pilot USAF, Reese AFB, Tex., 1977—78, instr. pilot T-37, 1979—82; pilot F-15 USAF Bitburg

Air Base , Germany, 1982—84; student test pilot sch. USAF, Edwards AFB, Calif., 1985; test pilot USAF , 1985—89; postgrad. studies U.S. Naval War Coll. , Newport, RI, 1989—90; astronaut NASA Johnson Space Ctr., Houston, 1990—. Decorated Disting. Flying Cross USAF, 4 Space Flight medals NASA; recipient David B. Barnes award, USAF Test Pilot Sch., 1989. Mem.: Soc. Exptl. Test Pilots, Exptl. Aircraft Assn., Assn. Space Explorers (v.p.). Achievements include 4 space flights; over 7000 flight hours in 60 types of civil and military aircraft; approximately 40 days spent in space. Office: Astronaut Office/CB Johnson Space Ctr. Houston TX 77085

PREDDY, RAYMOND RANDALL, retired newspaper publisher, educator; b. Texarkana, Ark., Feb. 1, 1940; s. Raymond Watson and Dorothy Belle (Long) P.; m. Sarah Elizabeth Mitchell, Nov. 20, 1965; children: Lewis, Tiffany. BS, Northwestern U., 1961, MS in Journalism, 1962. Copy editor Louisville Courier-Jour., 1965-69; with Dayton (Ohio) Daily News, 1969-74, asst. city editor, 1971, met. editor, 1971-74; systems mgr. Dayton Newspapers, Inc., 1974-76; bus. mgr. Waco (Tex.) Tribune-Herald, 1976-77, asst. pub., 1977-78; pub. Waco Tribune-Herald, 1978-96. Part time journalism instr. Baylor U., Waco. Pres. Waco United Way, 1986, Waco Found., 1984-86, Waco Symphony Assn., 1985-86. Served with USN, 1962-65; capt. Res. (ret.) Named Tex. Newspaper Leader of 1994; recipient Pat Taggart award from Tex. Daily Newspaper Assn. Mem.: Rotary. Presbyterian. E-mail: rrpreddy@aol.com.

PREECE, BARBARA G. librarian; b. Fall River, Mass., July 27, 1952; children: Ellen, Molly. MA, U. Minn., 1979. Coord. tech. and automated svcs. Shawnee Libr. Sys., Carterville, Ill., 1981—85; cataloger So. Ill. U.-Morris Libr., Carbondale, 1985—93, asst. access svcs. libr., 1993—98, dir. for sys. svcs., 1998—2000, acting assoc. dean for tech. and automation svcs., 1999—2000; exec. dir. Boston Libr. Consortium, 2000—. Vis. asst. libr. U. Calif., Davis, 1989—90. Contbr. articles to profl. jours. Mem.: ALA. Office: Boston Library Consortium 700 Boylston St. Rm. 317 Boston MA 02117 Office Fax: 617-262-0163.

PREECE, LYNN SYLVIA, lawyer; b. Birmingham, Eng., June 13, 1955; d. Norman and Sylvia Florence (James) Preece. LLB, Leeds (Eng.) U., 1976; postgrad., Washington U., St. Louis, 1978-79; JD, Loyola U., 1981. Bar: Ill., 1981. Assoc. Barnes Richardson, Chgo., 1980-86; from assoc. to ptnr. Burditt & Radzius, 1986-88; ptnr. Katten Muchin & Zavis, 1988-96, Baker & McKenzie, Chgo., 1996—. Adj. prof. John Marshall Law Sch., 1998—. Contbr. articles to profl. jours. Chair customs com. Chgo. Bar Assn., 1986-87, Am. Bar Sect. Internat. Law, Washington, 1993-95, practitioners workshop bd., 1995-97; sec., dir. Women in Internat. Trade, Chgo., 1986-89, British Am. C. of C., Chgo., 1990; dir. Chgo. Internat. Sch., 1994-96. Recipient Gold medal Duke of Edinurghs award Scheme, London, 1973. Mem.: ABA (program officer, coun. mem., newsletter editor 1996—98), Internat. Bar Assn., Ct. Internat. Trade Bar Assn. Avocations: gardening, dogs. Office: Baker & McKenzie Ste 3500 130 E Randolph Dr Chicago IL 60601-6342 E-mail: Lynn.S.Preece@Bakernet.com.

PREEG, ERNEST HENRY, manufacturers alliance executive; b. Englewood, N.J., July 5, 1934; s. Ernest W. and Claudia T. Preeg; m. Florence L. Tate, May 12, 1962; 1 child, Terri E. BS in Marine Transp., N.Y. State Maritime Coll., 1956; MA in Econs., New Sch. for Social Rsch., 1961, PhD, 1964. Officer Mcht. Marine, Am. Export Lines, 1956-61; lectr. econs. Bklyn. Coll., 1962-63; fgn. svc. officer Dept. State, Washington, 1963-88; amb. to Haiti, 1981-83; Scholl chair in internat. bus. Hudson Inst., Washington, 1988-99. Author: Traders and Diplomats, 1969, Economic Blocs and U.S. Foreign Policy, 1974, the Evolution of a Revolution, 1981, Haiti and the CBI, 1984, The American Challenge in World Trade, 1988, The Tied Aid and Credit Issue, 1989, Neither Fish Nor Foul: U.S. Economic Aid to the Philippines, 1991, Cuba and the New Caribbean Economic Order, 1993, Trade Policy Ahead, 1995, Traders in a Brave New World, 1995, The Haitan Dilemma, 1996, From Here to Free Trade, 1998, Feeling Good or Doing Good with Sanctions, 1999, The Trade Deficit, The Dollar, and The U.S. National Interest, 2000. Coun. Fgn. Rels. fellow, 1967-68. Mem. Am. Fgn. Svc. Assn. Office: Mfrs Alliance 1525 Wilson Blvd Arlington VA 22209 E-mail: epreeg@mapi.net.

PREER, JAMES RANDOLPH, science educator; b. Monahans, Tex., May 22, 1944; s. John R. Jr. and Louise B. (Brandau) P.; m. Jean H. Lyon, June 24, 1967; children: Genevieve L., Stephen R. AB, Swarthmore (Pa.) Coll., 1965; PhD, Calif. Inst. Tech., 1970. Woodrow Wilson teaching intern, 1969-71; asst. prof. chemistry Fed. City Coll., Washington, 1969-73; asst. prof. interdisciplinary sci. U. D.C., 1973-76, assoc. prof. interdisciplinary sci., 1976-79, prof. interdisciplinary sci., 1979-80, acting chairperson, 1979-80, 86-89, prof. environ. sci., 1980—, asst. provost acad. programs and rsch., 1997-99, assoc. provost acad. programs & rsch., 1999-2000. Vis. scholar Inst. Environ. Studies, U. Wis., Madison, 2000-2001. Co-author: Integrated Science, 1976, 88; contbr. over 30 articles to profl. jours. Asst. scoutmaster Boy Scouts Am., Washington, 1990-93, chmn. troop com., 1993-95; bd. dirs. Beauvoir Sch., Washington, 1983-86. Woodrow Wilson Found. fellow Columbia U., 1965-66, NSF fellow Calif. Inst. Tech., 1966-69, MIT, 1976-77; U. D. C. grantee, 1978-98. Mem. Am. Chem. Soc., Phi Beta Kappa, Sigma Xi. Office: Dept Biol & Environ Scis 4200 Connecticut Ave NW Washington DC 20008-1122

PREER, JEAN LYON, information science educator; b. Rochester, N.Y., June 25, 1944; d. Henry Gould and Helen Corinne (McTarnaghan) Lyon; m. James Randolph Preer, June 24, 1967; children: Genevieve, Stephen. BA in History with honors, Swarthmore Coll., 1966; MLS, U. Calif., Berkeley, 1967; JD with highest honors, George Washington U., 1974, PhD, 1980. Bar: D.C. 1975. With Henry E. Huntington Libr., San Marino, Calif., 1967-69; Woodrow Wilson Found. teaching intrn Fed. City Coll., Washington, 1969-70; cons. Inst. for Svcs. to Edn., Silver Spring, Md., 1981-82; vol. edn. divsn. Nat. Archives, Washington, 1981-89; adj. prof. U. D.C., 1984-85, Cath. U. Am., Washington, 1985-87, asst. prof. sch. libr. and info. sci., 1987-92, assoc. prof., 1993—, assoc. dean., 1991-93, 94-98, acting dean, 1993-94, 99; adj. assoc. prof. George Washington U., 1985-87. Vis. scholar, U. Wis., Madison, Sch. Libr. and Info. Studies, 2000-01. Contbr. articles to profl. jours. Mem. governing bd. Nat. Cathedral Sch., Washington, 1987—91; bd. dirs. Westmoreland Vol. Corps, 1997—2000; mem. strategic planning com. D.C. Pub. Libr., Washington, 1998—99. Fellow Nat. Acad. Edn., 1984-85; grantee Nat. Endowment for Humanities. Mem. Order of Coif, Beta Phi Mu. Home: 2900 Rittenhouse St NW Washington DC 20015-1524 Office: Cath U Am Sch Libr And Info Sci Washington DC 20064-0001 E-mail: preer@cua.edu.

PREGERSON, HARRY, federal judge; b. L.A., Oct. 13, 1923; s. Abraham and Bessie (Rubin) P.; m. Bernardine Seyma Chapkis, June 28, 1947; children: Dean Douglas, Kathryn Ann. BA, UCLA, 1947; LL.B., U. Calif.-Berkeley, 1950. Bar: Calif. 1951. Pvt. practice, Los Angeles, 1951—53; Assoc. Morris D. Coppersmith, 1952; ptnr. Pregerson & Costley, Van Nuys, 1953—65; judge Los Angeles Mcpl. Ct., 1965—66, Los Angeles Superior Ct., 1966—67, U.S. Dist. Ct. Central Dist. Calif., 1967—79, U.S. Ct. Appeals for 9th Circuit, Woodland Hills, 1979—. Faculty mem., seminar for newly appointed distr. Judges Fed. Jud. Center, Washington, 1970—72; mem. faculty Am. Soc. Pub. Adminstrn., Inst. for Ct. Mgmt., Denver, 1973—; panelist L.A. chpt. FBA, 1989, Calif. Continuing Edn. of Bar, 9th Ann. Fed. Practice Inst., San Francisco, 1986, Internat. Acad. Trial Lawyers, L.A., 1983; lectr. seminars for newly-appointed Fed. judges, 1970—71. Author: over 450 published legal opinions. Mem. Community Rels. Com., Jewish Fedn. Coun., 1984—, Temple Judea, Encino, 1955—; bd. trustees Devil Pups Inc., 1988—; adv. bd. Internat. Orphans Inc., 1966—, Jewish Big Brothers Assn., 1970, Salvation Army, Los Angeles Met. area, 1988—; worked with U.S. Govt. Gen. Svcs. to establish the Bell Shelter for the homeless Child Day Care Ctr., the Food Partnership and Westwood Transitional Village; bd. dirs. Marine Corps Res. Toys for Tots Program, 1965—, Greater Los Angeles Partnership for the Homeless, 1988—. 1st lt. USMCR, 1944—46. Decorated Purple Heart, Medal of Valor Apache Tribe; recipient Promotion of Justice Civic award, City of San Fernando, 1965, award, San Fernando Valley Jewish Fedn. Coun., 1966, Profl. Achievement award, Los Angeles Athletic Club, 1980, Profl. Achievement award UCLA Alumni Assn., 1985, Louis D. Brandeis award, Am. Friends of Hebrew U., 1987, award of merit, Inner City Law Ctr., 1987, Appreciation award, Navajo Nation and USMC for Toys for Tots program, 1987, Humanitarian award, Los Angeles Fed. Exec. Bd., 1987—88, Grateful Acknowledgement award, Bet Tzedek Legal Svcs., 1988, Commendation award, Bd. Suprs. Los Angeles County, 1988, Others award, Salvation Army, 1988. Mem.: ABA, Marines Corps Res. Officers Assn., State Bar Calif., San Fernando Valley Bar Assn., L.A. County Bar Assn., Am. Legion (Van Nuys Post), DAV (Birmingham chpt.). Office: US Ct Appeals 9th Cir 21800 Oxnard St Ste 1140 Woodland Hills CA 91367-7919*

PREGMON, STEPHEN KENNETH, music educator, musician, musician; b. Scranton, Pa., July 1, 1944; s. Stephen and Matilda Marie (Walczak) Pregmon; m. Janice Bond, Dec. 30, 1968 (div. July 1983); m. Amy Kleis, Aug. 17, 1986; 1 child Mark Robert. BS in Music Edn., Mansfield State U., Pa., 1966; MS in Music Edn., Mansfield State U., 1972; postgrad., Ithaca Coll., N.Y., 1981—82. Cert. tchr. N.Y. Orch./string tchr. Royalton-Hartland Ctrl. Schs., Middleport, NY, 1966—2001; ret., 2001. Guest condr. all county orchs., area all-state orch. in N.Y. and Va. and Allegheny Arts Spring String Festival; profl. musician guitar, jazz/pop. Mem.: Niagara County Music Educators Assn. (pres. 1991—92, v.p. for orch. 1970—2001), N.Y. State Sch. Music Assn. Home: 56 Lindhurst Dr Lockport NY 14094

PREIK, MICHELLE LETITIA PETRUNA, engineer; b. McKees Rocks, Pa., Sept. 11, 1951; d. Charles P. and Elizabeth L. (Butler) Petruna. BS in Metall. Engring., U. Pitts., 1973. Cert. lead quality sys. auditor, Registrar Accreditation Bd. Quality assurance engr. Westinghouse Electric Corp., Pitts., 1974-77, process devel. engr., 1977-78, materials devel. engr., 1979; quality assurance engr. Parsons, Brinckerhoff, Quade & Douglas, 1979-81; sr. quality assurance engr., cons. Energy Cons., Inc., 1981-83; sr. quality assurance engr. Battelle Meml. Inst., Columbus, Ohio, 1983-85; quality assurance mgr. McGraw-Edison Power Systems, Zanesville, 1985-88; cons., 1988; lead engr. Rochester (N.Y.) Gas & Electric Corp., 1988-97; lead quality auditor Underwriters Labs., Inc., Melville, NY, 1997—. Mem. Am. Soc. Quality Control (cert. quality engr.), Am. Soc. Metals. Avocations: photography, art. Home and Office: 9498 Babcock Blvd Allison Park PA 15101-2039

PREIS, CARL OTTO, company executive, mechanical engineer; b. Bklyn., Jan. 14, 1927; s. Otto and Madeline Adele Preis; m. Vera Marie Mayer, Aug. 2, 1952; children: Carl Ernest, Brenda Marie. Student, Cornell U., 1950-51; BME, Poly. U., Bklyn., 1957. Registered profl. engr., N.Y. WTS engr. Republic Aviation, Farmingdale, N.Y., 1951, missile design engr. Missile divsn. N.Y.C. and Hicksville, 1951-58; with Hazeltine Corp., Little Neck, 1959, shock and vibration cons. Green Lawn, 1959-64; CEO, Preis Mayer Corp., Baldwin, 1965-87, Copace Corp., Baldwin, 1968—. Cons. engr., Baldwin, 1955—; operator Timber Hill Farm, Presque Isle, Maine. Editor Atlantic Rock Artisans Newsletter, 1970-80. Night school instr. Baldwin Adult Edn., 1970-80; past pres. Rep. Social Club, Baldwin. With USNR, 1942-46. Mem. Am. Assn. for Artificial Intelligence, N.Y. Soc. Profl. Inventors, Pi Tau Sigma (hon.), Phi Sigma Kappa. Achievements include patent for variable frequency vibration absorber. Home and Office: 2249 Charing Cross Rd Baldwin NY 11510-3048

PREISER, WOLFGANG FRIEDRICH ERNST, architect, educator, consultant, researcher; b. Freiburg, Germany, June 26, 1941; came to U.S., 1967; s. Gerhard Friedrich and Ursula Helene (von Huelsen) P.; m. Cecilia M. Fenoglio, Feb. 16, 1985; children: Johanna, Timothy, Andreas, Nicholas. Student, Vienna Tech. U., 1963; diploma in Engring., Architecture, U. Karlsruhe, 1967; M.Arch., Va. Poly. Inst. and State U., 1969; PhD in Man-Environ. Relations, Pa. State U., 1973. Architect, Germany, Austria, Eng., 1960-66; prof. architecture Va. Poly. Inst. and State U., Pa. State U., U. Ill., U. N.Mex., U. Cin., 1970—; research architect constrn. engring. research lab. U.S. Army, 1973-76; co-dir. Inst. Environ. Edn., U. N.Mex., 1976-86; dir. Ctr. for R & D, U. N.Mex., Albuquerque, 1986-90; dir. research Archtl. Research Cons. Inc., 1976—. Lectr. ednl., profl. and civic groups worldwide; v.p. faculty club U. N.Mex., 1976-78; pres. Internat. Club, Va. Poly. Inst. and State U., 1968-69; rschr. in field. Editor, author 14 books on facility programming, post-occupancy evaluation, design review, pub. housing, universal design, and design rsch.; contbr. over 75 articles in field to books and profl. jours. Trustee Cin. Chamber Orch., 1992-98, v.p., 1995-98. Recipient Career award Environ. Design Rsch. Assn., 1999, Ann. Rieveschl award, U. Cin., 1999, MCB Univ. Press (U.K.) award for excellence, 1998, Faculty Devel. award for rsch. U. Cin., 1992, Faculty Achievement award, 1995, Pogue/Wheeler Traveling award, 1993, Dean's Spl. award, 1994, Finland's Inst. Tech. award, 1966, awards Am. Iron and Steel Inst., 1968, Progressive Arch. Ann., 1985, 89, undergrad. teaching award U. Ill., 1976, hon. mention 1st Kyoto award Internat. Coun. of Soc. for Indsl. Design, 1979; Fulbright fellow, 1967, 87, Ford Found. fellow, 1968, Nat. Endowment for Arts fellow, 1979, 82; grad. fellow U. Cin., 1996. Mem. Soc. Human Ecology (pres. 1980-86), Environ. Design Research Assn. (vice chmn. 1974-76, sec. 1973-74), Nat. Acad. Scis. (chmn. com. on programming and post-occupancy evaluation, bldg. research bd., 1985-86), U. Cin. Grad. Fellows (elected), Phi Kappa Phi. Office: U Cin Coll Daap Sch Architecture Cincinnati OH 45221-0001 E-mail: wolfgang.preiser@uc.edu.

PREISS, JACK, biochemistry educator; b. Bklyn., June 2, 1932; s. Erool and Gilda (Friedman) P.; m. Karen Sue; children: Jennifer Ellen, Jeremy Oscar, Jessica Michelle. BS in Chemistry, CCNY, 1953; PhD in Biochemistry, Duke U., 1957. Scientist NIH, Bethesda, 1960-62; asst. prof. dept. biochemistry, biophysics U. Calif., Davis, 1962-65, assoc. prof., 1965-68, prof., 1968-85, chair dept. biochemistry, 1971-74, 77-81; prof. dept. biochemistry Mich. State U., East Lansing, 1985-2000, univ. disting. prof., 2001—, chair dept., 1985-89, Univ. Disting. Prof., 2001—. Mem. editorial bd. Jour. Bacteriology, 1969-74, Arch. Biochem. Biophysics, 1969—, Plant Physiology, 1969-74, 77-80, assoc. editor, 1980-92, editor, 1993-95; editor Jour. Biol. Chemistry, 1971-76, 78-83, 94-99, 2000-04, Plant Physiol. Biochemistry, 1997—; 16th loomis lectr. Iowa State U., 1997-98. Recipient Camille and Henry Dreyfus Disting. scholar award Calif. State U., 1983, Alexander von Humboldt Stiftung Sr. U.S. Scientist award, 1984, Award of Merit, Japanese Soc. Starch Sci., 1992, Disting. Faculty Mem. award Mich. Assn. Governing Bds. of State Univs., 1997, Mich. Scientist of Yr. award Impressions 5 Mus., 1997, award lectr. Spanish Biochem. Soc., 2000; Alsberg-Schoch Meml. lectr. Am. Assn. Cereal Chemists, 1990, Nat. Sci. Coun. lectr. Republic of China, 1988; Guggenheim Meml. fellow, 1969-70, Japan Soc. for Promotion of Sci. fellow, 1992-93; grantee NIH, 1963-97, NSF, 1978-89, Dept. of Energy, 1993—, USDA, 1988—. Mem. AAAS, Am. Chem. Soc. (Charles Pfizer award in enzyme chemistry 1971), Biochem. Soc., Am. Soc. Biol. Chemists and Molecular Biology, Am. Soc. Microbiologists, Am. Soc. Plant Physiologists, Soc. for Complex Carbohydrates, Protein Soc., Pan Am. Soc. Biochemistry and Molecular Biology (sec. gen. 1994-96, vice chmn. 1997-99, chmn. 2000-2002). Office: Mich State Univ Dept Of Biochemistry & Molecular Biology East Lansing MI 48824 E-mail: preiss@msu.edu.

PREISS-HARRIS, PATRICIA, music educator, composer, pianist; b. N.Y.C., May 19, 1950; d. Fredric H. and Madeline (Robbins) P.; m. Eric A. Lerner, Nov. 1970 (div. 1975); m. William H. Harris, Aug. 13, 1995. BA, Harvard U., 1973; MFA, Calif. Inst. Arts, 1987. Performer, bassist Carla Bley Band, Willow, N.Y., 1977-78; instr. piano, composition The Hall Sch., Pittsfield, Mass., 1983-84; instr. music Santa Monica (Calif.) C.C., 1989; tchr. piano The Hackley Sch., Tarrytown, N.Y., 1991; tchr. piano and composition Fraioli Sch. of Music, Greenwich, Conn., 1991—2002; accompanist SUNY, Purchase, N.Y., 1991-95; performer, pianist Gary Wofsey Jazz Orchestra, 1996—, The Jones Factor Big Band, 1999—. Pvt. piano tchr., NY, 1980—, Conn., 1980—, Mass., 1980—84; pianist Greenwich Regency Hyatt Hotel, 1995—; solo and ensemble pianist, 1980—; accompanist Blue Notes vocal ensemble, 2000—; attendee Cummington (Mass.) Cmty. of Arts, 1981. Performer Trust in Love, 1981; composer, pianist Jamaica's Album, 1984; composer Messages (piano & flute), 1980, Invocations (women's choir, medieval instruments), 1981, Complete Enlightenment (woodwinds, spkr.), 1986. Performance grantee Cambridge (Mass.) Arts Coun., 1977, Artists grantee No. Berkshire Coun. on Arts, 1983 Home: 162 Toms Rd Stamford CT 06906-1031 E-mail: patti@pattipreiss.com.

PREKSIN, OLEG, bank executive, consultant; b. Moscow, Russia, July 28, 1951; s. Mikhail Preksin and Zinaida Preksina; m. Elena Rulnova Preksina, Jan. 3, 1973; children: Anna Preksina, Olga Preksina. Qualified Economist, Acad. Fin. , Moscow, 1973; PhD East-West Trade and Fin. , USA and Can. Inst. Russian Acad. Sci., Moscow, 1978. Economist, mgr. Bank Fgn. Trade USSR, Moscow, 1972—86; sr. analyst Coun. of Ministers, 1987—88; dep. chmn. Donau Bank, Vienna, 1988—92; dir. Russian Fedn., mem. bd. dirs. European Bank Reconstruction and Devel., London, 1992—96; head London office Russian Inward Investment Promotion Ctr., 1996—98; mng. dir. Russian Fin. and Banking Union, Moscow, 2002—, Euroinvest Group, London, 2002—. Mng. dir. other comml. and non-profitable orgns. in various countries , 2002—. Mem.: EBRD Cir., Com. Fin. and Monetary Issues Russian Parliament (mem. expert coun. 2000—02), Com. Credit Instns. and Fin. Markets (mem. expert coun.), Nat. Club (Moscow), Inst. Dirs. (London), Reform Club. Office Fax: 0044 201 839 3066.

PREM, F. HERBERT, JR. lawyer; b. N.Y.C., Jan. 14, 1932; s. F. Herbert and Sybil Gertrude (Nichols) Prem; m. Patricia Ryan Prem, Nov. 18, 1978; children from previous marriage: Julia Nichols, F. Herbert III(dec.). AB, Yale U., 1953; JD, Harvard U., 1959. Bar: N.Y. 1960. Assoc. Whitman & Ransom, N.Y.C., 1959-66, ptnr., 1967-93, co-chmn. exec. com., 1988-92, chmn., 1993; chmn. Whitman Breed Abbott & Morgan LLP, 1993-99, of counsel, 2000; vol. atty. The Legal Aid Soc., 2000—. Bd. dirs. Fuji Photo Film U.S.A., Inc., Fujifilm Med. Sys. U.S.A., Inc., Seiko Instruments Am., Inc. Bd. dirs. Bagaduce Music Lending Libr., Inc., 1988—95, pres., 1989—93; bd. dirs. The HealthCare Chaplaincy, Inc., InterFaith Neighbors, Inc., Legal Aid Soc., N.Y.C., 1969—73, Cmty. Action for Legal Svc., Inc., 1967—70, treas. Lt. (j.g.) USNR, 1953—56. Mem. ABA, Assn. of Bar of City of N.Y. (sec. 1967-69), N.Y. State Bar Assn., Am. Law Inst. (life), Union Club, Yale Club. Episcopalian.

PREM, KONALD ARTHUR, physician, educator; b. St. Cloud, Minn., Nov. 6, 1920; s. Joseph E. and Theresa M. (Willing) P.; m. Phyllis Edelbrock, June 14, 1947; children: Mary Kristen, Stephanie, Timothy. BS, U. Minn., 1947; M.B., 1950, MD, 1951. Diplomate: Am. Bd. Ob-Gyn (with spl. competence in gynecologic oncology). Intern Mpls. gen. Hosp., 1950-51; fellow dept. obstetrics and gynecology U. Minn., Mpls., 1951-54, instr., 1955-58, asst. prof., 1958-60, assoc. prof., 1960-69, prof., 1969-93; prof. emeritus, 1993—; dir. div. gynecologic oncology U. Minn., 1969-83, head dept. obstetrics and gynecology, 1976-84; prof. dept. surgery, 1993-96. Served to capt. USAR, 1941-46; brig. gen. M.C. USAR (Ret.). Decorated Legion of Merit. Mem. Am. Coll. Ob-Gyn, Am. Gynec. and Obstet. Soc., Central Assn. Ob-Gyn, Hennepin County Med. Soc., Soc. Pelvic Surgeons, Minn. Ob-Gyn Soc., Soc. Gynecologic Oncologists, Internat. Soc. Gynecologic Pathologists, Soc. Gynecologic Surgery, Minn. Acad. Medicine, Am. Radium Soc., Am. Assn. Pro-Life Ob-Gyn. Roman Catholic. Home: 15660-16 Place N Plymouth MN 55447-2497

PREMACHANDRA, BHARTUR NARASIMHAIENGAR, endocrinology educator, researcher; b. Bangalore, Mysore, India; came to U.S., 1955; s. Bhartur and Seshammal Narasimhaiengar; m. Ashalatha Anantram, Aug. 4, 1963; children: Padmavathi Nartan, Yoganand Naveen. PhD, U. Mo., 1958; DSc, U. Bombay, 1981. Rsch. assoc., asst. prof. U. Mo., Columbia, 1956-60; rsch. assoc. Jewish Hosp., St. Louis, 1960-62; radiation safety officer VA Med. Ctr./Jefferson Barracks, 1962-69, rsch. endocrinologist, 1962-95; dir. geriatrics and endocrinology dept. psychology Washington U., 1966-71, rsch. prof., 1967—; dir. Thyroid Splty. Lab., Inc., 1991—. Manuscript cons. Endocrinology, Jour. Clin. Endocrinology and Metabolism; Sci., Am. Jour. Medicine; rsch. proposal cons. VA/EPA, 1982—. Contbr.: (book) Hormones in Normal & Abnormal Human Tissues, 1981, Autoimmunity & the Thyroid, 1985; contbr. articles to Endocrinology, Jour. Clin. Endocrinology & Metabolism. Kiepe fellow U. Mo., 1958-59, recipient Curator's award, 1958-60. Fellow Royal Inst. Chemistry; mem. Am. Thyroid Assn., Endocrine Soc., Physiol. Soc. Achievements include research in thyroid hormone binding and amyloidosis; patent for radioimmunoassay technique. Home: 5 Blaytonn Ln Saint Louis MO 63124-1109 Office: Thyroid Splty Lab Inc 2900 Lemay Ferry Rd Ste 114 Saint Louis MO 63125-3915

PREMACK, ANN J. writer; b. Shanghai, China, Jan. 5, 1929; interned in Japanese detention ctr., 1943-45; came to the U.S., 1945; d. John Joseph James and Mae Victoria Parker; m. David Premack, Oct. 26, 1951; children: Ben, Lisa, Tim. BS with distinction, U. Minn., 1951. Author: Why Chimps Can Read, 1975; co-author (with D. Premack)): The Mind of An Ape, 1983; co-editor: Causal Cognition: A Multidisciplinary Debate, 1995; co-author (with D. Premack)): Original Intelligence: Unlocking the Mystery of Who We Are, 2002; contbr. Avocation: owning and running an avocado grove. Home: 6163 Heatherton Dr Somis CA 93066-9716 E-mail: dpremack@aol.com.

PREMACK, DAVID, psychologist; b. Aberdeen, S.D., Oct. 26, 1925; s. Leonard B. and Sonja (Liese) P.; m. Ann M. James, Oct. 26, 1951; children: Ben, Lisa, Timothy. BA, U. Minn., 1949, PhD, 1955. Rsch. assoc. Yerkes Labs. Primate Biology, Orange Park, Fla., 1955; rsch. assoc., asst. prof. psychology U. Mo., Columbia, 1956-58, assoc. prof., 1959-62, prof., 1963-64, U. Calif., Santa Barbara, 1965-75; vis. prof. Harvard U., 1970-71; prof. U. Pa., 1975—. Artist-in-residence Yaddo, Saratoga Springs, N.Y., 1955; fellow Van Leer Jerusalem Inst., 1980, Inst. for Advanced Study, Berlin, 1985-86; vis. scientist Japan Soc. for Promotion Sci., 1980; univ. rsch. lectr. U. Calif., Santa Barbara, 1973; mem. sci. gov. bd. Fyssen Found., Paris, 1989—; assoc. neurosci. rsch. program, La Jolla, Calif., 1991—. Author: Intelligence in Ape and Man, 1976, (with Ann James Premack) The Mind of an Ape, 1983, Gavagai! Or the Future History of the Animal Language Controversy, 1986 (with Dan Sperber and Ann James Premack) Causal Cognition: A Multidisciplinary Debate, 1995, (with Ann James Premack) Original Intelligence: The Architecture of the Human Mind, 2002, (with Ann Premack) The Cognitive Gap: The Architecture of Human Need, 2002; mem. editl. bd. Jour. Exptl. Psychology: Animal Processes, 1976—, Cognition, 1977—, Brain and Behavior Sci., 1978—, Jour. Cognitive Neurosci. Served with U.S. Army, 1943-46. Ford Found. teaching intern, 1954; USPHS postdoctoral fellow, 1956-59; Social Sci. Research Council fellow, summer 1963; Center for Advanced Study in Behavioral Scis. fellow, 1972-73; Guggenheim fellow, 1979-80; grantee NSF, 1961— , USPHS, 1960-80; recipient Kenneth Craik Research award St. John's Coll.-Cambridge U., 1987, Internat. Sci. prize Fyssen Found., Paris, 1987. Fellow AAAS; mem. Soc. Exptl. Psychologists. Home: 6163 Heatherton Dr Somis CA 93066-9716 also: CREA, Ecole Polytechnique 1 rue Descartes 75005 Paris France E-mail: dpremack@aol.com.

PREMEAUX, SHANE RICHARD, marketing educator; b. Gueyden, La., Mar. 13, 1954; s. Percy Donat and Florence Mary Premeaux; m. Jennifer Lynn Brandlein; 1 child Paige Elizabeth. BS in Acctg., McNeese State U., 1976, MBA, 1977; PhD in Mktg., U. Ark., 1982. Asst. prof. mktg. Northwestern La. U., Natchitoches, 1981-82, N.E. La. U., Monroe, 1982-84, Southeastern U., Hammond, La., 1984-85; prof. mktg. McNeese State U., Lake Charles, 1985—. Reviewer Bus. Jour., Jour. Bus. Strategies; cons. in field. Author: Personal Selling: Function, Theory, and Practice, 4th edit., 1998, Supervision, 3d edit., 1998, Human Resources Management, 8th edit., 2002, Management and Organizational Behavior, 1990, Management Concepts and Practices, 5th edit., 1990, Management Concepts and Practices, 8th edit., 2000, among others; contbr. over 60 articles to profl. and acad. jours. Recipient numerous grants. Mem. Assn. Grad. Bus. Dirs., McNeese U. MBA Assn., McNeese U. Alumni Assn., U. Ark. Alumni Assn., Southwestern Mktg. Assn., Soc. for Advancement of Mgmt., Sigma Iota Epsilon, Alpha Mu Alpha, Delta Nu Alpha, Tau Kappa Epsilon. Republican. Roman Catholic. Office: McNeese State U Coll Bus PO Box 92135 Lake Charles LA 70609-0001

PREMO, PAUL MARK, oil company executive; b. Syracuse, N.Y., Nov. 20, 1942; s. Matthias George and Kathryn (Whitbread) P.; m. Mary Catherine Hennessy, June 19, 1965; children— Deborah, Mark BS in Chem. Engring., Manhattan Coll., Riverdale, N.Y., 1964; S.M. in Chem. Engring., MIT, 1965. Chem. engr. Chevron Research, Richmond, Calif., 1965-69; fin. analyst Chevron Corp., San Francisco, 1969-72, coordinator, mgr. supply and distbn., 1972-79; mgr. petroleum regulations Chevron USA, 1979-81, sec.-treas., 1981-85, mgr. property tax adminstrn., 1985-86, mgr. natural gas regulatory affairs, 1986-92; exec. cons. Resource Mgmt. Internat., San Rafael, Calif., 1992-95; v.p. Foster Assoc., Inc., San Francisco, 1996-98; prin. Energy Econs. Consulting, Mill Valley, Calif., 1998—. Dir. Ky. Agrl. Energy Corp., Franklin Trustee Calif. Tax Found., 1985— Mem. Calif. State C. of C. (tax com.), Western Oil and Gas Assn., Am. Petroleum Inst. (property tax com.), Natural Gas Supply Assn., Inst. Property Taxation, Calif. Taxpayers Assn. (bd. dirs.

1985—), MIT Alumni Assn., Commonwealth (San Francisco), Sigma Xi, Tau Beta Pi. Avocations: sailing, investments. Home: 310 Hazel Ave Mill Valley CA 94941-5054 Office: 310 Hazel Ave Mill Valley CA 94941-5054 E-mail: paulpremo@msn.com.

PRENDERGAST, CAROLE LISAK, musician, educator; b. Chgo., Mar. 15, 1949; d. Chester Matt and Emily Julie (Krupa) Lisak; m. Joseph Thomas Prendergast, Oct. 19, 1974; children: Karin, Colin. MusB, DePaul U., 1971; MusM, St. Joseph's Coll., Rensselaer, Ind., 2002. Tchg. cert. K-14, Ill. Substitute organist St. Adalbert Ch., Chgo., 1965-76; music tchr. Chgo. Pub. Schs., 1971-74; music dir. St. Adalbert Ch., 1976-88; freelance musician, 1988—; choir accompanist St. Luke Ch., River Forest, Ill., 1993—, music dir., 2000—. Piano tchr., Chgo., 1970—. Chairperson welcome com. Queen of Martyrs Ch., Evergreen Park, Ill., 1990—. Ill. state scholar, 1968-71, DePaul scholar, 1968. Mem. Am. Guild Organists, Nat. Assn. Pastoral Musicians, Music Tchrs. Nat. Assn., Chgo. Fedn. Musicians, Chgo. Area Suzuki Tchrs., Suzuki Assn. of the Ams. Roman Catholic. Avocations: gardening, travel, antique collecting, sewing. Home: 10417 S Hamlin Ave Chicago IL 60655-3115 Office: St Luke Ch 528 Lathrop River Forest IL 60305

PRENDERGAST, CURTIS WALKER, journalist; b. Stockton, Calif., Oct. 21, 1915; s. Arthur Curtis and Catherine Lois (Walker) Prendergast; m. Elizabeth Clarke Prendergast, Apr. 8, 1944; children: Catherine, James, David, Sarah. AB in Philosophy, Stanford U., 1937; degree in Oriental langs., U. Calif., Berkeley, 1946; student, U. Colo.; grad., USN Japanese Lang. Sch., 1945. Bur. chief Time mag., Tokyo, 1954—57, Johannesburg, 1957—59, Paris, 1960—68, London, 1968—72; assoc. editor Time Europe, Paris, 1973; bur. chief Time mag., N.Y.C., 1974—77. Bd. dirs. World Press Freedom Com., Reston, Va., exec. com., Va. Co-author: The World of Time Inc., 1986; author: Easy Gardens, 1981; co-author: The First Aviators. Prin. drafter Charter for a Free Press World Press Freedom Com. to UNESCO. Lt. USN, 1942—46. Mem.: Time-Life Alumni Soc. (co-founder, past pres.). Avocation: carpentry. Home: 4970 Sentinel Dr Bethesda MD 20816

PRENDERGAST, GEORGE C. molecular biologist, researcher; b. Phila., Aug. 25, 1961; s. George A. and Mary C. P.; m. Kristine Kushmeider, Oct. 25, 1986. BA magna cum laude, U. Pa., 1983; MS, Yale U., 1984; PhD, Princeton U., 1989. Postdoctoral fellow NYU Med. Ctr. Am. Cancer Soc., 1989-91; sr. rsch. biochemist Am. Cancer Soc. Merck and Co., Inc., West Point, Pa., 1991-93; asst. prof. Wistar Inst., U. Pa., Phila., 1993-97, assoc. prof., 1997—2001; sr. dir. cancer rsch. DuPont Pharms. Co., Glenolden, 1999—2001; sr. investigator Lankenau Inst. Med. Rsch., 2002—; prof. Thomas Jefferson U., Phila., 2002—. Assoc. editor jour. Cancer Rsch.; contbr. articles to profl. jours.; patentee in field. Recipient Jr. Faculty award Am. Cancer Soc., 1995—, Biomed. Scholar award Pew Charitable Trusts, 1995-99, Rsch. award NIH, 1995—, CaPCURE Prostate Cancer award, 1996, 97; Pfizer traveling fellow, 1997. Mem. Am. Assn. Cancer Rsch. Office: Thomas Jefferson U Lankenau Inst Med Rsch Dept Pathology Anatomy and Cell Biol 100 Lancaster Ave Wynnewood PA 19096 Office Fax: 610-645-8090. Business E-Mail: prendergastg@mlhs.org.

PRENDERGAST, KENNETH LEE MICHAEL, JR. career officer; b. Macdill Air Force Base, Fla., Sept. 16, 1956; s. Kenneth Lee and Pauline Ann (Hall) P.; m. Naomi Sue Kincade, Aug. 6, 1976; children: Melissa Ann, Robert Anthony. BA, Jacksonville State U., 1986; BS, U. N.Y., 1986; MA, U. Fla., 1990; MPA, Troy State U., 1997. Enlisted U.S. Army, 1978, commd. 2d lt. mil. police corps, 1982; advanced through ranks to lt. col., 1997; exec. officer Company D 1st Battalion, Ft. McClellan, Ala., 1983; aide de camp to dep. comdg. gen., M.P. sch. commandant, 1984-85; ops. tng. officer Provost Marshal's Office U.S. Army WESTCOM, Ft. Shafter, Hawaii, 1987; co. commdr. U.S. Army Support Commd., 1988-89; ops. officer Provost Marshal's Office U.S. Army Law Enforcement Command, Hawaii, 1989; fgn. area officer U.S. Embassy, Kinshasa, Zaire, 1991, Yaounde, Cameroon, 1992-93; internat. officer instr. U.S. Army Command and Gen. Staff Coll., Ft. Leavenworth, Kans., 1993; MP long range plans officer 89th Mil. Police Brigade, Ft. Hood, Tex., 1994-95; exec. officer 720th Mil. Police Battalion, 1995-96; Am. Polit. Sci. Assn. congrl. fellow Senator Bob Graham, Washington, 1996-97; chief of plans and ops. office Chief of Legis. Liaison Office of Sec., U.S. Army, 1997-98; dir. legis. strategy Washington, 1998-99; bn. comdr. 19th Mil. Police Bn., Seoul, 1999—2001; provost marshal Fort Meade, MD, 2001—. Vol. coach youth football, soccer, baseball, 1974—; leader Boy Scouts Am., Ft. Hood, 1989—, mem. com., 1994-96. Decorated Legion of Merit. Mem. VFW, Ret. Officers Assn., Korean-Am. Assn., Assn. U.S. Army, 720th Mil. Police Battalion Reunion Assn., Mil. Police Regimental Assn., Fgn. Area Officer Assn. (founding), U. Fla. Nat. Alumni Assn. (life), Jacksonville State U. Alumni Assn. (life), Am. Polit. Sci. Assn., Am. C. of C. in Korea, Alpha Kappa Delta. Roman Catholic. Avocations: sailing, scuba diving, water-skiing, skydiving, travel. E-mail: co19mPBn@hotmail.com., kenneth.prendergast@us.army.mil.

PRENDERGAST, THOMAS A. investments and management consultant; b. Dec. 10, 1933; m. Mary Alice Peinado; children: Elizabeth Jane Mettler, Laura Ann Gordon. BS, Fordham U., 1955; postgrad., U. Tex., El Paso, 1960. CPA, Tex. Pvt. practice acctg., 1957-61; v.p. fin. Farah Mfg., Inc., 1961-71; chmn. bd. Billy the Kid, Inc., 1971-81, Jetco, 1972-74, Fashion Enterpreses, Inc., 1982-84, Air Cargo Equipment Corp., 1983-88, investments, mgmt. cons.; chmn. bd. El Paso Gibson's, Inc., 1988—92; chmn. Sunland Audio Ltd. Co., 1994—98, N.Am. Bender, Inc., 1995—2000. Chmn. bd. dirs. Baron Chem., Inc., Clinitech, Inc., 1986-91, Steel Corp. Tex., Texzona Industries, Inc., True Blue Sky, Inc.; bd. dirs. Market Guide Inc., Air Cargo Inc., Fischback and Moore Inc., Double Eagle Petroleum, Inc; chmn. Market Guide, 1997-99. Composer various music works; author poetry, film criticsm; contbr. articles on computer software digital printing to industry jours. Founder, pres. bd. trustees El Paso Community Coll, 1969-82. Home: 725 Montoya Oak El Paso TX 79932

PRENDERGAST, WILLIAM JOHN, ophthalmologist; b. Portland, Oreg., June 12, 1942; s. William John and Marjorie (Scott) P.; m. Carolyn Grace Perkins, Aug. 17, 1963 (div. 1990); children: William John, Scott; m. Sherryl Irene Guenther, Aug. 25, 1991. BS, U. Oreg., Eugene, 1964; MD, U. Oreg., Portland, 1967. Diplomate Am. Bd. Ophthalmology. Resident in ophthalmology U. Oreg., Portland, 1970-73; pvt. practice specializing in ophthalmology, 1973-82; physician, founder, ptnr. Eye Health NW (formerly Oreg. Med. Eye Clinic), 1983—; also bd. dirs.; founder, pres. (Focus Group) Inc. Focus Group Inc., Ophthalmic Clinic Networking Venture, Portland, 1992—. Clin. asst. prof. ophthalmology Oreg. Health Sci. U., 1985—; dir. Eye Health Ptnrs. Med. Optometric Managed Eye Care Venture, 1998. Vol. surgeon, Hosp. de la Familia, Nuevo Progreso, Guatamala, 2001, vol. surgeon N.W. Med. Teams, Oaxaca, Mexico, 1989, 90. With USPHS, 1968-70. Fellow Am. Acad. Ophthalmology; mem. Met. Bus. Assn., Multnomah Athletic Club, Mazamas Mountaineering Club, Portland Yacht Club, Phi Beta Kappa, Alpha Omega Alpha. Avocations: yacht racing, mountaineering. Office: Eye Health NW 1955 NW Northrup St Portland OR 97209-1614 E-mail: prenderw@omec.ehnpc.com.

PRENG, DAVID EDWARD, management consultant; b. Chgo., Sept. 30, 1946; s. Edward M. and Frances (Maras) P.; m. JoAnne Ferzoco, Dec. 6, 1969; children: Mark, Laura, Stephen, Michael. BS, Marquette U., 1969; MBA, DePaul U., 1973. Supr. Shell Oil Co., Houston, 1969—73, Chgo., 1969—73; contr. Litton Office Products, Houston, 1973—74; v.p. Addington & Assocs., 1976—77; sr. assoc. Energy divsn. Korn/Ferry Internat., 1977—78; v.p. Kors Marlar & Assocs., 1978—80; pres. Preng & Assocs., 1980—85, Preng Zant & Assocs., 1985—87, Preng & Assoc., 1987—. Bd. dirs. Citizens Nat. Bank of Tex. Mem. Sugar Creek Country Club. Home: 607 Chevy Chase Cir Sugar Land TX 77478-3601

PRENGLE, HERMAN WILLIAM, JR. chemical engineer, educator; b. Pa., Nov. 6, 1919; s. Herman William and Irene (Smith) P.; m. Ruth Hamilton, Dec. 6, 1941; children: Pixie Bernice Irene, Karl William, Scott Hamilton. BS, Carnegie-Mellon U., 1941, MS, 1947, DSc, 1949. Registered profl. engr., Tex. Rsch. engr. Linde Air Products Co., Tonwanda, N.Y., 1941; sr. engr. Shell Oil Co., Houston, 1949-53; assoc. prof. U. Houston, 1953-59, prof., 1959-97, prof. emeritus, 1997—, chmn. chem. engring. dept., 1958-61, assoc. dean Cullen Coll. Engring., 1981-85, dir. MChE program chem. engring. dept., 1985-97. Vis. scholar chemistry dept. Cambridge (Eng.) U., 1971-72, Corpus Christi Coll., 1988, Darwin Coll., 1990; cons. chem. and petroleum industries U.S. Govt., 1958—; panel mem. peer rev. of rsch. U.S. EPA, Washington, 1975-97. Contbr. articles to profl. jours. Chmn. Charter Commn., Friendswood, Tex., 1970-71; mem. Nat. Rep. Com., Washington, 1980—; mem. Rep. Presdl. Task Force, Washington, 1983—; mem. U.S. Com. Battle Normandy Mus., Caen, France, 1988—. Lt. col. U.S. Army, 1941-46, ETO. Decorated Bronze Star with oak leaf cluster; recipient Kittinger Tchg. award U. Houston Cullen Coll. Engring., 1971, award of Merit, Pollution Engring. Mag., Chgo., 1976, Tchg. Excellence award Haliburton Found., 1989, 92, 94, 96. Fellow Am. Inst. Chemists; mem. AIChE, Am. Chem. Soc., Royal Chem. Soc. (London), Army-Navy Club, Brotherhood of St. Andrew, Sigma Xi, Tau Beta Pi, Phi Kappa Phi. Episcopalian. Achievements include 3 patents (with others) for ozone-UV advanced oxidation prodess for water borne toxic compounds; invention (with other) of ammonium hydrogen sulfate (AHS) and duplex AHS solar energy storage process; invention (with others) of infrared radiometry spectroscopy method (IRSM) for remote sensing of temperatures, gradients and pollutant concentrations from stationary emission sources; invention (with others) of the hydrogen peroxide-VisUV process (HP/VisUV) for treatment of hazardous water borne substances and gaseous emissions; invention and patent (with others) for improved apparatus for fractional distillation of multi-component hydrocarbon mixtures. Home: 105 Sandpiper Cv Georgetown TX 78628-4809

PRENSKY, ARTHUR LAWRENCE, pediatric neurologist, educator; b. N.Y.C., Aug. 31, 1930; s. Herman and Pearl (Newman) P.; m. Sheila Carr, Nov. 13, 1969. AB, Cornell U., 1951; MD, N.Y. U., 1955. Diplomate: Am. Bd. Psychiatry and Neurology. Intern Barnes Hosp., St. Louis, 1955-56; resident and research fellow in neurology Harvard U., Mass. Gen. Hosp., Boston, 1959-66; instr. neurology Harvard Med. Sch., 1966-67; mem. faculty Washington U. Sch. Medicine, St. Louis, 1967—, prof. pediatrics and neurology, to 1975, Allen P. and Josephine B. Green prof. pediatric neurology, 1975-2000, prof. emeritus of neurology, 2000—; pediatrician St. Louis Children's Hosp.; neurologist Barnes and Allied Hosps., Jewish Hosp., St. Louis. Author: (with others) Nutrition and the Developing Nervous System, 1975; editor: (with others) Neurological Pathophysiology, 2d edit, 1978, Advances in Neurology, 1976; mem. editorial bd. Pediatric Neurology, 1984-90, Jour. Child Neurology, 1985—. Served with USAF, 1957-59. Fellow Am. Acad. Neurology; mem. Am. Neurol. Assn., Am. Soc. Neurochemistry (mem. council 1973-77), Central Soc. Neurol. Research (pres. 1977-78), Child Neurology Soc. (pres. 1979-80, Hower award 2000), Am. Pediatric Soc., Internat. Child Neurology Assn., Japanese Soc. Child Neurology, Profs. Child Neurology (pres. 1984-86) Home: 15 Monarch Hill Ct Chesterfield MO 63005-4004 Office: 400 S Kingshighway Blvd Saint Louis MO 63110-1014

PRENTICE, JAMES STUART, energy company executive, chemical engineer; b. Louisville, Feb. 4, 1944; s. John Edward and Helen (Staples) P.; m. Mary Joan Kelly, July 24, 1945; children: Holly Michelle, Craig Edward (dec.), Brian Andrew. BChemE, U. Louisville, 1966; MS, Northwestern U., 1967. Rsch. engr. Esso Rsch. and Engring. Co., Baytown, Tex., 1967-71; engr., supr. ops., mkt. mgr. to plant mgr. No. Petrochem. Co., Morris and Des Plaines, Ill., 1971-82, v.p. mfg. Omaha, 1982-85; sr. v.p. corp. planning HNG/Internorth, 1985-86; sr. v.p. adminstrn. and human resources Enron Transp. Svcs., Houston, 1986-87; exec. v.p. Enron Liquid Fuels, 1987-89; sr. v.p. Enron Gas Pipeline Group, 1989-93; sr. v.p., chief tech. officer Enron Ops. Corp., 1993-95, sr. v.p. human resources, 1995-96; pres. Enron Clean Fuels Co., 1996—2001; sr. v.p. Eott Energy Liquids, 2001—. Patentee in field. Bd. dirs. St. Joseph Hosp. Found., Child Advocates, Inc., CanCare, St. Joseph Hosp. Mem. AIChE, Lyons Fedn. Bd., Lakeside Country Club. Roman Catholic. Avocations: tennis, golf. Office: EOTT Energy Liquids BLP 5422 PO Box 4666 Houston TX 77210-4666 E-mail: James_Prentice@eott.com.

PRENTICE, TIM, sculptor, architect; b. N.Y.C., Nov. 5, 1930; s. T. Merrill and Theodora (Machado) P.; m. Marie Truesdale Bissell, Aug. 23, 1960; children: Nora L., Phoebe A. BA, Yale U., 1953, M.Arch., 1960. Gen. partner Prentice & Chan, Ohlhausen, Architects and predecessor, N.Y.C., 1966-74; adj. prof. archtl. design Columbia U., 1974-80. One-man shows include Inst. Arch. and Urban Studies, N.Y.C., 1975, Paul Mellon Arts Ctr., Wallingford, Conn., 1983, Aldrich Mus., Ridgefield, Conn., 1989, Bruce Mus., Greenwich, Conn., 1989, Maxwell Davidson Gallery, N.Y.C., 1990, 1992, 1994, 1997, 2000, 2002, Mattatuck Mus., Waterbury, Conn., 1990, Neville Sargent Gallery, Chgo., 1991, Robischon Gallery, Denver, 2000, 2002, exhibited in group shows at New Britain Mus. Am. Art, 1978, Carlson Art Gallery U. Bridgeport, 1978, Indpls. Mus. Art, 1978, Conn. Painting, Drawing and Sculpture Today, 1977, Parsons-Dreyfuss Gallery, N.Y.C., 1980, Am. Acad. and Inst. Arts and Letters, San Diego, 1993, Anderson Gallery, 1992, Soma Gallery, San Diego, 1993, Chgo. Cultural Ctr., 1993, Fitchburg (Mass.) Art Mus., Chattanooga, Ohio, 1995, Yale U., New Haven, 1995, The Discovery Mus., Bridgeport, 1999, Robischon Gallery, 1999, St. Gaudens Site, Cornish, Minn., 2002, Represented in permanent collections Am. Express Co., N.Y.C., AT&T Long Lines, Bedminster, N.Y., Henry St. Settlement, N.Y.C., major commns., , , , , , , . Served to lt. (j.g.) USNR, 1954-58. Dept. State cultural exchange grantee, 1963-64 Fellow AIA (pres. N.Y. chpt. 1973-74); mem. Nat. Council Archtl. Registration Bds., Mcpl. Arts Soc. N.Y. (pres. 1974-76) Clubs: Century Assn. Studio: 129 Lake Rd West Cornwall CT 06796-1402 E-mail: timprentice@mac.com.

PRENTKE, RICHARD OTTESEN, lawyer; b. Cleve., Sept. 8, 1945; s. Herbert E. and Melva B. (Horbury) P.; m. Susan Ottesen, June 9, 1974; children: Catherine, Elizabeth. BSE, Princeton U., 1967; JD, Harvard U., 1974. Assoc. Perkins Coie, Seattle, 1974-80, ptnr., 1981—, CFO, 1989-94. Author: School Construction Law Deskbook, 1989, rev. 2d edit. 1998; contbr. articles to profl. jours. Pres., trustee Seattle County Day Sch., 1990-95; trustee Pocock Rowing Found., 1996—. With USN, 1967-70. Fellow Leadership Tomorrow, Seattle, 1985-86. Mem. ABA, Wash. State Bar Assn. (mem. jud. screening com. 1985-91, chmn. 1987-91), Seattle-King County Bar Assn. (chmn. jud. task force 1990-93), Am. Arbitration Assn. (arbitrator 1988—), Princeton U. Rowing Assn. (pres. 1993—, trustee 1976—), Rainier Club, Princeton Club Wash. (trustee 1986—, pres. 1990-92), Seattle Tennis Club. Avocations: art, carpentry, travel, rowing, sports. Office: Perkins Coie 1201 3rd Ave Fl 40 Seattle WA 98101-3029

PREOBRAZHENSKY, ALEXANDER ANATOLIYEVICH, biochemist; b. Chita, Russia, Sept. 29, 1946; s. Anatoliy Nikolayevich and Magdalina Sergeyevna (Knyaginicheva) P.; m. Ekaterina Sergeyevna Grigoriyan, Mar. 14, 1970 (div. Jan. 1981); 1 child, Elena; m. Olga Stefanovna Zakharova, Dec. 22, 1984; 1 child, Sergei. Student, Moscow State U., 1970, PhD in Biology, 1976, DSc, 1996. Rsch. asst. Inst. for Protein Rsch., Pouschino, Russia, 1970-72; rsch. assoc. A.N. Bach Inst. of Biochemistry, Moscow, 1975-86, sr. scientist, 1986—. Grantee Ministry of Sci. and Tech., 1989, Russian Found. for Fundamental Rsch., 1994, 97, Internat. Sci. Found. Mem. Russian Biochem. Soc., N.Y. Acad. Scis. Avocations: hunting, tourism. Office: 2540 Olentangy River Rd Columbus OH 43202-1505

PREONAS, GEORGE ELIAS, lawyer; b. Dayton, Ohio, Oct. 5, 1943; s. Louis D. and Mary (Drakos) P.; m. Aileen Strike, June 1, 1944; children: Annemarie, Michael, Stephen. BA, Stanford U., 1965; JD, U. Mich., 1968. Bar: Ill. 1968, Nev. 1969, Calif. 1974. Ptnr. Seyfarth, Shaw, Fairweather & Geraldson, L.A., 1968—. Mem. ABA, L.A. County Bar Assn., Calif. Bar Assn., Ill. Bar Assn., Nev. Bar Assn. Office: Seyfarth Shaw 2029 Century Park E Ste 3300 Los Angeles CA 90067-3019

PRESANT, SANFORD CALVIN, lawyer, educator, writer, tax specialist; b. Buffalo, Nov. 15, 1952; s. Allen and Reeta Presant; children: Jarrett, Danny, Lauren; m. Nancy Loeb. BA, Cornell U., 1973; JD cum laude, SUNY, Buffalo, 1976; LLM in Taxation, Georgetown U., NYU, 1981. Bar: N.Y. 1977, D.C. 1977, U.S. Tax Ct. 1977, U.S. Ct. Claims 1978, Calif. 1992, U.S. Supreme Ct. 1982. Staff atty. SEC Options Task Force, Washington, 1976-78; assoc. Barrett Smith Schapiro, N.Y.C., 1978-80, Trubin Sillcocks, N.Y.C., 1980-81; ptnr. Carro, Spanbock, Fass, Geller, Kaster, 1981-86, Finley, Kumble, Wagner, Heine, Underberg, Manley, Myerson & Casey, N.Y.C., 1987, Kaye, Scholer, Fierman, Hays & Handler, N.Y.C., 1987-95, Battle Fowler LLP, L.A., 1995-2000, Ernst & Young, L.A., 2000—; nat. dir. real estate tax strategies, opportunity funds Ernst & Young LLP, 2000—. Adj. assoc. prof. real estate NYU, 1984—; frequest lectr. in tax law; regular TV appearances on Nightly Business Report, Pub. Broadcasting System, 1986-88; co-chmn. NYU Conf. Fed. Taxation of Real Estate Transactions, 1987, PLI Advanced Tax Planning for Real Estate, 1987, PLI Ann. Real Estate Tax Forum, 1999—; conf. chmn. various confs. in field. Author: (with others) Tax Aspects of Real Investments, 2002, Understanding Partnership Tax Allocations, 1987, Realty Joint Ventures, 1980-86, Tax Sheltered Investments Handbook-Special Update on Tax Reform Act of 1984, Real Estate Syndication Handbook, 1986, Real Estate Syndication Tax Handbook, 1987, The Tax Reform Act of 1986, 1987, The Final Partnership Nonrecourse Debt Allocation Regulations, 1987, Taxation of Real Estate Investments, 1987, Understanding Partnership Tax Allocations, 1987, Tax Aspects of Environmental (Superfund) Settlements, 1994, The Proposed Publicly Traded Partnership Regulations, 1995, others. Kripke Securities Law fellow NYU, 1976. Mem. ABA (nat. chmn. audit subcom. of tax sect. partnership com. 1984-86, partnership tax allocation subcom. chmn. 1986-90, nat. chmn. partnership com. 1992-94, chmn. task force publicly traded partnerships 1995—, others), N.Y. State Bar Assn. (tax sect. partnership com. 1980—), Assn. of Bar of City of N.Y. Republican. Jewish. Office: Ernst & Young LLP Ste 1800 2049 Century Park E Los Angeles CA 90067-3119 Fax: 310-284-7970. E-mail: sanford.presant@ey.com.

PRESBY, J. THOMAS, financial advisor, arbitrator; b. Newark, Feb. 15, 1940; s. George and Shirley (Kandel) P.; m. Elaine Merle Smith, Aug. 19, 1961; children: Philip, Terry, Mona. BSEE, Rutgers U., 1961; MS in Indsl. Adminstrn., Carnegie-Mellon U., 1963. CPA, Ohio, N.Y. Ptnr. Touche Ross, N.Y.C., 1972-76; regional ptnr. Touche Ross Internat., Paris, 1976-79, nat. dir. client svcs., 1979-81, exec. dir. internat., 1981-82, ptnr.-in-charge fin. svcs. ctr., 1982-90, mng. ptnr. Ea. Europe, Brussels, 1990-94, chief exec. officer Europe, Paris, 1991-95; COO Deloitte Touche Tohmatsu Internat., N.Y.C., 1995—, dep. chmn., 1997, chief staff, mem. exec. group, 1999—. Mem. bus. adv. coun. Grad. Sch. Indsl. Adminstrn., Carnegie-Mellon U., Pitts., 1984— ; trustee Rutgers U., New Brunswick, N.J., 1985-90, Coll. Ins., N.Y.C., 1986-89; bd. dirs. French Am. Found., German Marshall Fund. Mem. AICPA, Ohio Soc. CPAs, N.Y. Soc. CPAs, Harmonie Club. Avocations: antique autos; racquetball; squash, motorcycling. Home: 6 Holton Ln Essex Fells NJ 07021-1709 Office: Deloitte Touche 1633 Broadway New York NY 10019-6708 E-mail: tpresby@deloitte.com.

PRESCHLACK, JOHN EDWARD, management consultant; b. N.Y.C., May 30, 1933; s. William and Anna M. (Hrubesch) P.; m. Lynn A. Stanley, Dec. 29, 1962; children: John Edward Jr., James S., David C. BSEE, MIT, 1954; MBA, Harvard U., 1958. Ptnr. McKinsey & Co., Inc., N.Y.C., London, Düsseldorf, Germany, 1958-73; pres. ITEK Graphic Products Co., Lexington, Mass., 1973-77; pres., CEO Gen. Binding Corp., Northbrook, Ill., 1977-83; pres. Roberts & Porter, Inc., Des Plaines, 1984-86; sr. dir. Spencer Stuart, Chgo., 1987-96; chmn., pres. Jepcor, Inc., Lake Bluff, 1996—. Bd. dirs. Blyth Industries, Greenwich, Conn., 1989—. Trustee Chgo. Hort. Soc., 1979—; chmn. Lake Forest (Ill.) Planning Commn., 1982-88; alderman City of Lake Forest, 1990-96, mayor, 2002—; mem. devel. com. MIT, 1986-92. Lt. USAF, 1954-56. Recipient Corp. Leadership award MIT, 1978. Mem. Onwentsia Club, Chgo. Club, John's Island Club. Republican. Roman Catholic. Avocations: tennis, golf, boating, travel. E-mail: jepcor@aol.com. *Focus on what's right, not who's right; be honest and candid in dealing with others; don't get hung up on who gets credit for what you've done; select and reward outstanding people.*

PRESCOTT, BARBARA LODWICH, educational administrator; b. Chgo., Aug. 15, 1951; d. Edward and Eugenia Lodwich; m. Warren Paul Prescott, Dec. 2, 1979; children: Warren Paul Jr., Ashley Elizabeth. BA, U. Ill., Chgo., 1973, MEd, 1981; MA, U. Wis., 1978; postgrad., Stanford U., 1983-87. Cert. tchr., learning handicapped specialist, cmty. coll. instr., Calif. Grad. rschr. U. Ill., Chgo., 1979-81; learning handicapped specialist St. Paulus Luth. Sch., San Francisco, 1981-83; grad. rsch. asst. Sch. Edn. Stanford (Calif.) U., 1983-87, writing cons. for law students, 1985-86; learning handicapped specialist/lead therapist Gilroy Clinic Speech-Hearing-Learning Ctr., Crippled Children's Soc., Santa Clara, Calif., 1988-89; ednl. dir. Adolescent Intensive Resdl. Svc. Calif. Pacific Med. Ctr., San Francisco, 1989-95; exec. dir. Learning Profiles, South Lake Tahoe, Calif., 1995—. Instr. evening San Jose City Coll., 1988-92. Contbr. articles to profl. jours.; author: Proceedings of Internat. Congress of Linguistics, 1987; editor: Proceedings - Forum for Research on Language Issues, 1986; author videotape: Making a Difference in Language and Learning, 1989. Recipient Frederick Bork Teaching Trainee award San Francisco State U., 1983; Ill. State scholar, 1973. Mem. Calif. Assn. Pvt. Specialized Edn. and Svcs., Phi Delta Kappa (v.p. 1984-86), Pi Lambda Theta (sec. 1982-83), Phi Kappa Phi, Alpha Lambda Theta. Office: 2075 W Roosevelt Rd Wheaton IL 60187-6028

PRESCOTT, DAVID MARSHALL, biology educator; b. Clearwater, Fla., Aug. 3, 1926; s. Clifford Raymond and Lillian (Moore) P.; m. Gayle Edna Demery; children: Lavonne, Jason, Ryan. BA, Wesleyan U., 1950; PhD, U. Calif., Berkeley, 1954. Asst. prof. UCLA Med. Sch., 1955-59; biologist Oak Ridge (Tenn.) Nat. Lab., 1959-63; prof. U. Colo. Sch. Medicine, Denver, 1963-66; prof. molecular, cell and devel. biology U. Colo., Boulder, 1966-80, Disting. prof. molecular, cell and devel. biology, 1980—2002, Disting. prof. emeritus, 2002—. Pres. Am. Soc. Cell Biology, 1966. Author: Cell Reproduction, 1976, Cancer: The Misguided Cell, 1986, Cells, 1988; also numerous rsch. reports; editor: Methods in Cell Biology, 15 vols., 1963-78. Adv. com. March of Dimes, 1979-90. Recipient von Humboldt prize Fed. Republic Germany, 1979; grantee NIH, 1985-95, 97-2002, Nat. Found. Cancer Rsch., 1985-89, NSF, 1990-91, 95—; John Simon Guggenheim Meml. Found. fellow, 1990-91. Fellow Am. Acad. Arts and Scis.; mem. NAS, Soc. Protozoologists (pres. 1995-96). Avocations: numismatics, gardening. Home: 285 Brook Pl Boulder CO 80302-8031 Office: Univ Colo Campus Box 347 MCDB Biology Boulder CO 80309-0347

PRESCOTT, EDWARD C. economist, educator; Regents prof. U. Minn. Econ. adviser Fed. Res. Bank, Mpls. Recipient Erwin Plein Nemmers prize in Econ. Office: Univ Minn Dept Econ 1035 Heller Hall 271 19th Ave S Minneapolis MN 55455 Office Fax: 612-204-5515.

PRESCOTT, JANELLE, medical and surgical nurse, emergency room nurse, psychiatric nurse; b. Uniontown, Pa., Jan. 5, 1965; d. Robert Lee and Pauline (Marcinek) Smith; m. Marvin Levi Prescott, Oct. 14, 1989; children: Aaron Michael, Rebekah Anne. Diploma, Uniontown Hosp. Sch. Nursing, 1988, Finesse Finishing Sch., Uniontown, 1986. RN, Pa. Nurse Uniontown Hosp., 1988-2000, Ga. Regional Hosp. Savannah, 2000—01, Pa.-Uniontown Hosp. , 2001—. Ind. herbal distributor Advantage Mktg. Sys. Mem. U.S. Friendship Ambs., 1987—. Home: 81 Delaware Ave Uniontown PA 15401

PRESCOTT, JOHN MACK, biochemist, retired university administrator; b. San Marcos, Tex., Jan. 22, 1921; s. John Mack and Maude (Raborn) P.; m. Kathryn Ann Kelly, June 8, 1946; children: Stephen Michael, Donald Wyatt. BS in Chemistry, S.W. Tex. State Coll., 1941; MS in Biochemistry and Nutrition, Tex. A&M U., 1949; PhD in Biochemistry, U. Wis., 1952. Lab. asst. Dow Chem. Co., Freeport, Tex., 1942-43; faculty Tex. A&M U., College Station, 1946-49, 52-85, prof. biochemistry, 1959-85, dean Coll. Sci., 1970-77, v.p. for acad. affairs, 1977-81, dir. Inst. Occupational and Environ. Medicine, 1981-87, prof. med. biochemistry, 1981-85, prof. emeritus, 1985—, spl. asst. to dep. chancellor for biotech. devel., 1987-88; research asst. U. Wis.-Madison, 1949-51, U. Tex., Austin, 1951-52; vis. prof. Harvard Med. Sch., 1982. Contbr. articles profl. jours. Mem. Tex. Bd. Examiners in Basic Scis., 1974-79, mem. Tex. State Bd. Edn., 1984-88. Served to lt. USAAF, 1943-46; lt. col. USAF Res., 1946-68. Mem. Am. Soc. for Biochemistry and Molecular Biology, Soc. for Exptl. Biology and Medicine, Sigma Xi, Phi Lambda Upsilon. Home: 31 Forest Dr College Station TX 77840-2337 E-mail: jmscott1@juno.com.

PRESCOTT, LAWRENCE MALCOLM, medical and health science writer; b. Boston, July 31, 1934; s. Benjamin and Lillian (Stein) P.; m. Ellen Gay Kober, Feb. 19, 1961 (dec. Sept. 1981); children: Jennifer Maya, Adam Barrett; m. Sharon Lynn Kirshen, May 16, 1982; children: Gary Leon Kirshen, Marc Paul Kirshen. BA, Harvard U., 1957; MSc, George Washington U., 1959, PhD, 1966. Nat. Acad. Scis. postdoctoral fellow U.A. Army Rsch., Ft. Detrick, Md., 1965-66; microbiologist/scientist WHO, India, 1967-70, Indonesia, 1970-72, Thailand, 1972-78; with pub. rels. GCI, Hill & Knowlton, Aventis, Astra Zeneza, others, 1984—; cons. to internat. orgns. San Diego,

1978—. Author manuals; contbr. articles in diarrheal diseases and lab. scis. to profl. jours., numerous articles, stories, poems to mags., newspapers, including Living in Thailand, Jack and Jill, Strawberry, Bangkok Times, Spring, 1977-81; mng. editor Caduceus, 1981-82; pub., editor: Teenage Scene, 1982-83; pres. Prescott Pub. Co., 1982-83; med. writer numerous jours. including Modern Medicine, Dermatology Times, Drug and Market Devel., P&T, Clinical Cancer Letter, Anesthesiology News, Arzte Zeitong, Australian Doctor, Inpharma Weekly, Chronicle of Cardiovascular and Internal Medicine, Ophthalmology Times, Pharmacy Practice News, Body Positive, AIDS Update, Medical Allert, Infectious Diseases, Urology Times, Genetic Engineering News, Medical Week, Gastroenterology and Endoscopy News; author: Curry Every Sunday, 1984. Home and Office: 18264 Verano Dr San Diego CA 92128-1262

PRESCOTT, PERRY DON, psychology educator, counselor; b. Jasper, Ala., Mar. 15, 1952; s. Howard J. and Mary Lou Prescott; m. Hazel Ann Prescott, June 12, 1975; children: Justin H., Nigel A., Trevor G. BS, U. Ala., 1974, MA, 1978, PhD, 1984. Asst. prof. psychology Miss. Coll., Clinton, 1988-89; asst. prof. counseling U. Ga., Athens, 1989-90, U. Guam, Mangilao, 1990-91; pvt. practice Tuscaloosa, Ala., 1991-92; asst. prof. psychology McNeese State U., Lake Charles, La., 1992-93; counselor, tchr. State of Ala. Schs., Jasper, Double Springs, 1993-97; PACE psychology prof. Navy program Ctrl. Tex. Coll., San Diego, 1997—. Cons. Profl. Counseling Svcs., Jasper, Ala., 1994, Walker Regional Hosp., Jasper, 1994. Contbr. articles to profl. jours. including Ala. Assn. Counselors Jour., Jour. Reading. With USAR, 1972-78. Named one of Outstanding Young Men in Am., Jaycees, 1982. Mem So. Assn. Coll. Student Adminstrs. (com. 1986-87), William Glasser Inst. (cert.), Phi Delta Kappa, Kappa Delta Pi. Avocations: travel, foreign languages, reading. Home and Office: 11531 Shalom Rd Duncanville AL 35456-2533

PRESCOTT, PETER SHERWIN, writer; b. N.Y.C., July 15, 1935; s. Orville and Lilias (Ward-Smith) P.; m. Anne Courthope Kirsopp Lake, June 22, 1957; children: David Sherwin, Antonia Courthope. AB magna cum laude, Harvard, 1957. Editor E.P. Dutton Co., N.Y.C., 1958-67; lit. editor, syndicated columnist Women's Wear Daily, 1964-68; mem. faculty Pubs. Sch. for Writers, 1965-66; lit. editor, columnist Look mag., 1968-71; book critic Newsweek mag., N.Y.C., 1971-91, sr. writer, 1978-91; lectr. U.S. State Dept., 1978; adj. prof. Grad. Sch. Journalism, Columbia U., 1979-86. Vis. prof. Barnard Coll., 2001, 02. Author: A World of Our Own: Notes on Life and Learning in a Boys' Preparatory School, 1970, Soundings: Encounters with Contemporary Books, 1972, A Darkening Green: Notes from the Silent Generation, 1974, The Child Savers: Juvenile Justice Observed, 1981, Never in Doubt: Critical Essays on American Books, 1972-85, 1986, The Norton Book of American Short Stories, 1988. Mem. Dem. town Com., New Canaan, 1969-72, 1999-2001; constable Town of New Canaan, 1969-73; bd. dirs. Authors Guild Found., 1970-95, pres., 1971-93; exec. bd. Authors League Fund, 1987—, 1st v.p., 1994-97, pres., 1997—; trustee New Canaan Libr., 1998-01. With USAR, 1958-64. Recipient George Polk award criticism, 1978, 1st prize Robert F. Kennedy Book Awards, 1981; fellow Guggenheim Found., 1977, NEH, 1993. Mem. PEN Am. Center (exec. bd. 1974-76), Authors League Am. (exec. bd. 1974-76), Assn. Literary Scholars and Critics, Authors Guild (exec. bd. 1971-91), Nat. Book Critics Circle (exec. bd. 1973-75, 92-93), Century Assn., Harvard Club (N.Y.C.), Phi Beta Kappa. E-mail: pprescott@nyc.rr.com.

PRESCOTT, RICHARD CHAMBERS, writer; b. Houston, Apr. 1, 1952; s. Chambers Richard and Dorothy Mae (Bashara) P.; m. Sarah Elisabeth Grace, Oct. 13, 1981. Author: The Sage, 1975, Moonstar, 1975, Neuf Songes (Nine Dreams), 1976, 2nd edit., 1991, The Carouse of Soma, 1977, Lions and Kings, 1977, Allah Wake Up, 1978, 2nd edit., 1994, Night Reaper, 1979, Dragon Tales, 1983, Dragon Dreams, 1986, 2nd edit., 1990, Dragon Prayers, 1988, 2nd edit., 1990, Dragon Songs, 1988, 2nd edit., 1990, Dragon Maker, 1989, 2nd edit., 1990, Dragon Thoughts, 1990, Tales of Recognition, 1991, Kings and Sages, 1991, Dragon Sight: A Cremation Poem, 1992, Three Waves, 1992, Years of Wonder, 1992, Dream Appearances, 1992, Remembrance Recognition and Return, 1992, Spare Advice, 1992, The Imperishable, 1993, The Dark Deitess, 1993, Disturbing Delights: Waves of The Great Goddess, 1993, The Immortal: Racopa and the Rooms of Light, 1993, Hanging Baskets, 1993, Writer's Block and Other Gray Matters, 1993, The Resurrection of Quantum Joe, 1993, The Horse and the Carriage, 1993, Kalee Bhava: The Goddess and Her Moods, 1995, The Skills of Kalee, 1995, Because of Atma, 1995, Measuring Sky Without Ground, 1996, The Goddess And The God Man, 1996, Kalee: The Allayer of Sorrows, 1996, Living Sakti, 1997, The Mirage and the Mirror, 1998, Inherent Solutions to Spiritual Obscurations, 1999, The Ancient Method, 1999, Quantum Kamakala, 2000; contbr. articles and essays to profl. publs.

PRESCOTT, WILLIAM BRUCE, minister; b. Denver, Dec. 30, 1951; s. William Rex and Betena Naomi (Fletcher) P.; m. D. Kylene Winters, Nov. 24, 1973; children: William Doyle, Candice Joy. BS in Corrections, U. Albuquerque, 1973; MDiv, Southwestern Bapt. Sem., 1978, PhD, 1986. Ordained minister in Bapt. Ch., 1976. Youth minister Sandia Bapt. Ch., Albuquerque, 1974-75; pastor Clairette (Tex.) Bapt. Ch., 1976-79; instr. philosophy and religion Tarrant County Jr. Coll. NW Campus, Ft. Worth, 1984-86; pastor Easthaven Bapt. Ch., Houston, 1987-98; exec. dir. Mainstream Okla. Baptists, 1998—. Adj. prof. Southwestern Bapt. Theol. Sem., HBU Extension, Houston, 1987-90; police chaplain Houston Police Dept., 1987-94; trustee S.E. Area Ministries, Houston, 1988-98, exec. bd. 1997-98, v.p. 1998; mem. exec. bd. Union Bapt. Assn., 1987-98, Bapt. Gen. Conv. Tex., 1993-98, Tex. Bapts. Committed, 1990-98; coord. coun. Coop. Bapt. Fellowship, 1994-97, mem. Tex. exec. com., 1996-98, Tex. steering com., 1994-98; spkr. confs. in field. Book reviewer to Southwestern Jour. Theology; radio talk show host, Religious Talk, 1999—; editor: The Mainstream Messenger, 1998—. Served on Bapt. Gen. Conv. Tex. Com. Distinctives Com., 1994-98, Exec. Bd. Nominating Com., 1996, Com. on Conv. Arrangements, 1997; CBF Theol. Edn. Ministry Group , 1994-95, Bapt. Principles Ministry Group, 1995-98, Adminstrv. Coun. Structure Com., 1996, Adv. Coun., 1996-98, Info. Systems Mgmt. Project Team, 1996-97, chmn. Bapt. Bapt. Distinctives Partnership Team, 1995-97; trustee San Andres U., San Andres Island, San Andres Found. Named one of Outstanding Young Men of Am., Jaycees, 1984. Mem. ACLU, Am. Acad. Religion, Ams. United for Separation Ch. and State (pres. Houston chpt. 1997-99, nat. adv. coun. 1997—, editor First Amendment Advocate Newsletter, 1999—), So. Bapt. Alliance, Baptists Committed, People for the Am. Way, Concord Coalition, Whitsett Soc., Interfaith Alliance. Democrat. Home: 1706 Kiamichi Rd Norman OK 73026-5924 Office: Mainstream Okla Baptists 205 E Main St Norman OK 73069-1304

PRESECAN, NICHOLAS LEE, environmental and civil engineer, consultant; b. Indpls., Sept. 4, 1940; s. Nicholas Eli and Dorothy Lee (Moore) P.; m. Joan Westin, Nov. 11, 1940; children: Julie Marie, Mary Lee, Anne Westin. BSCE, Purdue U., 1963; MS in Engring., U. Calif., Berkeley, 1967. Registered profl. engr., 35 states; cert. value specialist. Project engr. San Bernardino County (Calif.) Flood Control, 1963, Engring. Sci. Inc., Arcadia, Calif., 1968-70, office mgr. Cleve., 1970-72, v.p., chief engr., 1972-81, v.p. internat. divsn. Arcadia, 1981-84, group v.p., 1984-87; sr. v.p. Parsons Engring. Sci. Inc., Pasadena, Calif., 1987—. Industry adv. bd. Sch. Engring. and Tech. Calif. State U., L.A., 1986-99. Contbr. articles to profl. jours. Commr. Archtl. Commn., Claremont, Calif., 1980-86; councilman Claremont City Coun., 1986-94; mayor City of Claremont, 1989-92; mem. Pasadena Tournament of Roses Assn., 1980-96, L.A. 2000 Environ. Com., 1987-88; pres. Claremont Hills Conservation Corp., 1997—; mem. adv. com. San Gabriel Valley Water Quality Authority, 2002-. With USMC, 1963-67. Recipient Disting. Engring. Achievement award Inst. for Advancement of Engring., 1993. Fellow ASCE (mem. internat. adv. com. 1987-90); mem. NSPE, Am. Acad. Environ. Engrs., Am. Water Works Assn. (life), Water Environ. Fedn., Soc. Am. Value Engrs., Rotary. Republican. Avocations: skiing, hiking, fishing, boating, writing. Home: 727 E Alamosa Dr Claremont CA 91711-2008 Office: Parsons Engring Sci Inc 100 W Walnut St Pasadena CA 91124-0001

PRESENT, DANIEL H. physician; b. N.Y.C., Apr. 3, 1934; s. Israel Present and Bertha (Hirsch) Newman; m. Jane W. Present, Oct. 20, 1956; children: Tracy, Stephanie Present Podolak, Douglas. BA magna cum laude, Syracuse U., 1955; MD magna cum laude, SUNY, Bklyn., 1959. Diplomate in internal medicine and gastroenterology Am. Bd. Internal Medicine. Intern Mt. Sinai Med. Ctr., N.Y.C., 1959-60, resident in internal medicine, 1962-64, resident in gastroenterology, 1964-66, mem. staff, 1966—, attending physician, 1987—; clin. prof. medicine Mt. Sinai Sch. Medicine, 1987—. Writer, producer ednl. videotapes; contbr. chpts. to books, more than 100 articles to profl. jours. Capt. U.S. Army, 1960-62. Master: Am. Coll. Gastroenterology; mem.: Am. Gastroenterol. Assn. (disting. clinician), Phi Beta Kappa. Office: 12 E 86th St New York NY 10028-0506

PRESKA, LORETTA A. federal judge; b. 1949; BA, Coll. of St. Rose, 1970; JD, Fordham U., 1973; LLM, NYU, 1978; LHD (hon.), Coll. of St. Rose, 1995. Assoc. Cahill, Gordon & Reindel, N.Y.C., 1973-82; ptnr. Hertzog, Calamari & Gleason, 1982-92; fed. judge U.S. Dist. Ct. (so. dist.) N.Y., 1992—. Mem. N.Y. State Bar Assn., N.Y. County Lawyers Assn., Fed. Bar Coun., Fordham Law Alumni Assn. (v.p.). Office: US Courthouse 500 Pearl St Rm 1320 New York NY 10007-1316

PRESKA, MARGARET LOUISE ROBINSON, education educator, administrator; b. Parma, N.Y., Jan. 23, 1938; d. Ralph Craven and Ellen Elvira (Niemi) Robinson; m. Daniel C. Preska, Jan. 24, 1959; children: Robert, William, Ellen Preska Steck. BS summa cum laude, SUNY, 1957; MA, Pa. State U., 1961; PhD, Claremont Grad. Sch., 1969; postgrad., Manchester Coll., Oxford U., 1973. Instr. LaVerne (Calif.) Coll., 1968-75, asst. prof., asso. prof., acad. dean, 1972-75; instr. Starr King Sch. for Ministry, Berkeley, Calif., summer, 1975; v.p. acad. affairs, equal opportunity officer Minn. State U., Mankato, 1975-79, pres., 1979-92; project dir. Kaliningrad (Russia) Mil. Re-Tng., 1992-96; disting. svc. prof. Minn. State U., Winona, 1993—, pres. Inst. for Effective Tchg., 1993-96; owner BuildaBikeInc.com, 2000—. Bd. dirs. XCEL Energy Co., Norwest Corp., Exec. Sports Inc., 1996-98; pres. emerita Minn. State U., Mankato, 1992—; provost, CEO AbuDhabi Campus, Zayed U., United Arab Emirates, 1997-99. Pres. Pomona Valley chpt. UN Assn., 1968-69, Unitarian Soc. Pomona Valley, 1968-69, PTA Lincoln Elem. Sch., Pomona, 1973-74, Nat. Camp Fire Boys and Girls, 1986-88; mem. Pomona City Charter Revision Commn., 1972; chmn. The Fielding Inst., Santa Barbara, 1983-86; bd. dirs. Elderhostel Internat., 1983-87, Minn. Agrl. Interpretive Ctr. (Farmam.), 1983-92, Am. Assn. State Colls. and Univs., Moscow on the Mississippi - Minn. Meets the Soviet Union; nat. pres. Campfire, Inc., 1985-87; chmn. Gov.'s Coun. on Youth, Minn., 1983-86, Minn. Edn. Forum, 1984; mem. Gov.'s Commn. on Econ. Future of Minn., 1985—, NCAA Pres. Commn., 1986-92, NCAA Cost Cutting Commn., Minn. Brainpower Compact, 1985; commr. Great Lakes Govs.' Econ. Devel. Coun., 1986, Minn Gov.'s Commn. on Forestry. Carnegie Found. grantee Am. Coun. Edn. Deans Inst., 1974; recipient Outstanding Alumni award Pa. State, Outstanding Alumni award Claremont Grad. Sch., YWCA Leader award 1982, Exch. Club Book of Golden Deeds award, 1987; named One of top 100 alumni, SUNY, 1895-1985, 1985, Hall of Heritage award, 1988, Wohelo Camp Fire award, 1989. Mem. AAUW (pres. Mankato 1990-92), LWV, Women's Econ. Roundtable, St. Paul/Mpls. Com. on Fgn. Rels., Am. Coun. on Edn., Am. Assn. Univ. Adminstrs., Rotary, Benedicts Dance Club, Horizon 100. Unitarian Universalist. Home: 3573 Bailey Ridge Bay Woodbury MN 55125 Office: 4156 Pre Emption Rd Himrod NY 14842-9734 E-mail: mpreska@mediaone.net.

PRESKI, BRIAN JOSEPH, lawyer; b. Phila., Apr. 25, 1965; s. Henry John and Dolores (Domanski) Przybyszewski; m. Kelly Ann McKeon, June 2, 1989; children: Dennis, Lauren. BA, St. Joseph's U., 1987; JD, Widener U., 1992. Bar: Pa. 1992. Asst. dist. atty. Dist. Atty.'s Office, Phila., 1989-95; chief counsel jud. com. Ho. of Reps., Harrisburg, Pa., 1995-2001, chief of staff to majority leader, 2001—. Republican. Roman Catholic. Office: Ho of Reps Majority Leaders Office 110 Main Capitol Harrisburg PA 17120 E-mail: bpreski@pahousegop.com.

PRESLEY, BRIAN, investment company executive; b. Evansville, Ind., Dec. 28, 1941; s. Harry and Ruth P.; m. Mary Nell Minyard, Aug. 17, 1972; children: Debra, Cynthia, David, Jeffrey, Clark, Gregory, Steven. BSBA, U. Evansville, 1963; MBA, Mich. State U., 1964; diploma, Wharton Sch., U. Pa., 1995. Market rsch. analyst Stanley Works, New Britain, Conn., 1964-68; tax shelter coord. F.I. Dupont, Memphis, 1968-73; v.p. Bullington Schas, 1973-75; pres., mng. ptnr. Presley Assocs., 1965-93; pres., CFO CSG, Inc., 1975—. Gen. ptnr. various real estate and oil and gas partnerships, 1974-1986; pres. Cooper St. Group Securities, Inc., 1983-86 ; divsn. mgr. Advantage Capital Corp. (divsn. SunAmerica, Inc.), 1986-89, reg. v.p., 1989, CEO 1990-94, mng. dir., mktg. strategist, 1995; pres. Presley Adv. Inc., 1995—, pub. Presley Adv. Letter; instr. fin. divsn. continuing edn. Memphis U. Bd. dirs. Apt. Coun. Tenn., 1980-86, sec.-treas., 1982-83; pres. Memphis Apt. Coun., 1983; mem., U. Evansville Nat. Alumni Bd., 1988-91; prodr. 2 daily radio stock market commentary shows, 1988; fin. commentator Sta. WEVU-TV (ABC), Ft. Myers/Naples, 1988-89; host syndicated radio show for sr. citizens, 1979-81; mem. found. bd. Fla. Gulf Coast U., 2001—. Mem. Leadership Charlotte; chmn. Charlotte County Econ. Devel. Coun., 1999-2002, Angels Found. Charlotte County Fla., Inc.; pres. Enterprise Charlotte Found., 2002—. Mem. Internat. Assn. Fin. Planners (broker dealer adv. coun. 1993-97), Admirals Club (life, bd. dirs.), Naples Jazz Soc. (chmn. bd. dirs.), Naples Sailing and Yacht Club (bd. dirs.), Pi Sigma Epsilon, Beta Gamma Sigma, Tau Kappa Epsilon Alumni Assn. (pres. Memphis area 1979-80). Presbyterian. Home: Acorn Ranch 35600 Bermont Rd Punta Gorda FL 33982-9511 Office: 726 1st Ave N Naples FL 34102-6006

PRESLEY, DALE MARK, electrical engineer; b. Port Arthur, Tex., May 30, 1947; s. Henry Joseph and Jewel Alice P.; m. Nancy Sue Harless, Nov. 26, 1970; children: Micah Shawn, Ryan Matthew. BEE, Lamar U., 1969. Reg. profl. engr., Tex. Quality assurance engr. LTV Aerospace, Grand Prairie, Tex., 1969-73; project engr. Bethlehem Steel Corp., Beaumont, 1973-86; dry dock operator, foreman Bethlehem Sabine Shipyard, Port Arthur, 1986-88; sr. design engr. Matrix Engring., Inc., Beaumont, 1988-96; project sr. elec. engr. Fluor Daniel, Inc., Orange, Tex., 1997-98; sr. staff engr. Petrocon Engring., Inc., Beaumont, 1998—. Author: Way Truth: Life-Revelation of the Creator LORD Jesus Christ, 1997, Daniel/Zechariah and the Creator Lord Jesus Christ, 2000. Bible tchr. First Bapt. Ch., Bevil Oaks, Tex., 1982—2002, ordained deacon, 1983. Avocations: boating, fishing, hiking. Home: 135 Pinevale Way Sour Lake TX 77659-9264

PRESLEY, JOHN WOODROW, academic administrator; b. Jonesboro, Ark., Mar. 24, 1948; s. Marvin Woodrow and Willa Louise (Taylor) P.; m. Katherine Bailey Harrison, Oct. 17, 1978. BSE, Ark. State U., 1970; MA, So. Ill. U., 1972, PhD, 1975; postgrad., Johns Hopkins U., 1976, U. Tex., 1980. Asst. prof. Augusta State U., 1974-77, assoc. prof., 1978-84, prof., 1984-89, chmn. Freshman English, 1974-76, chmn. developmental studies, 1976-78, asst. v.p. for acad. affairs, 1988-89; assoc. dean faculty Lafayette Coll., Easton, Pa., 1989-90, acting provost, dean faculty, 1990-91, assoc. provost, dean faculty, 1991-92; dean Coll. of Arts, Scis. and Letters U. Mich., Dearborn, 1992-99; provost, v.p. acad. affairs SUNY at Oswego, 1999—. Presenter in field. Author: The Robert Graves Letters and Manuscripts at Southern Illinois University, 1976, (with W.M. Dodd) Breakthrough: From Reading to Writing, 1981, To Be Exact: A Handbook for Revision, 1982, (with M.G. Kramer) The Prentice-Hall Workbook for Writers, 1983, 4th edit. (with M.G. Kramer and D. Rigg), 1985, 5th, 1988, 6th, 1990, How Like A Life, 1987, (with N. Prinsky) The World of Work, 1987, (with A.I. Philbin) Technical Communications: Method, Application, Management, 1989; contbg. author: The Prentice-Hall Handbook for Writers, 9th edit., 1985, Sparking Connections: Spoken and Written Communications, 1985, Speech Exercises for Basic Writers and Others, 1987; assoc. editor Gravesiana: The Journal of the Robert Graves Society, 1996-2000, gen. editor, 2001-; contbr. articles to profl. jours. NDEA fellow, 1972. Mem. Phi Kappa Phi. Home: 41 Garden Dr Oswego NY 13126-6103 Office: SUNY 702 Culkin Hall Oswego NY 13126-3525 E-mail: presley@oswego.edu.

PRESLEY, KEVIN PATRICK, minister of music; b. Springfield, Mo., June 19, 1964; s. Robert Lee and Darylene Delane P.; m. Robyn Michelle Maloy, Dec. 30, 1989; 1 child, Kirk Ian. BS in Music, S.W. Baptist U., 1986; M in Sacred Music, Southern M in Sacred Music, M in Music, Voice Performance, Southern Meth. U., 1989. Commd. min., deacon United Meth. Ch., 2000. Minister of music First United Meth. Ch., Celina, Tex., 1987-89, Peachtree City (Ga.) United Meth. Ch., 1989-94, Emmanuel United Meth. Ch., Memphis, 1994—. Treas. Fellowship of United Meth. in Music, Worship and other arts, North Ga. Conf., 1991-94. Designer, dir. musical program Building the City, 1997, For the Journey, 1998, Honour Bound, 1999, A Generation of Faith, 2000, This Is Our Story, 2001, Seek First, 2002; performer Carnegie Hall, 1996, Internat. Ch. Music Festival, Coventry, Eng., 1998, Internat. Ch. Music Festival, Bern, Switzerland, 2001. Singer Atlanta (Ga.) Symphony Chorus, Chamber Chorus, 1991-93; co-leader Metro Memphis Children's Choir Festival, 1995. Mem. Am. Choral Dirs. Assn., Chorister's Guild (exec. bd. mem. 1992-94). Avocations: travel, architecture, desktop publishing-design, health and fitness. Office: Emmanuel United Methodist 2404 Kirby Rd Memphis TN 38119-6621 E-mail: kirkian@earthlink.net., kpresley@emmanuelmemphis.org.

PRESLEY, PAULA LUMPKIN, editor; b. Des Arc, Ark., June 8, 1938; d. Herbert Eugene and Clara Erline (Jones) Lumpkin; m. Clifton Jay Presley, Apr. 19, 1958 (div. Mar. 1988); children: Richard Jay, Steven James, Susan Jean. BA in History, Truman State U., Kirksville, Mo., 1985, MA, 1989; MLS, U. Iowa, 1991. Copy editor Sixteenth Century Jour., Kirksville, 1982—; asst. editor Thomas Jefferson U. Press, 1986-91, assoc. editor, 1991-98; dir., editor-in-chief Truman State U. Press (formerly Thomas Jefferson U. Press), 1998—; owner Paula Presley Editl. Svcs. Editor (Keywords newsletter): Am. Soc. Indexers, 1997—98; editor: Editing History newsletter, 1996—97; contbr. ; co-editor: Habent sua libelli or, Books Have Their Own Destiny, 1998. Mem.: ALA, AAUW (pres. 1996—97), Conf. Hist. Jours., Calvin Studies Soc., Soc. for Scholarly Pub., Am. Soc. Indexes (newsletter editor 1997—98), Intertel, Am. Mensa, Kirksville Rotary Club. Democrat. Presbyterian. Avocations: book indexing, research in printing, incunabula, religious history/theology. Home: 820 E Meadow Ln Kirksville MO 63501-2568

PRESMANES, WILLA SUMMEROUR, behavioral health systems evaluator; b. Baton Rouge, Jan. 12, 1948; d. William Henry and Mildred Katherine (Hazen) Summerour; m. Gregory T. Presmanes, Dec. 26, 1970; 1 child, Alison. BA in Psychology, U. Ga., 1970; MEd in Counseling Psychology, Ga. State U., 1976, MA in Psychology, 1981. Psychiat. asst. Northside Hosp. Mental Health Ctr., Atlanta, 1971-74; program evaluator Ga. Mental Health Inst., 1976-79; dir. rsch. and statis. analyst DeKalb Bd. Health, Decatur, Ga., 1979-93; behavioral health program analyst DeKalb Cmty. Svc. Bd., 1993—. Seminar leader Millinaire DNA (Dollars, Number, Attitude), 2000—. Author: State of Ga. Comprehensive Service Plans, 1989, Balanced Service System Plans, 1978, Behaviorally Anchored Rating Scales, 1981, Quality Assurance Monitoring, 1977, Georgia Role Functioning Scale, 1982, Outcomes and Accountability Alert: Outcomes Measuring Daily Living Activities, 2000; co-author: Research on Social Work Practice Reliability and Validity of the Daily Living Activities Scale: A Functional Assessment Measure for Serious Mental Disorders, 2000; pub.: Internat. Soc. Quality in Health Care 14th Book of Abstracts, 1997. Mem. Dunwoody United Meth., Atlanta, 1984—, children's cancer cure rsch. vol. Egleston Hosp. Recipient award for publ. Joint Commn. on Accreditation of Healthcare Orgns. Nat. Libr., 1998. Mem. Tri Delta Alumni Soc., Renaissance Inst. Achievements include research in mental health outcomes. Avocations: mountaineering, healthcare, nutrition, exercise. E-mail: willap@dekcsb.org.

PRESMEG, NORMA CHRISTINE, mathematics educator, researcher; b. Germiston, Transvaal, South Africa, Oct. 12, 1942; came to U.S., 1990; d. Christian Brandt and Erika Eunice (De Barzellini) Parnell; m. Christopher Raymond Presmeg, July 8, 1978 (div. June 1989); children: Charmaine, Justine, Neale. BSc, Rhodes U., Grahamstown, South Africa, 1962; BSc with honors, U. Natal, Durban, South Africa, 1963, BEd, 1969, MEd, 1980; PhD, Cambridge U., 1985. Tchr. Natal Edn. Dept., 1965-82; lectr. U. Durban-Westville, 1986-90; asst. prof. dept. curriculum and instrn. Fla. State U., Tallahassee, 1990-94, assoc. prof., 1994-2000, math. edn. program leader, 1995-97, 99-00; prof. Ill. State U., Bloomington, 2000—. Cons. Leon County Schs., Fla., 1990-2000 Contbg. author: Mathematics Education and Culture, 1986; editor, author: Mathematics Education for Pre-Service and In-Service Teachers, 1991; editor: Educational Studies in Mathematics, 2000—; contbr. articles to profl. jours. Ch. leader Christian Sci. Ch., Margate, South Africa, 1978-82, 1st reader, Durban, 1986-90. Scholarship Univ.'s for the U.K., 1983-85, scholar Human Scis. Rsch. Coun., 1983-85; grantee U. Durban-Westville, 1987-89, Dade County Math. Project, 1996-2000; co-chair Am. Ednl. Rsch. Assn. Spl. Interest Group: Rsch. in Math. Edn., 2000-2002. Mem. Nat. Coun. Tchrs. of Maths., Math. Assn. Am. Avocations: music, environmental societies. Office: Ill State U Math Dept Stevenson Hl Normal IL 61790-4520 E-mail: npresmeg@ilstu.edu., npresmeg@msn.com.

PRESNIAKOV, ALEXANDER, painter, sculptor, inventor, novelist, writer; b. San Francisco, June 28, 1963; s. Alexander Alexandervich and Nina (Hanova) P. Student, Acad. of Art Coll., San Francisco, 1979-82. Curator Gen. Svcs. Adminstrn., Washington, 1983; artist, 1984-85, San Francisco, 1986—. Songwriter Hilltop Records, L.A., 1996—, Amerecord, L.A., 1996—, Premier Melodies, N.Y.C. Commd. to paint life-size portraits of Prince Charles, Princess Diana, Miss Dame Barbara Cartland, 1982, Amb. Gerald Posner Carmen, 1983, life-size portraits of presdl. candidates for 1985 Polit. Conservative Action Conf., Sheraton Hotel, Washington; series Women in Love Cycle, 1986—; inventor Manshield Deflector, 1983; commissioned to paint life-size portrait of Pres. Ronald Reagan, 1983; author 3 novels, including Eagle's Nest, 2001; screenwriter. Recipient Literary Excellence award Iliad Press, 1995; named Prof. and Corr. Academician Dept. Arts Accademia Internazionale, Italy. Mem. Internat. Soc. Poets (disting. mem., Hall of Fame 1997-98), Legion of Honor Mus., De Young Mus., Gallery Marabella (hon.). Republican. Russian Orthodox. Achievements include creation of artistic ideal, Ultrafictorilization, utilized in all U.S. gov. Agys., 1983. Avocations: tennis, golf, equestrian. Home: 775 42d Ave San Francisco CA 94121

PRESS, AIDA KABATZNICK, former editor, writer, poet; b. Boston, Nov. 18, 1926; m. Newton Press, June 5, 1947; children: David, Dina Press Weber, Benjamin Presskreischer. BA, Radcliffe Coll., 1948. Reporter Waltham (Mass.) News-Tribune, 1960-63; freelance writer, 1960-63; editl. cons. Mass. Dept. Mental Health, Boston, 1966-72; Waltham/Watertown reporter Boston Herald Traveler, 1963-70; dir. news and publs. Harvard Grad. Sch. Design, Cambridge, Mass., 1972-78; publs. editor Radcliffe Coll., 1978-81, dir., editor of publs., 1981-83, editor Radcliffe Quar., 1971-93, dir. pub. info., 1983-93; cons. editor Regis Coll. Alumnae Mag., Weston, Mass., 1994. Editor emerita Radcliffe Quar., 1993—; contbr. articles to newspapers and mags. Recipient Publs. Distinction award Am. Alumni Coun., 1974, Top 5 coll. Mag., Coun. for Advancement and Support of Edn., 1984, Top 10 Univ Mags., 1991, Gold medal Coll. Mags., 1991, Alumnae Achievement award Radcliffe Coll., 1994, Radcliffe Coll. Presdl. Commendation, 1992. Mem. Phi Beta Kappa. Avocations: hiking, playing recorder.

PRESS, CHARLES, retired political science educator; b. St. Louis, Sept. 12, 1922; s. Otto Ernst and Laura (Irion) P.; m. Nancy Miller, June 10, 1950; children: Edward Paul, William David, Thomas Leigh, Laura Mary. Student, Elmhurst (Ill.) Coll.; B of Journalism, U. Mo., 1948; MA, U. Minn., 1951, PhD, 1953. Faculty N.D. Agrl. Coll., 1954-56; dir. Grand Rapids Area Study, 1956-57; with Bur. Govt., U. Wis., 1957-58; faculty Mich. State U., East Lansing, 1958-91, prof. polit. sci., 1964-91; emeritus, 1991—; chmn. dept. Mich. State U., 1966-73. Cons. Mich. Constl. Conv., 1962-63; supr. Ingham County, 1966-72; tchr. summers, London; tchr. U. N.S.W., Sydney, Mich. State U. Author: Main Street Politics, 1962, (with Charles Adrian) The American Government Process, 1965, Governing Urban America, 1968, 5th edit., 1977, American Politics Reappraised, 1974, (with Kenneth VerBurg) States and Community Governments in a Federal System, 1979, 3d edit., 1991, American Policy Studies, 1981, The Political Cartoon, 1982, (with others) Michigan Political Atlas 1984, (with Kenneth VerBurg) American Politicians and Journalists, 1988, (with Kenneth VerBurg) (weekly newspaper column) The Pros and Cons of Politics. Sec. Ingham County Bd. Health, 1983-93; chmn., mem. East Lansing Bd. Rev., 1966-86; bd. dirs. Urban League, 1971-73; mem. East Lansing Housing and Urban Devel. Commn., 1988-93. Served with AUS, 1943-45. Recipient Disting. Prof. award Mich. State U., 1980, Alumni Merit award Elmhurst (Ill.) Coll., 1995. Mem. Am. Polit. Sci. Assn., Midwest Polit. Sci. Assn. (pres. 1974-75), So. Polit. Sci. Assn., Mich. Conf. Polit. Scientists (pres. 1972-73), Nat. Municipal League, B.S.I. Home: 987 Lantern Hill Dr East Lansing MI 48823-2831 Office: Mich State U 315 S Kedzie Hall East Lansing MI 48824-1032 E-mail: pressc@pilot.msu.edu.

PRESS, CHRISTOPHER E. health facility administrator; b. Dec. 4, 1952; BBA magna cum lade, Ohio U., 1976; MBA magna cum laude, U. Cin., 1980. V.p., sr. v.p. Franciscan Health Sys., Cin., 1980-89, Northside Hosp., Atlanta, 1989-97; ptnr. Morgan Healthcare Cons., LLC, 1998—. Adj. faculty Rollins Sch. Pub. Health, Emory U.; bd. dirs. Bettercare, Inc., Cin., Ga. 1st, Cin. Speech and Hearing Ctr.; cons. Jewish Hosp., Cin., 1989, Mayo Clinic, Rochester, Minn., 1987; presenter in field. Author: Building Market Strength Through DRGs, 1994; mem. editl. bd. Frontiers of Health Mgmt.; contbr. articles to profl. jours. Bd. dirs. Metro Atlanta YMCA, 1997—, Ctrl. Perimeter Partnership, Atlanta, 1996-98, Luth. Camp. Assn., 2000--. Fellow Am. Coll. Healthcare Mktg., Am. Coll. Healthcare Execs. (examiner); mem. Transp. Mgmt. Assn., U. Cin. Coll. Bus. Adminstrn. Alumni Assn. (charter pres.), Beta Gamma Sigma, Phi Kappa Phi. Home: 1165 Redfield Rdg Atlanta GA 30338-3729 Office: Morgan Cons LLC 5555 Glenridge Connector Atlanta GA 30342

PRESS, FRANK, geophysicist; b. Bklyn., Dec. 4, 1924; s. Solomon and Dora (Steinholz) Press; m. Billie Kallick, June 9, 1946; children: William Henry, Paula Evelyn. BS, CCNY, 1944, LLD (hon.) , 1972; MA, Columbia U., 1946, PhD, 1949; DSc (hon.) , 28 univs. Rsch. assoc. Columbia U., 1946—49, instr. geology, 1949—51, asst. prof. geology, 1951—52, assoc. prof., 1952—55; prof. geophysics Calif. Inst. Tech., 1955—65, dir. seismol. lab., 1957—65; prof. geophysics, chmn. dept. earth and planetary scis. MIT, Cambridge, 1965—77, inst. prof., 1981; sci. advisor to pres., dir. Office Sci. and Tech. Policy, Washington, 1977—81; pres. NAS, 1981—93, pres. emeritus, 2000—; Cecil & Ida Green sr. fellow Carnegie Inst. of Washington, 1993—97; ptnr. Washington Adv. Group, 1996—. Mem. Pres.'s Sci. Adv. Com., 1961—64, Com. on Anticipated Advances in Sci. and Tech., 1974—76, Nat. Sci. Bd., 1970—76; mem. lunar and planetary missions bd. NASA; participant bilateral scis. agreement with Peoples Republic of China and USSR; mem. U.S. delegation to Nuc. Test Ban Negotiations, Geneva and Moscow; prof. emeritus MIT, 2000—. Author (with M. Ewing, W.s. Jardetsky): Propagation of Elastic Waves in Layered Media, 1957; author: (with R. Siever) Earth, 1986; author: Understanding Earth, 2001; author: (contbr.) articles to over 160 publs. Decorated cross of Merit Germany, Legion of Honor France; named Sherman Fairchild Disting. scholar, Calif. Inst. Tech., 1994, A.D. White prof., Cornell U.; recipient Columbia medal for Excellence, 1960, Pub. Svc. award, U.S. Dept. Interior, 1972, Gold medal, Royal Astron. Soc., 1972, Pub. Svc. medal, NASA, 1973, Japan prize, Sci. and Tech. Found. Japan, 1993, Pupin medal, Columbia U., 1993, Nat. medal of Sci., Pres. U.S., 1994, Philip Hauge Abelson prize, AAAS, 1995, Lomonosov Gold medal, Russian Acad. Sci., 1998. Mem.: NAS, Engring. Acad. Japan (fgn. assoc.), Acad.Scis. Russia (fgn. mem.), Royal Soc. U.K., French Acad. Scis., Am. Philos. Soc., Seismol. Soc. Am. (pres. 1963), Soc. Exploration Geophysicists, Am. Geophys. Union, Geol. Soc. Am. (councilor), Am. Acad. Arts and Scis. Office: Ste 616 South 2500 Virginia Ave Washington DC 20037-1901 E-mail: fpress@theadvisorygroup.com.

PRESS, FRED, artist; b. Boston, Oct. 14, 1919; s. Samuel and Rose Press; m. Alice Bernadette, Nov. 4, 1942; children: David, Peter, Christopher. Student, Vesper George Sch. Art, Boston, 1938-39. Founder, chief designer sculpture collection Contemporary Arts, Inc., Boston, 1937-62; tchr. Vesper George Sch. Art, 1945—50; chief designer, exec. v.p. sales agy. N.Y.C., 1951—70; freelance in design field, 1970—85. Mem. Mass. Art Commn. One-man shows include Stuart Art Gallery, Boston, 1947, Jaffrey Civic Ctr., 1989, Granary Gallery, Martha's Vineyard, Mass., 1990, exhibited in group shows at NAD, N.Y.C., Delgado Mus. Art, New Orleans, Springfield Art League, Mass., Pan Am. Soc., Boston, Conn. Acad. Fine Arts, Allied Artists, N.Y., Vose Galleries, Boston, Boston Mus. Fine Arts, Silvermine Guild Artists, Conn., Mus. Contemporary Art, Boston, Ky. Derby Mus., Nat. Art League, Olin Art Ctr., Hoyt Inst. Fine Arts, Sharon Arts Ctr., Represented in permanent collections Worcester (Mass.) Art Mus., prin. works include 2 Bronze Reliefs, U.S. Navy Meml., Washington, individual pvt. collections; featured in Am. Artist Mag., Christian Sci. Monitor, Dance Mag.; author: (book) Sculpture at Your Fingertips, 1961; mng. editor: Ofcl. 6th Air Force Mag., 1944—45. Tech. sgt. USAF, 1942—45. Recipient ann. award for soap sculpture, Proctor and Gamble Co., 1936—39, 1st prize for Slave sculpture, Delgado Mus. Art, 1946; scholar, HS Commerce. Home: 262 Hadley Rd Jaffrey NH 03452

PRESS, MICHELLE, editor; b. Memphis, Nov. 22, 1940; d. Sam and Rana (Cohen) Appelbaum; m. Robert Press, June 18, 1960 (div. 1965) BA, New Sch. for Social Research, 1967. Tchr. U.S. Peace Corps, Malawi, Africa, 1962-64; copy editor Japan Quar., Tokyo, 1967-71; asst. editor Am. Scientist, New Haven, 1971-78, mng. editor, 1978-80, editor, 1981-90; mng. editor Scientific American, N.Y.C., 1990—. Mem. Am. Soc. Mag. Editors, Century Assn., Conn. Acad. of Arts and Scis. Office: Scientific American 415 Madison Ave Fl 11 New York NY 10017-1179

PRESS, WILLIAM HENRY, astrophysicist, computer scientist; b. N.Y.C., N.Y., May 23, 1948; s. Frank and Billie (Kallick) P.; m. Margaret Ann Lauritsen, 1969 (div. 1982); 1 dau., Sara Linda; m. Jeffrey Foden Howell, Apr. 19, 1991; 1 son, James Howell. AB, Harvard Coll., 1969; MS, Calif. Inst. Tech., 1971, PhD, 1972. Asst. prof. theoretical physics Calif. Inst. Tech., 1973-74; asst. prof. physics Princeton (N.J.) U., 1974-76; prof. astronomy and physics Harvard U., Cambridge, Mass., 1976-98, chmn. dept. astronomy, 1982-85; dep. lab. dir. Los Alamos Nat. Lab., 1998—. Mem. numerous adv. coms. and panels NSF, NASA, NAS, NRC; vis. mem. Inst. Advanced Study, 1983-94; mem. Def. Sci. Bd., 1985-89, sci. adv. com. Packard Found., 1988—, program com. Sloan Found., 1985-91; chmn. adv. bd. NSF Inst. Theoretical Physics, 1986-87; mem. Computer Sci. and Telecomm. Bd., 1991-96; U.S. del. IUPAP Gen. Assembly, 1996; cons. MITRE Corp., 1977—; trustee Inst. Def. Analysis, 1988—, exec. com., 1990—; chief naval ops. Exec. Panel, 1994-2000. Author: Numerical Recipes, 1986; contbr. articles to profl. jours. Sloan Found. research fellow, 1974-78 Fellow: Am. Phys. Soc., Am. Acad. Arts and Scis.; mem.: NAS, Coun. on Fgn. Relations, Assn. for Computing Machinery, Internat. Soc. Relativity and Gravitation, Internat. Astron. Union, Am. Astron. Soc. (Helen B. Warner prize 1981), Coun. on Fgn. Rels. Office: Los Alamos Nat Lab MS A-121 Los Alamos NM 87545-0001

PRESSER, CARY, research engineer; b. Bklyn., June 20, 1952; s. Harry and Regina Deborah (Lieberman) P.; m. Karen Leslie Antonoff, Feb. 27, 1977; children: Yona Ruth, Aliza Miriam. BSc in Aerospace Engring., Poly. U., 1974, MSc in Aero. Engring., 1976; DSc in Aero. Engring., Technion-Israel Inst. Tech., 1980. Tchg. fellow Poly. U., 1974-75; tchg. instr., rsch. asst. Technion-Israel Inst. Tech., Haifa, 1975-80; rsch. engr. Nat. Inst. Stds. and Tech., Gaithersburg, Md., 1980—, group leader high temperature processes, 1994-99, group leader thermal and reactive processes, 1999—. Mem. modeling and simulation subcom., interagency propulsion com. Joint Army-Navy-NASA-Air Force, 1999—. Contbr. articles to profl. jours. Recipient Silver medal, U.S. Dept. Commerce, 1991, SMART Bonus award, 1992, Sustained Superior Performance award, Nat. Inst. Stds. and Tech., 1983—89; fellow Lady Davis grad. fellow, Technion-Israel Inst. Tech., 1975—76. Fellow: ASME (com. heat transfer in energy sys. heat transfer divsn. 1986—, com. acad. and indsl. rsch. fuels and combustion techs. divsn. 1995—), AIAA (assoc.; propellants and combustion tech. com. 1987—90, terrestrial energy sys. tech. com. 1992—, computational fluid dynamics com. on stds. 1997—, Best Paper award terrestrial energy sys. tech. com. 1994, Best Paper award propellants and combustion tech. com. 1987, 1989); mem.: AIChE, ASTM (stds. and methods of particle size measurements 1991—, chmn. subcom. reference materials 1992—95, subcom. on internat. cooperation on terminology, com. on particle size measurements, subcom. on liquid particle measurements), AAAS, Optical Soc. Am., Instrument Soc. Am., Combustion Inst. (symposium program rev. subcom. 1989—), Assn. Orthodox Jewish Scientists, Inst. Liquid Atomization and Spray Sys. (diesel and automotive sprays tech. com. 1997—, computational and modeling tech. com. 1997—), N.Y. Acad. Scis., Am. Assn. Aerosol Rsch., Am. Chem. Soc., Sigma Xi (admission com. NIST chpt. 1990—93), Tau Epsilon Phi, Sigma Gamma Tau. Office: Nat Inst Stds and Tech 100 Bureau Dr Stop 8360 Gaithersburg MD 20899-8360 E-mail: cpresser@nist.gov.

PRESSER, HARRIET BETTY, sociology educator; b. Bklyn., Aug. 29, 1936; d. Phillip Rubinoff and Rose (Gudowitz) Jabish; m. Neil Nathan Presser, Dec. 16, 1956 (div.); 1 child, Sheryl Lynn. BA, George Washington U., 1959; MA, U. N.C., 1962; PhD, U. Calif., Berkeley, 1969. Statistician Bur. Census, Washington, 1959; research assoc. Inst. Life Ins., N.Y.C., 1962-64; lectr. demography U. Sussex, Brighton, England, 1967-68; staff assoc. Population Council, N.Y.C., 1968-69; asst. prof. sociomed. scis. Columbia U., 1969-73, assoc. prof. sociomed. scis., 1973-76; prof. sociology U. Md., College Park, 1976—99, dir. Ctr. on Population, Gender, and Social Inequality, 1988—2001, disting. faculty rsch. fellow, 1993-94, disting. univ. prof., 1999—; fellow in residence Netherlands Inst. for Advanced Study in Humanities & Social Sci., Wassenaar, The Netherlands, 1994-95. Fellow Ctr. for Advanced Study in the Behavioral Scis., Stanford, Calif., 1986-87, 91-92; bd. dirs. Population Reference Bur.; cons. Nat. Inst. for Child Health and Human Devel., 1975—; scholar-in-residence Russell Sage Found., N.Y.C., 1998-99,2000; resident scholar Bellagio Study and Conf. Ctr., Rockefeller Found., 2000; acad. visitor Gender Inst. London Sch. Econs and Polit. Scis. Editl. bd. Time and Soc., 1991-95, Social Forces, 1984-87, Signs, 1975-85; assoc. editor Jour. Health and Social Behavior, 1975-78. Nat. Inst. for Child Health and Devel. grantee, 1972-78, 83-88, Population Coun. grantee, 1976-79, NSF grantee, 1982-83, 90-94, 2000—, Rockefeller Found. grantee, 1983-85, 88-94, William and Flora Hewlett Found. grantee, 1989—, Andrew W. Mellon Found. grantee, 1994-95, W. T. Grant Found., 1996-99. Mem. Population Assn. Am. (bd. dirs. 1972-75, 2nd v.p. 1983, 1st v.p. 1985, pres.-elect 1988, pres. 1989), Am. Pub. Health Assn. (council mem. population sect. 1976-79), Am. Sociological Assn. (coun. mem. at large 1990-93, chmn., coun. mem. population sect. 1978-83), Sociological Research Assn. (elected). Office: U Maryland Dept Sociology College Park MD 20742-0001

PRESSER, JANICE, business executive; b. N.Y.C., Feb. 14, 1946; m. Barry S. Perlman; 2 children. BA, CCNY, 1967; BSN, Columbia U., 1978; MA, Hunter Coll., 1981; PhD, Union Inst., 1990. Pres., CEO The Gabriel Inst., Phila. Libertarian candidate for N.J. House, 1995, 97; Libertarian candidate for U.S. House 3rd dist., N.J., 1996, 98; chair N.J. Libertarian Party, 1998-99. Office: The Gabriel Inst 1601 Market St Ste 1500 Philadelphia PA 19103-2301 E-mail: jpresser@thegabrielinstitute.com.

PRESSER, STANLEY, sociology educator; b. Bklyn., Feb. 18, 1950; s. Sidney and Sydonia (Cohen) P.; m. Yan Yu; 1 child, Solomon Zhi-Qian. AB, Brown U., 1971; PhD, U. Mich., 1977. Rsch. investigator Survey Rsch. Ctr., U. Mich., 1977-78, head field office, 1981-83; rsch. assoc. Inst. Rsch. Social Sci., U. N.C., 1978-81; dir. Detroit Area Study, U. Mich., 1983-85; assoc. dir. sociology program NSF, 1985-87, dir., 1987-88; prof. sociology U. Md., 1989—; dir. Survey Rsch. Ctr., 1989-2000. Vis. prof. sociology U. Md., 1988-89; dir. joint U. Md. and U. Mich. program in Survey Methodology, 1992-96; bd. overseers Nat. Opinion Rsch. Ctr. Gen. Social Survey, 1984-85, 93-97; spl. cons. Nat. Econ. Rsch. Assocs., 1986-89; cons. U.S. Dept. Justice, 1995, Dept. Commerce, 1991, GAO, 1988-89, EEO Commn., 1985, NOAA, 1991-94, State of Alaska Atty. Gen., 1989-92. Co-author: Questions and Answers in Attitude surveys, 1981, Survey Questions: Handcrafting the Standardized Questionaire, 1986; editor Pub. Opinion Quar., 1993-97; co-editor: Sourcebook of Harris National Surveys, 1981, Survey Rsch. Methods, 1989; mem. editl. bd. Pub. Opinion Quar., 1983-87, Sociol. Methods and Rsch., 1980-83, Social Psychology Quar., 1979-82; contbr. articles to profl. jours. Fellow Am. Statis. Assn.; mem. Am. Assn. Pub. Opinion Rsch. (pres. 1993-94). Office: U of Md Sociology Dept College Park MD 20742-1315

PRESSER, STEFAN, lawyer, educator; b. Bklyn., Apr. 30, 1953; s. Sidney and Sydonia (Cohen) P.; m. Sandra B. Sherman, Sept. 21, 1988; children: David, Natania, Rachel Sherman-Presser. BA in Sociology magna cum laude, Yale U., 1976; JD, NYU, 1979. Staff counsel Civil Rights Bur. N.Y. State Office of the Atty. Gen., 1979-80; staff counsel Greater Houston chpt. ACLU, 1981-84; legal dir. ACLU of Pa., Phila., 1985—. Clin. adj. prof. Temple U. Sch. Law, 1990—, founder, co-dir. pub. interest scholars program, 2000—; vis. lectr. Bryn Mawr Coll. Grad. Sch. of Social Work & Social Rsch., 1997, 98, 2000. Co-author: The Rights of Single People, 1985. Recipient award for meritorious svc. in field of corrections Prison Soc., 1994, Liberty Bell award Bar Assn. Lehigh County, 1996, Andrew Hamilton award Phila. Bar Assn. 1997, Pres.'s meritorious svc. award NAACP, Phila., 1999; named Disting. Advocate, Support Ctr. for Child Advocates, Phila., 1996; Root-Tilden scholar NYU Sch. Law, 1976-79; Arthur Garfield Hays fellow, 1978-79. Jewish. Office: ACLU of Pa 125 S 9th St Ste 701 Philadelphia PA 19107-5194 Business E-Mail: spresser@aclupa.org.

PRESSER, STEPHEN BRUCE, lawyer, educator; b. Chattanooga, Aug. 10, 1946; s. Sidney and Estelle (Shapiro) P.; m. Carole Smith, June 18, 1968 (div. 1987); children: David Carter, Elisabeth Catherine; m. ArLynn Leiber, Dec. 13, 1987; children: Joseph Leiber, Eastman Leiber. AB, Harvard U., 1968, JD, 1971. Bar: Mass. 1971, D.C. 1972. Law clk. to Judge Malcolm Richard Wilkey U.S. Ct. Appeals (D.C. cir.), 1971-72; assoc. Wilmer, Cutler & Pickering, Washington, 1972-74; asst. prof. law Rutgers U., Camden, N.J., 1974-76; vis. assoc. prof. U. Va., 1976-77; prof. Northwestern U., Chgo., 1977—, class 1940 rsch. prof., 1992-93, Raoul Berger prof. legal history, 1992—, assoc. dean acad. affairs Sch. Law, 1982-85. Prof. bus. law Kellogg Grad. Sch. Mgmt., Northwestern U., Chgo., 1992—. Author: (with Jamil S. Zainaldin) Law and Jurisprudence in American History, 1980, 4th edit., 2000, Studies in the History of the United States Courts of the Third Circuit, 1983, The Original Misunderstanding: The English, The Americans and the Dialectic of Federalist Jurisprudence, 1991, Piercing the Corporate Veil, 1991, revised ann., (with Ralph Ferrara and Meridith Brown) Takeovers: A Strategist's Manual, 2d edit., 1993, Recapturing the Constitution, 1994, (with Douglas W. Kmiec) The American Constitutional Order: History, Cases, and Philosophy, 1998; assoc. articles editor Guide to American Law, 1985. Trustee Village of Winnetka, Ill., 2000—; mem. acad. adv. bd. Washington Legal Found. Recipient summer stipend NEH, 1975; Fulbright Sr. scholar Univ. Coll., London Sch. Econs. and Polit. Sci., 1983-84, Inst. Advanced Legal Studies, 1996; Adams fellow Inst. U.S. Studies, London, 1996; assoc. rsch. fellow Inst. U.S. Studies, 1999—. Mem. Am. Soc. Legal History (bd. dirs. 1979-82), Am. Law Inst., Univ. Club Chgo. (bd. dirs. 1997-99, sec., 1999), Legal Club Chgo., Reform Club (London), Arts Club Chgo. Office: Northwestern U Law Sch 357 E Chicago Ave Chicago IL 60611-3069 E-mail: s-presser@law.northwestern.edu.

PRESSEY, JANICE ELIZABETH, youth evangelist, writer; b. Balt., July 22, 1953; BS in Corp. Comms., U. Balt., 1994; MA in Liberal Studies, Coll. Notre Dame of Md., 1997; EdD in Urban Ednl. Leadership, Morgan State U., 2002. Cert. notary pub. Chmn. affirmative action/equal employment opportunity U.S. Postal Svc., 1978-96; motivational speaker, 1985—; founder The Coll. Workshop, 1996—; pres., owner Comms. Enhancement Cons., 1998—. Intern WSHW-TV, 1993; adj. prof. New Balt. City C.C., 1994—; co-host WorldViews TV mag., 1994—; segment prodr. Balt. Cable Access Corp., 1996—; faculty devel. cons., book reviewer Simon and Schuster Edn. Group, 1998—. Presenter numerous workshops and keynote speeches. Mem. fin. com. Union Bapt. Ch., 1981—, mem. budget com., co-chmn. Annual Women's Day; lobbyist Action for the Homeless, Child First Campaign; vol., kitchen crew asst. Helping Up Mission; coord. resume workshops P.A.T.H. Homeless Shelter; vol., counselor, motivational speaker Walbrook H.S.; vol. mentor Women Entrepeneurs of Balt., Inc. Recipient Woman of Yr. award Union Bapt. Ch., Faithful Svc. award Union Bapt. Ch.; Frank A. Decosta scholar, Md. State Del. scholar, Fed. Exec. Employees Assn. scholar, U.S. Postal Svc. scholar. Mem. Internat. Honor Ednl. Soc., Balt. Theater Alliance, Coll. Notre Dame of Md. Alumnae Assn., Delta Sigma Theta (cert. of recognition, mem. mental health awareness com.), Kappa Delta Pi (Theta XI chpt.). Home: 2539 W Lafayette Ave Baltimore MD 21216-4728

PRESSLEY, FRED G., JR. lawyer; b. N.Y.C., June 19, 1953; s. Fred G. Sr. and Frances (Sanders) P.; m. Cynthia Denise Hill, Sept. 5, 1981. BA cum laude, Union Coll., 1975; JD, Northwestern U., 1978. Bar: Ohio 1978, U.S. Dist. Ct. (so. dist.) Ohio 1979, U.S. Dist. Ct. (no. dist.) Ohio 1985, U.S. Dist. Ct. (ea. dist.) Wis. 1980, U.S. Ct. Appeals (6th cir.). Assoc. Porter, Wright, Morris & Arthur, Columbus, Ohio, 1978-85, ptnr., 1985—. Bd. dirs. Columbus Area Leadership Program, 1981-84, Franklin County Bd. Mental Retardation and Devel. Disabilities, Columbus, 1989-97, Union Coll., Schenectady, N.Y., 1992—. Recipient Civic Achievement award Ohio Ho. of Reps., 1988. Mem. ABA. Avocations: jogging, golf, basketball, military history. Office: Porter Wright Morris & Arthur 41 S High St Ste 2800 Columbus OH 43215-6194

PRESSLEY, JAMES RAY, electrical engineer; b. Ft. Worth, July 14, 1946; s. Loy Dale and Dorothy Helen (Foust) P.; m. Barbara Kay McMillin, Oct. 9, 1968 (div. 1981); children: James Foust Pressley, Kreg Milam Pressley; m. Susan Marie Straw, Apr. 27, 1985 (div.); children: Shaye Eugene Straw, Rebecca Alycen Straw, Rachel Leilani Straw. BSEE, U. Tex., Arlington, 1970. Registered profl. engr., Alaska, Hawaii, Oreg., Wash., Guam. Designer, draftsman Romine & Slaughter, Ft. Worth, 1967-71; engr. Crews MacInnes & Hoffman, Anchorage, 1971-73, O'Kelly & Schoenlank, Anchorage, 1973-75, Theodore G. Creedon, Anchorage, 1975-77; v.p. Fryer, Pressley Elliott, 1977-80, Fryer/Pressley Engring., 1980-91, FPE Roen Engrs., Inc., 1991-98; also chmn. bd., 1991-95; v.p., bd. dirs., 1991—; v.p., bd. dirs., mgr., prin. in charge Anchorage ofc. PDC, Inc. Cons. Engrs., 1998—. Mem. elec. constrn. and maintenance industry evaluation panel, 1982-96. Mem.: NSPE, IEEE, Am. Soc. Quality, Nat. Fire Protection Assn., Internat. Assn. Elec. Insps., Illuminating Engring. Soc. (sustaining). Office: PDC Inc Cons Engrs 1231 Gambell St Anchorage AK 99501 E-mail: jimpressley@pdceng.com.

PRESSLEY, JENNIFER L. accountant; b. Decatur, Ill., Apr. 1, 1973; d. Jerry Lynn and Karen Waye Pressley. AS in Bus., Richland C.C., Decatur, 1992; BA in Acctg., Ill. State U., 1995. CPA, Ill.; cert. mgmt. acct. Acctg. analyst Archer Daniels Midland Co., Decatur, 1995—, dept. coord. for United Way, 1998, 99. Cons. Jr. Achievement, 1999. Mem. Inst. Mgmt. Accts. (cert., v.p. comm. 1997—), Ill. CPA Soc., Decatur Area Young Bus. Profls. Avocations: running, crocheting, rollerblading, baking. Office: Archer Daniels Midland 4666 E Faries Pkwy Decatur IL 62526-5666

PRESSLY, JENNINGS G. radiologist; b. Nashville, Sept. 16, 1947; s. James Boyce and Florence Gillem P.; m. Anna Dunson, Feb. 2, 1948; children: Anna, Catherine, Elizabeth. BA, U. N.C., 1969; MD, Med. U. S.C., 1973. Dir. vasc. radiology Greenville (S.C.) Hosp., 1978-82, chair dept. radiology, 1981-91; dir. radiology Hillcrest Hosp., Simpsonville, S.C., 1991—. Mem. Radiol. Soc. N.Am., Am. Coll. Radiology, S.C. Med. Assn., S.C. Radiologists Assn., S.C. Assn. Radiology, Am. Inst. Ultrasound in Medicine. Office: Radiology Assocs 527 SE Main St # 669 Simpsonville SC 29681-3215

PRESSLY, THOMAS JAMES, history educator; b. Troy, Tenn., Jan. 18, 1919; s. James Wallace and Martha Belle (Bittick) P.; m. Lillian Cameron, Apr. 30, 1943; children: Thomas James II, Stephanie Suzuki. AB, Harvard U., 1940, AM, 1941, PhD, 1950; LLD (hon.), Whitman Coll., 1981. Instr. history Princeton U., 1946-49; asst. prof. U. Wash., 1949-54, assoc. prof., 1954-60, prof., 1960-87, prof. emeritus, 1987—. Vis. assoc. prof. Princeton U., 1953-54, Johns Hopkins U., 1969-70 Author: Americans Interpret Their Civil War, 1954; editor: (with W. H. Scofield) Farm Real Estate Values in the United States, 1965, (with others) American Political Behavior, 1974, Diary of George Templeton Strong (abridged), 1988, (with Glenn M. Linden) Voices From the House Divided, 1995, (with Maclyn P. Burg) The Great War At Home and Abroad, 1999. Served with AUS, 1941-45. Ford Found. Faculty fellow, 1951-52; Center for Advanced Study in Behavioral Scis. fellow, 1955-56 Mem. Am. Hist. Assn., So. Hist. Assn. (editorial bd. Jour. So. History 1973-77), Orgn. Am. Historians. Home: 4545 E Laurel Dr NE Seattle WA 98105-3838 Office: U Wash Dept History PO Box 353560 Seattle WA 98195-3560

PRESSMAN, GABE STANLEY, television reporter; b. N.Y.C., Feb. 14, 1924; s. Benjamin and Lena (Rifkin) P.; m. Emma Mae Kracht, Nov. 8, 1953 (div. 1967); children: Mark, Elizabeth, Margaret; m. Vera Elisabeth Olsen, Apr. 1, 1972; 1 child, Michael. BA in History, NYU, 1946; MS in Journalism, Columbia U., 1947. Reporter Peekskill (N.Y.) Star, 1941-42, Newark Evening News, 1947; corr. Overseas New Agy., N.Y.C., 1948-49; reporter World-Telegram Sun, 1949-54, WRCA and WRCA-TV, NBC, N.Y.C., 1954-72, WNEW-TV, N.Y.C., 1972-80, WNBC-TV, N.Y.C., 1980—; anchor News Forum. Served to lt. (j.g.) USN, 1943-46, PTO. Mem. N.Y. Press Club (1st v.p. 1988-97, pres. 1997-00), Inner Circle (pres. 1990). Office: WNBC 30 Rockefeller Plz Fl 2 New York NY 10112-0036

PRESSMAN, JACOB, rabbi; b. Phila., Oct. 26, 1919; s. Solomon David and Dora (Levin) P.; m. Marjorie Steinberg, June 14, 1942; children: Daniel Joseph, Joel David, Judith Sharon. BA, U. Pa., 1940; MHL, Jewish Theol. Sem., 1944, Dr.Hebrew Letters, 1960, Dr. Humane Letters, 1979. Ordained rabbi, 1945. Rabbi Forest Hills Jewish Ctr., N.Y.C., 1944-46, Congregation Sinai, L.A., 1946-50, Temple Beth Am, L.A., 1950—85. Dir. Bonds of Israel, L.A., 1988-90, city chmn., 1990-91; vice chmn. bd. govs. L.A. Jewish Fedn. Coun., 1988—; founder U. Judaism, L.A. Hebrew High Sch., Herzl Sch., Camp Ramah at Ojai, Akiba Acad., Rabbi Jacob Pressman Acad. Mem. Rabbinical Assembly Western Region (pres. 1954-56), Bd. Rabbis So. Calif. (pres. 1958-61). Office: Temple Beth Am 1039 S La Cienega Blvd Los Angeles CA 90035-2507 E-mail: jpress6511@aol.com. *God is. God is good. His creation is good, and so, mankind, being of His creation is good. As an act of grace, God gives man the power to choose between good and evil in his ways, and with even greater grace gives man the awareness that he has this choice. Man is perfectible. His perfect stage, the Messianic era, is coming; but it will always be coming, never at a moment in time to arrive, but always inviting us to progress to newer and higher goals personally and as a society, each new mountaintop of human progress toward that nobler future merely opens our eyes to visions of even greater and more God-like human life.*

PRESTAGE, JAMES JORDAN, university chancellor; b. Deweyville, Tex., Apr. 29, 1926; s. James J. and Mona (Wilkins) P.; m. Jewel Limar, Aug. 12, 1953; children— Terri, James Grady, Eric, Karen, Jay BS cum laude, So. U., Baton Rouge, 1950; MS, U. Iowa, 1955, PhD, 1959. Instr. biology Prairie View Coll., Tex., 1955-56; asst. prof. So. U., Baton Rouge, 1959, assoc. prof. biology, 1959-61, prof. biology, 1961—, dir. computer sci. ctr., 1968-71, 72-73, dean acad. affairs, v.p. acad. affairs, 1973-81, exec. v.p., 1981-82, chancellor, 1982-85, univ. disting. prof. emeritus, 1985—; univ. disting. prof. biology Dillard U., New Orleans, 1987—. Chair divsn. natural scis. Dillard U., 1990-97; asst. dir. La. Coordinating Council for Higher Edn., Baton Rouge, 1971-72; mem. commn. on scholars Ill. Bd. Higher Edn., 1975-82; mem. com. on off-campus instrn. La. Bd. Regents, 1975—; mem. La. Data Processing Council, Baton Rouge, 1979-82; vis. prof. biology Dillard U., New Orleans; trustee Am. Coll. Testing Program, 1983—; faculty assoc. Danforth Found., 1966-70. Mem. exec. bd. Istrouma council Boy Scouts Am.; vice chmn. bd. trustees Greater Mt. Carmel Baptist Ch., Baton Rouge; bd. dirs. Capital Area United Way, Baton Rouge. Served with USN, 1944-46, 50-52; ETO, Korea Named Most Outstanding Faculty Mem., So. U., 1966-67; Nat. Med. Fellowships fellow U. Iowa, Iowa City, 1956-59; NIH grantee, 1960-65 Mem. Conf. Acad. Deans So. States. NAACP, Sigma Xi, Alpha Chi, Alpha Phi Alpha (chpt. pres.), Sigma Pi Phi Democrat. Avocations: fishing; reading; gardening. Home: 2145 77th Ave Baton Rouge LA 70807-5508 Office: So Br PO Box 9222 Baton Rouge LA 70813

PRESTAGE, JEWEL LIMAR, political science educator; b. Hutton, La., Aug. 12, 1931; d. Brudis L. and Sallie Bell (Johnson) Limar; m. James J. Prestage, Aug. 12, 1953; children— Terri, James, Eric, Karen, Jay. BA, So. U., Baton Rouge, 1951; MA, U. Iowa, 1952, PhD, 1954; LHD (hon.), U. D.C., 1994, Loyola U., Chgo., 1999; LLD (hon.), Spelman Coll., 1999. Assoc. prof. polit. sci. Prairie View (Tex.) Coll., 1954-55, 56; assoc. prof. polit. sci. So. U., 1956-57, 58-62, prof., 1962—, chairperson dept., 1965-83; disting. prof. emeritus Prairie View Coll., 1989—; dean pub. policy and urban affairs So. U., 1983-89; prof. polit. sci. Prairie View U., 1989-90; dean Benjamin Banneker Honors College, Prairie View (Tex.) Coll., 1990-98, prof. political sci., 1998—; disting. prof. emeritus polit. sci. Benjamin Banneker Honors Coll., 2000—. Chmn. La. adv. com. to U.S. Commn. on Civil Rights, 1975-85; mem., chmn. nat. adv. coun. on women's ednl. programs U.S. Dept. Edn., 1980-82; vis. prof. U. Iowa, 1987-88. Author: (with M. Githens) A Portrait of Marginality: Political Behavior of the American Woman, 1976; contbr. articles to profl. jours. Rockefeller fellow, 1951-52; NSF fellow, 1964; Ford Found. postdoctoral fellow, 1969-70 Mem. NAACP, Am. Polit. Sci. Assn. (v.p. 1974-75, Frank Goodnow award 1998), So. Polit. Sci. Assn. (pres. 1975-76, Manning Daver award 1998), Nat. Conf. Black Polit. Scientists (pres. 1976-77), Nat. Assn. African Am. Honors Programs (pres. 1993-94), Am. Soc. for Pub. Adminstrn. (pres. La. chpt. 1988-89, nat. exec. coun. 1989-90), Policy Studies Orgn. (exec. coun. 2000), Links Inc., Alpha Kappa Alpha. Home: 11114 Wortham Blvd Houston TX 77065 Office: So Univ PO Box 125 Prairie View TX 77446-0125 *Commitments which guide my life are: (1) maximum* *development of personal potential through pursuit of excellence in all endeavors; (2) fair play, respect, compassion and quest of community in relations with fellow human beings; (3) utilization of personal talents in the interest of removing impediments to the good life "for all persons"; (4) pursuit of truth as the pervasive concern in academia; and (5) transmission of the above as priority goals to all with whom I have contact.*

PRESTBO, DARLENE (MARTHA DARLENE PRESTBO), clinical social worker; b. Ft. Wayne, Ind., May 3, 1941; d. Lake Osborn and Lorena Martha (Ford) Parrish; m. John Andrew Prestbo, Aug. 14, 1965; children: Bradford Jonathan, Laura Christine. BS in Speech, Northwestern U., 1963; MSW, U. Ill., 1971. Lic. clin. social worker; bd. cert. diplomate in clin. social work; cert. hypnotherapist Carrier Found.; cert. therapeutic touch practitioner Healing Assocs. Tchr. English, drama Garrett (Ind.) H.S., 1963-64; instr. Internat. Bus. Coll., Ft. Wayne, Ind., 1964-65; actress Acad. Playhouse, Chgo., 1967; caseworker Chgo. Dept. Pub. Aid, 1967-69; therapist Bowen Ctr. for Abused Children, Chgo., 1971-73; pvt. practice Summit, N.J., 1974-77, Bay Village, Ohio, 1978-81, Montgomery Twp., N.J., 1982—. Lectr., workshop leader various cmty. groups, also radio and TV appearances, Chgo., cen. and no. N.J., 1973—. Author: (book) Where Love Is Needed, 1991; author, editor: (book) Breaking the Shackles of Shame, 1993; contbr. poetry to anthologies; photographs exhibited in galleries, N.J., Pa., 1990—. Bd. trustees Montgomery Arts Coun., Montgomery Twp., 1993-97; deacon Nassau Presbyn. Ch., Princeton, N.J., 1991-93. Mem.: Creative Artists Guild, Acad. Cert. Social Workers, 1860 House Cultural Ctr. (performing arts com., trustee). Avocations: gardening, theater performance, women's spirituality, photography, poetry readings. Office: Montgomery Knoll 39 Tamarack Cir Skillman NJ 08558-2019

PRESTBO, JOHN ANDREW, newspaper editor, journalist, author; b. Northwood, N.D., Sept. 26, 1941; s. Oscar Bernt and Jeanne (Schol) P.; m. Darlene Parrish, Aug. 14, 1965; children: Bradford Jonathan, Laura Christine. BS, Northwestern U., 1963, MS, 1964. Reporter, writer Wall Street Jour., Chgo., 1964-74, staff editor, Page 1 N.Y.C., 1974-75, commodities editor, 1975-77, bur. chief Cleve., 1977-81, markets editor N.Y.C., 1984—, editor Dow Jones Indexes, 1993—; v.p. editorial Dow Jones Radio 2, Inc., Princeton, N.J., 1981-83. Author: Sleuthing, 1976; co-author: (with Frederick C. Klein) News and the Market, 1974, (with Douglas R. Sease) Barron's Guide to Making Investment Decisions, 1994, 2nd edit., 1998, The Wall Street Jour. Book of Internat. Investing, 1997; editor: This Abundant Land, 1975, Dow Jones Commodities Handbook, 1976-79, The Dow Jones Guide to the World Stock Market, 1994-98, The Market's Measure, 1999. Served with USAFR, 1966-73. Recipient Econ. Reporting award Ind. Natural Gas Assn., U. Mo., 1967; recipient Achievement-bur. writing award G.M. Loeb, 1968 Home: 14 Charleston Dr Skillman NJ 08558-1801 Office: 4300 Rte 1 Monmouth Junction NJ 08852 E-mail: john.prestbo@dowjones.com.

PRESTI, GERALYN MARIE, lawyer; b. Cleve., July 15, 1955; d. Joseph Carl Presti and Josephine Joanne Ambrogio; m. John Reid Sedor, Aug. 16, 1980; 2 children. BMus, Ohio U., 1979; M of Social Sci. Adminstrn. magna cum laude, JD, Case Western Res. U., 1988. Bar: Ohio 1989. Music therapist Bellefaire, Cleve., 1978-79, The Cleve. Music Sch. Settlement, Cleve., 1979-84; dep. gen. counsel Forest City Enterprises, Inc., 1989—. Admissions counsellor Case Western Res. U., Cleve., 1993-96, adv. bd. LLM degree fgn. students, 1998—; rsch. asst., law prof. Forest City Enterprise, Inc., Cleve., 1994-96. Trustee Homeowners Assn., Bentleyville, Ohio, 1992-94; v.p. bd. trustees Cleve. Music Sch. Settlement, 1999—; co-chmn. ann. fund U. Sch., Shaker Heights, Ohio, 1998—; dir. Ohio U. Sch. of Music, Athens, 1985-86; project mem. Reorgn. of the Cuyahoga County Dept. Human Svcs., Cleve., 1985. Recipient Greater Cleve. Woman of Profl. Excellence award YWCA, 1996. Mem. Greater Cleve. Gen. Counsel Assn., Order of the Coif. Avocations: pianist, travelling, art, reading, films. Office: Forest City Enterprise Inc 50 Public Sq Cleveland OH 44113-2267

PRESTIA, MICHAEL ANTHONY, accounting executive; b. S.I., N.Y., Oct. 6, 1931; s. Anthony and Antoinette (Folino) P.; m. Nancy Ferrandino, July 4, 1959 (div. May 1970); 1 child, Anthony; m. Janet Swanson, July 22, 1987 (dec. May 4, 2002). BA, NYU, 1953, MBA, 1956. CPA, N.Y. Sr. accountant Gluckman & Schacht, CPAs, N.Y.C., 1953-60; chief financial officer Franklin Broadcasting Co., N.Y.C., 1960-63; chief accountant asst. to bus. officer, sec. Cooper Union for Advancement Sci. and Art, N.Y.C., 1963-66; bus. officer Inst. Pub. Adminstrn., N.Y.C., 1966-71, controller, 1971-78, treas., 1978-84; cons. taxation and tax planning, 1959—. Served with AUS, 1953-55. Mem. AICPA, N.Y. State Soc. CPAs. Home: 53-06 Francis Lewis Blvd Flushing NY 11364-1633 Office: 445 5th Ave New York NY 10016-0109

PRESTIGIACOMO, CHARLES JOSEPH, neurosurgeon, educator; b. N.Y.C., Feb. 14, 1967; s. Franco and Francesa Paola (Calderone) P.; m. Cynthia M. Rinker, June 22, 1991; children: Rachel Diane, Laura Marie, Michelle Elizabeth. BS in Biology, Georgetown U.; MD, Columbia U., 1993. Resident in neurosurg. surgery Columbia-Presbyn. Med. Ctr., N.Y.C., 1993-2000; endovascular fellow Beth Israel Med. Ctr., 2000; asst. prof. dept. neurol. surgery and radiology U. Medicine and Dentistry NJ, Newark. Contbr. articles to med. jours. Mem. ACS (candidate), Am. Acad. Neurol. Surgeons, Congress Neurol. Surgeons. Roman Catholic. Avocations: building wooden ship models, photography, military technology, books, collecting wine, astronomy. Office: Neurol Inst of NJ U Med and Dentistry NJ 90 Bergen St Ste 8100 Newark NJ 07107 E-mail: cjp9@optonline.net.

PRESTON, ANDREW JOSEPH, pharmacist, drug company executive; b. Bklyn., Apr. 19, 1922; s. Charles A. and Josephine (Rizzutto) Pumo; m. Martha Jeanne Happ, Oct. 10, 1953; children: Andrew Joseph Jr., Charles Richard, Carolyn Louise, Frank Arthur, Joanne Marie, Barbara Jeanne. BSc, St. John U., 1943. Cert. bus. intermediary Internat. Bus. Brokers Assn. Mgr. Press Club, Bklyn. Nat. League Baseball Club, 1941-42; purchasing agt. Drug and Pharm. divsn. Intrassind, Inc., 1947; chief pharmacist Hendershot Pharmacy, Newton, N.J., 1949; agt. Bur. of Narcotics, U.S. Treasury Dept., 1948-49; owner Preston Drug & Surg. Co., Boonton, N.J., 1949-86; CEO Preston Pharmaceutics, Inc., Butler, 1970-80, Preston Bus. Cons., Inc., Kinnelon, 1987—. Commr. N.J. State Bd. Pharmacy, 1970—72, pres., 1973; organizer State of N.J. Drug Abuse Spkrs. Program, 1970—76; chmn. Morris County Drug Abuse Coun., 1969—70; lectr. drug abuse and narcotic addition various cmty. orgns., 1968—78; mem. adv. bd. Nat. Cmty. Bank, Boonton, 1973. Contbr. Chmn. bldg. fund com. Riverside Hosp., Boonton, 1963; mem. exec. com. Gov. Tom Kean Ann. Ball, 1985—86; chmn. Pharmacists of N.J. for election of Pres. Ford, 1976, Pharmacists for Gov. Tom Kean, 1981—84, N.J. Pharmacists for Reagan/Bush, 1984; mem. exec. com. Morris County Overall Econ. Devel. Com., 1976—82; chmn. Pharmacists for Fenwick, 1982; v.p. Kinnelon Rep. Club, 1980; Rep. com. Kinnelon, 1990; mem. adv. com. to Congressman Dean Gallo on Pres. Clinton's Health Security Plan, 1994; mem. Morris County (N.J.) Rep. Fin. Com., 1972; pres. Ronald Reagan N.J. Re-Election Adv. Bd., 1984. Lt. (j.g.) USNR, 1943—46. Recipient Bowl Hygeia award, Robbins Co., 1969, Pres.'s award, E.R. Squibb, 1968, Square Club award, N.J. Pharm., 1969, Andrew J. Preston award for Polit. Action established in his honor, 1999. Mem.: VFW, Morris-Sussex Pharmacists Soc., Morris County Pharm. Assn., N.J. Pub. Health Assn., Pharmacists Guild N.J., Pharmacists Guild Am. (pres. N.Y. divsn. 1946—47), Inst. Bus. Appraisers, Internat. Bus. Brokers Assn., N.J. Narcotic Enforcement Officers Assn., Internat. Narcotic Enforcement Officers Assn., Nat. Cmty. Pharmacists Assn., N.J. Pharm. Assn. (econs. com. 1960—65, pres. 1967—68, Oscar Singer Meml. award 1987, William H. McNeil award 1994, Presdl. Citation award 2000), Am. Pharm. Assn., St. John's Alumni Assn., N.J. Assn. Realtors, Nat. Assn. Realtors, Morris County Bd. Realtors, Am. Legion, Smoke Rise Club, KC, Elks. Roman Catholic. Home and Office: 507 Pepperidge Tree Ln Kinnelon NJ 07405-2223

PRESTON, ANN ELIZABETH, media and communication educator; b. Chisholm, Minn., June 6, 1955; d. William Martin and Elizabeth Ann (Krause) Baldwin; m. John Carr Preston, Mar. 24, 1976; children: Rachel Ann, Sarah Elizabeth. BA, U. Winnipeg, Man., Can., 1979; BS, Moorhead (Minn.) State U., 1981; MS, N.D. State U., 1985; PhD, Ohio U., 1992. Info. officer Orgn. for Cooperation in Overseas Devel., Winnipeg, 1979-85; instr. N.D. State U., Fargo, 1984-85, U. Wis., Superior, 1985-87; tchg. assoc. Ohio U., Athens, 1987-89; asst. prof. St. Bonaventure (N.Y.) U., 1989-92, N.D. State U., Fargo, 1992-96; assoc. prof. Quincy (Ill.) U., 1996—2001; prof. St. Ambrose U., Davenport, Iowa, 2001—. Publs. cons. Inst. for Democracy in Edn., Athens, 1988-89; rsch. assoc. Ohio U. Coll. Osteo. Medicine, Athens, 1987-90; mktg. mem. ARC, Olean, N.Y., 1990-92; chair adv. bd. KDSU, Fargo, N.D., 1993-96. Contbr. articles to profl. jours. Co-founder, mktg. dir. Dakota Radio Theatre, Fargo, 1993-96. Grantee Can. Consulate, 1994, N.D. State U., 1995, C-Span, 1991, St. Bonaventure U., 1990. Mem. Assn. for Edn. in Journalism and Mass Comm. (chair media and disability 1997-98), Popular Culture Assn. Home: 1935 N Perry St Davenport IA 52803-2920

PRESTON, BRUCE MARSHALL, lawyer, educator; b. Trinidad, Colo., Feb. 24, 1949; s. Marshall Caldwell and Juanita (Killgore) P.; m. Mariannina Erra, Aug. 10, 1974; children: Charles Marshall, Robert Arthur. BS summa cum laude, Ariz. State U., 1971; MA, U. Ariz., 1972, JD, 1975. Bar: Ariz. 1975, U.S. Ct. Appeals (9th cir.) 1976, U.S. Ct. Claims 1983, U.S. Tax Ct. 1983, U.S. Supreme Ct. 1983; cert. fin. planner. Atty. Maricopa County Office of Pub. Defender, Phoenix, 1975-84; ptnr. Simonsen & Preston, 1985-86, Simonsen, Preston, Sargeant & Arbetman, Phoenix, 1986; atty. office of atty. gen. State of Ariz., 1987-90; assoc. Broening, Oberg and Woods, Phoenix, 1989-96, ptnr., 1997—. Judge pro tem Mcpl. Ct., Phoenix, 1984-86; licensee in sales Ariz. Dept. Real Estate, Phoenix, 1981-87; adj. faculty Phoenix Coll. for Fin. Planning, Denver, 1984-87, Maricopa County Community Coll. Dist., Phoenix, 1985-87, Ariz. State U. Coll. of Bus., Tempe, 1986-87, Ottawa U., Phoenix, 1986. Chmn. com., treas., pres. bd. dirs. Kachina Country Day Sch., 1982-90; bd. dirs. Family Svc. Agy., Phoenix, 1988—, treas., 1990-91; bd. dirs. Clearwater Hills Homewoners Assn., Paradise Valley, Ariz., 1989—, v.p., 1990, treas., 1991; bd. dirs. Phoenix Boys Choir, 1989-90. Mem. Ariz. Assn. Def. Counsel, Ariz. Bar Assn. (cert. specialist criminal law 1982-84), Maricopa County Bar Assn., Ariz. State U. Coll. Liberal Arts Alumni Assn. (bd. dirs. 1978-80, 87-88), Phi Kappa Phi. Avocations: computers, skiing, boating, running. Home: 7247 N Black Rock Trl Paradise Valley AZ 85253-2802 Office: Broening Oberg & Woods 1122 E Jefferson St Phoenix AZ 85034-2224 E-mail: bmp@bowwc.com.

PRESTON, CHARLES GEORGE, lawyer; b. Nov. 11, 1940; s. Charles William and Gudveig Nicoline (Hoem) P.; m. Hilde Delphine van Stappen, Mar. 12, 1970; children: Charles William, Stephanie Delphine, Christina Nicoline. BA, U. Wash., 1963, MPA, 1968; JD, Columbia U., 1971. Bar: Wash. 1971, D.C. 1981, U.S. Dist. Ct. D.C. 1981, U.S. Dist. Ct. (we. dist.) Wash. 1971, U.S. Ct. Appeals (9th cir.) 1972, U.S. Ct. Appeals (4th cir.) 1979, U.s. Ct. Appeals (5th and D.C. cirs.) 1978, U.S. Ct. Appeals (2d cir.) 1980, U.S. Ct. Appeals (11th cir.) 1981, U.S. Supreme Ct. 1977, U.S. Ct. Claims 1982, U.S. Ct. Appeals (1st cir.) 1984, U.S. Ct. Appeals (3d, 6th and 7th cirs.) 1987, Va. 1987, U.S. Dist. Ct. (ea. dist.) Va. 1989, U.S. Dist. Ct. (we. dist.) Wash. 1971, U.S. Dist. Ct. (no. dist.) Calif. 1981, U.S. Bankruptcy Ct. Va. 1990. Assoc. Jones, Grey, Bayley & Olson, Seattle, 1971-72; atty., asst. counsel for litigation Officer of Solicitor U.S. Dept. Labor, 1972-76, Washington, 1976-81; atty. Air Line Pilots Assn., 1981-82; mng. ptnr. MacNabb, Preston & Waxman, 1981-86, Preston & Preston, Great Falls, Va., 1986-95, Charles G. Preston, P.C., 1995—. Pres. Preston Group, Inc. 1989-98; lectr. seminars. Mem. Wash. State Bar, D.C. Bar Assn., Va. Bar Assn., Tng. Law Inst. (pres. 1985-95), Gt. Falls Bus. and Profl. Assn. (pres. 1990), The Serbian Crown, Va. (pres. 1989-99). Office: Charles G Preston PC 774C Walker Rd Great Falls VA 22066-2639 E-mail: preston.law@verizon.net.

PRESTON, CHARLES MICHAEL, lawyer; b. Balt., Oct. 11, 1945; s. Carlton Edward and Jeannette Thorn (Baker) P.; m. Carol Ann Armacost, June 21, 1969 (div. Dec. 1978). BA, Western Md. Coll., 1967; JD, U. Balt., 1970. Bar: Md. 1970, U.S. Dist. Ct. Md. 1972, U.S. Supreme Ct. 1974, U.S. Dist. Ct. (trial bar) 1984. Law clk. to Hon. E.O. Weant, Jr., Westminster, Md., 1970-71; assoc. Hoffman & Hoffman, 1972-75; ptnr. Hoffman, Hoffman & Preston, 1976-77, Hoffman, Stoner & Preston, Westminster, 1978-79; ptnr., v.p. Stoner, Preston & Boswell Chartered, 1980—. Rev. bd., panel mem. Atty. Grievance Commn., Annapolis, Md., 1978-95; mem. Md. Ct. Appeals Commn. on alternate dispute resolution, 1998-2000, adv. bd., Md. Mediation and Conflict Resolution Office (co-chair, Circuit Courts Com.), 2001-, Md. Ct. of Appeals Task Force on Professionalism, 2002-. Contbr. articles to profl. jours. Mem. Carroll County Gen. Hosp., Westminster, 1983—; trustee Raymond I. Richardson Found., Middleburg, Md., 1979-93; bd. dirs. Carroll County Agrl. Ctr., Westminster, 1975—; dir. N.W. dist. ARC, Balt., 1987-95; trustee Balt. Opera Co., 1998-2001. With U.S. Army, 1970-71. Fellow Md. Bar Found. (dir. 1998-), Am. Bar Found.; mem. ABA (del. ho. of dels., 1997-2000), Md. State Bar Assn. (treas. 1991-96, bd. govs. 1985-86, 91-2000, pres.-elect 1997, pres. 98), Carroll County Bar Assn. (pres. 1985), Pro Bono Resource Ctr. Md. (bd. dirs. 1997-2000), Elks. Presbyterian. Avocations: snow skiing, ice skating, woodworking, music, travel. Office: Stoner Preston & Boswell PO Box 389 188 E Main St Westminster MD 21157-5017

PRESTON, DAVID RAYMOND, lawyer; b. Harlingen, Tex., Feb. 12, 1961; s. Raymond C., Jr. and Janet (Bowman) P. BS, U. Fla., 1983, MS, 1985, PhD, 1989; JD, George Mason Sch. Law, 1996. Bar: Calif., U.S. Patent and Trademark Office. Postdoctoral rsch. U.S. Army, Frederick, Md., 1989-90; patent examiner U.S. Patent and Trademark Office, Washington, 1990-94; tech. devel. specialist Nat. Cancer Inst., NIH, Bethesda, Md., 1994-96; intern for Judge Rader U.S. Ct. Appeals (fed. cir.), Washington, 1995; patent attorney Campbell & Flores, San Diego, 1996-97; asst. patent counsel Aurora Bioscis. Corp., 1997-98; pres. David R. Preston & Assocs., 1999—. Judge internat. sci. fair U.S. Patents and Trademark Office, 1991. NIH fellow, 1987, Pres.'s fellow Am. Soc. Microbiology, 1988. Mem. AAAS, ABA, Am. Intellectual Property Law Assn., Fed. Cir. Bar Assn., San Diego Intellectual Property Law Assn. Republican. Avocations: tennis, golf, skiing, surfing, windsurfing. Office: David R Preston & Assocs 12625 High Bluff Dr Ste 205 San Diego CA 92130- E-mail: preston@drpna.com.

PRESTON, DEBRA SUE, counselor, educator; b. Lansing, Mich., Mar. 28, 1964; d. Thomas Michael and Nancy Jean (Dickenson) P. BSW, East Carolina U., 1986, MA in Edn., 1989; CAGS, Va. Tech., 1994, PhD, 1995. Lic. sch. counselor; lic. profl. counselor; nat. cert. counselor; nat. cert. career counselor; cert. social worker. Sch. counselor Roanoke Rapids Schs., Roanoke, N.C., 1989-91, social worker, 1992-93; pub. rels. specialist Va. Tech., Blacksburg, 1993-95; adj. prof. W.Va. Grad. Sch., Beckley, 1994-95; asst. prof. U. N.C., Pembroke, 1995—. Mem. state tng. team State Occupl. Info. Coordinating Com., Raleigh, N.C., 1995—; pres. NCACES, 1998—. Author monthly letter Counselor's Corner, 1993-95. Mem. ACA, Chi Sigma Iota (pres., sec., faculty advisor). Home: 4730 Dunrobin Dr Hope Mills NC 28348-8515 Office: U NC-Pembroke 1 University Rd Pembroke NC 28372-8699

PRESTON, JAMES YOUNG, lawyer; b. Atlanta, Sept. 21, 1937; s. James William and Mary Lou (Young) P.; m. Elizabeth Buxton Gregory, June 13, 1959; children: Elizabeth P. Carr, Mary Lane P. Lennon, James Brenton Preston. BA in English, U. N.C., 1958, JD with high honors, 1961. Bar: N.C. 1961. Assoc. to ptnr. Parker, Poe, Adams & Bernstein L.L.P. and predecessors, Charlotte, N.C., 1961—. Pres. Charlotte Area Fund, 1968, Cmty. Sch. of Arts, 1976-78; pres. Arts and Sci. Coun. Charlotte/Mecklenburg, Inc., 1986-87, chair The Nat. Conf. for Cmty. and Justice, Charlotte, 1996-99, Wildacres Leadership Initiative, 1994—; vice chair N.C. Dance Theatre, 1995-97. Mem. ABA (ho. dels. 1988-92, 95-97), N.C. State Bar (pres. 1987-88), Am. Law Inst., Nat. Conf. Bar Presidents (exec. coun. 1989-92), Phi Beta Kappa, Phi Eta Sigma. Democrat. Episcopalian. Avocations: travel, tennis, profl. and civic activities. Office: Parker Poe Adams Bernstein LLP 3000 Three Wachovia Ctr 401 S Tryon St Ste 3000 Charlotte NC 28202 E-mail: jimpreston@parkerpoe.com.

PRESTON, LETRICIA ELAYNE, financial planner; b. El Paso, Tex., Oct. 19, 1947; d. Leon A. and Doris (Jones) Curry; m. Elisha I. Preston, May 22, 1965 (div.); children: Rhonda E. Eastman, Stacy A. Milburn Student, El Paso C.C. Lic. real estate broker. Sec. S.I.C. Fin. Co., El Paso, 1966-67; sec., credit investigator, asst. cashier First City Nat. Bank, 1967-79; real estate agt. Allied Agts., 1979-80, Coldwell Hovious, El Paso, 1980-83; asst. v.p. First Fin. Savs., 1983-86; sec. Kelly Svcs., 1986-87; sales-securities br. mgr. First Investors Corp., 1987-93; br. mgr. Linsco Pvt. Ledger Corp., 1993—. Avocations: dancing, travel, reading, bowling, crossword puzzles. Office: Linsco Pvt Ledger Corp 1790 N Lee Trevino Dr Ste 303 El Paso TX 79936-4525

PRESTON, MARK I. retired investment company executive; b. May 16, 1938; s. Samuel P. and Fay (Zelig) P.; children: Meredith, Laurence. BS, Syracuse U., 1959. Gen. mgr. AD-Allure Industries Inc., N.Y.C., 1962-64; pres. Marlin Mfg. Corp., 1965-68; acct. exec. Walston, Inc., 1969-72; v.p. DuPont, Walston, Inc., N.Y.C. and Washington, 1973, Legg Mason Wood Walker, Inc., Balt., 1974-81, sr. v.p. mktg., 1981-85, sr. v.p., dir. of sales, 1986-90, sr. v.p., 1991—2001, also bd. dirs. Pres. Baltimore County Gen. Hosp. Found., 1983-84; v.p. Safety First Club Md., 1982-90; trustee Baltimore County Gen. Hosp., 1983-88, pres. parent bd., 1988-90; bd. dirs. blood svcs. bd. ARC Md., Balt. Opera Co., 1996-97. Mem. Internat. Assn. Fin. Planners (cert.), Sparrows Point Country Club, Bond Club (pres. 1984). Home: 186 Clinton Ave Falmouth MA 02540

PRESTON, MARTHA SUE, pharmaceutical company executive; b. Cheverly, Md., Oct. 15, 1952; d. George Millard and Martha Lee Preston. BA in Biology cum laude, Lycoming Coll., 1974; postgrad., U. Md., 1981-85, Am. U. Lab. asst biology dept Lycoming Coll., Williamsport, Pa., 1973-74; biologist arthritis and rheumatism br. NIH, Bethesda, Md., 1974-75, biologist nutrition and endocrinology lab., 1975-80; biologist divsn. blood and blood products FDA, 1980-88; mgr. regulatory affairs Baxter Healthcare Corp., Glendale, Calif., 1988-90; mgr. quality and regulatory Trancel/Neocrin, Santa Ana, 1990-92; dir. quality and regulatory Medarex Corp., Princeton, N.J., 1992-93; v.p. quality and regulatory Alpha Therapeutic Care, L.A., 1993-2000; sr. v.p. quality and regulatory Connetics Corp., Palo Alto, Calif., 2000—01; v.p. global regulatory affairs Chiron Corp., Emeryville, 2001—. Chmn. regulatory affairs Am. Blood Resources Assn., Anapolis, Md., 1993-95. Author: (book chpt.) AIDS Safety of Blood and Blood Products, 1988; contbr. articles to profl. jours. FDA award 1984, 88. Office: Chiron Corp 4560 Horton St M/S U-201 Oakland CA 94608-2916

PRESTON, RICHARD ARTHUR, historian; b. Middlesbrough, England, Oct. 4, 1910; s. Frank and Florence Rachel (Carter) P.; m. Marjorie Fishwick, Sept. 2, 1939; children— David Frank, Carol Jane, Peter Eric. BA, Leeds U., 1931, MA, 1932, Dip.Ed., 1933; PhD, Yale U., 1936; LL.D., Royal Mil. Coll. Can., 1977. Mem. faculty U. Toronto, 1936-38, U., Coll. South Wales, 1938-45, U. Toronto, 1945-48; mem. faculty Royal Mil. Coll. Can., Kingston, 1948-65, prof. history, to 1965, Duke U., Durham, N.C., 1965-80, 1st N.K. Boyd prof. history, 1980—, dir. Can. studies, 1973-79. Author: Gorges of Plymouth Fort, 1953, Men in Arms, 1956-91, Royal Fort Frontenac, 1958, Kingston Before the War of 1812, 1958, Canada in World Affairs, 1959-61, 1965, Canada and Imperial Defense, 1967, Canada's R.M.C, 1969, For Friends at Home, 1974, Defence of the Undefended Border, 1977, Perspectives in the History of Military Education and Professionalism, 1980, the Squat Pyramid: Canadian Studies in the U.S. 1980, To Serve Canada, 1991. Served with RAF, 1940-45. Commonwealth Fund fellow, 1933-36; Can. Coun. fellow, 1963-64; Social Sci. Rsch. Coun. fellow, 1963-64; Guggenheim fellow, 1972-73; recipient Achievement award City Kingston, 1959, Can. Confedn. medal, 1967, Queen's Jubilee medal, 1975, Donner medal, 1977, No. Telecom. Internat. Can. Studies award and Gold medal, 1983, Kingston Hist. Soc. Centennial award, 1994. Mem. Can. Hist. Assn (pres. 1961-62), Assn. Can. Studies U.S. (founding pres. 1971-72), Am. Mil. Inst. Home: Olsen # 245 2701 Pickett Rd Durham NC 27705-5648

PRESTON, RICHARD MCKIM, lawyer; b. Balt., June 2, 1947; s. Wilbur Day Jr. and May Virginia (Honemann) P.; m. Trisa Jean Thompson, Apr. 28, 1961. BA, Washington & Lee U., 1969, JD cum laude, 1976; MA cum laude, Fairleigh Dickinson U., 1973. Assoc. vomBaur, Coburn, Simmons & Turtle, Washington, 1976-79, Seyfarth, Shaw, Fairweather & Geraldson, Washington, 1979-82, ptnr., 1982—. Mng. ptnr. Constrn. Group, 1987—; bd. govs. Washington Bldg. Congress, 1997—. Contbr. articles to profl. publs., chpt. to book. Bd. advisors Jubilee Support Found., Washington, 1989—; mem. Washington & Lee Law Coun., Lexington, Va., 1986-93. Mem. River Bend Golf and Country Club, Sankaty Head Golf Club, Metro. Cub (D.C.). Office: Seyfarth Shaw Fairweather 815 Connecticut Ave NW Washington DC 20006-4004

PRESTON, ROBERT BRUCE, retired lawyer; b. Cleve., Feb. 24, 1926; s. Robert Bruce and Erma May (Hunter) P.; m. Agnes Ellen Stanley, Jan. 29, 1949; children— Robert B., Patricia Ellen Preston Kiefer, Judith Helen Preston Yanover. AB, Western Res. U., 1950, JD, 1952. Bar: U.S. Dist. Ct. (no. dist.) Ohio 1953, U.S. Ct. Appeals (6th cir.) 1959, U.S. Supreme Ct. 1964. Assoc. Arter & Hadden, Cleve., 1952-63, ptnr., 1964-93; ret., 1994. Dir. Service Stampings Inc., Willoughby, Ohio Vice pres. Citizens League Cleve., 1965; chmn. Charter Rev. Com., Cleveland Heights, Ohio, 1972; mem. Zoning Bd. Appeals, Cleveland Heights, 1974-76 Mem. Ohio Bar Assn., Greater Cleve. Bar Assn. Republican. Presbyterian. Avocations: tennis, fishing, travel. Home: 117 Manor Brook Dr Chagrin Falls OH 44022-4163 Office: Arter & Hadden 1100 Huntington Bldg Cleveland OH 44115

PRESTON, ROBERT KEVIN, software quality engineer; b. Danville, Ky., Dec. 13, 1959; s. Jopat and Dorthy Ann (Edwards) P.; m. Patricia Ann Adkins, May 24, 1986; children: Ryan Adkins, Ray Edward, Nichelle Alyson. BS, Eastern Ky. U., 1982; MS, U. Ala., 1990; quality and reliability engr., U.S. Army Intern Training Ctr., 1983. Software quality engr. U.S. Army Missile Command, Redstone Arsenal, Ala., 1983-85; lead software quality engr. Gen. Electric, Huntsville, 1985-90; sr. software analyst Hilton Systems Inc., 1990-94; sr. software systems analyst MTA, Inc., 1994-96; sr. software quality assurance engr. Lockheed-Martin Missiles & Space, 1996—. Part-time instr. Southern Inst. of Tech., Huntsville, 1984-85; assn. mem. grad. faculty U. Ala., Huntsville, 1990—. Sunday sch. tchr., Hillwood Bapt. Ch., Huntsville, 1987—, choir mem., 1986—, deacon, 1994—. Mem. Focus Users Group (sec. 1994-96). Avocation: woodworking. Home: 10001 Todd Mill Rd SE Huntsville AL 35803-1719 Office: Lockheed Martin PO Box 70017 Huntsville AL 35807-7001

PRESTON, SAMUEL HULSE, demographer; b. Morrisville, Pa., Dec. 2, 1943; s. Samuel H. and Dora (Berrell) P.; m. Winnifred de Witt, June 19, 1965; children: Samuel, Andrew, Benjamin, Leah. BA in Econs., Amherst Coll., 1965; PhD in Econs., Princeton U., 1968. Asst. prof. demography U. Calif., Berkeley, 1968-72; dir. Ctr. for Demography U. Wash., Seattle, 1972-77; chief, population structure sect. UN, N.Y.C., 1977-79; prof., dir. Population Studies Ctr. U. Pa., Phila., 1979-88, dean, Sch. Arts & Scis., Frederick J. Warren prof. demography, 1998—. Author: Patterns of Urban and Rural Population Growth, 1980, (with M. Haines) Fatal Years, 1991, (with M. Guillot and P. Heuveline) Demography, 2000. Fellow AAAS, Am. Acad. Arts and Scis, Am. Statis. Assn.; mem. NAS, Inst. Medicine, Am. Philos. Soc., Population Assn. Am. (pres. 1984, Irene B. Tauber award for Excellence in Demographic Research 1983), Internat. Union for Sci. Study of Population (council 1981-88). Methodist. Home: 234 Walnut Ave Wayne PA 19087-3445 Office: Univ Pa Sch Arts and Scis Dean's Office Philadelphia PA 19104

PRESTON, SEYMOUR STOTLER, III, manufacturing company executive; b. Media, Pa., Sept. 11, 1933; s. Seymour Stotler and Mary Alicia (Harper) P.; m. Jean Ellen Holman, Sept. 8, 1956; children: Courtney J., Katherine E., Alicia D., Shelley S. BA, Williams Coll., 1956; MBA, Harvard Coll., 1958. With Pennwalt Corp., Phila., 1961-89, exec. v.p. in charge of chems. and equipment ops., worldwide, 1975-77, pres., COO, 1977-89; pres., CEO Elf Atochem N.Am., Inc. (formerly Atochem N.Am.), Phila., 1990-93. Chmn. AAC Engineered Sys. Inc., 1994—; bd. dirs. Scott Specialty Gases, Inc., Albermarle Corp., Tufco Techs., Inc. Trustee Shipley Sch., Bryn Mawr, Pa., 1976-88, Phila. Orch. Assn., 1992-95, Wistar, 1997—; trustee Acad. Natural Scis., 1980—, chmn., 1995-2000, pres., CEO, 2000—; bd. mgrs. Franklin Inst., Phila., 1980-92; bd. dirs. Lawrenceville (N.J.) Sch., 1982-99, Wistar Inst., 1997—, Barra Found., 1998—. 1st lt. USAF, 1958-61. Mem. Soc. for Chem. Industry, Greater Phila. C. of C. (bd. dirs. 1979-94), Radnor Hunt Club (Malvern, Pa.).

PRESTON, THOMAS LYTER, crisis management, violence consultant; b. Carrollton, Ky., Sept. 25, 1934; s. Thomas Jefferson and Mary Lyter (Robertson) P.; m. Carolyn Louise Points, June 1, 1957; 1 son, Matthew Thomas. AB in Journalism, U. Ky., 1956; postgrad., U. Wash., 1958. Editor The News-Democrat, Carrollton, 1956-57; pub., pres. The Cynthiana (Ky.) Pub. Co., 1959-68; pres. Preston Pub. Rels., Lexington, Ky., 1968-75; pres., chief exec. officer The Preston Group, Inc., 1975-97; chmn. of bd., 1991-97; princ. Preston Global, Versailles, KY, 1997—. Spl. asst. to the Gov.,

Commonwealth of Ky.; commr. Ky. Dept. Pub. Info., Frankfort, 1971-74; spl. asst. to U.S. Senate, Washington, 1975; adj. prof. U. Ky., Lexington, 1976-81, 99, 2001, Ea. Ky. U., Richmond, 1979, 99, 2001; lectr. Fla. State U., Tallahassee, 1989; bd. visitors Dept. Pub. Rels. Fla. State U., 1990—, Sch. Pub. Rels. Ea. Ky. U., 1990—; developer corp. strategies in counterterrorism and workplace violence; bd. dirs. Am. Founders Bank, 200, Frankfort, Ky., founding dir.; mem. nat. courts and cmty. com. Nat. Ctr. State Courts; leader seminars in crisis control, reputational mgmt., corporate terrorism and workplace violence response. Contbr. articles to profl. publs. Mem. Ky. Coun. on Higher Edn., 1963-67; mem. Ky. Emergency Response Commn., 2001—; mem. adv. coun. Eastern Ky. U. Coll. Bus. and Tech., 2000—. 1st lt. U.S. Army, 1956-59, 61. Recipient First Lifetime Achievement award for pub. rels./crisis mgmt. U. Ky., 2000. Mem. Coll. Fellows Pub. Rels. Soc. Am. (accredited, chmn. East ctrl. dist., 1989-90, pres. tho oughbred chpt. 1987-88), Am. Negotiation Inst. (adv. bd. 1999-2002), Am. Soc. Indsl. Security Profls., Counselors Acad., Fla. Pub. Rels. Assn. (chmn. 1998), Internat. Assn. of Counterterrorism and Security Profls., The Lafayette Club (bd. dirs. 1988-94). Avocations: golf, collecting antique golf equipment and memorabilia. Office: 100 United Dr Ste 3B Versailles KY 40383-1497 E-mail: tpglobal@qx.net.

PRESTON, THOMAS RONALD, English language educator, researcher; b. Oct. 31, 1936; s. Thomas and Marie Katherine (Nettlow) P.; m. Mary Ruth Atkinson, June 4, 1960; children: Lorel, Mary, Thomas BA, U. Detroit, 1958; MA, Rice U., 1960, PhD, 1962. Asst. prof. English Duquesne U., Pitts., 1962-63; Asst. prof. English U. Fla., Gainseville, 1963-67; assoc. prof., chmn. dept. Loyola U., New Orleans, 1967-69; prof., chmn. dept. U. Tenn., Chattanooga, 1969-73, U. Wyo., Laramie, 1973-82; prof., dean arts and scis. U. North Tex., Denton, 1982-92, prof. English, 1992—. Chmn. Wyo. Council for Humanities, Laramie, 1976-77 Author: Not in Timon's Manner, 1975; editor U. Ga. edit. of Smollett's Humphry Clinker, 1990; contbr. articles on 18th century lit. to profl. jours. Recipient John W. Gardner award Rice U., 1962; George Duke Humphrey award U. Wyo., 1982; NEH grantee, 1979; Am. Council of Learned Socs. grantee, 1980 Mem. Am. Soc. for 18th Century Studies, South Ctrl. Soc. for 18th Century Studies (pres. 1986-87). Democrat. Anglican. Office: U North Tex Dept English Box 311307 Denton TX 76203 E-mail: trpatlake@cs.com.

PRESTON, WILLIAM LEON, family practice; b. Salina, Kans., Nov. 19, 1947; s. Billie Wirth and Mary May Preston; m. Rebecca Cecilia Preston, June 19, 1971; children: William Andrew, Ellen Marie. BA in Physics, Kans. Wesleyan U., 1968; MD, U. Colo., 1972. Diplomate Am. Bd. Family Physicians. Resident West Suburban Family Practice, Oak Park, Ill., 1972-75; assoc. dir. Family Practice Ctr., LaGrange, 1975-79; med. dir. Wholistic Health Ctr., 1979-80; sr. ptnr. Preston Family Practice, Western Springs, Ill., 1980—. Med. dir. St. Thomas Hospice, Hinsdale, Ill., 1980—. Lay leader First United Meth. Ch., Western Springs, 1992-1999. Fellow Am. Acad. of Family Physicians; mem. Nat. Hospice Orgn., Am. Coll. of Sports Medicine. Republican. Methodist. Avocations: photography, music, martial arts. Office: Preston Family Practice 4479 Central Ave Western Springs IL 60558-1714 E-mail: billcmq@aol.com.

PRESTOPNIK, RICHARD JOHN, electronics and computer educator; b. Little Falls, N.Y., Nov. 23, 1951; s. John William and Frances (Grabowski) P.; m. Jan Sponenberg, June 16, 1973; children: Nathan Richard, Emily Kate, Adam Christopher. AAS in Elec. Tech., Mohawk Valley C.C., 1971; B Engring. Tech. in Elec. Engring., Rochester Inst. Tech., 1974; MSEE in Computer Engring., Syracuse U., 1982. From jr. engr. to sr. assoc. engr. IBM, Endicott, NY, 1974-80; from asst. to assoc. prof. elec. tech. dept. Fulton-Montgomery C.C., Johnstown, 1980-89, prof., 1989-95, acting dean career edn., 1995-96, dean bus. and tech., 1996-99, prof., 2001—; dir. NASA-Fulton-Montgomery C.C. Spatial Info. Tech. Ctr., 2000—01; advisor Spatial Info. Tech. Ctr., 2001—. Coll. rep. on bd. dirs. Fulton-Montgomery, Schoharie Pvt. Industry Coun.; participant long distance learning project Gloversville High Sch.; mem. tech. prep. steering com. Fulton County Econ. Devel. Corp.; v.p. CPT Assocs., Inc., computer and electronic cons., 1983-85; book reviewer Prentice-Hall, Inc. Revision author: The Encyclopedia of Integrated Circuits, 2d edit., 1987; author: The Microprocessor IC Reference Manual, 1989, Digital Electronics: Concepts and Applications for Digital Design, 1990, also lab. manual, 1990; also articles. Faculty grantee SUNY Rsch. Found., 1986, faculty excellence grantee Fulton-Montgomery C.C., 1992, numerous others; NASA/ASEE faculty fellow in aeronautics and space rsch., 1995, 96; recipient V.P. Gore's Nat. Performance Rev. Hammer award, 1997. Mem. IEEE, Am. Soc. Engring. Edn. (Outstanding Educator award St. Lawrence sect. 1990), N.Y. State Engring. Tech. Assn. Avocations: golf, hiking, travel. Office: Fulton-Montgomery CC 2805 State Highway 67 Johnstown NY 12095-3749 E-mail: rprestop@fmcc.suny.edu.

PRESTOWITZ, CLYDE VINCENT, economist, researcher; b. Wilmington, Del., Sept. 6, 1941; s. Clyde Vincent and Lillian (Lang) Prestowitz; m. Carol Ann Jay, Mar. 29, 1964; children: Anne, Clyde, Brian. BA, Swarthmore Coll., 1963; MA, U. Hawaii, 1965; MBA, U. Pa., 1980. Mgr. market devel. Scott Paper Co., Phila., 1968—72, dir. planning Europe Brussels, 1972—76; v.p. Japan Egon Zehnder Internat., Tokyo, 1976—78; dir. mktg. Am. Can Co., Greenwich, Conn., 1978—79; pres. Prestowitz Assocs., New Canaan, 1979—81; dep. asst. sec. internat. econ. policy U.S. Dept. Commerce, Washington, 1981—82, acting asst. sec. internat. econ. policy, 1982—83, counselor to sec., 1983—86; Wilson fellow, 1986—87; sr. assoc. Carnegie Endowment for Internat. Peace, Washington, 1987—89; pres. Econ. Strategy Inst., 1989—. Vice-chmn. Pacific Basin Econ. Coun., 1989—; vice chmn., presdl. com. U.S./Pacific Trade and Investment Policy. Republican. Presbyterian. Home: 10420 Masters Ter Potomac MD 20854-3862 Office: Econ Strategy Inst 1401 H St NW Ste 560 Washington DC 20005-2110

PRESTRIDGE, PAMELA ADAIR, lawyer; b. Delhi, La., Dec. 25, 1945; d. Gerald Wallace Prestridge and Louis Baugh and Peggy Adair (Arender) Martin. BA, La. Poly. U., 1967; M in Edn., La. State u., 1968, JD, 1973. Bar: U.S. Dist. Ct. (mid. dist.) La. 1975, U.S. Dist. Ct. (so. dist.) Tex. 1982, U.S. Ct. Appeals (5th cir.) 1982, U.S. Supreme Ct. 1990. Law clk. to presiding justice La. State Dist. Ct., Baton Rouge, 1973-75; ptnr. Breazeale, Sachse & Wilson, 1975-82, Hirsch & Westheimer P.C., Houston, 1982-92; pvt. practive, 1992—. Counselor Big Bros./Big Sisters, Baton Rouge, 1968-70; legal cons., bd. dirs. Lupus Found. Am., Houston, 1984-93; bd. dirs. Quota Club, Baton Rouge, 1979-82, Speech and Hearing Found., Baton Rouge, 1981-82, The Actors Workshop, Houston, 1988-93, Tex. Satsang Soc., 2000—; active Tex. Accts. and Attys. for the Arts. Recipient Pres.'s award Lupus Found. Am., 1991, cert. of appreciation Assn. Atty. Mediators, 1992, Outstanding Profl. Woman of Houston award Fedn. Profl. Women, 1984. Mem. ABA, La. Bar Assn., Tex. Bar Assn., Houston Bar Assn., Houston Bar Found., Assn. Atty. Mediators (bd. dirs. 1994-96, Citation for Outstanding Mems. 1993), Profl. Atty.-Mediators Coop. (v.p. 1994, bd. dirs. 1994-96, pres. 1995), Phi Alpha Delta. Eckankar. Avocations: acting, ultralite flying. Home: 1701 Hermann Dr Unit 407 Houston TX 77004-7345 Office: 3300 Phoenix Tower PO Box 130987 Houston TX 77219-0987

PRESTWOOD, ALVIN TENNYSON, lawyer; b. Roeton, Ala., June 18, 1929; s. Garret Felix and Jimmie (Payne) P.; m. Sue Burleson Lee, Nov. 27, 1974; children: Ann Celeste Prestwood Peeples, Alison Bennett, Cynthia Joyce Lee Koplos, William Alvin Lee, Garret Courtney. BS, U. Ala., 1951, LLB, 1956, JD, 1970. Bar: Ala. 1956, U.S. Ct. Appeals (6th and 11th cirs.) 1981, U.S. Supreme Ct. 1972. Law clk. Supreme Ct. Ala., 1956-57; asst. atty. gen. Ala., 1957-59; commr. Ala. Dept. Pensions and Security, 1959-63; pvt. practice Montgomery, Ala., 1963-65, 77-82; ptnr. Volz, Capouano, Wampold, Prestwood & Sansone, 1965-77, Prestwood & Rosser, 1982-85, Capouano, Wampold, Prestwood & Sansone, 1986-94, Volz, Prestwood & Hanan, Montgomery, 1995—. Chmn. Gov.'s Com. on White House Conf. on Aging, 1961; mem. adv. com. Dept. Health, Edn. and Welfare, 1962; sec. Nat. Coun. State Pub. Welfare Adminstrs., 1962 Mem. editl. bd. Ala. Law Rev., 1955-56; contbr. articles to profl. jours. Pres. Morningview Sch. P.T.A., 1970; chmn. Am. Nursing Home Assn. Legal Com., 1972; bd. dirs. Montgomery Bapt. Hosp., 1958-65; chmn. bd. mgmt. East Montgomery YMCA, 1969; chmn. deacons Cloverdale Bapt. Ch., 1994-95, 98. 1st lt., inf. AUS, 1951-53. Decorated Combat Inf. Badge.; recipient Sigma Delta Kappa Scholastic Achievement award U. Ala. Sch. Law, 1956, Law Day Moot Ct. award U. Ala. Sch. Law, 1956 Mem. ABA (chmn. com. on jud. performance and conduct 1996, chmn. Judiciary's Image Evaluation Task Force 1996-2000), Ala. Bar Assn. (chmn. adminstrv. law sect. 1972, 78, 83, 97), Montgomery County Bar Assn. (chmn. exec. com. 1971), Farrah Order Jurisprudence, Eleventh Cir. Jud. Conf., Am. Judicature Soc., Kappa Sigma. Home: 1431 Magnolia Curv Montgomery AL 36106-2043 Office: Volz Prestwood & Hanan 350 Adams Ave Montgomery AL 36104-4204 E-mail: attys@bellsouth.net.

PRESUTTI, ROBERT MICHAEL, secondary education educator; b. Niagara Falls, N.Y., Mar. 18, 1939; s. Michael F. and Anna M. P.; m. Rosamond C. Siegwarth, Aug. 3, 1963 (div. 1973); m. Patricia E. Kowalski, Dec. 20, 1975; children: Matthew T., Rebecca C. Goris. BS, Niagara U:., 1961; MA, SUNY, Buffalo, 1974. Tchr. Niagara Falls Schs., 1961-64, Lewiston-Porter Ctrl., Youngstown, N.Y., 1964-94. Commrs. panel tenure dismissal State Edn. Dept., Albany, N.Y., 1974-90; grader Ednl. Testing Svc., Princeton, N.J., 1984-94; cons. Coll. Bd. Advanced Placement, Princeton, 1988-94. Mem. bd. edn. Lewiston-Porter Ctrl. Sch., Youngstown, 1994-2000, pres., 1998-2000. Mem. Am. Fedn. Tchrs., N.Y. State United Tchrs., Lewiston-Porter United Tchrs. (pres. 1980-84), Alpha Kappa Psi (pres. 1960-61). Avocations: skiing, reading, cooking, wine. Home and Office: 718 Tuscarora St Lewiston NY 14092

PRESZLER, SHARON MARIE, psychiatric home health nurse; b. L.A. d. Rudolph Edward Wirth and Bertha Marie (Thornton) Paddock; m. Alan Preszler, Aug. 31, 1966; children: Brent, Alison. BS in Nursing, Loma Linda (Calif.) U., 1963, MS in Marriage and Family Counseling, 1978. RN, Calif., Idaho; cert. pub. health nurse. Team leader med. fl. Loma Linda U. Hosp., 1963-64; office nurse Dr. Lowell Johnson, Redlands, Calif., 1964-65, Dr. H. Glenn Stevens, Loma Linda, 1965-72; team leader women's oncology Loma Linda U. Hosp., 1974-75; pub. health nurse Riverside County Pub. Health, Hemet, Calif., 1975-78; nurse, staff psychologist Dept. Health and Welfare, Idaho Falls, Idaho, 1989-91, Boise, 1991-92; psychiat. nurse Cmty. Home Health, 1992-94, Mercy Home Health & Hospice, Nampa, Idaho, 1995-99; hospice nurse, home health nurse Mercy Med. Ctr., 1995-99, personal care supr. nurse for medicaid, 1996—; case mgr. Assisted Living of Idaho, 2001, Ada Can, 2001—. Instr. YWCA, Bartlesville, Okla., 1984-88; tchr. Bartlesville Pub. Sch., 1984-88, Heritage Retirement, Boise, 1994. Contbr. to Focus, 1986. Mem. Am. Assn. Marriage and Family Therapy, Sigma Theta Tau. Avocations: reading, tennis.

PRETLOW, THOMAS GARRETT, physician, pathology educator, researcher; b. Warrenton, Va., Dec. 11, 1939; s. William Ribble and May (Tiffany) P.; m. Theresa Pace, June 29, 1963; children: James Michael, Joseph Peter, David Mark. AB, Oberlin Coll., 1960; MD, U. Rochester, 1965. Intern U. Hosps., Madison, Wis., 1965-66; fellow McArdle Lab., 1966-67; rsch. assoc. Nat. Cancer Inst., Bethesda, Md., 1967-69; asst. prof. pathology Rutgers Med. Sch., Piscataway, N.J., 1969-70; assoc. prof. pathology U. Ala., Birmingham, 1971-73, prof. pathology, 1974-83, prof. biochemistry, 1982-83; vis. prof. pathology Harvard Med. Sch., Boston, 1983-84; prof. pathology Case Western Res. U., Cleve., 1983—, prof. oncology, 1987—, prof. environ. health scis., 1991—, prof. urology, 1994—. Cons. NIH, Bethesda, 1976-2000, Am. Inst. Cancer Rsch., 1995-98; chmn. pathobiolog y 2 prostate cancer grant reviewer U.S. Army, 1998, 99. Mem. editl. bd. Cell Biophysics, Cambridge, Mass., 1978-82; editor: Cell Separation: Methods and Selected Applications, 5 vols., 1982, 83, 84, 87, Biochemical and Molecular Aspects of Selected Cancers, 2 vols., 1991, 94. Mem. exec. bd. Birmingham coun. Boy Scouts Am., 1979-83, Greater Cleve. coun. Boy Scouts Am., 1984-90. Served to lt. comdr. USPHS, 1967-69. Recipient Rsch. Career Devel. award Nat. Cancer Inst., 1973-78; grantee for cancer rsch. Mem. Am. Assn. Pathologists, Am. Assn. Immunologists, Internat. Acad. Pathology, Am. Soc. Clin. Oncology, Am. Assn. Cancer Rsch., Serra Club (pres. Birmingham chpt. 1982-83). Avocations: camping, fishing, Boy Scouts, classical music, biking. Home: 3061 Chadbourne Rd Cleveland OH 44120-2446 Office: Inst of Pathology Case Western Reserve U Cleveland OH 44106 E-mail: tgp3@po.cwru.edu.

PRETTYMAN, ALFRED EMERSON, English language and social and behavioral sciences educator, publishing executive; b. Balt., Feb. 15, 1935; s. Edward Augusta and Helen P.; m. Julia Poussaint (div.); children: Meryl, Evan; m. Kathleen Conwell, Dec. 25, 1987 (dec.); m. Susan Stedman, Aug. 17, 1997. BS, Hamilton Coll., 1956; postgrad., Cornell U., 1959, Antioch U. Coll. exec. editor Harper & Row Pub., N.Y.C., 1966-70, sr. editor, trade, 1969-71; founder, pres. Emerson Hall Pub., 1973-80; asst. prof. Rutgers U., New Brunswick, N.J., 1989-98, Rockland C.C., SUNY, Suffern, NY, 1988—98; co-founder, pres. Pretty-Steady Prodns., N.Y.C., 1992—; asst. prof. Ramapo Coll. N.J., 1999—. Chair bd. The Nyack (N.Y.) Ctr., 1996—98, exec. dir., 1999—2001; cons. N.E. Humanities, Washington, 1970—73, N.E. Arts, Washington, 1970—72; elector Nat. Medal Lit., N.Y.C., 1980; co-chair lit. N.Y. State Coun. Arts, 1970; judge Nat. Book Awards, N.Y.C., 1980. Editor: U.S.: National Civics in a Mosaic Democracy 1996, 98, U.S.: The Intercultural Nation, 1999; prodr. Ogun's Fire: The Sculpture of Melvin Edwards, 1993; contbr. articles to profl. jours. Recipient Excellence In Comm. award Creative and Editl. Black Achievement, 1983. Mem.: Assn. Study Africana Philosophy (co-founder 1977—). Avocations: tennis, cooking, gardening, fly fishing, singing. Home and Office: 215 W 98th St Apt 12-b New York NY 10025-5635

PRETTYMAN, ELIJAH BARRETT, JR. lawyer; b. Washington, June 1, 1925; s. Elijah Barrett and Lucy Courtney (Hill) P.; children by previous marriage: Elijah Barrett III, Jill Savage Lukoschek. BA, Yale U., 1949; LLB, U. Va., 1953. Bar: D.C. 1954, U.S. Supreme Ct. 1957. Pvt. practice, Washington, 1955—; law clk. to Hon. Justices Jackson, Frankfurter and Harlan U.S. Supreme Ct., 1953-55; assoc. Hogan & Hartson, Washington, 1955—63, ptnr., 1964—2001, of counsel, 2002—; inspector gen. Dist. of Colo., 1998—99. Spl. asst. to Atty. Gen. U.S., 1963, White House, 1963-64; also Pres.'s rep. to Interagy. Com. on Transport Mergers; spl. cons. subcom. to investigate problems connected with refugees and escapees U.S. Senate Judiciary Com., Vietnam, 1967-68; outside cons. to subcom. on oversight and investigations, Ho. of Reps. com. on internal and fgn. commerce, 1978; spl. cons. for ABSCAM investigation to Com. on Standards of Ofcl. Conduct, U.S. Ho. of Reps., 1980-81; trustee emeritus, past exec com. Am. U., Washington; past trustee, mem. exec. com. Washington Journalism Ctr.; past adv. com. Media Law Reporter. Author: Death and the Supreme Court, 1961 (Edgar Allan Poe award); Editor: (with William E. Jackson) The Supreme Court in the American System of Government (Justice Robert H. Jackson), 1955; contbr. articles to profl. jours. Past corp. mem. Salvation Army; past mem. adv. com. Procedures of Jud. Coun., D.C.; past mem. adv. bd. Inst. Comm. Law Studies, Cath. U.; bd. govs. St. Albans Sch., 1957-63, 65-72, chmn., 1965-67; past mem. nat. adv. com. Nat. Inst. for Citizen Edn. in Law; bd. dirs., past pres. PEN/Faulkner Found.; v.p., chmn. publ. com., exec. com. Supreme Ct. Hist. Soc.; past internat. adv. group Toshiba Corp.; past commr. Supreme Ct. Jud. Fellows Commn. With AUS, 1943-45. Recipient Pub. Achievement award Common Cause, 1999, Justice Potter Stewart award Coun. for Ct. Excellence, 2000, disting. pub. svc. award D.C. 1999. Fellow: ABA; mem.: D.C. Cir. Hist. Soc. (pres. 2000—), Am. Acad. Appellate Lawyers (past pres.), Am. Judicature Soc. (vice chair exec. com.), Met. Washington Bd. Trade, DC Bar Assn. (bd. govs., Lawyer of Yr. award 1998), DC Bar (1st pres. 1972—73, bd. govs. 1973—74, jud. evaluation com.), DC Bar Found. (pres. 1983—84), Jud. Conf. DC Cir., Am. Coll. Trial Lawyers, Chevy Chase Club, Met. Club, Alfalfa Club, Barristers Club, Lawyers Club (past pres.). Methodist (past dir. ch.). Home: 2737 Devonshire Pl NW #424 Washington DC 20008-5148 Office: Columbia Sq 555 13th St NW Washington DC 20004-1109

PRETTYMAN-BAKER, SHEILA, pediatrics, neonatal nurse; b. Dayton, Ohio, May 22, 1957; d. Gene Clifton and Betty Jean (Rasnick) Prettyman; m. Stephen Ray Baker, Feb. 4, 1989; 1 child, Mollie Lynn. AS, Kettering Coll. Med. Arts, 1978, AD in Emergency Med. Tech., 1985. Cert. emergency med. technician-paramedic. Nursing supr. Bethany Luth. Village, Centerville, Ohio; neonatal intensive care nurse Franciscan Hosp., Dayton; charge nurse Mercy Hosp., Fairfield, Ohio; pediat. office nurse Oakwood; IV nurse educator St. Elizabeth Hosp., Dayton; mem. IV team Children's Med. Ctr., 2000—, staff nurse IV team; staff nurse neonatal intensive care Kettering (Ohio) Med. Ctr.

PREUHS, ROBERT RICHARD, social sciences educator; b. Sheboygan, Wis., Mar. 18, 1970; s. Richard Clarence Preuhs and Ann Christine Waters; m. Jennifer Lynn Warnken, June 22, 1996. BA, Hamline U., 1992; MPA, U. N.Mex., 1996; MA, U. Colo., 1999, PhD, 2001. Com. clk. Minn. State Senate, St. Paul, 1993; tchg. asst. U. Colo., Boulder, 1996—2001; lectr. U. Denver, 2001—, U. Colo., 2002—. Mem. mentor bd. Grads. Polit. Sci., Boulder, 1997—2001. Contbr. articles to profl. jours. Campus coord. Brown for Pres., St. Paul, 1992; chair Minn. Young Dem. Farmer Labor Party, 1993. Fellow Robert Stover, U. Colo., 1996—97; grantee, 2001. Mem.: Midwest Polit. Sci. Assn., Am. Polit. Sci. Assn., Sierra Club. Avocations: hiking, cooking, camping, running.

PREUS, DAVID WALTER, bishop, minister; b. Madison, Wis., May 28, 1922; s. Ove Jacob Hjort and Magdalene (Forde) P.; m. Ann Madsen, June 26, 1951; children: Martha, David, Stephen, Louise, Laura. BA, Luther Coll., Decorah, Iowa, 1943, DD (hon.), 1969; postgrad., U. Minn., 1946-47; BTh, Luther Sem., St. Paul, 1950; postgrad., Union Sem., 1951, Edinburgh U., 1951-52; LLD (hon.), Wagner Coll., 1973, Gettysburg Coll., 1976; DD (hon.), Pacific Luth. Coll., 1974, St. Olaf Coll., 1974, Dana Coll., 1979, Tex. Luth. Coll., 1994; LHD (hon.), Macalester Coll., 1976. Ordained to ministry Luth. Ch., 1950; asst. pastor First Luth. Ch., Brookings, S.D., 1950-51; pastor Trinity Luth. Ch., Vermillion, 1952-57; campus pastor U. Minn., Mpls., 1957-58; pastor Univ. Luth. Ch. of Hope, 1958-73; v.p. Am. Luth. Ch., 1968-73, pres., presiding bishop, 1973-87; exec. dir. Global Mission Inst. Luther Northwestern Theol. Sem., St. Paul. Disting. vis. prof. Luther-Northwestern Sem., St. Paul, 1988-94; Luccock vis. pastor Yale Div. Sch., 1969; chmn. bd. youth activity Am. Luth. Ch., 1960-68; mem. exec. com. Luth. Council U.S.A.; v.p. Luth. World Fedn., 1977-90; mem. cen. com. World Council Chs., 1973-75, 80-90; Luth. del. White House Conf. on Equal Opportunity Chmn. Greater Mpls. Fair Housing Com., Mpls. Council Chs., 1960-64; Mem. Mpls. Planning Commn., 1965-67; mem. Mpls. Sch. Bd., 1965-74, chmn., 1967-69; mem. Mpls. Bd. Estimate and Taxation, 1968-73, Mpls. Urban Coalition; sr. public adv. U.S. del. Madrid Conf. of Conf. on Security and Cooperation in Europe, 1980-81; bd. dirs. Mpls. Inst. Art, Walker Art Center, Hennepin County United Fund, Ams. for Childrens Relief, Luth. Student Found., Research Council of Gt. City Schs., Urban League, NAACP; bd. regents Augsburg Coll., Mpls. Served with Signal Corps AUS, 1943-46, PTO. Decorated comdr.'s cross Royal Norwegian Order St. Olav, Order of St. George 1st deg. Orthodox Ch. of Georgia (USSR), 1989; recipient Regents medal Augustana Coll., Sioux Falls, S.D., 1973, Torch of Liberty award Anti-Defamation League, 1973, St. Thomas Aquinas award St. Thomas U., Pax Christi award St. John's Univ/. Collegeville, Minn., 1997.

PREUSS, AXEL KURT, biologist, educator; b. Munich, May 7, 1959; s. Kurt G. and Margot P.; m. Grace M. Ogawa, Oct. 7, 1998. MSc, Max Planck Inst., Germany, 1987, PhD, 1990. Postdoctoral Hoffmann LaRoche, N.J., 1990-92, Cornell U., N.Y.C., 1992-93; instr. NYU, 1993-94; scientist Kyoto U., Japan, 1994-96; sr. scientist EPFL, Switzerland, 1996—; instr. Mt. Sinai Med., 2000. Cons. World Inst., Osaka, Japan, 1994—. Contbr. articles to profl. jours. including Cytotechnology. Grantee Nestle, 2000; fellowship Japan Tobacco, 1994, Nat. Stroke Assn., 1993. Mem. AAAS, Assn. Internat. Bus. Achievements include patent in biochip, cell culture device, high through put screening. Avocation: investing. Home: 106 Central Park S 6C New York NY 10019 Office: Mt Sinai Physiology Biophys dept Rm 10-02 1425 Madison Ave New York NY 10029

PREUSS, ROGER E(MIL), artist; b. Waterville, Minn., Jan. 29, 1922; s. Emil W. and Edna (Rosenau) P.; m. MarDee Ann Germundson, Dec. 31, 1954 (dec. Mar. 1981). Student, Mankato Comml. Coll., Mpls. Sch. Art. Emeritus instr. seminar Mpls. Coll. Art and Design; emeritus Mpls. Inst. Arts Speakers Bur.; former judge ann. Goodyear Nat. Conservation Awards Program; founder U.S. Fed. Roger Preuss Waterfowl Prodn. Area, LeSueur County, Minn., 1997; former advisor Wildlife Forever Nat. Fish-Art Contest. Painter of nature art; one-man shows include: St. Paul Fine Art Galleries, 1959, Albert Lea Art Center, 1963, Hist. Soc. Mont., Helena, 1964, Brotherhood Fine Arts Ctr., 1965, Bicentennial exhbn., Le Sueur County Hist. Soc. Mus., Elysian, Minn., 1976, Merrill's Gallery of Fine Art, Taos, N.Mex., 1980; exhbns. include: Mpls. Inst. Art Msa exhibit, 1946, Midwest Wildlife Conf. Exhbn., Kerr's Beverly Hills, Calif., 1947, Laguna Art Mus., Calif., 1947, Joslyn Meml. Mus., Omaha, 1948, Hollywood Fine Arts Center, 1948, Minn. Centennial, 1949, Federated Chaparral Authors, 1951, Nat. Wildlife Art, 1951, 52, N.Am. Wildlife Art, dir. exposition, 1952, Ducks Unltd. Waterfowl exhibit, 1953, 54, St. Paul Winter Carnival, 1954, St. Paul Gallery Art Mart, 1954, Harris Fine Arts Center, Provo, Utah, 1969, Galerie Internationale, N.Y.C., 1972, Holy Land Conservation Fund, N.Y.C., 1976, Faribault Art Ctr., 1981, Wildlife Artists of the World Exhbn., Bend, Oreg., 1984, U. Art Mus., U. Minn., Mpls., 1990, Rochester Art Ctr., 1991, Minn. Hist. Soc.-Hill House, 1992, Bemidji Art Ctr., 1992, Jack London Ctr., Dawson City, Yukon Territory, Can., 1992, Weyerhaeuser Meml. Mus., Little Falls, Minn., 1995, Minn. Valley Nat. Wildlife Refuge Ctr., Bloomington, 1995, Sagebrush Artists Exhbn., Klamath Falls, Oreg., 1995; represented in permanent collections: Demarest Meml. Mus., Hackensack, N.J., Smithsonian Instn., N.Y. Jour. Commerce, Mont. Hist. Soc., Inland Bird Banding Assn., Minn. Capitol Bldg., Mont. State U., Wildlife Am. Collection, LeSueur Hist. Soc., Voyageurs Nat. Park Interpretive Ctr., Krause-Hartig VFW Post, Mpls., Nat. Wildlife Fedn. Collection, Minn. Ceremonial House, U.S. Wildlife Svc. Fed. Bldg., Fort Snelling, Minn., Crater Lake Nat. Park Visitors Ctr., VA Hosp., Mpls., Luxton Collection, Banff, Alta., Can., Internat. Inst. Arts, Geneva, Mont. Capitol Bldg., People of Century-Goldblatt Collection, Lyons, Ill., Harlem Savings Collection, N.Y.C., Weisman Art Mus., Mpls., Minn. Vets. Home, Mpls., Blauvelt Art Mus., Oradell, N.J., Roger Preuss Art Collection, Augustana Ctr. for Western Studies, Sioux Falls, S.D., Minn. Mus. Am. Art, St. Paul, U. Minn. Art Mus., C.M. Russell Mus., Great Falls, Mont., Le Sueur County Courthouse, Le Center, Minn., others, numerous galleries and pvt. collections; designer: Fed. Duck Stamp, U.S. Dept. Interior, 1949, Commemorative Centennial Pheasant Stamp, 1981, Gold Waterfowl medallion Franklin Mint, 1983, Gold Stamp medallion Wildlife Mint, 1983, 40th Anniversary Commemorative Fed. Duck Stamp etching, 1989; panelist: Sportsman's Roundtable, Sta. WTCN-TV, Mpls. (emeritus), from 1953; author: Is Wildlife Art Recognized Fine Art?, 1986; contbr.: Christmas Echos, 1955, Wing Shooting, Trap & Skeet, 1955, Along the Trout Stream, 1979; contbr. Art Impressions mag., Can., Wildlife Art, U.S.; also illustrations and articles in Nat. Wildlife and over 300 essays on North American animals, others.; assoc. editor emeritus: Out-of-Doors mag.; compiler and artist: Outdoor Horizons, 1957, Twilight over the Wilderness, 1972, 60 limited edition prints Wildlife of America, from 1970; contbr. paintings and text Minnesota Today; creator paintings and text Preuss Wildlife Calendar; inventor: paintings and text Wildlife Am. Calendar; featured artist Art West, 1980-84, Wildlife Art; featured in films Your BFA- Care and Maintenance, Black Ducks Along the Border. Del. Nat. Wildlife Conf.; bd. dirs. emeritus Voyageurs Nat. Park Assn., Deep-Portage Conservation Found.; bd. dirs. Wetlands for Wildlife U.S.A.; active Wildlife Am.; co-organizer, v.p., bd. dirs. Minn. Conservation Fedn., 1952-54; mem. U.S. Hospitalized Vets. Venison Program, 1957—; trustee Liberty Bell Edn. Found.; Waseca Arts Coun.; founder, dir. Roger Preuss Conservation Preserve for Study of Nature, 1990—; adv. Wildlife Forever. With USNR, World War II. Recipient Stamp Design award U.S. Fish and Wildlife Svc., 1994, Minn. Outdoor award, 1956, Patron of Conservation award, 1956, award for contbns. conservation Minn. Statehood Centennial Commn., 1958, 1st award Am. Indsl. Devel. Coun., citation of merit VFW, award of merit Mil. Order Cootie, 1963, merit award Minn. Waterfowl Assn., 1976, silver medal Nat. SAR, 1978, Svcs. to Arts and Environ. award Faribault Art Ctr., 1981, Ptnrs. for Wildlife award U.S. Fish and Wildlife Svc., 1994; named Wildlife Conservationist of the Yr., Sears Found.-Nat. Wildlife Fedn. program, 1966, Am. Bicentennial Wildlife Artist, Am. Heritage Assn., 1976; hon. mem. Ont. Chippewa Nation of Can., 1957; named Knight of Mark Twain for contbns. to Am. art Mark Twain Soc., 1978; named to Water, Woods and Wildlife Hall of Fame, named Dean of Wildlife Art, 1981, Hon. Ky. Col.; recipient hon. degree U.S. Vets. Venison program, 1980, Western Am. award significant contbns. to preservation arts and history No. Prairie Plains, Augustana Coll. Ctr. for Western Studies, Sioux Falls, S.D., 1992, Pub. Svc. award for outstanding contbns. to Am. conservation and environ. U.S. Dept. Interior, 1996; named creator first signed, numbered photolithographic print pub. in N.Am., 1959; documented Colorado Springs Fine Arts Ctr., 1993, colleague of Frederick R. Weisman Mus., Mpls., 1994; grantee NEH, 1995, Prairie Lakes Arts Coun., 1995. Fellow Internat. Inst. Arts (life), Soc. Animal Artists (emeritus), N.Am. Mycol. Assn., Nat. Wildlife Fedn. (nat. wildlife week chmn. Minn.), Minn. Ducks Unltd. (bd. dirs. emeritus), Minn. Artists

Assn. (v.p., bd. dirs. 1953-59), Outdoor Writers Am. (emeritus), Soc. Artists and Art Dirs. (emeritus), Am. Artists Profl. League (emeritus), Mpls. Soc. Fine Arts, Wildlife Soc., Minn. Mycol. Soc. (pres. emeritus, hon. life mem.), Le Sueur County Hist. Soc. (hon. life mem.), Minn. Conservation Fedn. (hon. life), Wildlife Artists World (charter mem., emeritus internat. v.p., chmn. fine arts bd.), Internat. Platform Assn. (emeritus), Great Lakes Outdoor Writers (emeritus), The Prairie Chicken Soc. (patron), Mission Oceanic Arctic, 1992, Minn. Press Club (emeritus), Explorers Club (N.Y.C., emeritus), Silver Lake Sports (hon.). Office: care Wildlife Am PO Box 580004-a Minneapolis MN 55458-0004 *With a modicum of natural skills in painting and writing, my basic goal throughout all my work has been to help people appreciate and understand nature. If I as a naturalist am a small voice for our world's waters, woods, and wildlife, if I have influenced many children and adults to become more environment conscious, if my art brings to others a measure of joy, then my best aspirations for my creations have been fulfilled.*

PREVE, ROBERTA JEAN, librarian, researcher; b. Wilmington, Del., Feb. 27, 1954; d. Burton Hugo Sanders and Betsy (Kan) Klein; m. Thomas Alan Preve, Sept. 23, 1978; children: Stephanie Jean, Melanie Marie. BA, U. N.H., 1975; MLS, Simmons Coll., 1985. Rschr. U. N.H., Durham, 1974-75; rsch. asst. Eikonix Corp., Burlington, Mass., 1976-79; asst. cashier, credit dept. mgr. Dania (Fla.) Bank, 1980-83; rsch. assoc. Ctr. for Strategy Rsch., Cambridge, Mass., 1984-86; info. svcs. Braxton Assocs., Boston, 1986-87; mktg. adminstr. Summit Tech., Waltham, Mass., 1987-91; mgr. market rsch. AT&T Capital Corp., Framingham, 1991-95; mgr. Bus. Info. Ctr. Raytheon Co., Lexington, 1995—. Co-owner T&R Pest Mgmt., Attleboro, Mass., 1988-95. Mem. Spl. Librs. Assn., New England Online (dir., logistics chair 1986-90), Beta Phi Mu. Avocations: hiking, reading, needlework, sports. Office: Raytheon Co Bus Info Ctr 141 Spring St Lexington MA 02421-7899

PREVIATO, EMMA, mathematics educator; b. Badia Polesine, Veneto, Italy, Nov. 29, 1952; came to U.S., 1978; d. Pierluigi and Bice (Costato) P. Laurea in Math., U. Padua, Italy, 1974; MA in Math., Harvard U., 1979, PhD in Math., 1983. Assoc. prof. U. Padua, 1974-78; teaching fellow Harvard U., Cambridge, Mass., 1978-83; asst. prof. dept. math. Boston U., 1983-92, assoc. prof., 1992-98, prof., 1998—. Reviewer Math. Revs., Ann Arbor, Mich., 1985—; sci. scholar Bunting Inst. Radcliffe Coll., 1995-96; vis. prof. Math. Scis. Rsch. Inst., Berkeley, Calif., 1991. Author: (with R. Donagi, B. Dubrovin and E. Frenkel) Integrable Systems and Quantum Groups, 1996; editor: Advances in Algebraic Geometry Motivated by Physics, 2001. Swedish Royal Soc. fellow, Stockholm, 1986-87, English Sci. Engring. Rsch. Ctr. fellow, London, 1987-88; recipient award NSF, Princeton, 1984-85. Mem. Am. Math. Soc., London Math. Soc. Roman Catholic. Avocation: literary criticism. Office: Boston U 111 Cummington St Boston MA 02215-2411 E-mail: ep@bu.edu.

PREVOR, RUTH CLAIRE, psychologist; b. N.Y.C., June 20, 1944; d. Gustav and Greta (Dreifuss) Strauss; m. Sydney Joseph P., July 4, 1963; children: Joy, Grant, Jed. BA, U. P.R., 1966; PhD, Caribbean Ctr. of Postgrad., Studies, San Juan, 1988. Cert. forensic psychologist, critical incident stress debriefing. Asst. dean Caribbean Ctr. of Postgrad. Studies, 1986-87; dir. prenatal edn. Ashford Meml. Hosp., San Juan, 1987; pvt. practice, 1984—; advisor, field faculty Vt. Coll., Norwich U., 1990-91. V.p. bd. trustees Carlos Albizu U., San Juan and Miami campuses, 2001—. Bd. dirs. Jewish Cmth. Ctr., Miramar, P.R., 1986—, pre-sch., 1990—; pres. Home and Sch./St. John's Prep., San Juan, 1980-81, P.R. chpt. Hadassah Sch., 1972-74; presdl. adv. com., 1990-92. Mem. Am. Psychol. Assn., Assn. of Psychology of P.R. (hon. award 1984), Caribbean Counselors Assn., Caribe Hilton Club, Nat. Assn. Children with Learning Disabilities, Nat. Register Health Svc. Providers in Psychology. Jewish. Office: Ashford Medical Ctr San Juan PR 00907-1510

PREVOST, EDWARD JAMES, paint manufacturing executive; b. Baie Comeau, Que., Can., May 26, 1941; s. Omer and Jeanne (Ouellet) P.; m. Anna Marie Murphy, June 20, 1964; children: Marc, Louise, Eric. Luc. BA in History with honors, Loyola Coll., Montreal, Que., 1962; MBA, U. Western Ont., London, 1964. Cert. Advt. Agy. Practitioner. Account exec. J. Walter Thompson Co. Ltd., Montreal, 1964-66; successively account exec., account supr., group mgr. and v.p. Cockfield Brown & Co. Ltd., 1966-69; gen. mgr. CJRP Radio, Quebec City, 1969-71; exec. v.p., chief operating officer Mut. Broadcasting Ltd., 1971-72, pres., chief operating officer, 1973; exec. v.p. Civitas Corp. Ltd., Montreal, 1973-74, pres., chief exec. officer, 1974-82, also chmn. bd. operating cos., 1974-82; pres., chief exec. officer La Brasserie O'Keefe Limitée, 1983-89; sr. v.p. Carling O'Keefe Breweries of Can. Ltd., 1983-89; pres., chief exec. officer, dir. SICO Inc., Longueuil, Can., 1989-91; pres., CEO Para Inc., Brampton, Can., 1991-97; pres. Prevost & Assocs./Prevost et Associés Mergers & Acquisitions, 1998—. Can. Assoc. Einhorn Assocs., Inc. Bd. dirs. BBM Bur. Broadcasting Measurement, 1971-78; mem. Montreal Bd. Trade; treas., vice chmn.-elect Can. Paint & Coatings Assn., 1994—, chmn., 1995-97. Gov. Can. Advt. Found., 1982; chmn. Telefilm Can., 1983-86; chmn. Montreal Heart Inst. Rsch. Fund, 1979-81, exec. com. 1981-86. Mem. bd. dirs. L'Assn. des Brasseurs du Que. (chmn. 1984-86), Province Que., Can., C. of C., Can. Assn. Broadcasters (dir. 1975, vice Chmn. radio 1976-77, chmn. 1978-79, past chmn., mem. exec. com. 1980-81), Inter-Am. Assn. Broadcasters Uruguay (sec., past treas.), Young Pres. Orgn. (chmn. Que. chpt. 1987), Assn. des MBA du Que. (chmn. 1985-86), Credit Valley Golf and Country Club (Mississauga, Ont.). Clubs: St.-Denis (Montreal), Western Bus. Sch. (Montreal) (founding pres. 1972), Royal Montreal Golf. E-mail: eprev@globalserve.net.

PREVOTS, NAIMA, art educator, writer; b. N.Y.C., May 27, 1935; d. Reuben and Rae (Donchin) Wallenrod; m. Martin Wallen, Aug. 26, 1979; children: Becky, Aaron. BA, Bklyn. Coll., 1955; MA, U. Wis., 1960; PhD, U. So. Calif., 1983. Prof. Am. U., Washington, 1967-84, 88—; dir./curator Hollywood Bowl Mus., L.A., 1984-88. Cons./panelist NEA, 1979—90, Dept. Edn., 1979—91, Kennedy Ctr., 1988—95. Author: (book) Sound Waves, 1985, A Vision for Music, 1986, Dancing in the Sun, 1987, American Pageantry, 1990, Dance for Export: Cultural Diplomacy and the Cold War, 1998. Panelist Calif. & D.C. Arts Commns., 1976—94; chair D.C. chpt. Alliance for Arts, 1976—78. Fellow NEH, 1987, Fulbright, 1987, Sr. Fulbright, 2001—. Mem.: CORD (bd. dirs.), Fulbright Assocs. (bd. dirs. 1989—96), European Union Erasmus Dance Exts., Phi Beta Kappa. Democrat. Jewish. Avocations: reading, travel. Home: 5219 Massachusetts Ave Bethesda MD 20816-2702 Office: Am U 4400 Massachusetts Ave NW Washington DC 20016-8003

PREVOZNIK, STEPHEN JOSEPH, retired anesthesiologist; b. McAdoo, Pa., June 21, 1929; s. John George and Mary Margaret (Ficek) P.; m. Rita Agnes Kellett, Aug. 20, 1955; children— Mary Therese, Stephen Joseph, John Cyril, Michael Edward, Margaret Anne, Rita Marie, Thomas William, Jean Marie. R.N., St. Joseph Hosp. Sch. Nursing, Phila., 1951; BS, U. Notre Dame, 1955; MD, U. Pa., 1959. Intern Fitzgerald Mercy Hosp., Darby, Pa., 1959-60; resident in anesthesia U. Pa., Phila., 1960-62; practice medicine specializing in anesthesiology, 1962-94; mem. staff U. Pa. Hosp.; prof. anesthesia U. Pa., 1977-94, dir. clin. activities, 1971-89; ret., 1994. Chmn. Residency Rev. Com. for Anesthesiology, 1991-93. Contbr. to textbooks on anesthesiology. Mem. AMA, Am. Soc. Anesthesiologists, Pa. Soc. Anesthesiologists, Phila. Soc. Anesthesiologists (pres. 1975-77), Internat. Anesthesia Rsch. Soc., Assn. Univ. Anesthesiologists (exec. coun. 1977-79, sec. 1981-84, dir. anesthesiology pain mgmt. program 1992-94). Home: 204 N Concord Ave Havertown PA 19083-5021 *No one does everything by himself; someone is always there to provide a helping hand. As one progresses and matures, he finds many opportunities to repay what he has received. Without this repayment, the chain is broken and that life is without meaning.*

PREWITT, CHARLES THOMPSON, geochemist; b. Lexington, Ky., Mar. 3, 1933; s. John Burton and Margaret (Thompson) P.; m. Gretchen B. Hansen, Jan. 31, 1958; children: Daniel Hansen. SB, MIT, 1955, SM, 1960, PhD, 1962. Research scientist E.I. DuPont De Nemours & Co. Inc., Wilmington, Del., 1962-69; assoc. prof. SUNY, Stony Brook, 1969-71, prof., 1971-86, chmn. dept. earth and space scis., 1977-80; dir. Geophys. Lab., Carnegie Inst. of Washington, 1986-98, mem. rsch. staff, 1998—. Sec.-treas. U.S. Nat. Com. for Crystallography, Washington, 1983-85, 99—; gen. chmn. 14th Meeting of Internat. Mineral. Assn., Stanford, Calif., 1986; chmn. NRC/Nat. Acad. Scis. com. on physics and chemistry of earth materials, 1985-87; mem. bd. govs. Consortium for Advanced Radiation Svcs.; co-dir. NSF Ctr. for High Pressure Rsch., 1991—. Editor: (jour.) Physics and Chemistry of Minerals, 1976-85; contbr. more than 170 articles to profl. jours. Bd. dirs. Internat. Ctr. for Diffraction Data, 1998-2002. Capt. USAR, 1956-65. NATO sr. postdoctoral fellowship, 1975, Churchill overseas fellowship, 1975, Japan Soc. for Promotion of Sci. fellowship, 1983; named Disting. Vis. Prof. Chemistry, Ariz. State U., 1983. Fellow Mineral. Soc. Am. (pres. 1983-84), Am. Geophys. Union; mem. Geol. Soc. Am., Am. Crystallographic Assn., Materials Rsch. Soc., Mineral. Soc. Gt. Britain and Ireland, Cosmos Club. Office: Carnegie Inst Geophys Lab 5251 Broad Branch Rd NW Washington DC 20015-1305

PREWITT, KENNETH, political science educator, foundation executive; b. Alton, Ill., Mar. 16, 1936; s. Carl Kenneth and Louise (Carpenter) P.; children: Jennifer Ann, Geoffrey Douglas. BA, So. Meth. U., 1958; MA, Washington U., St. Louis, 1959; PhD, Stanford U., 1963. Prof. polit. sci. U. Chgo., 1964-80, chmn. dept. polit. sci., 1975-76; dir. Nat. Opinion Rsch. Ctr., 1976-79; pres. Social Sci. Rsch. Coun., N.Y.C., 1979-85, 95-98; sr. v.p. Rockefeller Found., 1985-95; dir. U.S. Census Bur., Washington, 1998-2001; dean grad. faculty New Sch. U., N.Y.C., 2001—02; Carnegie Prof. of Public Affairs School of International and Public Affairs, Columbia Univ., 2002—. Vis. scholar U. Nairobi, Kenya, 1968-71; bd. dirs. Washington U., So. Meth. U., Energy Found., Ctr. Advanced Study Behavioral Scis. Author: Political Socialization, 1969, Ruling Elites, 1973, Labryrinths of Democracy, 1973, Introduction to American Government, 1983, 6th edit., 1991. Guggenheim fellow, 1983; fellow Center Advanced Study in Behavioral Scis., 1983; recipient Officer's Cross of Order of Merit, Rep. of Germany. Fellow AAAS, Am. Acad. Arts and Scis.; mem. Am. Polit. Sci. Assn., Coun. on Fgn. Rels.

PREWITT, WILLIAM CHANDLER, financial executive; b. Phila., Aug. 23, 1946; s. Richard Hickman and Jean Mary (Simpkins) Prewitt; m. Karen Ruth Padgett, May 15, 1971. BA in History, Transylvania Coll., 1968; cert., Coll. Fin. Planning, 1985; MS in Fin. Planning, Coll. for Fin. Planning, 1991. Dist. exec. Cen. N.C. Coun., Albemarle, 1971-74, Transatlantic Coun., Heidelburg, Fed. Republic Germany, 1974-78; field dir. Dutchess City Coun., Hyde Park, N.Y., 1978-80; prin. Prewitt Properties, Charleston, S.C., 1980—, William C. Prewitt Cert. Fin. Planner, Charleston, 1986—; registered rep. First Investors Corp., 1982-83. Lectr. Coll. of Charleston, 1987—, Trident Tech. Coll., Charleston, 1987—, Charleston So. U. Sec. Hist. Ansonborough Neighborhood Assn., Charleston, 1987—90, v.p., 1999, pres., 1999—2000; bd. dirs. Christian Family Y, 1991—99, pres., 1995—97; treas. South Carolinians to Limit Congl. Terms, 1991—2000; deacon 1st Presbyn. Ch., Rockingham, NC, 1972—74; elder 1st Scots Ch., Charleston, 1990—93, meml. fund trustee, 1999—2000. 1st lt. Res. USMC, 1968—71. Named One of 300 Best Fin. Advisors, Worth Mag., 1996, 1997, 1998, One of 120 Best Fin. Advisors for Drs., Med. Econs. Mag., 1998, 1999, 2000. Mem.: SCV, SAR (chpt. treas. 1996—), Nat. Assn. Personal Fin. Advisors (pres. region 1994-96, chmn. ethics and stds. com. 1996-99, nat. bd. dirs. 1996-99), Internat. Assn. Fin. Planners (registry 1986-92), Inst. Cert. Fin. Planners, S.C. Soc. Cert. Fin. Planners (pres. 1985-87, chmn. bd. dirs. 1988-90), Société Francaise (sec. 1999-2001, pres. 2001—), Navy League (pres. 1992, chmn. bd. 1993, Charleston coun.), Internat. Churchill Soc., Rotary (bd. dirs. 2000—02). Republican. Avocation: Avocations: sailing, historic restorations. Home: 33 Hasell St Charleston SC 29401-1604 Office: 15 Broad St Charleston SC 29401-3001

PREWOZNIK, JEROME FRANK, lawyer; b. Detroit, July 15, 1934; s. Frank Joseph and Loretta Ann (Parzych) P.; m. Marilyn Ruth Johnson, 1970; 1 child, Frank Joseph II. AB cum laude, U. Detroit, 1955; JD with distinction, U. Mich., 1958. Bar: Calif. 1959. Pvt. practice, Calif., 1960-91. Served in U.S. Army, 1958-60. Mem. ABA, State Bar Calif. Republican. Home: Fisher Cove PO Box 120017 Big Bear Lake CA 92315-8913

PREY, BARBARA ERNST, artist; b. Jamaica, N.Y., Apr. 17, 1957; d. Herbert Henry and Margaret (Joubert) Ernst; m. Jeffrey Drew Prey, Jan. 11, 1986; children: Austin William Ernst Prey, Emily Elizabeth Prey. BA with honors, Williams Coll., 1979; MDiv, Harvard U., 1986. Sales staff Tiffany and Co., N.Y.C., summer 1977; intern Met. Mus. Art, summer 1979; pers. asst. Prince Albrecht Castell, Castell, Germany, 1980-81; with modern painting dept. Sotheby's Auction House, N.Y.C., 1981-82; sales asst. Marlborough Gallery, 1982; tchg. asst. Boston Coll., 1984, Harvard U., Cambridge, Mass., 1984-85; vis. lectr. Tainan (Taiwan) Coll. and Sem., 1986-87; artist Oyster Bay, N.Y., 1987—. Artist-in-residence Westminster Sch., Simsbury, Conn., 1998; art juror Washington and Jefferson Coll., Washington, Pa., 1990; presenter in field. Illustrator: Boys Harbor Cookbook, 1988, A Dream Became You, A City Grows Up, 1991, (cover) Am. Artist Mag., summer 1994, Barbara Ernst Prey: Watercolors, 1998; exhibited in group shows including Mus. Fine Arts, Nassau County, N.Y., 1988, Nat. Arts Club N.Y.C., 1988, Gallery One, Rockland, Maine, 1992, Williams Coll., Williamstown, Mass., 1993, Johnstown (Pa.) Art Mus., 1993, Blair Art Mus., Holidaysburg, Pa., 1993, Phila. Mus. of Art Gallery, 1995, Westmoreland Mus. Am. Art, Greensburg, Pa., (Best in Show award), 1996, Museum of the Southwest, Midland, Tex., Farnsworth Museum of Art, Rockland, Maine, 1997, Guild Hall Mus., East Hampton, N.Y., 1998, Portland (Maine) Mus. of Art, 1998, U.S. Embassy, Prague, 2002, others; one-woman shows include Harvard-Yale-Princeton Club, Pitts., 1991; represented in pvt. collections including Pres. and Mrs. George Bush Farnsworth Mus. Art; displayed 1997 Holiday Card on 80,000 screens worldwide Bloomberg Bus. News; solo exhibit Jensen Fine Arts, N.Y.C., 1999, 2001; featured on Fox TV News, 1999. Class agt. Williams Coll., Williamstown, Mass., 1981-91; bd. mem. Citizens Libr., Washington, 1992-93; active 1st Presby. Ch., Oyster Bay, N.Y. Fulbright scholarship Fulbright Assn., Germany, 1979-80; grantee Roothbert Fund, Chataugua, N.Y., 1982-84, Ch. History award Gordan-Conwell Sem., S. Hamilton, Mass., 1984, Henry Luce Found., Taiwan, 1986-87. Mem. Pitts. Watercolor Soc. (Jean Thoburn award 1994), Nat. Mus. Women in the Arts. Avocations: tennis, skiing, bird watching, reading, cross county skiing. Home and Office: 22 Pearl St Oyster Bay NY 11771-2305

PREY, JEFFREY DREW, minister; b. Pitts., Mar. 10, 1958; s. William Arthur and Shirley Ann Prey; m. Barbara Elizabeth Ernst, Jan. 11, 1986; children: Austin, Emily. Student, Cornell U., 1976; BA, Gordon Coll., 1980; MDiv, Gordon-Conwell Theol. Sem., 1984; DMin, Pitts. Theol. Sem., 1996. Ordained Presbyn. minister. Project mgr. Merritt & Harris, Inc., N.Y.C., 1984-86; vis. lectr. Tainan (Taiwan) Theol. Coll. & Sem., 1986-87; pastor Bethel Presbyn. Ch., Prosperity, Pa., 1988-96, First Presbyn. Ch., Oyster Bay, N.Y., 1996—. Lectr. New Testament, Waynesburg (Pa.) Coll., 1989-90. Speaker City Mission, Washington, Pa., 1990-93; bd. trustees Green Vale Sch., 1999—. Republican. Avocations: tennis, swimming, white water rafting. Home: 22 Pearl St Oyster Bay NY 11771-2305 Office: First Presbyn Ch 60 E Main St Oyster Bay NY 11771-2411

PREYER, NORRIS WATSON, history educator; b. Greensboro, N.C., Feb. 9, 1926; s. William Yost Preyer and Mary Norris Richardson; m. Kathryn Jeanette Cobb, Dec. 15, 1950; children: Norris Watson Jr., Janet McFadyen Nelson. BA, U. N.C., 1947; MA, U. Va., 1950, PhD, 1954. Asst. prof. history Guilford Coll., Greensboro, N.C., 1953-57, Queens Coll., Charlotte, 1957-58, prof. history, 1958-62, chair dept. history, 1959-90, Dana prof. history, 1962-90, Dana prof. emeritus, 1990—. Bd. dirs. Piedmont Fin. Co. Author: Hezekiah Alexander and the Revolution in the Backcountry, 1987 (Book award N.C. Soc. Historians 1988), The Preyer Boys, 2000; contbr. articles to profl. jours. Bd. dirs. Textile History Soc., 1962-65, Sci.Mus., Inc., Charlotte, 1973-79, Presbyn. Hist. Soc., 1985-91, Mecklenburg Hist. Soc., 1994-2000, cons. Mus. New South, 1990—; mem. adv. com. Spirit Sq. Ctr. for Arts and Edn., 1995-98; bd. dirs. Latta Place, Inc., Charlotte, 1972-75, 85-91, 92-95, 97-2002, pres., 1994-95; elder Myers Park Presbyn., Ch., Charlotte; mem. planning group Charlotte-Mecklenburg Cultural Task Force, 1974-75; bd. visitors Queens Coll., 1997—, Sharon Towers, 1999—; bd. dirs. Charlotte Mus. Art History, 2002—. Named Danforth Assoc., Danforth Found., 1962-68; NEH fellow Newberry Libr., Chgo., 1979. Mem. Orgn. Am. Historians, So. Hist. Assn., Soc. for the History of the Early Am. Republic, N.C. Hist. Soc., Presbyn. Hist. Soc., Mecklenburg Hist. Assn. Democrat. Avocations: tennis, fishing, travel. Home: 960 Cherokee Rd Charlotte NC 28207

PREYSZ, LOUIS ROBERT FONSS, III, management consultant, educator; b. Quantico, Va., Aug. 1, 1944; s. Louis Robert Fonss, Jr. and Lucille (Parks) P.; m. Patricia Dianne Yelland; children: Louis Robert Fonss IV, Christine Elizabeth, Michael Anthony, Daniel Timothy. BA, U. Wis., 1968; MBA, U. Utah, 1973; postgrad., Rutgers U., 1983; grad., Command and Gen. Staff Coll., Ft. Leavenworth, Kans., 1986. Tchg. and rsch. asst. U. Utah, Salt Lake City, 1972-73; mktg. and pers. officer Security 1st Nat. Bank of Sheboygan, Wis., 1973-76; mktg. dir. 1st Nat. Bank Rock Island, Ill., 1976-77; asst. v.p., mktg. sales mgr. 1st Nat. Bank Birmingham, Ala., 1977—78; v.p. mktg. mgr. Sun 1st Nat. Bank Orlando, Fla., 1978—80; pres. Preysz Assocs., 1980—. Assoc. prof. mgmt. and banking Flagler Coll., St. Augustine, Fla., 1982—; faculty U. Wis., Sheboygan, 1973-76, Fla. Inst. Tech., 1976-77, St. Ambrose Coll., Davenport, Iowa, 1976-77, U. Ctrl. Fla., 1979-81, Columbia (Mo.) Coll., 1981-82; mem. tng. and profl. devel. coun. Bank Mktg. Assn., 1976-78, chmn., 1978; mem. mktg. and pub. rels. com. Wis. Bankers Assn., 1975; v.p. Ala. Automated Clearing House Assn., 1977-78; spkr. in field; host to daily FM radio program Money Issues. Author: How to Introduce a New Service, 1976, Energy Efficiency Programs and Lending Practices for Florida's Financial Institutions, 1980, Credit Union Marketing, 1981, An Effective Management Structure for Multi-Bank Holding Companies, 1983, Credit Union Strategic Marketing, 1993; contbg. editor: Target Market, an Instructional Approach to Bank Cross Selling of Services, New Accounts Training Manual, 1977, Tested Techniques in Bank Marketing, 1977; contbg. author: Rapid Debt Reduction Strategies, 1990, The Debt Free Army, 1993; mem. editl rev. bd. SAM Advanced Mgmt. Jour.; contbr. articles to mags. Mem. Rep. Presdl. Task Force, 1982-86, Rep. Nat. Com., 1980-89, 2000, Rep. Nat. Com. Victory, 2000; mem., chmn. George W. Bush for Pres.; mem. Nat. World War II Meml.; bd. dirs. Cath. Charities Bur. Inc., 1988-89, v.p., 1989; bd. dirs. United Way St. Johns County, 1989-95, chmn., 1991-95; bd. dirs., treas., deacon Grace Cmty. Ch., 1996-99; charter mem. U.S. Com. for Battle Normandy Mus., 1989, Reagan Presdl. Libr.; fin. chair for Billy Graham Crusade, Jacksonville Crusade. Capt. U.S. Army, 1968-72; officer Fla. Army N.G. Fellow Soc. Advancement Mgmt. Honor Soc. (internat. v.p., bd. dir., cons., Mgmt. Excellence award 1990); mem. U. Wis. Alumni Assn., U. Utah Alumni Assn., N.G. Officers Assn. Fla., N.G. Assn. U.S., U.S. Holocaust Meml. Mus. (charter mem.), Nat. Trust Hist. Preservation, Civil War Soc., St. Augustine Officers Club, Rotary (Paul Harris fellow), Civil War Preservation Trust, Phi Gamma Delta. Republican. Baptist. Office: PO Box 1027 Saint Augustine FL 32085-1027 E-mail: preyszlr@flagler.edu., mosserrs@aol.com.

PREYSZ, SANDRA, music educator; BA, U. Utah, 1973. Cert. tchr. music, profl. piano Music Tchrs. Nat. Assn. Pvt. piano tchr., Salt Lake City, 1977—. Mem. Utah Music Tchrs. Assn. (state bd. dirs., membership chair 1995—), Utah Fedn. Music Club (state bd. dirs., Jr. Festival chmn. 1999—). Avocations: skiing, sailing, tennis.

PRIBANIC, VICTOR HUNTER, lawyer; b. McKeesport, Pa., Apr. 7, 1954; s. John Edward and Marlene Cecilia (Hunter) P. BA, Bowling Green State U., 1976; JD, Duquesne U., 1979. Bar: Pa. 1979, U.S. Dist. Ct. (we. dist.) Pa. 1979, U.S. Ct. Appeals (3d cir.) 1979, U.S. Supreme Ct. 1989, U.S. Ct. Claims 1990. Asst. dist. atty. Office of Dist. Atty., Pitts., 1980-82; law clk. to presiding justice Pa. Ct. Common Pleas, 1982-85; pvt. practice Pitts. and McKeesport, 1982—; pres. Pribanic & Pribanic, P.C., 1987—. Mem.: ATLA, Million Dollar Adv. Forum, Roscoe Pound Found., Acad. Trial Lawyers Allegheny County, Pa. Trial Lawyers Assn., Nat. Assn. Criminal Def. Lawyers. Democrat. Roman Catholic. Home: 100 Victoria Dr Mc Keesport PA 15131-1224 Office: 1735 Lincoln Way White Oak PA 15131-1715 Address: 513 Court Pl Pittsburgh PA 15219-2002

PRIBBENOW, PAUL C. higher education administrator, consultant; b. Decorah, Iowa, Jan. 18, 1957; s. Jerome Carroll and Elsie Mae (Zellmer) P.; m. Ann F. Raney, Sept. 4, 1982 (div. Sept. 1995); m. Abigail G. Crampton, Apr. 27, 1996. BA, Luther Coll., Decorah, 1978; AM in Divinity, U. Chgo., 1979, PhD in Ethics, 1993. Cert. fund raising exec. Dir. devel. Sch. Art Inst. Chgo., 1985-89; assoc. dean Sch. Social Svc. Adminstrn., U. Chgo., 1989-91, Div. Sch., U. Chgo., 1991-93; v.p. Sch. Art Inst. Chgo., 1993-96; dean for coll. advancement Wabash Coll., Crawfordsville, Ind., 1996-2001, rsch. fellow Ctr. Inquiry in Liberal Arts, 2001—02; pres. Rockford (Ill.) Coll., 2002—. Mem. faculty Sch. Art Inst. Chgo., 1993-96, Spertus Coll., Chgo., 1990-96, De Paul U., 2000—. Contbr. articles to profl. jours.; editor 2 books. Mem. vis. com. Div. Sch., U. Chgo., 1996—; sec. bd trustees Wabash Coll., 1998-2001. Mem. Assn. Fundraising Profls. (Pres.'s award for profl. leadership 1994), Coun. for Advancement and Support of Edn. Democrat. Lutheran. Avocation: reading. Office: Rockford Coll 5050 E State St Rockford IL 61108 E-mail: president@rockford.edu.

PRIBBLE, EASTON, artist; b. Falmouth, Ky., July 31, 1917; s. Thaddeus Sewell and Louise Ella (Parker) P. Student, U. Cin., 1941. Ind. tchr., N.Y.C., 1950-57; instr. painting and history of art Munson-Williams-Proctor Inst., Utica, N.Y., 1957—. Instr. history of art Utica Coll., Syracuse U., 1960-74 One-man exhbns. include Pinacotheca Gallery, N.Y.C., 1947, 48, Alan Gallery, N.Y.C., 1953, 55, 59, Hamilton Coll., Clinton, N.Y., 1975, Munson-Williams-Proctor Inst. Mus. Art, 1957, 76, 82, Kirkland Art Ctr., Clinton, N.Y., 1988, Rome (N.Y.) Art Ctr., 1990, Utica Coll. of Syracuse U., 1997; represented in permanent collections Sheldon Swope Art Mus., Savannah Coll. of Art and Design Mus. of Art, Whitney Mus. Am. Art, Hirschorn Mus. and Sulpture Garden, Smithsonian Instn., Parrish Mus., Southampton, N.Y., Munson-Williams-Proctor Inst. Mus. Art., Fallingwater (Frank Lloyd Wright House), Mill Run, Pa., Hudson River Mus., Yonkers, N.Y., Everson Mus., Syracuse, N.Y., Emerson Gallery, Hamilton Coll., The Farnsworth Mus. Art, Rockland, Maine, Colgate U. Art Gallery, Hamilton, Savannah Coll. of Art and Design. Fellow Yaddo, Saratoga Springs, N.Y., 1954, 55, 68 Mem. Artists Equity. Home: 24 Rose Pl Utica NY 13502-5614 Office: Munson-Williams-Proctor Inst 310 Genesee St Utica NY 13502-4764

PRICE, ALAN THOMAS, business and estate planner; b. Balt., Nov. 11, 1949; s. Alvah Thompson and Doris Elaine (Cole) P.; m. Page Angela Jennings, Sept. 1978 (div. 1980); m. Lauren Ann St. Clare, Aug. 12, 1983 (div. 1992); m. Melissa Renee Ballistreri, Nov. 1997. BS, U. N.C., 1972. CLU; chartered fin. cons.; cert. estate and bus. analyst, fin. planner; registered fin. planner. Mgmt. trainee Sears, Atlanta, 1972-73; ins. agt. Aetna Life & Casualty, 1973-76, Pilot Life/New Eng. Life, Virginia Beach, Va., 1976-81; owner, pres. Page II Prodns., Inc., Norfolk, 1981—. Founding prin. 1s Fin. Resources, 1989; veteran judge Miss U.S.A. Pageant System. Fin. columnist News-Herald, 1985-86. Active Mus. Marine Scis., Virginia Beach, 1986—, Hope Found., Windsor, N.C., 1987—, Va. Stage Co., Va. Pops Orch. Named Man of Yr., Pilot Life, Tidewater, Va., 1978, 79, 80. Fellow Life Underwriter Tng. Coun.; mem. Million Dollar Roundtable (life and qualifying), Internat. Assn. Registered Fin. Planners, Am. Coun. Ind. Life Underwriters, Am. Soc. CLU's, Internat. Assn. Fin. Planning (dir. 1987-88), Inst. Cert. Fin. Planners, Nat. Assn. Life Underwriters, Sales and Mktg. Execs., Ct. of the Table, Tidewater Estate Planning Coun., Tidewater Builders Assn., Cen. Bus. Dist. Assn., Hampton Roads C. of C. Methodist. Avocations: painting, fishing, reading, interior decorating, sports. Home: 2645 River Rd Virginia Beach VA 23454-1224 Office: First Fin Resources Page II Prodns 2645 River Rd Virginia Beach VA 23454-1224

PRICE, ALFRED LEE, lawyer, mining company executive; b. Little Rock, May 19, 1935; s. Dewey Ernest and Dorothy Ava (Cooper) P.; m. Magdalena Torres, June 20, 1958; children: Gregory L., Ana Maria. BA, Hendrix Coll., 1956; JD, Tulane U., 1967. Bar: La. 1967, Miss. 1974, D.C., U.S. Supreme Ct., 1980, U.S. Tax Ct., 1977, cert. arbitrator, mediator, Am. Arbitration Assn. and Better Bus. Bureau. Office mgr., dir. personnel Petroleum Helicopters Co., Lafayette, La. and New Orleans, 1956-67; atty. Offshore Navigation and Petroleum Helicopters Co., New Orleans, 1967-74; gen. counsel First Miss. Corp., Jackson, 1974-93, corp. sec., 1988-93; commr. Miss. Employment Commn., 1994—2002. Arbitrator Am. Arbitration Assn., 1998—. Mem. Jackson C.of C., chmn. legislative com., 1991-94. Recipient Arbitrator of Yr., Better Bus. Bureau, 1998. Mem. ABA, La. Bar Assn., Miss. Bar Assn., Hinds County Bar Assn., Miss. Mfrs. Assn. (bd. dirs.), Miss. Econ. Coun. (chmn. tort reform com.), River Hills Club. Methodist.

PRICE, ALICE LINDSAY, writer, artist; b. Augusta, Ga., Oct. 21, 1927; d. William Lloyd and Orlana Jerome (Gould) P. BA in Art English Lit., Okla. State U., 1949; MA in English, U. Tulsa, 1970. Mus. asst. Philbrook Art Mus., Tulsa, 1949-51; recreation supr. U.S. Army Europe, 1951-54; neighborhood ctr. dir. City of Monterey (Calif.) Parks and Recreation Dept., 1955-59; art gallery dir., co-owner Gallerie Quais de la Roquette, Arles, France, 1960-62; program dir. City of Tulsa (Okla.) Parks and Recreation Dept., 1963-69; instr. English lit. and creative writing Holland Hall Sch., Tulsa, 1970-86; artist-in residence Okla. State Arts Coun., Oklahoma City, 1986-91; scholar in residence Tulsa City-County Libr. of NEH, Tulsa/Washington, 1988, 90, 91; pub. HCE Publs./ Riverrun Press, Tulsa, 1974—. Acquisitions editor Coun. Oak Books, Tulsa, 1986-89; lectr. Gilcrease Inst., Tulsa, 1984, 86, 90, 94, Trumpeter Swan Soc., Mpls., 1997, Kans. State U., Manhattan, 1997. Author: (poetry) Faces of the Waterworld, 1970, Our Dismembered Shadow, 1981 (Pegasus award 1981); author/illustrator Swans of the World: Nature, Hist., Myth, Art, 1994 (Feldman award 1993), Cranes: The Noblest Flyers in Natural History and Cultural Lore, 2001. Bd. edn. chair Swan Lake Waterfowl Soc., Tulsa, 1986—; mem. lit. arts com. Arts and Humanities Coun., 1990—; creative writing workshop dir. Tulsa Ctr. Phys. Ltd., Tulsa, 1990. First pl. Folger scholarship Kans. City Art Inst., 1945; grantee Arts and Humanities Coun., 1990, 92. Mem. Trumpeter Swan Soc., Author's Guild, Pen West, Internat. Wild Waterfowl Assn., Tulsa Artists Coalition (First Pl. 1997), Living Arts (poetry coord. 1978-85), Phi Beta Kappa. Avocations: traveling, listening music, photography. Office: HCE Pubs/Riverrun Press 3113 S Florence Ave Tulsa OK 74105-2407

PRICE, ANNE ATCHISON, interior designer; b. Charleston, S.C., Aug. 11, 1943; d. James William and Patricia (Stokes) Atchison; m. James Bullock Price, Feb. 24, 1966; children: David Eugene, Laura Anne, Jamye Lynn. Grad. high sch., Charleston. Corp. sec., treas. Noah Corp., Aiken, S.C., 1981-89; v.p. WV Hydro, Inc., 1986-; owner, operator Interior By Anne, 1988-. Episcopalian. Avocation: aviation.

PRICE, ARTIS J. retired secondary education educator; b. Hoopeston, Ill., Dec. 10, 1929; d. John William and Marian Elizabeth (Moore) Little; m. Harry Mackey Price, Nov. 28, 1958; 1 child, Kathryn Elizabeth. BS, Purdue U., 1952; postgrad., U. Colo., 1955, Northwestern U., 1958. Cert. tchr. h.s. English, Spanish, speech and phys. edn., Ill. Tchr. English, Spanish and speech Onarga (Ill.) H.S., 1952-53; tchr. English and Spanish Reavis H.S., Oak Lawn, Ill., 1953-58; tchr. phys. edn. Niles Twp. H.S., Skokie, 1958-59; substitute tchr. Libertyville (Ill.) H.S., 1959-97; tchr. water ski clinics Chgo. Boat Show, 1960-97, Midwest Boat Show, Chgo., 1960-97. Tchr. water ski clinics Boy Scouts, Girl Scouts, Lions Club, Chgo. and suburbs, 1961-98; mem. adv. bd. Lambs Farm Retarded Facility, Libertyville, 1965-68; nutrition cons. Dr. Harry Price, Northbrook, Ill., 1964-98; cons., editor Diamond Video Prodns., Libertyville, 1976-99. Editor: Water Skiing with Champions, 1969. Vol., Adlai Stevenson Presdl. Campaign, Chgo., 1953-54; founder Ann. Lambs Show Tournament, 1965-99. Recipient 49 Nat. 1st Place Championships, U.S.A. Water Ski, 1957-2001, 4 World 1st Place Championships, 1984, award of distinction U.S.A. Water Ski Hall of Fame, 1998. Mem.: Am. Water Ski Ednl. Found. (award of distinction 1998), U.S.A. Water Ski Assn., Lambs Water Ski Club (hon.; pres. 1965—70), Diamond Lake Water Ski Club (hon.; pres. 1959—64). Christian. Home: 1660 Blackwelder Rd De Leon Springs FL 32130-3914

PRICE, BETTY JEANNE, choirchime soloist, writer; b. Long Beach, Calif., June 12, 1942; d. Grant E. and Miriam A. (Francis) Sickles; m. Harvey H. Price, Aug. 6, 1975; children: Thomas Neil Gering, Timothy Ray (dec.), Pamela Kay (dec.). Degree in Acctg., Northland Pioneer Coll., Show Low, Ariz., 1977. Youth missionary Open Bible Standard Missions, Trinidad, 1958-59; typographer Joel H. Weldon & Assocs., Scottsdale, Ariz., 1980-89; exec. chief acct. Pubs. Devel. Corp., San Diego, 1991-93; coord. music and worship College Ave. Bapt. Ch., 1994-95; ChoirChime soloist, 1986—; exec. acct. Advance Reprographics, San Diego, 1996—, 1996—. Author: 101 Ways to Fix Broccoli, 1994, ABC's of Abundant Living, 1995; co-author: God's Vitamin C for the Spirit, 1995, Bounce Back, 1997, You Can Bounce Back Too, 1998, Pathway of Love, One Man's Remarkable Journey, 2002. Dir. GHFC Handbell Choir. Mem.: San Diego Cash Flow Assn. (founder), Christian Writers Guild. E-mail: pricecan@juno.com.

PRICE, BRENDA CHLOÈ, artist, entrepreneur; b. Hockley County, Tex., Mar. 15, 1945; d. Thomas Irby and Mildred Ruth (Bryant) P.; 1 child, Amber Lacy Belcher. Student, West Tex. State U., 1963-64; BS in Art Edn., Tex. Tech. U., 1967; postgrad., La. Tech. U., 1978-97. Art tchr. Taos (N.Mex.) Valley Sch., 1983-89; artist Gallery Rodeo, Taos, 1991-92, Gallery Touchstone, Taos, 1992—; innkeeper, owner Touchstone B & B, 1994—; art tchr. Hurst-Euless-Bedford Sch., Rogers Sch. Okla. City, Okla. Mus. Art. Author: Inside the Wind, 1983; one woman shows include Barnes and Boughton/Gallery 3017, Oklahoma City, 1981, Lutz/Bergerson Gallery, Taos, 1981, Gallery of Fine Art, Oklahoma City, 1982, Ea. Hills Country Club, Albuquerque, 1982, Okla. Art Mus., Oklahoma City, 1983, The Actors' Playhouse, L.A., 1983, Scharf Gallery, Santa Fe, 1983, 84, 85, The Redroom, L.A., 1984, Bent St. Studio, Taos, 1988, 25 Yr. Retrospective, Centinel Bank, Taos, 1989, Goettler-Smeltzer Gallery, Albuquerque, 1990; group shows include Taos Today, 1986, 88, 89, Hollywood Arts Coun., 1988, Spring Arts Celebration, Taos, 1989, 90, 91, 92, 93, 94, 95, 96, 97, People's Choice, Taos, 1988, Artists of Taos, 1988, 89, 90, and many others. Advisor Med. Arts Found., Taos, 1994—; bd. dirs. for the arts Taos Med. Svcs. Found. Mem. Okla. Watercolor Soc. (past pres.), Nat. Mus. of Women in the Arts. Home and Office: PO Box 1885 0110 Mabel Dodge Ln Taos NM 87571

PRICE, CAROLINE LEONA, personnel consulting company executive; b. N.Y.C., Dec. 13, 1947; d. Richard Gustave and Ruth Leonora (Kling) Schlegel; m. Harold Edmond Price, Sept. 27, 1969; children: Jonathan (dec.), Matthew. AA, Concordia Jr. Coll., Bronxville, N.Y., 1967; student, Wagner Coll., Bregenz, Austria, 1967-68; BA, CUNY, 1969. Tchr. Dept. Def. Sch. Sys., Brindisi, Italy, 1970-71; prin. social welfare exec. Putnam County Dept. Social Svcs., Brewster, N.Y., 1971-75; pers. dir. to patent trader, Mt. Kisco, 1976-77; tchr. English as fgn. lang. Arbeiterkammer, Feldkirch, Austria, 1978-84; office mgr. Peachtree Temps., Inc., Peachtree City, Ga., 1984-85; office adminstr. Chip & Dale, 1985-87; rsch. dir. Borman/Gray, Atlanta, 1987-88; owner, prin. Caprice Cons., Peachtree City, 1988-94, 97—; assoc. Ward Howell Internat., Atlanta, 1994-97. Founding chair So. Conservation Trust, Inc., 1993-95. Chair Peachtree City Planning Commn., 1986-92, McIntosh Recreation Complex Bond Commn., Peachtree City, 1989; mem. Fayette County Solid Waste Com., Fayetteville, Ga., 1989-90, Fayette County Bicentennial Com., 1986; candidate Fayette County Bd. Commrs., 1990; mem. City Coun., Peachtree City, 1992-97; founding mem. Peachtree City Compassionate Friends, 1990; bd. dirs. West Fayette YMCA, 1991-95; chmn. Keep Fayette Beautiful, 1998. Mem. Atlanta Researcher's Roundtable (sec. 1989-90, pres. 1996), Am. Bus. Women's Assn. (pres. McIntosh charter chpt. 1989-90, Woman of Yr. award 1990), Regional Leadership Inst. (Atlanta regional commn.). Lutheran. Home: 2403 Ashford Park Peachtree City GA 30269-1448

PRICE, CHARLES H., II, former ambassador; b. Kansas City, Mo., Apr. 1, 1931; s. Charles Harry and Virginia (Ogden) P.; m. Carol Ann Swanson, Jan. 10, 1969; children: Caroline Lee, Melissa Marie, Charles H., C. B., Pickette. Student, U. Mo., 1951-53; LLD (hon.), Westminster Coll., 1984; LLD (honoris causa), U. Mo., 1988; LHD, Baker U., 1991; DSc (hon.), U. Buckingham, Eng., 1993. Chmn. bd., dir. Price Candy Co., Kansas City, 1969-81, Am. Bancorp., Kansas City, 1973-81; chmn., chief exec. officer Am. Bank & Trust Co., 1973-81; Am. ambassador to Belgium Brussels, 1981-83; Am. ambassador to U.K. London, 1983-89. Chmn. bd. Americanc, Inc., St. Joseph, Mo., 1989—92, pres., CEO, Mo., 1990—92; bd. dirs. Merc. Bank Kansas City, Mo., 1992—96, now bd. dirs., Mo.; bd. dirs. U.S. Industries Inc. Bd. dirs. St. Luke's Hosp., Kansas City, 1970-81, hon. dir., 1989—, advisor Heart Inst. com.; bd. dirs. Midwest Rsch. Inst., Kansas City, chmn., 1990-93. Hon. fellow Regent's Coll., London, 1986; recipient William Booth award Salvation Army, 1985, World Citizen of Yr. award Mayor of Kansas City, 1985, Trustee Citation award Midwest Rsch. Inst., 1987, Disting. Svc. award Internat. Rels. Coun., 1989, Mankind award Cystic Fibrosis Found., 1990, Gold Good Citizenship award SAR, 1991, Chancellor's medal U. Mo. Kansas City, 1992, William F. Yates medallion William Jewell Coll., 1996. Mem.: White's Club, Swinley Forest Club, River Club, Castle Pines Country Club, Eldorado Country Club, Brook Club, Cypress Point Club, Los Angeles County Club, Kansas City Country Club, Sigma Alpha Epsilon. Republican. Episcopalian. Office: 1 W Armour Blvd Ste 300 Kansas City MO 64111-2087

PRICE, CHARLES R., JR. advertising executive; Chmn. Price/McNabb Inc., Charlotte, N.C. Office: Price/McNabb Inc Unit 500 1001 S Morehead Square Dr Charlotte NC 28203-4270*

PRICE, CHARLES STEVEN, lawyer; b. Inglewood, Calif., June 10, 1955; s. Frank Dean Price and Ann (Rounds) Bolling; m. Sandra Helen Laney, Feb. 26, 1983; children: Katherine Laney, Courtney Ann, Diana Emily. BA, U. Calif., Santa Barbara, 1976; JD, U. Chgo., 1979. Bar: Ariz. 1980, U.S. Dist. Ariz. 1980, U.S. Ct. Appeals (9th cir.) 1982. Assoc. Brown & Bain P.A., Phoenix, 1979-85, ptnr., 1985-96, Allen & Price P.L.C., Phoenix, 1996-2000, Allen, Price & Padden, Phoenix, 2000—. Office: Allen Price & Padden PLC 3131 E Camelback Rd Ste 110 Phoenix AZ 85016-4597 E-mail: price@aplaw.com.

PRICE, CLIFFORD WARREN, retired metallurgist, researcher; b. Denver, Apr. 22, 1935; s. Warren Wilson and Vivian Fredricka (Cady) P.; m. Carole Joyce Waterman, June 14, 1969; children: Carla Beth, Krista Lynn Price. MetE, Colo. Sch. Mines, 1957; MS, Ohio State U., 1970, PhD, 1975. Design engr. Sundstrand Aviation-Denver, 1957-60; materials specialist Denver Rsch. Inst., 1960-63; sr. metallurgist Rocky Flats div. Dow Chem. Co., Golden, Colo., 1963-66; staff metallurgist Battelle Columbus (Ohio) Labs., 1966-75; sr. scientist Owens-Corning Fiberglas, Granville, Ohio, 1975-80; metallurgist Lawrence Livermore (Calif.) Nat. Lab., 1980-93; retired, 1993. Contbr. articles to profl. jours. Battelle Columbus Labs. fellow, 1974-75. Mem. Metall. Soc. AIME, Microscopy Soc. Am. (treas. Denver 1961-62), Am. Soc. for Metals Internat. Achievements include research on electron, scanning probe and optical microscopy, secondary ion mass spectroscopy, deformation, fracture and recrystallization mechanisms in metals, recrystallization kinetics. E-mail: cwprice@home.com.

PRICE, DANIEL MARTIN, lawyer; b. St. Louis, Aug. 23, 1955; s. Albert and Edith S. (Werner) P.; m. Kim Ellen Heebner, July 15, 1984; children: Emma Rachel, Joseph Armin, Joshua Simon. BA, Haverford Coll., 1977; diploma in law, Cambridge U., 1979; JD, Harvard U., 1981. Bar: D.C. 1981, Pa. 1987. Assoc. Drinker, Biddle & Reath, Phila., 1981-82, 86-89; dep. gen. counsel Office of U.S. Trade Rep., Washington, 1989-92; ptnr. Powell, Goldstein, Frazer & Murphy, 1992—. Atty., adviser Dept. State, Washington, 1982-84; dep. agt. U.S. Iran-U.S. Claims Tribunal, Hague, The Netherlands, 1984-86; lectr. Haverford Coll., 1982; mem. adv. bd. Can.-U.S. Law Inst. Articles editor Harvard Law Rev., 1980-81; contbr. articles to profl. jours. including Am. Jour. Internat. Law, Internat. Lawyer, Internat. Fin. Law Rev., Harvard Internat. Law Jour., others. Mem. Bush-Cheney Transition Team, 1999—2000. Am. Keasbey scholar Cambridge U., 1977-78. Mem. ABA, Internat. Bus. Forum (legal adv. bd. 1987-89), Am. Arbitration Assn. (panel arbitrators), Internat. C. of C. (arbitrator), Orgn. for Internat. Investment (counsel), Coun. on Fgn. Rels., Phi Beta Kappa. Office: 1001 Pennsylvania Ave NW Washington DC 20004-2505

PRICE, DAVID ALAN ALAN, biochemistry researcher; b. N.Y.C., NY, July 16, 1948; s. Marvin and Helen Jane (Douglass) P.; m. Rebecca Kyle Bouton, June 22, 1974; children: Franklin Douglass, Anne MacRae, Samuel Hinsdale, Nathaniel Bouton. BS, The Cooper Union, 1970; PhD, Fla. State U., 1977. Rsch. asst. Fla. State U., Tallahassee, 1975-81; asst. rsch. scientist Whitney Lab., St. Augustine, Fla., 1981-89, assoc. rsch. scientist, 1989-97; vis. rsch. scientist Mt. Sinai Med. Ctr., N.Y.C., 1997-98; dir. life scis. applicaitons devel. BioTraces, Inc., Research Triangle Park, N.C., 1998—. Vis. assoc. rsch. prof. Mt. Sinai Med. Ctr., New York, 1997—98. Author: (ca 70 articles in scientific journals) Science, Journal of Neuroscience, and others, 1977. Mem. Am. Chem. Soc., Soc. Neurosci., Internat. Peptide Assn. Achievements include fundamental studies on neuropeptides in lower animals, co-discovery (with Michael J. Greenberg) of neuropeptide FMRFamide. Office: Biotraces Inc 2 Davis Dr Research Triangle Park NC 27709

PRICE, DAVID EUGENE, congressman, educator; b. Johnson City, Tenn., Aug. 17, 1940; s. Albert Lee and Elna (Harrell) P.; m. Lisa Beth Kanwit, July 27, 1968; children: Karen Elizabeth, Michael Edmond. BA, U. N.C., 1961; BD, Yale U., 1964, PhD, 1969. Legis. aide to U.S. senator from Alaska, 1963-67; prof. Duke U., Durham, N.C., 1973-86; mem. U.S. Congress from 4th N.C. dist., Washington, 1987—; mem. appropriations com., budget com. Exec. dir. N.C. Dem. Party, Raleigh, 1979-80, chmn., 1983-84, mem. 1983—; staff dir. nat. com. on presdl. nomination Dem. Party, 1981-82 Author: Bringing Back the Parties, The Commerce Committees, Who Makes the Laws, The Congressional Experience: A View From the Hill. Mem. Am. Polit. Sci. Assn., Soc. for Values in Higher Edn., Phi Beta Kappa. Lodges: Kiwanis. Baptist. Avocations: jogging, music. Home: 2200 N Lakeshore Dr Chapel Hill NC 27514-1726 Office: US Ho of Reps 2162 Rayburn Ho Office Bldg Washington DC 20515-3304*

PRICE, DONALD ALBERT, veterinarian, consultant; b. Bridgeport, Ohio, Dec. 25, 1919; s. Arthur David and Louise Ann (Knellinger) P.; m. June Loree Fleming, July 16, 1945; children: Karen Price Privett, Benita Price Esposito, Donna Price Rocap. Grad., Elliott Sch. Bus., 1938; DVM, Ohio State U., 1950. Lic. veterinarian, Ohio, Ill., Tex. Adminstrv. asst. Wheeling (W.Va.) Steel Corp., 1938-41; counselor psychol. dept. Ohio State U., Columbus, 1946-48, lab. asst. vet. parasitology dept., 1948-50; mem. rsch. faculty Tex. A&M U., Sonora, 1950-55; ptnr. San Angelo Vet. Hosp., Tex., 1955-58; assoc. editor AVMA, Chgo., 1958-59, editor-in-chief, 1959-72, exec. v.p., 1972-85; cons., adj. prof. Tex. A&M U., College Station, 1985—. Capt. USAAF, 1941-46 Recipient Disting. Alumnus award Coll. Vet. Medicine, Ohio State U., 1966 Fellow Am. Med. Writers Assn.; mem. AVMA (Svc. Commendation award 1984, Appreciation award, 1984, CEO 1972-85), Ill. Vet. Med. Assn. (hon. life), Mich. Vet. Med. Assn. (hon. life), Tex. Vet. Med. Assn. (disting. life), Am. Equine Practitioners Assn. (hon.), Am. Assn. Sheep and Goat Practioners (hon.), Am. Animal Hosp. Assn. (hon., Merit award 1983), Bexar County Vet. Med. Assn. (hon.), Masons, Phi Eta Sigma, Phi Zeta, Alpha Psi Republican. Presbyterian. Avocations: woodworking, ranching. Home and Office: HC-1 Box 174-A Hunt TX 78024 E-mail: joyspringranchbb@hotmail.com.

PRICE, DOUGLAS ARMSTRONG, chiropractor; b. Pitts., Feb. 17, 1950; s. Walter Coachman and Janet (Armstrong) P.; m. Ann Georgette Martino, Jan. 31, 1989; 4 children. BA, Brown U., 1972; D Chiropractic, Life Chiropractic Coll., Atlanta, 1983. Diplomate Am. Bd. Chiropractic Examiners; cert. rehab. doctor; life extension physician; ind. med. examiner, Fla. Owner, CEO Applied Biomech. and Musculoskeletal Rehab., Tampa, 1989—, All Am. Chiropractic Clinic; pvt. practice Tampa, 1984—, Manalapan, Fla., 1994-96; clin. dir. Camber Clinics, South Tampa, Haines City, 1999—2001, Fla. Pain, Trauma, and Injury Clinics, Tampa, 2001—. Dir. Myofascial Therapy Found. Author: Protocols for Practioners Utilizing Myofascial Trigger Point Treatment, 1998; prodr. therapeutic exercise video for cervical and lumbar rehab.; contbr. articles to profl. jours. Magnetic Resonance Imaging fellow; named to Brown U. Athletic Hall of Fame; Southeastern Masters Champion Shotput, Discus, 1990-91. Fellow: Am. Gerontology Assn., Chiropractic Rehab. Assn., Am. Coll. Sports Medicine; mem.: APHA, Hillsborough County Chiropractic Soc. (bd. dirs. 1990—93, pres. 1992—93), Fla. Chiropractic Assn., Am. Chiropractic Assn., KC (trustee). Democrat. Roman Catholic. Achievements include research in Russian stimulation applications in low back rehabilitation; application of micro and interferential currents with utilization of manual myofascial release techniques, use of micro and interferential currents with manual treatment of myofascial pain syndromes. Home: 90 W Davis Blvd Tampa FL 33606-3535 E-mail: douglasmyodoc@aol.com.

PRICE, EDGAR HILLEARY, JR. business consultant; b. Jacksonville, Fla., Jan. 1, 1918; s. Edgar Hilleary and Mary Williams (Phillips) P.; m. Elise Ingram, June 24, 1947; 1 son, Jerald Steven. Student, U. Fla., 1937-38. Mgr. comml. flower farm, 1945-49, Fla. Gladiolus Growers Assn., 1949-55; exec. v.p. Tropicana Products, Inc., Bradenton, Fla., 1955-73, dir. div. govt. and industry regulations, to 1979; dir.; exec. v.p. Indsl. Glass Co., Inc., 1963-73; pres., chmn. bd. Price Co., Inc., cons., 1973—. Dir. emeritus F.P.L. Group, Inc.; past chmn. Fla. Citrus Commn., Fla. Gov.'s Freeze Damage Survey Team, Spl. Commn. for Study Abolition Death Penalty; bd. dirs. Fla. Power and Light Co., Fla. Fair Assn., Fla. Citrus Expn., Fla. Fruit and Vegetable Assn., G.T.E. Fla., Fla. Cyprus Gardens, Ellis Bank Co.; past chmn. Joint Citrus Legis. Com.; past mem. Fla. Plant Bd., Fla. Bd. Control, Fla. Legis. Coun.; exec. com. Growers and Shippers League Fla., Fla. Agrl. Council, Spl. Health Agrl. Research and Edn.; past pres., chmn. bd. Fla. Hort. Soc. Past chmn., commr. census 12th Jud. Circuit; mem. Gov. Fla. Com. Rehab. Handicapped, Fla. Commn. on Ethics, 1976-77, Presdl. Inaugural Fin. com., 1977, Ea. 5th Circuit U.S. Jud. Nominating Commn., 1977—, Fla. Senate from 36th Dist., 1958-66; past chmn. Manatee County Bd. Sch. Dist. Trustees, Local Housing Authority Bradenton, Bradenton Sub. Std. Housing Bd., Bradenton Charter Adv. Com.; del. Dem. Nat. Conv., 1960, dist. del., 1964; past trustee, mem. exec. com. Stetson U.; former trustee New Coll., Aurora Found. Served to 1st lt. USAAF, 1941-45. Named Boss of Yr., Nat. Secs. Assn., 1959, Man of Yr. for Fla. agr. Progressive Farmer mag., 1959; recipient merit award Am. Flag Assn., 1962, Gamma Sigma Delta, 1965, leadership award Fla. Agrl. Ext. Svc., 1963, Outstanding Senator award Fla. Radio Broadcasters, 1965, Allen Morris award s most valuable mem. Fla. Legislature, 1965, Most Valuable Mem. award Fla. Senate, St. Petersburg Times, 1965, Brotherhood award Sarasota chpt. NCCJ, 1966, Disting. Citizen award Manatee County, 1970, Disting. Alumnus award U. Fla., 1972, Svc. to Mankind award Sertoma Internat., 1976, Goodwill Disting. Citizen award, 1979, Crystal Shield award Salvation Army, 1996; inducted into Fla. Agrl. Hall of Fame, 1992, Tampa Bay Bus. Hall of Fame, 1992. Mem. Fla. C. of C. (bd. dirs. emeritus and past chmn.), Manatee C. of C. (past pres.), Fla. Hort. Soc. (past pres., chmn. bd.), Fla. Flower Assn., ARC Clara Barton Soc., Blue Key (hon.), Omicron Delta Kappa (hon.), Kiwanis (pres. 1955), Sigma Alpha Epsilon. Home: 3009 Riverview Blvd W Bradenton FL 34205-3420 Office: PO Box 9270 Bradenton FL 34206-9270 *The turning point in my life came at the age of 32 when I accepted Jesus Christ as my personal Lord and Saviour. I believe every person should live his life up to the fullest extent of his God-given talents and ability. I think we have a responsibility to "pay our dues" for the privilege of living in a free land by being actively involved in our government.*

PRICE, EDWARD WARREN, aerospace engineer, educator; b. Detroit, Dec. 6, 1920; s. Frank E. and Elizabeth Alleyne (Rattray) P.; m. Mary Kate Howard, June 21, 1952; children: Douglas Brian, Alison Tamara, Carolyn Louise. *Ed Price's ancestors lived in Almont, Michigan. He is the second of three brothers (Duane and George), who grew up in Pontiac, Michigan until moves to California (1929), Arizona (1929-33), and California (1934). The brothers all graduated from the Pasadena Junior College, California. Duane pursued research on brain chemistry at Columbia University. George became a biology teacher at Harbor Junior College, Los Angeles, California. Ed and his family lived in China Lake, California (1944-74). In 1974, the family moved to Atlanta, Georgia, where his daughters graduated from the University of Georgia. His son moved back to China Lake.* BA in Physics, Math, UCLA, 1948. Ballistician Calif. Inst. Tech., Pasadena, 1941-44; physicist U.S. Naval Weapons Ctr., China Lake, Calif., 1946-74; prof. aerospace engring. Ga. Inst. Tech., Atlanta, 1967-68, 74—. V.p. tech. AIAA, mem. Am. Acad. Scis.-Nat. Rsch. Coun. Space Shuttle Booster Redesign Rev. Panel, 1986-89; cons. in field. *Professor Price started his career in rocket propulsion at Cal Tech, Pasadena in 1941 in the wartime solid rocket program. He continued his research at the Navy's new China Lake, California center, 1944-74, focusing on propellant combustion and combustor stability in 1948. He organized in 1960 and led the Aeorthermochemistry division at that laboratory until his retirement at age 55 in 1974. At that time he continued his research as a professor in the School of Aerospace Engineering at Georgia Tech, Atlanta. Since his retirement in 1991 he has continued consulting and combustion research part-time at Georgia Tech.* Contbr. articles to profl. jours. With USNR, 1944-46. Recipient Pub. Svc. award, Astronauts award NASA, 1987. Fellow AIAA (Rsch., Pendrary, Goddard awards 1966, 71, 76); mem. AAAS, Nat. Acad. Engring., Combustion Inst., Sigma Xi. Achievements include numerous contributions to science in areas of rocket propulsion and combustion. Home: 5058 Highpoint Rd NE Atlanta GA 30342-2313 Office: Ga Inst Tech 225 North Ave Mail Code 0150 Atlanta GA 30332

PRICE, ELY, dermatologist; b. N.Y.C., Aug. 9, 1932; s. Jacob and Mary (Flattau) P.; m. Ilona Brodie, Apr. 30, 1989; children from previous marriage: Jeremy, Andrew. BS cum laude, CCNY, 1953; AM, Ind. U., 1956; MD, U. Lausanne, Switzerland, 1964. Diplomate Am. Bd. Dermatology. Intern Brookdale Hosp. Med. Ctr., Bklyn., 1964-65, resident internal medicine, 1965-66; fellow Mt. Sinai Hosp., N.Y.C., 1965-66; resident in dermatology Kings County Hosp., Bklyn., 1966-69; practice dermatology Bay Ridge Skin and Cancer Dermatology, P.C., 1969—; attending-in-charge, head dermatology Maimonides Med. Ctr., 1985—; clin. assoc. prof. dermatology SUNY Sci. Ctr., 1985—. Cons. in medicine Luth. Med. Ctr., Bklyn., 1988—; cons. in dermatology Victory Med. Hosp., Bklyn., 1989—. Fellow ACP, Am. Acad. Dermatology, Am. Soc. Dermatol. Surgery, N.Y. Acad. Medicine. Avocation: golf. Home: 674 W Fingerboard Rd Staten Island NY 10305-2631 Office: Bay Ridge Skin & Cancer Dermatology PC 9921 4th Ave Brooklyn NY 11209-8347 E-mail: elyilona@aol.com.

PRICE, ERNEST HOWELL, retired family practice physician, administrator; b. Madison, Fla., July 31, 1925; s. Ernest Cooper and Maude Marion (Yates) P.; m. Margaret Ann Barber, Sept. 29, 1945; children: John Howell, Michael Ernest, David Alan, James Dale. BS, Creighton U., 1948; MD, U. Nebr., Omaha, 1952. Diplomate Am. Bd. Family Practice. Intern Charles T. Miller Hosp., St. Paul, 1952-53; pvt. practice Portland, Oreg., 1953-92; med. dir. Aetna-Medicare Oreg./Alaska, 1989-97. Mem. cmty. adv. bd. Providence Portland Med. Ctr., 1979-85, pres. med. staff, 1978; trustee Blue Cross-Blue Shield Oreg., Portland, 1983-92. Mem. exec. com. Oreg. Divsn., Am. Cancer Soc., Portland, 1960-62; mem. med. adv. com. Vis. Nurse Assn., Portland, 1970-84; trustee Multnomah Found. for Med. Care, Portland, 1973-78; chmn. supervisory coun. Health Profls. Program, Oreg., 1996-97. 2nd lt. USAAF, 1943-45. Recipient Presdl. citation Multnomah County Med. Soc., 1980, 82, Svc. award, 1981. Mem. AMA, Am. Acad. Family Practice, Oreg. Med. Assn. (sec.-treas. 1986-87), Oreg. Acad. Family Practice, Med. Soc. Met. Portland (pres. 1977), Alpha Omega Alpha. Avocations: fishing, hunting, travel. Home: 2909 SE Bay Point Dr Vancouver WA 98683-3799 E-mail: Ehprice@aol.com.

PRICE, FRANK, motion picture and television company executive; b. Decatur, Ill., May 17, 1930; s. William F. and Winifred A. (Moran) P.; m. Katherine Huggins, May 15, 1965; children: Stephen, David, Roy, Frank. Student, Mich. State U., 1949-51. Writer, story editor CBS-TV, N.Y.C., 1951-53, Columbia Pictures, Hollywood, Calif., 1953-57, NBC-TV, Hollywood, Calif., 1957-58; producer, writer ZIV-TV, 1958, Universal Television, Universal City, 1959-64, v.p., 1964-71, sr. v.p., 1971-73, exec. v.p. in charge of production, 1973-74, pres., 1974-78; v.p., dir. MCA, Inc., 1976-78; pres. Columbia Pictures Prodn., 1978-79; chmn., chief exec. officer Columbia Pictures, 1979-84, also bd. dirs.; chmn. MCA Motion Picture Group, 1984-86; chmn., chief exec. officer Price Entertainment Inc., 1987-90; chmn. Columbia Pictures, 1990-91; chmn., chief exec. officer Price Entertainment, 1991—; prodr. The Tuskegee Airmen, 1996. With USN, 1948-49. Recipient Peabody award, 1996, NAACP Image award, 1996. Mem. Writers Guild Am., West. Office: Price Entertainment Inc 527 Spoleto Dr Pacific Palisades CA 90272-4517

PRICE, FREDRIC VICTOR, physician, educator, medical researcher; b. Wilmington, Del., Nov. 4, 1957; s. Martin Burton and Mollie (Saline) P.; m. Ellen S. Wilson, Nov. 30, 1985; children: George, Olivia. BA, Yale U., 1980; MD, U. Louisville, 1986. Diplomate Am. Bd. Ob-Gyn.; cert. gynecologic oncologist. Intern, resident in ob-gyn. U. Pitts., 1986-90; fellow in gynecologic oncology Yale U., New Haven, 1990-92; asst. prof. U. Pitts., 1993-98; attending physician Magee-Womens Hosp., Pitts., 1992—; pres. Pitts. Gynecol. Oncology, Inc., 1998—; pvt. practice Inc. Med. Practice, 1998—. Peer reviewer Obstetrics and Gynecology, L.A., 1996—, Gynecologic Oncology, San Diego, 1994—; grant reviewer FDA, Rockville, Md., 1995, Calif. Dept. Pub. Health, Sacramento. Contbr. articles to profl. jours. Felix Rutledge fellow M.D. Anderson Cancer Ctr., Houston, 1989; recipient Clin. Oncology award Am. Cancer Soc., 1991, Bristol-Myers Squibb Clin. Rsch. award Bristol-Myers Oncology, 1995, Nat. Faculty Recognition award Com. Resident Edn.

in Ob-Gyn., 1997. Fellow ACS, Am. Coll. Obstetric Gynecology; mem. Am. Soc. Clin. Oncology, Soc. Gynecol. Oncologists, Am. Cancer Soc. (bd. dirs. Southwestern Pa.). Office: 4221 Penn Ave Ste 505 Pittsburgh PA 15224-1389 E-mail: pitgo@nauticom.net.

PRICE, GLANVILLE, writer, French language educator; b. Rhaeadr, Wales, June 16, 1928; s. John Edmond and Bessie Price; m. Christine Winifred Thurston, Aug. 18, 1954; children: Gareth Charles, Christopher Iwan, Eluned Catrin, Steven Trefor. BA, U. Wales, Bangor, 1949, MA, 1952; doctorate, U. Paris, 1956. Lectr. in French U. St. Andrews, Scotland, 1958-64, U. Leeds, Eng., 1965-66; prof. French U. Stirling, Scotland, 1967-72, U. Wales, Aberystwyth, 1972-92, rsch. prof., 1992-95, prof. emeritus, 1995—. Vis. prof. U. Calif., Berkeley, 1982; bd. govs. Ctr. Info. on Lang. Teaching and Rsch., 1971-77; mem. Broadcasting Coun. for Wales, 1980-84. Author: The Present Position of Minority Languages in Western Europe, 1969, The French Language: Present and Past, 1971, (with Kathryn F. Bach) Romance Linguistics and the Romance Languages: A Bibliography of Bibliographies, 1977, The Languages of Britain, 1984, (revision) L. S. R. Byrne and E. L. Churchill, A Comprehensive French Grammar, 1986, An Introduction to French Pronunciation, 1991; editor: William, Count of Orange: Four Old French Epics, 1975, The Celtic Connection, 1991, Encyclopedia of the Languages of Europe, 1998, Languages in Britain and Ireland, 2000; editor: The Yr.'s Work in Modern Lang. Studies, 1972-75, co-editor, 1975-92, (with C. Lupu) Hommages offerts à Maria Manoliu-Manea, 1994. Mem. Soc. for French Studies, Philol. Soc. (coun. 1973-79, 84-87), Modern Humanities Rsch. Assn. (gov. com. 1972—, chmn. 1979-90). Office: Univ of Wales Dept of European Languages Aberystwyth SY23 3DY Wales

PRICE, GRIFFITH BALEY, JR. lawyer; b. Lawrence, Kans., Aug. 15, 1942; s. Griffith Baley and Cora Lee (Beers) P.; m. Maria Helena Martin, June 29, 1968 (div.); children: Andrew Griffith, Alexandra Helena; m. Nancy Culver Rhodes, Aug. 17, 1997; 1 child, Carolyn Rhodes. AB (cum laude), Harvard U., 1964; LLB, NYU, 1967. Bar: N.Y. 1967, D.C. 1991, U.S. Ct. Appeals (6th cir.) 1975, U.S. Ct. Appeals (2nd cir.) 1978, U.S. Ct. Appeals (3d, 5th and 11th cirs.) 1981, U.S. Ct. Appeals (fed. cir.) 1984, U.S. Supreme Ct. 2001. Assoc. Dewey, Ballantine, Bushby, Palmer & Wood, N.Y.C., 1967-75; ptnr. Milgrim Thomajan & Lee, 1976-86; of counsel, ptnr. Finnegan, Henderson, Farabow, Garrett & Dunner, LLP, Washington, 1987—. Adj. prof., lectr. George Washington U. Law Ctr., Washington, 1989—93; mem., chair pub. adv. com. U.S. Patent and Trademark Office, 1999—; lectr., spkr. in field. Author: (with others, treatise) Milgrim on Trade Secrets, 1986; contbr. articles to publs. Root-Tilden scholar NYU Law Sch., 1964-67. Mem. ABA (intellectual property sect., com. chmn.), Internat. Trademark Assn. (bd. dirs., com. chmn.), Am. Intellectual Property Law Assn. (bd. dirs., com. chmn.), Licensing Execs. Soc., N.Y. Athletic Club, Harvard Club (Washington), Nat. Press Club, Cosmos Club. Presbyterian. Office: Finnegan Henderson Farabow Garrett & Dunner LLP 1300 I St NW Ste 700 Washington DC 20005-3314 E-mail: gbprice@finnegan.com.

PRICE, GRIFFITH BALEY, mathematician, educator; b. Brookhaven, Miss., Mar. 14, 1905; s. Walter Edwin and Lucy (Baley) P.; m. Cora Lee Beers, June 18, 1940; children: Cora Lee, Griffith Baley, Lucy Jean, Edwina Clare, Sallie Diane and Doris Joanne (twins). BA, Miss. Coll., 1925; MA, Harvard U., 1928, PhD, 1932; LLD (hon.), Miss. Coll., 1962. Instr. math. Union Coll., Schenectady, N.Y., 1932-33, U. Rochester, 1933-36, Brown U., Providence, 1936-37; asst. prof., assoc. prof., then prof. math. U. Kans., Lawrence, 1937-75, prof. emeritus, 1975—, chmn. dept. math., 1951-70. Exec. sec. Conf. Bd. Math. Scis., Washington, 1960-62. Author: Linear Equations and Matrices (with others), 1966, Sets, Functions, and Probability (with others), 1968, History of Department of Mathematics of University of Kansas, 1976, Multivariable Analysis, 1984, An Introduction to Multicomplex Spaces and Functions, 1991; contbr. articles to rsch. jours. Civil. ops. analyst USAAF, 1943-45, Eng. Mem. AAAS, Am. Math. Soc. (editor 1950-57), Math. Assn. Am. (pres. 1957-58, award Disting. Svc. 1970), N.Y. Acad. Scis., Cosmos Club, Sigma Xi. Achievements include pioneering development of operations research. E-mail: gbprice@ku.edu.

PRICE, HARRIETT KINLOCH, community volunteer, writer; b. Springfield, Mo., Dec. 31, 1922; d. Arthur Earl and Nellie Mae (Watson) Kinloch; m. Douglas Corbelt Heimburger, Sept. 2, 1942 (dec. Sept. 1951); m. Richard Harvey Price, Sept. 2, 1953; children: Dick Jr., Robert B., Cynthia H., James C., Bruce H. BA, U. Dayton, 1946. Braille writer Braille Assn., Wichita, Kans., 1961-62; pres. of bd. Youthville, Newton, 1975-76. Author: From Dreams to Reality, 1981, Yavapai Language and Coloring, 1985, Dr. Oscar Fryer: A Drury Treasure, 1995. Co-hostess for Mrs. Boris Yeltsin, 1992. Named Trustee of Yr. U. Meth. Ch., 1976; recipient Workhorse award The Kans. Americard, 1974, Kans. Brotherhood award Nat. Conf. of Christian and Jews, 1976. Home: 78 Via Verde St Wichita KS 67230-1604

PRICE, HARRY MACKEY, dentist; b. Harvey, Ill., Mar. 14, 1927; s. Charles Bradlaugh and Ethyl (Mackey) P.; m. Artis Jane Litte, Nov. 28, 1958; 1 child, Kathryn Elizabeth. BDS, DDS, U. Ill., Chgo., 1954. Instr. water skiing Paw Paw Lake Ski Sch., Coloma, Mich., 1941-43; pvt. practice dentistry Northbrook, Ill., 1954-98; tchr. crown and bridge U. Ill., Chgo., 1984-56; instr. ski clinics Chgo. Boat Show Inc., 1960-98, O'Hare Midwest Show, Chgo., 1960-98; owner, prodr. TV Diamond Prodns., Libertyville, Ill., 1960-2001; owner boat sales Diamond Lake Marine, DeLeon Springs, Fla., 1960-2001; cons. sale of dental practices Northbrook, 1998—. Performer, diver Adolph Kieter Aquacades, 1947-64; hydroponic adv. MidWest Hydrophonics, Gurnee, Ill., 1964-67; tech. advisor Nat. Safety Coun. Movies, Washington, 1970-72. Co-author: Water Skiing with Champions, 1969; prodr. Wet and Wild Waterskiing, 1985, How to Barefoot Ski, Creating Miniatures, 1987. Speaker water skiing, Lions Clubs, Chgo. area, 1950-99; speaker water skiing Boy and Girl Scouts Am., Chgo. area, 1950-99, instr. ski clinics, 1960-98; adv. bd. Lamb's Retarded Facility, Libertyville, 1960-65, founder water ski shows, 1965-99; vol. Water Ski Ednl. Found., Winter Haven, Fla., 1983—. With USN, 1944-46. Recipient 35 nat. titles U.S.A. Water Ski, 1959-2001, 3 world titles, Fla., 1985; named 1st in all age groups U.S. Water Ski, Bakersfield, Calif., 1998-99. Mem. Diamond Lake Ski Club (hon. pres. 1959—), Am. Water Ski Ednl. Found. (benefactor, chmn. video 1983—), U.S.A. Trix (bd. dirs.), Ill. Dental Soc. (life), U.S. Water Ski Assn., Am. Water Ski Edn. Found. (Nat. award of Distinction 1992). Methodist. Avocations: water skiing, aerobatics, racquetball, tower diving. Home and Office: Diamond Prodns 1660 Blackwelder Rd De Leon Springs FL 32130

PRICE, HARVEY RAYMOND, safety, environmental health services administrator; b. Ochsenfurt, Germany, Apr. 27, 1947; s. Randall Dean and Annemarie (Biesecke) P.; m. Elizabeth Ann Panoske, May 29, 1974; 1 child, Joseph Raymond Dean. AAS, Cen. Tex. Coll., 1979; BS, U. Ctrl. Tex., 1981; MA, Webster U., 1991; MS, Regis U., 1995. Cert. protection officer; cert. fraud examiner, cert. healthcare protection adminstr., healthcare risk mgr. Enlisted USMC, 1966; transfered to U.S. Army, 1969; investigative supr., spl. agt. Criminal Investigative Divsn., 1979-82, spl. agt. supr., 1982-86, dir. exec. protection Europe, Mid. East, Africa, 1986-89, spl. agt. in charge, 1989-91, retired, 1991-94; dir. safety and risk mgmt. Regional West Med. Ctr., Scottsbluff, Nebr., 1991-94; environ. care cons. St. Joseph Hosp., Denver, 1994—. Chmn. safety com., hazardous materials com., disaster com. Regional West Med. Ctr., 1991-94. Active Local Emergency Planning Commn., Scottsbluff, 1991, Hazardous Waste Planning Commn., Scottsbluff, 1991. Decorated Bronze Star with two bronze oak leaf clusters, Air medal with three bronze oak leaf clusters, 1970-72; Airborne badge (Germany); Cross of Gallantry (Vietnam). Mem. Internat. Assn. Healthcare Safety and Security, Assn. Cert. Fraud Examiners, Am. Soc. Indsl. Security, Am. Soc. Healthcare Risk Mgrs., Retired Officers Assn., Masons, Shriners, Alpha Phi Sigma. Episcopalian. Avocations: swimming, skiing, hiking, reading. Office: Hosp Shared Svcs 1395 S Platte River Dr Denver CO 80223-3467

PRICE, HENRY ESCOE, broadcast executive; b. Jackson, Miss., Oct. 13, 1947; s. Henry E. Price Sr. and Alma Kate (Merrill) Noto; m. Maria Diane Harper, Apr. 8, 1972; children: Henry E. III, Norman Harper. BS in Radio, TV, Film, Journalism, U. So. Miss., 1972. Announcer, news dir. Sta. WROA Radio, Gulfport, Miss., 1967-69; comml. producer Sta. WJTV-TV, Jackson, 1969-73; prodn. mgr. Sta. WAAY-TV, Huntsville, Ala., 1973-77, Sta. WPEC-TV, West Palm Beach, Fla., 1977-79; dir. promotion Sta. WPTV-TV, Palm Beach, 1979-81; TV cons. Frank Magid Assoc., Marion, Iowa, 1981-83; dir. advt. and promotion Sta. WJLA-TV, Washington, 1983-84; v.p., dir. programming Sta. WUSA-TV, Gannett TV, 1984-88; pres., gen. mgr. Sta. WFMY-TV, Gannett TV, Greensboro, N.C., 1988-91, Sta. KARE-TV, Mpls., 1991-96; v.p., gen. mgr. Sta. WBBM-TV, CBS TV Stas., Chgo., 1996—. Pres. Carolina News Network, 1988-91; adj. faculty media mgmt. Ctr. Northwestern U., 2000—. Vice chair, bd. dirs. The Courage Ctr., Mpls.; regional dir. Nat. Conf.; mem. exec. com., bd. dirs. The Minn. Orch.; Pacesetter program chair Mpls. United Way Campaign; active Twin Cities Dunkers, Twin Cities Comm. Coun., 11 Who Care. Mem. Chgo. C. of C. (bd. dirs.), Ill. Broadcasters Assn. (bd. dirs.). Avocations: furniture design and constrn., reading, walking, bicycle riding. Home: PO Box 11847 Winston Salem NC 27116-1847 Office: Sta WBBM-TV CBS Television 630 N Mcclurg Ct Chicago IL 60611-4495

PRICE, HUMPHREY WALLACE, aerospace engineer; b. San Antonio, Sept. 25, 1954; s. Humphrey Rodes and Ruth (Wallace) P. BS in Engring., U. Tex., 1976, MS in Engring., 1978. Rsch. asst. nuclear reactor lab. U. Tex., Austin, 1976; nuclear engr. EDS Nuclear, Inc., San Francisco, 1977-78; engr. Jet Propulsion Lab., Pasadena, 1978-82; rsch. engr. SW Rsch. Inst., San Antonio, 1982-84; tech. group leader Jet Propulsion Lab., Pasadena, Calif., 1984-89; configuration engr. Cassini spacecraft NASA, 1989-93; system engr. Pluto Spacecraft, 1994-97; sys. engr. Mars Sample Return Mission, 1998-2000; mgr. Solar Sail Tech. Devel., 2000—. Cons. Am. Rocket Co., Camarillo, Calif., 1986-87; mem. tech. staff World Space Found., Pasadena, 1980-97. Patentee in field; contbr. to tech. papers in field. Mem. AIAA (sr.). Avocations: wind surfing, skiing, scuba diving. Office: HW Price Cons PO Box 454 La Canada Flintridge CA 91012-0454 E-mail: hoppyprice@netscape.net.

PRICE, JACK C. association administrator; Student, Weber State Coll. Various positions to dep. dir. distbn. Ogden Air Logistics Ctr., Hill AFB, Utah, 1953—88, ret., 1988; various positions to nat. pres., chmn. bd. Air Force Assn.; sustaining life mem., trustee Aerospace Edn. Foun., 1984—, v.p., 1994—96, pres., 1998—, chmn. bd., 2000—. Nat. dir., chmn. Air Force Assn. 50th Anniversary of Air Force Steering Com.; chmn. futures planning com. Aerospace Edn. Found.; aerospace industry cons. on solid rocket motor systems. With USAF, Korea. Office: c/o Aerospace Edn Found 1501 Lee Hwy Arlington VA 22209-1198*

PRICE, JAMES GORDON, physician, educator; b. Brush, Colo., June 20, 1926; s. John Hoover and Rachel Laurette (Dodds) Price; m. Janet Alice McSween, June 19, 1949; children: James Gordon II, Richard Christian, Mary Laurette, Janet Lynn. BA, U. Colo., 1948, MD, 1951. Diplomate charter Am. Bd. Family Practice . Intern Denver Gen. Hosp., 1951—52; practice medicine specializing in family medicine Brush, 1952—78; prof. family practice U. Kans. Med. Ctr., 1978—93; chmn. dept. U. Kans. Med. Center, 1982—90, exec. dean, 1990—93, prof. emeritus in family practice, 1993—. Dir., pres. Am. Bd. Family Practice , 1979; mem. Inst. Medicine of NAS, 1973—. Med. editor: Gen. Learning Corp., 1973—92, mem. editl. bd.: Med. World News, 1969—79; editor: Am. Acad. Family Physician Home Study Self Assessment Program, 1978—83; columnist: Your Family Physician, 1973—90. Trustee Family Health Found. Am., 1970—82; vol. physician St. Jude's Hosp., St. Lucia, West Indies, 1998—99. With USNR, 1943—46. Fellow: Am. Acad. Family Physicians (charter, pres. 1973); mem.: Alpha Omega Alpha, Phi Beta Kappa. Home: 12205 Mohawk Rd Shawnee Mission KS 66209-2137

PRICE, JAMES EDWARD, industrial engineer; b. St. Louis, Feb. 14, 1946; s. Robert Eugene and Cleo Burnice (Boldwyn) P.; m. Helen Rita Huff, Sept. 16, 1972 (div. Mar. 1995); children: Gregory Scott, Elizabeth Ann, Chrystal Dawn Price Fritz; m. Kim Leigh Koenig, Aug. 1997. Student, S.W. Mo. State U., 1966-67, Western Ky. U., 1968-69. Staff engr. Haywood divsn. Genesco, Nashville, 1967-71; dir. tng. Imperial Reading Corp., Lynchburg, Va., 1971-72; supt. premium divsn. King Louie Internat., Kansas City, Mo., 1972-75; pres. MER Cons., Louisville, 1975-79; gen. mgr. outer wear divsn. Londontown Corp., Eidersburg, Md., 1979-84; dir. engring. bike divsn. Colgate, Knoxville, Tenn., 1984-85; pres. Price & Assocs., Houston, 1985—. Adv. bd. Knoxville Bus. Coll., 1994-95. Patentee in field. Pres. Sevierville (Tenn.) br. Ch. of LDS, 1981-91, Gamaliel Area JayCees, 1970, Louisville Businessmen Assn., 1979; nat. bd. dirs., nat. chmn. bd., CEO Newborns in Need, 1999-2001. Named Hon. State Senator, Ky., 1971. Republican. Avocations: golf, tennis, singing. E-mail: paiinc@juno.com.

PRICE, JAMES TUCKER, lawyer; b. Springfield, Mo., June 22, 1955; s. Billy L. and Jeanne Adele Price; m. Francine Beth Warkow, June 8, 1980; children: Rachel Leah, Ashley Elizabeth. BJ, U. Mo., 1977; JD, Harvard U., 1980. Bar: Mo. 1980. Assoc. firm Spencer Fane Britt & Browne, Kansas City, 1980-86; ptnr. Spencer Fane Britt & Browne LLP, 1987—, chair environ. practice group, 1994—, mem. exec. com., 1997—. Mem. Brownfields Commn., Kansas City, 1999—; mem. steering com. Kansas City Bi-State Brownfields Initiative, 1997—. Contbr. to monographs, other legal publs. Mem. ABA (coun. sect. environ, energy and resources 1992-95, vice chmn. solid and hazardous waste com. 1985-90, chmn. 1990-92, chmn. brownfields task force 1995-97, vice chmn. environ. transactions and brownfield com. 1998-2000), Mo. Bar Assn., Kansas City Met. Bar Assn. (chmn. environ. law com. 1985-86), Greater Kansas City C. of C. (co-chair Brownfields Working Group, 1996-98, chmn. energy and environ. com. 1987-89). Office: Spencer Fane Britt & Browne LLP 1000 Walnut St Ste 1400 Kansas City MO 64106-2140 E-mail: jprice@spencerfane.com.

PRICE, JOE (JOE ALLEN), artist, former educator; b. Ferriday, La., Feb. 6, 1935; s. Edward Neill and Margaret (Hester) P. BS, Northwestern U., 1957; postgrad., Art Ctr. Coll., L.A., 1967-68; MA, Stanford U., 1970. Free-lance actor, artist, N.Y.C., 1957-60. Freelance illustrator, actor, L.A., 1960-68; freelance comml. artist, San Carlos, Calif., 1968-69; package designer Container Corp. Am., Santa Clara, Calif., 1969; prof. studio art and filmmaking, chmn. dept. art Coll. San Mateo, Calif., 1970-94. One-man shows include Richard Sumner Gallery, Palo Alto, Calif., 1975, San Mateo County Cultural Ctr., 1976, 82, Tahir Galleries, New Orleans, 1977, 82, Kerwin Galleries, Burlingame, Calif., 1977, Edits. Gallery, Melbourne, Australia, 1977, Ankrum Gallery, Los Angeles, 1978, 84, Edits. Ltd. West Gallery, San Francisco, 1981, Miriam Perlman Gallery, Chgo., 1982, San Mateo County Arts Council Gallery, 1982, Candy Stick Gallery, Ferndale, Calif., 1984, Assoc. Am. Artists, N.Y.C. and Phila., 1984, Gallery 30, Burlingame, 1991, San Mateo, 1984, Triton Mus. Art, Santa Clara, Calif., 1986, Huntsville (Ala.) Mus. Art, 1987, Gallery 30, San Mateo, 1988-97, Concept Art Gallery, Pitts., 1991, Eleonore Austerer Gallery, San Francisco, 1995, Vault Gallery, Sonora, 1995; exhibited in groups shows at Berkeley Art Ctr., Calif., 1976, Burlingame Civic Art Gallery, 1976, Syntex Gallery, Palo Alto, Calif., 1977, Gump's Gallery, San Francisco, 1976, 77, Nat. Gallery of Australia, 1978, Sonoma County Gallery, 1979, Gov. Dummer Acad. Art, Byfield, Mass., 1979, Miss. Mus. Art, 1982, C.A.A. Galleries, Chautauqua, N.Y., 1982, Huntsville Mus. Art, 1983, Tahir Gallery, New Orleans, 1983, Hunterdon Art Ctr., N.J., 1984, Editions Galleries, Melbourne, Australia, 1988, Van Stratten Gallery, Chgo., 1988, 6th Internat. Exhbn., Carnegie-Mellon U., Pa., 1988, Forum Gallery, Jamestown, N.Y., 1988, 5th Internat. Biennale Petite Format de Papier, Belgium, 1989, 4th Internat. Biennial Print Exhibit, Taipei Fine Arts Mus., People's Republic China, 1990, Interprint, Lviv '90, USSR, 1990, New Orleans Mus. Art, 1990, Internat. Print Triennale, Cracow, Poland, 1991, 15th Ann. Nat. Invitational Drawing Exhbn. Emporia State U., Kans., 1991, Haggar U. Gallery, U. Dallas, 1991, Directions in Bay Area Printmaking: Three Decades Palo Alto Cultural Ctr., 1992, Am. Prints: Last Half 20th Century, Jane Haslem Gallery, Washington, 1992, Wenniger Graphics, Boston, 1993, Eleonore Austerer Gallery, San Francisco, 1994, Triton Mus. Art, Santa Clara, 1994, Mobile Mus. Art, 1995, Huntsville (Ala.) Mus. Art, 1995, J.J. Brookings Gallery, San Francisco, 1996, 1997, Grisham Cornell Gallery, Decatur, Ala., 1996, St. Francis Festival of the Arts Invitational, San Francisco, 1996, The Vault Gallery, Sonora, 1997, 98, Heritage Bank Gallery, San Jose, 1998, Arches Paper "Printed on Paper" Competition (touring, 1st pl. winner), 1998, Kautz Internat. Vineyards Nat. Art Exhibition, Murphys CA, 1998, Audubon Artists 56th Ann. Exhibition, N.Y.C., 1998; represented in permanent collections San Francisco Mus. Modern Art, Achenbach Found. Graphic Arts, San Francisco, Phila. Mus. Art, New Orleans Mus. Art, Portland Mus. Art, Maine, The Libr. of Congress, Washington. Huntsville Mus. Art, Midwest Mus. Am. Art, Ind., Cracow Nat. Mus., Poland, Cabo Frio Mus., Brazil, Nat. Mus. Am. Art, Smithsonian Inst., Washington, actor: (movies) The Princess Diaries, 2000, Wicked, Hudson Theatre Mainstage, Los Angeles, 2001, Borderlands, 2002, The Clinic, 2002; co-star: (TV series) Frasier, 2000—; guest star (Chinese TV show) NY Blues, 2002. Recipient Kempshall Clark award Peoria Art Guild, 1981, Paul Lindsay Sample Meml. award 25th Chautauqua Nat. Exhbn. of Am. Art, 1982, 1st Ann. Creative Achievement award Calif. State Legislature/Arts Coun. San Mateo County, 1989. Mem. Am. Color Print Soc., Audubon Artists (Louis Lozowick Meml. award 1978, Silver medal of honor award 1991), Boston Printmakers (Ture Bengtz Meml. award 1987), Calif. Soc. Printmakers (mem. council 1979-81), Los Angeles Printmaking Soc., Phila. Print Club (Lessing J. Rosenwald prize 1979), Arts Council of San Mateo County, Ctrl. Sierra Arts Coun., Theta Chi. Democrat. Office: 6221 Cartwright Ave North Hollywood CA 91606-3801 E-mail: joeaprice@earthlink.net. *Personal philosophy: In being an artist, I do not wish to be just a "recorder" of my time, what I see, what I think. To me, the joy of art is in expressing the love of being an artist, for in loving without shame, without fear, and without doubt one transcends to the moment and speaks with integrity. For the rest of my life I wish to reflect on what life is, and to have the courage to create that which touches not only men's eyes, but their hearts and spirits. I seek the profound truth of what it is to be human and the universal truth of what is means to be creative in expressing the love of being.*

PRICE, JOE SEALY, retired law enforcement officer; b. Coleman, Tex., Feb. 27, 1933; s. Joe Collin and Thelma Lou (Boyd) P.; m. Peggy Littlefield LaBuff, June 1954 (div. 1955); 1 child, Roy Earl LaBuff; m. Elizabeth Earldeen Eddins, June 8, 1956; children: Joe Sealy Jr., Michael Raymond, Robert Wayne. Student, Lee Coll., 1982; BS in Law Enforcement Adminstrn., Pacific Western U., 1985; grad., Law Enforcement Mgmt. Inst., 1993. cert. master peace officer Tex. Com. on Law Enforcement Officer Standards Edn. Asst. mgr. Guardian Fin. Corp., Houston, 1954-55; mgr. Installment Credit Corp., 1955-56; dep. constable Montgomery County Constable Office, Splendora, Tex., 1956-58; dep. sheriff Montgomery County Sheriff's Dept., Conroe, 1958-59; chief dep. sheriff Kendall County Sheriff's Dept., Boerne, 1959-60; warrant officer City of Houston Police Dept., 1960-69; dep. sheriff Harris County Sheriff's Dept., Houston, 1969-73; patrolman Galena Park (Tex.) Police Dept., 1973-74, detective sgt. criminal investigation divsn., 1975-85, chief detectives, 1985-89, sgt., shift comdr. patrol divsn., 1989-90, detective sgt. criminal investigation divsn., 1990-94, lt. criminal investigation divsn., 1994-96, lt. patrol divsn., 1996-97; ret., 1997. Mem. swine auction com. Houston Livestock Show and Rodeo, 1987; bd. dirs. Trinity Valley Trailriders for Boys Harbor, Houston, 1986-87. Served with USN, 1950-53. Named Detective of the Yr., 100 Club, 1981. Mem. Galena Park Police Assn. (pres. 1975-85), Tex. Mcpl. Police Assn. (v.p. 1981, bd. dirs. 1975-87), Harris County Organized Crime Unit, Metro Crime Coun., Combined Law Enforcement Assn. of Tex. (bd. dirs. 1986-93), Masons (32 degree), Shriners, Arabian Knights. Avocations: horseback riding, hunting, fishing, table tennis, sports. Home: 1909 Fm 1942 Rd Crosby TX 77532-6348 Office: Galena Park Police Dept 2000 Clinton Dr PO Box 46 Galena Park TX 77547-0046 E-mail: jspricesr@juno.com.

PRICE, JOHN ALEY, lawyer; b. Maryville, Mo., Oct. 7, 1947; s. Donald Leroy and Julia Catherine (Aley) P.; m. Deborah Diadra Gunter, Aug. 12, 1995; children: Theodore John, Joseph Andrew. BS, N.W. Mo. State U., 1969; JD, U. Kans., 1972. Bar: Kans. 1972, U.S. Dist. Ct. Kans. 1972, U.S. Ct. Appeals (10th cir.) 1972, Tex. 1984, U.S. Ct. Appeals (5th cir.) 1984, U.S. Supreme Ct. 1987; cert. civil trial law Tex. Bd. Legal Specialization. Law clk. U.S. Dist. Ct. Kans., Wichita, 1972-74; from assoc. to ptnr. Weeks, Thomas and Lysaught, Kansas City, Kans., 1974-82; ptnr. Winstead, Sechrest & Minick, Dallas, 1982-96, litigation sect. coord., 1990-92, intellectual property sect. litigation coord., 1993-95; gen. counsel Travelhost Inc., 1996—, Club Co., Inc., 1999-2001. Pres. Umansys, Inc., Dallas, 2000—; spl. prosecutor Leavenworth County Office Dist. Atty., 1970-71, Sedgwick County Office Dist. Atty., Wichita, Kans., 1971-72. Author: Our Boundless Self (A Call to Awake), 1992, A Gathering of Light: Eternal Wisdom for a Time of Transformation, 1993; co-author: Soular Reunion: Journey to the Beloved, 1998; editor (mag.) Academic Analyst, 1968-69; assoc. editor U. Kans. Law Rev., 1971-72, Dallas Bus. Jour.; contbr. articles to profl. jours. Co-dir. Douglas County Legal Aid Soc., Lawrence, Kans., 1971-72; co-pres. Northwood Hills PTA, Dallas, 1984, Westwood Jr. H.S. PTA, 1989-90; founder New Frontiers Found., 1993; co-founder Wings of Spirit Found., 1994, dir., v.p. 1994—. Mem. ABA, Kans. Bar Assn. (mem. task force for penal reform; Pres.'s Outstanding Svc. award 1981), Tex. Bar Assn., Pro Bono Coll., State Bar Tex., World Bus. Acad., Inst. Noetic Scis., UN Assn. (human rights com. Dallas chpt. 1991-93, bd. dirs. 1991-93), Campaign for the Earth (chpt. coord. Global Report 1991-92, coord. govt. and polit. area 1991-92), Blue Key, Order of Coif, Phi Delta Phi, Sigma Tau Gamma (v.p. 1968-69). Mem. Unity Ch. Office: Travelhost Inc 10701 N Stemmons Fwy Dallas TX 75220-2419 E-mail: japrice@travelhost.com. *We create our reality every moment of existence. Our limitations are those we choose to accept.*

PRICE, J(OHN) DOUGLAS, human services administrator; b. Waynesboro, Pa., Sept. 5, 1952; s. John C. Price and Lois P. Fetters; m. Lois G. Myslinski, June 6, 1973 (div. June 1978) children: Mark Price, Sean Price; m. Lydia V. Wittman, Apr. 29, 2000; 1 child, Amanda Wittman. BA, U. Pa., 1974; MSW, Temple U., 1976. Lic. social worker, Pa. Br. office dir. Luth. Family and Social Svc. of Nebr., Ogallala, 1976-78; program dir., Area Agy. on Aging Northeastern Colo. Assn. Local Govts., Ft. Morgan, 1978-81, exec. dir., 1981-86; cmty. devel. grants officer County of Adams, Brighton, Colo., 1986-88, dir. cmty. outreach, 1988-90, dir. social svcs., 1990-95; human svcs. adminstr. County of Franklin, Chambersburg, Pa., 1995—. Mem. Healthy Cmtys. Partnersihp Greater Franklin County, Chambersburg, 1995—, Franklin County CareerLink, 1999—. Bd. dirs. Diakon Luth. Social Ministries, Topton, Pa., 2001—. Named one of Outstanding Young Men of Am., Nat. Jr. C. of C., 1982; recipient Pres.'s award, Pa. Assn. County Human Svcs. Adminstrs., 2002. Mem. NASW, Nat. Assn. County Human Svcs. Adminstrs. (bd. dirs. 2000-01, treas. 2002), Nat. Network Social Work Mgrs., Am. Pub. Human Svcs. Assn. (bd. dirs. local coun. 2001-02), Pa. Assn. County Human Svcs. Adminstrs. (pres. 1999-2001), Rotary Internat. (club pres. 1994-95, Paul Harris fellow 1997). Lutheran. Avocations: performing arts, travel, cycling, golf.

PRICE, JOHN EDWARD, religion educator; b. Chgo., Mar. 7, 1942; s. Edward Price and Carolyn Maxine Polachek; m. Julia Valeriyevna Shvartser; children: Larissa Marie, James Thomas, Elizabeth Suzanne, Victoria Ivana. BA, Univ. of St. Mary of the Lake, 1964, STB, 1966, STL, 1968. Lic. dir. religious edn. Tchr. Mother of God Sch., Waukegan, Ill., 1968-69; tchr., chmn. religion dept. Holy Trinity High Sch., Chgo., 1969-70; coord. religious edn. Transfiguration Ch., Wauconda, Ill., 1970-75; dir. religious edn. St. Athanasius Ch., Evanston, 1975-91, Ch. of St. Mary, Lake Forest, 1991—. Catechist resource person Archdiocesan Office of Religious Edn., Chgo., 1977-80; field supr. Mundelein Coll. and Inst. Pastoral Studies, Chgo., 1979-80, 84; team mem. North Ctrl. Evaluation, Chgo., 1984; presenter, lectr. Archdiocese of Chgo., 1979, 80, 84, 85, mem. Dir. Religious Edn. Cert. Commn., 1997—. Author: (filmstrip) Learning Right and Wrong, 1978, (testing svc.) Religious Education Diagnostic Survey, 1983; contbr. articles to religious publs. Del. Ill. White House Conf. on Librs. and Info. Svcs., Springfield, 1978. Mem. Cath. Theol. Soc. Am., Religious Edn. Assn., Nat. Assn. Parish Coords. and Dirs., Chgo. Assn. Religious Educators (treas. 1979-82, Care award 1983). Avocations: religious art, fishing, scuba diving, bicycling, poetry. Home: 737 E Glendale Rd Libertyville IL 60048-3329 Office: St Mary's Religious Edn Ctr 185 E Illinois Rd Lake Forest IL 60045-1915 E-mail: dre@restmary.com.

PRICE, JOHN RANDOLPH, writer; b. Alice, Tex., Feb. 12, 1932; s. John Randolph and Eva Mae (Boney) P.; m. Janis Bryant Price, June 20, 1953; children: Susan Lynn, Leslie Anne. BS, U. Houston, 1957; PhD (hon.) , Emerson Inst., 2001. Dir. advt. Gates Radio Corp., Quincy, Ill., 1957-62; v.p. Sander Rodkin, Ltd., Chgo., 1962-64; exec. v.p. Stewart, Price, Tomlin, Inc., 1964-67; v.p. Goodwin, Dannenbaum, Littman & Wingfield, Inc., Houston, 1967-70; pres. O'Neill, Price, Anderson, Fouchard, Inc., 1970-74, John Price & Co., Houston, 1974-79, Arnan, Inc., Austin, 1979-81; chmn. bd. The Quartus Found. Inc., Boerne, Tex., 1981—. Author: The Superbeings, 1981, The Manifestation Process, 1983, The Planetary Commission, 1984, Practical Spirituality, 1985, With Wings as Eagles, 1987, The Abundance Book, 1987, Prayer, Principles & Power, 1987, A Spiritual Philosophy for the New World, 1990, Empowerment, 1992, The Angels Within Us, 1993, Angel Energy, 1995,

Living a Life of Joy, 1997, The Success Book, 1998, The Wellness Book, 1998, The Meditation Book, 1998, The Love Book, 1998, The Jesus Code, 2000, The Alchemist's Handbook, 2000, Removing the Masks That Bind Us, 2001. Staff sgt. USAF, 1952-56. Recipient Joseph S. Cullinan award U. Houston, 1956, Grand Prix Best Consumer Mag. Advt. award, 1970. Mem. Internat. New Thought Alliance (Humanitarian award 1992, Joseph Murphy award 1994). Achievements include organizer of first annual World Peace day on December 31, 1986. Office: The Quartus Found Inc PO Box 1768 Boerne TX 78006-6768

PRICE, JOHN RICHARD, lawyer, law educator; b. Indpls., Nov. 28, 1934; s. Carl Lee and Agnes I. P.; m. Suzanne A. Leslie, June 22, 1963; children: John D., Steven V. BA with high honors, U. Fla., 1958; LL.B. with honors, NYU, 1961. Bar: Calif. 1962, Wash. 1977, U.S. Ct. Appeals (9th cir.), U.S. Dist. Ct. (we. dist.) Wash. Assoc. McCutchen, Doyle, Brown & Enersen, San Francisco, 1961-69; prof. law U. Wash., Seattle, 1969-97, dean, 1982-88; of counsel Perkins Coie, 1976—. Author: Contemporary Estate Planning, 1983, Price on Contemporary Estate Planning, 1992, 2d edit., 2000, Conflicts, Confidentiality and Other Ethical Issues, 2000. Served with U.S. Army, 1953-55 Root-Tilden fellow NYU Sch. Law, 1958-61 Fellow Am. Coll. Trust and Estate Counsel (former regent); mem. ABA, Am. Law Inst., Internat. Acad. of Estate and Trust Law, Order of Coif, Phi Beta Kappa. Congregationalist. Home: 3794 NE 97th St Seattle WA 98115-2564 Office: 1201 3rd Ave Ste 4800 Seattle WA 98101-3029 E-mail: pricj@perkinscole.com.

PRICE, JOHN ROY, JR. financial executive; b. N.Y.C., Dec. 20, 1938; s. John Roy and Pauline Bernice (Milnes) P.; m. Victoria Scott Pohle, Dec. 19, 1970 (div. 1982); 1 child, Matthew Roy; m. Marion Cobb Hardie, Oct. 1, 1988 (div. 1996); m. Svetlana Sergeyeva, July 11, 1999. BA, Grinnell Coll., 1960, Queens Coll., Oxford (Eng.) U., 1962, MA, 1965; JD, Harvard U., 1965. Assoc. Casey, Lane & Mittendorf, N.Y.C., 1965-67; v.p. Bedford-Stuyvesant D & S Corp., 1967-68; spl. asst. to Pres. U.S., Washington, 1969-71; assoc. Donaldson, Lufkin & Jenrette, N.Y.C., 1971-72; v.p. Mfrs. Hanover Trust, 1972-75, Mfrs. Hanover Corp., N.Y.C., 1975-80, sr. v.p. non-bank subs., 1980-83, sr. v.p., sec., 1983-87; mng. dir. Mfrs. Hanover Trust Co., 1987-88, Mfrs. Hanover Securities Corp., 1988-92; mng. dir. govt. affairs Chem. Bank, 1992-96, Chase Manhattan, 1996—. Bd. dirs. Am. Trust for Oxford, 1990-94; chmn. Bklyn. Acad. Music Cmty. Devel. Corp.; dir. Prin. Fin. Group (formerly Bankers Life Co.), Bankers Assn. for Fgn. Trade, 1990-97, pres., 1994-95, Nat. Fgn. Trade Coun., 1991—; pres. Am. for Oxford, 1987-99, chmn., 1999—. Nat. chmn. Ripon Soc., 1967-68; trustee Grinnell Coll., 1970— ; bd. dirs. New Communities Corp., 1976-77; mem. exec. panel Chief of Naval Ops., 1972-79. Rhodes scholar; named Disting. Friend of Oxford, 2000. Mem. Council Fgn. Relations, Phi Beta Kappa. Clubs: Harvard (N.Y.C.). Home: 3144 Granite Rd Woodstock MD 21163-1004

PRICE, JONATHAN G. geologist; b. Danville, Pa., Feb. 1, 1950; s. A. Barney and Flora (Best) P.; m. Elisabeth McKinley, June 3, 1972; children: Alexander D., Argenta M. BA in Geology and German, Lehigh U., 1972; MA, U. Calif., Berkeley, 1975, PhD, 1977. Cert. profl. geologist. Geologist Anaconda Copper Co., Yerington, Nev., 1974-75, U.S. Steel Corp., Salt Lake City, 1977, Corpus Christi, 1978-81; rsch. assoc. Bur. Econ. Geology, U. Tex., Austin, 1981-85, rsch. sci., 1984-88, program dir., 1987-88; dir. Tex. Mining & Mineral Resources Rsch. Inst., 1984-88; dir., state geologist Nev. Bur. Mines & Geology, U. Nev., Reno, 1988-92, 95—. Staff dir. Bd. on Earth Scis. & Resources Nat. Rsch. Coun., Washington, 1993-95; asst. prof. Bucknell U., Lewisburg, 1977-78; chair We. States Seismic Policy coun., 1998-2002. Author, editor: Igneous Geology of Trans-Pecos Texas, 1986. Vol. instr. CPR and first aid ARC, 1983-95, bd. dirs. Sierra Nev. chpt., 1991-92. German Acad. Exch. Svc. fellow U. Heidelberg, 1972-73; recipient Explorer award Am. Geol. Inst., 1995. Fellow Geol. Soc. Am., Soc. Econ. Geologists (nat. pres. 2003); mem. Am. Inst. Profl. Geologists (Nev. sect. pres. 1992, nat. pres. 1997, John T. Galey Sr. Meml. pub. Svc. award 1999), Assn. Am. State Geologists (pres. 2000-01), Mineral. Soc. Am., Phi Beta Kappa. Office: Nev Bur Mines & Geology UNR Ms 178 Reno NV 89557-0088 E-mail: jprice@unr.edu.

PRICE, JOSEPH HUBBARD, lawyer; b. Montgomery, Ala., Jan. 31, 1939; s. Aaron Joseph and Minnie Jule (Reynolds) P.; m. Cynthia Winant Ramsey, Sept. 14, 1963 (div. 1980); children: Victoria Reynolds, Ramsey Winant; m. Courtney McFadden, Apr. 25, 1980. AB, U. Ala., 1961; LLB, Harvard U., 1964; postgrad., London Sch. Econs., 1964-65. Bar: Ala. 1964, D.C. 1968. Law clk. to justice Hugo L. Black U.S. Supreme Ct., Washington, 1967-68; assoc. Leva, Hawes, Symington, Martin & Oppenheimer, 1968-71; v.p. Overseas Pvt. Investment Corp., 1971-73; ptnr. Leva, Hawes, et. al., 1973-83, Gibson, Dunn & Crutcher, Washington, 1983—. Mem. CARE Com. Washington; mem. adv. com. Hugo Black Meml. Libr., Ashland, Ala. Capt. U.S. Army, 1966-67, Vietnam. Decorated Bronze Star; Frank Knox Meml. fellow London Sch. Econs., 1964-65. Mem. ABA, Am. Soc. Internat. Law, Supreme Ct. Hist. Soc., Phi Beta Kappa, Met. Club. Home: 3104 Cathedral Ave NW Washington DC 20008-3419 Office: Gibson Dunn & Crutcher 1050 Connecticut Ave NW Ste 900 Washington DC 20036-5306

PRICE, JOSEPH MICHAEL, lawyer; b. St. Paul, Dec. 2, 1947; s. Leon and Rose (Kaufman) P.; m. Louise Rebecca Braunstein, Dec. 19, 1971; children: Lisa, Laurie, Julie. BA, U. Minn., 1969, JD, 1972. Bar: Minn. 1972, U.S. Dist. Ct. Minn. 1974. Ptnr. Faegre & Benson, Mpls., 1972—. Mem. Minn. Bar Assn., Hennepin County Bar Assn. Home: 4407 Country Club Rd Minneapolis MN 55424-1148 Office: Faegre & Benson 2200 Wells Fargo Ctr 90 S 7th St Ste 2200 Minneapolis MN 55402-3901 E-mail: jprice@faegre.com.

PRICE, KATHLEEN MCCORMICK, book editor, writer; b. Topeka, Dec. 25, 1932; d. Raymond Chesley and Kathleen (Shoffner) McCormick; m. William Faulkner Black, Aug. 25, 1956 (div. 1961); 1 child, Kathleen Serena; m. William Hillard Price, Aug. 13, 1976. BA, U. Colo., Denver, 1971. Book reviewer Denver Post, 1971-78; book editor San Diego Mag., 1978-92. Cons. editor St. John's Cathedral, Denver, 1985-95. Author: There's a Dactyl Under My Foot, 1986, The Lady and the Unicorn, 1994, From Vision to Vestment, 2001. Dir. Colo. Episcopal Vestment Guild. Fellow Phi Beta Kappa; mem. PEN, Denver Women's Press Club, Denver County Club, La Garita Club. Episcopalian. Home: 27 Crestmoor Dr Denver CO 80220-5853

PRICE, LEW PAXTON, writer, engineer, scientist; b. Takoma Park, Md., Dec. 19, 1938; s. Raymond Miller and Clarene Pearl (Morris) P.; m. Sherrie Darlene Sellers, June 25, 1960 (div. Apr. 1979); children: Terilyn Ann, Heather Rae, Crystal Alene. BS, U.S. Air Force Acad., Colorado Springs, Colo., 1960. Hon. Ho-O Ryu Bushido 6th Dan Master. Electronics engr. Pacific Telephone, Sacramento, 1965-66, engrng. coord., bldgs., 1966-85; pres., design engr. Condor Aeroplane Works, Ltd., 1983-85; engrng. coord. Tuttle Engrng. and Constrn. Consultants, El Dorado Hills, Calif., 1989-92; scientist, flute design cons., writer, flutemaker Fair Oaks, Garden Valley, 1977—. Cons. flute design. Author: The Cosmic Stradivarius, 1974, Aquarian Anastasis, 1975, The Music of Life, 1984, Dimensions in Astrology, 1986, Native North American Flutes, 1990, Secrets of the Flute (Math, Physics & Design), 1991, Creating & Using the Native American Love Flute, 1994, Creating & Using Grandfather's Flute, 1995, The Oldest Magic (Prehistory & Influence of Music), 1995, Creating & Using Older Native American Flutes, 1995, Creating & Using Smaller Native American Flutes, 1995, Creating & Using the Native American Concert Flute, 1996, More Secrets of the Flute, 1997, Creating and Using Larger Native American Flutes, 1998, Creating and Using the Largest Native American Flutes, 1998, Creating and Using Very Small Native American Flutes, 1998, Behind Light's Illusion (7 book series), 1999, 2000, 2001; author, programmer: (computer program) Flute Design (Native American), 1996. Co-advisor Aviation Explorers, archery/space/sci. merit badge instr./examiner, Boy Scouts Am., North Highlands, Calif., 1968-70; panelist United Crusade, Sacramento, Calif., 1971; rifle/pistol/shotgun safety instr. NRA, Fair Oaks, Calif., 1970-72. Capt. USAF, 1960-65. Mem. No. Calif. Flute Circle (co-organizer 1996), Oreg. Native Am. Flute Circle (hon.). Avocations: flying, singing, flute playing, hiking, archery. Home and Office: PO Box 88 Garden Valley CA 95633-0088

PRICE, LIA SCOTT, writer; BA in Journalism, U. Calif., Santa Cruz, 1990. Writer Norris Theater, L.A., 2002—; prodr. Tritan-Northstar Entertainment, Hollywood, Calif., 2000—; screenwriter Act Full Time Hollywood, 2000—; author Pumpkin Pub., L.A., 1997—. Author: (novels) Ghostwriter, 2002, The Frog Asylum, 2001, (short stories) Without Wings, 2001, (novels) The Guardian, 2000; co-author: (book) Body and Blood, 1997; contbr. short story Without Wings. Office: Pumpkin Pub PMB 335/POB 7000 Rolling Hills Estates CA 90274 Business E-Mail: princesslia@hotmail.com.

PRICE, LINDA RICE, community development administrator; b. Norman, Okla., Sept. 17, 1948; d. Elroy Leon and Esther May (Wilson) Rice; m. Michael Allen Price, May 17, 1970 (div. June 1998); children: Justin R, Mathew Lyon, David F. BA in Am. History, U. Okla., 1970, M. Regional and City Planning, 1975. Dir. U. Okla. Crisis Ctr., Norman, 1969-70; cardiopulmonary technician Bethany Med. Ctr., Kansas City, Kans., 1970-72; mgr. congressional campaign Barsotti for Congress, 1972; planning intern City of Seminole (Okla.), 1973-74, City of Tecumseh (Okla.), 1974-75; planner I City of Norman, 1975-76, planner II, 1975-80, community devel. coord., 1980-96, revitalization mgr., 1996—. Adj. prof. U. Okla., Norman, 1986-93; cons. in field, Norman, 1980—. Past pres., mem. LWV Norman, 1979—; chmn. Norman Arts & Humanities Coun., 1983—86; v.p. Oakhurst Neighborhood Assn., 1991—94; bd. dirs. Women's Resource Ctr., 1991—92; mem., past pres. bd. Thunderbird Clubhouse, 1992—95; bd. dirs. Ind. Living Svcs. for Youth, pres., 2001—02; gov.'s appt. Rural Housing Incentive Study Task Force, 2000. Named to Leadership Norman, Norman C. of C., 1992, for Exemplary Mgmt. Practice, The Urban Inst., 1989, for Outstanding Performance, HUD, 1988; recipient Citation of Merit, Okla. State Hist. Preservation, 1991, Spl. Recognition, Okla. Hist. Soc., 1991, John J. Gunther Blue Ribbon Practices in Cmty. Devel. award, 1997; Best of the Best Practice award HUD, 1999, 2 Best Practice awards, 1999, Okla. Best Practice award, 2000; named to Okla. Mcpl. League Honor Roll of Svc., 2001. Mem. Am. Inst. Cert. Planners (cert.), Am. Planning Assn. (sec. Okla. chpt. 1980-82), Planning and Women (regional coord. 1987-90), Assn. Cen. Okla. Govt. (areawide planning and tech. adv. com. 1979—), Nat. Cmty. Devel. Assn., (bd. dirs. 1998-99, state whip 1988-97, chair nat. membership 1994-96), Homeless Here Coalition, Social Svcs. Coordinating Coun. Democrat. Presbyterian. Avocations: softball, travel, music, reading, political activities. E-mail: linda.price.ci.norman.ok.us. Office: City of Norman PO Box 370 Norman OK 73070-0370

PRICE, LUCILE BRICKNER BROWN, retired civic worker; b. Decorah, Iowa, May 31, 1902; d. Sidney Eugene and Cora (Drake) Brickner; B.S., Iowa State U., 1925; M.A., Northwestern U., 1940; m. Maynard Wilson Brown, July 2, 1928 (dec. Apr. 1937); m. 2d, Charles Edward Price, Jan. 14, 1961 (dec. Dec. 1983). Asst. dean women Kans. State U., Manhattan, 1925-28; mem. bd. student personnel adminstrn. Northwestern U., 1937-41; personnel research Sears Roebuck & Co., Chgo., 1941-42, overseas club dir. ARC, Eng., Africa, Italy, 1942-45; dir. Child Edn. Found., N.Y.C., 1946-56. Participant 1st and 2d Iowa Humanists Summer Symposiums, 1974, 75. Del. Mid Century White House Conf. on Children and Youth, 1950; mem. com. on program and research of Children's Internat. summer villages, 1952-53; mem. bd. N.E. Iowa Mental Health Ctr., 1959-62, pres. bd., 1960-61; mem. Iowa State Extension Adv. Com., 1973-75; project chmn. Decorah Hist. Dist. (listed Nat. Register Historic Places); trustee Porter House Mus., Decorah, 1966-78, emerita bd. dirs., 1982—; participant N. Cen. Regional Workshop Am. Assn. State and Local History, Mpls., 1975, Midwest Workshop Hist. Preservation and Conservation, Iowa State U., 1976, 77; mem. Winneshiek County (Iowa) Civil Service Commn., 1978-87; rep. Class of 1940 Northwestern U. Sch. Edn. and Social Policy, 1986-88. Recipient Alumni Merit award Iowa State U., 1975, Cert. of Appreciation Iowa State U. Extension, 1988. Mem. Am. Coll. Personnel Assn., (life), ARC Overseas Assn. (life, nat. bd.), AAUW (life, mem. bd. Decorah, Named Gift award 1977), Nat. Assn. Mental Health (del. nat. conf. 1958), Norwegian-Am. Mus. (life, Vesterheim fellow), Internat. Platform Assn., Winneshiek County Hist. Soc. (life, cert. of appreciation 1984), DAR, Luther Coll. Heritage Club (life, pres.'s coun. 1993), Pi Lambda Theta, Chi Omega. Designer, builder house for retirement living. Avocation: remembering WWII. Home: 508 W Broadway St Decorah IA 52101-1704

PRICE, MICHAEL HOWARD, journalist, critic, composer, cartoonist, theatrical operator; b. Amarillo, Tex., Sept. 14, 1947; s. John Andrew and Thelma Adeline (Wilson) P.; m. Christina Renteria, Aug. 31, 1980. BA in Journalism, West Tex. State U., 1970. Edn. writer Amarillo Globe-News, 1968-74, fin. editor, 1974-76, city editor, 1976-77; adminstr. Amarillo Coll., 1977-80; bur. chief Ft. Worth Star-Telegram, 1980-83, features editor, 1983-85, film critic, 1985-98; dir. motion picture programming Sundance Sq. Entertainment Dist., Ft. Worth, 1998—2002; critic-at-large Ft. Worth Bus. Press, 2002—. Cons. journalism West Tex. State U., Canyon, 1977-90, Tex. Tech U., Lubbock, 1982-85; dirs. The Harvey Awards comic-book profls. awards, 1990—; syndicated columnist N.Y. Times News Svc., 1990-98; critic-in-residence Sta. KRLD Newsradio, Dallas-Ft. Worth, 1998—; columnist Fangoria mag., 2002—. Author: (CD-ROMs) A Century of Fantastic Cinema, 1995, Silver Screen Sensations, 1996; (albums) Cognitive Dissonance, 1994, The Last Temptation of Price, 1995, R. Crumb—The Musical, 1995, Swingmasters Revue, 1995, Claus & Effect, 1996, Diddy Wah Diddy, 1997, Big Hoedown Tonight!, 1999, From Hell to Texas, 1999, Arghlebargle, 2001; (books) Forgotten Horrors: The Definitive Edition, 1999, Forgotten Horrors II, 2001, Hollywood and the Piano, 2001, Spawn of Skull Island, 2002, Human Monsters in the Movies, 1994, Krime Duzzin't Pay, 1995, The Guitar in Jazz, 1996, Stitches, 1996, Frights Genuine & Fancied, 1996; (novels) The Prowler, 1989, Carnival of Souls, 1991, Holiday for Screams, 1992, Lon Chaney, Jr.: A Critical Biography, 1997; co-author: The Big Book of Biker Flicks, 2002; screen actor: Ramming Speed, 1997, Southern Fried Homicide, 1998, Beauty & the Beasts, 1998, Vincent Price: A Critical Biography, 1998, It's Christmastime at the Movies, 1998. Creative dir. Tex. Gridiron Show, Fort Worth, 1984-85, 92-93; pres. Ft. Worth Film Festival, Inc., 1997—. Grad. fellow in journalism U. Mo., 1975; inducted into Tex. Tornados Blues Hall of Fame, 1995. Mem. ASCAP, Soc. Profl. Journalists (bd. dirs. 1992-94), Soc. Film Critics. Office: Sundance Sq Mgmt 512 Main St Ste 1500 Fort Worth TX 76102-3922 E-mail: mprice@sundancesquare.com. *People who believe that writing is a glamour gig often ask, "How do you become a writer?" as if in search of some magical formula. The only answer is: "WRITE." For whatever purpose and however large or small a readership: WRITE.*

PRICE, NELSON (JOHN NELSON PRICE), author, journalist; b. Augusta, Ga., May 7, 1957; s. John Paul and Joy Gertrude (Scheck) P. BA in Journalism and Psychology, Ind. U., 1978. City hall reporter Lawrence (Kans.) Journal-World, 1978-79; fed. cts. reporter, social issues writer Fort Wayne (Ind.) Journal-Gazette, 1979-80; edn. writer Indpls. News, 1981-85; columnist, feature writer Indpls. Star-News, 1985—. Bd. dirs. The Sagamore, Indpls. Author: Indiana Legends: Famous Hoosiers from Johnny Appleseed to David Letterman, 1997, Indianapolis: Leading the Way, 2000, Legendary Hoosiers: Famous Folks from the State of Indiana, 2001; contbr. articles to profl. jours. Bd. dirs. Riley Area Revitalization Program, Indpls. Recipient Sagamore of the Wabash award Gov. Ind., 1995, Martin Luther King Jr. award Indpls. Edn. Assn., 1986, Best Sports Writing award Hoosier State Press Assn., 1994, Best Column award, 1994, Best Feature Story award, 1994, Best Personality Profile award, 1994. Mem. Soc. Profl. Journalists (awards), Mental Health Assn. Marion County (awards). Avocations: swimming, theater, travel, Olympic sports. Office: Indianapolis Star-News 307 N Pennsylvania St Indianapolis IN 46204-1899

PRICE, PAUL BUFORD, physicist, educator; b. Memphis, Nov. 8, 1932; s. Paul Buford and Eva (Dupuy) P.; m. JoAnn Margaret Baum, June 28, 1958; children— Paul Buford III, Heather Alynn, Pamela Margaret, Alison Gaynor. BS summa cum laude, Davidson Coll., 1954, DSc, 1973; MS, U. Va., 1956, PhD, 1958. Fulbright scholar U. (Eng.) Bristol, 1958-59; NSF postdoctoral fellow Cambridge (Eng.) U., 1959-60; physicist R&D Ctr., GE, Schenectady, 1960—69; prof. physics U. Calif., Berkeley, 1969—, Miller rsch. prof., 1972—73, chmn. dept. physics, 1987—91, McAdams prof. physics, 1990—92, dean phys. scis., 1992—2001, dir. Space Scis. Lab., 1979—85, prof., 2002—. Vis. com. Bartol Rsch. Inst., 1991-94; adv. bd. Indian Inst. Astrophysics, Bangalore, 1993-95; cons. to lunar sample analysis planning team NASA; space sci. bd. Nat. Acad. Scis.; adj. prof. physics Rensselaer Poly. Inst., 1967-68; vis. prof. Tata Inst. Fundamental Rsch., Bombay, 1965-66, U. Rome, 1983, 92; sci. assoc. Ctr. d'Etude Rsch. Nuclear, 1984; mem. polar rsch. bd. NAS; rschr. in space and astrophycs, nuclear physics; mem. U.S. Ice Core Working Groupo, 2002–. Author: (with others) Nuclear Tracks in Solids; Contbr. (with others) articles to profl. jours. Regional dir. Calif. Alliance for Minority Participation, 1993—. Recipient Disting. Svc. award Am. Nuclear Soc., 1964, Indsl. Rsch. awards, 1964, 65, E.O. Lawrence Meml. award AEC, 1971, medal for exceptional sci. achievement NASA, 1973; Sci. Symposium in honor of 65th birthday, Aug 23-24, 1997; John Simon Guggenheim fellow, 1976-77. Fellow: Am. Geophys. Union, Am. Phys. Soc., Indian Inst. Astrophysics (hon.); mem.: NAS (chmn. geophysics sect. 1981—84, sec. class phys.-math. scis. 1985—88, chmn. 1988—91), Bohemian Club. E-mail: bprice@uclink4.berkeley.edu.

PRICE, PAUL L. lawyer; b. Chgo., Apr. 21, 1945; s. Walter S. and Lillian (Czerepkowski) L.; m. Dianne L. Olech, June 3, 1967; children: Kristen, Kathryn. BBA, Loyola U., Chgo., 1967; JD with honors, Ill. Inst. Tech., 1971. Bar: Ill. 1971, U.S. Dist. Ct. (no. dist.) Ill., U.S. Ct. Appeals (7th cir.). Tax acct. Arthur Anderson & Co., Chgo., 1970—71; assoc. Doyle & Tarpey, 1971—75, Gordon & Assocs., Chgo., 1975—76; from assoc. to ptnr. Pretzel & Stouffer, Chartered, 1976—96; ptnr. Price, Tunney, Reiter, 1996—. With USMC, 1969-70. Fellow: Am. Coll. Trial Lawyers; mem.: ABA, Ill. Inst. Tech.-Chgo. Kent Coll. Law Alumni Assn. (pres. 1989—90), Assn. Def. Trial Attys., Lawyers for Civil Justice (bd. dirs. 1999—2001), Def. Rsch. Inst. (bd. dirs. 1999—2001), Fedn. Def. and Corp. Counsel (pres. 1999—2000), Ill. Assn. Def. Trial Counsel (pres. 1990—91), Soc. Trial Lawyers, Ill. Bar Assn. Roman Catholic. Office: Price Tunney Reiter 200 N Lasalle St Ste 3050 Chicago IL 60601-1014

PRICE, PAUL MARNELL, lawyer; b. Binghamton, N.Y., July 23, 1959; s. Paul B. and Rita E. (Marnell) P.; m. Teresa Lynn Doll, Sept. 26, 1987; children: Kayla Marie, Tyler Marnell. BS in Chemistry-Bus. cum laude, Scranton (Pa.) U., 1981; JD magna cum laude, Syracuse U., 1984. Bar: N.Y. 1985, Pa. 1995. Assoc. Levene, Gouldin & Thompson, Binghamton, 1984-87; mem. Hickey, Sheehan & Gates, P.C., 1987-95; prin. Law Office of Paul M. Price, N.Y., 1995—. Bd. dirs. United Way of Broome County, Inc., Broome County Bar Assn., Mothers and Babies Perinatal Network South Ctrl. N.Y. Inc. Mem. ABA, ATLA, N.Y. State Bar Assn., Broome County Bar Assn. Democrat. Roman Catholic. Avocations: Masters swimming, skiing. Office: Proctor Bldg 25 Main St Binghamton NY 13905-3121 E-mail: pmpesqlaw@aol.com.

PRICE, PETER WILFRID, ecology educator, researcher; b. London, Apr. 17, 1938; arrived in U.S., 1966; BSc with honors, U. Wales, Bangor, 1958-62; MSc, U. New Brunswick, Fredericton, 1964; PhD, Cornell U., 1970. Asst. prof. U. Ill., Urbana, 1971-75, assoc. prof., 1975-79; research ecologist Mus. No. Ariz., Flagstaff, 1979-80; assoc. prof. No. Ariz. U., 1980-85, prof. ecology, 1985-94, Regents' prof., 1994—. Author: Evolutionary Biology of Parasites, 1980, Biological Evolution, 1996, Insect Ecology, 3d edit., 1997; editor: A New Ecology, 1984, Evolutionary Strategies of Parasitic Insects, 1975, Plant-Animal Interactions, 1991, Population Dynamics, 1995, Effects of Resource Distribution on Plant-Animal Interactions, 1992, Macroevolutionary Theory on Macroecological Patterns, 2002. Guggenheim fellow, 1977-78; Fulbright Sr. scholar, 1993-94. Fellow Royal Entomol. Soc. (hon.); mem. NSF (panel mem. 1978-81, 91-93), Ecol. Soc. Am. (bd. editors 1973-76), Brit. Ecol. Soc., Entomol. Soc. Am. (Founders Award, 1993). Office: No Ariz U PO Box 5640 Flagstaff AZ 86011-5640

PRICE, REYNOLDS, novelist, poet, playwright, essayist, educator; b. Macon, N.C., Feb. 1, 1933; s. William Solomon and Elizabeth (Rodwell) P. AB summa cum laude (Angier Duke scholar), Duke, 1955; BLitt (Rhodes scholar), Merton Coll., Oxford U., Eng., 1958; LittD, St. Andrews Presbyn. Coll., 1978, Wake Forest U., 1979, Washington and Lee U., 1991, Davidson Coll., 1992; LittD, Elon Coll., 1996. Mem. faculty English Duke U., 1958—; asst. prof., 1961-68; assoc. prof., 1968-72; prof., 1972-77; James B. Duke prof., 1977—; acting chmn., 1983; writer in residence U. N.C., Chapel Hill, 1965, U. Kans., 1967, 69, 80, U.N.C., Greensboro, 1971; Glasgow prof. Washington and Lee U., 1971; faculty Salzburg Seminar, 1977. Author: A Long and Happy Life, 1962, The Names and Faces of Heroes, 1963, A Generous Man, 1966, Love and Work, 1968, Permanent Errors, 1970, Things Themselves, 1972, The Surface of Earth, 1975, Early Dark, 1977, A Palpable God, 1978, The Source of Light, 1981, Vital Provisions, 1982, Private Contentment, 1984, Kate Vaiden, 1986, The Laws of Ice, 1986, A Common Room, 1987, Good Hearts, 1988, Clear Pictures, 1989, The Tongues of Angels, 1990, The Use of Fire, 1990, New Music, 1990, The Foreseeable Future, 1991, Conversations with Reynolds Price, 1991, Blue Calhoun, 1992, Full Moon, 1993, The Collected Stories, 1993, A Whole New Life, 1994, The Promise of Rest, 1995, Three Gospels, 1996, The Collected Poems, 1997, Roxanna Slade, 1998, Learning a Trade, 1998, Letter to a Man in the Fire, 1999, A Perfect Friend, 2000, Feasting the Heart, 2000, Noble Norfleet, 2002. Recipient William Faulkner Found. award notable 1st novel, 1962, Sir Walter Raleigh award, 1962, 76, 81, 84, 86, award Nat. Assn. Ind. Schs., 1964, Roanoke-Chowan Poetry award, 1982; Guggenheim fellow, 1964-65; fellow Nat. Endowment for Arts, 1967-68, lit. adv. panel, 1973-76, chmn., 1976; recipient Nat. Inst. Arts and Letters award, 1971, Bellamann Found. award, 1972, Lillian Smith award, 1976, N.C. award, 1977, Nat. Book Critics Circle award, 1986, Elmer H. Bobst award, 1988, R. Hunt Parker award N.C. Lit. and Hist. Soc., 1991, Northcarolinana award, 1999. Mem. Am. Acad. Arts and Scis., Am. Acad. Arts and Letters, Phi Beta Kappa, Phi Delta Theta. Home: PO Box 99014 Durham NC 27708-9014 Office: care Harriet Wasserman Lit Agy Inc 137 E 36th St New York NY 10016-3528

PRICE, RICHARD, anthropologist, author; b. N.Y.C., Nov. 30, 1941; s. George Price and Gertrude (Swee) Jaffe; m. Sally Hamlin, 1963; children: Niko, Leah. AB in History and Lit. magna cum laude, Harvard U., 1963, PhD in Social Anthropology, 1970. From lectr. to assoc. prof. anthropology Yale U., New Haven, 1969-74; prof. anthropology Johns Hopkins U., Balt., 1974-87, chmn. dept., 1974-77, 79-85; Marta Sutton Weeks sr. fellow Stanford Humanities Ctr. Stanford (Calif.) U., 1989-90; fellow Shelby Cullom Davis Ctr. for Hist. Studies, Princeton U., 1992; Rockefeller fellow in humanities U. Fla., 1994. Vis. prof. U. Paris, 1985-87, U. Minn., Mpls., 1987-88, Ecole Pratique des Hautes Etudes, Paris, 2002; George I. Miller vis. scholar U. Ill., 1994; Dittman prof. Am. Studies, anthropology and history Coll. William and Mary, 1994—. Author: Maroon Societies, 1973, Saramaka Social Structure, 1975, The Guiana Maroons, 1976, Afro-American Arts of the Suriname Rain Forest, 1980, First-Time: the Historical Vision of an Afro-American People, 1983, To Slay the Hydra, 1983, Stedman's Narrative of a Five Years Expedition, 1988, Alabi's World, 1990, Two Evenings in Saramaka, 1991, The Birth of African-American Culture, 1992, Stedman's Surinam, 1992, Equatoria, 1992, On the Mall, 1994, Enigma Variations, 1995, The Convict and the Colonel, 1998, Maroon Arts: Cultural Vitality in the African Diaspora, 1999, Les Marrons en Guyane, 2002. Recipient Elsie Clews Parsons prize Am. Folklore Soc., 1984, Albert J. Beveridge award Am. Hist. Assn., 1991, Gordon K. Lewis Mem. award for disting. Caribbean scholarship, 1992, J.I. Staley prize, 1993; NEH grantee, NSF grantee, Fulbright grantee; John Simon Guggenheim Meml. fellow. Fellow Am. Anthrop. Assn., Royal Anthrop. Inst. Gt. Britain and Ireland, Royal Dutch Inst. Anthropology; mem. Am. Ethnological Soc., Phi Beta Kappa. Home: Anse Chaudière 97217 Anses d'Arlet Martinique Office: Coll William & Mary Dept Anthropology Williamsburg VA 23187 E-mail: rixsal@wm.edu.

PRICE, RICHARD HENRY, psychologist, educator; b. Clarence Alfred and Grace Gallavan Price; m. Mary Knowles Beecher, Aug. 22, 1964; children: Richard Henry, Margaret Beecher. BA, Lawrence Coll., 1962; PhD, U. Ill., 1966. Assoc. prof. Ind. U., Bloomington, 1966—72; prof. psychology U. Mich., Ann Arbor, 1974—, assoc. v.p. for rsch., 1996—97, dir. program on orgnl. studies, 2000—, sr. rsch. scientist Inst. for Social Rsch. Vis. prof. Stanford U., Palo Alto, Calif., 1972—73. Author: (book) Abnormal Behavior: Perspectives in Conflict, 1978, Principles of Psychology, 1982, Fourteen Ounces of Prevention, 1988, Person Environment Psychology, 1992, New Directions in Person Environment Psychology, 2000. Trustee Greenhills Sch., Ann Arbor, 1986—90, William T. Grant Found., N.Y.C., 1990—2002. Recipient Lela Roland Nat. Prevention award, Nat. Mental Health Assn., 1990, Internat. Rsch. Collaboration award, Soc. for Prevention Rsch., 2001. Fellow: APA (pres. divsn. 27 1984—85, Disting. Contbn. award Divsn. 27 1988), Am. Psychol. Soc.; mem.: Inst. Psychology, Chinese NAS. Office: Univ Mich Box 1248 580 Thompson St Ann Arbor MI 48106-1248

PRICE, ROBERT, electronics consultant; b. West Chester, Pa., July 7, 1929; s. Llewellyn Robert and Elise Maclay (Mirkil) P.; m. Jennifer Ann Livingstone Martin, Apr. 19, 1958; children: Stephen Livingstone, Colin Llewellyn, Edmund Hazleton. AB, Princeton U., 1950; ScD (Indsl. fellow 1950-52), MIT, 1953. Tech. dir. Sta. WPRU, Princeton (N.J.) U., 1949; engr. Philco Corp., Phila., 1950; mem. staff Lincoln Lab., MIT, 1951-65; mgr. Sperry Rsch. Ctr., Sperry Corp., Sudbury, Mass., 1965-77, staff cons. comm. scis., 1977-83; chief scientist M/A-COM Govt. Systems Div., Burlington, Mass., 1983-87, cons., 1987-88; cons. scientist Rsch. div. Raytheon Co., Lexington, 1988-93; pvt. practice cons., 1993—. Vis. lectr. U. Calif., Berkeley, 1962-63; adv. council dept. elec. engring. and computer sci. Princeton U., 1971-77; chmn. Mil. Communication Conf. Bd., 1985. Contbr. sci. hist. and litigation articles on spread spectrum techs.; patentee in spread spectrum communications and magnetic recording. Recipient Edwin Howard Armstrong achievement award, IEEE Comms. Soc., 1981, Ofcl. award citation, State Sen. Cert., Commonwealth of Mass., 1981, IEEE third Millennium medal, 2000; fellow Fulbright fellow in radio astronomy Australia, 1953—54. Fellow IEEE (gov. info. theory group 1967-70, 77-79, Info. Theory Soc. Golden Jubilee paper award 1998); mem. NAE, Internat. Union Radio Sci., Franklin Inst., Phi Beta Kappa, Sigma Xi. Achievements include the honor of Eagle Scout from the Boy Scouts of Am., 1953. E-mail: threeceepo@aol.com.

PRICE, ROBERT, lawyer, media executive, investment banker; b. N.Y.C., Aug. 27, 1932; s. Solomon and Frances (Berger) P.; m. Margery Beth Wiener, Dec. 18, 1955 (div.); children: Eileen Marcia, Steven. AB, NYU, 1953; LLD, Columbia U., 1958. Bar: N.Y. 1958, U.S. Dist. Ct. 1958, U.S. Ct. Appeals 1958, U.S. Supreme Ct 1958, ICC 1958, FCC 1958, IRS 1958. With R.H. Macy & Co., Inc., 1955-58; practiced in N.Y.C., 1958—; law clk. to judge U.S. Dist. Ct. (so. dist.) N.Y., 1958-59; asst. U.S. atty. So. Dist. N.Y., 1959-60; ptnr. Kupferman & Price, 1960-65; dep. mayor N.Y.C., 1965-66; exec. v.p., dir. Dreyfus Corp., 1966-69; v.p., investment officer Dreyfus Fund, until 1969; gen. ptnr. Lazard, Freres & Co., 1972-82; pres. N.Y. Law Jour., Nat. Law Jour.; pres., treas., dir. Price Comm. Corp., 1979—; chmn., pres., dir. PriCellular Corp., 1988-95; pres., dir. TLM Corp., 1989—2000. Mem. adv. com. Bankers Trust Co. N.Y.; dir. Holly Sugar Corp., Lane Bryant, Inc., Graphic Scanning Corp.; chmn. N.Y.C. Port Authority Negotiating Com. for World Trade Ctr., 1965-66; spl. counsel N.Y. State Joint Legis. Com. on Ct. Reorgn.; asst. counsel N.Y. State Joint Legis. Com. on N.Y. Banking Laws; mem. The N.Y. State Mcpl. Assistance Corp., 1996-2000; commr. N.Y. State Commn. of Investigations, N.Y.C., 2000—. Contbr. articles to profl. publs. Trustee CUNY, 1996-98; chmn. govt. and civil svc. divsn. United Jewish Appeal Greater N.Y., 1966; co-chmn. met. N.Y. blood drive ARC, 1966; campaign mgr. John V. Lindsay, Campaigns for Congressman, N.Y.C., 1958, 64, for Nelson A. Rockefeller Oreg. Rep. presdl. primary campaign, 1964, Lindsay campaign for mayor, N.Y.C., 1965; del. N.Y. Rep. State Conv., 1962, 66; del. Rep. Nat. Conv., 1988, 92, 96; lectr. Rep. Nat. Com., 1966; bd. dirs. Am. Friends Hebrew U.; past trustee Columbia U. Sch. Pharm. Scis. With U.S. Army, 1953-55. Recipient Yeshiva U. Heritage award, Pub. Svc. award Queens Catholic War Vets. Mem. ABA, FCC Bar Assn., Assn. Bar City N.Y., N.Y. State Dist. Attys. Assn., Coun. Fgn. Rels., Columbia Law Sch. Alumni Assn. (dir.), Scribes, Tau Kappa Alpha. Home: 25 E 86th St New York NY 10028-0553 Office: Price Communications Corp 45 Rockefeller Plz Ste 3200 New York NY 10111-0100 Fax: 212-397-3655.

PRICE, ROBERT DEMILLE, lawyer; b. N.Y.C., Oct. 11, 1915; s. Willard DeMille Price and Eugenia Reeve; m. Newell Potter, Aug. 15, 1940 (div. May 1946); 1 child, Jonathan; m. Ruth Bentley, July 5, 1946; children: Katharine, Susannah, Rebecca. AB in Econs. with honors, Cornell U., 1936; JD, Harvard U., 1940; MBA, Clark U., 1973. Bar: Mass. 1940, U.S. Dist. Ct. Mass. 1941, U.S. Ct. Appeals (1st cir.) 1976, U.S. Tax Ct. 1977, U.S. Supreme Ct. 1978. Assoc. Ropes & Gray, Boston, 1940-43, 1946-50; ptnr. Vaughan, Esty, Crotty & Mason, Worcester, Mass., 1950-53, Sibley, Blair & Mountain, Worcester, 1953-70, Corbin, Sarapas, Madaus & Arakelian, Worcester, 1970-73, Price & Madaus, Worcester, 1973-87; pres. Robert D. Price, PC, Holden, Mass., 1987—. Dir. Appian Way Pizza, Ltd., Worcester, 1951-61, Food Specialties, Inc., Worcester, 1951-61, James Monroe Wire and Cable Co., S. Lancaster, Mass., 1973—; mem. Fin. Com., Holden, 1989-95, conservation com., 1999—. Moderator (TV series) Am. Bar Assn. Jr. Bar Assn., 1947-50. Bd. dirs., treas. Friends Gale Free Librs., Inc., Holden, 1988—; mem. adv. bd. Met. Dist. Commn., 1990—96; pres. Humanist Chaplaincy at Harvard, 1995—; bd. dirs., sec. Humanist Assn. Mass., 1979—, Am. Humanist Assn., 1991—94; trustee AHA Humanist Found., 1999—. Lt. USNR, 1943. Mem. Mass. Bar Assn., Worcester County Bar Assn., Worcester Club (dir. 1953-56), Boston Athenaeum (propr. 1949—). Avocations: museum and art show, photography, alpine climbing, sailing. Office: 11 Malden St Holden MA 01520-1827

PRICE, ROBERT EBEN, judge; b. Waco, Tex., Jan. 13, 1931; s. Robert Eben and Mary Hamilton (Barnett) P.; m. Ann Hodges, June 4, 1954; children— Eben, Mary, Ann, Emily. BA, So. Methodist U., 1952, JD, 1954, LL.M., 1972; postgrad., Air War Coll., 1976. Bar: Tex. 1954, U.S. Supreme Ct., U.S. Ct. Mil. Appeals, U.S. Ct. Claims, U.S. Dist. Ct. (no. dist.) Tex. 1954. Mem. firm Taylor, Mizell, Price, Corrigan & Smith, Dallas, 1956-86; judge Dallas County Probate Ct. No. 2, 1986—. Lectr. continuing legal edn. program U. Houston Law Found., 1993—; lectr. law So. Meth. U. Law Sch., 1973—, faculty paralegal cert. program Sch. Continuing Edn., 1987—; lectr. practice skills program State Bar Tex., 1974—. Editor-in-chief: Southwestern Law Jour., 1953-54. Trustee and sec. St. Michael and All Angels Found.; bd. dirs. Downtown Ministry, Diocese of Dallas Episcopal; chmn. legis. and legal awareness subcom., vice chmn. Tex. Gov.'s Com. on Employment of Handicapped, 1978-82. Served as legal officer USAF, 1954-56; col. JAGC Res. ret. Fellow: Tex. Bar Found., Am. Coll. Trust and Estate Counsel (state membership com., fiduciary litigation com.); mem.: ABA (nat. conf. spl. ct. judges com. on probate and surrogates cts. 1992—), Tex. Coll. Probate Judges (mem. faculty), State Bar Tex. (lectr. profl. devel. program 1988—), Dallas Bar Assn., Coll. State Bar Tex., Nat. Coll. Probate Judges, Phi Delta Theta, Phi Eta Sigma, Phi Alpha Delta. Episcopalian. Home: 4300 Arcady Ave Dallas TX 75205-3704 Office: Probate Ct 2 ste 211 509 Main St Dallas TX 75202-3508

PRICE, ROBERT ERNEST, lawyer; b. Athens, Ohio, Dec. 24, 1954; s. Ernest and Cora (Pugh) P.; m. Linda Carol Jordan, Jan. 30, 1983; children: Sarah Catherine, David Ernest. BSBA, U. N.C., 1977, JD, 1980. Bar: U.S. Dist. Ct. (mid. dist.) N.C. 1982, U.S. Dist. Ct. (ea. dist.) N.C. 1987, U.S. Ct. Appeals (4th cir.) 1987, U.S. Supreme Ct. 1987. Assoc. Davis & Brewer, Clemmons, N.C., 1980-83; pvt. practice Rowland, 1984-86, 90—; ptnr. Price & McIntyre, 1987-89. Recipient Disting. Svc. award Robeson County Jaycees, 1989. Mem. Rowland C. of C. (sec.), Phi Beta Kappa, Phi Eta Sigma, Beta Gamma Sigma. Democrat. Presbyterian. Home and Office: PO Box 369 Rowland NC 28383-0369

PRICE, ROBERT IRA, coast guard officer; b. N.Y.C., Sept. 22, 1921; s. Alfred and Mary Edna (Schweitzer) P.; m. Virginia Louise Miller, June 20, 1946; children: Andrea Jean, Keven Virginia. BBA, CCNY, 1942; BS, U.S. Coast Guard Acad., 1945; postgrad., M.I.T., 1950-53. Registered profl. engr., D.C. Commd. ensign U.S. Coast Guard, 1945, advanced through grades to vice adm., 1978; asst. chief Mcht. Marine Tech. Div., Washington, 1965-67; chief planning staff Office Mcht. Marine Safety, 1967-71; capt. Port of Phila., 1971-73; chief Office Marine Environ. Washington, 1974-76; comdr. 11th Coast Guard Dist. Long Beach, Calif., 1976-78; comdr. Atlantic Area and 3d Coast Guard Dist. N.Y.C., 1978-81; ret., 1981; sr. v.p. J.J. Henry Co. (marine engrs.), N.Y.C., 1981-86; maritime cons., 1986—. Prin. U.S . negotiator to tech. programs Intergovtl. Maritime Consultative Orgn., UN, 1962-71 Contbg. author: Ship Design and Construction, 1980; Contbr. articles to profl. jours. Decorated D.S.M. with gold star, Legion of Merit with gold star, Meritorious Service medal with gold star, Coast Guard Commendation medal. Fellow Royal Instn. Naval Architects, Soc. Naval Architects (Land medalist 1982); mem. Sigma Xi. Clubs: Propeller, Army Navy, N.Y. Yacht.

PRICE, ROBERT OTIS, former mayor; b. Abilene, Kans., Jan. 4, 1932; s. Iru Paul and Irene Isabel (Parrish) P.; m. Dorothy Faye Price, Jan. 26, 1951 (dec. 1996); m. Sondra Boyd, Mar. 28, 1997; children: Fred Dennis, Donald Eugene. BA, U. Redlands, 1978. Patrolman, sgt., lt., capt. Bakersfield Police Dept., 1956-73, chief police, 1973-88; cons., troubleshooter, various cities, 1988-92; mayor City of Bakersfield, 1993—2001. Pres. Secret Witness Bd., 1980-83. Mem. Calif. Coun. on Criminal Justice, Sacramento, 1983-93; chmn. State Adv. Group on Juvenile Justice, Sacramento, 1988-93, Citizens Adv. Com., Fresno, Calif., 1993—, Youth Devel. Coalition, Bakersfield, 1993—, Econ. Devel. Discussion Group, Bakersfield, 1993—; chmn. western region Nat. Coalition Juvenile Justice and Delinquency Prevention, 1988-93; founder, cons. Youth Adv. Coun., Bakersfield, 1993—; founder Bakersfield Action Team, 1994. Sgt. U.S. Army, 1952-54. Recipient John W. Doubenmier award Am. Soc. Pub. Admins., 1978, Califf Morris award Calif. Probation, Parole and Corrections Officers Assn., 1982. Mem. Internat. Assn. Chiefs Police, Calif. Police Chiefs Assn., Calif. Peace Officers Assn., Calif. Council Criminal Justice, Kern County Police Chiefs Assn. (pres. 1979), Kern County Law Enforcement Admin. Assn. (pres. 1974). Republican. Avocations: photography, fishing, travel.*

PRICE, ROBERT STANLEY, lawyer; b. Phila., Jan. 21, 1937; s. Benjamin and Estelle B. (Muchnick) P.; m. Emilie W. Kirschbaum, June 27, 1965 (dec. Mar. 1998); children: Louise P. Kelly, Marianna R. BA, Kenyon Coll., 1958; LLB, Yale U., 1961. Bar: Pa. 1963, U.S. Dist. Ct. (ea. dist.) Pa. 1963, U.S. Ct. Appeals (3d cir.) 1963, N.Y. 1993. Assoc. Dechert, Price & Rhoads, Phila., 1961-63; asst tax atty. Smith, Kline & French, 1963-67; tax atty. Pa. Ctrl. Transp. Co., 1967-70; tax counsel IU Internat., 1970-72; ptnr. Townsend, Elliott & Munson, 1972-76, Pepper, Hamilton & Scheetz, Phila., 1977-86, Saul, Ewing, Remick & Saul, Phila., 1986-93; spl. cons. Saul, Ewing, Remick & Saul (now Saul Ewing LLP), 1994—2001. Ind. tax cons. Fischbein-Badillo-Wagner-Harding, N.Y.C., 1998—2001, Mintz, Levin, Cohn, Ferris, Glovsky and Popeo, P.C., N.Y.C., 2001—. Author: ABCs of Industrial Development Bonds, 1981, 5th edit., 1990; contbr. articles to legal jours. Served with U.S. Army, 1961-62. Mem. ABA (tax exempt fin. com.), Pa. Bar, Phila. Bar Assn., N.Y. Bar, Racquet Club Phila. (v.p. 1987-88), Alpha Delta Phi (pres. 1975-78). Office: Saul Ewing LLP 3800 Centre Sq W Philadelphia PA 19102 E-mail: rpricedj@earthlink.net.

PRICE, ROBERT V., JR. financial consultant; b. Washington, Dec. 4, 1946; s. Robert V. Price and Evelyn M. DuPree; m. Elizabeth J. Price, Apr. 27, 1968; children: Amy Pickerall, Valerie Price. Masters, Am. Coll., Bryn Mawr, Pa., 1997. Pres. Price Fin. Group, Waldorf, Md., 1969—, Four Star Products, Prince Frederick, 1997—. Mem. Alice Ferguson Found.; chmn. bd. Faith United Meth. Ch., Accokeek, Md., 1995. Recipient Harry Myer award Suburban Life Underwriters, 1993; named Man of Yr., Faith United Meth. Ch., 1999. Mem. Internat. Assn. Fin. Planners, Md. State Assn. Life Underwriters (pres. 1981, nat. committeeman, Paul Murphy award 1987), Greater Washington D.C. Soc. CLU ChFC (pres. 1992), Prince George Life Underwriters (bylaws chair, pres. 1976), Million Dollar Roundtable (life and qualifying mem.). Methodist. Avocations: tennis, poker. Office: Price Fin Group Inc 603 Post Office Rd Ste 206 Waldorf MD 20602

PRICE, RONALD JAMES, electrical products company executive; b. Wellsville, Ohio, Jan. 26, 1933; s. Thomas Pugh and Dorothy Maud (Saltsman) P.; m. Phyllis Eileen Mangan, Feb. 15, 1958; children: Penny Eileen, Deborah Lynn. BA in Math., Wooster Coll., 1953; BS in Mech. Engring., Ohio U., 1955. Registered profl. engr., Mich., Ohio, Pa. Sales engr. Westinghouse Corp., Detroit, 1957-62, dist. mgr., 1962-65, product mgr., standard control divsn. Beaver, Pa., 1965-68, sales mgr., 1968; v.p., gen mgr. Fife Fla. Electric Supply, Tampa, 1968-71; mktg. mgr. Westinghouse Control Products Divsn., Beaver, 1971-75, enging. mgr., 1975-77, mgr. mktg. and strategic planning Indsl. Control Bus. unit, 1977-78, acting gen. mgr. specialty transformer divsn. Greenville, Pa., 1976, control equipment group mktg. mgr., 1978-80; gen. mgr. Bryant divsn. Westinghouse Electric Corp., Bridgeport, Conn., 1980-83, gen. mgr. comml. divsn., distbn. and protection bus. unit, 1983-86, nat. sales mgr., 1986-89, v.p., 1989-92, ret., 1992. Vis. lectr. Mich. State U. MBA program. Author: Ask For the Order!, 1995. Trustee Beaver County Recreational Authority, 1972-76, mktg. dept. Indiana U. Pa., 1995—; mem. Coun. of 100, Tampa, 1969-71; pres. Beaver Civic Assn., 1977-80; chmn. Ft. McIntosh dist. Boy Scouts Am., Beaver, 1979-80; bd. assocs. U. Bridgeport, 1982-83; mem. alumni bd. Coll. Wooster; chmn. bd. dirs. Housing Opportunities Beaver County Inc., 1993-99. With U.S. Army, 1958. Recipient Bausch & Lombe Sci. award, 1950. Mem. NSPE, Nat. Elec. Mfrs. Assn. (indsl. control, systems sec., chmn. adv. com. for user needs), Elec. Coun. Fla., Nat. Assn. Elec. Distbrs. (spkr.), Nat. Assn. Mfrs. (industry spkr.), Am. Mgmt. Assn. (lectr.). Republican. Presbyterian. Home: 300 6th St Apt 11 Beaver PA 15009 E-mail: whs1949@@aol.com.

PRICE, RONNI FAY, therapist, social worker; b. N.Y.C., Apr. 2, 1954; BA, U. Miss., 1976; MSW, U. So. Miss., 1979. Cert. social worker. Asst. Head Start tchr. Lift, Inc., Tupelo, Miss., 1976-77; social worker Three Rivers Regional Ministry, 1977-78; counselor Alcorn County Youth Ct., Corinth, Miss., 1979-90; therapist, social worker Parkwood Counseling Svcs., 1990—. Task force mem. N.E. Miss. Foster Care Rev. Bd., Pontotoc, 1985-86, Alcorn County Foster Care Rev. Bd., Corinth, 1986-87, Regional Child & Adolescent Svc. System Program, Oxford, Miss., 1987. Active Corinth Jr. Aux., 1982-88, Jaycees, 1984-85; bd. dirs. Boy's Club, Corinth, Alcorn County Am. Cancer Soc., Corinth, 1983-85. Named Alcorn County Young Career Woman of The Yr. Business & Professional Women, 1983; recognized for being outstanding in field Nat. Juvenile Justice Assn., 1984. Mem. NASW, North Miss. Counseling Assn. Democrat. Methodist. Avocation: volunteer work. Office: Parkwood Couseling Svcs 3101 Oak Shadow Ln Pensacola FL 32504-4968

PRICE, ROSALIE PETTUS, artist; b. Birmingham, Ala. d. Erle and Ellelee (Chapman) Pettus; m. William Archer Price, Oct. 3, 1936. AB, Birmingham-So. Coll., 1935; MA, U. Ala., Tuscaloosa, 1967. Instr. Birmingham Mus. Art, 1967-70, Samford U., 1969-70; painter in watercolors, caseim, oil and acrylic. Solo shows include Samford U., 1964. Birmingham Mus. Art, 1966, 73, 82-83, Town Hall Gallery, 1968, 75, South Ctrl. Bell, 1977, Birmingham So. Coll., 1992, Altamont Sch., 1996; represented in permanent collections Birmingham Mus. Art, Springfield (Mo.) Art Mus., U. Ala. Moody Gallery of Art, Mobile (Ala.) Mus. Art, Huntsville (Ala.) Mus. Art, Randolph-Macon Woman's Coll. Maier Mus. Art, Wiregrass Mus. Art, Dothan, Ala., many others. Bd. dirs. Birmingham Mus. ARt, 1950-54, vice chair, 1950-51; trustee Birmingham Music Club, 1956-66, rec. sec., 1958-62. Recipient purchase awrd Watercolor USA, 1972; named to Watercolor USA Honor Soc., 1986. Mem. Nat. Watercolor Soc., Nat. Soc. Painters in Casein and Acrylic (W. Alden Brown Meml. award 1970, Joseph A. Cain Meml. award 1983), Birmingham Art Assn. (pres. 1947-49, Best Watercolor award 1950, Little House on Linden purchase award 1968), So. Watercolor Soc., Watercolor Soc. Ala. (Lassetter award 1968), La. Watercolor Soc., Jr. League of Birmingham (chmn. art com. 1947-50), Window Box Garden Club, Pi Beta Phi. Episcopalian. Home and Office: 502 Royal Tower Dr Birmingham AL 35209

PRICE, RUTHE GEIER, actress, writer, educator; b. New Brunswick, N.J., Dec. 16, 1922; d. Morris Payenson and Anne (Payenson) Dorfman; m. Arnold Geier, July 1, 1951 (div. Nov. 1976); children: Donald Lloyd, Michael Jay; m. Nathaniel Wolfred Price, Oct. 9, 1988. Student, State Tchrs. Coll., Trenton, N.J., 1941-43; BS in Edn., NYU, 1945, MA in Theater, 1946. Dir. Parker Playhouse, Plainfield, N.J., 1947, Newark Acad. Dramtic Art, 1948; asst. dir., theater chair Essex Conservatory, Newark, 1949-51; soc. editor Edison Jour., Miami, Fla., 1954; comptroller Nat. Ins. Cons., 1974-76; actress, 1977—; mng.editor Starbooks Inc., 1999—. Drama coach, Fla., 1990—; media cons., Fla., 1983—. Appeared in films including Let It Ride, Making Mr. Right, Italian Taxi Driver, The Bellboy, Hardly Working, Last Plane Out; TV appearances include Miami Sands, Miami Vice, The Sunset Gang; plays include Save Me a Place at Forest Lawn, Pocket Watch, Ladies in Retirement, Hamlet, You Can't Take it With You, The Male Animal, Blithe Spirit, Lady Precious Stream, As You Like It, Guest in the House, Godperson, Forty Carats, Medea, Skin of Our Teeth, Romeo and Juliet, A Choice to Make; hostess TV talk show Ruthe Geier Presents; hostess radio show Spotlight on Stars; Author: (book) Acting in On-Camera Commercials, 2001; contbr. poetry to Harper's mag. Recipient CLIO award, 1982, Emmy award, 1982, Addy award, 1982. Mem. AFTRA (columnist 1985-93, v.p. 1985-93), Screen Actors Guild (bd. dirs. 1990-93), Actors Equity Assn. Avocations: philately, reading, music, theater, travel. E-mail: writegal@bellsouth.net.

PRICE, STUART WINSTON, lawyer; b. Pasadena, Calif., Jan. 20, 1962; s. Frank Dean and Ann Browning (Rounds) P.; m. Lynne Marie Bowman, May 26, 1996. BA, U. Calif., Santa Barbara, 1983; JD, UCLA, 1986. Assoc. Drummy Garrett King & Harrison, Costa Mesa, Calif., 1986—91; assoc., ptnr. McDermott, Will & Emery, Newport Beach, 1991—99; assoc. Bryan Cave LLP, Irvine, 1999—. Office: Ste 1100 18101 Von Karman Ave Irvine CA 92612-0154

PRICE, SUSAN CAROLE, marketing and public relations professional; b. San Luis Obispo, Calif., Oct. 20, 1959; d. Whitlock Jones and Carole Ann (Soe) Wheeler. BA in Journalism, Colo. State U., 1982; MA in Communications, Western Ky. U., 1992. Data processing mgr. pub. rels. Eagle Computer Systems, 1984-85; comm. mgr. MPD Inc., Owensboro, Ky., 1986—90; owner Price Comm., San Luis Obispo, 1986—; mktg. dir. Info. Presentation Techs., Inc., 1992-93; mktg. support mgr. De Royal, 1993-97; mktg. comms. mgr. Shasbaugh, 1997-99. Lectr. Calif. Poly. State U., 1993—99. Democrat. E-mail: Sue4sea@aol.com.

PRICE, TERRY L. leadership studies educator; b. Taylorsville, NC, Dec. 27, 1966; s. Glenn Robert and Evelyn Yvonne Price; m. Lori L. Speagle, May 30, 1987; children: Harper Speagle-Price. AB summa cum laude, U. NC, 1989; M in Letters, U. Oxford, Eng., 1996; PhD, U. Ariz., 1998. Asst. prof. leadership studies Jepson Sch. Leadership Studies, U. Richmond, Va., 1998—. Contbr. articles to profl. jours. Recipient Emil R. Riesen prize in philosophy, 1993; fellow John M. Olin fellow, 1994. Mem.: Am. Philos. Assn., Phi Beta Kappa. Office: Jepson Sch Leadership Studies Univ Richmond Richmond VA 23173

PRICE, THEODORA HADZISTELIOU, individual and family therapist; b. Athens, Greece, Oct. 1, 1938; came to U.S. 1967; d. Ioannis and Evangelia (Emmanuel) Hadzisteliou; m. David C. Long Price, Dec. 26, 1966 (div. 1989); children: Morgan N., Alkes D.L. BA in History/Archaeology, U. Athens, 1961; DPhil, U. Oxford, Eng., 1966; MA in Clin. Social Work, U. Chgo., 1988; Diploma in Piano Teaching, Nat. Conservatory, Athens, 1958; student, Chgo. Greek Orthodox Diocesan Sch. Byzantine Music. Lic. clin. social worker; bd. cert. diplomate in clin. social work. Mus. asst. and resident tutor U. Sydney, Australia, 1966-67; instr. anthropology Adelphi U., N.Y.C., 1967-68; archaeologist Hebrew Union Coll., Gezer, Israel, 1968; asst. prof. classical archaeology/art U. Chgo., 1968-70; jr. rsch. fellow Harvard Ctr. Hellenic Studies, Washington, 1970-71; clin. social worker Harbor Light Ctr., Salvation Army, Chgo., 1988-89; therapist Inst. Motivational Devel., Lombard, Ill., 1989-90; caseworker Jewish Family & Community Svc., Chgo., 1989-90; staff therapist Family Svc. Ctrs. of South Cook County, Chicago Heights, 1990-91; pvt. practice child, adolescent, family therapy Bolingbrook, Ill., 1991—; dir. counseling svcs., clin. supr., psychotherapist The Family Link, Inc., Chgo., 1993; staff therapist Cen. Bapt. Family Svcs., Gracell Rehab., 1991, 91-92; casework supr., counselor Epilepsy Found. Greater Chgo., 1992-93; therapist children, adolescents and families dept. foster care Catholic Charities, 1993-94; individual and family therapist South Ctrl. Cmty. Svcs. Individual-Family Counseling Svcs., 1994-97. Lectr. in field; bd. mem., counselor Naperville Sch. for Gifted and Talented, 1982-84. Author: (monograph) Kourotrophos, Cults and Representations of the Greek Nursing Deities, 1978; contbr. articles to profl. jours. Meyerstein Traveling awardee, Oxford, Eng., 1963, 64; Eleutherios Venizelos scholar, 1962-65. Mem. NASW, Nat. Acad. Clin. Social Workers, Ill. Clin. Social Workers. Avocations: yoga, piano playing, dog training and therapy, hesychasm. Home and Office: 10 Pebble Ct Bolingbrook IL 60440-1557 *Nobody stands alone, for each of us partakes and contributes to universal energy and creation. Every thought or action has progressively timeless impact. Therefore, working in helping people is influencing the flow of creation.*

PRICE, THOMAS EMILE, investment company executive; b. Cin., Nov. 4, 1921; s. Edwin Charles and Lillian Elizabeth (Werk)P.; m. Lois Margaret Gahr Matthews, Dec. 21, 1970 (dec. Nov. 26 1988); 1 child by previous marriage, Dorothy Elizabeth Wood Price; stepchildren: Bruce Albert, Mark Frederic, Scott Herbert, Eric William Matthews. BBA, U. Tex., 1943; postgrad., Harvard U., 1944. Co-founder Pirce y Cia., Inc., Cin., 1946—; sec., 1946-75; treas., 1946—; pres., 1975—; also bd. dirs.; co-founder Price Paper Products Corp. (merger Price y Cia, Inc.), Cin., 1956; treas., 1956-75; pres., 1975-90; sec., 1956-75; also bd. dirs. Mem. Cin. Regional Export Expansion Com., 1961-63; bd. dirs. Ctrl. Acceptance Corp., 1954-55; founding mem. and dir. Cin. Royals Basketball Club Co., 1959-73. History columnist Tennis Talk Greater Cin., 1978-80. Referee Tri-State Tennis Championships, 1969-70, Nat. FAther-Son Clay Ct. Championships, 1974—, Tennis Grand Masters Championships, 1975-77, 80; vol. coach Walnut Hills High Sch. Boys Team, Cin. Jr. Davis Cup, 1968-78; co-founder Tennis Patrons of Cin., Inc., 1951, trustee, 1951-79, pres., 1958-63, 68; co-founder Greater Cin. Tennis Assn., 1979; participant in fundraising drives in Cin. Boys Amateur Baseball Fund; chmn. greater Cin. YMCA World Svc. Fund Drive, 1962-64; trustee Cin. World Affairs Inst., 1957-60, gen. chmn., 1959. 1st lt. USAAF, 1943-46, ETO. Elected to Western Hills High Sch. Sport Hall of Honor; named hon. Almaden Grand Master, 1980; Cin. Met. Tennis Tournament renamed Thomas E. Price Cin. Met. Tennis Tournament, 1991; nationally ranked boys 15, 1936, jr. tennis player, 1939. Mem. Cin. World Trade Club (pres. 1959), U.S. Trotting Assn., Cin. Hist. Soc., U.S. Lawn Tennis Assn. (trustee 1959-60, 62-64, chmn. Jr. Davis Cup com. 1960-62, founder Col. HJames H. Bishop award 1962), Ohio Valley Tennis Assn. (trustee 1948—, Gillespie award 1957, Dredge award 1973, pres. 1952-53, Tom Pirce award named in his honor at Jr. Davis Cup), Western Tennis Assn. (trustee 1951—, mem. championships adv. com. 1959-78, pres. 1959-60, Hall of Fame 1994, Melvin R. Bergman Disting. Svc. award 1989), Greater Cin. Tennis Assn. (named after and recipient Tom Price award), Assn. Tennis Profl. (nat. championships adv. 1979—), Cin. Country Club, Univ. Club, Cin. Tennis Club (hon., life, pres. 1957-58, adv. com. 1959—, Founders and Guardians award 1983), Indoor Tennis Club, Ea. Hills Indoor Tennis Club, Phi Gamma Delta. Republican. Presbyterian. Home: 3249 Epworth Ave Cincinnati OH 45211-7037 Office: Dixie Terminal Bldg Ste 216 Cincinnati OH 45202-3812 *Personal philosophy: Follow the Ten Commandments and the Golden Rule.*

PRICE, THOMAS FREDERICK, theatre educator; b. Salt Lake City, June 19, 1937; s. Thomas William P. and Caryl Susan Brown; children: Devin, Jennifer. BA in Drama, Pomona Coll., 1960; MA in Theatre, San Francisco State U., 1962; PhD in Drama, Stanford U., 1968; student, Columbia U. Rare Book Sch., 1983. Asst. prof. English U. of the Pacific, Stockton, Calif., 1968-70; asst. prof. drama U.S. Internat. U., Sch. Performing Arts, San Diego, 1970-74; archivist, curator The Philibrick Theatre Libr., Los Altos Hills, Calif., 1975-85; prof. English Tianjin (China) Normal U., 1985-87; adj. prof. theatre So. Oreg. State Coll., Ashland, 1991-92. Assoc. prof. English Tamnkang U., Taipei, Taiwan, 1993—; ednl. broadcaster (original staff) KPFA-FM, L.A., 1959—62, KSRO-FM, Ashland, Oreg., 1990—92; organizer west coast Gordon Craig retrospective Stanford U. Dept Spl. Collections, 1985. Author: Edward Gordon Craig Revisited, 1984, Edward Gordon Craig and the Theatre of the Imagination, 1985, Dramatic Structure and Meaning, 1992, rev. edit., 1999; editor: Critical Edition of the Jealous Wife and Polly Honeycombe by George Colman the Elder, 1997; contbr. articles to profl. jours. Recipient Taiwan Nat. Sci. Found., 1998, Disting. Tchr. award Tamkang U., 1998. Mem. Calif. Scholarship Fedn. (hon. life).

PRICE, THOMAS MUNRO, computer consultant; b. Madison, Wis., Oct. 2, 1937; s. John Edward and Georgia Winifred (Day) P.; m. Judith Ann Holm, Aug. 8, 1959; children: Scott Michael, Andrea Lynn. BS, Carroll Coll., Waukesha, Wis., 1959; MS, U. Wis., 1961, PhD, 1964. Prof. math. U. Iowa, 1964-77, U. Wyo., Laramie, 1978-79, computer user cons., 1979-85, MIS prof., 1985-89; computer cons., 1989—; home rebuilder Pecos, N.Mex., 1994-97; historic home renovator Yerington, Nev., 1997—. Contbr. articles to profl. jours. Home: Nordyke House 727 State Rt 339 Yerington NV 89447

PRICE, TOM, journalist; b. Pitts., May 26, 1946; s. H. Samuel and Anna Mae (Nicholson) P.; m. Susan Crites; 1 child, Julianna Margaret. BS in Journalism, Ohio U., 1968. Writer, editor Athens (Ohio) Messenger, 1968-73; freelance writer, 1973-75; politics writer Dayton (Ohio) Jour. Herald, 1975-82; corr. Washington bur. Cox Newspapers, Washington, 1982-96; freelance writer politics, govt., tech., bus. and edn., 1996—. Co-author: (with Susan Crites Price) The Working Parents Help Book, 1994 (Parent's Choice award, Scholastic Book Club selection), rev. edit., 1996, Working Solutions Internet Column; nat. newspaper columnist Working Parents Lifeline, 1996-98. Presbyterian. Avocations: photography, hiking, travel, reading.

PRICE, TOMMYE JO ENSMINGER, community health nurse; b. Shreveport, La., Oct. 10, 1943; d. Joe Pirkle and Edith Pipes (Whitmeyer) Ensminger; m. Murphy Briscoe Price, June 5, 1965; children: John Briscoe, Meredith Jo. BSN, Northwestern State U., 1965. Staff nurse Waterman Meml. Hosp., Eustis, Fla.; office nurse James C. Penrod, MD, Tallahassee; staff nurse Highlands (N.C.) Cashiers Hosp.; county coordinating nurse Miss. State Dept. of Health, Raleigh. Mem. ANA, Miss. Nurse's Assn. Home: PO Box 521 Raleigh MS 39153-0521

PRICE, TREVOR ROBERT PRYCE, psychiatrist, educator; b. Concord, N.H., Nov. 29, 1943; s. Trevor Alaric Price and Beatrice (Dinsmore) P.; m. Margaret Ann Bowring, June 8, 1991; children: Meghan Jennifer, Sara Brittany; children by previous marriage: Trevor Breton, Elizabeth Anne Price Pearson. BA, Yale U., 1965; MD, Columbia U., 1969. Diplomate Am. Bd. Psychiatry and Neurology (examiner 1985—), Am. Bd. Internal Medicine, Nat. Bd. Med. Examiners. Intern in medicine Med. Ctr. U. Calif., San Francisco, 1969-70; resident in internal medicine Med. Ctr. of U. Calif., 1972-74; resident in psychiatry Dartmouth Med. Sch., Hanover, N.H., 1974-77, asst. prof., assoc. prof. psychiatry and medicine, 1977-85; assoc. prof., prof. psychiatry U. Pa. Sch. Medicine, Phila., 1985-88; dir. psychiat. in-patient svcs. Hosp. of U. Pa., 1985-88; prof. psychiatry Med. Coll. Pa., Pitts., 1989-90, prof. psychiatry and medicine, 1991-95, tenured prof. psychiatry and medicine, 1993—2002; chmn. dept. psychiatry Med. Coll. Pa. and Hahnemann U., Pitts., 1989-95, sr. assoc. dean, 1993-95; pres. Allegheny Neuropsychiat. Inst. Allegheny Neuropsychiat. Inst., Pitts., 1992-94, exec. dir., 1994—; chmn. Dept. Psychiatry, Med. Coll. Pa. Hahnemann Sch. Medicine, Phila., 1995—2002; tenured prof. psychiatry and medicine Drexel U. Coll. Medicine, 2002—. Bd. dirs. Coll. Health Consortium, Inc., Phila., Highland Dr. Rsch. and Edn. Found., Yale Club Pitts., Pitts. Psychoanalytic Found., Med. Coll. Pa. Hosp.; mem. blue ribbon bd. Alzheimer's Disease Alliance, Western Pa., 1989-97; mem. governing bd. Med. Coll. of Pa. Hosp., 1999-2002. Mem. editl. bd. Convulsive Therapy, 1984-94, Jour. Neuropsychiatry and Clin. Neurosci., 1992—, Allegheny Gen. Hosp. Jour. Neurosci., 1992—, Seminars in Neuropsychiatry, 1995—; editl. reviewer 15 psychiat. and med. jours., 1978; contbr. chpts. to books and articles in profl. jours. Mem. N.H. Commn. on Laws Effecting Mental Health, 1974-75; bd. dirs. Advanced Studies Program, Friends of St. Paul's Sch., Concord, N.H., 1983-87. Recipient William C. Menninger award Ctrl. Neuropsychiat. Assn., 1977, Faculty Teaching award dept. psychiatry Dartmouth Med. Sch., 1984, Pres. award for Exceptional Achievement AHERF, 1994, numerous grants. Fellow Am. Psychiat. Assn., Am. Neuropsychiat. Assn. (bd. dirs. 1993-95, exec. dir. 1995); mem. Pa. Psychiat. Assn., Am. Coll. Psychiatrists, Am. Assn. Chairmen of Depts. Psychiatry, Soc. Biol. Psychiatry, Assn. for Acad. Psychiatry, Am. Assn. Dirs. Psychiat. Residency Tng., Assn. Acad. Psychiatry, Assn. Convulsive Therapy, Assn. Medicine and Psychiatry, Yale Club Pitts., H-Y-P Club Pitts. Avocations: fly fishing, tennis, reading, piano. Office: Ea Pa Psychiat Inst 3200 Henry Ave Rm 177 Philadelphia PA 19129-1137 also: Drexel U Coll Medicine Dept Psychiatry Philadelphia PA 19102-5087 *Life at its best is being continually challenged and fully engaged, yet not self-absorbed.*

PRICE, VIRGINIA ASHBAUGH, technical service director, workers compensation c; b. East Liverpool, Ohio, June 19, 1913; d. Theodore Reed Ashbaugh and Georgia Kate (Paul) Mackey; m. Joseph Clyde Price, Jan. 1, 1937 (dec. July 1972). Student, Ohio State U., 1963-64. Cert. profl. sec. Sec. Ohio Power Co., East Liverpool, 1930-37, Walter B. Hill, Atty., East Liverpool, 1937-38; sec., bookkeeper Price Electric Appliance Co., 1938-40; sec. Indsl. Commn. of Ohio, Columbus, 1940-44; sec., asst. treas. E.I. Evans & Co., 1944-72; mgr. actuarial dept. Gates McDonald, Hilliard, Ohio, 1972-75, mgr. customer rels., 1975-85, dir. tech. svc., 1985—. Contbr. articles to jours. in field. Trustee Nat. Ch. Residences, Columbus, 1982-95; mem. Rep. Nat. Com. Mem. Internat. Assn. Adminstrn. Profls. (chpt. pres. 1956, Ohio state pres. 1960, internat. treas. 1962, mem. cert. bd. 1965, trustee retirement ctr. 1970-74). Methodist. Avocations: ballroom dancing, choral and solo vocal music, bridge, cats. Home: 420A Alexandria Colony E Columbus OH 43215-1151 Office: GatesMcDonald 3455 Mill Run Dr Hilliard OH 43026-9079

PRICE, WALTER ERNEST, engineer; b. N.Y.C., Aug. 11, 1948; s. Obie and Marguerite (Smith) P.; m. R. Jean Hodge, July 28, 1972 (div. 1985); m. Carolyn Neal, Dec. 14, 1988. AA in Math., Bronx Community Coll., 1967; BEE, U. Dar Es Salaam, Tanzania, 1973; postgrad., Ga. Inst. Tech., 1980. Engring. assoc. Bell Labs., Atlanta, 1975-77; prin. engr. Computer Scis. Corp., Falls Church, Va., 1977-83; sr. engr. McDonnell Douglas Astronautics Co., St. Louis, 1980-81; assurance engr. Daniel, Mann, Johnson & Mendenhall, L.A., 1983-86, DKP, Balt., 1989—. Prin. Donaldson-Price Assocs., Ltd., Boston, 1981—. Mem. Audio Engring. Soc., Am. Soc. Quality Control (cert. reliability engr.), Sons Am. Legion. Avocation: yachting. Office: DKP 1 South St Ste 2200 Baltimore MD 21202-3281

PRICE, WILLIAM JAMES, IV, investment banker; b. Balt., Oct. 6, 1924; s. William James 3d and Frances (Robbins) P.; m. Marjorie Beard, Dec. 6, 1952; children: Marjorie, Jonathan Robbins, William James V, Juliet Robbins. BS, Yale U., 1949. Propr. Price & Co., 1949-52; with Alex. Brown & Sons, Balt., 1952-98, gen. partner, 1959-84, mng. dir., 1984-89. Trustee Washington Coll., St. Paul's Sch. for Girls. Served with inf. AUS, 1943—46, ETO. Decorated Bronze Star, Purple Heart with oak leaf cluster, Combat Infantry badge. Mem. Nat. Assn. Securities Dealers (bd. govs. 1964-66, vice chmn. 1966)

PRICE, WILLIAM RAY, JR. state supreme court judge; b. Fairfield, Iowa, Jan. 30, 1952; s. William Ray and Evelyn Jean (Darnell) P.; m. Susan Marie Trainor, Jan. 4, 1975; children: Emily Margret, William Joseph Dodds. BA with distinction, U. Iowa, 1974; postgrad., Yale U., 1974-75; JD cum laude, Washington and Lee U., 1978. Bar: Mo. 1978, U.S. Dist. Ct. (we. dist.) Mo. 1978, U.S. Ct. Claims 1978, U.S. Ct. Appeals (8th cir.) 1985. Assoc. Lathrop & Norquist, Kansas City, Mo., 1978-84, ptnr., 1984-92, chmn. bus. litigation sect., 1987-88, 90-92, exec. com., 1989-92; judge Supreme Ct. Mo., Jefferson City, 1992—, chief justice, 1999—2001. G.L.V. Zumwalt monitoring com. U.S. Dist. Ct. (we. dist.) Mo., Kansas City. Pres. Kansas City Bd. Police Commrs.; mem. Together Ctr. & Family Devel. Ctr., Kansas City; chmn. merit selection com. U.S. marshal Western Dist. of Mo., Kansas City; bd. dirs. Truman Med. Ctr., Kansas City. Rockefeller fellow, 1974-75; Burks scholar Washington & Lee U., 1976. Mem. Christian Ch. Office: Supreme Ct Mo PO Box 150 207 W High St Jefferson City MO 65102-0150

PRICE, WILLIAM W. engineer; b. Aug. 30, 1946; BSEE, Clarkson U., 1968; MSE, Rensselaer Polytechnic Inst., 1971. Cons. engr. GE Power Sys. Energy Cons., Schenectady, NY, 1968—.

PRICE, JR. DWIGHT RICHARD, musician, educator; b. Newton, Nc, June 15, 1960; s. Dwight Richard Price, Sr.; m. Pamela Grey Price, Apr. 0, 1999. BA, Lenoir-Rhyne Coll., Hickory, North Carolina, 1982. Band dir. Cannon Sch., Inc., Concord, NC, 2002—; music educator Pfeiffer U., Misenheimer, 2000—; trumpet player Legacy Brass, Charlotte, 1993—. Freelance trumpet player, Mounty Holly, NC, 1982—2002. Recipient Outstanding Jazz Soloist, U. of NC, 2001. Independent. Lutheran. Avocations: audio engineering, audio engineering. Home: 100 North Tanninger Road Mount Holly NC 28120 Personal E-mail: ricktrumpetman@aol.com.

PRICE BODAY, MARY KATHRYN, choreographer, small business owner, educator; b. Fort Bragg, N.C., May 20, 1945; d. Max Edward and Katharine (Jordan) P.; m. Les Boday (div. 1982); children: Shawn Leon Boday, Irmali Ferecho Boday; m. Richard A. Weil, May 1, 1986. BFA, U. Okla., 1968, MFA, 1970; studies with David Howard, 1972-74. Soloist dancer Mary Anthony Dance Co., N.Y.C., 1971-74, Larry Richardson Dance Co., N.Y.C., 1971-73; dancer Pearl Lang Dance Co., 1971-73, Gaku Dance Theater, N.Y.C., 1972-74; ballet mistress and soloist dancer St. Gallen Ballet, Switzerland, 1974-75; dancer, tchr. Zurich Ballet, Switzerland, 1975-76; asst. prof. U. Ill., Champaign-Urbana, 1976-79; artist-in-residence Cornish Inst., Seattle, 1979-80; pres. The Dance Works, Inc., 1981-90; dir. Seahurst Ballet, 1982-84; pres. The Dance Works, Inc., Erie, Pa., 1990-94; dir. dance dept., asst. prof. Mercyhurst Coll., 1990-94; dir. Peoria Ballet, 1994-99; asst. prof. Bradley U., Peoria, 1994—; dir. Ill. Ballet (formerly Ctrl. Ill. Ballet), 1999—. Tchr. Harkness Ballet N.Y., Mary Anthony Dance Sch., Zurich Ballet, Nat. Acad. Arts Ill., Jefferson High Sch. Performing Arts Portland, also choreographer; tchr. Summer Dance Lab.; choreographer Mary K. Price Dance Co., U. Ill., Nat. Acad. Arts, Cornish Inst., Seahurst Ballet; tchr. Kneeland Workshops, Port Townsend, Wash., 1988; tchr., co-dir. Kneeland Seminars, Las Vegas, Nev., Port Townsend, summers 1989, 90, Oklahoma City U., summer 1990, Am. Coll. Dance Festival, 1991, 92, 93; tchr. Pa. Gov.'s. Sch. of the Arts, 1991, 92, 94, David Howard summer seminar Mercyhurst Coll., summer 1992, David Howard Summer Workshop with Tulsa Ballet Theatre, 1993, 94, David Howard workshop Seattle tchrs., 1996, David Howard workshop U. Ill., 1997, David Howard-Western Mich. U., 1999; guest artist, asst. prof. Slippery Rock U., 1994; owner The Dance Works, Peoria, Ill., 1994—; guest artist, Southern Ballet Theatre, summer 2000, 2001, David Howard and Mary Price Boday Summer Intensives, Worcester, summer 2000, 2001, 2002. Choreographer 3 ballets Ballet Co. St. Gallen, 1988, dance concert Mary & Friends, Seattle, 1990, The Nutcracker for Warner Theatre Erie; co-choreographer The Nutcracker Ballet, 1991-93, Coppelia, 1993, The Little Mermaid of Lake Erie at the Warner Theater, 1994; choreographer Peoria Ballet, Nutcracker, Civic Ctr., 1995, 30 Yr. Gala, 1995, Alice in Wonderland, 1996, Little Mermaid of Lake Peoria, 1997; staged Swan Lake, 1999; choreographer Rudolph the Red Nose Reindeer at the Shrine Mosque, 2000; choreographer Rock Ballet and The Lion, Witch, and Wardrobe at the Peoria Civic Ctr. Theatre, 2001, Hansel and Gretel, 2002, Power of Dance, 2002. Outstanding Dancer award U. Okla., 1968; named one of Outstanding Young Women of Am., 1977. Address: 719 W Moss Ave Peoria IL 61606-1931

PRICER, WAYNE FRANCIS, counseling consultant; b. Bogue, Kans., Feb. 11, 1935; s. William C. and Lena I. (Hecke) P.; m. Alice M. Fitzpatrick, July 25, 1964; children: Wayne F. Jr., Elizabeth Anne. AB, Ft. Hays State U., 1957; MEd, U. N.D., 1963; postgrad., Wayne State U. Nat. cert. counselor; nat. cert. career counselor; nat. cert. sch. counselor; lic. prof. counselor Mich.; master career counselor. Tchr. Bogue (Kans.) Grade Sch., 1958-62; counselor Lamphere High Sch., 1963-64, 69-75; asst. prin. Page Jr. High, Madison Heights, Mich., 1964-68, prin., 1968-69; adj. counselor Oakland Community Coll., Bloomfield Hills, Mich., 1969—; dir. guidance Lamphere Schs., Madison Heights, 1975-99; adj. prof. Oakland C.C., 1969—; counseling cons. Royal Oak, Mich., 1999—. Bd. dirs., 2d v.p., v.p. Haviland Collectors Internat. Ednl. Found. Contbr. articles to prof. jours. Bd. dirs., 2d v.p. Haviland Collectors Internat., 1997—, Mich. Assn. Retired Sch. Personnel. Named Counselor of Yr. Oakland Counseling Assn., 1999, Lifetime Achievement award MCDA, 1999. Mem. ACA, Am. Mental Health Counselors Assn., Alliance for Ret. Americans, Assn. for Career and Tech. Edn., Assn. for Counselor Edn. and Supervision, Am. Coll. Counselors Assn., Am. Fedn. Tchrs., Am. Sch. Coun. Assn., Am. Vocat. Assn., Assn. for Adult Devel. and Aging, Assn. for Assessment in Counseling, Mich. Assn. for Adult Devel. and Aging, Mich. Assn. Coll. Admission Counselors, Mich. Counseling Assn., Mich. Assn. for Counselor Edn. and Supervision, Mich. Assn. for Measurement and Evaluation in Guidance (pres.), Mich. Assn. Specialists in Group Work, Mich. Career Devel. Assn. (treas. 1994—), Mich. Assn. Ret. Sch. Pers., Mich. Assn. Career and Tech. Edn., Mich. Mental Health Counselors Assn., Mich. Sch. Counselors Assn., Mich. Assn. for Humanistic Edn. and Develop., Mich. Assn. for Multi-Cultural Develop., Nat. Assn. Coll. Admission Counselors, Nat. Career Devel. Assn., Oakland Assn. for Counseling and Devel. (former pres.), Mich. Fedn. Tchrs., Suburban Assn. of Retired Sch. Personnel, Phi Delta Kappa. Office: 719 S Washington Ave Royal Oak MI 48067-3829

PRICER, WILBUR DAVID, electrical engineer, educator; b. Des Moines, July 22, 1935; s. Wilbur Ray and Mary Elizabeth (Berner) P.; m. Nancy Loizeaux, Oct. 10, 1964; children: Douglas, Amy, Timothy, Edward. AB in Physics, Middlebury Coll., 1959; BSEE, MSEE, MIT, 1959. Engr. IBM, Poughkeepsie, N.Y., 1959-70, sr. engr. East Fishkill, 1970-83, sr. mem. tech. staff Essex Junction, Vt., 1983-99; patent cons., 1999—. Adj. prof. elec. engring. U. Vt., 1984-90; pres. Solid State Cirs. Coun., 1980-81; program evaluator Accreditation Bd. for Engring. and Tech., 1990-95. Mem. editl. bd. Spectrum mag., 1990-92; editor Jour. Solid State Cirs., 1983-86; patentee in field. Fellow IEEE; mem. Internat. Solid State Cirs. Conf. (program chmn. 1976, chmn. 1988-96), Sigma Xi. Congregationalist. Home and Office: 5524 Spear St Charlotte VT 05445-9028 E-mail: pricer@wcvt.com.

PRICKETT, DAVID CLINTON, physician; b. Fairmont, W.Va., Nov. 26, 1918; s. Clinton Everett and Mary Anna (Gottschalk) P.; m. Mary Ellen Holt, June 29, 1940; children: David C., Rebecca Ellen, William Radcliffe, Mary Anne, James Thomas, Sara Elizabeth; m. Pamela S. Blackstone, Nov. 17, 1991. Student, Fairmont State Coll., 1940-42; AB, W.Va. U., 1944; MD, U. Louisville, 1946; MPH, U. Pitts., 1955. Pres. Prickett Chem. Co., 1938-43; acct. W.Va. Conservation Commn. Fed. Works Agy., 1941, 42; lab. asst., instr. chemistry W.Va. U., 1943; intern Louisville Gen. Hosp., 1947; surg. resident St. Joseph's Hosp., Parkersburg, W.Va., 1948-49; gen. practice, 1948-50, 55-61; physician USAF, N.Mex. and Calif., 1961-62, U.S. Army, Calif., 1963-64, San Luis Obispo County Hosp., 1965-66, So. Calif. Edison Co., 1981-84; assoc. physician indsl. and gen. practice Los Angeles County, Calif., 1967—; mem. staff Fairmont (W.V.) Gen. Hosp., 1955-60, Fairmont (W.V.) Emergency Hosp., 1955-60, St. Francis Hosp., L.A., 1970-71. Physician Bethlehem Mines Corp., Idamay, W.Va., 1956; resident physician Sedgwick County Hosp., Wichita, Kans., 1964-65; med. dir. South Gate plant GM, 1969-71; staff physician City of L.A., 1971-76; relief med. practice Appalachia summer seasons, 1977, 86, 88-97. Author: The Newer Epidemiology, 1962, rev., 1990, Public Health, A Science Resolvable by Mathematics, 1965; contbr. to publ. Med. officer USPHS, Navajo Indian Reservation, Tohatchi (N.Mex.) Health Ctr., 1953-55, surgeon, res. officer, 1957-59; pres. W.Va. Pub. Health Assn., 1951-52; sec. indsl. and pub. health sect. W. Va. Med. Assn., 1956; local and dist. health officer, W.Va., 1951-53; dist. health officer Allegheny County, Pa., 1957; med. adv. Boy Scouts Am., W.V., N. Mex. Served to 2d lt. AUS, 1943-46. Dr. Thomas Parran fellow U. Pitts. Sch. Pub. Health, 1955; named to Hon. Order Ky. Cols. Fellow Am. Pub. Health Assn; mem. AMA, Sons of Revolution, Am. Occupl. Med. Assn., Am. Acad. Family Physicians, Western Occupl. Med. Assn., Calif. Med. Assn., L.A. County Med. Assn., Am. Legion, Elks, Phi Chi. Address: PO Box 4032 Whittier CA 90607-4032

PRICKETT, GORDON ODIN, mining, mineral and energy engineer; b. Morris, Minn., Nov. 26, 1935; s. Glenn Irvin and Edna Margaret (Erickson) P.; m. Jean Carolyn Strobush, Oct. 8, 1958; children: Karen Joan Keating, Laura Jean, Glenn Thomas. B in Mining Engring., U. Minn., 1958, MS in Mineral Engring. and Econs., 1965. Registered profl. engr., Mo., Ill. U.S. Steel fellow U. Minn., Mpls., 1963-65; rsch. mineral engr. Internat. Minerals & Chem. Corp., Skokie, Ill., 1965-68; mgmt. sci. cons. Computer Mgmt. Cons., Northfield, 1968-71; mgr. tech. sys. Duval Corp., Tucson, 1971-77; dir. mgmt. info. sys. Arch Mineral Corp., St. Louis, 1977-78; supr. mine planning projects Peabody Coal Co., 1978-82; mgr. elec. tech. transfer, nuc. plant simulator, rsch. Union Electric Co., 1983-95. Tech. network advisor GordMett, Ltd., Aitkin, Minn., 1995—; presenter papers at industry confs; music and news program host Sta. KAXE-FM, Grand Rapids, Minn., 1997—. Contbr. articles to profl. jours.; columnist Aitkin Ind. Age, 1998—. Co-founder, chmn. Lake Forest-Lake Bluff (Ill.) Com. for Equal Opportunity, 1968-71; com. Confluence St. Louis, 1987-95; bd. dirs., officer ch. bds., polit. twp. and county orgn. Lake Forest, Tucson, St. Louis, Aitkin, Minn., 1968—; mem. Aitkin County Water Planning Task Force, 1997—, Onanegozie (Minn.) Regional Resource Conservation Devel. Coun., 1999—. Lt. USN, 1958-63, naval aviator, Cuba; to comdr. USNR, 1963-79. Mem. AIME (chair program com. 1958—), Assn. Quality and Participation (chair programs 1986-90), Norwegian Soc. St. Louis, LWV (charter mem. Brainerd Lakes unit, 1996—), Engrs. Club St. Louis (chair affiliated socs. and pub. affairs. 1987-88, 93-95), Heartland Poets. Avocations: fishing, canoeing, tennis, skiing, community band. Home and Office: Nord Lake 38639 337th Ln Aitkin MN 56431-2122

PRICKETT, GREGORY L. judge; b. Torrance, Calif., May 3, 1956; m. Laura Suzanne Arthur, Sept. 12, 1981; children: Jennifer, Sean. BA, U. So. Calif., L.A., 1978; JD, Southwestern U., 1981. Dep. dist. atty. L.A. County, 1981-83, Orange County, Santa Ana, Calif., 1983-91, sr. dep. dist. atty., 1991-95; mcpl. ct. judge Fullerton, 1995-98; judge Superior Ct., 1998—. Lectr. in field. Contbr. articles to profl. jours. Adv. bd. Canning Hunger, Orange, Calif., 1995—, Friends Ctr.-Azusa (Calif.) Pacific U., 1990—; chairperson missions com. S.W. Yearly Meeting, Whittier, Calif., 1998. Named Disting. Lectr. Calif. Dist. Atty. Assn., 1989. Mem. Am. Judges Assn. Mem. Evangelical Friends. Office: Superior Ct Judge 1275 N Berkeley Ave Fullerton CA 92832-1206

PRIDE, BENJAMIN DAVID, sales executive; b. Staten Island, N.Y., Sept. 20, 1952; s. Benjamin David and Evelyn Marie (Dann) P. BA, St. Francis Coll., Bklyn., 1974. Office mgr., prodn. estimator Leber Katz Ptnrs., N.Y.C., 1975-76; prodn. estimator, media planner, out-of-home media buyer, sports buyer Dancer, Fitzgerald & Sample, 1976-81; v.p. sports and promotion Backer, Spielvogel, Bates Worldwide, 1981-95, Zenith Media, N.Y.C., 1995-96; ptnr. Schineller & Pride, 1996-97; account exec. Newport Media, 1997-99; asst. mgr., sr. membership dir. UCC Total Home, Eatontown, NJ, 2001—. Divsn. capt. USCG Aux., 2000. Republican. Roman Catholic. Avocations: boating, fishing.

PRIDE, MIRIAM R. college president; b. Canton, China, June 6, 1948; d. Richard E. and Martha W. Pride; divorced. Grad., Berea College Found. Sch., 1966, College of Wooster, 1970; MBA, U. Ky., 1989. With sales room Boone Tavern Hotel Berea Coll., Berea, Ky., 1963-70; intern in administrn. in higher edn., head resident College of Wooster, Wooster, Ohio, 1970-72; accounts payable clerk, dir. Boone Tavern Hotel, head resident, dir. student activities Berea Coll., 1972-88; eligibility worker dept. human resources State of Ky., 1975-76; assistantship undergrad. advising coll. bus. U. Ky., 1987-89; asst. to pres. for campus life, v.p. for administrn., pres. Blackburn Coll., Carlinville, Ill., 1989—. Chmn. United Way Berea, Carlinville, 1989—92; fin. chmn. Carlinville Hosp., 1995—97; mem. Ill. Commn. on Status of Women; bd. dirs. Land of Lincoln Girl Scouts, 1993—2000, fin. chmn., 1995—2000, mem. nominating com., 2000—; bd. dirs. Carlinville Area Hosp., 1993—97, Assn. Presbyn. Colls. and Univs., Fedn. Ill. Colls. and Univs., 1993—, Federated Ch. Bd., 1998—2001. Mem. Carlinville C. of C. (bd. dirs.), Rotary (bd. dirs. 1996—). Mem. Federated Ch. Avocations: reading, walking, knitting. Office: Blackburn Coll Office of the President Carlinville IL 62626

PRIDEMORE, MILTON ERNEST, freelance/self-employed artist; b. Harlan, KY, Nov. 14, 1960; married. Portraiture. Home and Office: Ernie's Art 532 Sals Branch Road Evarts KY 40828 Business E-Mail: epridemore@kih.net.

PRIDHAM, THOMAS GRENVILLE, retired research microbiologist; b. Chgo., Oct. 10, 1920; s. Grenville and Gladys Etheral (Sloss) P.; m. Phyllis Sue Hokamp, July 1, 1943 (dec. Feb. 1994); children: Pamela Sue, Thomas Foster, Grenville Thomas, Rolf Thomas, Montgomery Thomas; m. Edna Lee Boudreaux, Mar. 6, 1995. BS in Chemistry, U. Ill., 1943, PhD in Bacteriology, 1949. Instr. bacteriology U. Ill., Champaign-Urbana, 1947; rsch. microbiologist No. Regional Rsch. Lab., USDA, Peoria, Ill., 1948-51, 53-65, U.S. Indsl. Chems., Balt., 1951-52; supr. tech. ops. Acme Vitamins, Inc., Joliet, Ill., 1952-53; sr. rsch. biologist U.S. Borax Rsch. Corp., Anaheim, Calif., 1965-67; supervisory rsch. microbiologist No. Regional Rsch. Ctr. USDA, Peoria, 1967-81, head agrl. rsch. culture collection No. Regional Rsch. Lab., 1967-81; ret., 1981. Cons. Mycogen Corp., San Diego, 1985-87; U.S. sr. scientist Fed. Republic Germany, Darmstadt, 1977. Contbg. author: Actinomycetales: The Boundary Microorganisms, 1974, Bergey's Manual of Determinative Bacteriology, 1974, Synopsis and Classification of Living Organisms, 1982; mem. editorial bd. Jour. Antibiotics, 1969-81; contbr. articles to Jour. Bacteriology, Applied Microbiology, Phytopathology, Actinomycetes, Mycologia, Devel. Indsl. Microbiology, Jour. Antibiotics, Internat. Bull. Bacteriological Nomenclature Taxonomy, Antibiotics Ann., Antimicrobial Agts., Chemotherapy, also others. With USNR, 1943-45, with Rsch. Res., 1945-54, lt. ret. Fulbright scholar, Italy, 1952; grantee Soc. Am. Bacteriologists, 1957. Fellow: Am. Acad. Microbiology; mem.: Alexander von Humboldt Assn. Episcopalian. Achievements include patents in fermentative production of riboflavin and of antibiotics; research in microbial culture collection technology and management, systematics of streptomycetes, industrial microbiology. Home: 38 Mayo Br/Brandy Keg Rd Prestonsburg KY 41653-8114

PRIDMORE, ROY DAVIS, government official; b. Gaffney, S.C., May 18, 1925; s. Davis Bailey and Ethel (Hughes) P.; m. Doris Hedy Glatzl, July 16, 1960; children: Lisa Ann, David Michael. Cert., Columbus U., Washington, 1949, Am. Inst., 1953, U.S. Dept. Agr. Grad. Sch., 1957. Pers. asst. Dept. Army, Fort Myer, Va., 1955-58; staff asst. D.C. Hwy. Dept., Washington, 1962-67; adminstrv. asst. Dept. Transp., 1958-62, adminstrv. officer, 1967-94, ret., 1994. Vice pres. Springboard Swim Club, Springfield, Va., 1984-85. Served with U.S. Army, 1946-47; mem. Res. (ret.) Decorated Legion of Merit. Democrat. Roman Catholic. Avocation: swimming, gardening.

PRIEBE, CEDRIC JOSEPH, JR. pediatric surgeon; b. N.Y.C., Feb. 7, 1930; s. Cedric Joseph and Mary Martha (O'Beirne) P.; m. Cynthia Amelia Cali, June 11, 1955; children: Diane Marie, Janice Marie, Cedric Joseph III, Catherine Marie, Michael Stephen, Gregory Paul, Marta Marcella. BS cum laude, Fordham U., 1951; MD, Cornell U., 1955. Surg. resident The Roosevelt Hosp., N.Y.C., 1955-60; pediatric surg. resident Ohio State U., Children's Hosp., Columbus, 1965-67; pediatric surgeon, asst. and assoc. prof. The Roosevelt Hosp., Colombia U., N.Y.C., 1967-79; chief pediatric surgery, prof. surgery La. State U., Charity Hosp., New Orleans, 1979-82; dir. surg. edn. Children's Hosp. of New Orleans, 1979-82; chief pediatric surgery, prof. surgery SUNY at Stony Brook, U. Hosp., 1982—. Sr. clin. trainee in cancer control NIH, Washington, 1963-65. Editl. cons. Jour. of Pediatric Surgery, Phila., 1994—; author: (with others) Neoplasia in Childhood, 1966; contbr. articles to profl. jours. Maj. USAF, 1956-65. Mem.: ACS, NY Soc. for Pediat. Surgery (v.p. 1976—78, pres. 1978—79), Children's Oncology Group, Pediat. Oncology Group (cancer control com. 1992—2000), Am. Pediat. Surg. Assn. (membership com. 1990—93, by-laws com. 1993—95, cancer com. 1996—99, 1996—99), Am. Acad. of Pediats. (publs. com. 1989—92, chair publs. com. 1992), Soc. for Surgery Alimentary Tract, Am. Burn Assn. Republican. Roman Catholic. Avocations: tennis, squash racquets, travel. Home: 9 Woodhull Cove Ln Setauket NY 11733-1643 Office: SUNY at Stony Brook HSC T 19 Stony Brook NY 11794-8191 E-mail: Priebe@surg.som.sunysb.edu., Priebe@optonline.net.

PRIEBE, DAVID JON, music educator; b. Madison, Minn., Aug. 4, 1945; s. Walter Ludwig and Imogene Elma Priebe. BA Music, Capital Univ. Conservatory of Music, Columbus, OH, 1963—67; MA Music Ed., Bowling Green State Univ., Bowling Green, OH, 1976. Nationally certified music instructor Ohio Music Edn. Assn., 1998. Choir dir. Waite H.S., Toledo, 1967—70; dir. choral music Norwood H.S., Cincinnati, 1970—75; choir dir. Greenville H.S., Greenville, 1975—76; elem. music instr. Greenville Schools, 1976—. Organist Darke County Oratorio Soc., Greenville, Ohio, 1980—85; organist/choir master St. Pauls Episcopal Ch., Greenville, Ohio, 1990—98; organist/pianist St. John Luth. Ch., Greenville, Ohio, 1998—2002; coach for greenville schools Interscholastic Track & Cross Country, Greenville, Ohio, 1994—2002; dir. 5th grade chorus East Elem., Greenville, Ohio, 1985—2002. Head of sportsmanship movement Greenville Schools, Greenville, Ohio, 1996—2002. Recipient Wall-Mart Tchr. of the Yr., Wall-Mart Found., Bentonville, AR, 2000, Sportsmanship Award, Ohio Athletic Assn., Columbus, OH, 2001. Mem.: Ohio Choral Directors Assn., Ohio Music Edn. Assn. (judge of adjudicated events 1995—2002), Music Educators Nat. Conf. (nationally cert. music instr.), Am. Guild of Organists. Lutheran. Achievements include received special citation from Ohio State Legislature for musicianship and teaching. Avocations: gardening, running, reading, cycling, weight lifting. Home: 1336 Jonquil Lane Greenville OH 45331 Office: East Elementary School 301 East Fifth Street Greenville OH 45331

PRIEBE, MARSHA L. family services counselor; b. Pierre, S.D., Sept. 23, 1952; d. Herbert and Kathryn (Buechler) Auch; m. Glenn D. Priebe, Nov. 9, 1974 (div. Feb. 1982), remarried Nov. 9, 1987; children: Andrew D., Christa L. ADN, Presentation Coll., Aberdeen, S.D., 1972; BS in Psychology, St. Joseph's Coll., North Windham, Maine, 1984; MEd in Counseling, S.D. State U., Brookings, 1990. Lic. prof. counselor, S.D.; nat. cert. counselor. Staff nurse Cmty. Bailey Hosp., Chamberlain, S.D., 1972-73; surg. nurse Sioux Valley Hosp., Sioux Falls, 1973-74; health/nutrition/mental health coord. South Ctrl. Child Devel., Lake Andes, 1975-85; program specialist, med. svcs. Dept. Social Svcs., Pierre, 1985, alternative care/home base provider Chamberlain, 1986-91; family svc. counselor St. Joseph's Indian Sch., 1991—. Health care specialist Westinghouse Health Systems, Denver, 1979-81, Am. Heritage Alliance, Denver, 1985; faculty trainer dept. social svcs. U. S.D., Vermillion,

1990-91. Mem. Brule County Child Protection Team, Chamberlain, 1988—; facilitator Cmty. Parenting Classes, Chamberlain, 1989-93. Recipient Outstanding Svc. award Child Welfare Tng. Inst., 1991, Head Start Program, 1985. Mem. ACA, S.D. Counseling Assn. Avocations: cooking, reading, fishing. Office: St Joseph Indian Sch PO Box 89 Chamberlain SD 57325-0089

PRIEM, RICHARD GREGORY, writer, information systems executive; b. Munich, Sept. 18, 1949; came to U.S., 1953; s. Richard Stanley and Elizabeth Teresa (Thompson) P. (both dec.); m. Janice Lynne Holland, July 27, 1976; children: Michael John, Matthew Warren (dec.), Kathryn Elizabeth. BS in Radio-TV-Film, U. Tex., 1970; MEd in Ednl. Tech., U. Ga., 1979; postgrad., Coll. William and Mary, 1981-82. Cert. fraud examiner. Radio personality, sales exec. KOKE, Inc., Austin, Tex., 1968-73; numerous positions including asst. prof. dept. behavioral scis. and leadership U.S. Mil. Acad., staff officer anti terrorism and inspector gen. U.S. Army, 1973-94; exec. v.p. It's Your Party, Herndon, Va., 1992-97; dep. divsn. mgr. Sci. Applications Internat. Corp., Vienna, 1994-97; pres., COO, Commerce Tech., Inc., Centreville, 1997—. Cons. Dallas Cowboys Football Club, 1981; scouting coord. Army Football, 1983-85; cons. in field of anti-terrorism. Contbr. articles to profl. jours. Mem. Assn. Cert. Fraud Examiners, Internat. Soc. for Performance Improvement, Phi Kappa Phi, Kappa Delta Pi. Home: 15386 Twin Creeks Ct Centreville VA 20120-3742 Office: Commerce Techs Inc PO Box 221254 Chantilly VA 20153-1254 E-mail: rpriem@commerce-tech.com.

PRIES, JANISE GOFF, counselor, secondary education educator; b. L.A., Oct. 3, 1949; d. Dean Carlson and Mercedes (Patakas) Goff; m. John T. Evans Jr., June 18, 1971 (div. 1986); children: John D., Jason R., Jacquelyn E.; m. Kim Henry Pries, May 15, 1993. BA, U. Colo., 1970; MEd, U. Tex., El Paso, 1996. Nat. certified counselor; lic. profl. counselor, Tex.; lic. profl. counselor supr., Tex.; cert. secondary edn., gifted and talented endorsement, Tex. Rector's sec. St. Francis-on-the-Hill Episcopal Ch., El Paso, 1987; music dir., English tchr. St. Clement's Episcopal Parish Sch., 1987-93; 8th grade lang. arts tchr. Morehead Mid. Sch., 1993-95, humanities tchr., 1996-97, H.E. Charles Mid. Sch., El Paso, 1995-96; counselor Rusk Elem. Sch., 1997-2000, Austin H.S., El Paso, 2000—; counselor in pvt. practice, 2001—. Vol. counselor Jewish Family and Children's Svcs., El Paso, 1996-97. Co-editor: Counselor Connection. Soprano, El Paso Pro Musica, 1990-93; dir. St. Clement's Honors Handbell Chorus, El Paso, 1989-93; aux. charter pres., soprano choir Bruce Nehring Consort, El Paso, 1993-95, 97-98; chmn. bd. deacons 1st Presbyn. Ch., El Paso, 1990-91, elder, 1992-94. Recipient Masons Mirabeau B. Lamar award Five Points Masonic Lodge, 2000. Mem. Am. Counseling Assn., Tex. Classroom Tchrs. Assn., Chi Sigma Iota. Avocations: reading, counted cross-stitch, singing. Office: Austin High Sch 3500 Memphis El Paso TX 79930 E-mail: jpries1@elp.rr.com., jgpries@episd.org.

PRIESAND, SALLY JANE, rabbi; b. Cleve., June 27, 1946; d. Irving Theodore and Rosetta Elizabeth (Welch) P. BA in English, U. Cin., 1968; B.Hebrew Letters, Hebrew Union Coll.-Jewish Inst. Religion, 1971, MA in Hebrew Letters, 1972; D.H.L. (hon.), Fla. Internat. U., 1973; DD (hon.), Hebrew Union Coll., 1997. Ordained rabbi, 1972. Student rabbi Sinai Temple, Champaign, Ill., 1968, Congregation B'nai Israel, Hattiesburg, Miss., 1969-70, Congregation Shalom, Milw., 1970, Temple Beth Israel, Jackson, Mich., 1970-71; rabbinic intern Isaac M. Wise Temple, Cin., 1971-72; asst. rabbi Stephen Wise Free Synagogue, N.Y.C., 1972-77, assoc. rabbi, 1977-79; rabbi Temple Beth El, Elizabeth, N.J., 1979-81, Monmouth Reform Temple, Tinton Falls, 1981—; chaplain Lenox Hill Hosp., N.Y.C., 1979-81. Author: Judaism and the New Woman, 1975. Mem. commn. on synagogue rels. Fedn. Jewish Philanthropies N.Y., 1972-79, mem. com. on aged commn. synagogue rels., 1972-75; mem. task force on equality of women in Judaism pub. affairs com. N.Y. Fedn. Reform Synagogues, 1972-75; mem. com. on resolutions Ctrl. Conf. Am. Rabbis, 1975-77, com. on cults, 1976-78, admissions com., 1983-89; chmn. Task Force on Women in Rabbinate, 1977-83, chmn. 1977-79, mem. exec. bd., 1977-79, com. on resolutions, 1989-92, chmn. com. conv. program, 1993-96; mem. joint commn. on Jewish edn. Ctrl. Conf. Am. Rabbis-Union Am. Hebrew Congregations, 1974-77; mem. task force on Jewish singles Commn. Synagogue Rels., 1975-77; mem. N.Y. Bd. Rabbis, 1975—, Shore Area Bd. Rabbis, 1981—; mem. interim steering com. Clergy and Laity Concerned, 1979-81; bd. dirs. NCCJ, N.Y.C., 1980-82, Jewish Fedn. Greater Monmouth County, trustee, 1988-2000, strategic planning commn., 1996—, hon. v.p., 2000—; trustee Planned Parenthood of Monmouth County, 1982-90; v.p. Interfaith Neighbors, 1988-96, pres., 1997—; mem. UAHC-CCAR Joint Commn. on Synagogue Affiliation, 1992—; bd. govs. Hebrew Union Coll.-Jewish Inst. Religion, 1993—; trustee Union Am. Hebrew Congregations, 1994-98. Cited by B'nai Brith Women, 1971; named Woman of Yr. Temple Israel, Columbus, Ohio, 1972, Woman of Yr. Ladies Aux. N.Y. chpt. Jewish War Vets., 1973, Woman for All Seasons N. L.I. region Women's Am. ORT, 1973, Extraordinary Women of Achievement NCCJ, 1978, Woman of Achievement Monmouth County Adv. Commn. on Status Women, 1988; recipient Quality of Life award Dist. One chpt. B'nai B'rith Women, 1973, Medallion Judaic Heritage Soc., 1978, Eleanor Roosevelt Humanities award Women's div. State of Israel Bonds, 1980, Rabbinical award Coun. Jewish Fedn., 1988, Woman of Leadership award Monmouth Coun. Girl Scouts U.S., 1991, The Woman Who Dares award Nat. Coun. Jewish Women, 1993, Women's Studies Diding. Alumnae award Friends of Women's Studies U. Cin., 1997. Mem. Hadassah (life), Ctrl. Conf. Am. Rabbis, NOW, Am. Jewish Congress, Am. Jewish Com., Assn. Reform Zionists Am., Jewish Women Internat. (life), Jewish Peace Fellowship, Women's Rabbinic Network, Nat. Breast Cancer Coalition, HUC-JIR Rabbinic Alumni Assn. (sec., treas. 1997-99, v.p. 1999-2001, pres. 2001—). Home: 10 Wedgewood Cir Eatontown NJ 07724-1203 Office: 332 Hance Ave Eatontown NJ 07724-2730 E-mail: spriesand@monmouth.com.

PRIEST, GEORGE L. law educator; b. 1947; BA, Yale U., 1969; JD, U. Chgo., 1973. Assoc. prof. U. Puget Sound, Tacoma, 1973-75; law and econ. fellow U. Chgo., 1975-77; prof. U. Buffalo, 1977-80, UCLA, 1980-81, Yale U., New Haven, 1981—. Dir. program in civil liability; John M. Olin prof. law and econs., 1986—. Mem. Pres.' Com. on Privatization, 1987-88. Office: PO Box 208215 New Haven CT 06520-8215

PRIEST, HARTWELL WYSE, artist; b. Brantford, Ont., Can., Jan. 1, 1901; d. John Frank Henry and Rachel Thayer (Gavet) Wyse; m. A.J. Gustin Priest, Aug. 4, 1927; children: Paul Lambert, Marianna Thayer. BA, Smith Coll. Former tchr. graphic art Va. Art Inst., Charlottesville. Former lectr. on prints and lithography; juror art exhbn. Unitarian Ch., 1993. One-woman shows include Argent Gallery, N.Y.C., 1955, 58, 60, 73, 77, 81, Va., 1969, 71, Nantucket, Mass., 1956, Ft. Lauderdale, Fla. Art Ctr., 1956, McGuffey Gallery, Charlotsville, Va., 1998; Pen & Brush, N.Y.C., 1973, 91, 97, invitational retrospective exhbn. McGuffey Art Ctr., Charlottesville, Va., 1984, Va., N.Y., 1984, 88; work represented in permanent collections Library of Congress Washington, Norton Gallery, Palm Beach, Fla., Soc. Am. Graphic Artists, Hunterdon County Art Ctr., Longwood Coll., Smith Coll., Va. Mus., Richmond, Carnegie Mellon U. and numerous others; solo exhbn. of prints McGuffey Art Ctr., Charlottesville, Va., 1988, 90, 93, Woodstock Artist Gallery, 1990, Soc. Am. Graphic Artists, 1988-89, 92, Bombay, 1989, U. Va. Hosp., 1989, Bergen Mus. Art and Sci., 1991; represented in group shows McGuffey Gallery, 1988, 94, Gallery Show, Richmond, Va., 1988, Nat. Assn. Women Artists, Florence, Italy, 1972, N.Y.C., 1989, 96, ann. show Ojibway Hotel Club, Pointe au Baril, Georgian Bay, Ont., Can., 1991, Soc. Am. Graphic Srts, N.Y.C., 1989, 92, Woodstock, N.Y. Art Assoc., 1990, McGuffey Art Ctr., Charlottesville, Va., 1990, 94, 98, Pen and Brush ann. Graphic Show, N.Y.C., 1991 (award for etching Spring, Ada Rosario Cecere Meml. award), Bergen Mus., N.J., 1991, Ojibway Club, Ont., Can., 1991; Pen and Brush Christmas exhbn., 1994-95, Showing of a Video, Harrisonburg, Va.; represented in traveling group shows Nat. Assn. Women Artists, Puerto Rico, 1987, India, 1989, N.Y.C., 1994; pvt. collection U. Va. Hosp., Charlottesville, 1989; subject of TV documentary Hartwell Priest: Printmaker, 1995. Recipient awards for lithograph Field Flowers, Longwood Coll., 1965, Nat. Assn. Woman Artists, 1965, lithograph West Wind, A Buell award, 1961, print Streets of Silence, T. Giorgi Meml. award, 1973, lithograph Blue Lichen, Pen & Brush, 1984, award for collage, 1985; 1st award for graphics Blue Ridge Art Show, 1985, Gene A. Walker award for print Glacial Rocks, 1986, award for print Blue Ridge Show, 1987, Philip Isenburg award for graphic PreCambrian Rock Pattern, 1988, Ada R. Cecere Meml. award Pen and Brush, 1991, Art award Piedmont Coun. Arts, 1993. Mem. Nat. Assn. Women Artists (Traveling Printmaking Exhbn. 1987-89), Pen and Brush, Soc. Am. Graphic Artists, Washington Print Club, 2d St. Gallery, Charlottesville, McGuffey Art Ctr. Avocations: walking, singing in choir, gardening, playing Bach and Mozart, playing recorder and piano. Home: 41 Old Farm Rd Charlottesville VA 22903-4725

PRIEST, PETER H. lawyer; b. Norwood, Mass., Sept. 12, 1955; s. William G. and Mary E. (Horne) P.; children: William, Sarah. BSEE, U. Maine, Orono, 1977; JD, U. Maine, Portland, 1980. Bar: N.Y. 1981, N.C., 1996, U.S. Dist. Ct. (so., ea. dists.) N.Y. 1981, U.S. Patent Office 1981, U.S. Ct. Appeals (Fed. cir.) 1987. Assoc. Davis, Hoxie, Faithfull, Hapgood, N.Y.C., 1980-88, ptnr., 1989-95; pvt. practice, Chapel Hill, N.C., 1995—. Mem. ABA, Am. Intellectual Property Law Assn., Fed. Cir. Bar Assn., Internat. Intellectual Property Soc., Union Internat. Avocats. Office: 529 Dogwood Dr Chapel Hill NC 27516-2807

PRIEST, ROBERT J. intercultural educator; b. Cochabamba, Bolivia, Mar. 20, 1957; s. Perry N. Priest and Lucy Anne McQuilkin; m. Kersten Bayt; children: Joseph, Shelly, Daniel, David. BA, Columbia Internat. U., 1975—79; MDiv, Trinity Evang. Divinity Sch., 1979—82; MA in Social Sci., U. Chgo., 1983—84; PhD in Anthropology, U. Calif., Berkeley, 1985—93. Asst. to assoc prof. Intercultural Studies Columbia Biblical Seminary and Grad. Sch. Mission, SC, 1990—99; assoc. prof. Intercultural Studies Trinity Evang. Divinity Sch., 1999—2002, dir. PhD Program Intercultural Studies, 2001—02. Grantee summer stipend, Louisville Inst., 2000, Wabash Ctr., 1999. Home: 30333 N Revere Dr Libertyville IL 60048 Office: Trinity Evang Divinity Sch 2065 Half Day Rd Deerfield IL 60015 Personal E-mail: robertjpriest@aol.com. Business E-Mail: rpriest@tiu.edu.

PRIEST, SHARON DEVLIN, secretary of state; b. Montreal, Quebec, Can. m. Bill Priest; 1 child, Adam. Tax preparer, instr. H & R Block, Little Rock, 1976-78; owner, founder Devlin Co., 1983-86; account exec. Greater Little Rock C. of C., 1990-94; mem. Little Rock Bd. Dirs., 1986, 90; vice mayor Little Rock, 1989-90, mayor, 1991-92; Sec. of State State of Arkansas, 1994—. Bd. dirs. Invesco Inc., New Futures. Bd. dirs., past pres. Metroplan (Environ. Svc. award 1982), YMCA, Southwest Hosp.; mem. Advt. and Promotion commn., Ark. Internat. Visitors Coun., Pulaski Are Transp. Svc. Policy Com., St. Theresa's Parish Coun., Exec. com. for Ark. Mcpl. League, Nat. League of Cities Trans. and Communications Steering Com. and Policy Com., adv. bd. M.M. Cohn., Little Rock City Beautiful Commn., 1980-86; former bd. dirs. Downtown Partnership, Southwest YMCA, 1984, 86, sec.; former mem. Community Housing Resource Bd., 1984-86, Pub. Facilities Bd. Southwest Hosp., 1985-86, Southwest Merchants' Assn., 1985—, 2d v.p., 1985; chmn. Little Rock Arts and Humanities Promotion Commn.; led petition dr. for appropriation for Fourche Creek Plan 7A. Recipient of the Fighting Back Freedom Fighter award, 1995, recipient of Environ. Svc. award from the Little Rock Metroplan Comm., 1982. Mem. Leadership Inst. Alumni Assn. (4 Bernard de la Harpe awards). Achievements include being selected by Arkansas Business as one of the Top 100 Women in Arkansas. Office: Office of Sec of State State Capitol Bldg 256 Little Rock AR 72201*

PRIESTLEY, HOLLY, education educator; b. Phila., Dec. 6, 1945; d. Vernard Fenel Delk and Florence Amelia Baker; m. William J. Priestley, May 24, 1986; 1 child from previous marriage, Aaron C. Stout. BS in Sci. Edn., Indiana U. of Pa., 1968; MEd in Sci. Edn., U. Pitts., 1975; EdD, Temple U., 1996. Tchr. Wilkinsburg (Pa.) Sch. Dist., 1971-75; sci. and math. tchr. Sch. Dist. Borough of Morrisville, Pa., 1977-99; instr. Holy Family Coll., Phila., 1985-89, Bucks County C.C., Newtown, 1989-93, Temple U., Phila., 1994-98, St. Joseph's U., Phila., 1998-99; instr. edn. U. Hawaii, Hilo, 1999—2000; assoc. rschr. Penn State Univ., 2000—. Co-author assessment tool Inquiry Matrix, 1998. Mem. Am. Edn. Rsch. Assn., Assn. for Edn. of Tchrs. of Sci., Hawaii Sci. Tchrs. Assn., Nat. Assn. Biology Tchrs., Nat. Coun. Tchrs. Math., Phi Delta Kappa. Avocations: greyhound adoption, gardening. Home: 1 W Water St Lock Haven PA 17745-1230

PRIETO, CHAR, humanities educator; b. La Hiniesta, Zamora, Spain, Oct. 17, 1954; arrived in U.S., 1979; d. Alfonso Prieto, Josefina Rodriguez; m. Dale Mattson; children: Raquel Mattson-Prieto, Eric Mattson-Prieto. BS in Edn., Ind. U. South Bend, 1989; MEd, Purdue U. Calumet, 1993; PhD of Spanish, Purdue U., 2000. Guest lectr. Purdue U., Calumet, Ind., 1990—94, tchg. asst. West Lafayette, 1994—96; prof. U. Notre Dame, Notre Dame, 1996—2001; asst. prof. Valparaiso U., Valparaiso, 2001—. Author: Four Spanish Authors, 2002, Between Two Worlds, 2002. Bd. dirs. Cmty. Concerts, Michigan City, Ind. Recipient First Pl. award, ESL in Adult Lit., 1996; grantee Jump Start grant, Info. Technologies, 2000. Mem.: Assn. Canadiense de Hispanistas, Modern Lang. Assn. Avocations: volleyball, gardening, travel. Office: Valparaiso Univ 109 Meier Hall Valparaiso IN 46383

PRIETO, VICTOR GERARDO, physician; b. Madrid, Spain, Feb. 14, 1963; arrived in U.S., 1991; MD, Alicante, Alicante, Spain, 1986; PhD, Barcelona, Barcelona, Spain, 1991. Diplomate in dermatopathology Am. Bd. Anat. Pathology. Resident pathology N.Y. Hosp., N.Y., 1993-94; fellow pathology Meml. Sloan Kettering, 1994-95; fellow dermatopathology N.Y. Hosp. Cornell Med. Ctr., 1991-93, 95-96; asst. prof. pathology Duke U., Durham, 1996-99; from asst. prof. to assoc. prof., chief dermatopathology U. Tex.-M.D. Tex. Anderson Cancer Ctr., Houston, 1999—. Mem. editl. bd.: Cutaneous Pathology, 1997—; contbr. articles to profl. jours. Recipient Fetter award Duke Univ., 1998, Callaway award, 1999. Fellow Am. Soc. Dermatology, Soc. for Investigative Dermatology; mem. U.S. and Canadian Acad. Pathology, Internat. Soc. of Investigative Dermatology, Am. Assn. Advancement Sci. Avocations: guitar, bicycling. Office: Univ Tex Anderson Cancer Ctr Dept Pathology Box 85 1515 Holcombe Blvd Houston TX 77030-4009 Fax: (713) 745-3740. E-mail: vprieto@mdanderson.org.

PRIGMORE, KATHRYN BRADFORD TYLER, architecture educator, architect; b. St. Albans, N.Y., Nov. 21, 1956; d. Richard Jerome and Shirley Virginia (Neizer) Tyler; m. James Craig Prigmore, June 20, 1986 (div. June 1992); children: Crystal Andrea, Amber Sheriesse. BS in Bldg. Sci., Rensselaer Poly. Inst., 1977, BArch, 1978; MS in Engring., Cath. U. Am., 1981. Registered architect, Va., NCARB. Intern architect VVKR Inc., Alexandria, Va., 1979-82; architect Robert A. Hawthorne, Architects, PC, Washington, 1982; project mgr. Robert Traynham Coles, Architect, PC, 1982-84; assoc. Segreti Tepper Architects, P.C., 1984-92; assoc. prof. dept. architecture Howard U., 1991—, assoc. dean Sch. Architecture and Planning, 1992-97, asst. dir. Sch. Architecture and Design, 1997-98, asst. dean Coll. Engring., Arch. and Computer Sci., 1998; sr. assoc. Einhorn Yaffee Prescott, Archs. and Engrs., 1998—. Chmn. Va. Bd. Archs., Profl. Engrs., Landsurveyors and Cert. Interior Designers and Landscape Architects, Landscape Archs. and Land Surveyors, 2001; chmn. com. exams Nat. Coun. Archtl. Registration Bds., 2000; mem. alumni adv. coun. Sch. Architecture, Rensselaer Poly. Inst., 1993—; mem. adv. bd. Dept. Arch. Hampton U.; guest spkr. in the field. Contbr. articles to profl. jours. Mem. adv. coun. No. Va. Urban League, 1980-81. Named to Outstanding Young Women in Am., 1983. Fellow AIA (Washington chpt. 1983—); mem. AAUW (mem. selected fellows selection panel 1995—), Nat. Orgn. Minority Archs., Black Women in Architecture and Related Professions (faculty advisor Howard U. chpt. 1992—). Episcopalian. Avocations: writing, gardening. Home: 8911 Union Farm Rd Alexandria VA 22309-3936 Office: Howard U Sch Arch and Design 2366 6th St NW Washington DC 20001-2323 E-mail: kprigmore@eypae.com.

PRIGOGINE, ILYA, physics educator; b. Moscow, Russia, Jan. 25, 1917; s. Roman and Julie (Wichmann) Prigogine; m. Marina Prokopowicz, Feb. 25, 1961; children: Yves, Pascal. Licencié en sciences chimiques, licencié en sciences physiques, Free U. Brussels, 1939, PhD, 1941, agrégé de l'Enseignement Supérieur en Chimie Physique, 1945; DHC (hon.) , U. Newcastle, Eng., 1966, U. Poitiers, France, 1966, U. Chgo., 1969, U. Bordeaux, France, 1972, U. de Liège, Belgium, 1977, U. Uppsala, Sweden, 1977, U de Droit, D'Economie et des Scis., d'Aix-Marseille, France, 1979, U. Georgetown, 1980, U. Cracovie, Poland, 1981, U. Rio de Janeiro, 1981, Stevens Inst. Tech., Hoboken, 1981, Heriot-Watt U., Scotland, 1985, Universidad Nacional de Educacion a Distancia, Madrid, 1985, U. Francois Rabelais de Tours, 1986, U. Beijing, People's Republic of China, 1986, U. Buenos Aires, 1989, U. Cagliari, Sardinia, Italy, 1990, U. Sienna, Italy, 1990; DSc (hon.) , Gustavus Adolphus Coll., 1990; Membre d'Honneur (hon.) , l'Academie Nationale d'Argenti, 1989, l'Academie des Sciences Naturelles de Republique Federale de Russie, 1991; Pres. d'Honneur (hon.) , l'Acad. Nat. des Scis. de Republique de San Marino, 1991; Membre d'Honneur (hon.) , l'Academie Chilienne des Scis., 1991, de l'Université de Nice-Sophia-Antipolis, Nice, France, 1991, de l'Univ. Philippines System, Quezon City, 1991, del'Université de Santiago, Chile, del'Université de Tucumán, Argentine, 1991; DHC (hon.) , Université Lomonosov de Moscow, Russia, 1993, L'Univ. de A L.I. Cuza IASI, Iasi, Romania, 1994, U. de San Luis, Argentina, 1994, U. de Palermo, 1994, Institut Nat. Polytechnique, Lorraine, France, 1994, SUNY, Binghamton, 1995, Vrije U. Brussel, Brussels, Belgium, 1995, Internat. Assn. U. Pres., Seoul, 1995; Doyen d'honneur Honoris Causa (hon.) , l'Institut Royal des Elites du Travail de Belgique Albert I, Brussels, 1995; DHC (hon.) , U. Valladolid, Espagne, 1995, l'Universite de Saint-Petersbourg, Saint-Petersbourg, Russia, 1995; Laurea ad honorem in philosophy (hon.) , U. degli Studi Inst. Filosofia, Urbino, Italy, 1996; DHC (hon.) , U. Salvador, Buenos Aires, 1996, U. Xanthi, Greece, 1996; Degree in Sci. and Applied Sci. (hon.) , Aristoteles U. of Thessaloniki, Thessaloniki, Greece, 1998; Degree (hon.) , Nat. Inst. Astrophysics, Optics & Electronics, Puebla, Mex., 1998; DHC (hon.) , Universidad Nacional Autonomade Mex., Mex., 1998; Degree (hon.) , Wesleyan U., Ill., 1998; DHC (hon.) , Wroclaw U. Tech., Wroclaw, Poland, 1998; numerous other honorary degrees (hon.) , 1998-2000. Prof. Free U. Brussels, 1947—; dir. Internat. Insts. Physics and Chemistry, Solvay, Belgium, 1959—; prof. physics and chem. engring. U. Tex., Austin, 1967—, dir. Ilya Prigogine Ctr. Studies Statis. Mechs./Complex Sys., 1967—; hon. dir. Internat. Inst. Rsch. U. del Salvador, Buenos Aires, 1999—. Hon. prof. U. Nankin, China, 1986; Ashbel Smith regental prof. U. Tex., Austin, 1984—; Dir.'s Disting. visitor Inst. for Advanced Study, Princeton (N.J.) U., 1993; conseiller spl. Commn. des Communautés Européennes, 1993; internat. advisor de l'Internat. Inst. Advanced Studies, Kyoto, 1994; hon. dir. Inst. Internat. Investigaciones Cientficas U. Salvador, 1996, hon. chmn., Greece, 96; mem. adv. bd. Kothari Ctr. Sci., Ethics and Edn. U. Delhi, 1995; mem. Internat. Info. Acad, Moscow, Moscow, 1996, Académie de Yuste-Fauteuil J.S. Bach, Moscow, 1996; hon. pres. Ctr. FI No Linear Sistemas Complejos U. Santiago, Chile, 1996—; with Ctr L.Am. Estudios U. Nacional San Luis, Argentina, 1994; with U. Lomonosov, Moscow, 1995, Haute Ecole Libre Ilya Prigogine, Brussels, 1996, Inst. Documentazione Ricerca Sull, Italy, 1996, Opere di Ilya Prigogine, CISST, Brugine, , Padova, Italy, 1996; Ilya Prigogine chair philosophy scis. U. Palermo, Argentina, 1996; pres. seminar Penser la Sci., U. Libre de Bruxelles, 1997; hon. pres. Inst. Philosophy, Naples, Italy, 1997; Prigogine lectr. U. Lombarde, Como, Italy, 1999; hon. prof. Internat. U. Albert Schweitzer, 2001; mem. internat. sci. adv. bd. UNESCO, 1996; numerous others; hon. prof. U. Ninking, China, 1986, Banaras Hindu U., Varasani, India, 1988; Ashbel Smith regimental prof. U. Tex., Austin, 1984—; Dir.'s Disting. visitor Inst. for Advanced Study, Princeton (N.J.) U., 1993; conseiller spl. Commn. des Communautes Europeennes, 1993; internat. advisor Internat. Inst. Advanced Studies, Kyoto, 1994; hon. dir. Inst. Internat. Investigaciones Cientificas U. Salvador, 1996; hon. chmn. Inst. Complex Sys., Thrace, Greece, 1996; mem. adv. bd. Kothari Ctr. Sci., Ethics and Edn., U. Delhi, 1995; mem. internat. Info. Acad., Moscow, 96; mem. Acad. de Yuste-Fauteuil J.S. Bach, Madrid, 1996; hon. pres.Ctr. FI No Linear Sistemas Complejos U. Santiago, Chile, 1996—; with Ctr. L.Am. Estudios, U. Nacional San Luis Argentina, 1994, U. Lomonosov, Moscow, 1995, Haute Ecole Libre Ilya Prigogine, Brussels, 1996, Inst. Documentazione Ricerca Sull, Italy, 1996, Opere di Ilya Prigogine, CISST, Brugine, Padova, Italy, 1996; Ilya Prigogine chair philosophy scis. U. Palermo, Argentina, 1996; pres. seminar Penser la Sci., U. Libre de Bruxelles, 1997; Prigogine lectr. U. Lombarde, Como, Italy, 1999; hon. prof. Internat. U. Albert Schweitzer, 2001; mem. internat. sci. adv. bd. UNESCO, 1996; numerous others. Author (with R. Defay): Traite de Thermodynamique, conformement aux methodes de Gibbs et de Donder, 1944, 1950; author: Etude Thermodynamique des Phenomenes Irreversibles, 1947, Introduction to Thermodynamics of Irreversible Processes, 1954, 1962, 1967; author: (translation) Russian, Serbo-Croatian, French, Italian and Spanish; author: (with A. Bellemans, V. Mathot) The Molecular Theory of Solutions, 1957; author: Nonequilibrium Statistical Mechanics, 1962; author: (with R. Herman) Kinetic Theory of Vehicular Traffic, 1971; author: (with R. Glansdorff) Thermodynamic Theory of Structure, Stability and Fluctuations, 1971; author: (with G. Nicolis) Self-Organization in Nonequilibrium Systems, 1977; author: From Being to Becoming--Time and Complexity in Physical Sciences, 1980; author: (translation) French, German, Japanese, Russian, Chinese, Italian, Romanian and Portuguese edits.; author: (with I. Stengers) Order Out of Chaos, 1983; author: La Nouvelle Alliance, Les Metamorphoses de la Science, 1979; author: (translations) German, English, Italian, Spanish, Serbo-Croatian, Romanian, Swedish, Dutch, Russian, Japanese, Chinese, Portuguese, Bulgarian, Greek, Korean, Polish, Danish, Turkish & Hungarian edits. Mem. sci. adv. bd. Internat. Acad. for Biomed. Drug Rsch., 1990; mem. adv. com. Internat. Coun. Human Duties, U. degli Studi di Trieste, Italy, 1996. Decorated comdr. Legion d'Honneur France, comdr. de L'Ordre de Leopold; named Viscount, King of Belgium, 1989; recipient Medaille de la Resistance, comdr. de l'ordre Leopold II, 1961, Grande Croix de l'Ordre de Leopold II, 1977, Medaille Civique de Premiere Classe, 1972, comdr. de l'Ordre Nationale du Merite, France, 1977, comdr. de l'Ordre des Arts et des Lettres, 1984, Titulaire de l' Ordre du Soleil Levant, avec Médaille d' Or et d' Argent, Japan, 1990, prix Francqui, 1955, Nobel prize in Chemistry, 1977, prix Solvay, 1965, Honda prize, 1983, Rumford Gold medal, Royal Soc. London, 1976, Karcher medal, Am. Crystallographic Assn., 1978, Descartes medal, U. Paris, 1979, award, Gravity Rsch. Found., 1988, prix Umberto Biancamano, 1987, Artificial Intelligence Sci. Achievement award, Internat. Found. for Artificial Intelligence, 1990, prix Summa de l'Universite Laval, Can., 1993, Medaille de l'Ecole Normale Superieure, Paris, 1995, Medaille Piotr Kapitza decernee par l'Academie des Scis. Naturelles de Russie, 1996—, Medaille d'Honneur de l'Inst. Phys. Chemistry, Polish Acad. Scis., 1996—, others; fellow RKG Found. Centennial, U. Tex., 1989—90. Fellow: Nat. Acad. Sci. India (hon.); mem.: Internat. Acad. Russia, Consejo Academico, Belorussian Acad. Sci., Conseil Consultatif Sci. Internat. de l'UNESCO, Internat. Soc. Theoretical Chem. Physics (hon. bd. mem.), Etranger ACad. Scis., Communautes Europeenne, Assemblee Europeenne Scis. Tech., World Inst. Sci., World Acad. Arts and Scis., Internat. Acad. Philosophy Sci., N.Y. Acad. Sci., Internat. Soc. Gen. Systems Rsch.. (pres.-elect 1988), Deutscher Acad. der Naturforscher Leopoldina (Cothenius medal 1970), Acad. Gottingen Germany, Royal Soc. Scis. Uppsala (Sweden), Korean Soc. Chemistry, NAS (assoc.), Ukrainian Nat. Acad. Sci., Am. Acad. Sci. (medal 1975), Royal Acad. Belgium (pres.), Osterreichische Acad. der Wissenschaften (corr.), Soc. Royale des Scis Liege Belgium (corr.), Korean Acad. Sci. and Tech. (hon.), Royal Acad. Medicine (hon.), Soc. Coreenne de Chimie (hon.), Royal Soc. Chemistry Belgium (hon.), Chem. Soc. Poland (hon.), Commn. Mondiale de la Culture et du Devel. de l'UNESCO (hon.), Acad. Nationale des Scis., des Lettres et des Arts de Modena (Italy) (hon.). Address: 67 Ave Fond Roy 1180 Brussels Belgium Office: Inst Internat Physics & Chem Campus Plaine ULB CP231 Bld du Triomphe 1050 Brussels Belgium also: U Tex Ilya Prigogine Ctr Robert Lee Moore Hall Studies Statis Mechanics Austin TX 78712 E-mail: annie@physics.utexas.edu., njockman@ulb.ac.be.

PRIJATELJ, CHARLES ANTHONY, music educator, musician; b. Pittsburgh, Pa., Mar. 11, 1960; s. Stanley and Mary Ann Prijatelj; m. Vicki Jo Prijatelj, June 28, 1986; children: Michael, Derek. BM, Duquesne U., Pittsburgh, PA, 1978—82; MM, Youngstown State U., Youngstown, OH, 1988—90. Teacher of Music K-12 PA, 1982. Marching band dir. Peters Twp. H.S., Peters Township, Pa., 1982—83; dir. of bands Mars Area H.S., Mars, 1983—. Pres. and founder Pa. Interscholastic Marching Band Assn, Pittsburgh, Pa., 1996—2001. Adjudicator Pa. Fedn. of Contest Judges, Pa. Mem.: Music Educators Nat. Conf., Pa. Music Edn. Assn. Methodist. Achievements include Music Program Was A National Semi-Finalist In 1999. Avocation: music. Home: 114 Ashmont Dr Butler PA 16002 Office: Mars Area High School 520 Rt 228 Mars PA 16046 Office Fax: 724-625-4477. Personal E-mail: cprijate@fyi.net.

PRILUTSKY, BORIS ISAAKOVICH, biophysicist; b. Moscow, June 19, 1957; s. Isaak Samuilovich and Taya Michailovna (Belkina) P.; 1 child, Anna. BS in Phys. Edn., Ctrl. Inst. Phys. Culture, 1978; BS in Applied Math., Moscow Inst. Electronic Engr., 1987; PhD of Biomechanics/Biology, Latvian Rsch. Inst. of, Traumatology and Orthopedics, 1990. Lectr., scientist Ctrl. Inst. Phys. Culture, Moscow, 1978-92; postdoctoral fellow U. Calgary, AB, Can., 1992-95, Ga. Inst. Tech., Atlanta, 1995-98, sr. rsch. scientist, 1998—. Cons. Peak Performance Tech., Inc., Englewood, Colo., 1994. Inventor in field;

contbr. articles to profl. jours. Fellow Alberta Heritage Found. Med. Rsch., 1993; recipient Gold medal USSR Ministry Higher Edn., 1977. Mem. AAAS, Can. Soc. Biomechanics, Am. Soc. Biomechanics (Young Scientist award 1995), Am. Soc. Neurosci. Avocations: reading, outdoor activities, sports. Office: Ga Inst Tech Dept Health 750 Ferst Dr Atlanta GA 30332-0110 Fax: 404 894-7593. E-mail: boris.prilutsky@hps.gatech.edu.

PRIMACK, ALICE LEFLER, librarian; b. Kent, Ohio, Feb. 14, 1939; d. Glenn Q. and Mary S. (Staley) Lefler; m. Robert B. Primack; children: Eric, Mary-Anne, Glenn. BS, Ea. Ill. U., 1961; MLS, U. Wis., 1962. Libr. intern Ohio State U., Columbus, 1962-63, reference, bot. and zool. librarian, 1963-64, head Pharmacy Libr., 1964-66; from asst. to assoc. librarian U. Fla., Gainesville, 1972-92, Univ. librarian, 1992—. Author: How to Find Out in Pharmacy, 1969, Finding Answers in Science and Technology, 1984, Journal Literature of the Physical Sciences, 1992. Mem. adv. bd. 4-H of Alachua County, Fla., 1989—; officer Unitarian-Universalist Fellowship of Gainesville; bd. dirs. Fla. Free Speech Forum, 1994—. Mem.: Spl. LIbrs. Assn. (pres. Fla. and Caribbean chpt. 1996—98). Democrat. Office: U Fla Marston Sci Libr Gainesville FL 32611

PRIMACK, BRIAN ADAM, physician; b. N.Y.C., Apr. 22, 1969; s. Aron and Karen (Margolis) Primack; m. Jennifer Hope Engel. BA magna cum laude and distinction in english, Yale U., New Haven, 1991; EdM, Harvard U., Cambridge, Mass., 1993; MD summa cum laude, Emory U., Atlanta, 1999. Lic. physician Pa., 2001. Counselor Yale U., New Haven, 1986—87; tchr. Am. Sch. of Niamey, Niamey, Niger, 1991—92; instr. math. U. Md., College Park, 1993—95; resident dir. Emory U., Atlanta, 1995—97; dean of students Exploration Summer Program, Wellesley, Mass., 2000; family practice resident UPMC St. Margaret Hosp., Pitts., 1999—2002; asst. prof. sch. medicine U. Pitts., 2002—. Actor: Gemini Theater Comedy Improvisation Troupe, 2001, Cloak and Dagger Dinner Theater, 2000, Murder Upon Request Theater Group, 1997, Romeo and Juliet, 1995, Joseph and the Amazing Technicolor Dreamcoat, 1990. Named Niger Nat. Champion, Jeux Mathematique Math. Competition, 1992; recipient Saybrook Fellows Prize, Yale U., 1991; fellow Robert W. Woodruff fellow, Emory U., 1995; grantee Scholarship and Grant to attend Patient Edn. conf., Soc. for Tchrs. of Family Medicine, 2000. Mem.: Am. Assn. of Family Physicians. Avocations: guitar, harmonica, piano, community service. Home: 2319 Eldridge St Pittsburgh PA 15217 Office: Univ Pitts Sch Medicine Dept Family Medicine 3518 Fifth Ave Pittsburgh PA 15261 Personal E-mail: brianprimack@yahoo.com.

PRIMEAU, KEITH, hockey player; b. Toronto, Nov. 24, 1971; Drafted Detroit Red Wings, 1990-97; right wing Carolina Hurricanes, 1997-99, Phila. Flyers, 1999—. Office: Phila Flyers First Union Ctr 1 Corse State Complex Philadelphia PA 19148*

PRIMEAUX, HENRY, III, automotive executive, author, speaker; b. New Orleans, Nov. 16, 1941; s. Henry Jr. and Ethel (Ritter) P.; m. Jane Cathrine Velcich, July 23, 1960; children: Joann Primeaux Longa, Lisa Primeaux Lotz, Henry Joseph. Student, La. State U., New Orleans, 1959-63. Compt. Jimco, New Orleans, 1965-66; owner, mgr. Picone Seafood, 1966-67; v.p. NADW Inc., Metairie, La., 1967-78, Am. Warranty Corp., L.A., 1978-80; pres. F&I Warranty Corp., Arlington, Tex., 1980-87; exec. v.p. F&I Mgmt. Corp., 1980-87; pres., CEO Primco Corp., 1987-91; owner Flavors Restaurant, Tulsa, Okla., Primeaux Mktg. Mng. ptnr. Crown Auto World, Bristow; founder, Pimeaux Family Found., 1998; mgr., Primeaux Family Dealerships; mng. ptnr., Primeaux Family Realty; cons., corr. Wards Auto Dealer, Detroit, 1987-95, weekly TV program Automotive Satellite TV Network; cons. Nissan Motor Co., L.A., 1988-89, Convergent div. Unisys, Hunt Valley, Md., 1988-90; cons. Mercedes-Benz N.Am.; exec. com. Okla. Workforce Investment Bd.; chmn. Tulsa Workforce Investment Bd. Writer Auto Age mag.; author: F&I Handbook. Mem. Rep. Task Force Okla. Workforce Devel. Com.; bd. dirs. John Starks Found., Boy Scouts U.S.; mem. nat. adv. bd. Automotive Yes Sch. to Work Initiative; mem. Okla. Sch. to Work Commn., bd. mem. Tulsa River Parks Commn.; bd. regents Okla. State U., Tulsa. With USN, 1959-61. Mem. Am. Internat. Automobile Dealers Assn., Assn. of F&I Profls. (bd. dirs. 1990—, pres. 1994), Nat. Auto Dealers Assn. (pres. Tulsa chpt. 1994, Time Quality Dealer of Yr. 1994), Okla. Amateur Sports Commn. (chmn.), Okla. State C. of C. (bd. dirs.), Met. Tulsa C. of C. (bd. dirs. 1998-2000). Roman Catholic. Home: 11716 S 66th East Ave Bixby OK 74008-2051 Office: Crown Bristow 901 S Roland Bristow OK 74010 E-mail: primeaux1@aol.com., crownhen@aol.com.

PRIMI, DON ALEXIS, advertising and public relations executive, railroad transportation executive; b. N.Y.C., Jan. 14, 1947; s. John Prosper, Sr. and Eileen Mary P.; A. in Advt., State U. N.Y., 1967; B.S. in Mktg. and Advt., Hofstra U., 1971; advanced astron. studies degree, Vanderbilt Mus. and Planetarium, 1967. Gen. mgr., Recreational Pub. Corp.; pres., owner Fantasia Trains/REE R.R. Equipment Exchange, 1980, Don Primi Designs, 1984, Rail Industries, Rail Fin. Corp., 1987, Gold Coast Ltd./Royal Rail, 1987, Rail Enterprises, 1990, LPA North Am., 1992, Alexis Daniels, 1992, Salon Promotions, 1992, Trans Fla. Express, Inc., 2001; cons. in field, ry. industry, brick and clay products industry; designer corp. identity programs. Recipient awards Printing Industries Met. N.Y., Gold Boli advt. awards, Kimberly-Clark Graphic excellence awards, Astrophotoawards. Mem. Assn. Ry. Progress Inst., R.R. Pub. Relations Assn., Nat. R.R. Assn. Passengers, Sales and Mktg. Execs., Astron Soc. L.I. (pres., pub. rel dir.), Rail Mktg. Club N.Y. Designs published in periodicals. Home: 4065 Old Settlement Rd Merritt Island FL 32952-6211 Office: 160 5th Ave New York NY 10010-7003 E-mail: dprail21@brevard.net.

PRIMM, DAVID JOHN, middle school educator; b. Des Moines, June 26, 1950; s. John Gerald and Nora Alice (Williams) P.; m. Linda Kay Huffman, Aug. 5, 1973; children: John, Heather. BS in Edn., Northwest Mo. State U., 1972, MA, 1976. Cert. tchr., Mo. and Iowa. Tchr. Maryville (Mo.) Sch. Dist., 1973—. Mem. Mo. State Tchrs. Assn., Maryville Pride Lions. Methodist. Avocations: reading, camping, restoring old farm tractors, woodworking. Home: 205 E Bentley St Ravenwood MO 64479-9124 Office: Maryville Sch Dist 1429 S Munn Ave Maryville MO 64468-2756

PRIMM, EARL RUSSELL, III, publishing executive; b. Rhinelander, Wis., Oct. 24, 1958; s. Earl Russell and Betty Joan (Dennis) P. AB in Classics (hon.), Loyola U. Chgo., 1980; MA in Libr. Sci., U. Chgo., 1990. Asst. to edn. dir. J.G. Ferguson Pub. Co., Chgo., 1981-84; prodn. mgr. Joint Commn. on Accreditation of Hosps., 1984-85; sr. editor J.G. Ferguson Pub. Co., 1985-87; asst. editor U. Chgo. Press., 1987-88; editorial dir. J.G. Ferguson Pub. Co., Chgo., 1988-89; project mgr. Children's Press, 1989-92; exec. editor Franklin Watts, Inc., Chgo., N.Y.C., 1992-95; editl. dir. Grolier Children's Pub., Danbury, Conn., 1995-97; pres. Editl. Directions, Inc., Chgo., 1997—. Mem. adv. bd. U. Chgo. Pub. Program, 1990-2000; judge Lambda Lit. awards, Washington, 1994-2000. Editl. chief: Career Discovery Encyclopedia, 1990, Favorite Children's Authors and Illustrators, 2002; editor: Civil Rights Movement in America, 2nd edit., 1991, Extraordinary Hispanic Americans, 1991. Mem. crisis counselor Nat. Runaway Switchboard, Chgo., 1985-88; Horizon's hotline counselor, Chgo., 1987-88; bd. dirs. Gerber/Hart Libr. and Archives, Chgo., 1992-94. Named Honors Sr. of Yr., Loyola U. Chgo., 1980; recipient Mertz Latin Scholarship key Loyola U. Chgo., 1980. Mem. Pub. Triangle, Chgo. Book Clinic, Am. Libr. Assn. Democrat. Home and Office: 1000 W Washington Blvd #147 Chicago IL 60607-2148

PRIMO, JOAN ERWINA, retail and real estate consulting business owner; b. Detroit, Aug. 28, 1959; d. Joseph Carmen and Marie Ann (Nash) P.; m. David James Yared, Sept. 20, 1997; 1 son, Benjamin Primo Yared. BA, Wellesley Coll., 1981; MBA, Harvard U., 1985. Acct. exec. Michigan Bell, Detroit, 1981-82, AT&T Info. Sys., Southfield, Mich., 1983; planning analyst Gen. Motors, Detroit, 1984; v.p. Howard L. Green & Assocs., Troy, Mich., 1985-89; prin., founder The Strategic Edge, Inc., Southfield, 1989—. Contbr. articles to profl. jours. Founders soc. mem. Detroit Inst. Arts, 1989—. Mem.: Internat. Coun. Shopping Ctrs. (faculty, seminar leader 1987—), Ivy Club Detroit (bd. dirs. 1994—, sec. 1995—99), Harvard Bus. Sch. Club Detroit (bd. dirs. 1994—98, v.p. 1995—96, exec. v.p. 1996—97), Wellesley Club Southeastern Mich. (pres. 1994—98). Republican. Avocations: antiques, travel, theatre, gourmet cooking. Home: 224 Woodwind Dr Bloomfield Hills MI 48304-2172 Office: The Strategic Edge 24333 Southfield Rd Ste 211 Southfield MI 48075-2849

PRIMOSCH, JAMES THOMAS, music educator, composer, musician; b. Cleve., Oct. 29, 1956; s. Edward Joseph and Rose Marie (Potochar) P.; m. Mary Marguerite Murphy, April 5, 1986. BA in Composition magna cum laude, Cleve. State U., 1978; MA in Composition, U. Pa., 1980; DMA in Composition awarded with distinction, Columbia U., 1988; studied piano privately with Lambert Orkis, Phila., 1978-80; studied composition with John Harbison, Tanglewood, 1984. Asst. prof. music U. Penn., 1988-94, assoc. prof. music, 1994—. Grad. assistantships Columbia-Princeton Electronic Music Ctr., 1982-84, 86-87, preceptorship Columbia U., 1984-85; residency Va. Ctr. Creative Arts, 1985, MacDowell Colony, 1988, Bellagio Conf. Ctr., 1992; regional vis. artist Am. Acad. in Rome, 1994; composer in residence Marlboro Music Festival, 1994. Composer of more than 40 compositions and 26 published works; compositions performed by L.A. Philharm., St. Paul Chamber Orch., Cleve. Chamber Symphony, N.Y. New Music Ensemble; compositions performed at Carnegie Hall, Dorothy Chandler Pavilion, Town Hall, Weill (Carnegie) Recital Hall, and many others; reviewer High Performance Rev. Mag., 1987-95. Recipient 3rd prize, People's prize Internat. Gaudeamus Competition, The Netherlands, 1977, Helen L. Weiss prize U. Pa., 1979, David Halstead prize U. Penn., 1980, 3rd prize Shreveport Symphony Composer's Competition, 1980-81, John H. Bearns prize, 1981, 1st. prize Holtkamp Organ Composition Contest, 1982, Eda and Boris Rappoport prize Columbia U., 1984, Tanglewood prize in Composition Berkshire Music Ctr., 1984, Cleve. Arts prize, 1992, Elise Stoeger prize Chamber Music Soc. Lincoln Ctr., 1999; recipient Mader Meml. Fund Recognition award, 1980, BMI Student Composers award, 1982; New Music Consort Composition Contest winner, 1987, League of Composers ISCM winner, 1988; Fine Arts scholar Cleve. State U., 1974-78, scholar Cleve. Fortnightly Music Club, 1976-78, Arthur Loesser Meml. scholar, 1977-78, Yale Composer's Workshop at Norfolk, 1981, Columbia U. scholar, 1981-82, Charles Ives scholar Am. Acad. Inst. Arts & Letters, 1985; U. fellow U. Penn., 1978-79, Composers Conf. Johnson Vt., 1979, 80, CBS Found. fellow U. Penn., 1979-80, Margaret Lee Crofts fellow Berkshire Music Ctr. Tanglewood, 1984, Guggenheim fellow, 1985, NEA, 1991-92, Goddard Lieberson fellow Am. Acad. Arts and Letters, 1993, Pew fellow in arts, 1996; ASCAP Found. Young Composers grant, 1984, 82, Meet The Composer grant 1980, 82, 85, 87, 89, 90, 94, 96, 97, Am. Music Ctr. Copying Assistance grant, 1985, 90, Penn. Coun. On The Arts, 1990, 98, Presser Found. grantee (2) U. Pa. Mem. BMI, Pi Kappa Lambda. Roman Catholic. Avocation: reading.

PRIMOV, GEORGE V. computer company executive; b. Plovdiv, Bulgaria, Aug. 9, 1954; s. Vesselin G. and Maria N. Primov; m. Diana N. Primov, July 6, 1980; children: Victor, Stephanie. MSc in Physics, Climent Ochridski U., Sofia, Bulgaria, 1981. Translator, various langs. pvt. cos., U.S., 1979—; tech. info. mgr. MachProject, Bulgaria, 1980-86; sr. expert sys. rschr. Microsys. Inst., Bulgaria, 1986-90; sr. network adminstr. Enter Corp., 1991-94; cons. Va., 1998-2000; sr. network engr. Washington (D.C.) Met. Transit Authority, 2001—. E-mail: primeg@ix.netcom.com.

PRIMPS, WILLIAM GUTHRIE, lawyer; b. Ossining, N.Y., Sept. 8, 1949; s. Richard Byrd and Mary Elizabeth (Guthrie) P.; m. Sophia Elizabeth Beutel, Aug. 25, 1973; children: Emily Ann, Elizabeth Armstrong, William Andrew. BA, Yale U., 1971; JD, Harvard U., 1974. Bar: N.Y., 1975. Assoc. LeBoeuf, Lamb, Leiby & MacRae, N.Y.C., 1974-82; ptnr. LeBoeuf, Lamb, Greene & MacRae, 1983—. Counsel to Bd. Zoning Appeals, Bronxville, 1988-89, chmn., 1989-91. Mem. class coun. Yale U., New Haven, 1986-91; trustee Village of Bronxville, 1991—, dep. mayor, 1995—; deacon Reformed Ch. Bronxville, 1989-94. Mem. ABA, N.Y. State Bar Assn., Assn. Yale Alumni (class rep. 1986-91), Yale Club, Bronxville Field Club. Republican. Home: 71 Summit Ave Bronxville NY 10708-1815 Office: LeBoeuf Lamb Greene & MacRae 125 W 55th St New York NY 10019-5369

PRINA, L(OUIS) EDGAR, journalist; b. West New York, N.J., Oct. 7, 1917; s. Louis Edgar and Marion (Duggan) P.; m. Frances Lee Lorick, Feb. 14, 1947; 1 dau., Lee Lorick II. AB, Syracuse U., 1938, MA, 1940. Copy editor, asst. night city editor N.Y. Sun, N.Y.C., 1946-48, Washington corr., 1948-50; nat. affairs writer Washington Star, 1950-66; mil. affairs writer/editor Copley News Svc., Washington, 1966-77, bur. chief, 1977-84, sr. corr., 1984-87; editor Navy mag., Washington, 1961-68; columnist Sea Power mag., 1968—. Author: The Political Virgin, 1958, Flew to South Pole for Overnight Visit, 1966. Served with USN, 1941-46, 51-53; capt. Res. (ret.). Recipient honorable mention-Heywood Broun award, 1956, Disting. Public Svc. award USN, 1965, Alfred Thayer Mahan award Navy League U.S., 1987, Copley Ring of Truth award, 1971, 74-76, 79, 80-81, Chancellor's Sr. Alumni award Syracuse U., 1998; nominated for Pulitzer Prize (twice). Mem. U.S. Naval Inst., Nat. Press Club (chmn. bd. govs.), White House Corrs. Assn., Explorers Club, Soc. Profl. Journalists (pres. Washington chpt., named to Hall of Fame 1999), Kappa Sigma, Phi Kappa Phi. Clubs: Gridiron, Chevy Chase, Met. of Washington. Roman Catholic. Home: 4813 Quebec St NW Washington DC 20016-3228 Office: The Metro Club Box 47 1700 H St NW Washington DC 20006-4689

PRINCE, ANDREW STEVEN, lawyer, former government official; b. Bklyn., Oct. 9, 1943; s. Milton S. and Beatrice M. (Ratkin) P.; m. Rochelle Moskowitz, July 4, 1973; children: Brett, Kenneth. BS, U.S. Naval Acad., 1965; MBA, JD, Harvard U., 1974. Bar: N.Y. 1975, U.S. Supreme Ct. 1980. Assoc. firm Shearman & Sterling, N.Y.C., 1974-81; dep. asst. sec. Navy Dept., Washington, 1981-86; exec. v.p., gen. counsel Urquhart and Co., Inc., McLean, Va., 1986-94; pres. BretKen Enterprises, 1994—; mng. dir. Nat. Capital Cos. LLC, Bethesda, Md., 1997-2000; mng. dir., COO HFS Capital LLC, McLean, Va., 2000—. Sec. Potash Import & Chem. Corp., N.Y.C., 1979-81; mem. panel of arbitrators Am. Arbitration Assn., N.Y.C., 1979—. Bd. dirs. Harvard Coop. Soc., Cambridge, Mass., 1972-74; bd. dirs. USO, Washington, 1982-86, N.Y.C., 1979-81. Served with USN, 1965-70; capt. Res., ret. Mem. Harvard Bus. Sch. Club, Washington, DC (bd. dir.), Mil Order World Wars (judge adv.), Naval Acad. Alumni Assn., Naval Acad. Found. (dir.). E-mail: aprince@hfscpa.com.

PRINCE, ANNA LOU, composer, music publisher, construction company executive; b. Isabella, Tenn., May 28, 1935; d. Ulysses Gordon and Della Carrie (Hawkins) P.; children: Sandra, Teresa, Vandi. Diploma, Carolina Sch. Broadcasting, 1966; Zion diploma, Israel Bible Sch., Jerusalem, 1970; diploma, S.W. Tech. Coll., 1970; student, United Christian Assn., 1976; MusD, London Inst. Applied Rsch., 1991; diplomatic diploma, Acad. Argentina de Diplomacia, 1993; PhD (hon.), Australian Inst. Coord. Rsch., Victoria, 1993; diploma of honors on internat. affairs, Inst. Des Affaires Internat., Paris, 1994. Lic. Bible tchr. United Christian Acad. Songwriter Hank Locklin Music Co., Nashville, 1963-70; entertainer 1982 World's Fair, Knoxville, Tenn., 1982; ptnr., owner Prince Wholesale Bait Co., Canton, N.C., 1976-82, Grad Builders, Canton, 1982-86, Prince TV Co., Canton, 1986—. Music pub. Broadcast Music, Inc., Nashville, 1982—; mem. prodn. staff, talent coord. (TV series) Down Home, Down Under, 1989-90. Songs recorded on RCA: I Feel a Cry Coming On, 1965 (#1 in Eng.), Best Part of Loving You, (#1 in Eng.), Anna, 1969 (Billboard 1970, recorded in Ireland 1974, hit in Europe and New Zealand); singer, composer I'm In Love With You, 1995; over 20 songs recorded to date; appeared Grand Ole Opry, 1970; exec. prodr., host TV talk show, Real Hereos of Country Music, 1989— (Emmy nomination 1997). Cand. for county commr. Dem. Party Macon County, N.C., 1984; bd. dirs. Macon County Taxpayers Assn., Inc., 1984, v.p., 1984-86; bd. dirs. Head Start, Topton, N.C., 1969-73. Nominated Disting. Women N.C., N.C. Coun. Coun. on Status of Women, 1984, Jefferson award WYFF TV and Am. Inst. for Pub. Svc., Outstanding Bus. Woman Small Bus. Adminstrn., 1984. Mem. BMI, Internat. Parliament Safety and Peace (life, dept. fgn. affairs, dep. mem. assembly), Nashville Songwriters Assn. Internat. (moderator, tchr. 1984-86), Country Music Assn., Reunion Profl. Entertainers, Fraternal Order Police, C. of C., Order of Knight of Templars (dame) Lofsensic Order (dame), Maison Internat. des Intellectuals. Democrat. Office: 313 Gallatin Rd S Madison TN 37115-4006

PRINCE, DAVID CANNON, lawyer; b. Hawkinsville, Ga., July 4, 1950; s. Carl Willis and Carobel (Cannon) P.; m. Mary MacIntyre, June 30, 1973. BA in Econs., Clemson U., 1972; JD, St. John's U., Jamaica, N.Y., 1980. Bar: N.Y. 1981, Ga. 1982, U.S. Dist. Ct. (no. dist.) Ga. 1982. Atty. enforcement SEC, Atlanta, 1981-86; regional counsel Shearson Lehman Bros. Inc., 1986-92; gen. counsel Robinson-Humphrey Co., Inc., 1992—. Capt. USAF, 1972-78. Mem. ABA (co-chairperson young lawyers div. 1986-88). Democrat. Avocations: sailing, running. Home: 1824 Lenox Rd NE Atlanta GA 30306-3031 Office: 3333 Peachtree Rd NE Atlanta GA 30326-1070

PRINCE, DON DAVID, automotive technician; b. Gastonia, N.C., Jan. 13, 1940; s. Ulysses Gordon and Della Carrie (Hawkins) P.; m. Pauline Phydella Flowers, May 24, 1960; children: David Alan, Landon Art, Barry Edmond. Cert. automotive technician. Owner, mgr. Precision Automotive Repair, Lowell, N.C., 1965-69; state vehicle insp. N.C. Hwy. Patrol, 1965-69; owner, mgr. Don's Automotive, Topton, 1969-71; svc. craftsman Kerley Pontiac, Lakeland, Fla., 1971-75; svc. technician Am. Honda, 1971-75; mechanic City of Lakeland Civil Svc., 1975-91. Author: The Three Dimensions of Existence, 1990, Twilight of the Ages, 1995; composer (songs) Heaven's Inspiration, 1996, Through the Shadow of the Cross, 1997, Beyond the Ages, 1997, Twilight of the Ages, 1997, Lyrics Live, 1998. Recipient Editors Choice awards Nat. Libr. Poetry for Lyrics, 1998, Poetry.com, 2000, Internat. Libr. Poetry, 2000. Avocations: racing, boating, antique cars, guns, inventions. Home: 3619 E Rd 542 Lakeland FL 33801 E-mail: Poldon1@juno.com.

PRINCE, DONNA JEAN, artist; b. L.A., Feb. 3, 1954; d. Robert Henry and Anna Marie (Estatico) P.; m. Donald James Molyneux, Sept. 2, 1989. BA with honors, Art Ctr. Coll. of Design, 1989. Key background painter Queen of the Universe Prodn., L.A., 1990, Disney TV Animation, N. Hollywood, 1995—; background painter Turner Publ., Hollywood, Calif., 1991, Hanna Barbera, Hollywood, 1991-92, Rich Animation, Burbank, Calif., 1993-94; tchr. Art Ctr. Coll. Design, 1997. Mem. neighborhood activist Friends of Washington Park, Pasadena, 1991-96, workshop presenter Neighborhoods USA Conf. Pasadena, 1994. Recipient Vol. award City of Pasadena Parks & Recs., 1995. Mem. Motion Picture Screen Cartoonists Guild, Friends of Washington Park (pres. 1991-94), Soc. of Illustrators (v.p. 1991). Democrat. Avocations: gardening, traveling, shopping, dancing, interior decorating. Home: 1277 N El Molino Ave Pasadena CA 91104-2839 Office: Disney TV Animation 5200 Lankershim Blvd Ste 600 North Hollywood CA 91601-3100

PRINCE, GEORGE EDWARD, retired pediatrician; b. Erwin, N.C., Nov. 25, 1921; s. Hugh Williamson and Helen Herman (Hood) P.; m. Millie Elizabeth Mann, Nov. 26, 1944; children: Helen Elizabeth, Millie Mann, Susan Hood, Mary Lois. MD, Duke U., 1944. Diplomate Am. Bd. Pediatrics, Am. Bd. Med. Examiners. Intern Boston Children's Hosp. Harvard Svc., Boston, 1944-45; resident pediatrics Children's Hosp., Louisville, 1945-47; instr. pediatrics U. Louisville, 1947; founder Gastonia (N.C.) Children's Clinic, 1947, pediatrician, 1947-86; pub. health physician Gaston County Health Dept., Gastonia, N.C., 1986-98, med. dir., 1995-98, ret., 1998. Chmn. bd. dirs. Carolina State Bank; bd. dirs. So. Nat. Bank, Gastonia, 1979-95, Hospice, Gastonia, 1987-92; organizer, dir. AIDS Adv. Coun., Gaston County, N.C., 1988-94; coord. N.C. chpt. Pediatric Rsch. in Office Setting, 1986-92. Contbr. articles to profl. jours. Mem. Gaston County Human Rels. Com., Gastonia, 1966; mem. Sch. Health Adv. Coun., Gaston County, 1980-97. Maj. USAF, 1955-57. Recipient Balthis Heart Assn. award, Gaston County, 1981, 1998, Good Amb. award, Health Dept., 1986, Family Adv. award, Commn. on the Family, Gaston County, 1995, commendation, City of Gastonia, 2001, Gaston County Bd. Commrs., 2001. Fellow Am. Acad. Pediatrics (pres. N.C. chpt. 1984-86); mem. AMA, N.C. Pediatric Soc. (hon., pres. 1970), N.C. Med. Soc., Gaston County Med. Soc. (pres. 1966), Rotary (pres. 1984), County Club (bd. dirs. 1975-76). Democrat. Methodist. Avocations: golf, flying, skiing, sailing, bridge. Home: 2208 Cross Creek Dr Gastonia NC 28056-8808

PRINCE, GREGORY SMITH, JR. academic administrator; b. Washington, May 7, 1939; s. Gregory Smith and Margaret (Minor) P.; m. Toni Layton Brewer; children: Tara Wyndom, Gregory S. III. BA, Yale U., 1961, M in Philosophy, 1969, PhD, 1973; cert. in teaching English as a Second Language, Georgetown U., 1961; DHL (hon.), LLD (hon.), Amherst Coll., 1991. Instr. New Asia Coll., Kowloon, Hong Kong, 1961-62, Chinese U., Kowloon, 1962-63, Yale China Assn., Kowloon, 1961-63, Woodberry Forest (Va.) Sch., 1963-65; dean summer programs Dartmouth Coll., Hanover, N.H., 1970-72, asst. dean faculty, 1972-78, assoc. dean faculty, 1978-89; pres. Hampshire Coll., Amherst, Mass., 1989—. Vice chair coun. on racial and ethnic justice ABA; bd. dirs. Mass Ventures. Producer: (film) A Way of Learning, 1988. Trustee Montshire Mus. Sci., Hanover, 1973-89, Washington Campus, 1978—; trustee, chmn. Univ. Press New England, Hanover, 1983-84; trustee, pres. Yale-China Assn., New Haven, 1969-84; bd. dirs. Five Colls., Inc., Amherst, 1989—; bd. dirs. Mass. Internat. Festival for Arts, 1994-98; chmn. bd. dirs. Assn. Ind. Colls. and Univs. Mass., 1994-95; chair commn. on accreditation Am. Coun. Edn.; bd. dirs. Mass. Nature Conservancy, 1996—; bd. dirs. Nat. Assn. Ind. Colls. and Univs., 1999-2001, Friendship House, 2002—. Coe fellow Stanford U., 1965, Woodrow Wilson fellow Yale U., 1966, NDEA fellow, 1967-70. Mem. Internat. Assn. of Chiefs Police Found. (bd. dirs. 1991-95), Nat. Assn. of Ind. Colls. and Univs. Democrat. Episcopalian. Home: 15 Middle St Amherst MA 01002-3009 Office: Hampshire Coll 893 West St Amherst MA 01002-3372

PRINCE, HAROLD, theatrical producer; b. N.Y.C., Jan. 30, 1928; s. Milton A. and Blanche (Stern) P.; m. Judith Chaplin, Oct. 26, 1962; children: Charles, Daisy. AB, U. Pa., 1948, DFA (hon.), 1971; LittD, Emerson Coll., 1971. Chmn. Performing Arts Libr., N.Y.C. Co-prodr.: Pajama Game, 1954-56 (Antoinette Perry award), Damn Yankees, 1955-57 (Antoinette Perry award), New Girl in Town, 1957-58, West Side Story, 1957-59, A Swim in the Sea, 1958, Fiorello, 1959-61 (Antoinette Perry award, Pulitzer prize), Tenderloin, 1960-61, A Call on Kuprin, 1961, They Might Be Giants, London, 1961, Side by Side by Sondheim, 1977; prodr.: Take Her, She's Mine, 1961-62, A Funny Thing Happened on the Way to the Forum, 1962-64 (Antoinette Perry award), Fiddler on the Roof, 1964-72 (Antoinette Perry award), Poor Bitos, 1964, Flora the Red Menace, 1965; dir., prodr.: She Loves Me, 1963-64, London, 1964, Superman, 1966, Cabaret, 1966-69 (Antoinette Perry award 1968), Zorba, 1968-69, Company, 1970-72 (Antoinette Perry award 1972), A Little Night Music, 1973-74 (Antoinette Perry award 1975), Pacific Overtures, 1976, A Doll's Life, 1982; co-dir., prodr.: Follies, 1971-72 (Tony award for directing), Faust, 1990; co-prodr., dir.: Candide, 1974-75 (Tony award for directing), Merrily We Roll Along, 1981; dir.: A Family Affair, 1962, Baker Street, 1965, Great God Brown, 1972-73, The Visit, 1973-74, Love for Love, 1974-75, Ashmedai, 1976, Some of My Best Friends, 1977, On The Twentieth Century, 1978, La Fanciulla Del West, 1978, Evita, London, 1979, N.Y.C., 1980, L.A., 1982, Australia, 1980, Chgo., 1980, Detroit, 1982, Sweeney Todd, The Demon Barber of Fleet Street, Broadway, 1979, London, 1980, Silverlake, 1980, Willie Stark, 1981, Candide, 1982, 94, 97, Madama Butterfly, 1983, Turandot, 1983, Play Memory, 1984, End of the World, 1984, Grind, 1985, Cabaret Revival, 1987, Roza, 1987, Phantom of the Opera, London, 1986, N.Y.C., (Antoinette Perry award) 1988, Kiss of the Spider Woman, Toronto, 1992, London, 1992, N.Y.C., 1993, Show Boat, Toronto, 1993, N.Y.C., 1994 (Tony award for directing), La Fanciula del West, Don Giovanni, N.Y. City Opera, 1989, Faust, Met. Opera, 1990, The Petrified Prince, 1994, (off broadway) Diamonds, 1984; adapter, dir. (off broadway) Grandchild of Kings, 1992, Candide, Broadway, 1997, Parade, Broadway, 1998; co-prodr: (films) The Pajama Game, 1957, Damn Yankees, 1958; dir.: (films) Something for Everyone, 1970, A Little Night Music, 1978, 3Hree, Phila. & L.A. Mem. coun. Nat. Endowment Arts; pres. League N.Y. Theatres, 1964-66; chmn. Performing Arts Libr., N.Y.C. Recipient 20 Antoinette Perry (Tony) Meml. awards, Critics Circle awards, Pulitzer prize, 1961, Best Mus. awards London Evening Std., Kennedy Ctr. Honors, 1994. Office: 10 Rockefeller Plz Ste 1009 New York NY 10020-1972

PRINCE, JOHN LUTHER, III, engineering educator; b. Austin, Tex., Nov. 13, 1941; s. John Luther and Glynda (Chollett) P.; m. Martha Ann Hight, Mar. 4, 1960; children: Cynthia Kay, John Luther IV, Alan Douglas, David William. BSEE, So. Meth. U., 1965; MEE, N.C. State U., 1968, PhD, 1969. Research engr. RTI, Res. Tri. Park, N.C., 1968-70; mem. tech. staff Tex. Instruments, Dallas, 1970-75; from assoc. prof. to prof. Clemson (S.C.) U., 1975-80; dir. R.A. Intermedics, Inc., Freeport, Tex., 1980-83; prof. U. Ariz., Tucson, 1983—. Acting dir. packaging scis. Semiconductor Rsch. Corp., 1991-92; cons. numerous semi-conductor and electronics cos., 1983—; dir. Electronic Packaging Lab., 1984-91, Ctr. for Electronic Packaging Rsch., 1991—, SEMATECH Ctr. of Excellence for Contamination and Defect Control, 1988-90. Contbr. articles to profl. jours. Named Ariz. Innovator of the Yr., 1992; NSF fellow, 1965-68. Fellow IEEE; mem. Am. Philatelic Soc. Lutheran.

Avocations: stamp collecting, classic cars, motorcycles. Home: 7542 N San Lorenzo Dr Tucson AZ 85704-3141 Office: U Ariz Dept Engineering Tucson AZ 85721-0001 E-mail: prince@ece.arizona.edu., jlpmhp@aol.com.

PRINCE, JULIUS S. (BUD PRINCE), retired foreign service reserve officer; b. Yonkers, N.Y., July 21, 1911; s. Julius and Clara B. (Rich) P.; m. Eleanora Molloy, July 6, 1943; children: Thomas Marc, Tod Ainslee (dec.), Richard M. Johnson. BA, Yale U., 1932; MD, Columbia U., 1938, M.P.H., 1948; Dr.P.H., Harvard, 1957. Intern Sinai Hosp., Balt., 1939-40; asst. resident medicine N.Y. U. div. Goldwater Meml. Hosp., 1941-42; dist. state health officer N.Y. State Dept. Health, Jamestown, 1948-58; chief pub. health div. USAID, Ethiopia, 1958-67; prin. investigator demonstration and evaluation project AID, Ethiopia, 1959-67; chief Africa div. Population and Humanitarian Affairs, Population Office, AID, Washington, 1967-73; dir. Africa Regional Population Office, Accra, Ghana, 1973-74; chief health, population and nutrition projects AID, Ghana, 1974-76; cons. internat. health APHA, 1977-78, Pacific Cons., Inc., 1978-82, RONCO Inc., 1982; pub. health specialist/sr. health advisor One Am., Inc., 1982-87; sr. pub. health and nutrition specialist Internat. Sci. and Tech. Inst. Inc., 1985-94; cons. on internat. health, 1985—. Report on sustainability of AID supported health, population and nutrition programs, Ghana, 1963-85, Ctr. Devel. Info. and Evaluation AID, 1988, Annotated History of AID-Supported Health and Nutrition Rsch.: From Outset to Present, Introduction and Background, AID Office Health, 1991, Compendium of Abstracts, 1985-92, rsch. by historically black colls. and univs. under AID Univ. Ctr./Rsch. and Univ. Devel. Linkages, 1985-92. Contbr. chpt. to book. Served from lt. to maj. M.C. Royal Canadian Army, 1942-46. Recipient Letter of Commendation, Adj. Gen. Can. Army, 1946, Superior honor award AID, 1968, Letter of Commendation, 1977 Fellow APHA (Lifetime Achievement award 1996), Soc. Applied Anthropology, Washington Acad. Scis., Royal Soc. Health, Am. Coll. Preventive Medicine; mem. AMA, N.Y. State Pub. Health Assn. (pres. 1957), Pan Am. Med. Assn., Am. Assn. World Health (emeritus mem. bd. dirs.), Internat. Soc. Hypertension in Blacks, Internat. Union for Sci. Study of Population, Population Assn. Am., Soc. Internat. Devel., Nat. Coun. Internat. Health (award 1992), World Med. Assn., Soc. Prospective Medicine, Can. Soc. Internat. Health. Home and Office: 7103 Pinehurst Pky Chevy Chase MD 20815-3144

PRINCE, KENNETH STEPHEN, lawyer; b. Newton, Mass., Jan. 28, 1950; s. Samuel and Edna L. Prince; m. Patricia Denning, Jan. 15, 1977 (dec. Nov. 1985); 1 child, Kenneth Stephen Jr.; m. Jane M. McCabe, Sept. 5, 1987; 1 child, Allison Pamela. BA, U. Pa., 1972; JD, Boston Coll., 1975. Bar: N.Y. 1976, Mass. 1975, U.S. Dist. Ct. (so. and ea. dists.) N.Y. 1978. Assoc. Shearman & Sterling, N.Y.C., 1975-83, ptnr., 1984—, antitrust group practice leader, 1992—. Mem. N.Y. Law Inst. (exec. com. 1984-96), Order of Coif. Home: 15 Dellwood Rd Darien CT 06820-2915 E-mail: kprince@shearman.com.

PRINCE, LARRY L. automotive parts and supplies company executive; b. 1937; With Genuine Parts Co., Atlanta, 1958—, v.p., then group v.p., 1977-83, exec. v.p., 1983-86, pres., chief oper. officer, 1986-90, chief exec. officer, 1989—, chmn. bd. dirs., CEO, 1990—, also bd. dirs. Office: Genuine Parts Co 2999 Circle 75 Pky NW Atlanta GA 30339*

PRINCE, LEAH FANCHON, art educator and research institute administrator; b. Hartford, Conn., Aug. 12, 1939; d. Meyer and Annie (Forman) Berman; m. Herbert N. Prince, Jan. 30, 1955; children: Daniel L., Richard N., Robert G. Student, U. Conn., 1957-59, Rutgers U., Newark, 1962; BFA, Fairleigh Dickinson U., 1970; postgrad., Caldwell Coll. for Women, 1973-75, Parsons Sch. of Design, N.Y.C., 1978. Cert. tchr. art, N.J. Tchr. art Caldwell-West Caldwell (N.J.) Pub. Schs., 1970-75; pres. Britannia Imports Ltd., Fairfield, N.J., 1979-89; tchr. religious studies Bohrer-Kaufman Hebrew Acad., Randolph, 1981-82; co-founder, corp. sec. Gibraltar Biol. Labs., Inc., Fairfield, 1970—; dir., co-founder Gibraltar Inst. for Rsch. and Tng., 1984—. Cons. Internat. Antiques and Fine Arts Industries, U.K., 1979-89; cons. in art exhibitry Passaic County Coll., Paterson, N.J., 1989-93; art curator Fairleigh Dickinson U., Rutherford, N.J., 1972-74; curator history of design Bloomfield (N.J.) Coll., 1990-91; lectr. nat. meeting Am. Soc. Microbiology, New Orleans, 1989; spkr. in field. Exhibited in group shows at Bloomfield (N.J.) Coll., 1990, Caldwell Women's Club, N.J., 1991, State Fedn. Women's Clubs Ann. Show, 1992 (1st pl. award 1992), Newark Art Mus., 1992, West (N.J.) Essex Art Assn., 1990, Somerset (N.J.) Art Assn. Ann. Juried Show, 1994, Mortimer Gallery, Gladstone, N.J., 1994 (1st pl. award 1998), Tewksbury His. Soc. (1st pl. award 1994), Tewksbury Hist. Soc., 2001; one-woman shows include Passaic County Coll., N.J., 1990, Caldwell Coll., N.J., 1990; author children's stories. Chair ann. juried art awards Arts Coun. of Essex Bd. Trustees, Montclair, N.J., 1984-90; chair fundraising Arts Coun. Essex County, N.J., 1989. Recipient 1st place award N.J. Tewksbury Hist. Soc., 1994, 98, Juried Art award Tewsbury Hist. Soc., 2001. Mem. AAUW, Soc. Childrens Book Writers & Illustrators, Somerset Art Assn., Nat. Mus. of Women in the Arts, Nat. League Am. Pen Women, Inc., Internat. Platform Assn., Barnegat Light Yacht Club. Republican. Avocations: boating, tennis, opera. Home: 5 Standish Dr Mendham Twp Morristown NJ 07960-3224

PRINCE, MATTHEW SPERRY, religious organization executive; b. Jacksonville, Fla., Sept. 29, 1928; s. Thomas Chafer and Abby Gail Prince; m. Beverly Ross Stanton, June 7, 1952 (div. Nov. 1977); children: Matthew Sperry Jr., David, Peggy, Patricia, Penny, Beverly; m. Judithe Seidell Boensch, June 30, 1979. BA, U. Tenn., 1949, JD, 1958; ThM, Dallas Theol. Sem., 1954. Pastor McKinney Meml. Ch., Ft. Worth, 1953-55, Bethany Bible Ch., Knoxville, Tenn., 1956-58; assoc. Ambrose, Wilson, Saulpaw, 1958-61; asst. to pres. Young Life, Inc., Colorado Springs, Colo., 1961-64; pvt. practice Knoxville, 1964-65; ptnr. Privette, Mann, Prince & Smith, 1965-69; pres. New Life, Inc., 1969—, Lewis Speary Chafer Theol. Sem., Knoxville, 2000—. Pres. Chafer Inst. Biblical Studies, 2000—. Author: Winning Through Caring, 1980. Chmn. Rep. Primary Election Commn., Knoxville, 1959-61. Named Tenn. Clergyman of Yr., Tenn. Christian Coalition, 1994. Baptist. Avocations: physical conditioning workouts, golf, playing instrumental music, barbershop quartet singing, gardening. Home: 1012 Edenbridge Way Knoxville TN 37923-6612 Office: New Life Inc 9040 Executive Park Dr Ste 222 Knoxville TN 37923-4671 E-mail: mattprince@IOL24.com.

PRINCE, MORTON BRONENBERG, physicist; b. Phila., Apr. 1, 1924; s. David H. and Jennie (Bronenberg) P.; m. Blanche E. Stern, June 15, 1947; 1 child, Judith Ann. AB, Temple U., 1947; PhD, MIT, 1951. Mem. tech. staff Bell Telephone Labs., Inc., Murray Hill, N.J., 1951-56; v.p., gen. mgr. Hoffman Electronics Corp., El Monte, Calif., 1956-61; with electro optical systems div. Xerox, Pasadena, Calif., 1961-69; pres. SSR Instruments Co., Santa Monica, 1970-74; v.p., gen. mgr. Meret Inc., 1974-75; with U.S. Dept. Energy, Washington, 1975-93. Contbr. chpts. to books, articles to profl. jours. Served with U.S. Army, 1943-46. Recipient Marconi premium Inst. Radio Engrs., Gt. Britain, 1959, Becquerel prize European Commn., 1994. Fellow IEEE; mem. Am. Phys. Soc., Internat. Solar Energy Soc. Clubs: Cosmos. Home: 7301 Coventry Ave Apt 601 Elkins Park PA 19027-2953

PRINCE, ROBB LINCOLN, manufacturing company executive; b. Duluth, Minn., June 30, 1941; s. Milton H. and Katherine (Lincoln) P.; m. Jacqueline H. Marik, June 19, 1965; children: Daniel, Deborah. BA in Econs., Carleton Coll., 1963; MBA in Mktg., U. Pa., 1965. With mktg. planning United Airlines, Chgo., 1965-72; dir. planning Jostens Inc., Mpls., 1973-74, treas., 1975-79, v.p., treas., 1979-95, ret., 1995; dir. FORTIS Mut. Funds, Analysts Internat. Corp. Trustee Hamline U. With USN, 1966-69. Office: 5108 Duggan Plz Edina MN 55439-1453

PRINCE, THOMAS RICHARD, accountant, educator; b. New Albany, Miss., Dec. 7, 1934; s. James Thompson and Callie Florence (Howell) P.; m. Eleanor Carol Polkoff, July 14, 1962; children: Thomas Andrew, John Michael, Adrienne Carol. BS, Miss. State U., 1956, MS, 1957; PhD in Accountancy, U. Ill., 1962. CPA, Ill. Instr. U. Ill., 1960-62; mem. faculty Northwestern U. Kellogg Grad. Sch. Mgmt., 1962—, prof. acctg. info. and mgmt., 1969—, chmn. dept. acctg. info. and mgmt., 1968-75; prof. health industry mgmt. Northwestern U., 1980—; cons. in field. Dir. Applied Research Systems, Inc. Author: Extension of the Boundaries of Accounting Theory, 1962, Information Systems for Management Planning and Control, 3d edit, 1975, Financial Reporting and Cost Control for Health Care Entities, 1992, Product Life-Cycle Costing and Management of Large-Scale Medical Systems Investments, 1997, Strategic Management for Health Care Entities: Creative Frameworks for Financial and Operational Analysis, 1998. Served to 1st lt. AUS, 1957-60. Mem. Am. Accounting Assn., Am. Inst. C.P.A.s, Am. Econ. Assn., INFORMS, AHA, HFMA, HIMMS, AUPHA, Fin. Execs. Inst., AAAS, Ill. Soc. C.P.A.s,, Inst. Mgmt. Acct., Alpha Tau Omega, Phi Kappa Phi, Omicron Delta Kappa, Delta Sigma Pi, Beta Alpha Psi. Congregationalist. Home: 303 Richmond Rd Kenilworth IL 60043-1138 Office: Northwestern U Leverone Hl Evanston IL 60208-2002 E-mail: t-prince@kellogg.northwestern.edu.

PRINCE, TIMOTHY PETER, lawyer; b. San Bernardino, Calif., July 11, 1965; s. Ralph H. and Alexine C. Prince. BA in Polit. Sci., U. Calif., Berkeley, 1987; JD, U. Calif., San Francisco, 1990. Bar: Calif., U.S. Dist. Ct. (ctrl. dist.) Calif. Asoc. Wilson, Borror, Dunn & Scott, San Bernardino, Calif., 1990-98; ptnr. Tomlinson, Nydam & Prince, 1998—. Law rev. editor Hastings Constnl. Law Quar., 1989-90; contbr. articles to profl. jours. Chmn. Citizens for Accountable City Govt., San Bernardino, 1997; bd. dirs. Am. Lung Assn. of the Inland Counties, 1993—96, sec., 1994—96; v.p. North End Neighborhood Assn., 1998—. Calif. Alumni scholar, 1983-87, Gannett Found. scholar, 1983-87. Mem.: Inland C's U. Calif. Berkley Alumni Club (pres. 1995), Rotary (chmn. youth and scholarship programs). Democrat. Presbyterian. Achievements include canidacy in primary and general elections for Mayor of San Bernardino; writing ordinance restricting tobacco use adopted by City Council of San Bernardino. Avocations: hiking, jogging, music, travel, politics. Office: Tomlinson Nydam & Prince 290 N D St Ste 807 San Bernardino CA 92401-1704

PRINCE, WILLIAM TALIAFERRO, retired federal judge; b. Norfolk, Va., Oct. 3, 1929; s. James Edward and Helen Marie (Taliaferro) P.; m. Anne Carroll Hannegan, Apr. 12, 1958; children: Sarah Carroll Prince Pishko, Emily Taliaferro, William Taliaferro, John Hannegan, Anne Martineau Thompson, Robert Harrison. Student, Coll. William and Mary, Norfolk, 1947-48, 49-50; AB, Williamsburg, 1955, BCL, 1957, MLT, 1959. Bar: Va. 1957. Lectr. acctg. Coll. William and Mary, 1955-57; lectr. law Marshall-Wythe Sch. Law, 1957-59; assoc. Williams, Kelly & Greer, Norfolk, 1959-63, ptnr., 1963-90; U.S. magistrate judge Eastern Dist. of Va., 1990-2000; ret., 2000; recalled Ct. of Appeals for 4th Cir., 2000—02, Ct. of Appeals for 10th Cir., 2002. Pres. Am. Inn of Ct. XXVII, 1987-89. Bd. editors: The Virginia Lawyer, A Basic Practice Handbook, 1966. Bd. dirs. Madonna Home, Inc., 1978-93, Soc. Alumni of Coll. William and Mary, 1985-88. Fellow Am. Coll. Trial Lawyers, Am. Bar Found., Va. Law found. (bd. dirs. 1976-90); mem. ABA (ho. of dels. 1984-90), Am. Judicature Soc. (bd. dirs. 1984-88), Va. State Bar (coun. 1973-77, exec. com. 1975-80, pres. 1978-79). Roman Catholic. Home: 1227 Graydon Ave Norfolk VA 23507-1006 Office: Walter E Hoffman US Courthouse 600 Granby St Ste 341 Norfolk VA 23510-1915 E-mail: WTPrince1@aol.com.

PRINCE, (PRINCE ROGERS NELSON), musician, actor; b. Mpls., June 7, 1958; s. John L. and Mattie D. (Shaw) Nelson; m. Mayte Garcia, 1996 (div., 2000); 1 son (dec.). Singer, songwriter, actor. Albums include For You, 1978, Dirty Mind, 1979, Controversy, 1981, 1999, 1983, film star and soundtrack Purple Rain, 1984 (Academy Award for best original score, 1984), Around the World in a Day, 1985 (Best Soul/Rhythm and Blues Album of the Yr., Downbeat readers poll, 1985), Parade, 1986, Chaos and Disorder, 1996, Sign O' the Times, 1987, Lovesexy, 1988, Batman: Motion Picture Soundtrack, 1989 (Soundtrack of Yr. award Playboy mag. readers' poll, Best Pop/Rock album Downbeat mag. readers' poll), (with the New Power Generation) Diamonds and Pearls, 1991, (symbol as title), 1992, Come, 1995, The Greatest Romance Ever Sold, 1999, 94 East, 2000, The Very Best of Prince, 2001, Beautiful Experience, 2001; films include Purple Rain, 1984 (Acad. award for best original score 1985), film star and soundtrack Under the Cherry Moon, 1986, film star and soundtrack Sign O' the Times, 1987; film appearance and soundtrack Graffiti Bridge, 1990 (ASCAP award for most performed songs from a motion picture, 1991); formerly mem. group Prince and the Revolution (Best Soul/Rhythm and Blues Group of Yr. Downbeat mag. readers poll 1985); composer Showgirls, 1995, Girl 6, 1996, The Gold Experience, 1995, Crystal Ball, 1998, Rave Un2 the Joy Fantastic, 1999, Bamboozled, 2000. Recipient 3 Grammy awards, 1985, Am. Music Achievement award for infuence on look and sound of the 80's, NAACP Spl. Achievement award, 1997; named Rhythm and Blues Musician of Yr. Down Beat mag. readers' poll, 1984, 1992.*

PRINCES, CAROLYN DIANE WILBON, educational director; b. Kansas City, Mo., Nov. 15, 1950; d. Will Lee (dec.) and Subemer Jean (Wiggins) Wilbon; m. Donald Louis Princes, July 15, 1972 (div.); children: Donald Jermaine, Aaron Jamelle Meade. BS in Psychology, U. Ill., 1973, MEd in Adminstrn. and Supervision, 1979; EdD in Curriculum and Instrn., U. Md., 1989; postdoc., U. Ghana, 1994, George Washington U., 1994. Cert. substitute tchr. K-12, Ill.; temporary cert. H.S. math., Ill. Asst. dir., acad. devel. specialist Frostburg (Md.) State U., 1980-86; admissions and records clk. Loyola U. Chgo., 1972-73; paralegal, asst. mgr. tng., instr. profl. tng. Chgo. Title and Trust Co., 1973-80; asst. dir. academic devel. spec., dir. student support svcs./disabled student svcs. Frostburg (Md.) State U., 1986-90; dir. African American Cultural Ctr., Indiana U. of Pa., 1990—. Mem. Act 101 Adv. Bd., Indiana, 1993—. Author: (book chpt.) ABCC Monograph, 1995; contbr. articles to profl. jours. and mags. Mem. Cmty. Rels. Adv. Bd., 1991-94; bd. dirs. Indiana County Day Care, 1993-96, Longstretch Youth Homes, Frostburg, 1983-86; bd. dirs., mem. edn. com. Human Resources Devel. Commn., Allegany County, Md., 1983-86; chair, instr. cultural arts program, NAACP, Cumberland, Md., 1983-86; chair United Negro Coll. Fund, Cumberland, 1983-85. Recipient Cert. of Appreciation, Mayor's Office of New Orleans, 1997, Dirs. Awd. for Instl. Membership, The Natl. Assn. of Black Culture, 1998, 99, Lifetime Achievement Awd., NAACP Indiana U. Pa. chpt., 1998, Trailblazer Awd., Black Stud. League, Indiana U. Pa., 98; co-recipient Excellence in Programming award Nat. Assn. Campus Activities, 1994, 95, 96, 97, 98, Multicultural Program award, 1993; Ebony and Ivory Outstanding Svc. Awd., SSDS grantee U.S. Dept. Edn., 1986, 90, Internat. Venture grantee Indiana U. of Pa., 1994, Social Equity grantee Pa. State Sys. of Higher Edn., 1992, 96, Edn. Svcs. Fee grantee Indiana U. of Pa., 1992-99. Fellow Nat. Coun. for Black Studies, 1994; WCBC Radio, Celebrity of the Day, Cumberland, 1988; mem. ASCD, Indiana County, Pa. NAACP, Indiana County PTA (gen. mem. 6th-grade dance com. 1997), Assn. for Black Culture Ctrs. (bd. dirs., chair of pub. rels. 1991—), Social Equity Com. Indiana U. of Pa., Pa. Black Conf. on Higher Edn. (editl. bd. jour. 1996-2001, chair program booklet com. 1999 ann. conf.). African Methodist Episcopalian. Avocations: dancing, aerobics, traveling, music. Office: Indiana U of Pa 1024 Washington St Indiana PA 15705-0001

PRINCIPE, MICHAEL LUIS, political science educator; b. Yakima, Wash., Dec. 22, 1952; s. Luis A. and Molly V. (Rider) P.; m. Lisa K. Principe (dec. Feb. 1982); children: Jacqueline, Crystal; m. Nancy L. Principe, Nov. 13, 1993; children: Michael Jr., Steven, Meghann, Camille. BA in Sociology, Whitman Coll., 1978; JD, U. Wash., 1983; PhD in Polit. Sci., U. Calif., Santa Barbara, 1992. Assoc. prof. polit. sci. William Paterson, Wayne, N.J., 1998—. Vis. prof. law Salmon P. Chase Coll. Law, Highland Heights, Ky., 1995-96; vis. scholar polit. sci. Santa Barbara City Coll., 1997-98; vis. scholar in constnl. law St. Edmund's Coll., Cambridge (Eng.) U., 1993—; assoc. mem. human rights sem. Columbia U., N.Y.C., 1998—. Author: Bill of Rights: A Comparative Constitutional Analysis, 2000; editor: American Government, Policy and Law, 2000. Fulbright Commn. scholar Inst. Internat. Edn., (New Zealand), 1990-91. Mem. N.E. Assn. Prelaw Advisors. Avocations: jogging, golf, hiking. Office: William Paterson U Dept Polit Sci 300 Pompton Rd Wayne NJ 07470

PRINCIPI, ANTHONY JOSEPH, federal official, lawyer; b. N.Y.C., Apr. 16, 1944; s. Antonio Joseph and Theresa (Princiotta) P.; m. Elizabeth Ann Ahlering, June 26, 1971; children: Anthony, Ryan, John BS, U.S. Naval Acad., 1967; JD, Seton Hall U., 1975. Commd. 2d lt. U.S. Navy, 1967, advanced through grades to comdr., 1984, line officer, 1967-72; atty. JAGC, San Diego, 1975-80; counsel Com. on Armed Service U.S. Senate, Washington, 1980-83, staff dir. Com. on Vet.'s Affairs, 1984—; dep. adminstr. congl. and pub. affairs VA, 1983-84; dep. sec. Dept. of Veterans Affairs, 1989-90; ptnr. Luce, Forward, Hamilton & Scripps, San Diego, 1990-95; sr. v.p., CEO Lockheed Martin IMS Integrated Solutions Co., Santa Clara, Calif., 1995-2001; sec. VA, Washington, 2001—. Decorated Bronze Star with combat "V", Vietnamese Cross of Gallantry, Navy Commendation medal with combat "V" (3); recipient Meritorious Service medal VA, 1983 Mem. ABA (chmn. subcom. gen. practice sect. 1985—) Republican. Roman Catholic. Avocations: gardening; skiing. Office: 810 Vermont Ave NW Washington DC 20420*

PRINDLE, ALLEN MERLE, economics educator; b. Black River Falls, Wis., July 11, 1947; s. Howard E. and Florence (Schlegel) P.; m. Nancy Robinson, Aug. 25, 1973; children: Edward, Justin. BS, U. Wis., River Falls, 1970; MS, Purdue U., 1972; PhD, Penn State U., 1977. Asst. prof. U. Md., College Park, 1976-81; economist USDA, Washington, 1981-82, U.S. A.I.D., Washington, 1982-83, Robinson Hybrids, Delaware, Ohio, 1983-87; assoc. prof., chmn. dept. bus., acctg. and econs. Otterbein Coll., Westerville, 1987-99, prof., 1999—. Contbr. articles to profl. jours. Speakers bur. Scioto River Valley Fedn., Delaware, 1991-92. Mem. Columbus Assn. Bus. Economists, Ohio Assn. Economists and Polit. Scientists, Ohio LEAD Alumni (sec. 1987-92), 4-H Alumni, IFYE Alumni. Office: Otterbein Coll Dept of Bus and Econs Westerville OH 43081

PRINDLE, WILLIAM ROSCOE, retired glass company executive; b. San Francisco, Dec. 19, 1926; s. Vivian Arthur and Harriette Alnora (Nickerson) P.; m. June Laverne Anderson, June 20, 1947; children— Carol Susan, William Alastair. BS, U. Calif., Berkeley, 1948, MS, 1950; Sc.D., M.I.T., 1955. Asst. tech. dir. Hazel-Atlas Glass Co., 1954-56; mgr. research Hazel-Atlas Glass div. Continental Can Co., Wheeling, W.Va., 1956-58, gen. mgr. research and devel., 1959-62; mgr. materials research Am. Optical Co., Southbridge, Mass., 1962-65; v.p. research Southbridge and Framingham, 1971-76; dir; research Ferro Corp., Cleve., 1966-67, v.p. research, 1967-71; exec. dir. Nat. Materials Adv. Bd., NRC-NAS, Washington, 1976-80; dir. adminstrv. and tech. svcs. R & D div. Corning Glass Works, N.Y., 1980-85, dir. materials rsch., 1985-87; assoc. dir. R & D, Engring. div. Corning Glass Works (now Corning, Inc.), 1987-90; div. v.p., assoc. dir. tech. group Corning Inc., 1990-92; ret. Pres. XII Internat. Glass Congress, 1980, Internat. Commn. on Glass, 1985-88. Served with U.S. Navy, 1944-46. Named Disting. Ceramist of New Eng., New Eng. sect. Am. Ceramic Soc., 1974, Toledo Glass and Ceramic award NW Ohio sect., 1986, Albert Victor Bleininger Meml. award Pitts. sect., 1989; Friedberg Meml. lecture Nat. Inst. Ceramic Engrs., 1990. Fellow Am. Ceramic Soc. (disting. life, pres. 1980-81), Soc. Glass Tech., Am. Soc. for Metals Internat.; mem. NAE, AAAS, Cosmos Club (Washington), Sigma Xi, Phi Gamma Delta. Home and Office: 1556 Crestline Dr Santa Barbara CA 93105-4611 E-mail: wprindle@aol.com.

PRING, ROBERT BRADFORD, financial consultant; b. St. Louis, July 22, 1951; s. Charles Branscombe Pring and A Helen Crosson Reim; m. Bernice Rosalyn Crisp, Oct. 25, 1975 (div. Dec. 2001); children: Robert Bradford III, Jennifer Christiane. BS in Agr., U. Mo., Columbia, 1973; postgrad., U. Mo., 1973. Lic. life, accident and health ins agt; cert. fin planner, stockbroker, registered investment advisor rep. Ptnr. Prings Nursery, St. Louis, 1973-74; dist. sales mgr. Curtis Circulation Co., Nashville, 1974-75, reg. mktg. mgr. Orlando, Fla., 1975-77, West Coast account exec. West Caldwell, N.J., 1977-79, div. mktg. supr. St. Louis, 1979-81; trust mktg. officer Commerce Bank, 1982-84; v.p. bus. devel./comml. lending Commerce Bank St. Charles County, N.A., St. Peters, 1984-91; v.p., comml. devel. officer Commerce Bank St. Louis, 1991-97; bus. mgr. program First State Bank St. Charles, St. Charles, 1997-2001; fin. advisor, investment mgr., personal fin. planning INVEST Fin. Corp., 2001—02. Prodr.: St. Charles County, A World of Opportunity, 1987; dir.: , 1987. Pres, chmn United Serv Handicapped, St Charles, 1988—89; treas bd dirs YMCA St Charles County, 1989—99, chmn bd dirs, 1991—92; treas Citizens St Charles County CC, 1990, co-chmn, 1991; bd dirs YMCA Greater Metropolitan St Louis, 1991—92, Mid-Am Theatre Co, St Charles, St Charles YMCA, 1985—2000; bd. dirs. St. Charles C.C. Found., 1995—, past chmn., v.p. fin. Recipient Meritorious Serv Award, United Servs Handicapped, 1989, Bell Vol Award, St Charles County Community Coun and Southwestern Bell, 1990. Mem.: Fin. Planning Assn., Inst. Cert. Fin. Planners, Greater St. Louis Soc. Cert. Fin. Planners (bd dirs 1990—91), St. Peters C. of C. (past dir, pres, chmn 1988, Disting Leadership Award 1990), Rotary (bd dirs St Charles chpt 1992). Presbyterian. Avocations: flying, soaring, water sports. Home and Office: 4164 Attleboro Ct Saint Charles MO 63304-5515 E-mail: rbpring@charter.net.

PRINGLE, LAURENCE PATRICK, writer; b. Rochester, N.Y., Nov. 26, 1935; s. Laurence Erin and Marleah Elizabeth (Rosehill) P.; m. Judith Malanowicz, June 23, 1962 (div. 1970); children: Heidi Elizabeth, Jeffrey Laurence, Sean Edmund; m. Alison Newhouse, July 14, 1971 (div. 1975); m. Susan Deborah Klein, Mar. 13, 1983; children: Jesse Erin, Rebecca Anne. BS in Wildlife Biology, Cornell U., 1958; MS in Wildlife Biology, U. Mass., 1961. Tchr. sci. Lima (N.Y.) Cen. Sch., 1961-62; editor Nature and Sci. mag. Am. Mus. Natural History, N.Y.C., 1963-70; free-lance writer, 1970—. Writer-in-residence Kean College, Union, N.J., 1985-86. Author: (children's books) Dinosaurs and Their World, 1968, The Only Earth We Have, 1969, From Field to Forest, 1970, In a Beaver Valley, 1970, One Earth, Many People, 1971, Ecology: Science of Survival, 1971, Cockroaches: Here, There, Everywhere, 1971, From Pond to Prairie, 1972, This Is a River, 1972, Pests and People: The Search for Sensible Pest Control, 1972, Estuaries: Where Rivers Meet the Sea, 1973, Into the Woods: Exploring the Forest Ecosystem, 1973, Follow a Fisher, 1973, Twist, Wiggle and Squirm: A Book about Earthworms, 1973, Recycling Resources, 1974, Energy: Power for People, 1975, City and Suburb: Exploring an Ecosystem, 1975, Chains, Webs and Pyramids: The Flow of Energy in Nature, 1975, Water Plants, 1975, The Minnow Family: Chubs, Dace, Minnows and Shiners, 1976, Listen to the Crows, 1976, Our Hungry Earth: The World Food Crisis, 1976, Death is Natural, 1977, The Hidden World: Life Under a Rock, 1977, The Controversial Coyote: Predation, Politics and Ecology, 1977, The Gentle Desert: Exploring an Ecosystem, 1977, Animals and Their Niches: How Species Share Resources, 1977, The Economic Growth Debate: Are There Limits to Growth?, 1978, Dinosaurs and People: Fossils, Facts and Fantasies, 1978, Wild Foods, 1978, Nuclear Power: From Physics to Politics, 1979, Natural Fire: Its Ecology in Forests, 1979, Lives at Stake: The Science and Politics of Environmental Health, 1980, What Shall We Do with the Land?: Choices for America, 1981, Frost Hollows and Other Microclimates, 1981, Vampire Bats, 1982, Water: The Next Great Resource Battle, 1982, Radiation: Waves and Particles/Benefits and Risks, 1983, Wolfman: Exploring the World of Wolves, 1983, Feral: Tame Animals Gone Wild, 1983, The Earth Is Flat—and Other Great Mistakes, 1983, Being a Plant, 1983, Nuclear War: From Hiroshima to Nuclear Winter, 1985, Animals at Play, 1985, Here Come the Killer Bees, 1986, Throwing Things Away: From Middens to Resource Recovery, 1986, Restoring Our Earth, 1987, Home: How Animals Find Comfort and Safety, 1987, Rain of Troubles: The Science and Politics of Acid Rain, 1988, Living in a Risky World, 1989, Nuclear Energy: Troubled Past, Uncertain Future, 1989, Bearman: Exploring the World of Black Bears, 1989, The Animal Rights Controversy, 1989, Saving Our Wildlife, 1990, Global Warming: Assessing the Greenhouse Threat, 1990, The Golden Book of Insects and Spiders, 1990, Killer Bees (rev. edit.), 1991, Batman: Exploring the World of Bats, 1991, Living Treasure: Saving Earth's Threatened Biodiversity, 1991, Antarctica: The Last Unspoiled Continent, 1992, The Golden Book of Volcanoes, Earthquakes, and Powerful Storms, 1992, Chemical and Biological Warfare: The Cruelest Weapons, 1993, revised edit., 2000, Oil Spills: Damage, Recovery, and Prevention, 1993, Jackal Woman: Exploring the World of Jackals, 1993, Scorpion Man: Exploring the World of Scorpions, 1994, Dinosaurs! Strange and Wonderful, 1995, Vanishing Ozone: Protecting Earth from Ultraviolet Radiation, 1995, Coral Reefs: Earth's Undersea Treasures, 1995, Dolphin Man: Exploring the World of Dolphins, 1995, rev. edit., 2002, Fire in the Forest: A Cycle of Growth and Renewal, 1995, Taking Care of the Earth: Kids in Action, 1996, Smoking : A Risky Business, 1996, An Extraordinary Life: The Story of a Monarch Butterfly, 1997, Nature! Wild and Wonderful, 1997, Everybody Has a Bellybutton: Your Life Before You Were Born, 1997, Elephant Woman: Cynthia Moss Explores The World of Elephants, 1997, Drinking: A Risky Business, 1997, One Room School, 1998, Explore Your Senses: SIGHT, 1999, Explore Your Senses: HEARING, 1999, Explore Your Senses: TASTE, 1999, Explore Your Senses: TOUCH, 1999, Explore Your Senses: SMELL, 1999, BATS! Strange and Wonderful, 2000, The Environmental Movement: From Its Roots to the Challenges of a New Century, 2000, Sharks! Strange and Wonderful, 2001, Global Warming: The

Threat of Earth's Changing Climate, 2001, A Dragon in the Sky: The Story of a Green Darner Dragonfly, 2001, Scholastic Encyclopedia of Animals, 2001, Strange Animals, New to Science, 2002, Crows! Strange and Wonderful, 2002, Dog of Discovery: A Newfoundland's Adventure with Lewis and Clark, 2002, (fiction) Jesse Builds a Road, 1989, Octopus Hug, 1993, Naming the Cat, 1997, (adult books) Wild River, 1972, Rivers and Lakes, 1985. Recipient Spl. Conservation award Nat. Wildlife Fedn., 1978, Eva L. Gordon award Am. Nature Study Soc., 1983, Orbis Pictus award Nat. Coun. Tchrs. English , 1998, Nonfiction award Washington Post/Childrens Book Guild, 1999. Mem.: The Authors Guild. Home and Office: PO Box 252 West Nyack NY 10994-0252

PRINGLE, LEWIS GORDON, marketing professional, educator; b. Lansing, Mich., Feb. 13, 1941; s. Gordon Henry and Lucile Roxana (Drake) P.; children: Lewis Gordon Jr., William Davis, Thomas Benjamin. BA, Harvard U., 1963; MS, M.I.T., 1965, PhD, 1969. Vice pres., dir. mktg. sci. BBDO, Inc., N.Y.C., 1968-73; asst. prof. mktg. Carnegie-Melon U., Pitts., 1973-74; exec. v.p., dir. rsch. svcs., corp. dir. BBDO, Inc., N.Y.C., 1978-91; exec. v.p. BBDO Worldwide, 1986-91; chmn., CEO BBDO Europe, 1986-91, LG Pringle and Assocs., 1992-95; Joseph C. Seibert prof. of mktg. Farmer Sch. Bus. Adminstrn., Miami U., Oxford, Ohio, 1995—. Bd. dirs. Yorktown U., prof.; mem. vis com. Sloan Sch. Mgmt., MIT. Author numerous articles in field. Active local Boy Scouts Am. Ford Found. fellow, 1967 Fellow Royal Statis. Soc.; mem. Market Rsch. Coun., Am. Psychol. Assn., European Soc. Mktg. and Opinion Rsch., Am. Mktg. Assn., Inst. Ops. Rsch. and Mgmt. Sci. Office: Silver Creek Farm 2858 N Stout Rd Liberty IN 47353

PRINGLE, MARY BETH, English language educator, writer; b. July 20, 1943; BA, U. Denver, 1964, MA, 1967; PhD, U. Minn., 1977. Prof. Wright State U., Dayton, Ohio, 1975—. Vis. lectr. Semester at Sea, U. Pitts., fall 1997, spring 2002; instr. U. Minn., Iowa State U., S.W. Mo. State U., U. Denver. Home: 8497 N Lebanon Pike Waynesville OH 45068 Office: Wright State U Dept English Dayton OH 45435 E-mail: marybeth.pringle@wright.edu.

PRINGLE, ORAN ALLAN, mechanical and aerospace engineering educator; b. Lawrence, Kan., Sept. 14, 1923; s. Oran Allan and Mae (McClell) P.; m. Billie Hansen, June 25, 1947; children— Allan, Billie, James, Rebecca. BS in Mech. Engring, U. Kan., 1947; MS, U. Wis., 1948, PhD, 1967. Registered profl. engr., Mo. Mech. engr. Black and Veatch (cons. engrs.), Kansas City, Mo., 1947-48; engr. Boeing Airplane Co., Wichita, 1952—; prof. U. Mo., Columbia, 1948—. Co-author: Engineering Metallurgy, 1957; contbr. articles to profl. lit. Bd. dirs. United Cerebral Palsy Boone County, Mo. Served with AUS, 1943-45. Ford Found. grantee. Mem. Am. Soc. M.E. (chmn. fastening and joining com., design engring. div.), Sigma Xi. Home: 1820 University Ave Columbia MO 65201-6004 Office: Dept Mech and Aerospace Engring U Mo Columbia MO 65201

PRINGLE, ROBERT MAXWELL, diplomat; b. N.Y.C., Nov. 12, 1936; s. Henry Fowles and Helena Huntington (Smith) P.; m. Barbara Ann Cade, Sept. 26, 1964; children: James Maxwell, Anne Elizabeth. BA, Harvard U., 1958; PhD, Cornell U., 1967. Dir. econ. policy staff Bur. African Affairs Dept. State, 1981-83; dep. chief mission Ouagadougou, Burkina Faso, 1983-85, Port Moresby, Papua New Guinea, 1985-87; ambassador to Mali, 1987-90; dir. cen. African affairs U.S. Dept. State, 1990-93; dir. ecology and terrestrial conservation U.S. Dept. of State, 1993-95; dir. sr. seminar U.S. Dept. State, 1995-96; dep. chief of mission Dept. State, Pretoria, 1996-99; prof. nat. security policy Nat. War Coll., 1999—2001. Author: Rajahs and Rebels: The Ibans of Sarawak under Brooke Rule, 1970, Indonesia and the Philippines: American Interests in Island Southeast Asia, 1980. Mem. Assn. Asian Studies, African Studies Assn. Avocations: photography, gardening, scuba diving. Home: 216 Wolfe St Alexandria VA 22314-3858 E-mail: pringler@post.harvard.edu.

PRINGLE, THOMAS HIVICK, sales executive; b. Ardmore, Okla., Aug. 22, 1945; s. William Cuthbert and Pauline (Gill) P.; m. Dina Soltzberg; 1 child, Thomas Anthony. Grad. high sch., Greensburg, Pa. Owner Mohawk Recreational Ctr., Latrobe, Pa., 1970-72, Poorhouse Pizza, Youngwood, 1970-72; mgr. Courtesy R.V., Las Vegas, 1977-79, Ace Auto Sales, Las Vegas, 1980-85; salesman Norm Baker Motors, 1986-90; sales mgr. Sterling Motors, 1990-91; gen. mgr. Sys. Supply, Inc., 1992-2000; owner Rapid Computer Supplies, Nev., 2000—. Author: Bar Table 9 Ball, 1994, The Three Lies, The Downfall of America, 1999. With U.S. Army, 1963-66. Mem. Christian Coalition. Republican. Avocations: pocket billiards, bible studies, oil painting. Home: 1340 Challenge Ln Las Vegas NV 89110-1760 Office: Rapid Computer Supplies 1340 Challenge Ln Las Vegas NV 89110-1760

PRINN, RONALD G. atmospheric science educator; b. Hamilton, New Zealand, June 11, 1945; BSc, U. Auckland, New Zealand, 1967, MSc with 1st honors, 1968; ScD, MIT, 1971. Asst. prof. MIT, Cambridge, Mass., 1971-76, assoc. prof., 1976-82, prof., 1982-93, Tepco prof., 1993—, head dept. earth, atmospheric and planetary scis., 1998—. Chair com. on earth sci. NAS, Washington, 1982-84; chair Internat. Global Atmospheric Chemistry Project, Stockholm, 1988-95. Recipient Vernadsky Meml. lectr. Russian Acad. Sci., Moscow, 1984. Fellow Am. Geophys. Union (Macelwane medal 1981), AAAS (chair atmospheric and hydrospheric scis. 1999). Office: MIT Bldg 54-918 Cambridge MA 02139

PRINS, BRANDON CHRISTOPHER, political scientist, educator; b. Balt., Jan. 11, 1971; s. Robert Prins, Mary Elizabeth Prins; m. Gloria Hernandez. PhD, Mich. State U., 1999. Asst. prof. Polit. Sci. U. New Orleans, 1999—; instr. Polit. Sci. Mich. State U., East Lansing, 1998—99. Contbr. Mem.: Internat. Peace Sci. Soc. Avocation: Avocations: travel, sports. Office: Dept Political Sci University New Orleans New Orleans LA 70148 Office Fax: 504-280-3838. Business E-Mail: bprins@uno.edu.

PRINS, CAROL, not-for-profit developer, consultant; b. N.Y.C., Aug. 23, 1940; d. J. Warner and Gertrude (Buttenwieser) Prins; m. John H. Hart, June 26, 1994; children from previous marriage: Jessica Eve(dec.) , Audrey, Joseph Stephen Patt. Student, Vassar Coll., 1958-59, Barnard Coll., 1962, Neighborhood Playhouse Sch., N.Y.C., 1962-64. Ptnr. Just Causes, Chgo., 1978-87; cons. in field, 1987—. Pres. The Jessica Fund, a pvt. family found., Chgo. Mem. nat. found. bd. NARAL; mem. nat. adv. bd. Santa Fe Opera; mem. women's bd. dirs. Am. Cancer Soc.; mem. costume com. Chgo. Hist. Soc.; mem. adv. bd. Aspen/Santa Fe Ballet; pres. nat. bd. dirs., trustee Georgia O'Keeffe Mus., Santa Fe; nat. bd. dirs. Art Inst. Santa Fe; bd. dirs. Goodman Theatre, Chgo., pres., 1993—, trustee, mem. exec. com.; bd. dirs. Chgo. Found. Women; trustee Neighborhood Playhouse Sch. Theatre, N.Y.C. Mem. The Arts Club, Standard Club of Chgo., Las Campanas (Santa Fe). Avocations: gardening, travel, writing poetry. Home: 1500 N Lake Shore Dr Chicago IL 60610-6657 E-mail: jessicafnd@aol.com.

PRINS, LAVONNE KAY, programmer analyst; b. Sibley, Iowa, Feb. 28, 1957; d. Henry Simon and Katherine (Schram) Prins; m. Dan Matthew Grose, Feb. 6, 1993 (div. Sept. 1997). BA, S.W. State U., Marshall, Minn., 1982; postgrad., Mankato (Minn.) State U., 1982-84. Instr. math. Mankato State U., 1982-84; computer operator Sathers, Round Lake, Minn., 1985; law records analyst ITT Consumer Fin. Corp., St. Louis Park, 1985-86; systems programmer Metaphor, Eden Prairie, 1987-89; pres. Ablazon Unltd. Inc., Ramsey, 1990—97; sr. systems programmer Health Risk Mgmt., Edina, 1989-91; software engr. Dimensional Medicine, Inc., Minnetonka, 1992-95; programmer analyst DynaMark Inc., Arden Hills, 1995-98; sr. programmer analyst United Hardware Distbg. Co., Plymouth, 1998; ind. contractor, 1999—; inspector Boston Sci. Corp., 2000—; pres. LaVonne's Home Businesses Inc., 2001—. Sgt. U.S. Army, 1975-79. Republican. Mem. Reformed Ch. in Am. Avocations: sponsoring needy children, studying foreign languages, writing, piano, travel. Home and Office: 8607 N Zinnia Way Maple Grove MN 55369-4626 Address: 8607 N Zinnia Way Maple Grove MN 55369-4626

PRINS, ROBERT JACK, retired academic administrator; b. Grand Rapids, Mich., Oct. 12, 1932; s. Jacob and Marie (Vanden Brink) P.; m. Ruth Ellen John, Oct. 10, 1950; children: Linda, Douglas, Debra, Nancy, Eric, Sarah. BA, Hope Coll., 1954; DBA, Coll. Emporia, 1974; DHL, Iowa Wesleyan U., 1999. With Mich. Bell Tel. Co., Detroit area, 1954-66; dir. devel. Bethesda Hosp., Denver, 1966-68; v.p. planning and devel. Park Coll., Parkville, Mo., 1969-70; chief adminstrv. officer Coll. of Emporia, Kans., 1970-75; dir. fin. and devel. The Abbey Sch., Canon City, Colo., 1975-79; dir. devel. Kirksville Coll. Osteo. Medicine, Mo., 1979-84; v.p. devel. McKendree Coll., Lebanon, Ill., 1984-86; pres. Iowa Weslyan Coll., Mt. Pleasant, 1986-99, pres. emeritus, 1999—; exec. dir. Internat. Student Svcs., Canon City, Colo., 1999—. Bd. dirs. Iowa Coll. Found., Iowa Commn. on Vol. Svc.; mem. Iowa Assn. Ind. Colls. and Univs.; former chmn., mem. bd. Potomak Worldwide, Taipei, Taiwan. Mem. Nat. Assn. Ind. Colls. and Univs., Coun. for Advancement and Support Edn.

PRINZ, RICHARD ALLEN, surgeon; MD, Loyola U., Chgo., 1972. Diplomate Am. Bd. Surgery, bd. dirs., 1994—. Intern Barnes Hosp., St. Louis, 1972-73, resident in surgery, 1973-74, Loyola U., Chgo., 1974-77, attending surgeon, 1980-93; staff Rush Presbyn.-St. Luke's Med. Ctr., 1993—; Helen Shedd Keith prof., chmn. dept. gen. surgery Rush U., 1993—. Mem. Am. Surg. Assn., Am. Assn. Endocrine Surgeons (pres. 1996), Midwest Surg. Assn. (pres. 1997), Western Surg. Assn. (treas. 1993-97). Office: Rush Presbyn/St Luke Med Ct 818 Professional Bldg 1725 W Harrison St Chicago IL 60612-3828 E-mail: rprinz@rush.edu.

PRINZE, FREDDIE, JR. actor; b. Mar. 8, 1976; Grad., La Cueva H.S., 1994. Actor: (TV series) Family Matters, 1994, ABC Afterschool Spl., 1996; (films) To Gillian on Her 37th Birthday, 1996, The House of Yes, 1997, I Know What You Did Last Summer, 1997, I Still Know What You Did Last Summer, 1998, She's All That, 1999, Wing Commander, 1999, Boys and Girls, 2000, Head Over Heels, 2001. Office: c/o BWR Pub Rels 6th Fl West Tower 9100 Wilshire Blvd Beverly Hills CA 90212

PRIOLEAU, DARWIN E. dance educator, choreographer; b. N.Y.C., May 10, 1949; p. E. Louis and Marietta Camilla Prioleau; m. Carl Victor Conrad, Dec. 19, 1992. BA, Bennett Coll., 1971; MA, NYU, 1981; EdD, U. Mass., 1999. Dancer Ed Kresley Jazz Co., N.Y.C., 1974-76; soloist, dancer Nat. Horne Dance Co., 1976-79; featured dancer, guest artist various dance cos. and off-Broadway prodns., 1977-81; artistic dir. Young Peoples Dance Co., 1978-81; assoc. prof. dance So. Meth. U., Dallas, 1981-88; head dance divsn. Kent (Ohio) State U., 1988-95, prof. dance, 1995—, asst. dean. Coll. Fine & Profl. Arts, 2001—. Dance coord. Internat. Ctr. for Integrative Studies, N.Y.C., 1975-81; artistic cons. Dallas Black Dance Theatre, 1983-88; trustee Am. Dance Guild, N.Y.C., 1993-95. Choreographer (commd. choreography) Dance Black Dance Theatre, 1983, 84, 88, 91, Dallas Theatre Ctr., 1985, 86, Dance Cleveland/Cain Pk., 1991, Opus II Dance Co., 1994, Ashland Regional Ballet, 2001; solo performer, Tex., N.Y.C., France, 1985-88; mem. editl. bd. Nat. Dance Edn. Jour.; contbr. articles to profl. jours. Mentor I Had A Dream Program, Dallas, 1986-88; quest tchr. Urban League, Akron, Ohio, 1994; adv. bd. Cleve. Sch. of the Arts, 1994-95; mem. Ohio Arts Coun., 2000, Arts Midwest, 2000, Columbus, 2000, Pitts. on Tour, 2000. Grantee NEA Arts Expansion Program, Washington, 1980, Vira I. Heinz Endowment, Pitts., 1994, Ohio Joint Programs in the Arts, Columbus, 1995. Mem. Nat. Assn. Schs. Dance, Internat. Black Dance Assn., Ams. for Arts. Nat. Dance Edn. Assn., Am. Assn. Higher Edn. Avocations: travel, hiking, jazz music. Home: 182 Gaylord Dr Munroe Falls OH 44262-1141 Office: Kent State Univ 266 Macca Kent OH 44242-0001 Fax: 330-672-4897. E-mail: dpriolea@kent.edu.

PRIOLEAU, SARA NELLIENE, dentist; b. Hopkins, S.C., Apr. 10, 1940; d. Willie Oree and Wilhelmina Illorah (Neal) P.; m. William F. McKeever, Aug. 31, 1969 (div. Mar. 1982); children: Kara, William P.; m. William R. Montgomery, Dec. 18, 1984; stepchildren: Sharon, Myra, John. BS, S.C. State U., 1960, MS, 1966; DMD, U. Pa., 1970. Rotating gen. dentist intern Phila. Gen. Hosp., 1970-71; staff dentist Comprehensive Group Health Ctr., Phila., 1971-72; dental dir. Hamilton Health Ctr., 1972-97; CEO Cmty. Dental Assocs., P.C., Harrisburg, 1976—; dental dir. Selinsgrove Ctr., 1999—2002. Cons. Region III Head Start, Phila., 1972—; dental dir. Healthmate HMO-Hamilton Health Ctr., Harrisburg, 1988-96, Healthmate HMO/Health Am., Harrisburg, 1996-97; v. p. bd. dirs. Harrisburg Area C.C., 1990-99, v.p., 1997-99; mem. adv. bd. Mellon Bank Commonwealth Region, Harrisburg, 1995—, Capital Area Math./Sci. Alliance, Harrisburg, 1995-99. Named to 50 Best Women in Bus., Dept. of Commerce and Econ. Devel., Harrisburg, 1997. Fellow Internat. Coll. Dentists; mem. ADA, Am. Assn. Women Dentists, Nat. Dental Assn., Pa. Dental Assn., Harrisburg Area Dental Soc. (v.p. 2000—), Soroptimist Internat. (past pres. Harrisburg chpt.), The Links Inc (past pres. Herrisburg chpt.). Republican. Baptist. Avocations: travel, golf, shopping. Home: 1094 Cardinal Dr Harrisburg PA 17111-3730 Office: Cmty Dental Assocs PC 2451 N 3rd St Harrisburg PA 17110-1902 E-mail: c-spriolea@state.pa.us.

PRIOR, BOYD THELMAN, management consultant; b. Tacoma, May 7, 1926; s. George Archie and Thelma Mary (Chambers) P. Student, U.S. Naval Acad., 1948-50; BA, Claremont Men's Coll., 1952; MBA, Harvard U., 1954. Sr. v.p., dir. The Lusk Corp., Tucson, 1954-60; v.p. sales & mktg. Horizon Land Corp., 1960-62; sr. v.p., dir. Gen. Devel. Corp., Miami, Fla., 1962-71; chmn., pres. Prior Assocs., Phoenix, 1971-74; mgmt. cons., dir. Am. Solar King Corp., Waco, Tex., 1982-85; pvt. practice Kerrville, Tex. and Boca Raton, Fla., 1974-82, Burleson, Tex., 1985; pvt. practice mgmt. cons. Burleson, Dallas/Ft. Worth, Phoenix, Miami, 1985—. Cons. Cob Select Sand & Gravel, Inc., 1986—, Resolution Trust, 1989-95. Recipient Cert. Appreciation Better Bus. Bur., 1971, 74. Republican. Episcopalian. Home and Office: 221 Meadow Oaks Dr Burleson TX 76028-2375

PRIOR, CORNELIUS B. JR. utilities company executive, financial consultant; b. Hartford, Conn., Feb. 26, 1934; s. Cornelius B. Sr. and Katherine (Daly) P.; m. Sandra Pierson; children: Elizabeth, Michael, Sarah. AB, Holy Cross Coll., 1956; LLB, Harvard U., 1962. Bar: N.Y. Assoc. atty. Sullivan and Cromwell, N.Y.C., 1963-68; gen. counsel Private Investment Co. for Asia, Tokyo, 1969-71; v.p. Drexel Firestone, N.Y.C., 1971-75; sr. v.p. Blythe Eastman Dillon, 1975-80; mng. dir. Kidder, Peabody and Co., 1980-87; chmn. V.I. Tel. Co., St. Thomas, 1987—; chmn. & CEO Atlantic Tele-Network, Inc., V.I. Bd. dirs. Atlantic Telenetwork Co., St. Thomas. Bd. dirs. Holy Cross Coll.; mem. vis. com. Harvard Law Sch.; chmn. Caribbean Assn. of Nat. Telephone Orgns.; mem. adv. bd. Peter Gruber Found. Served to lt (j.g.) USN, 1956-59. Fulbright scholar, 1962-63. Mem. Assn. Bar City of N.Y. Clubs: University (N.Y.C.). Roman Catholic. Office: Atlantic Tele-Network 19 Estate Thomas Havensight Saint Thomas VI 00801

PRIOR, JOAN, telecommunications industry executive; Pres., CEO Hydro One Telecom, Toronto, Canada. Bd. dirs. Hydro One Networks; acting sr. v.p., corp. gen. counsel, sec. Ontario Hydro, Canada. Office: Hydro One Telecom Inc North Tower 483 Bay St 13th Fl Toronto M5G 2P5 Canada

PRIOR, JOHN THOMPSON, pathology educator; b. St. Albans, Vt., Oct. 8, 1917; s. Thomas William and Pauline Thompson Prior; m. Elizabeth Titus Troy, July 24, 1948; children: Anne, Polly, John Jr., Thomas, Jeffrey, Timothy. BS, U. Vt., 1939, MD, 1943. Diplomate Am. bd. Pathology. Resident in pathology Binghamton (N.Y.) City Hosp., 1946-47; fellow in pathology Syracuse (N.Y.) U. Med. Coll., 1947-49; asst. prof. pathology SUNY, Syracuse, 1949-54, assoc. prof., 1954-63, prof., 1963-72, clin. prof. pathology, 1972—. Active ARC Blood Bank, Syracuse, 1966-70; pres. N.Y. State Assoc. Lab., Syracuse, 1959-60; med. dir. PSRO Ctrl. N.Y., Syracuse, 1983-84; mem. N.Y. Stat Hosp. Rev. & Planning Assn., Albany, 1980-82; bd. dirs. Am. Med. Peer Rev. Assn., 1985-90. Contbr. articles to profl. jours. Bd. dirs. Lung Assn. Ctrl. N.Y., Syracuse, 1994—. Col. M.C., U.S. Army, 1944-77. Decorated Bronze Star, Silver Star, Legion of Merit, Belgian Croix de Guerre; recipient William Hammond Citation, N.Y. State Jour. Medicine, N.Y.C., 1984, Disting. Alumnus award U. Vt., Burlington, 1994. Mem. Onondaga County Med. Soc. (pres. 1974, disting. svc. award 1981). Avocations: golf, tennis. Home: 4615 Pewter Ln Manlius NY 13104-9329

PRIOR, JOSEPH GERARD, priest, educator; b. Phila., Feb. 8, 1964; s. Hugh Joseph Prior and Rosemary Gertrude Phelan. MDiv, St. Charles Borromeo Sem., Wynnewood, Pa., 1989, MA, 1990; SSL, Pontifical Biblical Inst., Rome, 1997; STD, Pontifical Gregorian U., Rome, 1999. Assoc. pastor Our Lady of Good Counsel Parish, Southampton, Pa., 1990—92; tchr. St. James HS, Chester, 1992—93; assoc. prof. Sacred Scripture St. Charles Borromeo Sem., Wynnewood, 1999—, acad. dean Theology Divsn., 2000—. Mem.: Coll. Theology Soc., Soc. Biblical Literature, Cath. Biblical Assn. Home and Office: St Charles Borromeo Sem 100 E Wynnewood Rd Wynnewood PA 19096

PRIOR, MICHELLE, antiques dealer, caterer; b. Pasadena, Calif., May 27, 1955; d. Arthur Stephen Dutch Jr. and Helen Frances Stewart; m. Thomas Bethmann, Sept. 24, 1980 (div. June 1982); m. Ralph C. Prior III, July 23, 1988; 1 child, Devin Dutch McCarthy. BA, Calif. State U., Fullerton, 1976. Owner antique bus., Lake Forest, Calif., 1990—; owner catering bus. Fishes & Loaves, 1992—. Contbr. poems, short stories to numerous lit. publs. Chmn. newsletter Rancho Canada Elem. Sch. PTSO, Lake Forest, 1993—95; mem. Praise team Mission Hill Cmty. Ch., Rancho Santa Margarita, Calif., 1996. Recipient Blue Ribbons, Orange County Fair, 1991-98, divsn. winner, 1995. Republican. Home: 21525 Via Serpiente Lake Forest CA 92630-2612

PRIOR, WILLIAM ALLEN, electronics company executive; b. Benton Harbor, Mich., Jan. 14, 1927; s. Allen Ames and Madeline Isabel (Taylor) P.; m. Nancy Norton Sayles, July 7, 1951 (div. Oct. 1971); children: Stephanie Sayles, Alexandra Taylor, Robert Eames, Eleanor Norton; m. Carol Luise Becker-Ehmck, Oct. 30, 1971; children: Michael Becker-Ehmck, Jeffrey Renner. AB in Physics, Harvard Coll., 1950, MBA, 1954. Salesman IBM, Mineola, L.I., N.Y., 1950-52; sales engr. Lincoln Electric Co., Cleve., 1954-57; ptnr. Hammond Kennedy & Co., N.Y.C., 1957-66; v.p. The Singer Co., 1967-68; pres. Tansitor Electronics, Bennington, Vt., 1969-71, Aerotron Inc., Raleigh, N.C., 1971-82; v.p. J. Lee Peeler & Co., Durham, 1986-89; pres. Accudyne, Inc., Raleigh, 1990-99. Chmn. Royal Blue Capital, Inc., Raleigh; bd. dirs. NeoDyne, Inc., Raleigh. Cpl. USAAF, 1945-46, Germany. Mem. IEEE, North Ridge Country Club (Raleigh), Raleigh Racquet Club, Harvard Club of N.Y.C., 50 Group. Republican. Avocations: tennis, skiing, computer programming. Home: 329 Meeting House Cir Raleigh NC 27615-3133 E-mail: wprior@mba1954.hbs.edu.

PRIORE, ROGER L. biostatistics educator, consultant; b. Buffalo, Apr. 21, 1938; s. Anthony J. and Linda M. (DeMarchi) P.; m. Carol A. Cooper, Sept. 3, 1960; children— Howard W., Susan L., John D. BA, SUNY-Buffalo, 1960, MS, 1962; Sc.D., Johns Hopkins U., 1965. Jr. cancer research scientist Roswell Park Meml. Inst., Buffalo, 1960-65, sr. cancer research scientist, 1965-67, assoc. cancer research scientist, 1967-69, prin. cancer research scientist, 1974-79, dir. computer sci., 1979-83, dir. dept. biomath., 1983-91, dir. mgmt. info. systems, 1988-91; asst. rsch. prof. SUNY, 1966-68, assoc. rsch. prof., 1968-69, rsch. prof., dir. grad. studies in biometry, 1980-91; rsch. prof. Niagara U., 1968-91; cons. in stats. and computing, 1991—; clin. prof. dept. social and preventive medicine SUNY, Buffalo, 1991—; pres. Compustat Assocs., Inc., 1993—; clin. prof. dept. statistics SUNY, 1995—. Cons. Am. Joint Com. on Cancer, 1980-88. Contbr. articles to profl. jours. Mem. Am. Statis. Assn., Soc. for Epidemiol. Rsch., Sigma Xi Office: 342 Dan Troy Dr Buffalo NY 14221-3514

PRIORY, RICHARD BALDWIN, electric power industry executive; b. Lakehurst, N.J., May 15, 1946; s. Joseph Albert Jr. and Betty (Baldwin) P.; m. Joan Ellen Rourke, May 30, 1968; children: Jennifer Joan, Richard Baldwin Jr. BSCE magna cum laude, W.Va. Inst. Tech., 1969; MS in Engring., Princeton U., 1973; grad. utility exec. program, U. Mich., 1982; grad. advanced mgmt. program, Harvard U., 1991. Registered profl. engr., N.C., S.C. Design engr., project engr. Union Carbide Corp., 1969-72; asst. prof. structural engring. U. N.C., Charlotte, 1973-76; design engr. Duke Power Co., 1976-78, prin. engr., 1978-81, mgr. project mgmt. divsn., 1981-84, v.p. design engring., 1984-88, sr. v.p. generation and info. svcs., 1988-91, exec. v.p. power generation group, 1991-94, pres., COO, 1994-97; chmn., pres., CEO Duke Energy Corp. (formerly Duke Power Co.), 1997—. Bd. dirs. Duke Energy Corp., U.S. Airways, Dana Corp., EEI, AEIC; mem. Duke Fluor Daniel Mgmt. Com. Bd. visitors U. N.C., Charlotte; past chmn. bd. dirs. Charlotte-Mecklenburg Edn. Found.; pres., bd. trustees Discovery Place, Inc., 1992-93; past mem. Charlotte-Mecklenburg Pub. Broadcasting Found.; vice chmn. campaign drive United Way Ctrl. Carolinas, Inc., 1990; adv. coun. N.C. Alliance for Competitive Technologies. Mem. ASCE, Nat. Acad. Engring, Charlotte Engrs. Club. Avocation: golf. Office: Duke Energy Corp 526 S Church St Charlotte NC 28202-1802*

PRISANT, L(OUIS) MICHAEL, cardiologist; b. Albany, Ga., Dec. 25, 1949; s. Bennie Martin and Mozelle (Cosper) Prisant; m. Rose Corinth Trincher, June 28, 1975; children: Michelle Elizabeth, Louis Michael. BA, Emory U., 1971; MD, Med. Coll. Ga., 1977. Diplomate Am. Bd. Internal Medicine, Am. Bd. Cardiovasc. Diseases, Am. Bd. Clin. Pharmacology, Am. Bd. Forensic Medicine, Nat. Bd. Examiners, Am. Bd. Forensic Examiners, Am. Soc. Hypertension, cert. specialist in hypertension. Intern Med. Coll. Ga., Augusta, 1977-78, resident, 1978-80; chief med. resident, 1979-80; cardiology fellow Med. Coll. Ga., 1980-82, instr., 1982-83, asst. prof. medicine, 1983-89, assoc. prof. medicine, 1989-94, prof., 1994—, dir. cardiology fellowship tng. program, 1996—2001, dir. hypertension unit, 1999. Cons. in field; nat. and internat. lectr. in field. Contbr. . Grantee, FOE, 1989, Rorer, 1989, Am. Cyanamid, 1988, Sandoz, 1989—93, Merck, 1990—92, Squibb, 1991, Lorex, 1991, NIH, 1991, 1996, Lederle, 1993, Ciba-Geigy, 1995, Omedha, 1997, Smith-Kline-Beecham, 1997, Apothecon, 1996, Bristol-Meyer-Squibb, 1998, Novartis, 1999, HDI, 2000, Searle, 2000. Fellow: AMA (Physician's Recognition award 1982—2002), ACP, Am. Heart Assn. (coun. high blood pressure rsch.), Coun. geriatric Cardiology, Am. Coll. Chest Physicians, Am. Coll. Forensic Examiners, Am. Coll. Clin. Pharmacology, Am. Coll. Cardiology; mem.: AAUP, Richmond County Med. Soc., Med. Assn. Ga., Ga. Med. Care Found., Assn. for Advancement Med. Instrumentation (co-chmn. sphygmomanometer com.), Ga. Heart Assn., So. Med. Assn., Am. Soc. Internal Medicine, Am. Soc. Hypertension (CME com. 2000—03, nominating com. 2001—04), Am. Soc. Echocardiography, Am. Fedn. Clin. Rsch., Internat. Soc. on Hypertension in Blacks, Ahlquist Soc. (pres.), Tau Epsilon Phi, Alpha Phi Omega, Phi Delta Epsilon. Jewish. Avocation: computers. Office: Med Coll Ga Hypertension and Clin Pharmacology BI-50 Augusta GA 30912 E-mail: mprisant@mail.mcg.edu.

PRISBREY, REX PRINCE, retired insurance agent, underwriter, consultant; b. Washington, Mar. 18, 1922; s. Hyrum William and Susan (Prince) P.; m. Pinka Julieta Lucero, Nov. 16, 1943; children: Karol Sue Prisbey Lewallen, Pamela Blanche Prisbrey Ebert, Michael Rex. BA in Acctg., Denver U., 1949. CLU. Ptnr. Allen Stamm & Assocs., home builders, Farmington, N.Mex., 1949-52; acct. Linder Burke & Stevenson, Santa Fe, 1949-52; agt. State Farm Ins. Cos., Farmington, 1952-56, mgr. Phoenix, 1956-60, contractor, agt. Scottsdale, Ariz., 1960—. V.p., treas. Original Curio Store Inc., Santa Fe. Pres. Farmington Jr. C. of C., 1952; v.p. N.Mex. Jr. C. of C., 1953. 1st lt. USAAF, 1941-46, CBI. Decorated DFC, Air medal with oak leaf cluster; recipient Disting. Life Underwriter award Cen. Ariz. Mgrs. Assn., 1979. Mem. Am. Soc. CLU's, Scottsdale Assn. Life Underwriters (pres. 1980-81), Airplane Owners and Pilots Assn., Hump Pilots Assn. (life, speaker at meml. of Hump Flyers, Kunming, China 1993), Pinewood Country Club (bd. dirs., treas., v.p. 1985—), Civitans (pres. Scottsdale 1962-63). Avocations: flying, golf, photography. Home: 11859 N 80th Pl Scottsdale AZ 85260-5645

PRISCHING, MANFRED, sociology educator; b. Bruck Mur, Austria, Dec. 12, 1950; s. Karl and Margareth (Voggenhuber) P.; m. Roswitha Hribernig, Sept. 7, 1978; children: Margareth, Sebastian. JD, U. Graz, Austria, 1974; M Econs., U. Graz, 1977. Univ. asst., then lectr. U. Graz, 1976-87, lectr. dept. sociology, 1988—. Lectr., U. Limburg, Maastricht, The Netherlands, 1987-88; guest prof. Harvard U., 1995-96; sci. dir. Technikum Joanneum, Graz, 1997—. Author: Crises. A sociological analysis, 1986, Protest of Unemployed in Economic Crisis, 1988, Sociology Themes, Theories, Perspectives, 3d edit., 1995, Social Partnership, 1996, Pictures of the Welfare State, 1996, The McSociety, 1998; contbr. numerous articles to profl. jours. Mem. Austrian Acad. Scis. Roman Catholic. Home: Carnerigasse 12 A 8010 Graz Austria Office: Dept Sociology U Graz Universitaetsstrabe 15 A 8010 Graz Austria E-mail: manfred.prisching@kfunigraz.ac.at.

PRISCO, DOUGLAS LOUIS, physician; b. N.Y.C., Nov. 30, 1945; s. Frank James and Isabel (Gaetano) P.; m. Marianne Paula Mangano, Jan. 8, 1972; children: Jennifer Leigh, Douglas Louis, Dana Lauren, Andrew Michael. AB, Georgetown U., 1967; postgrad., NYU, 1967-68; MD, U. Rome, 1974. Diplomate Am. Bd. Internal Medicine, sub-bd. Pulmonary Diseases. Intern Mt. Sinai Svcs., Elmhurst, N.Y., 1974-75, resident in medicine, 1975-77, pulmonary medicine fellow, 1977-79; practice medicine specializing in pulmonary medicine N.Y.C., New Hyde Park, 1979-81; clin. asst. in medicine Bklyn. Hosp., 1979-81; pulmonary cons. and admitting physician Booth

Meml. Hosp. (now N.Y. Hosp. Med. Ctr. of Queens), Pkwy Hosp., Flushing Hosp. Med. Ctr.; admitting physician L.I. Jewish Hosp., New Hyde Park, Mt. Sinai of Queens, 1999—; chief pulmonary medicine Deepdale Gen. Hosp., 1980-93; clin. asst. Mt. Sinai Sch. Medicine, N.Y.C., 1977-79; physician adviser St. Barnabas Hosp., 1981-82; pres. Met. Pulmonary Assocs., P.C., 1980—, Met. Pulmonary P.C., 1985—; v.p. network devel. Parkway Hosp., 1997. Physician adv. to Queens County Profl. Standards Rev. Orgn., 1979-85; co-chmn. quality assurance com. downstate region Island peer Rev. Orgn., 1990—, vice chmn. pro-tem regional quality assurance com., N.Y., 1993—; bd. dirs. Queens County Profl. Standards Rev. Orgn., 1984-85, Fresh Meadows Med. Care, med. dir., 1997; chief pulmonary diseases Little Neck Cmty. Hosp. (formerly Deepdale Ge n. Hosp.), 1980-93, pulmonary chief, med. dir., 1993-96; pres. Med. Staff Soc., 1992—, mem. med. bd., 1993—; mem., cons. Queens div. Island Peer Rev. Orgn., 1985—; dir. pulmonary svcs. Astoria Med. Group, 1999—; dir. Fresh Meadows Care, 1997. Mem. Rep. Senatorial Inner Cir., 1990. Fellow Am. Coll. Chest Physicians; mem. ACP, Am. Lung Assn. Queens (bd. dirs. 1988—, honoree 1997), Queens County Med. Soc., Port Washington Yacht Club (former chmn. jr. activities 1987-88, fleet surgeon 1991-93, 95-97, bd.d irs. 1995-97), Capitol Hill Club, Integrated Delivery Systems of N.Y. (vice chmn., chmn. 1995—). Roman Catholic. Address: Ste 201 3003 New Hyde Park Rd New Hyde Park NY 11042-1214 E-mail: DLPMD@hotmail.com., dlpmd@aol.com.

PRISCO, FRANK J. psychotherapist; b. N.Y.C. s. Frank J. and Isabel (Gatano) P.; m. August Frances; children: Frank, Christian, Meredith. BS in History, NYU, 1964, MA in History and Psychology, 1972, PsyD in Psychoanalysis, 1980. Diplomate Am. Psychotherapy Assn., Am. Bd. Psychol. Specialties of Am. Coll. Forensic Examiners; cert. psychoanalyst, cert. med. hypnotherapist. Cons., staff therapist Creedmore Psychiat. Ctr.; faculty Psychanalytic Inst., L.I.; pvt. practice Ctr. for Modern Psychoanalytic Studies; instr. psychology N.Y.C. Bd. Edn. Trainer of trainers Conflict Mgrs. Program, N.Y.C.; discussion leader Gt. Books Found. Eucharistic min. Cath. Ch.; group leader Great Books Found. Recipient Soc. of Emil award. Mem. AAAS, Am. Psychol. Soc., Am. Assn. Guidance and Counseling, N.Y. Acad. Scis., Nat. Assn. Advancement Psychoanalysis, Am. Poetry Assn. (Poet Merit award 1988-90), Soc. Modern Psychoanalysis.

PRISCO, NICHOLAS ALLEN, hospital administrator; b. Englewood, N.J., Aug. 4, 1943; s. Nicholas T. and Ruth Esther (Allen) P.; m. Sarah Jane Watson, Aug. 16, 1969; children: Kimberly Anne, Ginger Marie, Nicholas Edwin. BA, U. Calif., 1967; M in Hosp. & Health Svcs. Adminstrn., Cornell U., 1973. Diplomate Am. Coll. Healthcare Execs. Asst. adminstr. Tompkins County Hosp., Ithaca, NY, 1973-75; CEO Little Falls Hosp., 1975-86, Sunbury Cmty. Hosp., Pa., 1986—2001. Capt. USAMSC, 1967-71, Vietnam. Avocations: fishing, watercraft. Office: Sunbury Cmty Hosp PO Box 737 Sunbury PA 17801-0737

PRISELAC, THOMAS M. health facility administrator; BA in Biology, Washington & Jefferson Coll.; MPH Health Svcs. Adminstrn. and Planning, U. Pitts. Asst. adminstr. Cedars-Sinai Med. Ctr., L.A., 1979—81, assoc. adminstr., 1981—82, sr. assoc. adminstr., 1982—83, v.p. adminstrn., 1983—85, sr. v.p. ops., 1985—91, exec. v.p., COO, 1991—94, pres., CEO, 1991—. Office: Cedars Sinai Med Ctr 8700 Beverly Blvd Rm 2628 Los Angeles CA 90048*

PRISSEL, BARBARA ANN, paralegal, law educator; b. Plum City, Wis., July 7, 1946; d. John Henry and Mary Ann Louise (Dankers) Seipel; m. Stephen Joseph Prissel, Dec. 16, 1967; children: Angela, Benjamin. Graduate with honors, Mpls. Bus. Coll., 1966; student, Moraine Park Tech. Coll., Wis., 1983—. Cert. interactive TV, adult edn. instr. Legal sec. Mott, Grose, Von Holtum & Hefferan, Mpls., 1966-67, Whelan, Morey & Morey Attys. at Law, Durand, Wis., 1967-70, Murry Law Office, River Falls, 1968-70, Potter, Wefel & Nettesheim, Wisconsin Rapids, 1970-71; sec. to adminstr. Moraine Park Tech. Coll., Fond du Lac, 1971-72; paralegal Kilgore Law Office, Ripon, 1985—. Chmn. legal adv. com. Moraine Park Tech. Coll., Fond du Lac, Wis., 1996-98, mem. adminstrv. assts. adv. com., 1984-86; mem. legal adv. commn. Moraine Park Tech. Coll., 1984—. Contbr. poems to newspapers. Ch. rep. Ch. Women United, Ripon, Wis., 1984-87; pianist Christian Women's Orgn., Ripon, 1985-95; pianist, organist Our Lady of Lake Ch., Green Lake, Wis., 1987—. Mem.: NAFE, Legal Profls. Assn. (East Ctrl. Wis. pres. 1994—95, chmn. edn1. lisison com., chmn. Day-In-Ct. 1999, sec. 1995—96, 2001—02, NALS Fedn. liaison 2000—02, Legal award of Excellence 1995—96), Wis. Assn. Legal Secs. (state legal ednl. liaison com. 1997—), Nat. Assn. Legal Secs. Roman Catholic. Avocations: teaching and playing piano, creative writing, cooking, swimming, exercising. Home: 129 Wolverton Ave Ripon WI 54971-1144 E-mail: prissel@powercom.net.

PRITCHARD, BETTY JEAN, retired art educator; b. Dana, Ind., Nov. 25, 1934; d. Terrence Ellis and Mary Ethel (Wishard) P. BS in Arts and Crafts, Ind. State U., 1957; MA in Art Edn. and Painting, Purdue U., 1972; postgrad., Ball State U., 1958, 66; postgrad. computer graphics works, Ind. U., Bloomington, 1985. Cert. pub. sch. tchr., supt., Ind., Ky., Ill. Art tchr. 1-12 Sheridan (Ind.) H.S., 1957-60; art tchr. 3-12 Danville (Ind.) City Schs., 1961-62; art tchr. 1-12 Brownsburg (Ind.) Comm. Schs., 1962-64; art tchr. 7-12 Blue River Valley S.C., New Castle, Ind., 1964-67; art tchr. 1-8 Twin Lakes Sch. Corp., Monticello, 1967-69; art tchr. 1-6 Tippecanoe Sch. Corp., Lafayette, 1972-75; art tchr., children's art Art Ctr. Sch., Albuquerque, 1977-78; tutor supr. Albuquerque Pub. Schs., 1977-78, art lab. asst., 1978-79; art tchr. 7-12 Attica (Ind.) Consolid. Schs., 1979-80; art tchr. 1-8 Southwest Parke C.S., Mecca, Ind., 1983-85; painting instr. Danville Area C.C., Ill., 1987-88; substitute tchr. Albuquerque Pub. Schs., 1989-2000; ret., 2000. One-artist and group shows of paintings at Purdue U., Jonson Gallery, U. N.Mex., Union Bldg., U. N.Mex., 1976, 77, 88. One-woman and group shows include Purdue U., Jonson Gallery, U. N.Mex., Union Bldg., U. N.Mex., 1976-78, Arts and Crafts Benefit. Mem. Neighborhood Watch, Bernalillo, N.Mex., 1995—97; mem. animal legal The Nature Conservancy; docent Albuquerque Mus.; vol. greeter Albuquerque Biol. Park. Grantee Wabash Valley Projects, Tippecanoe Arts Fedn. and Nat. Endowment of the Arts, Lafayette, 1987. Mem.: Nat. Wildlife Fedn., Doris Day Animal League, U.S. Defenders of Wildlife, The Wilderness Soc., Mus. of Albuquerque Found., Nat. Resources Def. Coun. Methodist. Avocations: animal rights and environ. issues, music, art. Home: 324 E Avenida Bernalillo Bernalillo NM 87004-9018

PRITCHARD, CLAUDIUS HORNBY, JR. retired university president; b. Charleston, W.Va., June 28, 1927; s. Claudius Hornby and Katherine (Ellison) P.; m. Marjorie Walker Pullen, Aug. 9, 1952; children: Virginia Aiken, Katherine Winston, Olivia Reynolds, Claudius V. BA, Hampden-Sydney Coll., 1950; MA, Longwood Coll., 1965; PhD, Fla. State U., 1971. Comml. loan teller Am. Nat. Bank and Trust Co., Danville, Va., 1950-53; asst. cashier Planters Bank & Trust Co., Farmville, 1953-55; asst. to pres. Hampden-Sydney (Va.) Coll., 1955-57, bus. mgr. and treas., 1957-67, v.p. devel., 1967-71; sr. budget analyst-edn. State of Fla., Tallahassee, 1971-72; pres. Sullins Coll., Bristol, Va., 1972-76; v.p. adminstrn. Maryville U., St. Louis, 1976-77, pres., 1977-92, pres. emeritus, 1992—. Adv. dir. Commerce Bank of St. Louis, 1982-92. Author: Col. D. Wyatt Aiken (1828-1887) South Carolina's Militant Agrarian, 1970; contbr. articles to profl. jours. Mem. bd. visitors Charleston So. U., 1993—; chmn. Summerville Comml. Design Rev. Bd., 1999—; bd. dirs. West St. Louis County UMCA, Chesterfield, Mo., 1985—92. With USNR, 1945—46. Fla. State U. fellow, 1969-70, Arthur Vining Davis fellow Am. Council on Edn., 1974. Mem. AAUP, SCV, Am. Assn. Higher Edn., So. Hist. Assn., S.C. Hist. Soc., Mo. Colls. Fund (bd. dirs., chmn. 1987-88), Mil. Order of the Stars and Bars, Ind. Colls. and Univs. Mo., Chesterfield C. of C. (pres. 1987, Chesterfield Citizen of Yr. award 1986), Rotary. Republican. Presbyterian.

PRITCHARD, COLIN, social work educator; b. Bradford, Yorkshire, Eng., Feb. 24, 1936; s. Sydney William and Doris (Barraclough) P.; m. Beryl Harrison, Sept. 15, 1962; children: Rebecca Anne, Claire Elizabeth. Postgrad. Diploma, U. Manchester, Eng., 1965; MA, U. Bradford, Eng., 1970; PhD, U. Southampton, Eng., 1996. Psychiat. social worker, West Riding, Eng., 1960-65; sr. prin. psychiat. social worker, 1965-70; lectr. U. Leeds, 1970-76; sr. lectr. U. Bath., Eng., 1976-80; found. chair social work U. Southampton, 1980—. Rsch. coord. JVC, London, 1976-80, chmn. SWEC Joint U. Coun. London, 1980-87; mem. CCETSW, London, 1982-87; mem. Southampton Health Authority, 1980-87; founding mem. Credit Union North Jersey; 1st pres. Fed. Credit Union, 1974-75. Author: Social Work, Reform and Revolution, 1978, Social Work and Adolescence, 1980, The Protest Makers - Anti-Nuclear Movement 1968-78, 1982, Suicide - The Ultimate Rejection, 1995, King David: War and Ecstasy, 2000, others; contbr. articles to profl. jours. and publs. Avocations: squash, family, friends, fell walking. Office: Mental Health Royal Southampton Hosp SO 14 099 Southampton England E-mail: cpl@soton.ac.uk.

PRITCHARD, DALTON HAROLD, retired electronics research engineer; b. Crystal Springs, Miss., Sept. 1, 1921; s. Cecil Harold and Marvie Prudence (Lofton) P.; m. Caroline Ann Hnatuk, Apr. 27, 1947; 1 child, Mary Ann Pritchard Poole. BSE.E., Miss. State U., 1943; postgrad., Harvard, MIT Radar Sch., 1943-44. Mem. tech. staff RCA Labs., Riverhead, N.Y., 1946-50, mem. tech. staff Princeton, N.J., 1950-75, fellow tech. staff, 1975-87. Session chmn., mem. program com. Internat. Conf. on Consumer Electronics, Chgo., 1980-85 Contbr. articles to profl. jours.; patentee in field. Mem. N.J. Gov.'s Sci. Adv. Council, Princeton, 1981-85. Served to capt. U.S. Army Signal Corps Decorated Bronze Star; recipient Eduard Rhein prize Edward Rhein Found., Berlin, Fed. Republic of Germany, 1980; Disting. Engring. fellow Miss. State U., 1991. Fellow IEEE (Vladimir Zworykin award 1977, David Sarnoff award 1981), Soc. Info. Display, Nat. Assn. Engrs., Nat. Acad. Engring., Sigma Xi, Tau Beta Pi, Kappa Mu Epsilon Republican. Baptist. Avocations: amatuer radio; tennis. Home: 3 Bent Tree Ln Hilton Head Island SC 29926-1906

PRITCHARD, HUW OWEN, chemist, educator; b. Bangor, Wales, July 23, 1928; s. Owen and Lilian Venetia (McMurray) P.; m. Margaret Ramsden, Nov. 3, 1956; children— Karen, David. B.Sc., U. Manchester, 1948, M.Sc., 1949, PhD, 1951, D.Sc., 1964. Asst. lectr. chemistry Manchester (Eng.) U., 1951-54, lectr., 1954-65; prof. chemistry York U., Ont., Can., 1965-97, prof. emeritus Can., 1997—. Contbr. articles to profl. jours. Fellow Royal Soc. Can. Office: Chemistry Dept York Univ Toronto ON Canada M3J 1P3 E-mail: huw@yorku.ca.

PRITCHARD, JAMES PATRICK, investment company executive; b. Buffalo, Mar. 2, 1960; s. Thomas Stanley and Marylou (Titus) P.; m. Jenny Margaret Howell, Aug. 23, 1986; children: James, Katherine, Laura. BA in Econ., Columbia U., 1982. CFP. Stockbroker Smith Barney, Scottsdale, Ariz., 1982-85; owner Pritchard Investment Mgmt., Durango, Colo., 1986—; CEO, founder Fundsearch.net, 1999, MyPortfolioPlanner.com, 2000, BuildYourOwn401K.com, 2000, iSharesAdvisor.com, 2000. Author: Evil Queen maliciousness, 2001, Every Boys Dream, 1998, The Gods, 1998, Kid Castle, 2001; pub.: Advantages of Indexing, 2000; performer Durango Snowdown Follies, 1999, 2000, 2001; actor: (movie) The Great West, 1995. Bd. dirs. Medina Meml. Hosp., 1988-93; v.p., bd. dirs. Medina Healthcare Found., 1990-93; pres. Chapman Hill Improvements Assn., Durango, 1993-98; co-founder/v.p. S.W. Colo. Youth Football Assn. Named to Kenmore East H.S. Athletic Hall of Fame, 1996. Avocations: writing, coaching football, handball, ice hockey, acting. Office: 556 Main Ave Durango CO 81301-5439 Fax: (970) 259-8909. E-mail: jim@pritchardinvestment.com.

PRITCHARD, KATHLEEN JO, not-for-profit association administrator; b. Milw., Feb. 6, 1951; d. Owen J. and Madelon (Coogan) P.; m. William A. Durkin Jr., Oct. 22, 1982; children: Elizabeth Durkin, Christine Durkin, W. Ryan Durkin. BA in Anthropology, U. Wis., Oshkosh, 1973; MA in Pub. Adminstrn., U. Wis., 1980; PhD in Polit. Sci., U. Wis., Milw., 1986. Rsch. analyst Wis. Coun. on Criminal Justice, Madison, 1974-77; planning analyst Wis. Dept. Health and Social Svcs., 1977-80; assoc. lectr. U. Wis., Milw., 1980-89; vis. asst. prof. Marquette U., 1986, 90-91; policy cons. dept. adminstrn. City of Milw., 1992; Outcomes Project dir. United Way of Greater Milw., 1992-96, dir. impact and evaluation, 1997—; chmn. United Way of Am. Forum on Outcomes II, 1997. Faculty advisor Model OAS, UN advisor, Milw., 1986-91; campus rep. spkr. Wis. Inst. for Study of War, Peace and Global Cooperation, Milw., 1989-90; mem. United Way Am. Task Force on Impact, 1995—; instr. Nat. Acad. Volunteerism, 1996. Contbr. articles to profl. jours. Dir. cmty impact United Way of Greater Milw., 1998; trustee Pub. Policy Forum, 2000—, NonProfit Mgmt. Fund, 2000—, NonProfit Mgmt. Edn. Ctr., 2000—; pres. Whitefish Bay Village, 2002—; mem. exec. steering com. Partnership for Healthiest Milw., 2001—. Recipient Alice Paul Dissertation award Women's Caucus for Polit. Sci., 1984; Grad. Sch. fellow U. Wis., Milw., 1983, fellow Kenyon Coll. Summer Inst., 1983. Mem. Am. Polit. Sci. Assn., Phi Kappa Phi (chpt. officer 1989). E-mail: kpritchard@uwaymilw.org.

PRITCHARD, NORMAN MACDONALD, pastor; b. Glasgow, Scotland, Nov. 19, 1945; came to U.S., 1996; s. Joseph Stasrk and Billie Macdonald (Kirkwood) Pritchard; m. Elizabeth Joan Clarke, July 5, 1969; children: Gillian E., Andrew M. MA with honors, U. Glasgow, 1968; BD with honors, Edinburgh, 1971, MTh, 1974; DMin, Fuller Theol. Sem., Pasadena, Calif., 1990. Ordained 1972. Asst. min. St. George's West Ch., Edinburgh, Scotland, 1971-74; min. St. Andrew's Ch., West Kilbride, Scotland, 1974-79; sr. min. The Scots Ch., Melbourne, Victoria, Australia, 1979-95; pastor, head of staff Kirk in the Hills, Bloomfield hills, Mich., 1996—. Author: Persistence of Faith, 1993; contbr. article to Scottish Jour. Theology. Dep. chmn. Scotch Coll. Coun., Melbourne, 1984—95. Avocations: squash, tennis. Office: Kirk in the Hills 1340 W Long Lake Rd Bloomfield Hills MI 48302 E-mail: revnmp@kirkinthehills.org.

PRITCHARD, SARAH MARGARET, library director; b. Boston, Feb. 8, 1955; d. Wilbur Louis and Kathleen Hunton (Moss) P.; m. Timothy John Brennan, Aug. 20, 1977 (div. 1993). BA, U. Md., 1975; MA in French, U. Wis., 1976, MLS, 1977. Intern Libr. Congress, Washington, 1977-78, reference specialist in women's studies, 1978-88, head microform reading rm., 1988-90; sr. program officer Assn. Rsch. Librs., 1990-91, assoc. exec. dir., 1991-92; acad. libr. mgmt. intern Coun on Libr. Resources Princeton U., N.J., 1991-92; dir. librs. Smith Coll., Northampton, Mass., 1992-99; univ. libr. U. Calif., Santa Barbara, 1999—. Editl. advisor Women's Rsch. and Edn. Inst., Washington, 1987-92; bd. dirs. Western Mass. Regional Libr. Sys., 1997-98; bd. dirs. U. Calif. So. Regional Libr. Facility, 1999—, Gold Coast Libr. Network. *Sarah Pritchard is widely active in regional and national library consortia and associations. She is the author of over fifty articles, reviews, and compilations and serves on many editorial boards and grant review panels. She has lectured and consulted in North America, Europe, and Asia on library management, electronic services, collection development, women's studies, and other professional issues.* Editor: The Women's Annual, 1984; compiler ARL Stats., 1990-92; contbr. articles to profl. jours.; mem. editl. bd. Jour. Acad. Librarianship, 1993-99, Portal: Librs. and the Acad., 2000—; contbg. editor Libr. Issues, 1994-99. Trustee Leroy C. Merritt Humanitarian Fund, 1991-94. Named Wis. Alumni Rsch. Found. fellow, 1975-77, Outstanding Alumna U. Wis. Sch. of Libr. and Info. Studies, 1997. Mem. ALA (chair machine assisted reference sect. 1986-87, chair women's studies sect. 1989-90, coun. 1990-98, 2000—, Equality award 1997), Nat. Women's Studies Assn., Cosmos Club. Democrat. Office: U Calif Davidson Libr Santa Barbara CA 93106

PRITCHARD, WILLIAM ROY, former university system administrator; b. Portage, Wis., Nov. 15, 1924; s. William Roy and Lillian Edith (Roberts) P.; m. Deanna Elaine Pritchard; children: Rosan June, William Roy, Caryl Jean, Alyn Evan, Cynthia Bedeau. Student, U. Wis., 1942-43; DVM, Kans. State U., 1946, DSc (hon.), 1970, Tufts U., 1988; PhD, U. Minn., 1953; JD, Ind. U., 1957; DSc (hon.), Purdue U., 1977, U. Guelph, 1998. Asst. prof. U. Wis., 1946-49; assoc. prof. U. Minn., 1949-53; prof. Purdue U., 1953-57; prof., head vet. sci. U. Fla., 1957-61; assoc. dir. Vet. Med. Rsch. Inst., Ia. State U., 1961-62; prof. U. Calif., Davis, 1962—, dean Sch. Vet Medicine, 1962-82; assoc. dir. Agrl. Expt. Sta., 1962-72; coord. internat. agrl. programs U. Calif. system, 1977-81. Vis. fellow Woodrow Wilson Sch. Pub and Internat. Affairs, Princeton, 1968-69; John Thomson lectr. U. Queensland, 1966; co-dir. nat. veterinary edn. program Duke U., 1987-92; spl. research hemmorrhagic diseases animals. Cons. Dept. Agr., Def. Dept., USPHS, VA, Calif. Dept. Health, FDA, 1962-97 ; bd. cons. agr. Rockefeller Found., 1962-66; nat. med. cons. surgeon gen. USAF, 1962-64; mem. FAO/WHO Expert Panel Vet. Edn., President's Sci. Advisory Com. Panel World Food Supply, 1966-67, President's Sci. Adv. Com. Panel Biology and Med. Sci., 1969-70, Joint Rsch. Com. Bd. Internat. Food and Agr. AID, 1977-81. With U.S. Army, 1942-44. Recipient Gov. Fla. award, 1961, Disting. Svc. award Kans. State U., 1963, Outstanding Achievement award U. Minn., 1976, Disting. Pub. Svc. award U. Calif., Davis, 1991, Gold Headed Cane award Am. Soc. Vet. Epidemiology, 1992. Mem. AAAS, APHA, Am. Vet. Med. Assn. (Internat. Vet. Congress award 1988), Nat. Acad. of Practice in Vet. Medicine (elected 1986), Am. Soc. Vet. Epidemiologists, Conf. of Pub. Health Vets. (hon. life), U.S. Animal Health Assn., Nat. Assn. State Univs. and Land-Grant Colls. (internat. affairs com. 1965-70), Order of Coif, Sigma Xi, Phi Zeta, Gamma Alpha. Home: 2409 Madrid Ct Davis CA 95616-0141

PRITCHETT, B(RUCE) MICHAEL, SR. economics educator, consultant; b. American Fork, Utah, Nov. 3, 1940; s. Melrose Jed and Lois (Watson) P.; m. Patricia Louise Sunderland, June 19, 1964; children: Bruce Michael Jr., Laura, Steven Louis. BS, Brigham Young U., 1965; MS, Purdue U., 1967, PhD, 1970. Bd. dirs. Pritchett Constrn. Co. Inc., Provo, Utah, 1954—; grad. instr. in econs. Purdue U., West Lafayette, Ind., 1967-68; asst. prof. econs. Brigham Young U., Provo, 1969-76, assoc. prof. econs., 1977-90, prof. managerial econs., 1990—. Cons. in field. Author: A Study of Capital Mobilization..., 1977, Financing Growth..., 1985, Applications of the GB2 Distribution in Modeling Insurance Loss Processes, 1990. NDEA fellow Purdue U., 1966-68, Krannert fellow Purdue U., 1968-69. Mem. Am. Econ. Assn., Western Econ. Assn., Nat. Assn. Bus. Economists. Office: Brigham Young U 614 Tanner Bldg Provo UT 84602

PRITCHETT, DEBORAH KAYE, artist; b. Fort Oglethorpe, Ga., Aug. 26, 1959; d. Fred Thomas Pritchett and Nellie Leola Bryant. A in Fine Arts, Young Harris Coll., 1979; BA, LaGrange Coll., 1981. Artist, typographer Omni Advt. and Graphics, LaGrange, Ga., 1982-89; asst. curator edn. Chattahoochee Valley Art Assn., 1989-90; social rsch. interviewer Medicare Current Beneficiary Survey Westat, Inc., Rockville, Md., 1991-2001. Instr. art workshops Chattahoochee Valley Art Assn., LaGrange, 1989-90. One-woman show LaGrange Coll., 1992, Young Harris Coll., 1998, LaGrange Coll. Alumni, 1999. Judge Student Art Competition, Murray County H.S., Chatsworth, Ga., 1998; vol. Whitfield-Murray Hist. Soc., Dalton, Ga., 2000, Sakes Alive, children's art mentor, Blue Ridge, 2002-. Recipient Best-in-Show Art Purchase award, Young Harris Coll., 1979, Smith Art Purchase award, Scroll award, LaGrange Coll., 1981, award, LaGrange Nat. XI, 1984; scholar Art, Young Harris Coll., 1979. Avocations: art history, genealogy, reading, web authoring. Home: PO Box 159 Eton GA 30724 Office: Show Industries Inc PO Drawer 2128 Dalton GA 30722 E-mail: dkp@southernmuse.com.

PRITCHETT, MICHAEL EUGENE COOK, lawyer; b. Louisiana, Mo., Mar. 14, 1960; s. Lloyd Thornton and Wanda Maxine P.; m. Lila Sue Cook, July 30, 1983; children: Andrew Jacob, Courtney Elizabeth. BA in Econs & Polit. Sci., U. Mo., 1982, MA in Econs., 1983, JD, 1986. Bar: U.S. Dist. Ct. (we. dist.) Mo., 1986, U.S. Ct. Appeals (8th cir.), 1989, U.S. Supreme Ct., 2000. Law clk. Supreme Ct. Mo., Jefferson City, 1986-88; assoc. Inglish, Monaco, Riner & Lockenvitz, 1988-89; asst. atty. gen. Mo. Atty. Gen.s Office, 1989—, chmn. CLE com., 2000—; deputy chief counsel Labor Dvsn., 2001—. Mem. Mo. Law Rev., 1984-86. Gregory fellow U. Mo., 1982-83. Mem. Mo. Bar Assn., Order of the Coif. Office: Atty Gen's Office PO Box 899 Jefferson City MO 65102-0899 E-mail: mike.pritchett@mail.ago.state.mo.us.

PRITCHETT, RUSSELL WILLIAM, lawyer, educator; b. Missoula, Mont., Feb. 16, 1951; s. Floyd Wiley and Mary Almeda (Brewer) P.; m. Meg Jesse Jacobson, June 23, 1974; 1 child, Arundel B. BA in History, U. Wash., 1974; JD, Northwestern Sch. of Law, 1977; LLM Maritime & Internat., U. London, 1979. Bar: Wash. 1978, Alaska 1979, U.S. Dist. Ct. Alaska 1979, U.S. Ct. Appeals (9th cir.) 1980, U.S. Dist. Ct. (we. dist.) Wash. 1984. In-house counsel Steamship Mut. Underwriting Assn., Ltd., London, 1978; assoc. Graham & James, Anchorage, 1978-81, Braun, Moriya, Hoashi & Kubota, Tokyo, 1981-83; pvt. practice Bellingham, Wash., 1983-95; ptnr. Pritchett & Jacobson, 1995—. Adj. prof. internat. trade Western Wash. U., Bellingham, 1986-98. Contbr. articles to profl. jours. Pres. Bellingham Maritime Found., 1985. Mem. Maritime Law Assn. U.S. (com. on fisheries 1985—, proctor), Am. Immigration Lawyers Assn. Avocations: cross country skiing, hiking. Home and Office: 870 Democrat St Bellingham WA 98226-8829 E-mail: PandJ@nas.com.

PRITCHETT, SAMUEL TRAVIS, finance and insurance educator, researcher, consultant; b. Emporia, Va., Dec. 18, 1938; s. Harvey Eugene and Mary (Brown) P.; m. Bertha Yates, Feb. 20, 1960; children: John Travis, Meri Katherine. BSBA, Va. Poly. Inst. and State U., 1960, MSBA, 1967; DBA, Ind. U., 1969. CLU, ChFC, CPCU. Claim rep. Equitable Life Assurance Soc., Richmond, Va., 1960-64, asst. div. claim mgr., 1964-65; asst. prof. bus. adminstrn. U. Richmond, 1969-70; asst. prof. ins. Va. Commonwealth U., Richmond, 1970-72, assoc. prof. ins., 1972-73; assoc. prof. fin. and ins. U. S.C., Columbia, 1973-76, prof. fin. and ins., 1976-99, J.H. Fellers prof., 1981-83, W.F. Hipp prof. ins., 1983-2000, program dir., chair banking, fin., ins. and real estate, 1977-83, 99-00, acad. dir. MBA program, 1993-95, disting. prof. finance and ins., 1999-2000, disting. prof. emeritus, 2000—. Vis. prof. ins. Ind. U., Bloomington, 1995-96; chmn. Risk Theory Soc., Columbus, Ohio, 1987-88; acad. dir. internat. exec. devel. program Bamerindus Seguros, Curtiba, Brazil, 1995. Author: Risk Management and Insurance, 7th edit., 1996, Stock Life Insurance Company Profitability, 1986, Individual Annuities as a Source of Retirement Income, 2d edit., 1982, An Economic Analysis of Workers' Compensation in South Carolina, 1994; assoc. editor Jour. Risk and Ins., 1982-86, editor, 1987-91; assoc. editor Fin. Svcs. Rev., 1989-95, 97-99; asst. editor Jour. Am. Soc. CLU and ChFC, 1993-98; mem. acad. rev. bd. Jour. Fin. Planning, 1990-91; mem. editl. bd. Jour. Bus. Rsch., 1976-83, Am. Jour. Small Bus., 1975-79; contbr. articles to profl. jours. Active S.C. Joint Ins. Study Com., 1981-86, 89-95. Mem. Am. Risk and Ins. Assn. (pres. 1980-81), Acad. Fin. Svcs. (pres. 1987-88), So. Risk and Ins. Assn. (pres. 1977-78), Fin. Mgmt. Assn., Profl. Ins. Agts. Found. (named Ins. Educator of Yr. 1989), Beta Gamma Sigma (pres. chpt. 1980-81), Gamma Iota Sigma (nat. trustee 1976-92). Home: 7740 Castleton Ln Columbia SC 29223-2508 Office: U SC Coll Bus Columbia SC 29208-0001 *Apply to others religious values such as honesty, humility, respect, and service. Cultivate a strong work ethic and select admirable mentors.*

PRITCHETT, THOMAS RONALD, retired metal and chemical company executive; b. Colorado City, Tex., Sept. 2, 1925; s. John Thomas and Meddie Omeira (Terry) P.; m. Mary Margaret Hallenbeck, Dec. 23, 1948; children: Rhonda Jean, Thomas Rand, Rebecca Ann. BS in Chemistry and ChemE., U. Tex., 1948, MS, 1949, PhD, 1951. Registered profl. engr. Calif. Rsch. chemist Def. Rsch. Lab., Austin, Tex., 1948-51, Monsanto Chem. Co., Dayton, Ohio, 1951-52; sect. head, rsch. investigator, asst. dir., tech. mgr. Kaiser Aluminum & Chem. Corp., Pleasanton, Calif., 1952-68, v.p., dir. rsch., 1968-89; metall. and corrosion cons. Alamo, Tex., 1989—. Contbr. articles to profl. jours. Mem. adv. bd. Sch. Engring. U. Calif.-Berkeley. Served with U.S. Army, 1944-46. Fellow Am. Soc. Metals; mem. AIME, Aluminum Assn. (chmn. tech. com. and acad. com.), Nat. Assn. Corrosion Engrs., Am. Chem. Soc., Electrochem. Soc., Materials Properties Council (bd. dirs.), Sigma Xi, Phi Lambda Upsilon. Home and Office: 325 Diana Dr ACC 403 Alamo TX 78516

PRITIKIN, JAMES B. lawyer, employee benefits consultant; b. Chgo., Feb. 18, 1939; s. Stan and Anne (Schwartz) P.; m. Barbara Cheryl Demovsky, Apr. 20, 1968 (dec. 1988); children: Gregory, David, Randi; m. Mary Szatkowski, July 7, 1990; 1 child, Peyton. BS, U. Ill., 1961; JD, DePaul U., 1965. Bar: Ill. 1965, U.S. Dist. Ct. (no. dist.) Ill. 1965, U.S. Supreme Ct. 1985; cert. matrimonial arbitrator. Pvt. practice, Chgo., 1965-68, 1984—; ptnr. Sudak, Grubman, Pritikin, Rosenthal & Feldman, 1969-80, Pritikin & Sohn, Chgo., 1980-84, Nadler, Pritikin & Mirabelli, Chgo., 1997—. Pres. Prepaid Benefits Plans Inc., Chgo., 1978—; exec. dir. The Ctr. for Divorce Mediation Ltd. Fellow Internat. Acad. Matrimonial Lawyers, Am. Acad. Matrimonial Lawyers (pres.-elect); mem. ABA, Am. Acad. Matrimonial Lawyers (pres. Ill. chpt.), Ill. Bar Assn., Chgo. Bar Assn. (cir. ct. Cook County liaison com.), Chgo. Pub. Schs. Alumni Assn. (v.p. 1984—). Office: 1 Prudential Plz 130 E Randolph Dr Chicago IL 60601-6207

PRITTS, KIM DEREK, state conservation officer, writer; b. Connellsville, Pa., Nov. 18, 1953; s. Harold Blaine and Janet Lorraine (Roth) P.; m. Rosanne Pritts; children: David, Brent, Kelly. BS, Pa. State U., 1978. Cert. mcpl. police tng.; cert. conservation officer. Police officer Royersford (Pa.) Police Dept., 1978-81; state conservation officer Pa. Fish and Boat Commn., Lancaster, 1981—. Competition judge Ethnic Minorities Screenwriting Competition, L.A., 1992-97; cons., expert Am. Ginseng. Author: The Mystery of Sadler Marsh, 1993, Ginseng: How to Find, Grow, and Use America's Forest Gold,

1995; author: (screenplay) Outlander (Christopher Columbus Discovery award), 1994. Mem. D.U.I. Coun. of Lancaster County. Cpl. USMC, 1972-74. Finalist, Am.'s Best Writing competition The Writers Found., 1994, 95. Mem. Conservation Officers of Pa., N.Am. Wildlife Enforcement Officers Assn., Pa. Sportsmen for the Disabled (Outstanding Svc. award 1992), Phila. Ind. Film Assn. Mem. Ch. of God. Avocations: hiking, photography.

PRITYCHENKO, BORIS VASILEVICH, physicist; b. Zabrama, Bryansk, Russia, Apr. 7, 1962; came to U.S., 1991; s. Vasily Alexeevich and Olga Dmitrievna (Tutunnick) P. Diploma in Engrng. and Physics, Kharkov (Ukraine) State U., 1985; MS in Physics, Mich. State U., 1996, PhD in Physics, 2000. Staff scientist Baksan Neutrino Obs., Inst. Nuclear Rsch. Moscow, Neutrino Village, Russia, 1985-91; vis. scientist CFPA, Ctr. Particle Astrophysics, U. Calif., Berkeley, 1991-94; rsch. asst. Cyclotron Lab., Mich. State U., East Lansing, 1994-2000; solution engr. Plumtree Software, Inc., San Francisco, 2000—. Health physicist Baksan Neutrino Obs., Inst. Nuclear Rsch. Moscow, Neutrino Village, 1989-91. Lt. Russian mil., 1984-86. Mem. Am. Phys. Soc., World Wildlife Fund. Achievements include starting a cold dark matter search program in USSR; development of high pressure and low background gaseous detectors; development of new methods for the fast neutron detection; experimental study of the "island of deformed nuclei;" avocations: mushroom hunting, recreational activities. Office: Plumtree Software Inc 500 Sansome St San Francisco CA 94111 E-mail: boris.pritychenko@plumtree.com.

PRITZKER, ELISA, painter, sculptor, educator, theater director; b. Rio Cuarto, Cordoba, Argentina, Dec. 10, 1955; came to US, 1993; d. Samuel and Esther (Maladetsky) P.; m. Leonardo Fabio Castria, Sept. 22, 1986 (div. Apr. 1994); 1 child, Jimena Castria; m. Enrique Rob Lunski, June 14, 1994. BA in Ceramic Arts, Sch. of Ceramics, Mar del Plata, Argentina, 1976; student in Theater Direction, Body Expression, Acting, Siembra Group, Mar del Plata, Argentina, 1983; MA in Visual Arts, Superior Inst. Visual Arts, Mar del Plata, Argentina, 1986. Prof. pottery, sculpture Superior Inst. Visual Arts, Mar del Plata, Argentina, 1983-88, prof. drawing Argentina, 1987-88; prof. drawing, visual arts Sch. Ceramics, Argentina, 1986-88; graphic art designer Alzamora S.A., Palma de Mallorca, Spain, 1991-93; prof. painting, pottery Ulster BOCES, Port Ewen, N.Y., 1995—. Artistic dir. Internat. Club YWCA, Kingston, N.Y.; founder, artistic dir. Highland (N.Y.) Cultural Ctr., curator, juror Nat. Juried Art Exhbn., 1994, juror of selection, 1995, co-chair creation peace park and monument, 1995; organizer, curator Ann. Juried Exhbn. UNISON, New Paltz, N.Y., 1994, prof. ceramics Arts & Learning Ctr.; curator Latin Am. show Latin Am. Studies SUNY, New Paltz, 1994; curator Global Sisters in Peace photography show SUNY, New Paltz, 1995. One woman exhbns. include Agora Art Gallery, Palma de Mallorca, Spain, 1989, Casa Argentina, Jerusalem, 1995, Lynn Prince Gallery, Poughkeepsie, N.Y., 1995; group exhbns. include 28th Pollensa Internat. Festival of Sculpture and Painting, Baleares, Spain, 1989, Colonya Art Gallery, Pollensa, Baleares, Spain, 1990, Es Cafeti, Palma de Mallorca, Spain, 1992, Manzana 50 Art Gallery, Palma de Mallorca, Spain, 1993, Middletown (N.Y.) Art Ctr. Arts Coun. Orange County, 1993, Putnam Arts Coun. Levine Art Ctr., Mahopac, N.Y., 1993-94, Mamaroneck Artists Guild, Inc. Westbeth Gallery, N.Y.C., 1994, Lynn Prince Gallery, Poughkeepsie, N.Y., 1994, Heritage Art Gallery, Poughkeepsie, N.Y., 1994, Fitton Ctr. Creative Arts, Hamilton, Ohio, 1995, Nassau Coliseum, 1995; represented in permanent collections La Pruna Art Gallery, Manzana 50 Art Gallery, La Luna Art Gallery, numerous pub. and pvt. collections; dir. Urban Theater, Palma de Mallorca, Spain, 1990-92. Mem. reflections program com. PTA, Highland, N.Y., 1994-95, 150th Anniversary com. Town of Lloyd, Highland, N.Y., 1995. Recipient Best Original Painting, Ecol. Soc., 1987, First award Galeria Praxis, 1988, award of Excellence Manattan Arts Internat. Cover Arts Competition, 1994, 2nd Place logo contest, Railroad Bridge Co., Inc., 1994, 4th prize ReviewArt Contest Columbia Pacific U., 1994, 1st prize, 1994, 2nd prize 1995. Mem. Nat. Mus. Women in the Arts. Avocations: photography, music, yoga. Office: Highland Cultural Ctr PO Box 851 Highland NY 12528-0851

PRITZKER, THOMAS JAY, hotel business executive; b. Chgo., June 6, 1950; s. Jay Arthur and Marian (Friend) P.; m. Margot Lyn Barrow-Sicree, Sept. 4, 1977; children— Jason, Benjamin, David. BA, MBA, Claremont Men's Coll, 1976; JD, U. Chgo., 1976. Assoc. Katten, Muchin, Zavis, Pearl and Galler, Chgo., 1976-77; exec. v.p. Hyatt Corp., 1977-80, pres., 1980—; chmn. Hyatt Corp., Hyatt Internat. Corp., 1999—, Hyatt Hotels Corp., 1980—; ptnr. Pritzker & Pritzker, Chgo., 1980—. Pres., chmn. bd. dirs. The Pritzker Orgn., 1998; bd. dirs. First Health Group, Royal Caribbean Cruises Ltd. Trustee Art Inst. Chgo. 1988—, U. Chgo. Mem. ABA, Ill. Bar Assn., Chgo. Bar Assn., Standard Club, Lake Shore Country Club. Clubs: Standard (Chgo.); Lake Shore Country (Glencoe, Ill.). Office: Hyatt Corp 200 W Madison St38th Flr Chicago IL 60606

PRITZL, KURT JOHN, philosophy educator, university dean, priest; b. Milw., Feb. 15, 1952; s. Raymond John and June Elizabeth (McGrath) P. BA, Marquette U., 1974; MA, U. Toronto, Ont., Can., 1975, PhD, 1982; MDiv, Dominican House Studies, Washington, 1991. Joined Dominican Order, Roman Cath. Ch., ordained priest, 1991. Instr. Cath. U. Am. Sch. Philosophy, Washington, 1980-82, asst. prof., 1982-86, assoc. prof., 1986—, interim dean, 1997-98, 99-2000, dean, 2000—. Regent of studies Dominican Province of St. Joseph, N.Y.C., 1993-97. Contbr. articles to profl. jours. Trustee Providence Coll., 1993—. Mem.: Soc. Ancient Greek Philosophy, Am. Cath. Philos. Assn. (exec. coun. 1994—97, Matchette award 1986), Am. Philos. Assn. Avocations. Home: 487 Michigan Ave NE Washington DC 20017 Office: Cath U Am Sch Philosophy Washington DC 20064 E-mail: pritzl@cua.edu.

PRIVER, MAURICE STERLING, retired obstetrician-gynecologist; b. L.A., Sept. 9, 1905; s. Aaron and Fannie (Levy) P.; m. Josephine Isenstein, Dec. 4, 1927 (dec. Aug. 1969); m. Cecille Roberta Finerman, Sept. 6, 1970; children: Robert S. (dec.). BA, U. So. Calif., L.A., 1932, MD, 1936. Intern L.A. Gen. Hosp., 1935-36; resident L.A. City Maternity, 1936-37; resident in ob-gyn. L.A. County Gen. Hosp., 1937-40; attending emeritus Midway Hosp. Med. Ctr., Calif., Cedars-Sinai Med. Ctr. Fellow ACOG (founding); mem. AMA, ACS, Am. Fertility Soc., Pan Pacific Surg. Soc. (sr. mem.), L.A. OB Gyn Soc.

PRIVETT, CARYL PENNEY, lawyer; b. Birmingham, Ala., Jan. 7, 1948; d. William Kinnaird Privett and Katherine Speake (Binford) Ennis. BA, Vanderbilt U., 1970; JD, NYU, 1973. Bar: Ala. 1973, U.S. Dist. Ct. (so. dist.) Ala. 1973, U.S. Dist. Ct. (no. dist.) Ala. 1974, U.S. Ct. Appeals (5th cir.) 1974, U.S. Ct. Appeals (11th cir.) 1981. Assoc. Crawford & Blacksher, Mobile, Ala., 1973-74, Adams, Baker & Clemon, Birmingham, 1974-76; asst. U.S. atty. no. dist. Ala. U.S. Atty.'s Office, U.S. Dept. Justice, 1976-92, 93-94, first asst. U.S. atty., 1992-93, U.S. atty., 1995-97, chief asst., 1997-98; pvt. practice Ala., 1998—; city prosecutor City of Mountain Brook, 1998—. Adj. prof. Cumberland Sch. Law Samford U., 1998—. Active Downtown Dem. Club, Birmingham; bd. dirs. Planned Parenthood Ala., Legal Aid Soc., Birmingham, 1986—88, pres., 1988; sec., founder Lawyers for Choice Ala., 1989—92; chair domestic violence com. City of Birmingham, 1989—91; sustaining mem. Jr. League Birmingham; active Photography Guild, Birmingham Mus. Art. Named, Outstanding Young Women Am., 1977, 1978; recipient Cert. in Color Photography, U. Ala. Birmingham, 1989, Commr.'s Spl. citation, Food and Drug Adminstrn. Mem.: ABA, Ala. Law Inst., Adminstrv. Dir., Ala. Dispute Resoulation Found., Ala. Acad. Atty. Mediators (v.p. 2001), Birmingham Bar Found. (pres. 2001), Birmingham Bar Assn. (exec. com. 1996-98), Ala. Bar Assn. (chmn. women in the profession com. 1997-99), Fed. Bar Assn. (pres. Birmingham chpt. 1979), Ala. Solution, Leadership Birmingham, Women's Network, Women's Fund, Altamont Alumni Assn., Summit Club. Presbyterian. Avocation: Avocation: photography. Home: 30 Norman Dr Birmingham AL 35213-4310 Office: 300 Union Hill Ste 220 Birmingham AL 35209 E-mail: carylprivett@mindspring.com.

PRIVITERA, JOSEPH F. retired foreign service officer, writer-researcher; b. N.Y.C., Feb. 22, 1914; s. Luigi and Grazia (Paparcuri) P.; m. Bettina La Marca, June 30, 1935; children: Joseph Henry, Stephen Louis. BS with honors, NYU, 1935, PhD, 1938; cert. phonetics course, U. Paris, 1936; cert., U. Mex., Mexico City, 1939. Instr. French, NYU, N.Y.C., 1938; asst. prof. Romance langs. St. Louis U., 1939-45; dir. Bi-Nat. Cultural Ctr., U.S. Dept. State, Sao Paulo, Brazil, 1945-47; fgn. svc. officer Am. Consulate Gen., 1947-50, Am. Embassy, Quito, Ecuador, 1950-52; dir. Italian broadcasts Voice of Am., U.S. Dept. State, N.Y.C., 1955-76; ret., 1976. Author: Charles Chevillet de Cahmpmeslé (1642-1701), 1938, The Latin American Front, 1945, Portrait of America, 1947, Perfil Cultural de America, 1951, (with wife) Language as Historical Determinant—The Normans in Sicily 1060-1200, 1995, Luigi Pirandello, His Plays in Sicilian, 2 vols., 1998, Beginner's Sicilian, 1998, A Treasury of Italian Cuisine (in Italian and English), 1998, Faustus in Love, And Other Poems in English and Other Tongues, 1998, Italy, An Illustrated History, 2000, Beginner's Italian, 2000, Sicily, An Illustrated History, 2001; translator, editor: Reference Grammar of Medieval Italian with a Dual Language Edition of The Thirty-One Poems of Dante's Vita Nova, 2001. Mem. Diplomats and Consular Officers Ret. Avocations: salon photographer, amateur flutist. Home and Office: 5818 Nevada Ave NW Washington DC 20015

PRIVMAN, VLADIMIR, physics educator; b. Lvov , Ukraine, Jan. 2, 1955; arrived in Israel, 1971; came to U.S., 1982; s. Lipa and Bronislava Privman; m. Marina Privman, May 22, 1980; children: Lior, Michael, Eve. BSc in Physics summa cum laude, Technion, Haifa, Israel, 1975, MSc in Physics, 1979, DSc in Physics, 1982. Rothschild fellow, rsch. assoc. Cornell U., Ithaca, N.Y., 1982-84; Bantrell rsch. fellow in physics Calif. Inst. Tech., Pasadena, 1984-85; prof. physics Clarkson U., Potsdam, N.Y., 1985—. Royal Soc. Guest Rsch. fellow U. Oxford, 1991-92. Co-author: (with N.M. Svrakic) Directed Models of Polymers, Interfaces and Clusters: Scaling and Finite-Size Properties, 1989; co-author, editor: Finite Size Scaling and Numerical Simulation of Statistical Systems, 1990, Nonequilibrium Statistical Mechanics in One Dimension, 1997. With Israel Def. Forces, 1975-78. Recipient Young investigator award, Petroleum Rsch. Fund, 1986; grantee NSF, Petroleum Rsch. Fund, SRC, USAF, U.S. Army Rsch. . Mem. Am. Phys. Soc., Am. Chem. Soc. Jewish. Office: Clarkson U Dept Physics Potsdam NY 13699-5820 E-mail: privman@clarkson.edu.

PRIVO, ALEXANDER, finance educator, department chairman; m. Elena Privo. BS, Touro Coll., N.Y.C., 1982; M Profl. Studies, New Sch. for Social Rsch., N.Y.C., 1985; MS in Edn., CUNY, 1988; PhD in Adminstrn. and Mgmt., Walden U., 1991. Cert. govt. fin. mgr.; cert. secondary tchr. math., ESL, social studies, bus., acctg., Russian, N.y. Dir. acctg. and fin. reporting Assoc. Retail Stores Inc., N.Y.C., 1982-85; tchr. acctg. N.Y.C. Bd. Edn., 1985—; prof., dept. bus. and econs. Touro Coll., 1987—; dean CUNY, 1987-90; chmn. dept. bus. econs. Touro Coll., 1991—. Coord. mentoring program CUNY and N.Y.C. Bd. edn., 1985-92; cons. and prof. Russian (former Soviet Union); exec. training program MBA Baruch Coll., CUNY, 1990—; coord. cooperative edn. program NYC BD. Edn./CUNY, 1992—. Curriculum devel. grantee. Mem. ASCD, Am. Acctg. Assn., Assn. Govt. Accts., Nat. Bus. Edn. Assn., Internat. Bus. Edn. Assn., Met. Bus. Edn. Assn., N.Y. Educators (doctorate), Am. Mgmt. Assn., Kappa Delta Pi. Home: 43-33 46th St Apt F15 Sunnyside NY 11104-2036

PRIZIO, BETTY J. volunteer, civic worker, property manager; b. L.A., Jan. 23, 1928; d. Harry W. and Irene L. (Connell) Campbell; divorced; children: David P., John W., Robert H., James R. AA in Social Sci., L.A. City Coll., 1949. Owner, mgr. indsl. bldgs. and condominiums, mktg. exec., Tustin, Calif., 1976—. Ind. mktg. exec., Melaleuca. Co-chair silent auction Am. Lung Assn., Santa Ana, 1997-2001, co-chair Big Breath Easy charity event; bd. dirs. Founders Chpt. Aux., Providence Speech and Hearing Ctr., 1986-88, aux. pres., 1986-89; vol. Western Med. Ctr. Aux., 1985-89, chmn. gift shop com., 1987-88, 2d v.p., 1992, aux. pres., 1999, jr. vol. adv., bd. dirs. fundraising group, scholarship com., Focus on Women com. 1990—, buyer for gift shop, 1998—, 4th v.p. gift shop, 1993, pres., 1999-2001; adv. coun. Chapman U., Orange, Calif., 1986-87; bd. dirs. Pres. Assocs., 1985-86, Chapman Music Assocs., 1986—, Santa Ana YWCA, 1976-77; adv. coun. Orange County chpt. Freedoms Found. at Valley Forge, 1985—; active United Meth. Ch., Olive Crest Treatment Ctr.; pres. Western Medicine Ctr. Disciplinary, 1999. Named Vol. of Yr. Gift Shop, 1999. Mem.: Tustin Hist. Soc. (bd. dirs. 1988—90), Western Med. Ctr. Aux. (life; pres. 1999, 2000, 2001, Col. of Yr. 1999). Republican. Avocations: gardening, arts and crafts, travel, photography. Home: 2522 N Tustin Ave Unit D Santa Ana CA 92705

PRIZZI, JACK ANTHONY, investment banking executive; b. Rochester, N.Y., July 5, 1935; s. Samuel Anthony and Mary Ann (Emanuele) P.; m. Geraldine A. Bias, Feb. 16, 1957 (div. 1971); children: Lynne Marie, Michael Vincent, Karen Annette; m. Serafina M. Iacono, Sept. 30, 1995. BS in Chemistry, Va. Mil. Inst., 1956; MS in Phys. Chemistry, U. Va., 1961, MBA, 1963. Chem. engr. E.I. duPont DeNemours & Co., Inc., Niagara Falls, N.Y., 1956-57; engr. Project Mercury, NASA, 1959; mgr. planning and devel. PPG Industries, Pitts., 1963-68; gen. mgr. Process Components Inc., Norfolk, Va., 1968-70; ptrn. Alan Patricof Assocs., N.Y.C., 1970-74, Beacon Ptnrs., N.Y.C., 1974-76, 77-79, Stuart Bros., N.Y.C., 1976-77; v.p. Walter E. Heller & Co.; exec. v.p. Heller Capital Svcs. Inc., N.Y.C., 1979-84; sr. v.p. DnC Am. Banking Corp., 1984-86; mng. dir. DnC Capital Corp., 1986-89; pres., CEO Jack A. Prizzi & Co., 1989-98. Founder, mng. prin. CoE Assocs., L.L.C., N.Y.C., 1998—; spl. ltd. ptnr. Harvest Ptnrs., 1993-97; bd. dirs. The Meridian Resource Corp.; instr. advanced grades N.Y. Power Squadron. Vol. Urban Cons. Group. Capt. U.S. Army, 1958-59. Grantee Office Naval Rsch., 1960, Calif. Rsch. Corp., 1960-61. Mem. Assn. for Corp. Growth, Am. Chem. Soc., Raven Soc., N.Y. Athletic Club. Office: CoE Assocs LLC 156 W 56th St Ste 1400 New York NY 10019-3800 E-mail: info@coeassociatesllc.com.

PRO, PHILIP MARTIN, judge; b. Richmond, Calif., Dec. 12, 1946; s. Leo Martin and Mildred Louise (Beck) P.; m. Dori Sue Hallas, Nov. 13, 1982; 1 child, Brenda Kay. BA, San Francisco State U., 1968; JD, Golden Gate U., 1972. Bar: Calif. 1972, Nev. 1973, U.S. Ct. Appeals (9th cir.) 1973, U.S. Dist. Ct. Nev. 1973, U.S. Supreme Ct. 1976. Pub. defender, Las Vegas, 1973-75; asst. U.S. atty. Dist. Nev., 1975-78; dep. atty. gen. State of Nev., Carson City, 1979-80; U.S. magistrate U.S. Dist. Ct. Nev., Las Vegas, 1980-87, U.S. dist. judge, 1987—2002, chief U.S. dist. judge, 2002—. Instr. Atty. Gen.'s Advocacy Inst., Nat. Inst. Trial Advocacy, 1992; chmn. com. adminstrn. of magistrate judge system Jud. Conf. U.S., 1993—. Bd. dirs. NCCJ, Las Vegas, 1982—, mem. program com. and issues in justice com. Mem. ABA, Fed. Judges Assn. (bd. dirs. 1992—, v.p. 1997-2001), Nev. State Bar Assn., Calif. State Bar Assn., Nev. Judges Assn. (instr.), Assn. Trial Lawyers Am., Nev. Am. Inn Ct. (pres. 1989-91), Ninth Cir. Jury (instructions com.), Nat. Conf. U.S. Magistrates (sec.). Republican. Episcopalian. Office: US Dist Ct 7015 Fed Bldg 300 Las Vegas Blvd S Ste 4650 Las Vegas NV 89101-5883 E-mail: Philip_Pro@nvd.uscourts.gov.

PROBASCO, CALVIN HENRY CHARLES, clergyman, college administrator; b. Petaluma, Calif., Apr. 5, 1926; s. Calvin Warren and Ruth Charlene (Winans) P.; m. Nixie June Farnsworth, Feb. 14, 1947; children— Calvin, Carol, David, Ruth BA cum laude, Biola Bible Coll., La Mirada, Calif., 1953; D.D. (hon.), Talbot Theol. Sem., La Mirada, 1983. Ordained to ministry, 1950. Pastor Sharon Baptist Ch., El Monte, Calif., 1951-58, Carmichael Bible Ch., 1958-97, pastor emeritus, 1997—; pres. Sacramento Bible Inst., Carmichael, 1968—. Mem. Ind. Fundamental Chs. Am. (rec. sec. 1978-81, pres. 1981-84, 1st v.p. 1987-88), Delta Epsilon Chi. Republican.

PROBASCO, DALE RICHARD, management consultant; b. Ogden, Utah, July 23, 1946; s. Robert Vere and Dorleen E. (Oppliger) P.; m. Joan Michele Takacs, Dec. 20, 1969 (div.); children: Todd Aaron, Brad Dillon; m. Vivian Jean Bennett, May 21, 1998. BS, Utah State U., 1975; MS, U. Phoenix, 1988. Inventory asst. Moore Bus. Form, Logan, Utah, 1973-75; systems engr. Electronic Data Systems, Dallas, 1975-76; start-up engr. Bechtel Corp., San Francisco, 1976-78; supr. project scheduling Toledo Edison Co., 1978-80; mgr. project controls Utah Power and Light Co., Salt Lake City, 1980-87, mgr. mktg. strategy, 1987-89; pres. Probasco Cons., Inc., West Jordan, 1989-90; dir. Navigant Cons., Inc., Chgo., 1990—. Contbr. articles to profl. publs. Pres. Emery County Little League, Castledale, Utah, 1981-84; coach Little League Baseball, West Jordan, Utah, 1985-86. With USN, 1965-72. Mem. Am. Pub. Power Assn., Nat. Rural Electric Coop. Assn. Lutheran. Avocations: computer programming, softball, basketball, music. E-mail: dale_Probasco@navignatconsulting.com.

PROBERT, DOROTHY WITTMAN, retired social worker; b. Ridgeway, Pa. d. William Edward and Marie (Ticknor) W.; m. Lionel W. Probert, June 15, 1946 (wid. June 1993); children: Susan Zaveruha, Sally Caldarazzo, William Probert, Marguerite Moller, Thomas Probert. BA, Pa. State U., 1944; MSW, Fordham Sch. Social Svcs., N.Y.C., 1967. Diplomate, Am. Psychotherapy Assn. Social worker Cath. Family Svcs., 1962-69; sch. social worker Trumbull (Conn.) Bd. Edn., 1969-73, Bridgeport (Conn.) Bd. Edn., 1973-99; ret., 1999. Mem. AARP, NEA, NASW, Acad. Cert. Social Workers, Assn. Ret. Tchrs. Conn., Lic. Clin. Social Workers, Conn. Edn. Assn., Bridgeport Edn. Assn., Greater Bridgeport Ret. Tchrs. Assn., Pa. State Alumni Assn. Roman Catholic. Home: 25 Denton Pl Stratford CT 06614-3409

PROBERT, EDWARD WHITFORD, foundation executive, volunteer; b. Orange, N.J., May 27, 1936; s. George Ernest and Ethel Loring (Whitford) P.; m. Ann Schuyler Linen, July 2, 1960; children: Edward Whitford Jr., Leslie P. Sirbaugh, David Linen. BA, Yale U., 1958; LLB, U. Va., 1961. With Morgan Guaranty Trust Co. of N.Y., N.Y.C., 1961-88, v.p., 1970-88, Fannie E. Rippel Found., Annandale, N.J., 1988-93, pres. Basking Ridge, NJ, 1994—95, pres., CEO, 1996—. Sec. Intersearch Inst., Inc., Annandale, N.J., 1989-93; bd. advisors Whitehead Inst. for Biomed. Rsch., Cambridge, Mass., 1996—. Co-chmn. capital campaign Jersey Battered Women's Svc., Morris Plains, N.J., 1996-99; chmn. capital campaign St. Peter's Episcopal Ch., Morristown, 2001—, bd. dirs., 2002-. Mem. Royal Dornoch Golf Club, Mountain Lake Club, Morristown Club and Morristown Field Club, Somerset Hills C.C. (bd. govs., golf chmn. 1981-90). Republican. Episcopalian. Avocations: golf, swimming, scuba diving, reading, singing. Home: Miller Rd New Vernon NJ 07976 Office: Fannie E Rippel Found 180 Mount Airy Rd Ste 200 Basking Ridge NJ 07920-2021 E-mail: rippel@gti.net.

PROBST, JOHN ELWIN, chaplain, minister; b. Klamath Falls, Oreg., Apr. 3, 1940; s. John Albert and Jocelyn Marlia (Tunnell) P.; m. Patty P. Maness, Jan. 13, 1975; children: Marla, Joni, Jessica. BTh, Internat. Bible Sem., Orlando, Fla. Ordained to ministry So. Bapt. Conv., 1969. Pastor 1st Bapt. Ch., Dorris, Calif., 1968-72; evangelist, Tex., 1972-74; youth pastor Salem Bapt. Ch., Rocky, Okla., 1975; pastor Retrop Bapt. Ch., Carter, 1975-79; supply pastor 1st Bapt. Ch., Hobart, 1975-79; interim pastor Mountain Heights So. Bapt. Ch., Leadville, Colo., 1979; missionary-evangelist, interim pastor Skyway Bapt. Ch., Glendale, Ariz., 1979-82; pastor 1st So. Bapt. Ch., Monrovia, Calif., 1982-85; chaplain Media Focus, Duarte, 1982—; interim pastor United Comty. Ch., Glendale, 1988-90; owner Probst & Assocs., 1991—. Revival leader; former mem. evangelism and search com. Estrella Assn., Ariz.; former br. mgr. Sherwin Williams Co.; writer, casting dir., producer Seven Star Prodn.; assoc. producer, writer, casting dir. Castel Prodns.; writer Esses Films; researcher, writer, asst. producer Nunn Prodns.; filming in Thialand Castel Prodns., 1987, telemarketer White Horse Prodns; pres. L.A. So. Bapt. Pastors Conf., 1983; ch. planter Philippine Crusade, 1983, 85; numerous others. With USAF, 1959-64. Mem. So. Calif. Motion Picture Coun. (life, Golden Halo awards 1985). Office: PO Box 618 Duarte CA 91009-0618 E-mail: MFocus@hotmail.com. *If I am able through sensitivity in prayer and loving devotion, to stay each day in the center of God's Will for my life-then I will accomplish exactly and only what He plans for me to do.*

PROBSTEIN, RONALD FILMORE, mechanical engineering educator; b. N.Y.C., Mar. 11, 1928; s. Sidney and Sally (Rosenstein) P.; m. Irene Weindling, July 30, 1950; 1 child, Sidney. BME, NYU, 1948; MSE, Princeton U., 1950, AM, 1951, PhD, 1952; ScD (hon.), Brown U., 1997. Rsch. asst. physics N.Y. U., 1946-48, instr. engrng. mechanics, 1947-48; rsch. asst. dept. aero. engrng. Princeton U., 1948-52, rsch. assoc., 1952-53, asst. prof., 1953-54; asst. prof. divs. engrng., applied math. Brown U., 1954-55, assoc. prof., 1955-59, prof., 1959-62; prof. mech. engrng. M.I.T., 1962—89, Ford prof. engrng., 1989-96, prof. mech. engrng., 1996—2001, emeritus prof. engrng., 1997—; Disting. prof. engrng. U. Utah, 1973; sr. partner Water Purification Assos., Cambridge, 1974-82; chmn. bd. Water Gen. Corp., 1982-83; sr. corp. tech. advisor Foster-Miller, Inc., 1983-91. Commr. commn. on engrng. and tech. systems NRC, 1980-83; sci. advisor to bd. Corrpro Cos., 1993-2001. Author: Hypersonic Flow Theory, 1959, Hypersonic Flow, Inviscid Flows, 1966, Water in Synthetic Fuel Production, 1978, Synthetic Fuels, 1982, Physicochemical Hydrodynamics, 1989, 2d edit., 1994; editor: Introduction to Hypersonic Flow, 1961, Physics of Shock Waves, 1966, Jour. PhysicoChem. Hydrodynamics, 1987-89; contbr. articles to profl. jours.; patentee in field. Guggenheim fellow, 1960-61; R.F. Probstein Lecture Series in Engrng. Sci., MIT, established 1999. Fellow Am. Acad. Arts and Scis. (councilor 1975-79), Am. Phys. Soc., ASME (Freeman award 1971), AIAA, AAAS; mem. NAS, NAE, Internat. Acad. Astronautics, Am. Inst. Chem. Engrs. Home: 5 Seaver St Brookline MA 02445-5714 Office: 77 Massachusetts Ave Cambridge MA 02139-4301 E-mail: rfprobst@mit.edu.

PROBSTFIELD, JEFFREY LYNN, cardiology educator, consultant; b. Fargo, N.D., June 27, 1941; s. George Berg and Alda Gail (Abbott) P.; m. Margaret Helen Belgum, Dec. 28, 1965; children: Erik, Kathryn, Cindy, Dawn, Shannon, Laura. BA, Pacific Luth. U., Tacoma, Wash., 1963; MD, U. Washington Sch. Medicine, Seattle, 1967. Attending physician U. Minn. Hosps., Mpls., 1972-78; asst. prof. medicine Baylor Coll. Medicine, Houston, 1978-84; spl. expert clin. trials branch NHLBI, DECA, Bethesda, Md., 1984-88, med. officer clin. trials branch, 1988-92; clin. prof. medicine Uniformed Svcs. U. Health Scis., 1991-93; cons. physician Fred Hutchinson Cancer Rsch. Ctr., Seattle, 1993—; prof. cardiology medicine U. Washington Sch. Medicine, 1994—, dir. clin. trials svc. unit cardiology, 1995—. Contbr. articles to profl. jours. Office: Fred Hutchinson Cancer Rsch Ctr 1100 Fairview Ave N # Mp557 Seattle WA 98109-4417 Fax: 206-667-4408. E-mail: jeffp@swog.fhcrc.org.

PROBUS, MICHAEL MAURICE, JR. lawyer; b. Louisville, Jan. 26, 1963; s. Michael Maurice and Jerilyn Ann (Burks) P.; m. Luz Marie Probus, May 22, 1985; children: Michael Julian, Lauren Michael. BA, U. Dallas, 1985; JD, U. Tex., 1988. Bar: Tex. 1988, U.S. Dist. Ct. (we. dist.) Tex. 1990, U.S. Ct. Appeals (5th cir.) 1993. Jud. law clk. to chief judge U.S. Dist. Ct. Tex., Houston, 1988-90; assoc. Law Offices of Michael A. Wash, Austin, Tex., 1990-97; pvt. practice, 1997—. Pro bono atty. Vol. Legal Svcs., Austin, 1994—. Mem.: Travis County Bar Assn. Democrat. Roman Catholic. Office: Law Office M Probus 100 Congress Ave Ste 1550 Austin TX 78701 E-mail: mprobusjr@msn.com.

PROCACCINO, JAMES DREW, computer scientist, educator; b. Princeton, N.J., Nov. 15, 1959; s. John Alan and Jean Ann Procaccino. BA, Ursinus Coll., 1982; BSc, Rider U., 1991, MBA, 1999; PhD, Drexel U., 2002. Prin., owner, Princeton, NJ, 1982—91; cons. Lawrenceville, 1998—. Graphics specialist Opinion Rsch. Corp., Princeton, 1996—98. Contbr. articles to profl. jours. Usher St. Ann's Roman Cath. Ch., Lawrenceville, 1990—. Avocations: photography, drums, graphic design. Home: 14 Temple Terrace Lawrenceville NJ 08648 Office: Rider University 2083 Lawrenceville Road Lawrenceville NJ 08648

PROCASKY, JOHN DAVID, secondary education educator; b. Kansas City, Mo., Feb. 14, 1963; s. David Edward Procasky and Elaine Joyce Tinney; m. Mary Irene Watner, July 30, 1988; children: Sean, BreAnna, Seth. BS, William Jewell, 1989. Cert. title 09, Ill. Sci. tchr. Jennings (Mo.) Jr. High, 1991-92, Smithton (Ill.) Grade Sch., 1992-2000, Cahokia (Ill.) H.S., 2000—. Instr. Kids On Campus, South Western Ill. Coll., Belleville, 1996-2002. Avocation: coaching sports. Home: 1921 Muren Blvd Belleville IL 62221 Office: 1700 Jerome Ln Belleville IL 62221

PROCHASKA, CHARLES ROLAND, aerospace engineer; b. Nampa, Idaho, Dec. 8, 1941; s. Roland William Anthony and Dorothy Helen (Harris) P.; m. Patricia Blessing Devlin, May 1, 1965 (div. May 1975); children: Roland Anthony, Meikle John, Peter Henry; m. Judith Diane Armstrong, May 16, 1975; stepchildren: Diane Elayne Petet (dec.), Gregg Andrew Petet. B. Aerospace Engring., U. Mich., 1965. Specialist engr. BCAC/BMS/BAC, Renton, Wash., 1965-79; sr. specialist engr. 767 div. Boeing Co., Everett, 1979-82; sr. specialist engr. Boeing Marine Systems, Renton, 1982-87; prin. engr. Sea Lance, Boeing Aerospace & Electronics, Kent, Wash., 1987-90; prin. engr. 777 div. Boeing Co. Cargo Systems, Renton, 1990-91; mgr. 777 divsn. Boeing Co. Cargo Furnishings, Everett, 1991-95, 777 divsn. Boeing Co. Insulation, Everett, 1994-95, Payloads, Boeing Co. Insulation-New Process, Everett, 1995-97; option mgmt. Boeing Co., 1997-98; mgr. Payloads, Boeing Co Emergency Equipment-Narrow Bodies, 1998-99, prin. engr. emergency equipment, 767 plane cabin interiors, 1999; prin. engr. Payload Concept Ctr., 1999—; master Deer Lagoon Grange, Langley, Wash., 2000—; asst. steward

Island County Grange, 2000—. Gen. chmn. 2d Aerospace Structures Design Conf., 1970. Scoutmaster troop 478 Boy Scouts Am., Auburn, Wash., 1983-91, cubmaster pack 478, 1980-83, round table commr. Green River dist., Seattle, 1981-84. Recipient Dist. Award of Merit, Chief Seattle coun. Boy Scouts Am., 1985. Mem. Seattle Profl. Engring. Employees Assn. (councilman 1967-72). Methodist. Achievements include patent for locking mechanism, patent pending for aircraft passenger cleansing system. Home: 3499 Smugglers Cove Rd Greenbank WA 98253-9764 Office: Boeing Co PO Box 3707 Seattle WA 98124-2207 E-mail: whidstar@whidbey.com., charles.r.prochaska@boeing.com.

PROCHASKA, FRANK JOSEPH, educator; b. Macolmb County, Mich., Apr. 20, 1939; s. Joseph Frank and Francis Katarina (Machacek) P.; m. Elfi Elisabeth Wortmann, Mar. 9, 1964; children— Gabriele, Stefanie. B.F.A., U. Notre Dame, 1961; postgrad. U. Colo.-Colorado Springs, 1973-78; M.A., Goddard Coll., 1980; Ph.D., Columbia Pacific U., 1982. Indsl. engr. Hq. Norad/Adcom, Colorado Springs, 1974-76, chief mgmt. engr., 1976-79; cons. Pro Systems, Inc., Colorado Springs, 1980-83; instr./prof. U. Colo., Colorado Springs, 1983— ; dept. chmn. indsl. mgmt. Colo. Tech. Coll., Colorado Springs, 1983— ; cons. in field. Contbr. articles to profl. jours. Served to capt. USAF, 1962-73. Recipient Pres. Cost Reduction award, Civil Profl. Excellence award USAF; mem. Inst. Indusl. Engrs. (pres. 1974), Personal Dynamics, Am. Mgmt. Assn., Performax Systems Internat., Assn. Humanistic Psychology. Address: 7648 Thunderbird Ln Colorado Springs CO 80919-2618

PROCHÁZKA, DAVID, librarian; b. Mishawaka, Ind., Oct. 27, 1956; s. Frank John and Mary Helen (Skolout) P.; m. George W. Crenshaw III, Oct. 26, 1985. BM in Music History, Chgo. Mus. Coll., 1987; MAL.I.S., Rosary Coll., 1993. Cataloging cons. Am. Osteopathic Assn., Chgo., 1991—92; sound recordings cataloger Northwestern U., Evanston, Ill., 1996—97. Co-composer: Operas Gilgamesh, 1988; composer: (incidental music) Music for Pearl S. Buck Stories, 1993—94; contbr. articles. Bd. dirs. Kulture Kids, Cleveland Heights, Ohio, 2000—. Grantee grant, Eugene M. Adler Found., 2001. Mem.: Acad. Libr. Assn. Ohio, Online Audiovisual Catalogers, Inc., Music O.C.L.C. Users Group. E-mail: davidp@uakron.edu.

PROCHNOW, DOUGLAS LEE, lawyer; b. Omaha, Jan. 9, 1952; s. Albert Delmer and Betty Jean (Wood) P. BA with high distinction, U. Nebr., 1974; JD, Northwestern U., 1977. Bar: Ill. 1977, U.S. Dist. Ct. (no. dist.) Ill. 1977, U.S. Ct. Appeals (7th cir.) 1989, U.S. Supreme Ct. 2000. Assoc. Wildman, Harrold, Allen & Dixon, Chgo., 1977-84, ptnr., 1985—. Spl. asst. corp. counsel City of Chgo., 1986—87. Bd. dirs. Chgo. chpt. Prevent Child Abuse Am. Mem. ABA, ATLA (assoc.), Ill. Bar Assn., Chgo. Bar Assn., Soc. Trial Lawyers, Def. Rsch. Inst., Am. Health Lawyers Assn., Phi Beta Kappa, Phi Eta Sigma. Home: 1230 N State Pky Apt 6D Chicago IL 60610-2261 Office: Wildman Harrold Allen & Dixon 225 W Wacker Dr Chicago IL 60606-1224 E-mail: prochnow@wildmanharrold.com.

PROCHNOW, HERBERT VICTOR, JR. lawyer; b. Evanston, Ill., May 26, 1931; s. Herbert V. and Laura (Stinson) P.; m. Lucia Boyden, Aug. 6, 1966; children: Thomas Herbert, Laura. AB, Harvard U., 1953, JD, 1956; A.M., U. Chgo., 1958. Bar: Ill. 1957, U.S. Dist. Ct. (no. dist.) Ill. 1961. With 1st Nat. Bank Chgo., 1958-91, atty., 1961-70, sr. atty., 1971-73, counsel, 1973-91, with adminstrv. asst. to chmn. bd., 1978-81; pvt. practice, 1991—. Author: (with Herbert V. Prochnow) A Treasury of Humorous Quotations, 1969, The Changing World of Banking, 1974, The Public Speaker's Treasure Chest, 1986, The Toastmaster's Treasure Chest, 1988; also articles in legal publs. Mem.: Am. Soc. Internat. Law, Chgo. Bar Assn. (chmn. com. internat. law 1970—71), Ill. Bar Assn., ABA, Chgo. Club, Lawyers Club (Chgo.), Harvard Club (N.Y.C.), Univ. Club (Chgo.), Econ. Club, Onwentsia, Phi Beta Kappa. Home: 949 Woodbine Pl Lake Forest IL 60045-2275 Office: 155 N Michigan Ave Chicago IL 60601-7511

PROCHNOW, JAMES R. lawyer; b. Hutchinson, Minn., Sept. 22, 1943; BA, Hamline U., 1965; JD, William Mitchell Law Sch., 1969. Bar: Minn. 1969, U.S. Supreme Ct. 1973, Colo. 1975. Staff civil divsn. Dept. Justice, Washington, 1973-74; legal counsel to Pres. The White House, 1974; ptnr. Baker & Hostetler, Denver, Patton Boggs, 1995—. Mem.: Direct Selling Assn., Am. Herbal Products Assn., Colo. Bar Assn., Denver Bar Assn. Office: Patton Boggs 1660 Lincoln St Ste 1900 Denver CO 80264-1601

PROCHNOW, LAURIE LYNN, management recruitment executive; b. Wausau, Wis., Dec. 7, 1954; d. Harlan Lloyd and Betty Ann Allman; m. Randall J. Prochnow, May 31, 1975; children: David, Betty Ann. AA, North Ctrl. Tech. Coll., 1993. Cert. sr. acct. mgr. MRI Internat. Acct. rep. Mgmt. Recruiters of Wausau, LLC, 1990-94, pres., 1994—. Named to Top 10 Entrepreneurs, Wausau Daily Herald, 1999. Mem. Soc. for Human Resource Profls., Assn. for Info. Tech. Profls. (chair 1995—), Wausau Area C. of C. Office: Mgmt Recruiters of Wausau LLC 3309 Terrace Ct Wausau WI 54401-3952

PROCHNOW, THOMAS HERBERT, lawyer; b. Chgo., May 29, 1967; s. Herbert Victor Jr. and Lucia (Boyden) P. AB, Harvard U., 1989; postgrad., U. London, 1989; student, U. Paris, Sorbonne, 1990; JD, Yale U., 1993. Bar: N.Y. 1994, U.S. Dist. Ct. (so. and ea. dists.) N.Y. 1994, U.S. Ct. Appeals (fed. cir.) 1998. Assoc. Debevoise & Plimpton, N.Y.C., 1993-99; assoc. counsel intellectual property NHL Enterprises, L.P., 1999—2001, sr. counsel legal and bus. affairs, 2001—. Contbr. chpt. to book, articles to profl. jours. Vol. atty., asylum program Lawyers Com. for Human Rights, N.Y.C., 1994-99. Recipient award of Excellence, Vol. Lawyers for the Arts, 1996. Mem.: ABA (intellectual property sect.), Internat. Trademark Assn. (internet com.), Assn. of Bar of City of N.Y. (com. copyright and literary property, internet law com.). Office: NHL Enterprises LP 47th Fl 1251 Ave of Americas New York NY 10020-1192

PROCIDANO, MARY ELIZABETH, psychologist, educator; b. New Rochelle, N.Y., Apr. 1, 1954; d. John D'Arge and Dorothy Diane (Utter) P.; m. Stephen Anthony Buglione, Aug. 9, 1986; children: Daniel Stephen, Katherine Mary, Anne Elizabeth. BS summa cum laude with honors, Fordham U., 1976; PhD, Ind. U., 1981. Lic. psychologist. Assoc. instr. Ind. U., Bloomington, 1979-80; intern in clin. psychology Inst. of Living, Hartford, Conn., 1980-81; asst. prof. Fordham U., Bronx, N.Y., 1981-90, asst. chair psychology dept., 1984-87, chair Inst. Rev. Bd. for Protection of Human Subjects, 1986-94, assoc. prof., mem. faculty senate, 1992-96, 99—, also mem. coll. coun. and various coms., advisor, chair psychology dept., 1997—; pvt. practice clin. psychology Scarsdale, 1992—. Assoc. dean Fordham U. Grad. Sch. of Art's and Scis., 1996, chair dept. psychology, 1996—. Cons. editor Jour. of Personality and Social Psychology, 1989—; contbr. articles and chpts. to profl. and scholarly jours. and books. Faculty fellow Fordham U., 1990; rsch. and faculty devel. grantee Fordham U. Mem. Am. Psychol. Assn., Ea. Psychol. Assn., Assn. for Advancement Behavior Therapy, Phi Beta Kappa, Sigma Xi, Psi Chi. Roman Catholic. Avocations: gardening, hiking, cooking. Office: Fordham U Dept Psychology Bronx NY 10458

PROCKNOW, MARGOT, artist; b. Galesburg, Ill. d. Ross Lincoln and Beulah Ellen (Gillard) Freeman; m. Lloyd L. Henze, Nov. 1953 (div. Dec. 1960; children: Steven Eric, Michael Ross; m. Jene Tremayne Procknow, Sept. 8, 1962; 1 child, Heidi Jene. Student, U. Wis., 1951-53. Artist NASCO, Inc., Ft. Atkinson, Wis., 1960-61; artist/illustrator freelance, Ft. Worth, 1961-77; custom designer fine jewelry, 1977-89; artist M.E. Procknow Fine Art, 1987—. Artist; painting inluded in Creative Watercolor, 1996, In Watercolor: People, 1996; painting inluded in Nat. Women's Caucus for Art newsletter, 1991. Mem. Natural Resources Def. Coun., 1970—. Mem. Nat. League Am. Pen Women, Nat. Mus. Women in the Arts, Soc. Watercolor Artists, Soc. Art of the Imagination, Internat. Soc. Exptl. Artists, Planetary Soc., Planned Parenthood, NOW. Avocations: reading, rocks, comparative religions, nature studies, science. Home: 1201 Cozby St E Fort Worth TX 76126-3601 E-mail: madmoggy@mindspring.com.

PROCKOP, DARWIN JOHNSON, biochemist, physician; b. Palmerton, Pa., Aug. 31, 1929; s. John and Sophie (Gurski) Prockop; m. Elinor Sacks, Apr. 15, 1961; children: Susan Elizabeth, David John. AB, Haverford Coll., 1951; MA, Oxford U., 1953; MD, U. Pa., 1956; PhD, George Washington U., 1962; DSc (hon.) (hon.) , U. Oulu, Finland, 1983, U. So. Fla., 1993. Investigator NIH, 1957—61; assoc., asst. prof., asso. prof., prof. medicine and biochemistry U. Pa., Phila., 1961—72; prof., chmn. dept. biochemistry U. Medicine and Dentistry of N.J. (Rutgers Med. Sch.), Piscataway, NJ, 1972—86; prof., chmn. dept. biochemistry and molecular biology Jefferson Med. Coll., Phila., 1986—96, dir. Jefferson Inst. Molecular Medicine, 1986—96; prof., dir. Ctr. for Gene Therapy, MCP/Hahnemann Med. Coll., 1996—2000; prof., dir. Ctr. Gene Therapy Tulane U. Med. Ctr., New Orleans, 2000—. Contbr. Served with USPHS, 1958—61. Named hon. companion, U. Manchester, 1999; recipient Disting. Alumnus award, George Washington U., 1991, U. Pa., 1994, Hopkins Meml. medal , Brit. Biochem. Soc, 1998; fellow Fulbright Found., 1951—53; grantee, NIH, 1961—. Mem.: NAS, Am. Assn. Physicians, Am. Soc. Clin. Investigation, Am. Soc. Biol. Chemists, Acad. Finland, Inst. Medicine, Alpha Omega Alpha, Phi Beta Kappa. Achievements include research in on collagen and gene therapy. Home: 291 Locust St Philadelphia PA 19106-3913 Office: Ctr Gene Therapy Tulane U Med Ctr 1430 Tulane Ave New Orleans LA 70112-2699 E-mail: dprocko@tulane.edu.

PROCTER, JOHN ERNEST, former religious publishing company executive; b. Gainesboro, Tenn., July 23, 1918; s. Leon and Mary (Poteet) P.; m. Jane Sprott, May 23, 1941; children: Mary Carol, Valere Kay. Student, Vanderbilt U., 1940-41, U. Miami (also extension div.), 1943-44, U. Tenn., 1946-50; LL.D. (hon.), Ohio No. U., 1971; D.L. (hon.), Ky. Wesleyan Coll., 1981. With Methodist Pub. House, Nashville, 1945-83, v.p., pub., 1964-70, pres., pub., 1970-83. Dir. 3d Nat. Bank, Nashville. Bd. dirs. Tenn Council on Econ. Edn. Served to capt. USAAF and USAF, 1944-45, 50-52. Decorated Certificate of Valor; Air medal with 7 oak leaf clusters; D.F.C. Mem. Adminstrv. Mgmt. Soc. (past pres. Nashville, area. sec.-treas. 1967-68, Merit Key award 1961, Diamond Merit award 1967), Nashville C. of C. (past mem. bd. govs.), Assn. Am. Pubs. (past dir.) Clubs: Golf Club of Tenn., Belle Meade Golf & Country. *The modest success I have achieved is the result of an intense commitment to intellectual honesty, sensitivity to the needs of my associates, the setting of challenging and realistic goals, striving for efficiency by doing things right and being effective by doing the right things, always with faith in myself and my associates.*

PROCTOR, CONRAD ARNOLD, physician; b. Ann Arbor, Mich., July 14, 1934; s. Bruce and Luena Marie (Crawford) P.; m. Phyllis Darlene Anderson, June 23, 1956; children: Sharon Darlene Proctor Heimbach, Barbara Jan Brown, David Conrad, Todd Bruce. MD, U. Mich., 1959, MS, 1964. Cert. Am. Bd. Otolaryngology. Intern St. Joseph Mercy Hosp., Ann Arbor, 1959-60; jr. clin. instr. Univ. Hosp., 1961-63, sr. clin. instr., 1963-65; chief dept. otolaryngology Munson Army Hosp., Ft. Leavenworth, Kans., 1965-67; mem. attending staff William Beaumont Hosp., Royal Oak, Mich., 1967—. Instr. Am. Acad. Otolaryngology, Washington, 1968-82, guest examiner, Chgo., 1978-79; Midwest dir. Macrocellular Cellular Phone Sys., 1990—. Author: Current Therapy in Otolaryngology, 1984-85; (booklet) Dietary Treatment of Meniere's Syndrome, 1983, Hyperinsulinemia and Tinnitus, 1988; (manual) Hereditary Sensorineural Hearing Loss, 1978, Etiology, Treatment of Fluid Retention in Meniere's Syndrome, 1992; (med. jour.) Abnormal Insulin Levels and Vertigo, 1981. Dir. Christian edn. Bloomfield Hills (Mich.) Bapt. Ch., 1969-72, fin. chmn., 1975-78, Sunday sch. tchr., 1967—. Served to capt. U.S. Army, 1965-67. Recipient 1st pl. award for med. rsch. Students Am. Med. Assn., 1959, Merit award Am. Acad. Otolaryngology, 1978; holder 5 world records Internat. Game Fish Assn. Mem. AMA, Mich. State Med. Assn., Oakland County Med. Assn., Am. Bd. Otolaryngology, ACS, Triological Soc., Otosclerosis Study Group, Internat. Game Fish Assn. (Nat. Fresh Water Fishing Hall of Fame), Am. Legion, U.S. Tennis Assn., U.S. Golf Assn., Panangling Ltd. (Chgo.), Victors and Presidents Club (Ann Arbor), Audubon Soc., Phi Eta Sigma, Phi Kappa Phi, Phi Beta Kappa. Republican. Avocations: baseball, football, tennis, Arctic exploration, fishing. Home: 3543 Riverside Dr Auburn Hills MI 48326-4309 Office: 3535 W 13 Mile Rd Royal Oak MI 48073-6710

PROCTOR, DICK, member of parliament; Grad. in Journalism, Carleton U. With newspaper, Toronto, Canada, Edmonton, Canada, CBC-TV; mem. 37th parliament House of Commons, Ottawa, Canada. Chair New Dem. Party caucus House of Commons, critic for agr. and agri-food. Office: House of Commons Rm 315 East Block Ottawa ON K1A 0A6 Canada also: 11 Hochelaga St W Moose Jaw SK S6H 2E9 Canada*

PROCTOR, DONALD FREDERICK, otolaryngology educator, physician; b. Red Bank, N.J., Apr. 19, 1913; s. Frederick R. and Gertrude (Chauncey) P.; m. Janice Carson, June 10, 1937; children: Douglas, Nan. AB, Johns Hopkins, 1933, MD, 1937. Diplomate: Am. Bd. Otolaryngology. With otol. lab. Johns Hopkins Hosp., 1937-38, mem. otolaryn. house staff, 1938-40; resident otolaryngology Balt. City Hosps., 1940-41; pvt. practice otolaryngology Balt., 1941-56; asso. prof. otolaryngology Med. Sch., Johns Hopkins, 1946-51, 58-73, prof. anesthesiology, 1951-55, 77-84, asst. prof. physiology, laryngology and otolaryngology, 1955-58, 77-84, prof. laryngology and otology, 1973-84, prof. environ. health sci., 1965-84, prof. emeritus, 1984—, chief bronchoscopic clinic, 1962-66, chief research program air hygiene, dept. environmental medicine, 1955—. With dept. physiology U. Rochester, 1946-47; fellow anesthesiology U. Pa., 1951-52 Author: Anesthesia and Otolaryngology, 1957, Tonsils and Adenoids in Childhood, 1960, Nose Paranasal Sinuses and Ears in Childhood, 1962, Breathing, Speech, and Song, 1980; editor: Respiratory Defense Mechanisms, 1977, The Nose, Upper Airway Physiology and Atmospheric Environment, 1982, A History of Breathing Physiology, 1995; author articles, book chpts. deafness, respiration, air hygiene, air polllution, mucous membrane. Fellow A.C.S., Am. Acad. Otolaryngology; mem. Am. Bronchoesophagol. Assn., Am. Indsl. Hygiene Assn., Air Pollution Control Assn., Am. Physiol. Soc., Phi Beta Pi, Sigma Xi. Clubs: 14 West Hamilton Street (Balt.). Home: Roland Park Place 615 830 W 40th St Baltimore MD 21211-2116

PROCTOR, JESSE HARRIS, JR. political science educator; b. Durham, N.C., Sept. 3, 1924; s. Jesse Harris and Rosa Belle (Rogers) P.; m. Ella Jane Callahan, Mar. 27, 1948; children: Edward Sidney, Thomas Christopher, Kenneth Stuart. AB, Duke U., 1948; MA, Fletcher Sch. Law and Diplomacy, 1949; PhD, Harvard U., 1955. Instr., asst. prof. polit. sci. MIT, 1949-56; asst. prof., assoc. prof. polit. sci. Am. U. in Cairo, 1956-58, vis. prof., 1991-92; asst. prof., then assoc. prof. and prof. polit. sci. Duke U., 1958-70; Charles A. Dana prof. polit. sci. Davidson (N.C.) Coll., 1970-91, prof. emeritus, 1991—, chmn. dept. polit. sci., 1972-89. Vis. assoc. prof. polit. sci. U. Coll., Nairobi, Kenya, 1964-65; vis. prof. polit. sci., U. Dar es Salaam, Tanzania, 1969-70; Fulbright lectr. St. Stephen's Coll., Delhi U., India, 1982-83 Editor: Islam and International Relations, 1965; contbg. author: Federalism in the Commonwealth, 1963, The Aftermath of Sovereignty, 1973, Prospects for Constitutional Democracy, 1976; Contbr. articles to profl. jours. Served with USAAF, 1943-46. Mem. Phi Beta Kappa, Pi Sigma Alpha, Omicron Delta Kappa. Home: 53 Wagon Trail Black Mountain NC 28711

PROCTOR, JULIAN, oncologist; b. Cheltenham, Eng., Mar. 20, 1942; arrived in U.S., 1976; s. Ian Robert and Jean Gertrude Proctor; m. Monique Mohl, June 15, 1980; children: Danielle, Owen. MBBS, London U., 1967, PhD, 1973. Diplomate Am. Bd. Therapeutic Radiology. Lectr. pathology Meml. U. Med. Sch., St. Johns, Canada, 1973, McGill U. Med. Sch., Montreal, Canada, 1973—76; sr. scientist NCI Cancer Inst. Mc Gill, 1973—76; chief tumor immunobiology lab. Allegheny Gen. Hosp., Pitts., 1976—82; asst. prof. oncology/ radiology Johns Hopkins Med. Sch., Balt., 1983—86; chief clin. radiation oncology Jameson Hosp., Newcastle, Pa., 1987—. Cons., chair QAC radiation oncology Highmark, Pitts., 2001—. Contbr. articles to profl. jours., chapters to books; sci. reviewer: jours. in field. Coach Beaver (Pa.) Ice Hockey Start, 1995—96; hockey coach Mohawk Warrior H.S., Lawrence County, 1997—2001; soccer coach Laurel Recreation, 2000, 2001. Fellow Gordon Jacobs Rsch., Royal Marsden Hosp., London, 1969—72, Nat. Cancer Inst., Washington, 1979—81. Fellow: Royal Soc. Medicine; mem.: AMA, N.Y. Acad. Scis., Reticule Entothelial Soc., Am. Soc. Clin. Oncology, Am. Soc. Therapeutic Radiology, Am. Coll. Radiology (accredited radiation oncology surveyor). Achievements include patent for method for screening anti tumor agents of the reticule endothelial stimulant class; resolution of soil seed hypothesis and mechanical theory of mitostatic spread. Avocations: bow hunting, fly fishing, ice hockey, skiing. Office: Jameson Hosp 1211 Wilmington Ave New Castle PA 16105 Fax: 724-656-4181.

PROCTOR, KENNETH DONALD, lawyer; b. Balt., Apr. 28, 1944; s. Kenneth Chauncey and Sarah Elizabeth (Kent) P.; m. Judith Danner Harris, Aug. 2, 1969; children: Kenneth Scott, Kent Harris, Janet Cameron BS, Lehigh U., 1966; JD, U. Md., 1969. Bar: Md. 1969, U.S. Dist. Ct. Md. 1970, U.S. Supreme Ct. 1974, U.S. Ct. Appeals (4th cir.) 1980. Law clk. to judge Md. Ct. Appeals, 1969-70; assoc. Miles & Stockbridge, Balt., 1970-73, 74-76, ptnr., 1976-81, Towson, 1981-96; asst. atty. gen. State of Md., Balt., 1973-74. Trustee Gilman Sch., Balt., 1982-85. Mem. ABA, Md. Bar Assn., Baltimore County Bar Assn. Democrat. Episcopalian. Office: K Donald Proctor PA 102 W Pennsylvania Ave Ste 505 Towson MD 21204-4542 E-mail: kdproctor@proctorlaw.com.

PROCTOR, LEONARD RAY, otolaryngologist, educator; b. Romulus, Mich., Dec. 26, 1929; s. Harvey Robert and Florence Caroline (Leimback) P.; children: James D., Alexander J., Thomas W. Student, U. Mich., 1948-51; MD, Wayne State U., 1955. Diplomate Am. Acad. Otolaryngology. Intern Huntington Meml. Hosp., Pasadena, Calif., 1955-56; resident in otolaryngology U. Chgo., 1956-61, NIH fellow in otology, 1961-62, assoc. prof. surgery, 1970-76; attending physician Los Angeles County Hosp., L.A., 1962-63, Oakwood Hosp., Dearborn, Mich., 1963-70; asst. clin. prof. Coll. Medicine Wayne State U., Detroit, 1963-70; assoc. prof. otolaryngology Johns Hopkins U., Balt., 1976—. Mem. coun. Med. Sch. Johns Hopkins U., 1981-85. Contbr. articles to med. publs.; patentee air stimulator, biphasic vestibular test method. Capt. U.S. Army, 1957-59, Germany. Rsch. grantee NIH, 1966-92, USPHS, NIMH, Neurosensory Interdisciplinary Rsch. Program, Schering Corp., Lilly Corp. Mem. Assn. for Rsch. in Otolaryngology, Am. Neurotology Soc., Am. Otologic Soc., Barany Soc., Triological Soc. Unitarian Universalist. Avocations: tennis, golf. Office: 1212 York Rd Bldg C Rm 202 Lutherville MD 21093-6240

PROCTOR, RICHARD J. geologist, consultant; b. L.A., Aug. 2, 1931; s. George Arthur and Margaret Y. (Goodman) P.; m. Ena McLaren, Feb. 12, 1955; children: Mitchell, Jill, Randall. BA, Calif. State U., L.A., 1954; MA, UCLA, 1958. Engring. geologist, Calif.; cert. profl. geologist Am. Inst. Profl. Geologists. Chief geologist Met. Water Dist., L.A., 1958-80; pres., cons. geologist Richard J. Proctor, Inc., Arcadia, Calif., 1980-95. Vis. assoc. prof. Calif. Inst. Tech., Pasadena, 1975-78. Co-author: Citizens Guide to Geologic Hazards, 1993; editor: Professional Practice Guidelines, 1985, Engineering Geology Practice in Southern California, 1992. Pres., dir. Arcadia Hist. Soc., 1993-96. Fellow Geol. Soc. Am. (Burwell Meml. award 1972); mem. Assn. Engring. Geologists (pres. 1979), Am. Inst. Profl. Geologists (pres. 1989, Van Couvering Meml. award 1990, hon. mem. 1992), Am. Geol. Inst. (sec.-treas. 1979-83).

PROCTOR, RICHARD JEROME, JR. business educator, accountant, expert witness; b. N.Y.C., Oct. 6, 1941; s. Richard Jerome and Edith (Decker) P.; m. Elfriede N. Neundorfer, Aug. 19, 1967; children: Courtney, John, David. BS, Columbia U., 1963, MBA, 1970. CPA, N.Y., Conn.; cert. valuation analyst, cert. govt. fin. mgr.; diplomate Am. Bd. Forensic Acctg. Sr. acct. Arthur Andersen, N.Y.C., 1970-72; dir. acctg. N.Y. Stock Exchange, 1972-75; chief fin. officer Executrans, Greenwich, Conn., 1975-77; dir. planning Irvin Industries, Stamford, 1977-79; asst. prof. acctg. and taxation U. Hartford (Conn.), 1979-82; prof. and dept. chairperson Ancell Sch. Bus. Western Conn. State U., Danbury, 1983—. Pvt. practice, 1979—; cons., expert witness in field. Mem. AICPA, Conn. Soc. CPAs (Disting. Authors award 1983, 92), Nat. Assn. Cert. Valuation Analysts, Inst. Bus. Appraisers, Am. Acctg. Assn., Inst. Mgmt. Accts., Am. Bd. Forensic Acctg. (diplomate). Home: 31 Cooper Hill Rd Ridgefield CT 06877-5903 Office: Western Conn State U 181 White St Danbury CT 06810-6826

PROCTOR, RICHARD MACFARLANE, art educator, artist, writer, gallery owner; b. Detroit, Feb. 27, 1936; s. Edgar Elmer and Kathryn Isobel (Macfarlane) P. Student, Henry Ford Community Coll., 1954-55; BS in Art Edn., Mich. State U., 1959, MA in Painting, 1962. Teaching credential K-12. Art tchr. Dearborn (Mich.) Pub. Schs., 1959-60; teaching asst. Mich. State U., East Lansing, 1960-61, acting instr., 1961-62; instr. U. Wash., Seattle, 1962-64, asst. prof., 1964-69, assoc. prof., 1970-92, assoc. prof. emeritus, 1992—. Co-owner, gallery dir., design cons. Childers/Proctor Gallery, Langley, Wash., 1983—. Author: Principles of Pattern for Craftsmen and Designers, 1969; (with others) Surface Design for Fabric, 1984 (Merit prize for tech. writing 1986), Principles of Pattern Design, 1990. Exhibited in group shows at Mus. of Contemporary Crafts, N.Y.C., Seattle Art Mus., Detroit Art Inst., Henry Art Mus., Kresge Art Ctr., East Lansing, Kerns Gallery, Eugene, Oreg., Contemporary Crafts Gallery, Portland, Seattle U., Northwest Craft Ctr. and Gallery, Wichita (Kansas) Art Assn., Kittredge Gallery, Tacoma, Cornell U., Ithaca, N.Y., Alberta Coll. of Art, Cranbrook Acad. of Art, Wash. State Capitol Mus., Yaw Gallery, Birmingham, Mich., Greenville County Art Mus., S.C., Cerulean Blue Gallery, Seattle, Cheney Cowles Meml. Mus., Spokane, Bellevue Art Mus., Richard White Gallery, Seattle, Childers/Proctor Gallery, Smithsonian Instn. (travelling exhibition); represented in collections Seattle/Tacoma Internat. Airport, Unigard Ins. Group Hdqrs., Rainier Bank, Seattle, Peoples Bank, Bellevue, Safeco Ins. Hdqrs., Seattle Waterfront Banners, 1979. Bd. dirs., founding mem. Island Arts Council, Langley, 1979—, Whidbey AIDS Support Fund; chmn. Design Review Bd. City of Langley, 1985—; mem. Island County AIDS Task Force, 1992—. Mem. AAUP, N.W. Designer Craftsmen (pres. 1968-70), Surface Design Assn. (N.W. reg. rep. 1984-87), N.W. Orchid Soc. (v.p. 1987—). Clubs: Useless Bay Golf and Country (Langley). Democrat. Episcopalian. Avocations: orchid grower, swimmer, diarist. Home: 118 Goodell Ln PO Box 667 Langley WA 98260-0667 Office: U Wash Sch of Art Dm 10 Seattle WA 98195-0001

PROCTOR, RICHARD OWEN, historian, public health administrator, army officer; b. Austin, Tex., Nov. 18, 1935; s. William Owen and Arlene Gertrude (Holdeman) P.; m. Martha June Whitlock, Nov. 19, 1955; children: Tanya Marie, Sheilia Renee, Michael Lee, Terry Glen, Richard Lowell, Roger Owen. BA, Oklahoma City U., 1957; MS, MD, Baylor U. Coll. Medicine, Houston, 1964; MPH and TM, Tulane U., 1970; diploma, U.S. Army War Coll., 1983; MS in History, Tex. A&M U., Commerce, 2001. Diplomate Am. Bd. Pediatrics, Am. Bd. Preventive Medicine. Commd. capt. U.S. Army, 1964, advanced through grades to brig. gen.; instr. Imperial Ethiopian Coll. A&M Arts, Alemaya, 1957-59; dep. comdr. U.S. Army Hosp., Kagnew Station, Ethiopia, 1967-69, U.S. Army Med. Lab., Ft. Sam Houston, Tex., 1973-75; instr. U.S. Army Acad. Health Scis., 1975-77; surgeon U.S. Army VII Corps, Moeringen, Fed. Republic Germany, 1978-81; prof., chmn., comdt. of students Uniformed Svcs. U. of Health Scis., Bethesda, Md., 1981-82; comdr. Raymond Bliss Army Community Hosp., Ft. Huachuca, Ariz., 1983-85; surgeon U.S. Army Tng. and Doctrine Command, Ft. Monroe, Va., 1985-88; comdg. gen. William Beaumont Army Med. Ctr., El Paso, Tex., 1988-91; dir. pub. health Region 6 Tex. Dept. Health, Houston, 1991-96; co-owner, rancher Whispering Oaks, Tex., 1985—; instr. U.S. history Tex. A&M U., Commerce. Cons. WHO/PAHO, Bolivia, 1971; lectr. on medicine, anthropology, theology, history; past adj. or clin. faculty positions Baylor U., Tulane U., U. Tex., Tex. A&M U. Author: (with others) Principles of Pediatrics: Healthcare of the Young, 1978, Current Pediatrics Diagnosis and Treatment, 1978, 80, Primary Pediatric Care, 1987, 3d edit., 1997, Comprehensive Adolescent Health Care, 1992; author multiple articles on viremia with Sabin polio vaccines. Asst. scout master Boy Scouts Am., Bowie, Md., 1971-73; scout committeeman Boy Scouts Am., Moeringen, 1978-81. Decorated D.S.M., Legion of Merit (twice); recipient scholarship Broadhurst Found., Tulsa, 1953-57; rsch. fellow NIH, 1960-61; Tropical Medicine fellow La. State U., 1970. Fellow Am. Acad. Preventive Medicine, Am. Acad. Pediatrics; mem. Nat. Eagle Scout Assn., Tex. State Hist. Soc., Tex. Oral Hist. Soc., Tex. Archaeological Soc., Okla. Hist. Soc., Tex. and S.W. Cattle Raisers Assn. Methodist. Avocations: conservation, living history. Home: RR 4 Box 1193 Paris TX 75462-9708

PROCTOR, ROBERT NEEL, history educator; b. Corpus Christi, Tex., June 25, 1954; s. Norman Neel Proctor and Eugenia K. (Milton) P.; children: Jonathan N. Proctor, Geoffrey R. Schiebinger. BS in Biology, Ind. U., 1976; MA in History of Sci., Harvard U., 1977, PhD History of Sci., 1984. Instr. and teaching fellow biology, history of sci. Harvard U., Cambridge, Mass., 1976-84; Andrew Mellon postdoctoral fellow history of sci. program Stanford (Calif.) U., 1984-86; faculty mem./organizer program in sci., tech. and power Eugene Lang Coll., New Sch. for Social Rsch., N.Y.C., 1986-90; assoc. prof. dept. history Pa. State U., University Park, 1990-93, prof. history, 1993-2000, disting. prof. history, 2000—. Vis. asst. prof. history Va. Poly. Inst. and State U., Blacksburg, summer 1984; vis. lectr. dept. history U. Calif.-Berkeley, Fall 1985. Author: Racial Hygiene: Medicine Under the Nazis, 1988, Value-Free Science? Purity and Power in Modern Knowledge, 1991, Cancer Wars: How Politics Shapes What We Know and Don't Know About Cancer, 1995, The Nazi War on Cancer, 1999. Recipient Disting. Alumni Svc. award Ind. U., 1975, Viseltear prize, 1999; Fulbright grad. scholar, Free U., Berlin, 1980-81; NSF grad. fellow, 1976-79, Charlotte W. Newcombe doctoral dissertation fellow, 1982-83, Andrew Mellon postdoctoral fellow, Stanford U., 1984-86, Ctr. for Advanced Study in the Behavioral Scis. summer fellow, 1986, George A. and Eliza Gardner Howard Found. fellow, 1989-90, Max Planck Inst. for History of Sci. fellow 1999-2000; NEH summer stipend, 1989; grantee ACLS, 1989, Nat. Ctr. Human Genome Rsch, 1992-93; sr. scholar in residence U.S. Holocaust Meml. Mus., 1994. Mem. Am. Acad. Arts and Scis., Phi Beta Kappa. Office: Pa State U Dept History 108 Weaver Bldg University Park PA 16802-5500

PROCTOR, SAMUEL, history educator; b. Jacksonville, Fla., Mar. 29, 1919; s. Jack and Celia (Schneider) P.; m. Bessie Rubin, Sept. 8, 1948; children: Mark Julian, Alan Lowell. BA, U. Fla., 1941, MA, 1942, PhD, 1958. Mem. faculty U. Fla., Gainesville, 1946—, prof. history and social scis., 1963-74, disting. service prof. history, 1974—, Julien C. Yonge prof. Fla. history, 1976—, univ. historian, 1953—, dir. Samuel Proctor Oral History Program, 1968—. Curator History Fla. State Mus.; dir. Doris Duke Southeastern Indian Oral History Program, Ctr. for Study of Fla. History and Humanities. Author: Napoleon Bonaparte Broward, Florida's Fighting Democrat, 1950, Florida Commemorates the Civil War Centennial, 1962, Florida One Hundred Years Ago, 1966, Florida History Preservation Planning, 1971, Gator History: History of the University of Florida, 1986, The University of Florida, 1990, N.B. Broward, 1993; editor, author introduction: Dickison and His Men: Reminiscences of the War in Florida, 1962; series editor: Bicentennial Floridiana Facsimile Series; editor: Eighteenth Century Florida and Its Borderlands, 1975, Eighteenth Century Florida and the Carribean, 1976, Eighteenth Century Florida, Life on the Frontier, 1976, Eighteenth Century Florida and the Revolutionary South, 1977, Eighteenth Century Florida and the Impact of The American Revolution, 1978, Tacachale, Essays on the Indians of Florida and Southeastern Georgia during the Historic Period, Jews of the South; assoc. editor: Fla. Hist. Quar., 1962-64, editor, 1963-93; contbr. articles to profl. jours. Served with U.S. Army, 1943-46. Mem. Fla. Blue Key, Phi Beta Kappa, Tau Epsilon Phi, Pi Kappa Phi, Phi Alpha Theta. Democrat. Jewish. Home: 2235 NW 9th Pl Gainesville FL 32605-5201

PROCTOR, SONDRA GOLDSMITH, musician; b. Kansas City, Kans., Aug. 5, 1942; d. J. Davis and Lucille (Riddle) Goldsmith. BA in Music Edn., Am. U., 1962, MEd in Music Edn., Psychology, 1966. Choral dir. pub. schs., Montgomery County, Md., 1962-79; assoc. condr., organist, pianist, accompanist Paul Hill Chorale & Washington Singers, Washington, 1971-96; adminstr., tchr., condr. Cmty. Arts Program, Bethesda, Md., 1976—; dir., founder Circle Singers, Inc., Washington, 1982—; dir. choral activities, condr. in residence Am. U., 1986-91. Dir. music and arts, organist Westmoreland Congl. United Ch. Christ, Bethesda, Md., 1976—; nat., internat. organ recitalist, instr., 1984—. Mem. Alain Found. (sec.-treas. 1987—), Am. Guild Organists (dean D.C. chpt. 1998-2000), Am. Choral Dirs. Assn. (pres. ea. divsn. 1982-84), D.C. Fedn. Musicians. Avocations: painting, reading, museums. Office: Westmoreland Congl United Ch Christ One Westmoreland Cir Bethesda MD 20816

PROCTOR, WILLIAM LEE, college chancellor; b. Atlanta, Jan. 27, 1933; s. Samuel Cook and Rose Elizabeth (Nottingham) P.; m. Pamela Evans Duke; children: Samuel Matthews (dec.), Priscilla Nottingham. BS, Fla. State U., 1956, MS, 1964, PhD, 1968. Tchr. Seminole County Pub. Schs., Longwood, Fla., 1956-57, 58-62, Orange County Fla. Pub. Schs., Orlando, 1957-58; athletic coach Fla. State U., Tallahassee, 1962-65, asst. dean men, 1965-67, grad. fellow, 1967-68; supt. of schs. Rock Hill (S.C.) Sch. Dist. #3, 1968-69; dean of men U. Ctrl. Fla., Orlando, 1969-71; pres. Flagler Coll., St. Augustine, Fla., 1971-2001, chancellor, 2001—. Cons. on higher edn. policy Heritage Found., Washington, 1983—, Fla. Bd. Edn., 2001—; mem. Commn. on Colls., So. Assn. Colls. and Schs., 1995-2000; dir. Tchr. Edn. Accreditation Coun. Vice-chmn. Fla. Edn. Stds. Commn., 1995-2001; bd. dirs. Penney Retirement Cmty., chmn., 1991—; bd. dirs. Vicar's Landing Retirement Cmty., pres., 1992-95, bd., 1990-96; trustee, chmn. Fla. Sch. for Deaf and Blind, St. Augustine, 1984-2001; mem. adv. coun. Salvation Army, St. Johns County; mem. devel. coun. First Coast Work Force, 1998-2001; active Bus./Higher Edn. Partnership, 2000—; chmn.-elect Communities in Schs., St. Johns County, Fla., 2001—. Recipient Disting. Educator award Fla. State U. Coll. Edn., 1989, Phil Carroll award Soc. for Advancement Mgmt., 1990, Disting. Svc. award Fla. Sch. for Deaf and Blind, 1990, Patrick Henry Medallion patriotic achievement Mil. Order of World Wars, 1991, Stetson S Club Achievement award, 1993, Order of the South So. Acad. Letters, Arts, and Scis., Excellence in Mgmt. award Soc. for Advancement of Mgmt., 2000, Lifetime Edn. Achievement award, 2001, Disting. Svc. award Fla. Assn. Colls. and Univs., 2002; named to Fla. State U. Athletic Hall of Fame, 1988, Order of La Florida, 2001. Mem. Am. Assn. Pres. of Ind. Colls., State Hist. Assn., Ind. Colls. and Univs. of Fla. (legis. chmn. 1974-77, vice chmn. 1976-77, chmn. 1978-79), Rotary (pres. 1978-79, govs. dist. 697 1988-89). Republican. Presbyterian. Avocations: history, jogging, karate. Office: Flagler Coll Office of the Chancellor PO Box 1027 Saint Augustine FL 32085-1027 E-mail: proctorw@flagler.edu.

PROCYSON, MARY G. WALTON, critical care nurse; b. Coatesville, Pa., May 4, 1948; d. Marvin O. and Florence G. (Johnson) W.; m. Michael Procyson, 1991. Diploma in Nursing, Brandywine Hosp. Sch. Nursing, Coatesville, 1970. RN, Pa.; CCRN. Critical care nurse Brandywine Hosp., Coatesville, Pa., 1970-82, Coatesville VA Med. Ctr., 1982-85, 86-87, Wilmington (Del.) VA Med. Ctr., 1985-86, 91—, Chester County Hosp., West Chester, Pa., 1987-91; ind. contractor as critical care nurse, 1994-95. Mem. AACN (cert.). Home: 520 Main St Parkesburg PA 19365-1014

PRODAN, JAMES CHRISTIAN, university administrator; b. Columbus, Ohio, Jan. 4, 1947; s. Nicholas Mackley and Muriel Eileen (Bennett) P.; m. Carol Ann Cochran, Mar. 4, 1994; children: Christopher, Tana. BS, Ohio State U., 1969; MMus, Catholic U. Am., 1972; DMA, Ohio State U., 1976. Musician U.S. Army Band, Washington, 1969-72; asst. prof. U. Akron, Ohio, 1975-79; prof. U. N.C., Greensboro, 1979—. Assoc. dean sch. music U. N.C., 1989—. Bd. dirs. Vol. Ctr., Greensboro, 1989-95, 99—; worship and music com. Christ Luth. Ch., 1988. Mem. Nat. Assn. Schs. Music, Internat. Double Reed Soc. (libr., exec. com.), Nat. Assn. Coll. Wind and Percussion Instrs., Music Educators Nat. Conf., N.C. Music Music Educators Assn., Coll. Music Soc., Music Tchrs. Nat. Assn., Intrnat. Soc. for Music Edn. Republican. Methodist. Home: 5510 Rutledge Dr Greensboro NC 27455-1258 Office: U NC Greensboro Sch Music Box 26167 Greensboro NC 27402 E-mail: j_prodan@uncg.edu.

PRODAN, JOHN, aviation executive; b. Orange, N.J., Nov. 17, 1924; s. Vasile and Cleda Blanche (Neville) P.; m. Ruth Jennie Larson, Dec. 29, 1945; children: Susan Ruth, Robert John, John Vernon, Donald Albert, Karen Ruth, Nancy Ann. BS in Aero. Engring., U. Ill., 1948; MS in Aero. Engring., MS in Instrumentation Engring., U. Mich., 1954; MBA, UCLA, 1980. Registered comml. pilot, cert. flight instr. Commd. 2d lt. USAF, 1943, advanced through grades to lt. col., 1966, squadron commdr. and asst. dep. wing commdr. Vietnam, 1971-72, asst. program dir. and mgr. shuttle program, 1972-74, ret., 1974; research pilot and engr. S.D. Sch. Mines and Tech., Rapid City, 1978-80; chief test pilot, sr. engr. Kohlman Systems Research, Lawrence, Kans., 1982-84; pres., chief engr. AV-CON, Rapid City, 1980—; sr. v.p. Highland Mfg. Inc., 1988-89. Vis. lectr. workshop on Meteorol. and Environ. Inputs to Aviation Systems, 1978-85; adj. prof. Embry-Riddle Aeronautical U., Ellsworth AFB, S.D., 1988—. Contbr. articles and reports to profl. jours. Treas. First Bapt. Ch. Alamogordo, N.Mex., 1958-61, First So. Bapt. Ch., Canoga Park, Calif., 1974-78. Decorated D.F.C., Legion of Merit with one oak leaf cluster, Meritorious Service medal, Air medal with six oak leaf clusters; named Disting. Alumnus, U. Ill., 1980. Mem. Soc. Exptl. Test Pilots (chmn. weather subcom. 1980-84, sect. sec. 1984-85), AIAA, Soc. Automotive Engrs. (flight test com.), Tau Beta Pi, Sigma Tau. Republican. Baptist. Avocations: flying, swimming, golf, restoring old cars. Home and Office: AV-CON 1100 Kings Rd Rapid City SD 57702-7718 E-mail: jprodan@enetis.net.

PROEBSTING, EDWARD LOUIS, JR. retired research horticulturist; b. Woodland, Calif., Mar. 2, 1926; s. Edward Louis and Dorothy (Critzer) P.; m. Patricia Jean Connolly, June 28, 1947; children: William Martin, Patricia Louise, Thomas Alan (dec.). BS, U. Calif., Davis, 1948; PhD, Mich. State U., 1951. Asst. horticulturist Wash. State U., Prosser, 1951-57, assoc. horticulturist, 1957-63, horticulturist, 1963-93, supt. Irrigated Agrl. Rsch. and Ext. Ctr., 1990-93; ret., 1993. Vis. prof. Cornell U., Ithaca, N.Y., 1966; vis. scientist Hokkaido U., Sapporo, Japan, 1978, Victoria Dept. Agr., Tatura, Australia, 1986—. Contbr. numerous articles to profl. jours. Scoutmaster Boy Scouts Am., Prosser, 1963-76, dist. chmn., 1976-78. Served to lt. USNR, 1943-46, 52-54. Recipient Silver Beaver award Boy Scouts Am.; fellow Japan Soc. Promotion Sci., Sapporo, 1978, Res. Bank. Australia, 1986. Fellow AAAS, Am. Soc. Hort. Sci. (pres. 1983-84, sci. editor jour. 1993-98). Methodist. Avocations: backpacking, native plants. Home: 1929 Miller Ave Prosser WA 99350-1532

PROEFROCK, CARL KENNETH, academic medical administrator; b. Curtis, Ill., Mar. 30, 1928; s. Carl Robert and Anna Lorraine (Hagel) Proefrock; m. Margaret Muntz (dec. Apr. 1984); 4 children ; m. Janelle Dillon, Sept. 8, 1988 (dec. Sept. 2001). BA, Carthage Coll., Kenosha, Wis., 1949; MDiv, Chgo. Luth. Theol. Sem., 1953. Sr. com. orgn. specialist N.Y.C. Housing and Devel. Adminstrn., 1966-68; exec. dir. Model Cities Program, Manchester, n.H., 1968-70, Health Assn. Rochester and Monroe (N.Y.), 1970-73, Mahoning Shenango Area Health Edn. Network, Youngstown, Ohio, 1973-78; spl. asst. to dean Northeastern Ohio Univs. Coll. Medicine, Rootstown, 1978-79; v.p. Med. Coll. Ohio, Toledo, 1979-88, sr. v.p. govtl. affairs, 1988-93; pres. KPA Assocs., Inc., 1993—. V.p. Found. for Applied Rsch., Washington, 1976; chmn. adv. bd. Ohio AHEC, Columbus, 1976; program adminstr. Ohio Statewide Area Health Edn. Ctr., Toledo, 1988-93. Mission organizer, 1953-59; sr. pastor, 1960-65; mem. budget allocation com. United Appeal, Youngstown, 1975-78; mem. dist. planning coun. Ohio Dept. Mental Health, Youngstown, 1977-78; chmn. Toledo Area Coun. Tech., 1986; spl. asst. to clergy All Saints Parish, Pawleys Island, S.C., 1998-2000. Mem. Nat. Area Health Edn. Ctrs. Assn. (bd. dirs. 1988-95), Nat. Assn. Univ. Rsch. Adminstrs., Soc. Rsch. Adminstrs., Internat. Assn. Univ. Rsch. Parks, Soc. Univ. Patent Adminstrs., Nat. Assn. Health Manpower Edn. Systems, Northeastern Ohio Med. Educators Assn. (bd. dirs.), Rotary. Episcopalian. Home: 189 Rose Hill Dr Pawleys Island SC 29585-7254 Office: KPA Assocs PO Box 194 Pawleys Island SC 29585-0194 E-mail: kenkpa@webtv.net.

PROEHL, GERALD T. pharmaceutical executive; Grad., SUNY; MA in Exercise Physiology, Wake Forest U.; MBA, Rockhurst Coll., Kansas City, Mo. From product mgr. to v.p. Hoechst Marion Roussel, Inc.; v.p. mktg. and bus. devel. Santarus, Inc., San Diego, 1999—2000, pres., COO, 2000—02, CEO, 2002—. Office: Santarus Inc 10590 W Ocean Air Dr San Diego CA 92130*

PROENZA, LUIS M. academic administrator, biology educator; b. Mexico City, Dec. 22, 1944; s. Luis and Sara Maria (Gonzalez) P.; m. Theresa Anne Butler, July 2, 1983. BA in Psychology, Emory U., 1965; MA in Psychology, Ohio State U., 1966; PhD in Neurobiology, U. Minn., 1971. Prof., dir. vision rsch. lab. U. Ga., Athens, 1971-87, asst. to pres., 1984-86, univ. liaison for sci. and tech. policy, 1986-87; study dir. NAS Com. on Vision, Washington, 1977-79; vice chancellor rsch., dean grad. sch., prof. biology U. Alaska, Fairbanks, 1987-92, acting v.p. acad. affairs and rsch., 1992-94; v.p. rsch., dean grad. sch., prof. biol. scis. Purdue U., W. Lafayette, Ind., 1994-98; pres., prof. biology U. Akron, Ohio, 1999—. Vice chmn., commr. U.S. Arctic Rsch. Commn. 1992-96, adv. bd., 1990-92, 97-98, chmn. exec. resources bd., 1994; pres. Arctic Rsch. Consortium U.S., 1988-90, past pres., 1991-92; mem. Nat. Biotech. Policy Bd., NIH, 1990; mem. vision com. NRC, NAS, 1979-82, study dir. 1977-79; advisor to gov. sci. and tech. policy State of Alaska, 1991-94; acad. adminstrn. fellow Am. Coun. Edn., 1983-84; rsch. fellow neuropsychology lab. U. Minn. Med. Sch., 1968-71; cons. rsch. assoc. dept. neurology and physiology U. Utah, 1972; sr. rsch. fellow IC2 Inst. U. Tex., 1998—; vis. asst. prof. neurosensory lab. SUNY, Buffalo, 1972; asst. prof. psychology U. Ams., Mex., 1967-68; dep. dir. Russian-Am. Sci. Ctr., ARKTIKA, Magadan, 1990-94; mem. exec. mgmt. com. Am. Polar Svcs., 1989-94; cons. in field. Co-editor: (with J.M. Enoch and A. Jampolski) Clinical Applications of Visual Psychophysics, 1981, (with J.E. Dowling and C. Atwell) Nutrition, Pharmacology and Vision, 1982; contbr. articles and abstracts to profl. jours. including Psychonomic Sci., Physiology and Behavior, Vision Rsch., Jour. Gen. Physiology, many others; spkr. in field; reviewer numerous jours. Mem. exec. com. Akron Regional Devel. Bd., 1999—, Nat. Assn. State Univs. and Lang-Grant Colls. Commn. on Urban Agenda, 1999—; mem. steering com. Clusters of Innovation, 1999—, Coun. on Competitiveness, 1999—; mem. adv. coun. Emory U. Grad. Sch. Arts and Scis., 1995-98, Lafayette Ctr. Med. Edn., 1998; mem. Greater Fairbanks C. of C., 1987-94; mem. Commonwealth North, Anchorage, 1987-94; mem. exec. com. Assn. Grad. Schs., Assn. Am. Univs., 197-98, nominating com., 1995; trustee Akron Tomorrow, 1999—; bd. trustees Northeastern Ohio Univs. Coll. Medicine, 1999—, Akron Civic Theatre; bd. dirs. Akron Roundtable, 1999—, Akron/Summit County and Visitors Bur., Inter-Univ. Coun. Pres., Inventure Pl., N.E. Ohio Coun. Higher Edn., Northeastern Ednl. TV Ohio, Inc., Fairbanks Indsl. Devel. Corp., 1988-94, Greater Lafayette Progress, 1995-98, exec. com.; bd. visitors Air U., 1999—. Grantee Nat. Eye Inst., 1973-76, 76-81, 81-86, 86-91, State of Alaska, 1989, NIH, 1989-90, 90-91, 91-92, Alfred P. Sloan Found., 1995-98, U. S. Army Corp. Engrs., 1992-97, NSF, 1988-93, U.S. Dept. Edn., 1995-96; fellow Ohio State U., 1965-66; recipient Rsch. Career Devel. award Nat. Eye Inst., 1976-83, commendation Alaska State Legislature, 1992, Richard M. Griffith Meml. award So. Soc. for Philosophy and Psychology, 1976. Mem. Nat. Coaliton for Advanced Mfg. (bd. dirs. 1999—), Union Club (Cleve.), City Club (Cleve.), Rotary, Golden Key, Phi Beta Delta, Sigma Xi. Avocation: sailing Apogee (44 ft. sailing vessel built by Dr. Proenza and his wife) around Great Lakes region and East Coast of U.S. Home: 465 Burning Tree Dr Akron OH 44303 Office: U Akron Buchtel Hall Akron OH 44325-4702 Fax: 330-972-8652. E-mail: proenza@uakron.edu.

PROFAIZER, JOSEPHINE E. elementary education educator; b. Rock Springs, Wyo., Sept. 2, 1951; d. Joseph and Enrica (Filippi) P. BS, U. Wyo., 1973; MEd, Utah State U., 1983. Cert. tchr., Wyo. Tchr. 3d grade Sweetwater Sch. Dist. 1, Rock Springs, 1973-79, tchr. kindergarten, 1980, tchr. 2d grade, 1980-89, tchr. Title 1 reading and math., 1989—. Bd. dirs. Internat. Tirolean Trentino Orgns. N.Am., 1991-95. Recipient Outstanding Young Educator award Rock Springs Jaycees, 1980. Mem. NEA, Wyo. Edn. Assn., Sweetwater Edn. Assn. (Tchr. of Yr. 1994-95), Tyrloean Trentini Wyo. (sec. 1986-91, newsletter editor 1989-92, 94-99, pres. 1991-95, v.p. 1999—), Delta Kappa Gamma (sec. 1982-84, v.p. 1990-92, treas. 1994-98), Beta Sigma Phi (sec. 1990-91, v.p. 1993-94, pres. 1996-98, treas. 1999—). Roman Catholic. Avocations: travel, reading, collecting Hummel and Anri figurines, gardening.

PROFETA, SALVATORE, JR. chemist; b. Phila., May 1, 1951; m. Catherine Mary Cherry, Sept. 20, 1980; children: Luisa, Theresa. BA, Temple U., 1973; PhD, U. Ga., 1978. Fellow chemistry dept. Fla. State U., Tallahassee, 1979-80; fellow pharm. chemistry dept. U. Calif., San Francisco, 1980-81, teaching fellow, 1981-82; instr. chemistry dept. La. State U., Baton Rouge, 1982-84; sr. scientist Allergan Pharms., Inc., Irvine, Calif., 1984-87; project mgr. computational chemistry Glaxo Rsch. Inst., Research Triangle Park, N.C., 1987-90, head chemistry systems, 1990-93; dir. N.C. Supercomputing Ctr. Rsch. Inst. at MCNC, 1993-95; prin. computational chemist Monsanto, St. Louis, 1996-2000; dir. computational chemistry and structural biology Millennium Pharm., Cambridge, Mass., 2000—02. Cons. CADD-CAMM Smith, Kline & French, Phila., 1980-82, Squibb Rsch. Inst., Princeton, N.J., 1982-84; allocation com. N.C. Supercomputing Ctr., 1989-94. Mem. editl. bd. Jour. Molecular Graphics, 1989-2000; contbg. editor Chem. Design Automation News, 1991-2000; contbr. articles to Jour. Am. Chem. Soc. NSF fellow, 1976-78; Petroleum Rsch. Found. grantee, 1984-88. Fellow N.Y. Acad. Scis.; mem. Am. Chem. Soc. Achievements include patents in anticancer drug design; co-author MM1, MM2, MM3 and AMBER molecular mechanical force fields. E-mail: sprofetajr@netscape.net.

PROFFIT, WILLIAM ROBERT, orthodontics educator; b. Harnett County, N.C., Apr. 19, 1936; s. Glenn Theodore and Edna Marie (Queener) P.; m. Sara Thomas, Sept. 20, 1953; children: Lola Ann, Edward Thomas, Glenn Theodore. BS, U. N.C., 1956, DDS, 1959; student, Campbell Coll., Buies Creek, N.C., 1952-53; PhD, Med. Coll. Va., 1962; MS, U. Wash., 1963; FDS, Royal Coll. Surgeons, 1990. Am. Bd. Orthodontics. Investigator Nat. Inst. Dental Research, Bethesda, Md., 1963-65; asst. prof. orthodontics U. Ky., Lexington, 1965-68, assoc. prof., 1968-71; prof. U.Ky., 1971-73; prof. orthodontics U. Fla., Gainesville, 1973-75; prof., chmn. dept. orthodontics U. N.C., Chapel Hill, 1975—, Kenan prof., 1992. Cons. NIH, Bethesda, 1974, 76— Author: Contemporary Orthodontics, 1986, 3d edit., 2000; co-author: Surgical Correction of Dentofacial Deformity, 1980, Surgical-Orthodontic Treatment, 1990, Contemporary Trreatment of Dentofacial Deformity, 2003; contbr. articles to sci. jours. Served to lt. comdr. USPHS, 1963-65. Fulbright research scholar U. Adelaide, Australia, 1972 Mem. Am. Assn. Orthodontists (council on research 1970-76), ADA, Internat. Assn. Dental Research, Phi Beta Kappa Democrat. Presbyterian. Home: 620 Rock Creek Rd Chapel Hill NC 27514-6716 Office: U NC Sch Dentistry Dept Orthodontics Chapel Hill NC 27599-7450 E-mail: william_proffit@dentistry.unc.edu.

PROFFITT, JOHN RICHARD, business executive, educator; b. Grand Junction, Colo., Sept. 12, 1930; s. Hillus D. and Joy Elaine (Lindsay) P.; m. Claire Boyer Miller, May 8, 1965 (div. 1992); children: Cameron Lindsay, William Boyer. BA in Edn., U. Ky., 1953, MA in Polit. Sci., 1961; postgrad., U. Mich., 1959-65. Asst. dean of men, instr. polit. sci. dept. U. Ky., Lexington, 1957-59; teaching fellow U. Mich., Ann Arbor, 1961-63, 63-65; asst. dir. Nat. Commn. on Accrediting, Washington, 1966-68; dir. accreditation and eligibility staff U.S. Dept. HEW, 1968-75; dir. divsn. eligibility and agy. evaluation U.S. Dept. Edn., 1975-80, dir. divsn. instnl. and state incentive programs, 1980-82; pres. The Clairion Corp., Bethesda, Md., 1982-84, Nat. Asbestos Removal, Inc., Beltsville, 1985-90, Commonwealth Environ. Svcs., Inc., Alexandria, Va., 1987-91, also chmn. bd. dirs.; chmn. Internat. Environ. Engrs., Inc., 1991-92; pres. Canterbury Internat., Vienna, 1992-95; cons., 1995-99; v.p. E-Pass Techs., Inc., McLean, Va., 1999—. Cons. Conn. State Commn. Higher Edn., Hartford, 1967, Am. Coun. Edn., Washington, 1970; cons. U.S. Dept. Hew, 1967, 68; mem. study steering com. Am. Vocat. Assn., Washington, 1968; exec. sec. Nat. Adv. Com. on Accreditation and Instnl. Eligibility, Washington, 1968-80; mem. gen. com. Nat. Study Sch. evaluation, Alexandria, 1970-78; mem. task force Edn. Commn. of the States, Denver, 1972; subcom. chmn. Fed. Interagy. Com. on Edn., Washington, 1974-76; lectr., presenter profl. confs. Co-author: Accreditation and Certification in Relation to Allied Health Manpower, 1971; contbg. author: Health Manpower: Adapting in the Seventies, 1971, Accreditation in Teacher Education, 1975, Transferring Experiential Credit, 1979; contbr. articles to profl. and govtl. agy. publs., 1968-79. V.p., bd. dirs. Nat. Accreditation Coun. for Agys. Serving the Blind, N.Y.C., 1985; pres., chmn. bd. dirs. Found. for Advancement of Quality Svcs. for the Blind, Alexandria, 1988. 1st lt. USAF, 1953-55, Japan and Korea. Higher edn. fellow Univ. Mich., 1959. Mem. Optimist Club (Lexington, Ky.), Club Internat. (Chgo.), Island Club (Hobe Sound, Fla.), Thoroughbred Club Am. (Lexington), Tower Club (Vienna, Va.), Sigma Nu. Democrat. Episcopalian. Avocations: conservation, animal welfare, travel, antiques, art. Home: 515 Beall Ave Rockville MD 20850-2106 E-mail: John.Proffitt@e-pass.com.

PROFFITT, KEVIN, archivist; b. Hamilton, Ohio, Dec. 24, 1956; s. Henry C. and Marjorie O. (Elam) P.; m. Joan Moriarity, May 17, 1986. BA, Miami U., Oxford, Ohio, 1979; MA, Wright State U., 1980; MLS, U. Ky., 1998. Archivist Am. Jewish Archives, Cin., 1981—. Contbr. articles to profl. jours. Mem. Soc. Am. Archivists, Acad. Cert. Archivists (cert.), Midwest Archives Conf., Soc. Ohio Archivists (pres. 1987-89). Office: Am Jewish Archives 3101 Clifton Ave Cincinnati OH 45220-2404

PROFFITT, WALDO, JR. newspaper editor; b. Plainview, Tex., Oct. 8, 1924; s. Waldo and Susan Ann (Smith) P.; m. Marjorie Baltzegar, Sept. 14, 1946 (div. 1963); children: Ann Herbert, Deborah, Geoffrey Harrison, Laurence Scott; m. Anne Collier Greene, Feb. 6, 1966; 1 child, Robert Waldo. BA cum laude, Harvard U., 1948. Reporter Bangor (Maine) Commercial, 1948-50; assoc. dir. Harvard News Office, Cambridge, Mass., 1952-54; city editor Charlotte (N.C.) News, 1954-58; mng. editor Journal, Lorain, Ohio, 1958-61; editorial dir. Sarasota (Fla.) Herald-Tribune, 1961-84; editor, 1984-98; columnist Sarasota-Herald Tribune, 1998—. Lt. U.S. Army, 1943-46, ETO, lt. USAF, 1950-52. Mem. Am. Soc. Newspaper Editors, Fla. Soc. Newspaper Editors (pres. 1978). Democrat. Unitarian Universalist. Home: 1581 Hillview Dr Sarasota FL 34239-2047 Office: Sarasota Herald-Tribune PO Box 1719 Sarasota FL 34230-1719

PROFICE, ROSENA MAYBERRY, elementary school educator; b. Natchez, Miss., Oct. 8, 1953; d. Alex Jr. and Louise V. (Fuller) Mayberry; m. Willie Lee Profice, Feb. 12, 1977; children: Jamie Martez, Alesha Shermille. BS in History, Jackson State U., 1974, MS in Elem. Edn., 1975, Edn. Splty. in Elem. Edn., 1977. Cert. elem. reading and social studies tchr., Miss. Tchr. reading Ackerman (Miss.) H.S., 1975-76, North Hazlehurst (Miss.) Elem. Sch., 1976-79; tchr. reading and elem. edn. Natchez-Adams Sch. Sys., Natchez, 1979—. Mem. NEA, Miss. Assn. Educators, Nat. Alliance Black Sch. Educators, Natchez Assn. for the Preservation of Afro-Am. Culture, Linwood Circle Ruritan Club (bd. dirs. 1992-93, sec. 1994-95), Zion Hill #1 Bapt. Ch. Democrat. Baptist. Avocations: reading, travel, shopping. Home: 11 Elbow Ln Natchez MS 39120-5346 E-mail: rprofice@edmail.com.

PROFILET, STEPHEN BONNER, engineer; b. Cairo, U.S., Dec. 26, 1926; s. Louis Emile and Julia Greenwell (Twyman) P.; m. Doris Anne Wallace, May 6, 1950; children: Theresa, Stephen, Cynthia. BEE, Cornell U., 1949; BCE, Rensselaer Polytechnic Inst., 1954. Registered profl. engr., N.Y., Md. Pub. works officer Civil Engr. Corps USN, Kodiak, Alaska, 1949-51, contract adminstrn. officer Moffett Field, Calif., 1951-53; asst. pub. works officer Clarksville (Tenn.) Ordnance Base, 1954-56; asst. res. officer in charge of constrn. USAF Base, Zaragoza, Spain, 1957-58; asst. pub. works officer Naval Air Sta., Pensacola, Fla., 1958-61, USMC Base, Camp Lejeune, N.C., 1961-64; staff officer hdqtrs. USN, Washington, 1964-67, ret., 1967; sr. engr. Washington Suburban Sanitary Commn., Hyattsville, Md., 1967-69, various positions to chief engr. Laurel, 1969-92, ret. Cons., Ft. Washington, Md., 1992—. Mem. ASCE (life), Am. Water Works Assn., KC (life). Republican. Roman Catholic. Achievements include supervision of a one billion dollar water/sewer program for Washington Suburban Sanitary Commission. E-mail: sprofilet@erols.com.

PROKASY, WILLIAM FREDERICK, academic administrator; b. Cleve., Nov. 27, 1930; s. William Frederick and Margaret Lovinia (Chapman) P.; m. Pamela Pearson; children: Kathi Lynn, Cheryl Anne; stepchildrenm: Lisa Wier, Kevin Wier. BA, Baldwin-Wallace Coll., 1952; MA, Kent State U., 1954; PhD, U. Wis., 1957. Grad. asst. Kent State U., 1953-54; W.A.R.F. fellow U. Wis., 1954-55, teaching asst., 1955-57; asst. prof., then asso. prof. Pa. State U., 1957-66; prof. psychology, chmn. dept. U. Utah, 1966-69, Disting. rsch. prof., 1971-72, dean social and behavioral sci., 1968-70; dean U. Utah (Coll. Social and Behavioral Sci.), 1970-79; acting dean U. Utah (Grad. Sch. Social Work), 1979-80; prof. psychology dean Coll. Liberal Arts and Scis., U. Ill., Champaign-Urbana, 1980-88; prof., v.p. for acad. affairs U. Ga., 1988-98. Cons. in field. Editor: Classical Conditioning, 1965, (with A.H. Black) Classical Conditioning II, 1971, (with D. Raskin) Electrodermal Responding in Psychological Research, 1973, Psychophysiology, 1974-77; editor (with I. Gormezano and R. Thompson) Classical Conditioning III, 1986; assoc. editor Learning and Motivation, 1969-76; cons. editor Jour. Exptl. Psychology, 1968-80. Trustee Utah Planned Parenthood Assn., 1977—80; Utah bd. dirs. ACLU, 1978—80; v.p., bd. dirs. Champaign-Urbana Symphony, 1986—88; mem. bd. advisors Ga. Mus. of Art, 1989—, U. Ga. Performing Arts Ctr., 1998—; mem. bd. visitors U. Ga. Librs., 1998—; treas. Friends Ga. Mus. Art, 2000—, v.p., 2001—; mem. Athens-Clarke County Libr. Bd., 1999—; treas. Athena Opera Co., 2001—; pres. Friends Ga. Mus. Art, 2002; Del. Utah Dem. Conv., 1968—70, 1972—74; bd. dirs. Friends Ga. Mus. Art, 1999—. Recipient Alumni Merit award Baldwin Wallace Coll., 1992, Disting. Alumni award Piedmont Coll., 1998, U. Ga. Alumni award of excellence, 1998; NSF sr. postdoctoral fellow, 1963-64. Fellow AAAS, Am. Psychol. Assn. (chmn. bd. sci. affairs 1977-78, coun. of reps. 1980-86, bd. dirs. 1983-86, bd. ednl. affairs 1993-96); mem. Fedn. Behavioral, Pyschol. and Cognitive Scis. (v.p. 1984-85, pres. 1985-87), coun. of Sci. Soc. Pres.'s (exec. bd. 1987-91, chmn.

1990), Psychonomic Soc., Coun. Rsch. Librs. (bd. dirs. 1990-96), NASULGC (exec. com. coun. on acad. affairs 1995-96), Am. Assn. Higher Edn., Soc. Psychophysiol. Rsch. (bd. dirs. 1978-84, pres. 1982-83), Utah Psychol. Assn. (exec. bd. 1968-70, pres. 1971-72), Assn. Advancement Psychology (bd. dirs. 1982-83), Sigma Xi (pres. U. Utah chpt. 1972-73), Phi Kappa Phi. E-mail: wprokasy@arches.uga.edu.

PROKOPIS, EMMANUEL CHARLES, computer company executive; b. Peabody, Mass., July 5, 1942; s. Charles Emmanuel and Stevia (Kassotis) P.; m. Mary Catherine Dudeck, Dec. 6, 1969; children: Peter Matthew, Christina Eve. BBA, U. Mass., 1966. Mgr., pricing, budgeting, acctg. The Mitre Corp., Mass., Va., 1969-74; mgr. contracts liaison Pratt & Whitney Aircraft, Conn., Fla., 1974-78; mgr. fin. planning, corp. office United Techs. Corp., Hartford, Conn., 1978-81, contr. magnet wire and insulation div. Fort Wayne, Ind., 1981-83, v.p. fin., chief fin. officer The Mostek Corp. (subs.) Carrollton, Tex., 1983-85; sr. v.p. fin. and ops., chief fin. officer The Lotus Devel. Corp., Cambridge, Mass., 1985-87, fin. mgr. mfg. and engring., 1987-91; v.p. budgeting Digital Equipment Corp., 1991-92; exec. v.p. MAST Industries, 1992, Ziff Comm., 1992-93; v.p. corp. contr. Digital Equipment Corp., 1994-96; COO, CFO, treas. IONA Technologies, Cambridge, 1996-97, COO, 1997-99. 1st lt. U.S. Army, 1966-69, Vietnam. Decorated Bronze Star. Greek Orthodox.

PROKOPY, JOHN ALFRED, government consultant; b. Phila., May 23, 1926; s. John A. and Mary Genevieve (Frushour) Prokopy. Diploma, Bentley Coll. (formerly, Bentley Sch. Acctg. and Fin.), 1950; BBA, Northeastern U., Boston, 1956. Chief acct. gen. contractors, Boston, 1950-56; contr. Peters & Co., Inc., 1956-61; purchasing sys. analyst Dept. Def., 1961-90, termination contracting officer, 1990-94; ret., 1994. Bd. dirs., past pres. Fed. Credit Union, Boston, 1971—78; lectr. to profl. assns., 1975—; govt. cons. in contract adminstrn., terminations, mediation and arbitration, 1988—. Contbr. articles to profl. jours. Fellow: Am. Arbitration Assn. (mediator, arbitrator 1992—), Nat. Contract Mgmt. Assn. (cert. profl. contract mgr.). Home: 5 School St Apt 3 Salem MA 01970-2306

PROKURAT, MICHAEL, theology studies educator, minister; b. Detroit, Feb. 8, 1950; s. Michael Alexis and Mary Catherine Prokurat; m. Margaret L. Gogol, Aug. 8, 1970; children: Natalie Kaiser, Melanie Gogol-Prokurat, Tatiana Moody. BA, U. Mich., 1970; MDiv, St. Vladimir Orthodox Theol. Sem., Crestwood, N.Y., 1973; PhD, Grad. Theol. Union, Berkeley, Calif., 1988. Ordained deacon Orthodox Ch. Am., 1973, ordained priest Orthodox Ch. Am., 1974. Lectr. Pacific Luth. Theol. Sem., Berkeley, 1977-83; lectr. Late Vocations Program Orthodox Ch. Am., San Francisco, 1980-83, dir. Late Vocations Program, 1988-91; lectr. U. Calif., Berkeley, 1989-90, Dominican Coll., San Rafael, 1991; mem. adj. faculty Pacific Luth. Theol. Sem., Berkeley, 1991-94; assoc. prof. sacred scripture U. St. Thomas, Houston, 1994—. Pastor St. Michael Ch., Concord, Calif., 1974—83, St. Nicholas Ch., San Anselmo, Calif., 1989—94; organizer Orthodox Inst., Berkeley, 1980—83; chancellor Diocese Midwest Orthodox Ch. Am., Chgo., 1983—86; vis. scholar in religion U. Houston, 1996—97. Author, translator: book On the Edge of the World, 1992; co-author: Historical Dictionary of the Orthodox Ch., 1996, (book) Bible in the Churches, 1998; editor: Parish Bylaws, 1985; contbg. author: Encyclopedia of Monasticism, 2000, contbg. author: book Interpreting Together, 2001. Rep. World Coun. Chs., Geneva, 1987, 1997, Nat. Coun. Chs., Chgo., 1986; trustee Orthodox Inst., Berkeley, 1980—83; mem. com. Scoba Transl. Com., Brookline, Mass., 1994—96. Decorated Gold Cross Holy Synod Orthodox Ch. Am., Patriarchal Cross Patriarch Alexis Russia, Berkeley; named Lilly lectr., Eli Lilly Endowment, St. Vladimir Sem., N.Y., 1992; recipient cert., Holy Land Seminar, Jerusalem, 1978. Mem.: Soc. Bibl. Lit., Cath. Theol. Soc. Am., Cath. Bibl. Assn. Am., Am. Schs. Orietnal Rsch., Am. Acad. Religion. Avocations: fishing, hiking, boating, camping. Office: U St Thomas Sch Theology 9845 Memorial Dr Houston TX 77024-3407 E-mail: prokurat@stthom.edu., prokurat@msn.com.

PROM, STEPHEN GEORGE, lawyer; b. Jacksonville, Fla., July 8, 1954; s. George W. and Bonnie M. (Porter) P.; divorced; children: Ashley Brooke, Aaron Jacob, Adam Glenn; m. Charlotte Rutter. AA in Polit. Sci. with high honors, Fla. Jr. Coll., 1974; BA in Polit. Sci. with high honors, U. Fla., 1977, JD with honors, 1979. Bar: Fla. 1980, U.S. Dist. Ct. (mid. dist.) Fla. 1980, U.S. Dist. Ct. (no. dist.) Fla. 1981, U.S. Tax Ct. 1982, U.S. Ct. Appeals (11th cir.) 1985, U.S. Supreme Ct. 1985. Assoc. Rogers, Towers, Bailey, Jones & Gay, Jacksonville, 1979-83, Foley & Lardner, Jacksonville, 1983-86; ptnr. Christian & Prom, 1986-87, Prom, Korn & Zehmer, P.A., Jacksonville, 1987-95, Brant, Moore, MacDonald & Wells, P.A., 1995-2001, Akerman, Senterfitt & Eidson, P.A., 2001—. Sr. mgmt. editor U. Fla. Law Rev., 1978-79. Mem. Leadership Jacksonville, 1984, Jacksonville Cmty. Coun. Inc., 1985-86; bd. dirs. Mental Health Resource Ctr., Jacksonville, 1984-87, Mental Health Resource Foun., Jacksonville, 1985-87, Mental Health Found., Inc., 1987-89, mem. cmty. bd., 1989-91; bd. dirs. Youth Crisis Ctr., Jacksonville, 1984-86, Young Profls. Bd. Multiple Sclerosis Soc., 1988-89; bd. dirs. The Team, Inc., 1992-94; vol. Jacksonville, Inc., 1993-96, Jacksonville Found., Inc., 1993-96, Positively Jacksonville!, Inc., 1993-95, We Care of Jacksonville, Inc., 2002—. Mem. ABA (tax, health law sects.), Fla. Bar Assn. (tax, health law sect., bd. govs. young lawyers sect. 1983-87), Jacksonville Bar Assn. (chmn. health law sect.), Am. Acad. Healthcare Attys., Am. Hosp. Assn., Nat. Health Lawyers Assn., Fla. Acad. Healthcare Attys. (bd. dirs. 1994-97), Jacksonville Sailing Found., Inc. (bd. dirs. 1997—), N.E. Fla. Sailboat Rating Assn., Inc. (bd. dirs. 1997-98, chair 1998), Epping Forest Yacht Club (bd. govs., vice commodore), Ponte Vedra Club, North Fla. Cruising Club, Phi Beta Kappa, Phi Theta Kappa, Phi Kappa Phi. Republican. Baptist. Avocations: sailing, surfing, weightlifting, tennis, jogging. Office: Akerman Senterfitt & Eldson PA 50 N Laura St Ste 2500 Jacksonville FL 32202 E-mail: sprom@akerman.com.

PROMINSKI, EILEEN ALICE, school nurse, educator; b. Winona, Minn., Oct. 11, 1938; d. Donald W. and Florence (Berzinski) Anderson; m. James Prominski, Sept. 22, 1962; children: Geneane, Maria Lynn. BSN, Coll. Saint Teresa, 1960; postgrad., U. Ill., Champaign, 1982-83, Northern Ill. U., 1969-70, 82, DePaul U., 1968-69; MEd, Nat. Coll. Edn., 1983; postgrad., St. Xavier Coll., Chgo., 1992, Nat. Louis U., 1995, No. Ill. U., 1995, Aurora U., 1996, Triton Coll., 1997. RN, Ill., Minn., Iowa; cert. sch. nurse, Ill.; tchr., Ill.; cert. instr. emergency med. svcs. for children. Nursing instr. Mercy Hosp. Sch. Nursing, Cedar Rapids, Iowa, 1960-61; nurse ob-gyn. St. Mary's Hosp., Duluth, Minn., 1961-62; nursing instr. West Suburban Hosp. Sch. Nursing, Oak Park, Ill., 1963-65; health educator Proviso West High Sch., Hillside, 1965-73; tchr. nursery sch. TreeView Sch., 1980-82; sch. nurse Dist. #41, Glen Ellyn, Ill., 1982—. P.E.P. grantee, 1995. Mem. Glen Ellyn Edn. Assn., Coun. of Cath. Women (pres. 1986-87, 87-88, v.p. 1982-83, 85-86).

PROMISEL, NATHAN E. materials scientist, metallurgical engineer; b. Malden, Mass., June 20, 1908; s. Solomon and Lyna (Samwick) P.; m. Evelyn Sarah Davidoff, May 17, 1931; children: David Mark, Larry Jay. BS, M.I.T., 1929, MS, 1930; postgrad., Yale U., 1932-33; D.Engring. (hon.), Mich. Tech. U., 1978. Asst. dir. lab. Internat. Silver Co. Meriden, Conn., 1930-40; chief materials scientist and engr. Navy Dept., Washington, 1940-66; exec. dir. nat. materials adv. bd. Nat. Acad. Scis., 1966-74; cons. on materials and policy, internationally, 1974—. Mem., chmn. NATO Aerospace Panel, 1959-71; U.S. rep. (materials) OECD, 1967-70; U.S. chmn. U.S./USSR Sci. Exch. Program (materials), 1973-77); hon. guest USSR Acad. Scis.; permanent hon. pres. Internat. Conf. Materials Behavior; mem. Nat. Materials Adv. Bd.; adv. com. Oak Ridge Nat. Lab., Lehigh U., U. Pa., U.S. Navy Dept. Labs., U.S. Congress Office Tech. Assessment. Contbr. 65 articles to profl. publs.; contbr., editor: Advances in Materials Research, 1963, Science and Technology of Refractory Metals, 1964, Science, Technology and Application of Titanium, 1970; other books. Named Nat. Capitol Engr. of Yr. Coun. Engring. and Archtl. Socs., 1974; recipient Outstanding Accomplishment awards Navy Dept., 1955-64, Nat. Materials Advancement award, Fedn. Materials Socs., 1994; annual hon. lectr. Electrochem. Soc., 1970. Fellow AIME (hon. mem., ann. disting. lectr. Metall. Soc. 1984), Soc. Advanced Materials and Process Engring., Am. Soc. Materials Internat. (pres. 1972, hon. mem., Carnegie lectr. 1967, ann. hon. lectr. 1984), Brit. Inst. Materials; mem. NAE, ASTM (hon., ann. disting. lectr. 1964), Fedn. Materials Soc. (pres. 1972-73, 1st Decennial award 1982), Soc. Automotive Engrs. (chmn. aerospace materials divsn. 1959-74), Alpha Sigma Mu (hon.). Inventor in electroplating, 1930-40; metall. devels., 1941-66. Home and Office: Hyatt Classic Residence 8100 Connecticut Ave Apt 1406 Chevy Chase MD 20815-2820 *Ten key words and phrases for a professional career: identified goals, long range vision, can-do attitude, integrity, objectivity, understanding and tolerance, faith and trust, professionalism, dedication and perseverance, sense of humor.*

PROMISLO, DANIEL, lawyer; b. Bryn Mawr, Pa., Nov. 15, 1932; s. Charles and Pearl (Backman) P.; m. Estelle Carasso, June 10, 1961; children: Mark, Jacqueline, Steven. BSBA, Drexel U., 1955; JD magna cum laude, U. Pa., 1966. Bar: Pa. 1966. Pres., owner Hist. Souvenir Co., Phila., 1957—; assoc. Wolf, Block, Schorr & Solis-Cohen, 1966-70, ptnr., 1977-94, exec. com., 1987-89, of counsel, 1994—, mng. dir., 1997-2001; founder, pres. dir. Inst. for Paralegal Tng., 1970-75, cons., 1975-77. Editor: Corporate Law, 1970, Real Estate Law, 1971, Estates and Trusts, 1971, Civil Litigation, 1972, Employee Benefit Plans, 1973, Criminal Law, 1974; contbr. articles to profl. jours. Bd. dirs. Phila. Drama Guild, 1977-95, chmn., 1982-86; bd. dirs. Phila. Israel Econ. Devel. Program, 1983-88, Inst. for Arts in Edn., 1990-93, WHYY, Inc., 1994—, vice-chmn., 1995-96, chmn., 1996-97; bd. dirs. U.S. Physicians, Inc., 1995-98; trustee Resource Asset Investment Trust (now RAIT), 1997—; bd. advisors Drexel U. Coll. Arts & Scis. Mem. Order of Coif, Drexel U. 100, Blue Key, Phi Kappa Phi. Democrat. Jewish. Avocations: movies, basketball, tennis. Office: Wolf Block Schorr & Solis-Cohen 1650 Arch St Fl 22 Philadelphia PA 19103-2097 E-mail: dpromislo@wolfblock.com.

PRONESTI, ROSA C. artist; b. W. Nantmeal Twp., Pa., Aug. 27, 1932; d. Salvatore Maria and Frances (Bavuso-Volpe) P. Student, Hussian Art Sch., Phila., 1954. With Deco Art, Phila., 1950-51; asst. artist Fliesher Art Meml., 1951-68; mech. artist William F. Bird Studio, 1952-65, Designers Frank Nofer Inc., Phila., 1968-85. One-woman shows include Cathedral Village Retirement Home, Andora, Pa., 1996, 98, Stone Harbor Cathedral Village, 1993-99, Jewish Comm. Centennial, 2001; group shows include Atlantic City (N.J.) Art Ctr., 1997-2001, Long Beach Island Miniature Show, 1985-2001 Surf City, N.J., Yellow Springs Art Show, Chester Springs, Pa., 1997-01, Ocean City Libr., 2002. Mem. Atlantic City Art Ctr., Nat. Mus. Women in the Arts, Del. Artist Guild, Woodmere Mus. Art, Phila. Water Color Soc. Roman Catholic. Home: 28 N Frontenac Ave Margate City NJ 08402-1853

PRONKO, PETER PAUL, physicist; b. Peckville, Pa., Mar. 29, 1938; s. Stephen and Mary (Mizerak) P.; m. Diana M. Dumas, Mar. 27, 1967; children: Andrea, Jocelyn. BS, U. Scranton, 1960; MS, U. Pitts., 1962; PhD, U. Alta., Edmonton, Can., 1966. Asst. prof. U. Scranton, 1967-68; rsch. assoc. McMaster U., Hamilton, Ont., Can., 1968-72; physicist Argonne Nat. Lab. (Ill.), 1972-80; chief scientist Universal Energy Systems, Dayton, Ohio, 1980—; dir. materials lab. divsn. Universal Energy Systems, Dayton, Ohio. Contbr. articles to profl. jours., patentee in processing and tech. materials. Mem. IEEE, Am. Phys. Soc., Materials Rsch. Soc. Home: 2070 Stewart Rd Xenia OH 45385-8938 Office: Universal Energy Systems Inc 4401 Dayton Xenia Rd Dayton OH 45432-1894

PRONZINI, BILL JOHN (WILLIAM PRONZINI), writer; b. Petaluma, Calif., Apr. 13, 1943; s. Joseph and Helene (Guder) P.; m. Marcia Muller. Coll. student, 2 years. Author: 60 novels (including under pseudonyms), 4 books of non-fiction, 10 collections of short stories, 1971—; first novel, The Stalker, 1971; editor 80 anthologies; contbr. numerous short stories to pubs. Recipient 6 scroll awards Mystery Writers Am., Life Achievement award Pvt. Eye Writers Am., 1987. Office: PO Box 2536 Petaluma CA 94953-2536 E-mail: pronhack@sbcglobal.net.

PROPER, MICHAEL CHARLES, cardiologist, educator; b. N.Y.C., Mar. 26, 1943; s. Morton and Miriam (Gitelson) P.; m. Hope Ann Ratzan, Dec. 20, 1964; children: David Matthew, Diana Ellen. BS magna cum laude, CUNY, 1963; MD, NYU, 1967. Diplomate Am. Bd. Internal Medicine, Am. Bd. Cardiovasc. Diseases. Intern Bellevue Hosp., N.Y.C., 1967-68, resident, 1968-69, Jackson Meml. Hosp., Miami, Fla., 1969-70; fellow in cardiology Mt. Sinai Hosp., Miami Beach, 1970-71, Yale-New Haven Hosp., 1973-74; cardiologist Cooper Hosp. Univ. Med. Ctr., Camden, N.J., 1975-94; clin. asst. prof. medicine Robert Wood Johnson Med. Sch., Piscataway, 1980-90, clin. assoc. prof. medicine, 1990-94. Hosp. affiliations include Our Lady of Lourdes Hosp., Camden, 1978—, West Jersey Hosp. Sys., Marlton, Voorhees, Camden, Berlin, 1975—, assoc. chief divsn. cardiology, 1994-96, chief divsn. cardiology Marlton divsn., 1985-95, exec. com. Marlton divsn., 1986-8, 1992-94; Underwood Meml. Hosp., Woodbury, N.J., 1995—; clin. as st. prof. medicine Jefferson Med. Coll., Phila., 1984-90; trustee Cooper Hosp., Camden, 1981-90; mem. various other hosp. svc. coms.; lectr. in field. Contbr. articles to profl. jours. Advisor Heart Day, Greenbriar Restaurant, Cherry Hill, N.J., 1990. Maj. USAF, 1971-73. Jonas Salk scholar CUNY. Fellow Am. Coll. Chest Physicians, Am. Coll. Cardiology; mem. AMA, ACP, Am. Heart Assn., Camden County Heart Assn., Med. Soc. N.J., Camden County Med. Soc., Phila. Coll. Physicians, Alpha Omega Alpha Honor Soc. Avocations: biking, gardening, cooking, sports. Office: Assoc Cardiovasc Cons 63 Kresson Rd Ste 101 Cherry Hill NJ 08034

PROPHETT, ANDREW LEE, political science educator; b. Lynchburg, Va., Mar. 1, 1948; s. Elisha and Evatna (Gilliam) P. BS in History, Hampton U., 1970; MEd in Social Studies, U. Ill., 1972; postgrad., U. Va., 1986-91. Cert. tchr., N.J. and Va. Tchr. U.S. and African history Camden (N.J.) H.S., 1970-85; tchr. social studies Randolph-Henry H.S., Charlotte Court House, Va., 1986-99, dept. chair social studies, 1992-99; instr. polit. sci. and African-Am. history Southside Va. C.C., Keysville, 1988-99; instr. social studies Chesterfield (Va.) County Pub. Schs., 1999—. Mem. Campbell County (Va.) Sch. Bd., 1992-95; chmn. edn. com. Staunton River Adv. Commn., Randolph, Va., 1994-96; summer participant Armonk Inst. Study Tour of Germany, 1995. Pres. Campbell County NAACP, Rustburg, 1992—; mem. youth adv. bd. Gethsemane Presbyn. Ch., Drakes Branch, Va., 1994—, deacon, 1995-97, elder, 1997—; mem. study tour of Israel, Va. Dept. Edn., 1997; chmn. Task Force on Racism, Presbytery of the Peaks; participant study tour of Spain and Morocco, summer 1997, study tour of Athens and the Greek Islands, summer 1998, study tour of Turkey, summer 1999; lay commr. 211th Gen. Assembly Presbyn. Ch. U.S.A., Ft. Worth, 1999. Recipient Excellence in Tchg. award Southside Va. Cmty. Coll., 1994, Tchr. Recognition award Charlotte County Edn. Found., Inc., 1997, disting. leadership award Campbell County NAACP, 1999, Cmty. Svc. award Lynchburg chpt. Nat. Conf. Cmty. and Justice, 1999. Mem. NEA, Va. Edn. Assn., Va. Geog. Soc., Phi Delta Kappa. Democrat. Presbyterian. Home: 5407 Houndmaster Rd Midlothian VA 23112-6522

PROPP, STEVEN H. analyst; b. Berkeley, Calif., Oct. 2, 1955; s. Harry and Dorothy S. Propp. BA, Calif. State U., Sacramento, 1978. Analyst Pub. Employees' Retirement Sys., Sacramento, 1979—. Author: Work, Death and Taxes, 2000, Tattered Pilgrims, 2001, Inquiries: Philosophical, 2002. Avocations: music, reading. E-mail: Stevenhpropp@hotmail.com.

PROPPER, MICHAEL WALLES, psychiatrist, educator; b. Metairie, La., Jan. 5, 1954; BA in French Lang. and Lit., Yale U., 1975; MD, Tulane U., New Orleans, 1979. Intern surgery dept. Highland Alameda Med. Ctr., Oakland, Calif., 1979-80; resident anatomic pathology Cedars-Sinai Med. Ctr., L.A., 1980-81; staff physician U. So. Calif. Student Health Ctr., 1983-87; resident, 1981-83, chief resident in psychiatry UCLA Neuropsychiat. Inst. and West L.A. VA Med. Ctr., 1987-90; pvt. practice psychiatry L.A., 1990-95; staff pschiatrist VA Med. Ctr., Nashville, 1995—; asst. clin. prof. Vanderbilt U. Sch. Medicine, 1995—. Asst. clin. prof. UCLA Sch. Medicine, 1990—94; med. dir. Mental Health Svcs. Clinica Para Las Americas, 1990—94; faculty, cert. trainer Bayer Inst. Healthcare Comm., West Haven, Conn., 1998—. Founder, prodr. Euphoria! The Theatre. Mem.: AMA, Nashville Acad. Medicine, Am. Acad. on the Physician and Patient, Am. Psychiat. Assn. Office: VA Med Ctr 1310 24th Ave S MC 116A Nashville TN 37212-2637

PROPST, CATHERINE LAMB, biotechnology company executive; b. Charlotte, N.C., Mar. 10, 1946; d. James Pinckney and Eliza Mayo (Mills) P. BA magna cum laude, Vanderbilt U., 1967; M of Philosophy, Yale U., 1970, PhD, 1973. Head microbiology div. GTE Labs., Waltham, Mass., 1974-77; various mgmt. positions Abbott Labs., North Chgo., Ill., 1977-80; v.p. rsch. and devel. Ayerst Labs., Plainview, N.Y., 1980-83; v.p. rsch. and devel. worldwide Flow Gen. Inc., McLean, Va., 1983-85; pres. and chief exec. officer Affiliated Sci. Inc., Ingleside, Ill., 1985-97; pres., CEO Tex. Biotech. Found., Hempstead, Tex., 1997—. Vis. prof. genetics U. Ill., Chgo., 1989-90; founder and exec. dir. Ctr. for Biotech., Northwestern U., 1990-95; pres., Ill. Biotechnology Ctr., 1995-97; bd. dirs. several cos.; bd. dirs., mem. sci. adv. bd. Keystone Symposia on Molecular and Cellular Biology, 1997—. Author and editor: Computer-Aided Drug Design, 1989, Nucleic Acid Targeted Drug Design, 1992; contbr. articles to profl. jours. Named to Outstanding Working Women in the U.S., 1982; recipient many sci. and bus. awards. Fellow Soc. Indsl. Microbiology (bd. dirs. 1990-93), Nat. Coun. Biotech Ctrs. (bd. dirs. 1995-97); mem. AAAS, Nat. Wildlife Fedn., Consortium for Plant Biotech. Rsch. (bd. dirs. 1994-99), Phi Beta Kappa, Sigma Xi. Episcopalian. Avocations: horseback riding, skiing, raising Black Angus and Black Brangus cattle. Office: Texas Biotech Found PO Box 17 Hempstead TX 77445-0017 Fax: 979-826-9710.

PROPST, MICHAEL TRUMAN, pathologist; b. Lebanon, Oreg., July 3, 1940; s. Lynn Edward and Vera Ruth (Forbes) P.; m. Susan Jean Joesting, Dec. 26, 1974; children: Christopher M., Andrew J., Matthew A., Michael Jonathan, Edwin Cam. BS, Oreg. State U., 1962; MD, U. Oreg., 1966. Diplomate Am. Bd. Pathology. Pathologist Humana Hosp., Anchorage, 1974—84; med. examiner State of Alaska, 1975—94; med. dir. Physicians Med. Lab., 1984—94; chief med. examiner State of Alaska, 1994—2001. Served to maj. USAF, 1971-74. Fellow Coll. Am. Pathologists, Am. Soc. Clin. Pathologists, Am. Acad. Forensic Scientists, Royal Soc. Medicine (Gr. Britain), ; mem. Nat. Assn. Med. Examiners. Lutheran.

PROROK, BARTON CHARLES, materials scientist; b. Pitts., July 12, 1968; s. Thomas Martin Prorok, V. Wanda Prorok. BS Ceramic Sci. & Engring., Pa. State U., 1991; MS Metallurgy, U. Ill., Chgo., 1993; MS Materials Sci. & Engring., U. Pitts., 1996; PhD Materials Engring., U. Ill., Chgo., 2001. Rsch. asst. Argonne Nat. Lab., Ill., 1991—2000; postdoctoral rsch. asst. Northwestern U., Evanston, 2000—02; asst. prof. materials sci. Auburn U., Ala., 2002—. Office: Materials Rsch and Edn Ctr Auburn U 201 Ross Hall Auburn AL 36849-5341 Business E-Mail: prorobc@eng.auburn.edu.

PROSKY, ROBERT JOSEPH, actor; b. Phila., Dec. 13, 1930; s. Joseph and Helen (Kuhn) Porzuczek; m. Ida Mae Hove, June 4, 1960, children: Stefan, John, Andrew Student, Temple U., Am. Theatre. Appeared at Arena Stage, Washington, 23 years including roles in Death of a Salesman, Twelfth Night, Enemy of the People, Galileo; appeared on Broadway in Moonchildren, View from the Bridge, Glengarry Glen Ross (Tony award nominee 1985), A Walk in the Woods, 1988 (Tony award nominee 1988, Best Actor award Outer Critics Circle, toured USSR and Lithuania 1989), Camping with Henry and Tim; films include Thief, 1981, Lords of Discipline, 1983, Christine, 1983, The Natural, 1984, Broadcast News, 1987, Outrageous Fortune, 1987, Things Change, 1988, Gremlins II, 1988, Something About Love, 1990, Green Card, 1990, Life in the Food Chain, 1990, Far and Away, 1992, Hoffa, 1992, Life on the High Wire, 1992, Rudy, 1992, Last Action Hero, 1993, Mrs. Doubtfire, 1993, Miracle on 34th Street, 1994, Scarlet Letter, 1995, Dead Man Walking, 1995, The Chamber, 1996, Mad City, 1997, Dudley-Do-Right, 1998, Swing Vote, 1999, Detox, 1999; TV appearances include role of Sgt. Jablonski in Hill Street Blues, The Murder of Mary Phagan, 1988, Home Fires Burning, 1988, From the Dead of Night, 1989, Heist, 1989, Dangerous Pursuit, 1990, Johnny Ryan, 1990, The Love She Sought, 1990, Double Edge, 1992, Teamster Boss: The Jackie Presser Story, 1992; role of Pat in Veronica's Closet, Danny, 2001, D-Tox, 2002, NBC 75th Anniversary Special, 2002; narrator Lifestories; mem. first Am. co. to tour Soviet Union, 1972., former mem. Arena Stage Repertory Company. Joseph Jefferson award nominee, 1985; recipient Drama Desk award, 1985, Helen Hayes award, 1995, Am. Express Tribute to an Am. Actor, 1998.*

PROSNITZ, DAVID J. finance company executive; b. Newark, June 27, 1948; s. Henry Marcus and Elaine Esther (Hendricks) P.; m. Lori Kim, July 20, 1986; children: Joseph, Hannah, Miriam. BA, Clark U., 1970; MA, New Sch. Social Rsch., 1973; PhD, U. Chgo., 1978. Rsch. analyst Mayor's Office, Chgo., 1978-81; pres., owner Personnel Planners, Inc., 1981—. Author: Common Differences, 2002. Coach Am. Youth Soccer Orgn., Skokie, Ill., 1994-99; treas. Friday night group Anske Emet Synagogue, Chgo., 1986-88. Mem. Assn. Unemployment Tax Orgns. Republican. Jewish. Avocations: anthropology of religion, reading, basketball. Office: Personnel Planners Inc 913 W Van Buren St Ste 3A Chicago IL 60607-3528

PROSNITZ, LEONARD R. radiologist; b. Apr. 9, 1936; BA, Amherst Coll., 1957; MD, SUNY, N.Y.C., 1961. Prof. Yale U., New Haven, 1969-83, Duke U., N.C., 1983—, chmn. radiol. oncology dept., 1983-96. Contbr. articles to profl. jours. Office: Duke U Med Ctr Radiation Oncology Dept PO Box 3085 Durham NC 27710-0001 E-mail: prosnitz@radonc.duke.edu.

PROSPER, PIERRE-RICHARD, federal agency administrator; b. Denver, 1963; BA, Boston Coll.; JD, Pepperdine U. Bar: Calif. Dep. dst. atty. L.A. County, 1989—94; asst. U.S. atty. State of Calif., ctrl. dist., 1994—96; war crimes prosecutor U.N. Internat. Criminal Tribunal for Rwanda, 1996—98; spl. asst. to asst. atty. gen. for criminal divsn. State Dept.; spl. counsel, policy adviser Office of War Crimes, 1999—2001; amb. at large for war crimes issues U.S. Dept. of State, Washington, 2001—. Recipient Alumni award of Excellence, Boston Coll., 1999, Dist. Alumnus award, Pepperdine U. Sch. Law Alumni, 2000; fellow Wasserstein fellow, Harvard U., 2000—01. Office: US Dept of State Ambassador at large for War Crimes Issue 2201 C St NW Washington DC 20520-7512 Office Fax: 202-736-4495.

PROSPERI, DAVID PHILIP, public relations executive; b. Chgo., June 20, 1953; BSBA, U. Ill., 1975; MBA in Internat. Bus., George Washington U., 1983. Moving cons. Fed. Safety Moving & Storage, Elmhurst, Ill., 1975-79; press aide 1980 Reagan for Pres. campaign, Los Angeles, 1979-80, Reagan-Bush Campaign, Alexandria, Va., 1980-81; asst. press sec. to the Pres. White House, Washington, 1981-82; mgr. govt. affairs The Superior Oil Co., 1982-84; press sec. U.S. Dept. Energy, 1985; asst. to sec. dir. pub. affairs U.S. Dept. Interior, 1985-88; asst. sec. transp. U.S. Dept. Transp., 1989-90; sr. v.p., asst. to pres. and CEO, Chgo. Bd. Trade, 1990-95, sr. v.p., 1995—, sr. v.p., asst. to pres., CEO, 1996—. Bd. dirs. Corp. Pub. Broadcasting, 1992-93. Republican. Roman Catholic. Avocations: basketball, tennis, spending time with family. Office: Chgo Bd Trade 141 W Jackson Blvd Ste 600A Chicago IL 60604-2992 E-mail: dpro72@cbot.com.

PROSPERI, LOUIS ANTHONY, lawyer; b. Altoona, Pa., Jan. 12, 1954; s. Louis Alfred and Ann Francis (DiDimenico) P.; m. Susan Lynn Irwin, Sept. 14, 1985. BS in Bus. Adminstrn. summa cum laude, Georgetown U., 1975; JD cum laude, Harvard U., 1978. Bar: Pa. 1978, U.S. Dist. Ct. (we. dist.) Pa. 1978, U.S. Ct. Appeals (Fed. cir.) 1985, U.S. Ct. Fed. Claims, 1985, U.S. Tax Ct. 1979. From assoc. to ptnr. Reed, Smith, Shaw & McClay, Pitts., 1978-94; pvt. practice Law Office Louis A. Prosperi, 1994—. Mem. Allegheny County Bar Assn., Pitts. Tax Club. Clubs: Longue Vue (Verona, Pa.). Republican. Roman Catholic. Avocations: golf, tennis, paddle tennis, cross-country skiing. Home: 3036 Grassmere Ave Pittsburgh PA 15216-1862 Office: Law Office of Louis A Prosperi Grant Bldg 310 Grant St Ste 3601 Pittsburgh PA 15219-2305 E-mail: laprosperi@acba.org.

PROSPERO, DEREK, graphics designer, educator; b. Bronx, NY, Oct. 5, 1979; s. Louis Sgandurra, Debra Sgandurra. Sr. graphic artist Liquigem, West Palm Beach, Fla., 1998—2001, Fastac, West Palm Beach, 2000—. Instr. New Eng. Inst. Tech., West Palm Beach, Fla., 2001—. Author: Verse, 1996; featured in. Mem.: Nat. Assn. of Photoshop Profl. (Photoshop Guru award 2000, 2001). Independent. Avocations: wildlife, music, cinema, art, technology. Personal E-mail: studio@derekprospero.com.

PROSSER, C. LADD, physiology educator, researcher; b. Avon, N.Y., May 12, 1907; s. Clifford James and Izora May (Ladd) P.; m. Hazel Blanchard, Aug. 25, 1934; children— Jane Ellen, Nancy Ladd, Loring Blanchard AB, U. Rochester, 1929; PhD, Johns Hopkins U., 1932; hon. degree, Clark U., 1975. Asst. prof. physiology Clark U., Worcester, Mass., 1934-39; asst. prof physiology U. Ill., Urbana, 1939-47, assoc. prof. physiology, 1947-52, prof. physiology, 1952-74, prof. emeritus, 1975—. Asst. sect. chief Metallurgy Lab. U. Chgo., 1943-46; vis prof. U. Hawaii, U. Wash., U. Mass., Ariz. State U. Author: Adaptational Biology, 1986; author, editor: Comparative Animal Physiology, 1st edit., 1951, 4th edit. 1991; contbr. numerous articles to profl. jours. Guggenheim fellow, 1963-64; Fulbright fellow, 1971-72 Fellow Am. Acad. Arts and Scis.; mem. Nat. Acad. Scis., Soc. Gen. Physiologists (pres.

1958-59), AAAS (v.p. 1960), Am. Soc. Zoologists (pres. 1961), Am. Physiol. Soc. (pres. 1969-70), Bavarian Acad. Sci. Unitarian Universalist. Avocations: music; gardening. Home: 101 W Windsor Rd Urbana IL 61802-6663 Office: U Ill 524 Burrill Hall Urbana IL 61801

PROSSER, FRANKLIN PIERCE, computer scientist; b. Atlanta, July 4, 1935; s. Edward Theron and Eunice (McDaniel) P.; m. Brenda Mary Lau, June 16, 1960; children: Edward, Andrea. BS, Ga. Inst. Tech., 1956, MS, 1958; PhD, Pa. State U., 1961. Prof. computer sci. Ind. U., Bloomington, 1969-99; asso. dir. Wrubel Computing Center, 1969-81, chmn. dept. computer sci., 1971-77, 87-93, spl. asst. for acad. computing, 1979-81; v.p. Logic Design, Inc., 1982-92. Cons. Lockheed Theoretical Physics Lab., Palo Alto, Calif., 1967 Home: 1200 S Longwood Dr Bloomington IN 47401-6072 Office: Ind U Dept Computer Sci Bloomington IN 47405

PROSSER, JOHN MARTIN, architect, educator, urban design consultant; b. Wichita, Kans., Dec. 28, 1932; s. Francis Ware and Harriet Corinne (Osborne) P.; m. Judith Adams, Aug. 28, 1954 (dec. 1982); children: Thomas, Anne, Edward; m. Karen Ann Cleary, Dec. 30, 1983; 1 child, Jennifer. BArch, U. Kans., 1955; MArch, Carnegie Mellon U., 1961. Registered architect, Kans., Colo. Architect Robinson and Hissem, Wichita, 1954-56, Guirey, Srnka, and Arnold, Phoenix, 1961-62, James Sudler Assocs., Denver, 1962-68; ptnr., architect Nuzum, Prosser and Vetter, Boulder, 1969-73; from asst. prof. to prof. U. Colo., Boulder and Denver, 1968—, acting dean, 1980-84, dean, 1984, dir. environ. design Boulder, 1969-72, dir. urban design, 1972-85. Cons. John M. Prosser Assocs., Boulder and Denver, 1974—; vis. prof. urban design Oxford Poly., Eng., 1979; vis. critic Carnegie Mellon U., U. N.Mex., Colo. Coll.; pres. Denver chpt. AIA, 1983; prin. investigator Fitsimmons-U. Colo. Health Scis. City Rsch. Study, 1997-99. Author, narrator PBS TV documentary Cities Are For Kids, Too, 1984; prin. works include (with others) hist. redesign Mus. Western Art,Denver (design honor 1984), Villa Italia, Lakewood, Colo., Denver, Auraria Higher Edn. Ctr., Pueblo C.C. campus plan and new acad. facilities, comprehensive campus plan Denver U., Ft. Lewis Coll., Westminster Golf Course Cmty., Denver Botanic Gardens 20-Yr. Concept Plan, Colo. Coll. Historic Preservation Plan, Buffalo Hills Ranch Golf Course Cmty., Fountain Valley Sch., Regional Urban Design and Campus Planning, Ctrl. Colo. Springs Strategic Urban Design and Planning, 2001—, Interguest Corp. Park Urban Plan, 1999—. Bd. dirs. Denver Parks and Recreation Bd., 1987-93, 96—; chmn. design rev. bd. univs. Colo., Boulder, Denver, Aurora, and Colorado Springs, 1981—; mem. archtl. control com. Denver Tech. Ctr., 1984—. Meridian Internat. Bus. Ctr., 1984—, DTC West, 1991—, Denver Internat. Bus. Ctr., 1993—, Nat. Renewable Energy Lab., 1995—, Buffalo Hills Ranch, 1996—; planning cons. Denver Internat. Airport Environs. Devel. Projects, Fitzsimons $5 Billion Redevel.; Nucleus co-founder U. Colo. Real Estate Ctr., 1989-2000. Capt. USAF, 1956-59. Co-recipient 2d place nat. award Am. Soc. Interior Designers, 1984, honor award Colo. Soc. Architects, 1984. Mem. Urban Land Inst., Denver Country Club (bd. dirs. 1984-88, pres. 1986-87). Democrat. Avocation: Arlberg ski. Home: 1620 Monaco Pky Denver CO 80220-1643 Office: U Colo 1200 Larimer St Denver CO 80204-5310 E-mail: jmpros@aol.com.

PROSSER, MICHAEL HUBERT, communications educator; b. Indpls., Mar. 29, 1936; s. Marshall Herbert and Clydia Catharine (O'Dea) P.; m. Carol Mary Hogle, Nov. 27, 1958 (div. 1983); children: Michelle Ann Prosser-Evans, Leo Michael, Louis Mark; m. Joan Ann Kirkeby, Dec. 6, 1986. BA, Ball State U., 1958, MA, 1959; PhD, U. Ill., 1964. Tchr. Latin Urbana (Ill.) Jr. High Sch., 1960-63; asst. prof. speech SUNY, Buffalo, 1963-69; assoc. prof. speech Ind. U., Bloomington, 1969-72; prof. rhetoric and comm. U. Va., Charlottesville, 1972-2001, chair, 1972-77, prof. emeritus, 2001—; William A. Kern prof. in comm. Rochester Inst. Tech., 1994-98. Disting. vis. prof. comm. Rochester Inst. Tech., 1998-2001; adj. prof. SUNY, Brockport, 1998-99; chair AFS Global Awareness Day, U. Va., 1983-90, RIT Global Awareness Day, 1995-98, Intercultural Comm.; confs. at Rochester Inst. Tech., 1995-97, 99, 2000-01; vis. lectr. comm. Queens Coll. CUNY, 1966, 67; vis. assoc. prof. speech Calif. State U., Hayward, 1971; vis. prof. curriculum Meml. U. Newfoundland, St. John's, 1972, St. Paul U. and U. Ottawa (Can.), 1975; cons. intercultural comm. U.S. Info. Agy., Washington, 1977; disting. vis. prof. speech Kent (Ohio) State U., 1978; Fulbright prof. English, U. Swaziland, Kwalusene, 1990-91; fellow New Coll. U. Va., 1990-94; professorial lectr. George Washington Univ., 1994; Gannett lectr. Rochester Inst. Tech., 1995, 2000, Kern lectr., 1995-98; prof. comm. Yangzhou U., China, 2001—. Author: The Cultural Dialogue, 1978 (translated into Japanese 1982); co-author: Diplomatic Discourse: International Conflict at the United Nations: Addresses and Analysis, 1997; editor: An Ethic for Survival: Adlai Stevenson Speaks on International Affairs, 1936-65, 1969, Sow the Wind, Reap the Whirlwind: Heads of State Address the United Nations (2 vols.), 1970, Intercommunication Among Nations and Peoples, 1973; co-editor: Readings in Classical Rhetoric, 1969, Readings in Medieval Rhetoric, 1973, Civic Discourse: Multiculturalism, Cultural Diversity, and Global Communication, 1998, Civic Discourse: Intercultural, International and global Media, 1999; series editor Civic Discourse for the Third Millennium, 1998— Ablex Pub. Co. Mem. Haiti commn. Cath. Diocese Richmond, 1989-93; bd. dirs., v.p. Assn. Rochester UN, 1996-97, pres., 1997-98; pres. Rochester Area Fulbright Chpt., 1995-97; mem. Spotlight on Scholarship Nat. Comm. Assn., Atlanta, 2001. Recipient Disting. Alumnus award Ball State U., 1978.Prosser-SITARIM award of excellence in internat. comm. theory, 2000. Mem. AAUP, Internat. Soc. for Intercultural Edn., Tng. and Rsch. (pres. 1984-86, Citizen of World 1986, Outstanding Sr. Interculturalist 1990), Internat. Comm. Assn. (v.p., Disting. Svc. award 1978), UN Assn. U.S.A., Fulbright Assn., Nat. Comm. Assn., UN Assn. of Rochester (bd. dirs., v.p., pres.), Am. Field Svc. (pres. intercultural programs 1982-86, Charlottesville), Assn. for Edn. in Journalism and Mass Media. Democrat. Roman Catholic. Avocations: social justice and peace advocacy, youth, travel. Office: Rochester Inst Tech Coll of Liberal Arts 92 Lomb Memorial Dr Rochester NY 14623-5604 Fax: 716-475-7732. E-mail: MHPGPT@rit.edu.

PROSSER, MICHAEL JOSEPH, college librarian; b. Syracuse, N.Y., May 9, 1948; s. Palmer Adelbert and Viola Mary (Clairmont) P. AA, Riverside (Calif.) City Coll., 1971; BA in History, Calif. State Coll., San Bernardino, 1977; MSLS, U. So. Calif., L.A., 1981. Cert. cmty. coll. instr., librarian, Calif. Libr. clk. Riverside C.C., 1968-81, learning resources asst., 1981—. Author: California and the Pacific Plate: A Bibliography, 1979. Tutor, Queen of Angels Ch., Riverside, 1985—, facilitator/patrons, 1985—; photographer. With U.S. Army, 1969-71. Mem. ASCD, Internat. Soc. Poets, Calif. Libr. Assn. Democrat. Roman Catholic. Home: 6800 Palos Dr Riverside CA 92503-1330 Office: Riverside Cmty Coll 4800 Magnolia Ave Riverside CA 92506-1242

PROSSER, ROBERT ARTHUR, retired research scientist; b. N.Y.C., Mar. 16, 1925; s. Joseph Watrous and Edna Prosser; m. Laila Vittands, Feb. 1958; children: Louise, Thomas, Joseph. BS, Haverford Coll., 1949; PhD, U. Pa., 1960. Rsch. scientist U.S. Army Natick (Mass.) Soldier Ctr., 1962-2000. Contbr. articles to sci. jours., including Textile Rsch. Jour., Analytical Chemistry, Exptl. Mechanics, Jour. Applied Polymer Sci., Jour. Macromolecular Sci., Jour. Applied Physics. Served with inf. U.S. Army, World War II, ETO. Decorated Combat Infantryman's Badge, Purple Heart. Lutheran. Achievements include patents for in field. Avocation: gardening. Home: 93 Beatrice Ln Holliston MA 01746

PROSSER, WESLEY LEWIS, advertising and public relations executive; b. Dodge City, Kans., Oct. 28, 1938; s. Wesley Lewis and Sarah Arvilla (Ellis) P.; m. Doris Jean Russell, Apr. 29, 1972 (dec. Nov. 1986). BA, Okla. State U., 1959. Advt. coordinator Aero-Commander, Inc., Oklahoma City, 1962-65; copy coordinator Farmland Industries, Inc., Kansas City, Mo., 1965-72; copy supr. Fletcher/Mayo/Assocs. Inc., St. Joseph, 1972-74; advt. and pub. relations dir. Agchem Abbott Labs., North Chicago, Ill., 1974-76; account exec. Rumrill & Hoyt, Inc., Rochester, N.Y., 1976-77; account rep. Vangard Communications Inc., St. Louis, 1977-78; v.p., client group supr. Bozell & Jacobs, Inc., Chgo., 1978-84; account supr. McKinney/Mid America, 1984-85; mgr. advt. and pub. rels. Inter Innovation LeFebure Inc., Cedar Rapids, Iowa, 1986-89; mgr. bus. devel. Fanning Advt. Agy. Inc., Davenport, 1989-91; dir. mktg. comm. Farm Bus. Software Sys., Inc., Aledo, Ill., 1991-96. Prodr. interactive promotional presentation on computer diskette; contbr. articles to profl. jours. Vol. Jackson County Rep. Party, Kansas City, Mo., 1969, Salvation Army, Dodge City, Kans., 1997-2000. 1st lt. USAF, 1959-61. Recipient 1st Place award Nat. Premium Execs., 1969, Objectives and Results award Am. Bus. Press, 1980, 81, 83, several others. Mem. Nat. Agrimarketers Assn. (1st Place Best in Advt. award 1974), Bus. and Profl. Advertisers Assn., Assn. Agrl. Computing Cos. (presenter seminars), Sports Car Club Am. Methodist. Avocations: aviation, summer water sports, creative writing. Home: 725 Alpine Dr Sherrard IL 61281-9339 Office: FBS Systems Inc 1855 55th Ave Aledo IL 61231-8610

PROST, SHARON, federal judge; b. Newburyport, Mass., May 24, 1951; m. Kenneth F. Greene, June 24, 1984; 1 child, Matthew Prost-Greene. BS, Cornell U., 1973; MBA, George Washington U., 1975, LLM in Taxation, 1984; JD, Am. U., 1979. Bar: D.C. Labor rels. specialist Office of Personnel Mgmt., 1973-76; with Gen. Acctg. Office, 1976-79; trial atty. Fed. Labor Rels. Authority, 1980-83; atty. chief counsel's office Dept. of Treasury, 1983-84; assoc. solicitor Nat. Labor Rels. Bd., 1984-89; chief minority labor counsel Senate Com. on Labor and Human Resources, 1989-93; minority chief counsel Senate Com. on the Judiciary, 1993—2001; judge U.S. Court of Appeal , Federal Cir., 2001—. Office: U.S. Court of Appeals - Federal Cir. 717 Madison Pl, NW Washington DC 20439*

PROTHEROE, WALTER JAMES, JR. environmental engineer, researcher; b. Miami, Fla., Dec. 18, 1957; s. Walter James Protherole, Lise Martha Detruit. BS in Environ. Engring., Columbia So. U., 1999. Registered environ. mgr., Nat. Registry Environ., cert. ergonomics compliance dir., Columbia So. Univ., lic. radiation safety officer, Nev. Sr. field svc. engr Cameca Instruments, Inc., Stanford, Conn., 1985—94; syst. engr. Energy-Micro-Analytical Cons., Inc., Houston, 1994—. Indep. rschr. Energy-Micro-Analytical Cons., Inc., Houston, 1997—2002. Mem.: Soc. Luminescence Microscopy and Spectroscopy, Geol. Soc. Am. Methodist. Avocation: travel. Office: Energy-Micro-Analytical Consultant Inc 8711 Beau Monde Houston TX 77099-1107 Personal E-mail: corvos@aol.com.

PROTHRO, JERRY ROBERT, lawyer; b. Midland, Tex., Dec. 22, 1946; s. Jack William Prothro and Nita Marie (Stovall) Milligan; m. Leslie Joan Lepar, Aug. 15, 1970 (div. 1994); children: Laura Kay, Evan Jackson. BA, Southwestern U., 1969; JD, U. Tex. Sch. Law, 1972. Lawyer, capt. U.S. Army, JAGC, 1972-76; ptnr. Turpin, Smith & Dyer, Midland, 1975-85, Boyd, Sanders, Wade, Cropper & Prothro, Midland, 1985-91; pvt. practice Dallas and Midland, Tex., 1991—. Mem. admissions com. M/O div. U.S. Dist. Ct. for Western Dist. Tex., 1987—; speaker in field. Treas., v.p. Southwestern U. Alumni Bd., Georgetown, Tex., 1980-90, pres.-elect, 1991, pres., 1992-94; trustee, Southwestern U., 1992-94; adminstrv. bd. First United Meth. Ch., Midland, 1989-96; vice chmn. Permian Basin AIDS Coalition Bd., 1994; active Midland County Hist. Commn., 1980-85. Named Univ. scholar Southwestern U., 1969; recipient Disting. Svc. medal U.S. Army, 1974. Mem. Midland County Young Lawyers (pres. 1979-80), Midland County Bar Assn., 5th Cir. Bar Assn., Pi Kappa Alpha Social Frat., Blue Key Leadership Frat., Pi Gamma Mu Social Sci. Frat. Methodist. Avocations: antique collecting, camping, men's movement activity. Home: Ste 211 4021 Cole Ave Dallas TX 75204 Office: 3626 N Hall Ste 820 Dallas TX 75219 E-mail: prothro@swbell.net.

PROTIGAL, STANLEY NATHAN, lawyer; b. Wilmington, Del., June 3, 1950; s. Bernard Protigal. BS in Aircraft Maintenance Engring., Northrop U., 1973; JD, Vt. Law Sch., 1978. Bar: U.S. Patent Office 1977, D.C. 1978. Assoc. Sixbey F. & L., Arlington, Va., 1978-79, atty., 1979-82; patent atty. Allied-Signal Bendix Aerospace, Teterboro, N.J., 1982-88; patent counsel Micron Tech., Inc., Boise, Idaho, 1988-94; pvt. practice, 1994-96, Seattle, 1996-98; assoc. Sabath and Truong, San Jose, Calif., 1998—. Mem. IEEE, Mensa. Avocations: pvt. pilot, bicycling, skiing.

PROTOKOWICZ, NORA JANE, nursing administrator; b. Jersey CIty, N.J., June 21, 1954; d. Maurice Joseph and Jane Catherine (Kealy) Monti; m. Daniel John Protokowicz, May 1, 1977; children: Jill Marie, Elizabeth Nora. BSN, U. Del., 1976; MSN, Widener U., 1997. RN Del., Pa. Staff nurse Hosp. U. Pa., Phila., 1976-77, Wilmington (Del.) Med. Ctr., 1977-80, asst. head nurse, 1980-82, head nurse, 1982-85; nurse mgr. Med. Ctr. Del., Newark, 1985—. Instr. Am. Heart Assn., Newark, 1990—. Mem. AACCN, ANA, Sigma Theta Tau. Home: 106 Rockland Cir Wilmington DE 19803-4542 Office: Christiana Hosp PO Box 6001 Newark DE 19718-0001

PROTTER, MURRAY A. mathematician, educator; b. New York, Ny, Feb. 13, 1918; s. Aaron and Bertha Keller Protter; m. Ruth Rotman Protter; children: Barbara, Philip. BA, U. Mich., Ann Arbor, 1933—37, MA, 1937—38; Ph.D, Brown U., Providence, RI, 1945—45. Prof. math U. Calif., Berkeley, Calif., 1953—. Author: of more than 14 books in math and advanced math. Achievements include research in Approximately fifty papers on research in math. Home: 1515 Oxford Street Berkeley CA 94709 Personal E-mail: mhprotter@email.com.

PROUD, ROBERT DONALD (ROBERT PAYTON), radio station executive, broadcaster; b. Cleve., Nov. 1, 1949; s. Lloyd Donald and Eleanore Matilda (Cihon) P.; m. K. Diane Siler, Feb. 17, 1979; 1 child, James S. Owen. Grad., Cleve. Inst. Broadcasting, 1969; student, U. N.Mex., 1982, Instituto Bilinque Cultural, 1989-90. Program dir. Sta. WGCL-FM, Cleve., 1972-74; ops. mgr. Sta. WRBR-FM, South Bend, Ind., 1974-75, Sta. XEROK, Juarez, Mex., 1975-77; program dir. Sta. WZZP-FM, Cleve., 1977-78; gen. mgr. Sta. KELP, El Paso, Tex., 1978-82; sales mgr. Sta. KAMZ-FM, 1982-86; gen. mgr. Stas. KAMA/KAMZ-FM, 1982-86; dir. nat. sales Thrash Broadcasting, El Paso, Lubbock, Tex., 1987-88; gen. mgr. Sta. KVIV, El Paso, 1987-89; v.p., gen. mgr. Sta. KEZB, Tex., 1989-91; gen. mgr. Sta. KFRR, Denver, 1991-92; gen. sta. mgr. KQQK, Houston, 1992-95; v.p., gen. mgr. Entravision Comm., Dallas, 1995—. Bd. dirs., chmn. communications Am. Heart Assn. Mem. El Paso Assn. Radio Stas. (pres. 1981), Tex. Assn. Broadcasters, Denver Area Radio Broadcasters. Office: 5307 E Mockingbird Ln Ste 500 Dallas TX 75206-5118

PROUGH, RUSSELL ALLEN, biochemistry educator, university official; b. Twin Falls, Idaho, Nov. 5, 1943; s. Elza Leroy and Beulah Elsie (Huddleston) P.; m. Betty Marie Ehlers, Dec. 26, 1965; children: Jennifer Sally, Kimberly Marie. BS in Chemistry, Coll. of Idaho, 1965; PhD in Biochemistry and Biophysics, Oreg. State U., 1969. Postdoctoral fellow VA Hosp., Kansas City, Mo., 1969-72; instr. biochemistry U. Tex. Southwestern Med. Sch., Dallas, 1972-73, asst. prof. biochemistry, 1973-77, assoc. prof. biochemistry, 1977-82, prof. biochemistry, 1982-86, U. Louisville Sch. Med., 1986—, chmn. dept., 1986-2000, vice dean rsch., assoc. v.p. rsch., 1998—. Mem. NIH Toxicology Study Sect., 1984-88, State of Nebr. Smoking Disease and Cancer Rsch. Program, 1984-91, NIEHS rsch. com., 1999—. Assoc. editor Drug Metabolism and Disposition, 1994—. Recipient Rsch. Career Devel. award USPHS. Mem. Am. Soc. Biochemistry and Molecular Biology, Am. Assn. Cancer Rsch., Am. Soc. Pharmacology and Exptl. Therapeutics, Internat. Soc. for Study of Xenobiotics, Sigma Xi. Lutheran. Office: U Louisville Dept Biochemistry and Molecular Biology Louisville KY 40292-0001 E-mail: russ.prough@louisville.edu.

PROULX, (EDNA) ANNIE, writer; b. Norwich, Conn., Aug. 22, 1935; d. George Napolean and Lois Nellie (Gill) Proulx; m. James Hamilton Lang, June 22, 1969 (div. 1990); children: Sylvia Marion Bullock Clarkson, Jonathan Edward Lang, Gillis Crowell Lang, Morgan Hamilton Lang. BA cum laude, U. Vt., 1969; MA, Sir George Williams U., Montreal, Can., 1973; DHL (hon.), U. Maine, 1994. Author: Heart Songs and Other Stories, 1988, Postcards, 1992 (PEN/Faulkner award 1993), The Shipping News, 1993 (Chgo. Tribune Heartland award 1993, Irish Times Internat. Fiction award 1993, Nat. Book award for fiction 1994, Pulitzer Prize for fiction 1994), Accordion Crimes, 1996 (Dos Passos prize for lit. 1996), Brokeback Mountain, 1998 (Nat. Mag. award 1998); contbr. more than 50 articles to mags. and jours.; editor: Best American Short Stories of 1997. Recipient Dos Passos prize for Lit., Longwood Coll., 1997, Ambassador Book award English Speaking Union, 2000, Best Fiction 1999 Book award The New Yorker, 2000; Kress fellow Harvard U., 1974, fellow Vt. Coun. Arts, 1989, NEA, 1991, Guggenheim Found., 1992; rsch. grantee Inter.-U. Ctr., 1975; resident Ucross Found., 1990, 92. Mem. PEN Am. Ctr., Phi Beta Kappa, Phi Alpha Theta. Avocations: canoeing, reading, fishing. Home: 37 Kelly Creek Rd Centennial WY 82055*

PROULX, DONALD A, retired science educator; b. Milwaukee, Wis., May 27, 1939; s. Philip Charles Proulx and Virginia Mary Mueller; m. Mary Jean Ross, July 27, 1968; children: Donald A Proulx, Jr, William R. BS, U. Wisconsin-Milwaukee, Milwaukee, WI, 1961; PhD, U. California-Berkeley, Berkeley, CA, 1965. Asst. prof. (anthropology) U Mass, Amherst, Mass., 1965—71, assoc prof. (anthropology), 1971—79, chairman-dept anthropology, 1975—78, prof., 1979—2002, director-latin am. studies, 1980—92, chairman-dept anthropology, 1999—2000, prof. emeritus, 2002—. Author: (book) An Analysis of the Early Cultural Sequence in the Nepena Valley, Peru, The NASCA (with Helaine Silverman). 1st lt USAR, 1961—65, Us. Mem.: Am. Assoc for Advancement of Sci., Am. Anthrop. Assoc. Soc. for Am. Archaeology. Home: 11 Laurel Ln Amherst MA 01002 Office: U Mass Dept Anthropology Machmer Hall Amherst MA 01003 Office Fax: 413-545-9494. E-mail: proulx@anthro.umass.edu.

PROUNTZOS, TINA, investment banker; b. N.Y.C., Jan. 12, 1971; BS in Fin., NYU, 1992. Analyst Brenner Securities Corp., N.Y.C., 1991-93; assoc. Southcoast Capital Corp. (formerly Brenner Securities Corp.), 1993-96; prin. Loewenbaum & Co. Inc. (formerly Southcoast Capital Corp.), 1997-98; v.p. Ladenburg Thalmann & Co., 1998-99, dir., 1999-2000; mng. dir. THCG, Inc., 2000-2001; dir. Morgan Lewis & Co. Inc, 2001—. Office: Morgan Lewis & Co Inc 600 5th Ave New York NY 10020 E-mail: tprountzos@mlga.com.

PROUT, CARL WESLEY, retired history educator; b. Bakersfield, Calif., Apr. 19, 1941; s. George Hecla and Ruth (King) P. BA, U. Calif., Santa Barbara, 1964, MA, 1965; postgrad., U. Tenn., Knoxville, 1968-71, Am. U., Cairo, 1974, U. So. Calif., 1981, Ain Shams U., Cairo, 1981. Instr. history Santa Barbara Coll., 1965-66, U. Tenn., Knoxville, 1968-71; instr. Orange Coast Coll., Costa Mesa, 1966-68, asst. prof., 1971-73, assoc. prof., 1973-75, prof., 1975-2001, prof. emeritus, 2001—; retired, 2001. Adj. prof. U. at Sea, 1996—; treas. Willmore Corp., 1980-81, sec., 1984-85, v.p., 1985-86, pres., chmn., 1988-89, also bd. dirs.; group facilitator Coastview Meml. Hosp., Long Beach, 1986-89. Research and publs. in field. Pres., chmn. bd. Alamitos Heights Improvement Assn., 1979-80, bd. dirs., 1980-82; mem. East Long Beach Joint Coun., 1979-80, Local Coastal Planning Adv. Com., 1979-80; preservation bd. Palm Springs Hist. Site, 1994-2002; mem. Palm Springs Hist. Soc.; founding pres. Palm Springs Hist. Site Preservation Found., 1997-2002. Recipient Salgo Outstanding Tchr. award, 1974-76. Mem. Writers Guild Palm Springs (v.p. 1996-98). *Personal philosophy: Honesty, Openmindedness, Willingness = How to succeed in life!.*

PROUT, CAROLYN ANN, controller, personnel administrator; b. Clare, Mich., Jan. 18, 1947; d. Aaron Eugene and Alice Marie (Fall) Prout; m. Stanley George Lyon, July 13, 1968 (dec. May 1971); children: Lori Anne Lyon (dec.), Jamie Lynn Lyon Pier (dec.); m. Dennis Karl Hunt, Jan. 1975 (div. Nov. 1977); 1 child, Julie Marie Baldwin; m. Arthur Roy Przybylowicz, Nov. 3, 1979 (div. Jan. 1998). Cert. acctg., Lansing Bus. U., 1965; BBA summa cum laude, Davenport Coll., 1998. Bank teller Citizens Bank & Trust, Rosebush, Mich., 1965-68; bookkeeper, sec. Doyle & Smith P.C., Lansing, 1968-74; legal sec. Foster, Swift, Collins & Coey P.C., 1974-79; mgr. office ARC, 1979-81; controller, personnel adminstr. Mich. Protection & Advocacy Service, 1981-88; bus. adminstr. White, Przybylowicz, Schneider & Baird, P.C., Okemos, Mich., 1988-98; faculty sec. Thomas M. Cooley Law Sch., 1998—. Vol. bookkeeper Citizens Alliance to Uphold Spl. Edn., Lansing, 1977-79; coord. bingo IHM Sch., Lansing, 1979-80; mem. St. Casimir Christian Svc., Lansing, 1981-84, chairperson, 1983-84; eucharistic min., 1987-2001; bd. dirs. Immaculate Heart of Mary Sch., Lansing, 1977-80; vol. Ingham County chpt. Am. Cancer Soc., 1989—, Nokomis Learning Ctr., 1990-97; vol. ARC, 1998-2000, WKAR-Radio Talking Book, 1999-2000. Honors scholar Thomas M. Cooley Law Sch., 2001—. Democrat. Roman Catholic. Avocations: sewing, travel, photography. Office: Thomas M Cooley Law Sch 300 S Capitol Ave Lansing MI 48933-2020 E-mail: lynnprzy@att.net.

PROUT, GEORGE RUSSELL, JR. medical educator, urologist; b. Boston, July 23, 1924; s. George Russell and Marion (Snow) P.; m. Loa Katherine Wheatley, Oct. 17, 1950; children: George Russell III, Elizabeth Louise. Student, Union Coll., 1943, DSc (hon.), 1990; MD, Albany Med. Coll., 1947, DSc (hon.), 1988; MA (hon.), Harvard U., 1969. Intern Grasslands Hosp., Valhalla, N.Y., 1947-48; asst. resident in surgery, 1948-50; surg. resident Grasslands Hosp., Valhalla, N.Y., 1948-50; resident N.Y. Hosp., N.Y.C., 1952-56; asst. attending physician Meml. Ctr. for Cancer and Allied Disease, 1956-57; asst. clinician in surgery James Ewing Hosp., 1956-57; assoc. prof., chmn. div. urology U. Miami, 1957-60; prof., chmn. div. urology Med. Coll. Va., 1960-69; chief urol. svc. Mass. Gen. Hosp., Boston, 1969-89; prof. surgery Harvard Med. Sch., 1969-89, emeritus prof. surgery, 1989—; hon. urologist Mass. Gen. Hosp., 1989—. Chmn. Adjuvants in Surg. Treatment of Bladder Cancer; mem. adv. task force Nat. Cancer Inst., 1968—, cons., 1990—; expert cons. divsn. surveillance, 1991—; Finland coop. ATBC study, 1991—; chmn. Nat. Bladder Cancer Group, 1973—86. Editor-in-chief: Urologic Oncology, 1994—2000. With USNR, 1950-52. Fellow ACS, Acad. Medicine Toronto (corr.); mem. AMA, AAUP, Am. Urol. Assn., Can. Urol. Assn., Japanese Urol. Soc. (hon.), Am. Cancer Soc., Soc. Surg. Oncology, Soc. Univ. Urologists, Dallas So. Clin. Soc. (hon.), Am. Assn. Genitourinary Surgeons, Soc. Pediat. Urology, Soc. Urol. Oncology, Soc. Internat. Urologists, Soc. Basic Urol. Rsch., Alpha Omega Alpha. Address: 1800 River Watch Ln Annapolis MD 21401-2009 also: 224 Corsair Rd Duck Key FL 33050 E-mail: druroncsal@aol.com.

PROUT, ROBERT STEPHEN, criminal justice educator; b. June 24, 1944; Degree in law, LaSalle Ext. U., Chgo., 1967; BA, Muskingum Coll., 1969; MEd, Ohio U., 1970; PhD, Ohio State U., 1972. State trooper Ohio Hwy. Patrol, Akron, Ohio, 1965-68; coord. Muskingum Tech. Coll., Zanesville, 1969-72; dept. chair criminal justice St. Cloud (Minn.) State U., 1972—96, 2002—, dir. grad. program criminal justice, 1988—. Adj. faculty St. John's U., Coll. St. Thomas, U. Louisville; chmn. Govs. Com. on Crime Prevention-Region D, Minn., 1976-77. Author: Meeting Ohio's Law Enforcement Needs, 1973; contbr. articles to profl. jours. Recipient Tchr. of Yr. award, 1988. Office: St Cloud State U 241 Stewart Hall Saint Cloud MN 56301 E-mail: prout@stcloudstate.edu.

PROVASEK, EMIL FRANK, JR. small business owner; b. Ft. Worth, Aug. 11, 1957; s. Emil F. and Rema Maxine (Dennis) P. BSEE, U. Tex.-Arlington, 1979. Sr. microwave systems engr. Gen. Dynamics Corp., Ft. Worth, 1979-91; mgr. Causey's Rare Coins, 1991—. Pres. ACLU, Fort Worth chpt.; bd. advisors Tarrant County Lesbian and Gay Alliance. Mem. IEEE, ACLU (bd. dirs.), Am. Numismatic Assn., Tex. Coin Dealer Assn. (bd. dirs.), Eta Kappa Nu. Roman Catholic. Avocations: broadcast history, preservation of historical broadcast and electronic equipment. Home: PO Box 150411 Fort Worth TX 76108-0411 Office: 1806 Layton St Fort Worth TX 76117-5437

PROVENCHER, STEPHEN WILFRED, computational physicist, consultant; b. Worcester, Mass., Nov. 3, 1942; s. Wilfred Oscar and Geraldine Cecilia (Casey) P. AB, Clark U., 1964; PhD, Yale U., 1967. Asst. prof. chemistry Dartmouth Coll., Hanover, N.J., 1967-70; program coord., sr. scientist European Molecular Biology Lab., Heidelberg, W.Ger., 1978-85; staff scientist Max Planck Inst., Gottingen, W.Ger., 1973-78, sr. staff scientist W.Ger., 1985-2000; pres. Stephen Provencher Sci. Software Inc., Oakville, Ont., Can., 2000—. Cons. European Community, Brussels, 1984—. Contbr. articles to profl. jours. Mem. AAAS, IEEE, Soc. Indsl. and Applied Math., Am. Chem. Soc., Assn. for Computing Machinery, Phi Beta Kappa, Sigma Xi. Home: 48 Chancery Ln Oakville ON L6J 5P6 Canada E-mail: sp@s-provencher.com.

PROVENCHER-KAMBOUR, FRANCES, international search consultant, public relations executive; b. Exeter, N.H., Apr. 22, 1947; d. Roger Arthur and Josette Marguerite (Camus) Provencher; m. Benjamin C. Ryder, Apr. 12, 1969 (div. Mar. 1979); 1 child, Tiffany Nicholas; m. Edward S. Kambour, Dec. 27, 1988. BA, U. N.H., 1969; exec. MBA (partial), U. N.C., 1990-91. Clk. typist, edtl. asst. U.S. Embassy, Moscow, 1964-65; asst. editor Durham (N.H.) Advertiser, 1965-69; assoc. editor Kaman Aerospace Corp., Bloomfield, Conn., 1970-71; publs. editor The Hartford Ins. Group, 1974-76; pub. rels. cons. Fran Ryder Assocs., Farmington, 1976-78; pub. rels. account exec. Shailer Davidoff Rogers, Inc., Fairfield, 1978-80; sr. account exec. Creamer Dickson Basford, Inc., Hartford, 1980-83; account group mgr., account exec. Spiro & Assocs., Phila., 1983-84, v.p., assoc. pub. rels. dir., 1984-85; sr. v.p.

pub. rels. LSGE Advt. Inc., Avon, Conn., 1985-87; v.p. corp. comm. Wondriska Assocs., Farmington, 1987-88; pres. The Kambour Co., Raleigh, N.C., 1988-92; dir. pub. rels. & mktg. The PBC Co., Research Triangle Park, 1993-94, The Kambour Co., Westmoreland, NH, 1994—; cons. MEI Search Consultancy, LLC, an MRI affiliate, Keene, N.H., 2001—. Translator: The Cogito in Edmund Husserl's Phenomenology, 1969. Founder The Art Guild, 1975; bd. dirs. Parent's Assn., Hartford Sch. Ballet, 1982-83, U. Conn. Found., 1996-99, dir. emeritas, 1999—, Cheshire Med. Ctr./Dartmouth-Hitchcock Clinic Cmty. Adv. Coun., 1997-2001, trustee, 1999—; incorporator, 1995-97; incorporator Monadnock Cmty. Found., 2000--, Monodnock Family Svcs., 1996--. Recipient Gold Quill awards Internat. Assn. Bus. Communicators, 1974, Nat. Safety Coun. award, 1985, Paul Harris Fellow award, Rotary Internat., 1997. Mem. Pub. Rels. Soc. Am. (accredited, bd. dirs. 1980-88, 90-2001, assembly del. 1987-88, spl. commendation 1985, mem. Counselors Acad. 1982-92, 94-99, Yankee chpt. pres. 1998-99, nat. presdl. citation for leadership 1993), Elm City Rotary Club (bd. dirs. 1995-2000). Republican. Congregationalist. Address: 4 Dutton Rd Westmoreland NH 03467-4201 E-mail: kambour@monad.net.

PROVENSEN, ALICE ROSE TWITCHELL, artist, author; b. Chgo. d. Jay Horace and Kathryn (Zelanis) Twitchell; m. Martin Provensen, Apr. 17, 1944; 1 child, Karen Anna. Student, Art Inst. of Chgo., 1930-31, U. Calif., L.A., 1939, Art Student League, N.Y., 1940-41; D.H.L. (hon.), Marist Coll., 1986. With Walter Lanz Studios, Los Angeles, 1942-43; OSS, 1944-45. Exhibited (with Martin Provensen) Balt. Mus., 1954, Am. Inst. Graphic Arts, N.Y., 1959, Botolph Group, Boston, 1964; exhibited one person shows: Henry Feiwel Gallery, N.Y.C., 1991, Children's Mus., Washington, 1991, Moscarelle Mus. Art, Williamsburg, Va., 1991; books represented in Fifty Books of Yr. Selections, Am. Inst. Graphic Arts, 1947, 48, 52 (The Charge of the Light Brigade named Best Illustrated Children's Book of the Yr. N.Y. Times 1964, co-recipient Gold medal Soc. Illustrators 1960); author/illustrator: books including Karen's Opposites, 1963, Karen's Curiosity, 1963, What is a Color?, 1967, (with Martin Provensen) Who's In the Egg, 1970, The Provensen Book of Fairy Tales, 1971, Play on Words, 1972, My Little Hen, 1973, Roses are Red, 1973, Our Animal Friends, 1974, The Year at Maple Hill Farm, 1978, A Horse and a Hound, A Goat and a Gander, 1979, An Owl and Three Pussycats, 1981, Town and Country, 1984, Shaker Lane, 1987, The Buck Stops Here, 1990, Punch in New York, 1991 (Best Books N.Y. Times 1991), My Fellow Americans, 1995, Count On Me, 1998 (Book of the Yr. by Parenting Mag. 1998), The Master Swordsman, 2001, The Magic Doorway, 2001; illustrator: (with Martin Provensen) children's books including Mother Goose Book, 1976, Old Mother Hubbard, 1977, A Peaceable Kingdom, 1978, The Golden Serpent, 1980, A Visit to William Blake's Inn, 1981 (Caldecott honor book 1981), Birds, Beasts and the Third Thing, 1982, The Glorious Flight, 1984 (Caldecott medal 1984), The Voyage of the Ludgate Hill, 1987; also textbooks. Inducted into Soc. of Illustrators' Hall of Fame, 2000.

PROVENZANO, DOMINIC, information specialist; b. N.Y.C., Jan. 25, 1951; s. Nicholas Patrick and Evelyn Provenzano; children: Saverio, Carmela, James. BA, Hobart Coll., Geneva, N.Y., 1972; MS in Fgn. Svc., Georgetown U., 1976; MS, L.I. U., 1978; MA, NYU, 1987. CFP; cert. security analyst. Rschr. The White House, Washington, 1981-82, Time, Inc., N.Y.C., 1982-87; asst. prof. Suffolk C.C., Selden, N.Y., 1987-91; rsch. specialist Wasserstein Perella & Co., N.Y.C., 1991-93, mgr. info. svcs., 1994-96; rsch. assoc. Russell Reynolds, 1996-97; dir. rsch. D.S. Wolf Assocs. Inc., 1997-98; fin. advisor Prudential Securities, Melville, N.Y., 1998—. Contbr. articles to profl. jours. Named to Outstanding Young Men of Am., 1982. Mem. Beta Phi Mu., Pi Gamma Mu. Roman Catholic.

PROVINE, JOHN CALHOUN, retired lawyer; b. Asheville, N.C., May 15, 1938; s. Robert Calhoun and Harriet Josephine (Thoms) P.; m. Martha Ann Monson, Aug. 26, 1966 (div. Jan. 1975); m. Nancy Frances Lunsford, Apr. 17, 1976 (div. Mar. 1996); children: Robert, Frances, Harriet. AB, Harvard U., 1960; JD, U. Mich., 1966; MBA, NYU, 1972, LLM in Taxation, 1975. Bar: N.Y., Tenn., U.S. Dist. Ct. (so. and ea. dists.) N.Y., U.S. Ct. Appeals (2nd and 6th cirs.), U.S. Dist. Ct. (mid. dist.) Tenn., U.S. Supreme Ct. From assoc. to ptnr. White & Case, N.Y.C., 1966-74, ptnr., 1974-81, 92-94, Jakarta and Ankara, 1982-91; counsel Dearborn & Ewing, Nashville, 1982-94; ret., 1994. Lt. USN, 1960-63. Mem. ABA, N.Y. Bar Assn., Tenn. Bar Assn., Assn. of Bar of City of N.Y. Avocations: bluegrass music, rural activities. Home and Office: 6630 Manley Ln Brentwood TN 37027-3401 E-mail: jprovine@compuserve.com.

PROVINE, LORRAINE, mathematics educator, retired; b. Altus, Okla., Oct. 6, 1944; d. Claud Edward and Emmie Lorraine (Gasper) Allmon; m. Joe A. Provine, Aug. 14, 1966; children: Sharon Kay, John David. BS, U. Okla., 1966; MS, Okla. State U., 1988. Tchr. math. U.S. Grant High Sch., Oklahoma City Schs., 1966-69; tchr. East Jr. High Sch., Ponca City (Okla.) Schs., 1969-70; tchr. Ponca City High Sch., 1978-79, 81-96; lectr. dept. math. Okla. State U., Stillwater, 1996-99. Mem. NEA, Coun. for Exceptional Children, Internat. Soc. Tech. in Edn., Math. Assn. Am., Nat. Coun. Tchrs. Math., Sch. Sci. and Math. Assn., Okla. Edn. Assn., Okla. Coun. Tchrs. Math., Assn. Women in Math., Ponca City Assn. Classroom Tchrs. (treas. 1983-86, 91-96), Okla. Assn. Mothers Clubs (life, state bd. dirs. 1977-87, pres. 1984-85), Delta Kappa Gamma (Delta chpt. treas. 1996-98, Gamma state essay com. 1999—, Eta chpt. treas. 2000—). Republican. Baptist. Avocations: reading, knitting, sewing. Home: 1019 Greenway Cir Norman OK 73072-6125 E-mail: lorraineprovine@mmcable.com.

PROVIS, TIMOTHY ALAN, lawyer; b. Chgo., July 13, 1948; s. William Harold Sr. and Dorothy Louise P. BA, U. Wis., 1974; JD, Santa Clara U., 1981. Bar: Calif. 1982, U.S. Dist. Ct. (no. dist.) Calif. 1982, U.S. Ct. Appeals (9th cir.) 1983, U.S. Supreme Ct. 1987, U.S. Ct. Appeals (7th cir.) 1992, Wis. 1992, U.S. Dist. Ct. (we. dist.) Wis. 1995, U.S. Dist. Ct. (ea. dist.) Wis. 1996. Atty. pvt. practice, Madison, Wis., 1982—. Sgt. USAF, 1968-71. Office: 1920 Birge Ter Apt 1 Madison WI 53705-2372

PROVORNY, FREDERICK ALAN, lawyer, educator; b. Bklyn., Sept. 7, 1946; s. Daniel and Anna (Wurm) P.; m. Nancy Ileene Wilkins, Nov. 21, 1971; children: Michelle C., Cheryl A., Lisa T., Robert D. BS summa cum laude, NYU, 1966; JD magna cum laude, Columbia U., 1969. Bar: N.Y. 1970, U.S. Supreme Ct. 1973, D.C. 1975, Mo. 1977, Md. 1987, Calif. 1989; CPA, Md., Mo. Law clk. to Judge Harold R. Medina U.S. Ct. Appeals (2d cir.), N.Y.C., 1969-70; asst. prof. law Syracuse (N.Y.) U., 1970-72; assoc. Debevoise, Plimpton, Lyons & Gates, N.Y.C., 1972-75, Cole & Groner P.C., Washington, 1975-76; with Monsanto Co., St. Louis, 1976-86, asst. co. counsel, 1978-86; pvt. practice Washington, 1986-89; ptnr. Provorny & Jacoby, 1989-91; counsel Shaw, Pittman, Potts & Trowbridge, 1991-93; ptnr. Tydings & Rosenberg, Balt., 1993-94; pvt. practice, 1994-95, Washington, 1995-98; Harold R. Tyler prof. of law and tech., dir. Sci. and Tech. Law Ctr., Albany (N.Y.) Law Sch., 1998—; pres. Empire State Venture Group, Inc., 2001—. Lect. Bklyn Law Sch., 1973-74; adj. prof. U. Balt. Sch. of Law, 1996-98; pres. Sci. and Tech. Assocs., Inc., 1986-91. Contbr. articles to profl. jours. Trustee Christian Woman's Benevolent Assn. Youth Home, 1979-83. Mem. ABA, Am. Law Inst., Am. Arbitration Assn. (panel comml. abitrators), Philo-Mt. Sinai Lodge 968, Masons, Beta Gamma Sigma. Jewish. Home: 11803 Kemp Mill Rd Silver Spring MD 20902-1511 Office: Albany Law School 80 New Scotland Ave Albany NY 12208-3494

PROVOST, LURA-SWIFT, civic volunteer; b. Bklyn., May 14, 1938; d. Donald Edgar and Marguerite (Belshaw) Swift; m. Pierre Eusebe Provost IV, June 18, 1960; children: Pierre Eusebe V, Normand Thomas, Paul Raymond. BA, Skidmore Coll., 1960; MEd, Boston U., 1963. Cert. tchr., Mass. Substitute tchr. Westwood (Mass.) Schs., 1975-85. Pres. parents aux. Roxbury Latin Sch., West Roxbury, Mass., 1982; bd. dirs. Westwood Hist. Soc., 1990—, pres., 1997-; vestry mem. St. John's Ch., Westwood, 1991-94; pres. bd. dirs. Family Svc. Dedham, Mass., 1991-93. Mem. Fox Hill Garden Club, Mass. Horticulture Soc., Garden Club Am. (treas. Boston com. 2002-). Episcopalian. Avocations: gardening, tennis, genealogy. Home: 68 Milk St Westwood MA 02090-1735

PROVOST, RHONDA MARIE, nurse anesthetist; b. Quincy, Mass., Sept. 13, 1948; d. John Stanley and Roberta Adelaide (Tangstrom) P. RN, Quincy City Hosp. Sch. Nursing, 1969, cert. nurse anesthetist, 1971; BS, George Washington U., 1982; MSN, Samuel Merritt Coll., 1997. Cert. RN anesthetist. Staff anesthetist, instr. Children's Hosp. Med. Ctr., Boston, 1971-77; staff anesthetist George Washington U. Med. Ctr., Washington, 1977-78; dir. Sch. of Anesthesia New Eng. Med. Ctr. Hosp., Boston, 1978-79; staff anesthetist Kaiser-Permanente Med. Group, Redwood City, Calif., 1979-88, chief anesthetist, 1988-89, Santa Rosa, Calif., 1989-91, staff anesthetist, 1991—. Freelance anesthetist Pregnancy Counseling Ctr., San Jose, Calif., 1983-84, Plastic Reconstructive Ambulatory Ctr., Los Altos, Calif., 1984-85; treas. Specific Publs., Inc., 1983-97, v.p., sales dir., 1991-97. Co-author: Indoor Exercise Book, 1981, Advanced Indoor Exercise Book, 1982, Feeling Fit in Your Forties, 1986; contbr. articles to profl. jours.; TV race commentator 2d Ann. Manila Internat. Marathon, 1983. Sec. bd. dirs. Grant Ave. Condominium Owners Assn., Palo Alto, Calif., 1984, v.p. bd. dirs., 1985; med. dir. Napa Valley Marathon, 1996--. Mem. Am. Assn. Nurse Anesthetists, Calif. Assn. Nurse Anesthetists, Toastmasters, Sigma Theta Tau Internat. Roman Catholic. Avocations: triathletics, marathons, piano, snow skiing, sailing. Home: 7050 Giusti Rd Forestville CA 95436-9637 Office: The Permanente Med Group 401 Bicentennial Way Santa Rosa CA 95403-2149

PROVUS, BARBARA LEE, executive search consultant; b. Washington, Nov. 20, 1949; d. Severn and Birdell (Eck) P.; m. Frederick W. Wackerle, Mar. 29, 1985. Student, NYU, 1969-70; BA in Sociology, Russell Sage Coll., 1971; MS in Indsl. Rels., Loyola U., Chgo., 1978; postgrad., Smith Coll., 1971. Sec. Booz, Allen & Hamilton, Chgo., 1973-74, mgr. tng., 1974-77, dir. rsch., 1977-79, cons. search, 1979-80; mgr. mgmt. devel. Federated Dept. Stores, Cin., 1980-82; v.p. Lamalie Assocs., Chgo., 1982-86; prin., founder Sweeney, Shepherd, Bueschel, Provus, Harbert & Mummert, Inc., 1986-91; founder Shepherd Bueschel & Provus Inc., 1992—. Bd. dirs. Anti-Cruelty Soc., Chgo., 1990—, pres., 1996-97; trustee Sage Colls., Troy, N.Y., 1999-2000. Mem. Assn. Exec. Search Cons. (dir. 1989-92), The Chgo. Network (bd. dirs. 1993—, chair 2002--), Econ. Club Chgo. Avocations: collecting rubber bands, modern art, baseball. Home: 3750 N Lake Shore Dr Chicago IL 60613-4238 Office: Shepherd Bueschel & Provus Inc 401 N Michigan Ave Ste 3020 Chicago IL 60611-4257

PROWN, JULES DAVID, art historian educator; b. Freehold, N.J., Mar. 14, 1930; s. Max and Matilda (Cassileth) P.; m. Shirley Ann Martin, June 23, 1956; children: Elizabeth Anderson, David Martin, Jonathan, Peter Cassileth, Sarah Peiter. AB, Lafayette Coll., 1951, DFA (hon.), 1979; AM, U. Del., 1956, Harvard U., 1953, PhD, 1961. Dir. Hist. Soc. Old Newbury, Newburyport, Mass., 1957-58, Old Gaol Mus., York, Maine, 1958-59; asst. to dir. Harvard U., Fogg Art Mus., Cambridge, Mass., 1959-61; instr. to Paul Mellon prof. history of art Yale U., New Haven, 1961-99, Paul Mellon prof. emeritus history of art, 1999—, curator Am. art, 1963-68; vis. lectr. Smith Coll., Northampton, Mass., 1966-67; dir. Yale Ctr. for Brit. Art, New Haven, 1968-76, sr. rsch. fellow, 1999—; assoc. dir. Nat. Humanities Inst., 1977. Trustee Whitney Mus., N.Y.C., 1975-94; mem. editorial adv. bd. Am. Art-Smithsonian, Washington, 1986-2001, On Common Ground, 1993—; mem. vis. com. Harvard U. Art Museums, 1993-98. Author: John Singleton Copley, 2 Vols., 1966, American Painting from Its Beginnings to the Armory Show, 1969, The Architecture of the Yale Center for British Art, 1977, American Artifacts: Essays in Material Culture, 2000, Art as Evidence: Writings on Art and Material Culture, 2002, (catalogue) American Art from Alumni Collections, 1968; editor (with Kenneth Haltman) American Artifacts: Essays in Material Culture, 2000, Art as Evidence: Writings on Art and Material Culture, 2002. Recipient George Washington Kidd award Lafayette Coll., 1986, recipient Iris Found. award for outstanding contbns. to the decorative arts, 2001, Lawrence A. Fleischman award for scholarly excellence in the field of Am. Art History, 2001. Fellow The Athenaeum of Phila. (hon.); mem. Am. Antiquarian Soc., Coll. Art Assn. (Disting. Tchg. of Art History award 1996), Am. Studies Assn., Conn. Acad. Arts & Scis., Walpole Soc., Royal Soc. Arts. Office: Yale U History of Art Dept PO Box 208272 New Haven CT 06520-8272 Business E-Mail: jules.prown@yale.edu.

PRPICH, MICHAEL FRANK, food company manager; b. Harbor City, Calif., Sept. 20, 1971; s. Nicholas Frank Prpich and Donna Jean O'Donnell; m. Cynthia Reneé Prpich, Dec. 18, 1993 (div. Oct. 1997); m. Loretta Faye Prpich, Nov. 28, 1998; children: Eric Glenn Barr, Morgan Destin Barr, Bethany Anna Faye. BS in Math., Ark. Tech. U., 1997. Dock worker Tyson Valley Distbn. Ctr., Russellville, Ark., 1990, checker, 1990-91, inventory control, 1991, 92, forklift operator, 1991-92, 92-95, lead, 1995-97; plant supr. Tyson Dardanelle, 1997-98, process improvement mgr., 1998—. Republican. Avocations: computers, racquetball, spending time with family. Home: 1116 N 7th St Dardanelle AR 72834-3122 E-mail: prpichm@tyson.com.

PRUCE, RHODA POSNER, social worker; b. N.Y.C., Sept. 4, 1944; d. Louis and Anna (Konovitch) Kfare; m. Gary H. Posner, June 27, 1965 (div. Jan. 14, 1989); children: Joseph, Michael; m. Morton S. Pruce, Aug. 22, 1999. BA, Hunter Coll., 1965; MEd, Johns Hopkins U., 1975; MSW, U. Md., 1980. Lic. social worker. Caseworker Family & Children's Svcs., Towson, Md., 1980-86; dir. Gestalt Therapy Ctr., Balt., 1983—; dept. dir. Jewish Family Svcs., 1991—2000. Bd. dirs. Mid-Atlantic Assn. for Tng. and Consulting, Washington, 1990-96; prof. devel. com. NASW, Balt., 1988—. Contbr. articles to profl. jours. Mem. NASW, Nat. Coun. Jewish Women, Nat. Coalition Bldg. Inst. Internat. (local assoc.). Democrat. Jewish. Avocation: square dancing. Home: 6117 Benhurst Rd Baltimore MD 21209-3804 Office: Gestalt Therapy Ctr Balt 6117 Benhurst Rd Baltimore MD 21209-3804

PRUCHA, JOHN JAMES, geologist, educator; b. River Falls, Wis., Sept. 22, 1924; s. Edward Joseph and Katharine (Schladweiler) P.; m. Mary Elizabeth Helfrich, June 12, 1948; children— David, Stephen, Katharine, Carol, Mark, Barbara, Margaret, Christopher, Anne, Andrew. Student, Wis. State U., River Falls, 1941-43; Ph.B., U. Wis., 1945, Ph.M., 1946; MA, Princeton, 1948, PhD, 1950. Asst. prof. geology Rutgers U., 1948-51; sr. geologist N.Y. State Geol. Survey, 1951-56; rsch. geologist Shell Devel. Co., 1956-63; prof. geology Syracuse U., 1963-90, prof. emeritus, 1990—, chmn. dept., 1963-70, 88-89, dean Coll. Arts and Scis., 1970-72, vice chancellor acad. affairs, 1972-85; pres. Syracuse U. Press, 1973-85, bd. dirs., 1985-90. Author: Basement Tectonics of Rocky Mountains, 1965, Structural Behavior of Salt, 1967, Stratigraphy and Structure of Southeastern New York, 1959, Fracture Patterns, 1979, Zones of Structural Weakness, 1992, (with Norman A. Foss) Kinnickinnic Years, 1993. Trustee Le Moyne Coll., 1971-78; bd. dirs. Everson Mus. Art, Syracuse, Syracuse, 1974—, pres., 1978-80; bd. dirs. Cultural Resources Coun., 1977-83, v.p., 1980-81; mem. regents vis. com. N.Y. State Mus., 1993-96. Recipient John Mason Clarke medal N.Y. State Geol. Survey, 1990. Fellow AAAS, Geol. Soc. Am.; mem. Am. Assn. Petroleum Geologists, Am. Geophys. Union, N.Y. State Coun. Profl. Geologists. Home: 112 Ardsley Dr Syracuse NY 13214-2110 Office: Syracuse Univ 204 Heroy Geology Lab Syracuse NY 13244-0001

PRUDEN, ANN LORETTE, chemical engineer, researcher, management consultant; b. Norfolk, Va., Sept. 3, 1948; d. James Otis and Elora Maie Pruden; m. Alan Todd Royer, Aug. 13, 1983; children: James Sebastian Royer, Annabelle Grace Royer. BS in Chemistry, Maryville (Tenn.) Coll., 1970; MA in Chem. Engring., Princeton (N.J.) U., 1978; PhD, 1981. Chemist Mobil Rsch. and Devel. Corp., Princeton, N.J., 1970-73, rsch. chemist, 1973-76, rsch. engr., 1980-86; sr. rsch. engr. Mobil Chem. Co., 1986-92, supr. Edison, 1992-97, lab. mgr., 1997-2000, tech. mgmt. team, 1997-2000; prin. Inventive Strategies, 2000—. Mem. Quality Director's Network, Indsl. Rsch. Inst., Washington, 1992-98. Contbg. author: Photocatalytic Purification and Treatment of Water and Air, 1993; contbr. articles to profl. jours. Fellow Mobil R&D Corp., Princeton, N.J., 1976-79. Mem.: Inst. Mgmt. Cons., Am. Soc. Quality, Am. Chem. Soc., AIChE. Achievements include research in heterogeneous catalysis, organizational effectiveness. Avocations: gardening, textile handwork. E-mail: pruden@inv-strat.com.

PRUDEN, WESLEY (JAMES PRUDEN), newspaper editor, columnist; b. Jackson, Miss., Dec. 18, 1935; s. James Wesley and Anne (Wilder) P.; m. Ann Fontaine Rice, Oct. 15, 1960 (div. 1961). Student, U. Ark.-Little Rock, Little Rock, 1954-55. Sportswriter Ark. Gazette, Little Rock, 1953, asst. state editor, 1954-56; reporter The Comml. Appeal, Memphis, 1956-63; fgn. corr. The Nat. Observer, Washington, 1963-77; free-lance journalist, 1977-82; chief polit. corr. The Washington Times, 1982-84, dep. mng. editor, 1984-87, mng. editor, 1987-92, editor-in-chief, 1992—. Author: Vietnam: The War, 1965. Ark. del. to Dem. Nat. Conv., L.A., 1960. With USAF, 1957-58, Ark. Air Nat. Guard, 1954-63. Recipient H.L. Mencken prize Balt. Sun, 1991. Mem. Am. Soc. Newspaper Editors, Sigma Delta Chi. So. Bapt. Office: The Washington Times 3600 New York Ave NE Washington DC 20002-1996

PRUDEN, WILLIAM BAILEY, JR. retired chemistry educator; b. Elizabeth City, N.C., Oct. 14, 1936; s. William Bailey and Johnola Augusta (Staton) P.; m. JoAnne Jones (div. 1965); children: Eric, Ellen, Denice. BS, Hampton U., 1958; postgrad., Temple U., 1974-75, Drexel U., 1978. Profl. teaching cert., N.J., Ohio. Chief rsch. asst. Jefferson U., Phila., 1960-61; lab. technician Hannahman U., 1961-62; tchr. Va. Pub. Schs., Norfolk-Portsmouth, 1962-67; tng. instr. Polaris Weapons Sys. USN, Virginia Beach, Va., 1968-69; tchr. Phila. Sch. Dist., 1969-88; ret., 1988. Inventor in field. Lt. U.S. Army, 1958-59. Mem. Nat. Sci. Tchrs. Assn., Phila. Fedn. Tchrs. Democrat. Episcopalian. Avocations: reading, writing, fishing, hunting. Home: 5131 Catharine St Philadelphia PA 19143-2614

PRUD'HOMME, ALBERT FREDRIC, securities company executive, financial planner; b. New Rochelle, N.Y., Dec. 19, 1952; s. Albert O. and Rita R. (Moshier) P.; m. LuAnn Winfield, June 29, 1985 (div.); children: Cherilyn, Alicia. BA, Mercer U., 1975. Chartered underwriter, 1999. Sales rep. Met. Life Ins. Co., N.Y.C., 1975-82; sales agt. Ohio Nat. Life, Cin., 1977-92; pres. The Scepter Securities Inc., Charlotte, N.C., 1982-91; with Wall St. Capital, The Advisors Group, and Acacia Fin. Group, 1991-98; mktg. dir. Ballantyne Planning Group, MetLife, 1998—. Bd. dirs. Lyons Fin. Group Advisors, Inc. Pres. Belmont Abbey Coll. Athletic Found., 1985-87; bd. dirs. Charlotte Youth for Christ. With U.S. Army, 1972-74. Recipient Estate Planning award Winthrop Coll., 1981. Mem. Fin. Planning Assn. (cert. 1985), Nat. Assn. Ins. & Fin. Advisors, Charlotte Soc. Inst. CFPs (pres. 1994-95). Democrat. Presbyterian. Home: 2119 Bon Villa Way Fort Mill SC 29708-8549 E-mail: APrudhomme@MetLife.com.

PRUELLAGE, JOHN KENNETH, lawyer; b. St. Louis, Feb. 4, 1941; s. John H. P. and Bertha Kunkel; m. Patricia Marré, Dec. 30, 1966 (div. Apr. 1993); children: Jill Shannon Pruellage Hunt, John Kenneth, Jr., William Marré; m. Vicky L. Fehl, Aug. 29, 1993. BS, St. Louis U., 1962; JD, U. Mo., 1965; LLM, George Washington U., 1968. Tax staff Coopers & Lybrand, St. Louis, 1965-66; ptnr., chmn. Lewis, Rice & Fingersh, LLC, 1970—. Bd. dirs. Unity Health Sys., St. Louis. Bd. dir. St. Anthony's Med. Ctr., St. Louis, 1996—; trustee St. Louis U., 1998—. Capt. USAF, 1966-70. Mem. ABA, Mo. Bar Assn., St. Louis Bar Assn., Noonday Club (v.p., bd. dirs. 1996—), Old Warson Country Club (v.p., bd. dirs. 1997—). Office: Lewis Rice Fingersh LLC 500 N Broadway Ste 2000 Saint Louis MO 63102-2147

PRUETT, JAMES WORRELL, librarian, musicologist; b. Mt. Airy, N.C., Dec. 23, 1932; s. Samuel Richard and Gladys Dorne (Worrell) P.; m. Lilian Maria-Irene Pibernik, July 20, 1957; children— Mark, Ellen. BA, U. N.C., Chapel Hill, 1955, MA, 1957, PhD, 1962. Mem. faculty U. N.C., Chapel Hill., 1961-87, prof. music, 1974-87, music librarian, 1961-76, chmn. dept. music, 1976-86; chief music div. Library of Congress, Washington, 1987-95. Vis. prof. U. Toronto, 1976; cons. in music, 1995—. Editor: Studies in the History, Style and Bibliography of Music in Memory of Glen Haydon, 1969; author: Research Guide to Musicology, 1985. Contbr. profl. jours., encys. Newberry Library fellow, summer 1966 Mem. Internat. Musicol. Soc., Am. Musicol. Soc. (chpt. chmn. 1964-66, mem. coun. 1974-77), Music Libr. Assn. (pres. 1973-75, editor jour. 1974-77), Cosmos Club (Washington). Home: 343 Wesley Dr Chapel Hill NC 27516-1520

PRUGH, GEORGE SHIPLEY, lawyer; b. Norfolk, Va., June 1, 1920; s. George Shipley and Florence (Hamilton) P.; m. Katherine Buchanan, Sept. 27, 1942; children: Stephanie Dean, Virginia Patton. AB, U. Calif., Berkeley, 1941; JD, U. Calif., San Francisco, 1948; postgrad., Army War Coll., 1961-62; MA, George Washington U., 1963. Bar: Calif. 1949, U.S. Supreme Ct. 1954. Legal advisor U.S. Mil. Assistance Command, Vietnam, 1964-66; legal adviser U.S. European Command, Stuttgart, Ger., 1966-69; Judge Adv., U.S. Army Europe, Heidelberg, Ger., 1969-71; Judge Adv. Gen. Washington, 1971-75; ret., 1975. Prof. law Hastings Coll. Law, U. Calif., San Francisco, 1975-82 Author: (with others) Law at War, 1975; (play) Solferino; contbr. articles to profl. jours. Mem. Sec. Def. Task Force on Racial Discrimination in Adminstrn. Mil. Justice, 1973; mem. U.S. del. Diplomatic Conf. on Law of War, Geneva, 1974, 75. 2d lt. U.S. Army; maj. gen. JAGC, 1971. Decorated D.S.M. with oak leaf cluster, Legion of Merit with oak leaf cluster. Mem. ABA, Am. Judicature Soc., Internat. Soc. Mil. Law and Law of War (hon. pres.), Civil Affairs Assn. (hon. dir.), Selden Soc., Calif. Bar, Order of Coif, Bohemian Club, Army and Navy Club (Washington), Phi Delta Phi. Episcopalian.

PRUIS, JOHN J. business executive; b. Borculo, Mich., Dec. 13, 1923; s. Ties J. and Trientje (Koop) P.; m. Angeline Rosemary Zull, Sept. 14, 1944; children: David Lofton, Daniel J., Dirk Thomas. BS, Western Mich. U., 1947; MA, Northwestern U., 1949, PhD, 1951; Litt.D. (hon.), Yeungnam U., Taegu, Korea, Ind. State U.; LL.D. (hon.), Ball State U., U. So. Ind.; DHL (hon.), Keuka Coll. Tchr. pub. schs., Mich., 1942-43; supervising tchr. Campus Sch., Western Mich. U., 1947-48; instr. speech U. No Ia., 1951-52; from asst. prof. to assoc. prof. speech So. Ill. U., 1952-55; mem. faculty Western Mich. U., 1955-68, sec. bd. trustees, 1964-68, v.p. adminstrn., 1966-68; pres. Ball State U., 1968-78; v.p. corp. rels. Ball Corp., 1978-88. Cons., examiner North Central Assn., 1959-78; also bd. dirs. N. Central Assn. V.p. Country dr. chmn. Kalamazoo Cmty. Chest, 1964; bd. dirs. Kalamazoo chpt. Am. Cancer Soc., 1963-68, Del. County United Way, Muncie Symphony Assn., Ball Meml. Hosp., Big Bros./Big Sisters, Ind. Legal Found.; trustee U. So. Ind., 1985-90; exec. v.p. George and Frances Ball Found. With USNR, 1943-46; capt. Res., ret. Mem. Am. Assn. Higher Edn., Speech Communication Assn., Muncie C. of C., Blue Key, Rotary, Phi Delta Kappa, Omicron Delta Kappa, Beta Gamma Sigma Presbyterian.

PRUITT, ALICE FAY, mathematician, engineer; b. Montgomery, Ala., Dec. 17, 1943; d. Virgil Edwin and Ocie Victoria (Mobley) Maye; m. Mickey Don Pruitt, Nov. 5, 1967; children: Derrell Gene, Christine Marie. BS in Math., U. Ala., Huntsville, 1977; postgrad., Calif. State U., Northridge, 1978-79. Instr. math. Antelope Valley Coll., Quartz Hill, Calif., 1977-78; space shuttle engr. Rockwell Internat., Palmdale, 1979-81; programmer, analyst sci. support svcs. Combat Devel. and Experimentation Ctr., Ft. Hunter-Liggett, 1982-85; sr. engrng. specialist Loral Vought Sys. Corp., Dallas, 1985-92; dir. concepts and analysis, advanced sys. engrng. Nichols Rsch. Corp., Huntsville, Ala., 1992-99; sr. sys. engr. Computer Sci. Corp., 1999—. Active DeSoto (Tex.) Coun. Cultural Arts, 1987-89. Mem. AAUW (sch. bd. rep. 1982, legal advocacy fund chairperson 1989-91), Toastmasters, Phi Kappa Phi. Republican. Methodist. Avocations: dancing, gourmet cooking. Office: PO Box 400002 4090 S Memorial Pky Ste A Huntsville AL 35815-1502 E-mail: afpruitt@comcast.net., apruitt@csc.com.

PRUITT, ANNE LORING, academic administrator, education educator; b. Bainbridge, Ga., Sept. 19, 1929; d. Loring Alphonzo and Anne Lee (Ward) Smith; m. Harold G. Logan; children: Leslie; stepchildren: Dianne, Pamela, Sharon, Ralph Pruitt, Jr., Harold, Minda, Andrew Logan. BS, Howard U., Washington, 1949; MA, Columbia U., N.Y.C., 1950, EdD, 1964; HumD hon., Ctrl. State U., Wilberforce, Ohio, 1982. Counsel for women Howard U., 1950-52; tchr., dir. guidance Hutto H.S., Bainbridge, 1952-55; dean students Albany State Coll., Ga., 1955-59, Fisk U., Nashville, 1959-61; prof. edn. Case Western Res. U., Cleve., 1963-79; prof. ednl. policy and leadership Ohio State U., Columbus, 1979-95, prof. emeritus, 1995—; assoc. dean Ohio State U. Grad. Sch., 1979-84; assoc. provost Ohio State U., 1984-86, dir. Ctr. for Tchg. Excellence, 1986-94; dean in residence Coun. Grad. Schs., Washington, 1994-96, scholar in residence, 1996—. Cons. So. Regional Edn. Bd., Atlanta, 1967-78, So. Edn. Found., Atlanta, 1978-87. Author: New Students and Coordinated Counseling, 1973, Black Employees in Traditionally White Institutions in the Adams States 1975-77, 1981, In Pursuit of Equality in Higher Education, 1987; co-author: (with Paul Isaac) Student Services for the Changing Graduate Student Population, 1995, (with Jerry Gaff and Richard Weibl) Building the Faculty Weekend: Colleges and Universities Working Together, 2000. Bd. trustees Urban League, Cleve., 1965-71, Ctrl. State U., 1973-82, Case Western Res. U., 1978—, Columbus Area Leadership Program, 1988-91; bd. dirs. ARC, Cleve., 1978-79, Am. West Airlines Found., 1992-95; mem. adv. com. USCG Acad., New London, Conn., 1980-83; Ohio State U. rep. to AAUW, 1989-94; univ. co-chairperson United Way, 1990-91; trustee

Marburn Acad., 1991-95; mem. Columbus 1992 Edn. Com., 1988-92; mem. edn. subcom. Columbus Found., 1991-94; mem. exec. com. Renaissance League, 1992-94; mem. vis. panel on rsch., Ednl. Testing Svc., 1996—; mem. Commn. on Future Clemson U., 1997-98; bd. dirs. Black Women's Agenda, Inc., 1997-98, pres. 1998—; deacon People's Congregational United Ch. of Christ, 1998—. Recipient Outstanding Alumnus award Howard U. Alumni Assn., 1975; Am. Council on Edn. fellow, 1977; named one of Am.'s Top 100 Black Bus. and Profl. Women Dollars & Sense Mag., 1986; recipient Disting. Affirmative Action award Ohio State U., 1988; named Sr. Scholar Am. Coll. Personnel Assn., 1989, Woman of Achievement award YMCA, 1993. Mem. NSF (mem. com. on equal opportunities in sci. and engring. 1989-95), Am. Coll. Pers. Assn. (pres. 1976-77), Coun. Grad. Schs. in U.S. (chairperson com. on minority grad. edn. 1980-84), Am. Ednl. Rsch. Assn., Ohio Assn. Counselor Edn. (pres. 1966-67), Links Inc., Cosmos Club.

PRUITT, BASIL ARTHUR, JR. surgeon, retired army officer; b. Nyack, N.Y., Aug. 21, 1930; s. Basil Arthur and Myrtle Flo (Knowles) P.; m. Mary Sessions Gibson, Sept. 4, 1954; children: Scott Knowles, Laura Sessions, Jeffrey Hamilton. AB, Harvard U., 1952, postgrad., 1952-53; MD, Tufts U., 1957. Diplomate Am. Bd. Surgery (bd. dirs. 1982-88). Intern Boston City Hosp., 1957-58, resident in surgery, 1958-59, 61-62; commd. capt., M.C. U.S. Army, 1959, advanced through grades to col., 1972; resident Brooke Gen. Hosp., Ft. Sam Houston, Tex., 1962-64; chief clin. divsn. Inst. Surg. Rsch., 1965-67; chief profl. services 12th Evacuation Hosp., Vietnam, 1967-68; comdr., dir. U.S. Army Inst. Surg. Research, Brooke Army Med. Center, Ft. Sam Houston, 1968-95, ret., 1995; clin. prof. gen. surgery U. Tex. Health Sci. Ctr., San Antonio, 1996—; prof. surgery Uniformed Svcs. U. of the Health Scis., Bethesda, Md., 1978—. Mem. surgery, anaesthesiology and trauma study sect. NIH, 1978-82; mem. Shriners Burns Adv. Bd., 1985-92, Shriners Med. Adv. Bd., 1992-95, Shriners Rsch. Adv. Bd., 1996—, mem. Shriners Clin. Outcomes Studies Adv. Bd., 1999—; merit rev. bd. for surgery VA, 1990-93. Author med. books; contr. chpts. to textbooks, articles to profl. jours.; mem. editl. bd. Jour. Trauma, 1975-94, editor, 1995—; mem. edit. bd.: Archives Surgery, 1981-93, Consultations in Surgery, Correspondence Society of Surgeons, Collected Letters, 1978—, Circulatory Shock, 1985-93, Jour. Burn Care and Rehabilitation, 1984-87, Jour. Investigative Surgery, 1987-97, Shock Research, 1993—, Current Opinion in Surgical Infections, 1993—, Sepsis, 1996—, Injury, 1998—, Turkish Jour. Trauma, 2002—, English edit. Chinese Jour. Traumatology, 1998—. Decorated Bronze Star, Legion of Merit, Disting. Svc. medal; recipient ISS/SIC Danis prize, 1995, Am. Surgical Assn. Medallion, 1998, G. Whitaker Internat. Burns prize, 2000. Fellow: ACS (pre and postoperative care com. 1969—79, vice chmn. 1973—75, gov. 1973—79, com. on trauma 1974—84, internat. rels. com. 1983—93, chmn. 1987—89), Am. Coll. Critical Care Medicine (disting. investigator award 2000); mem.: No. Am. Burm Soc. (pres. 1993—94, 1993—94), Shock Soc. (clin. counselor 1995—98), Internat. Surg. Group, Surg. Infection Soc. (recorder 1980—84, pres. 1985—86), Assn. Acad. Surgery, Internat. Soc. Surgery, Surg. Biol. Club III, Am. Assn. Surgery Trauma (recorder 1976—80, pres. 1982—83), Halsted Soc. (pres. 1985—86), So. Surg. Assn. (pres. 1985—86), Western Surg. Assn. (dist. rep. 1984—88, pres. 1993—94), Tex. Surg. Assn., Am. Surg. Assn. (2d v.p. 1980—81, pres. 1999—2000), Soc. Univ. Surgeons, Am. Trauma Soc. (pres. Tex. divsn. 1974—75, dir. 1974—, sec. 1986—88, v.p. 1988—90, pres.-elect 1990—92, pres. 1992—94), Smoke Burn and Fire Assn. (adv. coun.), Internat. Soc. Burn Injuries (nat. rep. 1974—82, co-chmn. disaster planning com. 1982—86, pres.-elect 1990—94, pres. 1994—98), Am. Burn Assn. (pres. 1975—76), Mediterranean Club Burns and Fire Disasters (regional rep. Ams.), Surgeons' Travel Club. Home: 402 Tidecrest Dr San Antonio TX 78239-2517 Office: U Tex Health Sci Ctr Dept Surgery 7703 Floyd Curl Dr San Antonio TX 78229-3900 also: Editl Office Jour Trauma 7330 San Pedro Ste 654 San Antonio TX 78216-6236

PRUITT, BRAD ALEXANDER, business executive; b. Lubbock, Tex., May 3, 1967; s. William Alvis and Cherolyne Louise (Northam) P.; m. Kay Elizabeth Williams, Dec. 29, 1987. BBA in Acctg., Abilene Christian U., 1989. CPA, Tex. Staff auditor Weaver and Tidwell CPAs, Ft. Worth, 1989-90; sr. acct. Dal-Tile Corp., Dallas, 1990-93, acctg. mgr., 1993-95; v.p., treas. Thermo-Serv, Inc., plastics mfr. and dist., 1996—. Mem. AICPA, Inst. Mgmt. Accts. Mem. Ch. of Christ. Avocations: golf, basketball, reading, travel. Home: 6201 Turtle Cove Ct Arlington TX 76018-3133 Office: Thermo-Serv Inc 3901 Pipestone Rd Dallas TX 75212-6017

PRUITT, DEAN GARNER, psychologist, educator; b. Phila., Dec. 26, 1930; s. Dudley McConnell and Grace (Garner) P.; m. France Juliard, Dec. 27, 1959; children: Andre Juliard, Paul Dudley, Charles Alexandre. AB, Oberlin Coll., 1952; MS, Yale U., 1954, PhD, 1957. Postdoctoral fellow U. Mich., 1957-59; rsch. assoc. Northwestern U., 1959-61; asst. prof., then assoc. prof. U. Del., 1961-66; Disting. prof. emeritus SUNY, Buffalo, 2001—, assoc. prof., then prof., Disting. prof. emeritus, 1966-2001, dir. grad. program in social psychology, 1969—73, Disting. prof. emeritus, 1976—77, 1985—88, 1998—2001; vis. faculty George Mason U., 2001—. Author: Negotiation Behavior, 1981, (with J. Z. Rubin and S.H. Kim) Social Conflict, 1986, 94; (with P.J. Carnevale) Negotiation in Social Conflict, 1993; editor; (with R.C. Snyder) Theory and Research on the Causes of War, 1969, (with K. Kressel) Mediation Research, 1989. Grantee Office Naval Rsch., 1965, NIMH, 1969, NSF, 1969, 74, 76, 80, 83, 86, 88, 93, Guggenheim Found., 1978-79. Fellow APA, Am. Psychol. Soc., Soc. for Psychol. Study Social Issues; mem. Internat. Assn. for Conflict Mgmt. (pres. 1990-92, Lifetime Achievement award 1997), Internat. Soc. Polit. Psychology (v.p. 1984-85, Harold D. Lasswell award 1992), Phi Beta Kappa, Sigma Xi. Home: 9006 Friars Rd Bethesda MD 20817-3320 Office: George Mason U Inst Conflict Analysis and Resolution Fairfax VA 22030-4444 E-mail: dean@pruittfamily.com.

PRUITT, GEORGE ALBERT, college president; b. Canton, Miss., July 9, 1946; s. Joseph Henry and Lillie Irene (Carmichael) P.; m. Pamela Young; 1 child, Shayla Nicole. BS, Ill. State U., 1968, MS, 1970, DHL (hon.), 1994; PhD, Union Grad. Sch., Cin., 1974; D Pub. Svc. (hon.), MA (hon.), Bridgewater State Coll., 1990; LLD (hon.), Ill. State U., 1994; DHL (hon.), SUNY Empire State Coll., 1996. Asst. to v.p. for acad. affairs Ill. State U., Normal, 1968-70, dir. high potential students program, 1968-70; dean students Towson State U., 1970-72; v.p., exec. asst. to pres., assoc. prof. urban affairs Morgan State U., 1972-75; v.p., prof. Tenn. State U., 1975-81; exec. v.p. Council for Advancement Experiential Learning, Columbia, Md., 1981-82; pres. Thomas A. Edison State Coll., Trenton, 1982—. Commn. on ednl. credit and credentials, labor/higher edn. coun. Am. Coun. on Edn.; advisor group XII, Nat. Fellowship program W.K. Kellogg Found., 1990-94, advisor group XV, 1995-99; bd. dirs. SEEDCO; nat. adv. com. on instnl. quality and integrity U.S. Dept. Edn., 1994—; bd. dirs. Sun Nat. Bank, Vineland, N.J. Past chair Mercer County Chamber of Commerce; chair Union Inst., Cin., 1989—97, Rider U., Lawrenceville, NJ; bd. dirs. N.J. Assn. Colls. and Univs. Recipient Resolution of Commendation Bd., Trustees Morgan State U., 1975, Outstanding Svc. to Edn. award Tenn. State U., 1981, Gubernatorial citation Gov. of Tenn., 1981, Good Guy award George Washington coun. Boy Scouts Am., 1991, Humanitarian award NCCJ, 1992, Educator of Yr. award Black N.J. Mag., 1993, Disting. Alumni award Ill. State U., 1996; apptd. hon. mem. Gen. Assembly Tenn., 1981, hon. mem. U.S. Congress from 5th Tenn. dist., 1981; named ofcr. of the Most Effective Coll. Pres. in U.S., Exxon Edn. Found. Study, 1986; named to Coll. of Edn. Hall of Fame, Ill. State U., 1995; named Mercer Co. N.J. Citizen of Yr., Mercer Co. C. of C., 1997. Mem. Coun. for Advancement Exptl. Learning, Am. Assn. State Colls.and Univs., Coun. for Advancement and Support of Edn., Am. Coun. Edn., Mid. States Assn. Colls. and Schs. (accreditation evaluator commn. on higher edn.), Mercer County C. of C. (chmn.). Office: Thomas Edison Coll 101 W State St Trenton NJ 08608-1101

PRUITT, ROSANNE HARKEY, nursing educator, human services researcher; b. Charlotte, N.C., Aug. 3, 1952; d. Martin L., Jr. and Lucille Clark (Wayland) H.; m. John Crayton Pruitt, Aug. 10, 1974; children: Crayton Smith, Martin Curtis. BSN, Emory U., Atlanta, 1974; MN, U. S.C., 1979; PhD, U. Md., 1989. RN, S.C. Family nurse practitioner Nat. Health Svc. Corps, Calhoun Falls, S.C., 1979-81; asst. prof. U. Md., Balt., 1984-89; prof. Clemson (S.C.) U. Sch. Nursing, 1990—. Part-time family nurse practitioner Clemson U. Nursing Ctr., 1990—, Columbia, Md., 1983-87, NIH Occupational Health, Bethesda, Md., 1988-89. Contbr. articles to profl. jours. Recipient grants for rsch. in health promotion. Mem. ANA, Am. Acad. Nurse Practitionrs, Nat. Orgn. Nurse Practitioner Faculty, S.C. Nurses Assn., Cmty. Health Coun., Sigma Theta Tau (rsch. grantee 1988-89). Home: 117 Carter Hall Dr Anderson SC 29621-1976

PRUITT, STEPHEN WALLACE, finance educator; b. Indpls., Feb. 3, 1957; s. Harry Wallace and Dorothy (Thorp) P.; m. Mary Melinda Settle, Dec. 19, 1981; children: Rebecca Elizabeth, Victoria Barrick. BS in Mgmt., Purdue U., 1979; MBA in Fin., Ohio State U., 1980; PhD in Fin., Fla. State U., 1987. Internat. cash mgr. Marathon Oil Co., Findlay, Ohio, 1980-81; fin. analyst Nat. Svc. Industries, Crawfordsville, Ind., 1981-83; asst. prof. fin. U. Miss., Oxford, 1986-88, Ind. U., Bloomington, 1988-93; assoc. prof. fin. U. Memphis, 1993-96, prof. fin., 1996-2000; Arvin Gottlieb/Mo. chair in bus. econs. and fin. U. Mo., Kansas City, 2000—. Cons. in field. Contbr. articles to profl. jours. Bd. dirs. Art Mus. U. Memphis, 1995-2000; founder, pres. Memphis Print Club, 1995-2000. Mem. So. Fin. Assn., Fin. Mgmt. Assn. Republican. Baptist. Avocation: collecting art and antiques. Office: U Mo Henry W Bloch Sch Bus & Pub 5100 Rockhill Rd Kansas City MO 64110-2481 Home: 5316 W 140th St Overland Park KS 66224

PRUNA, LAURA MARIA, lawyer; b. La Habana, Cuba, Apr. 23, 1954; came to U.S., 1961; d. Max and Martha Luz P. BBA, U. Miami, 1976; JD, Fla. State U., 1988. Bar: Fla. 1989, U.S. Ct. Appeals (11th cir.), U.S. Ct. Mil. Appeals, Ill. 1989. Law clk. Dept. Profl. Regulation, State of Fla., Tallahassee, 1987-88; atty. Carl Di Bernardo, P.A., South Miami, Fla., 1989-90, Pruna & Milian, Miami, 1991-93, Pruna Law Offices, Miami, 1993—. Atty., Fundacion Centro Americana, Miami, 1997-98. Mem. Colombian Am. Bar (bd. dirs. 1997-98), Cath. Lawyers Guild (pres. 1989-92). Republican. Avocations: fishing, reading. Office: Pruna Law Offices 2525 SW 3d Ave Ste 205 Miami FL 33129-2057 E-mail: pruna@lawyer.com., prunaesq@aol.com.

PRUSA, JAMES GRAHAM, association executive; b. Cleve., Dec. 1, 1948; s. James Leonard and Mary LaVerne (Graham) P.; m. Patricia Ann Thwaits, June 20, 1971 (dec. 1975); m. Karen Beth Adamo, Nov. 30, 1980; children: Nathasha Clare, Shamus Graham. BS, Calif. State Poly. U., 1975; postgrad., U. Santa Clara, 1977-79, Stanford U., 1984. Golf course supt. China Lake NWC Golf Course, China Lake, Calif., 1975-77; golf course mgr. Pasatiempo, Inc., Santa Cruz, 1977-82; assoc. exec. dir. Golf Course Supt. Assn. Am., Lawrence, Kans., 1982-87; adminstr., chief staff exec. Nat. Office Machine Dealers Assn., Kansas City, Mo., 1987-90; gen. mgr., COO Ridgemark Golf and Country Club Resort, Hollister, Calif., 1990-93; exec. dir. Diving Equipment & Market Assn., Laguna Hills, 1993—. Contbr. articles to profl. jours.; tech. editor Golf Course Mgmt.; pubr. Spokesman mag. With USN, 1967-71, Calif. N.G. 1971-72. Decorated Air medal. Named Alumnus of the Yr., Calif. Poly. Hort. Dept., 1984. Mem. Am. Soc. Assn. Execs., Golf Writers Assn. Am., U.S. Golf Assn., Club Mgrs. Assn. of Am., Rotary Internat. Republican. Roman Catholic. Avocations: golf, writing, photography, personal computers, snow skiing. Office: Diving Equipment & Market Assn 3750 Convoy St Ste 310 San Diego CA 92111-3741 Address: 653 Lincoln St Red Bluff CA 96080-3730

PRUSAK, MAXIMILIAN MICHAEL, lawyer; b. Granite City, Ill., Mar. 22, 1943; s. Max Emil and Catherine Theresa (Jakich) P.; m. Carolyn Irene Pinkel, July 2, 1966; children: Scott Michael, Stephanie K. BS in Math., U. Ill., 1965, JD, 1968. Bar: Ill. 1968, U.S. Dist. Ct. (so. dist.) Ill. 1973. Staff atty. Atty.'s Title Guaranty Fund, Champaign, Ill., 1968-69; ptnr. Goldsworthy, Fifield & Prusak, Peoria, 1973-80, Nicol, Newell, Prusak & Winne, Peoria, 1980-83, Prusak & Winne, Peoria, Ill., 1983-88, Prusak, Winne & Wombacher, Peoria, 1988-93, Prusak & Winne, Ltd., Peoria, 1993—. Contbr. articles to profl. publs. Bd. dirs. Human Svc. Ctr., Peoria, 1970's, Friendship House, Peoria, 1980, Southside Mission, Peoria, 1988-89; pres. adminstrv. bd. 1st United Meth. Ch., Peoria, 1990—. Capt. USAF, 1969-73. Mem. Ill. State Bar Assn. (chmn. law office cons. sect. coun. 1997-98) , PeoriaCounty Bar Assn. (bd. dirs. 1982, 94, 98, 99, v.p. 1999, pres. 2000), Union League Club Chgo., Ill. Valley Yacht Club. Avocations: computers, sailing, reading. Home: 5821 N Mar Vista Dr Peoria IL 61614-3850 Office: Prusak & Winne Ltd 704 Jefferson Bldg 331 Fulton St Peoria IL 61602-1499 E-mail: mprusak@mtco.com.

PRUSICK, VINCENT ROGER, orthopaedic surgeon; b. Dec. 26, 1954; BS in Biochemistry, Mich. State U., 1976; MD, U. Mich., 1980. Diplomate Am. Bd. Orthopaedic Surgery. Surg. resident William Beaumont Hosp., Royal Oak, Mich., 1980-86; orthopaedic surgeon Gt. Lakes Orthopaedic Ctr., Traverse City, 1986—. Chief orthopaedic sect. Munson Med. Ctr., 1997-99. Patentee in field including lumbar back exerciser Ab-Fit; contbr. articles to profl. jours. Fellow Am. Acad. Orthopaedic Surgeons; mem. AMA, Mich. Med. Soc., Mich. Orthpaedic Soc. (pres. 1996-97), N.Am. Spine Soc., Alpha Omega Alpha, Phi Kappa Phi. Home: 10517 S West Bay Shore Dr Traverse City MI 49684-5229

PRUSINER, STANLEY BEN, neurology and biochemistry educator, researcher; b. Des Moines, May 28, 1942; s. Lawrence Albert and Miriam (Spigel) Prusiner; children: Helen Chloe, Leah Anne. AB cum laude, U. Pa., 1964, MD, 1968, DS (hon.) , 1998; PhD (hon.) , Hebrew U., Jerusalem, 1995, René Descartes U., Paris, 1996; DS (hon.) , Dartmouth Coll., 1999; DS, U. Liege, 2000; MD (hon.) , U. Bologna, Italy, 2000; DSc (hon.) , Pa. State U., 2001; DSc (hon.) , U. Liege, 2000. Diplomate Am. Bd. Neurology. Intern in medicine U. Calif., San Francisco, 1968—69, resident in neurology, 1972—74, asst. prof. neurology, 1974—80, assoc. prof., 1980—84, prof., 1984—, prof. biochemistry, 1988—, acad. senate faculty rsch. lectr., 1989—90, prof. virology Berkeley, 1984—, dir. Inst. for Neurodegenerative Diseases, 1999—; founder, chmn. bd. dirs. InPro Biotech. LLC, South San Francisco, Calif., 2001—. Mem. neurology rev. com. Nat. Inst. for Neurodegenerative Diseases, NIH, Bethesda, Md., 1982—86, Bethesda, 1990—92; mem. Coun. Nat. Inst. Aging, NIH, Bethesda, Md., 2001—; mem. sci. adv. bd. French Found., L.A., 1985—, chmn. sci. adv. bd., 1996—; mem. sci. rev. com. Alzheimer's Disease Diagnosic Ctr. & Rsch Grant Program, State of Calif., 1985—89; chmn. sci. adv. bd. Am. Health Assistance Found., Rockville, Md., 1986—2000, hon. mem. bd. dirs., Md., 2001—; mem. spongiform encephalopathy adv. com. FDA, 1997—2001; mem. adv. bd.Family Survival Project for Adults with Chronic Brain Disorders, San Francisco, 1982—90; mem. adv. bd. San Francisco chpt. Alzheimer's Disease and Related Disorders Found., 1985—91. Editor: The Enzymes of Glutamine Metabolism, 1973, Slow Transmissible Diseases of the Nervous System, 2 vols., 1979, Prions--Novel Infectious Pathogens Causing Scrapie and CJD, 1987, Prion Diseases of Humans and Animals, 1992, Molecular and Genetic Basis of Neurologic Disease, 2d edit., 1997, Prions Prions Prions, 1996, Prion Biology and Diseases, 1999; contbr. more than 300 articles to profl. jours. Trustee U. Pa., 2000—, Congregation Sherith Israel, San Francisco, 1999—2002. Lt. comdr.19 USPHS, 1969—72. Recipient Leadership and Excellence for Alzheimer's Disease award, NIH, 1990—97, Potamkin prize for Alzheimer's Disease Rsch., 1991, Presdl. award, 1993, Med. Rsch. award, Met. Life Found., 1992, Christopher Columbus Discovery award, NIH and Med. Soc. Genoa, Italy, 1992, Charles A. Dana award for pioneering achievements in health, 1992, Dickson prize for outstanding contbns. to medicine, U. Pitts., 1992, Max Planck Rsch. award, Alexander von Humboldt Found. and Max Planck Soc., 1992, Gairdner Found. Internat. award, 1993, Disting. Achievement in Neurosci. Rsch. award, Bristol-Myers Squibb, 1994, Albert Lasker award for Basic Med. Rsch., 1994, Caledonian Rsch. Found. prize, Royal Soc. Edinburgh, 1995, Paul Ehrlich and Ludwig Darmstaedter award, Germany, 1995, Paul Hoch award, Am. Psychopathol. Assn., 1995, Wolf prize in medicine, 1996, ICN Virology prize, 1996, Victor and Clara Soriano award, World Fedn. Neurology, 1996, Pasarow Found. prize in neurosci., 1996, Charles Leopole Mayer prize, French Acad. Scis., 1996, Keio Internat. prize for med. rsch., 1996, Baxter award, Am. Assn. Med. Colls., 1996, Louisa Gross Horwitz prize, Columbia U., 1997, Nobel prize in medicine, 1997, K.J. Zulch prize, Gertrude Reemtsma Found., 1997, Benjamin Franklin medal, Franklin Inst., 1998, Jubilee medal, Swedish Med. Soc., 1998, Prize Lecture medal, U. Coll. London, 1999, Sir Hans Krebs medal, Fedn. European Biochem. Socs., 1999, Ellen Browning Scripps medal, 2000; fellow Alfred P. Sloan Rsch. fellow, U. Calif., 1976—78; grantee Med. Investigator grantee, Howard Hughes Med. Inst., 1976—81, grantee for excellence in neurosci., Senator Jacob Javits Ctr., NIH, 1985—90. Fellow: AAAS, Royal Coll. Physicians, Am. Acad. Arts & Scis., Am. Soc. Microbiology; mem.: NAS (Inst. Medicine, Richard Lounsbery award for extraordinary achievements in biology and medicine 1993), Protein Soc. (Amgen award 1997), Royal Soc. London, Am. Philos. Soc., Am. Soc. Molecular Biol. Biochemistry, Am. Soc. Cellular Biology, Am. Soc. Cell Biology, Genetics Soc. Am., Am. Soc. Human Genetics, Soc. Neurosci., Am. Chem. Soc., Am. Soc. Biochemistry and Molecular Biology, Am. Soc. Clin. Investigation, Am. Neurol. Assn., Am. Soc. Virology, Am. Soc. Neurochemistry, Am. Soc. Neurochemistry, Am. Assn. Physicians, Am. Acad. Neurology (George Cotzias award for outstanding rsch. 1987, Presdl. award 1993, Disting. Achievement award 1998), Bohemian Club, Concordia Argonaut Club (bd. dirs. 1997—).

PRUSINSKI, JAN RICHARD, civil engineer; b. Detroit, Oct. 13, 1958; s. Richard C. and Virginia A. (Komorski) P.; m. Carol Lee Yates, June 28, 1980; children: Lara Jan, Alexander Yates. BS in civil engr., U. Mich., 1980; postgrad., George Washington U., 1981; MBA, U. Houston, 1987. Registered profl. engr. Tex. Engr. Bechtel Power Corp., Gaithersburg, Md., 1980-81, Houston Lighting & Power, Houston, 1981-82, 1982-83, engring. supr., 1984-87, sr. budget analyst, 1987-89, sr. mktg. analyst, 1989-91, project supr., 1991-95; mgmt. cons., 1995-96; program mgr. Portland Cement Assn., 1996—2001; exec. dir Slag Cement Assn., Tex., 2001—. Contbr. articles to profl. jours. Cons., tchr. Jr. Achievement, Houston, 1989-91. Mem. ASCE, Am. Concrete Inst. (various com. 1991—), Tex. Coal Ash Utilization Group (chmn. mktg. com. 1991-96), Am. Coal Ash Assn., Am. Concrete Pavement Assn., Nat. Concrete Bridge Coun., Environ.Coun. Concrete Orgns., Beta Gamma Sigma. Achievements include recycled thermoplastic polymer concrete patent, sulfate resistant fly ash concrete patent, immured concrete foundation system for steel utility poles patent. Avocations: tennis, running, golfing, personal computing, coaching children's sports. E-mail: jprusinski@slagcement.org.

PRUSOFF, WILLIAM HERMAN, biochemical pharmacologist, educator; b. N.Y.C., June 25, 1920; s. Samuel and Mary (Metrick) P.; m. Brigitte Auerbach, June 19, 1948 (dec. Apr. 1991); children— Alvin Saul, Laura Ann. BA, U. Miami, Fla., 1941; MA, Columbia U., 1947, PhD, 1949. Research assoc., instr. pharmacology Western Res. U., 1949-53; mem. faculty Yale Med. Sch., 1953—, prof. pharmacology, 1966-90, prof. emeritus. sr. rsch. scientist, 1990—, acting chmn. dept., 1968. Cons. in field, 1965— Mem. Am. Assn. Cancer Rsch., Am. Chem. Soc., Am. Soc. Biol. Chemists, Am. Soc. Pharmacology and Exptl. Therapeutics, Soc. Chinese Bioscientists in Am., Sigma Xi, Internat. Soc. for Antiviral Rsch. Achievements include rsch. in virology, photochemistry, mechanism drug action, synthesis potential drugs; synthesized Idoxuridine; developed (in collaboration with D.T.S. Lin) Stavudine for therapy of AIDS. Home: De Forest Dr Branford CT 06405 Office: Yale U Sch Medicine New Haven CT 06510 E-mail: William.Prusoff@yale.edu.

PRUSSIN, JEFFREY A. management consultant; b. Bklyn., Aug. 11, 1943; s. Samuel and Shirley (Solomon) P.; m. Judith H. May; children: Aaron Justin, Leya Monique. AB, UCLA, 1965; MA, Johns Hopkins U., 1967. Dir. edn. and tng. Group Health Assn. Am., Washington, 1971-72; mgr. prog. devel. Health System div. Westinghouse, Columbia, Md., 1972-73; prin. Health Care Orgn., Delivery & Fin. System, Kensington, 1973-80; exec. asst. for policy Bur. Health Facilities, HHS, Washington, 1980-81; exec. v.p. Comprehensive Am. Care, Miami, Fla., 1981-84; sr. v.p. Internat. Med. Ctrs., 1984-86; pres. Health Sys. Devel. Corp., South Miami, Fla., 1986-99, J&JP Funding Corp., Jacksonville, 1990-99. Cons. in field; lectr. in field; adj. prof. U. Miami, Fla., 1982-99; vis. asst. prof. Oreg. State U., Eugene, 1970; adj. asst. prof. Linfield Coll., Oreg., 1969-70, Portland State U., 1969-70. Contbr. numerous articles to profl. jours.; author: Health Maintenance Organization Legislation in 1973-74, 1974, Employee Health Benefits: HMOs and Mandatory Dual Choide, 1976, Results of a State-of-the-Art Review of Health Assurance for the Elderly, 1979, (with Judith M. Prussin), Health Services and the Elderly: A Comprehensive, Annotated Bibliography, 1982, (with Jack C. Wood), Topics in Health Care Financing: Private Third Party Reimbursement, 1975. Mem. Fla. Assn. Health, Maint. Orgns. (pres. 1985-86), Group Health Assn. Am. Office: J & JP Funding Corp PO Box 600580 Jacksonville FL 32260-0580 E-mail: jprus1234@aol.com.

PRUSTY, RABIN, environmental engineer; b. Cuttack, India, Oct. 6, 1939; MS, M of Environ. Engring., W.Va. U., 1979. Lab. tech. Tech. Testing Lab., Charleston, W.Va., 1979—83; environ. engr. Dept. Natural Resources, 1984—87; engr. IV Dept. Environ. Protection, Tallahassee, 1987—. Contbr. ; developer: Web site www.nettally.com/prusty/mcs.htm. Named Internat. Scientist of Yr., 2001. Achievements include research in multiple chemical sensitivity, electromagnetic fields, environ. pollution control, effect of pollution on humans, environ. illness, toxicology, alternate medicine, genetic engring. Address: PO Box 20517 Tallahassee FL 32316-0517

PRUTER, KARL HUGO, bishop; b. Poughkeepsie, N.Y., July 3, 1920; s. William Karl and Katherine (Rehling) P.; m. Nancy Lee Taylor, 1943; children: Hugo Jr., Robert, Karl, Stephen, Maurice, Katherine, Nancy Tenney. BA, Northeastern U., 1943; M.Div., Lutheran Theol. Sem., Phila., 1945; MA in Edn., Roosevelt U., 1963; MA in History, Boston U., 1968. Guest lectr. Landerziehungsheim, Stein, Germany, 1964—65; ordained priest Christ Catholic Ch., 1965; pastor Ch. of the Transfiguration, Boston, 1965—70; bishop Christ Cath. Ch., 1967—. Author: The Theology of Congregationalism, 1953, The Teachings of the Great Mystics, 1969, A History of the Old Catholic Church, 1973, The People of God, 1975, The Jewish Christians in the United States, 1985 Address: Cathedral of Prince of Peace Highlandville MO 65669

PRUTER, ROBERT DOUGLAS, editor; b. Phila., July 1, 1944; s. Hugo Rehling and Nancy Lee (Taylor) P.; m. Margaret Franson; 1 child, Robin Franson. BA, Roosevelt U., 1967, MA, 1976; MLS, Dominican U., 2000. Asst. editor New Std. Ency., Chgo., 1969-74, assoc. editor, 1974-79, sr. editor, 1979-96; sr. rsch. assoc. Planning Comms., 1996-97; asst. editor Charles D. Spencer & Assocs., Chgo., 1997-98, assoc. editor, 1999-2001; govt. documents lib. Lewis U., Romeoville, Ill., 2001—. Author: Chicago Soul, 1991, Doowop: The Chicago Scene, 1996; editor: Blackwell Guide to Soul Recordings, 1993; adv. editor Popular Music and Society, 1995—; rhythm and blues editor Goldmine Mag., 1984—. Mem. adv. com. Chgo. Blues Festival, 1992—. Served U.S. Army, 1967-69, Vietnam. Mem.: NARAS, Soc. Midland Authors, Chgo. Hist. Soc., Ill. Hist. Soc., N.Am. Soc. for Sport History. Democrat. Avocations: collecting records, sports history rsch.

PRUTZMAN, LEWIS DONALD, lawyer; b. Phila., Nov. 1, 1951; s. L. Donald and Caroline (Butler) P.; m. Deborah Sorace, May 24, 1975 (div. 1998); children: Sarah, Stephen; m. Elizabeth Clement, July 7, 1998. AB, Harvard Coll., 1973; JD, NYU, 1976. Bar: Pa. 1976, N.Y. 1977, U.S. Dist. Ct. (so. and ea. dists.) N.Y. 1977, U.S. Dist. Ct. (ea. dist.) Pa. 1977, U.S. Ct. Appeals (9th cir.) 1979, U.S. Supreme Ct. 1980, U.S. Ct. Appeals (2d cir.) 1983. Law clk. to judge U.S. Dist. Ct., Phila., 1976-77; assoc. Cravath, Swaine & Moore, N.Y.C., 1977-84; ptnr. Stecher Jaglom & Prutzman, 1984-2000, Tannenbaum Helpern Syracuse & Hirschritt LLP, 2000—. Dir., v.p. Respect for Law Alliance, Inc. Mem.: N.Y. State Bar Assn. (co-chair intellectual property com. of internat. law and practice). Office: 900 3rd Ave New York NY 10022-4728 E-mail: prutzman@tanhelp.com.

PRUZAN, IRENE, arts administrator, music educator, flutist, marketing and public relations specialist; b. Watertown, N.Y., Jan. 3, 1949; d. John Edward and Esther (Coahn) P.; m. Charles G. Ullery, Jan. 30, 1972 (div. 1978); m. Charles Robert Freeman, May 20, 1988. Student, U. Ariz., 1966-68; MusB, U. So. Calif., 1971; postgrad., San Francisco State U., .1972-74, U. Minn., 1976-80. Tchr. flute, coach chamber music MacPhail Ctr. for Arts, U. Minn., Mpls., 1976-85, coordinator instrumental music, 1978-81, program dir. instrumental music, 1982-85, div. head of programs, 1985-86; regional dir. Music On The Move, Inc., Valley Cottage, N.Y., 1986-87; pres. Music On the Move Minn., Inc., St. Paul, 1987—. Founding mem. Crocus Hill Trio, 1976—; pub. rels. cons. Sch. of Music, U. Minn., 1991; faculty Nat. Music Camp, Interlochen, Mich., 1983, 84; cons. edn. and festival Ordway Music Theatre, St. Paul, 1985-87; mgr. Sartory String Quartet, Mpls., 1986-93; developer numerous master classes. Writer teaching materials for flute. Mem. Ariz. Chamber Orch., Tucson, 1967, San Gabriel (Calif.) Symphony, 1968-71; extra player St. Paul Chamber Orch., 1977-91; bd. dirs. Twin Cities Friends of Chamber Music, 1982-89; organizer German jazz residency USIA, Minn. and Wis., 1986; cons., program dir. Young Audiences Minn., Mpls., 1986-88; mem. edn. com. Orlando Philharmonic, 2000-. Mem. Nat. Flute Assn. (dir. mktg. 1987-90), Twin Cities Musicians Union. Avocation: tennis.

PRUZANSKY, JOSHUA MURDOCK, lawyer; b. N.Y.C., Mar. 16, 1940; s. Louis and Rose (Murdock) P.; m. Susan R. Bernstein, Aug. 31, 1980; 1 child, Dina Gabrielle. BA, Columbia Coll., 1960, JD, 1965. Bar: N.Y., 1965, U.S. Dist. Ct. (ea. and so. dists.) N.Y., 1968, U.S. Supreme Ct., 1980. Ptnr. Scheinberg, DePetris & Pruzansky, Riverhead, N.Y., 1965-85, Greshin, Ziegler & Pruzansky, Smithtown, 1985-2000, Pruzansky & Besunder, LLP, Islandia, 2001—. Mem. exec. coun. N.Y. State Conf. Bar Leaders, 1984—, chmn., 1988-89; mem. grievance com. Appellate Divsn. 10th Judicial Dist., 1992-96; mem. adv. bd. Ticor Title Guarantee Co., 1992-2001; mem. L.I. adv. bd. HSBC Bank, 1995—; dir. N.Y. State Com. for Modern Cts., 1998—; mem. adv. task force N.Y. Dept. State Corps., 1998—. Mem. bd. visitors Columbia Law Sch., 1998—; chair bd. visitors Touro Law Sch., 1998—; dir., sec. L.I. Mus., 1998—. Fellow ABA Found., N.Y. State Bar Found. (bd. dirs. 1994—); mem. ABA (ho. of dels. 1997—, probate and real property sect., standing com. on solo and small firm practitioners 1998-2000, N.Y. state del. Caucus of State Bar Assns.), N.Y. State Bar Assn. (ho. dels. 1982—, pres. 1997-98, exec. com. 1992-99, spl. com. women and law 1986-91, task force on small firms 1991-92, spl. com. on MDP 1999-2000, nominating com. 1999-2000, chair 2000-01, trusts and estates sect., gen. practice, elder law sects.), Suffolk County Bar Assn. (bd. dirs. 1979-89, pres. 1985-86), N.Y. County Lawyers Assn., Nassau County Bar Assn. Office: Pruzansky & Besunder LLP One Suffolk Sq Ste 315 Farmingville NY 11749 E-mail: pruzansk@villagenet.com.

PRUZZO-HAWKINS, JUDITH JOSEPHINE, office manager; b. Oklahoma City, July 11, 1945; d. Joseph Michael and Mary Amelia (Reinhart) Engel; m. Neil Alan Pruzzo, Aug. 20, 1966 (dec. Sept. 1991); children: Maria Pruzzo Richards, Eric Alan, Brian Samuel, Lisa Michelle; m. Robert James Hawkins, Dec. 9, 1995. BS in Pharmacy, Southwestern Okla. U., 1968. Registered pharmacist, Mo., Okla., Tex.; cert. by Coun. Homeopathy, 1994. Nurse's aide Valley View Hosp., Ada, Okla., 1963-64; pharmacy technician Gibson Pharmacy, 1966; pharmacist Trinity Luth. Hosp., Kansas City, Mo., 1968-69, Rsch. Hosp., Kansas City, 1969-73, East Town Osteo. Hosp., Dallas, 1973; office mgr., profl. homeopath Neil A. Pruzzo, DO, P.A., Richardson, Tex., 1975-91; profl. homeopath, nutritional counselor Pruzzo Clinic, Inc., 1992-95; classical homeopath Environ. Health Ctr., Dallas, 1995—; owner Highland Meadows Constrn., 1996—. Lectr., presenter homeopathy and weight loss. Mem. Dallas Symphony Assn., 1992—, Stradivarious patron, 1994—. Women's Bowling Assn. scholar, 1963; named Ada Dist. Dairy Princess, Okla. Dairy Princess Contest, 1965. Mem. Nat. Ctr. Homeopathy, Homeopathic Assn., Naturopathic Physicians (assoc.), Southwestern State U. Alumni Assn. (life), Tex. Soc. Homeopathy (sec.-treas. 1997—, chmn. annual meeting 1997, 99), Kappa Epsilon (life, v.p. 1967-68). Avocations: classical music, aerobic walking, reading, competitive ballroom dancing, travel. Home: 4303 Shadow Glen Dr Dallas TX 75287-6828 Office: Environ Health Ctr - Dallas Inc 8345 Walnut Hill Ln Ste 220 Dallas TX 75231-4205 Fax: (972) 931-2685.

PRYBUTOK, VICTOR RONALD, business educator; b. Phila., Sept. 25, 1952; s. Albert and Dorothy (Welt) P.; m. Gayle Linda Trofe, Apr. 11, 1987; children: Alexis Nicole, Sara Kellie. BS, Drexel U., Phila., 1974, MS in BioMath and Environ. Health, 1976, 80, PhD Environ. Analysis and Applied Stats., 1984. Tchr. math. Sch. Dist. Phila., 1976-78; lectr. stats. Drexel U. Coll. Bus. and Adminstrn., 1980-84; sr. biostatistician Campbell Soup Co., Camden, N.J., 1984-85; asst. prof. quantitative methods Drexel U. Coll. Bus. and Adminstrn., 1985-91; dir. Drexel U. Ctr. for Quality and Productivity, 1986-91; assoc. prof. mgmt. sci. U. North Tex., Denton, 1991-96, dir. Ctr. for Quality and Productivity, 1991—, prof. mgmt. sci., 1997—2001, doctoral program dir. Coll. Bus. Adminstrn., 2000—, Regents prof. mgmt. sci., 2001—. Adj. asst. prof. Drexel U., 1984-85, Phila. Coll. Textiles and Sci., 1984-85; cons. Pa. Health Care Cost Containment Coun., Harrisburg, 1987, 88; cons. to dept. rsch. nursing Thomas Jefferson U., Phila., 1989-92. Contbr. more than 50 articles to profl. jours., over 50 conf. procs., presentations and internal reports. Mentor to gifted child Phila. Sch. System, 1988-89. Fellow HEW, 1978-80. Mem. (sr.) Am. Soc. for Quality (cert. quality engr., quality auditor, quality mgr., Phila. sect. exec. bd. 1990-91, Irwin S. Hoffer award), Delaware Valley Partnership for Quality and Productivity (founder). Avocations: running, investments. Office: U North Tex Dept Bus Computer Sys Box 305249 Denton TX 76203-5249 E-mail: prybutok@unt.edu.

PRYCE, DEBORAH D. congresswoman; b. Warren, Ohio, July 29, 1951; BA cum laude, Ohio State U., 1973; JD with honors, Capital U., 1976. Bar: Ohio 1976. Former asst. city prosecutor, asst. city atty., first asst. city prosecutor, Columbus, Ohio; former judge Franklin County Mcpl. Ct.; mem. U.S. Congress from 15th Ohio dist., Washington, 1993—; mem. rules com.; mem. select com. on homeland security. Republican. Presbyterian. Avocation: skiing. Office: US Ho Reps 221 Cannon Ho Office Bldg Washington DC 20515-0001*

PRYCE, JONATHAN, actor; b. North Wales, June 1, 1947; Appearences include (stage) Liverpool Everyman, 1972, Nottingham Playhouse-Comedians, Comedians, 1977 (Tony award, Theatre World award), Hamlet (Olivier award), Macbeth, The Caretaker, 1981, Accidental Death of an Anarchist, 1984, Miss Saigon, 1991 (Tony award, Olivier award), Oliver, 1995, My Fair Lady, 2001; (films) Voyage of the Damned, 1976, Breaking Glass, 1980, Loophole, 1981, Praying Mantis, 1982, The Plowman's Lunch, 1983, Something Wicked This Way Comes, 1983, Brazil, 1985, The Doctor and the Devils, 1985, Haunted Honeymoon, 1986, Jumpin Jack Flash, 1986, Hotel London, 1987, Man On Fire, 1987, The Adventures of Baron Munchausen, 1988, Consuming Passions, 1988, The Rachel Papers, 1989, Glengarry Glen Ross, 1992, The Age of Innocence, 1993, Shopping, 1994, A Business Affair, 1994, Carrington, 1996 (Best Actor award Cannes Film Festival 1995), Evita, 1996, Tomorrow Never Dies, 1997, Regeneration, 1997, Ronin, 1998, Stigmata, 1999, Very Annie Mary, 2001, Unconditional Love, 2001; (TV movie) Barbarians at the Gate, HBO, 1993 (Emmy nomination, Supporting Actor - Miniseries or Special, 1993), David, 1997, Confessions of an Ugly Stepsister, 2002. Address: Julian Belfrage Assocs 46 Albermarle St London WIX 4pp England also: UTA 9560 Wilshire Blvd Beverly Hills CA 90212

PRYDE, PHILIP RUST, geography educator; b. Pittsfield, Mass., Jan. 8, 1938; s. David Russell Pryde and Viola Rust. MA, U. Wash., 1965, PhD, 1969. Prof. San Diego State U., 1969-2001. Author: Conservation in the Soviet Union, 1972, San Diego: An Introduction to the Region, 1976, 92, Nonconventional Energy Resources, 1983, Environmental Resources and Constraints in the Former Soviet Republics, 1995. Bd. dirs. San Dieguito River Valley Regional Pk., 1989—, San Diego County Water Authority, 1985-91. With U.S. Army, 1960-63. Fulbright fellow, 1995. Mem. Nat. Coun. for Geog. Edn. (bd. dirs. 1998-2001). Avocations: photography, travel, mountaineering. Office: San Diego State U Dept Geography 5500 Campanile Dr San Diego CA 92182

PRYOR, CAROL GRAHAM, obstetrician, gynecologist; b. Savannah, Ga. m. Louis O.J. Manganiello, June 11, 1950; children: Carol Helen, Victoria Manganiello Mudano. AB, Ga. Coll., 1943; MD, Med. Coll. Ga., 1947. Rotating intern City Hosps., Balt., 1947-48; asst. resident pathology Baroness Erlanger Hosp., Chattanooga, 1948; intern. obstetrics City Colls., Balt., 1949; coll. physician Ga. State Coll. for Women, Milledgeville, Ga., 1949-50; resident obstetrics City Hosps., Balt., 1950-51; asst. resident gynecology Univ. Hosp., 1951-52, sr. resident ob-gyn. Augusta, Ga., 1952; pvt. practice ob-gyn., 1952—; chmn. ob-gyn. St. Joseph Hosp., 1997—. Chair ob-gun. dept. St. Joseph Hosp., Augusta. Mem., former pres. Iris Garden Club, Augusta; mem. coun. on maternal and infant health State of Ga., Atlanta, 1981-90; mem. edn. found. AAUW, 1961-63, state v.p., br. pres., 1963-65. Recipient Cert. of Achievement-Community Leadership, Ga. div. AAUW, 1982; named Med. Woman of Yr., Ga. br. 51 Am. Med. Women's Assn., 1961; Heritage Award, GA Coll. and State U., 2001 Fellow am. Coll. Surgeons (1st woman mem. Ga. chpt. 1956), Am. Coll. Ob-Gyn.; mem. AMA, Richmond County Med. Soc., So. Med. Assn., So. Surg. Congress, Delta Kappa Gamma. Democrat. Methodist. Office: 2316 Wrightsboro Rd Augusta GA 30904-6220 E-mail: cpryor@jetbn.net.

PRYOR, DIXIE DARLENE, elementary education educator; b. Anderson, Ind., May 22, 1938; d. Thurman Earle and Alice D. (Watson) Rinker; m. Charles Lee Pryor, Mar. 13, 1958; children: Charles A., Deborah Lee Pryor Evans, Laurinda Ann Pryor Owen. BS, Ball State U., 1967, MEd, 1974. Tchr. Anderson (Ind.) Pub. Schs., 1967-72, Wawasee Cmty. Sch. Corp., Syracuse, Ind., 1972—97, ret. Bd. dirs. Internat. Palace Sports-Scholarship, North Webster, Ind., chair scholarship com., 1996-97, 98-99. Bd. dirs. North Webster Day Care, sec., 1998-2000; bd. dirs. Cardinal Ctr., Inc., Warsaw, Ind., 1996—, sec. bd., 1998; bd. dirs. Kosciusko Co. Found., chmn. scholarship program; trustee Webster United Meth. Ch., chmn. edn. Named Outstanding Mem. Tippkee Reading Coun., 1995, Outstanding Educator Honor Srs., 1995; recipient Ind. State Reading Assn., 1995. Mem.: Ind. Reading Assn. (pres. 1994—95, chair state reading conf. 1996—, Outstanding Mem. award 1996, 2000), Kiwanis (com. chair North Webster 1988—, sec. 1996—97, bd. dirs. 1997—2001). Republican. Methodist. Avocations: travel, reading. Home: 4630 E Armstrong Rd Leesburg IN 46538-9588 Office: PO Box 324 North Webster IN 46555 E-mail: ddpryor@kconline.com.

PRYOR, FREDERIC L. economist, educator; b. Apr. 23, 1933; s. Millard H. and Mary S. Pryor; m. Zora Prochazka, Mar. 26, 1964; 1 child, Daniel. BA, Oberlin (Ohio) Coll., 1955; PhD, Yale U., 1962. Prof. econs. Swarthmore (Pa.) Coll., 1967—98. Rsch. dir. Pa. Tax Commn., 1979-81. Author: The Communist Foreign Trade System, 1963, Public Expenditures in Communist and Capitalist Nations, 1968, Property and Industrial Organization in Communist and Capitalist Nations, 1973, The Origins of the Economy, 1977, A Guidebook to the Comparison of Economic Systems, 1985, Revolutionary Granada, 1987, The Political Economy of Poverty, Equity and Growth: Malawi and Madagascar, 1990, The Red and the Green: The Rise and Fall of Collective Agriculture, 1992, Economic Evolution and Structure, 1995, The Future of U.S. Capitalism; co-author: Who's Not Working and Why, 1999. Trustee Tougoloo Coll., 1981—. Office: Swarthmore College Ave Swarthmore PA 19081-1390 E-mail: fpryor1@swarthmore.edu.

PRYOR, HAROLD S. retired college president; b. Overton County, Tenn., Oct. 3, 1920; s. Hubert S. and Ethel (Stockton) P.; m. LaRue Vaughn, June 26, 1946. BS, Austin Peay State U., 1946; MA, George Peabody Coll., 1947; Ed.D., U. Tenn., 1951. Instr. George Peabody Coll., Vanderbilt U., 1946-47, E. Tenn. State U., 1947-49, U. Tenn., Knoxville, 1949-51; head dept. edn. Austin Peay State U., 1952, dir. tchr. edn., 1954-68; pres. Columbia (Tenn.) State Community Coll., 1968-84, now pres. emeritus, 1984—. Dir. First Farmers and Merchants Nat. Bank, Columbia, 1970— , First Farmers and Mchts. Corp., 1982— ; Columbia State Found., 1971— . Contbr. articles to profl. jours. With U.S. Army, 1943-46. Grantee Dept. Labor; Grantee HEW. Mem. NEA, Tenn. Coll. Assn. (past pres.), Tenn. Edn. Assn., Am. Assn. Higher Edn., Comparative Edn. Soc., Graymere Country Club, Kiwanis, Kappa Delta Pi, Phi Delta Kappa. Democrat. Presbyterian.

PRYOR, HUBERT, editor, writer; b. Buenos Aires, Argentina, Mar. 18, 1916; (parents Am. citizens); s. John W. and Hilda A. (Cowes) P.; m. Ellen M. Ach, 1940 (div. 1959); children: Alan, Gerald, David. Grad., St. George's Coll., Argentina, 1932; student, U. London, Eng., 1934-36. Corr. in S.Am. for United Press, 1937-39; pub. relations rep. Pan Am. Airways in Buenos Aires, 1939-40; reporter N.Y. Herald Tribune, 1940-41; writer, dir. short-wave newsroom CBS, 1941-46; asst. mng. editor Knickerbocker Weekly, 1946-47; sr. editor Look mag., 1947-62; creative supr. Wilson, Haight & Welch, 1962-63; editor Science Digest, 1963-67; mng. editor Med. World News, 1967; editor NRTA Jour. Modern Maturity, 1967-82; editl. dir. Dynamic Years, 1977-82; publs. coord. Modern Maturity, Dynamic Years, 1982-84; editl. cons., writer, 1985—. Author: Soul Talk, 1995, Eleanor of Palm Beach, 2002. Lt. USNR, 1943-46. Mem. Am. Soc. Mag. Editors, Author's Guild, Overseas Press Club. Home: 3560 S Ocean Blvd Palm Beach FL 33480-5772

PRYOR, JERRY DENNIS, corporate professional; b. Cin., Apr. 11, 1952; s. Cicero and Pauline (Estill) P. BA in History, Lincoln U., 1978. Collector, mgmt. trainee Gem Savs. & Loan, Dayton, Ohio, 1978-81; loan mgr. Maj. Fed. Savs. & Loan, Cin., 1981; acct. receivable mgr. Sonitrol of Cin., 1983-84; sr. adjuster Cen. Trust Bank, Cin., 1984-86; collector Robert Half/ Accountemps, 1986-97; founder Cin. Empowerment Corp., 1998—. Owner J.D. Pryor & Assocs., 1981—. Treas. Avondale Cmty. Coun.; mentor Taft H.S. and Bloom Middle Sch.; bd. dirs. Avondale Redevel. Corp.; vice chmn. cmty. devel. adv. bd. City of Cin., chmn. housing com.; bd. dirs. Nasus Inc. Honoree Am. Chem. Soc., 1969. Mem. Am. Inst. Banking, MBA Execs. Inc., Real Estate Investor Assn., Am. Inst. Constructors Inc., Civitan Club, Dayton Lodge. Democrat. Baptist. Avocations: softball, basketball, reading, chess. Home: 3455 Knott St Cincinnati OH 45229-2930 Office: Robert Half/Accountemps 201 E 5th St Cincinnati OH 45202-4117 E-mail: jdpryor@one.net., jpryor@stpubs.com.

PRYOR, LOIS MARIE, management consultant; b. Oakland, Calif., Apr. 16, 1950; d. Arthur William and Lila Marie (Carlin) P. BA, U. Calif., Berkeley, 1971, postgrad., 1981. Instr. English and chem. engring. Grad. Sch. Edn., U. Calif., Berkeley, 1974-83; pres., co-founder Echols & Pryor Tech. Comms., Inc., San Francisco, 1981-92; owner, pres. Pryor Comm., Sausalito, Calif., 1992—. Cons., trainer Support Ctr., San Francisco, 1985—; cons., tchr., mem. steering com. Bay Area Writing Project, Berkeley, 1980-84. Co-editor: Borzoi College Reader, 1980; author manual Borzoi College Reader, 1980, also over 200 workshop manuals, 1981—. Vol., Marin Humane Soc., 1992—. U. Calif. Regents fellow, 1976, 81; U. Calif. English dept. scholar, 1970. Mem. AAUW, NAFE, Inst. Mgmt. Cons., Sierra Club. Avocations: painting, hiking, reading, travel, art history. Office: Pryor Comm 1001 Bridgeway Ste 130 Sausalito CA 94965-2158

PRYOR, MARK LUNSFORD, state attorney general; b. Fayetteville, Ark. m. Jill Pryor; children: Adams, Porter. BA in History, U. Ark., 1985, JD, 1988. Pvt. practice Wright, Lindsey & Jennings, Little Rock, 1988—97; mem. Ark. Ho. of Reps., 1990, chmn. Freshman Caucus, mem. judiciary com., com. on aging and legis. affairs; atty. gen. State of Ark., 1999—. Office: Office of Attorney General 200 Tower Bldg Little Rock AR 72201*

PRYOR, RICHARD, actor, writer; b. Peoria, Ill., Dec. 1, 1940; s. Leroy and Gertrude (Thomas) Pryor; m. Jennifer Lee, June 8, 2001; children: Elizabeth Ann, Richard, Rain, Stephen, Gelsey, Franklin. Grad. high sch. Appeared on: Ed Sullivan, Merv Griffin and Johnny Carson television shows in 1960s; appeared in motion pictures The Busy Body, 1967, The Green Berets, 1968, Wild In The Streets, 1968, The Phynx, 1970, Dynamite Chicken, 1970, Lady Sings the Blues, 1972, Hit, 1973, Wattstax, 1973, The Mack, 1973, Some Call It Loving, 1973, Uptown Saturday Night, 1974, Adios Amigos, 1976, The Bingo Long Travelling All-Stars and Motor Kings, 1976, Car Wash, 1976, Silver Streak, 1976, Greased Lightning, 1977, Which Way is Up?, 1977, Blue Collar, 1978, California Suite, 1978, The Wiz, 1978, Richard Pryor Live in Concert, 1979, The Muppet Movie, 1979, Wholly Moses, 1980, In God We Trust, 1980, Stir Crazy, 1980, Bustin' Loose, 1981, Some Kind of Hero, 1982, The Toy, 1982, Superman III, 1983, Richard Pryor Here and Now, 1983, Brewster's Millions, 1985, Critical Condition, 1987, Moving, 1988, See No Evil, Hear No Evil, 1989, Harlem Nights, 1989, Another You, 1991, Lost Highway, 1996, Mad Dog Time, 1996; writer, producer, dir. Jo Jo Dancer Your Life Is Calling, 1986; writer scripts for Flip Wilson; co-writer TV spls. for Lily Tomlin, 1973 (Emmy award); movie script Blazing Saddles, 1973 (Am. Writers Guild award, Am. Acad. Humor award), Lily, 1974 (Am. Acad. Humor award); recorded That Nigger's Crazy, 1974 (Grammy award, certified Gold and Platinum album), Bicentennial Nigger, 1976 (Grammy award); star Richard Pryor Show, NBC-TV, 1977; owner Richard Pryor Enterprises, Inc., Los Angeles, 1975—. Served with U.S. Army, 1958-60. Recipient Grammy award, "...and It's Deep Too!", 2002. Mem. Nat. Acad. Rec. Arts and Scis., Writers Guild Am. Office: Indigo Prodns care Jennifer Lee 4900 Valjean Ave Encino CA 91436-1336

PRYOR, RICHARD J. physicist, researcher; b. Pitts., Aug. 25, 1940; m. Rebecca Pryor. PhD, U. Pitts., 1970. Sr. scientist, physicist, Albuquerque, 1989—. Mem.: Am. Phys. Soc. Office: Sandia Nat Labs Mail Stop 1109 Albuquerque NM Personal E-mail: rjpryor@earthlink.net Business E-Mail: rjpryor@sandia.gov.

PRYOR, RICHARD WALTER, telecommunications executive, retired air force officer; b. Poplar Bluff, Mo., Nov. 6, 1932; s. Walter V. and Mary (Clifford) P.; m. Barbara LeCompte, Feb. 19, 1955; children: Richard, Susan Davis, Robert, William. B in Gen. Studies, U. Nebr., Omaha, 1972; MA, Webster Coll., St. Louis, 1975; grad., U. No. Colo., 1975. Commd. 2d lt. USAF, 1953, advanced through grades to maj. gen., 1982, ret., 1982, instr. Acad., DVMT engr. space and missile systems, chief of staff Communication Services; mgr. worldwide def. communication system Def. Communications Agy., 1980-81; pres. ITT World Communications, N.Y.C., 1982-84, ITT Indsl. Transmission Co., N.Y.C.; sr. v.p. engring. ops. ITT Communication Services GP; pres., gen. mgr. ITT Christian Rovsing-Copenhagen DK, 1984-86; chmn. Christian-Rovsing Inc., Tulsa; exec. v.p. Electronic Data Systems (EDS) Comm. Corp., Dallas, 1986-89; pres., COO IMM Corp.-Interdigital AMEX, Phila., 1989-92; chmn., CEO. officer Ultranav Corp, Dallas, 1992—; chmn. Prism Video, 1994—; pres. Trans-Tech Holdings Corp., 1996—; pres., CEO Unison Corp., 1998—, Video Net, Addison, Tex. Dir. RPost, L.A., 2000—. Contbr. articles to tech. publs. Assoc. dir. Boy Soucts Am., N.Y.C., 1983. Recipient Cert. of Appreciation Okla. Mental Health Assn., 1979, Kansas City Lions Club, 1974. Mem. Armed Forces Communications and Electronics Assn. (pres. N.Y.C. 1983, nat. dir.), Air Force Assn., Oklahoma City Soc. Profl. Engrs., Canoe Brook Country Club, Army-Navy Club, Phi Alpha Theta. Republican. Roman Catholic. Home: 7802 Mason Dells Dr Dallas TX 75230-2418 Office: Video Net Ste 705 16475 Dallas Pkwy Addison TX 75001

PRYOR, SHANNON PENICK, otolaryngologist; BA, Williams Coll., 1989; MD, Tulane U., 1993. Diplomate Am. Bd. Otolaryngology. Intern, resident Johns Hopkins Med. Instns., 1993-98; with NIDCD/NIH, Rockville, Md. Vol., Grillo Health Info. Ctr., Boulder, Colo., 2000. Fellow Am. Acad. Otolaryngology-Head and Neck Surgery; mem. AMA (del., Ho. of Dels., Chgo., 2000—, alternate, 1995-99). Office: NIDCD/NIH 5 Research Ct 2A-37 Rockville MD 20850

PRYOR, SHEPHERD GREEN, III, lawyer; b. Fitzgerald, Ga., June 27, 1919; s. Shepherd Green Jr. and Jeffie (Persons) P.; m. Lenora Louise Standifer, May 17, 1941 (dec.); m. Ellen Wilder, July 13, 1984; children from previous marriage: Sandra Pryor Clarkson, Shepherd Green IV, Robert Stephen, Patty Pryor Smith (dec.), Alan Persons, Susan Lenora. BSAE, Ga. Inst. Tech., 1947; JD, Woodrow Wilson Coll. Law, Atlanta, 1974. Bar: Ga. 1974, U.S. Dist. Ct. (no. dist.) Ga. 1974, U.S. Ct. Appeals (5th cir.) 1974, U.S. Ct. Appeals (11th cir.) 1982, U.S. Supreme Ct. 1977; registered profl. engr., Ga. Comml. pilot engr. Hartford Accident and Indemnity Co., 1947-56; nuclear engr. Lockheed Ga. Co., 1956-64, research and tech. rep., 1964-76; real estate salesman Cole Realty Co. and Valient Properties, 1955-74; sole practice law Atlanta, 1974—. Past pres. Loring Heights Civic Assn.; past mem. Sandy Springs Civic Assn. Devonwood Br.; former trustee Masonic Children's Home of Ga.; bd. advisors Reinhardt Coll.; mem. North Springs Homeowners Assn.; chmn. Bd. Equalization Fulton County, Ga. Capt. U.S. Army, 1942-45, USAFR, 1942-55. Mem. Ga. Bar Assn., Ga. Trial Lawyers Assn., Mensa, Intertel, Soc. Automotive Engrs., Assn. Old Crows, The Old Guard of the Gate City Guard (past commandant), Masons, Shriners, Sigma Delta Kappa, Pi Kappa Phi, Kappa Kappa Psi. Republican. Methodist. Address: 135 W Spalding Dr NE Atlanta GA 30328-1912

PRYOR, TOMMI THORNBURY, marketing professional; b. Pikeville, Ky., Oct. 21, 1950; BS in Speech and Journalism, U. Wis., 1972; MA in Comms. Studies, U. Mo, Kansas City, 1980. Registered lobbyist Calif., 2001. Various mktg. positions to CEO Infobahn Industries, Inc., Orange County, Calif., 1995—97; CEO TLC Comms., Ltd., 1998—2002. Dir. Family Entertainment Am., Inc., Laguna Beach, Calif., 1988—90. Co-author: (novels) Assassins of the Pont d'Alma, 1997, (TV series) On the Hill, 1992, (films) Blood Chit, 1992. Mktg. profl. Reagan-Bush '84, Washington, 1983—84, Nat. Com. to Draft Pat Robertson for Pres., Washington, 1987—88. Named an Outstanding Young Career Woman of Ea. Kans., Kansas City Bus. and Profl. Women's Clubs, 1976; named to Order of Ky. Cols., Gov. of Ky., 1997. Mem.: Nat. Rep. Club. Avocation: writing, gourmet cooking, travel, antiquing.

PRYOR, WILLIAM DANIEL LEE, humanities educator; b. Lakeland, Fla., Oct. 29, 1926; s. Dahl and Lottie Mae (Merchant) P. AB, Fla. So. Coll., 1949; MA, Fla. State U., 1950, PhD, 1959; postgrad., U. N.C., 1952-53; pvt. art study with Florence Wilde; pvt. voice study with Colin O'More, Anna Kaskas; pvt. piano study with Waldemar Hille and audited piano master classes of Ernst von Dohnànyi. Asst. prof. English, dir. drama Bridgewater (Va.) Coll., 1950-52; grad. tchg. fellow humanities Fla. State U., Tallahassee, 1953-55, 57-58; instr. English U. Houston, University Park, Houston, 1955-59, asst. prof. University Park, 1959-62, assoc. prof., 1962-71, prof., 1971-97, prof. emeritus, 1997. Vis. instr. English, Fla. So. Coll., Lakeland, MacDill Army Air Base, Tampa, Fla., 1951, Tex. So. U., 1961-63; vis. instr. humanities, govt. U. Tex. Dental Br., Houston, 1962-63; lectr. The Women's Inst., Houston, 1967-72; lectr. humanities series Jewish Cmty. Ctr., Houston, 1972-73; originator, moderator TV and radio program The Arts in Houston Stas. KUHT-TV and KUHF-FM, 1956-57, 58-63. Contbg. author: National Poetry Anthology, 1952, Panorama das Literaturas das Americas, vol. 2, 1958-60; assoc. editor Forum, 1967, editor, 1967-82; contbr. articles to profl. jours.; dir. Murder in the Cathedral (T.S. Elliot), U. Houston, 1965; performed in opera as Sir Edgar in Der Junge Lord (Henze), Houston Grand Opera Assn., 1967; played the title role in Aella (Chatterton), Am. premiere, U. Houston, 1970. Bd. dirs., founding mem. Houston Shakespeare Soc., 1964-67; bd. dirs., founding mem., program annotator Houston Chamber Orch. Soc., 1964-76; narrator Houston Symphony Orch., Houston Summer Symphony Orch., Houston Summer Symphony Orch., Houston Chamber Orch., U. Houston Symphony Orch., St. Stephen's Music Festival Symphony Orch., New Harmony, Ind.; narrator world premier of the Bells (Jerry McCathern), 1969, U. Houston Symphony Orch., 1969, Am. premier Symphony No. Seven, Antartica (Vaughn-Williams), Houston Symphony Orch., 1967, L'Histoire du Soldat (Stravinski), U. Houston Symphony Orch., 1957, Am. premier Babar the Elephant (Poulenc-Francais), Houston Chamber Orch., 1967, Le Roi David (Honegger), 1979, Voice of God in opera Noye's Fludde (Britten), St. Stephen's Music Festival, 1981; bd. dirs., program annotator Music Guild, Houston, 1960-67, v.p., 1963-67, adv. bd., 1967-70; bd. dirs., founding mem., Contemporary Music Soc., Houston, 1958-63; mem.-at-large, bd. dirs. Houston Grand Opera Guild, 1966-67; mem. repertory com. Houston Grand Opera Assn., 1967-70; bd. dirs. Houston Grand Opera, 1970-75, adv. bd. 1978-79; mem. cultural adv. com. Jewish Cmty. Ctr., 1960-66; bd. dirs. Houston Friends Pub. Libr., 1962-67, 73-75, 1st v.p., 1963-67; adv. mem. cultural affairs com. Houston C. of C., 1972-75; adv. bd. dirs. The Wilhelm Schole, 1980-98, Buffalo Bayou Support Com., 1985-87, bd. dirs. The Moores Sch. Music Soc., 1998—; charter mem. 1927 Soc. U. Houston, 1998—; bd. dirs. U. Houston Retiree Assn., 1999-2001, v.p., 2000-2001.; founding bd. dirs. Internat. Dohna'nyi Rsch. Ctr., Inc., 2002-. Recipient Master Tchg. award Coll. Humanities and Fine Arts U., Houston, 1980, Favorite Prof. award Bapt. Student Union, U. Houston, 1991. Mem. MLA, Coll. English Assn., L'Alliance Francaise, English-Speaking Union, Alumni Assn. Fla. So. Coll., Fla. State U., Am. Assn. U. Profs., South Ctrl. MLA, Conf. Editors Learned Jours., Coll. Conf. Tchrs. English, Nat. Coun. Tchrs. English, Am. Studies Assn., Shepard Soc. Rice U., Century Club, Fla. S. Coll., President's Club, James D. Westcott Legacy Soc., Fla. State U., Phi Beta (patron), Phi Mu Alpha Sinfonia, Alpha Psi Omega, Pi Kappa Alpha, Sigma Tau Delta (Outstanding Prof. English U. Houston chpt. 1990), Houston Philos. Soc., Tau Kappa Alpha, Phi Kappa Phi, Caledonian Club (London), Century Club (Fla. Southwestern Coll.), James Westcott Soc. of Pres's Club (Fla. State U.). Episcopalian. Avocations: tennis, racquetball, swimming, traveling. Home: 2625 Arbuckle St Houston TX 77005-3929 Office: U Houston Dept English U Park 3801 Cullen Blvd Houston TX 77004-2602 *My commitment is to the humanities. I believe that the most important thing that a teacher can do is to help a student to stand on his/her own intellectual hind legs; to help him/her to learn how to aquire facts; to help him/her to learn how to organize and utilize these facts in intelligent, responsible ways.*

PRYOR, WILLIAM HOLCOMBE, JR. state attorney general; b. Mobile, Ala., Apr. 26, 1962; s. William Holcombe Sr. and Laura Louise (Bowles) Pryor; m. Kristan Camille Wilson, Aug. 15, 1987; children: Caroline Elizabeth, Victoria Camille. BA in Legal Studies with honors, U. of La. (now N.E. La. U.), Monroe, 1984; JD with honors, Tulane U., 1987. Law clk. U.S. Ct. Appeals (5th cir.), Judge John Minor Wisdom, New Orleans, 1987—88; assoc. Cabaniss, Johnston, Gardner, Dumas & O'Neil, Birmingham, Ala., 1988—91, Walston, Stabler, Wells, Anderson & Bains, Birmingham, 1991—95; dep. atty. gen. State of Ala., Montgomery, 1995—97, atty. gen., 1997—. Adj. prof. Samford U. Cumberland Sch. Law, Birmingham, 1989—94. Bd. student editors: Tulane Law Rev., 1985—86, editor-in-chief: , 1986—87, bd. adv. editors: , 1995—. La. nat. com. Young Rep. Nat. Fedn., 1984—86; mem. Ala.

Rep. Exec. Com., 1994—95. Mem.: Order of Coif, Omicron Delta Kappa, Phi Kappa Phi. Roman Catholic. Office: Office Atty Gen 11 S Union St Montgomery AL 36130-2103 E-mail: billpryor@ago.state.al.us.*

PRYSBY, CHARLES LEE, political science educator; b. Olympia, Wash., May 11, 1945; s. Charles C. and Rose G. Prysby; m. Anita D. Ebert, June 17, 1967; children: Nicole D., Michelle D. BS in Polit. Sci., Ill. Inst. Tech., 1966; PhD in Polit. Sci., Mich. State U., 1973. NDEA fellow Mich. State U., East Lansing, 1966-69, instr., 1969-71, U. N.C., Greensboro, 1971-73, asst. prof., 1973-78, assoc. prof., 1978-92, prof., 1992—, dept. head, 1993—2002. N.C. state mgr. News Election Service, N.Y.C., 1980-92; N.C. state mgr. Voter News Svc., 1996. Co-author: Voting Behavior: 1972 Election, 1975, Voting Behavior: 1976 Election, 1978, Political Choices, 1980, Voting Behavior: 1980 Election, 1981, Voting Behavior: 1984 Election, 1985, Voting Behavior: 1988 Election, 1989, Political Behavior and the Local Context, 1991, Voting Behavior: 1992 Election, 1993, Voting in Presidential Elections 1972-92, 1995, Voting Behavior: 1996 Election, 1997, Voting Behavior: 2000 Election, 2002; contbr. articles to profl. jours. and edited vols. NEH summer seminar fellow, 1978, 83. Mem. N.C. Polit. Sci. Assn. (past-pres. 1984-85), Am. Soc. Pub. Adminstrn. (coun. mem. Piedmont Triad chpt. 1984-85), Am. Polit. Sci. Assn., Southern Polit. Sci. Assn., Midwest Polit. Sci. Assn. Home: 1910 Milan Rd Greensboro NC 27410-2948 Office: Univ NC at Greensboro Dept Polit Sci Greensboro NC 27402-6170 E-mail: prysby@uncg.edu.

PRYSESKI, GARY MICHAEL, secondary school educator; b. Balt., Mar. 15, 1946; s. Charles and Eleanor (Lentowski) P.; m. Joan Cody, June 21, 1969; children: Grant Michael, Charles Cody. BS, Towson State U., 1968; MS, Morgan State U., 1975; cert. in advanced studies, Johns Hopkins U., 1979; EdD, U. Md., 1989. Adminstr. Old Mill High Sch., 1985-88, Wilde Lake Mid. Sch., Columbia, Md., 1988-91, Hammond Mid. Sch., 1991-93; adminstr., staff devel. specialist Mount View Middle Sch., Marriotsville, Md., 1993—. Adj. prof. Johns Hopkins U., admin. Dunloggin Mid. Sch.; staff specialist Md. State Dept. Edn. Mem. NEA, ASCD, Nat. Assn. Secondary Sch. Prins., Md. Assn. Secondary Sch. Prins., Nat. Middle Sch. Assn., Md. Assn. Supervision and Curriculum Devel., Md. Middle Sch. Assn., Md. Tchrs. Assn., Nat. Coun. Social Studies, Am. Ednl. Research Assn., Mont. Hist. Soc., Custer Battlefield Preservation Com., Phi Delta Kappa. Democrat. Roman Catholic. Home: 8 Weston Ct Lutherville Timonium MD 21093-6342 Office: 9129 Northfield Rd Ellicott City MD 21042-5903

PRZEKOP-SHAW, SUSAN, lawyer; b. Grand Rapids, Mich., July 1, 1952; d. Charles Peter P. and Stella Anastasia Niedzwiecki; m. William Francis Shaw, Sept. 3, 1977; children: William, Jonathan, Michael. BS in Pharmacy, U. Mich., 1975; postgrad., U. Tenn., 1977; JD, Thomas Cooley Law Sch., 1979. Bar: Mich.; registered pharmacist. Drug analyst Upjohn Drug Co., Portage and Ann Arbor, Mich., 1974; pharmacy intern, pharmacist Meijer Thrifty Acres Pharmacy, Grand Rapids, Ypsilanti, Lansing, Mich., 1972-81; analyst funds adminstrn. silicosis and disease fund Bur. Workers Compensation Dept. Labor State of Mich., Lansing, 1977-78; student liaison for com. on advtsg. cert., specialization State Bar Mich., 1977-78; assoc. Sinas, Dramis, Brake, Boughton, McIntyre & Reising, P.C., 1979-89; asst. atty. gen. corrections divsn. Mich. Dept. Atty. Gen., 1989-97, mem. litigation adv. bd., 1992-98, asst. atty. gen. Mich. Civil Svc. Commn., 1997—. Legal advisor gov.'s adv. group on mental health and corrections Office of Gov. State of Mich., Lansing, 1991-93; mem. labor and employment sect. State Bar Mich. Prodr. plays Lansing Catholic Ctrl. Drama Dept. Prodns., 1998-2000. Chairperson pub. rels. com. Boys and Girls Club Lansing, 1985-87, bd. dirs., 1985-91, sec., 1987-88, first v.p., 1988-90, pres., 1989-90; co-chairperson, raffle ticket chairperson St. Gerard Cath. Ch., Lansing, 1989—, mem. edn. commn. 1993-2000, chairperson parent-student activity day, 1993-2000, chairperson fin., 1993-95, co-chairperson fin. Parish Spring Festival, 1998; orgn. com. Greater Lansing Susan G. Komen Found., 2000, bd. dirs. Greater Lansing Affil. 2001—; mem. Lansing Cath. Ctr. Bd. Edn., 2001—. Fellow Mich. State Bar Found.-State Bar Mich., 1998. Mem. Nat. Assn. Attys. Gen. (spkr. on consent decrees and injunctions 1992, constitutionality of prison litigation reform act 1997), Mich. Trial Lawyers Assn. (bd. dirs. 1983-85). Avocation: theatre. Home: 5914 Claremont Ct Lansing MI 48917-5125 Office: 120 N Washington Sq Ste 300 Lansing MI 48933-1617 Fax: (517) 373-6434. E-mail: przekopshaws@michigan.gov.

PRZEMIENIECKI, JANUSZ STANISLAW, engineering executive, former government senior executive and college dean; b. Lipno, Poland, Jan. 30, 1927; came to U.S., 1961, naturalized, 1967; s. Leon and Maria (Sarnacka) P.; m. Stefania (Fiona) Rudnicka, July 17, 1954; children: Anita, Christopher. BS, U. London, 1949, PhD, 1958; diploma in Aeros., Imperial Coll. Sci. and Tech., 1953; DSc in Engring., U. London, 1988; hon. doctorate Honoris Causa, Warsaw U. Tech., 1999. Registered profl. engr., Ohio. Head structural R & D sect. Bristol Aircraft Ltd., Eng., 1954-61; from assoc. prof. to prof. mechanics Sch. Engring., Air Force Inst. Tech., Wright-Patterson AFB, Ohio, 1961-66, from asst. dean, assoc. dean rsch. to dean, 1966-89, sr. dean, 1970-95; pres. Astra Technologies, Inc., Fla., 1996—. Cons. in field. Author: Theory of Matrix Structural Analysis, 1968, Mathematical Methods in Defense Analyses, 3d edit., 2000, Defense Analyses Software, 1991; assoc. editor: Jour. Aircraft, 1970-71; editl. bd.: Internat. Jour. Numerical Methods in Engring., 1969-75; editor: Mechanics of Structural Systems (textbook series) 1973-89; editor: Critical Technologies for Nat. Defense, 1991, Acquisition of Defense Systems, 1993; contbr. articles to profl. jours. Chmn. bd. trustees The Air Force Inst. Tech. Found., Ohio, 1987-88, trustee, 1993-95; trustee Engring. and Sci. Found. of Dayton, 1984-95. Decorated Polish Underground Army Cross, Warsaw Uprising Cross, Armed Forces medal; recipient USAF superior performance award, 1965, exceptional civilian svc. decoration, 1978, Presdl. rank of Meritorious Exec., 1981, Disting. Exec., 1982, Outstanding Engr. award Dayton Engring. and Sci. Found., 1986, Outstanding Civilian Svc. medal, 1995, Comdrs. Cross of the Polonia Restituta Order by Pres. of Poland, 1995, Disting. Svc. award, Am. Inst. of Polish Culture, 1997. Fellow Royal Aeros. Soc. (Usborne Meml. prize 1959), AIAA (editor-in-chief ednl. series 1981—, Pendray medal 1992), City and Guilds of London Inst.; mem. Am. Soc. Engring. Edn., Ohio Acad. Sci., Polish Inst. Arts and Scis., Tau Beta Pi. Home: 510 Pennyroyal Pl Venice FL 34293-7233

PRZYBILLA, CARRIE ELLEN, art curator; b. St. Cloud, Minn., Sept. 24, 1960; d. Arthur and Anne Przybilla; m. Rogers Barry. BA in Art History, U. Minn., 1982; MA in Art History and Mus. Studies, U. So. Calif., 1988. Curatorial asst. Fisher Gallery, U. So. Calif., L.A., 1982-84; curatorial asst. Mus. Contemporary Art, Chgo., 1984-85, vis. curator, 1987; art curator Univ. Mus., Ill. State U., Normal, 1985-86; asst. curator High Mus. Art, Atlanta, 1988-90, assoc. curator, 1990-95, curator, 1995—. Mem. Am. Assn. Mus., Coll. Art Assn. Office: High Mus of Art 1280 Peachtree St Atlanta GA 30309

PRZYBYLSKI, SANDRA MARIE, speech pathologist; b. Berwyn, Ill. d. Raymond and Julie Marie (Vocelka) Hammers; m. James Przybylski; children: Eric, Sara. BS, U. Iowa, 1968; MA, U. Ill., 1971. Cert. clin. speech pathologist; speech/lang., educable mentally retarded education, learning disabilites and elem. tchr., life, Mo. Speech, lang. pathologist LaPlata (Mo.) Sch. Dist., 1974-87, Maysville (Mo.) Sch. Dist., 1990-92, Bucklin (Mo.) Sch. Dist., 1992—. Named to Disting. Svc. Registry-Speech and Hearing, 1990. Mem. Am. Speech, Lang., Hearing Assn., Autism Soc. Am., Mo. State Tchrs. Assn., Mo. Speech, Lang. and Hearing Assn. E-mail: sprzy@hotmail.com., sprzybylski@bucklin.k12.mo.us.

PRZYGODZKI, RONALD MIECZYSLAW, pathologist, researcher; b. Chgo., Sept. 25, 1961; s. Matthew and Irena Przygodzki; m. Eva Maroszek, Oct. 20, 1984; children: Roman A., Isabela K. MD, Warsaw (Poland) Med. Acad., 1985. Diplomate in anat. and clin. pathology, molecular genetic pathology Am. Bd. Pathology. Anatomic pathologist Warsaw Med. Acad., 1985-87; anatomic and clin. pathologist U. Ill., Chgo., 1988-89, Brown U./R.I. Hosp., Providence, 1989-92; fellow in surg. and pulmonary pathology Armed Forces Inst. Pathology, Washington, 1993-95, staff clin. and rsch. pathologist, 1995—; molecular biology fellow Nat. Cancer Inst./NIH, Bethesda, Md., 1993-95. Author: (chapter) State of the Art Reviews - Pathology, 1996, International Agency for Research on Cancer, WHO, 1997, A Practical Atlas of Pseudomalignancy, 1997; contbr. articles to profl. jours. Recipient Pathologist in Tng. award, 1993, 96. Fellow AAAS, Internat. Assn. for Study Lung Cancer (Young Investigator award 1994); mem. AMA, U.S. and Can. Acad. of Pathology (Stowell-Orbison award 1993). Roman Catholic. Achievements include application of molecular technique on difficult and rare archival human samples; establishment of molecular techniques for patient prognostication of survival and tumor recurrence in cases with colon, lung, liver, brain, pancreatic and mediastinal malignancies. Avocations: model and steam railroading, computer programming, tai chi chuan. Office: Armed Forces Inst Pathology 1413 Research Blvd Rockville MD 20850 E-mail: gizbab@aol.com., przygodz@afip.osd.mil.

PRZYPYSZNY, JOHN CASIMIR, surgeon; b. Chgo., Apr. 21, 1928; MD, U. Ill., 1953. Diplomate Am. Bd. Surgery. Intern St. Mary Nazereth Hosp., Chgo., 1953-54; resident gen. surgery Hines VA Hosp., Maywood, Ill., 1957-61; pvt. practice surgery Chgo., 1962—. Attending surgeon St. Mary Nazereth Hosp., Chgo., 1965—. Mem. ACS, AMA. Office: 2222 W Division St Ste 225 Chicago IL 60622-2989

PRZYTYCKI, JOZEF HENRYK, mathematician, educator; b. Warsaw, Poland, Oct. 14, 1953; s. Jakub and Roza (Awrach) P.; m. Teresa Maria Szczepanek, June 19, 1984; children: Tomasz, Pawel. MS, Warsaw U., 1977, Habilitation, 1994; PhD, Columbia U., 1981. Postdoctoral fellow Toronto U., Canada, 1987-88; mem. Inst. for Advanced Study, Princeton, NJ, 1990; prof. math. George Washington U., Washington, 1999—. Adj. prof. Warsaw U., 1982-86; vis. asst. prof. U. B.C., Vancouver, Can., 1986-87, vis. assoc. prof., 1988-89; vis. scholar Mich. State U., East Lansing, 1989; assoc. vis. prof. Univ. Calif., Riverside, 1990-92; vis. assoc. rsch. mathematician U. Calif., Berkeley, 1994-95. Assoc. editor: The Jour. of Knot Theory, 1995—; contbr. articles to profl. jours. Recipient prize of pres. Warsaw U., 1989, Kuratowski's prize, 1983. Mem. AAAS, Polish Math. Soc. (Marcinkiewicz prize 1977), Polish Acad. Sci. (Kuratowski prize 1982), Am. Math. Soc., Math. Assn. Am. Office: George Washington U 2201 G St NW Funger 428 Washington DC 20052-0001 E-mail: przytyck@gwu.edu.

PSALTIS, HELEN, medical and surgical nurse; b. Rockford, Ill., Nov. 27, 1931; d. Harry and Martha (Triantafelakis) P. Diploma, St. Margaret Hosp., Hammond, Ind., 1953; BSN, DePaul U., 1961; MS in Health Edn., Purdue U., 1971; MSN, Purdue U., Calumet, Ind., 1988. RN, Ind., cert. sch. nurse, Ind. Staff nurse U. Ill. Hosp., Chgo., 1959—61, U. Chgo. Hosp., Billings, 1962; sch. nurse Pub. Sch. City of E. Chgo., Ind.; asst. supr., staff nurse, instr. St. Catherine Hosp., East. Chgo.; instr., head nurse, staff nurse St Margaret Hosp., Hammond. Mem. ANA, Nat. League for Nursing, Sigma Theta Tau. Home: 4303 Ivy St East Chicago IN 46312-3026

PSENKA, ROBERT EDWARD, real estate developer, behavioral scientist; b. Canton, Ohio, Sept. 13, 1935; s. Nicholas Charles Psenka and Julia Ella Boldizsar; children: Robert Nicholas, Eric Joseph, Rene Yvette. BA in Sociology, Kent State U., 1962, MA in Sociology, 1963; MA in Health Adminstrn., San Jacinto Coll., Pasadena, Tex., 1972. Lic. health care adminstr. skilled nursing facilities. Planning cons. U.S. Ho. of Reps., Washington, 1962-65; dir. Health and Welfare Planning and Rsch. Coun., Youngstown, Ohio, 1965-68; CEO Health Devel. & Rsch. Assocs., Inc., 1968-82, Rolzcad Industries, Inc., Houston, 1983-89; adminstr. Psenka Family Investment Mgmt. Trust, Rancho Mirage, Calif., 1973—; chief exec. Conv. Mgmt. Am., Inc., 1994—. Author: Region IX Community Mental Health Centers Guide To Development, 1964, Skilled Nursing Facilities, An Operations Guide, 1972, The Cluster Home Concept, A Guide to Devlopers, 1979 (novel) Fiction Collections, 1987, Passenger, 1986. Mem. Rep. Nat. Com., 1985; advisor Cmty. Chest, Youngstown, 1965, Child and Adult Mental Health Ctr., Youngstown, 1965; cons. Mayor Hon. Walter G. Sanders, City of West Wendover, 1996—. With JAGC, U.S. Army, 1959-61. Hosp. expansion and cmty. mental health ctr. grantee HEW, 1963. Mem. Internat. Auto Appraisers Soc. (antique automobile appraiser), Calif. Friends Native Ams., Rolls Royce Enthusiasts (London), Social Sci. Honor Soc. Republican. Mem. Ch. of Christ. Avocations: collecting and restoring antique Rolls Royce automobiles, writing poetry..

PSIHARIS, NICHOLAS See HARRICE, NICHOLAS CY

PSILLOS, SUSAN ROSE, artist, educator; b. Bethpage, N.Y., Feb. 15, 1960; d. Reginald and Gloria Barbara Psillos; 1 child, Jennifer Rose. Student, Alfred U., 1978-80; Tchg. Degree in Art, L.I. U., Southampton, 1996. Substitute tchr. art Shoreham-Wading River Sch. Dist., Shoreham, N.Y., 1992—; tchr. arts and crafts Round-out Shoreham-Wading River Sch., 1995-96; tchr. art Bellport (N.Y.) H.S., 1997-98; art tchr. Raynor Country Day Sch., Speonk, N.Y., 1998—, Plainview-Old Bethpage Sch. Dist., 1999—. Guest spkr. in field. Exhibited sculptures at Smithtown (N.Y.) Mus., 1995, 96-97, Bellemeade Gallery, 1992, Knickerbocker Gallery, N.Y.C., 1997, Studio 88, Hampton Bays, N.Y., 1999, Hampton Bays Pub. Libr.; exhibited paintings at Ambiente Gallery, 1991-92, Smithtown Twsp. Art Mus., 1995, 96, Doweling Coll., 1997. Advisor Partnership for Survival, Smithtown, 1991—; bd. dirs., pub. rels. person Sexual Abuse Survivors, Smithtown,1991—. Recipient Art Judge's award Parrish Art Mus., 1976, Outstanding award Sch. Visual Arts, 1976, Profl. Recognition Day award, 1996, Child Abuse & Neglect Family Violence Vol. award Town of Brookhaven. Mem. NOW, N.Y. Art Tchrs. Assn., Artist Support Group. Avocations: cooking, gardening, fine arts, painting, sculpture.

PSOMIADES, HARRY JOHN, political science educator; b. Boston, Sept. 8, 1928; s. John and Koula (Yalmanides) P.; m. Dorothy Smith, Aug. 18, 1962 (dec. Aug. 27, 1984); children— Kathy Alexis, Christine Anne. BA, Boston U., 1953; M.Internat. Affairs, Columbia U., 1955; cert., Middle East Inst., 1956, PhD (Ford Found. fellow), 1962; Litt.D. (hon.), Holy Cross/Hellenic Coll., 1985. Lectr. govt. Columbia U., 1959-65, asst. dean Grad. Sch. Internat. Affairs, 1959-65, dir. Carnegie Endowment Fellowships in Diplomacy, 1959-71; assoc. prof. polit. sci. Queens Coll., City U. N.Y., 1965-69, prof., 1970—, chmn. dept. polit. sci., 1967-71, dep. exec. officer Ph.D. program in polit. sci., 1975-76, program dir. seminar on the modern Greek state, 1976—; dir. Center Byzantine and Modern Greek Studies, 1976—. Cons. faculty U.S. Army Command and Gen. Staff Coll., 1968-86; U.S. Dept. State Fgn. Service Inst., 1968-71; mem. screening com. Fgn. Area Fellowships Program for Asia and Middle East Joint Com., Social Sci. Research Council and Am. Council Learned Socs., 1967-69 Author: Greece and Turkey: Mutual Economic Interests, 1964, (with Thomas Spelios) A Pictorial History of the Greeks, 1967, The Eastern Question: The Last Phase, 1968,2d edition,2000, (with T.A. Couloumbis) Foreign Interference in Greek Polics: An Historical Perspective, 1976, (with A. Scourby) The Greek American Community in Transition, 1982, (with R.S. Orfanos) Education and Greek Americans: Proccess and Prospects, 1987, (with S. Thomadakes) Greece, The New Europe and the Changing International Order, 1993, (with Van Cufoudakis) Greece and the New Balkans: Challenges and Opportunities, 1999, (with Sam Tsemberis) Greek American Famiilies: Traditions and Transformations, 1999; editor: Jour. Modern Hellenism, 1984—; contbr. articles to profl. jours. Served with U.S. Army, 1946-50; to col. USAR, 1950-83. Hon. fellow Soc. Macedonian Studies, Thessaloniki, Greece, 1970—; named Comdr. Order of Honor The Republic of Greece, 1996. Fellow Middle East Studies Assn. N.Am.; mem. Am. Polit. Sci. Assn., Middle East Inst., Modern Greek Studies Assn. (mem. exec. com. 1972-76), Phi Beta Kappa. Greek Orthodox. Home: 440 Riverside Dr New York NY 10027-6828 Office: Dept Polit Sci Queens Coll Flushing NY 11367

PSUTY, NORBERT PHILLIP, marine sciences educator; b. Hamtramck, Mich., June 13, 1937; s. Phillip and Jessie (Proszykowski) P.; m. Sylvia Helen Zurinsky, June 13, 1959; children: Eric Anthony, Scott Patrick, Ross Phillip. BS, Wayne State U., 1959; MS, Miami U., Oxford, Ohio, 1960; PhD, La. State U., 1966. Rsch. assoc. Coastal Studies Inst., La. State U., Baton Rouge, 1962-64; instr. geography and dept. geology U. Miami, Coral Gables, Fla., 1964-65; asst. prof. geography U. Wis., Madison, 1965-69; assoc. prof. geography and geol. scis. Rutgers U., New Brunswick, N.J., 1969-73, prof., 1973—2002, chmn. dept. marine and coastal scis. N.J., 1991-99, prof. marine and coastal scis., geog., geol. scis., 1989—2002, dir. Marine Scis. Ctr. N.J., 1972-76, dir. Ctr. for Coastal and Environ. Studies, 1976-90; assoc. dir. Inst. Marine and Coastal Scis., 1990—2002; prof. emeritus Rutgers U., 2002—. Mem. sci. com. Thalassas, Vigo, Spain, 1985—; dir. Sandy Hook Coop. Rsch. programs, Rutgers U., 2002—. Co-author: Living with the New Jersey Shore, 1986, Coastal Dunes, 1990, Coastal Hazard Management, 2002; mem. editl. bd. Coastal Mgmt., 1981—, Jour. Coastal Rsch., 1987—, Jour. of Coastal Conservation, 1996—; contbr. numerous articles to scholarly jours., chapters to books, monographs. Mem. Water Policy Bd., East Brunswick, NJ, 1981—83, N.J. Shoreline Adv. Bd., Trenton, 1984—86; chmn. N.J. Gov.'s Sea Level Rise Com., 1987—90; mem. N.J. State Beach Erosion Commn., 1994—99; referee U.S.A. Volleyball. Recipient Disting. Pub. Svc. award Pres. of Rutgers U. 1988; numerous grants including NSF, Nat. Park Svc., EPA, Office Naval Rsch., Nat. Sea Grant Program, NOAA, 1961—. Mem.: AAAS, N.J. Acad. Sci. (pres. 1982), Internat. Geog. Union (editor newsletter 1984—96, vice chair commn. on coastal environment 1988—92, chmn. commn. on coastal systems 1992—96, editor newsletter 2002—), Coastal Soc. (pres. 1980—82), Assn. Am. Geographers (Honors award 1993), Profl. Assn. Volleyball Ofcls. (chair N.J. bd. 2000—). Avocations: gardening, reading. Office: Rutgers U Inst Marine & Coastal Scis Cook Campus New Brunswick NJ 08903 E-mail: psuty@imcs.rutgers.edu.

PTAK, FRANK STANLEY, manufacturing executive; b. Chgo., Apr. 23, 1943; s. Frank J. and Stella R. (Los) P.; m. Karen M. Novoselsky, May 2, 1971; children: Jeffrey B., Jacquelyn F., Russell E. BSc, De Paul U., 1965. CPA, Ill. Sr. auditor Arthur Young & Co., Chgo., 1965-69; sr. rsch. cons. Kemper Fin. Svcs., 1969-71; asst. sec., mgr. acquisitions Sara Lee Corp., 1971-73, asst. treas., 1973-74, asst. to chmn., 1974, v.p. planning, 1974-75; bus. devel. mgr. ITW Conex, Des Plaines, Ill., 1975-77; mktg. mgr. ITW Shakeproof, Elgin, 1977-78, group pres., 1977-78, ITW Metal Components Cos., Glenview, 1978-91; exec. v.p. Global Automotive Components ITW Corp., 1991-95, vice-chmn., 1996—. Bd. dirs. Heller Fin., Kemper Ins., Snap-On Inc.; adv. coun. DePaul U. Coll. Commerce, Chgo., 1998. Patentee in field. Mem. AICPA, Assn. Corp. Growth, ITW Patent Soc. Jewish. Home: 849 Edgewood Ct Highland Park IL 60035-3714 Office: Illinois Tool Works 3600 W Lake Ave Glenview IL 60025-5811 E-mail: fptak@itw.com.

PTAK, JOHN, talent agent; b. San Diego, Sept. 23, 1942; s. John and Doris Elizabeth P.; m. Margaret Elizabeth Black, May 21, 1981; 1 child, Hillary Elizabeth. BA, UCLA, 1967. Theatre mgr., booker Walter Reade Orgn., Beverly Hills, Calif., 1967-69; adminstrv. exec. Am. Film Inst., 1968-70; talent agent Internat. Famous Agy. (now ICM), L.A., 1971-75, William Morris Agy., Beverly Hills, 1976-91, Creative Artists Agy., Beverly Hills, 1991—. Co-chmn. Am. Film Inst. Ctr. for Film & Video Preservation, L.A., 1991—; mem. Nat. Film Preservation Bd., Washington, 1992—. Bd. dirs. Motion Pictures and T.V. Fund Found., 1996—, Nat. Film Preservation Found., 1997—. Avocations: tennis, travel. Office: Creative Artists Agy 9830 Wilshire Blvd Beverly Hills CA 90212-1825

PTALIS, DONALD L. telecommunications company executive, entrepreneur; b. Bronx, N.Y., Nov. 18, 1942; s. David and Mildred P.; m. Sandra Ptalis, Oct. 11, 1964; children: Peri A. Mendelson, Dov King. BME, CCNY, 1964. Pres., CEO, Oceanography Unltd., Inc., Paterson, N.J., 1969-76; group exec. IPCO Corp., White Plains, N.Y., 1976-78; v.p. Poloron Products, Inc., Harrison, 1978-81; v.p., gen. mgr. N.J. Office Supply, Whippany, N.J., 1981-84, Lubin Bus. Interiors, New Haven, 1984-87; pres., CEO, Desks, Inc., N.Y.C., 1987-93; pres. Masque Sound and Recording Corp., Moonachie, N.J., 1995-97; pres., CEO, Aridal, Inc., Emerson, 1992—. Bd. dirs. Global Telecomm. Solutions, Marlton, N.J., 1995—. Author: Oceanography, 1970. Named Entrepreneur of Yr., N.J. Soc. Bus. Execs. Avocations: golf, fishing. Home: 16 Ross Ave Emerson NJ 07630-1516 Office: Aridal Inc 142 Main St Nyack NY 10960-3002 E-mail: donptalis@aol.com.

PTASINSKI, CAROL MARY, nurse, educator; b. Chgo., Aug. 21; d. Edmund J. and Sophie (Siudyla) Truszkowski; m. Steve F. Ptasinski, June 20, 1981; children: Jennifer, Thomas. AAS, Truman Coll., Chgo., 1979; BSN, DePaul U., Chgo., 1982; MS in Nursing, St. Xavier U., 1996, MBA, 2002. Adminstr. Royal Home Health Inc., Chgo., 1985-86; ICU charge nurse MacNeal Hosp., Berwyn, Ill., 1986-87; staff nurse auditor Nat. Health Care Rev., Woodland Hills, Calif., 1987-88; staff nurse/spl. procedures St. Mary of Nazareth Hosp., Chgo., 1988-95, with dept. of continuous quality improvement and risk mgmt., 1993-96; quality mgr. Vencor Hosp., Northlake, Ill., 1996-97, asst. adminstr. clin. ops., 1997-98; clin. educator Glenbrook Hosp., Glenview, 1998—. Mem. AACN, DePaul Alumni Assn., St. Xavier Nursing Alumni Assn., Sigma Theta Tau. E-mail: cptasinski@hotmail.com.

PTASYNSKI, HARRY, geologist, oil producer; b. Milw., May 26, 1926; s. Stanley S. and Frances V. (Stawicki) P.; m. Nola G. Whitestine, Sept. 15, 1951; children: Ross F., Lisa Joy. BS, Stanford U., 1950. Cert. profl. geologist; cert. petroleum geologist. Dist. geologist Pure Oil Co., Amarillo, Tex., 1951-55, Casper, Wyo., 1955-58; ind. geologist, oil prodr., 1958—. With USN, 1943-46, PTO. Mem. Am. Assn. Petroleum Geologists, Am. Inst. Profl. Geologists, Ind. Petroleum Assn. Am. (v.p., bd. dirs. 1976-85), Ind. Petroleum Assn. Mountain States (v.p., bd. dirs. 1976-80, Rocky Mountain Oil and Gas Assn. (bd. dirs., exec. com. 1980-96). Republican. Episcopalian. Avocations: tennis, trout and salmon fishing, western history, golfing. Home: 1515 Brookview Dr Casper WY 82604-4895 Office: 123 W 1st St Ste 560 Casper WY 82601-2483 E-mail: hptasyn@trib.com.

PTASZKOWSKI, STANLEY EDWARD, JR. civil engineer, structural engineer; b. N.Y.C., June 11, 1943; s. Stanley Edward and Elsie Helena (Heihs) P. AAS, Acad. Aeronautics, Flushing, N.Y., 1967; BS in Civil Engring., U. Mo., 1975. Registered profl. engr., Tex., profl. sanitarian, Tex. Engr. Brown & Root, Inc., Houston, 1975-79; sr. engr. Marathon Marine Engring. Co., 1979-84, Gen. Dynamics, Ft. Worth, 1984-91, Bridgefarmer & Assocs., Dallas, 1991-93; prin. Pasko Consultants, Arlington, Tex., 1993—; mgr. spl. projects Raytheon Svc. Co., Ft. Worth, 1994—. Mem. NSPE, Tex. Soc. Profl. Engrs., Soc. Profl. Bldg. Designers (cons.). Lutheran. Avocations: lic. pvt. pilot, golf, racquet ball. Home: 2002 Park Hill Dr Arlington TX 76012-1926

PTRCIK, JOHN FERDINAND, writer; b. Passaic, NJ, Mar. 26, 1956; s. Eugene Vincent and Helen Ann Petrik; m. Mary Louise Hinzmann, Apr. 6, 2002. AB in Philosophy, Middlebury Coll., 1977; MA in Philosophy, U. Chgo., 1980. Commd. 2d lt. U.S. Army, 1981, advanced through grades to maj.; platoon leader, staff officer, battery comdr. 1st Battalion, 32d Field ARty., Hanau, Germany, 1981—85; combat trainer Nat. Tng. Ctr., Ft. Irwin, Calif., 1986—89; instr., asst. prof. U.S. Mil. Acad., West Point, NY, 1989—92; resigned U.S. Army, 1992; lectr., dir. advising Rockhurst Coll., Kansas City, Mo., 1992—97; writer Noesis, Inc., Arlington, Va., 1998—. Mem. bd. advisors N.Y.C. semester Fordham U. , 1996—97. Author: Academic Opportunities, 1996, (textbook module) How to Study Philosophy, 2001. Fellow, U. Chgo., 1978. Mem.: Am. Philos. Assn., Naval Inst. (life), Am. Cath. Philos. Assn. (life), Naval Order, Phi Beta Kappa. Roman Catholic. Office: Noesis Inc 4200 Wilson Blvd Ste 900 Arlington VA 22203-1300

PUANGSUVAN, SOMPORN, surgeon, consultant; b. Rajburi, Thailand, 1941; came to U.S., 1967; s. Boon and Sanguan P.; m. Chintana Chanvitayapongs, Mar. 18, 1978; children: Nick, Neesann. MD, Chiengmai (Thailand) Hosp. U., 1966. Diplomate Am. Bd. Surgery. Intern St. Clares Hosp., N.Y.C., 1967-68; resident Aultman Hosp., Canton, Ohio, 1968-69, Tuskegee (Ala.) VA Hosp., 1969-73; pvt. practice, Caruthersville, Mo., 1979—. Attending physician Pemiscot County Meml. Hosp., Hayti, Mo., chief surgery 1994, surg. cons. 1979—. Fellow ACS. Office: 418 Ward Ave Caruthersville MO 63830-1451

PUCCI, MARK LEONARD, public relations professional; b. Irvington, N.J., Mar. 14, 1947; s. James and Anna (Pagach) P.; m. Patricia Ann Powers, Feb. 1, 1974. BBA, Memphis State U., 1971. Music editor River City Rev., Memphis, 1972-74; comml. producer Mid-South Concerts, 1973-74; freelance writer, 1973-74; nat. publicity dir. Capricorn Records, Macon, Ga., 1974-79; owner, pres. Mark Pucci Assocs., Atlanta, 1979-91; v.p. publicity and media rels. Capricorn Records, Nashville, 1991-95; pres., owner Mark Pucci Media, Atlanta, 1996—. Mem.: AMA, Blues Found. Avocations: fishing, basketball, baseball. Office: 5000 Oak Bluff Ct Atlanta GA 30350-1069 E-mail: mpmedia@aol.com.

PUCCIATTI, SANDRA MILSTEIN, opera company director; b. Phila., June 14, 1952; d. Harvey Jack Milstein and Beverly Goldberg; m. Joseph Robert Pucciatti, Oct. 2, 1977; 1 child, Rachel Shabana. MusB summa cum laude, Temple U., 1974; MA, Coll. N.J., 1980. Co-founder, adminstr. The Boheme Club, Inc., Trenton, N.J., 1981-89; co-founder, music dir. Boheme Opera Co. N.J., 1989-95, mng. dir., 1995—. Piano and ensemble coach N.J.

Gov.'s Sch. of Arts, Ewing, N.J., summers 1993-2000; program coord. Inside Opera program Boheme Opera N.J., Mercer County, 1999—. Co-dir. Congregation Beth Chaim Choir, Princeton Junction, N.J., 1980—. Mem. Opera Am., N.J. Art Pride, Trenton Torch Club. Avocations: chamber music, gardening, lecturing about opera medium. Home: 108 Fetter Ave Trenton NJ 08610-3510 Office: Boheme Opera NJ 1 Municipal Dr Hamilton NJ 08619-3809 E-mail: jrspuce@aol.com.

PUCCINELLI, ANDREW JAMES, lawyer; b. Elko, Nev., July 21, 1953; BA cum laude, U. of the Pacific, 1975, JD, 1978. Bar: Nev. 1978. Ptnr. Puccinelli & Puccinelli, Elko, Nev., 1978—. Bus. law adj. prof. No. Nev. C.C., 1982-93; legal advisor Nev. Home Health Svcs., 1980-88. Bd. dirs. Nev. Legal Svcs., 1986-93. Mem. ATLA, Nev. Trial Lawyers Assn., Nev. State Bar Assn. (bd. govs. 1993-2000, v.p. 1996-97, pres.-elect 1997-98, pres. 1998-99, No. Nev. disciplinary bd. 1988-93, CLE com. 1981-85), Elko County Bar Assn. (pres. 1985-86), Phi Delta Phi. Office: Puccinelli & Puccinelli 700 Idaho St Elko NV 89801-3824 Home: 2090 Sawyer Way Elko NV 89801

PUCEK, ANTHONY J. psychiatric nurse practitioner; Cert. nurse practitioner in psychiatry, N.Y., cert. specialist adult psych/mental health nursing. Mem. Am. Psychiat. Nurses Assn., N.Y. State Coalition of Nurse Practitioners. E-mail: junctiona@aol.com.

PUCEL, ROBERT ALBIN, electronics research engineer; b. Ely, Minn., Dec. 27, 1926; s. Joseph and Theresa (Francel) P.; m. Catherine Ann Silva, June 30, 1952; children: Robert W., James J., Valerie A., Marc R., David J. BS, MS, MIT, 1951, DSc, 1955. With rsch. div. Research div. Raytheon Co., Lexington, Mass., 1955-93, staff mem. microwave tube group, 1951-55, solid state physics group, 1955-65, project mgr. microwave semicondr. group, 1965-70, cons. to microwave semicondr. group, 1970-74, cons. scientist semicondr. group, 1974-93; pres. RCP Cons., Needham, Mass., 1994—. Lectr. on monolithic microwave integrated circuits Editor: Monolithic Microwave Integrated Circuits, 1985; contbg. author: Advances in Electronics and Electron Physics, vol. 38, 1975, Gallium Arsenide Technology, 1985. Served with USNR, 1945-46. Recipient Excellence in Technology award Raytheon, 1988. Fellow IEEE (life); mem. Microwave Theory and Techniques Soc. (editorial rev. bd., nat. lectr. 1980-81, Microwave prize 1976, Microwave Career award 1990), Nat. Acad. Engring., Electron Devices Soc. Inventor low-distortion FET; co-inventor Spacistor, Overlay FET.

PUCHTA, RANDOLPH E. lawyer; b. Hermann, Mo., May 31, 1928; s. Everett Adam and Marie Katherine (Sexauer) P.; m. Eunice Marie Rohlfing, Apr. 7, 1951 (wid. Apr. 1995); children: Kristine Marie Puchta-Brown, Timothy John Puchta, Matthew Paul Puchta; m. Lois Lydia Verena Hoerstkamp, July 28, 1996. BA, U. Mo., 1950, JD, 1955. Pvt. practice, Hermann, Mo., 1955-78; prosecuting atty. Gasconade County, 1957-67, assoc. cir. judge, 1978-98, sr. assoc. cir. judge, 1998—. Chmn. Gasconade County Rep. Cen. Com., Mo., 1950-51; dir. Hermann Indsl. Devel. Corp., Hermann, 1956—, Gasconade County Hist. Soc., Hermann, 1980s—, Emmaus Homes, Inc., 2000—; mem. numerous other orgns. Served USAF, 1951—53, Korean War, ret. as lt. col. USAF, 1978. Named to Outstanding Young Men of Mo., Jaycees, 1961; recipient Disting. Svc. award Jaycees, Hermann, 1961. Mem. Mo. Bar Assn., 20th Cir. Bar Assn., Gasconade County Bar Assn., U. Mo. Alumni Assn. Republican. Mem. United Ch. of Christ. Avocations: reading, mil. history, gardening, woodworking, antique collecting. Home: PO Box 231 Hermann MO 65041-0231 Office: Sr Assoc Cir Judge Hermann MO 65041 E-mail: ranlo@ktis.net.

PUCK, THEODORE THOMAS, geneticist, biophysicist, educator; b. Chgo., Sept. 24, 1916; s. Joseph and Bessie (Shapiro) Puckowitz; m. Mary Hill, Apr. 17, 1946; children: Stirling, Jennifer, Laurel. BS, U. Chgo., 1937, PhD, 1940. Mem. commn. airborne infections Office Surgeon Gen., Army Epidemiol. Bd., 1944-46; asst. prof. depts. medicine and biochemistry U. Chgo., 1945-47; sr. fellow Am. Cancer Soc., Calif. Inst. Tech., Pasadena, 1947-48; prof. biophysics U. Colo. Med. Sch., 1948—, chmn. dept., 1948-67, disting. prof. dept. medicine, 1986—; founder, dir. Eleanor Roosevelt Inst. Cancer Research, 1962-95; Disting. rsch. prof. Am. Cancer Soc., 1966—. Nat. lectr. Sigma Xi, 1975-76 Author: The Mammalian Cell as a Microorganism: Genetic and Biochemical Studies in Vitro, 1972. Mem. Commn. on Physicians for the Future. Recipient Albert Lasker award, 1958, Borden award med. rsch., 1959, Louisa Gross Horwitz prize, 1973, Gordon Wilson medal Am. Clin. and Climatol. Assn., 1977, award Environ. Mutagen Soc., 1981, E.B. Wilson medal Am. Soc. Cell Biology, 1984, Bonfils-Stanton award in sci., 1984, U. Colo. Disting. Prof. award, 1987, Henry M. Porter medal, 1992; named to The Colo. 100, Historic Denver, 1992; Heritage Found. scholar, 1983; Phi Beta Kappa scholar, 1985; Fogarty Internat. scholar NIH, 1997. Fellow Am. Acad. Arts and Scis.; mem. Am. Soc. Human Genetics, Am. Chem. Soc., Soc. Exptl. Biology and Medicine, AAAS (Phi Beta Kappa award and lectr. 1983), Am. Assn. Immunologists, Radiation Research Soc., Biophys. Soc., Genetics Soc. Am., Nat. Acad. Sci., Tissue Culture Assn. (Hon. award 1987), Paideia Group, Santa Fe Inst. Sci. Bd., Phi Beta Kappa, Sigma Xi. Achievements include pioneering contributions to establishment of somatic cell approaches to mammalian cell genetics, to the identification and classification of the human chromosomes; measurement of mutation in mammalian cells; demonstration of the camp-induced reverse transformation reaction and the genome exposure defect in cancer; development of quantitative approaches to mammalian cell radiobiology. Office: Eleanor Roosevelt Inst Cancer Rsch 1899 Gaylord St Denver CO 80206-1210 *Our age is threatened by distorted emphasis on power, material wealth, and competitiveness, and by an explosive increase in population which exceeds our traditional regulative capacities. But it also holds promise for new and profound understanding of ourselves - of our basic human biological intellectual and emotional needs. There is room for hope.*

PUCKETT, ALLEN WEARE, health care information systems executive; b. Pasadena, Calif., Mar. 17, 1942; s. Allen Emerson Puckett and Betty Jane (Howlett) Ward; m. Joan Adrienne Roth, Apr. 10, 1965 (div. 1980); children: Glenn A., Tod A.; m. Laura Treadgold, July 10, 1992. BS, U. Calif., Berkeley, 1963; JD, Harvard U., 1966. Bar: Calif. 1966. Prin. McKinsey & Co., San Francisco, 1966-78; pres. Atman Corp., 1979-83; v.p. VWR Sci., 1980-83, Univar Corp., Seattle, 1984-85; sr. v.p. fin. VWR Corp., 1986-90, Momentum Distbn. Inc., Seattle, 1990; v.p. cen. ops. Eldec Corp., Lynnwood, 1990-92; exec. v.p. Phycom Corp., 1993-2000, HealthGnostics, Inc., 2000—01; prin. Gordian Solutions LLC, 2001—. Bd. dirs. Washington Dental Svcs. Recipient Nathan Burkan prize ASCAP, 1966. Mem.: Wash. Athletic Club. Avocations: skiing, scuba diving, music. Home: 1624 38th Ave E Seattle WA 98112-3134

PUCKETT, C. LIN, plastic surgeon, educator; b. Burlington, N.C., Oct. 19, 1940; s. Harry W. and Lula C. Puckett; m. Florence Elizabeth Loy, June 18, 1961 (div. 1976); children: Loy C., Lisa A., Leslie A.; m. Patricia Louise Wells, June 17, 1984 (div. 1994); 1 child, Harry James; m. Teresa G. Teel, Nov. 24, 1995. MD, Bowman Gray Sch. Medicine, 1966. Assoc. in surgery Duke U. Med. Ctr., Durham, N.C., 1971-73; assoc. prof., head divsn. plastic surgery U. Mo. Med. Ctr., Columbia, 1976-81; prof., head attending plastic surgeon U. Mo. Med. Ctr., Truman VA Hosp., 1982—. Editl. bd. (jour.) Jour. Plastic & Reconstructive Surgery, 1994—2000; contbr. articles. Fellow: ACS (gov. 1992-98); mem.: Assn. Acad. Chmn. Plastic Surgery (bd. dirs. 1985-, pres. 1987-88), So. Med. Assn., Plastic Surgery Rsch. Coun., Mo. Chpt. ACS, Internat. Microsurg. Soc., Am. Trauma Soc., Am. Soc. Surgery of the Hand, Am. Bd. Plastic Surgery (cert., bd. dirs. 1988-94, chmn. 1993-94), Am. Soc. Plastic Surgeons, Inc. (bd. dirs. 1985-, asst. sect. 1988, trustee 1990, chmn. 1992, parliamentarian 1993, various to pres. 1999-2000), Am. Cleft Palate Assn., Am. Assn. Plastic Surgeons (trustee 1995-98), Am. Assn. hand Surgery (bd. dirs. 1982-84, chmn. nominating com. 1985, v.p. 1987, pres.-elect 1988, pres. 1988-89), AMA, Alpha Omega Alpha, Sigma Xi. Republican. Avocation: breeding Quarter horses, Angus cattle. Office: U Mo Divsn Plastic Surgery 1 Hospital Dr Columbia MO 65212-0001 E-mail: puckettc@health.Missouri.edu.

PUCKETT, ELIZABETH ANN, law librarian, law educator; b. Evansville, Ind., Nov. 10, 1943; d. Buell Charles and Lula Ruth (Gray) P.; m. Joel E. Hendricks, June 1, 1964 (div. June 1973); 1 child, Andrew Charles; m. Thomas A. Wilson, July 19, 1985. BS in Edn., Eastern Ill. U., 1964; JD, MS in L.S., U. Ill., 1977. Bar: Kans. 1978, Ill. 1979. Acquisitions/reader services librarian U. Kans. Law Library, Lawrence, 1978-79; asst. reader services librarian So. Ill. U. Law Library, Carbondale, 1979-81, reader services librarian, 1981-83; assoc. dir. Northwestern U. Law Library, Chgo., 1983-86, co-acting dir., 1986-87; dir./assoc. prof. South Tex. Coll. Law Library, Houston, 1987-89; dir./prof. South Tex. Coll. Law Libr., 1990-94, U. Ga. Law Libr., Athens, 1994—. Co-author: Evaluation of System-Provided Library Services to State Correctional Centers in Illinois, 1983; co-editor Uniform Commercial Code: Confidential Drafts, 1993. Mem. ABA, Am. Assn. Law Librs. (mem. exec. bd. 1993-96). Avocations: reading, antiques. Office: U Georgia Law Libr Athens GA 30602-6018 E-mail: apuckett@arches.uga.edu.

PUCKETT, ELSBETH CAMILLE, b. Dayton, Ohio, Apr. 25, 1946; d. Hollis Elwood and Elsbeth (Burnham) P. B of Design, U. Fla., 1968. Mem. coll. fashion bd. Levy's Dept. Store, Savannah, Ga., 1965-68; sr. designer Ivan Allen Co., Atlanta, 1968—. Pres. Ga. State Bd. Archs. and Interior Designers, 2001-02; coord., speaker profl. meetings. Sec., mem. bd. Woodmont Landing Homeowners Assn. Recipient Salute to Women of Achievement, YWCA, Atlanta, 1986; Interior Design Gov. Appointee Ga. State Bd. Architects and Interior Designers, 1992-2002. Mem. Am. Soc. Interior Designers (2d v.p. Ga. chpt. 1987, 1st v.p. 1988, treas. 1989, pres. 1991-92, Medalist award 2002), Atlanta Lawn Tennis Assn. (flight coord.), Nat. Coun. for Interior Design Qualification (chmn. S.E. regional jury 1984-89, master juror ctr. coord. of grading 1990-92, exam. dir. intraprofl. affairs, dir. intraprofl. affairs exec. bd. 1994-95, advising dir. 1996, coun. mem. 1997-2002, chmn. atem validation com. 2001-02, Louis Tregre award 1993), Ga. Alliance for Interior Design Profls. (pres. 1993). Republican. Presbyterian. Avocations: tennis, reading, travel. Home: 6107 Woodmont Blvd Norcross GA 30092-2758 Office: Ivan Allen Furniture Co 730 Peachtree St Ste 200 Atlanta GA 30308 Fax: 404-760-8753. E-mail: cpuckett@ivanallen.com.

PUCKETT, HELEN LOUISE, retired tax consulting company executive; b. Ripley, Ohio, Oct. 29, 1934; d. Joseph and Gladys Muriel (Madden) Haney; m. Marvin R. Puckett, May 26, 1953 (dec.); children: Steven W., Thomas J. Grad., Columbus Bus. U., 1971. Office mgr., sec.-treas. Al-Win Tng., Inc., West Jefferson, Ohio, 1971—, agt., 1977—99; ret., 1999. Notary pub., 1975-88. Sunday sch. tchr. London (Ohio) Ch. of Christ, pres. Women's Fellowship, 1979-81. Mem. London Bus. and Profl. Women (pres.), Coover Soc., Cornerstone Club at Madison County Hosp. Office: 485 Glade Run Rd West Jefferson OH 43162-9581

PUCKETT, PAUL WALTER, lawyer; b. Honolulu, July 31, 1946; s. Paul James and Jean Haruko (Tsuda) P.; m. Peggy Hope, Nov. 29, 1969; children: Christopher, Paul Casey, Curtis James. BA, Colo. U., 1971, JD, 1974. Bar: Colo., U.S. Dist. Ct. Colo., U.S. Ct. Appeals (10th cir.). Right-of-way coord. Colo.-Ute Elec. Co., Montrose, 1975-76; pvt. practice Gunnison & Crested Butte, Colo., 1976-86, Denver, 1986-92; asst. prosecutor Glendale, Colo., 1988-92; asst. city atty. City and County of Denver, 1992—. Bd. dirs. Rocky Mountain Ski Assn., Denver, 1978-82; pres., bd. dirs. Concerned Lawyers, Inc., Wheat Ridge, Colo., 1987-92; bd. dirs., v.p. Mile High Coun. on Alcohol and Drug Abuse, Denver, 1990-92. Home: 2701 S Utica St Denver CO 80236-2102 Office: City Atty's Office 303 W Colfax Ave Ste 500 Denver CO 80204-2623

PUCKETT, RICHARD EDWARD, artist, consultant, retired recreation executive; b. Klamath Falls, Oreg., Sept. 9, 1932; s. Vernon Elijah P., Leona Belle (Clevenger) P.; m. Velma Faye Hamrick, Apr. 14, 1957 (dec. 1985); children: Katherine Michelle Briggs, Deborah Alison Bolinger, Susan Lin Rowland, Gregory Richard. Student, So. Oreg. Coll. Edn., 1951-56, Lake Forest Coll., 1957-58, Hartnell Jr.Coll., 1960-70; BA, U. San Francisco, 1978. Acting arts and crafts dir., Ft. Leonard Wood, Mo., 1956-57; arts and crafts dir., asst. spl. svcs. officer, mus. dir. Ft. Sheridan, Ill., 1957-59; arts and crafts dir. Ft. Irwin, Calif., 1959-60, Ft. Ord, 1960-86; dir. arts and crafts br. Art Gallery, Arts and Crafts Ctr. Materials Sales Store, 1960; opening dir. Presidio Monterey Army Mus., 1968; dir. Model Army Arts and Crafts Program. One-man shows include Seaside City Hall, 1967—86, 2002, Ft. Ord Arts and Crafts Ctr. Gallery, 1967, 1973, 1979, 1981, 1984, 1986, Presidio of Monterey Art Gallery, So. Oreg. Art Assn., Salinas Valley Art Gallery, Glass on Holiday, Gatlinburg, Tenn., 1981, 1982, Del Messa Gallery, Carmel, Calif., 1998, So. Oreg. Art Gallery, Medford, 2000, also pvt. collections, designed and opened first Ft. Sheridan Army Mus., one-man shows include Walter Avery Gallery Seaside City Hall, 2002. Recipient 1st pl. Dept. Army and U.S. Army Forces Command awards for programming and publicity, 1979-81, 83-85, 1st and 3d pl. sculpture awards Monterey County Fair Fine Arts Exhibit, 1979, Comdrs. medal civilian svcs., 1986, other awards, Golden Acad. award, Internat. Man of Yr. award, 1991-92. Mem. Monterey Peninsula Art Mus. Assn., Salinas Fine Arts Assn. (pres. 2000-), So. Oreg. Art Assn., Ft. Ord Alumni Assn., Salinas Valley Art Assn. (pres. 2000—). E-mial. Home: 210 San Miguel Ave Salinas CA 93901-3021

PUCKETT, ROBERT MARION, clergyman; b. June 17, 1926; BA, Mercer U., 1954; BD, Colgate Rochester Div. Sch., 1957; postgrad., U. Chgo., 1957-58; D Ministry, Princeton Theol. Sem., 1980. Ordained minister Am. Bapt. Ch., 1944, Internat. Coun. of Cmty. Chs., 1944. Min. small rural chs., Ga., Tenn., Fla., 1947-54; Immanuel Congl. Ch., Ontario, N.Y., 1954-57; 1st Bapt. Ch., East Aurora, 1964-67; Norris (Tenn.) Religious Fellowship, cmty. ch., 1967-94; assoc. min. South Ch.-Cmty. Bapt., Mt. Prospect, Ill., 1957-59, Scarsdale (N.Y.) Cmty. Bapt. Ch., 1959-64; min. visitation Tellico Village Cmty. Ch., Loudon, Tenn., 1994—. Pres. Internat. Coun. Cmty. Chs., 1987-89; mem. Morehouse Coll. Preachers, Morehouse Coll., 1988. Editor Pastor's Jour., 1984-94, Inclusive Pulpit, 1996—. Faculty fellow Colgate Rochester Divinity Sch., 1957-58, Melvin Jones fellow Internat. Lions Club, 1994. Home and Office: 177 Chahyga Way Loudon TN 37774-2801 E-mail: tvpuckett@aol.com.

PUCKETT, RUBY PARKER, nutritionist, hospital administrator, consultant, author; b. Dora, Ala., Nov. 26, 1932; d. John Franklin Parker and Ethel V. (Short) Tuggle; m. Larry Willard Puckett, July 2, 1955; children: Laurel Lynn Puckett Brown, Hollie Kristina Puckett Walker. BS in Food and Nutrition, Auburn (Ala.) U., 1954; postgrad. in vocat. edn., U. Fla., 1970, 80; MA in Health Sci. Edn., Cen. Mich. U., 1976. Registered dietitian. Dietetic intern Henry Ford Hosp., Detroit, 1955; staff dietitian VA Hosp., Houston, 1955-56; dietitian Matty Hersee Hosp., Meridian, Miss., 1957-58; asst. dir. U. Miss. Med. Ctr., Jackson, 1960-61; dir. dietetics Ft. Sanders Presbyn. Hosp., Knoxville, Tenn., 1961-63, Waterman Meml. Hosp., Eustis, Fla., 1963-68; dir. food and nutrition U. Fla. Shands Hosp., Gainesville, 1968-95; pres. Square One Cons. Service, 1979-85; pres., owner Food Svc. Mgmt. Cons., 1995—. Mem. adv. com. on jr. coll. dietetic programs Fla. Dept. Edn., 1967-69; mem. nominating com. Southeastern Hosp. Conf. for Dietitians, 1969, sec., 1974-75; pres. Field Agy. Nutrition, 1970; instr. U. Fla., 1972-73, 82-85, mem. clin. and community coordinated undergrad. dietetic program adv. bd., 1974-89; instr. Santa Fe Jr. Coll., Gainesville, 1977-81; mem. adv. com. Marquis Library Soc., Inc., 1974; mem. health project rev. com. North Cen. Fla. Planning Council, 1974-76; mem. adv. bd. U. Fla. Clin. and Community Coordinated Undergrad. Dietetic Progar mem. nutrition adv. com. Sunland Tng. Ctr., Gainesville, 1975-76; named to White House Conf. on Food and Nutrition, 1976, Senate Select Com. on Food and Nutrition, 1976; mem. com. on animal products NRC Adv. Bd. on Mil. Pers. Supplies, 1978-81; site evaluator dietetic programs in colls and univs. Commn. on Accrediation Dietetic Edn., 1999—; mem. adv. bd. various corps. Co-author: Food Service in Health Care Facilities, 1988, Basic Nutrition and Diet Modification Shands Hospital, 1992, Managing Foodservice Operations, 1992, HACCP The Future Challenge, 4th edit., Nutrition Diet Modification Meal Patterns, 4th edit., Disaster and Emergency Preparedness for Food Service Operations, 2002; author: Dietary Managers Course by Correspondence, 9 edits., Nutrition for the Elderly, Safety, Sanitation and Security for Food Services Operation; mem. editl. adv. com.: Stokes Report, 1980—84, editl. advisor: Food Management: Topics in Clinical Nutrition, 1988—, editl. advisor: Aspen's Focus, 1984—91, editl. advisor: Aspen's Hosp. Nutrition and Foodservice Forms; contbr. numerous articles to profl. jours. ; spkr., seminar leader, developer nutrition and older adult distance edn.course. Bd. dirs. U. Fla. Credit Union, 1978—, v.p., 1980—81, pres.-elect, 1981—82, chmn. bd., 1982—83, chmn. bd., 1998; chmn. Shands Hosp. chpt. United Way, 1978, mem. budget and allocations com., 1983—, mem. speakers bur., 1985—86; mem. adv. bd. Harvest Gainesville, 1991—93, Children's Miracle Telethon, 1992—95; adv. bd. Sta. WRUF Pub. Radio, 1988; profl. adv. bd. Shands Home Care; vol. Mothers Supporting Daus. with Breast Cancer, 2000—; bd. dirs. Fla. 4-H, 2000; mem. Sexual Phys. Abuse Bd.; election clk. Alachua County (Fla.) Elections, 2000—; bd. dirs. North Fla. Regional Vocat. Sch. Named Alumni of Yr., Auburn U. Sch. Home Econs., 1985, Disting. Ind. Study Course award, 1986, 1990, Disting. Woman, Alachua County, Fla., 1992; named to Woodlawn H.S. Hall of Fame, 1982, Fla. Women's Hall of Fame, 1986; recipient Community Leader award, Sta. WRUF-FM, 1972, Ivy award, Restauranteurs of Distinction, 1980, Disting. Pace Setter award, Roundtable for Women in Foodservice, 1984, Award of Distinction, Sch. Human Svc., Auburn U., 1991. Mem.: Fla. Coun. on Aging (sec. nutrition sect. 1974—76, adv. bd. 1974—76, chmn. 1974—76), Nat. U. Continuing Edn. Assn. (disting. ind. study course 1986), Nutrition Edn. Soc. (liaison with industry com. 1974, legis. com. 1974, charter), Dietary Mgr. Assn. Found. (steering com.), Am. Soc. Hosp. Food Service Adminstrs. (edn. com. 1968—71, nomination com. 1978, chmn. publ. com. 1981—82, chmn. legis. com. 1984, bd. dirs.), Gainesville Dietetic Assn. (v.p. 1969, pres. 1970, 1976), Fla. Dietetic Assn. (sec. 1968—70, pres. 1973—74, chmn. by-laws com. 1985, del. 1985—87, numerous other offices), Am. Dietetic Assn. (pres. practice group 41 1982—84, area III coord. 1985—88, 1989—, chair practice group mgmt. in food and nutrition svc. 2001, numerous other offices, medal 1996, Excellence in Mgmt. Practice award 1994, Medallion for Profl. Cmty. and Career Achievement), Internat. Gold and Silver Plate Soc. (sec. bd. trustees 1983—85), Gainesville Woman's Club, Ivy Soc., Altrusa, Pi Lambda Beta, Kappa Sigma Phi. Democrat. Mem. Lds Ch. Avocations: whitewater rafting, hiking, gardening. Office: 5200 NW 43d St Ste 102-302 Gainesville FL 32606 Fax: 352-371-6160. E-mail: puckerp@juno.com.

PUCKETT, TERRY GAY, art educator, artist; b. Amarillo, Tex., Aug. 18, 1938; s. Howard Ezra and Alice (Maltsberger) P.; div.; children: Augusta Brook Gallagher Rosser, William Howard Bengamin Gallagher. BFA, Tex. U., 1960; MA, West Tex. A&M U., 1973, Tex. U., San Antonio, 1988. Illustrator Oil Well Svcs. Mag., Dallas, 1962; instr. art S.W. Ctr. for Arts and Crafts, San Antonio, 1966-78; prof. art St. Philip's Coll., 1982-99, prof. emeritus, 1999—. Curriculum developer telecourse and internet classes in art; organizer, workshop leader Texturas de San Miguel, San Miguel de Allende, Mexico, 1991—97, Paint/Sketch Guatemala, Antiqua, 1997, Antiqua, 2001; organizer, workshop leader drawing classes Paloma Studios, 2001, 02; adj. instr. Ctr. for Spirituality in Art, 2000—01. Exhibitions include Springfield (Mo.) Art Mus., 1994, Watercolor USA, 1994, Nat. Coll. Soc. Stocker Ctr. Gallery, 1997, Arrowmount Sch. of Art, Gattlingburg, Tex., 1997, Windows to My World, 1998, Internat. Exhbn. Enamel, Buenos Aires, 2001, St. Philip's Coll., 1999, U. Colo., Colorado Springs, 2001, U.S. Embassy, Nassau, Bahamas; contbr. articles to profl. jours. Guest artist Creativity Week, HEB Found., Laekey, Tex., summers 1980—; organizer The Olmos Park Art Walk, 2000, 01, 02. Recipient First prize The Ctr. for Spirituality and the Arts, 1993, Best of Show, 1996, Pres.'s award San Antonio Art League Mus., 1993, Sponsors award, 1994, Tchg. Excellence award Nat. Inst. Staff and Orgnl. Devel., 1998. Mem. Tex. Watercolor Soc. (v.p. 1997-99), San Antonio Art League (awards chair 1998-99), Enamelist Soc., Soc. Layerists in Multimedia. Episcopalian. Avocation: collecting Latin American folk art. E-mail: tpuckett@txdirect.net.

PUCKETT, TONY GREG, lawyer; b. Oklahoma City, Mar. 28, 1961; s. Tony Gene and Sandra Claire P.; m. Jennifer Ann Tubb, Aug. 8, 1987. BA, Colo. Coll., 1983; JD with distinction, U. Okla., 1988. Bar: U.S. Supreme Ct., 10th Cir. Ct. Appeals, 8th Cir. Ct. Appeals, U.S. Dist. Ct. Okla. (we. dist.), U.S. Dist. Ct. Okla. (no. dist.), U.S. Dist. Ct. Okla. (ea. dist.), U.S. Dist. Ct. Tex (No. Tex. dist.). Law clk. Lytle Soule & Curlee, Oklahoma City, 1986-88, assoc., 1988-92, shareholder, 1993-97, McAfee & Taft, Oklahoma City, 1998—. Author: Supreme Court Broadens Liability for Harassment, 1998, Supreme Court Dicples Same-Sex Sexual Harassment Issue, 1998; contbg. author: Age Discrimination in the Workplace: A Primer for Human Resources Professionals, 1999. Trustee McAfee & Taft Found., Oklahoma City, 1998-99. Mem. ABA (labor and employment law sect.), Okla. Bar Assn. (labor and employment sect., chmn. 1997-98), Okla. County Bar Assn., Okla. Assn. Muncipal Attys., Soc. for Human Resources, Optimist Club Republican. Presbyterian. Office: McAfee & Taft 211 N Robinson Ave Ste S1000 Oklahoma City OK 73102-7103 E-mail: tony.puckett@mcafeetaft.com.

PUCKETT, W. GREER, engineer; b. Oak Ridge, Tenn., Apr. 20, 1952; s. James Beverly and Jane (Greer) P. BS, U.S. Naval Acad., 1975. Design engr. Ford Motor Co., Dearborn, Mich., 1979-80; field engr. Westinghouse, Groton, Conn., 1980-84, Dunoon, Scotland, 1984-85, Westinghouse/Northrop Grumman, Groton, 1985-96; project mgr. Northrop Grumman, Sunnyvale, Calif., 1996-99, field engr. Bangor, Wash., 1999-2000, sr. field engr. Sunnyvale, Calif., 2000—. Bd. dirs. Southeastern Conn. AIDS Project, New London, 1989-93, 1995-96, Concern Inc., New London, 1994-96, Kitsap Human Rights Network, Silverdale, Wash., 1999-2000; contbg. mem. Human Rights Campaign, Washington, 1991-98, Dem. Nat. Com., Washington, 1996—. Served U.S. Navy 1975-78. Recipient Appreciation award Southeastern Conn. AIDS Project, 1996, Westinghouse Marine Divsn. Quality Ach. award, 1989. Democrat. Presbyterian. Avocations: collecting art and antiques, playing bridge, walking, reading, doing volunteer work. Home: 4661 Albany Cir Apt 112 San Jose CA 95129 Office: 401 E Hendy Ave Sunnyvale CA 94086-5100 E-mail: greerp1975@aol.com.

PUCKETTE, STEPHEN ELLIOTT, mathematics educator, mathematician; b. Ridgewood, N.J., Oct. 18, 1927; s. Charles McDonald and Elizabeth Argyle (Gettys) P.; m. Upshur Smith, June 22, 1957; children: Robert B. E., Miller S., Emily E., Charles McD., Charlotte Elliott. BS, U. of the South, 1949; MS, Yale U., 1950, MA, 1951, PhD, 1957; DSc (hon.), U. of the South, 1998. Asst. prof. math. U. of the South, Sewanee, Tenn., 1956-64; vis. asst. prof. math. U. Ga., Athens, 1962-63; assoc. prof. math. U. Ky., Lexington, 1966-69; dean of arts and scis., prof. U. of the South, Sewanee, Tenn., 1969-79; prof. associé U. Nationale, Cote d'Ivoire, Côté d'Ivoire, Ivory Coast, 1979-80; prof. math. U. of the South, Sewanee, Tenn., 1980-93, prof. emeritus, 1993—; vis. prof. U. N.C., Chapel Hill, 1986-87. Vis. lectr. Math. Assn. Am., Washington DC, 1967-77. NSF faculty fellow, Yale U., 1964-65; Fulbright scholar (France), 1952-53; Fulbright lectr. (Ivory Coast), 1979-80. Mem. Am. Math. Soc., Société Mathématique de France, Deutsche Mathematiker-Vereinigung, London Math. Soc. Democrat. Episcopalian. Home: Morgan's Steep Sewanee TN 37375 Office: U South Dept Math Sewanee TN 37375 E-mail: stephen.puckette@sewanee.edu.

PUDER, JANICE, special education educator; b. Phila., Apr. 6, 1950; d. Allen Thrasher and Dorothy Ruth (Mathis) P.; 1 foster child, Corienna Gallagher. AA, Pasadena (Calif.) City Coll., 1970; BA, U. Calif., Chico, 1973, postgrad., 1973-74, U. Pacific, 1982; MA in Spl. Edn., Santa Clara U., 1996; postgrad., U. San Diego, 2000. Cert. elem., secondary, and spl. edn. tchr., Calif.; cert. adapted phys. edn. specialist. Tchr. New Covenant Christian H.S., Palo Alto, Calif., 1977-81; spl. edn. tchr. Sunnyvale (Calif.) Christian Jr. and Sr. H.S., 1981-82; adapted phys. edn. and cons. to spl. edn. local plan area 3 Santa Clara County Office Edn., 1983-92, adapted phys. edn. specialist, 1992—. Vol. Christian Counseling. Mem. PEO. Avocations: Bible study, reading, sports, advocate (guardianship) for foster daughter. E-mail: janp@earthlink.net.

PUDERBAUGH, KATHLEEN ANNETTE, maternal/women's health nurse practitioner; b. Bremerton, Wash., May 20, 1950; d. Albert William and Martha Annette (Palmer) Rapp; m. Michael R. Puderbaugh, Apr. 25, 1970; children: Brian, Michael. Assoc Tech. Arts, AS in Nursing, Olympic Coll., Bremerton, 1971; student, Seattle U., 1968, City U., Bellevue, Wash., 1987; BSN, U. Wash., 1992, MN, 1994. RN, Calif., Wash.; cert. ob-gyn. nurse practitioner, adult nurse practitioner ANCC. Nurse Kaiser Permanente Med. Group, Oakland, Calif., 1972-74, Swedish Hosp. Med. Ctr., Seattle, 1975-80; ob-gyn nurse practitioner Dr. Gary L. Rogers, Bellevue, 1980-93; women's health care nurse practitioner Harborview Med. Ctr., Seattle, 1994-95, Dr. Estelle Yamaki, Federal Way, Wash., 1995—. Mem.: Assn. Registered Nurse Practioners United of Washington State, Nurse Practioners in Women's Health, Nat. Assn. Nurse Practioners, Am. Coll. Nurse Prationers, Obstetric & Neonatal Nurses, Assn. Women's Health.

PUDLO, FRANCES THERESA, human resources specialist; b. Hartford, Conn., Jan. 17, 1948; d. Alexander and Eve Antoinette (Paczkowski) P. AS in Secretarial Sci., U. Hartford, 1974; postgrad., St. Joseph Coll., 2001. Sec. United Techs. Corp., East Hartford, Conn., 1966-74; asst., sec. Richard M.

Bissell, Jr., Farmington, 1974-94; adminstrv. officer DeWolfe New Eng., Avon, 1994-97; office mgr. Painting & Decorating, Inc., New Britain, 1997—. Co-author: Reflections of a Cold Warrior: From Yalta to the Bay of Pigs, 1996. Bd. dirs. Friends of Hill-Stead Mus., Farmington, Conn., 1994—, sec. 2000—; mem. SS Cyril & Methodius Sch. Bd., chmn. alumni and pub. rels. com. 2000—; mem. World Affairs Coun., 1996—; sec. 100th ann. com. SS Cyril and Methodius Ch., Hartford, 1997—, eucharistic min., 2000—. Avocations: reading, cooking, gardening, ancient history, travel. Home: 33 Worthington Rd Glastonbury CT 06033

PUDLO, VIRGINIA MARY, medical surgical nurse; b. Hartford, Conn., Jan. 22, 1951; d. Alexander and Eve Antoinette (Paczkowski) P. AS in Secretarial Sci., U. Hartford, 1974; BSN, St. Joseph Coll., 1988, MA in Human Devel./Gerontology, 1999. RN, Conn.; cert. med.-surg. nursing ANCC. Exec. sec. Pratt & Whitney Aircraft divsn. United Techs. Corp., East Hartford, Conn., 1969-85; clin. nurse I med.-surg. orthopedic/rehab. unit Hartford Hosp., 1988-93, clin. nurse II surg. unit, 1993-96, with preadmission testing ctr., 1996-2001, case coord., 2001—. Staff nurse coun. Hartford Hosp., rep., 1989-97, sec., 1993-97, acting pres., 1996-97. Tchr. calligraphy East Hartford Adult Edn., 1983-96; parish nurse program coord. SS Cyril & Methodius Ch., 1998— (stewardship com., 1999—); coord. Legislative Advocacy for Human Rights, 2000, Parish Coun. Com., 2001; eucharistic min., 2000—. Recipient Linda Richards-June Long Nursing award for Leadership Excellence Hartford Hosp., 1994. Mem. Nat. Assn. Orthopedic Nurses, Conn. Nurses Assn., Conn. Valley Calligraphers (libr. 1993—), Sigma Theta Tau (Upsilon chpt., mem.-at-large 1992), Sigma Phi Omega. Avocations: calligraphy, sewing, leather-work, woodworking, cooking. Home: 33 Worthington Rd Glastonbury CT 06033-1372

PUDWILL GORIE, DOMINIC L. astronaut; b. Lake Charles, La., May 2, 1957; m. Wendy Lu Williams; children: Kimberly, Andrew. BS in Ocean Engring., U.S. Naval Acad., 1979; MS in Aviation Systems, U. Tenn., 1990. Commd. ensign USN, 1981, advanced through grades to capt.; pilot Attack Squadron 46, USS America, 1981—83, Strike Fighter Squadron 132, USS Coral Sea, 1983—86; test pilot Naval Air Test Ctr., 1988—90; with Strike Fighter Squadron 87, USS Roosevelt, 1990—92; with U.S. Pace Command, Colorado Springs, 1992—94; astronaut NASA, Houston, 1994—, with Astronaut Office, spacecraft communicator Mission Control. Decorated DFC with Combat "V", 2 Air medals, 2 Space Flight medals, 2 Navy Commendation medals with Combat "V", Navy Achievement medal; named Strike Fighter Wing Atlantic Pilot of Yr. Achievements include logged over 5,200 flight hours in over 30 different aircraft; over 600 carrier landings; logged over 32 days in space; pilot STS-91 (1998), STS-99 (2000); crew comdr. STS-108 (2001). Avocations: skiing, bicycling, fishing, golf. Office: Astronaut Office/CB NASA Johnson Space Ctr Houston TX 77058*

PUENTE, ANTONIO E. psychologist, educator, scientist; b. Habana, Cuba, Feb. 14, 1956; s. Antonio A. and Sylvia (Llanso) P.; m. Linda Newman, June 11, 1977; children: Kirsta, Antonio, Lucas. AA, Fla. Jr. Coll., Jacksonville, 1971; BA, U. Fla., 1973; PhD, U. Ga., 1978. Diplomate Am. Bd. Profl. Neuropsychology. Asst. prof. neuroanatomy St. George's U. Sch. Medicine, Grenada, W.I., 1978-79; clin. psychologist N.E. Fla. State Hosp., Macclenny, Fla., 1979-81; clin. neuropsychologist Wilmington, NC, 1982—; prof. psychology U. N.C., 1981—. Author: Neuropsychological Assessment of the Spanish Speaker, Handbook of Neuropsychological Assessment, others; editor: Neuropsychology Review. Mem. AMA (current procedural terminology panel 1994—, Health Care Financing Adminstrn. medicare coverage adv. com. 1999—), APA (coun. of reps. 1994-2000, pres.-elect divsn. neuropsychology 2001, Karl Heiser award 1995), Nat. Acad. Neuropsychology (pres. 1991, disting. svc. award 2000), N.C. Psychol. Assn. (pres. 1990), N.C. Psychol. Found. (founding pres. 1991). Republican. Roman Catholic. Avocations: surfing, tennis. Home: 1916 Lunar Ln Wilmington NC 28405-4211 Office: U NC Wilmington Dept Psychology Wilmington NC 28403 E-mail: puente@uncwil.edu.

PUENTE, JOSE GARZA, safety engineer; b. Cuero, Tex., Mar. 19, 1949; s. Roque Leos and Juanita Vela (Garza) P.; m. Francisca Rodriguez Estrada, Sept. 7, 1969; 1 child, Anthony Burk. BA, West Tex. A&M U., 1972; postgrad., U. Ariz., 1980; grad., U.S. Army Transp. Courses, 1972, 78, Command and Gen. Staff Coll., 1992, grad., 1999. Cert. U.S. Coun. Accreditation in Occupl. Hearing, Audiometric Technicians of Am. Indsl. Hygiene Assn.; cert. pub. mgr., Ariz. Asst. gen. mgr. Am. Transit Corp., Tucson, 1972-75; pub. transp. supt. City of Tucson, 1975-77, asst. safety coord., 1977-81; safety coord. City of Mesa, Ariz., 1981-88; corp. safety dir. Am. Fence Corp., Phoenix, 1988-89; safety adminstr. Ariz.-ADOT, 1989-98; safety mgr. ADP Marshall, Raleigh, N.C., 1998, ADP Marshall Lucent Tech., Norcross, Ga., 1998-99; tech. cons. Bell South projects Liberty Mut., 1999—. Owner La Paz Gospel Supplies & Gift shop, Tucson, 1979-80. Mem. Tucson Child Care Assn., 1973-74; mem. citizen task force Sunnyside Sch. Bd., 1977; mem. minority selection for Hispanic seatbelt program vendor Gov.'s Office of Hwy. Safety, 1989—; mem. Mayor's Task Force on Seatbelt Awareness, City of Mesa, 1988-89. Lt. Col. USAR, 1971-99. Recipient Excellence award Ariz. Safety Assn., 1984; fellow Advanced Mgmt. Seminar Urban Mass Transp. Adminstrn., Northeastern U., 1976-77. Mem. Am. Soc. Safety Engrs. (pres. Ariz. chpt. 1990-91, Safety Profl. of Yr. 1984), Inc. Mex.-Am. Govtl. Employees (charter), Ariz. Safety Engrs., Ariz. Mcpl. Safety Assn. (Profl. of Yr. 1986), Nat. Coun. of La Raza), Internat. Order DeMolay (charter), Toastmasters. Republican. Baptist. Home and Office: 5434 Culzean Way Suwanee GA 30024-4129 Office: 1750 Beaver Ruin Rd Ste 500 Norcross GA 30093-2805 Fax: 770-831-6504. E-mail: jose.puente@libertymutual.com.

PUERNER, JOHN P. newspaper publishing executive; b. Aruba, Dutch West Indies, Jan. 13, 1952; BA, MBA, U. of Colo. V.p., dir. mktg. and devel. Chgo. Tribune; pres., pub. The Orlando Sentinel, Fla., 1993-99, Los Angeles Times, Calif., 2000—. Office: Los Angeles Times The Times Mirror Co Times Mirror Sq Los Angeles CA 90053-0001*

PUESCHEL, SIEGFRIED M. pediatrician, educator; b. Waldenburg, Germany, July 28, 1931; came to U.S., 1961; naturalized, 1971; widowed. Student, Braunschweig Coll., Germany, 1953-55, Leibniz Coll., Tubingen, Germany, 1955-56, U. Tubingen, Germany, 1955-57, Free U., Berlin, 1957-58, U. Freiburg, Germany, 1958; MD summa cum laude, Med. Acad., Dusseldorf, Germany, 1960; MPH, Harvard U., 1967; PhD, U. R.I., 1985; JD, So. New Eng. Sch. Law, 1996. Diplomate Am. Bd. Pediatrics, Am. Bd. Med. Genetics. Intern Mercer Hosp., Trenton, N.J., 1961-62; jr. resident in pediatrics Children's Hosp., Honolulu, 1962-63; asst. resident in pediatrics Children's Hosp. Med. Ctr., Boston, 1963-64, asst. in mental retardation, 1967-68, assoc. in mental retardation, 1968-75, dir. Down Syndrome Program, 1970-75, dir. PKU Clinic, 1972-75; sr. resident in pediatrics Montreal Children's Hosp., 1964-65, fellow in biochemical genetics/metabolism, 1965-66; assoc. physician R.I. Hosp., Providence, 1975-79, dir. child devel. ctr., 1975-94, dir. PKU and Amino Acid Program, 1975—, dir. Down Syndrome Program, 1978—, physician, 1979—. Instr. pediatrics Harvard U., Cambridge, Mass., 1968-74, asst. prof. in pediatrics, 1974-75, lectr. in pediatrics, 1975—; asst. prof. in pediatrics Brown U., Providence, 1975-77, assoc. prof. in pediatrics, 1977-85, prof. in pediatrics, 1985—; consulting pediatrician Waltham (Mass.) Hosp., 1968-75; cons. in genetics Lying in Hosp., Boston, 1969-75, Women and Infants Hosp., Providence, 1975—; cons. Devel. Evaluation Clinic Children's Hosp. Med. Ctr., Boston, 1975—; mem. prevention of mental retardation com. Internat. League of Socs. for Persons with Mental Handicaps; mem. rsch., prevention and program svc. com. Assn. for Retarded Citizens U.S.; mem. nat. conf. on rsch. perspectives in down syndrome Nat. Inst. Child Health and Rehab. Svcs.; mem. state-of-the-art conf. on down syndrome Office Spl. Edn. and Rehab. Svcs. U.S. Dept. Edn.; mem. nat. adv. child health and human devel. coun. NIH, Washington; mem. sub-com. on tng., edn. and quality assurance-tech. assistance Devel. Disabilities Coun., R.I.; mem. med. adv. com. Spl. Olympics. Author chpts. to books; mem. editl. bd. Down Syndrome Papers and Abstracts for Profls., Exceptional Parents, Down's Syndrome: Rsch. and Practice; reviewer numerous jours.; contbr. articles to profl. jours. Grantee Mass. Dept. Health, 1968, Vigneron Meml. Fund, 1984-85, Charlotte Taylor Fund, 1985-86, Dept. Health and Human Svcs., 1982-86, March of Dimes Nat. Found., 1987-89, Sigma-Tau Pharm., Inc., 1990-93; recipient Recognition award March of Dimes, 1976, Recognition award Blackstone Valley chpt. R.I. Assn. for Retarded Citizens, 1979, Fogarty Founders award, 1988, Edn. award Muscular Dystrophy Assn., 1985, 86, Muscular Dystrophy Tchg. award, 1988, Recognition award Devel. Ctr. for Handicapped Personsn-Utah State U., 1986, Down Syndrome Assn. of Greater Cin. award, 1986, Colegion John Langdown Down award Mexico City, 1987, Disting. Rsch. award Assn. for Retarded Citizens of U.S., 1990, Conn. Down Syndrome Assn. award, 1991, Sindrome de Down award Asociación Down de Monterrey (Mexico), 1994. Fellow Am. Acad. Pediatrics, Am. Coll. Med. Genetics (founder); mem. AAAS, Am. Assn. Mental Retardation (Profl. Contbn. award 1991), Am. Acad. Cerebral Palsy and Devel. Medicine, Am. Pediatric Soc., Am. Soc. Human Genetics, Nat. Down Syndrome Congress (past pres., Recognition for Disting. Svc. award 1980, Mid-Hudson Valley award 1983, Achievement in Rsch. award 1988, Outstanding Physician award 1991), N.Y. Acad. Sci., R.I. Med. Soc., New Eng. Regional Genetics Group, Soc. Inherited Metabolic Disorders, Down Syndrome Soc. R.I. (award 1985), Assn. for Children with Down Syndrome (bd. dirs.). Office: RI Hosp Child Devel Ctr 593 Eddy St Providence RI 02903-4923

PUETZ, PAMELA ANN, human resources executive; b. Lawrence, Mass., Aug. 17, 1949; d. Gregory and Eleanor Christine Bedrosian; m. Tracy Barnum Braun, Jan. 26, 1974 (div. 1985); 1 child Susannah ; m. Dan Lee Puetz, May 31, 1986. AS, Fisher Jr. Coll., Boston, 1969; BS in Mgmt. with high distinction, Babson Coll., Wellesley, Mass., 1973. Br. mgr. First Security Bank of Utah, N.A., Salt Lake City, 1974-76; bus. mgr. U.S. Ski Team, Inc., Park City, 1976-77; banking specialist Tracy Collins Bank, Salt Lake City, 1980-83; instr. Fitness Inst., LDS Hosp., 1983-85; owner/operator Grapevine Svcs., Redondo Beach, Calif., 1987-88; human resources adminstr. PacifiCare Health Systems, Inc., Cypress, 1988-89, human resources analyst, 1989-91, human resources project mgr., 1991-93, human resources mgr., 1993—94; sr. mgr. human resources systems Mattel, Inc., El Segundo, 1994-95; sr. cons., HRIS mgr. PacifiCare Health Systems, Inc., Cypress, 1995-96; dir. HR/Payroll Sys., Santa Ana, 1996—. Mem. Internat. Human Resources Info. Mgmt. Assn., Soc. for Human Resources Mgmt., World Art Work. Avocations: scuba, snow skiing. E-mail: Pam.Puetz@phs.com.

PUFFER, RICHARD JUDSON, retired college chancellor; b. Chgo., Aug. 20, 1931; s. Noble Judson and Lillian Katherine (Olson) P.; m. Alison Foster Cope, June 28, 1952; children— Lynn, Mark, Andrew. Ph.B., Ill. Wesleyan U., 1953; MS in Edn, Ill. State U., 1962; PhD (Roy Clark Meml. scholar), Northwestern U., 1967. Asst. plant supt. J.A. Olson Co., Winona, Miss., 1957-59; tchr. Leroy Community Unit Dist. (Ill.), 1959-60; tchr., prin. Community Unit, Dist. 7, Lexington, Ill., 1960-62; asst. county supt. schs. Cook County, 1962-65; dean arts and scis. Kirkwood Community Coll., Cedar Rapids, Iowa, 1967-69; v.p. Black Hawk Coll., Moline, Ill., 1969-77, pres., 1977-82, chancellor, 1982-87; pres. The Ark Computer Ctr., 1989-92. Dir. W. Ctrl. Ill. Ednl. TV Corp., Springfield, Ill., 1977-87; cons. examiner North Central Assn., 1978-87. Editor: Cook County Ednl. Digest, 1962-65. Bd. dirs. Cedar Rapids Symphony, 1967-69, United Way of Rock Island and Scott Counties, Ill., 1978-80, Unitarian Universalist Dist. of Mich., 1995-98; bd. dirs., sec. West Shore Unitarian Universalist Congregation, 1996-99; sec., treas. Ill. Ednl. Retirement Cts., 1987-91; vice-chmn. Illini Hosp. Bd., 1988-93, chmn., 1993-95; bd. dirs. Illowa coun. Boy Scouts Am., 1979-83, v.p., 1981-83. With USNR, 1953-57. Mem. Rotary (pres. 1975-76, East Moline, Ill.), Green Medallion, Blue Key, Phi Delta Kappa, Pi Gamma Mu. Home and Office: 6191 Grace Ave Ludington MI 49431-8629

PUFONG, MARC-GEORGES, political scientist, educator; b. Galim, Western Province, Cameroon, Dec. 2, 1958; s. Zacharia Kuoh and Christine Yiba Pufong. BS in Comm. & Politics, U. Tex., 1982—85; student, Ind. U., 1986—89; MA Policy Studies Telecommunications, So. Ill. Telecomm., 1997; PhD , So. Ill. U., 1995. Assoc. istnr. Ind. U., Bloomington, 1986—89; tchg. asst. So. Ill. U., Carbondale, Ill., 1989—93; prof. pub. law and polit. sci. Valdosta (Ga.) State U., 1994—. Vis. prof. Austin Peay State U., Clarkesville, Tenn., 1996; vis. prof. law and polit. sci. European Coun. of U. Sys. Ga., Paris, 2000. Contbr. articles. Fellow, So. Ill. U., 1993—94. Mem.: Am. Judicature, Ga. Polit. Sci. Assn., So. Polit. Sci. Assn., Am. Polit. Sci. Assn., Rsch. Com. Comparative Jud. Sys. (1995), Pi Sigma Alpha. Office: Valdosta State Univ 1500 N Patterson St Valdosta GA 31698-0035

PUGA, FRANCISCO JAVIER, cardiac surgeon; b. Mexico City, Oct. 10, 1942; came to U.S., 1967; s. Carlos and Maria Luisa Puga; divorced; children: Francis, Alex, Luis. BS, Colegio Franco-Ingles, 1959; MD, U. Nacional Autonoma Mex., 1966. Diplomate Am. Bd. Surgery, Am. Bd. Thoracic Surgery. Intern Stamford (Conn.) Hosp., 1967; resident in gen. surgery Mayo Grad. Sch. Medicine, 1968-72, resident in thoracic and cardiovasc. surgery, 1972-75; staff cardiac surgeon, chief surg. rsch. Inst. Nacional Cariologia, Mexico City, 1975-76; staff thoracic & cardiovasc. surgeon Scott & White clinic, Temple, Tex., 1976-77, Mayo Clinic, Rochester, Minn., 1977—. Mem. AMA, ACS, Am. Coll. Cardiology, Am. Assn. Thoracic Surgery, Congenital Heart Surgeons Soc., Soc. Thoracic Surgeons, Am. Acad. Pediatrics. Roman Catholic. Office: Mayo Clinic 200 1st St SW Rochester MN 55905-0002

PUGACH, MARLEEN CAROL, education educator; b. Englewood, N.J., Apr. 22, 1949; d. Paul Irving and Lillian (Rosenstein) P.; m. William Havens Rickards, June 21, 1978; children: Lev Ian, Anna Yael. BA with distinction, Mt. Holyoke Coll., South Hadley, Mass., 1971; MS in Edn., U. So. Calif., L.A., 1974; PhD, U. Ill., 1983. Asst. prof. U. Ill., Urbana, 1984-85; asst. prof. edn. U. Wis., Milw., 1986-89, assoc. prof., 1989—. Mem. disting. bd. advisors Tchrs. Coll. Press Spl. Edn. Series. Editor: (with R. Clift and W. Houston) Encouraging Reflective Practice in Education, 1990, (with H. Barnes and L. Beckum) Changing the Practice of Teacher Education, 1991; contbr. articles to profl. jours., chpts. to books. U.S. Dept. Edn. peer collaboration grantee, 1985-88. Mem. Am. Ednl. Rsch. Assn., Coun. for Exceptional Children (exec. bd. tchr. edn. div. 1988-91). Office: U Wis PO Box 413 Milwaukee WI 53201-0413

PUGACH, NEIL LEWIS, neurologist; b. Englewood, N.J., Aug. 22, 1953; s. Paul and Lillian (Rosenstein) P.; m. Monica Terry Deitell, July 5, 1986; 1 child, Joseph. AB, Conn. Coll., 1975; MD, Boston U, 1980. Diplomate Am. Bd. Psychiatry and Neurology. Pvt. practice neurology, L.A., 1988-95, Chesapeake, Va., 1995—. Asst. clin. prof. UCLA Sch. Medicine, 1990-95. Mem. Am. Acad. Neurology, Am. Heart Assn. Avocations: martial arts, jazz music. Office: 300 Medical Pkwy Ste 212 Chesapeake VA 23320-4985

PUGAY, JEFFREY IBANEZ, mechanical engineer; b. San Francisco, June 26, 1958; s. Herminio Salazar and Petronila Pugay. BSME, U. Calif., Berkeley, 1981, MSME, 1982; MBA, Pepperdine U., 1986, MS in Tech. Mgmt., 1991. Registered profl. engr., Calif. Engring. asst. Lawrence Berkeley Nat. Lab., 1978-80; assoc. tech. staff Aerospace Corp., L.A., 1981; tech. staff Hughes Space & Comm. Co., El Segundo, Calif., 1982-85, from project engr. to project mgr., 1985-95; mgr. spaceway program mktg. Hughes Comm. Inc., Long Beach, 1995-97, dir. bus. devel., 1997-99, Hughes Network Sys, El Segundo, 1999; dir. strategic devel. BroadStream Comms. Corp., San Diego, 1999-2000; v.p. LCC Internat., Inc., Mission Viejo, 2000—. Active ARC Emergency Svcs. White House Fellow regional finalist, 1991, 92. Mem. ASME, Soc. Competitor Intelligence Profls., Am. Mgmt. Assn., L.A. World Affairs Coun., Make A Wish Found., Pi Tau Sigma, Delta Mu Delta. Republican. Roman Catholic. Avocations: racquetball, scuba diving, sailing, backpacking, volleyball. Home: 13600 Marina Pointe Dr #707 Marina Del Rey CA 90292 Office: LCC Internat Inc 27401 Los Altos Mission Viejo CA 92691

PUGH, ARTHUR JAMES (JAY PUGH), retired department store executive, consultant; b. Glen Morrison, W.Va., Sept. 24, 1937; s. Arthur James and Mary Pugh; m. Sharon Hubacher, Sept. 26, 1961; children: James Gregory, Mary Elizabeth. BSBA, W.Va. U., 1959; Master of Retailing, U. Pitts., 1960. Mgmt. trainee, buyer Woodward & Lothrop, Washington, 1960-71, v.p., 1971-77, sr. v.p., 1977-80, exec. v.p., 1980-87, Coun. of Better Bus. Bur., Arlington, Va., 1987-90, bd. dir.; cons., bd. dir. Fairfax, Va., 1990—. Trustee, chmn. audit com. Calvert Mut. Funds, Washington, 1983—; bd. dirs. Acacia Capital Corp., Washington; bd. dirs., exec. com. compensation com., chmn. investment com. Acacia Fed. Savs. Bank, Falls Church, Va. Chmn. bd. dirs. Better Bus. Bur. Met. Washington, 1987. Mem. Rotary Found. of Washington (pres. 1990-91), Nat. Retail Mchts. Assn. (bd. dirs. 1986), W.Va. U. Alumni Assn. (bd. dirs. 1993-98), Fairfax Country Club (bd. dirs. 1990-92), Rotary Club of Washington (Rotarian of Yr. 1982, pres. 1984). Republican. Presbyterian. Avocations: tennis, running, skiing. Home and Office: 4823 Prestwick Dr Fairfax VA 22030-4533 E-mail: jaypugh@prodigy.net.

PUGH, CHRISTINA ANNE, poet, educator; b. Buffalo, Feb. 18, 1966; d. Walter Davis and Sybil Humphries P. BA in English and French, Wesleyan U., 1988; PhD in Comparative Lit., Harvard U., 1998; MFA in Creative Writing, Emerson Coll., 2001. Tutor in lit. Harvard U., Cambridge, Mass., 1994-98, lectr. in lit., 1998-2001; instr. poetry workshop Grub St. Writers Group, Somerville, 2000; instr. honors program Emerson Coll., Boston, 1999-2001; asst. prof. creative writing CUNY, Coll. S.I., 2001—. Asst. to the dir. Blacksmith House Reading Series, Cambridge, 2000-01; panel chair Poetics of Space Conf., SUNY Binghamton, 2000; organizer grad. student conf. Comparative Lit. Dept. Harvard U., coord. Ford Found. Rsch. Group, 1994-96. Contbr. poetry to profl. publs. Ruth Lilly Poetry fellowship Poetry mag., 2000, Whiting fellowship for the humanities Whiting Found., 1997-98; recipient Grolier Poetry prize Ellen La Forge Meml. Found., 2000, Scott prize for excellence in modern langs. Wesleyan U., 1988; nominee Pushcart Prize, 2001. Mem. MLA, Internat. Assn. of Philosophy and Lit., Am. Comparative Lit. Assn. Office: CUNY Coll S I English Dept Bldg 25 Rm 218 2800 Victory Blvd Staten Island NY 10314 E-mail: cpugh@gis.net.

PUGH, DANIEL WILBERT, theatre educator, costume designer; b. Bluffton, Ind., Sept. 6, 1945; s. Ralph Moody and Doris L. (Baker) P. BA in Drama, Butler U., 1968; MFA in Costume Design, Goodman Sch. Drama, Chgo., 1974. Writer-contbr. Nat. Sch. Dress Design, Americana Corp., Mundelein, Ill., 1969-72; faculty asst. over costume design Northeastern Ill. State Coll., Chgo., 1968-71; costume designer U. Chgo. Court Theatre, 1971-78; design cons. Landes Costumes Co., Indpls., 1980—94; assoc. prof. emeritus theatre Butler U., 1971-2000; freelance costume designer Landes costumes by Rachel, 2000—. Rschr. Internat. Flat Pattern Repository and Exch., 1993—. Costume, constrn. designer, play dir. (theatrical prodns.) Diamond Lil (1st prize, Meml. award for outstanding theater design Nat Costumers Assn. 1983), An Erte Montage (Grand Internat. prize Nat Costumers Assn. 1984), A Clown Couple (1st prze comedy, Meml. award for outstanding comedy costume Nat. Costumers Assn., 1985), Mrs. Higgins and Eliza/My Fair Lady (Grand Internat. prize Nat. Costumers Assn., 1989), a' la Pompadour (Landes Meml. award for outstanding theater design Na. Costumers Assn. 1996), Carnival of Venice, 1997 (1st pl. award theater category, Landes Meml. award for outstanding theater design), Dona Lucia & Amy from Charlie's Aunt (1st prize theater category, runner-up best of show), Meml. award for excellence in theater design, Nat. Costumers Assn., 1998, walking and dinner dresses for Nora of A Doll's House (1st prize theatre category, Landes Meml. award for Excellence in theatre design, 2d runner-up Best of Show Nat. Consumers Assn. 1999), 2 dresses for Camille (1st prize theater category Landes Meml. award for excellence theater costume design Nat. Costumers Assn. 2001). Nominated for costume design citation, The Tempest, Joseph Jefferson Com., Court Theatre, Chgo., 1977; fellow Butler U., 1993-94, 96-97; Creative Renewal Arts fellow Arts Coun. Indpls., 1999-2001. Mem. Costume Soc. Am., Nat. Costumers Assn. (affiliate), U.S. Inst. Theatre Tech., Nat. Model Railroaders Assn., Circus Fans Assn. Am. Avocations: model railroading, collecting antiques, antique sewing machines for historic/vintage embroidery and embellishment, antique/old comml. garment patterns, elephants. Home: 515 E 36th St Indianapolis IN 46205-3503 Office: Landes Costumes by Rachel 811 N Capitol Ave Indianapolis IN 46204 E-mail: danlpugh@ameritech.net.

PUGH, DAVID EDWARD, lawyer; b. Union, N.Y., July 3, 1950; s. William and Arline (Loudenburg) P.; m. Karin L. Brooks, Sept. 27, 1980; children: Jonathan, Brian, Catherine. Student, Syracuse U., 1968-69; BA, SUNY, Binghamton, 1972; JD, Bklyn. Law Sch., 1975. Bar: N.Y. 1976, U.S. Dist. Ct. (ea. and so. dists.) N.Y. 1977; cert. family mediator, Fla. Sole practice, N.Y.C., 1976-81; assoc. Wallman & Kramer, 1981-83, ptnr., 1984-92, Warshaw, Burstein, Cohen, Schlesinger & Kuh, LLP, N.Y.C., 1992-94; counsel Banks Pickett Gruen & Shapiro, LLP, Mt. Kisco, N.Y., 1994-97, Randal G. Lawrence & Assocs., Katonah, 1997-99; negotiator Steven A. Bagen & Assocs., Gainesville, Fla., 1999; tng. coord. Gainesville Ford, 2000—. Lectr. Women's Survival Space, Bklyn., 1978-81; cons. Playcare, Inc., Katonah, N.Y., 1983—. Mem. ABA (family law sect.), N.Y. State Bar Assn. (family law sect.), Assn. Trial Lawyers Am., N.Y. Trial Lawyers Assn. Republican. Presbyterian. Home: 1429 NW 48th Ter Gainesville FL 32605-4566

PUGH, DOROTHY GUNTHER, artistic director; b. Memphis, May 8, 1951; Grad. magna cum laude, Vanderbilt U., 1973; studied with Raymond Clay, studied with Donna Carver, studied with David Howard; student, Royal Acad. Dancing, London. Founder, artistic dir. Ballet Memphis, 1985—. Recipient Woman of Achievement award for Initiative, 1987, Gordon Holl Artistic Adminstr. of Yr. award State of Tenn., 1999; featured as one of city's influential citizens in Memphis Mag. Office: Ballet Memphis PO Box 3675 Cordova TN 38088-3675*

PUGH, EMERSON WILLIAM, electrical engineer; b. Pasadena, Calif., May 1, 1929; s. Emerson Martindale and Ruth Hazel (Edgin) P.; m. Elizabeth Burnam Russell; children: William Russell, Sarah Elizabeth, David Emerson. BS in Physics, Carnegie Mellon U., 1951, PhD in Physics, 1956. Asst. prof. physics Carnegie Mellon U., Pitts., 1956-57; with IBM, 1957-93, rsch. staff mem. rsch. div., Poughkeepsie, N.Y., 1957-61, engring. mgr. components div., 1962-65, group dir. data processing group, Harrison, N.Y., 1965-66, dir. tech. planning rsch. div., Yorktown Heights, N.Y., 1966-68, asst. to v.p. IBM Corp., Armonk, N.Y., 1968-71, rsch. mgr. rsch. div., Yorktown Heights, 1971-85, mgr. tech. history, 1985-93. Vis. scientist IBM Lab., Zurich, Switzerland, 1961-62; mem. United Engring. Trustees Bd., N.Y.C., 1986-92; mem. Engring. Soc. Libr. Bd., N.Y.C., 1986-89; trustee Chalres Babbage Found., 1990—, Samuel Morse Hist. Site, 1998-99. Author: Principles of Electricity and Magnetism, 1960, Memories That Shaped an Industry, 1984, IBM's Early Computers, 1986, IBM's 360 and Early 370 Systems, 1991, Building IBM, 1995; also articles; 10 patents. Fellow IEEE (v.p. 1986-87, pres. 1989, chmn. friends com. Ctr. for History Elec. Engring. 1991-94, chmn. history com. 1995-98, dir. found. bd. 1996—, pres. found. bd. 2000—), AAAS, Am. Phys. Soc. Home: 3 Rock St Cold Spring NY 10516-2911

PUGH, FRANKLIN DAVID, band director; s. Leonard Wayne . and Doris Ann P.; m. Stephanie Marie Edwards, Dec. 20, 1992. BS in Music Edn., BA in Music Performance, Elon Coll., N.C., 1992. Cert. tchr. Va. Gen. music tchr., elem. band tchr., asst. band dir. Alleghany County Schs., Sparta, NC, 1995—96; band dir. Ft. Chiswell Mid. Sch., Max Meadows, Va., 1996—, Ft. Chiswell High Sch., 1996—, chair fine arts dept., 1998—. Mid. sch. devel. team fine arts rep. Wythe County Pub. Sch., Wytheville, Va., 2001—02; mem. Wytheville C.C. Cmty. Band. Composer: Appalachian Sunrise for Band, 1999. Mem. praise and worship team New Covenant Fellowship Ch., Wytheville, Va., 1998—2002. Mem.: Wythe County Edn. Assn., Va. Music Educators Assn. Avocation: reading. Office: Ft Chiswell High Sch #1 Pioneer Tr Max Meadows VA 24360 Office Fax: 276-637-6316.

PUGH, GEORGE WILLARD, law educator; b. Napoleonville, La., Aug. 17, 1925; s. William Whitmell and Evelyn (Foley) P.; m. Jean Earle Hemphill, Sept. 6, 1952; children: William Whitmell III, George Willard, David Nicholls, James Hemphill. BA, La. State U., 1947, JD, 1950; J.S.D., Yale U., 1952; Dr. h.c., U. Aix-Marseille III, France, 1984. Bar: La. 1950. Instr. La. State U. Law Sch., 1950, mem. faculty, 1952-94, prof. law, 1959-94, Julius B. Nachman prof. law, 1984-94; prof. law emeritus, 1994—. Faculty summer session abroad U. Thessaloniki Greece summer 1974, Aix-en-Provence, France, 1985, 91; mem. faculty summer program U. San Diego, Paris, 1977; part-time rsch. cons. La. State Law Inst., 1953-54; 1st jud. administr. Jud. Coun. Supreme Ct. La., 1954-56; vis. prof. U. Tex., summer 1961; vis. Doherty prof. law U. Va., 1966-67; mem. faculty orientation program in Am. law Assn. Am. Law Schs., 1968, law teaching clinic, summer 1969; vis. prof. U. Aix-Marseille III, France, 1983, fall 1987, U. Catholique de Louvain, Belgium, fall 1987; cons. La. State U.S. Vietnam Legal Adminstrn. Project, 1969 Author: Louisiana Evidence Law, 1974, supplement, 1978; co-author: Cases and Materials on the Adminstration of Criminal Justice, 2d edit., 1969, Handbook on Louisiana Evidence Law, 1989, 14th edit., 2002; coord., reporter Code of Evidence for La., 1981-95. Bd. dirs. Legal Aid Soc. Baton Rouge, 1965-89, chmn., 1963-64; adv. bd. St. Alban's Episcopal Student Ctr., La. State U., 1965-68, 70-72. Served with AUS, World War II. Fellow Comparative Study Adminstrn.

Justice, 1962-65 Mem. Am., La., Baton Rouge bar assns., Order of Coif, Omicron Delta Kappa, Lambda Chi Alpha. Democrat. Episcopalian. Home: 167 Sunset Blvd Baton Rouge LA 70808-5073

PUGH, GRACE HUNTLEY, artist; b. Schenectady, N.Y., Sept. 25, 1912; d. Grant and Grace La Vallée (Lake) Huntley; m. Cresson Pugh, Sept. 21, 1940; 1 child, Gigi Grace Huntley Pugh Sundstrom. Student, Wellesley Coll., 1930-32; BA, Barnard Coll., 1934; postgrad., Nat. Acad. Design, 1934-36, Art Students League, 1938. Head art dept., artist in residence Briarcliff Jr. Coll., Briarcliff Manor, N.Y., 1936-40; mem. staff directions in Am. painting exhibit Carnegie Inst., Pitts., 1942-44; asst. art dir. Young & Rubicam Inc., N.Y.C., 1946-50; painting instr. Westchester County Workshop, White Plains, N.Y., 1961-63. Chair fine arts and exhbn. Mamaroneck (N.Y.) Libr., 1950-88; co-chair Emelin Theatre Street Fair, Mamaroneck, 1975-81; fine arts advisor, artist in residence Village of Mamaroneck, 1977—. Exhibited oil and watercolor paintings in numerous group and one-woman shows including Nat. Acad. Design, N.Y.C., 1957, N.Y. State Painters, N.Y. State bldg. in World's Fair, 1965, Franklin & Marshall Colls., 1974, Carnegie Inst., 1950, Canton Art Inst., Ohio, 1995, Canton (Ohio) Art Inst., 1995, Kinderhook (N.Y.) Lib., 1971 many others; Editor Mamaroneck Historical Society Newsletter, 1980—. Charter pres. Mamaroneck Hist. Soc., 1980-82, trustee emerita, 1980—; 1st chair Landmarks Adv. Com. Village of Mamaroneck, 1982-92, co-chair cherry blossom festival centennial com., 1993—; trustee Friends of Wildlife Sanctuary, Rye, N.Y., 1990—; founding pres. Mamaroneck Artists Guild, 1953-55; founding sec. Westchester Soc. Archeol. Inst. of Am., 1976-78. Day named in her honor Village of Mamaroneck, 1982, 91. Mem. Am. Watercolor Soc., Rockport Art Assn. (Longfellow award 1944), Federated Conservationists of Westchester County (Cert. of Appreciation 1991), DAR (conservation chair 1982-88). Republican. Episcopalian. Avocations: swimming, gardening, community service, research, sailing. Home: 823 Stuart Ave Mamaroneck NY 10543-4122

PUGH, JESSIE TRUMAN, minister; b. Noble, La., Oct. 28, 1923; s. Jessie Trulonzer and Lucy (Sanderson) P.; m. Bessie Byrl Halbrooks, Aug. 10, 1944; children: James Terry, Datha Jo, Nathanael Brent. BTh, Tex. Bible Coll., 1971; DD, Berean Christian Coll., 1973; D Christian Lit., Christian Life Coll., 1985. Ordained to ministry United Pentecostal Ch. Internat. Youth sec. Tex. Dist., 1940, pres. youth camps, 1954; instr. Tex. Bible Coll., Houston, 1962-67; pastor various chs., 1944-67; gen. dir. home missions U.S. and Can., 1967-74; pastor 1st Pentecostal Ch., Odessa, Tex., 1974—; pres. Christian Life Coll., Stockton, Calif., 1980-82; dist. supt. Tex. dist. United Pentecostal Ch., 1983—, mem. gen. bd., 1985—. Speaker camp meetings and convs.; host lectr. Pastor's Round Table, 1997—; overseas lectr. Contbr. articles to profl. jours.; hosy Pastor's Round Table, 1997—. Home: 1500 Tanglewood Ln Odessa TX 79761-1824 *I am increasingly impressed that the real issues of life are moral. All racial and physical maladies have roots in neglected moral and spiritual principles. Thus to uphold and propagate such is to have lived well.*

PUGH, JOHN ROBERT, chancellor, former state health administrator; b. New Orleans, Dec. 20, 1945; s. Edward Nicholls and Yvonne Marie (Duplantier) P.; m. Margaret Louise McMullen, Aug. 26, 1975; children— Margaret Elizabeth, John Robert. BA in Philosophy, Baylor U., 1967; M. in Social Work, U. Tex.-Austin, 1970. Program dir. McLaughlin Youth Ctr., Anchorage, 1973-78; dep. dir. Alaska Div. Social Services, Juneau, 1978-80; dir. Alaska Family and Youth Services, 1980-83; dep. commr. Alaska Dept. Health and Social Services, 1983, commr., 1983-86; dean, Sch. of Education Univ. Alaska Southeast, 1986-95, chancellor, 1995—. Cons., lectr. in field Mem., Blue Ribbon Commn. for Revision of Children's Code, 1975-77; supt. Sunday Sch., No. Light United Ch., Juneau, 1979— ; mem. Gov.'s Council for Handicapped and Gifted, 1980-84; mem. precinct com. Greater Juneau Democratic Com., 1983— ; bd. dirs. Alaska State Fin. Corp., 1985— ; coach Juneau Little League, 1984— . Served to capt. USAF, 1969-73 Mem. Nat. Assn. Social Workers (pres. 1975-76), Am. Pub. Welfare Assn., Am. Correctional Assn., Alaska Pub. Employees Assn. (pres. 1977-79), Acad. Cert. Social Workers (cert.) Methodist. Avocations: fishing, outdoor sports. Office: U Alaska Southeast 11120 Glacier Hwy Juneau AK 99801*

PUGH, JOYE JEFFRIES, educational administrator; b. Ocilla, Ga., Jan. 23, 1957; d. Claude Bert and Stella Elizabeth (Paulk) Jeffries; m. Melville Eugene Pugh, Sept. 21, 1985. AS in Pre-law, S. Ga. Coll., 1978; BS in Edn., Valdosta State Coll., 1980, MEd in Psychology, Guidance and Counseling, 1981; EdD in Adminstrn., Nova U., Ft. Lauderdale, Fla., 1992. Cert. tchr., adminstr., supr., Ga. Pers. adminstr. TRW, Inc., Douglas, Ga., 1981-83; recreation dir. Ocilla (Ga.), Irwin Recreation Dept., 1983-84; exec. dir. Sunny Dale Tng. Ctr., Inc., Ocilla, 1984-96; employment cons. TPS Staffing and Recruiting, Douglas, Ga., 1997-98; mgr. Global Employment Solutions, Inc., 1999—. Pres. and registered agt. Irwin County Resources, Inc., Ocilla, 1988-97, Camelot Ct., Inc., 1994-97. Author: Antichrist-The Cloned Image of Jesus Christ, 1999; contbr. articles on handicapped achievements to newspapers, mags. (Ga. Spl. Olympics News Media award, 1987, Assn. for Retarded Citizens News Media award, 1988). Mem. adv. bd. Area 12 Spl. Olympics, Douglas, Ga., 1984-88, bd. dirs., 1995-2000; pres. Irwin County Spl. Olympics, 1984-97, mem. adv. task force Spl. Olympics Internat. for 6-7 yr. olds, 1995—; bd. dirs. Ga. Spl. Olympics, 1995-98, 98-99, mem. comm. and mktg. com., 1995-96, mem. nominations com., 1997-98, outreach and edn. com., 1999-2000; exec. dir., fund raising chmn. Irwin Assn. for Retarded Citizens, Ocilla, 1984-97; arts and crafts chmn. Ga. Sweet Tater Trot 5k/1 Mile Rd. Races, 1993-97; founder, chmn. Joseph Mascolo Celebrity Events, 1985—; vol. Am. Heart Assn., 2000—. Recipient Spirit of Spl. Olympics award Ga. Spl. Olymics, Atlanta, 1986, Award of Excellence Ga. Spl. Olympic Bd. Dirs., 2000, Cmty. Svc. award Ga. Assn. for Retarded Citizens, Atlanta, 1987, Govs.' Vol. award Ga. Vol. Awards, Atlanta, 1988, Presdl. Sports award AAU, Indpls., 1988, Humanitarian award Sunny Dale Tng. Ctr., Inc., Ocilla, 1988, Golden Poet award New Am. Poetry Anthology, 1988, Outstanding Coach-Athlete Choice award Sunny Dale Spl. Olympics, Ocilla, 1992, Dist. Coach award, 1993, Outstanding Unified Sports Ptnr. of Yr. award, 1995, Coach of Yr. award, 1996; carried Olympic Torch, Ocilla, Ga., 1996; Ga. Spl. Olympics State Gold medalist Golf Unified Team, 1996, State Silver medalist Unified Table Tennis Team, 1996, State Bronze medalist Master's Unified Softball Team, 1995. Mem. DAR (Author-Educator-Humanitarian award Nathaniel Abney chpt. 2000), Mut. Unidentified Flying Object Network (Ga. state sect. dir., asst. state dir., cons. 1994—), Ga. State Assn. for Retarded Citizens, Ctrs. Dirs. Ga., Ocilla Rotary Club (program dir. 1995-97, bd. dirs. 1995-97, sec. 1996-97), Sunny Dale Unified Track Club (founder 1991), Sunny Dale Ensemble (founder), Ocilla/Irwin County C. of C., Irwin Assn. Retarded Citizens Inc. Baptist. Avocations: playing musical instruments, jet skiing, weight lifting, dancing, singing. Home: 201 Lakeside Cir Douglas GA 31535-6629 Office: Global Emp Solutions Inc 1214 Peterson Ave N Ste A Douglas GA 31533-2836 Fax: 912-383-7067.

PUGH, KEITH E., JR. lawyer; b. L.A., Mar. 17, 1937; s. Keith Emerson and Serena (Reynolds) P.; m. Kathleen Perry, Aug. 28, 1958 (div. Mar. 1973); children— Linda, Lisa, Scott; m. Pamela Carolyn Winberry, May 20, 1973; children— Alexander, Caroline Student, Principia Coll., 1955-58; JD, U. So. Calif., 1962. Bar: Calif. 1962, D.C. 1969, U.S. Supreme Ct. 1976, U.S. Ct. Internat. Trade 1983, U.S. Ct. Appeals (fed. cir.) 1994. Dep. atty. gen. antitrust sect. Office Calif. Atty. Gen., San Francisco, 1962-65; assoc. Broad, Busterud & Khourie, 1965-66. Office Joseph Alioto, San Francisco, 1966-68, Howrey & Simon, Washington, 1968-69, ptnr., 1970-98, also mem. mgmt., 1980-98. Mem. State Bar Calif., D.C. Bar Assn., Annapolis Yacht Club, Ocean Reef Yacht Club, Phi Delta Phi. Avocation: boating. Home: 24 Dockside Ln PMB # 443 Key Largo FL 33037-5277 E-mail: kpugh87801@aol.com.

PUGH, KYLE MITCHELL, JR. musician, retired music educator; b. Spokane, Wash., Jan. 6, 1937; s. Kyle Mitchel, Sr. and Lenore Fae (Johnson) P.; m. Susan Deane Waite, July 16, 1961; children: Jeffray, Kari. BA in Edu., East Wash. U., 1975. Cert. tchr., Wash. Tuba player Spokane Symphony Orch., 1958-63; rec. assoc. Century Records, Spokane, 1965-73; tuba player World's Fair Expo '74, 1974; bass player Russ Carlyle Orch., Las Vegas, 1976, Many Sounds of Nine Orch., northwest area, 1969-81; band tchr. Garry Jr. High School, Spokane, 1976-79, Elementary Band Program, Spokane, 1979-96; bass player Doug Scott Cabaret Band, 1982-91. Dept. head Elem. Band Dept., Spokane, 1984-89. Editor (newsletter) The Repeater, 1987 (Amateur Radio News Svc. award 1987); extra in movie Always, 1989. Active in communications Lilac Bloomsday Assn., Spokane, 1977. Served to E-5 USNR, 1955-63 Recipient Disting. Service award Wash. State Commn., 1974, Nev. Hollerin' Champ Carl Hayden Scribe, 1979. Mem. Am. Fedn. Musicians (life), Spokane Edn. Assn. (rec. sec. 1987), Music Educator's Nat. Conf., Am. Radio Relay League (asst. dir. 1987), Ea. Wash. Music Educator's Assn. (pres. 1978-79), Dial Twisters Club (pres. 1979-80), VHF Radio Amateurs (dir. 1980-83), Elks. Avocations: ham radio operator, model railroading, photography. Home: 5006 W Houston Ave Spokane WA 99208-3728

PUGH, RANDALL SCOTT, lawyer; b. Jamestown, N.Y., Mar. 31, 1950; s. H. Theodore and Jeanne M. (Crossley) P.; m. Christie s. Sept. 3, 1978; 1 child, Theodore Clifford. BA, Hobart Coll., 1972; JD, U. Richmond, 1976. Bar: Va. 1976, U.S. Dist. Ct. Va. 1982, U.S. Bankruptcy Ct. 1982. Law clk. to justice Supreme Ct., Richmond, Va., 1976-77; asst. county atty. Prince William County, Manassas, 1977; assoc., ptnr. Whitticar, Sokol, Ledbetter & Haley, Fredericksburg, 1978-87; prin. R. Scott Pugh, 1987—. Pres. Lawyer Assistance and Support Svc., Fredericksburg, 1987—; dep. county atty. Spotsylvania County, Va., 1988-90; instr. criminal law Rappahannock Criminal Justice Acad., 1978-90. Editor Cir. Writer, 1991—. Bd. dirs. Rappahannock Boy Scouts Am., Fredericksburg, 1982-86, Big Bros. & Sisters, 1978-81; chmn. Spotsylvania County Dem. Com., 1987-91; mem., chair Spotsylvania County Sch. Bd., 1993-96; mem. Spotsylvania County Bd. of Zoning Appeals, 1997—, now vice chair; television host and panelist Rappahannock Rev., 1997—2002. Mem. ABA, Va. Trial Lawyers Assn. (pres.-elect), Fredericksburg Area Bar Assn., Fredericksburg C. of C. (legal counsel), Fredericksburg Area Jaycees (bd. dirs. 1978-82), Hobart Coll. Alumni, U. Richmond Alumni Assn. Democrat. Methodist. Avocation: computers. Office: PO Box 999 9108 Courthouse Rd Spotsylvania VA 22553-1902

PUGH, RICHARD CRAWFORD, lawyer; b. Phila., Apr. 28, 1929; s. William and Myrtle P.; m. Nanette Bannen, Feb. 27, 1954; children: Richard Crawford, Andrew Lembert, Catherine Elizabeth. AB summa cum laude, Dartmouth Coll., 1951; BA in Jurisprudence, Oxford (Eng.) U., 1953; LLB, Columbia U., 1958. Bar: N.Y. 1958. Assoc. firm Cleary, Gottlieb, Steen & Hamilton, N.Y.C., 1958—61, ptnr., 1969—89; disting. prof. law U. San Diego, 1989—, univ. prof., 1998—99. Mem. faculty Law Sch. Columbia U., 1961-89, prof., 1964-69, adj. prof., 1969-89; lectr. Columbia-Amsterdam-Leyden (Netherlands) summer program Am. law, 1963, 79; dep. asst. atty. gen. tax div. U.S. Dept. Justice, 1966-68; Cons. fiscal and fin. br. UN Secretariat, 1962, 64. Editor: Columbia Law Rev., 1957—58; co-editor (with W. Friedmann): Legal Aspects of ment, 1959; editor (with others): siness Enterprises, 2002; co-editor: International Law, 2001, Taxation of International Transactions, 2001, International Income Taxation: Code and Regulations, 2002—. Served with USNR, 1954-56. Rhodes scholar, 1951-53. Mem. ABA, Am. Law Inst., Am. Coll. Tax Counsel, Am. Soc. Internat. Law, Internat. Fiscal Assn. (pres. U.S. br. 1978-79). Home: 7335 Encelia Dr La Jolla CA 92037-5729 Office: U San Diego Sch Law Alcala Park San Diego CA 92110-2429 E-mail: rpugh@sandiego.edu.

PUGH, RODERICK WELLINGTON, psychologist, educator; b. Richmond, Ky., June 1, 1919; s. George Wilmer and Lena Bernetta (White) P.; m. Harriet Elizabeth Rogers, Aug. 29, 1953 (div. 1955). BA, Fisk U., 1940; MA, Ohio State U., 1941; PhD, U. Chgo., 1949. Diplomate: Am. Bd. Profl. Psychology. Instr. Albany (Ga.) State Coll., 1941-43; psychology trainee VA, Chgo., 1947-49; lectr. Roosevelt U., 1951-54; staff clin. psychologist VA Hosp., Hines, Ill., 1950-54, asst. chief psychologist for psychotherapy, 1954-58, chief clin. psychology sect., 1958-60, supervising psychologist, coord. psychol. internship tng., 1960-66; pvt. practice clin. psychology Chgo., 1958—; assoc. prof. psychology Loyola U., 1966-73, prof., 1973-88, emeritus prof. psychology, 1989—. Cons. St. Mary of the Lake Sem., Niles, Ill., 1965-66, Ill. Div. Vocational Rehab., 1965-82, Center for Inner City Studies, Northeastern State U., Chgo., 1966-67, VA Psychology Tng. Program, 1966— , Am. Psychol. Assn. and Nat. Inst. Mental Health Vs. Psychologists Program, 1966-89; juvenile problems research rev. com. NIMH, 1970-74; cons. Center for Minority Group Mental Health Programs, 1975-77, cons. psychology edn. br., 1978-82; lectr. U. Ibadan, Nigeria, 1978; Mem. profl. adv. com. Div. Mental Health, City of Chgo., 1979-82; mem. adv. com. U.S. Army Command and Gen. Staff Coll., 1981-83 Author: Psychology and the Black Experience, 1972; Contbr.: chpt. in Black Psychology, 1972; Cons. editor: Contemporary Psychology, 1975-79; contbr. articles to profl. jours. Sec. bd. trustees Fisk U., 1968-78. Served to 2d lt. AUS, 1943-46, ETO. Vis. scholar Fisk U., 1966, vis. prof. in psychology, 1994. Fellow Am. Psychol. Soc., Am. Psychol. Assn. (nat. adv. panel to Civilian Health and Med. Program of Uniformed Services 1980-83, joint coun. on profl. edn. in psychology 1988-90); mem. Midwestern Psychol. Assn., Ill. Psychol. Assn. (chmn. legis. com. 1961, council mem. 1960-62, Disting. Psychologist award 1988, Outstanding Contbn. to Profession of Psychology award 2001), Soc. for Psychol. Study Social Issues, Assn. Behavior Analysis, AAUP, Sigma Xi, Alpha Phi Alpha, Psi Chi. Home: 5201 S Cornell Ave Chicago IL 60615-4207 Office: Loyola U 6525 N Sheridan Rd Chicago IL 60626-5344 E-mail: 72752.47@compuserve.com.

PUGH, THOMAS DOERING, architecture educator, educator; b. Jacksonville, Fla., May 27, 1948; s. William Edward Jr. and Lina Lillian (Doering) P.; m. Virginia Margaret McRae, June 14, 1972; children: Rachel McRae, Jordan Faith, Nathan Calder. B in Design, U. Fla., 1971, MA in Architecture, 1974. Asst. prof. architecture U. Ark., Fayetteville, 1976-78; pres. Thomas D. Pugh Constrn. Co., Inc., Ark., 1978-87; assoc. prof. Fla. A&M U. Sch. Architecture, Tallahassee, 1987—; interim dir. Inst. Bldg. Scis. Fla. Argl. and Mech. U., 1991-93, dir., 1993—. Vis. rsch. fellow Tech. U. Eindhoven, The Netherlands, 1993-94; chmn. radon adv. bd. Fla. State U. Sys., 1988-94; mem. Fla. Coordinating Coun. on Radon Protection; juror Progressive Arch.-AIA Nat. Archtl. Rsch. Awards, 1995; mem. rsch. policy bd. AIA/Assn. Collegiate Schs. of Arch., 1996—; mem. edn. com. Odyssey Sci. Ctr., Tallahassee, 1995—. Bd. dir. Tallahassee Habitat for Humanity, 1987-92; crew leader Habitat for Humanity Internat., Americus, Ga., 1988, 90. Recipient Bronze medal Fla. Assn. AIA, Gainesville, 1975; Named Vol. of Yr. Tallahassee Dem. and Vol. Tallahassee, Inc., 1991. Mem. ASCE (sec. spl. task com. radon mitigation 1990-91), Assn. Collegiate Schs. Architecture (coun. on archtl. rsch. 1994). Democrat. Lutheran. Avocations: sailing, woodworking. Office: Fla A&M Univ Sch Architecture 1936 S Martin Luther King Jr B Tallahassee FL 32307-4200 E-mail: tpugh@famusoa.net.

PUGLIA, FRANK ALAN, academic administrator; b. Hammond, Ind., Jan. 2, 1955; s. Frank Albert and Beulah Wanda Puglia; m. Mary Lydia Puglia, Mar. 18, 1978; 1 child Stefanie Marie. BS in Bus. Edn., U. Ariz., 1977; MBA, U. Phoenix, 1983; cert. instr. entrepreneurship, EDGE U. Cert. cmty. coll. tchr., Ariz. V.p. mktg., pub. rels. Frater Inc., Mesa, Ariz., 1978-83; owner, pres. Splty. Promotions Inc., Chandler, 1983-85, Gt. Western Fragrances Inc., Mesa, 1985-95; dean of students Phoenix Therapeutic Massage Coll., 1996—98; coord. Elderhostel Cen. Ariz. Coll., Apache Junction, 1998-2000, dir. Ariz. State Prison Campus Florence, 2000—. Contbr. articles, photography to profl. jours. Chmn., founder East Pinal county Golf Tournament, Gold Canyon, Ariz., 2000—. Mem. Cen. Ariz. Coll. Support Staff Assn. (v.p. 1999-2001, pres. 2001—), Learning in Retirment Assn. of Ariz. (v.p. 2000-01), Cen. Ariz. Sr. Assn. (chmn., founder, 2000—). Avocations: golf, photography, writing. Office: Cen Ariz Coll 800 E Butte Ave Florence AZ 85232 E-mail: frank_puglia@centralaz.edu.

PUGLIESE, ANTHONY PAUL, construction company executive, educator; b. Phila., Oct. 4, 1942; s. Henry and Philomena (Strate) P.; m. Joyce Elaine Daily, Sept. 26, 1970; children: Marc, Alicia. BS in Acctg., Temple U., 1966. Vice pres. constrn. lending People's Bond & Mortgage Co., Phila., 1964-70; pres. J & A Properties, Inc., Mt. Laurel, N.J., 1970-79; constrn. mgr. Ciotti Constrn. Co., Reading, Pa., 1979-83; owner, mgr. Pugliese Homes Inc., 1983-96, ret., 1997; ind. constrn. cons., 1996—. Cons. Kardon Investment Co., Phila., 1967-70; prof. constrn. mgmt. Pa. State U., 1989-93. Mem. Nat. Home Builders Assn., Pa. Home Builders Assn. (chmn. edn. com.), Home Builders Assn Berks County (past pres.), Nat. Fedn. Ind. Bus., Berks County C. of C., Exeter Golf Club (bd. dirs. 1986-88). Democrat. Roman Catholic. Avocations: golf, physical exercise. E-mail: pugliaj@bigfoot.com.

PUGLIESE, MARIA ALESSANDRA, psychiatrist; b. Phila., Sept. 16, 1948; d. Peter Francis and Ida Agnes (Rosa) Pugliese; m. J. Paul Hieble, Sept. 14, 1985. BS, Chestnut Hill Coll., 1970; MD, U. Pa., 1974. Diplomate Am. Bd. Psychiatry and Neurology; with added qualifications in addiction psychiatry. Intern in pediatrics Children's Hosp. of Phila., 1974-75; resident in psychiatry Inst. Pa. Hosp., Phila., 1975-78, attending psychiatrist, 1978-97, Malvern (Pa.) Inst., 1982—, Pa. Hosp., 1997—. Office: 111 N 49th St Philadelphia PA 19139-2718 E-mail: mariadoc2@cs.com.

PUGLIESE, PAUL JONES, cartographer; b. N.Y.C., Nov. 7, 1941; s. Anthony and Julia (Jones) Pugliese; m. Elaine Winston; children: Cassandra, Elisa, Peter, Jeffrey. Cartographer Harcourt Brace Jovanovich, N.Y.C., 1964-76; mayor Village of Ocean Beach, N.Y., 1994-98; chief of cartography Time mag., N.Y.C., 1976-97; pres. Gen. Cartography, Inc. Lectr. in field. Cartographer (maps) U.S. Holocaust Mus.; cartographer for numerous authors. Planning bd. chmn. Town of Cortlandt, N.Y. Fellow Am. Congress on Surveying and Mapping, Am. Geog. Soc.; mem. Assn. Am. Geographers, Can. Cartgraphic Assn. (Award of Distinction 1996). Home: 6 Corwin Ct Dix Hills NY 11746-8314

PUGNO, PERRY ALAN, family physician, educator; b. San Bernardino, Calif., Apr. 28, 1948; s. Piero and Vanda Diane (Boggio) P.; m. Terry Gail Ren, June 20, 1970; children: Andrew, Joseph, Benjamin. BA with highest honors, U. Calif., Riverside, 1970; MD, U. Calif., Davis, 1974; MPH, Loma Linda U., 1983. Intern Ventura Gen. Hosp., 1975, resident family practice, 1976-77; sr. surgeon USPHS, 1977-78; resident dir. Riverside (Calif.) Gen. Hosp., 1978-80, dir. Trauma Ctr., 1980-82; resident dir. Mercy Med. Ctr., Redding, Calif., 1983-94, Mercy Healthcare, Sacramento, 1994-99. Edn. dir. U. Conn., 1982-83; faculty U. Calif. Davis, 1983—. Fellow Am. Acad. Family Physicians, Am. Coll. Emergency Physicians; mem. Assn. Family Practice Resident Dirs. (pres. 1996-97), Soc. Tchrs. Family Medicine, U. Calif. Davis Alumni Assn. (pres. 1997-99). Republican. Roman Catholic. Office: Am Acad Family Physicians 11400 Tomahawk Creek Pkwy Leawood KS 66211-2672

PUGSLEY, FRANK BURRUSS, lawyer; b. Kansas City, Mo., Apr. 3, 1920; s. Charles Silvey and Emma (Burruss) P.; m. Aline East, May 7, 1943; children— John, Susan Pugsley Patterson, Nancy Pugsley Young BS in Mech. Engring, U. Tex., Austin, 1942; JD, DePaul U., Chgo., 1950. Bar: Ill. 1950, Tex. 1953, U.S. Supreme Ct. 1960. Engr. Gen. Electric Co., Schenectady, 1946-50, patent atty., 1950-52; assoc. Baker & Botts, Houston, 1952-60, ptnr., 1960-84, sr. ptnr., 1974-84. Lectr. Southwestern Legal Found., Practising Law Inst., Bur. Nat. Affairs Conf. Contbr. articles to legal jours. Trustee West Univ. Methodist Ch., Houston, 1959-65; bd. dirs. St. Stephens Episcopal Day Sch., 1960-62; adminstrv. bd. St. Luke's United Meth. Ch., 1981-83. Served to lt. USNR, 1942-46. Fellow Tex. Bar Found.; mem. ABA (chmn. intellectual property law sec. 1980-81), Am. Intellectual Property Law Assn. (pres. 1966-67), Tex. Bar Assn. (chmn. intellectual property law sect. 1960-61), Houston Bar Assn., Petroleum Club, Frisch Auf! Valley Country Club, Friars. Home: 3602 Nottingham St Houston TX 77005-2221

PUGSLEY, MICHAEL KENNETH, cardiac pharmacologist, research scientist; b. Burnaby, B.C., Can., Aug. 28, 1967; came to U.S., 1995; s. Kenneth Richard and Mary Agnes Pugsley; m. Suzanne Pugsley, Aug. 23, 1997. BSc, U. B.C., Vancouver, 1989, MSc, 1992, PhD, 1995. Postdoctoral rsch. fellow U. Calif., Irvine, 1995-98; rsch. scientist II Xoma (US) LLC, Berkeley, Calif., 1998-2000, sr. scientist, 2001—. Cons. Nortran Pharms., Vancouver, 1995-98, Chem. Works of Gedeon Richter, 1994-98; vis. rsch. fellow Australian Nat. U., Canberra, 1993. Editor, author: Methods in Cardiac Electrophysiology, 1997, Methods in Vascular Pharmacology, 2000; mem. editl. bd. Jour. Pharmacology and Toxicology Methods, Cardiovasc. Toxicology; contbr. articles to profl. jours. including Circulatory Shock, Brit. Jour. Pharmacology, European Jour. Pharmacology, Jour. Pharmacol. & Toxicol. Methods, Cardiovasc. Rsch., Cardiovasc. Drug Revs., Biochemica Biophysica Acta, Life Scis., Clin. and Exptl. Cardiology, Pharmacol. Rsch. Grantee Heart & Stroke Found. (Can.), 1992, 93, 94; recipient scholarship B.C. Med. Svcs. Found., 1994, Sci. Coun. B.C., 1994; postdoctoral fellow Med. Rsch. Coun. Can, 1995-98. Mem.: Internat. Complement Soc., Internat. Soc. for Heart Rsch., Western Pharmacology Soc. (pres.-elect), Brit. Pharmacol. Soc., Cardiac Electrophysiology Soc., Am. Assn. for Lab. Animal Sci., Safety Pharmacol. Soc., Am. Heart Assn. Avocations: walking, ice hockey, reading, skiing, golfing. Home: 201 Sunspring Ct Pleasant Hill CA 94523-4706 Office: Xoma (US) LLC Dept Pharmacol & Toxicol 2910 7th St Berkeley CA 94710-2700 Fax: 510-841-7805.

PUGSLEY, ROBERT ADRIAN, law educator; b. Mineola, N.Y., Dec. 27, 1946; s. Irvin Harold and Mary Catherine (Brusselars) P. BA, SUNY-Stony Brook, 1968; JD, NYU, 1975, LLM in Criminal Justice, 1977. Instr. sociology New Sch. Social Rsch., N.Y.C., 1969-71; coord. Peace Edn. programs The Christophers, 1971-78; assoc. prof. law Southwestern U., L.A., 1978-81, prof., 1981—, Paul E. Treusch prof. law, 2000-01. Adj. asst. prof. criminology and criminal justice Southampton Coll.-Long Island U., 1975-76; acting dep. dir. Criminal Law Edn. and Rsch. Ctr., NYU, 1983-86; bd. advisors Ctr. Legal Edn. CCNY-CUNY, 1978, Sta. KPFK-FM, 1985-86; founder, coord. The Wednesday Evening Soc., L.A., 1979-86; vis. prof. Jacob D. Fuchsberg Law Ctr. Touro Coll., L.I., N.Y., summers, 1988, 89; lectr. in criminal law and procedure Legal Edn. Conf. Ctr., L.A., 1982-96; prof., dir. Comparative Criminal Law and Procedure Program U. B.C., Vancouver, summers, 1994, 98, 99, 2000, 01, 02; chair pub. interest law com. Southwestern U., 1990-2001; lectr. legal profl. responsibility West Bar Rev. Faculty, Calif., 1996-98; legal analyst/commentator for print and electronic media, 1992—. Creative advisor Christopher Closeup (nationally syndicated pub. svc. TV program), 1975-83; host Earth Alert, Cable TV, 1983-87; prodr., moderator (pub. affairs discussion program) Inside L.A., Sta. KPFK-FM, 1979-86, Open Jour. program, Sta. KPFK-FM, 1991-94; contbr. articles to legal jours. Founding mem. Southwestern U. Pub. Interest Law com., 1992—; mem. L.A. County Bar Assn. Adv. Com. on Alcohol & Drug Abuse, 1991-95, co-chair, 1993-95; mem. exec. com. non-govtl. orgns. UN Office Pub. Info., 1977; mem. issues task force L.A. Conservancy, 1980-81, seminar for law tchrs. NEH UCLA, 1979; co-convenor So. Calif. Coalition Against Death Penalty, 1981-83, convener, 1983-84; mem. death penalty com. Lawyer's Support Group, Amnesty Internat., U.S.A.; founding mem. Ch.-State Coun., L.A., 1984-88; bd. dirs. Equal Rights Sentencing Found., 1983-85, Earth Alert, Inc., 1984-87; mem. adv. bd. First Amendment Info. Resources Ctr., Grad. Sch. Libr. and Info. Scis., UCLA, 1990—; mem. coun. Friends UCLA Libr., 1993—, pres., 1996—; mem. adv. bd. Children Requiring a Caring Kommunity, 1998—. Robert Marshall fellow Criminal Law Edn. and Rsch. Ctr., NYU Sch. Law, 1976-78. Mem. Am. Legal Studies Assn., Am. Soc. Polit. and Legal Philosophy, Assn. Am. Law Schs., Inst. Soc. Ethics and Life Scis., Soc. Am. Law Tchrs., Internat. Platform Assn., Internat. Soc. Reform of Criminal Law, The Scribes. Roman Catholic. Office: Southwestern U Sch Law 675 S Westmoreland Ave Los Angeles CA 90005-3905 E-mail: rpugsley@swlaw.edu.

PUHL, JENNIFER LOUISE, music teacher, pianist, organist; b. San Angelo, Tex., Dec. 16, 1946; d. William Lewis and Dorothy Marcelene (Smith) Bradford; m. Stephen Vincent Puhl, July 11, 1970; 1 child, Stephanie Noel. BA, Pepperdine U., 1967. Piano tchr. choral conductors guild Yamaha Music Edn., Buena Park, Calif., 1966-68; organist, dir. St. Paul's Presbyn. Ch., Anaheim, 1970-79, St. Andrew's Episcopal Ch., Irvine, 1980-82; organist Univ. United Meth. Ch., 1982-2000, St. Anne's Cath. Ch., Santa Ana, Calif., 1991-98, St. Barbara Cath. Ch., Santa Ana, 2000—. Choir accompanist Orange and Capistrano Schs., So. Calif. United Meth. Chorale accompanist Brit. tour, 1999. Mem. Choral Condrs. Guild, 1980-82, mem. Music Tchrs. Assn. Calif. (registrar 1994-99, dean 2000-2002), Nat. Piano Guild, Am. Guild Organists (sub-dean 1999). Home: 14672 Oak Ave Irvine CA 92606-2165

PUJARA, SUBHASH S. radiologist; b. Mahisa, Gujarat, India, Apr. 24, 1946; came to U.S., 1970; s. Somabhai and Manguben S.; married; children: Priya, Vishal. MB BChir, B.J. Med. Coll., Ahmedabad, Gujarat, 1969. Intern Civil Hosp., Ahmedabad, 1969-70, L.I. Jewish Hosp., Jamaica, N.Y., 1972-73; radiology resident St. Vincent Hosp., N.Y.C., 1973-76; nuclear medicine fellow U. Ala., Birmingham, 1976-78; assoc. radiologist Cmty. Hosp., Andalusia, Ala., 1978-85; staff radiologist Dorn VA Hosp., Columbia, S.C., 1985-89, Sterling Med. Co. DDEAMC, Ft. Gordon, Ga., 1989-93, 98—, Ft. Bragg/Fayetteville, N.C., 1994-96, Ft. Jackson (S.C.) Montcrief Hosp., 1996-98. Mem. Am. Coll. Radiology, Radiol. Soc. N.Am. Avocations: music, biking, tennis, reading. Home: 55 Old Still Rd Columbia SC 29223-3012 Office: DDEAMC Dept Radiology Fort Gordon GA 30905

PUKEL, CLIFFORD STUART, physician; b. Bronx, N.Y., Nov. 15, 1955; s. Bayas William and Pearl (Buchholtz) P.; m. Victoria Perry; children: Zachariah, Jacob. BA in Biology, Queens Coll. CUNY, 1979; MD, U. Miami, 1991. Rsch. technician Sloan-Kettering Inst. for Cancer Rsch., N.Y.C., 1980-83, rsch. asst., 1983-85; rsch. assoc. dept. medicine U. Miami, Fla., 1985-87; resident dept. internal medicine U. W.Va., Charleston, 1991-94; fellow hematology, oncology, instr. medicine Dartmouth-Hitchcock Med. Ctr., Lebanon, N.H., 1994-97; pvt. practice Wichita, 1997-99, Eau Claire, Wis., 2000—; asst. prof. clin. medicine U. Kans. Sch. Medicine, Wichita, 1998-99, U. Wis. Sch. Medicine, Madison, 2000—. Vis. scientist Escola Paulista de Medicina, Sao Paulo, Brazil, 1984. Contbr. articles to profl. jours. Free Sons of Israel scholar, 1974, N.Y. State Regents scholar, 1974, U. Miami Med. Sch. scholar, 1990. Jewish. Achievements include patent for Method for Detecting the Presence of GD3 Ganglioside; notable findings on role of gangliosides in human cancer, on role of cytokines in diabetes mellitus.

PULANCO, TONYA BETH, special education educator; b. Portland, Oreg., Apr. 17, 1933; d. Anthony Lorenzo and Adelfa Elizabeth (Dewey) P. BA, San Jose State U., 1955; MA, Columbia U., 1966. Occupl. therapist Langley Porter Hosp., San Francisco, 1958-60; writer ednl. sub-contracts Columbia U., N.Y.C., 1961-64; from tchr. to dir. edn. Gateway Sch. N.Y., 1965—. Mem. Assn. for Children with Learning Disabilities, Am. Occupl. Therapy Assn., Japanese Am. Citizens League. Avocations: tap dancing, walkathons, silversmithing, jazz, opera. Office: Gateway Sch NY 236 2d Ave New York NY 10003

PULASKI, LISA VALERIA, graphic designer; b. Guatemala City, Guatemala, Feb. 12, 1973; d. Stephen John and Valerie A. (Karolkiewicz) P. BA in Art, Va. Polytechnic Inst. and State U., Blacksburg, 1995. Graphic designer The New Virginians, Blacksburg, 1992-95; graphics and prodn. mgr. Laszlo & Assocs., Inc., Washington, 1996-97; graphic designer Datamat Sys. Rsch. Inc., 1997; ind. graphic designer, 1997-98; freelance designer, 1998—. Chair pub. rels. Chi Delta Svc. Sorority, Blacksburg, 1994-95. Recipient 1st Place award BIC Pen Corp., 1995. Mem. Women in Comms., Inc. Avocations: walking, painting, outdoors. E-mail: lisa_design@yahoo.com.

PULAY, PETER, chemist; b. Veszprem, Hungary, Sept. 20, 1941; s. Kalman Pulay and Lenke Zambo; m. Agnes Kovacs; children: Robert B., Emoke K. MS, Eotvos U., Budapest, Hungary, 1963; PhD, U. Stuttgart, Germany, 1970; Doctorate honoris causa (hon.) , Eotvos U., Budapest. Assoc. prof. Eotvos U., Budapest, 1975—80; vis. prof. U. Tex., Austin, 1980—82; prof. U. Ark., Fayetteville, 1982—84, Roger B. Bost prof. chemistry, 1984—. Pres. Parallel Quantum Solutions, LLC, Fayetteville, 1997—. Recipient Citation Classic, Current Contents, 1988, Creativity award, NSF, 1991, Alexander von Humboldt Sr. Scientist award, Alexander v. Humboldt Found., Germany, 1996. Mem.: Am. Chem. Soc., Hungarian Acad. Sci., Internat. Acad. Quantum Molecular Scis. (medal 1982). Achievements include research in molecular electronic structure theory and the ab initio calculation of molecular properties: energies, geometries, inrared, Raman and NMR spectra. Avocations: hiking, gardening, telescope making. Home: 1824 Applebury Pl Fayetteville AR 72701 Office: U Ark Chemistry Dept Chemistry Bldg Fayetteville AR 72701 Office Fax: 479-575-4049. Business E-Mail: PULAY@UARK.EDU.

PULEC, JACK LEE, otolaryngologist; b. Crete, Nebr., July 12, 1932; s. Anton and Antonette (Divoky) Pulec; m. Marlene Berniece Aron, Nov. 10, 1951; 1 child, Marilyn Louise. BA, U. Nebr., 1955, MD, 1957; MS, U. Minn., 1962. Diplomate Am. Bd. Otolaryngolgy. Intern Bishop Clarkson Meml. Hosp., Omaha, 1957-58; resident in ob-gyn. U. Nebr., 1958-59; resident in otolaryngology Mayo Found., 1959-62; fellow in neurol-otology L.A. Found. Otolaryngology, 1963-64; otologist Hosp. Good Samaritan, L.A.; otolaryngologist St. Vincent's Hosp., Children's Hosp., L.A., Cedars-Sinai Hosp., L.A., Hollywood Presbyn.-Queen of Angels, L.A., L.A. County Gen. Hosp.; clin. prof. otolaryngology Loma Linda Med. Ctr., U. So. Calif. Cons. Mayo Clinic, Rochester, 1963-69; ptnr. Otologic Med. Group, L.A., 1969-76; pres. Pulec Ear Clinic, L.A., 1976—. Editor: Meniere's Disease, 1968; editor-in-chief Ear, Nose and Throat Jour., 1992—. Fellow Am. Acad. of Otolaryngic Allery, Am. Acad. of Otolaryngology-Head and Neck Surgery (Practitioner Excellence award 1998), Am. Coll. Surgeons, Am. Laryngological, Rhinological and Otological Soc., Am. Neurotology Soc., Am. Otological Soc., Royal Soc. of Medicine, L.A. County Med. Assn. (pres. Met. dist. 1990-91, councilor 1993—), Banany Soc. (Sweden), Calif. Med. Assn. (del. 1988—), AMA, Neurotological and Equilibriometric Soc. (Germany), Otosclerosis Study Club (pres.-elect 1996-97, pres. 1997-98). Office: 1245 Wilshire Blvd Ste 503 Los Angeles CA 90017-4805

PULEO, FRANK CHARLES, lawyer; b. Montclair, N.J., Nov. 25, 1945; s. Frank and Kathren (Despenzerie) P.; m. Alice Kathren Leek, June 1, 1968; children— Frank C., Richard James. B.S.E., Princeton U., 1967; J.D., N.Y.U., 1970. Bar: N.Y., 1971. Ptnr., Milbank, Tweed, Hadley & McCloy, N.Y.C., 1970— . Mem. ABA (mem. com. on fed. regulation securities), N.Y. State Bar Assn. Office: Milbank Tweed Hadley & McCloy 1 Chase Manhattan Plz Fl 49 New York NY 10005-1413

PULGRAM, ERNST, linguist, philologist, Romance and classical linguistics educator, writer; b. Vienna, Austria, Sept. 18, 1915; came to U.S. 1939, naturalized 1943; s. Sigmund and Gisela (Bauer) P.; m. Frances McSparran, Nov. 29, 1985. Dr. Phil. in Romance and Classical Philology, U. Vienna, 1947, Dr. phil. honoris causa, 1990; PhD in Comparative Linguistics, Harvard U., 1946. Asst. prof. Union Coll., Schenectady, N.Y., 1946; asst. prof. U. Mich., Ann Arbor, 1948-51, assoc. prof., 1951-56, prof., 1956—, H. Keniston disting. prof. romance and classical linguistics, 1979-86, prof. emeritus, 1986—. Vis. prof. U. Florence, Italy, 1956-57, U. Cologne, Germany, 1970, U. Heidelberg, Germany, 1972, U. Regensburg, Germany, 1975, U. Vienna, 1977, Internat. Christian U., Tokyo, 1982, U. Innsbruck, Austria, 1983, U. Munich, Germany, 1987; lectr. numerous univs., internat. linguistic congresses; cons. Sch. Langs. and Linguistics, Georgetown U., Washington Author: Theory of Names, 1951, The Tongues of Italy, 1958, Introduction to Spectrography of Speech, 1959, Syllable, Word, Nexus, Cursus, 1970, Latin-Romance Phonology, Prosodics and Metrics, 1975, Italic, Latin, Italian: 600 B.C.-A.D. 1250, 1978, Practicing Linguist, Essays 1950-1985 (2 vols.), 1986; editor: Studies Presented to Joshua Whatmough, 1957, Romanitas: Studies in Romance Linguistics, 1984; contbr. autobiographical sketch in First Person Singular III, 1998; contbr. articles to profl. jours.; author revs.; mem. editorial bd. Current Issues in Linguistic Theory (Amsterdam), Mich. Germanic Studies, Jour. Linguistics and Philology, Mediterranean Language Rev. Served to pvt. inf. U.S. Army, 1942-44; PTO Fellow Am. Council of Learned Socs., 1951-52, 59-60, Guggenheim Found., 1954-55, 62-63; recipient Henry Russell award U. Mich., 1951, Festschrift, Amsterdam, 1980 Mem. Linguistic Soc. Am. (exec. com., com. on appointment of hon. mems., program com.), Internat. Linguistic Assn., Internat. Phonetics Assn., Linguistic Assn. Can. and the U.S. (founding mem., pres. 1978-79) Avocations: collecting drawings and watercolors; hiking; swimming. Home: 1050 Wall St Ann Arbor MI 48105-1974

PULGRAM, WILLIAM LEOPOLD, architect, space designer; b. Vienna, Austria, Jan. 1, 1921; came to U.S., 1940; s. Sigmund and Gisela (Bauer) P.; married, Jan. 12, 1952; children: Deirdre, Laurence, Anthony, Christopher. BS, Ga. Inst. Tech., 1949, BArch, 1950; postgrad., Ecole des Beaux Arts, Fontainebleau, France, 1951. Archtl. designer various firms, Atlanta, 1951-58; assoc., chief interior design FABR&P, 1958-63; exec. v.p., gen. mgr. Associated Space Design Inc., 1963-70, pres., chief exec. officer, 1971-85, chmn., chief exec. officer, 1985-86, chmn. emeritus, 1986-88; architect, cons., 1988—. Cons. UN, 1986; com. mem. NAS, 1980-84; lectr. at colls., univs., U.S. and abroad. Author: Designing the Automated Office, 1984, Japanese transl., 1985; contbr. articles to jours. in field. Mem., lectr. High Mus. Art, Atlanta, 1970—. With U.S. Army, 1943-46. Named to Hall of Fame, Interior Design mag., 1986. Fellow AIA (chmn. interiors 1978-84, archt. res. coun. AIA Found. 1983-85); mem. Architects, Designers and Planners for Social Responsibility (nat. bd. dirs. 1989-93), Am. Soc. Interior Designers, Atlanta C. of C., Atlanta City Club, Lake Lanier Sailing Club. Mem. Unitarian Universalist Ch. Home and Office: W L Pulgram FAIA Cons 4317 E Conway Dr NW Atlanta GA 30327-3528 E-mail: pulgramga@mindspring.com.

PULIAFITO, CARMEN ANTHONY, ophthalmologist, healthcare executive; b. Buffalo, Jan. 5, 1951; s. Dominic F. and Marie A. (Nigro) P.; m. Janet H. Pine, May 19, 1979 AB cum laude, Harvard Coll., 1973, MD magna cum laude, 1978; MBA, U. Pa., 1997. Diplomate Am. Bd. Ophthalmology. Intern Faulkner Hosp., Tufts U. Sch. Medicine, 1978-79; resident Mass. Eye and Ear Infirmary, Boston, 1979-82, retina fellow, 1982-83; instr. Harvard Med. Sch., 1983-85, asst. prof., 1985-89, assoc. prof., 1989-91, dir. divsn. continuing edn. dept. ophthalmology, 1989-91; dir. Bascom Palmer Eye Inst., Miami, 2001—. Vis. scientist MIT Regional Laser Ctr., Cambridge, 1982—, asst. prof. health scis. and tech. program, 1987-89, assoc. prof., 1989-91; mem. staff Mass. Eye and Ear Infirmary, Boston, 1983; dir. Morse Laser Ctr., Mass. Eye and Ear Infirmary, 1986-91, dir. New Eng. Eye Ctr., 1991-2001; prof., chmn. dept. ophthalmology Tufts U. Sch. Medicine, 1991-2001, prof. ophthalmology and health mgmt., 1997-2001; adj. prof. biomed. engring. Tufts U., 1991—; chmn. med. bd. New Eng. Med. Ctr. Hosps., 1994-95, ophthalmologist in chief, 1991-2001; assoc. examiner Am. Bd. Ophthalmology, 1990—; sr. v.p. for network devel. Lifespan, 1997-2001; prof., chmn. dept. ophthalmology U. Miami Sch. Medicine, 2001—; med. dir. Anne Bates Leach Eye Hosp., 2001—. Author: (with D. Albert) Foundations of Ophthalmic Pathology, 1979, (with R. Steinert) Principles and Practice of Ophthalmic YAG Laser Surgery, 1984, Lasers in Surgery and Medicine: Principles and Practice, 1996, (with M.R. Hee, J.S. Schuman and J.G. Fujimoto) Optical Coherence Tomography of Ocular Diseases, 1996, (with E. Reichel) Atlas of Indocyanine Green Angiography, 1996; editor-in-chief Lasers in Surgery and Medicine, 1987-95, Ophthalmic Surgery and Lasers, 1995—; contbr. about 120 articles to profl. jours. Pres. Am. Soc. for Laser Medicine and Surgery, 1994-95; v.p. Mass. Soc. Eye Physicians and Surgeons, 1994-96; assoc. examiner Am. Bd. Ophthalmology, 1990—; retina trustee Assn. Rsch. in Vision and Ophthalmology, 1995—. Recipient Richard and Hinda Rosenthal award in visual scis., 1994, Man of Vision award Boston Aid to the Blind, 1993, Leon Goldman award Biomed. Optics Soc., 1993, I Migliori award Pirandello Lyceum of Mass., 1994. Fellow Am. Acad. Ophthalmology, Am. Soc. for Laser Medicine and Surgery (pres. 1994-95); mem. Assn. Rsch. in Vision and Ophthalmology (pres.-elect 1998-99, pres. 1999-2000, immediate past pres. 2000-2001), Mass. Soc. Eye Physicians and Surgeons (v.p. 1994-96). Roman Catholic. Home: 9321 SW 63rd Ct Miami FL 33156-1814 Office: Bascom Palmer Eye Inst 900 NW 17th St Miami FL 33136 Fax: 305-326-6308. E-mail: cpuliafito@miami.edu.

PULIDO, MIGUEL ANGEL, mayor; b. Mexico City, Mex., 1956; m. Laura Pulido; children: Miguel Robert, David, Isabel. BSME, Calif. State U., Fullerton. Dir. computer program McCaughey & Smith Energy Assocs., v.p.; mem. Santa Ana (Calif.) City Coun., 1986—; mayor City of Santa Ana, 1994—. Mem. Santa Ana Redevel. Agy.; bd. dirs. Orange County Transp. Authority, mem. 1st dist. Bd. dirs. Calif. Workforce Investment, Bowers Mus., Discovery Sci. Ctr. Orange County, Pacific Symphony Orch., UCI Found., Fed. Inter-Govtl. Policy Adv. Com. Trade. Avocations: chess, backgammon, tennis, music, guitar. Office: Office Mayor & City Coun 20 Civic Ctr Plaza PO Box 1988 Santa Ana CA 92702-1988 E-mail: mpulido@ci.santa-ana.ca.us.

PULIN, CAROL, fine arts organization administrator; b. Cleve., Apr. 24, 1950; BA, U. Fla., 1972; MA, U. Tex., 1974, PhD, 1984. Curator fine prints The Libr. Congress, Washington, 1983-92; dir. Am. Print Alliance, Peachtree City, Ga., 1992—. Grant reviewer NEA, Rockefeller Found., Smithsonian Found., McDowell Colony, others, 1984—; sr. editor Contemporary Impressions, 1993—; curator exhibits Paradise Endangered: The New World in Contemporary Prints, 1993; curator traveling exhibits Estampes Quebecoises, 1990-92, Edges and Interfaces, 1996-98, On/Off/Over the Edge, 2001—; co-curator internet exhibit Scrolling the Page: Artists' Books From Around the World, 1999—; curator print portfolio and traveling exhbn. Sept. 11 Meml. Portfolio. Editor: Guide to Print Workshops, 1993, 95, 99; series editor: American Printmakers: A Smithsonian Series, 1990-92; author Introduction to Contents and Contexts: Lithography After 200 Years; co-author: Bertha Lum, 1991, Originals in the Age of Post-Modern Appropriation, 2001; contbr. articles to profl. jours. Samuel H. Kress Found. fellow, 1977-79, Renaissance Soc. Am. fellow, 1977. Office: Am Print Alliance 302 Larkspur Turn Peachtree City GA 30269-2210 E-mail: webmaster@printalliance.org.

PULITO, FRANCIS N. artist; b. Kensington, Conn., Jan. 12, 1920; s. Daniel I. and Victoria (Zappone) P.; m. Jean L. Lawrence, Nov. 3, 1945 (dec. 1989); children: Randy, Craig, Roger, Derek, Betsy. Grad. high sch., Berlin, Conn. Exhbns. of landscapes and seascapes U.S. and internat., especially along Eastern Seaboard and with galleries in Washington and the Northeast. Charter mem. Cmty. Art League Kensington, 1955—. With U.S. Army, 1942-45, ETO. Decorated Bronze Star, Silver Star. Mem. Lions (Berlin). Democrat. Avocations: outdoors, fishing, hiking, athletics. Home: 737 Lower Ln Berlin CT 06037

PULITZER, ROSLYN KITTY, social worker, psychotherapist; b. Bronx, N.Y., Apr. 25, 1930; d. George and Laura Eleanor (Holtz) P. BS in Human Devel. and Life Cycle, SUNY, N.Y.C., 1983; MSW, Fordham U., 1987; postgrad., Masterson Inst., N.Y.C., 1991. cert. in psychoanalytic psychotherapy of the personality disorders, Masterson Inst., N.Y.C.; lic. clin. social worker, N.Y. Clinic dir. Resources Counseling and Psychotherapy Ctr., N.Y.C., 1985-89; social worker, clin. supr. methadone maintenance treatment program Beth Israel Med. Ctr., 1989-97; psychotherapist pvt. practice, 1989—. Cons. therapist, clin. supr. Identity House, N.Y.C., 1980-97, exec. dir., 1985, clin. dir., 1993-94. Mem. regional adv. coun. N.Y. State Div. Human Rights, N.Y.C., 1975-76; mem. Community Bd. 6, N.Y.C., 1978-81; founder, legis. chmn. N.Y. State Women's Polit. Caucus, 1978-80. Mem. NASW, Acad. Cert. Social Workers, Soc. Masterson Inst., N.Y. Milton Erickson Soc. for Psychotherapy and Hypnosis (cert.). Avocations: photography, snorkeling. Home: 2742 La Silla Dorada Santa Fe NM 87505-6703 Fax: 505-438-2884. E-mail: imagesrkp@aol.com.

PULKKINEN, JYRKI TUOMO JUHANI, structural engineer; b. Paltamo, Finland, Sept. 25, 1963; s. Yrjo Kalle and Aino Johanna Pulkkinen; m. Karen Elaine Brautcheck, Oct. 24, 1993; 1 child, Erik Henri. MCE, U. Oulu (Finland), 1991; MBA, Eastern Mich. U., 2002. Registered profl. engr., Mich., Fla., Calif.; Eur. Ing. Structural engr. Makelainen & Raiha Engring., Kajaani, Finland, 1990; rsch. asst. VTT Bldg. Tech., Oulu, 1991; adminstrv. intern City of San Diego, 1992-93; project engr. Interclean Equipment Inc., Ann Arbor, Mich., 1993-94; project mgr. LWS Inc., 1994-96, Shimizu Am. Corp., Canton, Mich., 1997-98, Adminstrv. Controls Mgmt., Detroit, 1999—. Mem. Mich. Soc. Profl. Engrs., Assn. Finnish Civil Engrs. Avocations: photography, cars, model cars. Home: 2543 Meade Ct Ann Arbor MI 48105-1304 Office: Ste 2 525 Avis Dr Ann Arbor MI 48108

PULLEN, J(OHN) MARK, computer science and engineering educator; BSEE, W.Va. U., 1970, MSEE, 1972; DSc in Computer Sci., George Washington U., 1981. Registered profl. engr., W.Va. Assoc. prof. dept. elec. engring. U.S. Mil. Acad., West Point, N.Y., 1983-85; IEEE Congl. fellow U.S. Congl. Staff, Washington, 1985-86; program mgr. Def. Advanced Rsch. Projects Agy., 1986-88, dep. dir., 1989-91, program dir., 1991-92; assoc. prof. computer sci. (computer networking) George Mason U., Fairfax, Va., 1992—. Contbr. papers to conf. procs., profl. publs. Fellow IEEE (com. mem., vice chmn. Tech. Policy Coun., Harry Diamond award for Distributed Simulation-.commd. and ctrl. network 1995); mem. Assn. Computing Machinery, Armed Forces Comms.-Electronics Assn., Eta Kappa Nu, Phi Kappa Phi. Office: George Mason Univ Dept Computer Sci Fairfax VA 22030

PULLEN, MARGARET I. genetics physicist; b. Nebr., Sept. 13, 1950; d. Robert and Martha (Holtorf) P. AA, Stephens Coll., 1971; BA in Internat. Rels., Econs., Bus. & Trade, U. Colo., 1975; BS in Physics, Northeastern U., 1983; MS in Physics, Tufts U., 1984; postgrad., in applied phsics, U. Calif., 1984-86; postgrad., U. Colo. Med. Sci., 1990. Mathematician Lawrence Livermore Lab., Calif., 1987; entrepreneur, CEO Evergreen Applied Rsch. Inc., 1988—, patentee Gene Replication Techs. Mem. Biotech. Roundtable, Denver, 1987—, AIDS delegation to South Africa, 1997. Vol. Nat. Sports Ctr. for the Physically Disabled, Winter Park, Colo., 1988-92; AID del. to South Africa; invitee Harvard Med. Sch., 1997. Tufts U. grantee, U. Colo. grantee; Nat. Sci. fellow; Stephens scholar, Perry Mansfield Ctr. for the Preforming Arts scholar; recipient Cert. of Completion, Dirs.' Consortium, 2002. Mem.: DAR, Supercomputing Activity Group, Soc. Indsl. and Applied Math., Am. Phys. Soc. (mem. activity group on supercomputing). Achievements include developments in and applications of parallel processor computers and process, instrumentation for molecular synthesis. Office: Evergreen Applied Rsch Inc PO Box 1551 Aspen CO 81612-1551 E-mail: ear@sopris.net.

PULLEN, PENNY LYNNE, non-profit administrator, former state legislator; b. Buffalo, Mar. 2, 1947; d. John William and Alice Nettie (McConkey) P. BA in Speech, U. Ill., 1969. Tv technician Office Instnl. Resources, U. Ill., 1966-68; cmty. newspaper reporter Des Plaines (Ill.) Pub. Co., 1967-72; legis. asst. to Ill. legislators, 1968-77; mem. Ill. Ho. of Reps., 1977-93, chmn. ho. exec. com., 1981-82, minority whip, 1983-87, asst. minority leader, 1987-93; pres., founder Life Advocacy Resource Project, Arlington Heights, Ill., 1992—. Exec. dir. Ill. Family Inst., 1993-94; dir. Legal Svcs. Corp., 1989-93; mem. Pres.'s Commn. on AIDS Epidemic, 1987-88; mem. Ill. Goodwill Del. to Republic of China, 1987. Summit conf. observer as mem. adhoc Women for SDI, Geneva, 1985; mem. Nat. Coun. Ednl. Rsch., 1983—88; dir. Eagle Forum of Ill., 1999—; Del. Rep. Nat. Conv., 1984; mem. Rep. Nat. Com., 1984—88; Del. Atlantic Alliance Young Polit. Leaders, Brussels, 1977; pres. Maine Twp. Rep. Women's Club, 1997—99, Rep. Women of Park Ridge, 2001—. Recipient George Washington Honor medal Freedoms Found., 1978, Dwight Eisenhower Freedom medal Chgo. Captive Nations Com., 1977, Outstanding Legislator awards Ill. Press Assn., Ill. Podiatry Soc., Ill. Coroners Assn., Ill. County Clks. Assn., Ill. Hosp. Assn., Ill. Health Care Assn.; named Ill. Young Republican, 1968, Outstanding Young Person, Park Ridge Jaycees, 1981, One of 10 Outstanding Young Persons, Ill. Jaycees, 1981. Mem. DAR, Am. Legis. Exch. Coun. (dir. 1977-91, exec. com. 1978-83, 2d vice chmn. 1980-83), Com. on the Status of Women (sec. 1997—).

PULLEY, DOUGLAS BOYD, ophthalmologist; b. San Francisco, Apr. 1, 1942; s. Boyd Horace and Beth P.; m. Katherine Anne Bennion, June 25, 1966; children: Anne, Matthew, David, Susan, Stephen. BS, Brigham Young U., 1966; MD, UCLA, 1970. Diplomate Am. Bd. Ophthalmology. Intern UCLA, 1970-71; resident Jules Stein Eye Inst., 1973-76, Wadsworth V.A. Hosp., 1973-76; chief dept. ophthalmology Santa Teresa Cmty. Hosp., 1980-92; physician Spectrum Eye Ctrs., San Jose, Calif. Cons. surgery Guangzi Med. U., Nanning, China, 1988-90. Capt. U.S. Army, 1971-73. Fellow Am. Acad. Ophthalmology; mem. AMA, Calif. Med. Assn., Calif. Assn. Ophthalmology, Santa Clara County Med. Assn. Avocations: woodturning, orchids. Office: Spectrum Eye Physicians 393 Blossom Hill Rd Ste 265 San Jose CA 95123-1655

PULLEY, LEWIS CARL, lawyer; b. Oklahoma City, Aug. 19, 1954; s. Harriet Ruth (Meyers) P.; foster sons: Tuan Le, Chien Hoang. Student, Oxford U., England, 1974; BA with high honors, U. Okla., 1976; JD, Am. U., 1979. Bar: Pa. 1981, D.C. 1987, U.S. Ct. Mil. Appeals 1982, U.S. Ct. Appeals (D.C. cir.) 1985, U.S. Supreme Ct. 1985. Commd. 1st lt. USAF, 1982, advanced through grades to capt., 1982, judge advocate, 1982-88; atty. Def. Logistics Agy., Alexandria, Va., 1988-90; atty. EEO staff mass media bur. FCC, 1990-97, supr. atty. EEO staff mass media bur., 1997—, acting chief EEO staff mass media bur., 2001—. Contbr. over 500 articles to 11 newspapers and mags. (recipient Investigative Reporting award, Okla. City Gridiron Found., 1975, Media award for Econ. Understanding, Dartmouth Bus. Sch., 1980). Vol. Nat. Pub. Radio, Washington, 1989-90, Connections, 1990-98, White House, 1993-94; mem. Ams. for Med. Progress Ednl. Found. Ewing Found. fellow, 1975. Democrat. Jewish. Avocations: travel, collecting polit. paraphernalia. Office: FCC Mass Media Bur Policy Divsn 445 12th St SW Washington DC 20554

PULLIAM, FRANCINE SARNO, real estate broker, real estate developer; b. San Francisco, Sept. 14, 1937; d. Ralph C. Stevens and Frances I. (Wilson) Sarno; m. John Donald Pulliam, Aug. 14, 1957 (div. Mar. 1965); 1 child, Wendy; m. Terry Kent Graves, Dec. 14, 1974. Student, U. Ariz., 1955-56, U. Nev., Las Vegas, 1957. Airline stewardess Bonanza Airlines, Las Vegas, 1957; real estate agt. The Pulliam Co., 1958-68, Levy Realty, Las Vegas, 1976-76; real estate broker, owner Prestige Properties, 1976—. Importer, exporter Exports Internat., Las Vegas, 1984—; bd. dirs. Citicorp Bank of Nev.; mem. adv. bd. to Amb. to Bahamas Chic Hect.; property mgr. Prestigo Properties, 1992—. Bd. dirs. Las Vegas Bd. Realtors, Fedn. Internat. Realtors, Nat. Kidney Found., Assistance League, Cancer Soc., Easter Seals, Econ. Rsch. Bd., Children's Discovery Mus., New Horizons Ctr. for Children with Learning Disabilities, Girl Scouts, Home of the Good Shepard, St. Jude's Ranch for Homeless Children; pres., bd. dirs. Better Bus. Bur.; chmn. Las Vegas Taxi Cab Authority; pres. Citizens for Pvt. Enterprises. Mem. Las Vegas C. of C. (bd. dirs., developer). Republican. Roman Catholic. Office: 2340 Paseo Del Prado Ste D202 Las Vegas NV 89102-4341

PULLIAM, FREDERICK CAMERON, educational administrator; b. Mesa, Ariz., Jan. 5, 1936; s. Fredrick Posy and Nathana Laura (Cameron) P.; m. Deborah Jean Botts, June 1, 1979; 1 child, Sarah Elizabeth; children by previous marraige: Cameron Dale, Joy Renee. AA, Hannibal LaGrange Coll., 1955; AB, Grand Canyon Coll., 1958; MEd, U. Mo., 1966, EdS, 1976, EdD, 1981. Ordained to ministry So. Bapt. Conv., 1955. Tchr. Centerview (Mo.) Pub. Scsh., 1958-59; min. Bethel Bapt. Ch., Kansas City, Mo., 1959-61; adminstr. Fiti'uta Manu'a Sch., Am. Somoa, 1966-68; cons. in fin. Mo. State Tchrs. Assn., Columbia, 1969-79; supt. schs. Midway Heights C-VII, 1979-83; dir. elem. edn. Brentwood (Mo.) Pub. Schs., 1983-90; pres. Life Long Learning Sys. St. Louis, Mt. Vernon, Mo., 1989—; assoc. prof. edn. Mo. So. State Coll., 1990-99, dir. clin. and field experiences in tchr. edn., 1990-99. Pastor Patten Chapel and Miller (Mo.) United Meth. Chs., 1997-2001; founder, coord. Mo. Computer-Using Educators Conf., 1982-84; contbg. writer St. Louis Computing News, 1984-95; adj. asst. prof. ednl. studies U. Mo., St. Louis, 1986-90; adj. assoc. prof. grad. studies S.W. Bapt. U., 1991-98; cons. sch. fin., curriculum improvement. Contbr. articles to profl. jours. Mem. Columbia Am. Revolution Bicentennial Commn.; mem. edn. adv. com. Mo. Gov.'s Transition Team, 1992-93. Inst. Devel. Ednl. Activity fellow, 1969, 78-84. Mem.: ASCD (bd. dirs. 1984—90), Assn. Childhood Edn. Internat., Rotary Internat., Phi Delta Kappa (chpt. pres.). Home: 2416 Kayla Ln Mount Vernon MO 65712-1252 Office: Life Long Learning Sys St Louis 2416 Kayla Ln Mount Vernon MO 65712-1252 E-mail: cpulliam@hotmail.com.

PULLIAM, STEVE CAMERON, business owner; b. Martinsville, Va., May 1, 1948; s. Richard Cameron and Pauline Elsie (Haynes) P.; m. Sharon Elizabeth Richards, Nov. 25, 1972; children: Christina Elizabeth, Lindsay Anne. BS in Elec. Engring., Va. Poly. Inst. and State U., Blacksburg, 1971. With tech. mktg. program Gen. Electric, N.C., Mass, 1971-74, sales engr., 1974-77, product specialist Waukesha, Wis., 1977-79, mgr. sales support, 1979-81, area sales mgr. Tampa, Fla., 1981-83, dist. sales mgr., 1983-89, zone sales mgr., 1989-92; program mgr., 1992-94; owner Steve Pulliam Enterprises, Pisgah Forest, N.C., 1994-99; pres. Video Stop, Candler, NC, 1995—2001; exec. dir. United Way of Transylvania County, Brevard, N.C., 1999—. Bd. dirs. Tampa Unity, Inc., 1982-91; chmn. Juvenile Crime Prevention Coun., Transylvania County. Mem. Va. Tech. Alumni Assn., Rotary. Office: PO Box 53 Brevard NC 28712 E-mail: sisthtee@aol.com.

PULLING, THOMAS LEFFINGWELL, investment advisor; b. N.Y.C., May 1, 1939; s. T.J. Edward and Lucy (Leffingwell) P.; m. Lisa Canby, Sept. 14, 1962 (div. 1968); children: Elizabeth, Edward L.; m. Sheila Sonne, Mar. 12, 1970 (div. 1980);children: Victoria, Diana, Christopher; m. Eileen Kingsbury-Smith, Dec. 21, 1989. BA cum laude, Princeton U., 1961. Asst. treas. J.P. Morgan & Co. Inc., N.Y.C., 1962-68; v.p. N.Y. Securities Co., 1968-71, L.M. Rosenthal & Co., N.Y.C., 1971-76; mng. dir. Citigroup Asset Mgmt., 1976—. Bd. dirs. Henry Luce Found., 1988—, Woodlawn Cemetery, 1980—; trustee Long Island U., 1995—. With USMC, 1962-67. Mem.: Coun. on Fgn. Rels., Pilgrims of U.S. (N.Y.C.), The Brook Club (N.Y.C.), Univ. Club (N.Y.C.), La Gorce Country Club (Miami), Surf Club (Miami, Fla.), Piping Rock Club (Locust Valley, NY), Century Assn. Republican. Episcopalian.

PULLIS, JOE MILTON, business administration educator, writer; b. Ranger, Tex., Aug. 15, 1939; s. Richard Milton and Ima Helen (Rogers) P.; m. Cheryl Dean Thames, June 16, 1962; children: Robert Milton, Kevin Lance. BS, U. North Tex., 1960, MEd, 1961, EdD, 1966. Instr. bus. adminstrn. Tarleton State U., Stephenville, Tex., 1961-63; asst. prof. bus. adminstrn. U. North Tex., Denton, 1963-67; prof. bus. adminstrn. La. Tech. U., Ruston, 1967—, disting. prof., 1986—. Author (textbooks): Principles of Speedwriting, 1991, Speedwriting for the Medical Professions, 1996, Speedwriting for the Legal Professions, 1996, Notetaking and Study Skills, 1997. Named Phi Kappa Phi

Scholar of Yr., La. Tech. U., 1989. Mem. Nat. Bus. Edn. Assn., Am. Lung Assn. La. (bd. dirs. 1990—), Delta Pi Epsilon (chpt. pres. 1961—, bd. dirs. Rsch. Found., Little Rock, 1988-90), Beta Gamma Sigma (chpt. pres. 1968—). Avocations: tennis, golf, travel. Home: 1104 Mcdonald Ave Ruston LA 71270-4741 Office: La Tech U PO Box 3027 Ruston LA 71272-0001 E-mail: pullis@cab.latech.edu.

PULLMAN, MAYNARD EDWARD, biochemist; b. Chgo., Oct. 26, 1927; s. Harry and Gertrude (Atlas) P.; m. E. Phyllis Light, Sept. 12, 1948; children: H. Cydney, B. Valerie, Jacky Leigh. BS, U. Ill., 1948, MS, 1950; PhD (NIH fellow), Johns Hopkins U., 1953. Fellow in pediatrics Johns Hopkins Hosp., 1953-54; asst. Pub. Health Rsch. Inst., City N.Y., 1954-56, assoc., 1956-61, assoc. mem., 1961-65, mem., 1965-89, chief, 1973-87, assoc. dir., 1983-89; sr. rsch. scientist Coll. Physicians and Surgeons Columbia U., 1989-92, cons., 1997—. Vis. prof. biochemistry U. São Paulo (Brazil) Sch. Medicine, 1963-64; research assoc. prof. biochemistry Sch. Medicine NYU, 1966-76, research prof., 1976-90; biochemistry study section mem. NIH, 1969-73. Editorial bd.: Jour. Biol. Chemistry, 1967-71, 78-80. NIH grantee, 1956-85; Shubert Found. grantee, 1972-74. Fellow N.Y. Acad. Scis.; mem. AAAS, Am. Soc. Biol. Chemistry and Molecular Biology, Brit. Biochem. Soc., Am. Chem. Soc. Home and Office: 338 Archer St Freeport NY 11520-4233 E-mail: mep2658@aol.com.

PULLMAN, PHILIP NICHOLAS, author; b. Norwich, Norfolk, Eng., Oct. 19, 1946; s. Alfred Outram and Audrey Evelyn (Merrifield) P.; m. Judith Speller, Aug. 15, 1970; children: James, Thomas. BA, Oxford U., 1968. Tchr. Oxfordshire Edn. Authority, Oxford, Eng., 1972-88; lectr. Westminster Coll., 1988-96. Author: The Ruby in the Smoke, 1987 (Internat. Reading Assn. best book award 1988), Shadow in the North, 1988, The Tiger in the Well, 1991, Spring-Heeled Jack, 1991, The Broken Bridge, 1992, The White Mercedes, 1993, The Golden Compass (Guardian Children's Fiction award 1996, Carnegie medal 1996), The Subtle Knife, 1997, Clockwork or All Wound Up, 1998, I was a Rat!, 1999, The Amber Spyglass, 2000 (Whitlaread Book of Yr.). Avocations: music, drawing. Home: 24 Templar Rd Oxford OX2 8LT England

PULOS, WILLIAM WHITAKER, lawyer; b. Hornell, N.Y., Aug. 29, 1955; s. William Leroy and Juanita (Whitaker) P. BA magna cum laude Econs., Alfred U., 1977; JD, Union U., 1980. Bar: N.Y. 1982, U.S. Bankruptcy Ct. 1982, U.S. Supreme Ct. 1987. Pvt. practice, Alfred, NY, 1981-90. Adj. prof. law Alfred U., 1981-90; prof. bus. adminstrn. SUNY-Alfred, 1982-84; tutor Empire State Coll., 1982-85; atty. Town of Alfred, 1982-2000, Village of Almond (N.Y.), 1983-98, Town of West Almond (N.Y.), 1987-97, Town of Almond, 1990-98, Town of West Union (N.Y.), 1992-98, Town of Birdsall (N.Y.), 1993-97; mem. Allegany County and Steuben County Assigned Counsel Program for Indigent Defendants, 1982-85; spl. prosecutor Allegany County, 1984—; asst. counsel N.Y. State Assembly, 1980; hearing officer N.Y. state Small Claims Assessment Rev., 1983-87. Active Alfred Sta. Vol. Fireman's Assn., Inc., 1985-98, 2d chief, 1988-92, pres. 1994-96. Recipient Outstanding Young Man Am. award U.S. Jaycees, 1982, 86. Mem. ABA, ATLA, N.Y. State Bar Assn., Steuben County Bar Assn. Office: PO Box 337 70 Main St Hornell NY 14843-0337

PULSIFER, EDGAR DARLING, leasing service and sales executive; b. Natick, Mass., Jan. 11, 1934; s. Howard George and Elvie Marion (Morris) P.; m. Alice Minarik, Feb. 16, 1957 (div. Oct. 1979); children: Mark Edgar, Audrey Carol, Lee Howard; m. Barbara Ann Chuhak, Apr. 19, 1980. BSEE, MIT, 1955. With sales and service dept. Beckman Instruments, Fullerton, Calif., 1956-59; regional sales mgr. Hewlett Packard, Palo Alto, 1959-72, Gen. Automation, Anaheim, 1973-74; exec. v.p. Systems Mktg., Elk Grove Vlg., Ill., 1975-79; pres. Consol. Funding, Mt. Prospect, 1979—. Served as 1st lt. U.S. Army, 1956. Mem. MENSA, Coast Guard Auxiliary. Clubs: North Shore Country (Glenview, Ill.), Itasca (Ill.) Country. Republican. Episcopalian. Avocations: coins, stamps, curling, scuba diving, golf. Home: 3914 Dundee Rd Northbrook IL 60062 Office: Consol Funding Corp P O Box 801 Mount Prospect IL 60056-0801 E-mail: edgard@pulsifer.com.

PULST, STEFAN, neurologist, educator; b. Braunschweig, Germany, Jan. 1, 1945; MD, MHH, Hannover, Germany, 1979. Prof. medicine and neurobiology UCLA Sch. Medicine, 1987—. Sci. dir. Nat. Ataxia Found., Mpls., 1999—; founding chair sect. neurogenetics Am. Acad. Neurology, Mpls., 1999—. Author: (textbook) Neurogenetics, 2000; contbr. articles to profl. jours. Grantee, NIH, 1991—, Med. Br., U.S. Dept. Def., 1999—. Office: UCLA Sch Medicine 8631 W 3rd St Ste 1145E Los Angeles CA 90048

PULZ, GARY EDWARD, psychologist; b. Lakewood, N.J., Apr. 6, 1951; s. Edward Walter and Helen P.; m. Joanne Miriam Laukshtein, June 24, 1972; children: Kristian, Rein, Karalina, Daggi. BA, Mt. St. Mary's Coll., Emmitsburg, md., 1973; MA in Psychology, Jersey City State Coll., 1978, profl. diploma in Sch. Psychology, 1980. Nat. cert. sch. psychologist, N.J.; lic. profl. counselor, N.J. Probation officer Ocean County Probation Dept., Toms River, N.J., 1974-78; clin. psychologist Ocean County Mental Health Clinic, 1978-80; sch. psychologist Howell (N.J.) Twp. Schs., 1980-87; owner, operator Uncle Wills Pancake House, Beach Haven, N.J., 1974-95, Amber Apts. and Morningstar Band B, Beach Haven, 1995—; pvt. practice lic. profl. counselor N.J., 1999—. Sch. psychologist Stafford Twp. Schs., Manahawkin, N.J., 1987—. Contbr. articles to profl. jours. Organizer/mem. juv. conf. Ocean County Juv. Cts., Toms River, 1987—; mem. eucharistic minister com. St. Francis Ch., Beach Haven, N.J., 1995—; coach of softball and basketball Medford Youth Assn., N.J., 1995-97, LBI Youth Assn., Long Beach Island, N.J., 1990-95. Mem. Nat. Assn. Sch. Psychologists, N.J. Assn. Sch. Psychologists, N.Am. Master Psychologists, Nat. Assn. Mental Illness, N.J. Assn. Master Psychologists (pres. 1994—), Beach Haven Bus. Assn. (pres. 1990-95), N.J. Edn. Assn., Internat. Sch. Psychologists Assn., Mon/Ocean Sch. Psychologists Assn. (v.p. 1983-87). Republican. Roman Catholic. Avocations: Aikido, skiing, boating, travel, historical home renovations. Home: 125 Engleside Ave Beach Haven NJ 08008-1762 also: 24 Glen Lake Dr Medford NJ 08055-3104 Office: Stafford Twp Schs 1000 Mckinley Ave Manahawkin NJ 08050-2807 Fax: 609-978-5739. E-mail: garypulz@aol.com.

PUMARIEGA, ANDRES JULIO, medical educator, researcher; b. Matanzas, Cuba, Jan. 25, 1953; came to U.S., 1962; s. Andrès Augustin and America Maria (Mechoso) P.; m. JoAnne Buttacavoli, Dec. 26, 1975; children: Christina Marie, Nicole Marie. BS, U. Miami, Coral Gables, Fla., 1973; MD, U. Miami, Fla., 1976. Resident in psychiatry Duke U., Durham, N.C., 1976-78, fellow in child psychiatry, 1978-80; dir. child psychiatry consultation/liaison svc. Vanderbilt U., Nashville, 1980-83; dir. pediat. psychiatry consultation/liaison svc. Tex. Children's Hosp. Baylor Coll. Medicine, Houston, 1983-86; dir. divsn. child adolescent psychiatry U. Tex. Med. Bd., Galveston, 1986-91, dir. residency program, 1987-92; prof. neuropsychiatry and behavioral scis. U. S.C., Columbia, 1992-96, dir. divsn. child and adolescent psychiatry, 1992-96, vice-chmn. dept. neuropsychiatry and behavior sci., 1994-96; assoc. dir. William S. Hall Psychiat. Inst., 1992-96; prof. psychiatry and behavioral scis. East Tenn. State U., Johnson City, 1996—, chmn. dept. psychiatry and behavioral scis., 1996-2001, dir. divsn. child and adolescent psychiatry, 2001—. Examiner in child psychiatry and gen. psychiatry Am. Bd. Psychiatry and Neurology, Chgo., 1983—; co-investigator, mem. exec. com. Ctr. Cross-Cultural Rsch., Galveston, 1989-91; chmn. rsch. com. and exec. bd. S.C. Pub. Acad. Mental Health Consortium, 1994-96; chairperson Nat. Latin Behavioral Work Group, 1995—; chairperson Hispanic panel managed care initiative Ctr. for Mental Health Svcs. Abuse and MH Adminstrn., 1996—; cons. Ctr. for Substance Abuse Treatment USPHS, 1995-96; mem. nat. adv. coun. Ctr. Mental Health Svcs., Substance Abuse and Mental Health Adminstrn. U.S. Dept. Health and Human Svcs., 1997-2001. Editor: (with H. Vance) Clinical Assessment of Child and Adolescent Behavior, 2001; assoc. editor Jour. Child and Family Studies, 1996—; contbr. more than 200 articles and abstracts to sci. publs. Bd. dirs. Tex. Network for Children, Austin, 1986-88; mem. adv. coun. Ptnrs. Advocacy Network, 1990-92. Named site coord., grantee, Nat. Assn. State Mental Health Dir. Rsch. Fellowship, 1993—, Forest Pharm., 2000, co-prin. investigator, grantee, Ctr. for Cross-Cultural Rsch., NIMH, Bethesda, Md., 1988—92; named to Alumni Hall of Fame, U. Miami Sch. Medicine, 1999; recipient Minority Child Psychiatrist tng. grantee, 1988—92, Exemplary Psychiatrist award, Nat. Alliance for Mentally Ill, 1993, 1997, cert. of merit for beneficiary svc., Health Care Fin. Adminstrn., U.S. Dept. HHS, 1996; grantee, Fullerton Found., 1993—95. Fellow: Am. Psychiat. Assn., Acad. Psychosomatic Medicine, Am. Acad. Child Psychiatry (chmn. work group on sys. of care 1995—2001, chmn. cmty. psych. com. 2001—, Outstanding Mentor award 1994, Catchers in the Rye award 2001), Am. Acad. Pediat.; mem.: Tenn. Coun. Child and Adolescent Psychiatry (founding pres. 1996—97), Tex. Mental Health Assn. (mem. children's adv. com. 1991—92), Tenn. Soc. Child Psychiatry (sec. 1982—83, pres. 2001—), Bay Area Pediat. Soc. (pres. 1990—91), Soc. Profs. of Child Psychiatry, Am. Assn. Cmty. Psychiatrists (bd. dirs. 1996—, Ethics in Pub. Managed Care award 2000), Am. Coll. Psychiatrists, Nat. Mental Health Assn. (bd. dirs. 1999). Roman Catholic. Avocations: swimming, political history, public affairs. Home: 2 Roundtree Ct Johnson City TN 37604-1492 Office: East Tenn State U 107 Hillrise Hall PO Box 70567 Johnson City TN 37614-1707 E-mail: pumarieg@etsu.edu.

PUMARIEGA, JOANNE BUTTACAVOLI, mathematics educator; b. Coral Gables, Fla., May 27, 1952; d. Ciro Charles and Rosaria Frances (Calabrese) Buttacavoli; m. Andres Julio Pumariega, Dec. 26, 1975; children: Christina Marie, Nicole Marie. BA in Math. and Edn. magna cum laude, U. Miami, 1973, MA in Math., 1974; postgrad., U. Houston, 1991-92. Cert. secondary math. tchr., Tex., Fla., Tenn., N.C. Grad. tchg. asst. U. Miami, Coral Gables, 1973-74; substitute tchr. Dade County Pub. Schs., Miami, 1975; math. instr. Miami Dade C.C., 1975-76; math. and G.E.D. instr. Durham (N.C.) Tech. Inst., 1976-77; math. instr. Durham H.S., 1977-78, Durham Acad., 1978-80, Univ. Sch. of Nashville, 1980-83; pvt. practice math. instr. Houston, 1984-86; tutor Clear Lake Tutoring Svc., 1987-90; pvt. practice, S.A.T, lang. instr. League City, Tex., 1990-92; pvt. practice math. and S.A.T. instr. Johnson City, Tenn., 1996—; lang. instr. Nelson Elem. Sch., Columbia, 1993-96. Instr. fgn. langs. and math. Lonnie B. Nelson Elem. Sch., Columbia, S.C.; adj. faculty math. East Tenn. State U., 1999—. Co-author: (with F. Rodriguez & J. Pumariega) HIV/AIDS in Children and Adolscents, 1999. Chair bd. edn. St. Mary Parish, League City, 1988-90, lector, 1992, v.p. coun. Cath. Women, Johnson City, 1997-99; C.C.E. tchr. St. John Neumann Cath. Ch., Columbia, S.C. & Johnson City, Tenn., 1993-95, lector, 1992-96; lector St. Mary's Ch., Johnson City, 1996—; treas. St. Thomas More Women's Club, Houston, 1985-86; v.p., then pres. housestaff med. wives Duke U., Durham, N.C., 1978-80; mem. Wash./Unicoi/Johnson County Med. Aux., 1999-2002, asst. treas., 2002-. Recipient Above and Beyond award, East Tenn. State U., 2002. Mem. Newcomers of Greater Columbia (chmn. pub. rels. chpt. 1993,95), Newcomers of Greater Colo. (com. chair coord. 1994-95), Welcome Neighbors of Bay Area (v.p., program chmn. 1991-92), Washington/Unicoi/Johnson Co. Med. Aux. (chair pub. rels. com. 1999—), Tex. Med. Aux., Bay Area Med. Wives, East Tenn. State U. Women's Club (v.p. 1997-98, pres. 1998-99, parliamentarian 1999-2000), U. S.C. Faculty Women's Club (v.p. 1993-94, pres. 1994-95, parliamentarian, advisor 1995-96), Phi Kappa Phi, Kappa Delta Pi, Alpha Lamba Delta (Woman of Yr. 1972). Roman Catholic. Avocations: reading, public speaking, traveling. Home: 2 Round Tree Ct Johnson City TN 37604-1492 Office: East Tenn State U Dept Math PO Box 70663 Johnson City TN 37614-1701 E-mail: pumarieg@aol.com.

PUMP, BERNARD JOHN, finance company executive, consultant; b. Schenectady, N.Y., Feb. 23, 1960; s. Robert Franz and Mary Eileen (Dalton) P.; m. Karen Yi-Shui Kao, May 13, 1989; children: Rachel Elise, Ryan Bernard, Megan Eileen. BS in Econ. cum laude, U. Pa., 1984; MA in Econ., U. Chgo., 1994, MBA, 1995. CPA, Mass. Acct. Coopers & Lybrand, N.Y.C., 1984-87; mgr. fin. analysis Am. Express TRS, 1987-89; economist Lexecon, Inc., Chgo., 1991-96; ptnr. Deloitte & Touche LLP, 1996—. Fl. broker, trader evening session Chgo. Bd. Trade, 1995-97. Co-author: Proving Antitrust Damages, 1996. Mem. Inst. Mgmt. Accts. (cert.), Union League Club. Republican. Roman Catholic. Avocations: restoring antique watches and fountain pens, golf. Home: 1830 W Eddy St Chicago IL 60657 Office: Deloitte & Touche LLP 180 N Stetson Ave Fl 19 Chicago IL 60601-6779 E-mail: bpump@deloitte.com.

PUMPER, ROBERT WILLIAM, microbiologist, educator; b. Clinton, Iowa, Sept. 12, 1921; s. William R. and Kathrine M. (Anderson) P.; m. Ruth J. Larkin, June 24, 1951; 1 son. Mark. BA, U. Iowa, 1951, MS, 1953, PhD, 1955. Diplomate: Am. Soc. Microbiology. Asst. prof. Hahnemann Med. Coll., Phila., 1955-57; prof. microbiology U. Ill. Med. Sch., Chgo., 1957-92, prof. emeritus, 1992—, Raymond B. Allen Med. lectr., 1970, 74, 76, 87. Co-author: Essentials of Medical Virology; contbr. articles to profl. jours. Served with USAAF, 1942-46. Recipient Chancellors' award U. Ill., Bombeck award for excellence in med. edn., 1992. Mem. Tissue Culture Assn., Sigma Xi, Phi Rho Sigma. Lutheran. Home: 18417 Argyle Ave Homewood IL 60430-3007 Office: U Ill Med Sch Dept Microbiology 808 S Wood St Chicago IL 60612-7300

PUMPHREY, GERALD ROBERT, lawyer; b. Flushing, N.Y., May 31, 1947; s. Fred Paul and Anne (Afferman) P.; m. Joann DeLillo, Oct. 6, 1968; children: Gerald, Christopher, Elena. BBA, St. John's U., 1969, MBA, 1974; JD, Nova U., 1978. Bar: Fla. 1978. Assoc. Walden & Walden, Dania, Fla., 1978; v.p. legal svcs. Golden Bear, Inc., North Palm Beach, Jack Nicklaus & Assocs., Air Bear, Inc., also bd. dirs.; v.p., sec. Triple P., Inc., 1978-83; pvt. practice, 1983—. Bd. advdisor Benjamin Sch. Found. Athletics Assn., 1980-83; coord. Benjamin Sch. Found., Inc.; mem. golf com. St. Clare's Sch.; pres. Home and Sch. Assn., 1983-84; bd. dirs. Deaf Svc. Ctr. Palm Beach County Inc., 1988-89. Mem. ABA, Palm Beach County Bar Assn., North Palm Beach County Bar Assn. (pres. 1991-92), Palm Beach Gardens C. of C., Kiwanis (charter mem., bd. dirs. Palm Beach Gardens 1983-87), No. Palm Beaches C. of C. (counsel 1987—), Rotary North Palm Beach (bd. dirs. 1998—, pres. 2001—), Phi Alpha Delta. E-mail: pumph. Office: Ste 300 11000 Prosperity Farms Rd Palm Beach Gardens FL 33410-3462 Fax: 561-626-4824. E-mail: pumphreypa@aol.com.

PUNCH, NICHOLAS See PUNCH, WILLIAM

PUNCH, WILLIAM ANTHONY (NICHOLAS PUNCH), priest; b. Cobham, Surrey, Eng., Nov. 13, 1939; s. Julian William P. and Imelda Mildred Norfolk. Student, Dominican House of Studies, Canberra, Australia, 1962—68. Ordained priest Roman Cath. Ch., 1966. Provincial superior Dominican Religious Order, Canberra, Australia, 1981—88; preacher Thomas More Ctr., Webster, Wis., 1991—. Chmn. Clerical Major Superiors Orgn., Canberra, ACT, Australia, 1984—86. Named Queen scout, Boy Scouts of Australia, 1957. Home: 27781 Leef Rd Webster WI 54893 Office: Thomas More Ctr Peaching and Praying 27781 Leef Rd Webster WI Home Fax: 715-866-4277; Office Fax: 715-866-4277. Personal E-mail: tmcnick@attglobal.net. Business E-Mail: tmcnick@attglobal.net.

PUNDMANN, ED JOHN , JR. automotive company executive; b. St. Charles, Mo., Feb. 24, 1939; s. Ed J. Sr. and Ruth O. (Brehme) P.; m. Dolores Anne Lienau, June 15, 1963 (dec.); children: Mary Ann, Steven A., Susan K. BA, Westminster Coll., 1961. Jr. accountant Peat, Marwick & Mitchell, St. Louis, 1961-62; salesman Pundmann Ford, St. Charles, 1962-82, gen. mgr., 1982-92, pres., 1992—. Bd. dirs., chmn. First State Bank; bd. dirs. Mut. Fire Ins., St. Charles; mem. St. Charles City Tax Incremental Financing Commn., 1990-99; mem. Ford Motor Dispute Settlement Bd., 1993-94. Treas. St. Charles City Charter Commn., 1981; mem. St. Charles City Park Bd., 1981-82; chmn. St. Charles City Econ. Devel. Commn.; mem. St. Charles City Park Found. Bd., 1985—, also past pres.; St. Louis Regional Commerce and Growth Assn.; adv. bd. St. Charles County; mem. Handicapped Facilities Bd. St. Charles County, 1986-94, also past pres.; active St. Charles County Road Bd., 1996—; past pres. St. John United Ch. of Christ; bd. dirs. Emmaus Homes, 1981-91, Parkside Meadows Retirement Facility, 2001-; chmn. St. Charles City Charter Rev. Commn., 1991; bd. dirs. St. Charles Jaycee Village Retirement Home, 1980-90, Boone Ctr. Workshop, 1982-92, Parkside Found., 2001-, St. Charles City Schs. Found, 1995--; dist. chmn. Boy Scouts Am., 1979-82. Recipient Gov. of Mo. award, 1989, Mo. Time Quality Dealer award, 1995, United Ch. of Christ award, 1993, Jefferson award TV Sta. KSDK, St. Louis, 1996. Mem. Mo. Auto Dealers Assn. (bd. dirs. 1983—, treas. 1997-98, 2d v.p. 1998-99, 1st v.p. 1999-2000, pres. 2000-2001), Greater St. Louis Ford Dealers Assn. (past pres.), St. Charles C. of C. (past bd. dirs., pres., Citizen of Yr. award 1986, Small Bus. Person of Yr. 2002), Rotary (past pres.). Lodges: Rotary. Home: 3304 Lennox Dr Saint Charles MO 63301-0632 Office: Pundmann Ford 2727 W Clay St Saint Charles MO 63301-2566 E-mail: pundmann@nothnbut.net.

PUNT, LEONARD CORNELIS, educational services company executive; b. Bongondza, Zaire, Nov. 16, 1940; arrived in U.S., 1954, naturalized, 1960; s. Harry Marius and Clara VandeGevel Punt; m. Sarah Elizabeth Walton, Dec. 18, 1966; children: John, Amy, Brian. BA, Wheaton (Ill.) Coll., 1964; MEd, Loyola U., Chgo., 1981, Loyola U., 1981. Owner, dir. The Reading Tree Inc., Downers Grove, Ill., 1976—; v.p. Am. Bus. Comm., 1978—; owner, dir. The Reading Tree Inc., 1976—; v.p. Am. Bus. Comms., 1978—. Mem.: Naperville C. of C. Office: Reading Tree Inc 5117 Main St Ste D Downers Grove IL 60515-4654 E-mail: Readtree2@msn.com.

PUOTINEN, ARTHUR EDWIN, college president, clergyman; b. Crystal Falls, Mich., Sept. 7, 1941; s. Kaleva Weikko and Ines Pauline (Maki) P.; m. Judith Cathleen Kapoun, Aug. 8, 1964; children: Anne, Marjetta, Sara. AA, Suomi Coll., 1961; BA, Augustana Coll., Rock Island, Ill., 1963; MDiv, Luth. Sch. Theology, Chgo., 1967; MA, U. Chgo., 1969, PhD, 1973; MBA, Wake Forest U., 1984. Pastor Trinity Luth. Ch., Chgo., 1968-70; asst. prof. religion Cen. Mich. U., Mt. Pleasant, 1971-74; dean faculty Suomi Coll., Hancock, Mich., 1974-78; v.p. acad. affairs Lenoir-Rhyne Coll., Hickory, N.C., 1978-83; assoc. dean acad. affairs Roanoke Coll., Salem, Va., 1983-84; exec. dir. Luth. Ednl. Conf. of N.Am., Washington, 1984-88; pres. Grand View Coll., Des Moines, 1988-96; v.p., provost Finlandia U., Hancock, Mich., 1996—. Pastor ELCA No. Great Lakes Synod, Evang.-Luth. Ch. Am. Author: Finnish Radicals..., 1979; contbr. articles to books and jours. Grantee NEH, U.S. Dept. Edn. Democrat. Avocations: jogging, reading, travel. Home: 1404 Sugar Maple Ln Houghton MI 49931-2709 Office: Suomi Coll 600 Quincy St Hancock MI 49930-1806 E-mail: puotinin@mail.portup.com., apuotinen@accisd.k12.mi.us.

PUPPE, GERALD CLARENCE, trade association executive; b. Grafton, N.D., Sept. 1, 1938; s. Arthur G. and Bernice P. P.; m. Marsha J., Apr. 10, 1966; 1 child, Steven J. BS, N.D. State U., 1960; MS, So. Ill. U., 1975. Sales promotion specialist Fed. Crop Ins. Corp., Billings, Mont., 1964-66, divsn. dir. Washington, 1966-77, 82-86, Kansas City, 1977-82, dir. field underwriting, 1986-90, dir. underwriting divsn., 1990-93; v.p. Nat. Crop Ins. Svcs., Overland Park, Kans., 1993—. Lt. U.S. Army, 1961-63. Mem. Alpha Gamma Rho (grand pres. 1989-90). Home: 12804 El Monte St Leawood KS 66209-2313

PURCELL, ANN RUSHING, state legislator, office manager medical business; b. Reidsville, Ga., May 12, 1945; d. William Robert and Katie (Dasher) Rushing; m. Dent Wiley Purcell, May 26, 1966; children: Edwin Wiley, Mieke Ann, Mikki Marie. BS in Edn., Ga. So. Coll., 1966; hon. degree, Ga. Future Farmers Am., 1999. Cert. secondary tchr. Tchr. math. Evans (Ga.) High Sch., 1966-68; tchr. math., earth and sci. Beaumont Jr. High Sch., Lexington, Ky., 1969-70; substitute tchr. Tallahassee, 1970's; agt. Noblin Realty, 1970's; office mgr. Radiation Therapy Assocs., PC, Savannah, Ga., 1979—; state legislator Ho. of Reps. Ga. Gen. Assembly, Atlanta, 1991—. Author: Purcells of South Georgia and Other Related Families, 1976. Bd. dirs. Med. Assn. Ga. Polit. Action Com., Atlanta, 1988-89, Girl Scout Coun. Savannah, 1991-93, Ga. So. U. Found., 1992—; mem. adv. com. Effingham County Extension Svc., 1992—; Effingham County fin. chmn. State YMCA, 1991—, vice chmn. steering com., 1999, bd. dirs., 1999; mem. adv. com. Treutlin Home, 1999; bd. adv. Claxton Youth Detention Ctr.; bd. dirs. Effingham YMCA, 1999—. Hon. comdr. 165th Ga. Air Guard Airlift, 2000—; hon. mem. Civil Air Patrol, 2001—, Ga. State Patrol, 2001. Decorated WA-PO-HE award Ga. Nat. Air Guard; named Georgia's Legislator of Yr., Ga. Sch. Counselors Assn., 1996, Ga. Legislator of Yr., Coastal Conservation Assn. Ga., 1998; named to Hon. Ga. State Patrol, 2001; recipient Friend of Medicine award, Med. Assn. Ga., 1991, 1993, 1994, 1996, Guardian of Small Bus. award, Nat. Fedn. Ind. Bus., 1992, 1994, 1996, Commendation cert., Ga. Emergency Mgmt. Agy., 1995, Vol. of Yr. award, Effingham 4-H, 1998, nat. Am. hon. degree, Future Farmers Am., 1999, Friend of State 4-H award, 1999, svc. award, Effingham Recreation Dept., 2000, cmty. svc. award, Guyton Masonic Lodge, 2000, Hon. Family Consumer Cmty. Leaders of Ga. award, 2001. Mem. Aux. to the Med. Assn. Ga. (pres. 1985), Aux. to the Ga. Med. Soc. (pres. 1981-82), Ga. Salzburger Soc., Effingham County Pub. Ofcls. Assn., Rotary Internat., Ga. Peace Officers Assn. (hon.), Rincon Noon Lions Club, Exch. Club. Democrat. Methodist. Avocations: painting, genealogy, fishing. Home: 410 Willowpeg Way Rincon GA 31326-9157 Office: State Capitol SW Ste 401 Atlanta GA 30334-1600

PURCELL, BILL, mayor; b. Phila., Oct. 25, 1953; s. William Paxson Jr. and Mary (Hamilton) P.; m. Deborah Lee Miller, Aug. 9, 1986; 1 child, Jesse Miller. AB, Hamilton Coll., 1976; JD, Vanderbilt U., 1979. Bar: Tenn. 1979, U.S. Ct. Appeals (6th cir.) 1985, U.S. Supreme Ct. 1986. Staff atty. West Tenn. Legal Svcs., Jackson, Tenn., 1979-81; asst. pub. defender Metro Pub. Defender, Nashville, 1981-84, sr. asst. pub. defender, 1984-85; assoc. Lionel R. Barrett, P.C., 1985-86; ptnr. Farmer, Berry & Purcell, 1986-90; mem. Tenn. Ho. of Reps., 1986-96, also majority leader, 1990-96; dir. child and family policy ctr. Vanderbilt Inst. for Pub. Policy Studies, Vanderbilt U., 1996-99; mayor Met. Govt. of Nashville and Davidson county, 1999—. Hmn. select com. on children and youth Tenn. Gen. Assembly, 1989—96; exec. dir. Vanderbilt Legal Aid Soc., 1978—79; chmn. NCSL Assembly of State Issues, 1995; chmn. policy makers' program adv. bd. Danforth Found.; mem. adv. bd. U.S. Conf. of Mayors, 2001—. Mem. bd. advs., exec. com. U.S. Conf. Mayors, 2001—; exec. com. 6th Dist. Dems., Nashville, 1986—88; mem. Tenn. State Gen. Assembly, 1986—96, majority leader, 1990—96; chmn. human svcs. com. Nat. Conf. State Legislatures, Washington, 1993; mem. exec. com. Dem. Nat. Com. , 1994—97; chmn. Dem. Legislative Campaign Com., 1994—96. Toll fellow Coun. State Govts., 1988; named Legislator of Yr. Dist. Attys.' Gen. Conf. 1989, Tenn. Conservation League, 1991. Mem. ABA, Tenn. Bar Assn., Nashville Bar Assn. Methodist.

PURCELL, BRADFORD MOORE, publishing company executive; b. Garden City, N.Y., Oct. 1, 1929; s. William Lawrence and Margaret (Moore) P.; m. Louise Rauth, July 10, 1954; children: Margaret, Philip, Mark, Louisa, Christopher. BA, Williams Coll., 1951; MBA, Columbia U., 1957. Sr. v.p. devel. McGraw Hill, Inc., 1976-79, sr. v.p., 1979-81, group v.p. tng. systems, 1981-83, sr. v.p. mktg., 1983-85; pres. W.H. Smith Pubs Inc., N.Y.C., 1985-91; v.p. admin. and fin. Rsch. Books Inc., 1992. Served to 1st lt. USAF, 1951-53. Home: 106 Tantumorantum Rd Lyme CT 06371-3137 Office: Rsch Books Inc 38 Academy St # 1507 Madison CT 06443-2600 E-mail: brad@researchbooks.com.

PURCELL, CLIFFORD ANDREW, pathologist; b. Evansville, Ind., July 12, 1956; BS in Microbiology, U. Fla., 1985; MD, Ohio State U., 1989. Diplomate Am. Bd. Pathology. Resident in pathology U. Md., 1994; fellow Armed Forces Inst. Pathology, 1996. Mem. U.S. and Can. Acad. Pathology, Am. Coll. Clin. Pathologists, Coll. Am. Pathologists, Phi Beta Kappa. Office: Hays Pathology Lab 1300 E 13th St Hays KS 67601-2598

PURCELL, DALE, college president, consultant; b. Baxley, Ga., Oct. 20, 1919; s. John Groce and Agnes (Moody) P.; m. Edna Jean Rowell, Aug. 2, 1944; children: David Scott, Steven Dale, Pamela Jean; m. Mary Louise Gerlinger, Aug. 26, 1962; adopted children: Amelia Allerton, Jon Allerton. BA, U. Redlands, 1948, MA, 1949; postgrad., Northwestern U., 1951-52; LL.D., Lindenwood Colls., 1974. Topographer U.S. E.D., 1939; U.S. counter-intelligence agt., 1940-42; assoc. prof. Ottawa U., 1953-54, asst. to pres., 1954-58; gen. sec. Earlham Coll., 1958-61; dir. devel. U. So. Fla., 1961-63; exec. dir. Cancer Research Center, Columbia, Mo., 1963-65; pres. Westminster Coll., Fulton, 1973-76, Dale Purcell Assocs., 1972-92; a founding dir. Am. Sports Medicine Inst., Birmingham, Ala., 1987-92. Rep. cons. clients Hughston Sports Medicine Found., Columbus, Ga., Berry Coll., Mt. Berry, Ga., Hope Coll., Holland, Mich., William Woods Coll., Fulton, Mo., Eureka (Ill.) Coll., Cranbrook Insts., Bloomfield Hills, Mich., Penrose Hosp., Colorado Springs, Colo., Northwestern Coll., Orange City, Iowa, Centro Medico Docente, Caracas, Venezuela, Wayland Acad., Beaver Dam, Wis., Cen. Coll., Pella, Iowa, U. of Stirling, Scotland, U. Ottawa, Ont., Can., Washington & Lee U., Lexington, Va., Taylor U., Upland, Ind., Menninger Found., Topeka, Kans., Ill. Wesleyan U., Bloomington, Cox Med. Systems, Springfield, Mo., Nat. Council Family Rels. Mpls., Stephens Coll., Columbia, Mo., Hist. Savannah Found., Ga. Bd. visitors Berry Coll. Capt. USMCR, 1942-46, 52-53. Recipient Disting. Achievement award Berry Coll., 1974, medal Pres. of China, 1945, medal Pres. of Korea, 1953. Mem. Pi Kappa Delta (Alpha chpt.). Presbyterian (elder 1964—). Clubs: St. Louis (Clayton), Univ. (St. Louis and N.Y.C.), Litchfield County Ct. Home: Woodlands 120 Belden St Falls Village CT 06031-1124 E-mail: mlgp@discovernet.net.

PURCELL, ELIZABETH ANN, financial executive; b. Murphysboro, Ill., Aug. 1, 1951; d. John Thomas and Wilma Lucille (Wanstreet) P. BA, Rosary Coll., River Forest, Ill., 1973. Cert. fin. planner. Assoc. v.p. Investments A.G. Edwards & Sons, Inc., Chgo., 1976—. Mem. Internat. Assn. Fin. Planners. Home: 21 W Chestnut St Apt 904 Chicago IL 60610-3398 Office: 221 S Riverside Plz Chicago IL 60606

PURCELL, FENTON PETER, engineering consultant; b. Paterson, N.J., Nov. 23, 1942; s. Lee Thomas and Dorothy P.; BCE, Rensselaer Poly. Inst., 1965; m. Susan Duggan, Feb. 20, 1971; children: Aimee and Suzie (twins), Jacqueline. Engr., Lee T. Purcell Assocs., cons. engrs., Paterson, 1965-66, partner, 1969—; v.p. Fenton Corp., Paterson, 1970—; partner L.T.P.A. Partnership, Paterson, 1981—. Cons. World Bank, 1997—, Asian Devel. Bank, 1997—; bd. dirs. Ramapo Valley chpt. ARC, 1978—, 1st v.p., 1980. Served to capt. Med. Svc. Corps, U.S. Army, 1966-69. Decorated Army Commendation medal; registered profl. engr., N.J., N.Y. State, Pa., Mass.; lic. profl. planner, N.J.; diplomate Am. Acad. Environ. Engrs. Mem. Am. Water Works Assn., Water Pollution Control Fedn., N.J. Cons. Engrs. Coun., Am. Cons. Engrs. Coun., Rensselaer Soc. Engrs., N.J. Water Pollution Control Assn., Nat. Soc. Profl. Engrs., N.J. Soc. Profl. Engrs. Home: 4 Highview Ter Saddle River NJ 07458-2130 Office: Lee T Purcell Assocs Paterson NJ 07505

PURCELL, GEORGE RICHARD, artist, postal employee; b. Clayton, N.Y., May 4, 1921; s. George Thomas and Katherine Eileen (Eagan) P.; m. Mary Sutter, Apr. 3, 1961. BS, Niagara U., 1947; postgrad., Syracuse U., 1952-53, 55-56. With Eagan Real Estate, Syracuse, 1948-49; claims interviewer N.Y. State Divsn. Unemployment Ins., 1949-50, 52; with U.S. Postal Svc., Syracuse, 1957—, cert. classifier of mails, 1975-77, with registry dept., 1977—. Tutor in philosophy, 1971—. Exhibited in Ctrl. N.Y. Art Open, 1981, Drake Gallery, Fayetteville, N.Y., 1982, Assoc. Artists Gallery, Syracuse, 1983, 91, Fayetteville Art Festival, 1984, Recreation Generation Art Exhibit, 1982—, DeWitt (N.Y.) Libr., 1986-94, N.Y. State Fair, 1990, Art Telauc WCNY-TV, Syracuse, 1990-01, Cazenovia Coll. Art Auction, 1994, N.Y. State Fair Fine Art Exhibit, 1999. Founder, pres. Syracuse chpt. Cath. Med. Mission Bd., 1973-76, rep., 1976—; del. Presdl. Trust, 1992; active Cath. Near-East Welfare Assn., Book Mission Program, New Mems. Art Show Manlius Libr., 1991, Rep. Nat. Com., Heritage Found., Washington; dep. dir. gen. Internat. Biog. Assn., Cambridge, Eng. Served with U.S. Army, 1943-46. Decorated Legion de l'Aigle der Mer, Order of Holy Cross of Jerusalem, Order Knight Templars of Jerusalem, knight Order of Holy Grail, knight Lofsensischen Ursinius Orden, baron Royal Order of Bohemian Crown; N.Y. State War Svc. scholar, 1955. Fellow Australian Inst. Coordinated Rsch. (life); mem. Am. Biog Inst. (life assoc., rsch. bd. advisors nat. divsn., apptd. dep. dir.), Internat. Soc. Neplatonic Studies, World Jewish Congress, Soc. Ancient Greek Philosophy, Inst. des Hautes Etudes, Alliance Universelle pour la Pax (hon. prof.), Osterrichische Albert Sweitzer Gesselshaft, Acad. Maison des Internationale Intellectuels. Roman Catholic.

PURCELL, HENRY, III, real estate developer; b. Watertown, N.Y., Dec. 21, 1929; s. John Cecil and Elizabeth (Hathway) P.; m. L. Betty Collier; children: Robert William, Emmy Purcell Reynolds, Jenny Purcell Hawley. BS in Mil. Engring., U.S. Mil. Acad., 1953; MBA in Econs. and Fin., U. Utah, 1975; postgrad., Princeton, 1960-61; PhD in Bus., Kennedy Western U., 2001. Cert. Middle East specialist, Turkish linguist. Commd. 1st lt. U.S. Army, Augsburg, Republic of Germany, 1953, advanced through grades to lt. col., 1967, commdr. Co. K. 1st regiment, 5th infantry div. Fed. Republic of Germany, 1955-56, chief translation, U.S. Mil. Mission to Turkey Ankara, Turkey, 1957-59, batallion commdr., tng. div. Ft. Ord, Calif., 1965, sr. regimental adv. 7th ARVN regiment, 5th ARVN div. South Vietnam, 1966, adv. G3 plans, III Corps ARVN South Vietnam, 1966-67, with Middle East Plans div., U.S. Strike Commd. Fla., 1968-70, asst. chief staff, G5 101st Airborne/Ambl div. I Corps, South Vietnam, 1970, with G3Plans, Iv Corps ARVN South Vietnam, 1970, sr. regimental adv. 32d regiment South Vietnam, 1971, with war plans div., deputy chief of staff, ops., The Pentagon, 1971, Middle East Specialist U.S. Readiness command Fla., 1972-74, retired, 1974; Middle East specialist U.S. Attache's Office, Ankara, Istanbul, 1961-63; with Spacos, G3 Plans and nuclear weapons employment div. NATO, Izmir, Turkey, 1963-65; pres. Henry Purcell, Inc., Tampa, 1976—, Warn-a-Prowler Inc., Tampa, 1994—. Personal interpreter/Turkish translator for Lyndon B. Johnson. Pres. Nat. Sojourners, Tampa, 1969, 70, 72, Wilson Jr. High Sch. PTA, Tampa, 1977; commdr. Heroes of '76, Tampa, Fla., 1969, 70. Decorated DFC, Bronze Star for Valor with two oak leaf clusters, Cross of Gallantry, Gold Star, Silver Star (Vietnam), 10 Air medals, Army Commendation medal for valor with one oak leaf cluster with "V" device. Mem. Unified Constrn. Trades Bd., Nat. Assn. Realtors, Fla. West Coast Roofing Assn., Nat. Builders Assn., Greater Tampa C. of C. (com. of 100 1980—). Office: 825 W Platt St Tampa FL 33606-2251 E-mail: purcellh@aol.com., purcellh@warnaprowler.com.

PURCELL, JAMES FRANCIS, former utility executive, consultant; b. Miles City, Mont., May 13, 1920; s. Robert E. and Mary A. (Hickey) P.; m. Dorothy Marie Abel, Nov. 4, 1944; children— Angela, Ann, Alicia, Anita, Alanna, James Francis, Andrea, Adria, Michael, Gregory, Amara. AB magna cum laude, U. Notre Dame, 1942; MBA, Harvard U., 1943. With McGraw-Hill Pub. Co., N.Y.C., 1946-48; dir. public relations Am. Maize Products Co., 1948-51; public relations cons. Selvage & Lee, Chgo., 1951-53; with No. Ind. Public Service Co., Hammond, 1953—, v.p. public relations, 1961-75, sr. v.p., 1975-84, bd. dirs., chmn. environ. and consumer affairs com.; owner, pres. James F. Purcell and Assocs., 1984—. Chmn. bd. govs. Our Lady of Mercy Hosp., Dyer, Ind., 1979-83; past chmn. Hammond Community Chest drive; past mem. nat. president's council St. Mary's (Ind.) Coll.; bd. dirs. Catholic Charities, 1965-85; chmn. bd. dirs. Bishop Noll Found., 1988-90. Served to lt. USNR, 1943-46. Named Man of Year Notre Dame U., 1967 Mem. Pub. Rels. Soc. Am. (past pres. Hoosier chpt.), N.W. Ind. Assn. Commerce and Industry (v.p., dir. 1979-83), Newcomen Soc. N. Am., Briar Ridge Country Club (Schererville), Serra Club (past pres. Calumet region), Notre Dame Club, Harvard U. Bus. Sch. Club of Chgo. Office: 2842 45th St Highland IN 46322-2905

PURCELL, KAREN BARLAR, naturopathic physician, nutritionist, opera singer; b. Miami, Fla., Dec. 31, 1947; d. Raymond and Elita (Kitzmiller) Barlar; m. John A. Purcell, June 11, 1977 (div. Dec. 1986); 1 child, Carl; m. Roy Gene Autry, Dec. 31, 1987. MusB, U. Cin., 1969; MusM, New England Conservatory Music, Boston, 1971; post grad tng., Bastyr U., Seattle, WA, 1997-98; D in Naturopathy, Natural Health Acad. Healing Arts, Tenafly, NJ, 1992. Diplomate Am. Bd. Naturopathic Physicians, 1997, cert. master herbalist, Dallas; ordained to mininstry Progressive Universal Life Ch., 1998. Assoc. prof. U. Miami, 1974-77, Dade County Jr. Coll., Miami, 1974-77; pvt. practice, N.Y.C., 1990—. Assoc. prof. NYU, 1988-92, Strasberg Theater Inst., N.Y.C., 1988-92, UN Internat. Sch., N.Y.C., 1992-96; star mgr. Nature's Sunshine Products; profl. spkr. in field, 1990—. Author: Simplified Nutritional Handbook, 1996, How to Survive a Nuclear Disaster, 2002; opera singer, 1970—. Founder WINS Found. for the Learning Disabled, 1999—, Price-Mentors.Com, affordable web sites , 2002. Mem. Am. Naturopathic Med. Assn., Internat. and Am. Assn. Clin. Nutritionists, Internat. and Am. Assn. Counselors and Therapists, Nat. Spkrs. Assn. Avocations: botany, cooking, travel. Office: 666 West End Ave Ste 15S New York NY 10025-7357 E-mail: kbpurcell@aol.com.

PURCELL, KENNETH, psychology educator, university dean; b. N.Y.C., Oct. 21, 1928; s. Herman and Ann (Bulkin) P.; m. Claire Dickson Kepler, Dec. 17, 1949 (div. Dec. 1986); children: Kathleen Ann, Andrew Kepler; m. Marjorie Bayes, Jan. 17, 1987. BA, PhD, U. Nebr. Asst. prof. U. Ky., 1956-58; dir. behavior sci. div. Children's Asthma Research Inst.; asst. prof. U. Colo. Med. Center, 1958-68; prof., dir. clin. tng. psychology U. Mass., 1968-69, chmn. dept. psychology, 1969-70; prof. psychology U. Denver, 1970—, dean Coll. Arts and Scis., 1976-84, prof. psychology, 1984—94, prof. emeritus, 1994. Author papers in field. Served to 1st lt. AUS, 1953—56. Fellow Am. Psychol. Assn., Soc. Research Child Devel., AAAS, Colo. Psychol. Assn. (dir. 1962-64) Home: 3254 S Heather Gardens Way Aurora CO 80014-3666 Office: U Denver Coll Arts & Scis Denver CO 80208-0001

PURCELL, KEVIN BROWN, director of special services; b. Longview, Wash., Apr. 17, 1955; s. Wayne Donald and Joyce Elizabeth (Brown) P.; m. Carol Lynn Vincent, Mar. 29, 1980; children: Keelan Kathryn, Kelly Jean. BA, Western Wash. U., 1980; MS, Western Oreg. State Coll., Monmouth, 1986; degree in Ednl. Adminstrn., Portland (Oreg.) State U., 1989. Tchr. multiply handicapped Yamhill County Sch. Dist., McMinnville, Oreg., 1980-83; learning resource tchr. Newberg (Oreg) Sch. Dist., 1983-89, asst. prin., 1989-91; prin. Dayton (Oreg.) Sch. Dist., 1991-97, dir. spl. svcs., 1997-99, Newberg (Oreg.) Sch. Dist., 1999—. Mem. Nat. Assn. Elem. Prins., Assn. Supervision and Curriculum Devel., Oreg. Assn. Elem. Prins., Confedn. Oreg. Sch. Adminstrs. Democrat. Roman Catholic. Avocations: marathon running, skiing, swimming, reading, golf. Home: 2103 Haworth Ave Newberg OR 97132-1330 Office: Newberg Pub Schs 714 E 6th St Newberg OR 97132-3406 E-mail: purcellk@newberg.k12.or.us.

PURCELL, MARY LOUISE GERLINGER, retired educator; b. Thief River Falls, Minn., July 17, 1923; d. Charles and Lajla (Dale) Gerlinger; m. Walter A. Kuyawski, June 9, 1950 (dec. July 1954); children: Amelia Allerton, Joh Allerton; m. Dale Purcell, Aug. 26, 1962. Student, Yankton Coll., 1941-45, Yale Div. Sch., 1949-50, NYU, summer 1949; MA, Columbia U., 1959, EdD, 1963. Teenage program dir. YWCA, New Haven, 1945-52; dir. program in family rels. Earlham Coll., Richmond, Ind., 1959-62, asst. prof. sociology and psychology, 1959-62, conf. coord. undergrad. edn. for women, 1962; chmn. div. home and cmty. Stephens Coll., Columbia, Mo., 1962-73, chmn. family and cmty. studies, 1962-78; dir. Learning Unltd., continuing edn. for women, 1974-78; head dept. family and child devel. Auburn (Ala.) U., 1978-84, prof., 1978-88, chmn. search com. for v.p. acad. affairs, 1984, spl. asst. to v.p. acad. affairs, 1985-86, prof. emerita, 1988—. Developer course The Contemporary Am. Woman, 1962, cons., 1962; vis. prof. Ind. U. Summer Sch., 1970; cons. student personnel svcs. Trenton (N.J.) State Coll., 1958-59, 61. Contbr. articles to coll. bulls., jours. V.p. Falls Village-Canaan Hist. Soc. Alumni fellow Tchrs. Coll. Columbia U., 1959; recipient Alumni Achievement award Yankton Coll., 1975. Mem. AAUW, Am. Home Econs. Assn. (bd. dirs. 1967-69, chair 1st subject matter unit 1969, family rels. and child devel. sect. 1986-89), Groves Conf. on Family, Nat. Coun. Family Rels. (dir., chmn.-elect affiliated couns. 1981-82, chmn. 1982-84, nat. program chmn. 1977, chmn. film awards com., chmn. spl. emphases sect., bd. dirs., Ernest G. Osborne award for excellence in teaching 1979), Housatonic Camera Club (co-pres. 1996-2000), Delta Kappa Gamma. Congregationalist. Home: 120 Belden St Falls Village CT 06031-1124 E-mail: mlgp@discovernet.net.

PURCELL, PATRICK JOSEPH, newspaper publisher; b. N.Y.C., Nov. 9, 1947; s. Patrick Joseph and Sarah (Muller) P.; m. Maureen T. Shuart, Aug. 8, 1970; children: Kathleen, Erin, Patrick, Kerry. BBA, St. John's U., 1969; MBA, Hofstra U., 1977. Various supr. positions N.Y. Daily News, N.Y.C., 1969-80; assoc. pub. Village Voice, 1980-82; v.p. advt. N.Y. Post, 1982-83; v.p. sales and mktg. Skyband Inc., 1983; pres., pub. Boston Herald, 1984—, owner, 1994—; pub. The N.Y. Post, 1986-88; exec. v.p. News Am./Newspapers, 1986-90, pres., 1990-93, CEO, 1993-94; East Coast pres. Am. Ireland Fund, 1996—. Bd. dirs. Bay Bank, MetroWest Sub. Regional Bd., The Genesis Fund. Bd. dirs. NCCJ, Boston, 1984-86, Boy Scouts Am., Boston, 1984-85, Cath. Charitable Bur., Boston, 1984-86, John F. Kennedy Found.; mem. Greater Boston Assn. Retarded Citizens, 1984-86; chmn. Boston Against Drugs, 1988—; mem. White House Conf. for a Drug Free Am., 1987—. Mem. Boston Better Bus. Bur., Am. Newspaper Pub. Assn., New Eng. Newspaper Assn., Boston C. of C. (bd. dirs. 1984-86), Downtown Crossing Assn. (bd. dirs.) Clubs: Publicity, Ad (Boston). Roman Catholic. Avocations: jogging; skiing. Office: Boston Herald PO Box 2096 Boston MA 02106-2096*

PURCELL, PHILIP JAMES, financial services company executive; b. Salt Lake City, Sept. 5, 1943; m. Anne Marie Mc Namara, Apr. 2, 1964. BBA, U. Notre Dame, 1964; M.Sc. in Econs., London Sch. Econs. and Polit. Sci., U. London, 1966; MBA, U. Chgo., 1967. Mng. dir., cons. McKinsey & Co., Inc., Chgo., 1967-78; v.p. planning and adminstrn. Sears, Roebuck and Co., 1978-82; from pres., CEO, to chmn., CEO Dean Witter Discover & Co., N.Y.C., 1982-97; chmn., CEO Morgan Stanley (name changed from Morgan Stanley, Dean Witter & Co. 2002), 1997—. Dir. N.Y. Stock Exch., 1991-96; mem. coun. U. Chgo. Grad. Sch. Bus. Trustee U. Notre Dame. With USNR. Mem. Econ. Club Chgo., Chgo. Club, Links. Roman Catholic. Office: Morgan Stanley/Dean Witter & Co 1585 Broadway Ste 39th New York NY 10036-8200*

PURCELL, ROBERT HARRY, virologist, researcher; b. Keokuk, Iowa, Dec. 19, 1935; s. Edward Harold and Elsie Thelma (Melzl) P.; m. Carol Joan Moody, June 11, 1961; children: David Edward, John Leslie. BA in Chemistry, Okla. State U., 1957; MS Biochemistry, Baylor U., 1960; MD, Duke U., 1962. Intern in pediatrics Duke U. Hosp., Durham, N.C., 1962-63; officer USPHS, 1963; with Epidemic Intelligence Svc., Communicable Disease Ctr. Atlanta; assigned to vaccine br. Nat. Inst. Allergy and Infectious Diseases, Bethesda, Md., 1963-65; sr. surgeon Lab. Infectious Diseases, NIH, 1965-69, med. officer, 1969-72, med. dir., 1972-74, head hepatitis viruses sect., 1974-2001, co-chief, 2001—. Organizer, invited participant, speaker numerous nat. and internat. symposia, confs., workshops, meetings; temporary advisor WHO, 1967—; expert cons. in hepatitis U.S.—China, U.S.—Taiwan, U.S.—Japan, U.S.—Russia, U.S.—India, U.S.—Pakistan Bilateral Sci. Agreements; lectr. various virology classes. Reviewer numerous sci. jours.; contbr. 600 articles to profl. jours., chpts. to books; 20 patents in field. Recipient Superior Svc. award USPHS, 1972, Meritorious Svc. medal USPHS, 1974, Gorgas medal, 1977, Disting. Svc. medal USPHS, 1978, Disting. Alumni award Duke U. Sch. Medicine, 1978, Eppinger prize 5th Internat. FALK Symposium on Virus and Liver, Switzerland, 1979, Medal of City of Turin, Italy, 1983, Gold medal Can. Liver Found., 1984, King Faisal Internat. prize for Medicine, 1998, Rsch. Sci. award Hepatitis Found. Internats., 1999; named to Alumni Hall of Fame East Okla. State Coll., 1996. Fellow AAAS, Washington Acad. Scis., Am. Acad. Microbiology, Molecular Medicine Soc.; mem. Am. Epidemiology Soc., Am. Soc. Microbiology, Am. Soc. Virology, Soc. Epidemiol. Rsch., Infectious Diseases Soc. Am. (Squibb award 1980), N.Y. Acad. Scis., Am. Soc. Clin. Investigation, Assn. Am. Physicians, Am. Coll. Epidemiology, Am. Assn. Study of Liver Diseases (Disting. Achievement award 2000), Internat. Assn. Study and Prevention Virus Associated Cancers, Internat. Assn. Biol. Standardization, Internat. Assn. Study Liver, Soc. Exptl. Biology and Medicine (Disting. Scientist award 1986), Nat. Acad. Scis. (Washington chpt.). Office: NIH Lab Infectious Diseases 50 S Dr Msc 8009 Rm 6523 Bethesda MD 20892-8009 E-mail: rpurcell@niaid.nih.gov.

PURCELL, STEVEN RICHARD, international management consultant, engineer, economist; B of Mech. and Indsl. Engring., NYU Coll. Engring., 1950; MS in Indsl. Engring., Columbia U., 1951; EdM, Harvard U., 1968. Registered profl. engr., Can. Lectr. engring. NYU Coll. Engring., N.Y.C., 1948-50; gen. mgr. Dapol Plastics Co., Inc., Boston, 1956-58; gen. div. mgr. Am. Cyanamid Co., Sanford, Maine, 1958-61; sr. prin., mgmt. cons. investment banking Purcell & Assocs., N.Y.C., 1961-66; prof., chmn. Bristol Coll., Fall River, Mass., 1966-68; assoc. dean grad. faculty adminstrv. studies York U., Toronto, Ont., Can., 1969-71; chief economist Dept. Manpower and Immigration, Ottawa, Can., 1970-71; cons. Treasury Bd., 1971-72; dir. urban and internat. environ. policy Ministry of State for Urban Affairs Internat. Activities, 1973-74; mem. com. on challenges of modern soc. NATO, 1973-74; mem. sci., econ. policy com. OECD UN, 1973-74; prof. Grad. Sch. Bus. Adminstrn. and Econs. Algonquin Coll., 1974-76; advisor, cons. House of Commons, 1976-77; sr. prin. Purcell & Assocs., Internat. Mgmt. Cons., Washington, 1977-80, chmn., CEO, 1981—, Phoenix Internat. Capital Associates, Washington, 1981—; exec. dir. nat. coastal zone mgmt. adv. com. NOAA U.S. Dept. Commerce, 1980-81. Profl. lectr. Northeastern U. Grad. Sch. Bus. Adminstrn., Boston, 1953-56, U. Toronto, 1968-69, George Washington U. Grad. Sch. Bus. Adminstrn., Washington, 1979; vis. prof. Rensselaer Poly. Inst. Advanced Mgmt. Program, 1967, U. Ottawa Grad. Sch. Bus. Adminstrn., 1971-74; lectr. Council for Internat. Progress in Mgmt., N.Y.C., 1960, Royal Bank Can. Mgmt. Assn., Toronto, Ont., 1970; corp. appointment cons. Harvard U., Cambridge, Mass., 1967-68; cons. Govt. Venezuela, 1967-68, Can. Inst. Bankers, Toronto, 1969-70; internat. sr. adviser NASA, 1985-86, mem. nat. adv. bd. Ctr. for Nat. Policy; dir. Rental Resource Corp., 1986-89. Contbr. articles on indsl. orgn., sci. policy and fin. to profl. jours. Lt. AC, USNR, 1943-46. Mem. UN Assn., Soc. for Advancement of Mgmt. (pres. 1949-50, leadership award 1950), Tau Beta Pi, Alpha Pi Mu (v.p. 1949-50), Columbia Univ. Club (Washington, trustee 1982-84, chmn., sr. trustee 1984-85), Harvard Univ. Club. Office: 12904 Mayflower Ln Bowie MD 20720-3368

PURCELL, STUART MCLEOD, III, financial planner; b. Santa Monica, Calif., Feb. 16, 1944; s. Stuart McLeod Jr. and Carol (Howe) P. AA, Santa Monica City Coll., 1964; BS, Calif. State U., Northridge, 1967; grad., CPA Advanced Personal Fin. Planning Curriculum, San Francisco, 1985. CPA, Calif.; CFP. Sr. acct. Pannell Kerr Forster, San Francisco, 1970-73; fin. cons. Purcell Fin. Services, 1973-74, San Rafael, Calif., 1980-81; controller Decimus Corp., San Francisco, 1974-76, Grubb & Ellis Co., Oakland, Calif., 1976-78, Marwais Steel Co., Richmond, 1979-80; owner, fin. counselor Purcell Wealth Mgmt., San Rafael, 1981—. Exec. dir. www.norforprofits.com, 2000--; guest lectr. Golden Gate U., San Francisco, 1985—; leader ednl. workshops, Larkspur, Calif., 1984; speaker Commonwealth Club Calif., 1989, 91. Contbr. articles to newspapers and profl. jours. Treas. Salvation Army, San Rafael-San Anselmo-Fairfax, Calif., 1987—; chmn. fin. planners div. United Way Marin County, Calif., 1984; mem. fundraising com. Marin County March of Dimes, 1987—, Marin County Arthritis Found., 1988—; mem. Marin Estate Planning Council. Served to lt. (j.g.) USNR, 1968-76. Named Eagle Scout, 1959, Best Fin. Advisor Marin County Independent-Jour. newspaper, 1987, Top Producer Unimarc, 1986; recipient Outstanding Achievement award United Way, 1984; named to The Registry of Fin. Planning Practitioners, 1987. Mem. AICPA, Calif. Soc. CPAs, Nat. Speakers Assn., Internat. Assn. for Fin. Planners (exec. dir. North Bay chpt., San Francisco 1984), Internat. Soc. Pre-Retired Planners, Soc. CPA-Fin. Planners (dist. membership chmn. San Francisco 1986), Registry Fin. Planning Practitioners, Sigma Alpha Epsilon. Presbyterian. Avocations: travel, auto racing, skiing, gardening. Home: 45 Vineyard Dr San Rafael CA 94901-1228 Office: Purcell Wealth Mgmt 45 Vineyard Dr San Rafael CA 94901-1228 E-mail: topbuspro@attbi.com.

PURCHASE-OWENS, FRANCENA, human resources specialist, educator; b. Milw., Nov. 14, 1960; d. Johnny and Arlene (Roberts) Purchase. Cert., Mich. Profl. Sch. Modeling, 1980; AA cum laude, Milw. Stratton Coll., 1982; BS in Applied Liberal Studies, Western Mich. U., 1997, M in Ednl. Leadership, 2002. Investment mgmt. sec. M&I Bank, Milw., 1984-85; cons. United Devel. Corp., 1986-88; paraprofessional Grand Rapids (Mich.) Pub. Schs., 1990-92; temp. helper Dayton Hudson Fortune 500, Grand Rapids, Mich., 1990; customer svc. rep. Kent County Conv. and Visitors Bur., 1995; mktg. rschr. Wirthlin Worldwide, 1996-98; pres. Creative Works, 1988—, Francena Purchase Internat. Honor Soc., Kentwood, Mich., 1999—, Francena Purchase Internat. Applied Studies, Kentwood, 1999—, Purchase Bus. Inst., Kentwood, 1999—, Francena Purchase Internat. Applied Profl. Studies Soc., Kentwood, Mich., 2000—; prof. U. Wis. (Big 10 U. Sys.); adminstrv. asst. to Elizabeth Kubler-Ross Ga. State U., 1980. Sec. Mich. Nat. Bank, Grand Rapids, 1980-81, Internat. Mktg. dept. Am. Seating, Grand Rapids, 1980-81, Volt Tech. Svcs. engring. firm, Milw., 1980, sec. to various tep. cos. and positions; asst. exec. sec. Manpower Internat. Inc., Milw., 1982-84; cons. NASW; rschr., sec. United Devel. Corp.; human resource asst., computer programmer, sec. Patricia Stevens Coll., Milw., 1985-86; clerk-typist med. recors Spectrum Health (formerly Blodgett Meml. Med. Ctr.), Grand Rapids, 1979, telemarketer Weathermaster Indsutries, Inc., Milw., 1980; computer programming cons. Nat. Assn. Social Workers, Milw., 1980; office asst. to various cos. Access, Milw., 1980; asst.to pres. Alissia Cosmetics, Miss Black Pageant, 1980; legal sec. to attorney David Clowers, Milw., 1980, student asst. Ga. State U. Gerontology dept., Atlanta, 1980; student asst. Maln office, attendance office Ottawa Hills H.S., Grand Rapids, 1976-77, Fed. Govt. contract divsn., Grand Rapids, 19777-78; cashier Helen Smith's Market, Milw., 1972-73; clerk draft typist Ind. Libr. Life Ins. Co. claims dept., Grand Rapids, 1978-79; grad. asst. candidate Dale Carnegie course in Human Rels and Pub. Speaking; grad. student adv. bd. Western Mich. U., Kalamazoo, 2000; mem. Nat. Honor Soc. Iroquois Mid. Sch., 1974-75, Grand Rapids, Ottawa Hills H.S., 1976-79. Co-editor: Smoke Signal, 1975. Vol. United Way, Grand Rapids, 1990; reading condr. S.E. Neighborhood Assn., Grand Rapids, 1990; mem. literacy coun. Kent County Literacy Coun., Grand Rapids, 1991—, task force Dwelling Pl., Grand Rapids, 1999, First Call Help United Way, Grand Rapids, 1992; model Miss J. Fashion bd. Jacobson's Dept. store, East Grand Rapids Mich., 1979; finalist Miss Black Wis. pageant, Milw., 1981; bd. dirs. Program and Quality Com., Pers. Com., Fin. Com., Consumer Adv. bd., Touchstone innovaré mental health, Grand Rapids, 2000—, Kent County Cmty. Mental Health, 1999—; mem. Task Force Herkimer Apartment Projects, Weston Apartments Dwelling place of Grand Rapids, 1999; reading program asst. S.E. End Neigborhood Assn., Grand Rapids, 1993; rehab. asst. Kent Comty. Hosp. Complex, Grand Rapids, 1991; intake asst. Baxter Comty. Ctr., Grand Rapids, 1989; tutor Kent County Literacy Coun., Grand Rapids, 1988; facilitator trainer Employers Coalition for Healing Racism, Grand Rapids, 1997, Citizens Cirs. Resource Ctr., Grand Rapids, 1998, Ptnrs. in Pub. Edn., Grand Rapids, 1999, United Way Champions Diversity, Grand Rapids, 1999; project help tutor Iroquois Mid. Sch., Grand Rapids, 1975; student tutor Washington Elem., Kalamazoo, 1974; student rep. Bus. Office Edn. Club, 1978-79 (2nd place Extemporaneous Verbal Coms. 1978, 1st place second divsn. 1979, other leadership awards 1978-79); fundraiser Spl. Olympics Office Edn. Assn. Ottawa Hills H.S., 1978. Recipient shorthand awards taking dictation of 140 words per minute Milw. Stratton Coll., 1981-82, Century award typing 100 words per minute Milw. Stratton Coll., 1982, Machine Transcription award secretarial skills contest seventh place Milw. Area Tech. Coll., 1981, shorthand award Ottawa Hills H.S., 1979; Phillip Morris scholar Alverno Coll., 1981; Nontraditional Student grantee Western Mich. U., 1994, 2000, Thurgood Marshall Profl. Tuition grantee; Thurgood Marshall Assistanship scholar Western Mich. U.1989, 1998; 1st place speaker, 3rd place typist and secretarial job application Office Edn. Assn. Extemporaneous Speaking; 6th place with Letter of Recognition from Senator Berger of Wis. Milw. Area Tech. Coll., 1981; Internat. finalist theatre arts, Milw., 1986; noted as jr. achievement Ottawa Hills H.S., 1978, other different honors, awards, recognitions, accomplishments, etc. Mem. Am. Mgmt., Am. Soc. Tng. and Devel., Am. Cancer Soc. ProgramSoc. Human Resource Mgmt. (Superior Merit award), Phi Beta Lambda (sec. 1982), Mich. Jaycee, U.S. C. of C., Jr. Chamber Internat., Jaycess Networking and Leads, Alzheimers Assn., Am. Cancer Soc. Program, Profl. Bus. Leaders (sec.-elect), Profl. Secs. Internat., Office Edn. Assn., Phi Beta Lambda, others. Avocations: modern dancing, reading, tennis. also: PO Box 7421 Grand Rapids MI 49510-7421 Address: PO Box 7421 Grand Rapids MI 49510

PURCIFULL, DAN ELWOOD, plant virologist, educator; b. Woodland, Calif., July 1, 1935; s. Ernest Lee and Virginia (Margaroli) P.; m. Marcia Ann Weatherby, Sept. 7, 1966; children: Scott, Douglas. BS, U. Calif., Davis, 1957, MS, 1959, PhD, 1964. Asst. prof. plant pathology U. Fla., Gainesville, 1964-69, assoc. prof., 1969-75, prof., 1975-99, prof. emeritus, 2000—. Plant virus subcom. Internat. Com. for Taxonomy of Viruses, 1973-75, mem. potyvirus study group, 1987-93; mem. plant virology adv. com. Am. Type Culture Collection, 1993-99; mem. Internat. Legume Virus Working Group, 1999. Assoc. editor Phytopathology, 1971-73, Plant Disease, 1987-89; contbr. articles to profl. jours. Mem. Morningside Nature Center Commn., City of Gainesville, 1978-81, treas., 1981. With U.S. Army, 1957. Fellow AAAS, Am. Phytopathol Soc. (Lee Hutchins award 1981, Ruth Allen award 1992); mem. Fla. State Hort. Soc., N.Y. Acad. Sci., Am. Soc. Virology, U.S. Golf Assn., Nat. Wildlife Fedn., The Nature Conservancy, Sigma Xi, Gamma Sigma Delta. Home: 3106 NW 1st Ave Gainesville FL 32607-2504 E-mail: depurc@aol.com.

PURCIFULL, ROBERT OTIS, insurance company executive; b. Grinnell, Iowa, July 1, 1932; s. Chauncey O. and Mildred E. (Clendenen) P.; m. Mary G. White, Sept. 12, 1953; children: Jane, Robert Otis, Patricia, Elizabeth. BA, Grinnell Coll., 1954. C.L.U. With Occidental Life Ins. Co., Calif., 1960-78, 1st. v.p. charge agys., 1968-71, exec. v.p. sales, 1971-76; pres., chief exec. officer Transmerica Ins. Mgmt., Inc., Los Angeles, 1972-78, Countrywide Life Ins. Co., Los Angeles, 1973-76, dir., 1973-78; chmn. bd., pres. Plaza Ins. Sales Inc., San Francisco; pres., chief exec. officer Occidental Life of Can., 1977-78; pres., chief operating officer, dir. Penn Mut. Life Ins. Co., Phila., 1979-80. Sr. v.p. life divsn. Am. Gen. Corp., 1981-82; pres. Lincoln Am. Life Ins. Co., Am. Gen. Life Ins. Co. Del., Am. Gen. Life Ins. Co. Tex., Am. Amicable Life Ins. Co., Pioneer Am., 1982-84; vice chmn. Pioneer Security Life Ins. Co., 1982-84; pres., CEO Gulf Life Ins. Co., Interstate Fire Co., Jacksonville, Fla.,

1984-88, also dir.; pres. Am. Gen. Group Ins. Co. Fla., 1986-89; vice chmn. Gulf Life Ins. Co., 1988-91; chmn., CEO ROP & Assocs. Past pres. Vols. of Am., LA; trustee Life Underwriters Tng. Coun., Washington, 1975—78; campaign chmn. Jacksonville United Way, 1988, 1989, chmn., 1989—90; pres. Jacksonville U. Coun., 1992, 1993, Jacksonville Symphony Orch., 1993—94; chmn. bus. adv. coun. U. North Fla.; councilman City of Upper Arlington, Ohio, 1962—66; chmn. Conservative Order for Good Govt., San Diego County, Calif., 2001. Mem. Life Ins. Mktg. and Rsch. Assn. (bd. dirs. 1982-85). Home: 12285 Fairway Pointe Row San Diego CA 92128-3230

PURDES, ALICE MARIE, retired adult education educator; b. St. Louis, Jan. 8, 1931; d. Joseph Louis and Angeline Cecilia (Mozier) P. AA, Belleville Area Coll., 1951; BS, Ill. State U., Normal, 1953, MS, 1954; cert., Sorbonne U., Paris, 1964; PhD, Fla. State U., Tallahassee, 1976. Cert. in music edn., elem. edn., secondary edn., adult edn. Tchg. and grad. asst. Ill. State U., 1953-54; music supr. Princeton (Ill.) Pub. Schs., 1954-55; music dir. Venice (Ill.) Pub. Schs., 1955-72, secondary vocal music dir., 1955-72; coord. literacy program Venice-Lincoln Tech. Ctr., 1983-86, chmn. lang. arts dept., 1983-96; ret., 1996. Tchr. in space candidate, 1985. Mem. St. Louis chpt. World Affairs Coun., UN Assn., Nat. Mus. of Women in the Arts, Humane Soc. of Am.; charter mem. St. Louis Sci. Ctr., Harry S. Truman Inst.; contbr. Old Six Mile Mus., 1981, Midland Repertory Players, Alton, Ill., 1991; chair Cystic Fibrosis Spring Bike-A-Thon, Madison, Ill., 1981, Granite City, Ill., 1985. Named to Ill. Sr. Hall of Fame, 2001, Gov's Sr. Hall of Fame, 2001; recipient Gold medal, Nat. Senior Olympics, 1989, Sr. World Games, 1992, Generations of Success Alumni award, Belleville Area Coll., 1998, several scholarships. Mem.: AAUW, Am. Fedn. Tchrs. (pres. 1957—58), Ill. Adult and Continuing Educators Assn., Am. Choral Dirs. Assn., Ill. Music Educators Assn. (Svc. award 2002), Music Educators Nat. Conf., Ill. State U. Alumni Assn., Slavic and East European Friends (life), Fla. State Alumni Assn., Lovejoy Libr. Friends, Nat. Space Soc., Western Cath. Union, Croation Fraternal Union, St. Louis Numis. Assn., Friends St. Louis Art Mus., Archaeol. Inst. Am., Travelers Abroad (pres. 1966—68, 1989—), Madison Rotary Club (internat. amb., Humanitarian award 1975). Roman Catholic. Avocations: bowling, travel. Home: PO Box 274 Madison IL 62060-0274

PURDIE, TONYA MARIE THOMAS, school registrar; b. Dec. 23, 1968; m. Kelly Ryan Purdie, Apr. 23, 1988; children: Cierra S., Mariah S. BA in Bus., Westminster Coll., 1997, MBA, grad. cert. Info. Resource Mgmt., Westminster Coll., 1999. Webmaster, sales assoc. Semi Svc., Inc., Salt Lake City, 2000; registrar ITT Tech. Inst., Murray, Utah, 2001—. Home: 541 Echo Dr Murray UT 84123-5732 Office: ITT Tech Inst 920 W Levoy Dr Murray UT 84123 E-mail: tpurdie@itt-tech.edu.

PURDOM, PAUL WALTON, JR. computer scientist; b. Atlanta, Apr. 5, 1940; s. Paul Walton and Bettie (Miller) P.; m. Donna Armstrong; children: Barbara, Linda, Paul BS, Calif. Inst. Tech., 1961, MS, 1962, PhD, 1966. Asst. prof. computer sci. U. Wis.-Madison, 1965-70, asst. prof., 1970-71; mem. tech. staff Bell Telephone Labs., Naperville, Ill., 1970-71; assoc. prof., chmn. computer sci. dept. Ind. U., Bloomington, 1977-82, prof. computer sci., 1982—. Grant researcher FAW, Ulm, Germany. Author: (with Cynthia Brown) The Analysis of Algorithms; assoc. editor: Computer Surveys; contbr. articles to profl. jours. NSF grantee, 1979, 81, 83, 92, 94. Mem. AAAS, Soc. for Indsl. and Applied Math., Assn. Computing Machinery, Sigma Xi. Democrat. Methodist. Home: 2212 S Belhaven Ct Bloomington IN 47401-6803 Office: Ind U Dept Computer Science 215 Lindley Hall Bloomington IN 47405-4101 Business E-Mail: pwp@cs.indiana.edu.

PURDOM, THOMAS JAMES, lawyer; b. Seymour, Tex., Apr. 7, 1937; s. Thomas Exer and Juanita Florida (Kuykendall) P.; m. Betty Marie Shoemaker, May 31, 1969; 1 son, James Robert. Student, U. Syracuse, 1956-57, U. Md., 1958-59; BA, Tex. Tech. Coll., 1962; JD, Georgetown U., 1966. Bar: Tex. 1966, U.S. Supreme Ct. 1978, U.S. Ct. Appeals (5th cir.) 1983. Ptnr. Griffith & Purdom, Lubbock, Tex., 1966-67; asst. dist. atty. 72d Jud. Dist., 1967-68; county atty. Lubbock County, Tex., 1968-72; pres. Purdom Atchley & Pettiet, Lubbock, 1972—. Mem. com. for Vol. 5 pattern jury charges, 1988-97. Author: West's Texas Forms Vols. 16, 17, 18, 1984-96, Family Law, Texas Practice and Procedure, 1981. Served with USAF, 1956-60. RecipientSam Emison award Tex. Acad. Family Law Specialists, 2000. Fellow Tex. Bar Found.; mem ABA, Lubbock County Bar Assn. (bd. dirs. 1970, Disting. Sr. Lawyer award 2000), State Bar Assn. Tex. (sec. family law sect. 1974-75, chmn. family law sect. 1975-76, mem. examining commn. for family law specialization), Am. Acad. Matrimonial Lawyers (cert. family law, Tex. bd. legal specialization), Tex. Assn. Def. Counsel, Delta Theta Phi. Democrat. Baptist. Home: 3619 55th St Lubbock TX 79413-4713 Office: Purdom Atchley & Pettiet 6307 Indiana Ave Lubbock TX 79413-5713 E-mail: paplaw6307@aol.com.

PURDY, ALAN HARRIS, biomedical engineer; b. Mt. Clemens, Mich., Dec. 13, 1923; s. Harry Martin and Elinor (Harris) P.; m. Anna Elizabeth Sohn, Aug. 16, 1968 (dec.); children: Catherine, Charles, Susan, Harry; m. Margaret Josephine Kelley, Mar. 5, 1997. BSME, U. Miami, 1954; MS in Physiology, UCLA, 1967; PhD in Engring., U. Mo., 1970. Cert. clin. engr., Washington. Project engr. in acoustics Arvin Industries, Columbus, Ind., 1954-56, AC Spark Plug Co., Flint, Mich., 1956-60; asst. prof. engring. Calif. Poly. U., Pomona, 1960-62; assoc. dir. biomed. engring. U. Mo., Columbia, 1967-71; dep. assoc. dir., assoc. dir. Nat. Inst. for Occupational Safety and Health, Rockville, Md., 1971-81, scientist, biomed. engr. Cin., 1983-86; asst. dir. Fla. Inst. Oceanography, St. Petersburg, 1981-83; pres. Alpha Beta R & D Corp., San Marcos, Calif., 1986—. Cons. Smithy Muffler Corp., L.A., 1961-62, Statham Instruments, L.A., 1966; cons. faculty, Tex. Tech. U., Lubbock, 1972-73; lectr. U. Cin., 1980. Patentee in driving, acoustical and occupational safety fields. Pilot CG Aux., 1989-98. With USAF, 1942-43. Nat. Heart Inst. spl. fellow, 1963-67; Fulbright scholar, Yugoslavia, 1984. Mem. Acoustical Soc. Am., Biomed. Engring. Soc., Am. Inst. Physics, Exptl. Aircraft Assn., Aircraft Owners and Pilots Assn., DAV. Democrat. Home and Office: 941 Cycad Dr San Marcos CA 92078-5013 E-mail: ahpurdy@nethere.com.

PURDY, CAROL ANN, psychotherapist, conference coordinator, author; b. Long Beach, Calif., Jan. 5, 1943; d. Melvin Boyce and Kathryn Delia (Wilbur) Slaughter; m. John Allen Purdy, June 8, 1963; children: Laura Beth, Mark Robert, Sarah Ruth. BA, Calif. State U., Long Beach, 1964; MSW, Calif. State U., Sacramento, 1990. Cert. tchr., Calif; lic. clin. social worker. Tchr. Orange (Calif.) Unified Sch. Dist., 1964-67; freelance author, 1977—; social worker Tehama County Mental Health, Red Bluff, Calif., 1989-94; therapist in pvt. practice, 1994-99; conf. coord., play therapy supr. Kid Power Counseling and Tng. Ctr., 1995—, PlayTherapyCentral.com, 1995—. Lectr. in field; founder, trainer Kid Power Program Groups for High Risk Children, Red Bluff, 1989—. Author: Iva Dunnit and the Big Wind, 1985, Least of All, 1987, The Kid Power Program, 1989, Mrs. Merriwether's Musical Cat, 1994, Nesuya's Basket, 1997, Playing with Janet, 1999, Helping Them Heal, 1999. Mem. Assn. for Play Therapy. Avocations: music, gardening, language study, travel. Office: Kid Power 21432 Creekside Dr Red Bluff CA 96080 E-mail: carol@playtherapycentral.com.

PURDY, DENNIS GENE, insurance company executive, education consultant; b. Detroit, June 12, 1946; s. Culver and Tessie (Gillette) P.; m. Ardyce Maxine Wilcox, Aug. 9, 1969; children: Krista Rochelle, Steven Dennis. BS in Edn., Wayne State U., 1969; CLU, Am. Coll., Bryn Mawr, Pa., 1981; ChFC, Am. Coll., 1984. Cert. life underwriter tng. coun. fellow, 1989. Claims adjustor State Farm Ins., Southfield, Mich., 1969-71; pvt. practice Northville, 1971-73; claims rep. Farmers Ins. Co., Southfield, 1973-76, asst. tng. mgr. Aurora, Ill., 1976-78; life tng. mgr. Ohio State Life Ins., Columbus, 1978-80; sales adminstrn. mgr. Farmers Ins. Co., 1980-81, life tng. rep., 1981-86, life mktg. specialist, 1986-94, sr. claims rep., 1994-2000; pvt. practice, 2000—. Continuing edn. coord. for state of Ind., Farmers Ins. Group, Dublin, Ohio, 1990—; mem. pre-lic. adv. bd. State of Ohio, Columbus, 1992, mem. exam. rev. bd., 1992; field faculty mem. Life Underwriters Tng. Coun. Contbr. articles for internal publ., 1980—. Pres. Columbus Barbershop Chorus, 1989-90, v.p., 1991-92. Named Man of Yr. Columbus Barbershop Chorus, 1990. Mem. Nat. Assn. Life Underwriters, Am. Soc. CLUs and ChFCs., Columbus Assn. Life Underwriters. Avocations: music, swimming. Home and Office: 2129 Shirlene Dr Grove City OH 43123-4008

PURDY, DONALD GILBERT, JR. environmental and soil scientist, agronomist; b. St. Louis, Apr. 10, 1953; s. Donald Gilbert Purdy and Nelda Jean Bates Pierce; m. Janice Shirley Bogacki, Aug. 10, 1974; children: Erin Elizabeth, Justin Joseph. BS, U. Mo., 1975; MS, U. Nebr., 1981. Cert. profl. soil scientist/agronomist; registered environ. mgr. Insp. USDA-Agrl. Mktg. Svc., St. Louis, 1975-76; staff rsch. asst. U. Nebr., Lincoln, 1976-78; soil scientist Mo. Dept. Natural Resources, Jefferson City, Mo., 1978-80; project mgr. N. Am. Coal Corp., Dallas, 1980-89; sr. project mgr. SCI Environ. Inc., Chesterfield, Mo., 1989-91; asst. dir. ops. Environ. Mgmt. Corp., Creve Coeur, 1991—; pres. D. G. Purdy & Assocs., Inc., Manchester, 1991—. Contbr. articles to profl. jours. Mem. Am. Soc. Agronomy, Soil Sci. Soc. Am., Profl. Soil Scientist Assn. Tex., Mo. Assn. Profl. Soil Scientists, Am. Geol. Inst. Home: 1617 Woodside View Ln Ballwin MO 63021-5887 Office: D G Purdy & Assocs Inc 14422 Manchester Rd Manchester MO 63011-4045 E-mail: dgpurdy@myexcel.com.

PURDY, JAMES, writer; b. 1923; Ed., Spain. Editor, other positions, Cuba, Mexico. Author: Don't Call Me by My Right Name, 1956; 63, Dream Palace, 1956, 1980, Color of Darkness, 1957, Malcolm, 1959, 1980, paperback, 1987, The Nephew, 1960, , 1980, paperback, 1987, (play) Children is All, 1962, Cabot Wright Begins, 1964, Eustace Chisholm and The Works, 1967, An Oyster is A Wealthy Beast, 1967, Mr. Evening, 1968, Jeremy's Version, 1970, On the Rebound, 1970, (poems) The Running Sun, 1971, Collected Poems, 1990, (novel) I am Elijah Thrush, 1971; Sunshine is an Only Child, 1973, Sleepers in Moon Crowned Valleys, The House of the Solitary Maggot, 1974, Island Avenue, 1997, (play) Foment, 1997, (selected stories) Color of Darkness, Children is All, The Candles of Your Eyes, 1991, (fairy tale) Kitty Blue, 1993 (Eng. edit. The Netherlands); (novel) In a Shallow Grave, 1976; (plays and stories) A Day After the Fair, 1977; (recordings) Eventide, 63; Dream Palace, 1968, 1980; (novels) Narrow Rooms, 1978, Gertrude of Stony Island Avenue, 1998, Foment, 1997; (poetry) I Will Arrest the Bird that has No Light, 1978, Lessons and Complaints, 1978; Sleep Tight, 1978, Proud Flesh, 4 short plays, 1980; (novel) Mourners Below, 1981, The Berry-Picker, 1981, Scrap of Paper, 1981, Dawn, 1985, The Brooklyn Branding Parlors, 1986; (novel) On Glory's Course, 1983, (poems) Don't Let the Snow Fall, 1985, Are You in the Winter Tree?, 1987, (novel) In the Hollow of His Hand, 1986, (collected stories) The Candles of your Eyes, 1987, Garments the Living Wear, 1989, (fiction) Reaching Rose, 1994, (play) Ruthanna Elder, 1989, Moe's Villa & Other Stories, 2000, A Room All to Itself, 2002, Moe's Villa and Other Stories, 2002; subject of book: James Purdy (Stephen D. Adams), 1976, Collected Poems, 1990, (plays) In The Night of Time and Four Other Plays, 1992, A Day After the Fair, 1993, (novel) Out With The Stars, 1992, In the Night of Time and Four Other Plays, 1992, (plays) Foment, 1994, Brice, 1994, Where Quentin Goes, 1994, Gertrude of Stony Island Avenue, 1998 (novel), (play) Foment, 1998; intro. to Weymouth Sands (by John Cowper POWYS); contbr. article to Life Mag., 1965. Recipient Morton Dauwen Zabel Fiction award Am. Acad. Arts and Letters, 1993, Oscar Williams and Gene Durwood award for poetry and art, 1995; subject of The Not-Right House, Essays on the Books of James Purdy (Bettina Schwarzschild), 1969-70. Address: 236 Henry St Brooklyn NY 11201-4280

PURDY, JAMES AARON, medical physics educator; b. Tyler, Tex., July 16, 1941; s. Walter Bethel and Florence (Hardy) P.; m. Marilyn Janette Coers, Jan. 29, 1965; children: Katherine, Laura. BS, Lamar U., 1967; MA, U. Tex., 1968, PhD, 1971. Asst. rsch. scientist U. Tex., Austin, 1969-71; rsch. asst. M.D. Anderson Hosp. and Tumor Inst., Houston, 1968-69, fellow in med. physics, 1972-73; instr. physics Sch. of Medicine, Washington U., St. Louis, 1973-76, asst. prof., 1976-79, assoc. prof., 1976-83, chief physics sect., 1976—, prof., 1983—, assoc. dir. Radiation Oncology Ctr., 1987—. Mem. NIH Radiaton Study sect. Divsn. Rsch. Grantes, 1991-95; Landauer lectr., Oakland, Calif., 1991. Editor: Three Dimensional Treatment Planning, 1991, Advances in Radiation Oncology, 1992, 3D Radiation Treatment Planning and Conformal Radiation Therapy, 1995, A Practical Guide to 3D Planning and Conformal Radiation Therapy, 1999, 3-D Conformal and Intensity Modulated Radiation Therapy: Physics and Clinical Applications, 2001; sr. physics editor: Jour. Radiation Oncology, Biology, and Physics, 1996—. With USMC, 1961-64. Recipient William D. Coolidge award, 1997. Fellow Am. Assn. Physicists in Medicine (pres. 1985, Coolidge award 1997), Am. Coll. Radiology (ACR Gold Medal 2002), Am. Coll. Med. Physics (chmn. bd. chancellors 1990, Marvin M.D. Williams award 1996); mem. Am. Inst. Physics, Am. Bd. Med. Physics (vice chmn. 1988-92), Am. Bd. Radiology, Am. Soc. Therapeutic Radiology and Oncology (ASTRO Gold medal 2000). Methodist. Avocation: travel. Home: 1452 Lost Hollow Ct Chesterfield MO 63005-4423 Office: Washington Univ Sch of Medicine 660 S Euclid Ave Campus Box 8224 Saint Louis MO 63110-1093

PURDY, JEFFREY ELLISON, civil engineer; b. Haverford, Pa., June 13, 1956; s. Thomas E. and Carol (Bartlett) P.; m. Deborah Mitchell, Oct. 11, 1980; children: Laura, Adrienne. BSCE, Case Western Res. U., 1978; MS in Civil/Transp. Engring., U. Va., 1980. Registered profl. engr., Va., Pa., Md., Del. Engr. JHK & Assocs., Alexandria, Va., 1980-82, UTDC, Arlington, 1982-83; sr. assoc. Booz Allen & Hamilton, Phila., 1983-89; dir. transp. engring. Urban Engrs., Inc., 1989-92; mgr. IVHS programs Ebasco Infrastructure, 1992—95; sr. v.p. Edwards and Kelcey Inc., West Chester, Pa., 1995—; also bd. dirs. Contbr. articles to profl. jours. Mem. Sch. Bd., Germantown Friends Sch., Phila. Mem. ASCE, Inst. Transp. Engrs., Transp. Rsch. Bd. Office: Edwards and Kelcey Inc 1247 Ward Ave West Chester PA 19380

PURDY, JOHN EDGAR, manufacturing company executive; b. Detroit, June 17, 1919; s. William Everett and May Adeline (Fountain) P.; m. Elizabeth Anne Van Dyne; 1 child, Vannessa Anne. Grad. h.s., Mich. Founder, chmn. Dayton (Ohio) Showcase Co., 1947-87; pres. P-38 Nat. Assn., ret., 1987—. Capt. USAF, 1942-46. Decorated DFC with 2 oak leaf clusters, Purple Heart, Air medal with 6 oak leaf clusters. Mem. Am. Fighter Aces Assn. (pres. 1983-84), Am. Fighter Aces Mus. Found. (chmn. 1984-91), Nat. Aviation Hall of Fame (trustee 1978-86), Nat. Aviation Hall of Fame (bd. dirs. bd. of nominations), P-38 Nat. Assn. (pres. 1999-2001), Internat. Fighter Pilots Mus. Found. (trustee 1999—). Avocations: golf, aviation historian. Home: 6441 Far Hills Ave Dayton OH 45459-2725

PURDY, KEVIN MOORE, estate planner; b. Escondido, Calif., Jan. 26, 1952; s. Kenneth C. and Helen M. (Moore) P.; m. Janice M. Cook, May 12, 1982. BA in Philosophy, Psychology, U. Redlands, 1974. CFP. Pres. Timeline Pub., San Diego, 1980-90; estate planner Sagemark Cons., 1990—. Pub. speaker; digital artist. Author: A Brief History of the Earth and Mankind, 1986, A Brief History of Mankind, 1987. Fundraiser San Diego Hist. Soc., 1993-94. Avocations: photography, music, travel, investment analysis. Office: Sagemark Cons 4275 Executive Sq Ste 400 La Jolla CA 92037-9197 E-mail: kpurdy@home.com.

PURDY, LESLIE, community college president; b. Downey, Calif., Aug. 18, 1943; d. Hubert C. and Janice M. (Harker) Noble; m. Ralph Purdy, Aug. 23, 1969; children: Christopher Hugh, George Colin. BA cum laude, Occidental Coll., L.A., 1965; MAT, Oberlin (Ohio) Coll., 1966; EdD, UCLA, 1973. Tchr. Parma (Ohio) Sr. H.S., 1966; ombudsman/instr. social sci. Raymond Coll., U. of Pacific, Stockton, Calif., 1967-69; coord. spl. svcs. ERIC Clearinghouse for C.C.'s, L.A., 1970-74; sr. instrnl. designer Coastline C.C., Fountain Valley, Calif., 1974-84, adminstrv. dean, 1984-94, pres., 1994—. Bd. dirs. Intelecom, Pasadena, Calif.; bd. dirs., pres. Instrnl. Telecom. Coun., Washington, 1987-94; adv. bd. PBS "Going the Distance" program, Washington, 1993-96; cons. 94; adv. bd. PBS "Going the Distance" program, Washington, 1993-96; cons. Commn. on Innovation, Calif. Colls. Chancellor's Office, 1993-94. Editor: Reaching New Students Through New Technologies, 1983; instrnl. designer Psychology: The Study of Human Behavior, 1989 (Emmy 1990); exec. prodr. (telecourses): Universe: The Infinite Frontier, 1994 (Emmy 1994), Time to Grow, 1992 (Emmy 1992); contbr. articles to profl. jours. Mem. Orange County Forum, 1994—, Ctr. for Studies of Media and Values, L.A., 1990-95, Bread for the World, Washington, 1980—; bd. mem. West County Family YMCA, 1993-2000; bd. mem. Garden Grove Renaissance Found., 1998—; bd. mem. Orange County Nat. Conf. of Cmty. and Justice, 1997—, Orange County Workforce Investment Bd., 2000—; mem. adv. bd. Calif. C.C. Satellite Network, 2001-02. Recipient Emmy awards Am. Acad. TV Arts and Scis., 1987, 90, 92,. 95, Western Region award Instrn. Telecom. Coun., 1995; named one of Women of Distinction City of Garden Grove, 2001. Mem. Assn. of Calif. C.C. Adminstrs., Assn. Ednl. Comms. and Tech., Am. Assn. of Women in C.C.'s, UCLA Alumni Assn. (Doctoral Award in Edn. 1973). Presbyterian. Avocations: backpacking, gardening, conservation, choral singing. Office: Coastline Cmty Coll Office of Pres 11460 Warner Ave Fountain Valley CA 92708 E-mail: lpurdy@cccd.edu.

PURDY, TEDDY GEORGE, JR. programmer, analyst, researcher, consultant; b. Leadville, Colo., May 11, 1954; s. Teddy George and Geneva Ruth Purdy; m. Karen Ann Puleo, May 28, 1977 (div. Dec. 19, 1983); children: Christopher, Sarah. Student, Colo. U., 1972-75. Free-lance programmer/analyst, Boulder, Colo., 1975-84; pres., treas. IBEX Bus. Systems, Leadville, 1984—. Cons. Carlson Promotions, Mpls., 1987-91, Unidata, Inc., Denver, 1992, Household Fin., Chesapeake, Va., 1992—, Focus Tech., Dallas, 1992-98. Avocations: geology, biking, hiking, books, music.

PURÉ, ELLEN, biomedical researcher, educator; b. N.Y.C., Mar. 18, 1957; d. Joseph and Alicia Puré. AB, Washington U., St. Louis, 1977; PhD, U. Tex., Dallas, 1981. Postdoctoral fellow Rockefeller U., N.Y.C., 1982-84, asst. prof., 1984-92; assoc. prof. Wistar Inst., Phila., 1992-97, prof., 1998—; assoc. prof. U. Pa., 1992—98, prof., 1999—; dir. office acad. rev. Ludwig Inst. for Cancer Rsch., N.Y.C., 1997—. Sci. adv. com. Cancer Rsch. Inst., N.Y.C., 1984-2001, assoc. dir., 2002—; rev. coms. NIH, Bethesda, Md., 1991—. Mem. editl. bd. Jour. Exptl. Medicine, 1984-97, Jour. Immunology, 1994-97, Jour. Immunologic Methods, 1995—. Mem. Am. Assn. Immunology (membership com. 1982—). Office: Wistar Inst 3601 Spruce St Philadelphia PA 19104

PURI, ISHWAR KANWAR, engineering educator, researcher; b. New Delhi, Feb. 25, 1959; came to U.S., 1982; s. Krishan K. and Sushilla Puri; m. Beth R. Levinson, July 15, 1989; children: Shivesh, Sunil, Krishan. BSME, U. Delhi, 1982; MS in Engring. Sci., U. Calif., San Diego, 1984, PhD in Engring. Sci., 1987. Postdoctoral rsch. engr. U. Calif., San Diego, 1987-89, asst. rsch. engr., 1989-90; vis. asst. prof. U. Ill., Chgo., 1990-91, from asst. prof. to assoc. prof., 1991-94, prof., 1999—, dir. grad. studies, 1994-97, 99-00, dir. student transatlantic exch. program, 2000—, assoc. dean for rsch. and grad. studies, 2000-01, exec. assoc. dean engring., 2001—, dir. Ctr. Internat. Edn. and Rsch., 2001—. Disting. guest Inst. Energy Tech. Swiss Fed. Inst. Tech., Zurich, 1998, 99. Editor: Environmental Implications of Combustion Processes, 1993, Advanced Thermodynamics Engineering, 2001; contbr. articles to profl. jours. Fellow Stanford U. Ctr. Turbulence Rsch., 1992; Rsch. grantee NSF, NASA, U.S. Dept. Edn., Gas Rsch. Inst., EPA, DOE. Fellow ASME, AAAS (Environ. fellow 1993), AIAA (mem. terrestrial energy sources com. 1999—), Combustion Inst. Fax: 312-413-0447.

PURI, MADAN LAL, mathematics educator; b. Sialkot, Feb. 20, 1929; came to U.S., 1957, naturalized, 1973; s. Ganesh Das and S. W. P.; m. Uma Kapur, Aug. 24, 1962; 3 children. BA, Punjab U., India, 1948, MA, 1950, D.Sc., 1975; PhD, U. Calif. at Berkeley, 1962. Head dept. math. D.A.V. Coll., Punjab U., 1955-57; instr. U. Colo., 1957-58; teaching asst., research asst., jr. research statistician U. Calif. at Berkeley, 1958-62; asst. prof., asso. prof. math. Courant Inst., N.Y. U., 1962-68; vis. asso. prof. U. N.C., summers 1966-67; prof. math. Ind. U., Bloomington, 1968—. Guest prof. stats. U. Gottingen, West Germany, 1972, Alexander von Humboldt guest prof., 1974-75; guest prof. U. Dortmund, West Germany, 1972, Technische Hochschule Aachen, West Germany, 1973, U. Goteborg, Chalmers U. Tech., both Sweden, 1974; vis. prof. U. Auckland, N.Z., 1977, U. Calif., Irvine, 1978, U. Wash., Seattle, 1978-79, U. Bern (Switzerland), 1982, Va. Poly. Inst., 1988; disting. visitor London Sch. Econs. and Polit. Sci., 1991; vis. prof. U. Göttingen, Germany, 1991, June-July 1992; rsch. fellow Katholieke U., Nijmegen, The Netherlands, 1992; vis. prof. U. Des Scis. et Tech. de Lille, France, 1994, U. Basel, Switzerland, 1995—, U. New South Wales, Australia, 1996; vis. univ. fellow Australian Nat. U., Canberra, Australia, 1999; guest prof. U. Konstanz, Germany, 2000, U. Gottingen, 2001. Co-author: Non Parametric Methods in Multivariate Analysis, 1971, Non Parametric Methods in General Linear Models, 1985. Editor Statochastic Process and Related Topics, 1975, Statistical Inference and Related Topics, 1975, Non Parametric Techniques in Statistical Inference, 1970; co-editor: Nonparametric Statistical Inference, Vols. I and II, 1982, New Perspectives in Theoretical and Applied Statistics, 1987, Mathematical Statistics and Probability Theory, Vol. A, 1987, Statistical Sciences and Data Analysis, 1993, Recent Advances in Statistics and Probability, 1994, Asymptotics in Statistics and Probability, 2000. Recipient Sr. U.S. Scientist award, Humboldt Preis, 1974-75, 83, 2001, Rsch. award Humboldt Found., U. Göttingen, 2001. Fellow Royal Statis. Soc., Inst. Math. Statistics, Am. Statis. Assn.; mem. Math. Assn. Am., Internat. Statis. Inst., Bernoulli Soc. Math. Stats. and Probability. Office: Ind U Dept Math Rawles Hall Bloomington IN 47405

PURI, RAJENDRA KUMAR, business and tax specialist, consultant; b. Hoshiarpur, Punjab, India, Dec. 22, 1932; came to the U.S., 1965, naturalized, 1969; s. Harbans Lal and Satya Vati (Jerath) P.; children: Neena, Veena, Ram. BS, Agra U., 1952; diploma in Russian lang. and lit., U. Dehli, 1958; BA, U. Wash., 1968, MBA, 1969; MS in Taxation, Golden Gate U., 1982. Customs officer Govt. of India, New Delhi, 1955-60; asst. treas. Merc. Bank Ltd., 1960-65; mem. staff Peat, Marwick, Mitchell & Co., CPAs, Seattle, 1969-70; state examiner State of Wash., 1970-72, asst. supervising state examiner, 1972-74, supervising state examiner, 1974-77; sr. internal auditor Lockheed Corp., Sunnyvale, Calif., 1977-79; sci. programming analyst Lockheed Missile and Space Co., 1979-80, data processing specialist, 1980-84, sci. programming specialist, 1984-88; chief acct. Tex. Dept. Health, Austin, 1989-90; dir. internal audit, internal auditor Tex. Workers' Compensation Commn., 1990-95; bus. and tax cons., 1976—. Del. Wash. State Rep. Conv., 1976, Snohomish County Rep. Conv., 1976; Rep. nominee for state auditor, Wash., 1976; spl. advisor U.S. Congl. Adv. Bd., 1982-83. Mem. AICPA. Home: 2608 Hunlac Cove Round Rock TX 78681-7107 E-mail: rkpi_2000@yahoo.com.

PURI, RUCHIR, operations research specialist; b. Kanpur, India, Oct. 18, 1966; s. Desh Mitra and Uma P.; m. Rajshree Mehrotra, Nov. 11, 1994; children: Puri, Isha. BS in Engring., Regional Engring. Coll., Kurukshetra, India, 1988; MTech in Electrical Engring., Indian Inst. Tech., Kanpur, 1990; PhD in Electrical Engring., U. Calgary, Alb., Canada, 1994. Mem. sci. staff Bell-Northern Rsch., Ottawa, Ont., Canada, 1994-95; rsch. staff mem. IBM TJ Watson Rsch. Ctr., Yorktown Heights, N.Y., 1995—. Adj. asst. prof. Columbia U., N.Y.C., 2000—. Contbr. articles to profl. jours., chpts. to books; patentee in field. Mem. IEEE (Best Paper Citation of Synthesis award 1996, with ACM Design Automation fellowship award 1993, tech. program com. mem. internat. conf. on computer design 2000—). Office: IBM TJ Watson Rsch Ctr Rte 134 Yorktown Heights NY 10598-1846 Office Fax: 914-945-4469.

PURI, VINAY, pediatric neurologist; b. Chandigarh, India, June 12, 1969; came to U.S., 1990; s. Ved Mitter and Vinay Puri; m. Beth Puri, Oct. 10, 1998. MD, Kasturba Med. Coll., Manipal, India, 1989. Bd. cert. in pediat. and adult neurology. Resident in pediats. Henry Ford Hosp., Detroit, 1990-92; fellow in pediat. neurology Washington U., St. Louis, 1992—95; dir. pediat. neurology, mem. exec. bd. Kosair Children's Hosp., Louisville, 1996—. Assoc. prof. pediats. and neurology U. Louisville, 1997—. Fellow Child Neurology Soc., Am. Acad. Neurology. Office: Louisville Neurology Assocs 250 E Liberty St Ste 202 Louisville KY 40202-1534

PURIFICACION, DENNIS, secondary school educator, theologian; b. Manila, Philippines, July 24, 1974; , naturalized, 1987; s. Jaime and Evelyn. BA in Theology & Philos., U. of San Francisco, 1995; student, Pontifical Inst. for Marriage & Family, 1996; MA in Theology, The Cath. U. of Am., 1997; student, McGeorge Sch. of Law, 1998, U. of San Francisco, 1999—. Cert. Basic Catechist Cert. Diocese of Sacramento, 1999, Emergency Substitute Credential Vallejo Unified, 2001. Theology tchr. Chaminade Coll. Prep. Mid. Sch., Chatsworth, Calif., 1997—98, St. Patrick-St. Vincent H.S., Vallejo, 1998—. Adult adv. youth activities commn. City of Vallejo, Vallejo, 2001—; uniformed instr., advancement officer USN Sea Cadet Officer Corps (USN-SCC), Vallejo, 2001—02; catechist St. John's & St. Catherine's, Milpitas & Vallejo, Calif.; co-founder, vice chmn. youth acad. Pilipinos Engaged in the Appreciation of Cultural Edn., Vallejo, 1999—2001. Author: Hell's Captured Files YOU! Mag., 1994—99; actor: (plays) , 2002; commentator KDIA Radio, 2000—01. Mem. Chastity Task Force for No. Calif., Danville, Calif., Internat. Anti-Euthanasia Task Force, San Francisco; dep. dir. Bush-Keyes 2000, Provto, 2000; candidate Calif. State Senate, 2001—02; chmn. Calif. for Keyes for Pres. 2000, Los Gatos , Calif., 1999—2000; altar boy various Cath. Ch.;

bd. dir. Life Abortion Alternative Min., Vallejo. Lt. USNR, 1988—92. Recipient Mil. Excellence medals, Am. Legion, 1990, 1992. Mem.: Cath. League for Religious & Civil Rights, Acad. for Polit. Sci., Assn. for Supr. & Curriculum Devel., Filipino-Am. Educators Assn. of Calif., Fellowship of Cath. Scholars, Am. Cath. Philos. Assn. (assoc.), Alpha Sigma Nu, Phi Delta Kappa. Roman Catholic. Avocations: Karate, walking, travel, reading, friends. Home: 2902 Redwood Pkwy 31 Vallejo CA 94591 Home Fax: 707-647-1582. Personal E-mail: MrDennisP@aol.com .

PURINTON, MARJEAN D. English language educator, researcher; b. Tulsa, Nov. 14, 1953; d. Robert James and Neva Jean (Warren) P. BA English, U. Tulsa, 1975; MA English, U. Okla., 1977; PhD English, Tex. A&M U., 1991. Cert. secondary edn. instr., supr., adminstr. Instr. Caddo Magnet High Sch., Shreveport, 1980-86; teaching asst. Tex. A&M U., 1986-91, post-doctoral fellow, 1992; asst. prof. Westfield (Mass.) State Coll., 1992-95; assoc. prof. Tex. Tech. U., 1995—, mem. women's studies coun., grad. studies com., asst. prof., 1995-98, assoc. prof., 1998—, assoc. chair Eng. dept., 2002—, chair exec. coun. tchg. acad., 2002—. Advisor grad. studies English dept. Westfield State Coll.; rsch. assoc. Five Coll. Women's Studies Rsch. Ctr. Mt. Holyoke Coll., South Hadley, Mass., 1993-94; chair grad. studies com. Westfield State Coll; mem. grad. coun., women's studies group, sr. awards com. English Dept. Westfield State Coll.; libr. dir. search com. Westfield State Coll.; chmn. interdisciplinary studies in humanities session South Ctrl. Modern Lang. Assn., 1992-93; grad. student rep. Tex. A&M U., 1989-91, tester internat. students' English proficiency exams, Tex. A&M U., 1989-91; instrnl. cons. Ctr. for Teaching Excellence, Tex. A&M U., 1992; mem. exec. coun. Tex. Tech. U. Tchg. Acad. Author: Romantic Ideology Unmasked, 1994; contbr. articles to profl. jours. NEH grantee 1993, 2001, SCMLA grantee 1991; named U.S. Disting. Tchr., 1986; listed La. PTA Dist. Tchr. Svc. Memberscroll for Notable Leadership, 1985. Mem. MLA, NEA, South Ctrl. MLA, Byron Soc., Coll. English Assn., So. Ctrl. Soc. 18th Century Studies, Advancement of Women in Higher Edn. (chair steering com. for all univ. conf.), Keats-Shelley Assn., Phi Kappa Phi, Alpha Epsilon Lambda, Omicron Delta Kappa. Democrat. Anglican. Avocations: swimming, tennis, travel, bicycling, theatre. Office: Tex Tech U Dept English PO Box 3091 Lubbock TX 79452-3091 E-mail: mpurinto@ttacs.ttu.edu.

PURIS, MARTIN FORD, advertising agency executive; b. Chgo., Feb. 22, 1939; s. Martin and Virginia Lee (Farmer) Puris; m. Mary M. Herrmann; children: Kimberly Mayo, Jason Patterson, Mary Elizabeth. Student, DePauw U., 1961. With Campbell-Ewald Co., N.Y.C., 1962-64, Young & Rubicam, Inc., N.Y.C., 1964-66; v.p. Carl Ally, Inc., 1966-74; pres., CEO Ammirati & Puris, Inc., 1974-94; chmn., ceo, chief creative officer Ammirati, Puris, Lintas, 1995—99. Media advisor Pres. George Bush; dir. IPG Group, 1995—99; vice chmn. Sheltering Arms; mng. dir. New Things Investment Group. Author: Comeback: How Seven Straight-Shooting CEO's Turned Around Troubled Companies, 1999. Recipient awards Art Dir. Club, Copy Club, N.Y.C., Cannes Film Festival. Mem.: Devon Yacht Club, Union Club, Am. Yacht Club, Nantucket Yacht Club, N.Y. Yacht Club. Republican. Roman Catholic. Avocations: sailing, tennis, show jumping, hunting. Office: New Things LLC 35 W 35th St New York NY 10001

PURITZ, JOHN C. music educator; b. Coram, Ny, Apr. 9, 1970; s. Marc Steven Puritz and Francine Goldstein; m. Tricia J. Puritz, June 28, 1997; children: Sofia B. BA, Manhattanville Coll., Purchase, NY, 1993; MA, Sacred Heart U., Fairfield, CT, 2002. Cert. Teacher CT. Dir. of music Green Chimneys Children Svc., Brewster, NY, 1995—95; dir. of instrumental music Rippowam Magnet Mid., Stamford, Conn., 1995—99, Westhill H.S., Stamford, 1999—. Musician in one recording. Recipient Sporlight Tchr. Award, Stamford Bd. of Edn., 2002. Avocation: performing musician. Office: Westhill High School 125 Roxbury Road Stamford CT 06902 Personal E-mail: jpuritz@hotmail.com.

PURK, JANICE KAY, sociology and gerontology educator; b. Akron, Ohio, Aug. 26, 1950; d. Kenneth Louis and Helen Ruth Rech; m. James Dean Purk, May 13, 1973; children: Lee Ann Purk Steindl, Heather K. BS in Home Econs., Kent State U., 1972, MA in Family and Consumer Studies, 1990, PhD in Med. Sociology, 2000. Lic. social worker, Ohio; cert. in family and consumer studies. Tchr. home econs. Elyria (Ohio) City Schs., 1977; vocat. rehab. home economist Lorain County Bd. Mental Retardation, Elyria, 1977-79; adult protective social worker Lorain County Human Svcs., 1979-86; rehab. social worker Cmty. Health Ptnrs., Lorain, Ohio, 1986—; asst. prof. sociology and gerontology, coord. gerontology State U. West Ga., 2002—. Adj. prof. family and consumer studies Kent (Ohio) State U., 1992-95; adj. prof. sociology Lorain County C.C., 1993, 96-97, 99, mem. adv. vd., 1993-95; coord. Gerontology cmty. com. WWG; paper presenter in field to convs. and convs., 1991—. Contbr. articles to profl. jours., including Rehab. Nursing, Families in Society. Mem. bd. Lorain County Sr. Assessment, Elyria, Ohio, 1994—98, Lorain County Linking Employment, Awareness and Potentials for Disabled; vol. Ohio Reads Program; leader Lorain County Parkinson's Support Group; mem. Care-Net Ga. Mem. Am. Sociol. Assn., Nat. Coun. on Family Rels., Am. Assn. Family and Consumer Sci., Ga. Family and Consumer Sci. Assn., Fairfield Women's Assn., Delta Kappa Gamma. Lutheran. Avocations: swimming, handicrafts. Home: 9120 Tarnwood Dr Villa Rica GA 30180 Office: Univ Ga Carrollton GA E-mail: jpurk@excite.com.

PURKERSON, MABEL LOUISE, physician, physiologist, educator; b. Goldville, S.C., Apr. 3, 1931; d. James Clifton and Louise (Smith) P. AB, Erskine Coll., 1951; MD, U. S.C., Charleston, 1956. Diplomate Am. Bd. Pediat. Instr. pediat. Washington U. Sch. Medicine, St. Louis, 1961-67, instr. medicine, 1966-67, asst. prof. pediat., 1967-98, asst. prof. medicine, 1967-76, assoc. prof. medicine, 1976-89, prof., 1989-98, prof. emerita, 1998—, assoc. dean curriculum, 1976-94, assoc. dean acad. projects, 1994-98. Cons. in field. Editl. bd. Am. Jour. Kidney Diseases, 1981-87; contbr. articles to profl. jours. Mem. bd. counselors Erskine Coll., 1971-87; trustee St. Louis Symphony Orch., Erskine Coll., 2000—. USPHS spl. fellow, 1971-72. Mem. Am. Heart Assn. Coun. on the Kidney (exec. com. 1973-81), Am. Physiol. Soc., Am. Soc. Nephrology, Internat. Soc. Nephrology, Ctrl. Soc. Clin. Rsch., Am. Soc. Renal Biochemistry and Metabolism, Explorer's Club, Sigma Xi (chpt. sec. 1974-76). Home: 20 Haven View Dr Saint Louis MO 63141-7902 Office: Bernard Becker Med Libr Renal Div Dept PO Box 8132 Saint Louis MO 63110-1093 E-mail: purkerm@msnotes.wustl.edu.

PURKEY, THOMAS EUGENE, social worker; b. Dallas, Jan. 14, 1969; s. Walter Ross and Elizabeth (Kenner) Purkey. BA, Austin Coll., 1991; MA in Soc. Svcs. Adminstrn., U. Chgo., 1993. Campus mgr. Comtys. in Schs., Dallas, Inc., 1993-96, sr. program coord., 1996-97, network adminstr., 1996-97, United Way of Met. Dallas, 1997—. Recipient Arrow of Light, Boy Scouts of Am., Dallas, 1979, Eagle Scout, 1982. Mem. Nat. Assn. Social Workers, Nat. Eagle Scout Assn. Democrat. Methodist. Avocations: flying, boating, stamp collecting, computers. Home: 7210 Clemson Dr Dallas TX 75214-1719 Office: United Way of Met Dallas 901 Ross Ave Dallas TX 75202-1998

PURL, O. THOMAS, retired electronics company executive; b. East St. Louis, Ill., June 5, 1924; s. Ruthford Keith and Muriel Agnes (Thompson) P.; m. Martha Elaine Smalley, Feb. 21, 1948; children— Thomas Keith, Jeanne Marie Purl Elder. BS, U. Ill., 1948, BS, 1951, MS, 1952, PhD, 1955. Head high-power traveling wave tube sect., mem. tech. staff Hughes Research Lab., Culver City, Calif., 1955-58; sect. head, dept. mgr., group v.p., v.p. shareholder relations and planning coordination Watkins-Johnson Co., Palo Alto, 1958-86. Contbr. articles to profl. jours.; patentee in field. Chmn. career guidance com. Santa Clara Valley Joint Engring. Council, 1971-73; bd. dirs. Jr. Achievement of Santa Clara County, 1975-79. Served to 1st lt. USAAF, 1943-46. Fellow IEEE (chmn. Santa Clara Valley subsect. 1972); mem. Sigma Xi, Eta Kappa Nu, Phi Kappa Phi, Sigma Tau. Clubs: Commonwealth of Calif. Home: 466 La Mesa Dr Portola Valley CA 94028

PURMELL, ANN, children's writer, school presenter, inspirational speaker; b. Ann Arbor, Mich., Nov. 15, 1953; d. Burton George McGarry II and Helen Van Winkle McGarry; m. Bruce Hilary Purmell, July 6, 1974; children: Hilary Ann children: Michael McGarry. BSN cum laude, Ea. Mich. U., 1979. Sales clk. B. McGarry , Ann Arbor, 1965—77; pediat. psychiat. nurse Yorkwoods Ctr., Ypsilanti Regional Psychiat. Facility, 1979—86; geriatric sunstance abuse nurse Chelsea Cmty. Hosp., 1990—94; freelance writer Jackson Citizen Patriot Newspaper and Jackson Mag., 1999—2000. Author: (children's picture book) Apple Cider Making Days, 2002, (poem) In Other Words: An American Poetry Anthology, 1998, (writing contest) Woman's Day Magazine, 2001. Vol. Jr. League , Jackson, 1993—94. Episcopalian. Avocation: reading. Personal E-mail: annpurmell@mindspring.com.

PURMORT, AUDREY J. accountant, financial consultant; b. Jan. 12, 1975; d. Charles III and Barbara Loudon Purmort. BS, Butler U., 1997. CPA, Ill. Teller Van Wert Nat. Bank, 1990-93; librarian asst. Butler Sci. Libr., Indpls., 1993-97; actuarial asst. Allstate Ins. Co., Northbrook, Ill., 1995-97; auditor Arthur Andersen LLP, Chgo., 1997—2002; sr. fin. cons. Anthem Inc., Indpls., 2002—. Vol. Butler U. Into the Sts., Indpls., 1993—97, Chgo. Pub. Schs., 1998—2000, United Way, 1997. Edgar C. Seitz Sr. and Mabel B. Seitz Meml. scholar, 1996; grantee Pi Beta Phi Found., 1997. Mem. AICPA, Ill. CPA Soc., Inst. Mgmt. Accts. (scholar 1996). Avocations: running, volunteering, reading, travel. Office: Anthem Inc 120 Monument Cir M3SF Indianapolis IN 46204

PURNELL, CHARLES GILES, lawyer; b. Aug. 16, 1921; s. Charles Stewart and Ginevra (Locke) P.; m. Jane Carter; children: Mimi, Sarah Elizabeth, Charles H., John W. Student, Rice Inst., 1938-39; BA, U. Tex., 1941; student, Harvard Bus. Sch., 1942; LLB, Yale U., 1947. Bar: Tex. 1948. Ptnr. Locke, Purnell, Boren, Laney & Neely, Dallas, 1947-89, Locke, Purnell, Rain & Harrell, Dallas, 1989-90, of counsel, 1990-99, Locke, Liddell & Sapp, Dallas, 1999—. Exec. asst. to Gov. of Tex., Austin, 1973-75. Bd. dirs. Trinity River Authority of Tex., 1975-81; vice chmn. Tex. Energy Adv. Council, 1974. Served to lt. U.S. Navy, 1942-45; PTO. Mem. ABA, Tex. Bar Assn., Tex. Bar Found, Yale Club, Dallas Country Club, Dallas Petroleum Club, La Jolla (Calif.) Beach and Tennis Club. Episcopalian. Home: 1 Saint Laurent Pl Dallas TX 75225-8128 Office: Locke Lidell & Sapp 2200 Ross Ave Ste 2200 Dallas TX 75201-6776

PURNELL, MAURICE EUGENE, JR. lawyer; b. Dallas, Feb. 17, 1940; s. Maurice Eugene Sr. and Marjorie (Maillot) P.; m. Diane Blake, Aug. 19, 1966; children: Maurice Eugene III, Blake Maillot. BA, Washington and Lee U., 1961; MBA, U. Pa., 1963; LLB, So. Meth. U., 1966. Bar: Tex. 1966. Ptnr. Locke, Purnell, Boren, Laney & Neely, Dallas, 1966-87; shareholder Locke Purnell Rain Harrell PC, 1987-99; ptnr. Locke Liddell & Sapp LLP, 1999—. Bd. dirs. Leggett & Platt, Inc. Bd. dirs. Dallas Summer Musicals. Mem. ABA, Tex. Bar Assn., Tex. Bar Found., Dallas Bar Assn. Am. Judicature Soc., Dallas C. of C, Brook Hollow Golf Club. Home: 4409 S Versailles Ave Dallas TX 75205-3044 Office: Locke Liddell & Sapp LLP 2200 Ross Ave Ste 2200 Dallas TX 75201-6776

PURNELL, OLIVER JAMES, III, judge; b. Richmond, Va., Jan. 18, 1949; s. Oliver James Jr. and Margaret Helen (Hodges) P.; m. Cheryl Naomi Williams, June 30, 1973; children: Oliver James IV, Amy Susan. AA, U. Hartford, 1969; AB, Middlebury Coll., 1972; MSLS, Case Western Res. U., 1976; JD, Western New England Sch. Law, 1982. Bar: Conn. 1982, U.S. Dist. Ct. Conn. 1982. Dir., pharmacy libr. U. Conn. Sch. Pharmacy, Storrs, Conn., 1977-81; assoc. Lavitt, Hutchinson & Kaplan, Vernon, 1981-84, DuBeau & Ryan, Vernon, 1984-87, Howard, Kohn Sprague & Fitzgerald, Hartford, 1987-89; pvt. practice Vernon, 1989-92; reference libr. U. Conn. Sch. Law, Hartford, 1992-98; regional info. mgr. Lexis-Nexis, Vernon, 1998-99; judge Ellington Dist. Probate Ct., 1999—. Contbr. articles to profl. jours. Scoutmaster Boy Scouts of Am., Rockville, Conn., 1990—; trustee Rockville (Conn.) Pub. Libr.; corporator Ea. Conn. Health Network; mem. U. Hartford Alumni Coun. Recipient Eagle Scout award Boy Scouts of Am., 1964. Mem. Am. Assn. Law Libraries, So. New England Law Libr. Assn. (pres. 1998-99), Conn. Bar Assn. (pres. coun. of bar 1995-96), Tolland County Bar Assn. (pres. 1995-96), Nat. Coll. Probate Judges, Masonic Lodge, A.F. & A.M. (master Fayette Lodge 1970). Avocations: skiing, camping, hiking, church organist. Office: 6 Forestview Dr Vernon Rockville CT 06066-4807 E-mail: jpurnell3@att.net.

PURPURA, DOMINICK P. dean, neuroscientist; b. N.Y.C., Apr. 2, 1927; m. Florence Williams, 1948; children: Craig, Kent, Keith, Allyson AB, Columbia U., 1949; MD, Harvard U., 1953. Intern Presbyn Hosp., N.Y.C., 1953-54; asst. resident in neurology Neurol. Inst., 1954-55; Prof., chmn. dept. anatomy Albert Einstein Coll. Medicine, Yeshiva U., 1967-74, sci. dir. Kennedy Ctr., 1969-72, dir. Kennedy Ctr., 1972-82, prof., chmn. dept. neurosci., 1974-82, dean, 1984—. Stanford U., Calif., 1982-84. Mem. neurophysiol. panel Internat. Brain Rsch. Orgn., pres. 1987-98; v.p. med. affairs UNESCO, 1961—; chmn. internat. congress com. Internat. Brain Rsch. Orgn./World Found. Neuroscientists, 1983—. Mem. editorial bd. Brain Rsch., 1965-2000, editor-in-chief, 1975-2000; editor-in-chief Brain Rsch. Revs., 1975-2000, Developmental Brain Rsch., 1981-2000, Molecular Brain Rsch., 1985-2000, Cognitive Brain Rsch., 1991-2000. Served with USAAF, 1945-47 Fellow N.Y. Acad. Scis.; mem. Inst. Medicine of Nat. Acad. Scis., Nat. Acad. Scis., Am. Acad. Neurology, Am. Assn. Anatomists, Am. Assn. Neurol. Surgeons, Am. Epilepsy Soc., Am. Physiol. Soc., Assn. Research in Nervous and Mental Disease, Soc. Neurosci., Sigma Xi Office: Yeshiva U Albert Einstein Coll Medicine 1300 Morris Park Ave Bronx NY 10461-1926

PURPURA, PETER JOSEPH, museum curator, exhibition designer; b. Bklyn., Nov. 29, 1939; s. Salvatore and Vincenza (Scozzari) P. B in Indsl. Design, Pratt Inst., 1962. Package designer Walter Dorwin Teague Assocs., N.Y.C., 1961-65; exhibit designer Will Burtin, Inc., 1965-69; sr. exhibits designer Corning Glass Works, N.Y., 1969-71; assoc. exhibits dir. Met. Mus. Art, N.Y.C., 1971-72; exhibits dir. Mus. Sci., Boston, 1972-74; curator, dir. Explorers Hall, Nat. Geographic Soc., Washington, 1974-82; pres. Purpura & Kisner Inc., N.Y.C., 1983—. Vis. design instr. Cornell U., 1971; lectr. Parsons Sch. Design, 1988, Phila. U. for Arts, 1992, 93, 94, 95, 96; exhibn. design mgr. Forbes Mag., N.Y., 1996-2000. Recipient Gold medal award Internat. Film and TV Festival of N.Y., 1973, Edison award for excellence GE, 1985. Mem. Indsl. Designers Soc. Am. (v.p. Mid Atlantic chpt. 1978); Am. Assn. Museums. Office: Purpura & Kisner PMB # 144B 521 Logan Ave Laredo TX 78040-6633 E-mail: gpkisner@yahoo.com.

PURRENHAGE, CHARLES BRUCE, writer; b. Detroit, Oct. 21, 1946; s. William Edward Purrenhage and Margaret Dickson; m. Sandra Jean Postacchini, Dec. 21, 1973; 1 child Jennifer Lyn. BS, St. Joseph's Coll., Phila., 1968. Mng. editor, books Fgn. Policy Rsch. Inst., Phila., 1975—83; mng. editor Soc. Mag., New Brunswick, NJ, 1983—84; manuscript editor Princeton (N.J.) U. Press, 1984—85; freelance manuscript editor Sparta, 1985—99; writer, 2000—. Radioman 3d class USN, 1969—73, Pacific. Recipient Pan Am. medal, Pan Am. Assn. Phila., 1968; fellow Fulbright, U.S. Govt., Ecuador, 1968. Mem.: Mid. Atlantic Coun. L.Am. Studies, L.Am. Studies Assn., Am. Birding Assn. Home: 23 Lakeview Rd Sparta NJ 07871

PURRONE, SCOTT, physician assistant; b. Plainfield, N.J., Jan. 8, 1971; s. Robert Anthony and Christine (Leonard) P.; m. Samantha Louise Johnstone, Mar. 7, 1998. AA in Biol. Sci., Hillsborough C.C., 1991; BS in Physician Asst. Studies, Nova Southeastern U., 1996; MPAS, U. Nebr., 2002. Cert. Nat. Commn. on Certification of Physician Assts. Emergency dept. technician St. Joseph's Hosp., Tampa, Fla., 1991-94, 95-96, hyberbaric chamber attendant, 1993-94; physician asst. urgent care FirstCare Med. Treatment, Bradenton, 1996; physician asst. Family Medicine, Family Care, Lutz, 1996-98; physician asst. emergency medicine The Emergency Assocs. for Medicine/TEAM, Tampa, 1997-2000, Coastal Physician Svcs., Inc., Pompano Beach, Fla., 1999-2000, EMSA/InPhynet/TEAM, Ft. Lauderdale, 1999-2000, Fla. Emergency Physicians, Orlando, 1999—; physician asst. occupl. medicine Citibank Health Svcs., Brandon, 2000. Cons. State of Fla., Tallahassee; clin. asst. prof. physician asst. scis. Nova Southeastern U., 1999—. Fellow Fla. Acad. Physician Assts. (area rep. West Cent. Region 1996-98, asst. area rep. West Cen. Region 1998-2001, chair comm. com. 1998-2000), Am. Acad. Physician Assts., Soc. Emergency Medicine Physician Assts. (Marinelli scholar 1994, SEMPA scholar 1996); mem. So. Med. Assn. (assoc.). Roman Catholic. Avocations: skiing, computers, traveling. Office: PO Box 903 Oakland FL 34760 E-mail: pascott@pol.net.

PURSE, CHARLES ROE, real estate investment banker; b. Redhill, Surrey, Eng., May 19, 1960; came to U.S., 1960. s. James Nathanial II and Rolande Marie-Louise (Redon) P.; m. Carole Lynn Sadler, July 5, 1986; children: Hayley Elizabeth, Cameron James, Andrew Lang. BA, Dartmouth Coll., 1982; MBA, Northwestern U., 1985. Account officer Northern Trust Bank, Chgo., 1982-85; asst. v.p. Citicorp Real Estate, Inc., 1985-88; v.p. Citibank, Ltd., Sydney, Australia, 1988-91, Citibank Realty Investment Advisors, N.Y.C., 1991-94; sr. v.p. The Yarmouth Group, 1994-96; mng. dir. DRA Advisors, Inc., 1996-2000; dir. Real Estate Pvt. Fund Group, Credit Suisse First Boston, NYC, 2000—. Active alumni bd. Western Res. Acad., Hudson, Ohio. Mem. Pension Real Estate Assn., The Country Club (Cleve.), Cromer Golf Club (Sydney, Australia), The Hillsboro Club (Hillsboro Beach, Fla.), Fox Meadow Tennis Club (Scarsdale, N.Y.), Belle Haven Club. Republican. Avocations: golf, photography, skiing, tennis. Office: Credit Suisse First Boston 13th Fl Eleven Madison Ave New York NY 10010 E-mail: charles.r.purse@csfb.com.

PURSELL, CARROLL WIRTH, history educator; b. Visalia, Calif., Sept. 4, 1932; s. Carroll Wirth and Ruth Irene (Crowell) P.; m. Joan Young, Jan. 28, 1956 (dec. 1985); children: Rebecca Elizabeth, Matthew Carroll; m. Angela Woollacott, Dec. 20, 1986. BA, U. Calif., Berkeley, 1956, PhD, 1962; MA, U. Del., 1958. Asst. prof. history Case Inst. Tech., Cleve., 1963-65; asst. prof. U. Calif., Santa Barbara, 1965-69, asso. prof., 1969-76, prof., 1976-88; Adeline Barry Davee Disting. prof. history Case Western Res. U., Cleve., 1988—, chair history dept., 1998—. Mellon prof. Lehigh U., Bethlehem, Pa., 1974-76; vis. research scholar Smithsonian Instn., 1970 Author: Early Stationary Stem Engines in America, 1969, Military Industrial Complex, 1972, From Conservation to Ecology, 1973, White Heat, 1994, The Machine in America, 1995, American Technology, 2001. Fellow: AAAS; mem.: Am. Hist. Assn., Orgn. Am. Historians, Soc. History of Tech. (pres. 1990—92, pres. internat. com.for history of tech. 1998—2001, Leonardo da Vinci medal 1991), Phi Beta Kappa. Democrat. Office: Case Western Res U Dept History 11201 Euclid Ave Cleveland OH 44106-1717

PURSELL, CLEO WILBURN, church official; b. Ft. Worth, Feb. 16, 1918; d. Charles P. and Eltrie Lee (Tice) Dalton; m. Paul Edgar Pursell, Feb. 16, 1939 (dec. 1973). Grad. high sch. Ordained to ministry Nat. Assn. Free Will Bapts., 1939. Asst. pastor various chs., Okla., 1939-57. Pres. Okla. State Aux., First Okla. and First Mission Dists.; officer Calif. State Aux., 1960; 2nd v.p., youth chmn. Woman's Nat. Aux. Conv. 1946-48, 52-55, nat. study chmn., 1955-57, exec. sec.-treas., Nashville, 1963-85. Author: Missionary Education of Our Youth, 1955, Woman's Auxiliary Manual, 1965, Triumph Over Suffering, 1982, Death and Dying, 1982, Anne, You're Super, 1990; columnist: Words for Women Contact Mag., 1966-70; editor Co-Laborer, 1963-85, (newsletter) The Minister's Wife, 1965-94; contbr. articles to profl. jours. Prominent in youth work, Okla., 1939-57; tchr. dist. and state Sunday Sch. workshops. Mem. Women's Fellowship Federated Women's Missionary Socs. (treas. Bristow, Okla., 1955). Home: 60 Lester Ave Apt 749 Nashville TN 37210-4275

PURSER, DONALD JOSEPH, lawyer; b. Chgo., Apr. 21, 1954; s. Donald Cornelius and Mary Alice (Fashingbauer) P.; m. Ludmila Purser. BS, U. Utah, 1975; MS, Reid Coll., 1976; JD, George Mason U., 1980; postdoctoral, Georgetown U., 1981. Bar: Va. 1980, U.S. Tax Ct. 1980, U.S. Ct. Appeals (4th and 10th cirs.) 1980, Utah 1981, U.S. Supreme Ct, 1987; Nat. Bd. Trial Advocacy. Spl. agt. U.S. Dept. of State, Washington, 1976-80; law clk. to judge U.S. Dist. Ct., Alexandria, Va., 1980-81; assoc. Richards, Brandt, Miller & Nelson, Salt Lake City, 1981-83; sole practice, 1983-85; ptnr. Fowler & Purser, 1985-87, Purser & Edwards LLC, Salt Lake City, 1987—; owner Advent Wealth Strategies Group LLC. Judge pro tem Salt Lake County Cir. Ct., 1981-85; adj. faculty U. Phoenix, Salt Lake City, 1984—; advance staff office of v.p. of U.S., Washington, 1986; bd. dirs. Ameralex Risk Retention Group Chgo., Am. Western Life Ins. Co., Tarzana, Calif.; chmn. Rep. Congl. Dist. Utah. Active fin. com. Snelgrove for Congress campaign, 1988. Maj. JAGC, USAR. Mem. ABA (litigation sect., torts and ins. practice sect.), Am. Bd. Trial Advocates, Am. Inn of Ct. II (barrister), Phi Delta Theta, Delta Theta Pi. Clubs: Blue Goose (Salt Lake City), Utah Elephant. Lodges: K.C. Republican. Roman Catholic. Avocations: skiing, stock market, reading, Aikido. Home: 3054 Kennedy Dr Salt Lake City UT 84108-2123 E-mail: purserlaw@aol.com.

PURSEY, DEREK LINDSAY, physics educator; b. Glasgow, Scotland, Oct. 22, 1927; came to U.S., 1964; s. Henry Edwin and Margaret Martin (Lindsay) P.; m. Barbara Ann Parker, Aug. 4, 1962; 1 child, John BS, U. Glasgow, 1948, PhD, 1952. Asst. lectr. theoretical physics King's Coll., London, 1951-54; lectr. math. physics U. Edinburgh, Scotland, 1954-59; vis. lectr. UCLA, 1959-60; mem. sch. math. Inst. for Advanced Studies, Princeton, 1960-61; lectr. in theoretical physics U. Glasgow, Scotland, 1961-64; vis. prof. Iowa State U., Ames, 1964-65, prof. physics, 1965-93, emeritus prof. physics, 1993—. Vis. prof. UCLA, 1979-80. Contbr. articles to profl. jours. Fellow Royal Soc. Edinburgh, Am. Phys. Soc.; mem. AAAS, Presbyn. Assn. on Sci., Tech. and Christian Faith (sec.-treas. 1998-2002, pres. 2002—), Sigma Xi. Democrat. Presbyterian. Avocations: church-related activities, photography, music, reading, wilderness camping. E-mail: dlpursey@home.com.

PURSGLOVE, BETTY MERLE, computer software quality assurance tester; b. Pitts., Sept. 15, 1923; d. Earle E. and Merle A. (Smith) Baer; m. Larry A. Pursglove, June 30, 1944; children: Diana, Kathleen, Merry, Tanya, Yvonne. BS in Physics, U. Pitts., 1944; postgrad., Minn. U., 1945-47, Carnegie-Mellon U., 1947-49, W.Va. U., 1949-51, Mich. State U., 1968-69. Micro-pilot plant operator Minn. Mining and Mfg., St. Paul, 1944-46; cons. rsch. chemist Food Mach Co., Pitts., 1947-49; computer coder Dow Chem. Co., Midland, Mich., 1954; asst. entomologist pvt. collections, 1955-56; instr. chemistry Cen. Mich. U., 1958; head chem. dept. Midland Hosp., 1958-64; tchr. chemistry and physics parochial schs., Bay City, Mich., 1964; prin., chief exec. officer Crypticlear, Inc., Applegate, Oreg., 1965—2002. Leader Midland troup Girl Scout U.S., 1953-63. Mem. AAUW, Sigma Xi, Sigma Pi Sigma. Avocations: creative writing, performing in marching and concert bands, photography, genealogy, gardening. Home and Office: PO Box 3125 Applegate OR 97530-3125

PURSLEY, CAROL ROBERTS, admissions director; b. Montgomery, Ala., Dec. 11, 1965; d. Robert Edwin and Phyllis (Roberts) P. BA, Hartwick Coll., 1988; MEd, Boston U., 1995. Mktg. asst. Christie's, N.Y.C., 1990-95; mktg. assoc. United Distillers, Stamford, Conn., 1995-97; coord. spl. svcs., counselor St. Luke's Sch., New Canaan, 1997-99, dir. admissions, 1999—. Mem. ASCD, ACA. Roman Catholic. Avocations: running/racing, hiking, travel, mountain biking, baking. Home: Apt 1 51 Forest Ave Old Greenwich CT 06870-1510 E-mail: carolpursley@msn.com.

PURSLEY, MICHAEL BADER, electrical engineering educator, communications systems research and consulting; b. Winchester, Ind., Aug. 10, 1945; s. Bader E. and Evelyn L. (Bennett) P.; m. Lou Ann Hinchman, July 6, 1968; 1 child, Jessica Ann. BS, Purdue U., 1967, MS, 1968; PhD, U. So. Calif., 1974. Mem. tech. staff Hughes Aircraft Co., Los Angeles, 1967; engr. Northrop Co., Hawthorne, Calif., 1968; staff engr. Hughes Aircraft Co., Los Angeles, 1968-74; acting asst. prof. UCLA, 1974; asst. prof., then assoc. prof. elec. engring. U. Ill., Urbana, 1974-80, prof., 1980-93; Holcombe prof. elec. and computer engring. Clemson (S.C.) U., 1992—; assoc. Ctr. Advanced Study, 1980-81; vis. prof. UCLA, 1985; cons. U.S. Army, Huntsville, Ala., 1977, Ft. Monmouth, N.J., 1983-86, 91, ITT, Ft. Wayne, Ind., 1979—; pres. SIGCOM, Inc., 1986-90; prin. scientist Techno-Scis. Inc., 1990-96. Contbr. chpts. to books. Recipient Fred W. Ellersick award Comms. Soc., 1996, Tech. Achievement award Mil. Comm. Conf., 1999. Fellow IEEE (pres. info. theory group 1983, Centennial medal 1984, Millennium medal 2000); mem. Inst. Math. Stats. Office: Clemson U 303 Fluor Daniel Bldg Dept ECE Clemson SC 29634

PURSLEY, RICKY ANTHONY, communications analyst; b. Wareham, Mass., July 11, 1954; s. Gene Everett and Evelyn May (Silveira) P.; m. Susan Elizabeth Scott, Nov. 27, 1982 (div.); children: Carinda Elizabeth, Julia Rayner, Rianna Susan; m. Barbara Joan Lundblad, June 22, 2002. BA in Polit. Sci., Boston U., 1976; postgrad., Southwestern U., 1976-78. Notary public, D.C., 1991—. Law librarian Graham & James, Los Angeles, 1977-79; legal copy editor Arnold & Porter, Washington, 1980-85; rsch. libr., info. svcs. mgr. Fisher Wayland Cooper Leader & Zaragoza LLP, 1985-2000, law libr., 1985-97, accounts mgr., 1990; comms. analyst Shaw Pittman Potts & Trowbridge, 2000—. Jury commr. Circuit Ct. of Arlington County and City of Falls Church, Va., 1993. Bd. deacons Little Falls Presbyn. Ch., Arlington, Va., 1995-97, elder, mem. session, 1998—, clk. session, 1998—; mem. Nottingham Elem. Sch. PTA Capital Improvement Plan adv. com., 1995-98, legis. coord., 1996—; mem. Arlington, Va. Pub. Schs. Vocat., Career and Adult Edn. adv. com., 1996-2000, adv. coun. on Sch. Facilities and Capital Programs,

1996-2002. Named one of Outstanding Young Men in Am. U.S. Jaycees, 1978. Mem.: Am. Soc. Notaries, Law Librs.' Soc. Washington, Am. Assn. Law Librs. Democrat. Presbyterian. Avocations: music, writing, carpentry. Home: 2704 N Sycamore St Arlington VA 22207-1132 Office: 2300 N St NW Washington DC 20037-1128

PURSLEY-CROTTEAU, M. SUZANNE, psychiatric nurse, substance abuse professional; b. Augusta, Ga., Oct. 18, 1949; d. Norman B. and Florence M. (Morris) Pursley; m. Gary D. Crotteau, Aug. 24, 1985; 1 child, Elizabeth Ann. BSN, Med. Coll. Ga., 1977, MSN, 1981, PhD, 1995. RN Ga., cert. addiction snurse, adult psychiat. clin. nurse specialist. Psychiat. clin. nurse, asst. chief nurse, clin. specialist drug and alcohol Eisenhower Army Med. Ctr., Ft. Gordon, Ga., 1981-86, instr., 1984, 85, 86; dir. adolescent psychiat. substance abuse program Charter Hosp. Augusta, 1986-87; charge nurse chem. dependency unit, adminstrv. supr. Augusta Regional Med. Ctr., 1990-94; asst. prof. comty. health nursing Med. Coll. Ga., 1995-97, asst prof. mental health, psychiat. nursing, 1997-2000, assoc. prof., 2000-01; chief human subjects protection, reg. compliance and quality U.S. Army, Ft. Detrick, Md., 2001—. Instr. Augusta Coll., 1983, Med. Coll. Ga., Augusta, 1989-90, U. S.C., Aiken, 1991-94; cons. to chief U.S. Army Nurse Corps, Washington, 1986; cons. chem. dependency nurse liaison program Humana Hosp., Augusta, 1990-92; cons. staff devel. Behavioral Health Ctr., Univ. Hosp., Augusta, 1990-91. Maj. U.S. Army Res. Nurse Corps, 1979-86. E-mail: suzanne.pursley-crotteau@amedd.army.mil.

PURTLE, JEFFERY ALLAN, music educator; b. Bakersfield, Calif., Dec. 29, 1967; s. Mason Howard and Gertrude Mary Purtle; m. Mary Allye B. Gresham, Oct. 17, 1998. BMus, Calif. State U., Northridge, 1996. Pvt. practice, L.A., 1986—97, Greenville, SC, 1997—; owner First Call Entertainment, 1997—; prof. trumpet Clemson (S.C.) U., 1998—. Brass coach, pers. mgr. Greenville County Youth Orch., 1998—. Mem.: Internat. Tuba Euphonium, Internat. Trombone Assn., Internat. Trumpet Guild, Music Tchr. Nat. Assn., S.C. Assn. Christian Schs., S.C. Band Dirs. Assn., Am. Radio Relay League, Internat. Honor Soc. Republican. Presbyterian. Avocations: amateur radio, bicycling. Home: 30R Sweetbriar Rd Greenville SC 29615 Fax: 864-244-7376. E-mail: jeff@purtle.com.

PURTLE, JOHN INGRAM, lawyer, former state supreme court justice; b. Enola, Ark., Sept. 7, 1923; s. John Wesley and Edna Gertrude (Ingram) P.; m. Marian Ruth White, Dec. 31, 1951 (dec. 1995); children: Jeffrey, Lisa K.; m. Phyllis Kelly Purtle. Student, U. Central Ark., 1946-47; LLB, U. Ark., Fayetteville, 1950. Bar: Ark. 1950, U.S. Dist. Ct. (ea. dist.) Ark. 1950. Pvt. practice, Conway, Ark., 1950-53, Little Rock, 1953-78; mem. Ark. State Legislature, 1951-52, 69-70; assoc. justice Ark. Supreme Ct., 1979-90; ret. N000, Little Rock, 1990; pvt. practice, 1990—. Tchr., deacon Baptist Ch. Served with U.S. Army, 1940-45. Mem. ABA, Ark. Bar Assn., Am. Judicature Soc., Ark. Jud. Council. Democrat.

PURVES, SHERRILL J. neurologist; b. Montreal, Que., Can., July 2, 1946; d. John J. Swift and Gwen L. Woodburn; m. G. Barrie Purves, June 1, 1971; children: Erica, Carla, Alissa. BSc, McGill U., Montreal, 1967; MD, U. B.C., Vancouver, 1971, PhD in Physiology, 1976. Bd. cert. neurology. Neurologist, clin. assoc. prof., dir. epilepsy program U. B.C., Vancouver, 1983-92; neurologist Ctr. for Neuroscis. and Orthopedics, Sioux City, Iowa, 1992-95, 97—, MINCEP Epilepsy Care, Mpls., 1995-97. Adv. bd. mem. Epilepsy B.C., 1985-92; chmn. Can. Bd. Registered EEG Technologists, Can., 1987-91; lectr. Family Practice Residency, Sioux City, 1997—. Author: Treatment of Epilepsy, 1988; reviewer AAN Practice Parameters, 1995—. Bd. mem., fundraiser Sioux City Art Ctr., 1993—; educator Woodbury Med. Sioux City Alliance, 1997—; bd. mem., advisor Siouxland Mental Health Ctr., Sioux City, 1998—. Fellow Am. Acad. Neurology; mem. Am. Assn. Clin. Neurophysiology, Am. Epilepsy Soc., Can. Neurol. Assn., Can. Assn. Clin. Neurophysiology, Western EEG Soc. (past pres. 1988-89), Alpha Omega Alpha. Office: Ctr for Neuroscis Orthopedics and Spine 375 Sioux Point Rd Dakota Dunes SD 57049

PURVES, WILLIAM KIRKWOOD, biologist, educator; b. Sacramento, Oct. 28, 1934; s. William Kirkwood and Dorothy (Brandenburger) P.; m. Jean McCauley, June 9, 1959; 1 son, David William. BS, Calif. Inst. Tech., 1956; MS, Yale U., 1957, PhD, 1959. NSF postdoctoral fellow U. Tubingen, Fed. Republic Germany, 1959-60; Nat. Cancer Inst. postdoctoral fellow UCLA, 1960-61; asst. prof. botany U. Calif., Santa Barbara, 1961-65, assoc. prof. biochemistry, 1965-70, prof. biology, 1970-73, chmn. dept. biol. scis., 1972-73; prof. biology, head biol. sci. group U. Conn., Storrs, 1973-77; Stuart Mudd prof. biology Harvey Mudd Coll., Claremont, Calif., 1977-95, prof. emeritus, 1996—, chmn. dept. biol., 1985-95, chmn. dept. computer sci., 1985-90; adj. prof. plant physiology U. Calif., Riverside, 1979-85. V.p., sci. dir. The Mona Group LLC, 1996—. Author: Life, the Science of Biology, 1983, 6th edit., 2001. NSF sr. postdoctoral fellow U. London, 1967, Harvard U., 1968; vis. fellow computer sci. Yale U., 1983-84; vis. scholar Northwestern U., 1991; NSF rsch. grantee, 1962-83, 97-2001. Fellow AAAS; mem. Sigma Xi. Office: The Mona Group LLC 2817 N Mountain Ave Claremont CA 91711-1550 Fax: 909-626-7030. E-mail: bill_purves@hmc.edu.

PURVEZ, AKHTAR, otolaryngologist, anesthesiologist, pain management specialist, researcher; b. Srinagar, India, Apr. 1, 1958; s. Muzaffar Aazim and Padshah (Jan) Mir; m. Mudhasir Bashir; children: Ana Mir, Sama Mir. MB, BS, Govt. Med. Coll., Srinagar, India, 1981, M of Surgery with honors, 1986. Intern in surgery, ENT, medicine Govt. Med. Coll. Associated Hosps., Srinagar, 1981—82, resident house surgeon ENT, 1982—83, asst. surgeon ENT, 1983—84, postgrad. scholar ENT, 1984—86, registrar ENT, asst. surgeon, 1986—87; registrar ENT dept. otorhinolaryngology Hosp. Govt. Med. Coll., 1987—89. Fellow Internat. Coll. Surgeons; mem. AAAS, Assn. Otolaryngologists India, Internat. Anesthesia Rsch. Soc., Soc. for Cardiovasc., Pediatric and Ambulatory Anesthesia. Avocations: literature, mountaineering, riding, charities. Home: 1963 Arbor Ct Charlottesville VA 22911 E-mail: apurvez@hotmail.com.

PURVIS, GEORGE FRANK, JR. life insurance company executive; b. Rayville, La., Nov. 22, 1914; s. George Frank and Ann Mamie (Womble) P.; m. Virginia Winston Wendt, May 16, 1942; children: Virginia Reese (Mrs. William H. Freshwater), Winston Wendt, George Frank III. AA, Kemper Mil. Sch., 1932; LLB, La. State U., 1935; DHL (hon.), LLD (hon.), U. Southwestern La., 1997; DHL (hon.), U. S.W. La., 1997. Bar: La. 1935. Sole practice, Rayville, 1935-37; atty. Office Sec. State State of La., Baton Rouge, 1937-41, also dep. ins. commr., 1945-49; atty. La. Ins. Dept., also spl. asst. to atty. gen., 1937-41; with Pan-Am. Life Ins. Co., New Orleans, 1949—, exec. v.p., 1962-64, pres., chief exec. officer, 1964—, chmn. bd., 1969—, also bd. dirs. Pres., bd. dirs. Compania de Seguros Panamericana, S.Am.; pres. Pan-Am. de Colombia Compania de Seguros de Vida, S.A.; chmn., bd. govs. Internat. Ins. Seminars, Inc., 1984—; mem. Industry Sector Adv. Com. for Trade Policy Matters, 1986; lectr. ins. law Tulane U., New Orleans, 1949-56; bd. dirs. 1st Nat. Bank Commerce in New ORleans, Republic Airlines, Inc., 1st Commerce Corp., So. Airlines-Republic Airlines, Pan Am de Mex. Cos. de Seguros Sobre la Vida, S.A., 1964-88; dir. Northwest Airlines, 1986-87. Compiler, author: Louisiana Insurance Code, 1948; contbr. articles to profl. jours. Chmn. big donors com. New Orleans Christmas Seal Campaign, 1961, gen. campaign chmn., 1962, chmn. profl. group VIII, 1963; vice chmn. New Orleans United Fund campaign, 1965, gen. chmn., 1967; pres. Tb Assn. Greater New Orleans, 1967, La. State U. Found., 1967, YMCA, New Orleans, 1968—, Internat. House, 1977, Met. Area Com., 1979; geog. chmn. U.S. Savs. Bond Campaign, Greater New Orleans, 1971; mem. Bd. City Park Commrs., 1965-79, mem. bd. commrs. Port of New Orleans, 1979—, pres. bd. commrs., 1982; chmn. S.S. Huebner Found. Ins. Edn., 1977—, Bus. Task Force on Edn., Inc., 1980—; mem. adv. bd. Bapt. Hosp., 1985—, Salvation Army, 1986—; bd. dirs. Family Svc. Soc. New Orleans, Council for a Better La., New Orleans Philharm. Symphony Soc., Summer Pop Concerts, Bur. Govt. Rsch. New Orleans; mem. Govs. Cost Control Commn., 1981-89; trustee Greater New Orleans Found., 1987—, chmn. bd. trustees La. Ind. Coll. Fund Inc., 1987-88, mem. 1987—. Served with USNR, 1941-45. Decorated Order of Vasco Nunez de Balboa (Panama); named Alumnus of Yr., La. State U., 1975, role model Young Leadership Coun., 1993; recipient award Inst. for Human Understanding, 1975, Weiss Meml. award, 1976, Vol. Activist award, 1978, award of excellence Greater New Orleans Fedn. Chs., 1983, Disting. Svc. award Navy League, 1983, Humanitarian award Nat. Jewish Hosp./Nat. Asthma Ctr., 1984, internat. ins. award Internat. Ins. Adv. Coun., 1986, 1st ann. award for outstanding efforts in promoting trade with L.Am., Rotary Club, 1987, Hall of Fame award La. State U., 1987, Man of Yr. award Fedn. Ins. and Corp. Counsel, 1988, Integritas Vitae award Loyola U. of South, 1991, Bus. Hall of Fame award Jr. Achievement, 1993, cert. of appreciation La. Air N.G., 1995, Paul M. Hebert Law Ctr.'s Disting. Alumnus of 1998, La. State U., Exec. of Yr. award Bus. Assn. Latin Am. Studies, 1999, East Jefferson Gen. Hosp. Aux. Great Gentleman's award, 2000, Cert. of Life Membership award Salvation Army Bd., 2000; selected role model Young Bus. Leadership Coun., 1993; honored as a founding mem. in Soc. of St. Ignatius, Loyola U., 1996. Mem.: ABA, Internat. Trade Adminstrn. (industry sector and functional adv. coms. for trade policy matters), New Orleans Assn. Life Underwriters (award for Loyal and Unselfish Svc. to the Ins. Industry 1987), La. Assn. Legal Res. Life Ins. Cos. (pres. 1963—68), Ins. Econs. Soc. Am. (chmn. 1980—81), Health Ins. Assn. Am. (dir., chmn. 1970), Am. Life Conv. (past chmn. legal sect., exec. com., v.p. La., chmn. 1972), Assn. Life Ins. Counsel, Am. Judicature Soc., La. Law Inst., La. Bar Assn., C. of C. Greater New Orleans Area (dir., pres. 1970), Delta Kappa Epsilon (Disting. Alumnus award Zeta Zeta chpt. 2001), Omicron Delta Kappa, Phi Delta Phi. Episcopalian. Home: 5501 Dayna Ct New Orleans LA 70124-1042

PURVIS, JEFF, race car driver; Race car driver Joe Gibbs, Richard Childress Racing, Welcome, NC. Named Champion, World Series of Dirt, 1984, NDRA, 1984—85. Office: c/o Richard CHildress Racing 236 Industrial Dr Welcome NC 27374*

PURVIS, JOHN ANDERSON, lawyer, educator; b. Aug. 31, 1942; s. Virgil J. and Emma Lou (Anderson) P.; m. Charlotte Johnson, Apr. 3, 1976; 1 child, Whitney; children by previous marriage: Jennifer, Matt. BA cum laude, Harvard U., 1965; JD, U. Colo., 1968. Bar: Colo. 1968, U.S. Dist. Ct. Colo. 1968, U.S. Ct. Appeals (10th cir.) 1978. Dep. dist. atty., Boulder, Colo., 1968-69; asst. dir., dir. legal aid U. Colo. Sch. Law, 1969; assoc. Williams, Taussig & Trine, Boulder, 1969; head Boulder office Colo. Pub. Defender Sys., 1970-72; assoc., ptnr. Hutchinson, Black, Hill, Buchanan & Cook, Boulder, 1972-85; ptnr. Purvis, Gray, Schuetze and Gordon, 1985-98, Purvis, Gray & Gordon, LLP, 1999—2001, Purvis Gray LLP, 2001—. Acting Colo. State Pub. Defender, 1978; adj. prof. law U. Colo., 1981, 84-88, 94, others; lectr. in field; chmn. Colo. Pub. Defender Commn., 1979-89; mem. nominating commn. Colo. Supreme Ct., 1984-90; mem. com. on conduct U.S. Dist. Ct., 1991-97, chmn., 1996-97; chmn. Boulder County Criminal Justice Com., 1975-81. Recipient Ames award Harvard U., 1964, Outstanding Young Lawyer award Colo. Bar Assn., 1978, Dist. Achievement award U. Colo. Law Sch. Alumni Assn., 1997. Mem.: ATLA, Am. Bar Found., Colo. Bar Found., Trial Lawyers for Pub. Justice, Colo. Trial Lawyers Assn., Boulder County Bar Assn., Colo. Bar Assn. (chair litigation sect. 1994—95), Am. Coll. Trial Lawyers (state chmn. 1998—2000), Am. Bd. Trial Advs., Internat. Acad. Trial Lawyers, Internat. Soc. Barristers, Faculty of Fed. Advs. (bd. dirs. 1999—2001), Supreme Ct. Hist. Soc. (state chmn. 1998—). Democrat. Address: 1050 Walnut St Ste 501 Boulder CO 80302-5144

PURVIS, MARY CRAVEN, cosmetologist; b. Randolph County, N.C., Jan. 29, 1928; d. Artemas and Louada (Cox) Craven; m. Raymond Green Purvis, Aug. 7, 1946; children: Randy Craven, Carol Reynolds. Diploma, Continental Coll. Beauty Cult., 1951, tchrs. cert., 1984. Pub.: Descendants of Peter Craven Randolph County North Carolina, 1985, 280 Years with Peter Craven Family 1712-1993, 1995. Sec.treas. Craven Reunion of Randolph County, 1976-2001. Republican. Methodist. Avocation: genealogy research. Home: 406 N Highway 42 S Asheboro NC 27205-7924

PURVIS, RANDALL W. B. lawyer; b. Summit, N.J., Mar. 2, 1957; s. Merton B. and Marjory L. (Baker) P.; m. Robin Head Intemann Purvis; children: Zachary, Timothy, Andrew. BS, Ohio State U., 1979; JD, Georgetown U., 1982. Bar: Colo. 1983, U.S. Dist. Ct. Colo. 1983, U.S. Ct. Appeals (10th cir.) 1983. Pvt. practice, Colorado Springs, Colo., 1983—. Bd. dirs. Nova Resources Corp., Dallas, 1985-88; adj. prof. Colo. Coll. Councilman Colorado Springs City Coun., 1987-99, re-elected 1991, 95; mem. steering com. Nat. League of Cities, Washington; elder 1st Presbyn. Ch., Colorado Springs, 1987-91; bd. trustees Meml. Hosp. Colorado Springs, 1991-99. Mem. Colo. Bar Assn., El Paso County Bar Assn. (com. chmn. 1986), Colorado Springs C. of C. (com. chmn. 1986), Colorado Springs Bridge Club, Phi Beta Kappa. Republican. Avocations: bridge, woodworking. Office: 128 S Tejon Ste 402 Colorado Springs CO 80903-1520

PURVIS, RONALD SCOTT, financial counselor, real estate professional; b. Cleve., Apr. 17, 1928; s. Samuel Martin Jr. and Dorothea (Scott) P.; m. Lynne Willis, Dec. 20, 1963; children: Ward S., Blair P. Snyder, Heather Leigh Ann. *Glasgow son, Samuel, of Samuel and Elizabeth (Kidd) Purvis, County Tyrone, Ireland, arrived USA July 1871, wed Elizabeth Martin, a Scot of Aberdeen and Brooklyn, NY, who had Samuel Martin Purvis Sr. In Cleveland, OH, he wed Margaret Ann Evans, whose mother, Margaret Williams of Tredegar, Wales came solo in 1857 to Covington, KY. Forebear David Ward II was one of thirty-eight Lexington Minutemen. His granduncle was Gen. Artemas Ward, first C-in-C of the American Revolution. Katherine Washington wed Thomas Stanton, had Thomas II, who left London in 1635. Strong ancestors in CT yield England's William and Harry Windsor and Britain's first Queen, Boudicea.* BS, U.S. Naval Acad., 1953; B Individualized Study, George Mason U., 1984. CLU, Chartered Fin. Cons., registered gen. securities prin. Enlisted USN, 1946, advanced through grades to lt. comdr., 1966, hon. discharged, 1972; served in destroyer with task force 77 Korea, 1953; flight instr., 1955-56; vx-6 squadron pilot, parachutist in-charge U.S. Naval Support Force Team, Antarctica, 1956-58; to McMurdo and South Pole, 1957-58; in charge of all-weather fighter detachment, 1958-59; with Office of the CNO (Op-007) Navy Dept., 1960-63; aide to pres. Kennedy, 1961-63; in charge of ordnance Handling, Flight Deck of aircraft carrier in the Mediterranean, 1963-64; in charge of Pub. Affairs NAS, Jacksonville, Fla., 1965-67; in charge of 5 Def. Dept. Combat MoPic Teams, U.S. Mil. Assistance Command Vietnam, 1968-69; dir. internal rels. CNO (Op-007), 1969-72; gen. agt. Can. Life Assurance, Washington, 1972-88; pres. RSVP Realty, Annandale, Va., 1985-2000, Purvis Corp., Falls Church, 1986—. *A WWII merchant sailor, when his father returned from Fleet Air Wing Seventeen in the Philippines, he joined the Navy, won an appointment to Annapolis, volunteered for Army Parachute School, and served in a destroyer off Korea. After winning Navy wings, he was a flight instructor, volunteered for Antarctic exploration with Admiral Byrd. A pilot, he also led the search and rescue parachute team. In charge of a detachment of all-weather "banshee" jet fighters,he was appointed an Aide to President Kennedy. He flew over the Bay of Pigs, and was in charge of Defense Combat MoPic Teams in Vietnam. He became a Financial Services professional.* Del. Rep. Convs., Va., 1975—. Purvis Peak, Antarctic mountain, named in his honor. Mem. D.C. Soc., SAR (asst. registrar 1982-84, chaplain 1989-91, treas. 1991-92, state sec. 1992-94, sr. v.p. 1994-95, state pres. 1995-96, alt. nat. soc. trustee 1996-97, nat. soc. trustee 1997-98, registrar 1998-2000), Assn. Naval Aviation, Masons, Shriners. Avocations: skiing, flying, scuba diving, golf, dancing. Home: 27310 Baylys Neck Rd Accomac VA 23301 Office: Purvis Corp 3415 Lakeside View Dr Falls Church VA 22041-2454 E-mail: purvispeak@juno.com.

PURYEAR, ALVIN NELSON, management educator; b. Fayetteville, N.C., Apr. 6, 1937; s. Byron Nelson and Gladys (Bizzell) P.; m. Catherine Paulette Wiggins, Aug. 30, 1962; children: Pamela, Susan, Karen. BA, Yale U., 1960; MBA, Columbia U., 1962, PhD, 1966. Employee relations adviser Mobil Oil Corp., N.Y.C., 1965-66, fin. analyst, 1966-67; specialist computational systems Allied Chem. Corp., 1967-68; asso. prof. Grad. Sch. Bus. Adminstrn. Rutgers U., Newark, 1968-69; asso. prof. mgmt. Bernard M. Baruch Coll., N.Y.C., 1970-72, prof. mgmt., 1972—, Lawrence N. Field prof. entrepreneurship, 1999—, chmn. dept., 1978-79, dean coll., 1972-75, dir. Baruch/Cornell Indsl. and Labor Relations program, 1977-81; v.p. for orgn. and mgmt. Ford Found., 1980-82; 1st dep. comptroller City of N.Y., 1983-85. Chmn. bd. Broadcast Capital Fund Inc., 1993-95; bd. dirs. Green Point Fin. Corp., Bank of Tokyo-Mitsubishi Trust, Am. Capital Strategies Ltd.; dir. Greenpoint Savs. Bank, 1992—. Co-author: Black Enterprise, Inc, 1973; also articles. Trustee Barber-Scotia Coll., 1977-82, Loyola coll., Balt., 1976-82, Riverdale Country Sch., Bronx, 1980-92, chmn. bd., 1987-89, Grad. Sch. Polit. Mgmt., 1987-95, Pitts. Theol. Sem., 1989-92, 96-2000, Yale U., New Haven, 1994-96, Cmty. Svc. Soc. of N.Y., 1997—, Union Theol. Sem. & Presbyn. Sch. Christian Edn., 2001—; bd. dirs. Program Agy. United Presbyn. Ch., 1976-88, pres. 1983-86, Presbyn. Ch. U.S.A., 1987-97, chmn. 1991-93; active Presbyn. Investment and Loan Corp., 1996—, Yale Alumni Fund, 1977-82. John Hay Whitney fellow, 1960-61; Samuel Bronfman fellow, 1960-62 Mem. Acad. Mgmt., Assn. Yale Alumni (vice chmn. 1984-86, chmn. 1986-88), Am. Mgmt. Assn., Smithsonian Nat. Bd., Interracial. Coun. Bus. Opportunity (bd. dirs.). Presbyn. (elder).

PURYEAR, JAMES BURTON, college administrator; b. Jackson, Miss., Sept. 2, 1938; s. Harry Henton and Doris (Smith) P.; m. Joan Copeland, June 13, 1965; children: John James, Jeffrey Burton, Joel Harry. BS, Miss. State U., 1960, MEd, 1961; PhD, Fla. State U., 1969. Lic. profl. counselor, Ga. Assoc. dir. YMCA Miss. State U., Starkville, 1962-64; dir. YMCA, Miss., 1964-65; dir. fin. aid Fla. State U., Tallahassee, 1967-69; asst. dir. student affairs Med. Coll. of Ga., Augusta, 1969-70, dir. student affairs, 1970-86, v.p. student affairs, 1986-2000, v.p. emeritus, student affairs, 2000—. Mem. adv. bd. Ga. Fed. Bank, Augusta, 1978-85; deacon, 1971-, chmn. bd. First Bapt. Ch., Augusta, 1978-80; pres. Learning Disabilities Assn., Augusta, 1987, PTA, 1994, Band Assn.,1996; bd. dirs. Augusta Tng. Shop for Handicapped, 1994-98; mem. exec. bd., v.p. Boy Scouts Am., 1996-99. Yearbook Dedication MCG Student Yearbook, 1975; scholar Med. Coll. Ga., 1988; recipient Svc. to Mankind award Sertoma, 1988. Mem. Nat. Assn. Student Pers. (S.E. regional bd. 1985), Am. Coll. Pers. Assn., So. Assn. Coll. Student Affairs, Rotary (pres. 1978, dist. lt. gov. 1997-99, dist. gov. 2001-02, Paul Harris fellow 1985, Will Watt fellow). Baptist. Avocations: golf, photography, scouting.

PURYEAR, JEFFREY MERRILL, cultural association administrator; b. Lansing, Mich., Mar. 20, 1943; s. Oscar Donald and Lucille Anna (Battige) P.; m. Myriam Waiser, Dec. 17, 1994; 1 stepchild, Milena Flament. BA in Social Scis., Mich. State U., 1965; MA in Sociology, Duke U., 1967; PhD in Edn., U. Chgo., 1974. Instr. U. Chgo., 1972-73; program advisor The Ford Found., Santiago, Chile, 1973-78, Lima, Peru, 1973-78, program officer N.Y.C., 1979-85, rep. Lima, 1985-90; vis. scholar Stanford U., 1978-79; rsch. scholar NYU, 1990-92; program dir. Inter-America Dialogue, Washington, 1992—. Author: Thinking Politics, 1994; editor Education, Equity and Economics, 1995; contbr. articles to profl. publs. Fgn. Area fellow Social Sci. Rsch. Coun., Bogota, Colombia, 1971-72, U.S. Dept. Edn. fellow Chgo., 1969-71. Mem. Latin Am. Studies Assn., Comparative and Internat. Edn. Soc. Home: 3724 University Ave NW Washington DC 20016-5618 Office: Inter Am Dialogue 1211 Connecticut Ave NW Ste 510 Washington DC 20036-2706 E-mail: jpuryear@thedialogue.org.

PURYEAR, JOAN COPELAND, English language educator; b. Columbus, Miss., May 10, 1944; d. John Thomas and Mamie (Cunningham) Copeland.; m. James Burton Puryear, June 13, 1965; children: John James, Jeffrey Burton, Joel Harry. BA summa cum laude, Miss. State U., Starkville, 1965; MA, Fla. State U., 1969; EdD, U. Ga., 1987. Cert. tchr., Ga. Instr. English, Fla. State U., Tallahassee, 1965-69, Augusta (Ga.) State U., 1987-88; head English dept. Augusta Tech. Coll., 1989-93, chairperson gen. edn. and devel. studies, 1993-96, mem. dean's coun., mgmt. team, 1994—, dean allied health scis., gen. edn. and devel. studies, 1997—. Chmn. State Exec. Bd. English, Ga., 1990-92, East Ctrl. Consortium English, Ga., 1990-92; facilitator Total Quality Mgmt. Tech. Tng.; mem. exec. steering com. Continous Improvement Coun., 1996-02; mem. and co-chmn. Continuous Improvement Coun., 1996-97. Mem. Cmtys. in Schs., 1996—; trustee Augusta Tech. Inst. Found. Bd., 1996—; mem. founding bd. Junior Achievement, 2001-02; co-pres. Davidson Fine Arts Sch. PTA, 1995, co-pres. bd. assn., 1996; pres. Med. Coll. Spouse's Club, Augusta, 1972; dir. Women's Mission Orgn., First Bapt. Ch., Augusta, 1982, dir. youth Sunday Sch., 1992-98, chmn. 175th Anniversary, 1992, deacon, 1996—, vice moderator, 1998-99, mem. ministerial adv. com., 1992-2001, vice chmn. scholarship and edn. com., 2002-; mem. found. bd. Walton Rehab. Ctr. Mem.: Augusta South Rotary Club (pres.-elect 2001—), Phi Theta Kappa (advisor 1992—, Horizon regional award for outstanding advisor 1997). Baptist. Avocations: flower arranging, home decorating, reading, traveling. Office: Augusta Tech Coll 3116 Deans Bridge Rd Augusta GA 30906-3375

PURYEAR, RACHELLE MARIE, artist, educator; b. Washington, Aug. 27, 1947; arrived in Sweden, 1974; d. Reginald T. and Martina A. (Morse) P.; m. Håkan S. Lövgren, July 8, 1987. BA, Trinity Coll., 1969; MA, Ind. U., 1971. Curator Mus. Nat. Ctr. Afro-Am. Artists, Boston, 1972-74; asst. prof. Konstfackskolan-Coll. Arts, Crafts and Design, Stockholm, 1981-88; assoc. prof. Konsthögskolan-Royal Coll. Art, 1988-2000. Bd. dirs. Grafikskolan, Stockholm, Getfot Found., Stockholm. One-woman shows include Gallery Skånes Konst, Malmö, 1986, 92, Gallery Grafiska Sällskapet, Stockholm, 1985, Konstnärshuset, Stockholm, 1999, Tandsticksmuseet, Jonkoping, 2002, Trondheims Kunstmuseum, Norway, 1997; exhibited in group shows including Terry Dintenfass Gallery, N.Y.C., 1994, Spelman Coll. Mus., Atlanta, 1996, Museet for Fotokunst, Odense, Denmark, 1997. Grantee NEA, 1973, Swedish Art Coun., 1977, 80, 88, 91, 93, 97, 98, Rsch. grantee, 1990. Mem.: Grafikes Hus Found. (bd. dirs.), Soc. for Fine Art Prints (bd. dirs.), Swedish Art Soc. (bd. dirs.). Avocation: translating.

PURZE, JUDY SUZANNE, real estate executive, consultant; b. Chgo., Aug. 16, 1953; d. Gilbert and Marcia (Waldshine) P. BS in Bus., U. Colo., 1975; M in Internat. Bus., Am. Grad. Sch. Internat. Bus., Glendale, Ariz., 1976. Realtor Century 21, Phoenix, 1975-76; mgr. internat. site selection Britt and Frerichs, Chgo., 1976-78; sr. analyst Real Estate Rsch. Corp., 1978-80; devel. dir. Homart Devel. Co., 1980-83; real estate mgr. Best Products Co., Richmond, Va., 1983-84; real estate rep. Vol. Shoe Co., Hurst, Tex., 1984-87; real estate mgr. Montgomery Ward Co., Chgo., 1987-89; v.p. real estate Hit or Miss, Inc., Irving, Tex., 1989—. Mem. Internat. Assn. Corp. Real Estate Execs., Internat. Coun. Shopping Ctrs. Office: Hit or Miss Inc 4835 N O Connor Rd Ste 134-338 Irving TX 75062-2257

PURZYCKI, ROBERT HENRY, travel company executive, educator, writer, medical technician; b. Schenectady, N.Y., Feb. 12, 1944; s. Henry Stanley and Katherine Ellen (Krempa) P.; m. Jeanne Clair Semer, Aug. 11, 1979. AA, Hudson Valley Coll., Troy, N.Y., 1966; BA, U. South Fla., Tampa, 1968; postgrad., Crowell Coll. Inst., Arlington, Va., 1970, U. Madrid, 1972. Registered registered technician St. Clares Sch. X-Ray, 1964; cert. cert. travel agent Inst. Cert. Travel Agents. Travel agent Schenectady Travel, 1973—76; travel cons. Garber Travel Svc., Boston, 1976—85; sch. dir., instr. Uniglobe Travel Career Ctr., Salem, NH, 1985—87; sr. travel sch. instr. Travel Sch. Am., Boston, 1987—97; sr. instr. Travel Edn. Ctr., Cambridge, 1997—99; passenger svc. rep. MASSPORT, Boston, 1999—2000; mgr. opers. North Am. Albatross Travel Group, Hampton, NH, 2000—. Instr., grader Inst. Cert. Travel Agents, Wellesley, Mass., 1991—. Author: Destination Studies, 1997, Planning Itineraries, 1997, Sails for Profit, 1998. Petty officer 2nd USN, 1968—72. Mem.: Am. Registry Radiologic Techs. (registered technician), Am. Assn. Geographes, Elks. Mem. Universalist Ch. Avocations: hiking, swimming, collecting folk art, travel, writing. Home: One Capeview Rd Ipswich MA 01938

PUSATERI, JAMES ANTHONY, judge; b. Kansas City, Mo., May 20, 1938; s. James A. and Madeline (LaSalle) P.; m. Jacqueline D. Ashburne, Sept. 1, 1962; children: James A., Mark C., Danielle L. BA, U. Kans., 1960, LLB, 1963. Bar: Kans. 1963, U.S. Dist. Ct. Kans. 1963, U.S. Ct. Appeals (10th cir.) 1964. Assoc. Payne, Jones, Chartered, Olathe, Kans., 1963-65, James Cashin, Prairie Village, 1965-69; asst. U.S. atty. Dept. Justice, Kansas City, 1969-76; judge U.S. Bankruptcy Ct. Dist. Kans., Topeka, 1976—. Active Prairie Village City Coun., 1967-69. Mem. Kans. Bar Assn., Topeka Bar Assn., Nat. Conf. Bankruptcy Judges, Am. Bankruptcy Inst., Sam A. Crow Am. Inn of Ct.

PUSATERI, LAWRENCE XAVIER, lawyer; b. Oak Park, Ill., May 25, 1931; s. Lawrence E. and Josephine (Romano) P.; m. Eve M. Graf, July 9, 1956; children: Joanne, Lawrence F., Paul L., Mary Ann, Eva. JD summa cum laude, DePaul U., 1953. Bar: Ill. 1953. Asst. state's atty. Cook County, Ill., 1957-59; ptnr. Newton, Wilhelm, Pusateri & Naborowski, Chgo., 1959-77; justice Ill. Appellate Ct., 1977-78; ptnr. Peterson, Ross, Scloerb & Seidel, 1978-95; of counsel Peterson & Ross, 1996—2000. Pres. Conf. Consumer Fin. Law, 1984-92, chmn. gov. com., 1993-99; mem. Ill. Supreme Ct. Com. on Pattern Jury Instrns., 1981-96; mem. adv. bd. Ctr. for Analysis of Alt. and Dispute Resolution, 1999—; mem. U.S. Senate Jud. Nominations Commn. State Ill., 1993, 95; exec. dir. State of Ill. Jud. Inquiry Bd., 1995-96; panel chmn. Cook County mandatory arbitration, 1990—, judicate Am. Arbitration;

mem. Merit Selection Panel for U.S. Magistrate; lectr. law DePaul U., Chgo., 1962, Columbia U., N.Y.C., 1965, Marquette U., Milw., 1962-82, Northwestern U. Law Sch., Def. Counsel Inst., 1969-70; apptd. by U.S. Senator Paul Simon to Merit Screening Com. Fed. Judges, U.S. Atty. and U.S. Marshal, 1993, others; mem. task force indigent appellate def. Cook County Jud. Adv. Coun., 1992-95; mem. Ill. Gen. Assembly, 1964-68. Contbr. articles to profl. jours. Chmn. Ill. Crime Investigating Commn., 1967-68, chmn. Ill. Parole and Pardon Bd., 1969-70; bd. dirs. Ill. Law Enforcement Commn., 1970-72; chmn. Com. on Correctional Facilities and Services; exec. v.p. and gen. counsel Ill. Fin. Svcs. Assn., 1980-95; chmn. law forum Am. Fin. Svcs. Assn., 1975-76; mem. spl. commn. on adminstrn. of justice in Cook County, Ill. (Greylord Com.) 1984-90, bd. dirs. Chgo. Crime Commn., 1986-91; mem. Ill. Supreme Ct. Spl. Commn. on the Adminstrn. of Justice, Ill. Supreme Ct. Appointment, 1991. Served to capt. JAGC, AUS, 1955-58. Named One of Ten Outstanding Young Men in Chgo., Chgo. Jr. Assn. Commerce and Industry, 1960, 65; recipient Outstanding Legislator award Ill. Gen. Assembly, 1966. Mem. ABA (com. consumer fin. svcs. 1975-99, ho. dels. 1981-90, judicial adminstrn. divsn. 1980-95, mem. exec. com. lawyer's conf. 1994-95, mem. bench and bar rels. com. 1994-96, mem. adv. com. to Ill. State Del., Jud. Adminstrn. Divsn. in Recognition of Leadership in Improvement of Adminstrn. of Justice award 1993), Ill. State Bar Assn. (pres. 1975-76, com. on fed. jud. and related appointments; Abraham Lincoln Legal Writing award 1959, mem. adv. com., state del., 1994-99, bd. dirs., co-chmn. joint com. jud. compensation 2002-), Chgo. Bar Assn. (bd. mgrs. 1965-66), Fred B. Snite Found. (sec., counsel 1976-90), Gertrude and Walter Swanson Found. (sole trustee 1995—), Mid-Am. Club Chgo. Republican. Roman Catholic.

PUSCHEL, PHILIP P. textiles executive; m. Roberta J. Green. AB, Hamilton Coll., 1960; MBA, Stanford U., 1962. V.p. F Schumacher & Co., N.Y.C., 1971, pres., CEO, 1981, chmn. bd., CEO officer, 1989—, chmn. bd. With USN, 1962-65. Office: F Schumacher & Co 79 Madison Ave Fl 15 New York NY 10016-7802

PUSCHETT, JULES B. medical educator, nephrologist, researcher; b. Hazelton, Pa., Mar. 13, 1934; m. Diane Puschett; children: Mitchell, Lynne. BA magna cum laude, Lehigh U., 1955; MD, U. Pa., 1959. Intern Jackson Meml. Hosp., Miami, 1959-60; resident, fellow endrocrinology and metabolism Univ. Hosp., Balt., 1963-66; postdoctoral fellow in medicine NIH Inst. Arthritis and Metabolic Disease, Bethesda, 1966-68; fellow, renal-electrolyte sect. U. Pa. Sch. Medicine, Phila., 1966-68; rsch. assoc. VA Hosp., 1968-70, staff to chief renal-electrolyte sect. dept. medicine, 1968-73, clin. investigator, 1970-73; head renal-electrolyte divsn. Allegheny Gen. Hosp., Pitts., 1973-78; dir. renal-electrolyte divsn. fellowship tng. program U. Pitts. Sch. Medicine, 1976-78; chief renal-electrolyte divsn. dept. medicine U. Ark. for Med. Scis., Little Rock, 1979-80, U. Pitts. Sch. Medicine, 1980-90; interim chief sect. nephrology dept. medicine Tulane U. Sch. Medicine, New Orleans, 1990-92, prof. chmn. dept. medicine, 1990—, asst. dean network affairs, 1996—, Harry B. Greenberg, MD chair in internal medicine, 1999—. Instr. medicine U. Pa. Sch. Medicine 1967-79, assoc. in medicine 1969-70, asst. prof. medicine 1970-73; clin. assoc. prof. medicine U. Pitts. Med. Sch. 1973-78; prof. medicine U. Ark. Med. Scis. 1979-80; prof. medicine U. Pitts. Sch. Medicine 1980-90. Editor: The Diuretic Manual, 1984, Diuretics: chemistry, Pharmacology and Clinical Applications, 1984, Disorders of Fluid and Electrolyte Balance: diagnosis and Management, 1985, Diuretics II: Chemistry, Pharmacology and Clinical Applications, 1986, Diuretics III, 1989, Diuretics IV, 1993; contbr. over 170 articles to profl. jours.; spkr. and presenter in field; editl. bd. Am. Jour. Med. Scis., Am. Jour. Nephrology (sect. editor Physiology for the Nephrologist), Cardiovasc. Risk Factors, Internat. Jour. Artificial Organs, Southern Med. Jour. Chmn. 1st Ann. Kidney Ball, Nat. Kidney Found. of Western Pa., 1988, chmn. 2d Ann. Kidney Ball, 1989. With USN 1960-63. Recipient Gloria P. Walsh award for Tchg. Excellence, Graduating Class/Tulane U. Sch. Medicine, 1998; named Outstanding Tchr. Yr., Owl Club, Tulane U., 1991, 94; Coxe Meml. scholar Lehigh U., 1951. Fellow ACP; mem. AMA, AAAS, Am. Fedn. Clin. Rsch., Am. Soc. Artificial Internal Organs, Am. Soc. Nephrology (chmn. audit com. 1992), Nat. Kidney Found. (pub. policy com. 1989, vol. svc. award 1990), Internat. Soc. Nephrology, Am. Heart Assn. Coun. on the Kidney in Cardiovasc. Disease (chmn. subcom. on scientific confs. 1991-92, exec. com. 1991-95, long-range planning com. 1992-94, vice chair 1998-2000, chair-elect 1999-2000, chair 2000—), Am. Heart Assn. Coun. for High Blood Pressure Rsch., Am. Physiol. Soc., Fedn. Am. Socs. for Exptl. Biology, Am. Geriat. Soc., Ctrl. Soc. for Clin. Rsch., Soc. for Exptl. Biology and Medicine, Am. Soc. Clin. Pharmacology and Therapeutics, Am. Coll. Clin. Pharmacology, Endocrine Soc., Am. Soc. Renal Biochemistry and Metabolism, Am. Soc. Hypertension (Outstanding Tchr. Yr. 1986), Internat. Soc. Nutrition and Metabolism in Renal Disease, Am. Soc. Bone and Mineral Rsch., European Dialysis and Transplant Assn., Nat. Kidney Found. of Western Pa. (med. adv. com. 1981, chmn. 1981-83, Gift of Life award 1991), Nat. Kidney Found. of La. (mem.-at-large, trustee 1991), So. Med. Assn., So. Soc. Clin. Investigation (councilor 1992-94, sec.-treas. 1994-99, pres.-elect 1998-99, pres. 1999-2000), La. State Med. Soc., Orleans Parish Med. Soc. (membership com. 1993, long-range planning com. 1993), La. Soc. Internal Medicine, S.E. Clin. Club, Midwestern Salt and Water Club, Phi Beta Kappa, Alpha Epsilon Delta, Alpha Omega Alpha. Office: Tulane Univ Sch Medicine Dept Medicine SL 12 1430 Tulane Ave New Orleans LA 70112-2699 E-mail: jpusche@tulane.edu.

PUSEY, MAVIS IONA, artist, educator; b. Jamaica; Student, Art Students League, 1961-65, Birgit Sch. Workshop, London, 1967-68, Robert Blackburn Workshop, 1969-72, New Sch. for Social Rsch., 1974, 76, 87. Instr. painting New Sch. for Social Rsch., N.Y.C., 1973-88; asst. prof. painting and printmaking SUNY, Stony Brook, 1974-77; instr. intermediate painting Pa. Acad. Fine Arts, Phila., 1974-86; instr. printmaking and painting N.Y. State Summer Sch. of the ARts, 1978-79; instr. etching and painting Drew U., Madison, N.J., 1980-81; instr. studio art, art history and art appreciation Woodberry Forest (Va.) Sch., 1993—; lectr. in field. One-woman shows include Rainbow Art Found., N.Y., 1977, Franklin and Marshall Coll., Pa., 1979, New Sch. Assocs., N.Y.C., 1980, Korn Gallery, Drew U., Madison, 1980, Piedmont Va. C.C., 1993, St. Catherine's Sch., 1995, bozART Gallery, Charlottesville, Va., 1999; group exhbns. include Douglas Coll. Art Gallery, Rutgers U., New Brunswick, 1980, William Penn Meml. Mus., Harrisburg, Pa., 1983, City Gallery/2 Dept. Cultural Affairs, City of N.Y., 1983, Art Students League, 1986, 93, Lamar Dodd Art Ctr., LaGrange, Ga., 1991, Nat. Arts Club, 1993, others; traveling group exhbns. include Greenville (S.C.) Mus. Art, 1984, Metro-Dade Cultural Ctr., Miami-Dade Pub. Libr., 1988, The Artmobile, Miami-Dade Pub. Libr. Sys., 1991, Bronx (N.Y.) Art Ctr. and Gallery, 1992, Hillwood Art Mus., L.I. U., Bronxville, N.Y., 1992, others; represented in permanent collections Citibank, N.Y.C., First Nat. Bank Chgo., Chem. Bank, Tougaloo Coll., Miss., Mus. Modern Art, N.Y.C., numerous pvt. collections. Recipient Bryon Browne Meml. award Art Students League, 1963, Ford Found. Tuition award Art Students League, N.Y., 1964, Louis Comfort Tiffany Found. award, 1972, Louis Comfort Tiffany Found. Purchase award, 1974, Majors Travel Tour award S.I. Mus., 1975, Internat. Woman's Yr. award in recognition of outstanding cultural contbn. and dedication to women and art, 1976. Home: 20305 Gum Tree Rd Orange VA 22960-4125

PUSEY, STEVE, communications executive; married; 1 child. MBA, Harvard U. With British Telecom, Nortel Networks, Brampton, Canada, 1982—, pres. Europe, Middle East and Africa Canada. Office: Nortel Network 8200 Dixie Rd Ste 100 Brampton L6T 5P6 Canada

PUSEY, WALTER CARROLL, III, geologist, consultant; b. Upper Darby, Pa., Feb. 13, 1935; s. Walter Carroll Jr. and Elizabeth Foulke (Sharples) P.; m. Betsy Cantwell, Mar. 30, 1960; children: David, Steven, Anne. BA, Amherst Coll., 1960; PhD, Rice U., 1964. Cert. petroleum geologist. Mgr. worldwide exploration svcs. Conoco, Houston, 1964-93; prof. geology ESRI, U. S.C., Columbia, 1994-96, ESRI, U. Utah, Salt Lake City, 1996; cons., pres. Twin Lakes Resources, Houston, 1996-2000, cons., 2000—. Author, editor: Belize Shelf Carbonates, Clastics and Ecology, 1995. Served with U.S. Army, 1955-58. NSF grantee, 1959; NSF grad. fellow, 1960-64. Mem. Am. Assn. Petroleum Geologists (Citation of Excellence 1999), Geol. Assn. Am., Soc. Sedimentary Geology, Nat. Speleological Soc., Sigma Xi. Mem. Soc. Of Friends. Achievements include patent and liquid window concept which is widely used in the petroleum industry to describe thermal maturity of oil and gas source rocks. Avocation: photography. Home and Office: 5527 Honor Dr Houston TX 77041-6557 E-mail: wcpintx@aol.com.

PUSEY, WILLIAM ANDERSON, lawyer; b. Richmond, Va., Mar. 17, 1936; s. Paul H. and Vernelle (Barnes) P.; m. Patricia Powell, Sept. 3, 1960; children: Patricia Brent, William A. Jr., Margaret Glen. AB, Princeton U., 1958; JD, U. Va., 1962. Bar: Calif. 1963, Va. 1964, D.C. 1987. Assoc. McCutchen, Brown, et al, San Francisco, 1962-63; dep. dist. atty. Alameda County, Oakland, Calif., 1963-64; assoc., ptnr., sr. counsel Hunton & Williams, Washington, Fairfax and Richmond, Va., 1964—. Trustee Ea. Mineral Law Found., Morgantown, W.Va., 1985—, pres., 1987-88. Chmn. bd. dirs. Presbyn. Sch. Christian Edn., Richmond, 1984-85. Mem. Am. Horticultural Soc. (bd. dirs., sec., gen. counsel 1995-2001), Order of Coif, Phi Beta Kappa, Omicron Delta Kappa. Home: 3910 N Glebe Rd Arlington VA 22207-4340 Office: Hunton & Williams 1900 K St NW Washington DC 20006-1110

PUSHKAREV, BORIS S. research foundation director, writer; b. Prague, Czechoslovakia, Oct. 22, 1929; arrived in U.S., 1949, naturalized, 1954; s. Sergei G. and Julie T. (Popov) P.; m. Iraida Vandellos Legky, Oct. 20, 1973. BArch, Yale U., 1954, M.C.P., 1957. Instr. city planning Yale U., New Haven, 1957-61; chief planner Regional Plan Assn., N.Y.C., 1961-69, v.p. rsch., 1969-89, sr. v.p., 1989-90; adj. assoc. prof. NYU, 1969-79; chmn. Russian Rsch. Found. Study of Alternatives to Soviet Policy, 1981—. Bd. dirs. Russian Solidarists; lectr. New Humanitarian U., Moscow, 1993—2002. Author: (with Christopher Tunnard) Man-Made America, 1963; (with Jeffrey Zupan) Urban Space for Pedestrians, 1975, Public Transportation and Land Use Policy, 1977, Urban Rail in America, 1982, Russia and the Experience of the West, 1995; editl. bd. POSSEV; chmn. POSSEV Publ. Assn., Moscow, 1999--; contbr. articles to profl. jours. Recipient Nat. Book award (with C. Tunnard), 1964. Mem. Am. Assn. for Advancement of Slavic Studies. Russian Orthodox. Home: 770 Anderson Ave Apt 20F Cliffside Park NJ 07010-2172 E-mail: posevru@online.ru.

PUSHKARSKY, LOUIS PAUL, retired mathematics educator; b. Slovak Town, Ark., Aug. 17, 1922; s. Erasmm and Yadwiga (Petroczynski) P.; m. Clarice W. Pollard, Jan. 19, 1963; children: Larry, David. BS in Math. and sci., U. Ctrl. Ark., 1951; MA in Math., U. Ark., 1953. Head math. and sci. Bradford (Ark.) Schs., 1952-55; prof. math. North Ctrl. Mo. Coll., Trenton, 1955-89, prof. emeritus, 1989—, head math. and sci., 1955-89. Mem. Trenton City Coun., 1985-91. Sgt. USAAF, 1943-45. Mem. VFW (bd. dirs. Mo. dept. 1976-77, asst. insp. gen. 1980-81. mat. adc 1978, 98, chaplain ritual team 1995—, dist. adj. 1974—), DAV (comdr. 1999-2000), Elks (exalted ruler 1975), Alpha Chi. Avocations: observing nature, collecting music, gardening. Home: 169 E 7th St Trenton MO 64683

PUST, AUGUST B. government executive, artist; b. Ljubljana, Slovenia, Feb. 22, 1938; came to U.S., 1957; s. Franz Pust and Angela Terskan-Pust; m. Gloria A. Pust, Sept. 7, 1963; 1 child, Adriana A. Diploma, Cooper Sch. Art, 1961; grad. cum laude, Cleve. Advt. Club, 1967; Dr. Honoris Causa, Valachia U., Tergoviste, Romania, 1999. Staff artist La Salle Art Studio, Cleve., 1961-64; art dir., editor Penton Pub., 1964-70; art mgr., supr. Premier Indsl., 1970-74; adminstrv. asst. City of Cleve., 1974-85; project dir. Office of Mayor, Cleve., 1985-91, spl. asst. Columbus, Ohio, 1991-99, dir., 1999—. Mem. exec. com. Am. Nationalities Movement, Cleve., 1974-76. Exhibited art in group shows, Slovenia, 1985 (jury selection). Mem. exec. bd. Ohio Bicentennial Commn., Columbus, 1997-98; founding pres. Greater Cleve. Ethnographic Mus., 1974-76; regent Liberty U. Calif., Sacramento, 1999-2000; hon. mayor City of Cleve., 1986; sustaining mem. Ohio Rep. Party, Columbus, 1997—; mem. Victory Club, Rep. Nat. Com., Washington, 2000; mem. adv. com. Rep. Ethnic-Heritage Com., Cuyahoga County, 1997. Recipient Disting. Svc. medal Ohio N.G., 1996, Key of the City of Cleve., Mayor Voinovich White, 1989, 91, Martin Luther King Jr. award City Mayor/Coun., Cleve., 1991; named to Vitez-Hungarian Knightly Order, 1990; Internat. fellow Colo. Coll., 1990. Mem. Internat. Vis.'s Coun. (bd. trustees 1991—), Fedn. Asian Indian Assn. (hon.), All-Nations Festival Found. (chmn. 1985-89), Ohio Refugee and Immigrant Coun. (adv. bd. 1995—), U.S./UN Assn. (Bd. dirs. Columbus/N.Y.C. 1992—), Ohio Dept. LEdn./ESL Langs. (adv. bd. 1995—). Republican. Roman Catholic. Avocations: art, organic gardening, gourmet cooking. Home: 70 E 270th St Euclid OH 44132 Office: Gov's Office 77 S High St Columbus OH 43215

PUST, LADISLAV, physicist, researcher; b. Prague, Czech Republic, Mar. 3, 1953; s. Ladislav and Marie (Landova) P.; m. Renata Pustova, 1989; children: Daniela, Lucie. MSc in Engring., Czech Technical Univ., Prague, 1976; PhD, Inst. Physics, 1981. Rsch. asst. Rsch. Inst. Elec. Engring., Prague, 1975-76; rsch. fellow Ohio State U., Columbus, 1984-85; physicist Inst. Physics, Acad. of Scis. of Czech Republic, Prague, 1976-97; rsch. scientist dept. physics Wayne State U., Detroit, 1997-98; sr. rsch. staff Seagate Tech. Recording Heads, Mpls., 1998—. Contbr. numerous articles to profl. jours. Recipient scholarship Ohio State U., 1984. Mem. IEEE (sr.), Am. Phys. Soc., European Phys. Soc., Materials Rsch. Soc. Avocations: skiing, hiking. Home: 5695 S Park Dr Savage MN 55378 Office: SEAGATE RECORDING HEADS 7801 Computer Ave Bloomington MN 55435 E-mail: lpust@seagate.com.

PUSTILNIK, DAVID DANIEL, lawyer; b. N.Y.C., Mar. 10, 1931; s. Philip and Belle (Gerberholtz) P.; m. Helen Jean Todd, Aug. 15, 1959; children: Palma Elyse, Leslie Royce, Bradley Todd. BS, NYU, 1952, JD, 1958, LLM, 1959; postgrad., Air War Coll., 1976. Bar: N.Y. 1959, U.S. Supreme Ct. 1962, Conn. 1964. Legis. tax atty. legis. and regulations div. Office Chief Counsel, IRS, Washington, 1959-63; atty. Travelers Ins. Co., Hartford, Conn., 1963-68, assoc. counsel, 1968-73, counsel, 1973-75, assoc. gen. counsel, 1975-87, dep. gen. counsel, 1987-93. Mem. adv. coun. Hartford Inst. on Ins. Taxation, 1978-93, vice chmn., 1991-92, chmn., 1992-93. Grad. editor NYU Tax Law Rev., 1958-59. Trustee Hartford Coll. for Women, 1985-91; life sponsor Am. Tax Policy Inst.; dir. Congregation Beth Yam, 1996-99. Served to col. USAFR. Kenneson fellow NYU, 1958-59. Fellow Am. Coll. Tax Counsel; mem. ABA (chmn. ins. cos. com. 1976-78), Am. Coun. Life Ins. (chmn. co. tax com. 1982-84), Am. Ins. Assn. (chmn. tax com. 1979-81), Assn. Life Ins. Counsel (chmn. tax sect. 1991-93), Twentieth Century Club, Sea Pines Country Club (co-chair social com. 1997-99).

PUTATUNDA, SUSIL KUMAR, metallurgy educator; b. Santipur, W. Bengal, India, Jan. 31, 1948; came to U.S., 1983; s. Provat Chandra and Santi Kana Putatunda; m. Ivy M. George, June 7, 1984; children: Sujata, Shibani. BS, Instn. Engrs., Calcutta, 1975; MS, U. Mysore, India, 1979; PhD, Indian Inst. Tech., Bombay, 1983. Metallurgist Hindustan Copper Ltd., Khetri, Rajsthan, 1973-77; grad. rsch. asst. U. Mysore, Mangalore, India, 1977-79; R & D engr. Hindustan Electrographites, Bhopal, India, 1979-80; grad. rsch. asst. Indian Inst. Tech., Bombay, 1980-83; Fulbright scholar U. Ill., Urbana, 1983-84; assoc. prof. metallurgy Wayne State U., Detroit, 1985—. Govt. India scholar, New Delhi, 1977, 80; Fulbright fellow USIA, Washington, 1982. Mem. Am. Soc. Metals, The Metall. Soc., ASTM (editor spl. tech. pub. on fractography 1989), Iron and Steel Soc., Engring. Soc. Detroit. Home: 2732 Brady Dr Bloomfield Hills MI 48304-1725 Office: Wayne State U Coll Engring 5050 Anthony Wayne Dr Detroit MI 48202-3902 Fax: 313-577-3810. E-mail: sputa@chem1.eng.wayne.edu.

PUTCHAKAYALA, HARI BABU, engineering company executive; b. Maddirala, India, July 15, 1949; came to the U.S., 1978; s. Seshadri Chowdary and Sambrajyam (Penubothu) P.; m. Vijay Lakshmi, Aug. 9, 1976; children: Sashi Manohar, Gopi Krishna. BS in Chem. Engring., REC, Warangal, India, 1971; MS, BITS, Pilani, India, 1974; PhD, IIT, New Delhi, 1978. Registered profl. engr., Mich., Md., Calif., Pa., Mo. Trainee Fertilizer Corp., Bombay, 1971; environ. engr. Madison Madison Internat., Detroit, 1978-81, project coord., 1981-84, project mgr., 1984-89, v.p., 1990—, total quality officer, 1995—, also bd. dirs. Bd. dirs. Spack Inc., Bloomfield Hills, Mich. Contbr. articles to Canadian Jour. Chem. Engring. Rsch. fellow Univ. Grants Commn., 1974-78; recipient Cert. Boiler Efficiency Inst., 1981, U. Wis., 1986, 1992, Mich. State U., 1989, Ctr. for Hazardous Materials Rsch., 1990. Mem. AICE, NSPE, Am. Soc. for Quality Control, Am. Cons. Engrs. Coun., Project Mgmt. Inst. Achievements include development of design modification for incineration plants, O&M manuals for numerous water and wastewater facilities; design of wastewater treatment systems; research into energy and value engineering studies; capital improvement programs for public schools. Home: 654 Fox River Dr Bloomfield Hills MI 48304-1012 Office: Madison Internat 1420 Washington Blvd Detroit MI 48226-1718

PUTHENPURAKAL, JOSEPH MATHEW, information technology executive; b. Changanacherry, India, Feb. 12, 1949; came to U.S., 1978; s. Mathew Joseph and Teresa Mathew P.; m. Mary Jose Shirly, Aug. 21, 1977; children: Mathew Joseph, Thomas Joseph, Sherin Jose. BS, Kerala U., India, 1976; MS, Kerala U., 1978; AA, Dupage Coll., Glen Ellyn, Ill., 1982; BA, North Cen. Coll., Naperville, Ill., 1984; MBA, Thornwood U., Amsterdam, Netherlands, 1998; PhD, Thornwood U., Amsterdam, Netherlands, 2001. Software engr. AT&T Tech., Lisle, Ill., 1983-84; mem. tech. staff AT&T Bell Labs., Naperville, 1984-87; info. systems cons. Indecon, Inc., Chicago, 1987-89; pres. Chicagoland Star Telephone Co., 1988, Global Resources Co., Chgo., 1988—; with Jewel Info. Systems Group, Melrose Park, Ill.; pres. Optimum Techs. Inc., Lisle, 1992—. Trustee Rep. Presdl. Task Force, Washington, 1986. Mem. Data Processing Mgmt. Assn., Am. Entrepreneurs Assn., Internat. Traders. Avocations: reading, travel, swimming. Home: 1230 Golfview Dr Woodridge IL 60517 Office: Optimum Techs Inc 1230 Golfview Dr Woodridge IL 60517

PUTKA, ANDREW CHARLES, lawyer; b. Cleve., Nov. 14, 1926; s. Andrew George and Lillian M. (Koryta) P. Student, John Carroll U., 1944, U.S. Naval Acad., 1945-46; AB, Adelbert Coll., Western Res. U., 1949, JD, 1952. Bar: Ohio 1952. Practice law, Cleve.; instr. govt. Notre Dame Coll.; v.p. Koryta Bros. Coal Co., Cleve., 1952-56; supt. divsn. bldg. and loan assns. Ohio Dept. Commerce, 1959-63; pres., chmn. bd., CEO Am. Nat. Bank, Parma, Ohio, 1963-69; dir. fin. City of Cleve., 1971-74; dir. port control, 1974-78; dir. Cleve. Hopkins Internat. Airport, 1974-78. Mem. Ohio Ho. of Reps., 1953-56, Ohio Senate, 1957-58; dep. auditor, acting sec. Cuyahoga County Bd. Revision, 1970-71; mem. exec. com. Cuyahoga County Democratic Com., 1973-81, Assn. Ind. Colls. and Univs. Ohio, 1983-89; bd. govs. Sch. Law, Western Res. U., 1953-56; mem. exec. com. World Service Student Fund, 1950-52; U.S. rep. Internat. Pax Romana Congress, Amsterdam, 1950, Toronto, 1952; mem. lay advisory bd. Notre Dame Coll., 1968-90, trustee, 1990-93, hon. trustee, 1993—; mem. adv. bd. St. Andrew's Abbey, 1976-88 ; trustee Case-Western Res. U., Newman Found. No. Ohio, 1980-93, hon. trustee, 1993—; 1st v.p. First Cath. Slovak Union of U.S., 1977-80; pres. USO Council of Cuyahoga County, 1980-83. Voted an outstanding legislator Ohio Press Corrs., 1953; named to All-Star Legislative team Ohio Newspaper Corrs., 1955; named one of Fabulous Clevelanders Cleve. Plain Dealer, John Henry Newman honor Soc. Mem. Cuyahoga County, Cleve. Bar Assn., Nat. Assn. State Savs. and Loan Suprs. (past. nat. pres.), U.S. Savs. and Loan League (mem. legis com, 1960-63), Am. Legion, Ohio Mcpl. League (bd. trustees 1973), Parma C. of C. (bd. dirs., treas. 1965-67), Newman Fedn. (past nat. pres.), NCCJ, Catholic Lawyers Guild (treas.), Am. Ohio Bankers Assn., Am. Inst. Banking, Adelbert Alumni Assn. (exec. com.), Cathedral Latin Alumni Assn. (trustee 1952—), Internat. Order of Alhambra (internat. parliamentarian 1971—, past grand comdr., supreme advocate 1973), Amvets, KC, Pi Kappa Alpha, Delta Theta Phi (past. pres. Cleve. alumni senate, master inspector 1975). Office: 28 Pond Dr Cleveland OH 44116-1062

PUTMAN, DALE CORNELIUS, management consultant, lawyer; b. Ponca, Nebr., Apr. 29, 1927; s. Merle H. and Catherine V. (Sheahan) P.; m. Alice Anselmi, Sept. 8, 1951; children: Mark, Lee, Neil, Bruce, Kirk, Nancy, Wendy. BS, U. Nebr., 1949, LL.B., 1951. Bar: Nebr. 1951, Iowa 1951, Mo. 1977. Mgr. Interstate Assn. Credit Mgmt., Sioux City, Iowa, 1951-52; sec., legal counsel Metz Baking Co., 1953-66, v.p., 1966-69, exec. v.p., 1969-72, pres., 1972-76; chief operating officer Interstate Brands Corp., Kansas City, Mo., 1976-77, pres., dir., 1977-80, pres., chief exec. officer, 1980-84; chmn., chief exec. officer, pres., dir. Interstate Bakeries (formerly DPF, Inc.), 1980-84; pvt. practice mgmt. cons., 1984—. Served with U.S. Army, 1945-46. Knight, Order of the Holy Sepulchre of Jerusalem. Mem. KC (4th degree), Serra Interant. Republican. Roman Catholic. Home: 8405 Reinhardt Ln Shawnee Mission KS 66206-1316 E-mail: putman9752@aol.com.

PUTMAN, MICHAEL (JAMES PUTMAN), lawyer; b. San Antonio, May 12, 1948; s. Harold David and Elizaeth Finley (Henderson) P.; m. Kris J. Bird. BBA, S.W. Tex. State U., 1969; JD, St. Mary's U., 1972. Bar: Tex. 1972, U.S. Dist. Ct. (we. dist.) Tex. 1980, U.S. Ct. Appeals (5th and 11th cirs.) 1981; cert. personal injury trial law specialist Tex. Bd. Legal Specialization. Ptnr. Putman & Putman (Inc. 1981), San Antonio, 1972-81, officer, dir., 1981—. Mem. ATLA, State Bar Tex., Nat. Employment Lawyers Assn., Tex. Trial Lawyers Assn. (assoc. dir. 1995, dir. 1996-99, dir. emeritus 1999), Tex. Employment Lawyers Assn. (founding mem. 1998—), San Antonio Trial Lawyers Assn. (dir., officer 1975—, Am. Bd. Trial Advocates. Office: 310 S Saint Marys St Fl 27 San Antonio TX 78205-3113

PUTNAM, ADAM HUGHES, congressman, farmer, rancher; b. Bartow, Fla., July 31, 1974; s. William Dudley and Sara Elizabeth (Hughes) P. BS in Food and Resource Econs., U. Fla., 1995. Co-owner Dudley Putnam, Inc., Bartow, Fla., 1988—; mem. Fla. Ho. of Reps., Tallahassee, 1996-2000, 107th Congress from Fla. 12th dist., Washington, 2001—, mem. agrl. com., 1999—2000. Chmn. House Ag Com., 1999-2000. V.p. Fla. 4-H Found., 1997—. Mem. Fla. Cattlemen's Assn., Fla. Farm Bur., Bartow Kiwanis Club. Episcopalian. Avocations: hunting, fishing, reading. Office: US Ho of Reps 506 Cannon HOB Washington DC 20515

PUTNAM, ALLAN RAY, association executive; b. July 16, 1920; s. Carl Eugene and Alice (Atwood) P.; m. Marion S. Witmer, Aug. 8, 1942 (dec. Mar. 1993); children: Judith H., Robert W., Victoria, Christian; m. Ann K. Mossman, Sept. 10, 1994. BS in Econs., U. Pa., 1942. Mem. exec. staff Am. Electroplaters Soc., 1946-49; asst. exec. sec., pub. mag. Tool Engr. Am. Soc. Tool and Mfg. Engrs., 1949-59; mng. dir. ASM Internat., Materials Park, Ohio, 1959-84, sr. mng. dir., 1983-85; sec.-gen. World Materials Congress, 1986—. Prees. Nat. Assn. Exhibit Mgrs., 1955, Coun. Engring. and Sci. Soc. Execs., 1958; mgr. Am. Soc. Metals Found. Edn. and Rsch., 1963-85. Bd. govs., treas. Cape Cod Conservatory Music and Arts; bd. govs., pres. Cape Cod Symphony Orch. Served to capt. USAAF, 1942-46. Mem. ASTM, AAAS, NSTA (life), Am. Soc. Assn. Execs. (past dir.), Cleve. Conv. and Visitors Bur. (past dir.), Pres.'s Assn., Am. Mgmt. Assn., Metal Properties Coun. (past dir.), Franklin Inst., Internat. Iron and Steel Inst., Am. Iron and Steel Inst., S.E. Asia Iron and Steel Inst., Metals Soc. (London, hon.), Am. Assn. Cost Engrs., Associacao Brasileira de Metals, Italian Soc. Metallurgy, Chinese Soc. Metals, German Soc. Metals, Australasian Inst. Metals, Am. Nuclear Soc., Soc. Automotive Engrs., Soc. Mfg. Engrs., Cyrogenic Soc., Soc. for Advancement Materials and Process Engring., Am. Soc. Engring. Edn., Iron and Steel Inst. Japan (hon.), Metall. Soc., Greater Cleve. Growth Assn., Buckeye Trail Assn., Country Club (Pepper Pike, Ohio), Apalachian Mountain Club, Horseshoe Trail Club, Univ. Club (Washington), Orleans Yacht Club (bd. dirs.), Rotary (sec.). Home: 17 Pride's Path PO Box 2772 Orleans MA 02653-6772 E-mail: arputnam@capecod.net.

PUTNAM, FRANK WILLIAM, biochemistry and immunology educator; b. New Britain, Conn., Aug. 3, 1917; s. Frank and Henrietta (Holzmann) P.; m. Dorothy Alice Linder, Nov. 18, 1942; children— Frank William, Beverly Susan. BA, Wesleyan U., Middletown, Conn., 1939, MA, 1940; PhD, U. Minn., 1942; MA (hon.), Cambridge (Eng.) U., 1973. Instr., research asso. Duke U. Med. Sch., 1942-46; biochemist CWS, Camp Detrick, Md., 1946; asst. prof. U. Chgo., then assoc. prof. biochemistry, 1947-55; Lasdon research fellow Cambridge U., 1952-53; prof. biochemistry, head dept. U. Fla., 1955-65; prof. biology, dir. div. biol. scis. Ind. U., Bloomington, 1965-69, prof. molecular biology and zoology, 1972-74, disting. prof. molecular biology and biochemistry, 1974-88, prof. emeritus, 1989—. Bd. visitors Duke U. Med. Center, 1970-75; chmn. com. nomenclature of human immunoglobulins Internat. Union Immunol. Socs., 1971-76; chmn. basic sci. rev. bd. VA, 1972-76; chmn. cancer cause and prevention adv. com. Nat. Cancer Inst., 1974-75; sci. adv. com. Papanicolaou Cancer Research Inst., 1976-82; research rev. com. ARC, 1973-77; sci. com. Brussels Colloquium on Protides of Biol. Fluids, 1970-90; chmn. virus cancer program adv. com. Nat. Cancer Inst., 1975-77; sr. med. adv. group VA, 1976-80; council div. biol. scis. and Pritzker Med. Sch., U. Chgo., 1977-87; chmn. Assembly Life Scis. Nat. Acad. Scis., 1977-81; mem. U.S. Nat. Com. Biochemistry, 1973-79; pres. sci. adv. com. G.E.R.M.I., Lyon, France, 1981-87. Co-author, editor: The Plasma

Proteins, vol. 1, Isolation, Characterization and Function, 1960, vol. 2, Biosynthesis, Metabolism, Alterations in Disease, 1960, The Plasma Proteins, 2d edit., Structure, Function, and Genetic Control, Vol. 1, 1975. Vol. 2, 1975, Vol. 3, 1977, Vol. 4, 1984, Vol. 5, 1987; mem. editorial bd. Archives of Biochemistry and Biophysics, 1954-59, Science, 1968-82, Immunochemistry, 1972-75, Biomed. News, 1969-73, Fedn. Proc. 1958-63; Author numerous research papers. Trustee Argonne Univs. Assn., 1981-82; bd. govs. U. Chgo. Argonne Nat. Lab., 1983-89, chmn. Sci. and tech. com., 1983-87; bd. dirs. Radiation Research Found., 1981-87. Markle scholar med. scis., 1950-56; Guggenheim fellow, 1970; fellow Churchill Coll., Cambridge U., 1973— ; recipient Distinguished award teaching and research Wesleyan U., 1964, Distinguished Service award in medicine U. Chgo., 1968; Outstanding Achievement award U. Minn., 1974 Fellow AAAS, N.Y. Acad. Scis.; mem. Nat. Acad. Scis., Am. Acad. Arts and Scis. (Midwest council 1975-84), Pan-Am. Assn. Biomed. Scis. (sec.-gen. 1975-78), Japan Electrophoresis Soc. (hon.), Am. Inst. Biol. Scis. (life), Am. Soc. Biol. Chemists (sec. 1958-63), Soc. Exptl. Biology and Medicine, Am. Assn. Immunologists, Am. Chem. Soc. (chmn. div. biol. chemistry 1966-67), Soc. Peruana de Patologia (hon.), Fedn. Socs. Exptl. Biology (chmn. secs. com. 1958-63), Protein Soc., Internat. Soc. Thrombosis Haemostasis, Phi Beta Kappa, Sigma Xi, Phi Lambda Upsilon, Delta Sigma Rho. Clubs: Cosmos. Address: 5025 E Heritage Woods Rd Bloomington IN 47401-9314

PUTNAM, FREDERICK WARREN, JR. bishop; b. Red Wing, Minn., June 17, 1917; s. Frederick W. and Margaret (Bunting) P.; m. Helen Kathryn Prouse, Sept. 24, 1942; children: James Douglas, John Frederick, Andrew Warren. BA, U. Minn., 1939; M.Div., Seabury-Western Theol. Sem., 1942, D.D., 1963; postgrad., State U. Iowa, 1946-47, Mpls. Coll. of Art & Design, 1984-97. Ordained to ministry Episcopal Ch. as deacon, priest, 1942. Pastor in Windom and Worthington, Minn., 1942-43, Iowa City, 1943-47, Evanston, Ill., 1947-59, Wichita, Kans., 1960-63; Episc. chaplain State U. Iowa, 1943-47; suffragan bishop Episcopal Diocese, Okla., 1963-79; bishop Episcopal Ch. in Navajoland, 1979-83; asst. bishop Diocese of N.C., 1983, Diocese of Minn., 1983-89, 96-99; acting rector St. George's Episcopal, Pearl Harbor, Hawaii, 1984-85, 96, St. Clement's, Honolulu, 1986, St. John's, Kula, Maui, Hawaii, 1988, 98, St. Elizabeth's, Honolulu, 1990; interim rector St. Stephen's Episcopal Ch., Edina, Minn., 1991-92, Trinity Episcopal Ch., Pocatello, Idaho, 1994; vis. bishop Diocese of N.J., 1995. Bd. dirs. Kiyosoto Ednl. Experiment Program, 1954-91, Mobile Outreach Ministry, 1998—, v.p., 1989-91; cons. Oklahoma City Community Relation Commn., 1966-70; Pres. Okla. Conf. Religion and Race, 1963-67; v.p. Greater Oklahoma City Council Chs., 1966-67; nat. chaplain Brotherhood of St. Andrew, 1967-79, mem. brotherhood legion, 1972—; priest assoc. Order Holy Cross, 1942—; exec. com. Conf. Diocesan Execs., 1969-76, pres., 1972-74; mem. Okla. Commn. United Ministries in Higher Edn., 1970-79, pres., 1973-75; mem. nat. com. on Indian work Episc. Ch., 1977-80; chaplain Okla. Assn. Alcoholism and Alcohol Abuse, 1974-78; hon. life mem. Oklahoma City and County Criminal Justice Council, 1978—; Bechtel lectr. U. Denver, 1966. Editor: (pub.) Sharers Mag., 1957-63; contbr. articles to profl. publs. Founder, pres. Oklahoma City Met. Alliance for Safer City, 1971-78; Trustee Seabury-Western Theol. Sem., 1959-65, Episcopal Theol. Sem. Southwest, 1966-69, St. Simeon's Episcopal Home, 1963-79, St. Crispins Episcopal Conf. Ctr., 1963-79, Casady Sch., 1963-79, Holland Hall Sch., 1963-79, Episcopal Soc. Cultural and Racial Unity, 1967-70; trustee Neighborhood Services Orgn., treas., 1969; founder, 1st pres. Friends of Wichita Pub. Libr., 1962; bd. dirs. Minn. Photographic Exbn.; chmn. Mpls.-St. Paul Internat. Photog. Exhbn., 1987, 89; State Bd. Minn. Common Cause, 1989—, state chmn., 1993-95—; bd. dirs. Minn. Com. for Pub. Edn. Recipient Disting. Service award Evanston Jr. C. of C., 1952; Merit award Photog. Soc. Am. Fellow Coll. Preachers; mem. ACLU, Assoc. Parishes (pres. 1960-64), Mpls. Soc. Fine Arts (mem. photo coun.), Photog. Soc. Am., Am. Com. for KEEP (v.p. 1961-70, 90), Walker Art Ctr., Sierra Club, Met. Sr. Fedn., Audubon Club, Am. Assn. Ret. Persons, Minn. Hort. Soc., Hist. Soc. Episcopal Ch., Archaeol. Conservancy, Ancient Bibl. Manuscripts Ctr., Claremont, Calif., World Future Soc., Photographic Soc. Am. (assoc. 1989—, mem. v.p., 1995-97—), Twin Cities Assn. Camera Clubs (v.p. 1987), U. Minn. Alumni Assn., Minn. Hist. Soc., St. Paul Camera Club, Crosstown Camera Club, N.Am. Rights Fund., People for the Am. Way, Episcopal Peace Fellowship, Amnesty Internat., Greenpeace, Liturgical Conf., Living Ch. Found., Worldwatch Inst., Clan Douglas Soc., Northwest Racquet and Swim Club, Explorers Club, Phi Kappa Psi. Clubs: Normandale Tennis and Swim. Home: 5229 Meadow Rdg Edina MN 55439-1412

PUTNAM, GEORGE W., JR. retired army officer; b. Ft. Fairfield, Maine, May 5, 1920; s. George W. and Rae B. (Merrithew) P.; m. Elaine Anderson (dec. 1973); m. Claudine Mahin (div. 1995); m. Helen Guerin, 1995; children: James M., J. Glenn; stepchildren: Philip Mahin, Leslie Mahin. Enlisted man U.S. Army, 1941-42, commd. 2d lt., 1942, advanced through grades to maj. gen., 1970; comdg. gen. 1st Aviation Brigade, Vietnam, 1970, 1st Cav, Divsn., Vietnam, 1970-71; dir. Mil. Personnel Mgmt., Hdqrs. Dept. Army, Washington, 1971-75; comdg. gen. U.S. Army So. European Task Force, Vicenza, Italy, 1975-77, U.S. Army Phys. Disability Agy., Washington, 1977-81; ret. U.S. Army, 1981. Dir. Army Coun. Rev. Bds., 1977-81; pres. Nat. Capital Retiree Coun., 1982-85. Internat. judge 5th and 6th World Helicopter Championships, 1986, 89, 94, chief judge 7th World Championship, 1992; U.S. mem. Internat. Helicopter com. Fedn. Aeronautique Internationale, 1988-91, 93-95; bd. dirs. Army Aviation Mus. Found., 1987—, pres., 1993-96; chmn. bd. trustees Army Aviation Hall of Fame, 1996-2001. Inducted Army Aviation Hall of Fame, 1980. Mem. Nat. Aero. Assn. (sr. v.p. 1991-95, Fedn. Aero. Internat. Affairs (sr. v.p. 1995-98 and U.S. v.p. 1995-98), Army Aviation Assn. Am. (sr. v.p., pres. 1983-87, pres. scholarship found. 1991-93), Helicopter Club Am. (pres. 1988-90. recipient Elder Statesman of Aviation award, 1998). Home: 4106 N Richmond St Arlington VA 22207-4816 E-mail: gputj@aol.com.

PUTNAM, J. STEPHEN, financial executive; 3 children. BA, Bowdoin Coll., 1965. Pres. Raymond James Fin. Svcs. Inc., St. Petersburg, Fla. Sr. v.p. Raymond James & Assocs., Inc.; bd. dirs., exec. v.p. Raymond James Fin., Inc.; treas. Meerschaert Mut. Fund; v.p., bd. dirs. F.L. Putnam Securities. Bd. dirs., former chmn. bd. St. Joseph's Coll., North Windham, Maine; bd. dirs., former chmn. Citizens Scholarship Found. Am., Inc.; former pres. Palm Harbor (Fla.) Cmty. Svc. Agy.; former chmn. Boston Stock Exch., Nat. Assn. Securities Dealers, Inc. Decorated Bronze Star, Army Commendation medal. Mem.: Youth Soccer Assn. Office: Raymond James Fin Svcs Inc 880 Carillon Pkwy Saint Petersburg FL 33716-1100

PUTNAM, JOANNE WHITE, college financial aid administrator, bookkeeper; b. Chattanooga, Nov. 27, 1945; d. Joseph Mitchel and Virginia (Spencer) White; m. Richard Wocester Putnam, Dec. 23, 1967; children: Joseph Worcester, Charles Jason. BS, Emory U., 1967; MEd, We. Carolina U., 2001. Sci. programmer Lockheed Ga. Co., Marietta, Ga., 1967-71; bookkeeper Dr. Richard Worcester Putnam, Blairsville, 1973—; admissions staff Young Harris (Ga.) Coll., 1984-86, dir. fin. aid, 1986—. Contbr. articles to profl. jours. Mem. Union County Hist. Soc., 1980—, Creative Study Club, Atlanta, 1976—; youth advisor Sharp Meml. United Meth. Ch., 1991-93. Mem. Ga. Student Fin. Aid Adminstrs. (program com. 1989-90, nominating com. 1988-89), So. Assn. Student Fin. Aid Adminstrs., Nat. Assn. Student Fin. Aid Adminstrs., Garden Club of Ga. Inc. (chmn. hydroponics 1979-81, chmn. horticulture 1981-83, dir. laurel dist. 1983-85, chmn., advisor laurel dist. 1985—), Nat. Coun. State Garden Club Inc. (master flower show judge 1989—, landscape design critic 1985—, gardening cons. 1985—), Blairsville Garden Club (pres. 1977-79, awards and legislation chmn. 1989-93, chmn. by-laws com. 1999—). Avocations: flower arranging, gardening, walking. Home: PO Box 2059 Blairsville GA 30514-2059 Office: Young Harris Coll PO Box 247 Young Harris GA 30582-0247

PUTNAM, LLOYD ALAN, retired food products executive, apple specialist; b. Lyons, N.Y., May 1, 1922; s. Horace McKinley and Elizabeth G. (Lauster) P.; m. Mary Janet Taylor; children: Robert Wayne, William Taylor. BS in Agr., Cornell U., 1944. Asst. county agrl. agt., then county agrl. agt. Niagara County Extn. Svc., State of N.Y., Lockport, 1944-47; field rep., then sales mgr. Friend Mfr. Co., Gasport, N.Y., 1947-50; 1st exec. sec. Western N.Y. Apple Growers Assn., Rochester, 1950-55; 1st gen. mgr. Lake Ontario Fruit Growers Coop., Medina, 1955-62; sales mgr., then exec. v.p., gen. mgr. Sodus (N.Y.) Fruit Farm Inc., 1962-81; dir. agrl. ops. Nat. Fruit Product Co., Winchester, Va., 1981-90; ret. Nat. Fruit Products, 1990. Industry rep. on acad. rev. com. dept. agrl. econs. Cornell U., Ithaca, N.Y., 1970s, mem. food sci. adv. coun., chmn. adv. coun. Coll. Agrl. Life Scis., 1979-81; pres. Internat. Apple Inst., Washington, 1979-80; trustee Lockport (N.Y.) Savs. Bank, 1961-81; chmn. Empire State Coun. Agrl. Orgns.; advisor com. to develop consensus regulation for farm worker safety regulations U.S. EPA. Mem. bd. suprs. Frederick County, Winchester, Va., 1986-88; mem. steering com. for Vision 2020 long range planning com. City of Winchester and Frederick County. Recipient Golden Apple award N.Y. State Cherry Growers and Western N.Y. Apple Growers, 1989. Mem. Nat. Coun. Agrl. Employers (Ea. v.p. 1980-81, Svc. award 1991), N.Y. State Hort. Soc. (past pres.), Western N.Y. Apple Growers Assn. (past. pres.), N.Y. State Assn. Food Processors (past. pres.), N.Y. State Agrl. Businessmen's Assn. (past pres.), Internat. Apple Inst. (pres. 1979-80), Empire State Coun. Agrl. Orgns. (chmn.), Internat. Apple Assn. (bd. dirs.), Rotary, Kiwanis (pres. Lockport club 1963, bd. dirs. Winchester club), Suntree Country Club (pres. 1995-96). Republican. Methodist. Avocation: golf. Home: 834 Oak Forest Dr The Villages FL 32162-7453

PUTNAM, MARLENE EVANS, artist; b. Hartford, Conn., Nov. 2, 1941; d. Charles Evans and Adrienne Edmay Levasseur; m. Harold Barnes Putnam, Jr., Mar. 9, 1980. Student, U. Hartford, 1960-63, Mus. of Fine Arts, Boston, 1971-77. Profl. artist Rockport (Mass.) Art Assn., 1986—, North Shore Art Assn., Gloucester, Mass., 1980—, Internat. Soc. of Marine Painters, Bradenton, Fla., 1983—, Art of the Sea, Rockland, Maine, 1995—, Tequesta (Fla.) Galleries, 1986—; fellow Am. Artist Profl. League, N.Y.C., 1996—. One-woman shows include Elliott Mus., 1993, Vero Beach Mus. Art, 1992, Art of the Sea, S. Thomaston, Maine, 1995; permanant collections at Harvard Law Sch., Dartmouth Coll., Nat. Wildlife Refuge, Cape Canaveral, Fla., Fla. Supreme Ct., Elliott Mus., Stuart, Fla., Vero Beach Mus. Art. Recipient over 50 awards in Fla. and Mass. Fellow Am. Artist Profl. League; mem. Rotary. Democrat. Avocations: learning and playing the viola, reading, computers, gardening, hiking. E-mail: putnam2art@cs.com .

PUTNAM, MICHAEL COURTNEY JENKINS, classics educator; b. Springfield, Mass., Sept. 20, 1933; s. Roger Lowell and Caroline (Jenkins) P. AB, Harvard U., 1954, AM, 1956, PhD, 1959; LLD (hon.), Lawrence U., 1985. Instr. classics Smith Coll., Northampton, Mass., 1959-60; faculty classics Brown U., Providence, 1960—, prof., 1967—, chmn., 2000-2001, prof. comparative lit., 1980—, MacMillan prof. of classics, 1985—; acting dir. Ctr. for Hellenic Studies, Harvard U., 1961-62, sr. fellow, 1971-86; Townsend prof. classics Cornell U., 1985; Mellon prof.-in-charge Am. Acad. in Rome, 1989-91. Scholar in residence Am. Acad. in Rome, 1969-70, mem. classical jury, 1982-83, trustee, 1991—; assoc. univ. seminar on classical civilization Columbia U., N.Y.C., 1972—; mem. cath. Commn. on Intellectual and Cultural Affairs, 1969—; mem. adv. coun. dept. classics Princeton U., 1981-87, chmn., 1983-87; cons. Am. Coun. Learned Socs., 1987-89; mem. Inst. for Advanced Study, 1987-88; vis. scholar Phi Beta Kappa, 1994-95; councillor Assn. of Lit. Scholars and Critics, 1996-99. Author: The Poetry of the Aeneid, 1965, Virgil's Pastoral Art, 1970, Tibullus: A Commentary, 1973, Virgil's Poem of the Earth, 1979, Essays on Latin Lyric, Elegy and Epic, 1982, Artifices of Eternity: Horace's Fourth Book of Odes, 1986, Virgil's Aeneid: Interpretation and Influence, 1995, Virgil's Epic Designs, 1998, Horace's Carmen Saeculare, 2000; contbr. articles to profl. jours. Sole trustee Lowell Obs., Flagstaff, Ariz., 1967-87, bd. advisors, 1987—; trustee Bay Chamber Concerts, Camden, Maine, 1972-88, incorporator, 1988-94; mem. bd. cons. Portsmouth Abbey Sch., 1985-89; hon. sec. Keats-Shelley Meml. Assn., Rome, 1989-91. Rome Prize fellow Am. Acad. in Rome, 1963-64; Guggenheim Meml. fellow, 1966-67; sr. fellow NEH, 1973-74, cons. 1974-78, 87-90; Am. Council Learned Soc. fellow, 1983-84. Fellow Am. Acad. Arts and Scis. 1996—; mem. Am. Philol. Assn. (bd. dirs. 1972-75, mem. com. on award of merit 1975-78, chmn. 1977-78, 1st v.p. 1981, pres. 1982, del. Am. Coun. Learned Socs. 1984-87, Charles J. Goodwin award of merit 1971, fin. trustee 1997—), mem. Am. Philosophical Soc., 1998—; Archaeol. Inst. Am., Classical Assn. New Eng., Medieval Acad. Am., Vergilian Soc. Am. (trustee 1969-73, v.p. 1974-76), Accademia Nazionale Virgiliana, Acad. Lit. Studies, Art Club. E-mail: michael. Office: Brown U Dept Classics Providence RI 02912-1856 E-mail: michael_putnam@brown.edu

PUTNAM, PAUL ADIN, retired government agency official; b. Springfield, Vt., July 12, 1930; s. Horace Adin and Beatrice Nellie (Baldwin) P.; m. Elsie Mae (Ramseyer) June 12, 1956; children: Pamela Ann, Penelope Jayne, Adin Tyler II, Paula Anna. BS, U. Vt., 1952; MS, Wash. State U., 1954; PhD, Cornell U., 1957. Research animal scientist Agrl. Research Service, USDA, Beltsville, Md., 1957-66, investigation leader beef cattle nutrition, 1966-68, chief beef cattle research br., 1968-72; asst. dir. Beltsville Agrl. Research Ctr., 1972-80, dir., 1980-84; dir. cen. plains area Ames, Iowa, 1984-87; assoc. dir. mid. south area Stoneville, Miss., 1987-88; dir. mid south area, 1988-94; selectman Town of Springfield, Vt., 1996—2002. Contbr. articles to profl. jours. Recipient Kidder medal U. Vt.; Outstanding Performance awards USDA, also cert. merit; Danforth fellow; Borden fellow; Purina Research fellow. Fellow AAAS (rep. sect. O), Am. Soc. Animal Sci. (pres., North Atlantic sect., chmn. various coms., N.E. sect. Disting. Service award); mem. Am. Dairy Sci. Assn., Orgn. Profl. Employees USDA (pres. Beltsville chpt.), Council for Agrl. Sci. and Tech. Home: 36 Putnam Rd Springfield VT 05156-9115 E-mail: PPutnam@Vermontel.net.

PUTNAM, ROBERT ERVIN, chemist, consultant; b. Northampton, Mass., Oct. 18, 1927; s. Ervin Earl and Mary Gertrude (Connelly) P.; m. Caroline Wright, Aug. 23, 1952; children: David Earl, Mary Caroline, Robert Edward, Andrew Wright. BS in Chemistry, U. Mass., 1950; PhD in Organic Chemistry, U. Ill., 1953. Rsch. chemist E.I. du Pont de Nemours, Wilmington, Del., 1953-59, rsch. supr., 1959-65, sr. rsch. supr., 1965-67, Parkersburg, W.Va., 1967-78, rsch. lab. supt., 1978-82, rsch. mgr., 1982-85; adj. faculty Washington State C.C., Marietta, Ohio, 1985-95; pvt. practice, 1985-95. Alumni adv. coun. dept. chemistry U. Mass., Amherst, 1975-78; instr. chemistry Marietta Coll., 1982-89, adv. coun., 1989-95, dir. Inst. for Learning in Retirement, 1995-98. Editor Bull. Am. Friends of Puttenham, 1984—; contbr. 20 articles to profl. jours. With USNR, 1945-46. NSF fellow, U. Ill., 1952-53. Fellow AAAS; mem. Am. Chem. Soc. (chmn. Ohio Valley sect. 1976-78), Rsch. Soc. Am., Valley Renaissance Consort, Mid-Ohio Valley Aviation Assn., Sigma Xi, Gamma Alpha, Phi Lambda Upsilon. Democrat. Mem. Unitarian Ch. Achievements include patents on fluorine containing polymers and monomers, ion exchange resins; research on industrial processes for nylon, polyacetals, acrylics, rubber toughened plastics, fluorinated plastics. Address: 100 Alden Ave Marietta OH 45750-1138 E-mail: putnamr@charter.net.

PUTNAM, WILLIAM LOWELL, science association administrator; b. Springfield, Mass., Oct. 25, 1924; s. Roger Lowell and Caroline Piatt (Jenkins) P.; m. Joan Fitzgerald, Sept. 29, 1951 (dec. April 1993); children: Katherine Elizabeth Putnam Delaney, W. Lowell, Erica A. Broman; m. Katherine E. Flynn, Sept. 18, 1999. Grad., Harvard Coll., 1945. With Springfield C. of C., 1950-52; founder, chmn. Springfield TV Corp., 1952-84; with Carroll Travel Bur., 1984-98. Vice chmn. Assn. Maximum Svc. Telecasters, 1975-84; sec.-treas. NBC Affiliates, 1980-83. Sole trustee Lowell Obs., Flagstaff, Ariz.; chmn. Springfield Park Commn., 1991-95. 1st lt. U.S. Army, 1943-45. Decorated Silver Star, Bronze Star, Purple Heart. Mem. Assn. Canadian Mountain Guides (hon.), Alpine Club Can. (hon.), Appalachian Mountain Club (hon.), Am. Alpine Club (pres. 1974-76, treas. 1977-91, hon.), Internat. Union Alpine Clubs (Am. del., v.p.). Avocation: alpinism. Home and Office: Lowell Obs Flagstaff AZ 86001 E-mail: putnam@lowell.edu.

PUTNEY, LACEY EDWARD, state legislator; b. Big Island, Va., June 27, 1928; m. Elizabeth Harlow; children: Susan Powers, L. Edward Jr. BA, Washington & Lee U. Mem. Va. State Legis., 1962—, spkr. ho., 2000—, co-chair privileges & elections com., mem. appropriations com., mem. agrl. com., mem. rules com. Independent. Baptist. Office: Gen Assembly Bldg PO Box 406 Richmond VA 23218-0406*

PUTNEY, MARK WILLIAM, lawyer, utility executive; b. Marshalltown, Iowa, Jan. 25, 1929; s. Lawrence Charles and Geneva (Eldridge) P.; m. Ray Ann Bartnek, May 25, 1962 (dec. Feb. 2000); children: Andi Bartnek, William Bradford, Blake Reinhart. BA, U. Iowa, 1951, JD, 1957. Bar: Iowa 1957, U.S. Supreme Ct. 1960. Ptnr. Bradshaw, Fowler, Proctor & Fairgrave, Des Moines, 1961-72, of counsel, 1992-94; chmn., CEO. Bradford & Blake Ltd., Dakota Dunes, S.D., 1992—; pres., chmn., chief exec. officer Iowa Resources, Inc., 1984-90; chmn., chief exec. officer Iowa Power & Light Co., 1984-90, Iowa Gas Co., 1984-85, Midwest Resources Inc., 1990-92. Civilian aide to Sec. Army for Iowa, 1975-77; bd. dirs. Greater Des Moines YMCA, 1976-86, Boys' Home Iowa, 1982-86, Hoover Presdl. Libr. Assn., 1983—, U. Iowa Found., 1984—, Edison Electric Inst., 1986-89; bd. dirs. Greater Des Moines Com., 1984—, pres. 1988; bd. dirs. Assoc. Edison Illuminating Cos., 1988-93, pres., 1991-92; chmn. Iowa Com. Employer Support of Guard and Res., 1979-86; bd. dirs. Des Moines Devel. Corp., 1984-92, chmn., 1989-90. With USAF, 1951-53. Recipient Disting. Alumnus award U. Iowa, 1995. Mem. Iowa Utility Assn. (chmn. 1989, dir.), Des Moines Club (pres. 1977), Desert Forest Golf Club (Carefree, Ariz.), Masons, Shriners, Delta Chi, Phi Delta Phi. Republican. Episcopalian. Home: PO Box 19214 Reno NV 89511

PUTNEY, MARY LYNN, bank administrator, educator; b. N.Y.C., Feb. 26, 1948; d. Joseph John Berry and Evelyn Marie (Geoghegan) Schneir; m. Paul Michael McCaffery, May 18, 1968 (div. June 1976); children: Melissa Berry McCaffery, Paul David McCaffery; m. Frederick Bates Putney, May 30, 1992. MBA in Fin., Columbia U., 1982. Various positions Citibank, N.Y.C., 1974-85, v.p. fgn. exch., 1985-88, v.p. leveraged capital, 1988-92, mng. dir. pvt. banking, 1992-95, mng. dir. global equity, 1995—; adj. prof. Columbia Bus. Sch., 1986—. Dir. Sinter Metal Corp., Cleve.; mem. adv. bd. AIG Millenium Fund, Russia, CVC/Opportunity Ptnrs., Brazil. Contbr. articles to profl. jours. Dir. Project Renewal, N.Y.C., 1995—, Mary Knoll Sch. Theology, Ossining, N.Y., 1994-95. Mem. Emily's List, Women's Campaign Fund, Sleepy Hollow Country Club, Sea Pines Country Club, Beta Gamma Sigma. Avocations: golf, bridge. Office: Citibank NA 153 E 53rd St New York NY 10022-4611

PUTNEY, PAUL WILLIAM, lawyer; b. Phila., Feb. 6, 1940; s. R. Emerson and Dorothea (Schulz) P.; m. Joan E. High, June 9, 1961; children: Joanna E., Andrew E. AB, Princeton U., 1962; JD, Harvard U., 1965. BarP Pa. 1965, U.S. Dist. Ct. (ea. dist.) Pa. 1966, U.S. Supreme Ct. 1977, N.Y. 1988. Assoc. Dechert Price & Rhoads, Phila., 1965-73, ptnr., 1973—74, N.Y.C., 1977—, mng. ptnr., 1987—94; chmn. trust and estates dept., 1994—; dep. chief broadcast bur. FCC, Washington, 1974-77. Chmn. Phila. Presbytery Homes, Inc., 1987-93. Mem.: ABA. Office: Dechert Price & Rhoads 4000 Bell Atlantic Tower 1717 Arch St Philadelphia PA 19103-2793

PUTNEY, WAINSCOTT WALKER, lawyer; b. Pitts., Nov. 10, 1957; s. Charles Walker and Karen (Albright) P.; m. Sharon Lynn Smith, Apr. 11, 1982. BS in Physics, Va. Mil. Inst., 1978; JD, U. Tulsa, 1981; LLM, George Washington U., 1991. Bar: Fla. 1981, D.C. 1990, Va. 1993, U.S. Dist. Ct. (mid. dist.) Fla. 1981, U.S. Ct. Appeals (11th cir.) 1984, U.S. Dist. Ct. (so. dist.) Fla. 1985, U.S. Ct. Appeals (D.C. cir.) 1987, U.S. Dist. Ct. (ea. and we. dists.) Va. 1989, U.S. Ct. Appeals (4th cir.) 1993, U.S. Dist. Ct. (no. dist.) Okla. 1999, U.S. Ct. Appeals (10th cir.) 1999, U.S. Ct. Fed. Claims, 1989, U.S. Ct. Appeals (fed. cir.) 1990, U.S. Supreme Ct. 1985, Okla. 2001. Assoc. Sanders, McEwan, Mims & Martinez, Orlando, Fla., 1981-85; pvt. practice, 1985-89; trial atty. U.S. Dept. Justice, Washington, 1989-99; asst. U.S. atty. U.S. Atty.'s Office, Tulsa, 1999—. Bankruptcy trustee, Orlando, 1985-89; lectr. comml. law Mary Washington Coll., Fredericksburg, Va., 1997-99. Contbr. articles to profl. jours. Precinct committeeman Orange County Rep. Exec. Com., 1987-88. Recipient cert. of appreciation Legal Aid Soc., 1988. Mem. Fla. Bar Assn. (bd. govs. young lawyers divsn. 1991-93), IEEE.

PUTTER, DAVID SETH, lawyer; b. N.Y.C., Mar. 11, 1944; s. Norton Seth and Ruth Crystal P. Student, U. Granada, Spain, 1964; BA in Biology, Beloit Coll., Spain, 1965; JD, Syracuse U., 1968. Bar: Vt. 1970, N.Y. 1971, U.S. Dist. Ct. Vt. 1970, U.S. Ct. Appeals (2d cir.) 1975, U.S. Ct. Claims 1998. Atty. Putter & Carrington, Arlington, Vt., 1970-73; Bennington County pub. defender State of Vt., Bennington, 1973-76, law clk. to Superior Ct. judges Burlington, 1976-78, asst. atty. gen. Montpelier, 1979-81; with Putter & Unger, 1981-88; assoc. Saxer, Anderson, Wolinsky & Sunshine, 1988-2000; ptnr. Putter and Edson, LLP, 2001—; pvt. practice, 2002—. Contbr. articles to profl. jours. Acting Superior Ct. judge, 1997—; chair legal panel ACLU Vt., 1988—; sponsored advisor on assembly, free press, free speech USIA, Lusaka, Zambia, Kampala, Uganda, 1996. Recipient Jonathan Chase award ACLU Vt., 1991, 97. Avocations: hiking, camping, theater, travel, music (folk and rock). Home: 6 Towne St Montpelier VT 05602-4231 Office: 15 E State St Montpelier VT 05602-3010

PUTTER, IRVING, French language educator; b. N.Y.C., Dec. 3, 1917; s. Joseph and Anna (Schrank) P.; children— Paul Stephen, Candace Anne Putter. BA, CCNY, 1938; MA, State U. Iowa, 1941; PhD, Yale U., 1949. Mem. faculty U. Calif.-Berkeley, 1947-88; prof. French U. Calif. at Berkeley, 1961-88, chmn. dept., 1968-71, humanities research fellow, 1971-72, 78-79, 84-85. Author: Leconte de Lisle and His Contemporaries, 1951, The Pessimism of Leconte de Lisle: Sources and Evolution, 1954, The Pessimism of Leconte de Lisle: The Work and The Time, 1961, La Dernière Illusion de Leconte de Lisle: Lettres Inédites a Emilie Leforestier, 1968; also numerous articles.; editor, translator: Chateaubriand: Atala, René, 1952. Guggenheim fellow, 1955-56; Fulbright fellow, 1955-56 Home: 115 Saint James Dr Piedmont CA 94611-3603

PUTTERMAN, FLORENCE GRACE, artist, printmaker; b. N.Y.C., Apr. 14, 1927; d. Nathan and Jean (Feldman) Hirsch; m. Saul Putterman, Dec. 19, 1947. BS, NYU, 1947; MFA, Pa. State U., 1973. Founder, pres. Arts Unlimited, Selinsgrove, Pa., 1969—; curator Milton Shoe Collection, 1970—; artist in residence Title III Program Cultural Enrichment in Schs. Program, 1969-70; instr. Lycoming Coll., Williamsport, Pa., 1972-74, Susquehanna U., Selinsgrove, PA, 1984—. One-woman shows include Everson Mus., Syracuse, N.Y., 1976, Hagerstown, Md., 1978, Stuhr Mus., Grand Island, N.B., 1979, Muhlenburg Ctr. for the Arts, Pa., 1985, Harmon Gallery, Fla., 1985, The State Mus. of Pa., 1985-86, Segal Gallery, N.Y., 1986, Canton Inst. Fine Arts, Ohio, 1986, Fla. Biennial Polk Mus., Lakeland, Fla., 1987, 89, Artists Choose Artists, Tampa Mus., 1987, Auburn Works on Paper, 1987, Ala., Ruth Volid Gallery, Chgo., 1989, Polk Mus. Art, Lakeland, Fla., 1989, Lowe Gallery, Atlanta, 1990, Mickelson Gallery, Washington, 1990, Palmer Mus., Pa. State U., 1990, Payne Gallery, Moravian Coll., 1991, Everhart Mus., Scranton, Pa., 1991, Lowe Gallery, L.A., 1992, Center Gallery, Bucknell U., Pa., 1993, Lore Degenstein Gallery, Susquehanna U., Selinsgrove, Pa., 1993, Lowe Gallery, Atlanta, 1993, Down Roll Gallery, Sarasota, Fla., Gallery 10, Washington, Donn Roll Contemporary, Sarasota, Fla., 1996, Grand Central Gallery, Tampa Fla., 1997, Walter Wickiser Gallery, N.Y., Hodges-Taylor Gallery, Charlotte N.C., Ziegenfuss Gallery, Sarasota, Burroughs-Chapin Mus., Myrtle Bend, S.C., Lighthouse Gallery, Tequesta, Fla., 1998, Galerie Lumiere, Savannah, Ga., 1999, Walter Wickiser Gallery, N.Y., 1999, Ellen Noel Art Mus., Odessa, Tex., 1999, Spartansburg County Mus. Art, Spartansburg, S.C., 2000, Saginaw (Mich.) Art Mus., 2000, Art Mus., No. Mich. U., Marquette, Lancaster Mus. Art, 2001, Albany (Ga.) Art Mus., 2002; exhibited in group shows at Libr. Congress, Soc. Am. Graphic Artists, Ball State Drawing Ann., Muncie, Ind., Arts Club N.Y., Colorprint, U.S.A., Smithsonian Traveling Exhbn., Boston Printmakers, N.C. Print & Drawing, Chautauqua Nat., U. Dallas Nat. Print Invitational, Segal Gallery, Rutgers Drawing, Polk Mus., Tampa Mus., Sichaun Fine Art Inst., Mickelson Gallery, Harmon Gallery, Mus. Art U. Ariz., 1988, U. Del., Newark, 1988 Mid Am. Biennial, Owensboro Mus. Art, VCCA Exhbn. Mcpl. Gallery, Regensburg, Federal Republic of Germany, 1989, Erie (Pa.) Art Mus., 1990, 1990 twenty year survey Palmer Mus., Pa. State U., Univ. Park, Payne Gallery Moravian Coll., Bethlehem, Pa., 1991, Everhart Mus., Scranton, Pa., 1991, U. Del. Biennial, Phila. Watercolor Soc., Noyes Mus., N.J., 1992, Erie (Pa.) Mus., 1991, Mus. Fine Arts, Hanoi, 1991, Spanish Embassy, Madrid, 1992, Anita Shapolsky Gallery, N.Y., 1990, American Women's Artists, Foster Harman Gallery Sarasota, Fla., 1993, Humphrey Gallery, N.Y., 1992, Anita Shapolsky Gallery, N.Y., 1993, Fla. Printmakers, Miami, 1993, Fla. Artists Ringling Mus., 1994, Walter Wickiser Gallery, N.Y., 1995, Albany (Ga.) Mus. Art, 1997, Allentown (Pa.) Art Mus., 1998, Delmar Coll., Corpus Christi, Tex., 1998, Housatonic Mus. Art, Conn., 1998, Sarasota (Fla.) Biennial Ringling Mus., 2000, Tampa Mus. Art, 2001, Springfield (Mo.) Art Mus., 2002, Chattahoochee Valley Art Mus., 2002. Recipient award Silvermine Guild Conn. Appalachian Corridors, Arena, 1976, Gold medal of honor Audubon Artists ann. competition, Whitehead award Boston Printmakers, 1985, Shellenberg award Artists Equity, 1985, award N.C. Print & Drawing, 1985, award Chautauqua Nat., 1985, Johnson & Johnson award 3rd Ann. Nat. Printmaking Coun. of N.J., 1985, Purchase award N.J. State Mus.,

1987, Disting. Alumni award Pa. State U. Sch. Arts & Architecture, 1988, Ethel Klassen Meml. award Fla. Artists Group, 1992, Earl Horter award Phila. Watercolor Club, 1992, award of excellence, 1995, Stella Drabkin Meml. award Colorprint Soc., Award for Excellence Phila. Watercolor Club, 1996, Elizabeth Morse Meml. award Fla. Artists Group, 1996, Daniel Serra Y Navas Meml. award Audubon Artists, N.Y., 1996, Purchase award drawing annual Del Mar (Tex.) Coll., 1997, Purchase award Stockton (Calif.) Arts Commn., 1998, LaGrange Nat. Biennial, 2002; Va. Ctr. for the Creative Arts fellow, 1983-84; Nat. Endowment Arts grantee. Mem. Soc. Am. Graphic Artists (v.p.), Nat. Assn. of Women Artists (Nat. Medal of Honor, Elizabeth Blake award). *I examine the world through painting. I consider the act of art a spiritual experience. My work is informed by nature and visually recalled and then made permanent on paper or canvas. Maintaining a feeling of being in harmony with the world allows for periods of quiet meditation and creativity.*

PUTTERMAN, WILLIAM ZEV, foundation executive, television producer; b. Bronx, N.Y., Nov. 6, 1928; s. David Joseph and Amy Belle (Racoosin) P.; m. Anita Ruth Woien, Mar. 3, 1964 (div. 1971); children: Rachel Amy, Naomi Leah; m. Mary Elizabeth Kudlacik, Nov. 18, 1984. Student Colgate U., 1946-47; BA with honors in Philosophy, Syracuse U., 1949. Stage mgr. on Broadway, 1958; dir. Off-Broadway, 1960-61; with with Synanon found., 1962-64; prodr. Sta. KGO-TV, ABC, San Francisco, 1964-66; exec. prodr. Sta. KTTV, Metromedia, 1967-68; program cons. Sta. KABC-TV, ABC, L.A., 1969; dir. program devel. Metromedia TV, Inc., 1969-70; dir. nat. programs Sta. KQED, PBS, San Francisco, 1970-79; dir. comm. Werner Erhard and Assocs., 1980-83; v.p. program devel. Furia/Oringer Prodns., Inc., Sherman Oaks, Calif., 1984-86; supervising prodr. The Landsburg Co., L.A., 1986-88; pres. Zev Putterman Prodns., Tucson, 1989—; exec. dir. Amity Found., 1991—. Prodr. Alan Landsburg Prodns., L.A., 1972; vis. lectr. Calif. State U., Northridge, 1966; instr. U. Calif. Ext., Berkeley, 1972; lectr. Berkeley Film Inst., 1977, 79; mem. Norman Corwin student documentary program adv. bd. U. So. Calif., 1989—; U.S. del. Internat. Pub. TV Screening Conf., Milan, 1978. Prodr. On Location, Am. Broadcasting System, 1972, The Boarding House, PBS, 1975, Leukemia Soc.'s Televent '90, Nat. Leukemia Broadcast Coun., L.A., 1990; supervising prodr. Photoplay, 1986, 87; exec. prodr. Internat. Animation Festival, 1976, World Press, 1975-77, Music from Aspen/MoreMusic from Aspen spls., 1977, People vs. Inez Garcia, 1977, Turnabout, 1978, Transport of Delight, 1978, Black Filmmakers Hall of Fame spls., 1977, 78, Inside the Cuckoo's Nest, 1978; numerous others. Bd. dirs. Found. for Mideast Comm., 1985—, The Holiday Project, 1983-88, Am. Jewish Congress, 1985—, Marin Cmty. Workshop, 1977-78; mem. adv. coun. New Israel Fund, 1986—; bd. dirs. Chabad of No. Calif., 1975-84, chmn., 1984. Recipient Golden Eagle award for Vasectomy, Coun. for Internat. Non-Theatrical Events, 1973, for Private Lives of Americans, 1974, The Place for No Story, 1975, 13 Emmy awards, DuPont-Columbia award for "1985", 1970. Mem. NATAS, Nat. Assn. TV Program Execs., Nat. Assn. Fund Raising Execs., Internat. Documentary Assn., Theta Beta Phi. Democrat. Jewish. Avocations: arab-Jewish reconciliation, drug addict rehabilitation. Office: Amity Inc PO Box 32200 Tucson AZ 85751-2200

PUTTLITZ, DONALD HERBERT, medical microbiologist; b. Kingston, N.Y., Apr. 21, 1938; s. Adalbert Siegfried and Elizabeth Ann (Barthel) P.; m. Barbara Ann Dingman, July 19, 1969; children: Michelle, Brian, Laura. BS with distinction, SUNY, New Paltz, 1959; MS, SUNY, Albany, 1961; PhD, Cornell U., 1965. Diplomate Am. Bd. Med. Microbiology. Assoc. microbiologist Beth Israel Med. Ctr., N.Y.C., 1967-85; supr. microbiology Jamaica (N.Y.) Hosp., 1985-92; instr. physician asst. program Touro Coll., N.Y.C., 1986-88; supr. microbiology Sound Shore Med. Ctr. of Westchester, New Rochelle, N.Y., 1993-97. Mem. faculty Mt. Sinai Coll. Medicine, 1972-85. Mem. N.Y.C. Bd. Edn., 1997—. Predoctoral traineeship fellow NIH, 1964-65, postdoctoral traineeship fellow USPHS, 1965-67. Mem. Am. Soc. Microbiology, N.Y.C. Soc. Microbiology. Roman Catholic. Home: 116 Horace Harding Blvd Great Neck NY 11020-1107

PUTZEL, CONSTANCE KELLNER, lawyer; b. Balt., Sept. 5, 1922; d. William Stummer and Corinne (Strauss) Kellner; m. William L. Putzel, Aug. 28, 1945; 1 son, Arthur William. AB, Goucher Coll., 1942; LLB, U. Md., 1945, JD, 1969. Bar: Md. 1945. Social worker Balt. Dept. Pub. Welfare, 1945-46; atty. New Amsterdam Casualty Co., Balt., 1947; staff atty. Legal Aid Bur., 1947-49; mem. Putzel & Putzel, P.A., 1950-89; pvt. practice, 1989—; instr. U. Balt. Sch. Law, 1975-77, Goucher Coll., 1976-77. Chair character com. Ct. Appeals for 3d Cir., 1976-97. Author: A Practice Guide to Divorce, 1999, Representing the Older Client in Divorce, 1992. Active Md. Com. on Status of Women, 1972-76, Com. to Implement ERA, 1973-76; Pres. U. Md. Law Alumni Assn., 1978; bd. dirs. Legal Aid Bur., 1951-52, 71-73. Fellow Am. Acad. Matrimonial Lawyers (chair elder issues com. 1996); mem. ABA (co-chair elder issues com., mem. coun. sr. lawyers divsn. 1996-2000, editl. bd. 1996-99), Md. Bar Assn. (bd. govs. 1972-73, chmn. family law sect. 1978-79, chair sr. lawyers divsn. 2001—). Home: 7121 Park Heights Ave Unit 401 Baltimore MD 21215-1610 Office: 401 Washington Ave Ste 803 Towson MD 21204 E-mail: lawtowson@aol.com.

PUTZEL, MICHAEL, journalist, entrepreneur; b. Washington, Sept. 16, 1942; s. Max and Nell (Converse) P.; m. Ann Blackman, Feb. 23, 1974; children: Leila Elizabeth, Christof Blackman. BA, UNC in Polit. Sci., 1967. Reporter Charleston (W.Va.) Gazette, 1963-66; newsman AP, Raleigh, N.C., 1967-68, N.Y.C., 1968-69, war corr. Vietnam, 1969-72, reporter, 1972-79; asst. metro editor Washington Post, 1979; White House corr. AP, 1979-84, chief White House corr., 1984-87, chief of bur., 1987-90, diplomatic corr. Washington, 1990-91; Washington bureau chief Boston Globe, 1991-92, White House corr., 1993-94; columnist "Plugged In", 1994-95; founder, CEO Trysail, Inc., Washington, 1996—; founder, pres. Milestones Inc., 1999—2000; v.p. Continental Computer Corp., 2000—. Lectr. Georgetown U., Washington, 1999—. With USAR, 1964-65. Recipient AP Mgn. Editors citation, 1975, 81, Merriman Smith Meml. award White House Corr. Assn., 1986. Home: 4938 Quebec St NW Washington DC 20016-3231 Office: Continental Computer Corp 4200 Wisconsin Ave NW # 106-321 Washington DC 20016-2143

PUTZELL, EDWIN JOSEPH, JR. lawyer, mayor; b. Birmingham, Ala., Sept. 29, 1913; s. Edwin Joseph and Celeste (Joseph) Putzell; m. Dorothy Corcoran Waters, Aug. 5, 1967; children from previous marriage: Cynthia Putzell Reidy, Edwin Joseph, III. AB, Tulane U., 1935; LLB, Harvard U., 1938. Bar: N.Y. 1939, U.S. Supreme Ct. 1945, Mo. 1947. Atty. Donovan, Leisure, Newton & Lumbard, N.Y.C. and Washington, 1937-42; asst. dir., exec. officer Office of Strategic Svcs., 1942-45; asst. treas. Monsanto Co., St. Louis, 1945-46, asst. sec., atty., 1946-51, sec., 1951-77, dir. law dept., 1953-68, v.p., gen. counsel, 1963-77; ptnr. Coburn, Croft, Shepherd, Herzog & Putzell, 1977-79; of counsel Coburn, Croft & Putzell, 1979-96; mayor City of Naples, Fla., 1986-90; of counsel Thompson & Coburn, St. Louis, 1996—. Dir. St. Louis Symphony Soc., 1955—69; pres. The Conservancy, Inc., 1981—85, chmn. bd. dirs., 1984—85; pres. Social Planning Coun., St. Louis, 1954—57; vice chmn. Westminster Coll., 1976—79; chmn. Sta. KETC-TV, St. Louis, 1977—79; trustee St. Luke's Hosp., 1973—79; pres. Hospice of Naples (Fla.) Cmty. Found., Collier County., 2002—; bd. dirs. The Moorings, Inc., Fla., Collier/Naplescape, Inc., Greater Naples Civic Assn., Naples Bot. Garden; vice chmn. St. Louis County Bd. Police Commrs., 1964—72; Big Cypress Basin bd. S. Fla. Water Mgmt. Dist., 1985—86; chmn. Naples Airport Authority, 1979—83, 1993—97. Mem.: ABA, Assn. Gen. Counsel, Am. Soc. Corp. Secs. (pres. 1968—69), St. Louis Bar Assn., Mo. Bar Assn., Naples Area C. of C., Naples Yacht Club, Noonday Club, Forum Club (v.p. 1998—2000, pres. 2002—), Bogey Club, Port Royal Golf Club, Hole in the Wall Golf Club, Delta Sigma Phi, Phi Beta Kappa. Episcopalian. Home: 1285 Gulf Shore Blvd N Naples FL 34102-4911 E-mail: depnaples@aol.com.

PUYAU, FRANCIS ALBERT, retired physician, radiology educator; b. New Orleans, Dec. 1, 1928; s. Frank Albert and Rose Sue (Jones) P.; m. Geraldine Sally diBenedetto, June 6, 1951; children: Michael, Stephen, Jeanne Marie, Julie, Melissa. BS, Notre Dame U., 1948; MD, La. State U., 1952. Diplomate Am. Bd. Pediat., Am. Bd. Pediat. Cardiology, Am. Bd. Radiology. Intern Charity Hosp., New Orleans, 1952-53, resident in pediat., 1955-57; from instr. pediat. to prof. radiology and pediat. La. State U. Sch. Medicine, New Orleans, 1957-74, acting head dept. radiology, 1971-72, head dept., 1972-74; asst. prof. pediat. Vanderbilt U., 1961-68; fellow dept. diagnostic radiology Charity Hosp., New Orleans, 1968-70; prof. radiology and pediat. Tulane U. Sch. Medicine, 1974-97, prof. medicine, 1974-95, acting chmn. dept. pediat., 1976-78; cons. St. Tammany Hosps., Covington, La., 1968-81; dir. cardiac catherization lab. dept. cardiology Charity Hosp., New Orleans, 1970-85; staff radiologist Our Lady of the Lake Regional Med. Ctr., Baton Rouge, 1986-93. Mem. staff Hotel Dieu, New Orleans, 1973-80; head x-ray dept. Children's Hosp. of New Orleans, 1976-82. Contbr. articles to profl. jours. With USPHS, 1953-55. Fellow Am. Coll. Cardiology, Am. Coll. Radiology; mem. East Baton Rouge Med. Soc., So. Soc. Pediatric Research, Am. Coll. Radiology, La. Radiology Soc., New Orleans Radiology Soc. (pres. 1985), New Orleans Pediatric Soc., Soc. Chmn. Acad. Radiology Depts., Radiol. Soc. N.Am., Am. Roentgen Ray Soc., Assn. Univ. Radiologists, Southern Yacht Club (New Orleans), Alpha Omega Alpha. Roman Catholic. Home: 458 Shady Lake Pkwy Baton Rouge LA 70810-4322

PUZDER, ANDREW F. restaurant executive, lawyer; b. Cleve., July 11, 1950; s. Andrew F. and Winifried M. Puzder; m. Deanna L. Descher, Sept. 26, 1987. BA, Cleve. State U., 1975; JD, Washington U., 1978. Gen. counsel, exec. v.p. Fidelity Nat. Fin., Inc., 1978-96, CKE Restaurants, Inc., 1997-99; pres., chief exec. ofcr. Hardee's Food Systems, Inc., 1997—, CKE Restaurants, Inc., Anaheim, Calif., 2000—. Editor Washington U. Law Quarterly, 1977-78. Author of law upheld by U.S. Supreme Ct. in Webster v. Reproductive Health Svcs., 1989; founding dir. Common Ground Network for Life and Choice, 1993. Mem. State Bar Nev., The Mo. Bar, State Bar Calif., Phi Alpha Theta. Address: CKE Restaurants 401 W Karcher Way Anaheim CA 92801

PYATT, EVERETT ARNO, government official; b. Kansas City, Mo., July 22, 1939; s. Arno Doyne and Myrl Elizabeth (Osborn) P.; m. Susan Evelyn Kristal, Sept. 28, 1968; children: Jennifer, Laura, Jeffrey. B.E., BS, Yale U., 1962; MBA, U. Pa., 1977. Staff engr. office dir. def. research and devel. Office Sec. Def., Dept. Def., Washington, 1962-72; dir. acquisition planning Office Asst. Sec. Def. for Program Analysis and Evaluation, 1972-75; dir. logistics resources Office Asst. Sec. Def. for Installations and Logistics, 1975-77; prin. dep. asst. sec. for logistics Dept. Navy, Washington, 1977-79, prin. dep. asst. sec. for shipbldg. and logistics, 1981-84, asst. sec. for shipbldg. and logistics, 1984-89; exec. advisor Coopers & Lybrand, 1989—; pres. EV Ventures; dep. chief fin. officer Dept. Energy, 1979-81; dir. Dept. Energy (Office of Alcohol Fuels), 1980. Recipient Disting. Civilian Svc. medal USN, 1980-81, 87, Superior Civilian Svc. medal, 1981, Outstanding Svc. medal Dept. Energy, 1981, Pres.'s award of meritorious excellence, 1983, Disting. Civilian Pub. Svc. award Dept. Def., 1989; Office of Sec. Def. fellow, 1975-77. Mem.: IEEE, Yale Club. Home: 4560 25th Rd N Arlington VA 22207-4147 Office: Coopers & Lybrand 12902 Federal Systems Park Dr Fairfax VA 22033-4421

PYATT, KEDAR DAVIS, JR. research and development company executive; b. Wadesboro, N.C., May 20, 1933; s. Kedar D. and Frances (Hales) P.; m. Mary Mackenzie, June 2, 1956; children: Geoffrey, Kira, David, Rebecca. BS in Physics, Duke U., 1955; PhD in Physics, Yale U., 1960. With Gen. Atomic, San Diego, 1959-67; sr. v.p. Fed. sys. divsn. Maxwell Techs., 1967—, sr. v.p. just Sys. Divsn. Recipient Exceptional Pub. Svc. medal Dept. Def., 1985, Lifetime Achievement medal DSWA, 1997. Office: Maxwell Tech Sys Divsn 9210 Sky Park Ct San Diego CA 92123-4302 E-mail: bud@maxwell.com.

PYATT, LEO ANTHONY, real estate broker; b. Key Port, N.J., Oct. 20, 1925; s. Ralph James and Anna Regina (Kussmaul) P.; m. Geraldine Genevive Gibb, May 31, 1947; children: Steven Lee, Rebecca Lynn. Student, Franklin U., 1947-49. Salesperson Standard Oil Co., Columbus, Ohio, 1947-49, Borden Dairy Co., Columbus, 1950-57, Frito-Lay, Inc., Columbus, 1958-74; sec., treas. Snack Time, Inc., 1974-75; agt. N. NE Realty Co., 1976-86; owner-broker Pyatt's Rose Realty Co., 1986—. Mem. Citizens for an Alternative Tax System. With US Naval Air Force, 1943-46, PTO. Decorated D.F.C., Air medal with silver star, Philippine Liberation award. Roman Catholic. Avocations: writing, travel, reading. Home: 4400 Wanda Lane Rd Columbus OH 43224-1026 Office: Pyatts Rose Realty Co 4400 Wanda Lane Rd Columbus OH 43224-1026

PYDYNKOWSKY, JOAN ANNE, journalist; b. Ft. Riley, Kans., Oct. 2, 1951; d. Fredrick Albert and Mary Elizabeth (O'Connor) Gadwell; m. Michael Stanley Pydynkowsky, Mar. 14, 1981; children: Tricia Lynn Glotfelty, Deborah Findley, Alexandra. BA in Journalism, U. Ctrl. Okla., 1991, MEd in Journalism, 1993. Trust clk. Ill. Nat. Bank, Rockford, 1974-75; engring. aide Barber Colman, 1976-77; draftsperson Gen. Web, 1979-80, Keeson, Ltd., Rockford, 1981; editor Oklahoma City Marriage Encounter, 1988-89, 94-95; humor columnist UCO Vista, Edmond, Okla., 1990-91; city editor Guthrie (Okla.) Daily Leader, 1991-92; substitute tchr. Edmond (Okla.) Pub. Schs., 1993-94; with N.W. News, Piedmont, Okla., 1994-95, South Oklahoma City Leader, 1995-96; staff writer, columnist, reporter, photographer N.W. News, Piedmont-Surrey Gazette, Okarche Chieftain, Piedmont, 1996-97, 97-99; city editor Okarche Chieftain, 1996-98, asst. editor, 1998-99; staff writer, columnist, photographer El Reno (Okla.) Tribune, 1997; horsemanship/hunter/jumper trainer Red Tail Ranch, Piedmont, Okla., 1999-2000. Copywriter, cons., Edmond, 1991—, photographer, 1990—, cartoonist, 1984—, humorist, 1990—; columnist, contbg. writer N.W. News, Piedmont, Okla., 1994-95; reporter and assoc. editor: All About Kids/South Oklahoma City Leader, 1995-96. Artworks include: Turtle (cover), UCO Bus. Rev., winter 2000. Asst. leader Boy Scouts Am., Edmond, 1993-95; league coach Young Am. Bowling Alliance, Edmond, 1993-99; counselor Oklahoma City YWCA Rape Crisis, 1986-88; mem. Tiaras Jr. Women's Honor Soc., 1990-91; mem. selection com. Okla. Journalism Hall of Fame, 1990. Recipient awards State Fair of Okla., 1983-96, Feature Writing award Okla. chpt. Soc. Profl. Journalists, 1992-93, six awards including first place Entertainment, Sports feature, sports column, 1994-95, six awards including first place feature writing, 1995-96, five awards including first place feature writing, 1996-97, eight awards, 1997-98, first place Feature Writing award, State Fair of Okla. Better Newspaper Contest, 1995. Mem. Soc. Profl. Journalists (pres. U. Ctrl. Okla. chpt. 1990, treas. 1989, 91), Kappa Tau Alpha. Roman Catholic. Avocations: writing, photography, horsemanship, art. Home: 301 Reynolds Rd Edmond OK 73013-5121 E-mail: asliceofpy@msn.com.

PYE, GORDON BRUCE, economist; b. Oak Park, Ill., Oct. 30, 1933; s. Harold Charles and Florence Martha P. BS in Chem. Engring, M.I.T., 1955, PhD in Econs, 1963. Asst. prof. bus. adminstrn. U. Calif., Berkeley, 1963-66, assoc. prof., 1966-69, prof., 1969-72; econ. cons. Standard Oil Co. Calif. (name changed to Chevron Texaco Corp.), San Francisco, 1972-74; v.p., sr. economist Irving Trust Co., N.Y.C., 1974-78, sr. v.p., mgr. econ. research and planning div., 1978-89; prin. Gordon B. Pye Assocs., 1990—. Assoc. editor: Fin. Analysts Jour, 1972-89. Mem. Forecasters Club N.Y. (pres. 1980-81). Home: 230 E 50th St New York NY 10022-7702 E-mail: GBPye@aol.com.

PYE, LENWOOD DAVID, materials science educator, researcher, consultant; b. Little Falls, N.Y., May 16, 1937; s. Lenwood George and Elizabeth Marie Pye; m. Constance Lee Lanphere, Sept. 6, 1958; children: DeAnn, Lorie, Lisa, Brien. BS, Alfred U., 1959, PhD, 1968. Rsch. engr. PPG Industries, Pitts., 1959-60; rsch. scientist Bausch & Lomb, Rochester, N.Y., 1960-61, 62-64; prof. glass sci. N.Y. State Coll. Ceramics Alfred U., 1968—, dean N.Y. State Coll. Ceramics, 1996-2000, dir. Inst. Glass Sci. and Engring., 1984-96, dir. Industry-Univ. Ctr. Glass Rsch., 1986-96. Pres. Internat. Commn. on Glass, 1997-2000; bd. dirs. Schott Glass Technologies. 1st lt. U.S. Army, 1960-62. Recipient Dominick Labino lectr. award 1995, Phoenix award as Glassman of Yr., 1996, award for excellence in tchg. Am. Soc. Engring. Edn., 1980. Fellow Am. Ceramics Soc. (trustee 1992-95), U.K. Soc. Glass Tech.; mem. Acad. Ceramics, Optical Soc. Am., German Soc. Glass Tech. (hon.). Office: NY State Coll Ceramics Alfred Univ 2 Pine St Alfred NY 14802-1214 E-mail: pye@alfred.edu.

PYE, LUCIAN WILMOT, political science educator; b. Shansi, China, Oct. 21, 1921; s. Watts Orson and Gertrude (Chaney) P.; m. Mary Toombs Waddill, Dec. 24, 1944; children: Evelyn, L. Christopher, Virginia. BA, Carleton Coll., 1943, LLD, 1982; MA, Yale U., 1949, PhD, 1951. From instr. to asst. prof. polit. sci. Washington U., St. Louis, 1949-52; rsch. assoc. Yale U., 1951-52, Princeton, 1952-56; vis. lectr. Columbia U., 1956; faculty Mass. Inst. Tech., 1956-92, prof. polit. sci., 1960-92, Ford prof., 1972-92, chmn. sect., 1961-63; sr. staff mem. Mass. Inst. Tech. (Center Internat. Studies), 1956—. Vis. assoc. prof. Yale U., 1959-61; vis. prof. George Washington U., 1993, Balliol Coll., Oxford U., 1994, Fletcher Sch., Tufts U., 1994; chmn. com. comparative politics Social Sci. Rsch. Coun., 1963-73; assoc. Fairbank Ctr., Harvard U., 1995—; mem. adv. com. adminstr. AID, 1961-68; cons. Dept. State, 1962-68, NSC, 1968-72; trustee Asia Found., 1963—; gov. East-West Ctr., Honolulu, 1976-80; bd. dirs., v.p. Nat. Com. U.S.-China Rels. Author: Guerrilla Communism in Malaya, 1956, Politics, Personality and Nation Building, 1961, Aspects of Political Developments, 1966, Southeast Asia's Political Systems, 1967, The Spirit of Chinese Politics, 1968, Warlord Politics, 1971, China: An Introduction, 1972, Mao Tse-tung: The Man in The Leader, 1976, Dynamics of Chinese Politics, 1982, Asian Power and Politics, 1985; co-author: The Politics of the Developing Areas, 1960, The Emerging Nations, 1961; Editor: Communications and Political Development, 1963, Political Culture and Political Development, 1965, Political Science and Area Studies, 1975. 1st lt. USMCR, 1945-46. Fellow Center Advanced Study Behavioral Scis., 1963 Fellow Am. Acad. Arts and Scis., Am. Philos. Soc.; mem. Assn. Asian Studies (dir.), Am. Polit. Sci. Assn. (dir., pres. 1989), Council Fgn. Relations (dir.), Asia Soc. (dir.), Pilgrim Soc., Phi Beta Kappa. Clubs: Cosmos. Unitarian Universalist. Home: 72 Fletcher Rd Belmont MA 02478-2017 Office: Mass Inst Tech Dept Polit Sci Cambridge MA 02139 E-mail: pye@mit.edu.

PYERITZ, REED EDWIN, medical geneticist, educator, research director; b. Pitts., Nov. 2, 1947; s. Paul L. and Ida Mae (Meier) P.; m. Jane Ellen Tumpson, May 28, 1972; 2 children. SB in Chemistry, U. Del., 1968; AM, Harvard U., 1971, PhD in Biochemistry, 1972, MD, 1975. Diplomate Am. Bd. Internal Medicine, Am. Bd. Genetics. Intern Peter Bent Brigham Hosp., Boston, 1975-76; resident Peter Bent Bingham Hosp., 1976-77, Johns Hopkins Hosp., Balt., 1977-78; from instr. to prof. medicine and pediatrics Sch. Medicine, John Hopkins Hosp., 1977-93, chair dept. human genetics, 1994-00, prof. human genetics, medicine and pediatrics, 1994-01, MCP Hahnemann Sch. Medicine, 1993-00; prof. medicine and genetics U. Pa. Sch. Medicine, Phila., 2001—, chief divsn. med. genetics, 2001—. Dir. Inst. Genetics, Allegheny U. Health Sci., 1993-99; dir. Ctr. for Med. Genetics, Allegheny Gen. Hosp., 1995-2000; chief physician Md. Athletic Commn., Balt., 1978-93; med. adv. bd. Nat. Marfan Found., N.Y.C., 1982—, chmn. 1982-93, clin. care adv. bd., Nat. Neurofibromatosis Found., 1985—; med. adviser Alliance of Genetic Support Groups, 1994—; mem. rsch. adv. bd. Nat. Orgn. Rare Disorders, 1989-2000; mem. rsch. adv. com. Am. Heart Assn., 1996-98; mem. genetic adv. bd. Nat. Cancer Inst., 1996—. Co-editor Principles and Practice of Medical Genetics, 1992—; mem. editl. bd. New Eng. Jour. Medicine, 1993-96, JAMA, 1997-01; contbr. over 300 articles to profl. publs. NIH grantee. Fellow: ACP, Am. Coll. Med. Genetics (dir. 1992—94, pres.-elect 1995—96, pres. 1997—98, past pres. 1999—2000); mem.: AAAS, AMA, Am. Med. Accred. Program (spl. adv. com. 1998—2000), Assn. Profs. Human Med. Genetics (pres. elect 1998—99, pres. 2000—), Assn. Am. Physicians, Am. Soc. Clin. Investigation, Am. Fedn. Med. Rsch., Physician Consortium for Performance Improvement, Am. Heart Assn., Am. Soc. Human Genetics (chmn. program com. 1994—95). Office: Divsn Med Genetics Maloney 5 U Pa Sch Medicine 3400 Spruce St Philadelphia PA 19104-4283 E-mail: reed.pyeritz@uphs.upenn.edu.

PYFER, JOHN FREDERICK, JR. lawyer; b. Lancaster, Pa., July 25, 1946; s. John Frederick and Myrtle Ann (Greiner) P.; m. Carol Trice, Nov. 25, 1970; children: John Frederick III, Carol Lee. Grad. cum laude, Peddie Sch., 1965; BA in Polit. Sci. and Econs., Haverford Coll., 1969; JD, Vanderbilt U., 1972. Bar: Pa. 1972, U.S. Dist. Ct. (ea. dist.) Pa. 1973, U.S. Tax Ct. 1975, U.S. Supreme Ct. 1975, U.S. Dist. Ct. (mid. dist.) Pa. 1984, U.S. Ct. Appeals (3d cir.) 1986. Law clk. to presiding justice Ct. Common Pleas, Lancaster, Pa., 1972-74; assoc. Xakellis, Perezous & Mongiovi, 1972-76; founding ptnr. Allison & Pyfer, 1976-85; pres. Pyfer & Assocs., 1986-88, Pyfer & Reese, Lancaster, 1988—. Prof. para-legal tng. Pa. State Ext. Svc., 1989-93; fed. ct. mediator, 1992-2001. Contbr. articles to law revs., law treatises. Pres. Lancaster-Lebanon Coun., Boy Scouts Am., 1989—93, coun. commr., 1987—89, mem. nat. com., 1996—, exec. bd. N.E. region, 1998—, area pres., 2000—; bd. dirs. World of Scouting Mus.; achieved Eagle Scout , 1962; named Disting. Eagle Scout , 2001. Fellow Am. Bd. Criminal Lawyers, Lancaster Heritage Ctr. (sec. 2001—); mem. ABA (First prize Howard C. Schwab Nat. Essay Contest in Writing 1972), ATLA, SAR, Nat. Assn. Criminal Def. Lawyers, Pa. Trial Lawyers Assn., Pa. Criminal Def. Lawyers Assn., Am. Arbitration Assn., Pa. Bar Assn., Lancaster Bar Assn., Inns Ct. (founder, pres. W. Hensel Brown 1993-94), Christian Lawyers Soc., Train Collector Assn. (divsn. pres. 1984), Am. Orchid Soc. (affiliate pres. 1998), Lions Club (pres. 1980-82, 2000-01) (Willow Street, Pa.), Masons (Lancaster). Republican. United Ch. of Christ (elder, pres. 1989, 95). Home: 1100 Little Brook Rd Lancaster PA 17603-6116 Office: Pyfer & Reese 128 N Lime St Lancaster PA 17602-2951 E-mail: pyfer@redrose.net., law@pyferreese.com.

PYKE, RONALD, mathematics educator; b. Hamilton, Ont., Can., Nov. 24, 1931; s. Harold and Grace Carter (Digby) P.; m. Gladys Mary Davey, Dec. 19, 1953; children: Darlene, Brian, Ronald, Gordon. BA (hon.), McMaster U., 1953; MS, U. Wash., 1955, PhD, 1956. Asst. prof. Stanford U., Calif., 1956-58; asst. prof. Columbia U., N.Y.C., 1958-60; prof. math. U. Wash., Seattle, 1960-98, prof. emeritus, 1998—. Vis. prof. U. Cambridge, Eng., 1964-65, Imperial Coll., London, 1970-71, Colo. State U., Ft. Collins, 1979, Technion, Israel, 1988, 90, 92; pres. Inst. Math. Stats., 1986-87; mem. bd. math. scis. NRC/NAS, 1984-88, chmn. com. applications and theoretical stats., 1985-88. Editor Ann. Prob., 1972-75; contbr. articles to profl. jours. NSF grantee, 1961-91. Fellow Internat. Statis. Inst. (v.p. 1989-91), Am. Statis. Assn., Inst. Math. Stats. (pres. 1986-87); mem. Bernoulli Soc., Statis. Soc. of Can. Office: U Washington PO Box 354350 Seattle WA 98195-4350

PYKE, THOMAS NICHOLAS, JR. government science and engineering administrator; b. Washington, July 16, 1942; s. Thomas Nicholas and Pauline Marie (Pingitore) P.; m. Carol June Renville, June 22, 1968; children—Christopher Renville, Alexander Nicholas BS, Carnegie Inst. Tech., 1964; MS in Engring., U. Pa., 1965. Electronic engr. Nat. Bur. Standards, Gaithersburg, Md., 1964-69, chief computer networking sect., 1969-75, chief computer systems engring. div., 1975-79, dir. ctr. for computer systems engring., 1979-81, dir. ctr. programming sci. and tech., 1981-86; asst. adminstr. for satellite and info. services NOAA, Washington, 1986-92, dir. high performance computing and com., 1992-00, dir. The Globe Program, 1994—2002, chief info. officer, dir. high performance computing and comm., 2000—01; chief info. officer U.S. Dept. Commerce , 2001—. Organizer profl. computer confs., 1970-86; mem. Presdl. Adv. Com. on Networking Structure and Function, 1980, Interagy. com. on Info. Resources Mgmt., 1983-84, bd. dirs., 1984-87, vice chmn. 1986-87 (Exec. Excellence award 1991), chmn. Interagy. Working Group on Data Mgmt. for Global Change, 1987-93; speaker in field. Editorial bd. Computer Networks Jour., 1976-86; contbr. articles to profl. jours. Bd. dirs. Glebe Commons Assn., Arlington, Va., 1976-79, v.p., 1977-79; chmn. Student Congress, Carnegie Inst. Tech., 1963-64; mem. Task Force on Computers in Schs., Arlington, 1982-85; pres. Jamestown Elem. Sch. PTA, Arlington, 1983-84 Recipient silver medal Dept. Commerce, 1973, gold medal, 1995; award for exemplary achievement in pub. adminstrn. William A. Jump Found., 1975, 76, Presdl. Rank award of Meritorious Exec., 1988, 99; Westinghouse scholar Carnegie Inst. Tech., 1960-64; Ford Found. fellow U. Pa., 1964-66. Fellow Washington Acad. Scis. (Engring. Sci. award 1974); mem. IEEE (sr. mem.), Computer Soc. of IEEE (bd. govs. 1971-73, 75-77, vice chmn. tech. com. on personal computing 1982-86, chmn. 1986-87), AAAS, Assn. Computing Machinery, Sigma Xi, Eta Kappa Nu, Omicron Delta Kappa, Pi Kappa Alpha (chpt. v.p. 1963-64) Episcopalian. Office: 14th St and Constitution Ave NW Rm 5029 Washington DC 20230 E-mail: tpyke@doc.gov.

PYKE-REDLEY, GABELLA C. healthcare agency owner, medical/surgical and mental health nurse; b. Montego Bay, Jamaica, Sept. 11, 1945; d. Louis and Clementina C. (Grant) Pyke; m. Alban Redley, Dec. 22, 1962; children: Balfour G.A., Ann Marie, Maria C. AA, Malcolm X Coll., Chgo., 1972; BSN, Governors State U., Park Forest, Ill., 1984; MS in Nursing, Aurora (Ill.) U., 1988; postgrad., Nova U. Cert. CPR instr., trainer. Community health nurse Metro Home Health Care, Chgo.; nursing supr. employment Ill. State Psychiat. Inst.; mgr., owner Redley's Home Health Care Agy. Inc.; nurse practitioner Cook County Hosp., 1992—. Part-time clin. instr. Malcolm X Coll. Mem. Ill. State Edn. Profls. Home: PO Box 208753 Chicago IL 60620-8753 Office: PO Box 20753 Chicago IL 60620-0753

PYLE, BENJAMIN MALREY, investor; b. Apple Springs, Tex., Sept. 27, 1927; s. Uria Malrey Pyle, Nora Etta Burran; m. Mary Ellen Hartmann, Jan. 31, 1932; children: Malrey Nathan, Dwight Dana. BBA in Banking/Fin., U. Houston, 1960; postgrad., So. Meth. U., 1965—66; non-traditional degree, Beverly Hills U., 1985; MS in Econs., U. So. Calif.; MA, Liberty U., Lynchburg, Va., 1993. Banking exec., dir. Comml. Banking, Houston and Baytown, Tex., 1960—83; adminstrv. exec. Hill & Hill Transp., Houston, 1983—85; farm credit examiner Farm Credit Adminstrn., McLean, Va., 1986—87, asst. receiver Sugarland, Tex., 1988—91; entrepreneur/investor Baytown, 1994—. Bus. cons. Pyle Bros., Baytown, Tex., 1992—; adv. bd. So. Partison Mag., Columbia, SC, 1995—96. Contbr. articles. Polit. activist, precinct chmn. Rep. Party, Trinity County, Tex., 1998—; exec. bd. Episcop. Dioces. of Tex., Camp Allen, 1997—98; pres., bd. dirs. Civil War Round Table, Lufkin, Tex., 1999—; bd. regents Liberty U., 1994; mem. Trinity County Hist. Commn., 1991—; with U.S. Maritime Svc., 1944—46. With U.S. Merchant Marines, 1944—46, with USMC, 1946—57. Recipient Outstanding Leadership award, Mt. Zion Cemetery Assn. Mem.: SPJST (pres. 1977—94), Coll. of Bus. Adminstrn. Alumni U. Houston (charter). Republican. Episcopalian. Avocations: farming, ranching, hunting, lecturing. Mailing: 13529 FM 357 Groveton TX 75845-3203

PYLE, GERALD FREDRIC, medical geographer, educator; b. Akron, Ohio, Dec. 22, 1937; s. Russell Roy and Ruth (Martin) P.; m. Carole Wood, Aug. 29, 1959; children: Eric, Frances. BA, Kent State U., 1963; MA, U. Chgo., 1968, PhD, 1970. Cartographer Rand McNally, Chgo., 1962-64; rsch. geographer Ency. Brit., 1964-65; cartographer U. Chgo., 1965-70; from asst. prof. to prof. U. Akron, 1970-80; prof. geography and earth sci. U. N.C., Charlotte, 1980-98, prof. health promotion, 1995—, interim dir., 2001—. Vis. fellow Macquarie U., Sydney, Australia, 1988; rsch. dir. Ctr. for Urban Studies, Akron, Ohio, 1973—80; tech. dir. Akron Area Census File, 1974—80; vis. scholar U. SC, 1977; interim dir. health adminstrn. program U. NC, Charlotte, 2001—. Author: Heart Disease, Cancer and Stroke in Chicago, 1971, Spatial Dynamics of Crime, 1974, Applied Medical Geography, 1979, Diffusion of Influenza: Patterns and Paradigms, 1986, (with Shannon and Bashshur) The Geography of AIDS, 1990, (with shannon) Medical Atlas of the Twentieth Century, 1993; sr. editor Med. Geography, Social Sci. and Medicine, 1977-84; book rev. editor Social Sci. and Medicine, 1990—. Recipient Scholars medal First Citizens Bank, 1992; grantee Ill. Regional Med., 1969, Law Enforcement Adminstrn. Agy., 1972, 74, NSF, 1979, 82, Nat. Geog. Soc., 1988, NRC, 1995, Smart Start 1999-2001. Fellow Ohio Acad. Sci.; mem. APHA, Am. Coll. Epidemiology, Assn. Am. Geographers (Rsch. Honors S.E. divsn. 1994), Phi Kappa Phi. Democrat. Anglican. Achievements include research in spatial diffusion of infectious diseases and the location of health care delivery facilities. Home: 9801 Belt Rd Midland NC 28107-9057 Office: U NC Coll Health and Human Svcs 9201 University City Blvd Charlotte NC 28223-0002 E-mail: gfpyle@email.uncc.edu.

PYLE, HOWARD, lawyer, consultant; b. Richmond, Va., Feb. 1, 1940; s. Wilfrid and Anne Woolston (Roller) P.; children: Elizabeth Roller Ross, Howard. AB, Princeton U., 1962; JD, U. Va., 1967. Bar: Va. 1967, D.C. 1969. Career trainee CIA, Washington, 1967-69; adminstrv. asst. to Congressman Odin Langen, U.S. Ho. of Reps., 1969-70, to Congressman Hastings Keith, 1971; asst. to sec. Dept. Interior, 1971-73; Washington rep. Std. Oil Co. Ind., 1973-77; mgr. fed. pub. affairs R.J. Reynolds Industries, Inc., Winston-Salem, N.C., 1977-80; dir. fed. rels. Houston Industries, Washington, 1980-99; pres. HPYLE Cons., Alexandria, Va., 1999—. Bd. govs., pres. Episcopal Sr. Ministries, 1986-96; bd. dirs., pres. Friendship Terrace, 1986-96; chair commn. com. Princeton Club, Washington, D.C., chair D.C. area ann. giving. Capt. USNR, 1962-89, ret. Mem.: SAR, NRA, Fed. Energy Bar Assn., Va. Bar, DC Bar, Res. Officers Assn., Naval Res. Assn., Princeton Club of Washington (mem. coun. 1998—, chmn. comms. com., chair DC ann. giving), Va. Country Club, Delta Theta Phi. Republican. Episcopalian. Home: 125 N Lee St Alexandria VA 22314-3260 also: PO Box 19645 Alexandria VA 22320-0645 Office: HPYLE Cons Po Box 19645 Alexandria VA 22320-0645 E-mail: hpyle@alumni.Princeton.EDU., howard@hpyle.net.

PYLE, KENNETH BIRGER, historian, educator; b. Bellefonte, Pa., Apr. 20, 1936; s. Hugh Gillespie and Beatrice Ingeborg (Petterson) P.; m. Anne Hamilton Henszey, Dec. 22, 1960; children: William Henszey, Anne Hamilton. AB magna cum laude, Harvard U., 1958; PhD, Johns Hopkins U., 1965. Asst. prof. U. Wash., 1965-69, assoc. prof., 1969-75, prof. history and Asian studies, 1975—, dir. Henry M. Jackson Sch. Internat. Studies, 1978-88; pres. Nat. Bur. Asian Rsch., 1988—; vice chmn. Japan-U.S. Friendship Commn., 1989-92, chmn., 1992-95. Co-chmn. Joint Com. on U.S.-Japan Cultural and Ednl. Coop., 1992-95; vis. lectr. history Stanford U., 1964-65; vis. assoc. prof. history Yale U., 1969-70, Edwin O. Reischauer Meml. Lectr., 1997; Mansfield Freeman lectr. Wesleyan U., 2002. Author: The New Generation in Meiji, Japan, 1969, The Making of Modern Japan, 1978, rev. edit., 1996; editor: The Trade Crisis: How Will Japan Respond?, 1987, The Japanese Question: Power and Purpose in a New Era, 1992, rev. edit., 1996, From APEC to Xanadu, 1997; founding editor Jour. Japanese Studies, 1974-86, chmn. editl. bd., 1987-89, assoc. editor, 1989—. Bd. dirs. Maure and Mike Mansfield Found., 1979-88; bd. govs. Henry M. Jackson Found., 1983—; adv. bd. Japan Found., 1989-99, Japan-Am. Student Conf., 1991—. Recipient Japanese Imperial award 3d Class, Order of Rising Sun, 1999, The Henry M. Jackson award for disting. pub. svc., 2000; Ford Found. fellow, 1961-64; Fulbright-Hays fellow, 1970-71; Social Sci. Research Council-Am. Council Learned Socs. fellow, 1970-73, 77, 83-84 Mem. Assn. Asian Studies, Am. Hist. Assn., Coun. Fgn. Rels. Presbyterian. Home: 8416 Midland Rd Medina WA 98039-5336 Office: Henry M Jackson Sch Internat Studies U Wash Seattle WA 98195-0001

PYLE, R. MICHAEL, wholesale distribution executive, educator; b. Indpls., Oct. 2, 1948; s. Merrill Ernest Pyle Jr. and Virginia Ann (Mitchell) Gilson; m. Margaret Ann Johnson, Aug. 11, 1973; 1 child, Ian Scot. BA in English, Ind. U., 1976. V.p. Nat. Wine & Spirits Corp., Indpls., 1976—. Lectr. on wine, Ind., 1976—. T.V. host (series): Wine, What Pleasure, 1980-82; assoc. prodr. (4-part documentary): The Wines of California, 1981. Mem. Wine Educators Am. Avocations: book and film collecting. Home and Office: 6816 Sargent Rd Indianapolis IN 46256-2167

PYLE, ROBERT MILNER, JR. financial services company consultant; b. Orange, N.J., Oct. 24, 1938; s. Robert M. and Dorothy (Collings) P.; m. C. Page Neville, May 31, 1969; children: Cynthia Neville, Laura Collings. BA, Williams Coll., 1960; JD, U. Va., 1963. Bar: N.Y. 1964. Assoc. Mudge Rose Guthrie & Alexander, N.Y.C., 1963—68; with Studebaker-Worthington, Inc., 1968—77, sec., 1972—76, assoc. gen. counsel, 1974—77; with Singer Co., N.Y.C., 1977—79, corp. counsel, asst. to sec., 1977—78, sr. corp. counsel, asst to sec., 1979; v.p., counsel Am. Soc. Corp. Secs., Inc., N.Y.C., 1979—89, v.p., sec., counsel, 1989—91; v.p., sr. asst. sec. Am. Express Co., 1991—96, cons., 1997—. Career counseling rep. for Williams Coll., 1977—. Trustee Pingry Sch., Martinsville, N.J., 1972-74; trustee Arts Coun. Suburban Essex Inc., 1979-84, chmn. bd., 1981-84; bd. govs. Colonial Dances, Ltd., N.Y.C., 1970-74; bd. dirs. Millburn-Short Hills Hist. Soc., 1985-90, v.p., 1985-87; trustee Suburban Cmty. Music Ctr., 1985-87; mem. Millburn-Short Hills Rep. Mcpl. Com. Essex County, 1998—. Mem. ABA, Assn. Bar City N.Y., Am. Soc. Corp. Secs. (hon.), Pingry Sch. Alumni Assn. (pres. 1972-74, bd. dirs. 1966-78, cert. of merit 1968), Pilgrims U.S., Met. Squash Racquets Assn. (past treas.), No. N.J. Squash Racquets Assn. (sec., bd. trustees), Racquet and Tennis Club, Bay Head Yacht Club (N.J.), Short Hills Club, Hillsboro Club (Fla.), Sigma Phi, Delta Theta Phi, Pi Delta Epsilon. Republican. Episcopalian. Office: 16 Delwick Ln Short Hills NJ 07078-2021 E-mail: rmpylejr@aol.com.

PYLE, ROBERT NOBLE, public relations executive; b. Wilmington, Del., Oct. 23, 1926; s. Joseph Lybr and LaVerne Ruth (Noble) P.; m. Claire Thoron; children: Robert Noble Jr., Mark C., Nicholas A., Louis P. Crosier, Sarah P. Moore. BA, Dickinson Coll., 1948; postgrad., Wharton Sch., U. Pa., 1949, U. Minn. Pres. Robert N. Pyle, Inc., Wilmington, 1949-52; adminstrv. asst. to U.S. Congress, Washington, 1952-63; bus. and polit. cons. and lobbyist Robert N. Pyle & Assoc., 1970—; pres. Ind. Bakers Assn., 1981—. Sec./treas. Bulgarian Am. Bus. Ctr.; dir. Internat. Eye Found.; mem. Dickinson Coll. Coun. Contbr. numerous articles to profl. jours.; reporter covering Nurnburg Trials, Paris Peace Conf. for, Stars & Stripes, Europe, 1946. Part-time field man Rep. Nat. Congl. Com., 1959-74. With U.S. Army, 1945-46, ETO. Mem. City Tavern Club, Nat. Press Club, Kenwood Golf & Country Club. Presbyterian. E-mail: bpyleatindependentbaker.org. Home: 2613 Dumbarton Ave NW Washington DC 20007-3320 Office: 1223 Potomac St NW Washington DC 20007-3212

PYLE, THOMAS ALTON, instructional television and motion picture executive; b. Phoenix, Sept. 8, 1933; s. Thomas Virgil and Evelyn B. (Redden) P.; m. Victoria K. Bileck, Apr. 21, 1957; children: Pamela V., Brett T.; m. Marilyn Ann Miller, May 12, 2001. BA, Ariz. State U., 1956. Freelance unit mgr. theatrical motion picture industry, N.Y.C. and L.A., 1956-60; v.p. sales Depicto Films Corp., N.Y.C., 1960-65; prodr. John Sutherland Prodns., N.Y.C. and L.A., 1965-67; v.p. mktg. Audio Prodns. Ednl. Svcs., N.Y.C., 1967-71; exec. v.p. mktg. Data Plex Systems, 1971-74; divsn. pres., exec. prodr. Sterling Inst. Video Prodns., Washington, 1974-80; pres. Applied Video Concepts, Inc., 1980-83; pres., CEO Nat. Sci. Ctr. Found., Burke, Va., Augusta, Ga., 1983-85; exec. dir., CFO, CEO Network for Instrnl. TV, Inc., Reston, Va., 1987—, Phoenix, 1987—. Built 88 new TV channels for K-12 schs. in 13 states and D.C., 1997 started 1st highspeed wireless delivery of Internet to urban publ. schs., 1998 launched TeachersFirst.com an advertising supported free Internet svc. to K-12 teachers; launched TeachersAndFamilies.com, 2002; bd. dirs. Natl. ITFS Assn., So. Fla. Instrnl. TV, Inc., Del. Valley Ednl. Telecomms. Network, Inc., Instrnl. Opportunities, Inc., St. Louis, Mo., Cons. Wireless Cable Industry. Writer, dir., producer over 200 motion pictures; commd. for film Pres. John F. Kennedy, 1962; producer: (film) Pres. Lyndon B. Johnson, 1964. V.p. Dexter Park Assn., Spring Valley, N.Y., 1968-74, Solaridge Cluster Assn., Reston, Va., 1990. Recipient 27 awards from natl. and internat. film and video festivals, 2 Commendation awards White House, 1970, 2 Acad. award nominations. Mem. AAAS, Internat. Platform Assn., N.Y. Acad. of Scis. Republican. Presbyterian. Avocation: photography. Office: NITV West 34111 N 7th St Phoenix AZ 85085

PYLE, WALTER K. lawyer; b. Chgo. s. Garland K. and Agnes G. (O'Connor) P.; m. Frances S. Kaminer; children: Michael K., James B., Isaac David. JD, Loyola U., Chgo., 1964; postgrad, NYU, 1964-65. Bar: Ill. 1965, Calif. 1981, U.S. Supreme Ct. 1972, U.S. Ct. Appeals (1st cir.) 1979, U.S. Ct. Appeals (7th cir.) 1992, U.S. Ct. Appeals (8th cir.) 1977, U.S. Ct. Appeals (9th cir.) 1980, U.S. Dist. Ct. (no. dist.) Ill. 1965, U.S. Dist. Ct. (no. dist.) Calif. 1981, U.S. Dist. Ct. (ea. dist.) Calif. 1982, U.S. Dist. Ct. (cen. dist.) Calif. 1989, U.S. Dist. Ct. (so. dist.) Calif. 1991; cert. specialist appellate law and criminal law, State Bar Calif., Bd. Legal Specialization; bd. cert. civil trial advocate Nat. Bd. Trial Advocacy. Asst. state's atty. Criminal Div. Cook County (Ill.) State's Atty.'s Office, Chgo., 1967-69; asst. atty. gen. Ill. Atty. Gen.'s Office, 1969-78; pvt. practice law, 1978-80, San Francisco, 1981-88, Berkeley, Calif., 1988—. Arbitrator Alameda County (Calif.) Superior Ct., 1993—; judge pro tempore Alameda County (Calif.) Superior Ct., 1989—. Mem. ABA, Calif. Bar Assn., Ill. Bar Assn., Alameda County Bar Assn. (dir. 1992-93), DuPage County Bar Assn., Bar Assn. San Francisco, Chgo. Bar Assn., Calif. Appellate Def. Counsel (sec. 2002--), Calif. Assn. Toxicologists. Avocations: running, cooking. Office: 2039 Shattuck Ave Ste 202 Berkeley CA 94704-1150 E-mail: walt@wfkplaw.com.

PYLES, RODNEY ALLEN, archivist, county official; b. Morgantown, W.Va., June 21, 1945; s. Melford John and Luci L. (Scarcella) P.; m. Carol Louise Wrobleski, May 20, 1972; 1 child, Janessa Louise. BA, MA (Benedum scholar 1966-67, grad. research asst. 1967-68, grad. teaching fellow 1968-69), W.Va. U., 1967, 69. Instr. polit. sci. Alderson-Broaddus Coll., Philippi, W.Va., 1969-71; asst. curator W.Va. U. Library, 1971-77; dir. archives and history div. W.Va. Dept. Culture and History, 1977-85; dep. chief Assessor's Office Monongalia County, 1985-88; assessor Monongalia County, 1989—. Mng. editor: W.Va. History quar, 1977-85 Mem. Morgantown (W.Va.) Dem. exec. com., 1966-69, Monongalia County (W.Va.) Dem. exec. com., 1972-74; mem. Morgantown Libr. Bd., 1988-91; pres. Morgantown Hist. Landmarks Commn., 1986—; bd. dirs., trustee W.Va. Pub. Theatre, 1999—. Mem. Soc. Am. Archivists, Mid-Atlantic Regional Archives Conf., W.Va. Hist. Soc. (exec. sec. 1977-90), W.Va. Libr. Assn., Am. Assn. State and Local History (state awards chmn. 1980-85, state membership com. 1981-87), Monongalia Hist. Soc. (pres. 1986-88, bd. dirs. 1988—), W.Va. Polit. Sci. Assn. (treas. 1991—), W.Va. Assessors' Assn. (pres. 1992-93), KC (pres. bowling league 1995-96, 4th deg., faithful capt. 1996—, chancellor 1998-2000, dep. Grand Knight 2000-02, Grand Knight, 2002-), Sons of Italy (treas. 1995—). Roman Catholic. Home: 536 Harvard Ave Morgantown WV 26505-2157 Office: County Court House Rm 215 Morgantown WV 26505 E-mail: rpyles@sbccom.com.

PYLIPOW, STANLEY ROSS, retired manufacturing company executive; b. Coudersport, Pa., Apr. 4, 1936; s. Stanley Edward and Helen L. (Haskins) P.; m. Phyllis Beverly Moore, Dec. 1, 1956; children— David, James, Vicky, Kenneth, Sandra BBA in Acctg. cum laude, St. Bonaventure U., 1957. Various fin. positions Chicopee Mfg., New Brunswick, N.J., 1957-65; various positions to v.p., gen. mgr. Domestic Coatings div. Mobil Chem. Co., N.Y.C., 1965-73; asst. corp. controller Monsanto Co., St. Louis, 1974-76; controller, dir. planning Monsanto Comml. Products, 1976-79; sr. v.p., bd. dirs., chief fin. officer Fisher Controls Internat., Inc., 1979-92; ret., 1992; bd. dirs. RBA Group. Treas. Ulster Project, St. Louis. Treas., City of Town and Country, Mo., 1980-84; bd. dirs. Ecumenical Housing Prodn. Corp., St. Louis, 1980-90; mem. Acctg. Edn. Change Commn., 1992-96. Served to 1st lt., U.S. Army, 1958. Named Exec. of Yr., Profl. Secs. Internat., 1982 Mem. Inst. Mgmt. Accts. (pres. 1990-91, chmn. 1991-92), Fin. Execs. Inst., Bellerive Country Club, Silverthorn Country Club. Republican. Avocations: golf, fitness, spectator sports. Home: 5085 Golf Club Ln Brooksville FL 34609 also: 14006 Baywood Villages Dr Chesterfield MO 63017-3420 E-mail: stanpylipow@aol.com.

PYNE, WILLIAM JOSEPH, chemist; b. Boston, Jan. 30, 1923; s. Thomas Francis and Mary (Reidy) P.; m. Martha Ellen Cannon, July 3, 1954 (dec. Oct. 1991); children: Thomas, James, Kevin, Colleen, Patricia, Brian. BS, Boston Coll., 1948, MS, 1950; postgrad., Western Res. U., Cleve., 1953-57, Ohio State U., 1970. Instr. King's Coll., Wilkes-Barre, Pa., 1950-51; rsch. chemist Diamond Shamrock Co., Painesville, Ohio, 1952-66, sr. rsch. chemist, 1966-77, rsch. assoc., 1977-82; sr. rsch. assoc. Quatum Technologies, Twinsburg, 1984-85; corp. fellow in synthetic organic chemistry Rex Adv. Svcs., Painesville, 1985—. Lectr. in field. Contbr. articles to profl. jours.; patentee in field (20 U.S. and 36 fgn. patents). Mem Cmty. Devel. Com., Painesville, 1978. With U.S. Army, 1943-45. Recipient Squirrel award for patent Diamond Shamrock Co., 1982. Mem. Am. chem. Soc. (chpt. sec. 1976-77). Roman Catholic. Avocations: history, visiting Civil War battle fields. Home and Office: 257 Meriden Rd Painesville OH 44077-3733

PYOTT, DAVID EDMUND IAN, pharmaceutical executive; married; 4 children. Diploma in German and European Law, U. Amsterdam; MA, U. Edinburgh; MBA, London Bus. Sch. Numerous positions Sandoz Nutrition, Barcelona, 1980-90, gen. mgr., 1990-92; pres., CEO Sandoz Nutrition Corp., Mpls., 1992-95; head divsn. nutrition Sandoz Internat. AG, 1995-96, Novartis AG (merger Sandoz and Ciba), 1997; pres., CEO Allergan, Inc., Irvine, Calif., 1998—, chmn., 2001—. Bd. dirs. PhRMA, Avery Dennison Corp., Edwards Lifescis. Corp.; dir. Calif. Healthcare Inst.; mem. dirs.' bd., mem. exec. com. U. Calif. (Irvine) Grad. Sch. Mgmt. Mem. Pharm. Rsch. and Mfrs. Am. (bd. dirs., Allergan rep.), Pan Am. Assn. Ophthalmology (bd. dirs.), L.A. Bus. Advisors. Office: Allergan, Inc 2525 Dupont Dr Irvine CA 92612-1531*

PYSHER, ALAN GUY, nurse anesthetist; b. East Stroudsburg, Pa., Sept. 10, 1946; s. Kermit Joseph and Fern Elizabeth (Blake) P.; m. Branda Ann Petraitis, June 3, 1973 (div. 1984); 1 child, Lynn Claire. AAS, Northampton C.C., 1973; BA, Stephens Coll., 1984; MEd, U. So. Miss., 1988. RN; cert. registered nurse anesthetist. Nurse anesthetist Tinker AFB Hosp., Oklahoma City, 1981-84; chief nurse anesthetist Lajes Field Hosp., Azores, Portugal, 1984-85; asst. chief nurse anesthetist Kessler Med. Ctr., Biloxi, Miss., 1985-88; chief nurse anesthetist Cannon AFB Hosp., Clovis, N.M., 1988-91, Wilford Hall Med. Ctr., San Antonio, 1991-95; program dir. David Grant Med. Ctr., Fairfield, Calif., 1995-98; anesthesia element chief Wright-Patterson AFB, Dayton, Ohio, 1998-2000; comdr. surg. ops. squadron, dir. nurse anesthesia edn. Wilford Hall Med. Ctr., Lackland AFB, San Antonio, 2000—02; comdr. edn. and tng. squadron Wilford Hall Med Ctr., 2002—. Assoc. clin. prof. Uniformed Svcs. U. Health Scis., Bethesda, Md., 1998. Col. USAF, 1973— Mem. ANA, Am. Assn. Nurse Anesthetists, Assn. Mil. Surgeons U.S., Aerospace Med. Assn., Air War Coll. Alumni Assn., VFW, Purple Heart Assn. Rep. Lutheran. Avocations: golf, martial arts. Home: 8910 Shady Hls San Antonio TX 78254-5525 Office: 59th Med Wing Lackland AFB San Antonio TX 78233 E-mail: pyshera@aol.com.

PYSHER, ZANE KERMIT, counselor; b. Pen Argyl, Pa., Mar. 19, 1943; s. Kermit Joseph and Fern Elizabeth Pysher; m. Marcia Ann Cook, July 9, 1966; children: Erica Ann, Zane-Alan. BA, Albright Coll., 1965; MA, Kean Coll., 1970. Cert. tchr. English, History, N.J., Pa., Mass.; cert. student personnel guidance svcs. N.J., Pa. Tchr. English, reading Warren Hills Sch., Washington, 1965-69; counselor, dir. guidance Roxbury Twp. Schs., Succasunna, N.J., 1969—. Sec., pres. bd. edn. com. Good Shepherd Nursery Sch., Easton, Pa., 1996-98 Author: Book of Genealogy, 1997. Mem. ch. coun. Good Shepherd Luth. Ch., Easton, 1992—94, mem. ministry com., 2000—02. Recipient Morris County Tchr. Recognition award Morris County Assn. Sch. Administrators, 1999. Mem.: NEA, Roxbury Edn. Assn. (sch. rep. bldg. 1972—75, mem. scholarship com. 1978—2002, sch. test coord. 1987—2002), Morris County Guidance Assn., NJ Edn. Assn. Democrat. Lutheran. Avocations: photography, golf, bowling, sports cards collecting, coin collecting. Home: 2311 Ben Jon Rd Easton PA 18040

PYTELL, ROBERT HENRY, retired lawyer, former judge; b. Detroit, Sept. 27, 1926; s. Henry Carl and Helen (Zielinski) P.; m. Laurie Mazur, June 2, 1956; children: Mary Beth, Mark Henry, Robert Michael. JD, U. Detroit, 1951. Bar: Mich. 1952. Of counsel Pytell & Varchetti, P.C., Detroit, 1952-2001; asst. U.S. atty. Ea. Dist. Mich., 1962-65; judge Mcpl. Ct., Grosse Pointe Farms, Mich., 1967-85. With USNR, 1945-46. Mem. Am. Coll. Trust and Estate Coun., State Bar Mich. (mem. probate coun. probate sect. 1998-2000), Crescent Sail Yacht Club (Grosse Pointe), Delta Theta Phi. Roman Catholic. Office: 20100 Mack Ave Grosse Pointe Woods MI 48236

PYTKA, STEPHEN MILTON, office equipment executive; b. Ludlow, Mass., Apr. 29, 1947; s. Milton Ignatius and Jean Marie (Kmiecik) P.; m. Linda Rachel Madsen, May 25, 1969; children: Jonathan Stephen, Justin Stephen, Brendan Stephen. BSEE, Worcester Poly. Inst., 1968; MBA, Dartmouth Coll., 1977. Design engr. AT&T, Whippany, N.J., 1968-69, Kwajalein, Marshall Islands, 1970-71, Greensboro, N.C., 1969-70, Langdon, N.D., 1971-73; sys. engr. GE, Pittsfield, Mass., 1973-75; planning mgr. Xerox Corp., Rochester, N.Y., 1977-81; mktg. mgr. Wang Labs., Inc., 1982-83; exec. v.p. Cap. Internat., Marshfield, Mass., 1983—. Co-founder P&R Microtech, 1982-83; exec. v.p. BIS Cap Internat., 1983-89; pres., chief ops. officer BISCOM, Inc., 1990-96; v.p. The Onstott Group, 1997-98; chmn., CEO Streamware, Inc., 1998-2000; pres., CEO eChinaLink, 2000-01, Talksender, Inc., 2000-01; mem. exec. bd. WPI Venture Forum; bd. dirs. Distance Learning; trustee MV YMCA; bd. dirs. Streamware; mem. adv. bd. Mt. Vernon Strategies, eChinaLink; panelist MIT Enterprise Forum; trustee Andover YMCA; spkr. in field. Mem. Am. Mgmt. Assn., Soc. Photog. Scientists and Engrs., Andover Country Club. Republican. Roman Catholic. Home: 9 Langley Ln Andover MA 01810-4259 Office: eChinaLink 121 Brick Kiln Rd Chelmsford MA 01824

PYTTE, AGNAR, physicist, former university president; b. Kongsberg, Norway, Dec. 23, 1932; arrived in U.S., 1949, naturalized, 1965; s. Ole and Edith (Christiansen) Pytte; m. Anah Currie Loeb, June 18, 1955; children: Anders H., Anthony M., Alyson C. AB, Princeton U., 1953; AM, Harvard U., 1954, PhD, 1958. Faculty Dartmouth Coll., 1958—87, prof. physics, 1967—87, chmn. dept. physics and astronomy, 1971—75, assoc. dean faculty, 1975—78, dean grad. studies, 1975—78, provost, 1982—87; pres. Case Western Res. U., Cleve., 1987—99; adj. prof. physics Dartmouth Coll., 1999—. Rschr. in plasma physics; mem. Project Matterhorn Princeton U., 1959—60, U. Brussels, 1966—67, Princeton U., 1978—79; bd. dirs. Goodyear Tire & Rubber Co., A.O. Smith Corp. Bd. dirs. Accreditation Coun. for Grad. Med. Edn., 2000—, Sherman Fairchild Found., Inc., 1987—. Mem.: Am. Phys. Soc., Sigma Xi, Phi Beta Kappa. E-mail: agnar.x.pytte@dartmouth.edu.

PYUN, MATTHEW SUNG KWAN, lawyer; b. Honolulu, Mar. 21, 1937; s. Matthew S.K. and Elsie S.O. (Chee) P.; m. Mary Ann Kagawa, Feb. 26, 1959; children: Leslie S.H., Jane K. BBA, U. Hawaii, 1959; LLB, Drake U., 1963. Bar: Hawaii 1964, U.S. Ct. Appeals (9th cir.) 1964. Law clk., bailiff U.S. Dist. Ct. Hawaii, 1964; dep. corp. counsel City and County of Honolulu, 1965; atty. Legal Aid Soc. Hawaii, 1965-68; sole practice Honolulu, 1968—; judge Honolulu Dist. Ct. 1st cir., 1981-84. Per diem judge Dist. for 3rd cir. State of Hawaii. Mem. Rep. Nat. Com. Served with USAF, 1960-61. Mem. ABA, ATLA, Am. Judicature Soc., Honolulu Club, Phi Alpha Delta, Phi Kappa Pi. Episcopalian. Office: 615 Piikoi St Ste 1107 Honolulu HI 96814-3164

QADRI, YASMEEN, educational administrator, consultant; b. Hyderabad, India, June 12, 1955; came to U.S., 1979; d. Ghulam and Bilquees Mahmood; m. Najeeb Qadri, Oct. 8, 1978; children: Kamran, Farhan, Sumayya. BA, St. Francis Coll., Hyderabad, 1976; MA in Psychology, Osmania U., Hyderabad, 1978; MA in Social Sci., U. Ctrl. Fla., Orlando, 1991, EdD in Curriculum and Instrn., 1994. Tchr. Indian Embassy Sch. and Minaret-e-Jeddah, Jeddah, Saudi Arabia, 1981-84; asst. adminstr. Muslim Acad. Ctrl. Fla., Orlando, 1991-93, adminstr., 1993—, prin., 1994—. Profl. interaction Trinity Prep. Sch., Orlando, 1993—. Cons. NCCJ, Orlando, 1992—. Recipient Cert. of Appreciation, Orange County Pub. Schs., 1992, Islamic Coun. Calif., 1993. Mem. ASCD, Muslim Women's Assn., Kappa Delta Pi. Moslem. Avocations: counseling, multicultural education, cooking, tourism. Office: Muslim Acad Ctrl Fla 1005 N Goldenrod Rd Orlando FL 32807-8326

QI, JIANWEI, mechanical engineer, researcher; b. Wuxi, Jianhsu, China, Mar. 11, 1967; s. Guoqin Qi and Yaqin Huang; m. Xinwei Dong; children: Yun, Yuan. BS, Nanjing (China) U. Aeronautics and Astronautics, 1989; M.E., Zhejiang U., Hangzhou, China, 1991; PhD, Tsinghua U., Beijing, China, 1996. Rsch. asst. Inst. Fluid Engring., Zhejiang U., Hangzhou, China, 1989—91; rsch. and tching. asst. Tsinghua U., Beijing, 1992—94, lectr., 1995—96; engr. China Packaging Corp., 1996—97; jr. rschr. Nat. Inst. Advanced Indusl. Sci. and Tech., Tsukuba, Japan, 1998—2000; postdoctoral rschr. The Johns Hopkins U., Balt., 2000; rschr. U. of Md., College Park, 2000—. Sci. and tech. cons. Author: (Research Work) The First Prize in Advanced Sci. and Tech. by State Edn. Commn. China, 1996; contbr. articles to profl. jours. (The Excellent Engring Prize by Tsinghua U., 1996). Mem.: IMAPS, AAAS, ASME.

QI, MIN, economics educator; b. Anyue, Sichuan, China, Aug. 12, 1966; arrived in U.S., 1991; d. Guangsheng Qi and Guomei Zeng; m. Mingjie Wang, Apr. 11, 1991; children: Nancy L. Wang, Michelle L. Wang. B of Engring., Tsinghua U., Beijing, 1988, MBA, 1991; MA in Econs., Ohio State U., 1992, PhD in Econs., 1996. Fin. analyst Indsl. and Comml. Bank of China, Beijing, 1991; asst. prof. econs. Kent (Ohio) State U., 1996—2002, assoc. prof. econ., 2002—. Contbr. articles to profl. jours. Recipient Best Paper in Investments award Midwest Fin. Assn., 1998, 2d pl. award in fin. series competition Internat. Neural Network Soc. and IEEE Neural Network Coun., 1999; univ. fellow Ohio State U., 1991-92, Dice fellow, 1996; dissertation rsch. grantee Ohio State U., 1995. Mem. Am. Econ. Assn., Fin. Mgmt. Assn. Avocations: playing cards, gardening, swimming, music, movies. Office: Kent State U Coll Bus Adminstrn PO Box 5190 Kent OH 44242-0001

QI, SHOUHUA, English educator; b. Nanjing, Jiangsu, China, Feb. 10, 1957; came to U.S., 1989; s. Yingyao Qi and Huilan Ye; m. Xiaohong Wang, Apr. 26, 1982; 1 child, Frank Y. Doctorate, Ill. State U., 1993. Lectr. English Nanjing Tchs. U., China, 1986-88; asst. prof. English Harrisburg (Pa.) Area C.C., 1993-2000, Western Conn. State U., Danbury, 2000—. Adj. prof. humanities Pa. State U., Harrisburg, 1998-2000. Author: Success in Advanced English Writings: A Comprehensive Guide, 2000, Bridging the Pacific: Searching for Cross-Cultural Understanding Between the U.S. and China, 2000, Western Writing Theories, Pedagogies, and Practices, 2000, New Century Guide to Practical English Communication, 2000; co-author: Voices in Tragic Harmony: Essays on Thomas Hardy's Fiction and Poetry, 2001; translator: Pair of Blue Eyes, 1994, Well-Beloved, 1998, author short stories. Mem. MLA, Nat. Coun. Tchrs. English. Office: Western Conn State U Dept English Danbury CT 06810 E-mail: qis@wcsu.edu.

QIAN, CHUNJIANG, engineering educator, researcher; b. ZJG City, JiangSu, China, 1971; arrived in U.S., 1997; m. Qi Jiang, 1997. BS, Fudan U., Shanghai, China, 1991, MS, 1994; PhD, Case Western Res. U., 2001. Engr. TianLong Sci & Tech. Co., China, 1994—97; rsch. asst. Case Western Res. U., Cleve., 1997—2001; asst. prof. U. Tex. , San Antonio, 2001—. Mem. program com. 2002 IEEE CDC, 2002. Contbr. articles and sci. papers to profl. jours. Recipient Meritorious award, Consortium Math. and ITs, 1991; grantee Verhosek Fund, Case Western Res. U., 2000. Mem.: IEEE. Office: U Tex San Antonio 6900 N Loop 1604 West San Antonio TX 78249-0669

QIAN, HONG, mathematician, biologist; b. Shanghai, China, Sept. 26, 1960; s. Min Qian and Jinyan Zhang; m. Madeleine Yue Dong. BA in Astrophysics, Peking U., 1982; PhD in Biol. Scis. (Molecular Biology), Washington U., St. Louis, 1989. Rsch. assoc. Inst. Molecular Biology, U. Oreg., Eugene, 1990—92; rsch. fellow in chemistry Calif. Inst. Tech., Pasadena, 1992—94; adj. asst. prof. biomath. UCLA Sch. Medicine, 1994—97; asst. prof. applied math. and bioengrig. U. Wash., Seattle, 1997—. Fellow program in math. and molecular biology U. Calif., Berkeley, 1992—94; assoc. dir. Nat. Simulation Resource, Bioengrig. U. Wash., Seattle, 1997—. Office: U Wash Applied Math 412 Guggenheim Hall Seattle WA 98195-2420

QIAN, LIANFEN, statistician, educator; m. Qingchuan Yao; children: Jenny Yao. BS, Hangzhou U., 1984, MS, 1989; PhD, Mich. State U., 1996. Lectr. Hangzhou U., Hangzhou, China, 1984—91; tchg. & rsch. asst. Mich. State U., East Lansing, Mich., 1991—96; asst. prof. Fla. Atlantic U., Boca Raton, Fla., 1996—2002, assoc. prof., 2002—. Actuarial exam supr. Fla. Atlantic U., 1996—; stats. expert South Fla. Water Mgmt. Dist., Palm Beach, Fla., 1997—2001; cons. Fla. Atlantic U., 1996—. Author: (invention) Journal of Statistics Planning and Inference, 1998, [00b7]Journal of Statistical Computation and Simulation, 2000, Journal of Economic Botany, 2001, Congressus Numerantiu, 2000, Statistics & Probability Letters, 1996. Grantee Travel grant, NSF, ONR, NCI. Mem.: Internat. Biometric Soc., Inst. of Math. Stats., Am. Statis. Assn. (treas. 2001—, sec. 2000—01). Achievements include invention of in field. Office: Florida Atlantic University Department of Mathematical Sciences Boca Raton FL 33431 E-mail: lqian@fau.edu.

QIAN, XUEYU, physicist; b. Wengzhou, China, Aug. 1, 1943; arrived in U.S., 1980; m. Ping Zhu; children: Jun, Jiang, Tong. B in Physics, Beijing U., 1968; PhD in Physics, U. Mich., 1987. Head semiconductor divsn. Wenzhou Engrng. Sch., Zhejiang, 1970-74; lectr., rschr. U. Sci. and Tech., China, 1974-80; vis. scholar U. Mich., Ann Arbor, 1980-81, rsch. asst., 1981-87; rsch. assoc. U. Calif., Santa Barbara, 1987-88, Berkeley, 1988-90; tech. dir. Applied Materials, Santa Clara, Calif., 1990—2001, Novellus Systems, Inc., San Jose, 2002—. Author: (textbook) The Physics of Magnetic Recording, 1976; contbr. numerous articles to sci. publs.; patentee, inventor in field. Rsch. grantee Dept. Energy, 1981-87, Calif. Micro and Applied Materials, 1988-90. Mem. Am. Vacuum Soc. (No. Calif. chpt., editor plasma etch user's group 1996—). Office: Novellus Systems Inc 4000 N First St San Jose CA 95134 E-mail: xueyu_qian@novellus.com.

QIAN, ZHAOMING, critic, literature educator; b. Shanghai, China, July 25, 1944; s. Shaozhong Qian and Wenjing Chen; m. May Fang Wang, Jan. 1, 1969; children: Yuyan, Yuli. BA, Beijing Fgn. Studies U., 1967, MA, 1980; PhD, Tulane U., 1991. Instr. English, Beijing Fgn. Studies U., 1981-83, lectr. English, mng. editor, 1983-86, asst. dir. transl. studies, 1985-86; instr. English and Asian lit. Tulane U., New Orleans, 1986-91; asst. prof. English U. New Orleans, 1991-96, assoc. prof. English, 1996-2001, prof., 2001—. Author: Orientalism and Modernism: The Legacy of China in Pound and Williams, 1995, The Modernist Response to Chinese Art: Pound, Moore, Stevens, 2002; editor: 20th Century English and American Stories, 1987, Annotated Shakespeare: The Sonnets, 1990, 95, 98, Ezra Pound and China, 2002; contbr. articles to profl. jours. Yale Beineckefellow, 1992-93; Fellow NEH, 1998-99. Mem. MLA, South Ctrl. MLA, Ezra Pound Soc., William Carlos Williams Soc., Wallace Stevens Soc., Marianne Moore Soc. Office: U New Orleans Dept English New Orleans LA 70148-0001

QIAN, ZIFEN, artist, researcher; b. Shanghai, Dec. 30, 1957; came to U.S., 1987; s. Mingkong and Xuan Wu (Chen) Q.; m. Li Dai, Mar. 27, 1992; 1 child, Kristin. BA, Shanghai Normal U., 1983; MFA, Portland State U., 1989. Sr. artist Carol Wilson Fine Arts, Portland, 1992—; art instr. Pacific Northwest Coll. Art, 1989-95, Portland State U., 1987-89; art dir. Classic Clay Concept Inc., 1990-92; art editor Youth and Health mag. WHO, Shanghai, 1983-87; pres. Northwest Chinese Artists Assn., Portland, 1993-95; editor-in-chief World Arts Pub. Co., 1997—. Fine artist: (paintings, art philosophy) The Oregonian newspaper, 1987, Stepping Out Arts mag., 1988, (paintings in a book) Entertaining with Betsy Bloomingdale, 1994, (paintings prints) Carol Wilson Fine Arts, 1992—, (art experience) The Dictionary of World Chinese Artists Achievements, 1994. One-man exhbns. Denise Amato Galleries, 1989-98, Indigo Gallery, 1992, Portland State U. Gallery, 1989 (fine artist award), U.S. Nat. Bank Tower, 1987, Broderick Gallery, 2000, Internat. Artexpo, NYC, 2002, Dragon Gallery, NYC, 2002, Kavanaugh Art Gallery, West Des Moines, Iowa, 2002; group exhbns. include Shanghai Fine Arts Acad. Shows, 1982, 84, Across East China Nat. Art Show, 1986, San Francisco World Exposition, 1987, Pacific N.W. Coll. Art, 1992, Denise Amato Galleries, 1991, 93, 94, 96, 97, Emerly Fine Arts Gallery, 1997, Portland Art Mus., 1999; featured in The Washington Post, 1995, The Houston Chronicle, 1995, The Oregonian newspaper, 1987, (book) Always Bright (Paintings From 1970-1999), 1999; painting on cover of book Traditions and Encounters-A Global Perspective on The Past (From 1500 To The Present), 2000; represented in permanent collections at State Senate of Oreg., State House of Oreg., City Hall of Portland, Portland Christian Ctr., Portland Art Mus.; printing prints show in over 3,700 art galleries and gift stores, U.K., France, Finland, Italy, Germany, Denmark, Australia, N.Z., Japan, Can., U.S. Recipient Outstanding Painting award Lucil S. Welch Meml. Found., 1988. Avocations: creating poetry, singing, tennis. E-mail: lzwap@aol.com.

QIANG, XIAO, advocate; BS, U. Sci. and Tech. China; student, U. Notre Dame, 1986—89. Human rights worker Ind. Fedn. Chinese Students and Scholars, Washington; exec. dir. Human Rights in China, N.Y.C. Spkr. Chinese human rights UN Commn. on Human Rights, 1993—; lectr. in field in various countries. Office: Human Rights in China 350 Fifth Ave Ste 3309 New York NY 10118*

QIN, SHU, materials scientist; b. Beijing, China, May 21, 1950; arrived in U.S., 1986; d. Ni and Jin Zhang Qin; m. Fuping Zhai Qin, Jan. 21, 1978; 1 child Zhen. Diploma, Beijing Poly. U., 1976; MS, Tsinghua U., Beijing, 1982; PhD, Northeastern U., Boston, 1992. Asst. prof. Tsinghua U., Beijing, 1976—82; lectr. Beijing Inst. of Posts and Telcoms., 1982—86; rsch. scientist Lehigh U., Bethlehem, Pa., 1986—87; sr. scientist Northeastern U., Boston, 1992—97; prin. scientist Silicon Genesis Corp., Campbell, Calif., 1997—2000, Axcelis Technologies, Inc., Beverly, Mass., 2000—. Cons. Eaton Corp., Beverly, 1993—97. Contbr. Mem.: AAAS, IEEE (sr.), Materials Rsch. Soc. Achievements include patents for in field. Avocations: photography, sports, travel, classical music. Home: 47 francis St Apt 2 Malden MA 02148 Office: Axcelis Technologies Inc 108 Cherry Hill Dr Beverly MA 01915

QIN, SUOFU, biochemist; b. Jiangchuan, Yunnan, China, Aug. 26, 1964; s. Lianzhou Qin and Guizheng Li; m. Liqun Zhang, May 22, 1994; children: Jennifer, Jeffrey. PhD, Fukui Med. U., 1998. Teaching & rsch. asst. Shanghai Med. U., 1990-93; rsch. scientist NIH, Bethesda, Md., 1998—. Contbr. articles to profl. jours. Mem. AAAS, Am. Soc. Cell Biology. Office: LB/NHLBI/NIH Rm 2130 MSC 8012 50 South Dr Bethesda MD 20892 Fax: 301-496-0599. E-mail: qins@nih.gov.

QIU, LARRY DONGXIAO, economics educator; b. Luchun, Guangxi, China, Oct. 6, 1961; s. Peilung Qiu and Meijian Chen; m. Denise Jinglian Qiu, Jan. 9, 1987; children: Alice W., Jennifer Z. BS, Zhongshan U., Guangzhou, China, 1983; MA, U. B.C., Vancouver, Can., 1989, PhD, 1993. Asst. prof. Hong Kong U. Sci. and Tech., 1993-2001, assoc. prof., 2001—. Cons. Hong Kong Govt., 1996-98, Asian Devel. Bank, Manila, 1997-98. Contbr. articles to profl. jours. Mem. Am. Econ. Assn., Royal Econ. Soc., Econometric Soc., European Econ. Assn., Internat. Econs. and Fin. Soc. Avocations: tennis, soccer, music. Office: Dept Econs Hong Kong U Sci & Tech Kowloon Hong Kong Office Fax: 852 2358 2084.

QIU, PEIHUA, statistician, educator, statistician, researcher; b. Shanghai, China, Oct. 17, 1965; arrived in U.S., 1991; s. Hongde Ren, Qibao Li; m. Yan Zhang, May 7, 1977; 1 child Andrew Qiu Zhang. BS in Math., Fudan U., China, 1986; PhD, U. Wis., 1996. Asst. prof. Fudan U., Shanghai, 1989—91; sr. rsch. consulting statistician Ohio State U., Columbus, 1996—98; asst. prof. U. Minn., Mpls., 1998—2002, assoc. prof., 2002—. Contbr. chapters to books, articles to profl. jours. Recipient best paper winner of the 5th ISI competition for young statistician, Internat. Statis. Inst., 1991. Mem.: Bernoulli Soc., Inst. Math. Stats., Am. Statis. Assn. Home: 6768 Carlisle Curve Shakopee MN 55379

QIU, SIGANG, telecommunications engineer; b. Jan. 5, 1965; came to the U.S., 1994; s. Jian Shui Qiu and Qin Xiang Xu; m. Feng Zhou, Feb. 19, 1994; 1 child, Waveley Qiu. MS, Qufu (China) Normal U., 1989, U. Conn., 1996; PhD, U. Vienna, Austria, 2000. Cert. engr. N.C. Tchg. asst. U. Conn., Storrs, 1994-97; engr. Cirrus Logic, Raleigh, N.C., 1997-99; sr. engr. Intel, 1999—. Book referee Birkhauser Book Pub., Boston, 1997. Contbr. articles to profl. jours. Mem.: IEEE (jour. referee Trans. on Signal Processing 1994—), Am. Math. Soc., Soc. Photo-Optical Instrumentation and Engring. Avocations: walking, basketball, hiking. Office: Ambient Techs 110 Horizon Dr Raleigh NC 27615-4926 E-mail: sigang@ieee.org.

QIU, ZEYUAN, researcher, educator; b. Hubei, China, July 16, 1965; came to U.S., 1993; parents Jinmao Qiu and Shouxiang Liu; m. Mei Fu, June 25, 1993; children: Christina, Jeanna. BS, Ctrl. China Agrl. U., Wuhan, 1986; MS, People's U. China, Beijing, 1989; PhD, U. Mo., 1996. Lectr. People's U. of China, Beijing, 1989-93; rsch. asst. prof. U. Mo., Columbia, 1996—2001; asst. prof. N.J. Inst. Tech., Newark, 2002—. Contbr. articles to profl. jours. Mem. Am. Agrl. Econs. Assn., Soil and Water Conservation Soc., So. Agrl. Econs. Assn. Office: NJ Inst Tech 317 Cullimore Hall Newark NJ 07102-

QU, HAILIN, hospitality and tourism professional; b. Shanghai, China, Nov. 8, 1951; s. Gengming Qu and Renai Zhuo; m. Weifen Fang, Nov. 22, 1982; 1 child, Yi. AA, Shanghai Inst. Tourism, 1981; cert. mgmt. and microcomputer sci., Shanghai Jiaotong U., 1984; BS, No. Ariz. U., 1987; MS, Purdue U., 1989, PhD, 1992. Lectr. Shanghai Inst. Tourism, 1981-86; asst. prof. Hong Kong Polytechnic U., 1992-96; assoc. prof. San Francisco State U., 1996-99; prof. Okla. State U., 1999—, William E. Davis disting. chair, 1999—. Advisor URBIS Travers Morgan Ltd., Hong Kong, 1993-96; vis. fellow Hong Kong Poly. U., 1998, vis. chair prof., 2000—; vis. prof. Ecole Hoteliere, Lausanne, Switzerland, 1999. Editor: Pacific Tourism Rev., Australia, 19965, Jour. Quality Assurance in Hospitality and Tourism Mgmt., 19995, Jour. Travel and Tourism Mktg., 19995, Jour. Tchg. in Travel and Tourism, 19995; contbg. author: Tourism and Economic Development in Asia and Australasia, 1997; reviewer Jour. Hospitality and Tourism Rsch.; contbr. articles to profl. jours. Keynote or invited spkr. Asia-Bound Travel Congress, Hong Kong, 1996, China Nat. Tourism Adminstrn. Shanghai, 1993, 95, Hong Kong Peihua Edn. Found., 1995. Hon. lectr. U. Hong Kong, 1996; hon. prof. Beijing Inst. Tourism, 1993, China Tourism Mgmt. Inst., Tianjing, 1993, Hainan U., 2001, Shanghai Inst. Tourism, 2001. Mem. CHRIE/Washington, Travel and Tourism Assn. Avocations: reading, travel, classical music, tennis. Office: Okla State U 210 Hes Stillwater OK 74078-6120 E-mail: qhailin@okstate.edu.

QUAAL, WARD LOUIS, broadcast executive; b. Ishpeming, Mich., Apr. 7, 1919; s. Sigfred Emil and Alma Charlotte (Larson) Q.; m. Dorothy J. Graham, Mar. 9, 1944; children: Graham Ward, Jennifer Anne. AB, U. Mich., 1941; LL.D. (hon.), Mundelein Coll., 1962, No. Mich. U., 1967; D.Pub. Service, Elmhurst Coll., 1967; D.H.L. (hon.), Lincoln Coll., 1968, DePaul U., 1974. Announcer-writer Sta. WBEO (now sta. WDMJ), Marquette, Mich., 1936-37; announcer, writer, producer Sta. WJR, Detroit, 1937-41; spl. events announcer-producer WGN, Chgo., 1941-42, asst. to gen. mgr., 1945-49; exec. dir. Clear Channel Broadcasting Service, Washington, 1949-52, pres., chief exec. officer, 1964-74; v.p., asst. gen. mgr. Crosley Broadcasting Corp., Cin., 1952-56; v.p., gen. mgr., mem. bd. WGN Inc., Chgo., 1956; exec. v.p., then pres. WGN Continental Broadcasting Co. (now Tribune Broadcasting Co.), 1960-75; pres. Ward L. Quaal Co., 1975—; dir. Tribune Co., 1961-75; dir., mem. exec. com. U.S. Satellite Broadcasting Co., 1982-2000. Bd. dirs. Christine Valmy Inc.; chmn. exec. com., dir. WLW Radio Inc., Cin., 1975-81; co-founder, dir. Universal Resources Inc., 1961-86; mem. FCC Adv. Com. on Advanced TV Sys., 1988-96. Author: (with others) Broadcast Management, 1968, rev. edit., 1979, new edit. 1997; co-prodr. (Broadway play) Teddy and Alice, 1988. Mem., Hoover Commn. Exec. Br. Task Force, 1949-59; mem. U.S.-Japan Cultural Exchange Commn., 1960-70; mem. Pres.'s Council Phys. Fitness and Sports, 1983-93; bd. dirs. Farm Found., 1963-73; bd. trustees Hollywood (Calif.) Mus., 1964-78, MacCormac Jr. Coll., Chgo., 1974-80; chmn. exec. com. Council for TV Devel., 1969-72; mem. bus. adv. coun. Chgo. Urban League, 1964-74; bd. dirs. Broadcasters Found., Internat. Radio and TV Found., Sears Roebuck Found., 1970-73; trustee Mundelein Coll., 1962-72, Hillsdale Coll., 1966-72. Served as lt. USNR, 1942-45. Recipient Disting. Bd. Gov.'s award Nat. Acad. TV Arts and Scis., 1966, 87, Freedoms Found. award, Valley Forge, 1966, 68, 70, Disting. Alumnus award U. Mich., 1967, Loyola U. Key, 1970, Advt. Man of Yr. Gold medallion, Chgo. Advt. Club, 1968, Disting. Svc. award Nat. Assn. Broadcasters, 1973, Ill. Broadcaster of Yr. award, 1973, Press Vet. of Yr. award, 1973, Comm. award of distinction Brandeis U., 1973, Founder & Leadership award Broadcast Pioneers Libr., 1991; first recipient Sterling Medal, Barren Found., 1985, Lifetime Achievement award in broadcasting Ill. Broadcasters Assn., 1989, Lifetime Achievement award WGN TV 50th Anniversary, 1998; 1st person named to Better Bus. Bur. Hall of Fame, Council of Better Bus. Burs. Inc., 1975; named Radio Man of Yr. Am. Coll. Radio, Arts, Crafts & Scis., 1961, Laureate in Order of Lincoln, Lincoln Acad. Ill., 1965, Communicator of Yr., Jewish United Fund, 1969, Advt. Club Man of Yr., 1973; named to Delta Tau Delta Disting. Svc. Chpt., 1970; named one of top 100 mems. of Delta Tau Delta who has attained the highest levels of nat. achievement during 20th century, 1999; named to Broadcasting Mag. Hall of Fame, 1991; named one of top 100 contbrs. to broadcasting and cable in 20th century, Broadcasting and Cable Mag., 1999. Mem. NATAS (bd. govs. 1966-76, Silver Circle award 1993), Nat. Press Found. (bd. dirs. 1991-99), Nat. Assn. Broadcasters (bd. dirs. 1952-56), Fed. Comm. Bar Assn., Broadcast Music Inc. (bd. dirs. 1953-70), Assn. Maximum Svc. Telecasters Inc. (bd. dirs. 1952-72), Broadcast Pioneers (pres., bd. dirs. 1962-73), Broadcast Pioneers Libr. (pres. 1981-84), Broadcast Pioneers Ednl. Fund Inc., Broadcasters Found. (chmn. bd. 1996-99). Office: Ward L Quaal Co One Northfield Plaza Ste 300 Northfield IL 60093

QUACKENBUSH, CATHY ELIZABETH, secondary school educator; b. Carthage, N.Y., Sept. 20, 1949; d. James Adrian and Miriam June (Fickes) Seaman; m. Roger E. Quackenbush, March 31, 1973; 1 child, Thomas Bradford. AAS, SUNY, Morrisville, 1969; BS, SUNY, Albany, 1971, MS, 1976; attended, U. Ga., 1978, Cornell U., 1984, U. Calif., 1986, SUNY, Albany, 1986-87. Cert. tchr., N.Y. Tchr., 7th grade sci. Bethlehem Ctrl. Middle Sch., Delmar, N.Y., 1971-92; tchr., biology Bethlehem Ctrl. High Sch., 1992—. Bd. dirs. Bethlehem Opportunities Unlimited-Corp. for Substance Abuse Prevention, Delmar, 1983-91, 96-98; organizer and co-adv. Bethlehem Ctrl. Leadership Club, 1985-89; chair Middle Sch. Final Assessment Com., 1990-91, Middle Sch. Restructuring Com., 1991-92; organizer and leader Student Ednl. Tours to Kenya, East Africa, 1985, 89, 91, 94, 96, 98; rater and question writer for N.Y. State Regents Competency Exam in Sci., N.Y. State Edn. Dept., Albany, 1990-92. Sunday sch. tchr. Bethany Reformed Ch., 1988-92. N.Y. State Environ. Coun. and N.Y. State Outdoor Edn. Assn. grantee N.Y. State Outdoor Edn. Inst., 1979, NSF grantee DNA Inst. for Middle Sch. Tchrs., 1990, Human Genetics and Bioethics grantee Greenwall Found., 1993, Molecular Biology for Tchrs. grantee Howard Hughes Med. Inst., 1993, co-inst., 1994-98, 2001. Mem. Delta Kappa Gamma Soc. (sec. 1987-90, 2d v.p. 1990-92), Cornell Inst. for Biology Tchrs.(1996-2000). Avocations: traveling, sailing, motorcycling. Home: 25 Robinhood Rd Albany NY 12203-5133 Office: Bethlehem Ctrl High Sch 700 Delaware Ave Delmar NY 12054-2436

QUACKENBUSH, MARGERY CLOUSER, psychoanalyst, administrator; b. Reading, Pa., Apr. 30, 1938; d. Carl Brumbach and Katherine Elvina (Althouse) Clouser; m. Robert Mead Quackenbush, July 3, 1971; 1 child, Piet Robert. BA, Pratt Inst., 1960; MA, Calif. Grad. Inst., 1982; PhD in Psychoanalysis, Internat. U. Grad. Studies, N.Y.C., 2001. Cert. in psychoanalysis Ctr. for Modern Psychoanalytic Studies, 1992. Instr. Pratt Inst., Bklyn., 1978-79, Fash. Inst. of Tech., N.Y.C., 1980-81; counselor Wiltwyck, Bronx Ctr., 1981-82; adminstr. Nat. Assn. for Advancement of Psychoanalysis, N.Y.C., 1982—; pvt. practice in psychoanalysis, 1980—. Mem. Lenox Hill Dem. Club, N.Y.C., 1993-95; spkr. various cmty. groups, 1991—. Recipient Maison Blanche award, 1959, Miriam Berkman Spotnitz award, 1992. Mem. Nat. Assn. for Advancement of Psychoanalysis, Nat. Soc. DAR, Alumni Assn. of the Ctr. for Modern Psych. Studies (sec. 1992-94, Alumni Assn. program dir., v.p. 1995-98). Democrat. Avocations: reading, writing, golf, horseback riding. Home: 460 E 79th St Apt 14E New York NY 10021-1447 Office: Nat Assn Advancement Psychoanalysis 80 8th Ave # 1501 New York NY 10011-5126 E-mail: naap72@aol.com.

QUACKENBUSH, ROBERT DEAN, management consultant; b. Lansing, Mich., Oct. 12, 1947; s. Gerald G. and Margaret Lee (McLean) Q.; m. Donna Jean Cleary, Aug. 4, 1976; children: Dana McLean, Grant Robert. BA, Elmhurst Coll., 1969; postgrad., John Marshall Law Sch., 1969, 71. Mgmt. cons., Nineveh, Pa., 1982—. Instr. Washington and Jefferson Coll., 1982-85; dir. adv. and intermediary svcs. Internat. Profit Assocs., 2000—, sr. project mgr., 1993-2000, 2001-. Author: Lake Lauzon, 1991. With U.S. Army, 1970-71, Vietnam. Avocations: fishing, snorkeling, travel. Home and Office: PO Box 14 Nineveh PA 15353-0014

QUACKENBUSH, ROBERT MEAD, artist, author, psychoanalyst; b. Hollywood, Calif., July 23, 1929; s. Roy Maynard and Virginia (Arbogast) Q.; m. Margery Clouser, July 3, 1971; 1 child: Piet Robert. B of Profl. Arts, Art Ctr. Coll. of Design, Pasadena, Calif., 1956; grad., Ctr. Modern Psychoanalytic Studies, N.Y.C., 1991; MSW, Fordham U., 1994; PhD, Internat. U. Grad. Studies, 1999. Art dir. Scandinavian Airlines Sys., N.Y.C. and Stockholm, 1956-61; pvt. practice N.Y.C., 1961—; psychoanalyst/psychtherapist New Hope Guild Ctrs. for Emotionally Disturbed Children, Bklyn., 1994-2000. Educator Robert Quackenbush Studios, N.Y.C.; lectr. U.S., Europe, Middle East and South Am.; TV performer Ednl. TV; mem. faculty N.J. Ctr. for Modern Psychoanalysis. Author/artist: more than 180 books for young readers including; author: (novels) Robert Quackenbush's Treasury of Humor, 1990, Benjamin Franklin and His Friends, 1991, Evil Under the Sea, 1992, James Madison & Dolly Madison and Their Times, 1993, Arthur Ashe and His Match with History, 1994, Clara Barton and Her Victory Over Fear, 1995, Batbaby, 1997, (under pen name Richard Gobbletree) Treasure Hunt, 1997, Two Miss Mallard Mysteries: Surfboard to Peril and Stage Door to Terror, 1998, Daughter of Liberty, 1999, Flamenco to Mischief: A Miss Mallard Mystery , 2000, Miss Mallard's Case Book, 2000, Batbaby Finds a Home, 2001, Mishap in Kaiserslautern: A Miss Mallard Mystery, 2001; prodr.: (TV series) Dear Mr. Quackenbush and The Great American Storybook, 1988, The Miss Mallard Mysteries, 1999; Represented in permanent collections Whitney Mus., The Smithsonian Inst., numerous pvt. collections include. With U.S. Army 1951-53. Recipient 2 Citations for outstanding Troop Info. & Edn. instrn. from commdg. gen. 31st Inf. Divsn. 1953, 4 time winner Am. Flag Inst. award for outstanding contbn. to field of children's lit., 1976, 77, 81, 99, Edgar Allen Poe Spl. award, 1982, Gradiva award, 1998, Gold medal for disting. achievement by a mem. in art and lit. Holland Soc., 2000. Mem. Mystery Writers of Am., Authors' Guild, Authors' League of Am., Holland Soc. of N.Y., Nat. Assn. for Advancement of Psychoanalysis (trustee, v.p. pub. info., founder and chair Gradiva awards), Soc. Modern Psychoanalysts. Avocations: travel, antique restoration. Home: 460 E 79th St Apt 14E New York NY 10021-1447 Office: Robert Quackenbush Studios 223 E 78th St New York NY 10021-1222 E-mail: rqstudios@aol.com. *Humor became a key to survival in my family when I was growing up during the depression and World War II. Thus humor became the keynote of all the books I write and illustrate - I want young readers to know that as long as we keep our sense of humor, our spirits cannot be crushed. In my analytic practice I encourage children to verbalize their conflicts through art and writing projects.*

QUACKENBUSH, ROGER E. retired secondary school educator; b. Cooperstown, N.Y., Jan. 22, 1940; s. Eugene W. and Marion I. (Clark) Q.; m. Cathy E. Quackenbush, Mar. 31, 1973; children: Michele, Stacey, Thomas. BS, SUNY, Albany, 1961, MS, 1966; PhD, Columbia Pacific U., San Rafael, Calif., 1984; postgrad., numerous univs. Cert. permanent biology and gen. sci. tchr., N.Y. Tchr. gen. sci. and math Troy (N.Y.) Pub. Sch. System, 1961-64; tchr. earth sci. and biology Schuylerville (N.Y.) Cen. H.S., 1964-66; tchr. biology Bethlehem Cen. H.S., Delmar, N.Y., 1966-95; cons. advanced placement biology Niskayuna (N.Y.) H.S., 1995-96; instr. anatomy and physiology lab. Russell Sage Coll., Troy, N.Y., 1996-97. Mentor student tchrs., 1968-90; instr. Tchr. Expectation Student Achievement program, 1985-91; lectr. on marine mammals SUNY, Albany, 1986; instr. DNA Sci. and Tech. for h.s. students SUNY, Albany, 1996; lectr. on whales; workshop leader on use microcomputers in classroom; former mem. Mid States Commn. on Evaluation Local H.S.'s; past mem. adv. bd. Upstate N.Y. Jr. Sci. and Humanities Symposium; test writer Regents biology exams. N.Y. State Dept. Edn.; presenter/cons. N.Y. State Edn. Dept. alt. assessment writer's workshop, 1994; leader, naturalist for whale watch trips and Kenya safaris; presenter for DNA-molecular biology lab. techniques; presenter on use of Tex. Instruments calculator and the Calculator Based Lab. sys. in the sci. classroom; mem Select Seminar on Evaluating Tchrs., 1985; mem. Wells Conf. Regents Biology Syllabus Revision, 1991; faculty cons. AP Biology reading Coll. Bd. Advanced Placement Program, 1997-98; cons. DNA molecular biology technology Greater Capital Region Tchr. Ctr., 1988-97; instnl. animal care and use com. N.Y. State Health Dept., 1999-2001. Editor/writer of alternative assessments for N.Y. State Edn. Dept., 1993-94; contbr. articles to profl. jours.; author: Swahili Phrasebook, 1993. Hon. admisssions liaison officer USAF Acad., 1988. Recipient Excellence in Tchg. award, 1989, letter of commendation U. Chgo., 1978, MIT, 1985, U.S. Army, 1989, Tufts U., 1990, 94, 97, Tchr. of Yr. award Tufts U., 1985, Golub Tchr.-Scholar award SUNY, 1991, 96; Chpt. II grantee N.Y. State Dept. Edn., 1987, NSF grantee, 1965, 67, 68, 72, 87, 90, Future Directions, 1990, Greenwall Found., 1993, hon. mention Tandy Tech. Scholar award, 1994, Tandy Tech. Scholar prize for excellence in sci. tchg., 1995, Outstanding Tchr. award U. Chgo., 1995; named Hon. Grad. Marshal, 1991, 94, hon. N.Y. State Biology Mentor, 1995. Mem. NEA, Nat. Assn. Biology Tchrs., BALSA, Soc. Marine Mammalogy, Am. Cetacean Soc., Cetacean Soc. Internat., Sci. Tchrs. Assn. N.Y. State (past sect. dir., past state bd. dirs.), NEA of N.Y., Phi Delta Kappa. Home: 25 Robinhood Rd Albany NY 12203-5133

QUADAY-GRAY, AILENE DIANN, retired speech pathologist; b. Blue Earth, Minn., Aug. 26, 1937; d. Carl Frederick Quaday and Arlene Alice Bunting; m. Maurice Clayton Maine, Aug. 18, 1956 (div. May 1975); children: Keith Mauricé, Kevin Richard; m. Francis Moulton Gray Jr., May 7, 1989 (dec. Dec. 1994). BA, St. Cloud (Minn.) State U., 1971; postgrad., San Diego State U., 1979-81, various colls., 1971-85, West Hills and Fresno Pacific, 1987-94. Lic. speech pathologist, Calif.; cert. presch. tchr., Calif. Speech pathologist Comprehensive Health Ctrs., Inc., San Diego, 1981-82; speech pathologist pilot project Kings Rehab. Ctr., Inc., Hanford, 1983 summer; tchr., dir. First Luth Ch. Presch., 1983-85; speech specialist Fresno (Calif.) County Office of Edn., 1985-87, Kings County Office of Edn., Hanford, 1987-91, Reef-Sunset Unified Sch. Dist., Avenal, Kettleman City, Calif., 1991-94, Kingsburg (Calif.) Joint Union Charter Elem. Schs., 1994-2001; part-time presch. speech therapist Sanger (Calif.) Unified Sch. Dist., 2001—02. Cons. Headstart: Tech. Assistance Mgmt., 1971-72; speech therapist Job Share, Sanger, Calif., 2002-. Vice chmn. bd. edn. St. James Luth., San Diego, 1979-80; del. Consortium on County Health Needs, Wright County, Minn., 1972-75; advisor Wright County Minn. Commrs. on Handicapped, 1973-75; vol. children's waiting rm. Navy Hosp., Bremerton, Wash., 1976-77. Mem. Calif. Speech, Lang. and Hearing Assn. Democrat. Methodist. Avocations: playing flute, teaching language, reading, writing poetry. Home: 1551 6th Avenue Dr Lot 78 Kingsburg CA 93631-1731

QUADE, MARSHALL ROSS, transportation planner; b. Milw. s. Richard William and Shirley Ann Quade. BA in Polit. Sci., U. Wis., Milw., 1989, M of Urban Planning, 1992; mgmt. cert., Marquette U., 1997. Grad. rsch. asst. dept. urban planning U. Wis., Milw., 1990-91, grad. rsch. asst. Urban Rsch. Ctr., 1991-92; econ. devel./land use planner City of Brookfield, Waukesha, Wis., 1991-94; sr. transp. planner, analyst Wis. Dept. Transp., 1994-2000, dist. planning supr. Madison, 2000—. Planning, allocations, and monitoring vol. United Way Greater Milw., 1994-96; Future Cities Competition vol. Nat. Engrs. Week, Milw., 1994. Recipient Wis. Downtown Action Coun. Student

Project award, 1992, Site Sponsor award Goodwill Industries of S.E. Wis. and Greater Chgo., 1999. Mem. Am. Inst. Cert. Planners, Am. Planning Assn., Inst. Transp. Engrs. (affiliate dir. Wis. sect.), Assn. Commuter Transp.

QUADE, VICTORIA CATHERINE, editor, writer, playwright, producer; b. Chgo., Aug. 15, 1953; d. Victor and Virginia (Uryasz) Q.; m. Charles J. White III, Feb. 15, 1986 (div. Aug. 1996); children: Michael, David, Catherine. BS in Journalism, No. Ill. U., 1974. Staff reporter news divsn. The News-Tribune, LaSalle, Ill., 1975-77; staff writer news divsn. The News-Sun, Waukegan, 1977-81; staff writer ABA Jour., Chgo., 1981-85; mng. editor ABA Press, 1985-90, editor, 1990-2000, sr. editor, 1994-2000. Author: (poetry) Rain and Other Poems, 1976, Laughing Eyes, 1979, Two Under the Covers, 1981, (biography) I Remember Bob Collins, 2000; playwright Late Nite Catechism, 1993, (with Maripat Donovan) Room for Advancement, 1994, Mr. Nanny, 1997, (musical) Lost in Wonderland, 1998, (musical) Here Come the Famous Brothers, 2001; prodr. Late Nite Catechism, Mr. Nanny, Here Come the Famous Brothers, Christopher Carter Messes With Your Mind; contbr. to numerous anthologies and publs.; contbd. to: 20th Century Chicago: 100 Years, 100 Voices (contbd. the year 1953), owner/operator Crossroads Theater, Naperville, Ill. Recipient numerous awards from Soc. Nat. Assn. Publs., AP, UPI. Mem. Am. Soc. Bus. Press Editors (award), Chgo. Newspaper Guild (award), Am. Soc. Assn. Execs. (Gold Circle award 1989, 90). Avocations: traveling, photography.

QUAGLIARELLO, VINCENT JAMES, medical educator; b. Bklyn., Feb. 4, 1955; s. Marcy and Brigita Q.; m. Joyce Marino, July 16, 1977; children: James, Brigit, Timothy. BA, Johns Hopkins U., 1976; MD, Washington U., St. Louis, 1980. Intern, resident Yale New Haven (Conn.) Hosp., 1980-83, chief resident in medicine, 1983-84; fellow infectious diseases U. Va., Charlottesville, 1984-87; asst. prof. medicine Yale U. Sch. Medicine, New Haven, 1988-93, assoc. prof. medicine, 1993—2002, prof. medicine, 2002—, dir. med. student clerkship, 1989—, dir. infectious diseases fellowship, 1990—, clin. dir. infectious disease sect., 1990—. Contbr. over 40 articles to profl. jours. Coach Little League Baseball. Fellow Am. Coll. Physicians, Infectious Disease Soc. Am.; mem. Am. Soc. Microbiology. Roman Catholic. Office: Yale U Sch Medicine 800 LCI New Haven CT 06520

QUAIFE, MARJORIE CLIFT, retired nursing educator; b. Syracuse, N.Y., Aug. 21; Diploma in Nursing with honors, Auburn Meml. Hosp; BS, Columbia U., 1962, MA, 1978. Cert. orthopaedic nurse; cert. in nursing continuing edn. and staff devel.; BLS instr. Staff instr. Columbia Presbyn. Hosp., N.Y.C., 1968-97, ret., 1997. Content expert for computer assisted instrn. program-ctrl. venous catheters. Contbr. articles to numerous profl. publs. Mem. ANA, N.Y. State Nurses Assn., Nat. Assn. Orthopaedic Nurses, Nat. Assn. Nursing Staff Devel., Nat. Assn. Vascular Access Networks, Intravenous Nurses Soc., Sigma Theta Tau.

QUAINTANCE, ALICE LYNN, elementary school media specialist; b. Morristown, Tenn., July 20, 1958; d. Celton D. and Mary Lou (Scott) VanCleave; m. David Scott Quaintance, Aug. 2, 1980; children: Jennifer Lee, Allison Marie. BS, East Tenn. State U., 1980. Media specialist Surgoinsville (Tenn.) Elem. Sch., 1980-82, Clearwood Jr. H.S., Slidell, La., 1982-83, 84-86, tchr., 1983-84; media specialist Rose Park Mid. Sch., Nashville, 1987-88, Hermitage (Tenn.) Elem. Sch., 1988—; owner Just Acquaintances. Publicity chairperson Donelson/Hermitage (Tenn.) Neighborhood Assn., 1995-97; parent rep. Nashville Ballet Friends, 1997-99. Recipient Dalcon Arts in Schs. award Nashville Inst. for the Arts, 1992, Merit award Gov. Tenn., 1993, Acts of Excellence award Mayor of Nashville, 1994, Golden Apple award Metro Nashville Pub. Schs., 1996, Vol. of Yr. award Nashville Ballet, 1998. Mem. NEA, Tenn. Edn. Assn., Met. Nashville Edn. Assn., Delta Kappa Gamma (sec. 1993-97). United Methodist. Avocation: the Arts. Home: 3826 Pacifica Dr Hermitage TN 37076-1926

QUAINTON, ANTHONY CECIL EDEN, diplomat; b. Seattle, Apr. 4, 1934; s. Cecil Eden and Marjorie Josephine (Oates) Q.; m. Susan Long, Aug. 7, 1958; children: Katherine, Eden, Elizabeth. BA, Princeton U., 1955; BLitt, Oxford (Eng.) U., 1958. Research fellow St. Antony's Coll., Oxford, 1958-59; with Fgn. Service, State Dept., 1959-97; vice consul Sydney, Australia, 1960-62; Urdu lang. trainee, 1962-63; 2d sec., econ. officer Am. embassy, Karachi, Pakistan, 1963-64, Rawalpindi, Pakistan, 1964-66, 2d sec., polit. officer New Delhi, 1966-69; sr. polit. officer for India Dept. State, Washington, 1969-72; 1st sec. Am. embassy, Paris, 1972-73, counselor, dep. chief mission Kathmandu, Nepal, 1973-76; ambassador to Central African Empire, Bangui, 1976-78, Nicaragua, Managua, 1982-84, Kuwait, 1984-87; dir. Office for Combatting Terrorism, Dept. State, Washington, 1978-81; dep. insp. gen. Dept. State, 1987-89; ambassador Peru, 1989-92; asst. sec. of state for diplomatic security Dept. State, Washington, 1992-95, dir. gen. fgn. svc., 1995-97. Exec. dir. Una Chapman Cox Found., 1998-99; vis. lectr. Princeton U., 1998-99; pres., CEO Nat. Policy Assn., 1999—; mem. internat. policy com. U.S. Cath. Conf.; mem. adv. com. Inst. L.Am. Studies, Columbia U. V.p. Washington Lions Found., Pub. Diplomacy Found. English Speaking Union fellow, 1951-52; Marshall scholar, 1955-58; recipient Rivkin award, 1972, Herter award, 1984, Disting. Honor award Dept. State, 1997. Mem. Am. Acad. Diplomacy, Coun. on Fgn. Rels., Am. Fgn. Svc. Assn., Washington Inst. Fgn. Affairs, Lions Internat., Met. Club, Phi Beta Kappa. Home: 3424 Porter St NW Washington DC 20016-3126 Office: 1424 16th St NW Ste 700 Washington DC 20036-2240 E-mail: aquainton@npa1.org.

QUAKENBUSH, BRIAN CLAY, music educator; b. Burlington, N.C., Apr. 22, 1967; s. Calvin Wally and Alice (Purvis) Quakenbush; m. Jenny Ann Widder, May 28, 1994; 1 child Jason Widder. BS, East Tenn. State U., 1995. Band dir. Carroll County H.S., Hillsville, Va., 1996, Virginia H.S., Bristol, 1996—98, Heritage H.S., Lynchburg, 1998—. Adj. faculty, instr. trumpet Lynchburg Coll., Va., 2000—; counselor/instr. Va. Tech. Summer Music Camp, Blacksburg, 1997—; freelance musician. Recipient Outstanding Educator award, Va. Gov.'s Sch., 1998, 2000. Mem.: Music Educators Nat. Assn., NEA, Nat. Band Assn., Va. Band and Orch. Assn. Methodist. Avocations: jazz history, reading and exploring civil war history, music arranging, performing and listening to jazz. Home: 107 Stonehouse Dr Lynchburg VA 24502 Office: Heritage High Sch 3020 Wards Ferry Rd Lynchburg VA 24502

QUALE, ANDREW CHRISTOPHER, JR. lawyer; b. Boston, July 7, 1942; s. Andrew Christopher and Luella (Meland) Q.; m. Sally Sterling Ellis, Oct. 15, 1977; children: Andrew, Addison. BA magna cum laude, Harvard U., 1963, LLB cum laude, 1966; postgrad., Cambridge (Eng.) U., 1966-67. Bar: Mass. 1967, N.Y. 1971. Fellow Internat. Legal Ctr., Bogota, Colombia, 1967-68; cons. Republic of Colombia, 1968-69; assoc. Cleary, Gottlieb, Steen and Hamilton, N.Y.C., 1969-75; ptnr. Coudert Brothers, 1975-82, Sidley Austin Brown & Wood, N.Y.C., 1982—. Adj. prof. Sch. of Law U. Va., Charlottesville, 1976—88; cons. privatizations World Bank, UN, Harvard Inst. Internat. Devel., 1982—; bd. dirs. Bottell Stoeckel Assocs., Norfolk. Contbr. to profl. publs. Pres. Bronxville (N.Y.) Sch. Bd., 1991-93; founder, bd. dirs. Bronxville Sch. Found., 1991-95, 96—; bd. dirs. Coun. The Ams. Recipient Knox fellowship, 1966—67. Mem.: ABA, The Little Forum (co-chair Bronxville), Colombian-Am. Assn. (v.p., bd. dirs.), NY State Bar Assn., Assn. Bar City NY (chmn. Inter-Am. affairs com. 1982—85), Norfolk (Conn.) Country Club, Bronxville Field Club. Office: Sidley & Austin 875 3rd Ave Fl 14 New York NY 10022-6293

QUALE, JOHN CARTER, lawyer; b. Boston, Aug. 16, 1946; s. Andrew C. and Luella (Meland) Q.; m. Diane Zipursky, Jan. 19, 1992; children: Virginia Ann, Jane Harris, John Andrew; stepchildren: Rachel Goldman, Alisa Goldman. AB cum laude, Harvard U., 1968, JD cum laude, 1971. Bar: Mass. 1971, D.C. 1972. Assoc. Kirkland & Ellis, Washington, 1971-78, ptnr., 1978-83, Wiley, Rein & Fielding, Washington, 1983-96, Skadden, Arps, Slate, Meagher & Flom L.L.P., Washington, 1996—. Spkr. mass media trade groups. Contbr. articles to profl. jours. Trustee Fed. Comm. Bar Assn. Found., 1992-93. Mem. ABA, Fed. Comm. Bar Assn. (treas. 1982-83, 98-99, mem. exec. com. 1993-98), Barristers, Met. Club. Office: Skadden Arps Slate Meagher & Flom LLP 1440 New York Ave NW Ste 600 Washington DC 20005-6000 E-mail: jquale@skadden.com.

QUALLS, CHARLES WAYNE, JR. research pathologist; b. Oklahoma City, Feb. 8, 1949; s. Charles Wayne and Mary Opal (Howard) Q.; m. Cheryl Lynn Lightfoot, Aug. 9, 1969; children: Kerry Lynn, Julie Elizabeth. BS, Okla. State U., 1971, DVM, 1973; PhD, U. Calif., Davis, 1980. Diplomate Am. Coll. Vet. Pathologists. Postdoctoral fellow U. Calif., Davis, 1973-77; asst. prof. La. State U., Baton Rouge, 1977-82; assoc. prof. Okla. State U., Stillwater, 1982-87, prof. vet. pathology, 1988-99, acting head dept. vet. pathology, 1991-92, coord. grad. instrn. Coll. Vet. Medicine, 1996-99, adj. prof. vet. pathology, 1999—; sr. prin. pathologist GlaxoSmithKline, Research Triangle Park, N.C., 1999—; dir. molecular pathology and electron microscopy Glaxo Wellcome Inc., 1999-2001; project mgr., pathologist GlaxoSmithKline, 2001—. Dir. molecular pathology and electron microscopy. Mem. editl. bd. Jour. Toxicology and Environ. Health, Vet. Pathology, Bull. Environ. Toxicology; contbr. articles to profl. jours., chpts. to books. Grantee Dept. of Def., U.S. Army Rsch. and Engring. Program, EPA, others. Mem AVMA (student sponsor 1983-90), Soc. Toxicologic Pathologists, Soc. Toxicology, Phi Kappa Phi, Phi Zeta. Home: 4722 NC 57 Hurdle Mills NC 27541-9305 Office: GlaxoSmithKline Safety Assessment 5 Moore Dr Rm 9 3013 Research Triangle Park NC 27709

QUALLS, ROBERT GERALD, ecologist; b. Boone, N.C., May 20, 1952; s. Edward Spencer Qualls and Lynn Brown Heffner. MPH, U. N.C., 1981; PhD, U. Ga., 1989. Asst. rsch. prof. Duke U., Durham, N.C., 1989-96; assoc. prof. dept. environ. and rsch. sci. U. Nev., Reno, 1996—. Contbr. articles to profl. jours. NSF rsch. grantee, 1999, USDA rsch. grantee, 1997; NSF Dissertation Improvement awardee, 1985; recipient Internat. Assn. on Water Pollution Founders award for best paper in Water Rsch., 1986. Mem. Soil Sci. Soc. Am., Ecol. Soc. Am. Presbyterian. Achievements include development and validation of mathematical model of disinfection process in ultraviolet light reactors; demonstration of the means by which soluble organic nutrients are conserved within a natural forest ecosystem, others. Home: 5020 Ambrose Dr Reno NV 89509-2104 Office: U Nev MS 199 Dept Environ & Rsch Sci Reno NV 89557-0001 E-mail: qualls@unr.edu.

QUALLS, ROBERT L. manufacturing executive, banker, former state official, educator; b. Burnsville, Miss., Nov. 6, 1933; s. Wes E. and Letha (Parker) Q.; m. Carolyn Morgan, Feb. 10, 1979 (dec. July 1996); 1 child, Stephanie Elizabeth; m. Nancy Martin, Sept. 11, 1999. BS, Miss. State U., 1954, MS, 1958; PhD, La. State U., 1962; LLD, Whitworth Coll., 1974; DBA (hon.), U. of the Ozarks, 1984. Prof., chmn. div. econs. and bus. Belhaven Coll., Jackson, Miss., 1962-66, asst. to pres., 1965-66; asst. prof. finance Miss. State U., State College, 1967-69, adj. prof., 1969-73; sr. v.p., chmn. venture com. Bank of Miss., Tupelo, 1969-73; v.p. Wesleyan Coll., Macon, Ga., 1974; pres. U. of the Ozarks, Clarksville, Ark., 1974-79; mem. cabinet Bill Clinton Gov. of Ark., 1979-80; exec. v.p. Bank of America, Little Rock, 1980-85, chmn., CEO, dir. Harrison, 1985-86; pres., dir. First Bank Fin. Services, Inc., 1980-85, Advt. Assocs., Inc., 1980-85; pres., chief oper. officer Baldor Electric Co., Ft. Smith, Ark., 1986-91, CEO, 1992-97, vice chmn., 1998—2000, dir., mem. exec. com., 1987—. Mktg. cons. Ill. Central Industries, Chgo., 1964; mem. faculty, thesis examiner Stonier Grad. Sch. Banking, Rutgers U., 1973-86; mem. faculty Miss. Sch. Banking, U. Miss., 1973-78; course coordinator Sch. Banking of the South, La. State U., 1978-88, Banking Sch., Duke U., 1977; lectr. Southwestern Sch. Banking, So. Meth. U., 1983; adj. prof. bus. adminstrn. U. Central Ark., 1985-86; bd. dirs., mem. audit com. Bank of Ozarks. Author: Entrepreneurial Wit and Wisdom, 1986; co-author: Strategic Planning for Colleges and Universities: A Systems Approach to Planning and Resource Allocation, 1979; mem. editorial adv. bd.: Bank Mktg. Mag., 1984-86. Chmn. cmty. svc. and continuing edn. com. Tupelo Cmty. Devel. Found., 1972-73; mem. Miss. 4-H adv. coun., 1969; active Boys Scouts Am.; mem. Lee County Dem. Exec. Com., 1973-74; trustee Wal-Mart Found., 1975-79, Oklahoma City U., 1990-95; trustee, mem. exec. com. U. Ozarks, 1982-88, chmn. bd., 2000—; mem. Pres.'s Roundtable U. Ctrl. Ark., 1982-87; mem. exec. com. Coll. Bus. Adv. Bd., U. Ark., Little Rock, 1980-85; bd. dirs. U. Ark. Med. Sch. Found., 1991-97, Ark. Inst., 1991-94; chmn. bd. Petit Jean Youth Found., 2001--; mem. Clarksville Light and Water Commn., 2000-01; elder Clarksville Presbyn. Ch., 1997-2000. Lt. AUS, 1954-56. Found. for Econ. Edn. fellow, 1964; Ford Found. faculty research fellow Vanderbilt U., 1963-64; recipient Pillar of Progress award Johnson County, 1977 Mem. Am. Bankers Assn. (mktg. planning and rsch. com. 1972-73), Ark. Coun. Ind. Colls. and Univs. (chmn. 1978-79), Johnson County C. of C. (pres. 1977), Fort Smith C. of C. (dir. 1995-98), Blue Key, Omicron Delta Kappa, Delta Sigma Pi, Sigma Phi Epsilon (citation 1977), Beta Gamma Sigma, Masons (32 deg.), Clarksville Rotary (pres. 1979). Presbyterian. E-mail: nancy_qualls@msn.com.

QUALLS, STEVEN DANIEL, lawyer; b. Detroit, May 24, 1967; s. Hugh Pharris Qualls and Lenora Ann Allen; m. Elizabeth Lynn Crosier, June 21, 1990; children: Joshua Michael, Emily Elizabeth. BS, Tenn. Tech. U., 1992; JD, Nashville Sch. Law, 1996. Law clk. Cameron & Chaffin, Cookeville, Tenn., 1992-96, atty., 1996-98; atty., sr. ptnr. Qualls & Fry PLLC, 1998—. Mem. adv. bd. First Am. Nat. Bank, Cookeville, 1996-98; cons. Jackson Bank and Trust, Cookeville, 1996-98. Bd. dirs. Montessori Childrens Sch., Cookeville, 1993-98, Cancer Care Fund, Inc., 1999-2000, Putnam County Clean Commn., 2000-2001; treas. State Senate Charlotte Burks, Cookeville, 1998; active Dem. Party Putnam County, Cookeville, 1998; mem. Leadership Putnam Class of 2000; vice mayor Cookeville, 2002-. Mem. Noon Day Lions Clu b(v.p. 1996-98). Avocations: racquetball, tennis, golf. Home: 410 Concord Dr Cookeville TN 38501-3069 Office: Qualls Fry & Dunaway PLLC 16 S Washington Ave Cookeville TN 38501-3980 E-mail: squalls@citlink.net.

QUALSET, CALVIN O. plant genetics and agronomy educator; b. Newman Grove, Nebr., Apr. 24, 1937; s. Herman Qualset and Adeline (Hanson) Vakoc; m. Kathleen Boehler; children: Douglas, Cheryl, Gary. BS, U. Nebr., 1958, M Alumnus, 1997; MS, U. Calif., Davis, 1960, PhD, 1964. Asst. prof. U. Tenn., Knoxville, 1964-67; from asst. prof. to assoc. prof. U. Calif., Davis, 1967, prof., 1973-94, prof. emeritus, 1994—, chmn. dept. agronomy and range sci., 1975-81, 91-94, assoc. dean coll. agrl. and environ. sci., 1981-86; dir. Genetic Resources Conservation Program, 1985—. Sci, liaison officer U.S. Agy. Internat. Devel., Washington, 1985-93, mem. rsch. adv. com., 1989-92; mem. nat. plant genetic resources bd. USDA, Washington, 1982-88; bd. trustees Am. Type Culture Collection, 1993-99, Internat. Rice Rsch. Inst., 1999—. Contbr. over 200 articles to profl. jours. Fulbright fellow, Australia, 1976, Yugoslavia, 1984; recipient Pub. Plant Breeding award U.S. Coun. Comml. Plant Breeders, 1996, Charles Black award Coun. Agrl. Sci. and Tech., 2002. Fellow AAAS (chmn. agr. sect. 1992), Am. Soc. Agronomy (pres. 1994, agronomy honoree Calif. sect. 2001), Crop Sci. Soc. Am. (pres. 1989); mem. Soc. Conservation Biology, Soc. Econ. Botany, Genetic Soc. Am., Internat. Union Biol. Scis. (mem. U.S. nat. com. 2000—). Achievements include development of more than 15 cultivars of wheat, oat, triticale. Office: U Calif Genetic Res Conserv Prog One Shields Ave Davis CA 95616

QUAN, DENISE ALANE, music educator; b. L.A., Mar. 10, 1959; d. Olin Quan and Lois Wong Patterson. AA, L.A. City Coll., 1991; BA, BMus, U. So. Calif., 1994, MMus, 2001. Cert. tchr., Calif. Piano dept. chair Sat. Conservatory Music, L.A., 1992—; asst. lectr. U. So. Calif., 1994-96; music dept. chair, orch. and band dir. Virgil Mid. Sch., 1996—; instr. music dept. L.A. City Coll., 2001—. Bd. dir. Sat. Conservatory Music; adv. bd. L.A. City Coll. Music Dept., 1998—. Mem. L.A. City Coll. Alumni Assn., Phi Beta Kappa, Pi Kappa Lambda, Phi Kappa Phi. Avocations: reading, crossword puzzles, gardening, history, baking. Office: Virgil Mid Sch 152 N Vermont Ave Los Angeles CA 90004

QUANDT, JOSEPH EDWARD, lawyer, educator; b. Port Huron, Mich., May 21, 1963; s. Herbert Raymond and Mary Katherine (West) Q.; m. Christine Ann Reilly, Aug. 21, 1993. BA, Oakland U., 1990; JD, Thomas M. Cooley Law Sch., Lansing, Mich., 1993. Bar: Mich. 1994, U.S. Dist. Ct. (ea. and we. dists.) Mich. 1994. Exec. dir. Lord & Taylor, Sterling Heights, Mich., 1985-90; compliance and enforcement specialist Mich. Dept. Environ. Quality, Lansing, 1990-93, adv. bd., 1997—; assoc. Stowe, Draling & Boyd, Traverse City, Mich., 1993-94, Smith & Johnson, Traverse City, 1994-98; ptnr. Menmuir, Zimmerman, Kuhn, Taylor and Quandt, 1998—. Lectr., commentator Inst. CLE, Ann Arbor, Mich., 1994—; adj. prof. Thomas M. Cooley Law Sch., 1997—; co-chair environ. law sect. State Bar Mich. Contbr. articles to profl. jours. Bd. dirs. Involved Citizens Enterprises, Traverse City, 1995—. Mem. Nat. Honor Soc. for Polit. Scientists, Ancient Order Hibernians, Pi Sigma Alpha. Republican. Roman Catholic. Avocations: ice hockey, golf, fly fishing. Office: Zimmerman Kuhn Darling Boyd Taylor and Quandt PLC 122 W State St Traverse City MI 49684-2404

QUANDT, WILLIAM BAUER, political scientist; b. Los Angeles, Nov. 23, 1941; s. William Carl and Dorothy Elaine (Bauer) Q.; m. Anna Spitzer, June 21, 1964 (div. 1980); m. Helena Cobban, Apr. 21, 1984; 1 child, Lorna BA, Stanford U., 1963; PhD, MIT, 1968. Researcher Rand Corp., Santa Monica, Calif., 1968-72; staff mem. Nat. Security Council, Washington, 1972-74, sr. staff mem., 1977-79; assoc. prof. U. Pa., Phila., 1974-76; sr. fellow Brookings Instn., Washington, 1979-94; prof. govt. and fgn. affairs U. Va., Charlottesville, 1994—. Sr. assoc., Cambridge Energy Research Assocs., Mass., 1983-90. Author: Revolution and Political Leadership: Algeria, 1954-68, The Politics of Palestinian Nationalism, 1973, Decade of Decisions, 1977, Saudi Arabia in the 1980's, 1981, Camp David: Peacemaking and Politics, 1986, The United States and Egypt, 1990, Peace Process, 1993, revised edit., 2001, Between Ballots and Bullets, 1998. Social Scis. Research Council fellow, 1966; Council Fgn. Relations fellow, 1972; NDEA fellow, 1963 Mem. Council Fgn. Relations, Middle East Inst., Middle East Studies Assn. (pres. 1987-88). Avocations: tennis, travel, photography. edu. Home: 206 Alderman Rd Charlottesville VA 22903-1704 Office: U Va Dept Politics Cabell Hall 255 Charlottesville VA 22901 E-mail: wbq8f@virginia.edu.

QUANN, JOAN LOUISE, French language educator, real estate broker; b. Phila., Oct. 14, 1935; d. John Joseph and Pauline Cecelia (Karpink) Q. Diploma, U. Paris, 1963; BA in French, U. Pa., 1976; grad., Temple U. Real Estate Inst., 1988; MEd, Temple U, 1994. Lic. real estate broker. Exec. sec. to chief fgn. corr. Newsweek, Inc., Paris, 1964-70, internat. editorial asst. N.Y.C., 1971-73; exec. sec., adminstrv. asst. Richard I. Rubin & Co., Inc., Phila., 1977-91; tchr. French and English to speakers of other langs. The Sch. Dist. of Phila., Bd. Edn., 1991—. Judge of elections City of Phila., 1977-81. Mem. AAUW (2d v.p. membership 1985-87, bd. dirs., corr. sec. 1987-91, fin. com. 1993), Alliance Francaise, La Societe Francophone Arts et Loisirs (bd. dirs. 1988—), Am. Coun. on Tchg. of Fgn. Langs., Pa. Acad. Fine Arts, MLA of Phila. and Vicinity, Phila. Mus. Art (Asian adv. group 2000). Republican. Roman Catholic. Avocations: art history, reading, swimming, travel. Office: Sch Dist of Phila Bd Edn 21st St S Of The Pky S Philadelphia PA 19103

QUANSTROM, ROY FRED, non-profit organization executive; b. Gary, Ind., Mar. 4, 1934; s. Roy Fred and Isabella Mary (Ulrich) Q.; m. Shirley Ann Martin, June 11, 1955; children: Mark Roy, Joan Ardath Wood, Stephen Roy, Lynne Renee Dillman. AB, Ea. Nazarene Coll., 1956; MA, Olivet Nazarene U., 1968, DD, 1982. Cert. fundraising exec. Sys. analyst IBM, Cleve., 1961-64; minister First Ch. of the Nazarene, Avon Lake, Ohio, 1961-64; Brookfield, Ill., 1964-70; minister Hillcrest Ch. of the Nazarene, Pontiac, Mich., 1970-73; sr. minister First Ch. of the Nazarene, Port Huron, 1973-76; dir. devel. Olivet Nazarene U., Kankakee, Ill., 1976-82; sr. minister First Ch. of the Nazarene, Seymour, Ind., 1982-93; planned giving dir. The Salvation Army, Peoria, 1993—. Adv. bd. S.W. Ind. Dist., Salvation Army, 1990-93. Contbr. articles to profl. jours. Mem. Nat. Soc. Fund Raising Execs. (Ctrl. Ill. chpt.) Nat. Com. Planned Giving, Rotary, Lions. Avocations: sailing, hunting, fishing, mountain hiking, golf. Home: 4106 W Hollow Trace Dr Peoria IL 61615-2421 Office: The Salvation Army 401 NE Adams St Peoria IL 61603-4224 E-mail: Roy_Quanstrom@USC.salvationarmy.org.

QUANT, HAROLD EDWARD, retired financial services company executive, rancher; b. Aug. 21, 1948; s. Harold Atwell and Dorothy Ann Quant; m. Michelle Bumpers, June 27, 1982; children: Andrew, Angela, Emily. BSBA, San Jose State U., 1976. Account exec. Dun & Bradstreet, San Jose, Calif., 1970-81; pres. Telecredit Collection Svcs., Inc., L.A., 1981-85; v.p. FCA, Arlington, Tex., 1986-90; pres., CEO Creditwatch, Inc., 1990-2000, chmn. bd. dirs.; ret., 2000. Sgt. USMC, 1965-70, Vietnam. Decorated Bronze Star, Purple Heart. Mem. City Club. Republican. Mem. United Ch. of God. Avocation: horses.

QUANTRELL-MULLINS, BIANCA RODERT, interior architect; b. Koln, W. Ger., Aug. 4, 1937; came to U.S., 1959, naturalized, 1960; d. Josef Karl and Elsa (Corsi) Rodert; m. Carlisle A. Quantrell, Jr., 1959 (div. 1973); 1 child, Gilonne Corsi Quantrell; m. Henry Foster Mullins, Jr., June 22, 1974. Student World Congress Inst., Atlanta, 1984, London Sch. Econs., 1984. Interior archtl. designer Jova/Daniels/Busby, Atlanta, 1971-72, interior archtl. design project mgr., 1972-74; pres., chief exec. officer, chief operating officer Quantrell Mullins & Assocs., Inc., Atlanta, 1974— ; mem. bd. govs. World Trade Club, Atlanta, 1983— . Interior architect Lloyds Bank Internat. Ltd., 1981, Life Ins. Co. Ga., 1985; Dean Witter Reynolds, 1985, Nat. Westminster Bank, 1985, MCI Telecommunications, Ogilvy & Mather, 1985, IBM, 1985. Mem. Central Atlanta Progress, 1985. Named an Interior Design Giant, Interior Design Mag., 1984, 85. Mem. Soc. Internat. Bus. Fellows, AIA (profl. affiliate), Midtown Bus. Assn., German-Am. C. of C. (bd. dirs. 1983), Atlanta C. of C. (mem. internat. task force 1984—), British-Am. Bus. Group (bd. dirs. 1985), Belgian-Am. C. of C. Roman Catholic. Avocations: travel, the arts.

QUARLES, CARROLL ADAIR, JR. physicist, educator; b. Abilene, Tex., Nov. 24, 1938; s. Carroll Adair and Marguerite Marie (Vollmers) Q.; m. Sonja Gale Bandy, May 14, 1971; children: Jennifer Anne, John Patrick. BA, Tex. Christian U., 1960; PhD, Princeton U., 1964. Rsch. physicist Brookhaven Nat. Lab., Upton, N.Y., 1964-67; mem. faculty Tex. Christian U., Ft.Worth, 1967—, assoc. prof. physics Ft. Worth, 1970-76, prof. Ft.Worth, 1976—, W.A. Moncrief Jr. prof. physics, 1986—, chmn. dept. physics, 1978-84, 96-99, assoc. dean Coll. Arts and Scis. Ft.Worth, 1974-78. Mem. exec. com. Forum on Physics and Soc., 1999—2002. Contbr. articles to profl. jours. Mem. AAAS, Am. Phys. Soc. (sec.-treas. Tex. sect. 1993-99, vice chair 2002), Am. Assn. Physics Tchrs. (pres. Tex. sect. 1984), Sigma Xi, Phi Beta Kappa (pres. Delta of Tex. chpt. 1982-84). Roman Catholic. Office: Tex Christian U Dept Physics Fort Worth TX 76129-0001 E-mail: c.quarles@tcu.edu.

QUARLES, GREYSON, data processing executive; BA, Hampden-Sydney Coll.; MBA, Rutgers U. Mgr. Ernst & Young; pvt. practice tax cons. & fin. reporting; from v.p. fin. to exec. v.p. SAS Inst. Inc., Cary NC, 1982, exec. v.p. Office: SAS Institute Inc 100 SAS Campus Dr Cary NC 27513-2414*

QUARLES, JAMES LINWOOD, III, lawyer; b. Huntington, W.Va., Oct. 12, 1946; s. James Linwood Jr. and Beatrice (Hardwick) Q.; m. Sharon Taft, Dec. 20, 1969; children: Jessica, Matthew. BS cum laude, Denison U., 1968; JD cum laude, Harvard U., 1972. Bar: Mass. 1974, U.S. Dist. Ct. Mass. 1975, U.S. Ct. Appeals (D.C. cir.) 1975, U.S. Ct. Appeals (6th cir.) 1979, U.S. Supreme Ct. 1980, D.C. 1981, U.S. Ct. Appeals (2d cir.) 1981, U.S. Ct. Appeals (1st and 4th cirs.) 1983, Md. 1985, Va. 2000. Law clk. to presiding justice U.S. Dist. Ct. Md., Balt., 1972-73; with Watergate Spl. Pros. Force, Washington, 1973-75; from assoc. to sr. ptnr. Hale and Dorr, Boston and Washington, 1975—. Mem. Am. Law Inst. Democrat. Office: Hale & Dorr Ste 1000 1455 Pennsylvania Ave NW Washington DC 20004-1085 E-mail: james.quarles@haledorr.com.

QUARLES, MARY VIRGINIA, education union consultant; b. Nashville, Nov. 12, 1940; d. Chester Lew and Virginia Estelle (Cooper) Q. BA, Miss. Coll., 1962; MA, Fla. State U., 1970. Tchr. recruiter Brevard County Schs., Titusville, Fla., 1962-76; dir. Fontana/Chaffey UniServ, Calif., 1976-78, Cen. Wis. UniServ Council-West, Wausau, Wis., 1978—. Older children dir. Park Ave. Bapt. Ch., Titusville, Fla., 1970-73; Sunday Sch. dir. Calvary Bapt. Ch., Schofield, Wis., 1985-86, 1st Bapt. Ch., Wausau, 1986—. Experienced Tchr. fellow Fla. State U., 1970. Mem. Indsl. Rels. Rsch. Assn., AAUW, LWV, Fla. Teaching Profession div. NEA (bd. dirs. 1974-76), Sigma Tau Delta. Democrat. Avocations: reading, travel, sewing. Home: 726 N 1st Ave Wausau WI 54401-2960 Office: Cen Wis UniServ Council-West PO Box 158 Mosinee WI 54455-0158

QUARLES, PEGGY DELORES, secondary school educator; b. Dalton, Ga., July 14, 1947; d. Henry Lemuel and Mae Bradford (Hester) Q. BA, Trevecca Nazarene Coll., 1969; MEd, U. Ga., 1981; EdS, West Ga. Coll., 1987; EdD, Univ. Sarasota, 2001. English tchr. Darlington County Schs., Lamar, S.C., 1969-78, Murray County Schs., Chatsworth, Ga., 1978—. Mem. Shakespeare Inst., NEH, Washington, 1985, Writing Inst., Boulder, Colo., 1988, Italian Renaissance Inst., Del., Ohio and Florence, Italy, 1990, Women in Renaissance Inst., Richmond, Va., 1992; participant Armonk Inst. to Germany, 1998.

ARC, 1987—; mem. Dalton Little Theater, 1980—; bd. dirs. Friends of Libr., 1989—92; mem. NW Ga. Humane Soc. Named Teacher of Yr., Murray County Bd. of Edn., 1989, Murray County Schs., 2001—02. Mem. NEA, Nat. Coun. Tchrs. English, Ga. Coun. Tchrs. English (H.S. English Tchr. of Yr. 1994-95), Carpet Capital Running Club (pres. 1980-82, v.p. 1993-94), Lesche Lit. Club (v.p. 2001—). Avocations: running, travel, cooking, reading, attending plays.

QUARLES, RANDAL KEITH, lawyer, federal agency administrator; b. San Francisco, Sept. 5, 1957; s. Ralph Ray and Beverly Kay (Hulse) Q.; m. C. Hope Eccles, Sept. 13, 1997; children: Randal, Spencer. AB, Columbia U., 1981; JD, Yale U., 1984. Assoc. Davis Polk & Wardwell, N.Y.C., 1984-91; spl. asst. to sec. Dept. of Treasury, Washington, 1991-92, deputy asst. sec., fin. insts. policy, 1992-93; ptnr. Davis Polk & Wardwell, 1993—; Dep Under Secy Int Nat Affairs Dept Treasury, Washington, 2002—. Mem. fin. adv. com. Dole Presdl. Campaign, Washington, 1996. Mem. Yale Club, Salt Lake Country Club. Mem. Lds Ch. Avocations: aviation, skiing. Home: 116 E 63d St Apt 2C New York NY 10021 Office: Dept Treasury Under Secy for Int Affairs 1500 Pennsylvania Ave NW Washington DC 20220 E-mail: quarles@dpw.com.*

QUARLES, WILLIAM DANIEL, judge; b. Balt., Jan. 16, 1948; s. William Daniel and Mabel (West) Q.; m. Deborah Ann Grant, Oct. 7, 1969 (div. Aug. 1976); 1 child, Eloise; m. Mary Ann Pirog, Nov. 18, 2000. BS, U. Md., 1976; JD, Cath. U., 1979. Bar: D.C. 1979, Md. 1991. Law clk. to presiding judge U.S. Dist. Ct. Md., Balt., 1979-81; assoc. Finley Kumble, Washington, 1981-82; asst. U.S. atty. U.S. Dept. Justice, Balt., 1982-86; assoc., then ptnr. Venable, Baetjer, Howard & Civiletti, Washington, 1986-96, head litigation group, 1993-94; apptd. assoc. judge Cir. Ct. for Balt. City, 1996. Permanent mem. U.S. 4th Cir. Jud. Conf., Richmond, Va., 1986—; mem. D.C. Law Revision Commn., 1989-91; nominated to U.S. Dist. Ct., Dist. Md., 1992; mem. Md. Gov.'s Commn. on Volunteerism Svc., 1994-95, 96—. Author: Summary Adjudication: Dispositive Motions and Summary Trials, 1991. Coord. Presdl. Regional Task Force on Organized Crime and Drug Law Enforcement, 1984-85; lector St. Michael Roman Cath. Ch. Office: Circuit Court Bar for Baltimore City 111 N Calvert St Ste 324 Baltimore MD 21202-1910

QUARTERMAN, CYNTHIA LOUISE, lawyer; b. Savannah, Ga., Apr. 6, 1961; d. Rudolph V. and Bernice Q.; m. Pantelis Michalopoulos, Nov. 2, 1993. BS, Northwestern U., 1983; JD, Columbia U., 1987. Atty. Benson & McKay, Kansas City, 1987-88, Steptoe & Johnson, Washington, 1989-93; dep. dir. Minerals Mgmt. Svc., Dept. Interior, 1993-95, dir., 1995-99; ptnr. Steptoe & Johnson, 1999—. Mem. adv. bd. Inst. for Energy Law, co-chair ann. inst. Mem. ABA (vice chair sect. on environment, energy, resources, oil and natural gas exploration and prodn. com. 2002—), Energy Bar Assn. (chair environment and pub. lands com. 2002—), Women's Coun. Energy & Environment. Home: 1337 21st St NW Washington DC 20036-1503 E-mail: cquarter@steptoe.com.

QUARTON, WILLIAM BARLOW, broadcasting company executive; b. Algona, Iowa, Mar. 27, 1903; s. William B. and Ella B. (Reaser) Q.; m. Elnora Bierkamp, Aug. 24, 1935; 1 dau., Diane (Mrs. Waldo F. Geiger). Student, U. Iowa, 1921-22, George Washington U., 1923-25. Joined radio sta. KWCR, Cedar Rapids, Iowa, 1931; comml. mgr. radio sta. WMT, 1936, gen. mgr., 1943; exec. v.p. Am. Broadcasting Stas., Inc., 1959-68, chmn., 1968-70; chmn. bd. KWMT Inc., Ft. Dodge, Iowa, 1968-88, Cable Communications Iowa, Inc., 1971-83; pres. WMT-TV, Inc., 1959-68; chmn. adv. bd. CBS-TV Affiliates, 1960; Mem. bd. Iowa Ednl. Broadcasting Network, 1967-77; bd. govs. Pub. Broadcasting Service, 1973-78. Trustee Coe Coll., 1946-78; trustee, mem. exec. com. Herbert Hoover Presdl. Library; bd. regents State Iowa, 1965-71. Mem. Cedar Rapids C. of C. (pres. 1944), Nat. Assn. Broadcasters (chmn. TV bd. 1962-63, chmn. joint bd. 1963-64. Clubs: Ft. Lauderdale Country (Fla.), Coral Ridge Yacht (Ft. Lauderdale); Cedar Rapids Country. Lodges: Rotary. Home: 134 Kyrie SE Cedar Rapids IA 52403-1712 also: Plaza East 4300 N Ocean Blvd Fort Lauderdale FL 33308

QUARTUCCIO, MARYANN, insurance agent, home economist; b. San Jose, Calif., Aug. 26, 1957; d. Anthony Angelo and Catherine Elizabeth (Sunseri) Q. AA, San Jose City Coll., 1979; BS in Home Econs., Calif. Poly. State U., San Luis Obispo, 1984. Lic. ins. agt., Calif. Dept. head Marshall's Dept. Store, San Jose, Calif., 1977-80; food server Servomation Corp., Santa Clara, 1980-85; sr. customer svc. coord. Prudential Ins., Los Altos, 1985-90; personal lines account mgr. Alburger Basso Degrosz Ins. Svcs., Belmont, 1990-95; personal lines mgr. Bandar Covall Ins., San Mateo, 1995-96, Micheletti & Assocs., San Jose, 1997-99; personal lines mgr., claims mgr. Dorsey Hazeltine Wynne Ins., Palo Alto, 1999—2001; ins. agt. Allwest Ins. Brokers, Campbell, 2001—. Tchg. asst. for the disabled San Jose City Coll., 1978-79. Vol., Second Harvest Food Bank, San Jose, 1999. Mem. Peninsula Ins. Women's Assn. (2d v.p. 1996-97, various coms., Ins. Woman of Yr. 1995), Nat. Assn. Ins. Women, Italian Am. Heritage Found. Republican. Roman Catholic. Avocations: cooking/baking, culinary arts, catering, sports, interior decorating. Office: Allwest Ins Brokers 1700 S Winchester Blvd Ste 204 Campbell CA 95008 Home: Apt 71 4951 Cherry Ave San Jose CA 95118-2737

QUATRANO, ANNE, chef, restaurant owner; Grad., Calif. Culinary Acad., San Francisco. Chef, co-owner Bacchanalia, Atlanta, Floataway Cafe, Atlanta, Star Provisions, Atlanta; chef Grolier Club, NY, Bimini Twist, La Petit Ferme. Elected mem. James Beard Found. Office: 1198 Howell Mill Rd Atlanta GA 30301*

QUATTLEBAUM, WILLIAM FRANKLIN, lawyer; b. Bradenton, Fla., Apr. 10, 1953; s. Marion C. and Elizabeth Marie (Stephenson) Q. BS in Advt. and Comm. summa cum laude, U. Fla., 1975, JD, 1978. Bar: Fla., 1979. Atty. Fla. Dept. of Ins., Tallahassee, 1979-80; press sec. Richard Stone U.S. Senate Campaign, 1980; atty. Fla. Ho. of Reps., 1980-84; press sec., exec. asst. Fla. Dept. Banking and Fin., 1984-86; dep. mgr. Bob Graham U.S. Senate Campaign, 1986; asst. dir. Fla. Health Care for the Uninsured, 1987; adminstrv. law judge Fla. Div. Adminstrv. Hearings, 1987—. Mem. Fla. Blue Key Club (pres.), Omicron Delta Kappa, Kappa Tau Alpha. Avocations: writing, reading, music, computers. Office: Divsn Adminstrv Hearings 1230 Apalachee Pkwy Tallahassee FL 32301-3060

QUATTRONE-CARROLL, DIANE ROSE, clinical social worker; b. N.Y.C., July 18, 1949; d. Mario Anthony and Filomena (Serpico) Quattrone; m. Rene Eugene Carroll Jr., June 7, 1980; children: Jenna Cristine, Jonathan Rene. BA cum laude, Bklyn. Coll., 1971; MSW, Rutgers U., 1974. Lic. marriage and family counselor, lic. clin. social worker, N.J.; bd. cert. diplomate in clin. social work. Clin. social worker, field instr. Essex County Guidance Ctr., East Orange, N.J., 1974-82; exec. dir. Psychotherapy Info. and Referral Svc., Madison, 1982-87; pvt. practice Sparta, 1982—. Nat. Assn. Social Workers. Avocation: travel.

QUAY, GREGORY HARRISON, retired secondary school educator; b. Detroit, Dec. 4, 1937; s. Edward H. and Frances J. (Keena) Q. BS in Edn., Wayne State U., 1960, MEd, 1963, MA in Teaching Math., 1966. Certt. math., history and English tchr., Mich. Tchr. Detroit Pub. Schs., 1960-69; cons. Macomb County Intermediate Sch. Dist., Mt. Clemens, Mich., 1969-70; tchr. math. Warren (Mich.) Consol. Schs., 1970-99; ret., 1999—. Activities writer SRA Pub. Co., Chgo., 1970-71, summer assoc. U.S. Army Tank Automotive Command, Warren, 1986-91, 93-94, 96-97. Author: (manual) Photacoustics and Photoacoustic Spectroscopy, 1986, Thermal Wave Interferometry Applied to Thermally Thick Samples, 1988, A Theoretical Model for Thermal Wave Interferometry Applied to a Two-Layer Coating, 1989, One Dimensional Single Layer Photacoustic Theory, 1991, An Introduction to One Dimensional Dual Layer Thermal Wave/Photoacoustic Theory, 1996; co-author: An Introduction to One Dimensional Single Layer Thermal Wave/Photoacoustic Theory, 1994, Use of Advanced Ceramics for Bearings and Engine Wear Applications (An Advanced Technology Assessment Report), 1996, Ceramic and Metal Coatings for Improved Engine Performance (An Advanced Technology Assessment Report), 1997; contbr. articles to profl. jours. Usher Redeemer Bapt. Ch., Warren, 1969-95, asst. treas., fin. sec., 1972-82; usher Bethany Bapt. Ch., Clinton Twp., 1996—; mem. bd. edn. Macomb Christian Schs., 1983-85. Named Tchr. of Yr., Warren Consol. Schs., 1984. Mem. Nat. Coun. Tchrs. Math. (life, editl. referee 1978—), Mich. Coun. Tchrs. Math., Detroit Area Coun. Math. Tchrs. (v.p. 1969-70, treas. 1970-71, pres. 1971-72, co-founder Math. Field Day 1969, co-founder Myriad of Math. Merriment 1972). Avocations: reading, gardening, antique automobiles. Home: 14640 Talbot Dr Warren MI 48088-3825

QUAY, JOYCE CROSBY, writer; b. Dayton, Ohio, Aug. 8, 1928; d. Wilson Hill and Marianne (Mitchell) Crosby; m. John Grier Quay, Nov. 12, 1952; children: Peter Crosby, John Paul, Leslie Quay McMillan. Student, Simmons Coll., 1951, NYU, 1959-60. Ptnr. Quay Assocs., 1961-84. Author: Sam Walton, Founder of Wal-Mart (People to Know), 1994, Early Promise, Late Reward, 1995, (play) Double Destinies, 2000; contbr. articles to popular publs. Mem. Rep. Nat. Com., 1990, 94-95. Presbyterian. E-mail: jaconfer@aol.com.

QUAY, THOMAS EMERY, lawyer; b. Cleve., Apr. 3, 1934; s. Harold Emery and Esther Ann (Thomas) Q.; divorced; children: Martha Wyndham, Glynis Cobb, Eliza Emery; m. Winnifred B. Cutler, May 13, 1989. AB in Humanities magna cum laude (Univ. scholar), Princeton U., 1956; LLB (Univ. scholar), U. Pa., 1963. Bar: Pa. 1964. Assoc. Pepper, Hamilton & Scheetz, Phila., 1963-65; with William H. Rorer, Inc., Ft. Washington, Pa., 1965—, sec., counsel, 1974-79, v.p., gen. counsel, sec., 1979-88; v.p. legal planning and adminstrn. Rorer Group, 1988-90; counsel Reed Smith Shaw and McClay, Phila., 1991-93; v.p., gen. counsel Athena Inst., Chester Springs, Pa., 1993—. Bd. dirs. Main Line YMCA, Ardmore, Pa., 1971-73, chmn. bd., 1972-73; editor 10th Reunion Book Princeton Class of 1956, 1966, 25th Reunion Book, 1981—, class sec., 1966-71, class v.p., 1971-81, pres., 1981-86. Lt. (j.g.) USNR, 1957-60. Recipient Commendation award, Main Line YMCA, 1984. Mem. ABA, Pa. Bar Assn., Phila. Bar Assn., Pharm. Mfrs. Assn. (chmn. law sect. 1983), Pa. Biotech. Assn. (chmn. legis. com., mem. exec. com. 1991-93), Phila. Drug Exch. (chmn. legis. com. 1975-78), Cannon Club of Princeton U., Sharswood Law Club of U. Pa., Princeton Club of Phila. Democrat. Presbyterian. Office: 601 Swedesford Rd Ste 201 Malvern PA 19355-1573

QUDDUS, MOHAMMED TANVIR, electrical engineer, researcher; b. Comilla, Bangladesh, July 1, 1966; , U.S., 1995; s. Mohammed Abdul Quddus and Khodeja Begum; m. Farhana Hussain. BS, Bangladesh U. Engring. and Tech., Dhaka, 1991, MS, 1993; PhD, Ariz. State U., 1999. Lectr. Bangladesh U. Engring. and Tech., Dhaka, Bangladesh, 1991—93, asst. prof. Bangladesh, 1993—95; sr. staff engr. ON Semiconductor, Phoenix, 2000—. Contbr. articles to profl. jours. Pres. Bangladesh Student Assn., Ariz. State U., Tempe, Ariz., 1998—99. Recipient Pres. award, Govt. Bangladesh, 1984; scholar, Ariz. State U., 1997—98, 1999—2000. Mem.: IEEE, Phi Kappa Phi. Home: 1255 E University Dr #J275 Tempe AZ 85281 Office: ON Semiconductor 5005 E Mcdowell Rd Phoenix AZ 85008 Office Fax: 602-244-6008. Personal E-mail: tanvir@fastq.com. Business E-Mail: tanvir.quddus@onsemi.com.

QUEBBEMAN, ROBERT C. conductor, educator; b. Hinsdale, Ill., Oct. 9, 1948; s. Edward C.G. and Elizabeth M. Quebbeman; m. Sandra J. Quebbeman, June 26, 1971; children: Amanda, John. PhD Musical Arts, U. of Mich., Ann Arbor, Michigan, 1976; MA Music, No. Ill. U., DeKalb, Illinois, 1971, BS Edn., 1970. Educator SW Mo. State U., Springfield, Mo., 1986—, Minot State U., Minot, ND, 1976—86, Olivet Coll., Olivet, Mich., 1975—76, Sycamore H.S., Sycamore, Fla., 1971—74. Music dir. Springfield Regional Opera, Springfield, Mo., 1989—, Minot Cmty. Opera, Minot, Mo., 1976—86. Contbr. articles in professional journals. Elder educator Redeemer Luth. Ch., Springfield, Mo., 1983—86. Mem.: Am. String Teacher's Assn., Music Educator's Nat. Conf., Conductor's Guild. Avocations: reading, raquetball, raquetball. Office: Southwest Missouri State University 901 South National Springfield MO 65804 E-mail: robert.quebbeman@smsu.edu.

QUEBE, JERRY LEE, retired architect; b. Indpls., Nov. 7, 1942; s. Charlie Christopher and Katheryn Rosella (Hankins) Q.; m. Mary Lee Darby (div.); children: Chad, Tara; m. Julie Ann Gordon (div.); 1 child, Dana Ann; m. Lisbeth Jane Gray, Mar. 16, 1986. BArch, Iowa State U., 1965. Registered Ill., Calif., Wis. Mem. staff Hansen Lind Meyer, Iowa City, 1965-70, assoc., 1970-74, prin., 1975-77, prin., v.p. Chgo., 1977-86; exec. v.p. VVKR, Inc., Alexandria, Va., 1986-93; prin., sr. v.p. Perkins & Will, Chgo., 1994-96, also bd. dirs.; sr. v.p. RTKL Assocs. Inc., 1996—2002, ret., 2002. Chmn. Cedar Rapids/Iowa City Architects Council, 1974. Author: Drafting Practices Manual, 1978; contbr. articles to profl. jours. Pres. bd. dirs. Mental Health Assn. of Greater Chgo., 1990-95. Fellow AIA, Am. Coll. Healthcare Archs. (founder); mem. Am. Hosp. Assn., Chgo. Health Exec. Forum, Forum for Health Care Planning (bd. dirs. 1992-99). Avocations: photography, sports car racing, woodworking. Home: 43495 Trout Creek Road Soldiers Grove WI 54655-7090 E-mail: jquebe@rtkl.com.

QUEEN, DANIEL, acoustical engineer, consultant; b. Boston, Feb. 15, 1934; s. Simon and Ida (Droker) Q.; 1 child, Aaron Jacob. Student, U. Chgo., 1951-54. Quality control mgr. Magnacord, Inc., Chgo., 1955-57; project engr. Revere Camera Co., 1957-62; dir. engring. for Amplivox products Perma Power Co., 1962-70; prin. engr. Daniel Queen Assocs., 1970—; pres. Daniel Queen Labs., Inc., 1980—. Chmn. Am. Nat. Standards Subcom. PH7-6, 1969-84, mem. com. PH-7; mem. standards com. P8-5 Electronic Industries Assn., 1967-82. Contbr. editor Sound and Communications, 1973—; patentee in field; contbr. papers to profl. jours., also articles to trade and popular jours.; editorial bd. Jour. Audio Engring. Soc., 1978—. Bd. dirs. The Working Theatre. Recipient Technical Emmy award TV Acad. Arts and Scis., 1995. Fellow Audio Engring. Soc. (stds. mgr. 1980-2001, chmn. tech. coun. 1985-96, Citation 1998, Disting. Svc. award 2002); mem. IEEE (sr.), ASTM, AAAS, Am. Nat. Stds. Inst. (sec. com. S4 on audio engring.), Acoustical Soc. Am. (chmn. Chgo. regional chpt. 1976-78, mem. engring. acoustics com. 1974-97), Midwest Acoustics Conf. (pres. 1971-72), Chgo. Acoustical/Audio Group (pres. 1969-70), Assn. Ednl. Comms. and Tech., Soc. Motion Picture and TV Engrs. (audio rec./reprodn. com.), Am. Pub. Health Assn., Nat. Coun. Acoustical Cons., Inst. Noise Control Engring. Office: 143 University Ave Providence RI 02906 E-mail: master@dqueen.com.

QUEEN, JOYCE ELLEN, elementary school educator; b. Cleve., Mar. 17, 1945; d. Wilbur Raynor and Mae (Reid) Closterhouse; m. Robert Graham Queen, Mar. 17, 1973. BA in Biology, Macalester Coll., 1966; MS in Conservation and Natural Resource Mgmt., U. Mich., 1968. Cert. tchr. biol. and earth scis., Ohio. Exhibitor, docent, coord. Grand Rapids (Mich.) Pub. Mus., 1967-68; tchr., naturalist Rose Tree-Media (Pa.) Outdoor Edn., 1967, Willoughby-Eastlake (Ohio) Schs., 1969-70, Independence (Ohio) Schs., 1970-78; sci. tchr. grades 1-7, coord. sci. field trip Hathaway Brown Sch., Cleve., 1970—, primary sci. educator, 1970—, primary sci. dept. chair, 1999—. Designer Courtland Woods nature trail, 1986, designer sci. greenhouse, 1990-92; designer sci. classroom Van Dyke Architects/Hathaway Brown Sch., 1990-92; designer, coord. Dampeer Primary sci. courtyard, 1993, Oliva Herb Garden, 1998, Colini Landscape Design/Hathaway Brown Sch., Shaker Hts., Ohio; mem. ednl. adv. com. William G. Mather Vessel Mus., Cleve., 1992, Holden Arboretum, Kirtland, Ohio, 1992-97; workshop leader Lake Erie Islands Hist. Mus., South Bass Island, Ohio, 1992, H.B. Winter Sci. Symposium Workshop, 1994—; presenter Nat. Assn. Ind. Schs., Columbus, Ohio, 1993; workshop leader for schs. on garden design, sci. labs., and sci. discovery programs; youth divsn. judge Cleve. Botanic Garden Show, 1999, 2000, 2002. Contbr. articles to profl. jours. Design cons. Cleve. Bot. Garden and Floral Scape, 1998; active Belize (Ctrl. Am.) Tchrs. Workshop, 1994. Catalyst grantee Hathaway Brown Sch. Gt. Lks. Curriculum, 1991; recipient Environ. Edn. award Ohio Alliance for Environment, 1986, Presdl. Excellence in Elem. Sci. Tchg. award NSF, 1992, Sheldon Exemplary Equipment and Facilities award, 1992; Great Lakes Lighthouse Keepers Assn. scholar; Marine Ecology scholar Marine Resources, Inc., 1989; Internat. Space Sta. Conf. scholar, 2000; Maine Salt Marsh Ecology Curriculum scholar, 2001; Calif. Coastal Wetlands and Desert Study scholar, 2002. Mem. NSTA (recipient Exemplary Environ. and Facilities award with Sheldon Mfg. Co. 1992), Cleve. Regional Coun. Sci. Tchrs., Cleve. Coun. Ind. Schs., Cleve. Natural Hist. Mus., Cleve. Zool. Park, Ind. Sch. Assn. Ctrl. Sts., Internat. Pen Pal Exchange Progam. Presbyterian. Avocations: orchardist, naturalist, horticulturist. Office: Hathaway Brown Sch 19600 N Park Blvd Cleveland OH 44122-1899 E-mail: jqueen@hb.edu.

QUEEN, SALLY ANN CRANNELL, entrepreneur; b. Dallas, Feb. 25, 1949; d. Kenlen Bates Jr. and Eleanor Crannell; m. Bruce Fielding Queen, Apr. 20, 1968; children: Heather Leigh Queen Dennis, Christopher Dyer Queen. BS in Home Econs., U Ariz., 1983. Mgr. Wicker Rocker, Panama City, Fla., 1973-75, House of Fabrics, Alamogordo, N.Mex., 1984-86, Colonial Williamsburg (Va.) Found., 1987-95; owner Calico Queen, Fla., Ariz., Germany, 1975-83, Sally Queen & Assocs., Arlington, Va., 1995—. Creator: (video) Costuming at Colonial Williamsburg, 1995, (costume calendar) Reflections in Time, 1998. Fund raiser various wive's clubs, 1972—; dist. commr. Girl Scouts U.S., Germany, 1978-80. Named Outstanding new member Panama City C. of C., 1975. Mem. Peninsula Women's Network, Costume Soc. Am. (regional bd. dirs. 1992-96, nat. bd. dirs. 1993—, long range planning coord. 1994-96, regional v.p. 1996—), Kappa Omicron Nu, Phi Upsilon Omicron, Omicron Nu. Republican. Mem. Christian Ch. (Disciples Of Christ). Avocation: clothing and textile industry. Office: 2801 S Joyce St Arlington VA 22202-2248

QUEFFÉLEC, ANNE, pianist; b. Paris, Jan. 17, 1948; d. Henri and Yvonne Q.; m. Luc Dehaene, Oct. 5, 1983; children: Gaspard, Arthur. Baccalaureat of Philosophy, Paris, 1965; postgrad., Paris Conservatorie. Prin. works include 31 recordings, 1970—; performed in numerous concert tours worldwide. Decorated chevalier Legion of Honor; recipient 1st piano prize Paris Conservatory, 1965, 1st chamber music prize Paris Conservatory, 1966, 1st prize award Munich Internat. Piano Competition, 1968, finalist and prize winner Internat. Piano Competition, Leeds, Eng., 1969, Victoire de la Musique award, France, 1990; named Officer de l'ordre du Merite, 2002. Roman Catholic. Address: 15 ave Corneille 78600 Maisons-Laffitte France E-mail: annequeff@caramail.com.

QUE HEE, SHANE STEPHEN, environmental health educator; b. Sydney, Oct. 11, 1946; came to U.S., 1978; s. Robert and Beris (Byers) Que Hee. BS, U. Queensland, Brisbane, Australia, 1968, MS, 1971; PhD, U. Saskatchewan, Can., 1976. Registered profl. indsl. hygienist. Asst. prof. U. Cin., 1978-84, assoc. prof., 1984-89, U. Calif., L.A., 1989-94, prof., 1994—. Author: The Phenoxyalkanoic Acids: Chemistry, Analysis and Environmental Pollution, 1981, Biological Monitoring: An Introduction, 1993, Hazardous Waste Analysis, 1999; contbr. more than 140 articles to profl. jours. and book chpts. Sec. Lesbian Gay Acad. U., Cin., 1978-87, pres. 1988-89, facilitator Gay/Lesbian March Activists, Cin., 1987-89; pres. Lesbian Gay Health and Health Policy Found., L.A., 1994—. Postdoctoral fellow McMaster U., Hamilton, Ont., Can., 1976-78. Fellow Am. Inst. Chemists, Am. Indsl. Hygiene Assn.; mem. AAAS, Am. Coll. Toxicology, Am. Indsl. Hygiene Assn., Am. Chem. Soc., Am. Conf. Indsl. Govt. Hygienists, Am. Pub. Health Assn., N.Y. Acad. Scis. Avocations: civil rights, piano, writing, tennis, bridge, chess. Home: 923 Levering Ave Unit 102 Los Angeles CA 90024-6612 Office: UCLA Sch Pub Health Dept Environ Health Sci 650 Charles Young Dr S Los Angeles CA 90095-1772 E-mail: squehee@ucla.edu.

QUEHL, GARY HOWARD, consultant, association executive; b. Green Bay, Wis., Mar. 25, 1938; s. Howard and Virginia Babcock (Dunning) Q.; children: Scott Boyer, Catherine Mary. BA, Carroll Coll., 1960; MS, Ind. U., 1962, EdD, 1965; LHD, Buena Vista Coll., 1977, Davis and Elkins Coll., 1979; EdD (hon.), Columbia Coll., S.C., 1987. Asst. dean students Wis. State U., 1962; asst. dean coll. Wittenberg U., 1965-67; v.p., dean coll. Lindenwood Colls., St. Charles, Mo., 1967-70; exec. dir. Coll. Ctr. of the Finger Lakes, Corning, N.Y., 1970-74; pres. Coun. of Ind. Colls., Washington, 1974-86, Coun. for Advancement and Support of Edn., Washington, 1986-90, Quehl Assocs., 1990—. Cons. in field, 1990—. Editor, author books in field. Mem. secretariat Nat. Ctr. for Higher Edn.; bd. dirs. St. Norbert Coll., Carroll Coll., Muskingum Coll., Elmira Coll., Nat. Assn. Ind. Colls. and Univs., ind. sector, Cornell Coll. Mem. Am. Coun. Edn., Am. Conf. Acad. Deans, Nat. Panel for Women in Higher Edn., North Ctrl. Assn. Acad. Deans (past pres.) Mem. United Ch. Christ. E-mail. E-mail: quehl@queasso.com.

QUELER, EVE, conductor; b. N.Y.C. Student, Mannes Coll. Music, CCNY. Music dir. Opera Orchestra of N.Y., N.Y.C., 1969—. Music staff N.Y.C. Opera, 1958-70; assoc. condr. Ft. Wayne (Ind.) Philharm., 1970-71; founder, music dir. Opera Orch., N.Y., 1968; condr. Lake George Opera Festival, Glen Falls, N.Y., 1971-72, Oberlin (Ohio) Music Festival, 1972, Romantic Festival, Indpls., 1972, Mostly Mozart Festival, Lincoln Center, 1972, New Philharmonia, London, 1974, Teatro Liceu, Barcelona, 1974, 77, San Antonio Symphony, 1975; guest condr. Paris Radio Orch., 1972, P.R. Symphony Orch., 1975, 77, Mich. Chamber Orch., 1975, Phila. Orch., 1976, Montreal Symphony, 1977, Cleve. Orch., 1977 (Recipient Martha Baird Rockefeller Fund for Music award 1968, named Musician of Month Mus. Am. Mag. 1972), N.Y.C. Opera, 1978, Opera Las Palmas, 1978, Opera de Nice, 1979, Nat. Theatre of Prague, 1980, Opera Caracas, Venezuela, 1981, San Diego Opera, 1984, Australian Opera, Sydney, 1985, Kirov Opera, St. Petersburg, Russia, 1993, Hamburg Opera, Germany, 1994, Pretoria, South Africa, 1995, Hamilton, Ont., 1995, Hawaii Philharmonic, 1997, Hong Kong Sinfonietta, 1998, Hong Kong Philharmonic, 1999, Orch. dello Stato de Mexico, 1999-2002, Macau Festival, 2000, Festival Euro Mediteranneo, Italy, 2002; Opei Bonn, 1994-96; recording CBS Masterworks, 1974, 76, Hungaroton Records, 1982-85. Decorated Chevalier de l'ordre des Arts et des Lettres; named Woman in Music, N.Y.C., 2002. Office: Opera Orch 239 W 72nd St Ste 2R New York NY 10023-2734

QUELLA, JAMES ANDREW, merchant banker; b. Chgo., Feb. 3, 1950; s. Andrew Sylvester and Mary (Failla) Q.; children: Lindsay V., James S. BA, U. Wis., 1975; MBA, U. Chgo., 1981. Sales dir. Textron, Inc., Dallas, 1975-79; v.p. Strategic Planning Assocs., Washington, 1981-90; vice chmn. Mercer Mgmt. Consulting, N.Y.C., 1990-2000; bd. dirs. Mercer Mgmt. Cons., 1996-2000; mng. dir./sr. op. ptnr. DLJ Mcht. Banking Ptnrs./CSFB Pvt. Equity, 2000—. Bd. dirs. Merrill Corp., Advanstar, Inc., Von Hoffman Corp., Arcade Holdings. Co-author: Profit Patterns, 1999; contbr. articles to profl. jours. Vol./contbr. Hale House, N.Y.C., 1996—. Avocations: golf, skiing, biking, art collection, basketball. Home: 22 W 66th St Apt 12 New York NY 10023-6202 Office: DLJ Mcht Banking Ptnrs/ CSFB Pvt Equity 11 Madison Ave 16th Fl New York NY 10010 E-mail: QuellaJ@aol.com.

QUELLMALZ, FREDERICK, foundation executive, editor; b. N.Y.C., May 24, 1912; s. Frederick and Edith (Grant) Q.; m. Jayne Elizabeth Osten, May 29, 1942; children: Barbara Jayne Coffin, Carol Grant Arran, Patricia Ellen, Sandra Lee Erchinger, Tracy Louise Koziel. AB, Princeton U., 1934; grad., Woodrow Wilson Sch. Pub. & Internat. Affairs, 1934; B of Profl. Arts (hon.), Brooks Inst., 1968. Statis. asst. Pepperell Mfg. Co., 1934-40; dir. photographic activities N.Y. World's Fair, 1940; editor PSA Jour., 1939-52; exec. sec. Photographic Soc. Am., Phila., 1940-42; asst. to chief engr. U.S. Naval Ordinance Plant, York, Pa., 1942-45; exec. v.p. Profl. Photographers Am., Des Plaines, Ill., 1952-74; editor, pub. Profl. Photographer mag., 1953-74; exec. dir. Photog. Art and Sci. Found., Oklahoma City, 1965-94, pres., 1988-96; pres. Internat. Photog. Hall of Fame and Mus., Kirkpatrick Ctr., 1988-96. Trustee Winona Sch. Profl. Photography, 1953-75; amb. Oakton Community Coll.; mem. Oakton Found. Devel. Coun., 1996—; treas. Des Plaines Spl. Events Commn., 1999—. Named to Hon. Order Ky. Cols.; recipient Father Smyth Humanitarian award City of Des Plaines, Ill., 1991. Fellow Royal Soc. Arts (London); mem. Photo Soc. Am. (hon. mem., assoc.), Profl. Photographers Am. (hon. master of photography, photo craftsman), Cert. Assn. Execs., Am. Soc. Assn. Execs. (bd. dirs. 1963-66), Chgo. Soc. Assn. Execs. (life mem.), Internat. Assn. Exposition Mgrs. (life mem., cert. exposition mgr., bd. dirs. 1959-61), Wis. Soc. Assn. Execs. (sec. 1963, pres. 1965), Am. Soc. Photographers (hon. assoc.), Nat. Press Photographers Assn. (life), Royal Photographic Soc., Am. Society Medalists, Am. Assn. Retired Persons (treas. Des Plaines chpt. 1982, 83, 90, pres. 1984-85, tax-aide coord. 1980-97), Sister Cities Internat. (treas. local chpt. 1980-88, 93—, pres. 1989-93, treas. Ill. state chpt. 1986—), Elks, Princeton Club, York Camera Club, Bella Vista Country Club, Kappa Alpha Mu. Home and Office: 111 Stratford Rd Des Plaines IL 60016-2105

QUELLO, JAMES HENRY, government official; b. Laurium, Mich., Apr. 21, 1914; s. Bartholomew and Mary Katherine (Cochis) Q.; m. Mary Elizabeth Butler, Sept. 14, 1937; children: James Michael, Richard Butler. BA, Mich. State U., 1935, D of Humanities (hon.), 1977; D of Pub. Svc. (hon.), No. Mich. U., 1975. V.p., sta. mgr. Goodwill Stas., Inc., Detroit, 1947-72; v.p. Capital Cities Comm. Corp., 1968; commr. FCC, Washington, 1974—98. Comm. cons., Detroit, 1972-74; commr. Detroit Housing and Urban Renewal Commn., 1951-72 Contbr. articles to mags., newspapers. Bd. dirs. Greater Detroit Hosp. Assn.; trustee Mich. Vet. Trust Fund; mem. Gov.'s Spl. Commn.

on Urban Problems, Mich., Gov.'s Spl. Study Com. on Legis. Compensation, Mayor's Com. on Human Relations; bd. dirs. Am. Negro Emancipation Centennial; mem. exec. bd. Boy Scouts Am.; TV-radio chmn. United Found. Lt. col. AUS, 1940-45. Decorated Bronze Star with oak leaf cluster, Croix de Guerre (France); recipient Internat. Pres.'s award Nat. Assn. TV Program Execs., 1985, Silver Satellite award Am. Women in Radio and TV, 1988, 93, Sol Taishoff award Washington Area Broadcasters Assn., 1989, 93, Pub. Svc. award Fed. Comm. Bar Assn., 1993, Disting. Svc. award Media Inst., 1993, Golden Eagle Amb. award Pa. Assn. Broadcasters, 1993, Disting. Alumni award Mich. State U., Club Dir. award Detroit Adcraft Club, 1993, L.I. Coalition for Fair Broadcasting award, 1993, Nat. Disting. Svc. award Nat. Assn. Pub. TV, 1993, Obie award Ohio Ednl. TV Stas., 1993, Gold Eagle Leadership award Wireless Cable Assn. Internat., 1993, Pres. award Alaska Broadcasting Assn., 1994, Chmn. award Nat. Religious Broadcasters, 1994, Ga. Broadcasters award Broadcasters of Am., 1994, 1st Amendment award Radio & TV News Dirs. Found., 1994. Mem. Nat. Assn. Broadcaster (gov. liaison com. 1964-72, Keystone award 1990, Disting. Svc. award 1994, Honor award for protecting the technical integrity of radio and TV 1994, Broadcasting Cable Hall of Fame, 1995, Nat. Radio Hall of Fame 1996), Mich. Assn. Broadcasters (pres. 1958, legis. chmn. 1959-72, dir., Outstanding Mich. Citizen 1989, Pioneer award 1994, Ellis Island honor award 1997), Greater Detroit Bd. Commerce, Sigma Alpha Epsilon. Clubs: Adcraft (Detroit); Detroit Athletic, Army and Navy Country; Nat. Press (Washington). Office: FCC Wiley Rein and Fielding 1776 K St NW Washington DC 20006-2304 E-mail: j.Quello@wrf.com.

QUENBY, JEAN MARIE, clinical care specialist; b. Nov. 2, 1959; MSW, Mich. State U., 1988. Dir. Associated Family Svc., Flint, Mich., 1988-94; dist. mgr. Oakland Family Svcs., Pontiac, 1994-98; coord. Sparrow Hosp., Lansing, 1998—2000; clin. care specialist Foote Hosp., Jackson, 2000—. Office: 205 N East Ave Jackson MI 49202

QUENCER, ROBERT MOORE, neuroradiologist, researcher; b. Jersey City, Nov. 14, 1937; s. Arthur Bauer and Isabell (Moore) Q.; m. Christine F. Thomas, Sept. 16, 1972; children: Kevin, Keith. BS, Cornell U., 1959, MS, 1963; MD, SUNY, Syracuse, 1967. Diplomate Am. Bd. Radiology, Nat. Bd. Med. Examiners; cert. of added qualifications in neuroradiology. Intern Jackson Meml. Hosp., Miami, Fla., 1967-68; resident in radiology Columbia U., N.Y.C., 1968-71, fellow in neuroradiology, 1971-72; asst. prof. Downstate Med. Ctr., Bklyn., 1972-76; assoc. prof. U. Miami, 1976-79, prof., 1979-92, chmn., prof., 1992—, chief sect. neuroradiology, 1976-86, dir. divsn. magnetic resonance imaging, 1986-92, Robert Shapiro MD prof. radiology. Vis. prof. U. Tenn. Coll. Medicine, Memphis, 1982, Downstate Med. Ctr. Coll. Medicine, Bklyn., 1992, U. Vt. Coll. Medicine, Burlington, 1983, N.Y. Med. Coll., Valhalla, 1984, U. Va. Sch. Medicine, Charlottesville, 1984, U. Ky. Sch. Medicine, Lexington, 1985, Yale U. Sch. Medicine, New Haven, 1986, 2000, Columbia U. Sch. Medicine, N.Y.C., 1986, The Mayo Clinic & Found., Rochester, Minn., 1987, Med. Coll. Va., Richmond, 1988, U. Pa. Sch. Medicine, Phila., 1988, Harvard U. Sch. Medicine/Mass. Gen. Hosp., Boston, 1989, U. Conn., Farmington, 1990, Kumamoto, Japan, 1993, U. Man., Can., 1992, Mich. State U., 1996, Mt. Sinai Med. Ctr., 1997, Cornell U. Sch. Medicine, 1998, U. Minn., 2001, U. Ky., 2002; guest lectr. Asian Oceanic Soc. Neuroradiology, 2001, Internat. Med. Soc. Paraplegic, Lucerne, Switzerland, 2001; Phaler lectr. Phila. Roentgen Soc., 1995; dir. programs in dept. radiology U. Miami Sch. Medicine, 1984, 86, Med. Coll. Wis., 1990, 92, Kauai, Hawaii, 1991, Whistler, B.C., 1990; guest lectr. at ASEAN Congress of Radiology, Malaysia, 1992, Royal Australia Radiology Soc., Brisbane, 1993, Brazilian Congress Neurology, 1996, N.Y. Roentgen Soc., 1997, Somerset MR course, Torquay, U.K., 1998, Republic of China, 1999, Yale U., 2000, U. Minn., 2001; adv. cons. NIH, 1987, 90; sci. merit reviewer V.A., 1987; presenter, lectr. in field. Author: Neurosonography, 1988; dep. editor Am. Jour. Neuroradiology, 1984-96, editor-in-chief, 1998— ; assoc. editor for neuroimaging Yearbook of Neurology and Neurosurgery, 1991—; manuscript reviewer Am. Jour. Neuroradiology, 1984—, Paraplegia, 1989—, Radiographics, 1991—, Pediatrics, 1993—, Radiology, 1994—; mem. editl. bd. Jour. Clin. Neuro-Ophthalmology, 1980-90; contbr. articles to profl. jours. Pres. Am. Soc. Neuroadiology, 1994-95; prin. investigator NIH Grant on imaging/pathology of spinal cord injury. Lt. (j.g.) USN, 1959-61. Fellow Am. Coll. Radiology, Am. Soc. Neuroradiology (pres. 1994-95, program com. 1985-89, 92, editl. com. 1984—, publs. com. 1984—); mem. AMA, Radiol. Soc. N.Am. (program subcom. on neuroradiology 1990-94), Southeastern Neuroradiol. Soc. (founder, pres. 1980-81, examiner for bd. certification in radiology and neuroradiology, mem. Marconi med. adv. bd.), Dade County Med. Assn., Soc. Chmn. Acad. Radiology Depts., Fla. Radiol. Soc. (magnetic resonance com. 1991-92), Alpha Omega Alpha. Avocations: golf, travel. Office: U Miami 1150 NW 14th St Miami FL 33136-2137 E-mail: rquencer@med.miami.edu.

QUENEAU, PAUL ETIENNE, metallurgical engineer, educator; b. Phila., Mar. 20, 1911; s. Augustin L. and Jean (Blaisdell) Q.; m. Joan Osgood Hodges, May 20, 1939; children: Paul Blaisdell, Josephine Downs (Mrs. George Stanley Patrick). BA, Columbia U., 1931, BSc, 1932, M of Engring., 1933; postgrad., Cambridge (Eng.) U., 1934; DSc, Delft (Netherlands) U. Tech., 1971. With INCO, 1934-69; rsch. supt. Internat. Nickel Co., 1940-41, 46-48, v.p., 1958-69, chief tech. officer, tech. asst. to pres., 1960-66, asst. to chmn., 1967-69; vis. scientist Delft U. Tech., 1970-71; prof. engring. Dartmouth Coll., 1971-87, prof. emeritus, 1987—. Cons. engr., 1972—; vis. prof. U. Minn., 1974-75, U. Utah, 1987-91; geographer Perry River Arctic Expdn., 1949; chmn. arctic rsch. adv. com. USN, 1957; gov. Arctic Inst. N.Am., 1957-62; mem. engring. coun. Columbia U., 1965-70; mem. vis. com. MIT, Cambridge, 1967-70; mem. extractive metallurgy and mineral processing panels NAS; pres. Q-S Oxygen Processes Inc., 1974-79, also bd. dirs. Author: (with Hanson) Geography, Birds and Mammals of the Perry River Region, 1956; Cobalt and the Nickeliferous Limonites, 1971; editor: Extractive Metallurgy of Copper, Nickel and Cobalt, 1961; (with Anderson) Pyrometallurgical Processes in Nonferrous Metallurgy, 1965; The Winning of Nickel, 1967; contbr. articles to profl. jours.; patentee 500 internat. patents, 36 U.S. patents including processes and apparatus employed in the pyrometallurgy, hydrometallurgy and vapometallurgy of nickel, copper, cobalt, lead, zinc, iron and steel, extractive metallurgy oxygen tech. including INCO oxygen flash smelting, oxygen top-blown rotary converter, lateritic ore matte smelting, nickel high pressure carbonyl and iron ore recovery processes; co-inventor Lurgi QSL direct lead-making, QSOP direct coppermaking and nickelmaking reactors, Lurgi direct steelmaking reactors, and Dravo oxygen sprinkle smelting copper furnaces. Bd. dirs. Engring. Found., 1966-76, chmn. bd. dirs., 1973-75. With U.S. Army, 1942-45, ETO; col. C.E., AUS ret. Decorated Bronze Star, ETO medal with 5 battlestars, Army Commendation medal USAR, 1937-62; Evans fellow Cambridge U., 1934; recipient Egleston medal Columbia U., 1965, Fletcher award Dartmouth Coll., 1991, McGraw-Hill Chem. Engring. award for Personal Achievement in Chem. Engring., 1996. Fellow Metall. Soc. of AIME (dir. 1964, 68-71, pres. 1969, Extractive Metallurgy Lecture award 1977, Paul E. Queneau TMS Internat. Symposium on Extractive Metallurgy of Copper, Nickel and Cobalt 1993); mem. AIME (Douglas Gold medal 1968, v.p. 1970, dir. 1968-71, Henry Krumb lectr. 1984, keynote lectr. ann. meeting 1990), NAE, NSPE, Can. Inst. Mining and Metallurgy, Inst. Mining and Metallurgy U.K. (overseas mem. council 1970-80, Gold medal 1980), Sigma Xi, Tau Beta Pi. Office: Dartmouth Coll Thayer Sch Engring Hanover NH 03755

QUENNELL, NICHOLAS, landscape architect, educator; b. London, Sept. 30, 1935; s. Cecil William and Beatrice Irene Quennell; m. Grace Tankersley, Apr. 30, 1983. AA, Archtl. Assn., London, 1957; MLA, Harvard U., 1969. Registered architect, N.Y., Pa., N.J., Conn., U.K.; registered landscape architect, N.Y., N.J., Conn., Mass., N.C. Architect London County Coun., 1959-61, Jose Luis Sert, Cambridge, Mass., 1961-62, Lawrence Halprin & Assocs., San Francisco, 1962-65, Vollmer Assocs., N.Y.C., 1965-68; prin. Nicholas Quennell Assocs., 1968-79, Quennell Rothschild Assocs., N.Y.C., 1979-97, Quennell, Rothschild & Ptnrs., N.Y.C., 1998—. V.p. The Mcpl. Art Soc. (dir. 1978-85), N.Y.C., 1985-92, dir. The Archtl. League, N.Y.C., 1984-89. Bd. dirs. Nat. Assn. for Olmsted Pks., Washington, 1988-90, chmn., 1990-93; mem. Art Commn. of City of N.Y., 1992-97, pres., 1993-97. Fellow Am. Soc. of Landscape Architects; mem. Century Assn. Office: Quennell Rothschild and Ptnrs. 118 W 22nd St New York NY 10011-2416 E-mail: quennell@qrpartners.com.

QUENNEVILLE, JOEL, professional hockey coach; b. Windsor, Ont., Can., Sept. 15, 1958; m. Elizabeth Quenneville; children: Dylan, Lily, Anna. Hockey player, player coach St. John's Maple Leafs, 79-92; head coach Springfield Indians, Am. Hockey League, 1993-94; asst. coach Colo. Avalanche, 1995-96; head coach St. Louis Blues, NHL, 1997—. Named Most Valuable Defenseman, 1985, 86, Coach of Yr., NHL, 1999-2000. Office: Savvis Ctr 1401 Clark Ave Saint Louis MO 63103-2709*

QUENON, ROBERT HAGERTY, retired mining consultant and holding company executive; b. Clarksburg, W.Va., Aug. 2, 1928; s. Ernest Leonard and Josephine (Hagerty) Q.; m. Jean Bowling, Aug. 8, 1953; children: Evan, Ann, Richard. BS in Mining Engring., W.Va. U., 1951; LL.B., George Washington U., 1964; PhD (hon.), U. Mo., 1979, Blackburn Coll., 1983, W.Va. U., 1988. Mine supt. Consol. Coal Co., Fairmont, W.Va., 1956-61; mgr. deep mines Pittston Co., Dante, Va., 1964-66; gen. mgr. Riverton Coal Co., Crown Hill, W.Va., 1966-67; mgr. ops. coal and shale oil dept. Exxon Co., Houston, 1967; pres. Monterey Coal Co., 1969-76; sr. v.p. Carter Oil Co., 1976-77; exec. v.p. Peabody Coal Co., St. Louis, 1977-78, pres., chief exec. officer, 1978-83, Peabody Holding Co., Inc., St. Louis, 1983-90, chmn., 1990-91. Bd. dirs. Newmont Mining Co., Denver, Ameren Corp., St. Louis, Laclede Steel Co., St. Louis, Miss. Lime Co., Alton, Ill.; bd. dirs., chmn. Fed. Res. Bank St. Louis, 1993-95, dep. chmn., 1990-92; mem. coal industry adv. bd. Internat. Energy Agy., 1980—, bd. chmn., 1984-90; chmn. Bituminous Coal Operator's Assn., 1980-83, 89-91. Trustee Blackburn Coll., Carlinville, Ill., 1975-83, St. Louis U., 1981-91; pres. St. Louis Art Mus., 1985-88. Served with AUS, 1946-47. Recipient Eavenson award Soc. Mining, Metallurg. and Exploration, 1994, Erskine Ramsay award Am. Inst. Mining, Metallurg. and Petroleum Engrs., 1985. Mem. Am. Mining Congress (vice-chmn. 1980-91), Nat. Coal Assn. (chmn. bd. 1978-80), U.S. C. of C. (dir. 1982-88). Office: PO Box 11328 Saint Louis MO 63105-0128

QUENTEL, ALBERT DREW, lawyer; b. Miami, Fla., Nov. 27, 1934; s. Charles Edward Jr. and Alberta Amelia (Drew) Q.; m. Paula Staelin Hagar, Feb. 9, 1957 (dec. Mar. 1998); children: Albert D. Jr., Stephen C., Marshall Lee, Paul G., Peter E., Michael J. BA, U. Fla., 1956, JD with honors, 1959. Bar: Fla. 1959. Assoc. Mershon, Sawyer, Johnston, Dunwody & Cole, Miami, 1959-64, ptnr., 1965-71; prin., shareholder Greenberg Traurig P.A., 1971—. Editor-in-chief U. Fla. Law Rev., 1959; contbg. author: Florida Real Property Practice, 1965, Real Estate Partnerships Selected Problems and Solutions, 1991, Commercial Real Estate Finance, 1993. Mem. Gov.'s Growth Mgmt. Adv. Com., Tallahassee, 1985-87; bd. dirs. Nat. Parkinson Found., Miami, 1980-98, v.p., 1985-97. Mem. NRA (life 1989—), Am. Coll. Real Estate Lawyers, Fla. Bar Assn. (chmn. pub. rels. com. 1970-72, chmn. editorial com. jour. 1972-73), Lions (pres. Key Biscayne, Fla. club 1973), Miami Club (pres. 1991-92), Bath Club, Blue Key, Beta Theta Pi (pres. local chpt. 1954-55), Phi Eta Sigma, Phi Kappa Phi. Republican. Congregationalist. Avocations: reading, shooting, photography. Home: 825 Algeria Ave Miami FL 33134-2401 Office: Greenberg Traurig 1221 Brickell Ave Miami FL 33131-3224 E-mail: QuentelA@gtlaw.com.

QUERESHI, MOHAMMED YOUNUS, psychology educator, consultant; b. Haripur Hazara, Pakistan, Dec. 12, 1929; came to U.S., 1953; s. Mohammed Noor and Meryam Khatoon Q.; m. Nora Jane Knapp, May 27, 1958 (div. Nov. 1979); children: Ahmed, Amna, Shukria, Shawn; m. Farzana Kaukab, May 17, 1980; children: Ajmel, Sabeeha, Azem. PhD, U. Ill., 1958. Lic. psychologist, Wis.; diplomate Am. Bd. Psychol. Spltys. Asst. prof. psychology U. Minn., Duluth, 1960-62, U. N.D., Grand Forks, 1962-64; assoc. prof. psychology Marquette U., Milw., 1964-70, prof., 1970—, chmn. dept. psychology, 1971-77. Cons. psychologist. Author: Statistics and Behavior: An Introduction, 1980, 2d edit., 1991; contbr. articles to sci. and profl. jours. Pres. 81st St. Sch. PTA, 1968-70; merit badge counselor Milw. County coun. Boy Scouts Am., 1973-88; pres. Islamic Assn. Greater Milw., 1978-83. NIH grantee, 1962-69; Office of Edn. grantee, 1970-71; TOPS Club grantee, 1969-76. Mem. Am. Psychol. Assn., Psychometric Soc., Sigma Xi. Home: 2759 N 68th St Milwaukee WI 53210-1204 Office: Marquette U Schroeder Health Complex PO Box 1881 Milwaukee WI 53201-1881

QUESADA, ANTONIO RETTSCHLAG, mathematics educator; b. Melilla, Spain, Jan. 29, 1948; came to U.S., 1971; s. Antonio and Milagros (Rettschlag) Q.; m. Milagros Agostini, July 4, 1971; 1 child, Marival. Licenciado Math., U. Granada, Spain, 1971; MS, U. Fla., 1977, PhD, 1978. Intermediate and high sch. tchr., Granada, 1968-71; instr. Cath. U. of P.R., Ponce, 1971-74, asst. prof., 1974-75, 78-80, assoc. prof., chmn. math, 1980-84; assoc. prof. U. Akron, Ohio, 1984-95, prof., 1995—, coord. math. div., 1990-92. Collaborator Coll. Entrance Exam. Bd., San Juan, P.R., 1973-75, 81-82; co-founder, judge Math. Olimpiads, Ponce, 1978-84; bd. advisors P.R. Coun. Higher Edn., San Juan, 1980; cons. Prentice Hall Addison-Wesley, Tex. Instruments; presenter profl. meetings, U.S., Mex., Portugal, Spain, Colombia, Chile, Czech Republic, Greece and Austria, Argentina, Panama. Co-author: Basic Algebra, 1975, Precalculus with Graphing Calculators, 1994; mem. editorial bd. Buletin Cientifico Del Sur, Ponce, 1983-84; contbr. articles to profl. jours. in U.S., Portugal, Mex., U.K., and Spain. Bd. dirs. Sacred Heart High Sch., 1980-84, Fundacion Isolina Ferre, 1979-83. Grantee FPH, 1979, NSF, 1980, Martha H. Jennings Found., 1991, 92, Knight Found., 1994, 98, 2000, Eisenhower OBR, 1999, 2002, OBR Capital, 2002, OBR, 2001. Mem. Am. Math. Soc., Math. Assn. Am., Nat. Coun. Tchrs. Math., Pi Mu Epsilon. Office: U Akron Dept Math & Computer Scis Akron OH 44325-0001 Home: 659 Woodledge Dr Akron OH 44313-5913 E-mail: aquesada@uakron.edu.

QUESADA, BERNARD, English educator; b. Waynesburg, Pa., Feb. 18, 1971; s. Bernard and Mary (Cumberledge) Q. BS, West Va. Univ., 1993. Eng. tchr. Frederick Co. Pub. Schs., Frederick, Md., 1993—. Asst. football coach Brunswick H.S., 1994-99, asst. track coach, 1995-98. Roman Catholic. Avocations: reading, writing, book collecting.

QUESENBERRY, KENNETH HAYS, agronomy educator; b. Springfield, Tenn., Feb. 28, 1947; s. James William and Cora Geneva (Moore) Quesenberry; m. Joyce Ann Kaze; children: James Kenneth, Kendra Joyce. BS, Western Ky. U., 1969; PhD, U. Ky., 1975. D.F. Jones predoctoral fellow U. Ky., Lexington, 1972—75; asst. prof. U. Fla., Gainesville, 1975—80, assoc. prof. agronomy, 1980—86, prof. agronomy, 1986—. Contbr. articles to profl. jours. Chair So. Pasture and Forage Crop Improvement Conf., 1991. Served with U.S. Army, 1969—71, Vietnam. Fellow: Crop Sci. Soc. Am. (chair divsn. C-8 1993—94), Am. Soc. Agronomy. Democrat. Achievements include research in germplasm enhancement of forages with release of four cultivars of tropical grasses and three clovers and genetic transformation of clovers; specialist trifolium species germplasm. Avocations: sports, antique furniture refinishing. Office: U Fla PO Box 110500 Gainesville FL 32611-0500 E-mail: clover@mail.ifas.ufl.edu.

QUESNEL, GREGORY L. transportation company executive; b. Woodburn, Oreg., May 24, 1948; BA in Finance, U. Oregon; MA in Bus. Adminstrn., U. Portland; grad. Exec. Program in Bus. Adminstrn., Columbia U. Dir. fin. acctg. Consolidated Freightways, Portland, 1975-78, dir. mgmt. and cost acctg., 1978-86; fin. officer CF MotorFreight, Consolidated Freightways, 1986-89; v.p. acctg. Emery Worldwide, Consolidated Freightways, Scranton, Pa., 1989-91; exec. v.p., CFO CNF Transp. Inc., Palo Alto, Calif., 1991-97, pres., CEO, 1997—. Mem. Fin. Exec. Inst., Chief Fin. Execs. (conf. bds. coun., conf. bds. coun. of fin. execs.). E-mail: colvert.nancy@cnf.com.*

QUEST, DONALD O. neurological surgeon; b. St. Louis, Nov. 20, 1939; s. Oliver Harry and Elaine Elsie (Henderson) Q.; m. Ilona Maris, July 20, 1969; children: Wendy Elaine, Amy Ilona, Susan Elissa. BS, U. Ill., 1961; MD, Columbia U., 1970. Diplomate Am. Bd. Neurol. Surgery. Intern Mass. Gen. Hosp., Boston, 1970-71, resident, 1971-72, Neurol. Inst. N.Y., N.Y.C., 1972-76; attending neurosurgeon Downstate Med. Coll., Bklyn., 1976-78, Columbia U., N.Y.C., 1978—; chair. Am. Bd. Neurological Surgery, Houston. Past pres. Congress Neurosurgery, 1986-87; sec. Am. Bd. Neurosurgery, 1996—. Pres. Bd. Edn., N.J., 1980-86. Lt. USN, 1961-66. Mem. Neurol. Soc. Am., Am. Acad. Neurol. Surgery, Am. Assn. Neurol. Surgery, Congress Neurol. Surgeons, Soc. Neurol. Surgeons. Avocations: literature, music. Office: Neurol Inst NY 710 W 168th St New York NY 10032-2603*

QUEST, KRISTINA KAY, art educator, small business owner; b. Fort Atkinson, Wis., Sept. 22, 1952; d. Duane and Kiwa (Kikuchi) Tessman; m. Michael Charles Quest, July 28, 1973; children: Jennifer, Eric, Sarah. BS in Art Edn., U. Wis., 1992; student, U. Wis., Whitewater, 2002—. Lic. tchr., Wis. Substitute tchr., various cities, 1993-97, 99—; summer sch. tchr. Ft. Atkinson Sch. Dist., 1993-97; art tchr. 7th and 8th grade St. Pete's Luth. Sch., Helenville, Wis., 1997; tchr., kindergarten day care tchr. 1st Class Presch., Before Sch. Day Care at Prospect Elem., Lake Mills, 1997-99; owner The Oriental Quest, Oshkosh, 2000—, Back Acres Mobile Home Park, Oshkosh, 2000—. Past mem. Jefferson Arts Coun., bd. dirs., 1976-90; workshop fine arts fair judge Lakeside Luth. H.S., Lake Mills, Wis., 1991, 92; art fair judge for Fort Fest, Fort Atkinson, Crafters, 1993; owner mobile home park, Before/After Regular/Summer Sch. Day Care, Lake Mills Elem. Sch.; substitute tchr. Lake Mills (Wis.) Sch. Dist., Johnson Creek (Wis.) Sch. Dist. Author/illustrator: (book) Tiannamen Square, China's Dark Hours, 1987 (Juried Art Show 1993). Participant art donator AIDS Wellness Auction, The Globe, Oshkosh, 1999. Recipient art award Wis. Regional Arts Program/Waukesha Creative Arts League, Madison, 1993. Mem. Wis. Art Edn. Assn., Nat. Art Edn. Assn., Women in the Arts Nat. Mus., Japanese Am. Pub. Mus., U. of Wis.-Whitewater Alumni Assn., Student Tchr.'s Assn. Lutheran. Avocations: watercolor, sketching, painting, Japanese Sumi brush-stroke painting, block printing. Office: 105 Aztalan St Johnson Creek WI 53038-9666 E-mail: backacres@jefnet.com.

QUESTER, GEORGE HERMAN, political science educator; b. Bklyn., July 14, 1936; s. Jacob George and Elizabeth (Mattern) Q.; m. Aline Marie Olson, June 20, 1964; children: Theodore, Amanda. AB, Columbia U., 1958; MA, Harvard U., 1964, PhD, 1965. Instr., then asst. prof. govt. Harvard U., 1965-70; assoc. prof. govt. Cornell U., 1970-73, prof., 1973-82; prof. polit. sci. U. Md., College Park, 1982—. Vis. prof. U.S. Naval Acad., Annapolis, Md., 1991-93. Author: Deterrence Before Hiroshima, 1966, Nuclear Diplomacy, 1970, The Politics of Nuclear Proliferation, 1973, The Continuing Problem of International Relations, 1974, Offense and Defense in the International System, 1977, American Foreign Policy: The Lost Consensus, 1982, The Future of Nuclear Deterrence, 1986, The International Politics of Television, 1990, Nuclear Monopoly, 2000. Served with USAF, 1958-61. Fellow Center Advanced Study Behavioral Scis., 1974-75 Mem. Council Fgn. Relations, Inst. Strategic Studies, Am. Polit. Sci. Assn. Home: 5124 37th St N Arlington VA 22207-1862 Office: Univ Md 3140 Tydings College Park MD 20742-0001 E-mail: gqueste@gvpt.umd.edu.

QUESTROM, ALLEN I. retail executive; b. Newton, Mass., Apr. 13, 1941; s. Irving Allen and Natalie (Chadbourne) Q.; m. Carol Brummer, Sept. 9, 1967. BS, Boston U., 1964. From exec. trainee to div. mdse. mgr. Abraham & Straus, Bklyn., 1965-73; v.p., gen. mdse. mgr. home store Bullock's, L.A., 1973-74, sr. v.p., gen. mdse. mgr. all stores, 1974-77; exec. v.p. Bullock's div. Federated Dept. Stores, 1977-78, pres. Rich's div. Atlanta, 1978-80, chmn. bd., chief exec. officer, 1980-84, chmn. bd., chief exec. officer Bullock's/Bullocks Wilshire div., 1984-88, corp. exec. v.p. Cin., 1987-88, vice-chmn., 1988; also chmn., CEO Allied Stores Corp., 1990-97; pres., CEO Neiman Marcus Group Inc., Dallas, 1988-90; chmn., CEO Federated Dept. Stores Inc., Cin., 1990-97; chmn., pres., CEO Barneys New York, 1999—2000; chmn., CEO J.C. Penney Co., Inc., Plano, Tex., 2000—. Prin. AEA Investors Inc.; prin. Mellon Ventures. Avocations: skiing; golf; travel. Office: JC Penney Corp Inc 6501 Legacy Dr Plano TX 75024-3698*

QUETGLAS, MOLL JUAN, plastic and maxillofacial surgeon; b. Cuidadela, Menorca, Spain, Feb. 11, 1922; s. Honesto Quetglas Montserrat and Catalina Moll Coll; m. Conception Marimon Alvarez; children: Juan, Alfonso, Carlos. Degree, U. Barcelona, Spain, 1945; MD, U. Madrid, 1970. Diplomate Bd. Plastic Surgery, Bd. Maxillofacial Surgery and Plastic and Reconstructive Surgery, Bd. Gen. Surgery and Traumatology. Gen. practice medicine, Mahon, Spain, 1945-52; resident in gen. surgery Madrid, 1953-55; head surg. svc. Mil. Hosp., Larache, Morocco, 1955-59, Tenerife, Canary Island, 1960-61, Social Security, Madrid, 1962-84; head plastic surgery svc. Ctrl. Mils. Hosp., 1962-87; prof. U. Madrid, 1978-87. Dir. hosps. Social Security, 1968-71; mem. exec. com. I.S.A.P.S., 1975-76; prof. anatomy Med. Sch., Salamanca (Spain) U., 1972; asst. plastic surgery svc. Walter Reed Hosp., Washington, 1969. Author: Brief Handbook of Plastic and Aesthetic Surgery of the Face, 1971, Plastic Surgery: Three Steps in its Evolution, 1999; co-author: Treatise of Medical Rehabilitation, 1967, 2d edit., 1970, Iberoamerican Text of Plastic Surgery, 1986, 2d edit., 1994, Art of Aesthetic Plastic Surgery, 1989, Ualoracion de las Secuelas Traumaticas en el Aparato Locomotor, 1995, Rehabilitacion Media-Editorial Masson, 1996; dir., founder Spanish Jour. Plastic Surgery, 1968-76; hon. dir. Jour. Plastic Jour., 1983; editor: Facial Traumatology, 1983; dir. Jour. Ibero-L.Am. Jour. Plastic Surgery, 1975-2000; contbr. over 100 articles to med. jours.; co-translator (book) Aesthetic Rhinoplasty (written by Dr. Aiach). Col. M.C., Spanish Army, 1987. Recipient Ex-Combatiente, Donador de Sangre, Cruz de San Hermenegildo, Placa de San Hermenegildo, Cruz del Merito Militar, Spanish Army Min., medal Complutense U. Madrid. Mem. Internat. Confedn. Plastic Surgery, Spanish Soc. Plastic Surgery (mem. exec. com. 1969-71, pres. 1972-74), Plastic Surgery Soc. Ecuador (hon.), Plastic Surgery Soc. Argentina (hon.), Plastic Surgery Soc. Chile (hon.), Spanish Soc. Traumatology, Assn. Mil. Plastic Surgeons, Assn. Mil. Surgeons, Acad. Surgery Madrid, N.Y. Acad. Scis., Helenic Soc. Plastic Reconstructive Surgery, Revista Palstic Surgery Am. Ibero-Latinamerican (hon. dir.), Spanish Plastic Surgery Soc. (hon.). E-mail: cirplast@teleline.es., jquet@grupobbva.net.

QUIAN QUIROGA, RODRIGO CESAR, physicist; b. Buenos Aires, Mar. 21, 1967; arrived in Germany, 1996; s. Hugo Lope and Maria Celia (Capredoni) Q.Q. M Physics, U. Buenos Aires, 1993; PhD, Med. U. Lübeck, Germany, 1999. Tchg. asst. U. Buenos Aires, 1991-96; scholar dept. neurophysiology FLENI, Buenos Aires, Argentina, 1993-95, scholar dept. epilepsy Argentina, 1995-96; guest scientist Inst. Physiology Med. U. Lübeck, 1996-98; postdoctoral rschr. John von Neumann Inst. Computing Forschungszentrum JÜlich, 1998—2001; Sloan-Swartz fellow Sloan-Swartz Ctr. for Theoretical Neurobiology, Calif. Inst. Tech., Pasadena, 2001—. Recipient Sci.-Tech. Prodn. prize, U. Buenos Aires, 1994, Young Investigator award, Am. Epilepsy Soc., 2001. Office: Divsn Biology 139-74 Caltech Pasadena CA 91125

QUIAT, GERALD M. lawyer; b. Denver, Jan. 9, 1924; s. Ira L. and Esther (Greenblatt) Q.; m. Roberta M. Nicholson, Sept. 26, 1962; children: James M., Audrey R., Melinda A., Daniel P., Ilana L., Leonard E. AA, U. Calif., Berkeley, 1942; AB, LLB, U. Denver, 1948, changed to JD, 1970. Bar: Colo. 1948, Fed. Ct. 1948, U.S. Dist. Ct. Colo. 1948, U.S. Ct. Appeals (10th cir.) 1948, U.S. Surpeme Ct. 1970. Dep. dist. atty. City and Co. of Denver, Colo., 1949-52; partner firm Quiat, Seeman & Quiat, Denver, 1952-67, Quiat & Quiat (later changed to Quiat, Bucholtz & Bull, P.C.), 1968; pres. Quiat, Bucholtz & Bull & Laff, P.C. (and predecessors), Denver, 1968-85; pvt. practice, 1985—. Bd. dirs., past chmn. audit com. Guaranty Bank & Trust Co., Denver. Past trustee Holding Co.; pres., chmn. bd. dirs. Rose Med. Ctr., Denver, 1976—79; mem. Colo. Civil Rights Com., 1963—71, chmn., 1966—67, 1969—70, hearing officer, 1963—71; bd. dirs. AMC Cancer Rsch. Ctr., Denver, 1971—, chmn. bd., 1991—93, Am. Med. Ctr., 1993—95; mem. nat. civil rights com. Anti-Defamation League, hon. mem. nat. exec. com., hon. nat. commr.; chmn. Mountain State region, 1980—82; sec. treas. AMC Cancer Rsch. Ctr., 1999—; mem. exec. com., bd. mem. Mountain States region Anti-Defamation League. With inf. U.S. Army, 1942—45. Decorated Combat Infantry Badge, Bronze Star. Mem. ABA, Colo. Bar Assn., Colo. Trial Lawyers Assn. (pres. 1970-71), Am. Legion (comdr. Leyden-Chiles-Wickersham post 1 1955-56, past judge adv. Colo. dept.). Home: 5361 Nassau Cir E Englewood CO 80110-5100 Office: Penthouse Suite 1720 S Bellaire St Denver CO 80222-4304 E-mail: gqph@aol.com.

QUIAT, MARSHALL, lawyer; b. Denver, Mar. 10, 1922; s. Ira Louis and Esther Quiat; m. Ruth Laura Saunders, Nov. 26, 1950 (dec. Nov. 1995); 1 child, Matthew Philip; m. Jane Cooley, May 1, 1996. BA, U. Colo., 1947, JD, 1948. Bar: Colo. 1949, U.S. Dist. Ct. Colo. 1949, U.S. Ct. Appeals (10th cir.) 1968. Pvt. practice, Denver, 1949—. Judge Gilpin County (Colo.) Ct., 1956, 1st Jud. Dist. Ct., Golden, Colo., 1959; mem. com. on jud. reform Colo. Legis. Commn., 1958. Mem. Colo. Ho. of Reps., Denver, 1949-51; bd. dirs. Luth. Med. Ctr., Denver, 1961-87. 1st lt. F.A., U.S. Army, 1941-46, MTO, ETO.

Mem. Am. Radio Relay League (nat. bd. dirs. 1986-99, honorary v.p. 1999—), Pi Gamma Mu, Delta Sigma Rho, Phi Alpha Delta. Avocations: amateur radio, skiing, mathematics, history. Home: 714 Pontiac St Denver CO 80220-5540 Office: PO Box 200878 Denver CO 80220-0878 E-mail: quiat@msn.com.

QUICK, DANNY RICHARD, computer systems engineer; b. Millen, Ga., Aug. 7, 1948; s. John Francis and Olene (Crane) Q.; m. Donna Kay Nobles, Oct. 13, 1973; children: Dexter Brian, Debby Kim. Cert. data processing, Strayer Coll., Arlington, Va., 1989. Enlisted USAF, 1967, advanced through grades to sr. master sgt., 1984; chief Message Processing Br., Orgn. Joints Chiefs of Staff, Pentagon, Washington, 1984-88, ret., 1988; systems analyst Potomac Systems Engring., Annandale, Va., 1988-89; sr. systems cons. Wang Labs., Inc., Bethesda, Md., 1989-93; prin. systems engr. Computer Scis. Corp., Falls Ch., Va., 1993—2002; computer specialist Dept. of State, Washington, 2002—. Mem. methods & procedures panel U.S. Mil. Comm.-Electronics Bd., Washington, 1984-88, mem. call signs panel, 1984-88. Recipient Defense Meritorious Svc. medal Sec. Defense, Washington, 1987, Meritorious Svc. medal Sec. Air Force, Washington, 1980; named one of 50 Outstanding Airmen of Yr., Airforce Mil. Personnel Ctr., Randolph AFB, Tex., 1983-84. Mem. Am. Legion (exec. com. 1984-86, editor Post-O-Gram, 1983-84). Republican. Methodist. Achievements include the merge of the principal officers e-mail system and the foreign affairs information systems networks; led the Dept. of State test and deploy team in testing and deploying a Lotus Notes locally developed database program, which is installed on a Microsoft Windows NT LAN, for distributing inbound and transmitting outbound diplomatic telegrams, throughout the Department of State and at American embassies and consulates worldwide. Home: 4 Caledon Ct Stafford VA 22556-1608 Office: Dept of State IRM/OPS/MSO/MSP/TD 7374 Boston Blvd Springfield VA 22153-2804

QUICK, EDWARD RAYMOND, museum director, educator, curator; b. L.A., Mar. 22, 1943; s. Donald Russell Quick and Gertrude Ruth (Albin) Thornbrough; m. Ruth Ann Lessig; children: Jeannette Lee, Russell Raymond. BA, U. Calif., Santa Barbara, 1970, MA, 1977. Adminstr. supr. Civil Service, Santa Ana, Calif., 1971-75; sr. computer operator Santa Barbara Rsch. Ctr., 1975-77; asst. collections curator Santa Barbara Mus. Art, 1977-78; collections mgr. Montgomery (Ala.) Mus. Fine Arts, 1978-80; asst. dir. Joslyn Art Mus., Omaha, 1980-85; dir. Sheldon Swope Art Mus., Terre Haute, Ind., 1985-95, Berman Mus., Anniston, Ala., 1995-97; mus. curator National Archives, Washington, 1998-2000, William Clinton Presdl. Libr. and Mus., 2000—. Adv. Ind. Arts Commn., Indpls., 1986-91; mem. Arts in Pub. Places Commn., Terre Haute, Ind., 1986-93; pres. Friends Vigo County Pub. Libr., 1988-95, treas., 1990-93. Author: Code of Practice for Couriering Museum Objects, 1985, Gilbert Brown Wilson and Herman Melville's "Moby Dick", 1993, The American West in the Berman Collections, 1997, Cattle Drive, 1997; co-author: Registrars in Record, 1987. Bd. dirs. Vol. Action Ctr., Terre Haute, 1987-90, Terre Haute Cmty. Relief Effort for Environ. and Civic Spirit, 1989. With USAF, 1961-65, Air N.G., 1979-96. Mem. Am. Assn. Mus. (adv. 1994—, mgmt. and long-range planning com. 1994—), Assn. Ind. Mus., Am. Assn. State and Local History, Internat. Coun. Mus., Rotary Internat., Kiwanis Internat., Alpha Gamma Sigma. Avocation: museum administrative research. Office: Clinton Presl Materials Project 1000 La Harpe Blvd Little Rock AR 72201

QUICK, GARY, emergency physician; b. Apr. 17, 1945; MD, U. Pitts., 1972. Diplomate Am. Bd. Emergency Medicine. Med. dir. emergency dept. Barnes Hosp., St. Louis, 1987-93; chief sect. emergency medicine U. Okla., Oklahoma City, 1993-99, assoc. prof. dept. emergency medicine, 1999—. Editor: Mosby's Paramedic Textbook, 1995, 2nd edit., 2000. Fellow Am. Coll. Emergency Physicians (sec. sect. emergency ultrasound 1999--).

QUICK, JERRY RAY, academic administrator, retired; b. Gosport, Ind., July 3, 1939; s. Waldo C. and M. Marguerite (Goss) Q.; m. Elizabeth Ahlemeyer, June 10, 1962; children: Patrick, Andrew. BS, Ind. State U., 1961; MS, Ind. U., 1965. Tchr., coach MSD Washington Twp., Indpls., 1961-63; assoc. dir. housing Ind. State U., Terre Haute, 1963-75; asst. v.p. Ctrl. Mich. U., Mt. Pleasant, 1975-85; assoc. vice chancellor for bus. Vanderbilt U., Nashville, 1985-89; v.p. fin. and adminstrn. U. Ala., Huntsville, 1989-2000, ret., 2000, v.p. fin. and adminstrn. emeritus, 2000—. Mem. task force U.S. Dept. Edn., Washington, 1981-84; mem. accreditation teams So. Assn. Colls. and Schs., 1993—. Contbr. articles to profl. jours. and chpts. to books. Bd. dirs. Better Bus. Bur., Nashville, 1988-89, Better Bus. Bur., Huntsville, Ala., 1998-2000; mem. Mayor's Commn. on Efficiency, Nashville, 1988-89. Mem. Nat. Assn. Coll. and Univ. Bus. Officers (editl. bd. 1987-92), So. Assn. Coll. and Univ. Bus. Officers, Nat. Assn. Coll. Aux. Svcs., Ala. Assn. Coll. and Univ. Bus. Officers, Assn. Coll. and Univ. Housing Officers (pres. 1979-80), Huntsville C. of C., Huntsville Rotary Club. Avocations: farming, collecting and restoring antiques, travel, microcomputers. Home: 2513 Garth Rd SE Huntsville AL 35801-1422 E-mail: JRQ007@aol.com.

QUICK, PETER, former brokerage firm executive; married. BS in Engring., U. Va.; postgrad., Stanford U. With U.S. Clearing Corp., 1983-94, pres., 1990-94, Quick & Reilly Group, Inc., 1994-96, Quick & Reilly, Inc., N.Y.C., from 1996. Ofcl.; pres., dir., firm com. Am. Stock Exch.; bd. dirs., dir. depository trust Clearing Corp.; vice chmn. Security Industry Assn., N.Y. Dist.; Ins. Agy. Bd., NASD. Mem. nat. selection com. Jefferson scholar program U. Va. Mem. U. Va. Alumni Assn. (bd. mgrs.). Office: The American Stock Exch 86 Trinity Pl New York NY 10006

QUICK, THADINE NANETTE, executive secretary, writer; b. Chgo., Mar. 1, 1968; d. Dessie Brooks and Mosetta Tucker; m. Tony Lee Quick; children: DeMarcus Jockquay, Zaria Danielle. Student, Oakton Coll., 2000—. Cert. exec. adminstrv. sch. Author: (novel) Fiction Mainstream , 2001. Sgt. promotable U.S. Army, 1988—97, S.C. Decorated Arm Accommodation medal (3), Good Conduct award (3), Army Achievement award (3). Personal E-mail: tquickwriter@hotmail.com. Business E-Mail: tquick1@motorola.com.

QUICK, THOMAS CLARKSON, brokerage house executive; b. Westbury, N.Y., Feb. 26, 1955; s. Leslie Charles and Regina (Clarkson) Q. BS in Bus., Fairfield U., 1977. Br. mgr. Quick & Reilly Inc., Palm Beach, Fla., 1977-81; dir. The Quick & Reilly Group, N.Y.C., 1981-85; v.p. Quick & Reilly Inc., Palm Beach, 1981-86, pres., dir. N.Y.C., 1985-96, also bd. dirs.; pres., COO Quick & Reilly/Fleet Securities, Inc., 1996-98; also bd. dirs.; pres., COO Quick & Reilly Group Inc., 1998-2001. Trustee Security Industry Found. for Econ. Edn., Securities Industry Inst.; bd. dirs. Senesco Techs., corcoran.com., MindArrow Systems.com. Treas. Nat. Corp. Theater Fund, Alcoholism Coun. of N.Y.C; trustee U.S. Com.; bd. trustees Fairfield U.; mem. investment adv. bd. and endowment com. St. Jude Children's Rsch. Hosp., Memphis, 1986—; chmn. com. Wall Street Friends of St. Jude Children's Rsch. Hosp., 1979—, mem. endowment com.; bd. dirs. Best Buddies, Am. Ireland Fund. Mem. The Investment Assn. N.Y., N.Y. Stock Exch., Securities and Industry Assn. (econ. edn. com.), Am. Assn. of Sovereign Mil., Order of Malta, Young Pres.'s Orgn., Univ. Club, Friendly Sons of St. Patrick, Apawamis Country Club (Rye, N.Y.), The Beach Club (Palm Beach, Fla.), Chgo. Athletic Club., New York Yacht Club, Lotus Club, Lost Tree Club. Home: 291 El Vedado Way Palm Beach FL 33480 Office: Quick & Reilly Inc Fleet Securities 26 Broadway Fl 14 New York NY 10004-1801 E-mail: tquick@quick-reilly.com.

QUICK, WALTER CURTIS, music company executive; b. Bklyn., Jan. 10, 1962; s. Clarence and Della (Holder) Q.; 1 child, Sapphire Asia. BS, Fisk U., 1986. Gen. mgr. restaurant, Bklyn., 1982-84; resident dir. Upward Bound U. Pitts., Pitts., 1985-86; pres. Quick Del Music Co., N.Y.C.; C.D.P. Southland Corp., Falls Church, Va., 1987; mgr. Marriott Corp., Alexandria, 1988; marshall, coach football and track Falls Church High Sch., 1989-90; security specialist Downtown EMT dba Live, N.Y.C., 1997—; security specialist internal security Azure, Inc. Cons. security Downtown Enterprises, N.Y.C. Author: poems. Mem. Easter Seals, N.Y., Wilson Cancer Assocs., N.Y., Covenant House, N.Y. Links scholar. Mem. ACLU, Am. Assn. Retired Persons, Am. Fedn. T.V. and Audio Artists, Nat. Park Trust, Nat. Cancer Coalition, Screen Actors Guild, Smithsonian Instn. Home: 7002 Boulevard E # 38H West New York NJ 07093-4929 Office: Quick-Del Music 595A Decatur St Brooklyn NY 11233-2005

QUICK, WILLIAM THOMAS, author, screenwriter; b. Muncie, Ind., May 30, 1946; s. Clifford Willett and Della May (Ellis) Quick. Student, Ind. U., 1964-66. Pres. Iceberg Prodns., San Francisco, 1986—. Author: Dreams of Flesh and Sand, 1988, Dreams of God and Men, 1989, Yesterday's Pawn, 1989, Systems, 1989, Singularities, 1990; author: (as Quentin Thomas) Chains of Light, 1992, Ascensions, 1997; author: (as Margaret Allan) The Mammoth Stone, 1993, Keeper of the Stone, 1994, The Last Mammoth, 1995, Spirits Walking Woman, 1997; author: (as W.T. Quick) Star Control: Interbellum, 1996, American Gothic: Family, 1996, Sister of the Sky, 1998; co-author (with William Shatner): Quest for Tomorrow: Delta Search, 1997, Quest for Tomorrow: In Alien Hands, 1997, Quest for Tomorrow: Step Into Chaos, 1999, Quest for Tomorrow: Beyong the Stars, 2000; author (as Sean Kiernan): Roar, 1998, Roar: The Cauldron, 1998, Roar: The Talisman, 1998, Mortal Kombat: Noob Saibot, 1999, The Hollow Man, 2000, Planet of the Apes, 2001; co-author (with Richard Curtis): How to Get Your E-Book Published, 2001. Mem.: Authors Guild, Sci. Fiction and Fantasy Writers Am. Home and Office: 1558 Leavenworth St San Francisco CA 94109-3220

QUIDD, DAVID ANDREW, paralegal; b. Chicago Heights, Ill., Sept. 8, 1954; s. John Richard and Mary (Wingate) Q. BA in Polit. Sci., U. New Orleans, 1976; postgrad., La. State U., 1976-79; paralegal cert., U. New Orleans, 1990. Coord. vols. Carter/Mondale Re-election Commn., New Orleans, 1980; paralegal Kitchen & Montagnet, 1981-84, Herman, Herman, Katz & Cotlar, New Orleans, 1985-92; freelance paralegal Metairie, La., 1992—. Pres. Alliance for Good Govt., Jefferson Parish, La., 1982, Young Dems. La., 1975-77; mem. Jefferson Parish Dem. Exec. Com., 1983-87, 89-96, chmn., 1990-93, treas., 1994, vice chmn., 1995; mem. Dem. State Ctrl. Com., 1996—; chmn. Jefferson Dem. Alliance, 1997—. Mem. Nat. Fedn. Paralegal Assns. (primary rep. 1995-97, 2001—, secondary rep. 1998-2000), New Orleans Paralegal Assn. (treas. 1991-94), Gretna Hist. Soc. (parliamentarian 1998-2001, pres., 2002—). Roman Catholic. Avocation: jogging. Home: 1141 Papworth Ave Metairie LA 70005-2338

QUIE, PAUL GERHARDT, pediatrician, educator; b. Dennison, Minn., Feb. 3, 1925; s. Albert Knute and Nettie Marie (Jacobson) Quie; m. Elizabeth Holmes, Aug. 10, 1951; children: Katie, Bill, Paul, David. BA, St. Olaf Coll., 1949; MD, Yale U., 1953; PhD (hon.) , U. Lund, 1993. Diplomate Am. Bd. Pediat., Nat. Bd. Med. Examiners (mem.). Intern Hennepin County Hosp., 1953—54; pediatric resident U. Minn. Hosps., 1957—59; mem. faculty U. Minn. Med. Sch., 1959—, prof. pediatrics, 1968—99, prof. microbiology, 1974—99, assoc. dean of students, 1992—, Am. Legion meml. heart research prof., 1974—91, Regents prof., 1991; Regent's prof. emeritus, 1999—; interim dir. Ctr. for Biomed. Ethics U. Minn. Med. Sch., 1985—86; attending physician Hennepin County Hosp., 1959—91. Cons. U. Minn. Nursery Sch., 1959—91; chief of staff U. Minn. Hosp., 1979—84; vis. physician Radcliffe Infirmary, Oxford, England, 1971—72; mem. Adv. Allergy and Infectious Disease Coun., 1976—80; mem. pediat. com. NRC, 1978; mem. bd. sci. counselors Gamble Inst., 1985—90; vis. prof. U. Bergen, 1991; hon. prof. U. Hong Kong Med. Sch., 1995; vis. prof. pediat. Chubu Hosp., Nagasaki, Japan, 1996. Editl. bd. Pediat., 1970—76, Rev. Infectious Diseases, 1989—92. Pres. Fairview Found., 1998—99; bd. dirs. Ctr. for Victims of Torture. Med. officer USNR, 1954—57. Recipient E. Mead-Johnson award, Am. Acad. Pediat., 1971, Shotwell award, Hennipen Med. Soc., 2001; fellow Guggenheim, 1971—72, Alexander von Humboldt, 1986; scholar John and Mary R. Markle, 1960—65. Mem.: Eliz Glaser Pediat. AIDS Found., Minn. Acad. Medicine (pres. 1993—94), Assn. Am. Physicians, Am. Acad. Pediat., Minn. Acad. Pediat., Am. Soc. Clin. Investigation, Am. Pediatric Soc. (coun. 1976—83, pres. 1987—88), Soc. Pediatric Rsch., Infectious Diseases Soc. Am. (coun. 1977—82, pres. 1985, Bristol award 1994), Am. Soc. Microbiology, Am. Fedn. Clin. Rsch., Minn. Med. Found. (pres. 1986—88), N.W. Pediat. Soc., Inst. Medicine of NAS. Achievements include research in function of human leukocytes and international medical education and research. Home: 2154 Commonwealth Ave Saint Paul MN 55108-1717 Office: PO Box 293 Minneapolis MN 55440-0293 E-mail: quiex001@umn.edu.

QUIGG, CHRIS, physicist; b. Bainbridge, Md., Dec. 15, 1944; s. John Mitchell and Geneva Anne (Zimny) Q.; m. Elizabeth Kelley, Sept 2, 1967; children: David Michael, Katherine Kelley. BS in Physics, Yale U., 1966; PhD in Physics, U. Calif., Berkeley, 1970. From rsch. assoc. to assoc. prof. SUNY, Stony Brook, 1970-74; physicist Fermi Nat. Accelerator Lab., Batavia, Ill., 1974—. Editor: Annual Review of Nuclear & Particle Science, 1994--. Rsch. fellow, Alfred P. Sloan Found., 1974-78; named scholar-in-residence, Rockefeller Found., Bellagio, Italy, 1990. Fellow Am. Phys. Soc., AAAS. Office: Fermi Nat Accelerator Lab PO Box 500 Batavia IL 60510-0500 E-mail: quigg@fnal.gov.

QUIGLEY, HERBERT JOSEPH, JR. pathologist, educator; b. Phila., Mar. 6, 1937; s. Herbert Joseph and Mary Kathleen (Carney) G.; m. Jacqueline Jean Stocksdale, Nov. 28, 1965 (div. 1974); 1 child, Amelia Anne. BS in Chemistry, Franklin and Marshall Coll., 1958; MD, U. Pa., 1962. Diplomate Am. Bd. Pathology. Intern Presbyterias Hosp., NYC, 1962—66, resident, 1962—66; chief pathology Monroe County Hosp., Key West, Fla., 1966-68; from asst. prof. to assoc. prof. pathology Creighton U., Omaha, 1968-72, prof., 1972—; chief pathology svc. VA Med. Cr., 1968-88. Bd. dirs. Triton-Chito Inc., Omaha. Contbr. articles to profl. jours.; patentee in field. Bd. dirs., former pres., chmn. Nebr. Assn. Earth Sci. Clubs, Omaha, 1972—. Lt. comdr. USNR, 1966-68. Recipient career devel. award NIH, 1962-66, Borden prize for med. rsch. Borden Co., Inc., 1962; fellow NIH, Nat. Cancer Inst., 1958-62. Fellow Coll. Am. Pathologists, Am. Soc. Clin. Pathologists, Am. Inst. Chemists; mem. Nebr. Assn. Pathologists, N.Y. Acad. Scis. Republican. Roman Catholic. Avocations: paleontology, geology. Home: 9511 Mockingbird Dr Omaha NE 68127-2423 Office: VA Med Center 4101 Woolworth Ave Omaha NE 68105-1850

QUIGLEY, JEROME HAROLD, management consultant; b. Green Bay, Wis., Apr. 19, 1925; s. Harold D. and Mabel (Hansen) Q.; m. Lorraine A. Rocheleau, May 3, 1947; children: Kathy, Ross, Michael, Daniel, Mary Beth, Andrew, Maureen. BS, St. Norbert Coll., 1951. Pers. adminstr. Gen. Motors Corp., 1959-64; dir. indsl. rels. Raytheon Co., Santa Barbara, Calif., 1964-67; dir. pers. U. Calif., 1967-72; corp. dir. indsl. rels. Gen. Rsch. Corp., 1972-73; dir. indsl. rels. ISS Sperry Univac, 1973-75; corp. dir. indsl. rels. Four-Phase Systems, Inc., Cupertino, Calif., 1975; sr. v.p. human resources UNC, Annapolis, Md., 1975-86; pres. Profl. Guidance Assocs., Inc., 1986—. Aviator with USN, 1943-47. Mem. Am. Electronics Assn., Assn. Former Intelligence Officers, Scottsdale Civilian Police Acad., Machinery and Allied Products Inst., Assn. Naval Aviation, Tailhook Assn., Ariz. County Attys. and Sheriffs Assn., Marines' Meml. Assn., Ret. Officers Assn., AVCAD/NAVCAD Assn., Navy Aviation Mus. Found., Navy League, The Mist Spa and Tennis Club. Republican. Roman Catholic. Office: Profl Guidance Assocs Inc 7789 E Joshua Tree Ln Scottsdale AZ 85250-7962 E-mail: jerryq@gobi.com.

QUIGLEY, JOHN BERNARD, law educator; b. St. Louis, Oct. 1, 1940; s. John Bernard and Ruth Rosina (Schieber) Q. BA, Harvard U., 1962, MA, LLB, 1966. Bar: Ohio 1973, Mass. 1967, U.S. Dist. Ct. (so. dist.) Ohio 1976, U.S. Ct. Appeals (6th cir.) 1986, U.S. Supreme Ct. 1989. Research assoc. Harvard U. Law Sch., Cambridge, Mass., 1967-69; prof. law Ohio State U., Columbus, 1969—. Author: Basic Laws on the Structure of the Soviet State, 1969, The Soviet Foreign Trade Monopoly, 1974, Palestine and Israel: A Challenge to Justice, 1990, The Ruses for War: American Interventionism since World War II, 1992, Flight into the Maelstrom: Soviet Immigration to Israel and Middle East Peace, 1997, Genocide in Cambodia, 2000. Mem. Nat. Lawyers Guild (v.p. 1977-79), Am. Soc. Internat. Law, AAUP. Avocations: tennis, speed skating, violin. Office: Ohio State U Coll of Law Coll of Law 55 W 12th Ave Columbus OH 43210-1338

QUIGLEY, JOHN MICHAEL, economist, educator; b. N.Y.C., Feb. 12, 1942; BS with distinction, U.S. Air Force Acad., 1964; MSc with honors, U. Stockholm, Sweden, 1965; AM, Harvard U., 1971, PhD, 1972. Commd. 2d lt. USAF, 1964, advanced through grades to capt., 1968; asst. prof. econs. Yale U., 1972-74, assoc. prof., 1974-81; prof. pub. policy U. Calif., Berkeley, 1979—, prof. econs., 1981—, Chancellor's prof., 1997—, I. Donald Terner prof., 1999—, chmn. dept. econs., 1992-95; vis. prof. econs. and stats. U. Gothenberg, 1978. Cons. numerous govt. agys. and pvt. firms; econometrician Hdqrs. U.S. Air Force, Pentagon, 1965-68; research assoc. Nat. Bur. Econ. Research, N.Y.C., 1968-78; mem. com. on nat. urban policy NAS, 1985-93. Author, editor, contbr. articles to profl. jours.; editor in chief Reg. Sci. and Urban Econs., 1987—; mem. editl. bd. many sci. and sholarly jours. Fulbright scholar, 1964-65; fellow NSF, 1968-69, Woodrow Wilson, 1968-71, Harvard IBM, 1969-71, NDEA, 1969-71, Thord-Gray Am. Scandinavian Found. 1971-72, Social Sci. Research Council, 1971-72. Mem. Am. Econ. Assn., Econometric Soc., Regional Sci. Assn. (bd. dirs. 1986—), Nat. Tax Assn., Assn. for Pub. Policy and Mgmt. (bd. dirs. 1986-89, v.p. 1987-89), Am. Real Estate and Urban Econs. Assn. (bd. dirs. 1987-2001, pres. 1995-97). Home: 875 Hilldale Ave Berkeley CA 94708-1319 Office: U Calif 2607 Hearst Ave Berkeley CA 94720-7305 E-mail: quigley@econ.berkeley.edu.

QUIGLEY, KEVIN FRANCIS FLAHERTY, nonprofit organization executive; b. N.Y.C., Dec. 3, 1952; s. Martin S. and Katherine D. Quigley; m. Susan L.Q. Flaherty, Nov. 1, 1986. BA, Swarthmore Coll., 1974; MA, Nat. U. Ireland, Dublin, 1975; MIA, Columbia U., N.Y.C., 1981; PhD, Georgetown U., 1995. Budget examiner Office of Mgmt. and Budget, Office of Pres. of U.S., Washington, 1981-86; legis. dir. for Senator John Heinz U.S. Senate, 1986-89; dir. policy programs Pew Charitable Trusts, Phila., 1989-95; guest scholar Woodrow Wilson Ctr., Washington, 1995-97; v.p. Asia Soc., N.Y.C., 1997-99; exec. dir. Global Alliance for Workers and Cmtys., Balt., 1999—2001; counselor Ctr. for Global Devel., Washington, 2002—. Co-author: The Allies and East-West Conflict, 1989; author: For Democracy's Sake, 1997. Vice chmn. Inst. for Sustainable Cmtys., Burlington, Vt., 1999—, Adv. Com. on Fgn. Voluntary Aid, Washington, 1990-94. Mem. Coun. on Fgn. Rels. Home: Apt 910 1600 N Oak St Arlington VA 22209-2755 E-mail: kffquigley@juno.com.

QUIGLEY, LEONARD VINCENT, lawyer; b. Kansas City, Mo., June 21, 1933; s. Joseph Vincent and Rosemary (Cannon) Q.; m. Lynn Mathis Pfohl, May 23, 1964; children: Leonard Matthew, Cannon Louise, Daniel Pfohl, Megan Mathis. AB, Coll. Holy Cross, 1953; LL.B. magna cum laude, Harvard U., 1959; LL.M. in Internat. Law, NYU, 1962. Bar: N.Y. 1960. Assoc. Cravath, Swaine & Moore, N.Y.C., 1959-67; ptnr. Paul, Weiss, Rifkind, Wharton & Garrison, 1968—; gen. counsel Archaeol. Inst. Am., Boston. Served to lt. USN, 1953-56. Mem. ABA, Can. Bar Assn., N.Y. State Bar, Coun. Fgn. Rels., Assn. Bar City N.Y., Harvard Club (N.Y.C.), West Side Tennis Club (Forest Hills, N.Y.). E-mail: lquigley@paulweiss.com.

QUIGLEY, MARTIN SCHOFIELD, publishing company executive, educator; b. Chgo., Nov. 24, 1917; s. Martin Joseph and Gertrude Margaret (Schofield) Q.; m. Katherine J. Dunphy, July 2, 1946; children: Martin, Elin, William, Kevin, Karen, Patricia, John, Mary Katherine, Peter. AB magna cum laude, Georgetown U., 1939; MA, Columbia U., 1973, EdD, 1975. Reporter Motion Picture Herald, N.Y.C. and Hollywood, Calif., 1939-41; with overseas br. OWI, 1942; secret war work U.S. Govt., 1943-45; various editl. and mgmt. posts Quigley Pub. Co., Inc., N.Y.C., 1946—2001, pres., 1964-2001, chmn., 2001—; staff, dept. higher and adult edn. Tchrs. Coll., 1974-75; prof. higher edn. grad. courses Baruch Coll. CUNY, 1977-89; prof. higher edn. grad. courses Tchrs. Coll. Columbia U., 1979-80, 90; prof. higher edn. grad. courses Seton Hall U., 1981-82. Pres. QWS, Inc., 1975-80; ednl. cons.; cons. supt. schs. N.Y. Archdiocese, 1962-70 Author: Great Gaels, 1944, 2d edit. 1997, Roman Notes, 1946, Magic Shadows--the story of the origin of motion pictures, 1948, Government Relations of Five Universities in Washington, D.C., 1975, Peace Without Hiroshima-Secret Action at the Vatican in Spring of 1945, 1991, First Century of Film, 1995, A U.S. Spy in Ireland, 1999, Community College Movement in Transition, 2002; co-author: Catholic Action in Practice, 1962, Films in America, 1969; editor: New Screen Techniques, 1953. Pres. N.Y. Christian Family Movement, 1960-62, mem. nat. exec. com., 1960-65; founder, chmn. N.Y. Ind. Schs. Opportunity Project, 1965-77; pres. Found. Internat. Coop., 1960-65; bd. dirs. Will Rogers Inst., Motion Picture Pioneers; treas. Religious Edn. Assn. U.S. and Can., 1975-81, chmn., 1981-84; trustee Village of Larchmont, N.Y., 1977-79, mayor, 1980-84; mem. Laymen's Nat. Bible Assn., 1981—; trustee Am. Bible Soc., 1984—; bd. dirs. William J. Donovan Meml. Found., 1994-2001. Mem.: Larchmont Yacht. Roman Catholic. Home: 8 Pheasant Run Larchmont NY 10538-3423

QUIGLEY, PHILIP J. retired telecommunications industry executive; b. 1943; With Advanced Mobile Phone Svc. Inc., 1982-84, v.p., gen. mgr., Pacific region; with Pac Tel Mobile Access, 1984-86, pres., chief exec. officer; with Pac Tel Personal Communications, 1986-87, pres., chief exec. officer; exec. v.p., chief oper. officer Pac Tel Corp., 1987; ret. chmn., pres., chief exec. officer Pacific Telesis Group, San Francisco, 1997—; pres. Pacific Bell, 1987-94; bd. dirs. SRI Internat., Menlo Park, Calif., 1998—. Address: 2241 Forest View Ave Hillsborough CA 94010-6166

QUIGLEY, ROBERT CHARLES, insurance industry consultant; b. Phila., Feb. 2, 1949; s. James and Kathrine Regina (Kinckiner) Q.; m. Barbara Jeanne Browne, Apr. 17, 1971; children: Robert J., Michael J., Brian A., Jason T. BS in Acctg., Pa. State U., 1970. CPA, Pa. Sr. acct. Touche Ross & Co., Phila., 1970-72; dir. acctg. policy and rsch. Ins. Co. of N.Am., 1972-81; asst. treas. Reliance Ins. Co., 1981-85; v.p., treas. Mutual Fire Marine and Inland Ins. Co., 1985-86; owner Quigley & Assocs., Hatboro, Pa., 1987—. Team leader accreditation Nat. Assn. of Ins. Commrs., Kansas City, 1992—. Author: (with others) Property and Liability Insurance Accounting, 5th edit., 1991. With USMCR, 1967. Mem. AICPA, Soc. of Ins. Fin. Mgmt., Am. Arbitration Assn. (panelist 1987—). Republican. Presbyterian. Avocations: family, reading, writing. Office: PO Box 147 Hatboro PA 19040-0147 E-mail: RCQCPA@aol.com.

QUIGLEY, SCOTT PHILIP, investment banker; b. Whittier, Calif., Feb. 6, 1969; s. Philip John Quigley and Juliet Garibay Trueblood; m. Martha Munoz Quigley, Jan. 31, 1998. BA, UCLA, 1991; MBA, U. Mich., 1995. CPA, Calif. Sr. acct. Deloitte & Touche, San Francisco, 1991-93; investment banker, v.p. Bear, Stearns & Co., Inc., N.Y.C., 1995-99; investment banker, prin. Murphy Noell Capital, L.A., 1999—. Republican. Roman Catholic.

QUIGLEY, STEPHEN HOWARD, executive editor; b. Boston, May 29, 1951; s. John Joseph Sr. and Anne Margaret (O'Brien) Quigley; m. Suzanne Elizabeth Daley, July 21, 1980; children: Benjamin Parker, Theodore Hunter, Margaret Hunter. BA in French and Internat. Rels., Dartmouth Coll., 1973. Sales rep. Addison-Wesley Pub. Co., Inc., Reading, Mass., 1973-75, math. editor, 1975-81, regional sales mgr., 1981-85; sr. math. editor Scott, Foresman and Co., Chgo., 1985-88, PWS-KENT Pub. Co., Boston, 1988-95; exec. editor math. and stats. sci., tech. and med. pub. div. John Wiley and Sons, Inc., Marblehead, 1995—. Mem. Independence Day Celebration Commn., 1987—88; mem. Eveleth Sch. liaison Sch. PTA, Marblehead, Mass., 1989—90, vice chair sch. com., 1991—92, chair sch. comm., 1992—93; water safety chmn., bd. dirs. Greater Lynn chpt. ARC, 1978—81; leader Boy Scouts Am., Explorers Group, Marblehead, 1976—79; swim ofcl. Ill. High Sch. Ofcls. Assn., 1984—88; lector Star of Sea Ch., Marblehead, 1988—; dir. Goldthwait Reservation; vol. Marblehead Little Theatre, 2001—. Recipient Club of Yr. award, Darmouth Coll., 1988, Disting. Book award, Assn. Am. Publ., 2001. Mem.: ASCD, Nat. Coun. Tchrs. Math., Nat. Fedn. Interscholastic Ofcls. Assn., Am. Math. Assn. Two-Yr. Colls., Am. Statis. Assn., Math. Assn. Am., Am. Math. Soc., Friends of the Performing Arts, North Shore Friends in Pub. (founding group), Glenview C. of C. (mem. accreditation team 1988), Chgo. Dartmouth Club (pres. 1988—89), North Shore (Mass.) Dartmouth Club, Corinthian Yacht Club (rec. chair, operating com. 1997—2000), Rotary (bd. dirs. Boston 1990—95, Svc. award 1988). Republican. Roman Catholic. Avocations: swimming, sailing, skiing, tennis. Home: 10 Leicester Rd Marblehead MA 01945-1817 Office: 2 Hooper St Marblehead MA 01945-3431 Office Fax: 781-631-0271. Business E-Mail: squigley@wiley.com.

QUIGNEY, THERESA ANN, special education educator; b. East Cleveland, Ohio, June 19, 1952; d. James and Lenora Mary (McDonald) Q.; m. Joseph Carl Lang, July 23, 1983. BA, Notre Dame Coll., 1974; MEd, Cleve. State U., 1980; PhD, Kent State U., 1992. Cert. tchr. handicapped K-12; cert. ednl. adminstrv. specialist edn. of exceptional pupils; cert. ednl. supr.; cert. elem. prin.; cert. h.s. prin. cert. tchr. French K-12, Ohio. Spl. edn. tchr. Newbury (Ohio) Local Schs., 1974—80; county supr., specific learning disabilities and behavior handicaps Geauga County Bd. Edn., Chardon, 1980—86, 1987—88; asst. prof. spl. edn. West Chester (Pa.) U., 1992—93; asst. prof. edn. Heidelberg Coll., Tiffin, Ohio, 1993—94; assoc. prof. spl. edn. Cleve. State U.,

1994—. Spl. edn. program coord. Coll. of Edn. Cleve. State U., 2000—02; ednl. rschr. Contbr. articles to profl. jours. Vol. cons. Tchrs. for Action Rsch. South Euclid/Lyndhurst (Ohio) Sch. Dist., 1996—; past participant issues task force Ohio Coun. for Exceptional Children; past bd. mem. Camp Sue Osborne, Lake County; mem. steering com. State Improvement Grant (Edn.), 2000—. Grantee Ohio State Supt.'s Task Force on Spl. Edn., 1997, Cleve. State U. Coll. Edn., 1997, Am. Sch. Counselor's Assn.; recipient achievement recognition Assn. for Children and Adults with Learning Disabilities, Ohio, 1980. Mem. CEC, ASCD, Am. Ednl. Rsch. Assn., Learning Disabilities Assn., Mid-We. Ednl. Rsch. Assn., Coun. for Learning Disabilities, Kappa Delta Pi, Phi Delta Kappa, Pi Lambda Theta (vol. cons. Gamma Epsilon chpt. 1996—). Avocations: travel, writing, reading, sketching. Office: Cleveland State Univ Euclid Ave at E 24th St Cleveland OH 44115 E-mail: t.quigney@csuohio.edu.

QUIJADA, ANGÉLICA MARIA, elementary education educator; b. Tijuana, Mex., Mar. 22, 1963; came to U.S., 1967; d. Juan José Quijada and Paula (Magallanes) Garcia. AA, L.A. Harbor Coll., Wilmington, Calif., 1985; BA, Calif. State U., Carson, 1990, MA, 1993. Tchr. asst., tutor L.A. Harbor Coll., 1982-85; elem. tchr. asst., tutor Ambler Avenue Sch., Carson, 1985-90; bilingual elem. tchr. Hooper Avenue Sch., L.A., 1991—; mentor tchr. Hooper Avenue Elem. Sch., 1997—, mem. coordinated compliance rev. team, 1998. Jefferson cluster tchr. trainer dist. stds. L.A. Unified Sch. Dist., 1996—, tchr. trainer early literacy, 1997—; stakeholder Instrnl. Transformation Team, 1995-96; mem. pupil quality rev. team, 1995-96; co-chair local sch. leadership coun., 1998; mentor Latino Tchr. Project, U. So. Calif., 1993—. Counselor Pathfinders, Carson Seventh Day Adventist Ch., 1980; treas. Carson Spanish Seventh-Day Adventist Ch., 1994; pianist Harbor City Seventh Day Adventist Ch., 1995-96; mem. ednl. com. Lynwood Seventh Day Adventist Ch., 1999. Mem. TESOL, United Tchrs. L.A. (co-chmn. 1994, chpt. chmn. 1995-98). Democrat. Avocations: playing piano, photography, reading, playing softball, drawing. Home: 320 E 181st St Carson CA 90746-1815 E-mail: angieq@earthlink.net.

QUILLEN, CECIL DYER, JR. lawyer, consultant; b. Kingsport, Tenn., Jan. 21, 1937; s. Cecil D. and Mary Louise (Carter) Q.; m. Vicey Ann Childress, Apr. 1, 1961; children: Cecil D. III, Ann C. BS, Va. Poly. Inst., 1958; LLB, U. Va., 1962. Bar: Va. 1962, N.Y. 1963, Tenn. 1974. Atty. patent dept. Eastman Kodak Co., Rochester, N.Y., 1962-65; atty. patent sect. Tenn. Eastman Co. (divsn. Eastman Kodak), Kingsport, 1965-69, mgr. patent sect., 1969-72, mgr. licensing, 1972-74, sec. and asst. chief counsel, 1974-76, v.p., chief counsel, 1983-85; dir. patent litigation Eastman Kodak, 1976-82, dir. antitrust litigation, 1978-82, v.p., assoc. gen. counsel, 1986, sr. v.p., gen. counsel, dir., 1986-92; sr. adv. Putnam, Hayes, Bartlett and PHB Hagler Bailly, Washington, 1992-99; sr. advisor Cornerstone Rsch., 2000—. Mem. ABA, Va. State Bar, Am. Intellectual Property Law Assn., Va. Poly. Inst. Com. of 100, Assn. Gen. Counsel. E-mail: cquillen@cornerstone.com.

QUILLEN, CECIL DYER, III, lawyer; b. Rochester, N.Y., Aug. 15, 1963; s. Cecil Dyer, Jr. and Vicey Ann (Childress) Q.; m. Mary Stuart Humes, Oct. 20, 1990; children: Caroline, James C.D. AB magna cum laude, Harvard U., 1985; JD, U. Va., 1988. Bar: N.Y. 1989, D.C. 1991, U.S. Ct. Appeals (4th cir.) 1989. Law clk., Sr. Cir. Judge U.S. Ct. Appeals (4th cir.), Richmond, Va., 1988-89; assoc. Sullivan & Cromwell, N.Y.C., 1989-95, Linklaters, N.Y.C., 1995-96, ptnr., 1996—, ptnr. London office, 2000—. Spkr. various profl. confs. Notes editor Va. Law Rev., 1987-88. Mem. ABA, N.Y. State Bar Assn., Assn. Bar City of N.Y., Raven Soc., Order of Coif, Phi Beta Kappa. Office: Linklaters One Silk St London EC2Y 8HQ England

QUILLEN, LLOYD DOUGLAS, oil and gas executive; b. Red House, Ky., Sept. 9, 1943; s. Carter Livingston and Irene (Bolson) Q.; m. Leslie J. Johnsen (div. Jan. 1980); children: Tracey, David; m. Debra Gale Wagner, Aug. 7, 1982; children: Justin, Meghan, Bradley. BA, U. Ky., 1965, JD, 1969; student, Emory U., 1966-67. Bar: Ky., 1970, Tex., 1986. Atty. Phillips Petroleum Co., Denver, 1970-76; mgr. real estate and claims Phillips Petroleum Co. Euro. Afr., London, 1976-79; dir. govt. and comml. affairs Phillips Petroleum Co. & Subs., Lagos, Nigeria, 1979-82; mgr. internat. gas devel. Phillips Petroleum Co., Bartlesville, Okla., 1982-84; dir. laws and regulations Phillips 66 Natural Gas Co., 1984-88; mgr. bus. devel. and mktg. HUFFCO/VICO Indonesia Co., Jakarta, Indonesia, 1988-93; v.p. Lng Texaco Natural Gas Internat., 1997; sr. v.p. Texaco Global Gas and Power, 1997—2001; sr. LNG comml. advisor Chevron Texaco, 2002—. Cons. Govt. of Nigeria, Lagos, 1977-82; gas cons. LNG/Internat. Gas, Houston, 1993-97. Charter mem. Statue of Liberty Ellis Island Found., N.Y.C., 1983; pro bono counsel Landmark Preservation Coun., Bartlesville, 1986-87, Washington County Sr. Citizens, Inc., Bartlesville, 1987—, Pro Bono Coll. Tex. Bar, 1997-2000; cubmaster Boy Scouts Am. 1987—. Recipient Speak Out award Am. Petroleum Inst., 1972; named to hon. order Ky. Cols., 1969. Mem. Ky. Bar Assn., Tex. Bar Assn., Houston Vols. Lawyers Assn. Republican. Avocations: woodworking, gardening, sailing, scuba diving, travel. E-mail: dougquillen@netscape.net.

QUILLEN, WILLIAM TATEM, retired judge, lawyer, educator; b. Camden, N.J., Jan. 15, 1935; s. Robert James and Gladys Collings (Tatem) Quillen; m. Marcia Everhart Stirling, June 27, 1959; children: Carol Everhart, Tracey Tatem. BA, Williams Coll., 1956; LLB, Harvard U., 1959; LLM, U. Va., 1982; LLD (hon.), Widener U., 2002. Bar: Del. 1959. Assoc. Richards, Layton & Finger, Wilmington, Del., 1963—64; adminstrv. asst. to Gov. of Del., 1965; assoc. judge Superior Ct. of Del., 1966—73; chancellor State of Del., 1973—76; sr. v.p. Wilmington Trust Co., 1976—78; justice Supreme Ct. of Del., 1978—83; ptnr. Potter Anderson & Corroon, Wilmington, 1983—86; gen. counsel, v.p. Howard Hughes Med. Inst., 1986—91; sec. of state State of Del., Dover, 1993—94; assoc. judge Superior Ct. Del., Wilmington, 1994—2000. Mem. adj. faculty Widener U. Sch. Law, Wilmington, 1976—83, 1985—86, 1995—2000, disting. vis. prof. law, 1992—94, 2001—02. Trustee Widener U., 1979—91; Dem. candidate for gov. Del., 1984. With JAGC USAF, 1959—62. Mem.: ABA, Del. State Bar Assn., Wilmington Club, Phi Beta Kappa. Democrat. Presbyterian.

QUILLIAN, HENRY MILTON, III, lawyer; b. Atlanta, Nov. 16, 1962; s. Henry Milton Quillian Jr. and Crystal Evelyn (McRae) Allen; m. Celia Dean Patrick, June 22, 1985; children: Celia Elizabeth, Henry Milton IV. BSE, Duke U., 1985; JD, U. Ga., 1988. Bar: Ga. 1988, D.C. 1989, U.S. Patent and Trademark Office 1993, U.S. Supreme Ct. 1997. Atty. Smith, Gambrell & Russell, Atlanta, 1988-96; ptnr. Fellows, Johnson & LaBriola, LLP, 1996—. Author: Managing Construction Contracts, 1992; contbr. articles to mags. Elder, N.W. Presbyn. Ch., Atlanta, 1992—; coach Peachtree Rd. Meth. Ch., Atlanta, 1998-2000, Northside Youth Orgn., 2000. Mem ASME (Arthur L. Williston award 1985), Fed. Bar Assn. (pres. Atlanta chpt. 1995-96, chair nat. younger lawyers divsn. 1998-99, nat. exec. com. 1998-99, chair resolutions com. 2000-01), Atlanta Bar Assn. (constrn. sect. bd., sec. 2002—), Atlanta Lawyers Club, Constrn. Mgmt. Assn. Am. (bd. mem. South Atlantic chpt.). Avocations: inventing, investing, skiing, coaching, cars. Office: Fellows Johnson & LaBriola LLP 225 Peachtree St NE Ste 2300 Atlanta GA 30303-1731 E-mail: hquillian@fjl-law.com.

QUILLIAN, WARREN WILSON, II, pediatrician, educator; b. Miami, Fla., Jan. 21, 1936; s. Warren Wilson and Rosabel (Brown) Q.; m. Sallie Ruth Creel, July 26, 1958; children: Rutledge, Ruth, Warren C., Frances. MD, Emory U., 1961. Diplomate Am. Bd. Pediat. (examiner 1966—, bd. dirs. 1974-80, 1992-98, treas. 1978, v.p. 1979, pres. 1980). Intern in pediatrics Vandertilt U., Nashville, 1961-62; resident Children's Hosp. Med. Ctr., Harvard U., Boston, 1962-63; chief resident Grady Meml. Hosp., Emory U., Atlanta, 1963-64; pvt. practice, Coral Gables, Fla., 1966. Instr., asst. clin. prof., assoc. clin. prof., now clin. prof. pediat. U. Miami Med. Sch., 1966—; active staff, bd. dirs. Miami Children's Hosp.; active staff Jackson Meml. Hosp.; chief pediat. Doctors' Hosp.; mem. courtesy staff Mercy Hosp., Bapt. Hosp., South Miami Hosp.; chmn. health adv. com. Dade County Schs.; bd. dirs., v.p. Am. Bd. Pediat. Found., 1991-98; mem. adv. bd. McGlannon Sch.; cons. Fla. Div. Med. Svcs.; bd. dirs. Bank Coral Gables. Contbr. articles to med. jours. Hon. bd. dirs. Soc. for Abused Children of Children's Home Soc., Miami, 1980-84; mem. Coral Gables Code Enforcement Bd., 1986-88; team-sch. physician Coral Gables Sr. H.G., 1980-88; bd. dirs. Dade County March of Dimes, Miami, 1968-72; bd. advisors Dade County Assn. Retarded Children, 1968-76; trustee Emory U., 1991-97; mem. coun. ministries, youth coord., mem. fin. com., Sunday sch. tchr. United Meth. Ch. Coral Gables, 1966—; chair parrish rels. com.; mem. bd. advisors The Growing Place; mem. Citizens Bd. U. Miami, 1997—; v.p. Good Hope Equestrian Tng. Ctr. for Retarded, 1999—. Capt. M.C., U.S. Army, 1964-66. Recipient citation of merit Emory U., 1980, alumni commendation Miami Children's Hosp., 1983, Teaching award U. Miami Sch. Medicine, 1995, Winston Churchhill medal, 1999; named CGHS Athletic Hall of Fame, 1996, Wisdom Hall of Fame, 1998. Fellow Am. Acad. Pediat.; mem. AMA, Fla. Med. Assn. (sch. health com.), Fla. Pediat. Soc. (past chmn. sch. health com.), So. Med. Assn., Dade County Med. Assn. (sch. health com., continuing edn. com.), Empirical Soc. (past pres.), Soc. for Pediat. Rsch., So. Perinatal Soc., Greater Miami Pediat. Soc. (past pres., chmn. legis. and sch. health com.), Miami Med. Forum (past pres., Haverfield Cup 1985, Mansfield Trophy 1983, 88, 98), Sr. Soc. Emory U., Biscayne Bay Yacht Club (vice commodore, bd. govs.), DVS Sr. Honor Soc., Alpha Omega Alpha, Omicron Delta Kappa, Alpha Epsilon Upsilon, Phi Delta Theta. Democrat. Avocations: fishing, golf, boating. Office: 305 Granello Ave Coral Gables FL 33146-1806

QUILLIAN, WILLIAM FLETCHER, JR. retired banker, former college president; b. Nashville, Apr. 13, 1913; s. William Fletcher and Nonie (Acree) Q.; m. Margaret Hannah Weigle, June 15, 1940; children— William Fletcher III, Anne Acree, Katherine, Robert. AB, Emory U., 1935, Litt.D. (hon.), 1959; B.D., Yale, 1938, PhD, 1943; postgrad., U. Edinburgh, 1938-39, U. Basel, 1939; Day fellow from, Yale, 1938-39; Rosenwald fellow, 1940-41; LL.D., Ohio Wesleyan U., 1952, Hampden-Sydney Coll., 1978, Randolph-Macon Coll., 1967; D.H.L., Randolph-Macon Woman's Coll., 1978. Ordained to ministry Meth. Ch., 1942. Student asst. Stamford (Conn.) Presbyn Ch., 1936-38; del. Gen. Com. of World Student Christian Fedn., Bievres, France, 1938; discussion leader World Conf. Christian Youth, Amsterdam, Holland, 1939; pastor Clarendon (Vt.) Community Ch., summer 1940; asst. prof. philosophy Gettysburg Coll., 1941-43, prof., 1943-45; prof. philosophy Ohio Wesleyan U., 1945-52; pres. Randolph Macon Woman's Coll., 1952-78, pres. emeritus, 1978—; sr. v.p. Central Fidelity Bank, 1978-88; exec. dir. Greater Lynchburg (Va.) Community Trust, 1988-97; v.p., bd. dirs. Pride of Virginia Meats, Inc. Tchr. Garrett Biblical Inst., summer 1951. Author: The Moral Theory of Evolutionary Naturalism, 1945, Evolution and Moral Theory in America, Evolutionary Thought in America, 1950; Contbr. articles to philos. and religious jours. Pres. bd. dirs. United Way Cen. Va., campaign chmn., 1987; bd. dirs. Alpha Tau Omega Found., Lynchburg Gen. Hosp.; hon. life trustee Va. Found. Ind. Colls., pres., 1958-61. Mem. Assn. Va. Colls. (past pres.), So. U. Conf. (pres. 1967-68), So. Assn. Colls. for Women (pres. 1956), Nat. Assn. United Methodist Colls. and Univs. (pres. 1973), Am. Philos. Assn., Soc. for Values in Higher Edn. (mem. central com. 1945-48, chmn. 1947-48), Nat. Assn. Bibl. Instrs., AAUP, Greater Lynchburg C. of C. (dir. pres. 1979-80), Phi Beta Kappa., Omicron Delta Kappa, Alpha Tau Omega (dir. found.) Home: 501 Ves Rd Lynchburg VA 24503-2503

QUILLIGAN, EDWARD JAMES, obstetrician, gynecologist, educator; b. Cleve., June 18, 1925; s. James Joseph and Maude Elvira (Ryan) Q.; m. Betty Jane Cleaton, Dec. 14, 1946; children: Bruce, Jay, Carol, Christopher, Linda, Ted. BA, MD, Ohio State U., 1951; MA (hon.), Yale, 1967. Intern Ohio State U. Hosp., 1951-52, resident, 1952-54, Western Res. U. Hosps., 1954-56; asst. prof. obstetrics and gynecology Western Res. U., 1957-63, prof., 1963-65; prof. obstetrics and gynecology UCLA, 1965-66; prof., chmn. dept. Ob-Gyn Yale U., 1966-69, U. So. Calif., 1969-78, asso. v.p. med. affairs, 1978-79; prof. Ob-Gyn. U. Calif., Irvine, 1980-83, vice chancellor health affairs, dean Sch. Medicine, 1987-89; prof., chmn. ob.-gyn. dept. U. Wis., 1983-85; prof., chmn. Ob-Gyn Davis Med. Ctr. U. Calif., Sacramento, 1985-87, vice chancellor Health Scis., dean Coll. Med. Irvine, 1987-89, prof. ob-gyn, 1987-94, prof. emeritus ob-gyn., 1994; exec. dir. med. edn. Long Beach (Calif.) Meml. Health Svcs., 1995—. Contbr. articles to med. jours.; co-editor-in-chief: Am. Jour. Obstetrics and Gynecology. Served to 2d lt. AUS, 1944-46. Recipient Centennial award Ohio State U., 1970 Mem. Soc. Gynecologic Investigation, Am. Gynecol. Soc., Am. Coll. Obstetics and Gynecology, Sigma Xi. Home: 24 Urey Ct Irvine CA 92612-4077 E-mail: equilligan@home.com.

QUILLING, MICHAEL GENE, music educator, protective services official; b. Denver, Oct. 9, 1959; s. Vernie Gene and Helen Teresa Quilling; m. Rosanna Flores, July 17, 1982; children: Lance, Bradley. Bachelor's in Music Edn., We. Tex. State U., 1982. Cert. tchr. Tex., Kans., law enforcement Kans. Instrumental music educator Unified Sch. Dist. #457, Garden City, Kans., 1982—89; law enforcement officer Garden City Police Dept., 1989—91; instrumental music educator Unified Sch. Dist. #352, Goodland, 1991—99; law enforcement officer Goodland Police Dept., 1992—99; instrumental music educator Unified Sch. Dist. #363, Holcomb, 1999—. Dir.: N.W. Kans. League Honor Band, 1998, Ea. Colo. League Honor Band, 1998. Euphonium player Garden City Mcpl. Band, 1983—88, dir., 1988—89; trombone player Kans. Flatland Big Band, Colby, 1991—2002. Recipient Outstanding Tchr. award, Goodland Nat. Educators Assn., 1996. Mem.: Kans. Bandmasters Assn. (N.W. dist. rep. 1996—99), Kans. Music Educators Assn. (S.W. dist. pres. 2001—02), Phi Beta Mu. Conservative. Avocations: fishing, camping, jazz. Home: 405 Scotty Ln Holcomb KS 67851 Office: Unified Sch Dist # 363 600 N Jones Box 38 Holcomb KS 67851 Office Fax: 620-277-0240. Personal E-mail: quilling@pld.com. E-mail: mquillin@pld.com.

QUIMBY, FRED WILLIAM, pathology educator, veterinarian; b. Providence, Sept. 19, 1945; s. Edward Harold and Isabel (Barber) Q.; m. Cynthia Claire Connelly, Aug. 21, 1965; children: Kelly Ann, Cynthia Jane. VMD, U. Pa., 1970, PhD, 1974. Diplomate Am. Coll. Lab. Animal Medicine. Hematology fellow New Eng. Med. Ctr., Boston, 1974-75, instr. pathology, 1975-76, asst. prof., 1976-79; assoc. prof. pathology Cornell Med. Coll., N.Y.C., 1979-92, prof. pathology, 1993-2000. Dir. lab. animal medicine Tufts-New Eng. Med. Ctr., Boston, 1975—79; dir. Ctr. Rsch. Animal Resources Cornell U., Ithaca, 1979—2001; assoc. v.p., sr. dir., Lab. Animal Rsch. Ctr. Rockefeller U., 2001—. Editor Animal Welfare, 1992, Lab. Animal Sci., 1992-93, consulting editor, 1993-95; editor: Clinical Chemistry of Laboratory Animals, 2d edit., 1999, Laboratory Animal Medicine, 2d edit., 2002; guest editor Applied Animal Behavior Sci., 1997; chmn. editl. bd. ILAr News, 1988-91; contbr. over 120 sci. papers and abstracts. Chmn. Health, Rsch. and Safety Alliance of N.Y. State. Greenfield Trust scholar, 1966-70, N.H. Rural Rehab. Corp. scholar, 1966-70, U. Pa. scholar, 1969-70. Mem. Am. Vet. Med. Assn. (Charles River prize 1995), Am. Assn. Lab. Animal Sci. (pres. N.E. br. 1978-79, B. Trum award 1979), World Vet. Assn. (sec. exec. com. animal welfare 1990-96). Episcopalian. Home: Apt 24P 504 E 63d St New York NY 10021-7919 E-mail: quimby@rockefeller.edu.

QUIMPO, RAFAEL GONZALES, civil engineering educator; b. Altavas, Aklan, The Philippines, Mar. 23, 1939; came to U.S., 1963; s. Manuel and Consuelo (Gonzales) Q.; m. Vanida Suriyakham, Dec. 28, 1963; children: Rafael Jr., Veronica, Carlos-Manuel, Vanessa. BSc, Feati U., Manila, 1959; M Engring., SEATO Grad. Sch. Engring., Bangkok, 1962; PhD, Colo. State U., 1966. Civil engr. Amer-Asia Engring. Assocs., Bangkok, 1962-63; asst. prof. U. Pitts., 1966-70, assoc. prof., 1970-75, prof. civil engring., 1975—, chmn. civil and environ. engring., 1996—. Author: Hydrology and Hydraulics, 1992; contbr. articles to profl. jours. including Jour. of Hydrology, Water Resources Rsch., Jours. of ASCE. Mem. ASCE (com. chair 1991, 92, Outstanding Prof. award 1984), Am. Water Work Assn., Am. Geophys. Union. Achievements include pioneering research on the physical basis of stochastic models in hydrology; development of reliability methods for analyzing water distribution systems. Avocations: chess, piano, tennis. Office: U Pitts 940 Benedum Hl Pittsburgh PA 15261-0001

QUIN, JOSEPH MARVIN, oil company executive; b. Vicksburg, Miss., Aug. 18, 1947; s. Billy Henry Quin and Cele (Burdette) Peterson; m. Terry Gage, June 12, 1973; children: William C., Elizabeth G. BBA, U. Miss., 1969; MBA, U. Va., 1972. Dir. planning and devel. Ashland Chem. Co., Dublin, 1978-81, adminstrv. v.p., 1981-83; treas. Ashland Inc., 1983-87, adminstrv. v.p. fin., treas., 1987-92, sr. v.p., CFO, 1992—. Bd. dirs. Ky. Electric Steel Inc., Marathon Ashland Petroleum, LLC. Episcopalian. Office: Ashland Inc PO Box 391 Covington KY 41015-0391

QUIN, LOUIS DUBOSE, chemist, educator; b. Charleston, S.C., Mar. 5, 1928; s. Louis DuBose and Olga vonOven (Jatho) Q.; children: Gordon, Howard, Carol. BS, The Citadel, 1947; MA, U. N.C., 1949, PhD, 1952. Research chemist Am. Cyanamid Co., Stamford, Conn., 1949-50; research project leader FMC Corp., South Charleston, W.Va., 1952-54, 56; mem. faculty dept. chemistry Duke U., Durham, N.C., 1956-86, prof., 1967-81, James B. Duke prof. chemistry, 1981-86, chmn. dept., 1970-76; prof. chemistry U. Mass., Amherst, 1986-96, prof. emeritus, 1996—, head dept., 1986-94; adj. prof., disting. vis. prof. chemistry U. N.C., Wilmington, 1996—. Mem. Durham Human Relations Commn., 1978-81 Author: Heterocyclic Chemistry of Phosphorus, 1981, (with J.G. Verkade) Phosphorus-31 NMR Spectroscopy in Stereochemical Analysis, 1987, Phosphorus-31 NMR Spectral Properties in Compound Characterization and Structural Analysis, 1994, A Guide to Organophosphorus Chemistry, 2000. Served to 1st lt. U.S. Army, 1954-56. Fellow AAAS; mem. Am. Chem. Soc. Office: 124 White Oak Bluffs Stella NC 28582

QUIN, MARY PATRICIA, writer; b. Palmerston North, New Zealand, Sept. 2, 1953; came to U.S., 1976; d. Francis Xavier and Mollie Cowell (Little) Q. BSc with first class honors, U. Canterbury, Christchurch, New Zealand, 1976; PhD, Northwestern U., 1980; MBA, Harvard U., 1988. Metall. engr. Raychem Corp., Menlo Park, Calif., 1980-82, mgr. alloy rsch., 1982-84, metals mgr. Cergy-Pontoise, France, 1984-85; product mgr. Beta Phase, Inc., Menlo Park, 1985-86; dir. market and product planning Eastman Kodak Co., Rochester, N.Y., 1988-90, dir. U.S. nat. accounts, 1990-91; gen. mgr. Mid-Volume copier and printer products Office Imaging Divsn., Eastman Kodak Co., 1991-93; v.p. ops. and customer svc. Avid Tech., Inc., Tewksbury, Mass., 1993-94; dir. corp. bus. strategy Xerox Corp., Rochester, N.Y., 1995-96, v.p. strategy Prodn. Systems Group, 1996-98, v.p., gen. mgr. OEM bus. unit Office Document Products Group, 1998-99, v.p., gen. mgr. Color Solutions Bus. Unit, 1999—. Bd. dirs. Material Scis. Corp.; del. NGO Forum of UN 4th World Conf. on Women, Beijing, China, 1995. Vice chmn. bd. trustees Garth Fagan Dance, Inc., 1995-98; founder, chmn. 100 Heroines Project, 1996—; bd. dirs. Ctr. for Devel. and Population Activities, Washington, 1998—. Internat. Nickel Co. fellow Northwestern U., 1978; Baker Scholar Harvard Bus. Sch., Boston, 1988. Achievements include inventor NiTiV alloys with shape memory. Avocations: global women's rights, international travel.

QUINBY, HAROLD EUGENE, city councilman; b. St. Louis, July 19, 1929; s. Porter Harris Quinby and Ruth Elaine Dodendorf; m. Eunice Jean Davis, Mar. 18, 1950; children: Hal Eugene, Constance Louise. Grad. h.s., Seattle, 1947. Cert. leadership tng. Neighborhood commr. Boy Scouts Am., Seattle, 1953-55; lt. vol. fire dept. King County Fire Dist. 11, 1962-71; city councilman City of Mukilteo, 1994—2001. Adv. bd. Paine Field Cmty. Coun., Mukilteo, 1996-99, Snohomish County Mental Health, Everett, Wash., 1991-99, adv. bd. chmn. 1991-99; sign/advertise chair Save Our Cmty., Mukilteo, 1992-99; city councilman Mukilteo City, 1994-2001. Sgt. USMC, 1947—52, Korea. Democrat. Episcopalian. Avocations: model railroader, model airplanes, motor cycle tourer, antique cars. Office: City of Mukilteo 4480 Chennault Beach Rd Mukilteo WA 98275

QUINBY, LEE, humanities educator; b. Tampa, Fla., Oct. 29, 1946; d. Thomas Joseph and Miriam (Mays) Q.; div. Apr., 1977; children: Michael A. Miller, Paul J. Miller. BA, U. North Fla., 1977; MA, Purdue U., 1979, PhD, 1984. Donald R. Harter prof. Hobart and William Smith Coll., Geneva, 1984—, co-dir. Am. studies. Vis. endowed chair of millennium Rochester Inst. Tech., 1999-2001; bd. assocs. Ctr. Millennial Studies Boston U., 1996—; cons. on diversity women's studies programs, gender, cultural studies. Author: Freedom, Foucault and the Subject of America, 1991, Anti-Apocalypse, 1994, Millennial Seduction, 1999; co-editor: Feminism and Foucault, 1988; editor: Genealogy and Literature, 1995; guest editor: Womens Studies Qtrly., 2001. David Ross fellow, 1982-84, Sr. Fulbright Lectr. U. Athens, 1995; Mellon grantee, 1987. Mem. Am. United for Separation of Ch. and State, Am. Studies Assn., MLA. Office: Hobart and William Smith Coll Geneva NY 14456 E-mail: leequinby@aol.com.

QUINBY, WILLIAM ALBERT, lawyer, mediator, arbitrator; b. Oakland, Calif., May 28, 1941; s. George W. and Marge (Diaz) Q.; m. Marion Bach, Nov. 27, 1964; 1 child, Michelle Kathleen. BA, Harvard U., 1963; JD, U. Calif., San Francisco, 1967. Bar: Calif. 1967. V.p., dir., shareholder Crosby, Heafey, Roach & May, Oakland, Calif., 1967-96; mediator, arbitrator Am. Arbitration Assn. and AAA Ctr. for Mediation, San Francisco, 1996—. Bd. dirs. Haws Drinking Faucet Co., Berkeley, Calif.; mem. faculty Hastings Coll. Advocacy, San Francisco, 1980, instr. Boalt Hall Sch. Law, 1997; co-moderator Counsel Connect's Calif. ADR Discussion Group; lectr. currents devels. in banking arbitration and mediation; mem. fellowship rev. com. HEW; mem. panel disting. neutrals Ctr. for Pub. Resources, Inc.; mem. mediation panel Nat. Assn. Securities Dealers; trustee Nat. Pre-Suit Mediation Program; adj. prof. Hastings Coll. of the Law, U. Calif., 1998, 99. Author: Six Reasons--Besides Time and Money--to Mediate Rather Than Litigate, Why Health Care Parties Should Mediate Rather Than Litigate, Starting an ADR Practice Group in a Law Firm, Mediation Process Can Amicably Solve Business Disputes and Not a Gold Rush (But Silver, Maybe), ADR Practice in a Large Law Firm Produces No Overnight Bonanzas, Making The Most of Mediation (Effective Mediation Advocacy). Bd. dirs. Big Bros. East Bay, Oakland, 1983-87, Easter Seals Soc. East Bay, 1973; past bd. dirs. Oakland East Bay Symphony, Oakland Pub. Libr. Found.; chmn. bd. dirs. Bay Area Tumor Inst. Scholar Harvard U., 1962-63. Mem. ABA (sect. on dispute resolution, chair programs, mediation coms.), Calif. Bar Assn., Alameda County Bar Assn., Calif. Bus. Trial Lawyers Assn., Am. Arbitration Assn. (large, complex case panel, comml. mediation and arbitration panels), Oakland C. of C. (past bd. dirs., exec. com.), Alameda County Barristers Club (bd. dirs., pres. 1972), Harvard Club, San Francisco Calimari Club. Republican. Avocations: running, skiing, tennis, travel, gardening. Office: Wulff Quinby & Sochynsky Dispute Resolution 1901 Harrison St Ste 1420 Oakland CA 94612-3582 E-mail: wquinby@aol.com.

QUINCY, ALPHA ELLEN BEERS, school board president; b. Olympia, Wash., Oct. 15, 1924; d. George Howard and Grace Florence (Penrose) Beers; m. John J. Quincy, Nov. 12, 1942 (dec. Feb. 1987); children: Cheri Sue, John Jay. BE in Edn., Calif. State U., Sacramento, 1960; MA in Ednl. Adminstrn., U. Calif., Berkeley, 1966, postgrad., 1996—. Life cert. adminstrn., presch., K-12 and adult, elem. sch. adminstrn., elem. tchg. Tchr., resource tchr., vice prin., prin., dist. cons. Mt. Diablo Unified Sch. Dist., 1959-83; coord. Acad. Curriculum and Instrn. Leaders Assn. Calif. Sch. Adminstrs., 1985-89; cons. edn., spkr., writer, workshop leader, 1983—; exec. dir. San Ramon Valley Sch. Age Child Care Alliance, 1992-93; mem. Contra Costa County Bd. Edn., 1988—, pres., 1992, 96. Mem. Calif. Curriculum Devel. and Supplemental Materials Commn., State Bd. Edn., 1971-74; chair com. for reading and lit. Calif. Curriculum Devel. and Supplemental Materials Commn., State Bd. Edn., 1971-74, mem. English lang. arts adv. Calif. Assessment Program, 1971—. Contbr. articles to profl. jours. Bd. dirs. U. Calif. Berkeley, Inst. Sch. Adminstrs., 1979-88, Diablo Internat. Resources Ctr. Recipient Adminstr. of Yr. ann. award Assn. Calif. Sch. Adminstrs., Region 7, 1983. Mem. LWV (leader Lafayette unit 1985, edn. chairperson Diablo Valley 1987, chair nominating com. 1991, edn. chair 1989—), ASCD, Nat. Coun. Tchrs. English (writing awards com. 1990-92, ency. entry team, emeritus assembly), Calif. Assn. Tchrs. English (past bd. dirs., program chair 1990 ann. conf.), Ctrl. Coun. Tchrs. English (past bd. mem., curriculum study com. 1970—, conf. chmn. 1991, 96), Assn. Calif. Sch. Adminstrs. (past mem. mid. sch. com., C&I acad. coord. 1984-88), area VI scholarship chmn. 1990—), Calif. Sch. Bds. ASsn., Calif. County Bds. Edn , Contra Costa Sch. Bds. Assn., Calif. Retired Tchrs. Assn., East Contra Costa County Retired Tchrs. Assn. (program chair 1992-93, pres. 1995—), Nat. Women's Polit. Caucus, U. Calif. Berkeley Alumni Assn., Internat. Reading Assn., Calif. Reading Assn., Contra Costa Reading Assn., Commonwealth Club Calif., Concord Century Club, Home Group, Phi Delta Kappa, Delta Kappa Gamma. Home: 1529 Rancho View Dr Lafayette CA 94549-2231

QUINLAN, C. PATRICK, retired diplomat, educator; b. Canby, Minn., Oct. 20, 1922; s. Patrick James and Frances Loretta (Lawler) Q.; m. Louise B. Butala, May 20, 1950. BA cum laude, U. Minn., 1948; BS in Fgn. Svc., Georgetown U., Washington, 1949. Econ. officer U.S. Dept. State, Berlin, Ger., 1951-53, polit. officer Am. Embassy Karachi, Pakistan, 1953-55, rsch. analyst Washington, 1955-58, prin. officer Am. Consulate Kaduna, Nigeria, 1959-62, prin. officer Embassy Br. Office Sanaa, Yemen, 1964-66; polit. officer Am. Embassy U.S. Dept. State, Cairo, 1967-69; prin. officer Am. Consulate, Adana, Turkey, 1970-72; civil rights officer U.S. Office Econ. Opportunity,

Washington, 1970-72; prin. officer U.S. Embassy, Muscat, Oman, 1972-74, U.S. Consulate, Salzburg, Austria, 1974-78; diplomat-in-residence Oakland U., Rochester, Mich., 1979; lectr. U. Minn., 1980-85. Freelance columnist Mpls. Star and Tribune, St. Paul Pioneer Press, Edina Sun, Washington Report on Middle East, others. Mem. Am.-Arab Anti-discrimination Com. of Minn., 1990, Alex Odeh award, 1990; mem. St. Paul-Mpls. Com. on Fgn. Rels., 1983—; pres. Middle East Peace Now of Minn., 1984; leader internat. course Elder Learning Inst. U. Minn., 1996. Recipient Meritorious Honor award, U.S. Dept. State, Sanaa, 1965. Democratic Farm Labor Party. Roman Catholic. Avocations: downhill skiing, biking, swimming. Home: 5601 Dewey Hill Rd Apt 216 Minneapolis MN 55439-1925

QUINLAN, J(OSEPH) MICHAEL, lawyer; b. Rockville Centre, N.Y., Nov. 2, 1941; s. Joseph Charles Quinlan and Harriet Veronica (Gorman) Greene; m. Agnes Mary Quinlan, May 5, 1973; children: Kara Ann, Kristen Mary. BS in Social Sci., Fairfield U., 1963; JD, Fordham U., 1966; LLM, George Washington U., 1970. Bar: N.Y. 1966, D.C. 1967, Va. 1993, U.S. Ct. Mil. Appeals 1967, U.S. Supreme Ct. 1970. Exec. asst. to warden U.S. Penitentiary, Leavenworth, Kans., 1973-74; of counsel N.E. region U.S. Bur. Prisons, Phila., 1974-75, exec. asst. to dir. Washington, 1975-78; supt. Fed. Prison Camp, Eglin AFB, Fla., 1978-80; warden Fed. Correctional Inst., Otisville, N.Y., 1980-85; from dep. asst. dir. to dir. U.S. Bur. Prisons, Washington, 1985-92; dir. strategic planning Corrections Corp. Am., 1993-97; dir., bd. dirs. U.K. Detention Svcs., London, 1993-97; vice-chmn., bd. trustees Prison Realty Trust, 1997-99. 1st vice-chmn. bd. dirs. Horton Meml. Hosp., Middletown, N.Y., 1982-85; CEO Prison Realty Trust, 1997-99; pres. Corrections Corp of Am., 1999-2000, exec. v.p., COO, 2000—. Bd. advisors BI Inc., 2001—; adv. bd. Criminal Justice Alliance, 2001—. Lt. col. USAFR, 1966-93. Recipient SES Presdl. Disting. Rank award, 1988, SES Presdl. Meritorious Rank award, 1991, Exceptional Leadership award U.S. Atty. Gen., 1991, Nat. Pub. Svc. award Nat. Acad. Pub. Adminstrn./Am. Soc. Pub. Adminstrn., 1992, John Marshall award Dept. Justice, 1993. Fellow Nat. Acad. Pub. Adminstrn.; mem. ABA (corrections and sentencing com. 1985—), Am. Correctional Assn. (mem. prison industries com.), Nat. Com. Comm. Corrections, N.Y. Bar Assn., D.C. Bar Assn., Va. Bar Assn. Roman Catholic. Avocations: reading, family activities.

QUINLAN, KATHLEEN, actress; b. Pasadena, Calif., Nov. 19, 1954; Actress: (theatre) Taken in Marriage, 1979 (Theatre World award 1979), Accent on Youth, 1983, Les Liaisons Dangereuses, 1988, (feature films) One is a Lonely Number, 1972, American Graffiti, 1973, Lifeguard, 1976, Airport '77, 1977, I Never Promised You a Rose Garden, 1977, The Promise, 1979, The Runner Stumbles, 1979, Sunday Lovers, 1981, Hanky Panky, 1982, Independence Day, 1982, Twilight Zone: The Movie, 1983, The Last Winter, 1983, Warning Sign, 1985, Wild Thing, 1987, Sunset, 1988, Clara's Heart, 1988, The Doors, 1991, Trial by Jury, 1994, Apollo 13, 1995 (Acad. award nominee for best actress 1996), Zeus and Roxanne, 1997, Event Horizon, 1997, Lawn Dogs, 1997, A Civil Action, 1998, My Giant, 1998; (TV movies) Can Ellen Be Saved?, 1974, Lucas Tanner, 1974, Where Have All the People Gone?, 1974, The Missing Are Deadly, 1975, The Turning Point of Jim Malloy, 1975, The Abduction of Saint Anne, 1975, Little Ladies of the Night, 1977, She's in the Army Now, 1981, When She Says No, 1984, Blackout, 1985, Children of the Night, 1985, Dreams Lost, Dreams Found, 1987, Trapped, 1989, The Operation, 1990, Strays, 1991, An American Story, 1992, Stolen Babies, 1993, Last Light, 1993, Perfect Alibi, 1994, Breakdown, 1996, In the Lake of the Woods, 1996, The Doris Duke Story, 1998. Mem. Actors' Equity Assn., Screen Actors Guild.

QUINLAN, MICHAEL EDWARD, retired civil servant; b. Hampton, Eng., Aug. 11, 1930; s. Gerald A. and Roseanne (Corr) Q.; m. Mary Finlay, Aug. 7, 1965; children: Anthony, Jane, Matthew, Caroline. MA, Merton Coll., Oxford (Eng.) U., 1952. Under-sec. Cabinet Office, U.K., 1974-77; dep. sec. for policy Ministry of Defence, U.K., 1977-81; dep. sec. for industry Treasury, U.K., 1981-82; permanent sec. Dept. of Employment, U.K., 1983-88, Ministry of Defence, U.K., 1988-92; dir. Ditchley Found., U.K., 1992-99. Vis. prof. King's Coll., London, 1992-95; trustee Sci. Mus. U.K., 1992-2001; Pub. Policy scholar Woodrow Wilson Ctr., Washington, 2000. Author: Thinking About Nuclear Weapons, 1997, European Defence Corporation, 2001, also numerous articles on def. and other pub. policy issues. Flying officer RAF, 1952-54. Decorated Knight Grand Cross Order of Bath (U.K.). Roman Catholic. Avocations: golf, sports, music. Office: 3 Adderbury Pk Banbury Oxon OX17 3EN England E-mail: meq@adderbury03.fsnet.co.uk.

QUINLIN, MICHAEL PATRICK, public relations executive; b. Pitts., Nov. 26, 1952; s. John J. and Marie J. (Campbell) Q.; m. Colette M. Minogue, June 4, 1994; 1 child, Devin Patrick; 1 stepchild, W. Leo. BA in Liberal Arts, LaSalle Coll., 1974; MS in Journalism, Boston U., 1992. Chief copywriter Elsevier North Holland, N.Y.C., 1977-79; mktg. mgr. Ballinger Pub., Cambridge, Mass., 1979-82; pres. Quinlin Campbell Pub. Co., Boston, 1980—; mktg. cons. MIT Advanced Engring. Ctr., Cambridge, 1985-86; mayor's press officer City of Boston, 1986-88, mayor's Irish advisor, 1991-93; mktg. dir. City of Boston Parks Dept., 1988-94; comm. dir. Mass. Water Resources Authority, Boston, 1995-99; pres. Boston Irish Tourism Assn., 1999—. Author: Guide to Boston Irish, 1985, Guide to New English Irish, 3d edit., 1994; editor: Peace, Justice and Unity: Ireland's Unfinished Agenda, 1985. Founder, bd. dirs. Boston Book Fair, 1992-94, Irish Writers Series, Boston, 1993-94; vol. Dukakis for Pres. campaign, Boston, 1988, Ray Flynn Reelection Com., Boston, 1988, 92, Irish Ams. for Clinton/Gore, 1992; founding mem., pub. rels. dir. St. Patrick's Parade Com., Cambridge, 1995; founding mem. Boston Irish Famine Meml. Com., 1995; creator Boston Irish Heritage Trail. Grantee Mass. Coun. Arts and Humanities, 1987, Boston Arts Lottery, 1987, Boston Pub. Libr., 1995, Irish Am. Cultural Inst., 1995. Mem. Comhaltas Ceoltoiri Eireann (auditor 1985-90), Friends of Harvard Celtic Studies (exec. bd., pub. rels. dir.). Democrat. Roman Catholic. Avocations: music, writing, travel, gardening, running. Home: 20 Buckingham Rd Milton MA 02186-4418 E-mail: bostonirish@attbi.com.

QUINN, ALICE, literature educator; BA, Manhattanville Coll.; student in English Lit., NYU. Editor Alfred A. Knopf Pub. Firm, The New Yorker, 1987—. Dep. editor fiction dept. Columbia U., adj. prof. poetry; lectr. in field. Contbr. articles to profl. jours. Chmn. jury Kingsley & Tate Tufts Poetry Awards. Office: Sch of Arts Columbia U Mail Code 1808 305 Dodge Hall 2960 Broadway New York NY 10027*

QUINN, ANDREW PETER, JR. lawyer, insurance executive retired; b. Providence, Oct. 22, 1923; s. Andrew Peter and Margaret (Canning) Q.; m. Sara G. Bullard, May 30, 1952; 1 child, Emily H. AB, Brown U., 1945; LLB, Yale U., 1950. Bar: R.I. 1949, Mass. 1960, U.S. Tax Ct. 1960, U.S. Supreme Ct. 1986. Pvt. practice, Providence, 1950-59; ptnr. Letts & Quinn, 1950-59; with Mass. Mut. Life Ins. Co., Springfield, 1959—88, exec. v.p., gen. counsel, 1971-88; of counsel Day, Berry & Howard, Hartford, Conn. and Boston, 1988-99; retired, 1999. Pres., trustee MML Series Investment Fund, 1971-88; bd. dirs. Sargasso Mut. Ins. Co., Ltd., 1986-95, pres., 1986-89, chmn. bd. dirs., 1989-93. Trustee, MacDuffie Sch., 1974-87, chmn. bd., 1978-85; trustee Baystate Med., Springfield, 1977-80. Lt. (j.g.) USNR, 1944-46. Mem. ABA (co-chmn. nat. conf. lawyers and life ins. cos. 1973), Assn. Life Ins. Counsel (pres. 1983-84), Am. Coun. Life Ins. (chmn. legal sect. 1971), Life Ins. Assn. Mass. (chmn. exec. com. 1975-77), Brown U. Alumni Assn. (bd. dirs. 1969-72), N.Y. Yacht Club, Longmeadow Country Club, Dunes Club, Hillsboro Club, Colony Club (Springfield, Mass.), Conn. Valley Brown U. (past pres.). Home: 306 Ellington Rd Longmeadow MA 01106-1559

QUINN, ANTHONY, academic administrator; b. Toledo, June 30, 1972; s. Joe Willie and JoAnn (Harris) Quinn; m. Brandi LaShelle Cosper, Apr. 20, 2002; children: Braniya Cosper-Quinn. BA, Ohio State U., 1995; MA, U. Toledo, 2000. Pollster Peter D Hart Rsch., Inc., Toledo, 1998—99; academic skills coord. Lourdes Coll. Upward Bound, Sylvania, 1999—. Tutor U. Toledo Upward Bound, Toledo, 1996—99. Mem.: Mid-Am. Assn. Ednl. Opportunity Program Pers., Ohio Assn. Ednl. Opportunity Program Pers., Phi Alpha Theta, Omega Psi Phi. Baptist. Avocations: boxing collector, travel. Office: Lourdes College Upward Bound 6832 Convent Blvd Sylvania OH 43560 Home Fax: 419-531-1989. Personal E-mail: aquinn1972@aol.com.

QUINN, ART JAY, veterinarian, retired educator; b. Bennington, Kans., Aug. 2, 1936; s. Arthur Jess and Edith Mae (Reigle) Q. BS, Kans. State U., 1959, DVM, 1961. Diplomate Am. Coll. Vet. Ophthalmologists. Pvt. practice, Albuquerque, 1961-75; field rep. Am. Animal Hosp. Assn., Denver, 1968-69; prof. Coll. Vet. Medicine, Okla. State U., Stillwater, 1975-95, prof. emeritus, 1995—. Contbr. articles to profl. jours. Capt. U.S. Army, 1962-64. Recipient Small Animal Proficiency award, Kans. Vet. Med. Assn., 1961, Upjohn award, 1961, Western Region Practitioner award, AAHA, 1993, Meritorious Svc. award, Western Vet. Conf., 2002; grantee, Sarkey Found. grantee, 1981. Mem.: AVMA, Am. Coll. Vet. Ophthalmologists, Am. Animal Hosp. Assn. Democrat. Home: 210 Cedar Ln Diamond Head Sand Springs OK 74063-5309

QUINN, CHARLES NICHOLAS, journalist; b. Utica, N.Y., July 28, 1930; s. Charles Dunaway and Elsa (Zarth) Q.; children— Diana David, Ben, Jane. BA, Cornell U., 1951; MS, Columbia U. Sch. Journalism, 1954. Reporter Providence Jour., 1954-56, N.Y. Herald Tribune, 1956-62; corr. NBC News, N.Y.C., 1962-66, Washington, 1966-71, Rome, 1971-74; mng. editor, chief corr. NBC Radio News, Washington, 1978-80; corr. Ind. Network News, 1980-81; electronic media rep. Am. Petroleum Inst., 1981-91. Reported on hunger in U.S. on: Huntley-Brinkley Report, (co-recipient Emmy 1969). Served with arty. U.S. Army, 1951-53. Mem. Nat. Press Club (bd. govs. 1990-91).

QUINN, DAVID IAN, oncologist, pharmacologist, researcher; b. Orange, N.S.W., Australia, July 24, 1963; m. Claire Templeman, Oct. 23, 1993. MB, BChir with honors, U. New South Wales, Australia, 1986, PhD, 2000. Intern to resident St. Vincent's Hosp., Sydney, Australia, 1987-88, med. registrar Australia, 1989-91, oncology registrar Australia, 1992-93, sr. med. registrar Australia, 1993-94, clin. pharmacology registrar Australia, 1994, dir. clin. tng. Australia, 1996-99; lectr. medicine and pharmacology Southampton (Eng.) Univ. Hosp. Trust, 1995; asst. prof. clin. medicine Keck Sch. Medicine U. So. Calif., 2000—. Exec. mem. N.S.W. State Com., 1996-99; lectr. Sch. Physiology and Pharmacology, U. NSW, 1997—. Author: (with others) Avery's Drug Treatment, 1997. Recipient Nat. Health Med. Rsch. Coun. award, scholar, 1996-99, Disting. Contbr. award Postgrad. Med. Coun. NSW; Neil Hamilton Fairley postdoctoral fellow Nat. Health and Med. Rsch. Coun., 2000—, Vincent Fairfax Family fellow Royal Australasian Coll. Physicians, 2000-2001. Fellow Royal Australian Coll. Physicians; mem. Med. Oncology Group Australia, Australian Soc. Clin. & Exptl. Pharmacology and Toxicology, Univ. N.S.W. Med. Soc. (pres. 1984, clin. v.p. 1985), Am. Soc. Clin. Oncology. Avocations: rugby referee. Office: 1441 Eastlake Ave Ste 3453 Los Angeles CA 90089-0112 E-mail: diquinn@hsc.usc.edu.

QUINN, DENNIS B. English language and literature educator; b. Bklyn., Oct. 3, 1928; s. Herbert John and Thelma Leona (Warren) Q.; m. Eva M. Jensen, Aug. 13, 1952; children— Timothy, Monica, Alison. Student, Creighton U., 1948-50; BA in English, U. Wis., 1951, MA in English, 1952, PhD in English, 1958. Instr. English U. Kans., Lawrence, 1956-60, asst. prof. English, 1960-64, assoc. prof. English, 1964-68, prof. English, 1968—, dir. Pearson Coll., 1968-75, dir. integrated humanities program, 1971-79. Author: Iris Exiled: A Synoptic History of Wonder, 2002; contbr. articles. Served with U.S. Army, 1946-48; Japan Recipient student Fulbright award, Leiden, The Netherlands, 1955-56, research Fulbright award, Salamanca, Spain, 1962-63; H. Bernard Fink Outstanding Tchr. award U. Kans., 1965, H.O.P.E. Teaching award, 1969; NEH grantee, 1971; Kemper Tchg. fellow, 1997. Roman Catholic. Avocations: gardening, travel. Home: 1102 W 25th St Lawrence KS 66046-4441 Office: Univ Kansas Dept English Lawrence KS 66045-0001

QUINN, EDWARD FRANCIS, III, orthopedic surgeon; b. Washington, Apr. 28, 1944; s. Edward F. Jr. and Louise Q.; m. Audrey Dickinson; 1 child, Edward Francis IV. BS, U. Md., 1968, MD, 1969. Diplomate Am. Bd. Orthopedic Surgery, Am. Bd. Neurol. and Orthopedic Surgery, Am. Bd. Forensic Medicine, Am. Bd. Forensic Examiners. Intern Ohio State Univ. Hosp., Columbus, 1969-70; resident USN Hosp., Bethesda, Md., 1971-74; staff Milford (Del.) Meml. Hosp., 1975—, pres. med. staff, 1991-93, chief surgery, 1993—. Jkns. staff Beebe Hosp., Lewes, Del., 1975-92, 98—, Nanticoke Meml. Hosp., Seaford, Del., 1975-90, Kent Gen. Hosp., Dover, Del., 1981-90, 98—, attending staff, 1990-94. Bd. advisors So. Campus of Goldey Beacon Coll., 1987-91. Lt. comdr. USN, 1970-75. Fellow ACS, Am. Acad. Orthopaedic Surgery, Internat. Coll. Surgeons, Am. Coll. Forensic Examiners; mem. AMA, Med. Soc. Del., Sussex County Med. Soc., Am. Fracture Assn., Del. Soc. Orthopedic Surgeons (pres. elect 1997-99, pres. 1999—), So. Med. Assn., Med. Soc. Del. (v.p. 1998-99, pres. elect 1999-2000, pres. 2000—), Ea. Orthopaedic Assn., So. Orthopaedic Assn., Chemonucleolysis Adv. Bd., Milford Rotary Club, Rotary Internat. (Paul Harris fellow 1986), Am. Acad. Disability Evaluation Rsch. Physicians, Am. Legion, So. Del. C. of C. (bd. dirs. 1983-90). Republican. Avocations: boating, skiing, firearms, hunting. Office: Dickinson Med Bldg 800 N duPont Hwy Milford DE 19963-1006 E-mail: efquinn@dca.net.

QUINN, ELIZABETH ANNA, artist, art educator; b. Kittanning, Pa., Dec. 6, 1973; d. Duane LaRoy and Deborah Lynn Quinn. BFA in Fine Arts, Clarion U., 1996; MFA in Fine Arts, Ohio U., 1998, postgrad., 1998—. Cert. tchr., Pa. Program asst. spl. edn. dept. Clarion (Pa.) U., 1992-93, asst. to sec., 1993, asst. to dir. Sandford Gallery, 1994-96; tchg. asst., grad. asst. Ohio U., Athens, 1996-98; art tchr. Blackhawk Area H.S., Chipewa, PA., 2000—. Vis. artist Clarion U. and DuBois (Pa.) Area Schs., 1996; instr. various workshops and seminars, Clarion, Athens, 1996-98; artist educator Andy Warhol Mus.; adj. faculty Carlow Coll., Pitts. Author, designer (ednl. program) Beadworks, Athens, 1998; exhbns. nationally, locally, and internationally. Mem. art edn. grad. com. Ohio U., 1998. Lesser scholar Clarion U., 1996, Albert Murray scholar Ohio U., Athens. Mem. Gov.'s Inst. for Arts Educators. Avocations: outdoor activities, collecting antique furniture, creating. E-mail: quinnhuwarliz@hotmail.com.

QUINN, EUGENE FREDERICK, foreign service officer, clergyman; b. Oil City, Pa., Sept. 16, 1935; s. Frederick Anthony and Wilma (Scott) Q.; m. Charlotte Alison Smith, Aug. 25, 1965; children: Christopher Edward Vermilye, Alison Moore. AB, Allegheny Coll., 1957; MA in African studies, UCLA, 1966, MA in History, 1969, PhD in History, 1970; diploma in theol. studies, Va. Theol. Sem., 1974. Ordained to ministry Episcopal Ch., 1975. Info. officer Am. Embassy, Rabat, Morocco, 1958-59, cultural affairs officer Port-au-Prince, Haiti, 1959-61; country pub. affairs officer Ouagadougou, Upper Volta, 1961-63; field rep. Joint U.S. Affairs Office, Saigon, Vietnam, 1964-66; country pub. affairs officer Am. embassy, Yaounde, Cameroun, 1966-68, counselor embassy for press and cultural affairs Prague, Czechoslovakia, 1975-78; apptd. career mem. Sr. Fgn. Service with class of counselor, 1981, minister-counselor, 1986; dir. fgn. service personnel Voice of Am., Washington, 1981-83; dep. asst. sec. pub. affairs Dept. Transp., 1983-85; dir. Office Pub. Affairs Voice of Am., 1985-86; internat. coord. for Bicentennial U.S. Constn., dir.'s office U.S. Info. Agy., 1986-91; cons. internat. affairs, 1992—. Dir. rule of law programs, conf. on security and cooperation in Europe, Office of Dem. Instns. and Human Rights, Warsaw, 1993-95. Author: Federalist Papers' Reader, 1992, To Heal the Earth, 1994, Democracy at Dawn, Notes From Poland and Points East, 1998, Human Rights and You, 1998, French Overseas Empire, 2000, To Be A Pilgrim, The Anglican Ethos in History, 2001; editor: Diplomacy for the Seventies, 1969; mem. edit. bd. Fgn. Svc. Jour., 1972-75, Dept. State Open Forum Jour., 1982-83; contbr. articles to profl. jours., chpts. to books. Trustee N.J. Ednl. Consortium, 1970-72; coord. USIA Yorktown Bicentennial Activities, 1981; assisting clergyman St. Columba Ch., Washington, 1973-75, 78-81, Nat. Cathedral, Washington, 1981-82, 95-2001 , Grace Ch., Silver Spring, Md., 1981-82, Epiphany Ch., Washington, 1983, 86-92; chaplain Anglo-Am. Diplomatic Cmty., Prague, 1975-78, Warsaw, 1993-95; vicar St. James Ch., Bowie, Md., 1983-84; rector Christ Ch., Accokeek, Md., 1985, St. John's Ch., Pomonkey, Md.; assisting clergyman All Saints Ch., Chevy Chase, Md., 1981-82, 86-90; interim pastor Ch. of Holy Communion, Washington, 1992-93, St. Andrews Leonardtown, Md., 1998-99; chair environ. com. Episcopal Diocese of Washington Peace Commn., 1991-92; mem. Environ. Stewardship Team, Episcopal Ch., 1992-95. Recipient Meritorious Honor award USIA, 1964, 66, 85; Merit medal Republic of Vietnam, 1965, medal of honor, 1966 Mem. Cosmos Club (Washington). Clubs: Cosmos (Washington). Home and Office: 1175 Second Ave Salt Lake City UT 84103

QUINN, FRANCIS XAVIER, arbitrator, mediator, author, lecturer; b. Dunmore, Pa., June 9, 1932; s. Frank T. and Alice B. (Maher) Q.; m. Marlene Stoker Quinn; children: Kimberly, Catherine, Cameron, Lindsay, Megan, Savannah, Jackson Blair. BA, Fordham U., 1956, MA, 1958; STB, Woodstock Coll., 1964; MS in Indsl. Rels., Loyola U., Chgo., 1966; PhD in Indsl. Rels., Calif. Western U., 1966. Assoc. dir. Inst. Indsl. Rels. St. Joseph's Coll., 1966-68; Manpower fellow Temple U., 1969-74, asst. to dean Sch. Bus. Adminstrn., 1972-78. Arbitrator Fed. Mediation and Conciliation Svc., Nat. Mediation Bd., Am. Arbitration Assn., Nat. Assn. Railroad Referees, Dem. Nat. Steering Com.; ; apptd. to Rail Emergency Bd., 1975, to Fgn. Service Grievance Bd., 1976, 78, 80. Author: The Ethical Aftermath of Automation, 1963, Ethics and Advertising, 1965, Population Ethics, 1968, The Evolving Role of Women in the World of Work, 1969, Developing Community Responsibility, 1970; editor: The Ethical Aftermath Series; contbr. articles to profl. jours. Chmn. Hall of Fame com. Internat. Police Assn., 1990—, Tulsa City-County Mayor's Task Force to Combat Homelessness, 1991-92; mem. exec. bd. Tulsa Met. Ministries, 1990-92, Labor-Religion Coun. Okla., 1990—. Named Tchr. of Yr. Freedom Found., 1959; recipient Human Rels. award City of Phila.; inducted into Hall of Fame, Internat. Police Assn., 2000. Mem. Nat. Acad. Arbitrators (v.p. 1999-2001), Indsl. Rels. Rsch. Assn., Assn. for Social Econs., Soc. for Dispute Resolution, Am. Arbitration Assn. (arbitrator), Nat. Assn. Railroad Refs. (pres. 2000–, arbitrator), Internat. Soc. Labor Law and Social Security, Internat. Ombudsman Inst. Democrat. Home: 4213 Blackhaw Ave Fort Worth TX 76109-1618 E-mail: FXQ@prodigy.com.

QUINN, FRANCIS A. bishop; b. L.A., Sept. 11, 1921; Ed., St. Joseph's Coll., Mountain View, Calif., St. Patrick's Sem., Menlo Park, Calif., Cath. U., Washington, U. Calif., Berkeley. Ordained priest Roman Cath. Ch., 1946; ordained titular bishop of Numana and aux. bishop of San Francisco, 1978; bishop Diocese of Sacramento, 1979-94, bishop emeritus, 1994—. Office: 2110 Broadway Sacramento CA 95818-2518

QUINN, FRANCIS F. lawyer; b. Phila., Jan. 22, 1946; AB, St. Joseph's U., 1967; JD, U. Pa., 1971. Bar: Pa. 1972, N.J. 1993, N.Y. 1995, U.S. Supreme Ct. 1985. Law clk. to Hon. Daniel H. Huyett III U.S. Dist. Ct. (ea. dist.) Pa., 1971-73; ptnr. Lavin, Coleman, O'Neill, Ricci, Finarelli & Gray, Phila., 1973—. Mem. Phila. Bar Assn., Def. Rsch. and Trial Lawyers Assn., N.Y. Assn. Def. Counsel, Bar Assn. City of N.Y., N.Y. State Bar Assn. Office: Lavin Coleman Finarelli & Gray 767 3rd Ave Fl 7 New York NY 10017-2023

QUINN, HOLLI JO BARDO, social worker, educator; b. Muncy, Pa., Jan. 7, 1961; d. Emerson David and Beverly Bair Bardo; m. Joel Paul Quinn, Oct. 15, 1983; children: Tara Jo, Austin Paul. BA in Comm., Shippensburg U., 1982; MS in Bible, Phila. Bibl. U., 1997; MA in Religion, Temple U., 1999. Mktg. asst. Lower Bucks Cablevision, Levittown, Pa., 1984—87; English composition instr. Templet U., Phila., 1998, Bible instr., 1999; case worker Bucks County Head Start, Bensalem, 2001—. Impact study rep. Bucks County Head Start, Morrisville, Pa., 2002—. Author: Sacrifical Offerings, 1989, Fishing, 1995. Vol. A Woman's Place, Doylestown, Pa., 2002, Pennsbury Manor, Tallytown, 2002; spkr. Women's Ink, Phila., 1989. Recipient Discovery award in fiction, Bucks County C.C., 1989, Senatorial citation, Pa. Senate, 1992. Republican. Avocations: gardening, landscaping, writing, reading, swimming. Home: 2224 Bent Rd Langhorne PA 19053 Office: Bucks County Head Start Bensalem Ctr PO Box 1286 Bensalem PA 19020

QUINN, JACK, congressman, English language educator, sports coach; b. South Buffalo, N.Y., 1951; s. Jack Sr. and Norma Ide Q.; m. Mary Beth McAndrews, 1974; children: Jack III, Kara. BA, Siena Coll.; MA in Edn., SUNY, Buffalo. English language tchr. Orchard Park (N.Y.) Schs.; town councilman Town of Hamburg, N.Y., also town supv.; mem. U.S. Congress from 30th N.Y. Dist., 1993—; mem. transp. and infrastructure com., chmn. subcom. on railroads, mem. vet. affairs com. Recipient Humanitarian award Erie County for the Disabled, Pub. Svc. award Niagara Frontier Parks and Recreation Soc., Disting. Grad. award Nat. Cath. Elem. Schs. Assn., Bronze Good Citizen medal SAR, New Horizons award Drug Edn. of Internat. Assn. of Lions Club, Red, White and Blue award Am. Legion of N.Y., Honor medal Hilbert Coll., Fin. Reporting award Govt. Fin. Officer's Assn., Disting. Career Svc. award Siena Coll., 1995. Mem. Hamburg C. of C., Greater Buffalo C. of C., Buffalo KC, Hamburg Kiwanis Club. Republican. Roman Catholic. Office: US Ho Reps 2448 Rayburn Ho Office Bldg Washington DC 20515*

QUINN, JAMES BRIAN, business educator; b. Memphis, Mar. 18, 1928; s. Clarence A. and Henriette (Rein) Q.; m. Allie Brady James, Feb. 9, 1950; children— James Franklin, John Brady, Virginia Anne. BS in Engring, Yale, 1949; MBA, Harvard, 1951; PhD, Columbia, 1958; MA (hon.), Dartmouth, 1964. Rsch. adminstr. R&D Allen B. DuMont Labs., Inc., 1951-54; faculty marketing dept. U. Conn., 1954-57; faculty Amos Tuck Sch. Bus. Adminstrn., Dartmouth, 1957—, asst. dean, 1957-58, prof., 1964—. Vis. prof., lectr. Ctr. d' Etudes, Switzerlan, Monash U., Australian Grad. Sch. of Mgmt., U. Western Australia, Dalien U. in China; acad. dean Iternat. Mgmt. MBA Progam, Internat. U. Japan; mem. sci. and tech. bd. for Internat. Devel. Nat. Acad. Scis.; mem. spl. NAS teams on economics, planning, edn. for sci. and tech. in Colombia, Peru, USSR, People's Rep. of China; cons. to numerous leading U.S. and fgn. corps., U.S. and fgn. govts. and small enterprises; chmn. Nat. Acad. Engring coms. on Productivity of Info. Tech. in Svcs., Tech. in the Svcs. Sector, and Environ. Impact of Svcs. Author: Yardsticks for Industrial Research, 1959, Strategies for Change, 1980, (with H. Mintzberg and R. James) The Strategy Process, 1987, Technology in Services: Policies for Growth, Trade and Employment: Managing Innovation: Cases from the Services Sector, 1988, Intelligent Enterprise, 1992 (Am. Pub. Assn. Book of Yr. in Bus. and Scholarship, Am. Acad. Mgmt. Book of Yr.), Information Technology in the Service Economy, 1994, The Strategy Process: Concepts, Contexts, and Cases, 1995, Innovation Explosion, 1997; contbr. articles to profl. jours. including Harvard Bus. Rev., U.S. Acad. Mgmt. Jours.; creator of STRAT, TYCOON and Global TYCOON (computer strategy simulations). Recipient McKinsey Found. award, 1963, 68, 85; Ford Found. fellow, 1963-64; Sloan Found. fellow, 1967-68; Fulbright fellow, 1973, Outstanding Educator award, Acad. Mgmt., 1989, Best Article in U.S. Mgmt. Jours., 1992, 94, 97. Mem. AAAS. Home: 20 Low Rd Hanover NH 03755-2207 E-mail: j.brian.quinn@dartmouth.edu.

QUINN, JAMES W. lawyer; b. Bronxville, N.Y., Oct. 1, 1945; s. James Joseph Quinn and Marie Joan (Blossy) Tisi; m. Kathleen Manning, Kellianne, Christopher, Tierney, Kerrin. AB cum laude, U. Notre Dame, 1967; JD, Fordham U., 1971. Bar: N.Y. 1972, U.S. Dist. Ct. (so. and ea. dists.) N.Y. 1973, U.S. Ct. Appeals (2nd cir.) 1976, U.S. Supreme Ct. 1984, U.S. Ct. Appeals (3rd, 7th and 9th cirs.) 1985, U.S. Ct. Appeals (8th cir.) 1991. Assoc. Weil, Gotshal & Manges, N.Y.C., 1971-77, 78-79, ptnr., 1979—, Fleisher & Quinn, N.Y.C., 1977-78. Adj. assoc. prof. law Fordham U., N.Y.C., 1985-87. Co-author: Corporate Counsellors Deskbook, Litigating Complex Careers; editor: Fordham U. Law Rev., 1969—71; contbr. articles to profl. jours. Fellow Internat. Acad. Trial Lawyers, Am. Coll. Trial Lawyers; mem. ABA (litigation sect., co-chmn. subcom. alternate means of dispute resolution of com. corp. counsel, program chmn. trial practice com., sports and entertainment forum), Assn. of Bar of City of N.Y. (com. of state jurisdiction, com. on entertainment sports, com. on anti-trust regulation, chmn. sports law com.). Home: 1 Maple Way Armonk NY 10504-2602

QUINN, JANE BRYANT, journalist, writer; b. Niagara Falls, N.Y., Feb. 5, 1939; d. Frank Leonard and Ada (Laurie) Bryant; m. David Conrad Quinn, June 10, 1967; children— Matthew Alexander, Justin Bryant. BA magna cum laude, Middlebury Coll., 1960. Assoc. editor Insiders Newsletter, N.Y.C., 1962-65, co-editor, 1966-67; sr. editor Cowles Book Co., 1968; editor-in-chief Bus. Week Letter, 1969-73, gen. mgr., 1973-74; syndicated financial columnist Washington Post Writers Group, 1974—2001; contbr. fin. column to Women's Day mag., 1974-95; contbr. fin. column Good Housekeeping, 1995—; contbr. NBC News and Info. Service, 1976-77; bus. corr. WCBS-TV, N.Y.C., 1979, CBS-TV News, 1980-87, ABC-TV Home Show, 1991-93; contbg. editor Newsweek mag., 1978—. Host PBS personal fin. series Take Charge!, 1988. Author: Everyone's Money Book, 1979, 2d edit., 1980, Making the Most of Your Money, 1991, 2d edit., 1997, A Hole in the Market, 1994; contbr. Quicken Financial Planner, 1995. Mem. Phi Beta Kappa. Office: Newsweek Inc 251 W 57th St New York NY 10019-1802

QUINN, JARUS WILLIAM, physicist, former association executive; b. West Grove, Pa., Aug. 25, 1930; s. William G. and Ellen C. (DuRoss) Q.; m. Margaret M. McNerney, June 27, 1953; children: J. Kevin, Megan, Jennifer, Colin, Kristin. BS, St. Joseph's Coll., 1952; postgrad., Johns Hopkins U., 1952-55; PhD, Cath. U. Am., 1964. Rsch. assoc. physics Johns Hopkins U., 1954-55; staff scientist Rsch. Inst. Advanced Study, 1956-57; rsch. assoc. physics Cath. U. Am., 1958-60, instr., 1961-64, asst. prof., 1965-69; exec. dir. Optical Soc. Am., Washington, 1969-93; governing bd. Am. Inst. Physics, 1973-94; pres. Stellar Focus, Sunnyvale, Calif., 1994-95. Bd. govs. Am. Assn. Engring. Socs., 1990-93. Fellow Optical Soc. Am. (Distinguished Service Award, 1993), mem. Am. Phys. Soc., Am. Soc. Assn. Execs., Coun. Engring. and Sci. Soc. Execs. Home: 357 Fearrington Post Pittsboro NC 27312-8517 E-mail: optics2010@yahoo.com.

QUINN, JOHN ALBERT, chemical engineering educator; b. Springfield, Ill., Sept. 3, 1932; s. Edward Joseph and Marie (Von De Bur) Q.; m. Frances Wilkie Daly, June 22, 1957; children: Sarah D., Rebecca V., John E. BSChemE, U. Ill., 1954; PhDChemE, Princeton U., 1959. Mem. faculty chem. engring. U. Ill., Urbana, 1958-70; prof. U. Pa., Phila., 1971—, Robert D. Bent prof., 1978—, chmn. dept. chem. engring., 1980-85. Vis. prof. Imperial Coll. U. London, 1965-66; vis. scientist MIT, 1980; vis. prof. U. Rome/La Sapienza, 1992; mem. sci. adv. bds. Sepracor, Inc., Marlborough, Mass., 1984—, Whitaker Found., Mechanicsburg, Pa., 1987—; Mason lectr. Stanford U., 1981; Katz lectr. U. Mich., 1985; Reilly lectr. U. Notre Dame, 1987; Michael's lectr. MIT, 2001. Contbr. articles to profl. publs.; editl. advisor Jour. Membrane Sci., 1975—, Indsl. and Chem. Engring. Rsch., 1987-88, Revs. in Chem. Engring., 1980—; pioneer rschr. on mass transfer and interfacial phenomena. Sr. postdoctoral fellow NSF, 1965-66; Sherman Fairchild scholar Calif. Inst. Tech., 1985. Fellow AAAS, Am. Inst. Med. and Biol. Engring.; mem. NAE, AIChE (Allan P. Colburn award 1966, Alpha Chi Sigma award 1978), Am. Acad. Arts and Scis., Am. Chem. Soc., Internat. Soc. Oxygen Transport to Tissue, Sigma X, Phi Lambda Upsilon, Tau Beta Pi. Home: 275 E Wynnewood Rd Merion Station PA 19066-1627 Office: Univ Pa Towne Bldg 220 S 33rd St Philadelphia PA 19104-6393

QUINN, JOHN COLLINS, publishing executive, newspaper editor; b. Providence, Oct. 24, 1925; s. John A. and Kathryn H. (Collins) Q.; m. Lois R. Richardson, June 20, 1953; children: John Collins, Lo-anne, Richard B., Christopher A. AB, Providence Coll., 1945; MS, Columbia U. Sch. Journalism, 1946. Successively copy boy, reporter, asst. city editor, Washington corr., asst. mng. editor, day mng. editor Providence Jour.-Bull., 1943-66; with Gannett Co. Inc., Rochester, N.Y., 1966-90; exec. editor Rochester Democrat & Chronicle, Times-Union, 1966-71; gen. mgr. Gannett News Service, 1967-80, pres., 1980-88, v.p. parent co., 1971-75, sr. v.p. news and info., 1975-80, sr. v.p., chief news exec. parent co., editor USA TODAY, 1983-89; exec. v.p. Gannett Co., Arlington, Va., 1983-90; trustee Gannett Found., 1988-91; dep. chmn. Freedom Forum, 1991-97, trustee, 1991—. Named to R.I. Hall of Fame, 1975, Editor of Yr. Nat. Press Found., 1986; recipient William Allen White citation, 1987, Women in Communications Headliner award, 1986; Paul Miller/Okla. State U. medallion, 1988. Mem. AP Mng. Editors (past dir., nat. pres. 1973-74), Am. Soc. Newspaper Editors (dir., chmn. editorial bd., chmn. conv. program, nat. pres. 1982-83) Roman Catholic. Home: 365 S Atlantic Ave Cocoa Beach FL 32931-2719 Office: Freedom Forum 1101 Wilson Blvd Ste 2300 Arlington VA 22209-2265

QUINN, JOHN MICHAEL, physicist, geophysicist; b. Denver, May 8, 1946; s. Leonard Simon and Winifred Ruth (Doolan) Q.; m. Pamela Dagmar Shield, May 28, 1983. BS in Physics, U. Va., 1968; MS in Physics, U. Colo., 1982. Physicist U.S. Naval Rsch. Lab., Washington, 1967—73; prin. engr. Singer Simulation Products, Silver Spring, Md., 1973—74; rsch. physicist U.S. Naval Rsch. Lab, Washington, 1979—80; geophysicist U.S. Naval Oceanog. Office, Stennis Space Ctr., Miss., 1974—79, 1982—85, geophysicist, mathematician, 1985—95; rsch. geophysicist U.S. Geol. Survey, Denver, 1995—2002; ret., 2002; cons. Global Climate Change Inst. Investigator Polar Orbiting Geomagnetic Survey Experiment, 1990-94; prin. investigator Def. Meteorol. Satellite Program Polar Orbiting Geomagnetic Survey Ext., 1991-2002; chmn. com. on earth and planetary geomagnetic survey satellites Internat. Assn. Geomagnetism and Aeronomy, 1991-99, mem. internat. geomagnetic ref. field com., 1989-2002; U.S. del. UN Internat. Stds. Orgn., 2000-2002. Author: Epoch World Geomagnetic Model, 1985, 90, 95, 2000. With U.S. Army, 1968-71. Mem. Am. Geophys. Union, Am. Math. Soc., European Geophys. Soc., Math. Assn. Am. Achievements include creation of official Department of Defense world magnetic models which are used by military and civilian agencies for navigational purposes and basic rsch. of the earth's magnetic field; project coord. USN Project MAGNET; developed specialized remote geomagnetic sensing/modeling techniques to detect, in the lithosphere, magnetization due to meteorite impact shocks and hotspot basalt flows; engaged in geodynamo research, yielding high-resolution fluid-flow models at the core-mantle-boundary. Home: 2732 S Braun Way Lakewood CO 80228-4954 E-mail: mty_quinn@hotmail.com.

QUINN, JOHN PETER, lawyer, software designer; b. Bay City, Mich., Aug. 20, 1944; s. William Joseph and Helen Marie (Darland) Q.; m. Dana Elizabeth Hillman, June 1969 (div. 1974); 1 child, Adrianne; m. Sharon Margaret Goode, June 27, 1981; children: William, Catherine, Mary Margaret, John, Daniel. BS in Chemistry, Xavier U. La., New Orleans, 1968; JD cum laude, U. Mich., 1972. Bar: Mich. 1974, U.S. Dist. Ct. (ea. dist.) Mich. 1977, U.S. Ct. Appeal (6th cir.) 1977, U.S. Supreme Ct. 1985. Police officer Detroit Police Dept., 1973-74; counsel Detroit Bd. Police Commrs., 1974-76; chair bd. dirs. Quinn & Budaj, P.C., Detroit, 1977-85; asst. corp. counsel Detroit Law Dept., 1976-77, prin./supervising asst. corp. counsel, 1985—. Def. mediator Mediation Tribunal Assn., Detroit, 1995—; spkr. profl. seminars and confs. Contbr. articles to profl. jours. Chair bd. dirs. S.W. Alliance of Neighborhoods, Detroit, 1995—; founding mem. bd. dirs. S.W. Cmty. and Neighborhood Devel. Orgn., Detroit, 1990. With U.S. Army, 1968-70, Munich. Recipient Spirit of Detroit award Detroit City Coun., 1979. Mem. Detroit Bar Assn. (pub. adv. com., mediator, chair dist. ct. sect.), Assn. Def. Trial Counsel. Roman Catholic. Avocations: cottage living, camping, woodworking, classical languages. Office: City of Detroit Law Dept 1650 First Nat Bldg Detroit MI 48226

QUINN, LINDA VICTORIA, psychologist, consultant; b. Milw., Oct. 5, 1955; d. Lenord and Louise (Craig) Nixon; 1 child, Melaina Victoria Scott. BA, Mt. Mary Coll., Milw., 1989; MS, U. Wis., Milw., 1991, PhD, 1998. Cert. rehab. counselor. Residence counselor Oconomowoc Devel. Tng. Ctr., Milw., 1989-90; vocat. couselor Milw. Ctr. for Ind., 1991; rsch. asst. U. Wis., 1992; rehab. vocat. counselor Divsn. Vocat. Rehab., State of Wis., 1992-96; tng. group supr. Marquette U., 1996; counselor, therapist Counseling Ctr. Milw., 1995-97; project asst. U. Wis., Milw., 1996-97; psychology intern Grand Valley State U., Allendale, Mich., 1997-98; psychologist, coord. diverse student counseling U. Dayton, Ohio, 1998—. Adj. prof. U. Dayton, 1999—; mentor Grand Valley State U., Allendale, Mich., 1998. Contbr articles to profl. jours. Vol. Milw. Ctr. for Ind., 1991. Mem. APA (assoc.), Am. Coll. Pers. Assn., Counseling and Psychol. Svcs. (career devel. com. 1998—). Avocations: listening to jazz, travel, movies, reading. Office: U Dayton Counseling Ctr 300 College Park Dayton OH 45469-0001 E-mail: quinn@worf.udayton.edu.

QUINN, MICHAEL DESMOND, diversified financial services executive; b. Balt., Sept. 4, 1936; s. Michael Joseph and Gladys (Baldwin) Q.; m. Mary Annette McHenry, Apr. 11, 1961; children: Cailin A., Maureen K., Patricia B., Marianne P. BA, U. Md., 1970. With Weaver Bros., Inc. of Md., Balt., 1960—, investment v.p., corporate dir. interim loan dept., 1978-86; chmn. bd. Wye Mortgage Co., L.P., 1977—, Christiana Capital Group, Inc.; chmn., chief exec. officer Alliance Recovery Group, Inc., 1990—, Estate Trust Co., Inc.; faculty evening coll. Johns Hopkins U., Essex Community Coll., 1967—. Mem. gov.'s task force Md. Housing Ins. Fund; mem. Md. Health Claims Arbitration Panel; bd. visitors U. Md.; dist. adv. coun. U.S. Small Bus. Adminstrn. With USN, 1956-58. Mem. Md. Mortgage Bankers Assn. (pres. bd. govs.), Real Estate Bd. Greater Balt. (bd. dirs.), Home Builders Assn. Md., Md. Bankers Assn., Balt. Econ. Soc., N.Am. Soc. Corp. Planning, Soc. Cert. Sr. Advisors, Soc. Cert. Sr. Advisors, Greater Balt. Com., Ancient Order Hibernians, Balt Jr. Assn. Commerce (Richard Troja Meml. award 1967, Outstanding Young Man of Balt. 1969), Balt. County C. of C. (bd. dirs.). Home: 8207 Robin Hood Ct Baltimore MD 21204-1900 Office: 7400 York Rd Ste 300 Baltimore MD 21204-7502 E-mail: eti7400@aol.com.

QUINN, MICHAEL LLYN, construction executive; b. Chehalis, Wash., Apr. 2, 1952; s. Dick Wendell and Shirley Lee Quinn; m. Virginia Lynne Ahlgren; children: Shane, Scott. BSc in Engring. Constrn. Mgmt., Calif. State U., Sacramento, 1978. V. p. R. C. Hedreen Company, Seattle, 1981—90; v.p. E. Kent Halvorson Inc., Redmond, 1990. Fund raiser Muscular Distrophy, Seattle, 1990—2002. Avocations: cooking, running, travel. Office: E Kent Halvorson Inc. 9840 Willows Rd. Ste 200 Redmond WA 98052 Business E-Mail: Mike@ekhi.com.

QUINN, MICHAEL WILLIAM, public affairs educator; b. Detroit, Apr. 26, 1949; s. Hubert James and Carolee (Sproull) Q.; m. Deborah Cooper, Feb. 11, 1978; children: Michelle Diane, Brooks William. BA in Journalism, U. S.C., 1975, M in Mass Communications, 1976. Pub. info. officer USAR, Ft. Jackson, S.C., 1977-79, chief command info. div., 1979-85; pub. affairs officer IRS, Columbia, 1985-97, taxpayer advocate, 1997—2001, comms. br. chief, 2001—. Instr. Midlands Tech. Coll., Columbia, 1976-80; adj. prof. U. S.C., 1991—. Maj. USAR, 1968-2002. Democrat. Methodist. Office: IRS 1835 Assembly St Columbia SC 29201-2430 E-mail: mwquinn@aol.com.

QUINN, NIGEL WILLIAM TREVELYAN, scientist, engineer; b. Belfast, Northern Ireland, Nov. 28, 1955; , U.S., 1978; s. Stanley Quinn and Elaine Elizabeth Hayes. PhD, Cornell U., 1987. Registered profl. engr., Calif. Geol. scientist Berkeley (Calif.) Nat. Lab., 1990—; rsch. engr. U. Calif., 1999—2002. Convener Calif. Water and Environ. Modeling Forum, Sacramento, 2002—; bd. dirs. Internat. Symposium on Environ. Software Sys., Germany. Contbr. chapters to books, articles to profl. jours. Dir. UN Assn., Ames, 1978—81. Recipient Hunting Challenge Cup, Cranfield U., 1977. Mem.: Internat. Symposium Environ. Software Sys., Am. Water Resources Assn., Am. Geophysical Union, ASCE, Berkeley Yacht Club, Yolo Polo Club. Unitarian. Avocations: sailing, travel, polo. Home: 1123 Lochbrae Rd Sacramento CA 95815 Office: Berkeley Nat Lab 70A-3317H 1 Cyclotron Rd Berkeley CA 95815 Business E-Mail: nwquinn@lbl.gov.

QUINN, PAT (JOHN BRIAN PATRICK QUINN), professional sports team manager; b. Hamilton, Ont., Can., Jan. 29, 1943; s. John Ernest and Jean (Ireland) Q.; m. Sandra Georgia Baker, May 1, 1963; children: Valerie, Kathleen. BA in Econs., York U., 1972; JD, Del. Law Sch., 1987. Player Toronto Maple Leafs, Ont., 1968-70, Vancouver Canucks, B.C., Can., 1970-72, Atlanta Flames, 1972-77; coach Phila. Flyers, 1977-82, L.A. Kings, 1984-86; head coach Team Canada, 1986; pres., gen. mgr. Vancouver Canucks, 1987-97, head coach, 1990-97, Toronto Maple Leafs, 1997—. Player rep. NHL, Atlanta, 1973-77, bd. govs., 1987—. Named Def. Man of Yr., Vancouver Canucks, 1971, Coach of Yr. NHL, 1979-80, Coach of Yr., Sporting News, 1980, 92, Coach of the Yr. Hockey News, 1980, 92, Coach of the Yr. Acad. Awards of Sports, named to the Longest Unbeaten Record in Profl. Sports of 35 Games, 1979-80, named to the Best Record in the History of the Canucks Franchise, 1991-92; recipient Jake Milford award, 1994, Jack Diamond award, 1994. Roman Catholic. Avocations: sports, reading. Office: Toronto Maple Leafs 60 Carlton St Toronto ON Canada M5B 1L1*

QUINN, PAT MALOY, engineering company executive; b. Clay Ctr., Kans., May 28, 1932; s. Lawrence Maloy and Lois Shouse (Benjimen) Q.; m. Virginia Lois White, June 1, 1957; children: Michael Maloy, Jennifer Quinn Williams, Patrick Maloy, Amy Anne. BA in Literature, Kans. State U., 1954, BS in Civil Engring., 1960. Licensed engr., Kans., D.C., Va., N.Y., N.J., Pa., N.C., S.C., N.H., Ohio, Ill., Ind., Ky., W.Va. Civil engr. Schuab-Eaton, Manhattan, Kans., 1957-66, Louis Berger Internat., East Orange, N.J., 1966—, v.p., 1976-84, chief structural engr. Thailand, 1966-68, chief engr. Indonesia, 1968-72, project mgr. Peru, 1973, The Philippines, 1974, v.p. Iran, 1974-76, group v.p., ptnr., 1984—. 1st lt. U.S. Army, 1954-57, Germany. Mem. ASCE, ASME, NSPE. Office: Louis Berger Internat 1819 H St NE Ste 900 Washington DC 20002-4017

QUINN, PATRICK, tranportation executive; BA, U. Nebr., 1968, JD, 1971. From assoc. to ptnr. Nelson & Harding, Lincoln, Nebr., 1971-77; gen. counsel S.W. Motor Freight, Chattanooga, 1977-85; pres., co-chmn. U.S Xpress Enterprises, Inc., 1985—. Office: US Xpress Enterprises Inc 4080 Jenkins Rd Chattanooga TN 37421-1174

QUINN, PAUL C. psychologist, educator; b. Floral Park, N.Y., June 29, 1959; s. Neil and Mary Carden Q.; m. Laurie Anne Yarzab, Aug. 6, 1994. BSc magna cum laude, Brown U., 1981, PhD, 1986. Asst. prof. psychology U. Iowa, Iowa City, 1986-88; from asst. prof. to prof. psychology Washington & Jefferson Coll., Washington, 1988-2000, prof., 2000—. Author: (chpt.) Perceptual Development, 1998; assoc. editor Devel. Sci., 1998—, Child Devel., 2001—; mem. editl. bd. Devel. Psychology, 1997—, Jour. Exptl. Child Psychology, 1999—; contbr. articles to profl. jours. Hon. Univ. fellow Univ. Exeter, 1997; NSF grantee, 1999. Mem. APA, Am. Psychol. Soc., Psychonomic Soc., Cognitive Sci. Soc., Internat. Soc. Infant Studies, Soc. Rsch. Child Devel. (chair rev. panel 1999, 2001). Avocations: jogging, swimming. Office: Washington & Jefferson Coll 60 S Lincoln St Washington PA 15301 E-mail: pquinn@washjeff.edu.

QUINN, PHILIP LAWRENCE, philosophy educator; b. Long Branch, N.J., June 22, 1940; s. Joseph Lawrence and Gertrude (Brown) Q. AB, Georgetown U., 1962; MS, U. Del., 1967; MA, U. Pitts., 1968, PhD, 1970; MA (hon.), Brown U., 1972. Asst. prof. philosophy Brown U., Providence, 1969-72, assoc. prof. philosophy, 1972-78, prof. philosophy, 1978-85, William Herbert Perry Faunce prof. philosophy, 1982-85; John A. O'Brien prof. philosophy U. Notre Dame, South Bend, Ind., 1985—. Author: (book) Divine Command and Moral Requirements, 1978; editor Faith and Philosophy, 1990-95; co-editor: A Companion to Philosophy of Religion, 1997, The Philosophical Challenge of Religious Diversity, 1999; contbr. articles to profl. jours. Fulbright fellow, 1962-63; Danforth fellow, 1967-69. Mem. Am Philos. Assn. (sec., treas. ea. divsn. 1982-85, chmn. career opportunities com. 1985-90, exec. com. ctrl. divsn. 1987-90, v.p. ctrl. divsn. 1993-94, pres. 1994-95, chair ctrl. divsn. nominating com. 1995-96, acting chair Nat. Bd. of Officers 1995-96, chair 1996-99), Philosophy of Sci. Assn. (nominating com. 1984-86), Soc. Christian Philosophers (exec. com. 1981-84), Am. Acad. Religion (steering com. philosophy of religion sect. 1999--). Roman Catholic. Avocations: reading, swimming, film, theater . Home: 1645 W Turtle Creek Dr South Bend IN 46637-5660 Office: Univ Notre Dame Dept Philosophy Notre Dame IN 46556

QUINN, ROBERT NEAL, retired computer company executive, artist, freelance/self-employed writer; b. Bklyn., Feb. 8, 1927; s. Thomas Henry and Florence Quinn; m. Dolores Mae King, Sept. 20, 1952 (dec. Nov. 18, 1983); m. Barbara Joanne Hargis, July 5, 1984; children: Bonnie, Kimberly, Steven. Student, La. State U., 1947—48. Petty officer USN, 1943—52; field engr. IBM, Houston, 1952—59, Galveston, 1959—65, br. mgr. Beaumont, 1965—67, L.A., 1967—69, mgr. field ops. N.Y.C., 1969—71, br. mgr. Miami, Fla., 1971—73, Ft. Worth, 1973—83. Mgmt. devel. cons. IBM, 1973—83. Author: (anthologies) Fall From Innocence, 1997, Suddenly, 1998, Muscadine Vine and Clear CreekWater, 2002, Promises, 2002, (novels) Damon, 2001, Beyond the Looking Glass, 2002. Pres. Toastmasters, Galveston, 1968—69; chmn. bd. govs. Country Clubs of Am., 1996—2000. Recipient Adm.'s Commendation, USN, 1950. Mem.: Escort Aircraft Carriers Assn. of Am., Amphibious Sailor's Assn., Vets. of Underage Mil. Servicemen Orgn., Scribblers Writers Club. Avocations: writing, painting.

QUINN, RODNEY DAVID, neurologist; b. Champaign, Ill., Sept. 1, 1955; s. Paul Stanley and Doris Marilyn (Dormire) Q.; m. Roberta Rae Chiles, June 12, 1977; children: Rebecca, Philip, Sarah. BS in Biology, U. Mo., 1978, MD, 1980. Diplomate Am. Bd. Psychiatry and Neurology, Am. Bd. Clin. Neurophysiology, Nat. Bd. Med. Examiners. Cons. neurologist Springfield Neurol. Assocs., 1985-88; chmn. of neurology Cox Health Systems, Springfield, 1991-93, chief of staff, 1994; cons. neurologist Ferrell-Duncan Clinic, 1988—. Dir. Muscular Dystrophy Assn. Clinic, Springfield, 1985—, Clin. Neurophysiology Lab., Cox Health Systems, 1985—. Named to Hall of Fame Greater Ozarks chpt. Muscular Dystrophy Assn., 1995. Fellow Am. EEG Soc.; mem. Mo. State Neurol. Assn., Am. Acad. Neurology. Methodist. Avocations: musical performance acoustical stringed instruments, wilderness conservation management, astronomy. Office: Ferrell-Duncan Clinic PO Box 9007 Springfield MO 65808-9007 E-mail: rodney.quinn@coxhealth.com.

QUINN, SONDRA, science center executive; BA, Pa. State U., 1962; MEd, U. Pitts., 1965; postgrad., U. Calif., Berkeley, 1986. Pres. Orlando (Fla.) Sci. Ctr., Inc. Mem. Fla. Sci. Edn. Improvement Adv. Com.; advisor scholastic sci. project Scholastic, Inc.; former chair steering com. Ctrl. Fla. Non-Profit Group for Quality Improvement; mem. rev. panel NSH, NEH, Inst. Mus. Svcs., Dept. Energy, Fla. Divsn. Cultural Affairs Sci. Mus. Programs. Mem. bus. leadership Orlando City of Light Program; active Art Svcs. Coun., Boy Scouts Am., State of Fla. Task Force for Comprehensive Plan to Improve Math., Sci. and Computer Edn. Recipient Cmty. Leader of Yr. award, Woman of Yr. award in Arts and Culture Phi Delta Kappa, 1995, Key to City of Orlando, 1997. Mem. Getty Leadership Inst. (adv. com.), Giant Screen Theater Assn. (bd. dirs., chair mem. com., selection com.), Mus. Film Network (sec., bd. dirs.), U. Ctrl. Fla. Found. (bd. dirs.), Fla. Assn. Mus. (past bd. dirs., regional membership coord., head sci. sect., Mus. Svc. Lifetime achievement award 1996), Am. Assn. Mus. (bd. dirs. 1992-95, various coms.), Assn. Sci. and Tech. Ctrs. (bd. dirs., chair exhibit svcs. com., former chair new and developing mus. com., program com., human resources com., former v.p. small mus.). Office: Orlando Sci Ctr Inc 777 E Princeton St Orlando FL 32803-1291

QUINN, TIMOTHY CHARLES, JR. lawyer; b. Caro, Mich., Mar. 3, 1936; s. Timothy Charles and Jessie (Brown) Q.; m. Linda Ricci, June 21, 1958; children: Gina M., Samantha E., Timothy Charles III. BA, U. Mich., 1960; JD, Columbia U., 1963. Bar: N.Y. 1963, U.S. Dist. Ct. (so. and ea. dists.) N.Y. 1965, U.S. Ct. Appeals (2d cir.) 1967. Assoc. Clark, Carr & Ellis, N.Y.C., 1963-69, Casey, Tyre, Wallace & Bannerman, N.Y.C., 1969-71, Arsham & Keenan, N.Y.C., 1971, Conboy, Hewitt, O'Brien & Boradman, N.Y.C., 1972-74, ptnr., 1975-83, mem. exec. com., 1981-83; ptnr. Quinn, Cohen, Shields & Bock, 1983-88, Quinn & Suhr, White Plains, N.Y., 1988-95, Quinn, Marantis & Rosenberg, White Plains, 1995-97, Dickerson & Reilly, N.Y.C., 1997—. Arbitrator N.Y.C. Civil Ct., 1982-88 , Am. Arbitration Assn., N.Y.C., 1966—, 9th Jud. Dist., 1988—. Mem. ABA, N.Y. State Bar Assn., Westchester County Bar Assn., Assn. of Bar of City of N.Y., N.Y. State Trial Lawyers Assn., Nat. Assn. R.R. Trial Counsel, Conf. Freight Loss and Damage Counsel, N.Y. Law Inst., Def. Rsch. Inst., Westchester Country Club. Avocation: golf. Office: Dickerson & Reilly 780 3rd Ave New York NY 10017-2024 Address: 70 W Red Oak Ln White Plains NY 10604-3602 Home: 105B Pemberwick Rd Greenwich CT 06831-5012

QUINN, TIMOTHY ROBERT, dermatopathologist, consultant; b. Windsor, Ont., Can., Dec. 14, 1964; HBSc, McMaster U., 1988; MDCM, McGill U., 1992. Diplomate Am. Bd. Pathology, Am. Bd. Dermatopathology. Resident in pathology Mass. Gen. Hosp., Boston, 1993-96; fellow in dermatopathology Harvrd Med. Sch., 1996-97; dermatopathologist Pathology Svcs., Cambridge, Mass., 1997—. Office: Pathology Svcs 640 Memorial Dr Cambridge MA 02139-4853 E-mail: tquinn@pathsrv.com.

QUINN, TOM, communications executive; b. L.A., Mar. 14, 1944; s. Joseph Martin and Grace (Cooper) Quinn; children: Douglas, Lori, Shelby. BS, Northwestern U., 1965. Reporter, newswriter ABC Radio, Chgo. and L.A., 1965; reporter, prodr. Sta. KXTV, Sacramento, 1966; day editor City News Svc., L.A., 1966-68, chmn., 1980-85; pres. Americom Broadcasting, Inc., 1985—. Pres. Radio News West, L.A., 1968—70, Reno Radio Reps, 1998—, KFSO Radio, Fresno, 1995—98; dir. Southland News, L.A. Mem. governing bd. Tahoe Regional Planning Agy., 2002—; campaign mgr. Jerry Brown for Sec. State, L.A., 1970; dep. sec. state Calif. Sacramento, 1971—74; campaign mgr. Brown for Gov., L.A., 1974; sec. Calif. Dept. Environ. Affairs, Sacramento, 1975—79; chmn. Calif. Air Resources Bd., 1975—79, Tom Bradley Mayoral Campaign, 1985. Recipient Headliner of Yr. award Greater L.A. Press Club, 1978, Environ. Protection award Calif. Trial Lawyers Assn., 1979. Democrat. Office: # 1880 1900 Ave of the Stars Los Angeles CA 90067

QUINN, WILLIAM FRANCIS, lawyer, director; b. Rochester, N.Y., July 13, 1919; s. Charles Alvin and Elizabeth (Dorrity) Q.; m. Nancy Ellen Witbeck, July 11, 1942; children: William Francis, Stephen Desford, Timothy Charles, Christopher Thomas, Ann Cecily, Mary Kaiulani, Gregory Anthony. BS summa cum laude, St. Louis U., 1940; LL.B. cum laude, Harvard U., 1947. Bar: Hawaii 1948. Ptnr. Robertson, Castle & Anthony, Honolulu, 1947-57; gov. Ter. of Hawaii, 1957-59, State of Hawaii, Honolulu, 1959-62; ptnr. Quinn & Moore, 1962-64; exec. v.p. Dole Co., Honolulu., 1964-65, pres., 1965-72; ptnr. Jenks, Kidwell, Goodsill & Anderson, Honolulu, 1972-73, Goodsill Anderson & Quinn, 1973-82, Goodsill Anderson Quinn & Stifel, 1982-91; ret., 1991. Mem. sr. adv. bd. 9th Cir. Jud. Coun. Served with USNR, 1942-46. Decorated knight of Holy Sepulchre Order. Mem. Pacific Club (Honolulu). Republican. Roman Catholic. Home: 4340 Pahoa Ave Apt 13C Honolulu HI 96816-5023

QUINN, YVONNE SUSAN, lawyer; b. Spring Valley, Ill., May 13, 1951; d. Robert Leslie and Shirley Eilene (Morse) Quinn. BA, U. Ill., 1973; JD, U. Mich., 1976, MA in Econs., 1977. Bar: N.Y. 1978, U.S. Dist. Ct. (ea. and so. dists.) N.Y. 1978, U.S. Ct. Appeals (3d, 5th, 9th, 10th and D.C. cirs.) 1982, U.S. Ct. Appeals (2d cir.) 1992, U.S. Ct. Appeals (4th cir.) 1994, U.S. Supreme Ct. 1982. Assoc. Cravath, Swaine & Moore, N.Y.C., 1977-80, Sullivan & Cromwell, N.Y.C., 1980-84, ptnr., 1984—. Mem. ABA, Assn. of Bar of City of N.Y., India House Club. Office: Sullivan & Cromwell 125 Broad St New York NY 10004-2489

QUINONES, JOSE RAMON, JR. obstetrician-gynecologist, educator; b. N.Y.C., 1940; MD, U. P.R., 1963. Diplomate Am. Bd. Ob-Gyn. Intern USAF Hosp., Washington, 1963-64; resident in ob-gyn. Kings County-SUNY Downstate Med. Ctr., Bklyn., 1967-71; staff N.Y. Meth. Hosp. Bklyn., 1971—, Brookdale Hosp., Bklyn., 1985—2001. Clin. assoc. prof. SUNY Downstate. Fellow ACOG, ACS; mem. AMA. Office: Ste 103 6410 Veterans Ave Brooklyn NY 11234

QUINONES-D'BRASSIS, R. RAFAEL, civil engineer; b. San German, P.R., Aug. 16, 1937; s. Rafael Angel and Teresa (D'Brassis) Q.; m. Miriam Esther Rivera, Oct. 12, 1960 (div. 1982); children: Maria C., Rafael I., Lourdes M., Jose R.; m. Martha Otilia Neris, Oct. 22, 1982 (div. 1991); m. Buenaventura Bejarano, Apr. 11, 1993. BSCE, U. P.R., 1961; cert., Caribbean Acad. Mgmt., 1968. Cert. value engr., U.S. Army C.O.E., 1988; registered profl. engr. Ariz., Fla., P.R. Field engr. Maxon Constrn. Corp., Rincon, P.R., 1960-64, Austin Co., Barceloneta, 1967-68; project engr. Rexach Constrn. Co., Inc., San Juan, 1965-67; project mgr. Fuentes Concrete Pile Co., Bayamon, P.R., 1968-70, IBEC-Bland Constrn. Corp., Dorado, 1970-74; prin. R.R. Quinones-D'Brassis & Assoc., Mayaguez, 1974-80; liaison engr. Howard, Needles, Tammen & Bergendoff, Tampa, Fla., 1980-81, sr. civil engr., project mgr. Phoenix, 1981-91; area engr. HNTB Corp., Tampa, Fla., 1991-95; constrn. project mgr. St. Johns River Water Mgmt. Dist., Palatka, 1996—. Lectr. in field. Contbr. articles to profl. jours; inventor in field. Mem. ASCE, Lions, Rotary, KC. Avocations: computer, photography, golf, travel. Home: 607 S Moody Rd Apt 14B Palatka FL 32177-3955 Office: St Johns River Water Mgmt Dist PO Box 1429 Palatka FL 32178-1429

QUIÑONES KEBER, ELOISE, art historian, educator; b. L.A. d. Rudy Jr. and Margaret (Romero) Q. BA, Immaculate Heart Coll., 1966; MA, UCLA, 1967, Columbia U., 1979, PhD, 1984. Lectr. Columbia U., N.Y.C., 1984-86; prof. art history Baruch Coll., The Grad. Ctr., CUNY, 1986—. Author: Codex Telleriano Remensis: Ritual, Divination, and History in a Pictorial Aztec Manuscript, 1995 (Getty Grant Program Publ. Subvention award, 1992); co-author: Art of Aztec Mexico: Treasures of Tenochtitlan, 1983; editor: Chipping Away on Earth: Studies in Prehispanic and Colonial Mexico in Honor of Arthur J.O. Anderson and Charles E. Dibble, 1995, In Chalchihuitl in Quetzalli: Mesoamerican Studies in Honor of Doris Heyden, 2000, Representing Aztec Ritual: Performance, Text, and Image in the Work of Sahagún, 2002; co-editor: The Work of Bernardino de Sahagun: Pioneed Ethnographer of 16th-Century Aztec Mexico, 1988, Mixteca-Puebla: Discoveries and Research in Mesoamerican Archaeology and Art, 1994; contbr. articles to profl. jours. Mellon postdoctoral fellow Columbia U., 1984-86, fellow Ford Found./NRC, 1986-87, Am. Coun. of Learned Socs. fellow, 1987-88, 93-94, grantee, 1985, 95, NEH fellow, 1993-94, grantee, 1986, 91; grantee Am. Philos. Soc., 1986; fellow Guggenheim Found., 1998; recipient

Ralph Waldo Emerson award Phi Beta Kappa Soc., 1996. Mem. Coll. Art Assn., Assn. Latin Am. Art, Am. Soc. for Ethnohistory. Office: CUNY Baruch Coll Dept Art History 55 Lexington Ave Box B7-235 New York NY 10010-1703 E-mail: Eloise_Quinones-Keber@baruch.cuny.edu., EQuinones-Keber@gc.cuny.edu.

QUINSON, BRUNO ANDRE, publishing executive; b. Norwich, Conn., Jan. 1, 1938; s. Louis Jean and Suzanne Marie (Richard) Q.; m. Mary Ann Goodman, May 3, 1980; children by previous marriage: Timothy Bruno, Marc Albert (dec.), Christopher Louis; stepchildren: J. Geoffrey Taylor, Luke J. Taylor (dec.), Adam J. Taylor, Joshua P. Taylor. BA, Williams Coll., 1958; postgrad., NYU, 1960-61. Product mgr. Simon & Schuster, N.Y.C., 1960-65; pub., gen. mgr. Golden Press (div. Western Pub. Co., Inc.), 1965-70; pres. Larousse & Co., Inc., N.Y.C., 1970-82, also bd. dirs.; pres. trade and reference div. Macmillan Pub. Co., 1982-88; pres., chief exec. officer Henry Holt & Co. Inc., 1988-96. Bd. dirs. Millbrook Press, 1999—, The Frost Place, Music & More, Fitzhenry & Whiteside, Nat. Book Found., chmn., 1993-96; treas. Columbia Univ. Press, 1994—, vice chmn., 1997—; mem. exec. bd. MacMillan Ltd., 1995-96. Bd. dirs. Rye (N.Y.) Art Ctr., treas., 1973-74; bd. dirs. Northside Ctr. for Child Devel., 1981-89, chmn., 1987-89, mem. adv. bd., 1990—; bd. dirs. 1115 Fifth Ave. Corp., 1983-94, 96—, pres., 1998—; bd. dirs. Mus. of the City of N.Y., 1999—, Lycee Francais de New York, 1994-96, Vol. Cons. Group, 1997, Each Child a Reader Found., 1996; founding mem. Barrington Stage Co.; founding mem., bd. dirs. Interlaken Sch. Art, 1998-2001; mem. nat. adv. bd. Eudora Welty Found., 2002--. Decorated chevalier Des Arts et Lettres (France). Mem. Am. Assn. Pubs. (bd. dirs. 1991-95), Pubs.' Lunch Club (pres. 1990-93), Century Assn., Manhattan Theater Club (bd. dirs. 1991-97), Norfolk Country Club, The River Club. Office: 2 E 93rd St New York NY 10128-0610

QUINT, ARNOLD HARRIS, lawyer; b. Boston, Jan. 3, 1942; s. Milton and Esther (Kirshen) Q.; m. Susan Arenson, July 23, 1967; children: Edward, Michael. AB, Haverford (Pa.) Coll., 1963; LLB, Yale U., 1966. Bar: D.C. 1967. Supervisory atty. Power Commn., Washington, 1967-70; assoc. Hunton & Williams, 1970-74, ptnr., 1974—. Mem. ABA, Energy Bar Assn. (com. chmn. 1979-83, bd. dirs. 1989-92). Office: Hunton & Williams 1900 K St NW Washington DC 20006-1110 E-mail: aquint@hunton.com.

QUINT, BERT, journalist; b. N.Y.C., Sept. 22, 1930; s. George and Sadye (Slonim) Q.; m. Diane Frances Schwab, Apr. 10, 1975; children: Lara Gabrielle, Amy Frances. BS, NYU, 1952. Reporter Worcester (Mass.) Telegram, 1952-53, AP, 1953-54, N.Y. Herald Tribune, 1956-58; mag. editor, free lance corr. N.Y. Herald Tribune, Wall Street Jour., CBS News, others, Mexico City, 1958-65; corr. CBS News, 1965-93; adj. prof. broadcast journalism U. Colo., Boulder, 1993-97; journalist/anchor/writer TV Quint Colo. Inc.; writer, novelist, 1998—. Recipient Radio Reporting award Overseas Press Club, 1971. Mem. Soc. Profl. Journalists. Home and Office: 126 Annette Dr Portsmouth RI 02871-3704

QUINT, IRA, retail executive; b. N.Y.C., May 29, 1930; s. Theodore Isaac and Rebecca (Ginandes) Q.; m. Carol Ann Goldsmith (div. Feb. 1984); children: Susan Amy, Stephanie Ann. BS, NYU, 1951; MBA, Harvard U., 1954. Group nat. mdse. mgr. Sears Roebuck & Co., Chgo., 1954-78; pres. Colonial Corp. Am., N.Y.C., 1978-79; pres., CEO Venture Stores, St. Louis, 1979-81; exec. v.p. Montgomery Ward, Chgo., 1981-85; pres. Lane Bryant Stores, N.Y.C., 1985-90; pres., chief exec. officer Conston Corp., Phila., 1990-92; pres. Quint Consultancy, N.Y.C., 1992—; dir. Maggie Moos Internat., 2001—. Bd. dirs. MaggieMoos Internat. Mem.: Harvard (N.Y.C.). Home and Office: 130 E 67th St New York NY 10021-6136

QUINTANA, JOSE BOOTH, health care executive; b. Coral Gables, Fla., July 13, 1946; s. Jose Luis and Carmen Elaine (Booth) Q.; m. Mary Jo Gregg, Sept. 7, 1968; children: Stephanie Elizabeth, Meredith Caroline. BSBA, U. Fla., 1968; MHA, Duke U., 1974; PhD, U. Ala., 1984. Commd. 2d lt. USAF, 1969, advanced through grades to lt. col., 1985, resigned, 1989; dir. pers. and adminstrv. svcs. USAF Regional Hosp., March AFB, Calif., 1969-71, adminstrv. asst. hosp. svcs., 1971-72; adminstr. USAF Hosp., Ubon Royal Thai Air Base, Thailand, 1974, Kunsan Air Base, South Korea, 1974-75; dir. pers. and adminstrv. svcs. USAF Regional Hosp., Maxwell AFB, Ala., 1975, dir. patent info., 1975-76, dir. med. resource mgmt., 1976-78; chief med. readiness ops. divsn. Office of Surgeon, USAF in Europe, Ramstein AFB, West Germany, 1978-81; strategic planner, health affairs and plans divsn. Office Air Force Surgeon Gen., Bolling AFB, Washington, 1984-86, sr. health rsch. analyst, directorate med. plans and resources, 1986-89; health svcs. rsch. and devel. coord., rsch. svc. VA Med. Ctr., Birmingham, Ala., 1989—, exec. asst. to dir. (quality), 1991—, acute care mgr. surg. svc., 1997—; asst. prof. dept. health svcs. adminstrn. U. Ala., 1989—. Lectr. in field. Contbr. articles to profl. jours. Fellow ACHE; mem. Assn. Health Svcs. Rsch., Assn. Univ. Programs in Health Adminstrn., Acad. Mgmt., Phi Kappa Phi, Beta Gamma Sigma. Republican. Southern Baptist. Avocations: computers, bridge, bible study. Office: U Ala at Birmingham Dept Health Svcs Adminstrn Webb 512 1530 3d Ave S Birmingham AL 35294-3361 E-mail: quintana@uab.edu.

QUINTANILLA, ANTONIO PAULET, retired physician, educator; b. Feb. 8, 1927; came to U.S., 1963, naturalized, 1974; s. Leandro Marino and Edel Paulet Quintanilla; m. Mary Parker Rodriguez, May 2, 1958; children: Antonio Paulet, Angela, Francis, Cecilia, John. PhD, San Marcos U., 1948, MD, 1957. Assoc. prof. physiology U. Arequipa, Peru, 1960-63; assoc. in physiology Cornell U., N.Y., 1963-64; prof. physiology U. Arequipa, 1964-68; assoc. prof. medicine Northwestern U., 1969-80, prof., 1980-2000; ret., 2000. Chief renal sect. VA Lakeside Hosp., 1976-90; cons. nephrologist Northwestern Meml. Hosp., Evanston Hosp., 1990-98, sr. attending emeritus; lectr. nat. Ctr. Advanced Med. Edn., Chgo.; mem. adv. bd. Am. Fedn. Clin. Rsch. Contbr. articles on renal disease to med. jours.; author books in English and Spanish, poetry, short stories. Fellow ACP; mem. Ctrl. Soc. Clin. Rsch., Internat. Soc. Nephrology, Am. Soc. Nephrology, Am. Physiol. Soc. Home: 650 S River Rd Unit 411 Des Plaines IL 60016-8428 E-mail: a.p.quintanilla@worldnet.att.net.

QUINTANILLA-VILLANUEVA, ROSALINDA, economist; b. Monterrey, Mex., Feb. 22, 1955; came to U.S., 1978; d. Ernesto Quintanilla and Marina Villanueva. BA in Econs. with high honors, Inst. Tech. Monterrey, 1976; MA in Econs., U. Wis., Milw., 1979; PhD in Econs., U. Minn., 1988. Rsch. assoc. Econometric Unit Inst. Tech. Monterrey, 1976; cons. Grupo Indsl. ALFA, Monterrey, 1977; assoc. prof. econs. U. Autonoma Metropolitana, Mexico City, 1977-78; cons. World Bank, Washington, 1983—. Nat. Coun. Sci. and Technology fellow, 1978-82. Avocations: painting, pottery, stained glass, Mexican history. Office: World Bank 1818 H St NW Washington DC 20433-0001

QUINTANS, ALFREDO SISON, JR. thoracic and cardiovascular surgeon; b. Dagupan City, Philippines, Dec. 25, 1937; s. Alfredo L. Quintans, Sr. and Sotera S. Sison; m. Estrellita Tan Quintans: children: Armel, Alfredo III, Arlene Quintans Carr. MD, U. Santo Tomas, Manilla, Philippines, 1961. Diplomate Am. Bd. Gen. Surgery, Am. Bd. Thoracic Surgery; lic. surgeon, N.C., N.Y. Rotating intern St. Luke's Hosp., Newburgh, N.Y., 1963-64, surg. resident, 1964-66, chief surg. resident, 1966-67, 68-69, emergency room physician, 1969-70, attending thoracic and cardiovascular surgeon, 1972—; chief surg. resident Youngstown (Ohio) Hosp. Assocs., 1967-68; resident in thoracic and cardiovascular surgery VA Hosp./Duke U. Hosp., Oteen and Durham, N.C., 1970-72; pvt. practice thoracic and cardiovascular surgeon New Windsor, N.Y., 1972—; attending thoracic and cardiovascular surgeon Cornwall (N.Y.) Hosp., 1972—. Cons. VA. Hosp., Castle Point, N.Y. Fellow ACS, Am. Coll. Chest Physicians; mem. Am. Thoracic Soc. (N.Y. Trudeau Soc. chpt.), Soc. Thoracic Surgeons, N.Y. State Med. Soc., Med. Soc. County Orange, Mid-Hudson Surg. Soc., Inc. Home: 3212 Nys Route 9W New Windsor NY 12553-6756

QUINTERO, RONALD GARY, management consultant; b. Detroit, Jan. 5, 1954; s. John Urdiales and Jean Lorraine (Morton) Q.; m. Barbara Kay McDaniel, June 15, 1985; children: Jean Marie, Alexandra Lisa. AB, Lafayette Coll., 1975; MS, NYU, 1976, APC, 1978. CPA, CFA, CFP, cert. mgmt. acct., cert. fraud examiner, cert. insolvency, cert. turnaround profl.; accreditation in bus. valuation. Sr. mgr. Peat, Marwick, Mitchell & Co., N.Y.C., 1975-85; workout cons. Zolfo, Cooper & Co., 1985-87; assoc. Bear, Stearns & Co., Inc., 1987-88; prin. R. G. Quintero & Co., 1988—. Mng. dir. Chartered Capital Advisers, Inc., N.Y.C., 1988—; adj. prof. New Sch. for Social Rsch., N.Y.C., 1983-85; internat. lectr.; adj. prof. N.Y. Inst. Fin., N.Y.C., 1988—; instr. Ctr. for Profl. Edn., Berwyn, Pa., 1991—; leading provider CFA Sems. Author: (book and cassette) Mergers and Acquisitions, 1990; contbg. author several books; contbr. articles to profl. jours.; creator: Quintero Index of Bankrupt Stocks. Mem. AICPAs, Am. Bankruptcy Inst., N.Y. Soc. CPAs (chmn. com. 1990-91, Max Block Disting. Article award 1990, Outstanding Discussion Leader 1991), Turnaround Mgmt. Assn. (bd. dirs., exec. com.). Avocations: squash, softball, running, computers, reading. Office: R G Quintero & Co 145 4th Ave New York NY 10003-4906 E-mail: chartered@aol.com.

QUINTIERE, GARY GANDOLFO, lawyer; b. Passaic, N.J., Nov. 26, 1944; s. Benjamin and Sadie (Riotto) Q.; m. Judy Rosenthal, Aug. 16, 1966; children: Karen, Geoffrey. AB in Govt., Lafayette Coll., 1966; JD, George Washington U., 1969. Bar: Va. 1969, D.C. 1970. Law clk. to Judge Philip Nichols, Jr. U.S. Ct. Appeals (Fed. cir.), Washington, 1969-70; from assoc. to ptnr. Miller & Chevalier, 1970-85; ptnr. Morgan, Lewis & Bockius, 1985—. Mem. ABA, D.C. Bar Assn., Va. Bar Assn., Am. Coll. Employee Benefits Counsel. Avocations: tennis, skiing, golf. Home: 14 Mercy Ct Potomac MD 20854-4540 Office: Morgan Lewis & Bockius 1111 Pennsylvania Ave NW Washington DC 20004

QUINTO, ERIC TODD, mathematics educator; b. Indpls., May 10, 1951; s. Joel Leon and Mary Lorena (Zimmer) Q.; m. Judith Anne Larsen, Aug. 29, 1993; 1 child, Laura Beth. BA with honors, Ind. U., 1973; PhD, MIT, 1978. Asst. prof. to prof. Tufts U., Medford, Mass., 1978-92, prof., 1992—. Co-head Tufts Budget and Priorties com., 1995-98. Assoc. editor Jour. Fourier Analysis and Applications, 1994—; co-editor: Integral Geometry, 1990, Tomography, 1994, Ehrenpreis Conference, 1999; head editor: Radon transforms and tomography, 2000; contbr. articles to profl. jours. Vol. Boston Children's Hosp., 1989—; Leadership vol., 1998—. Grantee NSF, 1982-84, 87—, NIH, 1984-87; fellow Humboldt Stiftung, 1985, 92, 99. Mem. Am. Math. Soc., Math. Assn. Am., Assn. Women in Math., Phi Beta Kappa (chpt. pres. 1987-90). Office: Tufts Univ Dept Math Medford MA 02155 E-mail: equinto@tufts.edu.

QUINT-ROSE, MARYLIN IRIS, artist; b. Boston, Apr. 1, 1927; d. Julius Nathaniel Lewis and Helen Isabelle (Lipp) Quint; m. Sidney Rose, Oct. 30, 1948 (div. Sept. 1979). BS in Edn., Wheelock Coll., 1948; MFA, Bard Coll., 1985. Instr., designer Sch. of the Worcester Art Mus., 1966-79; prof. art U. New England, Biddeford, Maine, 1981-89, lectr. anatomy-art, 1990. Vis. artist Castleton (Vt.) State Coll., 1988; lectr. U. of Women, York, Maine, 1992; adv. bd. Skowhegan (Maine) Art Sch., 1989-90; guest curator Payson Gallery Art/Westbrook Coll., 1980; guest artist sculpture rev. bds. U. Mass., 1994; guest artist, lectr. Holy Cross, 1996, Portland Sch. Art, David Winton Bell Gallery, Brown U., 1987; guest artist, awards com. U. N.H., 1986; lectr. Castleton State Coll., 1988. One woman exhibits include Payson Gallery of Art, Westbrook Coll., Portland, Maine, 1981, Varley & Stevens Galleries, Portsmouth, 1985, Edith C. Blum Inst. Bard Coll., 1985, Kuhn Gallery, Cape Neddick, Maine, 1986, Castleton (Vt.) State Coll., 1988, Barn Gallery, Ogunquit, Maine, 1989, U. R.I., Kingston, 1993, Portland Mus. of Art, 1993, York Inst., Saco, Maine, 1998; exhibited in group shows at Barn Gallery, 1991, Cape Neddick Show House, 1991, Leopold-Hoesch Mus., Duren, Germany, 1992, Danforth Gallery, 1995, Ogunquit Mus. of Art, 1995, Maine Coast Artists, Rockport, 1996, Portland Mus. of Art, 1985, 96, Maine Coast Artists, 1997, O'Farrell Gallery, Brunswick, Maine, 2000, Ficker Libr., Camden Pub. Libr, 20000, others; work represented in permanent collections including Portland Art Mus., Citicorp Park, Champion Paper Co., Tom's of Main, A.G. Edwards, others. Active cmty. svc. program U. South Maine, Portland, 1989; panel meaning art Brick Store Mus., Kennebunk, Maine, 1988; lectr. Camden Pub. Libr., 1999. Recipient Bertha K. Barstow 1st prize Pittsfield Art Mus., 1958, 1960, 2d prize 1960; Macdowell Colony fellowship, 1987-88. Mem. Internat. Assn. of Hand Papermakers and Paper Artists, Maine Arts Commn. Avocations: landscape design poetry, workshops in painting, sculpture. Home: PO Box 54 Tenants Harbor ME 04860-0054

QUINT SEHAT, ARLENE, art history educator, curator, museum administrator; b. Chgo., Sept. 4, 1944; d. Milton and Ruth Quint; m. Kourosh Sehat, July 11, 1938. BA in Art History, U. Calif., 1966, MA in Art History, 1969, PhD in Art History, 1974. Asst. prof. Calif. State U., L.A., 1969-76, assoc. prof., 1976-79; fine arts mgmt. specialist, curator of collections U.S. gen. svcs. adminstrn. Washington, 1980-88; assoc. prof. Coll. Notre Dame, Balt., 1988-90; vis. assoc. prof. Lincoln U., Pa., 1993-95; lectr. in art history Morgan State U., Balt., 1994—. Vis. assoc. prof. HUC Skirball Mus., L.A., 1975-77; cataloger, rschr. NYU, N.Y.C., 1969; rschr. Los Angeles County Mus. Art, 1964-66; chancellor's tchr. fellow U. Calif., 1966-67; adj. prof. Towson U., Balt. Contbr. articles to profl. jours. R & D grantee Coll. Notre Dame, Balt. Mem. Am. Assn. Museums, Internat. Coun. Museums (mem. documentation working group, internat. coord. conservation documentation), Coll. Art Assn., Arts Club Washington (chmn. edn. and scholarship com., admissions and membership com.).

QUIRANTES, ALBERT M. lawyer; b. Cuba, Jan. 25, 1963; came to U.S., 1966; s. Alberto adn Haydee (Mendez) Q. B in Bus., U. Miami, Fla., 1984; JD, U. Fla., 1987. Bar: Fla. 1988, U.S. Dist. Ct. (so. dist.) Fla. 1990, U.S. Dist. Ct. (mid. dist.) Fla. 1990, U.S. Ct. Appeals (11th cir.) 1990, U.S. Supreme Ct. 1991, U.S. Dist. Ct. Ariz. 1991. Pub. defender Ct. 8th cir., Gainsville, Fla., 1988-89; pvt. practice Miami, Fla., 1989—; sr. ptnr. Ticket Law Ctr., P.A., Miami, Fla., 1990—. Mem. Fla. Traffic Ct. Rules Com., Tallahassee, 1991—. Mem. Fla. Assn. Criminal Def. Attys., Dade Bar (cts. com. 1992—, criminal cts. com. 1992—), Latin C. of C., Jaycees. Home and Office: 1800 NW 7th St Miami FL 33125-3504 E-mail: lawyer@ticketlawyer.com.

QUIRING, FRANK STANLEY, chemist, educator; b. Goessel, Kans., Sept. 2, 1927; s. Henry and Helen (Lehrman) Q.; m. Evelyn Ruth Wiebe, Aug. 16, 1950; children: Samuel, Sherwood, Natalie, Powell. BA, Bethel Coll., 1950; MA, U. Kans., 1957. Cert. tchr. Kans., Mo. Tchr. sci. Coldwater (Kans.) High Sch., 1950-51, Pretty Prairie (Kans.) High Sch., 1952-55; tchr. chem. Wyandotte High Sch., Kansas City, Kans., 1955-59, Clayton (Mo.) High Sch., 1959-91; lab. dir. NSF Summer Insts. Hope Coll., Holland, Mich., 1964-92; rsch. assoc. Washington U., St. Louis, 1967-68; rsch. chemist Monsanto U., 1976-77, 84-85. Cons. Coll. Bd. Adv. Placement Divsn., Princeton, N.J., 1966—, Ohaus Corp., Florham Park, N.J., 1986-90. Contbr. articles to profl. jours. With USN, 1945-46. Recipient Presdl. award NSF, 1984, Catalyst award Chem. Mfgs. Assn., 1973; Tandy Corp. Tech. scholar, 1990. Mem. NEA (pres. Clayton chpt. 1965-66), Am. Chem. Assn. (pres. St. Louis chpt. 1970-71), Am. Chem. Soc. (Conant award 1969), Nat. Sci. Tchrs. Assn. Mennonite. Avocations: hiking, tennis, church choir. Home: 32 Regal Crescent St North Newton KS 67117-8039 E-mail: fsq@southwind.net.

QUIRING, PATTI LEE, human resource consulting company executive; b. Indpls. d. Harold Woodrow and Flora Lee (Hoffman) Dulin; m. David Allen Niederhaus, June 1972; (div. May 1974); m. David Jonathon Quiring, Dec. 7, 1976; 1 child: Erin Ashley. AA, Ball State U., Muncie, 1972, BS, 1975; MBA, Ind. Wesleyan U., 1990. Profl. Sec. Summer employee P. R. Mallory and Co., Inc., Indpls., 1970, 1971; student asst. Ball State U., Muncie, Ind., 1970-72; adminstrv. asst. Ball Corp., 1972-74; student asst. Ball State U., 1975; adminstrv. asst. P. R. Mallory and Co., Inc., 1975-76; various mgmt. level positions Blue Cross and Blue Shield of Ind., Indpls., 1976-87; exec. recruiter Tech. Resource Group, 1988-91; pres. Quiring Assocs., Inc., 1991—. Co-facilitator Corp. Bd. Task Force, 1993—94; bd. dirs. Mega Sys. Inc. Co-chmn. venture com. United Way, 1991-93, mem. adv. com. women's divsn., 1991-94, bd. dirs., mem. exec. com., 1993-99, mem. goals and priorities com., 1993, vice chmn. agy. rels. cabinet 1993-94, chmn., 1995-98, co-chmn. campaign cluster, 1994-95, mem. campaign cabinet, 1995, N.E. area team leader, 1995; vol. Pan. Am. Games, Indpls., 1987; dir. alumni rels. Ball State U. Coll. Bus., Muncie, 1988-97, mem. alumni coun., 1994-97; bd. dirs. Heritage Place St. Citizens Ctr., Indpls., 1988-90, Indpls. YWCA, 1988-90, Feathercove Homeowners Assn., 1990-97, Geist Harbors Property Owner's Assn., 1994-97, Lawrence Twp. Found., 2000-01; corp. capt. Humane Soc., 1990-91; mem. mktg. com. Children's Mus., 1992-97, mem. bd. advisors, 1995—; mem. Equal Opportunity Adv. Bd., 1992-95, Indpls. BBB; bd. dirs. Lawrence Twp. Found., 2000—. Recipient Blue Cross award of Excellence, Indpls., 1985, City Ctr Vol. award, Indpls., 1985, Salute to Women of Achievement Individual award YWCA, 1993, Network of Women in Business Networker of Yr. award, 1993; named Blue Cross Bus. Women of Yr., Indpls. 1982, 86, Humane Soc. Outstanding Vol., Indpls., 1985. Mem. Ind. Assn. Pers. Svc. Bd., Network Women in Bus. (pres. 1993), Ind. C. of C. (small bus. coun. bd.), Nat. Assn. Pers. Svcs. (mem. bd.), Indpls. and Ind. C. of C. (bd. dirs.), Better Bus. Bur. Avocations: fishing, boating, arts, tennis. Office: Quiring Assocs Inc 7267 C Jessman Rd West Dr Indianapolis IN 46256

QUIRK, FRANK JOSEPH, management consulting company executive; b. N.Y.C., Feb. 27, 1941; s. Frank J. and Madeline B. Quirk; m. Betty Josephine Mauldin, Jan. 7, 1967; children: Laura Josephine, Katherine Elizabeth. BA, Cornell U., 1962, MBA, 1964. Assoc. Booz, Allen & Hamilton, Inc., Chgo. and Washington, 1967-72; exec. v.p. Macro Internat., Inc., Calverton, Md., 1972-79, pres., CEO, 1980-98, chmn., CEO, 1998—; exec. v.p. Opinion Rsch. Corp., Princeton, N.J., 1999—. Bd. dirs. Profl. Svcs. Coun., Opinion Rsch. Corp. Served to capt. U.S. Army, 1964-66. Capt. U.S. Army, 1964—66. Mem. Belle Haven Country Club. Home: 2110 Foresthill Rd Alexandria VA 22307-1128 Office: Macro Internat Inc 11785 Beltsville Dr Beltsville MD 20705-3121

QUIRK, GAIL ELIZABETH MANZ, community services administrator; b. Phila., Dec. 25, 1929; d. Erwin Christian and Ruth Agnes (Pope) Manz; m. Virgil Porter Quirk, Feb. 14, 1953; children: Susan Crawford, Alexander Johnson, Elizabeth Pope Quirk Wood, Caroline Manz Quirk Flacinski, Sarah Porter Quirk Mills, Nancy Stiles Quirk Cameron. BS in Art Edn., Kutztown U., 1951. Elem. art supr. Wilson Sch. Dist., Easton, Pa., 1951-53; agy. dir., chief exec. officer Oak Manor, Inc., St. Marys, Pa., 1975-91; bd. dirs. Tri-County Home Health Agy., St. Marys, 1972-81. Cadette-sr. leader Keystone Tall Tree council Girl Scouts U.S., 1969-74, calendar chmn., 1972-74; mem. charity ball com. Andrew Kaul Meml. Hosp. Aux., St. Marys, 1964-66; mem. Elk County Regional Health Ctr. Aux. Recipient Disting. Svc. cert. Am. Legion Pa., 1987. Mem. AAUW, Cath. Daus. Am., Assn. Retarded Citizens Pa., Internat. Tett Syndrome Assn. Assn. Retarded Citizens Elk County, Elk County Cursillo (St. Marys, dir. Spark Club 1975-2001). Republican. Roman Catholic. Avocations: genealogy, interior decorating, painting. Home: 828 Johnsonburg Rd Saint Marys PA 15857-3420

QUIRK, JOHN JAMES, investment company executive; b. N.Y.C., July 10, 1943; s. Francis J. and Madeline A. (Meizinger) Q.; m. Kathryn Anne O'Brien, Mar. 21, 1963; children: John James, Ashlin Carter, Merritt Andrew. BA, Georgetown U., 1965; MBA, U. Va., 1967. Asst. treas., mgr. corp. fin. dept. W.R. Grace & Co., N.Y.C., 1967-74; asst. v.p., asst. treas. City Investing Co., 1974-77, v.p., treas., 1978-81, sr. v.p., treas., 1982-85; chmn. bd. Quirk Carson Peppet Inc., 1985-98; prin. Churchill Capital, Inc., 1999—2001; mng. dir. Morgan, Lewis, Githens & Ahn, 2001—. Dir. Environmental Opportunities Fund., Ltd., Ameraparts Internat., Asche Transp., Inc., Oakleaf Waste Mgmt., LLC. Mem.: Racquet and Tennis; Wee Burn (Conn.). Home: 445 Hollow Tree Ridge Rd Darien CT 06820-3030 Office: 600 5th Ave Fl 19 New York NY 10020-2302 E-mail: jquirk@mlga.com.

QUIRK, KENNETH PAUL, accountant; b. Lake Charles, La., Aug. 29, 1953; s. Charles Patrick and Helen (Lejeune) Q.; m. Teresa Ann Tucker, Mar. 26, 1982 (div. Mar. 1988); 1 child, Heather Marie. BS in Acctg., McNeese State U., 1978; MBA, U. Phoenix, 1998. CPA, La.; cert. Microsoft product specialist in Windows NT 4.0., cert. info. tech. profl., AICPA, 2000. Staff acct. Quirk, Cargile, Hicks & Reddin, Lake Charles, 1979-80, Browning-Ferris Industries, Lake Charles, 1980-81, La. Savs. Assn., Lake Charles, 1981-90, Calcasieu Marine Nat. Bank, Lake Charles, 1990-96, Hibernia Nat. Bank, Lake Charles, 1996-97; pres. Acctg. Tech. Strategies, 1997—. Instr. U. Phoenix-Online, 1999—. Author fin. acctg. software sys. Mem. Young Men's Bus. Club, Lake Charles, 1986-90, Girl Scouts U.S., Lake Charles, 1989-90; bd. dirs. Ednl. and Treatment Coun., Inc., 2001—. Named 1st La. CPA to receive Innovative User of Tech. award La. Soc. CPAs and the Am. Inst. CPAs. Mem. AICPA (cert. 2000), Soc. La. CPAs (task force com. 2000—), Assn. for Computing Machinery, Computer Soc. IEEE, Kiwanis. Republican. Episcopalian. Avocations: jazz drumming, genealogy, hunting.

QUIRKE, LILLIAN MARY, retired art educator; b. West Haven, Conn., Oct. 1, 1928; d. Mortimer Francis and Ellen Louise (Bird) Q. BS, BA, So. Conn. U., 1950; MA, Long Beach State U., 1953; EdD, Columbia U., 1963. Cert. elem. and art tchr., Conn., Calif. Tchr. Long Beach (Calif.) Pub. Schs., 1950-54; jr. high art tchr. Army Dependents Sch., Frankfurt, Germany, 1954-55; art tchr. Navy Dependents Sch., Naples, Italy, 1955-56; art instr. So. Conn. U., New Haven, 1956-64, Foothill C.C., Los Altos, Calif., 1964-67; from art instr. to prof. DeAnza C.C., Cupertino, 1967-88; adj. prof. Queens (N.Y.) Coll., 1990-91. Author: The Rug Book, 1979; contbr. articles to profl. jours.; mem. editl. bd. Art Edn. mag., 1985-87. Active Dem. and Rep. Ctrl. Coms., San Jose, Calif., 1968-71; mem. arts rev. com. Cupertino Pub. Libr., 1977-81. Title IV grantee, 1967, grantee State of Calif., 1968, NDEA grantee U.S. Office Edn., 1966. Mem. Nat. Art Edn. Assn. (life, sec. Pacific chpt. 1954—, founder higher edn. sect. 1973), Calif. Art Edn. Assn. (rsch. chair 1969-72), Artists and Tech. (bd. dirs. 1984-88), Fla. Shore and Beach Preservation Assn. (founding bd. dirs. St. Johns First Coast chpt. 1996, sec.-treas. 1996-97, sec. 1996-98). Avocations: quilting, boating, cooking, computer graphics. Home: 5916 Rio Royalle Rd Saint Augustine FL 32080-7304

QUIRKE, TERENCE THOMAS, JR. genealogist, retired geologist; b. Mpls., Aug. 18, 1929; s. Terence Thomas and Anne Laura (McIlraith) Q.; m. Ruth Mary Carter, Jan. 18, 1958; 1 child, Grace Anne. BS, U. Ill., 1951; MS, U. Minn., 1953, PhD, 1958. Cert. genealogist Bd. for Cert. of Genealogists. Asst. prof. U. N.D., Grand Forks, 1958-60; rsch. geologist INCO Ltd., Thompson, MB, Can., 1960-70, regional mgr. Can., 1970-75; supervisory staff geologist Am. Copper & Nickel Co., Milw., 1975-79, sr. supervisory staff geologist Wheat Ridge, Colo., 1979-90; rsch. cons. Quirke, Quirke & Assocs., Golden, 1990—. Contbr. articles to profl. jours., numerous others. Pres. Colo. Genealogical Soc. Computer Interest Group, Denver, 1991-93; v.p. Colo. Genealogical Soc., 1997-99; bd. dirs. Wales, Ireland, Scotland, Eng. Family History Soc., 1998—; sec.-treas., bd. dirs. Genesee Water and Sanitation Dist., Golden, Colo., 1994-2000. Mem. Soc. Genealogists (London), Irish Genealogical Soc. Internat., Irish Genealogical Rsch. Soc., Ontario Genealogical Soc., Sussex Family History Group, Kent Family History Soc. Avocations: masters swimming, hiking. Home: 2310 Juniper Ct Golden CO 80401-8087 E-mail: T2quirke@aol.com.

QUIRMBACH, HERMAN CHARLES, economics educator; b. St. Paul, Oct. 6, 1950; s. William Herman and Elizabeth Lou (Ziegler) Q. AB in Govt. cum laude, Harvard U., 1972; AM in Econs., Princeton U., 1980, PhD in Econs., 1983. Assoc. economist, cons. Rand Corp., Santa Monica, Calif., 1981—; assoc. prof. econs. Iowa State U., Ames, 1990—. Contbr. articles to profl. jours. Treas. Story County Dem. Party, Ames, 1992-94; councilman 4th ward Ames City Coun., 1995—; pres. Iowa Civil Liberties Union, 2001—02, bd. dirs., 1996—2002; bd. dirs. Ames Mcpl. Utility Retirement Sys., 1996—, Ames Convention and Visitors Bur., 1997-99. Recipient Don Biggs award for polit. leadership, 1998-99. Mem. AAUP, ACLU, Am. League of Women Voters, Am. Econ. Assn., Econometric Soc., Ames C. of C., Appalachian Mountain Club, White Mountain Four Thousand Footer Club, Ames Kiwanis Club, Ames Patriotic Coun. Office: Iowa State Univ Econs Dept Heady Hall Ames IA 50011

QUIROGA, CESAR AUGUSTO, engineer; b. Bogota, Aug. 26, 1961; s. pedro Nel and Imelda Saavedra Q.; m. Tosca Olive Gonsalves, Sept. 25, 1987; children: Pamela, Sophia. Diploma in Civil Engring., Escuela Colombiana Ingenieria, Bogota, 1982; MSCE, La. State U., 1986, PhD, 1997. Registered profl. engr., Tex., La. Instr. Escuela Colombiana de Ingenieria, Bogota, 1982-88; project engr. Hidroestudios, 1983-84; project engr., prin. engr. Consultores Civiles e Hidraulicos, 1988-90; prin. engr., specialist Hidroestudios, 1990-92; grad. asst. La. State U., Baton Rouge, 1993-95, rsch. assoc., 1995-98; asst. rsch. engr. Tex. Transp. Inst., San Antonio, 1998-2001, assoc. rsch. engr., 2001—. Contbr. articles to profl. jours. Bd. dirs. Assn. Amigos de Colombia, San Antonio, 1999. Recipient Fulbright scholarship U.S. Info. Agy., 1984. Mem. ASCE, Inst. Transp. Engrs. (Best Tech. Paper award 1996), Transp. Rsch. Bd. (com. mem. 1996—), others. Office: Tex Transp Inst 1100 NW Loop 410 Ste 460 San Antonio TX 78213 E-mail: c-quiroga@tamu.edu.

QUIROZ, CAROLE ELIZABETH, nurse anesthetist; b. Passaic, N.J., Mar. 20, 1961; d. Masami Okada and Bette (Shizuko) Masuda; m. Richard Quiroz, Oct. 19, 1985; children: Richard Sean, Danielle Elizabeth, Bryan David. AAS, Fashion Inst. Tech., N.Y.C., 1980; BSN, Seton Hall U., 1985, MSN, 1994, Columbia U., 2000. Cert. ACLS; cert. med. surg. clin. nurse specialist, cert. nurse anesthetist ANCC; RN, N.J., N.Y.; lic. clin. nurse specialist, N.J. Staff nurse Overlook Hosp., Summit, N.J., 1985-86; ICU staff nurse Lenox Hill Hosp., N.Y.C., 1986-88, critical care nurse, 1988-93; nurse cardiothoracic post anesthesia care unit Morristown (N.J.) Meml. Hosp., 1992-93; nurse Critical Care Assocs., Montclair, N.J., 1990-93; adminstrv. supr. The Gen. Hosp. Ctr. at Passaic, 1993-94; nurse Advantage Healthcare, 1994-97; adj. prof. Seton Hall U., South Orange, N.J., 1994-97; tng. cons. Siemens Med. Sys., 1996—2000; nursing coord. Mountainside Hosp., 1999-2000; nurse anesthetist No. Valley Anesthesiology, 2000—. Presenter in field. Recipient Nursing Rsch. award Jersey Shore Med. Ctr., 1992. Mem. Am. Assn. Nurse Anesthetists, Sigma Theta Tau.

QUIST, GORDON JAY, federal judge; b. Grand Rapids, Mich., Nov. 12, 1937; s. George J. and Ida F. (Hoekstra) Q.; m. Jane Capito, Mar. 10, 1962; children: Scot D., George J., Susan E., Martha J., Peter K. BA, Mich. State U., 1959; JD with honors, George Washington U., 1962. Bar: D.C. 1962, Ill. 1964, U.S. Dist. Ct. (no. dist.) Ill. 1964, U.S. Supreme Ct. 1965, Mich. 1967, U.S. Dist. Ct. (we. dist.) Mich. 1967, U.S. Ct. Appeals (6th cir.) 1967. Assoc. Hollabaugh & Jacobs, Washington, 1962-64, Sonnenschein, Levinson, Carlin, Nath & Rosenthal, Chgo., 1964-66, Miller, Johnson, Snell & Cummiskey, Grand Rapids, 1967-72, ptnr., 1972-92, mng. ptnr., 1986-92; judge U.S. Dist. Ct. (we. dist.) Mich., 1992—. Bd. dirs. Wedgewood Acres-Ch. Youth Home, 1968-74, Mary Free Bed Hosp., 1979-88, Christian Ref. Publs., 1968-78, 82-88, Opera Grand Rapids, 1986-92, Mary Free Bed Brace Shop, 1988-92, Better Bus. Bur., 1972-80, Calvin Theol. Sem., 1992-93; bd. dirs. Indian Trails Camp, 1970-78, 82-88, pres., 1978, 88. Recipient Disting. Alumnus award George Washington U. Law Sch., 1998 Mem. Am. Indicature Soc., Mich. State Bar Found., Univ. Club Grand Rapids, Order of Coif, Am. Inns Ct. Avocations: reading, travel. Office: 482 Ford Fed Courthouse 110 Michigan St NW Grand Rapids MI 49503-2313 E-mail: Gordon_J_Quist@miwd.uscourts.gov.

QUIST, JEANETTE FITZGERALD, television production educator, choreographer; b. Provo, Utah, July 4, 1948; d. Sherman Kirkham and Bula Janet (Anderson) Fitzgerald; m. G. Steven Quist; children: Ryan, Amy, Michelle, Jeremy. Student, U. Redlands, Calif., 1970; BA, Brigham Young U., 1971; postgrad., Calif. State U., Riverside, 1972, Calif. State U., San Bernardino, 1973. Host, co-producer children's show PBS Sta. KBYU-TV, Provo, 1968-69; buyer ready to wear J.C. Penney & Co., Redlands, 1969-71; tchr. spl. reading program Fontana (Calif.) Elem. Sch. Dist., 1971-73; owner, choreographer Jeanette Quist Creative Dance, Tri Cities, Wash., 1975-79; owner, tchr. Dance Studio, Gridley, Calif., 1979-81; producer, instr. Butte Coll., Oroville, 1986—. Asst. producer Kate Knight Prodn. Co., Chico, Calif., 1987; video producer Gridley Sch. Dist., 1987-88; cmty. svcs. cons. Biggs-Gridley Meml. Hosp., 1999—. Prodr., editor promotional video Police Acad., 1986, commls. for Butte Coll., 1987—; prodr., dir. telecourse Interior Designer, 1988—; prodr., hostess TV talk shows Crossroads, 1988—, NVCA Today, BCTV Forum, 1991—; prodr. orientation video Butte Coll., 1989, 90, video series Intro to Telecommunications, video documentary on migrant edn. summer sch., 1994-98, video series on Recycling for Butte Environ. Coun., 1995, Early Alert video for Butte Coll., 1995, promotion video City of Chico, 1995, video Sports Events for Butte Coll., 1995—, video series on Small Bus. Devel. Ctr., 1996, video Work Tng. Ctr., 1996, Project Maestros, 1996, video for bilingual tchrs. recruitment Butte Coll. 1997, video documenting the American Dream: Unity in Diversity, Butte Coll., 1997, Sentencing Video for the Fed. Defs. Office, Ea. Dist. of Calif., 1998; choreographer Kaleidoscope, 1988, South Pacific, 1989, Fantasticks, 1990, Amahl and the Night Visitors, 1990, An Evening of Song and Dance, Butte Coll., 1991, Kiss Me Kate, Butte Coll., 1992, Hello Dolly, Chico Stake, 1992; prodr. videos for Butte Coll. Child Devel. Program, 1999, Multimedia Program, 2001, Radio TV Film Program, 2002, Environ. Hort. Program, 2002, EMT/Paramedics Program, 2002; choreographer Tumbleweeds, Butte Theatre, 1994, Joseph and the Amazing Technicolor Dreamcoat, Gridley H.S., 1999. State judge Miss. Am. Contest, Provo, 1968; 1st v.p. Friends of Libr., Gridley, 1988; chmn. Regional Fine Arts Festival Tri Cities, 1978; v.p. Gridley High Sch. Parent Club, 1990; chmn. 3D Expo Fine Arts Festival for Oroville, Gridley, and Butte Coll., 1991; cmty. svcs. cons. Biggs-Gridley Meml. Hosp., 1999—, organizer 50th anniversary celebration, 2000. Recipient Acad. Excellence award Butte Coll., 1993-94, What Would We Do Without You award, Butte Coll., 1998; Mask club scholar Brigham Young U., 1967; Project Maestro grantee, 1994, Svc. Learning grantee Butte Coll., 2002. Mem. AAUW (membership v.p. 1989-91, pres. 1997-99, com. for gender equity for Gridley br., Tech Trek chmn. Gridley br. 2001—), Butte County Arts Coun. (spl. com. 1986), Kaleidoscope Arts Coun., Am. Assn. Women in Cmty. Jr. Colls. Republican., Ch. of Jesus Christ Latter-day Saints. Avocations: family, theatre, music, camping, reading.

QUIVERS, ERIC STANLEY, physician; b. Winston-Salem, N.C., Oct. 27, 1955; s. William Wyatt and Evelyn Cecelia (Seace) Q.; m. Mara Carlos, Feb. 15, 1987; children: Micah Stanley, Lucas Sorrell. BS, Morehouse Coll., 1979; MD, Howard U., 1983. Cert. pediats., pediat. cardiology. Intern and resident in pediats. Howard U. Hosp., 1983-86, Dist. Columbia Gen. Hosp., 1983-86; staff pediatrician Park W. Med. Ctr., Balt., 1986-88; fellow in pediat. cardiology Mayo Clin., 1988-91; mem. cardiology faculty Children's Nat., Washington, 1991—. Dir. preventive cardiology, Children's Nat., Washington, dir. exercise lab., 1991—, transplant cardiologist, 1997—; adv. bd. Take AIM Prodns. Healthcare Forum Cardiology fellow, 1999. Mem. Am. Coll. Cardiology, Internat. Heart and Lung Transplantation Soc. Assn. of Black Cardiologist, Mid Atlantic Am. Coll. Sports Medicine. Office: Childrens Med Ctr Dept Pediat Cardiology 111 Michigan Ave NW Dept Pediat Washington DC 20010-2916

QUON, MALCOLM YEE, defence systems company executive; b. Greenwood, Miss., Sept. 3, 1960; s. Joe Wing and Sandra Quon; m. Melanie Chow; children: Mallery, Joseph. BBA in Computer Info. Systems, Delta State U., 1983. Exec. v.p. Vision Systems Internat. LLC, San Jose, Calif., 1999—. Capt. U.S. Army, 1983-88. Office: Vision Systems Internat LLC 2711 Orchard Pkwy San Jose CA 95134 E-mail: Malquon@cs.com.

QUON, MICHAEL JAMES, medical scientist, physician; b. Oakland, Calif., Apr. 26, 1960; s. Jimmie Earl and Helen (Tang) Quon; m. Huison Kim, June 22, 1985; children: Hana, James. BS in Biomed. Engring., Northwestern U., 1982, PhD in Biomed. Engring., 1987, MD, 1988. Diplomate Nat. Bd. Med. Examiners, Am. Bd. Internal Medicine. Resident in internal medicine U. Chgo., 1988—90; fellow in endocrinology NIH, Bethesda, Md., 1990—93, sr. clin. investigator, 1993—95, sr. investigator Nat. Heart, Lung and Blood Inst., 1995—. Contbr. . Comdr., 1990—. Mem.: ACP, Juvenile Diabetes Found. Internat., Coun. for High Blood Pressure, Am. Heart Assn., Am. Diabetes Assn. (Rsch. award grant 1994—). Avocations: piano, violin. Office: NIH NHLBI HEB 218 Bldg 10 Rm 8C Bethesda MD 20892-0001

QURAISHI, MOHAMMED SAYEED, retired health scientist, administrator; b. Jodhpur, India, June 23, 1924; came to U.S., 1946, naturalized, 1973; s. Mohammed Latif and Akhtar Jahan Q.; m. Akhtar Imtiaz, Nov. 12, 1953; children: Rana, Naveed, Sabah. B.Sc., St. John's Coll., 1942; M.Sc., Aligarh Muslim U., 1944; PhD, U. Mass., 1948. Sr. mem. UN, WHO Team to Bangladesh, 1949-51; entomologist Malaria Inst. Pakistan, 1951-55; sr. rsch. officer Pakistan Council Sci. and Indsl. Rsch., 1955-60; sr. sci. officer Pakistan AEC, 1960-64; assoc. prof. entomology U. Man., 1964-66, N.D. State U., Fargo, 1966-70, prof., 1970-74; chief scientist biology N.Y. State Sci. Svc., Albany, 1974-75; entomologist, toxicologist, chief pest control and consultation sect. NIH, Bethesda, Md., 1976-84; health scientist adminstr., exec. sec. microbiology and infectious disease rsch. com. Nat. Inst. Allergy and Infectious Diseases, 1984-88, sci. rev. adminstr. spl. revs., 1988-96, sci. rev. adminstr. AIDS clin. epidemiol. rsch. rev. br., 1996-2000; ret., 2000; sr. scientist Inst. Nuclear Sci., CENTO, Tehran, Iran, 1960-64; program mgr. interdepartmental contract Project THEMIS, Dept. Def., 1968-74. Cons. breast cancer rsch. program UIS Dept. Def., 2001; vis. scientist Harvard Sch. Pub. Health, 1995. Author: Biochemical Insect Control: Its Impact on Economy, Environment and Natural Selection, 1977; mem. editorial bd. Jour. Environ. Toxicology and Chemistry, 1981-84; author numerous sci. papers. Chmn. NIH Asian-Am. Cultural Assn., 1980—81; mem. Montgomery County Bd. Social Svcs., 2002. Recipient Sustained High Quality Performance award, 1980, Merit Pay Performance awards, 1984, 86, 87, Recognition and Appreciation of Spl. Achievement award NIH, 1988, Spl. Recognition award for Svcs. to NIH, Asian Am. Cultural Com., 1989, Appreciation in Recognition of Outstanding Support for Combined Fed. Campaign, 1991. Mem. Am. Chem. Soc., Soc. Environ. Toxicology and Chemistry (mem. publs. com. in charge spl. publs. 1982-84), Sigma Xi, Phi Kappa Phi. Home: 19813 Cochrane Way Gaithersburg MD 20879-1637 E-mail: sayeedquraishi@aol.com

QURAISHI, NISAR ALI, internist; b. May 15, 1946; s. Jehan Dad and Sahib Jan (Qureshi) Q.; m. Shahida Parveen, June 25, 1970;children: Abid, Zahid. MB BS, Dacca Med. Coll., Pakistan, 1969. Diplomate Am. Bd. Internal Medicine. House surgeon Dacca Med. Coll., 1969, sr. house physician, 1969-70; intern, resident Beekman Downtown Hosp., N.Y.C., 1970-74; pvt. practice, 1974—. Attending physician NYU Downtown Hosp., N.Y.C., 1974—; physician in charge exercise EKG, Mobil Oil Corp., N.Y.C., 1977-86; clin. asst. prof. medicine N.Y. Med. Coll., 1996—; attending physician St. Vincent's Hosp. and Med. Ctr. of N.Y., 1996—. Fellow Am. Coll. Physicians, Am. Soc. Internal Medicine; mem. AMA, N.Y. State Med. Soc., N.Y. County Med. Soc. Office: 303 Greenwich St New York NY 10013-3801 also: 1 Chopin Ct Jersey City NJ 07302-3240

QUREISHI, A. SALAM, computer software and services company executive; b. Aligarh, India, July 1, 1936; s. M.A. Jabbar and Saira (Sattar) Q.; m. Naheed Fatima; children: Lubna, Leila. BS in Physics and Math., Aligarh U., India, 1954; MS in Stats., Patna U., India, 1957. Mgr. applications IBM Corp., Palo Alto, Calif., 1961-67; founder, pres., chmn. bd. Optimum Sys., Inc., 1967-71; CEO Sysorex Internat., Inc., Mountain View, 1972—. Republican. Office: Sysorex Internat Inc 335 E Middlefield Rd Mountain View CA 94043-4028 Home: 925 Mountain Home Rd Woodside CA 94062-2519

QUTUB, MUSA YACUB, hydrogeologist, educator, consultant; b. Jerusalem, June 2, 1940; came to U.S., 1960; s. Yacub and Sarah Qutub; married; children: Hanhia, Jennan, Sarmad, Muntaser, Aya, Saif, Tasneem. BA in Geology, Simpson Coll., Indianola, Iowa, 1964; MS in Hydrogeology, Colo. State U., 1966; Ph.D in Water Resources, Iowa State U. Sci. and Tech., 1969. Instr. earth sci. Iowa State U., Ames, 1966-69; from asst. prof. to prof. Northeastern Ill., Chgo., 1969-80, prof. geography and environ. studies, 1980—. Cons. hydrogeology, Des Plaines, Ill., 1970— ; sr. adviser Saudi Arabian Ministry Planning, Riyadh, 1977-78; leader U.S. environ. sci. del. to People's Republic of China, 1984; pres., founder Islamic Info. Ctr. Am. Author: Secondary Environmental Science Methods, 1973; contbr. numerous articles to profl. jours.; editor Environ. Resource, Directory Environ. Educators and Cons. World. NSF grantee, 1970-71, 71-72, 72-73, 75, 76, Hew grantee, 1974, grantee Ill. Dept. Edn., 1970. Mem. AAAS, NSF (cons.), Am. Waterworks Assn., Am. Men and Women Sci., Nat. Assn. Geology Tchrs. (pres. central sect. 1974), Environ. Sci. Inst. (edn. com.), Internat. Assn. Advancement of Earth and Environ Sci. (pres. 1975—, founder), Ill. Earth Sci. Edn. (pres. 1971-73, founder), Phi Delta Kappa. Moslem. Avocations: tennis, track, cross country, soccer.

RAAB, IRA JERRY, lawyer, judge; b. N.Y.C., June 20, 1935; s. Benjamin and Fannie (Kirschner) R.; m. Regina Schneider, June 4, 1957 (div. 1978); children: Michael, Shelley; m. Katie Rachel McKeever, June 30, 1979 (div. 1991); children: Julie, Jennifer, Joseph; m. Gloria Silverman, Nov. 7, 1996; children: Jill, Todd, John. BBA, CCNY, 1955; JD, Bklyn. Law Sch., 1957; MPA, NYU, 1959, postgrad., 1961; MS in Pub. Adminstrn., L.I. U., 1961; MBA, Adelphi U., 1990. Bar: N.Y. 1958, U.S. Dist. Ct. (so. and ea. dists.) N.Y. 1960, U.S. Supreme Ct. 1967, U.S. Tax Ct. 1976, U.S. Ct. Appeals (2d cir.) 1977. Pvt. practice, Woodmere, N.Y., 1958-96; agt. Westchester County Soc. Prevention of Cruelty to Children, White Plains, 1958; counsel Dept. Correction City of N.Y., 1959, trial commr. Dept. Correction, 1976, asst. corp. counsel Tort divsn., 1963-70; staff counsel SBA, N.Y.C., 1961-63; counsel Investigation Com. on Willowbrook State Sch., Boro Hall, S.I., N.Y., 1970; gen. counsel Richmond County Soc. Prevention of Cruelty to Children, Boro Hall, 1970-81; pro bono counsel N.Y.C. Patrolmen's Benevolent Assn., 1974-81; rep. to UN Internat. Criminal Ct. , 1977-78; arbitrator Small Claims Ct. Day Cts., N.Y.C., 1970-96; arbitrator L.I. Better Bus. Bur., 1976-93, Nassau County Dist. Ct., 1978-93, arbitrator Small Claims Ct., 1978-96; spl. master N.Y. County Supreme Ct., 1977-96; judge N.Y.C. Parking Violations Bur., 1991-93. Small claims arbitrator N.Y.C. Civil Ct., 1970-96; arbitrator U.S. Dist. Ct. (ea. dist.) N.Y., 1986-96; lectr. cmty. and ednl. orgns.; instr. paralegal course Lawrence Sch. Dist., N.Y., 1982-84; law prof. Briarcliff Coll., Bethpage, N.Y., 1997. Chmn. Businessmen's Luncheon Club, Wall St. Synagogue, 1968-79; exec. sec. Cmty. Mediation Ctr., Suffolk County, 1978-80, exec. v.p., 1980-81; vice chmn. Woodmere Inc., Com., 1980-81; mem. adv. bd. Nassau Expressway Com., 1979-80; bd. dirs. Woodmere Mchts. Assn., 1979-80, v.p., 1979-83, chmn., 1984-93; candidate for dist. ct. judge Nassau County, 1987, 88, 89, 91, 93, 94, 2000; candidate for supreme ct. justice Nassau and Suffolk Counties, 1995, 98; elected judge Nassau County Dist. Ct., 1997-99; candidate for county ct., Nassau County, 1997; elected presiding judge dist. ct., 1999-2000; sec. Congregation Aish Kodesh, Woodmere, 1992—; elected justice Nassau County Supreme Ct., 2000. Recipient Consumer Protection award FTC, 1974, 76, 79, Recognition award Pres. Ronald Reagan, 1986, Man of Yr. award L.I. Coun. of Chambers, 1987, N.Y. State Ct. Reporters Assn., 1999. Mem. ABA (chmn. cts. and comty. com. 1988-93, exec. com. jud. adminstrn. divsn. lawyers conf. 1989-95), Am. Judges Assn. (rep. to UN 2000—, bd. govs. 1973-78, 82-88, 89-96, 97—, nat. treas. 1978-82, chmn. civil ct. ops. com. 1975-76, chmn. ednl. film com. 1974-77, editl. bd. Ct. Rev. mag. 1975-79, 82-86, chmn. spkrs. bur. com. 1976-77, chmn. legis. com. 1983-95, chmn. resolutions com. 1995-98, 2000—, chmn. jud. concerns com. 1997-99, historian 1988—, William H. Burnett award 1983), Am. Judges Found. (pres. 1977-79, chmn. bd. trustees 1979-83, treas. 1974-75, 76-77, trustee 1983-97, 2000—), Assn. Arbitrators of Civil Ct. City of N.Y. (past pres.), N.Y. State Bar Assn. (sec. dist., city, town and villages cts. com.), Nassau County Bar Assn. (criminal cts. com., matrimonial and family ct. com., ct. com., ethics com., Supreme Ct. com.), Profl. Group Legal Svc. Assn. (past pres.), Internat. Assn. Jewish Lawyers and Jurists (com. to draft Internat. Bill of Rights to Privacy 1982, coun. 1981-95, bd. govs. 1984-95), adv. bd. comty. dispute ctr. 1979-81), K.P. (past chancellor comdr.). Democrat. Home: 375 Westwood Rd Woodmere NY 11598-1624 Office: Supreme Court 100 Supreme Ct Dr Mineola NY 11501 Fax: 516-571-2555. E-mail: iraab@courts.state.ny.us.

RAAB, LAWRENCE EDWARD, English educator; b. Pittsfield, Mass., May 8, 1946; s. Edward Louis and Marjorie (Young) R.; m. Judith Ann Michaels, Dec. 29, 1968; 1 child, Jennifer Caroline. BA, Middlebury Coll., 1968; MA, Syracuse U., 1972. Lectr. Am. U., Washington, 1970-71; jr. fellow U. Mich. Soc. Fellows, Ann Arbor, 1973-76; prof. English Williams Coll., Williamstown, Mass., 1976—. Author: (poems) Mysteries of the Horizon, 1972, The Collector of Cold Weather, 1976, Other Children, 1987, What We Don't Know About Each Other, 1993 (National Book award nominee, 1993), The Probable World, 2000, Visible Signs: New and Selected Poems, 2003. Creative Writing fellow Nat. Endowment Arts, 1972, 84; recipient Bess Hokin prize Poetry mag., 1983; residencies at Yaddo, 1979-80, 82, 84, 86-90, 94, MacDowell Colony, 1993, 95. Office: Williams Coll English Dept Williamstown MA 01267

RAAB, SELWYN, journalist; b. N.Y.C., June 26, 1934; s. William and Berdie (Glantz) R.; m. Helene Lurie, Dec. 25, 1963; 1 dau., Marian. BA, Coll. City N.Y., 1956. Reporter N.Y. World-Telegram and Sun, N.Y.C., 1960-66; producer, news editor NBC-TV News, 1966-71; exec. producer WNET-News, 1971-74; reporter New York Times, 1974—2000. Author: Justice in the Back Room, 1967; co-author: Mob Laywer, 1994. Recipient award for best mag. consumer protection article U. Mo. Sch. Journalism, 1969, Deadline awards for excellence in television reporting Sigma Delta Chi, 1971, 73, 1st prize for excellence in television reporting N.Y. State A.P., 1973, Best Television Reporting award N.Y. Press Club, 1973, Heywood Broun Meml. award, 1974, Page One award Newspaper Guild of New York, 1975, Best Feature Story award N.Y. Press Club, 1984, N.Y.C. Patrolmen's Benevolent Assn. award, 1985. Address: c/o McIntosh & Otis 353 Lexington Ave New York NY 10016 E-mail: selraab@aol.com.

RAAB, SHELDON, lawyer, Bklyn. Nov. 30, 1937; s. Morris and Eva (Shereshevsky) R.; m. Judith Deutsch, Dec. 15, 1963; children: Michael Kenneth, Elisabeth Louise, Andrew John. AB, Columbia U., 1958; LLB cum laude, Harvard U., 1961. Bar: N.Y. 1961, U.S. Ct. Appeals (2d cir.) 1963, U.S. Dist. Ct. (so. and ea. dists.) 1967. Dep. asst. atty. gen. State of N.Y., 1961-63, asst. atty gen., 1963-64; assoc. Fried, Frank, Harris, Shriver & Jacobson and predecessor firm, N.Y.C., 1964-69, ptnr., 1970-81, inc. ptnr., 1981—. Mem. exec. com. lawyers' div. United Jewish Appeal, 1982—. Mem. ABA, Am. Law Inst., N.Y. State Bar Assn. (trial lawyers sect. 1968—), Assn. of Bar of City of N.Y. (adminstr. law com. 1968-71, spl. com. electric power and environment 1971-73, chmn. energy com. 1974-79, fed. cts. com. 1981-84, state superior cts. juris. com. 1985-88). Democrat. Office: Fried Frank Harris Shriver & Jacobson 1 New York Plz Fl 22 New York NY 10004-1980

RAABE, GERHARD KARL, epidemiologist; b. Flushing, N.Y., Feb. 24, 1948; s. Oscar Albert and Eugenie (Loehr) R.; m. Barbara Irene Douglas, Nov. 27, 1969; children: Andrew John, Emily Jean. BA in Biology, Hofstra U., 1969; MS in Computer Sci., Pratt Inst., 1971; DrPH, Columbia U., 1987. Sr. rsch. scientist N.Y. State Dept. Mental Hygiene, N.Y.C., 1970-77; med. systems analyst Mobil Oil Corp., 1977-79, indsl. med. advisor, 1979-81, mgr. epidemiology and med. info. svcs., 1982-89, dir. epidemiology and med. info. svcs. Princeton, N.J., 1990-97; dir. med. info. and health risk assessment Global Med. Svcs., Mobil Bus. Resources Corp., 1997-99; pres., prin. scientist occupl. and environ. health Health Risk Scis., Inc., New Hope, Pa., 1999—. Cons. spl. studies Cornell U. Med. Ctr., N.Y.C., 1973-77; cons. N.Y.C. Health Systems Agy., 1976; chmn. occupational health com. Fla. Phosphate Coun., Lakeland, 1979-85; reviewer profl. jours.; expert panelist WHO, IARC, U.S. EPA. Contbr. articles to profl. jours., chpts. to books. Fellow Am. Coll. Epidemiology (mem. policy com.); mem. AAAS, Soc. for Epidemiologic Rsch., Internat. Soc. for Environ. Epidemiology, Am. Statis. Assn., Am. Petroleum Inst. (chmn. epidemiology 1985-88, chmn. health and product stewardship 1996-2000), N.Y. Acad. Scis., Soc. for Risk Analysis, Indsl. Epidemiology Forum (chmn. 1991), Internat. Commn. on Occupl. Health. Republican. Lutheran. Avocations: science fiction, tennis. Home: 2215 Aquetong Rd New Hope PA 18938-1149 Office: Health Risk Scis Inc PO Box 189 New Hope PA 18938-0189 E-mail: gkraabe@cs.com.

RAABE, WILLIAM ALAN, tax writer, business educator; b. Milw., Dec. 14, 1953; s. William Arthur and Shirley (Semmann) R.; m. Nancy Elizabeth Miller, Mar. 1989; children: Margaret Elisabeth, Martin William. BS, Carroll Coll., 1975; MAS, U. Ill., 1976, PhD, 1979. Wis. Disting. prof. U. Wis., Milw., 1979-96; tax edn. cons. Price Waterhouse Coopers, N.Y.C., 1990—; prof., dir. acctg. programs Samford U., Birmingham, Ala., 1997-2001; founding dean Sch. Mgmt., disting. prof. Capital U., Columbus, Ohio, 2001—. Vis. assoc. prof. Ariz. State U., Tempe, 1985; vis. faculty Ernst & Young, N.Y.C., 1990—, Deloitte & Touche, N.Y.C., 1998—, Calif. CPA Found., 1986, AICPA, 1984-94, Wis. Bar Assn., 1992; developer Estate Tax Planner, McGraw Hill Software, N.Y.C., 1980-88; expert witness, 1985—; cons. corp. income tax State Ala., 1997-01, State of Wis., 1995, 99. Author West's Federal Taxation, 1985—, West's Federal Tax Research, 1986—, Income Shifting After Tax Reform, 1987, Multistate Corporate Tax Guide, 1985-96; contbr. articles to profl. jours. Bd. dirs., pres. Luth. High Sch. Assn. Milw., 1991-96, Bethesda Luth. Home, Watertown, Wis., 1989-91, Concord Chamber Orch., Milw., 1983-88; mem. Econ. Devel. Com., Wauwatosa, Wis., 1986-89; faculty athletic rep. to NCAA from U. Wis. Milw., 1990-96; mem. Milw. Symphony Chorus, Master Singers of Milw., Samford Master Singers, Samford Die Kantorei; vice chair faculty senate Samford U., 2000-01. Fellow Am. Acctg. Assn., Nat. Ctr. for Tax Edn. and Rsch., Wis. Inst. CPAs (Educator of Yr. 1987), Ala. Acctg. Educators Assn. (pres. 1999-2000). E-mail. Office: Capital Univ Sch of Mgmt 2199 E Main St Bexley OH 43209

RAAD, VIRGINIA, pianist, lecturer; b. Salem, W.Va., Aug. 13, 1925; d. Joseph M. and Martha (Joseph) R. BA in Art History, Wellesley Coll., 1947; spl. student, New Eng. Conservatory Music, 1947-48; diplôme, Ecole Normale de Musique, Paris, 1950; Doctorate with honors (French Govt. grantee 1950-52, 54-55), U. Paris, 1955; student, Alfred Cortot, Jeanne Blancard, Berthe Bert, Jacques Chailley. Artist in residence Salem (W.Va.) Coll., 1957-70; ind. concert pianist, 1960—; musician in residence N.C. Arts Council, at community colls., 1971-72. Adjudicator Nat. Guild Piano Tchrs., Nat. Fedn. Music Clubs; panelist, grant reviewer NEH, 1978-84, 92—; mem. com. Nat. Endowment Arts, 1978; Am. rep. Debussy Centennial Colloque, Paris, 1962. Perfomances, concerts, lectrs. master classes at West Ga. Coll., Carrollton, La Grange (Ga.) Coll., Columbus (Ga.) Coll., Young Harris (Ga.) Coll., U. Fla., Gainesville, Norton Gallery, Palm Beach, Fla., Alliance Française de Rollins Coll., Winter Park, Fla., Dixon Gallery and Gardens, Memphis, St. Jude Children's Rsch. Hosp., Memphis, Cleveland (Tenn.) State C.C., Sampson Tech. Inst., Clinton, N.C., Wayne C.C., Goldsboro, N.C., Brevard (N.C.) Coll., Ctrl. (S.C.) Wesleyan Coll., Ky. Wesleyan Coll., Owensboro, Berea (Ky.), Coll., Alice Lloyd Coll., Pippa Passes, Ky., Coll. of William and Mary, Williamsburg, Va., Eastern Mennonite Coll., Harrisonburg, Va., The Phillips Gallery, Washington, Trinity Coll., Washington, Manhattanville Coll., Purchase, N.Y., Elmira (N.Y.) Coll., Fordham U., N.Y.C., The Piano Tchrs. Congress of N.Y., Middlebury (Vt.) Coll., St. Anselm's Coll., Manchester, N.H., Mount St. Mary's Coll., Hooksett, N.H., Wellesley (Mass.) Coll., Curry Coll., Milton, Mass., So. Conn. State U., New Haven, Slippery Rock (Pa.) U., Seton Hill Coll., Greensboro, Pa., Alliance Française de Pitts. and U. Pitts., Channel 13 WQED (PBS) Pitts., Lincoln U., Oxford, Pa., The Grier Sch., Tyrone, Pa., Mount de Chantal Acad., Wheeling W.Va., Wheeling Jesuit Coll., among other colls. and univs.; contbg. author: Debussy et l'Evolution de la Musique au XX Siècle, 1965; author: The Piano Sonority of Claude Debussy, 1994; recording artist: EDUCO, 1995—; contbr. articles to profl. jours. Active Amnesty Internat. Urgent Action Network; alumna regional representative Wellesley Coll. Named Outstanding W.Va. Woman Educator Delta Kappa Gamma, 1965; included in Schlesinger Library on History of Women in Am. Radcliffe Coll., 1967; grantee Govt. France, Am. Coun. Learned Socs. Mem. Soc. Française de Musicologie, Am. Musicol. Soc. (regional officer 1960-65), Am. Coll. Musicians, Am. Soc. for Aesthetics (grant reviewer), Internat. Musicol. Soc., Music Tchrs. Nat. Assn. (adjudicator, musicology program chair 1983-87), W.Va. Music Tchrs. Assn., Coll. Music Soc., Audubon Activist, Alpha Delta Kappa (hon.). Republican. Roman Catholic. Avocations: hiking, gardening, birding. Address: 60 Terrace Ave Salem WV 26426-1116 E-mail: virginiaraad@aol.com.

RAADSCHELDERS, JOZEF CORNELIS NICOLAAS, political science educator; b. Uithoorn, The Netherlands, Dec. 14, 1955; came to U.S., 1998; s. Jozef Cornelis and Cornelia Petronella Maria (Van Boheemen) R.; m. Julie Lynn Bivin, July 14, 1990; children: Katherine, Glenn, John Jozef. BA, Tchrs. Coll., 1979; MA, U. Leiden, 1982, PhD, 1990. Rschr. U. Leiden, 1983-84, asst. prof., 1984-92, assoc. prof., 1992-98, U. Okla., 1998—, Henry Bellmon chair of pub. svc., 2000—. Author: Handbook of Administrative History, 1998, L'entourage administratif du pouvoir exécutif, 1998, Between Market and Government. An Administrative History of the National Union for Itinerant Trade, 1996, Waterboards in the Netherlands. An Administrative Science Exploration of the Institutional Development, 1993, The Fourth Power. The Civil Service in the Netherlands, 1992, Local Government History, 1992, Meso-Government in European Perspective. The "Randstad" Provinces out of touch?, 1992, Local Government Administrative Development 1600-1980: An Administrative History of Four North Holland Municipalities, 1990; contbr. articles to profl. jours. Sec., chmn. Youth Assn., The Hague, 1977-92. Mem. ASPA. Roman Catholic. Avocations: classical guitar, watercolor, reading. Home: 2912 Devonshire Dr Norman OK 73071-2119 Office: Dept Polit Sci U Oklahoma Dale Hall Tower Rm 318 Norman OK 73019-0001 E-mail: raadschelders@ou.edu.

RAAF, JOHN HART, surgeon, health facility administrator, educator; b. Portland, Oreg., Aug. 10, 1941; s. John E. and Lorene (Rardin) R.; m. Heather Neilson, June 15, 1965; children— Jennifer, John, Sabrina AB magna cum laude, Harvard U., 1963, MD cum laude, 1970; D.Phil., Oxford U., 1966. Diplomate Am. Bd. Surgery. Intern Mass. Gen. Hosp., Boston, 1970-71, resident in surgery, 1971-73, 75-77; research fellow Sloan-Kettering Inst., N.Y.C., 1973-75; fellow in immunology Meml. Hosp., 1973-74; faculty assoc. in surgery M.D. Anderson Hosp. and Tumor Inst., Houston, 1977-78, asst. prof. surgery, 1978-79, Cornell U. Med. Coll., N.Y.C., 1979-81; assoc. prof. surgery Meml. Sloan-Kettering Cancer Ctr., 1981-85; dir. Cleve. Clinic Cancer

Ctr., 1985-90; chmn. dept. surgery Meridia Huron Hosp., Cleve., 1991-94; chief surg. svc. VA Med. Ctr. Cleve., 1994-2001; prof. surgery Case Western Res. U., 1994—, vice chmn. dept. surgery, 1994-2001. Mem. selection coms. for Rhodes scholarships, Vt., 1969-71, New Eng., 1969-71, La., 1977, Tex., 1978, Ohio, 1989-94; mem. soft tissue sarcoma discussion group Nat. Cancer Inst., 1980; mem. clin. trials com. Nat. Cancer Inst., NIH, 1984-88 Co-author Meml. Sloan-Kettering Cancer Ctr. publs., 1980; also numerous articles, chpts., abstracts, letters, short papers, movies, med. photographs; editor: Diagnosis and Treatment of Soft Tissue Sarcomas, 1993; editor-in-chief Primary Care and Cancer, 1981-92; mem. editorial bd. Meml. Sloan-Kettering Cancer Ctr. Clin. Bull., 1979-82; assoc. editor Oncology mag., 1987-92; mem. editorial com. Cleve Clinic Jour. Medicine, 1987-90. Rhodes scholar Oxford U., Eng., 1963; nat. scholar Harvard U. Med. Sch., 1966-70; Am. Cancer Soc. postdoctoral scholar Harvard U. Med. Sch., 1969-70; ACS scholar Mass. Gen. Hosp., Boston, 1975-77; Am. Cancer Soc. jr. faculty clin. fellow, 1980-83 Fellow ACS; mem. Am. Assn. Cancer Research, Am. Assn. Endocrine Surgeons, Am. Soc. Clin. Oncology, Assn. Acad. Surgery, Assn. Am. Rhodes Scholars, Cen. Surg. Assn., Cleve. Surg. Soc., Soc. Surg. Oncology (publs. com. 1981-84, working group on edn. 1982, membership com. 2000), Transplantation Soc., Meml. Hosp. Alumni Soc. (chmn. program com. 1982), Cleve. Skating Club, Charaka Club (N.Y.C.). Home: 12501 Fairhill Rd Cleveland OH 44120-1017 E-mail: jhr101@ameritech.net.

RAAFLAUB, KURT ARNOLD, classics educator; b. Buea, Cameroon, Feb. 15, 1941; s. Fritz and Heidi (Ninck) R.; m. Deborah Dickmann Boedeker, July 14, 1978. MA, U. Basel, Switzerland, 1967, PhD, 1970. Asst. prof. ancient history Free U. Berlin, 1972-78, Brown U., Providence, 1978-80, assoc. prof. classics and history, 1980-83, prof., 1983—, John Rowe Workman Disting. prof. classics and humanistic tradition, 1989-92, David Herlihy Univ. prof., 2001—, chmn. dept. classics, 1984-89; co-dir. Ctr. for Hellenic Studies, Washington, 1992-2000, chmn. program in ancient studies, 2000—. Author: Dignitatis Contentio, 1974, Die Entdeckung der Freiheit, 1985; co-author: Studien zum Attischen Seebund, 1984, Aspects of Athenian Democracy, 1990, Ancient History: Recent Work and New Directions, 1997; editor or co-editor: Social Struggles in Archaic Rome, 1986, Between Republic and Empire: Interpretations of Augustus and His Principate, 1990, Athens and Rome, Florence and Venice: City-States in Classical Antiquity and Medieval Italy, 1991, Anfänge politischen Denkens in der Antike: Die nahöstlichen Kulturen und die Griechen, 1993, Studies in the Ancient Greek Polis, 1995, More Studies in the Ancient Greek Polis, 1996, Democracy 2500: Questions and Challenges, 1998, Democracy, Empire and the Arts in Fifth-Century Athens, 1998, War and Society in the Ancient and Medieval Worlds, 1999; contbr. articles to profl. jours. Mem. Historisches Kolleg Munich, 1989-90. Am. Coun. Learned Socs. fellow, 1983-84, Ctr. for Hellenic Studies fellow, 1976-77, NEH fellow, 1989; faculty fellow U. New England, Armidale, Australia, 1996. Mem. Philol. Assn., Assn. Ancient Historians, Am. Inst. Archaeology Avocation: music. E-mail: kurt. Home: 495 Lloyd Ave Providence RI 02906-4547 Office: Brown U Dept Classics Providence RI 02912-1856 E-mail: kurt_raaflaub@brown.edu.

RA'ANAN, URI (HEINZ FELIX FRISCHWASSER), international politics educator; b. June 10, 1926; married; 2 children. BA, MA, MLitt, Oxford U. Polit. journalist, 1950-57; positions in internat. diplomacy, 1958-64; sr. fellow Rsch. Inst. on Communist Afairs, Columbia U., N.Y.C., 1964-66, lectr. in govt., 1965-66; assoc. Ctr. for Internat. Studies MIT, Boston, 1966-76, vis. prof. polit. sci., 1966-68; prof. internat. politics, dir. Internat. Security Studies Fletcher Sch. Law and Diplomacy, Tufts U., 1967-87; univ. prof. Boston U., 1988—, dir. Inst. for Study of Conflict, Ideology and Policy, 1988—. Assoc. Davis Ctr. for Russian Studies, Harvard U.; cons. Nat. Inst. Justice and Temple U. Rsch. Program on Organized Crime, 1981-83, Battelle Columbus Labs./U.S. Army Ballistic Missile Def. Program, 1976-77, U.S. Senate Subcom. on Nat. Security, 1972; mem. Ronald Reagan's Fgn. Affairs and Def. Adv. Team, 1980. Author, editor 24 books; mem. editl. bd. Strategic Rev.; mem. adv. bd. Polit. Warfare; contbr. chpts. to numerous books, articles to profl. jours.; numerous appearances on TV and radio. Mem. Com. on Fgn. Rels., Am. Assn. Advancement of Slavic Studies. Office: Inst for Study of Conflict Ideology and Policy 141 Bay State Rd Boston MA 02215-1708 E-mail: raanan@bu.edu.

RAAS, DANIEL ALAN, lawyer; b. Portland, Oreg., July 6, 1947; s. Alan Charles and Mitzi (Cooper) R.; m. Deborah Ann Becker, Aug. 5, 1973; children: Amanda Beth, Adam Louis. BA, Reed Coll., 1969; JD, NYU, 1972. Bar: Wash. 1973, Calif. 1973, U.S. Dist. Ct. (we. dist.) Wash. 1973, U.S. Ct. Appeals (9th cir.) 1975, U.S. Supreme Ct. 1977, U.S. Tax Ct. 1983, U.S. Ct. Claims 1984. Atty. Seattle Legal Svcs, VISTA, 1972-73; reservation atty. Quinault Indian Nation, Taholah, Wash., 1973-76, Lummi Indian Nation, Bellingham, 1976-97, spl. counsel, 1997—; mem. Raas, Johnsen & Stuen, P.S., 1982—. Cons. Falmouth Inst., Fairfax, Va., 1992-2000, Nat. Am. Ind. Ct. Judges Assn., McLean, Va., 1976-80. Rules chmn. Whatcom County Dem. Conv., Bellingham, 1988, 92, 94, 96; bd. dirs. Congregation Beth Israel, Bellingham, 1985-2000, pres., 1990-92; mem. adv. com. legal asst. program Bellingham Vocat. Tech. Inst., 1985-91; trustee Whatcom County Law Libr., 1978-2002; pres. Vol. Lawyer Program, 1990-93, bd. dirs., 1988-94; pres. Cliffside Cmty. Assn., 1978-80, bd. dirs., 1977-89; bd. dirs. Friends Maritime Heritage Ctr., 1983-86, Samish Camp Fire Coun., 1988-94, pres. 1991-94, v.p., 1989-91, regional v.p. Union Am. Hebrew Congregations, 1986-93, nat. trustee, 1995—, exec. com., 1995-99, sec. Pacific N.W. region, 1993-95, pres., 1995-99. John Ben Snow scholar, NYU, 1969-70, Root-Tilden scholar, NYU, 1970-72. Mem. Wash. State Bar Assn. (trustee Ind. law sect. 1989-95, Pro Bono award 1991), Whatcom County Bar Assn. (v.p. 1981, pres. 1982, Pro Bono award 1991), Grays Harbor Bar Assn. (v.p. 1976). Home: 1929 Lake Crest Dr Bellingham WA 98226-4510 Office: Raas Johnsen & Stuen PS 1503 E St Bellingham WA 98225-3007

RAASH, KATHLEEN FORECKI, artist; b. Milw., Sept. 12, 1950; d. Harry and Marion Matilda (Schwabe) Forecki; m. Gary John Raash, June 13, 1987. BS, U. Wis., Eau Claire, 1972; MFA, U. Wis., Milw., 1978. One-woman and group shows include Sight 225 Gallery, Milw., 1979, 81, Nicolet Coll., Rhinelander, Wis., 1981, Messing Gallery, St. Louis, 1982, Arts Consortium, Cin., 1982, Ctr. Gallery, Madison, Wis., 1982, Otteson Theatre Gallery, Waukesha, Wis., 1982, Foster Gallery, Eau Claire, 1984, Duluth (Minn.) Art Inst., 1984, West Bend (Wis.) Gallery of Fine Arts, 1987, U. Wis., Waukesha Fine Arts Gallery, 1988, Mount Mary Coll., Milw., 1990, Cardinel Stritch Coll., Milw., 1991, West Bend Art Mus., 1995, Gwenda Jay Gallery, Chgo., 1995, Wis. Acad., Madison, 1996, Nicolet Coll., Rhinelander, Wis., 1997, Wausau (Wis.) Ctr. for Arts, 1998, Riveredge Galleries, Mishicot, Wis., 2000, Union Theater Gallery, Madison, 2000, Gallery 110, Plymouth, Wis., 2001, Bloomington (Minn.) Art Ctr., 2001, Mt. Seanrio Coll., Ladysmith, Wis., 2001, Regional Art Ctr., Eau Claire, 2002; exhibited in group shows at River Edge Galleries, Wis., 1990-91, 94-95, 2000, Peltz Gallery, Milw., 1990-94, 96-98, 2000-02, Minnetonka Ctr. Arts, Wayzata, Minn., 1996, Paine Art Ctr., Oshkosh, Wis., 1998, 2002, Woodward Gallery, N.Y.C., 2000-01; represented in permanent collections United Bank and Trust of Madison, Fine Arts Gallery U. Wis., Miller Brewing Co., Independence Bank Waukesha, Fed. Res. Bank, Mpls., Rhinelander Med. Ctr., U. Coll., Madison, Wis., Univ. Hosp. Recipient Purchase award, Madison Art Ctr., 1978, Honorable mention, Paine Art Ctr., 2001.

RAAT, WILLIAM DIRK, history educator; b. Ogden, Utah, July 1, 1939; s. Elmer William and Iris R.; m. Geraldine Koba, July 3, 1984; children: Kelly Corter, David Corter. AA, Weber Coll., 1959; BS, U. Utah, 1961, PhD, 1967. Asst. prof. history Moorhead (Minn.) State U., 1966-68, assoc. prof. history, 1968-70, SUNY, Fredonia, 1970-77, prof. history, 1977—99, prof. emeritus, 1999—, dir. internat. edn., 1982-84. Vis. prof. U. Utah, 1984-85. Author: Revoltosos, in English, 1981, in Spanish, 1986, Mexico: From Independence to Rev., 1982, Mexico's Sierra Tarahumara, 1986, Mexico and the U.S., 1992, rev. edit., 1996, Twentieth Century Mexico, 1986; contbr. 25 articles to profl. jours. Recipient James A. Robertson award Conf. on Lat. Am. History, 1968, Edwin Lieuwen Meml. prize Rocky Mt. Coun. on Lat. Am Studies, 1988. Mem. Conf. on Lat. Am. History, World History Assn., Phi Beta Kappa, Alpha Mu Gamma. Avocations: racquetball, golf. Home: 15849 W Grand Isle Way Surprise AZ 85374-4518

RABADEAU, MARY FRANCES, protective services official; b. Elizabeth, N.J., July 13, 1948; d. Russell John and Frances (Hanley) R. Student, Union Coll., 1967-69; MEd, Kean Coll., 1976. Officer City of Elizabeth Police Dept., N.J., 1978-82, detective, 1982-83, sgt., 1983-87, lt., 1987-91, capt., 1991-92, dir., 1993-95, dep. chief, 1994; chief N.J. Transit Police Dept., Maplewood, 1995—. Instr. Union County Police Acad. Trustee Blessed Sacrament Ch., Elizabeth, N.J., 1989-99; bd. acad. advisors N.J. state police grad. studies program Seton Hall U.; bd. trustees Benedictine Acad., Elizabeth, N.J. Named one of Outstanding Young Women in Am., 1983, Woman Leader N.J. Assn. Women Bus. Owners, 1997; recipient John H. Stamler Police Acad. Svc. award, 1992, Cert. of Recognition award YWCA, 1992, Disting. Grad. award Nat. Cath. Ednl. Assn., 1995; honoree Union County Commn. on the Status of Women, 1993, Hispanic Law Enforcement Assn. of Union County, 1995, Women Helping Women Recognition award Soroptimist Internat. Ams., 2001. Mem. NAACP, Internat. Assn. Chiefs of Police, N.J. State Chiefs of Police, Essex County Chiefs Assn., N.E. Assn. Women Police (cert., Merit award), Elizabeth Police Patrolman's Benevolent Assn., Elizabeth Police Superior Officers Assn. (treas. 1983-91, v.p. 1991), Am. Soc. Law Enforcement Trainers, Emerald Soc., Union County Urban League, Italian Law Enforcement Officers Assn., Fellas Inc. (hon.), Union County Men's Svc. Orgn., Nat. Assn. of Women Law Enforcement Execs. Democrat. Roman Catholic. Office: NJ Transit Police Dept 180 Boyden Ave Maplewood NJ 07040-2494 Home: 184 Riveredge Dr Chatham NJ 07928-3112

RABALAIS, JOHN WAYNE, chemist, physicist; b. Bunkie, La., Sept. 7, 1944; s. Stafford J. and Lurline S. Rabalais; m. Rebecca G. Guillory, Jan. 29, 1966; children: Dennis, Eva-Marie. BS in Chemistry, U. Southwestern La., 1966; PhD in Phys. Chemistry, La. State U., 1970. NATO postdoctoral fellow U. Uppsala, Sweden, 1970—71; asst. prof. U. Pitts., 1971—75; assoc. chmn. dept. chemistry U. Houston, 1978—82, assoc. prof., 1975—79, prof., 1979—81, Disting. Univ. Chair prof., 1981—88, Cullen Disting. prof. chemistry and physics, 1988—, joint appointment in dept. chemistry and physics, 1992—. Vis. faculty rschr. Sandia Nat. Lab., Albuquerque, 1983; rsch. scientist Copolymer R&D Co., Baton Rouge, 1966; cons. in field; lectr. in field; reviewer papers for numerous jours. Author: Principles of Ultraviolet Photoelectron Spectroscopy, 1977; co-author (with P. Nordlander): Proceedings of the 12th International workshop on Inelastic Ion-Surface Collisions, 1999; editor: Low Energy Ion-Surface Interactions, 1994; contbr. ; mem. editl. bd. Radiation Effects and Defects in Solids, 1990—94, Surface Sci., 1994—98, Chem. Physics Letters, 1980—88, Jour. Electron Spectroscopy and Related Phenomena, 1974—86. Named to La. State U. Hall of Distinction, 1989; recipient Esther Farfel award, U. Houston, 1993, Faculty Rsch. Excellence award, 1985—86, Tech. Writing award, Pitts. Chemists Club, 1973, Soc. Tech. Comm., 1976; grantee numerous grants including, Petroleum Rsch. Fund, NSF, Solar Energy Lab., U. Houston, Energy Inst., Dow Chem. Co., U.S. Army Rsch. Office, NAS, R.A. Welch Found., Tex. Instruments Co. Fellow: Am. Vacuum Soc.; mem.: AAAS, N.Y. acad. Sci., Tex. Acad. Sci., Soc. Applied Spectroscopy, Am. Phys. Soc., Am. Chem. Soc. (Southeastern Tex. sect. award 1983), Sigma Xi, Phi Lambda Upsilon. Achievements include patents for process for deposition of diamond films using low energy, mass-selected ion beam deposition; time-of-flight ion scattering spectrometer for scattering and recoiling for electron density and structure. Office: Univ of Houston 4800 Calhoun St Houston TX 77204-5641

RABASSA, CLEMENTINE CHRISTOS, humanities educator, translator; b. N.Y.C., July 31, 1932; d. Sotter and Mary (Legatos) Christos; m. Gregory Rabassa; 1 child, Clara C. BA cum laude, Hunter Coll., 1953, MA, 1958; PhD with distinction, Columbia U., 1971. Preceptor, instr. Spanish Columbia U., N.Y.C., 1963-66, instr. Spanish, 1964-66; from asst. prof. to assoc. prof. humanities Medgar Evers Coll., CUNY, 1973-79, prof. humanities, 1979-90, prof. humanities emerita, 1990—, coord. fgn. langs., 1976-79. Author: Demetrio Aguilera - Malta and Social Justice, 1980, En Torno a Aguilera - Malta, 1981, Summer II, a novella, 1999; co-editor Studies in Afro-Hispanic Lit., 1977-79; translator: Canticle for a Memory (Francisco Arriví), 1993, Emotions (Julio Ortega), 1999. Fellow Fulbright-Hays, 1963, NEH, 1971-72, Rockefeller Found., 1979-80, Gulbenkian Found., 1989; named to Hunter Coll. Hall of Fame, 1982. Mem. MLA, Am. Recorder Soc., Am. Assn. Tchrs. of Spanish and Portuguese, Am. LIt. Translators Assn., Alliance Françise, Renaissance Soc. Am., PEN Am. Ctr., Phi Beta Kappa, Sigma Delta Pi. Democrat. Greek Orthodox. Avocations: music, painting, writing. Home and Office: 140 E 72d St Apt 10B New York NY 10021-4243

RABASSA, GREGORY, Romance languages educator, translator, poet; b. Yonkers, N.Y., Mar. 9, 1922; married 1966. AB, Dartmouth Coll., 1945, Litt.D. hon., 1982; MA, Columbia U., 1947, PhD in Portuguese, 1954. Instr. Spanish Columbia U., 1947-52, assoc., 1952-58, asst. prof., 1958-63, assoc. prof. Spanish and Portuguese, 1963-68; prof. Romance langs. Queens Coll., CUNY Grad. Sch., Flushing, N.Y., 1968-86, Disting. prof., 1986—. Assoc. editor Odyssey Rev., 1961-64 Contbr. articles to profl. jours. Staff sgt. OSS, 1942-45. Decorated Croce al Merito di Guerra Italy, Order of San Carlos Colombia; recipient Nat. Book award for transl., 1967, transl. prize, PEN Am. Ctr., 1977, Gode award, Am. Transl. Assn., 1980, PEN transl. medal, 1982, Arts award, N.Y. Gov., 1985, transl. prize, Wheatland Found., 1988, lit. award, Am. Acad. and Inst. Arts and Letters, 1989, presdl. medal, Dartmouth Coll., 1991, Ivan Sandrof award, The Nat. Book Critics Cir., 1993, Lit. Lion award, N.Y. Pub. Libr., 1993, Mellon Humanities award, Loyola U., Chgo., 1995, Gabriela Mistral prize, Chile, 1996, Gregory Kolovakos award, PEN, 2001, John Steinbeck Writers award, Southampton Coll., 2002; fellow Fulbright-Hays fellow, 1965—66, NEH fellow, 1979—80, Guggenheim fellow, 1988—89. Mem. Renaissance Soc. Am., MLA, Am. Assn. Tchrs. Spanish and Portuguese, Latin Am. Studies Assn., Am. Lit. Translators Assn., Hispanic Soc. Am., Century Assoc., PEN Club, Phi Beta Kappa. Office: Dept of Hispanic Langs & Lits CUNY Queens College Flushing NY 11367

RABB, BRUCE, lawyer; b. Cambridge, Mass., Oct. 4, 1941; s. Maxwell M. and Ruth (Criedenberg) R.; m. Harriet Rachel Schaffer, Jan. 4, 1970; children: Alexander Charles, Katherine Anne. AB, Harvard U., 1962; Cert. d'Etudes Politiques, Institut d'Etudes Politiques, Paris, 1963; LLB, Columbia U., 1966. Bar: N.Y. 1966. Law clk. to judge U.S. Ct. Appeals (5th cir.), 1966-67; assoc. Stroock & Stroock & Lavan, N.Y.C., 1967-68, 71-75, ptnr., 1976-91, Kramer Levin Naftalis & Frankel LLP, N.Y.C., 1991—. Staff asst. to Pres. U.S., 1969-70; vice-chmn. Lawyers Com. Human Rights, 1977-95, nat. coun., 1996—; supr. bd. dirs. Agora-Gazeta, sp.zo.o., 1993-98, Agora-Druk, sp.zo.o., 1995-98; pub. mem. Adminstrv. Conf. U.S., 1982-86, 89-92, spl. counsel, 1986-88. Sec. Lehrman Inst., 1978-88; bd. dirs. Citizens Union of N.Y., 1981-87, 88-94, 95-2001, 02--, treas., 2002--; bd. dirs. Am. Friends of Alliance Israelite Universelle, 1987-2001, Human Rights Watch, 1987—, Welfare Law Ctr., 1997—; mem. Human Rights Watch/Ams., 1982—, Human Rights Watch/Helsinki, 1985-97, Fund for Free Expression, 1987-97, Human Rights Watch/Middle East and No. Africa, 1989—, vice chmn., 1990—; mem. internat. adv. com. Internat. Parliamentary Group for Human Rights in the Soviet Union, 1984-88, Prin. of the Coun. for Excellence in Govt., 1990—; adv. coun. Doctors of the World USA, 1996—, FilmAid Internat., 2000—. Mem. ABA (adv. panel Internat. Human Rights Trial Observer project), Am. Law Inst., Assn. of Bar of City of N.Y. (fed. legis., internat. law chair 1992-95, internat. human rights, civil rights, legal edn. and admission to bar, internat. trade coms., coun. on fgn. affairs), Harvard Club N.Y.C., Met. Club of Washington. Office: Kramer Levin et al 919 3rd Ave New York NY 10022-3902

RABB, GAEL CAUTION, mental health consultant; b. Nüernberg, Germany, Oct. 24, 1953; U.S. mil. dependent, came to U.S., 1965; d. Gustave Hamilton Jr. and Anne Grace (Richardson) Caution; m. Larry Lebby, Oct. 2, 1970 (div.); children: Lanir, Amanda; m. Moses Rabb Jr., Oct. 16, 1995; children: Mary Anne Grace. BA in Psychology, U. S.C., 1975, PhD in Clin. Psychology, 1984. Lic. ind. social worker. Fellow White House, Washington, 1980-81; dir. psychology Morris Village Alcohol and Drug Tx Ctr., Columbia, S.C., 1985; dir. health and human svcs. Office of the Gov., 1986; pres. Cautions Consults, Columbia, 1988—. Home: 2324 Washington St Columbia SC 29204-1862

RABB, GEORGE BERNARD, zoologist, conservationist; b. Charleston, S.C., Jan. 2, 1930; s. Joseph and Teresa C. (Redmond) R.; m. Mary Sughrue, June 10, 1953. BS, Coll. Charleston, 1951, LHD (hon.), 1995; MA, U. Mich., 1952, PhD, 1957. Teaching fellow zoology U. Mich., 1954-56; curator, coord. rsch. Chgo. Zool. Park, Brookfield., Ill., 1956-64, assoc. dir. rsch. and edn., 1964-75, dep. dir., 1969-75, dir., 1976—. Rsch. assoc. Field Mus., 1965—; lectr. dept. biology U. Chgo., 1965-89; mem. Com. on Evolution Biology, 1969—; pres. Chgo. Zool. Soc., 1976—; steering com. Species Survival Commn., Internat. Union Conservation of Nature, 1983—, vice-chmn. for N.Am., 1986-88, dep. chmn., 1987-89, chmn., 1989-96, vice-chmn. comms., 1997—; chmn. policy adv. group Internat. Species Info. System, 1974-89, chmn. bd., 1989-92; pres. bd. dirs. Chgo. Wilderness Mag., 1999—; v.p. Fauna and Flora Internat., 1998—; chmn. bd. Ill. State Mus., 1999—. Fellow AAAS; mem. Am. Soc. Ichthyologists and Herpetologists (pres. 1978), Herpetologists League, Soc. Systematic Zoology, Soc. Mammalogists, Soc. Study Evolution, Ecol. Soc. Am., Soc. Conservation Biology (council mem. 1986), Soc. for Integrative and Comparative Zoology, Soc. Study Animal Behavior, Am. Assn. Museums, Am. Soc. Naturalists, Am. Assn. Zool. Parks and Aquariums (dir. 1979-80), World Assn. Zoos and Aquariums, Am. Com. Internat. Conservation (chmn. 1987—), World Conservation Union (hon. mem.), Chgo. Coun. Fgn. Relations (Chgo. com.), Economic Club Chgo., Tavern Club, Sigma Xi. Office: Brookfield Zoo 3300 Golf Rd Brookfield IL 60513-1095

RABB, HARRIET SCHAFFER, government official, lawyer, educator; b. Houston, Sept. 12, 1941; d. Samuel S. and Helen G. Schaffer; m. Bruce Rabb, Jan. 4, 1970; children: Alexander, Katherine. BA in Govt., Barnard Coll., 1963; JD, Columbia U., 1966. Bar: N.Y. 1966, U.S. Supreme Ct. 1969, D.C. 1970. Instr. seminar on constl. litigation Rutgers Law Sch., 1966-67; staff atty. Center for Constl. Rights, 1966-69; spl. counsel to commr. consumer affairs N.Y.C. Dept. Consumer Affairs, 1969-70; sr. staff atty. Stern Çommunity Law Firm, Washington, 1970-71; asst. dean urban affairs Law Sch., Columbia U., N.Y.C., 1971-84, prof. law, dir. clin. edn., 1984-99, George M. Jaffen prof. law and social responsibility, 1991-99, vice dean, 1992-93; gen. counsel Dept. Health and Human Svcs., Washington, 1993—2001; v.p., gen. counsel Rockefeller U., 2001—. Mem. faculty employment and tng. policy Harvard Summer Inst., Cambridge, Mass., 1975-79 Author: (with Agid, Cooper and Rubin) Fair Employment Litigation Manual, 1975, (with Cooper and Rubin) Fair Employment Litigation, 1975. Bd. dirs. Ford Found., 1977-89, N.Y. Civil Liberties Union, 1972-83, Lawyers Com. for Civil Rights Under Law, 1978-86, Legal Def. Fund NAACP, 1978-93, Mex. Am. Legal Def. and Edn. Fund, 1986-90, Legal Aid Soc., 1990-93; mem. exec. com. Human Rights Watch, 1991-93; trustee Trinity Episcopal Sch. Corp., 1991-93. Office: Rockefeller U 1230 York Ave New York NY 10021*

RABB, MAXWELL M. lawyer, former ambassador; b. Boston, Sept. 28, 1910; s. Solomon and Rose (Kostick) R.; m. Ruth Creidenberg, Nov. 2, 1939; children: Bruce, Sheila Rabb Weidenfeld, Emily Rabb Livingston, Priscilla Rabb Ayres. AB, Harvard U., 1932, LLB, 1935; LLD (hon.), Wilberforce U., 1957; DHL (hon.), Mt. St. Mary's Coll., 1983; LLB (hon.), Pepperdine U., 1985, St. Thomas U., 1986; DHL (hon.), Hebrew Union Coll., 1990. Bar: Mass. 1935, N.Y. 1958. Mem. firm Rabb & Rabb, Boston, 1935-37; adminstrv. asst. to U.S. Senator H.C. Lodge Jr., Mass., 1937-43; adminstrv. asst. U.S. Senator Sinclair Weeks, 1944; legal and legis. cons. Sec. Navy Forrestal, 1946; practice law Boston, 1946-51; cons. U.S. Senate Rules Com., 1952; presdl. asst. to Pres. Eisenhower; sec. to Cabinet, 1953-59; partner Stroock & Stroock & Lavan, N.Y.C., 1959-81, of counsel, 1989-91, Kramer, Levin, Naftalis & Frankel LLP, N.Y.C., 1991—; amb. to Italy, 1981-89. Bd. dirs. Sterling Nat. Bank, Sister City Program City of N.Y., MIC Industries, Data Software Sys. Inc., Dwight Eisenhower Nat. adv. bd., Oak Tree Med. Sys., Inc. Exec. asst. campaign mgr. Eisenhower presdl. campaign, 1951-52; del. Republican Nat. Conv., 1952, 56, 76, 80; mem. exec. com. U.S. Commn. for UNESCO, 1959-60; chmn. U.S. del. UNESCO conf., Paris, 1958; mem. Coun. on Fgn. Rels., 1978—; pres. Congregation Emanu-El, N.Y.C., 1973-81; former mem. bd. advisors John F. Kennedy Sch. Govt., Harvard U. Sch. Pub. Health; trustee Cardinals Cooke and O'Connor Inner City Scholarship Fund, The Lighthouse, 1995—, Eisenhower Libr., George Marshall Internat. Ctr.; mem. bd. mgrs. Seamen's Ch. Inst.; mem. presdl. adv. panel on South Asian Relief assistance, 1971; mem. panel conciliators World Bank Internat. Ctr. for Settlement of Investment Disputes, 1967-73, U.S. rep., 1974-77; mem. Presdl. Commn. on Income Maintenance Programs, 1968-69; hon. chmn. bd. Am. Friends of Alliance Israelite Universelle; vice chmn. United Cerebral Palsy, Inc., Nat. Com. on Am. Fgn. Policy; mem. adv. bd. Auburn U. Served as lt. amphibious corps USNR, 1944-46. Decorated Commendatore Order of Merit, 1958, Grand Cross of Order of Merit (Italy), 1982, Commendation ribbon USN; Grand Cross of Order of Malta, 1989; Brandeis U. fellow. Mem. ABA, Am. Law Inst., Amb.'s Club of Reps. Abroad (hon. chmn.), Harvard Club (N.Y.C.), Harmonie Club (N.Y.C.), Army and Navy Club (Washington), Met. Club (Washington). Home: 480 Park Ave New York NY 10022-1613 also: Wilson Hill Rd Colrain MA 01340 Office: Kramer Levin Naftalis & Frankel LLP 919 3rd Ave New York NY 10022-3902

RABB, THEODORE K. historian, educator; b. Teplice-Sanov, Czechoslovakia, Mar. 5, 1937; came to U.S., 1956, naturalized, 1978; s. Oskar Kwasnik and Rose (Oliner) Rabinowicz; m. Tamar Miriam Janowsky, June 7, 1959; children: Susannah Rabb Bailin, Jonathan Richard, Jeremy David. BA, Queen's Coll. Oxford U., Eng., 1958; MA, Queen's Coll. Oxford U., 1962, Princeton U., 1960, PhD, 1961. Instr. Stanford U., 1961-62; instr. Northwestern U., 1962-63; asst. prof. Harvard U., 1963-67; mem. faculty Princeton U., 1967—, prof. history, 1976—. Vis. assoc. prof. Johns Hopkins U., 1969, SUNY-Binghamton, 1973-74; visitor Inst. Advanced Studies, Princeton, 1973, 82; mem. nat. bd. cons. NEH, Nat. Coun. History Edn. (chair); N.J. Com. for Humanities (chair); chief historian Renaissance Television Series; bd. dirs. Humanities West, Save Venice, Inc.; juror Rome Prize; cons. in field. Author: The Thirty Years War, 2d edit, 1972, Enterprise and Empire, 1967, The Struggle for Stability in Early Modern Europe, 1975, The Origins of Modern Nations, 1981, Renaissance Lives: Portraits of an Age, 1993, rev. edit., 2000, Origins of the Modern West, 1993, Jacobean Gentleman, 1998; co-author: The Western Experience, 8th edit., 2003, Peoples and Nations, 1982; editor: Jour. Interdisciplinary History, 1970—; co-editor: Action and Conviction in Early Modern Europe, 1969, The Family in History, 1973, Marriage and Fertility, 1981, Industrialization and Urbanization, 1981, Climate and History, 1981, The New History, 1982, Hunger and History, 1985, Population and Economy, 1986, Art and History, 1988, La Fame nella storia, 1991, Origin and Prevention of Major Wars, 1988. Bd. govs. Hebrew U. Fellow and/or grantee Folger Shakespeare Library, Am. Philos. Soc., Social Sci. Research Council, Am. Council Learned Socs., Guggenheim Found., NEH. Mem. Am. Hist. Assn. (chmn. com. quantitative rsch. history, chmn. nominating com.), Social Sci. History Assn. (exec. com., treas.), Am. Assn. Advancement Humanities (dir., sec.-treas.), Nat. Coun. History Stds., C.C. Humanities Assn. (steering com.), Royal Hist. Soc., Internat. Commn. History Parliamentary and Rep. Instns., Renaissance Soc. Am., Hakluyt Soc., Nat. Coun. History Edn. (chair), Historians Early Modern Europe, Conf. Brit. Studies. Office: Princeton University History Dept Princeton NJ 08544-0001

RABBANI, FARHANG, urologic oncologist; b. Tehran, Iran, Dec. 30, 1967; s. Mehdi and Parirokh Rabbani; m. Taghreed Almahmeed, Aug. 24, 1999. BSc in Math. with honors, U. B.C., Vancouver, Can., 1987, MD, 1991. Rotating intern St. Joseph's Hosp., London, Can., 1991-92; urology resident U. B.C., 1992-96; urol. oncology fellow Meml. Sloan-Kettering Cancer Ctr., N.Y.C., 1996-99, clin. asst. attending dept. urology, 1999—. Grants reviewer Med. Rsch. Coun., London, 1997-99. Cons. editor Prostate Cancer and Prostatic Diseases; contbr. articles to profl. jours., chpts. to books. Recipient Gov.-Gen. of Can. Gold medal, 1987. Fellow Royal Coll. Physicians and Surgeons Can.; mem. Am. Assn. Cancer Rsch., Am. Urol. Assn. (scholarship award western sect. 1995), Am. Soc. Clin. Oncology. Avocations: skiing, skating, programming. Office: Meml Sloan-Kettering Cancer Ctr Dept Urology 1275 York Ave New York NY 10021-6094

RABBANI, LEROY ELAZAR, physician, researcher; b. N.Y.C., June 12, 1958; s. Edward and Miriam Rabbani. AB in Biochemistry cum laude, Harvard Coll., 1980; MD, Columbia U., 1984. Diplomate Am. Bd. Internal Medicine subspecialty cardiovasc. disease. Intern, resident dept. medicine Columbia-Presbyn. Med. Ctr., N.Y.C., 1984-87, chief resident dept. medicine, 1987-88; clin./rsch. fellow in cardiology Brigham and Women's Hosp., Boston, 1988-91, assoc. physician, 1990-93; instr. in medicine Harvard Med. Sch., 1991-93; asst. attending physician Columbia-Presbyn. Med. Ctr., N.Y.C., 1993—; asst. prof. medicine Columbia U. Coll. Physicians and Surgeons, 1993-2000; dir. coronary care unit Columbia-Presbyn. Med. Ctr., 1999—, assoc. prof. clin. medicine, 2000—. Aid for impaired med. students com. Columbia U. Coll. Physicians and Surgeons, 1986-88, 94—, instnl. self-study task force, grad. med. edn. subcom., 1987-88; morbidity and mortality classification com. TIMI 4 (thrombolysis in myocardial infarction 4) Trial, Boston, 1992-93. Contbr. articles to profl. jours. Recipient Dr. Alfred Steiner award for med. student rsch. Columbia U. Coll. Physicians and Surgeons, 1982, Herbert J. Bartelstone award in pharmacology, Columbia U. Coll. Physicians and Surgeons, 1984, Physician-Scientist award NIH, 1991-96. Fellow Am. Coll. Cardiology, Am. Coll. Physicians, Coun. on Clin. Cardiology of Am. Heart Assn.; mem. AMA, AAAS, N.Y. Acad. Scis., Alpha Omega Alpha. Office: Columbia-Presbyn Med Ctr 161 Fort Washington Ave New York NY 10032-3713

RABBE, DAVID ELLSWORTH, oil company executive; b. Alexandria, Va., Dec. 17, 1955; s. Raymond Leed and Judith Ann (Ayers) R.; m. Maryann Degroot, Sept. 25, 1982; children: Lisa Ann, Chelsea Nicole, Jamison David. BCE, U. Md., 1979. Terminal trainee Amerada Hess Corp., Balt., 1980-81, terminal supt. Syracuse, N.Y., 1981-82, Roseton, 1982-83, Pennsauken, N.J., 1983-87, mgr. gas station maintenance Woodbridge, 1987-91; project mgr. Chem. Land Holdings, East Brunswick, 1991-92, mgr. environ. affairs Kearny, 1992-98, remediation dir., 1998-99, pres., 1999—. Mem. Md. Soc. Surveyors, World Affairs Counci. Republican. Episcopalian. Avocations: woodworking, sailing. Home: 33 Sorrel Run Mount Laurel NJ 08054-4819 E-mail: Davermxs@aol.com.

RABE, LAURA MAE, mathematician, educator; b. Cin., May 28, 1945; d. Howard Lawrence and Alberta Catherine (Held) R. BS, U. Cin., 1967, MS, 1972, supr. cert., 1982. Tchr. Colerain H.S., Cin., 1967-97, chairperson math. dept., 1980-97; tchr. Mt. St. Joseph Coll., 1997—. Presenter grant writing workshop Miami U., Oxford, Ohio, 1994; pressenter in field. Named Hixon Tchr. of Yr., 1996; grantee GTE, 1994-95, NSF, 1980, Dartmouth Univ., 1995, 96; Tandy Tech. scholar, 1995-96. Mem. NEA, Nat. Coun. Tchrs. Math., Ohio Coun. Tchrs. Math., Greater Cin. Coun. Tchrs. Math. Roman Catholic. Avocations: travel, camping, water skiing, snow skiing, photography.

RABE, RICHARD FRANK, dentist, lawyer; b. Crystal Lake, Iowa, May 19, 1919; s. Otto Henry and Agnes Marie (Juhl) R.; m. Barbara Jean McNeal, Mar. 15, 1946; children: Richard Frank, Mary Elizabeth, Kathleen Ann, Michelle. AA, Waldorf Coll., 1938; DDS, U. Iowa, 1942; JD, Drake U., 1952. Bar: Iowa 1952. Dentist pvt. practice, Des Moines, 1946—, atty., 1952—. Cons. Nat. Bd. Dental Examiners, 1955-60; chmn. Iowa Bd. Dental Examiners, 1962-63, Iowa Bd. Nursing Home Examiners, 1980-84; lectr. dental assns. throughout U.S. Contbr. articles to profl. jours. Fellow Am. Coll. Dentists; mem. ABA, ADA (vice chmn. coun. legis. 1977-78), Am. Acad. Dental Practice Adminstrn., Am. Inst. Parliamentation, Iowa Dental Study Club (past pres.), Iowa Dental Assn. (pres. 1972, trustee 1960-71), Iowa Bar Assn., Des Moines Dist. Dental Soc. (past pres.), Milw. Dental Rsch. Group, Ctrl. Regional Dental Testing Agy., Masons, Shriners, Des Moines Gold & Country Club, Psi Omega, Delta Theta Phi. Episcopalian. Avocations: sailing, flying. Home and Office: 3662 Ingersoll #406 Des Moines IA 50312 also: 6527 Bay Club Dr Fort Lauderdale FL 33308-1814

RABECS, ROBERT NICHOLAS, lawyer; b. Scranton, Pa., Mar. 19, 1964; s. Nicholas and Anne Marie (Stull) R. BA summa cum laude, U. Scranton, 1986; JD cum laude, Georgetown U., 1990. Bar: Pa. 1990, D.C. 1992. Assoc. Reed Smith Shaw & McClay, Washington, 1990-94, Hogan & Hartson, Washington, 1994—. Columnist Managed Healthcare News, Belle Meade, N.J., 1994-98. Fulbright scholar, 1986-87; NEH undergrad. fellow, 1985. Mem. ABA, Am. Health Lawyers Assn., Pa. Bar Assn. (health law com.), D.C. Bar Assn. (health law sect.), Alpha Sigma Nu. Roman Catholic. Home: 3401 38th St NW Apt 914 Washington DC 20016-3045 Office: Hogan & Hartson 555 13th St NW Washington DC 20004-1161 E-mail: rnrabecs@hhlaw.com.

RABEKOFF, ELISE JANE, lawyer; b. N.Y.C., June 26, 1959; d. Sidney and Natalie (Kaufman) R.; m. Christopher Gladstone, June 7, 1986; children: Katherine, Nicholas. AB, Princeton U., 1980; JD, Yale U., 1986. Bar: Pa. 1986, D.C. 1988, U.S. Dist. Ct. (fed. dist.) D.C. 1988. Legis. asst. Sen. D.P. Moynihan, Washington, 1980-83; law clk. judge Charle Robert Richey U.S. Dist. Ct. D.C., 1986—88; assoc. Shea & Gardner, 1988-93; v.p., gen. counsel Quadrangle Devel. Corp., 1993—. Bd. dirs. Chelsea Sch., Silver Spring, Md., 1990-95. Office: Quadrangle Devel Corp 1001 G St NW Washington DC 20001-4545 E-mail: eliserabekoff@quad1.com.

RABEN, NINA, molecular biologist, biochemist; b. Moscow, Russia, Jan. 13, 1945; came to the U.S., 1987; d. Anatoly S. and Liza M. (Vinogradsky) R.; m. Mark Belenky, Sept. 23, 1966; 1 child, Masha Belenky. MD, 1st Moscow (Russia) Med. Inst., 1967; PhD in Biochemistry, USSR Acad. Med. Sci., Moscow, 1973. Rschr. USSR Surgery Ctr., Moscow, 1968-73, sr. investigator, 1973-79; vis. assoc. Nat. Inst. of Diabetes, Digestive and Kidney Diseases, Bethesda, Md., 1987-90; vis. scientist Nat. Inst. of Arthritis and Musculoskeletal Diseases, 1990-94; rsch. chemist NIAMS, NIH, 1994-97, staff scientist, 1997—. Contbr. articles to profl. jours.; patentee in field. Mem. AAAS. Jewish. Home: 5455 Grove Ridge Way Rockville MD 20852-4648 Office: NIAMS NIH 9000 Rockville Pike Bethesda MD 20892-0001 E-mail: rabenn@arb.niams.nih.gov.

RABENS, STEVEN FISHER, dermatologist, educator; b. Chgo., Mar. 7, 1946; s. Jack I. and Leah (Fisher) R.; m. Wendy S. Rudin. BA, U. So. Calif., 1968, MD, 1970. Diplomate Am. Bd. Dermatology, Am. Bds. of Dermatology and Pathology. Intern L.A. County-U. So. Calif. Med. Ctr., L.A., 1970-71, resident in dermatology, 1971-74, chief resident in dermatology, 1973-74; from clin. instr. to assoc. clin. prof. U. So. Calif. Sch. Medicine, 1974-87, clin. prof. medicine, 1988-96, emeritus clin. prof., 1996—; pvt. practice, Encino, Calif., 1974-98; ret., 1998; hon. staff Encino Tarzana Regional Med. Ctr. Contbr. articles to profl. jours. Maj. USAR M.C., 1971-77. Named one of "The Best Doctors in Town", L.A. Mag., 1991. Fellow Am. Acad. Dermatology, Am. Soc. Dermatol. Surgery; mem. Calif. Med. Assn., L.A. County Med. Assn., L.A. Met. Dermatol. Soc. Office: PO Box 16755 Beverly Hills CA 90209-2755

RABENSEIFNER, HANNA CAMILLE, lawyer; b. Rymarov, Czechoslovakia, May 8, 1957; d. Slavoj V. and Vera L. (Valouch) Rabenseifner; m. John K. Pepper, Jr., Sept. 19, 1986 (div. Nov. 19, 1995). JD, U. Zurich, Switzerland, 1982; LLM, U. Miami, 1984, JD, 1987. Bar: Fla. 1988, U.S. Dist. Ct. (so. dist.) Fla. 1992. Contr. Internat. Bus. Corp., Miami, Fla., 1987-89; pvt. practice, 1989—. Office: Ste 730 905 Brickell Bay Dr Miami FL 33131-2925

RABENSTEIN, DALLAS LEROY, chemistry educator; b. Portland, Oreg., June 13, 1942; 8. Melvin Leroy and Rose Marie (Nelson) R.; m. Gloria Carolyn Duncan, Aug. 30, 1964; children: Mark, Lisa. BS, U. Wash., 1964; PhD, U. Wis., 1968. Lectr. U. Wis., Madison, 1967-68; research chemist Chevron Research Co., Richmond, Calif., 1968-69; from asst. prof. to prof. chemistry U. Alta., Edmonton, Can., 1969-85; prof. U. Calif., Riverside, 1985-97, chmn. dept. chemistry, 1989—92, 1998—2000, 2002—, dean Coll. Natural and Agrl. Scis., 1993-94, disting. prof. chemistry, 1997—. Vis. prof. U. Oxford, 1976-77, U. Western Ont., 1982; McElvain lectr. U. Wis., 1981; Dow lectr. U. B.C., 1988; Eli Lilly lectr., Ind. U., 1993; faculty rsch. lectr. U. Calif., Riverside, 2000. Contbr. articles to profl. jours. NIH and NSF grantee. Fellow AAAS, Chem. Inst. Can. (Fisher Sci. Lecture award 1984); mem. Am. Chem. Soc., Internat. Soc. Magnetic Resource. Avocations: reading, gardening, music. Home: 5162 Palisade Cir Riverside CA 92506-1521 Office: U Calif Dept Chemistry Riverside CA 92521-0001 E-mail: dallas.rabenstein@ucr.edu.

RABER, CONNER E. (ROARK RABER), counselor, administrative assistant; b. Springfield, Tenn., Feb. 25, 1949; d. Madison Conner and Dorothy Christine (Lowery) Roark; m. Dan Edward Raber, Aug. 26, 1972; children: Nicole Christine, Jefferson Dale. BS in Sociology, Ind. State U., 1971; M in Counseling, Edn., N.C. State U., Greensboro, 1991. Cert. counselor in edn. Caseworker Vigo County Dept. Pub. Welfare, Terre Haute, Ind., 1969-72; tchg. asst. Magnum Durham County Sch. Sys., Durham, N.C., 1982-84; caseworker Guilford County Dept. Pub. Welfare, Greensboro, 1984-89; counselor Randolph County Sch. Sys., Archdale, 1989-94; counselor, adminstrv. asst. Carey Ridge Elem. Sch. Westfield (Ind.) Washington Schs., 1994—. Mem. AIDS Coun. WWS, 1998, Sch. to Work (Learning to Living), 1998. Mem. Am. Counselor Assn., Nat. Student Assistance Assn., Ind. Sch. Counselor Assn. Baptist. Avocations: reading, walking. Home: 6291 Woodcrest Dr Avon IN 46123-7742 Office: Carey Ridge Elem Sch 16321 Carey Rd Westfield IN 46074-8925

RABIDEAU, MARGARET CATHERINE, retired media center director; b. Chgo., Nov. 24, 1930; d. Nicholas and Mary Agnes (Burke) Oberle; m. Gerald Thomas Rabideau, Nov. 27, 1954; children: Mary, Margaret, Michelle, Gregory, Marsha, Grant. BA cum laude, U. Toledo, 1952, MA in Ednl. Media Tech., 1978. Cert. tchr. K-12 media tech., supr. ednl. media, tchr. English and journalism, specialist in edn. Asst. dir. pub. rels. U. Toledo, 1952-55; publicity writer United Way, Toledo, 1974-75; tchr. Toledo Pub. Schs., 1975-80, libr., media specialist, 1980-90; dir. media svcs. Sylvania (Ohio) Schs., 1990—2002, ret., 2002. Task force to evaluate coll. programs Ohio Dept. Edn., 1987; on-site evaluation team, Hiram Coll., Ohio, 1991; north ctrl. evaluation team Northwestern Ohio, 1985—. Citizen task force Toledo/Lucas County Libr., Ohio, 1991, mem. friends of the libr., 1990—; task force Sta. WGTE-TV PBS Sta., Toledo, 1993; mem. tech. com. strategic plan Sylvania Schs., 1997; instr. U. Toledo, 1990—. Recipient Disting. Educator for Art Edn. award N.W. Ohio Art Edn. Assn., 1997; nmamed Educator of Yr., Sylvania Schs., 2001. Mem. ALA, U. Toledo Alumni Assn., Ohio Ednl. Libr. Media Assn. (N.W. dir. 1993—, vocat. dir. 1985-89, Libr. Media Specialist of Yr. 1993, disting. educator art edn. 1999), Am. Ednl. Comm. and Tech., Ednl. Leadership Assn. (bd. dirs.), Maumee Valley Computer Assn. (task force), Phi Delta Kappa (Outstanding Newsletter Nat. award 1990, pres. Toledo chpt., svc. key award, 1998). Avocations: running, travelling, cross stitching. Home: 1038 Olson St Toledo OH 43612-2828

RABIDEAU, MARILYN ANN, elementary education educator; b. Green Bay, Wis., Sept. 23, 1939; d. Henry John and Irma Tornow Fink; m. Kenneth Francis Rabideau, June 9, 1962; children: Neil Kenneth Rabideau, Laurie Ann Rabideau Kleisinger. BS in Edn., U. Wis., 1961; MEd, Nat. Louis U., 1996. Life license elem. sch. tchr. grades 1-8 Wis. Dept. Pub. Instrn. Elem. educator Janesville (Wis.) Pub. Schs., 1961-2001, retired, 2001. Pres. Rock County (Wis.) Ext. Homemakers, 1968-70; pres., coun. mem. Faith Luth. Ch., Janesville, 1983-88; officer, bd. dirs. Faith Lutheran Endowment Found., 1996-2002. Recipient Cert. of Excellence, Wis. Ctr. for Academically Talented Youth, Inc., Madison, 1995. Mem. Delta Kappa Gamma (chapter pres. 1998-2000, 2002—), Phi Beta Kappa. Avocations: writing, music, drawing, sports, handicrafts.

RABIDEAU, PETER WAYNE, university dean, chemistry educator; b. Johnstown, Pa., Mar. 4, 1940; s. Peter Nelson and Monica (Smalley) R.; m. Therese Charlene Newquist, Sept. 1, 1962 (div.); children: Steven, Michael, Christine, Susan; m. Jennifer Lee Mooney, Nov. 15, 1986; children: Mark, Leah. BS, Loyola U., Chgo., 1964; MS, Case Inst. Tech., Cleve., 1967; PhD, Case Western Res U, Cleve., 1968. Postdoctoral asst. U. Chgo., 1968-69, instr., 1969-70; asst. prof. Ind. U.-Purdue U., Indpls., 1970-73, assoc. prof., 1973-76, prof., 1976-90, chmn. dept. chemistry, 1985-90; dean Coll. Basic Scis. La. State U., Baton Rouge, 1990-99; dean Coll. Liberal Arts and Scis. Iowa State U., Ames, 1999—. Program officer NSF, 1988-89. Contbr. numerous articles to profl. jours. Recipient rsch. award Purdue Sch. Sci. at Indpls., 1982, Outstanding Alumnus award chemistry dept. Case Western U., 2001. Fellow AAAS; mem. Am. Chem. Soc. (chmn. Ind. sect. 1974, councilor 1981-90). Home: 3509 Valley View Rd Ames IA 50014-4615 Office: Iowa State U Coll Liberal Arts and Scis 202 Catt Hall Ames IA 50011-1301 E-mail: rabideau@iastate.edu.

RABII, PATRICIA BERG, b. Lynn, Mass., Nov. 7, 1942; d. Clarence Oscar and Naomi Ruth (MacHugh) B.; m. S. Rabii, Oct. 26, 1966 (div. 1988); children: Susan M., Elizabeth L. AA, Green Mtn. Coll., Poultney, Vt., 1962; BA cum laude, U. Pa., 1978. Cons. City of Phila., 1981; fin. svcs. officer U. Pa., Phila., 1981-90; asst. to exec. dir. Psi Upsilon Found., Paoli, Pa., 1990-92; parish adminstr. St. David's (Radnor) Episcopal Ch., Wayne, 1992-98; clergy sec. St. David's Ch., 1998—. Co-dir. career planning/pub. rels. Resources for Women, Phila., 1978-81. Counselor direct patient and care ARC, St. Louis, 1967-69; bd. dirs. Upper Merion PTA, 1976-78, Dental Clinic, King of Prussia, 1976-78; leader Girl Scouts U.S.A., King of Prussia, 1976-77, 80-81. Recipient ACT 101 Svc. award, Penn Cap, 1989. Mem. AAUW, U. Pa. Women's Club (bd. dirs. 1975-80, v.p. 1979-80). Avocations: golf, bridge, travel. Home: 5 Drummers Ln Wayne PA 19087-1503 Office: St Davids Radnor Episcopal 763 Valley Forge Rd Wayne PA 19087-4724

RABIL, ALBERT , JR. humanities educator, educator; b. Rocky Mount, N.C., May 8, 1934; s. Albert and Sophie Mae (Safy) R.; m. Janet Spain, Aug. 29, 1956; children: Albert III, J. Alison. BA, Duke U., 1957; MDiv, Union Theol. Sem., 1960; PhD, Columbia U., 1964. Instr. religion Trinity Coll., Hartford, Conn., 1964-65, asst. prof., 1965-68; asst. prof. hist. theology Chgo. Theol. Sem., 1969-71; assoc. prof. SUNY-Old Westbury, 1971-74, prof., 1974-77, disting. tchg. prof. humanities, 1977-98, emeritus prof., 1998. Program dir. NEH Summer Inst., 1992, 94, 95, 96, 98, 2000, 2001. Author: Merleau-Ponty, 1967 (Ansley award 1964), Erasmus and the New Testament, 1972, Laura Cereta, 1981, (with others) Her Immaculate Hand, 1983, Erasmus' Paraphrases of Romans and Galatians, 1983, Erasmus' Annotations on Romans, 1994; editor: Renaissance Humanism (3 vols.), 1988; editor, translator: Knowledge, Goodness, and Power, 1991, Henricus Cornelius Agrippa Declamation on the Nobility and Preeminence of the Female Sex, 1996; co-editor Renaissance Quarterly, 1992-97; series co-editor The Other Voice in Early Modern Europe, 1993—; mem. editl. bd. Soundings: An Interdisciplinary Jour., 1992-94. Travelling fellow Union Theol. Sem., 1960, Soc. for Values in Higher Edn., 1961; grantee Fulbright Found., 1961, NEH, 1974, 81, 94. Mem. Erasmus Rotterdam Soc. (mem. editl. bd. 1980—), Soc. for Values in Higher Edn. (bd. dirs. 1981-90), Renaissance Soc. Am. (bd. dirs. 1991-97). Democrat. Home and Office: 2305 Honeysuckle Rd Chapel Hill NC 27514-1716 E-mail: arabil@nc.rr.com.

RABIL, MITCHELL JOSEPH, lawyer; b. Smithfield, N.C., Sept. 19, 1931; s. Albert G. and Eva (Nassif) R.; m. Antoinette M. Olivry, Nov. 25, 1956 (div. Oct. 1986); children: Elizabeth, Nathalie, Marcus, Gregory; m. Dolores E. Bleam, Jan. 21, 1989; children: Susan Starr Vermes, Scott Starr. BS, Wake Forest Coll., 1953; LLB, Georgetown U., 1961. Bar: N.C. 1961, N.J. 1967, D.C. 1980, Pa. 1981, U.S. Tax Ct. 1962, U.S. Supreme Ct. 1979; CPA, N.J., N.C. Supervisory acct. GAO, Washington, 1956-60; fin. analyst, staff acct. SEC, 1960-62; tax atty. Office of Chief Counsel, IRS, Phila. and N.Y.C., 1962-66; assoc. Archer, Greiner, Hunter & Read, Camden, N.J., 1966-71; ptnr. Myers, Matteo, Rabil, Norcross & Landgraf, Cherry Hill, 1971-89, Montgomery, McCracken, Walker and Rhoads, Cherry Hill, 1989-95; sole stockholder, pres. Mitchell J. Rabil & Assocs., P.A., 1995-2000; mem. Rabil & Harris L.L.C., 1998-2000, Rabil & Ropka, L.L.C., 2000—. Mcpl. chmn. Riverton (N.J.) Rep. Com., 1976-83; chmn. area 2 Burlington County Rep. Com., 1976-82; bd. dirs. The Archway Programs, Inc., 1988-99, West Jersey Chamber Music Soc., 1990-91, Zurbrugg Meml. Hosp., 1991-93; mem. N.J. New Capital Sources Bd., 1996—. Served with AUS, 1953-55. Mem. ABA, AICPA, N.J. Bar Assn., Phila. Bar Assn., N.J. Soc. CPAs, Am. Assoc. Atty. CPAs (bd. dirs., past pres. Delaware Valley, Greater Phila., chpt. founder, past pres.), Cherry Hill C. of C. (bd. dirs. 1990-94), World Affairs Council Phila., Union League (Phila.), Riverton Country Club, Rotary Club Cherry Hill (pres. 1980-81, past dir.). Roman Catholic. Home: 107 Wayside Ct Delran NJ 08075-2000 Office: Ste 2B Bldg 2 1010 Kings Hwy S Cherry Hill NJ 08034-2524

RABIN, ALAN ABRAHAM, economics educator; b. N.Y.C., June 16, 1947; s. Sidney and Claire Rabin. BA, Hamilton Coll., 1969; PhD, U. Va., 1977. NSF trainee U. Va., 1970-71, 71-72; intern Coun. Econ. Advisors, 1971; asst. prof. Calif. State U., Northridge, 1973-74, Georgetown U., Washington, summer 1975; asst. prof. econs. U. Tenn., Chattanooga, 1977-81, assoc. prof., 1981-86, prof., 1986—. Contbr. articles to profl. jours. NDEA fellow, 1969-70; U. Tenn.-Chatanooga faculty rsch. grantee, 1982. Mem. Am. Econs. Assn., So. Econs. Assn., Atlantic Econs. Soc., We. Econs. Assn., U. Tenn. Chattanooga Coun. Scholars, Omicron Delta Epsilon. Jewish. Avocations: sports, stamp collecting, bridge. Home: 1175 Pineville Rd Apt 161 Chattanooga TN 37405-2653 Office: U Tenn-Chattanooga Dept Economics Chattanooga TN 37403 E-mail: alan-rabin@utc.edu.

RABIN, BRUCE STUART, immunologist, physician, educator; b. Buffalo, Jan. 25, 1941; s. Eli and Dorothy R.; children: Andrew L., Alison J. BA, Case Western Res. U., 1962; MD, PhD (NIH predoctoral fellow, 1967), SUNY, Buffalo, 1969. Diplomate Am. Bd. Med. Lab. Immunology. Asst. prof. pathology SUNY and Ctr. for Immunology, Buffalo, 1970-72, Sch. Medicine, U. Pitts., 1972-76, assoc. prof. pathology, 1976-86, prof. pathology, 1986—, prof. psychiatry, 1987—, dir. Brain, Behavior and Immunity Ctr., 1989—. Dir. divsn. clin. immunopathology Univ. Health Ctr. Pitts., 1972—, med. dir. clin. lab. svcs., 1985—; interim chmn. dept. pathology U. Pitts. Sch. Medicine, 1990-91; merit rev. bd. for immunology VA Central Office, 1980-83; study sect. NIMH, 1988-91; chair oversight com. program in complementary and alternative medicine. U. Pitts. Med. Health Sys.; med. dir. health enhancement program U. Pitts. Med. Ctr. Assoc. editor Clin. Immunology Newsletter, 1980, Brain Behavior and Immunity, Clin. Immunology and Immunopathology; contbr. sci. papers in field to profl. publs. Grantee Rsch. grant, NIH, 1973—. Mem. AAAS, Pitts. Pathology Soc., Am. Assn. Pathologists, Acad. Clin. Lab. Physicians and Scientists, Am. Acad. Allergy, Am. Assn. Immunologists, Am. Assn. Clin. Histocompatibility Testing, Am. Soc. Clin. Pathologists (clin. immunopathology coun. 1978-84, editor Clin. Immunology Check Sample Program), Am. Acad. Microbiology (com. on postdoctoral edn. 1980), Assn. Med. Lab. Immunologists (pres. 1988), Psychoneuroimmunology Rsch. Soc. (pres. 1995). Home: 6615 Forest Glen Rd Pittsburgh PA 15217-1823 Office: Presbyn-U Hosp Clin Immunopathology DeSoto & O'Hara Sts Pittsburgh PA 15213-2582 E-mail: bsr@pitt.edu.

RABIN, DAVID NEAL, radiologist; b. Chgo., Jan. 16, 1956; s. Harold and Nancy Rabin; m. Debbie Lynn Rabin, Apr. 16, 1989; 1 child, Perry. BS in Biology, Loyola U. Chgo., 1978; MD, U. Ill., Chgo., 1982. Lic. physician, Ill. Intern Ill. Masonic, Chgo., 1982-83; resident Rush Presbyn. St. Lukes, 1983-87; abdominal imaging fellow Mallinckrodt Inst. of Radiology, Washington U., St. Louis, 1987-88; radiologist Rush Presbyn. St. Luke's Med. Ctr., Chgo., 1988-89; asst. prof. radiology Rush Med. Coll., 1988-89; radiologist Highland Park (Ill.) Hosp., 1988-2000; asst. prof. radiology Northwestern U. Med. Sch., Chgo., 1992—; vice chair Evanston Northwestern Healthcare Radiology, 2000—. Mem. cardiac computed tomography med. adv. bd. GE, 1999—; lectr. U. Chgo., 1996—. Contbr. articles to profl. jours.; editor Annals of Improbable Research, 1995—. Mem. profl. edn. com. Am. Cancer Soc., Lake County, Ill., 1993-98; vol. faculty Coll. Lake County, 1990-2000. Mem. Am. Coll. Radiology (com. on edn. for ultrasound 1995—, ultrasound accreditation program reviewer 1995—, commn. on stds. and accreditation com. on small and/or rural practices 1998-2000), Radiol. Soc. N.Am. (com. on comm. chair 1997-99), Highland Park Ind. Practice Assn. (bd. dirs. 1994-2000), Evanston Ind. Practice Assn. (compensation com. 2000—02). Avocations: amateur radio, fishing, woodwork, photography, astronomy. Office: Evanston Northwestern Healthcare 718 Glenview Ave Highland Park IL 60035

RABIN, GILBERT, judge, lawyer; b. Tarrytown, N.Y., June 10, 1923; s. Charles and Jeanette (Kalman) R.; m. Zita Segall, June 18, 1950; children: Jill, Corey, Marni. LLB, N.Y. U., 1948, LLM, 1950; LLD (hon.) , Mercy Coll., 1981. Bar: N.Y. 1948. Assoc. Raphael & Conlon, N.Y.C., 1948-50; sr. ptnr. Rabin & Green, 1950-73; sole practice Yonkers, N.Y., 1974-82; judge, chief judge City of Ct. Yonkers, 1982-94; jud. hearing officer N.Y. Supreme Ct., 9th Jud. Dist., 1994—. Supr. jury selection Supreme Ct., Westchester County, NY; lectr. N.Y. State Jud. Sems.; legis. advisor Mem. N.Y. State Assembly, Yonkers, 1966—70; justice City of Yonkers, 1970—82. Co-founder Children's Hearing Edn. and Rsch., 1979—. Recipient numerous awards Israel Bonds, Big Bros., others. Mem. N.Y. State Bar Assn., West County Bar Assn., Yonkers Lawyers Assn., N.Y. State City Ct. Judges Assn., N.Y. State Magistrates Assn. Jewish.

RABIN, HERBERT, physicist, university official; b. Milw., Nov. 14, 1928; 2 children. BS, U. Wis., 1950; MS, U. Ill., 1951; PhD in Physics, U. Md., 1959. Physicist elec. div. U.S. Naval Research Lab., 1952-54, physicist solid state physics div., 1954-62, head radiation effects sect. optical materials br., 1962-67, head quantum optics sect., applied optics br., 1967-68, head quantum optics br., 1968-71, assoc. dir. research for space sci. and tech., 1971-77, asso. dir. research for space and communication sci. and tech., 1977-79; dep. asst. sec. of Navy for research, applied and space tech. Office of Navy Secretariat, Washington, 1979-83; dir. engring. research ctr., prof. elec. engring., assoc. dean Coll. Engring., U. Md., College Park, 1983—, interim dean coll. engring., 1999-2000. Dir. GRC Internat., 1988-98, Washington Aluminum Co., 1992-95, Yurie Sys. Inc., 1995-98, Neocera Inc., 1999—, VT Linx Multimedia Systems, Inc., 2000-02; vis. scietist Technisch Hochschule, Stuttgart, Germany, 1960-61; mem. staff physics dept.George Washington U., 1955-73; cons. Sch. Engring. of Sao Carlos, U. Sao Paulo, Brazil, 1964,, 70; trustee Nat. Technol. U., 1984-2000, life trustee, 2000—. Contbr. articles to tech. jours.; patentee in field Recipient Meritorious Civilian Svc. award USN, 1969, Disting. Civilian Svc. award, 1976, 93; Disting. Civilian Svc. award Dept. Def., 1979, cert. of commendation NASA, 1986, Centennial medal U. Md. Coll. Engring., 1994. Fellow Am. Phys. Soc., AAAS, Optical Soc. Am., AIAA; mem. IEEE (sr. mem.), Brazilian Acad. Scis. (corr.) Home: 7109 Radnor Rd Bethesda MD 20817-6332 Office: U Md Engring Rsch Ctr College Park MD 20742-0001

RABIN, JACK, lawyer; b. Aug. 19, 1930; s. Leo and Bertha Rabin; m. Roberta Edith Libson, Oct. 25, 1953; children: Keith Warren, Michael Jay, Adam Douglas. Student, Bklyn. Coll., 1948-50; LLB, Bklyn. Law Sch., 1953. Bar: N.Y. 1953, U.S. Tax Ct. 1960, U.S. Ct. Claims 1964, U.S. Supreme Ct. 1964, U.S. Ct. Appeals (2d cir.) 1968. Ptnr. Hoffberg, Rabin & Engler and predecessor firms, N.Y.C., 1968-82, Javits, Hinckley, Rabin & Engler, N.Y.C., 1982-84, Phillips, Nizer, Benjamin, Krim & Ballon, N.Y.C., 1984-94, counsel, 1994—. Arbitrator gen. comml. and constrn. panel Am. Arbitration Assn., 1968—; instr. Real Estate Inst., NYU, 1976-78; ct. apptd. mediator U.S. Dist. Ct. (so. dist.), N.Y., 1994—, N.Y. Supreme Ct., N.Y. County, 1999. Assoc. editor Bklyn. Law Rev., 1952, editor-in-chief, 1953, also author law rev. note. 1st lt. JAGC, U.S. Army, 1954-57, col. res., ret., 1983. Mem. N.Y. State Bar Assn., Res. Officers Assn. U.S. (pres. Rockland County chpt. 1967-68), B'nai B'rith (pres. New City, N.Y. 1965-66). Jewish. Home: Box 233 Goshen CT 06756-0233 Office: 10 W 66th St Ste 8G New York NY 10023 E-mail: sutleg@earthlink.net.

RABIN, JOEL PHILLIP, management consultant; b. N.Y.C., Nov. 29, 1944; s. Bernard Rabin and Selma (Paul) Koppel; 1 child, Melissa. BA in Sociology, CUNY, 1966, postgrad., 1967-70, Columbia U., 1974-77. Rsch. specialist Cath. Med. Ctr. of Bklyn. and Queens, N.Y.C., 1968-70; program evaluator Mt. Sinai Med. Ctr., 1970-74; onsite dir., med. evaluation team Yale U., 1974-76; project dir. Trans Urban East Orgn., 1976; program coord. Columbia U., 1977-78; sr. assoc. Am. Practice Mgmt., Inc., 1979-81; prin. Reynolds & Co., 1982—. Mem. N.Y. Soc. for Health Planning, Acad. Health Svcs. Mktg. of Am. Mktg. Assn. (exec. mem. 1987—). Home: 53 Greenwich Ave Apt 3 New York NY 10014-2754 Office: Reynolds & Co Inc 333 E 51st St New York NY 10022-6702 E-mail: joelrabin@aol.com.

RABIN, JOSEPH HARRY, marketing research company executive; b. Chgo., Dec. 12, 1927; s. Morris and Libby (Broder) Rabinovitz; m. Barbara E. Leader, Oct. 31, 1954; children: Marc Jay, Michelle Ann, Deborah Susan. BSc, Roosevelt U., 1950; MBA, DePaul U., 1951. Account exec. Gould, Gleiss & Benn, 1951-56; asst. dir. mktg. rsch. Paper Mate Co., Chgo., 1956-63; pres. Rabin Rsch. Co., 1963—. Pres. Mather H.S. Coun., 1972-74; mem. adv. coun. U. Toledo, 1976-77, Kellstadt Ctr. DePaul U., 1986-93; mem. adv. com. Bur. of the Census, 1978-83; bd. dirs. Market Rsch. Inst., 1973-75, Ner Tamid Synagogue, 1976—, Jewish Vocat. Svc., 1977-80. With AUS, 1946-47. Mem. Am. Mktg. Assn. (pres. Chgo. chpt. 1961-62, nat. dir. 1973-75, nat. v.p. mktg. rsch. 1978-79, nat. pres. 1981-82), Assn. Consumer Rsch., Am. Statis. Assn. (pres. Chgo. chpt. 1962-63), Am. Assn. Pub. Opinion Rsch. Home: 7061 N Kedzie Ave Chicago IL 60645-2846 Office: Rabin Rsch Co 150 E Huron St Chicago IL 60611-2999

RABIN, LAURA ALYSON, psychologist; b. Bethesda, Md., Sept. 4, 1970; d. Sheldon Rabin, Carol Rabin. BA, Northwestern U.; MS in Judaism in the Greco Roman Period, Oxford U., England; MA in Interdisciplinary Jewish Studies, Jewish Theol. Sem. Am.; PhD in Clin. Psychology, Fordham U. Cognitive neuropsychology rsch. asst. Stanford U., Palo Alto, Calif.,

1995—96; neuropsychology extern Long Island Jewish Med. Ctr., 1997—98; clin. psychology extern Lenox Hill Hosp., Ctr. Attention and Learning Disorders, 1998—99; cognitive rehabilitation specialist N.Y. U. Med. Ctr., Rusk Inst. Rehab. Medicine, New York, 1999—2001; clin. psychology intern Dartmouth Med. Sch., Hanover, NH, 2001—. Contbr. articles. Fellow Tchg. fellow, Fordham U., 1999—2001, Food and Drug Adminstrn, Oak Ridge Inst. Sci. and Edn. Rsch., 1997; scholar Presdl. scholar, Fordham U., 1996—99. Mem.: APA, N.Y. State Psychol. Assn., Soc. Neurosci., Internat. Neuropsychol. Soc., Psi Chi, Phi Kappa Phi. Jewish. Avocations: animation art, tennis. Home: 59 Wensley Drive Great Neck NY 11020 Personal E-mail: rabin@dartmouth.edu.

RABIN, MICHAEL DOV, technology consulting executive, research psychologist; b. N.Y.C., Apr. 10, 1958; s. Edward I. and Miriam (Stern) R.; children from a previous marriage: Jeremy S., Eve R. BA magna cum laude, Clark U., 1979; MS, Yale U., 1982, MPh, 1983, PhD, 1986. Asst. prof. in residence U. Conn. Health Ctr., Farmington, 1986-87; asst. prof. psychology SUNY, Purhase, 1987-88; rsch. psychologist Internat. Flavor & Fragrances, Union Beach, N.J., 1988-89; sr. tech. staff AT&T Bell Labs., Holmdel, 1989-96; product dir. Web Site Svcs. AT&T, Lincroft, 1996-97, dir. internet2 networked commerce svcs. Bridgewater, 1997-98; v.p. info. arch. IllusionFusion, Inc., N.Y.C., 1999; v.p. user rsch. and info. Arch., Rare Medium, Inc., NYC, 1999—2001; pres. Direct Perception, LLC, Englishtown, NJ, 2001—. Exec. com. Yale Macintosh Users Group, 1984-86; chmn. AT&T Human Factors and Behavioral Scis. Symposium, 1991; mem. AT&T Bell Lab. Behavioral Scis. Com., 1990-96; presenter in field. Patentee and patents pending relating to voice command control and voice recognition; editor The Desktop Jour. (Yale Macintosh Users Group), 1984-86; contbr. articles to profl. jours. N.Y. State Regents scholar, 1976; grantee Fragrance Rsch. Fund, 1986. Mem. Human Factors and Ergonomics Soc. (pres. met. chpt. 1993-94, exec. com. 1991-96, chmn. annual symposium 1993, Jerome H. Ely award for most outstanding article in Human Factors jour. 1996), Assn. for Computing Machinery, N.Y. New Media Assn., Sigma Xi, Phi Beta Kappa, Psi Chi, Sig Chi. Democrat. Jewish. E-mail: mdr@aya.yale.edu.

RABIN, MONROE STEPHEN ZANE, physicist; b. Bklyn., Dec. 19, 1939; s. Louis and Helen (Haspel) R.; m. Joan Greenblatt, Feb. 27, 1965; children: Elaine Judith, Carolyn Sandra. AB, Columbia Coll., 1961; PhD, Rutgers U., 1967. Physicist Lawrence Berkeley (Calif.) Lab., 1967-72; assoc. prof. physics U. Mass., Amherst, 1972-81, prof. physics, 1981—; vis. physicist Stanford Linear Accelerator Ctr., Palo Alto, Calif., 1979-80; vis. scholar Physics Dept. Harvard U., Cambridge, Mass., 1986-87; Soriano scholar in radiol. physics, radiation therapy dept. Mass. Gen. Hosp., Boston, 1986-87. Mem. oversight panel Proton Therapy Med. Facility, Mass. Gen. Hosp., Boston, 1991-96. Contbr. articles to Physical Rev., Physical Rev. Letters, Physics Letters, Nuclear Instruments and Methods. Mem. Am. Phys. Soc., Sigma Xi. Achievements include research in experimental particle physics, medical physics, cancer therapy using accelerated protons, ductal carcinoma in situ, intravascular brachytherapy, heavy-ion physics. Home: 21 Atwater Cir Amherst MA 01002-3205 Office: U Mass Dept Physics Amherst MA 01003 E-mail: rabin@physics.umass.edu.

RABIN, STEVEN BARRY, research scientist; b. Bay Shore, N.Y., Nov. 3, 1959; s. Stanley H. and Joan E. (Block) R.; m. Ruth P. Silver, June 27, 1993; children: Sarah, Daniel. BS, Hobart Coll., 1981; MS, Rice U., 1986, PhD, 1987. Staff scientist Phillips Petroleum Corp., Bartlesville, Okla., 1987-90; group leader, scientist Dionex Corp., Sunnyvale, Calif., 1990-96; rsch. scientist Alza Corp., Palo Alto, 1996-2000, mgr. devel. materials, 2001—. Judge Internat. Sci. Fair, Tulsa, 1990; team leader Santa Clara County AIDS Walk, San Jose, Calif., 1995, 97. Welch grad. fellow Robert O. Welch Found., Houston, 1984-87. Mem. Soc. for Applied Spectroscopy (mem. steering com. No. Calif. sect. 1995—), No. Calif. Spectroscopy Soc. (sec. 1996, chmn. elect program 1997, chmn. 1998-00, treas. 2000—), Pacific Conf. on Chemistry (session organizer/pres. 1996). Achievements include 5 patents in field; inventor and co-inventor of several techniques in ion chromatography. Avocations: birdwatching, hiking, bicycling. E-mail: steve.rabin@alza.com.

RABINER, LAWRENCE RICHARD, retired electrical engineer; b. Bklyn., Sept. 28, 1943; s. Nathan Marcus and Gloria Hannah (Bodinger) R.; m. Suzanne Login, June 23, 1968; children: Sheri Lynn, Wendi Beth, Joni Elizabeth BS, MS, MIT, 1964, PhD, 1967. Mem. tech. staff AT&T Bell Labs., Murray Hill, N.J., 1967-70, supr. human machine voice communications group, 1971-85, head speech rsch. dept., 1985-90, dir. info. principles rsch. lab., 1990-95, v.p. user experience rsch. divsn., 1995-96; v.p. Speech and Image Processing Svcs., 1995-98, rsch. v.p., 1998—2002. Author: Theory and Application of Digital Signal Processing, 1975, Digital Speech Processing, 1979, Multirate Digital Signal Processing, 1983, Fundamentals of Speech Recognition, 1993. Bd. dirs. Summit Jewish Community Ctr., N.J., 1985-90. Fellow NAE, NAS, IEEE (pres. ASSP Soc. 1974-75, Piori award 1980), Soc. award 1980, Centennial award 1984, Kilby medal 1999, Millenium award 2000), Acoustical Soc. Am. (Biennial award 1974, v.p. 1994-95). Republican. Jewish. Avocations: stamp collecting, bridge, racquetball. Home: 58 Sherbrook Dr Berkeley Heights NJ 07922-2346 E-mail: lrr@comcast.net.

RABINOF, SYLVIA, pianist, composer, author, educator; b. N.Y.C., Oct. 10, 1913; d. Morris and Fanny (Edelstein) Smith; m. Benno Rabinof, Sept. 16, 1943 (dec. Apr. 1976); m. Charles Rothenberg, Dec. 22, 1978 (dec. April 1992). Student, 3rd St Music Sch. Settlement, N.Y.C., NYU, Juilliard Sch. Music; MusD (hon.), Lincoln Meml. U., 1947; studied with Marguerite Valentine, Mary Emerson, Rudolph Serkin, Ignace Jan Paderewski, Simon Barere, Georges Enesco, Oscar Ziegler, James Bleeker, Charles Haubiel, Albert Stoessel, Philip James. Tchr. piano, improvisation, ensemble theory Juilliard Sch. Music; mem. faculty Brevard Music. Ctr. N.C. Converse Coll., Spartanburg, S.C., Round Top Music Festival, Tex., SUNY, Fredonia; lectr. in field. Author: (textbooks) Musicianship Through Improvisation, 1966, The Improviser, 1967, The Improvisers Key Guidebook, 1969; contbr. composers' biographies to NFMC Jr. Keynotes mag., 1971-98; composer: cantata The Deluge, Three Profiles for Piano, Suite for String Orchestra, children's operetta Hamlet the Flea; published piano arrangements for Warner Bros.; piano solo and duo recordings with Benno Rabinof include Beethoven violin and piano sonatas, violin gypsy classics, Vivaldi concerti, others; performances in Vienna, Zurich, London, Phila., Carnegie Hall, N.Y.C., Boston, Chgo., Toronto, Paris, Moscow, Athens, Rome, Milan, others. Mem. ASCAP, Nat. Fedn. Music Clubs (chair improvisation), Musicians Club N.Y. (pres. 1976-79) Home: 8220 Jog Rd Boynton Beach FL 33437-2938

RABINOVICH, MICHAEL, computer scientist; b. Leningrad, Russia, July 16, 1955; came to U.S., 1988; s. Semyon and Yevgenya (Treyster) R.; m. Irina Bam, Aug. 11, 1991; 1 child, Rebecca J. Diploma in Piano Performance, Rimski-Korsakov Coll. Music, Leningrad, 1978; Engring. Diploma, Leningrad Electrotech. Inst., 1979; MSc, U. Wash., 1991, PhD, 1994. Programmer engr. various industries, Leningrad, 1979-87; sr. programmer Sterling Software, Dylakor Divsn., Chatsworth, Calif., 1988-89; rsch. asst. U. Wash., Seattle, 1989-94; tech. staff AT&T Bell Labs, Murray Hill, N.J., 1994-96; prin. tech. staff mem. AT&T Labs., Florham Park, 1996—. Mem. program com. Internat. Conf. on Data Engring., 1998, Internat. Conf. on Distributed Computing Sys., 1999, Internat. Conf. on Very Large Databases, 2000, Internat. WorldWide Web Conf., 2000. Co-author: Web Caching and Replication, 2001; contbr. articles to profl. jours., chapters to books; patentee in field. Mem. IEEE Computer Soc., Assn. Computing Machinery. Achievements include research in internet performance, distributed protocols, workflow management systems. Home: 55 Cottage Pl Gillette NJ 07933-1701 Office: AT&T Labs 180 Park Ave Florham Park NJ 07932-1004

RABINOVICH, RAQUEL, painter, sculptor; b. Buenos Aires, Argentina, Mar. 30, 1929; came to U.S., 1967, naturalized, 1973; d. Enrique Rabinovich and Julia Dinitz; m. Jose Luis Reissig, Feb. 14, 1956 (div. 1981); children: Celia Karen, Pedro Dario, Nora Vivian. Student, U. Córdoba, Argentina, 1950-53, Sorbonne, Paris, 1957, U. Edinburgh, Scotland, 1958-59. Lectr. Whitney Mus., 1983-86, Marymount Manhattan Coll., 1984-90. Exhbns. include Hecksher Mus., Huntington, N.Y., 1974, Susan Caldwell Gallery, N.Y.C., 1975, CUNY Grad. Ctr., 1978, The Jewish Mus. Sculpture Ct., N.Y.C., 1979, Ctr. Inter-Am. Rels., 1983, Bronx Mus. Arts., N.Y.C., 1986, Fordham U. Lincoln Ctr., N.Y.C., 1985, Ams. Soc., 1990, Erik Stark Gallery, 1991, Montgomery Ctr., 1992, Trans-Hudson Gallery, 1993, Noyes Mus., 1994, Nelson Atkins Mus. Art., 1995, Intar Gallery, N.Y.C., 1996, U. Tex. Mus. Art, 1998, Trans Hudson Gallery, N.Y.C., 1998, 2000, Emergences project, 2001—, others; represented in collections World Bank Fine Art Collection, Washington, Univ. Art Mus., Austin, Cin. Art Mus., Walker Art Ctr., others. NEA fellow, 1991-92; grantee N.Y. State Coun. Arts, 1995—, Pollock-Krasner Found., 2001. Avocations: travel, music. Home: 141 Lamoree Rd Rhinebeck NY 12572-3013 E-mail: raquelrabinovich@aol.com.

RABINOVICH, SERGIO, physician, educator; b. Lima, Peru, Apr. 8, 1928; m. Nelly; children— Gina, Sergio, Norca, Egla. MD, San Fernando Med. Sch., U. San Marcos, Lima, Peru, 1953. Intern San Fernando Med. Sch., U. San Marcos, Lima, 1947-54; resident in medicine Grasslands Hosp., Valhalla, N.Y., 1954-57, Henry Ford Hosp., Detroit; prof., head dept. internal medicine U. Arequipa Med. Sch., 1960-61; asst. prof. dept. internal medicine U. Iowa, Iowa City, 1963-65, asst. prof., 1965-69; attending physician and cons. VA Hosp., Iowa City, 1965-73; assoc. prof. U. Iowa, 1969-73; prof., chief dept. medicine div. infectious disease So. Ill. U. Sch. Medicine, Springfield, 1973-96, prof., chmn. dept. medicine, 1974-88, pres. Faculty Coun., 1992-93, prof. emeritus, 1996. Author: (with I.M. Smith, S.T. Donta) Antibiotics and Infection, 1974. Fellow ACP, Infectious Disease Soc. Am.; mem. AMA, Am. Soc. Microbiology, N.Y. Acad. Sci., Am. Fedn. Clin. Research, AAAS, Am. Thoracic Soc., Ill. Thoracic Soc. (pres. 1978-79), Central Soc. Clin. Research, Sigma Xi. Office: So Ill U Sch Medicine 800 N Rutledge St Springfield IL 62794-9636

RABINOVITCH, BENTON SEYMOUR, chemist, educator emeritus; b. Montreal, Que., Can., Feb. 19, 1919; came to U.S., 1946; s. Samuel and Rachel (Schachter) R.; m. Marilyn Werby, Sept. 18, 1949; children: Peter Samuel, Ruth Anne, Judith Nancy, Frank Benjamin; m. Flora Reitman, 1980. BSc, McGill U., 1939, PhD, 1942; DSc (hon.), Technion Inst., Haifa, 1991. Postdoctoral fellow Harvard, 1946-48; mem. faculty U. Wash., Seattle, 1948—, prof. chemistry, 1957—, prof. chemistry emeritus, 1985—. Cons. and/or mem. sci. adv. panels, coms. NSF, Nat. Acad. Scis.-NRC; adv. com. phys. chemistry Nat. Bur. Standards. Author Antique Silver Servers, 1991, Contemporary Silver, 2000; former editor: Ann. Rev. Phys. Chemistry; mem. editorial bd.: Internat. Jour. Chem. Kinetics, Rev. of Chem. Intermediates, Jour. Phys. Chemistry, J. Am. Chem. Soc. (assoc. editor). Served to capt. Canadian Army, 1942-46, ETO. Nat. Research Council Can. fellow, 1940-42; Royal Soc. Can. Research fellow, 1946-47; Milton Research fellow Harvard, 1948; Guggenheim fellow, 1961; vis. fellow Trinity Coll., Oxford, 1971; recipient Sigma Xi award for original research, Debye award in phys. chemistry, 1984, Polanyi medal Royal Soc. Chemistry; named hon. liveryman Worshipful Co. of Goldsmiths, London, 2000. Fellow Am. Phys. Soc., Am. Acad. Arts and Scis., Royal Soc. London; mem. Am. Chem. Soc. (past chmn. Puget Sound sect., past chmn. phys. chemistry div., editor jour.), Faraday Soc. Achievements include rsch. in Unimolecular gas phase reaction and history and design of silver implements. Home: 12530 42nd Ave NE Seattle WA 98125-4621 Office: Univ Washington Chemistry Box 351700 Seattle WA 98195 Fax: 206-685-8665.

RABINOVITZ, JASON, film and television consultant; b. Boston, Aug. 17, 1921; s. Morris J. and Martha (Leavitt) R.; m. Frieda Pearlson, July 18, 1948; children: Abby, Judith, Daniel, Jonathan. BA magna cum laude, Harvard U., 1943, MBA with distinction, 1948. With Chase Nat. Bank, N.Y.C., 1948-49; asst. to sec.-treas. United Paramount Theatres, Inc., 1949-53; dir. Microwave Assocs., Burlington, Mass., 1952-54; asst. controller ABC, N.Y.C., 1953-56; adminstrv. v.p. ABC-TV Network, 1956-57; with Metro-Goldwyn-Mayer, Inc., 1957-69, treas., CFO, 1963, financial v.p., 1967-69; dir., exec. v.p., gen. mgr. Ency. Brit. Ednl. Corp., Chgo., 1971-73; sr. v.p., gen. mgr. Am. Film Theatre, N.Y.C., 1974-75; v.p., asst. to pres. Metro-Goldwyn-Mayer, Inc., Culver City, Calif., 1976-79, v.p. fin., 1979-83; sr. v.p. fin. and corp. adminstrn. MGM/UA Entertainment Co., 1983-84; cons. motion picture and TV, 1984—. Dir. Pacific Rim Entertainment, 1993-95. Dir. Am. Jewish Hist. Soc., 1994—96. Capt. U.S. Army, 1942—46. Decorated Bronze Star. Mem. Phi Beta Kappa, Phi Eta Sigma. Home: 1675 Stone Canyon Rd Los Angeles CA 90077-1912 E-mail: frjarab@earthlink.net.

RABINOVITZ, JOEL, lawyer, educator; b. 1939. A.B., Cornell U., 1960; LL.B., Harvard U., 1963. Bar: N.Y. 1963, Calif. 1981. Asst. prof. U. Fla., Gainesville, 1966-68; vis. assoc. prof. UCLA, 1968-69, acting prof., 1969-72, prof., 1972-79; vis. prof., NYU, 1976; dep. Internat. Tax Counsel, Dept. Treasury, 1980-81; ptnr. with Irell & Manella, L.A., 1981—. E-mail: jrabinovitz@irell.com. Office: Irell & Manella 1800 Avenue Of The Stars Los Angeles CA 90067-4212

RABINOWITCH, DAVID GEORGE, sculptor; b. Toronto, Ont., Can., Mar. 6, 1943; came to U.S., 1972; s. Joseph and Ruthe (Calverley) R.; m. Sheila Martin, June 1966 (div. 1981); m. Catrina Neiman, Mar. 14, 1983. BA, U. Western Ont., London, 1966. Instr. sculpture Yale U., New Haven, 1974-75; prof. sculpture Staatliche Kunstakademie Düsseldorf, Germany, 1984—. Sculptor in residence Atelier Calder, Saché, France, 1994. Sculptures include Box Troughs, 1963, Fluid Sheet Pieces, 1964, Gravitational Vehicles, 1965, Tubers and Wood Constructions, 1966-67, Phantoms, 1967, Sectioned Mass Constructions, 1968, Metrical Constructions, 1973—, Tyndale Constructions, 1974—, Construction of Vision Drawings, 1969—, Ottonian Drawings, 1977—, Collinasca Cycle (Woodcuts), 1991-92, Ecclesiastical furniture, windows, and tapestry for Notre Dame de Bourg, Digne, France, 1990-97, sculpture for Catrina Neiman, 2000, guesthouse Oliver Ranch, Geyserville, Calif., 2001. Recipient CAPS award N.Y. State Coun., 1974, Lynch-Staunton award of distinction Can. Coun., Ottawa, Ont., 1977; J.S. Guggenheim Meml. Found. fellow, N.Y.C., 1975, Nat. Endowment Arts fellow, Washington, 1986-87. Mem. Royal Can. Acad. Arts and Scis. Avocations: music. Studio: 175 E 2nd St # 5C New York NY 10009-8017

RABINOWITSH, STEVE, urban planner educator, city council member; b. L.A., Jan. 17, 1949; s. Jack and Xenia Rabinowtsh; m. Lynnie Shaub Herr, Apr. 19, 1980; children: Ni cholas, Jackson. BA in Polit. Sci., U. Colo., 1970, MA in Polit. Sci., 1973, M in Urban Planning, 1975. City planner City of Longmont, Colo., 1975-76; planning cons. Brisco, Maphis, Murray & Lamont, Boulder, 1976-78; regional planner Denver Regional Coun. of Govts., 1978-82; planning cons., 1983-85; instr. Santa Rosa (Calif.) Jr. Coll., 1986—. City coun. mem. City of Santa Rosa, 1998—; mem., chmn. Sonoma County Open Space Dist., 1990-98; exec. bd. Assn. of Bay Area Govts., Oakland, Calif., 1999—; mem. Santa Rosa Creek Com., 1990-99, chmn., 1997-99. Recipient Conservation Partnership award U.S. Nat. Park Svc., 1996, Merit award City of Santa Rosa, 1992, 99. Avocations: photography, travel, French, aerobics. Home: 1275 4th St PMB 178 Santa Rosa CA 95404-4041 Office: City of Santa Rosa PO Box 1678 Santa Rosa CA 95402-1678

RABINOWITZ, HOWARD K. physician, educator; b. Pitts., Sept. 25, 1946; s. Mac and Anne (Morgan) R.; m. Carol A. Gelles, Feb. 4, 1968; children: Elyse, Daniel J. Student, Rutgers Coll., 1964-67; MD, U. Pitts., 1971. Diplomate Am. Bd. Family Practice, Am. Bd. Pediatrics. From instr. to assoc. prof. Dept. Family Medicine Jefferson Med. Coll., Phila., 1976-90, vice chmn., 1990-95; prof., 1990—. Bd. dirs. Am. Bd. Family Practice, Lexington, Ky., pres., 1992-93. Contbr. articles to profl. jours. With USPHS, 1972-74. RWJ Health Policy fellow, 1993-94. Fellow Phila. Coll. Physicians; mem. AMA, Soc. Tchrs. Family Medicine, Am. Acad. Family Physicians. Office: Jefferson Medical College Dept Family Medicine 1015 Walnut St Ste 401 Philadelphia PA 19107-5005

RABINOWITZ, JACK GRANT, radiologist, educator; b. Monticello, N.Y., July 9, 1927; s. Abraham and Bessie (Sussman) R.; m. Rica Gedalia Arnon, Oct. 19, 1972; children— Antoine, Anne, Pierre, Yaron, Tal. BA, UCLA, 1949; MD, U. Berne, Switzerland, 1955. Diplomate: Am. Bd. Radiology. Intern Kings County Hosp., Bklyn., 1955-56, resident, 1956-59; instr. radiology Downstate Med. Center, Bklyn., 1960-61, asst. prof. radiology, 1967-70, prof. radiology, 1970-73; asst. radiologist Mt. Sinai Sch. Medicine, N.Y.C., 1962-65, asst. prof. radiology, 1965-66, asso. prof. radiology, 1966-67, prof., chmn. dept. radiology, 1978-95, prof., 1995—. Asso. attending radiologist Mt. Sinai Hosp., N.Y.C., 1965-67, dir. radiology, 1978— ; radiologist-in-chief Bklyn.-Cumberland Med. Center, Bklyn., 1967-70; dir. diagnostic radiology Kings County Hosp. Center, Bklyn., 1970-73; prof., chmn. dept. diagnostic radiology U. Tenn., Memphis, 1973-78; cons. in radiology VA Hosp., Bronx, N.Y. Author: Pediatric Radiology, 1978, Radiology for the Primary and Emergency Care of Physicians, 1981. Fellow Am. Coll. Radiology; mem. Radiol. Soc. N. Am., Am. Roentgen Ray Soc., Assn. Univ. Radiologists, AMA, Soc. Chmn. Acad. Radiology Depts., Tenn. Radiol. Soc., Tenn. Med. Soc., Memphis and Shelby County Med. Soc., Memphis Roentgen Soc. Office: Mt Sinai Hosp 1 Gustave L Levy Pl New York NY 10029-6500 E-mail: jack-rabinowitz@msnyu.health.org.

RABINOWITZ, JOAN KAREN, social worker; b. N.Y.C., Mar. 1, 1947; d. Charles and Lillian (Rand) R. BA, Hunter Coll., 1976; MSW, Fordham U., 1980. Cert. social worker, N.Y., ACSW. Med. social worker 32B-J Health Fund, N.Y.C., 1980-81; counselor Narco Freedom, 1981; mental health cons. Addiction Rsch. Treatment Corp., 1981-87; social worker St. Luke's Roosevelt Hosp., 1987—. Adj. prof. Columbia U., 1988-89. Mem. NASW. Avocations: travel, theatre, music, reading, swimming. Office: St Luke's Roosevelt Hosp 428 W 59th St New York NY 10019-1105

RABINOWITZ, MAYER ELYA, librarian, educator; b. N.Y.C., Jan. 31, 1939; s. Simcha Rabinowitz and Dvora (Resnikoff) Masovetsky; m. Renah Lee Levine, June 16, 1965; children: Adi, Dalya, Ayelet. BA, B in Hebrew Lit., Yeshiva U., 1960, MA, 1961; M in Hebrew Lit., Jewish Theol. Sem., 1965, PhD, 1974. Ordained rabbi, 1967. Instr. Jewish Theol. Sem., N.Y.C., 1970-74, asst. prof., 1974-76, dean students Tchrs. Inst., 1974-76, assoc. prof., 1976—; assoc. dean grad sch., 1976-79, dean grad. sch., 1979-88, libr. NY, 1988—2002. Mem. com. on Jewish law and standards Rabbinical Assembly, N.Y.C., 1978—; chair Joint Bet Din Conservative Movement, N.Y.C., 1990—. Author: Sefer Hamordekhai Gittin, 1990, Sefer Hemordekhai Megillah, 1997; contbr. articles to profl. jours. Mem. Assn. Jewish Studies, Assn. Jewish Librs. Office: Jewish Theol Sem 3080 Broadway New York NY 10027-4650 E-mail: marabinowitz@jtsa.edu.

RABINOWITZ, SAMUEL NATHAN, lawyer; b. Hazleton, Pa., Sept. 16, 1932; s. Morris M. and Bodia (Janowitz) R.; m. Barbara Cohen, Mar. 27, 1955; children— Fredric E., Mark I., Joshua A. BA, Pa. State U., 1955; JD, Temple U., 1959. Bar: D.C. 1959, Pa. 1960. Agt. IRS, Phila., 1956-60; sole practice, 1960-61; ptnr. Blank Rome Comisky & McCauley, LLP, 1961—. Mem. trust com. Continental Bank, Phila., 1983-91; faculty Temple U. Sch. Law Contbr. articles to profl. jours. Active Phila. Friends Boys Town Jerusalem; bd. dirs. Jerusalem Soc. Boys Town, Phila., Friends of Ben Gurion U. the Negev, Jewish Nat. Fund Coun., Phila., Fellow Am. Coll. Trust and Estate Counsel; mem. ABA, Pa. Bar Assn., Phila. Bar Assn. (chmn. probate and trust sect. 1985-86), Green Valley Country Club, Elkview Country Club, Locust Club, Pyramid Club, Golden Slipper, B'nai B'rith, Maccabi/USA Sports for Israel (exec. com., counsel). Home: 1161 Norsam Rd Gladwyne PA 19035-1419 Office: Blank Rome Comisky & McCauley LLP One Logan Sq 8th Fl Philadelphia PA 19103-6998

RABINOWITZ, STANLEY SAMUEL, rabbi; b. Duluth, Minn., June 8, 1917; S. Jacob Mier and Rose (Zeichik) R.; m. Anita Bryna Lifson, June 24, 1945; children: Nathaniel Herz, Sharon Deborah, Judith Leah. BA, State U. Iowa, 1939; MA, Yale U., 1950; M. Hebrew Lit., Jewish Theol. Sem., 1944, Doctor Hebrew Lit., 1971. Ordained rabbi, 1943; dir. United Synagogue, N.Y.C., 1943-46; rabbi B'nai Jacob Synagogue, New Haven, 1946-53, Adath Jeshurun Synagogue, Mpls., 1953-60, Adas Israel Synagogue, Washington, 1960-86, rabbi emeritus, 1986—. V.p. Rabbinical Assembly, N.Y.C., 1974-76, pres., 1976-78; vice chmn. B'nai B'rith Youth Commn., 1965-76; pres. Mercaz, 1977-83 Mem. Rabbinical Assembly Assn. of Ret. Rabbis (pres. 1996-98). Clubs: Cosmos (Washington). Home: 3115 Normanstone Ter NW Washington DC 20008-2732 Office: Adas Israel Synagogue 2850 Quebec St NW Washington DC 20008-5200

RABINOWITZ, WENDY, artist, art therapist; b. Chgo., Jan. 6, 1946; d. Sam and Geraldine Bernice (Bielsker) Rabens; m. F. Douglas Munson, Sept. 7, 1969 (div. Sept. 1989); children: Sara Tenaya Munson, Joanna Rebecca Munson; m. Jeffrey Borak, Sept. 24, 1989. BA, U. Ill., 1968; student, Art Inst. Chgo., 1969-71, Haystack Crafts Sch., Deer Isle, Mass., 1975. Cert. creative arts therapist. Creative arts therapist Pritzger Ctr. for Emotionally Disturbed Children, Chgo., 1967-69; co-head theater dept. U. Chgo. Lab. H.S., 1968-71; dir. theater, art, craft Stockbridge (Mass.) Sch., 1971-74; studio Judaic art-craft artist Living Threads, Chgo. and Lenox, Mass., 1970—; creative arts therapist Austen Riggs Ctr., Stockbridge, 1992-94, Kimball Farms, Lenox, 1992—. Founding mem. Chgo. Artists Coalition, Chgo., 1972; chairperson art com. adv. bd. Internat. Rsch. Inst. on Jewish Women, Brandeis U., Waltham, Mass., 1997—. Contbr. book chpt.: Embracing Judaism, 1999; featured interviewee (documentaries) Embracing Judaism, 1992, Grateful I Am, to You, 1999; one-woman shows include Concepts of Art, Lenox, 1995, 99; traveling exhibit of woven artwork of women in Torah, U.S. and Israel, 1991—. Mem. adv. bd. Cmty. Access to the Arts, Stockbridge, 1994—; chairperson Lenox Cultural Arts Coun., 1982—85; v.p., pres. Sisterhood Temple Anshe Amunim, Pittsfield, 1989—92; bd. dirs. Mass. Cultural & Pittsfield Cultural Coun., 1998—. Named to Archives of Nat. Women in Arts, Mus. of Washington, 1995; grantee Diane Trotterman Found., 1993. Mem.: Jewish Artist's Support Group (founding mem.), Am. Guild Judaic Artists (mem. ethics com. 1990—99). Jewish. Avocations: hiking, writing poetry, singing. Home: 405 E New Lenox Rd Pittsfield MA 01201-8312 Office: Living Threads 405 E New Lenox Rd Pittsfield MA 01201-8312 E-mail: wrshalom@aol.com.

RABINOWITZ, WILBUR MELVIN, manufacturing executive, consultant; b. Bklyn., Feb. 18, 1918; s. Harry A. and Caroline (Simmons) R.; m. Audrey H. Perlmutter, Apr. 30, 1944; 1 child, Michael B. PhB, Dickinson Coll., 1940; JD, Harvard U., 1943. Gen. mgr. J. Rabinowitz & Sons, Inc., Bklyn., 1945-67, pres., 1967-81, pres. emeritus cons., 1981-95. Pres. Met. Glass & Plastic Containers, 1967-81; trustee Mendeleyev U., Moscow, 1991—. Author: Almost Everywhere. Pres. Rabinowitz Found., N.Y.C., 1967—; trustee Dickinson Coll., Carlisle, Pa., 1975—. With AUS, 1943-45, ETO. Mem. Nat. Assn. Container Distbrs. (past pres.), U.S. Power Squadrons (past comdr.), Explorers Club. Home: 2800 S Ocean Blvd Apt Phlm Boca Raton FL 33432-8332

RABINS, PETER VINCENT, psychiatrist; b. Everett, Mass., Sept. 8, 1947; s. Alexander and Sylvia Rabins; m. Karen Jane Briefer. MD, MPH, Tulane U., 1974. Cert. medicine. Prof. psychiatry Johns Hopkins U., Balt., 1978—. Author: (book) The 36-hour Day, 1981. Office: Johns Hopkins Hosp 600 N Wolfe St Baltimore MD 21287 Office Fax: 410-614-1094.

RABIOLA, SAMUEL CHARLES, English educator; b. Omaha, Oct. 12, 1963; s. Sammy and Mary Frances (Tegeder) R.; m. Lori-Kay Bouza, June 20, 1987; children: Natalie Kay, Alyssa Nicole. BS, U. Nebr., 1987. Tchr. Nebr. Dept. Edn., Lincoln, 1987—, Kans. Dept. Edn., Topeka, 1987—. Tnr. Kans. State Dept. Edn., Topeka, 1992—. Mem. NEA, Nat. Coun. Tchrs. English.

RABIU, BADRU I.O. federal official; b. Lagos, Nigeria, Aug. 18, 1935; came to U.S., 1972; s. Ajoke and Ashiawu Rabiu Ayinla; div.; six children. Polit., labor specialist Am. Embassy, Lagos, 1951-72; dir. Liberty Immigration & Citizenship Svc., Bklyn., 1981—. Adminstrv. asst. Arlington (Va.) County, 1981-83; labor writer U.S. Dept. Labor, Washington, 1979-80. Contbr. articles to profl. jours. Mem. Rep. Nat. Com., Rep. Senatorial Inner Circle, Nigeria Muslim Orgn., UNO. Moslem. Home: 2840 Ocean Pkwy Apt 9E Brooklyn NY 11235-7956 Office: 1716 Mermaid Ave Brooklyn NY 11224-2622

RABKIN, MITCHELL THORNTON, physician, educator, hospital administrator; b. Boston, Nov. 27, 1930; s. Morris Aaron and Esther (Quint) Rabkin; m. Adrienne M. Najarian, June 24, 1956; children: Julia Margaret, David Gregory. AB magna cum laude, Harvard U., 1951, MD cum laude, 1955; DSc (hon.), Brandeis U., 1983; DPharm (hon.), Mass. Coll. Pharmacy, 1983; DSc (hon.), Curry Coll., 1989; DSc (hon.), Northeastern U., 1994; DHumLet (hon.), Salem (Mass.) State Coll., 1995. Intern Mass. Gen. Hosp., Boston, 1955—56, resident in internal medicine, 1956—57, 1959—60, chief resident, 1962, mem. staff, 1963—72, bd. consultation, 1972—80, hon. physician, 1981—; clin. fellow NIH, Bethesda, Md., 1957—59; gen. dir. Beth Israel Hosp., Boston, 1966—80, pres., 1980—96; CEO CareGroup, 1996—98; now disting. inst. scholar Carl J. Shapiro Inst. for Edn. and Rsch. Harvard Med. Sch. and Beth Israel Deaconess Med. Ctr., 1996—; principal Washington Advisory Group, 1999—. Asst. prof. medicine Harvard U., 1969—70, assoc. prof., 1971—83, prof., 1983—, pres. med. alumni coun., 2000—; bd. dirs. Duke U. Health Sys.; trustee NYU Sch. Medicine Found. With USPHS,

1957—59. Fellow: AAAS, ACP, Am. Acad. Arts and Scis.; mem.: Inst. Medicine of NAS, Mass. Health Data Consortium (chmn. 1999—), Conf. Boston Tchg. Hosps. (past chmn.), Assn. Am. Med. Colls. (chmn. 1996—97), Soc. Med. Adminstrs., Mass. Med. Soc., Century Assn. (N.Y.C.), Tavern Club Boston, Harvard Club of Boston. Jewish. Office: Beth Israel Deaconess Med Ctr/Harvard U Shapiro Inst Edn and Rsch 330 Brookline Ave Boston MA 02215-5400 E-mail: mrabkin@caregroup.harvard.edu.

RABKIN, PEGGY ANN, retired lawyer; b. Buffalo, Apr. 13, 1945; d. Anthony J. and Margaret G. (Catuzzi) Marano; m. Samuel S. Rabkin, June 29, 1969. BA, SUNY, Buffalo, 1967, MEd, 1970, MA, 1972, JD, PhD, 1975. Tchr. Buffalo Pub. Schs., 1967-69; grad. teaching asst. SUNY, Buffalo, 1969-72; case analyst U.S. Equal Employment Opportunity Com., 1974; dir. affirmative action U. Louisville, 1975-78, adj. prof. of law, 1976-77; atty. office for civil rights HEW, N.Y.C., 1978; sr. atty. for labor and employment Am. Home Products Corp., 1978-86, sr. atty., 1986—. Author: Fathers to Daughters, 1980; editor: Buffalo Law Rev., 1974-75; contbr. articles to profl. jours. Commr. Louisville & Jefferson Co. Human Relations Com., Louisville, 1977-78. Recipient Christopher Baldy fellow, SUNY at Buffalo Law Sch., 1974-75, Regents Coll. Scholarship N.Y. State Bd. of Regents, 1963-67. Mem. ABA, Assn. of Bar of City of N.Y., Am. Corp. Counsel Assn., Soc. of Human Resources Mgmt., U.S. C. of C. (labor com. 1991—). Avocations: skiing, reading, cooking, and nutrition.

RABÓ, JULE ANTHONY, chemical researcher, consultant; b. Budapest, Hungary; came to U.S., 1957; m. Sheelagh Ennis; children: Benedict, Sebastian. BSChemE, Poly. U., Budapest, 1946, DSc in Chemistry, 1949; D honoris causa, Polytech. U., Budapest, 1986. From asst. prof. to assoc. prof. Poly U., Budapest, 1946-54; assoc. dir. Hydrocarbon Rsch. Inst., 1951-56; rsch. assoc. Union Carbide Corp., Buffalo, 1957-60, rsch. mgr. Tarrytown, N.Y., 1960-72, corp. fellow, 1969-82, sr. corp. rsch. fellow, 1982—, UOP, Tarrytown, 1988—. Cons. in chemsitry and catalysis, Armonk, N.Y.; former mem. adv. bd. Ctr. for Advanced Materials, Lawrence-Berkeley Lab.; mem. adv. bd. dept. chemistry Lehigh U. Author: Zeolite Chemisty and Catalysts; former mem. editorial bd. Jour. Catalysis, Applied Catalysis; contbr. articles to profl. jours.; patentee in field. Recipient Kossuth award Govt. of Hungary, 1953, Excellence in Catalysis award N.Y. Catalysis Soc., 1982, Humboldt award, Fed. Republic of Germany, 1990. Mem. Am. Chem. Soc. (E.V. Murphree award 1988), Am. Catalysis Soc. (Eugene J. Houdry award 1989), Hungarian Acad. Sci. (Varga medal 1991), Am. Inst. Chemists (Chem. Pioneer award 1993).

RABOLD, BARBARA ANN, artist, writer, illustrator, systems analyst; b. Germantown, Ohio, Apr. 15, 1939; d. George Crone and Gertrude Faye (Marshall) Carr; divorced; children: Matthew Theodore, Teresa Marie. Student, Sinclair C.C., Dayton, Ohio, 1990-92. Former saleswoman House of Stuart Cosmetics, McNess Home Products, Sarah Coventry Jewelry, Amway Products. Choir dir. for 14 yrs.; distbr. nutraceuticals Mannatech, 1998; tchr. art W. Carrollton City Recreation. Exhibited in group shows at Miamisburg (Ohio) Art Gallery, 1970-87, Salem and Dayton Malls, Dayton, 1975-78, Beachmont Mall, Cin., 1975-78, Indpls. Mall, 1975-78. Vol. tutor West Carrollton Sch. Sys., 1970-78, Miami Valley Literacy Coun., Dayton, 1988-2000; pub. spkr.; discussion moderator Parents Without Ptnrs., Dayton, 1980-82, 89-90; asst. group leader Alzheimer Assn., Dayton, 1990; pastoral svc. vol. local hosp. Recipient 600 vol. hours. svc. award Miami Valley Literacy Coun., 1991, more than 600 svc. hours Southview Hosp. Avocations: swimming, reading, gourmet cooking, dancing, boating. Home and Office: 102 1/2 Home Ave West Carrollton OH 45449-1206

RABOLD, JEANETTE WADE, artist, researcher; b. Franklin, Ky., July 30, 1924; d. Avery and Chloe (James) Wade; m. Stanley Joseph Rabold; children: Alan L., J. Gregory, Mark B. Student, Art Students League, N.Y.C., 1969; BS in Art, Vanderbilt U., 1978, postgrad. in Art, 1978-79. Sub. tchr. Nashville Met. Schs., 1963-64; pvt. art tchr. Nashville, 1964-66; printmaker, photographer, 1966—. Exhibited in 10 one-woman shows; group juried shows include Brooks Mus. Art, Memphis, 1965, 75, 84, 86, 88, The Parthenon, Nashville, Cheekwood Mus. Art, Nashville (numerous awards) and other juried exhbns.; illustrator (stereo album) The Winner, 1965, (book cover) Prayer and Our Bodies, 1987; printmaking and figure drawing Internat. Miniature Exhbn., Clearwater, Fla., 1985, Madison, N.J., 1983; exhibitor, mem. Mus. Women in Arts, Washington, 1993. Activist Bringing Urban Recycling to Nashville Today, 1990-93; Against Landfill and Dumping on Native Am. Sacred Grounds, Nashville, 1991; activist, spkr. Oak Ridge Nuclear Protest, 1992; activist, mem. Sierra Club, 1980-96. Mem. Nashville Artist Guild (v.p. 1983-84, publicity dir. 1983-85, hospitality chmn. 1992-93), Inst. Noetic Scis., Tenn. Environ. Coun. Democrat. Avocations: reading, research, travel, whitewater rafting, backpacking. Home: 248 Cargile Ln Nashville TN 37205-3207

RABON, RONALD RAY, retail jewelry store chain executive; b. Dothan, Ala., Apr. 27, 1955; s. Billy R. and Mary E. (Bruner) R.; m. E. Marie Hall, Oct. 25, 1974 (div. Sept. 1985); 1 child, Courtney Marie; m. Sheri L. Smith, Dec. 28, 1989; 1 child, Skylar Nicole. AS, Wallace Community Coll., Dothan, 1975. Cert. in diamond grading and evaluation Gemologist Inst. Am. Payroll clk., ironworker Daniels Constrn., Dothan, 1973-75; estate planner R&R Ins. Agy., 1975-76; v.p. merchandising Wilbro Co. Inc., 1976-84; owner, pres. Courtney's Jewelers Inc., 1984-87, Knight DetectivE Agy., Dothan, 1986-88; sr. merchandiser Reliable Stores Inc., Columbia, Md., 1988-89; dir. merchandising Glennpeter Jewelers, Schenectady, 1989-91, v.p. merchandising, 1991-92, sr. v.p. adminstrn., 1992-96; chief fin. adminstr. Bailey's Jewelers, Rocky Mount, N.C., 1996-98; sr. v.p. adminstrn. Hoff Jewelers Inc., Minneapolis/St. Paul, Minn., 1998—2001; pres. Rabon Fin. Inc., Dothan, Ala., 2002—. Lt. gov. Ala. dist. Circle K Interntat., 1974-75, gov., 1975-76. Recipient awards U.S. Jaycees, Circle K Internat.; named Outstanding Young Men of Am., 1977. Mem. Nat. Assn. Jewelry Appraisers (charter). Republican. Baptist. Avocations: reading, music, computer programming. Office: Rabon Fin Inc 890 W Main St Ste 5 Dothan AL 36301 Home: 2998 Ross Clark Circle # Q98 Dothan AL 36301

RABON, WILLIAM JAMES, JR. architect; b. Marion, S.C., Mar. 7, 1931; s. Williams James and Beatrice (Baker) R.; m. Martha Ann Hibbitts, Mar. 7, 1987. BS in Arch., Clemson Coll., 1951; BArch, N.C. State Coll., 1955; MArch, MIT, 1956; postgrad., Inst. Urbanistico, Rome, 1957-58. Registered architect, Calif., N.C., Ohio, Pa., Ga. Designer archtl. firms, N.Y.C. & Birmingham, Mich., 1958-61; designer, assoc. John Carl Warnecke & Assocs., San Francisco, 1961-63, 64-66, Keyes, Lethbridge & Condon, Washington, 1966-68; prin. archtl. ptnr. A.M. Kinney Assocs. & William J. Rabon, Cin., 1968-85; v.p., dir. archtl. design A.M. Kinney, Inc., 1977-85; v.p., dir. programming svcs. Design Art Corp., 1977-85; sr. architect John Portman & Assocs., Atlanta, 1985-88; dir. archtl. design Robert & Co., 1988-89; design prin. Carlson Assocs., 1990-93; prin., dir. rsch. & med. facilities programming & design Rosser Internat., 1993-97, William J. Rabon, Arch., 1995—. Lectr. U. Calif., Berkeley, 1963-65; asst. prof. archtl. design Cath. U. Am., 1967-68; planning cons. Nat. Bur. Stds. Lab., China, 1982. Prin. works include Children's Hosp. Ambulatory Svc. Ctr., Cin., 1984, East and West fleet hdqrs. and Data Ctr. Librs. of Royal Saudi Arabian Navy, 1985, corp. hdqrs. The Drackett Co., Cin., 1983, corp. hdqrs. Brown & Williamson, Louisville, 1984, Children's Hosp. Med. Ctr. Ambulatory Svcs. Ctr., Cin., 1984, Olin Corp. Rsch. Ctr., Cheshire, Conn., 1985, Inst. Paper Sci. & Tech., Atlanta, 1989, Citicorp Data Ctr., Napa, Calif., 1992, Animal Sci. Complex, Athens, Ga., 1996, U. Ga. Vet. Sch., Bicontainment Ctr., Athens, 1997, Kaiser Tech. Ctr., Pleasanton, Calif., 1970 (Rsch. Devel. Lab. of Yr. award), Clermont Nat. Bank, Milford, Ohio, 1971, Pavilion Bldg Childre's Hosp. Med. Ctr., Cin., 1973 (Cin. AIA design award), EC&G, Hydrospace, Inc., Rockville, Md., 1970 (Potomac Valley AIA design award), Mead Johnson Park, Evansville, Ind., 1973 (Rsch. Devel. lab. of Yr. merit award), Hamilton County Vocat. Sch., Cin., 1972, Hdqrs. Lab. EPA, Cin., 1975, Arapahoe Chem. Co. Rsch. Ctr., Boulder, Colo., 1976 (Rsch. Devel. lab. of Yr. award 1976, Concrete Reinforced Steel Inst. Nat. Design award, Regional AIA Design award), Corp. Hdqrs. Ohio River Co., Cin., 1977, Children's Hosp. Therapy Ctr., Cin., 1981 (Cin. AIa design award 1978, award of merit Am. Wood Coun. 1981), Va. Hosp. addition, Cin. (Cin. ASHRAE Design award 1980), NALCO Chem. Co. Rsch. Ctr., Naperville, Ill., 1980 (Ohio and Cin. AIA design awards 1980, 81), Proctor and Gamble-Winton Hill Tunnel, Cin., 1978 (Ohio AIA design award), Toyota Regional Ctr., Blue Ash, Ohio (Ohio AIA and Ohio Masonry Coun. combined design award 1981), U. Cin. Med. Ctr. Lab., Cin., 1981, Children's Hosp. Ambulatory Svc. Ctr., Cin., 1984, East and West fleethdqrs. and Data Ctr. Librs. of Royal Saudi Arabian Navy, 1985, corp. hdqrs. The Drackett Co., Cin., 1983, corp. hdqrs. Brown & Williamson, Louisville, 1984, Children's Hosp. Med. Ctr. Ambulatory Svcs. Ctr., Cin., 1984, Olin Corp. Rsch. Ctr., Cheshire, Conn., 1985, Inst. Paper Sci. & Tech., Atlanta, 1989, Citicorp Data Ctr., Napa, Calif., 1992, Sci. Complex, Athens, Ga., 1996, Biocontainment Rsch. Ctr., Athens, Ga., 1998. 1st lt., co. comdr. AUS, 1951—53, Korea. Company awarded Presdl. Unit Citation; recipient Silver Star, Bronze Star for Valor, Bronze Star for Meritorious Svc., Purple Heart with bronze cluster; MIT Grad. scholar, 1956; Fulbright scholar, Italy, 1957-58. Mem. AIA, Nat. Coun. Archtl. Registration Bds. Office: William J Rabon Jr Architect 5290 W Bank Dr Marietta GA 30068-1701

RABOSKY, JOSEPH GEORGE, engineering consulting company executive; b. Sewickley, Pa., May 20, 1944; s. Mary Helen (Mayer) Rabosky; m. Suzanne Lazzelle, Aug. 23, 1969. BS, Pa. State U., 1966; MS in Engring., W.Va. U., 1969; MSCE, U. Pitts., 1973, PhD, 1984. Registered profl. engr., W.Va., Pa., W.Va., Ohio. Project engr. Chester Engrs., Coraopolis, Pa., 1969-70, mgr., 1989-92; project mgr. Calgon Corp., Pitts., 1970-73, sect. leader, 1979-85, mktg. mgr., 1985-86; sr. environ. specialist Mobay Chem. Corp., 1975-79; project engr. Morris Knowles, Inc., 1973-74; project mgr. Penn Environ. Cons., 1974-75; engrng. mgr. Baker/TSA, Inc., Pitts., 1986-89; pres. Aqua-Terra, Inc., Moon Twp., Pa., 1992-95, Rabosky & Assocs., South Heights, 1995—. Adj. prof. U. Pitts., 1985-88, Pa. State U.-Beaver, McKeesport and New Kensington campuses, 1985—. Mem. Am. Acad. Environ. Engrs. (diplomate, cert. water supply wastewater engr.), Western Pa. Water Pollution Control Assn. (officer 1984-94, pres. 1992-93), Internat. Water Conf. (mem. exec. bd. 1989-94, gen. chmn. 1992-93). Home: 104 Wynview Dr Moon Township PA 15108-1033 E-mail: JoeRa1Co@aol.com.

RABOY, NATHAN H. music educator, musician; b. Harvey, Ill., May 19, 1955; s. Sol and Marguerite Marvin Raboy; m. Joanna Martin Baruch, June 29, 1980 (div.); children: Rachel. BM, State U. Coll., Potsdam, NY, 1973—77. Teachers Certificate, Music K-12 NYC Bd. of Regents, 1977. Music tchr., strings, grades 3-12 Maine/ Endwell Ctrl. Sch. Dist., Endwell, NY, 1977—78, music tchr., strings, grades 6-12, 1978—. Sect. trombone Tri-Cities Opera, Binghamton, NY, 1978—, Binghamton Philharm., Binghamton, NY, 1980—; trombone So. Tier Brass Quintet, Binghamton, NY, 1985—. Mem.: Broome County Music Educators Assn. (dist. rep. 1997—2002), Am. String Teachers Assn., NY State Sch. Music Assn. D-Liberal. Achievements include Guest Conductorship, Broome County Music Education Association, grades 7-9; Guest conductorship, All County Orchestra three times; research in Learned to teach Braille Music; General Chairperson, BCMEA Festival III, 2000-2001 and Festival III Orchestra 2002-2003. Avocations: home construction and renovation, home construction and renovation, contradancing, contradancing, contradancing. Home: 6 Chestnut Street Binghamton NY 13905 Office: Maine Endwell Central School District 720 Farm To Market Road Endwell NY 13905 E-mail: nraboy@me.stier.org.

RABSON, ALAN SAUL, physician, educator; b. N.Y.C., July 1, 1926; s. Abraham and Florence (Shulman) Rabson; m. Ruth L. Kirschstein, June 11, 1950; 1 child Arnold. BA, U. Rochester, 1948; MD, SUNY, Bklyn., 1950. Intern Mass. Meml. Hosp., Boston, 1951—52; resident in pathology NYU Hosp., 1952—54, USPHS Hosp., New Orleans, 1954—55; pathologist Nat. Cancer Inst., Bethesda, Md., 1955—; prof. pathology Georgetown U. Med. Sch., 1974—, Uniformed Services U. Health Scis., 1978—, George Washington U., 1978—; dep. dir. Nat. Cancer Inst., Bethesda. Contbr. articles. Mem.: Am. Assn. Pathologists, Alpha Omega Alpha, Sigma Xi, Phi Beta Kappa. Address: NIH-National Cancer Institute 9000 Rockville Pike Bldg 31 Bethesda MD 20892-0001 Fax: 301-402-0338.

RABSTEJNEK, GEORGE JOHN, photomics executive; b. Queens, N.Y., June 14, 1932; s. George John and Rose Anna (Krasa) R.; m. Patsy Kidd, July 17, 1964; 1 child, Marley Ann. B in Indsl. Engring., Ga. Inst. Tech., 1954; postgrad., U. Conn. Sch. Law, 1960, NYU Sch. Bus., 1965-69; advanced mgmt. program, Harvard U., 1975. Dir. material mgmt. svcs. divsn. Harbridge House, Inc., Boston, 1965-69, v.p., group head, 1969-75, exec. v.p., 1975-76, pres., 1976-83, CEO, 1983-92, chmn., 1983-93, ret., 1993. Chmn. bd. dirs. R.P.W., Inc., Bluelight, Inc.; chmn. B.O.D. Ctr. for Tech. Commercialization, 2002; mem. exec. com. Keck Neural Prothesis Rsch. Ctr. Contbr. articles to profl. jours. Vice chmn. World Affairs Coun. Boston, 1988, pres., 1984-87; trustee Internat. Coord. Coun., Boston, 1984—; trustee Mass. Eye and Ear Infirmary, Boston, 1984—, vice chmn. bd. dirs.; mem. Draper Labs. Corp., 1994; mem. adv. bd. Town of Cohasset, Mass., 1975; chmn. nat. adv. bd. Ga. Inst. Tech., 1991-92; mem. exec. adv. bd. Ivan Allen Coll.; mem. bd. visitors Northeastern U.; chmn. bd. dirs. Ctr. for Tech. Commercialization. Comdr. USNR, 1954-75, ret. Recipient Disting. Alumni award Sch. Indsl. and Sys. Engring., Ga. Inst. Tech., named to Acad. Disting. Engring. Alumni. Mem. Am. Inst. Indsl. Engrs., Nat. Security Indsl. Assn. (v.p. 1987—), Nat. Def. Transp. Assn. (Def. Transp. award 1980), Assn. Naval Aviators, Navy League, Reynolds Soc. (chmn.), Nat. Security Industry Assn. (trustee 1990-93), Harvard Club, Algonquin Club (Boston), Cohasset Golf Club (Mass.), Cohasset Yacht Club, Cohasset Tennis and Squash Club, Mill Reef Club, Antigua, B.W.I., Comml. Club, F St. Club (Washington), Phi Kappa Sigma. Republican. Unitarian Universalist. Home: 181 Border St Cohasset MA 02025-2043

RABUFFO, JEFFREY VINCENT, urologist; b. Bklyn., June 16, 1939; s. Vincent Michael and Bernadette (Terhune) R.; m. Judith Moore, Aug. 11, 1963 (div. Feb. 1990); children: Paul, Mark, Courtney. BS, Georgetown U., 1961, MD, 1965. Lic. physician, Va., Conn.; diplomate Am. Bd. Urology. Intern Mercy Hosp., Buffalo, 1968-69; resident gen. surgery Providence Hosp., Washington, 1968-69; resident urology Georgetown U., 1969-73; v.p. Middletown (Conn.) Surg. Group, 1976-96; pres. med. staff Middlesex Hosp., Middletown, 1980-82; mng. ptnr. Kaimar Realty, 1985-97; pres. Conn. Surgicenter Inc., 1985-96; chmn. com. on bioethics Middlesex Hosp., Conn., 1992-99, dir. outpatient svcs., 1995-99; v.p. Middlesex Urology; chmn. bd. Middlesex Profl. Svcs., 1997—. Sr. attending physician sect. urology dept. surgery Middlesex Hosp.; assoc. physician dept. surgery div. urology U. Conn. Health Ctr.; mem. staff Rocky Hill Vets. Hosp., Elmcrest Psychiat. Inst., Student Health Svcs., Wesleyan U.; assoc. mem. dept. surgery U. Conn. Health Ctr.; clin. instr. dept. surgery U. Conn.; mng. ptnr. Middletown Profl. Park Ltd. Partnership I, II; med. bus. cons. Cromwell Imaging Ctr. Regional chmn. Lt. Gov.'s State Com. for U. Conn. for devel. Noether chair in Italian history. Named Physician of Yr., Family Practice Residency Program, Middlesex Hosp., Middletown, 1989. Fellow ACS; mem. AMA, Am. Urol. Assn., Am. Soc. Law Medicine and Ethics, Am. Coll. Physician Execs., Conn. State Med. Soc., Conn. Hosp. Assn. (state chmn. ethics working group on futility policies), Middlesex County Med. Soc. Home: 107 Skunk Misery Rd Higganum CT 06441-4437 Office: Middlesex Urology 520 Saybrook Rd Ste S101 Middletown CT 06457-4700

RABUN, JOHN BREWTON, JR. criminal justice agency administrator; b. Augusta, Ga., Aug. 16, 1946; s. John Brewton and Alsie Imor (Bateman) R.; m. Anna Betsy Park, Dec. 27, 1967; children: Kerry Kristin, John Candler. BA, Mercer U., 1967; postgrad., So. Bapt. Theol. Sem., 1967-70; MS in Social Work, U. Louisville, 1971. Cert. social worker, Ky., D.C. Exec. dir. Ky. Civil Liberties Union, Louisville, 1971-72; dir. Cmty. Residential Treatment Svcs., 1973-78; program mgr. Field Svcs., 1978-80, Exploited and Missing Child Unit, Louisville, 1980-84; v.p., COO Nat. Ctr. for Missing and Exploited Children, Washington, 1984—. Mem. Alderman's Task Force on Social Svcs., Louisville, 1982, Mayor's City Youth Commn., Louisville, 1983-84; trainer and/or cons. to numerous agys. in U.S., U.K., Can., Mex., Belgium, Germany, Austria, The Netherlands. Contbr. articles to criminal justice and healthcare publs. and books. Recipient Key to City of Louisville, 1983, Disting. Alumnus award U. Louisville, 1985, Russell L. Colling Lit. award Internat. Assn. for Healthcare Security and Safety, 1991; named hon. chief of police City of Louisville, 1982; Alumni fellow U. Louisville, 1999. Mem. ACLU, NASW, Nat. Sheriff's Assn., Nat. Coun. Juvenile and Family Ct. Judges, Internat. Juvenile Officers Assn., Acad. Cert. Social Workers, Internat. Assn. Healthcare Safety and Security, Am. Soc. Indsl. Security, Internat. Assn. Chiefs of Police. Baptist (deacon). Avocations: photography, hunting, fishing, Internet. Home: 13519 Oak Ivy Ln Fairfax VA 22033-1230 Office: Nat Ctr for Missing and Exploited Children 699 Prince St Alexandria VA 22314-3117

RABUN, JOHN S. forensic psychiatrist; b. Austin, Tex., Apr. 3, 1961; s. John S. and Josette Rabun; m. Peggy Grace Rabun, May 25, 1996; children: Brandon, Maura, Tristan. MD, U. Tenn., 1987. Diplomate Am. Bd. Neurology and Psychiatry with subspecialty in forensic psychiatry. Resident in psychiatry Washington U., St. Louis, 1987-91; forensic psychiatrist St. Louis State Hosp., 1991—; pvt. practice St. Louis, 1994—. Cons. Griffin Pers. Group, Inc., St. Peters, Mo., 1996—. Mem. Am. Psychiat. Assn., Am. Acad. Psychiatry and the Law, Eastern Mo. Psychiat. Soc. (sec.-treas. 1998-99). Office: Saint Louis State Hosp 5300 Arsenal St Saint Louis MO 63139-1463

RABUN, JOSETTE HENSLEY, interior design educator; b. Wichita Falls, Tex. m. John Stanley Rabun, June 4, 1960; children: John S. Jr., Julie Lynne. BEd, Midwestern State U., Wichita Falls, 1964; BS with honors, U. Tex., 1974; MS, U. Tenn., 1979, PhD, 1984; postdoctoral fellow, U. York, Eng., 1988. Registered interior designer. Grad. teaching asst. interior design and housing U. Tenn., Knoxville, 1978-79, instr. dept. textiles, merchandising and design, 1980-81, asst. prof., 1983-86, assoc. prof. textiles, retailing and interior design, 1988-96; prof., program coord. interior design Coll. of Architecture and Design, U. Tenn., 1997—; coord. interior design program Coll. Arch. and Planning, 1996—; asst. prof. interior design divsn. U. Tex., Austin, 1979-80; asst. prof. USIA faculty exch. program Yarmouk U., Irbid, Jordan, 1985; assoc. prof. dept. interior design Va. Commonwealth U., Richmond, 1987-88; interior designer Weiser/Cawley Interiors, Marietta, Ohio, 1975-76; ptnr. Design Affiliates, Inc., Knoxville, 1984; owner J.S. Rabun & Assocs., 1977-86, 88—. Interior design cons. Yarmouk U., Irbid, 1986; interior cons. Loudon Heritage Assn., 1990, Revitalization Project for Downtown Loudon/Madisonville, Tenn., 1990, Cmty. Design Ctr., Del Rio, Tenn., 1991, Renovation of Residence, Knoxville, 1993, Cmty. Design Ctr., Knoxville, 1990—; co-presenter seminars on hist. preservation, Slovakia, Rumania, and Poland; exhibit designer Internat. Inda, Washington, 1992, Nat. Home Bldg.'s Show, Las Vegas, 1993, McClung Mus., Knoxville, 1993, Ewing Gallery A & A Bldg., 1998; invited lectr.U. Beijing, 1998, Sischuan U., Cheng du, U. Hong Kong, 1998. Author: (with Robert Meden) Historic Preservation and Rehabilitation, 1992; contbr. chpt. (with Betty Treanor) Popular American Housing: A Reference Guide, 1995; contbr. articles to profl. jours., chpts. to books. Bd. visitors Found. Interior Design Edn. Rsch., 1984—, accreditation bd. & evaluation com., 1999—. Co-recipient State Historic Preservation award State Daus. of Colonial Wars, 1984; recipient teaching and pub. svc. award U. Tenn., 1982, Faculty Rsch. award Coll. Human Ecology, 1986, 2d pl. award Nat. Trust Student Competition, 1991; grantee U. N.H., Durham, 1984, Historic Preservation for Revitalization of Elizabethton and Erwin, Tenn., 1991, Mabry-Hazen Hist. Found., Knoxville, 1993, U. Tenn., 1994. Mem.: Illuminating Engr. Soc., Nat. Coun. Interior Design Qualification (item writer and team leader theory and history 1993—94, coord. identification and application 1994—98), Interior Design Educators Coun. (mem. tenure and promotion com. 1986—90, chairperson South region 1988—90, bd. dirs. 1988—90, fin. chairperson 1990, continuing edn. unit internat. conf. 1995, 1996, Presdl. citations 1991, 1994), Am. Soc. Interior Designers (mem. several state chpts. 1991—, Tenn. state bd. 1999—2001, rep. to Tenn. interior design coalition 2002—, award for hist. preservation 1990, state edn. award 1994, presdl. citation 2001), Nat. Coun. Preservation Edn., Nat. Trust Hist. Preservation, Omicron Nu, Phi Kappa Phi. Avocation: travel. Office: U Tenn Coll Arch and Design Coll Architecture & Planning 1715 Volunteer Blvd Knoxville TN 37996-2400 E-mail: jrabun1@utk.edu., rabunj1@earthlink.net.

RABUZZI, DANIEL D. medical administrator; b. Pitts., June 19, 1935; s. Daniel Ralph and Victoria (Bruni) R.; m. Kathryn Allen, June 11, 1958; children: Daniel, Matthew, Douglas. AB, Harvard Coll., 1957; MD, U. Pa., 1961. Diplomate Am. Bd. Otolaryngology. Instr. otolaryngology U. Md., Balt., 1967-68; asst. prof. SUNY, Syracuse, 1968-71, assoc. prof., 1971-77, prof., 1977-81, clin. prof. otolaryngology, 1984-97, emeritus prof., 1997—; prof., chmn. N.Y. Med. Coll. and N.Y. Eye & Ear Infirmary, N.Y.C., 1981-84. Pres. St. Joseph's Hops. Med. Staff, Syracuse, 1990-92; med. dir. Harrison Surgery Ctr., 1996—. Contbr. 55 articles to profl. jours., chpts. to books. Capt. U.S. Army, 1966-68. Fellow ACS; mem. Am. Soc. Head and Neck Surgery, Am. Acad. Otolaryngology, Am. Cancer Soc. (pres. County unit 1978-80), Onondaga County Med. Soc. (pres. 1987-88). Avocations: Roman archeology, European travel, golfing, historical readings. Office: Harrison Outpatient Surgery Ctr 550 Harrison St Ste 230 Syracuse NY 13202-3064

RABY, KENNETH ALAN, lawyer, retired army officer; b. Dec. 29, 1935; s. Carl George and Helen Josette (Milne) R.; m. Shirley Rae Nelson, June 2, 1957; children: Randolph Carlton, Shelly Ann. BA, U. S.D., 1957, JD, 1960; grad. with honors, Command and Gen. Staff Coll., 1975, U.S. Army War Coll., 1981. Bar: S.D. 1960, Ga. 1988, Supreme Ct. Ga., Supreme Ct. S.D., Ga. Ct. Appeals, U.S. Supreme Ct. Commd. 2d lt. U.S. Army, 1957, advanced through grades to col. JAGC, 1979, ret., 1987; dep. staff judge adv. Am. Divsn., Chu Lai, Vietnam, 1968-69; chief legal team U.S. Army Inf. Sch., Ft. Benning, Ga., 1969-71; chief mil. def. counsel U.S. v. Calley (My Lai Massacre trials), 1969—71; team chief, acting divsn. chief adminstrv. law divsn. Office JAG, Dept. Army, 1971-74; staff judge adv. Hdqs. 24th Inf. Divsn., Ft. Stewart, Ga., 1974-79; staff judge adv. U.S. Army Armor Ctr., Ft. Knox, Ky., 1979; chief criminal law divsn. Office of JAG, Washington, 1981-84; sr. judge Army Ct. Mil. Rev., Falls Church, Va., 1984-87; staff atty. Ga. Ct. Appeals, 1987—; chief mil. def. counsel U.S. vs. Calley (My Lai Massacre) U.S. Army, 1969—71. Former chmn., mem. Joint Service Com. on Mil. Justice, 1981-84; mem. Mil. Justice Act of 1983 Adv. Commn., 1984-87; army liaison to criminal law sect. ABA, 1981-84. Eagle Scout Boy Scouts Am., 1952—53. Decorated Legion of Merit, Bronze Star with oak leaf cluster, Meritorious Svc. medal with 2 oak leaf clusters, Joint Svc. Commendation medal, Air medal, Army Commendation medal with oak leaf cluster, Army Achievement medal. Mem.: FBA (chmn. law enforcement liaison com. 1986—87), Ga. Bar Assn., Assn. U.S. Army, Scottish Rite (32d degree, KCCH), Shriners, Masons, Order Ea. Star (worthy grand patron, grand chpt. Ga. 1999—2000), Theta Xi, Delta Theta Phi. Home: 575 Spender Trce Atlanta GA 30350-5017 Office: Staff Atty Ga Ct Appeals Jud Bldg Rm 336 Capitol Sq Atlanta GA 30334-9003 E-mail: alan.raby@juno.com.

RABY, WILLIAM LOUIS, writer, consultant; b. Chgo., July 16, 1927; s. Gustave E. and Helen (Burgess) R.; m. Norma Claire Schreiner, Sept. 8, 1956; children: Burgess, Marianne, Marlene. BSBA, Northwestern U., 1949; MBA, U. Ariz., 1961, PhD, 1971. Ptnr. VAR CPA Firms, 1950-76, Touche Ross & Co., N.Y.C., 1977-87. Pres. Ariz. State Bd. Accountancy, 1993-94; mem. Ariz. State Bd. Tax Appeals, 1994—, chmn., 1997-99; prof. acctg. emeritus Ariz. State U.; columnist Tax Notes mag., Arlington, Va., 1990—; cons. on video and audio tax edn. tapes Bisk Pub. Co., 1992—. Author: The Income Tax and Business Decisions, 1964, Building and Maintaining a Successful Tax Practice, 1964, The Reluctant Taxpayer, 1970, Tax Practice Management, 1974, Introduction to Federal Taxation, annually, 1980-91, Tax Practice Management: Client Servicing, 1986; editor: Raby Report on Tax Practice, 1986-96, PPC Guide To Successful Tax Practice, 1991; mem. editorial adv. bd. Practical Tax Strategies; contbr. articles to profl. jours. Mem. AICPA (chmn. fed. tax divsn. 1980-83, v.p. 1983-84, coun. 1983-90), Tax Ct. Bar. Presbyterian (elder, chmn. adv. coun. on ch. and soc. 1979-81). Office: PO Box 26846 Tempe AZ 85285-6846 E-mail: wlraby@cs.com.

RACE, GEORGE JUSTICE, pathology educator; b. Everman, Tex., Mar. 2, 1926; s. Claude Ernest and Lila Eunice (Bunch) R.; m. Annette Isabelle Rinker, Dec. 21, 1946; children: George William Daryl, Jonathan Clark, Mark Christopher, Jennifer Anne (dec.), Elizabeth Margaret Rinker. MD, U. Tex., Southwestern Med. Sch., 1947; MS in Pub. Health, U. N.C., 1953; PhD in Ultrastructural Anatomy and Microbiology, Baylor U., 1969. Intern Duke Hosp., 1947-48, asst. resident pathology, 1951-53; intern Boston City Hosp., 1948-49; asst. pathologist Peter Bent Brigham Hosp., Boston, 1953-54; pathologist St. Anthony's Hosp., St. Petersburg, Fla., 1954-55; staff pathologist Children's Med. Center, Dallas, 1955-59; dir. labs. Baylor U. Med. Center, 1959-86, chief dept. pathology, 1959-86, vice chmn. exec. com. med. bd., 1970-72; cons. pathologist VA Hosp., Dallas, 1955-71; adj. prof. anthropology and biology So. Meth. U., 1969; instr. pathology Duke, 1951-53, Harvard Med. Sch., 1953-54; asst. prof. pathology U. Tex. Southwestern Med. Sch.,

1955-58, clin. assoc. prof., 1958-64, clin. prof., 1964-72, prof., 1973-94, prof. emeritus, 1994—, dir. Cancer Center, 1973-76, assoc. dean for continuing edn., 1973-94, emeritus assoc. dean, 1994—. Pathologist-in-chief Baylor U. Med. Ctr., 1959-86, prof. biomed. studies Baylor Grad. sch., 1989-94; chmn. Baylor Rsch. Found., 1986-89; prof. microbiology Baylor Coll. Dentistry, 1962-68, prof. pathology, 1964-68, prof., chmn. dept. pathology 1969-73, dean A. Webb Roberts Continuing Edn., 1973-94; spl. advisor on human and animal diseases to gov. State of Tex., 1979-83. Editor: Laboratory Medicine (4 vols.), 1973, 10th edit., 1983; Contbr. articles to profl. jours., chpts. to textbooks. Pres., Tex. div. Am. Cancer Soc., 1970; chmn. Gov.'s Task Force on Higher Edn., 1981. Served with AUS, 1944-46; flight surgeon USAF, 1948-51, Korea. Decorated Air medal. Fellow Coll. Am. Pathologists, Am. Soc. Clin. Pathologists, AAAS; mem. AMA (chmn. multiple discipline research forum 1969), Am. Assn. Pathologists, Internat. Acad. Pathology, Am. Assn. Med. Colls., Explorer's Club (dir., v.p. 1993-2000), Sigma Xi, Alpha Omega Alpha. Home: 3429 Beverly Dr Dallas TX 75205-2928 Fax: 214-526-8607. E-mail: georgejrace@worldnet.att.net.

RACEVSKIS, ROLAND, language educator; b. Syosset, N.Y., Feb. 11, 1971; s. Karlis and Maija Racevskis; m. Lynnette Rondeau, June 14, 1997. PhD, U. Pa., 1997. Lectr. U. Pa., Phila, 1997—98; asst. prof. U. Iowa, Iowa City, 1998—. Author: (book) Time and Ways of Knowing Under Louis XIV: Molière, Sévigné, Lafayette, 2002. Office: Univ Iowa French and Italian 555 Phillips Hall Iowa City IA 52242

RACHELEFSKY, GARY STUART, medical educator; b. N.Y.C., 1942; BS, Columbia Coll., 1963. Intern Bellevue Hosp. Ctr., N.Y.C., 1967-68; resident in pediatrics Johns Hopkins Hosp., 1968-70, Ctr. Disease Control, 1970-72; fellow UCLA Med. Ctr., 1972-74; clin. prof., assoc. dir. A/I Tng. Program UCLA. Fellow Am. Acad. Allergy, Asthma and Immunology (bd. dirs., past pres.). Office: 11620 Wilshire Blvd Ste 200 Los Angeles CA 90025-1767 E-mail: rachruss@ix.netcom.com.

RACHELSON, JOYCE ANN, computer marketing company executive, consultant; b. Phila., Sept. 8, 1946; d. Abraham Rachelson and Mary (Gordon) Rachelson Levy; m. Harry Steven Lichter, Aug. 8, 1971 (div. June 1976). BA in History, Temple U., 1968. Jr. project dir. Herbert Epstein, Inc., N.Y.C., 1967-70, Data Probe, Inc., N.Y.C., 1970-73; dir. rsch. svc. Grey Advt., Inc., N.Y.C., 1973-82; dir. tng. and support Data Tab, Inc., N.Y.C., 1982-83; v.p. dir. product sales Computers for Mktg., Corp., San Francisco, 1983—. Vol. Phila. Assn. for Retarded Children, 1960-67. Recipient Vol. of Yr. award, 1964. Mem. Am. Mktg. Assn., Mktg. Rsch. Assn. (bd.dirs. 1991—, chair fundraising 1989—), Temple Har Zion Young Adults Club (pres. 1968-69). Avocations: European and Far Eastern travel, ancient history, foreign culture studies. Office: Computers for Mktg Corp 547 Howard St San Francisco CA 94105-3001

RACHETER, DONALD PAUL, political science educator; b. Pigeon, Mich., Apr. 1, 1947; s. Paul A. and Aleatha R. (Baur) R.; children: Annalese, Alena, Donald Paul Byron. BA, U. Mich., 1969; MA, U. Iowa, 1972, PhD, 1978. Instr. in polit. sci. Cen. U. of Iowa, Pella, 1976-79, asst. prof. polit. sci., 1979-86, assoc. prof., 1986-93, prof., 1993—; founder, exec. dir. Pub. Interest Inst. Iowa Wesleyan Coll., Mt. Pleasant, 1991-92, 95-98, v.p., 1992-95, pres., 1999—. Mem. Pre-Law Advisors Nat. Coun., 1990-91; mem. pre-law liaison panel Law Sch. Admissions Coun., 1990-92. Del. Rep. Nat. Conv., Dallas, 1984, candidate Rep. Presdl. Elector, 1988, 92, 96, 2000; bd. dirs. Iowans for Tax Relief, Muscatine, 1981—, Iowans for Right to Work, Des Moines, 1982-92, vice chmn., 1989-91, chmn., 1991-92; bd. dirs. Nat. Taxpayers Union Found., 1998—. 1st lt. U.S. Army, 1973-75, lt. col. USAR, 1975-96. Recipient Congressman Neal Smith award, 1991. Mem. Am. Polit. Sci. Assn. (editl. bd. 1989-93, sec./treas. undergrad. edn. sect. 1993-2002), Iowa Conf. Polit. Scientists (sec./treas. 1979-80, 84-85, 93-94, pres. 1980-81, 85-86, 94-95, 95-96, exec. sec. 1996-2001, Van Dyke award, 1998), Midwest Polit. Sci. Assn. (nominating com. 1987-88), Am. Mock Trial Assn. (co-founder, treas. 1986-90, v.p. 1990—, Ward Reynoldson award 1986), Midwest Assn. Pre-Law Advisors (bd. dirs. 1986-96, editor newsletter 1986-90, pres.-elect 1990-91, pres. 1991-92, parliamentarian 1990-96, sec. 1994-96), Iowa Assn. Scholars (pres. 1999—). Avocations: reading, travel. Home: 1013 Main St Pella IA 50219-1318 Office: Central Coll of Iowa Dept Polit Sci Pella IA 50219-1999 E-mail: racheterd@central.edu., racheter@limitedgovernment.org.

RACHIE, CYRUS, retired lawyer; b. Willmar, Minn., Sept. 5, 1908; s. Elias and Amanda (Lien) R.; m. Helen Evelyn Duncanson, Nov. 25, 1936; children: John Burton Rachie, Janice Carolyn MacKinnon, Elisabeth Dorthea Becker. Student, U. Minn., 1927-28; JD, George Washington U., 1932, William Mitchell Coll. Law, 1934. Bar: Minn. 1934, U.S. Supreme Ct. Atty. Minn. Hwy. Dept., 1934-43; spl. asst. atty. gen. Minn., 1946-50; counsel Luth. Brotherhood (fraternal life ins. co.), 1950-61; pvt. practice law Mpls., 1961-62; v.p., counsel Gamble-Skogmo, Inc., 1962-64; v.p., gen. counsel Aid Assn. Lutherans, Appleton, Wis., 1964-70, sr. v.p., gen. counsel, 1970-73; with Rachie & Rachie, 1973-83; pvt. practice Minn., 1983—2001; part-time spl. master Minn. 4th Jud. Dist., 1977; ret., 2001. One of eleven com. mems. planning 1957 Luth. World Fedn. in Mpls. Councillor Nat. Luth. Coun., 1959-66, sec., 1962-64, mem. exec. com., 1965-66; United Luth. Ch. in Am. del. to 4th Assembly Luth. World Fedn., Helsinki, 1963; past pres. Luth. Welfare Soc. Minn.; past chmn. Mpls. Mayor's Coun. on Human Rels.; chmn. finance United Fund drive, 1967-68; past mem. bd. dirs. Mpls. YMCA; trustee emeritus William Mitchell Coll. Law Augsburg Coll. With USNR, 1943-46. Recipient Disting. Alumnus award William Mitchell Coll. Law, 1987. Mem. ABA, Minn. Bar Assn., Am. Legion, Minn. Fraternal Congress (past pres.), Rotary. Lutheran. Home: 7500 York Ave S Apt 101 Minneapolis MN 55435-4736 *I always try to keep in mind that the Christian Cross consists of both vertical and horizontal lines. The vertical is the longest line and represents a direct line from all of us on the bottom to God on the top and we must commune with Him. The horizontal represents an encompassing line that takes in all of mankind. If my life activities do not include the implementation of both lines of the cross, I will not have a balanced and Christian life.*

RACHKO, BARBARA GAIL, artist; b. Paterson, N.J., Jan. 22, 1953; d. George and Dorothy Barbara (King) Rachko; m. Bryan C. Jack, June 16, 2001 (dec. Sept. 2001). BA, U. Vt., 1975. Lic. comml. pilot and Boeing 727 flight engr. One-woman shows include Capitol Hill Art League, Washington, 1992, Cunneen-Hackett Art Gallery, Poughkeepsie, N.Y., 1993, Art League Gallery, Alexandria, Va., 1993, NIH, Bethesda, Md., 1994, Howard C.C., Columbia, Md., 1995, Manhattanville Coll., Purchase, N.Y., 1995, 479 Gallery, N.Y.C., 1996, Watchung (N.J.) Arts Ctr., 1996, Sch. 33 Art Ctr., Balt., 1996, Brewster Arts, N.Y.C., 1996, Doll Andstadt Gallery, Burlington, Vt., 1998, 2000, Mercedes-Benz Manhattan Artspace, N.Y.C., 1998, Broadway Windows, N.y.C., 1998, Park Ave. Atrium, N.Y.C., 1999, La MaMa, La Galleria, N.Y.C., 2000, KL Fine Arts, Highland Park, Ill., 2000, Roanoke Coll., Salem, Va., 2001; group exhibits include Art Barn Gallery, Washington, 1989, 93, Nat. Arts Club, N.Y.C., 1990, 91, Salmagundi Club, N.Y.C., 1991, 92, Hoyt Inst. Fine Arts, New Castle, Pa., 1991, 93, Sumner Mus., Washington, 1991, Harmon-Meek Gallery, Naples, Fla., 1992, Pensacola (Fla.) Mus. Art, 1992, Foxhall Gallery, Washington, 1992, 93, Pleiades Gallery, N.Y.C., 1992, Muscarelle Mus., Williamsburg, Va., 1992, 94, Cardinal Gallery, Annapolis, Md., 1993, 94, 96, Andre Zarre Gallery, N.Y.C., 1993, Chrysler Mus., Norfolk, Va., 1994, Miami '94 Internat. Art Exposition, Miami Beach, Fla., Roger Lapelle Galleries, Phila., 1994, 479 Gallery, Phila., 1994, 95, Gallery Juno, N.Y.C., 1994, Butler Inst. Am. Art, Youngstown, Ohio, 1995, Emerson Gallery/McLean (Va.) Project for Arts, 1996, N.J. Ctr. for Visual Arts, Summit, N.J., 1995, 96, 97, 98, Brewster Arts Ltd., N.Y.C., 1996, 97, 98, 99, 2000, The Art Alliance, N.Y.C., 1996, 97, 98, 99, 2000, 01, 02, Chamot Gallery, Jersey City, 1997, 98, 99, William Paterson U., Wayne, N.J., 1998, N.Y. Law Sch., N.Y.C., 1998, The Hudson Guild, N.Y.C., 1999, Doll-Anstadt Gallery, Burlington, 1999, 2000, 01, Aljira, Newark, 2000, Polish Consulate, N.Y.C., 2000, Touchstone Gallery, Washington, 2000, Steve Stein Gallery, Sherman Oaks, Calif., 2000, 01, Gallery Bergelli, Larkspur, Calif., 2000, 01, 02, KL Fine Arts, Highland Park, Ill., 1999, 2000, 01, Margeaux Kurtie Modern Art, Madrid, N.Mex., 2002, Padulo Longstreth & Goldberg, Naples, Fla., 2002, Ind. State U., Terre Haute, 2002, Suffolk (La.) Mus., 2002, Ellipse Art Ctr., Arlington, Va., 2002, City Without Walls, Newark, 2000, 02, Seton Hall U., Newark, 2002, La Mama La Galleria, N.Y.C., 2002. Served to lt. USN, 1983-89, lt. comdr. USNR, 1989—. Served to lt. USN, 1983—89, lt. comdr. USNR, 1989—2000, comdr. USNR, 2000—. Mem. Nat. Artists Equity Assn., N.Y.C. Chpt. Artists Equity Assn., Women's Caucus for Art, Nat. Assn. Women Artists, Orgn. of Ind. Artists. Roman Catholic. Avocations: traveling, collecting traditional folk objects. Studio: 208 W 29th St Rm 605 New York NY 10001-5206 also: 1311 W Braddock Rd Alexandria VA 22302-2705 Home: 164 Bank St Apt 7A New York NY 10014

RACHLIN, ALAN SANDERS, lawyer; b. N.Y.C., Mar. 14, 1942; s. Irving Louis and Blanche (Klein) R.; m. Gail S. Kaufman, June 11, 1972 (dec. Apr. 1987); m. Charlotte D. Moslander, Aug. 15, 1992. BA, CCNY, 1965; MPA, CUNY, 1971; JD, N.Y. Law Sch., 1975. Bar: N.Y. 1976, U.S. Dist. Ct. (so. and ea. dists.) 1976, U.S. Supreme Ct. 1983. Atty. N.Y. State Dept. Ins., N.Y.C., 1976-79, sr. atty., 1979-81, assoc. atty., 1981-87, supervising atty., 1987-96, prin. atty., 1996—. With U.S. Army, 1966-67. Mem. ABA, Assn. Bar City N.Y., N.Y. State Bar Assn., N.Y. County Lawyers Assn., Med. Jurisprudence. Democrat. Jewish. Avocations: science fiction, mysteries. Office: NY State Ins Dept 25 Beaver St New York NY 10004-2310 E-mail: arachlin@ins.state.ny.us.

RACHLIN, ELLEN JOAN, fund administrative services company executive; b. N.Y.C., Sept. 29, 1957; d. Lauren David and Jean Karet R.; m. William G. Portnoy, Jan. 12, 1991. AB, Cornell U., 1979; MBA, U. Chgo., 1981; postgrad., Antioch Coll., 2001. Fixed income assoc. Citibank, N.A., N.Y.C., 1981-83; trader Govt. Arbitrage Co./Diversified Hedge Fund, 1983-86; mng. dir. S.G. Warburg & Co., 1986-95; co-head IBJI agt. dept. New Japan Securities/Aubrey G. Lanston & Co. Inc., 1995-99; sr. v.p. Deerfield Internat. Adminstrv. Svcs. Ltd., Nassau, Bahamas, 1999—. Co-author: Managing Fixed Income Portfolios, 1997, Perspectives on International Fixed Income Investors, 1998, Handbook of Portfolio Management, 1998. Mem. Poetry Soc. Am. (treas. 1994-99). Avocations: karate, writing. E-mail: ejrachlin@aol.com.

RACHLIN, HARVEY BRANT, author; b. Phila., June 23, 1951; s. Philip and Mazie (Drucker) R.; m. Marla Sivak Goldwert, June 28, 1987; 1 child, Glenn. BA in Biology, Hofstra U., Hempstead, N.Y., 1973. With music pub. cos., 1973—; owner Western Hemisphere Music Co., Ellipsis Music Mgmt. Co., Manhasset Hills, N.Y., 1975—, pres., 1982-92; mem. faculty Five Towns Coll., Seaford, 1978-84, Manhattanville Coll., Purchase, 1995—. Author: The Songwriter's Handbook, 1977 (N.Y. Pub. Libr. Book for Teen Age 1979-82); The Encyclopedia of the Music Business, 1981 (Outstanding Music Reference Source ALA 1981, ASCAP-Deems Taylor award 1982); Love Grams, 1983; The Money Encyclopedia, 1984 (Outstanding Fin. Reference Book, Libr. Jour., 1984, Ency. Britannica Home Libr. selection); The Kennedy's: A Chronological History 1823--, 1986; The Songwriter's and Musician's Guide to Making Great Demos, 1988 (N.Y. Pub. Libr. Book for Teen Age 1989); The Making of a Cop, 1991, The Songwriter's Workshop, 1991, The TV and Movie Business: An Encyclopedia of Careers, Technologies, and Practices, 1991 (Fireside Theatre Book Club main selection), The Making of a Detective, 1995, Lucy's Bones, Sacred Stones, and Einstein's Brain, 1996 (History Book Club selection; co-writer, cons. adapted as three-part TV mini-series History's Lost and Found (now daily series on The History Channel, named one of best books in print The Reader's Catalog), Jumbo's Hide, Elvis's Ride, and the Tooth of Buddha, 2000 (Book-of-the-Month Club's Quality Paperback Book Club selection); free-lance music journalist; contbr. Songwriter Mag., 1978—, Law and Order Mag., 1992—, Songwriter's Market, 1979, 80, 87, 92; guest on The Joe Franklin Show, 1977, 81, The Dinah Shore Show, 1978, The Sally Jesse Raphael Show, 1993, The Late Late Show with Tom Snyder, 1996; compositions performed L.I. Mandolin and Guitar Orch., 1988. Recipient Outstanding Reference Book of Yr. award, ALA, 1981, award, Libr. Jour., 1984, profiled in, N.Y. Times, 1982, Pro-Music, 1982, Valley Stream Herald, 1995, 1996, 1998, Writer's Market, 1994, Newsday, 1996, 1999, Sarasota Herald-Tribune, 1996, Coral Springs Forum, 1997, Boston Herald, 1997, L.I. Lifestyles, 2000, City Line News, 2001. Mem.: Am. Soc. Journalists and Authors. Home: 878 Warner Rd Valley Stream NY 11580-1526

RACHLIN, LEILA, lawyer; b. Boston, Dec. 8, 1965; d. Howard C. and Nahid Rachlin; m. Greg M. Zipes, Aug. 21, 1994. BA, Cornell U., 1988; JD, Fordham U., 1991. Bar: N.Y. 1992, U.S. Dist. Ct. (so. and ea. dist.) N.Y. 1992. Assoc. dir. continuing legal edn. Court TV, N.Y.C., 1991-92; assoc. Zeichner, Ellman & Kruase, 1992-94, Cleary, Gottlieb, Steen & Hamilton, N.Y.C., 1994-97; sr. corp. assoc. White & Case, LLP, 1998—. Rsch. asst., law jour. mem. Fordham Internat., 1989-91. Editor Cornell Praxis Literary mag., 1986-88. Mem. Vol. Lawyers for the Arts, 1995—. Mem. Assn. of the Bar of the City of N.Y., New York Women's Bar Assn., Corp. (mem. corp. and banking coms., liaison for lawyer mentor program). Avocations: museums, theater, film. Home: 1675 York Ave Apt 20L New York NY 10128-6757 Office: White & Case LLP 1155 Avenue Of The Americas New York NY 10036-2711 E-mail: LRachlin@whitecase.com.

RACHLIS, ARNOLD ISRAEL, rabbi, religion educator; b. Phila., Apr. 25, 1949; s. Burech and Pauline (Glanzberg) R.; children: Adam, Michael. BA, U. Pa., 1970; MA, Temple U., 1972; ordination, Reconstructionist Rabbinical Coll, 1975; BA (hon.), Ctrl. High Sch., Phila., 1966; DD, Reconstructionist Rabbinical Coll., 2000. Ordained rabbi, 1975. Asst. dir. Hillel Found., Temple U., Phila., 1972-74; lectr. Temple U., 1974-76; mem. faculty Spertus Coll., Chgo., 1976-85; rabbi Jewish Reconstructionist Cong., Evanston, Ill., 1976-91, Univ. Synagogue, Irvine, Calif., 1991—. Host Of Cabbages and Kings Program ABC-TV, Chgo., 1982-91 ; sr. fgn. affairs advisor Dept. State, Washington, 1985-86; vice-chmn. Mazon, A Jewish Response to Hunger, 1996-98; internat. bd. dirs. New Israel Fund; bd. dirs. U.S. Interreligious Com. for Peace in the Mid. East, U. Ill. Fund for Gerontology Rsch.; mem. adv. bd. China Judaic Studies Assn., Nanjing U., People's Republic of China, Ams. for Peace Now. Contbr. articles to profl. jours.; regular columnist Chgo. Jewish Sentinel; columnist Phila. Jewish Exponent, 1974-76; cons. for Judaica sect. Compton's Ency. Recipient Leadership Citation Jewish Reconstructionist Found., 1980; White House fellow, 1985-86, Leadership Greater Chgo. fellow, 1988-89; subject of award winning documentary film, The Legacy. Mem. Reconstructionist Rabbinical Assn. (pres. 1977-79), Chgo. Bd. Rabbis (pres. 1990-91), Chgo. Action for Soviet Jewry (adv. coun.), Chevra. Avocations: theatre, writing, hiking, foreign travel. Home: 4876 Paseo De Vega Irvine CA 92612-3323 Office: University Synagogue 4915 Alton Pkwy Irvine CA 92604-8606

RACHOFSKY, DAVID J. lawyer; b. Oceanside, N.Y., Nov. 17, 1936; s. Lester M. and Marjorie A.; m. Faith Allen; children: Robert, Patricia, Edward. BSEE, MIT, 1958; JD, Temple U., 1968. Bar: Pa., U.S. Dist. Ct. (ea. dist.) Pa., U.S. Tax. Ct., U.S. Ct. Fed. Claims, Pa. Supreme Ct. 1968. Ptnr. Dechert Price & Rhoads, Phila., 1968—. Lectr. law Temple U. Law Sch., 1976-95. Contbr. articles to profl. jours. With USAF, 1969-72. Mem. ABA, Phila. Bar Assn., Internat. Fiscal Assn. (chmn. mid-Atlantic region 1985-87, mem. coun. 1986—, mem. exec. com. 1992—, v.p., sec. 1992-96, exec. v.p. 1996-98, pres. 1998-2000). Office: Dechert Price & Rhoads 4000 Bell Atlantic Tower 1717 Arch St Lbby 3 Philadelphia PA 19103-2713

RACHOW, LOUIS A(UGUST), librarian; b. Shickley, Nebr., Jan. 21, 1927; s. John Louis and Mable (Dondlinger) R. BS, York Coll., 1948; MS in L.S., Columbia U., 1959. Librarian York Coll., Nebr., 1949-54; instr. library asst. Queens Coll., N.Y.C., 1956-57; serials acquisition asst. Columbia U. Law Library, 1957-58; asst. librarian Univ. Club, 1958-62; librarian Hampden-Booth Theatre Library at the Players, 1962-86, curator, 1986-88; library dir. Internat. Theatre Inst. U.S., 1989—. Cons. theatre sect. U. Calif., San Diego, new campuses program, 1964, Music Ctr. Operating Archives, Los Angeles, 1985; mem. library adv. bd. Eugene O'Neill Meml. Theatre Center, 1966—. Editor, compiler: Guide to Performing Arts, 1968; assoc. editor Am. Notes and Queries, 1971-74, asst. editor, 1967-71; mem. editorial adv. bd. Nat. Dir. for Performing Arts and Civic Ctrs.; editor Performing Arts series Gale Info. Guide, 1976-83, Theatre and Performing Arts Collections, 1981; contbr. articles and revs. to profl. jours. Mem. adv. bd. Am. Theatre Co., OKC Theatre Prodns. Served with AUS, 1954-56 Mem. Theatre Libr. Assn. (rec. sec. 1966-67, pres. 1967-72, 81-83, v.p. 1976-80, editor Broadside 1973-81), ALA, Spl. Librs. Assn. (sec.-treas. mus. group N.Y.C. chpt. 1964-66), N.Y. Libr. Club (pres. 1979-80), Am. Theatre Assn., New Drama Forum Assn. (pres. 1983-86), Am. Soc. Theatre Rsch., N.Y. Tech. Svcs. Librs., Archons of Colophon (convener 1982-83), Episcopal Actors Guild Am. (bd. dirs. 1976—), Drama Desk, Broadway Theatre Inst. Outer Critics Circle (treas. 1998—), Players Club, The Lambs Club. Home: 528 W 114th St New York NY 10025-7841 Office: Internat Theatre Inst/US 355 Lexington Ave New York NY 10017-6603 E-mail: lrachow@tcg.org.

RACHOW, SHARON DIANNE, realtor; b. St. Joseph, Mo., Apr. 12, 1939; d. Norman DeLos Zancker and Sylvia Lavina (Hawkins) Trouel; m. Thomas Eugene Rachow, Oct. 22, 1968; children: Todd A., Tiffany K. Student, So. Ill. U., 1969-72. Sec. Westab, Inc. (now Mead), St. Joseph, 1957-60, Seitz Packing Co., St. Joseph, 1960-66; exec. asst. to v.p., gen. mgr. Kansas City (Mo.) Chiefs, 1972; co-owner, mgr. Pool 'N Patio Plus, St. Joseph, 1973-84; realtor Coldwell Banker Gen. Realtors, 1984-93, RE/MAX, 1993—. Trustee Nat. Multiple Sclerosis Soc., Mid Am. chpt., Midland M.S. Express Br., 1993-98. Inductee ReMax Internat. Hall of Fame, 1999. Mem.: Real Estate Buyer's Agt. Coun. (accredited buyers rep. 1996—), Re/Max Mid-States Region (Mo. Top 100 1993—, Re/Max Internat. Hall of Fame), St. Joseph Regional Bd. Realtors (cert. residential specialist 1987, Multi-List com. 1993—2003, dir. 1994, forms com. 1994—2003, Top 10 grad. Realtor Inst. 1986, St. Joseph Top Residential Sales award 1986—), Multi Million Dollar Club (life). Republican. Lutheran. Home: 4211 Country Ln Saint Joseph MO 64506-2454 Office: RE/MAX of St Joseph Inc 1119 N Woodbine Rd Saint Joseph MO 64506-2434 E-mail: srachow@stjoelive.com.

RACHWAL, STANISLAW, chemist; b. Jodlowka, Cracow, Poland, Feb. 21, 1949; came to U.S., 1988; s. Czeslaw and Stanislawa (Przybys) R.; m. Bogumila Hurlak, Sept. 5, 1970; children: Piotr, Maria, Agnieszka, Katarzyna. MS in Organic Chemistry, Jagiellonian U., Cracow, 1973; PhD in Organic Chemistry, Jagiellonian U., 1978. Assoc. prof. Jagiellonian U., Cracow, 1981-87; leader rsch. group U. Fla., Gainesville, 1988-93; sr. rsch. scientist Pharmos Corp., Alachua, Fla., 1993-97; sr. scientist Neurogen Corp., Branford, Conn., 1998—. Contbr. articles to Jour. Organic Chemistry, Jour. Heterocyclic Chemistry, Synthesis, others. Mem. Am. Chem. Soc., Planetary Soc. Achievements include invention of a new methodology in organic synthesis of various types of compounds based on derivatives of benzotriazole. Office: Neurogen Corp 35 NE Industrial Rd Branford CT 06405-2844 E-mail: srachwal@msn.com.

RACICOT, MARC F. lawyer, former governor; b. Thompson Falls, Mont., July 24, 1948; s. William E. and Patricia E. (Bentley) Racicot; m. Theresa J. Barber, July 25, 1970; children: Ann, Timothy, Mary Catherine, Theresa, Joseph. BA, Carroll Coll., Helena, Mont., 1970; JD, U. Mont., 1973; postgrad., U. Va., 1973, Cornell U., 1977. Bar: Mont. 1973. Dep. county atty. Missoula (Mont.) County, 1976—77; bur. chief County Prosecutor Svcs. Bur., Helena, Mont., 1977—89; asst. atty. gen. State of Mont., 1977—89, spl. prosecutor for the Atty. Gen.'s Office, atty. gen., 1989—93, gov., 1993—2001; ptnr. Bracewell & Patterson LLP, Washington, 2001—. Elected chmn. of the Rep. Nat. Com., Jan. 2002. Founder Missoula Drug Treatment Program, 1977; active United Way, Helena; bd. visitors U. Mont. Sch. Law. Capt. U.S. Army, 1973—76. Named to Basketball Hall of Fame, Carroll Coll., 1982. Mem.: Mont. Bar Assn. Republican. Roman Catholic. Office: Republican National Committee 310 First St., S.E. Washington DC 20003*

RACINA, THOM (THOMAS FRANK RAUCINA), television writer, editor; b. Kenosha, Wis., June 4, 1946; s. Frank G. and Esther May (Benko) Raucina. B.F.A., Goodman Sch. Drama, Art Inst. Chgo., 1970, M.F.A. in Theatre Arts and Directing with honors, 1971. TV writer Hanna-Barbera Co., Hollywood, Calif., 1973-74, MTM Enterprises, Inc., Hollywood, 1974-76; head writer General Hospital ABC-TV, 1981-84; head writer Days of Our Lives NBC-TV, 1984-86, head writer Another World, 1986-88, co-head writer Generations daytime series, 1988-91, head writer syndicated Dangerous Women night-time TV series, 1991-92; assoc. head writer daytime TV series Santa Barbara, 1992-93. Author: Lifeguard, 1976, The Great Los Angeles Blizzard, 1977, Quincy, M.E., 2 vols., 1977, Kodak in San Francisco, 1977, F.M., 1978, Sweet Revenge, 1978, The Gannon Girls, 1979, Nine to Five, 1980, Tomcat, 1981, Secret Sex: Male Erotic Fantasies (as Tom Anicar), 1976, Magda (as Lisa Wells), 1981, Snow Angel, 1995, Hidden Agenda, 1997, Secret Weekend, 1999, The Madman's Diary, 2000, Never Forget, 2002; ghost writer: non-fiction The Happy Hustler (Grant Tracy Saxon), 1976, Marilyn Chambers: My Story (Marilyn Chambers), 1976, Xaviera Meets Marilyn (Xaviera Hollander and Marilyn Chambers), 1977; musical plays A Midsummer Night's Dream, music and lyrics, 1968, Allison Wonderland, music and lyrics, 1970, The Marvelous Misadventure of Sherlock Holmes, book, music and lyrics, 1971; TV scripts Sleeping Over segment of Family, ABC, 1978, Russian Pianist segment, ABC, 1979, 1 Child of the Owl, NBC After-Sch. Spl., 1979; contbr. articles to Playboy, Cosmopolitan, Penhouse, Oui, Los Angeles, Gentleman's Quar., Westways; West Coast editor: Grosset & Dunlap, Inc., N.Y.C., 1978—; lead writer for TV: Family Passions, 1993-94, Life's A Bitch!, 1994, Friends & Lovers, 1994; theatre dir., pianist, organist, composer. Recipient Emmy award nomination 1982, 83, 84, 85, 87; U.S. Nat. Student Assn. grantee, 1965 Mem. Authors Guild Am., Writers Guild Am. West. Democrat. Roman Catholic. Home: 2851 Calle Loreto Palm Springs CA 92264-6702 E-mail: racina@aol.com. *Nearly losing my life to the disease pancreatitis at sixteen years of age certainly opened my eyes to how precious the future was— I had a second chance, and I knew I'd been given talent for a reason: to use. I've since lived wanting to do it all, know it all, feel and experience all that life has to offer. I've no desire to write literature, but rather to entertain, and everything I write has that motivation as a core. If my storytelling ability moves just one person to laughter— or tears— I've accomplished all I set out to do.*

RACINE, DOUG, lieutenant governor; b. Burlington, Vt., Oct. 7, 1952; m. Roberta A. Harold. AB, Princeton U., 1974. U.S. senator from Vt., 1983-92; v.p. Racine's Jeep, Eagle, Isuzu, Inc.; lt. gov. State of Vt., Montpelier, 1997—. Office: Office of the Lt Gov State House Montpelier VT 05633-0001*

RACINE, LINDA JEAN, college health nurse; b. Chester, Pa., Dec. 8, 1948; d. Charles D. and Marion E. (Clark) Malloy; m. Eugene F. Racine, Oct. 19, 1968; children: Valerie, Danielle. A in Applied Sci., Delaware County C.C., Marple, Pa., 1971; BSN, Immaculata Coll., 2000. RN; cert. coll. health nurse, Pa. Dir. health svcs. Lincoln U., Pa. Mem. Am. Coll. Health Assn. (mid-Atlantic chpt.), Md. Coll. Health Nurses Assn., Southeastern Pa. Coll. Health Nurses Assn. (v.p. 1994, pres. 1995-97). Lutheran. Avocations: sailing, water skiing, reading, sewing. Office: Lincoln U Health Svc Lincoln University PA 19352

RACITI, CHERIE, artist; b. Chgo., June 17, 1942; d. Russell J. and Jacque (Crimmins) R. Student, Memphis Coll. Art, 1963-65; BA in Art, San Francisco State U., 1968; M.F.A., Mills Coll., 1979. Assoc. prof. art San Francisco State U., 1984-89, prof., 1989—. Lectr. Calif. State U., Hayward, 1974, San Francisco Art Inst., 1978; mem. artist com. San Francisco Art Inst., 1974-85, sec., 1980-81. One woman shows include U. Calif., Berkeley, 1972, Nicholas Wilder Gallery, Los Angeles, 1975, San Francisco Art Inst., 1977, Marianne Deson Gallery, Chgo., 1980, Site 375, San Francisco, 1989, Reese Bullen Gallery, Humboldt State U., Arcata, Calif., 1990, Mills Coll. Art Mus., Oakland, Calif., 1998; group shows include Whitney Mus. Art, 1975, San Francisco Sci. Fiction, The Clocktower, N.Y.C., Otis-Parsons Gallery, Los Angeles, 1984-85, San Francisco Art Inst., 1985, Artists Space, N.Y.C., 1988, Angles Gallery, Santa Monica, 1987, Terrain Gallery, San Francisco, 1992, Ctr. for the Arts, San Francisco, 1993, Santa Monica Coll., 1998, 25/25 25th Anniversary Exhbn., So. Exposure Gallery, San Francisco, 1999. Bd. dirs. New Langton Arts, 1988-92. Eureka fellow Fleishhacker Found., San Francisco; recipient Adaline Kent award San Francisco Art Inst., 1976, Djerassi resident, 1994, Tyrone Guthrie Ctr. resident, Ireland, 1995, Millay Colony for Arts resident 1999, Juror's award Art Coun. Inc. San Francisco. Office: San Francisco State U Art Dept 1600 Holloway Ave San Francisco CA 94132-1722 E-mail: craciti@sfsu.edu.

RACK, PHILIP D. engineering educator; PhD, U. Fla. Prof. Rochester (N.Y.) Inst. Tech., 1998—2001, U. Tenn., Knoxville, 2001—. Rsch. scientist Advanced Vision Techs., Rochester, NY, 1997—98. Mem.: Materials Rsch. Soc. Office: U Tenn 603 Dougherty Engring Bldg Knoxville TN 37996-2200 Business E-Mail: prack@utk.edu.

RACKERS, THOMAS WILLIAM, physicist, researcher; b. Ft. Thomas, Ky., Apr. 1, 1955; s. Paul William and Geraldine (Cox) R.; m. Thelma J. Cox, June 18, 1977; 1 child, Teresa Dawn. BA cum laude, Thomas More Coll., Ft. Mitchell, Ky., 1975; MS, Ohio State U., 1977, PhD, 1984. Rsch. assoc. dept. physics Ohio State U., Columbus, 1981-84; rsch. physicist rsch. and technol. dept. Naval Coastal Sys. Ctr., Panama City, Fla., 1984-91; rsch. physicist coastal rsch. and tech. dept. NSWC Coastal Systems Sta., 1992—; judge. AAV Junior Olympics in Tae Kwon Do, Orlando , Fla., 2000. Mem. exec. comms. North Am. Data Gen. Users Group, co-chmn. Cent. Ohio Users of Data Gen. Equipment, Columbus, 1981-84; ind. computer cons. Composed and recorded original music for local cmty. theater prodns., 1994—. Judge Three Rivers Sci. and Engring. Fair, Panama City, 1985-89, 99; vol., actor Kaleidoscope Theatre, Panama City, 1987-97, bd. dirs., 1994-97, Internet Web site adminstr., 1996-97; active mentor program Jr. Mus. Bay County, Fla., 1988-89; guitarist St. John the Evangelist Cath. Ch. Folk Choir, Panama City, 1984—, co-dir., 1990-94, dir., 1995-2001; sec. Long Glass Youth Bowling League, 1993-94; active sch. enrichment program, NSWC Coastal Systems Station, 1997—; senior staff. isntr. Tae Kwon Do Am. Martial Arts, Panama City Beach, Fla., 1998—. Mem. Mensa, Bay Line Model R.R. (Panama City condr. 1987-89), St. Andrews Bay NTRAK (chmn. 1989-90), Sigma Pi Sigma. Roman Catholic. Avocations: computers, electronic and folk music, Tae Kwon Do "3rd degree black belt", model railroading, science fiction. Home: 2012 Pattho Ln Lynn Haven FL 32444-5411 Office: NSWC Coastal Systems Sta Code R62 6703 W Highway 98 Panama City FL 32407-7000

RACKLEY, RAYMOND R. hospital administrator, consultant; b. Plattsburg, N.Y., July 10, 1962; s. R. Robert and Jeannette Rackley; m. Carmen Maria Fonseca; children: Cristina Rackley-Fonseca. MD, Case Western Res. U., 1989. Staff sect. voiding dysfunction and female urology Cleve. Clinic Found., 1997—2000, co-sect. head sect. voiding dysfunction and female urology, 2001—. Author: (Books) Book chapters,in Campbel,Practical Urodynamic-s,Urology Secrets, Laparoscopic urology, Voiding Dysfunction, Urologic Clinics of North America, Springer Verlag, 1995. Mem.: AUA. Office: Cleve Clinic Found 9500 Euclid Ave Cleveland OH 44195 Office Fax: 216-445-1894. Business E-Mail: rackler@ccf.org.

RACKLIN, BARBARA COHEN, fundraising consultant; b. N.Y.C., Dec. 3, 1950; d. Harry Cohen and Sheri Lillian (Greene) Cohen; m. Arthur Michael Racklin, Aug. 19, 1979; 1 child, Nicholas Michael. BA in Math., U. Tex., 1972; postgrad., U. LaVerne, 1981-82. Cert. histocompatability technologist, Am. Bd. Histocompatability and Immunogenetics. Asst. dir. transplant lab. Med. br. U. Tex., Galveston, 1974-76; transplant immunology specialist Montefiore Hosp., Bronx, N.Y., 1976-77; dir. pediat. immunology lab. Cedar Sinai Hosp., L.A., 1977-79; supr. pathology lab. City of Hope Nat. Med. Ctr., Duarte, Calif., 1979-82, rsch. specialist transplant lab., 1982-85; staff coord. vol. devel. City of Hope Deve. Ctr., L.A., 1986-88; coord. fin. devel. events ARC, Pasadena, Calif., 1995-99; co-owner benefit specialists Fundraising Cons., La Cañada, 1995-99; dir. devel. San Gabriel chpt. ARC, 1999—. Tour chmn. City of Hope Ann. Conv., Duarte, 1987, 89, 91. Contbr. or co-contbr. articles to profl. publs. Bd. dirs. City of Hope Med. Ctr., 1986-89, mem. bd. govs., 1991-93; mem. steering com. local parcel tax election, La Cañada, 1992, local sch. bd. election, 1995; mem. sch. bd. La Cañada Unified Sch. Dist., 1997—, clk. governing bd., 1999-2000; pres. La Cañada Coun. PTA, 1995-97, City of Hope Aux., 1988-90; bd. dirs. LCF Ednl. Found., past pres., v.p., 1991-97; sec. Children's Hosp. Aux., 1994-97; auditor 1st Dist. PTA, 1997; chairperson youth com. Pasadena Temple, 1996-97; v.p. governing bd. La Canada Unified Sch. Dist., 1998-99; bd. dirs. southwest reg. B'nai B'rith Youth Orgn.; participant Leadership Pasadena, 1999-2000. Recipient Hon. Svc. award La Canada Coun. PTA, 1996, Svc. award LCF Ednl. Found., 1995, Golden Apple award La Canada Unified Sch. Dist., 1996. Mem. NSFRE. Avocations: skiing, bowling, reading. Home: 4117 Dover Rd La Canada Flintridge CA 91011-4006 Office: ARC PO Box 91087 Pasadena CA 91109-1087

RACKOW, JULIAN PAUL, lawyer; b. Phila., Dec. 16, 1941; s. Lawrence Lionel and Blanche (Wachman) R.; m. Paulette Schorr, June 23, 1963; children: Jeffrey A., Andrea B. AB, Cornell U., 1963; JD, Harvard U., 1966. Bar: Pa. 1966, U.S. Dist. Ct. (ea. dist.) Pa. 1966. Assoc. atty. Goodis, Greenfield, Narin & Mann, Phila., 1966-69; ptnr., co-chmn. dept. real estate Blank, Rome, Comisky & McCauley, 1970—. Mg., em. exec. com., bd. dirs. Ctrl. Phila. Devel. Corp., 1990—, pres. 1996-2000, chmn., 2000—. Mem. Pa. Bar Assn., Phila. Bar Assn., Harvard Law Sch. Assn. Phila. (v.p., exec. com. 1991—), Am. Coll. Real Estate Lawyers. Avocations: tennis, travel, piano. Office: Blank Rome Comisky & McCauley One Logan Sq Philadelphia PA 19103-6998

RACUYA-ROBBINS, ANN ELIZABETH, artist; b. Spokane, May 14, 1949; m. Guy P. Racuya, Aug. 24, 1995. AA in Broadcast Engring. & Elecs., Merritt Coll., 1973; BA in Music Composition, Ea. Wash. U., 1971; MFA, Mills Coll., 1974. Dir. planning & info. Met. Mortgage & Securities, 1980-81, v.p. data processing, 1981-82. Artist-in-residence, N.Mex., 1988-91, United World Coll., Montezume, N.Mex., 1989-90; pres., prin. Images For Media, Inc., Santa Fe, N.Mex., 1993—; pres. Resonant Comm. Network, Inc., Kauai, Hawaii, 1977-83; landscape designer Waikomo Project, Kauai, 1978-79; instr. Merritt Coll., Oakland, Calif., 1976-77; founder La Puebla Inst., 2000. Exhibitions include Festival Internat. Radio Art, Madrid, 1991, Fuller Lodge Art Ctr., Los Alamos, N.Mex., 1991, Mus. N.Mex., 1993, Hartwood Art Ctr., 1998, others; editor, pub.: Yefief, 1993; ; author: The Inevolution of Grace Series, 2002. Mem.: Orgn. Women Arch. and Design Profls., Internat. League Women Composers, Coun. Lit. Mags. and Presses, Pub. Mktg. Assn., Internat. Alliance for Women in Music, N.Mex. Ctr. for Book (v.p. 1996—97), N.Mex. Book Assn. (v.p. 1996). Office: Images For Media Inc PO Box 8505 Santa Fe NM 87504-8505

RACZKA, TONY MICHAEL, artist; b. Pottsville, Pa., Jan. 16, 1957; s. Albert Joseph and Rosemary Bernadette Raczka; m. Virginia Boone, 1974 (div. 1984); 1 child, Mesika; m. Patricia Martinez, June 20, 1986; 1 stepchild, Cynthia. BFA, No. Ariz. U., 1978; MFA, No. Ill. U., 1980; postgrad., U. Calif., San Diego, 1991-92. Instr. art Southwestern Coll., Chula Vista, Calif., 1981-84, No. Ariz. U., Flagstaff, Ariz., 1983; registrar Mingei Internat. Mus. World Folk Art, San Diego, 1985-86; instr. art San Diego State U., 1987; asst. dir. Quint Gallery, San Diego, 1987; sr. mus. preparator U. Art Gallery, U. Calif., 1989-95. Presenter in field. One-man shows include Quint Gallery, 1982, 83, Paris Green Gallery, La Jolla, Calif., 1987, Queens Coll. Art Ctr., CUNY, Flushing, N.Y., 1999—; two person shows include Printworks, Chgo., 1982, 84; exhibited in group shows include Butler Inst. Am. Art, Youngstown, Ohio, 1983, 97, The Drawing Ctr., 1994, Meridian Gallery, San Francisco, 1995 (Best of Show 2d place), Coll. William and Mary, 1996, Trenton (N.J.) State Coll., 1996, Laguna (Calif.) Art Mus., 1997, Carnegie Mus. Art, 1997, U. Richmond, Va., 1996, 98, San Jacinto Coll., Houston, 1998 (Merit award), Palm Springs Mus., 1999, Weber State U., Ogden, Utah, 2000, Bradley U., Peoria, Ill., 2001, Anne Arundel C.C., Arnold, Md., 2002, Hofstra U. Mus., Hempstead, N.Y., 2002; author poetry. Recipient Pollock-Krasner Found. award, 2001. Mem. Internat. Soc. Phenomenology and Scis. of Life, San Diego Mus. Art. Home: 4430 42d St # 2 San Diego CA 92116 E-mail: RaczkaTony@aol.com.

RADA, ALEXANDER, university official; b. Kvasy, Czechoslovakia, Mar. 28, 1923; s. Frantisek and Anna (Tonnkova) R.; came to U.S., 1954, naturalized, 1959; M.S., U. Tech. Coll. of Prague, 1948; postgrad. Va. Poly. Inst., 1956-59, St. Clara U., 1966-67; Ed.D., U. Pacific, 1975; m. Ingeborg Solveig Blakstad, Aug. 8, 1953; children: Alexander Sverre, Frank Thore, David Harald. Head prodn. planning dept. Mine & Iron Corp., Kolin, Czechoslovakia, 1941-42; mgr. experimenting and testing dept. Avia Aircraft, Prague, 1943-45; sec.-gen. Central Bldg. Office, Prague, 1948; head metal courses dept. Internat. Tech. Sch. of UN, Grafenaschau, W.Ger., 1949-50; works mgr. Igref A/S, Oslo, 1950-51; cons. engr., chief sect. machines Steel Products Ltd., Oslo, 1951-54; chief engr., plant supr. Nelson J. Pepin & Co., Lowell, Mass., 1954-55; sr. project engr., mfg. supt. Celanese Corp. Am., Narrows, Va., 1955-60; mgr. mfg., facilities and maint. FMC Corp., San Jose, Calif., 1960-62; mgr. adminstrn. Sylvania Electronic Systems, Santa Cruz, Calif., 1962-72; asst. to pres., devel. officer Napa (Calif.) Coll., 1972-88; chief exec. officer NAVCO Pacific Devel. Corp., Napa, 1984-91; pres. NAVCO Calif. Co., 1991—; prof. indsl. mgmt. Cabrillo Coll., Aptos, Calif., 1963-72; mgmt. and engring. cons., 1972—. Pres. ARC, Santa Cruz, 1965-72, bd. dirs., pres., Napa, 1977-88; mem. Nat. Def. Exec. Res., U.S. Dept. Commerce, Washington, 1966—, chmn. No. Calif. region 9, 1981-88; mem. President's Export Council-DEC, San Francisco, 1982—. Recipient Meritorious Service citation ARC, 1972, Etoile Civique l'Ordre de l'Etoile Civique, French Acad., 1985; registered profl. engr., Calif. Mem. NSPE, Calif. Soc. Profl. Engrs., Am. Def. Preparedness Assn., Assn. Calif. Community Coll. Adminstrs., Nat. Assn. Corp. Dirs., World Affairs Council No. Calif., Czechoslovak Foreign Inst., Praha, 1993—, Phi Delta Kappa, Editor-in-chief Our Youth, 1945-48; co-editor (with P. Boulden) Innovative Management Concepts, 1967. Home and Office: 1019 Ross Cir Napa CA 94558-2118

RADA, GEORGE ANDREW, painter; b. Bayonne, N.J., May 4, 1934; s. John Andrew and Mary Margaret (Manly) R.; m. Joanne Christine Walsh, Oct. 17, 1963 (div. Oct. 1974); children: George Andrew, Jr., Kevin Michael; m. Jacqueline Joy Sferra, Oct. 31, 1992. BA in Eng. Lit., Classics, St. Peter's Coll., 1956; postgrad., Art Students League N.Y., 1959-61, Pratt Inst., 1968-69, Frank J. Reilly Sch., N.Y.C., 1961-63. Art dir. Gambi Publs., N.Y.C., 1966-72, Progressive Grocer Mag., N.Y.C., 1972-79; painter, illustrator Freelance Studio, 1975—; founder, dir. Multicultural Visions Through the Arts, 1992—. Instr. painting Marymount Coll., N.Y.C., 1990-91; fine arts edn. cons. N.Y.C. Bd. Edn., 1992—; lectr. Met. Mus. of Art, 1987—; advisory bd. Studio Mus. Harlem, 1998. Arts career counselor, N.J., Lambertville, 1968-72. 1st lt. U.S. Army, 1957-59; capt. N.J. Army Nat. Guard, 1962-72. Recipient Program Sponsorship, N.Y. Found. for the Arts, N.Y.C., 1996—, award Jersey Jour. medal Graphics Hudson Artists Guild, Jersey City, 1969, Grumbacher medal Hudson Artists Guild, Jersey City, 1968, Blue Cross Keys, St. Peter's Coll., Jersey City, 1955. Mem. Art Students League of N.Y. (life), Artist Talk on Art (pres. 2000—), Am. Soc. Classical Realists. Roman Catholic. Avocations: classical literature, history. Home: 233 E 69th St Apt 6M New York NY 10021-5447 E-mail: georgerada00@yahoo.com.

RADA, HEATH KENNETH, social service organization executive; b. Richmond, Va., Aug. 4, 1944; m. Peggy Joyce Fish; children: Margaret, Mary-Talmage. BS, Va. Commonwealth U., 1967; MA, Union Presbyn. Sch. of Christian Edn., Richmond, Va., 1970; EdD, N.C. State U., 1979. Tchr. 5th grade Henrico County Schs., Richmond, 1969-70; dean of students Southeastern C.C., Whiteville, N.C., 1970-74; assoc. prof. cmty. edn., dir. N.C. Ctr. for Cmty. Edn. Appalachian State U., Boone, 1975-80; pres. Presbyn. Sch. of Christian Edn., Richmond, 1980-92; CEO Greater Richmond chpt. ARC, 1993—2002, interim CEO, 1999, San Diego, 2002—. Cons., guest spkr., writer Presbyn. Ch., Com. on Theol. Edn., 1992-96; prof. adult edn. Nova U., 1980-82; cons., trainer ASTD, 1975-80; guest prof. Tri-Nat. Inst. Adult Edn., Chorley, Eng., 1978; cons. Bolivia Dept. Edn., La Paz and Cochabamba, 1976; cons., proposal reader U.S. Office of Edn., 1973-75. Co-author: Blessed are the Debonair: The Wit and Wisdom of Charles E.S. Kraemer, 1990. Bd. dirs. Sheltering Arms Rehab. Hosp., 1983-98, Coun. for Am.'s 1st Freedom; tchr., spkr., elder River Rd. Presbyn. Ch.; mem. adult edn. adv. bd. Va. Commonwealth U., 1986-91; trustee Collegiate Schs., Richmond, 1987-90; adv. cons. Richmond Cmty. H.S., 1985-90; mem. supt. search com. Va. Pub. Schs., Richmond, 1988; part-time educator, program cons. West Raleigh (N.C.) Presbyn. Ch., 1974-76; part-time Christian educator 1st Presbyn. Ch., Whiteville, 1971-74; guidance worker Meml. Found., Richmond, 1969-70; dir. ednl. and cultural enrichment programs The Sr. Ctr. and William Byrd Cmty. Ctr., Richmond, 1964-66; del. World Coun. of Chs. 7th Assembly, Canberra, Australia, 1991, Bicentennial Assembly, Lesotho, 1983; mem. N.C. Gov.'s Office of Citizen's Affairs Adv. Bd., 1978, N.C. Gov.'s Interagy. Adv. Bd., 1977-79; regent Barium Springs Home for Children. Named Ptnrs. Orgn. Leadership Harvard U., 1998, Henrico Hero, Henrico County Pub. Schs., Richmond, 1997; Paul Harris fellow Rotary, Richmond, 1990; recipient Margaret Bowen award St. Andrew's Coll., 1983, 1st N.C. Cmty. Educator of Yr. award N.C. Assn. Cmty. Edn. Mem. Nat. Conf. Community Justice (pres. bd. dirs. Richmond chpt., 1998 Humanitarian award). Avocations: music, skiing, swimming, drama, travel. Home: 107 Holly Dr Manakin Sabot VA 23103-3232 Office: ARC-Greater Richmond Chpt PO Box 655 420 E Cary St Richmond VA 23219-3816 E-mail: radah@usa.redcross.org.

RADA, RUTH BYERS, college dean, author; b. Los Angeles, Oct. 3, 1923; d. George and Gerda Marie (Lihm) Byers; children: Kaaren Ruth, Georgene Melanie. AB, U. So. Calif., 1944, MA, 1945; EdD, Nova U., 1976. Asst. dean instrn. and evening East L.A. Coll., 1964-69, dean instrn., 1969-70; dean student personnel L.A. Harbor Coll., 1970-73, East L.A. Coll., 1973-77, L.A. Mission Coll., 1977-83; prof. biol. sci. East L.A. C.C., 1945-69, ret., 1983. Author: Water Biology, 1950, (with others) Human Body in Health and Disease, 1969, Structure and Function of Human Body, 1970, Laboratory Manual for Introductory Microbiology, 1963. Mem. Calif. Cmty. and Jr. Coll. Assn. (area pres. 1973-74), Calif. Woman Adminstrs. Assn., Los Angeles Coll. Adminstrs. Assn. (sec. 1973-74), Phi Beta Kappa, Phi Kappa Phi, Pi Lambda Theta, Phi Sigma. Republican. Mem. Ch. of Religious Sci.

RADABAUGH, MICHELLE JO, sales executive; b. Ashland, Ohio, May 1, 1961; d. James L. and Natalie J. (Barnhart) Sonnett; m. Brett L. Radabaugh, Sept. 22, 1990; 1 child, Natalie M. Assoc. in Advt., Northwood Inst., 1983, BBA, 1984. Xerox operator Nolan, Norton, Inc., Lexington, Mass., 1984-85; instr. Stautzenberger Coll., Findlay, Ohio, 1986-88, acad. coord., 1988-90, acad. dean, 1990-93; sr. sales rep. Glencoe divsn. McGraw-Hill, 1993—2001; sales rep. sch. divsn. Houghton Mifflin, 2001—. With USN, 1986. Recipient Golden Eagle award, 1994, 95, 96; named Outstanding Educator, C. of C., Findlay, 1988. Mem. Nat. Bus. Edn. Assn. Republican. Avocations: softball coaching, cross stitching, reading.

RADACOVSKÝ, MÁRIO, dancer; b. Slovaquie; Student, Conservatory of Dance, Bratislava. Soloist Slovak Nat. Theater Ballet, Bratislava, 1988; prin. dancer Slovak Nat. Theater, 1989—91; soloist Czech Nat. Theatre , Brno, 1991—92; dancer Nederlands Dans Theater II, 1992, Nederlands Dans Theater I, 1994; prin. dancer Les Grands Ballets Canadiens de Montréal, 1999—. Participant Moscow Internat. Ballet Competition, 1988; guest dancer Nat. Theatre Prague, 1997; participant Internat. Ballet Competition, Osaka, Japan, 1991, The 10 Dancers Ensemble, Austria, 1994. Dancer (ballets) Giselle, Slovak Nat. Theater, Swan Lake, Sleeping Beauty, Giselle, Les Grands Ballets Canadiens de Montréal, The Nutcracker, Approximate Sonata, Without Words, Jardí Tancat, Perpetuum, Concerto Barocco, The Queen of Spades. Recipient 1st prize, Czechoslovakian Ballet Competition, 1990. Office: Les Grands Ballets Canadiens de Montreal 4816 rue Rivard Montreal QU Canada H2J 2N6*

RADANOVICH, GEORGE P. congressman; b. Mariposa, Calif., 1955; s. Joan and George F.; m. Ethie Weaver; 1 child, George King. BS in Agr. Bus. Mgmt., Calif. State Polytechnic U., 1978. Pres. Radanovich Winery, Mariposa, Calif., 1982—; chair County Planning Comm., 1986-87, county supr., 1988-92; mem. U.S. Congress from Calif. 19th dist., Washington, 1995—; mem. energy and com. com., resources com. Mem. Calif. Agrl. Leadership Program Class XXI, Rotary (Paul Harris Fellowship). Republican. Office: US Ho Reps 123 Cannon HOB Washington DC 20515*

RADCLIFF, WILLIAM FRANKLIN, lawyer, director; b. Fredericksburg, Ind., May 21, 1922; s. Samuel Pearl and Hester Susan (Sherwood) R.; m. Elizabeth Louise Doeller Haines, May 15, 1982; children— Forrest Lee, Stephanie Anne; foster children— Cheryl Lynn, Sandra Lee, Richard Alan, Lezlie Laverne; stepchildren— Mark David, Laura Louise, Pamela Lynn, Veronica Leigh. BA, Yale U., 1948; JD, Ind. U., 1951. Bar: Ind. 1951. With DeFur, Voran, Hanley, Radcliff & Reed and predecessors, Muncie, Ind., 1951—, ptnr., 1954—. Dir., mem. exec. com. Am. Nat. Bank and Trust Co., Muncie . Author: Sherman Minton: Indiana's Supreme Court Justice, 1996, Sagamore of the Wabash. Pres. Delaware County Mental Health Assn., 1962-63; founding mem. Ind. Mental Health Meml. Found., 1962, sec., 1962-84; bd. dirs. Delaware County Cancer Soc.; trustee Acad. Community Leadership. Served with AUS, 1940-46, PTO Mem. ABA, Ind. Bar Assn., Muncie Bar Assn., Muncie-Delaware County C. of C. (pres. 1972-73) Clubs: Muncie Tennis and Country (bd. dirs., sec.), Muncie, Delaware Country (pres. 1972-73), Exchange (pres. 1962) (Muncie). Lodges: Masons. Home: 1809 N Winthrop Rd Muncie IN 47304-2532 Office: 201 E Jackson St Muncie IN 47305-2832 *Be yourself. Do not try to be someone else. Use your God given talents to the best of your ability and be content with the success that such effort brings.*

RADCLIFFE, EDWARD BRUCE, entomologist; b. Rapid City, Can., Oct. 25, 1936; s. Thomas Reid and Helen Louise R.; m. Betty Loraine Pederson, Dec. 20, 1964; children: David Glen, Peter Michael. BSA, U. Manitoba, 1959; MS, U. Wis., 1961, PhD, 1963. Rsch. fellow U. Minn., St. Paul, 1963-64, rsch. assoc., 1964-65, asst. prof., 1965-70, assoc. prof., 1970-76, prof., 1976—. Author numerous scientific publs. Mem. AAAS, Entomol. Soc. Am., Entomol. Soc. Can., Potato Assn. of Am. Office: Dept Entomology/U Minn 219 Hodson Hall 1980 Folwell Ave Saint Paul MN 55108-6125 E-mail: radcl001@umn.edu.

RADCLIFFE, GEORGE GROVE, retired life insurance company executive; b. Balt., Nov. 12, 1924; s. George G. and Elsie (Winter) R.; m. Bettie Howell, Feb. 10, 1951 (div.); 1 child, Cynthia; m. Kathleen Moore Smith, 1991. BA, Johns Hopkins U., 1947; grad. Advanced Mgmt. Program, Harvard U. Grad. Sch. Bus. Adminstrn., 1962. With Balt. Life Ins. Co., 1947-89, v.p. treas., 1963-69, exec. v.p., 1969-72, pres., 1972-89, chief exec. officer, 1974-89, chmn. bd., 1980-89, pres., 1981-86, ret., chmn. bd. dirs. emeritus, 1989. Chmn. bd. trustees Johns Hopkins U., 1984-90, trustee, 1975-93, trustee emeritus, 1993—. Mem. Tred Avon Yacht Club, Talbot Country Club, Delta Upsilon. Methodist. Home and Office: PO Box 409 Oxford MD 21654-0409

RADCLIFFE, REDONIA (DONNIE RADCLIFFE), journalist, author; m. Robert C. Radcliffe; 1 child, M. Donnel Nunes. BA, San Jose (Calif.) State U., 1951. Reporter, women's editor, county editor The Salinas Californian, 1951-59; free-lance writer Europe, 1959-66; reporter Washington Star, 1967-72; reporter, columnist Washington Post, 1972-95. Author: Simply Barbara Bush: A Portrait of America's Candid First Lady, 1989, Hillary Rodham Clinton: A First Lady for Our Time, 1993, reissued as Hillary Rodham Clinton: The Evolution of a First Lady, 1999; contbr.: The Fall of a President, 1974, Guide to Washington, 1989. Trustee Calvert County (Md.) Libr.; bd. dirs. Nat. 1st Ladies' Libr. E-mail: redrad@erols.com.

RADDING, ANDREW, lawyer, educator; b. N.Y.C., Nov. 30, 1944; m. Bonnie A. Levinson, Oct. 7, 1972; children: Judith Lynne, Joshua David. BBA, CCNY-Baruch Sch., 1965; JD, Boston U., 1968. Bar: N.Y. 1968, Md. 1977, D.C. 1977, U.S. Supreme Ct. Grad. fellow Northwestern U. Sch. Law, 1968-69; asst. counsel U.S. Ho. of Reps. Select Com. on Crime, 1969-72; asst. U.S. atty. for Dist. Md., 1972-77; ptnr. Francomano, Radding & Mannes, Balt., 1977-80, Burke, Gerber, Wilen, Francomano & Radding, Balt., 1980-85, Blades & Rosenfeld P.A., Balt., 1985-97, Adelberg, Rudow, Dorf and Hendler LLC, Balt., 1997—. Mem. adj. faculty clin. practice skills, criminal law, fed. criminal practice U. Balt. Sch. Law, 1980—; mem. trial experience com. U.S. Dist. ct., 1986-88; apptd. by gov. State Adminstrv. Bd. of Election Laws, 1995-96; instr. professionalism course Md. State Bar Assn., 1999—. Bd. dirs. Copper Hill Condominium, 1979-82, pres., 1981-82; subcom. Md. Republican Conv., 1981; sen. C.M. Mathias Jud. Selection com., 1986, chmn. U.S. Dist. Ct. Bicentennial Program, 1989-90; mem. Mayor's Domestic Violence Coord. com., 2001—. Mem.: Nat. Arbitration Forum (arbitrator), U.S. Arbitration and Mediation (inquiry panel atty. grievance com. 1991—, mediator and arbitrator), Md. Inst. Continuing Profl. Edn. for Lawyers (bd. govs. 1987—92, peer rev. panel), U.S. Atty. Alumni Assn. Md. (pres. 1978—), Fed. Bar Assn. (Balt. chpt. pres. 1986—87), Balt. City Bar Assn. (jud. selection com. 1990—92, 1994—, chmn. 1996—97, exec. coun. 1998—99, co-chmn. membership com. 1999—2000, exec. coun. 2000—, chmn. 2002—), Md. Bar Assn., ABA. Jewish. Office: Adelberg Rudow et al LLC 2 Hopkins Plz Baltimore MD 21201-2930 E-mail: aradding@adelbergrudow.com.

RADEBOLDT-DALY, KAREN ELAINE, medical nurse; b. Bklyn., Mar. 3, 1944; d. Harry Phillip and Lillian Florence (Renton) McAnaney; m. Richard William Radeboldt, Aug. 19, 1968 (dec. Aug. 1985); children: Karyn, Kellianne, Kimberly, Kristi-Jo, Richard; m. William J. Daly, Sr., Jan. 22, 1995. Lic. practical nurse, Wyckoff Heights Sch. Nursing, Bklyn., 1968; RN, Orange County C.C., Middletown, N.Y., 1990. LPN, N.Y., RN, N.Y.; cert. med.-surg. nurse, N.Y. Nurses aide, lic. practical nurse Wyckoff Heights Hosp., Bklyn., 1967-90; staff nurse, med.-surg. nurse Westchester Med. Ctr., Valhalla, N.Y., 1990-96, staff nurse, trauma unit, 1996-98, staff nurse, critical care-trauma ICU, 1998—. Mem. Am. Jour. Nursing. Adventist. Avocations: reading, sewing, bowling, walking, motorcycle riding. Home: 101 Daly Rd Middletown NY 10940-7356

RADEMAKER, STEPHEN GEOFFREY, lawyer; b. Balt., July 18, 1959; s. Thomas Joseph and Ruth Virginia (Wentz) R.; m. Danielle Pletka; children: Andrew, Olivia, Sophia. BA with Highest Distinction, U. Va., 1981, JD, 1984, MA in Fgn. Affairs, 1985. Bar: Va. 1984, D.C. 1985. Assoc. Covington & Burling, Washington, 1984-86; law clk. to Hon. James L. Buckley U.S. Ct. Appeals (D.C. cir.), 1986; counsel to vice chmn. U.S. Internat. Trade Commn., 1986-87; spl. asst. to asst. sec. for Inter-Am. affairs Dept. State, 1987-89; assoc. counsel to Pres. of U.S. and dep. legal advisor to NSC, 1989-92; gen. counsel Peace Corps, 1992-93; Rep. chief counsel Com. Fgn. Affairs U.S. Ho. of Reps., 1993-95, chief counsel Com. Internat. Rels., 1995—. Recipient Raven award U. Va.,1984; S. Philip Heiner scholar U. Va., 1983. Mem. ABA (U.S. Govt. liaison for sect. internat. law and practice), Va. Bar Assn., D.C. Bar Assn., Phi Beta Kappa, Omicron Delta Kappa. Republican. Lutheran. Avocations: skiing, cycling, scuba diving. Office: US House Reps 2170 Rayburn St Com Internat Rels Washington DC 20515*

RADENTZ, MICHAEL GREY, recording engineer, producer, composer, musician; b. St. Louis, Jan. 11, 1963; s. Donald Erwin Adolph and Nancy Ellen Radentz; m. Joan M. Rideout, Dec. 3, 1988; children: Samuel Grey, Andrew Stewart. Recording engr. Clayton Studios Inc., St. Louis, 1982-88; asst. producer Dick Cavett Comedy Show Clayton Webster Corp., 1987-88; dir. audio prodn. Technisonic Studios Inc., 1988—; pres. JMR Holdindgs LLC, 2000—. Recipient Emmy award, 1995, 96, Addy award, 1995, 96, 97, Clio nomination, 1997. Lutheran. Office: Technisonic Studios Inc 500 S Ewing Ave # G Saint Louis MO 63103-2944 E-mail: earwax@technisonic.com.

RADER, DAVID, insurance company executive; BA, Ohio State U., 1968. Pres., CEO, dir. First Profls. Ins. Co., Jacksonville, Fla., 1999—. Office: FPIC Ins Group Inc Ste 800 1000 Riverside Ave Jacksonville FL 32204

RADER, DOTSON CARLYLE, author, journalist; b. Minn., July 25, 1941; s. Paul Carlyle and Lois (Schacht) R. Student, Columbia, 1962-68. Editor Defiance: A Radical Rev. (Warner Communications, Inc.), 1969-71; contbg. editor Evergreen Rev., 1969-73, Esquire, N.Y.C., 1973-77, N.Y. mag., 1977-80; cons. Nat. Com. for Lit. Arts at Lincoln Center, N.Y.C., 1980—. Mem. sponsoring bd. New Politics, 1972— ; host Free Time Show, WNET-TV, N.Y.C., 1972-73 Author: I Ain't Marchin' Anymore!, 1969, Government Inspected Meat and Other Fun Summer Things, 1971, Blood Dues, 1973, Tennessee: Cry of the Heart; An Intimate Memoir of Tennessee Williams, 1985; screenplay The Bronze Lily, 1974, The Dream's on Me: A Love Story, 1976, Miracle, 1978; novel Beau Monde, 1981; play (with Mike Miller) Shattered Glass, 1990; contbg. editor Parade Mag., 1984—. Mem. Student Peace Union, 1961-63, Students for a Democratic Soc., 1964-69, War Resisters League, 1970— ; pres. Humanitas, Columbia, 1963-67; vice chmn. Peoples Coalition for Peace and Justice, 1972. Named hon. ambassador State of W. Va., 1982; recipient award for nat. journalism Odyssey Inst., 1982, Spl. Olympics award for nat. journalism Joseph P. Kennedy Found., 1985 Mem. PEN, Overseas Press Club, The Dramatists Guild.

RADER, ELLA JANE See ASHLEY, ELLA JANE

RADER, LOUIS T. corporation executive, educator; b. Frank, Can., Aug. 24, 1911; came to U.S., 1934, naturalized, 1940; s. Italo and Louise (Bonamico) R.; m. Constance Wayland, Sept. 10, 1938; children— Louis Albert, John Newton. BS, U. B.C., 1933; PhD in Elec. Engring, Calif. Inst. Tech., 1938. Engr. Gen. Electric Co., 1937-45; prof., head dept. elec. engring. Ill. Inst. Tech., 1945-47; with Gen. Electric Co., 1947-59, gen. mgr. splty. control div., 1951-59; v.p., dir. ITT, N.Y.C., 1959-61; group v.p. U.S. Commercial, 1961—; pres. Univac div. Sperry Rand Corp., N.Y.C., 1962-64; v.p., gen. mgr. Indsl. Process Control div. Gen. Electric Co., 1964-69; prof. elec. engring. U. Va., 1969-82, prof. emeritus, 1982—, prof., Grad. Sch. Bus., 1969-82. Vis. com.

div. engring. and applied sci. Calif. Inst. Tech., 1968-75 Recipient Alumni distinguished service award Calif. Inst. Tech., 1966; Va. Engring. Found. award, 1982. Fellow IEEE; mem. Am. Soc. Engring. Edn., Nat. Acad. Engring., Sigma Xi, Tau Beta Pi, Beta Gamma Sigma, Eta Kappa Nu, Omicron Delta Kappa. Office: U Va Prof Emeritus Darden Grad Sch Bus PO Box 6550 Charlottesville VA 22906-6550 Home: 1009 Arapaho Path Schenectady NY 12302-3301

RADER, PATRICK NEIL, accountant; b. Oak Ridge, Tenn., May 16, 1952; s. Daniel Hurley Jr. and Mary Lou (Arms) R.; m. Deborah Lynn Bryant, Dec. 20, 1975 (div. May 1978); 1 child, Andrew Neil; m. Caroline Elizabeth Snow, Dec. 30, 1983; children: Laura Ashley, Mary Beth, Patrick Samuel. BSBA with high honors, U. Tenn., 1974, MBA, 1986. CPA, Tenn.; CFP; chartered mutual fund counselor; chartered retirement planning counselor; accredited asset mgmt. specialist. Fin. officer Union Carbide Corp., Oak Ridge, 1975-79, fin. mgr., 1979-84; capital acctg. mgr. Martin Marietta Corp., 1984-86, materials mgr., 1986-90, bus. mgr., 1990-94, sr. bus. analyst, 1995-97; bus. mgr. Lockheed Martin Energy Rsch. Corp., 1998—. Tech. advisor software devel. Co-author: (user's manual) Subcontract Guidelines, 1986. Mem. AICPA, Fin. Planning Assn. Baptist. Avocations: boating, reading.

RADER, PAUL ALEXANDER, minister, religious organization administrator; b. N.Y.C., Mar. 4, 1934; s. Lyell M. and Gladys Mina (Damon) R.; m. Kay Fuller, May 29, 1956; children: Edith Jeanne, James Paul, Jennifer Kay. BA, Asbury Coll., Wilmore, Ky., 1956; BD, Asbury Theol. Sem., 1959; LLD (hon.), Asbury Coll., Wilmore, Ky., 1984; ThM, So. Bapt. Theol. Sem., Louisville, 1961; D Missiology, Fuller Theol. Sem., 1973; DD (hon.), Asbury Theol. Sem., 1995. Ordained to ministry Salvation Army, 1961. Tng. prin. The Salvation Army, Seoul, 1973-74, edn. sec., 1974-77, chief sec., 1979-83, tng. prin. Suffern, N.Y., 1983-86, divisional comdr. for Ea. Pa. and Del. Phila., 1986-88, chief sec. ea. ter. N.Y.C., 1988, territorial comdr. U.S.A. western ter. Rancho Palos Verdes, Calif., 1989-94, gen., 1994-99; pres. Asbury Coll., 2000—. Adj. prof. Seoul Theol. Sem., 1980-82; trustee Asian Ctr. for Theol. Studies and Mission, 1980-83, Asbury Coll., 1988—; pres. The Salvation Army Calif. Corp., Rancho Palos Verdes, 1989-94. Recipient Alumnus A award Asbury Coll., 1982, Disting. Alumni award Asbury Theol. Sem., 1989; Paul Harris fellow Rotary Internat., 1989. Mem. Am. Soc. Missiology, Internat. Assn. Mission Studies. Address: Asbury Coll 1 Macklem Dr Wilmore KY 40390-1198

RADER, RALPH TERRANCE, lawyer; b. Clarksburg, W.Va., Dec. 5, 1947; s. Ralph Coolidge and Jeanne (Cover) R.; m. Rebecca Jo Vorderman, Mar. 22, 1969; children: Melissa Michelle, Allison Suzanne. BSME, Va. Poly. Inst., 1970; JD, Am. U., 1974. Bar: Va. 1975, U.S. Ct. Customs and Patent Appeals, 1977, U.S. Dist. Ct. (ea. dist.) Mich. 1978, Mich. 1979, U.S. Ct. Appeals (6th cir.) 1979, U.S. Dist. Ct. (we. dist.) Mich. 1981, U.S. Ct. Appeals (fed. cir.) 1983. Supervisory patent examiner U.S. Patent Office, Washington, 1970-77; patent atty., ptnr. Cullen, Sloman, Cantor, Grauer, Scott & Rutherford, Detroit, 1977-88; ptnr. Dykema, Gossett, 1989-96, Rader, Fishman & Grauer, Bloomfield Hills, Mich., 1996—. Contbr. articles to profl. jours. Mem. adminstrv. bd. 1st United Meth. Ch., Birmingham, Mich., 1980—. With U.S. Army, 1970-76. Mem. ABA, Am. Patent Law Assn., Mich. Patent Law Assn., Mich. Bar (governing coun. patent, trademark and copyright law sect. 1981-84), Engring. Soc. Detroit, Masons, Tau Beta Pi, Pi Tau Sigma, Phi Kappa Phi. Methodist. Home: 4713 Riverchase Dr Troy MI 48098-4186 Office: Rader Fishman & Grauer 39533 Woodward Ave Ste 140 Bloomfield Hills MI 48304-5098 E-mail: rtr@raderfishman.com.

RADER, RANDALL RAY, federal judge; b. Hastings, Nebr., Apr. 21, 1949; BA magna cum laude, BYU, 1974; JD with honors, George Washington U., 1978. Bar: D.C., U.S. Ct. Appeals (fed. cir.) 1990, U.S. Claims Ct., U.S. Supreme Ct. Legis. asst. to Congresswoman Virginia Smith U.S. Ho. of Reps., 1975—78; mem. staff Ways and Means Com. U.S. Ho. Reps., 1978—81; chief counsel subcom. on Constn. U.S. Senate Judiciary Com., 1981—86, chief counsel, staff dir. subcom. on patents, copyrights and trademarks, 1986—87; counsel to Senator Orrin Hatch, 1981—88; judge U.S. Ct. Claims, Washington, 1988—90, U.S. Ct. Appeals (fed. cir.), Washington, 1990—. Lectr. patent law U. Va. Sch. Law, 1993—99; lectr. trial advocacy, lectr. George Washington U. Nat. Law Ctr., Washington, 1993—97; lectr. comparative patent law Georgetown U. Law Ctr., Washington, 1998—99. Co-author: Patent Law, 1997; co-editor: Criminal Justice Reform, 1983; contbr. articles to profl. jours. Mem.: FBA. Office: US Ct Appeals Fed Cir 717 Madison Pl NW Ste 913 Washington DC 20439-0002*

RADER, STEVEN PALMER, lawyer; b. Charlotte, N.C., Dec. 30, 1952; s. Alvin Marion Jr. and Shirley Ninabelle (Palmer) R. AB, Duke U., 1975; postgrad., Stetson U., 1975-76; JD, Wake Forest U., 1978. Bar: N.C. 1978, U.S. Dist. Ct. (ea. dist.) N.C. 1979. Assoc. Wilkinson and Vosburgh, Washington, 1978-81; pvt. practice, 1981-88; spl. asst. to sec. N.C. Dept. Human Resources, Raleigh, 1988-89, asst. dir. office legal affairs, 1989-91, gen. counsel, 1991-93; ptnr. Wilkinson & Rader, P.A., Washington, 1993—. Commr. Nat. Conf. Commrs. on Uniform State Laws, 1985-93; gen. counsel N.C. Rep. Party, 1992-97; commr. N.C. Rules Rev. Commn., 1997-99. Mem., sec. City of Washington Human Rels. Coun., 1981-83; chmn. Beaufort County Rep. party, Washington, 1983-87, 1st Congl. Dist. Rep. party, N.C., 1985-92; v.p. East Main St. Area Neighborhood Assn., 1983-85, 1st v.p., Ocean Villas Homeowners Assn., 1999—; del. Rep. Nat. Conv., 1984, 88, 92; Presdl. elector from N.C., U.S. Electoral Coll., 2000. Mem. N.C. State Bar, 2d Jud. Dist. Bar, Beaufort County Hist. Soc. (v.p. 1981-85, pres. 1985-86). Lutheran. Avocations: boating, classic automobiles, travel. Home: PO Box 1901 Washington NC 27889-1901 Office: Wilkinson & Rader PA PO Box 732 Washington NC 27889-0732

RADER, WILLIAM DONALD, economics educator, university administrator; b. Chgo., July 12, 1929; s. William Joseph Rader and Martha Virginia (Neubauer) Johnson; m. Mary Louise Poss, June 22, 1957; children: Steven, Lucy. BS, No. Ill. U., 1956, MS, 1957; PhD, Purdue U., 1969. Project dir. U. Chgo., 1964-72; asst. prof. Northeastern Ill. U., Chgo., 1968-72; assoc. prof. Fla. State U., Tallahassee, 1972-77; prof. Ohio U., Athens, 1977—, asst. dean, 1980-86, dir. curriculum and instrn., 1986-93; ret., 1999. Author: Economics and Free Enterprise, 1982. With U.S. Army, 1951-53. Recipient George Washington medal, Freedoms Found., 1968. Mem. KC (treas. 1989-91, pres. 1987-88, v.p. 1985-87, sec. 1983-85). Home: 56 Briarwood Dr Athens OH 45701-1301

RADETZKI, MARIAN, economist, researcher; b. Poland, Dec. 8, 1936; Grad., Stockholm Sch. Econs., 1958; B of Social Anthropology, Stockholm U., 1961, lic. econs., 1969, D of Econs., 1972. Rschr. mktg. Volvo Co., 1959-60; dir. Coop. Mgmt. Tng. Inst. South and East Asia, New Delhi, 1961-66, Swedish Coop. Union and Wholesale Soc., 1961-66; dir. Found. Swedish Coop. Ctr. Stockholm, 1966-68; chief economist Intergovtl. Council Copper Exporting Countries, Paris, 1973-75; rschr. Inst. for Internat. Econ. Studies, Stockholm, 1975-89; dir. Studieforbundet Näringsliv och Samhalle Energy, 1989—99; prof. econs. U. Lulea, 1999—; sr. rsch. fellow Studieforbundet Näringsliv och Samhalle, Stockholm, 2001—. Vis. prof. mineral econs. Colo. Sch. Mines, 1986-91; prof. econs. U. Lulea, Sweden; cons. in field. Author: International Commodity Market Arrangements, 1970, Aid and Development, 1973, Financing Mining Projects in Developing Countries, 1979, (with Stephen A. Zorn) Mineral Processing in Developing Countries, 1980, Uranium, A Strategic Source of Energy, 1981, State Mineral Enterprises: An Investigation Into Their Impact on Internation Mineral Market, 1985, A Guide to Primary Commodities in the World Economy, 1990, Energy and Economic Reform in the Former Soviet Union, 1994, (with Leslie Dienes and Istvan Dobozi) Polish Coal and European Energy Market Integration, 1995, Fashions in the Treatment of Packaging Waste: An Economic Analysis of The Swedish Producer Responsibility Legislation, 2000, The Green Myth-Economic Growth and the Quality of the Environment, 2001, numerous others. Office: SNS PO Box 5629 11486 Stockholm Sweden E-mail: radetzki@sns.se.

RADEWAGEN, FRED, publisher, organization executive; b. Louisville, Mar. 20, 1944; s. Hobart Fred (dec.) and Mildred Lillian (Carlsen) R.; m. Amata Catherine Coleman, Dec. 4, 1971; children— Erika Catherine, Mark Peter, Kirsten Alexandra. BA, Northwestern U., 1966; MS, Georgetown U., 1968. Rsch. asst. Republican Nat. Com., Washington, 1967-68; dir. mgmt. services Republican Presdl. Campaign and Inaugural Com., 1968-69; liaison officer Trust Terr. Washington, 1969-71; staff coordinator for territorial affairs Dept. Interior, Washington, 1971-75; assoc. dir. govtl. and polit. participation programs C. of C. U.S., 1975-76, dir., 1976-79; dir. resource devel. Rep. Govs. Assn., Washington, 1979-81, dir. state and fed. relations, 1981-82; Washington rep. Gov. of Am. Samoa, 1982-85, 89-93; pub. Washington Pacific Report, 1982—; dir. Pacific Islands Washington office, 1984—; rep. Cook Islands, Washington, 1986-89. Pres. Washington and Pacific Assocs., 1975-84; staff exec. Bus. Alliance for Congl. Action, 1976-79; lectr. Insts. for Orgn. Mgmt., 1977-79; exec. dir. Nat. Chamber Alliance for Politics, 1977-79; mem. U.S. del. UN Trusteeship Coun., 1972, advisor U.S. del. to Com. of Twenty-Four, 1982-83; mem. Am. Samoa dels. to South Pacific Conf., 1982-83, 89, 91, Post-Forum Dialogue, 1991, UN Conf. on Environment and Devel., 1992; del. Am. Coun. Young Polit. Leaders, 1982-83, mem. alumni coun., 1984—, Russia and Georgia Presdl. Elections, 2000; exec. dir. U.S.- New Zealand Coun., 1995, sr. v.p., 1996-97, exec. dir. Micronesia Inst., 1998-2001; mem. Guam del. Coun. Micronesian Chief Execs. Summit, 1998. Mem. Alexandria Rep. City Com., 1979-80; del. Va. Rep. State Conv., 1981, 89, 93, 94, 2000; participant Rep. Nat. Convs., 1968, 80, 84, 88, 92, 96, 2000; past mem. Christian edn. com. Westminster Presbyn. Ch. Mem. Nat. Assn. Rep. Campaign Profls., Northwestern U. Alumni Assn. (past Washington bd. govs.), Washington Roundtable for Asian/Pacific Press, Nat. Capital Interfrat. Forum (past pres.), Nat. Eagle Scout Assn. (life), Mensa, Delta Tau Delta (past pres. Washington alumni). Clubs: Ill. State Soc. (past v.p.), Capitol Hill (life), Circumnavigators. Home: 103 E Luray Ave Alexandria VA 22301-2027 also: 1019 3rd St Rehoboth Beach DE 19971-1503 Office: PO Box 26142 Alexandria VA 22313-6142 E-mail: fredradewagen@mail.com.

RADFORD, DIANE MARY, surgeon, surgical oncologist; b. Irvine, Ayrshire, Scotland, Nov. 14, 1957; came to U.S., 1985; d. Sidney and Mary Margery (Parr) R. BSc with honors, Glasgow U., Scotland, 1978, MBChB, 1981; MD, Glasgow U., 1991. Jr. house officer Gartravel Gen. Hosp., Glasgow, 1981-82, Monklands Dist. Gen. Hosp., Airdrie, Scotland, 1982; sr. house officer Western Infirmary, Glasgow, 1982-83, Royal Infirmary, Edinburgh, Scotland, 1983-84; registrar Crosshouse Hosp., Kilmarnock, Scotland, 1984-85; fellow in surg. oncology Roswell Park Meml. Inst., Buffalo, 1985-87; resident in surg. St. Louis U. Hosp., 1987-91; instr. in surgery Wash. U., St. Louis, 1991-92; asst. prof. surgery Washington U., 1992-96; mem. Parkcrest Surg. Assocs., 1996—2001, St. Louis Cancer & Breast Inst., 1999—. Contbr. articles to profl. jours. Recipient 1st prize residents competition Mo. chpt. ACS, 1989. Fellow Am. Coll. Surgeons (bd. cert. gen. surgery), Royal Coll. Surgeons (Edinburgh); mem. Soc. Surg. Oncology, St. Louis Surg. Soc., St. Louis Met. Med. Soc., Roswell Pk. Surg. Soc. Office: St Louis Cancer & Breast Inst 450 N New Ballas Rd Ste 270 Saint Louis MO 63141-6835

RADFORD, RICHARD FRANCIS, religious organization administrator, author; b. Boston, Feb. 15, 1939; s. Richard H. and Lorraine R.; m. Lynne S. Radford, Aug. 20, 1966; children: Amy, Richard III. BA with honors, Boston State Coll., 1979; MEd, U. Mass., 1988, EdD, 1990. Cert. master addictions counselor, criminal justice specialist. Exec. dir. Middlesex Shelter, Lowell, Mass., 1987-90, Home for Now, Boston, 1991-93, Louison Chilo Ctr., Brockton, Mass., 1994-2000; dir. religious edn. St. Mary of Assumption Parish, Brookline, 2000—. Author: Drug Agent, 1991, Trooper, 1990, Having Been There, 1980, Golfer's Book of Trivia, 1988. Bd. dirs. Brookline Cooperative Housing Authority, 1988-90, Alcohol Edn. Inc., Boston, 1984-86; ordained deacon Archdiocese of Boston, 1988. Sgt. U.S. Army, 1959-62. Recipient Short Fiction award Nat. Coun. on Alcoholism, 1980, Tenets award Masons, 1990; named Father of Yr. Drizzle.com, 2000. Democrat. Roman Catholic. Avocations: golf, poetry.

RADFORD, R.S. lawyer, law educator; b. Independence, Kans., July 30, 1945; s. Lloyd Raymond and Arlene (Bacon) R.; m. Sharon L. Browne, Nov. 24, 1992; children: Jessica Siegel, Jacob Siegel. BS in Bus. Adminstrn., Rockhurst Coll., 1974; MA in Econs., U. So. Calif., 1976; JD, 1988. Bar: Calif. 1988, Supreme Ct. 1992. Prin. atty. Pacific Legal Found., Sacramento, 1988—; dir. progrm for jud. awareness, 1999—. Adj. prof. law U. Pacific McGeorge Sch. Law, Sacramento, 2001—. Contbr. numerous articles to profl. jours. Named Laywer of Yr. Calif. Lawyer, 1997 Office: Pacific Legal Found 10360 Old Placerville Rd Sacramento CA 95827 Fax: (916) 362-2932. E-mail: radford@mother.com., rsr@pacificlegal.org.

RADICE, BEATRICE ROSEMARIE, family nurse practitioner; b. Bklyn., Nov. 6, 1959; d. Anthony and Rosaria (Liosi) R. BSN, Downstate Med. Ctr., 1981; MSN, Pace U., 1993. Cert. family nurse practitioner. Staff RN Brookdale Hosp. Med. Ctr., Bklyn., 1982-83; staff RN surg. ICU/staffing Maimonides Med. Ctr., 1984-86; staff nurse emergency rm. Victory Meml. Hosp., 1986-89; nurse clinician North Shore U. Hosp., Manhasset, N.Y., 1989-92, Elderplan, Inc., Bklyn., 1992-94; FNP Luth. Med. Ctr., 1993; FNP occupl. health svc. The N.Y. Hosp., N.Y.C., 1994; FNP, Heartland Med., S.I., N.Y., 1995, Citibank, N.Y.C., 1995-97; FNP, supr. Health First, 1997-98; FNP, dir. student health svcs. N.Y.C. Tech. Coll., 1999—. Mem. Am. Coll. Health Assn., N.Y. State Nurses Assn. (presenter poster 1991, 92, legis. com. 1993-94), N.Y. State Coalition Nurse Practitioners (presenter poster 1993), N.Y. Acad. Medicine (presenter poster, spkr. 1998). Office: 300 Jay St # P104 Brooklyn NY 11201-1909

RADICE, FRANK J. communications executive; b. Washington, Dec. 13, 1949; m. Vida S. Radice, July 4, 1995. Student, U. Md., 1968-72. Film editor WRC/NBC-TV, Washington, 1971-72, ABC News, Washington, 1972, assignment editor, 1976, assoc. prodr. Good Morning Am., 1978, ops. prodr. World News Tonight, 1979-80; prodr. Nightline N.Y.C., 1980-83; program prodr. The Last Word ABC News, 1983; field dir. Entertainment Tonight Paramount Motion Pictures, 1984; prodr., developer Live At 5:00 WRC/NBC-TV, Washington, 1985; exec. prodr. Entertainment News, Cable News Network, N.Y.C., 1987-89; InterActive sr. producer/product devel., producer advt. and promotion ABC News, 1989-91; advt. mgr. WCBS-TV, 1991; v.p. advt. and promotion NBC Entertainment, 1996; sr. v.p. The NBC Agy., 2000—; exec. prodr. NBC In Flight, United Airlines. Pres. V&R Co., 1999 Exec. prodr. NBC in Flight, 2000; prodr. A Line in the Sand, War of Peace, War in the Gulf; writer, prodr., 1992; co-exec. prodr. (CD): The Best of The Today Show Summer Concerts, Vols. 1 and 2, NBC Records, 2000. Recipient award Coll. Emergency Physicians, 1983, Emmy award NATAS, 1984, 1990, 2 N.Y. Festival awards; Alfred I Dupont grantee Columbia U., N.Y.C., 1984, 91, Mobius award, 1998, Line Golden Eagle award 2002. Mem. Broadcast Music Inc. (writer affiliate), AFTRA, Nat. Assn. Broadcast Employees and Technicians, Internat. Alliance Theatrical and Stage Employees, Writers Guild Am., Dirs. Guild Am., Congressional Country Club, Friars (N.Y.C.). Democrat. Roman Catholic. Office: NBC Ste 1891E 30 Rockefeller Plz New York NY 10112-0002 E-mail: frank.radice@nbc.com.

RADIGAN, FRANK XAVIER, pharmaceutical company executive; b. Paterson, N.J., Apr. 13, 1933; s. John Joseph and Susan Clair (Brett) R.; m. Julia Lou Smith, Aug. 27, 1960 (div. Nov. 1988); children: Francis Gregory, Patricia Louise, Brett Frasier; m. Carol E. Berkley, June 26, 1992; children: Dana, Traci. AB in Sociology, Seton Hall U., 1955; MBA Mktg., U. Hartford, 1968. Asst. mgr. Beneficial Fin. Co., Newark, 1955-57; hosp. rep. Becton-Dickinson Co., Rutherford, N.J., 1957-58; dist. mgr. Merck Human Health Divsn., West Point, Pa., 1958-98, ret., 1998. Horse breeder, 1976—86. Active Greater Balt. SCORE; mem. Passaic County Dem. Com., 1955—56; chmn. St. John the Baptist Social Justice, New Freedom, Pa., 1981—85. Capt. USAR. Mem.: Md. Mental Health Assn. (legis. com. 1969—73), Balt. Pharm. Assn. (hon. pres. 1989), W.Va. Pharm. Soc., Md. Pharmacists Assn. (past chmn. indsl. rels. com., hon. pres. 1999—2000), Am. Mktg. Assn., Am. Pharm. Assn., Hopewell Fish and Game Assn., Bon Air Country Club, Lions (pres. Glen Rock 1975—76, 1986—88), Elks. Roman Catholic. Home: 2440 Bradenbaugh Rd White Hall MD 21161-9661 E-mail: fxr333@msn.com.

RADIN, ALEX, former association executive, consultant; b. Chattanooga, June 14, 1921; s. Joseph and Mollie (Pernat) R.; m. Sara Leah Gordon, Sept. 6, 1943 (dec. Nov. 20, 1964); children— Jay Jacob, William Gordon m. Carol Nita Schuman, Sept. 21, 1979 BA, U. Chattanooga, 1948. Reporter Chattanooga Times, Chattanooga, 1938-42; adminstrv. asst. Office of Price Adminstrn., Washington, 1942-43; adminstrv. analyst Dept. of State, 1945-48; asst. to gen. mgr. Am. Pub. Power Assn., 1948-51, exec. dir., 1951-86; pres. Radin & Assocs. Inc., 1986—. Cons. U.S. Senate Com. on Interior and Insular Affairs, Washington, 1959; mem. exec. com. Am. Nuclear Energy Coun., Washington, 1973-88; v.p. Consumer Fedn. Am., Washington, 1978-86; mem. So. States Energy Bd.'s Adv. Com. on TVA, 1986-87; chmn. Monitored Retrievable Storage Rev. Commn., 1988-89; rep., sec. U.S. Dept. Energy, Independent Mgmt. and Fin. Rev. of Yucca Mt. (Nev.) Project, 1994-95; mem. adv. bd. Ford Found. Energy Policy Project, 1973-74; bd. dirs. Consumer Energy Coun. Am., 1999—. Columnist, Pub. Power Mag.; contbr. articles to newspapers and mags. Mem. adv. bd. Dance Theatre of Harlem, N.Y.C., 1985—. Recipient Leland Olds award Western States Water and Power Consumers Conf., 1970, Philip Hart Disting. Consumer Svc. award Consumer Fedn. Am., 1985, Alex Radin Disting. Svc. award Am. Pub. Power Assn., 1986, named Disting. Alumnus of 2001 U. Tenn. Chattanooga, 2001. Mem. Alpha Soc. Clubs: Nat. Press. Democrat. Jewish. Avocations: photography; music; art; hiking. Home: 2510 Virginia Ave NW Apt 610N Washington DC 20037-1904 Office: Radin & Assocs Inc Ste 609 2510 Virginia Ave NW Washington DC 20037-1904 E-mail: alexradin@aol.com.

RADIN, BERYL AVIS, public administration and policy educator; b. Aberdeen, S.D., Nov. 15, 1936; d. Norman and Sophie (Edelman) R. BA, Antioch Coll., 1958; MA, U. Minn., 1963; PhD, U. Calif., Berkeley, 1973. Asst. prof. LBJ Sch. of Pub. affairs U. Tex., Austin, 1973-77; prof. pub. adminstrn. Washington Pub. Affairs Ctr., U. So. Calif., 1978-94, dir., 1982-85; prof. pub. adminstrn. and policy SUNY, Albany, 1994—2001; prof. govt. and pub. adminstrn. U. Balt., 2002—. Vis. prof. Fudan U., Shanghai, China, 1985; vis. fellow pub. policy program The Australian Nat. U., Canberra, 1985, 86, 88, 93; vis. prof. Grad. Sch. Pub. Policy, U. Calif., Berkeley, 1987; Fulbright lectr. to India, Indian Inst. Pub. Adminstrn., New Delhi, 1990; speaker, conf. presenter in field; cons. to numerous govt. agys. and govts.; cons. Office Asst. Sec. for Mgmt. and Budget, HHS. Author: Implementation, Change and The Federal Bureaucracy: School Desegretation Policy in HEW (1964-68), 1977, Linkages Between Civil Rights Enforcement and Operating Programs, 1980, Evaluation of the Planning Requirements Reform Demonstration Project, 1981; co-author: New Governance For Rural America: Creating Intergovernmental Partnerships, 1996, The Politics of Federal Reorganization: Creating the U.S. Department of Education, 1988, Serving Children and Families Effectively: How the Past Can Help Chart the Future, 1991, Beyond Machiavelli: Policy Analysis Comes of Age, 2000, The Accountable Juggler, 2002; contbr. chpts. to books and articles to jours. Asst. info. officer U.S. Commn. on Civil Right, 1963-65; policy analyst SSI Study Group, Social Security Adminstrn., 1975; sr. policy analyst Office of Asst. Sec. for Planning and Evaluation, 1977-78, Pres.'s Reorganization Project, Office of Mgmt. and Budget, 1978; asst. edn. dir. Phila. Joint Bd., Amalgamated Clothing Workers of Am., 1960-62; cons. Nat. Urban League, Ford Found., The Urban Inst., Nat. Urban Coalition, Civil Rights Dept., Survey of Race Rels. in Britain. Mem. ASPA (program com. 1993, bd. dirs. Nat. Capital Area chpt. 1983-85), Nat. Acad. Pub. Adminstrn., Assn. Pub. Policy Analysis and Mgmt. (program com. 1991, vice chair program com. 1992, pres. 1995-97), Am. Polit. Sci. Assn. (chair pub. adminstrn. program com. 1992, chair Gaus lecture com. 1994), Nat. Assn. Schs. Pub. Affairs and Adminstrn. (speaker 1988, mem. stds. com. 1982-85), Nat. Commn. on Poverty, Am. Jewish Congress, Ctr. for Women Policy Studies. Office: U Balt Sch Pub Affairs 1304 St Paul St Baltimore MD 21202

RADIN, CECILE HOROWITZ, artist; b. Worcester, Mass., June 10, 1904; d. Jacob and Jeanne (Bloch) Horowitz; m. Morris J. Radin, Apr. 10, 1932; children: Harley, Robert. Student, Worcester Art Mus., 1922-23, Boston Mus. Sch. Fine Arts, 1923-27. One-woman show U. Hartford (Conn.) Lincoln Theater, 1994; exhibited in group shows Wadsworth Atheneum, Hartford,1930, Conn. Acad. Fine Arts, Hartford, 1931, Grand Central Galleries, N.Y.C., 1931, Ind. Artists Boston, 1931, Worcester Mus. Fine Arts, 1933, New Britain (Conn.) Mus., 1962 (portrait prize), West Hartford Art League, 1972, 75, Essex (Conn.) Art Assn. Gallery, 1976, John Slade Mus., New Haven, 1977, Slater Meml. Mus., Norwich, Conn., 1979, 83, Temple Beth-El, West Hartford, 1984, Conn. Art Festival, Hartford, Northwestern C.C., Winsted, Atria Gallery, Hartford, 1987. Mem. Conn. Acad. Fine Arts, Women in Art (charter), West Hartford Art League, Salmagundi Club. Home: 781 Farmington Ave West Hartford CT 06119-1673

RADIN, SAM, lawyer, estate planner; b. N.Y.C., Aug. 1, 1951; s. Clarence and Marjorie (Rembar) R.; m. Pamela Anderson, Sept. 13, 1981; children: Clarence Anderson, Elizabeth Rebecca. BA, Columbia U., 1973; JD, Boston U., 1976. Bar: N.J. 1976, U.S. Dist. Ct. N.J. 1976, N.Y. 1978, U.S. Dist. Ct. (so. dist.) N.Y. 1978, U.S. Ct. Appeals (D.C. cir.) 1978, U.S. Supreme Ct. 1980. Assoc. Burns, Van Kirk, N.Y.C., 1976-79, Lovejoy Wasson successor to Burns, Van Kirk, N.Y.C., 1979-80; pvt. practice, 1980-84; v.p., gen. counsel Nat. Madison Group, Inc., 1984-99, pres., 1999—. Contbg. author: Executive Compensation Answer Book, 1998; contbg. author, editor: Estate and Retirement Planning Answer Book, 1999; also articles. Bd. dirs. Student Athletes Inc., N.Y.C., 1992-98, Westchester Conservatory Music, White Plains, N.Y., 1995-97; trustee Payomet Performing Arts Charitable Trust, 1999—, Nat. Lighthouse Ctr. and Mus., 2000—, pres., 2001—. Recipient Nathan Burkan Meml. prize ASCAP, 1975. Mem. ABA (subcom. on life ins. tax sect. 1996—), N.Y. State Bar Assn., Assn. Bar City N.Y., Assn. Advanced Life Underwriting, Comm. on Estate Taxation. Avocations: salt water fly fishing, collecting books, skiing, running. Home: 71 Greenacres Ave Scarsdale NY 10583-1442 Office: Nat Madison Group Inc 261 Madison Ave New York NY 10016-2401 E-mail: sradin@nationalmadison.com.

RADIN, SHULAMITH, materials engineer; b. Moscow, June 25, 1948; came to U.S., 1983; d. Samuel and Debora (Lifshist) Ryzhak; m. Alexander Radin, Aug. 1, 1970; 1 child, Michael. MD in Merallurgy, Moscow U. Steel & Alloys, 1969; PhD in Materials Sci., Nat. Inst. Aerocraft Materials, 1972. Sr. rsch. engr. All-Nat. Inst. Aericraft Materials, Moscow, 1972-75, project dir., 1975-80; rsch. assoc., sr. investigator U. Pa., Phila., 1986—. Inventor in field. Mem. Soc. Biomaterials.

RADKE, CLAYTON J. chemical engineer, educator; b. Bremerton, Wash., Aug. 3, 1944; s. Rynhold Johannes and Inez Margaret Radke; m. Darlene Madge Radke, May 23, 1968; children: Alyssa Jeaneen, Jonathan Windsor. BSChemE, U. Wash., 1966; PhDChemE, U. Calif., Berkeley, 1971. NSF overseas postdoctoral fellow U. Bristol, Eng., 1971-73; asst. prof. Pa. State U., University Park, 1973-76, U. Calif., Berkeley, 1976-81, assoc. prof., 1981-84, prof., 1984—. On sabbatical chem. engring. U. Minn., Mpls., 1982-83, MIT, Cambridge, Mass., spring 1999. Contbr. more than 160 articles to profl. jours. including Jour. Colloid and Interface Sci., Jour. Chem. Physics, Colloids and Surfaces, among others. Bd. dirs. The New Coll., Berkeley, Calif., 1999—. Mem.: AIChE (Chem. Engring. Excellence Acad. Tchg. award 1993—94), Internat. Soc. for Contact Lens Rsch., Assn. for Rsch. in Vision and Ophthalmology, Internat. Union Pure and Applied Chemistry, Soc. Petroleum Engring., Am. Chem. Soc. (councilor colloid divsn. 2001—). Office: U Calif Berkeley Dept Chem Engring 201 Gilman Hall Berkeley CA 94720-1472 E-mail: radke@cchem.berkeley.edu.

RADKE, DALE LEE, religious organization administrator, deacon, editor, pastor; b. Sheboygan, Wis., July 9, 1933; s. Alfred and Viola (Aschenbach) R.; m. Diane Jean Simon, Aug. 16, 1958; children: Laura Lee, Jay Ryan. AA, Concordia Wis., 1954. Store mgr. Badger Paint Stores, Milw., 1958-65; with sales dept. Hilton Co., Butler, 1965-67; with sales and customer service depts. Century Hardware, Milw., 1967-72; exec. dir. Greater Milw. Fedn. Luth. Chs. Mo. Synod, 1973-87, 90-92; exec. dir. Luth. of Wis., 1982-89; Wis. affiliate Am. Heart Assn., 1989; editor Badger Luth. newspaper, 1990-92; pastor Savior Luth. Ch.-AFLC. CEO Creative Concepts Comm. and Servant of the Savior; voice of God-Love Prayer Telephone, 1973—. Editor The Milw. Luth., 1982-89, South Wis. Dist. News, 1992-93; contbr. articles to clown mags. Pastor Luth. Free Ch.; chaplain Milw. Fire Dept.; chaplain Milwaukee County Sheriff's Dept., Wis. State Fair, BSA Southeastern Wis.; mem. Milw. Citizenship Commn., 1960-63; mem. religious leaders divsn. Nat. Safety Coun., Chgo., 1980-91, bd. dirs., 1987-89; mem. Milw. Safety Commn., 1970—; chair Park Watch; mem., comty. svc. dir. Nat. Safety Coun., 1990—; pres. Capital W. Neighborhood Assn.; interim dir. MADD, Milw., 1997-99; pres. Met. Milw. Civic Alliance Bd., 1997—; on-call chaplain Milw. Police Dept. Mem. Nat. Inst. Bus. and Indsl. Chaplains, Fire Fighters for Christ, Fed. Fire

Chaplains, Milw. Press Club, Milw. Jaycees (Outstanding Young Man of Yr. 1962), Variety Club, Kiwanis, various clown orgns. Lutheran. Home: 6410 W Melvina St Milwaukee WI 53216-2129 Office: PO Box 18024 Milwaukee WI 53218-0024 Fax: 414-461-7505.

RADKE, RODNEY OWEN, agricultural research executive, consultant; b. Ripon, Wis., Feb. 5, 1942; s. Edward Ludwig and Vera Ione (Phillips) R.; m. Jean Marie Rutsch, Sept. 1, 1963; children: Cheryl Lynn, Lisa Diane, Daniel E. BS, U. Wis., 1963, MS, 1965, PhD, 1967. Rsch. scientist Monsanto Agrl. Co., St. Louis, 1969-75, sr. rsch. group leader, 1975-79, rsch. mgr., 1979-81, mgr. rsch., 1981-93; pvt. practice cons., 1993—2002; ret., 2002—. Contbr. articles to profl. jours.; patentee in field. Served to capt. U.S. Army, 1967-69. Mem. Weed Sci. Soc. Am., North Ctrl. Weed Sci. Soc. Lutheran. Avocations: power boating, soccer, gardening, woodshop. Home and Office: 1119 Grand Prix Dr Saint Charles MO 63303-6313

RADKOWSKY, KAREN, advertising research specialist; b. Washington, Nov. 8, 1957; d. Lawrence and Florence (Kramer) R. BA, Columbia U., 1979. Rsch. analyst Cosmair, Inc., N.Y.C., 1979-82, sr. rsch. analyst, 1982-84; asst. rsch. mgr. Am. Express Co., 1984-85; account rsch. mgr. BBDO, Inc., 1985-88, v.p., assoc. rsch. dir., 1988-94, sr. v.p., assoc. rsch. dir., 1994-95; sr. v.p., rsch. dir. BBDO N.Y., 1995-99; sr. ptnr., dir. consumer rsch. Ogilvy & Mather, 2000—. Bd. dirs. Advt. RSch. Found., 2001—. E-mail: karen.radkowsky@ogilvy.com.

RADLAUER, PATRICIA THOMASINE, designer; b. N.Y.C., Feb. 15, 1940; d. John Joseph and Lucinda Mary (Hinphy) McLoughlin; m. David Max Radlauer, Oct. 6, 1959; children: Mark Alfred, Daniel John. Student Plaza Bus. Sch., 1956-57, New Sch. Social Research, 1957, Palau Studios, 1968-70, Suffolk Community Coll., 1970-72. Legal sec. Giamo & Nicolossi, N.Y.C., 1956; exec. sec. World Wide Auto Corp., N.Y.C., 1956-59; advt. and display Sterns, N.Y.C., 1959-62; pres. Interiors by Patricia, Inc., Centerport, N.Y., 1967-88; designer Designers Showcase, Nassau County, 1981-82. Committeeman Suffolk County Liberal Party, 1975. Mem. Am. Soc. Interior Designers (assoc.), Nat. Assn. Women in Constrn. Office: Interiors by Patricia Inc 8 Fort Salonga Rd Rt 25A Centerport NY 11721

RADLAUER, STEVE, freelance writer, journalist, producer, film producer; b. N.Y.C., Nov. 2, 1948; s. Marvin and Gladys (Steltzer) R.; m. Kerry K. Willis, June 7, 1985; 1 child, Kate. Student, Union Coll., Schenectady, N.Y.; BS, U. State of N.Y. Dir. A-Space, Toronto, Ont., Can., 1971-73; co-owner The Ritz Cafe, 1973-77; program dir. Dry Salvages Film Group, N.Y.C., 1978-85. Freelance writer articles for various pubs. incl. N.Y. Mag., Spy, Esquire, N.Y. Times, L.A. Times; co-author: Dan Quayle: Airhead Apparent, 1992, Special Moments, 1984, The Historic Shops and Restaurants of New York, 2002; editor-in-chief (online news comedy site) Today's Other News on American Online, 1996. Mem. Authors Guild. E-mail: steve@radz.org.

RADLER, FRANKLIN DAVID, publishing holding company executive; b. Montreal, Que., Can., June 3, 1942; m. Rona Lassner, Mar. 26, 1972; children: Melanie, Melissa. MBA, Queen's U., Can., 1967. Pres., chief oper. officer, dir. Hollinger Inc., Toronto; exec. v.p. Argus Corp. Ltd.; co-chair, publ. Chgo. Sun-Times, 1995—. Chmn. Am. Pub. Co., Jerusalem Post Ltd., Palestine Post Ltd. Office: Chgo Sun-Times 401 N Wabash Ave Chicago IL 60611-5642*

RADLER, MONTE PHILIP, lawyer; b. Torrington, Conn., Feb. 25, 1952; s. Albert Gabriel and Hazel Dawn (Schneider) Radler; m. Christine Anne Gatti, Aug. 22, 1982; children: Matthew Abraham Idan, Ethan Alexander. BA, Northwestern U., 1974; JD, U. Conn., 1978; MS, So. Conn. State, 1985. Bar: Conn. 1979, U.S. Dist. Ct. 1980, U.S. Supreme Ct. 1993. Fund raiser Nat. Assn. March of Dimes, Chgo., 1974-75; assoc. Albert E. Goring, Jr., P.C., Torrington, 1979-80, Goldman & Rosen, P.C., Bridgeport, 1980-82, McHugh & McKeon, P.C., Westport, 1982-85; sr. asst. pub. defender State of Conn., Stamford, 1985-98, supr. asst. pub. defender, 1998-2000, chief psychiat. def. unit, 2000—. Office: State of Conn Pub Defenders Office Psychiat Def Unit CVH PO Box 351 Middletown CT 06457-7023

RADMER, MICHAEL JOHN, lawyer, educator; b. Wisconsin Rapids, Wis., Apr. 28, 1945; s. Donald Richard and Thelma Loretta (Donahue) R.; children from previous marriage: Christina Nicole, Ryan Michael; m. Laurie J. Anshus, Dec. 22, 1983; 1 child, Michael John BS, Northwestern U., Evanston, Ill., 1967; JD, Harvard U., 1970. Bar: Minn. 1970. Assoc. Dorsey & Whitney, Mpls., 1970-75, ptnr., 1976—. Lectr. law Hamline U. Law Sch., St. Paul, 1981-84; gen. counsel, rep., sec. 163 federally registered investment cos., Mpls. and St. Paul, 1977—. Contbr. articles to legal jours. Active legal work Hennepin County Legal Advice Clinic, Mpls., 1971—. Mem. ABA, Minn. Bar Assn., Hennepin County Bar Assn. Clubs: Mpls. Athletic. Home: 4329 E Lake Harriet Pky Minneapolis MN 55409-1725 Office: Dorsey & Whitney 50 South 6th St Ste 1500 Minneapolis MN 55402 *A key to a successful and happy life is achieving a balance. Intellectual, academic and vocational goals are important, but their pursuit should be balanced with ample time spent with family and friends, travel and enjoying reading, music, art and sports. Don't be afraid to try something new; realize that education should be a lifelong pursuit. Much frustration can be avoided by realizing that life is full of trade-offs. You can't experience the joy of raising children and have the complete freedom of the child-free. Finally, while you should strive for perfection, be content with less. We are only human, and live in an imperfect, yet wonderful, world.*

RADNER, ROY, economist, educator, researcher; b. Chgo., June 29, 1927; s. Samuel and Ella (Kulansky) R.; m. Virginia L. Honoski, July 26, 1949 (dec. Apr. 1976); children: Hilary A., Erica H. (dec.), Amy E., Ephraim L.; m. Charlotte Virginia Kuh, Jan. 22, 1978. PhB with honors, U. Chgo, 1945, BS in Math., 1950, MS in Math., 1951, PhD in Math. Stats., 1956. Rsch. asst. Cowles Commn. for Rsch. in Econs. U. Chgo., 1951, rsch. assoc., 1951-54, asst. prof., 1954-55; mem. Cowles Found. for Rsch. in Econs. Yale U., New Haven, 1955-57, asst. prof. econs., 1955-57; assoc. prof. econs. and stats. U. Calif., Berkeley, 1957-61, prof. econs. and stats., 1961-79, chmn. dept. econs., 1966-69; Taussig prof. econs. Harvard U., Cambridge, Mass., 1977-78, vis. prof. Kennedy Sch. Govt., 1978-79; mem. tech. staff AT&T Bell Labs, Murray Hill, N.J., 1979-84, disting. mem. tech. staff, 1985-95; rsch. prof. econs. NYU, N.Y.C., 1983-95, prof. econs. and info. sys., 1995-96, L.N. Stern Sch. prof. bus., 1996—. Mem. com. on fundamental rsch. relevant to edn. NRC-NAS, 1976-77, mem. commn. on human resources, 1976-79; mem. assembly of behavioral and social scis. NRC, 1979-82, mem. com. on risk and decision making, 1980-81, mem. working group on basic rsch. in behavioral and social scis., 1985-86, mem. com. on info. tech. workforce, 1999-2000, mem. com. on geophys. and environ. data, 2001--; mem. panel on contingent valuation methology NOAA, U.S. Dept. Commerce, 1992-93; mem. steering com. Enjeux et Procedures de Decentralization Commisariat du Plan, Paris, 1992-95; mem. com. on Prevention of Nuclear War; mem. com. on Info. Tech. workforce NRC; also various other profl. coms., bds., panels. Author: (books, monographs) Notes on Theory of Economic Planning, 1963, (with D. Jorgenson and J.J. McCall) Optimal Replacement Policy, 1967, (with J. Marshack) Economic Theory of Teams, 1972, (with L.S. Miller) Demand and Supply in U.S. Higher Education, 1975, (with C.V. Kuh) Mathematicians in Academia, 1980; also articles on econ. theory, orgn. theory, econs. of edn.; co-editor: Decision and Organization, 1972, Education as an Industry, 1976, Information, Incentives and Economic Mechanisms, 1987, Perspectives on Deterrence, 1989, Bargaining with Incomplete Information, 1992; assoc. editor Mgmt. Sci., 1959-70, Econometrica, 1961-68, Jour. Econ. Theory, 1968—, Am. Econ. Rev., 1970-82, Games and Econ. Behavior, Econ. Theory, Rev. Econ. Design, Rev. Acctg. Studies. 2d lt. U.S. Army, 1945-48, PTO. William Cook scholar U. Chgo., 1944-45; fellow Ctr. Advanced Study in Behavioral Scis., Stanford, Calif., 1955-56, Guggenheim Found. fellow, 1961-62, 65-66, overseas fellow Churchill Coll., Cambridge U., Eng., 1969-70, 89. Fellow AAAS (disting. fellow), Econometric Soc. (v.p. 1970-72, pres. 1972-73), Am. Acad. Arts and Scis., Am. Econ. Assn. (disting. fellow); mem. NAS (chair econ. sect. 1994-97), Inst. Math. Stats. Avocations: music, hiking, cross-country skiing. Home: 3203 Davenport St NW Washington DC 20008-2211 Office: Stern Sch Business NYU KMC 8-87 44 W 4th St New York NY 10012-1126 E-mail: rradner@stern.nyu.edu.

RADNER, SIDNEY HOLLIS, retired rug company executive; b. Holyoke, Mass., Dec. 8, 1919; s. William I. Radner; m. Helen Jane Cohen, Dec. 12, 1946; children: William Marc, Richard Scott. Student, Yale U., 1941. Ret. pres. Am. Rug Co., Holyoke. Lectr., cons., investigator on crooked gambling to U.S. Armed Forces, FBI, Govt. of Can., state and mcpl. police squads; dir. Houdini Magical Hall of Fame, Niagara Falls, Ont., Can.; dir., organizer Ann. Ofcl. Houdini Seance; cons. to Houdini movie T.N.T., 1998. Author: Radner on Poker, Radner on Dice, Radner on Roulette and Casino Games, How to Detect Card Sharks; contbr. articles to profl. jours.; appeared in 1st TV series Turn of A Card, 1953, BBC Omnibus: Houdini, 1971, CNN, 1993-94, Tonight Show, 1956, Today Show, Merv Griffin Show, CNBC, PBS, CBC, In Search Of..., 1st TV series exposing crooked gambling techniques, 1956; cons., major participant Houdini TV spl. A&E, 1996, Discovery Channel documentary, 1997 (Telly award 1997); featured in Can. Discovery TV series on magic, 1998, History TV, Houdini segment, 2000; featured in travel TV spl., 2001; appeared in E network Houdini documentary, 1998; featured 2000 History Channel TV. Past pres. Holyoke C. of C.; co-founder Volleyball Hall of Fame; past bd. dirs. Greater Springfield (Mass.) Better Bus. Bur.; hon. curator, dir. Houdini Hist. Ctr., Appleton, Wis. Served with criminal investigation divsn. U S. Army, 1942-46. Inducted into Volleyball Hall of Fame, 1999. Mem. Soc. Am. Magicians (occult investigation com.), Internat. Brotherhood Magicians, Magic Circle London (mem. Inner Magic Circle), Magicians Guild (charter), Magic Collector's Assn. (charter, Honor award 1992), Houdini Club Wis. (hon.), Nat. Assn. Bunco Investigators, Profls. Against Confidence Crime, Acad. Magical Arts, Soc. Osaris (hon. mem.), China-Burma-India Vets. Assn. (life), Rotary, Masons, Shriners. Jewish. Home: 1050 Northampton St Holyoke MA 01040-1321 also: 3200 S Ocean Blvd 203C Palm Beach FL 33480 Office: 1594 Dwight St Holyoke MA 01040-2356

RADNOR, ALAN T. lawyer; b. Cleve., Mar. 10, 1946; s. Robert Clark and Rose (Chester) R.; m. Carol Sue Hirsch, June 22, 1969; children: Melanie, Joshua, Joanna. BA, Kenyon Coll., 1967; MS in Anatomy, Ohio State U., 1969, JD, 1972. Bar: Ohio 1972. Ptnr. Vorys, Sater, Seymour & Pease, Columbus, Ohio, 1972—. Adj. prof. law Ohio State U., Columbus, 1979-99. Contbr. articles to profl. jours. Bd. dirs., trustee Congregation Tifereth Israel, Columbus, 1975—, pres., 1985-87; trustee Columbus Mus. Art, 1995-98. Named Boss or Yr., Columbus Assn. Legal Secs., 1983. Fellow Am. Coll. Trial Lawyers; mem. ABA, Ohio State Bar Assn., Columbus Bar Assn., Def. Rsch. Inst., Internat. Assn. Def. Counsel. Avocations: reading, sculpture. Home: 400 S Columbia Ave Columbus OH 43209-1629 Office: Vorys Sater Seymour & Pease 52 E Gay St PO Box 1008 Columbus OH 43216-1008

RADOCHA, RICHARD FRANCIS, plastic surgeon; b. Coaldale, Pa., Feb. 3, 1953; MD, Hahnemann U., 1979. Diplomate Am. Bd. Surgery. Intern U. South Fla., Tampa, 1979-80, resident in gen. surgery, 1980-84; resident in plastic surgery Duke U., 1985-86; fellow in hand surgery U. Louisville, 1985; staff Gessler Clin., P.A., Winter Haven, 1985—, Winter Haven (Fla.) Hosp., 1987, Winter Haven Ambulatory Surgery Ctr., 1998, Bartow (Fla.) Meml. Hosp., 1989. Mem. AMA, Am. Coll. Surgeons, Am. Soc. Plastic and Reconstructive Surgeons, Fla. Med. Assn., Polk County Med. Assn., Southea. Soc. Plastic and Reconstructive Surgeons, Fla. Soc. Plastic Reconstructive Surgeons, Am. Soc. Aesthetic Plastic Surgeons. Home: 1225 Cypress Pt E Winter Haven FL 33884-3027 Office: Gessler Clinic PA 635 1st St N Winter Haven FL 33881-4191

RADOCK, MICHAEL, foundation executive; b. Belle Vernon, Pa., July 17, 1917; s. Nicholas M. and Pauline (Radich) R.; m. Helen Adelaide Hower, Sept. 2, 1944; children: Robert Hower, William Michael. AB magna cum laude, Westminster Coll., New Wilmington, Pa., 1942, LittD (hon.), 1965; MS in Journalism, Northwestern U., 1946; postgrad., Case Western Res. U., 1950-52. Reporter Fayette City (Pa.) Jour., 1937-39; corr. for Pa. newspapers, 1937-39; reporter, sports editor Charleroi (Pa.) Daily Mail, 1942; dir. news bur., asst. prof. journalism Westminster Coll., 1942-45; dir. pub. relations, prof. journalism Kent (Ohio) State U., 1945-53; with corp. pub. relations Ford Motor Co., Dearborn, Mich., 1953-61; established Inst. for Pub. Rels. Kent (Ohio) State U., 1947; v.p. univ. relations, prof. journalism U. Mich., Ann Arbor, 1961-81; sr. v.p. devel. and univ. relations, prof. journalism U. So. Calif., Los Angeles, 1981-82; v.p. resource devel. Aspen Inst. Humanistic Studies, N.Y.C., 1982-83; advisor to pres. C.S. Mott Found., Flint, Mich., 1983-90, cons., 1990—. Mem. faculty Harvard U. Inst. in Ednl. Mgmt., 1972, 73, Williamsburg Devel. Inst., 1979-81; vis. prof. journalism U. Wyo., Laramie, 1952, U. Kent, Canterbury, Eng., 1989; trustee Westminster Coll., 1972-82; mem. adv. bd. Chronicle of Non-Profit Enterprise, 1990—. Contbr. Handbook of Institutional Advancement, 1977, (books) Lesly's Public Relations Handbook, 1978, Public Relations Career Directory, 1987, 88, 89, 93, 95, Lesly's Handbook of Public Relations and Communications, 1990. Mem. Fulbright Bd. Fgn. Scholarships, Washington, 1972-74; mem. exec. bd. U. Mich., 1979-81, mem. bd. in control of intracollegiate athletics, 1961-81; trustee Glacier Hills Retirement Ctr., Ann Arbor, 1988-93, Ann Arbor Area Cmty. Found., 1989-92, Mich. Hist. Ctr. Found., 1990—; chmn. White House Sci. and Tech. Adv. Com. on Black Colls., Washington, 1986-88. Recipient Disting. Service award Kent State U., 1965, Frank Ashmore award for disting. service to edn. Am. Coll. Pub. Relations Assn., 1968-69; Disting. Service award for leadership in institutional advancement for minority colls. and univs., 1980. Fellow Pub. Rels. Soc. Am. (accredited); mem. Inst. for Pub. Rels. Rsch. and Edn. (bd. trustees 1980-84), Soc. of Profl. Journalists, Nat. Soc. Fund Raising Execs., Higher Edn. Roundtable. Republican. Presbyterian. Home: 1200 Earhart Rd # 344 Ann Arbor MI 48105-2768

RADOFF, LEONARD IRVING, librarian, consultant; b. Houston, Jan. 9, 1927; s. Morris Aaron and Jenny (Goldberg) R.; m. Lisel Ruth Ephraim, July 25, 1953; 1 child, Lesley Radoff Rappaport BA, Rice U., Houston, 1949; M.L.S., U. Tex., Austin, 1965. Cert. secondary sch. tchr., Tex. Tchr. math Aldine Ind. Sch. Dist., Houston, 1959-61, sch. librarian, 1961-63; head pub. services Abilene Pub. Library, Tex., 1964-65; library dir. Pasadena Pub. Library, 1966-70; chief br. services Houston Pub. Library, 1971-92, ret., 1992; library bldg. cons. Houston, 1975—. Treas. Literacy Vol. Am., Houston, 1984-85; mem. Northside Interests, Houston, 1982-85. Served with USN, 1945-46 Hoenthal scholar, 1948 Mem. Tex. Library Assn., ALA, Freedom to Read Found., Houston Great Books Council (leader trainer 1953-59, pres. 1967-69) Avocations: tutoring; listening to music; stamp collecting. Home: 4013 Gano St Houston TX 77009-4119

RADOGNO, JOSEPH ANTHONY, lawyer; b. Chgo., Dec. 7, 1958; s. Nunzio Concetto and Bernice M. Radogno; m. Randi Ellen Weinberg, Sept. 28, 1991; 1 child, Celestina Nicole. BA, U. Ill., 1980; JD, Ill. Inst. Tech., 1984. Bar: Ill. 1984. Counsel Allstate Ins. Co., Northbrook, Ill., 1989—.

RADON, JENIK RICHARD, lawyer; b. Berlin, Jan. 14, 1946; came to U.S., 1951, naturalized, 1956; s. Louis and Irmgard (Hinz) R.; m. Heidi B. Duerbeck, June 10, 1971 (dec. Sept. 1999); 1 child, Kaara H.D. BA, Columbia Coll., 1967; MCP, U. Calif., Berkeley, 1971; JD, Stanford U., Berkeley, 1971. Bar: Calif. 1972, N.Y. 1975, U.S. Ct. Appeals (2d cir.) 1975, U.S. Dist. Ct. (so. dist.) N.Y. 1975. Atty. Radon & Ishizumi, N.Y.C., Berlin and Tokyo, 1981—; counsel Walter, Conston, Alexander & Green, N.Y.C., 1991—, ptnr., 2000. Lectr. Polish Acad. Scis., 1980, Tokyo Arbitration Assn., 1983, Japan External Trade Orgn., 1983, 86, Japan Mgmt. Assn., 1983, 90, Japan Inst. Internat. Bus. Law, 1983-84, Va. Ctr. World Trade, 1985, UN Indsl. Devel. Orgn., Warsaw, 1987, Wichita World Trade Coun., 1987, Inst. Nat. Economy of Poland, 1987, Hungarian Econ. Roundtable, 1987, Tallinn, 1988, USSR Com. on Sci. and Tech., 1988, USSR Fgn. Trade Ministry, 1988, Tallinn Tech. Inst., 1988, Tartu State U., 1988, U. Ottawa, 1988-89, Palm Beach World Trade Coun., 1988, Fla. Atlantic U., 1988, Bus. Assn. Latin Am. Studies, 1989—, Assn. France-Poland, 1989, Russian and East European Studies Inst. Stanford U., 1989, Ukrainian Profl. Assn. N.Y. and N.J., 1989, Columbia U. Harriman Inst., 1989, Inst. East-West Security Studies, 1989, Friedrich-Schiller U. Jena, East Germany, 1990, East European Inst. Free U. Berlin, numerous others; bd. dirs. Gland Pharma Ltd., India, 1996—, HTM Sport, Estonia, 1993—; pub. Baltic Rev., 1993—, City Paper (Baltic), 1993—; mem. exec. com. Vetter Group, Germany; adj. mem. faculty/lectr. Stanford Sch. of Law, 2000—, Stanford Bus. Sch., 2000-02, Columbia Sch. Internat. Pub. Affairs, 2002--. Editor-in-chief Stanford Jour. Internat. Studies, 1970-71; contbr. The International Acquisitions Handbook, 1987, Negotiating and Financing Joint Ventures Abroad, 1989, How to Form and Manage Successful Strategic Alliances, 1990, Risks Management in International Business, 1991, Comrade Goes Private, 1992, Investing in Reform, 1991, Fordham Internat. Law Jour., 1996, various jours. in U.S., Germany, Canada. Active Am. Coun. on Germany, N.Y.C., 1978—; vice-chmn. U.S.-Polish Econ. Coun., 1989-93; mem. exec. com. Afghanistan Relief Com., N.Y.C., 1980-95; bd. dirs. Columbia Coll. Alumni Assn., 1988-92, nat. coun., 1996-98, Freedom Medicine, 1987-94, chmn., 1989-94; trustee Direct Relief Internat., Santa Barbara, Calif., 1987-89; founder and dir. Eesti and Eurasian Fellowship of Columbia U., 1990—; profl. Harriman Inst., 1993—; advisor Estonian Ministry of Economy, Reform and Justice, 1991-95; adv. Prime Min. of Crimea, Ukraine, 1994-95; advisor to Parliament Republic of Georgia, 1996-98, to Pres. of Georgia, 1999—; advisor Min. of Fin. of Georgia, 1998—, Georgian Internat. Oil Corp., 1998—; chmn. Estonian-Am. C. of C., 1990-93, Deutsche Stiftung fuer internationale rechtliche Zusammenarbeit, Estonia Commn., Beirat, 1992-94. Recipient Order of Honor award Republic of Georgia, 2000. Mem. ABA, Asia-Pacific Lawyers Assn., German-Am. Law Assn. Roman Catholic. Office: Radon & Ishizumi 269 W 71st St New York NY 10023-3701

RADOSH, MARY, sociology educator; b. Corning, N.Y., Feb. 11, 1953; d. James Elwin and Patricia O'Reilly Flannery; m. Jeffrey Radosh, May 27, 1978; children: Michael, Caitlin, Amy, Mary. BA, SUNY, Geneseo, 1976; MA, So. Ill. U., 1978, PhD, 1983. Asst. prof. sociology U. Minn., Morris, 1983-84; prof. sociology, dir. women's studies Western Ill. U., Macomb, 1984—. Author: Past, Present & Future of American Criminal Justice, 1996, Introduction to Criminology, 1999. Named Outstanding Working Woman of Ill., Bus. and Profl. Women, Chgo., 1992. Democrat. Unitarian Universalist. Home: 3201 W Adams Rd Macomb IL 61455-7754 Office: Western Ill Univ Dept Sociology Macomb IL 61455 also: RR 1 Macomb IL 61455-9801

RADOVITZKY, RAUL A. science educator, educator; b. Buenos Aires , Nov. 20, 1966; arrived in U.S., 1993; s. Roberto Radovitzky, Leticia Gerding; m. Flavia Cardarelli; children: Felipe, Benjamin. Grad. in civil. engring., U. Buenos Aires, 1991; PhD, Calif. Inst. Tech., 1998. Cert. civil engr., Argentina, 1991. Scientist Calif. Inst. Tech., Pasadena, 1998—2001; Charles Stark Draper asst. prof. aeronautics and astronautics MIT, Cambridge, 2001—. V.p. Simulation Techs., Inc. , La Canada, 1995—2001. Mem.: AIAA. Office: MIT 77 Massachusetts Ave Cambridge MA 02139 Personal E-mail: rapa@mit.edu. Business E-Mail: rapa@mit.edu.

RADTKE, DAWN ELEANOR, clinical social worker; b. Launceston, Tasmania, Australia, May 16, 1925; came to U.S., 1961; d. Harold Clyde and Thelma (Fenwick) Dridan; m. Donald G.E. Radtke, Jan. 3, 1970 (div. Jan. 1974). AM in Social Svcs., U. Chgo., 1966, AM in Sch. Social Svc. Adminstrn., 1968. Diplomate Am. Bd. Social Workers; diplomate in clin. social work NASW; lic. social worker. Tchr. South Australian Edn. Dept., Adelaide, 1946-50; dir. religious edn. Diocese of Adelaide, 1952-60, St. Mark's and St. Christopher's Chs., Milw., 1961-64; clin. social worker St. Michael's Hosp., 1968-70; pvt. practice, 1970-81, Fairhope and Mobile, Ala., 1982—. Co-author: Aging With Joy, 1988, From Worry to Wellness, 1990; columnist Dear Dawn Eleanor, 1982-86. Pres. Baldwin County Friends of Opera, Ala., 1990—; bd. dirs. Mobile Opera, Inc., 1990—. Fellow of the Maple Leaf, London, 1950-52; Nat. Coun. Episcopal Ch. fellow, 1964-66; U. Chgo. scholar, 1966-68. Mem. Acad. Cert. Social Workers (chair women's issues 1982-83, Lifetime Achievement award Ala. chpt. 1996), Am. Harp Soc. (treas. Cen. Gulf Coast chpt. 1989—), Ala. Soc. Clin. Social Work (treas. 1990-96). Avocation: travel. Home: 204 N Bayview St Fairhope AL 36532-2506 E-mail: ddradtke@aol.com.

RADTKE, RODNEY A. neurologist; b. Mendota, Ill., Mar. 11, 1956; s. Ernest John and Catherine Elizabeth R.; m. Sara Cullen Hushion, Aug. 29, 1987; children: Tyler, Justin, Lindsay. BS, Northwe. U., 1976, MD, 1980. Diplomate Am. Bd. Psychiatry and Neurology. From asst. to assoc. prof. medicine Duke U., Durham, N.C., 1986-99, prof. medicine, 1999—. Fellow Am. Acad. Neurology, Am. Clin. Neurophysiology Soc.; mem. Am. Bd. Clin. Neurophysiology (chmn. 1999—), Am. Epilepsy Soc., Epilepsy Found. (mem. profession adv. bd. coun. 1993—). Presbyterian. Office: Duke U Med Ctr Dumc 3678 Durham NC 27710-0001 E-mail: radtk002@mc.duke.edu.

RADUNSKY, ALEXANDER, designer, lighting; b. Moscow, Mar. 31, 1951; s. Victor and Maria (Rachmilevich) R.; m. Duka Bruni, Sept. 9, 1978; children: Lev, Vera. MS in Architecture, Moscow Inst. Architecture, 1975. Project architect Design Inst. Comml. Bldgs., Moscow, 1974-81; architect N.Y.C., 1981-84; lighting designer Howard Brandston Lighting Design, Inc., 1984-87; pres. Alexander Radunsky Design, Inc., 1987—. Lectr., critic Moscow Inst. Architecture, 1974-76. Mem. Internat. Assn. Lighting Designers (profl.), Illuminating Engring. Soc. N.Am. Avocations: photography, travel. Office: 160 5th Ave Ste 715 New York NY 10010-7003 E-mail: aradunsky@ardinc.net.

RADVIC, STEPHAN, international management consultant, linguist; b. Mar. 5, 1940; s. Melko and Theresa (Cini) MA in Internat. Mgmt., U. Tex.-Dallas, 1976. Profl. soccer player, 1963-65; CPA Arthur Young & Co., 1965-69; exec. asst. to Lamar Hunt, Hunt Oil Co., Dallas, 1969-73; v.p., controller, chief fin. officer, electronics group Rockwell Internat., London and Paris, 1973-79; v.p.-gen. mgr. Europe, United Technologies, Barcelona and Geneva, 1979-81; pres. Atlantic Group, Inc., Madeira Beach, Fla., 1981—; consulting firm specializing in offshore bus. devel. & multilingual negotiations; adj. prof. internat. mgmt. grad. sch. bus. U. Tampa, 1987-90; prof. internat. mgmt. Am. U. Rome, 1991-93; linguist with fluency in 7 languages, good comprehension of 4 others; mem. bd. dirs. various European corps.; head coach So. Meth. U., varsity soccer team, 1972; lectr. internat. corp. fin. grad. sch. U. Tex.-Dallas, 1976-77. Mem. AICPAs. Roman Catholic. Office: Atlantic Group Inc PO Box 1041 Noosa Heads Q4567 Australia

RADWAY, LAURENCE INGRAM, political science educator; b. Staten Island, N.Y., Feb. 2, 1919; s. Frederick and Dorothy (Segall) R.; m. Patricia Ann Headland, Aug. 20, 1949; children: Robert Russell, Carol Sinclair, Michael Porter, Deborah Brooke. BS, Harvard U., 1940, MA, 1948, PhD, 1950; M.P.A., U. Minn., 1943; MA (hon.), Dartmouth, 1959. Jr. economist OPA, 1941; intern U.S. Bur. Budget, 1941-42, Nat. Inst. Pub. Affairs, 1941-42; teaching fellow govt. dept. Harvard U., 1946-50; instr. govt. dept. Dartmouth U., 1950-52, asst. prof., 1952-57, assoc. prof., 1957-58, prof., 1958—, chmn. dept., 1959-62, 70-72, 77-80, dir. Comparative Studies Ctr., 1963-68. Cons. ODM, 1952; prof. Nat. War Coll., 1962-63; civilian aide to sec. army, 1962-70; mem. N.H. Ho. Reps., 1968-72 Author: (with John W. Masland) Soldiers and Scholars, 1957, Military Behavior in International Organizations, 1962, Foreign Policy and National Defense, 1969. Chmn. Hanover Democratic Com., 1954-56; mem. N.H. Dem. Com., 1958-60, chmn. Platform Conf., 1959, 60, chmn., 1975-77; chmn. Grafton County Dem. Com., 1956-58; mem. Dem. Nat. Com., 1975-77; Bd. dirs. N.H. World Affairs Council, 1955-81; bd. advisers Indsl. Coll. Armed Forces, 1958-62. Served from pvt. to capt., Transp. Corps AUS, 1943-46. Pub. Adminstrn. fellow U. Minn., 1940-42; Social Sci. Research Council fellow, 1957 Mem. Council Fgn. Relations, Internat. Inst. Strategic Studies, Am. Polit. Sci. Assn. (nat. council 1965-67), Royal Inst. Internat. Affairs, New Eng. Polit. Sci. Assn. (mem. com. 1959-60, pres. 1964-65), Phi Beta Kappa. Presbyterian. Home: 29 Pinewood Vlg West Lebanon NH 03784-3119 Home (Summer): Star Route Box 213 Edgartown MA 02539

RADYCKI, DIANE JOSEPHINE, art historian; b. Chgo., Dec. 4, 1946; d. Casimir Constantine and Sophie Jeanette Radycki; m. Sidney Tillim, June 27, 1998. BA, U. Ill., 1969; MA, Hunter Coll., 1976; PhD, Harvard U., 1993. Intern Busch-Reisinger Mus., Cambridge, 1984-85; guest-curator Fogg Mus., 1983, 87, 88; tchg. fellow Harvard U., Mass., 1987; instr. U. Houston, 1992-93, asst. prof., 1993-96, Moravian Coll., 1998—; dir. Payne Gallery, Moravian Coll., Bethlehem, Pa., 1999—. Transl. editor: Letters and Journals of Paula Modersohn-Becker, 1980. Agnes Mongan fellow, 1982-84, Fulbright fellow, 1989-91, AAUW fellow, 1991. Office: Moravian Coll Art Dept Bethlehem PA 18018

RADZEVICH, STEPAN PAVLOVICH, mechanical engineering educator; b. Bila Tserkva, Kiev, Ukraine, Feb. 19, 1953; s. Pavlo Stepanovich and Anna Pavlivna (Oblomiy) R.; m. Natalia Ivanivna Starikova, Oct. 22, 1982; children; Irina, Andrey. MS, Kyiv Polytech. Inst., Ukraine, USSR, 1976, PhD,

1982; DS, Tula Polytech. Inst., Russia, 1991; Hon. Doctor, Dnieprodzerzhinsk State Tech U, Ukraine, 1995. Asst. prof. Kiev Polytech. Inst., 1976-82, assoc. prof., 1982-91, prof., 1991-2000; dean mech. engring. faculty Dnieprodzerzhinsk State Tech. U., Ukraine, 1993-96; sr. gear design engr. New Venture Gear, Inc., East Syracuse , 2000—01. Vis. scholar Mich. State U., Ea. Lansing, Mich., 1993—98; prof. Kyiv Polytech. Inst., Ukraine, 1996—2000. Author: Fundamentals of Part Surface Generating, 2001, NC Machining of Sculptured Part Surfaces, 1991, Hobbin of Hardened Gears, 1985, Cutting Tools for NC Machin Tools, 1987, numerous others; co-author: Drilling of Plastics, 1980; contbr. over 400 articles to profl. jours.; patentee in field. Hon. inventor of Ukraine, 1989; recipient State prize by V.K. Seminsky, Pres. of Ukraine, 1990. Mem. ASME, Internat. Acad. Scis. and Arts, Nat. Ukrainian Com. on Theory of Mechanisms and Machines, Ukrainian Higher Edn. Acad. Scis., N.Y. Acad. Scis., Rotary Club. Avocations: winter bathing, history of sci. of engring., arts and culture, mil. history, music. E-mail: stephen_radzevich@hotmail.com.

RADZICKI, MICHAEL JOSEPH, economist; b. Chgo., Aug. 18, 1958; s. Richard Lee and Roberta Joan (Koziol) R.; m. Julie Elizabeth Vande Berg, Mar. 1981; children: Nathaniel Steven, Amanda Josephine, Benjamin Richard. BA, St. Norbert Coll., 1979; MA, U. Notre Dame, 1982, PhD, 1985. Prof. U. Notre Dame, Ind., 1985-90; prof. econs. Worcester (Mass.) Poly. Inst., 1990—. Founder, pres. Sustainable Solutions, Inc.; guest scholar Ctr. for Modeling, Nonlinear Dynamics and Irreversible Thermodynamics, Tech. U., Denmark, Lyngby, 1989. Mem. editl. bd. Jour. of Econ. Issues, 1991-93; assoc. editor Systems Dynamics Rev., 1986—; contbr. articles to profl. jours. Mem. Am. Econ. Assn., Assn. for Evolutionary Econs., System Dynamics Soc. (founder, policy coun. 1988-90, v.p. meetings 1992-94, sec. 1995—). Roman Catholic. Avocations: Motorcycling, distance running, karate (black belt). Home: 10 Blueberry Ln Sterling MA 01564-2143 Office: Worcester Polytechnic Inst 100 Institute Rd Worcester MA 01609-2280

RADZINOWICZ, MARY ANN, language educator; b. Champaign, Ill., Apr. 18, 1925; d. Arthur Seymour and Ann (Stacy) Nevins; m. Leon Radzinowicz, June 16, 1958 (div. 1978); children: Ann Stacy Radzinowicz Prior, William Francis Henry. BA, Radcliffe Coll., 1945; MA, Columbia U., 1947, PhD, 1953; MA (hon.), U. Cambridge, Eng., 1960. Prof. Vassar Coll., Poughkeepsie, N.Y., 1947-50, 52-59, Girton Coll., Cambridge, Eng., 1960-80, U. Cambridge, 1973-80, Cornell U., Ithaca, N.Y., 1980-90, Jacob Gould Schurman prof. English emeritus, 1990—. Mem. adv. bd. 2d, 3d, 4th Internat. Milton Symposia, 1985—. Author: Toward Samson Agonistes, 1978 (Hanford prize 1979), Milton's Epics and Psalms, 1989, Milton and the Tragic Women of Genesis, 1995 (Hanford prize); editor American Colonial Prose, 1984, Paradise Lost, Book VIII, 1974; mem. editorial bd. Milton Quarterly, 1981—, Christianity and Literature, 1989—. Mem. MLA, Renaissance Soc. Am., Milton Soc. Am. (honored scholar 1987), John Donne Soc. Home: Ballyconry House Ballyvaughan County Clare Ireland Office: Cornell U Dept English Lit Ithaca NY 14850 E-mail: manr@tinet.ie.

RAE, BARBARA JOYCE, former employee placement company executive; b. Prince George, B.C., Can., May 17, 1930; d. Alfred and Lottie Kathleen (Davis) Holmwood; m. George Suart, Feb. 14, 1984; children: Jamie, Glenn, John. MBA, Simon Fraser U., Burnaby, B.C., 1975, LLD (hon.), 1998. Chmn., CEO Adia Can., Ltd., Vancouver, B.C., 1953-95; also bd. dirs. Bd. dirs. emeritus Can. Imperial Bank Commerce, Grosvenor Internat. Ltd., Noranda, Inc.; dir. VLINX.Com., Can. Inst. Adv. Rsch., 1995-2001, KTCS Pub. Broadcasting; bd. govs. Multiple Sclerosis Soc., 1995—; mem. Fed. Task Force on Future of Can. Fin. Svcs. Sector, 1997-98; past chmn. B.C. Women's Hosp. Found., 1994-97. Chancellor Simon Fraser U., 1987—93; mem. Jud. Appts. .Com., 1988—90; commr. Triennial Commn. on Judges Salaeris and Benefits; mem. Premier's Econ. Adv. Coun., 1987—91; mem. Prime Minister's Com. on Sci. and Tech., 1989—94; gen. chmn. United Way Lower Mainland, 1987; chair Salvation Army Red Shield Vancouver Campaign, 1986; bd. dirs. Vancouver Bd. Trade, 1972—76; patron Can. Coun. Christians and Jews; mem. adv. bd. Salvation Army, 1985—. Decorated Order of Can., Order of B.C.; recipient Outstanding Alumnae award Simon Fraser U., 1985, Disting. Alumni Svc. award, 1995, Bus. Women of Yr. award Vancouver YWCA, 1986, West Vancouver Achievers award, 1987, B.C. Entrepreneur of Yr. award, 1987, Nat. Vol. award, 1990, Can. Woman Entrepreneur B.C. award, 1992. Home: 2206 Folkestone Way #3 West Vancouver BC Canada V7S 2X7 E-mail: brae@sfu.ca.

RAE, MATTHEW SANDERSON, JR. lawyer; b. Pitts., Sept. 12, 1922; s. Matthew Sanderson and Olive (Waite) R.; m. Janet Hettman, May 2, 1953; children: Mary-Anna, Margaret Rae Mallory, Janet S. Rae Dupree. AB, Duke, 1946, LLB, 1947; postgrad., Stanford U., 1951. Bar: Md. 1948, Calif. 1951. Asst. to dean Duke Sch. Law, Durham, N.C., 1947-48; assoc. Karl F. Steinmann, Balt., 1948-49, Guthrie, Darling & Shattuck, L.A., 1953-54; nat. field rep. Phi Alpha Delta Law Frat., 1949-51; research atty. Calif. Supreme Ct., San Francisco, 1951-52; ptnr. Darling, Hall & Rae (and predecessor firms), L.A., 1955—. Mem. Calif. Commn. Uniform State Laws, 1985—, chmn., 1993-94; chmn. drafting com. for revision Uniform Prin. and Income Act of Nat. Conf., 1991-97, Probate and Mental Health Task Force, Jud. Coun. Calif., 1996-2000. Vice pres. L.A. County Rep. Assembly, 1959-64; mem. L.A. County Rep. Ctrl. Com., 1960-64, 77-90, 2000—, exec. com., 1977-90; vice chmn. 17th Congl. Dist., 1960-62, 28th Congl. Dist., 1962-64; chmn. 46th Assy. Dist., 1962-64, 27th Senatorial Dist., 1977-85, 29th Senatorial Dist., 1985-90, sec. 53d Assembly Dist., 2000-; mem. Calif. Rep. State Ctrl. Com., 1966—, exec. com., 1966-67; pres. Calif. Rep. League, 1966-67; trustee Rep. Assocs., 1979-94, pres., 1983-85, chmn. bd. dirs., 1985-87. 2d lt. USAAF, WWII. Fellow Am. Coll. Trust and Estate Counsel; academician Internat. Acad. Estate and Trust Law (exec. coun. 1974-78); mem. ABA, L.A. County Bar Assn. (chmn. probate and trust law com. 1964-66, chmn. legis. com. 1980-86, chmn. program com. 1981-82, chmn. membership retention com. 1982-83, trustee 1983-85, dir. Bar Found., 1987-93, Arthur K. Marshall award probate and trust law sect. 1984, Shattuck-Price Meml. award 1990), South Bay Bar Assn., State Bar of Calif. (chmn. state bar jour. com. 1970-71, probate com. 1974-75; exec. com. estate planning trust and probate law sect. 1977-83, chmn. legis. com. 1977-89; co-chmn. 1991-92; probate law cons. group Calif. Bd. Legal Specialization 1977-88; chmn. conf. dels. resolutions com. 1987, exec. com. conf. dels. 1987-90), Lawyers Club L.A. (bd. govs. 1981-87, 1st v.p. 1982-83), Am. Legion (comdr. Allied post 1969-70), Legion Lex (bd. dirs. 1964-99, pres. 1969-71), Air Force Assn., Aircraft Owners and Pilots Assn., Town Hall (gov. 1970-78, pres. 1975), World Affairs Coun., Internat. Platform Assn., Breakfast Club (law, pres. 1989-90), Commonwealth Club, Chancery Club (pres. 1996-97), Rotary, Phi Beta Kappa (councilor Alpha Assn. 1983—, pres. 1996), Omicron Delta Kappa, Phi Alpha Delta (supreme justice 1972-74, elected to Disting. Svc. chpt. 1978), Sigma Nu. Presbyterian. Home: 600 John St Manhattan Beach CA 90266-5837 Office: Darling Hall & Rae LLP 520 S Grand Ave Fl 7 Los Angeles CA 90071-2645

RAEBER, JOHN ARTHUR, architect, construction consultant; b. St. Louis, Nov. 24, 1947; s. Arthur William and Marie (Laux) R. AA, Jefferson Coll., 1968; AB, Washington U., 1970, MArch, 1973. Registered architect, Calif., Mo.; cert. constrn. specifier; cert. Nat. Coun. Arch. Specification writer Hellmuth, Obata & Kassabaum, St. Louis, 1973-78, constrn. administr., 1978-79; mgr. of specifications Gensler & Assocs., San Francisco, 1979-82; ind. constrn. specifier, 1982—. Adj. prof. architecture Calif. Coll. Arts and Crafts, San Francisco, 1986—; access code advisor Constrn. Industry & Owners, 1982—; spkr., instr. seminars orgns., univs., 1982—; mem. Calif. State Bldg. Standards Commn. Accessibility Adv. Panel, Sacramento, 1981, Calif. Subcom. Rights of Disabled Adv. Panel, Sacramento, 1993; cons. Nat. Inst. Bldg. Scis., 1996—. Author: CAL/ABL: Interpretative Manual to California's Access Barriers Laws, 1982; co-author: (with Peter S. Hopf) Access for the Handicapped, 1984; columnist Constrn. Specifier Mag., 1988-95. Vol. Calif. Office Emergency Svcs. Safety Assessment, Sacramento, 1991—. Fellow AIA (San Francisco chpt. codes com., Calif. coun. codes and standards com., nat. masterspec rev. com. 1982-84, nat. codes com. corr.), Contrns. Specifications Inst. (cert., columnist newsletter San Francisco chpt. 1984-95, Ben John Small award for Outstanding Stature as practicing specifications writer 1994, pres. St. Louis chpt. 1978-79, pres. San Francisco chpt. 1993-94, tech. com., edn. com., publs. com., Specifications Proficiency award San Francisco chpt. 1989, Tech. Commendation award 1987); mem. Specifications Cons. in Ind. Practice (nat. pres. 1990-92, nat. sec./treas. 1988-90), Internat. Conf. Bldg. Officials, Phi Theta Kappa. Avocations: history, anthropology, sci. fiction. Home and Office: 3962 26th St San Francisco CA 94131-2002

RAEBURN, ANDREW HARVEY, performing arts association executive, record producer; b. London, July 22, 1933; arrived in U.S., 1964, Can., 1993; s. Walter Augustus Leopold and Dora Adelaide Harvey (Williams) R. BA in History, King's Coll., Cambridge U., Eng., 1958; MA, King's Coll., Camridge U., Eng., 1962; diploma (hon.) in music performance, Mt. Royal Coll., Calgary, Can., 1998. Mus. dir. Argo Record Co., London, 1959-64; asst. to music dir., program editor Boston Symphony Orch., 1964-73; dir. artists and repertory New World Records, N.Y.C., 1975-79; artistic adminstr. Detroit Symphony Orch., 1979-82; exec. dir. Van Cliburn Found. Inc., Ft. Worth, 1982-85; performing arts cons., 1985-93; exec. v.p. The Peter Pan Children's Fund, 1990-91; exec. dir. Esther Honens Internat. Piano Competition Found., 1993-95, pres., 1995-99, vice chmn., artistic dir., 1999-2001, pres., artistic dir., 2001—. Cons. music; radio and TV commentator; mem. faculty Boston U., 1966-67; condr. New World String Orch., 1978 Author record liner notes, Argo, RCA, Time-Life records, 1960-79, program notes, Boston Symphony Orch., 1968-73. Served with Royal Arty. Brit. Army, 1952-55; founding dean Prague Mozart Acad. 1992-93. Home: 702 235 Fifteenth Ave SW Calgary AB Canada T2R 0P6 Office: 601 8th Ave SW Ste 600 Calgary AB Canada T2P 1G5 E-mail: raeburn@honens.com., ahr@cadvision.com.

RAEBURN, JOHN HAY, English language educator; b. Indpls., July 18, 1941; s. Gordon Maurice and Katherine (Calwell) R.; m. Gillian Kimble, Aug. 18, 1963 (div. July 1979); children— Daniel Kennedy, Nicholas Kimble; m. Kathleen Kamerick, July 5, 1986. AB with honors, Ind. U., 1963; A.M., U. Pa., 1964, PhD, 1969. Asst. prof. U. Mich., Ann Arbor, 1967-74; vis. lectr. U. Iowa, Iowa City, 1974-75, assoc. prof., 1976-83, prof. English, 1983—; chmn. Am. Studies dept., 1983-85, 94-2000; chmn. English dept. U. Iowa, Iowa City, 1985-91; assoc. prof. U. Louisville, 1975-76. Author: Fame Became of Him: Hemingway as Public Writer, 1984; editor: (with others) Frank Capra: The Man and His Films, 1975 Mem. Am. Studies Assn., Orgn. Am. Historians. Democrat. Home: 321 Hutchinson Ave Iowa City IA 52246-2407 Office: U Iowa Dept Am Studies Dept English 701 Jefferson Building Iowa City IA 52242-1418 E-mail: john-raeburn@iowa.edu.

RAEDEKE, LINDA DISMORE, geologist, researcher; b. Great Falls, Mont., Aug. 20, 1950; d. Albert Browning and Madge (Hogan) Dismore; m. Kenneth John Raedeke, Dec. 26, 1971 (div. 1982); m. Charles Moore Swift, Jr., Mar. 14, 1992. BA in History, U. Wash., 1971, MS in Geology, 1979, PhD, 1982. Geomorphologist, park planner Corporacion Nacional Forestal and U.S. Peace Corps, Punta Arenas, 1972-75; glacial geologist Empresa Nacional del Petroleo, 1972-75; geologist FAO, UN, 1974, Lamont-Doherty Geol. Obs., COlumbia U., Tierra del Fuego, Chile, 1974-75; wetlands evaluation project coord. Wash. Dept. Agr., U. Wash., Seattle, 1975-76; curator Remote Sensing Applications Lab. U. Wash., 1976-77; exploration geologist Chevron Resources Co., Denver, 1981-84; rsch. geologist Chevron Oil Field Rsch. Co., La Habra, Calif., 1984-89; sr. compensation analyst Chevron Corp., San Francisco, 1989-90; staff geologist Chevron Overseas Petroleum, Inc., San Ramon, Calif., 1990-91, project leader, 1991-95, new ventures coord. for the far east, 1995-96; sr. staff analyst for planning Chevron Corp., 1996-98; coorr. upstream bus. Chevron Rsch. Tech. Co., 1998-99; group mgr. Integrated Labs., 1999—. Mem. adv. bd. Bay Area Earth Sci. Inst., 1999—, Montana State U. Coll. Tech., 2000—. Contbt. articles to profl. jours. Mem. Am. Geophys. Union, Geol. Soc. Am., Am. Assn. Petroleum Geologists (poster chmn. 1987, internat. chmn. 1996 meeting). Office: Chevron Rsch and Tech Co 100 Chevron Way Richmond CA 94801-2016

RAEDER, JOACHIM, geophysicist; b. Cologne, Germany, June 7, 1956; s. Hans and Edith Raeder; m. Renate Kraus; children: Rebecca, Timothy. Diploma in Geophysics, U. Cologne, Germany, 1984, PhD in Geophysics, 1989. Rsch. geophysicist UCLA, L.A., 1990—. Contbr. articles. Decadal rev. panel mem. NRC, Washington, 2001—02. Sgt. army, 1975—77, Germany. Recipient Group Achievement award, NASA, 1998. Mem.: Am. Geophys. Union. Home: 2128 Glyndon Ave Venice CA 90291 Office: IGPP/UCLA 405 Hilgard Ave Los Angeles CA 90095 Office Fax: 310-206-3051. Business E-Mail: jraeder@igpp.ucla.edu.

RAEDER, WILLIAM MUNRO, publishing executive; b. Boston, Dec. 3, 1935; BA, Boston U., 1960, MA, 1964. Agent Nat. Life Ins. Co. Vt., 1965-69; exec. dir. Fund Urban Negro Devel., Boston, 1969-71; pres., mgr. Aquarius Theatre, 1971-72; bus. cons., 1972-75; pres. Nat. Braille Press, 1975—. Office: Nat Braille Press 88 Saint Stephen St Boston MA 02115-4302

RAEL, HENRY SYLVESTER, SR. retired health administrator, financial and management consultant; b. Pueblo, Colo., Oct. 2, 1928; s. Daniel and Grace (Abeyta) R.; m. Helen Warner Loring Brace, June 30, 1956 (dec. Aug. 1980); children: Henry Sylvester Jr., Loring Victoria, Thomas Warner Bush. AB, U. So. Colo., 1955; BA in Bus. Adminstrn., U. Denver, 1957, MBA, 1958. Sr. boys counselor Denver Juvenile Hall, 1955-58; adminstrv. asst. to pres. Stanley Aviation Corp., Denver, 1958-61; Titan III budget and fin. control supr. Martin Marietta Corp., 1961-65; mgmt. adv. services officer U. Colo. Med. Center, 1965-72; v.p. fin., treas. Loretto Heights Coll., 1972-73; dir. fin. and adminstrn. Colo. Found. for Med. Care, 1973-86, Tri-County Health Dept., Denver, 1986-96; fin. cons., 1996—. Cons. Clayton Found.-Denver Headstart, 1996, Colo. Dept. Pub. Health and Environ., 1997, Hosp. Shared Svcs., 1997-98, U.S. Dept. Commerce Census, 2000, Census Enumerator, 2000, Fin. Planning Assn., 2000-01; instr. fin. mgmt., mem. fin. com. am. Assn. Profl. Standards Rev. orgn., 1980-85; speaker systems devel., design assns., univs., 1967-71. Mem. budget lay adv. com. Park Hill Elem. Sch., Denver, 1967-68, chmn., 1968-69; vol. worker Boy and Girl Scouts, 1967-73; bd. dirs. Community Arts Symphony, 1981-83, 85-87; controller St. John's Episcopal Cathedral, 1982-83; charter mem. Pueblo (Colo.) Coll. Young Democrats, 1954-55; block worker Republican Party, Denver, 1965-68, precinct committeeman, 1978-84; trustee Van Nattan Scholarship Fund, 1974-96; bd. dirs. Vis. Nurse Assn., 1977-84, treas., 1982-84. Served with USAF, 1947-53, res., 1954-61. Recipient Disting. Service award Denver Astron. Soc., 1968, Citation Chamberlin Obs., 1985; Stanley Aviation masters scholar, 1957; Ballard scholar, 1956. Mem.: Nat. Astronomers Assn. (exec. bd. 1965—97), Am. Assn. Founds. for Med. Care (fin. com. 1981—82), Denver Astron. Soc. (pres. 1965—66, bd. dirs. 1982—94), Colo. Pub. Employees Retirement Assn. (bd. dirs. 1993), Budget Execs. Inst. (sec. 1963—64, v.p. chpt. 1964—65), Hosp. Systems Mgmt. Soc., Assn. Systems. Mgmt. (pres. 1971—72), Whispering Pines of Denver Homeowners Assn. (pres. bd. dirs. 1998—2001, dir.-at-large 2001—), Brandy Chase Homeowners Assn. (bd. dirs. 1997), Delta Psi Omega, Epsilon Xi. Home: 7755 E Quincy Ave Apt 57 Denver CO 80237-2312

RAESSLER, KENNETH RAY, music educator; b. Highspire, Pa., Aug. 17, 1932; s. Rufus Ray and Grace Maty; m. Joyce Elaine Bond, Aug. 20, 1960; children: Laurie Elaine Raessler Denison, Todd Ray. BS, West Chester U., West Chester, PA, 1954; MM, Temple U., Philadelphia, PA, 1959; PhD, Mich. State U., East Lansing, MI, 1967. Music dir. Belvidere Sch. Dist., Belvidere, NJ, 1954—57; choral music dir. East Stroudsburg Area H.S., East Stroudsburg, Pa., 1957—61, Hatboto-Horsham H.S., Hatboro, 1962—63; assoc. prof. music Gettysburg Coll., Gettysburg, 1963—73; dir. music edn. Williamsport Area Sch. Dist., Williamsport, 1973—89; dir. sch. music Tex. Christian U., Fort Worth, Tex., 1989—2001, prof. music, 1989—2001. Cons. Wenger Corp., Owatonnia, Minn., 1991, Korg Corp., Los Angeles, Calif., 1991, Yamaha Corp., Grand Rapids, Mich., 1986—96. Author: (book) Aspiring to Excell; contbr. articles to profl. jours. Pres. Willismsport Rotary Club, Williamsport, Pa., 1985. Recipient Cmty. Svc. award, Williamsport Rotary Club, 1989. Mem.: Tex. Christian U. Faculty Senate (sec. 1996—98), Van Cliburn Found. (exec. bd. 1989—2002), Phi Mu Alpha Sinfonia (v.p. 2000—02). D-Conservative. Christian. Avocations: golf, swimming. Home: 4900 Westridge Villa #14 Fort Worth TX 76116 E-mail: k.raessler@tcu.edu.

RAETZ, CHRISTIAN R. H. biochemistry educator; b. Berlin, Germany, Nov. 17, 1946; BS in Chemistry, Yale U., 1967; MD, Harvard U., 1973, PhD. House officer Peter Bent Brigham Hosp., Boston, 1973-74; research assoc. Nat. Inst. Gen. Med. Scis., USPHS, Bethesda, Md., 1974-76; asst. prof. biochemistry U. Wis.-Madison, 1976-79, assoc. prof., 1979-82, prof., dir. Ctr. for Membrane Biosynthesis Research, 1982—87; exec. dir biochemistry Merck Rsch. Lab., Rahway, NJ, 1987—91, v.p. basic rsch., biochemistry and mircobiology, 1992—93; prof. chmn. of biochemistry Duke Univ. Med. Ctr., Durham, NC, 1993—. Mem. biochemistry study sect. NIH Contbr. numerous articles to profl. jours. Mem. editorial bd. Jour. Biol. Chemistry Recipient James Tolbert Shipley Research prize Harvard U. Med. Sch., 1973, Harry and Evelyn Steenbock Career Advancement award, 1976, Research Career Devel. award NIH, 1978-83, Dreyfus Tchr.-Scholar award, 1979; H. I. Romnes Faculty fellow U. Wis., 1984; NIH grantee Mem. Am. Soc. Biol. Chemists, Japanese Soc. Promotion Sci., Phi Beta Kappa, Alpha Omega Alpha Office: Duke U Dept Biochemistry 225 Nanaline H. Duke PO Box 3711, DUMC Durham NC 27710-0001 Home: 7411 Bill Poole Rd Rougemont NC 27572

RAEUCHLE, JOHN STEVEN, software engineer; b. Washington, Sept. 21, 1955; s. Richard Frank and Ruth Darlene (Fulton) R. BS, Tex. Christian U., 1978. Programmer Tex. Christian U., Ft. Worth, 1976-78, Warrex Computer Sys., Ft. Worth, 1978-79; sys. programmer Tandy Data Processing, 1979-84; sr. programmer, analyst Commodity News Svcs., Leawood, Kans., 1984-86, Logica Data Archs., St. Louis, 1986-89; computer analyst Credit Sys., Inc., 1989-95; sr. software engr. Master Card Internat., 1995—. Mem. St. Louis Ambassadors, 1989—98; active Boy Scouts Am., 1964—95. Recipient awrd of merit Boy Scouts Am., Commrs. Key, 1982. Mem. St. Louis Jaycees Found. (treas. 1990-94, 2001—, sec. 1994-96, 99-2001, pres. 1996-99), U.S. Jr. C. of C. Senate Found., Mo. Jr. C. of C. Internat. Senate (treas. 1997-98, v.p. 1998-99, pres. 1999-2000, chmn. bd. 2000-01), Mo. Jaycees (state officer 1989-94), Kansas City Jaycees (bd. dirs. 1985-87), Kansas City Jaycees Found., St. Louis Jr. C. of C. (pres. 1988-89). Democrat. Methodist. Avocations: camping, bowling, hiking. Home: 52 Country Creek Dr Saint Peters MO 63376-3041 Office: Master Card Internat 2200 Master Card Blvd O'Fallon MO 63366

RAEZ, LUIS ESTUARDO, physician; b. June 29, 1967; MD, Cayetano Heredia U., Lima, Peru, 1992. Resident in internal medicine U. Miami, Fla., 1993-96, resident in hematology and clin. oncology, 1996-99; practice hematology and oncology Sylvester Comprehensive Cancer Ctr., 1999—, co-chair thoracic oncology group, 2001—; asst. prof. medicine U. Miami, 1999—, asst. prof. epidemiology and pub. health, 2002—. Contbr. articles to med. and profl. jours.; presenter in field. Med. advisor Am. Cancer Soc. Fla. Keys. Fellow: ACP; mem.: Peruvian Med. Assn., Am. Soc. Clin. Oncology (Clin. Career Devel. award). Address: 1475 NW 12th Ave #3510 Miami FL 33136

RAFAIDUS, DAVID MARTIN, health and human services planner; b. Hamtramack, Mich., Jan. 4, 1956; s. George S. and Emilia Helen (Mazak) R. BS, Cen. Mich. U., 1978; M in Urban Planning, U. Mich., 1980; postgrad. pub. mgmt., Fla. Atlantic U., 1988; site evaluation, planning & devel., Harvard U., 1988. Mem. staff Mich. Mcpl. League, Ann Arbor, 1978-79; teaching fellow dept. urban and regional planning U. Mich., 1980; planner dept. cmty. devel. City of Lafayette, La., 1980-82, coord. zoning dept. planning and devel. mgmt., 1982-83, devel. mgr. dept. planning and devel. mgmt., 1983-86; county planner Palm Beach County Dept. Planning, Zoning & Bldg., West Palm Beach, Fla., 1986-96; sr. health and human svcs. planner Palm Beach County Cmty. Svcs. Dept., 1996—. Pres. br. 888 Jednota Cath. Slovak Union. Mem. Am. Planning Assn., Palm Beach County Planning Congress, World Future Soc., KC (4th degree), Lambda Chi Alpha. Roman Catholic. Home: 6073 Brandon St Palm Beach Gardens FL 33418-1486 Office: Palm Beach County Dept Cmty Svcs 810 Datura St West Palm Beach FL 33401-5204 E-mail: sudiafar@yahoo.com., drafaidu@co.palm-beach.fl.us.

RAFAJKO, ROBERT RICHARD, medical research company executive; b. Chgo., Sept. 3, 1931; s. Edward Michael and Mildred Eleanor (Simo) R.; m. Mary Ann Filipi, June 24, 1954 (div. 1979); children: Rorie Rae, Ronald Raymond, Robin Rene, Rod Richard, Rebecca Rae.; m. Anne Thorne Sloan, Jan. 26, 1982; 1 son, Andrew Sloan. BA, Coe Coll., 1953; MS, U. Iowa, 1958, PhD, 1960. Rsch. assoc. Merck Sharp and Dohme, West Point, Pa., 1960-61; rsch. scientist Microbiol. Assos., Bethesda, Md., 1961-66; v.p., gen. mgr. Med. Rsch. Cons., Rockville, 1966-69; v.p. R & D, N.Am. Biols., 1969-74; pres. Biofluids, Inc., 1974-99, Bonheur Inc., Keswick, Va., 1999—. Pres. Tysan Serum, Inc., Rockville, 1974-2000, Kytaron Inc, Rockville, 1987-99; breeder thoroughbred horses, 1980—. Contbr. 23 articles to profl. jours. Chmn. PVAAU Swimming Program, Washington, Md. and Va., 1973-76; bd. dirs. Montgomery County Swim League, Montgomery County, Md., 1968-76. Served with USAF, 1954-55. Mem. AAAS, N.Y. Acad. Scis., Am. Soc. Microbiology, Tissue Culture Assn., Am. Horse Council, Horsemans Benevolent and Protective Assn. Republican. Presbyterian. Avocations: scuba diving, photography, collecting stamps, travel. Home and Office: 1349 Queenscroft Keswick VA 22947-2731 Fax: 804-244-0863. E-mail: bonheur421@aol.com.

RAFAL, KEITH W.L. physician; b. N.Y.C., June 15, 1955; s. Stanley and Joyce Rafal; m. Teriann S. Rafal, Dec. 27, 1981; children: Lauren E., Allison L. BA in Psychology, SUNY, Albany, 1977; MD, Howard U., 1982. Diplomate Am. Bd. Phys. Medicine and Rehab. Intern Faulkner Hosp., Boston, 1982-83; resident in phys. medicine and rehab. Boston U. Med. Ctr., 1983-85; fellow in geriatric medicine Brown U./Roger Williams Gen. Hosp., Providence, 1986-87; med. dir. Cushing Hosp., Framingham, Mass., 1987-89; chief physiatrist, dir. geriats. Fairlawn Rehab. Hosp., Worcester, 1989-93; chief physiatrist, med. dir. Wellmark Health Care, Wellesley, 1993-95; assoc. med. dir. New Eng. Rehab. at Home, Woburn, 1995-97; med. dir. rehab. Greenery Rehab. Ctr., Boston, 1995—; co-owner, co-founder Alternative Care & Healing Ctr., Franklin, Mass., 1996—; med. dir. fibromyalgia program Rehab. Hosp. R.I., North Smithfield, 1999—. Med. dir. Rehab. Hosp. R.I.; mem. clin. faculty, asst. prof. U. Mass. Med. Sch., Worcester, 1987—93; mem. clin. faculty, instr. Tufts Med. Sch., Boston, 1994—, Harvard U., Boston, 1997—98; pres., founder Healing Choices, P.C., 2001—. Fellow Am. Acad. Pain Mgmt.; mem. Am. Holistic Med. Assn., Nat. Ctr. for Homeopathy, Am. Acad. Phys. and Med. Rehab. Avocations: playing the cello, nature walks, spending time with family. Office: Alternative Care and Healing Ctr 326 Union St Ste 2 Franklin MA 02038-2438

RAFALOFF, GARY B. financial company executive; b. Bklyn., Apr. 25, 1952; s. Ralph and Sara R.; m. Roberta Dianne Rafaloff, Aug. 4, 1974; children: Lauren, David, Chelsea. BS in Psychology, SUNY, Cortland, 1974; MS in Orgnl. Psychology, Stevens Inst. Tech., 1979. Sr. ptnr. Person.Paradigms, Inc., 1978-83; assoc. prof. Stevens Inst. Tech., Hoboken, N.J., 1979-83; pres. Rafaloff Assocs., N.Y.C., 1983-86; br. mgr. Advest Inc., 1986-93; sr. v.p. Shearson Lehman, 1993-94, Smith Barney Inc., N.Y.C., 1994-96; pres. RGR Fin. Corp., 1996—. Founder, dir. GoCollect.com Corp., N.Y.C., 1999—. Avocations: various sports, collecting, coaching children's sports. Office: RGR Fin Corp 575 Lexington Ave Fl 7 New York NY 10022-6102

RAFALOWSKI, RAYMOND VICTOR, printing and publishing executive; b. Pitts., Dec. 22, 1951; s. Joseph and Elizabeth Ann R.; m. Karen Marie Carson, Feb. 20, 1971; two children. Student, U. Pitts., 1973-78. Prepress mgr. Fisher Scientific Co., Pitts., 1974-79; sales rep. Phillips/Jacobs, Inc., 1979-84; br. mgr. PrimeSource, Inc., Cin., 1984-99, nat. accts. mgr., 1999—. Adv. D. Russell Lee Vocat. Schs., Hamilton, 1995—. Mem. Cin. Club Printing House Craftsmen (pres. 1993, Craftsman of Yr. 1996), 5th Dist. Assn. Printing House Craftsmen (gov. 1997, Craftsman of Yr. 1997), Printing House Craftsmen Internat. (sec./treas. 1998, vice chmn. 1999, internat. chmn. 2000). Home: 5976 N Turtle Creek Dr Fairfield OH 45014-5152

RAFEEDIE, EDWARD, senior federal judge; b. Orange, N.J., Jan. 6, 1929; s. Fred and Nabeeha (Hishmeh) R.; m. Ruth Alice Horton, Oct. 8, 1961; children: Fredrick Alexander, Jennifer Ann. BS in Law, U. So. Calif., 1957, JD, 1959; LLD (hon.), Pepperdine U., 1978. Bar: Calif. 1960. Pvt. practice, Santa Monica, Calif., 1960-69; mcpl. ct. judge Santa Monica Jud. Dist., 1969-71; judge Superior Ct. State of Calif., L.A., 1971-82; dist. judge U.S. Dist. Court (cen. dist.) Calif., 1982-96, sr. judge, 1996—. With U.S. Army, 1950-52, Korea. Office: US Dist Ct 312 N Spring St Ste 244P Los Angeles CA 90012-4704

RAFELSON, MAX EMANUEL, JR. biochemist, medical school administrator; b. Detroit, June 17, 1921; s. Max Emanuel and Lillian (Kay) R.; m. Trudy Diane Hellem, Mar. 31, 1973; children— Mark Thomas, Anne Elizabeth. BS, U. Mich., 1943; PhD, U. So. Cal., 1951. Postdoctoral rsch.

fellow U. Stockholm, Sweden, 1951-52; asst. prof. biol. chemistry U. Ill. Coll. Medicine, Chgo., 1953-55, assoc. prof., 1955-60, prof., 1961-70; assoc. dean biol. and behavioral scis. Rush Med. Coll., Rush-Presbyn.-St. Luke's Med. Center, 1970-71, v.p. info. scis., 1971-77, v.p., 1972—; prof. biochemistry Rush Med. Coll., 1972-90, prof. and chmn. emeritus, 1990—. John W. and Helen H. Watzek meml. chmn. biochemistry Presbyn.-St. Lukes Hosp., Chgo., 1961-70; vis. prof. U. Paris, France, 1960, 77-78, U. Ulm, Fed. Republic Germany, 1986; assoc. mem. commn. influenza Dept. Def., 1961—. Author: Basic Biochemistry, 1965, 68, 71, 80, Concise Biochemistry, 1996; contbr. articles on biochemistry, blood platelets, viruses, protein structure, endothelial cells and metabolism to profl. publs. Served with USNR, 1943-46. Mem. Am. Soc. Biol. Chemists, Biochem. Soc. (London), Am. Chem. Soc., AAAS, Nat. Acad. Clin. Biochemistry, Société de Chemie Biologique, Sigma Xi. Home: 9015 Stoneland Dr San Antonio TX 78230-4576

RAFEYAN, ROUEEN, psychiatrist, educator; b. Tehran, Iran, Oct. 1, 1961; came to U.S., 1979; s. Majid Rafeyan and Nezhat Babanoury; m. Helena Linda Hernandez, Feb. 15, 1991; 1 child, Ryan Michael. BA, Knox Coll., 1981; MD, U. Istanbul, Turkey, 1989. Cert. Am. Bd. Psychiatry & Neurology, 2001; Am. Bd. Psychiatry and Neurology. Resident U. Ill. Chgo., 1996; dir. outpatient clin. svcs., dir. med. student edn. Michael Reese Hosp., Chgo., 1996-99; med. dir. Rush Presbyn., 1997—; asst. clin. prof. psychiatry U. Ill., 1996—. Cons. Threshold Cmty. Mental Health Ctr., Chgo., 1996—. Mem. AMA, Am. Psychiatric Assn., Ill. Psychiatric Soc., Chgo. Med. Soc. Avocations: tennis, music, world history. Office: Michael Reese Hosp 2959 S Cottage Grove Ave Chicago IL 60616 E-mail: rafeyan@classic.msn.com.

RAFF, DANIEL MARTIN GORODETSKY, economist, economic and business historian, educator; b. Washington, Sept. 23, 1951; s. Morton Spencer and Miriam Susan (Gore) R.; m. Susan Claire Adelman, May 18, 1986; 1 child, Anna Amelia Gorodetsky. BA, New Coll., Sarasota, Fla., 1973; MPA, Princeton U., 1976; BPhil, Oxford U., 1978; PhD, MIT, 1987. Vis. lectr. econs. Brasenose Coll., Oxford, 1982; lectr. econs. Magdalen Coll., 1983-85; rsch. assoc. Harvard U. Grad. Sch. Bus. Adminstrn., Cambridge, Mass., 1986-87, asst. prof. bus. adminstrn., 1987-93; assoc. prof. mgmt. The Wharton Sch., U. Pa., Phila., 1993—. Vis. assoc. prof. bus. adminstrn. Columbia U., N.Y.C., 1992-94, lectr. in law, 1994; faculty rsch. fellow Nat. Bur. Econ. Rsch., Cambridge, 1988—. Contbr. articles to profl. jours., chpts. to books. Mem.: Bus. History Conf., Econ. History Assn., Am. Econ. Assn., Cliometric Soc., Am. Hist. Soc. Office: U Pa Wharton Sch Dept Mgmt Philadelphia PA 19104-6370

RAFF, MARTIN JAY, internist, infectious diseases educator, lawyer; b. Bklyn., Mar. 20, 1937; s. Henry B. and Anne (Regunberg) R.; m. Marjorie A. Rosen (div. 1975); m. Patricia Jean Donnelly; children: Eric Howard, Lori Ellen, Stacy Alison, Jason Hart, Evan Jerome, Joshua Michael. BA, Brandeis U., 1958; MS, U. Vt., 1960; MD with honors, PhD, Med. Br. U. Tex., Galveston, 1965; JD, U. Louisville, 1988. Bar: Ky. 1988; diplomate Am. Bd. Internal Medicine, subsplty. infectious diseases; lic. in medicine Tex., N.Y., Pa., Ky., Ind. Intern N.Y. Hosp.-Cornell U. Med. Ctr., N.Y.C., 1965-66, asst. physician, fellow in infectious diseases, 1966-67; asst. physician in medicine N.Y. Hosp., CUMC, Meml. Hosp. Cancer Allied Diseases, 1969-71; chief sect. infectious diseases, from asst. to assoc. to prof. medicine U. Louisville, 1971—, dir., coordinator clin. diagnosis, 1971-76, assoc. dept. microbiology, 1971-76, mem. grad. faculty, 1974, from asst. to assoc. prof. microbiology, 1977—, assoc. chmn. dept. medicine (clin. service), 1979-80; dir. med. teaching program, staff physician, cons. Jewish Hosp., Louisville, 1983-87; clin. chief med. service, staff physician, cons. U. Louisville and Humana Hosp. U., 1987—. Physician N.Y. State Narcotics Addiction Control Commn., 1969-71; staff physician Louisville Gen. Hosp., 1971-79, Louisville Meml. Hosp., 1975—; staff physician, cons. VA Med. Ctr., Louisville, 1971—; cons. Bapt. Hosp. Highlands, Humana Hosp. Surburban, Norton-Kosair-Children's Hosp., Sts. Mary and Elizabeth Hosp., St. Anthony Hosp., Clark County (Ind.) Meml. Hosp., Meml. Hosp. Floyd County (Ind.), 1972—, Merrell-Nat. Labs., 1973-81, Bapt. Hosp. East, Inst. Phys. Medicine Rehab. 1975—, Humana Hosp. Audubon, 1979—; chief clin. internal medicine U. Louisville Health Scis. Ctr. Author: infectious diseases sects. in various med. examination rev. books; contrb.various articles to profl. jours., 1968—. Advisor-cons. PRO-POWER, 1987-; mem. Met. Opera Guild, 1978-, City-County Bd. Health com. Swine Flu, 1976-77; sponsor Louisville Orch., 1977-; patron Louisville Ballet, 1979-, Ky. Opera Assn.; mem. Pres.'s Coun., 1982-; physician cons. Actor's Theatre Louisville, 1977-, Louisville Ballet, 1977-. Served with U.S. Army Med. Corps, 1967-69. NIH fellow, 1966-67. Fellow Am. Coll. Physicians, Infectious Diseases Soc. Am., Am. Coll. Chest Physicians, Am. Coll. Legal Medicine; mem. Internat. Soc. Chemotherapy, Internat. Soc. Aquatic Medicine, Inter-Am. Soc. Chemotherapy Inc., AAAS, AAUP, Nat. Found. Infectious Diseases, Ky. Bar.Assn., Ky. Med. Assn., Louisville Bar Assn., Jefferson County Med. Soc., Assn. Trial Lawyers Am. Avocations: Japanese antiques, philately, numismatics, opera, scuba diving. Home: 517 Ridgewood Rd Louisville KY 40207-1324 Office: U Louisville Sch Med Louisville KY 40292-0001 also: Univ Physicians Group 530 S Jackson St Louisville KY 40202

RAFF, SAMUEL JOSEPH, editor-in-chief; b. N.Y.C., Nov. 4, 1920; s. Nathan and Fannie (Sagman) R.; m. Lillian Ruth Buckner, Sept. 23, 1943 (dec. May 1969); children: Melvin Hunt Raff, Brian Lindsay Raff, Nina Fern Raff, Terri Eden Raff; m. Anna Christine Pryce Carriere, Nov. 18, 1972 (div. Oct. 1981); children: Sara Christianne, Franklin Pryce; m. Barbara M. Loeb, Dec. 13, 1986. BSME, CUNY, 1943; MS, U. Md., 1950, PhD, 1957. Editor-in-chief Computers & Ops. Rsch., Oxford, Eng., 1971—. Prof. George Washington U., Washington, 1985-87. Author: Microwave Systems Engineering Principles, 1977, The Humor in Everyday Phrases, 1995, The Legacy of the White Oak Laboratory, 2000; patentee in field. With USN, 1944-45. Republican. Jewish. Home and Office: 8312 Snug Hill Ln Potomac MD 20854-4057 E-mail: sraffcor@aol.com.

RAFFA, JEAN BENEDICT, author, educator; b. Lansing, Mich., Apr. 23, 1943; d. Ernest Raymond and Verna Lois (Borst) Benedict; m. Frederick Anthony Raffa, June 15, 1964; children: Juliette Louise, Matthew Benedict. BS, Fla. State U., 1964, MS, 1968; EdD, U. Fla., 1982. Tchr. Leon County Sch. Sys., Tallahassee, 1964-69; coord. children's programming WFTV, Orlando, 1978-80; cons. edn. Tchr. Edn. Ctr. U. Ctrl. Fla., 1980-89; writer Fla., 1989—; instr. Disney Inst., 1996. Adj. instr. U. Cen. Fla., 1977-85; vis. asst. prof. Stetson U., DeLand, Fla., 1988-89; cons. Lang. Arts Curriculum Com. Orange County Sch. Sys., 1983; CEO Inner World Encounters, Orlando, 1995—. Author: Introduction to Television Literacy, 1989, The Bridge to Wholeness: A Feminine Alternative to the Hero Myth, 1992, Dream Theatres of the Soul: Empowering the Feminine Through Jungian Dreamwork, 1994; contbr. articles to profl. jours., articles and meditations to religious jours. Mistress of ceremonies Young Authors' Conf., Orange and Volusia County Sch. Sys., 1984-85; cons. Young Authors' Conf. Orange and Seminole County Sch. Sys., 1985-89; judge Volusia County Pub. Schs. Poetry Contest, 1983, 84, Seminole County Pub. Schs. Lit. Mag., 1985-89; pres. Maitland (Fla.) Jr. H.S. PTA, 1986-87; pres., bd. dirs. Canterbury Retreat and Conf. Ctr. Episcopal Diocese Ctrl. Fla., 1988-90; chair edn. commn. Episcopal Ch. of the Good Shepherd, 1986-89; sr. warden Vestry of Episcopal Ch. of the Good Shepherd, 1988. Mem. Kappa Delta Pi, Phi Delta Kappa. Democrat. Avocations: antiques, horseback riding, travel, reading. Office: 17 S Osceola Ave Ste 200 Orlando FL 32801-2828

RAFFALLI, HENRI CHRISTIAN, retired commissioner and administrative law judge, educator, criminologist; married; 3 children. BA, St. John's U., Bklyn., 1951, JD, 1956; postgrad., CUNY, 1959-64, Columbia U., 1967-68, St. Lawrence U., Canton, N.Y., 1966. Bar: N.Y. 1957. With U.S. Army Mil. Intelligence Svc., Linz an der Donau, 1951-53; pvt. practice atty. Forest Hills, N.Y., 1957-64; mem. N.Y. State Divsn. of Parole, N.Y.C., 1964-87; commr. N.Y. State Bd. of Parole, 1987-98, ret., 1998, adminstrv. law judge, 1998-99. Mem. comm. faculty Am. Inst. Banking, N.Y.C., 1968-70; mem. faculty dept. criminal justice Nassau C.C., SUNY, Garden City, N.Y., 1985—; adj. assoc. prof. dept. criminal justice Sch. Health and Pub. Svc. C.W. Post Ctr. L.I. U., Greenvale, N.Y., 1971-85; lectr. in field. Author: The Battered Child: An Overview of a Medical, Legal and Social Problem, 1970, The Burden of Proof in Parole Violation Cases, 1970, The Fourth Amendment and Search and Seizure in the Parole Process, 1975, Manual for the Inspector General of the New York State Division of Parole, 1986, Code of Conduct for the New York State Division of Parole, 1986, Crimes and Criminals, A Collection of Case Summaries, 2002; contbg. author: Deviance, 1975; editor-in-chief N.Y. State Parole Jour., 1983; contbr. articles to profl. jours.

RAFFAY, STEPHEN JOSEPH, manufacturing company executive; b. McAdoo, Pa., Oct. 25, 1927; s. Stephen John and Stephanie (Severa) R.; m. Audree Eugenia Kuehne, Sept. 12, 1953; children: Andrea, Stephen, Leslie. BA, Columbia, 1950, MS, 1951. C.P.A., N.Y. Sr. accountant Arthur Andersen & Co., N.Y.C., 1951-56; asst. controller Emhart Corp., Farmington, Conn., 1956-61, asst. treas., 1961-63, treas., 1963-67, v.p. internat., 1967-72, v.p., group pres., 1972-79, exec. v.p., 1979-84, vice chmn., chief adminstrv. officer, 1984-87, dir., 1980-87; sr. v.p. Dexter Corp., Windsor Locks, 1987-90. Bd. dirs. Reflexite Corp., Fresnel Optics, Inc., United Plumbing Tech., Inc., Trust Co. Conn., Rossi Enterprises, Inc., EDAC Techs. Inc. Bd. dirs. Hartford Symphony Soc. With AUS, 1946-47. Mem. AICPA, Conn. Soc. CPAs. Office: 93 Westmont St W Hartford CT 06117-2929

RAFFEL, BURTON NATHAN, educator, poet, writer, translator; b. N.Y.C., 1928; married, six children. BA cum laude, Bklyn. Coll., 1948; MA, Ohio State U., 1949; JD, Yale U., 1958. Lawyer Milbank, Tweed, Hadley & McCloy, N.Y.C., 1958-60; editor Foundation News, 1960-63; instr. English SUNY, Stony Brook, 1964-65, asst. prof. of English, 1965-66, assoc. prof. English Buffalo, 1966-68; prof. English and Classics U. Tex., Austin, 1969-71; sr. tutor, dean Ont. Coll. Art, Toronto, Can., 1971-72; prof. English U. Denver, 1975-87; dir. Adirondack Mountain Found., 1987-89; Disting. prof. humanities and prof. English U. La., Lafayette, 1989—; assoc. prof. English U. Haifa, 1968—69. Lectr. English dept. Bklyn. Coll., 1950-51; instr. Ford Found. English Lang. Tchr. Tng. program in Indonesia, resident in Makassar, 1953-55; vis. prof. Humanities York U., Toronto, 1972-75, vis. prof. English Emory U., 1974; sr. editor, cons. McDonnell Douglas Computer-Based Systems Tng. Group, Denver, 1985-87; lectr. in law U. Denver, 1986-87. Author: The Development of Modern Indonesian Poetry, 1967, Mia Poems, 1968, The Forked Tongue: A Study of the Translation Process, 1971, Why Re-Create?, 1973, Four Humours, 1979, (film) The Legend of Alfred Packer, 1979, Robert Lowell, 1981, T.S. Eliot, 1982, Changing the Angle of the Sun-Dial, 1984, Grice, 1985, Evenly Distributed Rubble, 1985, Ezra Pound: The Prime Minister of Poetry, 1985, The Art of Translating Poetry, 1988, American Victorians: Exploration in Emotional History, 1984, Possum and Ole Ez in the Public Eye, 1985, After Such Ignorance, 1986, Man as a Social Animal, 1986, Artists All, 1986, Politicians, Poets, and Con Men, 1986, Founder's Fury, 1988, The Art of Translating Poetry, 1988, Founder's Fortune, 1989, From Stress to Stress: An Autobiography of English Prosody, 1992, The Art of Translating Prose, 1994, The Annotated Milton, 1999, Beethoven in Denver and Other Poems, 1999, numerous translations ; editorial bd. Oral Tradition, 1983—, Literature East and West, 1967-70; adv. editor The Literary Rev., 1987—; reviewer/writer Asian Wall St. Jour., 1978-85; contbr. numerous articles to profl. publs. Mem. Bar of the State of N.Y., The Nat. Faculty. Home: 203 S Mannering Ave Lafayette LA 70508-4829 Office: U La 255 Griffin Hall Lafayette LA 70504-0001 E-mail: bnraffel@earthlink.net.

RAFFEL, JEFFREY ALLEN, urban affairs educator; b. Bklyn., June 19, 1945; s. George A. and Renee (Lane) R.; m. Joanne Ruth Traum, Aug. 27, 1966; children: Allison, Lori, Kenneth. AB, U. Rochester, 1966; PhD, MIT, 1972. Asst. prof. U. Del., Newark, 1971-76, assoc. prof., 1976-82, dir. M Pub. Adminstrn. program, 1980-86, prof., 1982—, chair pub. mgmt. faculty, 1994-97, acting assoc. dean Coll. Urban Affairs and Pub. Policy, 1989, chair pub. mgmt. faculty, 1994—, dir. sch. urban affairs and pub. policy, 1997—. Pub. svc. fellow, spl. asst. to gov. for intergovtl. rels. State of Del., 1979-80; chair urban ednl. policy group Nat. Assn. State Univs. and Land Grant Colls., 1987-93; mem. state supt.'s adv. com. on tchr. recruitment, Del., 1988-91. Author: Politics of School Desegregation, 1980, Historical Dictionary of School Segregation and Desegregation, 1998; co-author: Systematic Analysis of University Libraries, 1969, Selling Cities: Attracting Homebuyers Through Schools and Housing Programs, 1995; mem. editl. bd. Pub. Productivity Rev., N.Y.C., 1984—; contbr. articles to urban affairs publs. Treas. Nottingham Swim Club, Inc., Newark, 1985-88; co-chair Gov.'s Task Force on Enhancing Ednl. Dollar, 1986-87; chair long-range planning com. and membership com. Delmarva coun. Boy Scouts Am., 1988-89; mem. Gov.'s Sch. Reform Partnership, Del, 1990—. Recipient cert. of recognition, NCCJ Greater Wilmington, 1980, numerous profl. and civic awards. Mem. ACLU (Del. chpt. sec. 1992—), Del. Assn. Pub. Adminstrn. (pres. 1981-82), Am. Soc. Pub. Adminstrn., Am. Edn. Rsch. Assn. Avocations: golf, reading. Home: 4 High Pond Dr Newark DE 19711-2597 Office: U Del Coll Urban Affairs Pub Policy Newark DE 19716

RAFFEL, LEROY B. real estate development company executive; b. Zanesville, Ohio, Mar. 13, 1927; s. Jacob E. and Anne M. (Oliker) R.; m. Shirley Balbot, Sept. 11, 1949; children: Kenneth, Janet, James, Nancy. BS, U. Pa., 1949. Pres. Raffel Bros., Inc., Youngstown, Ohio, 1949-78; ret., 1978; pres. York Mahoning Co., Youngstown, 1950-64, Arby's, Inc., Youngstown, 1964-70, chmn. bd., 1971-79; ret., 1979; pres. Brom Equity Devel., Inc., Miami, Fla., 1979—. Served with USNR, 1945-46. Home: 2141 NE 190th Ter North Miami Beach FL 33179-4352 Office: Brom Equity Devel Inc Ste 207 1380 NE Miami Gardens Dr Miami FL 33179-4709

RAFFELSON, MICHAEL, financial executive; s. Leo and Fay Rebecca Raffelson; m. Eileen Judith, Mar. 23, 1975; 1 dau., Elyse Lauren. BBA, CCNY, 1967; MBA, CUNY, 1969. Acct. Am. Metal Climax Inc., N.Y.C., 1967-69; fin. analyst Anaconda Co., 1971-74; sr. fin. analyst corp. staff Internat. Paper Co., 1975-76, bus. analyst white papers group, 1976-79, applications coord. paper and packaging mgmt. sys., 1979-81, mgr. mgmt. svcs. info. sys., 1981-85; mgr. ops. analysis and control info. svcs. The First Boston Corp., 1986-87, mgr. telecom. analysis and control, 1987-88, asst. v.p., 1988; v.p. Chase Manhattan Bank, 1988-2000, J.P. Morgan Chase and Co., N.Y.C., 2001—. Instr. fin. mgmt. edn. program Internat. Paper, 1977. Served with AUS, 1969-71. Mem. Phi Epsilon Pi (pres. chpt. 1966). Office: JP Morgan Chase and Co 575 Washington Blvd Jersey City NJ 10041

RAFFERTY, JAMES GERARD, lawyer; b. Boston, July 9, 1951; s. James John and Helen Christine (Kennedy) R.; m. Rhonda Beth Friedman, May 17, 1981; children: Jessica Faith, Evan Louis Quinn. BA, Brown U., 1974; MA, Princeton U., 1980; JD, Georgetown U., 1984. Bar: Md. 1985, D.C. 1985, U.S. Tax Ct. 1988, U.S. Ct. Appeals (4th cir.) 1989, U.S. Ct. Appeals (3d cir.) 1992. Assoc. Piper & Marbury, Washington, 1984-91, Pepper, Hamilton & Scheetz, Washington, 1991-92; founding ptnr. Harkins Cunningham, 1992—. Contbr. articles to legal jours. Brown U. Club of Boston scholar, 1969-70. Mem. ABA (chmn. com. on affiliated and related corps. tax sect. 1994-95). Roman Catholic. Avocation: golf. Office: Harkins Cunningham 801 Pennsylvania Ave NW Ste 600 Washington DC 20004-2664 E-mail: jrafferty@harkinscunningham.com.

RAFFERTY, JAMES PAUL, telecommunications executive; b. Hartford, Conn., Oct. 26, 1952; s. James Paul and Kathleen Marie (LeHane) R.; m. Lucinda Anne Link, Sept. 16, 1989. BS in Mgmt. Engring., Rensselaer Poly. Inst., Troy, N.Y., 1974, M in Mgmt. Engring., 1975. MIS analyst Burroughs, Danbury, Conn., 1977-80, MIS project leader, 1981-83, mgr. resource planning, 1984, materials mgr., 1985-86; product program mgr. Fujitsu, 1987-88, R&D mgr., 1989-92; pres. Human Comm., 1992-99; sr. product mgr. Brooktrout Tech., Needham, Mass., 2000—. Pub. industry newsletter Human Commn. Digest, 1992-99, Human Commn. Stds. Update, 1996-99; U.S. del. Internat. Telecomms. Union Study Group 8, 1993-2000, Study Group 16, 2000—; tchr. in field; chair Internet Engring. Task Force, 1997-2000; dir. Internat. Bus. Communicators Assn., 1999-2000. Editor Enterprise Computer Telephony Forum, 1995-2000; co-author: IETF RFC 2301, 2302, 2306; contbr. articles to profl. jours. Active Caucus of Conn. Dems., 1986; pres. Deer Ridge Condo Assn., Danbury, 1987-90. Recipient Computer Facsimile Industry award, 1996. Mem. Electronic Messaging Assn. (Disting. Svc. award 1998), Telecom. Industry Assn., Danbury Golf League (team capt. 1984-85), Alliance Francaise, Epsilon Delta Sigma. Avocations: golf, cooking, hiking, music, skiing. Office: Brooktrout Tech 410 1st Ave Needham MA 02494-2815 E-mail: jrafferty@humancomm.com., jraff@brooktrout.com.

RAFFIN, THOMAS A. physician; b. San Francisco, Jan. 25, 1947; s. Bennett L. and Carolyn M. Raffin; m. Michele Raffin, June 19, 1987; children: Elizabeth S., Ross Daniel, Jake Bennett, Nicholas Ethan. AB in Biol. Sci., Stanford Med. Sch., 1968, MD, 1973. Diplomate Am. Bd. Pulmonary Medicine, Am. Bd. Internal Medicine (also in Critical Care Medicine). Intern Peter Bent Brigham Hosp., 1973-75; fellow in respiratory medicine sch. medicine Stanford U., Stanford, Calif., 1975-78, med. fiberoptic bronchoscopy service dir. med. ctr., 1978—, acting asst. prof. sch. medicine, 1978-80, assoc. dir. med. ctr. intensive care units, med. dir. dept. respiratory therapy hosp., 1978—, assoc. prof. medicine sch. medicine, 1986-95, acting chief div. respiratory medicine, 1988—, chief div. pulmonary and critical care, 1990—, prof. medicine sch. of medicine, 1995—, Colleen and Robert Haas professorship in medicine/biomed. ethics, 1999—; co-dir. Stanford U. Ctr. for Biomed. Ethics, 1989—; co-founder Rigel Pharms., Inc., 1996—. Chmn. ethics com. Stanford U. Med. Ctr., 1987—; ptnr. Telegraph Hill Ptnrs., 2002. Author: Intensive Care: Facing the Critical Choices, 1988; contbr. articles to profl. jours. V.p. lung cancer com., No. Calif. Oncology Group, 1983-85; com. mem. NIH Workshop, 1984. Recipient Henry J. Kaiser Found. award, 1981, 84, 88, 97, Arthur L. Bloomfield award, 1981. Fellow ACP (rep. coun. subsplty. socs. 1986), Am. Coll. Chest Physicians (program com. mem. 1985-86); mem. AAAS, Am. Fedn. for Clin. Rsch., Am. Thoracic Soc., Santa Clara County Lung Assn. and Med. Soc., Calif. Med. Assn. (chmn. sect. chest diseases 1984-85), Soc. for Critical Care Medicine, Calif. Thoracic Soc. Jewish. Avocations: painting, gardening. Home: 13468 Three Forks Ln Los Altos CA 94022-2432 Office: Stanford U Med Ctr Dept Medicine Div Pul & Crit Care Med # H3151 Stanford CA 94305

RAFFO, SUSAN HENNEY, elementary education educator; b. Kendallville, Ind., Feb. 14, 1945; d. Gordon Theron and Sue (Kizer) Henney; m. Lawrence Albert Raffo, Feb. 19, 1977; children: Timothy, Kathleen. BS in Elem. Edn., Ball State U., 1967; M in Spl. Edn., San Francisco State U., 1972. Cert. elem. tchr., Calif. Tchr. East Noble Sch. Corp., Kendallville, Ind., 1967-68, Burlingame (Calif.) Sch. Dist., 1968-2000, Las Lomitas (Calif.) Sch. Dist., 2000—. Master tchr. San Francisco State U., 1970-95, U. Notre Dame de Namur, Belmont, Calif., 1980-95, instr. grad. edn. dept., 1996—. Registrar AYSO, Burlingame, 1987-94; bd. dirs. Burlingame Cmty. Edn. Found., 1989-95, sec., 1992-94. Recipient Svc. award PTA, 1989, J. Russell Kent award for innovative programs San Mateo County Sch. Bds. Assn., 1993; named Tchr. of Yr., Lions Club, 1993. Mem. Calif. Reading Assn., Alpha Delta Kappa, Phi Delta Kappa. Avocations: reading, fabric arts, golf. Office: La Entrada Sch 2200 Sharon Rd Menlo Park CA 94025-6796 E-mail: sraffo@llesd.k12.ca.us., sraffo@email.com.

RAFKIN, SCOT C. R. science educator; b. Perth Amboy, N.J., July 29, 1967; s. Denny and Sherrie Randell; m. Gina M. Rafkin, Nov. 18, 1995. PhD, Colo. State U., 1996. Author: (numerical model of Mars' atmosphere) The Mars Global and Regional Atmospheric Modeling System, 2001; contbr. Fellow faculty fellow, NASA ASEE, 1998; grantee numerous rsch. grants, NASA, 1999, 2000. Mem.: Am. Meteorol. Soc., Am. Geophys. Union, Am. Astron. Soc. (divsn. planetary sci.).

RAFSNIDER, GILES THOMAS, economics educator; b. Dayton, Ohio, Oct. 18, 1941; s. Lowell Bruce and Cyrilla Stella Katrina (Strothman) R.; m. Donna Jean Fry, Dec. 27, 1964; children: Erica Christine, Gillian Helene. Student, Deep Springs Coll., 1959-62, Oreg. State U., 1962-63; BS, Utah State U., 1965; MS, U. Nev., Reno, 1967; PhD, U. Mass., 1974. Rsch. dir. Ins. div. Nev. Dept. Commerce, Carson City, 1973-74; forest economist USDA Forest Svc., Broomall, Pa., 1974-78; agrl. economist Econ. Rsch. Svc., USDA, Ft. Collins, Colo., 1978-85; adj. assoc. prof. Colo. State U., 1978-85; assoc. prof. agrl. econs. U. Nebr., Lincoln, 1985-91; vis. assoc. prof. agrl. econs. U. Wyo., Laramie, 1992—. Adj. prof. Ecole Nationale d'Agriculture, Meknes, Morocco, 1987-91; cons. The World Bank, 1993—. Contbr. articles to profl. jours. Harry J. Loman fellow, Media, Pa., 1973-74. Mem. Am. Econ. Assn., Am. Mgmt. Assn., Western Agrl. Econ. Assn., Internat. Assn. Agrl. Econs. Greek Orthodox. Avocations: reading, fly fishing, making harps. Home: 1215 Garfield St Denver CO 80206-3514 Office: U Wyo Dept Agrl Econs Laramie WY 82071-3354

RAFT, CAROLE RUTH, real estate executive; b. N.Y.C., Apr. 29, 1940; d. Matthew Martin and Charlotte Helen (Adler) Klein; widowed; children: J. Scott, Jodi Raft. BS, Queens Coll., 1962. V.p. film distbrn. Henry Strauss Prodns., N.Y.C., 1957-60; producer, writer Rafilm Inc., N.Y.C., Ft. Lauderdale, 1960-80; prin. Carole Raft Properties, Lauderhill, Fla. Author: Rape of the Blindfolded Lady, 1979; free-lance writer poems, children's cards, etc. Mem. Fla. Motion Picature Assn., Fla. State Assn. Realtors (bd. dirs. 1988—), Ft. Lauderdale Assn. Realtors (bd. dirs. 1988—), Am. Soc. Tng. and Devel. Avocations: vol. work. Office: Carole Raft Properties 7654 N Nob Hill Rd Tamarac FL 33321-1869

RAFTER, JAMES JOSEPH, internist, retired; b. Jersey City, 1923; MD, Jefferson Med. Coll., 1949. Cert. internal medicine, 1965, recert. 1977, cardiovascular diseases, 1974. Intern USn Hosp., Jacksonville, 1949-50; resident Oakland VA Hosp., 1958-60; fellow cardiologist Presbyn. Med. Ctr., San Francisco, 1960-61; retired. Mem. Am. Coll. Cardiology, Am. Heart Assn.

RAFTER, SANDRA JOY, special education educator; b. Johnson City, N.Y., Dec. 10, 1940; d. Martin Francis and Gladys Irene (McCoy) R. BS, SUNY, Cortland, 1963; MA, SUNY, Binghamton, 1979; PhD, U. Iowa, 1985. Cert. tchr. English 7-12, spl. edn., nursery, kindergarten, elem., N.Y.; cert. secondary tchr., Iowa. Tchr. spl. edn. Broome Bd. Coop. Ednl. Svcs., Binghamton, 1966-67; tchr. kindergarten, elem. Whitney Point (N.Y.) Sch., 1969-78; tchr. spl. edn. Binghamton Sch. Dist., 1979-81; lectr. Briar Cliff Coll., Sioux City, Iowa, 1987; tchr. spl. edn. Afton (N.Y.) Sch., 1987-99; spl. edn. pvt. tchr. Binghamton, N.Y., 1999—. Adj. lectr. Binghamton U., 1987-91, vis. prof., 1992-93. Sec. Binghamton Police Chaplaincy Program, 1976; coord. Project Concern, Whitney Point, 1974. Mem. NEA. Roman Catholic. Avocations: creative writing, writing jokes, gardening.

RAGAN, ANN TALMADGE, media and production consultant, actor; b. Raleigh, N.C., July 6, 1951; d. Samuel Talmadge and Marjorie Lois (Usher) R.; m. L. Worth Keeter III, Aug. 22, 1992. Student, U. N.C., 1969-71, Finch Coll., 1972-73, New Sch. Social Rsch., 1973-74, Western Wash. U., 1978. Acct. estimator Benton & Bowles Inc., N.Y.C., 1971-72, media buyer, 1974-77; speechwriter, press aide Senator Robert Morgan, Washington, 1978-79; asst. producer John F. Murray Inc., N.Y.C., 1979-80; producer, sales dir. Grand Street Films, 1980-84; ind. producer for various clients, 1984-86; asst. pub. The Pilot, Inc., Southern Pines, N.C., 1986-96, also bd. dirs. Prodn. mgr. Anglo Am. Media Workshops, London, 1988—90; program adminstr. profl. tng. divsn. Directing Workshop for Women, TV Writers Workshop - Am. Film Inst., L.A.; mgr., exec. prodr. films, commls., audio books Blue Kiss, LLC. Contbr. articles to newspaper and jour. Mem. Roanoke Island Hist. Assn., Moore County arts coun., 1986-89. Mem.: SAG (conservatory com., rec. sec. 1997—), AFTRA, Women in Film, Women in Theatre (adminstrv. dir. 1995—97, treas. 1997—99, bd. dirs. 1997—99), Actors Equity Assn., Ind. Feature Project West, Kings and Clowns Ednl. Shakespeare Alliance (treas. bd. dirs. 1999—), Pi Beta Phi. Democrat. Methodist. Home and Office: 10542 Bloomfield St Toluca Lake CA 91602-2813 E-mail: bluekissllc@aol.com.

RAGAN, BETTY SAPP, artist, educator; b. Birmingham, Ala., Mar. 15, 1937; d. Robert William and Emma Mildred (O'Neal) Sapp; m. Thaxton Drew Ragan, Apr. 1958 (div. Aug. 1986); 1 child, Robert McClearan. BA cum laude, Birmingham-So. Coll., 1958; student, Allegheny Coll., 1971-72, Auburn U., 1980-83; MFA, Pratt Inst., 1985. Teachng asst. Pratt Inst., Bklyn., 1985; vis. asst. prof. dept. art Auburn U., 1985-89; asst. prof. dept. art U. Puget Sound, 1989-91, assoc. prof. photography and printmaking, dept. art, 1992—. Panel moderator Soc. for Photo Edn. N.W., Tacoma, 1993; co-curator But Is It Art, Tacoma, 1993. Exhibited photography in solo shows at Maude Kerns Gallery, Eugene, Oreg., 1995, Helen Smith Gallery, Green River C.C., Auburn, Wash., 1996, others; group shows include Hanson Gallery, New Orleans, 1980, Montgomery (Ala.) Mus. Fine Arts, 1981, Ga. State U., Atlanta, 1981, Park Ave Atrium, N.Y.C., 1985, Carnegie Art Ctr., Walla Walla, Wash., 1990, Definitive Image Gallery, Seattle, 1992, Seattle Ctr. Pavilion, 1993, San Diego Art Inst., 1993, Eagle Gallery, Murray, Ky., 1994, B St. Pier Gallery, San Diego, 1995, numerous others; artist/photographer various collage series; co-curator But Is It Art?, Tacoma, 1993. Recipient numerous awards for art including Merit award Fine Arts Mus. of the South, Mobile, 1983, Dirk Andrew Phibbs Rsch. award U. Puget Sound, Tacoma, 1994. Mem. Soc. for Photog. Edn., Soc. Photog. Edn./N.W. (sec. 1990-93), Artist Trust, Women's Caucus for Art, Coll. Art Assn., Seattle Women's Caucus for Art. Unitarian Universalist. Avocations: entomology, hiking, gardening, existential philosophy. Office: U Puget Sound Dept Art 1500 N Warner St Tacoma WA 98416-0001

RAGAN, CHARLES OLIVER, JR. lawyer; b. Knoxville, Tenn., Dec. 23, 1935; s. Charles Oliver and Jeanette (Butler) R.; m. Pauline Iona Kimsey, Apr. 19, 1958. BSBA, U. Tenn., 1958, JD, 1963. Bar: Tenn. 1964, U.S. Dist. Ct. (ea. dist.) Tenn. 1965; cert. consumer bankruptcy specialist. Staff atty. State of Tenn., Chattanooga, 1964-69; atty. Bean & Phillips, 1969-73; sr. ptnr. Ragan & Schulman, 1973-75, Ragan & Littleton, Chattanooga, 1975-80, Ragan & Wulforst, Chattanooga, 1980-84; pvt. practice, 1984—. Tenn. commnr. Nat. Conf. Commrs. on Uniform State Laws, 1976-80. Campaign treas. for Dem. candidates. Democrat. Methodist. Home: 185 Woodcliff Cir Signal Mountain TN 37377-3142 Office: 707 Georgia Ave Ste 300 Chattanooga TN 37402-2047

RAGAN, CHARLES RANSOM, lawyer; b. N.Y.C., Aug. 13, 1947; s. Charles Alexander Jr. and Josephine Forbes (Parker) R.; m. Barbara Thiel McMahon, Aug. 30, 1969; children: Alexandra Watson, Madeline McCue. AB, Princeton U., 1969; JD, Fordham U., 1974. Bar: N.Y. 1975, U.S. Ct. Appeals (3d cir.) 1975, Calif. 1976, U.S. Ct. Appeals (9th cir.) 1976, U.S. Dist. Ct. (no. dist.) Calif. 1976, U.S. Supreme Ct. 1981, U.S. Dist. Ct. (so. dist.) N.Y. 1982, U.S. Ct. Appeals (2d cir.) 1984. Law clk. to Hon. R.J. Aldisert U.S. Ct. Appeals (3rd cir.), 1974-76; assoc. Pillsbury, Madison & Sutro, San Francisco, 1976-81, ptnr., 1982-97, Palo Alto, 1997-2000, Pillsbury Winthrop, Palo Alto, San Francisco , 2001—. Mem. exec. com. 9th Cir. Judicial Conf., 1987-91; mem. Civil Justice Reform Act Adv. Group, No. Dist. Calif., 1995-99. Contbr. articles to profl. jours. Mem. San Francisco Bar Assn. (chair feds. cts. 1982-89). Avocations: biking, swimming, spectator sports. Office: Pillsbury Winthrop LLP 50 Fremont St San Francisco CA 94105

RAGAN, DAVID, publishing company executive; b. Jackson, Tenn., Aug. 26, 1925; s. Amos and Esther Lee (Tacker) R.; m. Violet Claire Sills, Dec. 27, 1948; children— David Nathaniel, Sarah Sills, Jennifer Leigh. BA in English, Union U., Jackson, 1947; M. Theatre Arts, Calif. Sch. Theatre, 1950. Radio writer Grand Central Sta., 1950; syndicated columnist Hollywood South Side, 1951; mng. editor Tele-Views mag., 1952; free-lance writer, 1952-57, 74-77, 82—; editor TV and Movie Screen Sterling Group, Inc., N.Y.C., 1957-61; mng. editor Motion Picture mag. Fawcett Pub. Co., 1961-64; editor TV Radio Mirror, Macfadden-Bartell Pub. Co., 1964-71; pub., editorial dir. Movie Digest, Words and Music, Planet mags. Nat. Periodical Publs. (Warner Communications), 1971-74; editorial dir. Photoplay, Motion Picture, TV Mirror mags.; Macfadden Women's Group, N.Y.C., 1977-79; entertainment editor Globe Nat. Weekly, 1979-82. Author: Who's Who in Hollywood 1900-1976, 1977, Movie Stars of the '30s, 1985, Movie Stars of the '40s, 1985, Mel Gibson: An Intimate Biography, 1985, Who's Who in Hollywood: The Largest Cast of Film Personalities Ever Assembled, rev., 1992; co-author: Richard Pryor: This Cat's Got Nine Lives, 1982; contbr. articles to profl. jours. Served with U.S. Army, 1952-54. Mem. Screen Actors Guild, TV Acad., Alpha Tau Omega, Tau Kappa Alpha. Republican. Presbyterian. Home: 1230 Park Ave New York NY 10128-1724

RAGAN, JAMES THOMAS, communications executive; b. San Diego, Mar. 15, 1929; m. Susan Held, Nov. 9, 1957; children: James, Maria, Carey, Andrew. BA, Oxford U., Eng., 1951, MA, 1955; elect. engring. vocat. cert., U. State of N.Y., 1954. With Gen. Electric Co., 1954-69; pres., chief operating officer Athena Communications Corp. subs. Gulf & Western Industries, Inc., N.Y.C., 1969-74; v.p. broadcast services Western Union Telegraph Co., 1974-76, v.p. satellite services, 1976-82, pres. Western Union personal communications corp., v.p. communication systems group, 1982-85; pres. Associated Info. Services Corp., 1985-86, Bunting, Inc., 1985-88; ptnr. Pierce Kennedy Hearth, 1988-91; CEO Nat. Lang. Assocs. Lanarea Pub., Guilford, Conn., 1990—. Patentee recreational sports equipment; author: The Ultimate Diet, The First Alaskans, A Guide to the Geography of the Native Languages, Cultures, Their Communities, and Populations, 1996. Pres. Wilton Pop Warner Football League, Wilton, Conn., 1972—73. Maj. USMCR, 1952—54, Korea. Mem.: Sachem's Head Assn. (v.p., pres., treas.), Racquet and Tennis Club NYC. Home: PO Box 1112 Green Valley AZ 85622 Office: Nat Lang Assocs PO Box 1112 Green Valley AZ 85622 E-mail: jtrnla@aol.com.

RAGAN, JAMES FRANCIS, economics educator; b. Independence, Mo., Apr. 10, 1949; s. James Francis Ragan and Helen Rita (Vitt) Henderson; m. Gail Carol Rosenkoetter, Dec. 30, 1972; children: Emily, Patrick, Laura. BA, U. Mo., 1971; MA, Washington U., St. Louis, 1972, PhD, 1975. Rsch. economist Fed. Res. Bank N.Y., N.Y.C., 1975-77; vis. scholar Fed. Res. Bank Kansas City (Mo.), 1980; asst. prof. Kans. State U., Manhattan, 1977-80, assoc. prof., 1980-85, prof. econs., 1985—, dept. head, 1990—. Vis. assoc. prof. Washington U., St. Louis, 1984-85. Author: Principles of Economics, 1990, 2d edit., 1993. NDEA grad. fellow, 1971-74, H.B. Earhart fellow, 1974-75; recipient E.S. Bagley Rsch. award Kans. State U., 1988, William Stamey Teaching award Kans. State U., 1989-90.

RAGAN, JOHN DAVID, writer, historian; b. Buffalo, Dec. 28, 1951; s. William Andrew and Mary Irene (Howley) R. BA in History, SUNY, Binghamton, 1975; magistere, U. Paris, 1981; MA in French, U. Cin., 1982; PhD in History, NYU, 2000. Waiter Cripple Creek Resort, Ester, Alaska, 1975-76, 78. 89, Chena Hot Springs, Fairbanks, 1988-92; processer Petersburg (Alaska) Fisheries, 1979, Pan Alaska Fisheries, Dutch Harbor, 1979; Nodwell tracked vehicle operator Halliburton Geophys. Svcs., Alaska, 1980-90; freelance writer Chelsea House Pubs., N.Y.C., 1987—; comml. fisherman Bristol Bay, Alaska, 1996. Author: Emiliano Zapata, 1989, The Explorers of Alaska, 1992. Ofcl. challenger Clinton-Gore Campaign, Hoboken, N.J., 1992. Devel. fellow NYU, 1987; scholar U. Cin., 1981, NYU, 1988. Mem. Soc. Amis Bibliotheque Arsenal, Soc. Amis Ismayl Urbain. Democrat. Avocations: travel, swimming, backpacking, motorcycling, biking. Home: PO Box 294 Ester AK 99725-0294

RAGAN, ROBERT ALLISON, private investment executive, financial consultant; b. Gastonia, N.C., Aug. 21, 1938; s. Caldwell and Jocelyn (Sikes) R. BS in Bus. Adminstrn., U. N.C., 1961; postgrad., Rutgers U., 1968. V.p. N.C. Nat. Bank (now Bank of Am.), Charlotte, 1961-81; pres., treas. R.A. Ragan & Co., Inc., 1981—. Dir. Carolina Mills, Inc., Maiden, N.C., 1977—. Author, pub.: The Ragans of Gastonia (1790-1995), 1995, The Textile Heritage of Gaston County, N.C. (1848-2000), 2000. Founder, pres. bd. govs. The Gaston Soc. of Mecklenburg County, Charlotte, NC; trustee, bd. visitors Darlington Sch., Rome, 1981—; trustee Daniel Stowe Bot. Gardens, Belmont, NC, 2001—; pres. bd. trustees Gaston County Mus. Art and History, Dallas, 1978—81, 1997—99. Mem. Charlotte City Club, DeBordieu Colony Country Club (Georgetown, S.C.), Linville (N.C.) Ridge Country Club. Republican. Presbyterian. Avocations: preservation and recording of local and North Carolina history, especially industrial history, travel. Home: 227 Fenton Pl Charlotte NC 28207-1913 Office: R A Ragan & Co PO Drawer 6158 Charlotte NC 28207-0001 also: 407 DeBordieu Blvd Georgetown SC 29440

RAGAN, STEPHEN C. academic administrator; b. Gadsen, Ala., Sept. 2, 1965; s. Larry F. Ragan and Linda C. Regan; m. Becky A. Roth. BA in History, U. of Mich., 1989. Campaign dir. Ea. Mich. U., Ypsilanti, 1991—96; dir. capital campaigns St. Joseph Mercy Health System, Ann Arbor, 1996—99; v.p. for univ. advancement Lawrence Tech. U., Southfield , 1999—. Alt. del. Rep. Nat. Conv., San Diego, 1996; bd. trustees United Meth. Retirement Communities, Ann Arbor, 1996—; chmn. bd. trustees Schoolcraft Coll., Livonia, 1991—2000; trustee, past v.p. UMRC Heritage Found. Republican. Methodist. Avocations: running, travel, reading. Office: Lawrence Technological University 21000 W ten Mile Rd Southfield MI 48075 Office Fax: 248-204-2207.

RAGAN, STEPHEN T. music educator; b. Honolulu, Feb. 8, 1961; s. Stephen W. and Emilie Ragan; m. Connie Christopher; 1 child Michael Stromenger 1 child Marie Stromenger 1 child Jessica. BS in Edn. - Composite Music, Valley City (N.D.) State U., 1987. Music dir. Drake Pub. Sch., Drake, ND, 1987—88, Hope Pub. Sch., Hope, 1988—91, Adams (N.D.) Pub. Schs., 1991—95; chair music dept., dir. choral activities Larimore (N.D.) Pub. Schs., 1995—2000; dir. choral activites Bagley (Minn.) H.S., 2000—. Adj. music faculty Lake Region State Coll., Devils Lake, ND, 1993—. Mem.: NEA, Music Educators Nat. Conf., Am. Choral Dirs. Assn. Episcopalian. Office: Bagley H S 1130 Main Ave N Bagley MN 56621 Personal E-mail: musicman@polarcomm.com. Business E-Mail: sragan@bagley.k12.mn.us.

RAGANS, ROSALIND DOROTHY, textbook author, retired art educator; b. Bklyn., Feb. 28, 1933; d. Sidney Guy Gordon and Beatrice (Zuckerman) Safier; m. John Franklin Ragans, July 31, 1965; 1 child, John Lee. BFA, CUNY-Hunter Coll., 1955; MEd, Ga. So. Coll., 1967; EdD, U. Ga., 1971. Cert. tchr. art, Ga. Tchr. art Union City (N.J.) Bd. Edn., 1956-62; tchr. 1st grade Chatham Bd. Edn., Savannah, Ga., 1962-64; instr. art Ga. So. U., Statesboro, 1964-69, asst. prof., 1969-76, assoc. prof., 1976-89, prof. emeritus, 1989—. Keynote speaker art edn. confs., Ind., 1987, 88, Ark., Wis., 1989, Md., 1990, others; presenter GA Art Edn. Conf., 1998, 2000, NAEA, 1999. Author: (textbooks) ArtTalk, 1988, 2d edit., 1994, 3d edit., 1999, Introducing Art, 1997, Exploring Art, 1990, 2d edit., 1997, Understanding Art, 1990, 2d edit., 1997, (sr. author) Art Connections K-5, 1997, 2d edit., 2000. Mem. Nat. Assn. Educators (life), Ga. Assn. Educators (life), Nat. Art Edn. Assn. (Southeastern Art Educator of Yr. 1991, Nat. Art Educator of Yr. 1992), Ga. Art Edn. Assn. (Ga. Art Educator of Yr. 1990), Pilot Club Internat. (Ga. dist., Ga. Profl. Handicapped Woman of Yr. 1988). Jewish. Avocation: painting.

RAGATZ, THOMAS GEORGE, lawyer; b. Madison, Wis., Feb. 18, 1934; s. Wilmer Leroy and Rosanna (Kindschi) Ragatz; m. Karen Christensen, Dec. 19, 1965; children: Thomas Rolf, William Leslie, Erik Douglas. BBA, U. Wis., 1957, LLB, 1961. CPA Wis.; bar: Wis. 1961, U.S. Dist. Ct. (ea. and we. dists.) Wis. 1961, U.S. Tax Ct. 1963, U.S. Ct. Appeals (7th cir.) 1965, U.S. Supreme Ct. 1968. Staff acct. Peat, Marwick, Mitchell & Co., Mpls., 1958; instr. Sch. Bus., U. Wis., Madison, 1958-60; formerly lectr. in acctg. and law Law Sch. U. Wis.; law clk. Wis. Supreme Ct., 1961-62; assoc. Boardman Suhr Curry & Field, Madison, 1962-64, ptnr., 1965-78, Foley & Lardner, Madison, 1978—, mng. ptnr., 1984-93, chmn. budget com., 1994-99. Dir. Sub-Zero Freezer Co., Inc., Mortenson, Matzell & Meldrem, Inc., Norman Bassett Found., Wis. Sports Found., United Way Found., Courtier Found.; dir., past pres. Wis. Sports Devel. Corp.; lectr. seminars on tax subjects. Author: The Ragatz History, 1989; contbr. Formerly dir. United Way, Meth. Hosp. Found; mem. U. Wis. Found., United Way of Dane County; former dir. United Way, Meth. Hosp.; mem. Wis. Found., United Way of Dane County; chmn. site selection com. U. Wis. Hosp.; bd. regents U. Wis., panel provision of legal svcs.; past pres. 1st Congl. Ch. Found.; bd. dirs. Met. YMCA, Madison, YMCA Found., Found. for Madison Pub. Schs.; pres. Bus. and Edn. Partnership, 1983—89, bd. dirs.; former moderator 1st Congl. Ch.; past pres. First Congl. Ch. Found.; former moderator 1st Congl. Ch.; chmn. site selection com. U. Wis. Hosp.; bd. regents U. Wis., panel provision of legal svcs.; bd. dirs. Met. YMCA, Madison, 1983—90, YMCA Found., Norman Bassett Found., Courtier Found.; pres. Bus. & Edn. Partnership, 1983—89, also bd. dirs. Fellow: Am. Bar Found.; mem.: ABA, Dane County Bar Assn. (pres. 1978—79, chmn. jud. qualification com., sec.), Wis. Inst. CPA, State Bar Wis. (sec. 1969—70, bd. govs. 1971—75, chmn. fin. com. 1975—80, chmn. tax sect., chmn. spl. com. on econs., chmn. svcs. for lawyers com.), Wis. Bar Found., Seventh Cir. Bar Assn., Am. Judicature Soc., Order of Constantine, Bascom Hill Soc., Order of Coif, Madison Club (pres. 1980—81), Madison Club House Corp. (pres. 1999—, bd. dirs.), Sigma Chi, Beta Gamma Sigma. Republican. Home: 3334 Lake Mendota Dr Madison WI 53705-1469 Office: Foley & Lardner PO Box 1497 Madison WI 53701-1497 also: Foley & Lardner 1st Wisconsin Ctr 777 E Wisconsin Ave Ste 3800 Milwaukee WI 53202-5302

RAGATZKI, PAUL A. internist, administrator, educator; b. Detroit, Nov. 18, 1960; s. Paul F. Ragatzki and Marie A. Kazyaka; m. Kelly Francis, Sept. 3, 1993; children: Stephanie, Mallory, Avery. BS in Chemistry magna cum laude, Oakland U., 1982; MD, Wayne State U., 1986. Diplomate Nat. Bd. Med. Examiners; lic. physician, Mich. Intern in internal medicine dept. internal medicine Wayne State U. Sch. Medicine, Detroit, 1986-87, resident in internal medicine dept. internal medicine, 1987-89; chief med. resident dept. internal medicine Harper Hosp., Wayne State U. Sch. Medicine, 1989-90, dir. hosp. based svcs. dept. internal medicine, 1990-99, asst. prof. medicine dept. internal medicine, 1990—2000, assoc. prof., 2002—, yr. III clin. coord. dept. internal medicine, 1992-94, phys. diagnosis yr. II coord. dept. internal medicine, 1992-95, dir. med. edn. dept. internal medicine, 1992-95, firm chief dept. internal medicine, 1994-97, mng. physician hosp. physician group, 1998-99; med. dir. Hosp. Physicians Group, 1999—2001, Mich. Hospitalists, 2002—. Pres. Hosp. Care Consultants, Health Care Sys. Design and Mgmt., Detroit, 1994—; affiliate assoc. prof. U. Detroit Mercy, 1999-01. Fellow ACP (Cert. of Achievement 1994, 95); mem. AMA, Am. Coll. Physician Execs., Nat. Assn. Inpatient Physicians, Alpha Omega Alpha. Roman Catholic. Avocation: golf. Home: 48051 Andover Dr Novi MI 48374-3469 E-mail: paular@mich.com.

RAGAVAN, ANPALAKI JEYABALASINKHAM, application developer, researcher; d. George and Thangaranee Veluppilai Jeyabalasingham; m. Ragavan Vinasithamby, July 1, 1993. BS(hon.) , U. Sri Lanka, 1985, MPhil (hon.) , 1989; MS (hon.) , U. Nev., 1996, postgrad. Cert. BASIC computer programmer, geographic info. sys., Visual Basic programmer, GIS and web design, well drilling with LS 100. Asst. prof. U. Sri Lanka, Kilinochchi, 1989—92; rsch. asst. Ind. State U., Tere Haute, 1992—93; software developer Bur. Labor Stats., Washington, 1996—99; rsch. asst. U. of Nev., Reno, 1999—. Grad. fellow U. Nev., Reno, 1993—96. Contbr. articles to profl. jours. (Excellence in Abstract Submission award Am. Jour. Pub. Health, 2001); author: (book) Introductory Statistics, Lab-Guide - SAS, 1st edition., 1993, (Nev.health divsn. quar. report) Impact Of Discharge Planning On Adherence to Treatment for Inmates with HIV/AIDS in Nevada, 2001, Surveillance Update:Discharge Planning For Inmates with HIV/AIDS in Nevada, 2002. Recipient Excellence in Abstract Submission, APHA, HIV/AIDS Sect., 2001, Cert. Of Appreciation, Nev. State Mental Health and Devel. Services, 2000, Overseas Devel. Adminstrn. scholarship, Govt. Of UK, 1986—89; grantee, State of Nev., 2002; scholar, Asian Inst. Of Tech. in Thailand, 1991, Ind. State U., 1992—93, U. of Nev., Reno, 1993—, Soroptimist Internat. of Reno, Sierra Nev. Region, 2000. Mem.: Am. Statis. Assn., Geol. Soc. Am., Alumni Assn. U. Nev. Mem. Lds Ch. Avocations: dancing, music, guitar, swimming, sports. Home: 3952 Clear Acre Ln Apt 278 Reno NV 89512 Office: U Nev Dept Health Ecology Reno NV 89512 Home Fax: 775-674-0397; Office Fax: 775-674-0397. Personal E-mail: ragavan@unr.edu. E-mail: ragavan@unr.edu.

RAGENT, BORIS, physicist; b. Cleve., Mar. 2, 1924; s. Samuel and Bertha (Lev) R.; m. Dorothy Kohn, Sept. 11, 1949; children— David Stefan, Lawrence Stanton, Jesse Ron. Student, Ohio State U., 1941-44; BSE.E., Marquette U., 1944; PhD in Physics, U. Calif., Berkeley, 1953. Registered profl. engr., Calif. Engr. Victoreen Instrument Co., Cleve., 1946-48; engr., physicist Radiation Lab., U. Calif., Berkeley, 1948-53; physicist Livermore, 1953-56, Broadview Research Corp., Burlingame, Calif., 1956-59, Vidya div. Itek Corp., Palo Alto, 1959-66, Ames Research Ctr., NASA, Moffett Field, 1966-87, San Jose (Calif.) State U. Found., 1987-98. Lectr. Stanford U., U. Calif. Extension. Served in USNR, 1944-46. Mem. AAAS, Am. Phys. Soc., Optical Soc. Am., Am. Geophys. Union, Sigma Xi. Office: Ames Research Ctr NASA Mail Stop 245-1 Moffett Field CA 94035 E-mail: ragent@ssa1.arc.nasa.gov.

RAGER, JOHN EWING, III, computer science educator; b. N.Y.C., July 16, 1956; s. John Ewing Jr. and Eleanor Anne (Stubbe) R. SB, MIT, 1977; SM, U. Chgo., 1978; PhD, Northwestern U., 1987. Lectr. math. U. Chgo., 1979-83; instr., then spl. lectr. in artificial intelligence Northwestern U., Evanston, Ill., 1984-88; asst. prof. computer sci. Amherst (Mass.) Coll., 1988—. Cons. in computer-related law, 1986—; assoc., Behavioral and Brain Scis., Princeton, N.J., 1988—. Contbr. articles to profl. publs. Mem. Assn. Computational Linguistics, Assn. Computing Machinery, Internat. Nueral Network Soc., Am. Assn. Artificial Intelligence, IEEE, Psycoloquy (editorial bd.), Phi Beta Kappa. Avocations: violin, genealogy. Office: Amherst Coll Dept Math and Computer Sci Amherst MA 01002

RAGGI, REENA, federal judge; b. Jersey City, May 11, 1951; BA, Wellesley Coll., 1973; JD, Harvard U., 1976. Bar: N.Y. 1977. U.S. atty. Dept. Justice, Bklyn., 1986; ptnr. Windels, Marx, Davies & Ives, N.Y.C., 1987; judge U.S. Dist. Ct. (ea. dist.) N.Y., Bklyn., 1987—. Office: US Courthouse 225 Cadman Plz E Brooklyn NY 11201-1818

RAGGIO, LOUISE BALLERSTEDT, lawyer; b. Austin, Tex., June 15, 1919; d. Louis F. and Hilma (Lindgren) Ballerstedt; m. Grier H. Raggio, Apr. 19, 1941; children: Grier, Thomas, Kenneth. BA, U. Tex., 1939; student, Am. U. Washington, 1939-40; JD, So. Methodist U., 1952. Bar: Tex. 1952, U.S. Dist. Ct. (no. dist.) Tex. 1958. Intern Nat. Inst. Pub. Affairs, Washington, 1939-40; asst. dist. atty. Dallas County, Tex., 1954-56; shareholder Raggio and Raggio, 1956—. Sec. Gov.'s Commn. on Status of Women, 1970-71; trustee Tex. Bar Found., 1982-86, chmn., 1984-85, chmn. fellows, 1993—, Dallas Women's Found., 1993—, Nat. Conf. Bar Founds., 1986-92. Recipient Zonta award, Bus. and Profl. Women's Club award, So. Meth. U. Alumni award, Woman of Yr. award Tex. Fedn. Bus. and Profl. Women's Clubs, 1985, award Internat. Women's Forum, 1990, Disting. Law Alumni award So. Meth. U., 1992; Disting. Trial Lawyer award, 1993, Outstanding Trial Lawyer award Dallas Bar Assn., 1993, Pacemaker award Nat. Bus. Women Owners Assn., 1994, Thomas Jefferson award ACLU, 1994, Courage award Women Journalists North Tex., 1995; inducted into Tex. Women's Hall of Fame, 1985. Fellow Am. Bar Found.; mem. ABA (chmn. family sect. 1975-76, Best Woman Lawyer award 1995), LWV (pres. Austin 1945-46), State Bar Tex. (chmn. family law sect. 1965-67, dir. 1979-82, citation for law reform 1967, Pres.'s award 1987, Sarah T. Hughes award 1993), Dallas Bar Found. (pres. fellow com. 1991), Am. Acad. Matrimonial Lawyers (gov. 1973-81, trustee found. 1992—), Bus. and Profl. Women's Club (pres. Town North 1958-59), Phi Beta Kappa (pres. Dallas chpt. 1970-71, 90-92). Unitarian Universalist. Home: 3561 Colgate Ave Dallas TX 75225-5010 Office: Raggio and Raggio 3316 Oak Grove Ave Ste 100 Dallas TX 75204-2338 *All things are possible in our expanding universe if we can tune in to the infinite power available to all of us. Our ancestors concentrated on the problems— let us be a part of the solutions so desperately needed in our complex and troubled world.*

RAGGIO, WILLIAM JOHN, state legislator; b. Reno, Oct. 30, 1926; s. William John and Clara M. (Cardelli) R.; m. Dorothy Brigman, August 15, 1948 (dec. Apr. 1998); children: Leslie Ann, Tracy Lynn, Mark William. Student, La. Poly. Inst., 1944-45, U. Okla., 1945-46; BA, U. Nev., 1948; JD, U. Calif. at Hastings, 1951. Bar: Nev. 1951, U.S. Supreme Ct. 1959. Atty., Reno and Las Vegas; asst. dist. atty. Washoe County, Nev., 1952-58; dist. atty., 1958-71; ptnr. firm Wiener, Goldwater, Galatz & Raggio, Ltd., 1971-72, Raggio, Walker & Wooster, Reno and Las Vegas, 1974-78, Raggio, Wooster & Lindell, 1978-92; sr. ptnr. Vargas & Bartlett, 1992-98; then Jones-Vargas (formerly Vargas & Bartlett), 1998—; mem. Nev. Senate, Washoe Dist. 3, Carson City, 1973—. Mem. Nev. Senate, 1973—, minority floor leader, 1977-81, 82-87, 91, majority flr. leader, 1987—; mem. legis. commn., vice chmn. criminal law and adminstrn. com. council State Govts., 1972-75; v.p., dir. Archon Corp. Mem. Nev. Am. Revolutionary Bicentennial Commn., 1975-81; mem. Republican State Cen. Com.; past nat. chmn., current dir. Am. Legislative Exchange Council, dir. Sierra Health Svcs.; republican candidate for U.S. Senate, 1970. Served with USNR, 1944-46; to 2d lt. USMCR, 1946-47. Named Young Man of Yr., Reno-Sparks Jr. C. of C., 1959, Alumnus of Yr. U. Nev. Reno, 2000, Civic Leader of Yr Greater Reno C. of C., Disting. Eagle Scout, 1989; named to Jr. Achievement of Nev. Hall of Fame, 1999, Reg. Trans. Commn. Hall of Fame; recipient Disting. Nevadan award, 1968, Fellows award The Salvation Army, Torch of Liberty award The Anti-Defamation League, SIR award Assoc. Gen. Contractors, 1995, Outstanding Svc. award Airport Authority of Washor County, Pres.'s medal UNLV, 2000. Fellow Am. Bd. Criminal Lawyers; mem. ABA (state chmn. jr. bar conf. 1957-60, ho. dels.) Am. Judicature Soc., Am. Coll. Trail Lawyers, Am. Bd. Trial Advocates, Am. Inns of Ct., Navy League, Air Force Assn., Nat. (nat. pres. 1967-68; named Outstanding Prosecutor 1965), Nev. State (sec. 1959, pres. 1960-63) Dist. Attys. Assn., NCJ (Brotherhood award 1965), Nev. Peace Officers Assn., Internat. Assn. Chiefs Police, Am. Leg. Exch. Coun. (nat. chmn. 1991-92), Coll. of Edn. U. Nev. (life), Am. Legion, Elks, Lion Club, Prospectors Club, Alpha Tau Omega, Phi Alpha Delta. Republican. Roman Catholic. Home: PO Box 281 Reno NV 89504-0281

RAGHAVAN, DEREK, oncologist, medical researcher and educator; b. , Aug. 11, 1949; came to U.S., 1991; m. Patricia Harrison; 2 children. MB, BS with honors, Sydney U., 1974; PhD, London U., 1984. Cert. Royal Australian Coll. Physicians, Fgn. Lic. Exam Coun., Ednl. Coun. Fgn. Med. Grads., Gen. Med. Coun. (U.K.), NSW Med. Bd. (Australia). Resident, registrar Royal Prince Alfred Hosp., Sydney, 1974-77; lectr., sr. registrar Royal Marsden Hosp., London, 1978-80; rsch. fellow Ludwig Inst. Cancer Rsch., 1978-80; med. rsch. specialist U. Minn., Mpls., 1980-81; sr. specialist med. oncology Royal Prince Alfred Hosp., Sydney, 1981-91; prof., chief solid tumor oncology and investigational therapeutics Roswell Park Cancer Inst. and SUNY, Buffalo, 1991-97; prof. medicine and urology U. So. Calif., L.A., 1997—, chief divsn. med. oncology, 1997—, assoc. dir. Norris Cancer Ctr., 1997—. Bd. dirs. Nat. Prostate Cancer Coalition; pres. med. staff Roswell Park Cancer Inst., Buffalo, 1995—96; chair VA Merit Rev. Bd. in Oncology, 1996—97; mem. oncology drug adv. com. FDA, 1996—2000; chair cancer clin. investigations review com. Nat. Cancer Inst., 1996—97; prof. medicine SUNY, Buffalo, 1991—97, prof. urology, 1996—97; chief divsn. med. oncology U. So. Calif., 1997, assoc. dir. U. So. Calif.-Norris Cancer Ctr., 1997—; mem. VA Merit Rev. Bd. for Prostate Cancer, 1998, NIH Support Cancer Ctr. Rev. Com., 2000—; mem. scientific adv. bd. Southwest Oncology Group, 1998—, bd. govs., 1998—, vice chair genitournairy com., 1998; vice chair genitouring cancer com. Radiation Therapy Oncology Group, 1995—97; mem. sci. adv. com. European Orgn. for Rsch. and Treatment of Cancer, 2000—, mem. external sci. audit com., 2001—; mem. external adv. bd. Comprehensive Cancer Ctr. U. Ala., Birmingham, 2002—. Editor: The Management of Bladder Cancer, 1988, Textbook of Uncommon Cancer, 1988, 2d edit. 1999, Principles and Practice of Genitourinary Oncology, 1997; assoc. editor Urologic Oncology, 1995—, Clin. Cancer Rsch., 1996—; mem. editl. bd. Jour. Clin. Oncology, 1990-94, European Jour. Cancer, The Prostate, The Breast, Prostate Cancer, Advances in Oncology, Abstracts in Hematology and Oncology, 1998-2000; mem. editl. bd. Oncology; bd. cons. Jour. Urology, 1996—; contbr. numerous articles to profl. jours. Rsch. grantee Nat. Health amd Med. Rsch. Coun., Australia, 1983-90; traveling fellow NSW Cancer Coun., Sydney, 1978; named Hospice Physician of Yr., Hospice of Buffalo, 1994. Fellow: ACP (sci. program com. 2000, MKSAP XI com. 1997—98), Royal Australian Coll. Physicians (chair specialist adv. com. in med. oncology 1988—90); mem.: Sydney U. Med. Soc. (pres. 1974), Med. Oncology Group Australia (chmn. 1988—90), Soc. Urologic Oncology, Am. Assn. Cancer Rsch., Am. Soc. Clin. Oncology (chair cancer comms. com. 1998—2000, liaison Am. joint com. on cancer 1995—2000, program com. 1999—2000, chair cancer comms. com. 1998—2000, AJCC liaison 1995—2000, mem. pub. issues com. 2000—). Avocations: tennis, squash. Office: U So Calif-Norris Cancer Ctr 1441 Eastlake Ave Los Angeles CA 90089-0001

RAGHAVAN, SRINIVASA RAMAMURTHY, chemical engineer, educator; s. Vaikom Narayanaswamy and Vasantha Ramamurthy; m. Sangeetha Chandran. B in Chemical Engring., Indian Inst. of Tech., Chennai, India, 1992; PhD in Chem. Engring., N.C. State U., 1998. Asst. prof. U. of Md., College Park, Md., 2001—. Contbr. scientific papers. Office: University of Maryland Department of Chemical Engineering College Park MD 20742-2111 E-mail: sraghava@eng.umd.edu.

RAGHU, RENGACHARI, alternative medicine, nutrition, biotechnology and chemistry consultant, agriculture consultant; b. Amur, Tamilnadu, India, Mar. 22, 1943; came to U.S., 1975; s. Rengachari Veeraraghavachari and Sakunthala Krishnaswamy Rengachari; m. Kamala Rengan, Dec. 1, 1972; children: Anand, Adithya. HMB, Hanemann Homeopathic Inst., Bangalore, India, 1963; MS, Annamalai U., Chidambaram, India, 1965; MBA, S.P. Mandalia's Inst., Bombay, 1973; PhD, Bhaba Atomic Rsch. Ctr., Bombay, 1974. Asst. mgr. Amoor (India) Estates, 1962-65; mgr. Sakunthala Chemists, Tiruvarur, India, 1962-65; sr. rsch. fellow TB Ctr, Madras, India, 1965-68; sr. sci. officer Bhaba Atomic Rsch. Ctr., Bombay, 1968-75; dir. rsch. divsn. ob-gyn. Meharry Med. Coll., Nashville, 1975-85; chief clin. chemistry Apollo Hosps., Madras, 1985-89; rsch. cons. Vanderbilt U., Nashville, 1988-89; chmn. clin. biochemistry Nat. Chiropractic Coll., Lombard, Ill., 1989-90; pres.

Internat. High Tech. Transfer, Nashville, 1990—. Contbr. over 50 articles to sci. publs.; inventor no-share syringe. Bd. dirs. March of Dimes, Nashville, 1979-83, Juvenile Diabetes Fedn., Nashville, 1983-85, Jr. C. of C., Nashville, 1981-83; mem. bd. trustees Hindu Cultural Ctr., Nashville, 1983-90; mem. commerce adv. com. State of Tenn., Nashville, 1980-84; intern Mr. Bob Clement, U.S. House of Reps., U.S. Congress, Washington, 1994; mem. nat. steering com. Davidson County, Nashville, State of Tenn. Clinton/Gore '96 Campaign. March of Dimes fellow, N.Y., 1975-78; rsch. grantee Nat. Cancer Inst., Washington, 1981-86. Fellow Indian Phytopathology Soc. (life); mem. Am. Clin. Chemists, Soc. Biol. Chemists, Soc. Exptl. Biol. Medicine, Soc. Pharmacology, Soc. Preventive Medicine. Home: 822 Kendall Dr Nashville TN 37209-4512 Office: Internat High Tech Transfer 822 Kendall Dr Nashville TN 37209-4512 Fax: 615-356-9142. E-mail: iswara@jackatak.theporch.com., raghukamalanadit@yahoo.com., arraghu@hotmail.com.

RAGINSKY, NINA, artist; b. Montreal, Apr. 14, 1941; d. Bernard Boris and Helen Theresa R.; 1 child, Sofya Katrina. BA, Rutgers U., 1962; studied painting with, Roy Lichtenstein; studied sculpture with, George Segal; studied Art History with Allan Kaprow, Rutgers U. Freelance photographer Nat. Film Bd., Ottawa, Ont., Can., 1963-81; instr. metaphysics Emily Car Coll. Art, Vancouver, B.C., Can., 1973-81; painter Salt Spring Island, 1989—. Sr. artist, jury Can. Coun.; selected Can. rep. in Sweden for Sweden Now Mag., 1979; tchr., lectr. in field, 1973—. One woman shows include Vancouver Art Gallery, Victoria Art Gallery, Edmonton Art Gallery, Art Gallery Ont., San Francisco Mus. Art, Acadia U., Nancy Hoffman Gallery, N.Y.C., Meml. U. Newfoundland Art Gallery; exhibited in group shows at Rutgers U., 1962, Montreal Mus. Fine Arts, 1963, Nat. Film Bd., Ottawa, 1964, 65, 67, 70, 71, 76, 77, Internat. Salon Photography, Bordeaux, France, 1968, Nat. Gallery Ottawa, 1968, Eastman House, Rochester, N.Y., 1969, Vancouver Art Gallery, 1973, 80, Mural for Conf. Ctr. Ottawa, 1973, Field Mus., Chgo., 1976, Edmonton Art Gallery, 1978, 79, Walter Philips Gallery, 1979, Glenbow Mus. Gallery, 1979, Harbour Front Community Gallery, 1980, Hamilton Art Gallery, 1980, Musée Maisil de St. Lambert, 1981, Mendel Art Gallery, 1981, Dunlop Art Gallery, Regina, Can., 1981, Vancouver Art Gallery, 2001; represented in permanent collections Nat. Film Bd. Stills divsn., Ottawa, Ont., Banff (Alta.) Sch. Fine Arts, Nat Gallery Ottawa, Can., George Eastman House, Rochester, NY, Wadsworth Atheneum, Conn., Edmonton Art Gallery, U. Victoria, B.C., various pvt. collections. Bd. dirs. Island Watch, Salt Spring Island, B.C., 1993; founder, coord. Salt Spring Island Ecosys. Stewardship Project, 1993; founder, coord. Salt Spring Island Waterbird Watch Collective, 1994—. Decorated officer Order of Can., 1985; recipient Kees Vermeer award for edn. and conservation Simon Fraser U., 1997. Mem.: Royal Can. Acad. Arts. Avocations: gardening, birding, subject of numerous pubs. Home and Office: 272 Beddis Rd Salt Spring Island BC Canada V8K 2J1

RAGLAND, BOB, artist, educator; b. Cleve., Dec. 11, 1938; s. Carey and Violet (English) R. Cert. Completion, Rocky Mount Sch. Art, Denver, 1968. Instr. painting and drawing Denver Pub. Libr., 1969-71, Eastside Action Ctr., Denver, 1969-71; artist-in-residence Model Cities Cultural Arts Ctr. Workshop, 1971-73; artist/tchr. KRMA-TV. Lectr. in field; vis. artist Denver Pub. Sch. for the Arts, 1993-96, Urban Peak Homeless Ctr., Denver, 1996; founding faculty mem. Auraria campus C.C. Denver, 1970-72; lectr. Afro-Am. art of the 60's and 70's; visual arts coord. City Spirit Project, Denver, 1978; instr. Gove Cmty. Sch., 1979-95, Met. State Coll., Denver, Arapahoe C.C., Littleton, Colo.; artist-in-residence Fred N. Thomas Career Edn. Ctr., Denver Pub. Schs., 1997—, Denver Athletic Club, summer 2000; vis. artist Summer Scholars Program, Denver, 1998; founder Non-Starving Artist's Project, Denver, 1996; art career coach 1980—; advisor Foothills Art Ctr., 1998. Exhibited in 16th Ann. Drawing Exhbn., Dallas Mus. Fine Art Traveling Exhbn., 1967, Tubman Gallery, Boston, 1981; one man shows at Cleve. State U., 1968, Denver Nat. Bank, 1980-81, Century Bank Cherry Creek, Denver, 1980-81; works in permanet collections at Denver Pub. Libr., Karamu House, Cleve., Irving St. Ctr. Cultural Arts Program, Denver; group exhbns. include Colo. History Mus., 1993, 94, 95, Savageau Art Gallery, 1995-96, Met. State Coll. Visual Arts Ctr., 1993, The Triumph of the Human Spirit Foothills Art Ctr., Golden, Colo., 1997, 1st Plymouth Congl. Ch., 2000; author: The Artists Survival Handbook or What to do till You're Rich and Famous, 1980; pub.: Colo. Gallery Guide, 1978—; contbr. Black Umbrella/Black Artists Denver. Chmn. Arts and Humanities Com., 1968-69. Inducted in Colo. 100, Denver Post, Colo. Hist. Soc., 1993; recipient Excellence in Arts award Denver Black Arts Festival, 1993, Recognition award KCNC-TV and Denver Ctr. Performing Arts, 1986. Mem. Colo. Black Umbrella. Home: 1723 E 25th Ave Denver CO 80205-5505

RAGLAND, JACK WHITNEY, artist; b. El Monte, Calif., Feb. 25, 1938; s. Jack Rider and Dorsey (Whitney) R.; m. Marilee J. Weaver, July 31, 1969; children— Roxanne, Natasha. BA, Ariz. State U., 1960, MA, 1964; postgrad., UCLA, 1961-64. Grad. asst. tchr. Ariz. State U., 1960-61; grad. teaching asst. UCLA, 1961-64; head art dept. Simpson Coll., Indianola, Iowa, 1964-76. Demonstrator Nat. Art Materials Trade Assn., Denver, 1993, Pasadena Conv. Ctr., 1994 One-man shows include Kleine Gallery, Vienna, Austria, Simpson Coll., Internat. Art Svc., Pan Pacific Hotel, San Diego, Lakes Art Center, Okaboji, Iowa; exhibited in group shows, Lyn Kottler Gallery, N.Y.C., Phoenix Art Mus., Tucson Festival Art, Talisman Gallery, Bartlesville, Okla., Exhibiting Artists Fedn., Poultney, Vt., Des Moines Art Center, Joslyn Mus. Art, Omaha, Lagerquist Gallery, Atlanta, Glez-Harkins Gallery, Palm Desert, Calif., Desert Pleine Air Show, La Quinta, Calif., San Diego, NAMTA Art Show, San Francisco, 1995, Christian Art Show Jubilee 2000, Fall Brook, Calif., Pleine Air San Diego/Calif. Art Club, 2000, La Quinta Festival, 2000, AKA Mai Gallery, Del Mar, Calif., Tirage Gallery, Alta Dena, Calif., Polson Gallery, Pasadena, Show Case Houses, Pasadena, Rancho Santa Fe, Calif., 1995, 96, Palm Springs Paradise, 2000; San Diego, 97, 98, 99; represented in permanent collections, Albertina Museum, Vienna, Kunstmus., Basel, Switzerland, Bibliothèque National, Paris, Los Angeles County Mus., Simpson Coll., Phoenix Art Mus., Ariz. State collection, Graphische Bundes Versuchsanstalt, Vienna, Austria, also pvt. collections, works include stained glass windows, Meth. Ch., Perry, Iowa.; works reproduced Applause mag, 1971, New Woman mag, 1974, Artists of Cen. and No. Calif., Vol. II, San Diego Better Homes and Gardens Lifestyles mag., 1995, San Diego Decorating mag., 1995, 98, Pasadena Showcase House Design Mag., 1995, San Diego Decor and Style, 1996, 97, 98, Sci. of Mind Mag., 1997, Desert Art Scene Mag., 2000. Recipient grand purchase prize Ariz. Ann. Art Show, 1961, 1st prize in prints Iowa State Fair, 1974, 1st prize So. Calif. Expn., Del Mar, 1st prize Fall Brook Art Assn., 2000; featured in Am. Artist mag. Oct. 1993. Mem. Calif. Art Club. Home: 5490 Rainbow Heights Rd Fallbrook CA 92028-9619 E-mail: jwragland@aol.com. *To capture the spiritual essence of a subject through form and color is the goal of my art.*

RAGLAND, KATHRYN MARIE, dancer, educator; b. Lakewood, Ohio, Nov. 22, 1948; d. Earl Albert and Alice Maxine (Outzs) R.; m. Donald Glen Rubright, Sept. 1, 1973 (div. 1977); m. Jack Victor Rutberg, Mar. 9, 1980 (div. 1988); 1 child, Jessica Erin; m. Johnny Anthony Vergona, Oct. 9, 1988; 1 child, David Sean; stepchildren: Danielle Evelyn Vergona, Jonathan Chaunch Vergona. AA, L.A. Valley Coll., 1971; BFA cum laude, U. Utah, 1973, MFA in Dance, 1975; MA in Marriage, Family and Child Counseling/Clin. Child Devel., Pacific Oaks Coll., 1993; postgrad., Fielding Inst., 2001—. Lic. marriage and family therapist. With Momentum Dance Co., L.A., 1975-77; dance specialist pub. schs., 1975-76; instr. Scripps Coll., Claremont, Calif., 1976-77; dir. dance Cypress (Calif.) Coll., 1978-85, instr. dance, 1978-85, 86—; owner, operator Gymboree, 1985-88. Mem. adj. faculty Antioch U., 1998—; faculty facilitator MA-CEL program Finding Grad. Inst.; dance instr. Hollywood (Calif.) Little Red Sch. House, 1985-89, sch. coun., 1997—, asst. head of sch., 2000—; dance instr. McGroarty Arts Ctr., 1992-97, bd. dirs., 1991-92, 97-2002; mem. arts assistance team L.A. Supt. Schs.; curriculum coun. L.A. H.S. Performing Arts, adv. bd., 1986—. Dance Resource Ctr., 1991-92; intern Julie Ann Singer Ctr. Therapeutic Sch., 1991-92; coord. infant devel. program Santa Clara Valley Child and Family Devel. Ctr., 1992-93; therapist Julia Ann Singer Ctr. Family Stress Program, 1994-95, Verdugo Mental Health Ctr., 1994—; crisis counselor Verdugo Disaster Recovery Program, 1994-95; trainer Project COPE, 1995-96; co-dir. Verdugo Creative Arts Group, 1995—; program coord. Atwater Park Ctr., 1996-97; coach Odyssey of Mind, 1998—, L.A. regional dir., 2002, bd. dirs., 2002—; adj. prof. Antioch U., 1998—; regional dir. La Barin. Author/choreographer Kitty Kats, 1986; choreography work includes Man of La Mancha, 1976-80, Pippin, 1981, Fiddler on the Roof, 1982, Music Man, 1983, Spanish Suite, 1983, A Funny Thing Happened on the Way to the Forum, 1984, Skaters Edge, 1984, Cartoon, 1984, Urban Primitive, 1985, Cabaret, 1985, Healings, 1987, Cloud Reveries, 1988, Guys and Dolls, 1988, The Lottery, 1988, Cabaret, 1989, Atmos, 1990, Damn Yankees, 1990, Conflict of Interest, 1990; author, dir., choreographer We Saved the Day, 1987, The Visit, 1988, Where the Wild Things Are, 1991, Evening's After Image, 1992, Hair, 1992, South Pacific, 1993, Hello Dolly, 1993, In Search of Quieter Times and Places, 1993, Fiddler on the Roof, 1994, Pajama Game, 1994, Nine, 1994, Testosteroni Baloney, 1994, Guys and Dolls, 1995, Into the Woods, 1995, Alice in Wonderland, 1996, Pirates of Penzance, 1997, Rags, 1997; dir. Courage of the Heart, 1998; dir./choreographer Bye Bye Birdie, 1998; choreographer Mikado, 1998, Sweeney Todd, 1999, Funny Thing Happened on the Way to the Forum, 1999, Jesus Christ Superstar, 1999, Oklahoma, 2000, Rocky Horror Show, 2000, Man of La Mancha, 2001, Joseph and the Amazing Technicolor Dreamcoat, 2001, Cabaret, 2002. Mem. So. Calif. steering com. Legis. Action Coalition Arts Edn.; den leader Cub Scouts, 1996-2000. Mem. AAHPERD, ASCD, AARP, Dance Resource Ctr., Calif. Dance Educators Assn. (v.p. 1980-82, legis. rep. 1982-86), Calif. Music Educators (legis. com. 1982-86), L.A. Area Dance Alliance, Faculty Assn. C.C., Calif. Assn. Health, Phys. Edn., Recreation and Dance, Calif. Assn. Marriage and Family Therapists, So. Calif. Assn. Edn. Young Children (bd. dirs. South Bay chpt.), Calif. Confedn. Arts, Calif. Learning Disabilities Assn., Calif. Elem. Edn. Assn., Josephson Inst. Ethics (mem. shared leadership coun. Millikin Middle Sch. 1994-96, mem. learn coun. Apperson Sch. 1994-95), Assn. Ednl. Therapists, Learning Disabilities Assn. L.A., Calif. Elem. Edn. Assn., Assn. Supervision Curriculum Devel. Democrat. E-mail: kaye@hlrsh.com.

RAGLAND, NAN HOWARD, minister; b. Memphis; d. Terry James Howard and Clara Mae Bright; m. Joe M. Ragland. BSN, Miss. Coll. Pres. Nan Ragland Ministries. Avocations: prayer, walking, working out. Office: Nan Ragland Ministries PO Box 77 Jackson MS 39205

RAGLAND, ROBERT ALLEN, lawyer; b. Bartlesville, Okla., Apr. 18, 1954; s. Thomas Martin and Joan Ethel (Murphy) R. BA, U. Md., 1976; JD, George Mason Sch. of Law, 1980. Dir. regulatory reform and govt. orgn. Nat. Assn. Mfrs., Washington, 1979-82, asst. v.p. taxation, 1983-86; mgr. congl. rels. The Clorox Co., Oakland, Calif., 1982-83; dir. tax rsch. U.S. C. of C., Washington, 1988-93. Chief tax counsel, mng. dir. Nat. Chamber Found., Washington, 1989-93; v.p. Wachovia Bank, 1995—, officer, 1995—. Author: Transportation Reform, 1980, Employee Stock Ownership Plans, 1989, Taxation of Foreign Source Income, Distributional Impact of Excise Taxes, Taxation of Intercorporate Profits, 1990, Jour. Regulation and Social Costs, 1990; editor Taxation of Intercorporate Profits, 1990, Jour. Regulation and Social Costs, 1992—, Jour. Regulation, 1992-93. Active Boy Scouts Am., Washington, 1967—, bd. dirs. nat. capital area coun.; dep. dir. duPont for Pres., 1987-88; v.p. Nat. Chamber Found. U.S. C. of C., 1989-93, dir., Liz Lerman Dance Exchange, 1993-2001, dir. Our House, Inc., 1988-2000. Republican. Roman Catholic. Home: 3510 Inverness Dr Chevy Chase MD 20815

RAGLAND, SAMUEL CONNELLY, industrial engineer, management consultant; b. Nashville, July 12, 1946; s. Julian Potter and Stella (Thompson) R.; m. Marilyn Margaret Oppelt, July 15, 1967; children: Sherry Anne, David Michael. BSBA, Ariz. State U., 1974; MBA, U. Phoenix, 1991. Indsl. engr. 1st Interstate Bank, Phoenix, 1966-76, Beckman Instruments, Scottsdale, Ariz., 1976-78; mgmt. analyst Ariz. Legis. Budget Com., Phoenix, 1978; indls. engr. mgmt. sys. ITT Courier Terminal Sys., Tempe, Ariz., 1978-81; project control adminstr. Gen. Host Corp., Phoenix, 1981; sr. cons. Arthur Young & Co., 1981-82; ops. analyst City of Phoenix, 1982-84; project leader Garrett Engine divsn. Allied-Signal Corp. (formerly Garrett Turbine Engine Co.), Phoenix, 1984-92; cons., program mgr. TRW, Mesa, Ariz., 1992-93; prin., owner Ragland Assocs., Scottsdale, 1994—; regional mgr. Granite Investments, Inc., 2001—. Exec. mgmt. cons. Gov.'s Office Excellence in Govt., State of Ariz., 1995-96, mgr. quality assurance Coxreels, Inc., 1996-97; ind. engring. cons. The Boeing Co., 1997-2001; indsl. engr. strategic planning Aviation Mgmt. Sys., 2000-2001; owner, Granite Investments, Inc.; dir. Mary Moppets of Highland Inc., 1977-81. Contbr. articles to profl. publs. Mem. Inst. Indls. Engrs. (sr. mem. ctrl. Ariz. chpt., dir. cmty. rels. 1983-85, dir. chpt. devel. 1985-86, v.p. 1986-87, pres. 1987-88, 99-2000, nat. chpt. devel. com. 1988-91), Assn. Sys. Mgmt. (divsn. dir. 1989-92, pres. 1992-93), Phoenix Philatelic Assn. Address: 11319 E Jenan Dr Scottsdale AZ 85259-3121

RAGLAND, TERA DENISE, music educator; b. Louisville, July 18, 1973; d. Robert Noble and Sharron Kay Jones; m. Gordon Ragland, May 29, 1999. B in Music Edn., Georgetown Coll., 1995; M in Music Edn., Murray State U., 1996. Asst. band dir. McLean County Schs., Calhoun, Ky., 1996—2001; music tchr. Russellville (Ky.) Ind. Schs., 2001—. Mem.: Ky. Music Educators Assn., Music Educators Nat. Conf. Republican. Baptist. Office: Russellville Mid Sch Russellville KY 42276 Business E-Mail: tragland@rville.k12.ky.us.

RAGLAND, TERRY EUGENE, emergency physician; b. Greensboro, N.C., June 14, 1944; s. Terry Porter and Virginia Lucile (Stowe) R.; m. Marguerite Elizabeth Morton, May 15, 1976; children: Kenneth John McConnell, Ryan Lee Ragland. BS, Cen. Mich. U., 1966; MD, U. Mich., 1970. Diplomate Am. Bd. Internal Medicine, Am. Bd. Emergency Medicine. Intern St. Joseph Mercy Hosp., Ann Arbor, Mich., 1970-71, internal medicine resident, 1974-77, chief resident internal medicine, 1975-76, emergency physician, 1977-2001, med. dir. emergency ctr., 1985-97, chief of staff, 1996-97, assoc. dir. dept. emergency svcs., 1997-2000; CEO Secure Care, Inc., 1992—; pres. Huron Valley Phys. Assn., 1997-2000. Clin. asst. prof. U. Mich., Ann Arbor, 1981—; examiner Am. Bd. Emergency Medicine, 1983-2001; med. dir. Life Support Services, Ann Arbor, 1983-92; mem. Mercy Health Plans Bd., 1999-2000. Contbr. chpts. to book. Lt. USN, 1972-74. Fellow Am. Coll. Emergency Physicians; mem. Am. Coll. Physicians, Nat. Assn. Emergency Med. Technicians, Mich. State Med. Soc. (alt. del. 1982-84, 89-90, del. 1991-94, mem. jud. commn. 1999—), Mich. Emergency Med. Technicians Assn., Washtenaw County Med. Soc. (pres. 1993). Democrat. Avocations: trout fishing, gardening, skiing.

RAGNO, NANCY NICKELL, educational writer; b. Phila., Sept. 2, 1938; d. Paul Eugene and Sara Jane (Mensch) Nickell; m. Joseph Diego Ragno, Aug. 25, 1961; 1 child, Michelle Angela. BA, Lebanon Valley Coll., 1960; MA, NYU, 1968. Cert. tchr., N.J. Tchr. N.J. pub. schs., 1961-68; project editor Prentice-Hall, Inc., Englewood Cliffs, N.J., 1968-70, Harcourt Brace Jovanovich, N.Y.C, 1970-72; sr. editor Silver Burdett Co., Morristown, N.J., 1972-76; editor, writer Houghton Mifflin Co., Boston, 1976-77; sr. editor J.B. Lippincott Co., Phila., 1977-79; sr. author Silver Burdett Ginn, Morristown, 1984—. Author: (textbook series) Silver Burdett English, 1984, World of Language, 1992, (sound filmstrip) The City and the Modern Writer, 1970, Buying on the Installment Plan, 1974. Bassoonist Harrisburg (Pa.) Symphony Orch., 1959, Plainfield (N.J.) Symphony Orch., 1976, Somerset (N.J.) County Orch., 1989, Princeton (N.J.) Community Orch., 1992. Mem. ASCD, Nat. Coun. Tchrs. English, Internat. Reading Assn., Am. Soc. Journalists and Authors, Textbook Authors Assn., Authors Guild, U.S. Power Squadron. Democrat. Mem. Ch. of Christ. Avocations: music, writing, boating. Home: 38 Tortoise Ln Tequesta FL 33469-1552

RAGO, ANN D'AMICO, university official, public relations professional; b. Pitts., Aug. 24, 1957; d. Jack and Florence (Zappa) D'Amico; m. John Thomas Rago, Aug. 31, 1984; children: Annie J., Emily J., John Henry. BA, Duquesne U., Pitts., 1979, MA, 1987. From communications assoc. to dir. pub. relations Duquesne U., 1979-89, coord. univ. relations, 1989-93, exec. dir. pub. affairs, 1993—, adj. prof. comm. Editor University Record, 1989 (silver medal). Bd. dirs. Support, Pitts., 1989-91; sch. dir. Carylnton Sch. Bd., Pitts., 1989-93, pres. sch. bd., 1990. Recipient Gold award for publs./external prospectus 9th Ann. Admissions Advt. Awards, 1994, Gold award for Total Pub. Rels. Campaign, 10th Ann. Admissions Advt. Awards, 1995, Gold award for Total Pub. Rels. Campaign, 11th Ann. Admissions Awards, 1996, 1st Place award in Category 35, Internal Pub. Rels. Campaign, Pitts. chpt. Women in Comm., Inc., 1996, Bronze Cert. for logo and letterhead for Duquesne U.'s Capital Campaign and cert. merit for Duquesne U.'s internal publ. 14th Ann. Admissions Advt. Awards, 1998. Mem. Pub. Rels. Soc. Am. (1st place award 1993), Internat. Assn. Bus. Communicators (award of excellence 1991, award of honor 1993, award of merit 1994), Am. Mgmt. Assn., Press Club Western Pa., Sigma Delta Chi. Office: Carlow Coll 3333 Fifth Ave Pittsburgh PA 15213 E-mail: rago@duq.edu.

RAGO, DOROTHY ASHTON, retired educator; b. N.Y.C., Oct. 10, 1925; d. Thomas Percy and Isabel (Seddon) Ashton; divorced, 1958; 1 child, Thomas Ashton. BA, Wellesley Coll., 1946; MA, Columbia U., 1964. Cert. early childhood edn. tchr., N.Y. Editor Alford Baby Group mags., N.Y.C., 1948-52; kindergarten tchr. N.Y.C. Bd. Edn., 1964-86, ret., 1986. Mem. vestry Chapel of St. John, Saunderstown, R.I., 1988-91; mem. Human Rights Com., North Kingstown, R.I., 1988-94; treas. Pettaquamscutt Hist. Soc., 1991-98; mem. exec. bd. Friends of Oceanography/GSO-URI, 1997—. Mem. South County Mus., South County Women's Club, Saunderstown Yacht Club, R.I. Wellesley Club. Republican. Episcopalian. Avocations: local history, bell ringing.

RAGO, THOMAS ASHTON, physical oceanographer; b. N.Y.C., Jan. 29, 1957; s. Louis Joseph and Dorothy (Ashton) R. BA, Amherst Coll., 1979; MS, U. R.I., 1986. Oceanographer Naval Postgrad. Sch., Monterey, Calif., 1987—. Contbr. articles to profl. publs. Mem. Am. Geophys. Union, Oceanography Soc., Aircraft Owners and Pilots Assn. Avocation: flying, ice hockey. Office: Naval Postgrad Sch Code OC/Rg 833 Dyer Rd Bldg 232 Monterey CA 93943-5192 E-mail: tarago@nps.navy.mil.

RAGON, ROBERT RONALD, clergyman; b. Flintstone, Ga., Sept. 10, 1939; s. Robert Emmett and Frances Cora (Stoner) R.; m. Judith Ann Ward, Apr. 27, 1962; children: Ronald Russell, Regina Renee. BS, U. Chattanooga, 1962; BDiv, MDiv, Columbia Theol. Sem., Decatur, Ga., 1967. Ordained to ministry Presbyn. Ch., 1967. Pastor Trion (Ga.) Presbyn. Ch., 1967-72; dir., pastor Chattooga County Presbyn. Ministries, Trion, 1971-72; pastor Brainerd Presbyn. Ch., Chattanooga, 1972—. Moderator Knoxville Presbytery, 1979-80; founder An Order of Slaves of Christ, Chattanooga, 1970; stated clk. Presbytery of S.E., 1990-93, moderator, 1995-96. Author: Covenant Agreement: O.S.C., 1970, The Journey, 1990. Trustee King Coll., Bristol, Tenn., 1983-86. Mem. Masons (Ga. chaplain 1980), KT (sec. 1991), Shriners, Kiwanis (bd. dirs. Chattanooga 1986-90). Republican. Avocation: investments. Home: 4229 Happy Valley Rd Flintstone GA 30725-2222 Office: Brainerd Presbyterian Church 1624 Jenkins Rd Chattanooga TN 37421-3249 E-mail: rjragon@earthlink.net., bpcepc@iol.com.

RAGONE, DAVID VINCENT, former university president; b. N.Y.C., May 16, 1930; s. Armando Frederick and Mary (Napier) R.; m. Katherine H. Spaulding, Dec. 18, 1954; children: Christine M., Peter V. S.B., MIT, 1951, S.M., 1952, Sc.D., 1953. Asst. prof. chem. and metall. engring. U. Mich., Ann Arbor, 1953-57, assoc. prof., 1957-61, prof., 1961-62; asst. dir. John J. Hopkins Lab for Pure and Applied Sci., also chmn. metallurgy dept. Gen. Atomic div. Gen Dynamics, La Jolla, 1962-67; Alcoa prof. metallurgy Carnegie-Mellon U., Pitts., 1967-69; assoc. dean Carnegie-Mellon U. (Sch. Urban and Pub. Affairs) 1969-70; dean Thayer Sch. of Engring., Dartmouth Coll., 1970-72, Coll. Engring., U. Mich., 1972-80; pres. Case Western Res. U., Cleve., 1980-87; vis. prof., dept. materials sci. and engring. MIT, Cambridge, 1987-88, sr. lectr. dept. materials sci. and engring., 1988-98; gen. ptnr. Ampersand Ventures, 1988-92, ptnr., 1992—. Trustee Mitre Corp. Mem. Nat. Sci. Bd., 1978-84; mem. tech adv. bd. U.S. Dept. Commerce, 1967-75; chmn. adv. com. advanced auto power systems Council on Environ. Quality, 1971-75; Trustee Henry Luce Found. Named Outstanding Young Engr., Engring. Soc. Detroit, 1957 Mem. Univ. Club (N.Y.C.), Longwood Cricket Club (Boston), Sigma Xi, Tau Beta Pi. Office: Ampersand Ventures 55 William St Wellesley MA 02481-4003

RAGOSTA, VINCENT A.F. judge; b. Providence, Feb. 12, 1924; s. Domenic and Rosa (Bottis) R.; m. Carmela C. Bruno, Oct. 3, 1953; children: Vincent Jr., Paul D., Dominic L., Peter J. BS in Acctg., U. R.I., 1949; JD, Boston Coll., 1951. Bar: R.I. 1951, U.S. Ct. Appeals (1st cir.) 1962. Asst. city solicitor City of Providence, 1953-66, city pros., 1953-60, commr. Bur. of Lics., 1977-78; assoc. judge Dist. Ct. R.I., 1978-86; assoc. justice Superior Ct. R.I., 1986—; pvt. practice Providence, 1952-77. State pres. Arthritis Found., 1978. Staff Sgt. U.S. Army, 1943-46, PTO. Recipient Star of Italian Solidarity award Rep. of Italy, 1973. Mem. ABA, ATLA, R.I. Bar Assn., Order Sons of Italy in Am. (state pres. 1971-77), Phi Kappa Phi, Beta Gamma Sigma. Roman Catholic. Avocations: physical fitness, travel, reading, sports. Home: 161 Gentian Ave Providence RI 02908-1131 Office: RI Superior Ct 250 Benefit St Ste 7 Providence RI 02903-2724

RAGSDALE, BERTHA MAE See KOLB, BERTHA MAE

RAGSDALE, GEORGE ROBINSON, lawyer; b. Raleigh, N.C., Mar. 26, 1936; s. George Young and Susan (Jolly) R.; m. Adora Prevost, Oct. 20, 1962; children: John Robinson, George Young II, Adora P. AB, U. N.C., 1958, LLB, 1961. Asst. to chief counsel U.S. Senate Subcom. on Constnl. Rights, Washington, 1961—62; law ptnr. Bailey & Ragsdale, Raleigh, NC, 1962—65; legal counsel to Dan K. Moore, Gov. of N.C., 1965—68; judge Superior Ct. of N.C., 1968—70; ptnr. Moore, Ragsdale, Liggett, Ray & Foley, 1970—86, LeBoeuf, Lamb, Greene & MacRae, N.Y.C. and Raleigh, 1987—93, Ragsdale, Liggett & Foley, Raleigh, 1994—. Lectr. N.C. Assn. Def. Counsel. Trustee U. N.C., Chapel Hill, 1979-87, vice-chmn. bd. trustees, 1983-84, chmn., 1984-85; trustee U. N.C. Endowment, 1980—, chmn., 1984-85; bd. dirs. U. N.C. Instnl. Devel. Found., Inc., 1985—, U. N.C.-Chapel Hill Found.; bd. visitors U. N.C., The Ednl. Found., Inc. Mem. ABA, N.C. Bar Assn., Wake County Bar Assn., Assn. Bar of City of N.Y., Def. Rsch. Inst., Raleigh C. of C., Kiwanis, Sphinx Club of Raleigh, Terpsichorean Club, Raleigh Execs. Club, Carolina Country Club, Biltman Forest Country Club. Episcopalian. Office: Ragsdale Liggett 2840 Plaza Pl PO Box 31507 Raleigh NC 27612

RAGSDALE, MARY ELLEN, interior designer; b. Henderson, N.C., Mar. 1, 1940; d. Horace Woodrow and Mary Livingston (Harris) Robertson; m. John H. Bowen, Mar. 10, 1957 (div. July 1976); children: John Walter, Ellen Anne (dec.); m. Robert Allen Ragsdale, Dec. 7, 1996. AA, U. Md., 1964; BA, U. N.C., Wilmington, 1982. Head bookkeeper ins. dept. N.C. Nat. Bank, Henderson, 1964-66; head bookkeeper Frazier Bros. Grocery, 1966-76; interior designer Interiors Unltd., Inc., Wilmington, N.C., 1978-82; mfrs.'s rep. Spandorfer-Zimmerman, Inc., Atlanta, 1982-84; owner, mgr. Ellen Robertson, Inc., Charlotte, N.C., 1984-94; exec. v.p. Robertson Sales Assocs., Milw. and Charlotte, 1984-94; interior designer Bernardand, Inc., N.Y.C., 1989-92, Furnitureland South, High Point, N.C., 1992-94, Burnett's Treasures, La Jolla, Calif., 1994-96; owner, pres., CEO Ragsdale Interiors, Inc., Phoenix, 1996—. Cons. Inndesign, Charlotte, 1984-86. Contbr. articles to profl. jours. and newspapers. Home life chmn. Henderson Jr. Woman's Club, 1966-78; adult leader 4-H Club, Henderson, 1964-70; vol. ARC, Charlotte, 1985-89, Big Sisters, Charlotte, 1985-89, Students Against Drunk Driving, Charlotte, N.Y.C., Milw., 1986-92; vol. Home Base Youth Svcs., Phoenix. Recipient award Daily Express, 1987, 88. Mem. Am. Soc. Interior Designers (mktg. com. ASID 1996-98), Friends of Faith House (bd. dirs. 1997-98), Bus. and Profl. Women's Club (New Bus. Woman of Yr. award 1988), Friends and Alumni U. N.C.-Wilmington, Phi Beta Kappa. Republican. Baptist. Address: PO Box 714 Appomattox VA 24522-0714 Fax: 602-877-2291. E-mail: azragsglendale@msn.com.

RAGSDALE, RICHARD ELLIOT, healthcare management executive; b. St. Louis, Dec. 20, 1943; s. Billie Oscar and Isabelle (Roques) R.; m. Anne Elizabeth Ward, Aug. 20, 1968; children: Richard, Kevin, Bethany. BBA, Ohio U., 1965; M in Internat. Commerce, Thunderbird Grad. Sch. Internat. Mgmt., 1968. Asst. treas. Chase Manhattan Bank, N.Y.C., 1968-73; v.p., treas. Hosp. Affiliates Internat., Nashville, 1973-80; v.p., treas., chief fin. officer INA Health Care Group, Dallas, 1980-81; sr. v.p., chief fin. officer, dir. Republic Health Corp., 1981-83, sr. exec. v.p., dir., 1983-85; chmn. Cmty. Health Systems Inc., Brentwood, Tenn., 1985-96, co-chmn., 1996-98; chmn. Great No. Health Mgmt., Ltd., London, 1986-89. Bd. dirs. RehabCare Group, Inc., St. Louis; chmn. ProMed Co. Mgmt. Co., Ft. Worth, Tex., 1994-98, chmn. exec. com., 1998—; dir. HealthMont, Inc., 2000—, chmn, 2002—; dir. Vanderbilt U. Tech. Co., 2001—, chmn., 2002-. Coach Spring Valley Athletic Assn., Dallas, 1985; trustee Watkins Inst., 1988-94; trustee Benton Hall Sch., 1988—, chair, 1991—; trustee Maryville Coll., 1990—, chair, 192—; chmn. Hosp. Authority of Metro Govt. Bd. Trustees, Nashville; dir. Nashville Zoo,

2000—. Recipient Thunderbird Disting Alumni award Entrepreneurship, 1990, Jonas Meyer Disting. Alumni award, 1993, Maryville Coll. medallion, 1999. Mem. Fedn. Am. Hosps. (legis. commn. 1984-95) Republican. Avocations: SCUBA diving, drag racing.

RAGSDELL, KENNETH MARTIN, engineering educator, consultant; b. Jacksonville, Ill., Sept. 3, 1942; s. Lois June Martin; m. Janet Anna Norton, Feb. 14, 1962; children: Keith, Thomas, Matthew. BS in Mech. Engring., U. Mo., Rolla, 1966, MS in Mech. Engring., 1967; PhD, U. Tex., 1972. Lic. profl. engr., Tex. Assoc. prof. mech. engring. Purdue U., West Lafayette, Ind., 1972—82; prof., dir. Design Optimization Lab. U. Ariz., Tucson, 1982—84; chair mech. and aerospace engring. U. Mo., Columbia, 1984—89, assoc. vice chancellor Rolla, 1989—92, prof. engring. mgmt., 1992—. Cons. GM; expert witness product design and safety. Co-author: Engineering Optimization, 1982. Mem. Rotary, Rolla and Columbia, 1985. Fellow: ASME. Office: Univ Mo Design Engring Ctr Rolla MO 65409

RAGUSEA, STEPHEN ANTHONY, psychologist, educator; b. N.Y.C., Mar. 26, 1947; s. Anthony S. and Marie (Giampietro) R.; m. Kathleen Fox, Aug. 14, 1971; children: Anthony, Adam. AA, Nassau Coll., Garden City, N.Y., 1967; BS, Bowling Green (Ohio) State U., 1969; D of Psychology, Baylor U., Waco, Tex., 1980. Diplomate Am. Bd. Profl. Psychology in Family Psychology, Am. Bd. Profl. Neuropsychology; lic. psychologist, Pa. Tchr. Dayton (Ohio) then Cedar Rapids (Iowa) Community Schs., 1969-76; cons. team for local sch. system Waco, Tex., 1976-77; therapist Meth. Home Children's Guidance Ctr., 1978-79, Heart of Tex. Mental Health/Mental Retardation Ctr., Waco, 1978-79; intern in psychol. svcs. Norristown (Pa.) State Hosp., 1979-80; cons. Altoona (Pa.) Hosp. Community Mental Health Ctr., 1981-82; interim dir. psychol. svcs. Nittany Valley Rehab. Hosp., Pleasant Gap, Pa., 1983-84; pres., CEO Centre Valley Mgmt., Inc., 1981-85; exec. dir. Psychol. Forensics, P.C., State College, Pa., 1984-2000; clin. dir. The Meadows Psychiat. Ctr., 1984-85; psychologist, dir. ops. Child, Adult, & Family Psychol. Ctr., State College, 1980—. Asst. prof. dept. individual and family studies Pa. State U.; adj. faculty dept. psychology Pa. State U.; cons. psychol. staff The Meadows Psychiat. Ctr.; psychol. staff rep. to med. staff, allied staff Centre Community Hosp.; bd. dirs. Penn PsyPac; presenter in field. Fellow APA, Am. Coll. Forensic Psychology, Cen. Pa. Psychol. Assn. (past-pres., chmn. profl. affairs com.), Pa. Bd. Psychology, Pa. Psychol. Assn. (past-pres. clin. div., chmn. hosp. practice com., fellow and pres. 1993-94), APA (del. from Pa. Coun. Reps. 1994-2000, chair state and provincial caucus 1997-2000); mem. Am. Soc. Clin. Hypnosis, Nat. Acad. Neuropsychologists.

RAHALL, NICK JOE, II (NICK RAHALL), congressman; b. Beckley, W.Va., May 20, 1949; s. N. Joe and Alice Rahall; children: Rebecca Ashley, Nick Joe III, Suzanne Nicole. BA, Duke U., 1971. Staff asst. U.S. Senator Robert C. Byrd, 1971-74; sales rep. Sta. WWNR, Beckley, 1974; pres. Mountaineer Travel Co., 1975-77, W.Va. Broadcasting, 1980—; mem. U.S. Congress from 3rd W.Va. dist., Washington, 1977—. Mem. transp. and infrastructure com., mem. resources com.; bd. dirs. Rahall Comm. Corp. Del. Dem. Nat. Conv., 1972, 74, 78, 80, 84, 88, 92, 96; W.Va. chmn. March of Dimes, 1979; mem. profl. adv. bd. Alsac-St. Jude Children's Rsch. Hosp. Named Young Man of Year, Beckley Jaycees, 1972; Outstanding Young Man in W.Va., W.Va. Jaycees, 1977; recipient Achievement award Logan Cripple Children Soc., 1978; Citizenship award K.C., 1978, Disting. Svc. award Am. Fedn. Govt. Employees W.Va., 1984, Young Dem. of Yr. Dem. Nat. Conv., 1980, Outfitter of Yr. Profl. Outfitters, 1987, Seneca award Sierra Club 1988, River Conservation award Am. River 1988; named Coal Man of Yr. Coal Industry News, 1979, W.Va. Son of Yr., W.Va. Soc. of Washington, 1996. Mem. NAACP, NRA, Elks, Moose, Masons (33d degree) Shriners. Presbyterian. Office: US Ho of Reps 2307 Rayburn Ho Office Bldg Washington DC 20515-4803 E-mail: nrahall@mail.house.gov.*

RAHARINAIVO, ANDRÉ LÉON, research executive, educator; b. Tananarive, Madagascar, Sept. 1, 1940; arrived in France, 1954; s. Ignace Léon and Marthe (Rasoazanamalala) R.; m. Christiane Martine Laurent, May 7, 1966 (div. June 1994); 1 child, Jacques Yves. Engr. mining and metallurgy, Ecole des Mines, Nancy, France, 1964; degree superior scientific studies, U. Nancy, France, 1964; PhD, U. Compiegne, France, 1982. Cert. engr. Head sect. Lab. Ctrl. Ponts et Chaussées, Paris, 1971-80, dep. head dept., 1980-83, sec. sci. coun., 1983-91, rsch. mgr., 1991—. Prof. U. Paris-Sud, Orsay, France, 1981; lectr. Ecole Nat. Ponts et Chaussées, Paris, 1977. Author: Fracture Mechanics and Mechanisms, 1990; patentee in field. Capt. Equipment, 1967-69, France. Mem. Ctr. Français Anticorrosion, Nat. Assn. Corrosion Engrs. Avocation: singing Gospel music. Home: 378 rue de Vaugirard F-75015 Paris France E-mail: andraha@aol.com.

RAHBAR, REZA, pediatric otolaryngologist; b. Isfahan, July 29, 1962; BA in Biology, Boston U., 1984; DMD, Tufts U., 1988, MD, 1993. Diplomate Am. Bd. Otolaryngology. Gen. surgeon New Eng. Med. Ctr., Boston, 1993—94, otolaryngologist, 1994—98; pediat. otolaryngologist Harvard U. Med. Sch./Children's Hosp., 1998—, attending physician, 2000—. Fellow: Am. Acad. Otolaryngology; mem.: ACS. Office: Children's Hosp 300 Longwood Ave Boston MA 02115

RAHE, MARIBETH SEMBACH, bank executive; b. Evanston, Ill., Oct. 3, 1948; d. Daniel F. and Boysie (Beebe) Sembach; m. Martin E. Rahe, May 31, 1975. BA, Bowling Green State U., 1970; postgrad., Ohio State U., 1970-72; MA in Internat. Mgmt., Am. Grad. Sch. Internat. Mgmt., 1974. Internat. banking officer Harris Bank, Chgo., 1974-77, asst. v.p. London, 1977-80; v.p. Morgan Guaranty Trust Co., 1980-83, N.Y.C., 1983-84; sr. rep. Sparebanken Oslo Akershus, 1984-85; v.p. Morgan Guaranty Trust Co., 1985-87, J.P. Morgan Investment Mgmt., N.Y.C., 1987-88; sr. v.p. Harris Bank, Chgo., 1988-91, dept. exec., 1991-94, sr. exec. v.p., 1994-95, vice chmn. bd., 1995-97; vice chmn. U.S. Trust Co. N.Y., 1997—. Bd. dirs. Trustmark Ins. Co., U.S. Trust Co., N.Y., Pasquinelli Constrn. Co. Bd. dirs. Rush Presbyn. Hosp.; mem. found. bd. com. of 200, chair devel. com.; mem. Fin. Svcs. Roundtable, The Chgo. Network, Women's Forum, Inc. Recipient Outstanding Alumni award Am. Grad. Sch., 1991. Mem. Am. Bankers Assn. (vice chmn. 1991-92, chmn. 1992-93, exec. com. pvt. banking, banking advisor 1993—), Com. of 200, Econ. Club, Chgo. Women's Network, Chgo. Club. Republican. Lutheran. Office: US Trust Co NY 114 W 47th St New York NY 10036-1510 Home: 269 Vine Ave Lake Forest IL 60045-1934

RAHE, RICHARD HENRY, psychiatrist, educator; b. Seattle, May 28, 1936; s. Henry Joseph and Delora Lee (Laube) R.; m. Laurie Ann Davies, Nov. 24, 1960 (div. Dec. 1990); children: Richard Bradley, Annika Lee. Student, Princeton U., 1954-57; MD, U. Wash., 1961. Diplomate Am. Bd. Psychiatry and Neurology. Chief resident in psychiatry U. Wash. Sch. Medicine, Seattle, 1965; rsch. psychiatrist USN, San Diego, 1965-75; commdg. officer Naval Health Rsch. Ctr., 1976-80; exec. officer Long Beach (Calif.) Naval Hosp., 1980-82; commdg. officer Guam Naval Hosp., Agana, 1982-84; prof. psychiatry Uniformed Svcs. U. of the Health Scis., Bethesda, Md., 1984-86, U. Nev. Sch. Medicine, Reno, 1986—. Dir. Mil. Stress Studies Ctr., Bethesda, 1984-86, Nev. Stress Ctr. Vets. Affairs Med. Ctr., Reno, 1986—. Contbr. numerous articles to sci. jours., chpts. to books; photographer prints and video. Dir. Nev. Mental Health Inst., Sparks, 1991-94. Capt. USN, 1965-86. Recipient Humanitarian award Vietnamese Refugee Com., 1974, Dept. of State award for treatment of Am. hostages held in Iran, 1981. Fellow Am. Psychiat. Assn.; mem. Am. Psychosomatic Soc. (past pres.), World Psychiat. Assn. (past. pres. mil. sect.). Avocations: hiking, skiing, swimming. Home: 3895 Chinook Creek Rd Reno NV 89509 Office: Code 151 C 1000 Locust St Reno NV 89502-2597

RAHFELDT, DARYL GENE, minister; b. Ames, Iowa, Feb. 16, 1947; s. Edward DeLos and Anna Henrietta (Borchert) R.; m. Marjorie Kay Johnson, Mar. 18, 1973; children: Emily Kathryn, Gretchen Amanda Arellanos. BS in Forestry, Iowa State U., 1969; MA in New Testament, Wheaton (Ill.) Coll., 1975; PhD in Bibl. Theology, Marquette U., 1987. Ordained to ministry Community Ch., 1988. Lay leader, tchr. Christian and Missionary Alliance, Wheaton, Ill., 1973-75, asst. pastor, youth pastor Fremont, Nebr., 1975-78, ch. planter, founding pastor Pullman, Wash., 1978-80; lay leader, tchr. Bapt. Gen. Conf., Brown Deer, Wis., 1981-88; sr. minister Community Ch., Rolling Meadows, Ill., 1988-2000, Shiloh Bapt. Ch., Edmonton, Alta., Can., 2000—. Seminar leader religion Marquette Continuing Edn. Program, Milw., 1983; instr. N.T. Carroll Coll., Waukesha, Wis., 1983; tchr. adult bible class Capitol Dr. Luth. Ch., Milw., 1986-87; spkr., bible tchr., leader in prayer and Christian unity movements. Bd. dirs., pres. Meadows Cmty. Svcs., 1995-2000; coun. ring mem. Nebr. Camp Farthest Out, 1997-2000. With U.S. Army 1969-72. Arthur J. Schmitt Found. fellow, 1983-84, Internat. Ministerial fellow, 1994--. Home: 14305 103d Ave NW Edmonton AB Canada T5N 0T1 Office: Shiloh Bapt Ch 10727 114th St Edmonton AB Canada T5H 3K1 *What we must believe if we are to have any hope for this life or the next is that God exists, and that he is in the business of turning evil into good.*

RAHHAL, DONALD K. obstetrician, gynecologist; b. Clinton, Okla., 1942; MD, U. Okla. Coll. Medicine, 1971. Diplomate Am. Bd. Ob.-Gyn. (bd. dirs. 1992-2000). Resident Indiana U. Hosp., Indpls., 1971-74; obstetrician-gynecologist Mercy Health Ctr., Okla. City, 1981—, chief of staff elect, 2002—; obstetrician-gynecologist Deaconess Hosp., 1981—; clin. prof. U. Okla. Coll. Medicine, 1981—. Dir. Am. Bd. Gynecology, 1992-2000. Mem. ACOG, AMA, Am. Bd. Med. Specialties (del.). Office: 4200 W Memorial Rd Ste 410 Oklahoma City OK 73120-8376

RAHIM, M. AFZALUR, management educator, editor; b. Bangladesh; s. Khalilur and Nazman Nessa (Khatun) R.; m. Masuda Rahim, Mar. 25, 1966; 1 child, Sayeed M. B Commerce with honors, Dhaka (Bangladesh) U., 1960, M Commerce, 1961; MBA, Miami U., Oxford, Ohio, 1968; PhD, U. Pitts., 1976. Assoc. prof. mgmt. Dhaka U., 1970-72, Youngstown (Ohio) State U., 1976-83; prof. mgmt. Western Ky. U., Bowling Green, 1983—; pres. Ctr. for Advanced Studies in Mgmt., 1988—. Author: Managing Organizational Conflict, 1992, 3d edit., 2001, Current Topics in Management, vol. 1, 1996, vol. 2, 1997, vol. 3, 1998, vol. 4, 1999, vol. 5, 2000, vol. 6, 2001, vol. 7, 2002; editor Internat. Jour. Conflict Mgmt., 1988—, Internat. Jour. Orgn. Analysis, 1990—. Fulbright scholar, 1966-68. Avocations: chess, stamps, soccer. Office: Ctr for Advanced Studies in Mgmt 1574 Mallory Ct Bowling Green KY 42103-1300 E-mail: mgt2000@aol.com.

RAHM, DAVID ALAN, lawyer; b. Passaic, N.J., Apr. 18, 1941; s. Hans Emil and Alicia Katherine (Onuf) R.; m. Susan Eileen Berkman, Nov. 23, 1972; children: Katherine Berkman, William David. AB, Princeton U., 1962; JD, Yale U., 1965. Bar: N.Y. 1966, D.C. 1986. Assoc. Paul, Weiss, Rifkind & Wharton, N.Y.C., 1965-66, 1968-69; asst. counsel N.Y. State Urban Devel. Corp., 1969-72, assoc. counsel, 1972-75; counsel real estate div. Internat. Paper Co., 1975-80; ptnr. Stroock & Stroock & Lavan, 1980-83, sr. ptnr., 1984—2001. Mem. legis. com. Real Estate Bd. N.Y., 1988—92; lectr. Old Dominion Coll., Norfold, Va., 1967—68, NYU, 1986—; mem. editl. bd. Comml. Leasing Law and Strategy, 1988—95; mem. N.Y.C. bd. advisors Commonwealth Land Title Ins. Co., 1996—2000. Contbr. articles to profl. jours. Fund raiser corp. com. N.Y. Philharm., N.Y.C., 1980-84; trustee Manhattan Sch. Music, 1989—, treas., 1991-94, chmn., 1994—; bd. dir. New Dramatists, Inc., 2001-, exec. com., 2001-. Mem. ABA (comml. leasing com. 1987-88, 94—, pub./pvt. devel. com. 1989—, real property sect.), Assn. of Bar of City of N.Y. (housing and urban devel. com. 1977-80, 81-84, real property com. 1989-92), Princeton Club. Democrat. Presbyterian. Avocations: music, reading, travel. Office: Stroock Stroock & Lavan 180 Maiden Ln Fl 17 New York NY 10038-4937

RAHM, GERALD DAVID, artist; b. Toledo, Oct. 20, 1951; s. Lawrence Joseph and Corinne Marie Rahm; m. Donna Lichtenstein. Mem.: Pastel Soc. Am. (award Pastel Soc. of West Coast 2000, Hahnemuhle award 1995), Calif. Art Club.

RAHM, SUSAN BERKMAN, lawyer; b. Pitts., June 25, 1943; d. Allen Hugh and Selma (Wiener) Berkman; m. David Alan Rahm, Nov. 23, 1972; children: Katherine, William. BA with honors, Wellesley Coll., 1965; postgrad., Harvard U., 1966-68; JD, NYU, 1973. Bar: N.Y. 1974, D.C. 1988. Assoc. Marshall, Bratter, Greene, Allison & Tucker, N.Y.C., 1973-81, ptnr., 1981-82, Kaye Scholer, LLP, N.Y.C., 1982—, ptnr. chair real estate dept., 1993-98, chair internat. practice group, 1999—. N.Y. adv. bd., Chgo. Title Ins. Co., 1995. Editor: New York Real Property Service, 1987. Bd. dirs. Girls Inc., 1989-93; mem. aux. bd. Mt. Sinai Hosp., N.Y.C., 1976-78. Recipient cert. of outstanding svc. D.C. Redevel. Land Agy., 1969, She Knows Where She's Going award Girls' Clubs of Am., 1987, Woman of Yr. award CREW.NY, 1999. Mem. ABA, Assn. Bar City N.Y., N.Y. Bar Assn. (real property law com., co-chmn. real-estate devel. . 1987-91), Am. Coll. Real Estate Lawyers, Comml. Real Estate Women N.Y. (bd. dirs. 1988-94, v.p. 1988-91, pres. 1991-93). Office: Kaye Scholer LLP 425 Park Ave New York NY 10022-3506

RAHMAN, MUHAMMAD ABDUR, mechanical engineer; b. Sylhet, Assam, India, Mar. 1, 1930; came to U.S., 1950; s. Haji Sajjad Ali Khan and Momotaj Khanom. BSME, U. Toledo, 1953, MSME, 1968; PhD in Engring., Calif. Coast U., 1985. Registered profl. engr., Calif. Mech. design engr. various cons. firms, L.A., 1955-61; aerospace engr. Douglas Aircraft Co., Santa Monica, Calif., 1962-63, N.Am. Aviation, Inc., L.A., 1963-64, NASA Manned Spacecraft Ctr. Gemini & Apollo Program Office, Houston, 1964-70; safety engr. U.S. Dept. Labor, OSHA, Washington, 1975-86; invention researcher Arlington, Va., 1987—. Contbr. articles to profl. jours. Mem. N.Y. Acad. Scis. Democrat. Moslem. Achievements include patent for solar energy collector, supersonic MHD generator system; copyrights for hypothesis on unified field theory and creation of the universe, on the gravitoenergy in the creation of cosmic matters in the space, on the mechanism of superconductivity, a note of caution for superconductivity in reference to permeability and permitivity, concentration on suggesting methods to build superconductors and biomedical engineering instrumentation for cancer in particular, others. Home and Office: 1805 Crystal Dr Apt 1013 Arlington VA 22202-4407

RAHMAN, MUSTAQUR, administrative officer; b. Mymensingh, Bangladesh, Jan. 2, 1954; came to U.S., 1976; s. Mohammad Abdul Bari and Akika Akhtar Khatun. BA with honors, Jahangirnagar (Bangladesh) U., 1974; BS, Western Ill. U., 1978; diploma in journalism, Dhaka (Bangladesh) U., 1975, MA, 1981; diploma in travel and tourism, Parks Coll., Denver, Colo., 1985; cert., Travel Careers Internat., N.Y.C., 2000. Field-in-charge Australian Bapt. Missionary Soc., Dhaka, 1974; field officer Coop. Asst. Relief Everywhere, 1976; clk. Talent Tree, Denver, 1984-85; light indsl. dept. Handy Andy, Chgo., 1986-88; shipping asst. Eden Staffing, N.Y.C., 1996; clerical asst. Temps Am., 1996; quality contr. CTI Ops., 1997; mgmt. asst. Top Job Personnel, 1997-98, ITR, Travel Navigator, USA, 1999; adminstrv. officer Checker Mgmt., N.Y.C., 2000—. Travel cons. Travel Helps, Dhaka, 1989-96. Contbr. over 200 commentaries to daily newspapers and weekly mags., Dhaka, Bangladesh. Min. God The Order of the Holy Spirit. Merit scholar Govt. Bangladesh, Dhaka, 1966-68, 68-70, 74-75. Avocations: stories, travel, photography, sports. Home: PO Box 215 New York NY 10156-0215

RAHMAN, RAFIQ UR, oncologist, educator; b. Mirali, Pakistan, Mar. 3, 1957; came to U.S., 1985; s. Rakhman and Bibi (Sana) Gul; m. Shamim Ara Bangash; children: Maryam, Hassan, Haider. BS, MB, U. Peshawar, Pakistan, 1980. Bd. cert. internal medicine, med. oncology, hematology; lic. physician Pa., Ala., Ky. House officer in internal medicine Khyber Teaching Hosp.-U. Peshawar, Pakistan, 1980-81, house officer in gen. surgery Pakistan, 1981, jr. registrar med. ICU Pakistan, 1983-84; jr. registrar internal medicine Khyber Teaching Hosp., 1981-82; sr. registrar internal medicine Khyber Teaching Hosp.-Lady Reading Hosp. & Postgrad. Inst., Peshawar, 1984-85; Audrey Meyer Mars fellow in med. oncology Roswell Park Cancer Inst., Buffalo, 1985-86; resident in internal medicine SUNY-Buffalo Gen. Hosp.-Erie County Med. Ctr.-VA Med. Ctr., 1986-88; chief resident in internal medicine SUNY-Buffalo-Erie County Med. Ctr., 1988; fellow in hematology and med. oncology SUNY-Buffalo-Roswell Park Cancer Inst., 1989-90; hematologist, med. oncologist Daniel Boone Clinic and Harlan A.R.H., 1991-92; clin. asst. prof. medicine U. Ky., 1991—; attending physician, hematology/med. oncologist Hardin Meml. Hosp., Elizabethtown, 1993—, chief medicine, 1996, pres. elect med. staff, 2001—02, pres. med. staff, 2002—. Tchr. med. students Med. Sch., SUNY; participant CALGB protocol studies Roswell Park Cancer Inst., investigator. Editor English sect. Cenna mag. Cenna; contbr. articles to profl. jours. Founder Cmty. Uplift Program, Pakistan. Mem. Ky. Med. Assn., Hardin County Med. Soc. Avocations: traveling, aeromodeling, swimming, studying political science and history. Home: 400 Briarwood Cir Elizabethtown KY 42701-6915 Office: 1107 Woodland Dr Ste 105 Elizabethtown KY 42701-2789

RAHMING, ETTA LORRAINE, social worker, consultant, psychotherapist; b. Bronx, Mar. 6, 1957; d. Henry Lewis and Irene (Linen) R. BA in Sociology, CCNY, 1979; MSW, Howard U., 1981. Lic. social worker, N.Y.; lic. counselor, N.Y. Investigative probation officer N.Y.C. Dept. Probation, 1981-85; social worker E.N.T.E.R. Alcoholism O.P.D., 1985-86; psychiat. social worker Bronx Lebanon Alcoholism O.P.D., 1986-88; clin. supr. residential treatment program E.N.T.E.R. Inc., 1988-89; supr. Comprehensive Employment Opportunity Support Ctr. Fedn. Employment Guidance Ctr., 1989-92; therapist Our Lady of Mercy Mental Health Clinic, Bronx, 1994—. Mem. NASW, Nat. Assn. Black Social Workers, Inc., N.Y. Fedn. Alcoholism Counselors, Nat. Black Alcoholism Coun., N.Y. Women in Criminal Justice. Home: PO Box 502220 Saint Thomas VI 00805-2220

RAHMING, JOHN CHRISTOPHER, investment company executive, consultant; b. Mt. Vernon, Ohio, Oct. 25, 1937; s. Norris Walton and Mary Katherine (Arndt) Rahming; m. Ann Gail Smith, June 12, 1959 (div. Aug. 1974); children: Charles, Jennifer; m. Penelope Watson Bevan, Dec. 17, 1988; 1 child Jason Bevan. BA, Harvard U., Cambridge, Mass., 1959; MBA, Harvard U., Boston, 1965. Mgr Citibank, N.Y.C. and Buenos Aires, 1966-70; v.p. Security Pacific Bank, London and L.A., 1970-76, Alexander Proudfoot, L.A., Paris, London, 1976-81; mng. dir. London Interstate Bank, 1981-88; ops. mgr. Inter-Am. Investment Corp., Washington, 1989-93, gen. mgr., 1993-99, cons., 2000—. Bd. dirs. Environ. Enterprise Assistance Fund, Ctrl. Am. Small Enterprise Investment Fund. Lt. USN, 1959-63. Mem. Met. Club, Harvard Club (N.Y.C.), Harvard Bus. Sch. Club, Roehampton Club (London). Avocations: sailing, skiing, golf, music, theater. Home: 1221 28th St NW Washington DC 20007-3362 Office: Inter-Am Investment Corp IDB Group 1300 New York Ave Nw Washington DC 20577

RAHN, ALVIN ALBERT, former banker; b. St. Paul, Apr. 8, 1925; s. Albert and Manda (Lau) R.; m. Helen Lyngen, June 10, 1950; children: Jennifer, Karen, Paul. BBA, U. Minn., 1949; postgrad., Stonier Sch. Banking, 1968. C.P.A., Minn. With income tax div. Minn. Dept. Taxation, 1949-61, asst. dir., 1957-61; with 1st Bank System Inc., Mpls., 1961-85, treas., 1969-85, chief fin. officer, 1973-74, sr. v.p., 1974-85. Served with USNR, 1943-46. Mem. Am. Inst. C.P.A.s, Minn. Soc. C.P.A.s, Fin. Execs. Inst. Home: 5601 Dewey Hill Rd Minneapolis MN 55439-1919

RAI, MAQBOOL AHMAD, civil engineer, consultant; b. Shorkot, Pakistan, Apr. 15, 1937; s. M. Bahadur and Bakht Bhari R.; m. Samra Rubina Rani, Feb. 2, 1966; 4 children. BS, MIE, MAWWA, MASCE. Asst. engr. Karachi Devel. Authority, 1963-68; dist. engr. Dist. Coun., Gujrat, Sargodha, 1968-69, Mianwali, Campbellpur, 1971-72; asst. mcpl. engr. Mcpl. Corp., Lahore, 1972-74, mcpl. engr. Gujranwala, Multan, Lahore, 1975-78; deputy dir. Lahore Devel. Auth.; mcpl. engr. Mcpl. Corp., Lahore, 1978-82; project engr. Hamad M. Al-Qahtany Est., Saudi Arabia, 1982-84; officer on spl. duty Punjab Local Govt. Bd.; mcpl. engr., chief engr. Mcpl. Corp., Lahore, 1984, mcpl. engr. Sialkot, Sheikhupura, 1984-87, Met. Corp., Lahore, 1987-91, superintending engr., 1991-93; chief engr. Mcpl. Corp., Rawalpindi, 1993-94, Faisalabad, 1994-95; additional dir. gen. inspections local govt. dept. Govt. of Punjab, 1995; chief engr. Met. Corp., Lahore, 1995-97. Recipient prizes in English and Perusian, German first class first with distinction, U. Karachi, Higher Level Appreciations and awards for meritorious svcs. in Engring. Realsm. Home: 232 Pak Block Allama Iqbal Town Lahore Pakistan

RAI, SATISH, finance company executive; Vice chair, fixed income portfolio mgmt. and rsch. TD Asset Mgmt. Inc.; sr. v.p. TD Bank Fin. Group, Toronto. Office: TD Bank Fin Group 45 Overlea Blvd Toronto ON Canada M4H 1C3*

RAIA, CARL BERNARD, commercial real estate executive and developer; b. Houston, Nov. 23, 1931; s. Sam B. and Mary F. (Barzilla) R.; m. Micheline Fauret, June 9, 1956 (dec. Oct. 1990); children: Marylyn, Carlene LoDuca, Carl B. Jr.; m. Mary Teresa Corsentino Pizzitola, Feb. 17, 2001. BS, U. Houston, 1954. Lic. realtor, Tex. Pres. Fonmeadow Devel., Inc., Houston, 1975—; v.p. Vulcan Properties, Inc., Investment Co., 1970; ptnr. M&R, Investment Co., 1970; owner Carl Raia Realty, Houston, 1964—; pres. RaiCom Realty, Inc., 1995—. Pres., chmn. bd. KSBJ Edn. Found., Humble, Tex., 1988-90. Chmn. Jesus Rally, Houston, 1979-81. With U.S. Army, 1954-57. Mem. Nat. Assn. Realtors, Tex. Assn. Realtors, Houston Assn. Realtors, Full Gospel Businessmen's Internat., Houston Cath. Charismatic Ctr., K.C. Roman Catholic. Office: 7211 Regency Square Blvd Houston TX 77036-3138

RAIGN, MICHAEL STEPHEN, lawyer; b. Glendale, Ariz., Mar. 11, 1960; s. Phillip Harry and Stephanie Elizabeth (Medoff) R.; m. Sherie Leslie Gee, July 2, 1995; 1 child, Kelsie Gee. BBA in Acctg., U. Tex., 1982, BA in Govt., 1983; JD, St. Mary's U., San Antonio, 1986. Bar: Tex. 1987; cert. in criminal law Tex. Bd. Legal Specialization, 1997. Prosecutor Bexar County Dist. Atty.'s Office, San Antonio, 1987-95; pvt. practice, 1995—. Player San Antonio Soccer Assn.; referee San Antonio Soccer Referee's Assn.; mental health master, 2002—. Candidate for bd. dirs. Edwards Aquifer Authority, San Antonio, 1996. Mem.: San Antonio Criminal Def. Lawyers Assn. (treas. 2001—02, dir. 1999—), Tex. Dist. and County Attys. Assn., Tex. Criminal Def. Lawyers Assn. Republican. Roman Catholic. Avocations: music, soccer, backpacking, photography, antiques. Office: 313 S Main Ave San Antonio TX 78204-1016

RAIJMAN, ISAAC, gastroenterologist, endoscopist, educator; b. Empalme, Sonora, Mex., July 6, 1959; came to U.S., 1985; s. Jose and Amalia (Langsam) R. MD, Nat. Autonomous U., Mexico City, 1985; postgrad., Nat. U. Houston, U. Wis., 1985. Diplomate Am. Bd. Internal Medicine, Am. Bd. Gastroenterology. Resident in medicine Mt. Sinai Hosp., Milw., 1986-88, chief resident, 1989; clin. fellow in therapeutic endoscopy Wellesley Hosp., Toronto, Ont., Can., 1992-93; rsch. fellow in gastroenterology U. Tex., Houston, 1989-90, clin. fellow, 1990-92, asst. prof. medicine, 1993-97, dir. therapeutic endoscopy, 1993-97, asst. prof. M.D. Anderson Cancer Ctr., 1993—2000, dir. ann. therapeutic endoscopy course, 1995-97; assoc. prof. Med. U. Tex., 2002—; dir. therapeutic endoscopy U. Tex., 2002—. Chair Ann. Therapeutic Endoscopy Meeting; chair gastroenterology and endoscopy sub. com., GI subcom. on endoscopic credentialing and quality assurance Hermann Hosp., Houston. Author: Pancreas, 1993, Bockus Textbook of Gastroenterology, 1993; also numerous articles; reviewer jours. in field. Mem. Am. Coll. Gastroenterology, Am. Gastroenterology Assn., Internat. Assn. Pancreatology, Am. Soc. Gastrointestinal Endoscopy, Am. Soc. Internal Medicine. Avocation: painting. Office: Digestive Assocs 6624 Fannin Ste 1640 Houston TX 77030 E-mail: iraijman@dahpa.com.

RAIKES, CHARLES FITZGERALD, retired lawyer; b. Mpls., Oct. 6, 1930; s. Arthur FitzGerald and Margaret (Hawthorne) R.; m. Antonia Raikes, Dec. 20, 1969; children: Jennifer Catherine, Victoria Samantha. BA, Washington U., 1952; MA, Harvard U., 1955, LL.B., 1958. Bar: N.Y. State 1959. Assoc. White & Case, N.Y.C., 1958-69; assoc. gen. counsel Dun & Bradstreet, Inc., 1969-72, v.p., gen. counsel, 1972-73, The Dun & Bradstreet Corp., N.Y.C., 1973-76, sr. v.p., gen. counsel, 1976-94, of counsel, 1994-95; ret., 1995. Cons. Bd. Govs. Fed. Reserve System, 1958-95. Served with U.S. Army, 1952-54. Woodrow Wilson fellow, 1952 Mem. Assn. Bar City of N.Y., Harvard Club, Phi Beta Kappa. Home: 26 Crooked Trl Norwalk CT 06853-1106

RAIKES, JEFF, information technology executive; B of Engring. and Econ. Systems, Stanford U. Software devel. mgr. Apple Computer Inc.; product mgr. Microsoft, Redmond, Wash., 1981, v.p. Worldwide Sales and Support Group, group v.p. Productivity and Bus. Svcs. Ptnr. Seattle Mariners Baseball Club, 1992—; bd. dirs. XO Comm. Inc.; mem. Sr. Leadership Team, Bus. Leadership Team, Microsoft. Mem. U. Nebr. Found.; trustee Wash. State U. Found.; leader Online Wash. State U. Initiative. Office: Microsoft One Microsoft Way Redmond WA 98052-6399*

RAIL, KATHY LYNN PARISH, accountant; b. Chewelah, Wash., May 21, 1951; d. John Edward and Margaret Irene (Seefeldt) Rail. BBA, Gonzaga U., 1984. CPA, Wash. Legal sec. Redbook Pub. Co., N.Y.C., 1974-75, Howard Michaelson, Esquire, Spokane, Wash., 1975-76; sec. Burns Internat. Security Svcs., 1977-79; sec. to contr. Gonzaga U., 1979-81, acctg. asst., 1981-82; staff acct. Martin, Holland & Petersen, CPA's, Yakima, Wash., 1984-87; acct., supr. Strader Hallet & Co., P.S., Bellevue, 1988-91; acct. Miller & Co., P.S.,

Woodinville, 1991-93; pres. Parish Rail, CPA, P.S., Redmond, 1993—. Treas. White Pass Ski Patrol, Nat. Ski Patrol Systems, Wash., 1987-90; editor, chmn. audit com. Mt. Spokane Ski Patrol, 1983-84. Mem. AICPA, Am. Soc. Women Accts. (charter, editor 1987), Wash. Soc. CPA (sec. Sammamish Valley chpt. 1990-92, pres. 1992-93, 93-94), Washington Soc. of Cert. Pub. Accts. (chair adv. coun. 1995-96, tax com., govt. affairs com., dir. 1996-98), Bus. and Profl. Women of Woodinville (treas. 1994-95), Northshore C. of C. Lutheran. Avocations: snow skiing, piano, golfing.

RAILA, FRANK ARTHUR, radiologist; b. Chgo., July 26, 1925; BS, Loyola U., Maywood, Ill., 1950, MD, 1957; MS, U. Ill., Chgo., 1953. Diplomate Am. Bd. Radiology, subspecialty neuroradiology. Intern Resurrection Hosp., Chgo., 1957-58; resident in radiology VA Hosp., Long Beach, Calif., 1963-66; prof. radiology U. Miss. Med. Ctr., Jackson. Mem. staff U. Miss. Med. Ctr., Jackson; alsp pvt. practice managed care/HMO. Co-author: (CD-ROM) Diagnostic Radiology, 1996; contbr. Youmans Neurological Surgery, 4th edit. Mem. St. Mark's Meth. Ch., Brandon, Miss. Lt. col. U.S. Army Res. Med. Corps., ret. Fellow Am. Coll. Radiology; mem. Am. Univ. Radiologists, New Zealand Med. Assn., Radiol. Soc. N.Am., So. Med. Assn., Am. Inst. of Ultrasound in Medicine, Soc. of Nuclear Medicine, Am. Ex-Prisoners of War, Am. Legion, Veterans of the Battle of the Bulge, Southeastern Neuroradiol. Soc., Am. Soc. Head and Neck Radiology, Am. Soc. Neuroradiology, Am. Soc. Pediat. Neuroradiology, Am. Soc. Spine Radiology, N.Am. Spine Soc. Office: Univ Radiologists Assocs U Miss Med Ctr Dept Rad 2500 N State St Jackson MS 39216-4500 E-mail: frankaraila@aol.com.

RAILSBACK, DAVID PHILLIPS, executive, former state official, lawyer; b. Newton, Mass., Aug. 21, 1950; s. David and Mary Ann (Phillips) R.; m. Elizabeth Stone, June 7, 1974; 1 child, Meredith. BS summa cum laude, Lehigh U., 1972; JD cum laude, Suffolk U., 1978; LLM, Boston U., 1982. Bar: Mass. 1978, R.I. 1979, U.S. Dist. Ct. R.I. 1979, U.S. Tax Ct. 1979, U.S. Dist. Ct. Mass. 1980. Law clk. R.I. Supreme Ct., 1978-79; assoc. Tillinghast, Collins, and Graham, Providence, 1979-81; exec. v.p., gen. counsel New Eng. Rd. Machinery Co., Fitchburg, Mass., 1981-91; asst. state treas. Commonwealth of Mass., 1991-92, dep. state treas., 1992-96; asst. dir. Mass. Lottery Commn., Braintree, 1996-98, CFO, 1997-98; gen. mgr. Sales Consultants of Southborough, Inc., Mass., 1998—. Treas., bd. dirs. Assabet Leasing Corp., Railsback Corp., New Eng. Rd. Machinery Co. Chmn. crusade com. R.I. chpt. Am. Cancer Soc., 1979-82; mem. Concord Republican Town Com., 1990-99. Mem. Nat. Fedn. Ind. Bus. (Mass. adv. bd. 1999—). Republican. Home: 42 Saw Mill Rd Concord MA 01742-2220 Office: PO Box 3176 Fayville MA 01745-0176 E-mail: dave@sales-consultants.com.

RAILSBACK, SHERRIE LEE, adoption search and reunion consultant; b. Phila., Mar. 12, 1942; children: Ricky, Cindy. BBA, U. Ky., 1981. Sales mgr. Marjo Cosmetics, Ft. Wayne, Ind.; asst. dir. patient fin. svcs. Riverside Meth. Hosp., Columbus, Ohio; cons. Railsback and Assocs., Long Beach, Calif.; adoption search/reunion cons., educator Searchers Connection, L.A. Mem.: ASTD, NAFE, Book Publicists So. Calif., Am. Adoption Congress, Nat. Spkrs. Assn., Toastmasters.

RAILTON, PETER ALBERT, philosophy educator; b. Elgin, Ill., May 23, 1950; s. Arthur Roy and Marjorie Elizabeth Marks Railton; m. Rebecca Jarvis Scott, Apr. 21, 1978; children: John Scott-Railton, Thomas Scott-Railton. AB magna cum laude, Harvard U., 1971; PhD, Princeton U., 1980. From asst. prof. philosophy to assoc. prof. U. Mich., Ann Arbor, 1979—90, prof. philosophy, 1990—, Nelson prof., 1999—2001, Perrin Collegiate prof., 2001—. Vis. prof. U. Calif., Berkeley, 1984-85, Princeton (N.J.) U., 1990; mem. Coun. for Philos. Studies, N.Y.C., 1992-94; rsch. assoc. Ecole Poly., Paris, 1995—. Co-editor, author: Moral Discourse and Practice, 1997; mem. editl. bd. Ethics, Utilitas; contbr. articles to profl. jours. Am. Coun. Learned Socs. fellow, 1988-89, 2000, NEH fellow, 1999, Guggenheim fellow, 2001-2002. Mem. Am. Philos. Assn. (various coms. 1978—), Am. Soc. for Polit. and Legal Philosophy, Philosophy of Scis. Assn. (various coms. 1978—). Office: U Mich Dept Philosophy 2215 Angell Hall Ann Arbor MI 48109

RAILTON, WILLIAM SCOTT, retired lawyer; b. Newark, July 30, 1935; s. William Scott and Carolyn Elizabeth (Guiberson) R.; m. Karen Elizabeth Walsh, Mar. 31, 1979; 1 son, William August; children by previous marriage: William Scott, Anne Greenwood. BSEE, U. Wash., 1962; JD with honors, George Washington U., 1965. Bar: D.C. 1966, Md. 1966, Va. 1993, U.S. Patent Office 1966. Assoc., then ptnr. Kemon, Palmer & Estabrook, Washington, 1966-70; sr. trial atty. Dept. Labor, 1970-71, asst. counsel for trial litigation, 1971-72; chief counsel U.S. Occupational Safety and Health Rev. Commn., 1972-77, acting gen. counsel, 1975-77; ptnr. Reed Smith LLP, Pitts., 1977—2002; commr. U.S. OSH Rev. Commn., 2002—; ret., 2002. Lectr. George Washington U. Law Sch., 1977-79, seminar chmn. Occupational Safety and Health Act, Govt. Inst., 1979-96; lectr. Practicing Law Inst., 1976-79; apptd. commr., chmn. U.S. Occupl. Safety and Health Rev. Commn., 2002. Author: (legal handbooks) The Examination System and the Backlog, 1965, The OSHA General Duty Clause, 1977, The OSHA Health Standards, 1977; OSHA Compliance Handbook, 1992; contbg. author: Occupational Safety and Health Law, 1988, 93. Regional chmn. Montgomery County (Md.) Republican party, 1968-70; pres. Montgomery Sq. Citizens Assn., 1970-71; bd. dirs., pres. Foxvale Farms Homeowners Assn., 1979-82; pres. Orchards on the Potomac Homeowners Assn., 1990-92; dir. Great Falls Hist. Soc., 1991-94; scoutmaster Troop 55 Boy Scouts Am., 1993-98. With USMC, 1953-58. Recipient Meritorious Achievement medal Dept. Labor, 1972, Outstanding Service award OSHA Rev. Commn., 1977, elected fell. Coll. Labor and Employment Lawyers, 1998. Fellow Coll. Labor and Employment Lawyers; mem. ABA (mgmt. co-chmn. occupational safety and health law com. 1995-98), Md. Bar Assn., Va. Bar Assn., Bar Assn. D.C. (vice chmn. young lawyers sect. 1971), Order of Coif, Sigma Phi Epsilon, Phi Delta Phi. Home: 10102 Walker Lake Dr Great Falls VA 22066-3502 also: East Tower 1301 K St NW # 1100 Washington DC 20005-3317 E-mail: srailton@reedsmith.com. *Lawsuits are won by pre-trial preparation. A litigator should be candid with his clients and honest in his dealings with associates, opponents and the courts; an attorney should also volunteer his service to the community of which he is a part.*

RAIMI, BURTON LOUIS, lawyer; b. Detroit, May 5, 1938; s. Irving and Rae (Abel) R.; m. Judith Morse, Mar. 31, 1963 (div. Mar. 1985); children: Diane L., and Matthew D. BA, Brandeis U., 1960; JD with honors, U. Mich., 1963; LLM, George Washington U., 1964. Bar: Mich. 1963, DC 1964, Fla. 1991, U.S. Ct. of Claims, U.S. Ct. Appeals (4th, 7th, 8th, 9th, 10th, 11th and DC cirs.), U.S. Supreme Ct. Atty. appelate ct. sect. NLRB, Washington, 1964-69; assoc. Morgan, Lewis & Bockius, 1969-71; dep. gen. counsel FDIC, 1971-78; ptnr. Rosenman and Colin, 1978-86, Dechert Price & Rhoads, Washington, 1986-93; shareholder McCaffrey & Raimi, P.A., Naples and Sarasota, Fla., 1994—. Speaker various insts. Mem. ABA (past chmn. bank receiverships subcom. of banking com.), D.C. Bar Assn. (past chmn. banking law com., com. on interest on lawyers trust accounts), Fla. Bar (fin. instns., securities coms.). Avocations: sailing, travel, golf, fishing. Home: 4452 Staghorn Ln Sarasota FL 34238-5626 Office: McCaffrey & Raimi PA 1800 2nd St Ste 753 Sarasota FL 34236-5900 Fax: 941-957-0449. E-mail: burt@moneylaw.com.

RAIMI, RALPH ALEXIS, mathematics educator; b. Detroit, July 25, 1924; s. Jacob and Sylvia (Krusner) R.; m. Sonya Lenore Drews, June 29, 1947; children: Jessica, Diana. BS in Physics, U. Mich., 1947, MS in Math, 1948, PhD, 1954. Faculty U. Rochester, N.Y., 1952—, prof. math., 1966—98, chmn. dept. sociology, 1983-86, assoc. dean for grad. studies Coll. Arts and Sci., 1967-75, profe. emeritus math., 1995—. Cons. in Math. Edn. State of Calif. Bd. Edn. and private ednl. founds. Author: Vested Interests, 1982, The Philomathic Debating Club, 1991; contbr. articles to mags., jours., newspapers. Served to 1st lt. USAAF, 1943-46. Fulbright Grad. fellow Paris, 1949-50; Lloyd postdoctoral fellow U. Mich., 1955-56; NSF grantee; Office of Naval Rsch. grantee. Mem.: Nat. Assn. Scholars, Nat. Coun. Tchrs. Math., Am. Math. Soc., Math. Assn. Am., Philomathic Debating Club, Am. Wine Soc. Home: 46 Glen Ellyn Way Rochester NY 14618-1502 *In my childhood I was told to be like everyone else, and not to take on airs. My relatives and teachers doubtless had a democratic virtue in mind, but their egalitarianism slowed my ambition. Books came from the library and not from the likes of me, I thought, and wealth was theft from the poor. Now I know better, but it is mostly too late.*

RAIMO, BERNARD (BERNIE RAIMO), lawyer; b. Kansas City, Mo., May 29, 1944; m. Sharon Marie Brady, Aug. 23, 1974; children: Sarah Elizabeth, Peter Bernard. BA, U. Notre Dame, 1965; MA, U. Md., 1967; JD with honors, George Washington U., 1972. Bar: D.C. Staff asst. to Sen. Stuart Symington, Mo., 1968-72; asst. corp. counsel D.C., Washington, 1972-76; legis. analyst Am. Petroleum Inst., 1976-78; counsel Permanent Select Com. Intelligence U.S. Ho. Reps., Washington, 1978-91, chief counsel Ho. Com. Standards of Official Conduct, 1991-95; minority counsel Ho. Com. Standards of Official Conduct, 1995-97; counsel to Dem. leader U.S. Ho. of Reps., 1997—. Office: Office of the Dem Leader H-204 The Capitol Washington DC 20515-0001 E-mail: bernard.raimo@mail.house.gov.

RAIMONDI, JOSEPHINE ANN, lawyer; b. Indpls., Dec. 03; d. Anthony Leonard and Catherine Ann (Mascari) R. BS, Georgetown U., 1980; JD, U. Mich., 1987. Staff acct. Arthur Andersen & Co., Chgo., 1980-81; cons. Peterson & Co., 1982-84; assoc. LeBoeuf, Lamb Greene & MacRae, N.Y.C., 1987-92; gen. counsel Midwest Employers Casualty Co., St. Louis, 1993-97; v.p., sr. counsel W.R. Berkley Corp., Greenwich, Conn., 1997—. Mem. Westport (Conn.) Young Women's League. Home: 473 Main St Westport CT 06880-2159 Office: WR Bekeley Corp 475 Steamboat Rd Greenwich CT 06830-6608 E-mail: jraimondi@wrberkley.com.

RAIMONDI, RUGGERO, opera singer; b. Bologna, Italy, Oct. 3, 1941; m. Isabel Maier, 1987. Studies with, Teresa Pediconi, Rome, Armando Piervenanzi. Debut in La Boheme, Spoleto, Italy, 1964; singer in major houses, Europe and U.S.; Met. debut in Ernani, N.Y.C., 1970; favorite roles include Don Giovanni, Philip II, Boris and Don Quichotte; recorded Verdi Requiem, Vespri Siciliani, La Boheme, Aida, Attila, Don Carlos, Macbeth, Simon Boccanegra, Don Giovanni, Boris Godunov, Tosca, Turandot, Barbiere di Siviglia, Mosè, Nozze di Figaro, Italiana in Algieri, Cenerentola, Il Viaggio a Reims, and others; appeared in films Don Giovanni (Joseph Losey), 1978, Six Characters in Search of a Singer (Maurice Bejart), 1983, Carmen (Francesco Rosi), 1986, others; opera prodn. since, 1986—. Decorated comdr. Arts et Lettres (France), chevalier Ordre de Malte, Grand Ufficiale della Repubblica Italiana, comdr. Mérite Culturel (Monaco); named Citizen of Honor, City of Athens, Greece. Office: 140 bis rue Lecourbe F-75015 Paris France

RAIN, LAWRENCE MICHAEL, medical/surgical nurse, writer; b. Alton, Ill., Jan. 9, 1958; s. Ilda Unila Webster; m. Michelle Kay Rain, June 22, 1989; 1 child Jesse Lee. Student, Lewis & Clark Coll. Author: Charisma and the Law (Torah), 2002. Avocations: church, family, Bible teaching and counseling, dirt bikes. Home: 37 E Acton Ave # 8 Wood River IL 62095 E-mail: michaelrain_2000@yahoo.com.

RAINAL, ATTILIO JOSEPH, electronics engineer, researcher; b. Marion Heights, Pa., Feb. 14, 1930; m. Violet Dorothy Robel, June 29, 1957; children: Valery, Eric. BS in Engring. Sci., Pa. State U., 1956; MSEE, Drexel U., 1959; D of Elec. Engring., Johns Hopkins U., 1963. Engr. Applied Physics Lab. Johns Hopkins U., Silver Spring, Md., 1955; engr. Martin Co., Balt., 1956-59; mem. rsch. staff Carlyle Barton Lab. Johns Hopkins U., 1959-64; mem. tech. staff R & D AT&T Bell Labs., Whippany and Murray Hill, N.J., 1964-83, mem. disting. tech. staff R & D, 1983—. Contbr. more than 40 articles to jours. including Rev. of Sci. Instruments, Electronics, Bell Systems Tech. Jour., Bell Labs. Tech. Jour. With USAF, 1948-52. Mem. IEEE (life), Info. Theory, Component, Hybrids and Mfg. Tech. Achievements include research on noise theory, signal detection and estimation, radiometry, radar, FM, first passage times of random processes, crosstalk, voltage breakdown, current carrying capacity of printed wires, performance limits of electrical interconnections; 12 patents, including balanced interconnections, and laser intensity modulation. Home: 28 Woodruff Rd Morristown NJ 07960-4620

RAINE, LAUREN, artist; b. Nyack, N.Y., Aug. 19, 1949; d. Florence Greene and Kent Pillsbury; 1 child, Shari Axelrod. BFA, U. Calif., Berkeley, 1973; MFA, U. Ariz., 1987. Dir. Rites of Passage Gallery, Berkeley, 1998-2000, The Spiral Dance, Tucson, 2000—; owner Rainwalker Masks, 1998—. Author: The Song of Medusa, 2000; artist, performer Masks of the Goddess, 1999, Spiderwoman's Web, 2000, Invocation to Fire, 1999, Hungry Ghosts of Albion, 1999; mask and costume designer (film) Tragos, 2000; artist mask series Ancestor Series, 1996. Democrat. Studio: Rainwalker Studios PO Box 1301 Benicia CA 94510 E-mail: laurenraine@msn.com.

RAINE, MARTIN FREDERICK, senior agricultural economist, investor, farmer; b. Mex. Dist. Fed., Mex., July 14, 1951; s. Philip and Alice Lolo (Weiss) R.; m. Emilla Maria Rodriguez-Arias, June 15, 1980; children: Tanya, Christine, Daniel. Student, Hobart Coll., 1969-70; BSC, Cornell U., 1973; cert., Tex. A&M U., 1975, U. Costa Rica, San Jose, 1978; MSc, London Sch. Econs., 1979. Dir. social devel. Presdl. House, San Jose, Costa Rica, 1975-78; project dir. UNICEF, San Carlos, Costa Rica, 1976-78; cons. Accion Internat., San Jose, 1979-80; agrl. economist World Bank U.S.A., Kenya, Ivory Coast, 1980-89, sr. agrl. economist San Jose, 1989-97, dir. Ruta World Bank project, 1996—. Owner, adminstr. Macadamia Farm, Limon, Costa Rica, 1991—. Tourism Bus., Limon, 1985-97, Tropical Crops Farm, Limon, 1977-86; mem. Housing & Consumer Coop., Ithaca, N.Y., 1972. Contbr. articles to profl. jours. Named hon. citizen State Tex. Legis., Austin; presented Key to City, Waco, Tex. Mem. South Caribbean Devel. Assn. Fin. Lutheran. Avocations: tropical forest hiking, scuba diving, tennis, stamp collecting. Office: RUTA Apto PO 211-2100 Guadalupe San José Costa Rica

RAINE, MELINDA L. library manager; b. Boston, Feb. 4, 1951; d. James Agee and Marjorie Elizabeth (Gilstrap) Raine; m. Stephen Richard Brogden, Jan. 1, 1983; 1 child, Nathan Raine Brogden. BA, U. Iowa, 1973, MA, 1974. Info. specialist Pub. Libr. Des Moines, 1974-82, libr. mgr., 1982-90; task force coord. Visio 2020 Project, Conejo Future Found., Thousand Oaks, Calif., 1991-92; mgr. engring. libr. Metters Industries, Camarillo, 1992-94; govt. publs. libr. Pepperdine U., Malibu, 1994-98, coord. info. resources, 1998—. Author: Options for Our Endangered Environment, 1992, Water: Liquid Gold, 1992, The Housing Crisis, 1992, Solid Ideas for Solid Waste, 1992; co-author (with Elizabeth parang and Trisha Stevenson): Redesigning Freshman Seminar Library Instruction Based on Information Comepetencies in Research Strategies, 2001. Mem. ALA, AAUW (pub. policy chair 1993-96, v.p. programming 1992-93), Calif. Libr. Assn., Calif. Acad. and Rsch. Librs. Office: Pepperdine U 24255 Pacific Coast Hwy Malibu CA 90263-4786

RAINER, RENATA URBACH, photographer, artist, educator, artist; b. Vienna, Austria, May 20, 1928; came to the U.S., 1940; d. Robert and Lola (Finkelstein) Urbach; m. George F. Rainer, Feb. 6, 1949; childen: Nina H. Price, Andrew A. Rainer. BA cum laude, CUNY, 1949; MA cum laude, Columbia U., 1967. Cert. art specialist grades K-12, N.Y. Graphic designer Newsweek mag., 1949-52; freelance graphic designer N.Y.C., 1952-65; art specialist Irvington Pub. Schs., N.Y., 1968; art specialist grades K-8 Pocantico Hills Pub. Sch., Sleepy Hollow, 1968-71; adj. asst. prof. Marymount Coll., Tarrytown, 1980-90; adj. assoc. prof. studio art and photography Manhattanville Coll., Purchase, NY, 1990—2001. Advisor Pelham (N.Y.) Art Ctr. Gallery, 1980-90, Rye (N.Y.) Arts Ctr. Gallery, 1994—; lectr. art history SUNY, Purchase, 1982-85; spkr. N.Y. Coun. for the Humanities, 1988-90; artist-in-residence Westchester Pub. Schs., 1990-94. One-woman shows include Bridge Gallery, White Plains, N.Y., 1981, Butler Gallery-Marymount Coll., Tarrytown, 1984, Hewlett Packard, Palo Alto, Calif., 1986, Hudson River Mus., Yonkers, N.Y., 1988, Benham Gallery, Seattle, 1997, Wainwright House, Rye, N.Y., 1997, Luchsinger Gallery, 1999, Greenwich Acad., Conn., 1999; curator 150 Years of American History by American Photographers, Pelham Art Ctr., N.Y., 1989, The Feminine Focus: Photographs of Women and Women Who Photograph, Greenburgh Town Hall, Elmsford, N.Y., 1991, Photography Now: Facts and Fantasies, Rye (N.Y.) Arts Ctr., 1994, 95, Of Time and the River, Hastings (N.Y.) Gallery, 1995, Pelham Arts Ctr., 1995, Faces Through the Lens: Time, Space and Matter, Rye Arts Ctr., 1998, Rye Arts Ctr., 2002; exhibited in group shows at Hopkins Ctr., Hanover, N.H., 1976, Hudson River Mus., Yonkers, 1977, Bridge Gallery, White Plains, 1978, Focal Point Gallery, City Island, N.Y., 1980, Fig Tree Gallery, Fresno, Calif., 1980, River Gallery, Irvington, N.Y., 1981, Pace U. Gallery, Briarcliff, N.Y., 1982, Photographics Gallery, New Canaan, Conn., 1984, Mus. Gallery, White Plains, 1985, Sarah Lawrence Coll., Bronxville, N .Y., 1988, Katonah (N.Y.) Gallery, 1988, Candace Perich Gallery, Katonah, 1997, Brownson Gallery, Purchase, N.Y., 1990-2000, Gallery on the Hudson, Irvington, 1998, Paramount Ctr. for the Arts, Peekskill, N.Y., 1999, Westchester Biennial 2000, Castle Gallery, Coll. New Rochelle, N.Y., 2000, Bridgewater/Lustberg & Blumenfeld, N.Y.C., 2000, Westchester Arts Coun. Gallery, 2001, Eestchester Cmty. Coll., Valhalla, N.Y., 2002; included in (with other publs.) Black & White Photography Manifest Visions, 2000; pub. collections include Libr. Rsch. Ctr. Nat. Mus. Women in Arts, Washington, 1990, Boca Raton Mus. Art, Fla., 1992, Lyndhurst Nat. Trust Hist. Preservation, Tarrytown, N.Y., 1996, Neuberger Mus. Art, Purchase, N.Y., 2000, Pfizer Art Coll., Purchase, 2000, Metromedia Fiber Network, Hdqrs. White Plains, 2001. Recipient Hist. Svcs. award for excellence Lower Hudson Conf. Hist. Agys. and Mus., 1988, No. Westchester Ctr. for the Arts award Mt. Kisco, 2000; grantee N.Y. Coun. for the Humanities, 1988. Mem. The Ground Glass (founder, past pres.), Photographic Adminstrs., Inc. Avocations: hiking, gardening, cross country skiing. Home: 11 Cottontail Ln Irvington NY 10533-1011 E-mail: grainer153@aol.com.

RAINER, REX KELLY, civil engineer, educator; b. Montgomery, Ala., July 17, 1924; s. Kelly Kenyon and Pearl (Jones) R.; m. Betty Ann Page, Aug. 28, 1945; children: Rex Kelly, John Kenyon. BS, Auburn (Ala.) U., 1944, MS, 1946; PhD, Okla. State U., 1967. Asst. engr. L. & N. R.R. Co., Cin., 1944-45; design engr. Polglaze & Basenberg, Birmingham, Ala., 1945-51; pres., chmn. Rainer Co., Inc., Orlando, Fla., 1951-62; prof. civil engring. Auburn U., 1962-67, head civil engring. dept., 1967; exec. v.p., 1980; hwy. dir. State of Ala., 1979-80, fin. dir., 1981-82; spl. asst. to gov. of Ala., 1981-82; dir. Office for Advancement Devel. Industry U. Ala., Birmingham, 1982-86; pres., cons. engr. Rex K. Rainer, Inc., 1982-98, ret., 1998. Cons. to ins. cos., constrn. engring. firms; mem. Ala. Bd. Registration Profl. Engrs. and Land Surveyors, 1977-89. Contbr. articles to profl. jours. Mem. Municipal Planning Bd., 1963-65, Indsl. Park Devel. Bd., 1969-71, So. Regional Edn. Bd., 1982-86. Served with AUS, 1943. Fellow ASCE (sec., treas. 1970, pres. Ala. chpt. 1976-77, chmn. Constrn. Rsch. Coun., chmn. hwy. div. publs. com.; Civil Govt. award 1981); mem. Assn. Gen. Contractors Am. (bd. dirs. 1955), Am. Soc. for Engring. Edn. (chmn. constrn. engring. com.), Am. Pub. Works Assn., Phi Kappa Phi, Tau Beta Pi, Chi Epsilon. Home: 2162 Watercrest Dr Auburn AL 36830

RAINER, WILLIAM GERALD, cardiac surgeon; b. Gordo, Ala., Nov. 13, 1927; s. Jamie Flournoy and Lula (Davis) R.; m. Lois Sayre, Oct. 7, 1950; children: Vickie, Bill, Julia, Leslie. Student, Emory U., Atlanta, Ga., 1943-44, U. Ala., 1944-45; MD, U. Tenn., Memphis, 1948; MS in Surgery, U. Colo., Denver, 1958. Diplomate Am. Bd. Surgery, Am. Bd. Thoracic Surgery. Intern Wesley Hosp., Chgo., 1949; gen. practice medicine Blue Island, Ill., 1950-52; resident Denver VA Hosp., 1954-59; practice medicine specializing in cardiac surgery Denver, 1960—. Bd. dirs. St. Joseph Hosp. Found., Denver; dinsting. clin. prof. surgery U. Colo. Health Sci. Ctr. Contbr. articles to profl. jours. Active Colo. Symphony Assn., Bonfils Blood Ctr.; dir. emeritus St. Joseph Hosp. Found. Bd. Lt. U.S. Army, 1952-54. Decorated Bronze Star; recipient Disting. Alumnus award U. Tenn. Health Sci. Ctr., 1992, Florence Sabin award U. Colo. Health Sci. Ctr., 1998. Mem. Soc. Thoracic Surgeons (sec. 1980-85, pres. 1989, historian 1996—, Disting. Svc. award 1998), Colo. Med. Soc. (pres. 1984-85), Denver Med. Soc. (pres. 1984), Denver Clin. & Pathology Soc., Am. Coll. Chest Physicians (pres. 1984), Am. Bd. Thoracic Surgeons (bd. dirs. 1982-88), Am. Surg. Assn., Am. Assn. Thoracic Surgery, Societé Internationale de Chirugie, Cactus Club. Avocations: photography, traveling. Office: 2005 Franklin St Ste 380 Denver CO 80205-5411 E-mail: wrainersjh828@pol.net.

RAINES, CHARLOTTE AUSTINE BUTLER, artist, poet; b. Sullivan, Ill., July 1, 1922; d. Donald Malone and Charlotte (Wimp) Butler; m. Irving Isaack Raines, Sept. 26, 1941; children: Robin Raines Collison, Kerry Raines Lydon. BA in Studio Arts magna cum laude, U. Md., 1966. One-woman show at Castle Theatre, 1988, C.T.V. Awards Hall, Md., 1993; exhbd. in numerous group shows including Corcoran Gallery, 1980, Md.'s Best Exhbn., 1986, Md. State House, 1990, four-artist video documentary, 1992, U. Md. Univ.-Coll. Gallery, 1996; artist publ. cover Writers' Ctr., 1997, Md. State House Print Exhbn., 1999, Washington Women Artists Millenium Show, 2001; represented in various pvt. collections and permanent collection at U. Md. Univ.-Coll.; selected works in U.S. Dept. State Arts in Embassies Program; contbr. poems to lit. publs. Mem. Artists Equity Assn., Writers' Ctr., Phi Kappa Phi. Avocations: piano, jogging, gardening. Office: 4103 Longfellow St Hyattsville MD 20781-1748

RAINES, FRANKLIN DELANO, finance company executive; b. Seattle, Jan. 14, 1949; s. Delno Thomas and Ida Mae Raines; m. Wendy Farrow. BA magna cum laude, Harvard U., 1971, JD cum laude, 1976; postgrad., Oxford U., 1971-73. Assoc. dir. Seattle Model Cities Program, 1972-73; assoc. Preston, Thorgrimson, Ellis, Holman & Fletcher, Seattle, 1976-77; asst. dir. White House Domestic Policy Staff, Washington, 1977-78; assoc. dir. U.S. Office of Mgmt. and Budget, 1978-79; v.p. Lazard, Freres & Co., N.Y.C., 1979-82, sr. v.p., 1983-84, ptnr., 1985—91; vice-chmn. Fannie Mae, Washington, 1991-96; dir. U.S. Office Mgmt. and Budget, 1996-98; chmn., CEO designate Fannie Mae, Washington, 1998, chmn., CEO, 1999—. Bd. dirs. AOL Time Warner, Pepsico, Pfizer, Inc., Fannie Mae. Former pres. bd. overseers Harvard U.; chmn. Fannie Mae Found.; Nat. Urban League; Enterprise Found.; Black Student Fund. Rhodes scholar, 1971. Mem. AAAS, Coun. Fgn. Rels., Nat. Acad. Social Ins., Washington State Bar Assn., D.C. Bar Assn., Bus. Coun. Avocations: running, golf.

RAINES, JEFF, biomedical scientist, medical research director; b. N.Y.C., Sept. 5, 1943; s. Otis J. and Mildred C. (Wetzler) Raines; children: Gretchen Christena, Victoria Jean. BSME, Clemson U., 1965; MME, U. Fla., 1967; MD, Harvard U., 1968; PhD in Biomed. Engring., MIT, 1972. Mem. staff MIT, Cambridge, Mass., 1968—70; biophysicist dept. surgery Mass. Gen. Hosp., Boston, 1972—77, dir. Vascular Lab., 1972—77; instr. surgery Harvard Med. Sch., 1973—77; preceptor Harvard/MIT Sch. Health Scis., 1976—77; rsch. dir., dir. Vascular Lab. Miami (Fla.) Heart Inst., Miami Beach, 1977—88; adj. prof. bioengring. U. Miami, Coral Gables, 1977—; prof. surgery U. Miami (Fla.) Sch. Medicine, 1977—. Prin. investigator series NIH programs and pharm. firms, 1977—; Harvard Travelling fellow lectr. in Europe, 1975. Contbr. numerous articles on biomechanics, cardiovasc. diagnosis, dynamics and instrumentation to sci. jours. Recipient Apollo Achievement award, NASA, 1969; fellow, NIH, 1972. Fellow: Am. Assn. of Physicists in Medicine, Am. Coll. Radiology, Am. Coll. Cardiology; mem.: ASME, AAAS, Cardiovasc. Sys. Dynamics Soc. (founding mem., editor 1976—, pres. 1980—82), Internat. Cardiovasc. Soc., Instrument Soc. Am., Biomed. Engring. Soc., New Eng. Cardiovasc. Soc., Am. Heart Assn., MIT Club, Harvard Club, Coral Gables Club, Kiwanis, Sigma Xi, Tau Beta Pi. Republican. Presbyterian. Achievements include patents for medical devices; development of mathematical models of arterial hemodynamics and clinical use of autotransfusion. Home: 6820 Granada Blvd Coral Gables FL 33146-3824 Office: Univ Miami Dept Surgery R-310 1611 NW 12th Ave Miami FL 33136-1005

RAINES, KAREN CORNELL, secondary education educator; b. Columbus, Ohio, Dec. 12, 1956; d. Stanley Buel and Ruth Ellen Cornell; m. Roger Dale Raines, July 5, 1980; children: Mary Katherine, Sandra Beth. MusB, W.Va. U., 1979, MMus, 1983; tchg. cert., William Carey Coll., Gulfport, Miss., 1996. Cert. tchr., Miss. Choral dir. Grace Luth. Ch., Long Beach, Miss., 1992-94, Christ United Meth. Ch., Long Beach, 1994-98; tchr. music Waveland (Miss.) Elem. Sch., 1996-98, North Bay Elem. Sch., Bay St. Louis, Miss., 1996-99; tchr. choral music Robert Smalls Mid. Sch., Beaufort, S.C., 1999—. Mem. dist. curriculum com. Bay/Waveland Schs., Bay St. Louis, 1997-99. Mem. choirs performing at Carnegie Hall, N.Y.C., 1997, internat. choral competition, Verona, Italy, 1999. Mem. Music Educators' Nat. Conf. Democrat. Methodist. Avocations: reading, community choral groups. Home: 109 Lakewood Dr Guyton GA 31312-6562 Office: Robert Smalls Mid Sch 43 W K Alston Dr Beaufort SC 29906-9432

RAINES, LOUIS EDWARD, school administrator; b. Balt., Nov. 24, 1965; s. Clarence William Raines and Nona Ann Raines-Dotson; m. Carmen Benninga, Dec. 29, 1989. BME, Kans. State U., 1994, M of Ednl. Adminstrn., 1996. Cert. instr. grade K-12, Kans.; cert. bldg. level adminstr., Kans. Prin. arranger, composer Frontier, Manhattan, Kans., 1984-89; freelance composer, arranger, 1989-94; dir. choral activities Concordia (Kans.) H.S., 1994-98, assoc. prin., 1998-2000, prin., 2000—. State resource specialist Kans. North Cen. Accreditation, Wichita; vis. team chair N. Ctrl. Accreditation, Wichita;

mem. legis. liaison com. United Sch. Adminstrs. Kans. Composer, 1999—: (songs) Country Christmas, 1987; arranger: (mus. medley) Nursery Rhyme Parade, 1992; studio arranger: (sound recs.) Won't Let Love Hurt Me Again, Bed of Roses, Second Wind, Something to Remember You By, 1988; performer with Kans. State Opera Theatre; edn. and polit. editor Open Directory Project. Sec./treas., Cloud County Dem. Party, Concordia, Kans., 2000—; ordained elder, deacon Presbyn. Ch., Louisville, Ky., 1993—; mem. Kans. State Choir, Manhattan, 1986-88, 92-94. Mem. Nat. Assn. Secondary Sch. Prins., United Sch. Adminstrs. of Kans., Kans. Assn. Secondary Sch. Adminstrs., Kans. Music Educators Assn. (choral chairperson no. cen. dist. 1995-97), Golden Key Nat. Honor Soc., Phi Kappa Phi. Democrat. Presbyterian. Avocations: public speaking, coin collecting, writing and arranging music, fishing. Office: Concordia H S 436 W 10th St Concordia KS 66901-4122 Fax: (785) 243-8805. E-mail: raines@dustdevil.com.

RAINES, TIM D. real estate corporation executive; b. Everett, Wash., May 8, 1950; s. Richard Thomas and Arvilla Mae (Chick) R.; m. Virginia N. McLaurin, July 21, 1977. BA, U. Ala., Tuscaloosa, 1968-72; MA, U. Ala., Birmingham, 1977; postgrad., U. Calif., Berkeley, 1976-77. Cmty. planner HUD, Birmingham, 1972-77, dir., program planning and eval. Atlanta, 1977-83, dir. regional housing ops. div., 1983-87; exec. v.p., COO Sanbury Corp., 1987-92; prin. Profit, Inc., 1992—. Pres. Stonington Homeowners Assn., Atlanta, 1980-83; patron Atlanta Ballet, 1978—; sponsor Pub. TV (WPBA), Atlanta, 1980—; mem. adv. bd. Salvation Army, 1997—; mem. Ga. Affordable Housing Coalition, 1993—. Recipient Cert. of Recognition William A. Jump Found., 1978. Mem. Am. Soc. Pub. Adminstrs., Am. Mgmt. Assn., Atlanta Zool. Soc. Avocations: travel, gardening, harmonica, juggling, custom cars. Home: 8315 Ison Rd Atlanta GA 30350-3129

RAINES, ZANDER DELL, publishing executive; b. Lebanon, Tenn., Aug. 12, 1951; s. Chanie Gray Raines, Jewel Dean Hall Raines; m. Carol Jo Crutcher; children: David Lee, William Ray, Rachael Michelle. Grad. Computer Programming and Bus. Adminstrn., ICS, 1976. Order handler Bapt. Sunday Sch. Bd., Nashville, 1969—73; contractor self-employed, Lebanon, 1973—83; adjustment rep. Lifeway Christian Resources, Nashville, 1983—. Exec. prodr. Apocalypse Prodns., Lebanon, 1989—. Author: The Word of God-A Layman's Look At The Bible, 1997, The Two Kingdoms-A Layman's Look At The Old Testament, 1997, One Nation Under God-A Layman's Look At American History, 1998. State chmn. Tenn. Christian Coalition, Nashville, 2002, mid. Tenn. chmn., 2001—02, Wilson County dir. Lebanon, 1991—2001. Baptist. Avocations: chess, guitar, computers. Home: 415 Lealand Ln Lebanon TN 37087 Office: Tenn Christian Coalition PO Box 23793 Nashville TN 37202 Personal E-mail: zdraines@peoplepc.com. Business E-Mail: zdraines@peoplepc.com.

RAINESS, ALAN EDWARD, psychiatrist, neurologist, educator; b. N.Y.C., Sept. 24, 1935; s. George W. and Ida Rainess; m. Alice Maree Haber, June 5, 1968; children: Alice Jeanne Rainess, James Alan (dec.). AB, Columbia Coll., 1957; MD, U. Paris, 1965. Diplomate Am. Bd. Psychiatry and Neurology. Intern Meadowbrook Hosp., East Meadow, L.I., 1965-66; resident in psychiatry N.Y. VA Hosp., N.Y.C., 1966-67; teaching fellow in psychiatry Harvard Med. Sch., Boston, 1967; chief resident in psychiatry Boston City Hosp., 1967; resident in psychiatry Walter Reed Med. Ctr., Washington, 1970-72; clin. dir. Noyes Divsn. St. Elizabeths Hosp., 1973-76; asst. chief psychiatry Andrews AFB Hosp., Camp Springs, Md., 1976-80, chief neurology, 1989-91; resident in neurology Wilford Hall USAF Med. Ctr., San Antonio, 1980-83; chief medicine and neuropsychiatry Air Univ. Hosp., Maxwell AFB, Ala., 1983-89, chief neurology, 1991-94; psychiatrist Manhattan Psychiat. Ctr., N.Y.C., 1994—97, 1999—2002, clin. dir., 1997-99; psychiatrist Prison Health Svcs., Riker's Island, 2002—. Asst. clin. prof. psychiatry Georgetown U. Med. Sch., Washington, 1974-79, NYU Sch. Medicine, 1997-2002; assoc. prof. neurology and asst. prof. psychiatry Uniformed Svcs. U. Health Scis., Bethesda, Md., 1989-94. Maj. U.S. Army, 1968-73, col. USAF, 1976-94, ret. Fellow: Am. Psychiat. Assn. (life); mem.: NYU-Bellevue Psychiatric Soc., Harvard Club of N.Y.C., Masons. Home: 345 E 93d St Apt 22H New York NY 10128-5522 Office: OBCC Riker's Island New York NY E-mail: alan.rainess@verizon.net.

RAINEY, BARBARA ANN, sensory evaluation consultant; b. Fond du Lac, Wis., Nov. 11, 1949; d. Warren and Helen Eileen (Ginther) Bradley; m. Phillip Michael Rainey, Sept. 5, 1970; 1 child, Nicolette. BS, Kans. State U., 1975. Group leader Armour & Co. R&D Ctr., Scottsdale, Ariz., 1976-80; owner Barbara A. Rainey Cons., Mi Wuk Village, Calif., 1980—. Mem. editl. bd. Jour. Sensory Studies, 1997—; contbr. articles to profl. jours. Kans. State Alumni fellow Kans. State U. Alumni Assn., 1990. Mem. ASTM, Inst. Food Technologists (prof. sensory divsn. sec. 1980-82, chmn. 1984-85, short course spkr. 1979-81, Ctrl. Valley subsect., treas. 1989-91, chmn.-elect./sec. 1991-92, chmn. 1992-93). Avocations: cooking, recipe development. Home and Office: PO Box 964 Mi Wuk Village CA 95346-0964 E-mail: barainey@inreach.com.

RAINEY, CLAUDE GLADWIN, retired health care executive; b. Enloe, Tex., Apr. 21, 1923; s. Claude C. and Pauline (Whitlock) R.; m. Peggy Ballard, July 27, 1947; children— Kathy Suzanne, David Claude, Mark Jeffery, Joel Allen, Peggy Jan, Susan Elise Student pub. health and adminstrv. medicine, Columbia U., 1961-62. Med. adminstrv., officer dept. medicine and surgery VA, Temple, Tex., 1946-51, med. adminstrv., officer dept. medicine and surgery Muskogee, Okla., 1951-56; med. adminstr. Fite Clinic, Lakeland Med. Ctr., 1956-59; hosp. adminstr. M.-K.-T. R.R. Employees Hosp. Assn., Denison, Tex., 1959-62, also sec., treas. trustee; hosp. adminstr., cons. Denison Hosp. Authority, Meml. Hosp., 1962-66; adminstr. Seton Hosp., Austin, Tex., 1966-74; exec. v.p. Fort Worth Osteo. Hosp., 1974-83; pres. Health Care of Tex., Inc., Fort Worth, 1983-88, ret. Pres. North Grayson County chpt. Am. Cancer Soc., 1960-66, bd. dirs., Tex., 1961— . Served with USNR, 1942-46 Fellow Am. Coll. Hosp. Adminstrs., Am. Coll. Osteo. Hosp. Adminstrs. (award of merit 1984); mem. Am. Hosp. Assn., Tex. Hosp. Assn., Am. Osteo. Hosp. Assn. (Disting. Service award 1985)

RAINEY, DEREK REXTON, educator, sculptor; b. Palo Alto, Calif., Nov. 7, 1949; s. Rexton Sylvester and Kathrine (Wiedenhoeft) R.; m. Christine McLeod, Nov. 29, 1975 (dec. Aug. 1996); children: Jocelyn, Britta, Rexton. BA in History, U. Mich., 1971. High steel painter, various locations, 1968-74; tchr. art Portage (Mich.) Ctrl. H.S., 1975-76, Portland (Mich.) Mid. Sch., 1977-80; tchr. art, history, psychology Portland H.S., 1980—. Illustrator: (book) Portage And Its Past, 1976; sculptor (bronze) Warcry—Mich. Vietnam Meml., Mt. Pleasant, 1994. Set designer, scenic painter Portland Players, Ionia Cmty. Theatre. Democrat. Avocations: running, frisbee, scuba diving, watercolor painting, travel. Home: 8473 Riverest Dr Portland MI 48875-9692 Office: Portland High Sch 1100 Ionia Rd Portland MI 48875-1035 E-mail: derekrainey@power-net.net.

RAINEY, GORDON FRYER, JR. lawyer; b. Oklahoma City, Apr. 26, 1940; s. Gordon F. and Esther (Bliss) R.; m. Selina Norman, Aug. 3, 1968; children: Kate, Melissa, Gordon III. BA in English, U. Va., 1962, LLB, 1967. Bar: Okla. 1967, Va. 1968. Assoc. Rainey, Flynn, Wallace, Ross & Cooper, Oklahoma City, 1967-68, Hunton & Williams, Richmond, Va., 1968-75, ptnr., 1975—. Chmn. of exec. com. Hunton & Williams; bd. dirs. Bon Secours Richmond Health Sys., Inc., SunTrust MidAtlantic, Colonial Williamsburg Co.; bd. visitors U. Va. Past pres. U. Va. Alumni Assn.; trustee Colonial Williamsburg Found., Va. Found. Ind. Colls.; mem. Gov. Gilmore's Blue Ribbon Comm. on Higher Edn.; campaign chmn. United Way of Greater Richmond, 1982, trustee, 1981-84; bd. dirs., past pres. Sheltering Arms Hosp., 1984; trustee Sheltering Arms Found.; chmn. Gov.'s Econ. Devel. Adv. Coun. Dist. 12; mem. Gov. Gilmore Transition Adv. Com.; mem. Gov.'s Adv. Com. for Va. Strategy on Econ. Devel.; mem. Bd. Housing and Cmty. Devel.; past mem. bd. govs. St. Catherine's Sch.; past chmn. bd. dirs. Leadership Met. Richmond.; mem. Mayor's Emergency Shelter Task Force, 1981; past pres., bd. dirs. Met. Bus. Found. 1st lt. U.S. Army, 1962-64, Korea. Recipient Disting. Grad. award Cascady Sch., Comm. and Leadership award toastmasters Internat., 1983. Mem. ABA (sect. on bus. law, banking law com., mem. com. on devel. in investment svcs.), Richmond Metro C. of C. (bd. dirs., past chmn.), Commonwealth Club, Country Club of Va., The Brook (N.Y.C.), Forum Club (Richmond). Republican. Episcopalian. Office: Hunton & Williams Riverfront Plz East Tower PO Box 1535 Richmond VA 23218-1535

RAINEY, JEAN OSGOOD, public relations executive; b. Lansing, Mich., Apr. 5, 1925; d. Earle Victor and Blanche Mae (Eberly) Osgood; m. John Larimer Rainey, Nov. 29, 1957 (dec. Oct. 1991); children: Cynthia, John Larimer, Ruth. Grad., Lansing Bus. U., 1942. Pub. rels. dir. Nat. Assn. Food Chains, Washington, 1954-59; v.p. pub. rels. Manchester Orgns., 1959-61; ptnr. Rainey, McEnroe & Manning, 1962-73; v.p. Manning, Selvage & Lee, 1973-79, pres. Washington div., 1979-84, sr. counsellor, 1985; owner Jean Rainey Assocs., 1986-87; sr. v.p. Daniel J. Edelman Inc., 1987-96; owner Jean Rainey Assocs., Washington, 1996—. Chmn. bd. Windward Mortgage, 1997—2001. Author: How to Shop for Food, 1972. Pres. Hyde Home and Sch. Assn., Washington, 1969-71; co-chmn. Nat. Adv. Com. for Reelection of the Pres., 1972; chmn. bd. trustees St. John's Presch., 1996-99; pres. Sherwood Forest Endowment Fund, 1995-97; adminstr. A Few Good Women-Advancing the Cause of Women in Govt., 1969-74, 97—; bd. dirs. Westchester Corp. Mem. Internat. Women's Forum, Pub. Rels. Soc. Am. (accredited, Hall of Fame 1999), Am. Women in Radio and TV (pres. Washington chpt. 1962-63, mem. nat. bd. 1963-65), Am. News Women's Club (pres. 1973-75) Clubs: City Tavern. Republican. Episcopalian. Home: 4000 Cathedral Ave NW Apt 250B Washington DC 20016-5279 Office: PO Box 251 Main Lobby W 4000 Cathedral Ave NW Washington DC 20016-5249 E-mail: jorainey@aol.com.

RAINEY, JOHN DAVID, federal judge; b. Freeport, Tex., Feb. 10, 1945; s. Frank Anson and Jewel Lorene (Hortman) R.; m. Judy Davis, Aug. 17, 1968; children, John David Jr., Jacob Matthew, Craig Thomas. BBA, So. Meth. U., 1967, JD, 1972. Bar: Tex. 1972, U.S. Dist. Ct. (no. dist.) Tex. 1974, U.S. Tax Ct. 1974, U.S. Ct. Appeals (5th cir.) 1981, U.S. Supreme Ct. 1981, U.S. Dist. Ct. (so. dist.) Tex. 1986. Assoc. Taylor, Mizell, Price, Corrigan & Smith, Dallas, 1973-79; ptnr. Gilbert, Gilbert & Rainey, Angleton, Tex., 1979-82, Rainey & LeBoeuf, Angleton, 1982-86; judge 149th Dist. Ct., Brazoria County, Tex., 1987-90, U.S. Dist. Ct. (so. dist.) Tex., 1990—. Bd. dirs. Angleton Bank of Commerce. Mem. City of Angleton Planning and Zoning Commn., 1981-84; mem. Angleton Charter Rev. Commn., 1984, chmn. 1982. Served with U.S. Army, 1969-70. Mem. ABA, State Bar Tex., Brazoria County Bar Assn. (pres. 1983-84). Lodges: Lions (pres. Angleton 1986-87). Methodist. Avocations: hunting, fishing, woodworking. Office: US Dist Ct 312 S Main St Rm 406 Houston TX 77901

RAINEY, KENNETH TYLER, English language educator; b. Memphis, Feb. 27, 1936; s. Andrew Laughlin Jr. and Gracie Ruth (Mullins) R.; m. Elaine Fitts, Jan. 1, 1960; children: Kenneth Tyler Jr., Timothy Andrew, Kevin Laughlin. BA, Miss. Coll., Clinton, 1958; AM, U. Mich., 1959; ThD, New Orleans Bapt. Sem., 1966; PhD, Ohio State U., 1976. Asst. prof. Eng. Miss. Coll., Clinton, 1965-70, Ohio State U., Lima, 1977-83, U. Memphis, 1983-89; prof. humanities and tech. comm. So. Poly. State U., Marietta, Ga., 1989—, disting. prof. tchg. and learning, 1997-98. Presenter, cons. in field; vis. prof. Magdeburg, Germany, 1997, 99, Koethen, Germany, 2001-02; proprietor Atlanta ProCom. Contbr. articles to profl. jours. Woodrow Wilson fellow, 1958-59; Nat. Endowment Humanities grant, 1981-82; Deutsche Akademisches Austansdienst fellow, 1999. Fellow Soc. Tech. Comm. (Jay Gould award for excellence in tchg. tech. comm. 1999, Disting. Chpt. Svc. award 1999, Excellence in Internat. Tech. Pubs. award 1992, 2001), Nat. Coun. Tchrs. English (conf. coll. composition and comm.), Assn. Tchrs. Tech. Writing. Baptist. Avocations: gourmet cooking, traveling in Europe. Home: 1194 Robert Ln Marietta GA 30062-4929 Office: So Poly State U 1100 S Marietta Pkwy SE Marietta GA 30060-2896 E-mail: krainey@newton.spsu.edu.

RAINEY, RON PAUL, artist manager; b. East Stroudsburg, Pa., Feb. 3, 1946; s. Donald Elmo Rainey and Genevieve Elinore (Kwiecinski) Rushin. Concert agt. Internat. Famous Agy. (now Internat. Creative Mgmt.), N.Y.C., 1969-71; v.p. concert dept. Agy. for Performing Arts, N.Y.C. and L.A., 1971-73; chmn., CEO, Magna Artists Corp., Los Angeles, 1974-81; pres., CEO, Ron Rainey Mgmt., Inc., Beverly Hills, Calif., 1981—, Raineyville Music Pub., Beverly Hills, 1991—; pres., CEO Marshall Tucker Entertainment, 1997—; owner, pres. Am. Artists corp., 1996—. Served with USN, 1967-68. Avocation: collecting baseball cards, antique books and music memorabilia, fine wines. Office: 315 S Beverly Dr Ste 407 Beverly Hills CA 90212-4301

RAINEY, TERRY LEE, music educator, director; b. Miami, Fla., June 5, 1967; choir dir. First Presbyn. Ch., Cedartown, Ga., 2000X. s. Terry Lee Sr. and Olivia Marilyn (Meyers) R.; m. Cindy Renea Bradshaw, Apr. 4, 1992; children: Terry L. III, Randy, Danielle. BS in Music Edn. magna cum laude, U. Ala., 1990; postgrad., Jacksonville State U., 1991; MEd in Music Edn., Ga. So. U., 1997. Cert. music tchr., Ga., Ala. Music instr. U. Ala., Tuscaloosa, 1989-90; dir. bands, music tchr. Wadley (Ala.) H.S. and Elem. Schs., 1990-91; dir. bands Albany (Ga.) Mid. Sch., 1991-92; music tchr., chorus dir. Sixes Elem. Sch., Canton, Ga., 1992-93; dir. bands, head music dept. McIntosh County Acad., Darien, 1993-98; dir. bands Cedartown H.S., 1998—2001; music tchr. Buchanan Elem. Sch., 2001—; choir dir. First Presbyn. Ch., Cedartown, Ga., 2000—. Choir dir. Darien United Meth. Ch., 1994-98. Composer vocal music, ch. hymn. Sunday sch. tchr. First United Meth. Ch., Wadley, 1991-92, Canton, 1992-93. U. Ala. scholar, 1987-90. Mem. Ga. Music Educators Assn., Phi Kappa Lambda, Phi Mu Alpha Sinfonia (pres. 1988-90, citation of excellence 1990). Avocations: computer games, travel, home renovation, walking. Office: Buchanan Elem Sch 215 College Cir Buchanan GA 30113

RAINEY, WILLIAM JOEL, lawyer; b. Flint, Mich., Oct. 11, 1946; s. Ralph Jefferson and Elsie Matilda (Erickson) R.; m. Cynthia Hetsko, June 15, 1968; children: Joel Michael, Allison Elizabeth. AB, Harvard U., 1968; JD, U. Mich., 1971. Bar: N.Y. 1973, Wash. 1977, Ariz. 1987, Mass. 1992, Kans. 1997, U.S. Dist. Ct. (so. and ea. dists.) N.Y. 1973, U.S. Ct. Appeals (2nd cir.) N.Y. 1973, U.S. Dist. Ct. (we. dist.) Wash. 1977, U.S. Supreme Ct. 1976, U.S. Ct. Appeals (9th cir.) Wash. 1978, U.S. Dist. Ct. Ariz. 1987, U.S. Dist. Ct. Mass. 1992. Assoc. atty. Curtis, Mallet-Prevost, Colt & Mosle, N.Y.C., 1971-76; atty., asst. corp. sec. Weyerhaeuser Co., Tacoma, 1976-85; v.p., corp. sec., gen. counsel Southwest Forest Industries Inc., Phoenix, 1985-87; sr. v.p., corp. sec., gen. counsel Valley Nat. Corp. and Valley Nat. Bank, 1987-91; v.p., gen. counsel Cabot Corp., Boston, 1991-93; exec. v.p., gen. coun., corp. sec. Fourth Fin. Corp., Wichita, Kans., 1994-96; sr. v.p., gen. counsel, corp. sec. Payless ShoeSource, Inc., Topeka, 1996—. Editor U. Mich. Jour. Law Reform, 1970-71 Bd. dirs. Big Bros./Big Sisters, 1994-96. Maj. USAR, 1970-91. Mem. ABA (chmn. task force 1984-91), Wash. State Bar Assn., State Bar of Ariz., Assn. Bank Holding Cos. (steering com. 1989-91, chmn. lawyers com. 1990-91), Harvard Club of Phoenix (bd. dirs. 1989-91). Avocations: backpacking, running, fishing, bicycling. Home: 901 Deer Run Dr Lawrence KS 66049-4731 Office: Payless ShoeSource Inc PO Box 1189 Topeka KS 66601-1189

RAINIER, ROBERT PAUL, publisher, professional society administrator; b. Adrian, Mich., Oct. 19, 1940; s. Paul Leslie and Mildred Sofia (Magdefrau) R.; m. Dorothy Krauss, May 28, 1966; children: Michele Carole, Kenneth Charles. BA, Northwestern U., 1962, MA, 1964. Various positions with mktg. and sales dept. McGraw Hill Book Co., N.Y.C., 1964-70, editor in chief humanities, 1974—79; edit. exec. CBS Coll. Pub., 1979—86, v.p., editor in chief, 1984-86; dir. publs. AICPA, 1986-97, dir. prof. devel., 1997-99, sr. cons. strategic devel., 1999—. Vestryman St. Johns Episcopal Ch., Larchmont, N.Y., 1987-90, fundraiser, 1988-89. Staff sgt. N.Y. N.G., 1964-70. Mem. The Dessoff Choirs (bd. dirs. 1993-97, pres. 2000—), Soc. Nat. Assn. Publs. (bd. dirs. 1988-94, pres. 1992-93). Democrat. Episcopalian. Avocations: music, sports. Home: 21 Summit Ave Larchmont NY 10538-2913

RAINIS, EUGENE CHARLES, banking executive; b. N.Y.C., Sept. 24, 1940; s. Charles William and Louise Theresa (Nold) Rainis; m. Jane Margaret Micucci, Nov. 28, 1964; children: Ellen, David, Mark. BS, Fordham U., 1962; MBA, U. Pa., 1964. Security analyst trainee Merrill, Lynch Pierce Fenner & Smith, N.Y.C., 1963-65; ptnr. Brown Bros. Harriman & Co., 1965—, also bd. dirs. Bd. dirs. Bio-Brite, Inc., Ultra-Strip, Inc. Trustee Fordham U., N.Y.C.; chmn. Xavier H.S.; trustee Robert Brunner Found., Several Sources Found., Gregorian U. Found. Mem.: Inst. Chartered Fin. Analysts, Knights of Malta, Down Town Assn. (N.Y.C.), Harbour Ridge Golf Club (Palm City, Fla.). Republican. Roman Catholic. Avocation: Avocations: fishing, golf. Office: Brown Bros Harriman & Co 59 Wall St New York NY 10005-2808

RAINONE, MICHAEL CARMINE, lawyer; b. Phila., Mar. 4, 1918; m. Ledena Tonioni, Apr. 10, 1944; children: Sebastian, Francine. LLB, U. Pa., 1941. Bar: Pa. 1944, U.S. Dist. Ct. Pa. 1944, U.S. Supreme Ct. 1956. Del. 3d cir. Jud. Conf., 1984-95. Bd. dirs. C.C., Phila. 1970-85; past pres. Nationalities Svc. Ctr., hon. bd. dirs.; commr. Fellowship Commn., 1973-82; internat. pres. Orphans of Italy, Inc., 2975-83; bd. dirs., mem. govt. rels. com. Mental Health Assn. Southeastern Pa., 1979-91; pres. Columbus Civic Assn. Pa., Inc., 1984-91; chmn. Lawyers' Biog. Com. Hist. Soc., U.S. Dist. Ct.; trustee Balch Inst. for Ethnic Studies, 1989-92; regional v.p. Nat. Italian-Am. Found.; pres. Seaview Harbor Civic Assn., 1990-95, pres. emeritus, 1996—; apptd. judge Final Law Sch. Trial Advocacy Program for the Northeast, 1996; counsel, v.p. Piccola Opera Com., Phila., 1997—; pres. Grad. Club, bd. dirs., 2000; task force chmn. Mazzei Nat. Constn. Ctr., 2001. Recipient Disting. Svc. award Nationalities Svc. Ctr., 1975, Man of Yr. award Columbus Civic Assn., 1969, Legion of Honor, Chapel of Four Chaplains, 1979, Bronze Medallion award, 1982, commendation Pa. Senate, 1982, Villanova Law Sch. Appreciation award 1993, Syracuse U. Achievement award 1994, Hon. Lifetime award KC, 1997; Resolution of Praise, pres. City Coun. of Phila., 1999. Mem. ABA (chmn. U.S. Surpeme Ct. admissions com. 2001), ATLA (Supervising Judge Advocacy award Phila. region 2000, supr. judge law sch. trial advocacy competition, 2000, Phila. chpt. emeritus chmn. of Justice Michael A. Musmanno award 2000), Internat. Acad. Law and Sci., Justinian Soc. (bd. govs. 1980-83, sr. lawyer award 2000), Pa. Bar Assn., Pa. Trial Lawyers Assn. (bd. govs. 1982-84), N.Y. Trial Lawyers Assn. (assoc.), Phila. Bar Assn. (bd. dirs. 1980-83, asst. sec. 1983, 84, chmn. emeritus Beccaria award, 1993—), Lawyers Club Phila. (pres. 1982-84, chmn. Centennial Celebration 2001), Phila. Trial Lawyers Assn. (pres. 1982-83, Disting. Svc. award 2000), Nat. Italian-Am. Bar Assn. (bd. govs. 1985-90, historian 1987-90, pres. 1991-93, bd. chmn. 1993-95, chmn. Supreme Ct. admissions com. 2000), Am. Arbitration Assn. (arbitrator 1950—), Sons of Italy (Man of Yr. award 1995). Home: 2401 Pennsylvania Ave Philadelphia PA 19130-3010 Office: 1530 Chestnut St Fl 4 Philadelphia PA 19102-2739

RAINS, M. NEAL, lawyer; b. Burlington, Iowa, July 26, 1943; s. Merritt and Lucille (Lepper) R.; m. Jean Baldwin, July 26, 1980 (div. 1995); children: Robert Baldwin, Kathleen Kellogg. BA in Polit. Sci. with honors, U. Iowa, 1965; JD, Northwestern U., 1968. Bar: Ohio 1968. Assoc. Arter & Hadden, Cleve., 1968-76, ptnr., 1976—2001, mem. exec. com., 1981-90, mem. mgmt. com., 1987-90, mng. ptnr., 1990-92; master bencher Inns of Ct., 1990—; ptnr. Frantz Ward LLP, Cleve., 2001—. Lectr. on profl. topics, including alternative dispute resolution, distbn. law, litigation practice and procedure, and antitrust. Contbr. articles to profl. jours. Former trustee Legal Aid Soc. Cleve.; trustee Cleve. Play House, mem. adv. coun., 1988—; trustee Citizens League Greater Cleve., Cleve. Art Assn. With U.S. Army, 1968-70 Fellow: Am. Bar Found.; mem.: ABA, Harold H. Burton Am. Inn Ct. (pres. 1999—2000), William K. Thomas Inn Ct. (pres. 1999—), Cleve. Bar Found. (trustee 1999—), Ohio Assn. Civil Trial Attys., Internat. Assn. Def. Counsel, Def. Rsch. Inst., Bar Assn. Greater Cleve. (chmn. young lawyers sect. 1975—76, cert. merit 1975), Ohio Bar Assn., Rowfant Club, City Club, Print Club (trustee 2001—), Cleve. Skating Club, Union Club, Phi Delta Phi, Omicron Delta Kappa, Phi Beta Kappa. Home: 18400 Shelburne Rd Shaker Heights OH 44118 Office: Frantz Ward LLP 55 Public Sq Cleveland OH 44113 E-mail: nrains@arterhadden.com.

RAINVILLE, ALICE JOHANNAH, dietitian; b. Spring Valley, Ill., Oct. 27, 1957; d. Jon Francis and Mary Johannah Ellis; m. Daniel Thomas Shannon, May 22, 1979 (dec. Mar. 1992); m. Richard Joseph Rainville, May 29, 1993; 1 child, Richard Ellis. BS in Instn. Mgmt., U. Ill., 1979; MS in Foods and Nutrition, Ill. State U., 1981; PhD in Pub. Health, U. Tex., 1996. Registered dietitian commn. on dietetic registration. Lectr. Ill. State U., Normal, Ill., 1981; cafe mgr. Lord and Taylor, Houston, 1982-83; supr. food svc. Klein (Tex.) Sch. Dist., 1983-86; dir. test kitchen USA Rice Coun., Houston, 1986-89; asst. prof. U. Tex., 1989-97, Ea. Mich. U., Ypsilanti, 1997—2000, assoc. prof., 2000—. Contbr. article to jour. Fellow ConAgra fellow in child nutrition, Sch. Food Svc. Found., 1998; scholar, Nat. Food Svc. Mgmt. Inst., 2000—. Avocations: reading, cooking, crafts. Office: Ea Mich U 206 Roosevelt Hall Ypsilanti MI 48197-2240

RAINVILLE, CHRISTINA, lawyer; b. N.Y.C., Feb. 7, 1962; d. Dewey and Nancy Rainville; m. Peter S. Greenberg, May 1994; children: Jeremy, Catharine. BS, Northwestern U., 1984, JD, 1988. Atty. Schnader Harrison Segal & Lewis, Phila., 1988—. Mem. ABA (pro bono publico award 1999), Nat. Assn. Criminal Def. Lawyers. Presbyterian. Office: Schnader Harrison et al 1600 Market St Ste 3600 Philadelphia PA 19103-7287 E-mail: trainville@schnader.com.

RAINVILLE, DONNA JEAN, administration executive; b. Providence, Aug. 15, 1947; m. Raymond Rainville. BA in Journalism, U. R.I., 1969, MA in Polit. Sci., 1975; MBA, Bryant Coll., 1986. Research asst. U. R.I., Kingston, 1969-70; asst. dir. Warwick (R.I.) Cmty. Action, 1971-73; dir. adminstrn. Childreach, R.I., 1974-86, v.p. fin. and adminstrn., 1987-93; pres. The Cons. Source, Inc., 1994—2002; prin. cons. Rainville and Assocs., 2000—02; v.p. non-for-profit group, investment mgmt. svcs. Citizens Bank, Providence, 2002—. Mem. com. profl. rels. R.I. Group Health Assn., Providence, 1975-85; mem. adv. com. Warwick Cmty. Action Health Ctr., 1973-80; bd. dirs. R.I. Health Service Coun., Providence. Chmn. nat. fundraising com. U. R.I., Kingston, 1988—89; bd. dirs. R.I. chpt. ARC, 1994—2001, sec., 1997—2001; bd. dirs. Big Sisters, 1997—, pres., 1999—2001; mem. Blue Shield Bd. Incorporators, Providence, 1978—82. Mem. Am. Mgmt. Assn., Adminstrv. Mgmt. Soc., Am. Soc. Pers. Adminstrn., Inst. Mgmt. Cons., N.E. Human Resource Assn. Clubs: Potowomut Golf.

RAINWATER, FREDDIE BARRETT, volunteer worker; b. Pensacola, Fla., Aug. 25, 1947; s. Barnard Sr. and Blanche L. Barrett; m. Crawford Rainwater, Jan. 24, 1970. BS, U. Tex., 1970, postgrad.; MS, U. S.C., 1972. Founder Favor House Spouse Abuse Shelter, Pensacola, Fla., 1979-85; co-organizer Manna Food Bank, 1981—; co-founder Friendship Scholarships, Gulf Breeze, Fla., 1989—. Mem. reorganizing bd. Wildlife Sanctuary N.W. Fla., Pensacola; pres. Panhandle Tiger Bay Club, Pensacola, 1999-2000; chmn. Escambia and Santa Rosa Counties George Bush for Pres. Campaign, Pensacola, 1979-80; reorganizer Santa Rosa County Rep. Party, Milton, Fla., 1979-80; chmn. Santa Rose County Party Reorgn., Milton, Fla. Recipient Svc. to Mankind award Liberty Sertoma Club, Pensacola, 1986, Liberty Bell award Escambia-Santa Rosa Counties Bar Assn., 1991, Cmty. Leader of Yr. award Pensacola C. of C., 1992, Woman of Yr. award Pensacola YWCA, 1987, award dedicated in her name Shelter for Abused Women, 1986. Home: 616 Baycliff Rd Gulf Breeze FL 32561 Fax: (850) 932-5124. E-mail: fbr@infi.net.

RAINWATER, JOAN LUCILLE MORSE, investment company executive; b. Chattanooga, Mar. 5, 1943; d. Robert Ora and Alma Lucille (Miller) M.; m. Percy Raymond Rainwater (div. 1987); children: Karen Sue, Steven Jay, Robin Rae, Linda Sue. Student, John Robert Powan Sch. Design, 1977-78, Corcoran Sch. Art, 1985-86, Nova U., 1980, 85, 87. Co-owner Rainwater Concrete, Lorton, Va., 1962-87, Undertaking Gallery, Occoquan, 1977-80; cons. in art edn. Occoquan Elem. Sch., Woodbridge, Va., 1969-73; owner Riverside Gallery, Occoquan, 1980-84, Joamen Investments, Occoquan, 1985—. Author: (poems) At Waters Edge, 1995. Founding mem. Hist. Occoquan, 1970, Women's Mus., Washington; pres., v.p. Woodbridge Art Guild, 1980-82. Recipient numerous awards for paintings, various juried shows Washington area, 1977-87. Mem. Unity Ch. Avocations: hiking, reading, esoteric studies. Office: Rainwater Investments 611 Queen St Alexandria VA 22314-2514

RAINWATER, JOYCE KELLEY, special education educator, consultant; b. Gainesville, Tex., Feb. 1, 1937; d. Emerson H. and Ruth (Sanders) Kelley; children: Kelley Lynn, Kathryn Lee. BSC, Tex. Christian U., 1959, BA in Edn., 1970; spl. edn. cert., E. Tex. U., 1973; postgrad., Tex. Woman's U. Cert. spl. edn. tchr. Adv. bd. Goodwill Industries, Ft. Worth; vol. United Way. Mem. Coun. Exceptional Children, Assn. for Children with Behavior Disorders, Ft. Worth Woman's Club, Tex. Christian U.Century Club, Chi Omega Alumni Assn. Mem. Christian Ch. (Disciples Of Christ). Avocations: reading, cooking, gardening. Home: Apt 1195 5218 Bryant Irvin Rd Fort Worth TX 76132-3870

RAIRDIN, CRAIG ALLEN, software company executive, software developer; b. Cedar Rapids, Iowa, Oct. 23, 1959; s. Ernie W. and Sherryl E. (Asklund) R.; m. Johnna L. Miller, Jan. 9, 1982. BS in Computer Sci. with distinction, U. Iowa, 1981. Software engr. Rockwell Internat., Cedar Rapids, 1982-88; divsn. dir. Parsons Tech., 1988-90, v.p., 1990-98; ind. software developer, 1999—; pres. Laridian, Cedar Rapids, 1999—. Cons. Creative Computer Systems, Cedar Rapids, 1987-90. Author: (software) Juliet, 1987, QuickVerse, 1988, Bible Illustrator, 1990, Standard Template for Electronic Publishing (STEP), 1995, PalmBible, 1998, PocketBible, 2000. Chmn. Area Liaison Com., Campus Bible Fellowship, Iowa City, 1983-90; precinct chmn. Linn. County Rep. Party, Cedar Rapids, 1986-90; founder Bible Software Industry Standards Group, 1995; vol. pilot Angel Flight Ctrl., 2001—. Republican. Christian. Avocations: church, amateur radio, flying.

RAISBECK, GORDON, systems engineer, consultant; b. N.Y.C., May 4, 1925; s. Milton Joseph and Marcelle (Ellinger) R.; m. Barbara Wiener, Dec. 22, 1948; children: Michael Norbert, Lucy Margaret, Alison Jane, Timothy Gordon, James Gregory. Rhodes scholar, Oxford (Eng.) U., 1947-48; BA, Stanford U., 1944; PhD, MIT, 1949. Registered profl. engr., Mass., Maine. Instr. M.I.T., Cambridge, 1948-49; mem. tech. staff Bell Telephone Labs., Inc., Murray Hill, N.J., 1949-61; dir. transmission line research Bell Telephone Labs., Inc. (now Lucent), 1954-61; mem. profl. staff research and devel. Advanced Research Projects Agy., Washington, 1959-60; mem. profl. staff Arthur D. Little, Inc., Cambridge, 1961-86, dir. systems engring., 1966-70, dir. phys. systems research, 1970-75, v.p. systems engring., 1973-86 , part-time 1982-86; cons. mgmt. of technol. innovation, 1982-94. Instr. Drew U., Stanford U., MIT. Contbr. articles to profl. jours.; author: Information Theory: An Introduction for Engineers and Scientists, 1964; patentee in field (22). Served to lt. (j.g.) USNR, 1944-46, ATO, PTO. Rhodes scholar, 1947 Fellow IEEE, Acoustical Soc. Am.; mem. Oceanic Engring. Soc. IEEE (sec. 1988-92), Engring. Mgmt. Soc. IEEE, N.Y. Acad. Scis., New Coll. Soc., Oxford Soc., Assn. Am. Rhodes Scholars, Amateur Chamber Music Players, Chamber Music Am., Sigma Xi. Democrat. Episcopalian. Home and Office: 40 Deering St Portland ME 04101-2212 also: Blanche Rd RR #1 Barrington Cape Negro NS Canada B0W 1E0 E-mail: raisbeck7@netscape.net.

RAISH, DAVID LANGDON, lawyer; b. Cleve., Mar. 12, 1947; s. John E. Raish and Roslyn V. (Skeels) Pettibone; m. Roslyn Anne Dinnick, Sept. 12, 1969; children: David Jr., Anne, Julia. BA, Yale U., 1969; JD, Harvard U., 1973. Bar: Mass. 1975, D.C. 1981. Law clk. to hon. James R. Browning U.S. Ct. Appeals-9th Cir., San Francisco, 1973-74; assoc. Ropes & Gray, Boston, 1974-82, ptnr., 1982—. Mem. ABA Tax sect. 1991—, mem. Employee Benefits Com., 1993—, mem. coun., 1999—, vice chair, 2002—. Author: Cafeteria Plans, 2000, Cash or Deferred Arrangements, 1997, Compensation and Benefits for Key Employees of Tax-Exempt Organizations, 1995; bd. advisors Jour. Taxation of Employee Benefits, 1990-2000. Tenor Tanglewood Festival Chorus. Office: Ropes & Gray One International Pl Boston MA 02110 E-mail: draish@ropesgray.com.

RAISIG, PAUL JONES, JR. lawyer; b. Jamestown, N.Y., June 21, 1932; s. Paul Jones and Marian Elizabeth (Christian) R.; m. Carolyn Virginia Sides, June 12, 1955; children: Dawn Virginia, Paul Christian, Anne Sibley. B.G.E., U. Nebr., 1961; MBA, U. Ala., 1965; JD, Campbell U., 1989. Bar: N.C., 1989, D.C. 1991, U.S. Supreme Ct. 1992. Commd. 2d lt. U.S. Army, 1953, advanced through grades to col., 1973, ret., 1977, served in Vietnam, 1963, btn. comdr., Vietnam, 1968; dep. dir. U.S. Army Reorganization, 1973; v.p. Armed Forces Relief and Benefit Assn., Washington, 1977-79; sr. cons. Dept. Def., 1979-80; exec. dir. Am. Fedn. Info. Processing Socs., Arlington, Va., 1980-84; v.p., dir. Designs, Ltd., Alexandria, 1985-86; ptnr. Barrington, Herndon & Raisig, P.A., Fayetteville, N.C., 1989-92. Adj. prof. bus. law and bus. mgmt. Campbell U., 1992-2001; cons. in field. Decorated Legion of Merit (4), Bronze Star medal (2), Air medal (5), Purple Heart (2), Meritorious Service medal, Army Commendation medal with V Device (3), Combat INf. badge. Mem. U.S. Council for World Communications, Beta Gamma Sigma. Home and Office: Buffalo Lake 325 Mallard Rd Sanford NC 27332-1142 *As we go about climbing the mountains in our lives, we must always remember to take the high road - for that is the only way to truly reach the top.*

RAISLER, MARY E. nurse; b. May 13, 1955; BSN, U. South Ala., 1998. RN, Fla. Med. svcs. mgr. Med. Ctr. Health Plan, Pensacola, Fla., 1987-90; quality assurance coord. Blue Cross/Blue Shield Fla., 1990-95; managed care dir. West Fla. Med. Ctr. Clinic, 1995-98; dir. managed care Bapt. Health Care, Inc., 1998—, denial recovery dir., 2000—. Vol. Big Bros./Big Sisters of Pensacola, 1996-99. Mem. Nat. Assn. Healthcare Quality, Fla. Assn. Health Care Quality (pres.-elect 1997-98, pres. 1998-99). Office: 1302 W Moreno St Pensacola FL 32501-2316

RAISSI, JOSEPH, financial planner; b. Mar. 22, 1962; m. Connie Bayless, May 31, 1980; children: Alexandria, Victoria, Juliette. Lic. ins. underwriter. Staff mgr., agent United Nat. Agy., Inc., St. Petersburg, Fla., 1983-88; v.p., treas. sales, svc. Continental Diversified Ins. Svcs., Inc., 1988; pres. Fin. Security Plan, Inc., 1990; CEO, pres. Joseph Raissi & Co., Inc., 1994; br. mgr., registered agt. Registered Br. of FFP, Securities Inc., 1994—. Reg. rep. FFP Securities, Inc., St. Petersburg, 1994, reg. investment advisor, agent FFP Advisory Svcs., Inc., St. Petersburg, 1994; founder The Shepherd Fin. Investment Group, 1996; spkr. in field. Contbr. articles to profl. jours. Mem. Inst. CFP, Optimist Internat. (charter). Avocations: travel, reading, tennis. Office: Joseph Raissi & Co Inc 1821 E 71st St #200 Tulsa OK 74136 Fax: 918-491-2055. E-mail: mbowlesattorney@aol.com.

RAISYS, VIDMANTAS A. toxicology educator, clinical chemist; b. Telsiai, Lithuania, Nov. 3, 1934; came to U.S., 1956; s. Vladas A. and Jadvyga Raisys; m. Maria Nijole Galbuogis, Aug. 4, 1962; children: Victor A., Rasa K. BS, Roosevelt U., 1962; MS, U. Ill., Chgo., 1965; PhD, SUNY, Buffalo, 1969. Diplomate in clin. and toxicological chemistry Am. Bd. Clin. Chemistry. Postdoctoral fellow U. Pa., Phila., 1969—71; prof. toxicology, dir. toxicology U. Wash., Seattle, 1971—, Wash. State toxicologist, 1976—90, head chemistry divsn., 1996—2001, prof. emeritus, 2001—. Contbr. over 100 articles and abstracts to sci. jours. Fellow Nat. Acad. Clin. Biochemistry, Am. Acad. Forensic Scis.; mem. Acad. Clin. Physicians and Scientists, Am. Assn. Clin. Chemistry, Internat. Assn. Therapeutic Drug Monitoring and Clin. Toxicology. Avocations: reading, skiing, classical music, fishing.

RAITT, BONNIE LYNN, blues singer, guitarist; b. Burbank, Calif., Nov. 8, 1949; Student, Radcliffe Coll. Performer blues clubs, East Coast; concert tours in Britain, 1976, 77; albums include Bonnie Raitt, 1971, Give It Up, 1972, Takin' My Time, 1973, Streetlights, 1974, Home Plate, 1975, Sweet Forgiveness, 1977, The Glow, 1979, Green Light, 1982, Nine Lives, 1986, Nick of Time, 1989 (Grammys 1990, Rock-Best Vocal Performance, Female, Pop-Best Vocal Performance, Female, Album of Yr.), I'm in the Mood (with John Lee Hooker) (Grammy 1990, Blues-Best Traditional Record), The Bonnie Raitt Collection, 1990, Luck of the Draw, 1991 (Grammy 1992, Rock-Best Vocal Performance, Female, Grammy for Best Duet with Delbert McClinton), Road Longing In Their Hearts, 1994 (Grammy award Best Pop Album), Road Tested, 1996, Fundamental, 1998, I Can't Make You Love Me, 1998, Silver Lining, 2002; songs include Something to Talk About (Grammy 1992, Best Pop Vocal Performance, Female), Good Man, Good Woman (with Delbert McClinton) (Grammy 1992, Rock-Best Vocal by a Duo or Group). Founding mem. Musicians United for Safe Energy, Rhythm and Blues Found.*

RAJ, RISHI, ceramics engineer, educator; b. Ambala City, Punjab, India, July 21, 1943; m. Jyotsna Raj; children: Arjun, Ravi. PhD, Harvard U., 1970. Prof. U. Colo., Boulder, 1971—75, Cornell U., Ithaca, NY, 1975—96, U. Colo., Boulder, 1996—. Recipient Alexander von Humboldt sr. scientist award, Alexander von Humboldt Found., 1992; fellow Guggenheim Fellow, Guggenheim Found., 1985; scholar John Matthias scholar, Los Alamos Nat. Lab., 1996. Fellow: Am. Ceramic Soc. (Associate Editor 1990—2001); mem.: ASME (Chair of the Materials Divison 2000—01).

RAJA, RAJENDRAN, physicist; b. Guruvayur, Kerala , India, July 14, 1948; s. P.K. Sreeveerarayan and Chandramathi Raja; m. Selitha Barbara Freundorfer; children: Anjali. BA with honors, MA with honors, Cambridge (Eng.) U., 1974; PhD, Cambridge (Eng.)U., 1974. Rsch. assoc. Fermilab, Batavia, Ill., 1975—78, assoc. scientist, 1978—83, scientist I, 1983—88, scientist II, 1988—. Monte Carlo convenor DO Expt., 1986—97, top quark physics convenor, 1990—94; head DO Software Support Group, 1986—93, DO Electron ID Group, 1989—94; head, emittance exch./ring coolers group Muon Collider/Neutrino Factory Collaboration, 2001—; spokesman Mipp Expt. Fermilab, Batavia, 2001—. Contbr. over 250 articles to profl. jours. Pres. Cambridge U. India Soc., 1969—70. Mem.: AAAS, Planetary Soc., Am. Phys. Soc. Home: 1304 Margate Ct Naperville IL 60540 Office: Fermi Nat Accelerator Lab PO Box 500 Batavia IL 60510 Office Fax: 630-840-6311. Business E-Mail: raja@fnal.gov.

RAJAB, MOHAMMAD HASAN, biostatistician, educator; b. Oct. 8, 1955; married; 2 children. BS in Agrl. Scis., Damascus (Syria) U., 1976; MS in Quantitative Genetics, Tex. A&M U., 1983, MS in Stats., PhD in Quantitative Genetics, Tex. A&M U., 1987. Instr. Coll. Agr., Damascus (Syria) U., 1976-80, asst. prof. quantitative genetics, 1987-90; tchg. asst. dept. stats. Coll. Sci., Tex. A&M U., College Station, 1986-87; vis. asst. prof. Tex. A&M U., 1990; rsch. sci. dept. stats. Coll. Sci., Tex. A&M U., 1990-93, asst. prof. dept. psychiatry-behavioral scis. Coll. Medicine, 1993-99, assoc. prof. dept. psychiatry, behavioral scis., 1999—. Vis. asst. prof. Inst. für Tierenranhrung, U. Bonn, Germany, 1990; co-investigator Coordinating Ctr. Partial Hospitalization of High-Risk Suicidal Youth Study, NIH, 1990-94, statistician ctrl. vein occlusion study, 1994-96; epidemiologist biostats. dept. Scott and White Hosp., Temple, Tex., 1993—; dir. effectiveness registry outcome rsch. unit Scott and White Hosp., 1997—presenter in field. Contbr. articles to profl. jours. Acad. scholar USAID, 1980; recipient Govt. award Damascus U., 1976. Mem. Am. Statis. Assn., Soc. Clin. Trials, Sigma Xi. Office: Texas A&M U Health Sci Ctr Biostatistics 2401 S 31st St Temple TX 76508-0001 E-mail: mhrajab@yahoo.com.

RAJAGOPAL, ARVIND, sociologist; b. New Delhi, India, Mar. 17, 1959; s. Puducode Chandra and Padma R.; m. Anupama P. Rao, Aug. 20, 1993. PhD, U. Calif., 1992. Mem. Sch. of Social Sci., Inst. of Advanced Studies, Princeton, N.J., 1998-99; assoc. prof. NYU, 1999—. Author: Politics After Television, 2001; co-author (with Robert Goldman): Mapping Hegemony, 1991; guest editor in field. Fellowship John D. and Catherine T. MacArthur Found., 1996-97. Office: NYU 239 Green St 7th Fl New York NY 10003

RAJAGOPAL, RAJ, mechanical engineer; BS in Mech. Engring., Ill. Inst. Tech., 1974, MS in Mech. Engring., 1975; graduate Exec. Devel. Program, U. Va., 1985, U. Ill., 1991. Metallurgist IIT Rsch. Inst., 1976—78, mgr. mfg. tech., 1978—84; from mgr. armor & materials to v.p. rsch. & engring. United Def. L.P., Arlington, Va., 1984—90, v.p. rsch. & engring., 1990—. Mem.: NSIA, ADPA, AUSA. Office: United Defense LP 1525 Wilson Blvd Ste 700 Arlington VA 22209-2444*

RAJAN, ASHVIN VARADA, mathematician, educator; s. Mudumbai and Malati Varadarajan. PhD, Johns Hopkins U., 1996. Vis. academic Johns Hopkins U., Baltimore, 1996—97; lectr. Princeton U., NJ, 1997—2001; instr. Loyola Coll., Baltimore, 2001—. Contbr. articles. Vol. math. tchr. The Learning Bank, Baltimore, 2001—02. Mem.: Am. Math. Soc. Avocations: western classical music, reading, travel. Office: Loyola Coll In Md 4501 N Charles St Baltimore MD 21210-2699

RAJENDREN, GOPALAN, biomedical researcher; b. Kollam, Kerala, India, Nov. 25, 1957; came to U.S., 1988; s. Krishnan and Bhargavi (Soumini) Gopalan; m. Laly Kaniyarathinkal; 1 child, Soumya Rajendren. MS, U. Kerala, 1981; PhD, Banaras Hindu U., Uttar Pradesh, India, 1986. Biomed. rschr. divsn. endocrinology Mt. Sinai Med. Ctr., N.Y.C. Contbr. articles to sci. jours., includign Jour. Neuroendocrinology, Neuroendocrinology, Brain Rsch., Molecular and Cellular Neurosci. Mem. AAAS, Soc. for Neurosci. E-mll. Office: Mt Sinai Med Ctr Div Endocrinology Box 1055 One Gustave L Levy Pl New York NY 10029 E-mail: rajeng01@doc.mssm.edu.

RAJKUMAR, AJAY, computer scientist, consultant; b. Jagadhri, Haryana, India, Aug. 4, 1962; came to the U.S., 1990; s. Rajkumar and Pushpa Rajkumar; m. Aradhana Goel, Feb. 9, 1996. BSc in Math. with honors, U. Delhi, India, 1984; M in Computer Applications, U. Poona, Pune, India, 1987; MS in Computer Sci., Utah State U., 1992; PhD in Computer Sci., NYU, 1999. Rsch. engr. Uptron India Ltd., Lucknow, India, 1987-90, Vigyan Inc., Hampton, Va., 1991-92; cons. AT&T Bell Labs., Murray Hill, N.J., 1993-95, mem. tech. staff, 1995-96, Lucent Tech., Bell Labs. Innovations, 1996, cons., 1997. Grantee NASA-Goddard Space Flight Ctr., Hampton, 1992, Dept of Energy, Hampton, 1992. Mem. Assn. for Computing Machinery. Avocations: hiking, traveling, reading. Office: 67 Whippany Rd Whippany NJ 07981-1406

RAJKUMAR, ROSHINI ANNE, reporter; b. Colombo, Sri Lanka, Nov. 6, 1970; arrived in U.S., 1972; d. Rajadurai and Concy Rajkumar. BA, Boston Coll., 1993; JD, U. Minn., 1997. Reporter KVLY-TV, Fargo, ND, 1998—99, KCCI-TV, Des Moines, 1999—2000, WTVF-TV, Nashville, 2000—02, WFTC-TV, Mpls., 2002—. Mem.: NATAS, Minn. State Bar Assn., IRE, Minn. Women Lawyers, Asian Am. Journalists Assn. Avocations: travel, photography, movies. Office: KMSP/WFTC 11358 Viking Dr Minneapolis MN 55344

RAJLICH, VACLAV THOMAS, computer science educator, researcher, consultant; b. Prague, Czech Republic, May 3, 1939; came to U.S., 1980; s. Vaclav and Marie (Janovska) R.; m. Ivana m. Bartova, Aug. 6, 1968; children: Vasik, Paul, John, Luke. MS, Czech Tech. U., Prague, 1962; PhD, Case Western Res. U., 1971. Rsch. engr. Rsch. Inst. for Math. Machines, Prague, 1963-67, scientist, 1971-75, mgr., 1975-79; vis. assoc. prof. computer sci. Calif. State U., Fullerton, 1980-81; assoc. prof. computer and communication sci. U. Mich., Ann Arbor, 1982-85; prof. Wayne State U., Detroit, 1985—, chair dept. computer sci., 1985-90. Vis. scientist Carnegie-Mellon U., Pitts., 1987, Harvard U., Cambridge, Mass., 1988. Contbr. articles to profl. jours. Recipient Chrysler Challenge Fund, 1988. Mem. Computer Soc. of IEEE, Assn. for Computing Machinery. Roman Catholic. Achievements include development of tools for software maintenance, program comprehension, software design methods, parallel grammars, graph rewriting, abstract state machines. Office: Wayne State U Dept Computer Sci Detroit MI 48202 E-mail: rajlich@cs.wayne.edu.

RAJSKI, PEGGY, film director, film producer; b. Stevens Point, Wis. Attended, U. Wis. Films include: (prodn. mgr.): Lianna, 1982, Almost You, 1984; (prodr., prodn. mgr.) The Brother From Another Planet, 1984, Matewan, 1987, (co-prodr., prodn. mgr.) Eight Men Out, 1988; (co-prodr.) The Grifters, 1990, (prodr.) Little Man Tate, 1991 (also 2nd. unit dir.), Used People, 1992, Home for the Holidays, 1995; (prodr. video) Bruce Springsteen's Glory Days; (dir.) Trevor, 1994 (Acad. award for Best Live Action Short Film).

RAJU, KANTHI PENMATCH, psychiatrist; BS, Miss. Coll., 1990; DO, UOMHS, Des Moines, 1994. Biomaterials lab tech. U. Miss. Sch. Dentistry, Jackson, 1990; physician resident U. Iowa, Des Moines, 1994-95, U. Tex. Southwestern Med. Ctr., Dallas, 1996-99; triage physician Charter Behavioral Health Care System, Plano, 1997-98; psychiatrist Dallas Metrocare Svcs., 1999—. Chief resident dept. psychiatry U. Tex. Southwestern Med. Ctr., Dallas, 1998-99. Contbr. articles to profl. jours. Scholar U. Miss., 1985, Memphis Acad. Arts, 1985. Mem. AMA, Am. Psychiat. Assn., Am. Osteo. Assn., Tex. Med. Assn. Democrat. Avocations: painting, reading. Office: Dallas Metrocare Svcs 4645 Samuell Blvd Dallas TX 75228-6885

RAJU, VASUDEVA, financial analyst; b. Bangalore, India, Feb. 1, 1961; came to U.S., 1985; s. Sreenivasa and Lalithamma Raju; m. Anitha P. Raju. B in Engring., Bangalore U., India, 1983; MBA, Clarion U. Pa., 1987; postgrad., Pace U., 1998—. Sales engr. Photophone Ltd., Bangalore, India, 1984-85; fin. analyst Thieme Assocs/Am. Heritage Mgmt. Corp., N.Y.C., 1992-96, Athos Group, N.Y.C., 1997—. Mem. Fin. Mgmt. Assn. Hindu. Avocations: swimming, jogging. Home: 30 Willis Ave Fl 2D Staten Island NY 10301-3115 Office: Athos Group 200 E 94th St Ph 12 New York NY 10128-3916

RAJYAGURU, MAHESH SHANTILAL, educator; b. Bhavnagar, India, Oct. 26, 1951; came to U.S., 1998; s. Shantilal and Manorama Rajyaguru; m. Usha M. Rajyaguru, Nov. 30, 1973; children: Purvi, Shital, Khushbu. MSc, PhD, Bhavnagar (India) U.; MEd, Surashtra U., Bhavnagar. Lectr. B. Ed. Coll., Bhavnagar, 1981-92, prin., 1992-96; reader Bhavnagar U., 1996-98, mem. exec. coun., 1995-96; cons. ednl. rsch., 1996—. Faculty Phoenix Coll., Chandler-Gilbert Coll. Avocations: reading, educational research, Indian cultural activities. Home: 16606 N 19th Pl Phoenix AZ 85022 E-mail: maraj_2001@yahoo.com.

RAJYAGURU, VRAJLAL LALJIBHAI, anesthesiologist; b. Jam Raval, India, Nov. 24, 1961; arrived in U.S., 1987; s. Laljibhai Kanji and Devkiben L. (Joshi) Rajyaguru; m. Kalpana S. Thanki, Mar. 12, 1986; children: Neal, Parth. MB, BS, M.P. Shah Med. Coll., India, 1986; MD, N.Y. Med. Coll., 1994. Diplomate Am. Bd. Anesthesiology (fellow). Intern in surgery St. Vincent's Hosp., N.Y.C., 1989-90; resident in surgery L.I. Jewish Med. Ctr., New Hyde Pk., 1990-91; resident in anesthesiology and pain mgmt. N.Y. Med. Coll., Valhalla, 1991-94; pvt. practice. Rschr. laser application in vascular surgery, 1989. Co-chmn. physician adv. bd. Nat. Rep. Congl. Com., 2001. Named Fla. Businessman of the Yr., Nat. Rep. Congl. Com., 2001. Fellow: Am. Bd. Disability Analysis, Am. Acad. Pain Mgmt., Am. Bd. Pain Medicine; mem.: AMA, Neuromodulation Soc. (advisor). Address: Advanced Pain Clin PO Box 3129 Kissimmee FL 34742

RAK, LINDA MARIE, elementary education educator, consultant; b. Dunkirk, N.Y. d. Felix Joseph and Helen (Dudek) Ruzycki; m. Joseph John Rak, Oct. 11, 1969; children: Joel, Seth. BA in Edn., SUNY, Fredonia, 1969, MS in Edn., 1974; postgrad., SUNY, Brockport, 1980-84, SUNY, Buffalo, 1988-90. Cert. reading and spl. edn. tchr., N.Y. Tchr. 1st grade Webster (N.Y.) Cen. Sch. Dist., 1969-72; tchr. kindergarten and reading Williamson (N.Y.) Cen. Sch. Dist., 1973-76; instr. in GED Orleans County Job Devel. Agy., Albion, N.Y., 1979-83; adult basic edn. coord. SUNY, Brockport, 1980-85; tchr. remedial reading, lang. arts coord. Kendall (N.Y.) Cen. Sch. Dist., 1985—; adj. prof. SUNY, Brockport, 2001. In-svc. presenter Kendall Elem. Sch., 1984-2002, reading recovery tchr., 1996—; workshop presenter Monroe #2 Orleans BOCES, Spencerport, N.Y., 1988-91; workshop presenter Genesee Wyoming BOCES, 1988-90, N.Y. State Whole Lang. Conf., 1993, Curriculum Devel., 1989-2001; reading recovery tng. BOCES Monroe #2 Orleans, 1996-97; adj. prof. dept. edn. and human devel. SUNY, Brockport, 2001--. Nursery sch. treas. AAUW, Orleans and Niagara Counties, N.Y., 1977-79; tchr. Sunday sch. St. Joseph's Ch., Lyndonville, N.Y., 1978-95, mem. parish coun., 1996—. Recipient Cert. of Appreciation, Congressman John J. La False, 1985; named Religious Educator of the Yr., Diocese of Buffalo, 1987. Mem. Internat. Reading Assn., Rochester Area Reading Coordinators (pres. 1992-96), Genesee Valley Devel. Learning Group (satellite rep. 1987-88), Lit. Vols. Orleans County (v.p. 1981-84, Outstanding Leadership award 1984), Somerset Hist. Soc., Reading Recovery Coun. Roman Catholic. Avocation: home restoration. Home: 64 N Main St # 329 Lyndonville NY 14098-9672 Office: Kendall Cen Sch Dist 1932 Kendall Rd Kendall NY 14476-9775 E-mail: lrak@kendallcsd.org.

RAK, LORRAINE KAREN, lawyer; b. Trenton, N.J., Jan. 8, 1959; d. Charles Walter and Lottie Mary (Debiec) R. BA in Polit. Sci., Seton Hall U., South Orange, N.J., 1981; JD, Cornell U., 1984. Bar: N.J. 1986, N.Y. 1986, U.S. Dist. Ct. N.J. 1986, U.S. Dist. Ct. (so. and ea. dists.) N.Y. 1988, U.S. Dist. Ct. (no. dist.) N.Y. 1991, U.S. Ct. Appeals (4th cir.) 1989, U.S. Ct. Appeals (2d cir.) 1990, U.S. Ct. Appeals (3d cir.) 1991. Assoc. Shearman & Sterling, N.Y.C., 1984-91, Robinson, St. John & Wayne, N.Y.C., 1992-93; dep. atty. gen. State of N.J., Newark, 1993—. Active Lawyers' Com. for Human Rights, N.Y.C. Mem. ABA, ACLU, LWV, Cornell Law Assn., Amnesty Internat., Polish Arts Club Trenton. Democrat. Roman Catholic. Office: 124 Halsey St Fl 5 Newark NJ 07102-3017 E-mail: raklor@law.dol.lps.state.nj.us.

RAKESTRAW, GREGORY ALLEN, lawyer; b. Findlay, Ohio, Jan. 20, 1949; s. Russell E. and Genevieve (Might) R.; m. Sandra Sue Steegman, July 17, 1971; children: Adam Edwin, Seth Allen, Ashley Marie. BA, Wittenberg U., 1971; postgrad., Ohio State U., 1972; JD with distinction, Ohio No. U., 1974. Bar: Ohio 1974, U.S. Dist. Ct. (no. dist.) Ohio 1974, U.S. Ct. Appeals (6th cir.) 1992. Assoc. Russell E. Rakestraw, Findlay, 1974-78; ptnr. Rakestraw & Rakestraw, 1978—. Referee Findlay Mcpl., 1974-75; spl. prosecutor Marion Twp., Hancock County, Ohio, 1976—. Contbr. to Ohio Divorce, 1981. Mem.-at-large Findlay City Coun., 1975-76, Hancock County Human Rights Commn., Findlay, 1978-84. Fellow Ohio State Bar Found.; mem. ABA, Ohio State Bar Assn., N.W. Ohio Bar Assn., Findlay-Hancock County Bar Assn. (past pres.), Assn. Trial Lawyers Am., Ohio Assn. Trial Lawyers, Internat. Platform Assn., Findlay AAA (bd. dirs.), Lambda Chi Alpha (past pres.). Republican. Lutheran. Avocations: sailing and power boating, building , remodeling. Home: 11595 County Road 40 Findlay OH 45840-9029 Office: Rakestraw & Rakestraw 119 E Crawford St Findlay OH 45840-4887

RAKIC, PASKO, neuroscientist, educator; b. Ruma, Yugoslavia, May 15, 1933; came to U.S., 1969; m. Patricia Goldman, 1969. MD, U. Belgrade, Yugoslavia, 1959, ScD in Neuroembryology, 1969. With inst. path. physiology Med. Sch. U. Belgrade, 1959-61, resident in neurosurgery, 1961-62; NIH research fellow neuropathology Harvard Med. Sch., Boston, 1962-66; asst. prof. Inst. Biol. Rsch., Belgrade, 1967-68; from asst. prof. to assoc. prof. neuropathology and neuroscience Harvard Med. Sch., 1969-77; prof. neurosci. Yale Med. Sch., New Haven, 1977-78, Dorys McConnell Duberg prof. neurosci., 1978—, also chmn. neurobiology sect. Author of 200 sci. papers and gen. books on brain orgn. and devel. Recipient Henry Gray award Am. Assn. Anatomists, 1996. Mem.: NAS, Am. Acad. Arts and Sci., Soc. Neurosci. (pres. 1996), Am. Phys. Soc. (Lashley award 1986, Fyssen internat. sci. prize 1992)., Inst. of Med. Office: Yale U Sch Medicine Sect Neurobiology 333 Cedar St New Haven CT 06510-3289*

RAKITA, LOUIS, cardiologist, educator; b. Montreal, Que., Can., July 2, 1922; came to U.S., 1951, naturalized, 1962; s. S. and Rose (Weinman) R.; m. G. Blanche Michlin, Dec. 4, 1945; 1 son, Robert M. BA, Sir George Williams Coll., Montreal, 1942; MD, C.M., McGill U., 1949. Diplomate: Am. Bd. Internal Medicine. Intern Montreal Gen. Hosp., 1949-50; resident in medicine Jewish Gen. Hosp., Montreal, 1950-51; fellow in medicine Alton Ochsner Med. Found., New Orleans, 1951-52; chief resident in medicine Cleve. City Hosp., 1952-53, Am. Heart Assn. fellow, 1954-55, Inst. for Med. Research, Cedars of Lebanon Hosp., Los Angeles, 1953-54; practice medicine specializing in internal medicine and cardiology Cleve., 1954—; instr. medicine Western Res. U., 1954-55, sr. instr., 1955-57, asst. prof., 1957-61, asso. prof., 1961-71; asst. vis. physician Cleve. City Hosp., 1954-57, vis. physician, 1957—; advanced fellow Cleve. Met. Gen. Hosp., 1959-61, dir. cardiology, 1966-87, immediate past dir., div. cardiology, 1987—; asso. div. of research in med. edn. Case Western Res. U., Cleve., 1969-75, prof. medicine, 1971-93, prof. emeritus medicine, 1993. Chmn. Phase IIA Cardiovascular com. Case Western Res. U., 1965-70, Faculty Senate Subcom. for Devel. and Evaluation of Ednl. Methods, 1969, chmn. Univ. Com. on Ednl. Planning, 1971-73, Faculty Coun. Sch. Medicine, 1979-80, Faculty Coun. Steering Com. Sch. Medicine, 1979-80, mem. bd. trustees Com. on Univ. Plans, 1971-73, Faculty Senate, Exec. Coun.; cons. in cardiology Luth. Med. Ctr., Cleve., 1970—, Crile VA Hosp., Cleve., 1969—; vis. cardiologist Sunny Acres Hosp., Cleve., 1973—; cardiologist rep. of del. to USSR, 1973. Author: (with M. Broder) Cardiac Arrhythmias, 1970, (with M. Kaplan) Immunological Diseases, 1972; Contbr. (with M. Kaplan) articles on cardiovascular diseases to profl. pubis. Served with RCAF, 1942-45. Recipient Research Career Devel. award USPHS, 1962-69, Saltzman award Mt. Sinai Med. Health Found., 1997. Fellow ACP (Laureate award Ohio chpt. 1992), Am. Coll. Cardiology, Royal Coll. Physicians and Surgeons Can. (cert.), Am. Heart Assn. (mem. exec. coun. N.E. Ohio chpt. 1972—, trustee 1969—, pres. N.E. Ohio chpt. 1972-74, coun. on clin. cardiology 1972—, chmn. various coms., v.p. North Ctrl. Region 1985-86, bd. dirs. 1985-86, hon. life trustee Northeast Ohio affiliate, vice chmn. task force on product licensing feasibility 1987—, Award of Merit 1987, Gold Heart award 1989); mem. AAUP, Am. Fedn. Clin. Rsch., Ctrl. Soc. Clin. Rsch., Soc. Exptl. Biology and Medicine, Cleve. Med. Libr. Assn. (trustee 1972—), Nat. Bd. Med. Examiners, The Press of Case Western Res. U. (adv. com. 1970), Nat. Heart and Lung Inst., Nat. Insts. Health (left ventricular assist device clin. trial program divsn. extramural affairs, data rev. bd. 1981—, adv. com. med. devices applications program 1971-75), Sigma Xi. Home: 24151 S Woodland Rd Cleveland OH 44122-3315 Office: 2500 Metrohealth Dr Cleveland OH 44109-1900

RAKO, JENNIFER S. lawyer; b. Bronx, N.Y., Aug. 25, 1963; d. Jules and Susan Rako; m. Thomas Paul Bernardo, Sept. 20, 1987; 1 child, Alexandra. BA, NYU, 1986; JD, Northeastern U., 1992. Bar: Conn. 1992, Mass. 1993. Assoc. Murtha Cullina Richter & Pinney, Hartford, Conn., 1992-95, Kirkpatrick & Lockhart LLP (formerly Warner & Stackpole LLP), Boston, 1995-2000; ptnr. Murtha Cullina Roche Carens & DeGiacomo, 2000—. Treas.

Citizens for Tom Bernardo, Chatham, Mass., 1997—; pres. Friends of Chatham Animals, Inc., 1998—; trustee Eldridge Pub. Libr., Chatham, 1998—; overseer Zoo New Eng., Boston, 1998—. Office: Murtha Cullina Roche Et Al 99 High St Boston MA 02110

RAKO, SUSAN, psychiatrist, author; b. Springfield, Mass., Sept. 4, 1939; d. Robert and Ann (Melnikoff) Mandell; 1 child, Jennifer Sarah. Student, Wellesley Coll., 1957-60; BS, U. Cin., 1961; MS in Film, Boston U., 1988; MD, Albert Einstein Coll. Medicine, 1966. Med. rsch. asst. neuroendocrinology Worcester Found. Experimental Biology, Shrewsbury, Mass., 1959; med. rsch. asst. May Inst., Cin., 1961-62; intern in medicine, surgery Mt. Auburn Hosp., Cambridge, Mass., 1966-67; resident in adult psychiatry Mass. Mental Health Ctr., Boston, 1967-69; tchg. fellow in psychiatry Harvard Med. Sch., 1967-69, clin. fellow in psychiatry, 1969-70; pvt. practice Newton, Mass., 1970—; clin. instr. psychiatry Harvard Med. Sch., Boston, 1970-75; resident in child and adult psychiatry Beth Israel Hosp., 1969-70; psychiatrist Mass. Mental Health Ctr., 1970-77, Newton-Wellesley Hosp., 1982. Cons. Cutler Counseling Ctr., Norwood, Mass., 1983, VA Hosp., San Juan, P.R., 1990-94; spkr. in field. Author: The Hormone of Desire: The Truth About Testosterone, Sexuality, and Menopause, 1996, 2d edit., 1999; co-editor: Semrad: The Heart of a Therapist, 1984; film maker Susan and Jenni, 1987. E-mail: susanrako@aol.com.

RAKOFF, JED SAUL, federal judge, author; b. Phila., Aug. 1, 1943; s. Abraham Edward and Doris Tobiah (Michell) R.; m. Ann Rosenberg, Aug. 4, 1974; children: Jena Lynn, Elana Beth, Keira Jan. BA, Swarthmore Coll., 1964; MPhil, Balliol Coll., Oxford U., Eng., 1966; JD, Harvard U., 1969. Bar: N.Y. 1971, D.C. 1983, U.S. Supreme Ct. 1986. Law clk. U.S. Ct. Appeals (3rd cir.), Phila., 1969-70; assoc. Debevoise, Plimpton, Lyons & Gates, N.Y.C., 1970-73; asst. U.S. atty. So. Dist. N.Y., 1973-80, chief bus. and securities fraud prosecutions U.S. Atty.'s Office, 1978-80; ptnr. Mudge Rose Guthrie Alexander & Ferdon, 1980-90, Fried Frank Harris Shriver & Jacobson, N.Y.C., 1990-96; judge U.S. Dist. Ct. (so. dist.) N.Y., 1996—. Lectr. in law Columbia Law Sch., 1988—. Author: (with S. Arkin et al) Business Crime, 6 vols., 1982, Criminal Defense Techniques, 6 vols., 1982, (with H. Goldstein) RICO: Civil and Criminal Law and Strategy, 1989, (with L. Blumkin and R. Sauber) Corporate Sentencing Guidelines,: Compliance and Mitigation, 1993; editor-in-chief Bus. Crimes Bull., 1994-95; columnist N.Y. Law Jour., 1985-95; contbr. numerous articles to law revs. Mem. exec. bd. N.Y. chpt. Am. Jewish Com., 1971-95. Fellow Am. Coll. Trial Lawyers (chmn. N.Y. State 1993-94), Am. Bd. Criminal Lawyers; mem. ABA, N.Y. State Bar Assn., Assn. of Bar of City of N.Y. (chmn. criminal law com. 1986-89), Fed. Bar Coun., N.Y. Coun. Def. Lawyers (dir. 1990-94). Democrat. Jewish. Office: U.S. Courthouse 500 Pearl St Rm 1340 New York NY 10007-1316

RAKOFF, VIVIAN MORRIS, psychiatrist, writer; b. Capetown, South Africa, Apr. 28, 1928; s. David Wilfred and Bertha Lillian (Woolf) R.; m. Gina Shochat, Nov. 27, 1959; children: Simon, Ruth, David. BA, U. Capetown, 1947, MA with 1st class honors, 1949; M.B.BS, U. London, 1957; diploma psychiat. medicine, McGill U., 1963. Intern St. Charles Hosp., London, 1957, Victoria Hosp., Capetown, 1958; resident Groote Schuur Hosp., 1959-61, Jewish Gen. Hosp., Montreal, 1961-62, Verdun Protestant Hosp., Montreal, 1961-62; staff psychiatrist Jewish Gen. Hosp., 1963-66, dir. research psychiatry, 1967-68; dir. postgrad. edn. dept. psychiatry U. Toronto, Ont, Can, 1968-75, prof. psychiat. edn. Ont., Can., 1975-80, prof., chmn. dept. psychiatry Can., 1980-90, prof. emeritus, 1990—; head dept. psychiatry Sunnybrook Hosp., Toronto, 1978-80; dir., psychiatrist-in-chief Clarke Inst. Psychiatry, Toronto, 1980-90. Author: plays Nonquasi, 1967; Mandelstam's Witness, 1975; editor: Psychiatric Diagnosis, 1977, A Method of Psychiatry, 1979. Fellow Royal Coll. Physicians and Surgeons, Am. Psychiat. Assn., Am. Coll. Psychiatrists; mem. Sigma Xi Jewish. Office: Clarke Inst Psychiatry 250 College St Toronto ON Canada M5T 1R8

RAKOV, VLADIMIR A. electrical and computer engineering educator; b. Semipalatinsk, Kazakhstan, USSR, Aug. 7, 1955; came to U.S., 1991; s. Alexander I. Rakov and Lidiya D. Yakovleva; m. Lioudmila D. Fateev, Feb. 21, 1974; 1 child, Serguei V. MS, Tomsk (Russia) Poly., 1977, PhD, 1983. Asst. prof. Tomsk Poly., 1977-79, rschr., sr. rschr., 1979-84, dir. lightning rsch. lab., 1984-94; assoc. prof. U. Fla., Gainesville, 1991-98, prof., 1998—. Guest prof. Tech. U. Vienna, Austria, 1998, Fed. Inst. Tech., Lausanne, Switzerland, 2001; chmn. tech. program com. on lightning Internat. Zurich Symposium on Electromagnetic Compatibility, 1997—; mem. steering com. Internat. Symposium on Lightning Protection, 1998—; mem. Internat. Commn. on Atmospheric Electricity, 1999—; mem. tech. com. Internat. Conf. on Lightning and Static Electricity, 2000—, mem. Underwriters Labs. Standards tech. panel, 2001--. Contbr. over 80 articles to profl. jours.; 31 patents in field. Recipient Inventor of USSR medal USSR State Com. for Inventions and Discoveries, 1996, Silver medal USSR Exhbn. Tech. Achievements, 1987, Rsch. Unit award Am. Soc. Engring. Edn., 1999. Mem. IEEE (sr., Pwer Engring. Soc. Prize Paper award 2001), Am. Geophys. Union (mem. com. atmospheric and space electricity 1996-2000, chmn. 2000—), Am. Meteorol. Soc. (mem. sci. and tech. com. atmospheric electricity 2001—), Soc. Automotive Engrs. Avocation: travel. Office: U Fla Dept ECE 553 Engring Bldg #33 Gainesville FL 32611-6130

RAKOVE, JACK NORMAN, history educator; b. Chgo., June 4, 1947; s. Milton Leon and Shirley (Bloom) R.; m. Helen Scharf, June 22, 1969; children: Robert, Daniel. AB, Haverford Coll., 1968; PhD, Harvard U., 1975. Asst. prof. history Colgate U., Hamilton, N.Y., 1975-80; from asst. to assoc. prof. history Stanford (Calif.) U., 1980-90, prof., 1990—, Coe prof. history and Am. studies, 1996—, prof. polit. sci., 1999—. Author: Beginnings of National Politics, 1979, James Madison and The Creation of the American Republic, 1990, Original Meanings, 1996 (Pulitzer prize for History, 1997), Declaring Rights, 1997; editor: Interpreting the Consitution, 1990, James Madison Writings, 1999, The Unfinished Election of 2000, 2001. Commr. Calif. Bicentennial Commn., 1986-87. With USAR, 1968-74. NEH fellow, 1985-86, Stanford Humanities Ctr. fellow, 1988-89, 2000-01. Mem. Am. Hist. Assn., Orgn. Am. Historians, Soc. Am. Historians, Am. Polit. Sci. Assn., Am. Acad. Arts & Scis., Am. Antiquarian Soc., Soc. History of New Early Am. Rep (pres. 2002). Office: Stanford U Dept History Stanford CA 94305-2024 E-mail: rakove@stanford.edu.

RAKOWER, JOEL A. business appraiser, litigation consultant; b. 1958; BA in Acctg., U. South Fla., 1980. CPA, N.Y., Fla. Ptnr. Goodman, Rakower & Agiato, Commack, N.Y., 1989-93; pres. Fin. Appraisal Svcs. Ltd., 1993—. Testified as expert witness numerous times in N.Y. and Conn.; lectr., seminar presenter to profl. and ednl. orgns. Author: Enhanced Earning Capacity: Understanding the Computations, 1993, Quantifying Celebrity Status, 1995, Reality, What a Concept, 2001; contbr. articles to profl. jours. Mem. Nat. Assn. Cert. Fraud Examiners (cert.), Fla. Inst. CPAs, Am. Soc. Appraisers, Inst. Bus. Appraisers, N.Y. State Soc. CPAs, Nat. Assn. Forensic Economists. Office: Fin Appraisal Svcs Ltd 366 Veterans Memorial Hwy Commack NY 11725-4387

RAKOWICZ-SZULCZYNSKA, EVA MARIA, molecular oncologist; b. Poznan, Poland, Nov. 22, 1951; came to U.S., 1984; d. Tadeusz and Wieslawa Maria (Hankiewicz) Rakowicz; married; 1 child, Adriana Maria. MS in Biochemistry, A. Mickiewicz U., Poznan, 1974; PhD in Biochemistry, Acad. Medicine, Poznan, 1977, DMS in Human Genetics & Molecular Biol., 1981. Asst. prof. Inst. Human Genetics, Poznan, 1978-82, assoc. dir., 1982-86, assoc. prof., 1982-89; assoc. scientist, lab. head Wistar Inst., Phila., 1984-90, rsch. asst. prof., 1991-92; assoc. prof. ob/gyn. U. Nebr. Med. Ctr., Omaha, 1992-2000, assoc. prof. Eppley Inst., 1993-95, assoc. prof. biochemistry, 1995—2000. Mem. Nat. Cancer Inst., Eppley Cancer Ctr., Omaha, 1995—2000; v.p. ViroTech LLC, 1996—; CEO, pres. Exec. Mgmt. LLC, Fla., 2000—. Author: Nuclear Localization of Growth Factors and of Monoclonal Antibodies, 1993; contbr. over 60 articles to sci. jours., including Am. Jour. Pathology, Carcinogenesis, others. Grantee Nebr. Dept. Health, 1993-95, Elsa U. Pardee Found., 1993-94, Olson Ctr. for Women's Health, 1993-98. Mem. AAAS, Am. Assn. Cancer Rsch., Am. Assn. Microbiology, Internat. Soc. for Preventive Oncology, Am. Assn. Clin. Chemistry, N.Y. Acad. Scis. Roman Catholic. Achievements include patents for Methods for Detecting Growth Factor Receptor Expression, Methods for Screening Monoclonal Antibodies for Therapeutic Use; patents for diagnosis and therapy of breast, gynecological and prostate cancer. Office: 3710 S Atlantic Ave Daytona Beach FL 32127 E-mail: emrakowi@hotmail.com.

RAKSAKULTHAI, VINAI, obstetrician, gynecologist; b. Rayong, Thailand, Mar. 20, 1942; came to U.S., 1968; s. Choosak and Ngo (Koo) R.; m. Vullapa Raksakulthai, Sept. 20, 1968; children: Vipavull, Vivian, Vipat. MD, Chieng-Mai Med. Sch., Thailand, 1966. Diplomate Am. Bd. Ob-Gyn. Intern New Britain (Conn.) Gen. Hosp., 1969; resident St. Joseph Mercy Hosp., Pontiac, Mich., 1970-72; practice medicine specializing in ob-gyn. Fredericktown, Mo., 1973—. Mem. Mo. Med. Assn., Mineral Area Med. Soc. Buddhist. Home: 201 Williams St Fredericktown MO 63645-1317 Office: 735 W Main Fredericktown MO 63645

RAKSIN, ALEX, reporter; b. Nov. 9, 1960; m. Victoria Hendrick; 1 child Tobias. BA in Journalism, U. So. Calif., 1984. Columnist LA Times, 1985—93, dep. book editor, 1993—96, editl. writer, 1996—. Freelance writer, 1984—93; instr. UCLA Ext., 1986—89; dir. Lit. awards PEN USA West, 1998—2000. Recipient Outstanding Media award for Editl. Writing, Nat. Alliance for Mentally Ill, 2001, Nat. Headliner award for Editl. Writing, Calif. Alliance for Mentally Ill, 2001, 1999, Aaron Price Child Health and Welfare Scholarship and Journalism award, 1999. Mem.: Nat. Conf. Editl. Writers, Nat. Com. Concerned Journalists, Nat. Book Critics Cir. Office: LA Times 202 W 1st St Los Angeles CA 90012*

RALEIGH, CECIL BARING, geophysicist; b. Little Rock, Aug. 11, 1934; s. Cecil Baring and Lucile Nell (Stewart) R.; m. Diane Lauster, July 17, 1982; children: Alison, Marianne, Lawrence, David. BA, Pomona (Calif.) Coll., 1956; MA, Claremont (Calif.) Grad. Sch., 1958; PhD, UCLA, 1963. Fellow Research Sch. Phys. Sci., Australian Nat. U., Canberra, 1963-66; geophysicist U.S. Geol. Survey, Menlo Park, Calif., 1966-80, program mgr. for earthquake prediction research program, 1980-81; dir. Lamont-Doherty Geol. Obs. and prof. geol. scis. Columbia U., Palisades, N.Y., 1981-89; dean Sch. Ocean and Earth Sci. and Tech. U. Hawaii, Honolulu, 1989—. CEO Ctr. for a Sustainable Future, Inc., 1996—; mem. Gov.'s Task Force on Sci. Tech., 1996-98; mem. NAS/NRC Ocean Studies Bd.; chmn. NAS/NRC Yucca Mountain Panel, High Tech. Devel. Corp.; bd. dirs. JOI, Inc. Author papers control earthquakes, rheology of the mantle, mechanics of faulting, crystal plasticity. Trustee Bishop Mus., 1997—. Recipient Interdisciplinary award U.S. Nat. Com. Rock Mechanics, 1969, 74; Meritorious Service award Dept. Interior, 1974; Barrows Dist. Alumnus award Pomona Coll. Fellow Am. Geophys. Union, Geol. Soc. Am. Democrat. Inventor formation fracturing method. Office: U Hawaii Sch Ocean Earth Sci & Tech Honolulu HI 96822

RALEY, BENNETT W. federal agency administrator; BS in Agrl. Bus., Colo. State U., 1979, JD, 1983. From assoc. to ptnr. Davis, Graham & Stubbs, Denver; shareholder Trout & Raley, P.C., 1983—90; gen. counsel No. Colo. Water Conservancy Dist.; spl. asst. atty. gen. N.Mex. Office of the State Engr. and Interstate Stream Commn.; asst. sec. water and scis. U.S. Dept. Interior, Washington, 2001—. Staff counsel U.S. Senator Hank Brown; chief counsel U.S. Senate Judiciary Subcom. on the Constn., Federalism and Property Rights; co-chair Fed. Water Rights Task Force. Office: US Dept Interior Water and Sci 1849 C St NW Washington DC 20240*

RALEY, JOHN W., JR. lawyer; b. May 23, 1932; s. John Wesley and Helen Thames; children: John Wesley III, Robert Thames. AB, Okla. Baptist U., 1954; JD, U. Okla., 1959. Bar: Okla. 1959, U.S. Supreme Ct. 1973, U.S. Ct. Appeals (10th cir.), 1962, U.S. Dist. (we. dist.) 1961, U.S. Dist. Ct. (no. dist.) 1988, U.S. Dist. Ct. (ea. dist.) 1989 Okla. Asst. U.S. atty. We. Dist. Okla. U.S. Dept. Justice, 1961-69; ptnr. Northcutt, Raley, Clark and Gardner, Ponca City, Okla., 1969-90; U.S. atty. Ea. Dist. Okla. U.S. Dept. Justice, 1990-97; of counsel Northcutt, Clark, Gardner & Hron, Ponca City, 1997—; municipal ct. judge, 2001—. Mayor of Ponca City, Okla., 1980-83. Capt. USNR, 1950-84, ret. Recipient George Washington Honor medal Freedoms Found. at Valley Forge, 1971, Spl. Initiative award U.S. Dept. Justice, 1994, Outstanding Alumni Achievement award Okla. Bapt. U., 1981, Outstanding Citizen award Ponca City, 1984. Fellow Am. Coll. Trial Lawyers; mem. ABA, Am. Bd. Trial Advs., Okla. Bar Assn. (mem. bd. govs.), Kay County Bar Assn. (pres. 1980), Am. Legion, Mason, Reserve Officers Assn., Naval Reserve Assn., VFW. Republican. So. Baptist. Office: 400 E Central Ave Ste 401 Ponca City OK 74601-5428 Address: PO Box 1412 Ponca City OK 74602-1412

RALL, JOSEPH EDWARD, physician; b. Naperville, Ill., Feb. 3, 1920; s. Edward Everett and Nell (Platt) R.; m. Caroline Domm, Sept. 28, 1944 (dec. Apr. 1976); children: Priscilla, Edward Christian. BA, North Central Coll., 1940, D.Sc. (hon.), 1966; MS, Northwestern U., 1944, MD, 1945; PhD, U. Minn., 1952; Dr. honoris causa, Faculty of Medicine, Free U. Brussels, Belgium, 1975; MD (hon.), U. Naples, 1985. Assoc. mem. Sloan Kettering Inst., N.Y.C., 1950-55; chief clin. endocrinology br. Nat. Inst. Arthritis, Metabolism and Digestive Diseases, NIH, 1955-62; dir. intramural research Nat. Inst. Arthritis, Diabetes, Digestive and Kidney Diseases, 1962-83; dep. dir. intramural research NIH, 1983-91; sr. investigator Nat. Inst. Diabetes and Digestive and Kidney Diseases, NIH, 1991; scientist emeritus NIH, 1995. Mem. NRC, 1960-65 Author numerous articles, chpts. in books on thyroid gland nuc. hormone receptors, and radiation. Chmn. Coun. of Scientists for Internat. Human Frontier Sci. Program, 1989-93. Served to capt. M.C. AUS, 1946-48. Recipient Van Meter prize Am. Goiter Assn., 1950, Fleming award, 1959, Outstanding Achievement award Mayo Clinic and U. Minn., 1964; Disting. Service award Am. Thyroid Assn., 1967; Disting. Service award HEW, 1968, Disting. Exec. rank, sr. exec. service, 1980, R.H. Williams Disting. Leadership award in endocrinology, 1983, Disting. Achievement award N.Y. Hosp., Cornell Med. Ctr., 1987; named Outstanding Alumnus N. Central Coll., 1966 Mem. NAS, AAAS, Am. Acad. Arts and Scis., Am. Soc. Clin. Investigation, Am. Phys. Soc., Endocrine Soc., Assn. Am. Physicians, Societe de Biologie (France), Royal Acad. Medicine (Brussels). Home: 3947 Baltimore St Kensington MD 20895-3913 Office: NIH Bldg 10 Rm 6C201 Bethesda MD 20892 E-mail: joseph_rall@nih.gov.

RALL, LLOYD LOUIS, civil engineer; b. Galesville, Wis., Dec. 7, 1916; s. Louis A. and Anna (Kienzle) R.; m. Mary Moller, July 12, 1952; children: Lauris, David, Christopher, Jonathan. BCE, U. Wis., 1940. Commd. 2d lt. U.S. Army, 1940, advanced through grades to col., 1972, engr. forward area strategic air force, 1944-45, ret., 1977, chief construct divsn. Far East forces, 1945-47, engr., mem. mil. survey mission Turkey, 1947, with office joint chiefs of staff, 1947-49, exec. officer R&D office chief engrs., 1949-51, asst. dist. engr. Seattle, 1952-54, dept. engr. Comm. Zone France, 1954-56, commanding officer 540th combat engr. group, 1956-57, prof. mil. sci. and tactics Mo. Sch. Mines and Metallurgy, 1957-60, dep. dir. topography office chief engrs., 1960-64, dir. geographic intelligence and mapping Ft. Belvoir, Va., 1964-66, dep. asst. dir. defense intelligence mapping, 1966-69, asst. dir. defense intelligence agy. mapping and charting, 1969-72; dir. Washington ops. Itek Optical Systems, Washington, 1977-91. Mem. nat. tech. adv. com. Antarctica Mapping, 1960-64. Decorated Legion of Merit with oak leaf cluster, Bronze star. Home: 301 Cloverway Alexandria VA 22314-4817

RALL, LOUIS BAKER, mathematician, educator, mathematician, consultant; b. Kansas City, Mo., Aug. 1, 1930; s. Louis Everett Rall and Jennie Mae Frantz; m. Mary Frances Landram, Mar. 1, 1952; children: Denise, Alyse. BS, U. Puget Sound, 1949; MS, Oreg. State U., 1954, PhD, 1956. Mathematician Shell Devel. Co., Emeryville, Calif., 1956—57; assoc. prof. Lamar U., Beaumont, Tex., 1957—60; prof. Va. Poly. Inst., Blacksburg, 1960—62, Math. Rsch. Ctr., Madison, Wis., 1962—85, assoc. dir., 1965—73; prof. U. Wis., 1969—95, emeritus prof., 1995—. Author: Nonlinear Operator Equations, 1969, Automatic Differentiation, 1981; editor: Error in Digital Computation 1 & 2, 1965. Cpl. U.S. Army, 1951—53, Korea. Recipient Rsch. professorship, Brit. Sci. Rsch. Coun., Oxford, Eng., 1972—73, Danish Natural Sci. Coun., Copenhagen, 1980, Rsch. Lectureship, Japan NSF, Matsuyama, 1988. Mem.: AM. Math. Soc., Soc. for Indsl. and Applied Math., Inst. for Math. and Its Applications.

RALL, WALDO, research management consultant; b. L.A., Mar. 20, 1924; s. Udo and Doris (Keiser) R.; m. Barbara Anthony, Aug. 12, 1950 (dec. 1978); children: Richard A., Victoria A.; m. Andree Fortier Campbell, June 27, 1985. BS, Washington U., St. Louis, 1944; MS, Ind. U., 1948, PhD, 1950. Jr. physicist Manhattan Dist., various cities, 1943-46; instr., asst. prof. Yale U., New HAven, Conn., 1949-56; asst. div. chief U. S. Steel Tech. Ctr., Monroeville, Pa., 1956-61, div. chief physics, 1961-75, mgr. analysis, planning, 1975-80, dir. contract rsch., 1980-85; cons. AISI, USS & DOE, Monroeville, 1985—. Contbr. articles to profl. jours. Chmn. of bd. C. of C., Monroeville, 1983. Mem. AAAS, Am. Phys. Soc., Nat. Contract Mgmt. Assn., Sigma Xi.

RALLI, CONSTANTINE PANDIA, lawyer; b. Bronxville, N.Y., Apr. 6, 1948; s. Pandia C. and Mary (Motter) R.; m. Alison Rhoads, Aug. 11, 1973; children: Pandia C., Christopher A. BA, Middlebury Coll., 1970; JD, Fordham U., 1973; LLM in Taxation, NYU, 1986. Bar: N.Y. 1974, U.S. Ct. Appeals (2nd cir.) 1974, U.S. Dist. Ct. (so. and ea. dists.) N.Y. 1975, U.S. Tax Ct. 1977, Fla. 1985, Conn. 1985, U.S. Dist. Ct. Conn. 1987. Assoc. Davis Polk & Wardwell, N.Y.C., 1973-81; ptnr. Hall, McNicol, Hamilton & Clark, 1981-88, LeBoeuf, Lamb, Greene & MacRae, N.Y.C., 1988—. Sec., bd. dirs. Fairfield-Maxwell Ltd., Campo Tankers SA, N.Y.C., 1987-95. Bd. dirs. Samaritan Counseling Ctr., Rye, N.Y., 1987-90, Rye Free Reading Room, 1990-93, Rye Presbyn. Ch., 1986-89. Mem. Union Club, Am. Yacht Club, Ekwanok Country Club (Manchester, Vt.). Republican. Presbyterian. Home: 11 Rockridge Rd Rye NY 10580-4130 Office: LeBoeuf Lamb Greene & MacRae 125 W 55th St New York NY 10019-5369 also: 411 Pequot Ave Southport CT 06490-1386

RALLO, DOUGLAS, lawyer; b. Orange, N.J., Nov. 22, 1953; s. Vito and Mary (Spiduro) Rallo. BA, Montclair (N.J.) State Coll., 1975; cert., Inst. Internat. and Comparative Law, 1977; JD, John Marshall Law Sch., 1978. Bar: Ill 1979, US Dist Ct (no dist) Ill 1979, US Ct Appeals (7th cir) 1979, US Dist Ct (ea dist) Wis 1995, Wis 1998, US Dist Ct (we dist) Wis 2001. Corp. lawyer Bendix Corp., N.Y.C., 1979-81; assoc. David T. Rallo & Assocs., Ltd., Chgo., 1981-83, Horwitz & Assocs., Ltd., Chgo., 1983-84, Semmelman & Bertucci Ltd., Lake Forest, Ill., 1984-98; pvt. practice Law Offices of Douglas Rallo, P.C., Libertyville, 1998—. Research asst A Functional Analysis of the Criminal Code Reform Act of 1978 for US Congress; panel atty Ill State Appellate Defender's Office, 1980; profiled in Newsweek mag, 1989, Chicago Tribune, 1989; tchr adult legal educ programs Libertyville High Sch, Ill., 1988—90, Mundelein High Sch, Ill., 1989; Notable cases include: Sherrod vs. Berry, 629F. Supp. 159 (1985) and 589F Supp. 433 (1984). Contbr. articles to profl jours. Vpres Lake County chpt NW Ill MADD, 1989—91; comnr Libertyville Youth Comn, 1990—94; bd dirs Civic Ctr Found, Libertyville. Mem.: Vernon Hills C of C, Mundelein C of C, Libertyville C of C, Lake County Bar Asn, State Bar Wis, Ill Trial Lawyers Asn, Ill State Bar Asn (lectr hedonic damages, civil practice procedure, sem expert witnesses 1989), Pi Sigma Alpha. Avocations: water sports, swimming, softball. Office: Law Offices Douglas Rallo P C 611 S Milwaukee Ave Libertyville IL 60048-3256

RALLO, HARRY, architect, artist; b. N.Y.C., Sept. 28, 1951; s. Angelo and Rose Rallo; m. Bridgette Louise Bruno, May 5, 1979; 1 child, Matthew Henry. Student, CUNY, 1968-69; BS in Architecture, CCNY, 1973, BArch, 1977; student, Palm Beach Armory Art Ctr., 1994-97; studied under Douglas Ferrin, West Palm Beach, Fla., 1997-98. Registered arch., N.Y., Conn., Fla. Project engr. Turner Constrn. Co., N.Y.C., 1973-87; prin. Harry Rallo, Arch., Deerfield Beach, Fla., 1987—. Editl. cartoonist Observer, North Broward, weekly newspaper, Deerfield Beach, 1993—. One-man shows include Cultural Arts Com., Lighthouse Point, Fla., 1995, Cultural Com., Deerfield Beach, 1995, Meml. Hosp., Hallandale, Fla., 1997; commns. include Wellington Forum, Fla., 1995, Ft. Lauderdale St. Patrick's Day Com., 1995, Roman Cath. Archdiocese, Miami, Fla., 1996, Fla. Urban Forestry Coun., 1995; exhbn. include (mural) Historic Stranahan House, Ft. Lauderdale, 2001; contbr. articles to various publs. Recipient 4th pl., Palm Beach Soc. Four Arts. Home and Office: PO Box 587 47 Greenwoods Rd E Norfolk CT 06058-1321 E-mail: artist@hrallo.com.

RALLO, JAMES GILBERT, fleet management company executive; b. Balt., Mar. 1, 1942; s. James Vincent and Thelma Mary (Hannahs) R.; m. Frances Elaine Petro, June 13, 1965; children: James Michael, Robert Francis. BS, U. Md., 1965; postgrad., George Washington U., 1967—. Mktg. trainee Chessie Sys., Balt., 1965-66; market analyst Bendix Corp., 1966-68, contract adminstr. N.Y.C., 1968-70; account exec. Peterson, Howell & Heather, Inc. (name changed to PHH Arval) PHH Vehicle Mgmt. Svcs., Hunt Valley, Md., 1970-75; regional mgr. Peterson, Howell & Heather, Inc., 1975-80, v.p. sales, 1980-83, v.p. sales and client rels., 1983-87, sr. v.p. sales and client rels., 1987-91, sr. v.p. client and industry rels., 1991-94, v.p. industry rels., 1994—. Bd. dirs., mem. fin. com. Towson YMCA, Md., 1981-93, mem. fundraising com., mem. budget com.; coach Cockeysville-Springlake Recreation Coun., 1973-82; advisor Jr. Achievement, 1975-76; fund solicitor United Way, 1983-84; v.p. NAFA Found., 1995—, chmn. affiliates com., 1995-97. Mem.: Am. Automotive Leasing Assn., Automotive Fleet and Leasing Assn. (conf. com. 1993—2001, v.p. 1999—2000, exec. v.p. 2000—01, pres. 2001—, nat. level affiliate trustee 2001—, dir. lessors and bd. mem., ednl. com.), Nat. Assn. Fleet Adminstrs. (bd. dirs. 1976—81, bd. govs. 1993—, chmn. affiliates com. 1995—97, co-chair edn. com. 1999—2001, affiliate chmn. intercounty chpt. 1976—80, affiliate trustee 2001—, Affiliate and Editl. Com. nat. level trustee, program com., Hon. award for disting. svc. 1997), Optimists Club (v.p. Springdale-Cockeysville 1982—84, chmn. fundraising com.). Avocations: skiing, coaching youth sports, antique/classic cars, reading, golf. Office: PHH Arval 307 International Cir Cockeysville Hunt Valley MD 21030-1334 E-mail: jim.rallo@phh.com.

RALLO, ROBERT FRANCIS, engineering executive; b. New Brunswick, N.J., Dec. 1, 1968; s. James G. and Frances (Petro) R. B Elec. Engring., Villanova (Pa.) U., 1990. Engring. mgr. Kyocera Solar, Inc., Scottsdale, Ariz., 1990—.

RALPH, DAVID CLINTON, communications educator; b. Muskogee, Okla., Jan. 12, 1922; s. Earl Clinton and Rea Jane (Potter) R.; m. Kathryn Juanita Wicklund, Nov. 29, 1947; children: David Randall, Steven Wicklund. AA, Muskogee Jr. Coll., 1941; BS in Theatre, Northwestern U., 1947, MA in Theatre, 1948, PhD in Speech, 1953. Lectr. Ind. U., Hammond, 1947-48; instr. speech U. Mo., Columbia, 1948-53; tchr. debate-forensics summer program for high sch. students Northwestern U., Evanston, Ill., 1949-51; asst. prof. speech Mich. State U., East Lansing, 1953-57, assoc. prof., 1957-64, prof. speech and theatre, 1964-68, prof. communication, 1968-94, prof. emeritus, 1994—, dir. comm. undergrad. program, 1968-88. Cons. on pub. speaking, 1948—. Co-author: Group Discussion, 1954, 2d edit., 1956, Principles of Speaking, 1962, 3d edit., 1975; contbr. articles to profl. jours., chpts. to books. Coach Jr. League Boys' Baseball, Lansing, Mich., 1958-74; mem. civilian aux. to Lansing Fire Dept., 1987—. Lt. USNR, 1942-46, PTO, ETO. Named Hon. State Farmer, Future Farmers Am., 1965; recipient Community Svc. award Mich. State U. Sr. Class Coun., 1979, Outstanding Faculty award, 1987, 91; Teaching Excellence award State of Mich., 1990. Mem. AAUP, Nat. Communication Assn., Cen. States Communication Assn., Golden Key (hon., faculty advisor), Omicron Delta Kappa. Democrat. Methodist. Avocations: model trains and fire engines. Office: Mich State U Dept Communication East Lansing MI 48824

RALSTON, ANTHONY, computer scientist, mathematician, educator; b. N.Y.C., Dec. 24, 1930; s. Alfred Joseph and Ruth (Bien) R.; m. Jayne Madeleine Rosenthal, Feb. 14, 1958; children: Jonathan, Geoffrey, Steven, Elizabeth. BS, MIT, 1952, PhD, 1956. Mem. tech. staff Bell Tel. Labs., 1956-59; lectr. U. Leeds, 1959-60; mgr. tech. computing Am. Cyanamid Co., 1960-61; assoc. prof. math. Stevens Inst. Tech., 1961-64, prof., 1964-65; dir. computer services SUNY, Buffalo, 1965-70, prof., 1965-95, chmn. dept. computer sci., 1967-80, prof. emeritus, 1995—. Bd. examiners Grad. Record Exam in Computer Sci., 1976-82; mem. computer sci. and tech. bd. NRC, 1976-79, math. sci. edn. bd., 1985-89; acad. visitor Imperial Coll., London, 1995—. Author: A First Course in Numerical Analysis, 1965, 2d edit., 1978, Introduction to Programming and Computer Science, 1971, Discrete Algorithmic Mathematics, 1991, 3d edit., 2003, Algorithms, 1997; editor: Ency. of Computer Science, 1976, 2d edit., 1982, 3d edit., 1992, 4th edit., 2000, ABACUS, 1983-88; co-editor: Mathematical Methods for Digital Computers, Vol. 1, 1960, Vol. 2, 1967, Vol. 3, 1977, The Influence of Computers and Informatics in Mathematics and Its Teaching, 1993. 2d lt. U.S. Army, 1957. Fellow AAAS, Royal Soc. of Arts, Assn. Computing Machinery (pres. 1972-74, mem. coun. 1968-76, Disting. Svc. award 1982); mem. Math. Assn.

Am. (bd. govs. 1984-87), Am. Fedn. Info. Processing Soc. (pres. 1975-76), Com. Concerned Scientists (bd. dirs.). Home: Flat 4 58 Prince Consort Rd London SW7 2BA England E-mail: ar9@doc.ic.ac.uk.

RALSTON, CHARLES PHILIP, educator; b. Seattle, July 2, 1951; s. Charles and Angeline Elizabeth Ralston; m. Camille Taylor, Dec. 20, 1980; children: Emily, Charles. BA, Whitman Coll., 1973; cert. tchr., U. Wash., 1978. Tchr. Holy Family Sch., Seattle, 1975-78, St. Mary Magdalen, Everett, Wash., 1978-2000, St. Therese Sch., Seattle, 2000—. Named Wash. and regional Tchr. of Yr., DAR, 1999. Mem. Nat. Trust for Hist. Preservation, Hist. Seattle Preservation, Mus. History and Industry. Roman Catholic. Avocations: house restoration, antique car restoration. Home: 1140 38th Ave Seattle WA 98122-5202 Office: St Therese Sch 900 35th Ave Seattle WA 98122

RALSTON, HENRY JAMES, III, neurobiologist, anatomist, educator; b. Berkeley, Calif., Mar. 12, 1935; s. Henry James and Sue Harris (Mahnke) R.; m. Diane Cornelia Daly, Oct. 29, 1960; children: Rachel Anne, Amy Sue. BA, U. Calif., Berkeley, 1956, MD, 1959. Intern Mt. Sinai Hosp., N.Y.C., 1959-60; resident in medicine U. Calif., San Francisco, 1960-61, prof., 1973—, chmn. dept. anatomy, 1973-97, chmn. acad. senate, 1986-88; spl. postdoctoral fellow U. Coll., London, 1963-65, lectr., 1981; asst. prof. anatomy Stanford (Calif.) U., 1965-69; assoc. prof. U. Wis., Madison, 1969-73; prof. anatomy U. Calif., San Francisco, 1973—, assoc. dean admissions, 2001—. Cons. NIH; mem. com. for future of anat. scis., Macy Found., 1977-80; vis. prof. French Med. Rsch. Inst.-INSERM, Paris, 1981-82; chair step I U.S. med. lic. examination com. Nat. Bd. Med. Examiners, 1992-96. With M.C. U.S. Army, 1961-63. Recipient Henry J. Kaiser award for excellence in tchg., 1978, Jacob Javits Neurosci. Investigator award NIH, 1988-95; USPHS grant, 1966—. Mem. AAAS, Soc. Neurosci., Soc. Study Pain, Am. Pain Soc., Am. Assn. Anatomists (pres. 1987-88, chmn. publs. com. 1989-91, Henry Gray award 1997), Am. Assn. Med. Colls. (adv. panel on biomed. rsch. 1996-99), Anat. Assn. Gt. Britain, Alpha Omega Alpha. Achievements include research in field of organization of mammalian nervous system studied by electron microscopy, mechanisms subserving pain in animals and humans. Office: U Calif Dept Anatomy PO Box 0452 San Francisco CA 94143-0452 E-mail: hjr@phy.ucsf.edu.

RALSTON, J. FRED, JR. internist; b. Fayetteville, Tenn., Apr. 25, 1954; s. Joseph Frederick Ralston and Clara Robertson Ralston-Wolfhard; m. Farris Lynch, Feb. 17, 1990; children: James David, Willis Farris. BA in Polit. Sci., Yale U., New Haven, Conn., 1976; MD, U. Tenn., Memphis, 1980. Diplomate Am. Bd. Internal Medicine. Resident in internal medicine Bapt. Meml. Hosp., Memphis, 1980-83; pvt. practice internal medicine Fayetteville, Tenn., 1983—; dir. CCU Lincoln Regional Hosp., 1984—. Active Lincoln County unit Am. Cancer Soc., Fayetteville, 1984-97, bd. dirs., pres., 1988-89; deacon, elder First Presbyn. Ch., Fayetteville, 1988-99; trustee Lincoln Regional Hosp., Fayetteville, 1989-2001. Fellow ACP; mem. AMA (Tenn. del., chair young physicians sect. 1991-92), Tenn. Med. Assn. (rural caucus 1984—, chair 1991-92, 1997-98, del. 1985—, comm. com. 1988-99, co-chair 1992-95, chair 1995-99, judicial coun. 1988-92, chair 1990-92, legis. com. 1992—, bd. trustees 1998-2001, chmn. bd. trustees 2000-01), Am. Soc. Internal Medicine (gov. Tenn. chpt. 2001—, publs. com. 2001-, vice chair, 2002-). Home: 51 Timberlake Dr Fayetteville TN 37334 Office: Fayetteville Med Assocs PC 207 S Elk Ave Fayetteville TN 37334 Office Fax: (931) 438-0069. E-mail: ralston@fayelectric.com.

RALSTON, JOANNE SMOOT, public relations counseling firm executive; b. Phoenix, May 13, 1939; d. A. Glen and Virginia (Lee) Smoot; m. W. Hamilton Weigelt, Aug. 15, 1991. BA in Journalism, Ariz. State U., 1960. Reporter The Ariz. Rep., Phoenix, 1960-62; co-owner, pub. rels. dir. The Patton Agy., 1962-71; founder, pres., owner Joanne Ralston & Assocs., Inc., 1971-87, 92—. Pres. Nelson Ralston Robb Comm., Phoenix, 1987—91, Joanne Ralston & Assocs., Inc., Scottsdale, 1991—, Kapaau, Hawaii, 2000—. Contbr. articles to profl. jours. Bd. dirs. Ariz. Parklands Found,. 1984-86, Gov.'s Coun. on Health, Phys. Fitness and Sports, 1984-86; mem. task force Water and Natural Resources Coun., Phoenix, 1984-86; mem. Ariz. Rep. Caucus, 1984—, others. Recipient Lulu awards (36) L.A. Advt. Women, 1964—, Gold Quill (2) Internat. Assn. Bus. Communicators, Excellence awards Fin. World mag., 1982-93, others; named to Walter Cronkite Sch. Journalism Hall of Fame, Coll. Pub. Programs Ariz. State U., 1987; named one of 25 Most Influential Arizonians, Phoenix Mag., 1991. Mem. Pub. Rels. Soc. Am. (counselor sect.), Internat. Assn. Bus. Communicators, Phoenix Press Club (pres. bd.), Investor Rels. Inst., Phoenix Met. C. of C. (bd. dirs. 1977-84, 85-91). Republican. Avocations: horses, skiing. Address: PO Box 808 Kapaau HI 96755-0808

RALSTON, JOSEPH W. career officer; b. Hopkinsville, Ky., Nov. 4, 1943; m. Diane Dougherty; children: Christopher, Paige, David, Sarah. Grad., Miami (Ohio) U., 1965; M in Pers. Mgmt., Ctrl. Mich. U.; student, Army Command and Gen. Staff Coll., Nat. War Coll. at Fort McNair, Harvard U. Commd. 2d lt. res. officer tng. corps. program USAF, 1965, advanced through grades to gen., 1995; comdr. in chief U.S., European Command, NATO Supreme Allied Force. Achievements include operational command at squadron, wing, numbered air force and major command, as well as a variety of influential staff and management positions including two terms as vice chairman of the Joint Chiefs of Staff. Office: Supreme Allied Comdr Europe CMR Box 7100 APO AE 09705

RALSTON, LENORE DALE, academic policy and program analyst; b. Oakland, Calif., Feb. 21, 1949; d. Leonard Earnest and Emily Allison (Hudnut) R. BA in Anthropology, U. Calif., Berkeley, 1971, MPH in Behavioral Sci., 1981; MA in Anthropology, Bryn Mawr Coll., 1973, PhD in Anthropology, 1980. Asst. rschr. anthropology inst. internat. studies U. Calif., Berkeley, 1979-82, rsch. assoc. Latin Am. Study Ctr., 1982-83, acad. asst. to dean Sch. of Optometry, 1990-95, prin. policy analyst, chancellor's office, 1995—; assoc. scientist, rsch. adminstr. Med. Rsch. Inst., San Francisco, 1982-85; cons. health sci. Berkeley, 1986-90. Mem. fin. bd. Med. Rsch. Inst., 1983-84; speaker in field. Co-author: Voluntary Effects in Decentralized Management, 1983; contbr. articles to profl. jours. Commr. Cmty. Health Adv. Com., Berkeley, 1988-90; vice chair, commr. Cmty. Health Commn., Berkeley, 1990-93; mem. bd. safety com. Miles, Inc., Berkeley, 1992-94. Grantee Nat. Rsch. Svc. Award, WHO, NIMH, NSF. Fellow Applied Anthropology Assn.; mem. APHA, Am. Anthropology Assn., Sigma Xi. Home: 1232 Carlotta Ave Berkeley CA 94707-2707 E-mail: ralston@uclink4.berkeley.edu.

RALSTON, PAULA JANE, nurse; b. Cedar Rapids, Iowa, Feb. 2, 1960; d. Paul Raymond and Martha Jane (Salato) R. BSN, Morningside Coll., Sioux City, Iowa, 1982; MA in Human Resource Devel., Webster U., 1994. Cert. med.-surg. nurse; cert. EMT, CPR instr. Commd. 2d lt. USAF, 1984, advanced through grades to maj., 1995; staff nurse Cass County Meml. Hosp., Atlantic, Iowa, 1982-84; staff nurse male med. USAF, Scott AFB, Ill., 1984-85, staff nurse female surg., 1985-86, staff nurse 1st Aeromed. Staging Flight, 1986-88, flight nurse, flight nurse instr, quality improvement coord. 57AES/375AES 57AES/375AES, 1991-95, officer in charge nursing staff devel. 10TFW Clinic RAF, Alconbury, 1988-90, charge nurse acute care clinic and 24 hour ambulance svc. Alconbury, 1988-90, ob-gyn. asst. charge nurse 50 TFW Hosp. Hahn AB, Fed. Republic Germany, 1990-91, nurse mgr. multi-svc. unit, officer in charge hosp. dietary dept, Misawa AB, Japan, 1995-96, exercise evaluation team chief Japan, 1995-97, chief, group edn. and tng., 1996-97, comdr. group edn. and tng. human resource devel., diagnostics and therapeutics flight comdr., med. readiness flight comdr. N.D., 1997-2000; dep. comdr. Med. Support Squadron, 1997-2000; diagnostics & therapeutics flight comdr. USAF, 1999-2000; clinical nurse, 2001—. Mem. coord Air Tatto USAF Air Show, RAF Alconbury, 1990; air festival coord. Misawa AFB, Japan, 1995-96; mem. hyperbaric med. team USAF, 1988-90, 10 T.F.W. Hosp. Desert Storm USAF, Incirlik, Turkey, 1991; instr. ARC, Preparation for Parenthood, Health Baby, Health Pregnancy, Cmty. First Aid & Safety; affil. faculty advanced cardiac life support; instr. pediat. advanced life suport, basic life support instr. trainer/affiliate faculty. USAF rep. for hosp. Fete Hinchingbrooke Hosp., Huntington, England, 1988—90; installation voting officer Grand Forks AFB Installation, 1998—; mem. Bury Ch. Eng. Band, 1988—90, Belleville (Ill.) Philharm. Orch., 1984—88, 1991—95; bd. govs. Nebr.-Iowa Circle K Dist., 1981—82, sec.-treas., 1980—81; 35th med. group change of command coord. USAF, 1995. Decorated Achievement medal, 1995, Commendation medal with two oak leaf clusters, Meritorious Svc. medal, Joint Svc. medal, 1990-1994, 15th Air Force Air Crew Excellence award, 1994; named Co. Grade Nurse of Yr., USAF in Europe, 1989. Mem. AACN, Nat. Nursing Staff Devel. Orgn., Assn. Women's Health, Obstetrics & Neonatal Nurses, Morningside Coll. Circle K Club (v.p. (1979-80), Sigma Theta Tau. Methodist. Avocations: violin, music, bike riding, volleyball, arts and crafts. Home: 8952 Audubon Ct Longmont CO 80503-8668 E-mail: pjralston@hotmail.com.

RALSTON, STEVEN PHILIP, portfolio manager, financial analyst; b. Trenton, N.J., Mar. 29, 1954; s. George and Edith Martha Ralston; m. Miriam Mercedes Font, July 14, 1979. BS, MIT, 1975. CFA. Account exec. Merrill, Lynch, Pierce, Fenner & Smith, Balt., 1979-80; security analyst Fidelity and Deposit Co. of Md., 1980-83; security analyst, v.p. First Nat. Bank of Md., 1983-95; dir. rsch. 1st Nat. Bank of Md., 1990-95; portfolio mgr., analyst, v.p. Gen. Accident, Phila., 1995-98; equity investment mgr., v.p. BlackRock, 1998—. Instr. Johns Hopkins U., Balt., 1985-87. Mem. Howard County Hist. Soc., Ellicott City, Md., 1969-92; mem. Lake Falls Improvement Assn., 1984-95, treas., 1987, pres., 1988; mem. Northwoods Assn., 1995—, bd. dirs. 1996—; mem. Springfield Twp. Hist. Soc., 1997—. Mem. Inst. Chartered Fin. Analysts, Balt. Security Analysts Soc. (bd. dirs., v.p. 1984-89), Fin. Analysts Phila., Fin. Analysts Fedn., Assn. for Investment Mgmt. and Rsch., Consumer Analysts Group N.Y. Avocation: auctions. Home: 515 Edann Rd Glenside PA 19038-1404 Office: BlackRock 100 Bellevue Pkwy Wilmington DE 19809 E-mail: spr515@aol.com.

RAM, CHITTA VENKATA, physician; b. Machilipatnam, India, Oct. 24, 1948; s. Chitta M. Row and Chitta (Cheruvu) Sarojini; m. Ashalata Ram, Feb. 17, 1979; children: Gita, Radha. B.Sci, Marathwada U., Aurangabad, India, 1966; MD, Osmania U., Hyderabad, India, 1972. Diplomate Am. Bd. Internal Medicine. Resident in internal medicine Brown U., R.I. Hosp., Providence, 1974-76; fellow in hypertension Hosp. U. Pa., Phila., 1976-77; faculty assoc. U. Tex. Southwestern Med. Ctr., Dallas, 1977-78, asst. prof., 1978-83, assoc. prof., 1983-89, prof. internal medicine, 1989—. Dir. Tex. Blood Pressure Inst., Dallas; dir. rsch. and edn. Dallas Nephrology Assocs.; dir. hypertension clinic Parkland Meml. Hosp., Dallas, hypertension unit St. Paul Med. Ctr., Dallas, dir. continuing med. edn. dept., 1996-98, chmn. instnl. rev. com., 1996-98, pres. med. staff, 1997-98; dir. Tex. Blood Pressure Inst., Dallas. Contbr. numerous articles to profl. jours. and chpts. to textbooks; editl. cons., reviewer numerous nat. and internat. jours. and pubs. Pres. Tex. IndoAm. Physician Soc., Dallas, 1988; trustee Dallas/Ft. Worth Hindu Temple Soc., Dallas, 1988. Named Outstanding Tchr. St. Paul Med. Ctr., 1982; recipient Mother of India award, 1992. Master ACP; fellow Am. Coll. Cardiology, Am. Coll. Chest Physicians (regent), Am. Coll. Clin. Pharmacology; mem. Am. Assn. Physicians from India (pres.-elect 1994-95, pres. 1995-96), Tex. Indo-Am. Physicians Soc.

RAMACHANDRAN, RAVI PRAKASH, engineering educator; b. Bangalore, India, July 12, 1963; s. Venkat and Kamala Ramachandran; m. Roopashri Seshadri; 1 child Ujwal Prithvi. B in Engring., Concordia U., Montreal, Can., 1984; M in Engring., McGill U., Montreal, 1986; PhD, McGill U., 1990. Postdoctoral fellow AT&T Bell Labs., Murray Hill, NJ, 1990—93; rsch. asst. prof. Rutgers U., Piscataway, 1993—97; assoc. prof. Rowan U., Glassboro, 1997—. Cons. Speakez Inc., Piscataway, 1997, Avenir Inc., Edison, NJ, 2000—01. Grantee, NSF, 1998—2000, 1999—2001, 2001—, Calif. Ptnrs. for Advanced Transit and Hwys., 2000—01. Office: Rowan U 201 Mullica Hill Rd Glassboro NJ 08028 Office Fax: 856-256-5241. Business E-Mail: ravi@rowan.edu.

RAMACHANDRAN, TARAKAD SUBRAMANIAM, neurologist, physician; b. Erode, Madras, India, Apr. 11, 1948; came to U.S., 1976; s. Eswaran and Aylam samiyer (Alamelu) S.; m. Melanie Dhandra, Nov. 9, 1980; children: Manoj, Arun, Devan. MBBS, Stanley Med. Coll., Madras, 1971, MD; MBA, SUNY, Binghamton. Diplomate Am. Bd. Psychiatry and Neurology, Am. Bd. Electroencephalography, Am. Bd. Electrodiagnostic Medicine. Prof. neurology, clin. prof. neurosurgery Health Sci. Ctr., Syracuse, N.Y.; chief neurology Crouse Hosp.; med. dir. Ctr. for Performing Arts Medicine. Maj. USAR, 1989-97. Fellow ACP, Am. Coll. Internat. Physicians, Am. Acad. Neurology, Royal Coll. Physicians (Can.); mem. Royal Coll. Physicians (Eng.), Royal Coll. Surgeons (Eng.), Royal Coll. Physicians (Edinburgh), Royal Coll. Physicians (Glasgow), Am. Coll. Forensic Medicine, Am. Coll. Pain Medicine, Am. Coll. Managed Care Medicine, Onondage Med. Soc. Home: 5210 Harvest Hill Dr Jamesville NY 13078-9308 Office: 1000 E Genesee St Ste 201 Syracuse NY 13210-1853

RAMACHANDRAN, VENKATANARAYANA DEEKSHIT, electrical engineering educator; b. Mysore, India, May 3, 1934; s. K.C. Venkatanarayana Deekshit and Subbamma Deekshit R.; m. Kamala Visweswaraiya, June 12, 1960; 1 child, Ravi P. BS, U. Mysore, 1953; B in Engring., Indian Inst. Sci., Bangalore, 1956, M in Electronics, 1958, PhD, 1965. Registered profl. engr. Sr. research asst. Indian Inst. Sci., 1958-59, lectr., 1959-66; asst. prof. N.S. Tech. Coll., Halifax, Can., 1966-69; prof. elec. engring. Concordia U. (formerly Sir George Williams Univ.), Can., 1971—; acting chmn. dept. elec. and computer engring. Montreal, various times; grad. program dir. dept., 1969-84. Adj. prof. U. Windsor, Ont., Can., 1983—, Ecole Tech. Superieure U. Quebec, Montreal, 1989—; mem. program com. Internat. Symposium on Operator Theory of Networks and Systems, 1975; vice chmn. Internat. Symposium on Circuits and Systems IEEE, Montreal, 1984, mem. tech. program com., 1987; internat. coordinator Internat. Conf. on Computers, Systems and Signal Processing, Indian Inst. Sci., 1984. Author papers in profl. jours., over 125 papers presented to confs., others. Named to Order of Engrs. of Que.; recipient Merit award Concordia Council on Student Life, 1981-82, Outstanding Contbn. award Engring. and Computer Sci. Assn., Concordia U., 1996. Fellow Inst. Electronics and Telecomms. India (edit. bd. jour. 1986), Inst. Engrs. India, Inst. Elec. Engrs. Eng., Engring. Inst. Can. (sec. Montreal chpt. 1979-80, centennial bd. 1983-84), IEEE; mem. Circuits and Systems chpt. IEEE (chmn. Montreal sect. 1978-84), Can. Soc. Elec. Engrs. (editor jour. 1983-85, editor bull. 1981-83), Am. Soc. Engring. Edn. (chmn. awards com. St. Lawrence chpt. 1987-88, Western Elec. Fund award 1983, Myril B. Reed Best Rsch. Paper award 1984, Outstanding Svc. 1993) Office: Concordia U Faculty of Engring 1455 de Maisonneuve Blvd W Montreal QC Canada H3G 1M8

RAMADAN, NABIH M. pharmaceutical company official, educator; b. Beirut, Lebanon, Feb. 3, 1960; came to U.S., 1985; s. Manih Fawzi Ramadan and Nadia Shaar; m. Cynthia Ann Ramadan, Mar. 26, 1988. BS in Biology and Chemistry, Am. U. of Beirut, Lebanon, 1980, MD, 1985. Resident in neurology U. Cin., Ohio, 1985-88; fellow in cerebrovascular disease Henry Ford Hosp., Detroit, 1988-90, dir. Ambulatory Headache Clinic, 1990-96, dir. Cerebrovascular Diseases Lab., 1990-96; dir. Cin. Headache Ctr., 1996-99; assoc. prof. neurology U. Cin., 1996-99; med. dir. Eli Lilly & Co., Indpls., 1999, rsch. advisor, 1999—. Adj. prof. neurology Ind. U. Med. Ctr., Indpls. Office: Eli Lilly & Co Lilly Corp Ctr Indianapolis IN 46285-0001

RAMAGE, MARTIS DONALD, JR. banker; b. Tupelo, Miss., Oct. 6, 1957; s. Martis Donald and Helen Frances (Estes) R. AA, Itawamba Jr. Coll., Fulton, Miss., 1978; BBA in Banking and Fin., U. Miss., 1980; grad., Mid South Sch. of Banking, 1989. Mgmt. trainee Peoples Bank & Trust Co., Tupelo, 1981-82, asst. cashier, 1983-89, asst. v.p., 1989-90, v.p., 1990-93, 1st v.p., 1993-2000, sr. v.p., 2000—02, divsn. v.p., 2002—. Sec. Peoples Holding Co., 1993-96, v.p., 1996—. Author: Our Ramage Family, 1986, Mississippi Society SAR 1909-1993, Tupelo, Mississippi, Tornado 1936, 1997; co-editor: The Peoples Bank & Trust Co-In Partnership with the Community, 1989; editor N.E. Miss. Hist. Geneal. Soc. Quar. Sec., treas. United Way of Greater Lee County, Tupelo, 1988-89, Leadership Lee; pres. Friends of Lee County Libr., 1995-97; bd. dirs. Brice's Battlefield Commn., Inc., 1995—, Tupelo Cmty. Concert, 1998—; trustee Miss. Dept. Archives and History, 1996—, Lee/Itawamba County Libr., 1998—; chmn. Christmas Festival Com., Tupelo, 1990-91; mem. Miss. rev. bd. Nat. Register Hist. Places, 1999—. Mem. SAR (trustee 1992-94, pres. Miss. 1991-92, Silver Good Citizenship medal 1990, sr. v.p. 1994—), SCV, Mil. Order of Stars and Bars, Am. Inst. Banking (pres. Tupelo chpt. 1986-87), Ole Miss. Alumni Assn. (bd. dirs. 1991-94), Bank Adm. Inst. (v.p. North Miss. chpt. 1990-94, pres. 1994-95), Tupelo Artist Guild (bd. dirs. 1993-98, sec. 1996-98), Miss. Hist. Soc. (bd. dirs. 1995-97), Itawamba Jr. Coll. Alumni Assn. (pres. 1982-83), Civitan Club, Masons. Home: 4218 Ridgemont Dr Belden MS 38826-9785 Office: Peoples Bank & Trust Co 209 Troy St Tupelo MS 38804-4827 Office Fax: 662-680-1338. E-mail: martyr@tsixroads.com.

RAMAKRISHNAN, VENKATASWAMY, civil engineer, educator; b. Coimbatore, India, Feb. 27, 1929; came to U.S., 1969, naturalized, 1981; s. Venkataswamy and Kondammal (Krishnaswamy) R.; m. Vijayalakshmi Unnava, Nov. 7, 1962; children: Aravind, Anand. B.Engring., U. Madras, 1952, D.S.S., 1953; D.I.C. in Hydropower and Concrete Tech, Imperial Coll., London, 1957; PhD, Univ. Coll., U. London, 1960. From lectr. to prof. civil engring., head dept. P.S.G. Coll. Tech., U. Madras, 1952-69; vis. prof. S.D. Sch. Mines and Tech., Rapid City, 1969-70, prof. civil engring., 1970—, dir. concrete tech. research, 1970-71, head grad. div. structural mechanic and concrete tech., 1971—, program coordinator materials engring. and sci. Ph.D. program, 1985-86, disting. prof., 1996—. Emeritus mem. TRB. Author: Ultimate Strength Design for Structural Concrete, 1969; also over 200 articles. Recipient Outstanding Prof. award S.D. Sch. Mines and Tech., 1980, 1st Rsch. award, 1994; Colombo Plan fellow, 1955-60. Mem. Internat. Assn. Bridge and Structural Engring., ASCE (vice chmn. constrn. div. publs. com. 1974), Am. Concrete Inst. (chmn. subcom. gen. considerations for founds., chmn. com. 214 on evaluation of strength test results, sec.-treas. Dakota chpt. 1974-79, v.p. 1980, pres. 1981, Robert Philio Rsch. Excellence award), Instn. Hwy. Engrs., Transp. Rsch. Bd. (chmn. com. on admixtures and curing, chmn. com. on mech. properties concrete), Am. Soc. Engring. Edn., NSPE, Internat. Coun. Gap-Graded Concrete Rsch. and Application, Sigma Xi. Address: 1809 Sheridan Lake Rd Rapid City SD 57702-4219 E-mail: vramakri@silver.sdsmt.edu. *To me, success is a coin with hard work on one side and perseverance with devotion on the other. No matter what—head or tails—the message is the same: keep on working. Goals in my life were pursuit of truth and beauty. The structures I have created, and my writings based on research have given me greater satisfaction than any wealth, position, or power.*

RAMALEY, JUDITH AITKEN, former university president, endocrinologist; b. Vincennes, Ind., Jan. 11, 1941; d. Robert Henry and Mary Krebs (McCullough) Aitken; m. Robert Folk Ramaley, Mar. 1966 (div. 1976); children: Alan Aitken, Andrew Folk. BA, Swarthmore Coll., 1963; PhD, UCLA, 1966; postgrad., Ind. U., 1967-69. Rsch. assoc., lectr. Ind. U., Bloomington, 1967-68, asst. prof. dept. anatomy and physiology, 1969-72; asst. prof. dept. physiology and biophysics U. Nebr. Med. Ctr., Omaha, 1972-74, assoc. prof., 1974-78, prof., 1978-82, assoc. dean for rsch. and devel., 1979-81; asst. v.p. for acad. affairs U. Nebr., Lincoln, 1980-82; prof. biol. scis. SUNY, Albany, N.Y., 1982-87, v.p. for acad. affairs, 1982-85, acting pres., 1984, exec. v.p. for acad. affairs, 1985-87; exec. vice chancellor U. Kans., Lawrence, 1987-90; pres. Portland (Oreg.) State U., 1990-97, U. Vt., Burlington, 1997—2001; asst. dir. edn. and human resources NSF, 2001—. Endocrinology study sect. NIH, 1981-84; cons.-evaluator North Cen. Accreditation, 1978-82, 89-90; regulatory panel NSF, 1979-82, bioadv. com., 1994-98; mem. Ill. Commn. Scholars, 1980-90; Vt. tech. coun. Gov.'s Bus. Adv. Coun., Vt. Bus. Roundtable, Com. on Econ. Devel., 1997-2001; presdl. prof. biomed. scis. Margaret Chase Smith Ctr. for Pub. Policy. Co-author: Progesterone Function: Molecular and Biochemical Aspects, 1972; Essentials of Histology, 8th edit., 1979; editor: Covert Discrimination, Women in the Sciences, 1978; contbr. articles to profl. jours. Bd. dirs. Family Svc. of Omaha, 1979-82, Albany Symphony Orch., 1984-87, mem. exec. com., 1986-87, 2d v.p., exec. com., 1986-87, Capital Repertory Co., 1986-89, Assn. Portland Progress, 1990-97, City Club of Portland, 1991-92, Metro Family Svcs., 1993-97, Campbell Inst. for Children, Portland Met. Sports Authority, 1994; vice-chair Ore. Campus Compact, exec. com. 1996-97, nat. adv. coun. Sch.-Work Opportunities, 1996—; bd. dirs. NCAA Pres. Commn., 1991, chair divsn. II subcom., 1994, joint policy bd., 1994; chmn. bd. dirs. Albany Water Fin. Authority, 1987; exec. com. United Way Douglas County, 1989-90; adv. bd. Emily Taylor Women's Resource Ctr., U. Kans., 1988-90; mem. Portland Opera Bd., 1991-92, Portland Leaders Roundtable, 1991-97; bd. devel. com. United Way of Columbia-Willamette, 1991-95; active Ore. Women's Forum, 1991-97, Portland Met. Sports Authority, Greater Burlington Industry Corp., 1998—; progress bd. Portland-Multnomah County, 1993-97. NSF grantee, 1969-83; fellow Margaret Chase Smith Ctr. for Pub. Policy. Fellow AAAS; mem. Nat. Assn. State Univs. and Land Grant Colls. (exec. com., mem. senate 1986-88, vice-chair commn. urban agenda 1992-94, chair 1995-97), Assn. Am. Colls. and Univs. (bd. dirs. 1995-98), ACE Commn. Govt. Rels., Kellogg Commn. on Future of State and Land-Grant Univs., Assn. Governing Bds. (Pres.'s Coun. 1998-2000), Endocrine Soc. (chmn. edn. com. 1980-85), Soc. Study Reprodn. (treas. 1983-85), Soc. for Neurosci., Am. Physiol. Soc., Am. Assn. Schs. and Colls., Am. Coun. on Edn. (chmn. commn. on women in higher edn. 1987-88, commn. on govt. rels., bd. dirs. 1999-2001), Assn. Portland Progress (bd. dirs.), Portland C. of C. (bd. dirs. 1995), Western Assn. of Schs. and Colls. (commr. 1994-97). Office: Edn and Human Resources Directorate Nat Sci Found 4201 Wilson Blvd Arlington VA 22230

RAMALINGAM, GANESAN, computer scientist; b. Srivilliputhur, India, Feb. 6, 1966; came to the U.S., 1987; s. R. and Kalavathi Ganesan; m. Rajalakshmi Ramalingam, Nov. 15, 1992; children: Ragini, Ramya. MS in Computer Sci., U. Wis., 1989, MA in Math., 1991, PhD in Computer Sci., 1993. Tchg. asst. U. Wis., Madison, 1987-88, rsch. asst., 1989-93; postdoctoral fellow IBM Rsch. Divsn., Yorktown Heights, N.Y., 1993-95, rsch. staff mem., 1995—. Author: Bounded Incremental Computation, 1996; contbr. articles to profl. jours. Achievements include patent for object model for Java. E-mail: rama@watson.ibm.com.

RAMALINGAM, SAKKARAIPPAN, oncologist, hematologist; b. Tirunelveli, Tamil Nadu, India, June 9, 1969; came to U.S., 1993; MB, BS, Kilpauk Med. Coll., Madras, India, 1992. Diplomate Am. Bd. Internal Medicine. Resident in internal medicine Wayne State U. Hosp., Detroit, 1993-96, chief med. resident, 1996-97; asst. prof. medicine Wayne State U., 1998—2000; staff physician Harper Hosp., 1997-2000; fellow hematology/oncology U. Pitts., 2000—. Recipient award Indian Med. Assn., 1990. Mem.: AACR, ASCO, AMA, ACP (assoc.). Avocations: music, reading. Home: 311 Bear Run Dr Pittsburgh PA 15237-1473 Office: 200 Lothrop St MUH 755 Pittsburgh PA 15213 E-mail: ramalingams@msx.upmc.edu.

RAMAMURTHY, BYRAVAMURTHY, computer engineer, educator; b. Chennai, Tamil Nadu, India, Apr. 3, 1971; arrived in U.S., 1993; BTech, Indian Inst. Tech., Madras, India, 1993; MS, U. Calif., Davis, 1995, PhD, 1998. Asst. prof. U. Nebr.- Lincoln, 1998—. Author: (book) Design of Optical WDM Networks: LAN, MAN and WAN Architectures., 2000, E-cient Design of Wavelength-Division Multiplexing (WDM)-Based Optical Networks., 1998; editor: IEEE Network Mag., 2000, Optical Networks Mag., 2002. Fellow Non-Resident Tuition, U. Calif., Davis, 1993-1998; scholar Nat. Talent Search, Govt. of India, 1989-1993. Mem.: IEEE, IEEE Comm. Soc. Office: U Nebr Lincoln 115 Ferguson Hall Lincoln NE 68588-0115 Business E-Mail: byrav@cse.unl.edu.

RAMAMURTMY, MOHAN K. meteorologist; b. Kumbakonam, India, June 29, 1956; came to U.S., 1980; p. K. and Mythili R.; m. Usha Ramamurthy. BS in Physics, U. Poona, Pune, India, 1977, MS in Physics, 1980; PhD in Meteorology, U. Okla., 1986. Rsch. asst. U. Okla., Norman, 1980-86; rsch. assoc. Fla. State U., Tallahassee, 1986-87; from vis. asst. prof. to asst. prof. U. Ill., Urbana, 1987-94, assoc. prof. Urbana-Champaign, 1994—. Mem. Am. Meteorol. Soc., Am. Geophys. Union, Sigma Xi. Office: Univ Ill 105 S Gregory St Urbana IL 61801

RAMANI, KANTI SHAMJI, civil engineer; b. Munjiasar, Gujarat, India, June 28, 1938; came to U.S. 1968; s. Shamjibhai Premjibhai and Raniben (Dholaria) Ramani; m. Shanta, Mar. 4, 1967; children: Manish, Rajni. BSCE, Gujarat U., India, 1962. Registered profl. engr., Pa. Engr. Capitol Engring., Dillsburg, Pa., 1968-69, J.B. Ferguson, Hagerstown, Md., 1969-70, Buchart-Horn, Inc., York, Pa., 1970-73, Greenhorne-O'Mara Inc., Riverdale, Md., 1973-76; chief civil engr. Williams and Sheladia, Inc., Mt. Rainier, 1976-78; engr. Ebasco, Inc., Atlanta, 1978-80; dept. head civil engring. Orba Corp., Mt.

Lakes, N.J., 1980-88; project mgr. VEP Assocs., Inc., Parsippany, 1988-95, BET Cons., E. Hanover, NJ, 1995—. Cons. E. Harris Assocs., Fredericks, Md., 1976-78, A.K. Data Corp., Randolph, N.J., 1986-88. Home: 26 Delbrook Rd Morris Plains NJ 07950-3141

RAMANI, RAJA VENKAT, mining engineering educator; b. Madras, India, Aug. 4, 1938; came to U.S., 1966; s. Natesa and Meenakshi (Srinivasan) Rajaraman; m. Geetha V. Chalam, July 9, 1972; children: Deepak, Gautam. BSc with honors, Indian Sch. Mines, Dhanbad, Bihar, 1962, DSc (hon.), 1997; MS, Pa. State U., 1968, PhD, 1970. Registered profl. engr., Pa., 1971; lic. first class mine mgr., 1965. Mining engr., mgr. Andrew Yule & Co., Asansol, West Bengal, India, 1962-66; grad. asst. Pa. State U., University Park, 1966-70, asst. prof., 1970-74, assoc. prof., 1974-78, prof. mining engring., 1978—, chmn. mineral engring. mgmt. sect., 1974—, head dept. mineral engring., 1987-98, George and Anne Deike chair in mining engring., 1997—. Chmn. com. post-disaster survival/rescue NAS, Washington, 1979-81; mem. health rsch. panel NAS Com. on the Rsch. Programs of the U.S. Bur. of Mines, 1994; mem. NAS Com. on Techs. for the Mineral Industries, 2000-01; mem. NAS Com. on Coal Waste Impoundments, 2001-2002; cons. UN, UN Devel. Program, Dept. Econ. and Social Devel., N.Y.C., 1983-97, World Bank, 1998-99; cons., expert panels U.S. Dept. Labor, 1979, 92, 96, HHS, 1977, 92, U.S. Dept. State, 1986, 87, U.S. Dept. Interior, 1995, Dept. Environ. Resources, Commonwealth of Pa., 1990, 92; co-dir. Generic Mineral Tech. Ctr. on Respirable Dust, U.S. Bur. Mines, 1983—, Nat. Mines/Land Reclamation Ctr., 1988—, Std. Oil Ctr. of Excellence on Longwall Tech., 1983-89; presenter in field. Sect. editor, author: Computer Methods for the Eighties, 1979, SME Mining Engineering Handbook, 1992; editor State-of-the-Art in Longwall-Shortwall Mining, 1981, Longwall Thick Seam Mining, 1988, Computers in Mineral Industry, 1994, Internat. Mine Ventilation Congress, 1997. Recipient Disting. Alumni award Indian Sch. Mines, Dhanbad, 1978, Ednl. Excellence award Pitts. Coal Mining Inst., 1986, Environ. Conservation award AIME, N.Y.C., 1990, Howard N. Eavenson award SME/AIME, N.Y.C., 1991, Robert Stefanko Best Paper award, 1993, Coal Divsn. Disting. Svc. award, 1993, Howard L. Hartman award, 1997, Percy H. Nicholls award AIME/ASME Joint Soc., 1994, Mineral Industry Edn. award Am. Inst. Mining Engrs., 1999, The Thornton medal Instn. Mining and Metallurgy, 2000; Fulbright scholar to Soviet Union Coun. Internat. Exch. of Scholars, Washington, , 1989-90; Henry Krumb lectr. AIME, 1994. Mem. Internat. Coun. for Application of Computers in the Mineral Industry (chmn. 1984-87, Disting. Achievement award 1989), Soc. Mining, Metall. and Exploration (Disting. Mem. 1989, pres. 1995), Mine Ventillation Soc. South Africa, Inst. for Ops. Rsch. and Mgmt. Scis. Achievements include research in health, safety, environmental and productivity aspects in underground and surface mining engineering. Home: 285 Oakley Dr State College PA 16803-1349 Office: Dept Mineral Engring Pa State U University Park PA 16802 E-mail: RVR@PSU.edu.

RAMANUJA, TERALANDUR KRISHNASWAMY, structural engineer; b. Mysore, Mysore, India, June 23, 1941; came to U.S., 1967, naturalized, 1979; s. Teralandur R. and Padmammal Krishnaswamy; m. Jayalakshmi Ramanuja, Jan. 18, 1971; children: Srinivasan, Rekha. BSCE, U. Mysore, 1962; MS in Structural Engring., U. Notre Dame, 1969. Registered profl. engr., Ill., Mich., Ind., N.Y. Sub-divisional officer Mil. Engring. Svcs., Bangalore, India, 1962-67; structural engr. Clyde E. Williams and Assocs., South Bend, Ind., 1969-73; head structural engring. dept. Ayres, Lewis, Norris & May, Cons. Engrs., Ann Arbor, Mich., 1973-76; sr. project mgr. Johnson & Anderson Cons. Engrs., Pontiac, 1976-78; supr. Bechtel Power Corp., Ann Arbor, 1978-85; supr. Shoreham Nuclear Power Sta. Lilco, N.Y.C., 1985-89; engring. supr. Clinton (Ill.) Power Sta. Ill. Power Co., 1989—2000. Fellow ASCE; mem. Am. Concrete Inst.; mem. Chi Epsilon. Achievements include structural and foundation design of facilities for fossil and nuclear power plants, water/waste treatment plants, petrochemical plants, pulp and paper mills and for heavy equipment/machinery for these plants; seismic and dynamic analysis of structures, systems and components in nuclear power plants. Home: 307 Birchwood Crossing Ln Maryland Heights MO 63043 Office: Ill Power Co Clinton Power Sta PO Box 678 Clinton IL 61727-0678

RAMAPRASAD, KACKADASAM RAGHAVACHAR, physical chemist; b. Dec. 8, 1938; came to U.S., 1965, permanent resident, 1971; s. Kackadasam Raghavachar and Saroja (Narasimhachar) R.; m. Rukmani Raghavachari, July 14, 1968; children: Saroja, Venkat. BS in Chemistry (hon.), U. Mysore, Bangalore, 1958; MS in Phys. Chemistry, NYU, 1971; PhD, 1972. Trainee Bhabha Atomic Rsch. Ctr. Tng. Sch., Bombay, India, 1958-59; rsch. asst., jr. sci. officer chemistry divsn., 1959-65; teaching fellow N.Y.C., 1965-71; duPont teaching asst., 1967-68; maitre-asst. dept. de chimie physique U. Geneva, 1972-73; chemist Ecole Poly-Technique Federale de lausanne, Switzerland, 1974; rsch. assoc. dept. chemistry Princeton (N.J.) U., 1974-77; rsch. assoc., mem. profl. rsch. staff dept. chem. engring., 1977-79; sr. scientist Chronar Corp., Princeton, 1979-89, Electron Transfer Techs., Inc., Princeton, 1990-93; staff scientist TRI-Princeton, 1993-96, sr. scientist, 1996-2001, sr. scientist, group leader, 2001—. Contbr. articles to profl. pubs. Recipient Founder's Day award N.Y.U., 1972. Mem. Am. Chem. Soc., Sigma Xi. Office: TRI/Princeton PO Box 625 Princeton NJ 08542-0625

RAMAPRASAD, SUBBARAYA, medical educator; b. Mysore, India, May 20, 1954; came to the U.S., 1980, naturalized, 1993; s. Puttaniah and Sharadamma Subbaraya; m. Padma, Sept. 28, 1987; 1 child, Sanjay. PhD, Indian Inst. Sci., 1979. Instr. U. Ark. Med. Scis., Little Rock, 1989-91, asst. prof., 1991-94, assoc. prof., 1995—. Peer rev. breast cancer rsch. Dept. of Def., 1999—2000. Contbr. articles to profl. jours. Recipient Ind. Investigator award Nat. Alliance Rsch. in Schizophrenia and Depression, 1999; grantee NIMH, 1994, Ark. Sci. Tech. Authority, 1991, 95, Dept. of Def., 1999. Mem. Internat. Soc. Magnetic Resonance Medicine, Am. Coll. Radiology, N.Y. Acad. Scis., Soc. Photooptical Instrumentation Engrs., Am. Assn. Diabetes Educators, Nebr. Radiol. Soc., Sigma Xi. Hindu. Avocations: travel, photography, bicycling, gardening. Home: 17626 Jefferson St Omaha NE 68135-3028 Office: U Nebr Med Ctr Dept Radiology Omaha NE 68198-1045 E-mail: sramaprasad@unmc.edu., sramaprasa@aol.com.

RAMASWAMI, DEVABHAKTUNI, chemical engineer; b. Apr. 4, 1933; s. Veeriah and Rangamma Devabhaktuni; m. Vijayalakshmi, June 30, 1967; 1 child, Srikrishna. BSc, Andhra U., 1953, MSc, 1954, DSc, 1958; PhD, U. Wis., 1961. Rsch. scholar Andhra U., Waltair, India, 1954-56, Indian Inst. Tech., Kharagpur, 1956-57; asst. prof. Benaras Hindu U., Varanasi, India, 1957-58; rsch. asst. U. Wis., Madison, 1958-61; rsch. engr. IBM Corp., San Jose, Calif., 1961-62; chem. engr. Argonne Nat. Lab., Ill., 1962—. Contbr. numerous articles to profl. jours.; patentee in field. Recipient Am. Chem. Soc. Disting. and Promising Asian in U.S. award Asia Found., 1960. Fellow AIChE. Avocation: photography.

RAMASWAMY, PREMA, pediatrician, cardiologist; b. India, June 11, 1964; came to U.S., 1991; s. Balkrishna and Indira R.; m. Sanjeev Dheer, Sept. 22, 1993; children: Meera, Nina. MBBS, Mahatma Gandhi Meml. Med Coll., Indore, India, 1987, MD, 1990. Diplomate Am. Bd. Pediatrics, Am. Bd. Pediatric Cardiology. Intern, resident Montefiore Med. Ctr.; fellow in pediat. cardiology N.Y. Hosp.-Cornell Med. Ctr., 1993—96; pediat. cardiologist Bklyn. Hosp., 1996-97, dir. pediat. cardiology, 1997-98; co-dir. pediat. cardiology Maimonides Med. Ctr., Bklyn., 1998—; mem. staff Luth. Med. Ctr., 1998—, Coney Island Hosp., Bklyn., 1999—. Office: Pediat Cardiology Maimonides Children Ctr 4802 10th Ave K-106 Brooklyn NY 11219-2919 Fax: 718-635-7906. E-mail: pramaswamy@maimonidesmed.org.

RAMAYYA, AKUNURI V. physics educator; b. Vijayawada, India, Aug. 15, 1938; came to U.S., 1960; s. Venkata Rao and Subbamma Akunuri; m. Palakodeti Krishna Ramayya, Aug. 22, 1965; children: Radhika, Sarat. BSc with honors, Andhra U., 1957, MS, 1958; PhD, Ind. U., 1964; PhD (hon.), U. Bucharest, Romania, 1999. Sr. rsch. assoc. Vanderbilt U., Nashville, 1969-70, asst. prof., 1970-75, prof. physics, 1980—. Rschr. dept. physics Delft (The Netherlands) Tech. U., 1970-71. Contbr. articles to profl. publs., including Physics Rev. C., Jour. Modern Physics, World Sci. Alexander von Humboldt sr. fellow, 1981-82. Fellow Am. Phys. Soc.; mem. Nuc. Physics divsn. of Am. Chem. Soc., Sigma Xi. Home: 1201 Gen MacArthur Dr Brentwood TN 37027 Office: Vanderbilt U Box 1807 Sta B Nashville TN 37235 E-mail: a.v.ramayya@vanderbilt.edu.

RAMBERG, PATRICIA LYNN, college president; b. Melrose Park, Ill., June 15, 1951; d. Roy Andrew and Elsie Elaine (Lossau) Fricke; children: Richard Lynn II, Caitlyn Elizabeth. BS in Bus. Adminstrn. magna cum laude, Elmhurst Coll., 1976; MA in Edn., U. St. Thomas, 1989. Assoc. dir. ops. Bank Mktg. Assn., Chgo., 1972-75; exec. dir. Soc. Tchrs. Family Medicine, Kansas City, Mo., 1975-78, Minn. Assn. Children with Learning Disabilities, St. Paul, 1979-80; sr. instrnl. designer Applied Learning Systems, Mpls., 1989-90; dir. Upper Midwest Conservation Assn., 1990-92; account exec. Dean Witter Reynolds, Inc., Bloomington, Minn., 1992-94; investment specialist FBS Investment Svcs., Inc., Mpls., 1994; v.p., dir. profl. devel. US Bank, 1994-98; pres., CEO Alfred Adler Grad. Sch., Hopkins, Minn., 1998—. Adj. faculty U. St. Thomas, St. Paul, 1990. Lutheran. Avocations: photography, horses. Home: 7136 W 113th St Bloomington MN 55438-2448 Office: Alfred Adler Grad Sch 1001 Highway 7 Hopkins MN 55305-4723

RAMBERG, WALTER DODD, architect; b. Charlotte, N.C., Feb. 17, 1932; s. Walter Gustav Charles and Julia Elisabeth (Lineberger) R.; m. Lucinda Jenifer Ballard, Nov. 25, 1961 (dec. 1989); children: Lucinda E.G., Jenny S.F., Julia E.L.; m. Seska Peck Dunne, Sept. 14, 1996. BA, Yale U., 1953, M.Arch., 1956. Fulbright fellow Kyoto (Japan) U., 1956-58; apprentice architect Paul Rudolph, New Haven, 1958-61; project designer Meyer & Ayers, Balt., 1961-63; partner Howe & Ramberg, Washington, 1963-65; prin. Walter Dodd Ramberg (Architect), 1965—. Prof. architecture Cath. U. Am., 1977—; mem. design adv. panel Balt. Dept. Housing and Community, 1973—; mem. bd. architecture rev. Baltimore County, 1986-89. Designer: N.W. Balt. High Sch, 1963 (P.A. Excellence in Design award); architect: Bridge for Washington Cathedral, 1965 (Excellence in Design award Washington Bd. Trade, AIA), Kidder Guest House, 1965 (1st Honor award Balt. AIA), Azrael House, 1969 (Honor award Balt. AIA), Cutts House, 1973 (Honor award Balt. AIA), Woody House, 1975 (Merit award Balt. AIA), Lineberger Meml. Library, 1976 (Merit award Nat. AIA, ALA); contbr. articles to profl. publs. Served to lt. USCGR, 1958-59. Mem. AIA (corp.), AAUP, Soc. Archtl. Historians. Clubs: Met. (Washington). Episcopalian. Home: 1651 Belfast Rd Sparks MD 21152-9788 Office: 1830 T St NW Washington DC 20009-7138

RAMBO, SYLVIA H. federal judge; b. Royersford, Pa., Apr. 17, 1936; d. Granville A. and Hilda E. (Leonhardt) R.; m. George F. Douglas, Jr., Aug. 1, 1970. BA, Dickinson Coll., 1958; JD, Dickinson Sch Law, 1962; LLD (hon.), Wilson Coll., 1980, Dickinson Sch. Law, 1993, Dickinson Coll., 1994, Shippensburg U., 1996, Widener U., 1999. Bar: Pa. 1962. Atty. trust dept. Bank of Del., Wilmington, 1962-63; pvt. practice Carlisle, 1963-76; from public defender to chief public defender Cumberland County, Pa., 1974-76; judge Ct. Common Pleas, Cumberland County, 1976-78, U.S. Dist. Ct. (mid. dist.) Pa., Harrisburg, 1979-92, chief judge, 1992-99; federal judge U.S. Dist. Ct., Harrisburg, 2000—. Asst. prof., adj. prof. Dickinson Sch. Law, 1974-76, mem. Jud. Conf. Com. on Adminstrn. of Magistrate Judges Sys., 1996-2002. Bd. govs. Dickinson Sch. Law., Pa. State U., 2000—. Mem. Phi Alpha Delta. Democrat. Presbyterian. Office: US Dist Ct Federal Bldg PO Box 868 Harrisburg PA 17108-0868

RAMBO, WAYNE HERBERT, English language and education educator; b. Camden, N.J., Aug. 1, 1947; s. Herbert Jordan and Gladys Marie (Savage) R.; m. Alice Carolyn Huber, Nov. 3, 1944; children: Theodore Yung-Kyo, Faith Yung Gin. BA, Clearwater Christian Coll., 1969; MA, Glassboro State Coll., 1976; EdD, Temple U., 1982; MA, West Chester U., 1999. Cert. sch. adminstr., Pa. Elem. prin. Phila. Assn. Christian Schs., 1969-72, dir. pub. rels., 1972-75; teaching asst. Temple U., Phila., 1975-79; rsch. grants analyst Inst. Exptl. Psychiatry, 1979—; prof. English, acad. skills Camden County Coll., Blackwood, N.J., 1986—; prof. adj. composition and lit. MCP-Hahnemann U., Phila., 1990—; assoc. prof. speech and devel. English Delaware County C.C., Media, Pa., 1997—. Adj. prof. comm. Rowan U., Glassboro, N.J., 1990—, Gloucester County Coll., Sewell, N.J., 1995—; adj. prof. speech and English, Salem (N.J.) Coll., 1991—; cons. Ednl. Testing Svc., Princeton, N.J., 1989—, N.J. Dept. Higher Edn., Trenton, 1991, N.J. Divsn. Vocat. Edn., Trenton, 1981-82; co-founder Camden County Adj. Fedn., 1994. Author: Developing Critical Thinking Skills Through Reading and Writing: Expanding Bloom's Taxonomy to Differentiate Between Consumptive and Productive Cognitive Behavior, 1982, Gunning Rambo Readability Writability, 1994; contbg. author: Paragraphy and Essays, 1993; author symposium in field. 1st pres. Marie J. Carrol Found., Merchantville, N.J., 1984; bd. dirs. Merchantville Bd. Edn., 1979—, pres., 1989-92. Avocations: restoration of historical homes, building trades, travel. Home: 37 Rogers Ave Merchantville NJ 08109-2528 Office: Gloucester County College 1800 Tanyard Rd Sewell NJ 08080 E-mail: drwhr@aol.com.

RAMCHANDER, SANJAY, finance educator; b. Madras, India, July 25, 1968; came to U.S., 1988; s. Ramchander and Chandra Ramchander; m. Jana T., July 5, 1996; children: Naitra, Jai. B in Comm., Osmania U., Hyderabad, India, 1988; MBA, St. Louis U., 1990; PhD, Cleve. State U., 1995. Rsch. asst. Cleve. State U., Dept. Fin., 1990-94; asst. prof. Coppin State Coll., Balt., 1994-97, Minn. State U., Mankato, 1997-00; assoc. prof. Marshall U., Huntington, W.Va., 2000-01, Colo. State U., Ft. Collins, 2001—. Instr. Cleve. State U., Dept. Fin., 1992-94; presenter in field; mem. scholar enhancement com. Minn. State U., 1998-99, tech. enhancement com., 1998-00, faculty advisor, 1997-2000. Fin. editor Internat. Jour. Bus. & Econs.; contbr. articles to profl. jours. Faculty Rsch. grant Minn. State U., 1999. Mem. Fin. Mgmt. Assn., Acad. Econ. and Fin., Am. Acad. Acctg. and Fin., Beta Gamma Sigma. Avocations: reading. E-mail: ramchander@mail.biz.colostate.edu.

RAMER, BRUCE M. lawyer; b. Teaneck, N.J., Aug. 2, 1933; s. Sidney and Anne S. (Strassman) R.; children: Gregg B., Marc K., Neal I. BA, Princeton U., 1955; LLB, Harvard U., 1958. Bar: Calif. 1963, N.J. 1958. Assoc., Morrison, Lloyd & Griggs, Hackensack, N.J., 1959-60; ptnr. Gang, Tyre, Ramer & Brown, Inc., L.A., 1963—. Exec. dir. Entertainment Law Inst., Law Ctr. of U. So. Calif.; bd. of councilors Law Ctr. U. So. Calif.; chmn., nat. bd. govs. Am. Jewish Com., 1995-98, nat. v.p., 1982-88, pres., 1998—, L.A. chpt., 1980-83, chair Western region, 1984-86, comty. svc. award, 1987, nat. pres., 1998—, adv. bd. Skirball Inst. on Am. Values, 1998—; chmn. Asia Pacific Rim Inst., 1989-98; trustee Loyola Marymount U., L.A. Children's Mus., 1986-89; vice chair United Way, 1991-93, corp. bd. dirs., 1981-93, chair coun. pres. 1989-90, mem. cmty. issues coun., 1989-90, chair discretionary fund distbn. com., 1987-89; bd. dirs., chair Geffen Playhouse, 1995-98, founding chair, 1998—; bd. dirs. L.A. Urban League, 1987-93, 96—, Jewish Fedn. Coun. of Greater L.A. (mem. Cmty. Rels. com., bd. dirs., exec. com.), Jewish TV Network, Sta. KCET-TV; mem., bd. dirs. Rebuild L.A., 1992-96; mem. bd. govs. Calif. Cmty. Found., 1988-98; recipient Ann. Brotherhood award NCCJs, 1990; mem. Fellows of Am. Bar Found.; mem. econ. strategy panel State Calif., 1997—; bd. dirs. Shoah Visual History Found., Righteous Persons Found., L.A. 2012 Bid Com. for the So. Calif. Olympic Games; bd. dirs. Jewish Fedn. Coun. Greater L.A., mem. exec. com., cmty. rels. com. Pvt. U.S. Army, 1958-59, 2d lt., 1961-62. Mem. ABA (mem. spl. com. jud. ind.), L.A. County Bar Assn., Calif. Bar Assn., Beverly Hills Bar Assn. (Exec. Dirs. award 1988, Entertainment Lawyer of Yr. award 1996), L.A. Copyright Soc. (pres. 1974-75), Calif. Copyright Conf. (pres. 1973-74), Princeton Club (pres. 1975-78). Office: Gang Tyre Ramer & Brown Inc 132 S Rodeo Dr Beverly Hills CA 90212-2415

RAMER, HAL REED, academic administrator; b. Kenton, Tenn., June 8, 1923; s. Claude Orion and Dixie Clayton (Carroll) R. BS, George Peabody Coll., 1947; MSW, U. Tenn., 1952; PhD, Ohio State U., 1963. Asst. dean men Ohio State U., Columbus, 1953-58, dir. internat. house, 1958-60, staff asst. to pres., 1960-62; asst. commr. State Dept. Edn., Nashville, 1963-70; founding pres. Vol. State C.C., Gallatin, Tenn., 1970—. Bd. dirs. Sumner Regional Health Sys., Inc. Com. mem. March of Dimes, Gallatin; Mem. adv. bd. First Union Bank Mid. Tenn., First Union Bank Mid. Tenn., Hendersonville; trustee Nashville United Way, 1970, Hiwassee Coll., 2001; bd. advisors Aquinas Coll., Nashville, 1967—; former chmn. Tenn. Fulbright-Hays Sch. Commn.; YMCA. With USAAF, 1943—45. Recipient Distinctive Svc. award Devel. Coun. Peabody Coll., Nashville, 1960s, Disting. Svc. award Tenn. Dept. Edn., 1970, Outstanding Leader award Vanderbilt U. chpt. Phi Delta Kappa, 1987, Gov.'s Svc. award State of Tenn., 1993, Sertoma Club Svc. to Mankind award, 1995-96, Disting. Alumnus award Peabody Coll., 1996, Disting. Svc. award Tenn. Bd. Regents, 1997, Svc. Awd. Amer. Assn. of Commty. Col., 1999, Otis Floyd Jr. Awd. for Excellence Tenn. COll. Pub. Rels. Assn., 1999; named Rotarian of the Yr., 1979; Paul Harris fellow Rotary Internat., 1981. Mem. Am. Legion, Coun. Pres. C.Cs. (chmn. state Tenn. 1988-89), Tenn. Coll. Assn. (pres. 1985-86), Nat. Alumni Assn. Peabody Coll. (pres. 1970-71, trustee), Tenn. Acad. Sci., Tenn. and Sumner County Hist. Socs. (bd. dirs.), English Speaking Union Internat. (Nashville chpt.), So. Assn. Colls. and Schs., Univ. Club Nashville, Gallatin and Hendersonville C. of C., St. Thomas Aquinas Soc., Torch Club, Alpha Tau Omega, Kappa Phi Kappa, Alpha Phi Omega, Phi Delta Kappa. Methodist. Avocations: antiques, antique cars, photography. Home: 120 Abbottsford Nashville TN 37215-2440 Office: Vol State CC Office of Pres 1480 Nashville Pike Gallatin TN 37066-3188

RAMER, JAMES LEROY, civil engineer; b. Marshalltown, Iowa, Dec. 7, 1935; s. LeRoy Frederick and Irene (Wengert) Ramer; m. Jacqueline L. Orr, Dec. 15, 1957; children: Sarah T., Robert H., Eric A., Susan L. Student, U. Iowa, 1953-57; MCE, Washington U., St. Louis, 1976, MA in Polit. Sci., 1978; postgrad., U. Mo., 1984—. Registered profl. engr., land surveyor. Civil and constrn. engr. U.S. Army C.E., Tulsa, 1960-63; civil and relocations engr. U.S. State Dept., Del Rio, Tex., 1964; project engr. H.B. Zachary Co., San Antonio, 1965-66; civil and constrn. engr. U.S. Army C.E., St. Louis, 1967-76, tech. advisor for planning and nat. hydropower coord., 1976-78; project mgr. for EPA constrn. grants Milw., 1978-80; chief arch. and engring. HUD, Indpls., 1980-81; civil design and pavements engr. Whiteman AFB, Mo., 1982-86; project mgr. maintenance, 1993—; soil and pavements engr. Hdqrs. Mil. Airlift Command, Scott AFB, Ill., 1986-88. Project mgr. AF-1 maintenance hangar; cattle and grain farmer, 1982—; pvt. practice civil-mech. engr., constrn. mgmt., estimating, cost analysis, cash flow, project scheduling, expert witness, profl. land surveying, Fortuna, Mo., 1988—2001; chief constrn. inspector divsn. design and constrn. State of Mo., 1992—93; project engr. Mil. Housing, 2001—; adj. faculty civil engring. Washington U., 1968—78, U. Wis., Milw., 1978—80, Ga. Mil. Coll., Whiteman AFB, Longview Coll., Kansas City; adj. rsch. engr. U. Mo., Columbia, 1985—86; project engr., quality control officer Korte Constrn. Co. Author (tech. writing operation and maintenance manuals.): fin. reports and environ. control plans, designs & builds tech. and indsl. models. Mem.: AAUP, NSPE, ASCE, Soc. Am. Mil. Engrs., Optimists Internat. Lutheran. Achievements include patents for in diverse art, 9 copyrights; development of solar waterstill, deep shaft hydropower concept. Home: 11147 Angel Rd Fortuna MO 65034-2167

RAMER, LAWRENCE JEROME, corporation executive; b. Bayonne, N.J., July 29, 1928; s. Sidney and Anne (Strassman) R.; m. Ina Lee Brown, June 30, 1957; children: Stephanie Beryl, Susan Meredith, Douglas Strassman. BA in Econs, Lafayette Coll., 1950; MBA, Harvard U., 1957; LLD (hon.), Lafayette Coll., 1992. Sales rep., then v.p. United Sheet Metal Co., Bayonne, 1953-55; with Am. Cement Corp., 1957-64; v.p. mktg. div. Riverside Cement Co., 1960-62, v.p. mktg. parent co., 1962-64; vice chmn. bd., chief exec. officer Clavier Corp., N.Y.C., 1965-66; exec. v.p., vice chmn. bd. Pacific Western Industries, Los Angeles, 1966-70; pres., chief exec. officer Nat. Portland Cement Co. Fla., 1975-89; chmn. bd. Sutro Partners, Inc., Los Angeles, 1977-89, Somerset Mgmt. Group, 1975-92, Luminall Paints Inc., Los Angeles, 1972-95; chmn. bd., CEO Bruning Paint Co., Balt., 1979—2000; chmn. bd., chief exec. officer Pacific Coast Cement Co., Los Angeles, 1979-90; pres., CEO Ramer Equities, Inc., 1990—2000, chmn., 2000—; chmn. bd. Scott Paint Co., Sarasota, Fla., 2000—. Chmn. Lee and Lawrence J. Ramer Family Found., 1986—; bd. dirs. Orbis Internat., N.Y.C., The Music Ctr., L.A., Canyon Ranch, Tucson, Music Ctr. Found., L.A.; bd. dirs. Ctr. Theatre Group-Mark Taper Ahmanson Theatres, L.A., pres. and chmn., 1987-97. Chmn. bd. trustees Lafayette Coll., Easton, Pa., 1992—2001, chmn., 1976—2001, bd. trustees, 1976—2001; trustee, chmn. bd. trustees Calif. Inst. Arts, Valencia, Calif.; bd. dirs. Non-Traditional Casting Project; nat. bd. govs. Am. Jewish Com., NY, assoc. chmn. bd. trustees; trustee Facing History and Ourselves; bd. dirs. United Friends of Children. Office: Ramer Equities Inc 1999 Ave Of Stars Ste 1090 Los Angeles CA 90067-4612 E-mail: ljramer@pacbell.com.

RAMES, DOUGLAS DWIGHT, civil engineer; b. Colorado Springs, Colo., Apr. 14, 1942; s. Dwight S. and Eleanor A. (Roach) R.; m. Audrey Joan Satter, Nov. 26, 1963; children: Steven D., Wendy M., Eydee J. BSCE, S.D. Sch. Mines & Tech., 1965; postgrad., Ind./Purdue U., 1989, Harvard U., 1995. Registered profl. engr., Colo. Project engr. Colo. Dept. of Hwys., Eagle, 1970-72, resident engr. Grand Junction, 1972-78, preconstrn. engr. Greeley, 1978-84, asst. dist. engr., 1984-88; region dir. Colo. Dept. Transp., 1988-98, ret., 1998. Commr. urban renewal City of Greeley, 1993-98; mgr. transp. The Sear-Brown Group, 1998—. Avocations: genealogy, travel, fishing, old roadsters. Office: Sear-Brown Group 209 S Meldrum St Fort Collins CO 80521-2603

RAMESH, KALAHASTI SUBRAHMANYAM, materials scientist; b. Tiruchi, Madras, India, Mar. 22, 1949; s. Subrahmanyam Veeraragaviah and Kuntala (Chinnaswami) Kalahasti; m. Atsumi Yoshida Ramesh, Jan. 30, 1990; children: Siva, Arjun. MS in Ceramic Engring., Benaras Hindu U., India, 1973; D in Engring., Tokyo Inst. Tech., 1986. Asst. rsch. mgr. Steel Authority India Ltd., Ranchi, Bihar, 1979-80; lectr. dept. ceramic engring. Benaras U., Varanasi, India, 1980-82; tech. mgr. ceramics div. TYK Corp., Tokyo, 1986-89; mgr. rsch. and devel. Mer Corp., Tuscon, Ariz., 1989; prin. scientist Battelle meml. Inst., Columbus, Ohio, 1989-93; sr. sci. Pacific N.W. Lab., Richland, Wash., 1993-97; pres. Pacific Rim Tech. Integration, Inc., 1997; sr. tech. specialist, sr. design engr. Sheldahl, Inc., Northfield, Minn., 1998—; sr. process engr. Thin Films Guardian Industries, Corsicana, Tex., 2000—02. Adj. prof. Navarro Coll., Corsicana, Tex., 2000—; adv. Internat. Bus. Svc., Tokyo, 1988-89; cons. HTP Inc., Sharon, Pa., 1989—, Pierce Leslie Cashew & Coffee Ltd., 1997—. Hi-Tech Internat. Cons., 1997—; mem. U.S. Dept. Energy Ceramics Adv. Com., Washington, 1991—; tech. dir. XTALONIX, Inc., Columbus, Ohio, 1993—; mem. Boreskov Meml. Conf. Catalyst and Catalysis Sci. and Engring., Russia, 1997; spkr. Japanese 5th Sci., Tech., and Info. Conf., Washington, 1997; sci. staff Indian Trail Acad., Kenosha Unified Sch. Dist., 2002—; assoc. lectr. U. Wis. at Parkside, 2002—; online faculty U. Phoenix. Worked with Mother Teresa, Calcutta, 1979; Panel mem. NSF on Materials and Mechanics, 1995; organized photographic exhbn. of Mother Teresa's work Tokyo, 1989. Mombusho rsch. fellow Ministry Edn. Japan, 1982-84, Max Planck Soc. fellow, 1989. Fellow Indian Inst. Ceramics, Inst. Ceramics U.K.; mem. Japan India Assn., Found. for Indsl. Rsch. (expert), N.Y. Acad. Scis. Hindu. Achievements include development of several ceramic refractories for iron, steel, catalysis material and catalytic combustion and gas turbine/enbine applications, thin films coatings and semiconductor thin films. Home: 9035 17th Ave Kenosha WI 53143-6806

RAMET, MIKA P. physician, researcher; b. Oulu, Finland, 1971; s. Veikko I. and Kerttu K. Ramet; m. Maria E. Yliraatikka, Feb. 9, 2001. MD, U. Oulu, Finland, 1990, PhD, 1998. Resident in pediat. Oulu U. Hosp., 1998—99; rsch. fellow Mass. Gen. Hosp., Boston, 1999—. Contbr. articles. Recipient Young Investigator award, Duodecim Found. Oulu, 2001; fellow Clin. Rsch. fellow-lFellow clinical research award, Soc. Pediat. RSch., 2000. Mem.: Fiinish Med. Assn., Duodecim Found.

RAMETTE, RICHARD WALES, chemistry educator; b. Hartford, Conn., Oct. 9, 1927; s. Joel Edward and Grace Margaret (Wales) R.; m. Lenora Kathryn Kelleher, Aug., 21, 1949; children: Cheryl Lee, James Edward, John Richard, David Joel, William Michael. BA, Wesleyan U., Middletown, Conn., 1950; PhD, U. Minn., 1954. Prof. chemistry Carleton Coll., Northfield, Minn., 1954-90, Laurence M. Gould prof. chemistry, 1971-90, prof. emeritus, 1990—. Sci. advisor FDA, Mpls., 1969-80. Author: Chemical Equilibrium and Analysis, 1981. Asst. scoutmaster Boy Scouts Am., Northfield, 1968-73; calligraphy instr. Northfield Arts Guild, 1974-80; sec. Unitarian Universalist Congregation Green Valley, 1998-2001, pres., 2001-2002. Recipient Chemistry Teaching award Mfg. Chemists, 1966, Analytical Chemistry Teaching award Am. Chem. Soc., 1991, Disting. Alumnus award Wesleyan U., 1995. Mem.: Am. Chem. Soc. (Analytical Chemistry Tchg. award, 50 yr. mem. award 2002). Home: 765 W Fountain Creek Dr Green Valley AZ 85614-3272 E-mail: rramette@carleton.edu.

RAMETTE, VINCENT ALFRED, legal information specialist; b. Angers, Maine et L, France, Nov. 17, 1965; s. Etienne Jean and Théodora Louise R.; m. Anne Yvonne Gabilly, Sept. 21, 1991; children: Maxime, Antoine. 1st cert., Cambridge, 1985; diploma, U. Paris V René Descartes, 1990. Info. mgr.

Berlioz & Co., Paris, 1990-97; comm. project mgr. Ahlstrom Paper Group, Vitry Sur Seine, France, 1997-98; info. mgr. Jeantet & Assocs., Paris, 1998—. Co-author (legal database) Le Doctrinal, 1993-97; contbr. articles to profl. jours.; spkr. legal info. mgmt. confs. Mem. Juriconnexion (assoc.). Office: Baker & McKenzie 32 ave Kleber 75116 Paris France E-mail: vramette@6sens.com.

RAMEY, AVA LORRAINE, policewoman, detective; b. Northumberland County, Va., Mar. 21, 1951; d. Homer Albert and Marilyn Orenette (Corbin) Campbell; m. Kenneth Lee Howard, Apr. 5, 1972 (div. Mar. 1981); m. Randall Russell Ramey, Aug. 6, 1981; children— Ryan Randall, Robert Ryan. Student Radford Women's Coll., 1969-70, D.C. U., 1970-72, U. Md., 1974-76. Tour guide Landmark Services, Washington, 1970-71; store detective Hecht Co., Washington, 1971-72; policewoman, detective Washington Met. Police Dept., 1972— ; owner, dir. Lord Mayor Acad., Capital Children's Mus., Washington, 1984— ; owner Mattapony Video, specializing in children's videos, Md., 1986— . Author: (children's book) Tarsha, 1975. Served with USAR, 1977-80. Named among Top Ten Coll. Girls in Am., Glamour mag., 1969. Mem. Exec. Female, Black Women in Law Enforcement, Com. Police Parents (pres. 1983-84). Avocation: white water rafting. Office: Lord Mayor Acad 800 3rd St NE Washington DC 20002-4314

RAMEY, CARL ROBERT, lawyer; b. Binghamton, N.Y., Feb. 15, 1941; s. Clinton W. and Hester May (Wisdom) R.; m. Maryan Sitzenkopf, Aug. 11, 1962 (div. Sept. 1987); children: Mark Alan, Christian David; m. Karen Reichard, Nov. 28, 1987. AB, Marietta Coll., 1962; MA, Mich. State U., 1964; JD, George Washington U., 1967. Bar: D.C. 1968, U.S. Dist. Ct. D.C. 1968, U.S. Ct. Appeals (D.C., 2d, 3d, 4th, 5th, 7th and 9th cirs.), U.S. Supreme Ct. 1972, Md. 1999. Assoc. McKenna, Wilkinson & Kittner, Washington, 1967-71, ptnr., 1971-86, Wiley, Rein & Fielding, Washington, 1986—. Contbr. articles to profl. jours., chpt. to Copyright Law Symposium, 1969; editorial staff George Washington Law Rev., 1965-67. Recipient First Prize award Nat. Nathan Burkan Meml. Writing Competition, ASCAP, 1969. Mem. ABA, Fed. Communications Bar Assn. (treas. 1977-78, co-chair editl. adv. bd. Fed. Comms. Law Jour. 1993-96), D.C. Bar Assn., Md. Bar Assn. Republican. Episcopalian. Avocations: skiing, tennis, boating, biking. Office: Wiley Rein & Fielding 1776 K St NW Washington DC 20006-2304 Home: 4543 Boone Creek Rd Oxford MD 21654-1434

RAMEY, CECIL EDWARD, JR. lawyer; b. Shreveport, La., Nov. 9, 1923; s. Cecil Edward and Blanche (Gwin) R.; m. Betty Loper, June 15, 1945; children— Martha L., L. Christine, Stephen E. BS summa cum laude, Centenary Coll., 1943; LLB, Yale U., 1949; postgrad., Tulane U., 1950-51. Bar: Wis. 1949, La. 1951. Assoc. Miller, Mack & Fairchild, Milw., 1949-50; mem. faculty Tulane U., 1950-54; assoc. Hargrove, Guyton, Van Hook and Hargrove, Shreveport, 1954-56, ptnr., 1956-63, Hargrove, Guyton, Van Hook and Ramey, Shreveport, 1963-73, Hargrove, Guyton, Ramey and Barlow, Shreveport, 1973-89, of counsel, 1989-94, Barlow and Hardtner, L.C., Shreveport, 1994-2001, Lemle Kelleher Barlow and Hardtner, Shreveport, 2001—. Adj. prof. Centenary Coll., 1992—98. Former chmn. Citizens Capital Improvements com. City of Shreveport; former mem. governing bd. Shreveport YMCA; former chmn. bd. trustees Broadmoor Meth. Ch., Shreveport, chmn. bd. stewards; former bd. dirs., former chmn. Shreveport-Bossier Found.; trustee Centenary Coll. With AC, U.S. Army, 1943-46. Named Shreveport's Outstanding Young Man of Yr., 1956, Mr. Shreveport, 1968; recipient Clyde E. Fant Meml. award community service United Way, 1979 Fellow Am. Coll. Trust and Estate Counsel; mem. ABA, La. Bar Assn., Shreveport Bar Assn., La. Law Inst., Shreveport C. of C. (pres. 1974), Centenary Coll. Alumni Assn. (past pres.), Shreveport Club, Order of Coif, Phi Delta Phi, Kappa Sigma. Clubs: Shreveport. Home: 139 Oscar Ln Shreveport LA 71105-3566 Office: Lemle Kelleher Barlow and Hardtner 401 Edwards St Shreveport LA 71101-3289 E-mail: cer@bandhlaw.com.

RAMEY, DENNY L. bar association executive director; b. Portsmouth, Ohio, Feb. 22, 1947; s. Howard Leroy and Norma Wylodine (Richards) R.; m. Jeannine Gayle Dunmyer, Sept. 24, 1971 (div. Nov. 1991); children: Elizabeth Michelle, Brian Michael. BBA, Ohio U., 1970; MBA, Capital U., 1976. Cert. assn. exec. Adminstrv. mgr. Transit Warehouse div. Elston Richards Storage Co., Columbus, Ohio, 1970-73; mgr. continuing profl. edn. Ohio Soc. CPA's, 1973-79; exec. dir. Engrs. Found. of Ohio, 1979-80; asst. exec. Ohio State Bar Assn., 1980-86, exec. dir., sec., treas., 1986—. Treas., exec. com., bd. dirs. Ohio Bar Liability Ins. Co., Columbus, 1986—; treas. Ohio State Bar Found., 1986—; treas. Ohio Legal Ctr. Ins., Columbus, 1988-91; sec. Ohio Printing Co., Ltd., 1991; v.p. Osbanet, Inc., 1993—; chmn. Lawriter LLC, 2000—; bd. dirs. OSBA.com, LLC. Mem.: Ohio Soc. Assn. Execs., Am. Soc. Assn. Execs., Nat. Assn. Bar Execs., Brookside Golf & Country Club, Scioto Country Club. Methodist. Avocations: tennis, golf, sports, music, wine appreciation. Office: Ohio State Bar Assn 1700 Lake Shore Dr PO Box 16562 Columbus OH 43216-6562 E-mail: dramey@ohiobar.org.

RAMEY, FELICENNE HOUSTON, dean; b. Phila. m. Melvin R. Ramey; 2 children. BS, Pa. State U., University Park, 1961; MS, Duquesne U., 1967; JD, U. Calif., Davis, 1972; MA, Calif. State U., Sacramento, 1978. Bar: Calif. Microbiologist Pa. Dept. Labs., Phila., Walter Reed Army Med. Ctr., Washington; chemist Calgon Corp., Pitts.; instr. Carnegie-Mellon U.; dep. atty. gen. Calif. Dept. Justice, Sacramento; clk. U.S. Dist. Ct. Calif.; asst. prof. Calif. State U. Sch. Bus. Adminstrn., assoc. prof., chmn. dept. behavior and environment, assoc. dean, prof., dean, 1997—; exec. officer U. Calif., Davis. Dir. litigation Human Rights Commn., Sacramento; bd. dirs. Legal Aid Soc., Sacramento mag.; vis. scholar Ga. Inst. Tech., 1981, Boston Coll., 1988. Mem. edn. com. Blacks for Effective Community Action, 1978—. ACE fellow U. Calif., Santa Cruz, 1992—. Mem. Calif. Agrl. Alumni Assn. (bd. dirs.), Western Bus. Law Assn. (pres., pres. elect, v.p., exec. sec. Calif. and Nev. chpts. 1983-89), Nat. Assn. Women Deans and Adminstrs., Sacramento Black C. of C. (edn. com. 1990—, bd. dirs. 1989—). Avocations: jogging, cross crounty skiing, reading. Office: Calif State U Coll Bus Adminstrn Sacramento CA 95819-6088

RAMEY, MARIANNE CLIFFORD, civil engineer; b. Peoria, Ill., Nov. 12, 1957; d. Lloyd Samuel and Lois Lucille (Staat) C.; m. Timothy J. Ramey, Aug. 22, 1981. BSCE, Purdue U., 1978; MBA, U. Houston, 1982. Registered profl. engr., Tex., Va., Md., Mo., Calif., N.Y., Miss., D.C., Colo., Fla., Minn., W.Va., Ky. Staff engr. Turner, Collie & Braden Corp., Houston, 1979-80; sr. engr. Espey, Huston & Assocs., 1980-84; regional dir. Washington office The Nielsen-Wurster Group, Inc., Fairfax, Va., 1984-86; regional dir. of engring. Marriott Corp., 1986-91; regional v.p. S.E. office The Nielsen-Wurster Group, Inc., Farifax, Va., 1991—. Mem. Harris County Mcpl. Utility Dist. 119 Bd. of Dirs., Houston, 1982-84. Mem. ASCE, NSPE, Project Mgmt. Inst., AACE APWA. Avocations: cooking, antique collecting, gardening. Home: 6519 Ryanlynn Dr Fairfax Station VA 22039-1517 Office: Nielsen-Wurster Group Inc 3211 Jermantown Rd Ste 212 Fairfax VA 22030-2844

RAMIG, ROBERT FRANKLIN, molecular virology educator; b. Scottsbluff, Nebr., Oct. 16, 1945; s. Robert E. and Lois F. R.; m. Carolyn M. Mingus Hollrah-Ramig, Dec. 31, 1993; children: Lisa Morel, Michael Ramig. BS, Oreg. State U., 1967, MS, 1969; PhD, U. Colo., 1973. Asst. prof. Baylor Coll. of Medicine, Houston, 1979-84, assoc. prof., 1984-91, prof., 1991—. Dir. grad. studies virology Baylor Coll. of Medicine, Houston, 1989—. Contbr. articles to profl. jours. Postdoctoral fellow Albert Einstein Coll. Medicine, 1973-75, Harvard Med. Sch., 1975-79; rsch. grantee Nat. Inst. of Allergy and Infectious Diseases, 1980—. Mem. AAAS, Am. Soc. for Microbiology, Am. Soc. for Virology. Avocations: photography, birding. Office: Baylor Coll of Medicine One Baylor Plz Houston TX 77030 E-mail: rramig@bcm.tmc.edu.

RAMIL, MARIO R. state supreme court justice; b. Quezon City, The Philippines, June 21, 1946; came to U.S., 1956; s. Quintin A. and Fausta M. (Reyes) R.; m. Judy E. Wong, Nov. 6, 1971; children: Jonathan, Bradley. BA in Polit. Sci., Calif. State U., Hayward, 1972; JD, U. Calif., San Francisco, 1975. Bar: Calif. 1976, Hawaii 1976, U.S. Dist. Ct. Hawaii, U.S. Dist. Ct. (no. dist.) Calif., U.S. Ct. Appeals (9th cir.). Law clk. San Francisco Neighborhood Legal Aid Found., 1973-75; legal counsel Sandigan-Newcomers Svcs., Inc., San Francisco, 1975-76; dep. atty. gen. Dept. Labor and Indsl. Rels., 1976-79; dep. atty. gen. civil rights div. State of Hawaii, 1980-88; staff atty. house majority atty.'s office Hawaii Ho. of Reps., 1980; pvt. practice, 1980-82; dep. atty. gen. adminstrv. div. State of Hawaii, 1982-84, ins. commr., 1984-86; dir. Hawaii State Dept. Labor and Indsl. Rels., Honolulu, 1986-91; of counsel Lyons, Brandt, Cook and Hiramatsu, 1991-93; assoc. justice Hawaii Supreme Ct., Honolulu, 1993—. Bd. dirs. Hawaii Youth-At-Risk, 1989; co-chair state conv. Dem. Party State of Hawaii, 1984; mem. Adv. Coun. on Housing and Constrn., State of Hawaii, 1981; pres., bd. dirs. Hawaii Non-Profit Housing Corp.; exec. sec., chmn. adminstrv. budget com. Oahu Filipino Community Coun.; bd. dirs, legal advisor Oahu Filipino Jaycees, 1978-81. Office: Ali'iolani Hale Hawaii Supreme Ct 417 S Kinga St Honolulu HI 96813-2902*

RAMIREZ, ARCHIMEDES, neurosurgeon, educator; b. Binakayan, The Philippines, Nov. 26, 1938; came to U.S., 1947; s. Francisco Mendoza and Mercedes (Parales) R.; m. Carol Domush, Mar. 19, 1944. BS in Chemistry, Va. Mil. Inst., 1961; MD, U. Va., 1966. Diplomate Am. Bd. Neurol. Surgery. Intern Saginaw (Mich.) Gen. Hosp., 1967; resident in gen. surgery Saginaw Coop. Hosps., Inc., 1971-72; resident in neurosurgery Walter Reed Army Med. Ctr., Washington, 1972-76; commd. 2d lt. U.S. Army, 1961, advanced through grades to col., 1984, gen. med. officer Vietnam, 1968-69, Ft. Story, Va., 1969-70; chief neurol. surgery Letterman Army Med. Ctr., San Francisco, 1976-79; chief neurosurgery svc. Marin Gen. Hosp., Greensbrae, 1981—; neurosurgeon "Desert Storm", Letterman Army Med. Ctr., San Francisco, 1990—91; ret. U.S. Army M.C., 1991. Cons. Letterman Army Med. Ctr., 1979-92; mem. admission com. U. Calif.-San Francisco Med. Sch., 1978-79; mem. clin. faculty dept. neurosurgery U. Calif.-San Francisco Med. Ctr., 1978—; cons. neurosurgeon Kaiser Hosp. Terra Linda, San Rafael, Calif., 2000—. Mem. AMA, Am. Assn. Neurol. Surgeons, Congress Neurol. Surgeons, Pan Pacific Neurosurgery Congress (adv. coun. 1986—), Calif. Assn. Neurol. Surgeons, San Francisco Neurol. Soc., Calif. Med. Assn., Marin Med. Soc. Avocation: golf. Office: Archimedes Ramirez MD Inc Ste 308 599 Sir Francis Drake Blvd Greenbrae CA 94904-1732 E-mail: abackdoc@mail.MSN.com.

RAMIREZ, GRACIELA, women's health nurse; b. Mission, Tex., Jan. 23, 1960; d. Jose Frias and Roselia (Ramos) Ramirez; m. Ricky C. Azevedo, Nov. 24, 1978 (div. 1997); children: Brianna, Ricky. ADN, AA, Sacramento (Calif.) City Coll., 1990. RN, Calif. Rep. admitting/emergency dept. Woodland (Calif.) Meml. Hosp., 1982-87; pathologist's asst. coroner's office Sacramento County, 1988-89; nurse's aide Woodland (Calif.) Meml. Hosp., 1989-90; perinatal nurse U. Calif. Med. Ctr., Sacramento, 1990-92; clin. nurse family birthing ctr. Clovis (Calif.) Community Hosp., 1992-97, Kaiser South Sacto. Perinatal Unit. Home: 336 Mount Whitney Dr Woodland CA 95695-5878 E-mail: crazychela@aol.com.

RAMIREZ, JULIO JESUS, neuroscientist; b. Bridgeport, Conn., Dec. 25, 1955; s. Julio Pastor and Elia Rosa (Cortes) R. BS in Psychology magna cum laude, Fairfield U., 1977; MA, Clark U., 1980, PhD in Biopsychology, 1983. Asst. prof. Coll. of St. Benedict, St. Joseph, Minn., 1981-85; vis. scientist MIT, Cambridge, Mass., 1985-86; asst. prof. Davidson (N.C.) Coll., 1986-89, assoc. prof. dept. psychology, 1989-96, prof. dept. psychology, 1996—. Vis. scientist Centre Nat. Recherche Scientifique, Strasbourg, France, summer 1982, U. Va., Charlottesville, summers 1983-92, 96, Ludwig-Maximillians-U., Munich, Summer 1988, Yale U., New Haven, spring 1991; cons. dept. neurosci. U. Va., Charlottesville, 1983-92, 96; panelist NSF, 1991-95, chair, 1994-95; panelist NIMH, 1992-97, chair, 1995-97; pres., co-founder Faculty for Undergrad. Neurosci., 1991-94. Contbr. articles to profl. jours. Mem. Habitat for Humanity, Davidson, 1989—, Union Concerned Scientist, Cambridge, 1987—; adv. action com. Project Kaleidoscope, Washington, 1993-97. Coun. on Undergraduate Rsch. fellow, 2000; named N.C. Prof. of Yr., Nat. Gold Medalist Coun. for Advancement and Support of Edn., 1989, MacArthur Asst. Prof., 1986-89, R. Stuart Dickson Prof.; recipient Rsch. award NIMH, 1992, 2000, NSF, 1991, 97, Nat. Inst. Neurol. Disorders and Stroke, 1987, 93, N.C. Bd. Sci. and Tech., 1987, Faculty for Undergrad. Neurosci. Career Achievement award, 2001. Mem. AAAS, APA, Am. Psychol. Soc., Coun. on Undergrad Rsch. (councilor 1992-97), Soc. Neurosci. Faculty for Undergrad. Neurosci. Democrat. Achievements include rsch. in lesion-induced axonal sprouting may contribute to recovery of function after central nervous system injury. Home: PO Box 26 Davidson NC 28036-0026 Office: Davidson Coll Dept Psychology Davidson NC 28036

RAMIREZ, MARIA C(ONCEPCIÓN), retired educational administrator; d. Ines and Carlota (Cruz) R. BA, U. Incarnate Word, San Antonio, 1966; MEd, U. Tex., Austin, 1979; postgrad., S.W. Tex. State U., San Marcos, 1980. Cert. elem. tchr., bilingual tchr., supr. Elem. tchr. regular and bilingual Edgewood Ind. Sch. Dist., San Antonio, 1966-69; elem tchr. regular and bilingual Austin (Tex.) Ind. Sch. Dist., 1969-74, bilingual program coord., 1974-89; instrnl. coord. Austin Ind. Sch. Dist., 1989-91, asst. prin., 1991—96, bilingual instrnl. coord., 1996-97; ret., 1997.

RAMIREZ, MARIO EFRAIN, physician; b. Roma, Tex., Apr. 3, 1926; s. Efren M. and Carmen (Hinojosa) R.; m. Sarah B. Aycock, Nov. 25, 1949; children: Mario, Patricia Ann, Norman Michael, Jaime Eduardo, Roberto Luis. Student, U. Tex., 1942-45; MD, U. Tenn., 1948. Diplomate Am. Bd. Family Physicians. Intern Shreveport (La.) Charity Hosp., 1949, resident; practice medicine specializing in family practice; pvt. family practice, 1950-75, Rio Grande City, Tex., 1975-93; owner, adminstr. Ramirez Meml. Hosp., Roma, 1958-75. Assoc. med. dir. South Tex. Blue Cross Blue Shield Tex., McAllen, 1993-95. County judge Starr County, Rio Grande City, 1969-78; chmn. South Tex. Devel. Coun., 1975-76, Tri-County Cmty. Action Coun., 1971-78; mem. coordinated bd. Tex. Colls. and Univs., 1979-85; mem. devel. bd. U. Tex., 1986—; presdl. appointee bd. regents Uniformed Svcs. U. Tex. Health Scis., 1985-92; mem. bd. regents U. Tex. Sys., 1989-95, vice chmn. bd., 1991-92. Recipient Spl. citation Surgeon Gen., 1967, Disting. Alumnus award U. Tex., 1975, 78, Achievement award Lab World, 1978, Presdl. citation U. Tex., 1979, Outstanding Alumnus award U. Tenn., 1991, Mirabeau B. Lamar medal Assn. Tex. Colls. and Univs., 1997; named Family Dr. of Yr., Good Housekeeping mag. and Am. Acad. Family Physicians, 1978, Border Texan of the Yr., 1995; honoree Founder's Day for contbns. to higher edn. U. Tex. Pan Am., 1989. Fellow Am. Acad. Family Physicians; mem. AMA (vice chmn. com. health care of poor 1971-75, Benjamin Rush Bicentennial award 1976, Council of Med. Services 1985-94), Tex. Med. Assn. (chmn. com. health care of poor 1971, Disting. Service award 1972, pres. 1979-80), Tex. Acad. Family Physicians (v.p. 1973, pres. 1975, Distinguished Service award 1967, Outstanding Leadership award 1975-76, v.p. Valley chpt. 1960-61, pres. 1961-62), Hidalgo-Starr Counties Med. Soc. (pres. 1964) Clubs: Lions, K.C, Rotary, Alhambra. Address: 212 W Pine Ridge Ln Mcallen TX 78503-3129

RAMIREZ, MARTIN RUBEN, architect, engineer, educator, cognitive scientist, consultant; b. San Luis Potosi, Mex., Aug. 17, 1962; s. Victorio Niño and Concepcion (Zuñiga) R.; m. Maureen Therese McDermott, July 27, 1991. BS, Northwestern U., 1984, MS, 1986, PhD, 1991. Asst. to v.p. engring. Perkins & Will, Chgo., 1980-84; cons. engr. Alfred Benesch & Co., 1985-86, Teng & Assocs., Chgo.; prof. engring. Johns Hopkins U., Balt., 1990-94; pres. I.D.E.A.S., Chgo., 1994—. Cons. Wiss-Jenney Elstner, Northbrook, Ill., 1985—86, Mitsubishi Heavy Industries, Hunt Valley, Md.; cons. to une 500 corps., govts., dists. and instns.; founder, dir. program on engring. Johns Hopkins U., Balt., 1993. Reviewer for several jours.; editor Needs Database. Recipient Fazlur Khan Meml. prize, 1986, Young Investigator award NSF, 1993; Lilly fellow, 1992; NSF grad. fellow, 1985. Mem. ASCD, ASCE (assoc.), ASME, Am. Edn. Rsch. Assn., Am. Soc. Engring. Edn. (chair Frontiers in Edn. Conf. 1993), U.S. Assn. for Computational Mechanics, IEEE Computer Soc., Am. Acad. Mechanics, Tau Beta Pi. Achievements include major innovations e-business usability, business strategy, learning, integration. Avocations: bicycling, cars, travel, music. Office: IDEAS 474 N Lake Shore Dr Chicago IL 60611 E-mail: ver2@yahoo.com.

RAMIREZ, RALPH HENRY, nurse, corporate executive; b. Oakland, Calif., Sept. 25, 1949; s. Hector Ramirez and Genevieve (Figueroa) Ingraham. BS in Nursing, San Jose State U., 1974; M in Health Svcs. Adminstrn., St. Joseph's Coll., 1995. RN; cert. critical care nurse. DON nursing Chgo. Ctr. Hosp., 1980-84; adminstr. Med. Profls. Supplemental Staffing, Chgo., 1984-85; pres. Progressive Svcs., 1985-92; v.p. Seville Internat. Tours, Inc., 1990—; pres. Progressive Health Svcs. Ctrs., Inc., 1992-94, Merchants Nat. Fin. and Mgmt., Houston, 1994-95; ops. mgr. Ravenswood Home Care, Chgo., 1995-98; cons. to adminstr. United Home Health Svcs., Homewood, 1998—. Contbr. articles to profl. jours. Sponsor nursing symposium, Chgo., 1991—; bd. dirs. AIDS Found. of Chgo., 1991—, chmn. Gala com., 1993, 94, Chase House, Chgo., 1998—; co-chair Bonaventure House Benefit, 1993. Mem. Am. Biog. Inst. (Disting. Leadership award for Outstanding Svc. to Nursing Profession, Golden Acad. award), Chgo. Nurses Assn., Ill. Nurses Assn., Sigma Theta Tau. Democrat. Episcopalian. Avocations: swimming, weight lifting. Home: 5218 N Kenmore Ave Apt 1N Chicago IL 60640-2400 Office: United Home Health Care 1806 Gottschalk Homewood IL 60430 E-mail: rhr950@21stcentury.net.

RAMIREZ, SANDRA LEIGH, ceramic artist, potter, educator; b. Chgo., Aug. 3, 1957; d. J.W. and Elizabeth L. (Smith) Snarr; m. Carlos J. Ramirez, June 7, 1980. BFA, U. S.C., 1979; M of Visual Arts, Ga. State U., 1983. Lic. dispensing optician. Instr. Atlanta Jewish Cmty. Ctrs., 1981-83, Steeple House Arts Ctr., Marietta, Ga., 1990-91; part-time instr. Kennesaw State Coll., 1989—, Westminster, 1995—. Pres. Raku Club, Ga. State U., Atlanta, 1983; art cons. Chamblee (Ga.) H.S., 1991; vis. artist S.C. Arts Coun., Columbia, 1979. One woman shows include Mary Vinson Meml. Libr., 1992; exhibited in group shows at Mus. of Art Columbia, 1979, Cortona, Italy, 1979, U. Ga., 1980, Chattahoochee Nature Ctr., Roswell, Ga., 1982 (Best in Show), Saks Fifth Ave., Atlanta, 1983, Portfolio Gallery, Atlanta, 1983, Praters' Mill Arts Festival, Dalton, Ga., 1984, Merchandise Mart, Atlanta, 1984, Creative Arts Guild of Dalton, 1985, Las Manos, Santurce, P.R., 1988, Kennesaw State Coll., Marietta, 1989, 90, Southern Air, Memphis, 1989, Arts and Crafts Nationwide, Paducah, Ky., 1990, Faculty Exhibition, Kennesaw State Coll, Marietta, Ga., 1990, 92, 93, Taco Bell Corp. Hdqs., Atlanta, 1990, Mountain Valley Fine Arts Exhbn., Guntersville, Ala., 1991, Steeple House Arts Ctr., Marietta, 1991, Atlanta Coll. Art, 1991, Arts Festival of Atlanta, Piedmont Park, Ga., 1991, 92, Aliya Gallery, Atlanta, 1991, Arts Place, Marietta, 1992, Atlanta Apparel Mart, 1992, Trinith Sch., Atlanta, 1992, Governors' Mansion, Atlanta, 1993, Avery Gallery, Marietta, 1993, Auxiliary of the Jewish Home of Atlanta, 1993, 94, Kennesaw Fine Arts Soc., 1993, Arts Place, 1993, Madison-Morgan Cultural Arts Ctr., 1994, Cobb YWCA, 1994, Tucson Arts Coalition, 1994. Vol. Cobb Arts Coun., Marietta, 1990; mem., adv. Nat. Humane Soc., Marietta, 1995—. Recipient Artist in Edn. grant Ga. Arts Coun., 1991. Mem. Nat. Art Edn. Assn., Am. Crafts Coun., Cobb Arts Coun., Ga. Educators Assn., Ga. Artists Registry, Visions. Avocations: painting, water sports, antiques. Home: 660 Stansell Dr Hartwell GA 30643-2592 Office: Kennesaw State Coll 1000 Chastain Rd NW Kennesaw GA 30144-5588

RAMIREZ, VICTOR E. judge; b. L.A., Feb. 25, 1942; s. Salvador Ramirez and Maria Battalan; married, July 7, 1996. BA, Pepperdine U., 1967, MA, 1969; JD, U. San Diego, 1973. Bar: Calif. 1973. Psychologist Grossmont H.S. Dist., La Mesa, Calif., 1969-73; pvt. practice law Escondido, 1973-79; mcpl. ct. judge San Diego County, Vista, 1979-98, superior ct. judge, 1999—. Chmn. bd. dirs. Hidden Valley Nat. Bank, Escondido, 1982—. Bd. dirs. North County Centro, San Marcos, Calif., 1979-82, Vibrant Learning, Vista, 1996—; organizer, bd. dirs. Becca Found., Carlsbad, Calif., 1986. Named Best Trial Judge of Yr., Consumers Atty., 1982, 84, 97, Best Rated Judge, San Diego Bar Assn., 1982-97. Mem. Calif. Judges Assn., North San Diego Bar Assn., La Raza Bar Assn. Avocation: public advocacy. Home: PO Box 1255 Solana Beach CA 92075-7255 Office: Superior Ct San Diego County 325 S Melrose Dr Vista CA 92083-6627

RAMIREZ, W. FRED, chemical engineering educator; b. New Orleans, Feb. 19, 1941; s. Walter Frederick and Elza Welch Ramirez; m. Marion Kneipp; children: Jennifer Louise, Karen Elizabeth, Ellen Christine. BS, Tulane U., 1962, MS, 1964, PhD, 1965. Asst. prof. dept. chem. engring. U. Colo., Boulder, 1965-70, assoc. prof., 1970-75, prof., 1975—, chmn. dept. chem. engring., 1971-79, 89-92, 1997-98, 2002—. Vis. scientist Institut Francaise du Petrole, Rueil-Malmaison, France, 1976-77; vis. prof. dept. chem. engring., MIT, Cambridge, Mass., 1985-86; vis. prof. depts. engring. and chem. engring. Cambridge (Eng.) U., 1992-93; vis. prof. dept. chem. engring. U. Newcastle, Australia, 2001-02; cons. Marathon Oil Co., Littleton, Colo., 1968-72, Dowell divsn. Dow Chem., Tulsa, 1980-85, Adolph Coors Co., Golden, Colo., 1988-89, others. Author: Process Simulation, Applications of Optimal Control Theory to Enhanced Oil Recovery, 1987, Comp. Methods for Process Simulation, 1989, 2d edit., 1997, Process Control and Identification, 1994; contbr. articles to profl. jours. Singer several local choral groups, Boulder, 1980—. Faculty fellow U. Colo., 1985, 92, 2001, Exch. fellow Acad. Sci., USSR, 1987, rsch. fellow Fulbright Found., France, 1976. Fellow AIChE; mem. Am. Soc. Engring. Educators. Avocations: jogging, travel. Office: U Colo Dept Chem Engring Boulder CO 80309-0424

RAMIREZ-ANGULO, JAIME, electrical engineer, educator; b. Mexico City, Feb. 18, 1952; s. Julio Ramirez-Gilbon, Concepcion Angulo Devars; m. Emma Santarriaga; children: Daniel Ramirez-Santarriaga, Andrea Ramirez-Santarriaga, Paola Ramirez-Santarriaga, Diana Ramirez-Santarriaga. PhD, U. Stuttgart, Germany, 1982. Cert. elec. engr. Prof. Nat. Inst. for Astrophysics, Optics and Electronics, Tonantzintla, Mexico, 1982—84; asst. prof. Tex. A&M U., College Station, Tex., 1984—90; prof. N.Mex. State U., Las Cruces, 1990—. Cons. NASA/ACE Ctr. NMHU, Las Vegas, N.Mex., 1996—2000. Contbr. articles to profl. jours. Fellow: IEEE. Home: 7309 Desierto Pais El Paso TX 79912 Office: NMex State Univ Box 30001/Dept 3-0 Las Cruces NM 88003-0001 Office Fax: 505-646-1435. Personal E-mail: jramirezangulo@aol.edu. Business E-Mail: jramirez@nmsu.edu.

RAMIREZ-DE LA O, ROGELIO, economist; b. Mexico City, July 7, 1948; s. Felipe and Carmen (De la O) Ramirez; m. Gabrielle Inches, Aug. 15, 1974 (div. Oct. 1982); 1 child, Vanessa. BA in Econs., Mex. Nat. U., Mexico City, 1974; PhD in Econs., Cambridge (Eng.) U., 1982. Sec. Mex. Bus. Coun. Internat. Affairs, Mexico City, 1972-74; economist Ctr. on Trannat. Corps., UN, N.Y.C., 1980-81; dir. gen. Ecanal SA, Mexico City, 1982-83, sole ptnr., 1984—. Advisor maj. internat. funds and fgn. investors, Mex.; bd. dirs. Grupo Modelo SA de CV; mem. supervisory bd. ABN-AMRO Bank, Mexico City. Author: Foreign Investment in Mexico, 1983, Mexico-US-Canada Free Trade Agreement, 1991, Economic Outlook of Mexico in the 1990s, 1990; contbr. articles to profl. publs. Nat. Coun. Sci. and Tech. grantee, 1977-80. Mem. British C. of C. of Mex. (bd. dirs. 1993—), United Oxford and Cambridge Univ. Club, Univ. Club Mex. Avocations: reading, water sports, music, theater, horseback riding. Home: Sierra Chalchihui 270 11000 Mexico City Mexico Office: Ecanal SA Rio Lerma 156 06500 Mexico City Mexico E-mail: rro@attglobalnet.

RAMIREZ-MIRELES, FERNANDO, electrical engineer; s. Fernando Ramirez Matuk and Maria Elia Mireles Tabares; m. Gina Miroslava Guerrero Barja; children: Tania Fernanda Ramirez Guerrero, Thalia Miroslava Ramirez Guerrero. BSc in Electronics Comm., Met. Autonomous U., Mexico City; MScEE, Ctr. for Rsch. and Advanced Studies of Nat. Polytechnic Inst., Mexico City; PhDEE, U. So. Calif. Intern Mex. Tel. Co., Mexico City, 1987—88; rschr. Ctr. for Rsch. and Advanced Studies Nat. Polytechnic Inst., 1988—92; rsch. asst. U. So. Calif., L.A., 1996—98; summer intern Torrey Sci. Corp., San Diego, 1997; mem. tech. staff Glenayre/Wireless Access, Santa Clara, 1998—99; comm. sys. engr. Aware, Inc., Lafayette, 1999—2001; sr. comm. sys. engr. Ikanos Comms., Fremont, 2001—. Cons. Nat. Bank Mex., Mexico City, 1991. Contbr. articles to profl. jours. and confs. Named Candidate to Nat. Rschr., Nat. Sys. Rschrs., Mex., 1993—94; named one of Best Students of Mex., Best Students of Mex. Orgn., 1989; recipient Fulbright Scholarship, Fulbright-Garcia Robles Commn., 1992—97, Universitarian Merit medal, Met. Autonomous Univ., Mex., 1987, Honorific Mention, IV Ericsson's Nat. Prize of Sci. and Tech., Mex., 1990. Mem.: IEEE (sr.), Soc. Hispanic Profl. Engrs., Tau Beta Pi. Achievements include co-inventor in three patent applications for DSL communications. Avocation: travel. Home: 1319 Montego 65 Walnut Creek CA 94598 Office: Ikanos Comms 47709 Fremont Blvd Fremont CA 94538 Personal E-mail: fernandomireles@yahoo.com. Business E-Mail: ramirezm@ieee.org.

RAMIREZ-RIVERA, JOSE, physician; b. Mayaguez, P.R., June 26, 1929; s. Jesus Ramirez and Nieves Rivera; m. Leila Suner, May 14, 1971; children: Federico, Steven, Sally, Juliette, Natasha, Leila. BA, Johns Hopkins U., 1949; MD, Yale U., 1953. Diplomate Am Bd Internal Med. Intern U. Md. Hosp., 1953-54; resident in medicine Univ. Hosp., Balt., 1954-55, fellow in hematology, 1958-59, resident, 1959; staff physician VA Hosp., 1960-67, assoc. chief of staff, 1962-68; asst. in medicine Johns Hopkins U., 1960-67, instr. in medicine, 1967-68; asst. prof. medicine U. Md., 1961-68; assoc. prof. Duke U., Durham, N.C., 1968-70; dir. med. edn. and clin. investigation Western

Region P.R., 1970-80; chief medicine Mayaguez (P.R.) Med. Ctr., 1971-82. Prof med Univ PR, San Juan, 1974—, dir univ med servs Med Sci Campus, 1982—86; prof med Univ Cent del Caribe, 1998—; dir Rincon Rural Health Project, 1975—82; assoc chief staff educ VA Med Ctr, San Juan, 1990—92; dir clin investigation La Concepcion Hosp, San German, 1996—. Contbr. articles to med jours. Bd dirs Soc Educ Suroeste. With USPHS, 1955—57. Fellow: ACP (pres. PR chpt. 1986—88), Coll. Chest Physicians, Royal Soc. Med (London); mem.: Puerto Rican Fedn Bioethics (bd. dirs. 1999—2002, pres. 2002—), Soc. Autores Puertorriguenos, PR Lung Assn. (bd. dirs. 1975—80), Casa Espanã (bd. dirs. 1998—), Alliance Francaise PR (v.p. 1995—96, pres. 1996—2000), PEN Club. Roman Catholic. E-mail: ramirj@hotmail.com.

RAMLO, SARA B. computer company executive; b. Fargo, N.D., Feb. 6, 1974; d. Robert A. Ramlo and Nancy A. Decker. BS, Truman State U., 1996; MPA, Syracuse U., 1997. Cons. Andersen Cons., Mpls., 1997-99; web strategist, mgr. IBM, N.Y.C., 1999—. Congrl. intern U.S. Senate, Washington, Fargo, N.D., 1994, 95, congrl. fellowship, 1997. Recipient Truman fellowship Harry S. Truman Found., 1995. Office: IBM 1133 Westchester Ave White Plains NY 10604 E-mail: ramlosa@us.ibm.com.

RAMM, DOUGLAS ROBERT, psychologist; b. New Haven, Dec. 11, 1949; s. Robert Frederick and Gladys (Torgrimson) R.; m. Barbara Stephens, Aug. 10, 1974; children: Jennifer, Jessica. BA, Ithaca Coll., 1972; MA, Duquesne U., 1974, PhD, 1979. Diplomate Am. Bd. Profl. Psychology; bd. cert. clin. psychologist Am. Bd. Profl. Psychology. Staff psychologist Westmoreland Hosp., Greensburg, Pa., 1976-79, chief clin. psychologist, dir. child & adolescent psychiat., 1979-82; pvt. practice, 1980—. Pres. Ethics, Inc., Ctr. for Sci. Study of Values and Morality, 1995-98; cons. U. Pitts., Pa. Bur. Vocat. Rehab., Westmoreland County Ct. of Common Pleas; past pres. Mental Health Assn. Westmoreland County. Author: Clinically Formulated Principles of Morality, 1996. Mem. APA, ASCD, Am. Philos. Assn., Pa. Psychol. Assn., Acad. Clin. Psychology, Soc. Personality Assessment, Nat. Acad. Neuropsychologists, Am. Bd. Med. Psychotherapists, Nat. Register Health Svc. Providers in Psychology, Am. Coll. Forensic Examiners (diplomate), Soc. Bus. Ethics. Methodist. Home: 319 Elm Dr Greensburg PA 15601-5714 Office: 225 Humphrey Rd Greensburg PA 15601-4571 E-mail: plato1211@aol.com.

RAMMING, MICHAEL ALEXANDER, retired school system administrator; b. St. Louis, Feb. 4, 1940; s. William Alexander and Emily Louise (Reingruber) R.; m. Susan Ray Oliver, July 9, 1962; children: Michael Murray, Todd Alexander. BS, Centenary Coll., 1963; MA, Washington U., St. Louis, 1968. Cert. adminstr. secondary schs., Mo. Teacher and coach Ladue Sch. Dist., St. Louis, 1963-88, adminstr., 1988—2002. Adj. prof. Lindenwood U., 2002—; cons. Ladue Sch. Dist., 2002—. Vol. Sr. Olympics, St. Louis, 1992, 93. Mem. Nat. Assn. Secondary Sch. Prins., Mo. Assn. Secondary Sch. Prins., Nat. Interscholastic Athletic Adminstrs. Assn., Mo. Interscholastic Athletic Adminstrs. Assn. (25 Yr. Svc. award). Avocations: tennis, walking, travel. Home: 18128 Dawns Trail Wildwood MO 63005 Office: Ladue Horton Watkins High Sch 1201 S Warson Rd Saint Louis MO 63124-1266 *As I look back I feel that participation in sports as a player, coach, and fan provided me with a wealth of leadership, community building, daring, sharing, and the ability to accept success and failure.*

RAMMLER, LINDA HOPE, human services consultant; b. Bklyn., July 10, 1955; d. Walter and Helen (Shymanski) R.; m. Mark S. Partin; children: Timothy James, Larissa Ellen, Elizabeth Kay, Benjamin Michael. BA, U. Conn., 1975; MEd, U. Hartford, 1982; PhD, Yale U., 2000. Tchr. aide Hartford Regional Ctr., Newington, Conn., 1974; human rights aide, recreation program instr. Mansfield (Conn.) Tng. Sch., 1976-78; instr. Manchester (Conn.) Community Coll., 1978-79; substitute tchr., program specialist John N. Dempsey Regional Ctr., Putnam, Conn., 1979-80; planning analyst then dir. planning and evaluation Dept. Mental Retardation, East Hartford, 1980-85; exec. asst. Univ. Affiliated Program, Storrs, 1986-87; coord. CARC v. Thorne study Rsch. Project on Deinstitutionalization, Phila., 1987-88; project co-dir. Consumer Survey Devel. Disabilities Coun., East Hartford, 1988-89; human svcs. cons. in disability issues and inclusive edn. Conn., 1985—; ptnr. Rammler & Wood Cons., LLC, 1995—. Part-time instr. Yale U., New Haven, 1989-97, Ctrl. Conn. State U., 1994, Tunxis CC, 2001; staff devel. instr. N.E. Area Regional Edn. Svc., Putnam, 1979; presenter programs to various orgns., including Conn. Psychol. Assn., Young Adult Inst. N.Y.C., New England Ednl. Rsch. Orgn., others. Mem. Middletown Co. Concerning People with Disabilities, Conn., 1990-91. Mem. ASCD, CEC (learning disabilities, mental retardation tchr. preparation divsn.), Brain Rsch. Network, Acad. Mental Retardation, Am. Assn. Mental Retardation (adminstrn. div.), Nat. Assn. Dual Diagnosis, Assn. Retarded Citizens of Conn., Conn. Coalition for Inclusive Edn., TASH (nat. org. and New Eng. chpt.). Home: 80 Toad Ridge Rd Middlefield CT 06455-1114 Office: 6 Way Rd Ste 301 Middlefield CT 06455-1080

RAMO, ROBERTA COOPER, lawyer; b. Denver, Aug. 8, 1942; d. David D. and Martha L. (Rosenblum) Cooper; m. Barry W. Ramo, June 17, 1964. BA magna cum laude, U. Colo., 1964; JD, U. Chgo., 1967; LLD, U. Mo., 1995, U. Denver, 1995; LHD (hon.), U. Colo., 1995; JD (hon.), Golden Gate U., 1996, U. S.C., 2001. Bar: N.Mex. 1967, Tex. 1971. With NC. Fund, Durham, 1967-68; nat. tchg. fellow Shaw U., Raleigh, N.C., 1968-70; mem. Sawtelle, Goode, Davidson & Troilo, San Antonio, 1970-72, Rodey, Dickason, Sloan, Akin & Robb, Albuquerque, 1972-74; sole practice law, 1974-77; dir., shareholder Poole, Kelly & Ramo, 1977-93; shareholder Modrall, Sperling, Roehl, Harris & Sisk, 1993—. Lectr. in field., bd. dirs. Merrill Lynch Asset Mgmt., Ednl. Credit Mgmt. Corp. Co-author: New Mexico Estate Administration System, 1980; editor: How to Create a System for the Law Office, 1975; contbg. editor: Tex. Probate Sys., 1974; contbr. articles to profl. jours., chpts. to books. Bd. dirs., past pres. N.Mex. Symphony Orch., 1977-86; bd. dirs. Albuquerque Cmty . Found., N.Mex. First, 1987-90, Santa Fe Opera, 2001-; bd. regents U. N.Mex., 1989-94, pres., 1991-93, chmn. presdl. search com., 1990; mem. steering com. World Conf. Domestic Violence, 1996-99; mem. Am. Law Inst. Coun., 1997—, exec. com., 2000—; mem. Martindale-Hubbell Legal Adv. Bd., 1996-2000; chmn. bd. Cooper's Inc., 1999—; founding bd. mem. Think N.Mex., 1998—; mem. Civitas Initiative, 1997—. Recipient Disting. Pub. Svc. award Gov. of N.Mex., 1993. Fellow: Am. Bar Found.; mem.: ABA (pres. 1995, bd. govs. 1994—97, chmn. London 2000 com., Asia Law Initiatives Coun. 1999—, others), Am. Arbitration Assn. (bd. dirs. 1997—, bd. trustees Global Ctr. Dispute Resolution Rsch. 1999—), Law Inst. Coun., Am. Judicature Soc. (bd. dirs. 1988—91), Am. Bar Retirement Assn. (bd. dirs. 1990—94), N.Mex. Bar Assn. (Outstanding Contbn. award 1981, 1984), Albuquerque Bar Assn. (bd. dirs., pres. 1980—81), Greater Albuquerque C. of C. (bd. dirs., exec. com. 1987—91). Address: Modrall Sperling Roehl Harris & Sisk PO Box 2168 Albuquerque NM 87103-2168

RAMO, SIMON, retired engineering executive; b. Salt Lake City, May 7, 1913; s. Benjamin and Clara ((Trestman)) Ramo; m. Virgina Smith, July 25, 1937; children: James Brian, Alan Martin. BS, U. Utah, 1933, DSc (hon.), 1961; PhD, Calif. Inst. Tech., 1936; DEng (hon.), Case Western Res. U., 1960, U. Mich., 1966, Poly. Inst. N.Y., 1971; DSc (hon.), Union Coll., 1963, Worcester Polytechnic Inst., 1968, U. Akron, 1969, Cleve. State U., 1976; LLD (hon.), Carnegie-Mellon U., 1970, U. So. Calif., 1972, Gonzaga U., 1983, Occidental Coll., 1984, Claremont U., 1985. With Gen. Electric Co., 1936—46; v.p. ops. Hughes Aircraft Co., 1946—53; with Ramo-Woolridge Corp., 1953—58; dir. U.S. Intercontinental Ballistic Missile Program, 1954—58, TRW Inc., 1954—85, exec. v.p., 1958—61, vice chmn. bd., 1961—78, chmn. exec. com., 1969—78, cons., 1978—; pres. The Bunker-Ramo Corp., 1964—66; chmn. bd. TRW-Fujitsu Co., 1980—83. Bd. dirs. Arco Power Techs.; vis. prof. mgmt. sci. Calif. Inst. Tech., 1978—; Regents lectr. UCLA, 1981—82, U. Calif. at Santa Cruz, 1978—79; chmn. Ctr. for Study Am. Experience, U. So. Calif., 1978—80; Faculty fellow John F. Kennedy Sch. Govt., Harvard U., 1980—84; mem. White House Energy Rsch. and Devel. Adv. Coun., 1973—75; chmn. Pres.'s Com. on Sci. and Tech., 1976—77; bd. advisors for sci. and tech. Repu. of China, 1981—84; chmn. bd. Aetna, Jacobs & Ramo Venture Capital, 1987—90, Allenwood Ventures, Inc., 1987—; advisor Axiom Venture Ptnrs., 1997—. Author: (novels) The Business of Science, 1988, other sci., engring. and mgmt. books. Life trustee Calif. Inst. Tech., Nat. Symphony Orch. Assn., 1973—83; trustee emeritus Calif. State Univs.; bd. govs., pres. Performing Arts Coun. Mus. Ctr. La., 1976—77; co-chair bd. overseers Keck Sch. Medicine, U. So. Calif., 1999—; Bd. dirs. L.A. World Affairs Coun., 1973—85, Mus. Ctr. Found., L.A., Calif., L.A. Philharm. Assn., 1981—84. Named to Bus. Hall of Fame, 1984; recipient IAS, 1956, award, Am. Inst. Elec. Engrs., 1959, Am. Iron and Steel Inst., 1968, Disting. Svc. medal, Armed Forces Comm. and Electronics Assn., 1970, medal of achievement, WEMA, 1970, awards, U. So. Calif., 1971, 1979, Kayan medal, Columbia U., 1972, award, Am. Cons. Engrs. Coun., 1974, medal, Franklin Inst., 1978, Aesculapian award, UCLA, 1984, Durand medal, AAIA, 1984, John Fritz medal, 1986, henry Townley Heald award, Ill. Inst. Tech., 1988, Nat. Engring. award, Am. Assn. Engring. Socs., 1988, Franklin-Jefferson medal, 1988, Howard Hughes meml. award, 1989, Air Force Space and Missile Pioneers award, 1989, Pioneer award, Internat. Coun. on Sys. Engring., 1997, Disting. pub. Svc. medal, NASA, 1999, Lifetime Achievement trophy, Smithsonian Inst., 1999, John F. Kennedy Astronautics award, Am. Astronautical Soc., 2000, John R. Alison award for indsl. leadership, Air Force Assn., 2000. Fellow: Am. Acad. Polit. Sci., Am. Acad. Arts and Scis., IEEE (Electronic Achievement award 1953, Golden Omega award 1975, Founders medal 1980, Centennial medal 1984); mem.: Nat. Acad. Engring. (founder, coun. mem. Bueche award), Internat. Acad. Astronautics, Pacific Coun. Internat. Policy, Coun. Fgn. Rels., Inst. advancement Engring., Am. Philos. Soc., Am. Phys. Soc., N.Y. Acad. Scis., Theta Tau (Hall of Fame laureate), Eta Kappa Nu (eminent mem. award 1966). Office: 9200 W Sunset Blvd Ste 801 Los Angeles CA 90069-3603

RAMO, VIRGINIA M. SMITH, civic worker; b. Yonkers, N.Y. d. Abraham Harold and Freda (Kasnetz) Smith; m. Simon Ramo; children: James Brian, Alan Martin. BS in Edn., U. So. Calif., DHL (hon.), 1978. Nat. co-chmn., ann. giving U. So. Calif., 1968-70, vice chmn., trustee, 1971—, co-chmn. bd. councilors Sch. Performing Arts, 1975-76, co-chmn. bd. councillors Schs. Med. and Engring. Vice-chmn. bd. overseers Hebrew Union Coll., 1972-75; bd. dirs. The Muses of Calif. Mus. Sci. and Industry, UCLA Affiliates, Estelle Doheny Eye Found., U. So. Calif. Sch. Medicine; mem. adv. coun. L.A. County Heart Assn., chmn. com. to endow Chair in cardiology at U. So. Calif.; vice chmn., bd. dirs. Friends of Libr. U. So. Calif.; bd. dirs., nat. pres. Achievement Rewards for Coll. Scientists Found., 1975-77; bd. dirs. Les Dames L.A., Cmty. TV So. Calif.; bd. dirs., v.p. Founders L.A. Music Ctr.; v.p. L.A. Music Ctr. Opera Assn.; v.p. corp. bd. United Way; v.p. Blue Ribbon-400 Performing Arts Coun.; chmn. com. to endow chair in gerontology U. So. Calif.; vice chmn. campaign Doheny Eye Inst,. 1986; co-chair, bd. overseers Keck Sch. Medicine U. So. Calif., 1999—. Recipient Svc. award Friends of Libr., 1974, Nat. Cmty. Svc. award Alpha Epsilon Phi, 1975, Disting. Svc. award Am. Heart Assn., 1978, Svc. award U. So. Calif., Spl. award U. So. Calif. Music Alumni Assn., 1979, Life Achievement award Mannequins of L.A. Assistance League, 1979, Woman of Yr. award Pan Hellenic Assn., 1981, Disting. Svc. award U. So. Calif. Sch. Medicine, 1981, U. So. Calif. Town and Gown Recognition award, 1986, Asa V. Call Achievement award U. So. Calif., 1986, Phi Kappa Phi scholarship award U. So. Calif., 1986, Vision award Luminaires of Doheny Eye Inst., 1994, Presdl. medallion U. So. Calif., 2002. Mem. UCLA Med. Aux., U. So. Calif. Pres.'s Cir., Commerce Assocs. U. So. Calif., Cedars of Lebanon Hosp. Women's Guild (dir. 1967-68), Blue Key, Skull and Dagger.

RAMOS, ALBERT A. electrical engineer; b. L.A., Feb. 28, 1927; s. Jesus D. and Carmen F. (Fontes) R.; B.S. in Elec. Engring., U. So. Calif., 1950, M.S. in Systems Mgmt., 1972; Ph.D., U.S. Internat. U., 1975; m. Joan C. Pailing, Sept. 23, 1950; children— Albert A., Richard R., James J., Katherine. With guided missile test group Hughes Aircraft Co., 1950-60; with TRW DSG, 1960-91, sr. staff engr. Norton AFB, San Bernardino, Calif., 1969-91, ret., 1991. Served with USNR, 1945-46. Registered profl. engr., Calif. Mem. IEEE, NSPE, Air Force Assn., Mexican-Am. Engring. Soc., Mexican-Am. Profl. Mgmt. Assn. (mem. administering commn. dept. community svcs.), Sigma Phi Delta, Eta Kappa Nu, Tau Beta Pi. Home: 8937 Napoli Dr Las Vegas NV 89117-1182

RAMOS, CARLOS E. law educator; b. Caguas, P.R., Oct. 20, 1952; s. Francisco E. and Olga (Gonzalez) R.; m. Lesbia Hernandez, July 30, 1988; children: Carlos Francisco, Isabel Maria, Macarena Eugenia. BA, U. P.R., 1974, JD, 1978; diploma, U. Stockholm, 1975; LLM, U. Calif., Berkeley, 1987. Bar: P.R. 1978, U.S. Dist. Ct. P.R. 1978, U.S. Ct. Appeals (1st cir.) 1979. Staff atty. P.R. Legal Svcs., San Juan, P.R., 1978-79; asst. prof. law InterAm. U. P.R., 1979-86, assoc. prof., 1986-93, dean, 1993-2000, prof. law, 1993—; exec. dir. Santurce Law Firm, San Jose, 1983-86. Co-author: Derecho Constitucional de Puerto Rico y los Estados Unidos, 1990, Teoria y Practica de la Litigacion en Puerto Rico. Mem. ABA, ATLA, Am. Judicature Soc., P.R. Bar Assn. Office: InterAm U PR Sch Law PO Box 70351 San Juan PR 00936-8351 E-mail: ceramos@inter.edu.

RAMOS, CATHERINE LEHR, musician, cellist; b. Cleve., Dec. 7, 1949; d. Joseph Martin and Joan (Kimnach) Lehr; m. Manuel Ramos, 1981; children: Mary Ann, Elizabeth, David. BMusic, Eastman Sch. Music, 1971; MMusic, Ind. U., 1974. Prin. cello San Diego Symphony, 1985-86; asst. prin. cello St. Louis Symphony, 1975—. Mem. cello faculty Rocky Montain Summer Conservatory, Steamboat Springs, summers 1997-; cellist Trio Cassatt, St. Louis, 1980-85. Recorded string trios by Taniev and Reger, 1984. Presbyterian. Office: St Louis Symphony 718 N Grand Blvd Saint Louis MO 63103-1079

RAMOS, CHARLES JOSEPH (JOE RAMOS), wealth management consultant; b. Orinda, Calif., July 29, 1960; s. Charles Pimentel Ramos Jr. and Louise Antoinette Troja; m. Christine H. Schulz, Sept. 25, 1994; children: Summer Erica, Drake Joseph. BS, U. Calif., Berkeley, 1982. CPA, Calif.; CFP; registered investment advisor SEC. CPA Arthur Andersen, San Francisco, 1982-85; sr. analyst Montgomery Securities, 1985-87; fin. cons. Ramos Fin. Group, 1987-96; pres., CEO Pvt. Capital Mgmt., Inc., Larkspur, 2002—; sr. mng. dir. The Pvt. Cons. Group., Inc., 2002—. Nat. adv. bd. Empowered Wealth, LLC; mem. Am. Skandia Adv. Coun., Eaton Vance Advisors Coun. Mem. AICPA, Internat. Bd. CFP, Nat. Assn. Life Underwriters, The Fin. Planning Assn., Nat. Assn. Securities Dealers, Marin Estate Planning Coun., San Francisco Estate Planning Coun., Million Dollar Roundtable (Top of the Table divsn.), Olympic Club. Republican. Office: The Pvt Consulting Group Ste 240 900 Larkspur Landing Cir Larkspur CA 94939-1757 Office Fax: (415) 464-9755. Business E-Mail: jramos@privateconsulting.com.

RAMOS, DIANE PATRIGNANI, management consultant; b. Uniontown, Pa., Apr. 20, 1949; d. Dominick and Angela (Faini) Patrignani; m. William Thomas Ramos, July 24, 1971; children: Zachary, Benjamin, Rebecca. BA, U. Pitts., 1971, MBA, 1977. Sales rep. Procter & Gamble, Pitts., 1971; pub. rels. IMA of N.Y., N.J., Conn., Albany, 1972-73; mgr. sales promotion Calgon divsn. Merk & Co., Pitts., 1973-78; dir. sales planning and promotion Smith Kline Beecham, 1978-90; pres. DPR Assocs., 1990—. Adj. prof. Duquesne U., Pitts., 1991—; mid. sch. coach Odyssey of the Mind, 1998-2000. Co-author: Hook 'Em: Speaking & Writing to Catch & Keep and Audience, 1996. Chair Twp. Parenting Workshop Series, Pitts., 1991-97; unit leader day camp Girl Scouts U.S., Pitts., 1997-99. Mem. Zonta Club Pitts. (pres.). Roman Catholic. Avocations: helping children with dyslexia, supporting fine arts preservation, piano lessons, mentoring. Office: DPR Assocs 1691 Pinetree Dr Pittsburgh PA 15241-2947

RAMOS, MIGUEL WILLIE, priest, educator; b. Regla, Havana, Cuba, Sept. 29, 1958; s. Juana Rita Olga Nebot, Maximo Orlando Ramos; m. Nilda Ramos, Mar. 18, 1958; children: Caesar. MA in History, Fla. Internat. U., 2001. Rschr. Caribbean percussions exhibit Hist. Mus. So. Fla., Miami, 1997—97, guest curator, 1998—2001; adj. prof. Fla. Internat. U., 1997—. Contbr. author Santeria Aesthetics in Contemporary Latin American Art, 1996; author: Ase Omo Osayín. . .Ewé Ayé, 1980, Dida Obi. . .Adivinación a Traves del Coco, 1982, Oro Egungun. . .Las Honras de Egungun, 1982; dir.: (mus. exhibit) At The Crossroads: Afrocuban Orisha Arts in Miami, 2001. Dir. cou. oriates Ch. of Lukumi Babalu Aye, 2001—02. Grantee Rsch. grant, Ford Found./Cuban Rsch. Inst., Fla. Internat. U., 1999. Mem.: Am. Hist. Assn., Cabildo Yoruba Omo Orisha, Inc. Mem. Lukumí Orisha. Avocations: field research, travel. Personal E-mail: Ilari@eleda.org.

RAMOS, ROSE MARY, retired elementary education educator; b. San Antonio, Aug. 8, 1942; d. Henry Barbosa and Bertha Alice (Cuellar) Gonzalez; m. Jesus Ramos Jr., Sept. 11, 1965; children: Rebecca Anne, Veronica Anne. BS in Elem. Edn., Our Lady of Lake U., San Antonio, 1965; MA in Edn., U. Houston, 1992. Cert. elem. educator, kindergarten, reading specialist, bilingual and ESL. Tchr. San Antonio Ind. Sch. Dist., 1965-89, Ft. Bend County (Tex.) Ind. Sch. Dist., 1989-2001; ret., 2001—. Acad. adv. com. Ft. Bend I.S.D., 1996. Mem. Fort Bend Women's Tex. Dem. Party. Mem. San Antonio Conservation Soc. Democrat. Roman Catholic. Avocations: reading, life sciences, writing. Home: 3614 Belle Grove Ln Sugar Land TX 77479-2257 E-mail: rmramos@houston.rr.com.

RAMOS, THEODORE SANCHEZ DE PIÑA, artist, educator; b. Oporto, Portugal, Oct. 30, 1928; s. Guillermo Sanchez de Piña and Patrocinio Ramos Garcia; m. Julia Nan Rushbury, Aug. 17, 1950; children: Julian Sanchez de Piña (dec. 1986), Adrian Henry, Benedict John, Dominic Salvador. Student, Colégio Araugo Lima, 1936—39, No. Poly. London, 1943-45, Hornsey Sch. Art, 1945-47; diploma in fine art, Royal Acad. Schs., London, 1949-54. Freelance portrait painter. Advisor on design and graphics Royal Acad. Arts, London; vis. lectr. fine art Royal Acad. Schs., 1954-75, Brighton Coll. Art, 1956-70, Harrow Sch. Art, 1960-69; cons. on graphics to numerous orgns. Illustrator Chinese art for Penguin Classics, poster and catalog design for Royal Acad.; represented in permanent collections Nat. Portrait Gallery, Royal Acad.; portraits include Anita Leslie and Lord Thorneycroft, Sir Henry Rushbury, Her Majesty the Queen, His Royal Highness The Duke of Edinburgh, Prince Charles, The Queen Mother. Recipient Royal Acad. Silver medal, 1953; titular Count of Codevilla. Mem. East India Club (life), Devonshire Club (life), Marylebone Cricket Club. Liberal. Roman Catholic. Home: Studio 3 Chelsea Farmhouse Milmans St London SW10 ODA England

RAMOS-CANO, HAZEL BALATERO, caterer, chef, innkeeper, restaurateur, entrepreneur; b. Davao City, Mindanao, Philippines, Sept. 2, 1936; came to U. S., 1960. d. Mauricio C. and Felicidad (Balatero) Ramos; m. William Harold Snyder, Feb. 17, 1964 (div. 1981); children: John Byron, Snyder, Jennifer Ruth; m. Nelson Allen Blue, May 30, 1986 (div. 1990); m. A. Richard Cano, June 25, 1994. BA in Social Work, U. Philippines, Quezon City, 1958; MA in Sociology, Pa. State U., 1963, postgrad., 1966-67. Cert. exec. chef, Am. Culinary Fedn. Faculty, tng. staff Peace Corps Philippine Project, University Park, Pa., 1961-63; sociology instr. Albright Coll. Sociology Dept., Reading, 1963-64; research asst. Meth. Ch. U.S.A., State College, 1965-66; research asst. dept. child devel. & family relations Pa. State U., University Park, 1966-67; exec. dir. Presbyn. Urban Coun. Raleigh Halifax Ct. Child Care and Family Svc. Ctr., 1973-79; early childhood educator Learning Together, Inc., Raleigh, 1982-83; loan mortgage specialist Raleigh Savings & Loan, 1983-84; restaurant owner, mgr. Hazel's on Hargett, Raleigh, 1985-86; admissions coord., social worker Brian Corp. Nursing Home, 1986-88, food svc. dir., 1989-90; regional dir. La Petite Acad., 1989-90; asst. food svc. mgr. Granville Towers, Chapel Hill, N.C., 1990-92; mgr. trainee Child Nutrition Svcs. Wake County Pub. Sch. System, Raleigh, 1993-94; food svc. dir. S.W. Va. 4-H Ednl. Conf. Ctr., Abingdon, 1994-95; caterer, owner The Eclectic Chef's Catering, 1995—; innkeeper, owner Love House Bed and Breakfast, 1996—; pres. Ramos-Cano Inc., 1996—; owner Withaus Hardware Restaurant, Abingdon, Va., 2002—; pres. Ramos-Cano Mgmt. Svcs., LLC, 2002—. Cooking instr. Wake Cmty. Tech. Coll., Raleigh, 1986-92; freelance caterer, 1964-95; chair Internat. Cooking Demonstrations Raleigh Internat. Festival, 1990-93. Pres. Wake County Day Care United Coun., 1974-75, N.C. Assn. Edn. Young Children (Raleigh Chpt.), 1975-76; bd. mem. Project Enlightenment Wake County Pub. Schs., 1976-77; various positions Pines of Carolina Girl Scout Council, 1976-85; chmn. Philippine Health and Medical Aid Com., Phil-Am Assn. Raleigh 1985-88 (publicity chmn.); elder Trinity Presbyn. Ch., Raleigh, 1979-81, bd. deacons, 1993-94; elder, session mem. Sinking Spring Presbyn. Ch., 1997—; treas. Abingdon Newcomers Club, 1997—, Presbyn. Women, Sinking Spring Presbyn. Ch., Abingdon, 1999—; master gardener Va. Tech. Master Gardeners Program, 1998—. Recipient Juliette Low Girl Scout Internat. award, 1953, Rockefeller grant Rockefeller Found., 1958-59, Ramon Magsaysay Presidential award, Philippine Leadership Youth Movement, 1957; Gov.'s Cert. Appreciation State N.C., 1990, Raleigh Mayor's award Quality Childcare Svcs., 1990, Recipient award for keeping hist. Abingdon beautiful Abington Kiwanis Club, 1997. Mem. Am. Culinary Fedn., Presby. Women, Raleigh, (historian 1975-76), Penn State Dames (pres. 1968-69). Democrat. Office: Victoria & Albert Inn 224 Oak Hill St Abingdon VA 24210 also: The Love House Bed and Breakfast 210 E Valley St Abingdon VA 24210 E-mail: v&ainn@naxs.com., lovehouse@naxs.com.

RAMOS-MOLL, ERVIN, career officer, federal agency administrator; b. Utuado, P.R., Apr. 4, 1947; s. Carlos Ramos and Balbina Moll; m. Ruth E. Ruiz-Aceuedo, June 6, 1972; children: Ervin, Jr., Carlos S., Mary M. BBA in Econs., InterAm. U., 1969, MBA in Mktg. Mgmt., 1974, MEd in Guidance, Counselling, 1976. Commd. 1st lt. U.S. Army, 1975, col., 1968—; mil. personnel supr. ROTC, RUM, Mayaguez, P.R., 1972-75; revenue officer IRS, 1975-80, group mgr., 1980-86, Hato Rey, P.R., 1986-91, chief field br. Ft. Lauderdale, Fla., 1991-95, Miami, 1995-99, chief special procedures br. Ft. Lauderdale, 1999—, SBSE terr. mgr. Miami. Dep. chief staff logistics 65 ARCOM, Ft. Buchanan, P.R., 1995-97; commdr. 265th USARF Sch. Brigade, Caquas, P.R., 1997-99, asst. chief of staff 143rd TRANSCOM, Orlando, Fla. Recipient Bronze Star, 1970. Avocations: stamp collecting, computers, electronics, science fiction. Office: IRS 51 SW 1st Ave Miami FL 33130 E-mail: ermoll@bellsouth.net, ervin.ramos@ml.irs.gov.

RAMOS-ZÚÑIGA, RODRIGO, neurosurgeon, educator; b. Autlan, Jalisco, Mex., July 13, 1962; s. Roberto and Dolores (Zúñiga) R.; m. Rocio Enriquez, Apr. 3, 1993; 1 child, Rodrigo. MD, U. de Guadalajara, 1986, degree in neurosurgery, 1992, MSc, 2000; PhD in Neuroscis., U. de Guadelajara. Tech. asst. U. Guadalajara, 1982-86, prof. physiology, 1986-99, prof. neurosci., 1999—, chmn. lab. of neuroscis. Prof. VGF Hosp., Guadalajara, 1992—; pres. sci. com. med. students U. Guadalajara, 1985, pres. bachelors. Author: Neurophysiology, 1998; editor Neurosciences Jour., 1997; contbr. articles to profl. jours. Recipient Nat. Young award in Scis. from Pres. of Mex., 1987. Mem. Mexican Soc. Exptl. Surgery (v.p.), Mexican Soc. Neurol. Surgeons (sci. advisor), Mexican Surg. Rsch. Soc., Am. Assn. Neurol. Surgeons, Am. Assn. Neurol. (internat. mem. cerebrovascular sect.). Avocations: music, poetry, camping, snorkeling. Office: Univ Guadalajara Victoria 1531 Guadalajara 44630 Mexico E-mail: rodrigor@cencar.udg.mx.

RAMP, MARJORIE JEAN SUMERWELL, civic worker; b. Kansas City, Mo., July 20, 1924; d. Walter Francis and Helen Louise (Nichols) Sumerwell; m. Floyd Lester Ramp, Sept. 4, 1948; children: David L., Sandra Jean, Paul F., Cheryl Louise. BS in Nursing Edn., U. Minn., 1948. RN, Minn. Instr. nursing edn. U. Minn., Mpls., 1948-50; adminstrv. asst. to assn. minister Western Res. Assn. of Ohio Conf. United Ch. of Christ, Cleve., 1983-85. Former chmn. hunger task force Ohio Conf. of United Ch. of Christ, moderator, 19 81-82, moderator West. Res. Assn., 1976-77, mem. nat. exec. coun., 1983-89; mem. United Ch. Bd. for World Ministries, 1971-82; past bd. dirs. Western Res. coun. Girl Scouts U.S.; nat. sec. Campaign for UN Reform, Washington, 1987-2000; pres. Greater Cleve.-Volgograd Oblast Alliance, 1998-99; coord., co-founder Richfield-Wolfach Twin City Program, 1970, bd. dirs., 1970-92; mem. numerous local and nat. peace groups; nongovtl. orgn. rep. Earth Summit, Rio de Janeiro, 1992, del. to UN commn. for sustainable devel.; bd. trustees Kendal at Oberlin Retirement Cmty. Recipient Golden Trefoil award We. Res. Coun. Girl Scouts U.S., 1972; named Outstanding Woman of Ohio Conf., Gen. Synod United Ch. of Christ, 1985. Mem. AAUW (pres. Oberlin chpt. 2001-), LWV, World Federalist Assn. (chmn. Ohio 1985—, bd. dirs., nat. exec. com. 1997—, vice-chmn. bd. dirs. 1999-), Delta Kappa Gamma (hon.). Home: 225 Hollywood St Oberlin OH 44074-1011 E-mail: msramp@oberlin.net.

RAMPERSAD, PEGGY A. SNELLINGS, sociologist; b. Fredericksburg, Va., Jan. 12, 1933; d. George Daniel and Virginia Riley (Bowler) Snellings; m. Oliver Ronald Rampersad, Mar. 19, 1955; 1 child, Gita. BA, Mary Washington Coll., Fredericksburg, 1953; student, Sch. of Art Inst. of Chgo., 1953-55; MA, U. Chgo., 1965, PhD, 1978. Grad. admissions counselor U. Chgo., 1954-57, adviser to fgn. students, 1958, dir. admissions Grad. Sch. Bus., 1959-63, rsch. project specialist Grad. Sch. Bus., 1970-78, pers. mgr. Grad. Sch. Bus., 1979-80, mgr. organizational devel. Grad. Sch. Bus., 1980-82, adminstr. dept. econs., 1983-95; cons. PSR Consulting, Chgo., 1995—. Cons. North Ctrl. Assn. Colls. and Secondary Schs., Chgo.,1964-70, Orchestral Assn. of Chgo. Symphony Orch., 1982, Chgo. Ctr. for Decision Rsch., 1982, Harvard U., 1993—. Exhibited paintings in juried shows at Va. Mus. Fine Arts, Art Inst.

Chgo., others; editor North Cen. Assn. Quar., 1972; contbr. articles to profl. jours. U. Chgo. grad. fellow, 1963-67. Mem. AAUW, Am. Econ. Assn., Am. Acad. Polit. and Social Sci., Art Inst. Chgo. (museum assoc.), Pi Lambda Theta (past pres.). Episcopalian. Avocations: painting and drawing, music--especially opera, reading, walking. Home and Office: 28 Seneca Ter Fredericksburg VA 22401-1115

RAMPOLLA, MAURA SMITH, public health professional; b. Phila., Apr. 12, 1968; d. Gerard Peter and Barbara McInnis Smith; m. Mark Stephen Rampolla, Oct. 3, 1998. BA in Polit. Sci., cert. African studies, Northwestern U., 1990; M in Pub. Health, U. N.C., 1996. Adminstrv. asst. Lassez et Associes, Paris, 1990; placement officer African-Am. Inst., N.Y.C., 1992-95; rsch. asst. Carolina Population Ctr., Chapel Hill, N.C., 1995-96; cons. Internat. Projects Assistance Svcs., Carrboro, 1996, Rsch. Triangle Inst., 1997; coord. health promotion Le Bonheur Children's Med. Ctr., Memphis, 1997-99; dir. edn. Memphis Regional Planned Parenthood, 1999; ind. cons., 2000—. Maternal and infant health com. mem. Shelby Regional Health Coun., Memphis, 1998-99; grant reviewer Women's Found. of Greater Memphis, 1998-99; advocacy chair, mem. Adolescent Pregnancy Prevention Coun., Memphis, 1997-99. ILAS Field Rsch. and Travel grant Tinker Found., 1996; fgn. lang. and area studies fellowship U.S. Dept. of Edn., 1996. Mem. Am. Pub. Health Assn. Avocations: scuba diving, hiking, singing. Home: 6400 Poplar Ave Apt E60 Memphis TN 38197-0100

RAMSAY, DAVID LESLIE, physician, dermatologist, medical educator; b. Rochester, N.Y., Apr. 25, 1943; s. Joseph Walter and Jean (Eastwood) R. AB in English with honors, Ind. U., 1965, MD, 1969; MEd, U. Ill., 1973. Diplomate Am. Bd. Dermatology. Assoc. faculty mem. Ind. U., Indpls., 1965-69; intern in medicine George Washington U. Med. Ctr., 1969-70; resident in dermatology NYU Med. Ctr., 1970-73; dir. dermatology residency tng. Nat. Naval Med. Ctr., Bethesda, Md., 1973-75; asst. prof. medicine Georgetown U., Washington, 1974-75; asst. prof. dermatology NYU, 1974-78, assoc. prof. dermatology, 1978-95, prof. dermatology, 1995—, senator, 1986-94, pres. faculty coun., 1988-90, dir. ednl. affairs dermatology, 1975—, dir. cutaneous lymphoma sect., 1975—. Author: Simulations in Dermatology, 1974; contbg. author: Adolescent Dermatology, Basic Mechanisms of Physiologic and Aberrant Lymphoproliferation in the Skin, Hematology and Oncology Clinics in North America; contbr. more than 25 articles to profl. jours. Pres., bd. dirs. One Fifth Ave. Apt. Corp., N.Y.C., 1978-80; trustee Bklyn. Acad. Music, 1989—. Lt. comdr. USN, 1973-75. NIH fellow U. Ill., 1972-73. Fellow ACP, Internat. Soc. Cutaneous Lymphomas, Am. Acad. Dermatology; mem. Am. Dermatologic Assn. Roman Catholic. Avocations: collecting visual art, swimming, reading. Home: One Fifth Ave New York NY 10003 Office: NYU Med Ctr 530 5th Ave New York NY 10036-5101

RAMSAY, DONALD ALLAN, physical chemist; b. London, July 11, 1922; s. Norman and Thirza Elizabeth (Beckley) Ramsay; m. Nancy Brayshaw, June 8, 1946 (dec. July 25, 1998); children: Shirley Margaret, Wendy Kathleen, Catharine Jean; m. Marjorie Craven Findlay, Apr. 13, 2000. BA, Cambridge (Eng.) U., 1943, MA, PhD, Cambridge (Eng.) U., 1947, ScD, 1976; D honoris causa, U. Reims, France, 1969; Filosofie hedersdoktor, U. Stockholm, Sweden, 1982. With divs. chemistry Nat. Research Council Can., Ottawa, Ont., 1947-49, with divs. physics, 1949-75; with Herzberg Inst. Astrophysics, 1975-87, sr. research officer, 1961-68, prin. research officer, 1968-87, guest worker, 1987—2001; rschr. emeritus Nat. Rsch. Coun. Can., 2002—. Vis. prof. U. Minn., 1964, U. Orsay, 1966, U. Stockholm, 1967, 71, 74, U. Calif., Irvine, 1970, U. Sao Paulo, 1972, 78, U. Bologna (Italy), 1973, U. We. Australia, 1976, Australian Nat. U., 1976, East China Normal U., Shanghai, 1987, Tex. Christian U., 1988, U. Wuppertal, Germany, 1988, U. Canterbury, Christchurch, New Zealand, 1991, Christchurch, 96, U. Ulm, Germany, 1992, Germany, 96, Germany, 97; emeritus researcher Steacie Inst. Molecular Scis. Editor: (with J. Hinze) Selected Works of Robert S. Mulliken, 1975; contbr. numerous articles on molecular spectra and molecular structure to profl. jours. Recipient commemorative medal for 125th anniversary Confederation Can., 1992, Alexander von Humboldt Rsch. award, 1993-95; decorated Queen Elizabeth Silver Jubilee medal. Fellow: Chem. Inst. Can. (Chem. Inst. Can. medal 1992), Am. Phys. Soc., Royal Soc. London, Royal Soc. Can. (life; treas. 1976—79, 1988—91, Centennial medal 1982); mem.: Order of Can. Mem. United Ch. of Canada (organist 1954-97). Club: Leander (Henley-on-Thames, Eng.). Home: 400 Laurier Ave E No 11 Ottawa ON Canada K1N 8Y2 Office: Nat Rsch Coun 100 Sussex Dr Ottawa ON Canada K1A 0R6 E-mail: donald.ramsay@nrc.ca.

RAMSAY, GUSTAVUS REMAK, actor; b. Balt., Feb. 2, 1937; s. John Breckinridge and Caroline V. (Remak) R. BA, Princeton U., 1958. Appeared in plays Hang Down Your Head and Die, 1964, Half A Sixpence, 1965, Lovely Ladies, Kind Gentlemen, Sheep on the Runway, 1970, On the Town, 1971, The Real Inspector Hound, After Magritte, 1972, Jumpers, 1974, Private Lives, 1975, Landscape of the Body, Dirty Linen, 1977, The Rear Column, 1978, All's Well That Ends Well, 1978, Every Good Boy Deserves Favor, 1980, Save Grand Central, 1980, The Winslow Boy, 1980-81, The Dining Room, 1982, as St. John Quartermaine in Quartermaine's Terms, 1983— (Obie award), Woman in Mind, 1988, The Devil's Disciple, 1988, Love Letters, 1989, Prin, 1990, Nick & Nora, 1991, St. Joan, 1993, The Moliere Comedies, 1995, The Heiress, 1995, Misalliance, 1997, Thief River, 2001; appeared in movies The Tiger Makes Out, The Stepford Wives, The Great Gatsby, The Front, Class, Simon, The House on Carroll Street, Mr. and Mrs. Bridge, Shadows and Fog, King of the Hill, Addicted to Love, Fever, 1998; TV movies The Dining Room, Heartbreak House, Kennedy, Liberty, Concealed Enemies, Dream House, Mellon, Lincoln and Seward, Dead Ahead: The Exxon Valdez Disaster, Truman. With U.S. Army, 1959-62. Democrat. Presbyterian. Home: 115 Central Park W New York NY 10023-4153

RAMSAY, KARIN KINSEY, publisher, educator; b. Brownwood, Tex., Aug. 10, 1930; d. Kirby Luther and Ina Rebecca (Wood) Kinsey; m. Jack Cummins Ramsay Jr., Aug. 31, 1951; children: Annetta Jean, Robin Andrew. BA, Trinity U., 1951. Cert. assoc. ch. edn., 1980. Youth coord. Covenant Presbyn. Ch., Carrollton, Tex., 1961-76; dir. ch. edn. Northminster Presbyn. Ch., Dallas, 1976-80, Univ. Presbyn. Ch., Chapel Hill, N.C., 1987-90, Oak Grove Presbyn. Ch., Bloomington, Minn., 1990-93; coord. ecum. ministry Flood Relief for Iowa, Des Moines, 1993; program coord. 1st Presbyn. Ch., Green Bay, Wis., 1994-95; owner, sole proprietor Hist. Resources Press, Corinth and Denton, Tex., 1994—. Dir. Godspell tour Covenant Presbyn. Ch., 1972-75; mem. Presbytery Candidates Com., Dallas, 1977-82, Presbytery Exams. Com. Dallas, 1979-81; clk. coun. New Hope Presbytery, Rocky Mount, N.C., 1989-90; creator, dir. Thee Holy Fools mime/musical group and This Is Me retreats. Author: Ramsay's Resources, 1983—; editor: Patton's Ill-Fated Raid, 2002; contbr. articles to jours. in field. Design cons. Brookhaven Hosp. Chapel, Dallas, 1977-78; elder Presbyn. Ch. U.S.A., 1982—; coord. Lifeline Emergency Response, Dallas, 1982-84. Mem. Internat. Platform Assn., Small Publisher's Assn. of N. Am., Writer's League of Tex. *Yesterday taught me the lessons which made today possible. Today is the challenging link between yesterday and tomorrow. Tomorrow is an opportunity built on the foundation of today. Today is special.*

RAMSAY, LOUIS LAFAYETTE, JR. lawyer, banker; b. Fordyce, Ark., Oct. 11, 1918; s. Louis Lafayette and Carmile (Jones) R.; m. Joy Bond, Oct. 3, 1945; children: Joy Blankenship, Richard Louis. JD, U. Ark., 1947; LLD (hon.), U. Ark., Fayetteville, 1988, U. Ark., Pine Bluff, 1992. Bar: Ark. 1947, U.S. Dist. Ct. Ark. 1947, U.S. Ct. Appeals (8th cir.) 1948, U.S. Supreme Ct. 1952. Of counsel Ramsay, Bridgforth, Harrelson & Starling and predecessor firm Ramsay, Cox, Lile, Bridgforth, Gilbert, Harrelson & Starling, Pine Bluff, Ark., 1948—; pres. Simmons First Nat. Bank, 1970-78, CEO, chmn. bd. dirs., 1978-83. Chmn. exec. com., bd. dirs. Blue Cross-Blue Shield of Ark., Usable Life Ins. Co.; chmn. exec. com. Simmons First Nat. Corp. Mem. bd. Econ. Devel. Alliance of Jefferson County; mem. ofcl. bd. First United Meth. Ch. With USAF, 1942-45, maj. Res., 1945-49. Recipient Disting. Alumnus award U. Ark., 1982, Outstanding Lawyer award Ark. Bar Assn./Ark. Bar Found., 1966, 87. Mem. ABA (mem. spl. com. on presdl. inability and vice presdl. vacancy 1966), Ark. Bar Assn. (pres. 1963-64), Ark. Bar Found. (pres. 1960-61, Joint Bar Assn.-Bar Found. Outstanding Lawyer award 1966, Lawyer Citizen award 1987), Ark. Bankers Assn. (pres. 1980-81), Pine Bluff C. of C. (pres. 1968), Rotary (pres. Pine Bluff 1954-55). Methodist. Office: Ramsay Bridgforth Harrelson & Starling 11th Fl Simmons 1st Nat Bldg 501 S Main St Pine Bluff AR 71601-4327 E-mail: firm@ramsaylaw.com.

RAMSAY, WILLIAM CHARLES, writer; b. N.Y.C., Nov. 6, 1930; s. Claude Barnett and Myrtle Marie (Scott) R.; m. Jane Coutant Evans, July 7, 1997; children from previous marriages: Alice, John, Carol Ramsay Scott, David. BA in English Lit., U. Colo., 1952; MA in Physics, UCLA, 1957, PhD in Physics, 1962. NFS postdoctoral fellow U. Calif., San Diego, 1962-64, asst. prof. Santa Barbara, 1964-67; tech. mgr. Systems Assocs., Inc., Long Beach, Calif., 1967-72; sr. environ. economist U.S. AEC, Bethesda, Md., 1972-75; tech. adviser U.S. Nuclear Regulatory Agy., Washington, 1975-76; sr. fellow Resources for the Future, 1976-83, Ctr. for Strategic and Internat. Studies, Washington, 1983-85; sr. staff officer NAS, 1985-86; freelance writer, editor, publ. Washington, Santa Barbara, 1986—. Cons. Vols. in Tech. Assistance, Arlington, Va., 1987-90, 98—, Internat. Resources Group, Washington, 1991. Author: Unpaid Costs of Electrical Energy, 1979, Bioenergy and Economic Development, 1985, (play) Agamemnon, Georgetown Theatre Co., 2000, (play reading) Felix's Baby, Kennedy Ctr., 2001; co-author: Managing the Environment, 1972, Energy in America's Future, 1979. Mem. adv. bd. Nat. Zoo, Washington. Buenos Aires Convention fellow, 1952, NSF fellow, 1962; NATO scholar, 1960, 62. Mem.: Internat. Assn. Energy Economists, Am. Astron. Soc., Am. Phys. Soc. Avocations: piano, musical composition. Home and Office: 115 Summit Ln Santa Barbara CA 93108-2323

RAMSBY, MARK DELIVAN, lighting designer and consultant; b. Portland, Oreg., Nov. 20, 1947; s. Marshall Delivan and Verna Pansy (Culver) R.; married; children: Aaron Delivan, Venessa Mercedes. Student, Portland (Oreg.) State U., 1966-67. With C.E.D., Portland, 1970-75; minority ptnr. The Light Source, 1975-78, pres., 1978-87; prin. Illume Lighting Design, 1987-90; ptnr. Ramsby, Dupuy & Seats, Inc., 1990-91; dir. lighting design PAE Cons. Engrs., Inc., 1991—. Pvt. practice cons. Portland, 1979—. Recipient Top 100 Outstanding Achievement award Metalux Lighting, 1981-85, 100% award, 1985, Edwin F. Guth award of merit, 1990, 95, 96, 99, 2001, Edison award of excellence, 1990, Edwin F. Guth award of excellence, 1993, 94, Paul Waterbury award of Merit, 1995. Mem. Illuminating Engring. Soc. Am. (sec.-treas. Oreg. sect. 1978-79, Oreg. sect. pres. 2002—, Oreg. Section and Regional and Internat. awards 1989, 90, 93, 94, Lighting Design awards), Internat. Assn. Lighting Designers. Lutheran. Avocations: lighting design, historical restoration, flyfishing, downhill skiing. Office: PAE Cons Engrs 808 SW 3d Ave Ste 300 Portland OR 97204-2426

RAMSDELL, RICHARD ADONIRAM, marine engineer; b. Hartford, Conn., Feb. 28, 1953; s. Robert Allen and Irene Ella (Lewis) R.; m. Vicki Lynn Pepin, July 1, 1978 (div. Mar. 1984); children: Eric Charles, Ryan Amber; m. Beverly Jane Tenken; children: Alexander Richard, Matthew Robin. BS in Marine Engring., Maine Maritime Acad., 1975. Plant operator Ga. Pacific, Woodland, Maine, 1975-77; 2d asst. engr. Farrell Lines, Inc., N.Y.C., 1977-83; steam plant foreman Jackson Lab., Bar Harbor, Maine, 1984-86; plant operator Babcock-Ultrapower Jonesboro, 1986-90; results, environ. engr. Maine Power Svcs., Bangor, 1990-92; plant engr. Babcock-Ultrapower West Enfield, Maine, 1992-95, Ebensburg (Pa.) Power Co., 1995—. Office: Ebensburg Power Co PO Box 845 Ebensburg PA 15931-0845 E-mail: ramsdell@penn.com., rramsdell@penn.com.

RAMSDEN, KAREN MCCOIN, writer; b. Knoxville, Tenn., Sept. 26, 1945; d. Bedford Hamilton Sr. and Kathryn Etolia (Hines) McCoin; m. Richard William Ramsden, Oct. 22, 1976; 1 child, Kathleen Hamilton. Student, Westminster Sch. for Girls, Atlanta, 1963, U. Hawaii, 1963; BS, U. Tenn., 1967, postgrad., 1975-76, Edn. for Ministry, Sewanee, Tenn., 1991-92, Precept Bible Study, Marietta, Ga., 1992—. Buyer Athletic House, Knoxville, 1969-70; tutor Minority Students Program U. Tenn., 1974; architectural/interior designer Design/Build, 1976-83; aide pub. rels. Christ the King Sch., Atlanta, 1987-89, also instr. guidance, 1988-89. Author: The Tablet of Destinies, 1988, (newsletters) Hotline, King's Kids, 1987-89; contbr. to newspaper Ga. Bull., 1987-89; editor, pub. (quar.) What's Ahead?, 1988; residential designer Hild House, Thomas House, 1977; contbg. editor, pub. (quar.) Stillpoint, 1990-91; contbg. essayist (quar.) The Direct Line, Johnson Ferry Bapt. Ch. Ministry, 1997—. Dir., vol. Playmobile, Knoxville, 1971-73. Recipient community recognition Knoxville News Sentinel, 1980. Mem. Jr. League Cobb-Marietta, Inc., Nine O'Clock Cotillion, Alpha Lambda Delta, Delta Delta Delta (alumni v.p. 1982). Avocations: phys. fitness, gourmet cooking, gardening, travel, conversation.

RAMSDEN, MARY CATHERINE, substance abuse specialist; Diploma, St. Joseph Mercy Hosp., 1966; postgrad., Mason City Jr. Coll., Kirkwood Community Coll. Cert. alcohol and drug counselor; RN Iowa, cert. chem. dependency nurse. Nursing supr. children's unit State Mental Health Inst., Cherokee, Iowa, 1966-69, Iowa Security Med. Facility, Oakdale, 1969; staff nurse psychiatry St. Luke's Meth. Hosp., Cedar Rapids, Iowa, 1969-74, asst. psychiat. nursing instr., 1970-74; mem. staff Sedlacek Treatment Ctr. Mercy Hosp., 1974-85; cons. drug and alcohol CareUnit, Jacksonville Beach, Fla., 1985-86; nursing mgr. adolescent chem. dependency unit Broadlawns Med. Ctr., Des Moines, 1987-88; tng. mgr. Div. Substance Abuse and Heath Promotion Iowa Dept. Pub. Health, 1988-91; clin. program dir. Forest City (Iowa) Treatment Ctr., 1991-92; facilitator Employee & Family Resources Enhancement Women Pr Iowa Correctional Instn. for Women, Mitchellville, 1992-97; cast mgmt. tng. coord. Employee & Family Resources, Des Moines, 1998-99; substance abuse cons., trainer, 1999—; sr. counselor Powell Chem. Dependency Ctr. Iowa Luth Hosp., 1999—. Mem. licensing rev. com. Iowa Bd. of Nursing. Author: (with others) Nurses Quick Reference, 1989. Lt. Cmdr. Nurse Corps USNR. Named Nurse Expert Coll. Nursing U. Iowa., 1985. Mem.: Iowa Corrections Assn., Nat. Consortium Chem. Dependence Nurses, Nat. Assn. Alcoholism and Drug Abuse Counselors, Res. Officers Assn. Home: 1519 Idaho St Des Moines IA 50316-2425 E-mail: mrrncd@yahoo.com.

RAMSDEN, SALLY ANN, pianist; b. Port Clinton, Ohio, Feb. 23, 1963; d. Donald Burlinson and Vera Edna (Smith) Ramsden. BMusic in Piano, MusB in piano, U. Wash., Seattle, 1986. Student accompanist U. Wash., Seattle, 1981-86, U. Tex., Austin, 1986-87; staff accompanist Cornish, Seattle, 1988—; studio accompanist Stephanie Dudash, Algona, Wash., 1990-96; staff accompanist Highline C.C., Des Moines, 1995—. Author: Igor Denshik Classical Piano, 1996; pianist: (solo performances) TCI Cable TV, 1996. Pianist for benefit dinner Northend Emergency Fund, Seattle; pianist for fundraisers Nature Conservancy, Seattle, Seattle Symphony. Recipient scholarship Kent Music Study Club, 1981, Nat. Sch. Choral award Kent Meridian H.S., 1981. Mem. Washington State Music Tchrs. Assn. Democrat. Avocations: study of classic English literature, classic films, early broadway musicals.

RAMSDEN, WILLA OLDHAM, retired scouting organization executive, writer, historian, consultant; b. San Diego, Nov. 27, 1911; d. William Henry Stillwell and Martha Ellen Estell; m. Clifton John Oldham (dec. Feb. 1984); m. Percy Herbert Ramsden (dec. Oct. 1993). Field dir. Girl Scout Coun., San Diego, 1934—39, asst. exec., 1945—49, exec. dir. Fresno, 1939—41, San Jose, 1942—44, Riverside, 1949—56; ret., 1956; self-employed feature writer, columnist Riverside, 1957—59; feature writer, columnist Boulder City, Nev., 1960—69, Carson CIty, 1970—; staff substitute City of Carson City, 1974—92, cons. pers., adminstrn., orgn., 1974—. Spkr. various civic and svc. clubs, schs., Nev., 1960—. Hannah Clapp Lecture Series, Carson City, 1999—2000; mem. panel Landmark Soc. series, Carson City, 2001; pres. Region XII Girl Scout Profls.; nat. bd. dirs. Girl Scout Profls.; apptd. Nat. Girl Scout staff establishment of Girl Scout troops in various locations. Contbr. over 500 articles to profl. jours., mags. and newspapers; contbr. (anthology) Light From a Thousand Campfires, 1953; weekly columnist: Mayor of Boulder City, Nev., 1963—64; author: pers. manuals and publicity articles, 1974—83, (publicity articles) Coop. Ext. Svc., U. Nev., Reno, 1974—83, Carson-Tahoe Hospital: The Story of a Caring Community, 1987, Carson City - Nevada's Capital City, 1991. Active Nev. State Mus., Carson City, 1972—; organizer Appaloosa Club Clark County, Las Vegas, 1960; docent Nev. State Mus., Carson City, 1972—75; mem. bicentennial commn. Carson City Centennial, 1974—78; mem. organizing com. Friends in Svc. Helping, 1977; chmn. All Carson City Ch. Women Leadership Conf., 1978, Western Nev. Sr. Conf., Carson City, 1985; mem. promotion staff for bd. suprs. Marriage Bur. Supr. and City Clk., 1991; mem. planning com. Nev. Women's Project, 1997—98; sustaining mem. Rep. Nat. Com., Washington, 1970—; mem. election bd. Riverside, 1956—59, Carson City, 1971—72; chmn. election bd., 1973—81; dep. election bd., 1982—92; active local Rep. campaigns; bd. deacons 1st Presbyn. Ch., Carson City, 1978—80, chair, 1979—80, 1986—88, organizer sr. Serving Others Loving Others program, deacon, 1978, founder sr. assistance program, 1982, chair social action com., 1982. Nominee Nev. Woman of Yr., 1970; named Hon. Life mem., Nat. Presbyn. Ch. USA, 1976; recipient Thanks badge, Nat. Bd. Girl Scouts U.S., 1957, cert. of appreciation, Nat. Appaloosa Horse Club, 1960, commendation cert., Carson City Centennial/U.S. Bicentennial Commn., City of Carson City, 1979, Ad hoc Recreational Vehicle Com, City of Carson City, 1987. Mem.: Rep. Women Carson City (bd. dirs.), Christian Writers Guild, Heritage Found. Republican. Presbyterian. Achievements include a special collection at the Getchell Library of University of Nevada-Reno of her correspondence, manuscripts and writing samples. Avocations: gourmet food study, classical music, travel, reading, computer contacts.

RAMSEY, BONNIE JEANNE, mental health facility administrator, psychiatrist; b. Tucson, Dec. 9, 1952; d. William Arnold Jr. and Doris Marie (Gaines) R. BS cum laude, U. S.C., 1971-75, MD, 1981. Diplomate Am. Bd. Psychiatry and Neurology; lic. child and adult psychiatrist S.C., N.C., Ga. Chief resident in psychiatry William S. Hall Psychiat. Inst., Columbia, S.C., 1983, unit dir. adolescent girls, 1986-89, chief child and adolescent in-patient program, 1989—, interim dir. child and adolescent div., 1989-92; interim chmn. child and adolescent div. dept. neuropsychiatry U. S.C., 1989-92; instr. Sch. of Medicine U. S.C., 1986-89, asst. prof. Sch. of Medicine, 1989-98, assoc. prof., 1998—. Mem. choir Trinity Meth. Ch., West Columbia, chair pastor parish rel.com., 1981—, vice chmn. bd. trustees, 1989—, trustee, 1990—, mem. at large adminstrn. bd., 1993—; adv. coun. Habitat for Humanity. Named one of Outstanding Young Women of Am., 1985. Fellow Am. Psychiat. Assn. (local sec.-treas., pres. 1981—); mem. AMA (del. residents physician sect. 1983, 84, 86, housing staff sect. 1988—), Am. Acad. Child Psychiatry, S.C. Med. Soc., Columbia Med. Soc., Palmetto Soc. United Way. Methodist. Office: William S Hall Psychiat Inst PO Box 202 Columbia SC 29202-0202

RAMSEY, CHARLES EUGENE, sociologist, educator; b. Paragon, Ind., Apr. 24, 1923; s. Sarcefield Dodson and Stella (Goss) R.; m. Alberta Mae Jordan, July 19, 1943; children— James D., Charles W., Jane E., Suzanne. BS, Ind. State Tchrs. Coll., 1947; MS, U. Wis., 1950, PhD, 1952. Faculty U. Wis., 1951-52, U. Minn., 1952-54, Cornell U., 1954-62, Colo. State U., 1962-65, prof. sociology U. Minn., Mpls., 1965-77; chmn. dept. sociology U. Tex., Arlington, 1977-83. Vis. prof. Inter-Am. Instn. Agrl. Sci., Costa Rica, 1961, Exptl. Sta., U. P.R., 1961-62; research cons. to various univs., agys. Author: (with Lowry Nelson and Cooley Verner) Community Structure and Change, 1960, (with David Gottlieb) The American Adolescent, 1965, Understanding the Deprived Child, S.R.A, 1967, Problems of Youth, 1967, (with D.J. McCarty) The School Managers: Power and Conflict in American Public Education, 1971, (with William A. Stacey) Social Statistics, 1992; also articles. Achievements include developing and testing theory of variations in community power structure, types of sch. bds., and roles of sch. supt., developed method of comparative measurement of level of living for different countries. Home: 1102 De Pauw Dr Arlington TX 76012-5339 Office: U Tex Dept Sociology Arlington TX 76004

RAMSEY, CHARLES H. protective services official; B in Criminal Justice, M in Criminal Justice, Lewis U.; grad., FBI Nat. Acad., Nat. Exec. Inst. Cadet Chgo. Police Dept., 1968, police officer, 1971, promoted through the to commdr. of patrol, detectives and narcotics units, dept. supt. bur. staff svcs., 1994; chief police Met. Police Dept., Washington, 1998—. Spkr. in field; adj. faculty mem. Northwestern U. Traffic Inst. Sch. Police and Command, Lewis U. Recipient Gary P. Hayes award, Police Exec. Rsch. Forum, 1994, Robert Lamb Humanitarian award, Nat. Orgn. Black Law Enforcement Exec., 2001, Civil Rights award, Internat. Assn. Chiefs of Police, 2001. Office: Govt of DC John A Wilson Bldg 1350 Pennsylvania Ave NW Washington DC 20004*

RAMSEY, DAN STEVEN, consultant, business executive; b. Rockford, Ill., Apr. 15, 1949; s. Marvin Eugene and Clara Judith (Johnson) R.; m. Martha Duffy, Dec. 30, 1972; 1 child, Sara Judith. BA, Rockford Coll., 1971. Admissions rep., resident dir. Rockford (Ill.) Coll., 1970-74; dir. admissions Centenary Coll., Shreveport, La., 1974-77, Nichols Coll., Dudley, Mass., 1977-80, dir. inst. advancement, 1980-86; dir. devel. New Britain (Conn.) Gen. Hosp., 1986-88; dean of coll. advancement Post Coll., Waterbury, Conn., 1988-89; v.p. inst. advancement LeMoyne Coll., Syracuse, N.Y., 1989-93; pres. TRG Svcs., DeWitt, NY, 1980—; exec. dir. The Loretto Found., Syracuse, 1994-96; upstate N.Y. ptnr. Am. Fund Raising Inst., 1987—; dir. planned giving Rochester Inst. Tech., 2001—. Comm. cons. C.W. Beggs & Assoc., Rockford, Ill., 1970, writer, fund raising cons. G. Frederick Co., bd. mem. R. M. Jones & Co., Bristol, Conn., 1978-82, pres., CEO TRG Svcs. and The Ramsey Group, DeWitt, 1980—. Author: Introduction To Fund Raising, 1993, Giving It Away in America, 1995. Com. mem. Manlius Pebble Hill Sch., DeWitt, 1991-96; bd. dirs. Child and Family Svc. of Ctrl. N.Y., 1994-96, Frank Hiscock Legal Aid Soc., 1994-96, bd. dirs. Leadership Greater Syracuse Alumni Assn. Mem. Assn. Fundraising Profls., Fin. Planning Assn., Nat. Coun. on Planned Giving, Coun. for Advancement and Support of Edn., Assn. for Healthcare Philanthropy, Greater Syracuse C. of C., Fair Haven Yacht Club. Republican. Avocations: sailing, computers, cooking, fishing, camping. Home: 313 Lansdowne Rd Syracuse NY 13214-2128 E-mail: ramseyd@trgservices.com.

RAMSEY, DAVID SELMER, retired hospital executive; b. Mpls., Feb. 19, 1931; s. Selmer A. and Esther D. (Dahl) R.; m. Elinor Corfield, Aug. 15, 1953; children— Scott, Stewart, Thomas BS, U. Mich., 1953, MS in Microbiology, 1954, M.H.A., 1962. Research asst. Detroit Inst. Cancer Research, 1954-60; asst. adminstr. Harper Hosp., Detroit, 1962-68, assoc. adminstr., 1968-72; exec. v.p. Iowa Meth. Med. Ctr., Des Moines, 1972-83, pres., 1983-93, Iowa Health Sys., 1993-95, Fine Wood Designs, 1996—. Avocations: golf, tennis, photography. Home: 25213 N Quail Haven Dr Rio Verde AZ 85263-7108

RAMSEY, DONNA ELAINE, librarian; b. Charlotte, N.C., Oct. 10, 1941; d. William A. Epps and Mabel P. (Brown) Tatum; m. Reginal E. Ramsey, Apr. 9, 1979 (dec. May 1985); children: Ona B., Reginald E. II. BA, Johnson C. Smith U., 1969; MLS, Atlanta U., 1971. Reference libr. Barber-Scotia Coll., Concord, N.C., 1971-73; libr. Friendship Jr. Coll., Rock Hill, S.C., 1973-77; serials libr. N.Mex. State U., Las Cruces, 1977-81; info. libr. El Paso (Tex.) Pub. Libr., 1981; libr. U.S. Army Air Def. Artillary Sch., Ft. Bliss, Tex., 1985-92, 97-99; chief libr. U.S. Army Air Defense Artillery Sch., 1999-2000; libr. U.S. Army Sgts. Maj. Acad., 1992-97, Van Noy Libr., Ft. Belvoir, Va., 2001—. Spl. edn. parents adv. coun. Socorro Ind. Sch. Dist., 1997-99. V.p. Blacks in Govt., El Paso, 1993-95. Mem. ALA (program format chair 1990-92, planning com. 1990-92, black caucus 1976—, San Francisco conf. program com. 1991-92, armed forces librs. roundtable pub. rels. chair 1997-2001, com. on accreditation 2002--, black caucus program com. 3d nat. conf.), Tex. Libr. Assn. (chair leadership devel. com. 1999-2000). Democrat. Episcopalian. Avocations: reading, writing, sewing. Home: PO Box 1045 Fort Belvoir VA 22060 E-mail: yellowspeak@yahoo.com., ramseyd@bliss.army.mil.

RAMSEY, DOUGLAS ARTHUR, journalist, writer, critic, foundation executive; b. Choteau, Mont., Oct. 3, 1934; s. Arthur Bailey and Edith Mae (Tash) R.; m. Charlene Rae Lindberg, July 29, 1961; children: Paul Douglas, Miles Damon (dec.). BA in Journalism, U. Wash., 1956. Reporter, copy editor Seattle Times, 1956; mgr. Far East Network, Iwakuni, Japan, 1958-60; anchor, news dir. KIMA-TV, Yakima, Wash., 1960-61; documentary prodr. KYW-TV, Cleve., 1962; anchor, reporter KOIN-TV, Portland, Oreg., 1963; anchor KATU-TV, 1963-66; instr. broadcast journalism Loyola U., New Orleans, 1968-70; anchor WDSU-TV, 1966-70, WPIX-TV, N.Y.C., 1970-73; chief corr. UP Internat. TV News, 1973-74; news dir. KSAT-TV, San Antonio, 1975-77, WDSU-TV, New Orleans, 1977-81, KGO-TV, San Francisco, 1981-83; v.p. Found. for Am. Comm., L.A., 1983-84, sr. v.p., 1984-99. Lectr. Ea. Europe and Germany, 1992—. Author: Jazz Matters: Reflections on the Music and Some of its Makers, 1989; editor: (with Dale Ellen Shaps) Journalism Ethics: Why Change?, 1986; contbg. author: Oxford Companion to Jazz, 2000; contbg. editor Tex. Monthly, 1974-96; columnist Dallas Morning News,

1988-90; contbr. articles to books and profl. jours. Capt. USMC, 1957-60. Recipient Emmy award Acad. TV Arts and Scis., 1981, Deems Taylor award ASCAP, 1997. Mem. Soc. Profl. Journalists, Soc. Environ. Journalists, Nat. Acad. Rec. Arts and Scis., Jazz Journalists Assn., Nat. Assn. Sci. Writers, Investigative Reporters and Editors, Radio TV New Dirs. Assn., Am. Soc. Newspaper Editors (project credibility task force), Assn. Edn. in Journalism and Mass Comm., AP Mng. Editors (2000 com.), UN Corr. Assn., Nat. Acad. Rec. Arts and Scis., Delta Upsilon. Avocations: trumpet, photography, running, wine, travel. Home and Office: 3714 W Chestnut Ave Yakima WA 98902-3619 E-mail: daramsey@charter.net.

RAMSEY, EDWARD LAWRENCE, judge; b. Dothan, Ala., Dec. 9, 1941; s. Joseph Robert and Hilda (Hawkins) R.; m. Pamela Thuss, 1971 (div. 1976); 1 child, Matthew Edward. Student, Emory U., 1960-62; BA, U. Ala., Tuscaloosa, 1965, JD, 1966. Bar: Ala. 1966, Calif. 1970, U.S. Ct. Appeals (5th and 11th cirs.) 1972. Dep. dist. atty. Office of Dist. Atty., San Diego, 1970-72; pvt. practice Birmingham, Ala., 1972-94; judge civil divsn. Cir. Ct. Jefferson County, 1995—. Capt. USMC, 1967-70. Mem. Exchange Club (past pres.). Republican. Episcopalian. E-mail: jdgramsey@juno.com.

RAMSEY, FOREST LEE, II, b. Ashland, Ky., Aug. 23, 1945; s. Helen Juanita and Virgil Hughes(Stepfather); m. Nita Lewis Stewart; children: Grady Stewart, Forest. BA in English, U. Ky., 1964—81. Cert. Sr. U.S. Army Rotary Wing Aviator 1975. Overseas deployment officer Sixth U.S. Army, San Francisco, 1987—89; deployment officer U.S. Forces Command, Fort McPherson, Ga., 1989—91; ops. officer, Overseas Deployment Eighth U.S. Army, Seoul, Republic of Korea, 1991—92; chief, Exercise Br., Ops. Div., Army Nat. Guard Nat. Guard Bur., Dept. Army, Arlington, Va., 1992—94, chief, ops. div., Army Nat. Guard, 1994—96, spl. projects officer, Counter-Terrorism, 1996—97; cons. The Conaway Group, Alexandria, 1997—2000; pres., mng. ptnr. R.A.M. & Assoc. LLC, Lexington, Ky., 2001—02. Sr. cons. Congl. Study on Weapons of Mass Destruction Preparedness - 1997, McLean, 1997—97. Col. Nat. Guard Bur. U.S. Army, 1992—97. Decorated Legion of Merit Sec. Army; nominee Officer Candidate Sch. Hall Fame, Comdr., Infantry Sch., Ft. Benning, GA, 2000. Mem.: Ky. Nat. Guard Assn. (life). Avocations: running, golf, reading, physical fitness. Home and Office: R.A.M. Assoc LLC 2228 Stone Garden Ln Lexington KY 40513-1340 E-mail: framseyii@aol.com.

RAMSEY, FORREST GLADSTONE, JR. retired engineering company executive; b. Wichita, Kans., Oct. 25, 1930; s. Forrest Gladstone and Anastasia Ruth (Linot) R.; m. Gwendolyn Moreton, June 22, 1953 (div. Jan. 1982); children: Deborah Jenkins, Rebecca Johnson, Susan Klopp, Diane Hayes, Forrest G. III, Mark, Kenneth; m. Carmen Bergen, Apr. 30, 1988. BS in Engring., U.S. Naval Acad., 1952; postgrad., Wichita State U., 1957-58, U. Colo., 1958-64. Commd. ensign USN, 1952, res., 1957; planner, engr. Boeing Corp., Wichita, Kans., 1957-58; engr., logistician Martin-Marietta, Denver, 1959-65; div. dir. Computer Scis., Washington, 1965-73; program dir. Systems Cons., 1973-76; CEO Am. Sys. Corp., 1976-92, chmn., bd. dirs., 1992-97; ret., 1997. Mem. Profl. Svcs. Coun. (vice chmn. 1990), Naval Submarine League (bd. dirs. 1982-90). Roman Catholic. Home: 1700 Stony Brook Rd Bedford VA 24523 E-mail: forrest.ramsey@1952.ism.com.

RAMSEY, FRANK ALLEN, veterinarian, retired army officer; b. Rocksprings, Tex., May 1, 1929; s. Reynolds Allen and June (Burdette) R.; m. Lucette C. Reboul, Jan. 1958; children: Randal R., Ramsay A.; m. 2d, Mary Lou Cain, June 1991. D.V.M., Tex. A & M U., 1954; grad., U.S. Army Command and Gen. Staff Coll., 1965, U.S. Army War Coll., 1972. Commd. 1st. lt. U.S. Army Vet. Corps, 1955, advanced through grades to brig. gen., 1980; chief vet. service Ft. Leonard Wood, Mo., 1958-61; acad. vet. U.S. Mil. Acad., West Point, N.Y., 1962-64; vet. staff officer U.S. Army Combat Devel. Command Med. Service, Ft. Sam Houston, Tex., 1965-67; asst. chief profl. programming and planning br. Office Surgeon Gen., Washington, 1967-68, chief profl. programming and planning br., 1968-71, chief food inspection policy office, 1972-73, sr. vet. staff officer, 1973-77; asst. chief of staff Vet. Service, 7th Med. Command, Army Europe and 7th Army, Heidelberg, W. Ger., 1977-80; asst. for vet. services to surgeon gen. and chief U.S. Army Vet. Corps, Hdqrs. Dept. Army, Washington, 1980-85; ret., 1985. Decorated Army Commendation medal, Legion of Merit with oak leaf cluster, D.S.M. Mem. AVMA, Assn. Fed. Veterinarians, Assn. Mil. Surgeons U.S., Assn. Equine Practitioners, Am. Assn. Food Hygiene Veterinarians, Conf. Pub. Health Veterinarians, Tex. Vet. Med. Assn. Lodges: Masons (32 degree). Presbyterian. Home: 8 El Norte Cir Uvalde TX 78801-4021

RAMSEY, INEZ LINN, librarian, educator; b. Martins Ferry, Ohio, Mar. 25, 1938; d. George and Leona (Smith) Linn; m. Jackson Eugene Ramsey, Apr. 22, 1961; children: John Earl, James Leonard. BA in History, SUNY, Buffalo, 1971, MLS, 1972; EdD in Audiovisual Edn., U. Va., 1980. Libr. Iroquois Ctrl. H.S., Elma, N.Y., 1971-73, Lucy Simms Elem. Sch., Harrisonburg, Va., 1973-75; instr. James Madison U., 1975-80, asst. prof., 1980-85, assoc. prof., 1985-91, prof., 1991-98; ret., 1998. Mem. Va. State Library Bd., Richmond, 1975-80; cons. in field. Author: (with Jackson E. Ramsey) Budgeting Basics, Library Planning and Budgeti;g; contbr. to Ency., articles to profl. jours.; project developer Internet Sch. Libr. Media Ctr.; project dir. Oral (tape) History Black Community in Harrisonburg, 1977-78; storyteller, puppeteer. Recipient Pierian Press's Libr. Hi Tech (periodical) award, 1998; rsch. grantee James Madison U., Harrisonburg, 1981, Commonwealth Ctr. State Va., 1989. Mem. ALA, Am. Assn. Sch. Librs., Assn. Edn. Comm. Tech. (exec. bd. DSMS 1989-98, DSMT Meritorious Svc. award 1998), Va. Ednl. Media Assn. (sec. 1981-83, citation 1983, pres. 1985-86, Educator of Yr. award 1984-85, Meritorious Svc. award 1987-88), Phi Beta Kappa (pres. Shenandoah chpt. 1980-81), Beta Phi Mu, Phi Delta Kappa. Home: 3215 S Torrey Pines Dr Las Vegas NV 89146-6529

RAMSEY, IRA CLAYTON, retired pipeline company executive; b. Quitman, Ga., May 13, 1931; s. James Redding and Ruth Frances (Treadaway) R.; m. Marianne Vinzant, Dec. 23, 1962; children: Clayton Hamilton, Robin Leigh. BBA, U. Ga., Atlanta, 1954; LLB, Atlanta Law Sch., 1950; postgrad., U. Tex., 1968, U. Pitts., 1973. With Plantation Pipe Line Co., Atlanta, 1948-96, asst. sec., 1967-70, treas., contr., 1970-90, v.p. fin., 1990-96. Life trustee Ga. Found. for Ind. Colls.; bd. dirs. KingsBridge Retirement Ctr., Inc. Baptist. Home: 780 Wesley Oak Rd NW Atlanta GA 30328-4738

RAMSEY, JAROLD WILLIAM, English language educator, author; b. Bend, Oreg., Sept. 1, 1937; s. Augustus S. and Wilma E. (Mendenhall) R.; m. Dorothy Ann Quinn, Aug. 16, 1959; children: Kate, Sophia, John. BA with honors, U. Oreg., 1959; Ph. D., U. Wash., 1966. Acting instr. U. Wash., Seattle, 1963-65; asst. prof. English U. Rochester, (N.Y.), 1965-70, assoc. prof., 1970-81, prof. (N.Y.), 1981-97; prof. emeritus, 1997—; dir. undergrad. rsch. U. Rochester, (N.Y.), 1990-96. Vis. prof. English U. Victoria, B.C., Can., 1974, 75-76; dir. NEH summer seminars on Indian lit., 1985, 88. Author: The Space Between Us, 1970, Love in an Earthquake, 1973 (Lillian Fairchild award 1973), Dermographia, 1982, Reading the Fire, 1983, rev. edit., 1999, Hand-shadows, 1989, (play) Coyote Goes Upriver, premier 1985, (cantata) (with Samuel Adler) The Lodge of Shadows, premiere 1988; editor: Coyote Was Going There, 1977, Nehalem Tillamook Tales, 1990, The Stories We Tell: Oregon Folk Literature (with Suzi Jones), 1994. Recipient Don Walker award Western Am. Lit., 1979, Borestone Mount Found. Best Poems award, 1972, 75, 76; Helen Bullis prize, 1984, Poetry prize Quar. Rev., 1989; Alumni Achievement award U. Oreg. Alumni Assn, 1990; Nat. Endowment Arts writing grantee, 1974, 76; Ingram Merrill Found. writing grantee, 1976 Mem. MLA (chair com. on lits. and langs. of Am. 1991-92), Assn. Study Am. Indian Lit. (pres. 1981), Am. Folklore Soc., Phi Beta Kappa Democrat. Home: 5884 NW Highway 26 Madras OR 97741-9543 E-mail: jwr1937@madras.net.

RAMSEY, JENNIFER CHRISTA, civil engineer, consultant, engineering executive; b. El Paso, Tex., Mar. 19, 1973; d. Daryll Robert and Carlon Ann Eagan; m. John Randall Ramsey, Feb. 6, 1960. BS in Civil Engring., Tex.A&M U., College Station, Tex., 1997. EIT 1997; cert. Indoor Air Quality Professional 2002, Asbestos Inspector 2002, Hazwoper 2002. Engr. assoc. I Bury and Pittman, Austin, Tex., 1997—98; project engr. Property Solutions, Inc., Dallas, 1998—99; cons., divsn. mgr. Rimkus Consulting Group, Inc., Irving, 1999—. Mem.: Am. Indsl. Hygiene Assn., North Tex. Sect. Am. Indsl. Hygiene Assn., Am. Indoor Air Quality Coun. Home: 3312 Pine Tree Cir Dallas TX 75234 Office: Rimkus Consulting Group Inc 1431 Greenway Dr Ste 900 Dallas TX 75234 Home Fax: 972-518-0011; Office Fax: 972-518-0011. Personal E-mail: jennifer.eagan@attbi.com. E-mail: jcramsey@rimkus.com.

RAMSEY, JERRY VIRGIL, educator, financial planner, radio broadcaster; b. Tacoma, July 24, 1940; s. Virgil Emory and Winifred Victoria (Carothers) R.; m. Elaine Sigrid Perdue, June 24, 1967; 1 child, Jason Perdue. BA in Elem. Edn., U. Puget Sound, 1967; MEd in Tchr. Tng. and Curriculum Devel., U. Wash., 1971; PhD in Econ. Geography Curriculum, Columbia Pacific U., 1985. Tchr. Tacoma Pub. Schs., 1967-95; fin. planner Primerica Corp., Tacoma, 1986-90, Waddell & Reed, Inc., Tacoma, 1990-93; N.Am. Mgmt., 1993-96; real estate investor, CEO Ramsey Properties, Gig Harbor, Wash., 1970-98; radio broadcaster KGHP, KJUN/The Country Gold Network, KMAS, 1990-96, KGY, 1996—; study skills specialist Sylvan Learning Ctr., 1995-98. Lectr. Pacific Luth. U., Tacoma, 1972-86. Precinct committee officer Pierce County Rep. Com., Tacoma, 1968-78, 95-2000. With USAF, 1959-62. Recipient Golden Acorn award PTA, 1975, Meritorious Tchg. award Nat. Coun. Geog. Edn., 1978, achievement award Rep. Nat. Com., 1985; grantee U.S. Office Edn., 1971. Mem. NEA (life), Fort Nisqually Found. (chmn. hist. site adv. coun. 1996—, founder Dr. Jerry V. and Elaine S. Ramsey Fund for Fort Nisqually Endowment 2000), Knife and Fork Club (pres. 1983), Kiwanis (pres. Tacoma 1982), Phi Delta Kappa. Methodist. Avocation: living history interpretation, real estate investing, management and education. E-mail: jvramsey@juno.com.

RAMSEY, JOANNE MARIE, data processing executive; b. Long Branch, N.J., Oct. 13, 1945; d. Erwin P. and Erna M. (Green) Forrest; 1 child, Cheryl. BS, Monmouth Coll., 1967; MS, Stevens Inst. Tech., 1971. Mem. tech. staff Bell Telephone Labs., Holmdel, N.J., 1967-71; programmer analyst Cooper Electric Supply Co., Middletown, 1971-73; sr. programmer Insco Systems Corp., Neptune, 1973-78; sr. programmer analyst Internat. Flavors and Fragrances, Hazlet, 1978-79; mgr. Bristol-Myers Squibb Co., Plainsboro, NJ, 1980—2002. Mem. NAFE, Am. Prodn. and Inventory Control Soc. Home: 424 E Highland Ave Atlantic Highlands NJ 07716-1710 E-mail: jmramsey4@comcast.net.

RAMSEY, JOHN ARTHUR, lawyer; b. Apr. 1, 1942; s. Wilbert Lewis and Lillian (Anderson) R.; m. Nikki Ann Ramsey, Feb. 9, 1943; children: John William, Bret Anderson, Heather Nicole. AB, San Diego State U., 1965; JD, Calif. Western Sch. Law, 1969. Bar: Colo. 1969, Tex. 1978. Assoc. Henry, Cockrell, Quinn & Creighton, 1969-72; atty. Texaco Inc., 1972-80; asst. to pres. Texaco U.S.A., 1980-81, asst. to divsn. v.p., 1981-82, divsn. atty. Denver, 1982-88; ptnr. Holland & Hart, 1989—. Editor-in-chief: Calif. Western Law Rev., 1969. Bd. dirs. Selective Svc., Englewood, Colo., 1972-76; chmn. coun. Bethany Luth. Ch., Englewood, 1976; mem. exec. bd. Denver Area coun. Boy Scouts Am., 1999—. Mem. ABA (vice-chmn. oil, natural gas exploration and prodn. com. sect. natural resource law 1983-88, chmn. 1989—, coun. sect. natural resources, energy and environ. law 1993). Republican. Office: Holland & Hart 8390 E Crescent Pkwy Ste 400 Greenwood Village CO 80111-2822

RAMSEY, JOHN TALTON, sales executive; b. Kansas City, KS, Jan. 21, 1951; s. John Talton and Helen Frances Ramsey; m. Charlene McMahon, May 25, 1974; children: Lesley Anne, Lindsey Marie. AA, Kansas City (Kans.) Jr. Coll., 1971; BA, U. Mo., 1973. Salesman Papercraft Inc., Pitts., 1973-75, Glenbrook Lab., Chgo., 1976; dist. salesperson Amity Leather Products Co., West Bend, Wis., 1976-96; salesman Major Cadillac, Kansas City, Mo., 1997-98, Gerson/Rothenberg & Schloss, Mission, Kans., 1998—. Mem. exec. bd. dirs. Shawnee Mission (Kans.) Area Coun., 1990-91, Shawnee Mission Found., 1998—; bd. dirs. Shawnee Mission Edn. Found., 1992-93; pres. Brookwood Homes Assn., Lenexa, Kans., 1986-88, Christa McAuliffe PTA, Lenexa, 1989-90; mem. coun. Lenexa City Coun., 1995—, coun. pres., 1997-98; assoc. mem. Kans. Calvary, 1998—; bd. dirs. United Cmty. Svcs. Johnson County, Park and Recreation Found. Johnson County. Named Parent that Makes a Difference Kansas City Chiefs, Shawnee Mission, 1991. Mem. Lenexa C. of C. Avocation: travel. Home: 15332 W 83rd Ter Lenexa KS 66219-1551 E-mail: jramsey@ci.lenexa.ks.us.

RAMSEY, KATHLEEN SOMMER, toxicologist; b. Port Washington, Wis., June 2, 1947; d. Harrison Wilson and June Kathleen (Hansen) Sommer; m. Glenn A. Ramsey, Oct. 4, 1975; 1 child David A. BA, Ripon Coll., 1969; PhD, U. Iowa, 1973. Diplomate Am. Bd. Toxicology; cert. mediator. Rsch. assoc. U. Wis., Milw., 1969; instr. Baylor Coll. Medicine, Houston, 1973-74, USPHS rsch. fellow, 1974-76; rsch. chemist Shell Devel. Co., 1976-77; toxicologist Shell Oil Co., 1977-80; dir., cons. toxicologist Toxicon Corp., Magnolia, Tex., 1980—. Environ. planner Houston-Galveston Area Coun., 2001—; mem. nat. adv. rsch. resources coun. NIH, Bethesda, Md.; bd. dirs. Reid Rd. Mcpl. Utility Dist., Houston; guest lectr. U. Tex. Sch. Pub. Health, Houston. Contbr. Paramedic Cy-Fair Vol. Fire Dept., Houston. Recipient Nat. Rsch. Svc. award, NIH. Mem.: NSTA, Am. Chem. Soc., Assn. Water (bd. dirs.), Am. Coll. Toxicology. Office: Toxicon Corp 101 S Copper Knoll The Woodlands TX 77381-0685

RAMSEY, LLOYD BRINKLEY, retired savings and loan executive, retired army officer; b. Somerset, Ky., May 29, 1918; s. William Harold and Mary Ella (Barnett) R.; m. Glenda Burton, Feb. 22, 1941; children: Lloyd Ann (Mrs. Kyle D. Wallace), Larry Burton, Judi Ramsey (Mrs. David E. Derr). AB, U. Ky., 1940; postgrad., Yale U., 1946, Command and Gen. Staff Coll., Ft. Leavenworth, Kans., 1949-50, U.S. Army War Coll., Carlisle Barracks, Pa., 1953-54, Harvard, 1961. Commd. 2d lt. U.S. Army, 1940, advanced through grades to maj. gen., 1968; bn. comdr. 7th Inf., 3d Inf. Div., 1944-45; instr. Inf. Sch., Ft. Benning, Ga., 1946-49; assigned Office G-2 Dept. Army Gen. Staff, 1950-53; sec. joint staff UN Far East Command, 1954-57; comdg. officer 1st Inf. Brigade, Ft. Benning, Ga., 1957-58; adv. Korean Army War Coll., 1959-60; with Office Chief Legis. Liaison, Dept. Army Gen. Staff, 1960-63, Office Asst. Chief Staff Force Devel., 1963-64; dep. comdr. Ft. Leonard Wood, Mo., 1964-65; dep. chief information, 1966-67; chief of staff Third Army, Ft. McPherson, Ga., 1967-68; div. comdr. Americal 23d Div., Vietnam, 1969-70; provost marshall gen. Army, Washington, 1970-74, ret., 1974; chmn. bd. McLean Savs. & Loan Assn., Va., 1974-88. Decorated D.S.M. with oak leaf cluster, Silver Star medal with two oak leaf clusters, Legion of Merit with oak leaf cluster, D.F.C., Bronze Star medal with three oak leaf clusters, Air medal with 16 oak leaf clusters, Army Commendation medal with oak leaf cluster, Purple Heart with four oak leaf clusters, Combat Inf. badge; mem. Order Brit. Empire; Croix de Guerre France; Vietnamese Nat. Order; Vietnamese Armed Forces Honor medal; Vietnamese Gallantry Cross with palm. Mem. Sigma Chi, Omicron Delta Kappa. Baptist. Home: 3624 Bowling Dr Salem VA 24153-8806 *Accept a man for what he is, not for what you want him to be.*

RAMSEY, LUCIE AVRA, small business owner, consultant; b. N.Y., Mar. 3, 1942; d. Albert and Mazie (Gordon) Miller; m. Charles Allen Ramsey, Feb. 3, 1968; children: Aaron Ramsey (dec.), Jacqueline Hartigan. BS, U. San Francisco, 1986. Cert. mediator, cert. ct. mediator County Riverside Dispute Resolution Ctr. Office mgr. Quicksilver Products Inc., San Francisco, 1962-66; exec. sec. Far West Lab. for Educ. Rsch. and Devel., San Francisco and Berkeley, Calif., 1966-68; office mgr. The Ark Pub. Co., Tiburon, 1973-75; adminstrv. asst. Nat. Coun. Jewish Women, San Francisco, 1979-80; asst. to the chief Tiburon Fire Protection Dist., 1980; exec. dir. Zionist Orgn. Am., San Francisco, 1980-87; asst. dir. Bay Area Coun. for Soviet Jews, 1987-89; exec. dir. Jewish Community Rels. Coun., Oakland, Calif., 1989-91; pres. Ramsey Cons., Mill Valley, 1991—. Leader first ever interreligious task force to the USSR. Author: Concerns of the Jewish Community 1930's/1970's. Civic organizer, planner, chairperson Marin County Clergy Group, San Rafael, Calif., 1975-79; asst. area dir. Am. Jewish Com., San Francisco Bay Area chpt., 1994-96. Democratic. Jewish. Avocations: reading, camping, traveling.

RAMSEY, MARGIE, librarian; b. Bay City, Tex., Aug. 29, 1921; d. Cyrus Otis Lansford and Myra Lenore Ferrell; m. Joe Bryan Ramsey, July 29, 1945; children: Ronald Lansford, Kevin Bryan. BA in Libr. Sci., Tex. State U., 1942. Cert. tchr., Tex. Libr. Talco (Tex.) Ind. Sch. Dist., 1942-44; sec. Consolidated Aircraft, San Diego, summer 1943; bookkeeper Lockheed Aircraft, Dallas, 1944; libr. Dallas Pub. Libr., 1944-45; sec. Steck Co., Austin, Tex., 1946-48; libr. U. Tex., 1948-51. Author, poet:. Vol. libr. Hyde Park United Meth., Austin, 1963—; vol. libr. Leander (Tex.) Ind. Sch. Dist., 1982-92; mem. The Internat. Libr. of Poetry. Named Outstanding Vol., Nat. Assn. Ptnrs. in Edn., Kraft-Disney, 1989. Fellow AAUW. Democrat. Avocations: teaching, camping, computers, reading, collecting rare books. Home: PO Box 99 Leander TX 78646-0099 E-mail: mramsey81@msn.com.

RAMSEY, MARTHA L. publisher; b. Memphis, Oct. 24, 1946; d. Brooks U. and Rebecca J. Ramsey. BA, Rhodes Coll., 1969; MA, Duke U., 1970. Mgr. creative svcs. AARP, Washington, 1976-90, dep. dir. comm., 1990-97, dir. publs., 1997—. Mem. Internat. Assn. Bus. Profls., Nat. Press Club, Mag. Pubs. Am. Office: AARP-Modern Maturity 601 E St NW Washington DC 20049-0003

RAMSEY, NANCY LOCKWOOD, nursing educator; b. L.A., Jan. 26, 1943; d. Jack Thanke and Virginia Lee (Slaughter) Lockwood; m. Gordon S. Ramsey, June 24, 1972; children: Douglas Lockwood, Kathryn Anne. BSN, Loma Linda U., 1966; MSN, Duke U., 1969; postgrad., Calif. State U., L.A., 1974. Cert. clin. nurse specialist. Staff nurse various hosps., 1966-82, 91-92, 99; clin. instr. Azusa (Calif.)-Pacific U., 1984, 1991; instr. U. N.C., Chapel Hill, 1960—70, Calif. State U., L.A., 1970—74; acting dir. nursing edn. Children's Hosp. L.A., 1974—75; prof. nursing L.A. City Coll., 1974—87, East L.A. Coll., Monterey Park, Calif., 1988—99; instr. lead tchr. Concorde Career Inst., Garden Grove , 2001; staff nurse Hospice Care of Calif., 2001—. Instr. pediatric nursing State Bd. Rev. Classes, L.A. and San Francisco, 1975-82; instr. statewide nursing program Calif. State U., Dominguez Hills, 1983-84. Author, editor: Child and Family Concepts of Nursing Practice, 1982, 87; contbr. articles to profl. jours. Mem. Sigma Theta Tau. Home: 1561 Berenice Dr Brea CA 92821-1802 Office: 377 E Chapman Ave Placentia CA 92870-5055

RAMSEY, NATALIE D. lawyer; b. Greeneville, Tenn., Dec. 6, 1959; d. William Trent and Nancy Elizabeth (Maupin) R. BS, U. Del., 1981; JD, Villanova U., 1984. Bar: Pa. 1984, U.S. Dist. Ct. (ea. dist.) Pa. 1985, U.S. Ct. Appeals (3rd cir. and 11th cirs.) 1989. Assoc. atty. Frederick L. Reigle, Esq. and Assocs., Reading, Pa., 1984-85, Montgomery, McCracken, Walker & Rhoads, LLP, Phila., 1985-93; ptnr. Montgomery, McCracken, Walker & Rhoads, 1993—, chair bankruptcy and reorgn. group, 1997—. Sec. East. Dist. of Pa. Bankruptcy Conf., 2000—; dir. Consumer Bankruptcy Advocacy Project. Contbr. articles to profl. jours. Bd. pres. Habitat for Humanity, 1997-2002. Mem. Comml. Law League (bd. pres.), Turnaround Mgmt. Assn. Presbyterian. Avocations: travel, reading. Office: Montgomery McCracken Walker & Rhoads LLP 123 S Broad St Fl 24 Philadelphia PA 19109-1099 E-mail: nramsey@mmwr.com.

RAMSEY, NORMAN F. physicist, educator; b. Washington, Aug. 27, 1915; s. Norman F. and Minna (Bauer) Ramsey; m. Elinor Jameson, June 3, 1940 (dec. Dec. 1983); children: Margaret, Patricia, Janet, Winifred; m. Ellie Welch, May 11, 1985. AB, Columbia U., 1935; BA, Cambridge (Eng.) U., 1937, MA, 1941, DSc, 1954; PhD, Columbia U., 1940; MA (hon.) , Harvard U., 1947; DSc (hon.) , Case Western Res. U., 1968, Middlebury Coll., 1969, Oxford (Eng.) U., 1973, DCL (hon.) , 1990; DSc (hon.) , Rockefeller U., 1986, U. Chgo., 1989, U. Sussex, 1990, U. Houston, 1991, Carleton Coll., 1991, Lake Forest Coll., 1992, U. Mich., 1993, Phila. Coll. Pharmacy & Sci., 1995, Colby Coll., 1998. Kellett fellow Columbia U., 1935—37, Tyndall fellow, 1938—39; Carnegie fellow Carnegie Inst. Washington, 1939—40; assoc. U. Ill., 1940—42; asst. prof. Columbia U., 1942—46; assoc. MIT Radiation Lab., 1940—43; cons. Nat. Def. Research Com., 1940—45; expert cons. sec. of war, 1942—45; group leader, assoc. div. head Los Alamos Lab., 1943—45; assoc. prof. Columbia U., 1945—47; head physics dept. Brookhaven Nat. Lab. of AEC, 1946—47; assoc. prof. physics Harvard U., 1947—50, prof. physics, 1950—66, Higgins prof. physics, 1966—86, Higgins prof. emeritus, 1986—. Sr. fellow Harvard Soc. Fellows, 1970—; Eastman prof. Oxford U., 1973—74; Luce prof. cosmology Mt. Holyoke Coll., 1982—83; prof. U. Va., 1983—84; dir. Harvard Nuc. Lab., 1948—50, 1952—53, Varian Assocs., 1963—66; mem. Air Forces Sci. Adv. Com., 1947—54; sci. advisor NATO, 1958—59; mem. Dept. Def. Panel Atomic Energy; exec. com. Cambridge Electron Accelerator; gen. adv. com. AEC. Author: Nuclear Moments and Statistics, 1953, Nuclear Two Body Problems, 1953, Molecular Beams, 1956, 1985, Quick Calculus, 1965, Spectroscopy with Coherent Radiation, 1998; contbr. articles Phys. Rev., other sci. jours. on nuclear physics, molecular beam experiments, radar, nuclear magnetic moments, radiofrequency spectroscopy, masers, nucleon scattering. Trustee Assoc. Univs., Inc., Brookhaven Nat. Lab., Carnegie Endowment Internat. Peace, 1962—85, Rockefeller U., 1977—90; pres. Univs. Rsch. Assocs., Inc., 1966—72, 1973—81, pres. emeritus, 1981—. Recipient Presdl. Order of Merit for radar devel. work, 1947, award, E.O. Lawrence and AEC, 1960, Columbia award for excellence in sci., 1980, medal of honor, IEEE, 1983, Rabi prize, 1985, Monte Ferst award, 1985, Compton medal, 1985, Rumford premium, 1985, Oersted medal, 1988, Nat. medal of Sci., 1988, Nobel prize for Physics, 1989, Pupin medal, Columbia Engring. Sch. Alumni Assn., 1992, Sci. for Peace prize, 1992, Einstein medal, 1993, Vannevar Bush award, 1995; fellow Guggenheim, Oxford U., 1954—55. Fellow: Am. Phys. Soc. (coun. 1956—60, pres. 1978—79, Davisson-Germer prize 1974), Am. Acad. Sci.; mem.: AAAS (chmn. physics sect. 1977), NAS, Am. Inst. Physics (chmn. bd. govs. 1980—87), Am. Philos. Assn., French Acad. Sci., Sigma Xi, Phi Beta Kappa (senator 1979—88, v.p. 1982—85). Home: 24 Monmouth Ct Brookline MA 02446-5634 Office: Harvard U Lyman Physics Lab Cambridge MA 02138

RAMSEY, PATRICIA PRUSAK, artist; b. Cleve., Dec. 1, 1952; m. Jeffrey Kent Ramsey, Oct. 3, 1992; children: William K. and Stephanie E. (twins). BFA, Atlanta Coll. Art, 1983. Fine artist Ramsack Studio, Atlanta, 1983-94, Roseburg, Oreg., 1994-99, Waynesville, N.C., 1999—. Tchr. Callenwolde Ctr., Decatur, Ga., 1983-94, Steeplehouse Ctr., Marietta, Ga., 1984-91. Artist, photographer. Dep. dir. Ga. Vol. Lawyers for Arts, Atlanta, 1985-88; juror Mablehouse, Mableton, Ga., 1990. Recipient Best of Show award Mablehouse, 1989, 1st place award Ga. Mountain Crafts, 1992, 94, Great Mom award Grolier Books, 1998, 99. Mem. Nat. Geog. Soc., Smithsonian Instn., Dalton Fine Arts Alliance (exhibiting artist), Fulton County Arts Coun. (artist in edn. 1992), Pinckneyville Arts Ctr. (instr. 1991), Neighborhood Art Ctr. (vis. artist 1983). Home: 265 Love Ln Waynesville NC 28786-3676

RAMSEY, PAUL GLENN, dean, internist; b. Pitts., 1949; MD, Harvard U., 1975. Diplomate Am. Bd. Internal Medicine. Intern Cambridge Hosp., 1975-76; resident in medicine Mass. Gen. Hosp., Boston, 1976-78, U. Wash., Seattle, 1980-81, fellow infectious diseases, 1978-80, prof., 1991—, chmn. dept. medicine, 1992-97; physician-in-chief U. Wash. Med. Ctr., 1992-97; v.p. for med. affairs, dean Sch. Medicine U. Wash., Seattle, 1997—. Mem.: IOM, AAAS, AAP, AFCR, ACP. Office: U Wash Sch Medicine PO Box 356350 Seattle WA 98195-6350

RAMSEY, PAUL RANDALL, music educator; b. Haleyville, Ala., Jan. 6, 1949; s. Johnnie B. and Velma H. Ramsey; m. Bobbie Jean Nix, Aug. 27, 1988; children: Mary, Melanie. BS Edn., Jacksonville State U., 1971; M Music Edn., Miss. State U., 1974. Cert. Music Education K-12, State of Georgia 1971. Dir. bands Model H.S., Rome, 1971—73; dir. of bands Ctrl. H.S., Carrollton, 1974—78, Haralson County H.S., Tallapoosa, 1989—. Composer: (concert band music) Sinfonia for Winds and Percussion, 2002. Mem.: Music Educators Nat. Conf., Ga. Music Educators Assn., Phi Mu Alpha Sinfonia (chpt. pres. 1970—71). Ch. Of Christ. Home: 108 Faye St Tallapoosa GA 30176 Office: Haralson County HS 1655 Georgia Hwy 120 Tallapoosa GA 30176 Home Fax: 770-574-7648. Personal E-mail: bandology@aol.com.

RAMSEY, PETER CHRISTIE, bank executive; b. N.Y.C., Oct. 1, 1942; s. Norman Carnegie and Rosalie Amelia (Christie) R.; m. Maryalice Ives, Nov. 15, 1969. BA, Brown U., 1964. Mgmt. trainee Irving Trust Co., N.Y.C., 1965-67; account exec. Hayden Stone, 1967-72; regional sales mgr. Autex, Inc., Chgo., 1972-78; v.p. Chase Manhattan, N.Y.C., 1978-99; pres. Ramsey Cons. Inc. Mem. coun. of chairs YMCA Greater N.Y., N.Y.C., 1987-90; chmn. bd. mgrs. McBurney YMCA, N.Y.C., 1980-92. Mem. Brown U. Club. Home: 345 E 80th St New York NY 10021-0644 E-mail: PRamsey345@aol.com.

RAMSEY, ROBERT LESLIE, oncologist; b. Vienna, June 15, 1946; MD, U. Chgo., 1972. Diplomate Am. Bd. Internal Medicine. Intern UCLA Med. Ctr., 1972-73, resident in Medicine, 1973-75, fellow in Hematology-Oncology, 1975-77; asst. dep. for health policy, asst. sec. of the Army The Pentagon, Washington. Office: The Pentagon Washington DC 20905

RAMSEY, SALLY ANN SEITZ, retired state official; b. Columbus, Ohio, Feb. 15, 1931; d. Albert Blazier and Mildred (Dodson) Seitz; m. Edward Lewis Ramsey, Apr. 11, 1953 (div. 1962); children: Edward Lewis, Sylvia Ann Mitchell. BA, Ohio State U., 1952, MA, 1955, postgrad., 1963-66; postgrad. St. Mary Coll.-Xavier, Kans., 1962. Rsch. engr., then sr. rsch. engr. N.Am. Aviation, Inc., Columbus, Ohio, and Downey, Calif., 1962-67; legis. intern State of Ohio, 1964-65; rsch. and info. officer Ohio Dept. Urban Affairs, Columbus, 1967-68; adminstrv. specialist Ohio Dept. Devel., Columbus, 1968; assoc. planner, then sr. planner Div. State Planning, Fla. Dept. Adminstrn., Tallahassee, 1968-76; econ. analysis supr., then econ. analyst Fla. Dept. Commerce, 1976-93; ret., 1993; congl. campaign cons., 1966. U.S. Econ. Devel. Adminstrn. fellow, 1978-79. Mem. ASPA, DAR, Fla. Econs. Club, Kappa Kappa Gamma, Pi Sigma Alpha. Episcopalian. Home: 3012 Obrien Dr Tallahassee FL 32309-2760

RAMSEY, SANDRA LYNN, psychotherapist; b. Camp LeJeune, N.C., Feb. 7, 1951; d. Robert A. and Lola J. (Hann) R.; m. Edward G. Schmidt, July 9, 1988 (div. 1998); children: Seth, Sarah, Anna, Rachel. Student, U. Calif., Long Beach, 1969-70, Orange Coast Coll., Costa Mesa, Calif., 1971-72; BA in Psychology with distinction, U. Nebr., 1987, MA in Counseling Psychology, 1989; postgrad., Inst. Study Human Sexuality, 1995, 96. Lic. mental health practitioner; cert. profl. counselor, marriage and family therapist. Vol. coord., client adv. Rape/Spouse Abuse Crisis Ctr., Lincoln, 1989-90; mental health therapist Health Am., HMO, 1991-94; pvt. practice, 1994—; adj. faculty S.E. Cmty. Coll., 1994—; dir. Crisis Mgmt. Internat. Adj. faculty S.E. Cmty. Coll; contract therapist Lincoln Pediatric Group, 1990-91, Family Svc. Assn., Lincoln, 1990-91, Cmty. Preservation Assocs., Lincoln, 1991-94; crisis mgmt. assoc. Crisis Mgmt. Internat.; dir. Crisis Recovery Cons.; presenter in field. Contbr. articles to profl. jours. Mem. Nebr. Domestic Violence Sexual Assault Coalition; vol. ARC Disaster Mental Health Svcs., nat. instr. mental health, 1997—; mem., vol. Nebr. Critical Incident Stress Debriefing team, Nebr. Consortium Health Edn. Programs, Lincoln-Lancaster County Emergency Svcs.; mem. Disaster Morticians Team Dist. 7. Portenier scholar U. Nebr., 1986-87. Mem. APA (assoc., divsn. 50 addictions), Am. Assn. Sex Educators, Counselors and Therapists, Assn. Pvt. Practice Therapists, Nebr. Assn. for Counseling and Devel., Sex Info. and Edn. Coun. of the U.S., Am. Mental Health Counselors Assn. (clin.), Golden Key, Am. Assn. Marriage and Family Therapists, Assn. Pvt. Practice Therapists, Internat. Critical Incident Stress Found., Nat. Assn. Forensic Counselors (cert.), Traumatology Inst. (cert.), Assn. Traumatic Stress Specialists, Harry Benjamin Internat. Gender Dysphoria Assn., Psi Chi. Avocations: gardening, reading, travel, pvt. pilot. E-mail: sandyram@aol.com.

RAMSEY, WILLIAM DALE, JR. marketing and technology consultant; b. Indpls., Apr. 14, 1936; s. William Dale and Laura Jane (Stout) R.; m. Mary Alice Ihnet, Aug. 9, 1969; children: Robin, Scott, Kimberly, Jennifer. AB in Econs., Bowdoin Coll., 1958. With Shell Oil Co., 1958-95; salesman Albany, N.Y., 1960; merchanding rep. Milton, 1961-63; real estate and mktg. investments rep. Jacksonville, Fla., 1963-65; dist. sales supr. St. Paul, 1965-67; employee rels. rep. Chgo., 1967-69; spl. assignment mktg. staff-adminstrn. N.Y.C.; recruitment mgr. to sales mgr. Chgo., 1970-75; sales mgr. Detroit, 1975-79; dist. mgr. N.J. and Pa. Newark, 1979-84; Mid-Atlantic dist. mgr. (Md., D.C., Va.), 1984-87; econ. advisor head office Houston, 1987-89; mgr. mktg. concepts head office, 1989-94; mgr. tech. head office, 1984-95; mng. ptnr. Ramsey Cons., 1995—. Dir. N.Am. Fin. Svcs., 1971-72; lectr., spkr. on energy, radio, TV appearances, 1972—; guest lectr. on bus. five univs., 1967-72; v.p., dir. Malibu East Corp., 1973-74; prin. Robotics Rsch. Consortium, 1991—; mem. Am. Right of Way Assn., 1963-65. Author: Corp. recruitment and Employee Relations Organizational effectiveness Study, 1969. Active Chgo. Urban League, 1971-75; mem. program com., bus. adv. coun. Nat. Rep. Congl. Com., 1981-87, rep. nat. com., 1994—, nat. Rep. senatorial com., 1997—; mem. Rep. senatorial adv. com., Gov.'s Coun. on Tourism and Commerce, Minn., 1965-67; mem. Founders Soc., Detroit Inst. Arts, 1978-80; bd. dirs. N.J. Symphony Orch. Corp., 1981-85; mem. Nat. Audubon Soc., 1997—; mem. B.R.A.S.S. orgn. Jacksonville Symphony Orch., 1999—. Capt. U.S. Army, 1958-60. James Bowdoin scholar Bowdoin Coll., 1958. Mem.: World Affairs Coun., Bowdoin Alumni Club, Nat. Trust Hist. Preservation, Md. Petroleum Coun. (mem. exec. com. 1984—87), Midwest Coll. Placement Assn., N.J. Petroleum Coun. (exec. com. 1979—84, vice chmn. 1982—84), Internat. Svc. Robot Assn., Nat. Audubon Soc., Met. Golf Assn. (N.Y.), Bethesda (Md.) Country Club, Houston Soc. Club, Kingwood (Tex.) Country Club, Morris County (N.J.) Golf Club, Ponte Vedra (Fla.) Club. Episcopalian. Achievements include patents in Method for Automated Refueling; Automated Refueling System; Customer Interface for Driver; three patents pending. Office: Ramsey Consulting PO Box 200 Ponte Vedra Beach FL 32004-0200

RAMSIER, PAUL, composer, psychotherapist; b. Louisville, Sept. 23, 1927; s. Paul and Lucie (Herrmann) R. PhD., N.Y.U., 1972; MSW, SUNY, Stony Brook, 1976. Composer, N.Y.C., 1950—; psychotherapist in pvt. practice, 1977—. Adj. prof. music N.Y.U., 1970—. Composer numerous musical compositions including Divertimento Concertante on a Theme of Couperin, 1965, Road to Hamelin, 1978, Eusebius Revisited, 1980, Silent Movie, 1985, Zoo of Dreams, 1994, Stargazer, 1995, Pavane, 1998, Bass Lullaby, 1999; pub. Boosey and Hawkes. Huntington Hartford fellow, 1960, MacDowell fellow, 1963, Yaddo fellow, 1970; NEA grantee, 1975; recipient Disting. Alumnus award U. Louisville, 1983, Composer award Internat. Soc. Bassists, 1995. Mem. ASCAP. Home and Office: 2323 Goldenrod St Sarasota FL 34239-5334

RAMSTAD, JIM, congressman, lawyer; b. Jamestown, N.D., May 6, 1946; s. Marvin Joseph and Della Mae (Fode) R. BA, U. Minn., 1968; JD with honors, George Washington U., 1973. Bar: N.D. 1973, D.C. 1973, U.S. Supreme Ct. 1976, Minn., 1979. Adminstrv. asst. to speaker Minn. Ho. Reps., 1969; spl. asst. to Congressman Tom Kleppe, 1970; pvt. practice law, Jamestown, 1973, Washington, 1974-1978, Mpls., 1978-90; mem. Minn. Senate, 1981-90, asst. minority leader, 1983-87; mem. U.S. Congress from 3rd Minn. dist., 1990—; adj. prof. Am. U., Washington, 1975-78. Bd. dirs. Children's Heart Fund, Lake Country Food Bank. Served as 1st lt. U.S. Army Res., 1968-74. Mem. Minn. Bar Assn., D.C. Bar Assn., N.D. Bar Assn., Hennepin County Bar Assn., U. Minn. Alumni Assn. (nat. dir.), Am. Legion, Wayzata C. of C., TwinWest C. of C., Com. Ways & Means, U. Minn. Alumni Club (past pres. Washington), Lions, Phi Beta Kappa, Phi Delta Theta. Republican. Office: 103 Cannon Ho Office Bldg Washington DC 20515-0001*

RAMSTEIN, WILLIAM LOUIS, manufacturing company executive; b. L.A., July 9, 1950; s. Robert James and Norma Elaine (Knapp) R.; m. Sue Ann Cooper, Oct. 9, 1983 (div. 1985). BSBA magna cum laude, Calif. State U., Northridge, 1975; MBA, U. So. Calif., 1984. CPA, Calif.; cert. internal auditor. Sr. internal auditor County of Los Angeles, L.A., 1975-78; mgmt. cons. Alexander Grant & Co., Van Nuys, Calif., 1978-80; head of acctg. sect. Hughes Aircraft Co., Missile Systems Group, Canoga Park, 1980-89; mgr. fin. reporting space and electronics group TRW Inc., Redondo Beach, 1989—, mgr. spl. projects and systems, space and electronics group, 1998-2001, mgr. fin. analysis, space and electronics group, 2001—. Fin. cons. Mem. AICPAs, Beta Gamma Sigma. Republican. Avocations: acting, body building, piano, singing, softball. Home: 4310 Torreon Dr Woodland Hills CA 91364-5434 Office: TRW Inc One Space Pk Redondo Beach CA 90278

RAMUNNO, THOMAS PAUL, management consultant; b. Chgo., Sept. 13, 1952; s. Anthony Michael and Dorothy (Buriak) R.; m. Deborah G. Pauline Benton, Jan. 31, 1976 (div. 1991); 1 child, Michael Thomas. BBA, U. Ga., 1974, MBA, 1978. Treas. Concept Inc., Atlanta, 1974-77; product mgr. Johnson-Johnson, Inc., 1978-80; dir. Rollins Inc., 1979-80; cons. Chase Econometrics, 1980-83; v.p. comml. svcs., dir. corp. product mgmt./mktg. Union Trust Co. Md., 1983-84; prin., exec. v.p. Mktg. Scis. Group, Inc., Hunt Valley, Md., 1984-85; v.p., dir. Citicorp, Chgo., 1985-86; sr. mgr. fin. instns. consulting group Deloitte & Touche, 1987-90; dir. cons. svcs. FSA, Inc., 1990-92; CEO Adv. Scis. Group, 1991-98; pres. IASG, 1990-98; ptnr. Info. Scis., Inc., 1996-98; v.p., practice leader Metagroup Cons., 1998-2000; ptnr. KPMG Cons., 2000—01; mng. ptnr. Scient, Inc., 2001—; CEO, mng. ptnr. EVP/Chicago, 2001—; mng. ptnr. St. Charles Group, 2002—. Home: 25 Commons Dr Palos Park IL 60464

RAN, SHULAMIT, composer; b. Tel Aviv, Oct. 21, 1949; came to U.S., 1963; m. Abraham Lotan, 1986. Studied composition with, Paul Ben-Haim, Norman Dello, Joio, Ralph Shapey; student, Mannes Coll. Music, N.Y.C., 1963-67. With dept. music U. Chgo., 1973—, William H. Colvin prof. music; composer-in-residence Chgo. Symphony Orch., 1990-97, Lyric Opera of Chgo., 1994-97. Compositions include 10 Children's Scenes, 1967, Structures, 1968, 7 Japanese Love Poems, 1968, Hatzvi Israel Eulogy, 1969, O the Chimneys, 1969, Concert Piece for piano and orch., 1970, 3 Fantasy Pieces for Cello and Piano, 1972, Ensembles for 17, 1975, Double Vision, 1976, Hyperbolae for Piano, 1976, For an Actor: Monologue for Clarinet, 1978, Apprehensions, 1979, Private Game, 1979, Fantasy-Variations for Cello, 1980, A Prayer, 1982, Verticals for piano, 1982, String Quartet No. 1, 1984, (for woodwind quintet) Concerto da Camera I, 1985, Amichai Songs, 1985, Concerto for Orchestra, 1986, (for clarinet, string quartet and piano) Concerto da Camera II, 1987, East Wind, 1987, String Quartet No. 2, 1988-89, Symphony, 1989-90, Mirage, 1990, Inscriptions for solo violin, 1991, Chicago Skyline for brass and percussion, 1991, Legends for Orch., 1992-93, Invocation, 1994, Yearning for violin and string orch., 1995, (opera) Between Two Worlds (The Dybbuk), 1995-97, Soliloquy, 1997, Vessels of Courage and Hope for orch., 1998, (flute concerto) Voices, 2000, Three Scenes for solo clarinet, 2000; commd. pieces include for Am. Composers Orch., Phila. Orch., Chgo. Symphony, Balt. Symphony, Chamber Soc. of Lincoln Ctr., Mendelssohn String quartet, Da Capo Chamber Players, Sta. WFMT, Lyric Opera Chgo.; composer and soloist for 1st performances Capriccio, 1963, Symphonic Poem, 1967, Concert Piece, 1971. Recipient Acad. Inst. Arts and Letters award, 1989, Pulitzer prize for music, 1991, Friedheim award for orchestral music Kennedy Ctr., 1992; Guggenheim fellow, 1977, 90. Office: U Chgo Dept Music 1010 E 59th St Chicago IL 60637-1512

RANALD, MARGARET LOFTUS, English literature educator, author; b. Auckland, N.Z., Sept. 5, 1927; came to U.S., 1952; d. Leonard R. and Geraldine (McGrath) Loftus; m. Ralph Arthur Ranald, Feb. 26, 1955; 1 child, Caroline Margaret. AB, U. N.Z., Wellington, 1949, MA honors, 1951; MA, UCLA, 1954, PhD, 1958. Jr. asst. Dept. Prime Min. Govt. N.Z., Wellington, 1944-52; asst. to sec. Princeton (N.J.) U., 1956-57; from instr. to asst. prof. Temple U., Phila., 1957-61; from asst. prof. to prof. CUNY, N.Y.C., 1961—. Assoc. bibliographer MLA, N.Y.C., 1958—; mem. assoc. faculty, mem. adv. com. Columbia U., N.Y.C., 1976—; vis. prof. UCLA, 1970-85, 98, tchg. asst., 1953-55. Author: The Eugene O'Neill Companion, 1984, Shakespeare and his Social Context, 1987, John Webster, 1989; assoc. editor (book series): International Bibliography of Theatre, 1985—. Fulbright fellow, 1952-54; sr. fellow Folger Shakespeare Libr., 1970-72. Mem. MLA, Am. Soc. Theatre Rsch. (exec. sec., v.p. 1976-83), Eugene O'Neill Soc. (coun., pres. 1996-2000), Shakespeare Soc. Am. (former rsch. asst.), Princeton Club N.Y. Avocations: music, drama, theatrical history, travel. Office: CUNY Dept of Eng 65-30 Kissena Blvd Flushing NY 11367

RANALD, RALPH ARTHUR, former government official, educator; b. N.Y.C., Nov. 25, 1930; s. Josef A. and Pearl R.; m. Margaret Florence Loftus, Feb. 26, 1955; 1 dau., Caroline. AB, UCLA, 1952, MA, 1954; AM, Princeton U., 1958; postgrad. (Carnegie fellow) Law Sch., Harvard U., 1961-62, 76-77, 99-2000; grad., Exec. Program Nat. and Internat. Security, 1978; PhD, Princeton U., 1962; JD, Fordham U., 1997. Bar: N.Y. Teaching asst. UCLA, 1952-54; univ. fellow, rsch. asst. Princeton (N.J.) U., 1956-59; asst. prof. Fordham U. Grad. Sch., N.Y.C., 1959-65; asst. dean acad. affairs, prof. Coll. Arts and Scis. NYU, 1965-69; prof. CUNY, 1969—; spl. policy asst. HEW, Washington, 1968-69, Office of Mgmt. and Budget, 1976-77; sr. cons. U.S. Dept. Def., 1969-70, 77-78; mem. staffs Dept. Def. and Army Gen. Staff U.S. Govt. Long Com., 1989, U.S. Dept. Def., 1995-96. Vis. prof. and cons. univs. including U. So. Calif., summers 1968-74, Calif. State U., UCLA, summers 1985, 98; vis. scholar Harvard Law Sch., 1999—. Author: Management Development in Government, 1979, George Orwell, 1965; contbr. reports, articles to publs. in law, govt. and edn. Treas. N.Y. State Com. for Pub. Higher Edn., 1975-78, mem. com., 1970—. 1st lt. U.S. Army, 1953-56, to col., 1977-78, res., 1978—. Recipient U.S. Legion of Merit, 1983; sr. fellow Am. Soc. Pub. Adminstrn. (selection com. for fellows, 1970-74); mem. Res. Officers Assn. U.S. (life), Harvard U. Law Sch. Assn., Assn. of Princeton U. Grad. Alumni, U.S. Army War Coll. Alumni Assn., John F. Kennedy Sch. of Govt. Alumni Assn., Princeton Club of N.Y., Army and Navy Club, Phi Beta Kappa. Home and Office: 239 Central Park W New York NY 10024-6038

RANAWEERA, SAMANTHA LALINDA, software engineer; b. Nuwara Eliya, Ctrl. Province, Sri Lanka, Sept. 3, 1972; s. Kalu Arachchige and Swarna Ranaweera; m. Nilmini Wedisinghe, Oct. 7, 1972. BS, U. Peradeniya, Sri Lanka., 1998; MSc in Computer Engring., U. Cin., Ohio, 1998—2000. CPA Chartered Inst. of Mgmt. Accountants, UK, Stage 1, 1995. Software developer Nat. Inst. Bus. Mgmt., Colombo, Sri Lanka, 1993—94; tchg. asst. U. of Cin., Cincinnati, Ohio, 1998—99, rsch. asst., dept. of elec., computer engring. and computer sci., 1999—2000; software engr. LSI Logic Corp., Colorado Springs, Colo., 2000—02. Sec. Elec. and Electronic Engring. Students Soc., U. of Peradeniya, Sri Lanka, 1996—97; mem. coun. Engring. Students Union, U. of Peradeniya, Sri Lanka, 1997—98; student mem. of the faculty bd. Faculty of Engring., U. of Peradeniya, Sri Lanka, 1997—98. Contbr. articles to profl.jours. Recipient U. Grad. Scholarship, U. of Cin., 1998/1999/2000, E.F. Bartholomeusz prize for best cumulative performance in freshman throug, U. of Peradeniya, 1998, Ananda Amarasinghe Meml. prize best performance in Engring., U., U. Peradeniya, 1994/1995, U. Scholarship for the best performance in engring., U. of Peradeniya, 1994/1995.

RANCE, QUENTIN E. interior designer; b. St. Albans, Eng., Mar. 22, 1935; came to U.S., 1981. s. Herbert Leonard and Irene Ann (Haynes) R.; m. India Adams, May 17, 1974. Grad., Eastbourne (Eng.) Sch. Art, 1960. Soft furnishings buyer Dickeson & French Ltd., Eastbourne, 1960-61, outside sales mgr., 1961-62; design dir. Laszlo Hoenig, Ltd., London, 1962-73; mng. dir. Quentin Rance Interiors Ltd., 1973-81; pres. Quentin Rance Enterprises, Inc., Encino, Calif., 1981—. Works featured in Designers West, 1983, Design House Rev., 1983, Profiles mag., 1987, Nat. Assn. Mirror Mfrs. Jour., 1988, Designer Specifier, 1990. Mem. Founders for Diabetic Research/City of Hope. Served with RAF, 1953-55. Recipient Hon. Mention award Nat. Assn. Mirror Mfrs., 1987, 1st Pl. Nat. Pub. Svc. award, Designer Specifier, 1990. Fellow Chartered Soc. Designers (Eng.); mem. Am. Soc. Interior Designers (profl., chpt. bd. dirs. 1983-87, 89-91, chmn. Awards 1983-85, admissions chmn. 1985—, Presdl. citations 1984, 87, 91, 95, 97), Knights of Vine. Avocations: bicycling, antiques, fine wines, philately, theatre. Home and Office: 18005 Rancho St Encino CA 91316-4214 Fax: 818-705-2213. E-mail: qerca@earthlink.net. *Personal philosophy: Good design is always there to be seen, there to be appreciated, and there for expanding one's own boundaries of creativity.*

RANCK, EDNA RUNNELS, academic administrator, researcher; b. Waterville, Maine, Aug. 24, 1935; d. Everett Elias and Edna May (King) Runnels; m. James Gilmour Ranck, June 30, 1971 (dec. May 1979); children: Matthew, Christopher, Joshua Duggan; m. Martin Fleischer, Apr. 19, 1982; stepchildren: Christina, Laura Ranck. BA cum laude, Fla. State U., Tallahassee, 1957; MDiv magna cum laude, Drew U. Theol. Sch., Madison, N.J., 1971, MEd in Edn. Adminstrn., 1978; EdD in Curriculum and Tchg., Columbia U., N.Y.C., 1986. Dir. Collinsville Child Care Ctr., Morristown, N.J., 1971-78; exec. dir. Children's Svcs. Morris County, 1980-84; co-mgr. N.J. Child Care Clearinghouse, Trenton; coord. N.J. Child Care Adv. Coun., 1987-92; dir. N.J. Office Child Care Devel., 1992; child care coord. N.J. Dept. Human Svcs., 1992-98, Nat. Assn. Child Care Resource & Referral Agys., Washington, 1998—. Adj. faculty Kean U. N.J., Union, 1983; dir. Sprout House Preschool, Chatham, N.J., 1984-87; mem. Morris County Human Svcs. Adv. Coun., Morristown, N.J., 1986-87, spkr. in field. Author: Dodge Foundation Project, 1984, Young Children, 1987, Our History, Our Vision: A History of the National Association of Child Care Rsource and Referral Agencies, 1997, monthly Policy Perspectives column, 2000—; contbr. articles and revs. to profl. jours. Exec. bd. Drew U. Alumni Assn. Theol. Sch., 1986-92; mem. Drew U. Alumni Study Commn., 1993, Non-Govt. Orgn. rep. to UN Internat. Fedn. Educative Cmtys., 1992-99; mem. history/archives panel Nat. Assn. for Edn. of Young Children. Recipient Volpe Commitment in Child Care award, N.J. Child Care Assn., 1991, Essex C.C. Early Childhood award, 1997, Aletha Wright award for Excellence in Early Edn., 1998. Mem. Internat. Assn. Presch. Edn. N.Am. (bd. dirs.), Child Care Action Campaign Panel, Acad. Child and Youth Care Workers, Nat. Assn. of Regulatory Adminstrn. (bd. dirs. 2000--), World Orgn. Presch. Edn. (bd. dirs. 2000—), Phi Beta Kappa, Pi Sigma Alpha. Republican. United Methodist. Avocations: writing, travel, swimming, clothing design, art collecting. Home: 4447 MacArthur Blvd NW Washington DC 20007-2564 E-mail: edna.ranck@verizon.net.

RANCOURT, JOHN HERBERT, retired pharmaceutical company executive, marine engineer; b. Troy, N.Y., Aug. 10, 1946; s. Charles Dennis and Helen Mary (Keadin) R.; divorced; children: Karen Mary, John Herbert, Alison Jane, Elizabeth Anne, Maureen Ellen. BS in Mgmt., Rensselaer Poly. Inst., 1968, MS in Mgmt., 1972, MBA, 1981. CPA, Ill.; cert. mgmt. acct. From asst. to dir. rsch. Rensselaer Poly. Inst., 1968-69; mgmt. trainee, buyer/purchasing agt., contr. rsch. divsn. Huyck Corp., Rensselaer, N.Y., 1969-74, corp. internat. project mgr. Wake Forest, N.C., 1974-76, adminstrv. svc. mgr. Formex divsn., 1976-77; sr. fin. analyst Abbott Labs., North Chicago, Ill., 1977-79, sect. mgr. sales acctg., 1979-80, mgr. fin. analysis, materials mgmt. divsn., 1980-82, mgr. fin. planning and analysis, pharm. products divsn., 1982-84, contr. TAP Pharms. subs., 1984-97; mng. prin. The Rancourt Group Internat., Libertyville, Ill., 1997—; dir. adminstrn. and fin. Jered Industries, Chelsea, Mass., 1999-2000, dir. adminstrn. and fin. marine svcs. divsn. Vancleave, 2000. Fin. cons. to entrepreneurs and Fortune 500 cos.; instr. acctg. Coll. of Lake County, Grayslake, Ill., part-time, 1981-85. Indian Guide/Princess Tribal leader YMCA, 1980-90; solicitor United Way, 1981, 83, 85, 87, 88-89, 90-91, mem. allocation panel, 1990-92. Mem. Nat. Assn. Accts., Am. Acctg. Assn., Am. Inst. CPAs, Ill. CPA Soc., Fin. Execs. Inst., Liberty Road and Track Club. Roman Catholic. Home: Apt D-12 5080 Gautier/Vanclave Rd Gautier MS 39553

RAND, AUSTIN STANLEY, biologist, researcher; b. Seneca Falls, N.Y., Sept. 29, 1932; s. Austin Loomer and Rheua Vaughn (Medden) R.; m. Patricia Jane Grubbs, June 24, 1961; children: Hugh, Margaret, Katherine. BA, De Pauw U., 1954; PhD, Harvard U., 1961. Biologist Smithsonian Tropical Rsch. Inst., Balboa, Ancon, Rep. of Panama, 1964-97. Cons. Nat. Geog., 1970—. Editor: Iguana of the World, 1982; contbr. articles to profl. jours. Mem. Assn. Tropical Biology, Am. Soc. Icthyologists and Herpetologists, Animal Behavior Soc. Home: 2504 De Witt Ave Alexandria VA 22301 Office: Smithsonian Tropical Rsch Inst Internat Ctr MRC 705 1100 Jefferson Dr Ste 3123 Washington DC 20560 E-mail: rands@stridc.si.edu.

RAND, CALVIN GORDON, arts and education consultant; b. Buffalo, May 15, 1929; s. George Franklin and Isabel (Williams) R.; m. Patricia Clemens Andrew, Aug. 18, 1951; children— Robin, Melissa, Jennifer, Lucinda, Elizabeth BA, Princeton U., 1951; MA, Columbia U., 1954; LHD (hon.), York U., Can., 1984. Head history dept. Riverdale Sch., N.Y.C., 1955-60; lectr. philosophy SUNY-Buffalo, 1961-68, acting dir. cultural affairs, 1968-71; founder, pres. The Niagara Inst., Niagara-on-the-Lake, Can., 1971-79; pres. Am. Acad. in Rome, N.Y.C., 1980-84; ind. producer, theatre and film cons., 1985-90. Founding chmn., dir. Shaw Festival Theatre, Niagara-on-the-Lake, 1964-78, bd. govs., 1979—; trustee Playwrights Horizons Theatre, N.Y.C., 1982-92; bd. dirs. Arts in Edn. Inst.; mem. N.Y. State Coun. on Arts, 1978-82, Arts Coun. Western N.Y., 1987-93; chmn. World Ency. Contemporary Theater; chmn. arts coun. SUNY, Buffalo, 1987-94, adj. prof. theater, 1988—. Contbr. articles to profl. jours. Bd. dirs. Burchfield-Penney Art Ctr., Buffalo, 1991—, vice-chair, 1999—; bd. dirs. Irish Classical Theater, 1993—, pres., 1998—; trustee Albright-Knox Gallery, Buffalo, 1976-80, 84-88, 90-94. Recipient spl. citation Ont. Arts Coun., 1976, Fellowship Fund award Niagara Inst., 1980, Centennial Arts award Nichols Sch., 1992, Red Jacket award, Erie County Hist. Soc., 2000, Walter B. Cooke award, 1997; named Man of Yr., Coun. World Affairs, 1976, Buffalo Courier Express, 1976, Arts Patron of Yr., Western N.Y. Arts Coun. and C. of C., 1989; Disting Non-Alumni, SUNY, Buffalo, Man of Yr., YMCA of Western NY; Vanier Cook fellow York U. Mem. Players Club, Princeton Club, Saturn Club.

RAND, CAROLYN, financial executive; b. Bedford, Ky., Dec. 12, 1938; d. John William and Sarah (Bray) R.; m. Leonard Paul Schwartz, May 1, 1970 (div. 1990); children: Sarah Roselyn, Daniel. Student, Hanover Coll., 1957-59; BS, U. Ky., 1961; cert. in merchandising, Tobe Coburn Sch., 1962. Cert. fin. planner. Exec. trainee, assoc. buyer Shillito's Dept. Stores, Cin., 1962-65; buyer, merchandiser Jacobson's Stores, Jackson, Mich., 1965-70; mgr. pro shop Colonial Racquet Club, Cin., 1976-82; rep. Chubb Securities, 1982-86; v.p. Spectrum Fin. Svcs., 1986—. Chmn. N.W. fundraising WCET pub. TV sta., Cin., 1980; chmn. fundraising Finneytown schs. PTA, Cin., 1980-82; pres., chmn. fundraising Kindervelt # 37, Cin., 1981-82; mem. ch. fin. com., 1994-95, ch. pledge chmn., 1994-96; active Cin. Art Mus.; fund raising com. Habitat for Humanity, 1996-97, Church Endowment Com., 1996—, chair, 1999—; co-chair, trustee Friendship Meth. Ch., Cin., 1996-2000, mem. fundraising leadership team, 2001; vol. and lectr. cmty. groups; mem. leadership team Friendship Meth. Ch., 2001-02, mem. fund raising com. Mem. Inst. Cert. Planners, Miami Valley Soc. Inst. CFPs (pres. 1987-88), Internat. Assn. Fin. Planners (bd. dirs. Cin. chpt., ethics chmn. 1988, program chmn. 1989), Newcomers Club (Wyoming, Ohio) (program chmn. 1986), Encore Book Club. Democrat. Methodist. Avocations: tennis, skiing, gardening. Office e-mail: crand@spectrum financial.net. Office: Spectrum Fin Svcs 10641 Techwood Cir Cincinnati OH 45242-2837

RAND, CHRISTOPHER EDWARD, music educator; b. Titusville, Fla., Aug. 10, 1959; s. Virginia Katherine Graf and William Jackson Rand; m. Elizabeth Rene Flynn; children: Alexis Christine. MusB, SUNY, Potsdam, 1981, MusM, 1986. Cert. Edn. N.Y., 1986. Resident dir. SUNY , Potsdam, 1981—86; dir. of music Dover Ctrl. Sch., Dover Plains, 1986—. Head percussion instr. Arlington Marching Band , Lagrangeville, NY, 1990—. Composer: (songs) Halfast Boogie, 1993. Recipient First Pl. Band award, Nat. Ajudicators Invitational-Dixie Classic- Va. Beach, VA, 1998. Master: Music Educators Nat. Conf.; mem.: Dutchess County Music Educators Assn. (v.p. 1993—94, gen. chmn. 1993—2000). Roman Catholic. Avocations: microelectronics, running, golf, gardening. Home: 82 Scenic Hills Drive Poughkeepsie NY 12603 Office: Dover Union Free School District Rt 22 Dover Plains NY 12522 Home Fax: 845-473-9369; Office Fax: 845-473-9369. Personal E-mail: bikoleg @ AOL.com. Business E-Mail: bikoleg@ aol.com.

RAND, HARRY ISRAEL, lawyer; b. N.Y.C., July 27, 1912; s. Samuel and Rose (Hirth) R.; m. Anna Tulman, Oct. 22, 1938; children: Steven, Deborah, Naomi. BS, CCNY, 1932; JD, NYU, 1936. Bar: N.Y. 1936, U.S. Supreme Ct. 1943, D.C. 1947, U.S. Dist. Cts. (so. and ea. dists.) N.Y. 1959, 60, U.S. Ct. Appeals (2d cir.) 1966. Atty. U.S. Pub. Works Adminstrn., 1938-39, U.S. Dept. Interior, 1939-43, U.S. Dept. Justice, 1943-48; pvt. practice Washington, 1948-58; mem. Weisman, Celler, Allan, Spett & Sheinberg, N.Y.C., 1959-67, Botein, Hays & Sklar, N.Y.C., 1967-89; counsel Herrick, Feinstein, 1990—. Mem. Assn. of Bar of City of N.Y., Am. Law Inst. Home: 66 Hillandale Rd Westport CT 06880-5319 also: 320 W 86th St New York NY 10024-3139 Office: Herrick Feinstein LLP Two Park Ave New York NY 10016 E-mail: hrand@herrick.com.

RAND, HARRY ZVI, art historian, poet; b. N.Y.C., Jan. 10, 1947; m. Jennifer Rand; 1 child, Leah Zoë. BA, CCNY, 1969; AM, Harvard U., 1971, PhD, 1974. Contbg. editor Arts mag., N.Y.C., 1975-91, 1975—; assoc. curator Nat. Mus. Am. Art, Washington, 1977-79, curator, 1979-93, chmn. dept., 1978-84, sr. curator, 1993-97; sr. curator cultural history Nat. Mus. Am. Hist., Smithsonian Inst., 1997—. Mem. adv. bd. Awards in Visual Arts, Winston-Salem, N.C., 1982-92, Austrian Internat. Art Inst., 1989—; arts advisor Virlane Found., New Orleans, 1980—; cons. NAS, 1983, Cosanti Found., 1989—, Exodus Found., 1992—, World Econ. Forum, 1992-94, World Bank, 1994-96. Co-author: The Genius of American Painting, 1973, Still Working, 1993, Vincent Pepi, 1995; author: Seymour Lipton, 1979, Arshile Gorky, 1981, 91, Recent Trends in Collecting, 1982, The Beginning of Things, 1983, Martha Jackson Meml. Collection, 1985, Der Maler Hundertwasser, 1986, 2001, Manet's Contemplation at the Gare Saint-Lazare, 1987, paperback edit. 1991, Paul Manship, 1989, Julian Stanczak, 1990, Hundertwasser, 1991, 92, Jochen Seidel, 1992, Color, 1993, The Clouds, 1996; hon. editor Leonardo mag., 1983—; patentee in field. N.Y. State Regents scholar, 1965-68; travelling fellow Harvard U., 1973, Andrew W. Mellon Found. fellow, 1976-77; Rockefeller Found. devel. grantee, 1982-83, Rsch. Opportunities grantee Smithsonian Instn., 1985, 86, 87, 88, 89, 90, 91, 92, 94, 95, Spl. Scholarly Studies grantee, 1987-95, Ednl. Outreach grantee, 1995. Fellow Explorers

Club; mem. World Art Coun. (steering com. Geneva 1992-96), World Soc. to Stop Trade Stolen Art (bd. dirs. 1994—). Home: 5511 Greystone St Chevy Chase MD 20815-5556 Office: Nat Mus Am History Washington DC 20560-0616

RAND, JOELLA MAE, retired nursing educator, counselor; b. Akron, Ohio, July 9, 1932; d. Harry S. and Elizabeth May (Miller) Halberg; m. Martin Rand (dec.); children: Craig, Debbi Stark. BSN, U. Akron, 1961, MEd in Guidance, 1968; PhD in Higher Edn. Adminstrn., Syracuse U., 1981. Staff nurse Akron Gen. Hosp., 1953-54; staff-head nurse-instr. Summit County Receiving, Cuyahoga Falls, Ohio, 1954-56; head nurse psychiat. unit Akron Gen. Hosp., 1956-57; instr. psychiatric nursing Summit County Receiving, Cuyahoga Falls, 1957-61; head nurse, in-service instr. Willard (N.Y.) State Hosp., 1961-62; asst. prof. Alfred (N.Y.) U., 1962-76, assoc. prof., assoc. dean, 1976-78, acting dean, 1978-79, dean, 1979-90, dean coll. profl. studies, 1990-91, prof. counseling, 1991-2000; ret., 2000. Cons. N.Y. State Regents Program for Non-Collegiate Sponsored Instrn., 1984; cons. collegiate programs N.Y. State Dept. Edn., 1985, Elmira Coll., 1991, U. Rochester, 1992-93; accreditation visitor Nat. League for Nursing, 1984-92; ednl. cons. Willard Psychiat. Hosp., 1992-93; mem. profl. practice exam. subcom. Regents Coll., 1990-95. Vol. Williard Drug Treatment Ctr., 1997—, bd. dirs.; mem. Zoning Bd., Williard, 2002—; bd. dirs. Five Point Correctional Facility; bd. dir. Romulus Bd. of Zoning Appeals, 2002—. Recipient Tchg. Excellence award Alfred U., 1977, Mary E. Gladwin Outstanding Alumni award Akron U. Coll. Nursing, 1983, Alfred Alumni Friends award, 1989, Grand Marshall commencement Alfred U., 1993, Vol. of Yr. award Willard Drug Treatment Ctr., 1999. Mem.: ACA (NAR rep. 2000—), Genesee Valley Edn. Com. (chair 1984—86), Western N.Y. League Nursing (bd. dirs. 1991—93), Genesee Regional Consortium (v.p.), N.Y. State Coun. of Deans (treas. 1984—88), N.Y. State Counseling Assn. (v.p.-elect profl. svcs. 1995—96, 1998—99, v.p. profl. svcs. 1996—98, 1999—2000), Sigma Theta Tau (treas. Alfred chpt. 1984—85). Avocations: boating, fishing, public speaking in areas of family and child abuse. E-mail: drand@rochester.rr.com.

RAND, KATHY SUE, public relations executive; b. Miami Beach, Fla., Feb. 24, 1945; d. William R. and Rose (Lasser) R.; m. Peter C. Ritsos, Feb. 19, 1982. BA, Mich. State U., 1965; MBA, Northwestern U., 1980. Asst. editor Lyons & Carnahan, Chgo., 1967-68; mng. editor Cahners Pub. Co., 1968-71; pub. rels. writer Super Market Inst., 1972-73; account supr. Pub. Communications Inc., 1973-77; divisional mgr. pub. rels. Quaker Oats Co., 1977-82; exec. v.p., dep. gen. mgr. Golin/Harris Communications, 1982-90; exec. v.p. Lesnik Pub. Rels., Northbrook, 1990-91; mng. dir. Manning, Selvage & Lee, Chgo., 1991—2002. Dir. midwest region NOW, 1972-74; mem. Kellogg Alumni Adv. Bd.; bd. dirs. Jr. Achievement of Chgo. Mem. Pub. Rels. Soc. Am. (Silver Anvil award 1986, 87), Pub. Club Chgo. (Golden Trumpet awards 1982-87, 90, 94, 95, 97, 98, 99, 2000), Northwestern Club Chgo., Kellogg Alumni Club, Beta Gamma Sigma. Home: 400 Riverwoods Rd Lake Forest IL 60045-2547 E-mail: ksrand@aol.com.

RAND, LAWRENCE ANTHONY, investor and financial relations executive; b. Bklyn., Nov. 19, 1942; s. Gerald M. and Elaine Shirley Rand; m. Madelon L., July 4, 1942; children: Allan, Joshua, Emily. AB with honors, Brown U., 1964; MA, NYU, 1965, PhD, 1998. Lectr. NYU, 1967, CUNY, 1968; analyst CIA, Langley, Va., 1967-68; account supr. Ruder & Finn Inc., N.Y.C., 1968-71; co-founder, sr. v.p. Kekst & Co., 1971—, also bd. dirs. Chmn., bd. dirs. ALS Assn., L.A., 1987-92. Bd. govs. N.Y. United Hosp., Port Chester; chmn. ethics com. Village of Rye Brook, 1993—2000, village trustee, 2000—02; bd. dirs. USA Tennis Found. Mem. City Athletic Club (bd. govs.), Brown U. Club, Bailiwick Club (Greenwich, Conn.). Office: Kekst & Co 437 Madison Ave 19th Fl New York NY 10022-7195 E-mail: lar@kekst.com.

RAND, MERTHEL LURETTA, family nurse practitioner; b. Lincoln, Nebr., June 18, 1945; d. Lloyd Oswald and Edith Margaret (Cook) Barnes; m. Wayne Dean Vorhies, Aug. 1, 1965 (div. Aug. 1979); children: Sondra Renae Brickell, Steve Allen Vorhies; m. Mark Lindsay Atwood, Mar. 30, 1986 (div. Apr. 1995); m. Philip D. Rand, Aug. 9, 1996. BS, Union Coll., 1967; BA, Augustana Coll., 1989; MS in Nursing, Andrews U., Berrien Springs, Mich., 1999. RN, Mich. Staff nurse McKennan Hosp., Sioux Falls, S.D., 1989-90, Sioux Valley Hosp., 1990-91, Dartmouth-Hitchcock Med. Ctr., Lebanon, N.H., 1991-96; home health nurse Arcadia Health, Lincoln, Nebr., 1996-99; nurse cons. Martin Luther Homes, Inc., 1997-98, Alpha Home Health Care, St. Joseph, Mich., 1999-2000; mem. float pool Lakeland Med. Ctr., 2000—01; with VA Clinic, Benton Harbor, Mich., 2001—. Seventh-day Adventist. Avocations: music, writing, camping, reading. Home: Apt # 2 4322 E Tudor Rd Berrien Springs MI 49103-9219 Office: VA Clinic 960 Agard St Ste 240 Benton Harbor MI 49022 E-mail: lurand@juno.com.

RAND, PETER, writer, editor, educator; b. San Francisco, Feb. 23, 1942; s. Christopher T.E. Rand and Margaret Aldrich Demott; m. Bliss I. Rand, Dec. 19, 1976; 1 child, James. Student, U. Calif., Berkeley; MA, Johns Hopkins U., 1975. Adv. fiction editor Antaeus, N.Y.C., 1970-73; editor Washington Monthly, 1974-75; instr. Columbia U., N.Y.C., 1976-91; preceptor Harvard U., Cambridge, Mass., 1997-98, Boston U., 1999—. Freelance editor, Belmont, Mass., 1994—. Author: Firestorm, 1969, The Time of the Emergency, 1977, The Private Rich, 1984, Gold from Heaven, 1988, China Hands, 1995; editor: Deng Xinoping, Chronicle of an Empire (by Ruan Ming), 1994, Scarlet Memorial, Tales of Cannibalism in Modern China (by Zheng Yi), 1996. Trustee Belmont Citizens Forum, 1999—. Grantee Creative Artists Performing Svcs., N.Y.C., 1977. Mem. PEN, J.K. Fairbank Ctr. for East Asian Rsch. (affiliate), Tavern Club. Avocation: tennis. Home: 35 Falmouth St Belmont MA 02478

RAND, ROBERT STEPHEN, electrical engineer, researcher; b. Worcester, Mass., Nov. 10, 1953; s. Raymond Stephen and Dorothy May Rand. PhD in Engrng. Physics, U. Va., Charlottesville, 2001. Scientist U.S. Army ERDC, Alexandria, Va., 1977—. Mem.: IEEE-GRS Soc. Business E-Mail: robert.s.rand@erdc.usace.army.mil.

RAND, ROBERT WHEELER, neurosurgeon, educator; b. L.A., Jan. 28, 1923; s. Carl W. and Catherine (Humphrey) R.; m. Helen L. Pierce, Dec. 17, 1949; children: Carl W., Richard P. Student, Harvard U., 1940-42, UCLA, 1942-44; MD, U. So. Calif., 1947; MS, U. Mich., 1951, PhD in Anatomy, 1952; JD, U. West L.A., 1974. Intern, resident in neurosurgery U. Mich., Ann Arbor, 1947-52; from instr. to prof. neurol. surgery UCLA, 1953-89; assoc. med. dir. John Wayne Cancer Inst., Santa Monica, Calif., 1989—. Expert witness malpractice cases Superior Ct. Author: Spinal Cord Tumors in Childhood, 1960, Microneurosurgery, 3d edit., 1985; contbr. articles to profl. jours.; inventor neuropledgets, thermomagnetic surgery coil system, microballoon for aneurysm occlusion, Malcolm-Rand graphite cranial frame, cobalt scalpel. Lt. comdr. USNR, 1943-46, 54-56. Recipient Profl. award UCLA, 1973. Fellow ACS; mem. AMA, Calif. Med. Assn., L.A. County Med. Assn., Am. Surg. Assn., Internat. Coll. Surgeons, Am. Assn. Neurol. Surgeons, Assn. Neurol. Surgeons, Soc. Neurol. Surgeons, Western Neurosurg. Soc., L.A. Country Club. Office: John Wayne Cancer Inst St John's Hosp 2200 Santa Monica Blvd Santa Monica CA 90404-2302

RAND, RUTH A. science and computer educator; b. Phila., Mar. 31, 1935; m. Dr. Wilfred Kolman, 1957, (dec. 1980); children: Marc, Ross, Rachel. AB, Swarthmore Coll., 1956; MS, U. Pa., 1964. Tchr. N.C. Sch. Sci. and Maths., 1981-82, Abington (Pa.) Friends Sch., Latin Sch. Chgo., 1984-92, Albuquerque Acad., 1992—. Rsch. asst. Dept. Physiology, Sch. of Medicine U. N.C., 1977-82; policy rsch. assoc. Eagleton Inst. Ruters U., 1972-73; sr. chemist Bur. Rsch. in Neurology and Psychiatry, Princeton, 1967-70; sci. cons. Video Dialog, 1989; participant Chem. Scis. in Modern World conf. Beckman Ctr. History of Chemistry U. Pa., 1990; facilitator Project 2061; founder Sigma Pi. Author: Understanding and Designing the Microcomputer Based Lab. 1987, Getting Started in Organic and Biochemistry, 1985, revised, 1987; contbg. editor: Modern Chemistry, 1989—; contbr. articles to profl. jours. Recipient Dreyfus Master Tchr. award Woodrow Wilson Nat. Fellowship Found., 1983, 93, Master Tchr. Leader award, 1989, Presdl. Edn. award State of Ill., 1986, Presdl. award for excellence in h.s. sci. tchg., 1987, State award IMPACT II: Creative Teaching Ideas, 1990, CBE award 1993, N. Mex. ACS Outstanding High Sch. Chem. award, 1995, Catalyst award for excellence in h.s. tchg., 1996, Outstanding Chemistry Tchr. award ACS Rocky Mountain Region, 2002; Einstein fellow, 1999. Home: 869 Tramway Ln NE # D Albuquerque NM 87122-1408 Office: Albuquerque Acad 6400 Wyoming Blvd NE Albuquerque NM 87109-3899

RAND, SIDNEY ANDERS, retired college administrator; b. Eldred, Minn., May 9, 1916; s. Charles William and Ida Alice (Pedersen) R.; m. Dorothy Alice Holm, Sept. 1, 1942 (dec. Jan. 1974); children: Peter Anders, Mary Alice; m. Lois Schiager Ekeren, Nov. 23, 1974. BA, Concordia Coll., Moorhead, Minn., 1938, DD (hon.), 1956; degree in theology, Luther Sem., St. Paul, 1943; LHD (hon.), Colo. Coll., 1976; LLD (hon.), Carleton Coll., 1980, St. Olaf Coll., 1980, Coll. of St. Scholastica, 1985; DTh (hon.), St. John's U., 1980; LHD (hon.), Augustana Coll., 1988; DD (hon.), Luther Coll., 1997. Faculty Concordia Coll., Moorhead, Minn., 1945-51; pres. Waldorf Coll., Forest City, Iowa, 1951-56; exec. dir. coll. edn. Am. Luth. Ch., Mpls., 1956-63; pres. St. Olaf Coll., Northfield, Minn., 1963-80; U.S. ambassador to Norway, Oslo, 1980-81; pres. Augustana Coll., Sioux Falls, S.D., 1986-87, 92-93, Suomi Coll., Hancock, Mich., 1990-91. Sr. cons. Minn. Pvt. Coll. Council, St. Paul, 1981-87. Pastor Nashwauk (Minn.) Luth. Ch., 1943-45; chmn. Fund for Theol. Edn., Princeton, N.J., 1984-87; mem. Gov.'s Tax Commn., Minn., 1984-86; chmn. Minn. Citizens for Ct. Reform, 1984-87. Decorated comdr. Norwegian Order of Merit, comdr. Norwegian Order of Merit with star, knight 1st Class Order of St. Olaf Kingdom of Norway; recipient Wittenberg award, 1996. Mem. AIA (hon.), Phi Beta Kappa. Home: Apt 1218 910 Cannon Valley Dr Northfield MN 55057

RAND, THOMAS HOWARD, pediatrician, consultant, medical educator; b. Ft. Lauderdale, Fla., Sept. 28, 1956; s. Howard Floyd and Lillian Louise (Planz) R.; m. Barbara Lawlis, Nov. 23, 1984; children: Kip, Devin, Tace. BS summa cum laude, U. of the South, Sewanee, Tenn., 1978; PhD in Microbiology, Vanderbilt U., 1983, MD with first class honors, 1984. Diplomate Am. Bd. Pediat., Am. Bd. Pediat. Infectious Disease, Nat. Bd. Med. Examiners. Resident in pediat. U. Wash., 1984-87; rsch. fellow Inst. Med. Sci., Adelaide, Australia, 1987-88; fellow Harvard Combined Program in Infectious Diseases, Boston, 1988-91; instr. pediat. Harvard Med. Sch., 1991-92; clin. asst. prof. dept. pediat., cons. family medicine U. Wash., Seattle, 1991—; pvt. practice pediat. Boise, Idaho, 1992—. Cons. communicable disease control Dept. Health and Welfare, State of Idaho, 1993—. Contbr. articles to profl. jours. Immunology fellow Irvington Inst., N.Y.C., 1989. Fellow Am. Acad. Pediat. Avocation: mountain climbing. Office: St Luke's Children's Ctr 100 E Idaho St Ste 315 Boise ID 83712-6267 Address: PO Box 965 Boise ID 83701-0965 E-mail: randfam@interplus.net.

RAND, WILLIAM, lawyer, former state justice; b. N.Y.C., Oct. 11, 1926; s. William and Barbara (Burr) R.; married; children: Alicia, Carley Coudert, William Coudert, Paula Burr. AB, Harvard U., 1948; LLB, Columbia U., 1951. Bar: N.Y. 1951, U.S. Dist. Ct. N.Y. 1951, U.S. Supreme Ct., 1958, U.S. Ct. Appeals (2d cir.) 1961, U.S. Ct. Appeals (4th cir.) 1985. Asst. dist. atty. New York County, 1954-59; asst. counsel to gov. of State of N.Y., 1959-60; assoc. Coudert Bros., N.Y.C., 1961-62, ptnr., 1963-98; justice N.Y. State Supreme Ct., 1962. Justice Village of Cove Neck, Oyster Bay, N.Y., 1974-98. Mem. exec. com. New York County Reps., 1968-72. Served with USN, 1944-46, PTO. Mem.: Racquet and Tennis Club (N.Y.C.), Piping Rock Club (Locust Valley, N.Y.). Home: 73 Cove Neck Rd Oyster Bay NY 11771-1821 Office: Coudert Bros Fl 43 1114 Avenue of the Americas New York NY 10036-7710 E-mail: paularand@aol.com., randw@coudert.com.

RANDA, JAMES PAUL, physicist, electrical engineer; b. Chgo., Jan. 26, 1947; s. John Joseph and Catherine Anne (Baier) R.; m. Susan Bulmann, June 12, 1980; 1 child, David. BS, Ill. Benedictine Coll., 1969; MS, U. Ill., 1970, PhD, 1974. Vis. asst. prof. Tex. A&M U., College Station, 1974-75; postdoctoral fellow U. Manchester, Eng., 1975-78; asst. prof. U. Colo., Boulder, 1978-83; physicist, sr. project leader Nat. Inst. of Stds. and Tech., 1983—. Lectr. physics dept. U. Colo., Boulder, 1985-89; lectr., cons. Productivity and Stds. Bd., Singapore, 2000; U.S. rep. to working group on radiofrequency quantities Internat. Com. of Weights and Measures, Sevres, France, 1999—. Editor: Quantum Flavordynamics, Quantum Chromodynamics, and Unified Field Theories, 1980; contbr. articles to profl. jours. Recipient Bronze medal, U.S. Dept. Commerce, 1992, 1999, award for best paper, IEEE Transactions on Electromagnetic Compatibility, 1992. Mem. IEEE, MTT Soc., EMC Soc. (tech. com., chair 1990-94), Am. Phys. Soc., Automated RF Techniques Group. Avocations: hiking, gardening, writing. Office: NIST 813-01 325 Broadway Boulder CO 80305-3328

RANDALL, ALAN JOHN, environmental economics educator; b. Parkes, N.S.W., Australia, Mar. 31, 1944; came to U.S. 1967; s. Leonard Wesley and Margaret (Love) Randall; m. Beverley Ann Hathaway, June 20, 1966; children: Glenn, Nicole. BS, U. Sydney, 1965, MS, 1969; PhD, Oreg. State U., 1970; Doctor (hon.) , U. orway, 1997. Rsch. economist NSW Dept. Agr., Australia, 1965-67; rsch. fellow Oreg. State U., Corvallis, 1968-70; asst. prof. N.M. State U., Las Cruces, 1970-74; prof. U. Ky., Lexington, 1974-85; vis. prof. U. Chgo., 1981; prof. Ohio State U., Columbus, 1985—, chmn. dept., 1999—. Environ. specialist Econs. Rsch. Group, Lansing, Mich. Author: Resource Economics, 1981, 2d edit. 1987, Valuation of Wildlands, 1984, Making the Environment Count, 1999; contbr. articles to profl. jours. Chmn. Nat. Rsch. Coun. panel, Washington, 1978-80, mem. panel, 1989-91, mem. standing com., 1995; mem. Coun. on Agrl. Sci. and Tech. Panel, 1988-90. Recipient Rsch. award of merit Gamma Delta Sigma, 1991, Sr. Rschr. award Ohio Agrl. Rsch. Devel. Ctr., 2000; univ. disting. scholar, 1997. Fellow Am. Agrl. Econs. Assn. (awards for excellence 1973, 81, 90); mem. Assn. Environ. and Resource Economists (award for publ. 1991), Am. Econ. Assn. Avocations: horse breeding, training, tennis, travel. Home: 6445 Freeman Rd Westerville OH 43082-8002 Office: Ohio State Univ 2120 Fyffe Rd Columbus OH 43210-1010

RANDALL, ARTHUR RAYMOND, building contractor; b. Hamden, Conn., May 14, 1927. Cert. consultant, Consultants Inst., Columbus, Ohio, 1986. Pres., owner Sherman Constrn. Co, Orange, Conn., 1949—; ptnr. Shoreline Shelving Co., 1985—, Farrell Food Systems, New Smyrna, Fla., 1990—. Cons., pres. N.E. Bldg. Cons., Orange, 1978—; environ. insp., mem. Environ. Assessment Assn. Mem. Am. Cons. League, Am. Soc. Home Insps., Race Brook Country Club. Home and Office: Sherman Constrn Co 61 Hampton Close Orange CT 06477-1934

RANDALL, BARBARA ANN, computer design engineer; b. Mpls., Oct. 19, 1958; d. Brayton Dean and Phyllis Virginia (Soley) Naused; m. Kevin Courtney Randall, Nov. 19, 1988. BS in Applied Math., U. Wis., Menomonie, 1981; MSEE, U. Minn., 1988. Computer programmer Mayo Found., Rochester, Minn., 1981-83, computer architecture analyst, 1983-85, computer design engr., 1985-92; lead project engr., 1993—. Contbr. rsch. articles of high speed cirs. and systems to profl. jours. Mem. IEEE Computer Soc., Internat. Electronics Packaging Soc. Avocations: hiking, canoeing, billiards, softball, volleyball. Office: Mayo Found 200 1st St SW Rochester MN 55905-0001

RANDALL, CATHERINE HORN, advocate; b. Davenport, Iowa, Jan. 5, 1947; d. Frank Walton and Catherine (Castle) Horn; m. Robert Quentin Randall, Dec. 27, 1969. BA, MacMurray Coll., Jacksonville, Ill., 1969. Tchr. North Green Sch. Dist., Whitehall, Ill., 1970-71; substitute tchr. Jacksonville (Ill.) H.S., 1972-73; staff writer MacMurray Coll., Jacksonville, 1973-75; alderman City of Jacksonville, 1987-91. Bd. dirs. Convocom. Pres. Jacksonville Theatre Guild, 1984-87; mem. adv. coun. Ill Sch. Visually Impaired, 1986-99; 1st v.p. Nat. Fedn. Blind Ill., 1986-96; mem. coun. Ill. State Libr., 1992-98; mem. alumni bd. MacMurray Coll., Jacksonville, 1993—, trustee, 1993—; treas. Jacksonville Ctr. Ind. Living, 1996-99; sec.-treas. Trinity Ch. Guild, 1996-97; pres. Ind. Network Ctr., 2000-01. Recipient Gwendelynne Williams Meml. award Nat. Fed. Blind Ill., 1991, Alexander J. Skrzybek award Ill. Libr. Assn., 1996. Mem. Friends in Council Literary Orgn., The History Class. Episcopalian. Home: 11 Pitner Pl Jacksonville IL 62650

RANDALL, CHANDLER CORYDON, church rector; b. Ann Arbor, Mich., Jan. 22, 1935; s. Frederick Stewart and Madeline Leta (Snow) R.; m. Marian Archias Montgomery, July 2, 1960; children: Sarah Archais, Elizabeth Leggett, Rebekah Stewart. AB in History, U. Mich., 1957; S.T.B. in Theology, Berkeley Divinity at Yale U., 1960; PhD in Hebraic Studies, Hebrew Union Coll., 1969; D.D. (honoris causa), Berkeley Divinity at Yale U., 1985. Rector St. Paul's Episcopal Ch., Richmond, Ind., 1967-71; rector Trinity Episcopal Ch., Ft. Wayne, 1971-88, St. Peter's Episcopal Ch., Del Mar, Calif., 1988-00. Bd. dirs. Living Ch. Found., Milw.; bibl. theologian Episcopal Ch. Stewardship, N.Y.C., 1985; alumni coun. Berkeley Divinity at Yale, New Haven, Conn., 1981-87; bishop's cabinet Diocese of No. Ind., South Bend, 1983-87. Author: Satire in the Bible, 1969, An Approach to Biblical Satire, 1990; contbr. articles to profl. jours. Founder Canterbury Sch., Ft. Wayne, 1977; commr. Ind. Jud. Qualifications Commn., Indpls., 1981-87; pres. Ft. Wayne Plan Commn., 1977; bd. dirs. Ft. Wayne Park Found., 1983-88; platform com. Ind. Republican Party, Indpls., 1974. Recipient Disting. Svc. medal U. Mich., 1981, Scheuer scholar Hebrew Union Coll., 1963-66, Liberty Bell award Ft. Wayne Bar Assn., 1988; named Sagamore of the Wabash, Gov. Ind., 1987. Mem. Am. Schs. Oriental Research, Yale U. Alumni Club (pres. 1982-88), Quest Club (pres.), Rotary Club, Chi Psi (nat. chaplain 1982). Republican. Avocations: college recruiting, genealogy. Office: St Peters Episcopal Church PO Box 336 Del Mar CA 92014-0336

RANDALL, CHARLES WILSON, gastroenterologist; b. Shreveport, La., Feb. 24, 1958; s. Charles Harry and Jane (Wilson) R.; m. Catheryne Louise Lee, Aug. 11, 1984; children: Fletcher Wilson, Elizabeth Mary Catheryne. BA, U. Tex., Austin, 1981; MD, U. Tex., Galveston, 1988. Diplomate Am. Bd. Internal Medicine, Am. Bd. Gastroenterology, Tex. Bd. Med. Examiners. Resident Vanderbilt U., Nashville, 1988-91; fellow in gastroenterology Washington U., St. Louis, 1991-93; clin. assoc. prof. medicine U. Tex. Health Sci. Ctr., San Antonio, 1994—; pvt. practice, 1993—; dir. divsn. gastroenterology St. Lukes Bapt. Hosp., 1996—2000. Former chmn. dept. medicine St. Luke's Hosp.; chmn. dept. gastroenterology Meth. Specialty and Transplant Hosp.; chief of staff Kindred Hosp. Contbr. articles to profl. jours., book chpt. Mem. AMA, ACP (preceptorship award 1996), Am. Gastroenterology Assn., Am. Coll. Gastroenterology, Am. Soc. Gastroenterology and Endoscopy, Tex. Soc. Gastroenterology and Endoscopy. Episcopalian. Avocations: fishing, scuba diving, weight training. Office: Gastroenterology Clin San Antonio 7940 Floyd Curl Dr Ste 1050 San Antonio TX 78229-3906 E-mail: gastroclinic2001@yahoo.com.

RANDALL, CHRISTOPHER K. psychology educator; b. Indpls., Nov. 14, 1966; s. (stepfather) Eugene W. and Judith V. Karstens; m. Tracie L. Baker, July 22, 1995. AB, Wabash Coll., Crawfordsville, Ind., 1989; MS, U. Ky., 1992, PhD, 1995. Rsch. scientist, instr. SUNY-Binghamton U., 1994-97; asst. prof. psychology Mt. Holyoke Coll., South Hadley, Mass., 1997-98; dept. chair, assoc. prof. psychology Troy State U., Montgomery, Ala., 1998—. Faculty cons. Ednl. Testing Svc., Princeton, N.J., 1997—. Mem. APA, Am. Psychol. Soc., Assn. Heads of Depts. of Psychology, Soc. for Tchg. of Psychology, Sigma Xi. Office: Troy State U PO Drawer 4419 Montgomery AL 36103-4419 E-mail: crandall@tsum.edu.

RANDALL, CLAIRE, church executive; b. Dallas, Oct. 15, 1919; d. Arthur Godfrey and Annie Laura (Fulton) R. AA, Schreiner Coll., 1948; BA, Scarritt Coll., 1950; DD (hon.), Berkeley Sem., Yale U., 1974; LHD (hon.), Austin Coll., 1982; LLD (hon.), Notre Dame U., 1984. Assoc. missionary edn. Bd. World Missions Presbyterian Ch., U.S., Nashville, 1949-57, dir. art Gen. Council Atlanta, 1957-61; dir. Christian World Mission, program dir., assoc. dir. Ch. Women United, N.Y.C., 1962-73; gen. sec. Nat. Coun. Ch. of Christ in U.S.A., 1974-84, ret., 1985; nat. pres. Ch. Women United, 1988-92. Mem. Nat. Commn. on Internat. Women's Yr., 1975-77, Martin Luther King Jr. Fed. Holiday Commn., 1985. Recipient Woman of Yr. in Religion award Heritage Soc., 1977; Empire State Woman of Yr. in Religion award State of N.Y., 1984; medal Order of St. Vladimir, Russian Orthodox Ch., 1984 Democrat. Episcopalian. Avocations: golf, swimming, painting, reading, music. Home: 10015 W Royal Oak Rd #120 Sun City AZ 85351-3114

RANDALL, CLIFFORD WENDELL, civil engineer, educator; b. Somerset, Ky., May 1, 1936; s. William Lesbert and Geneva (James) R.; m. Phyllis Amis, Aug. 15, 1959; children: Andrew Amis, William Otis. BSCE, U. Ky., 1959, MS in Sanitary Engrng., 1963; PhD in Environ. Health Engrng., U. Tex., 1966. Asst. prof. civil engring. U. Tex., Arlington, 1965-68; mem. faculty Va. Poly. Inst. and State U., 1968—, prof. civil engring., 1972-81; Charles Lunsford prof., 1981—; vis. prof. U. Cape Town, South Africa, 1983; chmn. environ. engrng. and scis. program Va. Poly. Inst. and State U., 1979-97. Lectr. Shanghai Archtl. and Mcpl. Engring. Inst., Wuhan Tech. U., 1987; dir. Occoquan Watershed Monitoring Program, 1971—; mem. U.S. nat. com. Internat. Water Quality, 1976-88, chair 1986-88, mem. 1992 IAWQ Biennial Conf. Com., chair conf. arrangements, Washington; tng. grant cons. EPA, 1970-71; cons. to industry, 1969—; WHO cons. to Nat. Environ. Engring. Rsch. Inst. India, 1983-84; Va. gov. appointee sci. and tech. adv. com. Chesapeake Bay Program; mem. sci. and tech. adv. com. Chesapeake Bay Program, 1984—, chmn. 1993-97; mem. nitrogen tech. adv. com. N.Y.C. Dept. Environ. Protection, 1994—; mem. blue ribbon panel wastewater treatment City of Atlanta, 1997—. Author tech. papers in field; co-author: Biological Process Design for Wastewater Treatment, 1980, Stormwater Management in Urbanizing Areas, 1983, Design and Retrofit of Wastewater Treatment Plants for Biological Nutrient Removal, 1992. Troop com. chmn. local Boy Scouts Am., 1978-82, chmn. dist. Camporee com., 1977; camp pres. Gideons Internat., 1976-78, 80, 95-97, state cabinet mem., 1985-88; vice moderator Highlands Bapt. Assn., 1980-81, moderator, 1982-83; mem. bd. deacons Blacksburg Bapt. Ch., 1971-74, 79-82, chmn., 1974. Lt. U.S. Coast and Godetic Survey, 1959-62. Ford Found. fellow, 1964-65; recipient citation Engrng. News-Record, 1988, Disting. Svc. award U.S. nat. com. Internat. Assn. Water Quality, 1989, Salute to Excellence Gov. of Md., 1994, Pub. Svc. award Va. Tech., 1996, Mathias medal for sci. excellence Chesapeake Rsch. Consortium and the Sea Grant Offices of Md. and Va., 1996, Dean's award Excellence Pub. Svc., Va. Tech. Engring., 1997; named Conservationist of Yr. Chesapeake Bay Found., 1986; AEC trainee U. Tex., 1963-65. Mem. ASCE (chmn. water resources mgmt. com. 1977, environ. engrng. rsch. coun. 1989-90, svc. award 1978, 80, meritorious tech. paper award 1969), Am. Water Works Assn. (cert. recognition for acad. excellence 1980, 89), Water Environ. Fedn. (bd. dirs. 1981-84, Morgan cert. of merit for full scale rsch. 1982, Bedell award 1983, svc. award 1984, Gordon M. Fair medal for excellence in engring. edn. 1998), Internat. Assn. Water Quality (Mem. gov. bd. 1986-88, USA rep. on sci. and tech. com. 1994—, mem. nutrient removal specialist group mgmt. com. 1990—, chmn. 1994-98), Va. Water Environment Assn. (v.p. 1974-75, pres. 1975-76), Assn. Environ. Engring. Profs. (sec.-treas. 1979-80, bd. dirs. 1978-80, 93-97, v.p. 1994-95, pres. 1995-96, past pres. 1996-97). Home: 1302 Crestview Dr Blacksburg VA 24060-5609 Office: Va Poly Inst & State U Dept Civil Engring 330 Norris Hall Blacksburg VA 24061

RANDALL, CRAIG, financial and business management consultant, accountant, computer specialist; b. Santa Monica, Calif., Oct. 29, 1957; s. Les Shepard and Marian Hand; m. Jeanne Runsvold, July 14, 1984. Student, Pierce Coll., 1975-76, Calif. State U.-Northridge, 1977-79. Asst. controller Becker CPA Rev., Encino, Calif., 1979-81; sr. staff acct. Kress and Goldstein, CPAs, Sherman Oaks, 1981-84; pres., chief exec. officer Bus. Computers Network, Inc., Woodland Hills, 1984—, Randall Accountancy Corp., Woodland Hills, 1984—. Office: Randall Accountancy A Profl Corp 21031 Ventura Blvd Ste 1101 Woodland Hills CA 91364-2254

RANDALL, DAVID JOHN, physiologist, zoologist, educator; b. London, Sept. 15, 1938; BSc, U. Southampton, 1960, PhD, 1963, FRSC, 1981. From asst. to assoc. prof. U. B.C., 1963-73, prof. zoology, 1973—, assoc. dean grad. studies, 1990-96, 2000; head biology and chemistry City U. Hong Kong, 2000-01; univ. grants coun. mem. Hong Kong Govt. Spl. Adminstrv. Region. Vis. lectr. Bristol U., 1968-69; vis. sci. Marine Labs U. Tex., 1970, Zool. Sta., Naples, Italy, 1973; NATO vis. sci. Acadia U., 1975, Marine Lab U. Tex., 1977; chief sci. Alpha Helix Amazon Expedition, 1976; mem. adv. bd. J. Comp Physiology, 1977-92, J. Exp. Biol., 1981-84; chmn. animal biol. comt. Nat. Res. Coun., Can., 1974; vis. prof. U. Nairobi, 1988, George Washington U., 1988-89, City U. Hong Kong, 1997; concurrent prof. Nanjing U., China, 1993—; external examiner U. Singapore, 1990-91, 2000-02; mem. UGC, Hong Kong, 2001-02. Assoc. editor: Marine Behavior Physiology. Recipient Award of Excellence Am. Fisheries Soc., 1994. Fellow Royal Soc. Can.; mem. Can. Soc. Zoologists (Fry medal 1993), Soc. Exp. Biologists. Office: City U Hong Kong Biol Chem Tat Chee Ave Kowloon Hong Kong Fax: 2788 7406. E-mail: bhrand@cityu.edu.hk.

RANDALL, FRANCES, technical writer; b. Frederick, Md., Oct. 6, 1924; d. George Birely and Ruth Carty Delaplaine; m. Myron William Randall, Apr. 10, 1949; children: George Elliott, Myron William Jr., Ruth Ann Randall, Eleanor Jane Randall Luttrell. BA, Hood Coll., 1945; MS, The Johns Hopkins U., 1947. Chemist U.S. Army lab., Frederick, Md., 1947-49; writer-historian The Frederick News-Post, 1965—; CEO The Frederick News-Post (Randall Family LLC), 2001—. Chmn. bd. dirs. The Randall Family LLC, 2001—. Author: (book) Mirror on Frederick, 1998. Bd. dirs. Cmty. Found. of Frederick Co., 1988-96. Recipient vol. yr., Cmty. Found., Frederick Co., 1993, Cmty. Svc. award, Ch. Transfiguration, Braddock Heights, Md., 1999, Thanks Badge, Penn Laurel Girl Scout Coun., 1988, Alumnae Achievement award Hood Coll., 1998, Woman of Distinction award Girl Scouts Am., 2000. Mem. Hood Coll. Alumnae Assn. (pres., sec.), Frederick Woman's Civic Club (publicity chair, pres.); bd. dirs. Penn Laurel Girl Scout Coun., Braddock Heights Cmty. Assn. Avocations: swimming, biking, photography, travel, grand children. Home: 6301 Jefferson Blvd Frederick MD 21703-5809

RANDALL, FRANCIS BALLARD, historian, educator, writer; b. N.Y.C., Dec. 17, 1931; s. John Herman, Jr. and Mercedes (Moritz) R.; m. Laura Regina Rosenbaum, June 11, 1957; children: David R., Ariane R. BA, Amherst Coll., 1952; MA, Columbia, 1954, PhD, 1960. Instr. history Amherst Coll., 1956-59; from instr. to asst. prof. history Columbia, 1959-61, vis. prof., 1967-68; humanities faculty Sarah Lawrence Coll., Bronxville, NY, 1961—2002, chmn., 1985—89, 1998—2001, trustee, 1971-76. Author: (with others) Essays in Russian and Soviet History, 1963, Stalin's Russia, an Historical Reconsideration, 1965, N.G. Chernyshevskii, 1967, Vissarion Belinskii, 1987, History Papers: A Teaching Life, 2000. Freedom rider civil disobedience to racism, 1961, war draft resistance arrests, 1967, 70. Fulbright fellow for study in India, 1965, Wye fellow, 1986. Mem.: AAUP (chpt. chmn. 1966—69), Am. Assn. for Advancement Slavic Studies, Am. Hist. Assn., Sigma Xi, Phi Beta Kappa. Home: 425 Riverside Dr Apt 10I New York NY 10025-7730

RANDALL, KARL W. aviation executive, lawyer; b. Mount Pleasant, Mich., Feb. 12, 1951; s. Herbert J. and Wilma E. (Worstell) R.; m. Natalie Kilmer Randall, Dec. 17, 1971; children: Adam B., Kara J. AA, Mich. Christian Coll., Rochester, 1971; BA, Oakland U., Rochester, 1977; JD, Wayne State U. Law Sch., Detroit, 1981. Bar: Mich., 1981, U.S. Dist. Ct., 1981, U.S. Ct. Appeals, 1983; cert. airport mgr., Mich., 1993. Quality contr. Staley SNO BOL Corp., Pontiac, Mich., 1971-72; engring. tech. Oakland Co. Drain Comm., 1972-83; sr. asst. corp. counsel Oakland County Corp. Counsel, 1983-93; mgr. aviation Oakland County Internat. Airport, Waterford, Mich., 1993—. Dir. Integrity Jour., Mt. Pleasant, 1980-98, Oakland County Coord. Child Care Coun., Waterford, 1992-97. Author, editor: (religious jour.) Integrity, 1982, 94-95. Mem. Rep. Com. Oakland County, 1988—, Exec. Club Oakland County, 1993—. Mem. Mich. Assn. Airport Execs. (exec.). Republican. Mem. Ch. of Christ. Avocations: physical fitness, motorcycling, jogging, golf, piano. Office: Oakland County Internat Airport 6500 Highland Rd Waterford MI 48327-1649 E-mail: randallk@co.oakland.mi.us.

RANDALL, KAY TEMPLE, accountant, retired real estate agent; b. Chattanooga, Sept. 23, 1952; d. James H. Temple and Hortense N. (Dailey) Goodner; m. Gary F. Goodner, Feb. 9, 1968 (div. July 1972); 1 child, Jeffrey F. Goodner; m. Rodney B. Randall, Oct. 3, 1987. Student, Chattanooga State Coll., 1970-77, 82-83, Am. Inst. Banking, 1977-79. Lic. real estate agt., Tenn., ret.; notary public, Tenn. Ins. rep. Colonial Life Accident and Health, Columbia, S.C., 1980-82; real estate appraiser, agt. Chattanooga, 1983-88; acct. Mr. Transmission of Chattanooga, Inc., 1987—; real estate agt. Chattanooga, 1989—. Adminstrv. asst. to legal profession, Chattanooga, 1972-75. Adv. bd. United Meth. Ch., Chattanooga, 1979-82, tchr., 1979-83; fellow cen. br. YMCA, Chattanooga, 1977-97. Fellow Walden's Club. Republican. Episcopalian. Avocations: collecting art, grandchildren. Home: 1858 Rivergate Ter Soddy Daisy TN 37379-5947 Office: Mr Transmission of Chattanooga Inc PO Box 1395 Soddy Daisy TN 37384-1395 E-mail: rodkayj@aol.com.

RANDALL, LILIAN MARIA CHARLOTTE, museum curator; b. Berlin, Feb. 1, 1931; came to U.S., 1938; d. Frederick Henry and Elizabeth Agnes (Ziegler) Cramer; m. Richard Harding Randall, Apr. 11, 1953; children: Christopher, Julia, Katharine. BA cum laude, Mount Holyoke Coll., 1950; MA, Radcliffe Coll., 1951, PhD, 1955; LHD (hon.), Towson State U., 1993; D of Arts (hon.), Mt. Holyoke Coll., 1998. Asst. dir. Md. State Arts Coun., 1972-73; curator manuscripts and rare books Walters Art Gallery, Balt., 1974-85, rsch. curator manuscripts, 1985-95; rsch. cons., 1995-97. Vis. lectr. dept. art history Johns Hopkins U., 1964-68; hon. vis. lectr. U. Mich., Ann Arbor; lectr. in field; bd. dirs. Digital Scriptorium: Electronic Access to Medieval Manuscripts; advisor Union Manuscript Computer Catalogue, 1996—. Author: Images in the Margins of Gothic Manuscripts, 1966; co-editor: Gatherings in Honor of Dorothy Miner, 1974, The Diary of George A. Lucas: An American Art Agent in Paris, 1909-1957, 1979, Illuminated Manuscripts: Masterpieces in Miniature, 1984, Medieval and Renaissance Manuscripts in the Walters Art Gallery, Vol. I, France, 875-1420, 1989, Vol. II, France, 1420-1540, 1992, Vol. III, Belgium, 1250-1530, 1997; contbr. articles to profl. jours. Mem. Williston Libr. com., 1988-89; reviewer, panelist NEH, 1980—. Grantee AAUW, 1953-54, ACLS, 1960, 65, Bunting Inst., 1961-63, Ford Found., 1967-69, Am. Philos. Soc., 1971, NEA, 1975, Samuel H. Kress Found., 1979, 81-84, NEH, 1977-84, 89-95; grantee publ. subsidy Md. State Arts Coun., 1972, Mcpl. Art Soc. Balt., 1972, Andrew W. Mellon Found., 1988, Getty Grant program, 1990-92, NEA Mus. program, 1992-93; recipient Festschrift, Walters Art Gallery, ed. Elizabeth Burin, 1996, Sesquicentennial award Mount Holyoke Coll., 1987. Fellow Medieval Acad. Am. (libr. preservation com., various coms. 1985-87, 90-93); mem. Internat. Ctr. Medieval Art (bd. dirs. 1978-82, 96-99), Coll. Art Assn. (Arthur Kingsley Porter prize 1957), Balt. Bibliophiles (bd. dirs. 1966-80, pres. 1980-83), Pyramid Atlantic (bd. dirs. 1985-88), Phi Beta Kappa, Grolier Club. Home: 370 Adams St Milton MA 02186-4233

RANDALL, LYNN ELLEN, librarian; b. Chgo., Oct. 10, 1946; d. Ward W. and Hazel A. (Nettles) R. BA, King's Coll., 1970; MA, Seton Hall U., 1973; MLS, Rutgers U., 1978. Libr. N.J. Inst. Tech., Newark, 1970-75; libr. dir. N.E. Bible Coll., Essex Fells, N.J., 1975-81; reference libr. Seton Hall U., South Orange, 1983-85; dir. libr. svc. Berkeley Coll., West Paterson, 1985-89; libr. dir. Caldwell Coll., 1989—, exec. dir. libr. svcs. Reference libr., instr. Morris (N.J.) County Coll., 1981-83; panelist/facilitator Middle State Self-Study Inst., 1996, 97. Mem. N.J. Libr. Assn. (pres. 1996-97). Office: Jennings Libr Caldwell Coll 9 Ryerson Ave Caldwell NJ 07006-6109

RANDALL, MALCOM, health care administrator; b. East St. Louis, Ill., Aug. 9, 1916; s. John Leeper and Merle Dorothy Randall; m. Christine Sheppard, Nov. 10, 1972 AB, McKendree Coll., 1939; M.H.A., St. Louis U., 1955; D of Pub. Svc. with honors, U. Fla., 1996. Chief br. office VA, St. Louis, 1946-49, asst. area dir. area office, 1949-53; spl. asst. to dir. VA Hosp., 1953-56, hosp. adminstr. Spokane, Wash., 1956-57, Chgo., 1957-58, Indpls., 1958-60, Wood, Wis., 1960-64, hosp. dir. Miles City, Mont., 1964-66; med. ctr. dir. and med. dist. dir. VA, Gainesville, Fla., 1966—, regional rep., 1991—; prof. health and hosp. adminstrn. U. Fla., 1966—. Pres. N. Cen. Fla. Health Planning Council; mem. Fla. State Health Planning Council; chmn. Gov.'s Commn. on Alzheimer's Disease; mem. Alachua County Emergency Med. Svcs. Coun.; bd. dirs. emeritus 1st Union Nat. Bank Fla., Regional Med. Programs; mem. editorial bd. Jour. Am. Coll. Health Care Execs.; cons. on health care Univ. Clin. Ctr., Ljubljana, Slovenia, 1982—, Ministry of Health, Hungary and Med. U. Debrecen, 1989—. Contbr. numerous articles to profl. jours. Bd. dirs. Civitan Regional Blood Ctr., Gainesville, 1970. Served to capt. USN, 1942-46 Recipient Presdl. Rank award Pres. U.S., 1983, Meritorious Svc. award U. Fla., 1984, Exceptional Svc. award, 1985, Exec. Performance award, 1986, all VA; named Citizen of Yr., Gainesville, 1977. Fellow Am. Coll. Health Care Execs. (council regents, VA liaison); mem. Inst. Medicine, Nat. Acad. Sci., Assn. Am. Med. Colls. (bd. dirs., council tchg. hosps.), Am. Health Planning Assn. (bd. dirs.), Am. Hosp. Assn. (governing council met. and fed. hosp. sect.). Clubs: Heritage. Lodges: Rotary. Home: 1617 NW 19th Cir Gainesville FL 32605-4092 Office: VA Med Ctr Archer Rd Gainesville FL 32608 E-mail: mran268075@aol.com. *A core set of values should be the base for all of your activities, both professional and personal.*

RANDALL, NEIL WARREN, gastroenterologist; b. White Plains, N.Y., Mar. 24, 1957; s. Leroy Bruce and Libby Cynthia (Brandt) R.; m. Linda Ilene Zell, Oct. 31, 1992. BA, U. Va., 1978; MD, U. Md., 1983. Diplomate Am. Bd. Internal Medicine with subspecialty in gastroenterology, geriatrics. Resident in internal medicine Ochsner Clinic, New Orleans, 1983-86; fellow in gastroenterology Tufts U., Boston, 1986-88; staff gastroenterologist Cleve. Clinic Fla., Fort Lauderdale, 1988-92, Geisinger Clinic, Danville, Pa., 1992-97, Pa. State Geisinger Health Sys., Danville, 1997-98; med. dir. gastrointestinal endoscopy Geisinger Health Sys., 1999-2000; gastroenterologist Gastroenterology Group of Naples, 2001—. Fellow ACP, Am. Coll. Gastroenterology; mem. Am. Soc for Gastroent. Endoscopy. Avocations: Theatre, Travel, Wine. Office: Gasterenterology Group of Naples 1064 Goodlette-Frank Rd Naples FL 34102-5449

RANDALL, PRISCILLA RICHMOND, travel executive; b. Arlington, Mass., Mar. 19, 1926; d. Harold Bours and Florence (Hoefler) Richmond; m. Raymond Victor Randall, Mar. 2, 1946; children: Raymond Richmond, Priscilla Randall Middleton, Susan Randall Geery. Student, Wellesley Coll., 1943-44; Assoc., Garland Coll., 1946; student, Winona State U., 1977-81. Pub. relations dir. Rochester Meth. Hosp., Rochester, Minn., 1960-69; dir. pub relations Sheraton Rochester, 1969-71; pres. Med. Charters, Rochester, 1970-75, Ideas Unltd., Rochester, 1969-77; chief exec. officer Randall Travel, 1977-89; pres. Randall Travel Delray, Delray Beach, Fla., 1989—. Pres. Bar Harbour Apts. Inc., Delray Beach, 1989, sec., bd. dirs., 2002; social com. chmn., 1999—, sec., 1993-99. Editor, Inside Story, 1960-69, Rochester Meth. Hosp. News, 1960-69; producer Priscilla's World, 1972-75. Pres. Rochester Meth. Hosp. Aux., 1957-59, Downtown Bus. Assn., Rochester, 1985; treas. Class of 1947 Wellesley (Mass.) Coll., 1997-2002. Recipient Woman of Achievement Bus. YWCA, Rochester, 1983, Golden Door Knob, Bus. and Prfl. Women, Rochester, 1979. Mem. Inst. Cert. Travel Agts. (life), Assn. Retail Travel Agts. (life, nat. bd. 1988-90, sec. to bd. 1988-90, sec.-treas. Arlington, Va. nat. bd. 1990), Am. Soc. Travel Agts., Pacific Area Travel Agts., Minn. Exec. Women in Travel, Cruise Line Internat. Assn. (master cruise counselor), Little Club (sec. 2002—, Gulfstream, Fla.) (sec. women's golf com. 1993-99, sec. bd. govs. 2002, treas. 2002), Hibiscus Garden Club (Delray Beach, Fla.) (pres., corr. sec.), Travelors Century Club (bd. govs.), Circumnavigator Club. Avocation: travel writing. Home: 86 Macfarlane Dr Apt 2C Delray Beach FL 33483-6901

RANDALL, RICHARD RAINIER, geographer; b. Toledo, July 21, 1925; s. Robert Henry and Maree (Gard) R.; m. Patricia Lee Spencer, June 9, 1962; children: Allison Maree, Susan Rebecca, Richard Rainier Jr. BA, George Washington U., 1949, MA, 1950; PhD, Clark U., 1955; postgrad., Graz U., Austria. Geog. analyst CIA, Washington, 1955-61; Washington rep. Rand McNally & Co., 1961-72; owner Randall Assocs., 1972-73; exec. sec. U.S. Bd. Geog. Names, 1973-93; geographer Def. Mapping Agy., 1973-93; ret., 1993; cons. on geog. names, 1993—. Convenor UN Working Group on Undersea and Maritime Feature Names, 1975-84; mem., prin. U.S. tech. advisor U.S. and U.K. Conf. on Geog. Names, 1976, 79, 81, 84, 86, 88, 92; dep. head U.S. del. UN Conf. on Geog. Names, 1977, head, 1982, 87, 92; 1st v.p. of 6th UN Conf. 92; prin. U.S. expert UN Group Experts on Geog. Names, 1975, 77, 79, 82, 84, 86, 87, 89, 92; pres. com. on geog. terminology Pan Am. Inst. Geography and History, 1973-77, pres. working group on geog. names and gazetters, 1981-94. Author: Place Names: How they Define the World—And More, 2001; contbr. articles to profl. jours.; inventor flexible fishhook V.p. North Cleveland Park Citizens Assn., Washington, 1968. With U.S. Army, 1943-46, ETO. Fulbright scholar, NRC, Austria, 1953-54. Mem. Am. Congress on Surveying and Mapping (dir. cartography divsn. 1973-75, dir. press rels. 1961-72, program dir. cartography divsn. ann. meeting 1967), Am. Geog. Soc., Assn. Am. Geographers (chmn. Mid-Atlantic divsn. 1978, dir. press rels. ann. conf. 1968), Am. Names Soc., Am. Austrian Soc. (v.p. 1955-57), Explorers Club, Cosmos Club. Republican.

RANDALL, ROBERT L(EE), ecological economist; b. Aberdeen, S.D., Dec. 28, 1936; s. Harry Eugene and Juanita Alice (Barstow) R. MS in Phys. Chemistry, U. Chgo., 1960, MBA, 1963. Market devel. chemist E.I. du Pont de Nemours & Co., Inc., Wilmington, Del., 1963-65; chem. economist Battelle Meml. Inst., Columbus, Ohio, 1965-68; mgr. market and econ. rsch. Kennecott Copper Corp., N.Y.C., 1968-74, economist, 1974-79, dir. new bus. venture devel., 1979-81; pres., mng. dir. R.L. Randall Assocs., Inc., 1981—; economist U.S. Internat. Trade Commn., Washington, 1983—. Founder, pres., exec. dir. The RainForest ReGeneration Inst., 1986—, ind. internat. press corr., 1997—, indsl. panel policy rev. of effect of regulation on innovation and U.S.-internat. competition U.S. Dept. Commerce, 1980-81; participant preparatory com. UN Conf. on Environ. and Devel., Rio de Janeiro, 1991; del. observer internat. negotiating com. UN Framework Conv. on Climate Change, 1991—. Contbg. author: Computer Methods for the 80's; sect. lead author, editor: World Energy Assessment, 2000; pub. reviewer intergovtl. panel on climate change Third Assessment Report; addresser 4th Internat. Greenhouse Gas Tech. conf., Interlaken, Switzerland, 1998; contbr. articles to profl. jours. Mem. Gay Activists Alliance, N.Y.C., 1971-75, chmn. state and fed. legislation com., 1975. Mem. AAAS (organizer ann. meeting Tropical Forest Regeneration Symposium), AIME (econ. coun., mineral econ. subsect.), Internat. Soc. Ecol. Health, Internat. Soc. Ecol. Economists, Am. Econ. Assn., Am. Statis. Assn., Am. Chem. Soc., Soc. Mining Engrs., Chemists Club of N.Y.C., Metall. Soc., N.Y. Acad. Scis., Nat. Econs. Club Washington (sec., reporter), Assn. Environ. and Resource Economists, Marine Biol. Assn. (Plymouth, Eng.), Wanderbirds Hiking Club (hike leader, treas.), Capital Hiking Club (hike leader, Washington). Home: 1727 Massachusetts Ave NW Washington DC 20036-2153 Office: US Internat Trade Com 500 E St NW Washington DC 20436-0003 E-mail: randall@usitc.gov. *Like thousands of organizations around the world, The RainForest ReGeneration Institute is trying to find a practical and effective way forward, through United Nations-sponsored treaty negotiations, appropriate national actions, and imaginative project work, on the ground, in local communities. Tropical rainforests must have recognizable community value if they are to be viable. Global value is not enough for the conservation of the tropical rainforests. Ultimate wisdom does not reside in any individual or organization. All must work together through every available forum and mechanism, and to create new modalities where those presently in existence are inadequate or ineffective.*

RANDALL, ROBERT QUENTIN, retired nursery executive; b. Jacksonville, Ill., May 1, 1945; s. William Orlando and Agnes Johanna (Bruins) R.; m. Catherine Horn, Dec. 27, 1969. BS in Biology, Ill. Coll., 1967. Lab. technician Passavant Meml. Hosp., Jacksonville, 1966-68; sect. head in vival prodn. Beecham Labs., Whitehall, Ill., 1968-79, safety dir., animal welfare dir., 1970-79; prin. Jacksonville Landscape Nursery, 1979-89, nurseryman, 1989-95; ret., 1995. Presenter programs on birding and the arts and crafts movement. Contbr. articles on birding to topical publs. Sec. Jacksonville Theatre Guild; elder, deacon, trustee 1st Presbyn. Ch., Jacksonville, Ill. Coll. Jacksonville area Alumni Assoc., 1989; bd. dirs. Friends of the Libr., 1991-95; bd. dirs. Quincy Preserves, 2000—, v.p., 2000—; mem. Ill. Coll. Blue Ribbon Task Force, 1995-96; treas. Nat. Fedn. Blind Ill., 1993-96; bd. dirs. CONVOCOM, 1997-2000, exec. com. 1998-2000; bd. dirs. Dana-Thomas House Found., 2000—. Mem. Jacksonville Kiwanis (bd. dirs. 1986-87), Morgan County Audubon Soc. (treas. 1989-91, pres. 1991-94), Ill. Audubon Soc. (bd. dirs.), Jacksonville Symphony Soc. (bd. dirs. 1994-99, pres. 1996-97), Ill. Coll. Alumni Assn. (bd. dirs. 1998—), Quincy Preserves (bd. dirs. 2000—). Avocations: birding, tennis, wildlife photography, travel, reading. Home: 11 Pitner Pl Jacksonville IL 62650-2266

RANDALL, ROGER DAVID, publishing executive; b. St. Charles, Minn., Dec. 24, 1953; s. Curtis Clark and Virginia Mae (Tollefson) Randall; m. Mary Barnard, Aug. 25, 1979; children: Sarah Louise, Clark Robinson. BA, Morningside Coll., 1976. Advt. dir. Nutra-Flo Chem. Co., Kay Dee Feed Co., Sioux City, Iowa, 1976-78; agrl. account svc. Lewis & Gilman, Phila., 1978-80, Creswell, Munsell, Fultz & Zirbel, Cedar Rapids, Iowa, 1980-81, Richardson, Myers & Donofrio, Inc., Balt., 1981-84; mktg. mgr. Farm Jour., Inc., Phila., 1984-85, v.p., 1986-89, v.p., pub., 1989-95, pres., 1995-99, CEO, 1999-2000, also bd. dirs.; pres., CEO AgWeb.com, 1999-2001; exec. v.p. Miller Meester, Inc., 2001—. Mem. bus. adv. com. Nat. Assn. Conser. Dist. Bd. dirs. Planned Parenthood Sioux City, 1977-78, Iowa Planned Parenthood Fedn., 1978, Sioux City Pub. Mus., 1977-78; trustee Old 1st Reformed Ch., 1994-95. Recipient Disting. Alumni award, Morningside Coll., 1997. Mem. Nat. Agri-Mktg. Assn. (pres. Chesapeake chpt. 1984, nat. awards agri. excellence 1988, exec. com. 1990-92, sec.-treas. 1992-93), Queen Village Neighbors Assn. (dir., treas. 1987-90, pres. 1994-95). Mem. United Ch. Of Christ. Office: 17 N Washington Ave Minneapolis MN 55401 Home: 4270 Norwood Ln N Minneapolis MN 55442

RANDALL, RONALD RAY, lawyer; b. Los Angeles, Aug. 4, 1939; m. Joanne Menu, Aug. 7, 1959 (div. July 1971); children: Marjorie, Ronald Jr., John; m. Jane Warriner, June 17, 2000. BSEE, U. Nev., 1961; JD, U. Calif., Berkeley, 1967. Bar: Calif. 1968, U.S. Dist. Ct. (so. dist.) Calif. 1968, U.S. Ct. Appeals (9th cir.) 1978, Tex. 1990. Assoc. Fowler, Knobbe & Martins, Orange, Calif., 1967-69; gen. counsel Gen. Automation, Inc., Anaheim, 1969-75; ptnr. Randall & Engle, Tustin, 1975-79; gen. counsel Smith Internat., Inc., Houston, 1979-90; v.p., gen. counsel, sec. Camco Internat., Inc., 1990—98; cons., 1998—.

RANDALL, SHEILA R. real estate company executive; b. Shelby, N.C., Oct. 14, 1955; d. Bobby Randall and Jo Ann (Baldwin) Peeler; m. David Tiller, Aug. 18, 1973 (div. July 1986); children: Matt, Carrie, Katie. Student, Trevecca Nazarene U., 1997—. Affiliate broker Folk-Jordan Realtors, Brentwood, Tenn., 1985-90; residential sales rep. Liberty Mus. Ins., Franklin, 1990-94; broker ERA-Adams Realtors, Brentwood, 1994-98; pres. HomeTrust Real Estate Investments, 1996-98; prin. broker First Home Builder's Realty, Gastonia, N.C., 1998—. Recipient numerous real estate sales awards. Mem. Charlotte Regional Realtors Assn., Gastonia C. of C., William County C. of C., Greater Nashville Assn. Realtors, Williamson County Assn. Realtors (edn. com. 1985-96). Baptist. Avocations: dancing, boating, reading. Office: First Home Builder's Realty Gastonia NC 28056

RANDALL, VERNELLIA, lawyer, nurse, educator; b. Gladewater, Tex., Mar. 6, 1948; d. Ernest and Pauline (Hall) R.; children: Tshaka, Issa. AA, Amarillo (Tex.) Coll., 1968; BS, U. Tex., 1972; MSN, U. Wash., 1978; JD, Lewis and Clark Coll., 1987. Bar: Oreg. 1987. Dir. acad. excellence program U. Dayton, Ohio, 1994—, prof. torts, health care law, women and the law, race/racism remedies, 1990; assoc. Bullivant, Houser, Bailey, Pendergrass & Hoffman, Portland, Oreg., 1987-90. Adj. prof. law Lewis and Clark Coll., 1988-90, Wright State Med. Sch., 1990—; vis. prof. Seattle U., 1995; dir. Inst. on Race, Health Care and the Law. Editor: website: Race and Racism in American Law, Race, Health Care and Law, Students Learning Legal Education, Gender and the Law. Bd. dirs. Oreg. Legal Svcs., 1988-90, Oreg. chpt. Am. Heart Assn., 1988-90, Mary Scott Nursing Home, Inc., 1998—; coord. working group on health World Conf. Against Racism. Mem. ABA (vice chmn. health ins. com. 1988-90, young lawyers health com. religious non-profit orgn., mem. sect. on individual rights, vice-chmn. com. on health rights), ANA, Am. Health Care Assn., Am. Assn. Law Schs. (sec. sect. on health care law 1995, sec., chair sect. law and medicine 1996, chmn. sect. health care law 1997, exec. com. sect. on tchg. methods, 1998-2001, chair-elect 2000, treas.-elect sect. on women and the law), Oreg. Bar Assn., Assn. Oreg. Black Attys., Oreg. Women Lawyers (bd. dirs. 1989-90), Multnomah County Bar Assn. (status of women com.), Thurgood Marshall Legal Soc. (continuing edn. 1992), Soc. of Am. Law Tchrs. (bd. dirs). Avocation: computers. Office: U Dayton Sch Law 300 College Park Ave Dayton OH 45469-0001 E-mail: randall@udayton.edu.

RANDALL, WILLIAM B. manufacturing company executive; b. Phila., Jan. 8, 1921; s. Albert and Ann (Fine) R.; m. Geraldine Kempson, Aug. 10, 1943; children: Robert, Erica Lynn, Lisa. Student, Rider Coll., Trenton, N.J., 1940-41. Gen. Sales mgr. Lowres Optical Mfg. Co., Newark, 1946-49; pres., founder Rand Sales Co., N.Y.C., 1949-58; gen. mgr. Sea & Ski Co. div. Botany Industries, Inc., Millbrae, Calif., 1958-61, pres., dir., 1961-66, v.p., 1961-65; pres. Renauld of France, Reno, 1967-68; chmn. bd. Renauld Internat., Reading, Pa., 1963-65; pres., chief operating officer Renauld Internat., Ltd., Burlingame and Reno, 1966-67; pres., chmn. bd. Randall Internat., Ltd., 1967-68; sr. exec. v.p. Forty-two Prods. Ltd., 1969-71; pres. Exec. Products Internat. Ltd., 1969-71, New Product Devel. Ctr., Carlsbad, Calif., 1971—; pres. Internat. Concept Ctr. Exec. Products Internat. Ltd., Irvine, 1971—, pres. Sun Research Ctr., 1974—; pres. La Costa Products Internat., 1975-86; mng. dir. merchandising La Costa Hotel and Spa, 1986-88; pres., chief exec. officer Randall Internat., Carlsbad, 1989—. Bd. dirs. Bank of La Costa, Garden Botanika. Served to 1st lt., navigator USAAF, 1942-45. Mem. Am. Mgmt. Assn., Nat. Wholesale Druggists Assn., Nat. Assn. Chain Drug Stores, Hon. Order Ky. Cols., Baja Beach and Tennis Club (bd. dirs.). Home: 7150 Arenal Ln Carlsbad CA 92009-6701 E-mail: billr@randallinternational.com. *I play to win. I like to win. And I hate good losers.*

RANDALL, WILLIAM SEYMOUR, leasing company executive; b. Champaign, Ill., July 5, 1933; s. Glenn S. and Audrey H. (Honnold) R.; m. Sharon Larsen; children: Steve, Cathy, Mike, Jennifer. BS, Ind. State U., 1959. Controller Amana Refrigeration Co., Iowa, 1966-70; div. controller Trane Co., Clarksville, Tenn., 1970-74, corporate controller La Crosse, Wis., 1974-79; v.p., chief fin. officer Sta-Rite Industries, Milw., 1979-82; pres., owner Profl. Staff Resources, Inc., 1982—. Served with AUS, 1953-55. Mem. Financial Execs. Inst. Lodges: Rotary. Home: 13365 Tulane St Brookfield WI 53005-7141 Office: 14430 W Bluemound Rd Ste 103 Milwaukee WI 53226

RANDALL-KEENEY, ELINOR, artist; b. Norwalk, Conn., July 3, 1932; d. David Judson and Mary Leslie (Fuller) Randall; m. James Hervey Keeney, June 13, 1953 (div. June 1974); children: Benjamin, Dorigen. BFA, Wayne State U., 1969. Instr. drawings horse anatomy Peacham (Vt.) Summer Programs, 1970-73; tchr. Graphic Arts Workshop, San Francisco, 1978-92; instr. art Nat. Inst. Art and Disabilities, Richmond, Calif., 1990-92; propr. Rung Rim Press, Plainfield, Vt., 1992—. Archivist Marshall Glasier Collection, Houghton Libr., Harvard U., Cambridge, Mass.; oral historian, photographer D.J. Gavin, founder Maritime Union, Tamiment Inst. Libr., N.Y.C., Alride Berard and His Logging Horse, Chester Grimes and His Logging Horse, Bailey-Howe Libr., Burlington, Vt. Illustrator: (books) Farewell Dundrennan, 1987, Beyond Hadrians Wall, 1989, The Bird Poems (Len Irving), 1995, The Skipping Stone, 1995; prints represented in collections Wayne State U., Detroit, Pushkin Mus., St. Petersburg, Russia, also pvt. collections. Bd. dirs. Winooski Valley Coop., Plainfield, 1994-97. Mem. Art Resource Assn. (bd. dirs.), Calif. Soc. Printmakers, Vt. Coun. Arts, Artists Equity. Home: Maple Hill PO Box 223 Plainfield VT 05667-0223

RANDAZZO, GARY WAYNE, newspaper executive; b. Georgetown, Tex., Sept. 23, 1947; s. Frank Birchmans and Edna Earle (Forbis) R.; m. Joyce Sue McNorton, Oct. 7, 1966; children: Gary Wayne Jr., Vanessa Rene, Michael Jason, Daniel Paul. BBA, U. Tex., 1974; MBA, Tex. A&I U., Corpus Christi, 1976. Instr. Del Mar Coll., Corpus Christi, 1974-76; bus. mgr. Corpus Christi Caller-Times, 1976-81; pres., pub. Huntsville (Tex.) Item, 1981-83; pres. Am. Property Data, Houston, 1984-87; gen. mgr. Health Care News, 1987-89; sr. v.p. sales and mktg. Houston Chronicle, 1989—. Chmn., bd. dirs. Leadership Houston; bd. dirs. Downtown Houston Assn., treas.; bd. dirs. Better Bus. Bur., Big Bros./Big Sisters. Mem. Kiwanis (bd. dirs.). Home: 9610 Oxted Ln Spring TX 77379-6600 Office: Houston Chronicle 801 Texas St Houston TX 77002-2996 E-mail: gary.randazzo@chron.com.

RANDAZZO, REBECCA ANN, nursing administrator; b. Bellevue, Pa., May 20, 1950; d. David E. and Mary Anna (Braham) Bickett; m. Andrew M. Randazzo, Nov. 10, 1973; children: Gwen, Janet. BSN, U. Evansville, 1972; MPA, Ind. U., Gary, 1991. RN, Ind., Ill. Staff nurse Good Samaritan Hosp., Vincennes, Ind., 1972-73, Clark County Hosp., Clarksville, 1973-75; staff nurse, shift coord. St. Anthony Med. Ctr., Crown Point, 1975-91; assoc. dir. nursing St. Anthony Home, 1991-96, DON, 1996-99; adminstr. transitional care Franciscan Homes and Cmty. Svcs., 1999—2001; dir. subacute svcs. St. Margaret Mercy Healthcare Ctrs., 2001—. Cons. Vale Hops., Valparaiso, Ind., 1990; mem. rehab. adv. bd. St. Anthony Med. Ctr., Crown Point, 1993-94. Mem. Am. Coll. Healthcare Execs., Ind. Assn. Health Care Quality (edn. com. 1991). Home: 10408 W 173rd Ave Lowell IN 46356-9575 Office: St Mary Mercy 5454 Hohlman Ave Hammond IN 46230-4802 E-mail: rebecca.randazzo@ssfhs.com.

RANDEL, DON MICHAEL, academic administrator, musicologist; m. Carol Randel; children: Amy Elizabeth Keating, Julia, Emily Catherine Pershing, Sally Randel Eggert. AB magna cum laude, Princeton U., 1962, MFA, 1964, PhD, 1967. With dept. music, dept. chair, vice provost Cornell U., 1968, assoc. dean Coll. Arts and Scis., dean Coll. Arts and Scis., 1991-95, provost, Given Found. prof. musicology, 1995-2000; pres. U. Chgo., 2000—. Editor: New Harvard Dictionary of Music, 1986, Harvard Biographical Dictionary of Music, 1996, Harvard Concise Dictionary of Music and Musicians, 1999. Recipient Hon. Woodrow Wilson fellow, Danforth Grad. fellow; Fulbright award. Fellow: Am. Acad. Arts and Scis.; mem.: Am. Philos. Soc. Office: U Chgo Adminstrn 502 5801 S Ellis Ave Chicago IL 60637-5418

RANDELL, CHRISLYN ELIZABETH, psychology educator; b. Lancaster, Pa., Aug. 11, 1964; d. Thomas Henry Fisher and Jeralyn Elizabeth Fenstermacher; m. James David Harlow, Oct. 4, 1986 (div. Feb. 1995); Kevin Andrew Randell, May 27, 2000. BA, Metro. State Coll. of Denver, 1986; MS, Colo. State U., 1990, PhD, 1997. Rsch. analyst Coors Brewing Co., Golden, Colo., 1990—94; faculty Metro. State Coll. of Denver, 1995—97; honorarium faculty U. Colo., 1997—98; postdoctoral rsch. assoc. Colo. State U., Ft. Collins, 2000—; asst. prof. psychology Metro. State Coll. Denver, 2001—. Adj. faculty Regis U., Denver, 1997—2000; vis. instr. Metro. State Coll. Denver, 1998—2000. Contbr. articles to profl. jours.; editor: Selected Readings in Psychology, 4th edit., 1999, 5th edit., 2000, 6th edit., 2001. Metro. State Coll. of Denver Profl. Devel. grantee, 1998, Colo. Scholars award, 1985; Assn. for Rsch. in Vision and Ophthalmology Travel fellow, 1999. Mem. Assn. for Rsch. in Vision and Ophthalmology, Am. Psychol. Soc. Avocations: gardening, travel, reading, hiking, camping. E-mail: randellc2@home.com.

RANDELL, CORTES W. news service executive; b. Wash., D.C., 1935; m. Joan. V. (Wirz) 1968; children: Cortes John, Christina Alexis. BSME, U. Va., 1959; student, Darden Sch., U. Va., 1962. Engr. Gen. Electric, N.Y., 1959-61, Internat. Telephone & Telegraph, Chgo., 1962-64; pres. Nat. Student Mktg., N.Y., 1964-71; cons. and trustee Wash. Trust, 1972-84; pres. Federal News Svc., Wash., D.C., 1984—. Author: Taking the Stand, Testimony of Oliver North, 1987, The National Press Club's Best Contemporary Speakers, 1995. Mem. Nat. Press Club, Yale Club. Avocations: offshore performance boating, ballooning, advising startup companies. Office: 620 National Press Building Washington DC 20045-1601 E-mail: cort.randell@verizon.net.

RANDELS, DAVID GEORGE, secondary school educator; b. Bryan, Ohio, Feb. 6, 1943; s. George D. and Doris L. Randels; 1 child, Kellie R. BS in Edn., Bowling Green State U., 1965, MusM, 1971. Instr., counselor Culver (Ind.) Mil. Acad., 1962-67; instr. music Port Clinton (Ohio) City Schs., 1965—. Tchr., drummer various jazz bands, 1960—; drummer Jamie Wight New Orleans Joymakers, 1980—. Drummer 6 recordings. Recipient Bryan High Sch. John Phillips Sousa Band award, 1961; named Outstanding Bandsman Bowling Green State U., 1965. Mem. Nat. Sch. Orch. Assn. Disting Svc. award 1994), U.S. Capitol Hist. Soc., Port Clinton Fedn. Tchrs. Lifetime Achievement award 1984), Music Educators Nat. Conf., Elks, Port Clinton Model Railroad Club (pres. 1975-82), Kappa Kappa Psi (pres. 1965), Phi Delta Kappa. Democrat. Avocations: model railroading, music, antique cars, camping, fishing. Home: PO Box 182 Port Clinton OH 43452-1901 Office: Port Clinton Mid Sch 110 E 4th St Port Clinton OH 43452-1901 E-mail: dave_randels@port-clinton.k12.oh.us.

RANDELS, ED L. lawyer; b. Albuquerque, Nov. 17, 1953; s. James L. and Betty J. (Ridgeway) R.; m. Kathryn J. Eddleman, July 11, 1975; children: Nancy L, Joshua L. BA, Mid-Am. Nazarene Coll., Olathe, Kans., 1975; JD, U. Kans., 1982. Bar: Kans. 1982, U.S. Dist. Ct. Kans. 1982, U.S. Ct. Appeals (10th cir.) 1994. Asst. county atty. Montgomery County, Indpendence, Kans., 1982-85, Miami County, Paola, 1985-86; asst. city atty. City of Wichita, 1986-92; asst. county counselor Sedgwick County, Wichita, 1992—. Law day dir. Miami County Bar Assn., Paola, Kans., 1985-86. Contbr. articles to profl. jours. Mem. ABA, Kans. Bar Assn., Wichita Bar Assn. (chair law in edn. com. 1999-2000, mem. mcpl. practice com.), Christian Legal Soc. (pres. Wichita chpt. 1998-99, 2000-01). Republican. Nazarene. Office: Sedgwick County Counselor 525 N Main St Ste 359 Wichita KS 67203-3731 E-mail: erandels@sedgwick.gov.

RANDHAWA, BIKKAR SINGH, psychologist, educator; b. Jullundur, India, June 14, 1933; came to Can., 1961, naturalized, 1966; s. Pritam S. and Sawaran K. (Basakhi) R.; m. Leona Emily Bujnowski, Oct. 8, 1966; children— Jason, Lisa. BA in Math., Panjab U., 1954, BT in Edn., 1955, MA in History, 1959; BEd, U. Alta., Can., 1963; MEd in Measurement and Evaluation, U Toronto, 1967, PhD, 1969. Registered psychologist. Tchr. secondary sch. math., Panjab, 1955-61; asst. headmaster, then headmaster, 1955-61; tchr. high sch. math. and sci. Beaver County, Riley, Alta., 1964-65, Camrose County, 1961-64, Edmonton (Alta.) Public Schs., 1965-67; tutor in math. for social sci. Ont. Inst. Studies in Edn., Toronto, 1968-69; mem. faculty U. Sask., Saskatoon, 1969-76, 77—, prof. ednl. psychology, 1977-2000, prof. emeritus, 2000—, asst. dean research and field services, 1982-87. Prof., coord. Visual Scholars' Program, U. Iowa, 1976-77; cons. in field. Contbr. articles profl. jours. Fellow APA, Am. Psychol. Soc. (charter), Can. Psychol. Assn.; mem. Am. Ednl. Rsch. Assn., Can. Ednl. Rsch. Assn. (pres. 1997-99), Can. Soc. Study Edn., Sask. Psychol. Assn., Phi Delta Kappa (pres. Saskatoon chpt. 1971, 85). Home: 14 Harwood Dr St Albert AB Canada T8N 5V5 E-mail: randy.randhawa@shaw.ca.

RANDHIR, TIMOTHY O. science educator; b. Mettupalayam, Tamil Nadu, India, Jan. 15, 1965; came to U.S., 1991; s. Kruparao and Shyamala Devi Onukuri; m. Reena Sargunar, July 24, 1991; children: Priyanka, Ashwin. PhD, Purdue U., 1995. Asst. prof. Tamil Nadu Agrl. U., Coimbatore, 1989—91; natural resource economist Purdue U., West Lafayette, Ind., 1995—97; asst. prof. U. Mass., Amherst, 1997—, dir. Water Resources Rsch. Ctr., 2002—. Svc. Learning fellow U. Mass., 1997. Fellow Soil and Water Conservation Soc. (Berg fellow 1997); mem. AAAS, Am. Water Resources Assn., Am. Agrl. Econs. Assn. Avocation: travel. Office: U Mass Holdsworth Hall Rm 320 Amherst MA 01003 Home: 100 Columbia Dr Amherst MA 01002 Fax: 413-545-3943. E-mail: randhir@forwild.umass.edu.

RANDI, JAMES (RANDALL JAMES HAMILTON ZWINGE), magician, writer, educator; b. Toronto, Aug. 7, 1928; naturalized U.S. citizen, 1987; s. George Randall and Marie Alice (Paradis) Zwinge. Student, Oakwood Collegiate Inst., Toronto, 1940-45; LittD (hon.), U. Indpls., 1995. Internationally known conjuror, investigator. Regent's lectr. UCLA, 1984; skeptical lectr. on paranormal subjects. Author: The Magic of Uri Geller, 1975 (with Bert Sugar) Houdini, His Life and Art, 1978, Flim-Flam, 1982, Test Your ESP Potential, 1983, The Faith Healers, 1987, The Magic World of the Amazing Randi, 1989, The Mask of Nostradamus, 1990, James Randi: Psychic Investigator, 1991, Conjuring, 1992, An Encyclopedia of Claims, Frauds, and Hoaxes of the Occult and Supernatural, 1995 (English, Chinese, French, Italian, Japanese, Korean, Norwegian, Polish and Spanish edits.); host TV spls. Recipient Blackstone award Internat. Platform Assn., 1983, 87, Forum award Am. Phys. Soc., 1988, Nat. Consumer Svc. award Nat. Coun. Against Health Fraud, 1988, Gold medal U. Ghent, Belgium, 1989, Humanist Disting. Svc. award Am. Humanist Assn., 1990, medal with golden wreath Hungarian Soc. for Dissemination of Scientific Knowledge, 1992; MacArthur Found. fellow, 1986, Spl. fellow Acad. Magical Arts and Scis., 1987; inducted into Soc. Am. Magicians Hall of Fame, 1988. Founding fellow Com. for Scientific Investigation of Claims of the Paranormal (exec. bd. dirs. 1973-91). Achievements include performing at White House, 1974. Home: 12000 NW 8th St Fort Lauderdale FL 33325-1406 Office: James Randi Ednl Found 201 SE 12th St Fort Lauderdale FL 33316-1815 E-mail: randi@randi.org. *We have entered the third millennium with quack medicine, Creation "Science," and other pseudo-scientific matters heedlessly and increasingly embraced by the public, and major TV programs feature performers who claim to "speak from the Dead." These con artists, feeding on the grief and vulnerability of their victims, are ignored, even tolerated, by our state and federal agencies.. Medieval notions and an anti-science movement threaten our very survival. We must reach out to our youth and develop in them a respect for critical thinking. Acceptance of "politically correct" attitudes as standards, and of unquestioning belief in obviously crackpot theories have brought us to a crisis in education. We need to adopt higher standards for our young people in respect to critical thinking. As we enter the new millenium, the one-million dollar prize offered by my Foundation for proof of any paranormal power is still unclaimed. Why?.*

RANDINELLI, TRACEY ANNE, magazine editor; b. Morristown, N.J., Apr. 6, 1963; d. Andrew R. and Patricia Ann (Brenner) R. BA in Comm., U. Del., 1985. Copywriter Macy's N.J., Newark, 1985-86; edit. asst. Globe Comms. Corp., N.Y.C., 1986-87; from asst. editor to assoc. editor Scholastic Math and DynaMath Mags. Scholastic, Inc., 1987-89, editor Scholastic Math Mag., 1989-95; mng. editor Zig Zag Mag. Games Pub. Group, 1995; sr. editor Contact Kids Mag./ Sesame Workshop, 1996-2001; freelance writer, 2001—. Mem. Soc. Children's Book Writers, Ednl. Press Assn. Am. (Disting. Achievement award feature articles divsn. 1991, 95, coverdesign 1996, how-to feature divsn. 1998, 99). E-mail: pen4kidz@aol.com.

RANDISI, ELAINE MARIE, accountant, educator, writer; b. Racine, Wis., Dec. 19, 1926; d. John Dewey and Alveta Irene (Raffety) Fehd; m. John Paul Randisi, Oct. 12, 1946 (div. July 1972); children: Jeanine Randisi Manson, Martha Randisi Chaney (dec.), Joseph, Paula, Catherine Randisi Carvalho, George, Anthony (dec.); m. John R. Woodfin, June 18, 1994. AA, Pasadena Jr. Coll., 1946; BS cum laude (Giannini scholar), Golden Gate U., 1978. With Raymond Kaiser Engrs., Inc., Oakland, Calif., 1969-75, 77-86, corp. acct., 1978-79, sr. corp. acct., 1979-82, sr. payroll acct., 1983-86; acting mgr. Lilli Ann Corp., San Francisco, 1986-89, Crosby, Heafey, Roach & May, Oakland, 1990-98. Initiated Minority Vendor Purchasing Program for Kaiser Engrs., Inc., 1975-76; corp. buyer Kaiser Industries Corp., Oakland, 1975-77; lectr. on astrology Theosophical Soc., San Francisco, 1979-99; mem. faculty Am. Fedn. Astrologers Internat. Conv., Chgo., 1982, 84. Mem. Speakers Bur., Calif. Assn. for Neurologically Handicapped Children, 1964-70, v.p., 1969; bd. dirs. Ravenwood Homeowners Assn., 1979-82, v.p., 1979-80, sec., 1980-81, mem. organizing com. Minority Bus. Fair, San Francisco, 1976; pres., bd. dirs. Lakewood Condominium Assn., 1984-87; mem. trustee Ch. of Religious Sci., 1992-95; treas. First Ch. Religious Sci., 1994-98, lic. practitioner, pres., 1990-91, sec., 1989-90. Mem. Am. Fedn. Astrologers, Calif. Scholarship Fedn. (life), Alpha Gamma Sigma (life). Home: 742 Wesley Way Apt 1C Oakland CA 94610-2339

RANDLE, ELLEN EUGENIA FOSTER, opera and classical singer, educator; b. New Haven, Oct. 2, 1948; d. Richard A.G. and Thelma Lousie (Brooks) Foster; m. Ira James William, 1967 (div. 1972); m. John Willis Randle, Dec. 24, 1983. Student, Calif. State Coll., Sonoma, 1970; studied with Boris Goldovsky, 1970; student, Grad. Sch. Fine Arts, Florence, Italy, 1974; studied with Tito Gobbi, Florence, 1974; student, U. Calif., Berkeley, 1977; BA in World History, Lone Mountain Coll., 1976, MA in Performing Arts, 1978; studied with Madam Eleanor Steber, Graz, Austria, 1979; studied with Patricia Goehl, Munich, Fed. Republic Germany, 1979; MA in Counseling and Psychology, U. San Francisco, 1990, MA in Marriage and Family Therapy, 1994, EdD in Internat. Multicultural Edn., 1998. Asst. artistic dir. Opera Piccola, Oakland, Calif., 1990-92; instr. African Am. culture and humanities Mission C.C., Santa Clara, 1997—; instr. Peralta C.C. Dist., Oakland, 1998—; psychotherapy intern, sr. peer counseling program City of Fremont, Calif., 1999-2000; psychotherapist, marriage family therapist intern Portia Bell Human Behavioral Health and Tng. Ctr., Concord, 2000—01; family facilitator EMQ Family and Children Svcs., Sacramento, 2002—. Instr. East Bay Performing Art Ctr., Richmond, Calif., 1986, Chapman Coll., 1986, Las Positas C.C., Livermore, Calif., 1999—; adj. prof. U. Phoenix, 1999-2000, adj. prof. U. Pheonix, Northern Calif., 2001-. Singer opera prodns. Porgy & Bess, Oakland, Calif., 1980-81, LaTraviata, Oakland, Calif., 1981-82, Aida, Oakland, 1981-82, Madame Butterfly, Oakland, 1982-83, The Magic Flute, Oakland, 1984, numerous others; performances include TV specials, religous concerts, musicals; music dir. Natural Man, Berkeley, 1986; asst. artistic dir. Opera Piccola, Oakland, Calif., 1990—. Art commr. City of Richmond, Calif. Recipient Bk. Am. Achievement award. Mem. Music Tchrs. Assn., Internat. Black Writers and Artists Inc. (life mem., local #5), Nat. Coun. Negro Women, Nat. Assn. Negro Musicians, Calif. Arts Fedn., Calif. Assn. for Counseling and Devel. (mem. black caucus), Nat. Black Child Devel. Inst., The Calif.-Nebraskan Orgn., Inc., Calif. Marital & Family Therapist Assn. (San Francisco chpt.), Black Psychotherpist of San Francisco and East Bay Area, San Francisco Commonwealth Club, Gamma Phi Delta. Democrat. Mem. A.M.E. Zion Ch. Avocations: cooking, entertaining. Home: 5314 Boyd Ave Oakland CA 94618-1112

RANDLE, JOHN, professional football player; b. Hearne, Tex., Jan. 12, 1967; Student, Trinity Valley C.C., Tex., Tex. A&I U. Defensive tackle Minn. Vikings, 1990—2000, Seattle Seahawks, 2001. Selected to Pro Bowl, 1993, 94; named to The Sporting News NFL All-Pro Team, 1994. Achievements tied AFC record for most sacks, 1994. Office: Seattle Seahawks 11220 NE 53rd St Kirkland WA 98033-3825*

RANDLE, THERESA, actress; b. L.A., 1967; Represented by Internat. Creative Mgmt., Beverly Hills, Calif. Appeared in films, including King of New York, 1990, The Five Heartbeats, 1991, Jungle Fever, 1991, Malcolm X, 1992, Sugar Hill, 1994, Beverly Hills Cops III, 1994, Bad Boys, 1995, Girl 6, 1996, Space Jam, 1996, Spawn, 1997. Address: Murphy Edward Mgmt 1740 Broadway Fl 15 New York NY 10019-4315

RANDLETT, ALICE LORRAINE, educator; b. Chgo., Jan. 1, 1940; d. Fred W. and Alice Blanche Schmatz; m. James David Randlett, Feb. 25, 1961 (div. Aug. 1974); 1 child, Christopher. BS, U. Wis., Stevens Point, 1964, MAT in English, 1974; MLS, Rosary Coll., 1969; PhD, U. Wis., Madison, 1988. Rsch. libr. Fed. Reserve Bank, Chgo., 1969-70; dir. tutoring-learning ctr. U. Wis., Stevens Point, 1991-93, libr., 1970—, coord. reading program, 1985-91,93—. Dir. Ctrl. Wis. Writing Project, Stevens Point, 1991-94; adj. prof. Cardinal Stritch Coll., Milw., 1994-95. Trainer Portage County Literacy Coun., Stevens Point, 1990-2000; bd. dirs. Mid-State Tech. Coll., 1995—. Mem. Nat. Coun. Tchrs. English, Internat. Reading Assn., Phi Kappa Phi, Beta Phi U. Democrat. Presbyterian. Avocations: travel, reading. Office: U Wis LRC Stevens Point WI 54481

RANDLETT, MARY WILLIS, photographer; b. Seattle, May 5, 1924; d. Cecil Durand and Elizabeth (Bayley) Willis; m. Herbert B. Randlett, Oct. 19, 1950 (div.); children: Robert, Mary Ann, Peter, Susan. BA, Whitman Coll., Walla Walla, Wash., 1947. Freelance photographer, 1949—. One-woman shows include Seattle Sci. Ctr., 1971, Western Wash. State U., 1971, Seattle Art Mus., 1971, Art Gallery Greater Victoria, 1972, Alaska State Mus., 1972, State Capitol Mus., 1983, Whatcom Mus. History and Art, Bellingham, Wash., 1986, Janet Huston Gallery, LaConner, Wash., 1990, Gov.'s Gallery, Office of Gov., Olympia, Wash., 1991, Stonington Gallery, Seattle, 1992, Valley Mus. Art, LaConner, 1992, Grad. Sch. Design Dept. Landscape Arch. Harvard U., Cambridge, Mass., 1996, Mus. N.W. Art, LaConner, 1998, others, exhibited in group shows at Am. Soc. Mag. Photographers, 1970, Whatcom Mus., Bellingham, Henry Gallery, Seattle, 1971, 1974, Royal Photg. Soc., 1979, Heard Mus., Phoenix, 1979, State Capital Mus., Olympia, Wash., 1983, 1984, 1988, 1989, 1993, Santa Fe Ctr. for Photography, 1987, Tacoma Art Mus., 1989, Helen Day Art Ctr., Stowe, Vt., 1989, Valley Mus. N.W. Art, LaConner, 1991, 1994, 1996—98, Allen Libr. U. Wash., Seattle, 1991, Wing Luke Asian Mus., 1991, Cheney Cowles Mus., Spokane, 1991, 1998, Security Pacific Gallery, Seattle, 1992, Benham Gallery, Seattle, 1993, Stonington Gallery, 1993, 1998, Rainier Club, Seattle, 1994, Port Angeles (Wash.) Fine Arts Ctr., 1994, Mus. History and Industry, Seattle, 1994, Whatcom Mus., Bellingham, 1994, Pacific N.W. Annual Bellevue Art Mus., Wash., 1995, Skagit Valley Hist. Mus., LaConner, 1995, Seattle Art Mus., 1996—98, Kirkland (Wash.) Arts Ctr., 1997, Bainbridge Arts and Crafts, Bainbridge Island, Wash., 1997, Lucia Douglas Gallery, Bellingham, 1997, Anchorage Mus. History & Art, 1997, Burke Mus. Natural History and Culture, Seattle, 1998, Henderson House, Turnwater, Wash., 1998, Whatcom Arco Exhibit Gallery, Bellingham, 1998, Sea First Gallery, Seattle, 1998, 1999, Citizens Cultural Ctr., Fujinomita, Japan, 1999, Mus. Am. Indian, N.Y.C., 1999, Cheney Cowels Mus., Spokane, 1999, J. Paul Horiuchi Seattle Asian Art Mus., 2000, Mus. NW Art, 2000, Seattle Art Mus., 2002, Whitney Mus. Am. Art, N.Y.C., 2002, High Mus., Atlanta, 2002, and numerous others, Represented in permanent collections Met. Mus., Nat. Collection of Fine Arts, Nat. Portrait Gallery, Washington State Libr., Manuscript divsn. U. Wash., Pacific Northwest Bell, Seattle, Swedish Med. Ctr., Whatcom Mus., Bellingham, Henry Gallery, Seattle, Wash. State Capitol Mus., Olympia, Phillips Collection, Wash.; works appeared in books The Master and His Fish (Roderick Haig-Brown), 1982, Theodore Roethke: The Journey to I and Otherwide (Neal Bowers), 1982, Mountain in the Clouds (Bruce Brown), 1982, Masonry in Architecture (Louis Redstone), 1982, Writings and Reflections from the World of Roderick Haig-Brown, 1982, Pike Place Market (Alice Shorett and Murray Morgan), 1982, The Dancing Blanket, (Cheryl Samuel), 1982, Collected Poems of Theodore Roethke, 1982, Spires of Form (Victor Scheffer), 1983, Assault on Mount Helicon (Mary Barnard), 1983, New as a Wave (Eve Triem), 1983, Sketchbook: A Memoir of the '30's and the Northwest School (William Cumming), 1983, Good Intentions (Jane Adams), 1985, Blackbirds of the Americas (Gordon Orians and Tony Angell), 1985, Historic Preservation in Seattle (Larry Kreisman), 1985, Down Town Seattle Walking Tours (Mary Randlett and Carol Tobin), 1986, Seattle, the Seattle Book, 1986, When Orchids Were Flowers (Kate Knap Johnson), 1986, Jacob Lawrence, American Painter, (Ellen Wheat), 1986, Manic Power: Robert Lowell and His Circle (Jeffrey Meyers), 1987, The Isamu Noguchi Garden Museum (Isamu Noguchi), 1987, Washington's Audacious State Capitol an its Builders (Norman Johnston), 1988, The Bloedel Reserve: Gardens in the Forest (Lawrence Kreisman), 1988, Washingtonians: A Biographical Portrait of the State on the Occasion of its Centennial, 1988, Directory of Literary Biography: Canadian Writers 1920-59, 2d series, 1989, Crafts of America, 1989, The Lone Tree Tragedy (Bruce Brown), 1989, Northwest Coast Handbook of North American Indians, 1990, Dancing on the Rim of the World, 1990, Openings, Original Essays by Contemporary Soviet and American Writers (eds. Robert Atwan, Valeri Vinokurov), 1990, George Tsutakawa (Martha Kingsbury), 1990, Contemporary American Poetry (ed. Al Polin Jr.), 1991, Natural History of Puget Sound Country (Arthur Kruckberg), 1991, Bones (Joyce Thompson), 1991, Cebu (Peter Basho), 1991, Catalogue of Historic Preservation Publications, 1992, Art in Seattle's Public Places (James Rupp), 1992, The Olympic Rainforest (Ruth Kirk with Jerry Franklin), 1992, Steelhead Fly Fishing (Trey Combs), 1992, Illustrated Guidelines for Rehabilitation Historic Buildings, 1993, A History of African American Artists (Bearden and Henderson), 1994, Childrens Literature Review Vol. 1, 1994, Invisible Gardens: The Search for Modernism the American Landscape (Walker and Simo), 1994, Seeing Seattle (Roger Sale), 1994, Reaching Home (Jay and Matson), 1994, Redesigning the American Lawn: A Search for Environmental Harmony (Gordone Geballe, Diana Balmari and F. Herbert Bormann), 1995, Reaching Home: Pacific Salmon, Pacific People (Foves, Jay and Matson), 1995, Carl F. Gould: A Life in Architecture and the Arts (T. William Booth and William H. Wuksib), 1995, Destination Zero (Sam Hamill), 1996, Market Sketchbook, 25th Anniversary Edition, 1996, Spririts of the Ordinary, 1997, Instrument of Change: Jim Schoppert 1947-1992, 1997, Looking for Edulabee Dix (Joann Ridley), 1997, Jack Lenor Larsen: A Memoir, 1998, Museo Nacional Centro de Arte Reina (Mark Tobey), 1998, Fountains Splash, and Spectacle: Water and Design from the Renaissance to Present (ed. Marilyn Symmes), 1998, Ghost Dancing (Anna Linzer), 1998, The Flower in the Skull (Kathleen Alcala), 1998, This Great Unknowing: Last Poems (Denise Levertov), 1999, Building Washington (Paul Dorpat, Genevier McCoy), 1999, The Wright Collection, Seattle Art Museum, 1999, Made to Last: Historic Preservation in Seattle and King County (Larry Kreisman), 1999, Isamu Noguchi: A Study of Space (Ana Maria Torres), 2000, The Tiger Iris (Joan Swift), 2000, The Eighth Lively Art (Wesley Wehr), 2000, All Powers Necessary and Convenient (Mark F. Jenkins), 2000, Ice Breakers: Alaska's Most Innovative Artists (Julie Decker), 2000, Over the Line: The Life and Art of Jacob Lawrence (Peter Nesbett and Michelle Dubois), 2000, Iridescent Light: The Emergence of Northwest Art (Delores Tarzan Ament), 2001, Messages from Frank's Landing, 2000, Leo Kenney: A Retrospective, 2000, Building for Learning: Seattle Public Schools History 1860-2000, 2001, Geology and Plant Life, 2001, and numerous others; works also appeared in newspapers and mags. Recipient Wash. State Gov.'s award for spl. commendation for contbns. in field of photography, 1983, Individual Artist award, King County Arts Commn., 1989, Lifetime Achievement award, Artist Trust, 2001, Matrix Table, Seattle Women of Achievement, 1999, Nancy Blankenship Pryor award, 2001; grantee, Nat. Endowment for Arts, 1976, Allied Arts Found., 2000. Mem. AIA (hon.), Am. Soc. Mag. Photographers. Home: PO Box 11238 Olympia WA 98508-1238

RANDMAN, BARRY I. real estate developer; b. Cin., Apr. 1, 1958; s. David I. and Marilyn June (Garfinkel) F. BBA in Fin., U. Denver, 1980. With acctg. dept. Rookwood Pottery & Celestial Restaurants, Cin., 1976-80; asst. to pres., head mktg. and real estate branching Great Am. Banks Inc., Miami, 1980-83; pres. Tower Mgmt. Inc., Cin., 1983-85, bd. dirs.; pres. Ohio Jet Svcs. Inc., 1983-85; v.p. Home State Fin. Svcs. Inc., 1984-85; pres. East Hill Devel. Corp., 1985—, B.I.R. Properties Inc., Cin., 1985—. Pres. Golden Devel. Corp., 1988-91, SRB Food Corp., 1988-92, Scarborough Devel. Corp., 1989, Redmont Devel Corp., 1990—, Eastridge, Inc., 1993-99, 613 Roce LLC, Hale Justis, LLC, 1999—. Mem. Jewish Welfare Fund, Cin., 1980. Avocations: skiing, tennis, gardening. Home: 2840 Ambleside Pl Cincinnati OH 45208-3357 Office: 2321 Kemper Ln Cincinnati OH 45206-2610

RANDOLPH, A(RTHUR) RAYMOND, federal judge; b. Riverside, N.J., Nov. 1, 1943; m. Eileen J. O'Connor, May 18, 1984; children: John Trevor, Cynthia Lee. BS, Drexel U., 1966; JD summa cum laude, U. Pa., 1969. Bar: Calif. 1970, D.C. 1973, U.S. Supreme Ct. 1973. Law clk. to Hon. Henry J. Friendly U.S. Ct. Appeals (2d cir.), N.Y.C., 1969—70; asst. to solicitor gen. U.S. Dept. Justice, Washington, 1970—73, dep. solicitor gen., 1975—77; ptnr. Sharp, Randolph & Green, 1977—83, Randolph & Truitt, Washington, 1983—87, Pepper, Hamilton & Scheetz, Washington, 1987—90; judge U.S. Ct. Appeals (D.C. cir.), 1990—. Spl. asst. atty. gen. State of Mont., 1983—90, State of N.Mex., 1985—90, State of Utah, 1986—90; adv. panel Fed. Cts. Study Com., 1989—90; spl. counsel Com. on Stds. Ofcl. Conduct, U.S. Ho. of Reps., 1979—80; adj. prof. Georgetown U. Law Ctr., 1974—78; exec. sec. Atty. Gen.'s Com. on Reform of Fed. Jud. Sys., 1975—77; com. on fed. rules evidence U.S. Justice Dept., 1972; chmn. Com. on Govtl. Structures, McLean, Va., 1973—74; adj. prof. law sch. George Mason U., 1992, disting. prof., 1998—; com. codes conduct Jud. Conf. U.S., 1992—95, chmn., 1995—98. Recipient Spl. Achievement award, U.S. Dept. Justice, 1971. Mem.: D.C. Bar Assn., Calif. Bar Assn., Am. Law Inst., Order of Coif. Office: E Barret Prettyman Courthouse US CT Appeals DC Cir 333 Constitution Ave NW Washington DC 20001-2866*

RANDOLPH, BRIAN WALTER, civil engineer, educator; b. Dayton, Ohio, Feb. 23, 1959; s. John Francis and Joan Mary (Botkin) R.; m. Clare Ellen Luddy, June 22, 1985; children: Brigid Luddy, Hannah Luddy, Beatrix Luddy. BSCE, U. Cin., 1982, MS, 1983; PhD, Ohio State U., 1989. Registered profl. engr., Ohio. Engr. Woolpert Cons., Dayton, 1979-82; rsch. asst. U. Cin., 1982-83; rsch. assoc. Ohio State U., Columbus, 1983-87; instr. U. Toledo, 1987-89, founding dir. Environ. Geotech. Lab., 1987—, asst. prof., 1989-93, assoc. prof. civil engring., 1993—97, dir. under grad. studies, 1994—97, prof., chmn. civil engring., 1997—. Contbr. articles to profl. jours., including Jour. Geotech. Engring., Jour. Transp. Engring., Transp. Rsch. Record; referee Jour. Engring. Edn., 1994—, Jour. Hazardous Materials, 1991—, Jour. Geotech. and Environ. Engring., 1990—. Grantee Ohio Dept. Transp./FWHA, 1989, 92, 93, 94, 96, GE, 1986, Sokkia Corp., 1992, Ohio Bd. Regents, 1989, NSF, 1993. Mem. ASCE (dept. heads coun. 1997-, Toledo Young Engr. of Yr. 1992), Am. Soc. Engring. Edn. (exec. bd. NEE com. 1990-91, Dow Outstanding Young Faculty award 1993), Toastmasters (edn. v.p. 1990-93), Sigma Xi, Chi Epsilon, Pi Mu Epsilon, Tau Beta Pi. Roman Catholic. Achievements include research on reliability analysis of groundwater flow and pavement parameters, permiability of course materials, and shear properties of soil and polymer interfaces. Office: Univ Toledo Dept Civil Engring 2801 W Bancroft St Toledo OH 43606-3390

RANDOLPH, CARL LOWELL, chemical company executive; b. Pasadena, Calif., May 30, 1922; s. Carl L. and Lulu (McBride) R.; m. Jane Taber, June 25, 1943; children: Margaret, Stephen. BA, Whittier Coll., 1943; MS, U. So. Calif., 1947, PhD, 1949; LLD, Whittier Coll., 1982; D in Pub. Svc. (hon.), U. Alaska, 1983. Prin. chemist Aerojet-Gen. Corp., 1949-57; v.p. U.S. Borax Rsch. Corp., Anaheim, Calif., 1957-63; asst. to pres. U.S. Borax & Chem. Corp., L.A., 1963-66, v.p., 1966-68, exec. v.p., 1968-69, pres., 1969-86, vice chmn., 1983-87. Trustee, chmn. bd. Whittier Coll., emeritus, 1969—; bd. dirs., chmn., Ind. Colls. So. Calif., 1982—. Lt. (j.g.) USNR, 1944-46. Mem. Phi Beta Kappa, Sigma Xi. Home: 3836 Bay Ln Anacortes WA 98221-8413

RANDOLPH, CHRISTOPHER CRAVEN, lawyer; b. Washington, May 26, 1956; s. William Barksdale and Elizabeth Page (Craven) R.; m. Linda Bubernak Dressler, June 6, 1982; children: Alexander Dressler, Brian Donovan. BA summa cum laude, U. Va., 1978; JD cum laude, Harvard U., 1982. Bar: D.C. 1983, N.Y. 1983. Assoc. Debevoise & Plimpton, N.Y.C., 1982-86, Washington, 1987-92; atty. advisor Agy. for Internat. Devel., 1992-95; investor, entrepreneur Vienna, 1995—2002; assoc. gen. counsel Peace Corps,

2002—. Editor Harvard Law Rev., 1980-82; contbr. articles to profl. jours. Mem. ABA, D.C. Bar Assn., Phi Beta Kappa. Republican. Episcopalian. Avocations: travel, reading, sports. Home: 2784 Marshall Lake Dr Oakton VA 22124-1148

RANDOLPH, DAVID, conductor; b. N.Y.C., Dec. 21, 1914; s. Morris and Elsie (Goodman) R.; m. Mildred Greenberg, July 18, 1948. BS, CCNY, 1936; MA, Tchrs. Coll., Columbia U., 1942. Music specialist OWI, N.Y.C., 1943-47. Adj. prof. music NYU, 1948-85, Mostly Mozart course, 1976-85; lectr. Town Hall, N.Y.C., 1955-60, Columbia U., 1957, Cosmopolitan Club, N.Y.C., 1962-63; pre-concert lectr. N.Y. Philharm., Avery Fisher Hall, 1964-86,Cleve. Orch., 1981, Vienna Symphony Orch., 1988; tchr. conducting Dalcroze Sch., 1948-49; music commentator Little Orch. Soc. Concerts and Broadcasts, 1950-62, Met. Opera Intermission Broadcasts; intermission commentator Lewisohn Stadium Concert Broadcasts, 1952-58; vis. prof. music SUNY, New Paltz, 1970-72, Fordham U., 1972-73; lectr. New Sch. for Social Rsch., 1973-90, IBM, N.Y.C., 1978-86, Beethoven Soc., 1977, 83; prof. music Montclair State Coll., Upper Montclair, N.J., 1973-87; guest condr. Rockland County (N.Y.) Ann. Choral Festival, 1972, 73; adviser film Music to Live By, mem. N.J. Arts Coun., 1967-70; mem. music com. Gov. N.J.'s Commn. to Study Arts, 1965; honored guest Handel Festival, Halle, Germany, 1991. Condr. Randolph Singers, 1944-62 (appeared on NBC Today, and Tonight Shows), concerts Town Hall, N.Y.C., Carnegie Recital Hall, recs. for Columbia, Vanguard, Westminster, Concert Hall Soc., CRI, Esoteric Records, United Choral Soc., L.I. N.Y., 1961-86, N.J. Ballet Orch., 1977, 83, Masterwork Chamber Orch., 1982, 83, The Philharmonia Orch. in Brahms' Requiem, London, 1988, Barge Concert, N.Y.C., 1987, 89; guest condr., Conn. Symphony Orch., 1961; condr. concert tour Spain with Am. choruses and Radio TV Orch. of Moscow, 1992; music annotator, CBS, N.Y.C., 1947-48; yearly choral seminar leader Mohonk Mountain House, 1986-95; music dir., condr. Masterwork Chorus and Orch., 1955-93, St. Cecilia Chorus and Orch., N.Y.C., 1965—; numerous performances at Carnegie Hall, Avery Fisher Hall, Lincoln Ctr., Kennedy Ctr. including Brahms' Requiem, Schicksalslied, Nänie, Mozart's Requiem, C Minor Mass, Vesperae de Confessore, Beethoven's Missa Solemnis, Symphony No. 9, Mass in C Major, Choral Fantasy, Bach's Mass in B Minor, St. John Passion, St. Matthew Passion, Christmas Oratorio, Magnificat, Haydn's St. Cecilia Mass, Paukenmesse, Lord Nelson Mass, Heiligmesse, Schöpfungsmesse, Michael Haydn's Requiem, Bruckner's Mass in E Minor, Requiem, Vaughan Williams' A Sea Symphony, Dona Nobis Pacem, Mass in G Minor, Hodie, Verdi's Requiem, Four Sacred Pieces, Honegger's King David, Elgar's The Music Makers, Corigliano's Fern Hill, Salieri's Mass in D, Purcell's The Fairy Queen, Mendelssohn's Elijah, Die erste Walpurgisnacht, Lobgesang, Lauda Sion, Poulenc's Gloria, Rutter's Gloria, Dvorak's Requiem, Te Deum, Kodaly's Te Deum, Berlioz' Requiem, Cherubini's Requiem, Schubert's Masses 5 and 6, Stabat Mater, Zelenka's Missa Dei Patris, Gounod's St. Cecilia Mass, Handel's Solomon, Israel in Egypt, Judas Maccabaeus and 171 complete performances of Handel's Messiah, Orff's Carmina Burana, Saint-Saëns' Requiem, Zimmermann's Psalmkonzert, Finzi's for St. Cecilia, In Terra Pax, Rachmaninoff's The Bells, Psalmkonzert, others; broadcaster: David Randolph Concerts, WNYC and numerous radio stas. of Nat. Assn. Ednl. Broadcasters, 1946-79, Young Audience telecasts, CBS-TV, 1958-59, series of candid rehearsals of Bach's Mass in B minor, PBS, 1967; host: weekly broadcasts Lincoln Ctr. Spotlight, Sta. WQXR, N.Y.C., 1966-67; regular guest critic First Hearing program Sta. WQXR, N.Y.C., and 68 other stas., 1986-95; author: This Is Music, 1964, 98, numerous album jacket notes; A New Music Made with a Machine, Horizon Magazine, 1959; editor: David Randolph Choral Series; writer, narrator: Instruments of the Orchestra, 1958, compact disc 1995, Stereo Review's Guide to Understanding Music, 1973; music critic, High Fidelity Mag., 1952-57; composer: A Song for Humanity, 1968, Andante for Strings, 1937, Edward; contbg. author: The N.Y. Times Guide to Listening Pleasure, 1968; analyzed Mendelssohn's Symphony No. 3 on records for Book of Month Club. Recipient 1st award for edn. by radio Ohio State Inst., 1948, 50, 51, Sylvania TV award, 1959, Disting. Alumni award Columbia U., 1982, cert. of appreciation Mayor of City of N.Y. at Carnegie Hall, 1991, Townsend Harris medal CCNY, 1996, Lifetime Achievement award Carnegie Hall, MidAmerica Prodns., 2000; St. Cecilia Chorus endowed David Randolph Disting. Artist-in-Residence Program at New Sch. in N.Y., 1996. Home: 420 E 86th St Apt 4-c New York NY 10028-6456 E-mail: david.randolph@att.net.

RANDOLPH, HARRY FRANKLIN, III (RANDY RANDOLPH), health facility administrator, educator, physician assistant; b. Vallejo, Calif., Nov. 5, 1946; s. Harry Franklin Jr. and Viola Vinnie (Snyder) R.; m. Candice Patricia Garrison, Dec. 30, 1970; 1 child, Brandon Todd. BS in Zoology, San Diego State U., 1969; BS, Baylor Coll. Med., 1977. Cert. physician asst. Staff rsch. assoc. U. Calif. San Diego, La Jolla, 1969-72; med. machine technician VA Hosp., San Diego, 1972-75; physician asst. So. Calif. Permanente Med. Group, 1977-79, So. Calif. HMO, San Diego, 1981-82, Scripps Clin. Med. Group, La Jolla, 1982-97; clin. prof., assoc. dir. Sch. Physician Asst. Studies Pacific U., Forest Grove, Oreg., 1997—. Chief physician extender sect. Scripps Clin. Med. Group, La Jolla, 1991-97, expert witness/pysician asst. practice, 1992—, chief physician assts. Green Hosp., 1994-97; med. legal cons. Contbr. articles to profl. jours.; editor Surg. Physician Asst., 1994—; mem. editl. bd. Perspectives on Physician Asst. Edn., 2000—. Mem. Health Sys. Agency Sub-area Coun. VI, El Cajon, Calif., 1980-81, San Diego Zool. Soc., 1985-97. Fellow Am. Acad. Physician Assts., Am. Assn. Surgical Physician Assts. (treas. 1994-97), Calif. Acad. Physician Assts. (hon., dir. at large 1984, chmn. continuing med. edn. com. 1984-86, v.p. 1985, chmn. prof. practice com. 1996, 97, Outstanding Achievement award 1985, Outstanding Svc. award, 1994, 97), Oreg. Soc. Physician Assts. Democrat. Avocations: camping, gardening, mountain biking, hiking. Office: Pacific U Sch Physician Asst Studies 2043 College Way Forest Grove OR 97116-1797 E-mail: randolph@pacificu.edu.

RANDOLPH, JACQUELINE GENEVA, military officer, writer, small business owner; b. Madrid, Spain, Aug. 4, 1965; d. James Edward and Dorothy May Randolph. BS in Acctg., Met. State Coll. of Denver, 1989; MS in Adminstrn., Ctrl. Mich. U., 1997; M in Comml. Aviation, Delta State U., 2001. Lic. Pvt. Pilot FAA, 1997. Commd. 2d lt. USAF, 1994, advanced through grades to capt., 1998; acctg. technician Air Force Acctg. and Fin. Ctr., Denver, 1985—89; tax examiner intern Colo. Dept. of Revenue, 1987; def. contract auditor Def. Contract Audit Agy., 1989—90; aircrew USAF, Pope Air Force Base, NC, 1991—94, nuclear missile launch officer Minot, ND, 1994—98; asst. prof. of aerospace studies Miss. Valley State Univ. , Itta Bena , Miss., 1998—2001, Delta State U., Cleve., 1998—2001; global positioning satellite operator, crew comdr. Schriever AFB, Colorado Springs, Colo., 2001—. Civil air patrol liason univ. & air force rotc Delta State U., Cleveland , 1998—2000, Miss. Valley State U., 1998—2000; prin., owner Geneva Real Estate LLC, Colorado Springs, 2002—; adv. bd. Christian Women's News , Colorado Springs, 2002—. Author: Deception's Guard, 2002; editor: Christian Women's News, 2002—. Victim adv. Vol. of Am. Battered Women's Shelter, Denver, 1990—91; tchr. Minot Adult Literacy Vol.s, Minot, ND, 1996—98; vol. Domestic Violence Crisis Ctr., Inc., 1996—98, Companion for Children, Minot, 1995—96; vol. mil. case worker ARC, Minot Air Force Base, 1996—97; organizer local outreach ministries Woodland Pk. Christian Ch., Woodland Pk., Colo., 2001. Decorated Air Medal US Air Force; recipient Citation of Honor, The Nat. Fedn. of Bus. & Profl. Women's Clubs, Inc., 1995. Mem.: Civil Air Patrol, Internat. Assn. of Women Pilots, Aircraft Owners & Pilot Assn., Colo. Mountain Club, Sierra Club. Avocations: aviation, travel, writing, hiking, community service.

RANDOLPH, JENNINGS, JR. (JAY RANDOLPH), sportscaster; b. Cumberland, Md., Sept. 19, 1934; s. Jennings and Mary Katherine (Babb) R.; m. Sue Henderson, May 28, 1966; children: Jennings, Brian Robert, Rebecca Sue. BA, Salem (W.Va.) Coll., 1963. Sports and promotion dir. Sta. WHAR, Clarksburg, W.Va., 1958-61; sportscaster Sta. KLIF, Dallas, 1963-66; Sta. KMOX, St. Louis, 1966-68; with Sta. KSDK-TV, 1968—, sports dir., 1968-88, spl. sports corr., 1988—, also on nationally televised broadcasts for various sports events including Sr. PGA tour; TV announcer Fla. Marlins Baseball Club, Ft. Lauderdale, 1993—2002. Interviewer analyst sr. PGA Tour CNBC; broadcaster coll. basketball ESPN regional TV; TV announcer St. Louis Cardinals, 1970-87, Cin. Reds., 1988; mem. NBC's broadcast staff for 1988 Olympics, Seoul, Korea and 1992 Summer Games, Barcelona, Spain; host nationally syndicated The Golf Show. Trustee Salem Coll., 1976-89. With U.S. Army, 1954-56. Inducted into Boys and Girls Clubs of Am. Hall of Fame, 1990 Mem. Nat. Assn. Sportscasters, Delta Tau Delta. Achievements include being an amateur golf champion. Home: 12021 Charter Oakpky Saint Louis MO 63146

RANDOLPH, JESSE See CASTILE, RAND

RANDOLPH, JUDSON GRAVES, pediatric surgeon; b. Macon, Ga., July 19, 1927; s. Milton Fitz and Abigail Theresa (Graves) R.; m. Susan Comfort Adams, June 14, 1952; children: Somers, Garrett, Judson, Adam, Comfort. BA, Vanderbilt U., 1950, MD, 1953. Intern in surgery U. Rochester, N.Y., 1953-54; asst. resident in pathology Vanderbilt U., 1954-55; asst. resident, then sr. resident in surgery Mass. Gen. Hosp., Boston, 1956-58; asst. resident in surgery Children's Hosp., 1955-56, sr. resident, then chief resident, 1958-61, asst. surgeon, 1961-63; teaching fellow to instr. surgery Med. Sch. Harvard U., 1960-63; jr. assoc. in surgery Peter Bent Brigham Hosp., Boston, 1961-63; surgeon-in-chief Children's Hosp., Washington, 1964-91; mem. faculty Med. Sch. George Washington U., 1964-91, prof. surgery and child health, 1968-91; prof. surgery Meharry Med. Coll., 1992-96. Cons. Nat. Naval Med. Ctr., NIH, Walter Reed Army Med. Ctr.; trustee Vanderbilt U., 1980—. Editor: Pediatric Surgery, 3d edit., 2 vols., 1979, 4th edit., 2 vols., 1985, The Injured Child, 1980; mem. editl. bd. Surgery, 1978-92; contbr. numerous articles to med. jours. With USNR, 1945-46, PTO. Mem. ACS (gov. 1969-75), AMA, Am. Acad. Pediats. (chmn. exec. com. surg. sect. 1974-75), Am. Assn. Thoracic Surgery, Am. Pediat. Surg. Assn. (gov. 1980—, pres. 1984), Washington Acad. Surgery (pres. 1989), Soc. U. Surgeons, Am. Surg. Assn., So. Surg. Assn., Am. Bd. Surgery (bd. dirs. 1973-79, diplomate), Alpha Omega Alpha (faculty), Cosmos Club (Washington), Belle Meade Club. Methodist.

RANDOLPH, KEVIN HOWARD, marketing executive; b. Seattle, July 6, 1949; s. Howard Amos and Betty Elaine (Leahy) R.; children: Heather, Lyndsay. BA, Wash. State U., 1972. Mgr. Computers for Mktg., L.A., 1972-74; data processing mgr. Parker Rsch., Pasadena, Calif., 1974-77; prin. Randolph & Assocs., L.A., 1977-79; v.p. Bank Am. Corp., San Francisco, 1979-87, Interactive Network, Mountain View, Calif., 1987-91; sr. v.p. ICTV, Santa Clara, 1991-93; pres. Randolphs.Com, Ephrata, Pa., 1993—; v.p. U.S. West Mrg., Inc., Benicia, Calif., 1993-94; exec. v.p., COO Interactive Video Enterprises, Inc., San Ramon, 1994-95; founder, pres., CEO Asia Online, Ltd., Hong Kong, 1999-2000. Cons. Randolph Home Ctr., Ephrata, Wash., 1972—. Mem. Am. Mktg. Assn., Am. Mgmt. Assn. Home: 309 3rd Ave SE Ephrata WA 98823 E-mail: kevin@randolphs.com.

RANDOLPH, LEONARD MCELROY, JR. career officer; b. Washington, Sept. 22, 1943; s. Leonard McElRoy and Jessie Marshall (Stockton) R.; m. Linda Fleming Raney, Aug. 1, 1987; children: Nathaniel Randolph, Brion Randolph, Holly Muterspaw-Randolph, Chad Muterspaw, Judd Muterspaw. *Wife, Linda F. Randolph, is a noted interior designer, having contributed to the enhancement of numerous USAF installations. She has led Officer's Wives Clubs and initiated spouse groups across the country. Her development of children's play groups at USAF bases has provided a much appreciated outlet for social and child development programs that include all ranks. Son, Brion V. Randolph, is a graduate of University of Tennessee, BS 1994, MS 1996; Chad R. Muterspaw was a football star at University of Dayton (Ohio) and graduated BEd, 1998; Judd A. Muterspaw is an employee of Greene County, Ohio; Nathaniel D. Randolph resides at home and is in fourth grade. Daughter, Holly E. Muterspaw-Randolph, is a college sophomore at Palm Beach Atlantic College in Florida.* BS in Biology, Marietta (Ohio) Coll., 1965; MS in Microbiology, Howard U., Washington, 1967; MD, Meharry Med. Coll., Nashville, 1972. Diplomate Am. Bd. Surgery, Am. Bd. Med. Mgmt., Am. Coll. Physician Execs.; cert. physician exec. Grad. tchg. asst. Howard U., Washington, 1966-67; rsch. microbiologist Georgetown U., 1966-67; chemistry tchr. Ballou H.S., 1967-68; Commd. 2d lt. USAF, 1972, advanced through grades to maj. gen., 1998, intern Miss., 1972-73, resident, 1973-77, gen. surgeon Bergstrom AFB, Tex., 1977-78, chief gen. surgery, 1978-80, chief surg. svcs., 1980-83, attending surgeon Wright-Patterson AFB, Ohio, 1983-84, dir. med. edn., 1984-85, chief med. officer Minot AFB, N.D., 1985-86, hosp. cmdr. George AFB, Calif., 1988-90, dep. command surgeon HQ Tactical Air Command Langley AFB, Va., 1990-91, forward command surgeon Desert Storm Riyahd, Saudi Arabia, 1990-91, med. ctr. comdr. Travis AFB, Calif., 1994-97; asst. prof. surgery Wright State U. Sch. Medicine, Dayton, Ohio, 1983-88; command surgeon U.S. Ctrl. Command, MacDill AFB, Fla., 1991-94, U.S. Transp. Command and Air Mobility Command, Scott AFB, Ill., 1997-99. Lead agt. DOD Health Svc. Region 10, 1994-97; spec. asst. to USAF Surg. Gen., 1999, dep. surgeon gen., 1999-2001; dep. exec. dir. Tricare Mgmt. Activity, Office of Under Sec. Def., Washington, 2001—; assoc. prof. surgery U. Calif. Dvis Sch. Medicine, 1995-97; assoc. prof. mil. medicine and surgery Uniformed Svcs. U. of Health Scis., 1995—. Contbr. emergency medicine Uniformed Svcs. U. of Health Scis., 1995—. Contbr. articles to profl. jours. Bd. trustees Marietta Coll., 2001—. Decorated Def. Superior Svc. medal for Operation Restore Hope, Legion of Merit Operation Desert Storm; selected for Boys State (Georgetown U.); escort for Pres. Dwight D. Eisenhower (Nat. Christmas Tree lighting, laying of wreath at tomb of Unknown Soldier); pres. Student Nat. Med. Assn., 1971-72; named Disting. Alumni of Yr., Nat. Assn. for Equal Opportunity in Higher Edn., 1999. Fellow ACS (bd. govs. 1996—), Am. Coll. Physician Execs. (disting. pres. 2000-2001), Am. Acad. Med. Adminstrs. (hon.); mem. Soc. Air Force Clin. Surgeons (bd. govs. 1996—), Assn. Mil. Surgeons of the U.S., Air Force Assn. (life), Christian Med. Assn., Aerospace Med. Assn., Alpha Omega Alpha, Beta Kappa Chi, Beta Beta Beta. Avocations: reading, lecturing, sports, writing. Office: Tricare Mgmt Activity Skyline 5 Ste 810 5111 Leesburg Pike Falls Church VA 22041-3206 Fax: 703-681-3665. E-mail: caprand@aol.com., randy.randolph@tma.osd.mil.

RANDOLPH, PAUL S. writer; s. Robert E. and Valeda Randolph; m. Elizabeth A. Van Cleve, Apr. 21, 1960; children: Paul T., Stewart N., Dean M. BS, U. Calif., Berkeley, 1984. Med. writer Otsuka Am. Pharm., Rockville, Md., 1996—2000; sr. med. writer Berlex Labs., Richmond, Calif., 2000—. Mem.: Drug Info. Assn. Conservative. Mem. Lds Ch. Avocations: soccer, motorcycling, Japanese culture. Office: Berlex Labs 2600 Hilldop Dr Richmond CA 94806

RANDOLPH, PENELOPE FRANCES, artist, educator; b. Salem, Mass., Jan. 28, 1965; d. Evan IV and Penelope Howland (Dixon) R.; m. Thomas Aldren Dingman Watson, July 22, 1995. BA in Visual and Environ. Studies, Harvard U., 1988, MEd in Art and Tech. in Edn., 1996. Prin. Randolph Design, Truro, Mass., 1990—; tutor Harvard U., Cambridge, 1990-97. Mem. vis. com. for arts Groton Sch., 1997—, St. Botolph Arts Found., 1997—. Bd. dirs. The Humanity Found., Tisbury, Mass., 1994-96. Grantee AAUW, Washington, 1994, Contemporary Artists' Ctr., North Adams, Mass., 1996, Mass. Cultural Coun., Boston, 1997; recipient Ann. Excellence award Print Mag., 1999. Fellow Women's Caucus for Art; mem. North Woods Club, St. Botolph Club (artist mem., Annual Artist award 1993). Avocations: fishing, running. Home: 45 Depot Rd PO Box 1004 Truro MA 02666-1004 E-mail: francie@wn.net.

RANDOLPH, ROBERT DEWITT, lawyer; b. Sligo, Pa., Mar. 6, 1929; s. DeWitt Lyman and Hazel Irene (McCall) R.; m. Betty Ann McElhattan, May 8, 1953 (dec. Aug. 1979); children: Douglas, Andrew; m. Susan Denise Hopkins, Oct. 15, 1988 BA, Westminster Coll., 1951; LLB, Harvard U., 1957. Bar: Ohio 1958, Pa. 1960, U.S. Supreme Ct. 1981. Assoc. Buckingham, Doolittle & Burroughs, Akron, Ohio, 1957-59, Rose, Houston, Cooper & Schmidt, Pitts., 1959-60, 61-65; fgn. svc. officer U.S. Dept. State, Washington, 1960-61; ptnr. Houston, Cooper, Speer & German, Pitts., 1965-70, Randolph & O'Connor, Pitts., 1970-74, Buchanan Ingersoll P.C., Pitts., 1974-93. Pres. Assn. Retarded Citizens Allegheny, Pitts., 1990-92. With U.S. Army, 1951-54. U.S. Army, 1951—54. Mem. Duquesne Club, St. Clair Country Club. Democrat. Presbyterian. Avocations: golf, skiing. Home: 750 Washington Rd Pittsburgh PA 15228-2051

RANDOLPH, ROBERT LEE, economist, educator; b. East St. Louis, Ill., Jan. 2, 1926; s. John Andrew and Willye (Smith) R.; m. Patricia Smith, June 13, 1954 (div. 1986); 1 dau., Heather Elizabeth. AB, DePauw U., Greencastle, Ind., 1948; MS, U. Ill., Urbana, 1954, PhD, 1958; postdoctoral student, Case Western Res. U., 1960, U. Mich., 1962. From instr. to assoc. prof. econs. Springfield (Mass.) Coll., 1958-65, chmn. dept., 1960-63, dir. eve. and summer schs., 1960-64; dep. exec. dir. Equal Employment Opportunity Commn., Washington, 1967-68; dep. assoc. dir. Job Corps, 1965-67; exec. v.p. Chgo. State U., 1969-73; pres. Westfield (Mass.) Coll., 1973-79; vice-chancellor Mass. State Coll. System, 1979-81; pres. Ala. State U., 1981-83; prof. econs. U. Montevallo, Ala., 1983-86; pres. Randolph Assocs., Birmingham, Ala., Boston, 1983-91, Hyannis, Mass., 1991—, State C.C., East St. Louis, Ill., 1993-95. Mem. Cape Cod Commn., Barnstable, Mass., 1996—; cons. to industry. Author articles, monographs. Vice pres. Springfield Urban League, 1962-66; bd. dirs. Wesson Hosp., Springfield, Holyoke (Mass.) Hosp., Sickle-Cell Anemia Found.; mem. Cape Cod Commn., 1996—. Served to lt. (j.g.) USNR, 1943-45, 50-51. Decorated Bronze Star; recipient Danforth Found. award, 1943; Republic Steel Found. award, 1961; Vice Pres.'s award excellence pub. service U.S. Govt., 1967; Outstanding Alumni award Lincoln High Sch., E. St. Louis, 1973, Alumni Svc. award U. Ill., 1990, DePauw U., 1991; Navy V-12 scholar, 1943-45; State of Ill. scholar, 1952-56; Bailey fellow, 1957-58, Carnegie fellow, 1962. Mem. Am. Assn. State Colls. and Univs. (chmn. personnel com. 1974-75), Am. Assn. Polit. and Social Scis., Am. Econ. Assn., Phi Delta Kappa, Alpha Phi Omega, Kappa Alpha Psi. Clubs: Quandrangle (Chgo.), Internat. (Washington), Cape (Cape Cod). Home: 101 John Joseph Rd Harwich MA 02645-2822 Office: 3225 Main St Barnstable MA 02630-1105

RANDOLPH, SOMERS, sculptor; b. Boston, May 25, 1956; s. Judson Graves and Susan Comfort (Adams) R.; m. Hillary Allen Fitzpatrick, Oct. 8, 2000. BA, Princeton U., 1979. Mem. adv. bd. Nashville African Am. Art Assn., 1994—; pres. bd. dirs. Visual Arts Assn. Nashville, 1995-96. Creating sculptures in stone for more than 20 yrs. Mem. Leadership Nashville, 1996—. Recipient Gov.'s award for Cmty. Svc., State of Calif., 1990. Mem. Nat. Sculpture Assn. Home: 1889 Conejo Dr Santa Fe NM 87505 Studio: 1889 Conejo Dr Santa Fe NM 87505-6114

RANDOLPH, STEVEN, retirement investment specialist; b. Nebr., Oct. 14, 1946; m. Sherri Hamrick, 1980 (div. 1989); children: David, John, Michelle; m. Kathleen Riley, 1991. BS, U. Nebr., 1971. Registered rep. Nat. Assn. Securities Dealers, SEC; lic. in variable annuities, ins. and disabilities. Rep. Real Estate Consulting Svcs., Inc., Newport Beach, Calif., 1971-86; fin. advisor Agy. Fin. Svcs., 1986—. With USMC, 1964-68, Vietnam. Mem. Nat. Assn. Securities Dealers, Nat. Assn. Life Underwriters (Nat. Sales Achievement award, Nat. Quality award), Million Dollar Round Table Club, Pres.'s Club (awards). Avocations: cooking, travel, watersports, sports cars. Home and Office: PO Box 9612 Newport Beach CA 92658-9612 Fax: (949) 768-2000.

RANDS, ROBERT LAWRENCE, archaeologist; b. Washington, May 13, 1922; s. John and Una Alice (Clingan) R.; m. Barbara Rathbone Cornett, Aug. 1948 (div. 1977); 1 child, Gordon Phillips; m. Elizabeth Lowry Vaughan, May 26, 1977 (dec. Oct. 18, 1990). BA in Anthropology, U. N.Mex., 1949; MA in Anthropology, U. Calif., L.A., 1949; PhD in Anthropology, Columbia U., 1952. Asst. prof. to prof. U. Miss., University, 1952-63; prof., asst. dir. rsch. lab. anthropology U. N.C., Chapel Hill, 1963-66; prof., curator Mesoamerican archaeology So. Ill. U., Carbondale, 1966-91; rsch. prof. So. Ill. U., Ctr. Archeol. Investigations, 1993—. Rsch. assoc. Univ. Mus., U. Pa., Phila., 1960-82; vis. scholar Dumbarton Oaks, Washington, 1975; rsch. collaborator Smithsonian Instn. Ctr. Materials Rsch. & Edn., Washington, 1987-93, 95-2000, Brookhaven Nat. Lab. Dept. of Chemistry, Upton, 1974-77, 80-83; ceremicist Proyecto de las Cruces Palenque Pre-Columbian Art Rsch. Inst., San Francisco, 1997-98. Co-editor: Man Across The Sea, 1971; co-author: Maya Sculpture, 1972. Fellow John Simon Guggenheim Found., 1956; grantee Inst. Andean Rsch., 1951, 59, Am. Philos. Soc., 1959, NSF, 1963, 67, 70, 75, Found. Advancement Mesoamerican Studies, 1998. Mem.: AAAS, Archeol. Inst. Am., Am. Anthrop. Assn., Soc. Am. Archaeology (Excellence in Ceramic Studies award 1998), Sigma Xi. Achievements include research in ceramic technology as a means of investigating trade and interaction in ancient Maya society; major archaeological expeditions Chiapas and Tabasco, Mexico. Home: 27898 Old Village Rd Mechanicsville MD 20659-4286

RANDZA, JASON MICHAEL, engineer; b. Ellwood City, Pa., June 18, 1963; s. Frank Anthony and Jean Ann (Tracy) R. BS in Aerospace Engring., Pa. State U., 1985; postgrad., Camp Cmty. Coll. Cert. pvt. pilot. Engr. Atlantic Rsch. Corp., Gainesville, Va., 1985-90; control rm. operator Hadson Power #11, Franklin, 1991; tng. coord. LG&E Westmoreland Southampton, 1991-96, plant engr., 1996-97, team leader, 1997—; process engr. SONY Electronics, Mt. Pleasant, Pa., 1997—. Mem. AIAA, Nat. Assn. Rocketry, Pa. State U. Alumni Assn., Tripoli Rocketry Assn., Am. Kitefliers Assn., U.S. Hang Gliding Assn., Tau Beta Pi, Sigma Gamma Tau. Republican. Roman Catholic. Avocations: rocketry, paragliding, kite flying, weight training, aerobics. Home: 152 Horse Shoe Bend Rd Acme PA 15610-1232 E-mail: Jason_Randza@am.sony.com.

RANEY, JEAN PUCKETT, art gallery director, artist; b. San Juan, P.R., May 11, 1954; d. Ralph Puckett and Jean Martha Martin; m. Dixon Flanary Raney, Sept. 11, 1982; children: Lauren Flanary, Dixon Flanary, Jr. BA in Polit. Sci., U. Ga., 1976. Cert.: Nat. Ctr. for Paralegal Tng. (legal asst.). Legal asst. Webb, Carlock, Atlanta, 1978—86; owner Wedding Wand, 1984—94, Jean Raney Studios, Atlanta, 1992—. Art instr. Jean Raney Studio, Atlanta, 1995—; tchr. art appreciation Austin Elem., Dunwoody, Ga., 1997—99; judge DeKalb County State of Ga. Reflections Contests, Atlanta, 1998, Atlanta, 99. Author: Paralegal Training Manual, 1980, Training and Procedures Manual for DFAA Gallery, 1995; co-author: Art Appreciation for Elementary Schools, 1996. Fundraiser United Way Atlanta, 1981; spl. events chair, fundraiser Ga. Trust for Hist. Preservation, 1979—81; mem., chair coms. Jr. League Atlanta, 1982—; PTA pres., bd. dirs. Austin Elem. Sch., Dunwoody, 1991—99; Egleston Hosp. creator and chmn. Downton Night "Mingle, Jingle & Jazz" Egleston Hosp. Festival Trees, 1979—86; mem. young careers and membership dr. High Mus. Art, Atlanta, 1978—81; co-chmn, mem. Dunwoody Twigs, 1989; mem. social com. Wyntercreek Neighborhood1989, 1989—90; Sunday Sch tchr. 5th and 6th grades St. Luke's Presbyn. Ch., Dunwoody, 1991—93; bd. dirs. Neighbors of Wyntercreek, 1999—2001. Named Selected Artist, So. Living Idea House, 2000, Featured Artist, Wesleyan Sch., 2001. Mem.: Ga. Assn. Legal Assts. (newsletter chmn., bd. dirs.), PACESETTERS (bd. dirs., sec., spl. events chmn.), Dunwoody Fine Arts Assn. (bd. dirs., vol., gallery dir. 1995—98), Wesleyan Arts Alliance (artist market chair 1999—), Colonial Dames. Methodist. Avocations: painting in Italy, skiing, reading, studying languages, camping. Office: Jean Raney Studios 5247 Wyntercreek Ct Atlanta GA 30338

RANEY, MIRIAM DAY, actress; b. Florence, S.C., Sept. 30, 1922; d. Lewie Griffith and Iola Lewis (Edwards) Day; m. Robert William Raney, Mar. 31, 1946 (div. Sept. 1976); children: Robert William Jr., Miriam, Kevin Paige, Megan. *Great-great-great grandfather, William Lewis of Horry County, South Carolina, ran supplies in his sloops, the Rattlesnake and the Scorpion, to Colonel, later Brigadier General, Francis Marion, during the Revolutionary War. Great-great-great grandfather, Richard Edwards, formerly of Virginia, fought under General Washington at Valley Forge during the Revolutionary War. He received a head wound and had gold trepanned into his skull. From then on, he was known as "Gold Dick" Edwards. After mustering out, he settled in the South Carolina Low Country. Grandsons of both fought for the Confederacy in the Civil War.* BSM in Voice, Music Edn., U. N.C., Greensboro, 1939-43; student, Julliard Sch. Music, 1942-43; BA in Music History and Lit., U. Ark., Little Rock, 1978-81; cert., Adam Roarke Film Actors Lab., Irving, Tex., 1989. Singing chorus N.Y.C. Ctr. Opera Co., 1943-44; understudy, singing chorus Oklahoma, Theater Guild, N.Y.C., 1944-45; ingenue lead Connecticut Yankee, Geosan Subway Cir., 1945; understudy, singing chorus Up In Central Park, Michael Todd, 1945-46. Beauty cons. Mary Kay Cosmetics, Inc., Dallas, 1993-98. Author: slide sound synchronized show Ark. Women in Music, 1982; composer, lyricist: The Bend and the Willow, 1982, Ballad of Petit Jean, 1983; stage appearances include Hedda Gabler (Reponde de Capite repertory), 1990, Time of Your Life (Cmty. Theatre of Little Rock), 1991, Our Town, 1991, Evening with Women II (Regional Theatre of Ctrl. Ark.), 1991; appeared in TV program Unsolved Mysteries, 1988; film Killing Time with Aunt Olene, 1988; also commercials tng. films, 1987-99; print model, Little Rock, Memphis, Ft. Worth, 1988-98. Named Illustrious Alumna, U. N.C. at Greensboro, 1945; recipient Thanks Badge Oachita Coun. Girl Scouts U.S., Little Rock, 1965. Mem. AAUW (Little Rock br. legis. com. 1973-79, program com. 1973-79, cultural interest rep. 1975-77, 96-98, state rep. for cultural interests 1976-78), Mus. Coterie, Cen. Ark. Guild of Organists (pres. student chpt. 1977-80). Democrat. Avocations: walking, birding, gardening, reading, movies. Home: 25 Valley Forge Dr Little Rock AR 72212-2613

RANGEL, CHARLES BERNARD, congressman; b. Harlem, N.Y., June 11, 1930; s. Ralph and Blanche (Wharton) R.; m. Alma Carter, July 26, 1964; children: Steven, Alicia. BS, NYU, 1957; JD, St. John's U. Sch. Law, 1960; LLD (hon.), Wagner Coll., 1982, Atlanta U., 1983, St. John's U., Mt. Sinai Sch. Medicine, NYU, Howard U., 1988, Hofstra U., 1989. Bar: N.Y. 1960. Asst. U.S. atty., So. Dist. N.Y., 1961-62; mem. N.Y. State Assembly, 1966-70, U.S. Congress from 15th N.Y. dist., Washington, 1971—. Ranking mem. ways and means com., subcom. on trade; mem. joint com. on taxation.; dep. Dem. whip Served with AUS, 1948-52, Korea. Decorated Bronze Star, Purple Heart (U.S.); Korean presdl. citations. Home: 40 W 135th St New York NY 10037-2504 Office: US Ho of Reps 2354 Rayburn Ho Office Bldg Washington DC 20515-0001

RANGEL, ROGER HENRIQUE, mechanical and aerospace engineering educator; b. Caracas, Venezuela, Apr. 15, 1958; came to U.S., 1981; s. Henrique Tulio Rangel and Bettina Bianchi. BS in Mech. Engring., Simon Bolivar U., Caracas, 1981; MS, U. Calif., Berkeley, 1983, PhD, 1985. Rsch. asst. U. Calif., Berkeley, 1982-85, asst. specialist Irvine, 1985-87, lectr. mech. engring., 1987-89, asst. rschr., 1987-89, asst. prof. mech. engring., 1989-93, assoc. prof. mech. engring., 1993-97, prof., 1997—. Sect. head (fluid/thermal) dept. mech. and aerospace engring., U. Calif., Irvine, 1993-99, undergrad. advisor 1994-98; cons., 1987—; vis. prof. U. Barcelona, Spain, 1999, 2000; engring. coord. Calif.-Catalonia Program, 1998—. Contbr. over 100 articles to profl. jours., confs., chpts. to books, including Internat. Jour. Heat and Mass Transfer, Combustion and Flame, and many others. Recipient internat. fellowship Italian Rsch. Coun., Naples, 1991, Generalitat of Catalonia, Spain, 1998, 99, grad. fellowship OAS, Berkeley, 1985; Arthur Gould Tasheira fellow, Berkeley, 1983. Mem. ASME (sr.), AIAA (Best Paper award in Microgravity and Space Processing 1999), Combustion Inst. Achievements include advanced fundamental understanding of droplet and spray systems for combustion and advanced materials applications. Office: Univ Calif Eg 4200 Irvine CA 92697-0001

RANGEL-RIBEIRO, VICTOR, writer; b. Porvorim, India, Oct. 3, 1925; s. Oscar and Maria Pulqueria Rangel-Ribeiro; m. Lea Vaz Rangel-Ribeiro, Sept. 18, 1954; children: Eva Maria, Eric Dev. BA, Bombay U., 1945; MA, Tchrs. Coll., N.Y.C., 1982. Asst. editor Nationan and Sunday Std., Bombay, 1949—53; lit. and Sunday editor Times of India, Bombay and Calcutta, 1953—54; copy chief J. Walter Thompson, Bombay, 1954—56; stringer music dept. NY Times, N.Y.C., 1956—59; copy chief Schoonover Advt., 1960—64; owner Orpheus Music Shop, 1964—73; music dir. Beethoven Soc. NY, 1978—79; tchr. various schs. and orgns., 1980—91; self-employed writer, 1991—. Freelance editor Free Press and other pubs., N.Y.C., 1981—91. Author: Baroque Music: Practical Guide, 1981, Tivolem, 1998 (Milkweed award, 98); co-author: Chamber Music, 1991. Vol. Vista program Lit. Vols. N.Y.C., 1982. Fellow, NY Found Arts, N.Y.C., 1991. Mem.: Mensa. Avocations: watercolor painting, photography, music. Home: 17228 83d Ave Jamaica NY 11432-2104

RANGNEKAR, VIVEK MANGESH, molecular biologist, researcher; b. Bombay, Dec. 17, 1955; s. Mangesh Vithal and Sanjivani (Dewoolkar) R.; m. Vidya Vivek Varsha Kulkarni, May 15, 1981; children: Vidyuta, Viraj. MSc, U. Bombay, 1979, PhD, 1983. Postdoctoral fellow U. Chgo., 1983-86; rsch. assoc. Rush Med. Ctr., Chgo., 1986-87; asst. prof. U. Chgo., 1988-91, U. Ky., Lexington, 1992-96, assoc. prof., 1996-99, prof., 1999—. Cons. NIH/NCI and Dept. of Def. Contbr. articles to profl. jours. including Jour. Biol. Chemistry , Nucleic Acids Rsch., Molecular Cell Biology, Nature Medicine, Cancer Research, Oncogene. Mem. AAAS, Am. Soc. Microbiology. Achievements include identification of Par-4 gene that causes cell death. Office: U Ky 800 Rose St Lexington KY 40536-0001

RANGREJ, RASHESH BIPINCHANDRA, hotel executive; b. Surat, Gujarat, India, May 7, 1958; s. Bipinchandra Nanabhai and Indiraben Bipinchandra Rangrej; m. Rashesh Rangrej Patel, June 26, 1978; children: Ira, Sheetal, Minaxi. BS in Chemistry, South Gujarat U., India, 1978; MBA, Inst. Psychotherapy and Mgmt. Scis., Mumbai, India, 2001; PhD in Fin. Mgmt., Staunton U., 2002; postgrad., U. Tex., 2002. Cert. hotel adminstrn., Microsoft certified sys. engr., cert. housekeeping mgmt., mktg. of hospitality svcs. Exec. dir. Rohit Jacquard Texturisers Pvt. Ltd., Surat, India, 1978—86; houskeeping tng. specialist Harrah's Casion, Atlantic City, 1989—92; gen. mgr. Super 8 Motel, San Antonio, 1995—, Microtel Inn & Suites, San Antonio, 1998—, Ganeshji, Inc, New Braunfels, 2001—, La Quinta Inn & Suites, New Braunfels, 2002—. Mgmt. adv. bd. mem. Super 8 Motels, Inc., Parsippany, NJ, 2002—. Author: (Book) Key To Success: Hospitality Empire, 2002. Named Outstanding Gen. Mgr. of Yr., Am. Hotel and Lodging Assn., 2001. Avocations: reading, computers, basketball, tennis, ping pong. Home: 3617 N Pan Am Expressway San Antonio TX 78219 Office: Super 8 Motel 3617 N Pan Am Expressway San Antonio TX 78219 Office Fax: 210-224-2092.

RANIERI, JOSEPH JOHN, English language educator; b. Jersey City, Jan. 2, 1943; s. Albert Joseph and Ann Stephanie R.; m. Nina Yurkina. BA, U. Notre Dame, 1965; MA, Columbia U., 1967. Cert. secondary sch. tchr. English and German, N.J.; cert. secondary sch. tchr. German, N.Y. Tchr. English and German Belleville (N.J.) Pub. Schs., 1967-68, Don Bosco H.S., Ramsey, N.J., 1968-69; substitute tchr. Jersey City (N.J.) Pub. Schs., 1969-76, tchr. H.S. English, 1976—. Mem. NEA, Nat. Coun. Tchrs. English, Am. Assn. Tchrs. German, N.J. Ednl. Assn., Jersey City Ednl. Assn., Hudson County Ednl. Assn., Secaucus Lions Club (pres. 1995—), Holy Name Soc. Roman Catholic. Avocations: opera, travel, sports. Office: Dickinson HS 2 Palisade Ave Jersey City NJ 07306-1202

RANIS, GUSTAV, economist, educator; b. Darmstadt, Germany, Oct. 24, 1929; s. Max and Bettina (Goldschmidt) R.; m. Ray Lee Finkelstein, June 15, 1958; children: Michael Bruce, Alan Jonathan, Bettina Suzanne BA summa cum laude, Brandeis U., 1952, hon. degree, 1982; MA, Yale U., 1953, PhD, 1956. Asst. adminstr. program and policy AID/Dept. of State, 1965-67; dir. Econ. Growth Ctr. Yale U., New Haven, 1967-75, prof. econs., 1964—, Frank Altschul prof. internat. econs., 1981—; dir. Yale Ctr. Internat. and Area Studies, 1996—. Ford Found. vis. prof. U. De Los Andes, Bogota, Colombia, 1976-77; Ford Found. vis. prof. Colegio de Mex., 1971-72; fellow Inst. for Advanced Study, Berlin, 1993-94; cons. World Bank, AID, Ford Found., ILO, FAO, Inter-Am. Devel. Bank. Author: (with John Fei) Development of the Labor Surplus Economy: Theory and Policy, 1964,; (with Fei and Shirley Kuo) Growth with Equity: The Taiwan Case, 1979; (with Keijiro Otsuka and Gary Saxonhouse) Comparative Technology Choice in Development, 1988; (with F. Stewart and E. Angeles-Reyes) Linkages in Developing Economies: A Philippine Study, 1990; (with S.A. Mahmood) Political Economy of Development Policy Change, 1992; (with John C. H. Fei) Growth and Development from an Evolutionary Perspective, 1997; editor: Taiwan: From Developing to Mature Economy, 1992, En Route to Modern Economic Growth: Latin America in the 1990s, 1994, Japan and the U.S. in the Developing World, 1997,; co-editor: The State of Development Economics, 1988, Science and Technology: Lessons for Development Policy, 1990; mem. editl. bd. Jour. of Internat. Devel., 1995—, Oxford Devel. Studies, 1996—. Trustee Brandeis U., 1967-93, chmn. acad. affairs com., 1986-93. Social Sci. Rsch. Coun. fellow, Japan, 1955-56. Mem. Am. Econ. Assn., Coun. Fgn. Rels., Overseas Develop. Coun. (mem. adv. com.). Home: 7 Mulberry Rd Woodbridge CT 06525-1716 Office: Yale Ctr Internat and Area Studies 34 Hillhouse Ave New Haven CT 06511-3704 E-mail: gustav.ranis@yale.edu.

RANK, EVERETT GEORGE, government official; b. Fresno, Calif., Dec. 1, 1921; s. Everett George and Evelyn Lydia (Dawson) R.; m. Evelyn Ingeborg Karschen, Apr. 30, 1948; children— Patricia, Judy, Ginny Student pub. sch., Clovis, Calif. Farmer, Fresno, 1946-81; chmn. Fresno County Agrl. Stblzn. and Conservation Service, 1959-69, Calif. Agrl. Stblzn. and Conservation Service, Berkeley, 1969-73; western regional dir. Agrl. Stblzn. and Conservation Service, Dept. Agr., Washington, 1974-76, adminstr., 1981-86. Pres. Clovis Unified Sch. Bd., 1959-72; bd. govs. U. Calif.-Fresno, 1977-81. Served with USN, 1941-45, PTO Mem. Masons (32 degree), Shriners. Republican. Baptist. Avocation: golf. Home: 11868 Old Friant Rd Fresno CA 93720-9701

RANK, LARRY GENE, retired banker; b. Auburn, Ind., July 14, 1935; s. Lloyd R. Rank and Elizabeth M. (Williamson) Jackson; m. Bette Whitehurst, May 2, 1959; children: Kevin, Karen Grad., Am. Inst. Banking, 1962, U. Balt., 1969, Grad. Sch. Banking, Brown U., 1975, Nat. Council Savs. Instns., 1985. Exec. v.p. Provident Bank Md., Balt., 1982-85, pres., chief operating officer, 1985-90, dir., 1984-90; mng. dir. Jannotta, Bray & Assocs. Inc., Balt., 1991-92; exec. dir. Big Bros. and Big Sisters Ctrl. Md. Inc., 1993-96. Assoc. cons. Drake, Beam, Morin, 1997-98. Bd. dirs. ARC, Ctrl. Md. chpt., 1984-98, chmn. bd., 1990-92, bd. dirs. Ctrl. Ariz. chpt., 1998—, nat. com. on nominations; bd. dirs. United Way of Ctrl. Md., Balt., 1990-92; chair Gov.'s Vol. Awards Selection com., 1989; chmn. Am. Heart Assn.-Heart Ball, 1989, bd. dirs. Am. Heart Assn.; chmn. bd. Neighborhood Housing Svcs.; bd. dirs. Goodwill Industries, 1989-98; vol. Valley Big Bros./Big Sisters, Phoenix; bd. dirs. N.W. Hosp. Ctr., 1985-98, chair sys. bd., 1997-98; bd. dirs. Big Bros./Big Sisters Ctrl. Md. Mem.: Villanova Club, Wildcat Club, Deacon Club Wake Forest. Lutheran. Avocations: golf, sports, books, travel. Fax: (480) 753-9437. E-mail: rank37@msn.com.

RANKAITIS, SUSAN, artist; b. Cambridge, Mass., Sept. 10, 1949; d. Alfred Edward and Isabel (Shimkus) Rankaitis; m. Robbert Flick, June 5, 1976 BFA in Painting, U. Ill., 1971; MFA in Visual Arts, U. So. Calif., 1977. Rsch. asst., art dir. Plato Lab., U. Ill., Urbana, 1971-75; art instr. Orange Coast Coll., Costa Mesa, Calif., 1977-83; chair dept. art Chapman Coll., Orange, 1983-90; Fletcher Jones chair in art Scripps Coll., Claremont, 1990—. Represented by Robert Mann Gallery, N.Y.C.; overview panelist visual arts Nat. Endowment for Arts, 1983, 84; selector Bingham Ednl. Trust, 1997-2002. One-woman shows include Los Angeles County Mus. Art, 1983, Internat. Mus. Photography, George Eastman House, 1983, Gallery Min. Tokyo, 1988, Ruth Bloom Gallery, Santa Monica, 1989, 90, 92, Schneider Mus., Portland, Ore., 1990; Ctr. for Creative Photography, 1991, Robert Mann Gallery, N.Y.C., 1994, 97, Mus. Contemporary Photography, Chgo., 1994, Mus. of Photographic Arts, 2000; represented in permanent collections MOCA, L.A., U. N.Mex. Art, Ctr. for Creative Photography, Mus. Contemporary Photography, Chgo., Santa Barbara Mus. Art, Los Angeles County Mus. Art, Mpls. Inst. Arts, San Francisco Mus. Modern Art, Art Inst. Chgo., Mus. Modern Art, Lodz, Poland, Princeton U. Art Mus., Stanford U. Art Mus., Contemporary Art Mus., Honolulu, Mus. Contemporary Photography, Art Inst. Chgo., others. Active art auction Venice Family Clinic, 1980—. Recipient Graves award in Humanities, 1985; Nat. Endowment for Arts fellow, 1980, 88, U.S./France fellow, 1989, Agnes Bourne fellow in painting and photography Djerassi Found., 1989; Durfee Chinese/Am. grantee, 2000-2001; City of L.A. Cultural Affairs grantee, 2001. Mem. Coll. Art Assn., Los Angeles County Mus. Art, Santa Monica Mus. Art. Studio: Studio 5 1403 S Santa Fe Ave Los Angeles CA 90021-2500 Home: 3117 N Lansbury Ave Claremont CA 91711-4146 E-mail: srankait@scrippscollege.edu.

RANKIN, ALFRED MARSHALL, JR. business executive; b. Cleve., Oct. 8, 1941; s. Alfred Marshall and Clara Louise (Taplin) R.; m. Victoire Conley Griffin, June 3, 1967; children: Helen P., Clara T. BA in Econs. magna cum laude, Yale U., 1963, JD, 1966. Mgmt. cons. McKinsey & Co., Inc., Cleve., 1970-73; with Eaton Corp., 1974-81, pres. materials handling group, 1981-83, pres. indsl. group, 1984-86, exec. v.p., 1986, vice chmn., chief oper. officer, 1986-89; pres., COO NACCO Industries, Inc., 1989-91, pres., CEO, 1991-94, also bd. dirs., chmn., pres., CEO, 1994—; bd. dirs. The Goodrich Co., Vanguard Group. Bd. dirs. B.F. Goodrich Co., Vanguard Group. Former pres., trustee Hathaway Brown Sch.; trustee Univ. Hosps. Cleve., Mus. Arts Assn., Univ. Circle, Inc., Cleve. Mus. Art, John Huntington Art Trust, Cleve. Tomorrow; past chairperson The Cleve. Found. Mem. Ohio Bar Assn. Clubs: Chagrin Valley Hunt, Union, Tavern, Pepper Pike, Kirtland Country (Cleve.); Rolling Rock (Ligonier, Pa.); Met. (Washington). Republican. Office: NACCO Industries Inc 5875 Landerbrook Dr Ste 300 Mayfield Heights OH 44124

RANKIN, ARTHUR DAVID, retired paper company executive; b. Bklyn., July 5, 1936; s. David Emerson and Elizabeth Howe (Smart) R.; m. Judith Ann Clark, Sept. 6, 1958; children: Debi Lynn Murlowski, Kristen Lori. BSChemE, 5-Yr. Cert. Pulp and Paper, MS in Pulp and Paper, U. Maine, Orono, 1960. Tech. svc. engr. Mead Corp., Chillicothe, Ohio, 1960-65; product engr. Jones div. Beloit Corp., Dalton, Mass., 1965-69; tech. asst. paper supt. Crown Zellerbach St. Francisville, La., 1969-71; stock prep. supr. Crown Zellerbach, St. Francisville, 1971-74; paper machine supt. Appleton Coated LLC, Combined Locks, Wis., 1974-84, steps project coord., 1984-85, sr. paper machine supt., 1986-88, sr. prodn. assoc., 1988-90, edn. and mill planning mgr., 1991-95, tech. and devel. mgr. Coated Free Sheet divsn., 1995-97, tech. dir. Locks mill, 1998-2001; ret., 2001. Instr. video U. Wis., Stevens Point, 1988, 89. Officer Jaycees, Waverly, Ohio, 1960-63, Chillicothe, Ohio, 1963-65, Pittsfield, Mass., 1965-69; bd. dirs. acad. adv. coun. U. Minn. Paper Sci. Sch., Mpls., 1988—; bd. dirs. U. Minn. Paper, 1988—; acad. adv. coun. paper sci. U. Wis., Stevens Point, 1987—, bd. dirs., 1990—. Mem. ASTM, TAPPI (Harris O. Ware award 2001), Nat. Paper Indsl. Mgmt. Assn. (bd. dirs. 1988, pres. 1993, treas. 1994-2001, Del Boutin award 1995, Glen T. Renegar award 2001), North Ctrl. Paper Indsl. Mgmt. Assn. (bd. dirs. 1977—). Republican. Congregationalist. Avocations: reading, golf, YMCA fitness center, wine collecting and study. Home: 1408 S Lee St Appleton WI 54915-3824

RANKIN, CLYDE EVAN, III, lawyer; b. Phila., July 3, 1950; s. Clyde Evan, Jr. and Mary E. (Peluso) R.; m. Camille Cozzone, Aug. 24, 1997; A.B., Princeton U., 1972; J.D., Columbia U., 1975; postgrad. Hague Acad. Internat. Law, 1975. Bar: N.Y., N.J., D.C., U.S. Supreme Ct. Law clk. to judge U.S. Dist. Ct. So. Dist. N.Y., 1975-77; assoc. Debevoise, Plimpton, Lyons & Gates, N.Y.C., 1977-79; assoc. Coudert Bros., N.Y.C., 1979-83, ptnr., 1984—. Trustee The Rensselaerville (N.Y.) Inst., 1989—, Coun. on Fgn. Rels., 1996—. Stone scholar, 1974. Mem. ABA, Assn. of Bar of City of N.Y., N.Y. State Bar Assn., D.C. Bar Assn., N.J. Bar Assn. Roman Catholic. Club: Amateur Comedy (N.Y.C.). Contbr. article to legal jour. E-mail: rankinc@coudert.com. Office: Coudert Bros 1114 Ave of Americas New York NY 10036-7703

RANKIN, DAVID THERON, education administrator; b. New Orleans, July 7, 1953; s. Manly Whitfield and Dorothy Nadine Rankin; m. Sept. 7, 1991. MEd, Va. Commonwealth U., 1992. Tchr. history, social studies Bath County Pub. Schs., Hot Springs, Va., 1987-91; libr. Chesterfield (Va.) County Pub. Schs., 1992-97, instrnl. tech. specialist Libr. Media Svcs., 1997—2002, mgr. media svcs. and curriculum delivery, 2002—. Mem. ALA, AASL, Va. Ednl. Media Assn. Avocations: cave diving, horseback riding, bicycling, camping, hiking. Office: Chesterfield County Pub Schs 4003 Cogbill Rd Richmond VA 23234 Fax: 804-275-2873.

RANKIN, ERIC DREW, clinical social worker, educator; b. Brooklyn, New York City, NY, July 15, 1954; married. PhD, University of Chicago, Chicago, Illinois, 1981—85. Associate Professor & Section Chief WVU Department of Psychiatry, Morgantown, WV, 1994—2002, Assistant Professor, 1988—94. Fellow: Gerontological Society of America. Achievements include first to in the field of Alzheimer's rsch. Office: WVU Department of Psychiatry 930 Chestnut Ridge Road Morgantown WV 26506-9137 Office Fax: (304) 293-8724. Business E-Mail: erankin@wvu.edu.

RANKIN, GENE RAYMOND, lawyer; b. Madison, Wis., Sept. 29, 1940; s. Eugene Carleton and Mildred Florence (Blomster) R.; m. Katherine E. Hundt, Aug. 25, 1979; 1 child, Abigail Hundt. BS, U. Wis., 1966, MS in Planning, 1973, JD, 1980. Bar: Wis. 1980, U.S. Dist. Ct. (we. dist.) Wis. 1980, U.S. Ct. Appeals (7th cir.) 1992. Systems analyst U. Wis. Primate Research Ctr., Madison, 1967-72; planner Dane County Regional Planning Commn., 1973-79; pres. Mendota Rsch., 1978—; with Risser and Risser, Madison, 1980-89; dir. land regulation and records dept. Dane County, 1984-89; pvt. practice Wis., 1989—; dir. bd. examiners Wis. Supreme Ct., 1994—. Planning cons., Madison, 1973-77; guest lectr. land use, ethics and admiralty law Law Sch. U. Wis., 1982, 86, 93, 94, 95, 96, guest lectr. land econs. Planning Sch., 1973-81; guest lectr. various legal subjects U. Wis. Ext., 1988—. Author: Historic Preservation Law in Wisconsin, 1982; The First Bite at the Apple: State Supreme Court Takings Jurisprudence Antedating First English, 1990; (with others) Boundary Law in Wisconsin, 1991; contbr. articles to profl. jours. Bd. dirs. Madison Trust for Hist. Preservation, 1984-87, Madison Zoning Bd. Appeals, 1986-94, Dane County Humane Soc., 1988-90, Dane County Housing Devel. Corp., 1975-79; spl. counsel City of Fitchburg, 1983-84, Nat. Trust for Hist. Preservation, 1989-90, City of Shullsburg, 1990-98; gen. counsel Cat Fanciers' Assn. Midwestern Region, 1990-95, Hist. Madison, Inc., 1981—, Wis. Lead Region Hist. Trust, Inc., 1992—; mem. legis. coun. Spl. Com. on Condo. Issues, Madison, 1984-85; commr. and vice-chmn. Dane County Housing Authority, 1979-84; chmn. Wis. Chamber Orch. Bd., 1979-81; state chmn. McCarthy 1976 campaign, Madison, 1974-76. With USCGR, 1958-60. Fellow Nat. Endowment for the Arts and Humanities, 1972; Olympic finalist for Internat. 470 yachting competition, 1976. Mem. Am. Planning Assn., Urban Land Inst., Urban and Regional Info. Sys. Assn., Wis. Bar Assn. (bd. dirs., treas., founder environ. law sect.), Dane County Bar Assn., Coun. Bar Admission Adminstrs., U. Wis. Hoofers Sailing Club (vice commodore 1972), Meml. Union Club, U.S. Yacht Racing Union, Downtown Madison Rotary, Ixion. Avocations: sailing, racquet sports, music, skating, motorcycling. Home: 2818 Ridge Rd Madison WI 53705-5224 Office: 715 Tenney Bldg 110 E Main St Madison WI 53703-3395

RANKIN, GRAHAM M. educator, consultant; b. Detroit, Sept. 10, 1933; s. Paul T. and Dorothea (Callback) R.; m. Lois Clements, Dec. 16, 1955; children: Stuart James, Krista Lois. BS, Wayne State U., 1954, MEd, 1962; MA in Teaching Math., U. Detroit, 1967. Cons. on math. and sci. El Dorado County Schs., Placerville, Calif., 1971-82, assoc. supt., 1976-77; ind. contractor Kelsey, 1982-1984; tchr. Black Oak Mine Schs., Garden Valley, 1984-94. Corr. instr. U. Calif., Berkeley, 1969-96; instr. U. Calif. Ext., Davis, 1974-76, Cosumnes River Coll., Placerville, 1981—. Mem. El Dorado Commn. on Aging. With CIC, U.S. Army, 1956-58. Grantee NSF, 1966; fellow Gen. Telephone and Electronics, 1987. Mem. NEA, Sons in Retirement. Avocations: mechanics, travel, family. Home: 6181 Shoo Fly Rd Kelsey CA 95667-7423

RANKIN, HELEN CROSS, cattle rancher, guest ranch executive; b. Mojave, Calif; d. John Whisman and Cleo Rebecca (Tilley) Cross; m. Leroy Rankin, Jan. 4, 1936 (dec. 1954); children— Julia Jane, Patricia Helen Denvir, William John. A.B., Calif. State U.-Fresno, 1935. Owner, operator Rankin Cattle Ranch, Caliente, Calif., 1954— ; founder, pres. Rankin Ranch, Inc., Guest Ranch, 1965—; mem. sect. 15, U.S. Bur. Land Mgmt.; mem. U.S. Food and Agrl. Leaders Tour China, 1983, Australia and N.Z., 1985; dir. U.S. Bur. Land Mgmt. sect. 15. Pres., Children's Home Soc. Calif., 1945; mem. adv. bd. Camp Ronald McDonald. Recipient award Calif. Hist. Soc., 1983, Kern River Valley Hist. Soc., 1983. Mem. Am. Nat. Cattlemen's Assn., Calif. Cattlemen's Assn., Kern County Cattlemen's Assn., Kern County Cowbelles (pres. 1949, Cattlewoman of Yr. 1988), Calif. Cowbelles, Nat. Cowbelles, Bakersfield Country Club, Bakersfield Raquet Club. Republican. Baptist. Office: Rankin Ranch Caliente CA 93518

RANKIN, JACQUELINE ANNETTE, communications expert, educator; b. Omaha, May 19, 1925; d. Arthur C. and Virdie (Gillispie) R. BA, Calif. State U., L.A., 1964, MA, 1966; MS in Mgmt., Calif. State U., Fullerton, 1977; EdD, U. LaVerne, Calif., 1981. Tchr. Rowland H.S., La Habra, Calif., 1964-66, Lowell H.S., La Habra, 1966-69, Pomona (Calif.) H.S., 1969-75; program asst. Pomona Adult Sch., 1975-82; dir. Child Abuse Prevention Program, 1985-86; exec. dir. child abuse prevention Calif. Dept. Pub. Svc., 1985-87; instr. Ind. U., Purdue U., 1993; assoc. prof. speech Ball State U., Muncie, Ind., 1993-94; instr. No. Va. U., 1994—, trainer Loudoun campus, 1996. Faculty evening divsn. Mt. San Antonio C.C., 1966-72; asst. prof. speech Ball State U., Muncie, Ind., 1993; instr. No. Va. U., Alexandria, Annandale, Manassas, Woodbridge, 1995—; assoc. faculty dept. comm. and theatre, Ind. U., Purdue U., Indpls., 1993; trainer internat. convs., sales groups, staffs of hosps., others; spkr., writer, trainer, lectr., cons. in field. Columnist: Jackie's World, Topics Newspapers; author: Body Language: First Impressions, Body Language in Negotiations and Sales, Body Language in Love and Romance, Body Language of the Abused Child, 1999, Using body Language That Kids Trust, Ten Tips for Evaluating Body Language of the Abused Child; contbr. articles. Mem. Fairfax County Dem. Com.; mem. adv. coun., mem. nat. capital chpt. bd. dirs. ARC. Mem. Internat. Platform Assn., Pi Lambda Theta, Phi Delta Kappa. Home and Office: 7006 Elkton Dr Springfield VA 22152-3330 E-mail: jacki.rankin@verizon.net.

RANKIN, JAMES PATRICK, financial services company executive; b. Morris Plains, N.J., Jan. 25, 1957; s. Bernard James and Carol Joyce (Cooper) R.; m. Rebecca R. Samuel, May 11, 1989. BS, U. Calif., Davis, 1980; postgrad., U. Calif., Berkeley, 1981-83; MBA, Harvard U., 1986. Asst. v.p. Wells Fargo Bank, San Francisco, 1979-88; v.p. T. Rowe Price, L.A., 1988-93; v.p., chmn. oper. com. Founders Asset Mgmt., Denver, 1993-98; v.p. customer support FOLIOfn Investments, LLC, Vienna, 1999-2000; sr. mng. dir. product mgmt. EquiServe, Jersey City, 2000—. Mem. Harvard Bus. Sch. Club Boston. Avocations: skiing, cycling, travel. Office: EquiServe 150 Royal St Canton MA 02021 Home: Apt 7I 780 Boylston St Boston MA 02199-7807 E-mail: rankinjp@yahoo.com.

RANKIN, JAMES WINTON, lawyer; b. Norfolk, Va., Sept. 9, 1943; s. Winton Blair and Edith (Griffin) R.; m. Donna Lee Carpenter, June 25, 1966 (dec.); children— Thomas James, William Joseph, Elizabeth Jeanne; m. JoAnne Katherine Murray, Feb. 11, 1978. AB magna cum laude, Oberlin Coll., 1965; JD cum laude, U. Chgo., 1968. Bar: Ill. 1968, U.S. Dist. Ct. (no. dist.) Ill. 1969, U.S. Ct. Appeals (7th cir.) 1971, U.S. Ct. Appeals (5th cir.) 1979, U.S. Supreme Ct. 1975, Calif. 1986. Law clk. U.S. Dist. Ct. (no. dist.) Ill., 1968-69; assoc. Kirkland & Ellis, Chgo., 1969-73, ptnr., 1973—. Mem. ABA, Order of Coif, Mid-Am. Club, Univ. Club, Mich. Shores Club, Kenilworth Club, Ephriam Yacht Club. Presbyterian. Home: 633 Kenilworth Ave Kenilworth IL 60043-1070 Office: Kirkland & Ellis 200 E Randolph St Fl 54 Chicago IL 60601-6636

RANKIN, JASON RICHARD, customer service administrator; b. Morristown, Tenn., Jan. 26, 1972; s. Richard Wayne Rankin and Barbara Sue Kirk. AS in Bus., Walters' State C.C., Morristown, 1994; BS in MGmt., Carson-Newman Coll., Jefferson City, Tenn., 1997; MBA, U. Tenn., Chattanooga-Knoxville, 2000. Customer svc. rep. Philips Consumer Electronics, Jefferson City, 1994—96, planning specialist accessories, 1996—97, product support specialist, 1997—99, bus. analyst svc. contracts, 1999—2000, mgr. customer svc. adminstrn. and analysis Knoxville, 2000—. Baptist. E-mail: jrrankin@aol.com.

RANKIN, JIMMIE R. neuroscience nurse; b. Auburn, Calif., May 22, 1941; s. Gilbert O. and Wilma E. (Robertson) R. MSN, U. Calif., San Francisco, 1989; BSN, SUNY, 1983; BA, U. Calif., Berkeley, 1969; BS in Psychology, ASN, SUNY, Albany, 1977; ThD, St. Thomas Inst., 2001. Staff nurse Neurol. Inst., N.Y.C.; ind. nurse, prin. Dry Bones Nursing BBS, Dry Bones Press, San Francisco; dir. nursing Pacific Coast Hosp. Mem. AANN. Home: PO Box 597 Roseville CA 95678-0597 Office: Dry Bones Press PO Box 597 Roseville CA 95678-0597 E-mail: jrankin@drybones.com.

RANKIN, KEVIN ROBERT, securities broker, financial executive; b. Chgo., May 14, 1971; s. Robert A. Rankin and Marilyn P. (Ludewig) O'Brien. BS in Accountancy, U. Ill., 1993. CPA, Ill. Auditor Deloitte & Touche, Chgo., 1992-94; contr., CFO Access Fin. Group, Inc., 1994—. Mem. AICPA, Ill. CPA Soc., Phi Kappa Theta (treas. Beta Delta alumni bd.). Republican. Roman Catholic. Avocations: golf, softball. Office: Access Financial Group Inc 118 N Clinton St Ste 250 Chicago IL 60661-2304

RANKIN, RACHEL ANN, retired media specialist; b. High Point, N.C., Mar. 8, 1937; d. Benjamin Carl and Anne Jane (Robinson) Mixson; m. Thomas M. Rankin, July 30, 1961; 1 child, Rachel Roxanne Lineberry. AA, Mars Hill Coll., 1957; BA, Wake Forest U., 1959; MLS, U. S.C., 1977. Caseworker Rockingham County Welfare, Reidsville, N.C., 1959-61, Berlin Am. Sch., 1967-69, Albemarle County Schs., Charlottesville, Va., 1970-72, Lexington County Schs., Ballentine, S.C., 1973-76; tchg. asst., student tchr. supr. Sch. Edn. U. S.C., Columbia, 1976-77; sch. media specialist Montgomery County Schs., Rockville, Md., 1977-99; ret., 1999. Mentor for new librs./media specialists Montgomery Pub. Schs., 2001—. V.p. Berlin Am. PTA, 1967—68; del. European Conf. PTAs, Garmisch, Germany, 1968; mem. planning com. N.C. Cherry Blossom Ball, Washington, 1983; co-coord. support group Am. Cancer Soc., 1988—89; People to People del. to China, 1998; bd. dirs. Fourth Presbyn. Sch., Potomac, 2002—. Named Most Outstanding Tchr., Jackson Burley Sch., Charlottesville, 1972; recipient ofcl. citation Ho. of Dels., Md. Gen. Assembly, 1983, 96. Mem. NEA (life), Soc. Sch. Librs. Internat. (del. 1983), Am. Assn. Sch. Librarians (del. Montgomery County 1982, 90, 92, 97),

Am. Cancer Soc. (dist. chair crusades 1988-90), Md. Ednl. Media Orgn., Montgomery County Ednl. Media Specialists Assn. (treas. 1981-82, v.p. 1982-83, pres. 1983-84), Montgomery County Edn. Assn., N.C. State Soc. of Washington (bd. govs. 1984-86), Delta Kappa Gamma (sec. Sigma chpt. 1988-91, v.p. 1996-98, pres. 1998-2000). Democrat. Presbyterian. Home: 15219 Red Clover Dr Rockville MD 20853-1645 E-mail: rankint@starpower.net.

RANKIN, ROBERT ARTHUR, journalist; b. Richmond, Va., May 31, 1949; s. Arthur Norton and Martha Louise (Rountree) R.; m. Janis Johnson, May 11, 1979 (div. Apr. 2001); 1 child, Benjamin John. BA in Polit. Sci., Randolph Macon Coll., 1971; MA in Govt., U. Va., 1974; Walter Bagehot fellowship, Columbia U., 1978-79. Reporter Richmond News Leader, Va., 1972-75; reporter Congl. Quar., Washington, 1975-78; editorial writer Miami Herald, Fla., 1980-85, Phila. Inquirer, 1985-87; nat. corr. Washington bur. Knight Ridder Newspapers, 1987-99, govt. and politics editor, 2000—. V.p. Civic Assn. Hollin Hills, Alexandria, Va., 1991-92. Co-recipient Pulitzer prize for editorial writing 1983, Olive Branch award N.Y.U. Ctr. for War, Peace and The News Media, 1990; recipient 1st prize Va. Press Assn., 1974; best editorial award Phila. chpt. Sigma Delta Chi, 1987. Mem. White House Corres. Assn. (bd. govs., 1996-98), Nat. Press Club. Office: Knight Ridder Newspapers 700 National Press Building Washington DC 20045-1701

RANKIN, SCOTT DAVID, artist, educator; b. Newark, Mar. 21, 1954; s. Clymont J. and Jean L. (Lane) R.; m. Linda K. Piemonte, Sept. 3, 1989 (div. Apr. 2000). BFA, Tyler Sch. of Art, Phila., 1976; MFA, UCLA, 1980. Asst. prof. U. Iowa, Iowa City, 1985-86, U. Chgo., 1986-94; assoc. prof. Ill. State U., Normal, 1994—. Video cons. Math. Edn. Rsch. Project, L.A., 1991-93, 3d internat. math. and sci. study UCLA dept. psychology, 1994-95, 98-99. Prodr., dir.: (videotapes) Fugue, 1985, This and that (version 1), 1987, (version 2), 1990, The Pure, 1993, Wire, 1998, Flow, 2000, Central, 2001. Regional media arts fellow Nat. Endowment for Arts, 1984, visual artist's fellow Ill. Arts Coun., 1989, 90, visual artist's fellow Nat. Endowment for Arts, 1990, 93. E-mail: sdranki@ilstu.edu.

RANKIN, WILLIAM PARKMAN, educator, former publishing company executive; b. Boston, Feb. 6, 1917; s. George William and Bertha W. (Clowe) R.; m. Ruth E. Gerard, Sept. 12, 1942; children: Douglas W., Joan W. BS, Syracuse U., 1941; MBA, NYU, 1949, PhD, 1979. Sales exec. Redbook mag., N.Y.C., 1945-49, This Week mag., N.Y.C., 1949-55, adminstrv. exec., 1955-60, v.p., 1957-60, v.p., dir. advt. sales, sales devel. dir., 1960-63, exec. v.p., 1963-69; gen. exec. newspaper divsn. Time Inc., 1969-70; gen. mgr. feature svc. Newsweek Inc., 1970-74, fin. and ins. advt. mgr., 1974-81; prof., asst. to dir. Walter Cronkite Sch. Journalism & Telecomm., Ariz. State U., Tempe, 1981-98, prof. emeritus, also bd. dirs., 1998—. Lectr. Syracuse U., NYU, Berkeley Sch. Author: Selling Retail Advertising, 1944, The Technique of Selling Magazine Advertising, 1949, Business Management of Consumer Magazines, 1980, 2d edit., 1984, The Practice of Newspaper Management, 1986. Mem. Dutch Treat Club. Home: 2625 E Southern Ave C-18 Tempe AZ 85282-7615 Office: Ariz State U Walter Cronkite Sch Journalism and Mass Tempe AZ 85287-1305

RANKINE, V.V. sculptor, painter; b. Boston, July 27, 1920; d. Auguste and Hetty (Hemenway) Richard; m. John Magruder, 1945 (div. 1950); 1 child, John Magruder; m. Paul Scott Rankine, 1952 (div. 1969); 1 child, David Scott; m. Rufus King, Nov. 23, 1973. Student, Amedee Ozenfant Sch., N.Y.C., 1940-41, Black Mt. Coll., 1942-43. Dir. dept. art Madeira Sch., Greenway, Va., 1967-70; artist-in-residence Inst. Man and Sci., Rensselaer, N.Y., summer 1968; instr. humanities art Hunter Coll. H.S., N.Y.C., 1970-71; instr. painting and drawing U. Md., College Park, 1979-81. One-woman shows include Fraser's Stable Gallery, Washington, 1978, Corcoran Gallery Art, Washington, 1978, No. Va. C.C., 1978, Women Artists Ea. L.I., East Hampton, N.Y., 1979; group exhbns. include Corcoran Gallery Art, Washington, 1954, 55, 58, 67, Betty Parsons Gallery, N.Y.C., 1966-81, Mus. Modern Art, N.Y.C., 1966, 30th Corcoran Biennial, Washington, 1967-68, Four Americans, Axiom Gallery, London, 1968, Painting and Sculpture Today, Indpls., 1965; work rep. in Nat. Mus. Am. Art, Washington, Corocoran Gallery Art, Washington, Oklahoma City Mus., Indpls. Mus. Art, Woodward Found., Washington, Guild Hall Mus., East Hampton, N.Y. Recipient Painting prize Corcoran Gallery, 1955, Maurice Tuchman Juror award Corcoran Gallery Art, 1978. Home: 3524 Williamsburg Ln NW Washington DC 20008-1207

RANKIN-SMITH, PAMELA, photographer; b. Kansas City, Kans., Jan. 12, 1918; d. Dexter Leon and Ruth Dee (Millard) Rankin; m. George W. Witcher, 1943 (div. 1945); 1 child, Vann Leigh Witcher; m. A. Arthur Smith, 1968 (dec. 1968). Diploma, Dallas Little Theater, 1936; student, U. Tex., 1937-41; lic. in real estate, New Sch., N.Y.C., 1954. Real estate agt., N.Y.C., 1954-96. Flower arranger Ikebana Flowers The Met. Mus. Art, Patrons Lounge, N.Y.C., 1988—2002. Author: Perfectly Candid, 1994, Ikebana the Art of Japanese Flower Arrangements, 1998; one-woman photography shows include Soho/Stieglitz Gallery, N.Y.C., 1978, La Galerie, Paris, 1979, Donnell Libr., N.Y.C., 1979, Fed. Hall, N.Y.C., 1978, Nikon House, N.Y.C., 1980, Overseas Press Club, N.Y.C., 1980, Le Gallery, Kent, Conn., 1981, Camera Club N.Y., N.Y.C., 1985. Mem. Friend of PEN, Photographic Adminstrs., Inc., Actors Equity Assn., Am. Soc. Media Photographers, Mcpl. Art Soc., Circle of Confusion, Soc. Scribes. Avocations: oriental painting, decoupage, calligraphy, ikebana. Home: 150 E 69th St New York NY 10021-5704 Fax: 861-6836.

RANKS, ANNE ELIZABETH, retired elementary and secondary education educator; b. Omaha, June 10, 1916; d. Salvatore and Concetta (Turco) Scolla; m. Harold Eugene Ranks, Aug. 20, 1955 (dec.). B in Philosophy, Duchesne Coll., Omaha, 1937; MA, Creighton U., 1947. Tchr. Good Shepherd Parochial H.S., Omaha, 1937-38, St. Benedicts H.S., Omaha, 1938-39, Omaha Pub. Schs., 1939-81. Pres. women's divsn. Dem. Cen. Com., Nebr.; chmn. Gov.'s Profl. Practices Commn. Nebr., 1938-39; vol. Bergan-Mercy Hosp., Omaha, 1980-86, 99—, hosp. mem. aux. bd. dirs., 1985-86; vol. Saddleback Hosp., Laguna Hills, Calif., 1989-91; bd. dirs. Sylvia Tischhauser CRTA divsn. Scholarship Found., 1989-94; mem. bd. dirs. Saddleback Valley Ednl. Found., 1990-92; bd. dirs. Orange County Diocesan Coun. Cath. Women, 1989-90, 2d v.p., 1990-94; vol. Bergan Mercy Hosp., 1998-2001. Mem. AAUW (v.p. Laguna Hills br. 1988-91), Nebr. Edn. Assn. (bd. dirs. 1957-60, pres. dist. II 1960-62), Omaha Edn. Assn. (bd. dirs. 1950-55), Womens Club, Cath. Daus. Regent Omaha Ct. (rec. sec. Lake Forest, Calif. Ct. 1988-90), Coll. Club of Leisure World (v.p. 1990-95), Nat. Ret. Tchrs. Assn., Nebr. Ret. Tchrs. Assn., Local Ret. Tchrs. Assn., Cath. Daus.

RANLET, PHILIP HENRY, historian, educator; b. N.Y.C., Jan. 17, 1953; s. Donald John and Elizabeth Ranlet. BA summa cum laude, Fordham U., 1975; MA, Columbia U., 1976, MPhil, 1978, PhD, 1983. Adj. lectr. Hunter Coll., CUNY, N.Y.C., 1982-83, adj. asst. prof., 1983-86,87-2000, substitute asst. prof., 1987, 2001. Author: The New York Loyalists, 1986, 2nd edit., 2002, Enemies of the Bay Colony, 1995; contbr. articles, revs. to profl. jours. N.Y. State Regents scholar, 1971-75; Herbert H. Lehman grad. fellow, 1975-79; Can. Studies Rsch. Program rsch. grantee, 1979.

RANNEY, AUSTIN (JOSEPH RANNEY), political science educator; b. Cortland, N.Y., Sept. 23, 1920; s. Frank Addison and Florence Edith (Ranney) R.; m. Elizabeth Mackay (div. Oct. 1975); m. Nancy Boland; children: Joseph, Douglas, Gordon, David. BS, Northwestern U., 1941, LLD (hon.), 1995; MA, U. Oreg., 1943; PhD, Yale U., 1948, DSS (hon.), 1985; LLD (hon.), SUNY, 1986, Northwestern U., 1995. Statistician Douglas Aircraft Corp., Chgo., 1942-44; instr. Yale U., New Haven, 1945-47; from instr. to prof. U. Ill., Urbana, 1947-63; prof. U. Wis., Madison, 1963-76; resident scholar Am. Enterprise Inst., Washington, 1976-86; prof. U. Calif., Berkeley, 1986-91, prof. emeritus, 1991—, chmn. dept. polit. sci., 1987-90. Author: The Doctrine of Responsible Party Government, 1954, Governing, 1958, Curing the Mischiefs of Faction, 1975, Channels of Power, 1983. Mem. Presdl.-Congl. Commn. on Polit. Activity Govtl. Employees, Washington, 1967-68, Dem. Nat. Com. Commn. on Party Structure, Washington, 1969-72, Commn. on Presdl. Debates, Washington, 1980-88; chmn. Gov.'s Commn. on Registration and Voting Participation, Madison, Wis., 1964, social sci. rsch. coun. Com. on Govtl. Processes, 1964-71, coun. on social scis. policy Yale U., 1983-88. Recipient Wilbur Lucius Cross medal Yale U. Grad. Sch., 1977; sr. rsch. fellow NSF, 1970, John Simon Guggenheim fellow, 1974, fellow Ctr. for Advanced Study in Behavioral Scis., 1978. Mem. Am. Polit. Sci. Assn. (pres. 1975-76), Am. Acad. Arts and Scis. (v.p. 1981-84). Home: 990 Regal Rd Berkeley CA 94708-1430 Office: Univ Calif Dept Polit Sci Berkeley CA 94720-0001 E-mail: ranney@socrates.berkeley.edu.

RANNEY, CARLETON DAVID, plant pathology researcher, administrator; b. Jackson, Minn., Jan. 23, 1928; s. Carleton Oran and Ada Elizabeth (Harriman) R.; m. Mary Kathryn Ransleben, July 16, 1949; children: David Clayton, Mary Elizabeth. AA, Chaffey Jr. Coll., Ontario, Calif., 1952; BS, Tex. A&M U., 1954, MS, 1955, PhD, 1959. Plant pathologist Crops Rsch. Div. Agrl. Rsch. Svc. USDA, College Station, Tex., 1955-58, Stoneville, Miss., 1958-70, investigations leader Beltsville, Md., 1970-72; area dir. Ala. No. Miss. area Agrl. Rsch. Svc. USDA, Starkville, Miss., 1973-78, area dir. Delta States area Stoneville, 1978-84, area dir. Mid-South area, 1984-87; asst. dir. Miss. Agrl. and Forestry Exptl. Stas., 1987-94, head Delta br. sta., 1987-94, emeritus plant pathologist, 1994—. Adj. prof. agronomy Miss. State U., 1970-94; sr. exec. svc. USDA, Stoneville, Miss., 1984-87; adv. bd. Belt Wide Meetings Nat. Cotton Coun., Memphis, Tenn., 1987-96. Contbr. articles to profl. jours. Sect. advisor SE2 Order of Arrow, Boy Scouts Am., Miss. and West Tenn., 1973-83; pres. Delta Area coun. Boy Scouts Am., Clarksdale, Miss., 1990-91; v.p. Leland Habitat for Humanity, 1995-2000, bd. dirs. 2000—. Recipient Silver Beaver Boy Scouts Am., 1981, Disting. Svc. Order of Arrow, 1983, Superior Svc. award USDA, 1981, Cert. of Merit, 1983. Mem. Agron. Soc. Am., Nat. Cotton Disease Coun. (sec. 1959-60, chmn. 1961-62), Lions (pres. Leland club 1995-96), Sigma Xi, Alpha Zeta, Phi Kappa Phi. Methodist. Achievements include development of fungicide control seedling diseases; definition of relationship of microclimate to boll rot of cotton; development of non-mercurial seed treatments. Office: Delta Rsch & Ext Ctr PO Box 197 Stoneville MS 38776-0197

RANNEY, HELEN MARGARET, physician, educator; b. Summer Hill, N.Y., Apr. 12, 1920; d. Arthur C. and Alesia (Toolan) Ranney. AB, Barnard Coll., 1941; MD, Columbia U., 1947; ScD, U. S.C., 1979, SUNY, Buffalo, 1996. Diplomate Am. Bd. Internal Medicine. Intern Presbyn. Hosp., N.Y.C., 1947—48, resident, 1948—50, asst. physician, 1954—60; practice medicine specializing in internal medicine, hematology, 1954—70; instr. Coll. Phys. and Surg. Columbia, 1954—60; from assoc. prof. to prof. medicine Albert Einstein Coll. Medicine, 1960—70; prof. medicine SUNY, Buffalo, 1970—73, U. Calif., San Diego, 1973—90, chmn. dept. medicine, 1973—86, Disting. physician vet. adminstr., 1986—91; cons. Alliance Pharm. Corp., 1991—. Master: ACP; fellow: AAAS; mem.: NAS, Am. Acad. Arts and Scis., Am. Assn. Physicians, Harvey Soc., Am. Soc. Hematology, Am. Soc. for Clin. Investigation, Inst. Medicine, Alpha Omega Alpha, Sigma Xi, Phi Beta Kappa. E-mail: hranney@ucsd.edu.

RANNEY, MARY ELIZABETH, business executive; b. Louisville, Nov. 10, 1928; d. James William and Erna Marie Katerina (Hansen) Connell; m. Glen Royal Ranney, July 26, 1947; children: Darleen Diane Ranney Bowie, Nancy Elizabeth Ranney Pieratt. Student, Monmouth Coll., 1946-47. Cert. profl. sec., nursing asst. Nursing asst. Monmouth (Ill.) Hosp., 1957-63; asst. in fin. Bd. Pub. Instrn. Collier County, Naples, Fla., 1964-68; sec. 1st Nat. Bank, Bonita Springs, 1969-71; founder, dir. Planned Parenthood, Naples, 1972-76; writer Am. Hibiscus Soc., 1977-82; owner Tree Gallery, Naples and Ft. Myers, 1983—. Tchr., seedling judge Am. Hibiscus Soc., 1977-79. Author: (brochure) Abortion, 1976; solo performance Fiddler on the Roof, 1976. Chair Fla. Assn. for Repeal Abortion Laws, Lee and Collier County, 1972; founder Abortion Referral Svc. S.W. Fla., 1972-75; founder, dir. Accordion Band, Naples, 1974-79, Floridian Accordion Band, Ft. Myers, 1989-91; founding officer Naples Concert Band, 1972-79; sponsor Am. hibiscus shows, Naples, 1973-81; founder, cdr. City of Ft. Myers String Band, 1998—. Recipient Prominent Woman of Cmty. award Naples Star, 1977, 78, 79, Mover of 70's award Naples NOW Mag., 1980, Shaker, Mover and Star award Naples NOW Mag., 1983, Life Work Feature award Naples Star, 1981, Great Achiever award Naples Star, 1982. Mem. NOW (charter nat. pres. 1975-77), Am. Hibiscus Soc. (life, founder Ranney chpt. 1973—, editor Show Chair Manual 1979, Judges Manual 1980, Pres. Svc. award 1979, Hibiscus of Yr. 1980, 82), Meml. Soc. S.W. Fla. (pres. 1975-77). Democrat. Avocations: musician, seamstress, biker, walker, dancer. Home: 3164 Palm Beach Blvd Fort Myers FL 33916-1579

RANNEY, RICHARD RAYMOND, dental educator, researcher; b. Atlanta, July 11, 1939; s. Russell Ballou and Maureen Joan (Bannon) R.; m. Beverly Anne Toton, June 10, 1961 (div.); children: Christine Marie, Kathleen Anne; m. Patricia Marie DeNoto, Feb. 25, 1969; children: Maureen Frances, Russell Christopher. DDS, U. Iowa, 1963; MS, U. Rochester, 1969; D (hon.), U. Buenos Aires, 1995. Asst. prof. periodontology U. Oreg., 1969-72; assoc. prof. periodontics Va. Commonwealth U., Richmond, 1972-78, prof., 1978-86, dir. grad. periodontics, 1972-76, chmn. dept. periodontics, 1974-77, asst. dean rsch. and grad. affairs, 1977-84, asst. dean rsch., 1984-86; dir. Clin. Rsch. Ctr. Periodontal Diseases, 1978-86; prof. Sch. Dentistry U. Ala., Birmingham, 1986-91, dean, 1986-89; prof., dean U. Md., Balt., 1991—. Contbr. chpts. to books, articles to profl. jours. With USPHS, 1963-66. Nat. Inst. Dental Rsch. grantee, 1970-86. Fellow AAAS, Internat. Coll. Dentists, Am. Coll. Dentists; mem. ADA, Am. Acad. Periodontology, Internat. Assn. Dental Rsch. (pres. 1995-96, basic rsch. periodontology award 1985), Am. Assn. Dental Rsch. (pres. 1990-91), Am. Assn. Dental Schs., Sigma Xi, Omicron Kappa Upsilon. Office: U Md 666 W Baltimore St Baltimore MD 21201-1510 E-mail: rranney@dental.umaryland.edu.

RANNEY, SANDRA KAY, artist, humanities educator; b. Tucson, June 17, 1948; d. Gail Hamilton and Beverly Jean (Crawford) Cowell. BA in Social Scis., Nyack Coll., 1972; M Humanities, U. Richmond, 1985; PhD in Comparative Arts, Ohio U., 1995. Tchg. assoc., lectr. Ohio U., Athens, 1985-90; prof. Pittsburg (Kans.) State U., 1990-96, Ind. Wesleyan U., 1999. Exec. dir. Kokomo (Ind.) Art Assn., 1999. Scholar U. Richmond, 1984-85, Ohio U., 1987; doctoral fellow Ohio U., 1985-89; grantee Pittsburg State U., 1994, NEH, 1982. Mem. Assn. for Integrated Studies, Coll. Art Assn. Avocations: art, music, drama. Home: 503 Rainbow Cir Kokomo IN 46902 E-mail: drsranney@mymailstation.com.

RANSCHBURG, HERBERT JOSEF, economist; b. Vienna, Austria, Sept. 22, 1919; came to U.S., 1940; s. Frank and Martha (Adler) R.; m. Marilyn Goldstein, Mar. 22, 1950; children: Nina, Glenda. BA in Econs., Queens Coll., 1949; MA in Econs., NYU, 1950, PhD, 1958. Dir. rsch., v.p., sec., sr. rsch. analyst Citizens Budget Commn., N.Y.C., 1952-82; mgmt. auditor, adminstrv. staff analyst Office of Comptr. City of N.Y., 1983-91; rsch. assoc. Ednl. Priorities Panel, N.Y.C., 1992-95. Asst. adj. prof. Queens Coll., N.Y.C., 1949-91. With U.S. Army, 1943-46. Home: 11 Shari Ct Hicksville NY 11801-1813

RANSDELL, TOD ELLIOT, pharmaceutical, parenteral and in vitro diagnostics validation specialist; b. Imperial, Nebr., May 17, 1953; s. Merrill Guy and Rosalie E. Ransdell. BS in Botany, Mont. State U., Bozeman, 1977; grad., Mont. State Police Acad., 1978. Seasonal protective divsn. ranger USNPS, 1975-78; police officer Dillon (Mont.) Police Dept., 1979-80; dept. mgr. Woolco, Bozeman, Mont., 1980-83; lab. coord. Skyland Sci. Svcs., Inc., 1983-86; sales assoc. S&P Office Supply, 1986-87; validation specialist Skyland Sci. Svcs., Inc., 1987-92, sr. validation specialist, 1992, Genetics Sys. Corp./Sanofi, Redmond, Wash., 1992-2000, Genetic Sys. Corp./Bio-Rad Labs., Redmond, 2000—, QA documentation specialist 3. Cons. Skyland Sci. Svcs., Inc., Bozeman, Mont., 1987-92. Bd. advisors Jour. Validation Tech., 1996—. Order of Arrow, brotherhood, chpt. chief Boy Scouts Am. (life rank), 1973; pres. Bozeman (Mont.) Jaycees, 1983, 85, Crime Stoppers, 1982; mem. Benevolent and Prtective Order of the Elks, Bozeman, Mont. 1989-94. Mem. NRA, Orgn. Regulatory and Clin. Assocs., Union of Concerned Scientists, Inst. Validation Tech., Inst. Validation U.K., Parenteral Drug Assn., , Bozeman Jr. C. of C., Internat. Soc. Pharm. Engring., Inst. for Environ. Sci. and Tech. (sr.), Nature Conservancy, Greenpeace, Am. Assn. for the Furtherance of Cmty. Office: Genetic Sys Corp/Bio-Rad Labs 6565 185th Ave NE Redmond WA 98052-5039 E-mail: tod_ransdell@bio-rad.com., todransdell@attbi.com.

RANSEL, DAVID LORIMER, history educator; b. Gary, Ind., Feb. 20, 1939; s. Joseph A. and Patricia (Lorimer) R.; m. Therese Holma; children: Shairstin, Annaliisa. BA, Coe Coll., 1961; MA, Northwestern U., 1962; PhD, Yale U., 1969. Instr. Tollare Folkhogskola, Boo, Sweden, 1959-60; asst. instr. Yale U., New Haven, 1966-67; instr. U. Ill., Urbana, 1967-69, asst. prof., 1969-73, assoc. prof., 1973-81, prof., 1981-85, Ind. U., Bloomington, 1985—, Robert F. Byrnes prof. history, 2001—, dir. Russian and East European Inst., 1995—. Author: The Politics of Catherinian Russia, 1975, Mothers of Misery, 1988, Village Mothers: Three Generations of Change in Russia and Tataria, 2000; editor: The Family in Imperial Russia, 1978, Imperial Russia: New Histories for the Empire, 1998; editor/translator: Village Life in Late Tsarist Russia, 1993; editor Slavic Rev., Urbana, 1980-85, Am. Hist. Rev., Bloomington, 1985-95; bd. editors The History of the Family: An International Quarterly, Historisk Tidskrift, Kritika, Explorations in Russian and Eurasian History. Guggenheim fellow, 1989-90, Wilson fellow, 1989-90, NEH fellow, 1998-99; Fulbright-Hays grantee, 1979, 90, Irex grantee, 1990, 93. Mem. Am. Hist. Assn. (mem. gov. coun. 1985-95, mem. fin. com. 1989-95), Am. Assn. for Advancement of Slavic Studies (bd. dirs. 1979-85, mem. fin. com. 1980-85, chmn. com. on status of women 1991-93, mem. Irex program com. 1995-99). Avocations: classical guitar, sailing, running. Office: Ind Univ Russian/East European Inst 565 Ballantine Hall Bloomington IN 47401-5017 E-mail: ransel@indiana.edu.

RANSFORD, SHERRY, secondary education educator; b. Pitts., June 1, 1948; d. Herbert Earl Jr. and Cora Olive (Kraus) Ransford; m. David K. Frink, Mar. 21, 1970 (div. 1982); children: Jason R., Amanda M.; m. Thomas A. Myers, Dec. 11, 1982 (div. 1996); 1 child, Benjamin J. BA in English, Allegheny Coll., 1970; MA in English, Western Mich. U., 1987. Tutor, manuscript editor Allegheny Coll., Meadville, Pa., 1969-70; asst. buyer Kaufmann's Dept. Store, Pitts., 1970-72; tchr. Baldwin Community United Meth. Ch. Nursery Sch., 1978-83; lit. editor, non-traditional instr. Kalamazoo Coll., 1983-87; instr. Western Mich. U., Kalamazoo, 1988-92, 97—; tchr. Kalamazoo Pub. Schs., 1992—. Instr. C.C. of Allegheny County, Pitts., 1982-83; part-time instr. Kalamazoo Valley C.C., 1983—, asst. to dean instrn., 1986-88; instr. Acad. Talented Youth Program, Kalamazoo, 1984—; task force leader Kalamazoo Pub. Schs., 1990—. Contbr. articles to profl. jours. Chmn. grant com. Arts Coun. Greater Kalamazoo, 1984-94; v.p., sec., chmn. coms. parent-cmty. adv. coun. Kalamazoo Pub. Schs., 1986-92; mem. adult leadership corps Boy Scouts Am., Kalamazoo, 1987-89; bd. dirs. Civic Theatre, 1992-95; advisor lit. mag., 1991-93; coach Mock Trial Team, 1994-98, 2001; advisor Nat. Honor Soc., 2001—. Recipient Outstanding Educator award, Kalamazoo County, 1987, 1992, 1994—98, 2001—02, Ednl. Ptnr. award, Kalamazoo County Edn. Assn., 2001. Mem. NEA, AAUP, Mich. Edn. Assn., Nat. Coun. Tchrs. of English. Methodist. Home: 534 Pinehurst Blvd Kalamazoo MI 49006-3050 Office: Kalamazoo Pub Schs 1220 Howard St Kalamazoo MI 49008-1871

RANSIL, BERNARD J(EROME), research physician, methodologist, consultant, educator; b. Pitts., Nov. 15, 1929; s. Raymond Augustine and Louise Mary (Berhalter) R. BS, Duquesne U., 1951; PhD in Phys. Chemistry, Cath. U. Am., 1955; MD, U. Chgo., 1964. NRC-NAS postdoctoral fellow Nat. Bur. Stds., Washington, 1955-56; cons. heat div. thermodynamics sect. Nat. Bur. Standards, 1956-62; cons. NASA exobiology project, 1962-68; rsch. assoc. and dir. diatomic molecule project, Lab. Molecular Structure and Spectra, physics dept. U. Chgo., 1956-63; intern Harbor Gen. Hosp., UCLA, Torrance, Calif., 1964-65, Guggenheim fellow, 1965-66; from rsch. assoc. in medicine to assoc. prof. in medicine Harvard Med. Sch., Boston, 1966-96; from rsch. assoc. and clin. fellow to clin. assoc. Harvard II and IV Med. Svcs., 1966-74; core lab. scientist Clin. Rsch. Ctr. Thorndike Meml. Lab Boston City Hosp., Boston, 1966-74; asst. physician Beth Israel Hosp., 1974-96, sr. physician, 1996—; dir. Core Lab. Clin. Rsch. Ctr., 1974-94, Data Analysis Lab., 1989-94; cons., and mentor, rsch. ops. Beth Israel Hosp., Boston, 1994-96; cons. and mentor, computational stats. dept. neurology Beth Israel Deaconess Med. Ctr., 1996—. Statis. computing cons. Boston City Hosp. and Beth Israel Hosp., 1966-96; cons. Prophet project NIH, Bethesda, Md., 1971-88, exec. com., 1986-91, Howard Hughes Med. Inst., Boston, 1979-80, Coop. Cataract Rsch. Group, Boston, 1981-83, Mass. Alzheimer's Disease Rsch. Ctr., 1992-94; guest lectr. med. ethics Seton Hall U., 1971—; vis. scientist Rockefeller U., 1985, Scripps Rsch. Found., 1986, Calif. State U., 1986, U. Pitts. Med. Sch., 1987. Author: Abortion, 1969, Background to Abortion, 1979; editor: Life of a Scientist: Autobiography of Robert S. Mulliken, 1989, (videocassettes) Elements of Statistics and Data Analysis, 1985; contbr. biography of R.S. Mulliken to Nobel Laureates in Chemistry, 1973; contbr. numerous articles on computational chemistry, med. topics, computational stats. to sci. jours., also book revs. to Boston Globe, other periodicals, essays and poetry to The Critic. Recipient alumni rsch. award Cath. U. Am., 1969, Duquesne U. centennial award, 1978; endowment of Vernon F. Gallagher chair for intergration sci., philosophy and theology Duquesne U., 1999. Mem. numerous profl. socs. Home: 226 Calumet St Boston MA 02120-3303 E-mail: bransil@caregroup.harvard.edu.

RANSIN, DAVID WAYNE, lawyer; b. St. Louis, Dec. 7, 1956; BSBA, U. Mo., Columbia, 1979, JD, 1982. Bar: Mo. 1982, Ill. 1984, U.S. Supreme Ct. 1987. Assoc. Freeman & Fredrick, Springfield, Mo., 1982-86, Woolsey & Fischer, Springfield, 1986-89; pvt. practice, 1989—. Mem. ATLA, Mo. Assn. Trial Lawyers, Springfield Metro. Bar Assn. Avocation: outdoors. Office: Law Office 1650 E Battlefield Ste 140 Springfield MO 65804-3733 E-mail: david@ransin.com.

RANSOHOFF, RICHARD MILTON, neurologist, researcher; b. Cin., Aug. 18, 1946; s. Jerry Nathan and Sue (Westheimer) R.; m. Margaret Seidler, Mar. 26, 1988; children: Amy Julia, Lena Jane. BA, Bard Coll., 1968; MD, Case Western Reserve U., 1978. Diplomate Am. Bd. Psychiatry and Neurology, Am. Bd. Internal Medicine. Resident in internal medicine Mt. Sinai Hosp., Cleve., 1978-81; resident in neurology The Cleve. Clinic Found., 1981-83, chief resident in neurology, 1983-84, mem. assoc. staff in neurology, 1984-93, mem. asst. staff in molecular biology Rsch. Inst., 1989-94, mem. staff neurology dept., 1993—, mem. staff in molecular biology Lerner Rsch. Inst., 1994—97, mem. staff in neurosciences. Lerner Rsch. Inst., 1994—; prof. dept. med. virology, immunology and molecular genetics Ohio State U. Health Sci. Ctr., Cleve. Clinic Found., 1997—2001; postdoctoral fellow in molecular biology Case Western Reserve U., Cleve., 1984-89. Mem. neurology C study sect., Washington, 1995—98; cons. Rsch. Ctr. for AIDS Dementia, Johns Hopkins U., 1998—; mem. clin. adv. bd. LeukoSite, Inc., Cambridge, Mass., 1998—2000; project dir. Nat. Inst. Neurol. Diseases and Stroke, Washington, 1999—; mem. sci. adv. bd. ChemoCentryx, Santa Clara, Calif., 2001—. Co-author: Transcriptional Regulation in the Interferon System, 1997; co-editor: Cytokines in the CNS, 1996; editor: Chemokines in the CNS, 2002; sect. editor: Jour. Immunology, 2002—, editl. bd.: Jour. of Neuroimmunology, 1998—, editl. bd.: Ency. Neurol. Scis., 1999—; contbr. more than 135 articles to profl. jours. Chair profl. adv. com. Nat. Multiple Sclerosis Soc., N.E. Ohio, 1985-95, trustee, 1985-97, mem. med. adv. bd. Nat. Multiple Sclerosis Soc., N.Y.C. 1996—, mem. peer rev. com. B, 2003—; mem. corp. Hathaway Brown Sch., Shaker Heights, Ohio. Grantee NIH, Washington, 1988—, Harry Weaver Neurosci. scholar Nat. Multiple Sclerosis Soc., N.Y.C., 1987-92; recipient Physicians Rsch. Tng. award Am. Cancer Soc., N.Y.C., 1984-86, Clin. Investigator Devel. award Nat. Inst. Neurol. and Communicative Diseases and Stroke, Washington, 1988-93, John and Samuel Bard award for Sci. and Medicine, 2002. Mem.: Am. Assn. Immunologists, Am. Assn. Neurology, Am. Neurol. Assn. (mem. sci. program com. 1996—98). Office: Lerner Rsch Inst NC-30 Cleve Clinic Found 9500 Euclid Ave Cleveland OH 44195-0001 E-mail: ransohr@ccf.org.

RANSOM, DAVID MICHAEL, retired ambassador; b. St. Louis, Nov. 23, 1938; s. Clifford Fredic and Inez Natalie (Green) R.; m. Marjorie Ann (Marilley) Ransom; children: Elizabeth Inez, Katherine Hope, Sarah Grace. AB, Princeton U., 1960; MA, Johns Hopkins Sch. of Advanced Internat. Studies, 1962; student, The Nat. War Coll., 1982-83. With U.S. Dept. State, Yemen, Iran, Lebanon, Saudi Arabia, 1965-71, nat. security coun. staff White House Washington, 1971-73; dep. chief mission Am. Embassy, Sana'a, Yemen Arab Rep., 1975-78; dir., dept. dir. near east divsn. internat. security affairs Office of Sec. of Def., U.S. Dept. of Def., Washington, 1978-82; dep. chief mission Am. Embassy, Abu Dhabi, United Arab Emirates, 1983-85, dep. chief of mission Damascus, Syria, 1985-88; country dir. Arabian Peninsula-Near East Bur., U.S. Dept. State, 1988-90, country dir. Greece, Turkey, Cyprus-European Bur., 1990-93; amb. to Bahrain, Am. Embassy, Manama, 1994-97;

ret., 1997; prin. DM Ransom Assocs., Washington, 1997—. 1st lt. inf. USMC, 1962-65. Mem. Met. Club (Washington). Episcopalian. Avocations: scuba diving, canoeing, skiing. Home and Office: 2269 Cathedral Ave NW Washington DC 20008-1510

RANSOM, EVELYN NAILL, language educator, linguist; b. Memphis, Apr. 20, 1938; d. Charles Rhea and Evelyn (Goodlander) Naill Ransom; m. Gunter Heinz Hiller, June 7, 1960 (div. Mar. 1964). AA, Mt. Vernon Jr. Coll., 1958; BA, Newcomb Coll., 1960; MA, N.Mex. Highlands U., 1965; PhD, U. Ill., 1974. Cert. secondary tchr., N.Mex. Instr. Berlitz Sch. Langs., New Orleans, 1961; tchr. MillerWall Elem. Sch., Harvey, L.A., 1961-62; teaching asst. N.Mex. Highlands U., Las Vegas, 1963-64; instr. U. Wyo., Laramie, 1965-66; teaching asst. U. Ill., Urbana, 1966-70; prof. English lang. Ea. Ill. U., Charleston, 1970-93; vis. prof. in linguistics No. Ariz. U., Flagstaff, 1990-91, adj. faculty, 1993-94, Ariz. State U., Tempe, 1995-98; retired. Referee Pretext: Jour. of Lang. and Lit., Ill., 1981, S.W. Jour. Linguistics, 1999; co-chair roundtable Internat. Congress of Linguistics, 1987; linguistics del. People to People, Moscow, St. Petersburg, Prague, 1993, China, 1998; dissertation reader SUNY, Buffalo, 1982; vis. scholar UCLA, 1977; conductor workshop LSA summer inst. Author: Complementation: Its Meanings and Forms, 1986; contbr. articles to profl. publs. Organizer Prairie Women's Cir., Champaign, 1981-83. Nat. Def. Fgn. Lang. fellow, 1969; grantee Ea. Ill. U., 1982, 87, 88, NSF, 1988. Mem. Linguistic Soc. Am., Linguistic Assn. S.W. (jour. referee 1999). Avocations: computer applications for the humanities, chess, motor-homing. Home: 201 E Southern Ave # 135 Apache Junction AZ 85219-3740

RANSOM, KEVIN RENARD DORTCH, investment banker; b. Detroit, Sept. 24, 1964; s. Donald Lewis and Etta Mae (Dortch) R. B in Econs., Morehouse Coll., 1988. Fin. analyst Goldman Sachs & Co., N.Y.C., 1987-88, Merrill Lynch & Co., N.Y.C., 1988-89; freelance journalist KDR & Assocs., 1989-90; fiscal analyst Mich. State Legislature, Lansing, 1990-92; dir. fiscal analysis Detroit City Coun., 1992-95; v.p. First of Mich. Investment Bank, Detroit, 1995—. Cons. Lansing C.C., 1990—. Editor: Neighborhood Economic Development Strategies, 1990. Mem. Dem. Nat. Com. Mem. Nat. Assn. Securities Profls., Morehouse Nat. Alumni Assn., Kappa Alpha Psi. Democrat. Baptist. Avocations: weight lifting, basketball. Home: 5159 W Outer Dr Detroit MI 48235-1358

RANSOM, PERRY SYLVESTER, civil engineer; b. Atlanta, July 3, 1929; s. Perry Sylvester and Eva James (Smith) R.; m. Wilma Ruth Cone, June 1, 1951; children: Beverly Kay, Barbara Ann. BSCE, Auburn U., 1958. Registered profl. engr., La., Miss., Ala.; cert. land surveyor, La., Miss. Asst. timekeeper Swift & Co., Montgomery, Ala., 1947-51; trainman Atlantic Coast Line RR, 1951-58; lab. mgr. A.W. Williams Inspection Co., Mobile, Ala., 1958-60; owner, CEO Cons. Engrs., Inc., Biloxi, Miss., 1960—. Mem. Civitan Club, Mobile, 1959, Rotary Internat., Moss Point, Miss., 1965; pres. Gulf Coast chpt. Miss. Engring. Soc., Biloxi, 1965-66, chmn. Pepp sect., Jackson, 1967-68; bd. dirs. Miss. sect. ASCE, Jackson, 1972-74. With U.S. Army, 1951-53. Named Boss of Yr., Miss. Nat. Sec. Assn., 1975-76, for Outstanding Svc., Miss. Engring. Soc., 1966, Outstanding Supporter, Boys Clubs Am., Biloxi, 1991; recipient Cert. of Appreciation, Boys Clubs Am., Biloxi, 1990. Mem. Miss. Cons. Engrs. Coun., Aircraft Owners and Pilots Assn., VFW (Merit/Disting. Svc. 1989), Masons (life). Republican. Baptist. Home: 711 Twin Oaks Dr Ocean Springs MS 39564-4221 Office: Cons Engrs Inc 430 Caillavet St Biloxi MS 39530-2050

RANSOM, VICTOR HARVEY, engineering educator; b. King Hill, Idaho, Mar. 23, 1932; s. Harvey Edgar and Edna Jessie (Honess) R.; m. Mary Ann Pierce, July 20, 1975 (div. June 1974); children: JoEllen Kay, Vickie Ann, Darin Victor; m. Delrie G. Gridley, July 6, 1974; children: Jessica Delrie, Natasha Lynn. BSChemE, U. Idaho, 1955; PhD, Purdue U., 1970. Registered profl. engr., Calif. Engr. Rocketdyne Divsn., Canoga Park, Calif., 1955-59; rsch. engr. Aerojet Gen. Corp., Sacramento, 1959-73; sci. and engring. fellow Idaho Nat. Engring. Lab., Idaho Falls, 1973-90; head sch. of nuclear engring. Purdue U., West Lafayette, Ind., 1990-98, prof. nuclear engring., 1998—2001; nuclear engr. ISL, Inc., Idaho Falls, 2001—02; mem. ACRS U.S. Nuclear Regulatory Com., 2002—. Cons. State of Maine, 1996-99, Scientech, 1994-2001, U.S. Nuclear Regulatory Commn., Washington, 1991-2001, Idaho Nat. Engring. Lab., Idaho Falls, 1990-2001, Argonne Nat. Lab., Chgo., 1992-2001. Named to Alumni Hall of Fame U. Idaho, 1991. Fellow Am. Nuclear Soc. (chair T-H divsn. 1988, 1999, tech. achievement award 1999); mem. ASME, ASEE, Sigma Xi, Phi Eta Sigma, Sigma Chi. Achievements include development of the RELAP5 computer code for simulation of the transient response of Nuclear Powerplants under accident conditions. Avocations: skiing, auto mechanics. Home: 3035 Hamilton St West Lafayette IN 47906-1155 Office: Purdue U NUCL 140 Lafayette IN 47907 E-mail: ransom@ecn.purdue.edu.

RANSOME, ERNEST LESLIE, III, retail company executive; b. Riverton, N.J. s. Percy A. and Clarice (Frishmuth) R.; m. Nancy Ellis Clark, Aug. 16, 1947 (div. Jan. 1984); children: Leslie Ransome Hudson, Elizabeth Ransome, Jane Ransome Bromley; m. Myradean Alcott, Feb. 12, 1984. AB in Econs., Princeton U., 1947; LLD, U. St. Andrews, Scotland, 2001. Ins. exec. Johnson & Higgins, Phila., 1947-48; asst. to dean Princeton (N.J.) U., 1948-50; asst. treas. Giles & Ransome, Bensalem, Pa., 1950-55, v.p. adminstrn., 1955-69, exec. v.p., 1969-82, vice chmn., 1982-88, chmn. bd., 1988—; v.p. Ransome Airlines, Pa., 1966-86. With Mannington Mills, Salem, N.J., chmn., 1991-92. Mem. Zoning Bd. Borough of Riverton, N.J., 1965-69; bd. trustees Riverton Library, 1959-79; campaign chmn. Zurbrugg Hosp., Riverside, N.J., 1971. 2d lt. USMC, 1944-46. Mem. Pine Valley Golf Club (pres. 1977-88, chmn. 1988-2001), Royal and Ancient Golf Club (St. Andrews, Scotland). Republican. Episcopalian. Avocation: golf.

RANTA, RICHARD ROBERT, university dean; b. Virginia, Minn., Nov. 18, 1943; s. V. Robert and Bernice (Smith) R.; 1 child, Erick H.; m. Carol Crown. AS, Hibbing (Minn.) Community Coll., 1963; BS, U. Minn., 1965; MA, Cornell U., 1967; PhD, U. Iowa, 1974. Floor dir. Sta. KDAL-TV, Duluth, Minn., 1964-65; asst. prof. U. Va., Charlottesville, 1969-72, U. Memphis, 1972-75, assoc. prof., 1975-91, prof., 1991—, interim dean Univ. Coll., 1975, asst. v.p. academic affairs, 1976-78, dean Coll. Comm. and Fine Arts, 1977—; gen. mgr. High Water Records, Memphis, 1980—. Bd. dirs. Concerts Internat., Memphis, pres., 1988-90; TV cons., free-lance producer, 1973—; mem. Rec. Hall of Fame selection panel Nat. Rec. Acad., L.A., 1986-2000. Assoc. prodr.: (TV program) Nat. Arthritis Telethon, 1985-90; Rec. Acad. graphics and prodn. coord. Grammy Awards TV program, 1983—; author articles in Communication Adminstrn. Bull., 1977—, editl. bd., 1991—, exec. com., 1996-2000. Chmn., v.p. Tenn. Humanities Coun., Nashville, 1980-82; v.p. Memphis Devel. Found., 1983-86; bd. dirs. Leadership Memphis, 1987-90, 94-97, chmn. mktg. com., 1987-90, chmn. selection com., 1994-95; bd. dirs. Life Blood, Memphis, 1984-92; treas. Memphis-Shelby County Film and TV Commn., 1986-98, chair, 1999-2002, bd. dirs., 2002--; mem. Tenn. Film, Entertainment and Music Commn., Nashville, 1987-97, chmn., 1993-95; chmn. bd. dirs. Crime Stoppers Memphis Assn., 1993-95; chmn. Memphis Arts Festival, 1992-94;bd. dirs. Tenn. Arts Commn., 2000--. Recipient Edn. Operational Models grant Ednl. Testing Svc., 1975, Communication Lab. grant HEW, 1976, Disting. Alumnus award Minn. Cmty. Coll. System, 1984, Alumni Cmty. Svc. award Leadership Memphis, 1997. Mem. NARAS (v.p. 1986-88, 92-93, chmn. edn. com. 1983—, trustee 1982-86, 88-92, 93-97, pres. Memphis chpt. 1984-86, bd. govs. 1978-98), So. States Comm. Assn. (pres. 1987-88, fin. bd. 1985-87, 93-95, exec. dir. 1995—), Tenn. Speech Comm. Assn. (pres. 1986-87, editor Communicator 1993—), Nat. Comm. Assn. (vice chmn., then chmn. exptl. learning com. 1979-83, mem. fin. and adminstrn. coms. 1989-93, chmn. fin. com. 1991-93), So. Arts Fedn. (bd. dirs. 1994-2000), Internat. Coun. Fine Arts Deans (parliamentarian 1996-2000), Tenn. Arts and Scis. Deans Assn. (chair 1997-98), Advt. Fedn. (bd. dirs.), Delta Sailing Assn. Club (sec. 1984-2000), Rotary (pres.-elect Memphis). Avocations: sailing, tennis, photography. Office: U Memphis Coll Communication & Fine Ar Memphis TN 38152-0001 E-mail: rranta@memphis.edu.

RANU, HARCHARAN SINGH, biomedical scientist, administrator, orthopaedic biomechanics educator; b. Lyallpur, India; came to U.S., 1976; s. Jodh Singh and Harnam Kaur R. BSc, Leicester Poly., Eng., 1963; MSc, U. Surrey, Guilford, Eng., 1967, Cambridge (Eng.) U., 1972; PhD, Middlesex Hosp. Med. Sch. and Poly. of Cen. London, 1975; diploma, MIT, 1984. Chartered engr., Eng. Med. scientist Nat. Inst. Med. Rsch. of the Med. Rsch. Coun., London, 1967-70; rsch. fellow Middlesex Hosp. Med. Sch. and Poly. of Cen. London, 1971-76; rsch. scientist Plastics Rsch. Assn. of Great Britain, Shawbury, Eng., 1977; asst. prof. Wayne State U., Detroit, 1977-81; prof. biomed. engring./orthopaedic biomechanics biomaterials La. Tech. U., Ruston, 1982—; prof., chmn. dept. biomechanics N.Y. Coll. Osteo. Medicine, Old Westbury, 1989-93; prof., asst. to pres. and dir. doctoral program Life Coll., Marietta, Ga., 1993—; dir. tng. Rehab. Rsch. and Devel. Ctr., 1983-85; mem. La. Tech. U. Libr. Com., 1983-85; chmn. design competition Assn. Biomed. Engrs.; mem. steering com. So. Biomed. Engring. Confs., 1983—; chmn. tech. in health care conf. U. Cambridge, 1985; chmn. Internat. Symposium on Bioengring., Calcutta, India, 1985; dir. orthopaedic biomechanics rsch. labs., staff Nassau County Med. Ctr., Long Island, 1989—; prof., asst. to pres., dir. doctoral program Life Coll., Marietta, Ga., 1993—. Mem. biomed. engring. faculty com. La. Tech. U., faculty com., rsch. awards com., grad. studies com., grad. faculty, acad. bd. dirs; vis. scientist Dryburn Hosp., Durham, Eng., 1985-87, cons., 1988—; vis. prof. U. Istanbul, 1982, Lab. de Recherch Orthopediques, Paris, 1985—, Kings Coll. Med. Sch. U. London, 1989—, Indian Inst. Tech., New Delhi, Postgrad Inst. Med. Edn. and Rsch., Chandigarh, India, 1989—, Inst. Biol. Physics USSR Acad. Sci., Moscow, 1990, Polytech. Ctrl. London, 1991—; adj. prof. Coll. Physicians and Surgeons Columbia U., N.Y.C., 1988—, Inst. Biol. Physics USSR Acad. Sci., Moscow, 1990, N.Y. Coll. Podiatric Medicine, 1991—, CUNY, 1992—; cons. Lincoln Gen. Hosp., Ruston, La., 1982-85, La. State U. Med. Ctr., Shreveport, 1982—, St. Luke's and Roosevelt Hosp. Ctr., N.Y., 1988—, Foot Clinics N.Y., 1991—, Vets. Affairs Med. Ctr., N.Y., 1992—, various biomed. rsch. & legal corps., U.S., U.K.; mem. media resource svc. Inst. Pub. Info., N.Y., 1989—; med. scientist, cons. NATO, 1982—; presenter, lectr., dir. organizer numerous sci. orgns. and nat. & internat. confs.; external examiner for doctoral candidates All India Inst. Med. Scis., New Delhi, Indian Inst. of Tech., New Delhi, Banaras Hindu U., Varanasi, India, 1994—; vis. prof. U. Buenos Aires, Pontific Cath. U. Chile, Fed. U. Rio de Janeiro, numerous others. Author: Rheological Behavior of Articular Cartiliage Under Tensile Loads, 1967, Effects of Ionizing Radiation on the Mechanical Properties of Skin, 1975, Effects of Fractionated Doses of X-irradiation on the Mechanical Properties of Skin--A Long Term Study, 1980, Effects of Ionizing Radiation on the Structure & Physical Properties of the Skin, 1983, 3-D Model of Vertebra for Spinal Surgery, 1985, Application of Carbon Fibers in Orthopaedic Surgery, 1985, Relation Between Metal Corrision & Electrical Polarization, 1989, The Distribution of Stresses in the Human Lumbar Spine, 1989, Medical Devices & Orthopaedic Implants in the United States, 1989, Spinal Surgery by Modeling, 1989, Multipoint Determination of Pressure-Volume Curves in Human Intervertebral Discs, 1993, Evaluation of Volume-Pressure Relationship in Lumbar Discs Using Model and Experimental Studies, 1994, A Mechanism of Laser Nuclectomy, 1994, Microminiaturization in Laser Surgery in Vivo Intradiscal Pressure Measurements in Lumbar Intervertebral Discs, 1994, An Experimental and Mathematical Simulation of Fracture of Human Bone Due to Jumping, 1994; editor The Lower Extremity, 1993—; guest editor IEEE Engring. in Medicine & Biology, 1991; mem. editorial bd. Med. Instrumentation, 1988—, Jour. Biomed. Instrumentation & Tech., 1988—, Jour. Med. Engring. & Tech., 1989—, Jour. Med. Design & Material, 1990—, Jour. Long-Term Effects Med. Implants, 1991—, Biomed. Sci. & Tech., 1991—; reviewer Jour. Biomechanics, 1981—, Clin. Biomechanics, 1984—, Jour. Biomed. Engring., 1981, Phys. Therapy, 1990—, IEEE Biomed. Transactions, 1991—, Jour. Engring. in Medicine, 1989—; contbr. articles to profl. jours. Faculty advisor India Students Assn. Wayne State U., 1980. Recipient Edwin Tate award U. Surrey, 1968, Third Internat. Olympic Com. World Congress On Sprots Scis. award, Atlanta, 1995; numerous rsch. grants. Fellow ASME (bioengring. com. 1990—, award L.I. chpt. 1991), Biol. Engring. Soc. (London) (President's prize 1984), Instn. Mech. Engrs. (chmn. revv. bd. for corp. memberships, James Clayton awards 1974-76); mem. AAAS, Am. Coll. Sports Medicine, Am. Soc. Biomechanics (edn. com. 1990—), Orthopaedic Rsch. Soc., Biomed. Engring. Soc., India Assn., India Assn. North La., Inst. Physics and Engring. in Medicine. Sikh. Achievements include research in microfracture simulation of human vertebrae under compressive loading, laserectomy of the human nucleus pulposus and its effect on the intradiscal pressure, pressure-volume relation in human intervertebral discs, in vitro and in vivo intradiscal pressure measurements before and after laserectomy of the human nucleus pulposus, gait analysis of a diabetic foot, bioengineering in the millennium, bioengineering-building the future of biology and medicine, bioengineering the cutting edge of biology and medicine in the millennium, in vivo micro-fracture simulation in Indian Olympic field hockey players, relief from low-back pain in sports by infusion of saline into the human nucleus pulposus and establishing the pressure-volume relationship, clinical applications of bioinstrumentation for better health, fifth IOC World Congress on sports sciences, micro-fracture simulation in tennis players, human gait analysis normal and pathological, simulation of micro-fracture injury in female gymnasts-an in vivo study. Office: Life Coll Sch Grad Studies Marietta GA 30060 E-mail: drhsranu@yahoo.com.

RANUM, OREST ALLEN, historian, educator; b. Lyle, Minn., Feb. 18, 1933; s. Luther George and Nada (Chaffee) R.; m. Patricia McGroder, July 4, 1955; children— Kristin, Marcus BA, Macalester Coll., St. Paul, 1955; MA, U. Minn., 1957, PhD, 1961. Asst. prof. U. So. Calif., 1960-61; asst. prof. Columbia U., N.Y.C., 1961-63, assoc. prof., 1963-69; prof. history Johns Hopkins U., Balt., 1969-99; ret., 1999. Mem., chmn. GRE Ednl. Testing Service, Princeton, 1973-78 Author: Richelieu and Councilors, 1963; Paris, Age of Absolutism, 1968; Artisans of Glory, 1981, The Fronde, 1993. Recipient Bronze medal City of Tours, France, 1980. Mem. Am. Hist. Assn., Soc. French Hist. Studies, Inst. de France (corr.), Académie des Sciences Morales et Politiques (Paris; corr. 1989), Société de l'Histoire de France, Collège de France (internat. chair 1994-95). Home: 208 Ridgewood Rd Baltimore MD 21210-2539 Office: History Dept Johns Hopkins U Baltimore MD 21218 E-mail: pranum@compuserve.com.

RAO, ABDUL SOHAIL, transplant surgeon, immunologist, researcher; b. Karachi, Sind, Pakistan, Jan. 1, 1958; came to U.S., 1981; s. Majid Khan and Saeeda Majid (Fareed) R.; m. Rukhsana Sohail Bukhari, Oct. 12, 1983; children: Rida, Raoul, Rameez. MD, Dow Med. Coll., Karachi, 1983; MA, Boston U., 1990; DPhil, U. Oxford, Eng., 1993. Instr. Dow Med. Coll., 1983-85, Aga Khan U., Karachi, 1985-87; rsch. fellow Harvard Med. Sch., Boston, 1989-90; clin. instr. U. Oxford, 1990-92; dir. sect. of med. informatics Thomas E. Starzl Transplantation Inst., Pitts., 1993-2000, dir. sect. of cellular transplantation, 1995-2000, assoc. dir. translational rsch., 1994-2000, dir. rsch. adminstrn., 1994-2000, vice chair protocol com., 1994-2000; mem. exec. com. Pitts. Transplantation Inst., 1994-01; sr. assoc. dean rsch. and biomed. grad. studies MCP Hahnemann U. Sch. Medicine, Philadelphia, 2001—. Asst. prof. U. Pitts., 1993—; prof. ad honorarium U. Antiouqia, Medellin, Columbia, 1995-2000. Contbr. over 200 articles to profl. jours. Rsch. grantee British VC Com., 1990-92, BenVenue Pharm., 1994-96, Cancer Rsch. Treatment Found., 1996—, NIH, 1996—; recipient Outstanding Professorship award Govt. of India, 1998. Mem. AAAS, British Soc. Immunology, British Transplantation Soc., Pakistan Physiol. Soc., Pakistan Med. Assn., Cell Transplantation Soc., Transplantation Soc., Am. Soc. Transplant Surgeons, Am. Soc. Transplant Physicians. Home: 34 Dominion Dr Marlton NJ 08053 Office: MCP Hahnemann U Sch Medicine Mail Stop 400 245 N 15h St Philadelphia PA 19102-1192 E-mail: asr27@drexel.edu.

RAO, CH. V. endocrinologist, educator; b. Bantumelli, India, Dec. 26, 1941; came to U.S., 1964; m. Vijayalakshmi, Oct. 10, 1971; children: Naveen Rao, Satish Rao. B of Vet. Sci., Andhra Vet. Coll., Tirupathi, India, 1964; MS, Wash. State U., 1966, PhD, 1969. Rsch. asst. Wash. State U., Pullman, 1964-69; rsch. assoc. Albert Einstein Coll. Medicine, Bronx, N.Y., 1969-70, Cornell U. Med. Coll., N.Y.C., 1970-72; asst. prof. U. Louisville, 1972-76, assoc. prof., 1976-79, prof., 1979—. Cons. numerous local, nat. and internat. orgns., 1972—. Contbr. over 600 articles and abstracts to profl. jours. Recipient Pres.'s award for Outstanding Scholarship, U. Louisville, 1987, numerous rsch. grants NIH, 1976—. Mem. Am. Soc. Biol. Chemistry and Molecular Biology, Am. Soc. Cell Biology, Am. Fertility Soc., Soc. Study of Reproduction, Soc. Gynecologic Investigation, Endocrine Soc., Am. Physiol. Soc., Sigma Xi. Achievements include pioneering research in molecular reproductive biology and medicine. Office: Univ Louisville Med Dental Rsch 511 S Floyd St Bldg 438 Louisville KY 40202-1825

RAO, DABEERU C. epidemiologist, educator; b. Apr. 6, 1946; came to U.S., 1972; s. Ramarao Patnaik and Venkataratnam (Raghupatruni) R.; m. Sarada Patnaik, 1974; children: Ravi, Lakshmi. BS in Stats., Indian Statis. Inst., Calcutta, 1967, MS, 1968, PhD, 1971. Rsch. fellow U. Sheffield, Eng., 1971-72; asst. prof., geneticist U. Hawaii, Honolulu, 1972-78, assoc. prof., geneticist, 1978-80; assoc. prof., dir. divsn. biostats. Washington U. Med. Sch., St. Louis, 1980-82, prof. depts. biostats., psychiatry and genetics, 1982—. Adj. prof. math., 1982—, dir. div. biostats., 1980—. Author: A Source Book for Linkage in Man, 1979, Methods in Genetic Epidemiology, 1983, Genetic Epidemiology of Coronary Heart Disease, 1984; editor-in-chief Genetic Epidemiology jour., 1984-91; contbr. articles to profl. jours. Grantee NIH, 1978—. Mem. Am. Statis. Assn., Am. Soc. Human Genetics, Internat. Genetic Epidemiology Soc. (pres. 1996), Behavior Genetics Assn., Soc. Epidemiol. Rsch., Biomed. soc. Office: Washington U Sch Medicine Divsn Biostats Box 8067 660 S Euclid Ave Saint Louis MO 63110-1010 E-mail: rao@wubios.wustl.edu.

RAO, DESIRAJU BHAVANARAYANA, meteorologist, oceanographer, educator; b. Visakhapatnam, India, Dec. 8, 1936; came to U.S., 1960, naturalized, 1974; s. Desiraju Sreeramulu and Desiraju Hanumayamma Adavikolanu; m. Padmavati Kavuru; children: Desiraju Pramila, Desiraju Kavitha. B.Sc., Andhra U., Waltair, India, 1956, M.Sc., 1959; MS, U. Chgo., 1962, PhD, 1965. Rsch. scholar Indian Naval Phys. Labs., Cochin, 1959-60; postdoctoral fellow Nat. Center Atmospheric Rsch., Boulder, Colo., 1965-67; rsch. scientist marine scis. br. Can. Dept. Energy, Mines and Resources, Ottawa, Ont., 1967-68; asst. prof. atmospheric sci. Colo. State U., Ft. Collins, 1968-71; assoc. prof. energetics, also Center Gt. Lakes Studies, U. Wis.-Milw., 1971-74, prof., 1974-76; head phys. limnology and meteorology group Gt. Lakes Environ. Rsch. Lab., NOAA, Ann Arbor, Mich., 1975-80; adj. prof. limnology and meteorology U. Mich., 1977-80; head oceans and ice br. Lab. for Atmospheric Sci., Goddard Space Flight Ctr., NASA, Greenbelt, Md., 1980-84; chief marine prediction br. Nat. Meteorol. Ctr., NOAA, Washington, 1984-95; chief Ocean Modeling Br., Nat. Ctrs. Environ. Prediction NOAA, 1995—. Adj. prof. meteorology U. Md., College Park, 1981—; cons. in field. Contbr. articles on atmospheric, oceanic and lake dynamics to sci. jours. Fellow Am. Meteorol. Soc. (v.p. Denver chpt. 1969-70); Mem. Am. Soc. Limnology and Oceanography, AAAS, Internat. Water Resources Assn. (charter), Am. Geophys. Union, Internat. Assn. for Gt. Lakes Research, The Oceanography Soc. (charter), Sigma Xi. Home: 13101 Hugo Pl Silver Spring MD 20906-5916 Office: 5200 Auth Rd Rm 209 Suitland MD 20746-4304 E-mail: dbrao@ncep.noaa.gov.

RAO, IDUPULAPATI MADHUSUDANA, plant nutritionist, plant physiologist; b. Mandadam, Andhra Pradesh, India, July 1, 1951; s. Idupulapati Nageswara Rao and Rajya Lakshmi (Jammula) Idupulapati; m. Kusuma Kumari Yarlagadda, June 9, 1973; children: Madhuri, Subhashini. BS, Andhra U., Waltair, India, 1971; MS, Bhopal (India) U., 1973; PhD, Sri Venkateswara U., Tirupati, India, 1978. Rsch. assoc. U. Hyderabad, India, 1978-79; plant physiologist Internat. Crops Rsch. Inst. for Semi-Arid Tropics, Hyderabad, India, 1979-80; rsch. assoc. U. Ill., Chgo., 1981-82, Urbana, 1983-84; rsch. plant physiologist U. Calif., Berkeley, 1985-86, asst. specialist, 1987-88; plant nutritionist Internat. Ctr. for Tropical Agr., Cali, Colombia, 1989—. Vis. sci. BTI at Cornell U., Ithaca, N.Y., 1982; assoc. editor Jour. Environ. Quality, 2000—. Contbr. articles to profl. jours. Rsch. grantee BMZ-GTZ, 1991. Mem. Am. Soc. Plant Physiology, Am. Soc. Agronomy, Crop Sci. Soc. Am., Soil Sci. Soc. Am., N.Y. Acad. Scis. Avocations: playing tennis, watching sports. Home: Mandadam P. Mangalagiri 522503 India Office: Internat Ctr for Tropical Agr A.A. 6713 Cali Colombia

RAO, JAGANMOHAN BOPPANA LAKSHIMI, electrical engineer; b. Raghavapuram, India, Aug. 6, 1936; came to U.S. 1961; s. Satyanarayana and Subbarao (Challagulla) Boppana; m. Krishna K. Koganty, May 18, 1960; children: Ravi, Madhu, Sushma. MSEE, U. Wash., 1963, PhD in Elec. Engring., 1966. Asst. rsch. engr. Radiation Lab., U. Mich., Ann Arbor, 1966-68; staff engr. Northrop Corp., McLean, Va., 1968-70; asst. prof. Savannah (Ga.) State Coll., 1970-71; rsch. assoc. NASA Goddard Space Flight Ctr., Greenbelt, Md., 1971-73; electronics engr. Naval Rsch. Lab., Washington, 1974—. Contbr. articles to profl. jours. Pres. Greater Washington Telugu Cultural Soc., 1977-78. Recipient Spl. Achievement award IEEE/Antennas and Propagation Soc., 1969, pub. award, Naval Rsch. Lab., 1998. Fellow IEEE (chpt. chmn. 1986-87), Sigma Xi. Achievements include patents on bicollimated dual reflector antenna and on voltage controlled ferroelectric lens phased array. Home: 9004 Acredale Ct College Park MD 20740-4001 E-mail: rao@radar.nrl.navy.mil.

RAO, JIAN YU, physician, cancer biologist, educator; b. Xingguo, Jiangxi, China, Feb. 16, 1964; s. Youfar Rao and Yuanqiao Ding; m. Pingping Shuang Gu, Jan. 20, 1987; children: Andrew William, Elizabeth Ann. MD, Shanghai Med. U., 1984. Diplomate Am. Bd. Pathology. Rsch. investigator Cancer Inst. Chinese Acad. Med. Scis., Beijing, 1984-87; asst. rsch. prof. U. Okla. Health Scis. Ctr., 1993-94; intern, resident, cytopathology fellow UCLA Med. Ctr., 1994-98, asst. rschr., 1995-99, asst. prof., 1999—. Co-author: Molecular Epidemiology, 1993, Moleculary Pathology of Early Cancer, 1999; contbr. articles to profl. jours. Recipient Young Investigator award Internat. Soc. Analytic Cytology, 1992, Richard F. Dwyer and Elaine W. Dwyer award Jonsson Comprehensive Cancer Ctr., 1995; Provost's Rsch. fellow U. Okla. Health Scis. Ctr., 1987; Rsch. grantee Nat. Cancer Inst. NIH, 1993. Mem. AMA, Internat. Soc. Preventive Oncology, Am. Soc. Clin. Pathologists, Sigma Xi. Achievements include patent for Cell Analysis Method Using Quantitative Fluorescence Image Analysis. Office: UCLA 10833 Le Conte Ave Los Angeles CA 90095-3075 Fax: 310-206-5178.

RAO, K.V.R. MOHAN See KOTTAMASU, MOHAN RAO

RAO, NANNAPANENI NARAYANA, electrical engineer; b. Kakumanu, Andhra Pradesh, India; m. Sarojini Jonnalagadda, June 10, 1955; children: Vanaja, Durgaprasad, Hariprasad. BSc in Physics, U. Madras, India, 1952; DMIT in Electronics, Madras Inst. Tech., 1955; MSEE, U. Wash., 1960, PhD in Elec. Engring, 1965. Acting instr. elec. engring. U. Wash., 1960-64, acting asst. prof., 1964-65; asst. prof. elec. engring. U. Ill., Urbana, 1965-69, asso. prof., 1969-75, prof., 1975—, assoc. head elec. and computer engring., 1987—. Cons. Fakultas Teknik, Univ. Indonesia, Jakarta, 1985-86, 87. Author: Basic Electromagnetics with Applications, 1972, Elements of Engineering Electromagnetics, 5th edit., 2000; contbr. numerous articles to profl. jours. Recipient Engring. award Telugu Assn. N.Am., 1983, Excellence in Edn. award, 1999, Fakultas Teknik award Universitatas Indonesia, 1986. Fellow IEEE (Undergrad. Teaching award 1994); mem. Am. Soc. Engring. Edn. (AT&T Found. award for excellence in instrn. engring. students 1991), Internat. Union Radio Sci. (U.S. Commn. G). Achievements include contributions to engineering education in the United States and abroad. Home: 2509 S Lynn St Urbana IL 61801-6841 Office: U Ill Dept Elec & Computer Engring 1406 W Green St Urbana IL 61801-2918 E-mail: rao@ece.uiuc.edu.

RAO, P. SYAMASUNDAR, pediatric cardiologist; b. Ullibhadra, India, Sept. 21, 1941; came to U.S., 1966; s. P.V.B. Krishna Rao and P. Savithramma; m. P. Hymavathi, Mar. 27, 1966; children: Vijay K. Patnana, Madhavi Patnana, Radkhika N. Patnana. Intermediate degree in Arts and Scis., Andhra U., Visakhapatnam, India, 1958; MBBS, Andhra Med. Coll., Visakhapatnam, 1964, diploma in child health, 1966. Diplomate Am. Bd. Pediats, Am. Bd. Pediat. Cardiology. Asst. prof. Med. Coll. Ga., Augusta, 1972-75, assoc. prof., 1975-79, prof. pediats., 1979-82, assoc. dir. pediat. cardiology, 1976-82; cons. pediat. cardiologist King Faisal Specialist Hosp., Riyadh, Saudi Arabia, 1982-87, chmn. pediats. Saudi Arabia, 1986-87; prof., head pediat. cardiology U. Wis. Med. Sch., Madison, 1987-94; prof., dir. pediat. cardiology St. Louis U. Sch. Medicine, 1994-98, prof. pediats., 1998—. Author: Tricuspid Atresia, 1982, 2d edit., 1992, Transcatheter Therapy in Pediatric Cardiology, 1993; contbr. over 250 articles to profl. jours., 40 chpts. to books. Recipient award for outstanding contbn. to pediat. cardiology Telugu Assn. N.Am., John Lind's Lectr. award Swedish Pediat. Assn.,1 992, Meritorious Svc. award Wis.-Nicaragua Ptnr., 1993, Outstanding Scientist award Am. Assn. Cardiologists of Indian Origin, 1996. Fellow Am. Coll. Cardiology (councillor Mo. chpt. 1997), Am. Acad. Pediats., Soc. Cardiac Antiography (mem. pediat. cardiology com. 1996); mem. Am. Pediat. Soc., Soc. Pediat. Rsch., Am. Heart Assn. Avocations: tennis, movies. Office: St Louis U Sch Medicine 1465 S Grand Blvd Saint Louis MO 63104-1003 E-mail: rapos@slu.edu.

RAO, POTARAZU KRISHNA, government executive; b. Andhra Pradesh, India, Mar. 26, 1930; s. Satyanarayana and Annapoorna (Mullapudi) P.; m. Rukmani Krutivinti, Aug. 5, 1954; children: Ramanarayan, Sreedhar. BS, Andhra U., 1950, MS, 1952, Fla. State U., 1957; PhD, NYU, 1968. Meteorologist Can. Meteorol. Svc., Montreal, Can., 1960-61; rsch. phys. scientist Nat. Oceanic and Atmospheric Adminstrn./Nat. Environ. Satellite Data and Info. Svc., Washington, 1961-74, chief atmospheric energetics br., acting dir., 1976-80, chief satellite applications lab., 1980-86, dir. office of rsch. and applications, 1986-96; chief scientist for satellite and info. svcs. Nat. Oceanic and Atmospheric Adminstrn., 1996—; program dir., weather modification NSF, 1971-72; advisor on satellite programs World Meteorological Orgn., Geneva, 1974-76. Bd. dirs. Nat. Oceanic and Atmospheric Adminstrn. Climate and Global Change Program, Washington; adv. bd. Coop. Inst. for Rsch. in Atmospheres, Ft. Collins, Colo., 1986—. Editor: Weather Satellites, 1990; contbr. articles to profl. jours. Founder, trustee Sri Siva Vishnu Temple, Lanham, Md. Fellow Am. Meteorol. Soc., Royal Meteorol. Soc. (U.K.), N.Y. Acad. Scis. Hindu. Avocations: tennis, photography. Home: 15824 Buena Vista Dr Rockville MD 20855-2658 Office: NESDIS/NOAA NOAA Science Ctr 1335 E West Hwy Silver Spring MD 20910-3225

RAO, RAMA KRISHNA R. pharmaceutical company executive; b. Tanuku, Andhra P., India, Nov. 20, 1955; came to U.S., 1998; s. R.R. and Satyavani R. (Gudipati) R.; m. Kavitha Advikolanu, May 19, 1996. B in Tech., Indian Inst. Tech., Delhi, 1977; Postgrad. Diploma in Mgmt., Indian Inst. Mgmt., Calcutta, 1981; MBA, INSEAD, Fontainebleu, France, 1989. Asst. mgr. Metal Box India, Calcutta, 1977-84; exec. asst. to gen. mgr. Bank of Bahrain & Kuwait, Bahrain, 1985-88; fin. assoc. Eli Lilly, Geneva, credit and customer svc. mgr., 1993-94, fin. mgr. Africa, 1994-95; mgr. (global treasury) Gems Eli Lilly, Brussels, 1995-97; fin. advisor corp. fin. and investment banking Lilly Corp. Ctr., Indpls., 1998-99; CFO, fin. mgr. PC/NS Lilly USA, 1999—2001; fin. dir. intercontinental region Novartis Oncology Bus. Unit, East Hanover, NJ, 2001—. Alumni mem. panel for INSEAD interviews, Belgium, U.S., 1995-99. Contbr. journalist Students' Newsletter, IIT, Delhi, co-editor Students' Newsletter, I.I.M., Calcutta, INSEAD, Fontainebleu, France. Vol. Samaritans/Befrienders, Bahrain, 1987, 88; donor of blood Red Cross/Crescent, India, Belgium, U.S., Bahrain, 1974-97. Recipient First prize Nat. Young Mgrs. Competition, All India Mgmt. Assn., 1983. Mem. AMA, Assn. Investment Mgmt. and Rsch., Inst. Mgmt. Accts. Hindu. Avocations: travel, military history, foreign policy. E-male. E-mail: rama.rao@pharma.novartis.com.

RAO, RAMACHANDRA ADISESHAPPA, civil engineering educator; b. Kanakapura, Karnataka, India, Oct. 23, 1939; came to U.S., 1962; s. Adiseshappa Nagappa and Jayalakshmi (Gopaliah) R.; m. Mamatha Shama, Aug. 26, 1971; children: Malini Bhagavathi, Karthikeya Adisesha, Siddhartha Shankara. BE, U. Mysore, 1960; MSCE, U. Minn., 1964; PhD, U. Ill., 1968. Asst. prof. Purdue U., West Lafayette, Ind., 1968-73, assoc. prof., 1973-80, prof., 1980—. Cons. in field., 1971—. Co-author: Dynamic Stochastic Models from Empirical Data, 1976. NRAC Sr. Rsch. fellow, Chnstchurch, New Zeeland, 1977-78. Hindu. Home: 426 Forest Hill Dr West Lafayette IN 47906-2316 Office: Purdue U Sch Civil Engring Civil Engring Bldg West Lafayette IN 47907

RAO, SATISH, medical educator, physician scientist; MB BS, Osmania Med. Coll., Hyderabad, India, 1978; PhD, U. Sheffield, Eng., 1987. Intern in surgeyr North Manchester (Eng.) Gen. Hosp., 1979-80; house physician in internal medicine Newcastle Gen. Hosp., Newcastle upon Tyne, Eng., 1980; sr. house officer Sunderland Gen. Hosp., U.k., 1980-82; registrar Dist. Hosp., York, Eng., 1982-84; clin. rsch. fellow, hon. med. registrar in gastroenterology Royal Hallamshire Hosp., Sheffield, Eng., 1984-85, sr. registrar in gastroenterology Eng., 1985-86, clin. rsch. fellow in gastroenterology Eng., 1986-87; registrar in gastroenterology, therapeutics fellow Royal Liverpool (Eng.) Hosp., 1987-88; cons. physician City Hosp., Nottingham, Eng., 1991; asst. prof. medicine dept. internal medicine U. Iowa Coll. Medicine, Iowa City, 1991-97, assoc. prof., 1987—2002, prof. medicine, 2002—; dir. neurogastroenterology and GI motility U. Iowa Health Care. Cons. physician, gastroenterologist Apollo Hosps., Pramila Nursing Home, Durgabhai Deshmukh Hosp., Hyderabad, 1989-90; reviewer numerous jours. in field. Co-editor: Developments and Controversies in Gastrointestinal Motility; editor: Gastrointestinal Motility. Tests and a Problem-Oriented Approach, 1999, Disorders of Anorectum, 2001; patentee device for simulating artificial stool, multi sensor anorectal manometry catheter with surface electromyography; contbr. chpts. to books, more than 100 articles to profl. jours. Recipient Jubilee meeting rsch. prize N. Eng. Gastroenterology Soc., 1987, Clin. Rsch. award Am. Gastroenterology Assn., Smith Kline French-Beecham, 1993. Fellow Royal Coll. Physicians; mem. Am. Motility Soc., Am. Coll. Gastroenterology, Am. Gastroenterology Assn. (chair colonic motility and sensation rsch. forum 1999, mem. nerve, gut, motility abstract selection com. 1998, chair constipation focused rsch. update 1999), Ctrl. Soc. Clin. Rsch., Brit. Soc. Gastroenterology. Office: U Iowa Hosps 4612 JCP 200 Hawkins Dr Iowa City IA 52242-1009 E-mail: satish-rao@uiowa.edu.

RAO, SETHURAMIAH LAKSHMINARAYANA, demographer, United Nations official; b. Mysore, Karnataka, India, Apr. 28, 1942; came to U.S., 1967; s. Ramakrishniah Sethuramiah and Bhageerathi; m. Sudha Bagur Viswanath, Aug. 1, 1971; children: Rekha, Kumar. MSc, U. Mysore, 1963; MPH, U. N.C., 1968; cert., U. Mich., 1969; PhD, U. Pa., 1971. Cert. Demographic Tng. and Rsch. Ctr., Bombay. Asst. prof. Brown U., Providence, 1971-73; UN adviser Govt. of Sri Lanka, Colombo, 1974-77; chief population and devel. UN Population Fund, N.Y.C., 1978-82, chief policy br., 1982-90, country dir. Addis Ababa, Ethiopia, 1991-92, dep. dir. info. & extern rels. N.Y.C., 1992-95, dir. tech. and evaluation divsn., 1995-97, dir. divsn. adminstrn. fin. and mgmt., 1998-2000, dir. strategic planning & coord. divsn., 2001—. Sec. UN Population Fund segment of UN Devel. Program/UN Population Fund exec. bd.; leader UN tech. missions to several countries. Author: Socio-Religious Factors in Fertility, 1973; co-author: Population Problems of Sri Lanka, 1977, Population Program Experience, 1991; contbr. articles to profl. jours. V.p. Mysore Self Reliance Assn., Mangalore, 1963-65, Indo-Am. Forum for Polit. Edn., N.Y., 1989-90; founder, pres. New Eng. Kannada Koota, Providence, 1972-73. Recipient several acad. honors and gold medals, U. Pa., 1971, U. Mysore, 1961, 63. Mem. Delta Omega, Internat. Union for the Scientific Study of Population. Avocations: traveling, debate, bridge playing. Home: 143 Nelson Rd Scarsdale NY 10583-5811 Office: UN Population Fund 220 E 42nd St New York NY 10017-5806 E-mail: rao2108@aol.com.

RAO, SRINATH JAYRAM, electronics professional; b. Mangalore, Karnataka, India, Aug. 18, 1948; s. Jayram Javali and Sita Jayram (Prabhu) R.; m. Mangala Kamath; children: Nishant, Mohnish. B Tech with honors, IIT, Bombay, 1970; Diploma in Mgmt., All India Mgmt. Assn., Delhi, 1984. Cert. in human rels. and mgmt. field. Mktg. engr. Blue Star, Ltd., Bombay, 1970-76; product mgr. Philips, Teheran, Iran, 1977-79, product sales mgr. Bombay, 1979-89; dir. Fountainhead Electronics, Pvt. Ltd., 1989—; proprietor Fountainhead Solutions, San Antonio, 1997—. Founder, bd. dirs. Giants Group, Bombay, 1985-96, pres. 1986. Fellow Inst. Mktg. Mgmt., Inst. Electronics and Telecomms.; mem. Computer Soc. India, Instrument Soc. of India (life), Indian Cryogenics Coun. (life). Avocations: environ. issues, music, family activities, info. technology. E-mail: sjrao@fountainheadsolutions.com.

RAOOF, AMEED MOHAMMED SAEED, anatomist; b. Baghdad, Iraq, Aug. 20, 1952; s. Mohammed Saeed and Selima Shaker (Mahmood) R.; m. Samar Ghanim Ismail, Apr. 10, 1978; children: Saja, Duna, Khalid, Sarah. Diploma med. edn., U. Dundee, 1991, PhD in Anatomy, 1984; MSc in Anatomy, U. Baghdad, 1980, MB ChB, 1977. Lectr. Coll. of Medicine, Baghdad, 1978-80; tutor U. Dundee, 1983-84; asst. prof. Coll. of Medicine, Abha, Saudi Arabia, 1985-95, assoc. prof. Saudi Arabia, 1996-98; lectr. U. Mich. Sch. Medicine, Ann Arbor, 1998—. Head med. edn. Office Coll. Medicine, Abha, 1988-92; mem. coll. rsch. com., 1994—, mem. acad. com., 1986—, head computer ctr., 1990—. Contbr. articles profl. jours. Recipient Cert. of Recognition, Deanship of Admission, 1990, 1991, 1992, 1993, Elizabeth Crosby award, 2001, U. Mich. award for humanism in med. edn., 2001. Mem.: Assn. Am. Med. Colls., Internat. Soc. Plastination, Am. Assn. Clin. Anatomy, Am. Assn. Anatomy, Internat. Assn. Med. Sci. Educators, Assn. Med. Edn. Europe, Internat. Brain Rsch. Orgn., Royal Microscopical Soc., Assn. for Study of Med. Edn., AAAS. Achievements include description for the first time the complete histochemical profile of the Ochocerca fasciata worm; description of human fetal spinal cord length changes using room-temperature plastination technique; distribution of acetylcholinesterase enzyme in the camel's brain, histology and ultrastructure of the camel's lacrimal gland; choice factor for med. students' admission to U. Mich. Med. Sch., intro. of integrated clin. tchg. to anatomy. Address: 3808 Med Sci II Ann Arbor MI 48109-0608

RAPAPORT, RITA, artist, sculpture, painter; b. N.Y.C., May 25, 1918; d. Mandel E. and Birdie (Shapiro) Cohen; m. Alexander Rapaport, Oct. 13, 1940 (widowed June 1983); children: Anne, Marshall, Judith; m. Leon L. Wolfe, Mar. 15, 1986. BA, N.Y.U., 1940. Artist-in-residence Westchester Holocaust Commn. Manhatanville Coll. Purchase N.Y., 1990—. Prin. works include Gate of Remembrance, 1992. Mem. Nat. Orgn. Women, Dem. Party, B'nai Brith Haddassah, Mamaroneck Artists Guild, Hudson River Mus., Metro. Mus., Hudson River Contemporary Artists, Jewish Mus. N.Y., Nat. Holocaust Mus. Jewish. Avocations: swimming, photography, gardening, interior decorating. Home: 15 Tompkins Rd Scarsdale NY 10583-2839

RAPAPORT, SAMUEL I. educator, physician; b. Los Angeles, Nov. 19, 1921; s. Hyman and Bertha (Krupnick) R.; m. Joyce Mildred Cooperman, Oct. 3, 1950; children: Susan Rapaport Braunwald, Sally Rapaport Hartinian, Mark Hyman, Bruce Allen. Student, UCLA; MD, U. So. Calif., 1945. Diplomate: Am. Bd. Internal Medicine (mem. bd. 1973-80, bd. govs. 1976-80, sec.-treas., chmn. hematology subcom. 1978-80). Intern Los Angeles County Hosp., 1945; resident medicine VA Hosp., Long Beach, Calif., 1948-50, chief hematology sect., 1950-57; asso. prof. medicine U. Calif. at Los Angeles Med. Center, 1957-58; mem. faculty U. So. Calif. Sch. Medicine, 1958-74, head hematology div. dept. medicine, 1958-74, prof. medicine, 1964-74; head hematology div. Los Angeles County-U. So. Calif. Med. Center, 1958-74; chief med. service San Diego VA Hosp., 1974-78; prof. medicine U. Calif., San Diego, 1974-96; prof. emeritus, 1996—; vice chmn. dept. medicine U. Calif., 1974-78, co-head hematology-oncology div., 1978-87, prof. pathology, 1980-93; dir. Hematology Lab., U. Calif.-San Diego Med. Ctr., 1980-87. Cons. hematology tng. grants study sect. Nat. Inst. Arthritis and Metabolic Diseases, 1968-71; mem. med. adv. coun. Nat. Hemophilia Found., 1970, 77— ; chmn. adv. com., div. blood diseases and resources Nat. Heart, Lung and Blood Inst., 1980-82, mem. adv. coun., 1989-93; mem. hematology study sect. NIH, 1984-88, chmn. study sect., 1977-88. Author: Introduction to Hematology, 1971, 2d edit., 1987; also papers in field. Chmn. coun. on thrombosis Am. Heart Assn., 1995-97. Served with USAAF, 1946-48. Spl. fellow Nat. Heart Inst., U. Oslo, 1964-65; Fulbright research scholar U. Oslo, 1953-54; fellow Sackler Inst. for Advanced Study, Tel Aviv U., 1983; recipient Disting. Sci. Achievement award Coun. on Arteriosclerosis, Thrombosis, and Vascular Biology Am. Heart Assn., 2001. Master ACP (John Phillips Meml. award for outstanding work on clin. medicine 1996); mem. Assn. Am. Physicians, Am. Soc. Hematology (pres. 1977), Western Soc. Clin. Rsch. (pres. 1966), Am. Fedn. Clin. Rsch. (chmn. Western sect. 1960), Am. Soc. Clin. Investigation, Western Assn. Physicians (pres. 1973) Home: 7887 Lookout Dr La Jolla CA 92037-3951

RAPA RAFANIELLO, HELEN MARIE, forensic scientist; b. Bklyn., Oct. 26, 1965; d. Carlo Alberto Rapa and Bernice Ann Walsh; m. Gary Francis Rafaniello, Aug. 29, 1992; children: Carl Michael Rafaniello, Melissa Ann Rafaniello. BS, St. Joseph's Coll., 1987; MS, John Jay Coll. CUNY, 1991. Lab. rsch. technician N.Y. Blood Ctr., N.Y.C., 1991-92; forensic analyst Office of Chief Med. Examiner of N.Y.C., 1992-96, forensic scientist, 1996—. Liaison for dept. of forensic biology Office of Chief Med. Examiner, Kings County Dist. Atty.'s Sexual Assault Task Force, Bklyn., 1999—. Mem. Northeastern Assn. Forensic Scientists, N.Y. Microscopical Soc. Office: Office of Chief Med Examiner of NYC 520 1st Ave New York NY 10016

RAPER, CHARLES ALBERT, retired management consultant; b. Charleston, W.Va., Aug. 18, 1926; s. Kenneth B. and Louise (Williams) R.; m. Margaret Ann Weers, Dec. 26, 1947; children: Kathleen, Josephine, Charles. Student, Okla. State U., 1945; BS, U. Ill., 1949. Sales mgr. Meyer Furnace Co., Peoria, Ill., 1949-54; v.p. mktg. Master Consol., Inc., Dayton, Ohio, 1954-61; mgmt. cons. McKinsey & Co., Inc., Chgo., 1961-67; v.p. mktg. Gen. Portland Inc., Dallas, 1967-69, pres., also dir., 1969-75; v.p., gen. mgr. Scholl Inc., Chgo., 1975-81; pres. Oxford Group of Sara Lee, 1981-84; mgmt. cons. McKinsey & Co., 1984—. Vice chmn. devel. bd. U. Tex. at Dallas; exec. bd. Circle 10 council Boy Scouts Am.; Svc. Corp. of Ret. Execs. counselor. Served with USN, 1944-46. Mem. Dallas C. of C. (chmn. bd. dirs. 1974—), Sales Execs. Club, Cherokee Country Club, Chattooga Club, Atlanta Mallet Club (pres.), Phi Gamma Delta. Methodist. Home: 301 Townsend Pl NW Atlanta GA 30327-3035

RAPER, JULIA TAYLOR, pediatric and neonatal nurse; b. Bermuda, B.W.I., Mar. 25, 1963; d. Rodney Sr. and Barbara Taylor; m. Bruce Scott Raper, Dec. 3, 1988. BSN, East Carolina U., 1986; MS in Nursing, Duke U., 1988. Cert. neonatal resuscitation program instr., BCLS instr., PALS regional faculty. Staff nurse neonatal ICU Pitt County Meml. Hosp., Greenville, N.C.; edl. nurse specialist Children's Hosp. U. Health Sys. Ea. Carolina. Mem. adj. faculty East Carolina U. Sch. Nursing. Contbr. articles to profl. jours. Mem. Pitt County Child Fatality Team. Mem. Nat. Assn. Neonatal Nurses, Nat. Nursing Staff Devel. Orgn., Sigma Theta Tau. E-mail: jraper@pcmh.com.

RAPER, WILLIAM BURKETTE, retired college president; b. nr. Wilson, N.C., Sept. 10, 1927; s. William Cecil and Beulah Maybelle (Davis) R.; m. Rose Mallard, Aug. 19, 1951; children: Olivia, Kristie, Burkette, Elizabeth, Stephen (dec.), Laura. AB, Duke U., 1947, MDiv, 1951; MS (Kellogg fellow), Fla. State U., 1962; LLD, Atlantic Christian Coll. (now Barton Coll.), 1960. Ordained to ministry Free Will Baptist Ch., 1946; pastor Hull Rd. Free Will Bapt. Ch., Snow Hill, N.C., 1951-55; pres. Mt. Olive (N.C.) Coll., 1954-95, ret. pres. emeritus, 1995. Dir. Wachovia Bank and Trust Co., 1979-97; promotional dir. Free Will Bapt. State Conv. N.C., 1953-54; pres. council Ch.-Related Colls. N.C., 1966-67; mem. N.C. Edn. Assistance Authority, 1972-76; sec. Ind. Coll. Fund of N.C., 1976-78; Mem. N.C. Gov.'s Com. on Hwy. Traffic Safety, 1968; regional coordinator U.S. Office Edn. Program with Developing Instns., 1968-70; dir. Edn. Professions Devel. Act Grant for Strengthening Devel. in Pvt. Two-Year Colls., 1970-72; trustee N.C. Coll. Found., 1977-94; adv. com. Ind. Coll. Presidents, U. N.C. Recipient Disting. Service award Mt. Olive Jr. C. of C., 1961; named N.C. Young Man of Year, 1961 Mem. Am. Assn. Community and Jr. Colls. (commn. on legislation 1963-66, cons. 1968-71, chmn. commn. on student personnel 1970-71), N.C. Assn. Ind. Colls. and Univs. (exec. com. 1967-70, 76-77, 83-85), N.C. Assn. Colls. and Univs. (pres. 1969-70), Masons. Democrat. Office: Mt Olive Coll Office of Pres Emeritus Mount Olive NC 28365 E-mail: wraper@exchange.moc.edu.

RAPHAEL, ALBERT ASH, JR. lawyer; b. N.Y.C., June 4, 1925; s. Albert Ash and Clare (Schindler) R.; m. Dorothy Buck, Oct. 7, 1960; 1 child, Bruce William. AB, Yale U., 1947; LL.D., Harvard U., 1950. Bar: N.Y. 1950, Vt. 1972. Mem. firm Gallert, Hilborn & Raphael, N.Y.C., 1950-60, Alter, Lefevre, Raphael, Lowry, and Gould, N.Y.C., 1960-78; individual practice Waitsfield, Vt., 1972-86, 95-00; ptnr. Raphael and Ware, 1986-95. Dir. various real estate cos. Mem. bd. zoning appeals, Waitsfield, 1974-83, selectman, 1976-82, chmn. bd. selectmen, 1981-82 Mem. Waitsfield Planning Commn., 1996—. Served with F.A., AUS, 1943-46. Mem. Vt. Bar Assn., Assn. of Bar of City of N.Y. Home: PO Box 1149 Waitsfield VT 05673-1149 Office: PO Box 1149 200 Raphael Rd Waitsfield VT 05673 E-mail: aar@madriver.com.

RAPHAEL, COLEMAN, business consultant; b. N.Y.C., Sept. 16, 1925; s. Morris and Adella (Leav) R.; m. Sylvia Moskowitz, Feb. 28, 1948; children—Hollis, Gordon. B.Civil Engring., CCNY, 1945; M.C.E., Poly. Inst. Bklyn., 1951, PhD in Applied Mechanics, 1965. Structural research engr., test research engr. Republic Aviation Corp., 1945-47; instr. mech. engring. Pratt Inst., Bklyn., 1947-51; from sr. research engr. to mgr. space systems div. Republic Aviation Corp., 1951-65; gen. mgr. space and electronics systems div., then v.p. Fairchild Hiller Corp., Germantown, Md., 1965-70; with Atlantic Rsch. Corp., Alexandria, Va., 1970-86, chmn. bd., 1980-86, SJI Industries, 1968-70; dean bus. sch. George Mason U., Fairfax, Va., 1986-91; ret., 1991; bd. mem., prin. owner Applied Bus. Systems, Bethesda, Md., 1990-98; dir. GEICO, Envipco. Bd. dirs. ENVIPCO (chmn. 1995), Fairfax, Va.; founder, chmn. Night Owl Security, Landover, Md., Geico, Chevy Chase, Md., 1981-92; mem. engring. adv. com. Montgomery Coll., Md., 1968-69, George Washington U., 1977-82; mem. Gov. Va. Task Force Nuclear Power Plants, 1969; chmn. energy com. Gov. Md. Sci. Adv. Coun., 1974-76; bd. visitors U. Pitts., 1980-82. Author textbook, papers, reports in field. Chmn. U.S. Bond drive, Alexandria, 1975-76; chmn. adv. com. Montgomery County Bldg. Codes, 1976-77. Recipient Citizenship award Montgomery County Press Assn., 1967, Disting. Service award Montgomery County C. of C., 1969, Disting. Citizenship award State of Md., 1970, Washington Bus. Hall of Fame, 1998. Mem. AIAA (chmn. mgmt. com. 1976), Aircraft Industries Assn., Nat. Space Club, disting Alumus, Poly. Inst. of Bklyn., 1982. Home: 508 Hermleigh Rd Silver Spring MD 20902-1608 E-mail: colesyl@att.net.

RAPHAEL, JUDITH, artist, educator; b. Chgo., May 6, 1938; d. Theodore and Malvene Raphael; m. Robert Gordon, 1964 (div. 1977); children: Leslie Gordon, Alex Gordon; m. Tony Phillips, June 4, 1980. Student, Sch. of Art Inst. of Chgo., 1956—58; BFA, U. Miss., Oxford, 1960; MA, Northwestern U., 1962. Assoc. prof. Moraine Valley C.C., Palos Hills, Ill., 1969—2000; vis. artist Sch. of Art Inst. of Chgo., 1977—. Vis. artist, panelist Oxbow, Saugatuck, Mich., 1999, Saugatuck, 2001, U. Wis., Riverfalls, 1977, St. Johns U., Collegeville, Minn., 1978, U. Chgo., 1986, U. Ind., Gary, 1994. Exhibitions include ARC Gallery, Chgo., 1978, Chgo. Cultural Ctr., 1989, Gwenda Jay Gallery, Chgo., 1991, 1993, 55 Mercer Gallery, N.Y.C., 1995, Lyons Wier Gallery, Chgo., 1996, 1998, exhibited in group shows at Art Inst. of Chgo., 1962, Frumkin and Struve Gallery, Chgo., 1980, Springfield (Mo.) Art Mus., 1985, McClean County Arts Ctr., Bloomington, Ill., 1990, DeCordova Mus. and Sculpture Park, Lincoln, Mass., 1993, New Art Ctr. Newton, Mass., 1995, Rockford (Ill.) Art Mus., 1997, Artemesia Gallery, Chgo., 2000, Carlson Tower Gallery, North Park U., 2000, Printworks Gallery, 2000, Lyons Wier Packer Gallery, 2001, collections, . Recipient Springfield Mus. prize, 1986; fellow Visual Arts fellow, Arts Midwest/NEA, 1993, resident fellow, Rockefeller Found., Bellagio, Italy, 1999, Yaddo, Saratoga Springs, N.Y., 1998, Marie Walsh Sharpe Art Found. fellow, 1994—95; grantee, Ill. Arts Coun., 1987, 1990, 2002. Home: 807 W 116th St Chicago IL 60608 Office: Sch of Art Inst of Chgo 112 S Michigan Ave Chicago IL 60603

RAPHAEL, MARTIN GEORGE, research wildlife biologist; b. Denver, Oct. 5, 1946; s. Jerome Maurice and Alys (Salmonson) R.; m. Susan Williams, August 4, 1967; 1 child, Samantha Marie. BA, Sacramento State U., 1968; BS, U. Calif., Berkeley, 1972, MS, 1976, PhD, 1980. Staff research assoc. U. Calif., Berkeley, 1974-80, assoc. specialist, 1980-84; project leader USDA Forest Svc., Laramie, 1984-89, Olympia, Wash., 1989—; adj. prof. U. Wyo., Laramie, 1986-89. Adj. assoc. prof. U. Wash., 1998—; cons. ecologist Pacific Gas and Electric Co., San Ramon, Calif., 1981-84. Contbr. articles to sci. jours. Mem. Ecol. Soc. Am. (editl. bd. Ecol. Applications 1994-98), Soc. for Conservation Biology, Am. Ornithologists' Union, Cooper Ornithol. Soc. (chmn. membership com. 1985-90, asst. sec. 1986—, bd. dirs. 1989-92, 2001—), The Wildlife Soc. (local pres. publs. com. 1983-84, assoc. editor Wildlife Soc. Bull. 1987-90), Phi Beta Kappa, Sigma Xi, Sigma Pi. Avocations: sailing, skiing, photography. Home: 2422 44th Ave NW Olympia WA 98502-3558 Office: Pacific NW Rsch Sta 3625 93rd Ave SW Olympia WA 98512-9193 E-mail: mraphael@fs.fed.us.

RAPHAEL, NAN HELENE, musician; b. Passaic, N.J., Apr. 2, 1955; d. Jerome B. and Barbara (Bodek) R. MusB, Susquehanna U., 1977. Substitute flutist Kennedy Ctr. Opera House Orch., Washington, 1981; flutist R&R Flute and Guitar Duos, 1983-86; guest soloist Boca Raton (Fla.) Pops, 1987; solo piccolo U.S. Army Field Band, Washington, 1977—; flute and piccolo musician Prevailing Winds, Annapolis, Md., 1985—. Booking agt. Prevailing Winds, Annapolis, 1985—. Arranger overture and flute/piccolo pieces for Prevailing Winds, 1986-88. Vol. D.C. Jewish Community Ctr., Washington, 1987—. Mem. Piccolo Soc., Washington Flute Soc., Hist. Soc. of Washington, Sigma Alpha Iota. Jewish. Avocations: swimming, baking, travel, gardening, movies, collecting flute player figurines. Home: 233 Kentucky Ave SE Apt 12 Washington DC 20003-2316

RAPHAEL, SALLY JESSY, talk-show host; b. Easton, Pa., Feb. 25, 1942; children: Allison (dec.), Andrea; m. Karl Soderlund; 2 step-daughters, 1 adopted son, also foster children. BFA, Columbia U. Anchored radio program Jr. High Sch. News Sta. WFAS-AM, White Plains, N.Y., 1955; host of cooking program WAPA-TV, San Juan, P.R., 1965-67; radio and television broadcaster Miami and Ft. Lauderdale, Fla., 1969-74; host Sta. WMCA-Radio, N.Y.C., 1976-81; talk show host NBC Talk-net, 1982-88, ABC Talkradio, N.Y.C., 1988-91; syndicated TV talk-show host, 1983—. Part-time owner of a perfume factory, 1964-68; owner of an art gallery, 1964-69; owner, The Wine Press, N.Y.C., 1979-83; ind. producer TV films, 1991 Author: (with M.J. Boyer) Finding Love, 1984, (with Pam Proctor) Sally: Unconventional Success, 1980; film appearances include: She-Devil, 1989, Resident Alien, 1990, The Addams Family, 1991, The Associate, 1996, Meet Wally Sparks, 1996, (TV movie) No One Would Tell, 1996; TV appearances include: Murphy Brown, Dave's World, The Nanny, The Tonight Show, Nightline, Diagnosis Murder, Conspiracy of Silence, Touched By An Angel, Sabrina the Teenage Witch, John LaRoquette Show; co-exec. producer (mini-series) The 3rd Twin, 1997 (film cameo) Double Whammy, 2000. Recipient Bronze medal, Internat. Film & Television Festival of NY, 1985; Emmy award as outstanding talk-show host, daytime, 1988, Emmy award for outstanding talk show, 1989. Office: USA Studios The Sally Show Fl OF2 15 Penn Plz New York NY 10001-2010

RAPHAELSON, ARNOLD HERBERT, economist, educator; b. Worcester, Mass., Oct. 13, 1929; s. Louis and Celia (Ostroff) R.; A.B. in English, Brown U., 1950; M.S. in Journalism, Columbia U., 1951; M.A. in Econs., Clark U., 1956, Ph.D., 1960; m. Ruth Camann, July 4, 1951; children— Marc, Jonathan, Joshua. City staff reporter Worcester Telegram, 1953-55; lectr. part-time Clark U., 1957-58; asst. prof. econs. U. Maine, 1958-60, asso. prof., 1960-66; counsel Subcom. on Intergovtl. Relations, U.S. Senate, 1964-65; asso. prof. econs. Temple U., Phila., 1966-70, prof., 1970— ; cons. to govt. agys., 1964— . Mem. Upper Dublin (Pa.) Ednl. Adv. Com., 1972-78. Served with U.S. Army, 1951-53. Mem. Am. Econ. Assn., Health Econs. Research Orgn. Jewish. Contbr. articles on health econs. to profl. jours.

RAPHAELSON, JOEL, retired advertising agency executive; b. N.Y.C., Sept. 27, 1928; s. Samson and Dorothy (Wegman) R.; m. Mary Kathryn Hartigan, Aug. 20, 1960; children: Matthew, Katherine, Paul. BA, Harvard U., 1949. Copywriter Macy's, N.Y.C., 1950-51, BBDO, N.Y.C., 1953-58; with Ogilvy & Mather, Inc., 1958-94, sr. v.p., dir., 1966-75, mem. exec. com., 1970-75, creative cons. Europe, 1975-76, exec. creative dir., 1976-82; sr. v.p. internat. creative svcs. Ogilvy & Mather Worldwide, 1982-92, spl. assignments as editor, writer, speechwriter, cons., 1993-94, ret., 1995. Lectr. bus. writing Am. Assn. Advt. Agys., other bus. orgns. Author: (with Kenneth Roman) How To Write Better, 1978, Writing That Works, 1981, rev. expanded edit., 1992, 00; editor: The Unpublished David Ogilvy, 1986, Viewpoint (co. jour.), 1983-94; contbr. Harvard Bus. Rev., other bus. publs. Cons. Lyric Opera Chgo., Exec. Svc. Corps, Chgo.; bd. dirs. Fairfield Found., Fairfield Pub. Gallery, Sturgeon Bay, Wis. With U.S. Army Signal Corps, 1951-53. Home: 20 E Cedar St Apt 12C Chicago IL 60611-5115 E-mail: joelr28@aol.com.

RAPIER, PASCAL MORAN, chemical engineer, physicist; b. Atlanta, Jan. 11, 1914; s. Paul Edward and Mary Clare (Moran) R.; m. Martha Elizabeth Doyle, May 19, 1945; children: Caroline Elizabeth, Paul Doyle, Mollie Clare, John Lawrence, James Andrew. BSChemE, Ga. Inst. Tech., 1939; MS in Theoretical Physics, U. Nev., 1959; postgrad., U. Calif., Berkeley, 1961. Registered profl. engr., Calif., N.J. Plant engr. Archer-Daniels-Midland, Pensacola, Fla., 1940-42; group supr. Dicalite div. Grefco, Los Angeles, 1943-54; process engr. Celatom div. Eagle Picher, Reno, 1955-57; project mgr., assoc. research engr. U. Calif. Field Sta., Richmond, 1959-62; project mgr. sea water conversion Bechtel Corp., San Francisco, 1962-66; sr. supervising chem. engr. Burns & Roe, Oradell, N.J., 1966-74; cons. engr. Kenite Corp., Scarsdale, N.Y., Rees Blowpipe, Berkeley, 1960-66; sr. cons. engr. Sanderson & Porter, N.Y.C., 1975-77; staff scientist III Lawrence

Berkeley Lab., 1977-84. Bd. dirs. Newtonian Sci. Found.; v.p. Calif. Rep. Assembly, 1964-65; discoverer phenomena faster than light, origin of cosmic rays and galactic red shifts. Contbr. articles to profl. jours.; patentee agts. to render non-polar solvents electrically conductive, direct-contact geothermal energy recovery devices; contbr. Marks' Standard Handbook for Mechanical Engineers, 10th edit., 1996. Mem. Am. Inst. Chem. Engrs., Gideons Internat., Lions Internat., Corvallis, Sigma Pi Sigma. Home: 8015 NW Ridgewood Dr Corvallis OR 97330-3026 *Personal philosophy: Adopt a primary causal principle in your life and your work will not go unrewarded. Seek a guiding principle for your life, and find your efforts well rewarded in an infinite, ever-expanding universe.*

RAPKA, JAMES RICHARD, electronics engineer; b. Bethesda, Md., July 23, 1959; s. John Benjamin and Joan (Muller) R. BSEE, Rutgers U., 1981, MSEE, 1987. Registered profl. engr., N.J. Electronics engr. Object Recognition Sys., Princeton, N.J., 1981-85, Lucent Technologies, Holmdel, 1985-2000, Village Networks, Inc., Eatontown, 2000—. Mem., panelist Wisdom Soc., San Marcos, Calif., 1995. Mem. IEEE, N.J. Soc. Profl. Engrs. Avocations: electronics, philosophy, tennis, bicycling. Home: 313 Century Way Manalapan NJ 07726-8773 Office: Village Networks Inc 246 Industrial Way West Eatontown NJ 07724 E-mail: jrr123@aol.com.

RAPOPORT, ANATOL, peace studies educator, mathematical biologist; b. Lozovaya, Russia, May 22, 1911; emigrated to U.S., 1922, naturalized, 1928; s. Boris and Adel (Rapoport) R.; m. Gwen Goodrich, Jan. 29, 1949; children: Anya, Alexander, Charles Anthony. PhD, U. Chgo., 1941; DHL, U. Western Mich., 1971; LLD, U. Toronto, 1986; DS, Royal Mil. Coll. Can., 1995; Ehrendoktor, U. Bern, Switzerland, 1995. Faculty dept. math. Ill. Inst. Tech., 1946-47; com. math. biology U. Chgo., 1947-54; fellow Ctr. Advanced Study Behavioral Scis., Stanford, 1954-55; asso. prof. Mental Health Research Inst., prof. math. biology U. Mich., 1955-70; prof. psychology and math. U. Toronto, 1970-80; dir. Inst. for Advanced Studies, Vienna, 1980-83; prof. peace studies U. Toronto, 1984—. Author: Science and the Goals of Man, 1950, Operational Philosophy, 1953, Fights, Games, and Debates, 1960, Strategy and Conscience, 1964, Prisoner's Dilemma, 1965, Two-Person Game Theory, 1966, N Person Game Theory, 1970, The Big Two, 1971, Conflict in Man Made Environment, 1974, Semantics, 1975, The 2 x 2 Game, 1976, Mathematische Methoden in den Sozialwissenschaften, 1980, Mathematical Models in the Social and Behavioral Sciences, 1983, General System Theory, 1986, The Origins of Violence, 1989, Decision Theory and Decision Behavior, 1989, Canada and the World, 1992, Peace: An Idea Whose Time Has Come, 1992, Gewissheiten and Zweifel, 1994, Uverennost' i Somnenia, 1999, Certainties and Doubts, 2000; editor: General Systems, 1956—77. Served to capt. USAAF, 1942-46. Fellow Am. Acad. Arts and Scis.; mem. Am. Math. Soc., Internat. Soc. Gen. Semantics (pres. 1953-55), Canadian Peace Research and Edn. Assn. (pres. 1972-75), Soc. for Gen. Systems Research (pres. 1965-66), Sci. for Peace (pres. 1984-86) Home: 38 Wychwood Park Toronto ON Canada M6G 2V5

RAPOPORT, BERNARD, life insurance company executive; b. San Antonio, July 17, 1917; s. David and Riva (Feldman) Rapoport; m. Audre Jean Newman, Feb. 15, 1942; 1 child Ronald B. BA, U. Tex.-Austin, 1939. Chmn. bd., CEO Am. Income Life Ins. Co., Waco, Tex., 1951-99, cons., 1999—, founder and chmn. emeritus, 2002—; pres., chmn. bd., 2000-01. Chmn bd regents Univ Tex, 1991; apptd by pres adv comt for trade policy and negotiations, 1994—. Mem Nat Coun Crime and Delinquency, San Francisco, 1979—, Union Am Hebrew Congreagations, 1981—, Nat Hispanic Ctr Advanced Studies and Policy Analysis, Oakland, Calif., 1981—, Jerusalem Found, New York, NY, 1979—, Hebrew Union Col, Cincinnati, Ohio, 1980—; assoc mem Univ Cancer Found, Houston, 1976—, Jt Ctr Polit and Econ Studies, 1987—; chmn Negro Col Fund, Waco, 1979—80, United Way Waco, 1982—83; trustee Paul Quinn Col, Waco, 1963—90, Boy's Club Waco, 1982—; chmn bd regents Univ Tex, 1993—97; bd dirs Library of Congress Trust Fund, Washington, 1998—. Recipient Horatio Alger Award, 1999. Fellow: City of Jerusalem. Democrat. Jewish. Avocations: tennis, politics, reading. Home: 2332 Wendy Ln Waco TX 76710-2011 Office: PO Box 21900 Waco TX 76702-1900 E-mail: brapoport@ailins.com.

RAPOPORT, BERNARD ROBERT, lawyer; b. N.Y.C., Jan. 18, 1919; s. Max and Rose (Gerard) R.; m. Robyrta Wechter, May 31, 1959; 1 son: Michael. AB, Cornell U., 1939, JD, 1941. Bar: N.Y. 1941, Fed. Ct. (so. dist.) 1946. Assoc. firm Proskauer, Rose, Goetz, Mendelsohn, N.Y.C., 1941-50; gen. counsel M. Lowenstein Corp., N.Y.C., 1950-86, bd. dirs., 1961-86, treas., 1975-86, sec., 1970-86; dir., treas., sec. Leon Lowenstein Found. Served to capt. Signal Corps, U.S. Army, 1942-45. Mem. ABA, Assn. of Bar of City of N.Y. Address: 910 5th Ave New York NY 10021-4155

RAPOPORT, JUDITH, psychiatrist; b. N.Y.C., July 12, 1933; d. Louis and Minna (Enteen) Livant; m. Stanley Rapoport, June 25, 1961; children: Stuart, Erik. BA, Swarthmore Coll., 1955; MD, Harvard U., 1959. Lic. psychiatrist. Cons., child psychiatrist NIMH/St. Elizabeth's Hosp., Washington, 1969—72; clin. asst. prof. Georgetown U. Med. Sch., 1972—82, clin. assoc. prof., 1982—85, clin. prof. psychiat., 1985—; med. officer biol. psychiatry br. NIMH, Bethesda, Md., 1976—78, chief, child mental illness unit, biol. psychiat. br., 1979—82, chief, child psychiatry lab. of clin. scis., 1982—84, chief, child psychiatry div. intramural rsch. programs, 1984—; prof. psychiatry George Washington U. Sch. Med., Washington, 1979—; prof. pediat. Georgetown U., 1985—. Cons. in field. Author: (non-fiction) The Boy Who Couldn't Stop Washing, 1989 (best seller literary guild selection , 1989), Childhood Obsessive Compulsive Disorder, 1989. Fellow: Am. Acad. Child Psychiatry, Am. Psychiat. Assn.; mem.: Inst. Medicine, D.C. Psychiat. Assn. Home: 3010 44th Pl NW Washington DC 20016-3557 Office: NIMH Rm 3N202 10 Center Dr Bldg 10 Bethesda MD 20892-0001 E-mail: rapoport@helix.nih.gov.

RAPOPORT, RONALD JON, journalist; b. Detroit, Aug. 14, 1940; s. Daniel B. and Shirley G.; m. Joan Zucker, Sept. 2, 1968; children— Rebecca, Julie. BA, Stanford U., 1962; MS, Columbia U., 1963. Reporter Mpls. Star, 1963-65; asso. editor Sport mag., 1965-66; sports reporter AP, N.Y.C., San Francisco, 1966-70, Los Angeles Times, 1970-77; sports columnist Chgo. Sun-Times, 1977-88, Los Angeles Daily News, 1988-95; sports commentator Weekend Edit. Nat. Pub. Radio, 1986—; dep. sports editor Chgo. Sun-Times, 1996-98, sports columnist, 1998—. Author: (with Chip Oliver) High for the Game, 1971, (with Stan Love) Love in the NBA, 1975, (with Jim McGregor) Called for Travelling, 1979; editor: A Kind of Grace: A Treasury of Sportswriting by Women, 1994, (with Betty Garrett) Betty Garrett and Other Songs, 1998, See How She Runs: Marion Jones and the Making of a Champion, 2000. Served with U.S. Army Res., 1963.

RAPOPORT, SONYA, artist; b. Boston; d. Louis Aaron and Ida Tina (Axelrod) Goldberg; m. Henry Rapoport; children: Hava Rapoport de Fereres, David, Robert. Student, Mass. Coll. Art, 1941-42; BA, NYU, 1945; MA, U. Calif., Berkeley, 1949. Bd. dirs. LEONARDO, Jour. Internat. Soc. Arts, Scis. and Tech.; mem. adv. com. Berkeley Art Mus. U. Calif. One-woman shows include Calif. Palace Legion of Honor, 1963, Peabody Mus., Harvard U., 1978, N.Y.C. Pub. Libr., 1979, New Sch. Social Rsch., N.Y.C., 1981, NYU Grad. Sch. Bus. Adminstrn., 1982, Sarah Lawrence Coll., Bronxville, N.Y., 1984, Kuopio Mus., Finland, 1992, exhibited in group shows at Union Gallery San Jose (Calif.) State U., 1979, Ctr. Visual Arts, Oakland, Calif., 1979, Walker Art Ctr., Mpls., 1981, Nat. Libr., Madrid, 1982, SUNY Libr., Purchase, 1983, Otis Art Inst. Parsons Sch. Design, L.A., 1984, Cleve. Inst. Art, 1984, SIGGRAPH, 1998, N.Y. Digital Salon, 1995, 1996, 1997, 1998, Copenhagen Film Festival, 1996, Scotland Photo Biennial, 1997, Mill Valley Film Festival, 1997, Internat. Symposium Electronic Art, Mpls., 1993, 1995, 1996, 1999, others, Buenos Aires Biennial, 2002, Represented in permanent collections Mus. Modern Art, N.Y.C., Stedelijk Mus., Amsterdam, Inpls. Mus. Art, Grey Art Gallery, NYU, San Francisco Mus. Modern Art, San Jose State U. Found.-Union Gallery, Crocker Art Mus., Sacramento, Hall of Justice, Hayward, Calif.; book artist: book Shoe-Field, book artist: book Chinese Connections, book artist: book About Me, book artist: book Objects on My Dresser, book artist: interactive book Gateway to Your Ka, book artist: interactive book Your Fate is in Your Feet, book artist: interactive book Digital Mudra2; prodr.: A Shoe-In, Biorhythm, Coping with Sexual Jealousy, (computer assisted interactive installations) The Animated Soul, Digital Mudra, Transgenic Bagel; contbr. articles to profl. publs. Home: 6 Hillcrest Ct Berkeley CA 94705-2805 E-mail: sonyarap@lmi.net.

RAPP, CHRISTIAN FERREE, retired textile home furnishings company executive; b. Paradise, Pa., July 3, 1933; s. Christian F. and Mildred May (Peters) R.; m. Mary Yvonne Kirchner, June 25, 1953; children: Pamela, Linda, Christian. BS, Drexel U., 1961; postgrad., NYU, 1964-67. Cert. mgmt. acct. Bd. dirs., v.p. fin. Gamon-Calmet Meter Corp., Cin., 1963-73, Mack Shirt Corp., Cin., 1974-77; bd. dir., sr. v.p., CFO Louisville Bedding Co., 1978-2000. Treas. polit. campaign for Ky. Senate, 1976. With U.S. Army, 1953-56. Mem. Fin. Execs. Inst. (v.p. 1986—), Nat. Assn. Accts., Phi Kappa Phi. Home: 2316 Mohican Hill Ct Louisville KY 40207-1147 E-mail: rapp2316@bellsouth.net.

RAPP, GEORGE ROBERT (RIP RAPP), geology and archeology educator; b. Toledo, Sept. 19, 1930; s. George Robert and Gladys Mae (Warner) R.; m. Jeannette Messner, June 15, 1956; children: Kathryn, Karen. BA, U. Minn., 1952; PhD, Pa. State U., 1960. Asst. then assoc. prof. S.D. Sch. Mines, Rapid City, 1957-65; assoc. prof. U. Minn., Mpls., 1965-75, prof. geology and archeology Duluth, 1975-95, dean Coll. Letters and Sci., 1975-84, dean Coll. Sci. and Engring., 1984-89, dir. Archeometry Lab., 1975—; Regents' prof. geoarchaeology, 1995—. Prof. Ctr. for Ancient Studies, U. Minn., Mpls., 1970-93, prof. interdisciplinary archaeol. studies, 1993—; cons. USIA, Westinghouse Corp., Exxon Corp., Ford Found. Author, editor: Excavations at Nichoria, 1978, Troy: Archeological Geology, 1982, Archeological Geology, 1985, Excavations at Tel Michal, 1989, Encyclopedia of Minerals, 1989, Phytolith Systematics, 1992, Geoarchaeology, 1998, Artifact Copper Sources, 2000; mem. editl. bd. Jour. Field Archeology, 1976-85, Jour. Archeol. Sci., 1977-79, Geoarcheology Jour., 1984-92, Am. Jour. Archeology, 1985-92. NSF postdoctoral fellow, 1963-64, Fulbright-Hayes sr. rsch. fellow, 1972-73. Fellow AAAS (chmn. sect. E, 1987-88, nat. coun. 1992-95), Geol. Soc. Am. (Archeol. Geology award 1983), Mineral. Soc. Am.; mem. Nat. Assn. Geology Tchrs. (pres. 1986-89), Soc. for Archeol. Sci. (pres. 1983-84), Assn. Field Archeology (pres. 1979-81), Archaeol. Inst. Am. (Pomerance medal 1988), Sigma Xi (bd. dirs. 1990-98). Avocation: classical music, exercise, nutrition. Office: U Minn-Duluth Archaeometry Lab Duluth MN 55812

RAPP, GERALD DUANE, lawyer, manufacturing company executive; b. Berwyn, Nebr., July 19, 1933; s. Kenneth P. and Mildred (Price) R.; children: Gerald Duane Jr., Gregory T., Amy Frances Wanzek. BS, U. Mo., 1955; JD, U. Mich., 1958. Bar: Ohio bar 1959. Practice in, Dayton, 1960—; ptnr. Smith & Schnacke, 1963-70; asst. gen. counsel Mead Corp., Dayton, 1970, v.p. human resources and legal affairs, 1973, v.p., corp. sec., 1975, v.p., gen. counsel, corp. sec., 1976, v.p., gen. counsel, 1979, sr. v.p., gen. counsel, 1981-91, counsel to bd. dirs., 1991-92; of counsel Bieser, Greer & Landis, 1992—. Pres. R-J Holding Co., Weber Canyon Ranch, Inc. Sr. editor U. Mich. Law Rev., 1957-58. Past chmn. Oakwood Youth Commn.; past v.p., bd. dirs. Big Bros. Greater Dayton; mem. pres.'s visitors com. U. Mich. Law Sch.; past trustee Urbana Coll.; past pres., trustee Ohio Ctr. Leadership Studies, Robert K. Greenleaf Ctr., Indpls.; past pres. bd. trustees Dayton and Montgomery County Pub. Libr.; past. mem. bd. visitors Law Schs. of Dayton. 1st lt. U.S. Army, 1958-60. Mem. ABA, Ohio Bar Assn., Dayton Bar Assn., Moraine Country Club, Dayton Racquet Club, Dayton Lawyers Club, Met. Club Washington, Phi Kappa Psi, Phi Delta Phi, Beta Gamma Sigma. Presbyterian. Office: 108 Green St Dayton OH 45402-2835 Fax: 937-224-0403.

RAPP, JOANNA A. retired geriatrics nurse, mental health nurse; b. Youngsville, Pa., Nov. 22, 1920; d. Wade Hampton and Edith (Hodges) Brazee; m. Ellsworth G. Rapp, Nov. 6, 1976; children: Sallie Angel, Suzanne Herzing. Diploma, Meadville (Pa.) City Hosp., 1941; BS in Nursing Edn., Western Res. U., 1947. Field team nurse Bur. Occupational Health; staff nurse USPHS Hosp., Anchorage; supr. Hale-Makua, Mauia, Hawaii; instr. John Howard Forensic Psychiat. Hosp., Washington; DON, Twinbrooke So. Nursing Facility, Edinburg, Tex., until 1995; ret., 1995. 1st. Lt. ANC, 1944-46. Named Dist. Nurse of Yr. Home: Mission, Tex. Died Nov. 26, 2000.

RAPP, LYNN BLAIR, obstetrician-gynecologist, educator; b. N.Y.C., Mar. 25, 1950; MD, U. Padova, Italy, 1983. Diplomate Am. Bd. Ob-Gyn. Resident ob-gyn. S.I. (N.Y.) U. Hosp., 1984-88, attending ob-gyn., 1988—. Attending St. Vincent's Med. Ctr., Richmond, 1992—; attending ob-gyn. Victory Meml. Hosp., Bklyn.; clin. instr. ob-gyn. SUNY Health Sci. Ctr., Bklyn. Fellow ACOG, ACS, Bklyn. Gynecol. Soc.; mem. AMA, Am. Fertility Soc., Am. Assn. Gynecol. Laparoscopists, Med. Soc. State N.Y., Acad. Medicine Richmond.

RAPP, MICHAEL THOMAS, emergency physician; b. Chgo., 1945; MD, Northwestern U., 1969; JD, George Washington U., 1975. Intern Northwestern Meml. Hosp., Chgo., 1969-70; resident Georgetown U. Hosp., Washington, 1972-73; emergency physician Arlington (Va.) Physician Group Ltd., 1973—2001; chief dept. emergency medicine Arlington (Va.) Hosp., 1981-99; emergency physician George Washington U. Med. Faculty Assocs., 2001—. Mem. nat. alumni bd. Northwestern U. Med. Sch., 1998—; chmn. practicing physicians adv. coun. Dept. HHS, 2001—. Mem.: AMA, Am. Coll. Legal Medicine, Am. Coll. Emergency Physicians (bd. dirs. 1993—2001, v.p. 1997—98, pres.-elect 1998—99, pres. 1999—2000, immediate past pres. 2000—01). Office: 8101 Hinson Farm Rd #318 Alexandria VA 22306

RAPP, PAUL ERNEST, science educator; b. Chgo., Sept. 2, 1949; s. John Henry and Mary Katherine (Hendershot) R; m. Dorrie Louise Tholke, June 11, 1970 (div. 1982). BS, U. Ill., 1972; PhD, Cambridge U., Eng., 1975. Fellow Caius Coll., Cambridge, 1975-79; asst. prof. Med. Coll. Pa., Phila., 1979-82, assoc. prof., 1982—. Vis. prof. U. Western Australia, Perth, 1988, Bryn Mawr (Pa.) Coll., 1989. Broadcaster radio and TV Australian Broadcasting Co., CBC, PBS; contbr. articles in profl. sci. jours. Recipient James scholar U. Ill., Urbana, 1967, Churchill Found. scholar, Cambridge, 1972. Fellow Cambridge Philos. Soc.; mem. Am. Math. Soc., Soc. Math. Biology. Avocations: viola, piano. Office: Med Coll Pa 3300 Henry Ave Philadelphia PA 19129-1191

RAPP, RICHARD TILDEN, economist, consultant; b. Miami, Fla., Nov. 30, 1944; s. Melville Benjamin and Rachel (Marx) R.; m. Wilma J. Levin, Aug. 20, 1967; children: Ethan, Sandra. BA cum laude, Bklyn. Coll., 1965; MA, U. Pa., 1966, PhD, 1970. Asst. prof. SUNY, Stony Brook, 1970-75, assoc. prof. econ. history, 1976-77; pres., chief exec. officer Nat. Econ. Research Assocs., Inc., White Plains, N.Y., 1977—. Cons. on internat. trade and competition econs. Author: Industry and Economic Decline in Seventeenth-Century Venice, 1976, Trade Warfare and the New Protectionism, 1986; co-author: European Economic History, 1975. Nat. adv. bd. Santa Fe Opera, 1989—. Kent fellow Danforth found., 1968-70; Fulbright fellow, 1968-69. Mem. Am. Econ. Assn., Inst. for Advanced Study. Home: 52 Whippoorwill Lake Rd Chappaqua NY 10514-2314 Office: Nat Econ Rsch Assocs Inc 50 Main St White Plains NY 10606-1901

RAPP, ROBERT ANTHONY, metallurgical engineering educator, consultant; b. Lafayette, Ind., Feb. 21, 1934; s. Frank J. and Goldie M. (Royer) R.; m. Heidi B. Sartorius, June 3, 1960; children: Kathleen Rapp Raynaud, Thomas, Stephen, Stephanie Rapp Surface. BSMetE, Purdue U., 1956; MSMetE, Carnegie Inst. Tech., 1959, PhDMetE, 1960; D (hon.), Inst. Polytech., Toulouse, France, 1995. Asst. prof. metall. engring. Ohio State U., Columbus, 1963-66, assoc. prof., 1966-69, prof., 1969—, M.G. Fontana prof., 1988-95, Univ. prof., 1989-95, disting. univ. prof. emeritus, 1995—. Vis. prof. Ecole Nat. Superior d'Electrochimie, Grenoble, France, 1972-73, U. Paris-Sud, Orsay, 1985-86, Ecole Nat. Superior de Chimie, Toulouse, France, 1985-86, U. New South Wales, Australia, 1987; Acta/Scripta Metallurgica lectr., 1991; rsch. metallurgist WPAFB, Ohio, 1960-63. Editor: Techniques of Metals Research, vol. IV, 1982, High Temperature Corrosion, 1984; translator Metallic Corrosion (Kaesche), 1986; bd. rev. jour. Oxid. Metals; contbr. numerous articles to profl. jours. Decorated chevalier des Palmes Academiques; recipient Disting. Engring. Alumnus award Purdue U., 1988, B.F. Goodrich Collegiate Inventor's award, 1991, 92, Ulrick Evans award Brit. Inst. Corrosion, 1992; Guggenheim fellow, 1972; Fulbright scholar Max Planck Inst. Phys. Chemistry, 1959-60, Linford award for Disting. Tchg.,The Electrochem. Soc., 1998. Fellow: Nat. Assn. Corrosion Engrs. (W.R. Whitney award 1986), Electrochem. Soc. (HTM Divsn. Outstanding Achievement award 1992, Linford Tchr. award 1998), Mining Metals and Materials Soc. (R.F. Mehl medal 2000), Am. Soc. Metals Internat. (B. Stoughton award 1968, Howe gold medal 1974, gold medal 2000); mem.: Nat. Acad. Engring., French Soc. Metals and Materials (hon.). Lutheran. Home: 1379 Southport Dr Columbus OH 43235-7649 E-mail: bobheidirapp@msn.com., rapp.4@osu.edu.

RAPP, ROBERT NEIL, lawyer; b. Erie, Pa., Sept. 10, 1947; m. Sally K. Meder; 1 child: Jeffrey David. BA, Case Western Res. U., 1969, JD, 1972; MBA, Cleve. State U., 1989. Bar: Ohio 1972, U.S. dist. Ct. (no. dist.) Ohio 1973, U.S. Ct. Appeals (6th crct.) 1981, U.S. Supreme Ct. 1980. Assoc. Metzenbaum, Gaines & Stern, Co., L.P.A., Cleve., 1972-75; ptnr. Calfee, Halter & Griswold, 1975—. Adj. prof. law Case Western Res. U., 1975—78, 1994—98, Cleve. Marshall Coll. Law, Cleve. State U., 1976—82; practitioner-in-residence Cornell U. Law Sch., 1993; mem. legal adv. bd. Nat. Assn. Securities Dealers, 1992—96; mem. market ops. rev. com. Nasdaq Stock Market, 1996—; arbitrator, practitioner mediator Nat. Futures Assn. Contbr. numerous articles to law jours. Mem. ABA (sect. bus. law: mem. com. fed. regulation of securities, subcom. broker-dealer regulation, sect. litigation: mem. com. securities litigation), Am. Arbitration Assn. (securities arbitrator, mem. comml. adv. coun. Cleve. region), Ohio State Bar Assn. (elected mem. coun. dels. 1976-82, corp. law com. 1980—), Cleve. Bar Assn. (chmn. young lawyers sect. 1976-77), assoc. mem. cert. grievance com., sect. securities law: exec. coun. 1980-85, chmn. govt. liaison com. 1980-81). Office: Calfee Halter & Griswold LLP 1400 McDonald Investment Ct Cleveland OH 44114-2688 E-mail: rrapp@calfee.com.

RAPP, STEPHEN JOHN, international prosecutor; b. Waterloo, Iowa, Jan. 26, 1949; s. Spurgeon John and Beverly (Leckington) R.; m. Donna J.E. Maier, 1981; children: Alexander, Stephanie. AB cum laude, Harvard U., 1971; JD with honors, Drake U., 1973. Bar: Iowa 1974, U.S. Dist. Ct. (no. and so. dists.) Iowa 1978, U.S. Ct. Appeals (8th cir.) 1979, U.S. Supreme Ct. 1979. Rsch. asst. Office of U.S. Senator Birch Bayh, Ind., 1970; community program asst. HUD, Chgo., 1971; mem. Iowa Ho. Reps., 1972-74, 79-83, Coun. to Majority Caucus, Iowa Ho. Reps., 1975; staff dir., counsel subcom. on juvenile delinquency U.S. Senate, Washington, 1977-78; ptnr. Rapp & Gilliam, Waterloo, 1979-83; pvt. practice, 1983-93; U.S. atty. U.S. Dist. Ct. (no. dist.) Iowa, 1993—2001; sr. prosecuting atty. United Nations Internat. Crime Tribunal for Rwanda, 2001—. Del., mem. com. Dem. Nat. Conv., 1976, 80, 84, 88, 92; mem. Dem. Nat. Adv. Com. on Econ., 1982-84, chmn. Black Hawk Dem. Com., 1986-91; mem. Iowa Dem. Com., 1990-93, chair 2d C.D. Dem. Com., 1991-93. Mem. ABA, Iowa Bar Assn., Order of Coif. Methodist. Home: 219 Highland Blvd Waterloo IA 50703-4229 Office: K-708 UN-ICTR PO Box 6016 Arusha Tanzania E-mail: rapp@un.org.

RAPPAPORT, ALAN FRED, clinical psychologist; b. N.Y.C., Nov. 20, 1946; s. Sol and Edith (Drutman) R.; m. Liza E. Peguero, Dec. 27, 1981. BA, Seton Hall U., 1968; MA, U. Conn., 1969; PhD, Pa. State U., 1971. Cert. clin. psychologist, marital therapist, N.J.; cert. in treatment of alcohol and other psychoactive substance abuse disorders. Assoc. prof. Montclair (N.J.) State Coll., 1971-73; psychotherapist N.Y.C., 1973-78; clin. dir. Cmty. Mental Health Assocs., Parsippany, N.J., 1978&. Cons. psychologist Stress Release Ltd., N.Y.C., 1972-75; adj. prof. Montclair State Coll., 1978-79. Author: (with others) Marriage and Family Therapy, 1974, Couples in Conflict, 1974, Treating Relationships, 1976. Program dir. Holistic Health Inst. N.J., 1983-85. Fellow Am. Coll. Psychology; mem. APA, N.J. Psychol. Assn. Office: Cmty Mental Health Assoc 3599 Route 46 Parsippany NJ 07054-1015

RAPPAPORT, ANNA M, actuary; b. New Orleans, Sept. 15, 1940; d. Ludwig Guckenheimer, Gertrude Guckenheimer; m. Peter Plumley; 1 child Jennifer Rappaport Royce. MBA, University of Chicago, Chicago IL, 1985. Actuarial Analyst New York Life, New York, NY, 1958—62; Senior Vice President Standard Security Life, 1962—73; Vice President Equitable Life Assurance Society of the US, 1976; Principal William M. Mercer, Incorporated, Chicago, Ill. President Society of Actuaries, Schaumburg, IL, 1997—98; Member of the Board The Actuarial Foundation, Schaumburg, IL, 2000—, National Academy of Social Insurance, Washington, 2001—. Bd. dirs. Wiser, 2000—; Board Member Metro Chicago Information Center, Chicago, 1997—; Member The Chicago Network, IL, 1994. Avocation: Watercolor painting; snorkeling, bridge. Office: Mercer Human Resource Cons 10 South Wacker Drive Chicago IL 60606-7485 Office Fax: 312 902-7626. Business E-Mail: anna.rappaport@mercer.com.

RAPPAPORT, CAREY MILFORD, electrical engineering educator; b. Tokyo, Jan. 9, 1959; came to U.S., 1964; s. Paul Julian and Evelyn Rappaport; m. Ann Welke Morgenthaler, Nov. 12, 1989; children: Sarah Nason, Brian Hampton. BSEE, BS in Math., MSEE, EngEE, MIT, 1982, PhD, 1987. Asst. prof. elec. and computer engring. Northeastern U., Boston, 1987-93, assoc. prof., 1993-2000, prof., 2000—. Cons. AJ Devaney Assocs., Boston, 1987—; co-founder Berry Rappaport Assocs., Newton, Mass., 1990—, NSF Ctr. for Subsurface Sensing and Imaging Systems. Author: Progress in Electromagnetics Research, Vol. I, 1989; contbr. articles to profl. jours.; patentee in field. Recipient MIT K.T. Compton award, 1985. Mem. IEEE (sr., H.A. Wheeler award 1986), Sigma Xi, Eta Kappa Nu. Avocations: skiing, bridge, backpacking, chess, swimming. Office: Northeastern U 302 Stearns Boston MA 02115 E-mail: rappaport@neu.edu.

RAPPAPORT, CHARLES OWEN, lawyer; b. N.Y.C., May 15, 1950; s. Edward and Edith (Novick) R.; m. Valerie B. Ackerman, Oct. 11, 1987; children: Emily Randle, Sarah Elisabeth. BA, Columbia U., 1970; JD, NYU, 1975. Bar: N.Y. 1976. Assoc. Simpson, Thacher & Bartlett, N.Y.C., 1975-82, ptnr., 1982—. Office e-mail: c. Home: 26 N Moore St Apt 4W New York NY 10013-2436 Office: Simpson Thacher & Bartlett 425 Lexington Ave 14th Fl New York NY 10017-3954 E-mail: crappaport@stblaw.com.

RAPPAPORT, CLAUDIA DIANE, social worker, educator; b. San Antonio, Oct. 24, 1950; d. Burton Frederick and Betty Jean (Reaves) R. BA in Sociology summa cum laude, U. Tex., Austin, 1973, MS in Social Work, 1975; PhD, U. Tex. Med. Br., Galveston, 1996. Lic. master's social worker; cert. advanced clin. practitioner. Social worker pediatrics and perinatology dept. U. Tex. Med. Br., Galveston, 1975-83, social work supr. maternal and child health svcs., 1983-93; med. social worker Tex. Dept. Health, 1993-96, asst. dir. social work, 1996-2000; mem. clin. adj. faculty Sch. Nursing U. Tex. Med. Br., Galveston, 1984-96, instr. physician's asst. studies program, 1984-96; asst. prof. social work, field work coord. Tarleton State U., 2000—. Numerous lectrs. and presentations to profl. confs. and seminars. Contbr. essays to profl. publs. Vol. Austin State Hosp., 1972-73; founder, bd. dirs. Hospice of Galveston County, 1980-90, Gulf Coast Coalition for Prevention Child Abuse, Galveston, 1987-2000, Family Outreach of So. Galveston County, 1990-2000, Literacy Edn. and Parenting, 1987-99; bd. dirs. Candlelighters, Galveston, 1989-96, Family Outreach of Coryell County, 2000—; mem. profl. adv. bd. March of Dimes, Houston, 1988-91; mem. exec. bd. Family Outreach Am., 1992—. Recipient Svc. award, Hospice of Galveston County, 1989, 1990, Tex. Dept. Health, 1997, Tex. Leadership award, Prevent Child Abuse Tex., 2002. Mem. NASW (sec. Galveston unit 1982-88, chmn. 1981-82, mem. planning com. 1980-89, 91-95), Acad. Cert. Social Workers, Nat. Assn. Perinatal Social Workers (conf. planning com. 1982), Phi Beta Kappa, Phi Kappa Phi, Alpha Kappa Delta. Avocations: photography, needlepoint, reading, music. Home: 1007 Clairidge Ave Killeen TX 76549-3611 Office: 1901 S Clear Creek Rd Killeen TX 76549 E-mail: c.rappaport@att.net., rappaport@tarleton.edu.

RAPPAPORT, GEORGE LEE, communications executive, retired; b. Trenton, N.J., Dec. 19, 1920; s. Morris and Gertrude (Scull) R.; m. Mary Virginia Page, June 11, 1947; children: Robert Davis, Ross Lee. Student, Pa. Acad. Fine Arts, 1939-40, Pratt Inst., 1945-46, Art Ctr. Coll. Design, 1946-47. Asst. art dir. Dozier, Graham, Eastman, L.A., 1948-49; art dir. Edward J. Robinson, 1949-50, Anderson-McConnell, L.A., 1950-53; art dir., creative dir. Calkins & Holden, N.Y.C., L.A., 1953-63; pres., owner George Rappaport Graphic Design Cons., L.A., 1963-67; head creative TV group Carson/Roberts, 1967-70; mng. dir. Lee Lacy, Ltd., London, 1970-72; founder, chmn. bd. Multi Media Presentations, Culver City, Calif., 1972-85; ret., 1985. Bass player Trenton Symphony, 1937-41, MCA Orch., 1944-45. Art dir., designer (advertisements) Voice of Free Choice (Gold medal, 1964), Elizabeth Stewart Swimwear (Gold medal, 1965). Served with USAF, 1941-44. Numerous awards from Art Dirs. Clubs of N.Y.C., L.A. and Chgo. including Distinctive Merit award, Art Dirs. Club N.Y., 1943, Communications Arts Mag., 1963.

Mem. L.A. Art Dirs. Club (life mem., pres. 1956-57, medal 1964, 65), Soc. Art Ctr. Coll. of Design Alumni (pres. 1962-63), Nat. Acad. Jazz (pres. 1987-88), Acad. TV Arts and Scis. Democrat. Unitarian Universalist. Avocations: tennis, playing with community symphony and small jazz combos.

RAPPAPORT, LINDA ELLEN, lawyer; b. Freeport, N.Y., Jan. 12, 1952; d. William Jay and Marcia Ann (Wiland) Rappaport; m. Leonard Chazen, June 1, 1980; 1 child Matthew Ross Chazen. BA, Wesleyan U., Middletown, Conn., 1974; JD, NYU, 1977. Bar: N.Y. 1977. Law clk. Chief Judge James S. Holden U.S. Dist. Ct. Vt., Rutland, 1978; assoc. Shearman & Sterling, N.Y.C., 1979-85, ptnr., 1986—, elected mem. policy com., 1995—. Bd. dirs. N.Y. Women's Found., N.Y.C., 1995—2001, AIESEC Internat., N.Y.C., 1994—2000. Mem.: Bar Assn. City of N.Y. (employee benefits com. 1986—, employment law com. 1986—). Office: Shearman & Sterling 599 Lexington Ave Fl 13 New York NY 10022-6069 E-mail: lrappaport@shearman.com.

RAPPAPORT, MARGARET M.W.E. psychologist, physician, author, pilot, consultant; b. Nov. 16, 1947; d. Leo J. and Marie L. (Rischle) Williams; m. Herbert Rappaport; children: Amanda, Alexander. BA, U. Buffalo; MA, SUNY; PhD, MD, U. Colo. Zone Perfect cert. instr. Prof., rschr. U. Dar es Salaam, Tanzania; with Rappaport Assocs., Phila., 1974-94; exec. dir. Inst. for Parent/Child Svcs., 1978-94. Mem. adj. faculty Temple U., Phila., 1974-94; aviation safety counselor FAA; aviation cons.; nat./internat. spkr. Pres. Reach New Heights, Inc.; founder Fit to Fly. Trustee Cape Cod Healthcare Found.; chmn. Cape Cod devel. com. Vis. Nurse Assn. Mem. AAUP, Nat. Profl. Spkrs. Assn., Cosmopolitan Club, Orleans Yacht Club. Home: PO Box 1845 Orleans MA 02653-1845 E-mail: rappaportmm@prodigy.net.

RAPPAPORT, MARTIN PAUL, internist, nephrologist, educator; b. Bronx, N.Y., Apr. 25, 1935; s. Joseph and Anne (Kramer) R.; m. Bethany Ann Mitchell; children: Karen, Steven; stepchildren: Aaron Cole, Kevin Cole. BS, Tulane U., 1957, MD, 1960. Diplomate Am. Bd. Internal Medicine, Nat. Bd. Med. Examiners. Intern Charity Hosp. of La., New Orleans, 1960-61, resident in internal medicine, 1961-64; pvt. practice internal medicine and nephrology, Seabrook, Tex., 1968-72, Webster, 1972-98; internist Univ. Med. Group, Houston, 1998; mem. courtesy staff Mainland Ctr. Hosp. (formerly Galveston County Meml. Hosp.), Texas City, 1968-96, Bapt. Meml. System, 1969-72, 88-98; mem. staff Clear Lake Regional Med. Ctr., 1972-98; cons. staff St. Mary's Hosp., 1973-79; cons. nephrology St. John's Hosp., Nassau Bay, Tex.; fellow in nephrology Northwestern U. Med. Sch., Chgo., 1967—68; clin. asst. prof. in medicine and nephrology U. Tex., Galveston, 1969—; part-time physician dept. family medicine outpatient clinics U. Tex. Med. Br., 2000; locum tenens, 2000—. Lectr. emergency med. technician cours e, 1974-76; adviser on respiratory therapy program Alvin (Tex.) Jr. Coll., 1976-82; cons. nephrology USPHS, 1979-80. Served to capt. M.C. U.S. Army, 1961-67. Fellow ACP, Am. Coll. Chest Physicians; mem. Internat., Am. Socs. Nephrology, So. Med. Assn., Tex. Med. Assn., Tex. Soc. Internal Medicine (bd. govs. 1994-96), Am. Soc. Artificial Internal Organs, Tex. Acad. Internal Medicine, Harris County Med. Soc., Am. Geriatrics Soc., Bay Area Heart Assn. (bd. govs. 1969-75), Clear Lake C. of C., Rotary, Phi Delta Epsilon, Alpha Epsilon Pi, Tulane Alumni Assn. Home: 15913 Malibu W Willis TX 77318-6784

RAPPAPORT, MICHAEL PAUL, columnist; b. San Diego, Dec. 11, 1949; s. Norman Lewis and Yvonne Naomi Rappaport; m. Leslie Ann Rappaport, Apr. 19, 1975 (div. May 1982); m. Nicole Jacqueline Rappaport, Nov. 2, 1992; children: Pauline Nicole Borderies, Virgile Georges Borderies. AS, No. Va. C.C., Annandale, 1976; BS, George Mason U., 1981. Asst. sports editor Alexandria (Va.) Gazette, 1979-81, Gastonia (N.C.) Gazette, 1982-83; sportswriter Anderson (S.C.) Ind. Mail, 1983-84, St. Louis Globe Dem., 1984-86; sports editor, columnist Greeley (Colo.) Tribune, 1986-88; sportswriter, columnist Reno Gazette Jour., 1988-90; sportswriter Inland Valley Daily Bull., Ontario, Calif., 1990-96, metro columnist, 1996—. Co-author: (e-book) The Woman in the Box, 2000; creator website mikerappaport.com, 2000. Recipient Sweepstakes Writing award Soc. Profl. Journalists Inland Calif. Chpt., 1997, Writing award for best local column, 2001-; named Sportswriter of Yr., South Atlantic League, 1982, 83. Mem. Nat. Soc. Newspaper Columnists, Nat. Press Club, Greater L.A. Press Club, Sigma Phi Epsilon (life, chpt. pres. 1981). Roman Catholic. Avocations: reading, golf, films, rotisserie baseball. Home: 1234 Fernside Dr La Canada Flintridge CA 91011 Office: 2041 E 4th St Ontario CA 91764-2605 E-mail: m_rappaport@msn.com.

RAPPAPORT, NORMAN HARVEY, plastic surgeon; b. Phila., Apr. 23, 1947; s. Herbert and Ruth Rappaport; m. Deborah Ann Finn, Oct. 2, 1982; children: Jonathan David, Betsy, William. BA, LaSalle Coll., 1969; DDS, Temple U., 1972; MD, Hahnemann Med. Coll., 1975. Diplomate Am. Bd. Plastic Surgery. Resident in gen. surgery Abington (Pa.) Meml. Hosp., 1975-78; fellow in hand surgery U. Pa., Phila., 1978; resident in plastic surgery Baylor Coll. Medicine, Houston, 1978-80; clin. assoc. prof. surgery Baylor Coll. Surgery, 1994—. Contbr. articles to profl. jours. Fellow: ACS; mem.: AMA, Houston Surg. Soc. (pres. 2001), Tex. Soc. Plastic Surgeons, Tex. Med. Assn., N.Am. Burn Soc., Houston Soc. Plastic Surgeons (pres. 2002), Harris County Med. Soc., Am. Assn. Hand Surgeons, Am. Assn. Plastic Surgeons, Am. Soc. for Aesthetic Plastic Surgery, Am. Soc. Plastic Surgeons (bd. dirs. 1998—2000), Plastic Surgery Ednl. Found. (bd. dirs. 1994—2000), Am. Soc. Maxillofacial Surgeons (pres. 2000), Omicron Kappa Upsilon. Home: 5202 Huckleberry Ln Houston TX 77056-2712 Office: 6560 Fannin St Ste 1812 Houston TX 77030-2775 E-mail: nhr@hcps.cc.edu.

RAPPAPORT, STUART RAMON, lawyer; b. Detroit, Apr. 13, 1935; s. Reuben and Zella (Golechen) R.; m. Anne M. Plotnick; children: Douglas, Erica Rappaport Witt. BA in History, U. Mich., 1956; JD, Harvard U., 1959. Bar: Calif. 1962. Trial lawyer, chief trials, bur. chief, chief. asst. pub. defender L.A. County Pub. Defender's Office, L.A., 1962-87; pub. defender Santa Clara County, San Jose, Calif., 1987-95; pvt. practice, 1995—. Mem. standing adv. com. on criminal law Jud. Coun. Calif., San Francisco, 1993—; mem. discipline evaluation com. State Bar of Calif. Contbr. articles to profl. jours. Recipient Lifetime Achievement award Calif. Attys. for Criminal Justice. Mem. Calif. Pub. Defenders Asn. (pres. 1982-83, Lifetime Achievement award), L.A. County Pub. Defenders Assn. (pres.). Democrat. Jewish. Address: 1415 Arch St Berkeley CA 94708 E-mail: sturap@mcn.

RAPPAPORT, SUSAN ELIZABETH, English language educator; b. Wakeenie, Kans., Feb. 15, 1953; d. Fred and Susan Louise (Gwin) Thornburg; m. Ronald Irvin Rappaport, Feb. 16, 1977; children: Erick, Scott. BA, U. Okla., 1975. Cert. English tchr. Tchr. English Washington (Okla.) H.S., 1975-77, Highland East Mid. Sch., Moore, Okla., 1978-83, June Shelton Sch. and Evaluation Ctr., Dallas, 1984-89; content mastery aide Coppell (Tex.) Mid. Sch., 1991-92; tchr. English Lakeview Mid. Sch., The Colony, Tex., 1992-95; tchr. English and reading Arbor Creek, Carrollton, 1995—. Multicultural activities coord. Lakeview Mid. Sch., The Colony, 1994-95; mentor tchr. Arbor Creek Mid. Sch., Carrollton, 1995—, bldg. leadership team, 1995—, sponsor Nat. Jr. Honor Soc., 1996-98. Active Project Graduation, Coppell (Tex.) H.S., 1998, Culture Dept., Soka Gakkai Internat., Dallas, 1998. Grantee Lewisville Ind. Sch. Sys., 1997. Mem. ASCD, Internat. Reading Assn., Nat. Coun. Tchrs. English, Nat. Mid. Sch. Assn. Avocations: reading, gardening.

RAPPAPORT, ZVI HARRY, neurosurgeon; b. Munich, Federal Republic Germany, June 25, 1949; arrived in Israel, 1980; s. Aron and Sarah (Silberberg) R.; m. Isabelle Klein, Dec. 19, 1978; children: Yael, Maya, Ron. BA, Columbia Coll., 1969; MD, U. Pa., 1973. Diplomate Am. Bd. Neurol. Surgery. Surg. resident Columbia-Presbyn. Med. Ctr., N.Y., 1973-74; resident in neurosurgery NYU Med. Ctr., 1974-78; fellow in physiol. neurosurgery Westchester County Med. Ctr., Valhalla, N.Y., 1979; sr. neurosurgeon Sheba Med. Ctr., Tel Hashomer, Israel, 1980-83, Hadassah U. Med. Ctr., Jerusalem, 1983-89; chmn. dept. neurosurgery Rabin Med. Ctr., Petach Tikva, Israel, 1989—. Asst. prof. neurosurgery NYU Med. Sch., 1978-79; sr. lectr. in neurosurgery Hebrew U., Jerusalem, 1985-90; assoc. prof. neurosurgery Tel Aviv U., 1991—. Contbr. articles to profl. jours. Served as med. officer Israel Def. Forces, 1985—. Recipient research prize Am. Heart Assn., 1970. Mem. Israel Neurosurg. Soc. (pres. 1993-97), Am. Assn. Neurosurgery, Congress Neurol. Surgery, Internat. Assn. for Study Pain, Academia Euroasiana, European Soc. Pediatric Neurosurgery, World Soc. Functional & Stereotactic Neurosurgery. Jewish. Office: Rabin Med Ctr Dept of Neurosurgery Petah Tiqwa 49100 Israel E-mail: zhr1@internet-zahav.net.

RAPPÉ, TERI WAHL, piano educator; b. Missoula, Mont., Apr. 4, 1945; d. Charles Franklin and Mary Evelyn (Beaver) Wheeler; m. Bruce Dennis Wahl, June 20, 1964 (div. 1982); 1 child, Maradee; m. Gerald Alan Rappé, Sept. 19, 1987; stepchildren: Rick, Susan. BMus with honors, U. Mont., 1971. Cert. secondary tchr. Wash.; nat. cert. music tchr. Piano instr., Missoula, Mont., 1962-72, Wenatchee, Wash., 1972—, Wenatchee Valley Coll., 1976—; ch. organist Ctrl. Christian Ch., Wenatchee, 1982-90; ch. pianist First Ch. of God, 1990—. Accompanist Columbia Chorale, Wenatchee, 1984—98, Appleaires, Wenatchee, 1998—, Apollo Club, 2001—; percussionist Wenatchee Valley Symphony. Performer with Wenatchee Valley Symphony, 1992—, Am. Guild of Organists, 1992-99. Mem. Wash. State Music Tchrs. (pres. 1998-00), Pi Kappa Lambda, Mu Phi Epsilon. Avocations: reading, backpacking, snowshoeing. Home: 227 Grover Ct Wenatchee WA 98801-1811

RAPPLEYE, RICHARD KENT, financial executive, consultant, educator; b. Oswego, N.Y., Aug. 10, 1940; s. Robert Edward and Evelyn Margaret (Hammond) R.; m. Karen Tobe Greenberg, Sept. 7, 1963; children: Matthew Walker, Elizabeth Marion. AB, Miami U., Oxford, Ohio, 1962; postgrad., Boston U., 1962-63; MBA, U. Pa., 1964; postgrad., DePaul U., 1965-66; MRA, U. Detroit-Mercy, 1997. CPA, Ill. Auditor DeLoitte Haskins & Sells, Chgo., 1962-67, mgmt. cons., 1967-71; controller United Dairy Industry Assn., Rosemont, Ill., 1971, dir. fin. and adminstrn., 1971-73, exec. v.p., 1973-74; asst. to exec. v.p. Florists' Transworld Delivery, Southfield, Mich., 1974-75, group dir. fin. and adminstrn., 1975-80; asst. treas. Erb Lumber Co., Birmingham, 1980, v.p. fin., chief fin. officer, 1981-83; v.p., sec.-treas. C.S. Mott Found., Flint, 1983-2000, v.p. field svcs., 2000—. Lectr. U. Mich., Flint, 1987-91, 98-99; cons. in field; instr. Oakland U., Rochester, Mich., 1981-83; bd. dirs. Treas. Council Mich. Founds, 1986-92, 96—. Trustee Mich. State Bar Fedn., 2001—. Mem. AICPAs, Mich. Assn. CPAs, Theosophical Soc., Masons, Rotary. Unitarian Universalist. Home: 503 Arlington St Birmingham MI 48009-1639 Office: CS Mott Found 2000 Town Center Ste 1900 Southfield MI 48075 E-mail: rrappleye@mott.org.

RAPPOLT, GEORGE ALLEN, software engineer; b. Elizabeth, N.J., Oct. 11, 1950; s. John Paul and Elisabeth (Allen) R.; m. Hannah Tabitha Tuckerman, Sept. 29, 1973; children: Ethan Amita Arundel, Pelé Alethea Tara, Amanda Sophia Dierdre. BS in Biology with honors, Calif. Inst. Tech., Pasadena, 1972; MA, Clark U., 1976, PhD in Psychology, 1982. Asst. prof. psychology Holy Cross Coll., Worcester, Mass., 1982-83; tech. rev. mgr. Internat. Bur. of Software Test, Marlborough, 1984-85; software engr. Phoenix Techs., Norwood, 1986-89; software engr., contractor The Registry, Wellesley, 1990-91; software engr. Tenberry Software, Natick, 1992-97, Hologic Inc., Bedford, 1997—. Cons. Human-Tech. Systems, Weston, Mass., 1983-86; cons. software engr. Atlantic Microsystems, Salem, N.H., 1989, Computer Corp. of Am., Cambridge, Mass., 1991. Mem. IEEE, Assn. for Computing Machinery. Home: 134 Marked Tree Rd Needham MA 02492-1625

RAPS, GENA, pianist; b. Cleve., June 21, 1941; d. Louis Raps and Pola (Tannenbaum) Geier; divorced; 1 child, Symra Cohn. BA, Bklyn. Coll., 1964; MMA, MS, Juilliard Sch. Music, 1968. Mem. piano faculty Mannes Coll. Music, N.Y.C., 1970—; with Sarah Lawrence Coll., 1984-85. Pianist recs./CDs of Dvorak Waltzes, Dvorak Slavonic Dances, Mozart, Complete 4-Hand Music, (CD)(with Julie Andrews and Peter Schickele) Mother Goose and More, Louise Farrenc, 12 Etudes, Op. 41, 2001; author: The Bach Book, 1995; author, prodr.: (CD) Play Bach!, 1996; producer, author children's play Look Who's Back, 1997; concert performer, U.S. and Europe. Tchg. fellow Juilliard, 1968; writing grantee The New Sch., 1991, producing grantee, 1992. Home: 537 Manhattan Ave New York NY 10027-5215

RAPSON, RICHARD L. history educator; b. N.Y.C., Mar. 8, 1937; s. Louis and Grace Lillian (Levenkind) R.; m. Susan Burns, Feb. 22, 1975 (div. June 1981); m. Elaine Catherine Hatfield, June 15, 1982; 1 child, Kim Elizabeth. BA, Amherst Coll., 1958; PhD, Columbia U., 1966. Asst. prof. Amherst (Mass.) Coll., 1960-61, Stanford (Calif.) U., 1961-65, U. Calif., Santa Barbara, 1965-66; from assoc. prof. to prof. history U. Hawaii, Honolulu, 1966—, founder, dir. New Coll., 1968-73. Bd. dirs. Semester at Sea, U. Pittsburgh, 1979—; psychotherapist, Honolulu, 1982—. Author: Individualism and Conformity in the American Character, 1967, Britons View America, 1971, The Cult of Youth, 1972, Major Interpretations of the American Past, 1978, Denials of Doubt, 1980, Cultural Pluralism in Hawaii, 1981, American Yearnings, 1989; co-author: (with Elaine Hatfield) Love, Sex and Intimacy: Their Psychology, Biology and History, 1993, Emotional Contagion, 1994, Love and Sex: Cross-Cultural Perspectives, 1995, Rosie, 2000; mem. editl. bd. Univ. Press Am., 1981—. Woodrow Wilson fellow, Wilson Found., Princeton, 1960; Edward Perkins scholar, Columbia U., 1961; Danforth tchr., Danforth Found., St. Louis, 1965; recipient E. Harris Harbison for Gifted Teaching award, Danforth Found., 1973, Outstanding Tchr. award Stanford U. 25th Reunion Class, 1992. Mem. Am. Hist. Assn., Orgn. Am. Hist., Nat. Womens Hist. Project, Phi Beta Kappa, Outrigger Canoe Club, Honolulu Club. Avocations: squash, travel, classical music. Office: U Hawaii Dept History 2530 Dole St Honolulu HI 96822-2303

RAR, ANDREI, research scientist; b. Novosibirsk, Russia, May 19, 1961; s. Aleksandr and Valentina (Okhrimenka) R.; m. Nadejda Furova; children: Rostislav, Ekaterina. M, Novosibirsk State U., 1983; PhD, U. Hokkaido, Sapporo, Japan, 1996. Rschr. Inst. for Catalysis, Novosibirsk, 1983-93; vis. rschr. Inst. for Applied Solid State Physics, Germany, 1996-97, Nat. Rsch. Inst. for Metals, Tsukuba, Japan, 1997—99; postdoctoral rschr. Materials for Info. Tech. U. Ala., Tuscaloosa, 1999—2001; postdoctoral rschr. U. Tenn., Knoxville, 2001—. E-mail: arar@mit.va.edu.

RARDON, LARRY L. lawyer; b. Arcadia, Fla., Oct. 4, 1946; s. Wayne V. and Nellie Rardon; m. Hilda M. Rardon, Dec. 12, 1986; children: Shawn, Adria. BA, U. South Fla., 1968; JD, Stetson U., 1971. Bar: Fla. 1971. Specializing in trial work Rardon, Rodriguez & Anthony, PA, Tampa, Fla. Office: 3918 North Blvd Tampa FL 33603

RARICH, ANNE LIPPITT, management and organizational development consultant; b. New Haven, Apr. 8, 1943; d. Gordon L. and Phyllis (Parker) Lippitt; m. Thomas D. Rarich, June 26, 1965; children: Kirsten Ruth, Diana Lynn. BA, Baldwin-Wallace Coll., Berea, Ohio; MEd, Springfield (Mass.) Coll. NLP practitioner. Field dir. Mystic Side G.S. Coun., Medford, Mass., 1965-67; field dir., trainer Shabonee G.S. Coun., Moline, Ill., 1967-69; prin. Learning Exch., Concord, Mass., 1976—; v.p. mktg. and sales orgn. Renewal Inc., 1980-84; human resources devel. Digital Equipment Corp., Maynard, Mass., 1986-91; dir. human resource devel. Liberty Mutual Ins., Boston, 1992-94; field mgr. Carlson Learning Co., Mpls., 1989—. Leadership devel. for bd. Mass. LWV, Boston, 1983-85; adj. faculty Bentley Coll.; presenter in field. Contbg. author: When the Canary Stops Singing, Women's Perspective on Transforming Business, 1993, Open Letter to Our Daughters, 1997; contbr. articles to profl. jours. Pres. League of Women Voters, Concord, 1979-81; chmn. sch. com., Concord, 1983-89, Edn. Collaborative of Greater Boston, 1985-86; founder, past pres. Network for Women's Lives, Concord, 1991-95; bd. dirs. New Eng. Women's Fund, 1997, 99, 2000, Living Values Edn. Program, Inc., v.p. 2000-01; mem. adult basic edn. adv. bd. Mass. Bd. Edn. Recipient Outstanding Working Woman award Working Woman Mag., 1980, Boston YMCA, 1981. Mem.: ASTD (v.p. 1979—98), Concord C. of C., Nat. Assn. Bus. Coaches, Internat. Coaching Fedn. (pres. 2002—), Soc. for Human Resource Planning, World Bus. Acad. (program coord. 1990—92). Mem. UCC Ch. Home: 315 College Rd Concord MA 01742-5418 Office: Learning Exchg 315 College Rd Concord MA 01742-5418 E-mail: annerarich@aol.com.

RARIDON, RICHARD JAY, computer specialist; b. Newton, Iowa, Oct. 25, 1931; s. Jack Allison and Letha Helen (Woods) R.; m. Mona Marie Herndon, May 28, 1956; children— Susan Gayle, Ann Chaney. BA, Grinnell Coll., 1953; MA, Vanderbilt U., 1955, PhD, 1959. Assoc. prof. phys. sci. Memphis State U., 1958-62; rsch. scientist Oak Ridge Nat. Lab., 1962-92; cons. ORNL, 1992—. Environ. specialist Coop. Sci. Edn. Center, Oak Ridge, 1971-72 Contbr. articles to profl. jours. Radiol. Physics fellow AEC, 1953-55 Fellow AAAS, Tenn. Acad. Sci. (pres. 1971); mem. Assn. Acads. Sci. (sec.-treas. 1972-76, pres. 1977), Sigma Xi. Home: 111 Columbia Dr Oak Ridge TN 37830-7720 Office: Oak Ridge Nat Lab Oak Ridge TN 37831 E-mail: raridon@hotmail.com.

RAS, ZBIGNIEW WIESLAW, computer science educator; b. Warsaw, Poland, June 17, 1947; s. Stanislaw and Helena A. (Baczalska) R.; m. Margareta Gozdawa-Gizycka, Sept. 1970 (div. Oct. 1976); 1 child, Pawel; m. Joanna Wapinska, Sept. 1987; 1 child, Anna. MA in Math., U. Warsaw, 1970, PhD in Computer Sci., 1973. Rsch. assoc. math. dept. Columbia U., N.Y.C., 1975-76; asst. prof. computer sci. Jagiellonian U., Poland, 1976-78, U. Warsaw, 1974-83; assoc. prof. computer sci. dept. U. Tenn., Knoxville, 1985-86, U. N.C., Charlotte, 1981-88, prof. computer sci., 1988—. Co-author: Intelligent Systems: State of the Art and Future Directions, 1990; co-editor-in-chief Jour. Intelligent Info. Systems; assoc. editor Fundamenta Informaticae Jour. Mem. Assn. for Computing Machinery, Am. Assn. for Artificial Intelligence, Computer Soc. of IEEE. Office: U NC Computer Sci Dept Charlotte NC 28223

RASBURY, JULIAN GEORGE, financial services company executive; b. Houston, July 10, 1957; s. Julian George and Willie Ann (Stringer) R.; m. Kathleen Ellen Price, Nov. 10, 1984; 1 child, Lisa Dawn. BBA in Acctg., U. Tex., 1980. CPA Tex. Bd. Pub. Accountancy, Austin, 1993—; cert. funds specialist Inst. Funds Specialists, La Jolla, Calif., 1994—; gen. securities rep. NASD, Rockville, Md., 1992—, gen. securities prin., 1992—, registered investment advisor, 1993—, fin. & ops. prin., 1994—; pres. JGR Cons. Svcs., Lakeway, Tex. Co-author: Professional Standards in Cafeteria Plan Administration, 1993. Mem. Big Bros., Pleasant Hill, Calif., 1987. Mem. AICPA, Tex. Soc. CPAs, Employers Coun. on Flexible Compensation (exec. com. 1992-93), Cafateria Plan Adv. Coun., U. Tex. Alumni Assn. Republican. Baptist. Avocations: golf, water skiing, snow skiing, raquetball. Office: JGR Cons Svcs 2303 RR-620 S Ste 135-222 Austin TX 78734

RASCH, ELLEN MYRBERG, cell biology educator; b. Chicago Heights, Ill., Jan. 31, 1927; d. Arthur August and Helen Catherine (Stelle) Myrberg; m. Robert W. E. Rasch, June 17, 1950; 1 son, Martin Karl. PhB with honors, U. Chgo., 1945, BS in Biol. Sci., 1947, MS in Botany, 1948, PhD, 1950. Asst. histologist Am. Meat Inst. Found., Chgo., 1950-51; USPHS postdoctoral fellow U. Chgo., 1951-53, rsch. assoc. dept. zoology, 1954-59; rsch. assoc. Marquette U., Milw., 1962-65, assoc. prof. biology, 1965-68, prof. biology, 1968-75, Wehr disting. prof. biophysics, 1975-78; rsch. prof. biophysics East Tenn. State U., James H. Quillen Coll. Medicine, Johnson City, 1978-94, interim chmn. dept. cellular biophysics, 1986-94, prof. anatomy and cell biology, 1994—. Mem. Wis. Bd. Basic Sci. Examiners, 1971-75, sec. bd., 1973-75. Contbr. articles to various publs. Recipient Rsch. Career Devel. award, 1967-72, Tchg. Excellence and Disting. award Marquette U., 1975, Kreeger-Wolf vis. disting. prof. in biol. sci. Northwestern U., 1979. Mem. Royal Microscopic Soc., Am. Soc. Cell Biology, Am. Soc. Zoologists, Am. Soc. Ichthyologists and Herpetologists, The Histochem. Soc., Phi Beta Kappa, Sigma Xi. Home: 1504 Chickees St Johnson City TN 37604-7103 Office: East Tenn State Univ Dept Anatomy & Cell Biology PO Box 70582 Johnson City TN 37614-0582

RASCHE, ROBERT HAROLD, banker, retired economics educator; b. New Haven, June 29, 1941; s. Harold A. and Elsa (Bloomquist) R.; m. Dorothy Anita Bensen, Dec. 28, 1963; children: Jeanette Dorothy, Karl Robert. BA, Yale U., 1963; A.M., U. Mich., 1965, PhD, 1966. Asst. prof. U. Pa., Phila., 1966-72; assoc. prof. econs. Mich. State U., East Lansing, 1972-75, prof., 1975-98, prof. emeritus, 1999—; sr. v.p., dir. rsch. St. Louis Fed. Res. Bank, 1999—. Vis. scholar St. Louis Fed. Res., 1971-72, 76-77, 94-98, San Francisco Fed. Rsch. Bank, 1985, Bank of Japan, Tokyo, 1990; disting. vis. prof. econs. Ariz. State U., Tempe, 1986; rsch. assoc. Nat. Bur. Econ. Rsch., Cambridge, Mass., 1982-91; mem. Mich. Gov. Coun. Econ. Advisers, 1992-96; mem. Shadow Open Market Com., 1973-98. Mem. Am. Econs. Assn. Lutheran. Home: 14531 Radcliffeborough Ct Chesterfield MO 63017-5626 Office: Fed Res Bank St Louis Rsch Divsn PO Box 442 Saint Louis MO 63166-0442 E-mail: rasche@msu.edu.

RASCO, KAY FRANCES, antique dealer; b. Rienzi, Miss., Nov. 13, 1925; d. Robert Franklin and Sophia Agnes (Kinningham) Dilworth; m. H. Manfred Ray, July 9, 1943 (div. 1950); 1 child, Manfred Ray; m. Lavon Rasco, Mar. 22, 1951; children: Francine, Karen. BA, U. Miss., 1948, MA, 1953; PhD, Northwestern U., 1966. Instr. English Western Ill. U., 1953-54, 56-60, Northwestern U., 1960-61; lectr. De Paul U., Chgo., 1969, 71-74; master tchr. English Yale U., New Haven, summers 1963,64, 66,67; tchr. English New Trier High Sch., Winnetka, Ill., 1961-69, 71-73; assoc. prof. English Am. U., Cairo, 1969-71; prof. drama Al Azhar U., 1976-77; sales assoc. Merrill Lynch Realty, Evanston, Ill., 1973-76, 78-83, mgr. area sales, 1983-89; owner Sarah Bustle Antiques, 1989—. Mem. Rotary Internat. (pres. Evanston Lighthouse Rotary 1999-2000). Home: 1211 Hinman Ave Evanston IL 60202-1312 Office: 821 Dempster St Evanston IL 60201-4303

RASCOE, PAUL STEPHEN, librarian, researcher; b. Corpus Christi, Tex., July 7, 1954; s. Stephen Thomas and Barbara Jean (Butler) R. BA, U. Tex., Arlington, 1975, U. Tex., Austin, 1976, M Libr. Info. Sci., 1983; MA, U. London, 1977. Govt. documents and electronic info. svcs. libr. U. Tex., Austin, 1985-96, libr., 1978-85, libr. govt. documents maps and electronic info. svcs., 1996—. Dir. rsch. Weissmann Travel Reports, Austin, 1990-96. Avocation: travel. Office: U Tex Austin Documents Collection Gen Librs PCL 2.400 Austin TX 78713-7330

RASCON, ALFRED, federal agency administrator; B Mgmt. and Liberal Studies. Commd. 2d lt. U.S. Army, ret.; with immigration and naturalization svc. Dept. Justice, with drug enforcement adminstrn., with internat. criminal police orgn.; dir. Selective Svc. System, Arlington, Va., 2001—. Decorated medal of Honor. Office: Selective Svc System 1515 Wilson Blvd Arlington VA 22209-2425*

RASCÓN, ARMANDO, artist; b. Calexico, Calif., Dec. 9, 1956; s. Reynaldo and Maria (Herrera) R. BFA Coll. Creative Studies, U. Calif., Santa Barbara, 1979. Owner Terrain Gallery, San Francisco, 1988—. Guest faculty dept. art U. Calif., Davis, 1988, Calif. Coll. Arts and Crafts, Oakland, 1991, dept. art practice U. Calif., Berkeley, 1995; juror, panelist Artist Trust Fellowship Grants, Visual Arts, Seattle, 1994; lectr. N.Y. Mus. Modern Art, 1995; panelist LEF Found. Orgn. Grants, Cambridge, Mass., 1996, Nev. State Coun. on the Arts Grants, Carson City, 1996, 97; v.p. San Francisco Art Commn., 1996-97; presenter various lectrs., panels, workshops, confs. One-man shows include Randolph Street Gallery, Chgo., 1991, INTAR, N.Y., 1994, San Diego Mus. Contemporary Art, 1997, Blue Star Art Space, San Antonio, 1998, Newark Mus., 2002. Bd. dirs. New Langton Arts, San Francisco, 1988-92; vice-chair Art Commn. City of San Francisco, 1997. Recipient Hazel S. Lagerson scholarship U. Calif., Santa Barbara, 1975, fellowship grant in painting Nat. Endowment for Arts, Washington, 1987, Adaline Kent award San Francisco Art Inst., 1994, Goldie award in visual art San Francisco Bay Guardian, 1994; U.S. Mexico Fund for Culture grantee, 1999; Calif. Arts Coun. Artist fellow, 1999. Home and Office: 165 Jessie St Fl 2 San Francisco CA 94105-4010

RASENICK, MARK, biophysicist, educator; b. Chgo., Sept. 5, 1949; s. Maurice Milton and Eleanore Ruth (Fox) Rasenick; m. Helene Joy Shambelan; 3 children. BA, Case Western Res., 1971; PhD, Wesleyan U., Middletown, Conn., 1977; postdoctoral fellow, Yale U., 1977—81. Various edn. positions to assoc. prof., dept. physiology and biophysics U. Ill./Chgo. Coll. Medicine, 1988—93, dir. grad. studies, 1990—96, prof., 1993—, dir. biomed. neurosci. tng. program, 1995—; Robert Wood Johnson Health Policy fellow Sen. Com. on Health Edn., labor and pensions, 1999—2000. Program dir. U.S. Nat. Student Assn., Washington, 1971—72; mem. sci. panels NSF, 1989—92; mem. U.S. Mil. Rsch. Command Breast Cancer Rev. Panel, 1997—; reviewer jours. in field. Editor (editl. bd.): (jour.) Neuropsychopharmacology, 2002—. Recipient Rsch. Scientist award, NIMH, 1992—97, Rsch. Scientist Devel. award Level II, 1987—92, rsch. grant, Sigma Xi, 1976. Mem.: Union Concerned Scientists, Soc. Neurosci., Am. Soc. for Cell Biology, Am. Soc. Biol. Chemistry and Molecular Biology, AAAS, Sigma Xi. Office: Dept Physiol and Biophys Coll Med Univ Ill 901 Wolcott M Chicago IL 60612

RASERA, ROBERT L. physics educator; b. N.Y.C., July 25, 1939; s. Louis and Dorothy Jeannette R.; m. Paula J. Rasera, June 10, 1961; children: Renee Rasera Cornett, Roy Louis. BS, Wheaton Coll., Wheaton, Ill., 1960; PhD, Purdue U., 1965. Rsch. assoc. Purdue U., West Lafayette, Ind., 1965; asst. prof. of physics U. Pa., Phila., 1966-71; assoc. prof. of physics U. Md., Balt.,

1971-81, prof. of physics, 1981—, assoc. chair, dept. physics, 1996—. Guest prof. Inst. for Radiation and Nuclear Physics, U. Bonn, Germany, 1965-66. Office: Dept Physics Univ Md Balt County 1000 Hilltop Cir Baltimore MD 21250

RASH, WAYNE, JR. journalist; b. Erie, Pa., Mar. 2, 1948; s. Wayne and Elizabeth Rash; m. Carolyn Louise Hall, Nov. 25, 1972; children: Julia Leigh, Wayne III, Brittany Lynne. BA, Lynchburg (Va.) Coll., 1980. Dep. commr. revenue City of Lynchburg, 1976-80; prin. Am. Mgmt. Systems, Inc., Arlington, Va., 1984-92; pres. Wayne Rash & Assocs., 1990—; columnist InternetWeek, 1992—2002, mng. editor tech., 1998-2000, editor/events, 2000-01, sr. contbg. editor, 2001—02; contbg. editor CNet/2DNet, 2001—, 3D Times, 2001—. Mem. review bd. Infoworld, 1990-94, contbg. editor, 2002—. Author: The Novell Connection, 1989, The Executive Guide to Local Area Networks, 1989, WordPerfect Office 3.0: The Basics, 1991, Politics on the Nets, 1997; columnist Byte Mag., 1988-92, cons. editor, 1992-95; columnist The Star Ledger, Newark, 1996-98, OS/2 Mag., 1994-96, Windows NT Mag., 1995-96; cons. editor Byteweek, 1988-92, Computer Digest, 1986-91; editor Byte Information Exchange, 1984-2001, The Washington Post Computer Showcase, 1992-93; contbr. The Washington Post, 1994—; editor Tech Report/The Washington Post, 1996-97; sr. tech. editor, columnist InternetWeek, 1996-98; contbg. editor Plane and Pilot, 1995—, CNET.@DNET, 2001—, SD Times, 2001—. Pres. Kings Park West Civic Assn., Fairfax, Va., 1986-88; active Citizens Adv. Coun. on Nat. Space Policy, Studio City, Calif., 1986—; dir. tech. policy Commonwealth Policy Inst. Network. Lt. USN, 1980-84. Mem. Nat. Press Club, Lions (program chmn. Brookville-Timberlake chpt., Lynchburg 1976-80), Aircraft Owners and Pilots Assn., Am. Flying Club, Exptl. Aircraft Assn., Am. Radio Relay League, Va. Amateur Radio Emergency Svc. Episcopalian. Avocations: amateur radio, scuba diving, writing, foreign travel, flying. E-mail: wayne@rash.org.

RASHBA, ALLAN M. obstetrician-gynecologist, educator; b. Pitts., 1939; MD, Albert Einstein Coll. Medicine, 1964. Diplomate Am. Bd. Ob-Gyn. Intern U. Va. Hosp., Charlottesville, 1964-65; surg. resident Bronx Mcpl. Hosp. Ctr., N.Y.C., 1965-66; resident in ob-gyn. Boston Hosp. Women, 1968-71; staff Brigham and Womens Hosp., Boston. Clin. instr. ob-gyn., Harvard U. Med. Sch., Boston. Fellow ACOG.

RASHBA, EMMANUEL IOSIF, physicist, educator; b. Kiev, Ukraine, Oct. 30, 1927; came to U.S., 1991; s. Iosif Ovsei and Rosalia (Mirkine) R.; m. Erna Kelman, July 13, 1957; 1 child, Julia. Diploma with Honor, U. Kiev, Ukraine, 1949; PhD, Ukrainian Acad. Scis., 1956; DSc, Ioffe Inst. Physics and Tech., Leningrad, 1963; Prof. Theoretical and Math. Physics, Acad. Scis. Russia, 1967. Jr. and sr. scientist Inst. Physics, Ukrainian Acad. Scis., Kiev, Ukraine, 1954-60, head theoretical divsn. Inst. Semicondrs., 1960-66; head divsn. of theory of semiconductors, prin. scientist Landau Inst. for Theoretical Physics, Acad. Sci. Russia, Moscow, 1966-97; prof. Moscow Inst. for Physics and Tech., 1967-82; rsch. prof. dept. physics U. Utah, Salt Lake City, 1992—2000, SUNY, Buffalo, 2001—. Vis. scholar CNRS, Grenoble, France, 1987, U. Stuttgart, Germany, 1988, U. Warsaw, Poland, 1989, Inst. for Sci. Interchange, Turin, Italy, 1990, Internat. Ctr. for Theoretical Physics, Trieste, Italy, 1990, Racah Inst. for Physics, Hebrew U., Jerusalem, 1991; adj. prof. Dartmouth Coll., 2000—. Co-author: Collection of Problems in Physics, Russian edit. 1978, 2d edit., 1987, English edit., 1986, Japanese edit., 1989; Spectroscopy of Molecular Excitons, Russian edit. 1981, English edit. 1985; assoc. editor Jour. Luminescence, 1985—; editl. bd. Letters to the Jour. of Exptl. and Theoretical Physics, 1967-88; contbr. some 200 sci. and rev. articles to profl. jours. Recipient State prize in sci. Govt. of USSR, 1966, A.F. Ioffe prize Acad. of Scis. of the USSR, 1987, ICL prize Internat. Conf. on Luminescence and Optical Spectroscopy of Condensed Matter, 1999, Alan Berman award Naval Rsch. Lab., 2001. Fellow Am. Phys. Soc. Achievements include research in electron theory of solids, especially prediction of the effect of electric field on electron spin dynamics important for growing field of spintronics; proposed the concepts of giant oscillator strengths of bound excitons and coexistence of free and self-trapped states; initiation of mechanics of growing elastic bodies in civil engineering. Home: 123 Adeline Rd Newton MA 02459-2742 Office: SUNY Dept Physics 239 Fronczak Hall Buffalo NY 14260 E-mail: erashba@mailaps.org

RASHEED, KHALID, business executive; b. Karnal, Punjab, India, Aug. 2, 1935; came to U.S., 1968; s. Ghulam and Sabila Rasheed; m. Samra Rasheed, June 2, 1968; children: Maha R., Saba, Iram. Student, Lawrence Coll., Murree, Pakistan, 1948-51; BS, Forman Christian Coll., Lahore, Pakistan, 1955; PhD, U. Heidelberg, Germany, 1964. Sr. rsch. officer Pakistan Coun. of Rsch., Karachi, 1966-68; postdoctoral fellow U. Mich., Ann Arbor, 1964-65; sect. head synthesis Ansul Co., Madison, Wis., 1971-72, Weslaco, Tex., 1972-82; mgr. synthesis Witco Corp., Houston, 1987-97; group mgr., strategic chemistry CK Witco Corp., Dublin, 1997—. Contbr. articles to profl. publs. Grad. scholarship Deutsche Akademische-austauch Stipendium, 1960. Mem. Am. Chem. Soc., Am. Oil Chem. Soc., N.Y. Acad. Sci. Avocations: golfing, reading in history, history of science and economics. Office: CK Witco Corp 5777 Frantz Rd Dublin OH 43017-1524 Home: 1747 Berkoff Dr Sugar Land TX 77479-5506

RASHID, RICHARD F. information technology executive; Degree with hon., Stanford U., 1974; MSc in Computer Sci., U. Rochester, 1977, PhD in Computer Sci., 1980. Prof. computer sci. Carnegie Mellon U., Pitts., 1979—91; from mem. staff to v.p. rsch. Microsoft, Redmond, Wash., 1991—94, v.p. rsch., 1994—. Office: One Microsoft Way Redmond WA 98052-6399*

RASHKIND, ALAN BRODY, lawyer; b. N.Y.C., June 6, 1947; s. Julian and Eleanor (Brody) R.; m. Suzette DeBell, July 9, 1972; children: Graham Brody, Douglas Cormack. BA, Randolph-Macon Coll., 1969; JD, U. Va., 1972. Bar: Va. 1972, U.S. Dist. Ct. (ea. dist.) Va. 1972, U.S. Ct. Appeals (4th cir.) 1980, U.S. Supreme Ct. 1992. Assoc. Furniss, Davis and Sachs, Norfolk, Va., 1972-75; ptnr., shareholder Furniss, Davis Rashkind and Saunders P.C. and predecessors, 1976—. Mem. faculty Va. State Bar Law Sch., 1996-99, State Bar Professionalism Course, 2000—. Co-author: Virginia Insurance Case Finder, 1st edit., 1994, 2d edit., 2002; contbr. articles to profl. jours. Trustee Randolph-Macon Coll., Ashland, Va., 1991—, pres. Soc. of Alumni, 1987-89; trustee, mem. exec. com. Chesapeake Bay Acad., Virginia Beach, Va., 1989—, vice chmn., 1996-2002, chmn., 2002—. Fellow Va. Law Found.; mem. ABA, Va. State Bar Assn., Va. Bar Assn., Fed. Bar Assn., Norfolk-Portsmouth Bar Assn., Virginia Beach Bar Assn., Va. Assn. Def. Attys., Def. Rsch. Inst., Fedn. Def. and Corp. Counsel, Boyd-Graves Conf., (chmn. 1995-97), I'Anson-Hoffman Inn of Court (master of the bench 1987-94). Office: Furniss Davis et al 6160 Kempsville Cir Norfolk VA 23502-3933

RASHKIND, PAUL MICHAEL, lawyer; b. Jamaica, N.Y., May 21, 1950; s. Harvey and Norma (Dorfman) Rashkind; m. Robin Shane Rashkind, Dec. 20, 1975; children: Adam Charles, Noah Hamilton, Jennifer Elizabeth. AA, Miami-Dade Jr. Coll., 1970; BBA, U. Miami, Coral Gables, Fla., 1972, JD, 1975. Bar: Fla. 1975, D.C. 1981, N.Y. 1981, U.S. Dist. Ct. (so. dist.) Fla. 1975, U.S. Ct. Appeals (5th cir.) 1976, U.S. Supreme Ct. 1978, U.S. Dist. Ct. (mid. dist.) Fla. 1979, U.S. Ct. Appeals (2d and 11th cirs.) 1981, U.S. Ct. Appeals (4th and 6th cirs.) 1986, U.S. Dist. Ct. (no. dist.) Fla. 1987, U.S. Dist. Ct. (no. dist.) Calif. 1989; diplomate Nat. Bd. Trial Advocacy-Criminal Law (bd. examiners), bd. cert. Criminal Trial Law, Fla. Bar. Asst. state atty. Dade County State Attys. Office, Miami, Fla., 1975-78, chief asst. state atty. in charge of appeals, 1977-78; atty. Sams, Gerstein & Ward, P.A., 1978-83; ptnr. Bailey, Gerstein, Rashkind & Dresnick, 1983-92, supr. asst. Fed. Defender Chief of Appeals, 1992—. Spl. master Ct. Appointment, Miami, 1982-83; arbitrator Dade County Jail Inmates Grievance Program, Miami, 1981-92; mem. Fla. Bar Unauthorized Practice of Law Com. C, 11th Jud. Cir., Miami, 1980-84, Fed. Ct. Practice Com., 1992—; mem. So. Dist. Fla. Fed. Ct. Rules Com., 1996—. Contbr. articles on ethics and criminal law to profl. jours. Pres., bd. dirs. Lindgren Homeowners Assn., Miami, 1981-86. Fellow: Am. Bd. Criminal Lawyers (bd. govs. 1980—86); mem.: ATLA, ABA (ethics com. criminal justice sect. 1979—92, vice chmn. 1985—87, chmn. 1987—89, ethics advisor to chair 1992—97, criminal justice sect. coun. 1998—, vice chair criminal justice sect. 2001—), Soc. Bar and Gavel, Nat. Assn. riminal Def. Lawyers, Acad. Fla. Trial Lawyers (chmn. criminal law sect. 1985—86, diplomate 1986—), Fla. Assn. Criminal Def. Lawyers (Miami pres. 2002—, v.p. 2001—02, bd. dirs. 1992—2000), Dade County Bar Assn., D.C. Bar Assn., N.Y. Bar Assn., Fla. Bar Assn. (commn. on lawyer professionalism 1988—89, criminal law cert. com. 1989—94, standing com. on professionalism 1989—94), Hon. Order Ky. ols., Iron Arrow, Delta Theta Phi, Phi Rho Pi, Pi Sigma Alpha, Tau Kappa Alpha, Delta Sigma Rho, Omicron Delta Kappa. Democrat. Jewish. Office: Fed Pub Defender's Office SD FL 150 W Flagler St Ste 1500 Miami FL 33130-1555 E-mail: paul@rashkind.com.

RASHVAND, HABIB FALARI (FREIDOON RASHVAND), engineer, researcher; b. Qazvin, Tehran, Iran, Jan. 9, 1946; arrived in Eng., 1975; s. Mohamed and Khanum (Yakubi) R.; m. Elizabeth Elmes, Mar. 7, 1981; children: Leila, Cyrus. BS, Tehran U., Iran, 1969, MS in Elec. Engring., 1970; MSc, U. Kent, Canterbury, Eng., 1977, PhD, 1981. Div. engr. Iran Telecom Rsch. Ctr., Tehran, 1971-75; lectr. U. Zambia, Lusaka, 1981-83; rsch. mgr. Racal Milgo Ltd., Basingstoke, Eng., 1983-89; sr. rsch. officer Technophone Ltd., 1989-90; prof. C&W Telecommunication Coll., London, 1990-2000; dir. advanced comm. systems, prof. Coventry (Eng.) U., 2000—. Vis. rsch. fellow U. Southampton, Eng., 1988-89; vis. lectr. Portsmouth (Eng.) Polytechnics, 1987-88; cons. innovation and mktg., orgnl. re-structuring ICT. Editor IEEE Comms., 1996—; contbr. articles to profl. jours. Mem. The Engring. Coun., Basingstoke, 1988-89. Mem. Inst. Elec. Engrs., IEEE (sr. mem.), Internat. Telegraph and Telephone Consultative Com. Home: 78 Starbold Crescent Knowle Solihul West Midlands England E-mail: h.rashvand@iee.org.uk.

RASI, HUMBERTO MARIO, educational administrator, editor, minister; b. Buenos Aires, Argentina, Mar. 23, 1935; came to U.S., 1962, naturalized, 1968; s. Mario and Gertrudis Frida (Heyde) R.; m. Julia Cuchma, Feb. 28, 1957; children— Leroy Mario, Sylvia Beatrice. BA, Instituto Superior del Profesorado, Buenos Aires, 1960; MA, San Jose State U., 1966; PhD, Stanford U., 1971; D honoris causa, U. Peruana Union, Peru, 1999, U. Adventista del Plata, Argentina, 2001. Ordained to ministry Seventh-day Adventist Ch., 1980. Mem. faculty Instituto Florida, Buenos Aires, 1957-61; asst. editor Pacific Press Publ. Assn., Mountain View, Calif., 1962-66; asst. prof., assoc. prof. modern langs. Andrews U., 1969-76, prof., dean Sch. Grad. Studies, 1976-78; chief editor internat. publs. Pacific Press Publ. Assn., 1978-83, v.p. editorial devel., 1984-86; assoc. world dir. edn. Gen. Conf. Seventh-day Adventists, Silver Spring, Md., 1987-90, world dir. edn., 1990—. Exec. dir. Inst. for Christian Teaching, 1987—; bd. dirs. Andrews U., Loma Linda U., Adventist Internat. Inst. Advanced Studies. Author: The Life of Jesus, 3 vols., 1984—85; contbg. editor: Handbook of L.Am. Studies, Libr. of Congress, 1972—82; editor: Comentario Biblico Adventista, 7 vols., 1978—90; co-editor: Meeting the Secular Mind, 1985; founder, editor-in-chief: Coll. and Univ. Dialogue, 1989—, editor; compiler: Christ in the Classroom, 30 vols., 1991—; contbr. articles. NEH postdoctoral fellow Johns Hopkins U., 1975-76. Mem. Instituto Internacional de Literatura Iberoamericana. Office: 12501 Old Columbia Pike Silver Spring MD 20904-6601

RASIC, JANKO, architect; b. Zagreb, Croatia, Nov. 2, 1938; came to U.S., 1951; m. Carol Van Brunt, May 30, 1968; children: Timothy, Carolyn. BA, Princeton U., 1959, MFA in Arch., 1961. Registered architect, N.Y., N.J. Architect archeol. excavations NYU, 1961-64; archtl. designer Harrison & Abramovitz, N.Y.C., 1964-67; prin. architect Janko Rasic Assocs., 1969—. Cons. Met. Coun. Housing, N.Y.C., 1968-75, UN Orgn. for Overseas Office Facilities, 2000—. Prin. works include renovation of Henri Bendel bldg., N.Y.C., Coca-Cola bldg., Maxim's Restaurant, Pierre Cardin Gallery and the design of numerous facilities for over forty internat. and domestic banking instns. Mem. mayor's panel architects, N.Y.C., 1968-72; assoc. Real Estate Bd. N.Y., 1978—; mem. N.Y.C. Com. on Water Conservation, 1989—. Recipient design award Hackley Sch., Builders Assn. Westchester, 1970, Nat. Design award Monsanto Corp., 1993; Guggenheim fellow, 1964-65. Mem. AIA (chmn. ednl. facilities com., 1973-74), Adminstrv. Mgmt. Soc. (bd. dirs. 1982-83), Park Assn. N.Y. (design com. 1970), Quogue Assn. (bd. dirs. 1984-86, pres.), Group for South Fork (L.I., N.Y) (bd. dirs. 1986—).

RASIN, RUDOLPH STEPHEN, corporate executive; b. Newark, July 5, 1930; s. Simon Walter and Anna Rasin; m. Joy Kennedy Peterkin, Apr. 11, 1959; children: Rudolph Stephen, James Stenning, Jennifer Shaw Denniston. BA, Rutgers Coll., 1953; postgrad., Columbia U., 1958-59. Mgr. Miles Labs., Inc., 1959-61; devel. mgr. Gen. Foods Corp., White Plains, N.Y., 1961-62; asst. to pres., chmn. Morton Internat. Inc., Chgo., 1962-72; pres. Rasin Corp., 1971—, Alliance Brands, LLC. Bd. dirs. Ctr. for Def. Info., 1972—, Geneva Lakes Conservancy, Gatherings Waters Land Trust. With USAF, 1954—56. Mem. Hinsdale Golf Club, Mid Am. Club (Chgo.), Lake Geneva Country Club, Williams Coll. Club (N.Y.C.), Chgo. Club. Mem. United Ch. of Christ. Home: 179 E Lake Shore Dr Chicago IL 60611 Office: Rasin Corp 21 S Clark St Chicago IL 60603

RASKA, KAREL FRANTISEK JULIAN, JR. pathologist, virologist, educator; b. Prague, Czech Republic, May 26, 1939; arrived in U.S., 1965; s. Karel Raska and Helena (Heller) Raskova; m. Jana Dostalova, Feb. 18, 1960; children: Karel III, Francis. MD, Charles U., Prague, 1962; PhD in Biochemistry, Czechoslovak Acad. Scis., Prague, 1965. Diplomate Am. Bd. Pathology (anatomic and clin., immunopathology). Fellow Yale U. Sch. Medicine, New Haven, 1965—66; assoc. Waksman Inst. Microbiology, New Brunswick, NJ, 1966—67; scientist Czech Acad. Sci., Prague, 1967—68; prof. microbiology and pathology Rutgers Med. Sch., Piscataway, NJ, 1968—82; profl. pathology, lab. medicine, microbiology U. Medicine and Dentistry-Robert Wood Johnson Med. Sch., New Brunswick, 1982—; prof., chmn. dept. lab medicine and pathology U. Medicine and Dentistry NJ Med. Sch., Newark, 1989—92; chmn. dept. lab medicine and pathology St. Peter's U. Hosp., New Brunswick, 1992—. Bd. dirs. U. Diagnostic Labs., Piscataway, 1984—96; cons. Newark Beth Israel Med. Ctr., Newark, 1991—2001, E. Orange (NJ) VA Med. Ctr., 1991—; vis. prof. Charles U. Med. Sch., Prague, 1993—94. Contbr. articles to profl. jours., chapters to books. Trustee NJ Organ Sharing Network, Springfield, 1991—2000. Lt. Czechoslovak Air Force, 1962—63. Grantee, NIH, 1975—93, Damon Rynyon-Walter Winchell Cancer Rsch. Fund, 1975, NJ Commn. Cancer Rsch., 1985—86, 1994—95. Mem.: Am. Soc. Cell Biologists, Am. Soc. Virology, NJ Soc. Pathology, Assn. Univ. Pathologists, Internat. Acad. Pathology, Am. Assn. Cancer Rsch., Am. Soc. Clin. Immunology, Am. Assn. Immunology, Am. Soc. Investigative Pathology. Avocations: skiing, boating. Office: St Peters Univ Hosp Dept Lab Medicine & Pathology 254 Easton Ave New Brunswick NJ 08901

RASKIN, EDWIN BERNER, real estate executive; b. Savannah, Ga., Mar. 19, 1919; s. Isaac and Hannah (Berner) R.; m. Rebecca Kornman, Nov. 13, 1946; Children: Susan, Joan. BBA, Tulane U., 1940. Cert. property mgr., counselor of real estate, Inst. Real Estate Mgmt. Pres. Superior Shoe Co. and Nat. Shoe Co., Savannah, Ga., 1946-50, A.L. Kornman Co., Nashville, 1947-54; from pres. to sr. chmn. Edwin B. Raskin Co., 1954-99; chmn. Raskin Holdings, 2000—. Served to capt. USAAF, 1942-46. Mem. Greater Nashville Assn. Realtors, Tenn. Assn. Realtors, Nat. Assn. Real Estate Bds., Inst. Real Estate Mgmt. (past pres. middle Tenn. chpt.), Hillwood Country Club (Nashville), Rotary, Nashville City Club (past pres.), Cumberland Club. Home: 419 Ellendale Ave Nashville TN 37205-3401 Office: Raskin Holdings 5210 Maryland Way Brentwood TN 37027-5065

RASKIN, FRED CHARLES, transportation and utility holding company executive; b. N.Y.C., Sept. 11, 1948; s. Harry and Isabel (Wexler) R.; m. Lorraine Mary Sabourin, Apr. 25, 1974; children: Elizabeth Harris, Alexander Eastwood. BS, Syracuse U., 1970; JD, NYU, 1973. Bar: R.I. 1973, Mass. 1974; CPA, Ohio. Assoc. counsel Fleet Nat. Bank, Providence, 1973-75, Bank of Boston, 1975-78; asst. gen. counsel Eastern Enterprises, Boston, 1978-79, treas., 1979-81, v.p., treas., 1981-84; sr. v.p. fin. Eastern Assoc. Coal Co., Pitts., 1984-87; exec. v.p. Midland Enterprises, Inc., Cin., 1987-90, pres., 1991-98; pres., COO Eastern Enterprises, Weston, Mass., 1998-2000; CEO Woods Hole, Martha's Vineyart and Nantucket Steamship Authority, 2002—. Instr. Boston U., 2001—. Mem. Boston Heart Found., Greater Boston Diabetes Soc. Office: Eastern Enterprises 201 Rivermoor St West Roxbury MA 02132-4994

RASKIN, JONATHAN D. psychologist; b. Bklyn. s. Sherman and Paula Diane (Fishbach) Raskin; m. Shay A. Humphrey, Dec. 19, 1992; children: Ari Melissa, Noa Emily. AB in Psychology, Vassar Coll., Poughkeepsie, N.Y., 1990; MS in Counseling Psychology, U. Fla., 1992, PhD in Counseling Psychology, 1995. Lic. psychologist, N.Y. Predoctoral intern Emory U., Atlanta, 1994-95; asst. prof. psychology Tenn. State U., Nashville, 1995-96, SUNY, New Paltz, 1996—2001, assoc. prof., 2001—. Co-editor: Constructions of Disorder, 2000, Studies in Meaning, 2002; pres.: N.Am. Personal Construct Network, 2000—, book rev. editor: Jour. Constructivist Psychology, —. Mem.: APA (sec. divsn. 32 1999—2002), N.Am. Personal Construct Network (steering com.). Office: SUNY New Paltz 75 S Manheim Blvd New Paltz NY 12561-2400

RASKIN, JOY LYNN, art educator, silversmith; b. Manchester, N.H., May 3, 1967; d. Joel Barry and Judith Helena Raskin. BFA, RISD, 1990; MFA, U. Mass., Dartmouth, 1993. Instr. jewelry, silversmithing N.H. Inst. Art, Manchester, 1996—. Juror Am. Craft Coun., Highland, N.Y., 1998—. Exhibns. include Soc. Arts and Crafts, Boston, 1991, League N.H. Craftsmen, Brookfield Crafts Ctr., Conn. Office: PO Box 1422 Concord NH 03302-1422

RASKIN, MICHAEL A. retail company executive; b. N.J., Feb. 26, 1925; s. Harry and Elizabeth Rose (Furstenberg) R.; m. Mary Bonetta Whalen, June 12, 1948; children: Robin Raskin Crowell, Hillary Raskin Maass, Mary Allison Sullivan. AB, Pa. State Coll., 1947; MBA, Columbia U., 1948. With Abraham & Straus, 1949-65; successively mdse. v.p., dir. stores, sr. v.p. Abercrombie & Fitch, N.Y.C., 1966-68; exec. v.p. Dayton's div. Dayton Hudson Corp.; pres. Jos. Magnin Co., San Francisco, 1978—. Chmn., CEO, bd. dirs. Imnar Corp., San Francisco, Info. Please; chmn. exec. com. Acajoe Internat.; bd. dirs. Fortune Almac, Canterbury Cuisine, Cultural Devel. Assocs., HELP Inc., Express Yourself Through Art, Inc., Munsingwear, Inc., B&B Acceptance Corp. Bd. dirs. Amyotrophic Lateral Sclerosis Assn.

RASKIN, NEIL HUGH, neurology educator; b. N.Y.C., Jan. 16, 1935; s. Sidney and Bette Raskin; children: Keith, Alexis. AB, Dartmouth U., 1956; MD, Harvard U., 1959. Diplomate Am. Bd. Psychiatry and Neurology. Intern in medicine Bellevue Hosp./Columbia Med. Divsn., N.Y.C., 1959-61; asst. resident, resident, chief resident Neurol. Inst. N.Y., 1961-64, rsch. fellow in metabolic brain disease, 1964-65; rsch. assoc. NIH, 1966-68; asst. in neurology Coll. Physicians and Surgeons, Columbia U., N.Y.C., 1963-65; chief neurology U.S. Naval Hosp., Phila., 1965-66; sr. surgeon USPHS, Bethesda, Md., 1966-68; asst. prof. neurology U. Calif., San Francisco, 1968-73, assoc. prof. neurology, 1973-79, prof. neurology, 1979—. Attending neurologist Moffitt, San Francisco Gen., Ft. Milley VA Hosps., San Francisco, 1968—; dir. outpatient svcs. Moffitt Hosps., San Francisco, 1977-87; vice chmn. dept. neurology U. Calif., San Francisco, 1977—; vis. prof. U. Mich., U. Oreg., 1991, Cornell U., Harvard U., U. Chgo., Northwestern U., UCLA, 1992, Case Western Res. U., Montreal Neurol. Inst., U. Man., U. B.C., U. N.Mex., Hahnemann U., 1993, St. Louis U., U. Colo., 1994, Dartmouth Med. Sch., U. Pitts., Ind. U., 1996, U. Ark., U. Utah, 1997; invited lectr., Pan-Am. Neurol. Congress, 1975, Headache, Florence, Italy, 1980, World Fedn. Neurology, Kyoto, Japan, 1981, Internat. Symposium on Migraine, London, 1982, Internat. Headache Congress, Munich, 1983, Brazilian Neurol. Congress, Sao Paolo, 1988, Leeds Castle Workshop on Migraine, 1985, World Fedn. Neurology, Buenos Aires, 1997, among others. Author: Headache, 1988, (with O. Appenzeller) Headache: Major Problems in Internal Medicine, 1980; mem. editl. bd. Archives Neurology, 1969—, Neurology, 1969—, New Eng. Jour. Medicine, 1969—, Archives Internal Medicine, 1969—, Rsch. and Clin. Studies in Headache, 1976-81, Comprehensive Therapy, 1976-93, Headache, 1980—, The Medicine Group, 1986—, Cephalalgia, 1986—; contbr. articles to profl. jours. Fellow Am. Acad. Neurology; mem. AAAS, Am. Soc. for Neurochemistry, Am. Neurol. Assn., San Francisco Neurol. Soc., Assn. for Rsch. in Nervous and Mental Diseases, Internat. Assn. for the Study of Pain (panel on headache 1981—), Rsch. Group on Migraine and Headache of the World Fedn. Neurology, Am. Assn. for the Study of Headache (pres. 1994-96, bd. dirs. 1985—), Internat. Headache Soc., Stroke Coun., Am. Heart Assn., Phi Beta Kappa. Office: U Calif San Francisco 505 Parnassus Ave San Francisco CA 94143-0001

RASKIN, NOEL MICHAEL, thoracic surgeon; b. Bklyn., May 29, 1947; s. Rubin and Pauline (Sturm) R.; m. Deborah M. Axelrod, Feb. 27, 1987; children: Max, Ben. BA, NYU, 1969; MD, N.Y. Med. Coll., 1977. Intern St. Vincent's Hosp., N.Y.C., 1977-78; resident SUNY, Stony Brook, 1978-82; fellow in cardio-thoracic surgery U. Miami, Fla., 1982-84, fellow in thoracic oncology, 1984-85; attending surgeon Beth Israel Med. Ctr. and Cabrini Med. Ctr., N.Y.C., 1985-2001; chief thoracic surgery Cabrini Med. Ctr., 1985-2001; thoracic surgeon Kriser Lung Cancer Ctr., N.Y.C., 1989; attending surgeon Dover (N.J.) Gen. Hosp., 1989-91; surgeon pvt. practice N.Y.C., 1992—; chief thoracic surgeon Met. Hosp. Ctr., 2001—. Columnist, Med. Herald. Fellow ACS, Am. Coll. Chest Physicians; mem. Am. Assn. Physician and Surgeons, Soc. Thoracic Surgeons, Gen. Thoracic Surg. Club. Office: Met Hosp Ctr 1901 1st Ave Rm 12A4 New York NY 10029 E-mail: nraskinmd@medtower.com.

RASKIND, LEO JOSEPH, law educator; b. Newark, Nov. 2, 1919; s. Isaac and Fannie (Michelson) R.; m. Mollie Gordon, June 14, 1948; children— Carol Inge, John Richard. AB, UCLA, 1942; MA, U. Wash., 1949; PhD (Fulbright fellow), London Sch. Econs., 1952; LL.B., Yale, 1955. Faculty Stanford Law Sch., 1955-56; lectr., research asso. Yale Law Sch., 1956-58; faculty Vanderbilt Law Sch., 1958-64, Ohio State U. Coll. of Law, 1964-70, U. Minn., 1970-90. Vis. tchr. NYU, 1964, 83, U. Tex., 1964, U. Utah, 1967, So. Meth. U., 1973, U. N.C., 1978, Lyon III, 1984, Kiel U., 1988; vis. prof. Bklyn. Law Sch., 1991—2002, Coll. Law, U. Tenn., Knoxville, 1994, Law Sch., U. Calif., Davis, 1995, U. Minn., 1998. Co-author: Casebook Corporate Taxation, 1978, Casebook Antitrust Law, 2001; mem. adv. bd. BNA jour. Served to capt. AUS, 1942-46. Mem. Am. Law Inst. Office: Bklyn Law Sch 250 Joralemon St Brooklyn NY 11201-3700

RASKY, HARRY, producer, director, writer; b. Toronto, Ont., Can., May 9, 1928; emigrated to U.S., 1955; s. Louis Leib and Pearl (Krazner) R.; m. Ruth Arlene Werkhoven, Mar. 21, 1965; children: Holly Laura, Adam Louis. BA, U. Toronto, 1949, LLD, 1984. Reporter No. Daily News, Kirkland Lake, Ont., 1949; news editor-producer Sta. CHUM, Toronto, 1950, Sta. CKEY, 1951-52; co-founder new documentary dept. CBC, 1952-55; assoc. editor Saturday Night Mag., 1955; producer-dir-writer Columbia Broadcasting Corp., 1955-60, NBC-TV, N.Y.C., 1960-61, ABC-TV, N.Y.C., 1963-69, CBC-TV, Toronto, 1971-78; pres. Harry Rasky Prodns., N.Y.C. and Toronto, 1971—, Maragall Prodns., Toronto, 1978—. Guest lectr. film and TV at various univs., colls.; lectr. U. Toronto, York U. Creator (films) Raskymentary (Emmy 1978, 86, San Francisco Film Festival 1978, Grand prize N.Y. TV-Film Festival 1978, Jerusalem medal 1975), Travels Through Life with Leacock, 1976, The Peking Man Mystery, 1978, Arthur Miller on Home Ground, 1979 , (TV films) Hall of Kings (Emmy, 1965), producer, dir. , writer (films) Next Year in Jerusalem, 1973, The Wit and World of G. Bernard Shaw, 1974, Tennessee Williams South, 1975 , Homage to Chagall-The Colours of Love, 1977 (200 internat. prizes including Oscar nomination Emmy , 1986), Stratasphere, The Mystery of Henry Moore, Karsh: The Searching Eye , (plays) Tiger Tale, 1978, The War Against the Indians , 1992 (Humanities prize, Great Plains Film Festival, Lincoln, Nebr., Golden Hugo award Chgo. Film Festival), Prophecy , 1994 (Golden Angel, honored by Smithsonian, Jerusalem Found.), William Hutt: A Fortunate Man, 1997, Christopher Plummer: King of Players, 1988 ; author: (memoirs) Nobody Swings on Sunday-The Many Lives of Harry Rasky, 1980, Tennessee Williams a Portrait in Laughter and Lamentation, 1986, Karsh: The Searching Eye, 1986, To Mend the World, 1987, Stratas: An affectionate tribute, 1988 , Book 2001: The Song of Leonard Cohen, The Great Teacher, 1989, Robertson-Davies-The Magic Season, 1989; (19 hour retrospective of films including documentaries) Rasky's Gallery: Poets, Painters, Singers and Saints, CBC, 1988, The War Against the Indians, 1993 (12 Internat. awards, adopted Huron Nation title Keeper of the Flame, The Three Harrys, 1999). Mem. YMCA; mem. adv. coun. Univ. Coll./U. Toronto. Recipient honors City of Venice, Italy, 1970, Golden Eagle, Grand prize N.Y. Intenat. TV and Film Festival of N.Y., 1977, Cert. of Merit, Acad. Motion Picture Arts and Scis., 1984, Red Ribbon, Am. Assn. Film and Video, N.Y.C., 1988, Blue Ribbon, Am. Film Festival, Emmy award, 1990, Moscow award for cultural contbn. to 20th Century USSR, 1991, Retrospective of Films, 1990, Golden Hugo award Chgo. Film Festival, 1993; named Best Non-Fiction Dir., Dirs. Guild Am., N.Y.C. and L.A., 1988, hon. Mayor N.Y.C., 1977, City of Toronto, 1979; Harry Rasky Day named in his honor, City of Toronto, 1988; Moscow Film Festival honoree, 1991; adopted by Huron Indians, named Keeper of the Spirit, adopted by Ojibway Tribe, named Mountain Eagle. Mem. Writers Guild Am. (best non-fiction dir. 1986), Dirs. Guild Am., Writers Union Can., Am.,

Acad. TV Arts and Scis., Assn. Can. TV and Radio Artists, Producers Assn. Can., Acad. Motion Picture Arts and Scis., Overseas Press Club, Acad. of Can. TV and Film Can. (lifetime achievement award 1992), PEN (Toronto), Nat. Arts Club. Jewish. Avocations: swimming, lecturing. Home: 15 Gregory Ave Toronto ON Canada M4W 2X7 Office: care CBC Box 500 Terminal A Toronto ON Canada M5W 1E6 *I have tried to find the positive forces in life and out of them create works of art of a lasting nature with the idea of improving the lives of others. This, plus the adventure of passing on the tradition of my father and his, is my life.*

RASLEAR, THOMAS GREGORY, psychologist; b. N.Y.C., Nov. 25, 1947; s. John W. and Catherine (Turchin) R.; m. Lois T. Keck, Aug. 7, 1971. BS, CCNY, 1969; PhD, Brown U., 1974. Asst. prof. Wilkes Coll., Wilkes-Barre, Pa., 1975-79; rsch. psychologist Walter Reed Amy Inst. Rsch., Washington, 1979-89, sr. rsch. psychologist, 1989-93; engring. psychologist Fed. R.R. Adminstrn., 1993—. Lectr., presenter in field. Bd. editors Jour. of the Exptl. Analysis of Behaviour, 1989-92; author numerous publs. in field including Proceedings of the XXIV Internat. Congress of Psychology, Vol. 6: Learning; co-author: Understanding Economic Behavior, Animal Learning and Behaviour, 16, Physiology and Behavior, 43, others; contbr. articles to profl. jours.; guest reviewer Jour. of Exptl. Psychology: Animal Behavior Processes, Animal Learning and Behavior, Jour. of Comparative Psychology. Maj. U.S. Army, 1979-89. Rsch. fellow USPHS, 1970-72, N.Y. State Regents fellow, 1969-70. Mem. IEEE, Am. Psychol. Soc. (charter), Am. Psychol. Assn., Acoustical Soc. Am., Ea. Psychol. Assn., AAAS, Sigma Xi, Phi Beta Kappa. Achievements include development and validation of procedures for measuring subjective magnitudes in non-verbal subjects, including non-human animals; testing for toxic effects of drugs and electromagnetic radiation in non-humans; management of research program on human factors and safety in railroad operations; represents the Federal Railroad Adminstration as a human factors expert on the North American Rail Alertness Partnership, the Railroad Safety Advisory Committee (Locomotive Cab Working Conditions Group), The Department of Transportation Human Factors Coordinating Committee, and the Transportation Research Board Human Factors Workshop Planning Committee. Home: 1408 Woodman Ave Silver Spring MD 20902-3905 Office: Fed RR Adminstrn Office of Rsch and Devel RDV-32 400 7th St SW Washington DC 20590-0001

RASMUS, JOHN CHARLES, trade association executive, lawyer; b. Rochester, N.Y., Dec. 27, 1941; s. Harold Charles and Myrtle Leota (Dybevik) R.; m. Elaine Green Reeves, Mar. 19, 1982; children: Kristin, Stuart, Karin. AB, Cornell U., 1963; JD, U. Va., 1966. Bar: Va. 1970, U.S. Supreme Ct. 1974. Spl. agt. Def. Dept., Washington, 1966-70; v.p., adminstrv. officer, legis. rsch. counsel U.S. League Savs. Instns., 1970-83; asst. to exec. v.p. Nat. Assn. Fed. Credit Unions, 1983-84; sr. fed. adminstrv. counsel, mgr. regulatory & trust affairs Am. Bankers Assn., 1985—. Trustee The Appraisal Found. Mem. ABA, FBA (disting. svc. award 1980, 82, past chmn. long range planning com., past chmn. coun. fin. instns. and economy), Univ. Club, Exchequer Club, Masons. Home: 303 Kentucky Ave Alexandria VA 22305-1739 Office: Am Bankers Assn 1120 Connecticut Ave NW Washington DC 20036 E-mail: jrasmus@aba.com.

RASMUSON, BRENT J. photographer, graphic artist, lithographer; b. Logan, Utah, Nov. 28, 1950; s. Eleroy West and Fae (Jacobsen) R.; m. Tess Bullen, Sept. 30, 1981; children: John, Mark, Lisa. Grad. auto repair and painting sch., Utah State U. Pre-press supr., ptnr. Herald Printing Co., Logan, 1969—80; profl. drummer, 1971-75; owner, builder auto racing engines Valley Automotive Specialties, 1971-76; exec. sec. Herald Printing Co., 1980—89; owner Brent Rasmuson Photography, Logan, 1986—, Temple Picture Classics, Logan, 1996—. Author photo prints of LDS temples: Logan, 1987, 95, 98, 2000, Manti, 1989, 2000, Jordan River, 1989, 96, 98, 2000, Provo, 1990, 2001, Mesa, Ariz., 1990, 96, Boise, Idaho, 1990, 96, 2000, Salt Lake Temple, 1990, 96, 2001, Idaho Falls, 1991, 94, 2000, St. George, 1991, 93, 2000, Portland, Oreg., 1991, 96, 97, 2000, L.A., 1991, 96, 97, 2000, Las Vegas, Nev., 1991, Seattle, 1992, Oakland, Calif., 1993, 94, Ogden, 1992, 2001, Bountiful, 2002, Mt. Timpanogos, 2002; author photo print: Statue of Angel Moroni, 1994; author photos used to make neckties and watch dials of LDS temples: Salt Lake, Manti, Logan, L.A., Oakland, Seattle, Las Vegas, Mesa, Portland, St. George, Jordan River, scenic tie Mammoth Hot Springs in Yellowstone Park, 1995; landscape scenic photographs featured in Best of Photography Ann., 1987, 88, 89, also in calendars and book covers; author photo print of Harris Rsch., Inc. Internat. Hdqrs. (recipient 1st prize nat. archtl. photo competition); designer several bus. logos. Mem. Internat. Platform Assn., Assoc. Photographers, Internat. Freelance Photographers Orgn., Nat. Trust Hist. Preservation, Nat. Air and Space Soc. Republican. Mem. Lds Ch. Avocations: landscape design, travel, reading, numismatics, philately. Home and Office: 66 W 100 N Logan UT 84321-4506

RASMUSON, EDWARD BERNARD, banker; b. Aug. 27, 1940; s. Elmer Edwin and Lile Vivian Rasmuson; m. Cathryn Elaine Robertson, Sept. 11, 1969; children: Natasha Ann, Laura Lile, David Edward. BA, Harvard U., 1962. Mgmt. trainee Brown Brothers Harriman, 1963, Chem. NY, 1964; asst. cashier Nat. Bank Alaska, Anchorage, 1964—66, asst. v.p., 1966—68, v.p., 1968—73, pres., 1973—85, chmn. bd. dirs., 1986—. Bd. regents U. Alaska, 1975—89; mem. Rasmuson Found., 1973—; past trustee Sheldon Jackson Coll.; past pres. Anchorage United Way; Hon. Consul of Sweden State of Alaska. Mem.: World Bus. Coun., Young Pres.'s Orgn., Harvard Club (N.Y.C.), Rainier Club, Seattle Yacht Club, Wash. Athletic Club, Metropolitan Club, Pioneers Club Am., Explorers Club, Elks, Rotary. Office: Wells Fargo Bank Alaska PO Box 100600 Anchorage AK 99510-0600

RASMUSSEN, CAREN NANCY, hospital executive; b. Ft. Riley, Kans., July 7, 1950; d. Stanley Junior and Katherina Wilhelmina R. AAS, Grand Rapids Jr. Coll., 1970; BS, U. Md., 1977; MS, Johns Hopkins U., 1997. Cert. profl. contracts mgr. Contract specialist Kadena Air Base, Okinawa, 1979-81; med. sec. Walter Reed Army Med. Ctr., Washington, 1970-72, sec. procurement, 1972-76, contract specialist, 1976-79, 81-84, procurement analyst, 1984—, sr. contracting specialist, 1988—. Fellow NAFE; mem. Nat. Contract Mgmt. Assn. Democrat. Avocations: photography, stamp collecting, gardening, travel. Home: 18632 Clovercrest Cir Olney MD 20832-3057 Office: Nat Cancer Inst Rsch Contracts br Rockville MD 20852

RASMUSSEN, DAVID L. lawyer; b. Rochester, N.Y., Apr. 20, 1958; s. Verlin L. and Betty B. Rasmussen; m. Debra J. Rasmussen, Oct. 8, 1993. BS in Bus., Miami U., 1980; JD, Syracuse U., 1985. Bar: N.Y. 1986, U.S. Dist. Ct. (we. dist.) N.Y. 1986, U.S. Dist. Ct. (no. dist.) N.Y. 1989, U.S. Supreme Ct. 1997, U.S. Ct. Appeals (2d cir.) 2000. Internal auditor Union Pacific R.R., Omaha, 1980-82; assoc. Lacy Katzen Ryen & Mittliana, Rochester, 1985-87, Harris Beach LLP, Rochester, 1987-92, ptnr., 1993—. Avocations: skiing, mountain biking, kayaking. Office: Harris Beach LLP 99 Garnsey Rd Pittsford NY 14534

RASMUSSEN, DOUGLAS JOHN, lawyer; b. Mt. Clemens, Mich., Jan. 18, 1941; s. Kenneth Edward and Laura Jean (Fletcher) R.; m. Andrea Marie Smart, Aug. 22, 1964; children: Mark Douglas, Michael Andrew. BBA, U. Mich., 1962, MBA, JD, 1965. Bar: Mich. 1965, U.S. Dist. Ct. (ea. dist.) Mich. 1965, U.S. Tax Ct. 1973, U.S. Ct. Appeals (6th cir.) 1973. Assoc. Clark Hill plc, Detroit, 1965—73; mem., 1973—; CEO, 1994-2000. Trustee Community Found. for S.E. Mich., Holley Found., bd. dirs. S.E. chpt. ARC, Detroit, 1987—, chmn., 1994-96; bd. dirs. YMCA of Metro Detroit, chmn., 1992-93; unit chmn. United Way, Detroit, 1987-92; bd. dirs. Detroit Symphony Orch., 1999—, Friends of Detroit Pub. Libr., 2000—, pres., 2001-. Recipient Outstanding Vol. award Mich. Chpt. Nat. Assn. Fund Raising Execs., 1988, Fundraiser Yr. award Nat. ARC, 1997, Stanley S. Kresge award Rotary Club. Fellow Am. Coll. Trust and Estate Counsel (regent 1987-93); mem. ABA, State Bar Mich., Internat. Acad. Estate and Trust Law, Fin. and Estate Planning Coun. Met. Detroit (pres. 1986-87), Detroit Athletic Club (bd. dirs. 1992, pres. 1997), Econ. Club Detroit (bd. dirs. 1999—). Republican. Presbyterian. Avocations: music, photography, Nordic skiing, golf. Home: 466 Lakeland St Grosse Pointe MI 48230-1655 Office: Clark Hill PLC 500 Woodward Ave Ste 3500 Detroit MI 48226-3435 E-mail: drasmussen@clarkhill.com.

RASMUSSEN, GUNNAR, engineer; b. Esbjerg, Denmark, Nov. 23, 1925; s. Karl Sigurd and Frederikke Valentine (Gjerulff) R.; m. Hanna Hertz, June 27, 1973; children: Jan, Lise, Per, Thue. Student, Aarhus Teknikum, Denmark, 1950. Mgr. quality control Brüel and Kjaer, Nerum, Denmark, 1950-54, with devel. div. Denmark, 1955-69, with product planning div. Denmark, 1969-74, with innovation div. Denmark, 1975-93; engr. GRAS Sound and Vibration, Vedbaek, Denmark, 1993—. Lectr. Danish Tech. U., Copenhagen, 1974-79, Med. Air Force Acad., Jegersborg, Denmark, 1978-79; examiner Danish Engring. Acad., Copenhagen, 1972—, Chalmers Tech. U., Gothenburg, Sweden, 1984-85. Editor: Intensity Measurements, 1989; inventor measurement microphones, accelerometers; contbr. articles to profl. jours. Chairman Audio Engring. Soc. Denmark, Cophenhagen, 1976. Recipient Danish Design prize for microphones, 1962, medal for contbn. to intensity techniques SETIM, 1990. Fellow Acoustical Soc. Am., Can. Acoustical Soc., Danish Medico Tech. Soc.; mem. Internat. Union Pure and Applied Physics (vice chmn. internat. commn. on accoustics), Danish Acoustical Soc. (bd. dirs.), Internat. Electronical Commn., Internat. Orgn. for Standarization. Home: Hojbjerggardsvej 15 2840 Holte Denmark Office: GRAS Sound & Vibration Skelstedet 10 B DK-2950 Vedbaek Denmark

RASMUSSEN, HARRY PAUL, horticulture and landscape educator; b. Tremonton, Utah, July 18, 1939; s. Peter Y. and Lorna (Nielsen) R.; m. Mary Jane Dalley, Sept. 4, 1959; children: Randy Paul, Lorianne, Trent Dalley, Rachelle. AS, Coll. of So. Utah, 1959; BS, Utah State U., 1961; MS, Mich. State U., 1962, PhD, 1965. Rsch. scientist Conn. Agr. Expt. Sta., New Haven, 1965-66; rschr., instr. Mich. State U., East Lansing, 1966-81; chmn. dept. horticulture and landscape architecture Wash. State U., Pullman, 1981-88; dir. Utah Agrl. Expt. Sta. Utah State U., 1988—. Assoc. v.p. Utah State U., Logan, 1992-99, 2002—. Contbr. articles to profl. jours., chpts. to books. Mem. bd. control YMCA, Lansing, Mich., 1976; mem. coun. Boy Scouts Am., Lansing, 1980; stake pres. Ch. of Jesus Christ of Latter Day Saints, Lansing, 1973-81. NDEA fellow, 1961-65. Fellow Am. Soc. Horticulture Sci.; mem. AAAS, Scanning Electron Microscopy (chmn. plant sect. 1976-83, chmn. exptl. sta. com. on orgn. and policy 1996-97). Home: 1949 N 950 E Logan UT 84341-1813 Office: Utah State U 225 Agr Sci Bldg Logan UT 84322-0001

RASMUSSEN, JAY BECK, education educator, consultant; b. Bemidji, Minn., Feb. 3, 1953; s. L.V. and Jean M. R.; m. Roberta Ann Hernandez, Feb. 28, 1987; children: Nina, Conor. BS in Elem. Edn., Fla. State U., 1975; MA in Ednl. Adminstrn., U. Minn., 1986. Cert. elem. tchr., Minn. Tchr. Rice Lake (Wis.) Pub. Schs., 1977-79, teaching prin., 1979-85; assoc. prof. North Ctrl. Bible Coll., Mpls., 1985—. Contbr. articles to profl. jours. Recipient Pres.'s award for rsch. and innovative ideas North Ctrl. Bible Coll., 1992; Norine Odland Endowment award in children's lit., 1995. Mem. Internat. Reading Assn., Minn. Reading Assn., Nat. Coun. Tchrs. English, Minn. Assn. Tchrs. Edn., Minn. Sci. Tchrs. Assn., Phi Delta Kappa. Avocations: licensed fishing guide, tennis, canoeing, backpacking, travel. Office: North Ctrl Bible Coll 910 Elliot Ave Minneapolis MN 55404-1322

RASMUSSEN, JOHN OSCAR, nuclear research scientist; b. St. Petersburg, Fla., Aug. 8, 1926; s. John Oscar and Hazel (Ormsby) R.; m. Louise Brooks, Aug. 27, 1950; children— Nancy, Jane, David, Stephen. BS, Calif. Inst. Tech., 1948; PhD, U. Calif. at Berkeley, 1952; MA (hon.), Yale U., 1969. Mem. faculty dept. chemistry U. Calif., Berkeley, 1952-68, 73-91, prof. chemistry, 1971-91, ret., 1991, mem. research staff, 1952-68; sr. rsch. assoc. Lawrence Berkeley Nat. Lab., 1972—. Prof. chemistry Yale U. 1969-73; asso. dir. Yale Heavy Ion Accelerator Lab., 1970-73; vis. research prof. Nobel Inst. Physics, Stockholm, 1953; vis. prof. Inst. Nuclear Sci. U. Tokyo, 1974, Fudan U., Shanghai, 1979, hon. prof., 1984. Contbr. articles on radioactivity, nuclear models, heavy ion reactions. Served with USN, 1944-46. Recipient E.O. Lawrence Meml. award AEC, 1967; NSF sr. postdoctoral fellow Niels Bohr Inst., Copenhagen, 1961-62, NORDITA fellow, 1979, Guggenheim Meml. fellow, 1973, Alexander von Humboldt sr. rsch. fellow Tech. U. Munich, 1991. Fellow Am. Phys. Soc., AAAS; mem. Am. Chem. Soc. (Nuclear Applications in Chemistry award 1976), Fedn. Am. Scientists (chmn. 1969). Office: Lawrence Berkeley Nat Lab MS 70 319 Berkeley CA 94720-0001

RASMUSSEN, JULIE SHIMMON, cellist, educator; b. Aberdeen, S.D., June 3, 1940; d. George Barr and Clara (Lange) Shimmon; m. Frederick Robert Rasmussen, Apr. 1, 1961 (div. May 1971). BMusic, Ind. U., 1963; MEd, U. Fla., 1967. Cert. tchr., Fla. Coord. music Bradford County Sch. Bd., Starke, Fla., 1965-68; tchr. Duval County Sch. Bd., Jacksonville, Fla., 1968-69, community edn., 1972-79, program devel., 1979—; master tchr. Clay County Sch. Bd., Orange Park, Fla., 1969-72; facilitator, mem. planning com. Duval County Sch. Bd., Jacksonville, 1985-86. Grant writer in ednl. areas, 1979—. Com. mem. Jacksonville Community Coun., Inc., 1973; cellist Jacksonville Symphony, 1963-65; tech. asst. Arts Assembly of Jacksonville, Inc., 1979-82; mem. Cummer Art Gallery, Jacksonville, 1983; bd. dirs. YWCA, 1986; active Resource Devel. Assistance Program Com. for Vol. Jacksonville, 1986—. Recipient Little Red Schoolhouse award Fla. Dept. Edn., 1977-78, Sense of Community award Duval County Community Edn., 1979; Internat. String Congress grantee Musician's Union, 1961. Mem. Fla. Edl. Rsch. Assn., Pi Kappa Lambda, Phi Delta Kappa, Kappa Delta Pi (parliamentarian 1985-86). Democrat. Lutheran. Club: Pilot. Avocations: physical fitness, jogging, swimming, cycling, psychology. Home: 2950 Saint Johns Ave Apt 18 Jacksonville FL 32205-8719 Office: Duval County Sch Bd 1701 Prudential Dr Adminstrn Bldg 2d Fl Jacksonville FL 32207

RASMUSSEN, KATHLEEN MAHER, nutritional sciences educator; b. Dayton, Ohio, Mar. 1, 1948; AB, Brown U., 1970; MSc, Harvard U., 1975, ScD, 1978. Registered dietitian. Tchr. sci. Cape Hatteras Elem. Sch., Buxton, NC, 1971-72; analytical chemist Berkley Machine Works, Foundry Co., Norfolk, Va., 1972-73; rsch. assoc. dept. nutrition Harvard U., Boston, 1978; instr. div. nutritional scis. Cornell U., Ithaca, N.Y., 1981-83, asst. prof., 1983-88, assoc. prof., 1988-96, assoc. dir. grad. affairs, 1992-95, prof., 1996—, assoc. dean, sec. Univ. Faculty, 1997-2000. Com. mem. NAS, Washington, 1988-96; Pew faculty scholar in nutrition Nat. Ctr. Sci. Rsch., Meudon-Bellevue, France, 1989-90. NIH trainee, 1974-80; NIH grantee, 1984-90, 87—, 93—, 2001—, various other grants and awards, 1982-85, 88-89, 89-92, 92-94, 93-96, 97-99. Mem. Am. Soc. Nutrition Scis., Am. Soc. Clin. Nutrition, Brit. Nutrition Soc., Internat. Soc. for Rsch. in Human Milk and Lactation. Office: Cornell U Div Nutritional Sci 111 Savage Hall Ithaca NY 14853-6301 E-mail: kmr5@cornell.edu.

RASMUSSEN, RICHARD ROBERT, lawyer; b. Chgo., July 5, 1946; s. Robert Kersten Rasmussen and Marisa Bruna Batistoni; children: Kathryn, William. BS, U. Oreg., 1970, JD, 1973. Bar: Oreg. 1973. Atty. U.S. Bancorp, Portland, Oreg., 1973-83, 95-00, v.p. law divsn., 1983-87, mgr. law divsn. 1983-95, sr. v.p., 1987-95, mgr. corp. sec. divsn., 1990—95; exec. v.p., gen. counsel, sec. West Coast Bancorp, Lake Oswego, 2000—. Mem. editl. bd. Oreg. Bus. Law Digest, 1979-81, Oreg. Debtor/Creditor newsletter, 1980-84; contbr. articles to profl. jours. Chmn. mgmt. com. YMCA of Columbia-Willamette, Portland, 1978-79; bd. dirs. Camp Fire, 1988-89, v.p., 1990-91; bd. dirs. Portland Repertory Theatre, 1994-96. Mem. ABA, Oreg. State Bar Assn. (chmn. corp. counsel com. 1979-81, debtor/creditor sect. 1982-83; sec. com. on sects. 1982-83), Multnomah County Bar Assn., Am. Bankers Assn. (bank counsel com. 1996-99), Founders Club (Portland), Beta Gamma Sigma. Clubs: Founder's (Portland). Avocations: mountaineering, white-water rafting, tennis, basketball. Office: West Coast Bancorp 5335 Meadows Rd Ste 201 Lake Oswego OR 97035

RASMUSSEN, ROBERT DEE, retired real estate appraiser; b. Lincoln, Kans., Dec. 24, 1936; s. Sam and Kristena (Andersen) R.; m. Beverly Bert Rowden, Mar. 22, 1959; children: Robert Denis, Kay Lynn. B Gen. Edn., U. Nebr., 1965; MA, Ariz. State U., 1970. Cert. gen. real estate appraiser, Fla. Commd. USAF, 1957, advanced through grades to col., 1978, fighter pilot various locations, 1956-75, comdr. 59th Tactical Fighter Squadron Fla., 1975-77, chief Europe/Nato Plans Washington, 1978-80, vice-comdr. 474th Tactical Fighter Wing Nellis AFB, Nev., 1980-81; chief of plans U.S. European Command Joint Chiefs of Staff, Stuttgart, Germany, 1981-84; dir. joint matters Hdqrs. Tactical Air Command USAF, Langley AFB, Va., 1984-86, ret., 1986; appraiser, cons. Appraisal House Inc., Ft. Walton Beach, Fla., 1987-94; gen. appraiser Niceville, 1994-2000; ret., 2000. Dir. U.S. Power Squadrons, Ft. Walton Beach, 1988-90. Decorated DFC, Legion of Merit. Mem. Ret. Officers Assn., Am. Assn. Ind. Investors, Porsche Club Am. (v.p. Germany region 1983-84, pres. North Fla. region 1989, 97, dir. 1988-94), Mid-Bay Rotary Club (charter, dir. 1995-96). Avocations: boating, hunting, fishing, sports cars.

RASMUSSEN, THOMAS VAL, JR. lawyer, small business owner; b. Salt Lake City, Aug. 11, 1954; s. Thomas Val and Georgia (Smedley) R.; m. Donita Gubler, Aug. 15, 1978; children: James, Katherine, Kristin. BA magna cum laude, U. Utah, 1978, JD, 1981. Bar: Utah 1981, U.S. Dist. Ct. Utah 1981, U.S. Supreme Ct. 1985, U.S. Ct. Appeals (10th cir.) 1999. Atty. Salt Lake Legal Defender Assn., Salt Lake City, 1981-83, Utah Power and Light Co., Salt Lake City, 1983-89; of counsel Hatch, Morton & Skeen, 1989-90; ptnr. Morton, Skeen & Rasmussen, 1991-94, Skeen & Rasmussen, Salt Lake City, 1994-97; pvt. practice, 1997—. Co-owner, developer Handi Self-Storage, Kaysville, Utah, 1984-93; instr. bus. law Brigham Young U., Salt Lake City, 1988-90. Adminstrv. editor Jour. Contemporary Law, 1980-81, Jour. Energy Law and Policy, 1980-81. Missionary Ch. of Jesus Christ of Latter-Day Sts., Brazil, 1973-75. Mem. Utah, Salt Lake County Bar Assn., Intermountain Miniature Horse Club (pres. 1989, 2d v.p. 1990), Phi Eta Sigma, Phi Kappa Phi, Beta Gamma Sigma. Avocations: tennis, scuba diving, showing horses, travel, collecting art. Home: 3094 Whitewater Dr Salt Lake City UT 84121-1561 Office: 4659 Highland Dr Salt Lake City UT 84117-5137

RASMUSSON, EUGENE MARTIN, meteorology researcher; b. Lindsborg, Kans., Feb. 27, 1929; s. Martin Erick and Alma Sophia (Nelson) R.; m. Georgene Ruth Sachtleben, Aug. 7, 1960; children: Mary, Ruth, Elizabeth, Kristin. BS, Kans. State U., 1950; MS, St. Louis U., 1963; PhD, MIT, 1966. Forecaster Nat. Weather Service, St. Louis, 1956-64; rsch. meteorologist Geophysical Fluid Dynamics Lab, Princeton, N.J., 1964-70; chief, rsch. div. Ctr. for Experiment Design, NOAA, Washington, 1970-79; chief, diagnositc br. Climate Analysis Ctr., NOAA, Camp Spring, Md., 1979-86; sr. rsch. scientist U. Md., College Park, 1986-99, rsch. prof. emeritus, 1999—. Mem. numerous coms. and panels U.S. Nat. Res. Coun., World Climate Rsch. Program-UNESCO; Starr Meml. lectr. MIT, 1994; Benton Meml. lectr. Johns Hopkins, 1998. Contbr. numerous articles to profl. jours. 1st Lt. USAF, 1951-55. Recipient Silver medal, U.S. Dept. Commerce, Washington, 1973, Adminstr. award, Nat. Oceanic and Atmospheric Adminstrn., Washington, 1983. Fellow Am. Meteorol. Soc. (Jule Charney award 1989, coun. 1993-95, Horton lectr. 1996, pres. 1998), Am. Geophys. Union; mem. AAAS, NAE. Lutheran. Avocations: travel, history, gardening. Office: U Md Dept Meteorology College Park MD 20742-0001 E-mail: erasmu@atmos.umd.edu.

RASMUSSON, THOMAS ELMO, lawyer; b. Lansing, Mich., Dec. 5, 1941; s. William and Mary Jane Rasmusson; m. Alice Wolo, Oct. 1, 1989; children: David, Jane. BA, Mich. State U., 1963; JD, U. Mich., 1966; MA, Fletcher Sch., 1988. Bar: Mich. 1967, U.S. Ct. Appeals (6th cir.) 1982, U.S. Supreme Ct. 1982. Law clk. to presiding justice Mich. Supreme Ct., Lansing, 1966-68; asst. prosecutor Ingham Prosecutor's Office, 1968-72, criminal divsn. chief, 1972-75; spl. prosecutor Ingham County, 1975-76; pvt. practice, 1975—. Fulbright prof. U.S. Info. Svc., Washington, 1986-88; cons. U.S. AID, Monrovia, Liberia, 1989-90; contractor U.S. Dept. of State, Monrovia, 1987-90; adj. prof. Cooley Law Sch., Lansing, 1991-97; rsch. assoc. program on negotiation Harvard U., Cambridge, 1987-88; mem. Ct. Rule Com., Lansing, 1979-81. Editor: Jurisprudence and System Science, 1986, Interactive Systems, 1988, (series) Liberian Law Reports, 1988-90; contbr. articles to profl. jours. Chair fin. Ingham Rep. Party, Lansing, 1994-98, mem. exec. com., 1994—; mem. 8th Congl. Com., Lansing, 1997—; trustee Lansing C.C., 1998—; dir. Case Credit Union, Lansing, 1996; dir. MyWebConnect ISP, Lansing, 1998—. Recipient Outstanding Svc. award U.S. Edn. Found., 1987; grantee U.S. Edn. Found., 1987. Mem. AAAS, State Bar Mich. Republican. Methodist. Avocations: physics, history of science. Home: 1818 Redbud Lansing MI 48917 Office: Rasmusson and Assoc 2201 E Grand River Lansing MI 48912

RASOR, DORIS LEE, retired secondary education educator; b. Gonzales, Tex., June 25, 1929; d. Leroy and Ora (Power) DuBose; m. Jimmie E. Rasor, Dec. 27, 1947; children: Jimmy Lewis, Roy Lynn. BS summa cum laude, Abilene (Tex.) Christian U., 1949. Part-time sec. Abilene Christian U., 1946-50; sec. Radford Wholesale Grocery, Abilene, 1950-52; tchr. Odessa (Tex.) High Sch., 1967-98. Author play: The Lost Pearl, 1946. Recipient Am. Legion award, 1946. Mem. AAUW, Classroom Tchrs. Assn., Tex. Tchrs. Assn., NEA, Tex. Bus. Educators Assn., "W" Club for Women, Alpha Delta Kappa (pres. 1976-78), Alpha Chi. Ch. of Christ. Avocations: reading, cooking, camping, fishing. Home: 3882 Kenwood Dr Odessa TX 79762-7018 E-mail: drjrasor@apex2000.net.

RASS, HANS HEINRICH, politics educator; b. Norderney, Preussen, Germany, Apr. 29, 1936; s. Reinhard Johann and Elisabeth Margarete (Buse) R. Diploma, Freie U., Berlin, 1965, promotion, 1974. Asst. lectr. Otto-Suhr Inst. Freie U., Berlin, 1968-73; lectr. and sr. lectr. Tech. U., Braunschweig, Fed. Republic of Germany, 1973—. Author: Einführung in das Politische System Grossbritanniens, 1973, Britische Aussenpolitik, 1929-31, 1975; contbr. articles to profl. jours. Mem. Royal Inst. Internat. Affairs (assoc.). Avocations: classical music, books, cycling, wine, tea. Home: Niedersachsenstrasse 23 D-21423 Winsen/Luhe Germany Office: Tech Univ Wendenring 1-3 D-38114 Braunschweig Germany

RASS, REBECCA RIVKA, writer, English language educator; b. Tel Aviv, Israel, Dec. 9, 1936; came to U.S., 1971; d. Meir Mithya Wilcher and Rachel Berger-Wilcher; m. Izzy Abrahami; 1 child, Enid. BA, Empire State Coll., 1977; MFA, Bklyn. Coll., 1979. Lectr. CCNY, 1971-77, Queens Coll., N.Y.C., 1979-87, Hofstra U., L.I., 1980-86, Manhattan C.C., N.Y.C., 1985—; prof. English Pace U., 1978—. Author: From A to Z, 1969, 70, From Moscow to Jerusalem, 1976, The Fairy Tales of My Mind, 1978, The Mountain, 1982, From A to Z, 1984, World War I & II, 1984, The Fairy Tales of My Mind, 1985, The Mountain, 1988, Ursula Le Guin: The Left hand of Darkness, 1989, Simon de Beauvoir's: The Second Sex, 1990, The Writer Within--A Guide for Creative Writing, 1993, Woman, First Person Singular, 1995, The Way of Woman, 1996, Charlie Tar, 1997, In the Image of Woman, 1998, The Fifth Season, 1998. To Run with Words, 2000, Flowering Bones, 2002; contbr. short stories to anthologies, articles and features to mags., jours., newspapers; one woman sculpture shows include Tzavta Gallery, Tel Aviv, Pace U. Gallery, 1982,2001, Arbel Gallery, Tel Aviv, 1989, Bertha Urdang Gallery, N.Y.C., Lee-Nijhof Gallery, Amsterdam, 1993, Nurit Levy Gallery, Tel Aviv, 1994; group shows include Williamsburg Art and Hist. Ctr., N.Y., 1998, Pace U. Gallery, 2001. Recipient ACUM award Soc. Writers and Composers of Israel, 1995, Fiction award Crative Artists Pub. Svcs., 1981, Israeli Prime-Minister prize for lit., 2001. Home: 54 West 16th St Apt 14C New York NY 10011 also: 14 Bloch St Apt 10 64161 Tel Aviv Israel

RASSAI, RASSA, electrical engineering educator; b. Tehran, Oct. 15, 1951; d. Farjollah and Farideh (Mofakhami) R. BSEE with high honors, U. Md., 1973, MSEE, 1975, PhD, 1985. Sr. engr. Traycor Electronics Co., Arlington, Va., 1975; project engr. Iran Electronics Industry, Tehran, 1977-79; lectr. U. Md., 1980, 81-91, George Washington U., Washington, 1980-82, George Mason U., Fairfax, Va., 1982; rschr. elec. engring. dept. U. md., 1986-92; prof. No. Va. C.C., Annandale, 1986—, program head engring./elec. engring. tranfer program, 1991. Contbr. articles to profl. jours.; patentee remote telephone links. Mem. NOW Democrat. Avocations: reading, philosophy. Home: 6628 Medinah Ln Alexandria VA 22312-3117

RASSAS, BEVERLY, educator, consultant; b. Weehawken, N.J., Aug. 11, 1929; d. Abraham and Bessie (Bloch) Edelson; m. Harold Leonard Rassas, June 17, 1951; children: Ellen Rassas Cohn, Richard Frederick, Glen Aaron. BBA in Econs. and Psychology, Upsala Coll., East Orange, N.J., 1951; MS in Edn., Monmouth U., 1972. Home instr. Long Branch (N.J.) Bd. Edn., 1967-68, supplemental instr., 1970-72, instr. ESL, 1970-72, spl. edn. tchr., 1972; adminstrv. asst., instr. Monmouth Edn. Svcs., Long Branch, 1968-70; guidance counselor Long Branch H.S., 1973-94; ednl. cons. Long Branch, 1991—; adj. prof. Monmouth U., West Long Branch, 1995—. Chmn. curriculum com. Middle States Evaluation, Long Branch, 1989-90, mem. vis. com., Lodi, N.J., 1984, steering com., Long Branch, 1989. Pres. West End PTA, Long Branch, 1962; pres., treas. City of Long Branch Joint PTAs, 1963-64; pres. Hebrew Ladies Aux. Monmouth Med. Ctr., 1966, treas., 1967; mem. safety coun. City of Long Branch, 1967-72. Recipient Outstanding

Mem. award Student Coun., Long Branch H.S., 1980, Citation Vis. Com., Middle States Evaluation. Mem. ACA, N.J. Assn. Coll. Counselors, N.J. Counselors Assn., Monmouth County Sch. Counselors Assn. (Award of Svc. 1974). Jewish. Avocations: needlecraft, reading, travel, athletic events. Home: 595 Woodgate Ave Long Branch NJ 07740-5031

RASSBACH, HERBERT DAVID, marketing executive; b. Glen Ridge, N.J., Mar. 23, 1944; s. Merrill Augustus and Ruth Bruce (Sims) Rassbach. BS, Del. State Coll., 1971; MBA, Drexel U., 1979. Prodn. planning mgr. Standard Brands Chem. Industries, Edison, N.J., 1971-74; order fulfillment mgr. P Q Corp., Valley Forge, Pa., 1974-77, mkt. devel. project mgr., 1977-82; market mgr. Willson Safety Products, Reading, 1983-85; pres. HDR Group, mktg. and mgmt. cons., Wayne, 1986—. Guest speaker Wharton Sch. U. Pa., 1988, Temple U., Phila., 1989, Wharton Club, 1995. Media comms. bd. Upper Merion Twp., 1989, vice-chmn., 1990, 1992—2002, chmn., 1991, committee-man, 1977. Mem. Drexel U. Alumni Assn. (v.p. Montgomery County chpt. 1988-91), Alpha Kappa Mu, Delta Mu Delta. Democrat. Avocations: golf, tennis, running, travel, American history. Home: 635 Mallard Rd Wayne PA 19087-2346 Office: HDR Group PO Box 2164 Southeastern PA 19399-2164 E-mail: hdrassbach@hdrgroup.com.

RASSULO, DONNA MARIE, nurse, poet, writer, television producer; b. Boston, Jan. 18, 1951; d. Donald and Eleanor (Kadish) Guay; m. John A. Rassulo, June 20, 1981; children: Garret John, Nicole Darcy. Diploma, Shepard-Gill Sch. Practical Nursing, 1978; cert., Inst. Children's Lit., 1990. LPN, Mass. Model, cons. Reflections Unlimited, Amherst, Mass., 1974; med. sec. Mass. Gen. Hosp., Boston, 1969-78, staff nurse, acute medicine, 1978-1990, staff nurse, pediatric intermediate care, 1990-94; staff nurse Common-wealth Care, Inc., Newton, 1994—, Quantum Care Network, Inc., Newton, 1995—, Harvard Vanguard Med. Assocs., Medford, 1997-99; sch. nurse Adventures Pre Sch., Belmont, 1999—2002; pre-op coord. Acton (Ma.) Med. Assoc., 2002. Mem. Long Ridge Writers Group, West Redding, Conn., 1991-99. Author numerous poems; co-producer (with Marjorie Harrison) Clay Pit Pond Prodns., 1991—, Parent 2 Parent Show; contbr. articles to profl. jours. Mem. Neonatal ICU Parent Support Inc., Newton, Mass., 1989—, Parent Care, Inc., Alexandria, Va., 1990—. Recipient Disting. Poet award Spar-rowgrass Poetry Forum, 1990, Golden Poet award World of Poetry Press, 1990. Mem. LPNs Mass., Nat. Fedn. LPNs. Democrat. Roman Catholic. Avocations: needlepoint, horseback riding. Home: 78 Seminole Rd Acton MA 01720

RAST, MARK PETER, b. Syracuse, N.Y., Mar. 25, 1957; s. Max F. and Theresa M. (Winter) Rast; m. Kristie Lea McCollum; children: Ezekiel, Luke, Rosemary, Jacob. BA in Philosophy, U. Calif., Davis, 1979; BA in Physics, U. Calif., Santa Cruz, 1987; PhD in Astrophysical, Planetary, and Atmospheric Scis. Scis., U. Colo., 1992. Cert. pvt. pilot. Rsch. assoc. Joint Inst. Lab. Astrophysics, Boulder, Colo., 1992—93; rsch. fellow U. Leeds, Leeds, England, 1993, 1993—93; postdoctoral fellow Advanced Study Program/Nat. Ctr. Atmospheric Rsch., Boulder , Colo., 1993—95; rsch. assoc. Joint Inst. Lab. Astrophysics, Boulder, 1995—97; scientist High Altitude Observatory / Nat. Ctr. Atmospheric Rsch., Boulder , 1998—2002. Author: An Artificial Phenomenological Ensemble, 1979; contbr. articles to profl. jours., chapters to books. Stakeholder Erie Stakeholder's Assessment Process, Erie, 2000—01. Roman Catholic. Avocations: surfing, hang-gliding, gardening. Office: High Altitude Observatory PO Box 3000 Boulder CO 80307-3000 Office Fax: 303 497 1589. Business E-Mail: mprast@ucar.edu.

RASTAFARI, YUSUF BENYHMN, writer, educator; b. N.Y.C., Feb. 22, 1962; s. Alphornso Stanley and Shirley (Jones) Allen; m. Theresa Wells Smart, July 22, 1986; children: Mannashiim, Yahmnselah. Student, Wilberforce U., 1983-85, Edison State Coll. Poet laureate P.R.O.M.E.S.A., Inc., N.Y.C., 1976-77, West Side High Sch., N.Y.C., 1977-81; writer-in-residence Wilber-force (Ohio) U., 1983-85, Paul Robeson High Sch., N.Y.C., 1989-90, Children's Arts Carnival, N.Y.C., 1987-88, Grosvenor Neighborhood House, N.Y.C., 1988-90, P.J. Hill Elem. Sch., Trenton, N.J., 1991-92; columnist Am. Black Male Mag., N.Y.C., 1987-91. Creative dir. The Ark of Arks Edn. 360, Trenton, N.J., 1991-92; chmn. Ryiechus Reign Prodns., 1991-92; assoc. writer Columbia U. Intercultural Resource Ctr., 1991-92. Author: Black be Nimble, 1980, From Patritos to Hatriots, 1981; author 5 plays. Orator December Twelfe Movement, Harlem, 1987-90, N.A.Y.S.A. Youth Orgn., Harlem, 1986-90, Ethiopian Coptic Synagogue, 1986-89; messenger Nu-Form Holistic Health Svcs., Harlem, 1987—. Recipient Poet-Columnist award Wilberforce U., 1984, Playwright's award, 1984, Most Talented award, 1985, Coptic award Ethiopian Coptic Synagogue, 1987, Speaker's award Paul Robeson High Sch., 1989. Avocations: writing, reading, music, mystics-interpretation. Home: 101 Ferry St Trenton NJ 08611-2825

RASTALL, GEORGE RICHARD, music educator; b. Nottingham, Eng., Dec. 5, 1940; s. Hedley Nightingale and Margaret Ellen Rastall; m. Jane Elizabeth Oakshott, Aug. 11, 1978; children: Eleanor Jane, James Richard, William. BA, Christ's Coll., Cambridge, Eng., 1963, MusB, 1964, MA, 1967; PhD, Manchester (Eng.) U., 1968. Asst. lectr. U. Leeds, 1967-70, lectr., 1970-84, sr. lectr., 1984-96, reader in hist. musicology, 1996—, dean learning and tchg. faculty arts, 1997-2000, faculty, performing arts, 2001—. Chmn NE Early Music Forum, 1992—, Leeds Baroque Orch, 2000—. Editor (ed dir): Boethius Press, 1973—82; author: (book) The Notation of Western Music, 1983, Music in Early English Religious Drama I, 1996, Music in Early English Religious Drama II, 2001. Fellow: Soc Antiquaries; mem.: Royal Musical Asn, Soc Plainsong and Medieval Music (treas 1994—97). Office: Sch Music Univ Leeds Leeds LS2 9JT England Office Fax: 0113 233 2581. E-mail: g.r.rastall@leeds.ac.uk.

RASTEGAR, FARZAD ALI, investment banker; b. Teheran, Iran, June 25, 1956; arrived in U.S., 1980; s. Morteza and Rabeeh (Baghai-Kermani) Rastegar. BS with honors, Royal Sch. Mines, U. London, 1977; MBA, Columbia U., 1982. Asst. v.p. Phoenix Earth Resources Corp., San Francisco, 1982-83; v.p. Capital Properties Inc., N.Y.C., 1984-85, also bd. dirs.; exec. v.p. Asian Oceanic Real Estate Corp., 1986-87; dir. Berkeley Capital Advisors, Ltd., 1994—; spl. cons. Wellsford Group, 1988-94; chmn. SunLeigh plc, London, 1998—2002; dep. chmn. Ronson plc; chmn. Maclaren (USA) Inc. Bd. dirs. RENAFA Inc., Atlanta, Apax Ptnrs. & Co., Corp. Fin. Ltd., London, 1996—98. Lt. Imperial Iranian Army, 1977—79. Mem.: Royal Sch. Mines Assn., Engring. Coun. U.K., Instn. Mining and Metallurgy, Nat. Alumni Assn. Columbia Bus. Sch. (bd. dirs. 1984—88), Columbia Club N.Y. (bd. dirs.). Office: Berkeley Capital Advisors Ltd 4 Testa Place South Norwalk CT 06854-4638

RASTEGAR-DJAVAHERY, NADER E. private equities investor; b. Tehran, Iran, May 12, 1953; came to U.S., 1982; s. Morteza and Rabe'eh (Baghai-Kermani) R.; m. Soheila Gharai, Apr. 1979; children: Roya Z., Scheherazade B., Maryam A. BSc, U. Wis., 1976; MBA, Iran Ctr. Mgmt. Studies, 1979. Pres. Shahgard Indsl. Co., Tehran, 1977, Renafa, Inc., Atlanta, 1984—. Contbr. articles to various publs. Active various profl., historical, philatelical and environ. socs. and groups. Lt. Iranian Armed Forces, 1977-78. Avocations: historical research, social welfare, environmental issues, philatelics.

RASTOGI, AMIT, internist; b. Badaun, India, Apr. 5, 1973; s. Vinay Krishna and Alka Rastogi. MD, All India Inst. Med. Scis., New Delhi, 1995. Clk. All India Inst. Med. Scis., New Delhi, 1995, jr. resident orthop., 1996-97; intern in internal medicine St. Barnabas Med. Ct., Livingston, N.J., 1997-98, resident in internal medicine, 1998-2000; fellow in med. genetics Sch. Medicine Johns Hopkins U., Balt., 2000—. Recipient rsch. scholarship dept. medicine St. Barnabas Med. Ctr., Livingston, 1998-99. Assoc. mem. ACP. Hindu. Avocations: reading, travel, swimming, badminton, playing music. Home: 3 Aspen Tree Ct Apt 201 Baltimore MD 21209-2367 Office: Johns Hopkins Hosp 600 N Wolfe St Baltimore MD 21287-0005 E-mail: rastogia@hotmail.com.

RASTOGI, ANIL KUMAR, medical device manufacturer, executive; b. India, July 13, 1942; came to U.S., 1969, naturalized, 1978; s. R.S. and K.V. Rastogi; m. Anjali Capur, Mar. 18, 1970; children: Priya, Sonya. BS with honors, Lucknow U., 1963, MS, 1964; PhD in Polymer Sci., McGill U., 1969. Mem. staff Owens-Corning Tech. Ctr., Granville, Ohio, 1969-87, lab. supr., 1975-76; lab. mgr. materials tech. labs Ownes-Corning Tech. Ctr., Granville, Ohio, 1976-79; lab. mgr. product devel. labs. Owens-Corning Tech. Ctr., 1979-80, research dir., 1980-83, dir. corp. diversification portfolio, 1983-87; v.p. Mead Imaging, Miamisburg, 1987-89; pres. Mead Cycolor Div., Dayton, 1989-92; v.p., gen. mgr.infusion systems div. Pharmacia Deltec, Inc., St. Paul, 1992-93, exec. v.p., 1993-94; COO SIMS Deltec, Inc., St. Paul, 1994-95; pres., COO, Sabratek Corp., Niles, Ill., 1995-98; pres., CEO, NOMOS Corp., Sewickley, Pa., 1998—2002; v.p. entrepeneurship and tech. commercialization Drexel U., Phila., 2002—. Mem. adv. bd. Central Ohio Tech. Coll.; lectr., cons. in field. Author of 15 bus. and tech. publs.; patentee in field. Bd. dirs. Licking County Family Services Assn.; bd. dirs. Tech. Alliance of Central Ohio; v.p. local United Way; bd. dirs. and treas. Columbus Bus. Tech. Ctr.; mem. Overview Adv. Com. Strategic Hwy. Research Program. Fellow NRC Can., 1966-69 Mem. AAAS, Am. Mgmt. Assn., Am. Chem. Soc., Soc. Plastics Engrs., Comml. Devel. Assn., Med. Alley (bd. dirs.), Health Ind. Mfrs. Assn., Nat. Infusion Therapy Alliance (bd. dirs.), Toastmasters (past pres.), Rotary, Sigma Xi. Home: 414 Heights Dr Gibsonia PA 15044-6031 Office: Drexel U. 3141 Chestnut St Philadelphia PA 19104-2875

RAS-WORK, ANDENET T. software company executive; b. Addis Ababa, Ethiopia, May 28, 1963; s. Terrefe Ras-Work and Berhane Asfaw; m. Eleni Zaude Gabre-Hadhin, Sept. 17, 1993; children: Zega, Yared. Internat. bacca-laureate, Internat. Sch. Geneva, Switzerland, 1981; BSEE, UCLA, 1985; MBA, INSEAD, Fontainebleau, France, 1989. Engr., project mgr. Ascom, Bern, Switzerland, 1986-89; European program mgr. Hewlett Packard, Geneva, 1990-95, E-commerce group mgr. Santa Clara, Calif., 1995-2000; pres., CEO Semantix Corp., Herndon, Va., 2000—. Founde,r pres., African Enterprise Group, Geneva, 1992-95. Inventor, innovator, patentee Writing Utensils, 1998. Coun. mem., Leadership Mountain View, Calif., 1997-99. Recipient cert. Congl. Recognition, 1997. Mem. Scharnhorst Racing Club (exec. 1989—). Home: 3842 Macomb St NW Washington DC 20016 Office: Semantix Inc Ste 150 13530 Dulles Technology Dr Herndon VA 20171 Fax: (703) 793-1937; (202) 244-5941. E-mail: araswork@yahoo.com.

RATANAWONGSA, BOONLUA, ophthalmologist; b. Lomsak, Thailand, Nov. 29, 1936; came to U.S., 1971; s. Bhutha and Boonpun R.; m. Ratana, July 4, 1965; children: Rithi, Boosara, Neda. MD, Siriraj Med. Sch., Bangkok, 1962. Diplomate Am. Bd. Ophthalmology. Resident in ophthalmology Greater Balt. Med. Ctr., 1965-69; asst. prof. Siriraj Med. Sch., Bangkok, 1970-71; pvt. practice Charles Cole Meml. Hosp. Med. Ctr., Coudersport, Pa., 1971-79, Med. Arts Bldg., Olean, N.Y., 1978—. Fellow ACS, Am. Acad. Ophthalmol-ogy; mem. AMA. Avocations: golfing. Office: Med Arts Bldg Olean 2223 W State St Olean NY 14760-1938

RATCH, JERRY, writer; b. Chgo., Aug. 9, 1944; s. Otto Joseph Jr. and Bess Ratch; m. Sherry Karver, Mar. 18, 1990. BA, U. Ill., 1967; MFA, U. Calif., Irvine, 1970. Mem. staff paint store/warehouse Precision Tech. Coatings, Berkeley, Calif., 1975-79; salesman, 1979-80, Mason-McDuffie, 1980-85, 89-95, Coldwell Banker, Berkeley, 1985-89, 95-00, Red Oak Realty, Berkeley, 2001—. Author (poetry books) Puppet X, 1976, Hot Weather, 1982, Light, 1989, (novel) Wild Dreams of Reality, 2001. Home: 6065 Chabot Rd Oakland CA 94618 Office: Red Oak Realty 2983 College Ave Berkeley CA 94705

RATCHESON, ROBERT ALLAN, neurological surgeon; b. Chgo., Aug. 24, 1940; s. Maurice and Kate (Davidow) Ratcheson; m. Peggy Steiner, June 20, 1964; children: Alexey, Rachael Weissman, Abigail. Student, Miami U., 1961; BS, Northwestern U., 1962, MD, 1965. Diplomate Am. Bd. Neurol. Surgery. Asst. prof. Washington Sch. of Medicine, St. Louis, 1973-77, assoc. prof., 1977-81; Harvey Huntington Brown, Jr. prof., dir. Divsn. Neurol. Surgery U. Hosps. of Cleve., 1981-91, Harvey Huntington Brown prof., chmn., 1991—. Editl. bd. Jour. of Neurosurgery, 1992—, chmn. 2000-01; contbr. articles to profl. jours. With USPHS, 1967-69. Mem. Am. Assn. Neurol. Surgeons (bd. dirs. 1997—, sec. 2000—, William P Van Wagenen fellow 1972-73), Soc. Neurol. Surgeons (treas. 1996-2001, pres. 2001-2002), Neurol. Soc. Am. (pres. 2000—), Congress Neurol. Surgeons (pres. 1985-86). Avocation: fly fishing. Office: Univs Hosps of Cleve 11100 Euclid Ave Cleveland OH 44106-1736

RATCHFORD, ROGER LIONEL, retired secondary education educator; b. Norwalk, Conn., Oct. 18, 1933; s. Francis Thomas and Irene Audrey (Sharkany) R.; m. M. Gail Gruber, Aug. 10, 1963; children: Moira, Michael, Brendan. AB, Coll. of the Holy Cross, 1955; MA, Fairfield U., 1966; EdD, Nova Southeastern U., 1989. Cert. Latin, French, English, computers. Tchr. Woburn (Mass.) High Sch., 1956-58, Fairfield (Conn.) Prep Sch., 1958-97. Adj. prof. Fairfield (Conn.) U., 1980-81; golf coach, Fairfield Prep, 1965—. Author: Improving Writing in Secondary Schools, 1989. Pres. Soc. to Advance the Retarded, Norwalk, 1975-77, 85-87, bd. dirs., 1969-91. Recipient Conn. Disting. Svc. award in Golf Nat. Fedn. of Intersch. Coaches, 1989, Coaching award Sportsmen of Westport (Conn.), 1986. Mem. ASCD, Computer Assisted Lang. and Instrn. Consortium, Nat. High Sch. Coaches Assn. (regional Golf Coach of Yr. award 1986, 89, 93, nat. Golf Coach of Yr. award 1996), Am. Assn. Tchrs. French, Coun. of Lang. Tchrs., Conn. Assn. for Retarded Citizens (bd. dirs. 1972-89, Vol. of Yr. 1988), Nat. Coun. Techrs. of English, U.S. Golf Assn., Met. Opera Guild. Republican. Roman Catholic. Avocations: golf, walking, electronics, opera. Home: 12 Adams Ln Norwalk CT 06850

RATCLIFF, CARTER GOODRICH, writer, art critic, poet; b. Seattle, Aug. 20, 1941; s. Francis Kenneth and Marian Elizabeth (Carter) R.; m. Phyllis Derfner, Jan. 28, 1976. BA, U. Chgo., 1963. Dir. poetry workshop St. Mark's Poetry Project, N.Y.C., 1969-70; editorial assoc. Artnews, 1969-72; advisory editor Art Internat., Lugano, Switzerland, 1970-75; instr. modern and contem-porary art and art theory The Sch. of Visual Arts, N.Y.C., 1972-83; instr. modern and contemporary art Phila. Coll. of Art, 1973; instr. art history NYU Sch. of Continuing Edn., 1973-75; contbg. editor Saturday Review, N.Y.C., 1980-82, Art in America, N.Y.C., 1976—; mem. editorial adv. com. Sculpture, Washington, 1992—. Vis. prof. post-war Am. art SUNY, Purchase, 1983-84; vis. prof. modern and contemporary art and art theory Pratt Inst., Bkyn., 1984-85; vis. prof. art criticism and theory Hunter Coll., CUNY, 1985-86, 95-96, vis. prof. dept. art, 1996—. Author: (books, poetry), Fever Coast, 1973, Give Me Tomorrow, 1983; (books) John Singer Sargent, 1982, Andy Warhol, 1983, Robert Longo, 1985, Komar and Melamid, 1989, Gilbert and George: The Singing Sculpture, 1993, The Fate of a Gesture: Jackson Pollock and Post War American Art, 1996, paperback edit., 1998, Out of the Box: The Reinvention of Art, 1965-1975, 2001; (essays) Joseph Cornell, 1980, Willem de Kooning: The North Atlantic Light, 1983, Roy Lichtenstein, 1989, Barnett Newman, 1991, Gilbert & George, 1993, Ellsworth Kelly, 1996, Francis Bacon, 1998, William Blake, 2001; contbg. editor Art in America, 1976—, Art on Paper, 2001—; contbr. over 350 articles on art to mags. and catalogs including The Times Lit. Supplement, The L.A. Times Book Rev., Art in America, Art Internat., Artnews, Archtl. Forum; lectr. at many instns. including Met. Mus., N.Y.C., Mus. Modern Art, N.Y.C., Whitney Mus. Am. Art, Pratt Inst., U. So. Calif., U. Chgo., Detroit Inst. Art, San Francisco Art Inst. Recipient of the Frank Jewett Mather award for art criticism Coll. Art Assn., 1987; Poets Found. grantee, 1969, NEA Arts Critics grantee, 1972, 76; Guggenheim fellow, 1976. Home and Office: 26 Beaver St New York NY 10004-2311 E-mail: ratcliff1@earthlink.net.

RATCLIFFE, J. RICHARD, lawyer; b. Pawtucket, R.I., Aug. 15, 1956; s. J. Richard and Edith J. (Kerrigan) R.; m. Margaret M. Pfeiffer, Aug. 27, 1988; children: James, Nicholas. BA, Providence Coll., 1978; JD, Washington U., 1981. Bar: R.I. 1981, Mass. 1981, U.S. Dist. Ct. R.I. 1982, U.S. Ct. Appeals (1st cir.) 1982, U.S. Dist. Ct. Mass. 1983. Law clk. R.I. Supreme Ct., Providence, 1981-83; assoc. Zisson & Veara, Boston, 1983-86; pvt. practice, 1987; asst. atty. gen. R.I. Dept. Atty. Gen., Providence, 1988-95; assoc. Temkin & Assocs. Ltd., 1995-98; ptnr. Ratcliffe Burke & Harten LLP, 1999—. Mem. R.I. Bar Assn. (chair criminal bench bar com. 1995—, mem. ho. of dels. 1997—), Common Cause (mem. gov. bd.), Save The Bay, The Haitian Project (sec. 1990—), Am. Inns of Ct. Avocations: tennis, skiing. Home: 7 Holly Ln Cumberland RI 02864-3328 Office: Ratcliffe Burke & Harten LLP 1600 Financial Plz Providence RI 02903 E-mail: jrratcliffe@ratburke.com.

RATCLIFFE, SANDRA M(ARGUERITE), convention manager; b. Winter Haven, Fla. d. Jennings Duncan and Marguerite Alice Ratcliffe. BA, Columbia U., 1977; postgrad., CUNY, 1977-79. Prodn. coord. Alt. Current, N.Y.C., 1981-85; prodr. Concept/N.Y., 1985-88; v.p. Kaufman Films, 1989-92; sr. mgr. convs. Pfizer Inc., 1993—. Cons. The N.Y. Festivals, N.Y.C., 1991-94. Exec. prodr.: (film) Romeo & Julia, 1991. Bd. dirs. Abingdon Theater Co., N.Y.C., 1993—. Health Care Exhibitors Assn., 2001—. Mem. Health Care Business-women's Assn. Office: Pfizer Inc 235 E 42nd St New York NY 10017-5755

RATH, ALAN T. sculptor; b. Cin., Nov. 25, 1959; s. George and Carolyn R. BSEE, MIT, 1982. One-man exhbns. include San Jose (Calif.) Art Mus., 1990, Dorothy Goldeen Gallery, Santa Monica, Calif., 1990, 92, Walker Art Ctr., Mpls., 1991, Mus. Contemporary Art, Chgo., 1991, Carl Solway Gallery, Cin., 1991, Inst. Contemporary Mus., Honolulu, 1992, Ctr. Fine Art, Miami, Fla., 1992, Galerie Hans Mayer, Dusseldorf, Germany, 1992, Hiroshima (Japan) City Mus. Contemporary Art, 1994, Worcester (Mass.) Art Mus., 1994, John Weber Gallery, N.Y.C., 1994, Haines Gallery, San Francisco, 1995, 96, 98, Contemporary Art Mus., Houston, 1995, Aspen Art Mus., Colo., 1996, Dorfman Projects, N.Y.C., 1998, Yerba Buena Ctr. for the Arts, San Francisco, 1998, Site Santa Fe (N.Mex.), 1998, Mus. of Art, Austin, Tex., 1999, Scottsdale Mus. of Contemporary Art, 1999; group exhbns. include Visiona, Zurich, 1989, Ars Electronica, Linz, Austria, 1989, L.A. Contemporary Exhbns., 1989, Mus. Folkwang, Essen, Germany, 1989, Cite des Arts et des Nouvelles Technologies, Montreal, 1990, Stadtmuseum Siegburg, Siegburg, Germany, 1990, San Francisco Mus. Modern Art, 1990, 95, 98, Denver ArtMus., 1991, Whitney Am. Art, N.Y.C., 1991, Alvar Alto Mus., Jyvaskyla, Finland, 1992, Internat. Ctr. Photography, N.Y.C., 1992, Padigilione d'Arte Contemporanea, Ferrara, Italy, 1992, John Weber Gallery, N.Y.C., 1993, Spiral Art Ctr., Tokyo, 1994, Aldrich Mus. of Contemporary Art, Ridgefield, Conn., 1995, Otso Gallery, Espo Finland, 1996, LaLonja, Palma de Malloren, Spain, 1996, Kunsthalle, Vienna, 1998, L.A. Mus. Contemporary Art, 1999, Taipei ICA, Taiwan, 2001, Bienal de Valencia, Spain, 2001. Grantee NEA, 1988; Guggenheim fellow, 1994. Office: IKON 830 E 15th St Oakland CA 94606-3631

RATH, ED, artist, educator; b. Mpls., Nov. 17, 1952; s. Edwin A. and Verna A. Rath; m. Laura E. Gisondo; children: Rachel, Jacob. BFA, Mpls. Coll. Art & Design, 1974; MFA, Yale U., 1976. Artist, N.Y.C., 1977-2000. Instr. in drawing Parsons Sch. Design, N.Y.C., 1985-88; tchg. artist P.S. 8 Elem. Sch., Bklyn., 1991-2000. Solo shows include Art Galaxy, N.Y.C., 1980, Vassar Coll. Gallery, 1987, WEBO Gallery, N.Y.C., 1991, Gallery B.A.I., N.Y.C., 1994, Landmark at East View, Tarrytown, N.Y., 1996, Hunt Gallery, Webster U., St. Louis, 2000, 55 Mercer Gallery, N.Y.C., 2001; group exhbns. include Marymount Manhattan Coll. Gallery, 1990, Kingsborough Coll. Gallery, 1993-94, Salina (Kans.) Art Ctr., 2000, River Styx Poetry Mag. Benefit Show, St. Louis, 2001; commns. include 2 works at P.S. 7, Bklyn., 1999. Avocations: graphoanalysis, fishing, stamp collecting, bicycling. E-mail: edrathbrooklyn@aol.com.

RATH, FRANCIS STEVEN, lawyer; b. N.Y.C., Oct. 10, 1955; s. Steven and Elizabeth (Chorin) R.; m. Denise Stephania Thompson, Aug. 2, 1980. BA cum laude, Wesleyan U., Middletown, Conn., 1977; JD cum laude, Georgetown U., 1980; postgrad., Harvard U., 1999-2000. Bar: D.C. 1980, U.S. Dist. Ct. D.C. 1981, U.S. Ct. Appeals (D.C. cir.), 1981, U.S. Supreme Ct. 1987, Va. 1988. Atty., advisor Comptr. of the Currency, Washington, 1980-84; assoc. Verner, Liipfert, Bernhard, McPherson & Hand, 1984-85; founding mem. Wolf, Arnold & Monroig (merged with Burnham, Connolly, Oesterly & Henry), 1986-88; pvt. practice Great Falls, Va., 1989—. Internat. cons. Fried, Frank, Harris, Shriver and Jacobson, 1991-95; counsel Seward & Kissel, Washington, 1995-98; of counsel, Squire Sanders & Dempsey, Washington, 1998—. Editor: Law and Policy in Internat. Bus., 1979-80; contbg. author Business Ventures in Eastern Europe and Russia; contbr. articles to profl. jours. Trustee Dunn Loring (Va.) Vol. Fire Dept., 1986. Mem. ABA, D.C. Bar Assn., Va. Bar Assn., Bar of U.S. Supreme Ct., U.S. Combined Tng. Assn. (legal com. 1989-91, 96-99, safety com. 1990-91, 96-99, bd. govs. 1995-98). Home and Office: 1051 Kelso Rd Great Falls VA 22066-2032 E-mail: frath@fsrpc.com.

RATH, HOWARD GRANT, JR. lawyer; b. L.A., Sept. 2, 1931; s. Howard Grant and Helen (Cowell) R.; m. Peyton McComb, Sept. 13, 1958 (dec. Apr. 1984); children: Parthenia Peyton, Francis Cowell; m. Dorothy Moser, Aug. 29, 1986. BS, U. Calif., 1953; JD, U. So. Calif., 1958. Bar: Calif. 1959, U.S. Dist. Ct. (cen. dist.) Calif., 1959, U.S. Ct. Claims 1974, U.S. Tax Ct. 1960. Assoc. O'Melveny & Myers, L.A., 1959-66; tax counsel, dir. tax adminstrn., asst. treas. Northrop Corp. L.A., 1966-74; sr. tax ptnr. Macdonald, Halsted & Laybourne, L.A., 1974-86, Hill & Weiss, L.A., 1986-90; ptnr. Lewis, D'Amato, Brisbois & Bisgaard, L.A., 1990—; dir. Rath Packing Co., Waterloo, Iowa, 1966-81. 1st lt. U.S. Army, 1953-55. Mem. State Bar Calif., L.A. County Bar Assn., L.A. Yacht Club, The Athenaeum, Order of Coif, Phi Beta Kappa. Republican. Episcopalian. E-mail: rath@ldbb.com. Office: Lewis Brisbois Bisgaard & Smith 221 N Figueroa St Ste 1200 Los Angeles CA 90012-2646 E-mail: rath@lbbslaw.com.

RATH, THOMAS DAVID, lawyer, former state attorney general; b. East Orange, N.J., June 1, 1945; s. Harvey and Helen R.; m. Christine Casey, Dec. 18, 1971; children— Erin, Timothy. AB, Dartmouth Coll., 1967; JD, George-town U., 1971. Bar: N.J. 1971, N.H. 1972, U.S. Supreme Ct. 1978. Law clk. Judge Clarkson Fisher, U.S. Dist. Ct. N.J., 1971-72; atty. criminal div. Office of Atty. Gen., State of N.H., 1972-73, asst. atty. gen., 1973-76, dep. atty. gen., 1976-78, atty. gen., 1978-80; ptnr. Orr & Reno, P.A., Concord, N.H., 1980-87, Rath & Young, P.A., Concord, 1987-91; founding ptnr. Rath, Young, Pignatelli & Oyer, P.A., 1991—. Polit. analyst WHDH-TV, Boston, WGBH Pub. TV, Boston, WENH, N.H. Pub. TV, WBUR-Boston Radio; chief strategist Alex-ander for Pres.; vice chmn. of bd. Primary Bank, 1995-97; pres. Play Ball, N.H., 1994—; commentator, polit. analyst WMUR-TV and Yankee Network; bd. dirs. Assoc. Grocers New England, Chubb Am. Fund. Host State of the State, Yankee Cable Network; co-host Close-Up, WMUR-TV. Chmn. cam-paign Warren B. Rudman for U.S. Senate, 1980, 86; bd. overseers Aquinas House, Dartmouth Coll., com. on trustees Rockefeller Ctr. Bd. Visitors; bd. oversers Dartmouth Med. Sch.; nat. dir. Baker Exploratory Com., 1986-87; sec. bd. trustees Concord Hosp.; treas. N.H. Rep. party, 1981-93; trustee DWC, 1981-87, chmn., 1982-86; mem. Baker Exploratory Com., 1986-87; trustee Concord Hosp., 1980-86; sr. nat. cons. Dole for Pres.; del. Rep. Nat. Conv., 1984, 88, 92, rules com., 1988, 92, N.H. committeeman, 1996—; Rep. nat. committeeman State of N.H., 1996; bd. dirs. New Eng. Coun., 1997. Mem. Nat. Assn. Attys. Gen. (vice-chmn. Eastern region, vice chmn. standing com. on energy), N.H. Bar Assn. (Spl. Pres. award 1992). Clubs: Dartmouth Coll. (v.p. Merrimack County). Roman Catholic. Office: Rath Young and Pignatelli One Capital Plaza PO Box 1500 Concord NH 03302-1500 E-mail: tdr@rathlaw.com.

RATH-BECKMANN, ANNETTE, librarian; b. Bielefeld, Germany, Aug. 1, 1951; Degree in History, Georg-August U., Göttingen, Germany, 1977. Cert. in library sci. Chief librarian Staats und Universitätsbibliothek Bremen, Germany, 1993—. Office: Staats und Universitatsbibliothekstr 28359 Bremen Germany Fax: 0049 421-2182614. E-mail: rathb@suub.uni-bremen.de.

RATHBONE, SUSAN WU, social services administrator; b. Hofei, Anhwei, China, Oct. 29, 1922; came to U.S., 1946; d. Chung Liu and Jin Ban (Gung) Wu; m. Frank Harold Rathbone, Aug. 20, 1945; children: Frank, Edward George. BA, CUNY, 1984. Tchr. Second Sch., Chungking, China, 1941-42; founder Chinese-Am. Bus. Women's Assn., Flushing, N.Y., 1990; founder, chair Chinese Immigrants Soc. Inc., 1984—, Queens Chinese Woman's Assn., Flushing, 1984—. Editor Women's Voice mag., 1995—. Recipient Susan B. Anthony award NOW, 1987, Ethnic New Yorker award City of N.Y., 1984, Cmty. Svc. award NAACP, 1994, Gov.'s Woman of Distinction award N.Y. State, 1994, Cmty. Svc. award Newsday, 1995, China Jour. award, 1995, Svc. award Chinese Am. Planning Council, 1995, Asian Am. for Equality award, 1996, Cmty. Leadership award Pres. Borough Queens, 1997. Mem. Anhui Provincial Assn. (founder, hon. life pres.), Nat. Women's Polit. Caucus, Univ. Women. Avocation: writing. Home: 26-10 Union St Flushing NY 11354 Office: PO Box 1656 Flushing NY 11354-7656

RATHBUN, EDWIN DAVID, physician; b. Kansas City, Mo., June 13, 1936; s. Harold Vernon and Minnie Belle (Stanton) R.; m. Katherine Glynnten Burke, Aug. 20, 1960 (div. Oct. 1967); m. Suzanne Matkin, JDec. 16, 1967; children: Daniel F., David A., Douglas B. AB, U. Kans., 1958, MD, 1962. Diplomate Am. Bd. Family Practice. Family practitioner Fountain King Hartley, Wichita, Kans., 1964-66; pvt. practice Liberal, 1966-87; asst. prof. Tex. Tech Med. Sch., Odessa, 1987-90, asst. clin. prof., 1990-91; assoc. prof.

Tex. Tech. Med. Sch., 1995—99; assoc. clin. prof. Tex. Tech Med. Sch., 1991-95; family practitioner Primary Care Clinic, 1990—. Chief of staff Southwest Med. Ctr. Liberal, Kans., 1977, Family Practitioners Hosp. and Clinic, Iraan, Tex., 1999—. Contbr. articles to profl. jours.; photographer various mags. Counsellor Kans. Med. Soc., Topeka, 1984-87, vice speaker of house, 1986. Recipient award Family Practice News, 1986, MD Mag., 1995. Mem. AMA, Am. Acad. Family Practice, Tex. Acad. Family Practice, Tex. Med. Assn. Avocations: bicycling, photography, flying. Home: 98 Chukar Run Odessa TX 79761-2244 Office: Iraan Clinic PO Box 337 Iraan TX 79744-0337

RATHBUN, JOHN WILBERT, American studies educator; b. Sioux City, Iowa, Oct. 24, 1924; s. Wilbert W. and Paulina Amanda (Baldes) R.; m. Mary Regina Walsh, Aug. 2, 1947 (div. Sept. 19, 1985); children: Mary Walsh, John Philip. Ph.B., Marquette U., Milw., 1951, MA, 1952; PhD, U. Wis., 1956. Mem. faculty Calif. State U., Los Angeles, 1956—, prof. English/Am. studies, 1959—, chmn. dept. Am. studies, 1969-75, prof. emeritus, 1991—. Author: American Literary Criticism, 1800-1860, vol. 1, 1979, (with Harry Hayden Clark) American Literary Criticism, 1860-1905, vol. 2, 1979, Literature and Literary Analysis, 1983; (with Monica Grecu) American Literary Critics and Scholars, 1800-1850, vol. 1, 1987, 1850-1880, vol. 2, 1880-1900, 1988, vol. 3, 1988; contbr. articles to profl. jours. Served with AUS, 1943-46. Recipient Service citation Calif. State U., Los Angeles, 1977, Univ. Meritorious Achievement award, 1986; Fulbright fellow Romania, 1979-81. Mem. Am. Studies Assn. (council 1974), So. Calif. Am. Studies Assn. (pres. 1973), Coll. English Assn. So. Calif. (pres. 1966-67), MLA. Democrat. Office: 5151 State University Dr Los Angeles CA 90032-4226

RATHBURN, MARY JOANNE, communication educator; b. Green Bay, Wis., July 17, 1935; d. Harry J. and Gladys E. (Adrians) Butnick; m. Wesley Edward Rathburn, July 14, 1956; children: Randall A., Judie A., Joseph A., James J., John M., Mary A. BA in English, Coll. St. Scholastica, 1956; MEd in Reading, U. Wis., Oshkosh, 1973. Tchr. English Seymour (Wis.) Pub. Schs., 1956-57; tchr. English and reading St. Joseph's Acad., Green Bay, 1958-83; instr. comm. and reading N.E. Wis. Tech. Coll., 1983—. Cons. Ctr. for Edn. and Workforce Competitiveness, U. Wis., Green Bay, 1997. Asst. editor Wis. State Reading Jour., 1972. Pres. AAUW, Green Bay, 1963-65, Bayland Reading Assn., Green Bay, 1978-80. Mem. Internat. Reading Assn., Nat. Coun. Tchrs. English, Assn. Bus. Comm., Assn. Tech. Writing Tchrs. Avocations: depression glass, linens, Victorianna collecting, reading, family activities. Office: NE Wis Tech Coll 2940 W Mason St Green Bay WI 54313-5012

RATHER, DAN, broadcast journalist; b. Wharton, Tex., Oct. 31, 1931; m. Jean Goebel; children: Dawn Robin, Dan M. BA in Journalism, Sam Houston State Tchrs. Coll., Huntsville, Tex., 1953; student, U. Houston, South Tex. Sch. Law. Instr. journalism Sam Houston State Coll., for 1 year; later worked for U.P.I. and Houston Chronicle; with CBS, 1962—; joined staff of radio Sta. KTRH (CBS affiliate), Houston; staying about 4 years as news writer, reporter, and later, as news dir.; became dir. news and pub. affairs with CBS Houston TV affiliate KHOU-TV, in the late 1950's; became White House corr., 1964; and then transferred to overseas burs., including chief of London bur., 1965-66; then worked in Vietnam; returned to White House position in fall of 1966; appearing nightly on segments of CBS Evening News; became anchorman-corr. for CBS Reports, 1974-75; co-editor 60 Minutes, CBS-TV, 1975-81; anchorman Dan Rather Reporting, CBS Radio Network, 1977—; anchorman, mng. editor CBS Evening News with Dan Rather, 1981—. Co-editor show Who's Who, CBS-TV, 1977; anchor 48 Hours, 1986—; anchored numerous CBS News spl. programs. Author: (with Gary Gates) The Palace Guard, 1974, (with Mickey Herskowitz) The Camera Never Blinks, 1977, The Camera Never Blinks Twice: The Further Adventures of a Television Journalist, 1994, (with Peter Wyden) Memoirs, I Remember, 1991; editor Our Times, 1994. Recipient numerous Emmy awards; honors include dedication of Dan Rather Comm. Bldg., classroom facility Sam Houston State U., Huntsville, Tex. Office: CBS News 524 W 57th St New York NY 10019-2924*

RATHER, LEE, psychologist, educator; b. San Francisco, Sept. 9, 1948; s. Lelland Joseph Rather and Eleanor Edith Knight; m. Stefanie Nickel, Jan. 5, 1996. BA in History, Stanford U., 1971; MA in Clin. Psychology, Antioch U., 1984; PhD in Clin. Psychology, Calif. Sch. Profl. Psychology, 1988; grad., Psychoanalytic Inst. No. Calif., 1998. Pvt. practice, San Francisco, 1986—; psychologist Children's Hosp. Psychiat. Svcs., 1987—89; staff psychologist Cmty. Counseling and Edn. Ctr., Fremont, 1989—94; dir. tng. Westside Lodge, San Francisco, 1993—95, Juvenile Probation Svcs., Marin County, 1996—97. Mem. adj. faculty Calif. Sch. Profl. Psychology, Alameda, 1991—; mem. core faculty Psychoanalytic Inst. No. Calif., San Francisco, 1999—2002; clin. supr. Pacific Grad. Sch. Psychology, Palo Alto, Calif., 1991—92. Contbr. articles to profl. jours. Mem.: APA, Internat. Fedn. Psychoanalytic Edn., Nat. Register Health Svc. Providers in Psychology. Office: 2504 Clay St San Francisco CA 94115

RATHER, LUCIA PORCHER JOHNSON, library administrator; b. Durham, N.C., Sept. 12, 1934; d. Cecil Slayton and Lucia Lockwood (Porcher) Johnson; m. John Carson Rather, July 11, 1964; children: Susan Wright, Bruce Carson. Student, Westhampton Coll., 1951-53; AB in History, U. N.C., 1955, MS in Library Sci., 1957; PhD in History, George Washington U., 1994. Cataloger Library of Congress, Washington, 1957-64, bibliographer, 1964-66, systems analyst, 1966-70; group head MARC Devel. Office, 1970-73, asst. chief, 1973-76, acting chief, 1976-77, dir. for cataloging, 1976-91. Chmn. standing com. on cataloguing Internat. Fedn. Library Assns., 1976-81; sec. Working Group on Content Designators, 1972-77; chmn. Working Group on Corp. Headings, 1978-79, Internat. ISBD Rev. Com., 1981-87. Co-author: the MARC II Format, 1968. Recipient Libr. Congress Disting. Svc. award, 1991, Disting. Alumnus award U. N.C. Sch. Libr. and Info. Sci., 1992. Mem. ALA (Margaret Mann award 1985, Melvil Dewey award 1991), Phi Beta Kappa. Democrat. Presbyterian. Home: 10308 Montgomery Ave Kensington MD 20895-3327

RATHER, SHARI ANNE, social worker; b. Neenah, Wis., Oct. 13, 1948; d. Michael Eugene and Gloria Margaret (Hubert) Curran; m. Richard J. Rather, July 10, 1971; children: Michael, Shannon, Kimberly, Ashley. BS, U. Wis., 1973. Dir. social svc. Appleton (Wis) Meml. Hosp., 1973-75, Marshfield (Wis.) Convalscent Ctr., 1975-76; social worker, cons. Colonial House, Colby, Wis., 1975-76; social worker S.D. Perinatal Assn., Sioux Falls, 1977-80; merchandiser Dayton Hudson Corp., S.D., 1984-86; patient svc. coord. Muscular Dystrophy Assn., 1987-88; social worker Waukesha County (Wis.) Dept. Human Svcs., 1988—, Wis. Assn. Nursing Home, Milw., 1988-92. Cons. Muscular Dystrophy Assn. ALS Support Group, Sioux Falls, 1987-88. Team mgr. Spring City Soccer Club, 1994-96; v.p. City Coun., 1989-90, pres., 1990- 91; chmn. Jr. League, Sioux Falls, 1982-88, Milw., 1988-91; mem. Pewaukee chpt. PTO, Wis. Juvenile Ct. Intake Assn., 1991—; treas. Horrace Mann PTA, 1987-88, Pewaukee Parent for Soccer Registrar, 1990-92; mem. Pewaukee Friends and Neighbors, 1991—; child advocacy com. Scan, 1994-95; active Prevention Network, 1997-98; pres. Pewaukee H.S. Booster Club, 1996-98; bd. dirs. Pewaukee Select Soccer Bd., 1996-00, registrar, 1997-00, treas., 1997-00; crisis intervention worker Waukesha County Dept. Health and Human Svcs., 1993-01; mem. Pewaukee PTO, 1988-97; field instr. social work U. Wis., 1994—. Named One of the Outstanding Women in Am., Sioux Falls, 1985. Mem. NASW, Nat. Perinatal Social Worker Assn., Beta Sigma Phi (pres. local chpt. 1985-87, pres. Xi Beta Xi chpt. 1989-90), Alpha Xi Delta. Republican. Roman Catholic. Avocations: tennis, needlework, soccer, children's activities. Home: N29w22051 Kathryn Ct Waukesha WI 53186-8856 Office: 500 Riverview Ave Waukesha WI 53188-3632

RATHERT, PETER, urologist; b. Oldenburg, Germany, Oct. 9, 1938; m. Helga Kuehn. Dr.med., U. Goettingen, Germany, 1966; prof., 1979. Chief dept. urology Krankenhaus Dueren, 1977—. Co-author: Urinary Cytology, 3d edit., 1995, Klinische Urologie, 1992, 2d edit. 2000. Mem. German Urol. Assn. (historian 1988), Am. Urol. Assn. Office: Roonstr 30 52351 Düren Germany E-mail: urologie@krankenhaus-dueren.de.

RATHI, MANOHAR LAL, pediatrician, neonatologist; b. Beawar, Rajasthan, India, Dec. 25, 1933; came to U.S. 1969; s. Bagtawarmal and Sitadevi (Laddha) R.; m. Kamla Jajoo, Feb. 21, 1960; children: Sanjeev A., Rajeev. MBBS, Rajasthan U., 1961. Diplomate Am. Bd. Pediats., sub-bd. Neonatal Perinatal Medicine; lic. physician, N.Y., Ill., Calif. Resident house physician internal medicine Meml. Hosp., Darlington, U.K., 1963-64; resident sr. house physician pediatrics Gen. Hosp., Oldham, U.K., 1964-65; dir. perinatal medicine Christ Hosp. Perinatal Ctr., Oak Lawn, Ill., 1974-98, attending physician Oakl Lawn, 1974—2000; assoc. prof. pediatrics Rush Med. Coll., Chgo., 1979—; cons. obstetrician Christ Hosp., Oak Lawn, 1976—2000; cons. neonatologist Little Co. of Mary Hosp., Evergreen Park, Ill., 1972—98, Palos Cmty. Hosp., Palos Heights, 1978—2002; chmn. Midwest Neoped Assocs., Oak Brook, 1997—. Cons./lectr. in field. Contbr. articles to profl. jours.; editor: Clinical Aspects of Perinatal Medicine, 1984, Vol. I, 1985, Vol. II, 1986, Current Perinatology, 1989, Vol. II, 1990; editor with others: Perinatal Medicine Vol. I, 1978, Vol. I, 1980, Vol. II, 1982. Hummell Found. grantee, 1976-77, WyethLab grantee, 1977-78; recipient Physicians Recognition award AMA, 1971-74, 91-92, Outstanding New Citizen's award State of Ill., 1978, Asian Human Svcs. of Chgo., 1988, Nitric Oxide Study by Ohmeda, 1994-95. Fellow Am. Acad. Pediats. (perinatal sect., Ill. chpt. treas. 1994-96); mem. AMA, Chgo. Med. Soc., Ill. Med. Soc., Chgo. Pediat. Soc., Med. Soc. County of Kings Bklyn., N.Y. Acad. Scis., Am. Thoracic Soc., Soc. Critical Care Medicine. Republican. Hindu. Office: Midwest Neoped Assocs Ltd 900 Jorie Blvd Ste 186 Oak Brook IL 60523-3808

RATHINAVELU, MADI, manufacturing executive; b. Pondicherry, India, Dec. 18, 1958; came to U.S., 1982; s. Rathinavelu Viswanathan and Subbulakshmi Rathinavelu; m. Kaliani, Mar. 24, 1990. B in Engring. with honors, U. Madras, 1982; MS in Mech. Engring., Ohio U., 1984; MBA, Gannon U., 1994. Mechanical engr. Corry (Pa.) Mfg. Co., 1984-86, engring. mgr., 1986-87; v.p., gen. mgr. Corry (Pa.) Laser Technology, Inc., 1987—. Mem. Am. Soc. for Mechanical Engrs., Soc. Automotive Engrs., Am. Soc. Metals Internat. (exec. com. 1988-90). Avocations: astronomy, gardening, travel. Office: Corry Laser Technology Inc 1530 Enterprise Rd Corry PA 16407-8574

RATHJE, JAMES LEE, broker; b. Davenport, Iowa, Nov. 23, 1947; s. Gilbert L. and Wanda L. (Henning) R.; m. Karen L. Mangels, May 15, 1980. BBA with distinction, U. Iowa, 1970, MBA with distinction, 1972. Plant acct. Container Corp. Am., Wilmington, Del., 1972-73; portfolio mgr. Davenport Bank and Trust, 1973-76; investment broker Loewi and Co., Davenport, 1976-78; fin. cons. A.G. Edwards and Sons, Inc., 1978—. With USAR, 1970-76. Republican. Lutheran. Avocations: basketball, baseball, golf, cycling. Home: 3861 Parkdale Dr Bettendorf IA 52722-1974 E-mail: jamesrathje@agedwards.com.

RATHJENS, GEORGE WILLIAM, political scientist, educator; b. Fairbanks, Alaska, June 28, 1925; s. George William and Jennie (Hansen) R.; m. Lucy van Buttingha Wichers, Apr. 5, 1950; children: Jacqueline, Leslie, Peter. BS, Yale U., 1946; PhD, U. Calif., Berkeley, 1951. Instr. chemistry Columbia U., 1950-53; staff weapons systems evaluation group Dept. Def., 1953-58; research fellow Harvard U., 1958-59; staff spl. asst. to Pres. U.S. for sci. and tech., 1959-60; chief scientist Advanced Research Projects Agy., Dept. Def., 1961, dep. dir., 1961-62; dep. asst. dir. U.S. ACDA, 1962-64, spl. asst. to dir., 1964-65; dir. weapons systems evaluation div. Inst. Def. Analyses, 1965-68; prof. dept. polit. sci. MIT, 1968-96, prof. emeritus, 1996—; sec.-gen. Pugwash Confs. on Sci. and World Affairs, 1997—. Fellow Am. Acad. Arts and Scis.; mem. Fedn. Am. Scientists (sponsor), Inst. Strategic Studies. Office: Mass Inst Tech 77 Massachusetts Ave Cambridge MA 02139-4301 also: Pugwash Am Acad Arts/Scis 136 Irving St Cambridge MA 02138-1929 E-mail: pugwash@amacad.org., gwrathje@mit.edu.

RATHKE, DALE LAWRENCE, community organizer and financial analyst; b. Rangely, Colo., Mar. 16, 1950; s. Edmann Jacob and Cornelia Ruth (Ratliff) R. BA, Yale U., 1971; MA, Princeton U., 1974, ABD, 1977. Dir. internal ops. Assn. of Cmty. Orgns. for Reform Now (ACORN), New Orleans, 1977—; CFO Citizens' Cons. Inc., 1979—; fin. dir. ACORN Housing Corp., 1984—, Affiliated Media Found. Movement, 1979—. Sec.-treas. Broad St. Corp., New Orleans, 1986—, Elysian Fields Corp., New Orleans, 1986—, Greenwell Springs Corp., New Orleans, 1989—, ACORN Fund, Inc., New Orleans, 1991—, ACORN Beneficial Assn., Inc., New Orleans, 1991—, Houston Orgn. and Support Ctr., 1992—, St. Louis Orgn. and Support Ctr., 1992—. Pres. Assn. for Rights of Citizens, New Orleans, 1980—, ACORN Cultural Trust, Inc., 1988—; active Overture to Cultural Season, 1987—, treas., 1999—; active New Orleans Mus. Art, 1990—; dirs., assoc. treas. Raintree Svcs., Inc., 1998—, Sante Fe Opera Guild, 1995—, Metrolitan Opera Guild, 1998—. Mem. Yale Club of N.Y.C., Princeton Club of N.Y.C., Metairie County Club. Avocations: 18th century French furniture, English country homes. Office: ACORN 1024 Elysian Fields Ave New Orleans LA 70117-8454

RATHKE, SHEILA WELLS, strategic and marketing consultant; b. Columbia, S.C., Aug. 9, 1943; d. Walter John and Betty Marie (McLaughlin) Wells; m. David Bray Rathke, Sept. 1966 (dec. 1997); 1 child, Erinn Michele. BA summa cum laude, U. Pitts., 1976, postgrad., 1976-77. Loan coord. Equibank, Pitts., 1961-65; office mgr. U.S. Steel Corp., 1966-70; various account and mgmt. positions Burson-Marsteller, 1977-87, exec. v.p., gen. mgr., 1987-94, CEO Can. ops. Toronto, Montreal, Ottawa, Vancouver, 1994-95; sr. v.p., dir. corp. devel. Young and Rubicam, Inc., N.Y.C., 1995-99, COO, 1999-2000; asst. provost strategic and program devel. U. Pitts., 2001—. Instr. Slippery Rock Coll., Pitts., 1984-85; adviser Exec. Report Mag., Pitts., 1986-88, A Better Chance, N.Y.C., 1996-2000, N.Y. Philharm., 1997-99. Trustee U. Pitts., 1976-80, mem. alumni bd. dirs., 1990-94; trustee Robert Morris Coll., 1992-95; bd. dirs. Vocat. Rehab. Ctr., 1987-93, Freewheelers, 1989-92, Pitts. Hist. Soc., River City Brass Band. Named Disting. Alumnus, U. Pitts., 1992, Legacy Laureate, 2000. Mem. Female Execs. Am., Am. Assn. Advt. Agys. (chair ea. region 1994-95), Pitts. Advt. Club (bd. dirs. 1988-91, pres. 1990), Alpha Sigma Lambda (charter). Avocations: skiing, reading, gardening, traveling, photography. Home: 1819 Sarah St Apt 2 Pittsburgh PA 15203 Office: U Pitts Cathedral of Learning Pittsburgh PA 15260- E-mail: sheilarathke@msn.com.

RATHKOPF, DAREN ANTHONY, lawyer; b. Lynbrook, N.Y., May 12, 1933; s. Arden Herman and Florence Marie (Gortikov) R.; m. Mira Torgersen, Mar. 30, 1963; children: Ann, Erika. BA, Columbia U., 1955, LLB, 1958. Bar: N.Y. 1958, U.S. Dist. Ct. (ea., so. dists.) N.Y. 1962. Assoc. Mendes & Mount, N.Y.C., 1961-62, Rathkopf & Rathkopf, N.Y.C., 1962-66, ptnr. Glen Cove, N.Y., 1966-81, Payne, Wood & Littlejohn, Glen Cove and Melville, 1982-98, of counsel Melville, Bridgehampton, Locust Vly, N.Y., 1999-2001, Farrell Fritz, P.C., Uniondale, Melville, N.Y., Bridghampton, Locust Valley, 2001—. Author: (with others) The Law of Zoning and Planning, 4th edit., 1977. Mem. N.Y. State Bar Assn., Nassau County Bar Assn. Home: 149 Turkey Ln Cold Spring Harbor NY 11724-1712 Office: Farrell Fritz PC 290 Broadhollow Rd Melville NY 11747-4818 E-mail: drathkopf@aol.com.

RATHMAN, WILLIAM ERNEST, lawyer, minister; b. Middletown, Ohio, Jan. 10, 1927; s. Ernest Daniel and Marguerite (Sebald) R.; m. Constance Schedler, Nov. 28, 1958; children: Marchie, William E. Jr. Grad., Phillips Exeter Acad., 1944; BA, Kenyon Coll., 1948; postgrad., Harvard U., 1950, Ohio State U. Coll. of Law, 1951, United Theol. Seminary, Dayton, Ohio, 1975. Bar: Ohio 1952; ordained to ministry Episc. Ch., 1975. Pvt. practice law, Middletown, Ohio, 1952-78; sr. ptnr. Rathman, Elliott & Boyd, 1979-84, Rathman, Combs, Schaefer, Valen & Kaup, Middletown, 1985-88, Rathman, Combs, Schaefer & Kaup, Middletown, 1989-95. Spl. counsel to County of Butler, 1956-64, City of Middletown, 1965-66, Ohio Atty. Gen., 1967-69; acting judge Middletown Mcpl. Ct., 1969-74. Pres. Middletown Community Found., 1972-76, Middletown Chamber Found., 1977-80, Butler County Park Commn., 1986-90; trustee-at-large Ohio Found. of Ind. Colls., Columbus, 1972-90; trustee, mem. exec. com. Middletown United Way, 1963-90; trustee Middleton Req. Hosp. Found., 1986-90; adv. bd. Middletown campus Miami U., 1984-90. With USN, 1944-46, capt. USAF, 1959, comdr. Am. Legion, 1965. Named Exec. Yr., Middletown chpt. Nat. Secs. Assn., 1969; recipient Outstanding Community Svc. award Middletown post Am. Legion, 1975, Outstanding Svc. award Parstoral Counselling Svc., 1983, Vol. of Yr. award Middletown Area United Way, 1986. Fellow Am. Coll. Trust and Estate Counsel; mem. ABA (estate tax com. 1966-69), Ohio Bar Assn. (coun. del. 1980-93), Butler County Bar Assn. (pres. 1980), Middletown Bar Assn. (pres. 1967), Fed. Bar Assn. (pres. Cin. chpt. 1975), Ohio State Bar Found. (trustee 1992-96, Ohio Supreme Ct. bd. commrs. on grievances and discipline 1996-99), Browns Run Country Club, Masons (Jefferson lodge, master 1959-60), Scottish Rite Valley of Cin. (treas. 1986, chmn. bd. 1990, 33d degree mason 1988—). Episcopalian. Home: 501 Thornhill Ln Middletown OH 45042-3750 also: 1924 S Beach Club Hilton Head Island SC 29928-3750 E-mail: crathman@aol.com.

RATHMANN, PEGGY, author, illustrator; b. St. Paul; BA in Psychology, U. Minn.; student, Am. Acad. Chgo., Atelier Lack, Mpls., Otis Parsons Sch. Design, L.A. Author: Ruby the Copycat (Most Promising New Author Cuffie award Pubs. Weekly 1991), Good Night, Gorilla (ALA Notable Children's Book 1994), Officer Buckle and Gloria (Caldecott medal 1996); illustrator: Bootsie Barker Bites, 1992. Office: Penguin Putnam Inc 345 Hudson St Fl 15 New York NY 10014-4502*

RATHNAM, LINCOLN YESU, investment company executive; b. Westfield, Mass., May 5, 1949; s. Punuri Yesu and Virginia Bertha (Libby) R.; m. Deborah Parrish Ford, Sept. 5, 981; children: Lincoln Edward, Sarah Virginia, Hope Alexandra. AB, Dartmouth Coll., 1971; DPhil, Oxford U., 1976. Chartered fin. analyst. Investment analyst CIGNA Corp., Bloomfield, Conn., 1979-84, Scudder, Stevens & Clark, Inc., Boston, 1984-96, mng. dir. Latin Am. group, 1989—; chmn. Schooner Asset Mgmt. Co., 1996-98; mng. dir. Vistech Corp., 1998—. Contbr. articles on internat. investing to profl. jours. Mem. Assn. Investment Mgmt. and Rsch., Boston Security Analysts Soc. Avocation: fishing.

RATHORE, ANURAG SINGH, chemical engineer; b. Bareilly, India, Apr. 25, 1973; came to U.S., 1994; p. Hamir Singh and Kamini Rathore; m. Bhawana Niranjan, Nov. 16, 1976. B of Tech. in Chem. Engring., Indian Inst. Tech., New Delhi, 1994; MSChemE, Yale U., 1995, PhD in Chem. Engring., 1999. Rsch. asst. Yale U., 1994-99; sr. process engr. Pharmacia, Chesterfield, Mo., 1999—. Contbr. articles to profl. jours. Mem. ACS, Indian Soc. Analytical Chemists, Capillary Electrophoresis Soc. New Eng. (mem. tech. bd. 1998—). Avocations: soccer, movies, reading. Home: 1735 Ardmore Creek Dr #4 Chesterfield MO 63017 Office: Pharmacia Co GG3K 700 Chesterfield Pkwy W Chesterfield MO 63017-1700

RATHORE, NAEEM GUL, retired United Nations official; b. Lahore, Punjab, Pakistan, Nov. 21, 1931; arrived in country, 1950; s. Jalaluddin and Zohra (Butt) R.; m. Carol Salima, Sept. 19, 1951; 1 child, Amna Elona. BS, Mich. U., 1952; MA in Polit. Sci., Columbia U., 1955, PhD in Internat. Affairs, 1965. Dir. personnel and adminstrn. UNRWA, Beirut, 1975-76; exec. sec. Internat. Civil Svc. Commn. UN, N.Y.C., 1980-81, sec. First Com., 1980-84, asst. dir. Office Under-Sec. Gen./Dept. Polit. Affairs, 1984-87, chief Div. of Palestinian Rights, 1987-89; spl. advisor, spkr. Punjab Assembly, Pakistan, 1994-95; coord. Pakistan Expatriates in UN Systems UN, N.Y.C., 1992-93, adviser to the Pakistan amb., and permanent rep. of Pakistan, 1994—; corporator Emerson Hosp., Concord, Mass., 1996—. Lectr. Pakistan studies Near and Middle East Inst., Columbia U., N.Y., 1954-55; prof., head dept. internat. affairs U. Islamabad, 1974; active numerous UN coms., panels and task forces with Office of Human Resources Mgmt., UN, including chmn. N.Y. Gen. Svc. Classification Appeals and Rev. Com., 1986-92; pres. FICSA, 1971-74; chmn. UN staff com., 1971-74; active External Exam. in Polit. Affairs (France, Japan, others); counselor, Minuteman Regional Program, Serving Health Info. Needs of Elders, Mass. Exec. Office of Elder Affairs, 1996—; mem. adv. bd. Maynard (Mass.) Adult Learning Ctr., 1997-98; discussion leader Concord Current Affairs Group, 1997—; discussant Great Decisions Coun. on Aging Town of Concord, 1997— advisor spl. projects, 1999—; advisor The Pakistani-Am. Congr., 1999—; del. Overseas Pakistani's Conv., Islamabad, Pakistan, 1999, Russian-Am. Seminar, Ufa, Bashkortostan, 1999; prin. advisor Pakistan Millieneum, 2000—. Author: In Defense of of the International Civil Service: Statements and Submission, 1974, United Nations Secretariat: Problems and Prospects, 1974, other publs. in field; contbr. articles to profl. jours. Chmn. internat. svc. projects Rotary Club Concord; adv. Carlisle Cmty. Chest, 2001—. Mem. Fedn. of Internat. Civil Svcs. (pres. 1971-74), Rotary Club Concord (chmn. internat. projects com.). Moslem. Avocations: reading, writing newspaper columns, horseback riding, scuba diving, swimming. Home: 1305 Elm St Concord MA 01742-2103 Fax: (978) 369-9548. E-mail: nrathore@aol.com.

RATHORE, UMA PANDEY, utilities executive; b. Mar. 5, 1950; d. O Nath and R Devi Pandey; m. Ram N.S. Rathore, Dec. 18, 1978; children: Dinesh, Rana. BS, Kanpur U., 1967, MS, 1969. Adviser Consul Gen. of Iceland to India, 1976-85; v.p. Nevaid Cons., 1974-82; with North Jersey Utilities, Mount Freedom, N.J., 1983—, pres. Sr. ptnr. Translantic Cons.; founder Maxim Imports, 1994—; ind. mgmt. cons.; bd. dirs. Revel Inc., N.Y. Mem. ethics bd. Randolph Twp., N.J., 1986-91, county and state rep. Shongum Sch. PTA, 1989—, mem. multicultural com., 1993-94; membership chmn. LWV, 1979-81, com. person Dem. dist. 3 Randolph Twp., 1992, 94, mem. ethics com., 1994, mem. com., 1995; mem. drug action com. Randolph Twp., 1994, 95, 96—; mem. Dem. task force N.J. Women's Polit. Caucus, 1994; county and state rep. Randolph Intermediate Sch. PTA, 1993-94, bd. edn. rep., 1996—; mem. PTA coun. Randolph Twp. Schs.; legis. chair Morris County Coun. PTA, 1997—, counselor Region I; mem. Morris Mus., Macculloch Hall, Frelinghuysen Arboretum; mem. Ctr. for Study of Presidency, 1997; mem. DBE, 1999. Mem. Internat. Platform Assn., Dau. Brit. Empire, Acad. Polit. Sci., Kiwanis Club Smithsonian, Libr. of Congress, Fgn. Policy Assn., N.Y. Acad. Scis., Nat. Trust Hist. Preservation, Nat. Wildlife Fedn. Democrat. Avocations: reading, jogging, hiking, mountaineering. Home and Office: 3 Hickory Pl Randolph NJ 07869-4528

RATHOUR, RAJENDRA SINGH, internist; b. Delhi, India; came to U.S., 1984; MB BChir, LLRM Med. Coll., 1978. Cert. in internal medicine. Intern Sinai Samaritan Med. Ctr., Milw., 1988-90; resident in internal medicine VA Med. Ctr., Asheville, N.C., 1990-92; fellow in endocrinology U. Wis. Hosp., Madison, 1986; staff St. Francis Hosp., Milw., 1992—, West Allis Meml. Hosp., 1996—, St Luke's Hosp., 1996—. Mem. ACP. Office: 3201 S 16th St Ste 1000 Milwaukee WI 53215-4532

RATHWELL, PETER JOHN, lawyer; b. Windsor, Ont., Can., Aug. 20, 1943; came to U.S., 1947; s. Harold Wilfred and Jean Isabel (Lucas) R.; m. Ann Wickstrom Williams, Sept. 10, 1977; 1 child, James Michael BA, U. Ariz., 1965, JD, 1968. Bar: Ariz. 1968. Assoc. Boettcher, Crowder & Schoolitz, Scottsdale, Ariz., 1972-73; ptnr. Snell & Wilmer, Phoenix, 1973—. Seminar lectr. Nat. Bus. Inst. , Inc., 1987—90, Ariz. Ann. Bankruptcy Symposium, 1995, 97, Am. Agri. Lawyers Assn., 1997, 99, Lormans Bus. Seminars, 2000—, Sterlin Edn. Sems., 2001—. Mem. exec. com. Jr. Achievement Ariz., Phoenix, 1980-92, 2000—, bd. advisors, 1980—; chmn. scholarship fund St. Mary H.S., 1982-91; mem., chmn. Phoenix Parks Bd., 1982-87; trustee Orme Sch., 1991—, chair devel. com., 1994—; treas., trustee Smith Scholarship Trust U. Ariz. Law Sch., 1985—. Capt. JAGC, USAF, 1969-72. Fellow State Bar Ariz. Found. (founding mem.), Maricopa County Bar Found. (founding mem.); mem. Am. Bankruptcy Inst., Ariz. Bar Assn. (bar counsel 1982-87, 97, chmn. discipline hearing com. 1987-93, mem. bankruptcy sect.), S.W. Bankruptcy Conf. (bd. advisors 1995—), Maricopa County Bar Assn. (seminar lectr. 1987), Comml. Law League Am., Phoenix Zoo Wildest Club in Town (founding mem. 1972). Republican. Avocations: fishing, raising cattle. Home: 4523 E Mountain View Rd Phoenix AZ 85028-5213 Office: Snell & Wilmer 1 Arizona Ctr Phoenix AZ 85004

RATI, ROBERT DEAN, data processing executive; b. Pittsburg, Kans., Jan. 8, 1939; s. Steve Julius Rati and Dorothy Bill (Rodebush) McWilliams; m. Margaret Fort Henry, June 7, 1969; children: Susan Margaret, Robert Henry. BA, U. Kans., 1961; MA, Northeastern U., Boston, 1970; MBA, Columbia U., 1973. Systems engr. IBM Corp., Boston, 1965-72; mgr. mgmt. services Arthur Young and Co., N.Y.C., 1973-75; mgr. client systems Touche Ross and Co., 1975-76; mgr. systems and programs Walker Mfg. div. Tenneco, Racine, Wis., 1976-78; mgr. data processing Schwitzer div. Household Internat., Indpls., 1979-87; mgr. mgmt. info. systems Nat. Machinery Co., Tiffin, Ohio, 1988-90; pres. Dunhill Profl. Search of Carmel (Ind.), 1990-97; mgr. Muncie MIS Power Transformer div. Asea Brown Boveri, Muncie, Ind., 1991-94; dir. info. svcs. State Lottery Commn. Ind., Indpls., 1995-97; mgmt. cons. Aerotek-Maxim Group, 1998-2000; project mgr. corp. info. tech. SBC-Ameritech, 2000—. Contbr. articles to fraternal orgs. publs. Mem. Rep. Com., Ramsey, N.J., 1972-74; treas. Rep. Club Ramsey, 1972-75; vice chmn. Swimming Pool Commn., Ramsey, 1972-74; bd. dirs., exec. com. Near Eastside Multi-Svc. Ctr., Indpls., 1984-87; fin. com. Carmel (Ind.) United Meth. Ch., 1984-87, adminstrv. bd., 1987-90. Lt. (j.g.) USN, 1961-64. Recipient Regional Mgrs. award, IBM Corp., 1967. Mem. SAR (pres. 1979), Soc. Ind. Pioneers (pres. 1996-98), Huguenot Soc. Ind. (pres. 1985-89), S.R. in State of Ill. (pres. 1980-82), Ind. Soc. Colonial Wars (gov. 1995-98), Gen. Soc. Sons of the Revolution (chmn. awards com. 1983-91, Gen. Pres. Commendation award 1985, 91), Pi Mu Epsilon. Republican. Avocations: genealogy, home computer. Home: 4919 Regency Pl Carmel IN 46033-5959 Office: SBC Ameritech 220 N Meridian St Rm 652 Indianapolis IN 46204

RATIU, INDREI STEPHEN PILKINGTON, management consultant; b. London, July 12, 1946; s. Ion Augustin Nicolae and Elisabeth Blanche (Pilkington) R.; m. Ioana Georgescu, Sept. 28, 1974 (div. 1991); 1 child, Alexandru; m. Ana Maria da Silva Byrd, July 18, 1998. MA, Cambridge (Eng.) U., 1969; MBA, European Inst. Bus. Adminstrn. (INSEAD), Fontainebleau, France, 1970. Scriptwriter BBC, London, 1967-69; coord. exec. devel. programs INSEAD, 1971-73, dir. ednl. tech., 1973-76; researcher cross-cultural learning London Bus. Sch., 1976-78; ind. mgmt. cons. personal devel. Paris, 1979-82; mng. ptnr. ICM, 1983-88; dir., cons. Regent House Properties, London, 1976—2000. Trustee Rainford Trust, Ratiu Family Found., Pro Patrimonio-Romanian Heritage Found. Co-author: Leaders sans Frontieres, 1988, The Great Challenge: An International Anthology of Political Cartoons, 1999; editor spl. issue on multicultural mgmt. devel. Jour. Mgmt. Devel., 1987. Avocations: healing, counseling. Home and Office: 8387 E Indian School Rd Scottsdale AZ 85251 E-mail: indrei@compuserve.com

RATKOWSKI, DONALD J. mechanical engineer, consultant; b. Cleve., July 29, 1938; m. Joyce Ellen Kotlarczyk, July 15, 1961; children: Rhonda, Tamyra, Cheryl, Randall. Student, Ariz. State U.; AAS, Alliance Coll., 1959, DSc (hon.), 1986. Sr. project engr. semiconductor products div. Motorola, 1960-70, 75-77; v.p. engring. Danker & Wohlk, 1970-75; founder, pres. Paragon Optical Inc., 1976-90; exec. v.p. Pilkinton Vision Care, 1987-90, cons., 1990-91; pres. DJR Resources Inc., Paradise Valley, Ariz., 1990—. Mem. adv. bd. Am. Sec. Coun., 1988-89; mem. steering com. Optometry Coll., Marcinkowski Acad. Medicine, Poland, 1989-91; founder Rigid Gas Permeable Lens Inst., 1985; speaker Nat. Contact Lens Examiners, 1984-91. Contbr. articles to profl. jours.; patentee in field. Sustaining mem. Rep. Nat. Com., 1983-90; mem. U.S. Congl. Adv. Bd., 1990. Recipient Alumnus of Yr. award Alliance Coll., 1985. Mem. Opticians Assn. Am. (assoc. mem. adv. coun. 1987-88), Contact Lens Soc. Am. (bd. dirs. 1986-88, founder scholarship program 1988, hon. chmn. steering com. edn. fund 1989-91), Contact Lens Mfrs. Assn. chmn. external communication com. 1981-90, bd. dirs. 1982-84, Trailblazer award 1987, program chmn. 1989-90, Leonardo DaVinci award 1990), Ariz. Soc. Plastic Engrs. bd. dirs. 1976-78, 83, v.p. 1980-81, pres. 1981-82), Sigma Tau Gamma (Outstanding Alumni award 1985). Home and Office: DJR Resources Inc 8105 N 47th St Paradise Valley AZ 85253

RATLIFF, CHARLES EDWARD, JR. economics educator; b. Morven, N.C., Oct. 13, 1926; s. Charles Edward and Mary Katherine (Liles) R.; m. Mary Virginia Heilig, Dec. 8, 1945 (dec. Oct. 2000); children: Alice Ann, Katherine Virginia, John Charles. BS, Davidson Coll., 1947; AM, Duke U., 1951, PhD, 1955; postgrad., U. N.C., Harvard, Columbia. Instr. econs. and bus. Davidson Coll., 1947-48, asst. prof., 1948-49; scholar econs. Duke, 1949-51; faculty Davidson (N.C.) Coll., 1951-60, prof., 1960—, chmn. dept. econs., 1966-83, Charles A. Dana prof., 1967-77, William R. Kenan prof., 1977-92, Kenan prof. emeritus, 1992—; prof. econs. Forman Christian Coll., Lahore, Pakistan, 1963-66, 69-70. Summer vis. prof. U. N.C. at Charlotte, 1958, 60, Appalachian State U., 1962, Punjab U., Pakistan, 1963-64, Kinnaird Coll., Pakistan, 1965, Fin. Svcs. Acad., Pakistan, 1966, NDEA Inst. in Asian History, 1968; lectr. U.S. Cultural Affairs Office, East and West Pakistan, 1969-70. Author: Interstate Apportionment of Business Income for State Income Tax Purposes, 1962, A World Development Fund, 1987, Economics at Davidson: A Sesquicentennial History, 1987; co-author textbooks; contbg. author: Dictionary of the Social Sciences, 1964, Distinguished Teachers on Effective Teaching, 1986, Those Who Teach, 1988, Britain-USA: A Survey in Key Words, 1991; mem. editorial bd. Growth and Change: A Journal of Urban and Regional Policy, 1993-99; contbr. articles to profl. jours. Mem. Mayor's Com. on Affordable Housing, Davidson, 1996-97, Mayor's Com. Comty. Rels., Davidson, 1973-80, chmn., 1973-78; mem. Mecklenburg County Housing and Devel. Commn., 1975-81; mem. exec. com. Mecklenburg Dem. Com., 1967-69, precinct com., 1967-69, 72-74, 89-99, issues com., 1979-99, nat. bd. dirs. Rural Advancement Fund Nat. Sharecroppers Fund, Inc., 1978-94, exec. com., 1981-94, treas., 1981-94; mem. Mecklenburg County Comty. and Rural Devel. Exec. Com., 1981-99; bd. dirs. Bread for the World, Inc., 1983-84, Pines Retirement Comty., 1990-99, Crisis Assistance Ministry, 1992-96, Davidson Coll. Devel. Corp., 1992-95, Our Towns Habitat for Humanity, 1996-98, Davidson Coll. Alumni Assn., 1997-99, Davidson Affordable Housing Coalition, 1997-99; bd. advisors Mecklenburg Ministries, 1992-99, Drs. for Global Health, 1996—; mem. planning com. Fla. Presbyn. Homes, Inc., 2000—, spiritual life com., 2000—, fine arts com, 2001—. With USN, 1944-46. Rsch. grant Ford Found., 1960-61, Fulbright-Hays grant, 1973; Rsch. fellow Inter-Univ. Com. Econ. Rsch. on South, 1960-61; recipient Thomas Jefferson award Davidson Coll., 1972, Gold medalist Prof. of Yr. award Coun. Advancement and Support of Edn., 1985, Tchg. Excellence and Campus Leadership award Sear Roebuck Found., 1991, Hunter-Hamilton Love of Tchr. award, 1992. Mem. AAUP, So. Econ. Assn. (exec. com. 1961-63, v.p. 1975-76, N.C. corr. So. Econ. Jour.), Am. Econ. Assn., So. Fin. Assn. (exec. com. 1966-68), Nat. Tax Assn. (chmn. interstate allocation and apportionment of bus. income com. 1972-74), Assn. Asian Studies, Fulbright Alumni Assn., Old Catawba Soc., Phi Beta Kappa, Omicron Delta Kappa (Teaching award 1991). Home: 29 Lake Hunter Dr Lakeland FL 33803-1288 E-mail: ceratliff@email.msn.com.

RATLIFF, EVA RACHEL, elementary education educator; b. Ada, Mich., Mar. 9, 1944; d. Vernon C. and Edith Rachel (Coffey) Loew; m. Wallace Francis Ratliff, July 27, 1968; children: Ronald, Shelia. BA, Ind. Wesleyan U., 1967; postgrad., East Tenn. State U., 1978, U. Tenn., 1977, 82, 85, 87; MA, Columbia U., 1992. Cert. tchr. music 1-12, classroom 1-9. Tchr. music N. Judson (Ind.)-San Pierre Schs., 1967-68, Mississnewa Community Schs., Gas City, Ind., 1968-69, Mercer County Schs., Harrodsburg, Ky., 1969-73; classroom tchr. Hawkins County Schs., Rogersville, Tenn., 1977-80, Knox County Schs., Knoxville, 1980—. Twenty-First Century Classrm. Tchr. of Tenn., 1994—; del. Tenn. Edn. Assn., Nashville, 1989-90. Mem. Knoxville Choral Soc., 1986—. Mem. Knox County Edn. Assn., Rotary Club of Knoxville (Outstanding Tchr. of Yr. 2000). Avocations: doll making, crocheting, church choir, crafts. Home: 8016 Wilnoty Dr Knoxville TN 37931-3453 Office: Sarah Moore Greene Magnet Tech Acad 3001 Brooks Rd Knoxville TN 37914-6270 E-mail: errat.@aol.com.

RATLIFF, JAMES CONWAY, investor, consultant; b. Evanston, Ill., Mar. 28, 1940; s. Harold Sugart and Marjorie (Elmore) R. BA, Mich. State U., 1967. Dir. food & beverage ops. Detroit Hilton, 1970-71; dir. food & beverage purchasing Hilton Hotels Corp., N.Y.C., 1972-77, corp. dir. procurement Beverly Hills, Calif., 1977-97; pres., owner Ratliff & Assocs., 1998—. Bd. dirs. Am. Inst. Food Distbn., Fair Lawn, N.J., 1985-96, treas., 1989-90, vice chmn., 1991-92, chmn., 1994-95; instr. Calif. State Poly. U., Pomona, 1987, 88. With U.S. Army, 1963-65. Mem. Food Svc. Purchasing Assn. Can. (hon.), Produce Mktg. Assn. (bd. dirs. 1986-88, v.p. 1989-90, sec.-treas. 1991, chmn. elect 1992, chmn. 1993, chmn. exec. com. 1994), Product Mktg. Assn. (chmn. foodsvc. divsn. 1989-90, bd. dirs. foodsvc. divsn. 1985-88), Nat. Restaurant Assn. Foodsvc. Purchasing Mgrs. (bd. dirs. 1977-81, chmn. 1981-83), Pacific Corinthian Yacht Club. Republican. Methodist. Avocation: tennis. Office: 6947 W 85th Pl Los Angeles CA 90045-2604

RATLIFF, JANICE KAY, legal administrator; b. Odessa, Tex., Aug. 11, 1949; d. Boyce Emery and Fay LaNell (Russell) Albert; m. Richard Wayne Ratliff, May 4, 1974; children: Ryan, Courtney, Ashlee. BS in Secondary Edn., Tex. Tech U., 1971. Cert. secondary tchr., Tex. Recreation counselor Wichita Falls (Tex.) Parks and Recreation Dept., 1967, Austin (Tex.) Parks and Recreation Dept., 1969; rehab. technician Tex. Rehab. Commn., Austin, 1971-76; co-owner, mgr. Locker Room, sporting goods store, Monahans, Tex., 1984-88; contract worker Calame, Linebarger & Graham, Odessa, 1983-88; area mgr., paralegal Linebarger Heard Goggan Blair Graham Peña and Sampson LLP, 1988—2001. Pres. Gifted and Talented Parents Orgn., Monahans, 1986; mem. local parent/tchr. orgn. Tatom Life; v.p. Band Booster Club, 1994-96, pres. 1997-98; Sunday sch. tchr. Ch. of Christ; vol. instr. Jr. Achievement, Odessa, Tex., 1998. Recipient dist. 1st place award for poetry Tex. Fedn. Women's Clubs, 1987. Mem. Tex. Assn. Assessing Officers (v.p. Permian Basin chpt. 1994-96, treas. 1999-2000), Rotary Internat. (bd. dirs. 1994-96, program chmn. 1994-95, sec. 1996-97, Paul Harris fellow), Wednesday Study Club (pres. 1986-88). Republican. Avocations: reading, travel, cooking, crafts. Home: 1119 Heritage Burkburnett TX 76354

RATLIFF, LOUIS JACKSON, JR. mathematics educator; b. Cedar Rapids, Iowa, Sept. 1, 1931; s. Louis Jackson and Ruth Sara (Sidlinger) R.; m. Georgia Lee Smith, May 9, 1996. BA, State U. Iowa, 1953, MA, 1958, PhD, 1961. Lectr. Ind. U., Bloomington, 1961-63, U. Calif., Riverside, 1963-64, asst. prof. math., 1964-67, assoc. prof., 1967-69, prof., 1969—. Author: Chain Conjectures in Ring Theory, 1978; assoc. editor Procs. of AMS, 1987-92, Comm. in Algebra, 1990-95; contbr. articles to profl. jours. 1st lt. USAF, 1953-57. NSF fellow, 1960-62, grantee, 1965-69, 71-88; recipient Disting. Teaching award, U. Calif.-Riverside, 1983. Mem. Am. Math. Soc., Phi Beta Kappa. Democrat. Seventh Day Adventist. Home: 22344 San Joaquin Dr W Sun City CA 92587-7849 Office: U Calif Dept Math Riverside CA 92521-0001 E-mail: ratliff@math.ucr.edu.

RATLIFF, ROBERT BARNS, JR. mechanical engineer; b. Narrows, Va., Oct. 24, 1950; s. Robert Barns and Rosemary (Simpson) R.; m. Marsha Meredith, Aug. 19, 1972; children: Lori Ann, Robert Barns III, Heather Michelle. BSME, Va. Tech, 1973. Registered profl. engr., N.C. Distbn. engr. Duke Power Co., Winston-Salem, N.C., 1973-76, distbn. svc. engr. Charlotte, 1976-77, supt. engring. Lenoir, 1977-79; gen. mgr. Pike Elec., Inc., Mt. Airy, 1979-86, asst. v.p., 1986-90, v.p., 1990-91, exec. v.p., 1991—. Mem. exec. coun. Old Hickory Coun. of Boy Scouts, Winston-Salem, 1985; mem. C. of C., Mt. Airy, 1992; mem. adminstrv. bd. Ctrl. United Meth. Ch., Mt. Airy, 1992; bd. dirs. N.C. FREE, John Locke Found. Mem. NSPE, Profl. Engrs. N.C., Internat. Soc. Arboriculture, Internat. Platform Soc., Mt. Airy C. of C. Methodist. Office: Pike Elec Inc PO Box 868 Mount Airy NC 27030-0868

RATLIFF, THOMAS ASBURY, JR. retired engineer; b. Phila., May 5, 1919; s. Thomas Asbury and Edna Dorothy (Overman) R.; m. Lucy Lila Graydon, Aug. 15, 1942; children: Deborah Ratliff Miller, Anne Ratliff Naberhaus. Registered profl. engr., Calif. Test technician GE, Cin., 1951; quality engr. Am. Standard Corp., 1951-54, asst. dir. rsch., 1956-58; chief inspector Gruen Watch Co., 1954-58; cons. Hyde Engring. Co., 1958-60, Badgett & Smith, Inc., Cin., 1963-67; sales mgr. Lehmann Corp., 1960-63; purchasing mgr. Access Corp., 1967-70; pres. Ratliff & Assoc., Inc., 1970-96; ret. Adj. prof. engring. U. Cin., 1998-2000. Author: Basic Statistics for Lab Workers, 1992, The Laboratory Quality Assurance System, 1993. Col. U.S. Army, 1940-72. Fellow Am. Soc. for Quality (various coms.). Republican. Mem. Soc. Of Friends. Avocation: collecting model cannons. Home: 755 Greenville Ave Cincinnati OH 45246-4608

RATLIFF, WILLIAM, lieutenant governor, civil engineer; b. Aug. 16, 1936; BS in Civil Engring., U. Tex., 1960. City mgr., Copperas Cove, Tex.; pvt. practice civil engr. Mt. Pleasant; mem. Tex. Senate Dist. 1, 1989—2000, chair fin. com., mem. edn. com., mem. adminstrn. com.; mem. internat. rels., trade and tech. com., others; lt. gov. of Texas, 2000—. Pres. Mt. Pleasant Indsl. Found.; mem. exec. com. N.E. Tex. Econ. Devel. Dist., Inc.; Sunday sch. tchr., lay reader, chair fin. com., bd. trustees Tennison Meml. United Meth. Ch. Sgt. USAR. Mem. Am. Consulting Engrs. Coun. (past pres.). Republican. Office: PO Box 12068 Austin TX 78711-2068*

RATNATHICAM, WIJAYAN SENTHINATHAN, surgeon; b. Colombo, Sri Lanka, 1946; MB, BS, Madras U., Vellore, India, 1972. Diplomate Am. Bd. Surgery. Resident in surgery Westchester County Med. Ctr., Valhalla, NY, 1975—79; pvt. practice Peeksill, 1979—. Dir. trauma, Hudson Valley Hosp., Peekskill. Fellow ACS; mem. Soc. Am. Gastrointestinal Endoscopic Surgeons, Med. Soc. State of N.Y. Office: 1985 Crompond Rd Cortlandt Manor NY 10567-4146

RATNER, BUDDY DENNIS, bioengineer, educator; b. Bklyn., Jan. 19, 1947; s. Philip and Ruth Ratner; m. Cheryl Cromer; 1 child, Daniel Martin. BS in Chemistry, Bklyn. Coll., 1967; PhD in Polymer Chemistry, Polytech. Inst. Bklyn., 1972. Fellow U. Wash., Seattle, 1972-73, from rsch. assoc. to assoc. prof., 1973-86, prof., 1986—. Wash. Rsch. Found. Endowed Prof. Bioengring., 2001—. Dir. U. Wash. Engineered Biomaterials NSF Engring. Ctr.; founder Asemblon, Inc. Editor: Surface Characterization of Biomaterials, 1989, Plasmas and Polymers, 1994-99, Biomaterials Science: An Introduction to Materials in Medicine, 1996, Characterization of Polymeric Biomaterials, 1997; mem. editl. bds. 9 jours. and book series; editor Jour. Undergrad. Rsch. in Bioengring., 1998—; contbr. over 300 articles to profl. jours. Recipient Faculty Achievement/Outstanding Rsch. award Burlington Resources Found., 1990, Perkin Elmer Phys. Electronics award for excellence in surface sci. Fellow Internat. Acad. Med. and Biol. Engring., Am. Inst. Med. Biol. Engring. (founder, pres. 2002-), Am. Vacuum Soc.; mem. AAAS, AIChE (C.M.A. Stine award 1998), Nat. Acad. Engring., Am. Chem. Soc., Internat. Soc. Contact Lens Rsch., Materials Rsch. Soc., Soc. for Biomaterials (pres. 1991-92, Clemson award 1989, fellow 1994), Biomed. Engring. Soc. Achievements include 15 patents in field. Office: U Wash Dept Bioengring PO Box 351720 Seattle WA 98195-1720 E-mail: ratner@uweb.engr.washington.edu.

RATNER, CARL JOSEPH, theater director; b. Memphis, Sept. 17, 1957; MusB, Oberlin Conservatory of Music, 1980. Intern Juilliard Sch., N.Y.C., 1980-81, N.Y.C. Opera, 1981-82; asst. dir. Lyric Opera Chgo., 1982-84; prodn. asst. San Francisco Opera, 1985-86; asst. dir. Metropolitan Opera, N.Y.C., 1989-90; artistic dir. Chamber Opera Chgo., 1985-93, Chgo. Opera Theater, 1994-99. Home: 421 W Melrose St Apt 22A Chicago IL 60657-3881 Office: Chicago Opera Theater 70 E Lake St Ste 540 Chicago IL 60601-5990

RATNER, DAVID LOUIS, retired law educator; b. London, Sept. 2, 1931; AB magna cum laude, Harvard U., 1952, LLB magna cum laude, 1955. Bar: N.Y. 1955. Assoc. Sullivan & Cromwell, N.Y.C., 1955-64; assoc. prof. Cornell Law Sch., Ithaca, N.Y., 1964-68, prof., 1968-82; prof. law U. San Francisco Law Sch., 1982-99, dean, 1982-89, prof. emeritus, 1999—. Exec. asst. to chmn. SEC, Washington, 1966-68; chief counsel Securities Industry Study, Senate Banking Com., Washington, 1971-73; vis. prof. Stanford (Calif.) U., 1974, Ariz. State U., Tempe, 1974, U. San Francisco, 1980, Georgetown U., Washington, 1989-90, U. Calif., Hastings, San Francisco, 1992; mem. Larkspur (Calif.) Planning Commn., 1992—. Author: Securities Regulation: Cases and Materials, 6th edit., 2002, Securities Regulation in a Nutshell, 7 edit., 2002, Institutional Investors: Teaching Materials, 1978. Fulbright scholar Monash U., Australia, 1981. Mem. Cosmos Club (Washington), Harvard Club of San Francisco (pres. 1999-2000), Phi Beta Kappa. Home and Office: 84 Polhemus Way Larkspur CA 94939-1928 E-mail: dlratner@aol.com.

RATNER, GERALD, lawyer; b. Chgo., Dec. 17, 1913; s. Peter I. and Sarah (Soreson) R.; m. Eunice Payton, June 18, 1948. PhB, U. Chgo., 1935, JD cum laude, 1937. Bar: Ill. 1937. Since practiced in, Chgo.; sr. ptnr. Gould & Ratner and predecessor firm, 1949—. Officer Henry Crown & Co., CC Industries, Inc., Material Svc. Corp., Freeman United Coal Mining Co., Mineral and Land Resources Corp.; lectr., writer on real estate law. Capt. AUS, 1942-46. Gerald Ratner Athletics Ctr. named in his honor, U. Chgo. Mem. ABA, Ill. Bar Assn., Chgo. Bar Assn., Order of Coif, Phi Beta Kappa. Home: 180 E Pearson St Apt 6205 Chicago IL 60611-2191 Office: 222 N La Salle St Ste 800 Chicago IL 60601-1086

RATNER, HAROLD, pediatrician, educator; b. June 19, 1927; s. George and Bertha (Silverman) R.; m. Lillian Gross, Feb. 4, 1961; children: Sanford Miles, Marcia Ellen. BS, CCNY, 1948; MD, Chgo. Med. Sch., 1952. Diplomate Nat. Bd. Med. Examiners, Am. Bd. Pediatrics. Intern Jewish Hosp. Med. Ctr. Bklyn., 1952-53, resident in pediat., 1953-55; pvt. practice Bklyn.; clin. instr. pediat. Downstate Med. Ctr. SUNY, N.Y.C., 1955-67, clin. asst. prof., 1967-69, clin. assoc. prof., 1969-87, lectr. pediat., 1987—; chief pediat. Greenpoint Hosp., Bklyn., 1967-80, pres. med. staff, 1970-71, 74-80, clin. assoc. prof., 1983-87, lectr., 1987—; dir. ambulatory svcs. Woodhull Med. and Mental Health Ctr., 1980-83; clin. asst. prof. pediat. NYU, 1987-90, 97—, clin. asst. prof. psychiatry, 1997—. Med. specialist Nathan Kline Inst. Psychiat. Rsch., Orangeburg, N.Y., Rockland Psychiat. Ctr., 1986-88, unit chief med. svcs., 1988-90; emeritus assoc. clin. dir., dir. medicine Manhattan Psychiat. Ctr., N.Y.C., 1990-98; mem. adv. coun. to pres. N.Y.C. Health and Hosp. Corp., 1970-71, 74-80, 81-83, sec., 1975, v.p., 1976-80. Contbr. articles to profl. jours. Mem. med. bd., bd. dirs. Camp Sussex; bd. dirs. Kings County Health Care Rev. Orgn., Bklyn., 1976-84, past co-chmn. hosp. rev. com., continuing med. edn., med. care evaluation com. Trustee Village Saddle Rock, N.Y., 1980—. Served with AUS, 1945-47. Fellow Am. Pediatric Soc., Am. Soc. Clin. Hypnosis, Royal Soc. Health, Bklyn. Pediatric Soc., Kings County Med. Soc.; mem. AMA, Soc. Clin. and Exptl. Hypnosis, Pan-Am. Med. Socs. Democrat. Jewish. Home and Office: 55 Blue Bird Dr New York NY 10035

RATNER, JAMES HENRY, dermatologist; b. El Paso, Tex., Mar. 31, 1945; s. Alfred A. and Adalaide M. (Moye) R.; m. Janice Dimenstein, June 30, 1968; children: Derek J., Andrea E. BS, Yale U., 1967; MD, Baylor Coll. Medicine, 1971. Diplomate Am. Bd. Dermatology, Am. Bd. Dermatology and Pathology in Dermatopathology. Intern in internal medicine St. Luke's Episcopal Hosp., Houston, 1971-72; resident in dermatology Dartmouth Med. Sch. Affiliated Hosps., Hamover, N.H., 1972-75; chief of dermatology U.S. Army Hosp., Ft. Polk, La., 1976-77; pvt. practice in dermatology Amherst, Mass., 1977—. Bd. dirs. Amherst (Mass.) Youth Hockey Assn., 1985-91, Greater Springfield (Mass.) Jr. Amateur Hockey Assn., 1989-91. Major, U.S. Army, 1976-77. Fellow Am. Acad. Dermatology, Mass. Acad. Dermatology (bd. dirs. 1989-93); mem. New Eng. Dermatol. Assn., Internat. Soc. Dermatology, Mass. Med. Soc. (alt. exec. councilor 1983-84). Office: 170 University Dr Ste 102 Amherst MA 01002-2272

RATNER, LORMAN ALFRED, history educator; b. N.Y.C., July 23, 1932; s. Mortimer Ratner and Lillian Becker; m. Nina V. Nutt, June 20, 1953 (dec. Feb. 1989); children: Wendy Ratner MacMullen, Todd, Joseph, Matthew; m. Paula T. Kaufman, Sept. 17, 1989. AB, Harvard Coll., 1954; MA, Cornell U., 1958, PhD, 1961. Asst. prof. Ithaca (N.Y.) Coll., 1959-61; from asst. prof. to assoc. prof. to prof. Lehman Coll., CUNY, Bronx, 1961-70, dept. chair, 1970-72, dean of planning and social scis., 1972-77; vice chancellor U. Wis., Kenosha, 1977-83; chancellor U. Wis. Ctrs., Madison, 1983-86; dean of arts and scis., prof. U. Tenn., Knoxville, 1986-96, prof. history, 1996-99, prof. emeritus, 1999; adj. prof. U. Ill., Urbana-Champaign, 1999—. Author: Powderkeg, 1968, James Kirke Paulding, 1993, Andrew Jackson and His Tenn. Lieutenants, 1997, others. Mem., pres. Bd. of Edn., N.Y., 1971-76. Home: 1609A Lakeside Dr Champaign IL 61821-5557

RATNER, MARCIA, research scientist; b. Hartford, Conn., June 24, 1960; d. William and Gertrude Chorches Ratner. BA in Psychology, Boston U., 1995, postgrad., 1996—. Rsch. asst. neurology Boston U. Sch. Medicine, 1994-96, editl. asst., 1996-98, rsch. assoc., 1998—; project mgr. Boston U., 1998—; instr. toxicology and forensic toxicology Boston U. Sch. Medicine, 2000—. Counselor Specialized Housing, Brookline, Mass., 1995-. Mem.: N.Y. Acad. Sci., Am. Conf. Govt. Indsl. Hygiene, Soc. Occupl. Environ. Health, Soc. Occupl. Health, Soc. for Neurosci., Mass. Neuropsychol. Soc., Am. Acad. Clin. Toxicology, Internat. Neurotoxicol. Assn., Combined Jewish Philanthropies, Psi Chi, Alpha Phi Omega. Jewish. Avocations: horseback riding, guitar, running. Office: Boston U Sch Medicine C-329 715 Albany St Boston MA 02118-2526 E-mail: marcia@bu.edu.

RATNER, MICHAEL D. lawyer; b. June 13, 1943; s. Harry and Anne (Spott) Ratner. BA, Brandeis U., 1966; JD magna cum laude, Columbia U., 1971. Bar: N.Y. 1971, U.S. Supreme Ct. 1983. Law clk. U.S. Dist. Ct. (so. dist.), N.Y.C., 1971-72; prof. NYU Law Sch., 1973-74; atty. Ctr. for Constl. Rights, 1978-85, legal dir., 1985-90. Adj. prof. Yale Law Sch., New Haven, Conn., 1990-95; spl. counsel for human rights Govt. of Haiti, 1996; lectr. Columbia Law Sch., 1999-2002, Yale Law Sch., 2000; pres. Ctr. Constl. Rights. Author: International Human Rights Litigation in U.S. Cours, 1997, Che Guevara and the FBI, 1997, The Pinochet Papers, 2000; contbr. articles to profl. jours. Named Trial Lawyer of Yr., Trial Lawyers for the Pub. Interest; Skelly Wright fellow Yale Law Sch., 2000. Mem. Nat. Lawyers Guild (pres. 1982-83). Office: Ctr Constitutional Rights 666 Broadway New York NY 10012-2317 E-mail: mratner@igc.org.

RATNER, ROCHELLE, writer, editor; b. Atlantic City, Dec. 2, 1948; d. Herman and Esther Ratner; m. Kenneth Thorp, Mar. 30, 1990. Student, New Sch. for Social Rsch., N.Y.C., 1969-71. Poetry columnist Soho Weekly News, N.Y.C., 1975-82; exec. editor Am. Book Rev., Normal, Ill., 1978—. Poetry reviewer Libr. Jour., N.Y.C., 1976—; editor N.J. Online%Reading Room, Jersey City, 1995-96; poetry cons. Israel Horizons, N.Y.C., 1988-97. Author: A Birthday of Waters, 1971, False Trees, 1973, The Mysteries, 1976, Pirate's Song, 1976, The Tightrope Walker, 1976, Quarry, 1978, Combing the Waves, 1979, Sea Air in a Grave Ground Hog Turns Toward, 1980, Hide and Seek, 1980, Practicing To Be A Woman: New and Selected Poems, 1982, Trying To Understand What It Means To Be a Feminist: Essays on Women Writers, 1984, Bobby's Girl, 1986, The Lion's Share, 1991, Someday Songs, 1992, Zodiac Arrest, 1995; Editor: Bearing Life: Women's Writings on Childlessness, 2000 (Susan Koppelman award 2000); transalator: Paul Colinet: Selected Prose Poems, 1975. Mem. PEN Am. Ctr., Authors Ghild, Nat. Writers Union, Nat. Book Critics Circle (v.p. for publs. 1999-2001, bd. dirs. 1995-2001). Avocation: computer related projects. Home and Office: 609 Columbus Ave New York NY 10024-1433 Fax: 212-769-0498. E-mail: rochelleratner@mindspring.com.

RATTI, RONALD ANDREW, economics educator; b. Neath, West Glamorgan, Wales, Oct. 10, 1948; came to U.S., 1970; s. Ronald Rudolph and Janet (Marshall) R. BA, U. Lancaster, 1970; MA, Case Western Res. U., 1972; PhD, So. Meth. U., 1975. Asst. prof. to assoc. prof. U. Mo., Columbia, 1975-85, prof. econs., 1985—, chmn. dept., 1982-89. Vis. scholar Fed. Res. Bank Kansas City, Mo., 1978, Fed. Res. Bank St. Louis., 1984-85; acad. visitor London Sch. Econs., 1985; vis. Fulbright prof. Korea U., Seoul, 1996, Korea Inst. Fin., 1997. Contbr. articles to profl. jours. Office: U Mo Dept Econs 118 Profl Bldg Columbia MO 65211-0001

RATTIE, MARGARET ELIZABETH (BETH RATTIE), educator; b. Mount Airy, N.C., Feb. 11, 1951; d. Joseph Jackson and Margaret Adelaide (Hill) R.; divorced; 1 child, Heather Elizabeth Cooke. BS, North Tex. State U., 1972; MS, Radford (Va.) U., 1986; Specialist, Appalachian State U., 1983. Cert. tchr., adminstr. Tchr. Patrick County Schs., Stuart, Va., 1972-79; asst. prin. Surry County Schs., Mount Airy, N.C., 1980-84; tchr. Osceola County Schs., Kissimmee, Fla., 1984-88, asst. prin., 1988—. Mem. Found. for Osceola Edn., Kissimmee, 1998—; mem. Arts for Complete Edn., Kissimmee, 1997—; facilitator So. Assn. Colls. and Schs., Atlanta, 1994—. Mem. Nat. Assn. Secondary Sch. Prins., Beta Sigma Phi (pres., treas.), Alpha Delta Kappa (pres. 1994-96), Phi Delta Kappa. Democrat. Baptist. Avocation: bowling. Home: 2733 Scarborough Dr Kissimmee FL 34744-5485

RATTIGAN, JOHN E., JR. lawyer; b. Quincy, Mass., July 3, 1957; m. Carole J. O'Shaughnessy, June 12, 1982; children: Christopher, Michael, Timothy. BA, Merrimack Coll., 1979; JD, U. Va., 1982. Bar: Mass. 1982, U.S. Dist. Ct. Mass. 1982, U.S. Ct. Appeals (1st cir.) 1982. Assoc. Palmer & Dodge LLP, Boston, 1982-89, ptnr., 1990—. Mem. adv. bd. MIT Ctr. for Real Estate, Cambridge, Mass., 1990-2001. Bd. dirs., mem. exec. com. Trust for City Hall Plz., Boston, 1995—, Downtown Crossing Assn., Boston, 1991—; mem. Mayor's Washington St. Adv. Com., Boston, 1997; mem. Linkage Commn., 2001; bd. dirs. Back Bay Assn., 2001—. Recipient Disting. Svc. award Downtown Crossing Assn., 1997. Mem. Order of Coif. Office: Palmer & Dodge LLP 111 Huntington Ave Boston MA 02199-7613 E-mail: jrattigan@palmerdodge.com.

RATTMAN, WILLIAM JOHN, electronics and electro-optic engineer; b. Springfield, Mass., Nov. 16, 1933; s. Frank William and Sylvia Mary (Berry) R.; m. Jayne Winona Crockett, Aug. 19, 1954; children: Joy Diane, Beth Jayene, Amy Cathryn. BSEE, U. Mass, 1955; MSEE, Northeastern U., 1961. Sr. engr. Raytheon Co., Bedford, Mass., 1955-63; prin. engr., 1967-72; engring. specialist Sylvania Applied Rsch. Lab., Waltham, Mass., 1963-67; mgr. R&D Electro Signal Lab., Inc., Rockland, 1972-86. Cons. electronics, electro-optics to mfg. firms. Patentee optical depth finder, contrast detector, low drive power wideband optical modulator, laser ablative printing system, photoelectric smoke detector, self diagnostic smoke detector. Co-chmn. Town of Needham United Way Campaign, 1973. Mem. Soc. Photo-Optical Instrumentation Egnrs., S. Yarmouth Hist. soc. (pres. 1974-75). Home and Office: 8603 S Bay Dr Orlando FL 32819-4948 E-mail: wrattman@aol.com.

RATTRAY, JAMES BAILEY, lawyer; b. Watertown, N.Y., July 26, 1950; s. Clifford M. and Dora M. (Bailey) R.; m. Paula Cataldi, Nov. 30, 1998. AB cum laude, Syracuse U., 1972; JD, Coll. William and Mary, 1975, MLT, 1982. Bar: Va. 1975, D.C. 1976. Assoc. firm Ernest C. Consolvo, Norfolk, Va., 1975; dep. city atty. City of Hampton, 1976—92; exec. dir. Hampton Redevel. and Housing Authority, 1992—2001; asst. office dir. Ga. Dept. Cmty. Affairs, Atlanta, 2002—. Instr. St. Leo Coll., Tidewater Center, Langley AFB, Va., 1982-99, Golden Gate U., Resident Ctr., Langley AFB, 1978-82, Hampton U., Va., 1985-90. Contbr. articles to profl. jours. Mem. ABA, D.C. Bar Assn., Va. Bar Assn., Local Govt. Attys. of Va., Nat. Assn. Housing and Redevel. Ofcls., Pub. Housing Authority Dirs. Assn. Episcopalian. Home: 1015 Lake Wind Wald Overlook Alpharetta GA 30005-9010 Office: Dept Cmty Affairs 60 Executive Park S Atlanta GA 30329-2231 E-mail: jbrattray@aol.com.

RATZER, MARY BOYD, secondary education educator, librarian; b. Troy, N.Y., Sept. 6, 1945; d. John Leo and Katherine M. (Van Derpool) Boyd; m. Philip J. Ratzer, July 30, 1972; children: Joseph, David. BA cum laude, Coll. of St. Rose, Albany, N.Y., 1967; MA, SUNY, Albany, 1968, MLS, 1981. Cert. secondary tchr., sch. libr. media specialist, N.Y. Secondary tchr. English, Shenendehowa Cen. Sch., Clifton Park, N.Y., 1968-85; sch. libr. media specialist Shendehowa Cen. Sch., 1985—. Coord., mentor tchr. intern program; lectr. SUNY Grad. Sch. Info. Sci. and Policy, Albany; frequent speaker at state-level confs., 1986—; mem. adv. bd. U. Albany Grad. Sch. Info. Sci. and Policy. Contbr.: N.Y. State Teacher Resource Guides for Learning Standards; contbr. articles to profl. jours. Recipient grants. Mem. ALA, N.Y. Libr. Assn., Nat. Coun. Tchrs. English, N.Y. Assn. for Supervision and Curriculum Devel., N.Y. State Acad. for Tchg. and Learning, BIRT, LUERT (past pres.). Home: 433 County Route 68 Saratoga Springs NY 12866-6636

RATZLAFF, DAVID EDWARD, minister; b. Kansas City, Mo., Mar. 12, 1938; s. John Henry and Amy May (Cathcart) R.; m. Shiela Paige Hickerson, June 9, 1958; children: Perry Dean, Kevin Lee, Kalista Kay. BA in Ministry, Nebr. Christian Coll., 1961; MDiv, Memphis Theol. Sem., 1991; DMin, Lake Charles Bible Coll., 1996. Ordained to ministry Christian Ch., 1962. Min. Christian Ch., Neligh, Nebr., 1959-67; owner, mgr. Kordsman Evangelistic Assn., Hiawatha, Kans., 1967-75; sr. min. Christian Ctr., 1970-72; salesman Saladmaster Co., Springfield, Mo., 1975-76; ops. coord. Blackwood Bros. Quartet, Memphis, 1976-79, 85; mgr. sales and svc. Elliot Impression Products, 1980-85; elder, tchr. Lindewood Christion Ch., 1985—; min. Bethany Christian Ch., Eads, Tenn., 1986-95; owner Soma Co., 1993-96; sales cons., fleet mgr., dealership coord. Midway Ford, Collierville, Tenn., 1996-99; customer rels. mgr. Landers Ford, 1999—2001; assoc. pastor Macon Christian Ch., Collierville, Tenn., 1997-99; sales clk. Hutton Chevrolet, 2001—. Program chair exec. commn. on ministry com. Christian Chs. (Disciples of Christ), Tenn., 1988—95, ch. cons., 1996; western area moderator, mem. gen. and exec. bds. Region of Christian Ch. of Tenn., 1991—93; small bus. founder, 1993; mem. pastoral adv. bd. Genesis Crisis Ctr., Memphis, 1994; cons. WYLT-FM Radio, Collierville, 1997—2001, WUVLL-AM Radio, Mobile, Ala., 1997—2001. Co-author: (songbook) Kordsman Presents, 1966; recorded and produced 6 long play albums, 1966-74. Bd. dirs. Memphis Family Link, 1985-86; mem. United Cerebral Palsy, 1983-86; asst. police chief City of Neligh, 1962-67, coordinator, 1965-67. Mem. Nat. Arts and Recording Artists, Collierville Ministerial Assn., Christian Ch. Ministers Memphis. Republican. Mem. Disciples Christ. Avocations: fishing, weight lifting, basketball, coaching baseball and softball. Home: 10674 Ral LaGrange Eads TN 38028

RATZLAFF, DONNA CHERYL, social worker; b. Enid, Okla., July 21, 1946; d. Waldo Orlando and Florence (Nightingale) R. BA, Okla. City U., 1968; MSW, Okla. U., 1975. Missionary United Meth. Ch., Philippine Islands, 1968-71; soc. svc. supr. United Meth. Childrens Home, Tahlequah, Okla., 1975-79; adminstr. Frances E. Willard Home, Tulsa, 1979-87; regional dir. Fla. United Methodist Ch. Home, St. Petersburg, 1987-91; exec. dir. United Meth. Coop. Ministries, 1991—. Sec., treas. Okla. Assn. Childrens Insts. and Agys., Tulsa, 1984-87; chairperson bd. S.E. Asian Preschool, St. Petersburg, 1989-91; pres. bd. Childs Park Outreach, Inc., 1993-97. Mem. NASW, Acad. Cert. Social Workers, Qualified Clin. Social Workers. Methodist. Avocations: gardening, travel. Home: 3835 35th Way S Apt 100 Saint Petersburg FL 33711-4373

RATZLAFF, KEITH ALAN, English educator; b. Henderson, Nebr., July 29, 1953; s. Dietrich Peter and Marie Ratzlaff; m. Treva Sue Reimer, Sept. 6, 1975. BA in English, Bethel Coll., Kans., 1976; MFA in Creative Writing, Ind. U., 1983. Asst. prof. English Quincy (Ill.) Coll., 1984; co-dir. Ctrl. Coll. Study Abroad, London, 1986-89; assoc. prof. English Ctrl. Coll., Pella, Iowa, 1993—. Author: (poetry) Man Under a Pear Tree, 1997 (Anhinga prize 1996), Across the Known World, 1997, New Winter Light, 1994 (Wm. and Kingman Page award 1994), Out Here, 1984. Recipient Theodore Roethke prize Poetry Northwest, 1996. Mem. Associated Writing Programs. Home: 306 Liberty Pella IA 50219 Office: Central Coll 812 University Pella IA 50219 E-mail: ratzlaffk@central.edu.

RATZLAFF, RUBEN MENNO, religion educator, minister; b. Burrton, Kans., Jan. 8, 1917; s. Henry and Julia (Foth) R.; m. Frances Irene King, Sept. 7, 1941; children: Keith Lowell, Paul Dennis, Mark Henry, Loren Lee; m. Doris Carr Arneson, Aug. 1, 1992. BA, Johnson Bible Coll., 1940; BD, Butler U., 1955, MA, 1959. Ordained to ministry Chs. of Christ, 1938. Min. Pleasant Hill Christian Ch., Hall, Ind., 1948-50, Christian Ch., Clermont, 1950-55, Kennard, 1955-59; prof. San Jose (Calif.) Christian Coll., 1959-98, prof. emeritus, 1998—. Ann. vis. lectr. Springdale Coll., Selly Oak Colls., Birmingham, Eng., 1985-97; vis. lectr. Zimbabwe Christian Coll., Harare, 1995, Philippine Coll. Ministry, Baguio City, 1998. Author: Ezra Nehemiah, 1982; contbr. articles to profl. jours. Served with USPHS, 1965—67. Recipient Hebrew award Hebrew Synagogue, 1950. Mem. Theta Phi. Home: PO Box 58 5315 Boise St Turner OR 97392-0058 *What amazes me most is that God the Almighty sends His Son to knock at our door, and wait with His hat in His hand while we decide whether to follow Him.*

RAU, DAVID EDWARD, financial and real estate consultant; b. Lincoln, Nebr., Sept. 27, 1956; s. Leo George and Anne Marie (Pavel) R.; divorced; children: Andrew David, Peter Nicholas, Victoria Anne. BBA, U. Ariz., 1978. CPA, Ariz., N.Mex. Sr. Peat Marwick Main, Albuquerque, 1978-82, supervising sr. Phoenix, 1982-83; asst. treas. Kroy Inc., Scottsdale, 1983-85; acct. Zolondek & Blumenthal, Phoenix, 1985; v.p., controller Del Webb Corp., 1985—2002. Bd. dirs. Ariz. Tax Rsch. Assn. Chmn. Phoenix chpt. walk Juvenile Diabetes Found., 1990, pres. 1992, 93, 94; mem. Ariz. Town Hall; advisor Phoenix Sky Harbour Ctr. Tech. Adv. Panel, 1987; treas. Drugs Don's Work in Ariz., 1994—. Mem. Ariz. Soc. CPAs, Albuquerque Jaycees (treas. 1981-82), Nat. Assn. Real Estate Cos. (tax com.), Ariz. C. of C. (bd. dirs.), Beta Alpha Psi. Republican. Roman Catholic. Avocations: skiing, fishing, family. Office: Del E Webb Corp 2231 E Camelback Rd Phoenix AZ 85016-3453

RAU, LEE ARTHUR, lawyer; b. Mpls., July 22, 1940; s. Arthur W. and Selma A. (Lund) R.; m. Janice R. Childress, June 27, 1964; children: Brendan D., Patrick C., Brian T. BSB, U. Minn., 1962; JD, UCLA, 1965. Bar: Calif. 1966, D.C. 1972, Va. 1986, U.S. Dist. Ct. D.C. 1973, U.S. Dist. Ct. (ea. dist.) Va. 1988, U.S. Ct. Mil. Appeals 1966, U.S. Ct. Appeals (D.C. cir.) 1972, U.S. Ct. Appeals (3d cir.) 1975, U.S. Ct. Appeals (6th cir.) 1980, U.S. Ct. Appeals (4th cir.) 1988, U.S. Supreme Ct. 1971. Trial atty. evaluation sect. antitrust div. U.S. Dept. Justice, Washington, 1965-66, appellate sect., 1970-72; assoc. Reed Smith Shaw & McClay, 1972-74, ptnr., 1975—2002; commr. Fairfax County Redevel. and Housing Authority, 2002—. Former mem. constl. and adminstrv. law adv. com. Nat. Chamber Litigation Ctr. Inc.; sec., bd. dirs. Old Dominion Land Co., Inc. Contbr. articles to profl. jours. Sec. bd. dirs. Reston Found., 1982-93; bd. dirs. Reston Interfaith Inc., 1973-89, pres, 1984-88; bd. dirs. Greater Reston Arts Ctr., 1988-96, pres., 1989-91, sec., 1991-95; mem. Washington Dulles Task Force, 1982-91; mem. exec. com. and ops. com. Fairfax-Falls Ch. United Way, mem. regional coun., 1988-92. Capt. JAGC, U.S. Army, 1966-70. Named Restonian of Yr., 1990; decorated Commendation with oak leaf cluster; recipient Best of Reston award. Mem. ABA (antitrust, adminstrv. law, corp. banking and bus., sci. and tech. sects.), D.C. Bar Assn. (past chmn. energy study group), Calif. Bar Assn., U.S. C. of C. (antitrust policy com.). Democrat. Lutheran. Home: 11654 Mediterranean Ct Reston VA 20190-3401

RAU, RALPH RONALD, retired physicist; b. Tacoma, Sept. 1, 1920; s. Ralph Campbell and Ida (Montgall) R.; m. Maryjane Uhrlaub, June 2, 1944; children: Whitney Leslie, Littie Elise. BS in Physics, Coll. Puget Sound, 1941; MS in Physics, Calif. Inst. Tech., 1943, PhD in Physics, 1948; LHD (hon.) , U. Puget Sound, 2002. Asst. prof. physics Princeton U., 1947-56; Fulbright research prof. physics Ecole Polytechnique, Paris, 1954-55; physicist Brookhaven Nat. Lab., Upton, N.Y., 1956-66, chmn. dept. physics, 1966-70, assoc. dir. for high energy physics, 1970-81. Adj. prof. U. Wyo.; vis. prof. MIT, 1984-88; staff scientist Desy Lab., Hamburg, Fed. Republic Germany, 1984-85. Trustee U. Puget Sound, 1978-84 Named Alumnus Cum Laude U. Puget Sound, 1968; recipient Alexander von Humboldt U.S. Sr. Scientist award 1988. Mem. Am. Phys. Soc., N.Y. Acad. Sci. Office: Brookhaven Nat Lab Upton NY 11973 E-mail: rau@bnl.gov.

RAUB, DONALD WILMER, minister, author; b. Quakertown, Pa., Dec. 24, 1931; s. Harvey Wilmer and Estella Martha (Bleam) R.; m. Dolores Jean Kern, Oct. 20, 1951; children: Diane, Donald, Deborah, Devlyn. DRE, Evang. Bible Sem., Lake Worth, Fla., 1987, ThD, 1999. Ordained minister Evang. Ch. Alliance, 1951. Evangelist Evang. Ch. Alliance, Bradley, Ill., 1951-58; pastor Troy (Ohio) Gospel Tabernacle, 1959-60; writer and photographer Quakertown (Pa.) Free Press, 1963-73; pastor East Rockhill Chapel, 1965—; with Merck & Co., West Point, Pa., 1968-94; ret., 1994. Advisor Lebanon (Pa.) Gospel Assn., 1992-94; lectr. in field. Author: I, Being of Sound Mind, 1988, 2d edit., 1989, Unusual Experiences and Special Moments, 1990, The Value of Christian Holiness, 1992; inventor fin. game: Independence, 1976; patentee in field; contbr. articles to profl. jours. Bd. dirs. Transylvania Bible Sch. (now Biblical Life Inst.), Freeport, Pa., 1957—, North Penn Symphony Orch. Soc., Lansdale, Pa., 1980-90; v.p. Transylvania, Inc., 1994-97, chmn. bd. dirs., 1997—. Mem. Songwriters of N.Am. (founder). Republican. Avocation: horticulture. Address: PO Box 224 Tylersport PA 18971-0224

RAUBICHECK, CHARLES JOSEPH, lawyer; b. N.Y.C., Oct. 9, 1946; s. Walter Alan and Catherine Gertrude (Fordrung) R.; A.B., Georgetown U., 1968; J.D., Georgetown U., 1971; m. Ann S. Macdonald, Feb. 18, 1978. Admitted to D.C. bar, 1971, N.Y. State bar, 1976; atty. Office Gen. Counsel FDA, Washington, 1971-75; ptnr. Frommer Lawrence & Haug LLP, N.Y.C., 2000—; adj. prof. N.Y.U. Sch. Law, N.Y.C., 1976—; elder Lafayette Ave. Presbyn. Ch., Bklyn., 2000—; trustee Riverside Ch., N.Y.C., 1993-94. Mem. ABA, N.Y. State Bar Assn. (chair food, drug, cosmetic law sect. 1986-88, 98-2000, vice-chair 1996—), Assn. Bar City N.Y., Union League Club (N.Y.C.).

RAUCH, ARTHUR IRVING, management consultant; b. N.Y.C., Sept. 18, 1933; s. David and Miriam (Frankel) R.; m. Roxane M. Spiller, Aug. 19, 1962 (div. 1977); children: David S., Janine B.; m. Lynn R. Saidenberg, Oct. 11, 1987. BA magna cum laude, Dartmouth Coll., 1954, MS, 1955. Chartered fin. analyst. Security analyst Lionel D. Edie & Co., N.Y.C., 1959-64; group dir. rsch. Eastman Dillon, Union Securities & Co., 1964-68; v.p., sr. analyst Laird, Inc., 1968-69, dir. rsch., 1969-71, sr. v.p., 1970-73; ptnr. Oppenheimer & Co., 1973-77; v.p. corp. devel. Rorer Group, Inc., Ft. Washington, Pa., 1977-84; v.p. corp. fin. Arnhold & S. Bleichroeder, Inc., N.Y.C., 1984-88; cons. corp. devel. ICN Pharms., Inc., 1988-89. Mem. investment com. Becker Fund, 1969-73. Exec. com. Dartmouth Class of 1954, 1968-79, 94—. Lt. (j.g.) USNR, 1956-59. Rufus Choate scholar Dartmouth Coll., 1951. Mem. N.Y. Soc. Security Analysts, Assn. Corp. Growth, Fin. Analysts Fedn. (corp. fin. com.), Phi Beta Kappa. Home and Office: 115 Central Park W Apt 9D New York NY 10023-4153 E-mail: arthurrauch@aol.com.

RAUCH, CHARLES FREDERICK, JR. retired university official and business educator; b. Lancaster, Ohio, Oct. 24, 1925; s. Charles Frederick and Mary Catherine (Getz) R.; m. Diane Matilda Wilcox, Jan. 1, 1951 (div. July 1974); 1 child, Frederick Whitman; m. Esther Eleze Nettles, Apr. 25, 1975. BS, U.S. Naval Acad., 1947; MSME, U.S. Naval Postgrad. Sch., Monterey, Calif., 1957; MBA, Ohio State U., 1980, PhD, 1981. Commd. ensign USN, 1947, advanced through grades to rear adm., 1972; comdg. officer nuclear submarines, New London, Conn., 1962-66; systems analyst, sr. naval advisor, spl. asst. Office Chief Naval Ops., Washington and Saigon, Vietnam, 1967-71, dir. human resource mgmt. programs Washington, 1971-76; ret., 1976; asst. prof. U. Maine, Orono, 1981-84, dir. fin. mgmt., 1984-92, v.p. bus. and fin., 1992-96, part-time faculty, 1999-2000; acting pres. Am. Univ., Bulgaria, 1992. Cons. to dep. asst. sec. def., Washington, 1976; cons. Maine Maritime Acad., Castine, 1982-84; bd. dirs. Audubon Expdn. Inst., treas., 1998-; mem. coun. Am. U., Bulgaria, 1997-2000. Contbg. author: Leaders and Managers: International Perspectives on Managerial Behavior and Leaderships, 1984. Bd. dirs. Bangor Symphony Orch., 1999—, pres., 2001—. Decorated D.S.M. with gold star. Mem. Maine Audubon Soc., Greater Bangor C. of C. (chmn. com. on univ.-cmty. rels. 1986-89, bd. dirs. 1988-92), Navy League (pres. Penobscot coun. 1998-2000), Bangor Rotary (treas. 1999—), Phi Kappa Phi, Beta Gamma Sigma. Episcopalian. Avocations: wildlife photography, woodcarving. Home: 102 Stillwater Ave Orono ME 04473-3410 E-mail: CFR@maine.edu.

RAUCH, GEORGE WASHINGTON, lawyer, director; b. Marion, Ind., July 18, 1919; s. George W. and Emma Asenath (Nolen) R.; m. Audrey M. Cranfield, Feb. 28, 1943 (div.); children: George Washington III, Nancy Lynn, Jane Nolen; m. Dorothy D. Farlow, June 26, 1970. BS, Ind. U., 1941; LL.B., U. Va., 1947. Bar: Ind. 1948, Ill. 1957, Mass. and Fla. 1972. Practice law Batton, Harker and Rauch (and predecessor firms), Marion, Ind., 1948-57; v.p., gen. counsel The Greyhound Corp., Chgo., 1957-61; mem. firm Hubachek & Kelly Ltd. and predecessor firms, 1961-82; pres. Hubachek & Kelly Ltd., 1972-80; of counsel firm Chapman and Cutler, Chgo., 1982-95; gen. counsel Household Finance Corp., 1967-78, dir., 1967-92, mem. fin. com., 1969-92, exec. com., 1972-92; dir. Edwards Engring. Corp., Constrn. Materials Co., Indsl. Air & Hydraulics Co., 1976-90, Burch Co., 1972-97, pres., 1975-97; dir. 1242 Lake Shore Dr. Corp., 1971-83, pres., 1973-74. Mem. Nat. Conf. Commrs. on Uniform Laws, 1955-57. Served as aviator USNR, 1941-45; lt. comdr. Mem. Raven Soc., Sankaty Head Golf Club (Nantucket, Mass.), Casino Club (Nantucket), Beach Club (Palm Beach, Fla.), Masons, Shriners, Phi Delta Phi, Delta Tau Delta. Home: 455 Australian Ave Palm Beach FL 33480-4532 also: 83 Baxter Rd Siasconset MA 02564

RAUCH, IRMENGARD, linguist, educator; b. Dayton, Ohio, Apr. 17, 1933; d. Konrad and Elsa (Knott) R.; m. Gerald F. Carr, June 12, 1965; children: Christopher, Gregory. Student, Nat. U. Mex., summer 1954; BS with honors, U. Dayton, 1955; MA, Ohio State U., 1957; postgrad. (Fulbright fellow), U. Munich, Fed. Republic Germany, 1957-58; PhD, U. Mich., 1962. Instr., German and linguistics U. Wis., Madison, 1962-63, asst. prof., 1963-66; assoc. prof. German U. Pitts., 1966-68; assoc. prof. German and linguistics U. Ill., Urbana, 1968-72, prof., 1972-79, U. Calif., Berkeley, 1979—. Author: The Old High German Diphthongization: A Description of a Phonemic Change, 1967, The Old Saxon Language: Grammar, Epic Narrative, Linguistic Interference, 1992, Semiotic Insights: The Data Do the Talking, 1998; editor: (with others) Approaches in Linguistic Methodology, 1967, Spanish edit., 1974, Der Heliand, 1974, Linguistic Method: Essays in Honor of Herbert Penzl, 1979, The Signifying Animal: The Grammar of Language and Experience, 1980, Language Change, 1983, The Semiotic Bridge: Trends From California, 1989, On Germanic Linguistics: Issues and Methods, 1992, Insights in Germanic Linguistics I: Methodology in Transition, 1995, Across the Oceans: Studies from East to West in Honor of Richard K. Seymour, 1995, Insights in Germanic Linguistics II: Classic and Contemporary, 1996, Synthesis in Diversity: Semiotics Around the World, 1997, New Insights in Germanic Liguistics I, 1999, II, 2001, III, 2002; editor of three series: Berkeley Insights in Linguistics and Semiotics, Berkeley Models of Grammars, Studies in Old Germanic Languages and Literatures. founder, co-editor Interdisciplinary J. for Germanic Linguistics and Semiotic Anaylsis; contributor articles to profl. jours. Named outstanding woman on campus U. Ill. Sta. WILL, 1975; recipient Disting. Alumnus award U. Dayton, 1985; research grantee U. Wis., summer 1966, U. Ill., 1975-79, Eastern Ill. U., 1976, Nat. Endowment Humanities, 1978, U. Calif., Berkeley, 1979— ; travel grantee NSF, Linguistics Soc. Am., 1972; Guggenheim fellow, 1982-83; IBM Distributed Acad. Computing Environment, 1986; NEH grantee, 1988; Festschrift: Interdigitations: Essays for Irmengard Rauch, 1999. Mem. Linguistics Soc. Am., MLA, Am. Assn. Tchrs. German (hon.), Society for Germanic Philogy, Philogical Assn. of the West Coast, Phonetics Assn., Semiotic Soc. Am. (pres. 1982-83), Semiotic Circle of Calif. (founder), Internat. Assn. for Semiotic Studies (pres., dir. 5th congress 1994), Alpha Sigma Tau, Delta Phi Alpha. Home: 862 Camden Ct Benicia CA 94510-3633 Office: U Calif Dept German Berkeley CA 94720-0001

RAUCH, JANET MELODIE, elementary school educator; b. Mpls., June 17, 1952; d. James Harlan and Myrna Luverne (Prinsen) R. BA, Wheaton Coll., 1974; MA in Tchg., Rockford Coll., 1980; cert. of advanced study, No. Ill. U., 1985. Cert. elem. tchr., spl. edn. tchr., Ill. Elem. sch. tchr. Christian Life Ctr. Sch., Rockford, Ill., 1974-80; remedial reading tchr. Washington Elem. Sch., Belvidere, 1980-99, Kishwaukee Elem. Sch., Belvidere, 1999—. Mem. NEA, Ill. Edn. Assn., Belvidere Edn. Assn. (bldg. rep. 1980-82), No. Ill. Reading Coun., Nat. Assn. Christian Schs., Alpha Delta Kappa (sec. 1994-96, v.p. 1996-98, chaplain 1998-2000). Avocations: church choral singing, flute, violin, guitar, travel. Home: 1112 Fox Chase Ln Rockford IL 61107-6214 E-mail: rauch.janet@mcleodusa.net.

RAUCH, JOHN KEISER, JR. architect; b. Phila., Oct. 23, 1930; s. John Keiser and Marjorie (Gretz) R.; m. Carol Pfaff, Mar. 11, 1953 (div. June 1978); children: John David, Charles Daniel, Kathryn Mari, Peter, Carol Anne; m. Carol A. McConochie, Jan. 10, 1981. Student, Wesleyan U., Middletown, Conn., 1948-51; BArch., U. Pa., 1957; grad. cert. program, Pa. Acad. Fine Arts, 2001. Draftsman Cope & Lippincott, Phila., 1957-60; architect Venturi and Short, 1960-64; partner Venturi and Rauch (Architects and Planners), 1964-79, Venturi, Rauch and Scott Brown, 1980-82, v.p., mng. prin., 1982-87, mgmt. cons., mediator, arbitrator, 1988-96; instr. U. Pa. Grad. Sch. Fine Arts, 1969-70, 89. Lectr. dept. architecture Princeton (N.J.) U., 1990-94. Trustee Found. for Architecture, 1977-84, mem. adv. com., 1994—; treas. Phila. Rehab., Inc., 1984-94; pres. Reading Terminal Market Pres. Fund, 1988-93, bd. dirs., 1994-2001; bd. dirs. United Cerebral Palsy Assn., 1988-91. Recipient Good Neighbor award Mellon/PSFS Bank, 1992. Fellow AIA (Firm award 1983, John Harbeson Disting Svc. Phila. Chpt. award 1992); mem. Pa. Soc. Architects. Democrat. Home: 620 Gate House Ln Philadelphia PA 19118-4303

RAUCH, KATHLEEN, computer executive; b. Franklin Square, N.Y., Oct. 30, 1951; d. William C. and Marian (Shull) R.; B.A., U. Rochester, 1973; M.A. in L.S., U. Mich., 1974; postgrad. N.Y. U., 1981-82. Media specialist Sutton (Mass.) Sch., 1974-76; program cons. Advanced Mgmt. Rsch. Internat., N.Y.C., 1976-79; pub. rels. cons., N.Y.C., 1979; pres. N.Y. chpt. NOW, N.Y.C., 1979-80; computer programmer Blue Cross/Blue Shield of Greater N.Y., N.Y.C., 1981-82; computer programmer analyst Fed. Res. Bank of N.Y., 1983-84; systems officer Citibank, N.A., 1984-85; systems analyst Fed. Res. Bank of N.Y., 1986-89; computer and children's libr. East Meadow (N.Y.) Pub. Libr., 1989-91; pres. Panorama Children's Videos, Inc., 1988-93; microcomputer specialist N.C. State U., 1992-93; prin., v.p. The Computer Lab., Inc., 1993—; prin., v.p., The Computer Lab of Atlanta, Inc., 1994-98. Adv. bd. SafeSkills, Durham, N.C., 1997-98; mem. Coun. on Entrepreneurial Devel., Research Triangle Park, N.C., 1996—. Mem. ALA, NOW (dir. pub. rels. N.Y.C. chpt. 1978, v.p. programs 1978, pres. 1979-80, chmn. bd. 1981, founding mem., sec. Svc. Fund NOW, N.Y.C. chpt. 1981, Raleigh, N.C. chpt.), Assn. for Women in Computing (v.p. membership 1984, exec. v.p. 1985, treas. 1986, mem.-at-large 1987, pres. 1988), Triangle Bus. and Profl. Guild, Friends of the JC Raulston Arboretum. Office: The Computer Lab Inc 2700 Gateway Centre Blvd Morrisville NC 27560-9137

RAUCH, LAWRENCE LEE, aerospace and electrical engineer, educator; b. L.A., May 1, 1919; s. James Lee and Mabel (Thompson) R.; m. Norma Ruth Cable, Dec. 15, 1961; children: Lauren, Maury Rauch. AB, U. So. Calif., 1941; postgrad., Cornell U., 1941; AM, Princeton U., 1948, PhD, 1949. Instr. math. Princeton U., 1943- 49; faculty U. Mich., 1949—, prof. aerospace engring., 1953-79, emeritus, 1979, chmn. instrumentation engring. program, 1952-63, chmn. computer, info. and control engring. program, 1971-76, asso. chmn. dept. elec. and computer engring., 1972-75; chief technologist telecommunication sci. and engring. div. NASA/Calif. Inst. Tech. Jet Propulsion Lab., 1979-85. Vis. prof. École Nationale Supérieure de L'Aéronautique et de l'Espace, Toulouse, France, 1970, Calif. Inst. Tech., Pasadena, 1977-85, U. Tokyo, 1978; cons. govt. and industry, 1946—; chmn. telemetering working group, panel test range instrumentation Research and Devel. Bd. Dept. Def., 1952-53; mem. exec. com. (Nat. Telemetering Conf.), 1959-64; Western Hemisphere program chmn. (1st Internat. Telemetering Conf.), London, 1963, program chmn., U.S.A., 1967; supr. air blast telemetering, Bikini, 1946; mem. project non-linear differential equations Office Naval Research, 1947-49; mem. research adv. com. on communications, instrumentation and data processing NASA, 1963-68. Author: Radio Telemetry, 1956; also numerous sci. articles and papers on radio telemetry. Recipient award for outstanding contbn. to WWII Army and Navy, 1947, award for outstanding contbn. to telemetering field Nat. Telemetering Conf., 1960; Donald P. Eckman award for disting. achievement in edn. Instrument Soc. Am., 1966; Pioneer award Internat. Telemetering Conf./USA, 1985. Fellow IEEE (spl. award contbns. radio telemetry 1957, adminstrv. com. profl. group space electronics and telemetry 1958-64), AAAS, Explorers Club; mem. Am. Math. Soc., AIAA, U. Mich. Research Club, Phi Beta Kappa, Sigma Xi, Phi Eta Sigma, Phi Kappa Phi. Achievements include patent in field; development of first electronic time-division multiplex radio telemetering system, of pre-detection recording; radio telemetry of first U.S. jet aircraft, of air blast over pressure for Operation Crossroads at Bikini Atoll; analysis of optimum demodulation of frequency-modulated signals. Address: 759 N Citrus Ave Los Angeles CA 90038-3401 E-mail: lawrence.l.rauch@jpl.nasa.gov.

RAUCH, PAUL DAVID, television producer; b. Jersey City; s. Harry and Ruth (Reyman) R.; children— Stacie Jennifer, Tyler Meade. Classical music corr. Yomiuri Shimbun, 1956-58; corr. Voice of Am., 1958; Supr. prodn. TV programs CBS-TV, 1958-59; supr. prodn. TV programs Procter & Gamble Co., 1960-70; v.p. in charge daytime and east coast primetime programming CBS-TV, 1970-72; exec. producer Another World, others NBC-TV, 1972-82; exec. TV producer Twentieth Century Fox, 1982-83; executive producer One Life To Live ABC-TV, 1983-91; exec. producer Santa Barbara NBC-TV, 1991-93; exec. producer 919 Fifth Ave CBS, 1994-95; producer Lover's Knot (feature film), 1995-96; developer Columbia-Tristar TV, FOX TV, USA cable TV, 1994-96; exec. producer Guiding Light CBS, 1996—. Exec. prodr., Run The Wild Fields (Showtime feature film, Emmy award 2001), 1999. Served with AUS, 1956-58 Recipient Emmy award Nat. Acad. TV Arts and Scis., 1975, 76, Emmy award nomination for Another World, NBC-TV, 1976-77, NBC Bicentennial Special, Rachel Jackson, 1976.

RAUCH, RUDOLPH STEWART, III, periodical editor, arts education executive; b. Bryn Mawr, Pa., July 5, 1943; s. Rudolph Stewart and Frances (Brewster) R.; m. Sheila Prentice, Oct. 31, 1972; children: Edward Prentice, Michael Brewster. BA, Princeton U., 1965. Corr. Time mag., N.Y.C., 1969-70, Bonn, W. Ger., 1970-71, Saigon, Vietnam, 1971-72, Rio De Janeiro, Brazil, 1972-74, Buenos Aires, Argentina, 1974-76, Atlanta, 1976-79, dep. chief of corrs. N.Y.C., 1979-80; asst. to chmn. bd. Time Inc., 1981-84, internat. dir. mag. devel., 1984-85; exec. editor N.Y. N.J. Conn. Real Estate, 1986-87; mng. editor Constitution, 1989-94; mng. dir. Met. Opera Guild, Inc., N.Y.C., 1994—; pub. Opera News, 1994—, editor, 1998—. Editor, pub. Opera News, 1998—. Edward R. Murrow Press fellow Council on Fgn. Relations, 1980-81 Mem. Coun. Fgn. Rels. Office: Met Opera Guild 70 Lincoln Center Plz Fl 6 New York NY 10023-6577 E-mail: rrauch@metguild.org.

RAUCHER, HERMAN, novelist, screenwriter; b. Bklyn., Apr. 13, 1928; s. Benjamin Brooks and Sophie (Weinshank) R.; m. Mary Kathryn Martinet, Apr. 20, 1960; children: Jacqueline Leigh, Jennifer Brooke. BS, NYU, 1949. Asst. trade ad mgr. 20th Century Fox Films, N.Y.C. and Los Angeles, 1950-54; copy dir. Walt Disney Studios, N.Y.C., 1954-55; copy supr. Calkins & Holden Advt., 1955-57; copy dir., v.p., dir. Reach McClinton Advt., 1957-63; v.p., creative dir. Maxon Advt., 1963-64; creative supr. Gardner Advt., 1964-65; v.p. advt., cons. Benton & Bowles Advt., 1965-67; freelance novelist, screenwriter, 1967—; pres. Bearfilm Prodns., 1971-96. Author: (novels and screenplays) Watermelon Man, 1970, Summer of '42 (nominated Acad. award for best original screenplay 1971, Writers Guild award nomination, Photoplay award), Ode to Billy Joe, 1975, A Glimpse of Tiger, 1972, (novel) Maynard's House, 1979, (screenplays) Sweet November, 1968, The Other Side of Midnight, 1977, Class of 44, 1972, Hieronymus Merkin (Best Original Screenplay award Writers Guild of Great Britain 1969), There Should Have

Been Castles, 1978, Ginger, 1995, ARA/Froom, 2001 also various dramas appearing on TV in Alcoa Hour, Studio One, Matinee Theatre, Goodyear Playhouse, (TV mini-series under pseudonym) Master of the Game, 1984, (TV pilot) Remember When, 1974; playwright: Harold, 1962, Two Weeks Somewhere Else, 1967, Red Lights and Dragons, 1996, Kitty Hawk (musical), 2000; contbg. editor: Greenwich Time; contbr. to book revs. to N.Y. Times. Served with U.S. Army, 1950-52. Mem. Writers Guild Am., Authors League Am., Am. Film Inst., Dramatists Guild, Acad. of Motion Picture Arts and Scis.

RAUCHWERGER, LISA, artist, illustrator; b. San Luis Obispo, Calif., Jan. 14, 1965; d. George Paul and Diane Fey (Levin) R. BA in Illustration magna cum laude, Calif. State U., Northridge, 1988. Art dir. Temple Judea, Tarzana, Calif., 1987-88; in-house illustrator Torah Aura Prodns., L.A., 1988-89; artist in residence Am. Jewish Congress Feminist Ctr., 1990-93; illustrator, designer Superstudio Design, Jerusalem, 1994; illustrator, graphic designer Art Scroll Printing Corp., N.Y.C., 1994-95; freelance artist/illustrator Cutting Edge Creations, L.A., Jerusalem, N.Y.C., Cleve., San Jose, 1979—. Tchr. papercutting and calligraphy at various schs. and confs. nationwide. Illustrator: A Mouse in Our Jewish House, 1990; author, illustrator: Chocolate Chip Challah, 1999; The Chocolate Chip Challah Activity Book, v.i,ii, 2001. Recipient Best of Show awrd Mid Rockland Arts Festival, N.Y., 1995. Mem. Am. Guild Judaic Art, Soc. Children's Book Writers and Illustrators, Nat. Mus. Women in the Arts (charter), Coalition for Advancement of Jewish Edn. Democrat. Avocations: hiking, archery, writing, cooking, music. E-mail: Rauchie@aol.com.

RAUCINA, THOMAS FRANK See RACINA, THOM

RAUDONIS, VALERIE CHRISTINE, lawyer; b. Nashua, N.H., July 30, 1953; d. Alphonse J. and Sophie C. (Raucykevich) R.; children: Ryan, Laura. BA, Boston Coll., 1975; JD, New England Sch. Law, Boston, 1978. Bar: N.H. 1978, U.S. Dist. Ct. N.H. 1978, U.S. Tax Ct. 1979, U.S. Ct. Appeals (1st cir.) 1979. Pvt. practice, Nashua, N.H., 1978—. Mem. part-time faculty Rivier Coll. Paralegal Studies, Nashua, 1984-86, 91-92, mem. adv. bd., 1993-2001, chairperson, 1999. Bd. dirs. Nashua Children's Assn., 1980-88, v.p., 1982-84, pres., 1984-85, assoc., 1988—; bd. dirs. YWCA, 1979-84, mem. YM-YW coun., 1981-84, 2d v.p., 1983-84; trustee Mt. St. Mary Sem., 1981-86, Tacy House, Inc., 1981-86; bd. dirs. Nashua Youth Coun., 1982-83, Adult Learning Ctr., 1995-2001; mem. N.H. Action Com. for Foster Children, 1983-86; mem. adv. com. to bd. dirs. Souhegan Theatre Coun., 1990-95; mem. St. Casimir's Ladies Guild, 1981-86. Recipient N.H. Young Career Woman, Nat. Fed. Bus. and Profl. Women, Catherine M. McAuley award. Fellow N.H. Bar Found.; mem. ABA (custody com. family law sect. 1983-84), N.H. Bar Assn. (chmn. com. on juvenile problems and family law 1980-81, 82-83, com. on needs of children 1984-85), Nashua Bar Assn. (pres. 2001), Nat. Fedn. Bus. and Profl. Women (chmn. young career woman com. 1982-83, 2d v.p. Nashua 1983-85, pres. 1985-86, N.H. Young Career Woman award 1982). Avocations: downhill skiing, children. Office: 7 Auburn St Nashua NH 03064-2615 E-mail: raudonislaw@aol.com.

RAUE, JORG EMIL, electrical engineer; b. Stettin, Germany, June 13, 1936; came to U.S., 1952; s. Ludwig and Liselotte (Barth) R.; m. Anke Volkmann, June 29, 1957; children: Monika Kay, Jennifer Faye. BSEE, Milw. Sch. Engring., 1961; MSEE, Marquette U., 1965, PhDEE, 1968. Mem. faculty Milw. Sch. Engring., 1961-68, chmn. dept., 1968-69; research engr. TRW Systems, Redondo Beach, Calif., 1969-76, mgr. dept., 1976-79; sr. research scientist TRW Electronic Systems, Rendondo Beach, Calif., advanced systems mgr., 1980-93; tech. cons., 1993—; chmn. dept. elec. engring. Calif. Polytech State U., San Luis Opispo, 1979-80. Mem. faculty Marquette U., Milw., 1968-69, Loyola U., Los Angeles, 1970-72, U. So. Calif., Los Angeles, 1983—. Contbr. articles to profl. jours. Served with U.S. Army, 1955-58. Recipient Disting. Tchr. award Milw. Sch. Engring., 1968; named Outstanding Alumnus Milw. Sch. Engring., 1985. Fellow IEEE; mem. Microwave Soc. of IEEE (sec. adminstrn. com. 1985—), Sigma Xi. Avocations: tennis, bicycling, flying. Home and Office: 28813 Rothrock Dr Palos Verdes Estates CA 90275-3060

RAUENHORST, GERALD, architectural engineer, construction and development executive; b. Mpls., Dec. 8, 1927; s. Henry and Margaret (Keltgen) R.; m. Henrietta Schmoll, Sept. 2, 1950; children: Judith, Mark, Neil, Joseph, Michael, Susan, Amy. BA, U. St. Thomas, 1948, LLD, 1971; BSCE, Marquette U., 1951, LLD (hon.) , 2001. Instr. civil engring. Marquette U., Milw., 1950-51; engr. Peter Rasmussen & Son, Oshkosh, Wis., 1951-52, Viking Constrn., Mpls., 1952-53; pres., founder Rauenhorst Corp. (name changed to Opus Corp.), 1953—, chmn. bd., CEO, 1982—, founding chmn., 2000—. Chmn. and CEO Opus Nat., L.L.C., 1997—; dep. chmn. 1991-93, chmn. bd. dirs. Fed. Res. Bank, Mpls., 94-95, dir., chmn. human resources com. ConAgra, Omaha, 1982-98; bd. dirs. Cornerstone Properties, Inc., N.Y., 1993-98. Mem. devel. com. Papal Found.; trustee U. St. Thomas; chmn. bd. trustees Marquette U., 1985—87, trustee emeritus; dir. emeritus Cath. Cmty. Found.; treas. Papal Found. Recipient Disting. Engring. award Marquette U., 1974, Ernst & Young Lifetime Achievement award/Entrepreneur of Yr., 1997; named Alumnus of Yr., Marquette U., 1969, Coll. of St. Thomas, 1978, Minn. Exec. of Yr., Corp. Report mag., 1983, Developer of Yr., NAIOP, 1992, No. 1 Developer in Country, Nat. Real Estate Investor mag., 1995; named to Minn. Bus. Hall of Fame, 1980. Mem. ASCE, NSPE, World Pres. Orgn., Minn. Soc. Profl. Engrs., Mpls. Club, Interlachen Club, Naples Yacht Club, Port Royal Club, Royal Poinciana Golf Club, Serra Club (past gov. dist. 7, past pres. Mpls.), Knight of Holy Sepulchre, Knight of St. Gregory, Triangle. Roman Catholic. Avocations: fishing, golf, pottery. Office: Opus Corp PO Box 59110 Minneapolis MN 55459-0110

RAUGHTON, JIMMIE LEONARD, education consultant, public administrator, urban planner; b. Knoxville, Tenn., Oct. 9, 1943; s. George L. and Ann (Simotes) R. BA in Urban and Regional Planning, U. No. Colo., 1974, MA, 1976; PhD, U. Colo., 1993. Mgr. Flexitran divsn. Gathers, De Vilbliss Archs. and Planners, 1966-68; asst. dir. planning City of Aurora, Colo., 1968-71; planner City of Lakewood, 1971-73, City of Boulder, 1973-74; instr. urban planning C.C. of Denver, 1974-76, divsn. dir. human resources and svcs., 1976-81, divsn. dir. sci. and tech., 1981-85; v.p. State of Colo. C.C., 1985—. Chmn. profl. adv. com. to Colo. Gov.'s Land Use Adviser, 1973; cons. Denver Regional Coun. of Govts. for Model Sign Code, 1973, City of Boulder Transp. Dept., 1975—; coord. devel. Rocky Mountain Energy and Environ. Tech. Ctr., 1980; exec. dir. Edn. Found. Colo., 1989-98; spkr. in field. Mem. exec. bd. Civic Ctr. Assn., Denver, 1973-75; supervisory com. Colo. State Employees Credit Union, 1986—; mem. bd. Support Sys. Consol., 1984, Bridge Industry, 1984-85; candidate Denver City Coun., 1975; bd. dirs. Plan Metro Denver, 1975-76, Four Corner Art Collection, 1973—. Recipient Citizen award of honor Assn. Beautiful Colo. Roads, 1972. Mem. ASTD, Am. Inst. Planners (mem. exec. bd. Colo. 1970-75, treas. 1972-73), Am. Soc. Planning Ofcls., Am. Vocat. Assn., Pi Alpha Alpha, Colo. City Mgrs. Assn. Home: 2501 High St Denver CO 80205-5565

RAUH, JOHN DAVID, manufacturing company executive; b. Cin., May 28, 1932; s. Carl J. and Grace (Stix) R.; m. Elizabeth Gibbons, June 19, 1954; children: Carol Miller (dec. 1991), Daniel Gibbons.; m. Mary Stoner, Dec. 23, 1984; children: Brooks Tomb, Howard Tomb. AB, Harvard U., 1954, MBA, 1956. Gen. mgr. Rauh Shirt Co., Cin., 1959-61, Clopay Corp., Cin., 1961-85, pres., 1972-75, chmn., CEO, 1975-85, also chmn. Adj. faculty mktg. Colby-Sawyer Coll., New London, N.H., 1989-92; fellow Kennedy Sch., Harvard, 1989. Pres. Charter Com. Greater Cin., 1969-76; canidate U.S. Senate, N.H., 1990, 92, 96; trustee Franklin Pierce Coll., 1993-2000; chair Childrens Alliance N.H., 1997—; dir. Common Cause, 1998—. 1st lt. Finance Corps. AUS, 1956-59. Home: 57 Old Bay Rd PO Box 2124 New Castle NH 03854 E-mail: jdrauh5@aol.com.

RAUH, RICHARD PAUL, architect; b. Covington, Ky., Mar. 27, 1948; s. Robert Paul and Pauline (Farmer) R.; m. Mary Darlene Bailey, Oct. 6, 1975. AB in History of Art, Columbia U., 1970; BArch, MArch, Harvard U., 1974; DMD, U. Ky., 1980. Registered architect, 30 states; lic. dentist, Ky., Va. Asst. prof. U. Ky. Coll. Architecture, Lexington, 1976-80, adj. asst. prof., 1980-81; prin. Carpenter/Rauh, 1978-80, Rabun Hatch Portman McWhorter Hatch & Rauh Architects, Atlanta, 1981-85, Richard Rauh & Assocs., Architects, Atlanta, 1984—. Cons. Macon (Ga.) Heritage Found., City of Cin., Tampa Preservation Bd., Battle House Found., Mobile Ala., City of Norwood, Ohio, St. Petersburg (Fla.) Preservation Inc., City of West Palm Beach, Booker Creek Preservation Inc. Works published in numerous books and mags.; works include Norfolk Hilton Hotel, Va., 1985, Omni Netherland Plaza Hotel Restoration, Cin., 1982-83, Bridgeport Plaza Hilton Hotel, Conn., 1985, Carew Tower Block restoration, Cin., 1983-91, master plan Gaines Ctr. for Humanities, U. Ky., Lexington, 1984, La Concha Hotel, Key West, Fla., 1986, Carolina Head Injury Ctr., Durham, N.C., 1987, Albany (Ga.) Holiday Inn Hotel, 1989, Shenandoah Head Injury Ctr., Manassas, Va., 1989, Kenner Toyo Products Gen. Offices, Cin., 1990, Cin. Club, 1991, Tower Pl.-Emery Arcade Restoration, Cin., 1991, urban Design Masterplan, Mobile, Ala., 1993, O'Neil Cinemas, Duluth, Ga., 1994, Julius Fleischmann Meml. Fountain and Fleischmann Cen. Bldg., Naples, Fla., 1999, Masterplan 3d St. South retail dist., Naples, Fla., 2000, Lila Ross Wilburn Bldg. restoration, Atlanta, 2001; author: (with David G. Wright) Design Courses at Schools of Architecture in Western Europe: A Documentary Study, 1975. Pres. Hist. South Hill Assn., Lexington, 1978-80; bd. dirs. Margaret Mitchell House iNc., 1987-92, pres. 1989, Preservation Actin, Washington, 1988—, City of Atlanta Neighorhood Planning unit, Buckhead Bd., 1992-96, Planning Adv. bd., 1992-96. Sheldon fellow Harvard U., 1974-75, Appleton fellow, 1974-75; recipient LUMEN excellence award Illuminating Engring. Soc. N.Am., 1985; Harvard Book award Harvard Club Cin., 1965; U.S. Dept. Interior grantee Ky. Heritage Commn., 1978, U.S. Dept. HUD Urban Devel. Action grantee, 1988; recipient honor awards Nat. Trust Hist. Preservation U.S., 1985, AIA South Atlantic Reg. coun., 1984, Ga. Assn. AIA, 1984, 88, 89, 94, Ga. young Arch. award 1988, Ky. Soc. Archs. AIA, 1986, Nat. award Soc. Am. Registered Archs., 1986, 89, 90, 94, Build Am. award AGC/Motorola, 1992, Greater Cin. Beautiful award City of Cin., 1984, Ohio Hist. Soc., 1987, Fla. Keys Preservation Bd., 1987, City of Miami Beach, 1990, Nat. Hist. Landmark Designation U.S. Dept. Interior, 1995, Atlanta Urban Design Commn., 2001. Mem. Art Deco Soc. Am., Harvard Club Ga., Harvard Club Ky., Filson Club (Ky.), Order Ky. Cols. Democrat. Presbyterian. Home: PO Box 20061 Atlanta GA 30325 Office: Richard Rauh & Assocs PO Box 18560 Atlanta GA 31126-0560 E-mail: rrauh@atlanta.com.

RAUHUT, HORST WILFRIED, research scientist; b. Duesseldorf, Germany, May 4, 1930; came to U.S., 1964; s. Gustav Adolf and Johanna (Klose) R.; m. Magdalena Winkel, July 16, 1957; children: Birgit, Monika, Michael Winfred. BSc, U. Bonn., Germany, 1954, MSc, 1956; D in Natural Scis., U. Munich, 1958. Lab. supr. Henkel of CIE, Duesseldorf, 1959-64; chemist Harry Diamond Lab., U.S. Army, Washington, 1964-68, Morton Internat., Woodstock, Ill., 1968-71, Acme Resin, Forest Park, 1971-73; rsch. scientist Dexter Electronic Materials, Olean, N.Y., 1973—. Dir., program coord. Plastics Engrs., Chgo., 1971-73; instr. Jamestown C.C., Olean, 1977; author, presenter tech. seminars, 1976-88. Author: Ueber Bicyclische Ketale mit Spiran-Struktur, 1958, Microelectronics Packaging and Processing Engrs. Tutorial on Epoxies, 1994; contbr. articles to sci. jours. Treas. Haskell Cmty., Cuba, N.Y., 1977-94, local historian, 1991. Named Outstanding New Citizen, Citizenship Coun. Met. Chgo., 1970. Mem. Am. Chem. Soc., Soc. Plastics Engrs. (dir. thermoset divsn. 1973-81, chmn. divsn. 1981-82, mem. internat. rels. com. 1973-84, thermoset divsn. award 1978, chmn.'s award 1982, award for significant contbn. to plastics industry 1988). Democrat. Achievements include Belgian, French and German patents for epoxy compositions, U.S. patents for foam sandwich structure, for flammable striker; research in areas of synthetic organic chemistry, adhesives/adhesion, ordnance, epoxy encapsulation compounds, low-stress technology and dielectric analysis. Avocations: photography, hiking, history. Home: 3551 Willow Rd Cuba NY 14727-9425 Office: Dexter Electronic Materials 211 Franklin St Olean NY 14760-1211

RAUHUT, JOHN FREDERICK, pastor; b. Chgo., Aug. 30, 1975; s. Herbert Herman and Alice (Krotochwil) R.; m. Anna Mae Weaver, Aug. 30, 1975; children: Eben, Anthony, Marcus. AB, Faith Coll., 1982; MDiv, Moravian Sem., Bethlehem, Pa., 1989. Ordained to ministry United Meth. Ch., 1988. Tchr. Hess Sch., Lititz, Pa., 1971-76, Gehmans Sch., Denver, 1976-78, Maranatha Sch., Watsontown, 1978-83, Bethel Sch., Egg Harbor, N.J., 1983-84; pastor Bethany/Ebenezer United Meth. Ch., Barnesville, Pa., 1985-89, Trinity United Meth. Ch., Middleburg, 1989-98, Ft. Loudon-Edenville United Meth. Ch., Saint Thomas, 1998—2002, St. Paul United Meth. Ch., Williamsport, 2002—. Pres. Middleburg Ministerium, 1990—98; dist. missions dir. Lewisburg Dist. Ministerium, 1993—. Advisor Cub Scouts, Middleburg, 1991-93; chaplain Reliance Hose Fire Co., Middleburg, 1994-98; mem. parents adv. com. Middleburg H.S., 1995-98; mem. Moravian Hist. Soc., Bethlehem, Pa., 1990—; co-dir. UN Seminar, 1999—. Home: 1127 Louisa St Williamsport PA 17701-1614 Office: 1427 Memorial Ave Williamsport PA 17701-1614

RAUL, ALAN CHARLES, lawyer; b. Bronx, N.Y., Sept. 9, 1954; s. Eugene and Eduarda (Müller-Mañas) R.; m. Mary Tinsley, Jan. 30, 1988; children: Caroline Tinsley, William Eduardo Tinsley, Alexander Tinsley. AB magna cum laude, Harvard U., 1975, MPA, 1977; JD, Yale U., 1980. Bar: N.Y. 1982, D.C. 1982, U.S. Ct. Appeals (D.C. cir.) 1982, U.S. Supreme Ct. 1988. Law clk. to judge U.S. Ct. Appeals (D.C. cir.), Washington, 1980-81; assoc. Debevoise & Plimpton, N.Y.C., 1981-86; White House assoc. counsel Pres. Reagan, Washington, 1986-88; gen. counsel Office Mgmt. and Budget, 1988-89, USDA, Washington, 1989-93; prin. Beveridge & Diamond P.C., 1993-97; ptnr. Sidley Austin Brown & Wood, 1997—. Cons. Reagan-Bush campaign, N.Y.C., 1984; mem. implementation task force Internet Corp. for Assigned Names and Numbers, 2000—. Author: (book) Privacy and the Digital State, 2001. Co-chairperson, co-founder Lawyers Have Heart; chmn. bd. USDA Grad. Sch., 1991-93; bd. dirs. Nationas Capital affiliate Am. Heart Assn., 1993-97, Greater Washington region, 2002--; treas., dir. Citizens Assn. Georgetown, 1993-97; mem. Nat. Policy Forum's Environ. Policy Coun.; mem. adv. coun. Atlantic Legal Found., 2001--. Recipient Disting. Achievement award Am. Heart Assn., 1991, Vol. of Yr. award, 1993, Lifetime Achievement award, 1999. Mem. ABA (coun. sect. internat. law and practice 1992-98, chmn. com. on nat. security and internat. law 1990-92, standing com. on election law 1995-99, sect. internat. law and practice govt. affairs officer 1996-98), Assn. of Bar of City of N.Y. (chmn. subcom. on Cen. Am. issues 1985, mem. com. on inter-Am. affairs 1983), Federalist Soc. (mem. nat. practitioners adv. coun., chair environ. and property rights practice group 1996-99), Coun. on Fgn. Rels. Office: Sidley Austin Brown & Wood 1501 K St NW Washington DC 20005 E-mail: araul@sidley.com.

RAULINAITIS, PRANAS ALGIS, electronics executive, consultant; b. Kaunas, Lithuania, May 13, 1927; came to U.S., 1954, naturalized, 1960; s. Pranas Viktoras and Paulina (Gervaite) R.; m. Angele Staugaityte, Oct. 4, 1952; 1 son, Pranas Darius. With Commonwealth Rys. of Australia, Melbourne, 1949-53; asst. to fin. acct. Kitchen & Sons, Pty. Ltd., 1953-54; v.p. photo divsn. Interphoto Corp., L.A, 1954-71; sr. v.p., sec. Craig Corp., L.A., 1971-87; pres. PAR Enterprises, Burbank, Calif., 1987—. Adviser Ministry Fgn. Affairs Republic of Lithuania, 1992. Former pres. Lithuanian Am. Coun., Inc. of Calif.; bd. dirs. Lithuanian-Am. assns.; founder, dir., v.p. Baltic Am. Freedom League; former mem. Am. Soc. Internat. Law. E-mail. Home and Office: PAR Enterprises 1501 W Riverside Dr Burbank CA 91506-3027 E-mail: raulalgis@juno.com.

RAULT, RAYMOND MARCEL, nephrologist; b. London, Mar. 26, 1940; s. Peter Gerard and Janet (Davison-Orr) R. MBBS, St. Mary's Hosp., London, 1967. Diplomate in internal medicine and nephrology Am. Bd. Internal Medicine. From asst. prof. to prof. U. Pitts., 1979—. Mem. Am. Soc. Artificial Internal Organs, Royal Coll. Physicians (U.K.). Roman Catholic. Avocations: antiquarian medical books, medical history, British history. Office: U Pitts 3550 Terrace St Pittsburgh PA 15213-2500 E-mail: rault@msx.dept-med.pitt.edu.

RAUP, DAVID MALCOLM, paleontology educator; b. Boston, Apr. 24, 1933; s. Hugh Miller and Lucy (Gibson) R.; m. Susan Creer Shepard, Aug. 25, 1956; 1 son, Mitchell D.; m. Judith T. Yamamoto, May 30, 1987. BS, U. Chgo., 1953; MA, Harvard U., 1955, PhD, 1957. Instr. Calif. Inst. Tech., 1956-57; mem. faculty Johns Hopkins U., 1957-65, assoc. prof., 1963-65; mem. faculty U. Rochester, 1965-78, prof. geology, 1966-78, chmn. dept. geol. scis., 1968-71, dir. Center for Evolution and Paleobiology, 1977-78; curator geology, chmn. dept. geology Field Mus. Natural History, Chgo., 1978-80, dean of sci., 1980-82; prof. geophys. sci. U. Chgo., 1980-95, chmn. dept., 1982-85, Sewell L. Avery disting. service prof., 1984-95; prof. emeritus, Sewell L. Avery disting. svc. prof. emeritus, 1995—. Geologist U.S. Geol. Survey, part-time, 1959-77; vis. prof. U. Tubingen, Germany, 1965, 72 Author: (with S. Stanley) Principles of Paleontology, 1971, 78, The Nemesis Affair, 1986, 2d edit., 1999, Extinction: Bad Genes of Bad Luck?, 1991; editor: (with B. Kummel) Handbook of Paleontological Techniques, 1965; contbr. articles to profl. jours. Recipient Best Paper award Jour. Paleontology, 1966; Schuchert award Paleontol. Soc., 1973; grantee Calif. Rsch. Corp., 1955-56, Am. Assn. Petroleum Geologists, 1957, Am. Philos. Soc., 1957, NSF, 1960-66, 75-81, Chem. Soc., 1965-71, NASA, 1983-95. Mem. AAAS, Am. Acad. Arts and Scis., Nat. Acad. Sci., Paleontol. Soc. (pres. 1976-77, medal 1997), Am. Soc. Naturalists (v.p. 1983), Am. Philos. Soc. Home: RR 1 Box 168-y Washington Island WI 54246-9753 E-mail: draup@itol.com.

RAUP, PHILIP MARTIN, retired agricultural economics educator; b. Timken, Kans., Jan. 4, 1914; s. James R. and Bertha (Smith) R.; m. Marian Getter, Feb. 1, 1941; children: Philip Martin, Martha J., Gordon E. AB, U. Kans., 1939; MS, U. Wis., 1942, PhD, 1949. Rsch. fellow Brookings Instn., Washington, 1941-42; chief land officer U.S. Office Mil. Govt. for Germany, Berlin, 1945-49; asst. prof. U. Wis., Madison, 1949-53; prof. agrl. econs. U. Minn., St. Paul, 1953, prof. emeritus, 1984—. Land tenure officer FAO, Rome, 1960-61; cons. World Bank, 1961-66; lectr. Inst. for Internat. Agr., Berlin, 1963, 64, 66, 85. Author: Land Tenure, 1956, Changing Structure of Europe, 1970. Cons. The Citizens League, Mpls., 1970—, Minn. Legislature, St. Paul, 1978, 85-87. Lt. USNR, 1942-45. Fellow Am. Agrl. Econs. Assn. (bd. dirs. 1975-79); mem. Com. on Fgn. Rels. Home: 1572 Fulham St Saint Paul MN 55108-1312 Office: U Minn 1994 Buford Ave Saint Paul MN 55108-6038

RAUP, RUTH ANN, human resources consultant; b. Balt., Sept. 2, 1955; d. Thales Cromwell and Ruth Irene (Shirk) Pumphrey; 1 child, Joshua Karl Raup. BA in French, U. Md. Balt. County, 1977, MA in Edn., 1990. Cert. in Orgn. Devel., Georgetown U. Customer support rep. Xerox Corp., Towson, Md., 1979-90; orgn. devel. cons., tng. developer Blue Cross Blue Shield, Owings Mills, 1990-93, staff devel. mgr., 1993-94, human resources bus. cons., 1994-97, Zurich Ins. Group, Balt., 1997-99; asst. dir. human resources CIGNA Healthcare, 1999-2000; cons. human resources & orgn. devel., 2000—. Mem. Soc. for Human Resource Mgmt., Mensa Internat., Phi Kappa Phi. Avocations: reading, classical music, gardening, interior decoration. E-mail: rraup@earthlink.net.

RAUSCH, HOWARD, information service executive; b. N.Y.C., June 29, 1928; s. Sol and Helen (Kartiganer) R.; m. Sidra Levine Cohn, Apr. 22, 1979. AB, Syracuse U., 1950. Reporter Phila. Bull., 1961; copy editor Wall St. Jour., 1961-63, N.Y. Times, 1963-64; editor, fgn. corr. McGraw-Hill, N.Y.C. and Moscow, 1964-68; pres. Advanced Tech. Publs., Inc., Newton, Mass., 1968-80; editor, pub. Laser Focus mag., 1968-80; editor, founder Energy Research, 1975-80; editor Electronic Business, 1980-82; founder, pub. Lightwave Jour., 1983-90; tech. dir. Optical Soc. Am., Washington, 1991-93; pres. Capital Access Info. and Cons. Svcs., 1993—. Home and Office: 2541 Waterside Dr NW Washington DC 20008-2820 E-mail: hrausch@capaccess.org.

RAUSCH, JOAN MARY, art historian; b. Calmar, Iowa, Dec. 25, 1937; d. Bernard Joseph and Irene Sophia (Wieling) Menne; m. Gerald William Rausch, Sept. 3, 1960; children: John Thomas, Jennifer Nicole Rausch. BS, Coll. St. Teresa, Winona, Minn., 1959; postgrad., U. Wis., LaCrosse, 1974-79; MA, U. Wis., Milw., 1982. Instr. nursing Mercy Hosp., Iowa City, 1960-63, St. Francis Hosp./Viterbo Coll., LaCrosse, 1966-71; rsch. asst. dept. art U. Wis., 1977-79, asst. dept. art history Milw., 1979-81; historic planner Southwest Regional Planning Commn., Platteville, Wis., 1982-83; pres. Archtl. Researches, Inc., LaCrosse, 1983—. Cons. historic preservation divsn. State Hist. Soc. Wis., 1983—, Wis. Dept. of Transp., Dist. 5, 1991-2002. Author: A Catalog of the Oyen Collection, 1979, Historic LaCrosse Architectural and Historic Record, 1984, Chippewa Falls, 1985, Watertown, A Guide to Its Historic Architecture, 1987; (with Joyce Mckay) Richland Center Wisconsin, Architectural and Historical Survey Report, 1988; (with Carol Cartwright) City of Mineral Point, Architectural and Historic Survey Report, 1992, LaCrosse Wisconsin: Architectural and Historical Survey Report, 1996, City of LaCrossse Heritage Tour, 1999, Village of North LaCross Heritage Tour, 1999, (with Carol Cartwright) Town of Jefferson, Leon and Wells, Monroe, Wis. Intensive Survey Report, 2000. Mem. Women's Polit. Caucus, 1972-78, coord., 1974-75. Recipienc Scholarship award Victorian Soc. in Am., 1981, Workshop award Ctr. for Art Criticism, Mpls., 1986. Mem. Soc. Archtl. Historians (pres. Wis. chpt. 1982-84), Nat. Trust Hist. Preservation (Preservation Forum(, Wis. Trust Hist. Preservation (charter, task force mem. 1986), Preservation Alliance of LaCrosse (bd. dirs. 1982-88, Heritage award 1989), LaCrosse County Hist. Soc. (hist. preservation com. 1992—, bd. dirs. 1994-97, Hixon Ho. com. 1994-2001). Avocations: painting, ceramics, landscape gardening, travel, swimming. Home and Office: Archtl Researches Inc W5722 Sherwood Dr La Crosse WI 54601-8442 E-mail: joanrausch@juno.com.

RAUSCH, JOHN DAVID, JR. political science educator; b. W. Reading, Pa., Mar. 15, 1967; s. John David, Sr. and Barbara Ann R.; m. Mary Scanlon, May 25, 1991. BA in Polit. Sci., U. Alaska, 1989; MA in Polit. Sci., U. Okla., 1992, PhD in Polit. Sci., 1995. Asst. prof. polit. sci. Fairmont (W.Va.) State Coll., 1994-98, West Tex. A&M U., Canyon, Tex., 1998—. Sec./treas. North Cen. W.Va. Cmty. Action Assn., 1997-98. Mem. Am. Polit. Sci. Assn. Democrat. Lutheran. Avocations: writing, computer sci. Office: W Tex A&M Univ PO Box 60807 Canyon TX 79016-0001 E-mail: jrausch@mail.wtamu.edu.

RAUSCH, PAUL MATTHEW, financial executive; b. Lafayette, Ind., Dec. 14, 1953; s. Richard Leo and Vernice Ruth (Rhoades) R. Student, Purdue U., 1976. County supr. Farmers Home Adminstrn., Richmond and Falmouth, Ky., 1979-87; loan officer spl. accounts team Farm Credit Svcs., LaPorte, Ind., 1987; br. mgr. Nat. Mortgage Corp., Merrillville, 1987-89; collection mgr. Greentree Acceptance, Lexington, Ky., 1989; county supr. Farmers Home Adminstrn., Springfield and Alamosa, Colo., 1990-96; v.p. Hershey (Nebr.) State Bank, 1996-98; fin. svcs. mgr. Coop. Fin. Assn. for Elsie, Chappell and Stapleton, Nebr., 1998-2000; econ. devel. fin. specialist West Ctrl. Nebr. Devel. Dist., Ogallala, 2001—. Bd. dirs. Internat. Children's Soc., Hooper, Colo., 1993-96. Pres. rural devel. Madison County, Richmond, 1980-85; bd. dirs. Mosca-Hooper Soil Conservation Dist., 1993-94, San Luis Valley Rural Devel. Coun., Alamosa, 1993-94. Recipient Dedication to Cmty. award Madison County, Richmond, 1983; named Ky. Col., Richmond, 1985. Mem. Nat. Parks and Conservation Assn., Am. Soc. Farm Mgrs. and Rural Appraisers, Nature Conservancy, Wilderness Soc., Sierra Club (agr. com. 1987-94), Kiwanis (bd. dirs. 1980-85). Avocations: music collecting, antiques and art collecting, Studebaker vehicle restoration, hunting, farming. Home: 16409 S Hershey-Dickens Rd Dickens NE 69132-9714 Office: 201 E 2d St Ste C Ogallala NE 69153 Fax: 308-284-6070. E-mail: prwcndd@lakemac.net.

RAUSCHENBERG, BRADFORD LEE, museum researcher; b. Atlanta, Sept. 11, 1940; BS in Archaeology and Biology, Ga. State Coll., 1963; MA in History, Wake Forest U., 1995. Archaeologist Ga. Hist. Commn., 1963-64; site supr., asst. Stanley South, State Archaeologist of N.C., 1964-66; antiquarian, asst. Dir. Restoration Old Salem, Inc., Winston-Salem, N.C., 1966-73; asst. to dir. Mus. Early So. Decorative Arts, 1973-76, rsch. fellow, 1976-87, dir. rsch., 1987-93, Mus. Early So. Decorative Arts and Old Salem, Inc., Winston-Salem, 1993—. Cons., lectr. in field. Author: British Regional Carving (1600-1640), and Furniture (1600-1800), 1984, Wachovia Historical Society: 1895-1995, 1995. With USCG, 1964-72. Recipient Halifax Resolves award, 1986; grantee NEH, 1972-81, Kaufman Americana Found., 1981-82. Mem. Am. Ceramic Circle (grantee), Orgn. Am. Historians, No. Ceramic Soc., So. Hist. Assn., Friends of Swiss Ceramic Circle, Regional Furniture Soc., Furniture History Soc., Soc. Hist. Archaeology, Soc. Post-Medieval Archaeology, Soc. Historians Early Am. Republic. Address: 221 Harmon Ct Winston Salem NC 27106-4613 Office: Mus Early So Decorative Arts PO Box 10310 Winston Salem NC 27108-0310

RAUSCHENBERG, DALE EUGENE, music educator; b. Youngstown, Ohio, Jan. 13, 1938; s. Marvin Wilson and Colyn May (Wilhide) R.; m. Theresa Mary Neustupa, June 3, 1964; children: David Edward, Daniel Eric, Catherine Marie. B Music Edn., Youngstown State U., 1960; M Music Performance, Ind. U., 1963. Music dir. Mercer (Pa.) County Schs., 1963-64, Cardinal Mooney High Sch., Youngstown, 1965-66; percussion instr. Youngstown State U., 1965-66; prof. music Towson U., Balt., 1966—. Percussionist

Youngstown Philharm., 1957-60, John Devol Orch., Culvermore, N.J., 1960; auxiliary percussionist Balt. Symphony Orch., 1967—; free-lance percussionist Md. Ctr. for Pub. Broadcasting, Balt., 1967—, Balt. Ctr. for Performing Arts, 1967—; prin. percussionist Balt. Opera Orch., 1989—. Composer Discussion, 1963, What?, 1964; arranger Tchaikowsky's Arabian Dance, 1986, Scott Joplin's Solace, 1986, Scott Joplin's Palm Leaf Rag, 1989; contbr. articles to profl. jours. Capt. USAR, 1960-69. Recipient 3d prize, 3d Ann. W.Va. U. Composition Symposium, 1960. Mem. Am. Fedn. Musicians, Percussive Arts Soc. (pres. Md. chpt. 1979—), Nat. Assn. Coll. Wind and Percussion Instrs., Am. Soc. Composers, Authors and Pubs., Phi Mu Alpha Sinfonia (pres. Delta Eta chpt. 1959-60). Avocations: chess, model railroading. Home: 29 Othoridge Rd Lutherville Timonium MD 21093-5412 Office: Towson U Dept Music York Rd Baltimore MD 21252-0001 E-mail: drauschenberg@towson.edu.

RAUSCHENBERG, MARY EDNA, accountant; b. Commerce, Tex., Oct. 7, 1959; d. Roy Anthony and Gretchen Margaret (Strasma) R. BSEd, Ohio U., 1981; M Acctg. Sci., U. Ill., 1983. CPA, Ohio, W.Va., Ill. Tax staff Arthur Andersen, LLP, Denver and Columbus, Ohio, 1983-86, tax sr. Columbus, 1986-88, tax mgr., 1988-93, sr. tax mgr., 1993-98, tax prin. Chgo., 1998—. Spkr. Nat. Assn. of Coll. and Univ. Bus. Officers, 1994-2002, AICPA, 2000-02. Treas. Seal of Ohio Girl Scout Coun., Columbus, 1997; trustee, chair fin. com. Chgo. coun. Girl Scouts U.S.A. Mem. AICPA (mem. tax tech. resource panel for tax-exempt orgns.), Ill. Soc. CPAs, Ctrl. Assn. Coll. and Univ. Bus. Officers (spkr. 1992—), Healthcare Fin. Mgmt. Assn., Phi Beta Kappa. Office: Arthur Andersen LLP 33 W Monroe St Chicago IL 60603-5300

RAUSEN, AARON REUBEN, pediatric hematologist, oncologist; b. Jersey City, June 30, 1930; s. David and Ruth (Schwartz) R.; m. Emalou Watkins, Apr. 7, 1968; children: David, Susan, Elisabeth. Degree, Dartmouth Coll., 1950; MD, SUNY, Bklyn., 1954. Intern, then resident in pediatrics Bellevue Hosp. Ctr., N.Y.C., 1954-56; chief resident in pediatrics Mt. Sinai Hosp., 1958-59, asst. assoc. and attending pediatrician, 1961-81; fellow in hematology Children's Hosp. and Harvard Med. Sch., Boston, 1959-61; chief of pediatrics City Hosp. Ctr., Elmhurst, N.Y., 1964-72; dir. pediatrics Beth Israel Med. Ctr., N.Y.C., 1972-81; dir. pediatric oncology NYU Med. Ctr., 1981-97; prof. pediatrics NYU Sch. Medicine, 1981—. Prof. pediat. Mt. Sinai Sch. Medicine, N.Y.C., 1971—81, professorial lectr., 1981—; dir. Stephen D. Hassenfeld Children's Ctr. for Cancer and Blood Disorders, N.Y.C., 1990—97, founding dir., 1997—; cons. Lenox Hill Hosp., N.Y.C., 1981—; vis. prof. Dartmouth Med. Sch., Hanover, NH, 1984—86; prin. investigator Children's Oncology Group, 1999—. Contbr. articles to profl. jours. Bd. dirs. N.Y.C. chpt. Am. Cancer Soc., 1984—, Nat. Childhood Cancer Found., 1992—, Children's Oncology Soc. N.Y., 1993—, Ovarian Cancer Rsch. Fund, 1994-99. Capt. Med. Corps, U.S. Army, 1956-58. Fellow Am. Acad. Pediatrics; mem. Am. Pediatric Soc., Am. Soc. Hematology, Am. Soc. Clin. Oncology, Am. Assn. Cancer Rsch., Am. Soc. Pediatric Hematology-Oncology, N.Y. Pediatric Soc. (pres. 1974), Yale Club N.Y.C., Phi Beta Kappa, Alpha Omega Alpha. Office: 317 E 34th St Fl 8 New York NY 10016-4974

RAUSHER, DAVID BENJAMIN, internist, gastroenterologist; b. Bklyn., Sept. 15, 1952; s. Herbert and Shirley Ruth R.; m. Judy A. Steinlauf, Aug. 8, 1976; children: Scott, Michael, Steven. BA, Hamilton Coll., 1973; MD, SUNY, Bklyn., 1977. Diplomate Am. Bd. Internal Medicine, Am. Bd. Gastroenterology. Resident Emory U. Hosps., Atlanta, 1977-80, fellow in gastroenterology, 1980-82; pres. Atlanta Ctr. for Gastroenterology, Decatur, Ga., 1982—; med. dir. Atlanta Endoscopy Ctr., 1994—. Chmn. diagnostic treatment ctr. DeKalb Med. Ctr., Decatur, Ga., 1985—, co-chief gastroenterology, 1995-97, chief sect. gastroenterology, 1998—. Office: Atlanta Ctr Gastro 2665 N Decatur Rd Decatur GA 30033-6125

RAUSSER, GORDON C(LYDE), agricultural and resource economics educator; b. Lodi, Calif., July 21, 1943; s. Elmer A. and Doyve Ester (Meyers) R.; children: Sloan, Stephanie, Paige. BS summa cum laude, Calif. State U., 1965; MS with highest honors, U. Calif., Davis, 1968, PhD with highest honors, 1971. Prof. econs. and agrl. econs. U. Calif., Davis, 1969-74; vis. prof. U. Chgo., 1972-74; prof. econs. and stats. Iowa State U., 1974-75; prof. bus. adminstrn. Harvard U., 1975-78; prof., chmn. dept. agrl. and resource econs. U. Calif., Berkeley, 1979-85, 93-94, Robert Gordon Sproul disting. prof., 1985—; dir. Giannini Found., 1984-86; dean nat. resources U. Calif., 1994-2000. Vis. prof. Hebrew U. and Ben-Gurion U., Israel, 1978; Ford Found. vis. prof., Argentina, 72; spl. cons. and sr. economist Coun. Econ. Advisors, 1986—87; chief economist AID, 1988—90; advisor econ. rsch. svc. U.S. Dept. Agr., 1978—80, 1986—88, Agr. Can., 1977—79, Bur. Agrl. Econs., Australia, 1987, U.S. Office Mgmt. and Budget, 1986; mem., chmn. planning com. Sch. Bus. Adminstrn. U. Calif., Berkeley, 1986—87, mem. adv. com. Agrl. Issues Ctr., 1984—85, mem. planning com. Agrl. and Natural Resources Program, 1986, mem. econs. programs evaluation com., 1987—88; mem. Citrus Planning Commn., Brazil, 1984; pres. Inst. for Policy Reform, Washington, 1989—94; prin., founder Law & Econ. Cons. Group, Berkeley, Washington, Chgo., N.Y.C., 1990—2000; sr. cons. Charles River Assocs., 2000—. Author numerous books including Macroeconomic Environment for U.S. Agricultural Policy, Alternative Agricultural and Food Policies and the 1985 Farm Bill, The Emergence of Market Economies in Eastern Europe, New Directions in Econometric Modeling and Forecasting in U.S. Agriculture, Dynamics of Agricultural Systems: Economic Prediction and Control, Quantitative Methods in Agricultural Economics, GATT Negotiations and the Political Economy of Policy Reform; editor: Decision-Making in Business and Economics, 1977-79, Am. Jour. Agrl. Econs., 1983-86. Mem. western nutrition ctr. coordinating com. U.S. Dept. Agr., 1980-83; mem. Arab-Am. Council for Cultural and Econ. Exchange, 1979-81; bd. dirs. Giannini Found. Agrl. Econs., 1979-84, mem. exec. com., 1979-84 ; mem. planning com. Berkeley Food Coop., 1980-83, planning com. for agrl. and food policy Resources for the Future, 1984-85; mem. adv. com. Calif. State Dept. Agriculture, 1982-84; bd. dirs. Am. Agrl. Econs. Awards. Grantee U.S. Dept. Agr., NSF, World Bank, Chgo. Merc. Exch., U.S. Bur. Mines; Fulbright scholar, Australia, 1987; Sr. fellow Resources for Future, 1984-85. Fellow: AAAS, Am. Agrl. Econs. Assn. (oustanding enduring rsch. contbn. com. 1982—84, outstanding PhD dissertation com. 1974—76, chmn. outstanding article com. 1983—86, Pub. Enduring quality award 1993, Disting. Policy Contbn. award 1993, rsch. awards of merit 1976, 1978, 1980, 1982, 1986, 1989, 1992, 1993, 1994, 2000, 2001), Am. Statis. Assn.; mem.: Western Agrl. Econ. Assn. (Best Pub. Rsch. award 1978, 1994, Outstanding Pub. Rsch. award 1994), Ops. Rsch. Soc., Math. Assn. Am., Econometric Soc., Am. Acad. Polit. and Social Sci., Am. Econ. Assn., Commonwealth (dir. agriculture study group 1983-84), Commonwealth Club (dir. agr. study group 1983—84), Alpha Zeta, Alpha Gamma Rho. Home: 661 San Luis Rd Berkeley CA 94707-1725 Office: U Calif Berkeley ARE 207 Giannini Hall Berkeley CA 94720-3310

RAUTAHARJU, PENTTI MATTI, research scientist, educator; b. Tuusniemi, Finland, Dec. 23, 1932; s. Emil Matti Rautaharju and Ellen Raatikainen; m. Meeri Maria Rautaharju, Aug. 5, 1956 (div. 1977); children: Anu, Tina, Mia; m. Farida Swaliha Razack, Oct. 14, 1982; children: Satu, Sherene, Riza. MD, Helsinki Sch. Medicine, Finland, 1957; PhD, U. Minn., 1962. Prof. dir. Heart Disease Rsch. Ctr., Dalhousie, Halifax, Can., 1963-90, Epicare Ctr., U. Alberta, Can., 1990-94, Winston Salem, N.C., 1994—. Contbr. articles to profl. jours. With Finnish Army, 1954. Fellow RCP, Am. Coll. Cardiologists; mem. Can. Cardiovascular Soc. (Outstanding Scientist 1984), Order of Finland. Avocations: writing poetry, woodcarving, gardening. Home: 5224 Mountain View Rd Winston Salem NC 27104 Office: Epicare Ctr 2000 West First St Winston Salem NC 27104 E-mail: frautaha@wfubmc.edu.

RAUWERDINK, WILLIAM JAY, accountant; b. Sheboygan, Wis., Mar. 3, 1950; s. Harvard M. and Dorothy M. (Duenk) R.; m. Ann Catherine Geske, July 14, 1979; 1 child, Margaret Allene. BBA, U. Wis., 1972; MBA, Harvard U., 1974. CPA, N.Y., Mich., Mass. Ptnr. Deloitte & Touche, Detroit, 1978—93; exec. v.p., CFO, treas., sec. The MEDSTAT Group, Inc., Ann Arbor, 1994—96, Lason, Inc., Troy, 1996—2000. Bd. dirs. Trinity Health Svcs., Novi, Mich., 1998—. Mem. Wis. Bus. Alumni Assn. (bd. dirs. 1980-89, pres. 1984-85), Renaissance Club (Detroit), Harvard Club (Boston). Clubs: Rennaisance (Detroit); Harvard (Boston). Office: 3172 Interlaken Orchard Lake MI 48323-1821

RAVAUX-KIRKPATRICK, FRANCOISE, language professional; b. Fes, Morocco, July 8, 1941; came to U.S., 1967; d. Gilbert Rondot and Simone (Martin) Amet; m. Jacques Ravaux, Oct. 15, 1960 (div. 1981); 1 child, Catherine; m. Peter Steven Kirkpatrick, June 16, 1990. MA in French, Mich. State U., East Lansing, 1969; PhD, 1973; DEA in Semiotics, U. Paris, 1981. Instr. French U. Richmond, Va., 1973-74; asst. prof., 1974-84; assoc. prof., 1984-91; prof., 1991—. Translator: The Pledge, 1990, The Dinner Party, 1993; editor (with A.J. Greimas): La Mode en 1830: Langage et Société, 2000. Named: Chevalier dans L'ordre des Palmes Académiques, Min. Nat. Edn., France, 1994, The Gaines Chair of Modern Fgn. Langs., U. Richmond, 1996. Mem. MLA, Semiotic Assn. Am., World Inst. Phenomenology. Avocations: acting, biking, flyfishing, travel. Home: 312 Rowland St Richmond VA 23220 Office: Dept Modern Language and Literature University of Richmond Richmond VA 23173

RAVDIN, LISA DAWN, neuropsychologist; b. Bklyn., Jan. 29, 1965; d. Richard Lloyd and Susan (Alpert) R.; m. David Neil Deutsch, Oct. 12, 1996; children: Hannah Ravdin Deutsch, Rachel Ravdin Deutsch. BS, Syracuse U., 1987; MD, Chgo. Med. Sch., 1992, PhD, 1994. Lic. psychologist, N.Y. Rsch. asst. North Shore U. Hosp., Manhasset, N.Y., 1987-88; clin. neuropsychology extern Rehab. Inst. Chgo., 1990-91, L.I. Jewish Med. Ctr.-Hillside Hosp., New Hyde Park, N.Y., 1991-93; intern West Haven (Conn.) VA Med. Ctr., 1993-94; neuropsychology fellow in neurology NYU Sch. Medicine/Hosp. for Joint Diseases, N.Y.C., 1994-95; Nat. Rsch. Svc. Award fellow neuropsychology in neurology N.Y. Presbyn. Hosp.-Weill Med. Coll. of Cornell U., 1995-97, dir. neuropsychology svc., 1997—. Co-dir. Women's Neurologic Health Initiative, N.Y.C., 1998. Contbg. author: Neuropsychology of Aging, 1997; contbr. articles to profl. jours. NIH/NINDS Career awardee, 1998, other grants. Mem. APA, Internat. Neuropsychol. soc., N.Y. Neuropsychology Group (bd. dirs. 1998—, treas. 1999—), Nat. Acad. Neuropsychology. Address: NY Presbyn Hosp/ Weill Med Coll of Cornell U 525 E 68th St New York NY 10021-4870

RAVECHÉ, ELIZABETH SCOTT, immunologist, educator; b. Stuttgart, Federal Republic of Germany, Nov. 21, 1950; (parents Am. citizens); d. Williard Warren and Justine (Dorney) Scott; m. Harold Joseph Raveché, Jan. 26, 1974; children: John, Justin, Bernice, Beth. BS, Seton Hill Coll., 1972; PhD, George Washington U., 1977. Rsch. scientist NIH, Bethesda, Md., 1972-79, sr. investigator, 1980-85; assoc. prof. immunology Albany (N.Y.) Med. Coll., 1985-89; prof. immunology U. of Medicine and Dentistry, Newark, 1989-96, prof., 1996—. Contbr. 14 chpts. to books, 75 sci. articles to profl. publs.; mem. editl. bd. Oncology Reports, Procs. Soc. Exptl. Biol. Medicine. Sec. PTA, Hoboken, N.J., 1991. Recipient Disting. Alumna Leadership award, Seton Hall Coll., 2002. Fellow Washington Acad. of Sci. (Outstanding Researcher award, 1983); mem. Am. Assn. Immunologists, Am. Assn. Pathologists, Am. Assn. Cancer Rsch. Office: Dept of Pathology U Medicine-Dentistry NJ 185 S Orange Ave Newark NJ 07103-2757

RAVECHÉ, HAROLD JOSEPH, university administrator, physical chemist; b. N.Y.C., Mar. 18, 1943; s. Harold Edward Raveche and Helen Patricia (DeVincent) Gravino; m. Elizabeth Marie Scott, Jan. 26, 1974; children—John Vincent, Justin Blaise, Bernice Helen, Elizabeth Ann. BA in Chemistry, Hofstra U., 1963; PhD in Phys. Chemistry, U. Calif.-San Diego, 1968. NRC postdoctoral assoc. Nat. Bur. Standards, Gaithersburg, Md., 1968-70, research chemist, 1970-78, chief thermophysics div., 1978-85; dean Sch. of Sci., prof. chemistry Rensselaer Poly. Inst., Troy, N.Y., 1985-88; pres. Stevens Inst. Tech., Hoboken, N.J., 1988—. Bd. dirs. Nat. West N.J. and Bancorp, Atlantic Energy Inc.; commr. of sci. and tech., N.J. Editor: Perspectives in Statistical Physics, 1980; contbr. articles to profl. jours. Pres. Potomac Highlands Citizens Assn., Md., 1978-80 Recipient Disting. Young Scientist of Yr. award Md. Acad. Scis., 1975, U.S. Sr. Exec. Service award Nat. Bur. Standards, 1983, Equal Employment Opportunity award Nat. Bur. Standards, 1984 Mem. AAAS (commn. on sci. edn. 1972-75), Am. Phys. Soc. (adv. council 1975-78), Soc. for Indsl. and Applied Math. (adv. bd. conf. on large-scale computational problems 1984-88), Am. Chem. Soc., Sigma Xi Roman Catholic. Avocations: hiking, swimming, skiing, music, theater. Office: Stevens Inst Tech Office of Pres Castle Point On Hudson Hoboken NJ 07030*

RAVEN, BERTRAM H(ERBERT), psychology educator; b. Youngstown, Ohio, Sept. 26, 1926; s. Morris and Lillian R.; m. Celia Cutler, Jan. 21, 1961; children: Michelle G., Jonathan H. BA, Ohio State U., 1948, MA, 1949; PhD, U. Mich., 1953. Rsch. assoc. Rsch. Ctr. for Group Dynamics, Ann Arbor, Mich., 1952-54; lectr. psychology U. Mich., 1953-54; vis. prof. U. Nijmegen, U. Utrecht, The Netherlands, 1954-55; psychologist RAND Corp., Santa Monica, Calif., 1955-56; prof. UCLA, 1956—, chair dept. psychology, 1983-88. Vis. prof. Hebrew U., Jerusalem, 1962-63, U. Wash., Seattle, U. Hawaii, Honolulu, 1968, London Sch. Econs. and Polit. Sci., London, 1969-70; external examiner U. of the W.I., Trinidad and Jamaica, 1980—, rsch. assoc. Psychol. Rsch. Ctr., 1993—; participant Internat. Expert Conf. on Health Psychology, Tilburg, The Netherlands, 1986; cons., expert witness in field, 1979—. Co-dir. Tng. Program in Health Psychology, UCLA, 1979-88; cons. World Health Orgn., Manila, 1985-86; cons., expert witness various Calif. cts., 1978—. Author: (with others) People in Groups, 1976, Discovering Psychology, 1977, Social Psychology, 1983, Social Psychology: People in Groups (Chinese edition), 1994; editor: (with others) Contemporary Health Services, 1982, Policy Studies Rev. Ann., 1980; editor: Jour. Social Issues, 1969-74; mem. editl. bd. Jour. of Criminology and Social Psychology, 2001--; contbr. articles to profl. jours. Guggenheim fellow, Israel, 1962-63; Fulbright scholar The Netherlands, 1954-55, Israel, 1962-63, Britain, 1969-70; recipient Citation from Los Angeles City Council, 1966, Rsch. on Soc. power by Calif. Sch. of profl. psychology, L.A., 1991; NATO sr. fellow, Italy, 1989. Fellow APA (chair bd. social and ethical responsibility 1978-82), Am. Psychol. Soc., Soc. for Psychol. Study of Social Issues (pres. 1973-74, coun. 1995-97, Kurt Lewin award 1998); mem. AAAS, Am. Sociol. Assn., Internat. Assn. Applied Psychology, Soc. Exptl. Social Psychology, Assn. Advancement of Psychology (founding, bd. dirs. 1974-81), Internat. Soc. Polit. Psychology (governing coun. 1996-98), Interam. Psychol. Soc., Am. Psychology-Law Soc. Avocations: guitar, travel, international studies. Home: 2212 Camden Ave Los Angeles CA 90064-1906 Office: UCLA Dept Psychology Los Angeles CA 90095-1563 E-mail: raven@ucla.edu.

RAVEN, FRANCIS HARVEY, mechanical engineering educator; b. Erie, Pa., July 29, 1928; s. Frederick James and Eleanor Elizabeth (Sopp) R.; m. Therese Mary Strobel, June 21, 1952; children: Betty, Ann Raven McCarthy, Paul, John, Mary Raven Mansmann, Cathy, Linda. BS in Math., Gannon Univ., 1948; BSME, Pa. State U., 1950, MSME, 1951; PhD, Cornell U., 1958. Design engr. Hamilton Standard div. United Techs., Hartford, Conn., 1951-54; instr. Cornell U., Ithaca, N.Y., 1954-58; asst. prof. mech. engring. U. Notre Dame, 1958-62, assoc. prof., 1962-66, prof., 1966—. Cons. microprocessor and computer control of robots and mech. systems; devel. Vector Loop Method (first analytical method for the design of mechanisms and cam systems.). Author: Automatic Control Engineering, 1961, 5th edit., 1995, Mathematics of Engineering Systems, 1966, Engineering Mechanics, 1973; pub. McGraw-Hill Book Co. Mem. ASME, Am. Soc. for Engring. Edn. (AT&T Teaching award 1968-69), Sigma Xi. Roman Catholic. Home: 52740 Brandel Ave South Bend IN 46635-1248 Office: U Notre Dame Dept Aerospace-Mech Engring Notre Dame IN 46556 E-mail: francis.h.raven.1@nd.edu.

RAVEN, LUISA ANTONIA, nurse, psychotherapist; b. N.Y.C., Sept. 25, 1939; d. Joseph A. and Mary Louise (Swann) R. BSN, St. Louis U., 1976; BA in Edn., Caldwell (N.J.) Coll., 1970; MSN, Columbia U., 1982. RN, N.J. Joined Order Sisters of St. Joseph of Peace, Roman Cath. Ch. Pvt. practice nurse psychotherapist, Englewood Cliffs, N.J.; instr. nursing Felician Coll., Lodi; clin. specialist psychiat. nursing Greystone Park (N.J.) Psychiat. Hosp.; staff nurse med./surg. psychiat. unit St. Mary's Hosp., Passaic, NJ. Adj. faculty Bergen C.C., Paramus, N.J. Mem. N.J. Nurses Assn. (Psychiat. Nurse of Yr. award 1984), Sigma Theta Tau, Alpha Sigma Nu. Home: 5 Oakdale Manor Apt B18 Suffern NY 10901-5700

RAVEN, ROBERT DUNBAR, lawyer; b. Cadillac, Mich., Sept. 26, 1923; s. Christian and Gladys L. (Dunbar) R.; m. Leslie Kay Erickson, June 21, 1947; children: Marta Ellen, Matt Robert, Brett Lincoln. AB with honors, Mich. State U., 1949; LLB, U. Calif., Berkeley, 1952. Bar: Calif. 1953. Assoc. Morrison & Foerster and predecessor, San Francisco, 1952-56, ptnr., 1956-94, sr. of counsel, 1994—; chmn. Morrison & Foerster (and predecessor), 1974-82. Mem. Jud. Coun. of Calif., 1983-87. Bd. dirs. Bay Area USO, 1964-73, pres., 1968-70; mem. San Francisco Mayor's Criminal Justice Coun., 1971-72; co-chmn. San Francisco Lawyer's Com. for Urban Affairs, 1976-78; bd. dirs. Lawyers Com. for Civil Rights Under Law, 1976-96. With USAAF, 1942-45. Decorated Air medal with oak leaf cluster. Mem. ABA (pres. 1989, mem. standing com. fed. judiciary 1975-80, chmn. 1978-80, chmn. standing com. on legal aid and indigent defendants 1981-83, chair standing com. dispute resolution 1991-93, chair sect. dispute resolution 1993-94), FBA, Am. Arbitration Assn. (bd. dirs. 1988-96), CPR Inst. for Dispute Resolution (mem. exec. com.), Internat. Acad. Trial Lawyers, State Bar Calif. (gov. 1978-81, pres. 1981), Bar Assn. San Francisco (pres. 1971), Am. Law Inst., Am. Bar Found., Am. Judicature Soc., Boalt Hall Alumni Assn. (pres. 1972-73), World Trade Club (San Francisco), Order of Coif. Democrat. Home: 1064 Via Alta Lafayette CA 94549-2916 Office: Morrison & Foerster 425 Market St San Francisco CA 94105-2482

RAVENAL, EARL CEDRIC, international relations educator, author; b. N.Y.C., Mar. 29, 1931; s. Alan M. and Mildred S. (Sherman) R.; m. Carol Bird Myers, May 26, 1956; children: Cornelia Jane, John Brodhead, Rebecca Eliza. BA, Harvard U., 1952; postgrad., U. Cambridge, Eng., 1952-53; M.M.P. diploma, Harvard Bus. Sch., 1958; MA, Johns Hopkins U., 1971, PhD, 1975. Treas. Elbe File & Binder Co., Inc., Fall River, Mass., 1955-64, pres., 1965-67; dir. Asian div. systems analysis Office Sec. Def., Washington, 1967-69; prof. internat. relations Johns Hopkins U. Sch. Advanced Internat. Studies, 1973-78, Georgetown U. Sch. Fgn. Service, Washington, 1976—. Mem. bd. advisors Ctr. for Def. Info., Washington, 1971-97, Ctr. for Study of Conflict, 1983—; bd. dirs. Critical Rev. Author: (with others) Peace with China?, 1971, (with others) Atlantis Lost, 1976, Never Again, 1979, Toward World Security, 1978, Strategic Disengagement and World Peace, 1979, NATO's Unremarked Demise, 1979, Defining Def., 1984, NATO: The Tides of Discontent, 1985, Large-Scale Foreign Policy Change, 1989, Designing Defense, 1991, Defending America in an Uncontrollable World, 2002; contbg. editor Inquiry Mag., 1976-85, Critical Rev., 1987—; contbr. articles to profl. jours. Advisor Democratic Presdl. Campaign, 1972; advisor Jerry Brown Presdl. Campaign, 1976, Libertarian Presdl. Campaigns, 1980, 84. Served with JAGC U.S. Army, 1953-55. Henry fellow U. Cambridge, 1952-53; mem. faculty Salzburg Seminar in Am. Studies, 1977; fellow Bellagio Ctr. Rockefeller Found., 1975, Woodrow Wilson Internat. Ctr. for Scholars, 1973, Washington Ctr. of Fgn. Policy Research, 1974; sr. fellow Cato Inst., 1985-91, 97—. Mem. Council Fgn. Relations, Am. Polit. Sci. Assn., Internat. Inst. Strategic Studies, Fed. Am. Scientists, Internat. Studies Assn. Clubs: Cosmos (Washington); Fed. City (Washington); Harvard (N.Y.C.); Signet (Cambridge, Mass.); Tred Avon Yacht (Oxford, Md.). Libertarian. Home and Office: 4439 Cathedral Ave NW Washington DC 20016-3562

RAVENEL, SHANNON, book publishing professional; b. Charlotte, N.C., Aug. 13, 1938; d. Elias Prioleau and Harriett Shannon (Steedman) R.; m. Dale Purves, May 25, 1968; children: Sara Blake, Harriett. BA, Hollins Coll., 1960. Mktg. asst., sch. dept. Holt, Rinehart & Winston, Inc., N.Y.C., 1960-61; edit. asst. Houghton Mifflin Co., Boston, 1961-64, editor, 1964-73; editorial cons. pvt. practice, St. Louis, 1973-90; sr. editor, co-founder Algonquin Books of Chapel Hill, 1982-91, editorial dir., 1992-2000; dir. Algonquin imprint Shannon Ravenel Books, 2001—. Series editor: Best American Short Stories, 1978-90; editor: Best American Short Stories of the Eighties, 1990, New Stories From the South, 1986—. Recipient Disting. Achievement award Coun. Lit. Mags. & Presses, N.Y.C., 1990. Mem. PEN Am. Ctr. Democrat. Office: Algonquin Books of Chapel Hill PO Box 2225 Chapel Hill NC 27515-2225 E-mail: shannonr@algonquin.com.

RAVENHOLT, REIMERT THOROLF, epidemiologist, researcher; b. Milltown, Wis., Mar. 9, 1925; s. Ansgar Benedikt and Kristine Henriette (Petersen) R.; divorced; children: Janna, Mark, Lisa, Dane; m. Betty Butler Howell, Sept. 26, 1981. BS, U. Minn., 1948, MB, 1951, MD, 1952; MPH, U. Calif., Berkeley, 1956. Bd. cert. preventive medicine. Intern USPHS Hosp., San Francisco, 1951-52; epidemic intelligence service officer USPHS Communicable Disease Ctr., Atlanta, 1952-54; dir. epidemiology and communicable disease div. Seattle-King County Health Dept., 1954-61; epidemiology cons. European area USPHS, Paris, 1961-63; assoc. prof. preventive medicine U. Wash. Med. Sch., Seattle, 1963-66; dir. Office of Population, AID, Washington, 1966-79, World Health Surveys, Ctrs. for Disease Control, 1980-82; asst. dir. epidemiology and research Nat. Inst. Drug Abuse, Rockville, Md., 1982-84; chief epidemiology br. FDA, 1984-87; dir. World Health Surveys, Inc., Seattle, 1987-93; pres. Population Health Imperatives, 1993—. *In Dr. Ravenholt's "Adventures in Epidemiology", www.ravenholt.com, he records his far flung activities during this half-century in the investigation and control of a fascinating array of infectious and chronic disease epidemics: diphtheria, typhoid, poliomyelitis, staphylococcal disease, smallpox, influenza, encephalitis, the many cancers and cardiovascular diseases of tobaccosis and last and most difficult, the global humanosis pandemic. As Director of the Office of Population for USAID during its most challenging years, Dr. Ravenholt won highest honors in recognition of his distinguished leadership in the development of worldwide assistance programs to deal with the challenge of excessive population growth.* Author/designer website dealing with epidemiology. Served with USPHS, 1951-54, 61-63. Recipient Disting Honor award AID, 1973, Hugh Moore Meml. award IPPF and Population Crisis Com., 1974. Fellow Am. Coll. Epidemiology, APHA (Carl Schultz award 1978), mem. Am. Coun. on Sci. and Health (bd. dirs.); mem. Cosmos Club (Washington). Independent. Home: 3156 E Laurelhurst Dr NE Seattle WA 98105-5333 E-mail: ravenrt@oz.net.

RAVEN-RIEMANN, CAROLYN SUE, actress, model, small business owner; b. Evergreen Park, Ill., Dec. 7, 1945; d. Eugene Alexander and Eloise Irene (McGhee) Raven; m. Herbert Friedrich Riemann, Aug. 1, 1981. BA, Northwestern U., 1967. Model, actress Mannequin Models, N.Y.C., 1969-86, several talent agts., 1969—; model Les Girls Ltd., N.Y.C., 1986-92, Johnston Models, Norwalk, Conn., 1986—; owner, pres. The OrchidPhile, Stamford, 1984—. Sec., treas. GearGrip, Inc., Stamford, 1983—; author, pub., owner OrchidPhile Log; spkr., lectr., author on orchids. Mem. SAG, AFTRA, Am. Orchid Soc. (accredited judge 1998—, edn. com, vice chair 1994—), Greater N.Y. Orchid Soc. (trustee 1993—), Internat. Phalaenopsis Alliance, Inc. (co-founder, sec. 1990-96, v.p. 1996-2000, pres. 2000—), Greater Westchester Orchid Soc., N.J. Orchid Soc., Ramapo Orchid Soc., Genessee Orchid Soc., Northwestern U. Alumni Assn., Tri Delta Sorority Alumnae Soc. Republican. Congregationalist. Avocations: orchids, spatial design for homes and living spaces, travel, Far East.

RAVENSTAHL, MATTHEW JOHN, art educator, secondary school educator; b. Pitts., May 26, 1970; s. Howard Melvin and Barbara Ann Ravenstahl; m. Laura Jean O'Shea, July 4, 1993; children: Maris, Seth. BS, Indiana U. Pa., 1993. Art tchr. South Lakes H.S., Reston, Va., 1994—. Exhibitions include. Recipient Robert Rauschenberg Art Tchrs. award, Robert Rauschenberg Found., Washington, 1999. Mem.: Washington Sculptors Group. Home: 795 Vanderbilt Terr Leesburg VA 20175

RAVER, MIKI, writer; b. N.Y.C., May 31, 1945; d. James Raver and Sophie Zimmerman; m. Martin Perlmutter, Feb. 17, 1980; 1 child, Sara Sasha. BS, Emerson Coll., 1968. Street worker Youth Svcs. Agy., N.Y.C., 1972-73; therapist Phoenix House, 1973-76; founding dir. Women's Success Teams, San Francisco, 1976-78; prodr. Tele-Pros, N.Y.C., 1982-87; videodisc prodr., post-prodn. supr. Videodisc Pub., 1983—84; talent agt. Grimme & Mitchell Talent Mgmt., San Francisco, 1988-95; ptnr. Hook-up!, 1995-98; dir. internat. editl. recruitment LookSmart, 1998-2001; leader Listen to Her Voice Workshops, 2001—; adult and sr. activities dir. Osher-Marin JCC, 2002. Author: Listen to Her Voice, 1998. Dir. adult programs Osher Marin Jewish Cmty. Ctr., 2001. Avocations: hiking, swimming. Home: 2866 Mckillop Rd Oakland CA 94602-1503

RAVERTY, AARON See RAVERTY, THOMAS

RAVERTY, THOMAS DONALD (AARON RAVERTY), anthropologist; b. Stillwater, Minn., Mar. 13, 1950; s. Donald Ernest and Verla Frances (Shanahan) Raverty. BA, U. Minn., 1972, MA, 1979, PhD, 1990; MA, St. John's U., Collegeville, Minn., 1977. Instr. St. John's U., Collegeville, Minn., 1975—90; tchg. asst. U. Minn., Mpls., 1978; editor Liturgical Press, Collegeville, 1991—. Commn. rep., bd. monastic interreligious dialogue Benedictine Internet Commn., Collegeville, Minn., 1997—98; anthropol. book cons. Fr. Philip Kaufman, O.S.B., Collegeville, Minn., 1989; sec. Bd. Monastic Interreligious Dialogue, Tibet, Nepal, India, 1994—99, anthropol. cons. phase VII exch., Nepal, India, 1995; presenter in field; bd. dirs. comm. com. St. Johns U. Alumni, 1999—. Book reviewer in field, 1976; editor: The Modern Catholic Encyclopedia, 1994, The Encyclopedia of American Catholic History, 1997. Judge Saint Cloud (Minn.) Area H.S. Bowl, 1986; vol. Saint John's Vol. Fire Dept., Collegeville, 1990—95. Recipient Poetry award, Minn. Public Radio, 1998. Fellow: Am. Anthropol. Assn.; mem.: Am. Benedictine Acad., Internat. Graphoanalysis Soc. (cert.), Internat. Biographical Centre Adv. Coun. (hon.). Roman Catholic. Avocations: poetry, music, walking, weightlifting, birdwatching. Home: PO Box 2015 St Johns Abbey Collegeville MN 56321-2015 Office: The Liturgical Press PO Box 7500 Collegeville MN 56321-7500 Fax: 320-363-3278. Business E-Mail: araverty@csbsju.edu.

RAVETCH, IRVING, screenwriter; b. Newark, Nov. 14, 1920; s. I. Shalom and Sylvia (Shapiro) R.; m. Harriet Frank Jr., Nov. 24, 1946. BA, UCLA, 1941. Screenwriter: (films) (with La Cava) Living in a Big Way, 1947, The Outriders, 1950, Vengeance Valley, 1951; (with Harriet Frank, Jr.) The Long, Hot Summer, 1958, The Sound and the Fury, 1959, Home from the Hill, 1959, The Dark at the Top of the Stairs, 1960, House of Cards, 1969, The Cowboys, 1972, Conrack, 1974, The Spikes Gang, 1974, Norma Rae, 1979 (Academy award nomination best adapted screenplay 1979), Murphy's Romance, 1985, Stanley and Iris, 1990; writer, prodr.: (with Frank) Hud, 1963 (Academy award nomination best adapted screenplay 1963, N.Y. Film Critics Circle award best screenplay 1963), Hombre, 1967, The Reivers, 1969; story: (with Frank) Ten Wanted Men, 1955. Recipient N.Y. Film Critics award, 1963, Writers' Guild Am. award, 1988; Oscar nomination for Hud, Acad. Motion Picture Arts and Scis., 1963, Norma Rae, 1979.

RAVIKUMAR, THANJAVUR SUBRAMANIAM, surgical oncologist; b. Madras, India, Mar. 12, 1950; came to U.S., 1976; s. P. and Rajamani Subramaniam; m. Srikala Kandaswamy, Sept. 8, 1975; 1 child, Shruti. MS, Madras Med. Coll., 1976; MD, U. Edinburgh, Scotland, 1978. Diplomate Am. Bd. Surgery. Surg. resident Maimonides Med. Ctr., Maimonides Hosp., Bklyn., 1976-80; surg. oncology fellow U. Minn. Hosps., Mpls., 1980-82; rsch. fellow Harvard Med. SCh., Boston, 1982-84, asst. prof. surgery, 1986-89, assoc. prof. surgery, 1989-90; asst. prof. surgery SUNY Downstate Med. Ctr., Bklyn., 1984-85; assoc. prof., chief surg. oncology Yale U. Sch. Medicine, New Haven, 1990—. Chmn. cancer com. Yale New Haven Hosp., 1991—; cancer program dir. Yale-China Assn., New Haven, 1992—; prof. surgery and molecular genetics Robert Wood Johnson Med. Sch., N.J., 1993-98; chief surgery, assoc. dir. Cancer Inst. of N.J., 1993-98; prof., chmn. dept. surgery Albert Einstein Coll. of Medicine, Montefiore Med. Ctr., N.Y., 1998—. Contbr. articles to profl. jours. Mandelberg traveling fellow Maimonides Med. Ctr., Bklyn., 1978. Fellow Royal Coll. Surgeons, Am. Coll. Cryosurgery; mem. Soc. Surg. Oncology (clin. trials and govt. rels. com. 1991—, James Ewing Found. award 1983), Soc. Univ. Surgeons, Am. Assn. Cancer Rsch. Achievements include first human clin. trial of isolated hepatic perfusion chemotherapy using a novel double balloon catheter for treating liver cancers, new approaches to treat tumors spread into liver with cryosurgery and laser surgery. Home: 239 E 79th St Apt 15B New York NY 10021-0816 Office: Albert Einstein Coll Medicine Montefiore Med Ctr 3400 Bainbridge Ave Fl 4 Bronx NY 10467-2404 E-mail: travikum@montefiore.org.

RAVITCH, DIANE SILVERS, historian, educator, author, government official; b. Houston, July 1, 1938; d. Walter Cracker and Ann Celia (Katz) Silvers; m. Richard Ravitch, June 26, 1960 (div. 1986); children: Joseph, Steven (dec.), Michael. BA, Wellesley Coll., 1960; PhD, Columbia U., 1975; LHD (hon.), Williams Coll., 1984, Reed Coll., 1985, Amherst Coll., 1986, SUNY, 1988, Ramapo Coll., 1990, St. Joseph's Coll., N.Y., 1991, Middlebury Coll., 1997, Union Coll., 1998. Adj. asst. prof. Tchrs. Coll., Columbia U., N.Y.C., 1975-78, assoc. prof., 1978-83, adj. prof., 1983-91; asst. sec. office ednl. rsch. and improvement U.S. Dept. Edn., Washington, 1991-93, counselor to the sec. edn., 1991-93. Vis. fellow Brookings Instn., Washington, 1993-94, non-resident sr. fellow, 1994—, editor papers on edn. policy, 1997—, Brown chair in edn. policy, 1997—; rsch. prof. NYU, 1994—; mem. Nat. Assessment Governing Bd., 1997—. Author: The Great School Wars, 1974, The Revisionists Revised, 1977, The Troubled Crusade, 1983, The Schools We Deserve, 1985, National Standards in American Education, A Citizens Guide, 1995, Left Back, 2000; author: (with others) Educating an Urban People, 1981; author: The School and the City, 1983, Against Mediocrity, 1984, Challenges to the Humanities, 1985, What Do Our 17 Year Olds Know?, 1987; editor: The American Reader, 1990; co-editor: New Schools for a New Century, 1997, City Schools, 2000, The Democracy Reader, 1992, Making Good Citizens, 2001; editor: Learning from the Past, 1995, Debating the Future of American Education, 1995. Chair Ednl. Excellence Network, 1988—91, 1994—96; trustee Nat. Humanities Ctr., 1999—2000, N.Y. Pub. Libr., N.Y.C., 1981—87, hon. life trustee, 1988—; trustee N.Y. Coun. on Humanities, 1996—; mem. Landmarks Preservation Commn., Southold, NY, 2000—02; bd. dirs. Woodrow Wilson Nat. Fellowship Found., 1987—91, Coun. Basic Edn., 1989—91, Thomas B. Fordham Found., 1998—, New Am. Found., 2000—. Recipient Award for Disting. Svc., N.Y. Acad. Pub. Edn., 1994, Wellesley Coll. Alumnae Achievement award, 1989; Guggenheim fellow, 1977-78; Phi Beta Kappa vis. scholar. Mem. Nat. Acad. Edn., Am. Acad. Arts and Scis., Soc. Am. Historians, N.Y. Hist. Soc. (trustee 1995-98), PEN Internat. Office: NYU 26 Washington Sqare E New York NY 10003-6644

RAVNAN, KARI LISE, musician; b. Lincoln, Nebr., Dec. 3, 1960; d. Audun Johann and Barbara Jane (Puckett) R. Student, Juilliard Sch., N.Y.C., 1977-78; MusB, Eastman Sch., Rochester, N.Y., 1981; student, Mozarteum, Salzburg, Austria, 1985-86. Founding mem. Prometheus Ensemble, London, 1983-85, Zennor String Trio, London, Vienna and Bergen, Norway, 1986-90; prin. cellist Bergen Philharmonic, 1984-89; founding mem. Borealis Ensemble, Oslo, 1989—; prin. cellist Norwegian Radio Orch., 1992-97, Trondheim Symphony Orch., 1997-99, Norwegian State Opera Orch., 1999—. Debut recital Phillips Collection, Washington, 1986; participant Marlboro (Vt.) Chamber Music Festival, 1981, 82, Open Chamber Music, Prussia Cove, Eng., 1983—. Recipient 1st prize Washington Internat. Competition, 1985. Avocations: hiking, scuba diving. Home: Gulleraasveien 14 0779 Oslo Norway

RAWAL, DARSHAN LAL, civil, structural engineer, consultant; b. India, Nov. 12, 1934; came to U.S., 1966; s. Saudagar Mal and Kaushalya Devi R.; m. Raj Kumari, Dec. 5, 1956; children: Upma, Bela, Neeru. BSCE, M.U. Aligarh, U.P. India, 1957; MSCE, Utah State U., 1967; M in Engring. Adminstrn., Ill. Inst. Technology, Chgo., 1977. Registered profl. engr., Ill.; registered structural engr., Ill. Sr. civil engr. Ill. Dept. Transp., 1967-73; sr. structural engr. Sargent & Lundy, Chgo., 1974-86, Brown & Root, Lombard, 1979-81; sr. engr. Ambitech Engring. Corp., Downers Grove, 1988—99, John Brown Engrs. & Constructor's, Chgo., 1991—94. Pres. Hindu Soc., Chgo., 1971-72; chmn. bd. trustees Hindu Soc., Medinah, Ill., 1993-96. Fellow ASCE. Hindu. Achievements include civil, structural design and preparation of drawings related to fossil/nuclear power plants, hwys./bridges, petro chem. and steel industries. Home: 2078 Audubon Dr Glendale Heights IL 60139-1808

RAWDIN, GRANT, lawyer, financial planning company executive; b. N.Y.C., Nov. 17, 1959; s. Eugene and Nona (Neubauer) R.; m. Laura S. Schecter; children: Alexander, Jacob, Jesse, Aaron, Rachel. BA, Temple U., 1981, JD, 1987. Bar: Pa. 1987, N.J. 1987; CFP, Colo. Tax acct. Hepburn Willcox Hamilton & Putnam, Phila., 1978-81; mgr. tax acctg. dept. Duane Morris, 1981-86; dir. personal fin. planning Duane Morris, LLP, 1986-87; pres. Wescott Finl. Adv. Group LLC subs. Duane Morris, 1987—, also bd. dirs. Mem. adj. faculty Coll. for Fin. Planning, Denver, 1987-95; lectr. Inst. Tax and Fiduciary Mgmt., 1988-95; bd. dirs. A. Pomerantz & Co., Inc., 1995, TRS, LLC, 1999-. Bd. dirs. Phila. Child Guidance Ctr., 1991-94; bd. dirs. Am. Poetry Ctr., 1989-97, pres. People's Emergency Ctr., 1995—; pres. PEC Found., 1996—. Mem. ABA, Phila. Bar Assn., Finl. Planners Assn. (bd. dirs. 1987-93). Home: 928 Frog Hollow Terr Rydal PA 19046 Office: Wescott Finl Adv Group LLC 1 Liberty Pl Philadelphia PA 19103-7396 also: 249 Royal Palm Way Ste 403 Palm Beach FL 33480-4334

RAWDING, MICHAEL, information technology executive; BA in Polit. Sci. & German, Middlebury Coll., Vt. With Unisys; from mgr. to corp. v.p. Microsoft, Redmond, Wash., corp. v.p. Asia region. Avocations: tennis, reading, travel, spending time with family. Office: One Microsoft Way Redmond WA 98052-6399*

RAWITCH, ALLEN BARRY, medical educator, university administrator; b. Chgo., Dec. 29, 1940; s. Sam and Jean Rawitch; m. Patricia Nan Rawitch, July 21, 1962; children: Bruce, David. BS in Chemistry, UCLA, 1963, PhD in Biol. Chemistry, 1967. Rsch. fellow U. Ill., Urbana. 1967-69; asst. prof. Kent (Ohio) State U., 1969-73, assoc. prof., 1973-75, U. Kans. Med. Ctr., Kansas City, 1975-80, prof., 1980—, asst. dean student affairs, 1999-2000, vice chancellor acad. affairs, dean grad. studies, 2000—. Vice chair biochemistry U. Kans. Med. Ctr., 1977-95, chair edn. coun., 1995-99 Editor Med. Biochemistry Question Bank, 1985-94; contbr. articles to profl. jours. Res. police officer capt. Overland Park Police Dept., 1979—. Rsch. grant NIH, 1971—, NSF, 1970, Am. Hear Assn., 1998—. Mem. Am. Soc. for Biochemistry and Molecular Biology, The Protein Soc., Am. Thyroid Assn., Sigma Xi. Avocations: amateur radio, woodworking, target shooting. Office: Office Acad Affairs U Kans Med Ctr 3901 Rainbow Blvd Kansas City KS 66160-0001

RAWITCH, ROBERT JOE, journalist, educator; b. L.A., Oct. 11, 1945; s. Sam and Jean (Reifman) R.; m. Cynthia Z. Knee, Oct. 27, 1968; children: Dana Leigh, Jeremy Aaron, Joshua Eric. BA in Journalism, Calif. State U., Northridge, 1967; MS in Journalism, Northwestern U., 1968. Reporter L.A. Times, 1968-80, asst. met. editor, 1980-82, editor Valley sect., 1982-83, suburban editor, 1983-89, exec. editor Valley and Ventura County edits., 1989-93; dir. editorial ops. Valley and Ventura County edits., 1993-95; v.p. Winner and Assocs., 1996—. Lectr. Calif. State U., Northridge, 1971-83, 95-96. Co-author: Adat Ari El, The First Fifty Years, 1988. Chmn. Calif. Freedom of Info. Com., 1978-79; pres. Calif. First Amendment coalition, 1991-93; found. bd. dirs. Temple Adat Ari El, 1987-92; bd. dirs. Calif. State U. Northridge Found., 1998—. Recipient Greater L.A. Press Club award, 1973, 75, 79, L.A. Jewish Youth of Yr. award United Jewish Fund, 1963, Clarence Darrow Found. award, 1979. Mem. Soc. Profl. Journalists (nat. bd. dirs. 1979-82), Calif. Soc. Newspaper Editors (pres. 1995-96), Medill Alumni Assn. (bd. dirs. 1994-2000), CSUN Journalism Alumni Assn. (bd. dirs. 2002—). Office: Winner & Assocs 16501 Ventura Blvd Encino CA 91436-2007

RAWLEIGH, FLOYD ERNEST, JR. music educator; b. Dansville, N.Y., June 2, 1962; s. Floyd Ernest and Minerva Jeanette (Hinds) Rawleigh; m. Janet Louise Cochran, July 6, 1985; children: Seth Vincent, Joshua Thomas. BS, Roberts Wesleyan Coll., Rochester, N.Y., 1984; MMus, Temple U., Phila., 1991. Cert. tchr. N.Y., 1984, Pa., 1991. Music tchr. Halley-Luzerne Ctrl. Schs., Lake Luzerne, NY, 1984—87; asst. prof. music Valley Forge Christian Coll., Phoenixville, Pa., 1988—91; dir. music First Bapt. Ch., Lansdale, 1993—96, Proclamation Presbyn. Ch., Bryn Mawr, 1992—93, Faith Reformed Presbyn. Ch., Quarryville, 1997—; tchr. Csehy Summer Sch. Music, Muncy and Langhome, 1985—; tchr. music Downingtown Area Sch. Dist., 1991—, curriculum leader, 1999—, music theater dir., 1997—. Bd. dirs. Cschy Summer Sch. Music, 1988—94. Named to Outstanding Young Men of Am., 1990. Mem.: Pa. Music Educators Assn., Am. Choral Dirs. Assn., Music Educators Nat. Conf. Home: 165 Beddington Ln Strasburg PA 17579

RAWLES, EDWARD HUGH, lawyer; b. Chgo., May 7, 1945; s. Fred Wilson and Nancy (Hughes) R.; m. Margaret Mary O'Donoghue, Oct. 20, 1979; children: Lee Kathryn, Jacklyn Ann. BA, U. Ill., 1967; JD summa cum laude, Ill. Inst. Tech., 1970. Bar: Ill., 1970, Colo. 1984, U.S. Dist. Ct. (cen. dist.) Ill. 1970, U.S. Ct. Appeals (7th cir.) 1983, U.S. Supreme Ct. 1973. Assoc. Reno, O'Byrne & Kepley, Champaign, Ill., 1970-73, ptnr., 1973-84; pres. Rawles, O'Byrne, Stanko & Kepley P.C., Champaign, 1984-98, pres., 1990-97; mem. student legal svc. adv. bd. U. Ill., Urbana, 1982—; hearing officer Ill. Fair Employment Practice Commn., Springfield, 1972-74; mem. rules com. U.S. Dist. Ct. for Ctrl. Dist. Ill., 1994—. Diplomate Nat. Bd. Trial Advocacy. Fellow Ill. State Bar Found., 1984. Mem. Ill. Bar Assn., Bar Assn. 7th Fed. Cir., Rules Com. U.S. Dist. Court (ctrl. dist. Ill.), Assn. Trial Lawyers Am., Ill. Trial Lawyers Assn., Colo. Trial Lawyers Assn., Kent Soc. Honor Men, Phi Delta Theta. Roman Catholic. Home: 6 Alice Dr White Heath IL 61884-9747 Office: Rawles O'Byrne Stanko & Kepley PC 501 W Church St Champaign IL 61820-3412

RAWLEY, ANN KEYSER, small business owner, picture framer; b. N.Y.C., July 11, 1923; d. Ernest Wise and Beatrice (Oberndorf) Keyser; m. James Albert Rawley, Apr. 7, 1945; children: John Franklin, James Albert. BA, Smith Coll., 1944. Owner Ann Rawley Custom Framing, Lincoln, Nebr., 1969—. Pres. Friends of Fairview, Lincoln, 1976, Lincoln City Ballet Co., 1983-84; bd. dirs. Lincoln Community Playhouse; mem. adv. bd. Nebr. Repertory Theatre. Mem. Nebr. Art Assn. (sec. 1976-77, life trustee). Republican. Episcopalian. Avocations: foreign travel, tennis, needle work; One of 3 inaugural mems. Nebr. Repertory Theater Hall of Fame. Home and Office: 2300 Bretigne Dr Lincoln NE 68512-1910

RAWLEY, JAMES ALBERT, history educator; b. Terre Haute, Ind., Nov. 9, 1916; s. Frank S. and Annie B. (Vanes) R.; m. Ann F. Keyser, Apr. 7, 1945; children: John Franklin, James Albert. AB, U. Mich., 1938, A.M., 1939; PhD, Columbia U., 1949. Instr., Columbia U., 1946-48; Instr. N.Y. U., 1946-51, Hunter Coll., 1951-53; asso. prof. to prof. Sweet Briar Coll., 1953-64, chmn. history dept., 1953-57, chmn. div. social studies, 1962-64; prof. U. Nebr., 1964-87, prof. emeritus, 1987—, chmn. history dept., 1966-67, 73-82, acting dean univ. libraries, 1984-85, honors MASUA lectr., 1984-85, Carl Happold Disting. prof., 1986-87; resident scholar Rockefeller Study and Conf. Center, Italy, 1977. Vis. prof. U. Hanover, 1990; mem. adv. bd. Salmon P. Chase Papers, Abraham Lincoln Prize. Author: Edwin D. Morgan: Merchant in Politics, 1811-1883, 1955, Turning Points of the Civil War, 1966, Race and Politics, 1969, The Politics of Union, 1974, The Transatlantic Slave Trade, 1981, Secession: The Disruption of the American Republic, 1844-1861, 1989, Abraham Lincoln and a Nation Worth Fighting For, 1996; editor: The American Civil War: An English View, 1964; editor: Lincoln and Civil War Politics, 1969; contbr.: Essays in American Historiography, 1960. Served to 1st lt. AUS, 1942-46. Recipient Outstanding Research and Creativity award U. Nebr., 1983, George Howard-Louise Pound Disting. Career award U. Nebr., 1991; NEH fellow Huntington Library, 1979 Fellow Royal Hist. Soc.; mem. Am. Hist. Assn., So. Hist. Assn., Nebr. State Hist. Soc. (past pres.), Orgn. Am. Historians, Soc. Am. Historians, Abraham Lincoln Assn. (bd. dirs.), Civil War Round Table Nebr. (charter pres. 1989-90), Lincoln Country Club, Phi Beta Kappa. Home: 2300 Bretigne Dr Lincoln NE 68512-1910 E-mail: jcanningalunl@as.unl.edu.

RAWLINGS, BOYNTON MOTT, lawyer; b. El Paso, Tex., Dec. 6, 1935; s. Junius Mott and Laura Bassett (Boynton) R.; m. Nancy Mary Peay, Aug. 24, 1962 (div. 1973); children: Laura Bassett, James Mott; m. Judith Reed, Dec. 10, 1977; 1 child, William Reed. AB, Princeton U., 1958; LLB, Stanford U., 1961; diploma, U. Strasbourg, France, 1963. Bar: Calif. 1962, D.C. 1980, Conseil Juridique Paris, 1973, Avocat Paris, 1992. Assoc. Broad, Busterud & Khourie, San Francisco, 1963-65, Homer G. Angelo, Brussels, 1966; assoc., ptnr. S.G. Archibald, Paris, 1967-74; ptnr. Boynton M. Rawlings, Paris, L.A., 1974-84, Kevorkian & Rawlings, Paris, 1984-90, Oppenheimer, Wolff and Donnelly, Paris, 1990-99, Rawlings & Giles LLP., Paris, 2000—. Contbr. articles to profl. jours. Mem. L.A. Bar Assn. (bd. dirs. sect. internat. law 1975-82), French Am. C. of C. L.A. (bd. dirs. 1985—). Republican. Episcopalian. Avocations: music, tennis, skiing, hiking. Office: Rawlings & Giles 53 Ave Montaigne 75008 Paris France also: The Farragut Bldg 500 17th St NW Ste 700 Washington DC 20006-4804

RAWLINGS, HUNTER RIPLEY, III, university president; b. Norfolk, Va., Dec. 14, 1944; married; 4 children. BA, Haverford Coll., 1966; PhD in Classics, Princeton U., 1970. Asst. prof. U. Colo., Boulder, 1970-75, assoc. prof., 1975-80, prof. classics, 1980-88, v.p. acad. affairs, rsch., dean System Grad. Sch., 1984-88; pres. U. Iowa, 1988-95; pres., prof. classics Cornell U., Ithaca, N.Y., 1995—. Chair Iowa Commn. on Fgn. Lang. Studies and Internat. Edn., 1988-91; bd. dirs. Tompkins County Trust Co. Author: The Structure of Thucydides' History, 1981; editor-in-chief: Classical Jour., 1977-83; contbr. articles to jours. Bd. dirs. Norwest Bank Iowa, N.A., 1988-95. Jr. fellow Ctr. Hellenic Studies, 1975-76. Fellow Am. Acad. Arts and Scis.; mem. Assn. Am. Univs. (exec. com. 1990-92), Am. Coun. on Edn. (bd. dirs. 1994-97), Nat. Fgn. Lang. Ctr. (mem. nat. adv. bd. 1995—). Address: 511 Cayuga Heights Rd Ithaca NY 14850-1421*

RAWLINGS, PAUL C. retired government official; b. Cave City, Ark., June 21, 1928; s. Otha A. and Leona (King) R.; m. Catherine Terral, 1951 (div. 1970); children: William A., Rebecca, Neal; m. Erma Martin, June 20, 1971 (div. Jan. 1997). Grad., Little Rock Jr. Coll.; LL.B., Ark. Law Sch., 1950. Bar: Ark. 1950. Practiced in, Little Rock, 1950, 52-73; adminstrv. law judge Office Hearings and Appeals, Social Security Adminstrn., HEW, Hattiesburg, Miss., 1973-92; ret. adminstrv. law judge sr. status, 1992; partner firm Terral, Rawlings, Matthews & Purtle, until 1973. Asst. atty. gen., Ark., 1955-56 Bd. dirs. Ark. Enterprises for Blind, 1964-67. Served with AUS, 1950-52. Mem. Ark. Bar Assn., Law Sci. Acad. Methodist (past chmn. bd. adminstrn., trustee). Club: Lion (past pres.). Home: 107 Swinging Bridge Dr Heber Springs AR 72543-8717

RAWLINGS, ROBERT HOAG, newspaper publisher; b. Pueblo, Colo., Aug. 3, 1924; s. John W. and Dorothy (Hoag) R.; m. Mary Alexandra Graham, Oct. 18, 1947; children: Jane Louise, John Graham, Carolyn Anne, Robert Hoag II. Student, Colo. U., 1943-44; BA, Colo. Coll., 1947. Reporter Pueblo Chieftain and Pueblo Star-Jour., 1947-51, advt. rep., 1951-62, gen. mgr., 1962-79, pub., editor, 1980—. Sec. Star-Jour. Pub. Corp., 1962-84, pres., 1984—; past chmn. bd. dirs. Colo. Nat. Bank, Pueblo; me. adv. bd. U.S. Bank. Bd. dirs. U.S. Air Force Acad. Found., U. So. Colo. Found.; pres. Robert Hoag Rawlings Found., So. Colo. Cmty. Found., Medal of Honor Meml. Com.; mem. Colo. Chem. Demilitarzation Citizens Adv. Commn. With USNR, 1942-46. Named Colo. Newspaper Person of Yr., 1989, Disting. Univ. Fellow Pres. Club U. So. Colo., 1993, Outstanding Citizen of Yr. Pueblo C. of C. 1994, Colo. Bus. Leader of Yr., Colo. Assn. of Commerce and Industry, 1994; recipient Outstanding Svc. to Univ. award U. So. Colo. Alumni Assn., 1993, Colo. Corp. Philanthropy award Nat. Philanthropy Assn., 1993, Louis T. Benezet award Colo. Coll. Alumni Assn., 1996, Living Legend award U. Colo., 1997, Outstanding Am. Achievement award U. So. Colo., 1997, Outstanding Svc. to Hispanic Cmty. award, U. So. Colo. and Pueblo Hispanic Edn. Found., 1999; named Donor of Yr. Nat. Assn. Univ. Athletic Devel. dirs., 1995, Creative Spirit award Pueblo United Way, 1998, Lifetime Svc. award Colo. Bd. Vet. Affaris, 2000, Medal of Valur, Congl. Medal Honor Soc., 2000; named to Pueblo Hall of Fame, 1999, The Pueblo Greater Sports Assn. Hall of Fame, 1999. Mem. Colo. Press Assn. (dir. 1963-66, 76-78, pres. 1985, chmn. bd. dirs. 1986, Golden rule Makeup awrd 1998), Rocky Mountain Ad Mgrs. (past pres.), Colo. AP (past pres.) Colo. forum, U. So. Colo. Found., Colo. Mental Health Inst., Rotary. Presbyterian. Home: 1401 Rancho Del Sol Pueblo CO 81008-2043 Office: The Pueblo Cheiftain Star Jour Pub Corp PO Box 4040 Pueblo CO 81003-0040

RAWLINGS, STEPHEN PAUL, engineer; b. Wolverhampton, Eng., Mar. 16, 1954; came to U.S., 1986; s. Douglas Haig Rawlings and Lilian May (Price) Jones; m. Karen Lesley Gardner, Aug. 23, 1975; children: Katie Lauren, Philippa Jane, Ashley Victoria. Tech. cert. prodn. and automation, Walsall (Eng.) Coll., 1977. Product designer Raydyot, Ltd., Cradley Heath, Eng., 1978-80; dir. engring. GKN Tech., Inc., Auburn Hills, Mich., 1980-91; v.p. engring. Dura Convertible Sys., Inc., Adrian, 1991—. Author papers in field. Mem. Soc. Automotive Engrs., Soc. Mfg. Engrs., Am. Welding Soc. Achievements include patents for convertible boot, for composite vehicle suspensions. Office: Dura Convertible Sys Inc 2011 W Beecher Rd Adrian MI 49221-8747

RAWLINS, CHRISTOPHER JOHN, publishing executive, director; b. Stoke-on-Trent, Staffordshire, Eng., Aug. 20, 1945; s. Jack and Evelyn Daphne (Douglas-Hamilton) R.; m. Mary Joan Goodchild, May 31, 1969; children: Sarah Elizabeth, Jeremy Mark, Penelope Jane. BSc (with honors), London U., 1968. Editorial asst. Soc. of Chem. Industry, London, 1968-71; asst. editor Acad. Press Ltd., 1971, IPC Sci. and Tech. Press, Guildford, Eng., 1971-75, mng. editor Eng., 1976-79, pub. Eng., 1979-80, pub. dir. Eng., 1980-82, Butterworth Scientific Ltd., Guildford, Eng., 1982-86; v.p., pub. dir Butterworth Pubs., Stoneham, Mass., 1987-92; pub. Kluwer Acad. Pub., London, 1992-93; v.p., jours. pub. Appleton & Lange, Norwalk, Conn., 1993-97; pub. specialist Jours. divsn. Nature Pub. Group, N.Y.C., 1997-2000. Independent pub., 2001—. Chmn. North Farnham Liberal Assn., Hale, Eng., 1973-75, 79-81, chmn. bd. of govs. Hale and Folly Hill First Schs., Eng., 1983-85. Mem. Internat. Soc. Cancer Gene Therapy (mem. exec. coun. 1999—, v.p. membership affairs 2001--), Assn. of Am. Pubs. (jour. com. 1987-92, 97—, Sci., Tech. and Med. Pubs. Group serials com. 1988-92, Best New Jour. Sci., Tech., Medicine award 1990), Pubs. Assn. (vice chmn. serials pubs. exec. 1985-86), Inst. of Materials, Royal Soc. Chemistry. Anglican. Avocations: sports, gardening, music, current affairs, photography.

RAWLINS, DONALD R. lawyer; b. Dyersburg, Tenn., Apr. 28, 1965; s. Dal M. and Rebecca S. Rawlins. BBA, U. Memphis, 1987; JD, Am. U., 1990. Bar: Tenn., 1990. V.p., asst. gen. counsel, asst. sec. AutoZone, Inc., Memphis, 1990—. Recipient Best Brief award ATLA, 1990. Office: AutoZone Inc 123 S Front St Memphis TN 38103-3618

RAWLINS, JAN, principal; b. Salt Lake City, July 2, 1961; d. Robert E. and Carol Anne (Boss) R. BS in Home Econs. Edn., Brigham Young U., 1985, MA in Ednl. Adminstrn., 1998. Tchr. family and consumer sci. Clearfield (Utah) High Sch., 1985-92; tchr. consumer sci., student govt. advisor Northridge High Sch., Layton, Utah, 1992-97; prin. Tolman Elem. Sch., Bountiful, 1997—. Mem. Am. Vocat. Assn., Nat. Assn. Vocat. Home Econs. Tchrs., Nat. Assn. Secondary Sch. Prins., Utah Assn. Vocat. Tchrs., Utah Assn. Student Couns. Avocations: antique collecting, Barbie doll collecting, walking, hiking. Office: Tolman Elem Sch 300 E 1200 N Bountiful UT 84010-4522 E-mail: jrawlins@admin.tolmnel.davis.k12.ut.us.

RAWLINS, STEVEN WAYNE, management consultant; b. Hopkinsville, Ky., Sept. 28, 1956; s. Malcolm Franklin and Frances Ann (Ledford) R.; m. Terri Machelle Rogers, July 21, 1979; children: Brandon Christopher, Jason Todd. AA, U. Ky., 1976; BS, U. Ala., 1983; MBA, Vanderbilt U., 1990. Asst. sec. Liberty Nat. Bank West Ky., Hopkinsville, 1976-82; systems mgr. White Hydraulics, Inc., Lafayette, Ind., 1982-84, acctg. mgr. Hopkinsville, 1984-86, contr., 1986-90, v.p. adminstrn., 1990-94; sr. ptnr. Rawlins Group Internat., 1994—. Bd. dirs. Western Ky. State Fair, 1986, Westwood Day Care Ctr., 1987-88. Democrat. Mem. Ch. of Christ. Club: Pennyrile Indsl. Mgmt. (sec.-treas. 1985-86). Avocations: hunting, boating, flying. Home: 3141 Canton Pike Hopkinsville KY 42240-1315 Office: Rawlins Group Internat 1910 S Virginia St Ste 203 Hopkinsville KY 42240-6009

RAWLINS, V. LANE, university president; b. Rigby, Idaho, Nov. 30, 1937; m. Mary Jo Rawlins, three children. BA in Economics, Brigham Young U., 1963; PhD in Economics, U of Calif., Berkeley, 1969. Faculty Wash. State U., Pullman, 1968-86, chair. economics, 1977-82, vice provost, 1982—86; vice chancellor, academic affairs U. of Alabama, 1986-91; pres. Memphis St. U., Memphis, 1991-00, Wash. State U., Pullman, Wa., 2000—. Office: Washington State U Office Pres PO Box 641048 Pullman WA 99164-1048*

RAWLINSON, HELEN ANN, librarian; b. Columbia, S.C., Mar. 30, 1948; d. Alfred Harris and Mary Taylor (Moon) R. BA, U. S.C., 1970; MLS, Emory U., 1972. Asst. children's librarian Greenville (S.C.) County Library, 1972-74, br. supr., 1974-76, asst. head extension div., 1976-78; children's room librarian Richland County Pub. Library, Columbia, 1978-81, sr. adult services librarian, 1981-82, chief adult services, 1982-85, dep. dir., 1985—. Mem. adv. com. S.C. Pre-White House Conf. on Libr. and Info. Svcs., chmn. program com. Recipient Outstanding S.C. Librarian award by S.C. Library Assn., 1998. Mem. ALA, S.E. Libr. Assn., S.C. Libr. Assn. (2d v.p. 1987-89, editl. com. 1993, chmn. pub. libr. sect. 1995), U.S.C. Thomas Cooper Soc. (bd. dirs., v.p., pres.-elect, pres.). Baptist. Home: 1316 Guignard Ave West Columbia SC 29169-6137 Office: Richland County Pub Libr 1431 Assembly St Columbia SC 29201-3101

RAWLINSON, JOHNNIE BLAKENEY, federal judge; b. Concord, NH, Dec. 16, 1952; BS in Psychology summa cum laude, NC A&T State U., 1974; JD, U. of Pacific, 1979. Private practice, Las Vegas, 1979—80; staff atty.

Nevada Legal Services, 1980; from dep. dist. atty. to asst. dist. atty. Clark County Dist. Atty.'s Office, 1980—98; judge U.S. Dist. Ct. Nev., 1998—2000, U.S. Ct. Appeals (9th cir.), 2000—. Office: 333 Las Vegas Blvd S Rm 7072 Las Vegas NV 89101*

RAWLINSON, JOSEPH ELI, foundation executive, lawyer; b. Delta, Utah, May 9, 1915; s. Eli Wilford and Dora Pearl (Day) R.; m. Elaine Millicent Andersen, June 2, 1947; children: James, Jolene, Nancy, Rex, Anina, Cheryl, Mark, Lisa, David. BS, U. Utah, 1936; JD, Loyola U., 1958. Bar: Calif. 1959; CPA, Calif. Agt. IRS, Wichita, 1938-52; acct. Serene Koster, Barbour, Calif., 1952-62; lawyer in pvt. practice, 1959; pres., CEO Fritz B. Burns Found., Burbank, 1980—. Recipient Silver medal Am. Inst. Accts., 1942. Office: Fritz B Burns Found 4001 W Alameda Ave Ste 203 Burbank CA 91505-4338 E-mail: josepheli@aol.com.

RAWLS, FRANK MACKLIN, lawyer; b. Suffolk, Va., Aug. 24, 1952; s. John Lewis and Mary Helen (Macklin) R.; m. Sally Hallum Blanchard, June 26, 1976; children: Matthew Christopher, John Stephen, Michael Andrew. BA in History cum laude, Hampden Sydney Coll., 1974; JD, U. Va., 1977. Bar: Va. 1977, U.S. Dist. Ct. (ea. dist.) Va. 1977, U.S. Ct. Appeals (4th cir.) 1977. Assoc. Rawls, Habel & Rawls, Suffolk, 1977-78, ptnr., 1978-91, Ferguson & Rawls, Suffolk, 1991-96, Ferguson, Rawls, MacDonald, Overton & Grissom PC, Suffolk, 1996-98, Ferguson, Rawls, MacDonald & Overton PC, Suffolk, 1999—2002, Ferguson, Rawls & Raines, P.C., 2002—. Sec., bd. dirs. Suffolk Title Ltd., 1986-95; bd. dirs Old Dominion Investors Trust, Inc. 1994—, Secure Title, Inc., 1996—. Deacon Westminster Reformed Presbyn. Ch., Suffolk, 1979-83, elder, clk. of session, 1984-91, 94-99; chmn. bd. dirs. Suffolk Crime Line, 1982-90, Suffolk Cheer Fund, 1982—, Covenant Christian Schs., Suffolk, 1982-84; bd. dirs. Norfolk Christian Schs., 1990—, v.p., 1998-99, pres., 1999—; pres. Parent Tchr. Fellowship, 1995-97, vice-chmn. steering com. for capital campaign, 1996-98, v.p., 1997-98; adv. bd. dirs. Salvation Army, Suffolk, 1977-95, chmn., 1989-90; chmn. Suffolk Com. on Affordable Housing, 1989-90; bd. dirs. Suffolk YMCA, 1988-90, Suffolk Youth Athletic Assn., 1999-2000. Mem. ATLA, Suffolk Bar Assn. (past pres.), Va. State Bar, Va. Bar Assn., Christian Legal Soc., Va. Trial Lawyers Assn., Suffolk Bar Assn. E-mail: frawls@frrlaw.com.

RAWLS, JOHN D. lawyer; b. Jacksonville, Fla., Sept. 16, 1943; s. Hugh Miller Sr. and Katherine (Dickenson) R. BA, Williams Coll., 1965; JD, Fla. State U., Tallahassee, 1974. Bar: Fla. 1975, La. 1986, U.S. Dist. Ct. (mid. dist.) Fla. 1975, U.S. Dist. Ct. (ea. dist.) La. 1986, U.S. Dist. Ct. (no. dist.) Fla. 1989, U.S. Dist. Ct. (we. dist.) La. 1996, U.S. Ct. Appeals (5th cir.) 1986. Assoc. Foerster & Hodge, Jacksonville Beach, Fla., 1975-78; ptnr. Thames, Rawls & Skinner, Jacksonville, 1978-80; pvt. practice, 1980-85; pres. At Your Svc. Supply Co., New Orleans, 1985-86; assoc. Oestreicher, Whalen & Hackett, 1986-87; pvt. practice, 1987—. Charter mem. Fla. Commn. on Ethics, Tallahassee, 1974-75. Mem. Fla. State U. Law Rev., 1973-74. Bd. dirs. Celebration '86, New Orleans, 1985-86; vol. NO/AIDS Task Force, New Orleans, 1986—; bd. dirs. La. Lesbian and Gay Polit. Action Caucus, New Orleans, 1987-89, Nat. Lesbian and Gay Law Assn., Washington, 1992-94, Supreme Ct. of La. Hist. Soc., New Orleans, 1992-96; founder, sec., bd. dirs. La. Electorate of Gays and Lesbians, New Orleans, 1993-96; chair La. Gov.'s Commn. on HIV and AIDS, Baton Rouge, 1994-95; unofcl. advisor on Gay and AIDS issues Gov. of La., Baton Rouge, 1992-96. Capt. U.S. Army, 1968-72, Vietnam. Nat. Merit scholar, 1961; Forum for Equality ACCLAIM award Outstanding Polit. Activist, 1999, Champion for Equality award La. Lesbian and Gay Polit. Action Caucus, 2000. Fellow: La. Bar Found.; mem.: La. Landmarks Soc., Inc. (trustee 2001—), New Orleans Bar Assn. Democrat. Episcopalian. Avocation: reading. Office: 400 Magazine St Ste 100 New Orleans LA 70130-2439

RAWLS, NANCY LEE STIRK, nursing educator; b. Upper Darby, Pa., Mar. 11, 1945; d. Leslie W. and Esther Ruth (Cooper) Stirk; m. William D. Rawls; children: Diane Leslie, William D. Diploma, Lankenau Hosp. Sch. Nursing, Phila., 1966; BSN, Med. U. S.C., 1981; MN, U. S.C., 1990. Unit supr. Meadow Haven Nursing Ctr., Rock Hill, S.C., 1981-82; office nurse Lentz-Ross, MD, P.A., 1982-87; pediatric clin. instr. York Tech. Coll., 1987-89; asst. prof. nursing Kennesaw State Coll., Marietta, Ga., 1991-95; clin. examiner for so. performance assessment ctr. N.Y. Regents Coll., Atlanta, 1994-96; dir. nursing program Chattahoochee Tech. Coll., Dallas, 1995—. Mem. Sigma Theta Tau, Phi Kappa Phi. E-mail: nrawls@chattcollege.com.

RAWNSLEY, HOWARD MELODY, physician, educator; b. Long Branch, N.J., Nov. 20, 1925; s. Walter A. and Elizabeth (Melody) R.; m. B. Eileen Fiddes, Sept. 5, 1967; children: Virgilia Ingram, Elizabeth Sue. AB, Haverford Coll., 1949; MD, U. Pa., 1952. Diplomate Am. Bd. Pathology (trustee 1988-96). Intern Hosp. U. Pa., 1952-53, resident, 1953-57; practice medicine, specializing in pathology Phila., 1957-75; mem. Wm. Pepper Lab., U. Pa., 1957-75, asst. dir., 1960-68, dir., 1968-75; assoc. dir. Clin. Research Ctr., 1962-67, acting dir., 1969— 70, asst. prof. pathology and medicine, 1960-65, assoc. prof., 1965-69, prof., 1969-75; prof. pathology Dartmouth Hitchcock Med. Ctr., Hanover, N.H., 1975-95, chmn. dept., 1980-87, sr. v.p. med. affairs, 1987-94, emeritus, 1995—. Cons. VA Hosp.; mem. exec. com. Am. Bd. Med. Spltys., 1998-2001. Chmn. bd. dirs. New Eng. Blood Svcs. ARC, 1996—2000, 2002—. With U.S. Army, 1944—46. Woodward fellow in chemistry, 1953-55 Mem. AMA, ARC (biomed. svcs. com. 1990-92), Pathology Soc. Phila. (pres.), Coll. Am. Pathologists (bd. govs. 1985-93), Am. Soc. Clin. Pathologists (Disting. Svc. award 1995). Home: 7 Haskins Rd Hanover NH 03755-2204 E-mail: hrawn@valley.net.

RAWSKI, CONRAD H(ENRY), humanities educator, medievalist; b. Vienna, Austria, May 25, 1914; came to U.S., 1939, naturalized, 1944; s. Stanislaus and Johanna (Buberl-Maffei) R.; m. Helen Orr, July 5, 1957; children: Thomas George, Judith Ellen Rawski Kleen. MA, U. Vienna, 1936, PhD, 1937; postgrad., Péter Pázmány Egyetem, Budapest, 1938-39, Harvard U., 1939-40; MS in Libr. Sci., Western Res. U., 1957. Lectr. in music U. Louisville, 1940; from asst. prof. to prof. music Ithaca (N.Y.) Coll., 1940-56; dir. grad. studies, dean Ithaca (N.Y.) Coll. Sch. Music, 1951-56; head fine arts dept. Cleve. Public Library, 1957-62; assoc. prof., prof. library sci., coordinator Ph.D. program in info. sci. M.A. Baxter Sch. Info. and Libr. Sci., Case Western Res. U., Cleve., 1957-80, prof., sr. rsch. scholar, 1980-85, prof. emeritus for life, dean emeritus, 1985. Music columnist Boston Evening Transcript, 1939-40, Ithaca Jour., 1943-50; lectr. in musicology, medieval studies, info. sci. Fellow Fund for the Advancement of Edn., Ford Found., 1952-53, Nat. Endowment for Humanities, 1979 Author: Petrarch: Four Dialogues for Scholars, 1967, Toward a Theory of Librarianship, 1973, Petrarch's Latin Prose Works and the Modern Translator, 1977, Introduction to Research in Information Science, 1982; translator, editor: Petrarch's Remedies for Fortune Fair and Foul, 5 vols., 1991, Petrarch to Boccaccio: The Griseldis Letters, 1994, Francisci Petrarchae lectoris Adminiculum: Late Antique and Medieval Latin Words in the Works of Petrarch, 1998; originator: A Petrarch System, 1994-2002; contbr. articles to profl. jours. Mem. Renaissance Soc. Am., Medieval Acad. Am., Soc. for Medieval Latin, ALA (nat. Beta Phi Mu award 1979), Am. Musicol. Soc., Wembley Club. Clubs: Rowfant of Cleve. Address: 17877 Lost Trl Chagrin Falls OH 44023-5835 E-mail: hrawski@earthlink.net.

RAWSKI, EVELYN SAKAKIDA, history educator; b. Honolulu, Feb. 2, 1939; d. Evan T. and Teruko (Watase) Sakakida; m. Thomas G. Rawski, Dec. 16, 1967. BA, Cornell U., 1961; MA, Radcliffe Coll., 1962; PhD, Harvard U., 1968. Asst. prof. history U. Pitts., 1967-72, assoc. prof., 1973-79, prof. history, 1980—; univ. prof., 1996—. Author: Agricultural Change and the Peasant Economy of South China, 1972, Education and Popular Literacy in Ch'ing China, 1979, The Last Emperors: A Social History of Qing Imperial Institutions, 1998; co-author: Chinese Society in the Eighteenth Century, 1987, Worshiping the Ancestors: Chinese Commemorative Portraits, 2001; co-editor: Popular Culture in Late Imperial and Modern China, 1985, Death Ritual in Late Imperial and Modern China, 1988, Harmony and Counterpoint: Chinese Music in Ritual Context, 1996. Grantee Am. Coun. Learned Socs., 1973-74; NEH fellow, 1979-80, Chinese Studies fellow Am. Coun. Learned Socs./Sci. Rsch. Coun., 1989, Guggenheim fellow, 1990, Woodrow Wilson Internat. Ctr. fellow 1992-93. Mem. Assn. Asian Studies (China-Inner Asia coun., bd. dirs. 1976-79, v.p. 1994-95, pres. 1995-96). Home: 5317 Westminster Pl Pittsburgh PA 15232-2120 Office: U Pitts Dept History Pittsburgh PA 15260 E-mail: esrx@pitt.edu.

RAWSON, CLAUDE JULIEN, English educator; b. Shanghai, Feb. 8, 1935; came to U.S., 1985; m. Judith Ann Hammond, July 14, 1959; children: Hugh, Tim, Mark, Harriet, Annabel. BA, Oxford (Eng.) U., 1955, MA, BLitt, 1959. English lectr. U. Newcastle, Eng., 1957-65; from lectr. to prof., chmn. dept. U. Warwick, Coventry, Eng., 1965-85, hon. prof. Eng., 1986—; George Sherburn prof. English U. Ill., Urbana, 1985-86; George M. Bodman prof. English Yale U., New Haven, 1986-96, Maynard Mack prof. English, 1996—. Vis. prof. U. Pa., Phila., 1973, U. Calif., Berkeley, 1980; chmn. Yale Boswell Papers, 1990—2001; del. for lang. and lit. Oxford U. Press, NY. Author: Henry Fielding and the Augustan Ideal, 1972, 2d edit., 1991, Gulliver and the Gentle Reader, 1973, 2d edit., 1991, The Charater of Swift's Sahir, 1983, Order from Confusion Sprung, 1985, 2d edit., 1992, (with F.P. Lock) Collected Poems of Thomas Parcell, 1989, Satire and Sentiment 1660-1830, 1994, 2d edit., 2000, (with H. B. Nisbet) Cambridge History of Literary Criticism, vol. 4: The Eighteenth Century, 1997, God, Gulliver, and Genocide, 2001; editor: Modern Lang. Rev. and Yearbook of English Studies, London, 1974-88; gen. editor: Cambridge (Eng.) History of Literary Criticism, 1983—, Unwin Critical Libr., London, 1974—, Blackwell Critical Biographies, 1985—, Basic Writings of Jonathan Swift, 2002, Cambridge Edition of the Works of Jonathan Swift, 2002. Recipient Cert. of Merit for Disting. Svc. Conf. of Editors of Learned Jours., 1988; Andrew Mellon fellow Clark and Huntington Libr., 1980, 90, Guggenheim fellow, 1991-92, Sr. Faculty fellow Yale U., 1991-92; NEH grantee, 1991. Fellow Am. Acad. Arts and Scis.; mem. Modern Humanities Rsch. Assn. (life mem., com. mem. 1974-88), Internat. Soc. 18th Century Studies, Am. Soc. for 18th Century Studies, Brit. Soc. for 18th Century Studies (pres. 1973-74), Grolier Club. Office: Yale U Dept English PO Box 208302 New Haven CT 06520-8302 E-mail: claude.rawson@yale.edu.

RAWSON, ELEANOR S. publishing company executive; m. Kennett Longley Rawson (dec.); children: Kennett Longley, Linda. V.p., exec. editor David McKay Co.; pres., editor-in-chief Rawson, Wade Publishers, Inc.; v.p. Scribner Book Cos.; pub. Rawson Assocs. (divsn. Macmillan Pub. Co.); v.p., chmn., pub. Rawson Assocs./Scribner/divsn. Simon & Schuster Consumer Grp; teaching staff Columbia U. Lectr. NYU, New Sch., N.Y.; organizer, panelist various writers' confs.; mem. exec. coun., nominating chair Am. Assn. Pubs., 1970-74. Former editorial staff writer Am. mag.; free-lance writer radio and mags., newspaper syndicates; fiction editor Collier's mag., Today's Woman. Trustee, past v.p. Museums at Stony Brook. Mem. Women's Nat. Book Assn., P.E.N., Am. Assn. Museums, Yale Club, Cosmopolitan Club, Old Field Club, Women's Forum, Women In Media, Women in Comms. Office: Rawson Assocs/Scribner 1230 Avenue Of The Americas New York NY 10020-1513

RAWSON, ERIC GORDON, optical engineer; b. Saskatoon, Sask., Can., Mar. 4, 1937; s. Donald Strathern and Hildred Iantha (Patton) R.; m. Zivile Anne Nalivaika, May 5, 1966; children: Carol, Dalia, Cliff. BA, U. Saskatchewan, 1959, MA. 1960; PhD, U. Toronto, Ont., 1966. Mem. tech. staff Bell Telephone Labs., Murray Hill, N.J., 1966-73; mem. rsch. staff Xerox PARC, Palo Alto, Calif., 1973-78, area mgr., 1978-94; prin. Rawson Optics, Inc., Brentwood, 1994-99, pres., CEO, 1999—. Bd. dirs., sec. Alamed. Corp., Palo Alto, 1991—. Editor: Book of Milestones Fiber Optics Local Area Networks, 1994; contbr. over 65 articles to profl. jours. Fellow Optical Soc. Am. (mem. engrng. coun. 1995—, Engrng. Excellence award 1990), Soc. Photo-Instrumentation Engrs.; mem. IEEE (sr.). Achievements include over 30 patents for optics and biomedical monitoring. Office: 763 Franklin Dr Brentwood CA 94513-6463 E-mail: ericrawson@rawsonoptics.com.

RAWSON, HARVE E. psychologist, writer; b. Webb CIty, Mo., July 25, 1934; s. Paul Charles and Florence Landon Rawson; m. Joyce Elaine Blossom, June 9, 1961; children: Paul Gerald, Reed Harve. BA, Antioch Coll., 1957; MA, Ohio State U., 1959, PhD, 1961. Rsch. specialist N.Am. Aviation Inc., Columbus, Ohio, 1961—63; prof. psychology Hanover (Ind.) Coll., 1963—94, prof. emeritus, 1994—; dir. children's svcs. Englishton Pk., Lexington, 1969—93; dean faculty Franklin (Ind.) Coll., 1994—96; vis. prof. psychology Miss. State U., Starkville, 1998. Grant reviewer Coun. Internat. Exch. Scholars, Washington, 2000—01. Author: Webb City, 2000, Around the World in 30 Years, 2001, Purposeful Parenting, 2002; contbr. over 40 articles to profl. jours. Pres. Lide White Boys and Girls Club, Madison, Ind., 1969, 1974, 1978, 1999—2001; v.p. Jefferson County Youth Shelter, 1992. Recipient Sagamore of the Wabash award, Gov. Ind., 1993; scholar, Fulbright Found., Bahrain, 1988—89, Fulbright Found., 1994. Mem.: Ind. Psychol. Assn. (pres. 1974—76, Cmty. Svc. award 1991, Disting. Acad. Psychologist award 1986—87), Traveler's Century Club. Achievements include traveling to over 140 countries. Home: 1820 Crozier Ave Madison IN 47250

RAWSON, JIM CHARLES, accountant, executive; b. Houston, Apr. 20, 1947; s. Charles Manly and Georgie (Kearse) R.; m. Linda Eidman, Arp. 12, 1968; children: John Erich, Susan Margaret. BBA, Tex. Christian U., 1969. CPA, Tex. Acctg. clk. Tenneco, Inc., Houston, 1969-71, Projects Am. Corp., Houston, 1971-74, office mgr., 1974-77, v.p., gen. mgr., 1977-82, pres., 1982—. Recipient Bronze award Am. Land Devel. Assn., 1985, Gold award, 1983, Silver award, 1983. Mem. Am. Inst. CPA's, Tex. Soc. CPA's (Houston chpt.), Sports Car Club of Am. Evangelical. Avocations: sports car racing, salt water fishing. Office: Projects Am Corp 6124 Beverlyhill St Houston TX 77057-6610

RAWSON, JOHN ELTON, neonatologist, educator; b. Okolona, Miss., Jan. 31, 1938; s. Elton Phlemuel and Marjorie Morgan Jones Rawson; m. Mary Crouch Rawson, June 23, 1962; children: Katherine Asbury Rawson Kronzer, Edwin Lauderdale. BS in Chemisty, Millsaps Coll., 1960; MD, U. Miss., 1965. Diplomate Am. Bd. Pediat., Am. Bd. Neonatology and Perinatal Medicine; lic. physician, Miss. Clin. assoc. prof. pediat. U. Miss. Sch. Medicine, Jackson, 1972—; attending neonatologist, chief newborn medicine Ctrl. Miss. Med. Ctr., 1978—; attending neonatologist Miss. Bapt. Med. Ctr., 1982—. Chmn. bd. dirs. Health Choice of Miss., Jackson, 1991-98, Integrity Health Plan, Inc., Jackson, 1995-98, State Watch, Inc., Jackson, 1988-96; chief of staff Meth. Healthcare, Inc., Jackson, 1994-95. Editor: Newborn Ventilation, 1976. State chmn. March of Dimes, Jackson, 1972-82; mem. vestry St. James Episcopal Ch., Jackson, 1975-78; trustee St. Andrew's Day Sch., Madison, Miss., 1978-89, Meth. Lebouner Found., Memphis, 1991-2000. Capt. USAF, 1968-70. Mem. Rotary (Paul Harris fellow 1984). Home: 1 Barrington Sq Jackson MS 39206-6123 Office: Ctrl Miss Med Ctr 1850 Chadwick Dr Jackson MS 39204 E-mail: jackrawson@hotmail.com.

RAWSON, ROBERT BRADLEY, science educator; b. Dayton, Ohio, Nov. 26, 1958; s. William Charles and Ellen Galvin Rawson; m. Karen Lingo, June 23, 1984; children: Andrew Christopher, Carolyn Michelle, Elizabeth Ellen, James Joseph. BA, U. Calif., Berkeley, 1982; MS, Calif. State U., Hayward, 1987; PhD, U. Tex. Southwestern Med. Ctr., Dallas, 1993. Mgr. Tandy Radio Shack, Mountain View, Calif., 1982-85; instr. Calif. State U., Hayward, 1986-87; rsch. asst. U. Tex. Southwestern Med. Ctr., Dallas, 1988-93, fellow, 1994-99, asst. prof. molecular genetics, 1999—. Contbr. articles to profl. jours. Mem. AAAS. Roman Catholic. Office: U Tex Southwestern Med Ctr 5323 Harry Hines Blvd Dallas TX 75390-9046

RAWSON, WILLIAM ROBERT, lawyer, retired manufacturing company executive; b. Montclair, N.J., Mar. 14, 1925; s. William Howard and Maude Elizabeth (Wheeler) R.; m. Elizabeth S. Crandall, Sept. 30, 1949 (dec. Oct. 2001); children— Shirley, Jean, Elizabeth. AB, Brown U., 1947; LL.B., N.Y. U., 1950. Bar: N.J. 1950, Ill. 1974. Practice of law, Bloomfield, N.J., 1950-52; legal asst. Thomas A. Edison Industries, West Orange, 1952-57; asst. counsel T.A. Edison div. McGraw-Edison Co., Elgin, Ill., 1957-67, v.p. adminstrn., div., 1967-72, asst. gen. counsel, 1972-77, corp. v.p. adminstrn., 1977-80, v.p. law, adminstrn. also corporate sec., 1980-85; corp. counsel L. Kaiser/Estech div. Vigoro Industries, Inc., Savannah, Ga., 1985-89. Dir. Chgo. Econ. Devel. Corp. Chmn. Millburn (N.J.) Planning Bd. and Bd. Adjustment, 1962-70, Millburn Red Cross, 1969-70; mem. twp. coun., dep. mayor Twp. of Millburn, 1970-72; v.p. Elgin (Ill.) United Way, 1978-79; bd. dirs. United Way Suburban Chgo., 1981-85; pres. Regional Adult Literacy Partnership, Savannah, 1990-91; pres., bd. dirs. The Landings Homeowners Assn., 1992-94, pres., 1992-93. Lt. (j.g.) USN, 1943-46. Mem. ABA, Ill. State Bar Assn., Am. Arbitration Assn. (arbitrator constrn. industry panel 1985—), Elgin C. of C. (v.p. 1978-79) Republican. Episcopalian. Home: 4 Sandsfield Way Savannah GA 31411-2511

RAWSTHORNE, DANIEL ANDREW, software engineering executive; b. Oakland, Calif., Mar. 29, 1953; s. Edgar A. and Alta (Holmes) R.; m. Grace C. Colby, June 6, 1975; children: Derek, Catherine. BS in Math., Harvey Mudd Coll., Claremont, Calif., 1975; PhD in Math., U. Ill., 1980. Sr. staff mem. Decisions and Designs, Inc., McLean, Va., 1985-87; dir. U.S. ops. Intelligent Applications (USA), Columbia, Mo., 1987; mgr. decision support systems BDM Internat., McLean, 1987-92; prin. software engr. BDM Air Safety Mgmt., 1993—97; ind. cons. Seattle, 1997—98; chief arch. Access Via, 1998—2001; ind. cons., 2001—. Contbr. articles to profl. jours., symposiums and seminars in field. Lt. col., Mil. Intelligence, U.S. Army, 1979-85, res., 1985—. Mem. Computer Soc. IEEE, Assn. Computing Machinery, Am. Assn. Artificial Intelligence, Math. Assn. Am., Am. Math. Soc., Moose. Achievements include development and design of software Roadmap Methodology used by Dept. of Energy for environmental management planning; development of aircraft tracking and safety algorithms currently in use in Southern California; acknowledged expert in software engineering including use cases, architecture, and agile processes. Home: 116 S 294th Pl Federal Way WA 98003-3625

RAY, ALBERT, family physician; b. N.Y.C., Aug. 8, 1948; s. Herman and Stella (Meritz) R.; m. Cheryl Antecol, Oct. 8, 1977; children: Heather, Erin, Samantha. BA, Bklyn. Coll., 1969; MD, Cath. U. Louvain, Belgium, 1976. Diplomate Am. Bd. Family Practice, Can. Coll. Family Physicians. Intern Meml. U. of Nfld., St. John's, Can., 1976; resident McGill U., Montreal, 1978; family physician SCPMG, San Diego, 1978—. Clin. prof. U. Calif., San Diego, 1978—; mem. cmty. faculty UCLA, USD, U. Calif., Davis, USC; mem. clerkship cmty. adv. bd. U. Calif., San Diego, 1995—; pres. profl. staff Kaiser Found. Hosp.; bd. dirs. So. Calif. Permanente Med Group; asst. chief family medicine Kaiser Permanente, San Diego. Author: Lecons d'Histologie, 1973; contbr. to profl. jours. Program chair adult edn. Congregation Beth Israel, 1995; bd. dirs. Temple Emanuel, San Diego, 1990, Agy. for Jewish Edn.; expert reviewer Med. Bd. Calif., 1995; spl. med. cons. Calif. Dept. of Corps., 1996. Named Family Physician of Yr., Calif. Acad. Family Physicians, 2002. Fellow: Am. Acad. Family Physicians; mem.: Calif. Acad. Family Physicians, San Diego Acad. Family Physicians, San Diego County Med. Soc. (councilor 2002—), Calif. Med. Assn. (alternate del. ho. of dels.), AMA. Avocations: golf, tennis, travel, antiques. Office: Kaiser Permanente 4405 Vandever Ave San Diego CA 92120-3315

RAY, ANNETTE D. business executive; b. Decatur, Ind., Mar. 24, 1950; d. Gilbert O. and Florence L. Hoffman; m. Richard M. Ray, Nov. 28, 1975 (dec. June 1999); children: Michelle Ann, Ellen Marie, Laura Leigh, David Richard, Ruth Anne. AA, Concordia Jr. Coll., Ann Arbor, Mich., 1970; BS, Concordia Tchrs. Coll., Seward, Nebr., 1972; attended, Ctrl. Fla. C.C., Ocala, 1974. Lic. real estate, Ind.; lic. tchr., Ind., Fla. Elem. tchr. St. John's Luth., Ocala, 1972-74; mgr. apt. complex Victoria Sq. Apts., Ft. Wayne, Ind., 1974-75; substitute tchr. East Allen County Schs., Allen County, 1976-79, Circut A Luth. Schs., Adams and Allen County, 1977-81; corp. sec., treas., office mgr. Heritage Wire Die, Monroeville, 1987—. Co-author, co-editor: 1928-1988 A Rememberance, 1988, Coming to America--32 Families 1597-1997. Vol. Monroeville C. of C., 1987—, Concerned Area Residents Quality Edn., Allen County, 1990—, Am. Cancer Soc., Allen County, 1991—, chairperson Celebrity Bagger Day, 1995, 96; bd. dirs. Hoagland (Ind.) Hist. Soc., 1985—, Hoagland Area Advancement Assn., 1999—. Lutheran. Avocations: remodeling old homes, reading, genealogy, gardening, floral arranging. Home: 16901 Berning Rd Hoagland IN 46745-9753 Office: Heritage Wire Die Inc 19819 Monroeville Rd Monroeville IN 46773-9113 E-mail: heritagewiredie@yahoo.com.

RAY, ARLISS DEAN, retired environmental consultant; b. Hot Springs, Ark., Apr. 3, 1929; s. Clyde E. and Gladys Lorraine (Wofford) R.; m. Ardyth Lee Sharman, Aug. 23, 1952 (dec. Feb. 1992); children: Sandra Lee, Nancy Lynn, Laurie Jean, James Clyde; foster child, Joseph T. Yannetti. BEngring., Yale U., 1951; MS, Oreg. State U., 1957; PhD, U. Calif.-Berkeley, Berkeley, 1962. Asst. prof. environ. engrng. Vanderbilt U., 1961-63; assoc. prof., then prof. U. Mo., Columbia, 1963-71; v.p. Woodward-Envicon, also Woodward Clyde Cons., Clifton, N.J., 1972-75; pvt. cons., 1975-77; co-founder, 1978; exec. officer environ. mgmt. and cons. EMANCO Inc., Houston, 1978-94; ret., 1994. Adv. EPA, NSF. Contbr. articles to profl. jours. Lt. (j.g.) USN, 1951—55, Korea. Recipient award merit Mo. Water Pollution Control Assn., 1967. Mem. ASCE, Am. Water Works Assn., Air Pollution Control Assn., Water Pollution Control Fedn., Sigma Xi, Tau Beta Pi, Chi Epsilon, Pi Mu Epsilon. Home: 500 Pakis St Apt 2B Hot Springs National Park AR 71913-6556 E-mail: adrsprings@prodigy.net.

RAY, BILLY JOHN, JR. music educator; b. Puyallup, Wash., Apr. 9, 1964; s. Billy John, Sr. and Leone Dorothy Ray; m. Claudette Ann Laycock, Mar. 31, 1990; children: Jazmyn, Kierstyn. BA in Edn., Ctrl. Wash. U., 1987. Instrumental music tchr. Ellensburg (Wash.) Sch. Dist., 1987—88, Endicott (Wash.) Sch. Dist., 1988—. Mid. sch. football asst. coach Endicott-St. John Mid. Sch., 1993—95, mid. sch. football head coach, 1996—; baseball asst. coach St. John (Wash.)-Endicott HS, 1996—97, softball asst. coach, 1997—. Mem.: Wash. Interscholastic Activities Assn. (mem. music com. 1997—), Wash. Music Educators Assn. Home: 104 E St Endicott WA 99125 Office: Endicott Sch Dist 308 School Dr Endicott WA 99125 Office Fax: 509-657-3521. E-mail: bray@endicott.wednet.edu.

RAY, BRADLEY STEPHEN, petroleum geologist; b. Ada, Okla., Feb. 15, 1957; s. Walter Lloyd and Betty Louise (McCurley) R. BS in Geology, Baylor U., 1980; MS in Geology, U. Tex., 1985. Cert. geologist. Asst. geologist Hunt Oil Co., Dallas, 1978, geologist, 1979-81; ind. oil and gas producer, 1981—. Chmn. adv. bd. Geol. Info. Libr. Dallas, 1988—; bd. dirs. Global Mapping Internat. Trustee Dallas Bapt. U., 1988-94, Criswell Coll., 1990-92; chmn. The Habitats Project, 1993—; mem. Peoples Info. Network. Mem. Am. Assn. Petroleum Geologists, Ind. Petroleum Assn. Am., Soc. Ind. Profl. Earth Scientists, Dallas Geol. Soc., Tex. Ind. Producers and Royalty Owners, Okla. Ind. Petroleum Assn., Geol. Soc. Am., Computer Oriented Geol. Soc., Nat. Stripper Well Assn., Energy Club, Oklahoma City Geol. Soc., Colbert-Tracht Club. Republican. Baptist. Home: 4925 Greenville Ave Ste 1348 Dallas TX 75206-4021 Office: 1348 One Energy Sq Dallas TX 75206

RAY, BRENDA ELLEN, small business owner; b. New York, N.Y., Oct. 18, 1946; d. Garland Henry Rogers, Ruth Ellen Rogers; m. Tom Ray, June 29, 1995; 1 child from previous marriage Ariel M. Martin. Student, CCNY, 1964—66, UCLA, 1987, student, 1996, student, 1998. Asst. prodn. Universal City Studios, Universal City, Calif., 1972—84; writer various publs., 1985—89; sales rep. Albertson Olds Dealership, Culver City, Calif., 1989—97; pres., CEO, writer The Very Idea, Inc., N.Y.C., 1997—. Author (article): Herald Publs., 1975—77; author: Poetry (Editors Choice award, 1997), Screenplay (Writers Digest award, 1998). Democrat. Avocations: dancing, reading, writing. Office: The Very Idea Inc 20 E 53rd St Ste 3A New York NY 10022

RAY, BRUCE DAVID, lawyer, writer; b. Denver, Dec. 19, 1955; s. John Denver Ray and Jane (Guiney) Mitchell; m. Faith Theofanus, Aug. 20, 1978 (div. 2001); children: Ellena, Constance, Christian, Zoe. BA magna cum laude, U. Colo., 1978; JD, Union U., Albany, N.Y., 1981. Bar: Colo. 1981. Spl. environ. counsel URS-Berger, San Bernardino, Calif., 1982-84; asst. regional counsel EPA, Denver, 1984-90; spl. asst. U.S. atty. U.S. Dept. Justice, 1987-90; assoc. gen. counsel Johns-Manville Corp., 1990—. Asst. editor Natural Resources and Environment, 1989—; contbr. articles to legal jours. First v.p. St. Catherine Greek Orthodox Ch. of S.E. Denver, 1994-95. Recipient bronze medal EPA, 1986, 91, gold medal, 1989, Environ. Excellence award, 1987, Best Article award, 1988, Roasch prize Albany Law Sch., 1981. Mem. ABA (sect. on environment, energy and resources law), Colo. Bar Assn. (environ. law coun. 1987—, chmn. 1995-96), Aurora Bar assn., Environ. Law Inst., Air and Waste Mgmt. Assn., Phi Beta Kappa. Avocation: German language and literature, modern Greek. Office: Johns-Manville 717 17th St Denver CO 80202-3330 E-mail: rayb@jm.com.

RAY, C. CLAIBORNE, editor, columnist; b. Clinton, Iowa, Jan. 14, 1947; d. Dennie Ezell and Elizabeth Kathryn (Smith) Ray; m. J. Robert Thompson, June 17, 1972 (div.). AB cum laude, Vassar Coll., 1968. Copy editor The Daily Bond Buyer, N.Y.C., 1968-70; feature edits. editor The American Banker, 1970-75; copy editor The New York Times, 1977-80, asst. to editor, 1980-87, asst. to sci. editor, 1987-97, columnist Science Questions and Answers, 1988—, met. obituary editor, 1998—. Author: The New York Times Book of Science Questions and Answers, 1997. Mem. P.E.O. Sisterhood (chpt. past pres.). Democrat. Episcopalian. Home: 164 Bond St Apt 1A Brooklyn NY 11217-2233 Office: The New York Times 229 W 43rd St New York NY 10036-3959

RAY, CARLOS See NORRIS, CHUCK

RAY, CHARLES AARON, foreign service officer; b. Center, Tex., July 5, 1945; m. Myung Wook Soe, Nov. 3, 1973; children: David Edward, Denise Ellen, Gayle Denene, Jason Andre. BSBA, Benedictine Coll., 1972; MS in Sys. Mgmt., U. So. Calif., 1981; MS in Nat. Security Strategy, Nat. War Coll., 1997. Commd. 2d lt. U.S. Army, 1965, advanced through grades to maj., ret., 1982; consular officer U.S. Consulate Gen., Guangzhou, China, 1983-84, chief consular sect. Shenyang, China, 1985-87, chief adminstrv. sect. Chiangmai, Thailand, 1988-91; spl. asst. to dir. Office Def. Trade Controls, Washington, 1991-93; dep. chief of mission Am. Embassy, Freetown, Sierra Leone, 1993-96; detailed to Nat. War Coll., Washington, 1996-97, Nat. Fgn. Affairs Tng. Ctr., Arlington, Va., 1997-98; consul gen. U.S. Consulate Gen., Ho Chi Minh City, Vietnam, 1998-2001; sr. seminar Nat. Fgn. Affairs Tng. Ctr., 2001—. Editl. cartoonist Spring Lake News, 1975-79; contbr. articles to Asia Mag., 1974-79; editor mag. Psyop Digest, 1976-78; exec. editor Def. Trade News, 1992-93. Avocations: taekwondo, softball, tennis, painting, poetry. Office: 14116 Saddle River Dr North Potomac MD 20878 E-mail: rayca@state.gov.

RAY, CHARLES ALBERT, photojournalist; b. Franklin County, Tenn., Feb. 9, 1928; s. Sherman Peaturney and Sona Arlena Ray; m. Betty Heringa, Dec. 10, 1950 (div. June 1965); m. Deborah Freshwater, Apr. 7, 1972 (div. Apr. 1980); m. Theresa Ann Bailey, Dec. 20, 1997; children: David Charles, Thomas Wesley. Student, Grand Rapids (Mich.) Jr. Coll., 1951—53, Bay City (Mich.) Jr. Coll., 1956—61. News cinematographer Sta. WWTV-TV, Cadillac, Mich., 1953—54, Sta. KWWL-TV, Waterloo, Iowa, 1955, Sta. WNEM-TV, Bay City, 1956—61, Sta. WGN-TV, Chgo., 1961—65, NBC News, Chgo., 1965—87; ret., 1987. Author: The Life of a Network Newsreel Cameraman, 2001;exhibitions include Charles Ray Photo Archives, Florida Gulf Coast U., 2002. Named Chgo. Cameraman of Yr., 1963, 1965, 1967; recipient numerous news awards. Mem.: Internat. Cinematographers Guild Local 600, Chgo. Press Photographers Assn., Nat. Press Photographers Assn. (News Film award). Avocations: photography, reading, writing, fishing. Office: PO Box 449 Sanibel FL 33957

RAY, CHARLES DEAN, neurosurgeon, spine surgeon, bioengineer, inventor; b. Americus, Ga., Aug. 1, 1927; s. Oliver Tinsley and Katherine (Broadfield) R.; children: Bruce, Marlene. AB, Emory U., 1950; MS, U. Miami, 1952; MD, Med. Coll. Ga., 1956. Diplomate Am. Bd. Neurol. Surgery, Am. Bd. Spine Surgery. Intern Bapt. Meml. Hosp., Memphis, 1956-57; resident, rsch. assoc. neurosurgery U. Tenn. Hosp., 1957-62; fellow, rsch. asst. Mayo Clinic and Found., Rochester, Minn., 1962-64; asst. prof. neurosurgery, lectr. bioengring. Johns Hopkins U. Med. Sch., Balt., 1964-68; chief dept. engring. F. Hoffmann-LaRoche, Basel, Switzerland, 1968-73; practice medicine specializing in neurosurgery Norfolk, Williamsburg, Va., 1973—. Lectr. U. Basel, 1968-73; dir. emeritus Inst. Low Back and Neck Care; med. dir. The Spine Program, Ea. Va. Med. Sch., Norfolk, Va.; pres. Am. Coll. Spine Surgery; mem. staff Sentara Hosps., Norfolk; clin. assoc. prof. medicine U. Minn., Mpls., 1973-73; v.p. med. rsch. Medtronic, Inc., Mpls., 1972-79; chmn. bd., pres. Cedar Devel. Corp., Cedar Surg., Inc., 1985—; bd. dirs. Herman Miller, Inc.; chmn. emeritus, med. dir. Raymedia, Inc., Mpls.; cons. in field. Author: Principles of Engineering Applied to Medicine, 1964, Medical Engineering, 1974, Lumbar Spine Surgery, 1988; contbr. over 350 articles to profl. publs. Chmn. com. materials and devices World Fedn. Neurosurg. Socs., 1977—, Cosmos Club, 1976—; vestry St. Martin's Episcopal Ch., Wayzata, Minn., 1976-79. With USN, 1945-49. Named Disting. Alumnus, Med. Coll. Ga., 1999; recipient Gold award for Best Med. Device Design of Yr. R&D 100, 2000. Fellow: ACS, Royal Soc. Health, Am. Coll. Spine Surgery (pres.); mem.: ASTM, IEEE (sr.), AMA (sr.), N.Am. Spine Soc. (past pres., chmn., Wiltse award 1999), Internat. Orgn. Standardization, Internat. Soc. Stereotaxic and Functional Neurosurgery, Am. Assn. Neurol. Surgeons (sr.), Pan-Am. Med. Assn. (life), Internat. Fedn. Med. Biol. Engring., West Germany Armed Forces Med. Soc., Congress Neurol. Surgeons, Mpls. Club, Sigma Xi. Achievements include over 50 U.S. patents and over 100 foreign patents. Home: 24 Harleston Green PO Box 5718 Snowmass Village CO 81615 Office: PO Box 2219 Yorktown VA 23692 Office Fax: 757-988-1778. E-mail: InveRay@aol.com.

RAY, CHARLES KENDALL, retired university dean; b. Boise City, Okla., Mar. 15, 1928; s. Volney Holt and Mamie (Burton) R.; m. Doris Derby, Aug. 26, 1951. BA, U. Colo., 1951; MA, Columbia, 1955, Ed.D., 1959. Teaching prin. Bur. Indian Affairs, Savoonga, Alaska, 1951-54; mem. faculty U. Alaska, 1957-93, prof. edn., 1960-93, dean Sch. Edn., 1961-80, dir. summer sessions, 1980-93. Author: A Program of Education for Alaska Natives, 1959, Alaskan Native Secondary School Dropouts, 1961. Mem. N.E.A., Phi Delta Kappa. Home: 2000 1st Ave Apt 2204 Seattle WA 98121-2171

RAY, CREAD L., JR. retired state supreme court justice; b. Waskom, Tex., Mar. 10, 1931; s. Cread L. and Antonia (Hardesty) R.; m. Janet Watson Keller, Aug. 12, 1977; children: Sue Ann (dec.), Robert E., Glenn L., David B., Marcie Lynn, Anne Marie. BBA, Tex. A&M U., 1952; JD, U. Tex., 1957; L.H.D. (hon.), Wiley Coll., Marshall, Tex., 1980. Bar: Tex. 1957. Practiced in, Marshall, 1957-59; judge Harrison County, 1959-61; justice 6th dist. Ct. Civil Appeals, Texarkana, 1970-80, Supreme Ct. Tex., 1980-90, ret., 1990; prin. C.L Ray, 1991—. Past pres. Marshall Jaycees, Marshall C. of C.; mem. Tex. Ho. of Reps., 1966-70; active local, regional, nat. Boy Scouts Am.; trustee Wiley Coll. Lt. col. USAF, 1952-54, Korea; ret. Recipient various Boy Scouts awards. Mem. State Bar Tex., N.E. Tex. Bar Assn. (past pres.), Rotary, Tex. Aggies. Democrat. Methodist. E-mails. Home and Office: 604 Beardsley Ln Austin TX 78746-4929 E-mail: clray@iamerica.net., CRAY7147@aol.com., clray@qbiz.com.

RAY, DAVID PAUL, lawyer; b. Eastport, Maine, July 21, 1952; s. Ralph S. and Fae B. Ray; m. Kay Loftus, Sept. 16, 1989; 1 child, Cyrilla Jane. BS, U. Maine, 1974; JD, Cornell U., 1977. Bar: Maine 1977, U.S. Dist. Ct. Maine 1977, U.S. Ct. Appeals (1st cir.) 1977. Assoc. Jensen, Baird, Gardner & Henry, Portland, Maine, 1977-80; counsel to Senator George J. Mitchell, U.S. Senate, Washington, 1980-82; ptnr. Amerling & Burns, P.A., Portland, 1982-97, Burns, Ray & DeLano, Portland, 1997-2000, Bernstein Shur Sawyer & Nelson, P.A., Portland, 2001—. Bd. dirs., v.p. Ctr. for Cultural Exch., Portland. Mem. ABA, Maine Bar Assn., Maine Bar Found. Office: Bernstein Shur et al 100 Middle St PO Box 9729 Portland ME 04104 E-mail: dray@mainelaw.com.

RAY, DOUGLAS KENT, newspaper executive; Pres., CEO Daily Herald/Sunday Herald, Arlington Heights, Ill., 1970—. Office: Daily Herald/Sunday Herald Paddock Publs PO Box 280 Arlington Heights IL 60006-0280

RAY, EDDYE ROBERT, occupational safety and health professional; b. Tulsa, Jan. 16, 1941; s. Samuel McKeel and Oteka Nathalee (Ammons) R.; m. Dorothy Christine Rohrer, Aug. 12, 1966; children: Robert Harold, William McKeel. BS in Chemistry, East Cen. State U., Ada, Okla., 1968. Cert. safety profl., hazardous material mgr., safety mgr.; registered environ. mgr. Safety inspector ARCO Chem. Co., Sand Springs, Okla., 1968-86; safety specialist ChemLink Petroleum Inc., 1986-88; pres. Seagull Enteprise and Assocs., Inc., Tulsa, 1988—. Instr. engring. extension Okla. State U., Stillwater, 1988—; fire tng. instr. Tex. A&M U., College Station, 1976—. Asst. scoutmaster Boy Scouts Am., Sand Springs, 1987—. With USAF, 1960-64. Mem. Am. Soc. Safety Engrs., World Safety Orgn., Okla. Safety Coun. (chmn. occupational com. 1987-88), Bowhunting Coun. Okla. (pres. 1983-87). Democrat. Baptist. Avocations: archery, bowhunting, hunting, fishing, little league soccer. Office: Seagull Enterprise Assocs 212 N Main St Sand Springs OK 74063-7645

RAY, EDWARD JOHN, economics educator, administrator; b. Jackson Heights, N.Y., Sept. 10, 1944; s. Thomas Paul and Cecelia Francis (Hiney) R.; m. Virginia Beth Phelps, June 14, 1969; children: Stephanie Elizabeth, Katherine Rebecca, Michael Edward. BA, CUNY, 1966; MA, Stanford U., 1969, PhD, 1971. Asst. prof. econs. Ohio State U., Columbus, 1970-74, assoc. prof., 1974-77, prof., 1977—, chmn. dept. econs., 1976-92, assoc. provost acad. affairs Office Acad. Affairs, 1992-93, sr. vice provost, chief info. officer Office Acad. Affairs, 1993-98, acting sr. v.p. and provost, 1997-98, exec. v.p., provost, 1998—. Cons. Dept. Labor, 1974-76, Dept. Commerce, 1977, AID, Office Tech. Assessment, winter 1982 Contbr. articles to profl. jours. Active Upper Arlington Civic Assn., Columbus, 1983—. Mem. Am. Econs. Assn., Phi Beta Kappa Home: 1977 Rosebery Dr Columbus OH 43220-3044 Office: Ohio State U Acad Affairs 203 Bricker Hall 190 N Oval Mall Columbus OH 43210-1321 E-mail: ray.1@osu.edu.

RAY, EVA KONIG, biomedical consultant; b. Zagreb, Yugoslavia; d. Franjo and Erna (Kohn) K.; children: Jude, Diane, David, Jean. BA, Cornell U., 1955; MA, PhD, Bryn Mawr Coll., 1973. Postdoctoral fellow dept. Ophthalmology Med. Sch. of U. Pa., Phila., 1972-74, rsch. assoc. Scheie Eye Inst., 1974-76; asst. prof. dept. biochemistry/physiology Med. Coll. of Pa., 1976-83, dean of women, 1980-83; technology cons. Steg, Ray and Assocs., Villanova, Pa., 1983—; v.p. Organica, Inc., 1994-96. Chairperson Gordon Rsch. Conf., Kingston, R.I., 1988, 90; chair sci. adv. bd. BRT Inc., Troy, N.Y., 1981-83. Mem. Montgomery County Commn. on Women and Families; Dem. committeeperson Lower Merion, Pa., 1985—92; bd. dirs., mem. advocacy com. ElderNet of Lower Merion-Narberth. Mem. Am. Soc. Microbiology, Am. Soc. Gravitational and Space Biology, Assn. Women in Sci., B'nai B'rith (bd. dirs. 2001—), Sigma Xi. Office: 1222 Prospect Hill Rd Villanova PA 19085-2115 E-mail: evaray1@aol.com.

RAY, EVELYN LUCILLE, arts facilitator, small meetings planner; b. Phila., Oct. 15, 1949; d. William and Erma Lucille (Chadrick) Ray. Sec. City of Phila., 1967, Free Libr. of Phila., 1972-77, Office of City Solicitor, Phila., 1977-81, Water Dept., Phila., 1981-87; program devel. creative cons. Accoutrements for the Arts, 1989, creative dir., 1993—, meeting planner for small meetings specializing in theme and site selection, 1995—. Comms. support Pa. Acad. of Fine Arts, Phila., 1987-88; creative cons. West Phila. Cultural Alliance, Phila., 1988-89; mem. adv. bd. Internat. Biog. Ctr., Cambridge, Eng., 1995—, Am. Biog. Inst., Raleigh, N.C., 1995—. Republican. Baptist. Avocations: travel, real estate: interior design and preservation, entertaining, classical music. Office: Accoutrements for the Arts 341 N Robinson St Philadelphia PA 19139-1125

RAY, FRANK ALLEN, lawyer; b. Lafayette, Ind., Jan. 30, 1949; s. Dale Allen and Merry Ann (Fleming) R.; m. Carol Ann Olmutz, Oct. 1, 1982; children: Erica Fleming, Robert Allen. BA, Ohio State U., 1970, JD, 1973. Bar: Ohio 1973, U.S. Dist. Ct. (so. dist.) Ohio 1975, U.S. Supreme Ct. 1976, U.S. Tax Ct. 1977, U.S. Ct. Appeals (6th cir.) 1977, U.S. Dist. Ct. (no. dist.) Ohio 1980, U.S. Dist. Ct. (ea. dist.) Mich. 1983, U.S. Ct. Appeals (1st cir.) 1986; cert. civil trial adv. Nat. Bd. Trial Advocacy. Asst. pros. atty. Franklin County, Ohio, 1973-75, chief civil counsel, 1976-78; dir. econ. crime project Nat. Dist. Attys. Assn., Washington, 1975-76; assoc. Brownfield, Kosydar, Bowen, Bally & Sturtz, Columbus, Ohio, 1978, Michael F. Colley Co., L.P.A., Columbus, 1979-83; pres. Frank A. Ray Co., L.P.A., 1983-93, 2000—, Ray & Todaro Co., LPA, Columbus, 1993-94, Ray, Todaro & Alton Co., L.P.A., Columbus, 1994-96, Ray, Todaro, Alton & Kirstein Co., L.P.A., Columbus, 1996, Columbus, Ray, Alton & Kirstein Co., L.P.A., 1996-98; sr. ptnr. Ray & Alton, L.L.P., 1998-2000. Mem. seminar faculty Nat. Coll. Dist. Attys., Houston, 1975-77; mem. nat. conf. faculty Fed. Jud. Ctr., Washington, 1976-77; bd. editors Man. for Complex Litigation, Fed. Jud. Ctr., 1999—; bd. mem. bar examiners Ohio Supreme Ct., 1992-95, Rules Adv. Com., 1995-99. Editor: Economic Crime Digest, 1975-76; co-author: Personal Injury Litigation Practice in Ohio, 1988, 91. Mem. fin. com. Franklin County Rep. Orgn., Columbus, 1979-84; trustee Ohio State U. Coll. Humanities Alumni Soc., 1991-93, Nat. Coun. Ohio State U. Coll. Law Alumni Assn., 1998—; mem. Legal Aid Soc. of Columbus Capital Campaign Fund Cabinet, 1998. Capt. inf. U.S. Army, 1976. Named to Ten Outstanding Young Citizens of Columbus, Columbus Jaycees, 1976; recipient Nat. award of Distinctive Svc., Nat. Dist. Attys. Assn., 1977. Fellow: Ohio Acad. Trial Lawyers (pres. 1989—90, Pres.'s award 1986), Ohio State Bar Found., Roscoe Pound Found., Am. Coll. Trial Lawyers, Internat. Soc. Barristers, Columbus Bar Found.; mem.: ATLA (state del. 1990—92), ABA, Franklin County Trial Lawyers Assn. (pres. 1987—88, Pres.'s award 1990), Ohio State Bar Assn. (com. negligence law 1990—97), Million Dollar Advs. Forum, Columbus Bar Assn. (pres. 2001—02, Profl. award 1987), Am. Bd. Trial Advs. (sec. Ohio chpt. 2002—), Inns. of Ct. (pres. Judge Robert M. Duncan chpt. 1993—94). Presbyterian. Home: 2030 Tremont Rd Columbus OH 43221-4330 Office: 175 S 3rd St Ste 350 Columbus OH 43215-5188 E-mail: far@raylaw.com.

RAY, GEORGE MICHAEL, music educator; b. Martinsville, Va., Nov. 30, 1946; s. Columbus Washington and Patricia Ramsey R.; m. Shirley Ann Ray, June 19, 1971. B. Music Edn., Va. Commonwealth U., Richmond, Virginia, 1969; MS in Music Edn., Radford U., Radford, Va., 1975; MS in Edn., Jacksonville State U., Jacksonville, Ala., 1995. Cert. postgrad. profl. cert. Va., A1 instrumental music Ala. Commd. U.S. Army, 1975; advanced through grades to master sgt. (1st sgt.); clarinet sect. leader 392d Army Band, Ft. Lee, Va., 1975—77; staff instr. U.S. Army Element Sch. of Music, Norfolk, 1977—79, concert band br. head Va., 1981—84, army advanced coursesconducting instr., 1984—86; project NCO skill qualification test devel. Sch. Music-Testing Devel., Virginia Beach, 1979—81; woodwind groupleader 3d Inf. Divsn. Band, Wuerzburg, Germany, 1986—89; woodwind groupleader/first sgt. 14th Army Band, Anniston, Ala., 1990—92; woodwind group leader/ops. supr. US Army Band Europe, Heidelberg, Germany, 1992—95; woodwind groupleader The Continental Army Band, Ft. Monroe, Va., 1995—96; tchr. Pittsylvania County Sch. Sys., Chatham, 1996—70; music tchr. Botetourt County Pub. Sch. Sys., Fincastle, 1970—75; math. chairperson Peninsula Christian Sch., Smithfield, 1996—99; instrumental music tchr. Patrick County Pub. Sch. Sys., Stuart, 1999—. Choir dir. Wesley Meth. Ch., Martinsville, Va., 1969—73, Buchanan Bapt. Ch., Buchanan, Va., 1973—74, First Christian Church(Disciples of Christ), Norfolk, 1978—85, St. Mark's United Meth. Ch., Hampton, 1995—99; clarinetist Tidewater Winds (Profl. Band in the Sousa Tradition), Norfolk, 1996—99; singer Norfolk Savoyard Light Opera Co., Norfolk, Va., 1982—85. Musician (conductor) all shore band; musician: (solo clarinetist) (clarinet concerto) Stamitz-Concerto in Bb, 1988 (performed with the Wuerzburg Musik Freunde, 1988). Mem.: NEA, NCOA, AMVET, Am. Recorder Soc., Music Educators Nat. Conf. Methodist. Avocations: reading, computer programming. Home: 108 Deerwood Tr Stuart VA 24171

RAY, GILBERT T. lawyer; b. Mansfield, Ohio, Sept. 18, 1944; s. Robert Lee Ray and Renatha (Goldie) Washington; m. Valerie J. Reynolds, June 14, 1969; children: Tanika, Tarlin. BA, Ashland Coll., 1966; MBA, U. Toledo, 1968; JD, Howard U., 1972. Assoc. O'Melveny & Myers, L.A., 1972-79, ptnr., 1980-2000, ret. ptnr., 2000—. Bd. dirs. HMS Host Co., Sierra Monolithins, Inc., Watson, Wyatt & Co. Bd. dir. HMS Host Co., Sierra Monolithins, Inc., Automobile Club of So. Calif., Haynes Found., Watson, Wyatt & Co. Mem. The Calif. Club, L.A. Country Club. Democrat. Office: O'Melveny & Myers 400 S Hope St Los Angeles CA 90071-2899

RAY, GORDON THOMPSON, communications executive; b. N.Y.C., Jan. 31, 1928; s. John Henry and Hama Thompson (Potter) R. m. Ingrid Ray; children: Stuart, John, Lawrence, Carl. BEE, Rensselaer Poly. Inst., 1954; PhD, Midwest Coll. Engring., 1983. With The Bell System, various locations, 1954-83; successively engr., chief engr. N.Y. Tel., Albany, Utica, Jamaica, White Plains, N.Y., Bklyn., 1983, asst. v.p. long range planning N.Y.C.; former mem. tech. staff Bell Tel. Labs., N.Y.C., Murray Hill and Holmdel, N.J.; engr. AT&T, N.Y.C. Dir. Bell Sys. Computer Seminar; del. CCITT, Body Planning Internat. Direct Distance Dialing; v.p. planning NYNEX Material Enterprises Co. subs. NYNEX Corp., 1983-84; sr. vp. NEC Am., Inc., Melville, N.Y., 1985-91, exec. v.p., 1992—; bd. govs. Electronic Industry Assn.; mem. bus. and industry ctr. SUNY, adv. bd. Marine Scis. Rsch. Ctr., Harriman Coll., Stonybrook, sci. and bus. coun. L.I. Rsch. Inst.; bd. dirs. NEC Am. Inc., NEC Rsch. Inst., Tel. Industry Assn., L.I. Assn., Summa Four Corp., Numerex Corp., L.I. Forum for Tech.; exec. com. Computer and Comm. Industry Assn., Nat. Comm. Forum. Trustee U.S. Coun. for Internat. Bus., N.Y. Hall of Sci.; mem. exec. com. Akron Golf Charities. With U.S. Army, 1946-49. Fellow Royal Soc. Arts; mem. AAAS, NSPE (sr. mem.), IEEE (sr. mem., computer and comm. info. policy com.), IEEE Comm. Soc. (past chmn. quality assurance mgmt. com., internat. comm. field award com.), N.Y. Acad. Scis., Am. Mgmt. Assn., Internet Soc. Office: NEC Am Inc 8 Corporate Center Dr Melville NY 11747-3112

RAY, H. M. lawyer; b. Rienzi, Miss., Aug. 9, 1924; s. Thomas Henry and Isabelle (Dunlap) R.; m. Merle Burt, Nov. 28, 1953 (dec. Dec. 1993); children: Howard Manfred, Mark Andrew. JD, U. Miss., 1949. Bar: Miss. 1949. U.S. atty. No. Dist. Miss., Oxford, 1961-81; pvt. practice law Corinth, Miss., 1949-61, Jackson, 1981-85, 90—; asst. atty. gen. State of Miss., 1986-90. Mem. Atty. Gen.'s Adv. Com. U.S. Attys., 1973-78, chmn., 1976; vis. lectr. UN, Asia and Far East, UN (Inst. for Prevention Crime and Treatment of Offenders), Tokyo, 1977; pros. atty. Alcorn County, Miss., 1956-57, 58-61; mem. Miss. Ho. of Reps., 1948-51; mem. Miss. Gov.'s Com. to Study Laws Regarding Use of Deadly Force on Fleeing Felons, 1982-83, Miss. Gov.'s Constl. Study Commn., 1985-86. Co-author: Miss. Workmens' Compensation Act, 1948. Chmn. Corinth-Alcorn County Airport Bd., 1959-61; trustee Alcorn County Public Library, 1959-62. Served with USAAC, 1943-45, ETO; with USAF, 1951-53. Recipient Corinth's Young Man of Yr. award, 1958 Presbyterian (elder). Clubs: Kiwanis (lt. gov. 1955-56, dist. chmn. 1956-57, pres. Corinth 1953-54). Home: 12 Windy Ridge Cove Jackson MS 39211-2904 Office: PO Box 13415 Jackson MS 39236-3415

RAY, JAMES ALLEN, research consultant; b. Lexington, ky., Feb. 21, 1931; s. Allen Brice and Elizabeth Logan (Simpson) R.; m. Mary Ruth Johnston, June 8, 1958; children: James Edward, Allen Bruce, John David. BS in Geology, U. N.C., 1958; MS, N.C. State Coll., 1962. Chief petrographic rsch. Master Builders divsn. Martin Marietta Corp., Cleve., 1959-73, asst. dir. rsch., 1973-77, dir. rsch., 1977-78, dir. rsch. and engring., 1978-79, v.p. rsch., 1979-80, v.p. creative rsch., 1980-82; cons., 1982—; pres. James A. Ray Corp., 1986—. Patentee in field. With USAF, 1951-55. REcipient Jefferson Cup, Martin Marietta Corp., 177. Mem. Am. Inst. Chemists, ASTM, ICRI, Res. Officers Assn. (life), NRA (life), Ret. Officers Assn. (life), Am. Concrete Inst., Internat. Cement Microscopy Assn. Republican. Home: 9891 Stamm Rd PO Box 460 Mantua OH 44255-0460 Fax: 330-527-4790. E-mail: raycorp@apk.net.

RAY, JAMES ARTHUR, speaker, writer; b. Honolulu, Nov. 22, 1957; s. Gordon Ray Arthur, Elaine Ray Joyce. With AT&T Sch. Bus., Atlanta, 1989—92; spkr. James Ray Internat., La Jolla, Calif., 1992—. Author: The Science of Success, 2000. Master: Nat. Spkrs. Assn. (cert. 2000). Avocations: exercising, hiking, travel. Office: James Ray Internat 7514 Girard Ave 1PMB544 La Jolla CA 92037 Office Fax: 858-459-9186. Business E-Mail: service@JamesRay.com.

RAY, JENNIFER JO, analytical chemist; b. Springfield, Ohio, Sept. 28, 1966; d. Joseph F. and Phyllis Jean (Hahn) Leach; 1 child, Bobbi Jo Ray. BS, Urbana (Ohio) U., 1988; MS, Wright State U., 1990. Rsch. chemist SOCHE/Wright Patterson AFB, WRDC/MLPJ, Dayton, Ohio, 1987-90; devel. chemist Scitex Digital Printing, Inc., 1991-99; analytical lab. mgr. Chem First Electronic Materials, 1999—. Emergency med. technician Arcanum (Ohio) Cmty. Rescue, 1993-98. Mem. AAAS, AOAC, Am. Soc. Quality, Am. Chem. Soc. (co-founder Dayton sect. Women Chemist Com. 1998), Assn. for Women in Sci. Republican. Roman Catholic. Avocations: reading, bicycling, camping. Office: Chem First Electronic Materials 1515 Nicholas Rd Dayton OH 45418 E-mail: jray@chemfirst.com.

RAY, JOE C. academic administrator, musician; b. Weleetka, Okla., Aug. 21, 1948; s. Lycurgus Harrel and Edna Ray; m. Colleen S. Dawson, May 31, 1969; 1 child Bret 1 child Joy Hicks. MusB in Edn., U. Okla., 1970; MusM, Ind. U., 1974. Band dir. Western Heights Pub. Schs., Oklahoma City, 1970—72; instr. of music Ind. State U., Terre Haute, 1974—76; dir. of instrumental activities Carson-Newman Coll., Jefferson City, Tenn., 1976—97; chair music divsn. Phillips U., Enid, Okla., 1997—98; dir. of bands Northeastern State U., Tahlequah, 1998—99; coord. spl. events Okla. State U., Stillwater, 1999—. Adminstrv. asst. Harvey Phillips Found., Bloomington, 1972—76; assoc. dir. Ind. U. Summer Music Clinics, Bloomington, 1974—75; dir. Bapt. Student Union, Bloomington, 1974—76; music dir. 1st United Meth. Ch., Dandridge, Tenn., 1977—78; piano accompanist Magna View Bapt. Ch., Jefferson City, Tenn., 1984—85; summer instrumental music coord. So. Bapt. Conv., Nashville, 1986—96; tubist Knoxville Brass Quintet, 1990—95; condr., chair, bd. dirs. Knoxville Concert Band, 1991—96; min. of music New Market (Tenn.) Bapt. Ch., New Market, 1993—98; prin. tuba Enid Symphony Orch., 1997—99; adv. bd. Tri-State Music Festival, Enid, 1997—98, Friends of Music, Stillwater, Okla., 2000—; bd. dirs. Stillwater Concert Band. Musician: (mus. performance) East Tennessee Professors' Tuba Trio, 1978; contbr. articles to profl. jours. Mem. Mcpl. Arts and Humanities Com., Stillwater, 1999—2001. Named Outstanding Music Educator, So. Bapt. Conv., 1993; recipient Ln. Bryant award for outstanding cmty. svc., Carson-Newman Coll., 1990. Mem.: Ind. U. Alumni Assn., Tubists Universal Brotherhood Assn., Music Educators Nat. Conf., Christian Instrumentalists and Dirs. Assn. (nat. pres. 1997—99). Conservative. Avocations: hiking, cycling. Office: Okla State U 060 Student Union Stillwater OK 74078 Office Fax: 405-744-2680. E-mail: rayjc@okstate.edu.

RAY, JOHN WALKER, otolaryngologist, educator, broadcast commentator; b. Columbus, Ohio, Jan. 12, 1936; s. Kenneth Clark and Hope (Walker) R.; m. Susanne Gettings, July 15, 1961; children: Nancy Ann, Susan Christy. AB magna cum laude, Marietta Coll., 1956; MD cum laude, Ohio State U., 1960; postgrad., Temple U., 1964, Mt. Sinai Hosp., Columbia U., 1964, 66, Northwestern U., 1967, 71, U. Ill., 1968, U. Ind., 1969, Tulane U., 1969. Diplomate Am. Bd. Otolaryngology. Intern Ohio State U. Hosps., Columbus, 1960-61, clin. rsch. trainee NIH, 1963-65, resident dept. otolaryngology, 1963-65, 66-67, resident dept. surgery, 1965-66, instr. dept. otolaryngology, 1966-67, 70-75, clin. asst. prof., 1975-82, clin. assoc. prof., 1982-92, clin. prof., 1992-2000, clin. prof. emeritus, 2000—; hon. staff, past chief of staff Good Samaritan Hosp., also Bethesda Hosp., Zanesville, Ohio, 1967—. Hon. active staff Meml. Hosp., Marietta, Ohio, 1992—; radio-TV health commentator, 1982—. Contbr. articles to sci. and med. jours.; collaborator with surg. motion picture: Laryngectomy and Neck Dissection, 1964. Past pres. Muskingum chpt. Am. Cancer Soc.; bd. dirs. Zanesville Art Ctr. Capt. USAF, 1961-63. Recipient Barraquer Meml. award, 1965; named to Order of Ky. Col., 1966, Muskingum County Country Music Hall of Fame. Fellow ACS, Am. Soc. Otolaryn. Allergy, Am. Acad. Otolaryngology-Head and Neck Surgery (past gov.), Am. Acad. Facial Plastic and Reconstructive Surgery; mem. AMA, Nat. Assn. Physician Broadcasters, Muskingum County Acad. Medicine (past pres.), Ohio Med. Assn. (del.), Columbus Ophthalmol. and Otolaryn. Soc. (past pres.), Ohio Soc. Otolaryngology (past pres.), Pan-Am. Allergy Soc., Am. Acad. Invitro Allergy, Am. Soc. Contemporary Medicine and Surgery, Acad. Radio and TV Health Commentators, Fraternal Order of Police Assocs., Internat. Bluegrass Music Assn., Phi Beta Kappa, Alpha Omega Alpha, Beta Beta Beta. Presbyterian. Home: 1245 East Dr Zanesville OH 43701-1445

RAY, MARIANNE YURASKO, social services administrator; b. Mpls., Sept. 25, 1934; d. Andrew George and Ann (Rusinko) Yurasko; m. Raymond Robert Ray, Nov. 22, 1962 (div. July 1980); children: Joel Christopher, Angela Christine. BA, U. Utah, 1956; student, U. Wash., 1975; MA, Pacific Lutheran U., 1978. Lic. mental health counselor Wash. Case worker, vol. agy. liaison State of Wash. Dept. Social and Health Services, Tacoma, 1963-65, 1971-79, 1983, child placement project dir. Olympia, 1979-80, casework supr. Child Protective Service Tacoma, 1980-81, foster home recruiter and licenser, 1981-83; owner, cons. Myray Focuses, Seattle, 1983—; pres. Delta Dynamics Inc., 1984-86. Mental health therapist Children's Indsl. Home, Tacoma, 1985-86, Good Samaritan Mental Health, Puyallup, Wash., 1986-87; part-time faculty Cen. Wash. U., Ellensburg, 1985—, Highline Community Coll., Midway, Wash., 1985-87, Renton (Wash.) Vocational Tech. Inst., 1985—,

Lake Washington Vocational Tech. Inst., Kirkland, Wash., 1985-96; dir. child abuse treatment Cath. Community Services, Seattle, 1987-96; cons. Tacoma Sch. Dist., 1985-86; presenter nat. conferences and workshops. Creator workshops: Humor Techniques for Stress Management in the Classroom, 1985, Humor in Stress Management: Applications in Helping Professions, 1987, Kicking the Holiday Blues, 1986, Humor for the Health of It, 1987, Laughing Matters--It Really Does!, 1984—, Relocation: What it means for the Employee and Family, 1984—, Humor in the Workplace for Higher Productivity and Team Building, 1984—, Laughter and Liberation in the Classroom to Promote Learning, 1987—, Creative Imagery in Relaxation Techniques, 1987—. Mem.: APA (assoc.), Pacific Northwest Speakers Assn., Pacific Northwest Orgn. Devel. Network (bd. dirs.). Avocations: oil painting, cooking, writing. Office: Myray Focuses Counseling/Consulting PO Box 98570 Des Moines WA 98198-0570 E-mail: myrayfocuses@hotmail.com.

RAY, MARY LOUISE RYAN, lawyer; b. Houston, Dec. 8, 1954; d. Cornelius O'Brien and Mary Anne (Kelley) R.; m. Marshall Ransome Ray, Jan. 30, 1982; children: Siobhan Elisabeth Kelley, Johanna Frances Morris, Jonathan Jordan Willson. BA with honors, U. Tex., 1976; JD, St. Mary's Univ., San Antonio, Tex., 1980. Bar: Tex. 1980, U.S. Dist. Ct. (so. dist.) Tex. 1981, U.S. Ct. Appeals (5th cir.) 1993, U.S. Supreme Ct. 1994. Assoc. Kelley & Ryan, Houston, 1980-82, R.W. Armstrong, Brownsville, Tex., 1982-83; ptnr. Armstrong & Ray, 1983-87; shareholder Ransome and Ray, P.C., 1987—. Bd. dirs. Brownsville Soc. for Crippled Children, 1984-95, pres., 1992-93; bd. dirs. Valley Zool. Soc., 1990—, sec., 2001-02; bd. dirs. United Way of Southern Cameron County, 1989-95, pres., 1994; bd. dirs. Crippled Children's Found., Brownsville, 1989—; bd. dirs. Episcopal Day Sch. Found., 1995—, pres., 1995—. Fellow Tex. Bar Found.; mem. Tex. Bar Assn., Cameron County Bar Assn. (bd. dirs. 1990-99, pres. 1998), Tex. Assn. Bank Counsel, Brownsville C. of C. (bd. dirs. 1998-99). Episcopalian. Office: Ransome & Ray PC 550 E Levee St Brownsville TX 78520-5343

RAY, MICHAEL EDWIN, lawyer; b. Charlotte, N.C., Dec. 13, 1949; s. Daniel Shaw Ray and Jane (Horne) Keziah; m. Janet Langston Jones, July 14, 1973; children: John Daniel, Jennifer Marjory. BA, Furman U., 1972; JD, U. S.C., 1978. Bar: N.C. 1978, S.C. 1978, U.S. Dist. Ct. (ea., mid. and we. dists.) N.C. 1978, U.S. Ct. Appeals (4th cir.) 1981, U.S. Ct. Appeals (Fed. cir.) 1989. Legal adminstr. Wyche Burgess Freeman & Parham, Greenville, S.C., 1973-75; assoc. Womble Carlyle Sandridge & Rice, PLLC, Winston-Salem, N.C., 1978-85, mem., 1985—. Editor-in-chief S.C. Law Rev., 1977-78. Bd. dirs. Piedmont Opera Theatre, Inc., 1997-98; S.C. Manpower Planning Coun., Columbia, 1971-72. T.B. Clarkson scholar Furman U., 1971-72. Mem. ABA, Internat. Bar Assn., N.C. Bar Assn., S.C. Bar Assn., Fed. Cir. Bar Assn. (bd. govs. 1994-97), Am. Intellectual Property Law Assn., Forsyth County Bar Assn., Furman U. Alumni Assn. (bd. govs. 1995-2000), Lex Mundi, Ltd. (dir. 1995-99, sec. 1996-97, chair-elect 1997-98, chair 1998-99, chair emeritus 1999-2000). Democrat. Presbyterian. Avocations: sailing, woodworking, music. Home: 4269 Stonehenge Ln Winston Salem NC 27106-3535 Office: Womble Carlyle Sandridge & Rice PLLC One W Fourth St Winston Salem NC 27101 E-mail: mray@wcsr.com.

RAY, PAUL RICHARD, JR. executive search consultant; b. Columbus, Ga., Nov. 6, 1943; s. Paul Richard and Sarah (Campbell) R.; m. Elizabeth Richards, June 29, 1968; children: Paul Richard III, John Ray, Alice Ray. BSBA, U. Ark., 1966; JD, U. Tex., 1969. Bar: Tex. 1970. Dir. mktg., various mktg. positions tobacco divsn. R.J. Reynolds Tobacco Co., Winston-Salem, N.C., 1969-78; cons. Paul R. Ray & Co., Ft. Worth, 1978, v.p., 1978-79, sr. v.p., 1979-83, exec. v.p., 1983-84, pres., 1984—, COO, 1984-86; CEO Ray & Berndtson, 1986-98, chmn. bd., CEO, 1998—. Bd. dirs. Cook-Ft. Worth Children's Med. Ctr., United Way Met. Tarrant County; liberal arts adv. bd. U. Tex.; dean's exec. adv. bd. U. Ark. Recipient Brite Divinity award Tex. Christian U. Mem. ABA, Assn. Exec. Search Cons. (chmn. 1995-98), Tex. Bar Assn., Young Pres.' Orgn., River Crest Country Club, City Club. Office: Ray & Berndtson Inc 301 Commerce St Ste 2300 Fort Worth TX 76102-4123

RAY, RANJAN, economist, educator; b. Calcutta, West Bengal, India, Aug. 16, 1949; s. Ajit Kumar and Dipti Ray; m. Maitraee Ray, July 20, 1988; 1 child, Ruchira. BA, U. Calcutta, 1969; MA, U. Delhi, 1971; PhD, London U., 1977. Lectr. U. Manchester, Eng., 1979-89; prof. Delhi Sch. Econs., 1989-95, U. Tasmania, Hobart, Australia, 1995—, head Sch. of Econs., 1995—. Head, Dept. of Economics Univ. of Tasmania, Hobart, 1995—2002. Contbr. numerous articles to profl. jours. Australian Rsch. Coun. grantee, 1997, 2000. Mem.: Intertl. Assoc. for Research in Income and Wealth. Office: U Tasmania Sch Econs Hobart 7001 Australia Home Fax: 61-3-62267587; Office Fax: 61-3-62267587. Personal E-mail: Ranjan.ray@utas.edu.au. Business E-Mail: Ranjan.ray@utas.edu.au.

RAY, RAYMOND B. federal judge; b. 1943; BA, U. South Fla., 1965; JD, U. Fla., 1971. Bar: Fla. Asst. U.S. atty. Dept. Justice, So. Dist. Fla., Miami, 1971-74; bankruptcy judge U.S. Bankruptcy Ct. (so. dist.) Fla., Ft. Lauderdale, 1993—. Comdr. USNR, 1961—85, ret. Office: US Courthouse Rm 306 299 E Broward Blvd Fort Lauderdale FL 33301-1944

RAY, REBECCA CELESTE, anthropologist, educator; b. Tampa, Fla., Sept. 6, 1967; d. William Wood Ray and Anna Jean Dickey. BA in Anthropology, U. Fla., 1988; MA in Cultural Resource Mgmt., U. Edinburgh, Scotland, 1991; PhD in Anthropology, U. N.C., 1996. Asst. prof. Miss. State U., Starkville, 1996—97, U. of the South, Sewanee, Tenn., 1998—. Bd. dirs. Silver Wolf Ctr. for Globa Anthropology. Author: Highland Heritage: Scottish Americans in the American South, 2001. Mem.: So. Anthropol. Soc. (councillor 2000—). Address: PO Box 3187 Sewanee TN 37375-3187

RAY, RICHARD STANLEY, accountant; b. Miami, Ariz., June 12, 1937; s. Milton Sevier and Anne Elizabeth (Mickelson) R.; m. Laura Ann Young, Apr. 11, 1963; children: Denise, Mark, Melanie, Laura, Jordon. AA, Ea. Ariz. Jr. Coll., 1957; BS in Acctg., Ariz. State U., 1962, MS in Acctg., 1964. CPA, Ariz. Staff acct. Deloitte, Haskins & Sells, Phoenix, 1963-65; controller AMECO, 1965-70, U-Haul Co., Phoenix, 1970-76; dir. audit svcs. Ariz. Pub. Service Co., 1976—. Advisor to bd. Credit Data of Ariz., Phoenix, 1981—, chmn. bd., 1980-81; dir. Arcoa Internat., Phoenix, 1973-76. Treas., bd. mem. Big Sisters of Ariz., Phoenix, 1972-78; dist. coun. Boy Scouts Am., Phoenix, 1982-84; stake pres. Mormon Ch., Tempe, Ariz. 1987-96. Grad. rsch. fellowship, Ariz. Bankers Assn., Phoenix, 1962. Mem. Am. Inst. CPA's, Ariz. Soc. CPA's (Acctg. Achievement award 1962), Ariz. State Bd. Accountancy (continuing profl. edn. com. 1986-94), Inst. Internal Auditors (bd. dirs. Phoenix 1994-98), Rotary (bd. dirs. 1997-98). Republican. E-mail: richard.ray@pinnaclewest.com.

RAY, ROBERT SCOTT, human resources specialist; b. Hattiesburg, Miss., Jan. 17, 1970; s. Billy Joe Ray, Bobby Nell Ray. BSc, U. So.Miss., 1992; MSc in Human Resources, Chapman U., 1997. Avionics technician USAF, Cannon AFB, N.Mex., 1992—96; health promotion specialist Ala. Phys. Therapy Assoc., Jackson, Ala., 1996—97; foreman Osmose, Buffalo, 1997—98; human resources labor rels. mgr. Howard Industries, Inc., Laurel, Miss., 1998—. Co. rep. United Way, Laurel, Miss., 1999—2001, Salvation Army Angel Tree Canned Food Drive, Laurel. Senior Airman USAF, 1992—96. Mem.: Miss. Mfr. Assn., So.Miss. Soc. Human Resources Mgmt., Soc. Human Resources Mgmt., Team Clydesdale Triathlon, USA Triathlon. Avocation: Triathlons, hunting, fishing. Office: Howard Industries Inc. 3225 Pendorf Rd Laurel MS 39441

RAY, ROGER BUCHANAN, retired communications executive, lawyer; b. Tampa, Fla., Aug. 12, 1935; s. Ralph Jackson and Virginia Marie (Stewart) R.; m. Mary Frye Gaillard, Dec. 27, 1957; children: Mary Katherine, Roger Buchanan Jr. BA in Acctg., U. South Fla., 1967; MBA with honors, U. Notre Dame, 1984; JD, Stetson U., 1991. Bar: Fla. 1992. Acct. Gen. Telephone Co. Fla., Tampa, 1959-67; internal audit mgr. GTE Service Co., N.Y.C., 1967-69; budget dir. Gen. Telephone Co. of S.E., Durham, N.C., 1969-74; v.p., controller Gen. Telephone Co. Mich., Muskegon, 1974-78; regional v.p. fin. GTE Service Corp., Westfield, Ind., 1978-82; v.p. fin. Gen. Telephone Co. Wis., 1982-84, Gen. Telephone Co. Ohio, 1982-84, Gen. Telephone Co. Pa., 1982-84, Gen. Telephone Co. Ill., 1982-84; v.p. fin., bd. dirs. Gen. Telephone Co. Mich., 1982-84, Gen. Telephone Co. Ind., 1982-84; v.p. fin., mem. exec. com., bd. dirs. GTE Communications Systems, Phoenix, 1985-87; asst. state's atty. 13th jud. cir. Tampa, Fla. bar, 1992; asst. state atty. 6th Jud. Cir., Pinellas County, Fla., 1992-96; ret., 1996. Lay eucharistic min., former vestry mem., former sr. warden Ch. of Ascension, Clearwater, Fla.; treas., bd. mem. Monaco Travelers. Mem. Fin. Execs. Inst., Notre Dame Alumni Assn., Kappa Alpha. Republican. Episcopalian. Avocations: jogging, motorhome travel, golf, reading, church work. Home: 2337 Kings Point Dr Largo FL 33774-1010

RAY, RONALD DUDLEY, lawyer; b. Hazard, Ky., Oct. 30, 1942; BA in Psychology and English, Centre Coll., 1964; JD magna cum laude, U. Louisville, 1971. Assoc. Greenebaum, Doll & McDonald, 1971-75, ptnr., 1975-84, 85-86, Ray & Morris, Louisville, 1986-89; mng. ptnr. Ronald Ray Attys., 1990—; dep. asst. sec. def. Pentagon, Washington, 1984-85. Adj. prof. law U. Louisville Sch. Law, 1972-80; commr. Presdl. Commn. on Assigment of Women in Mil., 1992. Author: Military Necessity & Homosexuality, 1993; sr. legal editor: Personnel Policy Manual, Bank Supervisory Policies, The Bank Employee Handbook, 1985-86; mil. historian. State fin. chmn. Nat. Fin. Com. for George Bush for Pres.; chmn. Vietnam Vets. Leadership Program in Ky., 1982-85, Ky. Vietnam Vets. Meml. Fund, 1985-91; trustee Marine Corps Command and Staff Found., 1985-92; mem. exec. com. State Cen. Com., Ky. Rep. Party, 1986-90; mem. Am. Battle Monuments Commn., 1990-94; chmn. Vets. for Bush in Ky., 2000; mem. Nat. Com. Vets. for Bush, 2000; spokesman Coalition of Am. Vets., 1998—, chmn., 1999—. With USMC, 1964-69; col. USMCR (ret.). Decorated Silver Star medal with gold star, Bronze Star medal, Purple Heart, Vietnamese Cross of Gallantry, Vietnamese Honor Medal; recipient Nat. Eagle award Nat. Guard Assn., 1985. Mem. Naval Inst. (life), Marine Corps Res. Officers' Assn. Home: Halls Hill Farm 3317 Halls Hill Rd Crestwood KY 40014-9523 E-mail: euniceray@aol.com.

RAY, ROSABELL HARRIET See BATTIN, R.

RAY, RUTH ALICE YANCEY, retired rancher, real estate developer; b. Birmingham, Ala., July 26, 1931; d. John Grayson and Ruth Ethel (Lutman) Yancey; (div. July 1986); children: Virginia Ruth, John Edward, William Arthur. Student, Fla. State U., 1949-50; BS, Appalachian State U., 1954; postgrad., Stetson U., 1966-67, Appalachian State U., 1962-63, Stetson U., 1964-67. Tchr. pub. schs., Nenana, Alaska, 1955-56; tchr. 1st Christian Ch., Clermont, Fla., 1965-67, Lake County Sch. Bd., Clermont, 1969-70; rancher Rays' Ranch, 1963-97; pvt. real estate developer, 1990—; substitute tchr. Buncombe County Asheville City Sch. Sys., 1999—. Chmn. Clermont Planning and Zoning Commn., 1973-81; mem. Heart of Fla. Girl Scout Coun., 1988—, life mem. Ctr. Fla. Gir. Scout Coun.; life mem. Friends of Cooper Mem. Libr., South Lake Art League; assoc. Sisters of St. Mary. Named Conservation Farmer of Yr., State of Fla., 1982. Mem. Lake County Farm Bur. (bd. dirs. 1977-81), Lake County Cattlemen's Assn. (v.p. 1979-81), Lake County Farmer's Home Adminstrn. (bd. dirs. 1984-88, 1990—, chmn. 1985, 88, 90-91), Nat. Cutting Horse Assn. (life), Am. Quarter Horse Assn., Am. Paint Horse Assn., E.S.A. Internat., Daus. of King (bio. sec.), Sigma Kappa. Republican. Episcopalian (sr. warden, eucharistic min.). Avocations: needlepoint, fishing, hiking, reading. Home and Office: 4575 NW Continental Pl Beaverton OR 97006 E-mail: raray415@aol.com.

RAY, SCOTT ALLEN, real estate company executive; b. Peoria, Ill., Apr. 9, 1969; s. William Allan and Norma Jean (Abernathy) R.; m. Stacey Lynn McDowall, Sept. 4, 1993; 1 child, Hayden Allen. BBA, Iowa State U., 1992, BS, 1994. CPA, Ark. Acct. Bailey Properties Mgmt., LLC, Little Rock, 1994-95, v.p. residential divsn., 1996-97, v.p., contr., 1998-99, exec. v.p., contr., 1999—, also bd. dirs.; exec. v.p., CFO Bailey Properties, LLC, 2000—. Bd. dirs. Bailey Properties LLC, Little Rock. Sr. airman USAF, 1989-94. Recipient Tng. Honor Grad., USAF. Mem. AICPA, Inst. Real Estate Mgmt., Cen. Ark. Soc. CPAs. Avocations: fishing, astronomy, golf, landscaping, reading. Office: Bailey Properties LLC 1400 W Markham St Ste 202 Little Rock AR 72201-1843 E-mail: sray@baileyapts.com.

RAY, SHIRLEY DODSON, educational administrator, consultant; b. Smithville, Tex., Sept. 20, 1929; d. Pickett James and Marjorie (Dietz) Dodson; m. John Davis Ray, Aug. 12, 1950; children: Ellen Ray Stauffer, Daniel Dodson, John Andrew. BA, Baylor U., 1950; MA, Tex. A&I U., 1964; postgrad., Corpus Christi State U. Cert. supt., mid. mgmt., elem. secondary edn., bus. Tchr., math. cons., coord. elem. instrn. Corpus Christi (Tex.) Ind. Sch. Dist., 1958-73; gen. cons. Ednl. Svcs. Ctr. Region II, Corpus Christi, 1973-78; curriculum dir. Calallen Ind. Sch. Dist., 1978-87, asst. supt. instructional svcs., 1987-92; ind. elem. cons., 1992—. Cons. Corpus Christi, 1992—; adj. prof. Corpus Christi State U., 1983—, Tex. A&M U., Kingsville, 1993—; mem. staff NSF, Tex. A&I U., 1973—. Author numerous booklets and pamphlets, math. workshops; writer on state com. for EXCET test for suprs. Mem. ASCD, Nat. Coun. Tchrs. Math. (mem. tchr. insvc. com.), Tex. Coun. Tchrs. Math. (past pres.), Tex. Assn. Suprs. Math. (past v.p.), Tex. ASCD (bd. dirs.), Assn. Tex. Profl. Educators, Phi Delta Kappa (past pres. Kingsville chpt.). E-mail: johnshirleyray@aol.com.

RAY, SIBA PRASAD, materials scientist, ceramics scientist; b. Dinhata, India, Jan. 4, 1944; came to U.S., 1969; s. Nilmony P. and Bina Pani Ray; m. Liplka Ray, May 28, 1977; children: Sourav, Leena. B of Engring., Calcutta (India) U., 1964; MS, Columbia U., 1970, D of Engring. Sci., 1974. Sci. officer Bhabha Atomic Rsch. Ctr., Bombay, 1964-68; rsch. assoc. Pa. State U., University Park, 1974-76; scientist Alcoa Labs., Alcoa Ctr., Pa., 1977-78, sr. scientist, 1978-82, sci. assoc. Alcoa Center, 1982-91, sr. sci. assoc., 1991-98; program leader materials devel. NGAP, Alcoa, 1999—. Cons. Alcoa Separations Tech., Warrendale, Pa., 1991, Electro Metallurgy and Electrochemistry Cons., New Kensington, Pa., 1992. Contbr. articles to Jour. Solid State Chemistry, J. Am. Ceramic Soc., Light Metals, Bull. Am. Ceramic Soc. Pres. Bengali Assn. Pitts., 1988. Mem. The Metall. Soc., Am. Ceramic Soc., Sigma Xi. Achievements include 29 patents in the area of inert elctrodes, ceramic composites and reaction sintering. Home: 6007 Pilgrim Ct Murrysville PA 15668-8533 Office: Alcoa Labs Alcoa Tech Ctr Alcoa Center PA 15069

RAY, STEPHEN ALAN, academic administrator, lawyer; b. Oklahoma City, Aug. 26, 1956; s. Thompson Eugene and Dorothea Hodges. BA summa cum laude, St. Thomas Sem., 1978; PhD, Harvard U., 1986; JD, U. Calif., Hastings, 1990. Bar: Calif. 1990, Mass. 1994. Assoc. Richards, Watson & Gershon, L.A., 1990—93; lectr. theology Boston Coll., Chestnut Hill, Mass., 1993—95; staff counsel Houghton Miffin Co., Boston, 1995—96; assoc. dean acad. affairs Harvard Law Sch., Cambridge, 1998—, dir. acad. affairs, 1996—98, asst. dean acad. affairs, 1998—2001. Vis. lectr. religion Harvard Divinity Sch., spring 1995; adv. bd. Harvard Native Am. Program, 1999—. Author: The Modern Soul, 1987. Vol. AIDS action com., Boston, 1994-96; atty. vol. AIDS Project L.A., 1991-93; Native Am. Adv. Com. on Repatriation, Peabody Mus., 1999—. Mem. ABA, Cherokee Nation Okla. Office: Harvard Law Sch Griswold Hall 207 Cambridge MA 02138 E-mail: aray@law.harvard.edu.

RAY, SUSANNE GETTINGS, counselor; b. Marietta, Ohio, July 20, 1937; d. Lewis B. and Reina Ashton Gettings; m. John W. Ray; children: Nancy Ann, Susan Christy. BS in Nursing, Case Western Res. U., 1960; MEd in Cmty. Counseling, Ohio U., 1987. Lic. profl. counselor. Staff nurse Cleve. Vis. Nurse Assn., 1960-61; sr. nurse Columbus (Ohio) Pub. Health Nursing Svc., 1962-64; founder, mgr. healthcare program Muskingum County (Ohio) Children's Svcs., 1972-76; spl. svcs. coord. Muskingum County Head Start, Zanesville, Ohio, 1979-85; clin. counselor Six County Mental Health Ctr., 1987-94; edn. coord. Safe/Response, 1995-97; counselor Paula Colman & Assocs., 1999—. Stephen min. Ch. Sch. tchr. Ctrl. Presbyn. Ch., elder, 1996-99; founder, coord. SAFE; bd. dirs. Eastside Cmty. Ministry; mem. Grads. and Headstart Health Adv. Bd.; bd. dirs., legis. chair Ohio Coalition of Sexual Assault; mem. edn. and svc. com. Cmty. Against Rape. Recipient various profl. and cmty. awards. Mem. Am. Counseling Assn., Ohio Counseling Assn., Sigma Theta Tau, Chi Sigma Iota. Office: Paula Colman & Assocs 860 Bethesda Dr Zanesville OH 43701-1800

RAY, SWAPAN KUMAR, molecular biologist; b. Chakdaha, W. Bengal, India, June 17, 1957; came to U.S., 1990; s. Somendra Chandra and Sefali Rani (Bhowmick) R. BS with hons., U. Calcutta, India, 1978, MS, 1980, PhD, 1989. Postdoctoral rsch. assoc. Brookhaven Nat. Lab., Upton, N.Y., 1990-92; postdoctoral fellow Med. U. S.C., Charelston, 1993, instr. medicine, 1994-95, rsch. scientist, 1997-98; instr. medicine Emory U., Atlanta, 1995-96; ast. prof. neurology Med. U. S.C., Charleston, S.C., 1998—. Contbr. over 100 articles to profl. jours. Recipient postdoctoral award NIH, 1990-92, 93, co-investigator award, 1997, co-investigator award, Am. Health Assistance Found., 1998. Mem. Soc. for Neurosci., N.Y. Acad. Sci., Am. Soc. for Biochemistry and Molecular Biology, Am. Assn. for Cancer Rsch., Am. Soc. Neurochem., Internat. Soc. Neurochem., Internat. Brain Rsch. Orgn. Achievements include research revealing that chemotherapeutic drugs (Ara-C, Mitoxantrone and Taxol) cause internucleosomal DNA fragmentation in leukemic cells; Bcl-xS expression induces differentiation in CML K562 cells; retinoids downregulate telomerase activity in AML and glioblastoma cells; calpain is activated and involved in apoptosis in Alzheimer's disease, Parkinson's disease, traumatic brain injury, spinal cord injury and EAE. Avocations: bird watching, classical music, gardening. Office: Dept Neurology Med U of SC 96 Jonathan Lucas St Ste 309 Charleston SC 29425-8900

RAY, TAMBER, lawyer; b. Valparaiso, Ind., Dec. 4, 1968; BA, Radford U., 1990; JD, Howard U., 1993; LLM in Intellectual Property, George Washington U., 1998. Bar: Va. 1994, D.C. 1999. Program dir. WVRU-FM, Radford, Va., 1987-90; pub. info. specialist FCC, Washington, 1990-91; legal intern Nat. Assn. Broadcasters, 1992-93; assoc. Besozzi, Gavin, Craven & Schmitz, 1994-96, Ginsburg, Feldman & Bress, Washington, 1996-98, Shook, Hardy & Bacon, Washington, 1998-99, Kraskin, Lesse & Cosson LLP, Washington, 1999—. Contbr. articles to profl. publs. Vestry mem. St. James' Episcopal Ch., Washington, 1996-98. Mem. Va. State Bar Assn., Fed. Comms. Bar Assn. (co-chair young lawyers com. 1995-96, exec. com. 1996-97). Office: Kraskin Lesse & Cosson LLP 2120 L St NW Ste 520 Washington DC 20037-1527 E-mail: tamberray@klctele.com.

RAY, TERRILL WYLIE, physical scientist; b. Wichita, Kans., Nov. 29, 1967; s. Robert Gibson and Marvaline Joyce (Bannon) R. Student, Wichita State U., 1985-86; BS in Geophys. Engring., Colo. Sch. of Mines, 1990; MS in Planetary Sci., Calif. Inst. Tech., 1993, PhD in Planetary Sci. and Geophysics, 1995. Summer geophysicist Unocal, Midland, Tex., 1990; rsch./tchg. asst. Calif. Inst. Tech., Pasadena, 1990-95; phys. sci. officer U.S. Arms Control and Disarmament Agy., Washington, 1995-99, U.S. Dept. State, Washington, 1999—. Mem. program com. Internat. Geosci. and Remote Sensing Symposium, Pasadena, 1994; mem. planning com. Global Environ. Monitoring Early in the Next Century, World Resources Inst./Calif. Inst. Tech., Washington and Pasadena, 1992-94. Judge Denver Met. Area Sci. Fair, 1987, Calif. State Sci. Fair, L.A., 1993-95. Recipient Meritorious Honor award U.S. Arms Control and Disarmament Agy., 1999, Franklin award U.S. State Dept., 2000; Grad. Rsch. fellow NASA, 1993-95, Planetary Geology and Geophysics Undergrad. Rsch. fellow, 1985. Mem. IEEE, Am. Geophys. Union, Soc. Exploration Geophysicists, Nat. Capital Area Skeptics. Avocations: softball, music, reading, writing, crocheting. Home: 3006 Furman Ln Apt 103 Alexandria VA 22306-1018 E-mail: geospam@telocity.com.

RAY, TIMOTHY BRITT, social worker, lawyer, administrator; b. New Orleans, June 13, 1939; s. Archibald Cole and Eliza Owen (Britt) R.; m. Constance Helen Abbott, Nov. 27, 1964; children: Michael Gregory Owen, Mary Eliza Rebecca. BA, Davidson Coll., 1961; MA, La. State U., 1963; MSW, W. Va. U., 1968; JD, U. Santa Clara, 1976. Bar: Ohio 1981. Chief psychiatric social worker Alameda County, Oakland, Calif., 1974-77; exec. dir. Toledo Legal Aid Soc., 1977-82; counselor youth Fla. Health and Rehabilitative Svcs., Miami, 1983-84; exec. dir. Dist. Ill. Mental Health Bd., Gainesville, Fla., 1984, Older Americans Coun., Gainesville, 1984-90; elderly housing mgr. Gainesville Housing Authority, 1990-92, med. social work supr. Olsten-Kimberly Quality Care, 1993-94; med. social worker Hospice of Marion County, Gainesville, 1994—. Chmn. health care services adv. com. Upjohn Co., Gainesville, 1986. Contbr. articles in profl. jours. Chmn. United Way Exec. Dirs. Coun., Gainesville, 1985; Alachua County rep. Dist. III Alcohol, Drug Abuse and Mental Health Planning Coun.; chmn. Adult and Elderly Svcs. Com., 1987-88; pres. Interagy. Coun., Gainesville, 1986; pres. bd. Bread of Mighty Food Bank, Inc., 1987-90; elder 1st Presbyn. Ch., Gainesville; bd. dirs. Alzheimers Assn., 1989-90, Cmty. with a Heart, Ocala, Fla., 1995—; active Fla. Coun. on Aging, Gainesville Human Rels. Adv. Bd., 1989-91; contbg. mem. Children's Def. Fund; grad. Leadership Gainesville XVII. Bd. govs. fellow, 1967. Mem. ABA, NASW, Acad. Cert. Social Workers, Fla. Consumer Action Network, Sierra Club, Phi Alpha Delta. Democrat. Presbyterian. Avocations: swimming, tennis. Home: 3321 NW 45th Ave Gainesville FL 32605-1459 E-mail: socrates286@cs.com.

RAY, TUHIN, computer engineer; b. London, Aug. 28, 1963; came to U.S., 1987; s. Natabar and Rekha (Bhattacharya) R. B of Engring., Delhi (India) U., 1985; MSEE, Mich. State U., 1989; MBA, Ind. U., 1995. Project engr. Allen Bradley Ltd., Sahibabad, India, 1985-87; grad. rsch. asst. elec. engring. dept. Mich. State U., East Lansing, 1987-89; mgr. applied engring. Total Control Products Inc., Melrose Park, Ill., 1989-92; advanced software engr. Delco Electronics, Kokomo, Ind., 1992-95, software project mgr., 1995-97; resident mgr. Delphi-D (India), 1997-99, program mgr., 1999—. Cons. Motorola Inc., Northbrook, Ill., 1988; teaching asst. De Paul U., Chgo., 1990-92. Capt. sch. and coll. field hockey, Delhi, 1981-84. Recipient Merit cert. Math. Olympiad, New Delhi, 1981, Appreciation award Monsanto Chemical, Sauget, Ill., 1990. Mem. IEEE (sr. mem.), Engring. Soc. Detroit. Avocations: windows programming, music, tennis, reading autobiographies. Office: Delco Electronics MS CT-601 PO Box 9005 Kokomo IN 46904-9005 also: 12427 Springbrooke Run Carmel IN 46033

RAY, VIRGINIA H.S. writer, columnist; b. Chicago, Ill., Aug. 4, 1931; d. Russell Horton and Cora Virginia Stafford; m. Wilson K. Ray, Nov. 8, 1952 (dec. Oct. 14, 2000); children: Virginia Ray Bouchillon. Writer, reporter South Bend Tribune, South Bend, Ind., 1953—58; free lance writer Lausanne, Switzerland, 1960—60, Tokyo, Tokyo, Japan, 1970—70, Kennebankport, Kennebankport, Maine, 1980—90; freel ance writer and corr. The York County Coast Star, Kennebank, 1990—90; free lance writer and corr. Biddeford Jour. Tribune, Biddeford, 1980—. Newsletter editor Jr. League of Pitts., Pittsburgh, Pa., 1960—60, Tokyo Am. Club, Tokyo, 1970—70. Active Pitts. Jr. League, Pittsburgh, Pa., 1960—60; chmn. Three Rivers Art Festival, 1962; active Kennebankport Hist. Soc., Kennebankport, Maine, 1990—90. Mem.: Brick Store Mus., Portland Jr. League. R-Consevative. Protestant. Achievements include development of founded a library in Fox Chapel, PA. Avocations: reading, history, travel, tennis. Home: #15 Pt Arandel PO 1144 Kennebunkport ME 04046-1144 Home Fax: 207-967-9865. Personal E-mail: nay@cybertours.com.

RAY, WILLIAM JACKSON, psychologist; b. Birmingham, Ala., Sept. 3, 1945; s. Norman M. and Mary K. Agnew; m. Judith Mebane, Aug. 22, 1987; children from previous marriage: Adam, Lauren. BA, Eckerd Coll., 1967; MA, Vanderbilt U., 1969, PhD, 1971; Fellow in med. psychology, Langley Porter Neuropsychiat. Inst., U. Calif. Med. Center, San Francisco, 1971-72. Prof., dir. clin. psychology tng. program Pa. State U., 1972—, dir. clin. trng., 1991-97. Author: (with R.M. Stern) Biofeedback, 1977, (with others) Evaluation of Clinical Biofeedback, 1979, (with R.M. Stern and C.M. Davis) Psychophysiological Recording, 1980, 2d edit. (with R.M. Stern and K. Quigley), 2000, Methods Toward a Science of Behavior and Experience, 1981, 6th edit., 2000, (with E. Susman & L. Feajous) Emotion, Cognition, Health and Development in Children and Adolescents, 1992, (with L. Michelson) Handbook of Dissociation, 1996 (Cornelia Wilbur award ISSD); series editor: Plenum Series in Behavioral Psychophysiology and Medicine. Recipient Nat. Media award Am. Psychol. Found., 1976, 78, Rsch. award Best Empirical Paper, SCEH. Mem. AAAS, APA, APS, Soc. Psychophysiol. Rsch. Office: Dept Psychology Pa State U University Park PA 16802 E-mail: wjr@psu.edu.

RAY, WILLIAM MELVIN, newsletter publishing consultant; b. Dutchmills, Ark., Mar. 13, 1935; s. William Estes and Verda Lou (Robbins) R.; m. Janet Drachman, June 6, 1969; children: Matthew Stephen, Susannah Brett. BA, U. Redlands, 1959. Reporter Sun-Telegram, San Bernardino, Calif., 1959-60; sports editor Times-Delta, Visalia, 1961-62; reporter Progress-Bull., Pomona, 1962-63; copy editor, reporter Newsday, Garden City, N.Y., 1963-65; news editor Nat. Petroleum News, McGraw-Hill, N.Y.C., 1966-71; Washington editor/chief editor Energy Newsletters, McGraw-Hill, 1972-80, v.p., gen.mgr., 1980-98, newsletter cons., 1998—. New product champion McGraw-Hill, N.Y.C., 1989-92, chmn. newsletter editl. bd., 1985-88, seminar spkr., 1985—. Author: Newsletter Publishing, 1990, Business Newsletter Promotion, 1991.

RAYBECK, DOUGLAS, anthropologist, educator; b. Jamestown, N.Y., Mar. 8, 1941; s. Joseph Anthony Raybeck and Evelyn (Jackson) Warfield; m. Peggy Ann Root, June, 1964 (div.); m. Karen Lynne Jones, Mar. 11, 1967; 1 child,

Alethea Joy. Student, Freiburg U., 1962; BA, Dartmouth Coll., 1964; postgrad., Sch. Oriental African Studies, 1967; PhD, Cornell U., 1975. Instr. in anthropology Kirkland Coll., Clinton, N.Y., 1970-75, asst. prof., 1975-76, assoc. prof., 1976-78, Hamilton Coll., Clinton, 1978-84, prof., 1984—, Christian A. Johnson Excellence in Tchg. prof., 1993-96. Various adminstrv. positions Hamilton Coll., 1978—; co-dir. Cognitive Assocs., Clinton, 1988—; cons. Bur. Labor Statistics, Washington, 1990. Author: Mad Dogs, Englishmen and the Errant Anthropologist, 1996, Looking Down the Road: A Systems Approach to Future Studies, 2000; co-author: Improving Student Memory, 1993, A Clash of Scientific Cultures, 1998, Improving Memory and Study Skills: Theory and Practice, 2001; co-editor: Deviance, 1991; mem. editl. adv. bd. Ethnic Groups, 1988-94, Cross Cultural Rsch., 1995—, Cognitive Technology 1996—; contbr. articles to profl. jours. Active E. Timor Action Network, 1992—. Rsch. grantee NIMH, 1968-70, Fulbright-Hays teaching and rsch. grantee, 1977. Mem. Am. Anthrop. Assn., Soc. for Cross Cultural Rsch., Soc. for Psychol. Anthropology, Sigma Xi. Democrat. Avocations: biking, science fiction, computers. Office: Hamilton Coll 198 College Hill Rd Clinton NY 13323-1218 E-mail: draybeck@hamilton.edu.

RAYBURN, CAROLE ANN (MARY AIDA RAYBURN), psychologist, researcher, writer, consultant; b. Washington, Feb. 14, 1938; d. Carl Frederick and Mary Helen (Milkie) Miller; m. Ronald Allen Rayburn (dec. Apr. 1970). BA in Psychology, Am. U., 1961; MA in Clin. Psychology, George Washington U., 1965; PhD in Ednl. Psychology, Cath. U. Am., 1969; MDiv in Ministry, Andrews U., 1980. Lic. psychologist, Md. Psychometrician Columbian Prep. Sch., Washington, 1963; clin. psychologist Spring Grove State Hosp., Catonsville, Md., 1966-68; pvt. practice, 1969, 71—; staff clin. psychologist Instl. Care Svcs. Div. D.C. Children's Ctr., Laurel, Md., 1970-78; psychologist Md. Dept. Vocat. Rehab., 1973-74; psychometrician Montgomery County Pub. Schs., 1981-85. Lectr. Strayer Coll., Washington, 1969-70; forensic psychology expert witness, 1973—; guest lectr. Andrews U., Berrien Springs, Mich., 1979, Hood Coll., Frederick, Md., 1986-88; instr. Johns Hopkins U., 1986, 88-89; adj. faculty Profl. Sch. Psychology Studies, San Diego, 1987; adj. asst. prof. Loyola Coll., Columbia, Md., 1987; cons. Julia Brown Montessori Schs., 1972, 78, 82—, VA Ctr., 1978, 91-93. Editor: (with M.J. Meadow) A Time to Weep and a Time to Sing, 1985; contbg. author: Montessori: Her Method and the Movement (What You Need to Know), 1973, Drugs, Alcohol and Women: A National Forum Source Book, 1975, The Other Side of the Couch: Faith of the Psychotherapist, 1981, Clinical Handbook of Pastoral Counseling, 1985, An Encyclopedic Dictionary of Pastoral Care and Counseling, 1990, Religion Personality and Mental Health, 1993; co-editor (with Violet Franks) Springer Focus on Women series; author copyrighted inventories Religious Occupational and Stress Questionnaire, 1986, Religion and Stress Questionnaire, 1986, Organizational Relationships Survey, 1987, Attitudes Toward Children Inventory, 1987, State-Trait Morality Inventory, 1987, Body Awareness and Sexual Intimacy Comfort Scale (BASICS), 1993, Inventory in Religionsness, 1996, Inventory on Spirituality, 1997, Sports, Exercise, Leadership and Friendship Questionnaire, 1997, Peace Inventory, Life Choices Inventory, 1998, Inventory on the Supreme and Work, 1999; cons. editor Profl. Psychology, 1980-83; assoc. editor Jour. Pastoral Counseling, 1985-90, guest editor, 1988; contbr. numerous articles to profl. jours. Bd. dirs. Psychologists Ethical Treatment of Animals. Recipient Svc. award Coun. for Advancement Psychol. Professions and Scis., 1975, cert. D.C. Dept. Human Resources, 1975, 76, cert. recognition D.C. Psychol. Assn., 1976, 1985; AAUW rsch. grantee, 1983. Fellow: APA (mem. editl. bd. Jour. Child Clin. Psychology 1978—82, divsn. psychology women chair task force on women and religion 1980—81, chair equal opportunity affirmative action divsn. clin. psychology 1980—82, clin. psychology women's sect. 1984—86, divsn. psychology issues in grad. edn. and clin. tng. 1988—, program chair 1991—94, pres. divsn. psychology of religion 1995—96, pres. 1995—96, divsn. on internat. psychology 2001, divsn. psychology of religion, psychology of women, clin. psychology, cons. psychology, gen. psychology 2002, psychotherapy, state assn. affairs, divsn. media psychology, Mentoring award divsn. clin. psychology, sect. of clin. psychology of women 1997, Mentoring award divsn. psychology of religion 1997, William C. Bier award divsn. psychology of religion 2000), Md. Psychol. Assn. (editor newsletter 1975—76, chair ins. com. 1981—83, pres. 1984—85, exec. adv. com. 1985—, chpt. recognition 1978), Am. Assn. Applied & Preventive Psychology (sec. 1992—93, chair fellows com. 1992—93), Am. Orthopsychiat. Assn.; mem.: Balt. Assn. Cons. Psychologists (pres. D.C. chpt. 1991—92), Assn. Practicing Psychologists Montgomery-Prince George's Counties (pres. 1986—88, editor newsletter 1990—, treas. 1996—98), Soc. Personality Assessment, Internat. Soc. Polit. Psychology, Psi Chi (hon.). Achievements include research on stress in religious professionals, women and stress, women and religion, pastoral counseling, state-trait morality inventory, leadership, clergy stress, psychotherapy, children, body image, intimacy, peacefulness, spirituality, life choices, religiousness, work. Address: 1200 Morningside Dr Silver Spring MD 20904-3149

RAYBURN, S. T. lawyer; b. Brookhaven, Miss., Aug. 26, 1947; s. Harry Newton and Margaret Elaine (Zeigler) R.; m. Elizabeth Hooker, June 6, 1970 (div. Nov. 1990); children: Andrew Newton, Thomas McCarver, Shelby Hooker; m. Paige Bruce, Feb. 1, 1992; children: Samuel Taylor, Samath Paige. BA, Miss. State U., 1970; JD cum laude, U. Miss., 1972. Bar: Miss. 1972, U.S. Dist. Ct. (no. dist.) Miss. 1972, U.S. Ct. Appeals (5th cir.) 1973, U.S. Supreme Ct. 1976, U.S. Ct. Appeals (11th cir.) 1981, U.S. Dist. Ct. (so. dist.) Miss. 1984. Assoc. Sumners & Hickman, Oxford, Miss., 1972-75; ptnr. Sumners, Hickman & Rayburn, 1975-89, Hickman, Rayburn & Goza, Oxford, 1989-92; shareholder Mitchell, McNutt, Threadgill, Smith & Sams, 1992-97; ptnr. Rayburn Law Firm, 1997—. Mem. character & fitness com. Miss. State Bd. Bar Examiners, 1990-99. Sec. Lafayette County Dem. Exec. Com., Oxford, 1976-80, chmn., 1980-88; chmn. Miss. Commn. Wildlife Conservation, Jackson, Miss., 1984-89. Mem. Miss. Bar Assn. (commr.), Miss. Def. Lawyers Assn., 3rd Cir. Bar Assn. (pres.), Intern Assn. of Def. Counsel, Def. Rsch. Inst., Oxford-Lafayette County C. of C. (pres.). Presbyterian. Avocations: boating, motorcycles. Home and Office: Rayburn Law Firm PO Box 430 Oxford MS 38655-0430

RAYBURN, TED RYE, newspaper editor; b. Manchester, Tenn., Dec. 16, 1956; s. Ted and Thelma (Taylor) R. BS in Mass Comm., Mid. Tenn. State U., 1986. State corr. Nashville Banner, Murfreesboro, Tenn., 1978-79; reporter, photographer, sports editor Murfeesboro Press, 1978-80; state corr. The Tennessean, Murfreesboro, 1979-80; copy editor Jackson (Tenn.) Sun, 1980-82, asst. copy desk chief, 1982-85; copy editor Tennessean, Nashville, 1985-90, page one editor, 1990—, asst. copy desk chief, 1994-97, news editor, 1997—. Avocations: film, literature, jazz music. Office: The Tennessean 1100 Broadway Nashville TN 37203-3134 E-mail: trayburn@tennessean.com.

RAYBURN, WILLIAM FRAZIER, obstetrician, gynecologist, educator; b. Lexington, Ky., Aug. 19, 1950; s. Charles Calvin and Charlotte Elizabeth (Ballard) R.; m. Pamela Rae Gilleland, Nov. 27, 1976; children: Lindsay Ann, Britany Beth, Drake Tanner. BS, Hampden Sydney Coll., 1971; MD, U. Ky., 1975. Diplomate Nat. Bd. Med. Examiners, Am. Bd. Ob.-Gyn. (examiner), Divsn. Maternal-Fetal Medicine. Intern family medicine U. Iowa Hosps. and Clinics, Iowa City, 1975-76; resident ob.-gyn. U. Ky. Med. Ctr., Lexington, 1976-79; fellow in maternal-fetal medicine dept. ob.-gyn. Ohio State U. Hosps., Columbus, 1979-81; asst. prof. ob.-gyn. U. Mich. Med. Sch., Ann Arbor, 1981-83, assoc. prof. ob.-gyn., 1983-86; assoc. prof. dept. ob.-gyn. and pharmacology U. Nebr. Coll. of Medicine, Omaha, 1985-88, prof. dept. ob-gyn. and pharmacology, 1988-92, U. Okla. Coll. Medicine, Oklahoma City, 1992-98, John W. Records endowed chair, 1992-98; prof. dept. ob/gyn U. N.Mex. Sch. Medicine, Albuquerque, 1998—, chair dept. ob/gyn, 1998—. Prof., ob-gyn dept. chair U. N.Mex. Sch. Medicine, Albuquerque, 1998—; chief of obstetrics U. Okla. Coll. of Medicine, Okla. City, 1992-98; dir. maternal fetal medicine dept. ob-gyn U. Mich. Med. Ctr., 1981-85, med. edn.; reviewer for Ob and Gyn., Am. Jour. Ob-Gyn., Jour. Reproductive Medicine, Internat. Jour. Gyn. and Ob., New Eng. Jour. Medicine, Jour. Maternal-Fetal Medicine, Jour. Maternal-Fetal Investigation; U. Nebr. Med. Ctr., 1985-92, U. Okla. Health Sci. Ctr., 1992—, Presbyn. Hosp., Okla. City, 1992-98, Univ. Hosp., Albuquerque, 1998—. Author: (books) Obstetrics/Gynecology: Pre Test Self Assessment and Review, 1982; (with others), Every Woman's Pharmacy: A Guide to Safe Drug Use, 1983, Obstetrics for the House Officer, 1984, 2d rev. edition, 1988, Every Woman's Pharmacy, 1984, The Women's Health and Drug Reference, 1993, Oklahoma Notes: Obstetrics and Gynecology, 1994, 2d. rev. edit., 1996, Obstetrics and Gynecology for the House Officer, 1996, 2d rev. edit., 2001; editor: (with F.P. Zuspan) Drug Therapy in Obstetrics and Gynecology, 1982, 3d rev. edit., 1992; symposia editor Diagnosis and Management of the Malformed Fetus, Jour. Reprod. Medicine, 1982, Operative Obstetrics, Clinics in Perinatology, 1983, Controversies in Fetal Drug Therapy, Clin. Obstetrics and Gynecology, 1991; contbr. more than 50 chpts. to books, more than 200 articles to profl. jours. including Am. Jour. Obstetric Gynecology, Obstetrics Gynecology, Jour. Reproductive Medicine, New Eng. Jour. Medicine and many others; also speaker and lectr. at sci. confs. and seminars and author of audio visual ednl. material for universities and in continuing med. edn.; contbr. over 150 abstracts at sci. meetings; reviewer for Ob. and Gyn., Am. Jour. Ob.-Gyn., Jour. Reproductive Medicine, Internat. Jour. Gyn. and Ob., New Eng. Jour. Medicine, Jour. Maternal-Fetal Medicine, Jour. Maternal-Fetal Investigation. Dir. maternal and infant care programs U. Nebr. Med. Ctr., Omaha, 1986-92; U.S. Pharmacopeia Conv. field reviewer, 1983—. Recipient Residents' prize paper award Ky. Ob.-Gyn. Soc., 1978, 79, Faculty Teaching award for Excellence, 1993, 94, 96, Rsch. Excellence award Soc. Perinatal Obstetricians, 1998. Fellow Am. Coll. Obstetricians and Gynecologists (Ephraim McDowell) prize paper award 2d pl. 1978, 1st pl. 1979, Searle-Donald F. Richardson Prize Paper award 1980, Best Doctors in Am., 1998, 2000); mem. Am. Coll. Obstetricians and Gynecologists, Am. Gynecol. and Obstet. Soc., Soc. Maternal Fetal Medicine, Assn. of Profs. in Gyn.-Ob., Soc. for Gynecol. Investigation, Teratology Soc., Neurobehavioral Teratology Soc., N.Mex. Med. Soc. Achievements include contributions to the knowledge of drug effcts on developing fetus and of principals of induction of labor and to the influence he has had on peers not only through teaching and patient care but through his extensive writing. Office: U New Mex Health Sci Ctr 2211 Lomas Blvd NE # Acc-4 Albuquerque NM 87106-2745 E-mail: wrayburn@salud.unm.edu.

RAYCHAUDHURI, AJITAVA, economist, educator; b. Calcutta, June 29, 1957; s. Amiya Kumar and Mira Raychaudhuri; m. Sarmistha Sen, Dec. 4, 1988; 1 child, Sreejata. BA, Jadavpur U., Calcutta, 1976, MA, 1978; PhD, American U., 1988. Lectr. in econs. Jadavpur U., Calcutta, 1981-89, reader in econs., 1989-98, prof. econs., 1998—. Visitor SOAS, London U., 1996; vis. prof. Indian Statis. Inst., Calcutta, 1997-98; guest lectr. Calcutta U., 1992-94. Author: India's Exports: An Analytical Study, 1997; editor: Globalisation and India: A Multi-dimensional Perspective, 2000, Economy of West Bengal: Problems and Prospects, 1996; contbr. articles to profl. jours. Fulbright scholar Yale U., New Haven, 1996-97. Mem. Indian Econometric Soc. (life), Bengal Econ. Assn. (life), Jadavpur Univ. Tchrs. Assn. (jt. sec. 1992-94). Avocations: travel, reading. Office: Jadavpur U Dept Econs Raja SC Mullick Rd Calcutta 700032 India E-mail: ajitava29@hotmail.com., ajitava1@vsnl.net.

RAYEVSKY, ROBERT, illustrator; b. Moscow, Russia, Nov. 7, 1955; came to U.S., 1979; s. Igor G. and Pauline (Rubin) R.; m. Kimberley Colton, Dec. 29, 1994; children: Miriam, Claire, Rafael. BFA in Graphic Design, Moscow Polygraphic Inst., 1978; BFA in Illustration, Parsons Sch. of Design, N.Y.C., 1982. Lectr. various schs. and univs. Illustrator: Janski and Wilhelm and Farmer Kohl's Horse (Sally Derby), 2002, The Eyes of the Unicorn (Teresa Bateman), 2002, Under New York (Linda Oatman High), 2000, Joan of Arc (Margaret Hodges), 1999, Squash It! (adapted by Eric A. Kimmel), 1997, The Sleepy Men (Margaret Wise Brown), 1996, The Talking Tree (hardcover reprint), 1995, Our King Has Horns, 1995, Bernal and Florida (retold by Eric A. Kimmel), Three Sacks of Truth (adapted by Eric A. Kimmel), 1993, Belling the Cat and Other Aesop's Fables, 1990, The Riddle (Adele Vernon), 1987, others; profl. publs. include Applied Arts, 1997, Step-By-Step Graphics, 1997, N.Y. Art Rev., others; shows include Illustrators Only Awards Show, N.Y.C., 1996, 99, R. Michelson Galleries, Mass., Child-At-Heart Gallery, Mass., Bologna Illustrators Annual, Italy, others; set designer The Strange Games, N.Y.C., Illustration W. Annual Show, 1995, 98-99, Soc. of Illustrators Exhibition's 1992, 94-96, 99, 2001, Illustrators 38, N.Y.C., 1996, Illustrators 41, N.Y.C., 1999; contbr. commercial illustrations newspapers and magazines, including N.Y. Times, Chgo. Tribune, Working Mother, Individual Investor. Home: 76 Marian St Northampton MA 01060-1119 E-mail: rayevsky@earthlink.net.

RAYLESBERG, ALAN IRA, lawyer; b. N.Y.C., Dec. 6, 1950; s. Daniel David and Sally Doris (Mantell) R.; m. Caren Thea Coven, Nov. 20, 1983; children: Lisa Maris, Jason Todd. BA, NYU, 1972; JD cum laude, Boston U., 1975. Bar: N.Y. 1976, U.S. Dist. Ct. (so. dist.) N.Y. 1976, U.S. Dist. Ct. (ea. dist.) N.Y. 1978, U.S. Tax Ct. 1981, U.S. Ct. Appeals (2d and 5th cirs.) 1982, U.S. Ct. Appeals (1st cir.) 1986, U.S. Ct. Appeals (9th cir.) 1996. Assoc. Orans, Elsen & Polstein, N.Y.C., 1975-77, Guggenheimer & Untermyer, N.Y.C., 1977-83, ptnr., 1983-85, Rosenman & Colin, N.Y.C., 1985—2002, co-chmn. litigation dept., 1998-99, chmn. litigation dept., 1999—2002; ptnr., sect. head litigation group Vinson & Elkins, N.Y.C., 2002—. Adj. instr. N.Y. Law Sch., 1980-83; instr. Nat. Inst. of Trial Advocacy; mem. adv. group comml. divsn., mem. mediation panel N.Y. State Supreme Ct.; mem. arbitration panel U.S. Dist. Ct. (ea. dist.) N.Y.; judge Nat. Moot Ct. Competition, 1980—. Bd. dirs. Fund for Modern Cts., 1994—. Mem. ABA, Fed. Bar Coun., Assn. Bar City N.Y., N.Y. County Lawyers Assn. (bd. dirs. 1995-98, 99-2002, fed. ct. com. 1988—, appellate ct. com. 1990—, co-chmn. appellate ct. com. 1992-93, chair appellate ct. com. 1993-96), N.Y. County Lawyers Assn. Found. (bd. dirs. 1998—), N.Y. State Bar Assn. (ho. delegates 1996-2000), Securities Industry Assn. (legal and compliance divsn) N.Y. Coun. Def. Lawyers, Town Club of Newcastle (mem. exec. com. 1987-91). Democrat. Jewish. Office: Vinson & Elkins 666 Fifth Ave New York NY 10103 E-mail: araylesberg@velaw.com., alan.raylesberg@verizon.net.

RAYMOND, ANNE, artist; b. Wash., DC, Feb. 11, 1949; m. Kenneth C. Olson. BFA, U. Tex., Austin, 1967—71. Prin. works include contemporary oils on canvas and monotypes, 1990—. Home and Office: 9 Rolling Wood Ln East Hampton NY 11937 Home Fax: 631-324-3064. Personal E-mail: araymond@optonline.net.

RAYMOND, ARTHUR JOSEPH, economics educator; b. Putnam, Conn., Feb. 18, 1949; s. Arthur J. Sr. and Rita E. (Tetreault) R.; m. Helene M. Lucas, July 18, 1982; 1 child, Samantha H. BSBA, Bryant Coll., 1971; MA in Econs., Tufts U., 1972, PhD in Econs., 1990. Instr. Washington & Jefferson Coll., Washington, 1976-81; vis. instr. Wheaton Coll., Norton, Mass., 1982; instr. Harvard U., Boston, 1983; asst. prof. Suffolk U., 1983-85; lectr. Tufts U., Medford, 1985-91; lectr. MBA program Babson Coll., Wellesley Hills, 1985-91; asst. prof. Muhlenberg Coll., Allentown, Pa., 1991—, dir. Dana Program, 1993—. Mem. editorial adv. bd. Dushkin Publ., Conn., 1988—; contbr. articles to profl. jours. Mem. Human Svcs. Adv. Bd. Tufts U. scholar, 1972-76; rsch. granee Muhlenberg Coll., 1992-94. Mem. Am. Econ. Assn., Am. Fin., Western Econ. Assn., World Affairs Coun. Avocations: golf, computers. Office: Muhlenberg Coll Econs Dept 2400 W Chew St Allentown PA 18104-5564

RAYMOND, BETTY JEAN, critical care nurse; b. Harriman, Tenn., Feb. 28, 1955; d. Charles E. and Elizabeth Jane (Crump) Raymond. Student, State Vo-Tech, Harriman, 1982, Roane State Community Coll. Staff nurse ICU, CCU, cardiac rehab. Chamberlain Meml. Hosp., Rockwood, Tenn.; charge nurse Spring City (Tenn.) Health Care; staff nurse intensive care-coronary care unit Loudon (Tenn.) County Meml. Hosp.; charge nurse Marshall Voss Health Care, Harriman, Tenn.; staff nurse McVoss Health CAre, 2000—01, Royal Care Health Care, Harriman, 2001, Maxim Healthcare Svcs., Knoxville, Tenn., 2001—. Staff nurse Roane County Ambulance Svc., staff nurse with pediat. nursing specialists, Nashville, 1992, Elk Valley Health Svcs., Fayetteville, Tenn., 1994, Covenant Health Svcs., Knoxville, Tenn.; staff nurse Loudon Healthcare Ctr., Tenn., 1998—. Home: 125 Stevens Cir Rockwood TN 37854-4616

RAYMOND, CATHERINE M. editor; b. Syracuse, N.Y., Jan. 15, 1950; d. Stewart W. and Delores M. Raymond; life ptnr. Paul C. Horton III; children: Jason Alfieri, Darcy Alfieri. BA with honors, U. So. Maine, 1990, MA, 1998. Adminstrv. asst. pres.'s office U. So. Maine, Portland, Maine, 1994—2000; rsch. editor Marshall Penn York Co., Inc., Syracuse, NY, 2001—. Avocations: photography, writing. Personal E-mail: craymond@twcnyrr.com. Business E-Mail: visencmaps@aol.com.

RAYMOND, DAVID WALKER, lawyer; b. Chelsea, Mass., Aug. 23, 1945; s. John Walker and Jane (Beck) R.; m. Sandra Sue Broadwater, Aug. 12, 1967 (div.); m. Margaret Byrd Payne, May 25, 1974; children: Pamela Payne, Russell Wyatt. BA, Gettysburg Coll., 1967; JD, Temple U., 1970. Bar: Pa. 1970, D.C. 1971, Ill. 1975, U.S. Dist. Ct. (no. dist.) Ill. 1981, U.S. Supreme Ct. 1974. Govtl. affairs atty. Sears, Roebuck and Co., Washington, 1970-74, atty. Sears Hdqrs. law dept. Chgo., 1974-80, asst. gen. counsel advt., trademarks and customs, 1981-84, asst. gen. counsel adminstrn., 1984-86, mgr. planning and analysis corp. planning dept., 1986-89, sr. corp. counsel pub. policy corp. law dept., 1989-90; assoc. gen. counsel litigation and adminstrn. law dept. Sears Mdse. Group, 1990-92, dep. gen. counsel, 1992-93, v.p., gen. counsel, 1993-95; v.p. law Sears Roebuck and Co., 1996; of counsel Winston & Strawn, Washington, 1996-2001; v.p., gen. counsel C-NAV Systems, Inc., Gettysburg, Pa., 2001—. Mem. staff Temple Law Quar., 1968-69, editor, 1969-70. Trustee No. Ill. U., 1996-98; mem. bd. visitors Christopher Newport U., 1999—; mem. bd. fellows Gettysburg Coll., 1999—. Mem.: ABA, Phi Alpha Delta. Presbyterian. Office: C-NAV Systems Inc 337 Carlisle St Gettysburg PA 17325

RAYMOND, DOROTHY GILL, lawyer; b. Greeley, Colo., June 2, 1954; d. Robert Marshall and Roberta (McClure) Gill; m. Peter J. Raymond, June 8, 1974. BA summa cum laude, U. Denver, 1975; JD, U. Colo., 1978. Bar: Conn. 1978, Colo. 1981. Assoc. Dworkin, Minogue & Bucci, Bridgeport, Conn., 1978-80; counsel Tele-Communications, Inc., Englewood, Colo., 1981-88; v.p., gen. counsel WestMarc Communications, Inc., Denver, 1988-91, Cable Television Labs., Inc., Boulder, Colo., 1991-96, sr. v.p., gen. counsel, 1996—. Mem. Am. Corp. Counsel Assn. (pres. 1990-91, Colo. chpt. dir. 1988-94), Colo. Assn. Corp. Counsel (pres. 1987), Sports Car Club Am. (nat. champion ladies stock competition 1981, 85, 86, 88). Avocations: sewing, reading, outdoor activities. Office: Cable Television Labs Inc 400 Centennial Pkwy Louisville CO 80027-1266

RAYMOND, DOROTHY SARNOFF, communications consultant, former actress and singer; b. N.Y.C. d. Jacob and Belle (Roossin) S.; m. Milton Harold Raymond, Mar. 15, 1957. BA, Cornell U., 1935. Cons. 5 adminstrns., over 12 years; cons. 5 adminstrns. U.S. Dept. State; founder, chmn. Dorothy Sarnoff Speech Dynamics and Communications Svcs. Inc. subs. Oglivy & Mather, N.Y.C., 1975—2000. Lectr., cons. nat. and internat. orgns., 1975—. Appeared in Broadway plays: Rosalinda, 1942, Magdalena, 1948, The King and I, 1951, My Darling Aida, 1953; debut in opera as Marquerite in Faust, Phila. Opera, 1942; leading roles with N.Y.C., Phila., L.A. and San Francisco Civic Light, New Orleans, St. Louis Mcpl., Salt Lake City operas include La Boheme, Tosca, Tales of Hoffmann, Carmen, Merry Widow, Fleidermaus, Pagliacci, New Moon, Chocolate Soldier, Great Waltz, Vagabond King; soprano soloist with various symphony orchs., soloist and guest on numerous TV programs incl. Ed Sullivan Shows, 1951—; author: Speech Can Change Your Life, 1970, Make the Most of Your Best, 1981, Never Be Nervous Again, 1988, contbr. articles to profl. jours. and mags. Mem. spl. med. adv. bd. N.Y. Cornell Hosp. Recipient Gold Medal of Honor award for disting. svc. to humanity Nat. Inst. Social Scis.; named Woman of Achievement Albert Einstein Med. Coll. Mem. Women's Forum, Women in Communication, Mortar Bd., Tower Club (Cornell U. chpt.), Lotos Club, N.Y. Hosp. Med. Adv. Bd. Home: 150 E 69th St New York NY 10021-5704

RAYMOND, EUGENE THOMAS, technical writer, consultant, retired aircraft engineer; b. Seattle, Apr. 17, 1923; s. Evan James and Katheryn Dorothy (Kranick) R.; m. Bette Mae Bergeson, mar. 1, 1948; children: Joan Raymond Hibbs, Patricia, Robin Raymond Flashman. BSME, U. Wash., 1944, postgrad., 1953-55. Registered profl. engr., Tex. Rsch. engr. The Boeing Co., Seattle, 1946-59, sr. group engr., 1959-63, 66-71, sr. specialist engr., 1971-81, prin. engr. flight control tech., 1982-88; project design engr. Gen. Dynamics, Fort Worth, 1963-66. Author: (book) Aircraft Flight Control Actuation System Design, 1993; aircraft editl. adv. bd. Hydraulics and Pneumatics mag., 1960-70; contbr. over 20 tech. papers and articles to profl. jours. Lt. USNR, 1943-46, 49-52. Recipient prize Hydraulics and Pneumatics mag. 1958. Mem. Engrng. Soc. Advancing Mobility on Land, Sea, Air and Space (cert. of appreciation, chmn. adv. bd. com. A-6 nat. com. for aerospace fluid power, actuation, and control tech. 1983-88, vice-chmn. com. 1986-88, cons.), Fluid Power Soc. (dir. N.W. region 1973-74), Puget Sound Fluid Power Assn., AIAA, Meridian Valley Country Club, Masons, Shriners, Beta Theta Pi. Lutheran. Achievements include 5 patents in Fluid Sealing Arrangements, Quasi-Open-Loop Hydraulic Ram Incremental Actuator with Power Conserving Properties, Rotary Digital Electrohydraulic Actuator, Two-Fluid Nonflammable Hydraulic System and Load-Adaptive Hydraulic Actuator System and Method for Actuating Control Surfaces; designed and developed mechanical systems for the XB-47 and B-52 jet bombers, 707 airliner and many other aircraft, including the X-20 Dyna-Soar dynamic soaring hypersonic space plane, the American SST, the rewinged Navy A-6 attack plane the B-2 Stealth Bomber and the Chinese XAC Y-7 commuter. Home: 13816 SE 251st St Kent WA 98042-6629 *Personal philosophy: I have always tried to act correctly, fairly, and truthfully and to set a good example for my children and my peers.*

RAYMOND, FRED DOUGLAS, III, lawyer; b. Phila., May 12, 1958; s. F. Douglas Jr. and Carolyn Sue (MacReynolds) R.; m. Elizabeth Tuan Partridge, June 28, 1980; children: Peter Randolph, Alexander Partridge, Louisa Woodward. AB cum laude, Harvard U., 1980; JD magna cum laude, U. Pa., 1985. Bar: Pa. 1985, U.S. Ct. Appeals (3d cir.) 1986. Comml. banker Fidelity Bank, Phila., 1980-82; jud. clk. U.S. Ct. Appeals (3d cir.), 1985-86; ptnr. Drinker, Biddle & Reath LLP, 1996-99, mng. ptnr., 2000—. Mktg. ptnr., 1996—. Contbr. articles to law jours. Bd. dirs. Children's Aid Soc., Pa., 1992—. Mem. Independence Hall Assn. (bd. dirs., sec. 1984—). Home: 8 Briar Rd Wayne PA 19087-2603 Office: Drinker Biddle & Reath LLP 1100 PNB Bldg 1 Logan Sq 18th & Cherry St Philadelphia PA 19103-6996 E-mail: fdr@dbr.com.

RAYMOND, GEORGE EDWARD, JR. (CHIP RAYMOND), operations research analyst; b. Monterey, Calif., Dec. 26, 1947; s. George Edward and Madeleine (Gordon) R.; m. Elizabeth B. Dees, Aug. 26, 1968 (div. Dec. 1980); children: Madeleine, Anna Marie, Katie; m. Barbara Ann Sullivan, July 7, 1990. BS, N.C. State U., 1972; MBA, George Mason U./Oxford U., 1995; grad., Naval Postgrad. Sch., 1993. Served to maj. U.S. Army, Ft. Belvoir, Va., 1972-82; sr. cons. KPMG Peat Marwick, Washington, 1982-85; sr. product mgr. Magnavox, Ft. Wayne, Ind., 1985-87; dir. econ. analysis U.S. Army Info. Sys. Software Ctr., Ft. Belvoir, 1987—. Adj. prof. George Mason U., 1997—. Editor: Resource Management for Software Development, 1990. Mem. Army Acquisition Corps. Recipient meritorious svc. award U.S. Army, 1982. Mem. IEEE, Am. Soc. Mil. Comptrollers, Assn. Computing Machinery, Order Ky. Cols. Republican. Roman Catholic. Avocations: skiing, SCUBA diving, sailing. Home: 11447 Meath Dr Fairfax VA 22030-5449 Office: USAISSC Software Ctr 6000 6th St Fort Belvoir VA 22060-5506

RAYMOND, GEORGE MARC, city planner, educator; b. Odessa, Russia, Jan. 1, 1919; came to U.S., 1937, naturalized, 1942; s. Mark J. and Rachelle (Schneiderman) R.; m. Kathleen E. Waid, Oct. 3, 1942 (div. Mar. 1978); 1 dau., Valerie M.; m. Lois Jean Gainsboro, Mar. 26, 1979. BArch, Columbia, 1946. Planning dir. Harrison, Ballard & Allen, Inc., N.Y.C., 1952-54; founder, pres. Raymond, Parish, Pine & Weiner, Inc., 1954-83; pres. George M. Raymond Assocs., 1983—; prof. planning, chmn. dept. city and regional planning Pratt Inst., Bklyn., 1959-75; founder, dir. Pratt Ctr. for Community Improvement, 1963-70. Lectr. planning Columbia U., 1955-58; lectr. planning and urban renewal New Sch. Social Rsch., 1967-72; pres. Assn. Collegiate Sch. Planning, 1968-69; chmn. Westchester County Housing Implementation Commn., 1992-93. Editor: Pratt Planning Papers, 1963-73, (with Astrid Monson) Pratt Guide to Housing, Planning and Urban Renewal for New Yorkers, 1965. V.p. Citizens Housing and Planning Coun. N.Y.C., 1967-86, N.Y. Assn. Environ. Profls., 1977-79; pres. Westchester Citizens Housing Coun., 1964-66, Met. Com. on Planning, 1950-51; founder, pres. Friends of Music Concerts, 1954-57, Spoken Arts Soc., 1966-67; past 1st v.p. Federated Conservationists Westchester County; past dir. Nat. Housing Conf., Phipps Houses, Wave Hill, Settlement Housing Fund; chmn. Westchester County Housing Opportunity Commn., 1994—; land use adv. com. N.Y. State Legis. Commn. on Rural Resources, 1992-98. Fellow: Am. Inst. Cert. Planners; mem.: Am. Planning Assn. (pres. NY met. chpt. 1983—85), Am. Soc. Cons. Planners (pres. 1968—70). Home: 192 Locust Ln Irvington NY 10533-2315 Office: 101 Executive Blvd Elmsford NY 10523-1316

RAYMOND, GINNY TERRY, social worker, educator; b. Vicksburg, Miss., Aug. 23, 1944; d. Joseph Ray and Alma Blanche (Smith) Terry; children: Jeanne-Marie Sidonie, Leslie Elise. BA, U. So. Miss., 1966; MSW, Tulane U., 1968; PhD, U. Denver. Cert., lic. grad. social worker. Psychiat. social worker DePaul Mental Health Ctr., New Orleans, 1968-69; sch. social worker Orleans Parish Sch. Bd., 1969-70; social worker Home of Holy Infancy, Austin, Tex., 1970-72; sr. psychiatr. social worker Indian Rivers Mental Health Ctr., Tuscaloosa, Ala., 1973-75; prof. sch. social work U. Ala., 1975—, chair BSW program, 1982-88, assoc. dean, 1998—. Mem. commn. on edn. policy Coun. on Social Work Edn., Washington, 1988—, bd. dirs.; cons. Family Counseling Svc., Tuscaloosa, 1980-82, Tuscaloosa City Sch. System, 1979. Contbr. articles to profl. jours. Pres. bd. dirs. Big Bros./Big Sisters Tuscaloosa County, 1983-86; v.p. bd. dirs. Parents Anonymous, Tuscaloosa, 1981-83; bd. dirs. Turning Point-Domestic Violence Prevention Agy. Frank R. Egan award Phi Alpha Social Work Honor Soc., 1990; named Outstanding Bd. Mem. Big Bros./Big Sisters, 1986. Mem. NASW, Acad. Cert. Social Workers, Coun. on Social Work Edn. Roman Catholic. Office: U Ala Sch Social Work PO Box 870314 Tuscaloosa AL 35487-0154

RAYMOND, GORDON H. engineering executive, consultant; b. New Britain, Conn., Nov. 26, 1919; s. Sherwood Henry and Helen Martindale (Hodge) R.; m. Shirley Jean Erickson, May 1, 1948; children: Kristin L., Karen W. BSEE, Worcester Polytechnic Inst., 1942. Registered profl. engr., Conn. Project engr. Philco Corp., Phila., 1942-50, Raymond Engring. Lab., Middletown, Conn., 1950-54; chief electrical engr. Alln D. Cardwell Co., Plainville, 1954-56; chief engr. Gray Mfg. Co., Hartford, 1956-62, Landers, Frary & Clark, New Britian, 1962-65; cons. Lunar Orbiter Space Program, 1965-66, G.H. Raymond Engring., Southington, Conn., 1980—; v.p. engring. Waring Products, New Hartford, 1966-69; dir. engring. Electrolux Corp., Greenwich, 1970-81. Part-time cons. VCMA Engring.-Tech. Com., New Product Designs, Engring. Mgmt., New Bus. Ventures. Contbr. articles to profl. jours. Mem. Rep. Town Com., Southington, 1963-75, Rep. Town Mtg., Southington, 1964-65; commr. Indsl. Devel. Commn., Southington, 1968-71; bd. deacons 1st Congl. Ch., Southington, sr. deacon, bd. trustees; sec. William Hatton Sch. PTA, pres.; corporator Bradley Meml. Hosp.; life scout Boy Scouts Am. Recipient Commendation award ASTM Com., Phila., 1981. Mem. IEEE (sr.), Phi Sigma Kappa (treas., bus. mgr. coll. yearbook). Avocations: boating, swimming, camping, videography, computers. Home: 1105 East St Southington CT 06489-3843 E-mail: gordray@alum.wpi.edu.

RAYMOND, JACK, journalist, public relations executive, foundation executive; b. Lodz, Poland, Oct. 6, 1918; s. Harry and Anna (Lange) R.; m. Gertrude Silverman, Oct. 6, 1946; children: David Alan, Judith. Student, CCNY, 1939. Sports writer N.Y. World-Telegram, 1934-38; ct. reporter, city editor, columnist N.Y. Daily North Side News, 1938-40; Corr. N.Y. Times, 1940-66, Berlin, 1946-47, Frankfurt, 1947-49, Bonn, 1949-52, Balkans, Belgrade, 1952-56, Moscow, 1956, Pentagon corr. Washington, 1956-66; pub. rels. exec., pres. Thomas J. Deegan Co., Washington and N.Y.C., 1966-70; v.p. Bryan Publs., N.Y.C., 1970-74; founding pres. Internat. Inst. for Environ. Devel., 1970; pres. Dialog divsn. J. Walter Thompson Co., 1973-75; pres. Jack Raymond & Co., Inc., N.Y.C., 1975-87, chmn., 1987-92; pres. JR Cons. Svc., Inc., 1987-96; acting comm. dir. Commonwealth Fund, 1987. Book reviewer The Villager, N.Y.C., 1970-74; cons. UN Conf. on Human Environment, 1972, Aspen Inst. Humanistic Studies, HABITAT, UN Conf. Human Settlements; adv. com. Ctr. for Environ. Info. UN Assn. U.S., 1975-78; mem. Rumanian-U.S. econ. coun. U.S. C. of C., 1973-75; project dir. 1987 Workshop Internat. Environ. Bur. Internat. C. of C.; cons. INFORM, 1989, The Rene Dubos Ctr. for Human Environments, 1989-2000; mem. adv. bd. Volvo Journalists Retreat Duke U., 1992; internat. adv. bd. Ctr. for Social Policy in Mid-East, 1983-91; mem. exec. bd. Ency. of Environment. Author: Power at Pentagon, 1964, Your Military Obligations and Opportunities, 1963, Robert O. Anderson: Oil Man/Environmentalist, 1988; co-author: This is Germany, 1950; editor Upton Nooz, 1942-43; combat corr. Stars and Stripes, news editor Naples and Rome edits., mng. editor Marseilles edit.; combat corr., war editor, editor Stars and Stripes mag. Paris edit., combat corr., news editor Frankfurt edit., 1943-45; also author articles. Trustee N.Y. Urban League, 1969-72; bd. dirs. Internat. Inst. Environ. Affairs, N.Y.C., 1970-74, pres., 1970-73; bd. dirs. Internat. Inst. Environment and Devel., London, 1974-89, mem. adv. coun., 1978-82, mem. exec. com., 1982-89; bd. dirs. Epoch B. Found., La Jolla, Calif., acting pres., 1977-85; trustee Moroccan-Am. Found., 1982-88; bd. overseers Heller Grad. Sch., Brandeis U., 1981-88; founding assoc. John J. McCloy Internat. Ctr., N.Y.C., 1986, bd. dirs., 1987-99; mem. adv. bd. Ctr. for East-West Dynamics, 1992-95, Volvo JNLSTS Retreat, Williamsburg, Va., 1992; With U.S. Army, 1942-45. Decorated 5 Battle Stars, Bronze Star, Purple Heart. Mem. Coun. on Fgn. Rels. Clubs: Overseas Press Am. (N.Y.C.) (pres. 1972-76), Century Assn. (N.Y.C.), Nat. Press (Washington). Office: 340 E 57th St New York NY 10022

RAYMOND, KAY E(NGELMANN), Spanish language educator, consultant; b. Cin., Feb. 1, 1939; d. Gerson Silas and Pauline Coleman (Early) Engelmann; m. Ralph Raymond II, Feb. 1, 1964 (div. Nov. 1977); 1 child Jennifer Kay Raymond-Judy. AB magna cum laude, Radcliffe Coll., 1961; MA, Brown U., 1964; PhD, Ind. U., 1983. Lectr. Boston U., 1965-68; lectr. Assumption Coll., Worcester, Mass., 1965-67; instr. Regis Coll., Weston, 1967-71; assoc. instr. Ind. U., Bloomington, 1972-83; lectr. Emporia (Kans.) State U., 1983-84; asst. prof. U. Ala. at Huntsville, 1984-89, Sam Houston State U., Huntsville, Tex., 1989-94, assoc. prof., 1995—, coord. fgn. langs., 1995-98. Advisor Internat. Hispanic Assn., Sam Houston State U., 1990—, Sigma Delta Pi, 1990—; vol. translator City of Huntsville, 1993-98. Named Top Prof Bapt. Student Ministry Sam Houston State U., 1996, Outstanding Advisor Internat. Hispanic Assn., 1996-97. Mem.: Tex. Fgn. Lang. Assn., Tex. Assn. Coll. and Univ. Lang. Suprs., Tex. Assn. Coll. Tchrs., Am. Coun. on the Tchg. of Fgn. Langs., Harvard Univ. Club Houston (schs. and scholarship com. 1997—), Sigma Delta Pi, Pi Delta Phi, Phi Sigma Iota. Home: 3644 Youpon Ln Huntsville TX 77340-8920 Office: Sam Houston State U Dept Fgn Langs PO Box 2147 Huntsville TX 77341-2147 E-mail: fol_ker@.shsu.edu.

RAYMOND, KENNETH NORMAN, chemistry educator, research chemist; b. Astoria, Oreg., Jan. 7, 1942; s. George Norman and Helen May (Dunn) R.; m. Jane Galbraith Shell, June 19, 1965 (div. 1976); children: Mary Katherine, Alan Norman; m. Barbara Gabriele Sternitzke, June 17, 1977; children: Gabriella Petra, Christopher Norman. BA, Reed Coll., 1964; PhD, Northwestern U., 1968. Asst. prof. chemistry U. Calif.-Berkeley, 1967-74, assoc. prof., 1974-78, prof., 1978—; vice chmn. dept. U. Calif. Berkeley, 1982-84, chmn., 1993-96. Mem. study sect. NIH, 1983; adv. com. NSF, 1985—87; co-chmn. bd. chem. scis. & tech. NRC, 2000—; co-founder Lamiphere, Inc., 2001. Editor: Bioinorganic Chemistry II, 1977; assoc. editor Biology of Metals, 1987-91; editl. bd. Inorganic Chemistry, 1976-86, Accounts Chem. Rsch., 1982-90, Inorganica Chemica Acta f-Block Elements, 1984-90, Jour. Coordination Chemistry, 1981—, Jour. Inorganic and Nuclear Chemistry, 1974-81, Jour. Am. Chem. Soc., 1983-95, Topics in Current Chemistry, 1981-97, Metals in Biology, 1993—, Jour. Supramolecular Chemistry, 1992—, Jour. Biol. Inorganic Chemistry, 1996—, Procs. NAS USA, 2002--; U.S. editl. advisor Springer-Verlag in Chemistry, 1972-91; contbr. articles to profl. jours.; author more than 400 papers, 11 patents in field. Alfred P. Sloan rsch. fellow, 1971-73; Miller rsch. prof., 1977-78, 96; Guggenheim fellow, 1980-81; recipient E.O. Lawrence award Dept. Energy, 1984, Humboldt Rsch. award for U.S. Scientists, 1992, 2000, Alfred R. Bader award Am. Chem. Soc., 1994, Vollum award Reed Coll., 2002. Mem. NAS, Am. Acad. Arts and Scis., Am. Chem. Soc. (chair divsn. inorganic chemistry 1996), Am. Crystallographic Soc., Sigma Xi. Democrat. Office: U Calif Berkeley Dept Chemistry Berkeley CA 94720-1460 E-mail: raymond@socrates.berkeley.edu.

RAYMOND, LAWRENCE WILLIAM, internist, pulmonary and occupational medicine physician; b. Buffalo, Feb. 14, 1935; s. John Joseph and Kathryn Marie (Dowd) R.; m. Nancy Saunders Raymond, June 6, 1964 (dec. Jan. 1982); m. Claire Patricia Degraw, Oct. 12, 1986; children: Susan, Christopher, John Gareth, Mary (dec.). BCE, Manhattan Coll., 1956; MS, Harvard U., 1957; MD, Cornell U. Med. Coll., 1964. Registered profl. engr. N.Y.; diplomate Am. Bd. Internal Medicine (Internal Medicine and Pulmonary Diseases), Am. Bd. Preventive Medicine. Med. intern Georgetown Hosp., Washington, 1964-65; rsch. physiologist Naval Med. Rsch. Inst., Bethesda, Md., 1965-67, 72-74; resident in internal medicine Nat. Naval Med. Ctr., 1967-70, chief pulmonary divsn., 1974-76; pulmonary fellow CVRI, U. Calif., San Francisco, 1970-72; chief respiratory care VA Med. Ctr., New Haven, 1976-79; asst. med. dir. Exxon, N.Y.C., 1979-94, assoc. med. dir. Houston, 1994-95; dir. prospective health East Carolina U., Greenville, N.C., 1992-94; dir. occupl. medicine Carolinas Med. Ctr., Charlotte, 1995—. Assoc. prof. pulmonary medicine Yale Sch. of Medicine, New Haven, 1976-79; clin. assoc. prof. pulmonary medicine Cornell U. Med. Coll., N.Y.C., 1979-85; adj. prof. pulmonary medicine Baylor Coll. of Medicine, Houston, 1992-97; clin. prof. family medicine U. N.C., Chapel Hill, 1995—. Co-patentee Sound level timer. Cons. pulmonary disease NIH Clin. Ctr., Bethesda, 1974-76; cons. occupl. medicine Carolinas Poison Ctr., Charlotte, 1996—. Capt. USN, 1965-76, USNR, 1977-95. Recipient Citation Benrus Corp., 1974. Fellow ACP, Am. Coll. Chest Physicians, Am. Coll. Occupl. and Environtl. Medicine; mem. Am. Physiol. Soc., Am. Thoracic Soc., Undersea and Hyperbaric Med. Soc. Roman Catholic. Avocations: fitness, tennis, symphonic and choral music. Office: Carolinas Med Ctr PO Box 32861 Charlotte NC 28232-2861

RAYMOND, LEE R. oil company executive; b. Watertown, S.D., Aug. 13, 1938; m. Charlene Raymond. BSChemE, U. Wis., 1960; PhDChemE, U. Minn., 1963. Various engring. positions Exxon Corp., Tulsa, Houston, N.Y.C. and Caracas, Venezuela, 1963-72, mgr. planning Internat. Co. divsn. N.Y.C., 1972-75, v.p. Lago Oil Netherlands Antilles, 1975-76, pres., dir. Lago Oil, 1976-79, pres. Exxon Nuc. Co. divsn., 1979-81, exec. v.p. Exxon Enterprises Inc. divsn., 1981-83, pres., dir. Esso Inter-Am. Inc. Coral Gables, Fla., 1983-84, sr. v.p., dir. N.Y.C., 1984-86, pres., dir., 1987-93, chmn., CEO, 1993-99; chmn., CEO & pres. Exxon Mobil Corp., Irving, Tex., 1999—. Bd. dirs. J.P. Morgan & Co., Inc., N.Y.C., Morgan Guaranty Trust Co. of N.Y., N.Y.C., Am. Petroleum Inst.; mem. nat. task force on minority high achievement in Coll. Bd. Bd. dirs. United Negro Coll. Fund, Project Shelter PRO-AM, 1991—, Dallas Citizens Coun., Jason Found. for Edn.; trustee Wis. Alumni Rsch. Found., 1987—, Bus. Coun. Internat. Understanding, Inc., 1988—; mem. Tri Lateral Commn., U. Wis. Found.; mem. innovations in medicine leadership coun. Southwestern Med. Ctr.; ptnr. emeritus N.Y.C. Partnership; active Am. Coun. on Germany, Dallas Com. Fgn. Rels., Dallas Wildcat Com., 1993. Mem. NAE, Am. Soc. Engring. (nat. adv. coun.), Am. Soc. Royal Bot. Garden (founder), Bus. coun., Bus. Roundtable, Nat. Petroleum Coun. (mem. nom. com.), Coun. Fgn. Rels., Singapore-U.S. Bus. Coun., Nat. Acad. Engring. (bd. dirs.), Am. Soc. Engring. Educators (nat. adv. coun. 1994), Occupl. Physicians Scholarship Fund (chmn. fundraising campaign 1995), Coll. Bd. (nat. task force on minority high achievement 1997).

RAYMOND, LISA, tennis player; b. Norristown, Pa., Aug. 10, 1973; d. Ted and Nancy Raymond. Student, U. Fla. Recipient 1 singles title Corel WTA Tour, 5 doubles titles, 1 grand slam title; singles finalist, Oklahoma City, 1997; doubles finalist Australian Open, 1997; 12 doubles semifinals, 4 doubles finals, 5 double wins, 8 singles quarterfinals, 1 doubles semifinal, 1 singles win; singles rank No. 17, winner Australian Open Grand Slam doubles, 2000, Wimbledon, 2001, U.S. Open Grand Slam doubles, 2001. Avocations: shopping, hanging out with friends, watching television, football, volleyball. Office: US Tennis Assn 70 W Red Oak Ln White Plains NY 10604-3602*

RAYMOND, SUSAN GRANT, sculptor; b. Denver, May 23, 1943; d. Edwin Hendrie and Mary Belle (McIntyre) G; m. Macpherson Raymond Jr., Aug. 18, 1967 (div. Mar. 1987); children: Lance Ramsay (dec.), Mariah McIntyre. BA in English, Cornell U., 1965; MA in Anthropology, U. Colo., 1968. Curator of anthropology Denver Mus. of Nat. History, 1968-71, contract artist, 1976-77, 79, 81, 83; instr. in anthropology U.S. Internat. U., Steamboat Springs, Colo., 1971-73. Sculpted monumental bronze sculpture for Littleton Colo., 1987, Vail, Colo., 1986, inspirational sculpture Childrens Hosp., 1977, diorama figures for Denver Mus. of Nat. History, 1971, 76, 77, 79, 81, 83, sculptures Routt Meml. Hosp, 1977, U. Denver, 1982, Craig Hosp. 1984, 94, 99, Lakewood Westernaires, 1984, Stonegate swimming hole, Scottsdale, 1989, 10th Mtn. divsn. Monument, Ft. Drum, N.Y., 1991, Ketring Park, Littleton, Colo., 1994, Denver Zoo, 1993, Tulsa Zoo, 1994, Ritchie Assocs., Wichita, Kans., 1993-94, 96, St. Joseph's Hosp., Denver, 1997, Zoo Atlanta, 1997; exhibited at Western Heritage Art Fair, Littleton, 1991, Sculpture in the Park, Loveland, Colo., 1993, 94, Nat. Western Stock Show Art Exhib., 1994-2002, Meml. Wall for Kent Denver Sch., 1998, Monument for City of Albuquerque, 1998; commn. sculpture Littleton (Colo.) Hist. Mus., 1999, Donor Alliance Monument at Hudson Gardens, Littleton, 1999, Monument for Wichita (Kans.) Strykers, 2000, Monument for Rigden Farm, Ft. Collins, 2001. Mem. Nat. Ski Patrol, 1965-75; bd. dirs. Tread of Pioneers Mus., Steamboat Springs, 1971-87. Recipient Maurice Hexter award Nat. Sculpture Soc., 1984, Art Castings award N. Am. Sculpture Exhibition, 1982, Summerart award Steamboat Springs Arts and Humanities, 1984; winner 10th Mountain Div. Monumental Sculpture at Ft. Drum, Watertown, N.Y., 1990: named hon. mem. 10th Mountain Division at work's completion, 1992. Avocations: skiing, riding, backpacking, tennis.

RAYMOND, URAL WAYNE, retired retail executive; b. Missoula, Mont., May 20, 1944; s. Ural Daniel and Fayetta Arilla Raymond. Student, U. N.C., 1969-70, U. Mont., 1962-66, 93-94. Enlisted man U.S. Army, 1966-69, 70-89; advanced through grades to master sgt. U.S. Army, 1985; ret., 1989; advt. mgr. Sears & Roebuck, Missoula, 1993-99; ret., 1999. Chmn. western dist. Am. Legion Baseball, Missoula, 1997—; pres. Friends of the Libr., Missoula, 1997-99. With U.S. Army, 1966-69. Decorated Bronze Star. Mem. Nev. Internat. Lic. Plate Soc. (treas. state br. 1998—). Democrat. Evangelical. Avocations: collecting license plates, collecting flags, baseball, collecting stamps, collecting coins. Fax: 406-549-5630.

RAYMOND, WILFRED J. priest, educator; b. Old Town, Maine, Mar. 5, 1944; s. Joseph Raymond and Lydia Belanger. BA in Phil., Stonehill Coll., 1967; MTh, U. Notre Dame, 1971. Ordained priest Roman Cath. Ch., 1971. Tchr. St. Joseph's, South Bend, Ind., 1970-71, Notre-Dame H.S., Bridgeport, Conn., 1972-74; recruiter Congregation of Holy Cross, 1974-79; campus minister Stonehill Coll., Easton, Mass., 1979-92, adminstr., 1985-90, asst. dean, 1985-90; asst. provincial Congregation of Holy Cross, Bridgeport, Conn., 1994-98; pastor St. Francis de Sales, Bennington, Vt., 1993-94; provincial supr. Congregation of Holy Cross, Bridgeport, Conn., 1998—; nat. dir. Family Theater Prodns., Hollywood, 2000—. Contbr. articles to profl. jours.; guest spkr.. Bd. dirs. King's Coll., Wilkes Barre, Pa., 1998—, Stonehill Coll., Easton, Mass., 1998—; chmn. bd. dirs. Holy Cross Family Ministries. Democrat. Home and Office: 7201 W Sunset Blvd Los Angeles CA 90046-3405 E-mail: wraymond@familytheater.org.

RAYMUND, STEVEN A. computer company executive; b. 1955; BS, U. Oreg., Georgetown U. Sch. Fgn. Svc. Pres., CEO, chmn. bd., dir. Tech Data Corp., 1981-2001, chmn., CEO, 2001—. Office: Tech Data Corp 5350 Tech Data Dr Clearwater FL 33760-3122*

RAYNAULD, ANDRE, economist, educator; b. Quebec, Que., Can., Oct. 20, 1927; s. Léopold and Blanche (Gauthier) R.; m. Michelle Nolin, Oct. 15, 1951; children: Francoy, Olivier, Dominique, Isabelle. BA cum laude, U. Montreal, 1948, MA in Indsl. Rels. magna cum laude, 1951; D. in Econs., U. Paris, 1954; D. in Econs. (hon.), U. Ottawa, 1976, U. Sherbrooke, 1976. Mem. faculty U. Montreal, 1954-71, founder, dir. Ctr. Econ. Research and Devel., 1970-72; vis. prof. U. Toronto, 1962-63; chmn. Economic Council Can., Ottawa, 1971-76; mem. Que. Nat. Assembly, Montreal, 1976-80; prof. U. Montreal, 1980-93, prof. emeritus, 1993—. Exec. com. Can. Social Sci. Rsch. Coun., 1961-63, 64-65; pres. Inst. Canadien Affaires Publiques, 1961-62; bd. govs. Can. Labour Coll., 1962-66; dir., exec. com. CBC, 1964-67; trustee CBC Pension Fund, 1967-70; pres. Soc. Canadienne de Sci. Economique, 1967-69; mem. Royal Commn. Bilingualism and Biculturalism, 1969-70, Can. Coun. Urban and Regional Rsch., 1971, Quebec Coun. Planning and Devel., 1971; chmn. com. inquiry French-lang. tchr.-tng. Western provinces Dept. Sec. State, 1971; mem. interfutures study group OECD, Paris, 1976-78; mem. bd. Inst. Rsch. Pub. Policy, 1980—; rsch. fellow Devel. Ctr. OECD, Paris, 1986—; invited prof. College de France, Paris, 1987. Author: Economic Growth in Quebec, 1961, The Canadian Economic System, 1967, La propriete des entreprises au Quebec, 1974, Institutions Economiques Canadiennes, 2d edition, 1977, Le financement des exportations, 1979, Government Assistance to Export Financing, 1984, The External Financing of Tunisia's Imports, OECD, 1988, Financing Exports to Developing Countries, OECD, 1992; co-editor: Economic Integration in Europe and North America, 1992, Labour Standards and International Competitiveness, 1998; co-author: L'Etat Providence des Entreprises, 1999; editor Can. Jour. Econs., 1965-70. Recipient ann. award des Diplomes de l'U. de Montreal, 1974; apptd. Officer of Order of Can., 1986; fellow Walter Levy Coun. on Fgn. Rels., Boston, 1977. Fellow Royal Soc. Can.; mem. Can. Econs. Assn. (pres. 1983-84), Am. Econs. Assn., Atlantic Econ. Soc. (disting. assoc.). Liberal. Roman Catholic. Home: 4820 Roslyn St Montreal QC Canada H3W 2L2 E-mail: raynaul@attglobal.net.

RAYNER, ARNO ALFRED, investment company executive, consultant; b. San Francisco, Sept. 23, 1928; BS in Econs., U. Calif., Berkeley, 1949, MBA, 1954. Security analyst Bank of Calif., San Francisco, 1950-54; various positions to sr. v.p. Indsl. Indemnity, 1954-74; v.p. internat. svcs. Bechtel Group, 1975-76; pres. Rayner Assocs., Inc., Mill Valley, Calif., 1977-99, chmn. bd., 1999—. Home: 7 Venado Dr Belvedere Tiburon CA 94920-1625

RAYNER, LINDA CALIX, financial analyst; b. Long Beach, Calif., Nov. 13, 1957; d. Charles Frank and Pearl Irene (Hofman) C. BS, U. So. Calif., 1979, MBA, 1982. Staff acct. Deloitte & Touche, L.A., 1979-80; program controller Northrop Grumman, Anaheim, Calif., 1983-88; sr. fin. analyst Restaurant Enterprises Group, Costa Mesa, 1988-89, Sys. One Corp., El Segundo, 1989-91; sr. new bus.analyst Elec. Data Sys., 1991—. Mem. NAFE, U. So. Calif. Marshall Bus. Alumni Assn., Beta Gamma Sigma. Avocations: investing, tennis, women's issues, fashion design. Office: Elec Data Sys 600 Anton Blvd Ste 1000 Costa Mesa CA 92626

RAYNER, WILLIAM ALEXANDER, retired newspaper editor, author; b. Winnipeg, Man., Can., Nov. 7, 1929; s. William and Annie Mitchell (McDonald) R.; divorced; 1 child, Robert William. Student Can. schs. Sports editor Trail Times, B.C., 1954-55; sportswriter Victoria (B.C.) Times, 1955-57, Vancouver (B.C.) Herald, 1957; copy editor, reporter Montreal (Que.) Star, 1957-58; asst. sports editor Vancouver Sun, 1958-62, copy editor, then slotman, 1962-74, news editor, 1974-83, systems mgr., 1983-88, ret., 1988; copy editor Toronto Globe & Mail, 1962. Author: Vancouver Sun Style Guide, 1976, Images of History - Twentieth Century British Columbia Through the Front Pages, 1997, British Columbia's Premiers in Profile-The Good, The Bad and the Transient, 2000, Scandal! 130 Years of Damnable Deeds in Canada's Lotus Land. Dir. B.C. Newspaper Found. Mem. Writers Union Can. E-mail: v3n4w5@aol.com.

RAYNOLDS, DAVID ROBERT, buffalo breeder, writer; b. N.Y., Feb. 15, 1928; s. Robert Frederick and Marguerite Evelyn (Gerdau) R.; m. May (Kean) Raynolds, May 12, 1951; children: Robert, Linda, Martha, Laura, David A.F. AB, Dartmouth Coll., 1949; MA, Wesleyan U., Middletown, Conn., 1955; predoctoral, Johns Hopkins Sch. Advanced Internat. Studies, Washington, 1956; grad., Nat. War Coll., Washington, 1973. Account exec. R.H. Morris Assoc., Newtown, Conn., 1949-50; fgn. svc. officer Dept. of State, Washington, 1956-76; pres. Ranch Rangers, Inc., Lander, Wyo., 1976—. Pres. Nat. Buffalo Assn., Ft. Pierre, S.D., 1987-88. Author: Rapid Development in Small Economies (Praeger); contbr. articles to profl. jours. Trustee, bd. dirs. Liberty Hall Found.; mem. steering com. Wyo. Bus. Alliance; mem. planning bd. Mus. of the Am. West. With U.S. Army, 1950—53. Recipient Meritorious Svc. Award, Dept. of State, Washington, 1966. Mem. The Explorers Club, Fremont County Farm Bur., Fgn. Svc. Assn., Am. Legion, Rotary, Elks. Republican. Episcopalian. Avocation: travel. Office: Table Mountain Group PO Box 1310 Lander WY 82520-1310

RAYNOLDS, HAROLD, JR. retired state education commissioner; b. Chgo., Feb. 7, 1925; s. Harold and Dorothy (Smith) R.; m. Ann Richards Ellis, June 1950 (div. 1968); children— Christopher, Timothy, Madeline, Dorothy, m. Patricia Adele Miller, Jan. 20, 1973 (dec. 1996). BS, Cornell U., 1948, MA, 1953; postgrad., NYU, 1968-69. Cert. supt. schs., N.Y., Maine, Alaska. Supt. schs. Cape Elizabeth Sch. Dist., Maine, 1969-74; supt. schs. Portland Sch. Dist., 1974-79; commr. edn. State of Maine, Augusta, 1979-83, State of Alaska, Juneau, 1983-86, Commonwealth of Mass., 1986-91; interim supt. Windsor Ctrl. Supervisory Union Sch. Dist., Woodstock, Vt., 1991-92, vice chair, 1993—; supt. Springfield (Vt.) Sch. Dist., 1994-97. Contbr. articles to ednl. jours. Mem. sch. com., Pomfret, Vt., 1993—; vice chair Windsor Ctrl. Supervisory Union Bd., 1993—; mem. Vt. Senate, 1965-66; chmn. Vt. Bd. Edn., Montpelier, 1963-68; trustee U. Maine, Orono, 1979-83; Dem. candidate for U.S. Congress, Vt., 1962. Staff sgt. U.S. Army, 1943-45, ETO. Mem. Am. Assn. Sch. Adminstrs., Chief State Sch. Officers, Phi Delta Kappa. Unitarian-Universalist. Avocations: reading; gardening; cross-country skiing; theater; music.

RAYNOLDS, WILLIAM F., II, lawyer; b. San Antonio, Feb. 7, 1948; s. William F. and Doris Raynolds; m. Kathryn Raynolds, July 11, 1987; children: Lisa Chipman, Mike Chipman, Casey Raynolds. BS, U. Tulsa, 1973, JD, 1976. Atty. Hood & Raynolds, Tulsa, 1987—. Adj. prof. legal assistant program U. Tulsa, 1993—, adj. prof. coll. law, 1995—. Editor Okla. Family Law Jour., 1995. Fellow Am. Acad. Matrimonial Lawyers; mem. ABA (family law sect.), Tulsa County Bar Assn. (family law sect., pres. 1993-97), Okla. Bar Assn. (family law sect.). Roman Catholic. Office: Hood & Raynolds 1914 S Boston Ave Tulsa OK 74119-5222 E-mail: hood_raynalds@compuserve.com.

RAYNOR, RICHARD BENJAMIN, neurosurgeon, educator; b. N.Y.C., Aug. 16, 1928; s. Murray and Mildred (Pitt) R.; m. Barbara Golob; children: Geoffrey, Michele. BSME, U. Mich., 1950; MD, U. Vt., 1955. Diplomate Am. Bd. Neurol. Surgery. Intern Mt. Sinai, N.Y.C., 1955-56; residency Neurol. Inst. Presbyn. Hosp., 1956-57, Nat. Hosp., London, 1957; residency neurosurgery Neurol. Inst. Presbyn. Hosp., 1958-62; assoc. in neurosurgery Coll. Physicians and Surgeons Columbia U., N.Y.C., 1965-77; clin. assoc. prof. NYU, 1977-2000, clin. prof., 1984—. Pvt. practice neurosurgery, N.Y.C., 1965—. Cons. editor Spine; contbr. over 50 articles to profl. jours., chpts. to books. Served as capt. U.S. Army, 1962-64. Fellow Am. Coll. Surgeons; mem. Cervical Spine Research Soc. (pres. 1986-87), Am. Assn. Neurol. Surgeons, Congress Neurol. Surgeons. Clubs: University (N.Y.C.). Avocations: skiing, squash. Office: 112 E 74th St New York NY 10021-3535

RAYSON, EDWIN HOPE, lawyer; b. Earlville, Ill., Jan. 13, 1923; s. Edwin H. and Lillian (Astley) R.; m. Evelyn Sherry Kirkland, Oct. 1, 1983; children: Jane Rayson Young, Edwin Hope III, G. Scott. AB, U. Tenn., 1944, LL.B., 1948. Bar: Tenn. 1948. Pvt. practice, Knoxville, 1948—; ptnr. Kramer, Rayson, Leake, Rodgers & Morgan, 1949—. Lectr. labor law U. Tenn. Coll. Law, 1951-71 Served to lt. (j.g.) USNR, 1944-46. Mem. Order of Coif, Sigma Chi, Omicron Delta Kappa. Home: 501 River Rd Loudon TN 37774-5583 Office: 25th Fl 1st Tennessee Plaza Knoxville TN 37901

RAYSON, GLENDON ENNES, internist, preventive medicine specialist, writer; b. Oak Park, Ill., Dec. 2, 1915; s. Ennes Charles and Beatrice Margaret (Rowland) R. AB, U. Rochester, 1939; MD, U. Ill., Chgo., 1948; MPH, Johns Hopkins U., 1965; MA, Northwestern U., 1965. Diplomate Am. Bd. Internal Medicine, Am. Bd. Preventive Medicine, Am. Bd. Forensic Medicine, Am. Bd. Forensic Examiners. Resident in internal medicine Presbyn.-St. Luke's Hosp., Chgo., 1953-56; physician-in-charge Contagious Disease Hosp., 1956-58, asst. med. supt., 1958-64; rsch. assoc. Sch. Hygiene and Pub. Health Johns Hopkins U., Balt., 1966-7l; internist Johns Hopkins Hosp., 1971-82, Columbia Free State Health Plan, Balt., 1984-91; pvt. practice, 1984—; with Neurodiagnostics Assocs., 1990—2001. Attending internist emergency rm. South Balt. Gen. Hosp., 1982-84; asst. prof. health sci. U. Ill., Chgo., 1958-64; fellow in gastroenterology and endocrinology Presbyn.-St. Luke's Hosp., 1956-58. Contbr. articles to med. jours., chpt. to book. Vol. physician, Vietnam, 1968, 7l, 72, 73; mem. Citizens Amb. Program Delegation to Vietnam, 1993. Capt. M.C., USAF, 195l-53. Fellow: Am. Geriatrics Soc., Am. Coll. Preventive Medicine; mem.: APHA, ACP-ASIM, AMA. Avocations: writing poetry, short stories, composing songs. Home: 337 Poplar Point Rd Perryville MD 21903-1803 Office: 218 N Charles St Apt 1407 Baltimore MD 21201-4024

RAYWARD, WARDEN BOYD, librarian, educator; b. Inverell, NSW, Australia, June 24, 1939; s. Warden and Ellie Rayward. BA, U. Sydney, 1960; diploma in libr., U. NSW, 1964; MS in L.S, U. Ill., 1965; PhD, U. Chgo., 1973. Asst. state library, NSW, 1961-64; research librarian planning and devel., 1970; lectr. Sch. Librarianship U. NSW, Sydney, 1971-72, head sch. Info., Libr. and Archive Studies, 1986-92, prof., 1986-00, dean Faculty Prof. Studies, 1993-96, prof. emeritus, 2000—; asst. prof. U. Western Ont., 1973-74, Grad. Library Sch. U. Chgo., 1975-77, assoc. prof., 1978-80, prof., 1980-86; dean U. Chgo. Grad. Library Sch., 1980-86; rsch. prof. U. Ill., Champaign, 2000—. Cons. NEH, 1976-79, U.S. Dept. Edn., 1981; bd. govs.

Charles Stuart U., 1994-96; bd. dirs. Internat. House-U. NSW, 1992-97; George A. Miller vis. prof. U. Ill., 1997-98; Leverhulme Trust vis. prof. Leed Met. U., 2002. Author: The Universe of Information: The Work of Paul Otlet for Documentation and International Organization, 1975 (also transl. Russian and Spanish); editor: The Variety of Librarianship: Essays in Honour of John Wallace Metcalfe, 1976, The Public Library: Circumstances and Prospects, 1978, Library Quar., 1975-79, Library History in Context, 1988, Libraries and Life in a Changing World: the Metcalfe Years 1920-1970, 1993; editor, translator: International Organization and the Dissemination of Knowledge: Selected Papers of Paul Otlet, 1990; editor Confronting the Future, University Libraries in the Next Decade, 1992, Developing a Profession in Librarianship in Australia: Travel Diaries and Other Papers of John Wallace Metcalfe, 1996; mem. internat. editorial adv. bd. World Book of Encyclopedia, 1990-97; contbr. articles to profl. jours. Coun. on Library Resources fellow, 1978, vis. fellow U. Coll. London, 1986, 90, Mortenson fellow U. Ill., 1992-93, Garfield fellow in hist. sci. lit., 2000. Mem. ALA, (hon.) Australian Library and Info. Assn., Bibliog. Soc. Australia and New Zealand, Am. Soc. for Info. Sci. Office: U Ill Grad Sch Libr and Info Scis 501 E Daniel St Champaign IL 61820-6211 E-mail: wrayward@alexia.lis.uiuc.edu.

RAYZMAN, VIKTOR LAZAREVICH, metallurgist, consultant; b. Odessa, Ukraine, Dec. 27, 1934; s. Lazar Yakovlevich Rayzman and Bella Khaskelevna Pokh; m. Emiliya Aleksandrovna Aturina, Aug. 23, 1959; 1 child, Andrey Aturin; m. Nina Nikolaevna Sabadash, Jan. 20, 1976. BS in Nonferrous Metallurgy, Mining Inst., Leningrad, 1957; PhD, All-Nat. Aluminum-Magnesium, Inst., Leningrad, 1978; D Tech. Scis., Mining Inst., St. Petersburg, 1990. Foreman of shift VAMI Pilot Plant, Leningrad, 1957-59, supr. of hydrothermal facility, 1959-74, dep. chief and chief of alumina dept., 1974-81, gen. technologist, 1981-90; sr. scientific collaborator VAMI, St. Petersburg, 1990-91; gen. dir. RosKazMet, Ltd., 1990-91, rep. Cleve., 1991-94; cons., author Encinitas, Calif., 1994-99. Cons. Alcoa, Pitts., 1993. Author: (books) Sodium Aluminate and Hydroaluminate, 1991, Alumina Production, 1998; patentee in field. Bd. dirs. Am. Assn. of Jews from the ex-USSR, N.Y.-Cleve., 1992-94. Democrat. Avocation: Russian poetry. Personal E-mail: viktorayzman@yahoo.com. E-mail: rayzmanviktor@hotmail.com.

RAZANI, BABAK, medical researcher; b. Tehran, Iran, Apr. 30, 1974; s. Arsalan and Seddigheh (Boroujerdi) R. BS, BA, U. Calif., Berkeley, 1996; PhD in Molecular Pharmacology, Albert Einstein Coll. Medicine, 2001. Rsch. asst. Ctr. for Functional Imaging, Lawrence Berkeley Lab., Berkeley, Calif., 1994-96; grad. student rschr. Albert Einstein Coll. Medicine, Bronx, NY, 1997—2001. Mem. editl. bd. Einstein Quar. Sci. Jour., 1998—. Active Einstein Spoons Shelter, Bronx, 1996-2000. NIH fellow, 1996—; Presdl. fellow U. Calif. Berkeley, 1995-96; recipient Julius Marmur Rsch. award, 2002. Mem. AMA, Med. Soc. State of N.Y. (mem. bd. info. tech. in medicine 1997-2001), Am. Soc. Cell Biology, Golden Key, Tau Beta Pi, Eta Kappa Nu, Sigma Xi. Avocations: running, camping/hiking, soccer, tennis. Home: 1935 Eastchester Rd Apt 12F Bronx NY 10461-2188 Office: Albert Einstein Coll Medicine 1300 Morris Park Ave Bronx NY 10461-1926 E-mail: razani@aecom.yu.edu.

RAZDAN, RAJ KUMAR, chemicals executive; b. Simla, India, Dec. 19, 1929; arrived in U.S., 1963; s. Dwarka Pershad and Parkash Rani (Raina) Razdan; m. Janet S. A. Ritchie, Aug. 4, 1956; children: Rikki, Roma. BS in Chemistry with honors, U. Delhi, 1948; PhD in Organic Chemistry, U. Glasgow, Scotland, 1954. Jr. sci. officer Nat. Chem. Lab., Poona, India, 1954-56; sr. scientist, rsch. & devel. Glaxo Labs., Greenford, Middlesex, England, 1956-58, factory mgr. Bombay, 1958-63; sr. scientist Arthur D. Little, Cambridge, Mass., 1964-70; co-founder, prin. scientist SISA Pharm. Labs., Inc., 1970-86; affiliate prof. Va. Commonwealth U. Sch. Basic Health Scis., 1987—; co-founder, CEO Organix, Inc., Woburn, Mass., 1986—. Cons., spkr. infield. Contbr. chapters to books, articles to profl. jours. Active Coll. Problems Drug Dependence, Inc., 1993—. Fellow Postdoctoral, U. Mich., 1963—64; scholar, Govt. of India, 1951—54. Mem.: AAAS, Royal Inst. Chemistry, Chem. Soc. London, Am. Chem. Soc. Achievements include patents in field. Office: Organix Inc 240 Salem St Woburn MA 01801-2029 E-mail: razdan@organixinc.com.

RÁZIM, WILLIAM WENDELL, former radio broadcasting producer; b. Union City, N.J., Sept. 8, 1916; s. Ferdinand Joseph and Irene Teresa (Schutzbach) R. BA, NYU, 1942, cert. in meteorology, 1943, postgrad. With Richards R&D, Jersey City, 1938-42; instr. chemistry Mohawk Coll., Utica, N.Y., 1946-47; tech. writer Westvaco Chem. Co., N.Y.C., 1947-49; tech. editor Drug Topics & Drug Trade News, 1951-52; writer, editor M.W. Kellogg Co., Jersey City, 1952; ednl. cons., 1952-70. Founder, host radio program Sci. for the People, 1950-59. Pioneer in science broadcasting; contbr. articles to profl. jours. 2nd lt. U.S. Army Air Forces, 1942-45. Avocations: botanical science, music. Home: 261 Hutton St Jersey City NJ 07307-4203

RAZNOFF, BEVERLY SHULTZ, education educator; b. Ft. Myers, Fla., Apr. 24, 1946; d. John William and Dora Lucille (Galloway) S.; m. Gregory Michael Raznoff, June 8, 1968; children: John Gregory, James William. BA, Fla. So. Coll., 1968; MEd, Fla. Atlantic U., 1974. Elem. educator Pine Grove Elem. Sch., Delray Beach, Fla., 1968-69; secondary educator Pompano Beach (Fla.) High Sch., 1969-70, Deerfield Beach (Fla.) High Sch., 1970-71; prof. Broward C.C., Ft. Lauderdale, 1974-82, Palm Beach C.C., Boca Raton, Fla., 1977-93, Fla. Atlantic U., Boca Raton, 1984, Truett-McConnell Coll., Cleveland, Ga., 1994—2001; dir. instr. Toccoa (Ga.) Regional Campus, 1994—2001. Advisor Phi Theta Kappa, South campus Palm Beach C.C., 1983—93, Toccoa Regional Campus-TMC, 1994—2001. Contbr. articles to profl. jours. Recipient Fred Baker Nat. award Phi Theta Kappa, Outstanding Advisor, Fla. region, 1992, Robertt Giles Disting. Advisor award, 1998, Continued Excellence award for Advisors, 2000. Mem. Fla. Comm. Assn. (pres. 1990-91, Tchr. of Yr. 1990, Most Disting. Advisor Ga. region 2001), Internat. Listening Assn., So. States Comm. Assn., Ga. Speech Comm. Assn. Avocations: reading, needlework, cooking, mountain living. Home: 307 Old Deer Path Way Cleveland GA 30528-4243 E-mail: 69charger@direcway.com.

RAZOUK, RASHAD ELIAS, retired chemistry educator; b. Dumiat, Egypt, Aug. 22, 1911; came to U.S., 1968; s. Elias A. and Martha A. (Israfil) R.; m. Emily S. Habib, Aug. 24, 1946 (dec. Dec. 1988); children: Reda R., Rami R.; m. Henrietta Doche, July 8, 1990. *Son Reda R., PhD Purdue U. 1977, is Vice Presidentof technology, research and development, at National Semiconductors, Santa Clara, California. He married Laila Ragai, PhD Purdue U. 1977, who works as corporate stragic consultant,formerly vice president and general manager of network divsion at Advanced Micro Devices, Sunnyvale, California. Son Rami R., PhD UCLA 1980, is general manager, computer systems division, of The Aerospace Corporation, El Segundo, California. He is married to Deborah Downs, PhD UCLA 1978, who works as a senior engineering specialist at the Aerospace Corporation, El Segundo, California.* BSc with honors, Cairo U., 1933, MSc, 1936, PhD, 1939. Asst. prof. Cairo U., 1939-46, assoc. prof., 1946-50; prof. chemistry, chmn. dept. Ain Shams U., Cairo, 1950-66; prof. Am. U. Cairo, 1966-68, Calif. State U., L.A., 1968-78, emeritus prof., 1978—; vice dean Faculty Sci. Ain Shams U., Cairo, 1954-60. Acting dir. div. surface and coll. chem. Nat. Rsch. Ctr., Cairo, 1954-68; vis. rsch. prof. U. So. Calif., 1965; cons. Lockheed Aircraft Co., L.A., 1971-73. Contbr. articles on adsorption, active solids, wetting and wettability, solid reactions, surface tension, and contact angles to profl. jours. Fellow Am. Inst. Chemists (emeritus); mem. Am. Chem. Soc. (emeritus), Royal Soc. Chemistry (life). Democrat. Roman Catholic. Home: 420 S Orchard Dr Burbank CA 91506-2738 E-mail: rrazouk@aol.com.

RAZZANO, FRANK CHARLES, lawyer; b. Bklyn., Feb. 25, 1948; s. Pasquale Anthony and Agnes Mary (Borgia) R.; m. Stephanie Anne Lucas, Jan. 10, 1970; children: Joseph, Francis, Catherine. BA, St. Louis U., 1969; JD, Georgetown U., 1972. Bar: N.Y. 1973, U.S. Dist. Ct. (so. dist.) N.Y. 1973, U.S. Dist. Ct. (es. dist.) N.Y. 1973, N.J. 1976, D.C. 1981, Va. 1984, U.S. Dist. Ct. N.J. 1976, U.S. Dist. Ct. Md. 1977, U.S. Dist. Ct. (no. dist.) Calif. 1981, U.S. Dist. Ct. D.C. 1982, U.S. Dist. Ct. (ea. dist.) Va. 1989, U.S. Dist. Ct. (we. dist.) Va. 1990, U.S. Ct. Appeals (2d cir.) 1973, U.S. Ct. Appeals (3d cir.) 1975, U.S. Ct. Appeals (D.C. and 5th cirs.) 1983, U.S. Ct. Appeals (4th cir.) 1984, U.S. Ct. Appeals (6th cir.) 1990, U.S. Ct. Appeals (8th and 9th cirs.) 2000, U.S. Supreme Ct. 1976. Assoc. Shea & Gould, N.Y.C., 1972-75; asst. U.S. atty. Dist. of N.J., Newark, 1975-78; asst. chief trial atty. SEC, Washington, 1978-82; ptnr. Shea & Gould, 1982-94, mng. ptnr., 1991-92; ptnr. Camhy Karlinsky Stein Razzano & Rubin, 1994-96, Dickstein, Shapiro, Morin & Oshinsky, Washington, 1996—. Lectr. in field; adv. bd. Securities Litigation Reform Act Reporter, Securities Regulation Law Jour.; adj. prof. law U. Md. Sch. Law. Civil law editor Rico Law Reporter; mem. adv. bd. Corp. Confidentiality and Disclosure Letter; hon. adv. com. Jour. Internat. Law and Practice, Detroit Coll. Law; contbr. articles to legal jours. Scoutmaster Vienna coun. Boy Scouts Am., 1984. Recipient spl. achievement award Justice Dept., 1977, spl. commendation, 1978, Outstanding Achievement award Detroit Coll. of Law, 1993. Mem. ABA (chmn. criminal law com., sect. bus. law 1996—), Va. Bar, D.C. Bar (chmn. litigation sect. 1987-89, vice-chmn. coun. sects. 1988-89), Assn. Securities & Exch. Commn. Alumni (pres. 1993-95), Phi Beta Kappa, Eta Sigma Phi. Roman Catholic. Home: 1713 Paisley Blue Ct Vienna VA 22182-2326

RAZZANO, PASQUALE ANGELO, lawyer; b. Bklyn., Apr. 3, 1943; s. Pasquale Anthony and Agnes Mary (Borgia) R.; m. Maryann Walker, Jan. 29, 1966; children: Elizabeth, Pasquale, Susan, ChristyAnn. BSCE, Poly. Inst. Bklyn., 1964; student law, NYU, 1964-66; JD, Georgetown U., 1969. Bar: Va. 1969, N.Y. 1970, U.S. Ct. Appeals (2d, 3d, 7th, 9th and fed. cirs.), U.S. Supreme Ct., U.S. Dist. Ct. (so., ea. and western dists.) N.Y., U.S. Dist. Ct. (we. dist.) Tex., U.S. Dist. Ct. Hawaii, U.S. Dist. Ct. Conn. Examiner U.S. Patent Office, 1966-69; assoc. Curtis, Morris & Safford, P.C., 1969-71, ptnr., 1971-91, Fitzpatrick, Cella, Harper & Scinto, 1991—. Guest lectr. U.S. Trademark Assn., Am. Intellectual Property Law Assn., Practicing Law Inst., NYU Law Ctr., ABA, N.Y. Intellectual Property Law Assn. Mem. bd. editors Licensing Jour., 1986—; mem. bd. editors Trademark Reporter, 1987—, book rev. editor, 1989-91, pub. articles editor, 1991-94, domestic articles editor, 1992-93, 95, editor-in-chief 1996—. Rep. committeeman Rockland County. Recipient Robert Ridgeway award, 1964. Mem.: FBA (chmn. patent law com. 1999—2002, bd. govs. 2002—), ABA (guest lectr.), Columban Laws Assn., Bar Assn. City N.Y., Italian Am. Bar Assn., Va. Bar Assn., N.Y. Coun. Bar Leaders (exec. coun. 1993—94), N.Y. Bar Assn., Am. Intellectual Property Law Assn., Internat. Trademark Assn. (bd. dirs. 1996—99), Licensing Exec. Soc. (chmn. N.Y. chpt. 1996—99), N.Y. Intellectual Property Law Assn. (bd. dirs. 1985—93, sec. 1988—91, pres. 1994—95), Shorehaven Golf Club, Minute Man Yacht Club, N.Y. Athletic Club. Republican. Roman Catholic. Address: 21 Covlee Dr Westport CT 06880-6407 also: 14 Deerwood Trl Lake Placid NY 12946-1834

RCLEMENT, LESLIE JOSEPH, JR. lawyer; b. Thibodaux, La., June 26, 1948; s. Leslie Joseph and Shirley Marie (Picou) C.; m. Sandra Ann Rome, June 18, 1971; children: Paul, Philip, Rebecca. BA, Nicholls State Coll., 1970; JD, La. State U., 1974. Assoc. Porteous, Toledano, Hainkel & Johnson, Thibodaux, 1974-76; ptnr. Boudreaux & Clement, 1976-78; sole practice, 1978—. Served to 1st lt. La. N.G., 1970-76. Mem. ABA, La. Bar Assn., Lafourche Parish Bar Assn., La. Trial Lawyers Assn. Republican. Roman Catholic. Office: 409 Canal Blvd Thibodaux LA 70301-3413 E-mail: clement@cajun.net.

RE, EDWARD DOMENIC, law educator, retired federal judge; b. Santa Marina, Italy, Oct. 14, 1920; s. Anthony and Marina (Maetta) R.; m. Margaret A. Corcoran, June 3, 1950; children: Mary Ann, Anthony John, Marina, Edward, Victor, Margaret, Matthew, Joseph, Mary Elizabeth, Mary Joan, Mary Ellen, Nancy Madeleine. BS cum laude, St. John's U., 1941, LLB summa cum laude, 1943, LLD (hon.), 1968; JSD, NYU, 1950; DPed (hon.), Aquila, Italy, 1960; LL.D. (hon.), St. Mary's Coll., Notre Dame, Ind., 1968, Maryville Coll., St. Louis, 1969, N.Y. Law Sch., 1976, Bklyn. Coll., CUNY, 1978, Nova U., 1980, Roger Williams Coll., 1982, Dickinson Sch. Law, Carlisle, Pa., 1983, Seton Hall U., 1984, Stetson U., 1990, William Mitchell Coll. Law, 1992, St. Francis Coll., Bklyn., 1993; L.H.D. (hon.), DePaul U., 1980, Coll. S.I., CUNY, 1981, Pace U., 1985, Am. U. of Rome, 1995; D.C.S. (hon.), U. Verona, Italy, 1987; JD (hon.), U. Bologna, Italy, 1988, U. Urbino, 1994. Bar: N.Y. 1943. Appointed faculty St. John's U., N.Y., 1947, prof. law, 1951-69, adj. prof. law, 1969-80, Disting. prof., from 1980; vis. prof. Georgetown U. Sch. Law, 1962-67; adj. prof. law N.Y. Law Sch., 1972-82, Martin disting. vis. prof., 1982-90; spl. hearing officer U.S. Dept. Justice, 1956-61; chmn. Fgn. Claims Settlement Commn. of U.S., 1961-68; asst. sec. ednl. and cultural affairs U.S. Dept. State, 1968-69; judge U.S. Customs Ct. (now U.S. Ct. Internat. Trade), N.Y.C., 1969-91, chief judge, 1977-91, chief judge emeritus, 1991—. Mem. Jud. Conf. U.S., 1986-91, adv. com. on appellate rules, 1976-88, com. on internat. jud. rels., 1994-97; chmn. adv. com. on experimentation in the law Fed. Jud. Ctr., 1978-81; mem. bd. higher edn. City of N.Y., 1958-69, emeritus, 1969—; Jackson lectr. Nat. Coll. State Trial Judges, U. Nev., 1970. Author: Foreign Confiscations in Anglo-American Law, 1951, (with Lester D. Orfield) Cases and Materials on International Law, rev. edit., 1965, Selected Essays on Equity, 1955, Brief Writing and Oral Argument, 6th edit., 1987, (with Joseph R. Re) 8th edit., 1999, (with Zechariah Chafee Jr.) Cases and Materials on Equity, 1967, Cases and Materials on Equitable Remedies, 1975; (with Joseph R. Re) Law Students' Manual on Legal Writing and Oral Argument, 1991; chpt., freedom in internat. soc. Concept of Freedom (editor Rev. Carl W. Grindel), 1955; Cases and Materials on Remedies, 1982, (with Joseph R. Re) 5th edit., 2000; contbr. articles to legal jours. Served with USAAF, 1943-47; col. JAGD, ret. Decorated Grand Cross Order of Merit Italy; recipient Am. Bill of Rights citation; Morgenstern Found. Interfaith award; USAF commendation medal; Distinguished service award Bklyn. Jr. C. of C., 1956 Mem. ABA (ho. of dels. 1976-78, chmn. sect. internat. and comparative law 1965-67), Am. Fgn. Law Assn. (pres. 1971-73), Am. Law Inst., Fed. Bar Coun. (pres. 1973-74), Am. Soc. Comparative Law (pres. 1969-91), Am. Justinian Soc. Jurists (pres. 1974-76), Internat. Assn. Jurists: Italy-USA (pres. 1991—), Internat. Assn. Judges (prin. rep. to UN 1993-2000), Scribes Am. Soc. Writers on Legal Subjects (pres. 1978). Home: 305 B 147th St Neponsit NY 11694 Office: 305 B 147th St Neponsit NY 11694

REA, ANN HADLEY KUEHN, social organization marketing administrator; b. Arlington, Va., Oct. 14, 1962; d. Alvin Henry Kuehn and Barbara Ann Schanzenbach; m. Burt Richard Rea, June 30, 1990; 3 children. BA in Communications, Va. Poly. Inst. & State U., Blacksburg, 1984; MA in Liberal Studies, Georgetown U., Washington, 1993. Desk asst., prodn. asst. ABC News, Washington, 1986—88; media/info. officer Embassy of Australia, 1988—90; mktg. dir. The Connection for Women & Families, Summit, NJ, 1992—2002. Mem. LWV. Episcopalian.

REA, ANN W. librarian; b. Jefferson City, Mo., Aug. 3, 1944; d. William H. and Ruby (Fogleman) Webb; m. Glen N. Rea, Sept. 28, 1974; children: Sarah, Rebecca. BA, U. Mo., 1966; MLS, U. So. Calif., 1968. Libr. St. Charles (Mo.) County Libr., 1967-71; libr. adult svcs. Paterson (N.J.) Free Pub. Libr., 1971-74; libr. Beal Coll. Libr., Bangor, Maine, 1983—. Treas. Bairnet; trustee Hammond St. Congl. Ch. Mem. MLA (scholarship and loan com.), Am. Libr. Assn., Maine Libr. Assn. Office: Beal Coll Libr 629 Main St Bangor ME 04401-6848 E-mail: annrea@maine.edu.

REA, BURT RICHARD, management consultant; b. Bryan, Tex., May 29, 1961; s. Billy Craig and Nancy Louise (Fisher) R.; m. Ann Hadley Kuehn, June 30, 1990; 3 children. BSEE, U. Ariz., 1984; MBA, U. Pa., 1991. Sr. mgr. Deloitte Consulting, N.Y.C., 1991—. Capt. U.S. Army, 1984-89. Mem. Inst. of Mgmt. Cons. Episcopalian. Office: Deloitte Consulting Two World Financial Ctr New York NY 10281-1414

REA, JAMES JASON, engineer; b. East Greenwich, R.I., Jan. 30, 1958; s. James Francis and Sharon (Meives) R.; m. Maria Anna Frauchiger, Mar. 24, 1995; children: James Erich, Timothy Mark. BS in Conservation Sci., Fort Lewis Coll., 1986; postgrad., U. Montana. Envriontl. coord. Benson Motin Greer Drilling Co., Farmington, New Mexico, 1987; health physics technician Chem-Nuclear Systems, Inc., Albuquerque, 1988-89; project mgr. Briggs Assocs. Inc., Rockland, Mass., 1989-91; cons. Arthur D. Little, Cambridge, 1991-95; environtl. cons. UBS, Zurich, 1996; mgr. environtl. risk engring. Zurich Ins. Co., 1997—. Contbr. articles to profl. publs. Mem. Health Physics Soc., Am. Chem. Soc., Am. Soc. of Safety Engrs, Am. Soc. of Testing Materials. Avocations: skiing, mountain climbing.

READ, ALLAN ALEXANDER, minister; b. Toronto, Ont., Can., Sept. 19, 1923; s. Alec P. and Lillice (Matthews) R.; m. Mary Beverly Roberts, Sept. 28, 1949; children— John Allan, Elizabeth Anne, Peter Michael, Martha Ruth. BA, U. Toronto, Can., 1946; Licentiate in Theology, Trinity Coll., Toronto, 1947, D.D., 1972, Wycliffe Coll., 1972; D.S.T. (hon.), Thornloe Coll., Sudbury, Ont., 1982. Ordained diaconate, 1948, priest, 1949, Anglican Ch. of Can.; lic. Diocese of Albany, N.Y., 1996—. Rector 7 chs. Diocese Toronto-Anglican Ch., Parish of East and West Mono, Ont., Can., 1947-54; rector Diocese of Toronto-Trinity Anglican Ch., Christ Ch. Vespra, Barrie, Can., 1954-72; founder Barrie East End Mission, Parish of St. Giles, 1954; chaplain Simcoe County Gaol, 1954-72; Suffragan bishop Diocese of Toronto-Anglican Ch., Toronto, Ont., Can., 1972-81; bishop Diocese of Ont., Kingston, Can., 1981-92. Canon St. James Cathedral, Toronto, 1957-61; mem., chmn. provincial synod rural chmn. com., 1953-63, Diocese of Toronto Exec. Com., 1959-71, Diocesan Com. Prayer and Evang., 1950-70, Ont. Guelph Agr. Coll. Planning Com. on Courses for Clergy in Rural Areas, 1950-54, Anglican Gen. Synod Com. on Ministry in Rural Areas, 1952-65; Diocesan Com. Corrections, 1950-72, Gen. Synod Com. Music and Hymn Book, 1965-71, chmn. and chaplin, Boy Scout Com., Barrie #1, 1954-71, Govt. of Ont. Dept. Lands and Forests adv. com. on reforestation, 1950-54, provincial synod, 1955-91, rural ch. unit gen. synod Anglican Ch. Can., 1959-89; archdeacon of Simcoe, 1961-72, Can. churchmn. bd. trustees; participant World Anglican Congress, Toronto, 1963; mem. Anglican World Wide Lambeth Conf., 1978, 88; dir. Anglican Found., Toronto; priest-in-charge St. Patrick's Cathedral, Trim, Ireland, 1992, Parish of Dunster Diocese of Bath and Wells, Eng., 1993, Parish of St. Ippolyts, Diocese St. Alban's, Eng., 1994, Parish of St. Mary the Virgin Westerham, Diocese of Rochester Eng., 1995, Cathedral of St. John and St. Patrick, Ch. of Ireland, Eire, 1956; hon. asst. St. George's Cath., Kingston, Ont., 1992—; assoc. priest St. Anne's Eastons Corners, 1998-2001, Merrickville and Beveritto Rapids, 1993—. Author: Unto The Hills, 1951; Shepherds in Green Pastures, 1953. Patron Grenville Christian Coll., Brockville, Ont., 1981—; mem., hon. pres. Can. Coll. Organists, Simcoe Br., 1954-71; hon. Reeve, Black Creek Pioneer Village, 1981-82; mem. Barrie and Dist. High Sch. Bd., 1961-70; exec. com. Alcohol and Drug Concerns, 1971-83; asst. organist Grace Ch.-on-the-Hill, Toronto, 1941-47; hon. asst. St. George's Cathedral, Kingston, 1991—. Recipient Rural Workers Fellowship award Episcopal Ch. U.S., 1952, Citizenship awards Gov. of Ont., 1980, 85, 90; named Citizen of Yr. City of Barrie, 1967; adopted by Mohawks, Bay of Quinte, Deseronto with Mohawk names Tehahswahthe:than=the one who lights the way. Mem. Rural Workers Fellowship (hon. pres. 1967—), Barrie Ministerial Assn. (sec. 1954-81). Home: 39 Riverside Dr RR 1 Kingston ON Canada K7L 4V1

READ, DALE GILBERT, endocrinologist, educator; b. Louin, Miss., Aug. 6, 1937; s. Webster B. and Laura Katherine (Gilbert) R.; m. Virginia Hall, Mar. 5, 1960; children: Laura, D. Gilbert Jr., Eva Marie. Student, Jones County C.C., Ellisville, Miss., 1955-57, Miss. State U., 1957-58; MD, U. Miss., 1962. Diplomate Am. Bd. Internal Medicine, Endocrinology and Metabolism. Resident internal medicine U. Miss. Med. Ctr., Jackson, 1962-63, 65-68; fellow endocrinology U. Ala. Med. Ctr., Birmingham, 1968-70; endocrinolgist Jackson Med. Clinic, 1971—. Asst. prof., clin. asst. prof., clin. assoc. prof. medicine U. Miss. Med. Ctr., Jackson, 1970—; dir. diabetes sect. Miss. Bapt. Med. Ctr., Jackson, 1990—. Capt. U.S. Army, 1963-65. Fellow ACP, Am. Coll. Endocrinology; mem. AMA, Am. Diabetes Assn., Am. Assn. Clin. Endocrinologists, Endocrine Soc. Methodist. Avocations: hunting, photography, tree farming. Office: Jackson Med Clinic 501 Marshall St Jackson MS 39202-1687

READ, DAVID THOMAS, physicist; b. Seattle, Sept. 17, 1947; s. John Paul and Louise Marie (Smyth) R.; m. Susan Marie Voss, Aug. 19, 1972; children—Michael, Philip, Elizabeth, Angela. B.S. in Physics, U. Santa Clara (Calif.), 1969; M.S. in Physics, U. Ill., 1971, Ph.D. in Physics, 1974. Postdoctoral physicist Nat. Bur. Standards, Boulder, Colo., 1975-76, physicist, 1977— , group leader, 1983-87. Contbr. articles to tech. jours., chpt. to book. Mem. Am. Phys. Soc., ASTM. Home: 3320 Longwood Ave Boulder CO 80305-7204 Office: Nat Inst Standards and Tech 325 Broadway St # 853 Boulder CO 80305-3337

READ, JAMES CARROLL, geneticist educator; b. Stephenville, Tex., Aug. 28, 1940; s. Edgar L. and LaRUe (Webber) R.; m. Patricia Ann Higgins, Mar. 24, 1969 (dec.); children: Tambria L., Heather L., Pattillo H., Jeannette L.; m. Bonnie Kay Zimmerman, Nov. 3, 2001. BS in agrl. edn., Tex. A&M Univ., 1966, MS plant breeding, 1969, PhD in genetics, 1971. Rsch. geneticist USDA ARS, Salinas, Calif., 1971-74; asst. prof. Tex. A&M Univ., Dallas, 1974-81, assoc. prof., 1981-99, prof., 1999—. Higher pvt. edn. task force Dallas Ind. Sch. Dist., 1978-81; cons. B. Johnson, Inc.,Dallas, 1987. Contbr. articles to profl. jours. Pres. Plano Lions Club, 1984, election judge Collin County, Plano, 1995; bd. dirs. Tex. Forage & Grassland Coun., 1992-95. Recipient NDEA fellowhip U.S. Gov., 1969. Mem. Am. Soc. Agronomy, Crop Sci. Soc. Am., Soc. for Range Mgmt., Am. Forage and Grassland Coun. (merit award 1999), Tex. Forage Workers (pres. 1994-95), Alpha Zeta, Phi Kappa Phi, Gamm Sigma Delta. Republican. Presbyterian. Avocations: golf, hunting. Office: Tex A&M Univ 17360 Coit Rd Dallas TX 75252-6502 E-mail: j-read@tamu.edu.

READ, SISTER JOEL, academic administrator; BS in Edn., Alverno Coll., 1948; MA in History, Fordham U., 1951; hon. degree, Lakeland Coll., 1972, Wittenburg U., 1976, Marymount Manhattan Coll., 1978, DePaul U., 1985, Northland Coll., 1986, SUNY, 1986, Lawrence U., 1997. Former prof., dept. chmn. history dept. Alverno Coll., Milw., pres., 1968—. Past pres. Am. Assn. for Higher Edn., 1976-77; mem. coun. NEH, 1977-84; bd. dirs. Ednl. Testing Svc., 1987-93, Neylan Commn., 1985-90; past pres. Wis. Assn. Ind. Colls. and Univs.; mem. Commn. on Status of Edn. for Women, 1971-76, Am. Assn. Colls., 1971-77. Bd. dirs. Jr. Achievement, State of Wis. Coll. Savs. Bd., Greater Milw. Com., YMCA, Profl. Dimensions, Wis. Found. Ind. Colls., 1990-99, Women's Philanthropy Inst., 1997-2000, Wis. Women Higher Edn. Leadership, 1997-2000. First recipient Anne Roe award Harvard U. Grad. Sch. Edn., 1980; recipient Morris T. Keaton award, Coun. for Adult and Experiential Learning, 1992; recipient Jean B. Harris award, Rotary; Paul Harris fellow, Rotary. Fellow Am. Acad. Arts and Scis., Wis. Acad. Arts and Scis. Office: Alverno Coll Office of Pres PO Box 343922 Milwaukee WI 53234-3922 E-mail: joel.read@alverno.edu.

READ, JOHN CONYERS, non-profit management consultant; b. N.Y.C., May 21, 1947; s. Edward Cameron Kirk and Louise (Geary) R.; m. Alexandra Gould, Mar. 30, 1968; children: Cameron Kirk, Trevor Conyers, Alexandra. AB, Harvard, 1969, MBA, 1971. Ops. rsch. analyst HEW, Washington, 1971-72; exec. asst. to dir. Cost of Living Council, 1973; chief econ. adviser to Gov. Mass., 1974; exec. asst., counselor to sec. labor Washington, 1975; asst. sec. labor for employment standards, 1976-77; dir. corp. employee rels., pers. Cummins Engine Co., Columbus, Ind., 1977-80, plant mgr., 1980-85; v.p. Midrange Engines, 1986-90; v.p., gen. mgr. engine group Donaldson Co., Inc., Mpls., 1990-92; exec. v.p., 1992-94; ptnr. Hidden Creek Industries, Mpls., 1996—; pres., CEO Heavy Duty Holdings, 1997-2000; pres. Read Ptnrs. Inc., 2001—02, Outward Bound U.S.A., Garrison, NY, 2002—. Cons. nat. productivity and energy policies; chmn. NAM Task Force on Wage and Price Policies, 1978-80; bd. dirs. MAC Equipment Co., Active Leasing Co. Author Ford Found. monograph on occupational disease and workers' compensation; contbr. articles to newspapers and mags. Trustee Nat. Ctr. Occupl. Readjustment, 1984-87; trustee N.C. Outward Bound Sch., dir., 1995—, chmn., 1997-2000; chmn. Charleston Pvt. Industry Coun., 1985; mem. plant closing task force U.S. Dept. Labor, 1986, mfg. task force NRC, 1989, critical industries task force Def. Dept., 1989. Mem. Nat. Assn. Mfrs. (bd. dirs., chair employee rels. com. 1993-95). Home: 2697 E Lake Of The Isles Pkwy Minneapolis MN 55408-1051

READ, MICHAEL OSCAR, editor, consultant; b. Amarillo, Tex., July 11, 1942; s. Harold Eugene and Madeline (Welch) R.; m. Jill Kay Vanderby, July 6, 1963 (div. Apr. 1967); 1 child, Rebecca Anne; m. Fawn Dale Barby, Apr. 10, 1977; 1 child, Nathan Michael. AA in Chemistry, Amarillo Coll., 1962; BA in Journalism, Tex. Tech. U., 1965. News editor Olton (Tex.) Enterprise, 1963-64; reporter, photographer Lubbock (Tex.) Avalanche-Jour., 1964-67, copy editor, 1967-70, city editor, 1970-72; copy editor Houston Post, 1972-74, systems editor, 1974-89, dir. news tech., 1989-95; electronic media content coord. Houston Chronicle, 1995-2000, web ops. and devel. editor, 2000—. Bd. dirs. Shell Employees Fed. Credit Union, Houston, 2001—, vice chmn., 2002—, supervisory com., 1996-2001; tchr. Let's Compute!, Stafford, Tex., 1985—; cons. Newspaper Pub. Sys., Stafford, 1989—; mem. joint Newspaper

Assn. Am.-Internat. Press. Telecomm. Coun. Com. Wire Svc. Standards; mem. adv. bd. Found. for Am. Comms. FACSNET; chmn. adv. com. Sch. of Mass. Comm., Tex. Tech U. Author weekly newspaper column, 1977—. Vol. United Way, Houston, 1973—; bd. dirs. Meadows (Tex.) Community Improvement Assn., 1985-95, Meadows Utility Dist., 1988-93, Meadows Econ. Devel. Corp., 1994-99. Named among Outstanding Alumni, Tex. Tech U. Sch. Mass Comms., 2001; Eldon Durrett scholar, 1961-65. Mem. Am. MENSA, Am. Philatelic Soc., Am. 1st Day Cov. Soc. (life), U.S. Chess Fedn. (life), Soc. Profl. Journalists (conv. com. 1989-90), Press Club of Houston. Avocations: philately, photography, gardening. Office: Houston Chronicle 801 Texas St Houston TX 77002-2996 Home: 215 Lakeside Blvd Sugar Land TX 77478-3957 E-mail: mike.read@chron.com.

READ, NICHOLAS CARY, lawyer; b. Florence, Italy, Nov. 9, 1951; came to U.S., 1952; s. Forrest Godfrey III and Virginia (Cary) R.; m. Anne Parker Renfro, May 16, 1976; children: Sarah, Joanna. BFA, U. N.C., 1974; MA in History, U. Va., 1979, JD, 1982. Bar: Mass. 1982, U.S. Dist. Ct. Mass. 1982. Assoc. Craig & Macauley, Boston, 1982-85; counsel N.E. Merchants Leasing Co., 1985-87; sr. counsel Boston Safe Deposit and Trust Co., 1987—. Office: Boston Safe Deposit & Trust Co 1 Boston Pl Boston MA 02108-4407

READ, PIERS PAUL, author; b. Beaconsfield, Eng., Mar. 7, 1941; s. Herbert Edward and Margaret (Ludwig) R.; m. Emily Albertine Boothby, July 29, 1967; children: Albert Nathaniel, Martha Marianna, William Edward, Beatrice Mary. BA, St. John's Coll., Cambridge U., 1962, MA, 1963. Sub-editor Times Lit. Supplement, 1963-64. Adj. prof. writing Columbia U., 1980; lit. panel mem. Arts Coun. Gt. Britain, 1974-76; gov. Cardinal Manning Boys Sch., 1985; chmn. Cath. Writers Guild, 1993-97. Author: (novels) Game in Heaven with Tussy Marx, 1966, The Junkers, 1968 (Sir Geoffrey Faber Meml. prize 1969), Monk Dawson, 1970 (Somerset Maugham award, Hawthornden prize 1970), The Professor's Daughter, 1971, The Upstart, 1973, Polonaise, 1976, A Married Man, 1980, The Villa Golitsyn, 1982, The Free Frenchman, 1986, A Season in the West, 1988 (James Tait Black Meml. prize), On the Third Day, 1990, The Patriot, 1995, Knights of the Cross, 1997, (non-fiction) Alive: The Story of the Andes Survivors, 1974 (Thomas More medal), The Train Robbers, 1978, Ablaze: The Heros and Victims of Chernobyl, 1993, The Patriot, 1996, Knights of the Cross, 1997, The Templars, 1999, The Gospel of St. John: The Story of the Son of God, 1999, Alice in Exile, 2001, (TV plays) Coincidence, The Family Firm, The House of Highbury Hill. Mem. Brit. bd. of Aid to Church in Need, 1988. Ford Found. fellow, 1963-64; Harkness fellow, 1967-68 Fellow Royal Soc. Lit.; mem. Soc. Authors (com. mgmt. 1972-74), Inst. Contemporary Arts (com. mgmt. 1972-74) Roman Catholic. Address: 50 Portland Rd W11 4LG London England E-mail: piersread@dial.pipex.com.

READ, RICHARD EATON, newspaper reporter; b. St. Andrews, Scotland, Sept. 3, 1957; s. Arthur H. and Katharine (Eaton) R.; m. Kim R. Kunkle, July 26, 1986; 1 child, Nehalem Kunkle-Read. BA in English, Amherst Coll., 1980; postgrad., Harvard U., 1996-97. Press sec. Mass. Commn. on State and County Bldgs., 1980; staff writer The Oregonian, 1981-86; fellow The Henry Luce Found./The Nation, Bangkok, Thailand, 1986-87; freelance writer Tokyo, 1987-89; Asia bur. chief The Oregonian, 1989-94; sec., 1st dir., 1st v.p. Fgn. Corrs. Club of Japan, 1990-93; internat. bus. writer The Oregonian, Portland, 1994-99, sr. writer internat. affairs, 1999—. Recipient Pulitzer prize for explanatory reporting, 1999, Overseas Press Club award for bus. reporting from abroad, 1999, Scripps Howard Found. award for bus. reporting, 1999, Blethen award for enterprise reporting Pacific Northwest Newspaper Assn., 1999, 2001, Oreg. Gov.'s award for achievement in internat. bus., 2000, Pulitzer prize for pub. svc., 2001, Unity award in media investigative reporting, Lincoln U., 2001, Blethen award, 2001, Bruce Baer award, 2001, Media Leadership award Am. Immigration Lawyers Assn., 2001; named Internat. Citizen of Yr. 1999 World Affairs Coun. Oreg., named Internat. Citizen of Yr. 2002 Oreg. Assn. Consuls Gen., Internat. Citizen of Yr., Oreg. Counsular Corps, 2001; Eisenhower Exch. fellow, Peru, 1997; Nieman fellow, 1996-97.

READDY, WILLIAM F. astronaut, retired military officer; b. Quonset Point, R.I., Jan. 24, 1952; s. Francis Readdy; m. Coleen Nevius; 3 children. BS in Aerospace Engring., USN Acad., Annapolis, 1974; Disting. grad., U.S. Naval Test Pilot Sch., 1980. Commd. ensign USN, Annapolis, 1974, advanced through grades to capt., retired, 2000; pilot A-6 Intruder USN , USS Forrestal, 1976—80; project pilot Strike Aircraft Test Directorate, 1980—82; test pilot instr. USN, Patuxent River, Md., 1982—84, carrier pilot USS Coral Sea, 1984—86, transferred to naval reserve, 1986; rsch. pilot, program mgr. Shuttle Carrier Aircraft NASA Ellington Field, Houston, 1986; astronaut NASA Johnson Space Ctr. , 1987—. Decorated Legion of Merit, Disting. Flying Cross; named Instr. of Yr., U.S. Naval Test Pilot Sch., 1984; recipient 3 Space Flight medals, NASA, Kamarov Diploma, Fedn. Aeronatique Internat., De La Vaux medal, World Record Cert. Achievements include over 7000 flight hours, 60 tpes of fixed wing and helicopters aircraft, 550 carrier landings, 3 space flights, 672 hours in space. Avocations: flying, reading, sailing, racquet sports. Office: Astronaut office/CB Johnson Space Ctr Houston TX 77058

READE, LEWIS POLLOCK, business executive, retired diplomat, engineer; b. N.Y.C., Nov. 1, 1932; s. Herman Ross and Dorothy Stella (Pollock) R.; m. Anne Carol Kulka, July 3, 1953 (div. Feb. 1968); children: Steven Gordon, Nicholas Edward; m. Margaret Ann Kilpatrick, Mar. 30, 1968; 1 child, Jonathan Collins. BS in Mech. Engrin., U. Miami, 1953; postgrad., Hofstra U., 1953-54, U. Balt., 1957-59, U. N.Mex., 1997—. Product engr. Sperry Gyroscope, Lake Success, N.Y., 1953-54; project engr. ARMA, Garden City, 1954-55; field engr. Westinghouse Electric Corp., Balt. & Rome, 1957-66; v.p. Westinghouse Learning Corp., Washington & Pitts., 1966-70; v.p. corp. planning & devel. Tyco Labs., Waltham, Mass., 1970-71; chmn., chief exec. officer, treas. Kellett Corp., Willow Grove, Pa., 1971-72; exec. v.p. Big Bros./Big Sisters of Am., Phila., 1973-80; mission dir. U.S. Agy. Internat. Devel., Kingston, Jamaica, 1982-85; sr. dep. asst. adminstr. Pvt. Enterprise Bur., Washington, 1985-86; mission dir. U.S. Agy. Internat. Devel., Amman, Jordan, 1986-90, Jakarta, Indonesia, 1990-92; dir. gen. U.S.-Asia Environ. Partnership, Washington, 1992-97; ret., 1997; pres., CEO Jordan-U.S. Bus. Partnership, Amman, 1998—. Bd. dirs. Vista de la Mont. Civic Assn. Sgt. US Army, 1955-57. Mem. Soc. Internat. Devel., Am. Fgn. Svc. Assn., Am. Club (Amman). Home: 42 Vista Montana Loop Placitas NM 87043-9518

READER, GEORGE G. retired internal-public health medicine educator; b. Bklyn., 1919; m. Helen Brown, May 23, 1942; 4 children. BA in Animal Biology, Cornell U., Ithaca, N.Y., 1940; MD, Cornell U., N.Y.C., 1943; ScD (hon.) , Drew U., 1988. Intern in medicine N.Y. Hosp., N.Y.C., 1944-45, resident and fellow in medicine, 1946—50, resident in hematology, 1950—51; instr. medicine Cornell U. Med. Ctr., 1951—52, from asst. prof. to prof., 1952—89, emeritus prof. medicine, 1989—, Livingston Farrand prof. pub. health, 1989—. Former advisor Social Security Adminstrn.; former chmn. human ecology study sect. NIH; former chmn. tech. com. on tng. White House Conf. on Aging; former cons. OEO, Office Sec. of HEW, Health Svcs. and Mental Health Adminstrn.; head transition task force health adv. coun. N.Y. State Dept. Health, 1974—84; former chmn. N.Y. State Task Force on Health of Sch. Age Child and Health Manpower; rep. Cornell U. Med. Ctr. in Health Planning for N.Y.C.; mem. master plan com. N.Y.C. Hosp. Coun. Mem. N.Y.C. Mayor's Organized Task Force for Health Planning; mem. local planning bd. representing N.Y. Hosp., Health Sys. Agy., N.Y.C. Scholar Regents scholar, Cornell U., 1940. Mem.: Inst. of Medicine (sr.), Skulls. Office: Cornell U/Weill Med Coll Dept Pub Health 1300 York Ave # 73 New York NY 10021-4805

READER, JONATHAN WHITTIER, sociology educator, consultant; b. N.Y.C., July 19, 1944; s. George Gordon and Helen (Brown) R. BA in Govt., Cornell U., Ithaca, N.Y., 1966, PhD in Sociology, 1981; MPA, N.Y.U., 1969. Lt. USPHS, Washington, 1968-70; cons. project office Linton, Mields & Costen, 1969-70; rsch. adminstr. Cornell U., Ithaca, 1972-80; prof. sociology Drew U., Madison, N.J., 1980—. Cons. Trans Century Corp., El Paso, Tex., 1969-70, Conf. Mayors, Washington, 1970, Stockton (N.J.) State U., 1970, Local 32B and J, N.Y.C., 1982-84, 88. Author, co-author some 20 scholarly articles, papers, revs. and rsch. reports on local govt. fiscal policy, corp. mergers, innovations in med. tech., other subjects; appeared in movie Meeting the Beautiful People, 1994. Bd. dirs. N.J. Cheetah, Mendham, 1998—, Conservation Fund. Dissertation fellow U.S. Dept. Housing and Urban Renewal. Mem. Am. Sociology Soc. Democrat. Avocations: tennis, dancing, theatre, American presidents, birding. Home: 42B Loantaka Way Madison NJ 07940 Office: Drew U 36 Madison Ave Madison NJ 07940 E-mail: JReader@Drew.edu.

READING, ANTHONY JOHN, physician, department chairman; b. Sydney, Australia, Sept. 10, 1933; s. Abe Stanley and Esma Daisy R.; m. Elisabeth Ann Hoffman, July 27, 1975; children— Wendy Virginia Elisabeth, Sarah Alexandra Jane. M.B., BS, U. Sydney, 1956; M.P.H., Johns Hopkins U., 1961, Sc.D., 1964. Intern Sydney Hosp., 1957-58; resident in psychiatry Johns Hopkins Hosp., Balt., 1965-68; asst. prof. psychiatry and medicine Johns Hopkins U. Sch. Medicine, 1968-73, assoc. prof. psychiatry, 1973-75, dir. psychiat. liaison service, 1974-75; dir. comprehensive alcoholism program Johns Hopkins Hosp., 1972-75; prof. U. South Fla. Coll. Medicine, 1975—, chmn. dept. psychiatry and behavioral medicine, 1975—2002, assoc. dean, 1993-96. Mem. AMA, AAAS, Am. Psychiat. Assn. Home: 1171 Shipwatch Cir Tampa FL 33602-5787 Office: 3515 E Fletcher Ave Tampa FL 33613-4706 E-mail: areading@hsc.usf.edu.

READING, ANTHONY JOHN, business executive, accountant; b. London, Aug. 8, 1943; came to U.S., 1993; m. Myra Elizabeth Steer, Aug. 27, 1966; 1 child, Jason. Chartered acct. Mng. dir., dir. mfg., dir. fin. Donaldson Co. Inc., Brussels, 1970-80; group exec. Thomas Tilling Plc, London, 1980-83; divisional group chief exec. BTR Plc, 1983-87; group mng. dir. Polly Peck Internat., 1987-89, Pepe Group Plc, London, 1989-90; divisional dir. Tomkins Plc, 1990-92, also bd. dirs.; chmn., CEO Tomkins Corp., Dayton, Ohio, 1992—. Chmn. Orgn. Internat. Investment, Washington. Named Mem. of Most Excellent Order of Brit. Empire, Her Majesty Queen Elizabeth II, 1978. Fellow Inst. Chartered Accts. Eng. and Wales, Inst. Mgmt. Eng.; mem. Naval and Mil. Club London. Avocations: music, golf, water sports. Office: Tomkins Corp 4801 Springfield St Dayton OH 45431-1084 E-mail: areading@tomkins-industries.com.

READING, JAMES EDWARD, transportation executive; b. Milw., June 26, 1924; s. James Edwards and Helen Marie (Boehm) R.; m. Ada Irene Kelly, May 24, 1944; children: Wendy Irene, James David, Christopher Kelly, Mary Katherine, Kevin Sinclair. Student, San Diego State U., 1942, Ga. Inst. Tech., 1944. With Union-Tribune Pub. Co., San Diego, 1942-59, dist. mgr., 1953-58, circulation promotion mgr., 1958-59; adminstrv. asst. to v.p. Copley Newspapers, La Jolla, Calif., 1959-60; dir. advt. and pub. rels. San Diego Transit System, 1960-67; dir. mktg. Calif. Motor Express, 1967-68; asst. to exec. v.p. Am. Transit Assn., Washington, 1968; v.p. Nat. City Mgmt. Co.; resident mgr. Regional Transit Service, Rochester, N.Y., 1968-74; asst. gen. mgr. ops. Regional Transit Dist., Denver, 1974-77; gen. mgr. Central Ohio Transit Authority, Columbus, 1977-85; dir. Santa Clara County Transp. Agy., San Jose, Calif., 1985-90; ind. cons. San Diego, 1990—. Treas. San Diego State U. Continuing Edn. Ctr., Rancho Bernardo; lectr. in field. Served with U.S. Army, 1943-46, ETO. Named Public Relations Man of Yr. Public Relations Club, San Diego, 1962; recipient Urban Mass Transp. Adminstrs. award for outstanding pub. service, 1980, 82; charter mem. Herbert Hoover H.S. Achievement Hall of Fame, San Diego, 1998; named to Rancho Bernardo Hall of Fame, 2000. Mem. Am. Pub. Transit Assn. (bd. dirs., past v.p., elected Hall of Fame 1995), Am. Legion, Rotary Club Rancho Bernardo (past pres.), Press Club of Rancho Bernardo (past pres.), Rancho Bernardo Spirit of Fourth (past pres.), Tau Kappa Epsilon. Republican. Roman Catholic. Home: 11728 Caminito Corriente San Diego CA 92128-4548

READING, PHYLLIS ANN, social welfare administrator; b. Seattle, Apr. 21, 1954; ADN, Shoreline C.C., Seattle, 1975; BSN, Seattle U., 1979; M Nursing in Adminstrn., U. Wash., 1988. RN, Wash., Calif. Relief charge nurse CCU Group Health Hosp., Redmond, Wash., 1979-81; relief supr. pheresis unit Puget Sound Blood Ctr., Seattle, 1981-83; coord. critical care Snoqualmie (Wash.) Valley Hosp., 1983-85, asst. adminstr., 1985-89; staff devel. specialist U. Wash. Med. Ctr., Seattle, 1989-93; edn. specialist AACN, Aliso Viejo, Calif., 1993-94, program devel. and meeting svcs. dir., 1994-96, dir. profl. devel., 1996-97, exec. dir., 1997-2000, program dir. Ctr. for Leadership Excellence, 1994-96, exec. prodr. satellite video confs., 1994-96; exec. dir. Nat. Assistance League, L.A., 2000—. Mem. nat. faculty tchg. improvement project sys. Kellogg Found., 1992. Mem. adv. bd. N.W. Emergency Physicians, Seattle, 1985-89; bd. dirs. Am. Cancer Soc., Kirkland, Wash., 1988-89. Mem. AACN

READY, CHRISTOPHER JAMES, accountant; b. Somerset, Mass., Aug. 3, 1966; s. Daniel F. and Dorothy T. (McViney) R.; m. Mary E. Durand, May 30, 1992. BS in Acctg. cum laude, U. Mass. Dartmouth, 1992; MBA with honors, Bryant Coll., 1998. Sr. acct. Furon Co., Bristol, R.I., 1992-95; cost acct. Uvex Safety, Inc., Smithfield, 1995-99; contr. Invensys Position Sensors, Woonsocket, 1999—. Mem. Inst. Mgmt. Accts., Beta Gamma Sigma. Avocations: golf, drums, drawing. Home: 92 Log Rd Harrisville RI 02830-1884 Office: Invensys Position Sensors 245 Railroad St Woonsocket RI 02895-3039

READY, ROBERT JAMES, financial company executive; b. Bridgeport, Conn., June 26, 1952; s. John Edward and Anne (Salata) R.; m. Margaret S. Neale, Aug. 23, 1975; children: Carolyn, Christopher and Steven (twins). AS, Housatonic Community Coll., 1972; BS, Babson Coll., 1974. CLU; chartered fin. cons.; registered fin. cons.; cert. ins. cons; cert. retirement cons.; cert. retirement adminstr. Agt. John Hancock Mut. Life Ins. Co., Hamden, Conn., 1975-77; broker Beardsley, Brown & Bassett Inc., Bridgeport, 1977-80; agt. Aetna Life and Casualty Ins. Co., Trumbull, 1980-83; v.p. Crestview Fin. Services Inc., Westport, 1983-2000, Crestview Securities Inc., Westport, 1983-2000, Crestview Investment Advisors Inc., Westport, 1983-2000; sr. v.p. ins. RDM Ins. Svcs. Inc., 2000—. Mem. Nat. Assn. Life Underwriters, Conn. Assn. Life Underwriters, Bridgeport Life Underwriters (bd. dirs. 1977), New Haven County CLU and Chartered Fin. Cons., Soc. of Fin. Svc. Profls. (Fairfield county chpt.). Roman Catholic. Avocations: golf, tennis, softball. Office: RDM Financial Group Inc 1555 Post Rd E Westport CT 06880-5602 E-mail: bready@rdmfinancial.com.

REAGAN, BARBARA BENTON, economics educator; BS with honors, U. Tex., 1941; MA in Stats., Am. U., 1947; MA in Econs., Harvard U., 1949, PhD in Econs., 1952. Econ. researcher Dept. Agr., 1942-47; sr. project leader Agrl. Research Service, Washington, 1949-55; prof. econs. Tex. Woman's U., Denton, 1959-67, So. Meth. U., Dallas, 1967-90, prof. emeritus, 1990—, chmn. dept., 1984-90, dir. interdisciplinary research project, 1969-70, dir. undergrad. studies econs. dept., 1972-75, assoc. dean Univ. Coll., 1975, asst. to pres. for student acad. services, 1975-76, pres. faculty senate, 1981-82, mem. exec. com., 1981-84; dir. Region IX Fed. Home Loan Bank, 1981-85; mem. Dallas Morning News Bd. Economists, 1982-88. Dir. Agrl. Rsch. Svc. Project, Dallas, 1970-71; mem. adv. bd. econs. USA Wharton Econometric Forecasting Assocs., 1983-85; mem. adv. bd. Nat. Women's Mus., Dallas, 1998—; reviewer NSF; disting. vis. prof. econs. Kenyon Coll., spring, 1979; bd. dirs. 1st Am. Savs. Bank, 1990-95, North Tex. Mesbic, 1991-93, Tex. Guaranteed Student Loan Corp., 1991-97, sec., exec. com., chmn. policy com., 1992-93, chmn. bd., 1993-95. Author: Economic Foundations of Labor Supply of Women, 1981; co-editor, contbg. author: Women in the Workplace: Implications of Occupational Segregation, 1976; editor, contbg. author: Issues in Federal Statistical Needs Relating to Women, 1979; bd. editors: Jour. Econ. Lit., 1977-79, Jour. Econ. Edn., 1984-92; referee profl. jours. contbr. articles to profl. publs. Mem. Nat. Adv. Food and Drug Coun., 1968-71; mem. adv. com. Nat. Rsch. Inst. on Family, 1973-76; nat. coord. on issues in fed. statis. needs for women Census Bur. Conf., 1978; mem. Tex. adv. bd. Tex Coastal Mgmt. Program, 1977-78; mem. adv. com. White House Conf. on Balance Nat. Growth and Econ. Devel., 1977-78; bd. dirs. League for Ednl. Advancement in Dallas, 1972-75; trustee, mem. instrnl. TV com. Pub. Comm. Found. North Tex., 1973-76; mem. North Tex. Coun. Govts.' Manpower Coun., 1972-74; mem. adv. bd. Women's Ctr. Dallas, 1975-79, 82-85, 95—, pres. 1981, bd. dirs. 1990-92; bd. dirs. Dallas Urban League, 1975-79, co-chmn. com. on skills bank, 1977-79; Leadership Am., 1989-90. Ferguson fellow Harvard U., 1947-49; named Outstanding Tchr., So. Meth. U. 1972; recipient Women's Ctr. Dallas award as one of Dallas Outstanding Women, 1980,So. Meth. U. M award 1972, Willis M. Tate award as outstanding faculty mem., 1982, Laurel award AAUW, 1983, Headliner award Dallas Press Club, 1985, 86, Disting. Alumna award Mary Baldwin Coll., 1986. Mem. Am. Econ. Assn. (chmn. sessions 1977, 80, chmn. com. on status of women in econs. profession 1974-78), Southwestern Social Sci. Assn. (exec. com. 1977-80, pres. 1978-79), Assn. Am. Colls. (faculty rep. 1984), Dallas Economists Club, Dallas C. of C. (com. on urban affairs 1975), Phi Beta Kappa (pres. So. Meth. U. chpt. 1975-76), Town and Gown Club (pres. 1986-87), The Dallas Summit (exec. com. 1990-92). Home: 8600 Skyline Dr Dallas TX 75243 Office: So Meth U Dept Econs Dallas TX 75275-0001 E-mail: breagan10@aol.com. *America's productivity can be improved greatly by making better use of its human resources. Equality of opportunity needs to become a reality.*

REAGAN, GARY DON, state legislator, lawyer; b. Amarillo, Tex., Aug. 23, 1941; s. Hester and Lois Irene (Marcum) R.; m. Nedra Ann Nash, Sept. 12, 1964; children: Marc Kristi, Kari, Brent. BA, Stanford U., 1963, JD, 1965. Bar: N.Mex. 1965, U.S. Dist. Ct. N.Mex. 1965, U.S. Supreme Ct. 1986. Assoc. Smith & Ransom, Albuquerque, 1965-67; ptnr. Smith, Ransom, Deaton & Reagan, 1967-68, Williams, Johnson, Houston, Reagan & Porter, Hobbs, 1968-77, Williams, Johnson, Reagan, Porter & Love, Hobbs, 1977-82; pvt. practice pvt. practice, 1982—; city atty. City of Hobbs, 1978-80, 97—, City of Eunice, N.Mex., 1980—; mem. N.Mex. State Senate, 1993-96. Instr. N.Mex. Jr. Coll. and Coll. of S.W., Hobbs, 1978-84; N.Mex. commr. Nat. Conf. Commrs. Uniform State Laws, 1993-96; adv. mem. N.Mex. Constl. Revision Commn., 1993-95. Mayor City of Hobbs, 1972-73, 76-77, city commr., 1970-78; pres., dir. Jr. Achievement of Hobbs, 1974-85; pres., trustee Landsun Homes, Inc., Carlsbad, N.Mex., 1972-84; trustee Lydia Patterson Inst., El Paso, Tex., 1972-84, N.Mex. Conf. United Meth. Ch., 1988—, Coll. S.W. Hobbs, 1989-2001; chmn. County Dem. Com., 1983-85. Mem. ABA, State Bar N.Mex. (coms. 1989-96, v.p. 1992-93, pres. 1994-95), Lea County Bar Assn. (pres. 1976-77), Hobbs C. of C. (pres. 1989-90), Rotary (pres. Hobbs 1985-86), Hobbs Tennis Club (pres. 1974-75). Home: 200 E Eagle Dr Hobbs NM 88240-5323 Office: 1819 N Turner Ste G Hobbs NM 88240-3834 E-mail: lglregan@nm.net.

REAGAN, HARRY EDWIN, III, lawyer; b. Wichita, Kans., Sept. 9, 1940; s. Harry E. II and Mary Elizabeth (O'Steen) R.; m. Marvene R. Rogers, June 17, 1965; children: Kathleen, Leigh, Mairen. BS, U. Pa., 1962, JD, 1965. Bar: Pa. 1965, U.S. Dist. Ct. (ea. dist.) Pa. 1965, U.S. Ct. Appeals (3d cir.) 1965. From assoc. to ptnr. Morgan, Lewis & Bockius, Phila., 1965-98. Chmn. Northhampton Twp. Planning Commn., Bucks County, Pa., 1974-79; mem. Warwick Twp. Planning Commn., 1980-95, chmn., 1994; supr. Warwick Twp., 1996-98; mem. San Miguel County (Colo.) Open Space Commn., 1998—, chmn., 2001—, Town of Telluride Open Space Commn., 1999—. Mem. ABA (labor sect.), Pa. Bar Assn. (labor sect.), Phila. Bar Assn. (labor sect.), Indsl. Rels. Assn. (pres. Phila. chpt. 1990-91). Republican. Presbyterian. Avocations: coaching rugby, skiing, raising horses, bicycling. Home and Office: 12350 McKenzie Springs Rd Placerville CO 81430

REAGAN, JAMES RAYMOND, safety and ergonomics consultant; b. Camden, N.J., Aug. 24, 1926; s. James Raymond and Anne Frances R.; m. Gloria Ann Smith Reagan, Jan. 2, 1950; children: Michael, Stephen, John, James, Elizabeth. BME, U. Del., Newark, 1949. Reg. profl. engr., Del.; cert. profl. ergonomist. Student opr., engr. DuPont, Chattanooga, 1949-53, line supv. Seaford, Del., 1953-56, sr. engr., 1956-58, group supv. of design, 1958-65, area supv., 1965-78, safety, health & environ. supv., 1978-88, ergonomics mgr. Wilmington, 1988-91, sr. cons., 1992—. Pres., prin. cons. Reagan Ergonomics, Palm Coast, Fla., 1991—. Author: Ergonomics Overview, 1998. Pres. Bulldog Boosters, Laurel. Del., 1974, Sussex (Del.) Engring. Soc., 1968. 1st lt. U.S. Army, 1944-47, WWII, 51-52, Korea. Recipient Environ. Respect awards (2) DuPont, Wilmington, 1990. Mem. VFW, KC, Am. Indsl. Hygiene Assn., Nat. Safety Coun., Human Factors and Ergonomics Soc., Irish Social Club, Am. Legion. Achievements include development of criteria for selecting ergonomist and training DuPont leaders and engineers in ergonomics. Home and Office: 119 Barrington Dr Palm Coast FL 32137-8870 also: DuPont Safety Resources 131 Continental Dr Ste 307 Newark DE 19713-4324

REAGAN, JANET THOMPSON, psychologist, educator; b. Sept. 15, 1945; d. Virgil Joe and Carrie mae (Alexander) Thompson; children: Natalia Alexandria, Robert Barry. BA in Psychology, Berea Coll., 1967; PhD in Psychology, Vanderbilt U., 1972. Mgr. rsch. and eval. Nashville Mental Health Ctr., 1971-72; mgr. eval. Family Health Found., New Orleans, 1973-74; asst. prof. dept. health systems mgmt. Tulane U., 1974-77; dir. eval. Project Heavy West, L.A., 1977-78; asst. prof. health adminstrn. Calif. State U.-Northridge, 1978-83; assoc. prof., dir. health adminstrn., 1983-87; prof., dir. health adminstrn., 1987—. Cons. in field. Contbr. to books, articles to profl. jours., papers to profl. assns. Mem. edtl. adv. bd. Jour. of Long Term Care Adminstrn. Mem. Am. Pub. Health Assn., Am. Coll. Health Care Adminstrn., Assn. Health Svcs. Rsch., Am. Coll. Health Care Execs. (com. on higher edn. 1987, chmn. 1991), Assn. Univ. Programs in Health Adminstrn. (task force on undergrad. edn. 1985-90, chmn. 1988-90, mem. bd. dirs. 1995, chmn. bd. dirs. 1998-99), Psi Chi, Phi Kappa Phi. Home: 9354 Encino Ave Northridge CA 91325-2414 Office: Calif State U Dept Health Sci Northridge CA 91330-0001 E-mail: janet.reagan@csun.edu.

REAGAN, JOSEPH BERNARD, retired aerospace executive, management consultant; b. Somerville, Mass., Nov. 26, 1934; s. Joseph B. and Helen Lowry R.; m. Dorothy Hughes; children: Patrick, Michael, Kevin, Kathleen, Brian, John, Maureen. BS in Physics, Boston Coll., 1956, MS in Physics, 1959; PhD in Space Sci., Stanford U., 1975; postgrad. exec. mgmt., Pa. State U., State College, 1981. Staff scientist, rsch. scientist, sr. scientist, scientist Lockheed Rsch. & Devel. Div., Palo Alto, Calif., 1959-75, mgr., 1975-84, dir., 1984-86, dep. gen. mgr., 1986-88, v.p., asst. gen. mgr., 1988-90; v.p. gen. mgr. Lockheed Missle and Space Co., 1991-96. Chmn. bd. dirs. Southwall Techs. Inc., Palo Alto. Contbr. articles to profl. jours. Bd. dirs. Tech. Mus., San Jose. Capt. U.S. Army, 1956-64. Recipient Career Achievement in Sci. award Boston Coll. Alumni Assn., 1993. Fellow AIAA (outstanding engr. San Francisco chpt. 1988); mem. Am. Geophys. Union, Nat. Acad. of Engring., Nat. Rsch. Coun. (mem. naval studies bd.). Republican. Roman Catholic. Avocations: computer and woodworking hobbies. Home and Office: 13554 Mandarin Way Saratoga CA 95070-4847 E-mail: jbr733@aol.com.

REAGAN, LARRY GAY, college vice president; b. Jackson, Tenn., Mar. 30, 1938; d. Larry Alfred and Ann Mabel (Welker) Lane. BA, Union U., 1959; MA, Tulane U., 1961; MS, Ea. Ky. U., 1971; EdD, Vanderbilt U., 1975. Instr. Ill. Coll., Jacksonville, 1961-63, Union Univ., Jackson, Tenn., 1963-64, Chipola Jr. Coll., Marianna, Fla., 1964-67; asst. prof. Campbellsville (Ky.) Coll., 1967-70; divsn. dir. arts and letters, dean acad. affairs Manatee C.C., Bradenton, Fla., 1972—; health educator Tenn. Dept. Pub. Health, Nashville, 1974-75; chair dept. Volunteer State C.C., Gallatin, Tenn., 1975-90, divsn. chair, prof., 1990-92; v.p. Shelby State C.C., Memphis, 1991-92. V.p. Nat. Inst. Leadership Devel., New Coll. Libr. Assn.; lectr. in China, England, and Mexico. Contbr. poems to profl. publs. Bd. dirs. Fla./Colombia Alliance, Marianna, 1964-67; trustee Christian Sr. Housing, Atlanta, 1990—; pres. Tenn. Assn. of Women in C.C.'s, Nashville, 1991-92; mem. Manatee Cultural Alliance, Bradenton, 1993—. Recipient citation award Mex. Sec. of Edn., 1983, award Nat. Inst. Leadership, 1989. Mem. AAUW, AAHPERD, LWV, Am. Assn. Women in C.C.'s (keynote speaker, regional dir., v.p.), Fla. Assn. Women in C.C.'s (bd. dirs. 1993—), Nat. Coun. Instrnl. Adminstrn., Rotary Club, Phi Kappa Iota. Home: 6605 Gulfside Rd Longboat Key FL 34228-1416 Office: Argosy U 5250 17th and Honore Sarasota FL 34235 E-mail: lgreagan@aol.com.

REAGAN, LAWRENCE PAUL, JR. systems engineer; b. Honolulu, Nov. 5, 1957; s. Lawrence Paul Sr. and Laura Louise (Sears) R.; m. Ann Marie Decker, Apr. 15, 1989; children: Lawrence P. III, Andrew Scott, Kelly Rene, Ryan Joshua. BS in Mech. & Aerospace Engring., Ill. Inst. Tech., 1979; MS in Acquisition & Contract Mgmt., West Coast U., Santa Barbara, Calif., 1986. Product engr. R.G. Ray Corp., Schaumburg, Ill., 1978-80; launch integration mgr. USAF Hqrs. Space Divsn., L.A. AFB, 1980-84; chief Titan program mgmt. USAF Aerospace Test Group, Vandenberg AFB, Calif., 1984-89; chief joint comm. br. USAF Pentagon, Washington, 1989-91; sr. sys. engr. Dynamics Rsch. Corp., Arlington, Va., 1992-96, dir. Md. ops. California, Md., 1996-97; fed. programs mgr. Info. Builders, Inc., Arlington, 1997-98, dir. fed. programs, 1998—. CEO Jacob's Well, Inc., Lexington Park, Md., 1993—. Contbr. papers to profl. publs. Named Outstanding Young Engr., Air Force

Assn. Mem. AIAA, Soc. Logistics Engring., Air Force Assn., Armed Forces Comms. Electronics Assn. Home: PO Box 22 Lusby MD 20657-0022 Office: Info Builders Inc 2300 Clarendon Blvd Ste 800 Arlington VA 22201-3382 E-mail: larry_reagan@ibi.com.

REAGAN, NANCY DAVIS (ANNE FRANCIS ROBBINS), volunteer, wife of former President of United States; b. N.Y.C., July 6, 1921; d. Kenneth and Edith (Luckett) Robbins; step dau. Loyal Davis; m. Ronald Reagan, Mar. 4, 1952; children: Patricia Ann, Ronald Prescott; stepchildren: Maureen, Michael. BA, Smith Coll., 1943; LLD (hon.), Pepperdine U., 1983; LHD (hon.), Georgetown U., 1987. Contract actress, MGM, 1949-56; films include The Next Voice You Hear, 1950, Donovan's Brain, 1953, Hellcats of the Navy, 1957; Author: Nancy, 1980; formerly author syndicated column on prisoner-of-war and missing-in-action soldiers and their families; author: (with Jane Wilkie) To Love a Child, (with William Novak) My Turn: The Memoirs of Nancy Reagan, 1989. Civic worker, visited wounded Viet Nam vets., sr. citizens, hosps. and schs. for physically and emotionally handicapped children, active in furthering foster grandparents for handicapped children program; hon. nat. chmn. Aid to Adoption of Spl. Kids, 1977; spl. interest in fighting alcohol and drug abuse among youth: hosted first ladies from around the world for 2d Internat. Drug Conf., 1985; hon. chmn. Just Say No Found., Nat. Fedn. of Parents for Drug-Free Youth, Nat. Child Watch Campaign, President's Com. on the Arts and Humanities, Wolf Trap Found. bd. of trustees, Nat. Trust for Historic Preservation, Cystic Fibrosis Found., Nat. Republican Women's Club; hon. pres. Girl Scouts of Am. Named one of Ten Most Admired Am. Women, Good Housekeeping mag., ranking #1 in poll, 1984, 85, 86; Woman of Yr. Los Angeles Times, 1977; permanent mem. Hall of Fame of Ten Best Dressed Women in U.S.; recipient humanitarian awards from Am. Camping Assn., Nat. Council on Alcoholism, United Cerebral Palsy Assn., Internat. Ctr. for Disabled; Boys Town Father Flanagan award; 1986 Kiwanis World Service medal; Variety Clubs Internat. Lifeline award; numerous awards for her role in fight against drug abuse. Address: 2121 Avenue Of The Stars Fl 34 Los Angeles CA 90067-5062*

REAGAN, RONALD WILSON, 40th President of the United States; b. Tampico, Ill., Feb. 6, 1911; s. John Edward and Nelle (Wilson) R.; m. Jane Wyman, Jan. 25, 1940 (div. 1948); children: Maureen E., Michael E.; m. Nancy Davis, Mar. 4, 1952; children: Patricia, Ronald. AB, Eureka Coll., 1932, MA (hon.), 1957. Actor GE Theatre, 1954-62; host TV series Death Valley Days, 1962-66; gov. State of Calif., 1967-74; businessman, rancher, commentator on public policy, 1975-80; Pres. of U.S., 1981-89. Sports announcer, motion picture and TV actor, 1932-66. Author: Where's The Rest of Me?, Speaking My Mind: Selected Speeches, 1989, An American Life: The Autobiography, 1990. Mem. Calif. State Rep. Ctrl. Com., 1964-66; del. Rep. Nat. Conv., 1968, 72; chmn. Rep. Gov. Assn., 1968-73; mem. presdl. Commn. CIA Activities Within U.S., 1975; bd. dirs. Com. Present Danger, Washington, 1977—; cand. for Rep. nomination for Pres., 1976. Served as capt. USAAF, 1942-45. Recipient Great Am. of Decade award, Va. Young Am. for Freedom, Man of Yr. Free Enterprise award, San Fernando Valley Bus. & Profl. award, 1964, Am. Legion award, 1965, Horatio Alger award, 1969, George Washington Honor medal, Freedoms Found. Valley Forge award, 1971, Disting. Am. award; inducted into Nat. Football Found. Hall of Fame, Am. Patriots Hall of Fame. Mem. SAG (pres. 1947-52, 59), Am. Fedn. Radio & TV Artists, Lions, Friars, Tau Kappa Epsilon. Republican. Address: 11000 Wilshire Blvd Fl 34 Los Angeles CA 90024-3602*

REAGAN, STEVAN RAY, cable company executive; b. Brockton, Mass., Dec. 5, 1956; s. Raymond William and Marion (Ames) R.; m. Darlene Elaine Coffey, Sept. 2, 1978; children: Susan Kelly, Debra Kate. BA in Comms., Worcester State Coll., 1978. Announcer WSRO Radio, Marlboro, Mass., 1979-80; prodn. supr. Worcester (Mass.) State Coll., 1980-81; prodn. mgr. New England Prime Cable Network, Woburn, Mass., 1981-83; freelance producer, dir. various, 1983-85; asst. gen. mgr., dir. ops. SportsChannel, Woburn, 1985—; freelance tech. dir. various, 1983-95, v.p. programming and ops., 1995-98, Fox Sports Net New Eng., Woburn, Mass., 1998—. Producer (TV) World Cup Skiing at Loon Mountain, N.H., 1989; producer, dir. (TV) Women's Pro Ski Tour, 1990; exec. producer Exptl. NBA Low Angle Broadcast, 1996, Exptl. Multiple Picture NBA Broadcast, 1997. Recipient Emmy award for exec. prodr. Hartford Whalers Hockey, 1993, Boston Celtics Basketball, 1997, Hockey East, 1998, Boston Celtics, 1999, News Feature, 2000. Mem. CTAM, Nat. Acad. Cable Programming., Nat. Acad. TV Arts and Scis. (bd. govs. Boston/New Eng. chpt. 1995-98). Avocations: golfing, reading. Office: Fox Sports New England 10 Tower Office Park Woburn MA 01801-2182 E-mail: sreagan@rainbow-media.com.

REAGLE, GEORGE LEWIS, government official; b. Nov. 30, 1942; m. Sherald Reagle; children: Kara, Christopher. BS in Psychology and Math., U. Md., 1966; postgrad., George Washington U., 1967-68, Iowa U., 1971-72. Dir. Office State Program Assistance Nat. Hwy. Traffic Safety Adminstrn., 1977, assoc. adminstr. traffic safety program, 1982-88, assoc. adminstr. enforcement, 1989; dir. Office Surface Transp. Nat. Transp. Safety Bd., 1990-93; assoc. adminstr. Office Motor Carriers Fed. Hwy. Adminstrn., Dept. Transp., Washington, 1993—; dir. Office Driver and Pedestrian Programs Nat. Hwy. Traffic Safety Adminstrn. Chmn. working group heavy freight vehicle issues Permanent Internat. Assn. Rd. Congresses. Office: Dept Transp Motor Carriers Fed Hwy Adminstrn 400 7th St SW Washington DC 20590-0001

REAL, CATHERINE WILLIAMS, lawyer; b. Detroit, Dec. 5, 1946; BA, Fla. Atlantic U., 1967, postgrad.; JD, Stetson U., 1978. Bar: Fla. 1979, U.S. Dist. Ct. (mid. dist.) Fla., U.S. Ct. Appeals (11th cir.). Staff dir. Fla. Senate, Tallahassee; asst. state atty. 13th Jud. Circuit, Tampa; mng. ptnr. Muga & Real, PA, 1981-98; pres. Catherine W. Real, P.A., 1998—; staff dir. health and rehab. svc. com. Fla. Senate, Tallahassee. Founder CourtWatch Hillsborough County Inc., Tampa, 1996—; bd. dirs. The Spring, Tampa. Recipient award for outstanding victim advocacy Victim's Voice, Tampa, 1993, 95; cert. of appreciation Ctr. for Women, Tampa, 1994, 96, Outstanding Vol. award, 1995. Mem. ATLA, Am. Acad. Trial Lawyers, Hillsborough County Bar Assn. Office: 2110 W Platt St Tampa FL 33606-1759

REALE, ANTHONY, pension investment consultant; b. Jersey City, Oct. 14, 1957; s. Salvatore and Concetta Reale. BS in Fin., St. Peter's Coll., 1979. Ops. asst. E.F. Hutton & Co., N.Y.C., 1979-80; compliance Prudential Securities, 1980-87; investment analyst Buck Cons., 1987-91; pension cons. JP Morgan, 1991—. Roman Catholic. Avocations: golf, music, coin collecting. Office: 3 Chase Metrotech Ctr Brooklyn NY 11245-0001 E-mail: anthony.reale@jpmorgan.com.

REALE, SARA JANE, museum education director; b. Jamestown, N.Y., Jan. 25, 1961; d. Irving Reuben and Frances Goldinger Wolinsky; m. David Anthony Reale, July 28, 1985; children: Michael Joseph, Lauren Rebecca. AS, Jamestown (N.Y.) C.C., 1983; BA, Fredonia (N.Y.) State U., 1985. Mus. tchr. Fenton History Ctr., Jamestown, N.Y., 1990-95, dir. edn. and pub. programming, 1995—. Adv. bd. Roger Tory Peterson Inst., Jamestown, 1997-2000; mem. Chautaugna County Visitors Bureau Motorcoach Com., 2002-; mem. curriculum devel. com. Robert H. Jackson Ctr., Jamestown, 2001—. Mem. AAUW. Avocations: travel, exercise, children's school activities, historical research. Office: 67 Washington St Jamestown NY 14701-6631 E-mail: reale@madbbs.com.

REALS ELLIG, JANICE, human resources and marketing executive; b. N.Y.C., May 14, 1946; d. Otto Peter and Anne (Briganti) Astolfi; m. Paul T. Reals, 1971 (div.); m. Bruce Robert Ellig, July 16, 1994; 1 child, Meredith Evans. BBA, U. Iowa, 1968; MA, Rider Coll., Princeton, N.J., 1978. Dir. Shareholders Mgmt., L.A., 1968-71; v.p. human resources Cooper Med. Ctr., N.J., 1971-80; dir. human resources Pfizer, N.Y.C., 1980-86; v.p. human resources Citibank, 1986-91; sr. v.p. mktg., human resources, adminstrn. Ambac Fin. Group, 1991-2000; prin. Heidrick & Struggles, 2000; mng. dir. Gould, McCoy & Chadick, 2000—. Chmn. bd. Women's Econ. Roundtable, N.Y.C., 1997—. Author: What Every Successful Woman Knows, 2001. Bd. dirs. Fountain House, N.Y.C., 1998—, Nat. Exec. Svc. Corp., N.Y.C., 1997—, WMCA of N.Y., U. Iowa President's Club, WMCA of N.Y.; dir. adv. coun. Bus. Sch., U. Iowa, Iowa City, 1998—; bd. dirs. Women in the State and House, Washington, 1994—; mem. bus. com. Met. Mus. Art, N.Y.C., 1994—; mem. Women's Forum, N.Y.C., 1998—; mem. adv. coun. Children's Aid Soc., N.Y.C., 1995—; mem. leadership cir. Women's Campaign Fund, N.Y.C., 1990—. Named Woman of Yr., Rhinelander's Children Ctr., 1999, Children's Aid Soc., 1999. Mem. Fin. Women's Assn., Econ. Club N.Y.C. Republican. Avocations: writing, gourmet cooking, reading, travel, tennis. Home: Apt 12G 10 Gracie Sq New York NY 10028-7052 Office: Gould McCoy Chadick 300 Park Ave New York NY 10022 E-mail: jrellig@gmcsearch.com.

REAM, BOB, political organization administrator; Chmn. Mont. Dem. Party, Helena, 1997—. Office: Mont Dem Party PO Box 802 Helena MT 59624-0802 Fax: 406-442-9534.*

REAM, DAVIDSON, law publications administrator, writer; b. Ossining, N.Y., May 2, 1937; s. Joseph H. and Anita (Biggs) R.; m. Judith Krampitz, Oct. 1, 1966; children: Michael E., Caitlin D. BA, Yale U., 1961; JD, U. Va., 1964; LLM, U. Calif., Berkeley, 1971. Bar: D.C. 1972. Spl. asst. Supreme Ct. of Pakistan, 1964-65; law program developer The Asia Found., San Francisco and Sri Lanka, 1966-69; rsch. atty. Continuing Edn. of the Bar, Berkeley, 1970-75; publ. dir. ABA, Chgo., 1975-78; publ. mgr. Callaghan & Co., Wilmette, Ill., 1978-83; publs. dir. Def. Rsch. Inst., Chgo., 1984—. Editor: Condemnation Practice in California, 1973, Landslide and Subsidence Liability, 1974, Attorney's Guide to Professional Responsibility, 1978, Products Liability Pretrial Notebook, 1989, Products Liability Defenses, 1992, Products Liability Defenses, 2001; editor For The Defense, 1984—. Pres. Ridgeville Assn., Evanston, Ill., 1977-81, Mental Health Assn., Evanston, 1992-95; alderman City of Evanston, 1983-87; bd. dirs. Dem. Party Evanston, 1978-90, First Night Evanston, 1995—. Mem. ABA, D.C. Bar Assn. Avocations: hiking, camping, travel, community affairs. Office: Def Rsch Inst 150 N Michigan Ave Chicago IL 60601-7553 E-mail: dream@dri.org.

REAM, JAMES TERRILL, architect, sculptor; b. Summit, N.J., Sept. 8, 1929; s. Merrill Jay and Catherine Ada (Terrill) R.; m. Joyce Kimball Johnson, June 9, 1953 (div. Dec. 1976); children— Claudia, Sarah, Benjamin, m. Nancy Ann Buford, Jan. 1, 1980; stepchildren— Kathleen, Ann Maguire BArch, Cornell U., 1953; postgrad., Pratt Inst., 1953-54, U. Rome, 1956-57. Registered architect. Assoc. W. C. Muchow Assocs., Denver, 1959-62; prin. Ream, Quinn & Assocs., 1962-66; v.p. design John Carl Warnecke & Assocs., San Francisco, 1966-69; prin., pres. James Ream & Assocs., Inc., 1969-78, Robbins and Ream Inc., San Francisco, 1978-83; prin. James Ream Architect, 1983—. Prin. archtl. works include Denver Convention Ctr., Currigan Hall, Pasadena Conf. Ctr., Stapleton Plaza Hotel, Vail Transp. Ctr. Bd. dirs. San Francisco Planning and Urban Rsch. Assn., 1977—; chmn. bd. dirs. San Francisco Heritage, 1984-91, pres., 1983-84. Served to 1st lt. USAF, 1954-56. Recipient citation for design in steel Am. Iron and Steel Inst., 1975; Honor award Am. Concrete Inst., 1975; Nat. Design award Prestressed Concrete Inst., 1983; Honor award for design in steel Am. Inst. Steel Constrn., 1970 Fellow AIA (honor award western region 1969, fellowship in design 1979, honor award for design excellence 1983, design cons. San Jose Arena). Democrat. Avocations: opera, theater, hiking, tennis. Office: 3385 Clay St San Francisco CA 94118-2006

REAMAN, GREGORY HAROLD, pediatric hematologist, oncologist; b. Akron, Ohio, Sept. 9, 1947; s. Harold J. and Margaret U. (D'Alfonso) R.; m. Susan J. Pristo, Sept. 7, 1974; children: Emily Margaret, Sarah Elizabeth. BS in Biology, U. Detroit, 1969; MD, Loyola U., Chgo., 1973. Diplomate Nat. Bd. Med. Examiners, Am. Bd. Pediatrics. Pediatric intern Loyola U. Med. Ctr., 1973-74; resident in pediatrics Montreal Children's Hosp., McGill U., 1974-76; clin. assoc. pediatric oncology br. Nat. Cancer Inst., NIH, Bethesda, Md., 1976-78, investigator pediatric oncology br., 1978-79; assoc. dept. hematology/oncology, attending physician Children's Nat. Med. Ctr., Washington, 1979-87, chmn. dept. hematology/oncology, 1987—, dir. med. spl. svcs., 1995—99, exec. dir. Ctr. for Cancer and Blood Disorders, 1999—2002; asst. prof. pediatrics Sch. Medicine and Health Scis. George Washington U., 1979-82, assoc. prof. pediatrics, 1982-87, prof. pediats., 1987-97, prof., 1997—. Assoc. chmn. Children's Cancer Group; chmn. Children's Oncology Group; v.p. sci. and med. affairs Nat. childhood Cancer Found.; bd. dirs., mem. med. affairs com., chmn., strategic planning com. Children's Oncology Svcs. of Met. Washington. Mem. editorial bd. Cancer Data Query, Nat. Cancer Inst., Jour. Clin. Oncology, Am. Jour. Pediat. Hematology Oncology, Cancer, The Oncologist; reviewer Blood, Jour. Clin. Oncology; assoc. editor: Cancer, 1990-2000; contbr. articles to profl. publs. Trustee Nat. Childhood Cancer Found., Arcadia, Calif.; bd. dirs. Am. Cancer Soc., Atlanta; trustee, chmn. patient care and profl. edn. coms. Leukemia Soc. Am. Lt. comdr. USPHS, 1976-79, Res., 1979—. Folger Summer scholar Am. Cancer Soc.; recipient Spl. Fellowship Rsch. award Leukemia Soc. Am., 1980-82; grantee DHHS, Nat. Cancer Inst., 1987—. Mem. Soc. Pediat. Rsch., Am. Soc. Hematology, Am. Pediat. Soc., Am. Fedn. Clin. Rsch., Am. Soc. Clin. Oncology, Am. Assn. Cancer Rsch., Am. Soc. Pediat. Hematology/Oncology, Washington Blood Club, Alpha Omega Alpha. Democrat. Roman Catholic. Home: 7306 Brennon Ln Chevy Chase MD 20815-4064 Office: Children's Nat Med Ctr 111 Michigan Ave NW Washington DC 20010-2916

REAMER, SHIRLEY JEAN, minister; b. South Bend, Ind., Aug. 15, 1935; d. John Lewis and Vivian Leora (Hammer) Helvey; m. Thomas Charles Reamer, June 22, 1956; children: Thomas Darwin, Trent Alan, Terry Michael, Traci Sue, Tricia Ann. Grad. high sch., South Bend, 1953; ThD, Shalom Bible Coll. and Sem., West Des Moines, Iowa, 1992. Ordained to ministry Full Gospel Fellowship, 1974. Dir. children's ministry Calvary Temple, South Bend, 1972-73; evangelist Full Gospel Fellowship, 1976—; founder, pastor Maranatha Temple, South Bend, 1981-83. Founder, pres. Women's Aglow Fellowship, Michiana, Ind., 1976-79; founder, dir. Prison Ministry-Aglow, Westville, Ind., 1976-77; founder, dir. Soup Kitchen/Care Ctr., Maranatha Temple, 1982—, Supplied Facilities for Ctr. for Homeless, 1984-87, dir. City March, 1989; mem. United Religious Community Task Force, South Bend, 1985. Author: Ministerial Ethics, 1984, Teaching Syllabus, 1985, Recruits for Christ, 1987, Teaching Syllabus, Genesis, The Beginning, 1994. Pres. In His Glorious Image, 1998. Recipient Spirit of Am. Women award J.C. Penneys, South Bend, 1988; named one of 16 Best Pastors, Charisma Mag., 1988. *Life, when valued as our most treasured possession, will be held as sacred and will always be found on a lighted path to direct the way of another.*

REAMS, BERNARD DINSMORE, JR. lawyer, educator; b. Lynchburg, Va., Aug. 17, 1943; s. Bernard Dinsmore and Martha Eloise (Hickman) R.; m. Rosemarie Bridget Boyle, Oct. 26, 1968 (dec. Oct. 1996); children: Andrew Dennet, Adriane Bevin. BA, Lynchburg Coll., 1965; MS, Drexel U., 1966; JD, U. Kans., 1972; PhD, St. Louis U., 1983. Bar: Kans. 1973, Mo. 1986, N.Y. 1996, Tex. 2002. Instr., asst. librarian Rutgers U., 1966-69; asst. prof. law, librarian U. Kans., Lawrence, 1969-74; mem. faculty law sch. Washington U., St. Louis, 1974-95, prof. law, 1976-95, prof. tech. mgmt., 1990-95, librarian, 1974-76, acting dean univ. libraries, 1987-88; prof. law, assoc. dean, dir. Law Libr. St. John's U. Sch. Law, Jamaica, N.Y., 1995-97, assoc. dean acad. affairs, 1997-98; prof., dir. law libr. and info. tech. St. Mary's U., San Antonio, 2000—, prof. law, 2000—. Vis. fellow Max-Planck Inst., Hamburg, 1995, 97, 98, 2001; vis. prof. law Seton Hall U., 1998-2000. Author: Author: Law For The Businessman, 1974, Reader in Law Librarianship, 1976, Federal Price and Wage Control Programs 1917-1979: Legis. Histories and Laws, 1980, Education of the Handicapped: Laws, Legislative Histories, and Administrative Documents, 1982, 1983; actor: Internal Revenue Acts of the United States: The Revenue Act of 1954 with Legislative Histories and Congressional Documents, 1983; author: Congress and the Courts: A Legislative History 1978-1984, 1984, University-Industry Research Partnerships: The Major Issues in Research and Development Agreements, 1986, Deficit Control and the Gramm-Rudman-Hollings Act, 1986, The Semiconductor Chip and the Law: A Legislative History of the Semiconductor Chip Protection Act of 1984, 1986, American International Law Cases, 2d series, 1986, Technology Transfer Law: The Export Administration Acts of the U.S., 1987, Insider Trading and the Law: A Legislative History of the Insider Trading Sanctions Act, 1989, Insider Trading and Securities Fraud, 1989, The Health Care Quality Improvement Act of 1989: A Legislative History of P.L. No. 99-660, 1990, The National Organ Transplant Act of 1984: A Legislative History of P.L. No. 98-507, 1990, A Legislative History of Individuals with Disabilities Education Act, 1994, Federal Legislative Histories: An Annotated Bibliography and Index to Officially Published Sources, 1994, Electronic Contracting Law, 1996, Health Care Reform, 1994, The American Experience: Clinton and Congress, 1997, The Omnibus Anti-Crime Act, 1997, The Law of E-SIGN: A Legislative History of the Electronic Signature in Global and National Commerce Act, 2001; co-author: Segregation and the Fourteenth Amendment in the States, 1975, Historic Preservation Law: An Annotated Bibliography, 1976, Congress and the Courts: A Legislative History 1787-1977, 1978, Federal Consumer Protection Laws, Rules and Regulations, 1979, A Guide and Analytical Index to the Internal Revenue Acts of the U.S., 1909-1950, 1979, The Numerical Lists and Schedule of Volumes of the U.S. Congressional Serial Set: 73d Congress through the 96th Congress, 1984, Human Experimentation: Federal Laws, Legislative Histories, Regulations and Related Documents, 1985, American Legal Literature: A Guide to Selected Legal Resources, 1985. Bd. trustees Quincy Found. for Med. Rsch. Charitable Trust, San Francisco. Fellow Am. Bar Foun.; recipient Thornton award for excellence Lynchburg Coll., 1986, Joseph L. Andrews Bibliog. award, 1995; named to Hon. Order Ky. Cols., 1992. Mem. ABA, Am. Law Inst., ALA, Am. Soc. Law and Medicine, Nat. Health Lawyers Assn., Am. Assn. Higher Edn., Spl. Librs. Assn., Internat. Assn. Law Libr. Coll. and Univ. Attys., Order of Coif, Phi Beta Kappa, Sigma Xi, Beta Phi Mu, Phi Delta Phi, Phi Delta Epsilon, Kappa Delta Pi, Pi Lambda Theta. Office: St Marys U Sch Law One Camino Santa Maria San Antonio TX 78228 E-mail: breams@stmarytx.edu.

REAMSNYDER, MARGARET ELIZABETH, nurse; b. Ottawa, Ohio, Dec. 5, 1923; d. Louis Henry and Minnie Mary (Mershman) Borgelt; m. Ross Allan Reamsnyder, July 4, 1948; children: Richard, Dennis, Thomas, Linda. Diploma, Toledo Hosp. Sch. Nursing, 1945; postgrad., Bowling Green State U., 1979. RN, Ohio. Operating room nurse Blanchard Valley Hosp., Findlay, Ohio, 1945-46, operating room supr., 1946-48, gen. duty nurse, 1965-66; sch. nurse Findlay City Schs., 1966-97; ret., 1997. Advisor med. careers club Findlay High Sch., 1966-86, com. mem. student affairs, behavior screening, 1985-87. Vol. ARC, Findlay, 1984—, Blanchard Valley Hosp. Aux., 2002. Mem. NEA-Ret., Ohio Edn. Assn.-Ret., Ohio Ret. Tchrs. Assn., Hancock County Ret. Tchrs. Assn. Lutheran. Avocations: reading, walking, crocheting, growing African violets. Home: 328 Warrington Ave Findlay OH 45840-6333

REAMY, MICHAELIN, marriage and family therapist, educator, consultant; b. N.Y.C., Feb. 20, 1938; d. Judson Reamy and Eleanor Stevens (McMichael) R.; m. James Donald Cowie, Aug. 29, 1959; children: Jennifer D., James J., David K., Laura S.; m. Richard Ward Stephenson, Aug. 31, 1979. B.S. with Distinction in Human Ecology, Cornell U., 1960; M.S.W., U. Ga., 1979; student of Carolyn Myss and Norm Shealy, cert. program in intuition and energy medicine. Cert. primordial sound meditation instr., 1996. Tchr. swimming, Conn., E. Africa, Lebanon, 1968-75; social work intern, grad. asst., Atlanta, 1978-79; dir. social services, assoc. dir. and coordinator family therapy adult treatment program Brawner Psychiat. Inst., Atlanta, 1980-82; dir. extramural tng., marriage and family therapist Atlanta Inst. Family Studies, 1982-87; Perspective Ctr. for Psychotherapy, 1988-98; Natural Color & Design, 1988—. Mem. Atlanta Com. Children, 1983-85; instr. Water Safety ARC, 1957—. Recipient DAR Citizen award, 1956; YMCA award for Disting. Service, White Plains, N.Y., 1958. Diplomate NASW; mem. Nat. Assn. Social Workers, Am. Assn. Marriage and Family Therapy (com. on supervision), Cornell U. Human Ecology Alumni Assn., Mortar Bd., Omicron Nu, Phi Kappa Phi. Contbr. articles to profl. jours. Kappa Phi. Contbr. articles to profl. jours. Office: Natural Color & Design PO Box Q Menlo Park CA 94026-6218 Home: 1115 Santa Cruz Ave Menlo Park CA 94025-5002

REANEY, JAMES CRERAR, dramatist, poet, educator; b. South Easthope, Ont., Can., Sept. 1, 1926; s. James Nesbit and Elizabeth Henrietta (Crerar) R.; m. Colleen Thibaudeau, Dec. 29, 1951; children: James Stewart, Susan Alice. BA, U. Toronto, 1948, MA, 1949, PhD, 1957; D.Litt., Carleton U., 1975. Asst. prof. English U. Man., 1949-60; prof. English U. Western Ont., London, 1960—. (Recipient Massey award for the Killdeer 1960, Chalmers award for best Can. play The St. Nicholas Hotel 1975); Author: Killdeer, 1960 (Massey award), Poems, 1972, Colours in the Dark, 1969, Masks of Childhood, 1972, Listen to the Wind, 1972, Apple Butter and Other Plays for Children, 1973; plays include The St. Nicholas Hotel, 1975 (Chalmers award for best Can. play), Sticks and Stones: The Donnellys Part I, 1973, The Donnellys Part II, 1974, Handcuffs: The Donnellys Part III, 1977, 14 Barrels from Sea to Sea, 1975, The Dismissal, 1978, Wacousta, 1980, King Whistle, 1982, I the Parade, 1983, The House by the Churchyard, 1985, Alice Through the Looking-Glass, 1994, Serinette (opera libretto), 1986, Crazy to Kill (opera libretto), Performance Poems, 1991; novels for children include: The Boy with an R on his Hand, 1963, Take the Big Picture, 1986, Box Social & Other Stories, 1996, Taptoo (opera libretto) 1999, Zamorna: The Story of Branwell Bronte (play) 1999; editor, pub.: Alphabet, 1960-70; contbr. articles to profl. jours. Decorated Order of Can. Fellow Royal Soc. Can.; mem. Playwrights Union Can., Can. Poetry League. Mem. New Democratic Party. Home: 276 Huron St London ON Canada N6A 2J9 Office: U Western Ont Agent Livingstone Cooke Inc 457A Danforth Ave Ste 201 Toronto ON Canada M4K 1P1

REARDEN, CAROLE ANN, clinical pathologist, educator; b. Belleville, Ont., Can., June 11, 1946; d. Joseph Brady and Honora Patricia (O'Halloran) R. BSc, McGill U., 1969, MSc, MDCM, 1971. Diplomate Am. Bd. Pathology, Am. Bd. Immunohematology and Blood Banking, Am. Bd. HIstocompatibility and Immunogenetics. Resident and fellow Children's Meml. Hosp., Chgo., 1971-73; resident in pediatrics U. Calif., San Diego, 1974, resident then fellow, 1975-79, asst. prof. pathology, 1979-86, dir. histocompatibility and immunogenetics lab., 1979-94, assoc. prof., 1986-92, prof., 1992—, head divsn. lab. medicine, 1989-94; dir. med. ctr. U. Calif. Thornton Hosp. Clin. Labs., 1993—. Prin. investigator devel. monoclonal antibodies to erythroid antigens, recombinant autoantigens; dir. lab. exam. com. Am. Bd. Histocompatibility and Immunogenetics. Contbr. articles to profl. jours.; patentee autoantigen pinch. Mem. Mayor's Task Force on AIDS, San Diego, 1983. Recipient Young Investigator Rsch. award NIH, 1979; grantee U. Calif. Cancer Rsch. Coordinating Com., 1982, NIH, 1983; scholar Nat. Blood Found. Mem. Am. Soc. Investigative Pathology, Am. Soc. Hematology, Am. Assn. Blood Banks (com. organ transplantation and tissue typing 1982-87, tech. com. 13 and 14 edit. tech. manual 1996-2002). Office: U Calif San Diego Dept Pathology 0612 9500 Gilman Dr La Jolla CA 92093-0612 E-mail: arearden@ucsd.edu.

REARDON, BEA, social worker; b. Queens, N.Y., July 10, 1955; d. James Joseph and Evelyn May R. BS in Social Work, Salem (Mass.) State Coll., 1979; MSW, Smith Coll., 1984. Bd. cert. diplomate in clin. social work. Clin. social worker Valley Adult Counseling Svc., Milford, Mass., 1984-86; clin. social worker, outpatient psychiatry Univ. Hosp., Boston, 1986-88; clin. social worker Tri City Mental Health Ctr., Medford, 1986-88, dir. children's outpatient program, 1988-90; pvt. practice social work Cambridge , 1987—99; pvt. practice social work Glouchester, 1996—. Mem. Soc. Clin. Social Work (pres. 1993-95). Avocations: yoga, meditation. Office: PO Box 888 Rockport MA 01966

REARDON, FRANK EMOND, lawyer; b. Providence, May 22, 1953; s. J. Clarke and Dorothy (Emond) R.; m. Deborah Walsh, Sept. 30, 1978; children: Kathleen Elizabeth, Brendan Francis, William James, Sean Patrick. BA, Holy Cross Coll., Worcester, Mass., 1975; JD, Suffolk U., 1978; MS, Harvard U., 1981. Bar: Mass. 1978, R.I. 1978, U.S. Dist. Ct. Mass. 1980, U.S. Dist. Ct. R.I. 1980, U.S. Supreme Ct. 1986. Counsel Nat. Assn. Govtl. Employment and Internat. Brotherhood Police Officers, Cranston, R.I., 1978-81; asst. gen. counsel Brigham and Women's Hosp., Boston, 1981-84; litigation counsel Risk Mgmt. Found. Harvard Med. Instns., Cambridge, Mass., 1984-87; ptnr. Hassan and Reardon, Boston, 1987—. Chmn. bd. dirs. St. Monica's Nursing Home, 1984-89, Med. Area Fed. Credit Union, 1984-89; clk., trustee Deaconess Glover Hosp., Needham, Mass.; ethics com. Boston Children's Hosp., 1993-96. Contbr. articles to profl. jours. Chmn. fin. com. Town of Needham, Mass.; mem. pres.'s council Coll. Holy Cross, 1985—. Beuilacqua scholar, 1978. Mem. ABA, Mass. Bar Assn. (chmn. health law sect. 1987—), Assn. Trial Lawyers Am., Am. Soc. Law and Medicine (cmty. rep. children's hosp. ethics com.). Democrat. Roman Catholic. Avocations: tennis, sailing, golf, writing. Home: 44 Sargent St Needham MA 02492-3434 Office: Hassan & Reardon 535 Boylston St Boston MA 02116-3720

REARDON, MARK WILLIAM, lawyer; b. Englewood, N.J., June 7, 1956; s. Matthew Francis and Rose Mary (Snyder) R.; m. Patricia Louise Powers, Apr. 19, 1985. BA, Knox Coll., 1977; JD, Seton Hall U., 1980. Bar: N.J. 1980, U.S. Dist. Ct. N.J. 1980, U.S. Ct. Mil. Appeals 1981, Wash. 1987, U.S. Supreme Ct. 1987, U.S. Ct. Appeals (fed. cir.) 1988, Ct. of Fed. Claims 1997,

Ill. 2001. Atty. The Boeing Co., Chgo., 1986—. Capt. JAGC, U.S. Army, 1981-86. Maj. JAGC USAR, 1986-95. Mem. ABA, Wash. Bar Assn. Republican. Roman Catholic. Avocations: jogging, swimming. Office: The Boeing Co 5003-1001 100 N Riverside Plz Chicago IL 60606-1596

REARDON, PATRICK THOMAS, newspaper reporter; b. Chgo., Nov. 22, 1949; s. David Joseph and Audrey Joanne (Thomas) R.; m. Catherine Shiel, Oct. 30, 1982; children: David Joseph Shiel, Sarah Catherine Shiel. BA in English, St. Louis U., 1971. Reporter, photographer Austinite/N.W. Passage, Chgo., 1972-73; reporter, editor City News Bur. Chgo., 1973-76, Suburban Trib, Chgo., 1976-81, Chgo. Tribune, 1981-91, book reviewer, 1985—, columnist, 1990—92, 2001—02, urban affairs writer, 1991-97, feature writer, 1997—. Author: Daily Meditation (with Scripture) for Busy Dads, 1995, Starting Out: Reflections for Young People, 2000; contbr. . Recipient Lisagor award Headline Club, Chgo., 1988, 91, 92, Feature Writing award Minn. Soc. Profl. Journalists, 2000. Roman Catholic. Home: 6220 N Paulina St Chicago IL 60660-1119 Office: Chgo Tribune 435 N Michigan Ave Ste 500 Chicago IL 60611-4066 E-mail: preardon@tribune.com., ptreardon@aol.com.

REARDON, PEARL RANCE, real estate executive, writer; b. Savanna La Mar, Westmoreland, Jamaica, Apr. 17, 1941; came to U.S., 1968; d. Hugh Lawrence Rance and Ada Louise (Mullings) Watson; m. Michael I. Phillips, June 9, 1962 (div. Sept. 1977); children: Karim Irving, Felita Alessandra; m. Michael John Reardon, May 24, 1980. Student, Howard Community Coll., 1974-77; MFA in Creative Writing, Am. U., 1996. Cert. real estate broker Grad. Real Estate Inst. Sr. sec. Nat. Coun. Cath. Men, Washington, 1968-69; exec. sec. Nat. Acad. Sci, 1969-71; sr. sec. Pres.'s Commn. on Population, 1971-72; exec. sec. Westinghouse Health System, Columbia, Md., 1972-76; adminstrv. group mgr. Price, Williams & Assocs., Silver Spring, 1976-78; assoc. broker Merrill Lynch Realty, 1977-81; pres. and CEO Pearl Properties, 1982-93; v.p. Croton Mgmt. Svcs., Washington, 1994—. Organizer Peoples Nat. Party, Linstead, Jamaica, 1966; founding mem. Jamaica Nat. Assn., Washington, 1969, sec. 1969-73. Mem. Nat. Assn. Realtors, D.C. Bd. Realtors, Authors Guild, Dramatists Guild. Avocations: writing, music, piano, reading, dancing, crafts. Office: Croton Mgmt Svcs PO Box 9650 Washington DC 20016-9650

REARDON, ROBERT IGNATIUS, JR. lawyer; b. N.Y.C., Nov. 28, 1945; s. Robert I. and Mildred (Lomax) R.; m. Lise Hofffman; children: Colleen Brooke, Kelly Elizabeth. BS in Econs., Boston Coll., 1967; JD, Fordham U., 1970. Bar: Conn. 1970, U.S. Dist. Ct. Conn. 1974, U.S. Ct. Mil. Appeals 1971, U.S. Ct. Appeals (2d cir.) 1974, U.S. Supreme Ct. 1974, U.S. Ct. Claims 1986. Ptnr. Shapiro & Reardon, P.C., New London, Conn., 1973-83; pres. Reardon Law Firm P.C., 1983—. State trial referee Conn. Superior Ct., 1985—. Chmn. Bd. Fin. Town of Waterford, Conn., 1974-79; mem. Bd. Edn. Town of East Lyme, Conn., 1981-84; trustee Eugene O'Neill Meml. Theater, Inc., 1978-84; active Conn. Commn. Pub. Trust, 1998—. Served as capt. USMC, 1970-73. Mem. ABA (award of achievement young lawyers sect. 1975), ATLA (bd. dirs. 1998—), Conn. Trial Lawyers Assn. (pres. 1997-98), Conn. Bar Assn. (bd. govs. 1979-81, ho. of dels. 1975-79), New London County Bar Assn. (mem. exec. com. 1975-79). Home: 95 Quarry Dock Rd Niantic CT 06357-1908 Office: 160 Hempstead St New London CT 06320-5638

REARDON, ROBERT J. minister; b. Pitts., June 19, 1933; s. John J. and Catherine Scheuble Reardon. BA in Philosophy, St. Vincent, 1955, MA in Religion, 1959; MEd, DuQuesne, 1964. Parochial vicar St. Francis Xavier, Pitts., 1959—65; chaplain Villa Maria (Pa.) H.S., 1965—67; prin. Quigley H.S., Baden, Pa., 1967—69; diocesan dir. CCD Diocese of Pitts., 1969—72; pastor St. Conrad, Butler, Pa., 1975—78, St. Louise De Madillal, Upper St. Clair, 1978—91, St. John Capistran, Upper St. Clair, 1991—. Judge marriage tribunal Diocese of Pitts., 1976—80, dean South Hills, 1984—99, mem. fin. coun., 1986—2001. Roman Catholic. Office: St John Capistran Ch 1610 McMillan Rd Pittsburgh PA 15241

REARDON, STEPHEN JAMES, JR. retired English speech educator; b. Butte, Mont., Nov. 6, 1929; s. Stephen James and Myrtle Agnes (MacKillican) R. PhB, Carroll Coll., 1952; MA in English, U. Wash., 1963. Tchr. English, speech Butte Jr. H.S., 1957-65; instr. English, speech Mont. State U., Bozeman, 1965-67; upward bound tchr. St. Michael's Coll., Colchester, Vt., summers 1968, 69; tchr. English West Jr. H.S., Butte, spring 1969, Butte H.S., Sch. Dist. No. 1, 1972-92. Speech coach Butte H.S., Sch. Dist. No. 1, 1973-85. Mem. Am. Legion Post No. 1, Butte, 1976—. With U.S. Army, 1955-57. Named Class AA Mont. Speech Coach of Yr., Mont. Forensic Educators Assn., 1978-79, 83-84, named to Hall of Fame, 1997; recipient Gold Star Excellence Tchg award Rivendell Psychiat. Ctr. and Mont. Eagle Comm., 1990-91, Golden Apple Excellence in Edn. award Butte C. of C., 1992; torchbearer in Bozeman for Winter Olympics, 2002. Mem. U.S. Judo Assn. (5th degree black belt 1999), U.S. Judo, Inc. (5th degree black belt 1999), U.S. Tomiki Aikido Black Belt Fedn. (1st degree black belt 1998), Butte Tchrs. Union Local 332, Butte Judo Club (dir. 1972-80, 82—), Butte Karate Club N.W. Tae Kwon Do Assn. (hon. black belt 1989). Democrat. Roman Catholic. Avocations: martial arts, skiing, swimming, writing. Home: 616 W Gold St Butte MT 59701-2363 E-mail: sreardonj@aol.com.

REARDON, SUSAN B. human resources executive; b. Chgo., Mar. 30, 1956; d. Thomas P. and Agnes M. (Browne) Duffy; m. Timothy J. Reardon, Apr. 24, 1982; children: Matthew D., Mitchell T. BA in Bus. Adminstrn. and Mgmt., Loyola U., Chgo., 1983. Adminstr. human resources tng. Inst. Fin. Edn., Chgo., 1976-79; asst. to founder and gen. mgr. Lyric Opera of Chgo., 1979-80; human resources generalist Trailer Train Co., Chgo., 1980-87; dir. human resources Whittman-Hart, 1987—, ptnr., 1993—. Named Woman of Destiny Destiny Inst., Chgo., 1990. Mem. Nat. Human Resources Assn. (bd. dirs., treas. 1986-87, orientation chmn. 1985-86), N.Y. Investment Club (founding ptnr., v.p. 1984), Chgo. Software Assn. Home: 228 S Waiola Ave La Grange IL 60525-2264 Office: Whittman-Hart 311 S Wacker Dr Chicago IL 60606-6627

REARDON, TIMOTHY P. lawyer; b. Milw., Dec. 11, 1962; s. James P. and Mary M. Reardon; m. Ann E. Horning, June 6, 1987; children: Patrick, Megan, Michael, Kevin. BS, Marquette U., 1985, JD, 1988. Bar: Wis. 1988. Atty. Reinhart, Boerner Van Deuren, Milw., 1988—. Author comment Marquette Law Rev., 1988. Bd. dirs. Auror Family Svc., Inc., 1998—. Mem. Marquette H.S Alumni Assn. (bd. dirs.). Office: Reinhart Boerner et al 1000 N Water St Ste 2100 Milwaukee WI 53202-3197 E-mail: treardon@reinhartlaw.com.

REASON, J. PAUL, naval officer; b. Washington, Mar. 22, 1941; s. Joseph Henry and Bernice (Chism) R.; m. Dianne Lillian Fowler, June 12, 1965; children: Rebecca, Joseph. BS, U.S. Naval Acad., 1965; MS, USN Postgrad. Sch., 1970. Cert. nuclear propulsion engr. Commd. ens. USN, 1965, advanced through grades to adm., 1996; naval aide to pres. The White Ho., Washington, 1976-79; exec. officer USS Miss., 1979-81; comdg. officer USS Coontz, 1981-83, USS Bainbridge, 1983-86; comdr. Naval Base, Seattle, 1986-88, Cruiser-Destroyer Group 1, 1988-90, Naval Surface Force Atlantic, 1991-94; dep. chief naval ops. plans, policy and ops. Dept. Navy, Washington, 1994-96; comdr.-in-chief U.S. Atlantic Fleet, 1996-99; retired, 1999; v.p. Syntek, Inc., Arlington, Va., 1999-2000; pres. Metro Machine Corp., Norfolk, 2000—. Decorated DSM, Legion of Merit, other mil. awards. Avocations: fishing, tennis.

REASONER, BARRETT HODGES, lawyer; b. Houston, Apr. 16, 1964; s. Harry Max and Macey (Hodges) R.; m. Susan Hardig; children: Matthew Joseph, Caroline Macey, William Harry, Olivia Lucille, Eloise Susan. BA cum laude, Duke U., 1986; Grad. Dipl., London Sch. Econs., 1987; JD with honors, U. Tex., 1990. Bar: Tex. 1990, U.S. Dist. Ct. (ea., so., we., and no. dists.) Tex. 1993, U.S. Ct. Appeals (5th cir.) 1993, U.S. Supreme Ct. 1997. Asst. dist. atty. Harris County Dist. Atty.'s Office, Houston, 1990-92; ptnr. Gibbs & Bruns, L.L.P., 1992—. Fellow Tex. Bar Found., Houston Bar Found.; mem. Am. Judicature Soc. (bd. dirs. 1994-99, exec. com. 1997-99), State Bar Tex. (jud. rels. com. 1999-2001), Houston Bar Assn. (bd. dirs.), Houston Young Lawyers Assn. (pub. schs. and pub. edn. com. 1994-99, chmn. pub. schs. and pub. edn. com. 1997-99, outstanding com. chair 1999), Houston Vol. Lawyers Program (bd. dirs.), Order of Barristers. Episcopalian. Office: Gibbs & Bruns LLP 1100 Louisiana St Ste 5300 Houston TX 77002-5215 E-mail: breasoner@gibbs-bruns.com.

REASONER, HARRY MAX, lawyer; b. San Marcos, Tex., July 15, 1939; s. Harry Edward and Joyce Majorie (Barrett) Reasoner; m. Elizabeth Macey Hodges, Apr. 15, 1963; children: Barrett Hodges, Elizabeth Macey Reasoner Stokes. BA in Philosophy summa cum laude, Rice U., 1960; JD with highest honors, U. Tex., 1962; postgrad., U. London, 1962—63. Bar: Tex., DC, NY. Law clk. U.S. Ct. Appeals (2d cir.), 1963—64; assoc. Vinson & Elkins, Houston, 1964—69, ptnr., 1970—, mng.ptnr., 1992—. Vis. prof. U. Tex. Sch. Law, 1971, Rice U., 1976, U. Houston Sch. Law, 1977; chair adv. group U.S. Dist. Ct. (so. dist.) Tex.; mem. adv. com. Supreme Ct. Tex. Author (with Charles Alan Wright): Procedure: The Handmaid of Justice, 1965. Trustee U. Tex. Law Sch. Found., Southwestern Legal Found., Rice U., Baylor Coll. Medicine; chair Tex. Higher Edn. Coordinating Bd., 1991; mem. Houston Annenberg Challenge Child Centered Schs. Initiative Bd., Houston, 1997—; bd. dirs. Houston Music Hall Found. Bd., 1996—. Named Disting. Alumnus, U. Tex., 1997, U. Tex. Sch. Law, 1998; fellow, Rotary Found., 1962—63. Fellow: Tex. Bar Found., ABA Found., Internat. Soc. Barristers, Am. Coll. Trial Lawyers, Internat. Acad. Trial Lawyers; mem.: ABA (chmn. antitrust sect. 1989—90), Am. Bd. Trial Advocates, Philos. Soc. Tex., Houston Philos. Soc., Houston Com. Fgn. Rels., Am. Law Inst., Assn. Bar City of NY, Houston Bar Assn., Century Assn. N.Y.C., Barristers, Cosmos Club (DC), Eldorado Country Club (Calif.), Houston Country Club, Castle Pines Golf Club (Colo.), Galveston Artillery Club, Chancellors, Phi Delta Phi, Phi Beta Kappa. Office: Vinson & Elkins 2800 First City Tower 1001 Fannin St Houston TX 77002-6760

REASONER, WILLIS IRL, III, lawyer; b. Hamilton, Ohio, Dec. 24, 1951; s. W. Irl Jr. and Nancy Jane (Mitchell) R.; m. Lana Jean Mayes, Apr. 19, 1975 (div. Sept. 1985); 1 child, Erick; m. Joan Marie Mogil, Dec. 30, 1985; children: Scott, Sally. BA in History, Ind. U., 1974; JD cum laude, U. S.C., 1978. Bar: Ohio 1978, U.S. Dist. Ct. (so. dist.) Ohio 1978, U.S. Dist. Ct. (no. dist.) Ohio 1979, U.S. Ct. Appeals (6th cir.) 1988, U.S. Ct. Appeals (1st cir.) 1991, U.S. Ct. Appeals (7th cir.) 1999. Assoc. Porter, Wright, Morris & Arthur, Columbus, Ohio, 1978-83; ptnr. Baker & Hostetler, 1983-94, Habash, Reasoner & Frazier, 1994—. Mem. ABA, Ohio Bar Assn., Columbus Bar Assn. Home: 4005 Redford Ct New Albany OH 43054-9500 Office: Habash, Reasoner & Frazier 471 E Broad St Ste 800 Columbus OH 43215-3854

REASOR, MARK JAE, pharmacology and toxicology educator; b. Evansville, Ind., Nov. 3, 1945; s. Chester Thomas Reasor and Catherine Lillian Drury; m. Mary Louise Comer, Aug. 19, 1967; children: Michael Andrew, Meredith Kathleen. BS in Agr., Purdue U., 1967; MA in Biochemistry, Duke U., 1969; PhD in Toxicology, Johns Hopkins U., 1976. Diplomate Am. Bd. of Toxicology. Asst. prof. pharmacology and toxicology W.Va. U., Morgantown, 1976-80, assoc. prof. pharmacology and toxicology, 1980-84, prof. pharmacology and toxicology, 1984—. Cons., pharm. industry, 1982—. Contbr. chpts. to books; co-editor: Toxicology of Newborn, 1984; assoc. editor Jour. of Toxicology and Environ. Health; contbr. over 100 articles to profl. jours. and conf. procs. Moderator, 1st Bapt. Ch., Morgantown, 1982, 97; mem. constrn. com. Habitat for Humanity, Morgantown, 1996, rep. Suncrest Neighborhood Assn., 1996. 1st lt., U.S. Army, 1969-71. Rsch. grantee NIH, , 1979, Am. Heart Assn., , 1989, Procter & Gamble Pharms., 1992. American Baptist. Avocations: racquetball, gardening, cooking, cross-country skiing. Home: 676 Kenwood Pl Morgantown WV 26505-2407 Office: West Virginia U PO Box 9229 Morgantown WV 26506-9223 E-mail: mreasor@hsc.wvu.edu.

REATH, GEORGE, JR. lawyer, mediator, arbitrator; b. Phila., Mar. 14, 1939; s. George and Isabel Duer (West) R.; children from a previous marriage: Eric (dec. 1995), Amanda; m. Ann B. Rowland, 1990. BA, Williams Coll., 1961; LLB, Harvard U., 1964. Bar: Pa. 1965, U.S. Dist. Ct. (ea. dist.) Pa. 1966, U.S. Ct. Appeals (3d cir.) 1996. Assoc. Dechert Price & Rhoads, Phila., 1964-70, Brussels, 1971-74; atty. Pennwalt Corp., Phila., 1974-78, mgr. legal dept., asst. sec., 1978-87, sr. v.p.-law, sec., 1987-89; sr. v.p., gen. counsel, sec. Elf Atochem N.Am., Inc. (formerly Pennwalt Corp.), 1990-92; sr. v.p., gen counsel, sec. Legal Triage Svcs., Inc., 1993-98; sr. v.p., gen. counsel, sec. Triage Mediation Svcs., Inc., 1999—. Bd. dirs. Internat. Bus. Forum, Inc., 1978-91; arbitrator Am. Arbitration Assn. Trustee Children's Hosp., Phila., 1974—, sec., 1980-81, vice chmn., 1984-97; bd. mgrs. Phila. City Inst. Libr., 1974—, treas., 1981-88, pres., 1989-99; bd. dirs. Phila. Festival Theatre for New Plays, 1983-94, Ctrl. Phila. Devel. Corp., 1987-93; bd. dirs. Bach Festival Phila., 1990-98, v.p., 1992-93; bd. dirs. Crime Commn. Delaware Valley, 1st vice chmn., 1992-94, chmn., 1994-96; exec. com., 1996—; bd. coun. mem. Episcopal Cmty. Svcs. 1999—, treas., 2000—. Mem.: ABA, Assn. for Conflict Resolution, Am. Corp. Counsel Assn., Phila. Bar Assn., Pa. Bar Assn., Am. Arbitration Assn., Penn Club, Winter Harbor Yacht Club, Penllyn Club, Phi Beta Kappa. Personal E-mail: greath@mindspring.com. Business E-Mail: gr@triagemediation.com.

REAUGH, O(RLAND) H. oil industry executive; b. Hanford, Wash., June 19, 1913; s. Harry Wallace Reaugh and Anna Charlotte Magnuson; m. Ruth Verne Davis, July 8, 1941 (dec. Sept. 1999); children: Dianne Reaugh Bauman, Harry Coleman; m. Mary Ann McMillan, June 17, 2000. BSChemE, Wash. State U., 1933. Reg. profl. engr., Tex. Engr. Gulf Oil Corp., 1933-48; dist. supt. McElroy Ranch Co., Breckenridge, Tex., 1948-51; ptnr. Ibex Co., 1951-54; v.p. Graridge Corp., 1954-66; sr. v.p. Petroleum Corp. Tex., 1966-83, States Inc., Breckenridge, 1983—, co-chmn., 1998—. Mem. sch. bd. Breckenridge Ind. Sch. Dist.; trustee Breckenridge Libr. & Fine Arts Found., 1989—. Capt. USAF, 1942-46. Mem. West Central Tex. Oil and Gas Assn. (dir., v.p.), Breckenridge C. of C. (pres. 1978). Democrat. Methodist. Home: 304 N Harding St Breckenridge TX 76424-3219 Office: Breck Operating Corp PO Box 911 Breckenridge TX 76424-0911

REAULO, ARTHUR ROBERT, mental health specialist, advocate; b. Troy, N.Y., May 11, 1952; s. Arthur R. Reaulo and Barbara Joyce Doyle. BA, SUNY, Albany, 1976; postgrad., Ctrl. Tex. U., 1978-80, Boston U., 1998-99. Cert. case mgr. Resident counselor Rehab. Support Svcs., Albany, 1988-91, case coord., 1991-93, sr. resident counselor, 1993-95, residential mgr., 1995-99; case mgr. Homeless and Travelers Aid Soc., 1999—. Residential mgr., cons. Rehab. Support Svcs., Albany, 1995—. Mem. Albany County Sexual Abuse Task Force, 1997—; advocate to lobby legislators to mental health issues Rehab. Support Svcs., Albany, 1988—. Mem. Internat. Assn. Psychosocial Practitioners. Democrat. Avocations: basketball, historical documentaries, watching classical movies/C-Span, attending monlthy county sessions. Home: 19th house Kaine Dr Albany NY 12203-3803

REAVES, BARRY RECO, minister; b. June 25, 1951; s. Millard Ray Reaves and Gertrude E. Burney; m. Darla Gilliam, May 25, 1990 (div. Sept. 1995); children: Derrick Pace, Barry II, Roberto Vito, Renika Darla; m. Glenda Ree Reaves, June 21, 1996. Lic. min. Maranatha House of Prayer, 1999; lic. ins. MBA & TWA Assurance. Pers. specialist U.S. Army, 1971-73; letter carrier U.S. Postal Svc., Richmond and Washington, 1984-98; ins. agt. Mil. Benefit Assn., Clarksville, Tenn., 1989-90; preacher Mem. of the Ministry, 1999—. Cons. Gospel Ministry, Clarksville, 1999-2001. Composer gospel music. Avocations: reading, writing, gospel music, singing. Home: 405 Cunningham Ln Clarksville TN 37042

REAVES, CHARLES DURHAM, investment company executive; b. Florence, S.C., June 1, 1935; s. Howard Meacham and Kathleen (Durham) R.; m. Gretchen Wuerdeman, May 4, 1963; 1 son, Mark Charles. BA magna cum laude, Furman U., 1956; LLB, U. Ala., 1961; LLM, Georgetown U., 1966; MBA, Emory U., 1981. Bar: Ala. 1961, Mass. 1967, D.C. 1970. Legal adv. to chmn. FTC, Washington, 1963-67; sec., assoc. counsel Paul Revere Life Ins. Co., Worcester, Mass., 1967-70; v.p., sec., gen. counsel Saunders Leasing System, Inc., Birmingham, 1970-74, Birmingham, Ala., 1974-80, sr. v.p. fin., sec., 1981-86; pres. Southeastern Asset Mgmt. Funds Trust, Memphis, 1986-93; exec. v.p., gen. counsel, chief compliance officer Longleaf Ptnrs. Funds, 1993—. Bd. dirs. ICI Mut. Ins. Co., Burlington, Vt. Bd. trustees Memphis Opera, 1993—. Capt. USAR, 1961-63. Decorated Army Commendation medal. Mem. ABA, FBA, Mass. Bar Assn., D.C. Bar Assn., Ala. Bar Assn., Ala. Assn. Corp. Counsel (pres. 1981-82), Fin. Execs. Inst. (dir. 1983-84), Rotary, The Club (Birmingham), Westwood Country Club (Vienna, Va.), Econ. Club of Memphis (dir. 1993-96), Crescent Club, Southwind Country Club (Memphis). Office: Southeastern Asset Mgmt Inc 6410 Poplar Ave Ste 900 Memphis TN 38119-4841 E-mail: creaves@llpf.com.

REAVES, RAY DONALD, civil engineer; b. Jacksonville, Ala., Aug. 6, 1935; s. William Ozzie and Josephine (Jackson) R.; m. Annette Baird, Dec. 18, 1959; children: Tanya Ann Walker, Ronald Ray. BS in Civil Engring., Auburn (Ala.) U., 1960; MBA, U. Utah, 1976; postgrad., U. Mo., Kansas City. Registered profl. engr., Okla.; diplomate Am. Acad. Environ. Engrs. Commd. 2d lt. USAF, 1961, advanced through grades to col., 1981; comdt. Airlift Ops. Sch., Scott AFB, Ill., 1980-82; dep. base comdr. Little Rock AFB, 1982-83; base comdr. Kunsan Air Base, Korea, 1983-84, Tinker AFB, Oklahoma City, 1984-85; dir. environ. mgr. Oklahoma City Air Logistics Ctr., Tinker AFB, 1985-89; ret. USAF, 1989; mgr. environ. engring. Oklahoma County, Oklahoma City, 1989-95, Okla. county engr., 1995—. Bus. Tech. Delegation Citizen to Citizen ambassador to Russia and Ukraine, 1992. Mem. ASCE, NSPE, Okla. Soc. Profl. Engrs. (citizen ambassador to Russia and Ukraine 1992), Midwest City C. of C., Rotary, Masons, Shriners. Avocations: golf, boating, tinkering.

REAVIS, HUBERT GRAY, JR. metal products executive; b. Winston-Salem, N.C., May 4, 1945; s. Hubert Gray and Marie (Long) R.; m. Brenda Todd, Oct. 19, 1969; children: Anna Caroline, Jennifer Rebecca. BS in Engring., N.C. State U., 1967. Metall. engr. Aluminun Co. Am., Alcoa, Tenn., 1967-73; divisional metall. engr. Aluminum Co. Am., Newburgh, Ind., 1973-79, product metall. engr. Pitts., 1979-86; quality assurance mgr. Aluminun Co. Am., Newburgh, Ind., 1986-88; tech. mgr. Aluminum Co. Am., 1988-96, mgr. materials devel. group, 1997—. Patentee in field. Mem. Aluminun Co. Am. Polit. Action, Pitts., 1979-86, Newburgh, 1986—. Recipient (3) Arthur Vining Davis awards. Mem. Am. Soc. for Metals, N.C. State Alumni Loyalty Fund, Phi Kappa Phi, Theta Tau, Alpha Sigma Mu, Tau Beta Pi. Office: Aluminum Co Am PO Box 10 Newburgh IN 47629-0010

REAVIS, LIZA ANNE, semiconductor executive; b. N.Y.C., July 27, 1959; d. William Ralph and Juliette (Bustillo y Zelaya) Bartlett; m. Paul H. Reavis, May 25, 1985. BA in Internat. Rels., Rice U., 1981; MBA, Georgetown U., 1988. Project asst. Latham, Watkins & Hills, Washington, 1982-83; assoc. mgr. countertrade Sears World Trade, 1983-85; export asst. Weadon, Dibble & Rehm, 1985-86; assoc. cons. Vanguard Comm. Corp., Palo Alto, Calif., 1988-90; bus. mgr. Teleport Comm. Corp., San Francisco, 1990-94; corp. divsn. contr. Nat. Semicondr. Corp., 1995—. Contbr. Project Open Hand, San Francisco, Calif. Disabled Vets. Assn., Am. Assn. for AIDS Rsch., San Francisco, 1990—; mem. Golden Gate Nat. Recreation Area, San Francisco, 1990—. Recipient Teleport Comms. Group Ann. Hero award, 1994; Presdl. scholar Dept. HEW, 1977. Mem. Acad. Polit. Sci., Club des Hiboux (sec. 1979-80), Commonwealth Club, Sierra Club, Cousteau Soc., Phi Beta Kappa, Beta Gamma Sigma (treas. San Francisco alumni chpt. 2001-02), Pi Delta Phi. Avocations: international cultures and politics, classical ballet, poetry, piano. Home: 2060 14th Ave San Francisco CA 94116-1310 Office: Mail Stop A1-465 2900 Semiconductor Dr Santa Clara CA 95051-0606 E-mail: liza.reavis@nsc.com.

REAVLEY, THOMAS MORROW, federal judge; b. Quitman, Tex., June 21, 1921; s. Thomas Mark and Mattie (Morrow) Reavley; m. Florence Montgomery Wilson, July 24, 1943; children: Thomas Wilson, Marian, Paul Stewart, Margaret. BA, U. Tex., 1942; JD, Harvard U., 1948; LLD, Austin Coll., 1974, Southwestern U., 1977, Tex. Wesleyan, 1982; LLM, U. Va., 1983; LLD, Pepperdine U., 1993. Bar: Tex. 1948. Asst. dist. atty., Dallas, 1948—49; mem. Bell & Reavley, Nacogdoches, 1949—51; county atty., 1951; with Collins, Garrison, Renfro & Zeleskey, 1951—52; mem. Fisher, Tonahill & Reavley, Jasper, Tex., 1952—55; sec. state Tex., 1955—57; mem. Powell, Rauhut, McGinnis & Reavley, Austin, Tex., 1957—64; dist. judge, 1964—68; justice U.S. Supreme Ct., 1968—77; counsel Scott & Douglass, 1977—79; judge U.S. Ct. Appeals (5th cir.), Austin, Tex., 1979—90, sr. judge, 1990—. Lectr. Baylor U. Law Sch., 1976—94; adj. prof. U. Tex. Law Sch., 1958—59, 1978—79, 1988—95. Chancellor S.W. Tex. conf. United Meth. Ch., 1972—93. Lt. USNR, 1943—45. Mem.: Masons (33 degree). Office: US Ct Appeals Homer Thornberry Judicial Bldg 903 San Jacinto Blvd Ste 434 Austin TX 78701-2450 E-mail: tmr@ca5.uscourts.gov.

REBANE, ALEKSANDER, physicist, educator; b. Tartu, Estonia, Aug. 19, 1958; s. Karl and Ljubov (Shagalova) R.; m. Kaire Vaimel, Dec. 18, 1981; children: Kadri, Aleksander. MS, Tartu U., 1981; PhD, Inst. Physics Tartu, 1985. Rsch. scientist Inst. Physics, Tartu, 1984-90; asst. Swiss Fed. Inst. Tech., Zurich, 1991-96; assoc. prof. Mont. State U., Bozeman, 1996—. Inventor in field; contbr. articles to profl. jours. Recipient Internat. Commn. for Optics prize, 1993, Discover Mag. Best Invention award, 1995, Ruzicka prize, 1996. Mem. Internat. Soc. Optical Engrs., Optical Soc. Am., German Phys. Soc. Office: Mont State U Dept Physics Bozeman MT 59717-0001 E-mail: rebane@physics.montana.edu.

REBANE, JOHN T. lawyer; b. Bamberg, Germany, Oct. 29, 1946; s. Henn and Anna (Inna) R.; m. Linda Kay Morgan, Sept. 22, 1972; children: Alexis Morgan, Morgan James. BA, U. Minn., 1970, JD, 1973. Bar: Minn. 1973. Atty. Land O'Lakes, Inc., Arden Hills, Minn., 1973-80, assoc. gen. counsel, 1983, v.p., gen. counsel, 1984—. Sec. Land O' Lakes Farmland Feed LLC; sec., dir. Land O' Lakes Internat. Devel. Corp. Mem. ABA, Minn. Bar Assn., Hennepin County Bar Assn., Nat. Coun. Farm Coop. (gen.coun. com. chmn.). Office: Land O'Lakes Inc PO Box 64101 Saint Paul MN 55164-0101 E-mail: jreba@landolakes.com.

REBAY, LUCIANO, Italian literature educator, literary critic; b. Milan, Italy, Apr. 23, 1928; came to U.S., 1955; s. Angelo and Pierina (Doniselli) R.; m. Martha Virginia Krauss, Aug. 2, 1952; children: Alexandra, Ilaria. Maturita classica Liceo Manzoni, Milan, 1946; Licence es lettres, U. Aix-en-Provence, France, 1951; PhD, Columbia U., 1960. Instr. Italian Columbia U., N.Y.C., 1957-60, asst. prof., 1960-63, assoc. prof., 1963-65, prof., 1965-73, Giuseppe Ungaretti prof. Italian lit., 1973—, chmn. Italian Dept., 1970-73; dir. Ctr. Italian Studies, 1985-88. Cons. to scholarly jours.; mem. Nat. Bd. Translators, Columbia U. Transl. Ctr. Author: Le origini della poesia di Giuseppe Ungaretti, 1962, Invitation to Italian Poetry, 1969, Alberto Moravia, 1970, Giuseppe Ungaretti, Gli scritti egiziani, 1909-1912, 1980, Montale, Clizia e l'America, 1982, Montale per amico, 1994, Montale: del dire e del non dire, 1998; editor: Giuseppe Ungaretti, Saggi e interventi, 1974, Jean Paulhan-Giuseppe Ungaretti, Correspondance, 1921-68, 1989. Guggenheim fellow, 1966-67; Am. Council Learned Socs. fellow, 1970-71; NEH fellow, 1980-81; Am. Philos. Soc. research grantee, 1970, 75 Mem. MLA, Am. Assn. Tchrs. of Italian, Associazione Internazionale per gli Studi di Lingua e Letteratura Italiana

REBB, KAREN MARLENE, music educator; b. Columbus, Ga. d. Glen Percival and Vivian Irene (Williams) Loken; 1 child, Michael John-Glen. BS in Music Edn., Elem. Edn., Grand Canyon U., 1981; MA in Music Edn., No. Ariz. U., 1986. Cert. tchr., Ariz.; cert. I, II, III Levels Orff cert. Tchr. Heatherbrae Elem. Sch., Phoenix, 1981-82, Park Meadows Elem. Sch., Phoenix, 1982-95, Arrowhead Elem. Sch., Glendale, Ariz., 1995—. Mem. adj. faculty Ottawa U., 1989—. Author: project Science of Music: Integrating the Arts and Technology, 1995. Mem. 1st Hist. Presbyn. Ch.; mem. site-based mgmt. team Park Meadows Sch., 1994, 95; mem. Dist. Strategic Planning Com., 1994; mem. dist. fine arts coun. writing Fine Arts Curriculum for Dist., Phoenix, 1995, 96. Recipient Ray Maben Scholar award Grand Canyon U., 1980, Ariz.; artist-in-residence grantee, 1989. Mem. NEA, Am. Orff-Schulwerk Assn., Ariz. Edn. Assn., Ariz. Orff-Schulwerk Assn. (sec., bd. dirs. 1990-92), Ariz. Music Educators Assn., Music Educators Nat. Conf. Avocations: playing piano, guitar, singing, reading, writing. Home: 19436 N 83rd Dr Peoria AZ 85382-8790

REBEC, GEORGE VINCENT, neuroscience researcher, educator, administrator; b. Harrisburg, Pa., Apr. 6, 1949; s. George Martin and Nadine (Bosko) R. AB, Villanova U., 1971; MA, U. Colo., 1974, PhD, 1975. Postdoctoral fellow U. Calif., San Diego, 1975-77; asst. prof. Ind. U., Bloomington, 1977-81, assoc. prof., 1981-85, prof. psychology, 1985—, dir. program in neural sci., 1985—, Chancellor's prof., 1999. Mem. rsch. rev. com. NIMH. Author: (with P.M. Groves) Introduction to Biological Psychology, 1988, 92; contbr. articles to profl. jours. Recipient Eli Lilly Tchg. award, 1978, Pres.' award Ind. U., 1990, Ind. U. Tchg. Excellence Recognition award, 1999, 2000; grantee NIDA, 1979—, NSF, 1985-96, NINDS, 1996—. Fellow AAAS, Am.

Psychol. Soc.; mem. Soc. for Neurosci. (chmn. Ind. U. chpt.), Internat. Brain Rsch. Orgn., Assn. Neurosci. Depts. and Programs (treas.). Roman Catholic. Avocation: sports. Office: Ind U Program in Neural Sci Dept Psychology Bloomington IN 47405

REBEIN, ROBERT BRIAN, English studies educator, writer; b. Dodge City, Kans., Sept. 1, 1964; s. William Joseph and Patricia (Lee) R.; m. Alyssa Chase, July 1, 1995; children: Alexandra Maria, Rowan Jakob. BA in English, U. Kans., 1988; MA in English, Exeter (Eng.) U., 1990; PhD in English, SUNY, Buffalo, 1995; MFA in Writing, Wash. U., 1997. Asst. prof. English Ind. U.-Purdue U., Indpls., 1998—. Author: Hicks, Tribes, and Dirty Realists: American Fiction After Postmodernism, 2001. Office: Ind U Purdue U Dept English 425 University Blvd Indianapolis IN 46202

REBEIZ, CONSTANTIN A. plant physiology educator, laboratory director; b. Beirut, July 11, 1936; came to U.S., 1969, naturalized, 1975; s. Anis C. and Valentine A. (Choueyri) R.; m. Carole Louise Conness, Aug. 18, 1962; children: Paul A., Natalie, Mark J. BS, Am. U., Beirut, 1959; MS, U. Calif. - Davis, 1960, PhD, 1965. Dir. dept. biol. scis. Agrl. Rsch. Inst., Beirut, 1965-69; research assoc. biology U. Calif. - Davis, 1969-71; assoc. prof. plant physiology U. Ill., Urbana-Champaign, 1972-76, prof., 1976—, dir. Lab. Plant Biochemistry and Photobiology, 1999—. Contbr. articles to sci. publs. plant physiology and biochemistry. Recipient Beckman Rsch. award, 1982, 1985, Funk award, 1985, Sr. Rsch. award, U. Ill., 1994, Presdl. Green Chemistry Challenge award, 1999, named One of 100 Outstanding Innovators, Sci. Digest, 1984—85; grantee John P. Trebellas Rsch. Endowment, 1986, C.A. and C.C. Rebeiz Endowment for basic rsch., 2000. Mem. Am. Soc. Plant Physiologists, Comite Internat. de Photobiologie, Am. Soc. Photobiology, AAAS, Lebanese Assn. Advancement Scis. (exec. com. 1967-69), Sigma Xi. Achievements include research on pathway of chlorophyll biosynthesis, chloroplast devel., bioengring. of photosynthetic reactors; pioneered biosynthesis of chlorophyll in vitro; duplication of greening process of plants in test tube, demonstration of operation of multibranched chlorophyll biosynthetic pathway in nature; formulation and design of laser herbicides, insecticides and cancer chemotherapeutic agents. Home: 301 W Pennsylvania Ave Urbana IL 61801-4918 Office: U Ill 240A Pabl Urbana IL 61801 E-mail: crebeiz@uiuc.edu. *Meaningful scientific discoveries are those that help humans achieve a better understanding of themselves, of their environment or of the universe at large, as well as those that contribute to the betterment of the human spiritual, psychological and physical condition.*

REBEL, JEROME IVO, financial planner; b. Cin., Aug. 22, 1949; s. Ivo Anthony and Loraine (Spieser) R.; m. Sharyn Senchesak, Sept. 26, 1992. A in Mech. Engring., Ohio Coll. Applied Sci., 1969; BBA in Fin., U. Cin., 1988. CFP. CFP Investors Diversified Svcs./Am. Express, Cin., 1981-86, Oxford Fin. Group, Cin., 1986—. Mem. Internat. Assn. Fin. Planning. Office: Oxford Fin Group 8044 Montgomery Rd Ste 400W Cincinnati OH 45236-2923 E-mail: jrebel@lnc.com.

REBELLO, MARLENE MUNSON, speech pathologist; b. San Jose, Calif., Oct. 15, 1948; d. Alfred Vernon and Rose Zita (Pereira) Nunes; m. Steven Del Munson, Mar. 21, 1970 (div. 1982); m. William Wayne Rebello, Dec. 5, 1992. BA, San Jose State U., 1970, MA, 1971; MS in Counseling, U. LaVerne, 1990. Speech pathologist Newark (Calif.) Unified Sch. Dist., 1971—; pvt. practice Fremont and Pleasanton, Calif., 1980—; speech pathologist Washington Hosp., Fremont, 1980-89. Ednl. cons. Fremont and Pleasanton, 1980—. Recipient Bank of Am. award, 1966, Cabrillo scholarship, Nat. Merit scholarship, 1966, Maria Leonard award Outstanding Sr. Grade Point Average, 1970; fellow VA, 1970. Mem. Calif. Speech and Hearing Assn., Pleasanton Sister City Assn. (v.p. 1996—), Newark Tchrs. Assn. (treas. 1971—), Save Our Sunol Found., Calif. Tchrs. Assn., Arthur & Elena Court Conservation Soc. Avocations: antique collecting, decorating, gourmet cooking. Home: 10579 Foothill Rd Sunol CA 94586-9464 E-mail: marspot@aol.com.

REBENACK, JOHN HENRY, retired librarian; b. Wilkinsburg, Pa., Feb. 10, 1918; s. Charles Lewis and Carrie (Fielding) R.; m. Dorothy Merle Treat, Oct. 31, 1942 (dec. Apr. 1971); children: Charles Edwin, Christine (Mrs. Clair N. Hayes III); m. Frances Strabley Krieger, May 6, 1972. AB, U. Pitts., 1942; BS in L.S, Carnegie Library Sch., 1947. Reference asst. Carnegie Library, Pitts., 1947-50; librarian Salem (Ohio) Pub. Library, 1950-53, Elyria (Ohio) Library, 1953-57; asst. librarian Akron (Ohio) Public Library, 1957-65, asso. librarian, 1965-67, librarian-dir., 1967-80. Dir. U.S. Book Exchange, Inc., 1972 Mem. United Community Council, Citizens' Com. Pub. Welfare, 1965-66, chmn. group work and recreation div., 1963-66, v.p., 1967-68, pres. conf. of execs., 1975-76; mem. steering com., planning div. United Way; mem. Akron Mayor's Task Force on Human Relations, 1962; mem. library com. President's Com. on Employment of Handicapped, 1967-80, chmn., 1973-80, mem. sch. library manpower adv. com., 1967-73; mem. coll. adv. com. U. Akron, 1972-85; mem. adv. council on fed. programs State Library of Ohio, 1975-79; Bd. visitors Grad. Sch. Library and Info. Sci., U. Pitts., 1968-74; mem. exec. bd. Gt. Trail council Boy Scouts Am., 1977-80; bd. dirs. Summit County unit Am. Cancer Soc., 1976— , pres., 1979-81; bd. dirs. Ohio div., 1981-91, chmn. pub. info. com., 1989-90, exec. com. 1988-91. With AUS, 1942-45. Recipient Newton D. Baker citation, 1968 Mem. ALA (chmn. personnel adminstrv. sect. 1966-67, chmn. bldgs. and equipment sect. 1971-73, chmn. legislation assembly 1976-77), Ohio Library Assn. (exec. bd. 1957-60, chmn. adult edn. round table 1963, chmn. legis. com. 1965-66, 70-72, 76-80, pres. 1966-67, Librarian of Year 1979, named to Hall of Fame 1989), Ohio Library Found. (privileged mem. 1980, privileged dir. 1988—), Carnegie Library Sch. Assn. (pres. 1961-63), U. Pitts. Grad. Sch. Library and Info. Sci. Alumni Assn. (exec. com. 1978-79, Disting. Alumnus award 1980), Am. Assn. UN (v.p. Akron chpt. 1960), Kiwanis Internat. Found. (Tablet of Honor 1997, George F. Hixson fellow 1998), Beta Phi Mu. Clubs: Torch (pres. 1968-69), Kiwanis (pres. Akron 1978-79). Congregationalist. Home: 2095 Brookshire Rd Akron OH 44313-5323

REBER, CALVIN HENRY, theological studies educator, minister; b. Lebanon, Pa., Apr. 30, 1915; s. Calvin Henry Reber and Stella Elizabeth Mease; m. Audrie Eleanora Fox, June 6, 1939 (dec. Dec. 1987); children: Vera Blinn, James. BA, Lebanon Valley Coll., 1936, DD, 1959; MDiv, United Theol. Sem., Dayton, Ohio, 1939; PhD, Columbia U., 1958. Ordained to ministry Meth. Ch., 1939. Missionary to China, United Brethren Ch., Hong Kong, 1939-41; pastor Evang.-United Brethren Ch., Palmyra, Pa., 1942-46, Missionary to China, Canton, 1946-48; assoc. exec. sec. Kwangtung Synod Ch. of Christ, 1948-51; mission prof. United Theol. Sem., 1951-83, adj. faculty, 1983-88. Vis. prof. Chung Chi Coll., Chinese U. Hong Kong, 1970-71. Author: Renewal Thru Mission, 1966; editor Telescore Messenger, 1990-94. Fellow Am. Assn. Theol. Schs., 1973. Mem. Assn. Profs. of Missions, Ea. Pa. Conf. of United Meth. Chs. Democrat. Avocations: photography, travel. Home: 248 Village Sq Chambersburg PA 17201-4000

REBER, CHERYL ANN, consultant, social worker, trainer; b. Cin., Feb. 7, 1956; d. Randland John and Marcella Catherine (Hollstegge) Reber; m. Michael Zaleltel. AA, Xavier U., 1976, BA, 1980. Lic. social worker. Social worker Altercrest, Cin., 1977-79, Hamilton County Dept. Human Svcs., Cin., 1979-85, adoption specialist, social worker, 1985-92, trainer, program developer, 1988-92; social worker, AIDS specialist Hospice of the Miami Valley, 1992-95; ind. trainer Inst. for Human Svcs., Cin., 1996—. Trainer Hamilton County Dept. Human Svcs., Cin., 1988-92; permanency planning cons. Ohio Dept. Human Svcs., 1995-2000, Mem. Cmty. Task Force on Adoption, Cin., 1989-91, 95—. Mem. S.W. Ohio Adoption Resource Exch., Beechmont Players. Democrat. Roman Catholic. Avocations: whitewater rafting, community theatre, primitive camping and exploration. E-mail: creber4129@aol.com.

REBER, ELEANORA ANN, archaeologist, educator, archaeometrist; b. Indiana, Pa., June 26, 1973; d. James Calvin and Clarice Klump Reber. BS, Beloit (Wis.) Coll., 1995; AM, PhD, Harvard U., 2001. Archaeol. field technician, Wis., 1995—96, Pa., 1995—96, Calif., 1995—96; field sch. supr. Ctrl. Miss. Valley Rsch. Inst., Collinsville, Ill., 1998—99; tchg. fellow Harvard U., Cambridge, Mass., 1998—99; lectr. U. N.C., Wilmington, 2001—. Contbr. articles to profl. jours. Fellow, NSF, 1996; grantee, 2000, Mellon Found., 1998. Mem.: Southea. Archaeology Conf., Am. Anthropol. Assn., Soc. Am. Archaeology. Achievements include development of archaeometric technique for identifying the presence of maize in absorbed pottery residues; analysis of contents of ancient pottery from the Mississippi Valley in North America. Avocations: fencing, reading, writing, history, travel. Office: U NC Wilmington 601 S College Rd Wilmington NC 28403 E-mail: reber@post.harvard.edu.

REBER, JOSEPH E. lawyer; b. Butte, Mont., Aug. 9, 1940; s. Joseph B. and Marie Terry (Tauriainen) R. BA in Hist., U. Mont., 1962, JD, 1965; LLM in Tax, NYU, 1982. Bar: Mont. 1965, U.S. Supreme Ct. 1970, N.Y. 1980, Calif. 1989. Law clk. Mont. Supreme Ct., Helena, 1965; ptnr. Heron & Reber, 1965-70; pvt. practice, 1970-80; assoc. various law firms, N.Y.C., 1980-84; v.p. Pension & Actuarial Co., Colorado Springs, Colo., 1984-89; gen. counsel Great Am. Life Ins., L.A., 1989-90; pvt. practice Marina Del Rey, Calif., 1990—. Presenter in field. Author: Trust and Tax Estate Planning, 1993; editor law rev. U. Mont., 1964-65; contbr. articles to Fin. Planning Mag., 1987-89. State chmn. Robert F. Kennedy for Pres., Mont., 1968, Senator Frank Church for Pres., 1976; del. platform com. Dem. Nat. Conv., 1976-80; active endowment steering com. L.A. Philharmonic, 1992—; dir. SOM Found., 1995—. Capt. USMSC, 1966-72. Mem. ABA (minorities vice-chmn., internat. law com. 1995—), Nat. Acad. Elder Law Attys., Calif. Bar Assn. (trust com. 1992—), Mont. State Hist. Soc. (v.p. 1979-80), Marina-Culver City Bar Assn. (pres. 1994-95), L.A. County Bar Assn. (ho. of dels.), Beverly Hills Bar Assn., N.Y. Bar Assn. Avocations: art, history, skiing, music, scuba.

REBER, RAYMOND ANDREW, retired chemical engineer; b. Bklyn., Apr. 16, 1942; s. Herbert and Dorothy Agnes (Schmidt) R.; m. Anita Jean Roe, June 22, 1963; children: Laura Jean Bucci, Paul Raymond, Jill Anita. BChemE, NYU, 1963, MChemE, 1966. Engr. M.W. Kellogg, N.Y.C., 1964-69; devel. engr., supr. Union Carbide, Tarrytown, N.Y., 1970-74, lic. bus. mgr., 1975-81, new bus. devel. mgr. Danbury, Conn., 1982-84, tech. mgr. Tarrytown, 1985-87; dir. of tech. UOP, 1988-93; exec. v.p., COO Balchem Corp., Slate Hill, N.Y., 1994-96, pres., CEO, 1997; cons., 1999—. Patentee in field. Commr. Montrose Improvement Dist., NY, 1970—; soccer referee, 1977—93; trustee No. Westchester Water Works, 1995—98, 1998—2001. Recipient Kirkpatrick award McGraw-Hill, 1967, 87. Mem. AIChE, NSPE. Episcopalian. Avocations: soccer, boating, table games, philatelist. Home: 10 Bonnie Hollow Ln Montrose NY 10548-1314

REBERG, ROSALIE, principal; m. Larry Alan Reberg, Aug. 16, 1975; children: Camden Ashleigh, Jacob Alan. BA, Holy Names Coll., 1971; MA with distinction, Calif. State U., Stanislaus, 1994. Elem. edn. tchr. Stanislaus Union Sch. Dist., Modesto, Calif., 1974-96; vice prin. Chrysler Elem. Sch., 1996-97; prin. Eisenhut Elem. Sch., 1997-99, Prescott Sr. Elem. Sch., Modesto, 1999-2000, Auberry (Calif.) Elem. Sch., 2000—. Classroom mgmt. mentor tchr., Stanislaus Union Sch. Dist., 1988-89. Mem. Tchrs. English to Spkrs. of Other Langs., Assn. Calif. Sch. Adminstrs. Avocations: reading, computers, languages. Office: Auberry Elem Sch 33367 N Auberry Rd Auberry CA 93602 E-mail: rreberg@sierra.k12.ca.us.

REBERT, JEPHREY LEE, transportation planner, musician; b. Carlisle, Pa., June 10, 1959; s. John Alton and Mary Anna (Feeman) R. BS, Pa. State U., 1982. Residential appraiser County of York, Pa., 1984-85; phys. and environ. planner York County Planning Commn., 1985-87, transp. planner, 1987-93, sr. transp. planner, 1993—. Musician, prodr.: audiotape Peace of Mind (Loose Cannons), 1995; musician: (CD) Colonial Pagoda (Namaste), 1997. Alumni mem. Pa. State Blue Band; treas., bd. dirs. Ctr. for Ind. Living Opportunities. Mem.: Inst. Transp. Engrs., Am. Planning Assn., Victory Athletic Assn., Phi Mu Alpha Sinphonia (Alpha Zeta chpt., alumnus). Avocations: anthropology, racquet sports, numismatics. Home: 59 N Lehman St York PA 17403-1116 Office: York County Planning Commn 100 W Market St York PA 17401-1332

REBHUN, JOSEPH, allergist, immunologist, medical educator; b. Przemysl, Poland, Oct. 7, 1921; came to U.S., 1950; s. Baruch and Serel R.; m. Maria Birkenhejm, Aug. 10, 1945; children: Lillian Friedland, Richard B.R., Donald. MD, U. Innsbruck, Austria, 1950; MS in Medicine, Northwestern U., 1954. Diplomate Am. Bd. Allergy and Immunology. Intern Barnert Meml. Hosp., Patterson, N.J.; resident in internal medicine Tompkins County Meml. Hosp. and Cornell U., N.Y., 1951-52; fellow in allergy Northwestern U. Med. Sch./Chidlren's Meml. Hosp., Chgo., 1952-54; fellow instr. Northwestern U. Med. Sch., 1954; asst. clin. prof. medicine Loma Linda U., 1957-93; clin. prof. medicine U. So. Calif., L.A., 1965-91, ret., 1998. Chief allergy Chgo. Eye, Ear, Nose and Throat Hosp., 1953-55; cons. Pacific State Hosp., Spadra Pomona Valley Cmty. Hosp., Pomona Casa Colina Hosp. Author: SOS, 1946, The Cry of Democracy for Help, God and Man in Two Worlds, 1985, The Embers of Michael, 1993, Crisis of Morality and Reaction to the Holocaust, 1998, Leap to Life: Triumph Over Nazi Evil, 2000; contbr. numerous articles to med. jours. Pres. Am. Congress Jews from Poland, 1969-70. Capt., U.S. Mil., San Francisco. Recipient honors City and County of L.A., L.A. Office Dist. Atty., Senate of State of Calif., all 1985. Fellow Am. Acad. Allergy (rsch. coun. 1960-65), Am. Coll. Allergy, Assn. Clin. Allergy and Immunology; mem. West Coast Allergy Soc., Calif. Allergy Assn., L.A. Soc. Allergy, L.A. Med. Assn., Calif. Med. Assn. E-mail: joerebhun@aol.com.

REBICEK, VINCENT STASS, interior designer, speciality store executive; b. Scranton, Pa., Sept. 5, 1922; s. Anthony and Catherine (Mikolayczak) R. Student at N.Y. Sch. Design, N.Y.C., 1940. Head interior decoration dept. Cleland-Simpson, Scranton, Pa., 1944-48; owner Vincent S. Rebicek-Distinctive Interiors, Scranton, 1948—; owner Things (specialty store), Scranton, 1967—. Contbr. articles to profl. jours. Mem. St. Stanislaus Polish Nat. Cath. Ch. Mem. Am. Soc. Interior Designers., Scranton C. of C. Republican. Home: 906 Taylor Ave Scranton PA 18510-1409 Fax: 570-342-2079.

REBIK, JAMES MICHAEL, otolaryngologist; b. Marshalltown, Iowa, July 10, 1953; s. Hubert James and Donna Jean (Grandgeorge) R.; m. Sue Ellyn Primmer, Dec. 22, 1979; children: Christopher James, Kristin Leigh, Robert James, Jonathan Michael. BA summa cum laude, U. No. Iowa, 1981; DO, Kirksville Coll. Osteo. Med., 1985. Diplomate Am. Osteo. Bd. Ophthalmology and Otorhinolaryngology, Nat. Bd. Med. Examiners for Osteo. Physicians and Surgeons; lic. physician, Mo., Iowa, Minn., Tex., Okla. Intern Kirksville (Mo.) Osteo Med. Ctr., 1985-86, resident otorhinolaryngology/oro-facial plastic surgery, 1986-90; otolaryngologist Landstuhl (Germany) Army Regional Med. Ctr., 1990-92; chief otolaryngology-head and neck surgery svc. Reynolds Army Community Hosp., Ft. Sill, Okla., 1992-94; pvt. practice Altus, 1998—. Cons. VA Med Ctr., Big Spring, Tex., 1996-98. Maj. M.C. U.S. Army, 1990-94. Recipient 1st degree brown belt Gup U.S. Tang Soo Do Moo Duk Kwan Fedn., 1979. Fellow: Am. Osteo. Coll. Otolaryngology-Head and Neck Surgery, Soc. Mil. Otolaryngologists; mem.: AMA, Okla. Osteo. Assn., Okla. Acad. Otolaryngology-Head and Neck Surgery, Tex. Osteo. Med. Assn., Pan-Am. Assn. Otorhinolaryngology-Head and Neck surgery, Christian Soc. Otolaryngology-Head and Neck Surgery, Am. Acad. Otolaryngology-Head and Neck Surgery, Am. Acad. Otolaryngic Allergy, Assn. Mil. Surgeons U.S., Am. Osteo. Assn., Mensa, VFW. Baptist. Avocations: jogging, medieval and WWII history, baroque and classical music. Home: 901 Trail Dr S Altus OK 73521-1032 Office: 1200 E Pecan St Altus OK 73521-6141 also: PO Box 1754 Vernon TX 76385-1754 E-mail: drjrebik@intellisys.net.

REBMANN, NINA SOPHIE, research scientist; b. Huntington, N.Y., Oct. 2, 1964; d. Leonard Jerome and Erika Hermine (Busch) DiGiovanni; m. Wilhelm F.J. Rebmann, Sept. 30, 1990; 1 child, Andreas Wilhelm. BA in Biology, Douglass Coll., 1989. Cert. mobile intensive care paramedic, N.J. Cardiovascular pharmacologist Wyeth-Ayerst Rsch., Princeton, N.J., 1990-91; rsch. asst. dept. psychology Princeton U., 1991-97; scientist Novartis Pharm., Summit, 1997—2001; assoc. chemist Aventis Pharms., Bridgewater, NJ, 2001—. Contbr. articles to profl. jours. Vol. Watchung Rescue Squad, N.J., 1986-92; EMT Muhlenberg Regl. Med. Ctr., Plainfield, N.J., 1987-93. Mem. N.J. Assn. for Lab. Animal Sci. (editor, trustee 1992—, sec.), Am. Acad. Scis., Soc. for Whole-Body Autoradiography, Am. Assn. for Lab. Animal Sci. Republican. Lutheran. Avocations: tennis, skiing, antiques, travel. Home: 2024 S Branch Rd Somerville NJ 08876-3918 Office: Aventis Pharms PO Box 6800-JR2 3318a Bridgewater NJ 08807 E-mail: nina.rebmann@aventis.com.

REBOLI, JOHN ANTHONY, publishing executive; b. Newark, Sept. 3, 1963; s. Eneo S. and Josephine M. (Lock) R. BA in Bus., So. Conn. State U., 1986; postgrad., Seton Hall U. Assoc. pub. to Eneo S. Reboli pub. Reboli Newspapers Inc., West Caldwell, N.J., 1986-89, Newspaper pub., 1989—. Reboli Pub. Co. properties include Fairfield Chronicle, Parsippany News, Morristown News, N.J. Wire Svc., Parsippany Wire Svc.; co-owner Cafe Ernesto's Restaurant, Parsippany, N.J.; owner corp. office and rental property mgmt. co. Real Estate Investment Properties, Inc. Author: (with others) Portfolio of Accounting Systems of for Small and Medium-Sized Businesses, 1992, 3rd edit. Mem. Hist. Soc., Alumni-Presdl. Soc. Mem. N.J. Assn. Pub. Accts., Nat. Soc. Pub. Accts., Nat. Soc. Tax Profls. Democrat. Roman Catholic. Office: Reboli Newspapers Inc PO Box 6123 West Caldwell NJ 07007-6123

REBOLJ, JOAN KALETTA, training and development professional; b. Cleve., Sept. 17, 1959; d. John and Betty (Werner) K.; m. John Adolph Rebolj, May 8, 1982; children: John Michael, Hannah Marie. BA, Notre Dame Coll. Ohio, 1980; MA, John Carroll U., 1983. Tchr. Lumen Cordium H.S., Bedford, Ohio, 1981-83; lectr. English John Carroll U., University Heights, 1983, Lakeland C.C., Kirtland, 1983-99. Lectr. English Cuyahoga (Ohio) C.C., 1983-85, 94-95, Ursuline Coll., Pepper Pike, Ohio, 1989-90. Book reviewer. Mem. Modern Lang. Assn. Democrat. Roman Catholic. Avocations: painting, gardening, needlework, internet. Office: Sirva 6070 Parkland Blvd Mayfield Heights OH 44124 E-mail: joan.rebolj@crscms.com.

REBOLLO-LOPEZ, FRANCISCO, territory supreme court justice; Justice Supreme Ct. of Puerto Rico, San Juan, 1992—. Office: Supreme Court PO Box 2392 San Juan PR 00902-2392*

REBSTOCK, THEODORE LYNN, chemist, educator, retired research scientist; b. Elkhart, Ind., June 24, 1925; s. Adolph Rebstock and Redna Dunkelberger; m. Barbara Jean Lee, Nov. 30, 1957; children: David Lynn, Donald Lee. BA, North Ctrl. Coll., Naperville, Ill., 1949; MS, Mich. State U., 1951, PhD, 1956. Instr. rsch. Mich. State U., East Lansing, 1951—56, asst. prof. agrl. chemistry, 1956—59, vis. prof., 1965; assoc. prof. chemistry Westmar Coll., Le Mars, Iowa, 1959—66, prof. chemistry, 1966—83, chmn. chemistry dept., 1963—83; mgr. R&D Lab. Harkers, Inc., 1984—90; ret., 1990. Dir. divsn. natural scis. Westmar Coll., Le Mars, Iowa, 1970. Contbr. articles to profl. jours. Fellow: AAAS; mem.: Am. Chem. Soc., Kiwanis Club (pres. 1993), Sigma Xi. Methodist. Avocations: golf, bowling, gardening, woodworking. Home: 1026 Sixth Ave SE Le Mars IA 51031

RECABO, JAIME MIGUEL, lawyer; b. Manila, Philippines, Oct. 6, 1950; came to U.S., 1969; s. Matthew M. and Luisa (De Leon) R.; children: James M., Danielle M.; m. Maureen Susan Ward, Dec. 1980; children: Matthew J., Maura E., Joseph A., Olivia M. BA, Fordham U., 1973, JD, 1988; MBA in Fin., St. John's U., 1977. Bar: N.Y. 1989, N.J. 1989, Conn. 1989. Bus. office mgr. Eger Nursing Home Inc., S.I., N.Y., 1974-77; sr. acct. Kingsbrook Jewish Med. Ctr., Bklyn., 1977-78; asst. compt. Jewish Home & Hosp. for the Aged, Bronx, N.Y., 1978-79; dir. fiscal svcs. Frances Schervier Home & Hosp., 1979-86; exec. v.p. finance & legal affairs Franciscan Health System N.Y., 1986-89; mgmt. cons., health and immigration atty. N.Y.C., 1989—; co-founder, exec. v.p., legal counsel Profl. Healthcare Assocs., Bronxville, N.Y., 1994—. Bd. dirs. Frances Schervier Home and Hosp., Bronx, 1987-90, Bklyn. United Meth. Ch. Home, 1991-94, Hudson Valley Med. Ctr. Found., Peekskill, N.Y., 1998—, Frances Schervier Housing Devel. Fund, 2000—; vice-chmn. NYAHSA Contrs. Com., N.Y.C., 1985-86, N.Y. Archdiocese Contrs. Coun., N.Y.C., 1980-83. Mem. ABA, Am. Immigration Lawyers Assn., N.J. Bar Assn., N.Y. Bar Assn., Conn. Bar Assn., Healthcare Fin. Mgmt. Assn., Nat. Health Lawyers Assn., Filipino Am. Lawyers Assn. Roman Catholic. Office: 34 Palmer Ave Bronxville NY 10708-3404 E-mail: JRecaboLaw@msn.com.

RECANATI, ELIAS ISAAC, retired shipping company executive; b. Thessaloniki, Greece, Mar. 30, 1932; came to U.S., 1951; s. Maurice and Lina (Capuano) Recanati; 1 child Maurice. BS, NYU, 1956, MBA, 1958. V.p. Maritime Overseas Corp. (now named OSG Ship Mgmt. Inc.), N.Y.C., 1956-99; ret., 1999. Past pres. The Am. Friends of the Jewish Mus. of Greece, N.Y.C., 1988-95; mem. Soc. Maritime Arbitrators, Inc. Mem.: N.Y. Athletic Club. E-mail: lre330@aol.com.

RECCHIA, CHRISTOPHER, state agency environmental administrator; b. Wantagh, N.Y., Nov. 29, 1958; s. Michael Anthony and Adele Alma (Gluck) R. BA in Zoology, U. Vt., 1980; M Studies in Environ. Law cum laude, Vt. Law Sch., 1982; M of Environ. Studies, Yale U., 1984. Rsch. technician dept. physiology and biophysics U. Vt. Coll. Medicine, Burlington, 1980-81; environ. intern The Conservation Found., Washington, 1983; environ. analyst Coastal Resource Mgmt. div. Conn. Dept. Environ. Protection, Hartford, 1984-85, sr. environ. analyst, 1985-89; mgr. environ. programs Conn. Resources Recovery Authority, 1989-91, dir. environ. programs, 1991-96; dep. commr. Vt. Dept. Environ. Conservation, 1997—2001, commr., 2001—. Tech. expert Solar Energy Rsch. Inst. and U.S. Dept. Energy, Washington, 1991—92; spkr. Inst. Clean Air Cos. Conf., 1996; Vt. del. New Eng. Gov.'s/Ea. Can. Premier's Mercury Task Force, 1998—, co-chair, 1999—2000; policy advisor mercury pollution NAFTA North Am. Commn. Environ. Cooperation, 1999; Vt. apptd. commr. on ozone transport commn. established under The Clean Air Act of 1990, 2000—; chair Mid-Atlantic-Northeastern Visibility Union, 2001—; bd. dirs. Randolph Devel. Rev. Bd. Mem. spkrs. bur. Union Concerned Scientists, 1987-97; commr. New Haven City Plan Commn., 1995-97; bd. dirs. New Haven Land Trust, 1985-97, v.p., 1989-90, 93-94, pres., 1995-97; mem. New Haven Environ. Adv. Coun., 1988-90, Vt. Natural Resources Coun., 1979-97; mem. intermodal concept devel. com. Conn. Dept. Transp., 1993-97; field guide, naturalist New Haven Land Trust Coastal Areas, Yale U. Coastal Mods, 1989-97. Mem. New Haven Preservation Trust (Merit award for home restoration 1992). Avocations: music, farming, skating, kayaking, bicycling, home renovation. Home: 854 Tatro Hill Rd Randolph VT 05060-9706 Office: Agy Natural Resources Dept Environ Conservation 103 S Main St Bldg 1 Waterbury VT 05671-9800

RECH, SUSAN ANITA, obstetrician, gynecologist; b. Summit, N.J., Nov. 5, 1957; d. William F. and Mary Jane (Crooks) R.; m. Marc R. Sarnow. BA in Biology, Swarthmore Coll., 1979; MD, U. Medicine Dentistry N.J., Newark, 1984. Diplomate Am. Bd. Ob-Gyn. Resident in ob-gyn. Temple U. Hosp., Phila., 1984-88; pvt. practice, Plattsburgh, N.Y., 1988—; chief dept. ob-gyn CVPH Med. Ctr., 1997-2000. Asst. clin. prof. dept. ob-gyn. U. Vt. Sch. Medicine, 1991—; dir. ob-gyn. tchg. program CVPH Med. Ctr., 1998—; bd. dirs. CVPH Med. Ctr., 1999—; mem. med. adv. bd. Planned Parenthood No. N.Y., Plattsburgh, 1989-98, Clinton County Health Dept., Plattsburgh, 1989-96; bd. dirs. Cmty. Providers, Inc., Plattsburgh, 1994-97. Active Newman Ctr., St. Mary's of the Lake Ch., Plattsburgh; mem. alumni coun. Swarthmore (Pa.) Coll., 1994-96; mem. Seton Cath. H.S. Sch. Bd., Plattsburgh, 1995-98. Rsch. grantee U. Medicine and Dentistry N.J., summer 1980. Fellow ACOG; mem. AMA, Am. Med. Women's Assn. (founding pres. Champlain Valley chpt. 1991), Assn. Women Surgeons, No. N.Y. Ind. Practice Assn. (bd. dirs. 1994-98), Champlain Valley Oratorio Soc. (soloist 1989—), Nat. Honor Soc. Avocations: choral singing, skiing, running, gardening, reading. Home: 15 Point Farm West Grand Isle VT 05458-7021 Office: Assocs in Ob-Gyn PC 210 Cornelia St Ste 201 Plattsburgh NY 12901-2318

RECHARD, PAUL ALBERT, retired civil engineering company executive, consultant; b. Laramie, Wyo., June 4, 1927; s. Ottis H. and Mary R. (Bird) R.; m. Mary Lou Roper, June 26, 1949; children: Robert Paul, Karen Ann. BS, U. Wyo., 1948, MS, 1949, CE, 1955. Registered land surveyor, Wyo.; registered profl. engr., Wyo., Utah, Mont., Colo., Calif., Nebr., S.D., N.Mex.; cert. profl. hydrologist Am. Inst. Hydrology; diplomate Am. Acad. Environ. Engrs. Hydraulic engr. U.S. Bur. Reclamation, Cody, Wyo. and Billings, Mont., 1949-54; dir. water resources Natural Resource Bd., Cheyenne, Wyo., 1954-58; prin. hydraulic engr. Upper Colorado River Commn., Salt Lake City, 1958-64; dir. Water Resources Rsch. Inst. U. Wyo., Laramie, 1964-81, mem. faculty dept. civil engring., 1964-82, prof., 1964-82; pres. Western Water Cons., 1980-2001, Hydrology Assocs., Laramie, 1978-80; ret. Western Water Consults., Inc., 2001. Owner Paul A. Rechard, P.E., Laramie, 1964-78. Editor: Compacts, Treaties and Court Decrees Affecting Wyoming Water, 1956; contbr. articles to tech. publs. Pres., Thayer Sch. PTA, Laramie, 1965; mem. Laramie City Planning Commn., 1974-80. Served with USNR, 1945-46. Recipient Wyo. Eminent Engr. award Tau Beta Pi, 1993; named Disting. Alumnus U. Wyo., 1998; named Outstanding Engr. Wyo. Engring. Soc., 1999. Fellow ASCE (life mem., pres. Wyo. sect. 1968); mem. Am. Soc. Testing Materials, NSPE, Am. Geophys. Union, Nat. Water Well Assn., Wyo. Engring. Soc. (pres. 1976, hon.), Am. Water Works Assn., Am. Water Resources Assn.,

U.S. Com. on Large Dams, Lions (pres. Laramie 1968), Masons, Sigma Xi (pres. Wyo. chpt. 1973), Phi Kappa Phi (pres. Wyo. chpt. 1969), Gamma Sima Delta, Sigma Tau (pres. Wyo. chpt. 1948, selected Wyo. Eminent Engr. 1993). Republican. Presbyterian. Home: 316 Stuart St Laramie WY 82070-4866 Office: Western Water Cons Inc 611 Skyline Rd Laramie WY 82070-8909

RECHCIGL, JACK EDWARD, soil and environmental sciences educator; b. Washington, Feb. 27, 1960; s. Miloslav and Eva (Edwards) R.; m. Nancy Ann Palko, Sept. 30, 1983; children: Gregory John, Kevin Thomas, Lindsey Nicole. BS, U. Del., 1982; MS, Va. Poly. Inst. and State U., 1983, PhD, 1986. Asst. prof. soil sci. U. Fla. Agrl. Rsch. and Edn. Ctr., Ona, 1986-91, assoc. prof. soil and environ. scis., 1991-96, prof. soil and environ. scis., 1996—; assoc. dir. Gulf Coast Rsch. and Edn. Ctr., U. Fla., Bradenton, 2000-01, dir., 2001—. Hon. prof. Czech Agrl. U., Prague, 1999. Editor: Soil Amendments and Environmental Quality, 1995, Soil Amendments: Impact on Biotic Systems, 1995, Use of By-Products and Wastes in Agriculture, 1997, Environmentally Safe Approaches to Crop Disease Control, 1997, Biological and Biotechnilogical Approaches to Insect Pest Management, 1999, Environmentally Safe Approaches to Insect Pest Management, 1999; assoc. editor: Jour. Environ. Quality, 1994-97, Soil and Crop Science Society of Florida, 1999; editor-in-chief: (book series) Agriculture and Environment, 1999—; contbr. chpts. to books, articles to Environ. Quality, Soil Sci., Soil Fertility, Water Quality. Recipient rsch. achievement award U. Fla., 1991, Rsch. Found. Professorship, 1999—, U. Del. Disting. Alumni award, 1999; rsch grantee TVA, 1984-86, Allied Signal, 1987—, So. Fla. Water Mgmt. Dist., 1987-90, 1999—, Fla. Inst. Phosphate Rsch., 1990—, USDA, 1992—. Fellow Am. Soc. Agronomy, Soil Sci. Soc. Am.; mem. Soil Sci. Soc. Am., Sigma Xi, Gamma Beta Phi, Gamma Sigma Delta, Phi Sigma. Achievements include research leading to the reduction of fertilizer recommendations in Florida, thereby helping to improve water quality; utilization of industrial organic and inorganic wastes (ex. phosphogypsum and granular biosolids) as potential fertilizers in agriculture. Home: 13511 4th Plz E Bradenton FL 34212-9682 Office: U Fla Gulf Coast Rsch and Edn Ctr 5007 60th St E Bradenton FL 34203-9511 E-mail: rechcigl@mail.ifas.ufl.edu.

RECHKOBLIT, OLGA A. biochemist, researcher; b. Moscow, July 9, 1974; arrived in U.S., 1996; d. Abram Yakovlevich Rechkoblit and Liliya Semenovna Yedvabnaya. MS in Chemistry, Moscow State U., 1996; MS in Biomolecular Chemistry, NYU, 1998, PhD in Chemistry, 2002. Rsch. and tng. asst. NYU, N.Y.C., 1996—2001; rsch. fellow Meml. Sloan-Kettering Cancer Ctr., 2001—. Contbr. sci. articles to profl. jours. Recipient Brigid G. Leventhal Young Investigator Scholar award Am. Assn. for Cancer Rsch.-Women in Cancer Rsch., 2001; Dean's dissertation fellow NYU, 2000-2001. Mem.: AAAS, Women in Cancer Rsch., Am. Chem. Soc., Am. Assn. for Cancer Rsch (assoc.). Avocations: ballroom dancing, downhill and cross-country skiing, running. Office: Meml Sloan-Kettering Cancer Ctr 1275 York Ave New York NY 10021 Office Fax: 212-616-3066. E-mail: olgarech@sbnmr1.mskcc.org.

RECHTIEN, JAMES JOSEPH, osteopath, educator; b. St. Louis, June 4, 1938; s. Joseph Elmer and Celene Margaret (LeClere) R.; m. Mary Ann Ryan, Nov. 2, 1968; children: Catherine, Matthew, Timothy. BSMetE, Purdue U., 1960; PhD, Northwestern U., Evanston, Ill., 1966; DO, Kirksville Osteopathic Coll., 1976. Diplomate Am. Bd. Osteopathic and Rehab. Medicine. Asst. metallurgist Argonne Nat. Lab., LeMont, Ill., 1966-72; asst. instr. Kirksville (Mo.) Osteopathic Coll., 1972-76; intern Detroit Osteopathic Hosp., 1976-77; pvt. practice Rogers City (Mich.) Med. Group, 1977-80; resident U. Mich., Ann Arbor, 1983-86; assoc. prof. osteopathic medicine Mich. State U., East Lansing, 1980-91, prof. osteopathic medicine, 1991—. Fellow Am. Acad. of Phys. Medicine and Rehab., Am. Osteopathic Coll. of Rehab. Medicine. Avocation: railroad history. Home: 2947 Crestwood Cir East Lansing MI 48823-6500 Office: Mich State U A434 E Free Hall East Lansing MI 48824 E-mail: rechtien@msu.edu.

RECHTIN, EBERHARDT, retired aerospace executive, retired educator; b. East Orange, N.J., Jan. 16, 1926; s. Eberhardt Carl and Ida H. (Pfarrer) R.; m. Dorothy Diane Denebrink, June 10, 1951; children: Andrea C., Nina, Julie Anne, Erica, Mark. BS, Calif. Inst. Tech., 1946, PhD cum laude, 1950. Dir. Deep Space Network, 1958-67; asst. dir. Calif. Inst. Tech. Jet Propulsion Lab., 1960-67; dir. Advanced Rsch. Projects Agy., Dept. Def., 1967-70, prin. dep. dir. def. rsch. and engring., 1970-71, asst. sec. def. for telecom., 1972-73; chief engr. Hewlett-Packard Co., Palo Alto, Calif., 1973-77; pres., CEO Aerospace Corp., El Segundo, 1977-87, pres.-emeritus, 1988; prof. U. So. Calif., 1988-94, emeritus prof., 1994—. Author: Systems Architecting. Creating & Building Complex Systems, 1991, The Art of Systems Architecture, 1997, Systems Architecting of Organizations, Why Eagles Can't Swim, 2000. Served to lt. USNR, 1943-56. Recipient maj. awards NASA, Dept. Def., USN, Disting. Alumni award Calif. Inst. Tech., 1984. Fellow AAAS, AIAA (Robert H. Goddard Astronautics award 1991), IEEE (Alexander Graham Bell award 1977), Internat. Coun. Sys. Engrs. (Pioneer award 1999); mem. Nat. Acad. Engring. (C&C prize Japan 1992), Tau Beta Pi, Eta Kappa Nu (eminent mem.). Home: 1665 Cataluna Pl Palos Verdes Peninsula CA 90274-2162 E-mail: ebrechtin@earthlink.net .

RECHTMAN, DAVID J. physician; b. N.Y.C., Nov. 10, 1955; s. Theodore and Esther K. R.; m. Michelle Felice Roth, Mar. 16, 1980; 1 child, Jason. BA, Yeshiva U., 1976; MD, SUNY, Bklyn., 1980. Instr. SUNY - Downstate Med. Ctr. Coll. of Medicine, Bklyn., 1985-86; mng. physician, med. affairs Baxter Healthcare Corp. - Hyland Divsn., Glendale, Calif., 1987-92; med. dir. Ribi Immunochem Rsch. Inc., Hamilton, Mont., 1995—; pres. PharmaMed. Cons., Internat., Missoula, 1995—; ptnr. Clin. Cons. Alliance, 1997—. Cons. Office of the Chancellor, Bd. Edn., N.Y.C., 1985-86, CDC, Atlanta, 1991. Contbg. author: Use of Intravenous Immune Globulin in Adults with HIV Disease, 1997; contbr. articles to profl. jours. Mem. AIDS adv. group, N.Y.C., 1984-86, AIDS task force, Am. Cancer Soc., N.Y.C., 1986; trustee Missoula City - County Pub. Libr., 1998—; mem. Congregation Har Shalom, v.p. 1994—. Mem. Internat. Immunocompromised Host Soc., Infectious Disease Soc. of Am., Am. Acad. Pharm. Physicians. Independent. Jewish. Avocations: reading, travel, photography, computers. Office: PharmaMed Cons Internat 5725 Eastwood Ln Missoula MT 59803-3015

RECHTZIGEL, SUE MARIE (SUZANNE RECHTZIGEL), child care center executive; b. St. Paul, May 27, 1947; d. Carl Stinson and Muriel Agnes (Oestrich) Miller; m. Gary Elmer Rechtzigel, Aug. 20, 1968 (div. Feb. 1982); children: Brian Carl, Lori Ann. BA in Psychology, Sociology, Mankato (Minn.) State U., 1969. Lic. in child care, Minn. Rep. ins. State Farm Ins. Co., Albert Lea, Minn., 1969-73; free-lance child caretaker, 1973-78; owner, dir. Lakeside Day Care, 1983—. Asst. Hawthorne Sch. Learning Ctr., Albert Lea, 1978-83. Mem. New Residents and Newcomers Orgn., Albert Lea, 1970—, past. pres.; asst. pre-sch. United Meth. Ch., Albert Lea, 1975-78, tchr. Sunday sch., 1976-80, tchr. Bible sch., 1980-85; active Ascension Luth. Ch., 1976-80. Mem. Freeborn Lic. Day Care Assn. (v.p. 1986, pres. 1987), AAUW (home tour 1977, treas. 1980-81), Bus. and Profl. Women, YMCA, Albert Lea Art Ctr. Clubs: 3M Families. Republican. Avocations: ceramics, calligraphy, painting, art, sewing. Home and Office: 1919 Brookside Dr Albert Lea MN 56007-2142

RECHY, JOHN FRANCISCO, writer; b. El Paso, Tex. s. Roberto Sixto and Guadalupe (Flores) R. BA, U. Tex., El Paso; student, New Sch. Social Research. Instr. creative writing UCLA, Occidental Coll., U. So. Calif. Author: City of Night, 1963, Numbers, 1967, this Day's Death, 1969, The Vampires, 1971, The Fourth Angel, 1973, The Sexual Outlaw, 1977, Rushes, 1979, Bodies and Souls, 1983, Marilyn's Daughter, 1988, The Miraculous Day of Amalia Gõmez, 1991, Our Lady of Babylon, 1996, The Coming of the Night, 1999, The Naked Cowboy, His Life and Adventures, 2002; (plays) Momma As She Became-Not As She Was, 1968, Rushes, 1978, Tigers Wild, 1986; (CD-Rom) Mysteries and Desire: Exploring the Worlds of John Rechy, 2000; contbr.: short stories and articles to Tex. Observer, The Nation, Village Voice, London mag., Saturday Rev., N.Y. Times Book Rev., L.A. Times, San Francisco Chronicle Books, Washington Post Book World, Phila. Inquirer, Contemporary Fiction, Big Table, others; also anthologies Chicano Voices, Black Humor, Urban Reader, Evergreen Rev. Reader, New Am. Story, The Moderns, Rediscoveries, Men on Men, others; trans.: stories and articles for Tex. Quar., Evergreen Rev. Served with AUS. Recipient Lifetime Achievement award PEN-USA-West, 1997, Pub. Triangle's William Whitehead award for lifetime achievement in lit., 1999, Longview Found. award for short story The Fabulous Wedding of Miss Destiny, 1960; Nat. Endowment for Arts grantee, 1976. Mem. Authors Guild, Tex. Inst. Letters, PEN, Nat. Writers Union.

RECINE, JUDY ANN, medical/surgical nurse; b. Trenton, N.J., Oct. 13, 1963; d. Donald Vito and Gail Patricia (Walsh) R. BSN, West Chester U., 1986. Cert. in intravenous therapy, CPR, epidural analgesia. Surg. staff nurse, mentor, charge nurse Grad. Hosp., Phila., 1986—. Mem. Med.-Surg. Nursing Soc. Phila. (pres.), Sigma Theta Tau Xi Delta (West Chester U. chpt.).

RECK, ANDREW JOSEPH, philosopher, educator; b. New Orleans, Oct. 29, 1927; s. Andrew Gervais and Katie (Mangiaracina) R.; m. Elizabeth Lassiter Torre, June 17, 1987. BA, Tulane U., 1947, MA, 1949; postgrad., U. St. Andrews, Scotland, 1952-53; PhD, Yale U., 1954; student, U. St. Andrews, Scotland, 1952-53, U. Paris, summers 1962, 64. Instr. English U. Conn., 1949-50; instr. philosophy Yale, 1951-52, 55-58; faculty Tulane U., 1958—, prof. philosophy, 1964—, chmn. dept., 1969-89, dir. Master Liberal Arts program, 1984—. Thomasfest lectr. Xavier U., Cin., 1970; Suarez Lectr. Spring Hill Coll., 1971; Niebuhr lectr. Elmhurst (Ill.) Coll., 1976; vis. prof. Fordham U., 1979; vis. scholar Hastings Ctr. (N.Y.), 1981; Woodruff lectr. Emory U., 1982; Fairchild lectr. U. So. Miss., 1982, 87: Matchette Found. lectr. Cath. U. Am., 1991, 95; Sr. Scholar Inst. Humane Studies, Menlo Park, Calif., 1982; vis. scholar Poynter Ctr., Ind. U., Bloomington, 1983; Tulane U. faculty rep. to bd. adminstrs. Tulane Ednl. Fund., 1988-91. Author: Recent American Philosophy, 1964, Introduction to William James, 1967, New American Philosophers, 1968, Speculative Philosophy, 1972; editor: George Herbert Mead Selected Writings, 1964, 2d edit., 1981, Knowledge and Value, 1972, (with T. Horvath, T. Krittek and S. Grean) American Philosophers' Ideas of Ultimate Reality and Meaning, 1993; co-editor Ultimate Reality and Meaning, Interdisciplinary Studies in the Philosophy of Understanding, 1990-98; mem. adv. editl. bd. Internat. Jour. World Peace, Trans. Charles Peirce Soc., Santayana edit. So. Jour. Philosophy, Library of Living Philosophers; editor History of Philosophy Quar., 1993-98. Served with AUS, 1953-55. Howard fellow, 1962-63, Liberty Fund grantee, 1982, Newcomb fellow, 1991-93; Fulbright scholar, 1952-53; Am. Coun. Learned Socs. grantee, 1961-62, Am. Philos. Soc. grantee, 1972, Huntington Libr. grantee, 1973, La. Ednl. Quality State Found. grantee, 1994-96, U.S. Info. Agy. grantee, Brazil, 1993. Mem.: La. Endowment for Humanities (bd. dirs. 1990—96), Internat. Soc. for Study of Human Ideas of Ultimate Reality and Meaning (bd. dirs. 1989—, treas. 2001—), Charles S. Peirce Soc. (sec.-treas. 1985—86, v.p. 1986—87, pres. 1987—88), Soc. Advancement Am. Philosophy (exec. com. 1980—82, 2001—, pres.-elect 1997—98, pres. 1998—2000, chair nominating com. 2002—), Metaphys. Soc. Am. (councillor 1971—75, pres. 1977—78, program com. 1989—90, chair program com. 1995—96), Coun. for Internat. Rsch. Scholars (philosophy screening com. 1974—77), Am. Coun. Learned Socs. (Am. studies adv. com. 1972—76), So. Soc. Philosophy and Psychology (treas. 1968—71, pres. 1976—77), Southwestern Philos. Soc. (exec. com. 1965—69, v.p. 1971—72, pres. 1972—73), Am. Philos. Assn. (program com. ea. divsn. 1969, adv. com. to program com. ea. divsn. 1994—97, nominating com. western divsn. 1975—76, 1981—82, mem., chair ad hoc com. on history 1992, 1996—), Tulane U. Emeritus Club (Outstanding Grad. of Class of 1947 award 1997), Alpha Sigma Lambda (hon. Theta chpt. of La.), Phi Beta Kappa (pres. Alpha of La. 1966—67). Home: 6125 Patton St New Orleans LA 70118-5832 Office: Tulane Univ Dept Philosophy New Orleans LA 70118 E-mail: areck@tulane.edu.

RECK, CARLEEN JOAN, social welfare administrator; b. St. Louis, June 4, 1937; d. William Alois and Clara S. Reck. BA, Notre Dame Coll., 1960; MA, U. Notre Dame, 1969; PhD, St. Louis U., 1978. Tchr., adminstr. Notre Dame H.S., Quincy, Ill., 1961-70, tchr. Cape Girardeau, Mo., 1976-77; coord. edn. coun. Sch. Sisters Notre Dame, St. Louis, 1970-76, provincial coun., vicar, 1991-99; exec. dir. dept. elem. schs. Nat. Cath. Ednl. Assn., Washington, 1977-86; supt. schs. Diocese Jefferson City, Mo., 1986-91; dir. Criminal Justice Min., Soc. St. Vincent de Paul, St. Louis, 1999—. Pres. bd. dirs. English Tutoring Project Immigrant/Refugee Children, St. Louis, 1998—; mem. adv. bd. Employment Connection, St. Louis, 2000—; bd. dirs. Coll. Notre Dame, Balt., 1995-2001. Recipient C. Albert Koob Merit award Nat. Cath. Ednl. Assn., 1986, Excellence in Ednl. Journalism award Ednl. Press Assn. Am., 1988; named one of 25 Most Influential Individuals in Cath. Edn., Peter Li Edn. Group, 1997. Mem. Mo. Assn. Social Welfare (chair corrections task force 1999—), Mo. Cath. Conf. (vice-chair corrections task force 1999—), Ea. Mo. Coalition Abolish Death Penalty (treas. 1999—), Consortium Jail Prison Ministers, Notre Dame H.S. Alumnae (Disting. Alumna award 1998), Sch. Sisters Notre Dame (tech. com. 1994—). Avocations: computers, gardening. Office: Criminal Justice Min SVDP 1408 S 10th St Saint Louis MO 63104

RECKFORD, SAMUEL PHILIP, investment banker; b. Chapel Hill, N.C., Feb. 18, 1961; s. Kenneth Joseph and Mary Stevens Reckford; m. Susan Spencer, June 10, 1985; children: Spencer, Samantha, Mary. BA, Dartmouth Coll., 1983. CFA. Mgr. Bear, Stearns & Co. Inc., N.Y.C., 1983-88, v.p., 1988-91, assoc. dir., 1991-98, mng. dir., 1998—. Pres., bd. trustees Hudson Sch., Hoboken, N.J., 1989—. Republican. Episcopalian. Home: 28 Ridge Ter Short Hills NJ 07078 Office: Bear Stearns & Co Inc 383 Madison Ave New York NY 10179 E-mail: sreckford@bear.com.

RECKLEIN, LINDA SUE, library administrator; b. St. Louis, Feb. 19; d. Clifford H. and Billie M. (Bader) Lincks; m. Dan S. Recklein, Sept. 4 1993; 1 stepchild, Allison Faith. BA in Psychology cum laude, U. Mo., St. Louis, 1972; MLS, U. Mo., 1977. Supr., para-profl. St. Louis County Libr., 1972-80; mgr. info. ctr., info. specialist Ralston Purina Co., St. Louis, 1980—. Mem. bus. adv. bd. cons. group Gale Rsch., Detroit, 1990—; team mem. spl. librs. delegation Citizen Ambassador Program of People to People Internat., Russia and Czech Republic, 1995. Distbr. campaign lit. for Dem. and Rep. parties; vol. phone support at campaign hdqs.; vol. solicitor ARC Corp. Assocs. Ann. Fund, 1994. Recipient Cert. of Leadership, YWCA, 1991; named Outstanding Young Woman of Am., 1981. Mem. NAFE, AAUW, Soc. Competitive Intelligence Profls., Spl. Librs. Assn. (chpt. bd. dirs. 1983-84), Women in Bus. Network (treas. 1982-83), Am. Mgmt. Assn., St. Louis Regional Library Network (edn. com., info-lib lunchtime topics task force 1984-86). Roman Catholic. Avocations: photography, travel, running, cooking, orienteering. Home: 637 Laven Del Ln Saint Louis MO 63122-1115 Office: Ralston Purina Co Checkerboard Sq Saint Louis MO 63164-0001

RECKTENWALD, FRED WILLIAM, city financial official; b. Fremont, Ohio, Dec. 24, 1946; s. Harold Louis and Geraldine Fern (Worthington) R.; m. Elaine Marie Denman, July 3, 1982. Acct. Henry Packing Co., Perrysburg, Ohio, 1969-70, Edward R. Moyer, CPA, Bellevue, 1970-71; ptnr. Singer and Recktenwald Acctg., Fremont, 1971-79; compt. Shortway Bus Lines, Inc., Toledo, 1979-80; city auditor City of Fremont, 1980—. Mem. Coastal Resources Adv. Coun., 1992-93. Pres. Sandusky County Improvement Bd., Fremont, 1988-89, sec., 1990-95; chmn. Fremont Revolving Loan Fund Bd., 1989—; adv. bd. Terra Tech. Coll., Fremont, 1985-98, Vanguard Vocat. Sch., Fremont, 1988-93; fin. com. St. Joseph's Parish, Fremont, 1986-88; v.p. Terra C.C. Found. Bd., 1999-2001, pres., 2001; mem. cen. com. Sandusky County Dems., 1996—. Mem. North Ctrl. Ohio Fin. Officers (pres. 1985), Ohio Govt. Fin. Officers Assn., Govt. Fin. Officers Assn. U.S. and Can. (Fin. Reporting Achievement award 1989, 90, 91, 92, 93) Mcpl. Treas. Am., Ctrl. Cath. Boosters (trustee 1977-78, treas. 1997-2001), KC, Elks, Moose, Pt. Clinton Yacht Club, Fremont Country Club. Democrat. Roman Catholic. Avocations: bowling, golf. Office: City of Fremont 323 S Front St Fremont OH 43420-3037 E-mail: fremontauditor@ezworks.net.

RECORD, PHILLIP JULIUS, columnist; b. Fort Worth, Jan. 12, 1929; s. Phillip Cross and Frances Virginia (McElwee) R.; m. Patricia Ann Edwards, Sept. 29, 1954; children: Christopher Phillip, Gregory Edwards, Timothy James. BA in Journalism, U. Notre Dame, 1950. Gen. reporter Lubbock Avalanche-Jour., Tex., 1950-54; copy editor, reporter Fort Worth Star-Telegram, 1954-67, asst. city editor, 1967-68, city editor evening edit., 1968-76, mng. editor, 1976-80, assoc. exec. editor, 1980-91, spl. asst. to pub., ombudsman, 1991-97, columnist, 1997—2001. Mem. mass comms. com. Tex. Tech. U., 1971—, chmn., 1990—92; journalism profl. in residence Tex. Christian U., 1999—. Mem. Friends of Ft. Worth Pub. Libr.; conciliation/arbitration bd. Cath. Diocese of Ft. Worth, 1994—, chair, 1996—, publs. adv. com., 1982—; bd. dirs. Tarrant County Mental Health Assn., 1990—95; dir. Freedom Info. Found., Tex., 1987—93; founding mem. Ft. Worth Theatre. With U.S. Army, 1950—52. Recipient Ethics award Tex. Christian U., 1991, others for reporting, photography and headline writing; named to Tex. Tech U. Mass Comms. Hall of Fame. Mem. ABA (nat. commn. on pub. understanding about law 1984-90, commn. on partnership programs 1990-93), Investigative Reporters and Editors Inc., Soc. Profl. Journalists (pres. 1983-84, bd. dirs. Found. 1980-2001, v.p. Found., 1991-94, bd. chair 1994-01, Wells Key 1991), Creative Thinking Assn., Orgn. News Ombudsmen (dir. 1994—, v.p. 1995-96, pres. 1996-97), Petroleum Club. Avocation: tennis. Home: 6144 Walla Ave Fort Worth TX 76133-3557 Office: Fort Worth Star-Telegram 6144 Walla Ave Fort Worth TX 76133 *As a journalist, I strive to be a servant of the truth and a servant of the people. As a follower of Jesus, I try to live my life as he would. But, being human, I fail frequently. But I try and I care. I think that makes me OK in God's eyes.*

RECORD, WILLIAM JOHN, librarian; b. N.Y.C., June 21, 1931; s. William and Betty (Collins) R.; m. Betty Lowrey, Oct. 7, 1950; children: Linda, William John, Jr., Michael, John. BA, George Peabody Coll. for Tchrs, 1961; MLS, Pratt Inst., 1965. Cert. pub. librarian, N.Y. State. Cataloger N.Y. Pub. Library, N.Y.C., 1963-66; cataloger Coll. Dentistry, NYU, 1966-67; achivist Sch. Medicine, NYU, 1967-68; librarian Milton Helpern Libr. Legal Medicine, N.Y.C., 1969-70, Fordham Hosp., Bronx, N.Y., 1973-76, Misericordia Hosp., Bronx, 1976-81, Assn. Vol. Surg. Contraception, N.Y.C., 1981-97, ret., 1997. Periodicals librarian Met. Hosp., N.Y.C., 1971-72. Editor Odyssey, pres. parents group phase III, Odyssey House, N.Y.C., 1970. With U.S. Army, 1947-58, Korea. Mem. Assn. for Population/Family Planning Libraries Internat. (pres. 1987-88), Med. Library Assn. Home: 437 E 80th St Apt 26 New York NY 10021-0611

RECTOR, CLARK ELLSWORTH, advertising executive; b. Pilot Mound, Iowa, Apr. 3, 1934; s. Guy Charles and Hazel Catherine (Forney) R.; m. Suzanne Swayze, Aug. 21, 1956; children: Clark Ellsworth, Jr., Leigh Ann, Curtis Allen. BA, Puget Sound, 1959; postgrad., Pacific Luth., 1961-62. Pres. Clark Rector & Assoc., Inc., Austin, Tex., 1967—. Trustee Nat. Sales & Mktg. Coun., Washington, 1980—, Inst. Residential Mktg., Washington, 1980-83, pres., 1983. Contbr. articles to profl. jours. Commr. Austin Housing Authority, 1973-77; dir. N.W. Austin Civic Assn., 1974-76; state committeeman Rep. Party of Tex., 1974-76; adv. coun. Small Bus. Adminstrn., San Antonio, 1972-76. With U.S. Army, 1952-55. Mem. Nat. Assn. Home Builders (Bill Molster award 1984), Sigma Chi. Republican. Methodist. Avocations: skiing, golf, photography. Home: 3809 Woodbrook Cir Austin TX 78759-8226 E-mail: crector1@juno.com.

RECTOR, JOHN MICHAEL, association executive, lawyer; b. Seattle, Aug. 15, 1943; s. Michael Robert and Bernice Jane (Allison) R.; m. Mary Kaaren Sueta Jolly, Feb. 8, 1977 (div. 1994); m. Carmen De Ortiz Nouri, 1994; children: Christian Phillip, Ciera Rose, Zachary Ryan. BA, U. Calif., Berkeley, 1966; JD, U. Calif., Hastings, 1969; PharmD (hon.), Ark. State Bd. Pharmacy, 1991. Bar: Calif. 1970, U.S. Supreme Ct. 1974. Trial atty. civil rights div. Dept. Justice, 1969-71; dep. chief counsel judiciary com. U.S. Senate, 1971-73, counsel to Sen. Birch Bayh, 1971-77, chief counsel, staff dir., 1973-77; confirmed by U.S. Senate as assoc. adminstr. to Law Enforcement Assistance Adminstn. and adminstr. of Office Juvenile Justice Dept. Justice, 1977-79; spl. counsel to U.S. Atty. Gen., 1979-80; dir. govt. affairs Nat. Assn. Retail Druggists, Washington, 1980-85, sr. v.p. govt. affairs, gen. counsel, 1986—. Chmn. adv. bd. Nat. Juvenile Law Center, 1973-77; mem. Hew panel Drug Use and Criminal Behavior, 1974-77; mem. cons. panel Nat. Commn. Protection Human Subjects of Biomed. and Behavioral Research, 1975-76; mem. bd. Nat. Inst. Corrections, 1977-79; chmn. U.S. Interdepartmental Council Juvenile Justice, 1977-79; mem. bd. com. civil rights and liberties Am. Democratic Action, 1976-80, Pres.'s Com. Mental Health-Justice Group, 1978; com. youth citizenship ABA, 1978-84; mem. Pharm. Industry Adv. Com.; exec. dir., treas. polit. action com. Nat. Pharmacists Assn., 1981—; exec. dir. Retail Druggist Legal Legis. Def. Fund, 1985—, founder, chmn. Washington Pharmacy Industry Forum; mem. numerous fed. narcotic and crime panels and coms.; owner Second Genesis, an antique and furniture restoration co. Mem. editorial bd. Managed Care Law; contbr. articles to profl. jours. Exec. com. small bus. and fin. couns. Dem. Nat. Com., 1988-92; dir. Dem. Leadership Coun.'s Network, 1989-92, bd. advisers, 1992-94, Clinton-Gore Washington Bus. adv. com.; bd. dirs. Small Bus. Legis. Coun., 1987—, sec., 1999, treas., 2000, chmn. elect 2001, chmn., 2002; bd. dirs. Nat. Bus. Coalition for Fair Competition, 1984—. Perry E. Towne scholar, 1966-67; mem. U.S. Atty. Gen.'s Honors Program, 1968-71; recipient Children's Express Juvenile Justice award, 1981. Mem. Calif. Bar Assn., Nat. Health Lawyers Assn., Am. Soc. Assn. Execs. (govt. affrs sect.), Washington Coun. Lawyers, Assn. of Former Senior Senate Aides, Vinifera Wine Growers Assn. Va. (life), Health R Us, Am. League of Lobbyists, Theta Chi. Democrat. Avocation: collecting antique furniture, books and documents. Office: Nat Assn Retail Druggists 205 Daingerfield Rd Alexandria VA 22314-2885

RECTOR, LIAM, university program director; b. Washington, Nov. 21, 1949; s. David Alan and Pauline Evelyn (Moss) Rector; m. Mary Cunningham, 1983 (div. 1992); 1 child Virginia ; m. Tree Swenson. Student, Montgomery Coll., 1968—69, San Francisco State U., 1970, U. Md., 1971—74, Corcoran Sch. Art, 1976; MA, Johns Hopkins U., 1978; MPA, Harvard U., 1992. Tchg. fellow Johns Hopkins U., Balt., 1977—78; dir. poetry programs Folger Shakespeare Libr., Washington, 1978—80; program assoc., co-dir. Acad. Am. Poets, N.Y.C., 1980—81; instr. creative writing and lit. Phillips Acad., Andover, Mass., 1981—82; poet-in-residence Goucher Coll., Towson, Md., 1982—83; co-dir., program assoc. Martha's Vineyard Poetry Workshop, Vineyard Haven, Mass., 1982—83; specialist lit. program Nat. Endowment for Arts, Washington, 1983—85; exec. dir. Associated Writing Programs Old Dominion U., Norfolk, Va., 1986—91; founder, dir. Bennington (Vt.) Writing Seminars, 1991—. Vis. instr. poetry, composition and lit. George Mason U., Fairfax, Va., 1982—83. Editor: The Day I Was Older: On the Poetry of Donald Hall, 1989, Fastening the Voice to the Page: On the Poetry of Frank Bidart, 2002; author: (poetry collection) The Sorrow of Architecture, 1984, American Prodigal, 1994; contbr. poetry and prose to mags. and lit. jours.; editor (freelance): The Smithsonian Assoc., 1986; editor: (at-large) (lit. jour.) Black Box, 1979—80; contbg. editor: Agni, 1992—; editor (poetry): Harvard Mag., 1994—96. Commr. Norfolk Commn. on Arts and Humanities, 1988—; bd. dirs. Red Balloon Day Care Ctr., 1985—86, Associated Writing Programs, v.p., 1995—97; panelist Va. Commn. on Arts, 1989—91; panelist arts coun. State of N.J., 1986; panelist for grants to emerging poets D.C. Commn. on Arts and Humanities, 1979; panelist Ill. Arts Coun., 1991. Recipient Friend to Writers award, PEN New Eng., 1998; fellow, Johns Hopkins U., 1977—78, Nat. Endowment for Arts, 1980, Vt. Coll., 1984, John Simon Guggenheim Meml. Found., N.Y.C., 1985—86, Somerville Arts Coun., 1997; grantee, Phillips Acad., 1982. Home: 300 E 34th St # 3-J New York NY Office: Bennington Coll Bennington Writing Seminars Bennington VT 05201

RECTOR, M. EUGENE, community pharmacist; b. Sequin, Tex., Aug. 16, 1950; m. Marcia A. Rector, May 15, 1982. AA, Blinn Coll., 1970; BS in Pharmacy, U. Tex., Austin, 1972; BA in Philosophy, U. Tex., Dallas, 1982, MS in Mgmt. and Adminstrn. Scis., 1985; PharmD, Broadmore U., Belize City, Belize, 1998. Staff pharmacist Baylor U. Med. Ctr., Dallas, 1973-81, Presbyn. Hosp., Dallas, 1981-86; dir. pharmacy Madison St. Joseph Health Ctr., Madisonville, Tex., 1986—. Fellow Am. Coll. Apothecaries (assoc.); mem. Am. Soc. Health-Sys. Pharmacists, Tex. Soc. Health-Sys. Pharmacists, Lions Club of Hilltop Lakes, Masons (Vickery Lodge 1351, Rogers Prairie Lodge 540 past master). Republican. Methodist. Avocations: hunting, ranching. Home: 16584 Fm 3 S Normangee TX 77871-3511 E-mail: gener@txcyber.com.

RECTOR, MARGARET HAYDEN, freelance/self-employed writer; b. Azusa, Calif., May 23, 1916; d. Floyd Smith and Anna Martha (Miller) Hayden; m. Robert Wayman Rector, Aug. 25, 1940; children: Cleone Rector Grabowski Black, Robin Rector Krupp, Bruce Hayden. AA, Citrus Jr. Coll., 1936; BA, Pomona Coll., 1938; postgrad., Stanford U., 1938-40, Columbia U., 1942-46, St. John's Coll., Annapolis, Md., 1946-56, U. So. Calif., 1959-65, UCLA, 1959-66. Mem. advt. staff Curt Wagner, Redondo Beach, Calif., 1957-67; writer Am. Home Mag., N.Y.C., 1942-46, House Beautiful Mag.,

N.Y.C., 1942-46; author children's books Grossmont Press, San Diego, 1974-76. Invited lectr. Crystal Cruises, 1997. Author: Norton and Gus, 1976; Alva, That Vanderbilt-Belmont Woman, 1992; editor: History of Citrus, 1994; playwright, screenwriter. Dem. organizer, Annapolis, Md., 1946-56; mem. UCLA affiliates; bd. dirs. Friends of Rsch. Libr. Mem. AAUW (life), PEN, Women in Film, Women in Theatre, UCLA Faculty Wives Writers Group, Surfwriters Palos Verdes Peninsula, First Stage, The Audrey Skirball-Kenis Theatre, Dramatists Guild, Authors Guild, Womens Internat. Ctr. in San Diego, Pomona Coll. Alumni, Stanford U. Alumni. Avocation: performing arts on stage, for TV, and at comedy clubs. Home: 10700 Stradella Ct Los Angeles CA 90077-2604

RECTOR, WILLIAM DAVID, civil engineer; b. Terre Haute, Ind., Sept. 19, 1953; s. Charles Marshall and Sharon Lynn (Reeve) R.; m. Phyllis Ann Trefry, Feb. 23, 1974; children: Matthew David, Jennifer Layne. AS, Ind. State U., 1973, BS, 1981. Illustrator Hyster Co., Danville, Ill., 1974-76; draftsman Teepak, Inc., 1976-79; sr. designer Bristol-Myers, Evansville, Ind., 1979-86; sr. civil engr. Aluminum Co. of Am., Newburgh, 1986-90; sr. project mgr. John Brown Engring. & Constructors, 1990; plant mgr. Ameriqual Foods, Inc., Evansville, 1991-97; v.p., co-owner Facility Mgmt. and Engring., Inc., Newburgh, Ind., 1997—2002; gen. mgr. Vanderburgh County Bldg. Authority, Evansville, 2002—. Pres. Eagle Land LLC, 2002—. Councilman Warrick County, Ind., 1989-92, precinct committeeman, 1984—, commr., 1996—; pres. Newburgh Storm Water Mgmt. Bd., 1988-96; bd. dirs. Warrick Pub. Edn. Found., 1990-96, Warrick County Park, 1993-96, Warrick County Sheriff Merit, 1993—; mem. Bd. of Zoning Appeals, Warrick County, 1988-89; asst. scoutmaster Boy Scouts Am., 1985-89. Named Outstanding Young Man in Am., 1989, 92. Mem. ASCE, Assn. Ind. Counties. Democrat. Lutheran.

RECUPERO-FAIELLA, ANNA ANTONIETTA, poet; b. Boston, Nov. 22, 1966; d. Vittorio and Anna Maria Recupero; m. Mark Stephan James Faiella, May 30, 1998. Cert. early edn., Wheelock Coll. Tchr. N. Bennet St. Sch., Boston, 1981-87; clk. Post Office, 1988—. Art coord. N. Bennett Sch., Boston, 1985-87; acting extra films and commls. Author: (poems) A View From the Edge, 1992, Dusting Off Dreams, 1994, Echoes From the Silence, 1995, Treasure the Moment, 1996, Whispers, 1996, Sensations, 1997; co-author: (poems) Distinguished Poets of Amercia, 1993, Outstanding Poets of 1994, 1994, Treasured Poems of America, 1995, Treasured Poems of America, 1996, Best Poems of the 90's, 1996, Best Poems of '97, 1997, Ten Years of Excellence, 1998. Recipient Editors Choice award Nat. Libr. Poetry, 1993, 94, 95, 96, 97, semifinalist, Discover G'Vanni's 500th Art Awd., 1992; scholar Mass. State Gen. Scholarship, 1985. Mem. Internat. Soc. Poets (disting. mem. adv. com. 1994), Nat. Mus. Women Arts, Point of Pines Assn. Democrat. Roman Catholic. Avocations: painting, writing poems, traveling, NASCAR racing, comedy. Home: 40 Bickford Ave Revere MA 02151-1723

RED, ARJA H. TURUNEN, economics educator; b. Rautalampi, Finland, Jan. 29, 1955; came to U.S., 1986; m. Arnold J. Red, Apr. 3, 1987. BS in Math., U. Helsinki, Finland, 1973, MS in Math., 1978, Lic. in Polit. Sci., 1981; PhD in Econs., U. Brit. Columbia, Can., 1985. Lectr. econs. U. Sydney, Australia, 1985; asst. prof. econs. U. Tex., Austin, 1986-93; assoc. prof. econs. U. New Orleans, 1994-99, prof. econs., 1999—. Editl. bd. Jour. Internat. Trade & Econ. Devel., 1996—; contbr. articles to profl. jours. Mem. Econometric Soc., Am. Econ. Assn., Soc. for Social Choice & Welfare. Home: 45500 Summerfield Rd Prairieville LA 70769-6617 E-mail: aturunen@uno.edu.

REDA, JAMES FRANCIS, business consultant; b. Bklyn., Aug. 27, 1953; s. Ralph Charles and Evelyn Susan (Buchan) R.; m. Susan Rosemary Hisnay, June 10, 1982 (div. Oct. 1993); 1 child, Jennifer Beryl; m. Deborah Linda Grannis, July 4, 1994; children: Jennifer Rose, James Francis Jr., Linda Victoria. BS in Indsl. Engring., Columbia U., 1981; MS in Mgmt., MIT, 1983. 1st class FCC lic. Indsl. engr. IBM Corp., Bklyn., 1980, East Fishkill, N.Y., 1981; process engr. Hewlett-Packard Co., Andover, Mass., 1982; bus. mgr. Wang Labs., Inc., Lowell, 1983-85; sr. product mgr. Honeywell Fed. Systems, Inc., McLean, Va., 1985-87; assoc. cons. Touche Ross & Co., N.Y.C., 1987; v.p., cons. The Bachelder Group, 1987-96; cons. Buck Cons., 1996-97, Hewitt Assocs., Atlanta, 1997-99; sr. mgr. Arthur Andersen LLP, 1999-2000; prin., practice leader Buck Cons., Inc., 2000—. Campaign advisor Friends of Vincent Gentile, Bklyn., 1994; exec. compensation adv. svcs., pres. Atlanta chpt. Nat. Assn. Corp. Dirs. With USN, 1971-77; lt. comdr. USCGR. Mem. Internat. Inst. Indsl. Engrs. (sr. mem., chpt. pres. 1979-81, Walter Rautenstrauch award 1981), Res. Officers Assn. (Top Grad. award 1983), Am. Compensation Assn., N.Y. Soc. Security Analysts (mem. com. shareholder rights and corp. governance), Assn. for Investment Mgmt. Rsch., Internat. Assn. Fin. Engring., U.S. Naval Inst., Armed Forces Comms. Assn., Ret. Officers Assn., Nat. Assn. Stock Plan Profls., Nat. Assn. Corp. Dirs. (pres. Atlanta chpt.), Naval War Coll. Found., Am. Legion, Tau Beta Pi, Alpha Pi Mu. Republican. Methodist. Avocations: spectator sports, exercise, travel, history, current events. Home: 4034 Willows Way Marietta GA 30062-5281 Office: Buck Cons Inc Ste 1200 200 Galleria Pkwy NW Atlanta GA 30339-8336 E-mail: jfreda@alum.mit.edu.

REDA, ROBERT SALVATORE, lawyer; b. Chgo., Feb. 23, 1962; s. Robert Charles and Elizabeth (Barrett) R.; m. Joyce Karen Bettinger, May 19, 1990. BA, Drake U., 1984; JD, John Marshall Law Sch., Chgo., 1988. Bar: Ill. 1989, U.S. Dist. Ct. (no. dist.) Ill. 1989, U.S. Dist. Ct. (no. dist. trial bar) Ill. 1991, U.S. Supreme Ct. 1993. Real estate broker Ill. Dept. Profl. Regulation, 1989; pvt. practice Chgo., 1989-91; pres. Reda & Assocs., P.C., 1991—; producer Ill. Dept. Ins., 1999. Arbitrator Cir. Ct. of Cook County, Ill., 1998-2000; bd. dirs. First 100 Group, Ltd., Chgo. 1989—; sec. Bibs Disposeables Corp., Chgo., 1998—; ptnr. Beatrice Assocs., Chgo., 1998—. Author: Battle the Expert and Win, 1995. Fellow Roscoe Pound Found.; mem. ATLA, Nat Inst. for Trial Advocacy, Ill. Bar Assn., Union League Club (mem. athletic com., trustee boys and girls club). Office: Reda & Assocs PC 53 W Jackson Blvd Ste 715 Chicago IL 60604-3668

REDBURN, AMBER LYNNE, nurse; b. West Plains, Mo., Jan. 4, 1963; d. Norris Bert and Chlora Ivene (Brickey) Cozort; m. Timothy Mark Redburn, Apr. 26, 1997; 1 child, Corby Lee. BSN, Rockhurst Coll. and Rsch. Coll. of Nursing, Kansas City, Mo., 1985. RN, Mo. Psychiat. staff nurse Cox Med. Ctr. North, Springfield, Mo., 1985; psychiat. technician Park Cen. Hosp., 1985-86; orthop. staff nurse St. John's Regional Health Ctr., 1986-97; comprehensive care nurse Ozarks Med. Ctr., West Plains, 1997-98, nurse educator, 1998, also former instr. BLS, 1998; short term BLS instr. South Ctrl. Area Vocat.-Tech. Sch., 1998. Mem. com. St. John's Med. Explorer Post 339, 1989-90, pres., 1990-91; mem. Greene County Rep. Party-TARGET, 1993-97; mem. Rep. Nat. Com., 1995-98; mem. com. S.W. Mo. Nurses Recognition Dinner, 1992-97, chair, 1994-97; mem. West Plains Adult Day Svcs., 1997. Mem. Mo. Nurses Assn. (corr. sec., past bd. dirs., 4th dist., mem. nominating com., med.-surg. spl. interest group 1993-98, sec. 1996-98, regional dir. region F 1994-96, Mo. Nurses Assn.-PAC com. 1996—, comm. com. 1995-99, state bd. dirs. 1997-99, membership and mktg. com. 1997-99, nursing practice com. 1999), Nat. Assn. Orthopedic Nurses, Rsch. Coll. Alumni Assn., Rsch. Coll. Honor Soc.

REDD, J. DIANE, professional fund raiser and grants management executive; b. Apr. 10, 1945; d. Robert Fountain and Lillian (Fitts) Redd. BS, W.Va. State Coll., 1967. Instr. bus. subjects Paterson (N.J.) Bus. Edn., 1967-68; with U. Medicine and Dentistry, Newark, 1968-89; adminstrv. asst. rsch. and sponsored programs, 1968-73; asst. dir. health edn., 1973-76; sr. devel. officer, 1976-79; asst. dir. devel., 1979-83; chief devel. and alumni affairs, 1983-89; dir. devel. founds., corps. and major gifts Planned Parenthood Fedn. Am., Inc., N.Y.C., 1989—2002; dir. devel. NAACP-LDF, Inc., 2002—. Mem. priorities com., devel. com. United Way of Essex and West Hudson, Newark, 1983-85; chmn. human resources com. Cmty. Adv. Bd., U. Medicine and Dentistry N.J., Newark, 1978-82; mem. rsch. bd. advisors Am. Biographical Inst., 1992—. Recipient Recognition of Achievement award Young Women of Am., Inc., Montgomery, Ala., 1979, Black Achiever award YMWCA, 1986. Mem. Coun. Advancement and Support of Edn., Nat. Soc. Fund Raising Execs., Ind. (cert., trustee, v.p., parliamentarian, sec.), Assn. Am. Med. Colls., Exec. Women N.J. (trustee, chmn. scholarship com.), Women in Fin. Devel., Consortium of Devel. and Alumni Profls. of Greater N.Y. Democrat. Office: Planned Parenthood Fedn of Am 810 7th Ave New York NY 10019-5818

REDD, MARY DELENA, social service administrator; b. East Gulf, W.Va., Jan. 24, 1943; d. John D. and Bettie Elizabeth (Hubbard) R. BA in Sociology, W.Va. State Coll., 1963; MS in Social Casework, Fordham U., 1967. Caseworker Soc. for Seamen's Children, Staten Island, N.Y., 1963-68; dir. social svcs. Bronx River Neighborhood Ctr., 1968-72; dir. Manhattan ctr. The Wiltwyck Sch., N.Y.C., 1972-76, coord. cmty. mentel health svcs., 1976-78; exec. dir. Steinway Child & Family Svcs., Inc., L.I., N.Y., 1978—. Cons. Bronx River Head Start Ctrs., 1977—; ajd. prof. Fordham U. Sch. Social Sci., N.Y.C., 1978-80. Dir. Riverbend Housing Co., Inc., 1993, pres., 1994; vice chair Multicultural Adv. Com., 1991; dir. UpperManhattan Empowerment Zone Devel. Corp., N.Y.C., 1995. Mem. N.Y. State Office Mental Health, Pan-Hellenic Coun. N.Y. (pres. 1980-84), Coalition of Vol. Mental Health Agys., W.Va. State Coll. Alumni Assn. (corr. sec. 1980-84), The Links, Delta Sigma Theta (N.Y. state coord. 1985-87). Democrat. Baptist. Avocations: reading, travel. Home: 2333 5th Ave # 1-hh New York NY 10037-1605 Office: Steinway Child & Family Svc 41-36 27th St Long Island City NY 11101

REDDAN, KENNETH, psychotherapist, social worker; b. Bklyn., Nov. 23, 1972; BSW, Alvernia Coll., 1996; MSW, Marywood U., 1998. Cert. social worker NY. Group leader Rehab. Specialists, Hawthorne, NJ, 1996—97; counselor Bergen Pines Hosp., Ridgewood, 1996—98; mental health clinician Barnert Hosp., Paterson, 1997—99; social worker Kintock Group, Newark, 1998—99; dir. Rehab. Counseling Assocs., Bklyn., 1997—; coord. Human Svc. Ctrs., 1999—. Exec. dir., program devel., founder NY Svc. Network, Bklyn., 2000—. Chmn. Hillsid Assn., Bklyn., 2001, Forward Thinking Philosophy Forum, Weehawken, NJ, 2001. Recipient Blessed Art Thou Among Women award of excellence, Alvernia Coll., 1996. Mem.: NASW, N.Y.C. Dept. Mental Health (mem. com. 2001—). Avocations: writing, inspirational speaking, volunteering, community organizing, historic restoration.

REDDEL, CARL WALTER, educational administrator; b. Gurley, Neb., May 31, 1937; s. Walter Julius and Friedora Regina (Sorge) R.; m. Colette Marie Antoinette Mansuy, Oct. 26, 1963; children: Eric, Damien. BSED, Drake U., 1959; MA in Russian Studies, Syracuse U., 1962; PhD in Russian History, cert. Russian Studies, Ind. U., 1973. Lectr. U. Md., Toul-Rosieres, France, 1963-66; instr. U.S.A.F. Acad., Colorado Springs, Colo., 1967-68, 71-72, asst. prof., 1972-73, assoc. prof., 1973-80; prof., head dept. history, postdoctoral fellow U. Edinburgh, 1981-82; prof., head dept. history U.S. Air Force Acad., 1982-99; pres., CEO Eisenhower World Affairs Inst., 1999-2000; pub. svc. fellow Gettysburg (Pa.) Coll., 2000-01; cons. coord. Dwight D. Eisenhower Meml. Commn., Washington, 2001—02, exec. dir., 2002—. Nat. coord., regional World History Assn., Phila., 1990-95; bd. editors, mem. Joun. Slavic Mil., London, 1988—; series editor Military Hist. Symposium Series, Colorado Springs, 1993—. Editor: Transformation in Russian and Soviet Military History, 1990; contbr. articles to profl. jours. Mem. Rotary Internat., 1994—. Served to brig. gen. U.S. Air Force, 1962-99. Recipient Young Faculty exch. Internat. Rsch. Exchs. Bd., Moscow State U., 1975; Woodrow Wilson fellow, 1959-60, Danforth Found. fellow, 1959-61. Mem.: Ctrl. Slavic Assn., World History Assn., Am. Assn. Advancement of Slavic Studies, Am. Hist. Assn. Lutheran. Home: 420 7th St NW Apt 809 Washington DC 20004-2214 Office: 1730 K St NW Ste 410 Washington DC 20006-3837 E-mail: eisenhower2@starpower.net.

REDDEN, HARRAL ARTHUR, JR. insurance agency executive; b. Neptune, N.J., Aug. 14, 1936; s. Harral A. and Evelyn Redden; m. Bernadine Tenreiro, July 30, 1983; children: Stephen D., Scott H. BA, Ursinus Coll., 1958. Owner, mgr. Redden Agy. (merged into Connelly, Campion, Wright, Inc.), Fair Haven, N.J., 1958-97; producing agt. Connelly, Campion, Wright, Inc., Belmar, 1997—. Instr. Brookdale C.C., 1972-80. Pres. Little Silver (N.J.) Cmty. Appeal, 1971—. 1st lt. USAR, 1963-70. Mem. Monmouth County Ind. Ins. Agts. Assn. (pres. 1966-67), Soc. C.P.C.U.'s (pres. Ctrl. Jersey chpt. 1968-69), Ind. Ins. Agts. N.J. (pres. 1982-83), Sea Bright Lawn Tennis Club (Rumson, N.J.). Republican. Methodist. Office: 186 Woods End Dr Little Silver NJ 07739

REDDEN, LAWRENCE DREW, lawyer; b. Tallassee, Ala., Dec. 16, 1922; s. A. Drew and Berta (Baker) R.; m. Christine U. Cunningham, Dec. 20, 1943. AB, U. Ala., 1943, LL.B., 1949. Bar: Ala. bar 1949. Since practiced in, Birmingham; asst. U.S. atty. No. Dist. Ala., 1949-52; partner firm Rogers, Howard, Redden & Mills, 1952-79, Redden, Mills & Clark, 1979—; Civilian aide for Ala. to sec. army, 1965-69. Mem. Ala. Democratic Exec. Com., 1966-74 Editor-in-chief: Ala. Law Rev, 1948. Trustee Ala. Law Sch. Found.; adv. council Cumberland Law Sch. Served with AUS, 1943-46; maj. gen. Res. ret. Decorated D.S.M.; recipient Outstanding Civilian Service medal Dept. Army, 1970 Fellow Am. Coll. Trial Lawyers, Internat. Soc. Barristers; mem. ABA, Am. Judicature Soc., Ala. Bar Assn. (pres. 1972-73), Birmingham Bar Assn. (past pres.), Ala. Law Inst. (mem. coun.), U. Ala. Law Sch. Alumni Assn. (past pres.), Phi Beta Kappa, Alpha Tau Omega, Omicron Delta Kappa. Baptist. Home: 2513 Beaumont Cir Birmingham AL 35216-1301 E-mail: ldr@rmclaw.com.

REDDEN, LINDA JOYCE, public relations professional; b. Nashville, Feb. 5, 1950; d. Joseph Edward and Bessie Mai (Carr) R. BA in History, Tenn. Tech. U., 1972; MS in Communications, U. Tenn., 1975. Photographer, Tenn. Tech. U., Cookeville, 1972-73; editor Hendersonville Star News, Tenn., 1975-76; editor, sales promotion exec. Am. Gen. Life and Accident Ins. Co., Nashville, 1975-85; communications coordinator Barge, Waggoner, Sumner & Cannon, Nashville, 1985-86, Ingram Industries Inc., 1987—; adminstrv. asst. Nashville Symphony Guild, 1987—. Editor: The Shield, 1980 (award Nat. Fedn. Press Women 1980). Bd. dirs. Mur-Ci Homes for Retarded, Nashville, 1984—; mem. Nashville Symphony Guild, 1987—. Mem. Pub. Relations Soc. Am., Internat. Assn. Bus. Communicators (sec. 1982), Tenn. Women's Press and Authors Club (treas. 1983-86), Phi Kappa Phi, Kappa Tau Alpha, Phi Alpha Theta. Avocations: reading, photography, cooking, swimming, travel. Home: 136 Island Dr Hendersonville TN 37075-4507 Office: Ingram Industries Inc 4400 Harding Rd Nashville TN 37205-2244

REDDEN, TAYLOR TILGHMAN, musician; b. Swarthmore, Pa., Mar. 2, 1946; s. O. Tilghman Redden and Virginia Dare (Martin) Martin-Redden. Artist diploma, Phila. Conservatory of Music, 1965; BA, BFA in Music, Phila. Music Acad., 1967. Artist, tchr. Phila. Settlement Music Schs., 1968—70; prof. piano Bryn Mawr Conservatory of Music, Bryn Mawr, Pa., 1971—. Mem.: Music Tchrs. N. Am. Home: 539 Cornell Ave Swarthmore PA 19081

REDDER, THOMAS JOSEPH, lawyer, judge, legislator, federal administrator, biotech executive; b. Marshall, Minn., June 18, 1955; s. Lester J. and Ardell S. (Hentges) R. BA, Colo. State U., 1978; JD, U. Colo., 1981. Bar: Colo. 1981, U.S. Dist. Ct. Colo. 1981, U.S. Ct. Appeals (10th cir.) 1982, D.C. 1983, U.S. Supreme Ct. 1985. Pvt. practice, Fort Collins, Colo., 1981-91. Mcpl. judge Wellington, Colo., 1983-88, Timnath, Colo., 1985-88; elected Colo. Ho. of Rep. 58th Gen. Assy., 1991-93; region VIII adminstr. U.S. Sml. Bus. Adminstrn., Denver, 1993-98; v.p. sales, mktg., bus. devel. Cytomation, Inc., Ft. Collins, Colo., 1999-2001; dir., bus. devel., Agilent Techs., Inc., Palo Alto, Calif., 2002-. Mem. advance staff White House, Washington, 1977, 78, 80, 93; staff asst. U.S. Senator Daniel Patrick Moynihan, Washington, 1977; advance staff Mondale for Pres., Washington, 1984; trip dir. for Dukakis/Bentsen presdl. campaign, Boston, 1988; Dem. nominee for U.S. House of Reps., 4th Congrl. Dist. of Colo., 1992. Mem. ABA, Colo. Bar Assn., Larimer County Bar Assn. Democrat. Roman Catholic. Home and Office: PO Box 9626 Fort Collins CO 80525-0503 E-mail: tjredder@aol.com.

REDDIEN, CHARLES HENRY, II, lawyer, corporate executive, consultant; b. San Diego, Aug. 27, 1944; s. Charles Henry and Betty Jane (McCormick) R.; m. Paula Gayle, June 16, 1974; 1 child, Tyler Charles. BSEE, U. Colo., Boulder, 1966; MSEE, U. So. Calif., 1968; JD, Loyola U., L.A., 1972. Bar: Calif. 1972, Colo. 1981, U.S. Dist. Ct. 1981. Mgr. Hughes Aircraft Co., 1966-81; pvt. practice, 1972—. Pres., broker R&D Realty Ltd., 1978-91; mem. spl. staff, co-dir. tax advantage group OTC Net Inc., 1981-82; pres., chmn. Heritage Group Inc., investment banking holding co., 1982-84, Plans and Assistance Inc., mgmt. cons., 1982-83, Orchard Group Ltd., investment banking holding co., 1982-84, J.W. Gant & Assocs., Inc., investment bankers, 1983-84; mng. ptnr., CEO J.W. Gant & Assocs., Ltd., 1984-85; chmn. bd. Kalamath Group Ltd., 1985-87, Heritage group Ltd. Investment Bankers, 1985-87; dir. Virtusonics Corp., 1985-92; v.p., dir. Heritage Fin. Planners Inc., 1982-83; pres., chmn. PDN Inc., 1987-89; pub., exec. v.p., dir. World News Digest Inc., 1987-90, LeisureNet Entertainment, Inc., 1989-90; chief exec. officer, Somerset Group Ltd., 1988-93, Inland Pacific Corp., 1989-91, World Info. Network, Inc., 1990-92, pres., CEO, chmn., Europa Cruises Corp., 1992-94; CEO, chmn. Casino World Inc., 1993-97, Miss. Gaming Corp., 1993-97; pres., chmn., CEO Chart Group Ltd., 1997—, SkyData Corp., 2000—; pres., Miss. Corrections, L.L.C. Contbr. articles to profl. jours. Pres. Diamondhead Business and Profl. Assn.; commr. Diamondhead Fire Dist. Recipient tchg. internship award, 1954. Mem. AIAA, IEEE (chmn. U. Colo. chpt. 1965), Calif. Bar Assn., Nat. Assn. Securities Dealers, Phi Alpha Delta, Tau Beta Pi, Eta Kappa Nu. Office: PO Box 6133 Diamondhead MS 39525-6002 E-mail: chartgroup@aol.com.

REDDIG, WALTER EDUARD, architect, master cabinet maker; b. Meldorf, Holstein, Fed. Republic Germany, Apr. 3, 1936; came to U.S., 1960; s. Ernst and Frieda (Probst) R.; m. Irma Andresen, May 6, 1961; children: Sara Birgit, Ralph Edward. Student, Trade Sch., Meldorf, 1953-56; cert. design technician, Masters Sch., Flensburg, Fed. Republic Germany, 1959, cert. interior architect, 1960. Registered architect, Mich., Va., Md., Tex., Ill., Pa., N.H., Fla. Interior designer J. Holleman Assocs., Birmingham, Mich., 1963-66; project coordinator Levine-Alpern Assocs., Detroit, 1966-69; design and project dir. F. Stickel Assocs., Troy, Mich., 1969-73; project designer Greimel, Malcomson & James, Detroit, 1973; pvt. practice architecture Farmington Hills, Mich., 1973—. Instr. Lawrence Tech. U. Coll. of Architecture and Design, Southfield, Mich., 1992— Contbr. articles to mags.; artist water colors. Appointed to Ad Hoc Hist. Dist. Com., Farmington Hills, 1979-81; vice chmn. Hist. Dist. Commn., Farmington Hills, 1981-91; artist in residence Farmington Area Arts Commn., 1984. Mem. AIA, Mich. Soc. Architects, Nat. Council Archtl. Registration Bd. (cert.). Clubs: Farmington Artist (pres. 1983-85). Lutheran. Avocations: painting, photography, music. Home and Office: 24003 Inkster Rd Farmington Hills MI 48336-3855

REDDING, BARBARA J. nursing administrator, occupational health nurse; b. Youngstown, Ohio, Jan. 5, 1938; d. Richard Howard and Helen N. (Price) Sterling; m. Philip L. Redding, Nov. 7, 1957; children: Cheryl L., Jeffrey A., Scott P. Diploma in nursing, Miami Valley Hosp., Dayton, Ohio, 1959; AA in Sociology, Miami U., Oxford, Ohio, 1984; postgrad., U. Cin. RN, Ohio; cert. EMT, CPR, BLS. Office nurse Dr. Stewart Adam, Dayton; primary nurse Miami Valley Hosp; adminstr. employee health Armco Steel Co., L.P., Middletown, Ohio; v.p. Redding Ins. Agy., Inc., 1993—. Instr. CPR, ARC. Mem. NAFE, Am. Assn. Occupational Health Nurses, Ind. Ins. Agts. Am., Inc. Home: 4501 Riverview Ave Middletown OH 45042-2938

REDDING, LEE SCOTT, economist; b. Ft. Knox, Ky., May 4, 1969; s. Joseph Michael and Nancy Kay (Brunner) R. BS in Math., Computer Sci., and with highest honors in Econs., U. Mich., 1986; MA in Econs., Princeton U., 1990, postgrad., 1988—. Merchandiser Chelsea (Mich.) Pharmacy, Inc., 1984-85; rsch. asst. dept. econs. U. Mich., Ann Arbor, 1985-87, teaching asst. dept. elec. engring., computer sci., 1986-87; rsch. asst. Environ. Rsch. Inst. Mich., 1986-88; asst. in instrn. dept. econs. Princeton U., 1990—. Slater scholar U. Mich., 1982, Coll. Lit., Sci., and Arts scholar, 1984; Princeton U. fellow, 1988. Libertarian. Office: Princeton U Dept Econs Princeton NJ 08544-0001

REDDING, RICHARD ELLSWORTH, psychologist; b. Miami, Fla., Sept. 17, 1964; s. Richard and Betty (Wellman) R. BA cum laude, Hampden-Sydney Coll., 1984; MS, Vanderbilt U., 1986; JD cum laude, Washington and Lee U., 1992; PhD, U. Va., 1997. Bar: Va. 92. Instr. Lehigh U., 1986-87; clin. psychologist PATH, Inc., Phila., 1987; sr. analyst, rsch. psychologist Pacer Systems, Inc., Arlington and Horsham, 1986-89; project dir. Human Tech., Inc., McLean, Va., 1989—; law clk. to Judge Farrell D.C. Ct. Appeals, Washington, 1992—93; asst. prof., assoc. dir. Inst. of Law, Psychiatry and Pub. Policy U. Va. Sch. Law, Charlottesville, 1998—2001; assoc. prof. law, dir. JD/PhD program in law and psychology Villanova (Pa.) U. Sch. of Law, 2001—; assoc. prof. clin. psychology Med. Coll. Pa.-Hahnemann U., Phila., 2001—. Mem. dissemination rev. panel U.S. Dept. Edn., Washington, 1989; vis. prof. U. Malaysia, 1995; vis. disting. fellow U. So. Queensland, Australia, 1994; sr. scientist Human Tech., Inc., McLean, Va., 1989-92; cons. McArthur Found., 1998-99; Frances Lewis law fellow Washington and Lee U. Sch. of Law, 1992. Author: A Trainer's Guide to Cognitive Task Analysis, 1991, Due Process Protections for Juveniles in Civil Commitment Proceedings, 1991, Applied Cognitive Task Analysis in Aviation, 1997; contbr. more than 50 articles to profl. and sci. jours. Mem. Am. Psychol. Assn. (assoc.), Am. Psychology-Law Soc., Human Factors Soc. Office: Villanova Univ School of Law 299 North Spring Mill Rd Villanova PA 19085-1597

REDDING, ROBERT HULL, writer; b. Hilo, Hawaii, Dec. 3, 1919; s. Emily Hull; m. Grace Margaret Feeny, July 14, 1956. Freelance writer, Sequim, Wash., 1977—. Sgt. USAF, 1942-46. Avocations: swimming, hiking. Home: 1301 S 3d St Apt 18D Sequim WA 98382

REDDING, ROGERS WALKER, physics educator, university official; b. Louisville, July 15, 1942; s. George Walker and Carolyn Lorraine (Rogers) R.; m. Jennie Ruth Fincher, Sept. 6, 1966 (div.); children: Jeffrey Walker, Jonathan Hull; m. Shirley Rubrecht, Aug. 24, 1991. BS, Georgia Tech., 1965; PhD, Vanderbilt U., 1969. Rsch. assoc. Nat. Bur. Standards, Washington, 1969-70; from asst. prof. to assoc. prof. North Tex. State U. (name now U. North Tex.), Denton, 1970-78, prof. physics, 1978-94, dept. chmn., 1980-87, dir. Tex. Acad. Math. and Sci., 1987-89, assoc. dean arts and scis., 1990-94; prof. physics, dean Coll. Arts and Scis. No. Ky. U., Highland Heights, 1994—, v.p. acad. affairs, provost. Disting. vis. prof. USAF Acad., 1989-90. Author: Exploring Physics, 1984; contbr. articles to profl. jours. Mem. Am. Phys. Soc., Am. Assn. Physics Tchrs., AAAS, Optical Soc. Am. Lodges: Kiwanis. Democrat. Avocations: handball, jogging, referee college football, little league coach. Home: 10501 Cheshire Ridge Dr Florence KY 41042-3197 E-mail: redding@nku.edu.

REDDISH, JOHN JOSEPH, management consulting company executive; b. Albany, N.Y., July 23, 1946; s. Leonard Frank and Marion Elizabeth (McElveney) R.; children: Jorin T., Adam Sledd, Lee Sledd, Nicholas Brendel. AB in Communication Arts, Fordham U., 1968; MSA, West Chester U., 1984. Cert. Inst. Mgmt. Cons. Pub. rels. asst. Civil Svc. Employees Assn., Albany, 1967-68; assoc. editor Edison Electric Inst., N.Y.C., 1968-69; dir. info. svcs. N.Y. State Nurses Assn., Guilderland, 1969-70; pres. RA Group, Inc., Advt. and Pub. Rels., Albany, 1970-77; v.p. The Presidents Assn. div. Am. Mgmt. Assocs., N.Y.C., 1977-78; pres. Advent Mgmt. Assocs. Ltd., Chadds Ford, Pa., 1978-92; pres., dir. Advent Mgmt. Internat., Ltd., 1992—. Mem. adv. bd. PAC Strapping Products, Inc., 1995—; spkr. in field. Author: New Techniques For Motivation and Discipline; contbr. articles to profl. jours. With Chester County Internat. Trade Coun., 1998—; trustee N.Y. Theol. Sem., 1988—98; bd. dirs. Focus Chs. of Albany, 1973—76; bd. deacons Emmanuel Bapt. Ch., 1974—77; bd. dirs. Kennett Symphony Orch., 1991—2001. Mem.: Nat. Spkrs. Assn. (dir. Mid-Atlantic chpt. 1999—, pres. 2001—), Am. Arbitration Assn. (mem. panel of arbitrators 1990—). Office: Advent Mgmt Internat Ltd 411 Old Baltimore Pike Chadds Ford PA 19317-9444

REDDY, GADDUM JAGAN MOHAN, surgeon; b. Nizamabad, India, Feb. 12, 1942; s. Gaddum Ganga and Gaddum Chandra (Devi) R.; m. Gaddum Sriranjani, Sept. 2, 1972; children: Gaddum H. Pavan, Gaddum Suman P., Gaddum Duemani P. MBBS, Osmania Med. Coll., Hyderabad, India, 1965. Diplomate Am. Bd. Surgery, Am. Bd. Thoracic Surgery. Chief of surgery VA Med. Ctr., Montgomery, Ala., 1976-79, Alexandria, La., 1979-81, Big Spring, Tex., 1988—. Am. Am. Assn. Physician Indian Origin, Internat. Soc. Endovascular Specialist, Assn. Vets. Adminstrn. Surgeons. Hindu. Avocations: reading, aerobic activity. Office: VA Med Ctr 300 W Veterans Blvd Big Spring TX 79720-5566

REDDY, GERARD ANTHONY, corporate training executive; b. N.Y.C., Sept. 25, 1958; s. Warren and Julia (O'Reilly) R.; m. Lorraine Bush, Feb. 20, 1994. BA in English Writing and Comms. Media, Queens Coll., 1981. Rsch. analyst John Blair and Co., N.Y.C., 1981—82, Katz Ind. TV Sales, N.Y.C., 1982—83; sr. rsch. analyst Seltel, 1983—84; sales presentation writer Capital Cities/ABC TV Sales, 1984—86; client svc. exec. A.C. Nielsen Co., 1986—87; rsch. mgr. off network programming MCA-TV, 1987—88; mgr. corp. tng. and instrn. Dale Carnegie Tng., 1989—96, major accounts bus. mgr.,

1996—97; tng. supr. Americhoice Inc., Newark, 1998; sr. tng. specialist The Dreyfus Corp., Uniondale, NY, 1999—2000; fin. advisor Am. Express Fin. Advisors Inc., Mitchel Field, 2000—. Mgr. Little League Our Lady Miraculous Medal, Ridgewood, N.Y., 1993, 94; campaigner Rudolph Guliani for Mayor, N.Y.C., Ridgewood, 1994. Mem. ASTD, Am. Soc. Quality Control, Am. Mgmt. Assn., Soc. Human Resource Mgmt. Avocations: script writing, motorcycle touring, meditation, jogging. Home: 3 Smith St East Rockaway NY 11518-1716 Office: The Dreyfus Corp 144 Glenn Curtiss Blvd Uniondale NY 11553-0144 Business E-Mail: gerard.a.reddy@aexp.com.

REDDY, J. NARASIMHA, mechanical engineering educator; b. Warangal, AP, India, Aug. 12, 1945; m. Aruna Reddy; children: Anita, Anil. BE in Mech. Engring., Osmania U., 1968; MS in Mech. Engring, Okla. State U., 1970; PhD in Engring. Mechanics, U. Ala., 1973. Rsch. scientist Lockheed Missiles & Space Co., 1974-75; asst. prof. U. Okla., 1975-78, assoc. prof., 1978-80; prof. mech. engring. Va. Poly. Inst. and State U., Blacksburg, Va., 1980-85, Clifton G. Garvin prof., 1986-92; Oscar S. Wyatt Jr. chair Tex. A&M U., College Station, 1992—, Univ. Disting. prof., 1998—. Author: Energy and Variational Methods in Applied Mechanics, 1984, Applied Funcational Analysis and Variational Methods in Engineering, 1986, An Introduction to the Finite Element Method, 1993, Mechanics of Laminated Composite Plates: Theory and Analysis, 1997, Theory and Analysis of Elastic Plates, 1999, (with others) Variational Methods in Theoretical Mechanics, 1976, A Mathematical Theory of Finite Elements, 1976, Advanced Engineering Analysis, 1982, Finite Element Analysis of Composite Laminates, 1992, The Finite Element Method in Heat Transfer and Fluid Dynamics, 1994, 2d edit., 2001, Practical Analysis of Laminated Composite Structures, 1995; editor-in-chief Mechanics of Composite Materials and Structures; mem. editl. bd. Jour. Applied Mechanics, Internat. Jour. Numerical Methods in Engring., Internat. Jour. Numerical Methods in Fluids; contbr. over 250 papers to profl. jours. Recipient Ralph R. Teetor Edn. award Soc. Automotive Engrs., 1976, Technical Achievement award NAE, 1995, Archie Higdon Disting. Educator award Am. Soc. Engring. Edn., 1997. Fellow ASME (Worcester Reed Warner medal 1992, Charles Russ Richards Meml. award 1995), ASCE (chair adv. com. engring. mechanics divsn., Walter L. Huber Civil Engring Rsch. prize 1983, Nathan M. Newmark medal 1998), AIAA (assoc.), Am. Acad. Mechanics, Aeronautical Soc. India, U.S. Assn. Computational Mechanics (pres.); mem. Internat. Assn. Computational Mechanics (co-editor of bulletin). Office: Texas A&M Univ Dept Mech Engring College Station TX 77843-3123 Fax: 979-862-3989.

REDDY, KAMBHAM RAJA, plant physiology educator; b. Ambuvari Palli, India, July 1, 1953; came to U.S., 1988; s. Kambi Kambham and Ammannamma (Reddy) R.; m. Anasuya Kambham, Feb. 9, 1982; 1 child, Sasank. BSc in Biology, S.V. U., Tirupati, India, 1975, MSc in Botany, 1977, PhD in Botany, 1984. Curator in botany S.V. U., 1977-88; prof. plant physiology Miss. State U., 1988—. Vis. scientist Govt. of India, 1988. Editor: Climate Change and Global Crop Productivity, 2000; contbg. author: Climate Change and Agriculture: Analysis of Potential International Impacts, 1995; contbr. articles to profl. jours., chpts. to books. Mem. Agronomy Soc. Am., Crop Sci. Soc. Am., Biol. Sys. Simulation Work Group, Gamma Sigma Delta (Rsch. award of merit 1995). Achievements include development of new theories and concepts in plant growth regulation and incorporated into a cotton simulation model GOSSYMX, used by cotton producers, consultants and researchers across the cotton belt; extensive contributions to the field of crop and climate change, environmental plant physiology and crop simulation modeling. Home: 505 Banyan Rd Starkville MS 39759-4348 Office: Mississippi State U Box 9555 Mississippi State MS 39762-9555

REDDY, KRISHNA NARAYANA, artist, educator; b. Chittoor, India, July 15, 1925; s. Narayana B. and Laksmamma R.; m. Judith Blum, June 30, 1967; 1 child, Aparna. Diploma in Fine Arts, Internat. U. Santiniketan, India, 1947; cert. in Fine Arts, Slade Sch. Fine Arts, U. London, 1952; student of Zadkine in sculpture, Academie Grande Chaumière, Paris, 1952-55; student of Marino Marini in sculpture, Academia di Belle Arti di Brera, Milan, 1956-57; specialist in Gravure, Internat. Ctr. for Graphics, Atelier 17, Paris, 1953-55; D.Litt. (hon.), S.V. Univ., India, 1984. Asst. dir. Internat. Ctr. for Graphics, Atelier 17, Paris, 1957—64, prof., co-dir., 1964—76; prof. art N.Y. U., N.Y.C., 1977—2001, dir. graphics and printmaking program, 1977—, prof. emeritus art and art edn., 2001—; lectr. art Arundale Montessori Tchrs. Tng. Center, 1948—49; dir. art dept. Coll. Fine Arts, Kalakshetra, Madras, India, 1947—49; vis. prof. Yale U. Summer Sch. Music and Art, 1978, Am. U., 1964, Kala Inst. Graphics, Berkeley, Calif., 1979, U. Calif., Santa Cruz, 1979. Andrew Mellon vis. prof. Cooper Union Sch. Art and Architecture, 1977; prof. U. Wis., Madison, 1973, U. Calif., Davis, 1970-71; guest prof. Yale U. Summer Sch. Music and Art, 1973 Author: Intaglio Simultaneous Color Printmaking: Significance of Materials and Processes, 1989, New Ways of Colour Printmaking, 1997; retrospective exhbns., Bronx Mus. Arts, 1981-82, Indian Council for Cultual Relations, Ministry of Culture and India Nat. Acad. Fine Arts, 1984-85, Museo del Palacio de Bellas Artes, Mexico City, 1988-89. Recipient Gagan-Abani Puraskar Nat. award Viswa-Bharati, 1983, Printmaker Emeritus award So. Graphics Coun. of Am., 2000; named Featured Guest Artist-Printmaker at the Northwest Print Coun. Ann. Meeting, 1985; Title of Padma Shree awarded by Pres. of India, 1972. Home: 80 Wooster St New York NY 10012-4347

REDDY, KRISHNA P. pathologist, laboratory director; b. P.V. Palli, India, Jan. 10, 1945; s. Pennabadi Gangi and P. Gangulamma Reddy; m. Aruna Reddy, Aug. 20, 1970; children: Syam, Kavitha. MD, Kurnool (India) Med. Coll., 1969; MS in Mathology, U. Ill., Chgo., 1976; MBA, No. Ill. U., 1997. Intern Ill. Masonic Hosp., Chgo., 1969-70, Govt. Gen. Hosp., Kurnool, 1968-69; resident in gen. surgery Ill. Masonic Hosp., Chgo., 1970-71; resident in pathology U. Ill., chgo., 1971-75; lab. dir., pathologist Kishwaukee Cmty. Hosp., DeKalb, Ill., 1977—, continuing med. edn. dept., 1982—. Chief of staff Kishwaukee Cmty. Hosp.; instr.Abraham Lincoln Sch. Medicine, U. Ill., Chgo., 1971-76, clin. instr., 1976-77; attending pathologist, U. Ill. Hosp., Chgo., 1975-76, Copley Meml. Hosp., aurora, Ill., 1976-77; dir. lab. dept. Kishwaukee Cmty. Hosp., DeKalb, 1977—; dir. lab. dept. KeKalb Clinic, 1989—, No. Ill. Univ. Health Svcs., DeKalb, 1989—; clin. asst. prof. U. Ill. Coll. Medicine, Rockford, 1997—. Contbr. articles to profl. jours. Trustee Heartland Blood Ctr., Aurora, Ill., 1982—, Kishwaukee Cmty. Hosp., 1989-90; pres. Hindu Temple of Greater Chgo., 1984-86, trustee, 1983-93, 2002—; chmn. Am. Telugu Assn., Naperville, 1991. Mem. AMA, Coll. Am. Pathologists, Am. Soc. Clin. Pathologists, Ill. State Med. Soc., DeKalb County Med. Soc., Am. Coll. Physician Execs., Am. Soc. Cytopathology, U. Ill. Alumni Assn. Office: Kishwaukee Cmty Hosp 626 Bethany Rd Dekalb IL 60115-4939 E-mail: Pennabad@msn.com.

REDDY, NALLAPU NARAYAN, economics educator; b. June 22, 1939; arrived in U.S., 58; s. Narasimha H. and Shantha N. Reddy; m. Saroja N. Nalladi, June 1, 1957; children: Lata, Mala. BS, Mich. Tech. U., 1961; MS, U. Mo., 1963; PhD, Pa. State U., 1967; MA, U. Notre Dame, 1973. Asst. prof. Clarkson U., Potstam, NY, 1967—72, assoc. prof., 1972—74; assoc. prof. econs. U. Mich., Flint, 1974—79, prof., 1979—, chmn. dept., 1981—84, 1993—99. Vis. fellow London Sch. Econs., 1981, Oxford (England) U., 1987; vis. prof. Washington U., St. Louis, 1994. Editor: Empirical Studies in Microeconomics, 1985; contbr. articles to profl. jours. Recipient Disting. Prof. Award for Teaching Excellence, 1979. Mem.: Western Econ. Assn., So. Econ. Assn., Ea. Econ. Assn., Am. Econ. Assn., Omicron Delta Epsilon., Phi Kappa Phi. Home: 6250 Kings Shire Rd Grand Blanc MI 48439-8656 E-mail: nreddy@umich.edu.

REDDY, RAMAKRISHNA L. physician, pathologist, consultant; b. India; came to U.S., 1983; m. Sarada L. Reddy. BSc, Andhra Loyala Coll., 1961; MBBS, Kurnool Med. Coll., 1968; MBA, U. Nebr., 1996. Bd. cert. anatomic and clin. pathology and blood banking/transfusion medicine; diplomate Am. Bd. Pathology. Med. officer AP State Health Svcs., Andhra Pradesh, India, 1968-69; tutor, asst. prof. physiology Kurnool (India) Med. Coll., 1969-83; resident pathology U. Ill., Chgo., 1984-88; fellow transfusion medicine U. Minn., Mpls., 1988-90; med. assoc. ARC Blood Svcs., St. Paul, 1990-91, med. dir. Omaha, 1991—. Fellow ACP; mem. AMA, Am. Soc. Apheresis, Am. Assn. Blood Banks (area chair 1993—). Office: ARC Blood Svcs 3838 Dewey Ave Omaha NE 68105-1148

REDDY, SATTI SETHU-KUMAR, physician, educator; b. Tadepalligudem, India, Jan. 9, 1958; arrived in U.S., 1995; s. Satti Paddi and Satti Parvati Reddy; m. Lalitha Padala, Jan. 6, 1986; children: Pranav, Suparna, Vishal, Pavitra. MD, Meml. U. Newfoundland, 1980. Bd. cert. in internal medicine and endocrinology, metabolism, and diabetes. Intern in internal medicine Meml. U. Nfld., 1980-82, resident in internal medicine, 1982-83; clin. fellow endocrinology U. Toronto, 1983-85; rsch. fellow Joslin Diabetes Ctr., Harvard Med. Sch., Boston, 1985-88; asst. prof. Dalhousie U., Halifax, N.S., Can., 1988-93, assoc. prof. Can., 1994—; mem. staff Cleve. Clinic, 1995—, chmn. dpet. endocrinology, diabetes and metabolism, 2000—. Contbr. articles to profl. jours. Co-chair Mayfield Schs. Sci. Ctr., Mayfield Heights, Ohio, 1996-99, Sci. Bond Issue, Mayfield Heights, 1998. Fellow ACP, Royal Coll. Physicians and Surgeons Can., Am. Coll. Endocrinology. Avocations: reading, music, tennis. Office: Cleve Clinic A53 9500 Euclid Ave Cleveland OH 44195-0001 E-mail: reddys@ccf.org.

REDDY, THIKKAVARAPU RAMACHANDRA, electrical engineer; b. Nellore, India, June 4, 1944; came to the U.S., 1979; s. Thikkavarapu Kota and Saraswathi T. (Sivareddy) R.; m. Padmavathi Reddy Kakuturu Thikkavarapu, Aug. 17, 1973; children: Lavanya T., Samatha T. BSEE, Osmania U., 1968; diploma in computer sci., Coll. Engring., Madras, India, 1978. Cert. profl. engr., chartered engr. Supervising engr. APSE Bd., Hyderabad, India, 1969-79; elec. design engr. Sargent & Lundy, Chgo., 1979-80; engr. Bechtel Corp., San Francisco, 1980-82, supr. Athens, Ala., 1989-92; sr. project engr. EGS, Inc., Huntsville, 1983-84; sr. start-up engr. Gilbert Commonwealth Co., Reading, Pa., 1984-86; cons. Quantum Resources, Decatur, Ala., 1986-87; prin. engr. Ebasco Svcs. Inc., N.Y.C., 1987-89; pres. LSP Internat. Inc., Huntsville, 1992—, LASA Internat., Huntsville, 1992—; project engr. Sargent & Lundy, Chgo., 1997—. Guest lectr. gen. interest and wide range of engring. issues; pres. Lasa Internat. Inc., Huntsville, 1992—. Author: Qualification of Electrical Distribution Components, 1984, Thermal Aging Techniques of Organic Materials, 1984, and others; contbr. articles to profl. jours.; guest lectr. on wide range of engring. issues. Mem. NSPE (Outstanding Profl. award 1991, Profl. Engr. of Yr. award 1996), IEEE (Meritorious Svc. award 1985), Commonwealth Engrs. Coun., Project Mgmt. Inst., Am. Telugu Assn. (life), Telugu Assn. N.Am. (life), Internat. Platform Assn., C. of C. Avocations: journalism, table tennis, anthropology, archaeology, classic and modern art, literature. Home and Office: 814 Reserve Champion Dr Rockville MD 20850 E-mail: trcreddy@hotmail.com.

REDDY, VARDHAN JONNALA, surgeon; b. Kollipara, India, Nov. 26, 1960; MBBS, Guntur Med. Coll., Andhra U., 1985. Diplomate Am. Bd. Surgery. Internist Robert Packer Hosp., Sayre, Pa., 1990-91; res. L.I. Jewish Med. Ctr., New Hyde Park, N.Y., 1991-95; fellowship Tex. Heart Inst., Houston, 1995-96; staff surgeon Glades Gen. Hosp., Belle Glade, Fla., 1996-98, chief surgery, 1998—99; cardiothoracic surgeon U. Miss., Jackson, Miss., 1999—2001, Shadyside Hosp., Pitts., 2001—. V.p. Med. Staff Assocs. of Glades Inc., 1998, pres., CEO Heartcom Inc., 1999. Mem. AMA, Internat. Coll. Angiology, Royal Coll. Surgeons Edinburgh (diplomate), Am. Coll. Angiology. Home and Office: 504 Greenbrier Ct Steubenville OH 43953-3335 E-mail: vardhanreddy@usa.net.

REDDY, VEMULA SHANTH, physician; b. Nizamabad, India, Jan. 11, 1948; came to U.S., 1975; s. Sudershan and Lakshmi Devi (Nalla) R.; m. Asha Latha Nalla, May 6, 1972 (dec. Aug. 2000); children: Varsha, Nitin. MD, Kakatiya Med. Coll., Warangal, India, 1970. Diplomate Am. Bd. Internal Medicine, Am. Bd. Geriatrics. House surgeon MGM Hosp., Warangal, India, 1971-72; postgrad. in medicine Osmania Gen. Hosp., Hyderabad, India, 1972-75; staff physician St. John Riverside Hosp., Yonkers, N.Y., 1975-76; resident in medicine Kingsbrook Jewish Med. Ctr., Brooklyn, 1976-79; pvt. practice Energy Basin Clinic, Hanna, Wyo., 1979-81; staff physician VA Hosp., Biloxi, Miss., 1981-87, Coatesville, Pa., 1987-95, Waco, Tex., 1995—. Fellow ACP. Hindu. Home: 2044 Oak Glen Dr Mc Gregor TX 76657-3449 Office: VA Hosp 4800 Memorial Dr Waco TX 76711-1329

REDDY, VIJAYA, emergency physician; b. Aug. 24, 1945; MBBS, Kasturba Med. Coll., India, 1969. Diplomate Am. Bd. Emergency Medicine. Emergency rm. physician St. Johns Riverside Hosp., Yonkers, N.Y., 1975—. Address: 45 Ridge Rd Dobbs Ferry NY 10522-3300 E-mail: vijayr@bellatlantic.net.

REDDY, YENAMALA RAMACHANDRA, metal processing executive; b. Polavaram, Andhra, India, Feb. 12, 1939; came to U.S., 1974; s. Y. Venkata and Y. Lakshamamma Reddy; m. Y. Uma Reddy, May 30, 1965; children: Y. Sharath, Y. Jay. BME, S.V. U., Andhra, 1961; M in Tech., IIT, Bombay, 1966, PhD, 1970. Lic. profl. engr., Wis. Asst. prof. IIT, Bombay, 1966-69; research and devel. mgr. Jyoti Pumps, Baroda, 1973-74; chief engr. Patterson Pumps, Toccoa, Ga., 1974-80; pres. R.B. Pump Co., Baxley, 1980—, U.B. Cons., Ga., 1980—. Pres. Falcon Castings, Inc., 1996, Eagle Motors, Inc., 1996. Contbr. articles to tech. jours. Postdoctoral fellow U. of Tech., Loughborough, Eng., 1970-73. Mem. ASME, IEEE, Am. Foundryman's Soc., Nat. Fire Protection Assn. Office: R B Pump Co 1 Dixie Dr # 557 Baxley GA 31513-6947

REDFERN, JOHN D. manufacturing company executive; b. 1935. Grad. Queen's U., Kingston, Ont., 1958, DEng (honoris causa), Carleton U., 1992. With Lafarge Can. Inc. (formerly Can. Cement Lafarge Ltd.), Montreal, 1977—, pres., chief exec. officer, 1977-84, chmn., 1985—; chmn. bd. parent co. Lafarge Corp., Reston, Va., 1985-88, vice-chmn., 1989-96. Office: Lafarge Can Inc 606 Cathcart Ste 800 Montreal QC Canada H3B 1L7

REDFIELD, DAVID ALLEN, chemistry educator; b. Grand Junction, Colo., Aug. 26, 1948; s. Donald Lee and Wilda Mae (Bean) R.; m. Sandra Kay Trandem, Dec. 13, 1969; children: Daniel, John, Jessica. BA, Point Loma Nazarene Coll., 1970; PhD, U. Nevada, Reno, 1974. Postdoctoral fellow U. Ill., Urbana, 1974-75; sr. rsch. chemist Olin Corp., New Haven, 1975-80; prof., chair dept. chemistry N.W. Nazarene U., Nampa, Idaho, 1980-99, dean Sch. Health and Sci., 1999—. Cons. Nyssa (Oreg.)-Nampa Sugar Beet Growers, 1982-2000, co-dir. Students Investigating Today's Environment. Participant Vallivue Band Parents, Caldwell, Idaho, 1991—, participant Vallivue Sch. Mission Setting Team, Caldwell, 1994-95; elected Vallivue Sch. Bd., 1998; trustee Vallivue Sch., 1998—. Recipient tchr. recognition program Nampa C. of C., 1989. Mem. Am. Chem. Soc., Idaho Acad. Sci. (treas. and pres. 1980-99). Nazarene. Avocations: backpacking, fishing, model trains. Office: N W Nazarene U 623 Holly St Nampa ID 83686-5855 E-mail: DARedfield@nnu.edu.

REDFORD, DONALD BRUCE, historian, archaeologist; b. Toronto, Ont., Can., Sept. 2, 1934; s. Cyril Fitzjames and Kathleen Beryl (Coe) R.; m. Susan Pirritano, Jan. 30, 1982; children: Alexander, Aksel; children by previous marriage: Christopher, Philip. BA, U. Toronto, 1957, MA, 1958; PhD, Brown U., 1965. Lectr. Brown U., 1960-61; lectr. U. Toronto, 1961-64, asst. prof. Egyptian history and language, 1965-67, asso. prof., 1967-69, prof., 1969-98; site supr. Brit. Sch. Archaeol. Excavations, Jerusalem, 1964-67; dir. Soc. Study Egyptian Antiquities Expdn. to, Karnak, Egypt, 1970-72, Akhenaten Temple Project, Luxor, Egypt, 1972—; research assoc. Univ. Museum, U. Pa., Royal Ont. Mus.; prof. classics Pa. State U., 1998—. Vis. prof. Ben Gurion U., Beersheva, Israel, 1986, U. Pa., 1995-96; dir. excavations Mendes and Ted Kedwa, Egypt, 1991—. Author: History and Chronology of the Egyptian 18th Dynasty, 1967, A Study of the Biblical Joseph Story, 1970, Papyrus and Tablet, 1973, The Akhenaten Temple Project, vol. I, 1977, Akhenaten, the Heretic King, 1984; Annals, King-Lists and Daybooks, 1986, The Akhenaten Temple Project, vol. II, 1988, Egypt, Canaan and Israel in Ancient Times, 1992. Killam grantee, 1975-79; Smithsonian Fgn. Currency grantee, 1973-76, 1979, Social Scis. Humanities Research Council Can. grantee, 1980—. Fellow Royal Soc. Can. Achievements include discovering Temple of Akhenaten at Luxor, 1976. Office: CAMS Weaver Bldg State College PA 16803 also: Pa State U Dept Classics & Mediterranean Studies 108 Weaver Bldg University Park PA 16802-5500 E-mail: dbr3@psu.edu.

REDFORD, ROBERT (CHARLES ROBERT REDFORD), actor, director; b. Santa Monica, Calif., Aug. 18, 1937; m. Lola Van Wegenen (div.); children: Shauna, Jamie, Amy. Student, U. Colo., Pratt Inst. Design, Am. Acad. Dramatic Arts; LHD (hon.), U. Colo., 1987; D (hon.), U. Mass., 1990. Owner ski resort Sundance, Provo, Utah. Pres., founder The Sundance Inst., 1981—. Stage appearances include: Tall Story, The Highest Tree, Sunday in New York, Barefoot in the Park; Films include: (actor) War Hunt, 1961, Situation Hopeless But Not Serious, 1965, Inside Daisy Clover, 1965, The Chase, 1966, This Property Is Condemned, 1966, Barefoot in the Park, 1967, Butch Cassidy and the Sundance Kid, 1969, Tell Them Willie Boy is Here, 1969, Little Fauss and Big Halsey, 1970, The Hot Rock, 1972, Jeremiah Johnson, 1972, The Way We Were, 1973, The Sting, 1973 (Academy award nominee), The Great Gatsby, 1974, The Great Waldo Pepper, 1975, Three Days of the Condor, 1975, A Bridge Too Far, 1977, The Electric Horseman, 1979, Brubaker, 1980, The Natural, 1984, Out of Africa, 1985, Legal Eagles, 1986, Havana, 1990, Sneakers, 1992, Indecent Proposal, 1993, Up Close and Personal, 1996, Anthem, 1997, Enredando sombras, 1998, Forever Hollywood, 1999, Spy Game, 2001, The Last Castle, 2001; (actor, exec. prodr.) Downhill Racer, 1969, The Candidate, 1972, All The President's Men, 1976; (exec. prodr.) Promised Land, 1988, Some Girls, 1988, She's the One, 1996, The Dark Wind, 1991, Slums of Beverly Hills, 1998, How to Kill Your Neighbor's Dog, 2000; (exec. prodr., narrator) Yosemite: The Fate of Heaven, 1989, Incident at Oglala, 1992 (TV) Independent's Day, 1998, Visions of Grace: Robert Redford and 'The Horse Whisperer' 1998 (Audience award); (dir.) Ordinary People, 1980 (Academy and Golden Globe Awards, Best Director); (dir., prodr.) The Milagro Beanfield War, 1988, Quiz Show, 1994, A River Runs Through It, 1993 (narrator); (prodr.), A Civil Action, 1998, The Legend of Bagger Vance, 2000. Recipient Audubon medal, 1989, Dartmouth Film Soc. award, 1990; Cecil B. Demille Golden Globe Award for Lifetime Achievement, 1994, Screen Actors Guild Awards for Life Achievement, 1996, Honoray award, Academy Awards, 2002. Office: 1223 Wilshire Blvd # 412 Santa Monica CA 90403-5400 also: Creative Artists Agy c/o David O'Conner 9830 Wilshire Blvd Beverly Hills CA 90212-1804*

REDHEAD, PAUL AVELING, physicist; b. Brighton, Eng., May 25, 1924; m. Doris Packman, 1948; children: Janet, Patricia. BA with honors in Physics, Cambridge (Eng.) U., 1944, MA, 1948, PhD, 1969. Sci. officer dept. naval ordnance Brit. Admiralty, 1944-45, svcs. electronics rsch. lab., 1945-47; rsch. officer NRC Can., Ottawa, Ont., 1947-69, dir. planning group, 1970-72, dir.-gen. planning, 1972-73, dir. div. physics, 1973-86, chmn. com. of lab. dirs., 1981-86, sec. sci. and tech. policy com., 1986-89, researcher emeritus, 1989—. Author: Physical Basis of Ultrahigh Vacuum, 1968, 2d edit., 1993; editor: Jour. Vacuum Scis. and Tech., 1969-74; contbr. numerous articles to profl. jours.; patentee in field. Fellow IEEE, Royal Soc. Can., Am. Phys. Soc., Am. Vacuum Soc. (past pres., Medard W. Welch award 1975); mem. Can. Assn. Physicists (medal for achievement in physics 1989). Home: 1958 Norway Crescent Ottawa ON Canada K1H 5N7 Office: Nat Rsch Coun Can Inst Microstructural Scis Ottawa ON Canada K1A OR6

REDICAN, KERRY JOHN, health education educator; b. Chgo., May 1, 1950; s. Albert and Catherine (Locelso) Quintiliani; m. Barbara Lee Willman, June 26, 1982; children: Kelly Nicole, Kyle James. BA, Calif. State U., 1971; MS in Pub. Health, UCLA, 1972; PhD, U. Ill., 1975; MPH, U. N.C., 1986. Cert. pub. health specialist. Asst. prof. U. Nebr., Lincoln, 1975-78, Ariz. State U., Tempe, 1978-81; assoc. prof. Va. Tech., Blacksburg, 1981—. Cons. Aramco, Saudi Arabia, 1978-80, ABT Assocs., Cambridge, Mass., 1980-82. Co-author: Health Today, 1986, Organization of School Health Program, 1986. Bd. dirs. Med. Clinic of New River Valley, Christiansburg, Va., 1984-86, Crisis Pregnancy Ctr., Blacksburg, 1988-91, Am. Lung Assn., Richmond, Va., 1989—. Mem. APHA, Am. Alliance Health Edn., Am. Sch. Health Assn., Va. Pub. Health Assn. Republican. Home: 1000 Auburn Dr Blacksburg VA 24060-8123 Office: Va Tech 104 WMH Blacksburg VA 24061

REDIGER, RICHARD KIM, lawyer; b. Glendale, Calif., Sept. 10, 1950; s. Richard Lee and Alba Clare (Burt) R.; m. Linda Lee Olsen, Mar. 21, 1981; children: Susan Elizabeth, Kathryn Rose, Erin Marie. BA, UCLA, 1975; JD, Loyola U., 1978. Bar: Calif. 1978, Colo. 1979, U.S. Ct. Appeals (9th and 10th cirs.) 1979, U.S. Dist. Ct. (cen. dist. L.A.) 1979, Utah 1993, U.S. Dist. Ct. Utah 1993. Assoc. Gray, Gorham & Paul, L.A., 1976-79; dep. dist. atty. 4th Jud. Dist., Colorado Springs, Colo., 1979-83; asst. atty. gen. Office Atty. Gen., Denver, 1983-84; assoc. Hall & Evans, 1984-88; of counsel George L. Vamos, 1988-89, Manville Corp., Denver, 1989-91, Cook & Fitch, Denver, 1992—. Spl. asst. county atty. El Paso County, 1983-84; spl. pros. 20th Jud. Dist., 1984; instr. State of Colo., 1981-83, lectr., 1984. Contbr. DUI/DWAI Manual State of Colorado, 1981. Mem. ABA, Colo. Bar Assn., Calif. Bar Assn., Utah Bar Assn., Denver Bar Assn., Salt Lake County Bar Assn. Avocations: vocal instruction and performance. Office: Cook & Fitch 7887 E Belleview Ave Ste 375 Englewood CO 80111-6057

REDING, JOHN ANTHONY, lawyer; b. Orange, Calif., May 26, 1944; AB, U. Calif., Berkeley, 1966, JD, 1969. Bar: Calif. 1970, U.S. Dist. Ct. (no., ctrl., ea. and so. dists.) Calif., U.S. Claims Ct., U.S. Supreme Ct. Formerly mem. Crosby, Heafey, Roach & May P.C., Oakland, Calif.; now ptnr. Paul, Hastings, Janofsky & Walker, LLP, San Francisco, global chmn. litigation dept. Mem. ABA (sects. on litigation, intellectual property, and natural resources, energy and eviron. law, coms. on bus. torts, internat. law, trial practice and torts and insurance), Am. Intellectual Property Law Assn., State Bar Calif. (sect. on litigation), Bar Assn. San Francisco, Assn. Bus. Trial Lawyers. Office: Paul Hastings Janofsky & Walker LLP 55 2d St 24th Fl San Francisco CA 94105-3441 E-mail: jackreding@paulhastings.com.

REDISH, EDWARD FREDERICK, physicist, educator; b. N.Y.C., Apr. 1, 1942; s. Jules and Sylvia Redish; m. Janice Copen, June 18, 1967; children: A. David, Deborah. AB, Princeton U., 1963; PhD, MIT, 1968. CTP fellow U. Md., College Park, 1968-70, from asst. prof. to assoc. prof., 1970-79, prof., 1979—, chmn. dept. phys. astronomy, 1982-85. Vs. scholar, U. Calif., Berkeley, 1999-00; vis. prof. Ind. U., Bloomington, 1985-86, U. Washington, Seattle, 1992-93; vis. fgn. collaborator CEN, Saclay, France, 1973-74; co-dir. Md. U. Project in Physics and Ednl. Tech., 1983-93, Comprehensive Unified Physics Learning Environment, 1989-96; mem. Nuclear Sci. Adv. Com., Dept. of Energy/NSF, 1987-90; mem. program adv. com. Ind. U. Cyclotron Facility, 1985-89, chmn., 1986-89; mem. Internat. Commn. on Physics Edn., 1993—, sec., 1999—. Author: (software) Orbits, 1989, The M.U.P.P.E.T, Utilities, 1994, The Comprehensive Unified Physics Learning Environment, 1994; editor: (conf. procs.) Computers in Physics Instrn., 1990, Internat. Conf. Undergrad. Physics Edn., 1997, Physics Edn. Rsch. Supplement to Am. Jour. Phys., 1999—; contbr. over 60 articles to profl. jours. Named Sr. Resident Rsch. Assoc., NAS-NRC, 1977-78; recipient Inst. medal Ctrl. Rsch. Inst. for Physics, 1979, Leo Schubert award Wash. Acad. Sci., 1988, Educator award Md. Assn. Higher Edn., 1989, Glover award Dickinson Coll., 1991, Forman award Vanderbilt U., 1996. Fellow AAAS, Am. Phys. Soc., Wash. Acad. Sci.; mem. Am. Assn. Physics Tchrs. (Robert A. Millikan medal 1998). Office: U Md Dept Physics College Park MD 20742-0001

REDKEY, EDWIN STORER, history educator; b. Washington, Sept. 19, 1931; s. William Henry and Lucille (Storer) R.; m. Nancy Lee Jenks, June 22, 1963; children: David Henry, Elizabeth. BA, U. Wash., 1954; BD, Princeton Theol. Sem., 1960; MA, Yale U., 1964, PhD, 1967. Asst. and acting chaplain Middlebury (Vt.) Coll., 1960-62; dean Trumbull Coll. Yale U., New Haven, 1965-68, asst. prof. history, 1967-68; assoc. prof. history U. Tenn., Knoxville, 1968-71, SUNY, Purchase, 1971-92, prof. history, 1992—, dean student affairs, 1971-78. Lectr. USIA, Asia, Africa, 1978. Author: Black Exodus, 1969; editor: Respect Black, 1971; editor: A Grand Army of Black Men, 1992. Trustee, Whitby Sch.-Am. Montessori Ctr., Greenwich, Conn., 1974-86, pres., 1983-86; bd. dirs. Old Greenwich Riverside Community Ctr., 1974-77. Lt. (j.g.) USN, 1954-57. Rsch. fellow Am. Coun. Learned Socs., 1977-78; scholar in residence Schomburg Ctr. Rsch. Black Culture, 1992-93. Mem. Orgn. Am. Historians, Am. Mil. Inst., Am. Acad. Religion. Democrat. Presbyterian. Office: SUNY Divsn Humanities Purchase NY 10577-1400 E-mail: eredkey@idsi.net.

REDLEAF, DIANE LYNN, lawyer; b. N.Y.C., Dec. 3, 1954; d. Paul David and Rhoda Eileen (Rosen) Redleaf; m. Anatoly S. Libgober, June 28, 1987; children: Brian Daniel, Jonathan Alan. BA, Carleton Coll., Northfield, Minn., 1976; JD, Stanford U., 1979. Bar: Ill. 1979, U.S. Ct. Appeals (7th cir.) 1989, U.S. Dist. Ct. (no. dist.) 1979. Staff atty. 18th St. Office, Chgo., 1979-81; staff atty. women's law project Legal Assistance Found. of Chgo., 1981-84, supr. children's law and policy project, 1984—. Lectr. child welfare law U. Chgo. Law Sch., 1994-96. Contbr. articles to profl. jours. Mem. Neon St. Adv. Bd., Chgo., 1988-90; founding mem. Ill. Task Force on Child Support, Chgo.,

1982—; coord. adv. bd. Children's Rights Project, Chgo., 1985-91; bd. dirs. Nat. Coalition Child Protection Reform, pres., 2000-01. Recipient Equal Justice award Legal Assistance Found. Chgo., 1990, 94. Mem. Chgo. Coun. Lawyers. Avocations: piano, violin.

REDLICH, MARC, lawyer; b. N.Y.C., Nov. 25, 1946; s. Louis and Mollie R.; m. Janis Redlich, Jan. 16, 1982; children: Alison, Suzanne, Rachel. BA, Queens Coll., 1967; JD, Harvard U., 1971. Bar: Mass. 1971, U.S. Dist. Ct. 1971, U.S. Ct. Appeals (1st cir.) 1974, U.S. Ct. Appeals (5th cir.) 1984. Assoc. Rubin & Rudman, Boston, 1971-75; mem., sr. dir. Widett, Slater & Goldman, 1975-84; prin. Law Offices of Marc Redlich, 1984—. Seminar chmn. Mass. Continuing Legal Edn., Inc., 1996. Mem. Mass. Bar Assn. (governing coun. civil litigation sect., participant/panelist chpt. 93A in the bus. context seminar 1996), Cambridge Bar Assn., Nat. Assn. Coll. and Univ. Attys., Harvard Sq. Bus. Assn. (bd. dirs. 1989-92, 93-94), Friends of Switzerland Inc. (bd. dirs. 1984—, assoc. pres. 1991-93, pres. 1993—), German Am. Bus. Club of Boston (exec. com. 1997-2001), Harvard Club Boston (co-chair music com. 1997-98, chair 1998—), Am. Council on Germany (Boston Chpt. Coord., 2001—) , Phi Beta Kappa. Office: Three Center Plz Boston MA 02108

REDLICH, NORMAN, lawyer, educator; b. N.Y.C., Nov. 12, 1925; s. Milton and Pauline (Durst) R.; m. Evelyn Jane Grobow, June 3, 1951; children: Margaret Bonny-Claire, Carrie Ann, Edward Grobow. AB, Williams Coll., 1947, LLD (hon.), 1976; LLB, Yale U., 1950; LLM, NYU, 1955; LLD (hon.), John Marshall Law Sch., 1990. Bar: N.Y. 1951. Practiced in, N.Y.C., 1951-59; assoc. prof. law NYU, 1960-62, prof. law, 1962-74, assoc. dean Sch. Law, 1974-75, dean Sch. Law, 1975-88, dean emeritus, 1992—. Judge Edward Weinfeld prof. law, 1982—; counsel Wachtell, Lipton, Rosen & Katz, N.Y.C., 1988—. Editor-in-chief Tax Law Rev., 1960-66; mem. adv. com. Inst. Fed. Taxation, 1963-68; exec. asst. corp. counsel, N.Y.C., 1966-68, 1st asst. corp. counsel, 1970-72, corp. counsel, 1972-74; asst. counsel Pres. Commn. on Assassination Pres. Kennedy, 1963-64; mem. com. on admissions and grievances U.S. 2d Circuit Ct. Appeals, 1978—, chmn., 1978-87. Author: Professional Responsibility: A Problem Approach, 1976, Constitutional Law, Cases and Materials, 1983, rev. edit., 1996, 2001, Understanding Constitutional Law, 1995, rev. edit., 1999; contbr. articles in field. Chmn. commn. on law and social action Am. Jewish Congress, 1978—, chmn. governing coun., 1996; mem. Borough Pres.'s Planning Bd. Number 2, 1959-70, counsel N.Y. Com. to Abolish Capital Punishment, 1958-77; mem. N.Y.C. Bd. Edn., 1969; mem. bd. overseers Jewish Theol. Sem., 1973—; trustee Law Ctr. Found. of NYU, 1975—, Freedom House, 1976-86, Vt. Law Sch., 1977-99, Practicing Law Inst., 1980-99; trustee Lawyers Com. for Civil Rights Under Law, 1976—, co-chmn., 1979-81; bd. dirs. Legal Aid Soc., 1983-88, NAACP Legal Def. Fund, 1985—, Greenwich House, 1987—. Decorated Combat Infantryman's Badge. Mem. ABA (coun. legal edn. and admissions to bar 1981—, vice chmn. 1987-88, chmn. 1989-90, equal opportunities in legal profession 1986-92, ho. of dels. 1991—), Assn. of Bar of City of N.Y. (exec. com. 1975-79, professionalism com. 1988-92), com. on capital punishment 1998—). Office: 51 W 52nd St Fl 30 New York NY 10019-6119

REDLIN, BRUCE MICHAEL, financial consultant; b. Milwaukee, June 13, 1952; s. Raymond Elmer and Elizabeth June R.; m. Lynn Marie, Aug. 7, 1976; children: Joseph, David. B in Bus. Adminstrn., U. Wisc., 1974, M in Bus. Adminstrn., 1975. CPA; cert. govt. fin. officer. Acct. Krueger, Feld & Co. CPA, Milwaukee, 1974-78; mgr. Kirchow, Krause & Co. CPA, 1978-80; ptnr. Hafner, Jurack & Co., 1980-82, Redlin & Co. CPA, Milwaukee, 1982—; fin. tech. dir. City of Merrill, Wisc., 1996—. Mem. coms., City of Merrill, Wisc., 1996—. Mem. Am. Inst. CPA's, Wisc. Inst. CPA's, Govt. Fin. Officers Assn., Lion's Club, Rotary Club, Kiwanis Club, Optimists Club. Avocation: physical fitness. Home: PO Box 146 Antigo WI 54409-0146 Office: Redlin CPA 6001 N 91st St Milwaukee WI 53225-1721 E-mail: bredlin@dwave.net.

REDMAN, BARBARA KLUG, nursing educator; b. Mitchell, S.D. d. Harlan Lyle and Darlien Grace (Bock) Klug; m. Robert S. Redman, Sept. 14, 1958; 1 child, Melissa Darlien. BS, S.D. State U., 1958; MEd, U. Minn., 1959, PhD, 1964; LHD (hon.), Georgetown U., 1988; DSc (hon.), U. Colo., 1991. RN. Asst. prof. U. Wash., Seattle, 1964-69; assoc. dean U. Minn., Mpls., 1969-75; dean Sch. Nursing U. Colo., Denver, 1975-78; VA scholar VA Cen. Office, Washington, 1978-81; postdoctoral fellow Johns Hopkins U., Balt., 1982-83; exec. dir. Am. Assn. Colls. Nursing, Washington, 1983-89, ANA, Washington, 1989-93; prof. nursing Johns Hopkins U., Balt., 1993-95; dean, prof. Sch. Nursing U. Conn., Storrs, 1995-98; dean Coll. Nursing Wayne State U., Detroit. Vis. fellow Kennedy Inst. Ethics, Georgetown U., 1993-94; fellow in med. ethics Harvard Med. Sch., 1994-95. Author: Practice of Patient Education, 1968—; contbr. articles to profl. jours. Bd. dirs. Friends of Nat. Libr. of Medicine, Washington, 1987—. Recipient Disting. Alumnus award S.D. State U., 1975, Outstanding Achievement award U. Minn., 1989. Fellow Am. Acad. Nursing. Home: 12425 Bobbink Ct Potomac MD 20854-3005 Office: Wayne State U 5557 Cass Ave Detroit MI 48202-3615

REDMAN, CINDA J. music educator; b. Lewiston, Idaho, May 21, 1945; d. Mackenzie Goold and Sara Kathryn Hamilton; m. Michael Redman, June 15, 1968; children: Jennifer Kathryn, Melissa Hope. MusB, U. So. Calif., 1968. Piano tchr. U. So. Calif. Prep. Sch., L.A., 1968-73; prodn. asst. Allen Ludden Prodn., Studio City, Calif., 1974, Dick Clark Prodn., Hollywood, 1975-77; pvt. practice, 1978-98. Author: Recipes for Remembrance, 1985; accompanist Wash. State Music Festivals, 1992—, Oreg. State Music Festivals, 1995—, Oreg. Baroque Festival, 1997—, Nat. Assn. Tchrs. Singing, 1997—, Coral Cross Ties, 1998—, Portland Symphonic Choir, 1999—; pianist Vancouver (Wash.) Symphony, 1995—. Mem. grant com. Children's Trust Aux., Vancouver, 1994—; bd. dirs. Vancouver Symphony, 2000—. Mem. Clark County Music Tchrs. Assn. (chmn. 1992-93, v.p. 2000—), Wauna Lake Club (social chmn. 1999—). Republican. Avocations: reading, fishing. Home and Office: 14711 SE 29th St Vancouver WA 98683-9261

REDMAN, ERIC, lawyer; b. Palo Alto, Calif., June 3, 1948; s. M. Chandler and Marjorie Jane (Sachs) R.; children: Ian Michael, Graham James; m. Heather Bell, 1996. AB, Harvard U., 1970, JD, 1975; BA, Oxford U., 1972, MA, 1980. Bar: Wash. 1975, U.S. Dist. Ct. (we. dist.) Wash. 1975, D.C. 1979, U.S. Ct. Appeals (9th cir.) 1981, U.S. Supreme Ct. 1983. Asst. U.S. senator W.G. Magnuson, Washington and Seattle, 1968-71, 74-75; assoc. Preston, Thorgrimson et al, Seattle, 1975-78, ptnr., 1979-82, Heller, Ehrman, White & McAuliffe, Seattle, 1983—. Author: Dance of Legislation, 1973; also book revs., articles. Office: Heller Ehrman White & McAuliffe 701 5th Ave Ste 6100 Seattle WA 98104-7098

REDMAN, ROBERT SHELTON, pathologist, dentist; b. Fargo, N.D., Aug. 1, 1935; s. Kenneth and Elizabeth Francis (McMillan) R.; m. Barbara Darlien Klug, Sept. 14, 1958; 1 child, Melissa Darlien Redman Johnson. Student, S.D. State U., 1953-55; BS, DDS, U. Minn., 1959, MSD, 1963; PhD, U. Wash., 1969. Cert. Am. Bd. Oral and Maxillofacial Pathology. Clin. asst. prof. sch. dentistry U. Minn., Mpls., 1963-64, assoc. prof., 1969-75; assoc. prof. sch. dentistry U. Colo., Denver, 1975-78; staff dentist, chief oral pathology rsch. lab. Dept. VA Med. Ctr., 1975-78, Washington, 1978—. Clin. assoc. prof. Balt. Coll. Dental Surgery U. Md., 1989—; cons. Children's Orthop. Hosp., Seattle, 1966-69; program specialist in oral biology Dept. VA, Washington, 1982-86; adj. scientist Nat. Inst. Dental and Craniofacial Rsch., NIH, 1997—. Contbr. 14 chpts. to books, over 95 articles to profl. jours.; mem. editl. bd. Jour. Dental Rsch., 1995-98, Biotech. and Histochemistry, 2000—. Mem. Biol. Stain Commn., 1999—. (bd. trustees, 2002-, Biol. Stain Com.) Capt. U.S. Army, 1959-61. Recipient Carl A. Schlack award Assn. Mil. Surgeons U.S., 1997. Fellow Am. Acad. Oral and Maxillofacial Pathology; mem. ADA, Am. Assn. Anatomists, Internat. Assn. Dental Rsch. (program chmn. salivary rsch. group 1982-86, sec.-treas. 1995-2001, Salivary Rschr. of the Yr., Salivary Rsch. Group 2001), Soc. for In Vitro Biology, Omicron Kappa Upsilon. Presbyterian. Achievements include discovery and naming of an unique minor salivary gland in the rat; documentation of the relationship between weaning and maturation of salivary glands, of mitotic division of well-differentiated salivary gland cells of all types, including acinar, ductal and myoepithelial cells, of constant cell cycle length and very low rate of apoptosis in salivary glands during development and into maturity; determination of mode of inheritance of benign migratory glossitis, co-developer method to maintain salivary gland acinar cells in culture and several cell lines of these cells. Office: Dept VA Med Ctr (151-I) Oral Pathology Rsch Lab 50 Irving St NW Washington DC 20422-0001 E-mail: oralpath@erols.com.

REDMAN, TIMOTHY PAUL, English language educator, author, chess federation administrator; b. Elmhurst, Ill., June 26, 1950; s. William Charles and Eileen Marie (Keenan) R. BA, Loyola U., Chgo., 1973; MA, U. Chgo., 1974, PhD, 1987. Instr. Loyola U., Rome, 1977, Ill. Inst. Tech., Chgo., 1980-84; lectr. English dept. Loyola U., 1982-84; lectr. U. Wis., Parkside, 1984-85; instr. Ohio State U., Lima, 1985-87, asst. prof., 1987-89, U. Tex., Dallas, 1989-91, assoc. dean, coll. master, 1991-92, assoc. prof., 1991-98, prof., 1998—. Author: Ezra Pound and Italian Fascism, 1991; editor: Official Rules of Chess, 3d edit., 1987. Trustee U.S. Chess Fedn. Cultural Trust, 2001—. Whiting fellow, 1981-82, NEH fellow, 1992-93. Mem. MLA, U.S. Chess Fedn. (past pres.), Nat. Coun. Tchrs. English, PEN U.S.A. West. Roman Catholic. Home: 3034 Brookshire Dr Plano TX 75075-7644 Office: U Tex Dallas Sch Arts & Humanities JO31 PO Box 830688 Richardson TX 75083-0688 also: US Chess Fedn 3054 US Rte 9W New Windsor NY 12553-7624 E-mail: redman@utdallas.edu.

REDMAN, VIOLET JANE, printer, writer, genealogist; b. Carlyle, Ill., Oct. 22, 1939; d. Elmer Raymond and Lorraine Ann (Sommers) Higgins; m. William Raymond Redman, Mar. 15, 1958; children: William Roderick, Jason Cole. Grad. h.s., Carlyle, Ill., 1957; student, Houston C.C., 1985. Printer, typesetter, writer News Pub. Co., San Benito, Tex., 1959-61; printer, typesetter Newspaper Printing Co., Tulsa, 1961-63, Houston Post, 1963-92; office mgr., tax preparer H & R Block, Houston, 1981-91; printer, typesetter U. Houston, 1992-93; printer, writer Yoakum (Tex.) Herald-Times, 1998. Freelance writer; chmn. Houston Typographical Union 87, 1963-93, Internat. Typgraphical Union, 1963-93; trustee Comm. Workers Am., Houston, 1990-93. Author, editor, pub.: A Pattern of Life, 1993, The Opened Door, 1994, Lafferty: Genealogy, History, Legend, Myth, 1995 (Award of Excellence 1996); contbr. articles to mag. The Community Messenger. Mem. Dewitt County Hist. Commn., Cuero, Tex., 1995-99; bd. dirs. Yoakum Heritage Mus., 1997—; treas., vice pres., pres., bd. dirs. Yoakum Cmty. Hosp. Aux., 1997—. Recipient Anna Ford Family Book Contest award of excellence Heart of Am. Geneal. Soc., 1996. Mem. Ill. Geneal. Soc., Clinton County Hist. and Geneal. Soc., Dewitt County Shutterbugs Camera Club (historian, editor newsletter), Dewitt Wildflower Assn., Dewitt County Hist. Mus., Hochheim (Tex.) Cmty. Club (pres., sec.). Methodist. Avocations: genealogy research, reading, writing, embroidery, photography. Home: Hwy 183 Hochheim TX 77967

REDMAN, WILLIAM WALTER, JR. realtor; b. Statesville, N.C., Oct. 15, 1933; s. William Walter and Mildred (Huie) R.; m. Elizabeth Ann Wilhelm, Dec. 28, 1956; children: Lisa Dawn, Kathryn Marlene, Adrienne Ann. Student, U. So. Calif., 1966; BS, Embry-Riddle Aeronat. U., 1972; postgrad., Jud. Coll., 1987. Enlisted U.S. Army, 1954, advanced trhough grades to lt. col., 1974, ret., 1974; dir. pub. rels. Northwestern State Bank, Statesville, 1974-76; pres. Redman Realty, 1976-92; mem. N.C. Senate from 26th Dist., 1978-87, minority leader, 1986-87; commr. pub. utilities State of N.C., 1987-95; chmn. N.C. Utilities Commn., 1995—. Exec. dir. N.C. Telecomm. Industry Assn.; exec. v.p. carolina Vas. Telephone Membership Assn.; mem. exec. com., vice chmn. com. on adminstrn., comm. com. Nat. Assn. Regulatory Utility Commrs.; chmn. bd. dirs. Nat. Regulatory Rsch. Inst., Ohio State U., 1993; mem. exec. com. Southeastern Assn. Regulatory Utilities Commrs.; past trustee Gardner-Webb Coll.; mem. bd. advisors Sch. Bus. Pub. Utility Regulatory Bd., N.Mex. State U.; dir. N.C. Solar Ctr.; past mem. N.C. Energy Policy Coun., N.C. Tax Rev. Bd.; bd. dirs. N.C. Child Advocay Inst., 1997, Assn. Excs. N.C. 1997—. Decorated DFC with oak leaf cluster, Bronze Star medal with two oak leaf clusters, Air medal with sixteen oak leaf clusters, Meritorious Svc. medal; recipient Valand award N.C. Mental Assns.; named to Inf. Officers Sch. Hall of Fame, Ft. Benning Ga., Disting. Mem. Regt., U.S. Transp. Corps, 1990; recipient Long Leaf Pine award, N.C. Mem. VFW (life), Ret. Officers Assn. (life), Nat. Assn. Adminstrv. Law Judges, Am. Legion (life), Raleigh Exec. Club, N.C. State U. Faculty Club, Rotary Club. Republican. Baptist. Address: 1320 Royalty Cir Statesville NC 28625-8230 E-mail: bredman@energyunited.net.

REDMON, CYNTHIA ANN, poet, songwriter; b. Royal Oak, Mich., Feb. 10, 1951; d. Martin Lewis and Mary Elizabeth (Andrews) Hook; m. Robert Carl Nelson, Sept. 18, 1971 (div. Apr. 1983); children: Jennifer, Christina, David; m. Robert Marx Redmon, Mar. 23, 1985; 1 child, Karl. Grad., h.S., 1969. With Buckley Security Svc. Contbr. poetry to 10 Best Poets of the 90s, Watermark Press, 10 Best Poets of the 90s, Nat. Library of Poetry, Poetic Voices of Am., 1998, The Best Poets, Nat. Library of Poets, 1991, others; pub. in numerous anthologies. Sgt. USAF, 1970-75. Recipient awards World of Poetry, 1991, 1997; named to Internat. Poetry Hall of Fame, 1997. Mem. Internat. Soc. Poets (life; bd. advisors), Charles F. Menninger Soc., Humane Soc. U.S. Avocations: cooking, reading, gardening, spirituality. Home: 4169 Old Brandon Rd Jackson MS 39208-3010

REDMON, ROSE MARIE, secondary school educator; b. Pasadena, Calif., Sept. 24, 1952; d. Earl Eugene and Rose Ellen (Jackson) R.; 1 child, Matthew Eugene. AA, Midway Jr. Coll., 1972; BS, SUNY, Brockport, 1973; MS, Emporia State U., 1981. Cert. secondary edn. tchr., Minn., N.Y. Educator Kansas City (Kans.) Pub. Schs., 1974-81; instr. U. Minn., Morris, 1981-82; educator Spl. Sch. Dist. 1, Folwell Jr., Mpls., 1982-83; educator, mid. sch. coord. Webster Open Sch., 1983-2000; mid. sch. coord. Jordan Park Sch. Extended Learning, 2000—. Bd. dirs. Grace Meth. Pre-sch., Mpls., 1988-96. Mem. NEA, ASCD, Am. Fedn. Tchrs., Mpls. Fedn. Tchrs., Nat. Coun. Tchrs. Math., Nat. Youth Leadership Coun., Secondary Edn. Task Force Mpls., Minn. Ednl. Effectiveness Project, Mpls. Edn. Assn. Democrat. Home: 2958 Knox Ave N Minneapolis MN 55411-1250 Office: Mpls Pub Schs 807 Broadway St NE Minneapolis MN 55413-2332 E-mail: rredmon@mpls.k12.mn.us.

REDMOND, CATHERINE, artist, educator; b. Jamestown, N.Y., 1943; Student, Cornell U., 1961-62; AB, SUNY, Binghamton, 1965; postgrad., Art Students League N.Y., 1969-74. Instr. The Art Students League N.Y., 1999-2000. Artist-in-residence The Vt. Coun. on the Arts, 1980-82; asst. prof. painting Cleve. Inst. Art, 1985-90; vis. asst. prof. Grad. Sch. Fine Arts The Pratt Inst., NYC., 1999-2002. One-woman shows include Blue Mountain Gallery, N.Y.C., 1985, 88, Bonfoey, Cleve., 1986, 91, The Butler Inst. Am. Art, Youngstown, Ohio, 1987, MB Modern, N.Y., 1996, 98, 99; group exhbns. include Blue Mountain Gallery, N.Y.C., 1991, Mansfield (Ohio) Art Ctr., 1992, Erector Square Gallery, New Haven, Conn., 1992, Babcock Galleries, N.Y., 1993, Gallery Dong Ho, Seoul, Korea, 1995, Gerald Peters Gallery, Santa Fe, 1996, Chuck Levitan Gallery, N.Y.C., 1996, MB Modern, N.Y.C., 1996, 98, Elise Goodheart Fine Art, Sag Harbor, N.Y., 1998, M.D. Modern, Houston, 1998, 99, Albright Knox Art Gallery, 1998, others; represented in permanent collections Ade Skunta and Co., Cleve., Amerada Hess Corp., N.Y.C., Am. Soc. for Metals, Art Students League N.Y., Butler Inst. Am. Art, Citibank N.Y., Cleve. Indians, Jones, Day, Reavis & Pogue, Cleve., Kemper Group, Luther Coll., Iowa, No. Trust Bank, Chgo., Progressive Ins. Corp., Cleve., The Reading Pub. Mus., Pa., 1999, numerous others. Trustee Vt. Alliance for Art in Edn., 1981, Warehouse Dist. Redevel. Corp., Cleve., 1985-87; cons. Vt. Children's Mag., 1981, 92; panel rev. mem. The Cleve. Pub. Theater Performance Art Festival, 1989; juror Pen and Brush, N.Y.C., 2002, Pitchberg Mus., Md., 2002. Home: 156 Chambers St New York NY 10007-3505 E-mail: RCathred@aol.com.

REDMOND, CHRISTOPHER JOHN, lawyer; b. Oakland, Calif., May 8, 1947; s. Owen Joseph and Josephine Alice (Hanswirth) R.; m. Rosalyn Lee Finney, June 8, 1970; children: Kirk, Renee, Megan. BA, U. Kans., 1968, JD, 1970. Bar: Kans. 1970, U.S. Dist. Ct. Kans. 1970, U.S. Ct. appeals (10th cir.) 1973, U.S. Supreme Ct. 1974. Mem. Husch & Eppenberger LLC, Kansas City, Mo., 1970—. Mem. U.S. delegation to UN Commn. on Internat. Trade Law. Assoc. editor Am. Bankruptcy Inst. Jour. Mem. ABA (chmn., subcom. internat. law, bus. bankruptcy com., 1995—), Wichita Bar Assn. (bd. govs.). Office: Husch & Eppenberger LLC 1200 Main St Ste 1700 Kansas City MO 64105-2100 E-mail: christopher.redmond@husch.com.

REDMOND, DONALD EUGENE, JR. neuroscientist, educator; b. San Antonio, June 17, 1939; s. Donald Eugene and Viola (Kellum) R.; m. Patricia Welder Robinson, Dec. 22, 1972; 1 child, Andy J. BA, So. Meth. U., 1961; MD, Baylor U., 1968; MAH, Yale U., 1987. Diplomate Am. Bd. Psychiatry and Neurology. With Lab. of Clin. Sci., NIMH, Bethesda, Md., 1973-74; assoc. chief clin. neurosci. unit Conn. Mental Health Ctr., New Haven, 1974-87; asst. prof. psychiatry Yale U., 1974-77, assoc. prof. psychiatry, 1978-87, prof. psychiatry, dir. neurobehavior lab., 1987—, dir. neural transplant program for neurol. diseases, 1987—; pres. St. Kitts Biomed. Rsch. Found., St. Kitts, W.I., 1983—, Axion Rsch. Found., Hamden, Conn., 1985—; prof. neurosurgery, 1993—. Contbr. articles to profl. jours.; patentee in field. With USPHS, 1972-74. Recipient Rsch. Scientist award NIMH, 1980-2001, Founds. Fund prize, 1981; grantee NIMH, 1974-91, Nat. Inst. Neurol. Diseases and Stroke, 1986—, others. Mem.: Internat. Soc. Motor Disturbances, Am. Soc. Neural Transplantation and Repair (coun. mem. 1994—, pres. 2002), Am. Coll. Neuropsychopharmacology, Am. Psychiat. Assn. Office: Neurobehavior Lab PO Box 3333 New Haven CT 06510-0333

REDMOND, JEFFREY ROBERT, author, journalist; b. Detroit, May 10, 1953; s. Robert Jerome Redmond and Ruth Audrenne Ward BA in History, Mich. State U., 1975, MA in History, 1988; postgrad., U. Calif., L.A., 1976-77; BBA in Internat. Bus., Davenport U., 1994. Secondary tchrs. cert. Mich. State U. Civil svc. U.S. Fed. Govt., Detroit, 1970's; substitute tchr. Grand Rapids (Mich.) Schs., 1980-85; cmty. edn. tchr. Kent Intermediate Schs., Grand Rapids, 1985-89; prodn. and sales svcs. Steelcase, Inc., 1989-93; acad. adminstrv. asst. Davenport Coll., 1993-96; libr. asst. Kent Dist. Libr., 1996-98; proofreader The Composing Rm., 1998-99; proofreader, typesetter Greatland, Inc., Walker, Mich., 1999-2000; advt. display asst. Corp. Color, Grand Rapids, 2000—02. Pub., editor NorthWoods Jour.; author of books, stories and articles. Cpl. USAR, 1971-73, active USNR, 1981. Grantee NEH, Steelcase Found., Soc. for the Advancement of Scandinavian Studies; scholar Sons of Norway Heritage Fund. Mem. Nat. Writers Assn., Nat. Writers Union, Nat. Fantasy Fedn., Sci. Fiction Writers of Earth, Soc. Profl. Journalists, Authors Guild, Authors League Am., Freelance Editl. Assn., Mich. Press Assn. Avocations: reading, writing, travel, movies, music. Home: 1335 Beechwood NE Grand Rapids MI 49505-3830 E-mail: redmondjeff@hotmail.com.

REDMOND, JOHN, oncologist; b. Tampa, Fla., July 21, 1944; s. John and Sara (Lee) R.; married; 1 child, Geoff. BS, West Point Acad., 1966; MD, Emory U., 1974. Diplomate Nat. Bd. Med. Examiners, Am. Bd. Internal Medicine. Chief hematology and oncology Walter Reed Meml. Hosp., Washington, 1987-90; dir. Rosenfeld Cancer Ctr. Abington (Pa.) Meml. Hosp., 1990—. Fellow ACP; mem. AMA, Am. Soc. Hematology, Am. Soc. Clin. Oncology, Am. Assn. Cancer Rsch., Phila. Coll. Physicians, Am. Assn. Cancer Edn., Pa. Med. Soc., Am. Cancer Soc. Avocation: cycling. Office: Abington Meml Hosp 1200 Old York Rd Abington PA 19001-3788 E-mail: redhoarse@aol.com.

REDMOND, PATRICIA ANN, lawyer; b. Phila., Mar. 17, 1950; d. John Charles and Mildred Muriel (Smith) R.; m. Jerry M. Markowitz, Oct. 19, 1985; 1 child, Lisa Dawn. BA, U. Miami (Fla.), 1975, JD, 1979. Bar: Pa. 1979, Fla. 1979, U.S. Dist. Ct. (so. dist.) Fla. 1980, U.S. Ct. Appeals (11th cir.) 1985. Assoc. Britton, Cohen, Kaufman, et al, Miami, 1980-81; pvt. practice law, 1981-92; atty., shareholder Stearns, Weaver Miller et al, 1992—. Lectr., advisor Legal Svcs., Greater Miami, 1985—; ethics panelist Nat. Conf. of Bankruptcy Judges, 1990; adj. prof. St. Thomas U. Sch. Law, U. Miami Sch. Law, 1999—; co-founder So. Dist. Fla. Bankruptcy Assistance Clinic, 2000-01. Recipient Fla. Bar Pres.'s Pro Bono award for the 11th Jud. Cir., 2002. Mem. ABA (co-chair subcom. on data collection and bankruptcy), Bankruptcy Bar Assn. So. dist. Fla. (pres. 1988-89, chmn. legal edn. com. 1990-91, chair pro bono clin. programs, vice-chair secured creditors subcom.), Norton Inst., Am. Bankruptcy Inst. (local rules com. 1990, 91), Comml. Law League (vice chmn. speaker bur.). Democrat. Avocations: cycling, running. Fax: 305-789-3395. E-mail: predmond@swmwas.com.

REDMOND, ROBERT, lawyer, educator; b. Astoria, N.Y., June 18, 1934; s. George and Virginia (Greene) R.; m. Georgine Marie Richardson, May 21, 1966; children: Kelly Anne, Kimberly Marie, Christopher Robert. BA, Queens Coll., 1955; MPA, CUNY, 1962; JD, Georgetown U., 1970. Bar: D.C. 1971, Va. 1974, U.S. Supreme Ct. 1974. Commd. 2d lt. USAF, 1955, advanced through grades to lt. col., 1972, ret., 1978; served as spl. investigations officer Korea, Vietnam, W. Germany; adj. prof., acad. dir. mil. dist. Washington Resident Ctr. Park U., Parkville, Mo., 1977—; pvt. practice Falls Church, Va., 1980—. Precinct capt. Fairfax County Rep. Party, Va., 1981-87; pres. PTO, Falls Church, 1984-86; bd. dirs. Chaconas Home Owners Assn., 1984—, Social Ctr. Psychiat. Rehab., 1987-93. Mem. ATLA, Va. Trial Lawyers Assn., Fairfax Bar Assn., Assn. Former Air Force Office Spl. Investigations Agts. (chpt. pres. 1984-86, nat. membership com. 1986—), Comml. Law League, Delta Theta Phi, K.C. (4th deg.). Roman Catholic. Home: 7802 Antiopi St Annandale VA 22003-1405 Office: Ste 900-N 7799 Leesburg Pike Falls Church VA 22043-2413 Address: PO Box 2103 Falls Church VA 22042-0103 E-mail: collectlaw@aol.com.

REDMOND-STEWART, AUDREY A. small business owner; b. Mt. Sterling, Ky., July 16, 1938; d. William and Jessette (Rhoades) Redmond; m. William Stewart, July 16, 1988. Office adminstr. St. Paul United Meth. Ch., Fresno, Calif., 1983-86; owner D.A. Cons., 1986—. Instr. Fresno Adult Program, 1983-88; instr. Leadership/Legis. 1997-99. Mem. Area Agy. on Aging, Fresno and Madera Counties, Calif. Mem. Am. Bus. Women (pres. Ponderosa chpt. 1994-95), Calif. Press League Assn. (pres. 1997-98), Am. Legion Aux. (v.p. 1997-98 , dist. pres. 1998-99, nat. legis. com. 1999—). Republican. Avocations: traveling, music, writing. Office: DA Cons PO Box 11545 Fresno CA 93774-1545

REDMONT, BERNARD SIDNEY, university dean, journalism educator; b. N.Y.C., Nov. 8, 1918; s. Morris Abraham and Bessie (Kamerman) R.; m. Joan Rothenberg, Mar. 12, 1940; children: Dennis Foster, Jane Carol. BA, CCNY, 1938; M.J., Columbia U., 1939; D.H.L., Fla. Internat. U., 1980. Reporter, book reviewer Bklyn. Daily Eagle, 1936-38; free lance corr. Europe, 1939, Mexico City, 1939-40; telegraph editor, editorial writer Herkimer (N.Y.) Evening Telegram, 1941-42; newswriter U.S. Office of Inter-Am. Affairs (Washington shortwave radio newscasts to Latin Am.), 1942-43, dir. News div., 1944-46; staff corr., bur. chief U.S. News & World Report, Buenos Aires and Paris, 1946-51; columnist Continental Daily Mail, Paris, 1951-53; chief corr. English Lang. World News Service Agence France-Presse, 1953-65; European corr. Paris news bur. chief Westinghouse Broadcasting Co., 1961-76; corr., bur. chief CBS News, Moscow, 1976-79, corr. Paris, 1979-81; prof. journalism, dir. broadcast journalism program, dean Boston U. Coll. Communication, 1982-86, dean emeritus, prof. journalism, 1986—, mem. adv. bd. Latin Am. journalism program, 1989—. Cons. Exec. Svc. Corps. of New Eng., 1991—, Internat. Exec. Svc. Corps, 1992—. Author: Risks Worth Taking: The Odyssey of a Foreign Correspondent, Univ. Press of Am., 1992, Friendly Moderation, 1997. Served with USMCR, 1943-44. Decorated Purple Heart, chevalier Legion of Honor (France); recipient award for advancement of journalism Columbia U., 1986, Townsend Harris medal for life achievement, 1991, Yankee Quill award for disting. contbns. to betterment of journalism, 1995; Pulitzer travel fellow; named to Commns. Hall of Fame CCNY, 2002 Mem. Overseas Press Club (award best radio reporting from abroad 1968, 73), Soc. Profl. Journalists, Nat. Press Club, Anglo-American Press Assn. of Paris (pres. 1961, treas. 1970-73, sec. 1974-76) Unitarian Universalist. *Life has more meaning when it affirms, with grace, the Yang and the Yin, reconciling opposites--independence, yet cooperative effort and community caring; courage and hard work, yet moderation and generosity; hatred of injustice, yet kindness,fairness and compassion.*

REDMOUNT, MELVIN BERR, chemical engineer, consultant; b. Lakewood, Pa., Oct. 11, 1926; s. Joseph and Sarah Redmount; m. Florence Constance Schweitzer, June 1, 1952; children: Esther Redmount-White, Ian H., Joel Joseph. BS, Pa. State U., 1948; M in Chem. Engring., Poly. Inst. of Bklyn., 1953. Devel. engr. Tidewater Oil Co., Bayonne, NJ, 1951—53; group leader Columbia Mineral Benfication Lab., N.Y.C., 1953—57; resident mgr. of devel. Speer Carbon Co., Niagara Falls, 1958—64, acting mgr. carbon products devel. St. Marys, Pa., 1964—67; dir. new products comml. devel. Airco Carbon, 1967—71, dir. forward planning and application engring., 1971—85; pres., prin. MBR Assocs., Ridgway, 1985—; cons. Showa Denko Carbon Co., Ridgeville, SC, 1988—. Author: Electrode Tip Analysis, 1986; contbg. author: Introduction to Carbon Technologies, 1997. Bd. dirs. Animal Protection Assn., Ridgway, 1994—. With USN, 1944—45. Grantee, Ctr. for

Metals Prodn., Pitts., 1984—85. Mem.: Am. Inst. Mining and Metall. Engring., Am. Chem. Soc. (sect. dir. 1966—67). Home and Office: MBR Assocs 310 Jackson Ave Ridgway PA 15853 E-mail: mbrassoc@penn.com.

REDNAM, KRISHNA RAO VENKATA, ophthalmologist; b. Visakhapatnam, India, Aug. 1, 1949; MD, Andhra Med. Coll., 1971. Diplomate Am. Bd. Ophthamology. Internist King George Hosp., Visakhapatnam, 1971-73, res. ophthamology, 1973-76; resident in surgery Jewish Hosp. and Med. Ctr., Bklyn., 1976-77; fellow in glaucoma Eye and Ear Infirmary, 1977-79; fellowship retina & citreous Ill. Eye and Ear Infirmary, Chgo., 1979-82; active staff St. Josephs Hosp., Kirkwood, Mo., 1983—; courtesy staff St. Lukes Hosp., Chesterfield, 1983—, Alexian Bros., St. Louis, 1984—, Lutheran Med. Ctr., St. Louis, 1985—; Courtesy staff St. Anthony Med. Ctr., 1985—; assoc. Depaul Med. Ctr., Bridgeton, Mo., 1985—; staff Out Patient Surg. Ctr., St. Louis, 1986—; assoc. St. Marys Eye Ctr., 1987—, 1988—; courtesy staff Christian Hosp., 1993—; provisional staff Mo. Bapt. Hosp., 1995—. Fellow ACS, Am. Acad. Ophthalmology, Internat. Coll. Surgeons; mem. AMA, Am. Assn. Opthamology. Office: St Louis Eye Clin 4530 Hampton Ave Saint Louis MO 63109-2238 also: St Louis Eye Clinic 135 W Adams Ave Kirkwood MO 63122-4043

REDO, DAVID LUCIEN, investment company executive; b. Lakewood, Ohio, Sept. 1, 1937; s. Joseph L. and Florence M. (Morse) R.; m. Judy L. Ijams, Aug. 4, 1962; children: Jenny, Mark. BSEE, U. Calif., Berkeley, 1961; MBA, U. Santa Clara, 1967. Registered investment advisor. Asst. engring. mgr. AT&T, N.Y.C., 1968-71; pension fund mgr. Pacific Telephone, San Francisco, 1971-77; mng. dir. The Fremont Group (formerly Bechtel Investments Inc.), 1977—; chmn., CEO Fremont Investment Advisors, Inc., 1986-2001; chmn. emeritus Fremont Mutual Funds, 2001—. Bd. dirs. The Fremont Group (formerly Bechtel Investments, Inc.) San Francisco, Fremont Investors, Inc., Sequoia Ventures Inc., San Francisco, Fremont Investment Advisors, Sit/Kim Internat. Investments; chmn., CEO Fremont Mutual Funds, 1998-2001. Chmn. investment com. U. Calif. Found., 1988—2001; mem. bd. advisors Sentinel Pension Inst., 1978—2001; trustee U. Calif., Berkeley, 1988—2001, trustee emeritus, 2001—. Mem.: Internat. Assn. Fin. Planners. Avocations: golf, traveling, reading, walking. Office: Fremont Investment Advisors 333 Market St Ste 2600 San Francisco CA 94105-2127 E-mail: dredo@fremontgroup.com.

REDO, S(AVERIO) FRANK, surgeon; b. Bklyn., Dec. 28, 1920; s. Frank and Maria (Guida) R.; m. Maria Lappano, June 27, 1948; children— Philip, Martha. BS, Queens Coll., 1942; MD, Cornell U., 1950. Diplomate: Am. Bd. Thoracic Surgery, Am. Bd. Surgery (pediatric surgery). Intern in surgery N.Y. Hosp., N.Y.C., 1950-51, asst. resident surgeon, 1951-56, resident surgeon, 1956-57, asst. attending surgeon, 1958-60, assoc. attending surgeon, 1960-66, surgeon in charge pediatric surgery, 1960, attending surgeon, 1966—; practice medicine specializing in surgery; clin. asso. prof. surgery Cornell U. Med. Coll., 1963-72, prof., 1972—. Author: Surgery in the Ambulatory Child, 1961, Principles of Surgery in the First Six Months of Life, 1976, Atlas of Surgery in the First Six Months of Life, 1977; contbr. articles to profl. jours.; patentee in field. Served to capt. USAAF, 1942-46. Fellow A.C.S., Am. Coll. Chest Physicians; mem. Harvey Soc., Pan Am. Med. Assn., Soc. Univ. Surgeons, Am. Acad. Pediatrics, Am. Fedn. for Clin. Research, Internat. Cardiovascular Soc., Am. Surg. Assn., Am. Assn. Thoracic Surgery, Soc. for Surgery Alimentary Tract, Am. Soc. Artificial Internat. Organs, Am. Acad. Pediatrics, Assn. Advancement Med. Instrumentation, Soc. Thoracic Surgeons, Internat. Soc. Surgery, N.Y. Gastroent. Soc., N.Y. Acad. Sci., N.Y. Cardiovascular Soc., N.Y. Acad. Medicine, N.Y. Soc. Thoracic Surgery, N.Y. Pediatric Soc., Med. Soc. County N.Y., Queens Coll. Alumni Assn. (gov. 1962—), Sigma Xi. Home: 435 E 70th St New York NY 10021-5342 Office: 525 E 68th St New York NY 10021-4870 E-mail: s.f.redo@aol.com. *My life is based on the principles of doing as much for others as possible and doing no harm; to offer advice only when asked; to apply myself unstintingly, but not selfishly, to my work; to learn from my mistakes; to strive for perfection; and to always have a project and a dream.*

REDSHAW, JAMES DOUGLAS, neurologist; b. Montreal, Que., Can., Aug. 5, 1952; s. Robert Leslie Redshaw and Dorothy Ann Levine; m. Evelyn Lee Downs, Dec. 28, 1979; children: Jeffrey Devin, Timothy Douglas. BSc in Biology, Laurentian U., Sudbury, Ont., Can., 1975; PhD in Med. Sci., McMaster U., Hamilton, Ont., 1980; MD, U. Calgary, Alta., Can., 1986. Postdoctoral fellow Alta. Heritage Found. for Med. Rsch., Calgary, 1980-86; med. resident internal medicine U. Calgary Med. Sch., 1986-87; resident in neurology U. Western Ont., London, 1987-89; clin. fellow in neurology U. Alta., Edmonton, Alta., 1989-91; neurologist Boise (Idaho) Neurol. Cons., 1991—. Mem. med. staff St. Alphonsus Med. Ctr./St. Lukes Med. Ctr., Boise, 1991—, chmn. dept. neurology/neurosurgery, Boise, 1997-99. Contbr. articles to profl. jours. Mem. profl. adv. bd. Epilepsy Found. Idaho, Boise, 1991—. Mem. Am. Acad. neurology, Idaho Med. Assn., Idaho Neurol. Inst. (bd. dirs. 1994-2000), Nat. Stroke Assn. Avocations: photography, snow skiing, water skiing. Home: 4155 W Quail Ridge Dr Boise ID 83703 Office: Boise Neurol Cons 999 N Curtis Rd Ste 506 Boise ID 83706

REDSTONE, SUMNER MURRAY, entertainment company executive, lawyer; b. Boston, May 27, 1923; s. Michael and Belle (Ostrovsky) R.; m. Phyllis Gloria Raphael, July 6, 1947; children: Brent Dale, Shari Ellin. BA, Harvard U., 1944, LLB, 1947; LLD (hon.), Boston U., 1994; LHD (hon.), N.Y. Inst. Tech., 1996. Bar: Mass. 1947, U.S. Ct. Appeals (1st cir.) 1948, U.S. Ct. Appeals (8th cir.) 1950, U.S. Ct. Appeals (9th cir.) 1948, D.C. 1951, U.S. Supreme Ct. 1952. Law sec. U.S. Ct. Appeals for 9th Circuit, San Francisco, 1947-48; instr. law and labor mgmt. U. San Francisco, 1947; spl. asst. to U.S. Atty. Gen., Washington, 1948-51; ptnr. Ford, Bergson, Adams, Borkland & Redstone, 1951-54; CEO Nat. Amusements Inc., Dedham, Mass., 1967—, pres., 1967—99, chmn. bd., 1986—, Viacom, Inc., N.Y.C., 1987—, CEO, 1996. Prof. Boston U. Law Sch., 1982, 85-86; bd. dirs. TV Acad. Arts and Scis. Found.; vis. prof. Brandeis U., Waltham, Mass.; lectr. Harvard Law Sch., Cambridge, Mass.; Judge on Kennedy Libr. Found., (sel. comm. John F. Kennedy Profile in Courage award). Chmn. met. divsn. NE Combined Jewish Philanthropies, Boston, 1963; mem. exec. bd. Combined Jewish Philanthropies of Greater Boston; mem. corp. New Eng. Med. Ctr., 1967—, Mass. Gen. Hosp. Corp.; trustee Children's Cancer Rsch. Found.; founding trustee Am. Cancer Soc.; chmn. Am. Cancer Crusade, State of Mass., 1984-86; Art Lending Libr.; sponsor Boston Mus. Sci.; chmn. Jimmy Fund Found., 1960; v.p., mem. exec. com. Will Rogers Meml. Fund; bd. dirs. Boston Arts Festival; bd. overseers Dana Farber Cancer Ctr., Boston Mus. Fine Arts; mem. presdl. adv. com. on arts John F. Kennedy Libr. Found., also judge ann. John F. Kennedy Profile in Courage Award com.; chmn. Corp. Commn. on Edn. Tech., 1996—, presdl. apptd. chmn., 1996. 1st lt. AUS, 1943-45. Decorated Army Commendation medal; named 1 of 10 Outstanding Young Men in New Eng., Boston Jr. C. of C., 1958; recipient William J. German Human Rels. award Am. Jewish Com. Entertainment/Comm. Divsn., 1977, Silver Shingle award Boston U. Law Sch., 1985, Variety New Eng. Humanitarian award, 1989, Golden Plate award Am. Acad. Achievement, 1993, 32d Ann. Salute to Excellence Program, 1993, Bus. Excellence award U. So. Calif. Sch. Bus. Adminstrn., 1994, The Stephen S. Wise award The Am. Jewish Congress, 1994, Man of Yr. award MIPCOM, the Internat. Film and Programme Market for TV, Video, Cable and Satellite, 1994, The Legends in Leadership award Emory U., 1995, Allan K. Jonas Lifetime Achievement award Am. Cancer Soc., 1995, Humanitarian award Variety Club Internat., 1995, Expeditioner's award N.Y.C. Outward Bound Ctr., 1996, Patron Arts award Songwriter's Hall Fame, 1996, Vision 21 award N.Y. Inst. Tech., 1996, Trustees award NATAS, 1997, Ripple of Hope award Robert F. Kennedy Meml., 1998, Humanitarian award Nat. Conf. Christians and Jews, 1998; named Communicator of Yr., B'nai B'rith Comm./Cinema Lodge, 1980, Man of Yr., Entertainment Industries Divsn. of UJA Fedn., 1988, Pioneer of Yr., Motion Picture Pioneers, 1991, Grad. of Yr., Boston Latin Sch., 1989, Honoree 7th ann. fundraiser Montefiore Med. Ctr., 1995, Hall of Fame award Broadcasting and Cable mag., 1995. Mem. ABA, Nat. Assn. Theatre Owners (chmn. bd. dirs. 1965-66, exec. comm. 1995—), Theatre Owners Am. (asst. pres. 1960-63, pres. 1964-65), Motion Picture Pioneers (bd. dirs.), Boston Bar Assn., Mass. Bar Assn., Harvard Law Sch. Assn., Am. Judicature Soc., Masons, Univ. Club, Harvard Club. Home: 98 Baldpate Hill Rd Newton MA 02459-2825 Office: Nat Amusements Inc PO Box 9126 Dedham MA 02027-9126*

REDWINE, JOHN NEWLAND, state legislator, physician; b. Pratt, Kans., Oct. 28, 1950; s. Albert Herold and Joyce Nadean (Durall R.; m. Barbara Ann Bomgaars, Dec. 27, 1975; children: John Newland II, William Merritt, Adam Boone. BA with honors, U. Kans., 1972; cert. med. technology, U. Tex. at Houston, 1974; DO, U. Health Scis., Kansas City, Mo., 1978. Diplomate Am. Bd. of Family Practice. Intern U. Hosp., Ctr. for Health Scis., Kansas City, Mo., 1978-79; family practice resident Siouxland Med. Edn. Found., Sioux City, Iowa, 1979-81; med. dir. Morningside Family Practice, 1981-95; v.p. St. Luke's Health Sys., Inc., 1995-2001; mem. Iowa Senate from 2nd dist., Des Moines, 1996—2003. Sr. aviation med. examiner FAA, 1979—95; clin. lectr. Iowa U. Coll. Medicine, Iowa City, 1983—95; past pres. Siouxland Med. Edn. Found., 1982—2001; past chmn. family practice St. Luke's Regional Med. Ctr., Sioux City, Iowa, pres.-elect, Iowa, 1993—95. Contbr. articles to profl. jours. Past v.p. Prairie Gold Area coun. Boy Scouts Am., Sioux City, bd. dirs. Mid.Am. coun., 1984—; bd. dirs. New Perspectives, Inc., 1996-2002, Sioux City Cmty. Sch. Dist., 1994-97, Crittenton Ctr., 2000—, Morningside Coll., 2000—; elected 2d dist. Iowa Senate, 1996-2003, asst. majority leader, 1998-2002. Recipient achievement award Upjohn Pharm. Co., Kansas City, 1978, Silver Beaver award Prairie Gold Area Coun., Boy Scouts Am., 1997, Pub. Ofcl. award Siouxland Dist. Health Dept., 1998, Leadership award Iowans for LIFE, 2000, Guardian of Small Bus. award Nat. Fedn. Ind. Bus., 2001, Iowa Friend of the Family award Christian Coalition Iowa, 2001, 02. Fellow Am. Acad. Family Physicians; mem. AMA, Am. Osteo. Assn., Iowa Med. Soc., Woodbury Med. Soc. (past pres.), Flying Physicians Assn. Republican. Avocation: politics. E-mail: jnredwine@hotmail.com.

REDWINE, ROBERT PAGE, physicist, educator; b. Raleigh, N.C., Dec. 3, 1947; s. Robert Word and Hazel Virginia (Green) R.; m. Jacqueline Nina Hewitt, Nov. 22, 1986; children: Keith Hewitt, Jonathan Hewitt. AB, Cornell U., 1969; PhD, Northwestern U., 1973. Rsch. assoc. Los Alamos (N.Mex.) Nat. Lab, 1973-77, staff sci., 1977-79; rsch. assoc. U. Berne, Switzerland, 1974-75; asst. prof. physics MIT, Cambridge, Mass., 1979-82, assoc. prof., 1982-89, prof., 1989—, dir. lab. nuclear sci., 1992-2000, dean for undergrad. edn., 2000—. Contbr. articles to profl. jours. Fellow AAAS, Am. Phys. Soc. Office: MIT Undergrad Edn Bldg 4-110 Cambridge MA 02139

REE, DONNA, social services administrator, educator; b. Pitts., Sept. 28, 1950; d. Anthony Paul and Raphalena (Gatto) Morelli; m. Ronald Ree, June 29, 1974. BA in Edn., Point Park Coll., 1971; MS in Spl. Edn., Duquesne U., 1973; postgrad., No. Ill. U., 1989—. Cert. elem. and spl. edn. tchr., Ill. Head tchr. Turtle Creek Valley Day Care, Pitts., 1971-74; tchr. Chgo. Sch. & Workshop, 1974-76; ednl. cons. Chpt. I, Chgo., 1976-79; dir. curriculum Ada S. McKinley Community Svc., 1979-82, dir. adminstrv. svcs., 1982-89, dir. quality assurance, 1989—. Pres. Edn. Resource Ctr., Chgo., 1982-83; sec. Near North Spl. Edn. Ctr., local sch. coun., 1999—. Mem. Am. Assn. on Mental Retardation, Nat. Coun. for Exceptional Children, Chgo. Coun. for Exceptional Children (treas. 1984-86, pres. 1986-87), Ill. Coun. for Exceptional Children (regional dir. 1987-90, pres.-elect 1991, pres. 1992-93, liaison 1997—, convention chair 1999-2000), Ill. Affiliation Pvt. Schs. for Exceptional Children (chmn. membership 1988-97), Chgo. Issues Assn. (chmn. 1990-97), Am. Soc. Quality, Phi Delta Kappa. Avocations: gourmet cooking, skiing, travel. Office: Ada S McKinley Community Svcs 725 S Wells St Chicago IL 60607-4521 E-mail: dree@adasmckinley.org.

REEB, SUE ELLEN, biochemist; b. Balt., Feb. 7, 1959; d. Thomas John and Catherine Jacqueline (Insley) R.; m. George Wesley Lee, Jr., July 16, 1976 (div. Nov. 1985). AA summa cum laude, Catonsville C.C., Balt., 1987; BS, Towson State U., 1993. Area supr. Pizza Hut of Md., Inc., Balt., 1979-81; regional mgr. Godfathers Pizza, Inc., Omaha, 1981-83; credit analyst Citicorp Fin. Inc., Towson, Md., 1983-84; fine wine cons. Kronheim Co., Inc., Balt., 1984-86; asst. sch. adminstr. O'Conor, Piper & Flynn, Inc., Timonium, 1986-88; analyt. chemist Analyte Labs., Balt., 1988-89; rsch. chemist E.I. DuPont de Nemours & Co., Inc., Newark, 1989; rsch. biochemist Martek Bioscis., Inc., Columbia, Md., 1989-94; biochem. engr. Cephalon, Inc., Beltsville, 1993-94; bioprocess engr. Human Genome Scis., Inc., Rockville, 1994-97; owner, pres. Sunflower Soapworks & Sundries, Gaithersburg, 1997; process devel. scientist Nat. Cancer Inst.-Frederick Cancer Rsch. & Devel. Ctr., 1997—. Author: (with others) Lipids, 1992; contbr. articles to profl. jours.; patentee in field. Recipient Small Bus. Innovative Rsch. Product of Yr. First Prize, 1995, Grand prize Tech. Utilization Found., 1995; Md. Indsl. Partnership grantee, 1990-92. Mem. Am. Oil Chemists Soc., Am. Diabetes Assn., Soc. Indsl. Microbiologists, Towson State Alumni Assn., Sierra Club, Upsilon Eta. Avocations: bicycling, scuba diving, flying, sea kayaking.

REECE, BETH PAULEY, commodities broker; b. Warsaw, June 4, 1945; d. Lester Elden and Genevene (Walter) Pifer; m. Gyle Barry Reece, June 20, 1987. BA, Grace Coll., 1967; interior design degree, Harrington Inst. Design, Chgo., 1995; summer student, Oxford and Cambridge, Eng., 1987, 95, 97; Trinity Coll., Dublin, 1999, U Edinburgh, 2001; grad., Inst. Spiritual Companionship, 2000—02. Cert. Inst.. Companionship Cert., 2002. Grain trader, hedger Ctrl. Soya Inc., Ft. Wayne, Ind., 1973-82; account exec. ACLI Internat. Inc., Chgo., 1982-83; account exec., hedger Ctrl. States Enterprises, Ft. Wayne, 1983-84; account exec. Stotler & Co., Chgo., 1984-89, LaSalle Brokerage Inc., Chgo., 1989—. Mem. Nat. Futures Assn., Spiritual Dirs. Internat., Art Inst. of Chgo., Met. Club. Republican. Presbyterian. Avocations: reading, sailing, traveling. Home: 227 E Delaware Pl Apt 5C Chicago IL 60611-7758 E-mail: bethreece@aol.com.

REECE, DAVID BRYSON, information systems administrator; b. Phoenix, Aug. 5, 1953; s. Frank Williams and Margaret Leonora (Bryson) W.; div.; children: Ashley Cambridge, Christopher David. ADN, Phoenix C.C., 1974; Baccelaurette Sci. Wholistic Nursing, Westbrook U., 1991, Master Sci. Wholistic Nursing, 1992, PhD, 1993. V.p. Young Nursing Svc., Kingman, Ariz., 1987-89; CEO No. Ariz. Cons., Phoenix, 1987-92, Butterfield Health Systems, Phoenix, 1990-92; dean of nursing, co-founder Sch. Wholistic Nursing Westbrook U., Aztec, N.Mex., 1994-2000; co-founder Auditors Unlimited, Inc., Phoenix, 1997, bd. dirs., 1998-2000; prin. Reece & Assocs., 1999-2000. Alternative health nurse practitioner; Human Rights, 1997. Author: Minerals, Metals and Gemstones of the Holy bible, 1998, Wholistic Nursing Theory, 1998, Homeopathy: Introduction to Healthcre Proffesional, Computer: Internet and Int-anet Site Development, Database Administration Fraud & Abuse Analysis, Software Development, 1% Solution-Ergonomic Designs for the Exceptionally Tall and Big, 2000. Mem. Ariz. Assn. Healthcare Agys. (bd. dirs. 1988-90). Avocations: scuba diving, aviation soaring, mining, treasure hunting, archeology.

REECE, E. ALBERT, dean, obstetrician, gynecologist, perinatologist; b. Spanishtown, Jamaica, Jan. 3, 1950; came to U.S., 1969; s. Wilfred Anderson Reece and Daisy Lucinda (Price) Reece Batten; m. Sharon Andrea Blake, July 28, 1974; children: Kelie, Brynne, Sharon-Andrea II. BS with honors, L.I. U., 1973; MD, NYU, 1978; ob/gyn specialty diploma, Columbia U., 1982; maternal-fetal subspecialty diploma, Yale U., 1984. Diplomate Am. Bd. Ob-Gyn.; bd. cert. maternal-fetal medicine. Intern, resident Columbia U., Presbyn. Med. Ctr., N.Y.C., 1978-82; materal-fetal medicine fellow Yale U. Sch. Medicine, 1982-84, asst. prof. ob-gyn, 1984-87, assoc. prof. ob-gyn, 1987-90; prof., chmn. ob-gyn Temple U. Sch. Medicine, Phila., 1991—2001; dean, v.p. for med. sciences U. of Arkansas for Med. Sciences, Coll. of Med., 2002—. Elected Inst. Medicine, NAS, 1998. Co-editor Diabetes Mellitus in Pregnancy: Principles and Practice, 1st edit., 1988, 2nd edit., 1995, Medicine of the Fetus and Mother, 1992, 2nd edit., 1999, A Study Guide for Medicine of the Fetus and Mother, 1992, A Handbook of Medicine of the Fetus and Mother, 1995; co-author: Fundamentals in Obstetric and Gynecologic Ultrasonography, 1993; contbr. articles, abstract to profl. jours. in excess of 400. Mem. sci. adv. com. March of Dimes, 1993—; mem. sci. adv. bd. NIH-DC Infant Mortality Initiative, 1993—; mem. adv. com. Nat. Inst. Child Health and Human Diseases, NIH, 1994—; trustee Reading Rehab. Hosp., 1992—; mem. bioeffects com. AIUM, 1992-95. Grantee March of Dimes, 1985-87, Friedman Found., 1990-92, William Penn Found., 1989-93, Am. Diabetes Assn., 1991-93, NIH, 1992—. Fellow Am. Coll. Ob-Gyn., Coll. Physicians Phila.; mem. Am. Diabetes Assn. (coun. on diabetes in pregnancy), Am. Inst. Ultrasound in Medicine, Hellenic Perinatal Soc. Greece (hon.), Nat. Med. Assn. (exec. com. 1987-88, chmn. ob-gyn. sect. 1991-93), Nat. Acad. Scis. (Inst. Medicine), New Haven Obstet. Soc., Soc. for Gynecol. Investigation, Soc. Perinatal Obstetricians (leader diabetes spl. interest 1992-94, bd. mem. 1995—), Phila. Perinatal Soc. (program chair 1993—), Phila. Obstet. Soc. (mem. coun. 1992-94). Seventh-Day Adventist. Office: U of Ark for Med Sciences Sch of Med 4301 W Markham, Slot 551 Little Rock AR 72205*

REECE, MAYNARD FRED, artist, author; b. Arnolds Park, Iowa, Apr. 26, 1920; s. Waldo H. and Inez V. (Latson) R.; m. June Carman, Apr. 7, 1946; children: Mark A., Brad D. Privately educated. Artist Meredith Pub. Co., Des Moines, 1938-40; artist, asst., mus. dir. Iowa Dept. History and Archives, 1940-50. Artist: Fish and Fishing, 1963, Waterfowl of Iowa, 1943; watercolor Trout, Saturday Evening Post (award of Distinctive Merit 1962); watercolors 73 Fish, Life mag. (cert. of merit 1955); print of Water's Edge Canada Geese for Am. Artist Collection, Am. Artist Mag., 1985; author, artist: The Waterfowl Art of Maynard Reece, 1985, The Upland Bird Art of Maynard Reece, 1997. Chmn. Gov.'s Com. Conservation of Outdoor Resource, 1963-64; trustee Iowa Natural Heritage Found., Des Moines, 1979—; hon. trustee Ducks Unltd., Inc., 1983—; trustee J.N. "Ding" Darling Conservation Found., Inc., Des Moines, 1962—. Served with AUS, 1943-45. Recipient awards for duck stamps and others Dept. Interior, 1948, 51, 59, 69, 71; recipient award Govt. Bermuda, 1963, award Iowa Conservation Commn., 1972, 77, 80, 81, award Fish and Game Commn., Little Rock, 1982, 88, award Tex. Parks and Wild Life Dept., 1983, award Nat. Fish & Wildlife Found., 1988, award Wash. State Dept. Wildlife, 1989, award Idaho Dept. Fish & Game, 1998, 4 awards Ill. Dept. of Natural Resources, 1997-2000; named Artist of Yr. Ducks Unltd. Inc., 1973; chosen Master Artist 1989, Leigh Yawkey Woodson Art Mus., Wausau, Wis., 1989. Mem. Nat. Audubon Soc., Nat. Wildlife Fedn., Izaak Walton League Am. (hon. pres. 1974-75). Home and Office: 5315 Robertson Dr Des Moines IA 50312-2133

REECE, MONIQUE ELIZABETH, marketing, advertising and sales consultant; b. Eldora, Iowa, Jan. 12, 1960; d. Barry Lynne and Vera Marie (Powell) R.; m. Gordon Duane Myron, Mar. 14, 1992 (div. Apr. 2000); children: Morgan Reece, Isabella Monique. BSBA, Regis U., 1991. Mgr. regional advt. Silo, Inc., Denver, 1979-86; dir. mktg. LaserLand Corp., U.S.A., 1986-87; advt. mgr. King Soopers, 1987-90; supr. brand devel. Garrison-Lontine Advt., 1991; pres. Monique Myron and Assocs., Denver and La Jolla, Calif., 1991-94, MarketSmarter, Denver and San Diego, 1994-99; v.p. corp. devel. Tactical Mktg. Ventures, LLC, Denver, 1999—. Chmn. bus. partnership com. Colo. Mktg. Tech. Advt. Com., Denver, 1987-91; spkr. in field. Co-author: Market Smarter Not Harder, 1996. Mem. publ. rels. com. Make-A-Wish Found., Denver, 1989. Recipient 1st Place Advt. award Nat. Frozen Food Assn., 1988, 89, 90, award Retail Advt. Coun., 1990. Mem. NAFE, ASTD, Nat. Assn. Women Bus. Owners (bd. dirs.), Colo. Women's C. of C., La Jolla C. of C. (bus. profl. com. 1992-93), Denver Met. C. of C., U. Denver Marketing Advisory Bd. Avocations: skiing, running, triathlons, diving, reading. Home and Office: 401 Monaco Pkwy Denver CO 80220-6015 E-mail: moniquer@tmventures.com.

REECE, ROBERT MAYHALL, pediatrician; b. Indpls., Dec. 14, 1932; s. Ralph Cass and Maude Lucille (Mayhall) R.; m. Pamela Hattem (div. June 1986); m. Betsy Kyle, Sept. 10, 1988; children: David, Scott, Jennifer, Meredith. BS in Chemistry, U. Cin., 1954, MD, 1961. Diplomate Am. Bd. Pediatrics. Asst. prof. pediatrics U. Cin. Sch. Medicine, 1970-72; assoc. prof. pediatrics U. Ill., Rockford, 1972-74, Boston U. Sch. Medicine, 1974-89; prof. pediatrics Case-Western Reserve U., Cleve., 1992-93; clin. prof. pediatrics Tufts U. Sch. Medicine, Boston, 1993—; dir. inst. prof. edn. Mass. Soc. Prevention Cruelty to Children, 1993—. Mem. Gov.'s Coun. Child Abuse, Boston, 1983-89; mem. Spl. Commn. Violence Against Children, Boston, 1983-89. Author: Practical Strategies in Pediatric Diagnosis and Treatment, 1996; author/editor: Manual Emergency Pediatrics, 1992, Child Abuse Medical Diagnosis and Management, 1994; exec. editor Quar. Child Abuse Med. Update; editor: Treatment of Child Abuse: Common Ground for Mental Health, Medical and Legal Professionals, 2000, Child Abuse: Medical Diagnosis and Management, 2d edit., 2001. With U.S. Army, 1955-57. Fellow Am. Acad. Pediatrics (program chair child abuse sect. 1992-95, chair exec. com. sect. on child abuse and neglect, Child Abuse Ann. Sect. award 2000); mem. Am. Profl. Soc. on Abuse of Children (exec. com., 2d v.p. 1993-97, Outstanding Profl. in Child Abuse 1997). Democrat. E-mail: RMReece1@aol.com.

REECE, WANDA G. space station training engineer, writer; b. Tuscaloosa, Ala., June 21, 1956; d. James Elton and Mattie Lou (Keating) R. BA, U. Ala., Tuscaloosa, 1977; MA, U. Ala., 1981. News corr. Birmingham (Ala.) Post-Herald, The New York Times, N.Y.C.; assoc. editor Kentron Internat., Houston, Pickens County (Ala.) Herald, Sumter County (Ala.) Jour.; Spacelab tng. engr. and tng. adminstr. Teledyne Brown Engring., Huntsville, Ala.; engine ops. engr. Tec-Masters, Inc. Contbr. numerous news and feature articles to profl. jours. Recipient Scripps-Howard Found. award, 1981, 1st place writer's contest Randall House Publs., 1982, Internat. Cultural Diploma of Honor, 1990, Huntsville/Madison County Conv. and Visitors Bur. award, 1995; first recipient of Paul "Bear" Bryant Acad. scholar U. Ala., 1974. Assoc. fellow AIAA (first woman chmn. of Ala./Miss. sect., chmn. AIAA/ASTD tng. and simulation conf., missile and space reunion com., spl. citation award 1990, Martin Schilling award 1990, Engr. of Yr. 1988, Profl. of Yr. 1992, Ala./Miss. sect.); mem. NAFE, Nat. Space Soc., Am. Soc. Tng. and Devel., Soc. Profl. Journalists, Internat. Soc. Logistics, Kappa Tau Alpha, Sigma Delta Chi. Home: 6315D Madison Blvd Huntsville AL 35806

REECE-PORTER, SHARON ANN, international human rights educator; b. Cin., Nov. 28, 1953; d. Edward and Claudia (Ownes) Reece; divorced, 1981; children: Erika Lynn, Melanie Joyce. BS in Textiles and Clothing, Edgecliff Coll., 1975; cert. clerical computer, So. Ohio Coll., 1984; MEd in Gen. Edn., SUNY, Buffalo, 1994; PhD in Internat. Human Rights Devel., Brentwick U., London, 2000; EdD in Global Edn. (hon.), Australian Inst. Coordinated Rsch., Victoria, 1995. Cert. tchr., Ohio. Dept. supr., asst. buyer Mabley & Carew, Cin., 1975-76; claims adjuster Allstate Ins. Co., 1976-78; sales merchandiser Ekco Houseware, 1979-80; sales rep. Met. Life Inc., 1981-83; info. processing specialist GPA/Robert Half/Word Source, Cin., Dallas, 1985-87; tchr. adult edn. Princeton City Schs., Cin., 1984-90; with Rainbow Internat. Non-Profit Adult Ednl. Rsch. Ctr., Honolulu, 1990-98, Norfolk, Va., 1998—; edn. specialist rsch. found. SUNY, Buffalo, 1993. Prof. computer sci. So. Ohio Tech. and Bus. Coll., Cin., 1986-90; computer software tng. cons., 1987-89; part-time tchr. adult GED classes Adult Learning Ctr. Buffalo Bd. Edn., 1994-95; participant Am. Forum for Global Edn., Honolulu. Tutor U.S. div. Internat. Laubach Literacy, Clermont County, Ohio, 1984. Fellow Australian Inst. for Coordinated Rsch. (life); mem. NAFE, ASTD, Internat. DOS Users Group, Am. Ednl. Rsch. Assn., Nat. Assn. Women Bus. Owners, UN Assn., World Assn. Women Entrepreneurs, Assn. Baha'i Studies in Australia, Boston Computer Soc., Cin. Orgn. Data Processing Educators and Trainers, Internat. Platform Assn., Cin. C. of C. (cert. minority supplier devel. coun.) Baha'I. Home: 2941 Chilton Pl Virginia Beach VA 23456 Office: Rainbows Global Human Rights Inst 4221-125 Pleasant Valley Rd @ 172 Virginia Beach VA 23464 E-mail: Sharaocean@aol.com., SharonAnn@rainbowshumanrights.org.

REED, ALFRED, composer, conductor; b. N.Y.C., Jan. 25, 1921; s. Carl Mark and Elizabeth (Strasser) Friedman; m. Marjorie Beth Deley, June 20, 1941; children: Michael Carlson, Richard Judson. Student, Juilliard Sch. Music, 1946-48; MusB, Baylor U., 1955, MusM, 1956; MusD, Internat. Conservatory of Music, Lima, Peru, 1968. Exec. editor Hansen Publs., N.Y.C., 1955-66; prof. music U. Miami (Fla.) Sch. Music, 1966-93. Composer, arranger, N.Y.C., 1941-60; condr. Tri-State Music Festival, Okla., 1956-57, 60-66, 70, 73, Midwest Nat. Band Clinic, 1960-91, Bemidji (Minn.) Summer Music Camp, 1970-71, 75, Mid-East Instrumental Music Conf., Pitts., 1957-60, Can. Music Educators Assn., Edmonton, Alta., 1975; composer: Russian Christmas Music, 1944, Symphony for Brass and Percussion, 1952, Rhapsody for Viola and Orch, 1956, Choric Song, 1966, Titania's Nocturne, 1967, A Festival Prelude, 1962, Passacaglia, 1968, Music for Hamlet, 1973, Armenian Dances, 1974-75, Punchinello, Overture to a Romantic Comedy, 1974, Testament of an American, 1974, First Suite for Band, 1975, Othello, A Symphonic Portrait in Five Scenes, 1976, Prelude and Capriccio, 1977, Second Symphony, 1978, Siciliana Notturno, 1978, Second Suite for Band, 1978, The Enchanted Island, 1979, The Hounds of Spring, 1980, Third Suite for Band, 1981, Queenston Overture, 1982, Viva Musica!, 1983, A Little Concert Suite, 1983, El Camino Real, 1985, Centennial!, 1985, Three

Revelations from the Lotus Sutra, 1985, Golden Jubilee, 1986, A Christmas Celebration, 1986, Praise Jerusalem!, 1987, Third Symphony, 1988, Eventide, 1988, Golden Eagle, 1989, Curtain Up!, 1990, A Springtime Celebration, Hymn Variants, 1991, With Trumpets and Drums, 1991, Concertino for Marimba and Winds, 1991, 4th Symphony, 1992, Fourth Suite for Band, 1993, Evolutions, A Concert Overture, 1993, 5th Symphony, 1994, Fifth Suite for Band, 1995, Two Bagatelles, 1997, Concerto for Trumpet and Winds, 1997, Divertimento for Flute and Winds, 1997, Sixth Suite for Band, 1998, Millenium III, 1999, Sumus Futuro, 1999, Carto e Camdombe, 1999, Jidai (Year of Years!), 1999, Acclamation!, 1999, others. With AUS, 1942-46. Mem. ASCAP, Am. Bandmasters Assn., Am. Fedn. Musicians, Nat. Band Assn., Music Educators Nat. Conv. Home: 1405 Ancona Ave Miami FL 33146-1903 *As a composer, my desire has always been to achieve both a depth and intensity of communication between myself, my music and my audiences that would enable me to express something of value as regards myself and my time that, hopefully, would give rise to a deeply felt response on the part of my fellow human beings. I suppose this is true of the arts in general, and all artists, regardless of their medium of expression, but music, for me at least, has been the supreme expression of all time, for all men.*

REED, ALFRED DOUGLAS, university administrator; b. Bristol, Tenn., July 18, 1928; s. Roy Theodore and Elizabeth Brown (Tuft) R.; m. Emily Joyce Freeman, Mar. 18, 1950; children: Roy Frederick, Robert Douglas, David Clark, Timothy Wayne, Joseph William. AB, Erskine Coll., Due West, S.C., 1949. Reporter Citizen-Times, Asheville, N.C., 1949-51, city editor, 1953-60, mng. editor, 1962-63, assoc. editor, 1963-66, capital corr., 1959-66; asst. editor The Presbyn. Jour., Weaverville, 1951-52; assoc. editor Shelby (N.C.) Daily Star, 1961-62; dir. pub. info. Western Carolina U., Cullowhee, N.C., 1966-96, asst. to the chancellor, 1996—. Cons. Devel. Office, East Carolina U., Greenville, 1980; bd. dirs. Wachovia Bank and Trust Co., Sylva, N.C., 1969—. Author: Prologue, 1968, Decade of Development, 1984; exec. editor: Western, The Mag. of Western Carolina University, 1991-96. Mem. Asheville City Bd. Edn., 1958-62; vice chmn. bd. dirs. Sta. WCQS FM, Western N.C. Pub. Radio Inc., Asheville, 1978-88; bd. dirs., mem. exec. and fin. coms. Cherokee Hist. Assn., 1985—, Western N.C. Assn. Cmtys., 1985-2001, Jackson County Fund of N.C. Cmty. Found., 1991-93; mem. Hunter Libr. Adv. Bd., 1991-98, Pack Place Adv. Coun., Asheville, 1991-95. Recipient Paul A. Reid Disting. Svc. award Western Carolina U., 1980, Disting. Svc. award, 1996. Mem. Pub. Rels. Assn. Western N.C. (bd. dirs. 1988-98, treas. 1966-86), Coll. News Assn. Carolinas (bd. dirs. 1968-71, 80-82), Smoky Mountain Host Assn. (bd. dirs., 1st v.p. 1994-96, pres. 1996-98), Great Smoky Mountains Natural History Assn. (bd. mem. 1998-2002). Democrat. Presbyterian. Avocations: travel, stamps, gardening. Home: 931 University Heights Rd Cullowhee NC 28723-6953 Office: Western Carolina U Asst to Chancellor 408 Robinson Cullowhee NC 28723

REED, ANGELICA DENISE, sculptor, writer, illustrator; b. Murfreesboro, Tenn., Dec. 16, 1955; d. Keith Kenyon and Lester Faye (Todd) Reed; m. David Earl Myers, Apr. 19, 1975 (dec. Mar. 1978); m. John Gregory Bettis, May 11, 1979. Student, Mid. Tenn. State U., 1973-75, 77-78, UCLA, 1981-82, Venice Sculpture Studio, 1983-85, Brucchion Sch. of Art, Culver City, Calif., 1987-90. Artist-in-residence Reed Studio and Gallery, Venice, Calif., 1990-95, The Jerry Solomon Gallery, L.A., 1997, Belle Art Galleries, Inc. at Bel Age Hotel, West Hollywood, Calif., 2000—. Cons. Sweet Harmony Music, Sunset Beach, Calif., 1978-83, Bettis Paradise Music, Sunset Beach, 1978-85, John Bettis Music, L.A., 1983—, John Bettis Property Mgmt., L.A., 1986—. Sculptures, illustrations, home landscapings and pencil drawings exhibited in Calif., 1985—. Fundraiser Children's Hosp./Santa Monica Bay Aux., 1991, Nat. Acad. Songwriters, 1985, SEA Environ. Assn., Bonaventure Hotel, L.A., 1990, 91; mem. L.A. com. P.E.T.A. People for the Ethical Treatment of Animals, 1992; vol. St. John Hosp., 1998. Avocations: gymnastics, scuba diving, travel, animals, ballet. E-mail: adreed.reed@verizon.net.

REED, AUSTIN F. lawyer; b. Waterbury, Conn., Aug. 4, 1951; m. Mary Cincotta, Dec. 22, 1973; children: George, Patricia, Edward, John. AB in Econs. and Polit. Sci., Boston Coll., 1973; JD, U. Fla., 1975. Bar: Fla. 1976, Conn. 1982, Va. 1997. Atty. Fla. Pub. Employee Rels. Commn., 1976-77; sr. atty. Jack Eckerd Corp., 1977-81; assoc. Cummings & Lockwood, Stamford, Conn., 1981-87; asst. gen. counsel Pittston Co., Greenwich, 1987-89; v.p., gen. counsel Brink's, Inc., Darien, 1989-93; v.p., gen. counsel, sec. Pittston Co., Richmond, Va., 1994—. Office: Pittston Co 1801 Bayberry Ct PO Box 18100 Richmond VA 23226-8100

REED, BERENICE ANNE, art historian, artist, government official; b. Memphis; d. Glenn Andrew and Berenice Marie (Kallaher) R. BFA, St. Mary-of-the-Woods Coll., Ind., 1955; MFA in Painting and Art History, Istituto Pio XII, Villa Schifanoia, Florence, Italy, 1964; ind. art history rsch., Ctr. for Advanced Study in the, Visual Arts, Nat. Gallery of Art, Washington, 1998—. Cert. art tchr., Tenn. Comml. artist Memphis Pub. Co., 1955-56; arts adminstr., educator pub. and pvt. instns., Washington, Memphis, 1957-70; arts adminstr. Nat. Park Svc., 1970-73; mem. staff U.S. Dept. of Energy, Washington, 1973-81, U.S. Dept. Commerce, Washington, 1983-84, Exec. Office of the Pres., Office of Mgmt. and Budget, Washington, 1985; with fin. mgmt. svc. U.S. Treasury Dept., 1985—. Ind. art history rschr. Nat. Gallery of Art, Ctr. Advanced Study in Visual Arts, Washington, 1998—; cons. on art and architecture in recreation AIA, 1972-73; artist-in-residence St. Mary-of-the-Woods Coll., Ind., 1965; guest lectr. instr. Nat. Sch. Fine Arts, Tegucigalpa, Honduras, 1968; exec. com. Parks, Arts and Leisure Project, Washington, 1972-73; rschr. art projects, Washington, 1981-83. Developer (video) In Your Interest, 1992; TV interviewer Am. Fin. Skylink satellite programs, 1996-98. Bd. dirs. Am. Irish Bicentennial Com., 1974-76; advisor Royal Oak Found. Recipient various awards for painting; installed as Dama of Merit, Sacred Mil. Constantinian Order of St. George, Naples, 1997, awarded Star, 2001, installed as Dama, Order of St. Maurice and St. Lazarus, 2000; named one of 150 Women Who Made A Difference in 150 years of St. Agnes Acad., 2001. Mem. Soc. Woman Geographers, Nat. Soc. Arts and Letters, Ctr. for Advanced Study in Visual Arts, Art Barn Assn. (bd. dirs. 1973-83), Patrons of the Arts in the Vatican Mus., Irish Georgian Soc. Roman Catholic. Avocations: photography, performing arts. Home: PO Box 34253 Bethesda MD 20827-0253 Office: Dept Treasury Fin Mgmt Svc 401 14th St SW Washington DC 20024-2106

REED, CHRISTOPHER See KAHAN, SHELDON JEREMIAH

REED, CHRISTOPHER ROBERT, civil engineer; b. Charleston, W.Va., Feb. 12, 1948; s. Clarence Milton and Anne (Schaffner) R.; m. Mary Dandridge Kennedy, Mar. 4, 1983. Student, W.Va. Inst. Tech., 1966-70, 76-77, Ga. State U., 1973-74. Designer Sverdrup & Parcel, Charleston, 1970-72; assoc. project engr. Mayes, Sudderth & Etheredge, Atlanta, 1973-76; project mgr. Sverdrup & Parcel, Washington, 1976-79; estimator Deleuw, Cather/Parsons, 1979-80; project mgr. Parsons Brinckerhoff, McLean, Va., 1980-85; assoc. Loledermann Assocs., Inc., Rockville, Md., 1985-86, Post Buckley Schuh and Jernigan, Inc., Arlington, Va., 1986-89; assoc., dir. mcpl. engring. Lolderman Assocs., Inc., Rockville, 1989-90; mgr. CRS Donohue and Assocs., Inc., Fairfax, Va., 1990-92; asst. dist. location and design engr. VDOT, 1992-95, dist. location and design engr., 1995-96, Culpeper, Va., 1996-98, program mgr. Alexandria, 1998-2001; v.p. Michael Baker Jr., Inc., Richmond, 2001—. Bd. dirs. Ashland Bassats. Mem. ASTM, Constrn. Specifications Inst., Inst. Transp. Engrs., Am. Assn. Cost Engrs., Am. Ry. Engring. Assn., Soc. Am. Mil. Engrs., Am. Pub. Transit Assn., Capital Yacht Club (sec. 1988-89, vice commodore 1990, commodore 1991, chair com. 1999-2001), Corinthian Yacht Club (fleet capt. 1992, rear commodore 1993, vice-commodore 1998), Potomac River Yacht Club Assn. (sec. 2000-01, del. 2002). Home: 320 Culpeper St Warrenton VA 20186-3001 Office: Hillcrest Bldg Ste 101 1801 Bayberry Ct Richmond VA 23226 E-mail: piperreed@starpower.net.

REED, CLARENCE RAYMOND, retired association executive; b. Shamokin, Pa., Sept. 23, 1932; s. Benton Howard and Gerda Maude (Hoover) R.; m. Joan Ann Engle, June 25, 1955; children: Ann Elizabeth, Susan Engle. BA, U. Pa., 1954, MBA with distinction, 1958; grad., Stonier Grad. Sch. Banking, 1969. With Prudential Ins. Co. Am., 1954; with Robert Morris Assos., Phila., 1958-95, asst. sec., 1959-60, sec.-treas., 1960-74, exec. mgr., 1961-74, exec. v.p., 1974-95, mem. exec. com., 1980-95, pres., 1995—, also dir., 1995. Mem. faculty loan mgmt. seminar Ind. U., 1971-72, bd. dirs. Tredyffrin Twp. LibrFound., 2000—; chmn. Shares in Edn., 1968. Pres. Council Springfield (Pa.) Twp. Home and Sch. Assns., 1969-70. Served with AUS, 1954-56. Mem. Credit Assn. Delaware Valley, Am. Soc. Assn. Execs., Am. Mgmt. Assn., Cen. Home and Sch. Assn. (pres. 1966-67), Wharton M.B.A. Alumni Assn., Exchequer Club (chancellor 1984-85/Washington). Presbyterian (fin. sec. 1970, 79, ruling elder 1972-74, 83-85, 96-98, chmn. 50th anniversary com. 1974, trustee 1977-79). Home: 15 Long Rd Berwyn PA 19312-1211

REED, CONSTANCE LOUISE, materials management and purchasing consultant; b. Point Pleasant, W.Va. d. John Melvin Supple and Garnet L. Tooley; m. James Wesley Reed Jr., Sept. 20, 1985; children: Andrew James, Tatiana. Student, Ohio State U., 1974—76, Capital U., 1984—85. Buyer Abex Corp., Columbus, Ohio, 1971-79; maj. component buyer Grumman Corp., Delaware, 1979-81; purchasing mgr. Atlantic Richfield (ANATEC), Dublin, 1981-85; purchasing agt. Columbus Lodging, Inc., 1986-87, Monitronix Corp., Westerville, Ohio, 1988-89; contracts adminstr. Cellular Communications Inc., Worthington, 1989-90; dir. materials mgmt. Fibrebond Corp., Minden, La., 1991-92; v.p. C&P Mgmt. Cons., Powell, Ohio, 1985—. Mem. NAFE, Am. Mgmt. Assn., Nat. Assn. Purchasing Mgmt., Bus. and Profl. Women's Club. Republican. Roman Catholic. Avocations: writing, photography, bear collection. Home: 1245 Windham Dr Columbus OH 43220-4940

REED, D. GARY, lawyer; b. Covington, Ky., June 4, 1949; m. Mary Elizabeth Goetz, May 20, 1972; children: Mark, Stacey. BA, Xavier U., 1971; JD, Catholic U. Am., 1974. Bar: Ohio 1974, Ky. 1975, U.S. Ct. Appeals (6th cir.) 1975, U.S. Dist. Ct. (so. dist.) Ohio 1974, U.S. Dist. Ct. (ea. dist.) Ky. 1977, U.S. Dist. Ct. (we. dist.) Ky. 1980. Law clk. to judge U.S. Dist. Ct. (so. dist.) Ohio, Cin., 1974-75; assoc. Dinsmore & Shohl, 1976-82, ptnr., 1982-90; dir. legal svcs. Choice Care Health Plans, Inc., 1991-96; asst. gen. coun., 1996-97; ins. counsel Humana, Inc., Louisville, 1998—. Asst. sec. Choice Care Found., 1996-97. Contbg. author: Woodside, Drug Product Liability, vol. 3, 1987. Asst. sec. The Choice Care Found., 1996-97. Mem. ABA, Ky. Bar Assn., Ohio Bar Assn., Nat. Health Lawyers Assn., No. Ky. C. of C. (Leadership award 1988), Greater Cin. Coun. for Epilepsy (bd. dirs. 1990-97), Leadership No. Ky. Alumni Assn. Office: Humana Inc Insurance Cons-Law Dept 500 W Main St Ste 300 Louisville KY 40202-4268 E-mail: dgaryreed@aol.com., greed@humana.com.

REED, DANIEL A. computer science educator; BS in Computer Sci. summa cum laude, U. Mo., 1978; MS in Computer Sci., Purdue U., 1980, PhD in Computer Sci., 1983. Postdoctoral rsch. assoc. Purdue U., Ind., 1983; asst. prof. U. N.C., Chapel Hill, 1983-84; asst. prof. in computer sci. U. Ill., Urbana, 1984-88, assoc. prof. in computer sci., 1988-91, prof. in computer sci., 1991—, head computer sci., 1996—2001; sr. rsch. scientist Nat. Ctr. Supercomputing Applications, Champaign, Ill., 1995—2000, dir., 2000—, Nat. Computational Sci. Alliance, Urbana, 2000—. Vis. scientist IBM T.J. Watson Rsch. Ctr., 1990; vis. scholar Indonesian Second U. Devel. Project, Jakarta, 1990. Author: Multicomputer Networks: Message-Based Parallel Processing, 1987; editor: Sixth SIAM Conference on Parallel Processing for Scientific Computing, 1993, Debugging and Performance Tuning for Parallel Computing Systems, 1996, Scalable Input/Output: Achieving System Balance, 2001. Bd. dirs. Computing Rsch. Assn., 1998—, chair govt. affairs com., 1999-2001; chair Presdl. IT Adv. Commn. High end Software Rev. Subcom., 1998; mem. adv. com. NSF Computer and Info. Sci. and Engring., 1997-2000, chair high performance computing adv. subcom., 1998-2000. Recipient Presdl. Young Investigator award NSF, 1987-92. Mem. IEEE, ACM, AAAS, Internat. Fedn. Info. Processing (mem. working group WG10.3). Avocations: amateur astronomy, golf. Office: Nat Ctr Supercomputing Applications 152 Computing Apps Bldg 605 E Springfield Ave Champaign IL 61820 Fax: 217-244-8195. E-mail: reed@ncsa.uiuc.edu.

REED, DAVID BENSON, bishop; b. Tulsa, Feb. 16, 1927; s. Paul Spencer and Bonnie Frances (Taylor) R.; m. Susan Henry Riggs, Oct. 30, 1954 (div.); children: Mary, Jennifer, David, Sarah, Catherine; m. Catherine Camp Luckett, Apr. 15, 1984. AB, Harvard U., 1948; M.Div., Va. Theol. Sem., 1951, D.D., 1964, U. of South, 1972, Episc. Theol. Sem., Ky., 1985. Ordained deacon Episcopalian Ch., 1951. Missionary, Panama, 1951—58, Colombia, 1951—58; with Nat. Ch. Exec. Office, 1958—61; mission priest SD, 1961—63; bishop of Colombia, 1964—72, Ecuador, 1964—70; bishop coadjutor Diocese of Ky., Louisville, 1972—74, bishop of Ky., 1974—94; asst. bishop of Conn. Episcopal Diocese of Conn., Hartford, 1994—95; 1st pres. Anglican Council Latin Am., 1969—72; chmn. standing commn. on ecumenical relations Episcopal Ch., 1979—82; pres. Ky. Coun. Chs., 1988—91; exec. dir. Global Episcopal Mission, 1998—99. Mem. governing bd. Nat. Coun. of Chs. of Christ in U.S.A., 1982-91, mem. exec. com., 1985-91, sec., 1988-91; Anglican co-chmn. Anglican Orthodox Theol. Cons., 1984-94. Bd. dirs. Alliant Health Systems (formerly Norton Kosair Children's Hosp.), Louisville, 1979-94; trustee U. of the South, 1972-94, regent, 1979-82; chmn. Louisville United Against Hunger, 1980-84, 86-87; chmn. Presiding Bishop's Com. on Interfaith Rels., 1991-97. Mem. Harvard Club of Western Ky. (pres. 1992-94). Democrat. Home: 5226 Moccasin Trail Louisville KY 40207-1634

REED, DAVID GEORGE, entrepreneur; b. Alameda, Calif., July 19, 1945; s. David Francis and Anna Amelia Vangeline (Paulson) R.; m. Marianne Louise Watson, Apr. 7, 1971 (div. June 1975); m. Michele Ann Hock, June 28, 1989; 1 child, Casey Christine Michele. AA in Bus. Adminstrn., Diablo Valley Coll., Pleasant Hill, Calif., 1965; BA in Design and Industry, San Francisco State U., 1967, MBA in Mktg., 1969; cert. res. police officer, Los Medanos Coll., Pittsburg, Calif., 1977. Owner Western Furs, Ltd., Walnut Creek, Calif., 1963-72; mgmt. cons. Controlled Interval Scheduling, Rolling Hills Estates, 1972-73; owner Dave Reed's Texaco, Concord, 1973-76; mgmt. cons. Mgmt. Scheduling Systems, Houston, 1974-76, Thomas-Ross Assocs., Mercer Island, Wash., 1972-82; plant mgr. Bonner Packing, Morgan Hill, Calif., 1981; mfg. engr. Systron Donner, Concord, 1982-84, Beckman Instruments, San Ramon, Calif., 1984-90; owner Dave Reed & Co. Water Ski Sch., White Water Rafting, Chiloquin, Oreg., 1987—, Dave Reed & Co., design, market, mfg. Contender boats, Chiloquin, 1976—. Lectr. wildlife mgmt. Dave Reed & Co., Chiloquin, 1965—, lectr. mgmt. seminars, 1982—; coach Japanese Water Ski Team, Bluff Water Ski Club, Tokyo, 1984; fin. mgr. Japanese investors Dave Reed & Co., Chiloquin, 1986—, design and supply solar electric power sys., 1994—. Res. dep. sheriff Contra Costa County Sheriff's Dept., Martinez, Calif., 1977-80. With U.S. Army, 1969-71, Vietnam. Recipient Gold medal internat. freesytle wrestling Sr. Olympics, Fullerton, Calif., 1983. Mem. Am. Water Ski Assn. (Calif. state water ski champion 1977, 86, western region water ski champion 1977, silver medal nat. water ski championships 1977), Bay Area Tournament Assn. (chmn. 1968—), Diablo Water Ski Club (bd. dirs. 1968—). Republican. Avocations: water skiing, snow skiing, surfing, camping, fly fishing. Home: PO Box 336 Chiloquin OR 97624-0336

REED, DIANE MARIE, psychologist; b. Joplin, Mo., Jan. 11, 1934; d. William Marion and Olive Francis (Smith) Kinney; m. William J. Shotton; children: Wendy Robison, Douglas Funkhouser. Student, Art Ctr. Col., L.A., 1951-54; BS, U. Oreg., 1976, MS, 1977, PhD, 1981. Lic. psychologist. Illustrator J.L. Hudson Co., Detroit, 1954-56; designer, stylist N.Y.C., 1960-70; designer, owner Decor To You, Inc., Stamford, Conn., 1970-76; founder, exec. dir. Alcohol Counseling and Edn. Svcs., Inc., Eugene, Oreg., 1981-86, clin. supr., 1986, Christian Family Svcs., Eugene, 1986-87; pvt. practice, 1985-94; co-founder Reed Consulting, Bend, Oreg., 1995—2000. Evaluator Vocat. Rehab. Div., Eugene, 1982—; alcohol and drug evaluator and commitment examiner Oreg. Mental Health Div., 1981—86. Mem.: APA, Sunriver Area C. of. C. (bd. dirs. 1997—98), Bend C. of C., Lane County Psychol. Assn. (pres. 1989—90), Oreg. Psychol. Assn., Ctrl. Oreg. Llama Assn. (pres. 1999—2000), Sunriver Women's Club (comm. chair), Toastmasters Internat., Rotary (pres. 1997—98, Rotarian Yr. 1996—97, 1997—98), U. Oreg. Nat. Alumni (bd. dirs.). Avocations: photography, skiing, running, hiking, backpacking.

REED, EDDIE, pharmacologist; b. Hughes, Ark., Dec. 17, 1953; married; 1 child. BS magna cum laude, Philander Smith Coll., Little Rock, 1975; MD, Yale U., 1979. Diplomate Am. Bd. Internal Medicine, Nat. Bd. Med. Examiners. Commd. USPHS, 1978, advanced through grades to capt.; intern in internal medicine Stanford U. Hosp., Palo Alto, Calif., 1979-80, resident, 1980-81; clin. assoc. div. cancer treatment Nat. Cancer Inst., Bethesda, Md., 1981-83, investigator detailed to lab. cellular carcinogenesis, 1983-85, spl. asst. for pre-clin. sci. Office Dir., 1985-87, sr. investigator clin. pharmacology and med. br., 1987—2001, coord. ovarian cancer studies, 1988-91, head med. ovarian cancer sect. clin. oncology program, 1991—2001, chief clin. pharmacology br., 1993—2001, chief peritoneoscopy svc. med. br., 1987—, sr. attending physician clin. pharmacology and medicine brs., 1987—, sr. med. cons. medicine br., 1987—; dir. Mary Babb Randolph Cancer Ctr./W.Va. U., Morgantown, 2001—. Participant numerous seminars in field, 1984-95; chmn. ambulatory care com. NIH Clin. Ctr., 1989-93; mem. protocol com. Gynecologic Oncology Coop. Study Group, 1989-96, mem. tumor biology and applied sci. com., 1990-95; mem. com. on status of minorities in the intramural NIH, 1992-2001; mem. NIH Inter-Inst. Working Group on Breast and Gynecologic Tumors, 1993-2001; mem. sci. adv. bd. Nat. Ctr. for Toxicological Rsch., FDA, Jefferson, Ark., 1988-96; reviewer Jour. Nat. Cancer Inst., Cancer Rsch., Jour. Clin. Oncology, Jour. Clin. Investigation, Jour. Biol. Chemistry, Gynecologic Oncology. Mem. editl. bd. Yale Jour. Biology and Medicine, 1976-79, Oncology Reports, 1993—, Jour. Nat. Med. Assn., 1994—; contbr. numerous articles to med. jours. Recipient commendation medal USPHS, 1993; EEO spl. achievement award NIH, 1993, tech. transfer award, 1995. Mem. AAAS, Am. Fedn. Clin. Rsch., Am. Assn. Cancer Rsch., Nat. Med. Assn. (sci. coun., head basic sci. subsect. 1994—), Assn. for Acad. Minority Physicians, Environ. Mutagen Soc., Internat. Assn. Environ. Mutagen Socs., Ark. Med., Dental and Pharm. Assn., Gynecologic Oncology Group, Soc. Gynecologic Oncology, Alpha Kappa Mu, Beta Kappa Chi. Home: 901 Suncrest Pl Morgantown WV 26505-3310 Office: Mary Babb Randolph Cancer Ctr WVa U 1801 Health Scis S Morgantown WV 26506-9300

REED, EDWARD CORNELIUS, JR. federal judge; b. Mason, Nev., July 8, 1924; s. Edward Cornelius Sr. and Evelyn (Walker) R.; m. Sally Torrance, June 14, 1952; children: Edward T., William W., John A., Mary E. BA, U. Nev., 1949; JD, Harvard U., 1952. Bar: Nev. 1952, U.S. Dist Ct. Nev. 1957, U.S. Supreme Ct. 1974. Atty. Arthur Andersen & Co., 1952-53; spl. dep. atty. gen. State of Nev., 1967-79; judge U.S. Dist. Ct. Nev., Reno, 1979—, chief judge, now sr. judge. Former vol. atty. Girl Scouts Am., Sierra Nevada Council, U. Nev., Nev. Agrl. Found., Nev. State Sch. Adminstrs. Assn., Nev. Congress of Parents and Teachers; mem. Washoe County Sch. Bd., 1956-72, pres. 1959, 63, 69; chmn. Gov.'s Sch. Survey Com., 1958-61; mem. Washoe County Bd. Tax Equalization, 1957-58, Washoe County Annexation Commn., 1968-72, Washoe County Personnel Com., 1973-77, chmn. 1973; mem. citizens adv. com. Washoe County Sch. Bond Issue, 1977-78, Sun Valley, Nev., Swimming Pool Com., 1978, Washoe County Blue Ribbon Task Force Com. on Growth, Nev. PTA (life); chmn. profl. div. United Way, 1978; bd. dirs. Reno Silver Sox, 1962-65. Served as staff sgt. U.S. Army, 1943-46, ETO, PTO. Mem. ABA (jud. adminstrn. sect.), Nev. State Bar Assn. (adminstrv. com. dist. 5, 1967-79, lien law com. 1965-78, chmn. 1965-72, probate law com. 1963-66, tax law com. 1962-65), Am. Judicature Soc. Democrat. Baptist. Named in his honor Edward C. Reed H.S., Sparks, Nev., 1972. Office: US Dist Ct 400 S Virginia St Ste 606 Reno NV 89501-2182

REED, EVA SILVER STAR, chieftain; b. Vinita, Okla., Nov. 29, 1929; d. Robert Elbert Jones and Anna Mae (Campfield) Reed; m. Johnnie Silver Eagle Reed, June 10, 1946 (dec. Sept. 1982); children: Patty Deeanne, Lorrie Ann, Billy John. Sec. United Lumbee Nation of N.C. and Am., Fall River Mills, Calif., 1979-82, nat. head chieftain, 1982—, also bd. dirs. Bd. dirs., sec. Chapel of Our Lord Jesus, Exeter, Calif., 1974—2001, pres., Calif., 2001—; bd. dirs., sec. Native Am. Wolf Clan, Calif., 1977—; tchr. Indian beading and crafts, Calif., 1977—. Author, compiler: Over the Cooking Fires, 1982, Lumbee Indian Ceremonies, 1982, United Lumbee Deer Clan Cook Book, 1988; editor: (newspaper) United Lumbee Nation Times, 1981—. Mem. parent com. Title IV & Johnson O'Malley Indian Edn. Program, Tulare/Kings County, 1976-80, Shasta County, Calif., 1982-84. Recipient United Lumbee Nation of N.C. and Am.'s Silver Eagle award, 1991, also various awards for beadwork Intermountain Fair, Shasta County, 1982-96. Mem. United Lumbee Nation Hawk Soc. Avocations: writing, Indian beadwork, basket making, Indian crafts. Office: United Lumbee Nation of NC & Am PO Box 512 Fall River Mills CA 96028-0512

REED, FRANCES BOOGHER, writer, actress; b. Marion, Ky., May 29, 1938; d. Charles Boogher and Evelyn Shelby (Roberts) R.; m. José Joaquín Solís, June 1, 1957 (div. Sept. 1964); children: Julie, Michael Charles; m. Arnold Haslund, Jan. 30, 1965 (div. May 1967); 1 child, Elizabeth Evelyn Marie; 1 adopted child, Leni Ellis. BA in English and Spanish, U. Houston, 1960; MPH, U. P.R., 1970. Tchr. English as 2d lang. Author: A Dream With Storms, 1979, Thoughts, Feelings and Dreams, 1985, Black Mexican Necklace, 1990, TOEIC Test Guide, 1997, Miguel's Aztec Calendar, 1997, (with Koji Shimada) From Chocolate Bars to CEO, A MacArthur's Kid, 2000, (with Francisco Diaz Infante M.) Pockets and Jingles: Something for His Pockets, 2000; actress (television shows) General Hospital, Rescue-911, others, also movies. Mem. Am. Pub. Health Assn., Screen Actors' Guild, Mensa, Phi Kappa Phi. Democrat. Methodist. Avocations: teaching, dancing, reading. Home: 239 Beach City Rd Apt 2113 Hilton Head Island SC 29926-4713 also: PO Box 23481 Hilton Head Island SC 29925-3481 E-mail: ML888888@aol.com.

REED, FRANK FREMONT, II, retired lawyer; b. Chgo., June 15, 1928; s. Allen Martin and Frances (Faurot) R.; m. Jaquelin Silverthorne Cox, Apr. 27, 1963; children: Elizabeth Matthiessen Mason, Laurie Matthiessen Stern, Mark Matthiessen, Jeffrey, Nancy, Sarah Reed. AB, U. Mich., 1952, JD, 1957. Bar: Ill. 1958. Assoc. Byron, Hume, Groen & Clement, Chgo., 1958-61, Marks & Clerk, Chgo., 1961-63; pvt. practice law, 1963-78; dir. Western Acadia (Western Felt Works), 1960-75, chmn. exec. com., 1969-71. Author: History of the Silverthorn Family, 4 vols., 1982, Allen Family of Allen's Grove, 1983, Goddard and Ware Ancestors, 1987, Faurot Family, 1988; contbr. articles to The Am. Genealogist, 1972-73, 76-77. Rep. precinct capt., 1972-78; candidate for 43d ward alderman, 1975; bd. dirs., sec. Chgo. Found. Theater Arts, 1959-64; vestryman St. Chrysostom's Ch., 1975-79, mem. ushers guild, 1964-79, chmn., 1976-78; bd. dirs. North State, Astor, Lake Shore Dr. Assn., 1975-78, pres., 1977-78; bd. dirs. Cmty. Arts Music Assn. Santa Barbara, 1984-93, treas., 1988-93; bd. dirs. Santa Barbara Arts Coun., 1987-89. Cpl. AUS, 1952-54. Mem. ABA, Ill. Bar Assn., Racquet Club, Wausaukee Club (sec., dir. 1968-71, 92-94) (Chgo.), Birnam Wood Golf Club (Santa Barbara), Phi Alpha Delta. Episcopalian. Home: 1944 E Valley Rd Santa Barbara CA 93108-1428

REED, GEORGE ELLIOTT, surgeon, educator, dean; b. N.Y.C., Aug. 4, 1923; s. Morris and Mary R. Reed; m. Anne Miller Moore, 1995; children from previous marriage: Elizabeth E., George E. Jr. DVM, Cornell U., 1944; MD, NYU, 1951. Diplomate Am. Bd. Surgery, Am. Bd. Thoracic Surgery. Successively intern, resident, chief resident NYU Bellevue Med. Ctr., N.Y.C., 1951-56, Berg fellow in cardiovascular surgery, 1956-59; from asst. prof. to assoc. prof. surgery NYU, 1959-69, prof., 1969-78, N.Y. Med. Coll., Valhalla, 1978; pres. med. staff Westchester County Med. Ctr., 1989-93, med. dir. acting, 1992-95, med. dir., 1996—, dir. George E. Reed Heart Ctr., 1994—; pres. Med. Faculty Health Alliance, 1994—; vice dean N.Y. Med. Coll., 1996—; also bd. dirs. Westchester Health Care Corp., 1998—. Bd. dirs. Mid-Hudson Family Health Inst.; cons. surgery N.Y. State Dept. Health, Albany, 1963—90, VA, N.Y.C., 1969—78, Lenox Hill Hosp., N.Y.C., 1971—91, Kingston (N.Y.) Hosp., 1971—90; pres. Federated Faculty Practice Plan, 1996—99; adv. bd. Asian Cardiovasc. Thoracic Annals; presenter in field. Sect. editor: Heart Disease, mem. editl. bd.: Heart and Health Reports; contbr. articles to profl. jours., chapters to books. Pres. Eastview Found., 1992—. Fellow: ACS, Am. Coll. Cardiology; mem.: JSoc. Thoracic Surgeons, Am. Assn. Thoracic Surgery, Alpha Omega Alpha (faculty). Avocations: woodworking, landscape architecture. Office: Westchester Med Ctr Macy 128 Valhalla NY 10595 E-mail: reedg@wcmc.com.

REED, GEORGE FORD, JR. investment executive; b. Hollywood, Calif., Dec. 26, 1946; s. George Ford and Mary Anita Reed; B.A. in Econs. with honors, U. So. Calif., 1969, M.A., 1971; m. Kathryn Nixon, 1981. Analyst planning and research Larwin Group, Beverly Hills, Calif., 1971-72; with Automobile Club So. Calif., Los Angeles, 1972-76, supr. mgmt. info., research and devel., 1973-74, mgr. fin. and market analysis, 1975-81, group mgr. fin.

analysis and forecasting, 1981-86; pres. Reed Asset Mgmt. Co., Inc., Los Angeles, 1986—; instr. bus. and econs. Los Angeles Community Coll. Mem. population task force Los Angeles C. of C., 1974; mem. Gov. Calif. Statewide Econ. Summit Conf., 1974. Served with U.S. Army, 1969. Mem. Assn. Corp. Real Estate Execs., Fin. Execs. Inst., Nat. Assn. Bus. Economists, Western Regional Sci. Assn., Am. Mgmt. Assn., Am. Fin. Assn., So. Calif. Planners Assn., Rotary Internat., Omicron Delta Epsilon. Home: 1001 S Westgate Ave Los Angeles CA 90049-5905 Office: 10940 Wilshire Blvd Ste 1600 Los Angeles CA 90024-3940

REED, GEORGINE SZALAY, interior designer, art historian; b. Budapest, Aug. 26, 1928; came to U.S., 1947; d. Akos and Georgine (De Bobula) Szalay; m. Stephen Kent Biggs, Apr. 3, 1954 (div. 1957); m. Jonathan Duff Reed III, Dec. 3, 1962 (dec. 1971). BA, Vassar Coll., 1950; MA, U. Md., 1972. Cert. interior designer (residential and art installation). Curator of rsch., collection of photographs Dumbarton Oaks Ctr. of Byzantine Studies, Washington, 1963-68; exhbn. coord., designer Nat. Mus. Am. Art, Smithsonian Inst., 1974-91; pvt. practice interior designer Georgine Reed Design, 1991—. Exhbn. designer Hist. Soc. Washington, 1992. Designer: Joseph Cornell: Sources, Mus. Am. Art, 1981, Exhbns.: Am. Painters in Normandy, 1983, Treasures of Am. Folk Art, Mus. Am. Art, 1989. Mem. Am. Soc. Interior Designers, Nat. Assn. Mus. Designers, Nat. Trust for Hist. Preservation, Capitol Hill Restoration Soc. (hist. dist. com. 1990—). Avocations: cats, opera, cooking, Italy. Home and Office: Georgine Reed Design 161 Kentucky Ave SE Washington DC 20003-1447

REED, GLEN ALFRED, lawyer; b. Memphis, Sept. 24, 1951; s. Thomas Henry and Evelyn Merle (Roddy) R.; m. Edith Jean Renick, June 17, 1972; children: Adam Christopher, Alec Banjamin. BA, U. Tenn., 1972; JD, Yale U., 1976. Bar: Ga. 1976. Project dir. Tenn. Rsch. Coordinating Unit, Knoxville, 1972-73; assoc. Alston Miller & Gaines, Atlanta, 1976-77, Bordurant Miller Hishon & Stephenson, Atlanta, 1978-81, ptnr., 1981-85, King & Spalding, Atlanta, 1985—. Author: Practical Hospital Law, 1979. Legal adv. Ga. Gov.'s Commn. in Healthcare, 1994; gen. coun. Assn. Retarded Citizens, Atlanta, 1979—, bd. dirs., 1986—, pres., 1992-96; mem. adv. bd. CARE Atlanta, 1992—, chmn., 1994-99; v.p. Ga. Network for People with Devel. Disabilities, 1991-92; bd. dirs. Ctrl. Health Ctr., 1989-95; bd. dirs. Vis. Nurse Health Sys., 1992—, chmn., 1996-99; dean's coun. Sch. Pub. Health Emory U., Atlanta, 1998—, Ga. Partnership for Caring, 1999—, MedShare Internat., vice chmn., 1999—; with Ga. Comm. Support and Solutions, 2000—. Mem. ABA, Ga. Bar Assn., Am. Acad. Hosp. Attys. (bd. dirs. 1991-97, pres. elect 1997), Ga. Acad. Hosp. Attys. (pres. 1981-92), Am. Health Lawyers Assn. (bd. dirs. 1997-2000, pres. 1998-99), Phi Beta Kappa. Methodist. Office: King & Spalding 191 Peachtree St NE Ste 40 Atlanta GA 30303-1740 E-mail: gareed@kslaw.com.

REED, HOWARD ALEXANDER, historian, educator; b. Izmir, Turkey; s. Cass Arthur and Rosalind Christine (MacLachlan) R.; m. Shafiga Daulet, May 25, 1985; children from previous marriage: Seth Olcott, Heather MacLachlan, Deborah Lamont; stepchildren: Aylin, Sibel. Student, Phillips Acad., Andover, Mass., 1935-37, Wellington Coll., Berkshire, Eng., 1937-38; BA with honors, Yale U., 1942; MA, Princeton U., 1949, PhD, 1951; PhD (hon.), Hacettepe U., 1997. Instr. history Princeton U., 1949-50, Yale U., New Haven, also dir. Internat. Student Ctr., 1950-52; co-founder, asst. dir., prof. Inst. Islamic Studies, McGill U., 1952-55; dir. Inst. Internat. and Intercultural Studies, U. Conn., 1967-71, prof. history, 1967-89, prof. emeritus, cons., 1989—. Del. UNRRA and World Student Svc., Greece, 1946-47; program specialist internat. tng. and rsch. Ford Found., 1955-57; dir. coll. and youth programs Am. Friends Svc. Com., 1958-60; assoc. dir. Danforth Found., St. Louis, 1960-64; dir. Nat. Survey Non-Western Studies in Liberal Arts Colls. Dept. Edn., Assn. Am. Colls., 1963-64; exec. assoc. Edn. World Affairs, N.Y.C., 1964-67; participant internat. confs.; cons. Dept. State, U.S. A.I.D., World Bank, India, Oman, Turkey, various unvis., lectr. Author: Non-Western Studies in the Liberal Arts College, 1964, Issues and Opportunities in Turkish Education, 1991; contbr. author: Ency. Islam, 2d edit., 1954— , Foreign Affairs Bibliography, 1942-52, 55, Islam and the West, 1957, A Guide to Historical Literature, 1961, Ency. Americana, 1964-, General Education, Current Ideas and Concerns, 1964, The Emergence of the Modern Middle East, 1970, Expanding Dimensions of World Education, 1976, Internat. Ency. Higher Edn., 1977, Social and Economic History of Turkey (1071-1920), 1980, Islam in the Contemporary World, 1981, 2d edit. 1986, Contributions à l'histoire économique et sociale de l'empire ottoman, 1980, 83, The Oxford Encyclopedia of the Modern Islamic World, 1995; adv. editor: Muslim World, 1970-95; bd. adv. editors: The Middle East Jour, 1977—, Jour. Am. Studies Turkey, 1995—, Bull. of the Internat. Conf. on Higher Edn., 1997—; contbr. articles to profl. jours. Bd. dirs. Assn. Princeton Grad. Alumni, 1961-63, Lisle Fellowship, 1948-52, 58-60, 65-70, Pendle Hill, Wallingford, Pa., 1958-73, 75-86, Campus Christian Found., 1969-73, Univ. Senate, 1969-72, Am. Research Inst. Turkey, 1969-74, 77-79; co-founder Middle East Studies Assn., 1966, bd. dirs. 1977-80; trustee Friends World Coll., 1976-87; bd. overseers Moses Brown Sch., 1975-77; mem. exec. council Conf. Peace Research in History, 1972-75. Served to lt. (s.g.) USNR, 1942-46. Decorated Legion of Merit; D.S.C. (Gt. Britain); fellow Internat. Scholboy, 1937-38, Mid. East Inst., 1948-49, Rockefeller Found., 1949-50, 52, Ford Found., 1954, Fulbright fellow, 1970, 81, fellow Am. Coun. Learned Socs.-Social Sci. Rsch. Coun., 1977. Fellow Mid. East Studies Assn. (charter), Soc. Values in Higher Edn., Turkish Studies Assn. (co-founder 1970, sec.), Inst. Turkish Studies (hon.), AHEPA (hon.); mem. Am. Hist. Assn., Conf. on Peace Rsch. in History, Mid. East Inst. (Year 2000 award), Internat. Soc. Oriental Rsch., Brit.-Am. Alumni, Turkish Hist. Soc. (hon.), Assn. Turkish Am. Scientists (adv. bd.), Am.-Turkish Friendship Coun. (nat. adv. bd., Chmn.'s award in edn. 1991), Am.-Turkish Coun., Atatürk Soc. Am., Phi Beta Kappa, Phi Kappa Phi. Mem. Soc. Of Friends. Office: U Conn Dept History U-103 241 Glenbrook Rd Unit U-103 Storrs Mansfield CT 06269-2103

REED, JAKE, football player; b. Sept. 28, 1967; m. Vinita; 2 children, Jake Rashann, Jarvin O. Degree in Criminal Justice, Grambling State. Wide receiver New Orleans Saints, Metairie, La., 1991—. Named NFC Offensive Player of Month of Sept., 1997. Office: New Orleans Saints 5800 Airline Dr Metairie LA 70003*

REED, JAMES (JAMES RUDOLPH REED), foundation administrator; b. Mexico, Mo., Nov. 9, 1938; s. Charles W. and Virginia (Cooper) R.; m. Katie Nowinski, Mar. 12, 1961; children: Philip R., Holly A. Mgmt. trainee Southwestern Bell Telephone, St. Louis, 1960-62, mgr. Tulsa, 1962-64, dist. mgr. Oklahoma City, 1964-69, coll. rels. dir. St. Louis, 1969-72, comml. supr. Kansas City, Mo., 1972-73, divsn. mgr. San Antonio, 1973-92; exec. dir. Am. Heart Assn. So. Tex.Coun., 1992-98; pres. San Antonio Med. Found., 1999—. Bd. dirs. Govt. Pers. Mut. Life Ins. Co., San Antonio; adv. bd. Tex. Golf Mag., 1990-91. Chmn. Target 90 Goals for San Antonio, 1988-89; chmn. adv. bd. Salvation Army, San Antonio, 1981-82; devel. bd. U. Tex., San Antonio, 1991—; vice-chmn. United Way, San Antonio, 1976; dist. chmn. Alamo Area Boy Scouts Am., 1977; crusade chmn. Am. Cancer Soc., San Antonio, 1979; pres. Rsch. and Planning Coun., San Antonio, 1974-75; tri-chair NCCJ, 1991; pres. coun. U. Tex. Health Sic. Ctr. at San Anotnio. Recipient Alumni Achievement award Westminster Coll., 1991, Humanitarian award Nat. Jewish Ctr. for Immunology and Respiratory Medicine, 1991; named one of Outstanding Young Men of Am., 1976. Mem. World Affairs Coun. (exec. com. 1988-89), San Antonio Golf Assn. (vice chmn. 1988-89), Rotary (pres. 1983-84), Greater San Antonio C. of C. (chmn. 1990), Shriners, South Tex. C. of C. (vice-chmn. 1978-80), Oak Hills Country Club (pres. 1994), Tex. Club Assn. (pres. 2000). Presbyterian. Avocations: golf, travel. Home: 7317 Ashton Pl San Antonio TX 78229-4170 E-mail: Jimrreed@swbell.net.

REED, JAMES ELDIN, consultant, publisher, historian; b. Walla Walla, Wash., Mar. 13, 1945; s. Eldin Wallace and Mary Ellen (White) R.; m. Deborah Jane Addis, Apr. 14, 1983. AB, Ripon Coll., 1967; AM, Harvard U., 1968, MTS, 1971, PhD, 1976. Cert. mgmt. cons., 1984-89. Tchg. fellow Harvard U., Cambridge, Mass., 1972-77, dir. summer writing program, 1977-78; founder, pres., chmn. Addis & Reed Cons., Inc., Boston, 1977—; pub. ARC Publs., 1995—. Vis. scholar Harvard U., 1992-94, 96-98, 99—; rsch. assoc. North Pacific program Fletcher Sch. Law and Diplomacy, Medford, Mass., 1994-96; v.p., pres. Assn. Mgmt. Cons., Boston, 1985-89; founder, bd. dirs. Nat. Coun. Pub. History, Washington, 1980-83; participant internat. confs. in field. Author: The Missionary Mind and American East Asia Policy, 1983; contbg. author: Enhancing Global Governance, 2002; editor: American Canada Watch, 1995—; contbr. numerous articles, papers, and revs. to profl. publs., Christian Sci. Monitor, Boston Globe and other newspapers. Cons. House Agr. Com. Washington, 1978, House Judiciary Com., 1999-2000, invited witness Senate Judiciary Com., 1990, Ontario Coun. on Grad. Studies, 1999-2000; legis. dir. Asbestos Victims Campaign, Boston, 1987-90. Woodrow Wilson fellow, 1967-68, Harvard Grad. Prize fellow, 1967-68, fellow Newberry Libr., Chgo., 1965, Ctr. for Internat. Affairs, Harvard U., 1993-94. Mem. Am. Hist. Assn., Can. Inst. Internat. Affairs (pres. Boston br. 1998—), Boston Athenaeum, Harvard Club Boston, Phi Beta Kappa. Unitarian Universalist. Achievements include book on traditional Far East policy of U.S., monthly subscription newsletter on Can. and World Affairs, presentations and articles on Am. civilization, 25-year consultancy and creation of several nonprofit organizations. Avocation: French language. Home: 25 Holly Ln Brookline MA 02467-2156 Office: Addis & Reed Cons PO Box 85 Chestnut Hill MA 02467 E-mail: jimreed@post.harvard.edu.

REED, JAMES ANTHONY, hotel industry executive, consultant; b. Marion, Ohio, June 12, 1939; s. James E. and Sue (McCurdy) R. Student, Fla. State U., 1956-59, U. N.H., 1978. Food and beverage mgr. Caneel Bay Plantation, St. John, Virgin Islands, 1960-64; mgr. Mauna Kea Beach Hotel, Kamuela, Hawaii, 1964-72; v.p. C. Brewer & Co., Ltd., Honolulu, 1972-77, Dunfey Hotel Corp., Hampton, N.H., 1977-80, Marriott Hotels & Resorts, Calif., Hawaii and Asia, 1980-89; pres. The Reed Group, Irvine, Calif., 1989; gen. mgr. La Posada de Santa Fe, 1990-91, Hotel Santa Fe, 1991-93; asst. to pres. LaJolla (Calif) Beach and Tennis Club, Inc., 1993-95; pres. The Reed Group, Santa Fe, N.M., LaJolla, 1993—. Pres. Kilauea Volcano House Inc., Mackensie Hawaii Ltd., Augustine's Decor Spain; vice-chmn., bd. dirs. Picuris Pueblo Enterprises, cons. to Native Am. Tribes, hotels, resorts and restaurants. Named Outstanding Young Men of Am., 1969. Mem. Calif. Thoroughbred Breeders Assn., Calif. Hotel Assn., Community Leaders of Am., Appaloosa Horse Club. Home and Office: 7550 Eads Ave La Jolla CA 92037-4800 Fax: (858) 454-6640. E-mail: jimreed@cts.com.

REED, JAMES DAVID, retired minister, social worker; b. Sonora, Ark., Aug. 26, 1925; s. Fred Edwards and Lula (Caldwell) R.; m. Winnie Doss Brown, Aug. 24, 1949; children: David Doss, James Brown. BA, Ouachita Bapt. Coll., 1949; BD, Southwestern Bapt. Theol. Sem., 1958, MDiv, 1970. Ordained to ministry First Bapt. Ch., Arkadelphia, Ark., 1947. Pastor Brumley Bapt. Ch., Conway, Ark., 1947-50, Pine Grove Bapt. Ch., Little Rock, 1952-53; dir. Bapt. Student Union Ark. State Coll., Jonesboro, 1953-57; dir. student dept. St. Louis Bapt. Mission Bd., 1958-63; pastor Moline Bapt. Ch., St. Louis, 1963-70; social worker State of Arkansas, Little Rock, 1970-87; chaplain assoc. Bapt. Med. Ctr., 1983-98, ret., 1998. Chaplain Vets. Hosp., Little Rock, 1970-97. Sgt. USAAF, 1943-46, ETO. Baptist. Avocations: woodworking, genealogy. Home: 51 West Springhill Dr Greenbrier AR 72058-9237

REED, JAMES DONALD, journalist, author; b. Jackson, Mich., Oct. 7, 1940; s. Clair and Esther (Bryden) R.; m. Christine Flowers, June 14, 1969; children: Phoebe C., Alicia M., Gabrielle A. Student, Albion Coll., 1958-60; BA, Mich. State U., 1962; postgrad., SUNY-Stony Brook, 1967-69; MFA, U. Mont., 1970. Mem. faculty dept. creative writing U. Mass., 1970-75; dir. M.F.A. program, 1974; staff writer Sports Illustrated, N.Y.C., 1975-80; assoc. editor Time mag., 1980-90; sr. writer People mag., N.Y.C., 1990-91, sr. editor, 1991-93, sr. assoc. editor spl. issues, 1993—2001; contbg. editor Time Digital mag., 1997—; freelance journalist , 2001—. Author: (poetry) Expressways, 1970, Fatback Odes, 1973; (fiction) Free Fall, 1980; (with Christine Reed) Exposure, 1987. Guggenheim fellow, 1971

REED, JAMES EARL, protective services official; b. San Francisco, Mar. 21, 1957; s. Arlen Earl and Louise (Gibbs) R.; m. Jody Lynn Bales, Feb. 14, 1976 (div. Aug. 1978); 1 child, Darci Lynn; m. Donna Kaye Lewis, June 25, 1994. A in fire sci., Casper Coll., 1995. State cert. fire fighter I, II, III, state cert. fire svc. instr. I, state cert. fire prevention officer I. Shop worker, shop foreman, salesman Becker Fire Equipment, Casper, Wyo., 1975-78; safety equipment maintance Bell H2S Safety and Oilfield Safety Engring., 1978-80; tchr. outreach program Casper Coll., 1988-90; owner operator J.R.'s Custom Hand Planted Signs, 1980-93; capt. Casper (Wyo.) Fire Dept., 1978-93, comdr., 1993—; artist Images Studio, Casper, 1991—. Instr. CPR courses Am. Heart Soc., ARC, 1980—; instr. SCBA courses, 1983-85. Active fund raisers City/County Fire Fighters Burn Fund, 1982, 84—, fund raisers Muscular Dystrophy Assn., 1981, 82, 85-89, fund raisers March of Dimes, 1984, 85, 87, fund raisers Casper Mountain Racers Youth Olympics, 1985-87, Casper Event Ctr.'s "Spl. Christmas for Spl. Kids," 1984-87; mem. Wyo. chpt. Multiple Sclerosis Soc., 1994—. Named Firefighter of Yr. Casper Fire Dept., Casper Ladies Auxiliary, Am. Legion Regional and Post 2, 1984, Man in Blue, Casper Fire Dept., 1994. Mem. Casper Fire Fighters Assn. (entertainment com. 1980—, exec. com. 1988-90), City County Fire Fighters Burn Fund (trustee 1985-86, treas. 1986-89, sec. 1989-91, pres. 1992—). Republican. Seventh-day Adventist. Avocations: painting, alpine and water skiing, weight lifting, racquetball. Home: PO Box 2297 Casper WY 82602-2297

REED, JAMES WESLEY, social historian, educator; b. New Orleans, Oct. 17, 1944; married. BA, U. New Orleans, 1967; AM, Harvard U., 1968, PhD, 1974. Research fellow in history Schlesinger Library, 1973-75; prof. history Rutgers U., New Brunswick, N.J., 1975—; dean Rutgers Coll., Rutgers U., 1985-94. Author: From Private Vice to Public Virtue: The Birth Control Movement and American Society Since 1830, 1978. Office: Rutgers U Dept History Van Dyke Hall Rm 118 New Brunswick NJ 08901 E-mail: jwr@rci.rutgers.edu.

REED, JAMES WHITFIELD, physician, educator; b. Pahokee, Fla., Nov. 1, 1935; s. Thomas Reed and Chineater (Grey) Whitfield; married; children: David M., Robert A., Mary I., Katherine E. BS, W.Va. State Coll., 1954; MD, Howard U., 1963. Diplomate Am. Bd. Internal Medicine, Am. Bd. Endocrinology and Metabolism. Commd. U.S. Army, 1963; advanced through grades to col., 1981; resident in internal medicine Madigan Army Med. Ctr., Tacoma, 1966-69, chief endocrinology and metabolism, 1971-76, chief dept. clin. rsch., 1976-78; chief dept. medicine Eisenhower Army Med. Ctr., Augusta, Ga., 1978-81; assoc. prof. internal medicine edn. for FP program U. Tex. at Dallas, 1981-84; prof. medicine Morehouse Sch. Medicine, Atlanta, 1985—, chmn. dept., 1985-92, chmn. grad. med. edn., 1992-96, activity chmn., 1986-88, dir. internal medicine residency, 1992-98, dir. Clin. Rsch. Ctr., 1998-2000; postdoctoral fellow in endocrinology and metabolism U. Calif. Med. Ctr., San Francisco, 1969-71; assoc. chair, prof. medicine Morehouse Sch. Medicine, 1992—, chief endocrinology, 1992—. Dir. endocrinology, fellow Madigan Army Med. Ctr., 1976-78; dir. internal medicine residency program Eisenhower Army Med. Ctr., 1978-81, chmn. directorate of clin. investigation, 1978-81, dir. endocrinology fellowship program; med. cons. Tuskgee (Ala.) VA Hosp., 1985—; mem. nat. high blood pressure edn. com. NHLBI/NIH, Nat. Diabetes Mellitus Adv. Coun., Nat. Diabetes Adv. Bd., NHLBI working Com. on Hypertension and Diabetes; chmn. Sub Com. Special Population and Situations, chmn. subcom., mem. exec. com. Joint Nat. Commn. for Detection Evaluation and Treatment of High Blood Pressure. Author: Black Man's Guide to Good Health, 1994; contbr. articles to profl. publs. Med. advisor, chmn. March of Dimes, Pierce County, Tacoma, 1976-78; pres. Charles Drew Sickle Cell and Health Bd., Tacoma, 1976-78; mem. task force on cardiovascular risk reduction Am. Heart Assn. Decorated Legion of Merit; recipient Disting. Alumni award Nat. Assn. for Equal Opportunity in Higher Edn., 1988, Nat. Alumnus of Yr. award W.Va. State Coll., 1987; inducted into ROTC Hall of Fame, W.Va. State Coll., 1987. Fellow ACP, Am. Coll. Clin. Endocrinologist; mem. Assn. Profs. Medicine, Endocrine Soc., Internat. Soc. Hypertension in Blacks (v.p. 1986, pres. 1992—), Assn. of Program Dirs. in Internal Medicine, Am. Heart Assn. Task Force on Cardiovascular Risk, Alpha Phi Alpha. Democrat. Avocations: bowling, skiing. Home: 380 Mcgill Pl NE Atlanta GA 30312-1069 Office: Morehouse Sch Medicine 720 Westview Dr SW Atlanta GA 30310-1458 E-mail: reedj@msm.edu. *One cannot control the circumstance of one's birth, but with keen alertness and honest hard work there are no limits to what one can achieve. So hitch your wagon to a star and never lose sight of it.*

REED, JANE GARSON, eldercare/disability consultant; b. Cleve., Jan. 11, 1948; d. Joseph John Guzowski and Irene Sophie (Dominic) Garson; children: Craig Michael, Kevin Matthew. BBA magna cum laude, Baldwin Wallace Coll., 1977; MBA in Mgmt., Case Western Res. U., 1983; postgrad., Cleve. State U., 1991-97. CPA, Ohio. Sr. asst. acct. Deloitte, Haskins & Sells, Cleve., 1977-78; sr. corp. auditor White Motor Corp., Beachwood, 1979-81; instr. acctg. Cuyahoga C.C., Parma, 1981-82; ind. contractor State of Wash., Olympia, 1982-84; dir. fin. Nonprofit SNF, Cleveland Heights, Ohio, 1985-86; controller Proprietary SNF, Akron, 1986-87; lectr. mgmt. acctg. U. Akron, 1987-88; asst. prof. Baldwin-Wallace Coll., Berea, Ohio, 1989-94; pres. Athena Music, Inc. Lectr. advocacy and health policy change Cleve. State U., 2001—02. Asst. editor Ohio CPA Jour., 1997-99. Chair Trinity (Marymount) H.S. Reunion Com., 1990-91; vice-chair Com. for Advanced Edn. in Brunswick, 1995-96; mem. acctg. curriculum adv. com. Lorain County C.C.; bd. dirs. Greater Cleve. Brain Injury Coalition, 1997-2000; mem. Ohio Brain Injury Assn., 1996—, 2d v.p., 1999-2001. Mem. AICPA, Ohio Soc. CPAs (editl. bd. jour. com. 1992-95, task force on implementing quality edn. 1992-94, assurance svcs. com. 1998-2000, adv. coun. M.A.P. sect. 1999-2000), Inst. Mgmt. Accts. (faculty advisor to Baldwin-Wallace student chpt. 1990-94), Am. Soc. Women Accts. (pres. 1993-94), Medina County Writers Group (treas. 1998—). Methodist. Avocation: woodworking. Home and Office: 1254 Hadcock Rd Brunswick OH 44212-3018 E-mail: reed@brightdsl.net.

REED, JANINE REGALE, freelance writer, English composition and language educator; b. Chgo., Feb. 3, 1955; d. Orie James and Mildred Joyce (Marino) R.; m. William Jones Wheeler, Sept. 10, 1988; 1 child, Katherine Ann Reed Wheeler. BA in English, Calif. State U., Fresno, 1981; MA, Ind. U., 1984, PhD in English, 1990; postgrad., U. Ill., 1997-98. Assoc. instr. English Ind. U., Bloomington, 1982-85, 86-89; instr. English El Planetario, Morelia, Michoacan, Mex., 1985-86; asst. prof. English Mansfield U. Pa., 1990-93, Ohio Wesleyan U., Delaware, Ohio, 1993-95; freelance editor and tchr. Urbana, Ill., 1996-97; tchr. divsn. English as Internat. Lang. U. Ill., 1997-98; freelance writer New Haven, 1998-99; instr. Yale English Lang. Inst., 2000—. Grant writer, resource coord. Waverly Extended Family, New Haven,, 1999-2000. Contbr. articles to profl. jours. Vol., vol. coord. PTA, Urbana, 1996—98; parent rep. planning mgmt. team West Hills Sch., New Haven, 1998—2000, mem. bd. reps. PTO, 1999—2001; editor sch. newspaper West Hills Magnet Sch., 1998; clk., trustee Unitarian Soc. New Haven, 1999—2001, com. chair, 2001—. Democrat. Mem. Unitarian Universalist Ch. Avocations: choir singing, poetry writing, fitness walking, yoga, meditation. Home and Office: 110 Bellevue Rd New Haven CT 06511-2800 E-mail: janine.reed@yale.edu.

REED, JEFFREY GARTH, organizational psychologist, educator; b. Black Creek, Wis., Mar. 28, 1948; s. George Edward and Norma Groeling (Renneisen) R.; m. Sylvia F. Kollasch, Apr. 18, 1981; 1 child, Daniel Benjamin. BA in Polit. Sci., Muskingum Coll., 1970; MLS, U. Md., 1971; MA in Psychology, Towson State U., 1976; PhD in Psychology, Kans. State U., 1979; cert. in bus., NYU, 1983; cert. in program evaluation, U. Mass., 1977. Lic. psychologist, N.Y.; cert. project mgmt. profl. Asst. reference libr. Bucknell U., Lewisberg, Pa., 1971-73; rsch. asst. Towson State U., Balt., 1974-75; ednl. researcher Kans. State U., 1975-79; asst. prof. indsl. and orgnl. psychology SUNY, Geneseo, 1979-83; organizational cons. Rochester, N.Y., 1983-85; user interface developer Xerox Corp., Webster, 1985-89, user interface software design mgr., 1989-90, electronics and system software program mgr., 1991-92, process & planning mgr., 1993-94, mgr. scanning requirements strategies and planning, 1995-96, xerox planning and process mgr., 1996-98; assoc. prof. bus. adminstrn., dir. mgmt. program Marian Coll., 1998—. V.p. Marian Coll. Faculty Senate, 2001; participant Careers in Bus., NYU, 1983. Co-author: Library Use, 1983, 2d edit., 1992; assoc. editor: Awards, Honors and Prizes, 2d edit., 1972; also jour. articles. Bd. sec. Webster Montessori Sch., 1987-90; trustee Cobblestone Sch., Rochester, chair pers. com., 1993-98; chair bd. dirs. Marian Coll. Coffee House, 1998—. NIMH summer fellow U. Mass., 1977, ALA fellow, Dallas, 1971. Mem. APA, Soc. for I/O Psychology, Fond du Lac Human Resource Assn., Homeowners' Assn. (sec. and pres. 1991-94), Project Mgmt. Inst., Soc. Human Resource Mgmt., Fond du Lac Morning Rotary. Achievements include software patents. Home: 984 Buttermilk Creek Dr Fond Du Lac WI 54935-6119 Office: Bus Adminstrn Divsn Marian Coll 45 S National Ave Fond Du Lac WI 54935-4621

REED, JOAN-MARIE, special education educator; b. St. Paul, Sept. 8, 1960; d. William Martin Reed and Diana-Marie (Miller) Reed Moss. BA, U. Minn., 1982, BS, 1983; MEd, Tex. Woman's U., 1986. Cert. tchr., Tex. Tchr. emotionally disturbed Birdville Ind. Sch. Dist., Ft. Worth, 1984-86, Goose Creek Ind. Sch. Dist., Baytown, Tex., 1986-92, ctr. leader, 1992-93, dept. chairperson, 1987-91; tchr. emotionally disturbed Conroe (Tex.) Ind. Sch. Dist., 1993-94, Willis (Tex.) Ind. Sch. Dist., 1994-95, Jefferson County Pub. Schs., 1995—. Co-editor: New Teacher Handbook, 1986-87, Behavior Improvement Program Handbook, 1987-88. Mem. NEA, Coun. for Exceptional Children. Congregationalist. Avocations: reading, cooking, travel, running. Office: Sobesky Acad Adolescent Day Treatment Program 2001 Hoyt St Lakewood CO 80215-5101

REED, JOHN ADDISON, JR. European studies educator; b. Cleve. s. John Addison and Margaret Adelaide (Timmons) R.; m. Nancy Arlene Campbell, June 16, 1956; children: John Addison III, Elizabeth Scott, Jeffrey Jamison, Jamie Campbell. AB, Dartmouth Coll., 1954; MA, U. Mich., 1958; degree, U. Amsterdam, The Netherlands, 1959; ABD, George Washington U., Washington, 1991. Dep. dir. near east affairs Office Sec. Def., Washington, 1968-72, dir. African affairs, 1975-78; polit.-mil. attache U.S. Embassy, London, 1972-75, Bonn, Germany, 1982-85; sr. rsch. fellow Nat. Def. U., Washington, 1985-86; dep. NATO advisor to sec. of def. Dept. Def., 1986-89; prof. european studies Def. Intelligence Coll., 1989-92. Lectr. Presdl. Classroom, Washington, 1970-72; lectr. European and NATO policy Nat. Def. U., 1978-92; lectr. fgn. affairs and NATO policy Eckerd Coll., St. Petersburg, Fla., 1997—. Author: Germany and NATO, 1987. Recipient Presdl. Cross of Merit award Fed. Rep. Germany, 1987; Rufus Choate scholar, 1954. Mem. Acad. Sr. Profls. Dem. Avocations: fgn. affairs, geneology, hiking, cycling, vocal recitals. Home: 307 Newfane Hill Rd Newfane VT 05345-9508 E-mail: reedja@eckerd.edu., campreed@sover.net.

REED, JOHN ALTON, lawyer; b. Washington, June 29, 1931; s. John Alton and Emma Powers (Ball) R.; m. Louisa Wardman, June 6, 1953; children: Donna, Joanne, Deborah. AB, Duke U., 1954, LLB, 1956. Bar: Fla. 1956. Assoc. Fowler-White, Tampa, Fla., 1956-57; ptnr. Rush, Reed & Marshall, Orlando, 1957-67; judge Fla. 4th Dist. Ct. Appeal, 1967-73, chief judge, 1971-73; judge U.S. Dist. Ct. for Middle Dist. Fla., Orlando, 1973-84; ptnr., chmn. dept. litigation Lowndes, Drosdick, Doster, Kantor & Reed, 1985-99. Com. on standard civil jury instructions Fla. Supreme Ct., 1986-90. Bd. visitors Duke U. Law Sch., 1983—. Mem. ABA, Fla. Bar Assn., Orange County Bar Assn. Republican. Episcopalian. Home: 1847 Jessica Ct Winter Park FL 32789-5935 Office: PO Box 2809 215 N Eola Dr Orlando FL 32802

REED, JOHN E. producer, consultant; b. Torrance, Calif., Aug. 18, 1954; s. J.E. and Dorothy Charlene (Bitner) R.; m. Christine Elaine Haddon, Aug. 10, 1975 (div. Aug. 1980); m. Beth Walker, Sept. 16, 1988; 1 child, Kelly Kristen. Student, El Camino, Torrance, Calif., 1973; cert. in bus., UCLA, 1981. S.W. regional supr. Internat. Computer Equipment, L.A., 1973-77; sr. customer engr. Datapoint, Sherman Oaks, Calif., 1977-81; sr. sales engr. United Techs., L.A., 1981-86, U.S. West Info. Sys., Torrance, Calif., 1986-88; prodr. Music Room Pub., Redondo Beach, 1987-88; sr. sales engr. NEC Am., Gardenia, 1988-93; v.p. ops. Elixir Entertainment, Culver City, 1991-93; pres., prodr. Music Room Prodns., Redondo Beach, 1993—. S.W. regional supr. Internat. Computer Equipment, L.A., 1973-77. Prodr.: (video) Comedy at Warped Speed, 1992, (feature film) Shadow Warriors, 1996; co-prodr.: (TV series) Adventures of Virgil Badd, 1994 (Golden Halo award 1994), Universal Cops, 1996; CD's include: Rawk Dawg, 2001; prodr. sound design for interactive toys and CDROMS, 1997-2000, including 23 Barbie CDROMS, Amazing Ally, Playmates Toys, WWF Crushers, Amazing Amy, Amazing Maddie. Mem. ASCAP, BMI, Harry Fox, Am. Cinematech, Audio Engring. Soc. Office: Music Room Prodns PO Box 219 Redondo Beach CA 90277-0219 E-mail: mrp@aol.com.

REED, JOHN FRANCIS (JACK REED), senator; b. Providence, Nov. 12, 1949; s. Joseph Anthony and Mary Louise (Monahan) R. BS, U.S. Mil. Acad., 1971; M in Pub. Policy, Harvard U., 1973, JD cum laude, 1982. Bar: D.C. 1982, R.I. 1983. Commd. 2d. lt. U.S. Army, 1971, served with 82d Airborne

Div., 1973-77; asst. prof. U.S. Mil. Acad., West Point, N.Y., 1977-79; resigned U.S. Army, 1979; assoc. Sutherland, Asbill & Brennan, Washington, 1982-83, Edwards & Angell, Providence, 1983-89; mem. R.I. Senate, 1984-90, 102nd-104th Congresses from 2d R.I. dist., 1990-96; mem. judiciary com., mem. econ. and edn. opportunity com., regional whip for New Eng. Dem. del.; senator U.S. Senate, 1996—. Co-chair N.E.-Midwest Congl. Coalition.; mem. appropriations com. Armed Svcs. Banking, Housing, and Urban Affairs, Health, Edn., Labor and Pensions, vice-chmn. joint econ. com.; mem. Coun. Fgn. Rels. Author: (with others) American National Security, 1981. Recipient Disting. Svc. award AARP, 1989, John Fogarty award, 1990, Disting. Legislator award United Way Southeastern New Eng., 1988. Mem. ABA, R.I. Bar Assn., D.C. Bar Assn., Environ. and Energy Study Inst., Phi Kappa Phi. Democrat. Roman Catholic. Avocations: reading, hiking. Office: US Senate 320 Hart Senate Ofc Bldg Washington DC 20510-0001

REED, JOHN HATHAWAY, former ambassador; b. Fort Fairfield, Maine, Jan. 5, 1921; s. Walter and Eva Ruth (Seeley) R.; m. Cora Mitchell Davison, Mar. 24, 1944; children— Cheryl, Ruth. BS, U. Maine, 1942, LL.D. (hon.), 1960, Ricker Coll.; grad., Harvard Naval Supply Sch., 1944. Officer Reed Farms, Inc., Fort Fairfield, Maine, 1948-98; pres. Aroostook Raceway, Inc., 1958-59; adv. com. Fort Fairfield br. No. Nat. Bank of Presque Isle; mem. Nat. Transp. Safety Bd., Washington, 1967-75, chmn., 1969-75; ambassador to Sri Lanka Colombo, 1975-77; dir. govt. rels. Assoc. Builders & Contractors, Inc., Washington, 1978-81; ambassador to Sri Lanka and Republic of Maldives, 1982-85; cons. Dept. State, 1985-90; pvt. practice cons. Washington, 1990—. Chmn. Nat. Govs. Conf. Rep., 1966; rep. Fort Fairfield to Maine Legislature, 1954-56; mem. Senate, 1957-59, pres., 1959-60; gov. State of Maine, 1960-67. Pres. bd. Community Gen. Hosp., Fort Fairfield, 1952-54, No. Maine Fair, 1953-59; trustee Ricker Coll., 1953-60, Oak Grove Sch., Vassalboro, Maine; bd. advisors Coll. of Democracy, 1986—, chmn., 1991-2000. Served to lt. (j.g.) USNR, 1942-46. Mem. Am. Fgn. Svc. Assn., Coun. Am. Abassadors, Soc. Sr. Aerospace Execs. Inc. (bd. dirs. 1987-99, pres. 1988-91), Nat. Inst. Former Govs. (bd. dirs. 1992—), Am. Legion, VFW, Grange, Maine Assn. Agrl. Fairs (pres. 1956), Mil. Order of Carabao, Capitol Hill Club, Driving Club (Ft. Fairfield) (pres. 1950-53), Aeroclub of Washington, Internat. Aviation Club, Rotary, Masons, KP, Anah Temple Shrine. Republican. Congregationalist. Office: 410 O St SW Washington DC 20024-2239

REED, JOHN KENNEDY EMANUEL, elementary school teacher; b. Shelby, Tenn., July 9, 1966; s. Robert and Gail Patrick (Caple) R. AA in Tech. and English, Milw. Area Tech. Coll., 1989; student, Clark Atlanta U., 1990. Field agt. Blue Arrow Flexi-Force, Milw., 1988-93; team leader Washington Inventory Svcs., 1989; tech.paraprofl. tchr. Milw. Pub. Schs. Sys., 1993—. Sch. implementor Silver Spring Elem Sch., Milw., 1993, mentor coord., 1993, newspaper sr. editor, 1993-97, tech. coord., 1993—. Author and editor (games with books), Star Venture: RPG, 1991, Professor X: RPG, 1996. Mem. Celestial Defender Assn. (founder and CEO 1994—). Home and Office: Celestial Defender Assn 3832 W Nash St Milwaukee WI 53216-3034

REED, JOHN SHEDD, former railway executive; b. Chgo., June 9, 1917; s. Kersey Coates and Helen May (Shedd) R.; m. Marjorie Lindsay, May 4, 1946; children: Ginevra, Keith, Helen, Peter, John Shedd Jr. Student, Chgo. Latin Sch., Hotchkiss Sch.; BS in Indsl. Adminstrn., Yale U., 1939; grad., Advanced Mgmt. Program, Harvard U., 1955. With A.T. & S.F. Ry., 1939-83; test dept. asst., successively spl. rep. to gen. supt. transp. Chgo.; transp. insp. Amarillo, Tex.; trainmaster Slaton, Pueblo, Colo.; supt. Mo. div., Marceline, Mo.; asst. to v.p. Chgo., 1957-59; exec. asst. to pres., 1957-59; v.p. finance, 1959-64; v.p. exec. dept., 1964-67; pres., 1967-78; chief exec. officer, 1968-82; chmn. bd., 1973-83. Pres. Santa Fe Industries, Inc., 1968-78, chmn. bd. dirs., CEO Santa Fe So. Pacific Corp., 1987, chmn., 1987-88. Dir. Nat. Merit Scholarship Corp., 1996, past chmn.; trustee Shedd Aquarium, Chgo., 1996, past pres.; v.p., dir. Alliance Francaise de Chicago. With USNR, 1940-45. Mem. Chgo. Club, Old Elm Club, Shoreacres Club, Onwentsia Club (Lake Forest). Home: 301 W Laurel Ave # 112 Lake Forest IL 60045-1180 Office: 224 S Michigan Ave Ste 200 Chicago IL 60604-2591

REED, JOHN SHELTON, JR. sociologist, writer; b. Jan. 8, 1942; s. John Shelton and Alice (Greene) R.; m. Dale Volberg, July 11, 1964; children: Elisabeth Marshall, Sarah Greene. SB, MIT, 1964; PhD, Columbia U., 1971; LittD (hon.), U. of South, 1999, U. N.C., Wilmington, 2000. Mem. faculty U. N.C., Chapel Hill, 1969-2000, dir. Inst. Rsch. Social Sci., 1988-2000. Pitt prof. Am. history and instns. Cambridge (Eng.) U., 1996-97; Fulbright sr. lectr Hebrew U., Jerusalem, 1973-74. Author: The Enduring South, 1972, Whistling Dixie, 1990; editor So. Cultures, 1993—. Presdl. appointee Nat. Coun. on Humanities, 1987-92; mem. adv. com. U.S. Commn. Civil Rights, N.C., 1985-87. John Simon Guggenheim Found. fellow, 1977-78, Nat. Humanities Ctr., 1983-84, Ctr. Advanced Study in Behavioral Scis., 1990-91, 2000-01. Mem. Fellowship So. Writers (non-fiction prize 1995). Sociol. Rsch. Assn., So. Sociol. Soc. (pres. 1988-91), St. George Tucker Soc., So. Assn. Pub. Opinion Rsch. (pres. 1999), Cosmos Club (Washington). Episcopalian. Office: U NC Inst Rsch Social Sci Chapel Hill NC 27599-3355 Home: 820 Forest Ave Palo Alto CA 94301-2104

REED, JOHN SQUIRES, II, lawyer; b. Lexington, Ky., Mar. 20, 1949; s. John Squires and Mary Alexander (O'Hara) R.; m. Nancy Claire Battles, Dec. 29, 1973; children: Alexandra Simmons, John Squires III. AB in Polit. Sci., U. Ky., 1971; JD, U. Va., 1974. Bar: Ky. 1974, U.S. Dist. Ct. (we. dist.) Ky. 1975, U.S. Ct. Appeals (6th cir.) 1975, U.S. Dist. Ct. (ea. dist.) Ky. 1979, U.S. Supreme Ct. 1980, U.S. Ct. Appeals (fed. cir.) 1985. Assoc. Greenbaum Doll & McDonald, Louisville, 1974-79, ptnr., 1979-87, Hirn, Doheny, Reed & Harper, Louisville, 1987-96, Reed Weitkamp Schell & Vice PLLC, Louisville, 1996—. Mem. Leadership Louisville, 1982, treas., mem. exec. com. Leadership Louisville Alumni Assn., 1984, pres., 1985; bd. dirs. Econs. Am. in Ky., 1985—, Nat. Assn. Cmty. Leadership, 1986-91, treas., 1987-88, v.p., 1988-89, pres., 1989-90, Leadership Louisville Found., Inc., 1986-92, Greater Louisville Econ. Devel. Partnership, 1987-97; chair Leadership USA, Inc., 1997, Louisville Collegiate Sch., 1996—. 1st lt. U.S. Army, 1974. Mem. ABA (antitrust, intellectual property, litig. sects.), Ky. Bar Assn., Louisville Bar Assn. (bd. dirs. 1985-86, treas. 1988, sec. 1989, v.p. 1990, pres. 1992), Louisville Boat Club, Valhalla Golf Club, Phi Beta Kappa. Democrat. Presbyterian. Office: Reed Weitkamp Schell & Vice PLLC 2400 Citizens Plz Louisville KY 40202 E-mail: jreedrwsv@aol.com., jreed@rwsvlaw.com.

REED, JOHN THEODORE, writer, publisher; b. Camden, N.J., July 5, 1946; s. Theodore and Marion Theresa (Simonsick) R.; m. Margaret Ogden Tunnell, May 31, 1975; children: Daniel Tunnell, Steven Tunnell, Michael Tunnell. BS, U.S. Mil. Acad., West Point, N.Y., 1968; MBA, Harvard U., 1977. Salesman Pritchett & Co., Pine Hill and Collingswood, N.J., 1972-74; property mgr. Fox & Lazo Inc., Cherry Hill, 1974-75; writer Harcourt Brace Jovanovich, Boston, 1976-86; bank exec. Crocker Nat. Bank, San Francisco, 1977-78; writer, pub. Alamo, 1977—. Author: Apartment Investing Check Lists, 1978, Aggressive Tax Avoidance for Real Estate Investors, 1981, Aggressive Tax Avoidance for Real Estate Investors, 16th edit., 1998, How to Manage Residential Property for Maximum Cash Flow and Resale Value, 1995, How to Manage Residential Property for Maximum Cash Flow and Resale Value, 5th edit., 1998, How to Use Leverage to Maximize Your Real Estate Investment Return, 1984, 1986, How to Increase the Value of Real Estate, 1986, Office Building Acquisition Handbook, 1982, 1985, 1987, Residential Property Acquisition Handbook, 1991, How to Buy Real Estate for at Least 20% Below Market Value, 1993, How to Buy Real Estate for at Least 20% Below Market Value, 2d edit., 1996, Coaching Youth Football Defense, 1994, Coaching Youth Football Defense, 2d edit., 1996, John T. Reed's Real Estate Investor's Monthly Newsletter, 1986—, Coaching Youth Football, 1995—, Coaching Youth Football, 3d edit., 2000—, Football Clock Management, 1997—, Football Clock Management, 2d edit., 2001—, Aggressive Tax Avoidance for Real Estate Investors, 17th edit., 2001—, Youth Baseball Coaching, 2000—, How to Get Started in Real Estate Investment, 2000—, Gap-Air-Mirror Defense for Youth Football, 2000—, How to Buy Real Estate for Little or No Money Down, 2001—, Single-Wing Offense for Youth Football, 2001—, Fixers, 2002. Coach, Youth Flag Football, 1999. 1st lt. U.S. Army, 1968-72, Vietnam. Mem. Nat. Assn. Real Estate Editors, Am. Baseball Coaches Assn., Am. Football Coaches Assn., Nat. Youth Sports Coaches Assn., Nat. Fedn. Interscholastic Coaches Assn., Calif. Coaches Assn., Football Writers Assn., Profl. Football Rschrs. Assn., Nat. Single-Wing Coaches Assn. Avocations: reading, activities with family. Home and Office: 342 Bryan Dr Alamo CA 94507-2858

REED, JOHN WESLEY, lawyer, educator; b. Independence, Mo., Dec. 11, 1918; s. Novus H. and Lilian (Houchens) R.; m. Imogene Fay Vonada, Oct. 5, 1946 (div. 1958); m. Dorothy Elaine Floyd, Mar. 5, 1961; children: Alison A., John M. (dec.), Mary V., Randolph F., Suzanne M. AB, William Jewell Coll., 1939, LLD, 1995; LLB, Cornell U., 1942; LLM, Columbia U., 1949, JSD, 1957. Bar: Mo. 1942, Mich. 1953. Assoc. Stinson, Mag, Thomson, McEvers & Fizzell, Kansas City, Mo., 1942-46; assoc. prof. law U. Okla., 1946-49; assoc. prof. U. Mich., 1949-53, prof., 1953-64, 68-85, Thomas M. Cooley prof., 1985-87, Thomas M. Cooley prof. emeritus, 1987—; dean, prof. U. Colo., 1964-68, Wayne State U., Detroit, 1987-92, prof. emeritus, 1992—. Vis. prof. NYU, 1949, U. Chgo., 1960, Yale U., 1963-64, Harvard U., 1982, U. San Diego, 1993; dir. Inst. Continuing Legal Edn., 1968-73; reporter Mich. Rules of Evidence Com., 1975-78, 83-84; mem. faculty Salzburg Sem., 1962, chmn., 1964. Author: (with W.W. Blume) Pleading and Joinder, 1952; (with others) Introduction to Law and Equity, 1953, Advocacy Course Handbook series, 1963-81; editor in chief Cornell Law Quar., 1941-42; contbr. articles to profl. jours. Pres. bd. mgrs. of mins. and missionaries benefit bd. Am. Bapt. Chs. U.S.A., 1967-74, 82-85, 88-94; mem. com. visitors JAG Sch., 1971-76; trustee Kalamazoo Coll., 1954-64, 68-70. Recipient Harrison Tweed award Assn. Continuing Legal Edn. Adminstrs., 1983, Samuel E. Gates award Am. Coll. Trial Lawyers, 1985, Roberts P. Hudson award State Bar Mich., 1989. Fellow Internat. Soc. Barristers (editor jour. 1980—); mem. ABA (mem. coun. litigation sect.), Assn. Am. Law Schs. (mem. exec. com. 1965-67), Am. Acad. Jud. Edn. (v.p. 1978-80), Colo. Bar Assn. (mem. bd. govs. 1964-68), Mich. Supreme Ct. Hist. Soc. (bd. dirs. 1991—), Sci. Club Mich., Order of Coif. Office: U Mich Sch Law Ann Arbor MI 48109-1215 E-mail: reedj@umich.edu.

REED, JOSEPH WAYNE, American studies educator, artist; b. St. Petersburg, Fla., May 31, 1932; s. Joseph Wayne and Gertrude (Cain) R.; m. Kit Craig, Dec. 10, 1955; children: Joseph McKean, John Craig, Katherine Hyde Maruyama. BA, Yale U., 1954, MA, 1958, PhD, 1961. Rsch. asst. Yale Libr., 1956-57; instr. English Wesleyan U., Middletown, Conn., 1960-61, assoc. prof., 1967-71, prof., 1971—, chmn. dept., 1971-73, 75-76, 85-86, prof. English and Am. studies, 1987. Vis. lectr. Yale U., New Haven, 1974; lectr. U.S. dept. State and USIS, Can., India, Nepal, 1974; coord. cultural exch., New Delhi, Bombay, 1992; coord. music and writing workshop U. Va., Georgetown U., others. Author: English Biography in the Early Nineteenth Century, 1801-38, 1966, Faulkner's Narrative, 1973, Three American Originals: John Ford, William Faulkner, Charles Ives, 1984, American Scenarios, 1989; editor: Barbara Bodichon's American Diary, 1972, (with W.S. Lewis) Horace Walpole's Family Correspondence, 1975, (with F.A. Pottle) Boswell, Laird of Auchinleck, 1977, 2d edit., 1994; one-man shows include Portal Gallery, London, 1971, USIS Libr., New Delhi, 1974, 92, Addison/Ripley Gallery, Washington, 1987, 92, 95, 98. Chmn. Wesleyan Sesquicentennial, 1982; chmn. bd. trustees Yale Libr. Assocs., 1984-2000, hon. trustee, 2000—. Lt. (j.g.) USNR, 1954-56. Mem. Elizabethan Club, The Johnsonians (chmn. 1988). Democrat. Episcopalian. Home: 45 Lawn Ave Middletown CT 06457-3135 E-mail: jreed@wesleyan.edu.

REED, KARL, computer systems engineering educator; b. Melbourne, Victoria, Australia, Sept. 29, 1943; s. Alfred Albert Reed and Eileen (Soffer) Capocchi; m. Robin Ann Russell; children: Emma Jane, Joanna May. Assoc. diploma, Royal Melbourne Inst. Tech., 1965; MSc, Monash U., Australia, 1984. Rsch. engr. LM Ericsson, Sweden, 1969-71, Australia, 1971-76; tutor Monash U., 1976-78; lectr., sr. lectr. Royal Melbourne Inst. Tech., 1978-88, sr. vis. fellow, 1991-92; sr. lectr. LaTrobe U., Bundoora, Australia, 1989-93, assoc. prof. Australia, 1994—. Dir. Quantative Software Rsch. Australia, 1994—, Andehl Australian Intelligent Tools Program, 1989—. Chmn. Australian Computer Soc./Software Industry Com./Software Industry Assn., Australia, 1974-88. Fellow Australian Computer Soc. (hon. life mem., chmn. Victoria br. 1990, dir. tech. bd. 1989—); mem. Inst. Engrs. Australia, Software and Svc. Industry Fedn. Australia (hon. life, joint pres. 1986-87). Avocations: running, cooking, classical guitar. Office: AAITP LaTrobe U Bundoora Victoria Australia 3083

REED, KATHLYN LOUISE, occupational therapist, educator; b. Detroit, June 2, 1940; d. Herbert C. and Jessie R. (Krehbiel) R. BS in Occupational Therapy, U. Kans., 1964; MA, Western Mich. U., 1966; PhD, U. Wash., 1973; MLIS, U. Okla., 1987. Occupational therapist in psychiatry Kans. U. Med. Center, Kansas City, 1964-65; instr. occupational therapy U. Wash., Seattle, 1967-70; assoc. prof. dept. occupational therapy U. Okla. Health Scis. Ctr., Oklahoma City, 1973-77, prof., 1978-85, chmn. dept. occupational therapy, 1973-85; libr. edn. info. svcs. Houston Acad. Medicine Tex. Med. Ctr. Libr., 1988-97. Cons. to Okla. State Dept. Health, 1976-77, Children's Convalescent Ctr., Oklahoma City, 1977-80, Oklahoma City pub. schs., 1980-81; vis. scholars program Tex. Woman's U., 1991-94, adj. prof. Sch. Occupational Therapy, 1992-97, vis. prof., 1997—; prof. Houston Ctr. Author: (with Sharon Sanderson) Concepts of Occupational Therapy, 1980, 2d edit., 1983, 3rd edit., 1992, 4th edit., 1999, Models of Practice in Occupational Therapy, 1983, Quick Reference to Occupational Therapy, 1991, 2d edit., 2000, (with Julie Pauls) Quick Reference to Physical Therapy, 1996, (with S. Cunningham) Internet Guide for Rehabilitation Professionals, 1997, (with Sally Pore) Quick Reference to Speech-Language Pathology, 1999. Vol. crisis counselor Open Door Clinic, Seattle, 1968-72; mem. exec. bd. Seattle Mental Health Inst., 1971-72; Mem. Citizen Participation Liaison Council, Seattle, 1970-72. Recipient Award of Merit, Can. Assn. Occupational Therapists, 1988. Fellow Am. Occupl. Therapy Assn. (Merit award 1983, Slagle lecture award 1985, Svc. award 1985, 2001); mem. N.Am. Riding for Handicapped Assn., World Fedn. Occupl. Therapists, Coun. Exceptional Children, Okla. Occupl. Therapy Assn. (pres. 1974-76), Tex. Occupl. Therapy Assn., Med. Libr. Assn. (Rittenhouse award 1987, Acad. Health Info. Professions), Am. Occupl. Therapy Found., Assn. Advancement Rehab. Tech., Sensory Integration Internat., Neuro-Developmental Treatment Assn., Tex. Occupl. Therapy Found. (pres. 1998—), Pi Theta Epsilan, Sigma Kappa (Colby award 1994). Democrat. Home: 6699 De Moss Dr Houston TX 77074-5003 E-mail: klreeds3@juno.com.

REED, KEITH ALLEN, lawyer; b. Anamosa, Iowa, Mar. 5, 1939; s. John Ivan and Florence Lorine (Larson) R.; m. Beth Illana Kesterson, June 22, 1963; children: Melissa Beth, Matthew Keith. BBA, U. Iowa, 1960, JD, 1963. Bar: Ill. 1963, Iowa 1963. Ptnr. Seyfarth Shaw, Chgo., 1963—. Co-author: Labor Arbitration in Healthcare, 1981; co-editor: Chicagoland Employment Law Manual, 1994, Employment and Discrimination, 1996, Federal Employment Law and Regulations, 1989-99, 2001-; co-contbr. articles to Am. Hosp. Assn. publs., 1986-89. Trustee Meth. Hosp. Chgo., 1985—; mem. ad hoc labor adv. com. Am. Hosp. Assn., Chgo., 1980—; bd. dirs. Lyric Opera Chgo. Ctr. for Am. Artists, pres., 1983-86. Mem. ABA (dir. health law forum 1979-82), Chgo. Bar Assn. (chair labor and employment law com. 1996-), Union League Club Chgo. (bd. dirs. 1985-88), Sunset Ridge Country Club (Northbrook, Ill.). Republican. Methodist. Avocations: music, community theater, tennis, golf. Office: Seyfarth Shaw 55 E Monroe St Ste 4200 Chicago IL 60603-5863

REED, KIT, writer; b. San Diego; d. John Rich and Lillian (Hyde) Craig; m. Joseph Reed; children: Joseph, John, Katherine. BA in English, Coll. Notre Dame, Balt. Reporter St. Petersburg (Fla.) Times, New Haven Register; freelance novelist. Adj. prof. English Wesleyan U., 1974— ; USIS lectr. in India, 1974; lectr. Smithsonian, 1996. Author: Mother Isn't Dead, She's Only Sleeping, 1961, At War as Children, 1964, The Better Part, 1967, Mr. Da V. and Other Stories, 1967, Armed Camps, 1969, Cry of the Daughter, 1971, Tiger Rag, 1973, Captain Grownup, 1976, The Killer Mice, 1976, The Ballad of T. Rantula, 1979, Magic Time, 1980, Other Stories and The Attack of the Giant Baby, 1981, Story First, The Writer as Insider, 1982, Fort Privilege, 1985, The Revenge of the Senior Citizens Plus, 1986, Catholic Girls, 1987, Revision, 1989, Mastering Fiction Writing, 1991, Thief of Lives and Other Stories, 1992, (radio play) The Bathyscaphe, 1979, Little Sisters of the Apocalypse, 1994, Strait, 1995, J. Eden, 1996, Weird Women, Wired Women, 1998; (as Kit Craig) Gone, 1992, Closer, 1997, Some Safe Place, 1998, Seven for the Apocalypse, 1999, Short Fuse, 1999, @expectations, 2000. Co-dir. writers exch. for Indo-U.S. subcommn. on edn. and culture, 1990. Named New Eng. Newspaperwoman of Year, New Eng. Women's Press Assn., 1958, 59; grantee Abraham Woursell Found., 1966-71; Guggenheim fellow, 1964, Rockefeller fellow Aspen (Colo.) Inst. for Humanistic Studies, 1976. Mem. P.E.N., Writers Guild Am. East, Nat. Book Critics Circle (bd. dir. 1991-95), Century Assn., Authors League Fund (bd. dirs. 1998—). Democrat. Roman Catholic. Office: care Blauner Books Lit Agy 12 E 86th St Apt 633 New York NY 10028-0512

REED, LEON SAMUEL, policy analyst, writer, photographer; b. Warren, Ohio, July 6, 1949; s. Walter Charles and Lois Avalene (Botroff) R.; m. Margaret Smith, Dec. 27, 1975 (div.); m. Lois S. Lembo, Aug. 5, 1997; children: Samuel Currier, Stephen Walter, Catherine Lois. BA in Econs. and Journalism, Antioch Coll., 1971. Project dir. Coun. on Econ. Priorities, N.Y.C. and Washington, 1970-75; sr. mem. profl. staff Joint Com. on Def. Prodn., U.S. Congress, Washington, 1975-77; mem. profl. staff Com. on Banking, Housing and Urban Affairs, U.S. Senate, 1977-81; analyst TASC, 1981-82, mgr. contingency planning, 1982-85, mgr. instl. resources dept., 1985-91, dir. indsl. and mfg. scis. divsn., 1991-97; rsch. staff Inst. Def. Analyses, 1998—. Author: Military Maneuvers, 1975, Resource Management: A Historical Perspective, 1988; co-author: Guide to Corporations, 1973, Report of the National Critical Technologies Panel, 1991; contbr. Strategic Survey, 1981-82, The American Defense Mobilization Infrastructure, 1983; corr. Potomac Almanac, Fairfax/Springfield Connection; author numerous congressional and exec. br. reports, also mag. and jour. articles. Del. White House Conf. on Youth, 1971; writer, photographer Md. Soccer News, 1996—98, exec. editor, 1998—; pres. Randolph Civic Assn., 1978—80; v.p. North Bethesda Congress of Citizens Assns., 1983—84, pres., 1984—86; v.p. Md. State Youth Soccer Assn., 1998—; bd. dirs. Coun. on Econ. Priorities, 1971—73, Montgomery Soccer, Inc., 1994—, pres., 2001—. Inducted into Warren H.S. Alumni Hall of Fame, 1997; named MSI Coach of Yr., 1996. Office: 1801 N Beauregard St Alexandria VA 22311-1701 E-mail: lreed@ida.org.

REED, LEONARD NEWTON, secondary school educator; b. Alva, Okla., Feb. 27, 1952; s. Leonard S. and Vevian M. (Chew) R. BA, Northwestern Okla. State U., 1970, MA, 1980; postgrad., No. Ariz. U., 1982-89; cert. ESL, U. Phoenix, 1992. Cert. social sci. tchr., Ariz., Okla., ESL, Ariz. Tchr. social sci. Chinle (Ariz.) Unified Sch. Dist., 1974—, chair dept. social sci., 1982-91, 96—; night staff Diné Coll., 1988—. Student coun. advisor Chinle Unified Sch. Dist., 1975-76, 78-83, 84-93. Mem. com. Apache County (Ariz.) Dem. Party, 1980-88, 93-96, 2001—; state del. Ariz. Dem. Party, 1980; mem. Nat. Gay and Lesbian Task Force, 1976—. NEA (gay and lesbian caucus 1988—, rural and small caucus, 1986—), Ariz. Edn. Assn. (bd. dirs. 1984-88, 89-90, human rels. com. 1987-94, 95—, 99-2002, chair human rels. com. 1992-94, 99—, treas. N.E. adv. coun., Bill Hodge award 1989, first male co-chair gay, lesbian caucus 1995-2001, founder 1995-2001), Ariz. Student Coun. Advisors Assn., Chinle Edn. Assn. (past pres. 1979, 81, treas.). Home: PO Box 1678 Chinle AZ 86503-1678 Office: Chinle Unified Sch Dist # 24 PO Box 587 Chinle AZ 86503-0587 E-mail: lenny727@alva.ok.net.

REED, LESTER JAMES, biochemist, educator; b. New Orleans, Jan. 3, 1925; s. John T. and Sophie (Pastor) R.; m. Janet Louise Gruschow, Aug. 7, 1948; children: Pamela, Sharon, Richard, Robert. BS, Tulane U., 1943; D.Sc. (hon.), 1977; PhD, U. Ill., 1946. Rsch. asst. NDRC, Urbana, Ill., 1944-46; rsch. assoc. biochemistry Cornell U. Med. Coll., 1946-48; faculty U. Tex., Austin, 1948—, prof. chemistry, 1958—, Ashbel Smith prof., 1984-99, prof. emeritus, 1999—; rsch. sci. Clayton Found. Biochem. Inst., 1949—. Assoc. dir., Clayton Found. Biochem. Inst., 1962-63, dir., 1963-96. Contbr. articles profl. jours. Mem. NAS, Am. Acad. Arts and Scis., Am. Soc. for Biochemistry and Molecular Biology (Merck award 1994), Am. Chem. Soc. (Eli Lilly & Co. award in biol. chemistry 1958), Phi Beta Kappa, Sigma Xi. Home: 3502 Balcones Dr Austin TX 78731-5802 Office: U Tex Biochem Inst Experimental Sci Bldg 442 Austin TX 78712 E-mail: lreed@mail.utexas.edu.

REED, LOWELL A., JR. federal judge; b. Westchester, Pa., 1930; s. Lowell A. Sr. and Catherine Elizabeth R.; m. Diane Benson; four children. BBA, U. Wis., 1952; JD, Temple U., 1958. Bar: Pa. 1959, U.S. Dist. Ct. (ea. dist.) Pa. 1961, U.S. Ct. Appeals (3d cir.) 1962, U.S. Supreme Ct. 1970. Corp. trial counsel PMA Group, Phila., 1958-63; assoc. Rawle & Henderson, 1963-65, gen. ptnr., 1966-88; judge U.S. Dist Ct., 1988-99; sr. judge U.S. Dist. Ct., 1999—. Lectr. law Temple U., 1965-81, faculty Acad. Advocacy, 1988—, Pa. Bar Inst., 1972—. Contbr. articles to profl. jours. Elder Abington (Pa.) Presbyn. Ch.; past. mem. Pa. Senate Select Com. Med. Malpractice; past pres., bd. dirs. Rydal Meadowbrook Civic Assn.; bd. dirs. Abington Sch. Bd., 1971, World Affairs Coun. Phila., 1983-88; trustee Abington Health Care Corp., 1983-88, 90-93. Lt. comdr. USNR, 1952-57. Recipient Alumni Achievement award Temple U. 1988, Cert. of Honor, 2001. Mem. ABA, Phila. Bar Assn. (chmn. medico legal com. 1975, constl. bicentennial com. 1986-87, commn. on jud. selection and retention 1983-87), Temple Am. Inn of Ct. (pres. 1990-93, master of bench 1990—), Am. Judicature Soc., Temple U. Law Alumni Assn. (exec. com. 1987-90, 99—), Hist. Soc. U.S. Supreme Ct., Hist. Soc. U.S. Dist. Ct. Ea. Dist. Pa. Republican. Office: US Dist Ct 11614 US Courthouse Independence Mall W Philadelphia PA 19106

REED, MARK ARTHUR, educator, researcher; b. Suffern, N.Y., Jan. 4, 1955; s. Arthur Julius and Rita Margaret Reed; m. Elizabeth J. Schaffer; 1 child, Victor. BS in Physics with honors, Syracuse U., 1977, MS in Physics, 1979, PhD in Solid State Physics, 1983; MA (hon.), Yale U., 1990. Mem. tech. staff Ctrl. Rsch. Labs., Tex. Instruments, Dallas, 1983-88, sr. mem. tech. staff, 1988-90; prof. elec. engring. and applied physics Yale U., New Haven, 1990—, chmn. elec. engring. dept., 1995—2001, Harold Hodgkinson prof. engring. and applied sci., 1999—; chief tech. officer, dir. Molecular Electronics Corp., 1999—2001. Chmn., organizer of numerous confs. Contbr. 130 articles to profl. jours., chpts. to books; author 3 books; speaker in field. Recipient Kilby Young Innovator award, 1994, Disting. Alumni award Syracuse U., 2000, Fujitsu ISCS Quantum Device award, 2001, YSSA award for advancement of basic and applied sci., 2002; named one of Fortune Mag.'s 12 most promising young Am. Scientists. Mem. IEEE (sr.), Am. Phys. Soc., Optical Soc. Am., Sigma Xi. Achievements include pioneered investigation of "Quantum Dots" and Quantum devices; invention of resonant tunneling transistor; 17 patents for novel quantum effect and heterojunction devices; pioneered research on molecular electronic systems. Avocations: scuba, chess. Office: Molecular Electronics Corp PO Box 208284 New Haven CT 06520-8284

REED, MARY LOUISE. natural health professional; b. Spangler, Pa., July 26, 1957; d. Paul Peter Paranich and Beatrice Clara (Butler) Eckenrode; m. Paul Reed, Sept. 22, 1976 (div. May 1978); children: Nicole L., Jenard. Degree in acctg., Cambria-Rowe Bus. Coll., Johnstown, Pa., 1981; D of Naturopathy, Trinity Sch. of Health, Wiona Lake, Ind., 1997. Owner Mary's Herbs and Iridology, Patton, Pa. Author: The Moth and the Butterfly, 1987, Moweez, 1988; editor The Herbal Grapevine Newsletter, 1991—. Homemaking instr. Relief Soc., Altoona, 1997. Mem. Nat. Assn. Cert. Natural Health Profls. (cert.). Home and Office: Marys Herbs & Iridology 626 Donnelly Ave Patton PA 16668-1504

REED, MIRIAM BELL, legislative staff; b. N.Y.C., May 31, 1930; d. Samuel Dennis and Miriam Wilkes Bell; m. John Grady Reed, May 1, 1954; children: Roberta, Christine, Karen, Laura, Margaret, Abigail, Elisabeth. BA, Mount Holyoke Coll., 1952. Asst. to adminstrv. asst. Rep. Harlan Hagan, Washington, 1953-54; asst. to econ. prof. Littauer Sch. Pub. Adminstrn., Cambridge, Mass., 1954; producer, treas. Video Ed Prodns., Inc., Hyattsville, Md., 1974-90; Singapore testing coord. Malaysian Am. Commn. on Ednl. Exch., Singapore, 1991-92; legis. aide Del. Constance A. Morella, Annapolis, Md., 1978-86; legis. asst. Hon. Constance A. Morella, Washington, 1987-90, 92, 94-97; staff Friends of Connie Morella for Congress, 1999-2000. Cons. Acad. Arrangements Abroad, N.Y.C., 1974-99. Rsch. and writing of ednl. hist. videotapes, 1974-90 (Pratt Libr. award 1986). V.p., pres. bd. LWV, Bronxville, N.Y., 1957-74; mem. Montgomery County Commn. on the Humanities, 1985-88; mem. Montgomery County Com. to Celebrate Md.'s 350th Birthday. Mem. Montgomery County Hist. Soc. (dir. 1998—), C&O Canal Assn. (dir. 2000—). Avocations: swimming, hiking, backpacking. Home: 8221 Burning Tree Rd Bethesda MD 20817-2908 E-mail: mreed8221@aol.com.

REED, NANCY BOYD, English language and elementary education educator; b. Lodi, Calif., Oct. 10, 1946; d. Leo H. and Anna Gwen (Coombes) Boyd; m. Maurice Allen Reed, Dec. 22, 1966; 1 child, Scot Alastair. AA Recreational Adminstrn. with honors, Delta Coll., 1974; BA Recreational Adminstrn. with honors, Calif. State U., Sacramento, 1976, MA in Edn., English Lang. Devel., 1988; cert. computers in edn., U. Calif., Davis, 1984. Cert. multiple subject, phys. edn., computers in edn. teaching. Tchr. 4th grade Hagginwood Sch., Sacramento, 1980-81; tchr. 4th/5th grade impacted lang. Noralto Sch., 1981-88, bilingual resource tchr., 1988-91, tchr. English lang. devel., 1991-96, bilingual resource tchr., 1996-98; mentor tchr. North Sacramento Sch. Dist., 1992-95, bilingual resource tchr., 1996-98, English lang. devel. curriculum assoc., 1997-98, ednl. cons., 1998—; bilingual rsource tchr. Woodlake Sch., 2001—. Fellow, tchr./cons. No. Calif. Math. Project, U. Calif., Davis, 1985—. Dir. Jasmine Flower Dancers, Sacramento, 1984-96; comty. rep. Am. Host Found., Sacramento, 1976—. Named Outstanding Educator Capitol Svc. Ctr., 1992, Tchr. of Yr., Noralto Sch., North Sacramento Sch., 1996; scholar Fridtjof-Nansen-Akademie, Ingleheim, Germany, 1993, Adenauer Found., Berlin, 1982, 93. Mem. NEA, Nat. Vis. Tchrs. Assn. (bd. dirs. 1994—), Nat. Assn. Bilingual Edn., Nat. Coun. Tchrs. Math., Calif. Tchrs. Assn. (state coun. rep. 1995-96), North Sacramento Edn. Assn. (sec. 1986-88, v.p. 1988-90, pres. 1990-92, outstanding educator 1992). Avocations: travel, photography, camping. Home: 3665 Halter Ct Sacramento CA 95821-3266 Office: Woodlake Sch North Sacramento Sch Dist 700 Southgate Rd Sacramento CA 95815-1605 E-mail: nancyboydreed@hotmail.com.

REED, PAUL ALLEN, artist; b. Washington, Mar. 28, 1919; s. Charles Miler and Lula Rachael (Annadale) R.; m. Esther Kishter, July 10, 1939; children—Jean Reed Roberts, Thomas, Robert. Student, San Diego State Coll., 1936, Corcoran Sch. Art, 1937. Asst. art dir. USAF mag., N.Y.C., 1942-44; artist B.D. Adams Advt. Agy., Montclair, N.J., 1944-48; asst. art dir. M.F. Dreher Advt. Agy., N.Y.C., 1948-50; free lance graphics designer Washington, 1950-62; graphics dir. U.S. Peace Corps, 1962-71; asst. prof. Corcoran Sch. Art, 1971-81. Artist in residence Phoenix Art Mus., 1976; vis. artist Ariz. State U., Tempe, 1980. One-man shows include Corcoran Gallery Art, 1966, Washington U., 1967, Ariz. State U., 1971, Phoenix Art Mus., 1977, Am. U., 1997, Marymount U., 2002, Represented in permanent collections Hirshhorn Mus., Nat. Mus. Am. Art, N.C. Mus. Art, Corcoran Gallery, San Francisco Mus. Art, Detroit Inst. Art, others. Home: 3541 N Utah St Arlington VA 22207-4444

REED, RALPH EUGENE, JR. political party official; b. Portsmouth, Va., June 24, 1961; s. Ralph Sr. and Marcy R.; m. Jo Anne Young, 1987; children: Brittany, Ralph III, Christopher, Nicole. BA in History, U. Ga., 1985; D in Am. History, Emory U., 1991. Exec. dir. Christian Coalition, Chesapeake, Va., 1989-97; pres. Century Strategies, Strategies Cons. Co., Duluth, Ga., 1997—; chmn. Ga. Republican Party, 2001—. Founder Students for Am., Raleigh, N.C., 1984; lobbyist; spkr. in field. Address: Ga Repub Party 5600 Roswell Rd NE E Bldg Atlanta GA 30342 Office: Century Strategies 3235 Satellite Blvd Ste 575 Duluth GA 30096-9017*

REED, RAYMOND DERYL, architect; b. Alturas, Calif., Mar. 29, 1930; s. Russell Jacob and Nita Ferne (Wilcox) R.; m. Patricia Reinerth, Apr. 30, 1954; children— Kathryn, Russell, Ann, Andrea. B.Arch., Tulane U., 1953; M.Arch., Harvard U., 1958. Chmn. architecture and interior design dept. U. Southwestern La., 1958-64; head dept. architecture Iowa State U., 1964-70, dir. grad. research in architecture, 1970-73; mem. faculty Tex. A&M U., 1973—, prof. architecture, 1973—96; dean Tex. A&M U. (Coll. Architecture and Environ. Design), 1973-80, prof. emeritus, 1996—. Dir. Internat. Ctr. for Cybernetics and Informatics, 1990. Author: Sustainable Architecture, 1988, rev. edit, 1990; contbr. numerous articles on energy conservation and post petroleum architecture to research publs. Served with USNR, 1953-58. Mem. AIA, Nat. Council Archtl. Registration Bds., Am. Collegiate Schs. Architecture, Tex. Soc. Architects, La. Architects Soc. Home: 1601 Wolf Pen Ct College Station TX 77840-3169 Office: Tex A&M U Dept Architecture College Station TX 77843-0001

REED, REX RAYMOND, retired telephone company executive; b. Peterson, Iowa, Mar. 19, 1922; s. Charles Bernard and Dagmar Helen (Heick) R.; m. Rita Compton, Dec. 3, 1944; children: Julie, Nancy, Linda; m. Mary Connors, June 13, 1992. Student, Morningside Coll., 1940-41, Iowa State U., 1941-43, 46-47, U. Notre Dame, 1943-44; BS in Gen. Engring, Iowa State U., 1947. With Northwestern Bell Telephone Co. (various locations), 1947-60, 61-66, employee info. mgr., pub. relations dept. Omaha, 1957-58, gen. comml. mgr., comml. dept. N.D., 1958-60, asst. v.p. personnel and employment, 1961-62, asst. v.p. personnel Nebr. area, 1962-64, asst. v.p. personnel and labor relations, 1964-66; with AT&T Corp., N.Y.C., 1960-61, 66-84, dir. labor relations, personnel dept., 1966-71, v.p. labor relations, 1971-83, sr. v.p. labor relations, 1984; ret., 1984. Dir. Ind. Bell Telephone Co., Ill. Bell Telephone Co., First Investors Corp N.Y.C. Mem. Madison (N.J.) Bd. Edn., 1969-70, pres., 1971-75; Trustee Menninger Found., Topeka, 1979— , Morristown (N.J.) Meml. Hosp., 1977-95; bd. dirs. Nat. Urban Coalition, 1981-84. Served with USMC, 1943-46; to capt. 1951-53. Mem. Bus. Roundtable (chmn. labor-mgmt. com. 1976-77), Labor Policy Assn. (chmn. 1979-83), Inst. Collective Bargaining (bd. dirs. 1976-84), Orgn. Resources Counselors, Morris County Golf Club (Morristown, N.J., pres. bd. govs. 1991-92). Home: 259 Governors Dr Kiawah Island SC 29455-5751

REED, RICHARD JOHN, retired meteorology educator; b. Braintree, Mass., June 18, 1922; s. William Amber and Gertrude Helen (Volk) R.; m. Joan Murray, June 10, 1950; children: Ralph Murray, Richard Cobden, Elizabeth Ann. Student, Boston Coll., 1940-41, Dartmouth Coll., 1943-44; BS, Calif. Inst. Tech., 1945; ScD, MIT, 1949. Research staff mem. MIT, Cambridge, 1950-54; asst. prof. dept. atmospheric scis. U. Wash., Seattle, 1954-58, assoc. prof., 1958-63, prof., 1963-91, prof. emeritus, 1991—. Cons. U.S. Weather Service, Suitland, Md., 1961-62, European Ctr. for Medium Range Weather Forecasts, Reading, Eng., 1985-86; exec. scientist NRC, Washington, 1968-69; trustee Univ. Corp. for Atmospheric Research, Boulder, Colo., 1987-92. Served to lt. (j.g.) USN, 1942-46. Fellow AAAS, Am. Meteorol. Soc. (pres. 1972, Meisinger award 1964, Second Half Century award 1972, Charles Franklin Brooks award 1983, Carl-Gustaf Rossby Rsch. medal 1989, hon. mem. 1999), Royal Meteorol. Soc. (hon. mem.), Am. Geophys. Union; mem. NAS. Democrat. Unitarian Universalist. Office: U Wash Box 351640 Dept Atmospheric Scis Seattle WA 98195-1640 E-mail: reed@atmos.washington.edu., richandjreed1@attbi.com.

REED, ROBERT A. performing arts executive; Gen. mgr. Buffalo (N.Y.) Philharmonic; exec. dir. Tulsa Philharmonic Orch., Tulsa, Okla. Office: Tulsa Philharmonic 2901 S Harvard Ave Ste A Tulsa OK 74114-6100*

REED, ROBERT DANIEL, publisher; b. Pottsville, Pa., May 24, 1941; s. Robert Daniel R.; children: Robert Duane, Alan Andrija, Tanya. Purchasing mgr. Ogden Tech. Labs., Sunnyvale, Calif., 1962-69; mktg. mgr. Plaza Press, 1969-94; pub. R & E Pubs., Saratoga, Calif., 1966-94; founder Bob Reed Studios; ptnr. Reed's Mktg. Svcs.; co-founder Ceasefire USA; founder, pres. Green PR Internat. Mktg. Cons.; pres. Robert D. Reed Pubs. Co-founder Monterey Pacific Pub., 1997. Author: We Care Cookbook, 1974; pub. over 1150 books on human rights, ethnic history edn., criminology, AIDS, Alzheimers disease, teen suicide, also how-to, trade, and humor books; co-author 50 books on poverty, hunger, homelessness, abuse, sexual assault. With U.S. Army, 1959-61. Mem. Ctr. for Dem. Instns., Nat. Fedn. Ind. Bus., Calif. Inventors Coun., Smithsonian Instn., Soc. for Scholarly Pub., World Future Soc. Inventor electro mech.-electronics devices, creative humor products. Home: 750 La Playa St # 647 San Francisco CA 94121-3262 E-mail: 4bobreed@msn.com. *Spend your life doing what you like to do, by putting all your efforts into it. Don't be afraid to take a chance. Remember, if life gets dull-Risk it a bit.*

REED, ROBERT PHILLIP, lawyer; b. Springfield, Ill., June 14, 1952; s. Robert Edward and Rita Ann (Kane) R.; m. Janice Leigh Kloppenburg, Oct. 8, 1976; children: Kevin Michael, Matthew Carl, Jennifer Leigh, Rebecca Ann. AB, St. Louis U., 1974; JD, U. Ill., 1977. Bar: Ill. 1977, U.S. Dist. Ct. (ctrl. dist.) Ill. 1979, U.S.Ct. Appeals (7th cir.) 1983, U.S. Dist. Ct. (so. dist.) Ill. 1992, Colo. 1993. Intern Ill. Legislature, Springfield, 1977-78; assoc. Traynor & Hendricks, 1979-80; ptnr. Traynor, Hendricks & Reed, 1981-88; pvt. practice, 1988—. Pub. defender Sangamon County, Ill., Springfield, 1979-81; hearing examiner Ill. State Bd. Elections, Springfield, 1981-88; spl. asst. atty. gen. State of Ill., Springfield, 1983—; instr. Lincoln Land Community Coll., Springfield, 1988. Trustee Springfield Pk. Dist., 1985-89. Mem.: Attys Title Guaranty Fund, Inc., Colo. Bar Assn., Ill. State Bar Assn., Nat. Assn. Securities Dealers, Inc (arbitrator 1996—), Phi Beta Kappa. Roman Catholic. Office: 1129 S 7th St Springfield IL 62703-2418

REED, ROGER DUANE, maintenance electrician; b. Euclid, Ohio, May 29, 1968; s. David Andrew and Irene Reed; m. Lori Lynn Hjerpe, Sept. 9, 2000. AA, Lakeland C.C., 1998. Indsl. electrician Ardcor, Willoughby, Ohio, 1986-96; maintenance technician Aviation Product Support, Mentor, 1996-2000, E, H and S and maintenance technician, 2000—01; maintenance electrician Griffin Wheel Co., 2001—. Mem. Young Reps., Ashtabula County, Ohio, 1993-94. Mem. Columbus Outdoor Pursuits, Phi Theta Kappa. Republican. Avocations: cycling, church, reading. Home: 4278 Bearington Pond Dr Groveport OH 43125 E-mail: rd11reed@yahoo.com.

REED, RONALD ERNST, lawyer; b. Frankfort, Ky., Mar. 24, 1958; s. Thomas B. and Gerhild M. Reed; m. Lisa J. Hayden, Mar. 7, 1994; 1 child, Spencer Thomas. BA, U. Fla., 1980, JD, 1983. Bar: Fla. 1983, U.S. Dist. Ct. (mid. dist.) Fla. 1987. Asst. states atty. State Atty.'s Office, Jacksonville, Fla., 1983-86; ptnr. Fallin & Reed, 1986-87, Bullock, Childs, Pendley & Reed, P.A., Jacksonville, 1987—. Democrat. Methodist. Avocations: golfing, reading, sports. Office: Bullock Childs Pendley & Reed PA Ste 711 Blackstone Bldg 2333 E Bay St Jacksonville FL 32202 E-mail: rreed@bcprlaw.com.

REED, RONALD KEITH, oceanographer, researcher; b. Mountain Top, Ark., May 6, 1932; s. Thomas Vernon and Bessie Thelma Reed; m. Annemarie Hills, Oct. 13, 1965 (div. May 1990); stepchildren: Christopher M. Hills, Mark S. Hills. BS, Ark. Poly. Coll., 1958; MS, Oreg. State U., 1973. Oceanographer Coast & Geodetic Survey, Washington, 1958-63, Seattle, 1963-70, NOAA, Seattle, 1970—. Contbr. articles to profl. jours. With U.S. Army, 1954-56. Recipient Bronze medal U.S. Dept. Commerce, 1997. Mem. Am. Geophys. Union. Avocations: song writing, singing, photography. Home: 12417 NE 129th Ct # E14 Kirkland WA 98034-7437 Office: NOAA Pacific Marine Environ Lab 7600 Sand Point Way NE Seattle WA 98115-6349

REED, SALLY GARDNER, library director; BA in English, Colo. State U., 1979; MLS, No. Ill. U., 1981. Dir. North Hampton (H.H.) Pub. Libr., 1981-85, Ilsley Pub. Libr., Middlebury, Vt., 1985-93, Ames (Iowa) Pub. Libr., 1993-95; dir. librs. Norfolk (Va.) Pub. Libr., 1995—2001. Adv. com. product devel. Rsch. Pub., Inc., 1993-94; bd. trustees Bibliographic Ctr. Rsch., Aurora, Colo., 1994-95. Author: Small Libraries: A Handbook for Successful Management, 1991, 2d edit., 2002, Saving Your Library: A Guide to Getting, Using and Keeping the Power You Need, 1992, Library Volunteers: Worth the Effort!, 1994; editor: Creating the Future: Essays on the Future of Librarianship in an Age of Great Change, 1996, Speaking Out: Voices in Celebration of Intellectual Freedom, 1999, Making the Case for Your Library, 2001; contbr. articles to profl. jours. Bd. dirs. Sheldon Art History Mus., Middlebury, 1988-93, United Way Story County, Ames, 1994-95; mem. cabinet United Way Norfolk, 1996-97, chair city campaign, 1997. Recipient Recognition award Tidewater Area Minority Libr. Network, 1997, Am. Lib. Assoc. Herb & Virginia White award for Promoting Librarianship, 2000. Mem. ALA (exec. bd., intellectual freedom roundtable 1997-2001, chpt. coun. 1989-93, promotion task force 1989-91, planning budget assembly 1991, adv. com. office libr. outreach svcs. 1993-94, nat. libr. week com. 1993-95, presdl. com. pub. awareness 1994-96, councilor at large 1995—, chair membership com. 1996, resolutions com. 1997, bd. dirs. 1997—, exec. bd. 1997—), Pub. Libr. Assn., Libr. Adminstrn. Mgmt. Assn., Va. Libr. Assn. Office: Friends Libraries USA 1420 Walnut Ste 450 Philadelphia PA 19102-

REED, SAM, secretary of state; b. Portland, Oreg. m. Margie Reed, 1963; children: David, Kristen. BA, MA, Wash. State U. Cert. profl. elections officer. Exec. dir. Gov. Evans' Urban Affairs Coun.; Thurston County auditor; asst. sec. of state State of Wash.; dir. State Constl. Reform Commn.; sec. of state State of Wash., 2001—. Bd. mem. Fed. Election Commn. Voting System; internat. election observer, Rwanda, Uganda; mem. Wash. State Archives Adv. Com., Americorps Adv. Coun., Wash. State Election Admin. & Cert. Bd. Recipient Gov.'s Disting. Vol. award, Thurston County Citizen of the Year Disting. Svc. award. Mem.: Mainstream Reps. of Wash., Wash. State Assn. County Auditors, Olympia Kiwanis. Avocations: running, piano, arts, tennis. Office: 520 Union Ave SE PO Box 40220 Olympia WA 98504 E-mail: sreed@secstate.wa.gov.*

REED, SAMUEL ALLEN, III, secondary school educator; b. Patterson, N.J., Jan. 27, 1964; s. Samuel A. Reed, II and Lizzie Reed; m. Matlhatso-Kesupile Reed; children: Mpho, Thato, Kagiso. BA in Computer Sci., Cheyney State U., 1986; MBA, Atlanta U., 1988; MEd, Temple U., 1998. Sr. ops. officer Botswana Devel. Corp., 1988—91; bus. advisor Nat. Industries, Botswana, 1991—93; bus. dir. Logical Solutions, Botswana, 1993—96; after-sch. leader Free Libr. Phila., 1997—2000; tchr. Beeber Mid. Sch., Phila., 1998—. Mem. steering com. Phila. Writing Project, 2001—. Vol. Peace Corps, Botswana, 1988—91. Recipient Creative Classroom award, Disney Learning Partnership, 2001, Tchg. Tolerance award, So. Poetry Law Ctr., 2001; grantee, Phila. Art Edn. Partnership, 2001. Fellow: Phila. Writing Project; mem.: Nat. Coun. for Tchrs. English. Avocations: chess, poetry. Home: # 206 6355 Lancaster Philadelphia PA 19151 E-mail: sriii2000@aol.com.

REED, SCOTT WARREN, respiratory therapist, consultant; b. Hemet, Calif., May 16, 1949; s. Charles Addison and Miriam Jean (Larson) R.; m. Janis Darlene Rothenberg, June 1977 (div. 1986); m. Tiina Joensuu, Aug. 30, 1988; children: Warren, Sofia. BS in Biology, Calif. Poly. State U., 1971. Staff respiratory therapy, dir. Hemet Valley (Calif.) Hosp., 1972, 74, 75, 88; supr. respiratory therapy Loma Linda Community Hosp., 1974, 76, 79; staff respiratory therapy Children's Hosp., Dallas, 1981-82; dir., mgr. respiratory therapy Monte Vista (Colo.) Community Hosp., 1982-83; staff respiratory therapy King Fahad Hosp., Al Baha, Saudi Arabia, 1983-84, Riyadh (Saudi Arabia) Mil. Hosp., 1985-87, Dhahran (Saudi Arabia) Med. Ctr., 1987-88, San Juan Regional Med. Ctr., Farmington, N.Mex., 1988, 90; supr. respiratory therapy St. Joseph Hosp., Bellingham, Wash., 1990—. Bd. dirs. R.C. Computer Cons., Everson, Wash. Capt. USAR, 1972-80. Mem. Nat. Bd. Respiratory Care, Am. Assn. Respiratory Care. Avocations: photography, music, computers. E-mail: ScottReed3@aol.com.

REED, SHERMAN KENNEDY, chemical consultant; b. Chgo., Apr. 11, 1919; s. Frank Hynes and Helen Louise (Kennedy) R.; m. Octavia Bailey, Oct. 11, 1943; children: Martin Bailey, Holly Anne, Julie Marie Reed. BS with honors, U. Ill., 1940; PhD, Cornell U., 1949. Asst. instr. chemistry Cornell U., 1940-43; asst. research scientist Manhattan Project, N.Y.C., 1942-46; asst. prof. Bucknell U., Lewisburg, Pa., 1946-50; with FMC Corp., 1950—, mgr., asst. dir. research, 1950-60, divisional dir. research and devel., central research dir., 1960-76, v.p., 1976-82, cons., 1983—; dir. Avicon, Inc., 1970-82; pres., dir. FMC Gold Corp.; mng. dir. COGAS Devel. Co., 1975—; dir. Indsl. Research Inst., N.Y.C., Franklin Inst., Phila., 1976-83; chmn. bd. Franklin Research Ctr., 1976-83. Fellow Am. Inst. Chemists; mem. AAAS, Am. Chem. Soc., Assn. Research Dirs. (pres. 1973), Vero Beach Country Club. Clubs: Union League (Phila.); Nassau (Princeton, N.J.). Republican. Home and Office: 2300 Indian Creek Blvd W #C211 Vero Beach FL 32966-2400 E-mail: shermankreed@aol.com.

REED, STANLEY FOSTER, editor, author, publisher, lecturer; b. Bogota, N.J., Sept. 28, 1917; s. Morton H. and Beryl (Turner) R.; m. Stella Swingle, Sept. 28, 1940 (div. 1978); children: Nancie, Beryl Ann, Alexandra; m. Shirley Weihman, Sept. 28, 1985 (dec. Feb. 1988); m. Catherine Case Commander, Dec. 16, 1989 (div. 1991). Student, George Washington U., 1939-40, Johns Hopkins, 1940-41; MBA, Loyola U., Md., 1981. Registered profl. engr., D.C. With Bethlehem Steel Corp., Balt., 1940-41; cons. engr., 1942-44; founder, pres. Reed Research, Inc., Washington, 1945-62; pres. Reed Research Inst. Creative Studies, from 1951; founder, chmn. LogEtronics, Inc., 1955; founder, pres., chmn. Tech. Audit Corp., 1962; assoc. Mgmt. Analysis Corp., 1978-81; sr. cons. Hay Assocs., Phila., 1980-83; entrepreneur-in-residence Coll. Charleston, S.C.; editor, CEO Merger Central Inc., mergercentral.com. Co-chmn. semi-ann. Merger Week Northwestern U.; lectr. numerous U.S. and fgn. groups and instns. including Union Theol. Sem., U. Pa., Pa. State U., U. Colo., Georgetown U., Rensselaer Poly. Inst., Am. U., Claremont Coll., So. Meth. U., Pace U., Wayne State U., U. Oreg., U. Conn., St. John's U., Pepperdine U., Loyola Coll. of Md., San Francisco State U., U. Pitts., U. R.I., Marquette U., Vanderbilt U., Boston U., U. Cin., Gustavus Adolphus Coll., U. Mo., Mich. State U., Lehigh U., Calif. Inst. Tech., Denver U., George Washington U., Elmhurst Coll.; vis. fellow Wilton Pk. Conf., Eng., 1968 Author: The Art of M&A: A Merger/Aquisition/Buyout Guide, 1989, 3d edit., 1999, The Toxic Executive, 1993, The Art of M&A Deskbook, Dictionary and Casebook, 2000; founder, editor, pub.: Mergers and Acqusitions mag., 1965—, Dirs. and Bds. mag., 1976—; founder, editor, pub.: Campaigns and Elections mag., 1980; founder, pub. Global Bus. mag., 1985; contbr. articles to leading jours., chpts. to books; patentee. Bd. dirs. Nat. Patent Coun., 1970—; founder, chmn. ann Merger Week, Washington, 1973-77, Northwestern U., 1977-87; Entrepreneur-in-Residence, mem. adv. bd. Tate Ctr. Entrepreneurship, Coll. Charleston, S.C. Decorated officer Chef de Protocol, La Confrerie Chevaliers Tastevin. Mem. Soc. Naval Architects and Marine Engrs. (life), Am. Econ. Assn., Dictionary Soc. of N.Am., N.Y. Yacht Club. Home: 330 Concord St Apt 18G Charleston SC 29401-1511 E-mail: reeds@cofc.edu.

REED, STEPHEN RUSSELL, mayor; b. Chambersburg, Pa., Aug. 9, 1949; s. Galen Berkley Reed and Jane Louise. Student, Harrisburg Area C.C., Dickinson Coll. Rep. Pa. State House of Reps., 1974-80; commr. Dauphin Co., Pa., 1980-81; mayor/CEO City of Harrisburg, 1982—. Author 12 books and handbooks. Bd. dirs. numerous groups. Recipient Chapel of Four Chaplains award, 1998, Urban and Cmty. Forestry award, Pa. Forestry Assn., 1998, Disting. Leadership award, Pa. Planning Assn., 1999, Gov's. award Environ. Excellence, State Pa., Tree of Life award, Jewish Nat. Fund and numerous others. Office: City of Harrisburg 10 N 2nd St Rm 202 Harrisburg PA 17101-1683

REED, THOMAS LEE, II, minister, social worker, educator; b. Kansas City, Jan. 9, 1964; s. Thomas Lee and Kathleen E. (Green) R. BA in Preaching, Okla. Christian, 1986; BS in Edn., Mo. Southern State Coll., Joplin, 1994. Cert. elem. edn. Assoc. min Ch. of Christ, Nevada, Mo., 1986-89; music min. Plymouth, Ind., 1989; assoc. min. Nevada, Mo., 1990-98; clin. tchr. 3rd grade Mo. Sch. Dist., Joplin, 1992; practicum tchr. Early Childhood Devel. Ctr. MSSC, Mo., 1993; student tchr. 4th grade Web City (Mo.) Sch. Dist., 1994; social worker Pathways Comty. Behavioral Healthcare, El Dorado Springs, Mo., 1999—. Music dir. Ch. of Christ, Nevada, Mo., 1981—89, youth dir., Mo., 1990, youth min., Mo., 84, dir. religious edn., Mo., 1986—. Recipient Key Charitable Fund scholarship, 1993, Selected for Acad. fellowship Mo. So. State Coll., Oxford U., Eng., 1994. Mem.: Phi Eta Sigma. Mem. Churches of Christ. Avocations: music composition, writing, vocal performance, drawing, painting. E-mail: tomree@excite.com.

REED, THOMAS W. secondary education educator; b. San Jose, Calif., July 25, 1961; s. Marshall Walker and Joy Collette R.; m. Anna, Sept. 1, 1991; 1 child, Adam. BA in Phys. Edn., Calif. State U., 1986, MA in Edn., 1990. Long-term substitute tchr. Stateline (Nev.) Pvt. Sch., 1988; substitute tchr. Clovis (Calif.) Unified Sch. Dist., 1988-89, various sch. dists., Calif., 1989-90; 6th grade tchr. Sylvan Union Sch. Dist., Modesto, 1990-92; 7th grade tchr. Waterford (Calif.) Sch. Dist., 1992—. Coach football, 1992-99, basketball, 1992—; mentor tchr. 1997, 98; mem. negotiation team Calif. Mid. Sch. Phys. Edn. Workshop, Sacramento, 1996—, mentor leader, 1997, co-dir., 1999, mem. curriculum com., 2000—; instr., coord. Advancement Via Individual Determination. Mem. Cyclists Across U.S.A., 1987; CPR instr. Meml. Hosp., Modesto, 1998—; speech coord., scholarship chair Waterford Lions Club; vol. Habitat for Humanity. Mem. Calif. Assn. Health, Phys. Edn. & Dance (pub. rels. chair), Am. Alliance Health, Phys. Edn. & Dance, Nat. Ski Patrol (first aid instr.). Avocations: reading, skiing, family time. Home: 1524 W Roseburg Ave Modesto CA 95350-4859 Office: Waterford Unified Sch Dist 12916 Bentley St Waterford CA 95386-9017

REED, TONY NORMAN, aviation company executive; b. Odessa, Tex., Apr. 12, 1951; s. Norman W. and Naoma N. (Johnson) R.; 3 children. Pres. Trinity Aviation, Trinity Communication, Tyler, Tex., 1986-90; v.p. internat. mktg. Cardinal Aerospace, Inc., Independence, Mo., 1990-92; v.p. comml. programs Multinat. Enterprises, Inc., N.Y.C., 1992-93; internat. sales profl. Puritan-Bennett Aero Systems, Inc., Lenexa, Kans., 1993-98; dir. sales B/E Aerospace, 1998—. Bd. dirs. Missionary Aviation Svcs., Tyler. Mem. Aircraft Owners and Pilots Assn. Home: PO Box 1085 Blue Springs MO 64013-1085

REED, TRAVIS DEAN, public relations executive; b. Trinity, Tex., Sept. 27, 1930; s. Travis and Alma (Rains) R.; m. Caroline M. McDonald, June 15, 1957; children: Anne Reed Adams, Lisa Reed Lettau. Student, Tex. A&M U., 1948-51, U. Houston, 1951-53. Reporter Houston Post, 1951-53; Washington Bur. corr. McGraw-Hill Pub. Co., 1955-61, Boston Herald-Traveler, 1961-62; with Newhouse News Svc., Washington, 1962-79, chief corr., 1964-67, editor, 1967-79; pub. rels. cons., 1979—. 1st lt. U.S. Army, 1953-55. Mem. Nat. Press Club, Federal City Club, Gridiron Club, Army and Navy Club. Home: 37277 Branchriver Rd Purcellville VA 20132-1922 Office: T Dean Reed Co Madison Office Bldg 1155 15th St NW Ste 1003 Washington DC 20005-2706

REED, VANESSA REGINA, secondary education educator; b. Grenada, Miss., Oct. 4, 1965; d. Willie Mann and Elma Lee (Finley) R. BS in Social Sci. Edn., Miss. Valley State U., 1987; MA in History, Jackson State U., 1988; postgrad., Miss. State U., Meridian, 1991, 92. Cert. tchr. social sci. History tchr. Jackson (Miss.) State U., 1987-88; social studies tchr. Magnolia Mid. Sch., Meridian, 1988-93; U.S. history tchr. Kate Griffin Jr. H.S., 1993—. Sunday sch. tchr., dir. children's ch. Mt. Olive Bapt. Ch.; mem. Heroines of Jericho; chmn. Bridge Builders Ministry; mem. adv. bd. Freedom Rock Christian Fellowship Ch. Mem. Am. Fedn. Tchrs., Sigma Gamma Rho. Democrat. Avocations: traveling, geneology, reading. Office: Kate Griffin Jr HS 2814 Davis St Meridian MS 39301-5655

REED, VASTINA KATHRYN (TINA REED), child and adolescent psychotherapist, family development specialist; b. Chgo., Mar. 5, 1960; d. Alvin Hillard and Ruth Gwendolyn (Thomas) R.; 1 child, Alvin J. *Son Alvin Joseph is an Eagle Scout, and featured in Who's Who Among American High School Students 1996-97, 97-98, 98-99, 99-2000.Alvin is studying to become a Microsoft certified Systems engineer at Chicago's Computer Training Labs. He graduated with honorary Medal in Computer Science from Holy Trinity High School, year 2000. He became certified as an A+ computer professional from Comp TIA, Feb. 2002. Sister Delores Reed-Smith is a speech therapist with the Chicago Board of Education. Mother Ruth is retired from Carson Pirie Scott.* BA in Human Svcs. magna cum laude, Nat.-Louis U., Chgo., 1988; MA, Ill. Sch. Profl. Psychology, 1991; tng. cert., Applebaum Inst. Child Devel. First aid/CPR cert., ARC; cert. family devel. specialist. Tchr. early childhood edn. Kendall Coll. Lab. Sch., Evanston, Ill., 1983-85, Rogers Park Children's Learning Ctr., Chgo., 1983-85; child life therapist Mt. Sinai Hosp., 1988; child psychotherapist Nicholas Barnes Therapeutic Day Sch., 1989-90; presch. instr. YMCA, 1999-2000; crisis line counselor Washington Security Corp., 2000—02; family support specialist Maywood Head Start, 2000—; health care rep. Care Entrée, 2002—. Den leader Boy Scouts Am., Chgo., 1989-92, scoutmaster, 1992-2000, merit badge counselor, 1999—, troop advisor for Order of the Arrow; vision ptnr., co-labourers Christ Ministry; mem. Christ Outreach Deliverance Ctr. Ministry, 2001—. Recipient Cub Scouter award Boy Scouts Am., 1990, Scoutmaster award of merit, 1993, 94, Scouters Vet. award, 1994, Scouters Tng. award, 1995, Scoutmasters Key award, 1996, Okpik Cold Weather Camping cert., 1994-95, Outstanding Women of 20th Century medal, 2000, Boy Scout Woodbadge Tng. award, 2001. Mem. APA, Nat. Orgn. for Human Svc. Edn., Order of the Arrow, Ea. Stars (Hon. Lady status 1999—), Charles F. Menninger Soc. (patron), Phi Theta Kappa, Kappa Delta Pi. Democrat. Roman Catholic. Avocations: camping, cruising, classic movies, performing in ministry's ensemble. Home: 1872 S Millard Ave Chicago IL 60623-2542

REED, W. FRANKLIN, lawyer; b. Louisville, Dec. 30, 1946; s. William Ferguson and Stella Elizabeth (Richardson) R.; m. Sharon Ann Coss, June 16, 1973; children: Jonathan Franklin, William Brian, Carrie Ann. BA, Williams Coll., 1968; JD, Columbia U., 1971. Bar: N.Y. 1972, U.S. Dist. Ct. (so. dist.) N.Y. 1975, U.S. Ct. Appeals (2d cir.) 1975, Pa. 1982, U.S. Dist. Ct. (we. dist.) 1983. Assoc. Milbank, Tweed, Hadley & McCloy, N.Y.C., 1971-82, Reed Smith Shaw & McClay, Pitts., 1982-83; ptnr. Reed, Smith, Shaw & McClay, 1984—. With Instnl. Devel. Com., The Pitts. Cultural Trust. Mem. ABA, Pa. Bar Assn., Allegheny Bar Assn., Carnegie 100, Williams Coll. Alumni Soc. W.

Pa. (sec. 1983—), Rivers Club (Pitts.), St. Clair Country Club (Upper St. Clair, Pa.), Duquesne Club (Pitts.), Phi Beta Kappa. Democrat. Presbyterian. Avocations: fishing, golf. Home: 525 Miranda Dr Pittsburgh PA 15241-2039 Office: Reed Smith LLP 435 6th Ave Pittsburgh PA 15219-1886 E-mail: wreed@reedsmith.com.

REED, WALLACE ALLISON, anesthesiologist; b. Covina, Calif., May 19, 1916; s. Wallace Allison and Mary Julia (Birdsall) Reed; m. Maria Eva Wiemers, Jan. 20, 1938; children: Ellen E., Barbara R., Wallace J., Michael E., Kathryn L., Vikki T. AB, UCLA, Los Angeles, 1937; postgrad., U. Cologne, 1937-38; U. Freiburg, Breisgau, 1938-39; MD, U. So. Calif., 1944. Diplomate Am. Bd. Anesthesiology. Intern Santa Fe Coast Lines Hosp., Los Angeles, 1943-44; resident Los Angeles County Gen. Hosp., 1946-47, asst. to head dept. anesthesiology, 1946-47; clin. instr. surgery U. So. Calif. Sch. Medicine, 1946-47; practice medicine, specializing in anesthesiology Phoenix, 1948-89. Hon. staff mem. Good Samaritan Hosp., St. Joseph Hosp., Maricopa County Gen. Hosp.; mem. hon. staff Children's Hosp.; co-founder John L. Ford, M.D., Surgicenter, 1970; vice pres. Maricopa Found. for Med. Care, 1970-74, pres., 1975-76; mem. House Ways and Means Adv. Com.; adv. coun. Nat. Health Inst., 1975-76; mem. accreditation coun. for ambulatory health care Joint Commn. on Accreditation of Hosps., 1975-79; vice-chmn. Accreditation Assn. for Ambulatory Health Care, 1979-81, pres., 1981-83; mem. panel for study Nat. Health Ins., Congl. GAO; chmn. bd. Alterna Care Corp., 1984-87, now chmn. bd. emeritus; mem. adv. bd. Kino Inst., 1994-95. Bd. dirs. South Phoenix Montessori Sch., pres. bd., 1971-75, Alzheimer's Assn., Greater Phoenix chpt. 1998-2000, co-v.p. 2000; bd. dirs. Ctrl. Ariz. Health Sys. Agy., 1975-78; exec. dir. Surgictr. of Phoenix, 1987-97. Capt. M.C., AUS, 1944-46. Recipient Pinal award Ariz. Psychiat. Soc., 1967-68, Gerard B. Lambert Merit award for innovative ideas that improve patient care; John L. Ford M.D., 1972; recipient spirit of philanthropy award Alzheimer's Assn., 1996, Samba Disting. Svc. award, 2000. Fellow: Am. Coll. Anesthesiologists; mem.: AMA, Soc. for Advancement Geriatric Anesthesia (charter mem.), Guedel Assn. (pres. 1972), Am. Assn. Founds. for Med. Care (dir. 1970—74), Central Ariz. Physicians Svc. Assn. (pres. 1982—83), Maricopa County Med. Soc. (pres. 1964, dir., Salsbury medal 1967, 1971, Thomas Dooley medal 1970), Internat. Assn. Amb. Surgery (hon.), Soc. for Ambulatory Anesthesia (bd. dirs. 1985—87), Federated Amb. Surgery Assn. (pres. 1974—75, dir.), Acad. Anesthesiology (dir. 1966—72, pres. 1969), Ariz., Maricopa County Socs. Anesthesiologists, Am. Soc. Anesthesiologists, WarMer Rsch. Found., Seed Money for Growth Found. (pres. 1984—). Methodist. Home: 4716 N Dromedary Rd Phoenix AZ 85018-2939 Office: 1040 E Mcdowell Rd Phoenix AZ 85006-2622 E-mail: somnus4@cox.net.

REED, WALTER GEORGE, JR. osteopathic physician; b. Ardmore, Okla., Sept. 10, 1928; s. Walter George and Lillian Dorene (Gee) Reed; children: Jay Walter, David George, Kimberly Sue. BA, Phillips U., 1955; DO, Kansas City Coll. Osteopathy, 1959. Intern Des Moines Gen. Hosp., 1959—60; pvt. practice Oklahoma City, 1960-63, Atoka, 1963-80; flight surgeon USAF, Omaha, 1980-84, Lubbock, Tex., 1984-86; chief med. officer Army Health Clinic, McAlester, Okla., 1986-96; ret. USAF, 1996. Mayor City of Atoka, 1970s; v.p. Atoka Bd. Edn., 1970. Lt. col. USAF, 1980—86. Mem.: Assn. Mil. Surgeons U.S., Air Force Assn. (life), Okla. Osteo. Assn. (life), Assn. Mil. Osteo. Physicians and Surgeons (life; life), Ret. Officers Assn. (life; life), Masons (32d degree). Avocation: Avocations: flying, hunting, computers, auto mechanics, plate collecting. Home: 9921 N 110th East Ave Owasso OK 74055-4358 Address: PO Box 119 Owasso OK 74055-0119 Office: Slim Care Owasso OK 74055 also: Slim Care Tulsa OK 74135

REED, WILLIAM EDWARD, government official, educator; b. Columbia, La., July 15, 1914; s. William Reed and Virginia (Barnes) R.; m. Mattye Marie Scott, Aug. 27, 1942; children: Edwarda Marie (Mrs. Lucien L. Johnson), Carol Ann, Beverlyn Bernetiae. BS, So. U., 1937; MS, Iowa State U., 1941; PhD, Cornell U., 1946. County agrl. agt. Agr. and Home Econs. Extension Service, La. State U., 1937-41; lectr. soil sci. and chemistry So. U., 1942-47; agrl. research specialist U.S. Econ. Mission to Liberia, 1947-49; dean agr. Agrl. and Tech. Coll. N.C., 1949-61; mem. U.S. del. Russia; rep. ICA in Togo, 1961; asst. dir. AID Mission to Nigeria, 1961-68; mem. U.S. del. to UN Conf. on Application Sci. and Tech., 1963; dep. dir. AID Mission to Ethiopia, 1968-72; fgn. service officer in residence N.C. A. & T. State U., Greensboro, 1972-74, spl. asst. to chancellor for internat. programs, 1974-76, asso. dean research and spl. projects, 1976-78, dir. internat. programs, 1978-84; cons. in field, 1984—. State rep. Sisters Cities Internat. Mem. Nat. Planning Assn., Am. Fgn. Svc. Assn., Sigma Xi, Phi Kappa Phi, Beta Kappa Chi, Sigma Pi Phi, Gamma Sigma Delta, Beta Epsilon (trustee Boulé Found. 1964—). Episcopalian. Home: 2711 Mcconnell Rd Greensboro NC 27401-4534

REED, WILLIAM GERALD, consulting firm executive; b. Abington Twp, Pa., Feb. 25, 1941; s. Frank Hibbs and Evelyn Hower; m. Joan Derby, Jul. 16, 1966; children: Kris, Michael. BSME, Pa. State Univ., 1963, MSME, 1964. Profl. engr. Supr. United Tech., Windsor Locks, Conn., 1964-70; gen. mgr. Gen. Elec. Co., Schenectady, N.Y., 1970-85; sr. v.p., gen. mgr. Impell Corp., Berkeley, Calif., 1985; pres. Reed Ventures, Inc., Danville, 1985—. Dir. Barrier Systems, Inc., Carson City, Nev., 1986—; dir. Reed Ventures, Inc. Danville, Calif., 1985—, Thermal Technologies, Inc., Cambridge, Mass., 1986—, Hemedex Inc., Cambridge, Mass., 2000—. Inventor in field. Recipient Spl. CEO award Gen. Elec. Co., 1984. Avocations: basketball, gardening, photography. Office: Reed Ventures Inc 935 Blemer Rd Danville CA 94526-1501

REEDER, CLINTON BRUCE, economist, public policy consultant, farmer; b. Pendleton, Oreg., Apr. 22, 1939; s. O. Howard and Rachel B. (Porter) R.; n. Karen J. Durham, June 19, 1960; childre: Jeffrey T., Lori J., Paul D. BS, Oreg. State U., 1961, MS, 1963; PhD, Purdue U., 1966; postgrad., U. Oreg. Instr. agrl. econs. Purdue U., West Lafayette, 1963-66; contract mgmt. trainer Nat. Food Mfg. Corp., 1972-78; farmer Pendleton, Oreg., 1978—; mgmt. cons., 1968—; mktg. economist, bus. mgmt. specialist Dept. Agrl., Econs. & Extension Svc, Oreg. State U., Corvallis, 1966-78; econ. & pub. policy cons. Clinton B. Reeder & Assocs., 1968—; dir. Northwest Wheat Policy Project, 1992—, WestFork Natural Resources Rsch. Ctr., 1995—. Ombudsman Oreg. Agrl. Water Quality Mgmt. Program, 2000. Recipient Disting. Svc. award Oreg. Wheat Growers League, 1998, County Points of Light award Nat. Assn. Counties, 1992, Voice of Industry award, 1989, OFS Unity award, 1988; inducted into Hall of Fame, Coll. Agr., Oreg. State U., 1998. Republican. Avocations: reading, public service, writing, research. Home and Office: 47647 Reeder Rd Pendleton OR 97801-9226

REEDER, EDWARD CAMERON, association executive, clergyman; b. Beaufort, S.C., June 22, 1961; s. Edward Clayton, Jr. and Virgie Leola Reeder; m. Sherry Hicks Reeder, Dec. 5, 1986; children: Christian Till, Phoenix Hope. BA, Auburn U. Montgomery, Ala., 1989. Lic. minister Assemblies of God, 1992. Staff writer The Montgomery Advertiser, Ala., 1989—91; adminstrv. asst. Canaanland Boys Home, 1991—93; pub. info. specialist Ala. Bur. Tourism and Travel, Montgomery, 1993—2000; exec. dir. North Ala. Tourism Assn., Mooresville, 2000—. Mem.: Pub. Rels. Coun. Ala., Soc. of Am. Travel Writers (assoc.). Republican. Avocations: all sports, music, reading, living history, travel. Office: North Alabama Tourism Assn 25062 North St Mooresville AL 35649-1075 E-mail: info@almtlakes.org.

REEDER, F. ROBERT, lawyer; b. Brigham City, Utah, Jan. 23, 1943; s. Frank O. and Helen H. (Heninger) R.; m. Joannie Anderson, May 4, 1974; children: David, Kristina, Adam. JD, U. Utah, 1967. Bar: Utah 1967, U.S. Ct. Appeals (10th cir.) 1967, U.S. Ct. Appeals (D.C. and 5th cirs.) 1979, U.S. Ct. Mil. Appeals 1968, U.S. Supreme Ct. 1972. Shareholder Parsons, Behle & Latimer, Salt Lake City, 1968—. Bd. dirs. Holy Cross Found., 1981-90, chmn., 1987-90; bd. dirs. Holy Cross Hosp., 1990-93, treas., 1986-87, vice chmn., 1987-93; bd. dirs. Holy Cross Health Svcs. Utah, 1993-94, treas., 1993-94; bd. dirs. Sale Lake Regional Med. Ctr., 1995—, vice chmn., 1995-2000, chmn., 2000—; trustee Univ. Hosp. Found.; hon. col. Salt Lake City Police, Salt Lake County Sheriff. Served with USAR, 1967-73. Mem. ABA, Utah State Bar, Salt Lake County Bar (ethics adv. com. 1989-94), Cottonwood Country Club (bd. dirs. 1978-82, 83-86, pres. 1981-82), Rotary. Office: Parsons Behle & Latimer PO Box 45898 Salt Lake City UT 84145-0898

REEDER, JAMES ARTHUR, lawyer; b. Baton Rouge, June 29, 1933; s. James Brown and Grace (Britt) R.; m. Mary Leone Guthrie, Dec. 30, 1958; children: Mary Virginia, James Jr., Elizabeth Colby. BA, Washington and Lee U., Lexington, Va., 1955; LLB, U. Tex., 1960; JD, La. State U., 1961. Ptnr. Booth, Lockard, Jack et al, Shreveport, La., 1961-72; pres. and mgng. ptnr. Shreveport Broadcasting Co., 1972-86; CEO, mng. gen. ptnr. Radio USA Limited, Houston, 1986-89; pres. SW subsidiaries Sun Group, Inc., 1990-92; atty. Patton & Boggs, LLP, Washington, 1991-94; ptnr. Patton, Boggs LLP, 1994—. Dir. ABC Radio Sta. Affiliates adv. bd., N.Y.C., 1978-84. Dir. Boys Country, Houston, 1986-90; pres. Holiday in Dixie, Shreveport, 1968; chmn. Ambassadors Club, Shreveport, 1979. 1st Lt. U.S. Army, 1955-57. Named La. Outstanding Young Man, La. Jaycees, 1969. Mem. ABA (bd. dirs. young lawyers sect. 1967-68, Gavel awards com. 1980), La. Bar Assn. (pres. young lawyers sect. 1966, La. Outstanding Young Lawyer award 1968), D.C. Bar Assn., Tex. Bar Assn., Nat. Assn. Broadcasters, Houston Country Club, Allegro Club (Houston). Roman Catholic.

REEDER, OLIVER HOWARD, paint products manufacturing executive; b. Balt., Sept. 19, 1916; s. Charles Howard and Nannie Dryden (Kensett) R.; m. Nancy Hardcastle Fisher, Apr. 18, 1942; children: Nancy Fisher, Ellen Dryden. AB, Princeton U., 1939. With Balt. Copper Paint Co., Balt., 1939—, tech. dir., treas., 1939-47, pres., 1947—, chmn., 1959—; v.p. Balt. Copper Paint div. Glidden-Durkee Div. SCM Corp., 1969—; pres. Jotun-Balt. Copper Paint Co., Inc., 1974-76, v.p., 1976-81. Pres. Hosp. for Consumptives of Md., 1968-84, trustee, 1951-95, trustee emeritus, 1995—; trustee Gilman Sch., Balt., 1948-65, Walters Art Gallery, 1978-83, U.S. Frigate Constellation Found., 1976-89; trustee Johns Hopkins Hosp., 1957-87, trustee emeritus, 1987—, vice chmn. bd., 1986-87; trustee Md. Hosp. Laundry, 1970-89, pres., 1975-84. Fellow Am. Inst. Chemists; mem. Am. Chem. Soc., Soc. Naval Architects and Marine Engrs., Phi Beta Kappa, Sigma Xi. Home: 1300 Dulaney Valley Rd Baltimore MD 21286-1308

REEDER, ROBERT HARRY, retired lawyer; b. Topeka, Dec. 3, 1930; s. William Harry and Florence Mae (Cochran) R. AB Washburn U., 1952, JD, 1960. Bar: U.S. Dist. Ct. Kans. 1960, Kans. 1960, U.S. Supreme Ct. 1968. Rsch. asst. Kans. Legis. Council Rsch. Dept., Topeka, 1955-60; asst. counsel Traffic Inst., Northwestern U., Evanston, Ill., 1960-67, gen. counsel, 1967-92; exec. dir. Nat. Com. on Uniform Traffic Laws and Ordinances, Evanston, 1982-90. Co-author: Vehicle Traffic Law, 1974; The Evidence Handbook, 1980. Author: Interpretation of Implied Consent by the Courts, 1972. Served with U.S. Army, 1952-54. Mem. Com. Alcohol and Other Drugs (chmn. 1973-75). Republican. Methodist.

REEDER, THOMAS ALLEN, television writer; b. L.A., Oct. 15, 1946; s. Orlenzo Chester and Alice Elizabeth (Hendershot) R.; m. Sally Stephens, Apr. 25, 1969; children: Jennifer, Brian Thomas. AA, San Bernardino Valley Coll., 1966; BA, U. So. Calif., 1969. Writer Barney Miller ABC, Hollywood, Calif., 1975-79, producer Benson, 1979-80; writer M*A*S*H CBS, 1978; writer Cheers NBC, 1982-90, creative cons. Night Court, 1983-84, exec. script cons. Night Court, 1986-89, exec. script cons. Nurses, 1992-94; creative cons. Dave's World, CBS, 1995-97; exec. cons. Grace Under Fire, ABC, 1997-98; cons. prodr. Cosby, CBS-TV, 1998-2000; creative con. Frasier NBC-TV, 2000—. Coach YMCA Basketball, North Hollywood, Calif., 1983; mgr. Little League Baseball, Sherman Oaks, Calif., 1986-87. Mem. Acad. TV Arts & Scis. Mem. Christian Ch. Avocation: travel.

REED-GRAHAM, LOIS L. administrator, secondary education educator; b. Muscogee, Okla., Jan. 19, 1933; d. Louis G. and Bonnie (Hill) Reed; children: Harold Gibson, Kathryn Ann Graham. RN, San Diego County Hosp., 1957; BA, Calif. State U., Sacramento, 1972, MPA, 1978; postgrad., Calif. State U., Sacremento; EdD, U. Laverne. Tchr., adminstr., job developer CETA, Sacramento, 1972-78; bus. instr. Los Rios Community Coll., 1978-84; tchr. grade 6 Mark Hopkins Sch., 1984-89; acting adminstr. Fern Bacon Sch.; adminstr. Sacramento City Schs.; tchr. grades 7,8, mentor tchr. Fern Bacon Sch., Sacramento; asst. prin. secondary edn. Sacramento City Schs., 1989-93; elem. sch. prin. Theodore Judah Elem. Sch., Sacramento, 1993—; asst. supt. secondary, middle and K-8 schs. Sacramento City Unified Sch.; prin. Hubert Bancroft Elem. Sch., Sacramento. Cons. Prentice Hall Pub. Co. Contbr. articles to profl. publs. Mem. Calif. State Fair Employment and Housing Commn. Mem. AAUW (bd. dirs., pres. Sacramento chpt. 1990), Nat. Assn. Univ. Women (pres.) Home: 7408 Toulon Ln Sacramento CA 95828-4641

REEDY, EDWARD K. academic administrator; Dir. rsch. ops. Ga. Tech. Rsch. Inst., Atlanta, 1993—97, 1997—. Office: Ga Tech Rsch Inst Centennial Rsch Bldg 212 Atlanta GA 30332-0801

REEDY, HARRY LEE, financial services executive; b. Lebanon, Pa., Dec. 25, 1945; s. Harry Lee and Charlotte (Weedmark) R.; m. Linda Bartley, Nov. 7, 1970; children: Jennifer Beth, Sara Emily. BS in Indsl Engring., Pa. State U., 1967; MBA, U. Conn., 1977. Mgmt. asst. Bell Telephone Pa., Phila., 1967-70; field engring. rep. Travelers Cos., Hartford, Conn., 1971-72, ops. analyst, 1972-76, supervising ops. analyst, 1976-79, sr. mgmt. cons., 1979-83, adminstr. consumer affairs, 1983-85, asst. dir. consumer affairs, 1985-90; dir. corp. customer svc. John Hancock Fin. Svcs., Boston, 1990-91, dir. Ctr. for Quality, 1991-96; asst. v.p. quality State St. Corp., North Quincy, Mass., 1997-98, v.p., dir. quality, 1998—. Mem. consumer affairs com. Ins. Info. Inst., N.Y.C., 1988-90. Contbr. articles to trade publs. Participant Leadership Greater Hartford, 1985; bd. dirs., treas. Woodland Manor Condominium Assn., Manchester, Conn., 1986-87; bd. mgrs. Auburn Ct. Condominimum Assn., 2001—; bd. examiners Malcolm Baldridge Nat. Quality award, 1995-2000, sr. examiner, 1997-2000, panel of judges, 2002—; sr. examiner Mass. State Quality award, 1995-99, judge, 1999, New Hampshire Quality Award, 2002. With U.S. Army, 1968-70. Fellow Ins. Consumer Affairs Exch. (treas. 1985-87, v.p. 1987-88, pres. 1988-90), Soc. Consumer Affairs Profls. (v.p. New Eng. chpt. 1991-92); mem. Am. Coun. Life Ins. (consumer affairs com. 1987), Am. Soc. Quality Control, Am. productivity & Quality Ctr., Internat. Benchmarking Clearing House, Strategic Planning Inst., Mass. Coun. Quality (bd. dirs. 1998—, treas. exec. com. 1999—), Benchmarking Coun., Assn. Quality and Participation, Beta Gamma Sigma. Democrat. Avocations: photography, racquetball, swimming, reading. Home: 3 Auburn Ct # 2 Brookline MA 02446-6302 E-mail: hlreedy@statestreet.com.

REEDY, NANCY SUE, elementary school educator; b. Fort Riley, Kans., Sept. 22, 1963; d. David Boothe Cox, Judith Kay Cox; m. Darrell Lee Reedy, Dec. 20, 1986; children: Nathan, Kyle, Jordan. BS, Pensacola Christian Coll., 1985. Cert. cert. tchr. Tchr. elem. Lowndes Christian Acad., Valdosta, Ga., 1985—87, tchr. kindergarten, supr., 1987—88; tchr. elem. Canyon Creek Christian Acad., Richardson, Tex., 1993—2000, tchr. elem., supr., 2000—. Baptist. Home: 10700 Castle Dr Frisco TX 75035

REEDY-DEWEY, MADELINE ANNE, retired occupational therapist; b. Milw., Jan. 25, 1954; d. Samuel Smith and Louise Rita (Thomas) Reedy; m. Craig D. Dewey, Sept. 28, 1989. BS in Occupl. Therapy, U. Wis., Milw., 1978. Registered occupl. therapist, Wis. Dir. occupl. therapy Hillhaven, Shorewood, Wis., 1978-83, Colonial Manor, Glendale, 1983-85; Saturday/on-call occupl. therapist Northwest Gen. Hosp., Milw., 1981-84; chief occupl. therapist Silver Spring Convalescent Ctr., Glendale, 1985-86; dir. occupl. therapy Colonia Manor, 1986-91; rehab. clin. cons. Therapy Mgmt. Inc. Facilities, various locations, 1991-92; cons./instr. in edn. program W.H. Carter, Inc., Milw., 1994-95; instr. med. terminology and anatomy/physiology Concordia U., Mequon, 1996; ret., 1996; bd. dirs. Toner Tech Cartridge Services Inc., Panama City, Fla., 1996—. Clin. supr. occupl. therapy program U. Wis.-Milw., Milw. Area Tech. Coll., 1978-83; instr. U. Wis., Milw., 1978-83. Vol. Gulf Coast Cmty. Hosp., Panama City, Fla., 1985, St. Michael's Hosp., Milw., 1994, St. Francis Children's Ctr., Milw., 1996, Humane Soc. Bay County, Fla., 2000-01, Vocat. Rehab., Panama City, 2001. Mem. Am. Occupl. Therapy Assn., Wis. Occupl. Therapy Assn. Roman Catholic. Avocations: volunteer work, gardening, cooking. Home: 314 Massalina Dr Panama City FL 32401 E-mail: cdeweybc@att.net.

REEF, ARTHUR, industry business consultant; b. N.Y.C., Sept. 21, 1916; s. Herman and Eva (Van Panich) R.; m. Betty Olsen, Aug. 1995; children from previous marriage: Jennifer, Nancy. BA, CCNY, 1937; postgrad., U. Pa., 1937-38, Am. U., 1941-42, Sorbonne, U. Paris, 1949. With Ruder & Finn Internat., N.Y.C., 1955-57, Barnet & Reef, N.Y.C., 1957-64, AMAX, Inc., Greenwich, Conn., 1964-81, sr. v.p. and dir. office communications and pub. affairs, sr. cons. to exec. office Greenwich and N.Y.C., 1981-87. Dir. AMAX Australia Ltd.; trustee, chmn. U.S. com. Internat. Inst. Communications, 1979-81; bd. mem. World Environ. Ctr. N.Y., 1974-79, Ctr. for the Study of the Presidency; trustee Am. Coun. of Young Polit. Leaders; councillor Am.-Australian Bi-Centennial Commn. Fellow Inst. Mining and Metallurgy London, Acad. Internat. Bus.; mem. French Am. C. of C. (former councillor), Chaine des Rotisseurs (chevalier), Am. Food and Wine Inst., Fgn. Policy Assn. (assoc.), Overseas Press Club Am. (chmn. fgn. journalism com. 1958-63). Home: 2000 S Ocean Blvd Apt 608 Delray Beach FL 33483-6490

REEF, GRACE, government official; b. Portland, Maine; m. Don Green, Nov. 9, 1991; children: Megan, Jamie, Ryan. BA, Colby Coll., 1984. Legis. asst. Sen. George Mitchell U.S. Senate, Washington, 1984-94, legis. asst. Sen. Tom Daschle, 1995-97; dir. intergovt. affairs Children's Def. Fund, 1997-2001; subcom. staff dir. children and families Office of Senater Chris Dodd, 2001—. Office: Office of Senator Chris Dodd 448 Russell Bldg Washington DC 20510 E-mail: grace-reef@laser.senate.gov.

REEG, KURTIS BRADFORD, lawyer; b. St. Louis, Sept. 1, 1954; s. Jay Flory and Mary Louise (Braun) R.; m. Cynthia Diane Wable, June 25, 1994. BA cum laude, DePauw U., 1976; JD, St. Louis U., 1979. Bar: U.S. Dist. Ct. (ea. dist.) Mo. 1979, U.S. Dist. Ct. (so. dist.) Ill. 1981, U.S. Ct. Appeals (8th cir.) 1984, U.S. Ct. Appeals (7th cir.) 1986, U.S. Dist. Ct. Ariz. 1994, U.S. Ct. Appeals (2d cir.) 1994, U.S. Supreme Ct. 1994. Law clk. to presiding justice Ill. Appellate Ct. (5th dist.), Granite City, 1979-80; assoc. Coburn, Croft & Putzell, St. Louis, Mo. and Belleville, Ill., 1980-86, ptnr., 1986-91; ptnr., chmn. tort and ins. group, co-chmn. litigation dept. Gallop, Johnson & Neuman, L.C., St. Louis, 1991-98, mem. mgmt. com., 1991-98, mng. ptnr. Belleville, 1997-98; ptnr. Sonnenschein Nath & Rosenthal, St. Louis, 1998-2000, Kohn, Shands, Elbert, Gianoulakis & Giljum, LLP, St. Louis, 2001—02, Leritz, Plunkert & Bruning, P.C., St. Louis, 2002—. Nat. chmn. Products Liability Group; chmn. St. Louis Tort and Ins. Grp., instr. legal rsch. and writing St. Louis U., 1979-80. Mem. Police, Fire Commns., City of Town and Country, Mo., 1987-89; Rep. committeeman 24th ward, St. Louis, 1980. Mem. ABA, Ill. State Bar Assn., Mo. Bar Assn., Bar Assn. of Met. St. Louis, Internat. Assn. Def. Counsel, Mo. Orgn. of Defense Counsel, Fedn. Defense and Corp. Counsel, Def. Rsch. Inst., Midwest Environ. Claims Assn., Phi Alpha Delta, Pi Sigma Alpha. Republican. Avocations: hunting, fishing, golf, astronomy. also: 12720 Willowyck Dr Saint Louis MO 63146-3726 Office: Leritz Plunkert & Bruning PC 1 City Centre Ste 2001 Saint Louis MO 63101 E-mail: kreeg@leritzlaw.com.

REEL, DAVID MARK, museum curator, art historian; b. Pitts., Nov. 21, 1969; m. Stephanie L. Wolf. BA, Dickinson Coll., 1992; M in Arts Adminstrn., NYU, 1994. Rsch. specialist Pa. State Capitol Preservation Com., Harrisburg, 1991; cons. Sotheby's Auction Ho., N.Y.C., 1992; asst. curator, adminstr. Forbes Mag. Collection Forbes, Inc., 1993-98; mus. curator West Point (N.Y.) Mus. U.S. Mil. Acad., 1998—. Author: Guide to PA State Capitol, 1991, A Guide to Quarters 100, 1999 (Gold medallion, 1999); contbg. author: West Point/Points West, 2002. Bd. dirs. art alumni adv. coun. NYU, 1994—; trustee Friends Hermitage, Inc., Ho-Ho-Kus, NJ, 1997—2001. Sr. scholar Victorian Soc., 1996; named among People to Watch Times Herald Record, 2001. Mem. Am. Assn. Mus. (mem. curators com.), Nat. Assn. Corp. Art Curators, Army Mus. Assn., Am. Assn. State and Local History, Nat. Trust Historic Preservation. Office: West Point Mus Bldg 2110 US Mil Acad West Point NY 10996

REEMS, ERNESTINE C. minister; b. Oklamugee, Okla., July 07; d. Elmer E. and Matilda Cleveland; m. Paul E. Reems, June 14; children: Brandon, Brian. Hon. degree, Trinity Coll. Founder, evangelist Ernestine Reems Ministries, Oakland, Calif.; founder, sr. pastor Ctr. of Hope Cmty. Ch.; founder Ernestine C. Reems Internat. Ministries. CEO Lee Cleveland Manor, Hope Housing Devel., Oakland, Lee Reems Garden Hope Housing Devel., Oakland, Matilda Cleveland Hope Housing Devel. Transitional Housing, Oakland. Author: In the Storm, 1994; co-author: Fine Gold, 1999. Trustee Oral Roberts U., Tulsa. Named one of 15 Outstanding Women Preachers, Ebony mag., 1990's. Avocations: travel, reading, sports, cruises, social gatherings. Office: Ctr of Hope Cmty Ch 8411 Macarthur Blvd Oakland CA 94605-3553

REEN, TERRY PETER, social worker; b. Grand Rapids, Mich., Jan. 21, 1951; s. Peter and Frances (Boersma) R.; m. Joanne Martha Byloff, May 21, 1983; children: Peter Nicholas, Marc Forrest. AB, Hope Coll., 1973; MSW, Mich. State U., 1979. Cert. social worker, school social worker, Mich. Psychiatric aide Pine Rest Christian Hosp., Grand Rapids, 1973-79; activities dir. Birchwood Manor Nursing Home, Holland, Mich., 1976-77; sr. therapist Project Recovery, Kalamazoo, 1979-81; therapist Ennis and Assocs., Flint, Mich., 1981-83; outpatient therapist Ucer's Psychiatric Clinic, 1981-84, Oakland Psychol. Clinic, Flint, 1984—. Sch. social worker Birch Run (Mich.) Area Schs., 1984-85, Grand Blanc (Mich.) Area Schs., 1986—; instr. Mott C.C., Flint, 1989—; cons. Mott Middle Coll. High Sch., Flint, Our Community Cares, Grand Blanc, 1986-88; instr. Ea. Mich. U. Continuing Edn., Ypsilanti. Vol. probation officer, Ottawa County Probate Ct., Grand Haven, Mich., 1975-76; speaker, John Anderson for Pres. Campaign, Kalamazoo, 1979-80. Recipient scholarship, NIMH, Washington, 1977. Mem. NASW, Acad. Cert. Social Workers, Mich. Sch. Social Workers Assn. Presbyterian. Avocations: skiing, golf, tennis, racquetball, travel. Home: 2237 Rollins St Grand Blanc MI 48439-4352 Office: Grand Blanc Community Schs 11920 S Saginaw St Grand Blanc MI 48439-1402

REEP, EDWARD ARNOLD, artist; b. Bklyn., May 10, 1918; s. Joseph and Elsie (Abramson) R.; m. Karen Patricia Stevens, Dec. 9, 1942; children—Susan Kay, Cristine Elyse, Janine J., Mitchell Jules. Student, Art Center Coll. Design, 1936-41. Instr. painting and drawing Art Center Coll. Design, Los Angeles, 1946-50, Chouinard Art Inst., Los Angeles, 1950-69; prof. painting, chmn. dept., artist in residence E. Carolina U., 1970-85, prof. emeritus, 1985—. Cons. editor Van Nostrand Reinhold Pub. Co.; ofcl. war artist-corr. WWII, Africa and Italy. Author: The Content of Watercolor, 1968, A Combat Artist in World War II, 1987; shows include Whitney Mus. Am. Art Ann., N.Y.C., 1946-48, Los Angeles County Mus. Ann., 1946-60, Corcoran Gallery Art Biennial, Washington, 1949, Nat. Gallery Art, Washington, 1945, They Drew Fire, 2000, Mus. Modern Art, N.Y.C.; represented in permanent collections Los Angeles County Mus., U.S. War Dept., Grunwald Graphic Arts Collection, UCLA, Nat. Mus. Am. Art, Washington, Lytton Collection, Los Angeles, State of Calif. Collection, Sacramento. Guggenheim fellow, 1945-46; Nat. Endowment for Arts grantee, 1975 Mem. AAUP, Nat. Watercolor Soc. (past pres.), Watercolor USA Honor Soc. (lifetime achievement gold medal 1997). Democrat. Home: 9021 Crowningshield Dr Bakersfield CA 93311-1901 *I once was consumed by the desire to become an artist. I feel no differently today. There is work ahead. If I had set goals for myself I no longer can recall what they may have been; I go along painting as well or as inventively as I can. Never have I sacrificed living life as I feel I must for my art. My work is a reflection of my life— experiences real and imagined.*

REEP, ROBERT GREGG, mayor; b. Warren, Ark., June 17, 1954; s. Robert Ellis and Eloise (Galloway) R.; m. Beverly A. Holloway; 1 child, Robert Gregg, Jr. BA in Polit. Sci., U. Ark., Monticello, 1976. Dir. cmty. devel. City of Warren, 1975-86, mayor, 1987—. Mem. bd. dirs. YMCA. Mem. Lions. Home: 409 N Walnut St Warren AR 71671-2130 E-mail: greep@seark.net.

REES, CHARLES H. G. retired finance company executive, investor, consultant; b. Trenton, N.J., Mar. 6, 1922; s. Albert H. and Helen (Gallagher) R.; m. Nancy Thomas, Oct. 30, 1954; children: Liberty, Camilla, Nancy, Hilleary. BA, Princeton U., 1948. Salesman John A. Roebling's Sons Co., Trenton, 1948-50; staff officer CIA, Washington, 1951-54; assoc. J.H. Whitney & Co., N.Y.C., 1954-59; gen. ptnr. Whitcom Investment Co., 1967-85; with Whitney Comm. Corp., 1960-85, pres., 1982-85; ret., 1985. Trustee Riverside Rsch. Inst., N.Y.C. Capt. U.S. Army, 1942-46, 50-51. Capt. U.S. Army, 1942—46, capt. U.S. Army, 1950—51. Decorated Bronze Star. Mem. Brook Club, Pilgrims of N.Y.C., Ivy Club (Princeton, N.J.), Misquamicut Club, Watch Hill (R.I.), Union Club, Wadawanuck Yacht Club (Stonington). Republican. Home: 215 Farmholme Rd Stonington CT 06378-2205

REES, CLIFFORD HARCOURT, JR. (TED REES), association executive, retired air force officer; b. Newport News, Va., Dec. 11, 1936; s. Clifford Harcourt Sr. and Mary Evelyn (Brooks) R.; m. Joan Elizabeth Mittong, July

26, 1958; children— Clifford Harcourt III, Steven M., Daniel B., William B. BS in Fgn. Svc., Georgetown U., 1958; MS in Polit. Sci., Auburn U., 1969; grad., Air War Coll., Montgomery, Ala., 1978. Commd. 2d lt. U.S. Air Force, 1958; advanced through grades to lt. gen., 1988; later comdr. 421st Tactical Fighter Squadron, Udorn Royal Thai AFB, 1974-75; chief, house liaison office U.S. Ho. Reps., Washington, 1978-80; asst. col. assignments Randolph AFB, 1980-82; vice-comdr. Air Force Manpower and Personnel Ctr., 1982; dep. dir. legis. liaison Office Sec. Air Force, 1982-84, dir. legis. liaison, 1984-86; comdr. USAF Air Defense Weapons Ctr., Tyndall AFB, Fla., 1986-88; vice comdr. in chief USAF in Europe, Ramstein AB, Federal Republic of Germany, 1988-92, ret., 1992; founder, pres. Rees Group Cons.; pres. Air Conditioning and Refrigeration Inst., Arlington, Va., 1993—. U.S. rep. to v.p. Internat. Coun. Mil. Sports, Brussels, 1982-94. Decorated D.S.M. with one oak leaf cluster, DFC with one oak leaf cluster, Legion of Merit with one oak leaf cluster, Meritorious Svc. medal with one oak leaf cluster, Air medal with 11 oak leaf clusters USAF, Das Grosse Verdienstkreuz Mit Stern, Pres. Fed. Republic Germany, 1993; named Commander Order of Meritorious Svc. Mil. Sports Coun., 1993. Mem. Delta Phi Epsilon (v.p. membership 1957-58, nat. pres. 1984-86) Methodist. E-mial. Home: 2487 Oakton Hills Dr Oakton VA 22124-1530 Office: Air Conditioning & Refrigeration Inst # 200 4100 Fairfax Dr Arlington VA 22203-1629 E-mail: trees@ari.org.

REES, FRANK WILLIAM, JR. architect; b. Rochester, N.Y., June 5, 1943; s. Frank William and Elizabeth R. (Miller) R.; m. Joan Mary Keevers, Apr. 1, 1967; children: Michelle, Christopher. BS in Architecture, U. Okla., 1970; postgrad., Harvard U., Boston, 1979, 90; OPM, Harvard U., 1990; DArch, U. Hawaii, 2001. Registered architect, 39 states & D.C.; cert. Nat. Coun. Archtl. Registration Bds.; registered interior designer. Sales mgr. Sta. KFOM, Oklahoma City, 1967-70; project architect Benham-Blair & Affiliates, 1970-75; pres., CEO, founder Rees Assocs., Inc., 1975—. Pres., chmn. bd. Weatherscan Radio Network, Oklahoma City, 1973-78; chmn. bd. Weatherscan Internat., Oklahoma City, 1972-78; pres. Frontier Communications, Oklahoma City, 1980-84; chmn. architecture bd. U. Okla., Norman, 1988-91; bd. dirs. Century, Inc., Oklahoma City. Past pres. Lake Hefner Trails, Oklahoma City, Hosp. Hospitality House, Oklahoma City, Oklahoma City Beautiful; mem. Leadership Oklahoma City. Mem. AIA, Am. Assn. Hosp. Architects, Am. Healthcare Assn., Tex. Hosp. Assn., World Pres. Orgn. (chmn. 1997-98), Assisted Living Fedn. of Am., Am. Assn. Homes and Svcs. for the Agig. Home: 1104 Stone Gate Dr Irving TX 75063-4676 Office: Rees Associates Inc 3102 Oak Lawn Ave Ste 200 Dallas TX 75219-4279

REES, JAMES CONWAY, IV, historic site administrator; b. Richmond, Va., May 5, 1952; BA, Coll. William & Mary, 1974; MPA, George Washington U., 1978. Reporter, photographer Newport News Daily-Press, 1974; coord. radio and television programming The Coll. William & Mary, 1974-78; mng. editor The William & Mary Mag., 1978-82; promotions dir. Va. Shakespeare Festival, 1980; dir. annual giving and pub. info. The Coll. William & Mary, 1978-80, dir. annual support and corp. rels., 1980-81, dir. capital support, 1981-82; asst. dir. devel. Nat. Trust Historic Preservation, 1982-83, assoc. dir. devel., 1983; dir. devel. and comms. Historic Mount Vernon, 1983-85, assoc. dir., 1985-94, resident dir., 1994—; exec. v.p. Mount Vernon Inn, Inc., 1994—. Mem. bd. dirs. Va. Shakespeare Festival, Washington Area Chpt. WIlliam and Mary Alumni Soc. Mem. Nat. Trust for Historic Preservation, Friends of the Nat. Symphony, WETA Pub. Television. Mem. Am. Film Inst., Va. Assn. Mus. (pres. 1991-94). Methodist. Home: 710 A St NE Washington DC 20002-6032 Office: Mount Vernon Ladies Assn Mount Vernon VA 22121

REES, LANE CHARLES, industrial relations consultant; b. Longview, Tex., June 23, 1951; s. Holly Elias and Charlene Elizabeth (Quin) R.; m. Brenda Faye Anderson, July 1, 1978; children: Brian Andrew, Lauren Catherine. BBA in Mgmt. magna cum laude, Tex. A&M U., 1973, MEd in Ednl. Adminstrn., 1978. Pers. rep. Tex. A&M U., College Station, 1973-77; v.p. Brazos Gen. Svcs., Bryan, Tex., 1977-78; successively personnel office supr., wage and salary administrator, employee relations rep., sr. employee relations rep. ARCO, various cities, 1979-83, from sr. employee rels. rep. to employee rels. dir. Anchorage and Kuparuk, Alaska, 1983-87, dir. employee rels. Prudhoe Bay, 1987-90, dir. human resources dept. engring., 1990-94; sr. human rels. advisor Algeria and engring. exploration Arco Internat. Oil and Gas, Plano, Tex., 1994-99; pres. Human Resources Solutions, Inc., Dallas/Santa Rosa Beach, 1999—. Ptnr. Rees and Assocs., Anchorage and Tex., Fla., 1978—. Mem. editorial staff Conf. Leadership, 1978. Vice chmn. Rep. Party of Alaska, 1993-94, chair, 1994; vice-chmn. Walton Co. GOP exec. com., 1999—; mem. ctrl. com. State of Alaska, 1990-94; chmn. utility regulatory commn. municipality of Anchorage, 1989-91; mem. com. sec. United Meth. Com. Commn., Nashville, 1988-97; evangelism chmn., mem. adv. coun. St. John United Meth. Ch., Anchorage, 1986-91, chmn. adminstrv. bd., 1991-93; trustee Nat. Found. Evangelism, Lake Junaluksa, N.C., 1988—, exec. com., 1995—, chair-elect, 2001, chmn. 2002—; conf. lay leader Ala. Missionary Conf.-Meth. Ch., 1992-94; chmn. evangelism and mem. adminstrv. bd. 1st United Meth. Ch., Allen, Tex., 1995-97; mem. adminstrv. bd. Suncreek (Tex.) United Meth. Ch., 1997-99, adv. bd. Freeport United Meth. Ch., lay del. to ann. conf., 1995-2001; active Port Washington United Meth. Ch., 2001--; external advisor bd. internat. programs, George Bush Ctr., Tex. A&M U., 1996—; bd. dirs. Walton Co. C. of C., 1999—; commr. Walton County, 2000—; vice chair Walton Bd. County Commrs., 2000-01, chair, 2001----; mem. adv. bd. Walton Tourist Devel. Coun., 2001—; mem. adv. coun. U. West Fla. Coll. Bus., 2002--. Recipient Denman award Alaska Missionary Conf. of United Meth. Ch., 1989, Legis. citation State of Alaska, 1989. Mem. Acad. Mgmt., Tex. A&M U. Assn. Former Students (nat. councilman 1987-91, bd. dirs. 1996—), Am. Numismatic Assn., Alaska Soc. SAR (pres. 1989-90, trustee Nat. Soc. 1991-94, Silver Good Citizenship award 1989), Fla. Assn. Countries Trust (bd. dirs.), Phi Eta Sigma, Phi Kappa Phi, Sigma Iota Epsilon (pres. 1972-73), Beta Gamma Sigma. Avocations: golf, racquetball, reading, travel, coin collecting. Home: 323 Lakeview Dr Santa Rosa Beach FL 32459-6604

REES, MARTIN JOHN, astronomy educator; b. York, Eng., June 23, 1942; s. Reginald and Joan (Bett) R. MA, PhD, Cambridge (Eng.) U., 1967; DSc (hon.), Sussex (Eng.) U., 1990, Leicester (Eng.) U., 1993, Uppsala (Sweden) U., 1995, Keele (Eng.) U., 1995, Newcastle (Eng.) U., 1995, Copenhagen U., 1995, Toronto (Can.) U., 1997, Durham (Eng.) U., 1999, Oxford (Eng.) U., 2000. Rsch. fellow Calif. Tech. Inst., 1968; vis. rsch. fellow Inst. for Advanced Study, Princeton, N.J., 1969, 82, 96, 97; vis. scientist Harvard U., Cambridge, Mass., 1972, 87-90; Regents fellow Smithsonian Instn., 1984-87; prof. Sussex U., 1972-73; Plumian prof. astronomy Cambridge U., 1973-91; dir. Inst. Astronomy, Cambridge, 1977-91; rsch. prof. Royal Soc. Cambridge U., England, 1992—; astronomer royal, 1995—. Fellow King's Coll., Cambridge Univ., England, 1969—; hon. fellow Trinity Coll., 1995—, Jesus Coll., 1996—, Cardiff U., Wales, 1998; vis. prof. Harvard U., Princeton U., Calif. Tech., Imperial Coll., London, Leicester U., hon. prof., Imperial Coll., London; bd. trustees Brit. Mus., 1996—, Nat. Endowment for Sci., Tech. and Arts, 1998—2001, Inst. for Advanced Study, Princeton, 1998—. Kennedy Meml. Trust, England, 1999—, Inst. for Pub. Policy Rsch., 2001—. Author: (with M.C. Begelman) Gravity's Fatal Attraction, 1995, Perspectives in Astrophysical Cosmology, 1995, Before the Beginning, 1997, Just Six Numbers, 1999, Our Cosmic Habitat, 2001. Decorated officer Order of Arts and Letters (France); recipient Heinemann prize, Am. Inst. Physics, 1984, Gold medal, Royal Astron. Soc., 1987, Balzan prize, 1989, Robinson prize, 1990, Bruce medal, 1993, Knight Bachelor, 1992, Sci. Writing award, Am. Inst. Physics, 1996, Bower award, Franklin Inst., 1998, Rossi prize, AAS, 2000, Cosmology prize, Gruber Found., 2001. Fellow AAAS, Royal Soc. London, Royal Netherlands Acad. Arts and Scis., Indian Acad. Scis. (hon.), Russian Acad. Scis. (hon.), Swedish Acad. Scis., Am. Philosophy Soc.; mem. NAS (fgn. assoc.), Pontifical Acad. Scis., Academia Europea, Inst. Physics (Eng.) (Guthrie prize 1990—), Royal Astron. Soc. (pres. 1992-94), Brit. Assn. Advancement Sci. (pres. 1994-95), Norwegian Acad. Sci., Acad. Lincei (Rome). Anglican. Office: Inst Astronomy Cambridge England CB3 0HA

REES, NORMA S. academic administrator; b. N.Y.C., Dec. 27, 1929; d. Benjamin and Lottie (Schwartz) D.; m. Raymond R. Rees, Mar. 19, 1960; children— Evan Lloyd, Raymond Arthur BA, Queens Coll., 1952; MA, Bklyn. Coll., 1954; PhD, NYU, 1959; D of Arts and Letters honoris causa, John F. Kennedy U., 2001. Cert. speech-language pathology, audiology. Prof. communicative disorders Hunter Coll., N.Y.C., 1967-72; exec. officer, speech and hearing scis. grad. sch. CUNY, 1972-74, assoc. dean for grad. studies, 1974-76, dean grad. studies, 1976-82; vice chancellor for acad. affairs U. Wis., Milw., 1982-85, from 1986, acting chancellor, 1985-86; vice chancellor for acad. policy and planning Mass. Bd. Regents for Higher Edn., Boston, 1987-90; pres. Calif. State U., Hayward, 1990—. Chmn. Commn. Recognition of Postsecondary Accreditation, 1994-96; mem. adv. com. quality and integrity U.S. Dept. Edn. Contbr. articles to profl. jours. Trustee Citizens Govtl. Rsch. Bur., Milw., 1985-87; active Task Force on Wis. World Trade Ctr., 1985-87; bd. dirs. Am. Assn. State Colls. and Univs., 1995-97, Coun. of Postsecondary Accreditation, Washington, 1985-94, Greater Boston YWCA, 1987-90; mem. Calif. Sch. to Career Coun.; mem. Oakland Edn. Cabinet; mem. steering com. Econ. Devel. Alliance for Bus., Alameda County, 1995—; sec. edn. Nat. Adv. Com. Institutional Quality and Integrity, 1998—; bd. dirs. Bay Area World Trade Ctr., 2001—, Alameda County Health Care Found., 2002-. Fellow Am. Speech-Lang-Hearing Assn. (honors); mem. Am. Coun. Edn. (com. internat. edn. 1991-93), Am. Assn. Colls. and Univs. (chair task force on quality assessment 1991-92, mem. steering com. of coun. of urban met. colls. & univs. 1992—), Nat. Assn. State Univs. and Land Grant Colls. (exec. com. divsn. urban affairs 1985-87, com. accreditation 1987-90), Hayward C. of C. (bd. dirs. 1995-98), Oakland C. of C. (bd. dirs. 1997—). Office: Calif State Univ Hayward 25800 Carlos Bee Blvd Hayward CA 94542-3001 E-mail: nrees@csuhayward.edu

REES, PATRICIA GLINES, occupational health nurse, consultant, educator; b. Santa Maria, Calif., Aug. 28, 1945; d. Jack Holloway and Frances Ruth (Baril) Glines; m. Nov. 28, 1970 (div. July 1989); children: Eric Michael, Jennifer Lynne. BSN with honors, U. Calif., San Francisco, 1968; MSN, Clarkson Coll., Omaha, 1994. RN, Nebr., Calif.; cert. occupational health nurse-specialist; cert. BLS, CPR, first aid instr., hearing conservationist. Staff nurse Marin Gen. Hosp., Marin County, Calif., 1968-70; sch. health nurse Novato (Calif.) Unified Sch. Dist., 1968-70; obstetrics office nurse Oxon Hill, Md., 1971-72; vol. sch. health svcs. Sullivan Sch., Yokosuka, Japan, 1976-80; sch. health nurse, client svcs. rep. Vis. Nurse Assn., Omaha, 1987-89; occupational health nurse Armour Swift-Eckrich, 1989-91; dir. of client svcs. Advantage Health Sys., Inc., Kansas City, Mo., 1991-99; occupational health mgr. Omaha Steaks Internat., 1999—. Preceptor U. Nebr. Med. Ctr., Omaha, 1994-95; vol./instr. ARC, Omaha, 1989-96; presenter in field. Co-author: Cumulative Trauma Disorders, 1991, Case Management, 1994, Work Injury Management, 1996, Return to Work, 1997, Employee Education, 1997, Work Injury Management Software and Documentation, 1998; contbr. articles to profl. jours. Mem. Nebr. Safety Coun., Omaha, 1989-91, U.S. Swimming, Omaha, 1981-89. Named Pres.'s scholar, U. Calif., San Francisco, 1967—68; recipient Pvt. Res .Gold Choice award, Omaha Steaks. Mem. APHA, Am. Assn. Occupational Health Nurses (peer rev. com. 1994-2001), Nebr. Assn. Occupational Health Nurses (edn. com. 1995-96), Clarkson Honor Soc. (pres. 1994-96), Sigma Theta Tau, Alpha Xi Delta. Avocations: travel, miniatures, stitchery. Home: 1311 Beechwood Ave Papillion NE 68133-2509

REES, RAYMOND F. military officer; b. Pendleton, Oreg., Sept. 29, 1944; s. Raymond Emmett and Lorna Doone (Gemmell) R.; m. Karen Kristine Young, Nov. 1966 (div. Mar. 1974); children: Raymond Gordon, Christian Frederick; m. Mary Len Middleton, Dec. 30, 1977; 1 child, Carrie Evelyn. BS, U.S. Mil. Acad., 1966; JD, U. Oreg., 1976. Commd. 2d lt. U.S. Army, 1966; platoon leader, troop exec. officer, co. comdr. 2d Armored Cavalry Regiment, Bamberg, Fed. Republic Germany; troop comdr. 2-17 Cavalry 101 Airborn divsn., Camp Eagle, Vietnam, 1969; troop exec. officer 1-17 Cavalry 82 Airborn divsn., Ft. Bragg, N.C., 1972; resigned U.S. Army, 1973; with Oreg. Army Nat. Guard, 1973—, advanced through grades to maj. gen., 1990; asst. ops. officer Infantry Brigade; co. comdr. 2d Battalion, 162d Infantry, Corvallis, Oreg.; with 116th Armored Calvary Regiment, 1976-87; comdr. 116th cavalry regiment, adjutant gen. Oreg. Army Nat. Guard, 1987-91; dir. Army N.G., 1991-92; vice chief N.G. Bur., Washington, 1992-94; adjutant gen. Oreg. N.G., 1994-99; vice chief N.G. Bur., Washington, 1999—. Decorated Bronze Star, Legion of Merit, D.S.M., Def. Disting. Svc. medal. Mem. VFW, Adjutant Gen. Assn. U.S., Nat. Guart Assn. U.S., Assn. of U.S. Army, Oreg. Nat. Guard Assn., U.S. Armor Assn., Oreg. Bar Assn., Am. Legion, Mil. Order World Wars, West Point Soc. Oreg., 101st Airborne Div. Assn., 116th Armored Cavalry Assn., 41st Infantry Div. Assn., Elks. Office: Vice Chief 1411 Jefferson Davis Hwy Arlington VA 22202-3231

REES, THOMAS DYNEVOR, lawyer; b. S.I., N.Y., Sept. 25, 1949; s. Thomas and Caroline (Bridgman) R.; m. Josephine Stephanie Madej, Apr. 8, 1978; 1 child, Thomas D. III. AB in Polit. Sci., Stanford U., 1971; JD, U. Pa., 1975. Bar: N.Y. 1976, Pa. 1977, U.S. Supreme Ct. 1982. Assoc. Lovejoy, Wasson, Lundgren & Ashton, N.Y.C., 1975-77, Morgan, Lewis & Bockius, Phila., 1977-81; dep. gen. counsel Office of Gov. of Pa., Harrisburg, 1981-85; counsel High, Swartz, Roberts & Seidel, Norristown, Pa., 1985-86, ptnr., 1987—. CLE course planner, faculty mem. Pa. Bar Inst., 1990—; employment panel arbitrator Am. Arbitration Assn., Phila., 1991—. Solicitor Upper Merion Twp., King of Prussia, Pa., 1987-88, 90-95, Abington (Pa.) Twp., 1986-87; pres. Gladwyne (Pa.) Civic Assn,. 1995-97. Mem. ABA, Pa. Bar Assn. (chair mcpl. law sect. 1993-95), Montgomery County Bar. Assn. (co-chair employment law com. 1996-2000), King of Prussia C. of C. (solicitor 1996—, v.p., gen. counsel 1999—). Republican. Episcopalian. Office: High Swartz Roberts & Seidel LLP 40 E Airy St Norristown PA 19401-4803 E-mail: trees@highswartz.com.

REESE, ALFERD GEORGE, retired army civilian logistics specialist; b. Granville, N.D., Apr. 5, 1934; s. Ferdinand Emil and lola May (Boulds) R.; m. Donna Mae Berger, 1955 (div. 1972); children: Rick, Denise, Roxanna; m. Nelda Cecilia Pena, May 31, 1985; children: Nancy, Joyce, Alfred, Jeffrey, Jessica, James, Alicia. AS, Humphreys Coll., 1963; BS, U. State of N.Y., Albany, 1983; MPA, U. Colo., Colorado Springs, 1985; postgrad., Ga. State U., 1987-88; PhD, Columbia Pacific U., 1994. Inspector, mechanic Sharp Army Depot, Lathrop, Calif., 1958-66; equipment specialist various stations U.S. Army Aviation Systems Command, 1966-84, supervisory equipment specialist, 1984-88, supervisory logistics specialist St. Louis, 1988-93; ret. Civil Svc., 1993. Mem. com. Boy Scouts Am., Fed. Republic Germany, 1979-81. With USAF, 1953-57. Mem. Army Aviation Assn. Assn. (USAEUR Dept. Army Civilian of Yr. 1980, 81), Ctr. for the Study of the Presidency, Acad. Polit. Sci., Am. Soc. for Pub. Adminstrn., Nat. Rifle Assn. Avocations: golf, skiing, photography, painting. Home: 1590 Fairmount Dr Florissant MO 63033-2645

REESE, ANNETTE EVELYN, music educator; b. Waynesville, N.C., Sept. 23, 1958; d. James F. and Shirley Sharpe Robertson; m. Mark A. Reese, Nov. 22, 1980; children: Alana Riggle, Emily Riggle. MusB Edn., Mars Hill Coll., 1980; MEd, Belmont Abbey Coll., 1996. Cert. music educator K12. Elem. music specialist Marlboro County Schs., Bennettsville, SC, 1980—81; choral dir. North Gaston H.S., Dallas, 1981—85; dir. of bands East Gaston High/Stanley Mid. Sch., Mt. Holly/Stanley, 1985—95, Belmont Mid. Sch., Belmont, 1995—98, Olympic High/Kennedy Mid. Sch., Charlotte, 1998—. Pres. NC Bandmasters Assn., Charlotte, NC, 2000—, South Ctrl. Dist. Bandmasters, NCBA, Charlotte, NC, 1996—98; sec. NC Bandmasters Assn., Charlotte, NC, 1998—2000; band sect. chair, exec. bd. mem. NC Music Educators Assn., Raleigh, NC, 2000—. Contbr. articles to profl. jours. Troop leader Pioneer Girl Scout Coun., GSUSA, Gastonia, NC, 1996—2002. Mem.: NEA, N.C. Assn. Educators, Music Educators Nat. Conf., N.C. Bandmasters Assn. (pres. 2000—02, Excellence award 1996), N.C. Music Educators Assn. (band sect. chair 2000—02), Delta Omicron Profl. Music Frat. Mem. Evangelical Lutheran Ch. Of America. Avocations: needlework , music, travel. Office: Olympic High/Kennedy Mid Sch 4301 Sandy Porter Rd Charlotte NC 28273 E-mail: mrmsyuba@aol.com.*

REESE, CLAUDIA, artist; b. Des Moines, May 1, 1949; d. William Lewis and Louise (Weeks) R.; m. Phil Martin, 1988; 1 child, Taylor. Student, SUNY, Albany, summer 1967, 68, RIT, summer 1969; BA, Conn. Coll., 1971; MFA, Ind. U., 1974. Vis. artist Iowa Wesleyan Coll., Mt. Plesant, 1974-75, U. No. Colo., Greeley, 1976-77, The Sch. of the Art Inst. of Chgo., 1980, Purdue U., West Lafayette, Ind., 1980-81, La. State U., Baton Rouge, 1981, Brookhaven Coll., Dallas, 1990, N.Mex. State U., Las Cruces, 1992; dir., designer Cera-Mix Studio, Austin, Tex., 1982—. Subject of various articles in profl.. jours.; one woman shows include Purdue U., West Lafayette, Ind., 1981, Objects Gallery, San Antonio, 1982, Willingheart Gallery, Austin, Tex., 1984, R.S. Levy Gallery, Austin, 1987, S.W. Craft Ctr., San Antonio, 1988, Everson Mus., Syracuse, N.Y., 1988, Tokyo, 1989, 90, 91, Lyons-Matrix Gallery, Austin, 1997; exhibited in group shows Edits Ltd., Indpls., 1981, Berkeley-Lainson Gallery, Denver, 1981, Renwick Gallery, Smithsonian Instn., Washington, 1981, Wichita Art Mus., Kans., 1981, St. Mary's Coll., South Bend, Ind., 1981, Herron Sch. Art, Indpls., 1981, Craftsman's Gallery, Scarsdale, N.Y., 1982, ACVAA Juried Show, Austin, 1982, Elements Gallery, N.Y.C., 1982, Greenwich, Conn., 1983, Mattingly Baker Gallery, Dallas, 1983, Adesso, Chgo., 1983, Coll. Mainland, Tex. City, 1983, S.W. Tex. State U., 1983, New Stone Age Gallery, 1984, Willingheart Gallery, 1984, Maple Hill Gallery, Portland, Maine, 1984, Tex. Christian U., Ft. Worth, 1984, Laguna Gloria Art Mus., Austin, 1985, Carol Hooberman Gallery, Birmingham, Mich., 1985, John Michael Kohler Arts Ctr., Sheboygan, Wis., Elizabeth Fortner Gallery, Santa Barbara, Calif., 1985, 86, Kimbell Art Mus., Ft. Worth, 1986, Contemporary Arts Ctr., New Orleans, 1986, Aeteilers D'Art, Paris, 1986, Mendocino (Calif.) Arts Ctr., 1986, Kimbell Art Mus., Ft. Worth, 1986, N.Mex. State U., Carlsbad, 1987, Aspen (Colo.) Art Mus., 1987, Longview (Tex.) Mus. Invitational, 1988, North Hampton, Mass., 1988, Huntington Gallery at U. Tex., Austin, 1989, S.W. Univ. in Georgetown, 1989, Nat. Mus. Women in the Arts, Washington, 1989, Nat. Mus. Ceramic Art, Balt., 1990, La. State U., Baton Rouge, 1990, Laguna Gloria Art Mus., Austin, 1990, 91, Twist Gallery, Portland, Oreg., 1991, Virginia Breier gallery, San Francisco, 1991, Art Options, Santa Monica, Calif., 1991, Virginia Brier Gallery, San Francisco, 1991, Twist Gallery, Portland, Oreg., 1991, U. Tex., El Paso, 1992, Renwick Gallery, 1992, Mindscape Gallery, Evanston, Ill., 1992, Pittsburg Ctr. for the Arts, 1992, IO Gallery, New Orleans, 1993, Ruskin Place, Seaside, Fla., 1993, Martin Rathburn Gallery, San Antonio, 1995, Farmington Valley Art Ctr., Conn., 1996, Lyons-Matrix Gallery, 1997, Arlington Mus. Art, 1998, Irving Arts Ctr., Tex., 1998, U. Tex. San Antonio, 1999, San Antonio Mus. Art, 2000, numerous others; represented in permanent collections The Crescent Collection, Dallas, June Mattingly, Dallas, Bill Bostleman, Ft. Worth, Laurence Miller, Austin, Hadley Sleight, Austin, Marilyn Maxwell, Ft. Worth, Archer Huntington Mus. (now Blanton Mus. of Fine Art); commissioned work displayed at Austin Bergstrom Internat. Airport, S.E. Comm. Linr., Westbank Libr., St. Francis Hosp. for Chldrn., Los Angeles, Ch. of Conscious Harmony, Austin, Tex. Mem. Tex. Fine Arts Assn., Women and Their Work, Austin Visual Artists Assn. Democrat. Avocations: snow skiing, sailing, windsurfing, gardening. Office: Cera-Mix Studio 709 N Tumbleweed Trl Austin TX 78733-3240 Fax: 512-263-5019. E-mail: ceramix@io.com.

REESE, DELLA (DELOREESE PATRICIA EARLY), singer, actress; b. Detroit, July 6, 1931; d. Richard and Nellie Early; m. Vermont Adolphus Bon Taliaferro (div.); m. Leroy Basil Gray (div.); m. Franklin Thomas Lett, Jr. Student, Wayne U. Ordained to ministry Ch. Understanding Principles for Better Living Inc., April, 1987. Choir singer, 1938—, with Mahalia Jackson troupe, 1945-49, Erskine Hawkins, N.Y.C.; solo artist, 1957—; organized gospel group at Wayne U.; appearances include: (radio shows) with Robert Q. Lewis; (TV shows) Della, 1969, The Voyage of the Yes, 1972, Twice in a Lifetime, 1974, Cop on the Beat, 1975, Chico and the Man, 1974, 76-78, Nightmare in Badham County, 1976 (Emmy nomination), Roots: The Next Generation, 1979, It Takes Two, 1982, Charlie & Co., 1985, 86, The Kid Who Loved Christmas, 1990, The Royal Family, 1991, You Must Remember This, 1992, Touched By an Angel, 1994—, A Match Made in Heaven, 1997, Miracle in the Woods, 1997, Emma's Wish, 1998, The Secret Path, 1999, Having Our Say: The Delany Sisters' First 100 Years, 1999; spl. appearances with Jackie Gleason, Ed Sullivan, McCloud, 1971, Sanford and Son, 1972, Welcome Back, Kotter, 1975, The A-Team, 1983, Night Court, 1984, MacGyver, 1985, Designing Women, 1986, L.A. Law, 1986, Married People, 1990, Dream On, 1990, Picket Fences, 1992, Promised Land, 1996, Anya's Bell, 1999, The Moving of Sophia Myles, 2000; guest host The Tonight Show; actress (films) Let's Rock, 1958, Psychic Killer, 1975, Harlem Nights, 1989, A Thin Line Between Love and Hate, 1996, (plays) Same Time Next Year, Ain't Misbehavin, Blues in the Night, The Last Minstrel Show; recs. for Jubilee, RCA Victor Records, ABC Paramount Records, Jazz Ala Carte, AIR Co. (Grammy nomination 1987); author: Angels Along the Way, 1997, (voice) Dinosaur, 2000. Voted Most Promising Singer of Yr. 1957; recipient Image awards, 1996, 98-2000, Star on Walk of Fame, 1994. Office: William Morris Agy c/o Norman Brokaw 151 S El Camino Dr Beverly Hills CA 90212-2775 : The FTL Co Los Angeles CA

REESE, EDWARD JAMES, JR. computer scientist; b. San Antonio, Aug. 8, 1957; s. Edward James Sr. and Kathy (Veitch) R.; m. Pamelia Kay Oxendine, Sept. 28, 1979; children: Dawn Alicia, Paul Christopher. AAS in Avionics Systems Tech., C.C. of the Air Force, 1985, AAS in Tech. Instrn., 1986, AAS in Electronic Engring. Tech., 1990; BS in Computer Sci. summa cum laude, Park Coll., 1986; MS in Computer Sci., Midwestern State U., 1994. Cert. master instr.; cert. Oracle master Oracle Edn. Svcs., 1993; cert. Oracle Database adminstr. Chauncey Group Internat., 1996. Enlisted USAF, 1975, advanced through grades to master sgt., 1989, avionic systems technician 67 Tactical Recon Wing Tex., 1976-84, tech. instr. 423 Field Tng. Detachment, 1984-89, info. sys. supt. 82 Field Tng. Group Sheppard AFB, 1989-95, ret., 1995; database adminstr. Oracle Rockwell Automation, 1995—. Cubmaster pack 230 Boy Scouts Am., Wichita Falls, Tex., 1991-93. Mem. Internat. Oracle Users Group Am., Planetary Soc. Avocations: astronomy, scuba diving, private pilot. E-mail: ejreesejr@yahoo.com.

REESE, FRANCIS EDWARD, retired chemical company executive, consultant; b. Monaca, Pa., Nov. 3, 1919; s. Francis Edward and Vivian Iris (Hancuff) R.; m. Katherine Mary McBrien, June 29, 1946; 1 son, Francis Edward III. BS in Chem. Engring, Purdue U., 1941. Registered profl. engr., Pa. With Monsanto Co., St. Louis, research engr. plastics div., 1941-48, chief devel. engring. plastics div., 1948-53, asst. engr. plastics div., 1953-56, dir. engring. plastics div., 1956-59, asst. gen. mgr. plastics div., 1959-61, asst. gen. mgr. hydrocarbons div., 1961-65, asst. gen. mgr., hydrocarbons and polymers div., 1965-66, gen. mgr. internat. div., 1966-68, corp. v.p., 1968-74, gen. mgr., hydrocarbons and polymers div., 1966-71, gen. mgr. polymers and petrochems. div., 1971-73, gen. mgr. internat. div., 1973-74, dir., 1973-84, group v.p., 1974-79, sr. v.p., 1979-84. Pres. FTR Assocs., Inc.; mem. engring. found. adv. coun. U. Tex. Fellow AAAS, Am. Inst. Chem. Engrs.; mem. Am. Chem. Soc., Nat. Soc. Profl. Engrs., Soc. Chem. Industry, Tau Beta Pi, Phi Lambda Upsilon. Home: Rydal Park 271W 1515 The Fairway Rydal PA 19046-1435 Office: 801 Old York Rd Ste 316 Jenkintown PA 19046-1611

REESE, GEORGE W. federal agency administrator; b. Detroit; married; 2 children. BS, Lincoln U.; JD, George Washington U.; postgrad., U. Pitts. Sr. atty., atty. advisor Office Gen. Counsel NASA, Washington, with Office Gen. Counsel, 1977—, dep. gen. counsel, 1993—97, assoc. adminstr. equal opportunity programs, 1997—. Officer U.S. Army, Vietnam. Office: NASA Hdqrs Mail Code E 300 E St SW Washington DC 20546

REESE, HARRY EDWIN, JR. electronics executive; b. Balt., Oct. 27, 1928; s. Harry Edwin and Margery Lee (Stroud) R.; m. Elizabeth Syra Pfeiffer, Oct. 15, 1955; children: Clifford Owen, Susan Syra, Peter Eyre. BSEE, Tufts U., 1950; MS in Stats., Villanova U., 1960. Engr. Philco Corp., Phila., 1950-54; project engr. Burroughs Corp., Paoli, 1956-59, dept. mgr., 1959-65, GE Co., King of Prussia, 1965-69; group staff mgr. Burroughs Corp., Paoli, 1969-75, gen. mgr. Plainfield, N.J., 1975-82, corp. staff dir. Detroit, 1982-83; v.p. quality assurance Am. Electronic Labs., Inc., Lansdale, Pa., 1984—90, ret., 1990. Chmn. Charlestown Twp. Planning Commn., Pa., 1973-75. With U.S. Army, 1954-56. Fellow IEEE (life, pres. Reliability Soc. 1969-70, gen. chmn. Rams symposium 1968, chmn. bd. 1969, Centennial medal 1984); mem. Nat. Mgmt. Assn. (life, chmn. formation com. Am. Electronics Labs. chpt. 1985, Leadership award 1973, 86), Lake Hopatcong Yacht Club (commodore), Masons, Rotary (Paul Harris fellow, treas.). Republican. Episcopalian. Avocations: carpentry, architecture, boating, antiques, travel. Home: 17 Bass Rock Rd Hopatcong NJ 07843-1901

REESE, HAYNE WARING, psychologist, educator; b. Comanche, Tex., Jan. 14, 1931; s. Tom F. and Marion (Waring) R.; m. Patsy Atwood, Aug. 24, 1957 (div. Apr. 1967); children: Anne, William, Margaret; m. Nancy Mann, Dec. 16, 1967; 1 child, Bradley. Student, So. Meth. U., 1949-50; BA, U. Tex., 1953, MA, 1955; PhD, U. Iowa, 1958. Asst. prof. U. Buffalo, 1958-62; assoc. prof. SUNY-Buffalo, 1962-66, prof., 1966-67, U. Kans., Lawrence, 1967-70; Centennial prof. psychology W.Va. U., Morgantown, 1970-2000, dir. grad. tng. in life-span devel. psychology, 1973-2000, Centennial prof. emeritus, 2000—.

Mem. initial rev. groups div. research grants NIH, Washington, 1969-71, 74-78, 79-84 Author: Perception of Stimulus Relations, 1968, Basic Learning Processes in Childhood, 1976; co-author: Life-Span Developmental Psychology, 1977, Child Development, 1979; editor: Advances in Child Development and Behavior, 26 vols., 1969-2001; co-editor: Life-Span Developmental Psychology, 8 vols., 1973-97; assoc. editor: Jour. Exptl. Child Psychology, 1975-83, editor, 1983-97, mem. editl. bd. 1965-74, 98-2000. Served with U.S. Army, 1954. Fellow AAAS, Am. Psychol. Soc.; mem. AAUP, Soc. for Rsch. in Child Devel., Psychonomic Soc., Assn. for Behavior Analysis, Ea. Psychol. Assn., Internat. Soc. for Study Behavioral Devel. E-mail: hayneree@aol.com.

REESE, JASON RUSKIN, lawyer; b. Davenport, Iowa, Dec. 31, 1971; s. Jay Rodney and Margaret Lynne Reese; m. Jill Elizabeth Pilcher, Feb. 7, 1998; 1 child, Anja. BA in History, U. Ariz., 1994; JD, Ind. U., 1997. Bar: Ind. Atty. Hilbrich Cunningham & Schwerd, Highland, Ind., 1996-98, Ladendorf & Assocs., Indpls., 1998-2000; ptnr. Wagner Reese & Crossen. Mem. Ind. Trial Lawyers Assn., Lake County Bar Assn. (bd. dirs. 1997-98), Sagamore Am. Inn of Ct. (assoc. 1999—). Democrat. Presbyterian. Avocations: golf, tennis, basketball. Office: Wagner Reese & Crossen LLP Ste 1040 9000 Keystone Crossing Indianapolis IN 46240

REESE, JOAN CAROL, mediator, consultant, coach; b. Hershey, Pa., Aug. 25, 1947; 1 child, Byron T. Hogan. BS, Shippensburg U., 1968; postgrad. studies, Calif. State U., L.A., 1970-71; JD, Southwestern U., L.A., 1975; postgrad., U. Tex., 1997. Bar: Calif. 1975, Tex. 1993; Reiki master, tchr.; cert. instr. Nat. Guild Hypnotists. Tchr. Lower Paxton Sch. Dist., Harrisburg, Pa., Pasadena (Calif.) Sch. Dist.; adminstrv. asst., comml. paper buyer Transam. Investment Mgmt. Co., L.A., Calif., 1969-71; law clk. Am. Civil Liberties Union, 1974-75; pvt. practice law Beverly Hills, Calif., 1976-93; mediator and conflict resolution trainer, 1987—; pvt. practice law Brenham, Tex., 1993-98. Author: (poetry) Journey of Many Sojourns, 1993; (book) Practice Guide: Protect Your Rights to Health, Healing, Hypnotherapy, 1994; contbr. poems to anthologies of Nat. Libr. Poetry. Bd. dirs. Tex. Assn. Against Sexual Assault, Austin, 1997-98, Felicity House for Women in Recovery, L.A., 1987-89; organizer, chair Parents on Patrol Program, Brenham (Tex.) Ind. Sch. Dist., 1993-94; vol. political campaigns, pro bono legal counseling, mediation, stress and conflict mgmt. sems.; vol. women's prison project Calif. Inst. for Women, Chino through Loyola U., L.A. Office: PO Box 13 Roanoke VA 24002

REESE, JOHN H. electrical engineer, consultant; BSEE, U. Utah, 1962. From. mgr. to sr. technologist GTE Gov. Sys., sr. technologist; from dir. bus. devel. to dir. advanced tech. sys. & studies TRW, dir. advanced tech. sys. & studies; cons. Mem.: Nat. Security Indsl. Assn. (dir., sci. adv. bd.). Office: SAAL ASB 2511 Jefferson Davis Hwy Ste 11500 Arlington VA 22202-3911*

REESE, JOHN RATHBONE, investment banking executive; b. N.Y.C., Jan. 11, 1944; s. Willis Livingston Mesier and Frances (Stevens) R.; m. Hope Wells, Oct. 15, 1966; children: Victoria Stevens, Augusta Bliss. BA, U. Pa., 1965, MBA, 1967. V.p. Wood, Struthers & Winthrop, N.Y.C., 1969-78, pres., dir., 1978-85; ptnr. Lazard Freres & Co., 1986—. Trustee Cold Spring Harbor (L.I.) Lab., Green-Wood Cemetary, Bklyn.; bd. dirs., chmn. Internat. Tennis Hall of Fame, Newport, R.I., Holy Cross Monastery, West Park, N.Y., U. Pa. Athletic Alumni Bd.; vestry St. John's Ch., Cold Spring Harbor. Mem. N.Y. Soc. Security Analysts. Clubs: Wharton of N.Y., Down Town, Racquet and Tennis (N.Y.C.); Piping Rock (Locust Valley, N.Y.) (gov.). Home: 86 Shore Rd Cold Spring Harbor NY 11724-1102 ALSO: Owosso Corp The Triad Bldg 2200 Renaissance Bldg Ste 150 King Of Prussia PA 19406

REESE, JOHN ROBERT, lawyer; b. Salt Lake City, Nov. 3, 1939; s. Robert McCann and Glade (Stauffer) R.; m. Francesca Marroquin Gardner, Sept. 5, 1964 (div.); children— Jennifer Marie, Justine Francesca; m. Robin Ann Gunsul, June 18, 1988. AB cum laude, Harvard U., 1962; LLB, Stanford U., 1965. Bar: Calif. 1966, U.S. Dist. Ct. (no. dist.) Calif. 1966, U.S. Ct. Appeals (9th cir.) 1966, U.S. Dist. Ct. (cen. dist.) Calif. 1974, U.S. Supreme Ct. 1976, U.S. Dist. Ct. (ea. dist.) Calif. 1977, U.S. Ct. Appeals (6th cir.) 1982, U.S. Ct. Appeals (8th cir.) 1985, U.S. Ct. Appeals (10th cir.) 1992, U.S. Ct. Appeals (Fed. cir.) 1994. Assoc. McCutchen, Doyle, Brown & Enersen, San Francisco, 1965-74, ptnr., 1974—. Adj. asst. prof. law Hastings Coll. of Law, 1991; lectr. U. Calif., Berkeley, 1987, 92. Mem. editl. and adv. bds.: Antitrust Bull., Jour. Reprints for Antitrust Law and Econs., 1981—99. Bd. dirs. Friends of San Francisco Pub. Libr., 1981-87; bd. vis. Stanford U. Law Sch., 1983-86. Capt. U.S. Army, 1966-68 Decorated Bronze Star Mem. ABA, State Bar Calif., San Francisco Bar Assn., U.S. Supreme Ct. Hist. Soc., Ninth Jud. Cir. Hist. Soc., Calif. Acad. Appellate Lawyers, Order of the Coif. Avocations: aviculture, gardening. Home: 9 Morning Sun Dr Petaluma CA 94952-4780 Office: McCutchen Doyle Brown & Enersen 3 Embarcadero Ctr San Francisco CA 94111-4003

REESE, KATHERINE ROSE, music educator; b. Mannington, W.Va., July 27, 1937; m. Wallace Reese, July 29, 1955; children: Kyla O'Dell, Ann Landers. BA, W.Va. U., 1986. Cert. profl. music tchr. Artist tchr. of piano Fairmont (W.Va.) State Coll., 1986—. Address: RR 1 Box 122 Mannington WV 26582-9801

REESE, KIRK DAVID, lawyer; b. Rochester, Minn., Jan. 8, 1948; s. Orville Arnold and Alta Matilda (Borgen) R.; m. Shan G. Kovatch, Aug. 1, 1974; children: Nels E., Hannah M., Ingrid M. BA, Beloit Coll., 1970; JD, Ohio No. U., 1983. Bar: Wis. 1983, U.S. Dist. Ct. (we. and ea. dists.) Wis. 1985, U.S. Ct. Appeals (7th cir.) 1986. Instr. Ohio No. U., Ada, 1983-84; pvt. practice, Rhinelander, Wis., 1984-85, 91—; assoc. Eckert Law Office, 1985-91; commr. Oneida County Family Ct., 1991-2000. Rsch. editor Ohio No. U. Law Rev., 1981-82. Chmn. bd. dirs. White Pines Community Broadcasting, Rhinelander, 1991-2001, Rhinelander Soccer Assn., 1990-2001. Recipient Book award Am. Jurisprudence, 1983. Mem. Kiwanis. Office: PO Box A Rhinelander WI 54501-0076

REESE, LYMON CLIFTON, civil engineering educator; b. Murfreesboro, Ark., Apr. 27, 1917; s. Samuel Wesley and Nancy Elizabeth (Daniels) R.; m. Eva Lee Jett, May 28, 1948; children: Sally Reese Melant, John, Nancy. BS, U. Tex. at Austin, 1949, MS, 1950; PhD, U. Calif. at Berkeley, 1955. Diplomate: Registered profl. engr., Tex., La. Internat. Boundary Commn., San Benito, Tex., 1939-41; surveyor U.S. Naval Constrn. Bns., U.S., Aleutian Islands, Okinawa, 1942-45; field engr. Assoc. Contractors & Engrs., Houston, 1945; draftsman Phillips Petroleum Co., Austin, 1946-48; research engr. U. Tex., 1948-50; asst. prof. civil engring. Miss. State Coll., 1950-51, 53-55; asst. prof. U. Tex., Austin, 1955-57, assoc. prof., 1957-64, prof., 1964—, chmn. dept., 1965-72, Taylor prof. engring., 1972-81, assoc. dean engring. for program planning, 1972-79, Nasser I. Al-Rashid Chair, 1981-84; prin. Ensoft, Inc., 1985—. Contbr. articles to profl. jours. Served with USNR, 1942-45. Recipient Thomas Middlebrooks award ASCE, 1958; Joe J. King Profl. Engring. Achievement award, 1977, Offshore Tech. Conf. Disting. Achievement award for Individuals, 1985, Disting. grad. Coll. of Engring., U. Tex., Austin, 1985. Mem. ASCE (Karl Terzaghi lectr. 1976 Terzaghi award, 1983, Tex. sect. award of Hon. 1985, hon. mem. 1984—), Nat. Acad. Engring., Nat. Soc. Profl. Engrs. Baptist (deacon). Office: U Tex Dept Civil Engring Austin TX 78712-1104 Home: 11110 Tom Adams Dr Austin TX 78753-3302 E-mail: lymonreese@aol.com.

REESE, MARTHA GRACE, minister, lawyer; b. Newark, Feb. 27, 1953; d. John Gilbert and Louella Catherine (Hodges) R.; 1 child, Elizabeth Lang Harman. BA with high distinction, DePauw U., 1975; JD magna cum laude, Ind. U., 1980; MDiv magna cum laude, Christian Theol. Sem., 1989. Bar: Ind. 1980, U.S. Dist. Ct. (so. dist.) Ind. 1980, U.S. Ct. Appeals (7th cir.) 1981; ordained to ministry Christian Ch. (Disciples of Christ), 1989. Law clk. U.S. Dist. Ct. (so. dist.) Ind., 1980-82; assoc. Baker & Daniels, Indpls., 1982-83; ptnr. Wilson, Hutchens & Reese, Greencastle, Ind., 1984-86; interim assoc. regional min. The Christian Ch. in Ind. (Disciples of Christ), 1988-89; sr. min. Carmel (Ind.) Christian Ch. (Disciples of Christ), 1989-96; dir. The Bethany Project of the Christian Chs., 1996—. Cons. Lilly Endowment, Inc., 1989, 90. Steering com. Ind. Leadership Celebration, 1983-98; trustee Christian Theol. Sem., 1995-99. Mem. Phi Beta Kappa, Theta Phi. Home: 3942 N Delaware St Indianapolis IN 46205-2650

REESE, MONTE NELSON, agricultural association executive; b. Mooreland, Okla., Mar. 31, 1947; s. James Nelson and Ruby Edith (Bond) R.; m. Treisa Lou Bartow, May 25, 1968; children: Bartow Allan, Monica Lynnelle. BS in Agrl. Econs., Okla. State U., 1969. Staff asst. Wilson Cert. Foods, Oklahoma City, 1969-71; assoc. farm dir. Sta. WKY Radio and TV, 1971-73; radio-TV specialist Tex. A&M U., College Station, 1973; dir. agrl. devel. Oklahoma City C. of C., 1973-76; asst. exec. dir. Am. Morgan Horse Assn., Westmoreland, N.Y., 1976-77; v.p. pub. affairs Farm Credit Banks of Wichita, Kans., 1977-87; exec. dir. Coffey County Econ. Devel., Burlington, 1987-88; farm dir. Mid-Am. Ag Network, Wichita, 1988-89; CEO Cattlemen's Beef Promotion and Rsch. Bd., Englewood, Colo., 1989-96; exec. dir. Cattlemen's Beef Promotion & Rsch. Bd., CO, 1996-98, COO, 1998—. Lt. col. USAR, 1969—. Office: Cattlemens Beef Promotion Rsch Bd 9110 E Nichols Ave 303 Englewood CO 80112

REESE, NORMA CAROL, retired psychologist; b. Biloxi, Miss., Oct. 26, 1946; d. Virgil Stephen and Lila Mae (Shelton) Tatom; m. John Jay Reese, June 5, 1965 (div. Mar. 1983); children: Cher LeAnne, James Steven. AA in Psychology, Dade County Jr. Coll., Kendall, Fla., 1971; BS in Psychology, U. Miami, 1973; MS and PhD in Psychology, U. So. Miss., 1976. Lic. psychologist, Wis., Tex. Rsch. asst. NASA Lang. Rsch. Lab., Coral Gables, Fla., 1971-73; psychology instr. U. So. Miss., Hattiesburg, 1975-76, Grambling (La.) State U., 1976-78; clin. psychologist II Lake Charles (La.) Mental Health Ctr., 1979-83; tng. cons. Human Rels. Cons., Lake Charles, 1983-86; clin. dir. Grafton (N.D.) State Sch., 1986-89; dir. psychol. svcs. State Devel. Ctr., Grafton, 1989-95; ind. contractor, cons. psychol. svcs. Harley Residential Svcs. (name changed to Applied Behavioral Cons., Inc. 1990), Roseville, Minn., 1990-91; pvt. practice MYNDAK Moblie Cons., Minn. and N.D., 1990-95; program dir. for spl. needs Saint Coletta Sch., Jefferson, Wis., 1995-98, human rights and sexual health curriculum coms., 1995—2001; psychol. cons. Tex. Deer Oaks Geriatric Svcs., 1999-2000, Deer Oaks Mental Health Assocs., Harlingen, Tex., 2000-01. Dir. sexual health project for devel. disabled and mentally retarded N.D. Dept. Human Svcs., Grafton, 1989-95, dir. sex offender and treatment program devel. disabled offenders, 1986-87; mem. adj. faculty grad. clin. psychology dept. U. N.D., Grand Forks, 1994—; presenter in field. Author: The Bulletin of the Psychonomic Soc., 1975-76; author/cartoonist The Worm Runner's Digest, 1975-80. Freedom writer Amnesty Internat., Midwest, 1989; founding mem. Sexual Health Coalition Steel of N.D., 1990; nat. disaster mental health technician, chpt. family svc. worker Red River Valley chpt. ARC, 1993—; mentor Am. Assn. Mental Retardation, 1992—; vol. Red Cross Nat. Disaster Mental Health Team, 1993, Emilys List, 1993. Named Silver Knight candidate, art, Miami (Fla.) Herald News, 1965; nominated Profl. of the Yr., La. Assn. Retarded Citizens, Lake Charles, 1983. Mem. N.D. Psychol. Assn. (legis. action com. 1990-91, mem. disaster action com. 1993-94, mem. women in psychology 1995), Am. Assn. Mental Retardation (sec.-treas. N.D. chpt. 1991), Ft. Worth Psychol. Assn. Republican. Methodist. Avocations: boating, dance, art, travel. Home: 609 E Business Hwy 83 # 17 Alamo TX 70816

REESE, PATRICIA ANN, retired editor, columnist; b. Superior, Nebr., Mar. 14, 1954; d. Robert John and Billie Jo (Gooch) R. BS in Wildlife Ecology, Communications, Okla. State U., 1976. Proofreader Ada (Okla.) Evening News, 1976-77, reporter, 1977-81, wire editor, 1981-85, city editor, 1985-92, sects. editor, 1992, ret., 1992. Bd. dirs. Ada Arts and Humanities Coun., 1981-85, 92-95, 96—, historian, 1982-83, sec., 1983-85, 92-95, 96—, newsletter editor, 1996—, webmaster, 1998—; editor, webmaster Upward Bound Regional Math./Sci. Ctr., Ada, 1996—; webmaster Okla. Horseshoe Pitchers Assn., 1999—; charter mem. Seekers dept. Tanti Study Club, Ada, 1982. Recipient Carl Rogan News Excellence award Associated Press/Okla. News Execs., 1986, 90, 91, 92, Best Column award Okla. Natural Gas, 1991, Outstanding Adan in Arts award, 2000. Mem. Am. Mus. Natural History, Archaeology Inst. Am., Okla. Lupus Assn., Ada Cmty. Theatre II, Okla. Press Assn., Internat. Ceramic Inst., Soc. Environ. Journalists, Okla. Horseshoe Pitchers Assn. (webmaster 1999—). Democrat. Avocations: ceramics, painting, gardening, horses, the environment. Home: RR 4 Box 118 Ada OK 74820-9407 E-mail: fantasyfactory@compworldnet.com

REESE, WILLIAM ALBERT, III, psychologist, clinical neuropsychologist; b. Tabor, Iowa, Nov. 23, 1932; s. William Albert and Mary-Evelyn Hope (Lundeen) R.; m. Barbara Diane Windermere, Dec. 22, 1954 (dec. Jan. 1995); children: Judy, Diane William IV, Sandra-Siobhan, Debra-Anne, Robert-Gregory, Barbara-Joanne; m. Ruth Alice Moller, Sept 12, 1996. BA, U. Washington Reed Coll., 1955; M.Ed., U. Ariz., 1964, PhD, 1981; postgrad., Fielding Inst. Clin. Neuropsyc, 2000. Diplomate Am. Bd. Christian Psychology, Am. Bd. Forensic Psychologists; cert. in clin. neuropsychology. Clin. psychology cons. Nogales Pub. Schs., Nogales-Tucson, Ariz., 1971-79; clin. psychologist Astra-Found., N.Y.C., 1979-86, chief psychology svc., neuropsychiatry, 1980-89; chief psychologist Family Support Ctr. Community-Family Exception Mem. Svcs., Sonoita, Ariz., 1986-89, Psychol. Svc. Ctr., Mount Tabor, Iowa, 1989-95, Calif. Ctr. Health and Wellness, 1995—. Dir. religious Marriage and Family Life Wilderness Ctr., Berchtesgaden, W. Ger., summer, 1981-82; exec. sec. Astra Ednl. Found, 1975-79, bd. dirs, 1979—, EEO officer, 1978—. Author: Developing a Scale of Human Values for Adults of Diverse Cultural Backgrounds, 1981, rev. edit., 1988. Served with USAF, 1967-71, Vietnam. Decorated Bronze Star. Fellow in cons. psychology and holistic medicine Clin. Services Found., Ariz., 1979—. Fellow Am. Psychol. Soc., Am. Coll. Forensic Examiners, Clin. Neuropsychiatry and Neuropsychology, 1998; mem. APA, ACA, Internat. Neuropsychol. Assn., Calif. Psychol. Assn., Iowa Psychol. Assn., K.C., Los Padres Wilderness Ctr., Outdoor Club, Sierra Club, Skyline Estates Golf and Country Club (Tucson). Office: AstraWorldMedicineUSA dot com Integrated Med Ctr Wellness 798 Lighthouse Ave Ste 228 Monterey CA 93940-1010 E-mail: dr_reese@mail.com.

REESE, WILLIAM LEWIS, philosophy educator; b. Jefferson City, Mo., Feb. 15, 1921; s. William Lewis and Lillian Amelia (Fisher) R.; m. Louise Weeks, June 11, 1945; children: Claudia, Patricia, William Lewis III. AB, Drury Coll., 1942; B.D., U. Chgo., 1945, PhD, 1947; postdoctoral, Yale U., 1955-56. Asst. prof. philosophy Drake U., 1947-49, asso. prof. philosophy, 1949-57, head dept., 1954-57; asso. prof. philosophy Grinnell Coll., 1957-60; vis. prof. philosophy Iowa State U., 1958; prof. philosophy, chmn. dept. U. Del., Newark, 1960-67, dir. seminar in philosophy of sci., 1960-66, H. Rodney Sharp prof. philosophy, 1965-67; prof. philosophy SUNY-Albany, 1967-99, chmn. dept., 1968-74, 84, prof. philosophy emeritus, rsch. prof. philosophy, 1999—. Tully Cleon Knoles lectr. U. Pacific, 1962; del. U.S. Nat. Commn. for UNESCO, 1963; gen. mem. 4th East-West Philosophers Conf., 1964 Author, contbr.: Studies in C.S. Peirce, 1952, (with Charles Hartshorne) Philosophers Speak of God, 1953, 2d edit., 2000, The Ascent from Below, 1959, 2d edit., 2000, (with Eugene Freeman) Process and Divinity, 1964, Dictionary of Philosophy and Religion: Eastern and Western Thought, 1980, 3d edit., 1999, Freedom, 2000, Values, 2000; gen. editor: Philosophy of Science, The Delaware Seminar, vols. 1, 2, 1963, vol. 3, 1967; editor: Philosophy and World Religions: The Reader's Adviser, vol. 4, 1988, Fundamental Issues in Philosophy Series, 2000-75; editl. bd.: State of N.Y. Press, 1968-78; contbr. articles to profl. jours. Recipient Ford Found. Study award Argentina, 1967; Fulbright lectr. Argentina, summer 1971; Inst. Humanistic Studies fellow, 1977— Mem. AAUP, Am. Philos. Assn., Metaphysical Soc. Am. (sec.-treas. 1962-65) Mem. Christian Ch. (Disciples Of Christ). Home: Font Grove Rd Slingerlands NY 12159 Office: SUNY Dept Philosophy Albany NY 12222-0001 E-mail: wlr@albany.edu., reesewl@cs.com. *To have before one always the realistic sense that if one has been successful in one way one has failed in others, and that one's failures surely outnumber one's successes.*

REETZ, HAROLD FRANK, JR. industrial agronomist; b. Wat., Ill. s. Harold Frank and Evelyn Evedeen (Russell) R.; m. Christine Lee Kaiser, Aug. 25, 1973; children: Carrie, Wesley, Anthony. BS in Agrl. Sci., U. Ill., 1970; MS in Agronomy, Purdue U., 1972, PhD in Agronomy, 1976. Extension and rsch. specialist Purdue U., West Lafayette, Ind., 1974-82; regional dir. Potash & Phosphate Inst., Monticello, Ill, 1982—; v.p. Found. for Agronomic Rsch., 1996—. Cons. Control Data Corp., Mpls., 1978-82, Internat. Harvester Co., Chgo., 1979-82, Monsanto Agrl. Chem. Co., St. Louis, 1981-82; adj. prof. Crop Scis. U., Ill., 1999—. Author: Crop Simulation Model, CORNCROPS, 1976, several crops mgmt. computer programs; contbr. articles to profl. jours. Chmn. Ill. Com. for Agrl. Edn., 1987-89; mem. Ill. Groundwater Adv. Coun., 1988—2002; mem. Ill. Fertilizer Rsch. and Edn. Coun., Ill. Dept. Agr., 1989-98, Ill. Occupl. Skills Stds. Credentialing Coun., 2001—2002, Ill. Dept. Agr. Nutrient Mgmt. Com. Recipient Hon. mem. Hon. State Farmer Ill. Assn. FFA, Urbana, 1987; IFCA Spl. Recognition award Ill. Fertilizer and Chem. Assn., 1988, Site-Liner award Farm Chems., 1997, Alumni award of merit U. Ill., 2000. Fellow Crop Sci. Soc. Am., Am. Soc. Agronomy (Agronomic Industry award 2000); mem. Soil Sci. Soc. Am. (divsn. chmn. editl. bd., chmn. internat. cert. crop adviser exec. com. 1996-98), Ill. Assn. Vocat. Agrl. Tchrs. (hon. life 1989—), Gamma Sigma Delta (Merit award 2001). Methodist. Avocations: photography, travel, computers.

REEVE, FRANKLIN D. writer, literature educator; b. Phila., Sept. 18, 1928; m. Laura C. Stevenson, 1997; children: Christopher, Benjamin, Alison, Brock, Mark, Katharine, Margaret. AB, Princeton U., 1950; PhD, Columbia U., 1958; AM (hon.), Wesleyan, 1964. Instr., asst. prof. Columbia U., N.Y.C., 1952-61; assoc. prof. Wesleyan U., Middletown, Conn., 1962-66, adj. prof., 1967-87, prof., 1988—. Bd. govs., v.p. Poetry Soc. Am., 1976-84; bd. dirs., sec. Poets House, N.Y.C., Translation Ctr., N.Y.C., 1985-99; bd. dirs. New Eng. Poetry Club, 1996—; bd. govs. transl. Ctr., N.Y.C., 1980-94; mem. adv. panel Vt. Ctr. for Book; vis. prof. Oxford (Eng.) U., 1964, Columbia U., 1988, Marlboro Vt. Coll., 1999; vis. scholar, Moscow, 1961; mem. adv. panel Vt. Ctr. for the Book; vis. lectr. Yale U., New Haven, 1972-84; assoc. fellow Saybrook Coll., 1972—; lectr. poetry Ctr., N.Y.C., 1980-84; cons. in field. Author: Aleksandr Blok: Between Image and Idea, 1962, 1981, Robert Frost in Russia, 1964, 2001, The Russian Novel, 1966, 2002, The Red Machines, 1968, In the Silent Stones, 1968, Just Over the Border, 1969, The Brother, 1971, The Blue Cat, 1972, White Colors, 1974, The White Monk, 1989, (edited with Jay Meek) After the Storm, 1991, Concrete Music, 1992; editor: Winged Sprits, 1995, A Few Rounds of Old Maid and Other Stories, 1995, The Moon and Other Failures, 1999, The Urban Stampede and Other Poems, 2002. Recipient Lit. award Am. Acad.-Nat. Inst., 1970, Lifetime Golden Rose award New Eng. Poetry Soc., 1994. Office: Wesleyan U Lit Dept Wesleyan Sta Middletown CT 06459-0001

REEVE, IVAN LEON, physician; b. Sept. 2, 1930; BA, Pacific Union Coll., 1957; MD, Loma Linda U., 1961. Diplomate Am. Bd. Family Physicians, Am. Bd. Managed Care Medicine. Clin. asst. prof. family medicine Coll. Osteopathic Medicine, Pomona, Calif., 1998; mem. faculty Loma Linda (Calif.) U., 1998; physician Loma Linda Family Med. Group, 1999—. Fellow Am. Acad. Family Physicians (charter). Office: Loma Linda Family Med Group 11370 Anderson St Ste 1050 Loma Linda CA 92354-3450

REEVE, JOHN NEWTON, molecular biology and microbiology educator; b. Wakefield, W. Yorkshire, Eng., June 21, 1947; came to U.S., 1979; s. Arthur Newton and Lilian Elsworth (Tallant) R.; m. Patricia Margaret Watson, Sept. 21, 1967; children: Simon Arthur, Daniel John. BS with 1st class honors, U. Birmingham, Eng., 1968; PhD, U. B.C., Vancouver, Can., 1971. Rsch. scientist U. Ariz., Tucson, 1971-73, Nat. Inst. Med. Rsch., Mill Hill, London, 1973-74; rsch. dir. Max-Planck Inst., Berlin, 1974-79; prof. microbiology Ohio State U., Columbus, 1979—, chmn. dept., 1985—, Rod Sharp prof. microbiology, 1999—. Cons. Battelle Rsch. Lab., Columbus, 1982-87, Govt. of Bulgaria, Sofia, 1987, Promega Corp., Madison, Wis., 1990, Procter and Gamble Co., Cin., 1990; mem. sci. adv. bd. BioTrol. Inc., Chaska, Minn., 1986-90; Disting. vis. prof. U. Adelaide, Australia, 1984, U. Wyo., Laramie, 1988, U. Calcutta, India, 1989, Frei U., Berlin, 1991, U. Karachi, Pakistan, 1995, U. Concepcion, Chile, 1995; mem. governing coun. So. Petrochems. Corp., Chennai, India, 1999—. Named Disting. Rsch. Scholar Ohio State U., 1989. Mem. Am. Soc. for Microbiology (lectr. Found. for Microbiology 1987-88, 94-96. chair Div. K, microbial physiol. 1998-99, coun. 2000-2002, mem. U.S. nat. organizing com. for 2005 Internat. Congress of Microbiology Socs., 2002—). Office: Ohio State U Dept of Microbiology 484 W 12th Ave Columbus OH 43210-1214 Fax: 614-292-8120. E-mail: reeve.2@osu.edu.

REEVES, ANITA SUE WINDSOR, healthcare administrator; b. Oxford, Miss., Mar. 1, 1947; d. Alton Eugene and Mary Emma (Haney) Windsor; m. Johnny Lafayette Reeves Jr., Nov. 1, 1969; children: Ashley Renee, Lesley Windsor, Douglas Stephens. BA in Edn., U. Miss., 1969; MEd, La. State U., 1972. Cert. tchr., La. Tchr. Jackson (Miss.) Pub. Schs., 1969-71; profl. vol. Nat. Assn. Jr. Aux., Slidell, La., 1979-87; tchr. St. Tammany Parish Schs., 1981-83; dir. infant youth services Slidell Meml. Hosp., 1984, dir. cmty. rels., 1984-85, dir. women's ctr., 1985-87, dir. physician recruitment, 1985-87, dir. physician services, 1987-90; exec. dir. Women's Health Found. Am. Med. Internat., New Orleans, 1986-88; asst. chair for adminstrn. dept. ob-gyn. U. N.C. Sch. Medicine, Chapel Hill, 1990-91; asst. adminstr. Highland Med. Ctr., Lubbock, Tex., 1991-94; physician recruitment dir. Tex. Tech. U. Health Sci. Ctr. and Univ. Med. Ctr., 1994-95; adminstr. Lubbock Ind. Physician Assn., 1995-2000; exec. dir. Open Air MRI of Lubbock, 1997-2000; CEO Open Aire MRI, Ft. Smith, Ark., 2000—. Cons., spkr. in field. Project designer Vol. Coord. Ctr., 1983, bd. dirs., 1983-88; exec. dir. Women's Health Found., 1987-88; mem. gala com. Leukemia Soc. Am., 1989; founding bd., v.p. Women's Health Care Exec. Network, New Orleans, 1988-90, Network Speakers, 1992; sec. Lubbock Mentor Coun., 1993-96, Exec. Forum, 1994-96, Women's Fin. Forum , 1995-98. State La. grant, 1982; recipient Tex. Vol. award Tex. Dept. of Human Svcs., 1994, Commendation award Lubbock Mentoring Coun., 1995. Mem. NAFE, Am. Assn. Med. Colls., Nat. Assn. Jr. Aux. (Martha Wise award 1984, nat. com. woman 1982-87), Am. Coll. Healthcare Execs., Assn. for Mgrs., Ob-Gyn. Med. Group Mgmt. Assn., Assn. for Profl. Women Medicine, Slidell Panhellenic, Univ. Women's Club, Women's Health Found. La. (com. mem. 1989-96), Nat. Assn. Women's Health Profls., Lubbock C. of C. (healthcare com.), Phi Kappa Phi, Phi Mu. Republican. Avocations: reading, gourmet cooking, interior decorating, developing community progs., pub. speaking. Home: 10017 Essex Pl Fort Smith AR 72908 Office: 5701 Euper Lane Ste B Fort Smith AR 72903 E-mail: swrvs@aol.com., openairemrifs@aol.com.

REEVES, BARBARA, writer, educator; b. Wellington, Tex., Aug. 29, 1931; d. Edward Decatur Reeves and Ruth Caroline Rich; m. Stanley Kolaski, Jan. 15, 1956 (dec. Feb. 1987); children: Anne Marie, Linda Caroline, John Edward. Writing tchr. San Jacinto Coll. Sys., Houston, 1990—. Curriculum cons. San Jacinto Coll. South, Houston, 1998-2000; cons. and mentor in field. Authro: Georgina's Campaign, 1991, The Dangerous Marquis, 1993, The Much Maligned Lord, 1995, My Buffalo Soldier, 2000. Mem. Romance Writers Am. (founder chpt. 30, chairperson, fundraiser for literacy), Bay Area Writer's League (founder, chairperson). Democrat. Roman Catholic. Avocations: social historian, interior design, family history. E-mail: bkwriter@swbell.net.

REEVES, BRUCE, social worker; b. Centerville, Utah, Jan. 8, 1955; s. Leon W. and Maxine (Hodson) R. BA, U. Utah, 1979, MSW, 1983. Mental health caseworker Traveler's Aid Soc. Salt Lake, Salt Lake City, 1983-86; socialwork cons. Home Health Utah, Bountiful, 1985-86; victim svcs. counselor Salt Lake County Atty's. Office, Salt Lake City, 1986-87; mgr., cons. AIDS and employee assistance program Aetna and Human Affairs Internat., 1987-96; dir. social work and therapies Paracelsus Home Care & Hospice, 1996-98; registrar, bus. mgr. Awakening Spirit Massage Sch., L.C., 1998-99; mgr. Christus St. Joseph Villa, 1999-2001; med. social worker Harmony Home Care and Hospice, 1999-2001; owner, operator Satori Pers. Coaching and Cons., 1999—; exec. dir. Violence Intervention Project, Thief River Falls, Minn., 2001—. Health educator Health Horizons, L.C., 1996-98; presenter in field. Bd. dirs. Walk-ons, Inc., Salt Lake City, 1989-98, Gay and Lesbian Cmty. Ctr. Utah, Salt Lake City, 1998-99, Utah chpt. Gay Lesbian Straight Edn. Network, 1996-99; mem. appropriations com. United Way Greater Salt Lake, Salt Lake City, 1990-99, bd. assocs. Ririe-Woodbury Dance Co., Salt Lake City, 1991-95, human svcs. com. Utah Stonewall Ctr., Salt Lake City, 1992-95. Mem.: NASW, Am. Soc. Aging, Gay Lesbian Straight Edn. Network. Democrat. Avocations: dance, theatre, music, literature. Office: Violence Intervention Project PO Box 96 Thief River Falls MN 56701

REEVES, DAVID CHARLES, secondary educator, construction executive; b. Boston, Aug. 31, 1943; s. Charles Victor and Cecile Stella (Steiler) R.; m. Roberta Jean Strohmeier, 1972 (div. 1982); m. Laura Lee Brandle, Apr. 14, 1984; 1 child, Kelly Rochelle. BA in History, N.C. Wesleyan Coll., 1967; MS in Edn., Va. Tech., 1976. Cert. tchr. Va. State Bd. Edn. Tchr. Fairfax County Schs., McLean, Va., 1967-98, ret., 1998; pres. B&R Assocs., Great Falls. Head soccer coach McLean H.S., 1969-71, sponsor sr. class, 1970-90, chmn. faculty advisor, 1971-91, head baseball coach, 1976-86, chmn. shared governance, 1993-95, mem. McLeadership com., 1997-98. Recipient McLean H.S. Helen Dekter award, 1987, 88, 91, 93, 98; voted Tchr. of Yr. 23 times by h.s. sr. class. Mem. Assn. Fairfax Profl. Educators (bd. dirs. 1991—), Moose Lodge. Republican. Methodist. Avocations: fishing, flowers, woodworking. E-mail: davesfishing3@aol.com.

REEVES, DIANNE L. artist; b. Milw., Apr. 8, 1948; d. John J. and Bernice M. (Hendricksen) Kleczka; m. Robert A. McCoy, Oct. 15, 1983 (div. June 1988). BFA, U. Wis., Milw., 1968; student, Mus. Fine Arts, Houston, 1974-77, 83, Glassell Sch. Art, 1980-83. Instr. papermaking Glassell Sch. Art, 1984-85. One-woman shows include Women and Their Work Gallery, Austin, Tex., 1988, Moreau Galleries/Hamms Gallery, Notre Dame, Ind., 1991, The Martin Mus. of Art, Waco, Tex., 1996, Robert C. Williams Am. Mus. Papermaking, Atlanta, 2000, Diamond/Tanita Gallery, Portland, 2002; exhibited in group shows; author: From Fiber to Paper, 1991. Bd. dirs., sec. Friends of Dard Hunter, Inc., 1993-94. NEA/Tex. fellow Mid-Am. Arts Alliance, 1986; recipient awards for art work. Mem.: Nat. Mus. Women in the Arts, Nat. Assn. Women Artists, Tex. Fine Arts Assn., Women and Their Work, Inc., Internat. Assn. Hand Papermakers and Paper Artists (co-chair nominating com. 1993—94), Sierra Club. Avocations: archaeology/anthropology, camping, reading, travel, environmental issues. Home: 1103 S 3rd St Austin TX 78704-2301

REEVES, EDMUND HOFFMAN, III, food products executive; b. Easton, Pa., Sept. 14, 1949; s. Edmund Hoffman Jr. and Constance Irene (Bartholomew) R.; children: Courtney Ann, Edmund Hoffman IV, Brendan Gill. BA in Econs., Lynchburg Coll., 1972; MBA in Food Mktg., St. Joseph's U., Phila., 1979. With Am. Stores, Inc., 1972-81, Shaffer Clarke & Co., Inc., Old Greenwich, Conn., 1982—88, R.W. Frookies, Inc., 1988—90, Yankee Food Distributors, Ayer, Mass., 1990-92; v.p., gen. mgr. Am. Specialty Brands, Fargo, N.D., 1992-96; dir. U.S. sales Billy Bee Honey Products, Ltd., 1997-2000; v.p. sales & mktg. ZBI Foods, Inc., 2001—. Alumni bd. dirs. Lynchburg Coll. , 1989—91; asst. cubmaster, com. chmn. Boy Scouts Am., Trumbull, Conn. Mem. Nat. Food Distbr. Assn., Nat. Assn. Splty. Food Trade Republican. Episcopalian. Avocations: pvt. piloting, boating, woodworking, photography, antiques. Home: PO Box 320368 Fairfield CT 06432-0061 E-mail: reeves3@attglobal.net.

REEVES, GARY L. musician, educator; b. Muscatine, Iowa, Jan. 21, 1953; s. Harold Richard and Carol Marie Reeves; m. Deborah Ann Check. D of Mus. Arts, U. Iowa, 1986. Asst. prof. Oreg. State U., Corvallis, 1988—92; assoc. prof. So. Utah U., Cedar City, 1992—95; assoc. prof. U. S.D., Vermillion, 1995—. Horn player S.D. Symphony Orch., Sioux Falls, 1996—, Sioux City Symphony Orch., 1995—. Contbr. Mem.: Internat. Horn Soc. (Area Representative 1996—pres). Avocations: bicycling, automobile restoration. Home: 1909 Princeton Ave Vermillion SD 57069-7203 Office: U S D 414 E Clark St Vermillion SD 57069-2390 Home Fax: 605-677-5988; Office Fax: 605-677-5988. Personal E-mail: greeves@usd.edu. Business E-Mail: greeves@usd.edu.

REEVES, GENE, judge; b. Meridian, Miss., Feb. 27, 1930; s. Clarence Eugene and May (Philyaw) R.; m. Brenda Wages, Sept. 26, 1980. JD, John Marshall U., 1964; cert. judge spl. ct. jurisdiction; postgrad., U. Nev., 1995. Bar: Ga. 1964, U.S. Ct. Appeals (11th cir.) 1965, U.S. Supreme Ct. 1969. Ptnr. Craig & Reeves, Lawrenceville, Ga., 1964-71; sole practice, 1971-85; prin. Reeves Law Firm, 1985-94; judge City Ct., Lawrenceville, 1969-70, Magistrate Ct. of Gwinnett County, Ga., 1994—. Sgt. USAF, 1951-54. Mem. ABA, ATLA, GTLA, Am. Jud. Soc., Gwinnett County Bar Assn. (pres. 1970-72), Criminal Def. Lawyers Assn., Atlanta Bar Assn. Baptist. E0-mail: green-Wmindspring.com. Home: 221 Pineview Dr Lawrenceville GA 30045-6035 Office: 75 Langley Dr Lawrenceville GA 30045-6935 E-mail: GREEV@mindspring.com., gwinmag4@courts.dc.gwinnett.ga.us.

REEVES, JOHN CRAIG, religious studies educator; b. Fayetteville, N.C., Dec. 1, 1954; s. William Donald and Martha Suzanne (Robinson) R.; m. Lu Waggoner, Oct. 26, 1985; 1 child, Daniel Jesse. BA, U. N.C., 1976; MPhil, Hebrew Union Coll., Cin., 1986, PhD, 1989. Asst. prof. religious studies Winthrop U., Rock Hill, S.C., 1989-92, assoc. prof. religious studies, 1992-96; Blumenthal prof. Judaic studies U. N.C., Charlotte, 1996—. Author: Jewish Lore in Manichaean Cosmogeny, 1992, Tracing the Threads, 1994, Heralds of that Good Realm, 1996. Mem. Soc. Bibl. Lit., Am. Oriental Soc. Office: Dept Religious Studies U NC Charlotte Charlotte NC 28223

REEVES, JOHN DRUMMOND, English language professional, writer; b. Troy, N.Y., Dec. 8, 1914; s. Robert Brockway and Emma Caroline (Mausert) R.; m. Mary Markwick Moore, Sept. 1, 1951. AB, Williams Coll., Williamstown, Mass., 1937; AM, Columbia U., 1941. Instr. in Eng. Irving Sch., Tarrytown, N.Y., 1937-40, Horace Mann Sch., N.Y.C., 1940-41, 46-47; asst. prof. of classics and Eng. Whitman Coll., Walla Walla, Wash., 1956-62; assoc. prof. English Millikin U., Decatur, Ill., 1962-65; lectr. in Eng. Hofstra U., Hempstead, N.Y., 1965-73, ret., 1973. Author: Windows on Melville, 2001; contbr. articles to prof. jours. Lt. USNR, 1941-45, PTO. Mem. AAUP, Coll. Eng. Assn., Am. Coun. Learned Soc. (reg. assoc. 1957-59), Walla Walla Archaeol. Assn. (pres. 1959-62), SR (N.Y. state chpt.), Masons. Home: Newey Ln Brookhaven NY 11719

REEVES, JUDITH ANN, critical care nurse; b. St. Louis, July 29, 1955; d. Charles David Reeves and Patricia Ann (Westerhold) Tutin. Student, U. Mo., St. Louis, 1973-76; ADN, Meramec C.C., 1978; BSN, St. Louis U., 1981. RN, Mo.; cert. BLS instr., ACLS instr. Staff nurse, team leader Firmin Desloge Hosp., St. Louis, 1978; relief nurse Staff Builders, 1978-79; paramed. examiner Meditest, 1979-80; relief nurse Kimberly Nurses, 1978-80; asst. head nurse surg. ICU Barnes Jewish Hosp., BJC Health Sys. (formerly Barnes Hosp.), 1980-81, clin. instr., asst. head nurse surg. and cardiovascular ICU, staff nurse, charge nurse, 1981-93, staff nurse, charge nurse surgical and med. ICU, 1993-98; staff nurse cardiovascular recovery unit Mo. Bapt. Med. Ctr., BJC Health Sys., 1998—. Vacation Bible sch. tchr. St. John's Luth. Ch., St. Louis, 1969-74, Sunday sch. tchr., 1972-78; vol. Mo. Hist. Soc., 1979-80; judge regional competitions Mo. Speed Skating Assn., 1978-84; beginners coach Clayton Speed Skating Club, 1977-84. Mem. AACN Greater St. Louis Chpt. (past pres. St. Louis chpt., mem. symposium com., program com., pub. rels. com., membership com., symposium com. chair, adv. bd., rev. panel, strategic planning chair, nat. bd. adv. team mem. chpt./mem. awards review panel), Am. Heart Assn., St. Louis Soc. Critical Care Medicine (bylaws com. 1981), Mid Am. Transplant Assn. (adv. coun. 1989-91). Office: Mo Bapt Med Ctr 3015 N Ballas Rd Saint Louis MO 63131-2329

REEVES, LUCY MARY, retired school educator; b. Pewamo, Mich., July 2, 1932; d. Lavaldin Edgar and Marian S. (Lee) Hull; m. Walter Emery Reeves, Jan. 21, 1922. BS, Western Mich. U., Kalamazoo, 1965; postgrad., Western Mich. U., 1965-75. Tchr. Country Sch. One Room, Matherton, Mich., 1956-57, Ionia, 1957-58, Belding, 1958-62, Saranac, Belding, 1965, Belding (Mich.) Area Schs., 1965-89; ret., 1989. Vol. Frederick Meijers Garden, Grand Rapids, Point Man Internat. Ministries, Shiloh Cmty. Ch., United Meml. Health Ctr., Shiloh Cmty. Ch.; vol. United Meml. Health Ctr., Greenville. Mem. NEA, Mich. Edn. Assn., Belding Area Edn., Profl. Businesswomen's Assn. Avocations: computers, reading, travelling, sewing.

REEVES, NANCY ALICE, critical care nurse; b. Manhasset, N.Y., Aug. 19, 1965; d. Kenneth George and Jean Adele (Reincke) Leib. BSN, Hartwick Coll., 1988. RN, N.Y. Staff nurse intermediate care unit Mercy Med. Ctr., Rockville Center, N.Y., 1988-92, staff nurse CCU, 1992-99; office nurse Gary Friedman, MD, 1993-98, head nurse, 1998—, office mgr., 2001. Mem. AACN, ANA, Am. Heart Assn. (cardiovasc. nursing coun.), Am. Assn. Office Nurses, N.Y. State Nurses Assn., Empire State Keeshond Club, Alpha Omicron Pi. Avocations: needlework, collecting.

REEVES, PATRICIA HOUTS (TRISH REEVES), English and humanities educator; b. Columbia, Mo., Nov. 8, 1947; d. Joseph Kinyoun and Patricia (Collins) Houts; m. Jeremiah Early Krug Reeves, June 28, 1969 (div. Mar. 1989); children: Caroline Reeves Petrie, Jeremiah Krug Reeves. BJ, U. Mo., 1969; MFA, Warren Wilson Coll., Swannanoa, N.C., 1983. Editor New Letters Rev. of Books, Kansas City, Mo., 1986-88; adj. faculty creative writing U. Mo., 1988-91; adj. lectr. English and humanities Kansas City Art Inst., 1988-91; mem. faculty English and creative writing Haskell Indian Nations U., Lawrence, Kans., 1991—. Mem. adv. bd. BKMK Press, Kansas City, 1998—. Author: Returning the Question, 1989 (Cleve. State U. Poetry Ctr. prize), In the Knees of the Gods, 2001; co-editor (anthology) Decade, 1989-90. Fellow Yaddo Corp., Saratoga Springs, N.Y., 1987, Kansas Arts Commn., Topeka, 2001; creative writing grantee for individual artists NEA, 1988. Office: Haskell Indian Nations U 155 Indian Ave Lawrence KS 66046 E-mail: treeves@rossl.cc.haskell.edu.

REEVES, PEGGY LOIS ZEIGLER, accountant; b. Orangeburg, S.C., May 12, 1940; d. Joseph Harold and Lois Vivian (Stroman) Zeigler; m. Donald Preston Reeves, Sept. 9, 1961. Degree in Secretarial Sci., Coker Coll., 1960. Sec. Ladson Beach, CPA, Orangeburg, 1960-61; acctg. clk. Milliken & Co., Laurens, S.C., 1962-67, sec., 1967-73, mgmt. trainee, 1973, plant contr., 1973-74, 76-81, cost acctg. supr. Spartanburg, 1974-76, 81—. Chair bd. dirs. Enoree (S.C.)-Lanford Fire dist., 1982-98, treas., 1988—, sec., 1999-2000; mem. alumni exec. bd. Coker Coll., 1996-98, sec. alumni exec. bd., 1998-2000. H.L. Jones scholar Coker Coll., 1959-60. Mem. Inst. Mgmt. Accts. (sec. 1991-94, v.p. membership 1994-95, v.p. adminstrn. and fin. 1995-96, pres.-elect 1996-97, pres. 1997-98, v.p. adminstrn. and fin. 2002, sec. Carolinas Coun. 1998-2000, nat. svcs. com. 2000-02, nat. ethics com. 20022—), Profl. Secs. Internat. (v.p., rec. sec., Sec. of Yr. 1973). Baptist. Avocations: reading, collecting plates and antiques.

REEVES, PHILLIP A. school system administrator; b. Weleetka, Okla., Mar. 31, 1943; s. Plazie and Mary Louise Reeves; m. Charlene Kay Reeves, July 17, 1965; children: Phillip, Bonnie. BS, U. Tulsa, 1969, JD, 1975; MS, Calif. State U., San Bernardino, 1991, cert. in sch. adminstrn., 1999. Tchr. Nev. Pub. Schs., 1969—71; adminstr. Tulsa County schs., Tulsa, 1971—79; bus. owner, 1979—87; tchr. Barstow (Calif.) Pub. Schs., 1987—95; edn. adminstr. Victorville (Calif.) Pub. Schs., 1995—. Pres. Cometa (Okla.) C. of C., 1978—81, Barstow Sports Club, 1988—90, High Direct Adminstrs., Victorville, 1998—99. Staff sgt. USMC, 1961—66. Recipient Pub. Svc. award, Future Farmers Am., 1979—80. Mem.: 3d Marine Divsn. Assn. (Gold Star 1992), Nat. Assn. H.S. Adminstrs., Calif. Assn. Sch. Adminstrs., Nat. Order of Barristers. Republican. Avocations: scuba, golf, fishing. Home: 13916 Palomino Ct Victorville CA 92394 Office: Victor Valley Union HS Dist 14048 Cobalt Rd Victorville CA 92392 Office Fax: 760-955-3439. E-mail: stjoch@aol.com.

REEVES, RALPH BERNARD, III, publisher, editor; b. Raleigh, N.C., Apr. 2, 1947; s. Ralph Bernard Reeves Jr. and Frances Rhoda (Campbell) M.; m. Caroline Holton Green, Apr. 24, 1971 (div. 1986); children: Ralph B. IV, Daniel MacQuarrie; m. Katherine Drewry Reid, June 20, 1998. AB in History, U. N.C., 1970. Field coord. FMI Mgmt. Group, Raleigh, N.C., 1972-76; gen. mgr., v.p. The Leader Newspaper, Rsch. Triangle Pk., 1976-78; pres., pub., founder Spectator Pubs. Inc., Raleigh, 1978-98, Triad Bus., Greensboro, 1986-88, Triangle Bus., Raleigh, 1985-91, Spectator Pub., N.C. Architect, 1981-84; pres. Reeves Media, 1998—; pub., editor Metro Mag., 1999—. Editor: Mr. Spectator, 1978-98. 1st v.p. Mordecai Square Hist. Soc., Raleigh, NC, 1980—83; pres. Hilltop Home, 1982—84; chmn. Downtown Adv. Com., 1983—85; mem. Bus. Adv. Com. for N.C. Sec. of State, Raleigh, 1992—; bd. dirs. N.C. State U. Friends of Libr., Buy.com Carolina Classic Golf Tournament, Carolina Ballet. Gov.'s. Bus. award in the Arts and Humanities, 1986, Benjamin Fine award, 1991, AABP award Triangle Bus., 1st place award Feature Writing, 1991. Mem. Fifty Group, English Speaking Union (past pres. RTP br. 1988—), Carolina Co. Club, Sphinx Club. Republican. Episcopalian. Avocations: golf, history, travel. Home: 3066 Granville Dr Raleigh NC 27609 E-mail: reevesmedia@msn.com.

REEVES, ROSSER SCOTT, III, retired investment company executive; b. N.Y.C., Aug. 20, 1936; s. Rosser and Elizabeth (Street) R.; m. Colin McRae Squibb, Dec. 14, 1963; 1 dau., Elizabeth Robinson. Acad. degree with honors, Westminster Sch., 1954; postgrad., Yale, 1954-55; BS with honors in architecture, U. Va., 1961. Assoc. real estate firm Douglas L. Elliman & Co., N.Y.C., 1961-62; investment banker Lazard Freres & Co., 1962-67; founder, mng. partner R.S. Reeves & Co., 1967-68; sr. mng. partner Bacon, Stevenson & Reeves, 1968-70; chmn. bd. Quantum Corp., 1970-75; pres. Rosser Reeves Holdings, Ltd., 1975—; pres., chief exec. officer dir. Rosser Reeves, Inc., 1976—; pres. Charlie O Co., 1980-82; pres., chief exec. officer Tiderock Corp., Little Rock, 1990—. Founder, CEO The Recovery Found., 1992—; mem. N.Y. Stock Exch., 1967-69; mng. ptnr. Wall St. Leasing Assn., 1968-70; chmn. bd. Internat. Subsea Devel. Corp., N.Y.C., 1969-75, Mil. Armament Corp., N.Y.C., 1969-75. Trustee Youth Consultation Service, N.Y.C., 1968-72; bd. dirs. Ark. Symphony Orch., 1982-85, St. Charles Cmty. Assn., 1997—; chmn. St. Charles Lighting Improvement Dist., 1998—. Mem. Scarab. Clubs: Union League (N.Y.C.), Racquet and Tennis (N.Y.C.), N.Y. Stock Exchange Lunch (N.Y.C.); Little Rock (Ark.). Home: 14201 Orleans Dr Little Rock AR 72211-5549 E-mail: scottr@spiritus.org.

REEVES, THOMAS A. naturalist; b. Phila., Feb. 8, 1931; s. Frank Armstrong and Henrietta (Lewis) R.; m. Marjorie Jean Decker, Apr. 15, 1952 (dec.); children: Bruce, Susan; m. Helen Nichols, July 7, 1984. BS, Temple U., 1952. Sales rep. Nat. Biscuit Co. (Nabisco), 1952-91. Pres. Valley Forge Audubon, 1984-88; vol. guide J. Heinz Nat. Wildlife Refuge, Tinicum, Pa., 1977—, Tylor Arboretum, Media, Pa., 1980—. Recipient Silver Beaver award Boy Scouts Am., 1977, Vol. award Phila. Airport Hilton, Phila., 1997. Fellow Delaware Valley Ornithology Club; mem. Phila. Acad. Natural History. Republican. Lutheran. Avocations: bird watching, camping, botany. Home: 311 Wyndmoor Rd Springfield PA 19064-2328 Fax: (610) 544-4217. E-mail: tomrevs7@bellatlantic.net.

REEVES, TRACEY ELIZABETH, director; b. Ocala, Fla., Dec. 3, 1965; d. Edwin MacDowell and Elizabeth Ann (Dekle) R. BS, U. Fla., 1988, MEd, EdS, U. Fla., 1990, PhD, 2001. Dir. residence hall U. Fla., Gainesville, 1990-93, asst. dir. housing, 1993—. Mem. AACD, Nat. Assn. Student Pers. Adminstrs., Am. Coll. Pers. Assn., So. Assn. Coll. Student Adminstrs., Phi Theta Kappa, Phi Beta Kappa, Chi Sigma Iota. Avocation: volunteer work. Home and Office: Univ Fla Divsn Housing Murphree Area Office Gainesville FL 32612 E-mail: traceyr@housing.ufl.edu., traceyr@ufl.edu.

REEVES, VAN KIRK, lawyer; b. N.Y.C., May 14, 1939; arrived in France, 1967; s. William Harvey and Caroline (Buck) R.; m. Ann Murchison, June 24, 1967; children: Daisy Fiona, Evander James. BA, Harvard U., 1961, JD, 1964. Ptnr. Coudert Frères, Paris, 1973-95, Coudert Bros., N.Y.C., 1973-95, Porter & Reeves, Paris, 1995—. Mem. Ctr. du Droit de l'Art, Geneva, 1998—, Mona Bismark Found. Author: Confessions of an Art Lawyer, 1997, The Structure and Financing of Art Transactions, 1994; co-author: (with Dr. J. Boll) Auction Sales and Conditions, 1991. Bd. mem., v.p. Internat. Coun. Muss. Found., Paris, 1972-95; bd. suprs. Am. Tax Inst., London, 1978; bd. mem. Fabergè Arts Found., Washington, 1992. Mem. Inst. Internat. Bus. Law and Practice (assoc. mem.). Avocations: projects for the preservation of cultural heritage, hiking. Home: 8 Cité Nicolas Poussin 240 Blvd Raspail 75014 Paris France Office: Porter & Reeves 5 Rue Cambon 75001 Paris France

REEVY, ANTHONY WILLIAM, environmental organization administrator; b. Lubbock, Tex., Aug. 2, 1961; s. William R. and Carole M. Reevy; m. M. Caroline Weaver, June 23, 1990; 1 child M. Lindley. BS, NC State U., 1983, BS, 1985; MS, Miami U., Oxford, Ohio, 1988. Devel. assoc. MWWU-FM, Washington, 1987—89, corp. devel. mgr., 1989—90; dir. devel. WFAE-FM, Charlotte, NC, 1990—93, dir. corp. devel., 1993—94; dir. libr. devel. NC State U. Librs., Raleigh, 1994—. Author: Ghost Train!, 1999; co-author: Dr. of NC Railroad Strict, 2001; contbr. poems, articles, short stories to profl. publs. Mem.: CASE, Nat. Assn. Fund Raising Execs. Democrat. Mem. Soc. Of Friends. Avocations: travel, hiking, reading, raliroad history. Home: 7777 W Club Blvd Durham NC 27705 Office: U NC Carolina Environ Program CB # 1105 100 Miller Hall Chapel Hill NC 27599-1105 Office Fax: 919-966-9970. E-mail: tony-reevy@unc.edu.

REEVY, GRETCHEN MARIA, psychology educator; b. Cortland, N.Y., Oct. 17, 1964; d. William Robert and Carole May Reevy; m. Todd Royal Manning. AB in Psychology, U. N.C., 1986; PhD in Psychology, U. Calif., Berkeley, 1994. Lectr. psychology dept. Dominican Coll. , San Rafael, Calif., 1993—99; lectr. U. Calif., Davis, 1994; lectr. psychology dept. Calif. State U. , Hayward, 1994—. Grantee, Rand Corp., 1991. Mem.: APA, Soc. Psychol. Study of Social Issues, Western Psychol. Assn., Phi Beta Kappa, Psi Chi. Avocation: swimming. Office: Calif State U Psychology Dept Hayward CA 94542 Business E-Mail: greevy@csuhayward.edu.

REFAI, SHAHID, history educator; b. Baroda, Gujarat, India, Dec. 17, 1936; s. Zainulabedin Badruddin and Afzal Banu R.; m. Shama Banu Nagamia, May 19, 1963 (div. Mar. 1998); children: Irfan, Saba, Farah, Aslam; m. Sartaj Banu Kazi, Aug. 16, 1998. BA magna cum laude, MS U., Baroda, India, 1959, MA summa cum laude, 1962; PhD, Cambridge U., 1968. Asst. prof. Cen. Wash. U., Ellensburg, 1971-77; assoc. prof. Coll. St. Rose, Albany, NY, 1977-82, 84-88, prof. of history, 1988—. Vis. lectr. UCLA, 1969-70, U. Calif. Berkeley, 1971; adj. assoc. prof. Cen. Wash. U., Ellensburg, 1983-84; pres. N.Y. Conf. on Asian Studies, New Paltz, N.Y., 1999-2001, chmn. 2000. Contbr. essays to profl. publs. Gen. sec. Tri-City India Assn., Albany, 1985-88, bd. dirs., 1988-91; organizer and coord. Sunday Urdu Sch. of Albany, 1990-95; judge Nat. History Day, Inc., Seattle, 1984; panelist Assn. for Asian Studies, U. Mich., Ann Arbor. Recipient Lady Mountbatton award Cambridge, 1967, scholarship Bombay-Cambridge Soc., 1964-66, others. Avocations: rare book collecting, computers, Indian music, videography. Office: Coll of St Rose 432 Western Ave Albany NY 12203-1419 E-mail: refais@mail.strose.edu.

REFINSKI, JOSEPH ANTHONY, secondary education educator; b. Orange, N.J., July 7, 1954; s. Chester Walter and Antoinette (DeCarlo) R. BA in History, Seton Hall U., 1976, MA in Secondary Edn., 1978. Cert. tchr. social studies and history, N.J.; supr. cert., N.J. Tchr. Columbia High Sch., Maplewood, N.J., 1977-78; tchr. and coach Edison Jr. High Sch., Westfield, 1978-85, Verona (N.J.) High Sch., 1985-86, Costley Sch., East Orange, N.J., 1986—. Photographer and cons. N.J. Bicentennial Commn., Mahwah, 1987—; mem. civics consortium E.A. Coleton Inst., Rutgers U. Coord. nat. competition on Constitution and Bill of Rights, Washington, 1988, Nat. Commn. on U.S. Constitution, Calabasas, Calif., 1989; active in local Constitution Day projects, 1987, 88, N.J. Coun. Social Studies, Hands Across Am. State Com., 1986; closing ceremonies staff Liberty Weekend, 1986; tchr. edn. adv. com. Seton Hall U., 1992—; mem. Kodak ProPassport Network, Libr. Congress. Recipient East Orange Sch. Based Program award, 1987, Bicentennial Leadership award Ctr. for Civic Edn., Calabasas, 1989, Alumni Svc. award Seton Hall U., Nat. History Day award Am. Hist. Assn., 1991, N.J. We The People Citation, 1991; Constitution fellow, 1989, Thomas Jefferson fellow, 1991, Woodrow Wilson fellow, 1994, Tcrh. Outreach nat. devel. program (TORCH) presenter, 1995-99, USCHE Bd. Dirs., 1998, Tchr. of the Year, 1995, Excellence in Tchg. award, 1995. Mem.: ASCD, NY Times Learning Network (affiliate), Found. for U.S. Constn. (founding mem.), NJ Dept. Edn. (social studies content stds revision com.), Nat. Coun. for Edn. in Disciplines (history com.), Nat. Bd. for Profl. Tchg. Stds. (assessor, trainer), Fgn. Policy Rsch. Inst., NJ Coun. for History Edn., Am. Hist. Assn., Orgn. Am. Historians, Nat. Coun. Social Studies (del.), Seton Hall U. Alumni Assn. (pres. 1990—92, v.p. 1992—), Athletics Congress (mid. sch. com. NJ State Bar Assn.), Tau Kappa Epsilon, Kappa Delta Pi, Phi Alpha Theta. Roman Catholic. Avocations: photography, piano, guitar, historial celebrations. Home: 2094 Aldene Ave Scotch Plains NJ 07076-4649

REFO, PATRICIA LEE, lawyer; b. Alexandria, Va., Dec. 31, 1958; BA with high honors and high distinction, U. Mich., 1980, JD cum laude, 1983. Bar: Ill. 1983, Ariz. 1996, U.S. Dist. Ct. (no. dist.) Ill. 1988, U.S. Ct. Appeals (7th cir.) 1989, U.S. Ct. Appeals (11th cir.) 1990, U.S. Ct. Appeals (5th cir.) 1992, U.S. Ct. Appeals (9th cir.) 1998, Fed. Trial Bar (no. dist.) Ill. 1993, U.S. Dist. Ct. Ariz. 1996. Ptnr. Jenner & Block, Chgo., 1991-96, Snell & Wilmer L.L.P., Phoenix, 1996—. Mem. evidence rules adv. com., U.S. Jud. Conf. 2000—; mem. faculty Nat. Inst. Trial Advocacy, 1989—; bd. advisors Comml. Lending Liability News; lectr. ALI/ABA and Practicing Law Inst. on various subjects including trial advocacy and lender liability. Co-author: Class Action Controversies, 1989, Notice to Members of the Class, IICLE Class Actions Handbook, 1986, Closing Argument: A String of Pearls, Litigation, 1998. Dir. Ariz. Found. for Women, 1999—, Ariz. Acad. Decathlon Assn., 1998—, Legal Clinic for the Disabled, 1994-96, Chgo. Lawyers' Com. Civil Rights Under Law, 1987-91, Cabrini Green Legal Aid Clinic, 1987-91. Mem. ABA (chair sect. litigation 1990 annual meeting, co-chair sect. litigation Pro Bono com. 1990-93, dir. divsns. sect. litigation 1993-94, sec. sect. litigation 1994-98, mem. Ho. of Dels. 1998-2001, vice chmn. litigation 2001-02). Office: Snell & Wilmer LLP One Arizona Ctr Phoenix AZ 85004-2202

REGALADO, RAUL L. airport executive; b. L.A., Jan. 31, 1945; s. Raul and Antonia (Estavillo) R.; m. Helen Sutcliffe; children: Stephanie, Jennifer, Horst. BS, Embry-Riddle Aero. U., 1972. Mgr. airport City of Klamath Falls, Oreg., 1972-74, City of Fresno, Calif., 1974-79, Orange County, Santa Ana, 1979-80; dir. aviation San Jose (Calif.) Airport, 1980-89; aviation and parking cons. Raul Regalado & Assocs., 1989-2001; dep. dir. aviation Houston Dept. Aviation, 1991-95; market pres. airport properties APCOA, Inc., Vancouver, Wash., 1995-97, market pres. nat. sales Dallas, 1997-98; pres., CEO Met Nashville Airport Authority, 2001—. Capt. U.S. Army, 1966-71, col. USAR (retired). Decorated Legion of Merit, Bronze Star, DFC, Air medal with 49 oak leaf clusters, Meritorious Svc. medal, Army Commendation medal with 3 oak leaf clusters. Mem. Am. Assn. Airport Execs., Calif. Assn. Airport Execs. (pres. 1980-81), Airport Operators Coun. Internat. (bd. dirs. 1986-88), Vietnam Helicopter Pilots Assn., Ret. Officers Assn., Aero. Club No. Calif. (bd. dirs. 1982-91, pres. 1987-89), Quiet Birdmen. E-mail: raul_regalado@nashintl.com.

REGALMUTO, NANCY MARIE, small business owner, psychic consultant, therapist; b. Bay Shore, N.Y., Aug. 24, 1956; d. Antonio J. Jr. and Agnes C. (Dietz) R. Student, SUNY, Stony Brook. Sales mgr. Fire, Inc., Hempstead, N.Y., 1976-78; sports handicapper Red Hot Sport, J. Dime Sports, Diamond Sports, Hicksville, 1978—; small bus. owner, pres. Synergy (vitamin/nutritional product mfr. and distributor), Bellport, 1981—. Cons. on medicine, fin., past life, bus. readings, hypnosis, substance abuse, archeology, law enforcement investigations, family, counseling, inter-species comm., animal therapy, psychic surgery, healing, 1989—; lectr. in field, specializing in holistic remedies and therapies, 1989-91. Columnist Daily Racing Form, 1989-91; appeared on numerous TV programs, worldwide radio, mags., newspapers. Lectr., seminar leader, written about in numerous books. Min. Universal Life Ch., 1996, 97, Ch. of Inner Wisdom, 1996, 97. Mem. NAFE, Internat. Platform Assn., Horse Protection Assn., Therapeutic Riding for the Handicapped, World Wildlife Fedn. Office: 18 Woodland Park Rd Bellport NY 11713-2315

REGAN, CHARLOTTE CAME, real estate company executive; b. Salina, Kans., Apr. 10, 1941; d. Charles W. Marie A. (Gunzelman) Came; m. James V. Regan Jr., Feb. 24, 1962; children: Annette Regan Loyd, James V. III, John C., Joseph P. BBA, Marymount Coll. Kans., 1963. Cert. residential specialist. Savs. counselor Gibraltar Savs., Ft. Worth, 1977-78; broker/assoc., property mgr. Award Realtors, Inc., 1978-90; broker/assoc. Wm. Rigg Inc., 1990-93, Coldwell Banker, Salina, Kans., 1993-99; co-owner John Utsey Properties Inc., Ft. Worth, 1999—2002; owner, broker Sunflower Realty, Inc., 2002—. Membership chair Salina Bd. Realtors, 1996, 97, ednl. chair, 1996, 97, profl. stds. mem., 1996-97. 2d v.p. Kiwanis Internat., Salina, 1996, pres.-elect, 1997. Mem. AAUW (mem.-at-large), Women's Coun. Realtors (party chair, meetings chair 1991-92), Nat. Assn. Realtors Property Mgrs., Cert. Residential Specialist (Kans. chpt.), Salina Kiwanis Club (pres. 1997-98). Republican. Roman Catholic. Avocations: piano, bridge, decorating and refurbishing old homes. Home: 4351 Delarosa Ct Fort Worth TX 76126-2305 Office: Ste 5A 1020 Macon St Fort Worth TX 76102-4562

REGAN, DAVID, brain researcher, psychology and biology educator; b. Scarborough, Eng., May 5, 1935; arrived in Can., 1976; s. Randolph and Muriel Frances (Varley) R.; m. Marian Pauline Marsh, Aug. 15, 1959; children: Douglas Lawrence, Howard Michael. BSc, London U., 1957, MSc, 1958, PhD, 1964, DSc, 1974. Lectr. physics London U., 1960-65; reader neurosci. Keele U., Eng., 1965-75; prof. psychology Dalhousie U., Can., 1976-80, prof. physiology Can., 1980-84, assoc. prof. medicine Can., 1978-84, prof. medicine Can., 1984-87, prof. ophthalmology Can., 1980-87, prof. otolaryngology Can., 1980-84, Killam rsch. prof. Can., 1978-82; prof. engrng. Rutgers U., 1985-86; prof. psychology York U., Can., 1987—, prof. biology Can.; prof. ophthalmology U. Toronto, Ont., Can., 1987—. Retained inventor Wilkinson-Graviner Group, Eng., 1970-75; cons. Westinghouse,

Pitts., 1980-86; co-dir. human performance in space lab. Inst. for Space and Terrestrial Sci., York U., 1989—, disting. rsch. prof., 1991—; indsl. rsch. chair aviation vision Natural Sci. and Engring. Rsch. Coun. Can./Can. Aviation Electronics, 1993—; Spinoza profl. U. Amsterdam, The Netherlands, 1999. Author: Human Evoked Potentials, 1972, Human Brain Electrophysiology, 1989, Human Perception of Objects, 2000; editor: Spatial Vision, 1989, Binocular Vision, 1989, Vision Research, 1992; contbr. over 250 articles to profl. jours.; holder 8 patents. Recipient Forman prize for med. rsch., 1983, Prentice medal, 1990, Sir J.W. Dawson Medal, Royal Soc. Can., 1997, award of excellence Nat. Sci. and Engring. Rsch. Coun. Can., 2000; rsch. grantee NIH, NRC, Air Force Office Sci. Rsch., Nat. Scis. and Engring. Rsch. Coun. Can., Med. Rsch. Coun.; Killam fellow, 1990. Fellow: Optical Soc. Am., Royal Soc. Can.; mem.: Order Can., Netherlands Royal Acad. (fgn.), Am. Acad. Optometry, Royal Coll. Sci. (London) (assoc.), Assn. Rsch. in Vision and Ophthalmology, Soc. Clin. Electroretinography, Exptl. Psychology Soc. Avocations: cricket, walking, modern European history. Office: York U Dept Psychology 4700 Keele St North York ON Canada M3J 1P3

REGAN, DONALD THOMAS, financier, artist, lecturer; b. Cambridge, Mass., Dec. 21, 1918; m. Ann G. Buchanan, July 11, 1942. BA, Harvard U., 1940; LLD, Hahnemann Med. Coll. Hosp., 1968, U. Pa., 1972, Pace U., 1973, Middlebury Coll., 1999; DHL (hon.), Colgate U. With Merrill Lynch, Pierce, Fenner & Smith Inc. (and predecessor), 1946-81, exec. v.p., 1964-68, pres., 1968-70, chmn., chief exec. officer, 1971-80; chmn. bd., chief exec. officer Merrill Lynch & Co. Inc., 1973-81; sec. Dept. of Treasury, Washington, 1981-85; White House chief of staff, 1985-87. Vice chmn., dir. N.Y. Stock Exchange, 1972-75. Author: A View from the Street, 1972, For the Record, 1988. Chmn. bd. trustees U. Pa., 1974-78, life trustee, 1971-80. Lt. col. USMCR, World War II. Laureat Bus. Hall of Fame, 1981; Commdr. Legion of Honor. Mem. Army-Navy Club (Washington). Office: 266 Mclaws Cir Williamsburg VA 23185

REGAN, ELLEN FRANCES (MRS. WALSTON SHEPARD BROWN), ophthalmologist, educator; b. Boston, Feb. 1, 1919; d. Edward Francis and Margaret (Moynihan) R.; m. Walston Shepard Brown, Aug. 13, 1955. AB, Wellesley Coll., 1940; MD, Yale U., 1943. Intern Boston City Hosp., 1944; asst. resident, resident Inst. Ophthalmology, Presbyn. Hosp., N.Y.C., 1944-47, asst. ophthalmologist, 1947-56, asst. attending ophthalmologist, 1956-84; instr. ophthalmology Columbia Coll. Physicians and Surgeons, 1947-55, assoc. ophthalmology, 1955-67, asst. clin. prof., 1967-84. Mem. AMA, Am. Ophthal. Soc., Am. Acad. Ophthalmology, N.Y. Acad. Medicine, N.Y. State Med. Soc., Mass. Med. Soc., River Club. Office: PO Box 632 Tuxedo Park NY 10987-0632

REGAN, FRANCIS VINCENT, lawyer; b. Toronto, Ont., Can., Dec. 13, 1922; s. James Dennis and Irene Philomena (Duggan) R.; m. Barbara Jane Callahan, Apr. 26, 1947; children: Rosemary, Paul, Michael, Deborah, John, Mary Anne. BCom., U. Toronto, 1945; LLB, York U., 1949. Apptd. Queen's Counsel, Ont., 1964. Pvt. practice, Toronto, 1949—. Co-founder radio sta. C.K.S.L.-A.M., London, Ont., 1955, C.I.Q.M.-F.M., London, 1986. Pres. Toronto Dist. Liberal Assn., 1956-58, Liberal Bus. Men's Club of Toronto, 1961-63, The Ont. Club, Toronto, 1970-72; bd. dirs. Our Lady of Mercy Hosp., 1961-74, chmn., 1971-74; bd. dirs. St. John's Sch., Uxbridge, 1966-75, chmn., 1970-75; bd. dirs. Can. Opera Co., 1969-80; bd. dirs. Met. Toronto adv. bd. Salvation Army, 1980—, chmn., 1983-86. Named Knight Equestrian Order of Holy Sepulchre of Jerusalem, 1973, Knight Comdr. with Star Equestrian Order of Holy Sepulchre of Jerusalem, 1979. Mem. Can. Assn. of Knights of Sovereign Mil. Order of Malta (knight of magistral grace 1983, pres. 1992—, knight grand cross of magistral grace 1995), Venerable Order St. John (hon. life mem., grand priory of Can.), Ont. Club (hon. life mem.). Home: 611 Lonsdale Rd Toronto ON Canada M5P 1R8 Office: 65 Queen St W Ste 1507 Toronto ON Canada M5H 2M5

REGAN, FREDERIC DENNIS, cardiologist, internist; b. Newburyport, Mass., Aug. 21, 1921; s. Dennis and Catherine R. (Haley) R.; w. Margaret amary Regan. Student Syracuse U., 1940-42; M.D., U. Buffalo, 1945; children: Denise, Frederic, Michael. Intern, USPHS Hosp., S.I., N.Y., 1945-46, research fellow in cardiology, 1947, resident in medicine, dep. chief medicine, chief cardiac clinic, 1950-52; practice medicine specializing in cardiology and internal medicine; chief of medicine Richmond Meml. Hosp. and Health Ctr. (now S.I. Univ Hosp.), dir. medicine; instr. medicine N.Y. Hosp.; organizer, dir. Gateway State Bank. Diplomate Am. Bd. Internal Medicine. Fellow ACP, Am. Coll. Cardiology, N.Y. Cardiology Soc.; mem. Richmond County Med. Soc. (pres. 1961-62).

REGAN, JAMES RICHARD, JR. computer company executive; b. Hinsdale, Ill., Apr. 8, 1966; s. James Richard and Patricia Brahm Regan; m. Evonne Therese McGuire, May 17, 1997 (div. Apr. 2000). BA, U. Tex., 1989. Sys. engr. Dell Computer Corp., Austin, Tex., 1993-97, s.w. engring. mgr., 1997-99, s.w. product program mgr., 1999—. Democrat. Office: Dell Computer Corp 1 Dell Way Round Rock TX 78682

REGAN, MICHAEL PATRICK, lawyer; b. Bklyn., Feb. 22, 1941; s. Cornelius Francis and Marguerite (Cann) R.; m. Susan Ann Light, July 13, 1974; children: Michael Patrick, Brian Christopher, Mark Dennis. BA in English, U. Notre Dame, 1963; LLB, Albany Law Sch., Union U., 1967, JD, 1968. Bar: N.Y. 1967, Va. 1975. Assoc. Medwin & McMahon, Albany, N.Y., 1967-69; asst. dist. atty. Albany County, N.Y., 1969; corp. atty. Mohasco Corp., Amsterdam, N.Y., 1969-74; asst. gen. csl. Dan River Inc., Danville, Va., 1975, assoc. gen. counsel, 1981-84, assoc. gen. counsel, asst. sec., 1984, acting gen. counsel, asst. sec., 1988, gen. counsel, asst. sec., 1989, assoc. gen. counsel, asst. sec. Dan River Holding Co., 1984-88, acting gen. counsel, asst. sec., 1988, gen. counsel, asst. sec., 1989—; assoc. gen. counsel, asst. sec. Dan River Svc. Corp. of Va., 1984-88; gen. counsel, Wunda Weve Carpets, Inc., Greenville, S.C., 1990-93; pvt. practice, Danville, Va., 1990—. Clarinetist, saxophonist Tightsqueeze Philharm. Band; leader: The DanceNotes; sec. DanPac Polit. Action Com., 1976-89; prin. Danville Symphony Orch., 1998-. Mem. ABA, N.Y. State Bar Assn., Va. Bar Assn., Danville Bar Assn., Union Internat. des Avocats, Rotary. Home: 236 Cambridge Cir Danville VA 24541-5233 Office: 703 Patton St Danville VA 24541-1905

REGAN, MURIEL, librarian; b. N.Y.C., July 15, 1930; d. William and Matilda (Riebel) Blome; m. Robert Regan, 1966 (div. 1976); 1 child, Jeanne Booth. BA, Hunter Coll., N.Y.C., 1950; MLS, Columbia U., 1952; MBA, Pace U., N.Y.C., 1982. Post libr. US Army, Okinawa, 1952-53; researcher P.F. Collier, N.Y.C., 1953-57; asst. libr. to libr. Rockefeller Found., 1957-67; dep. chief libr. Manhattan Community Coll., l967-68; libr. Booz Allen & Hamilton, 1968-69, Rockefeller Found., N.Y.C., 1969-82; prin. Gossage Regan Assocs., Inc., 1980-95; pub. svcs. libr. Carlsbad (N.Mex.) Pub. Libr., 1995-2000. Dir. N.Y. Met. Reference and Rsch. Libr. Agy., 1988-95, Coun. Nat. Libr. and Info. Assns., 1991-95; cons. Librs. Info. Ctrs., Gossage Sager Assocs., 2001—. Elder First Presbyn. Ch. of Carlsbad, 1997-99, Stephan min., 2000—, deacon, 2002-. Mem. ALA, Spl. Librs. Assn. pres. 1989-90), Archons of Colophon, Altrusa. Avocations: cats, reading, playing piano, traveling. Home: 604 N Lake St Carlsbad NM 88220-5014 E-mail: murielregan@hotmail.com.

REGAN, PAUL JEROME, JR. manufacturing company executive, consultant; b. Ithaca, N.Y., Mar. 13, 1940; s. Paul Jerome and Mildred (Dempsey) R.; m. Barbara Ann Easton, Feb. 4, 1962 (dec. Nov. 1996); children: Paul J. III, Timothy Andrew, Allison Ann. BS, Cornell U., 1962, MBA, 1965. Pers. asst. Corning (N.Y.) Glass Works, 1963, pers. mgr., 1964-68, dept. mgr. mfg. State College, 1968-70, personnel devel. cons. Corning, 1970-72, prodn. supt. Wilmington, N.C., 1972-74, devel. mgr. Corning, 1974-77, corp. dir., 1977-83, v.p. human resources, 1983-86; sr. v.p. Corning Inc., 1986-93; ret. Mem. adv. bd. Cornell U., Ithaca, N.Y., 1970-82, lectr., 1977—; founding mem. Human Resource Planning Soc., 1974-93; dir. Corning Can. Inc., Toronto, 1983-93. Contbr. articles to books and profl. jours. including Human Resource Planning Soc. jour.; expert comment on exec. compensation and succession including Wall St. Jour., N.Y. Times, Bus. Week, Forbes. Mem. exec. bd. Thousand Islands Assn., Gananoque, Ont., Can., 1988—, pres., 1999—; chmn. Blue Ribbon Fund, Corning Hosp., 1989-93; mem. Rep. Nat. Com., Washington, 1984—; dir. State College C. of C., 1967-73, Half Moon Bay Found., dir. Friends of the 1000 Islands Mus., Inc., 2000—; chmn. Historic Thousand Islands Village Found., 1998—. Johnson Soc. fellow Cornell U., 1991; named Ky. Col., State of Ky., 1984, Adm. Thousand Islands Navy, 1999. Mem. Am. Compensation Assn. (regional chair 1978-81), Am. Acad. Polit. and Social Sci., Heron Soc. (life.), Cornell Club, Nat. Mus. Am. Indian (charter, membership com. 1991—), Antique Boat Mus., Save the River Com. (adv. 1982—), Menninger Found. (patron), Trust for Historic Preservation, Delta Phi (past pres.). Avocations: antique wooden boats, decoys, photographs, Inuit art, poetry.

REGAN, PETER FRANCIS, III, physician, psychiatry educator; b. Bklyn., Nov. 11, 1924; s. Peter Francis Jr. and Veronica (Tierney) R.; m. Laurette Patricia O'Connor, June 18, 1949; children: Peter, Stephen, William, Elizabeth, John, Carol. MD, Cornell U., Ithaca, N.Y., 1949. Diplomate Am. Bd. Psychiatry and Neurology, Nat. Bd. Med. Examiners. Intern in medicine N.Y. Hosp., 1949-50; asst. resident psychiatry Payne Whitney Psychiat. Clinic, 1950, 53-54, resident, 1954-56; asst. prof. psychiatry Cornell U. Med. Coll., 1956-58; prof., head dept. psychiatry U. Fla. Coll. Medicine, chief psychiat. svc. Univ. Teaching Hosp., 1958-64; prof. psychiatry SUNY, Buffalo, 1964-84, v.p. health affairs, 1964-67, exec. v.p. univ., 1967-69, exec. v.p., acting pres. univ., 1969-70, vice chancellor acad. programs, 1970-71; assoc. chief staff for edn. Buffalo VA Med. Ctr., 1979-84; prof. psychiatry U. Tex. Health Sci. Ctr., San Antonio, 1984-87, assoc. dean Sch. Medicine, 1986-87; assoc. chief staff for edn. San Antonio VA Med. Ctr., 1984-86, chief staff, 1986-87; dep. assoc. chief med. dir. for acad. affairs VA Cen. Office, Washington, 1987-88, assoc. chief med. dir. for acad. affairs, 1988-92; prof. emeritus / sen. cons. dept. psychiatry SUNY, Buffalo, 1992—; interim chair dept. psychiatry Med. U. S.C., 2001—02. Project dir. Ctr. for Ednl. Rsch. and Innovation, OECD, 1972-74. Author: (with F. Flach) Chemotherapy in Emotional Disorders, 1960, (With E. Pattishall) Behavioral Science Contributions to Psychiatry; contbr. articles to profl. jours. Capt. M.C. AUS, 1951-52. Fellow Am. Psychiat. Assn., Am. Coll. Psychiatrists (bd. regents 1986-95, 2d v.p. 1988, 1st v.p. 1989, pres.-elect 1990, pres. 1991); mem. AMA, Alpha Omega Alpha. Home: 900 Delaware Ave Apt 504 Buffalo NY 14209-2018 Office: SUNY Dept Psychiatry 462 Grider St Buffalo NY 14215-3021

REGAN, RICHARD JOSEPH, education educator, writer; PhD in Polit. Sci., U. Chgo., 1967. Prof. Fordham U., Bronx, NY, 1968—. Author: Just War, 1996; translator: The De Malo of Thomas Aquinas, 2001. Roman Catholic. Avocation: running. Home and Office: Spellman Hall Forham U. Bronx NY 10458 Fax: 718-817-5717.

REGAN, ROBERT CHARLES, English language educator; b. Indpls., Mar. 13, 1930; s. Francis Bernard and Alma Ophelia (McBride) R.; m. Katherine Jeanclos, Aug. 11, 1989; children by previous marriage: Christopher, Alison, Amelia. BA, Centenary Coll., 1951; MA, Harvard U., 1952; PhD, U. Calif., Berkeley, 1965. Instr. English, Centenary Coll., 1956-57; asst. prof. English, U. Va., 1963-67; Fulbright-Hays lectr. Am. civilization U. Montpellier, France, 1967-68; assoc. prof. English, U. Pa., Phila., 1968-82, prof., 1982-2000, undergrad. chmn. dept. English, 1978-80, 81-83, 89-90, dir. Penn-in-London program, prof. emeritus, 2000—. Lectr. Internat. Communications Agy., Morocco, Algeria, Jordan, 1980; vis. prof. King's Coll., London, 1983-84 Author: Unpromising Heroes; Mark Twain and His Characters, 1966, Poe: A Collection of Critical Essays, 1967; mng. editor: Am. Quar., 1969-72; mem. editl. bd. Mark Twain Papers, U. Calif., Berkeley, 1997—; contbr. articles to lit. jours. Served with USNR, 1952-56, 61-62. Woodrow Wilson fellow, 1962-63; Am. Philos. Soc. research grantee, 1970 Mem. Univ. Mews Assn. (pres. 1999-2001), Faculty Club U. Pa. (bd. govs. 1997-2001). Democrat. Episcopalian. Office: U Pa Dept English Philadelphia PA 19104

REGAN, SIRI LISA LAMBOURNE, gifted education educator; b. New Orleans; d. George William Hugh and Roma Schilling Lambourne; m. Stephen E. Regan, July 21, 1978; 1 child, Addie R.F.R. BA in English Edn., U. New Orleans, 1977, M in Edn. Curriculum and Instrn., 1981, postgrad. Cert. tchr., La. Tchr. Roosevelt Middle Sch., Kenner, La., 1977—. Presenter in field; dir., coord. La. Writing Project Jefferson Parish, 1989-90; co-dir. Greater New Orleans Writing Project Inst., 1990, audio-visual coord., 1992—, comuter project coord., 1995—; coord. Jefferson Dollars for Scholars, 1995—, LEAP Engring. program, 1997—, tech. coord., 1999—. Contbr. articles to profl. jours. Named Tchr. of Yr. for Jefferson Parish, Metairie Jaycees, 1987, Tchr. of the Yr. for State of La., La. Jaycees, 1988, La. Middle Sch. Tchr. of Yr., La. State Dept. Edn., 1989, Tchr. of Yr., Southeastern Regional Middle Sch., 1989; recipient Valley Forge Freedom Found. Educator's medal, 1989-90, Young Careerist award Jefferson Bus. and Profl. Women's Club, Key to City of Kenner, 1989. Mem. Nat. Assn. Bilingual Educators (cert.) Nat. Coun. Tchrs. English (cert.), Nat. Middle Sch. Assn., La. Middle Sch. Assn., Coun. Learning Disabilitis, Coun. Exceptional Children, S.E. La. Profl. Assn. Gifted and Talented, Kappa Delta Phi, Phi Delta Kappa, Alpha Theta Epsilon. Meth. Avocations: reading, needlework, cooking, woodworking, photography. Office: Roosevelt Mid Sch 3315 Maine Ave Kenner LA 70065-3806

REGAN, SUSAN GINSBERG, lawyer; b. N.Y.C., Oct. 20, 1947; d. Irwin Arthur and Sylvia (Rosen) Ginsberg; m. Neil A. Goldberg, Jan. 24, 1975 (div. May 1987); children: Jane Goldberg, Rafael Goldberg; m. Edward Van Buren Regan, Oct. 12, 1991. BA, U. Mich., 1969; JD, SUNY, Buffalo, 1974. Bar: N.Y. 1975. Asst. county atty. Erie County, Buffalo, 1975-78; ptnr. Magavern, Magavern & Grimm LLP, 1982-98; assoc. gen. counsel Vis. Nurse Svc. N.Y., N.Y.C., 1998—. Mem., chair establishment com. N.Y. State Pub. Health Coun., 1996—; clin. asst. prof. SUNY Sch. Medicine and Biomed. Scis., Buffalo, 1997—. Mem. Nat. Health Lawyers Assn., N.Y. State Bar Assn. (health law com., com. on profl. ethics, N.Y.C., 1984-87). Avocation: skiing. Office: Vis Nurse Svc NY 107 E 70th St New York NY 10021-5006 E-mail: sregan@mail1.vnsny.org.

REGAN, SUZANNE ELIZABETH, film and television educator; b. Portland, Maine, June 23, 1949; d. Francis John and Alice Volora (Ward) R.; m. Beryl Bellman, July 20, 1990; 1 child, Sarah Alice Regan Bellman. BA, Simmons Coll., 1971; MA, UCLA, 1974; PhD, U. Mass., 1981. Prof. comm. studies Calif. State U., L.A., 1978—. Presenter in more than 30 profl. confs. Editor Jour. of Film & Video, 1997-02; contbr. articles to profl. jours. Sarah Orne Jewett scholar Simmons Coll., Boston, 1970-71. Mem. Internat. Comm. Assn. (Nat. chpt.), Soc. for Cinema Studies, Univ. Film & Video Assoc. (sec. 1983-84, bd. dirs. 1985-86, 97-98). Office: Calif State U Dept Comm Studies 5151 State University Dr Los Angeles CA 90032-4226

REGAN, THOMAS JOSEPH, priest, educator; b. Waltham, Mass., Apr. 13, 1954; s. John C. and Sarah P. (Corbett) R. AB, Boston Col., 1976; AM, Fordham U., 1982, PhD, 1984; M in Divinity, Weston Sch., 1987. Ordained priest Roman Cath. Ch., 1987. Asst. prof. Fairfield (Conn.) U., 1988-93, assoc. prof., chair. Philosophy dept., 1993-2000, assoc. dean Coll. Arts & Scis., 2000—. Trustee St. Joseph's U., Phila. Mem. Soc. of Jesus (New England province), Jesuit Philosophical Assn. (pres. 1997-98), Alpha Sigma Nu (pres., chmn., nat. bd. dirs. 1991-97). Roman Catholic. Office: Fairfield U N Benson Rd Fairfield CT 06430-5195 E-mail: tjregan@mail.fairfield.edu.

REGAN, WILLIAM JOSEPH, JR. energy company executive; b. Bronx, N.Y., Mar. 7, 1946; s. William Joseph and Eleanor F. (Malone) R.; m. Mary Lee Wynn; children— Katrina Lee, Thomas Wynn, James William BS, U.S. Air Force Acad., 1967; MBA, U. Wis.-Madison, 1969, PhD, 1972. Asst. prof. Wayne State U., Detroit, 1971-75; with Nat. Bank Detroit, 1975-77; sr. bus. planner Am. Natural Resources Co., Detroit, 1977-78, dir. fin. planning, 1978-82, v.p., treas., 1982-85; v.p. corp. fin. United Svcs. Automobile Assn., San Antonio, 1986-88, sr. v.p., treas., 1988-95; v.p., treas. Entergy Corp., New Orleans, 1995-99; CFO Calif. Ind. Sys. Operator Corp., Folsom, Calif., 1999—. Home: 15181 De La Pena Cir Rancho Murieta CA 95683-9798 Office: 151 Blue Ravine Rd Folsom CA 95630 E-mail: wregan@calweb.com, wregan37@earthlink.net.

REGAZZI, JOHN HENRY, retired electronic distributor executive; b. N.Y.C., Jan. 4, 1921; s. Caesar B. and Jennie (Moruzzi) R.; m. Doris Mary Litzau, Feb. 16, 1946; children: Mark, Dale BBA, Pace Coll., 1951. CPA, N.Y. Mgr. Price Waterhouse, N.Y.C., 1946-62; comptroller ABC, 1962-70; sr. v.p., CFO Avnet, Inc., 1970-93; retired, 1993. Contbr. articles to profl. jours. Pres. bd. River Dell Regional High Sch., Oradell, N.J., 1962-65; trustee, treas. Oradell Pub. Library, 1970-79; councilman Borough of Oradell, 1979-88. Served as staff sgt. USAF, 1942-45 Mem. AICPA, Fin. Execs. Internat. Republican. Roman Catholic. Home: 8980 King John Ct Las Vegas NV 89149-3221

REGELBRUGGE, ROGER RAFAEL, steel company executive; b. Eeklo, Belgium, May 22, 1930; came to U.S., 1953, naturalized, 1961; s. Victor and Rachel (Roesbeke) R.; m. Dorcas Merchant; children: Anita, Marc, Laurie, Jon, Craig, Kurt, Christiane, Lauren, Roger Rafael Jr. BSME, State Tech. Coll., Ghent, 1951; BS in Indsl. Engring, Gen. Motors Inst., Flint, Mich., 1955; MSME, Mich. State U., 1964. Supr. product engring. dept. Gen. Motors Corp., Antwerp, 1955-58; chief devel. engr., then gen. mgr. Airmaster div. Hayes Industries Inc., Jackson, Mich., 1958-66; with Koehring Co., 1966-74, group v.p. internat. ops., 1969-74; exec. v.p. Korf Industries, Inc., Charlotte, N.C., 1974-77, chmn.; chmn., pres., CEO Georgetown Industries, Inc. (formerly Korf Industries, Inc.), 1977-95; chmn., CEO GS Industries Inc. (formerly Georgetown Industries), 1995-97, chmn., 1997-99. Bd. dirs. GS Industries. Mem. adv. coun. Coll. Engring. U. Notre Dame; trustee Belmont (N.C.) Abbey Coll.; bd. trustees Charlotte County Day Sch. Mem. ASME, Am. Soc. Automotive Engrs., Carmel Country Club, Tower Club (Charlotte), Georgetown Club (Washington). Roman Catholic.

REGELLO, TIMOTHY JAMES, civil engineer; b. Richmond, Calif., Feb. 20, 1959; s. Louis Joseph and Esther Marie (Marinelli) R.; m. Michelle Mutschler; 1 child, James Anthony; 1 stepchild, Benjamin Riley Wilson. AA, Palomar Community Coll., 1980; BSCE, U. Calif., Irvine, 1983; MBA, Nat. U., San Diego, 1986. Registered profl. engr., Calif.; cert. land surveyor in training, Calif. Jr. design engr. Civil Design Group, San Diego, 1983-84; design engr. O'Day Cons., Carlsbad, Calif., 1984-87; assoc. civil engr. City of San Marcos, 1987—. Treas. Encinitas (Calif.) Village Homeowners Assn., 1989-91; v.p. Cath. Alumni Club of San Diego, 1990-91. Mem. ASCE. Republican. Roman Catholic. Office: City of San Marcos Capital Improvements San Marcos CA 92069

REGENBOGEN, ADAM, judge; b. Steyer, Austria, June 12, 1947; s. William and Pauline (Feuerstein) R.; m. Paula Ruth Rothenberg, June 27, 1970 (div. Oct. 1992); children: Stacy, Candice; m. Helen Busuttil Drwal, Apr. 20, 1996; 1 stepchild, Jason A. Drwal. BA, Temple U., 1969; MSW, U. Pa., 1972; JD, Temple U., 1980. Bar: N.Y. 1983. Social worker VA, Coatesville, Pa., 1974-78, supr. Northport, N.Y., 1978-80, quality assurance dir., 1980-87; dir. quality assurance N.Y. State Office Mental Health, Willard, 1987-91; conciliator, acting judge N.Y. State Workers Compensation Bd., Binghamton, 1992-98; judge Binghamton, Norwich, Oneonta, Norwich, 1998—; pvt. practice N.Y., 1983-98; conciliator, acting judge Workers Compensation Bd., 1992-98, judge, 1998—. Organizer/incorporator Ithaca (N.Y.) Reform Temple, 1992; organizer Parents Without Partners, Ithaca, 1992. Recipient Pro Bono Svc. award Suffolk County Bar Assn., 1986. Mem. Tompkins County Bar Assn. Home: 14 Grant St Port Dickinson Binghamton NY 13901 Office: Workers Compensation Bd 44 Hawley St Binghamton NY 13901-4434 E-mail: adam.regenbogen@wcb.state.ny.us.

REGENER, CONNIE SUE, minister, religious commentator; b. Albany, Calif. d. Noble Morgan and Lelvina Opal Thompson; m. John Roland Regener, Feb. 1, 1974; children: Mark, Ryan (dec.). BA, Calif. State U., 1970; MDiv, Fuller Theol. Sem., 2000. Registered record adminstr.; cert. bereavement facilitator; cert. tchr., Calif.; ordained min. Evangelical Ch. Alliance, 2000. Med. record cons. Anderson Adminstrn. Record Cons., Santa Ana, Calif., 1991-93; instr. Capistrano-Laguna Beach Regional Occupl. Program, San Juan Capistrano, 1993-95, Saddleback Coll., Mission Viejo, 1994-96; pastor women's discipleship ministries First Bapt. Ch., Downey, 1996-98; interfaith dir. Nat. Conf. for Cmty. and Justice, Newport Beach, 2000—. Freelance writer L.A. Times; founding mem. Faith Cmtys. in Prevention, Santa Ana, 2000—; pvt. practice spiritual dir., Irvine, Calif. Leader Cmtys. of Faith Tour, Nat. Conf. for Cmty. and Justice, Newport Beach, 2000—. Recipient Humanitarian and Interfaith award, Islamic Soc. of Orange County and Coun. on Am.-Islamic Rels. Mem. Evangel. Press Assn., Mins. Assn., Evangel. Alliance, Rotary of Santa Ana. Home: 6 Amberwood Irvine CA 92604-3102 E-mail: cregener@cox.net.

REGENSTEINER, ELSE FRIEDSAM (MRS. BERTOLD REGENSTEINER), textile designer, educator; b. Munich, Apr. 21, 1906; came to U.S., 1936, naturalized, 1942; d. Ludwig and Hilda (Nelson-Bachhofer) Friedsam; m. Bertold Regensteiner, Oct. 3, 1926; 1 dau., Helga Regensteiner Sinaiko-Botts. Tchrs. degree, Deutsche Frauenschule, Munich, 1925; student, U. Munich, Inst. Design, Chgo. Instr. Hull House, Chgo., 1941-45, Inst. Design, Chgo., 1942-46; asst. prof. Sch. Art Inst. Chgo., 1945-57, prof., 1957-71, prof. emeritus, 1971—; textile designer for industry; partner Reg/Wick Studios, 1945-80; also lectr. Cons. Am. Farm Sch., Thessaloniki, Greece, 1972-78 Exhibited one man shows throughout U.S., 1946—; group shows include Art Inst. Chgo., 1997; represented in permanent collection, Art Inst. Chgo., Cooper-Hewitt Mus., N.Y.C.; Author: The Art of Weaving, 2d edit, 1981, 3d edit., 1986, German edit., 1987, Program for a Weaving Study Group, 1974, Weaver's Study Course- Sourcebook for Ideas and Techniques, 1982, 2d edit., 1987, Geometric Design in Weaving, 1986; written about in Else Regensteiner, Biography of a Weaver, 1997; contbr. articles to profl. mags. Recipient 1st prize for drapery and upholstery Internat. Textile Exhbn., 1946; five citations merit Am. Inst. Decorators, 1947, 48, 50; Regensteiner award Midwest Weavers Assn., 1980; Award of Merit in Textiles, The Textile Arts Ctr., Chgo., 1994. Fellow Collegium Craftsmen of Am. Crafts Coun.; mem. Am. Crafts Coun., Handweavers Guild Am. (bd. dirs. 1970-78). Address: 5550 South Shore Dr Apt 406 Chicago IL 60637-5031

REGENSTREIF, HERBERT, lawyer; b. N.Y.C., May 13, 1935; s. Max and Jeannette (Hacker) R.; m. Patricia Friedman, Dec. 20, 1967 (div. July 1968); m. Charlotte Lois Levy, Dec. 11, 1980; 1 child, Cara Rachael. BA, Hobart Coll., 1957; JD, N.Y. Law Sch., 1960; MS, Pratt Inst., 1985. Bar: N.Y. 1961, Ky. 1985, U.S. Dist. Ct. (ea. and so. dists.) N.Y. 1962, U.S. Dist. Ct. (ea. dist.) Ky. 1998, U.S. Tax Ct. 1967, U.S. Ct. Appeals (2d cir.) 1962, U.S. Supreme Ct. 1967. Ptnr. Fried & Regenstreif, P.C., Mineola, N.Y., 1963—; reservist atty. Fed. Emergency Mgmt. Agy., 1998-99. Cons. in field; arbitrator Dist. Ct., Nassau County, N.Y., 1989—, N.Y.C. Civil Ct., 1984-86; sec.-treas. Sta. WAHY-FM, Inc., 1998-2000. Contbr. articles to profl. jours. County committeeman Dem. Com., Queens County, N.Y., 1978-79. Mem. Bar Assn. Nassau County, Ky. Bar Assn., Phi Delta Phi, Beta Phi Mu, Hobart Club of N.Y. (gov. 1968-69).

REGENSTREIF, S(AMUEL) PETER, political scientist, educator; b. Montreal, Que., Can., Sept. 9, 1936; s. Albert Benjamin and Miriam Lillian (Issenman) R.; children: Anne Erica, Mitchell Chester, Jeffrey Gershon, Gail Aviva. BA, McGill U., 1957; PhD, Cornell U., 1963. Mem. faculty U. Rochester, 1961—, prof. polit. sci., 1971—; coordinator Can. studies program, 1967—. Editl. cons. Toronto Star, 1968-82, Chgo. Sun-Times, 1988-89; polit. cons. Bunting Warburg, Toronto, 1973-90, Coopers & Lybrand, Ltd., 1981-89, Loewen, Ondaatje, McCutcheon, 1991-94; prin. Policy Concepts Inc., Toronto; broadcaster CKO Radio Network, 1983-89; pvt. polit. cons. Author: The Diefenbaker Interlude: Parties and Voting in Canada, 1965; syndicated columnist: Toronto Star, 1963-82; contbr. articles to profl. jours. Served to lt. Canadian Army, 1957. Ford. Found. fellow, 1960; Can. Council fellow, 1960, 65; Canadian Royal Commn. on Bilingualism and Biculturalism grantee, 1964-66; recipient Edward Peck Curtis award U. Rochester, 1979 Mem. AAAS, Am. Polit. Sci. Assn., Can. Polit. Sci. Assn., Assn. Can. Studies in U.S., Phi Beta Kappa. Jewish. Home: 438C Browncroft Blvd Rochester NY 14609 Office: Univ Rochester Dept Polit Sci Rochester NY 14627 E-mail: peter.reguistreif@rochester.edu.

REGER, LAWRENCE LEE, trade association administrator; b. Lincoln, Nebr., June 23, 1939; s. Lawrence John and Bertha (Hergenrader) R. Student, U. Nebr., 1961; LL.B., Vanderbilt U., 1964. Bar: Nebr 1964. Asso. firm Crosby, Guenzel & Binning, Lincoln, 1964-70; gen. counsel Nat. Endowment Arts, 1970-72, dir. program devel. and coordination, 1972-78; dir. Am. Assn. Mus., Washington, 1978-86; pres. Heritage Preservation, 1988—. Mem. visual arts vis. com. U. Del., 1995—; mem. cultural property adv. com. USIA, 1996—2000; mem. bd. trustees St. Petersburg Internat. Preservation Ctr., 1996—; bd. dirs. Peck Stacpoole Found. Chmn. Nat. Humanities Alliance, 1982-86; bd. dirs. Nat. Musical Arts, 1990—. Recipient Forbes medal Am. Inst. Conservation, 2000. Home: 5010 Garfield St NW Washington DC 20016-3469 Office: Heritage Preservation 1730 K St NW Ste 566 Washington DC 20006-3847

REGES, MARIANNA ALICE, marketing executive; b. Budapest, Hungary, Mar. 23, 1947; arrived in U.S., 1956, naturalized, 1963; d. Otto H. and Alice M. Reges; children: Rebecca, Charles III. AAS with honors, Fashion Inst. Tech., N.Y.C., 1967; BBA magna cum laude, Baruch Coll., 1971, MBA in Stats., 1978. Media rsch. analyst Doyle, Dane, Bernbach Advt., N.Y.C., 1967-70; rsch. supr. Sta. WCBS-TV, 1970-71; rsch. mgr. Woman's Day mag., 1971-72; asst. media dir. Benton & Bowles Advt., 1972-75; mgr. rsch. and sales devel. NBC Radio, 1975-77; sr. rsch. mgr. Ziff-Davis Pub. Co., 1977-84; media mgr. Bristol-Myers Squibb Co., 1984—2001, Procter & Gamble Co., 2001—. Mem. Spanish Radio Adv. Coun., N.Y.C., 1986—88, Pan-European TV Audience Rsch. Mgmt. Com., 1988—. Mem. advisor Baruch Coll. Advt. Soc., 1975—; active First Presbyn. Ch., N.Y.C. Mem.: Advt. Rsch. Found., Radio and TV Rsch. Coun., Media Rsch. Dirs. Assn., Am. Advt. Fedn., Am. Mktg. Assn., Anthroposophical Soc., Nature Conservancy, Baruch Alumni Assn., Gilda's Club, Beta Gamma Sigma. Home: 626 E 20th St New York NY 10009-1509

REGESTEIN, QUENTIN RODNEY, psychiatrist; b. Port Chester, N.Y., Mar. 28, 1938; s. Quentin Walter and Mary Violante R.; m. Lois Wetzel, Oct. 24, 1970. AB, Dartmouth Coll., 1960; MD CM, McGill U., Montreal, 1964. Rotating intern Jewish Gen. Hosp., Montreal, 1964-65; resident in psychiatry Royal Victoria Hosp., 1965-66, Boston City Hosp., 1966-67, Peter Bent Brigham Hosp., Boston, 1967-68; neurophysiology investigator Aeromed. Rsch. Lab., Alamagordo, N.Mex., 1968-70; psychiatrist Brigham & Women's Hosp., Boston, 1970—. Med. adv. bd. Narcolepsy Network, Cin., 1992—; grant application reviewer NIH, Bethesda, Md., 1989, 94. Author: Sound Sleep (3 vols.), 1980; mem. editl. bd. N.Am. Menopause Soc., Cleve., 1999—; contbr. articles to profl. jours. Recipient Best Paper of Yr. award Am. Coll. Obs. Gyn., 1979. Mem. Am. Sleep Disorder Assn., Sleep Rsch. Assn., Old West Organ Soc. (bd. dirs. 1990—). Avocations: running, music, philosophy. Office: Brigham & Womens Hosp 75 Francis St Boston MA 02115

REGGIE, DORIS BOUSTANY, volunteer; b. Lafayette, La., July 18, 1930; d. Frem Frem and Beatrice (Joseph) Boustany; m. Edmund Michael Reggie, June 17, 1951; children: Ed Michael, Victoria, Denis, Gregory, Alicia, Raymond, Reggie. BS with honors, U. Southwestern La., 1950. Vice chairperson La. State Mus., 1984-88, 92-96, La. Endowment for Humanities, 1982-90, La. Gov.'s Mansion Commn.; mem. adv. com. Boustany Chair in Home Econs., U. Southwestern La.; chairperson Cleanest City Contest, Crowley, 1983, 84; chmn. Crowley, la. city lighting contest, 1980; mem. Dem. Nat. Com. La.; exec. com. La. Dem. Ctrl. Com.; mem. Acadia Parish Dem. Exec. com., 1976-92, La. Dem. State Ctrl. Com., 1976-92; mem. resolution com. Dem. Nat. Conv., 1984, mem. final platform com., 1988; mem. Dem. Nat. Fin. Com., 1980, 84, 88, 92; del. Dem. Nat. Conf., 1976, 80, 84, 88, 92, 96, La. Dem. Conv., 1976—; mem. La. Gov.'s Commn. on Children. Inducted in La. Ctr. for Women and Govt.'s Hall of Fame, 1997. Mem. Equestrian Order of Holy Sepulchre, Crowley Garden Club (pres. 1992-94), Crowley Tree Bd.

REGGIO, VITO ANTHONY, management consultant; b. Rochester, N.Y., Dec. 17, 1929; s. Salvatore and Carrie Angela (LoRe) R.; m. Mary Ann Dolores Pippie, Sept. 28, 1957; children: Salvatore, Angela. BS, Purdue U., 1952; postgrad. sch. modern langs., Middlebury Coll., 1948; postgrad. fellowship, U. Ky., U. Tenn. and U. Ala., 1952-53. Jr. engr. Rochester (N.Y.) Gas and Electric Co., 1950; designer/drafter Globe Constrn. Co., Rochester, 1951; rsch. analyst Commonwealth of Ky., Frankfort, 1952; orgn. & methods analyst, then wage adminstrn. specialist USN Dept. Indsl. Rels., Indpls., 1955-56; cons. mgmt. engr. to project mgr. to account exec. Bus. Rsch. Corp., Chgo., 1956-60; sr. cons. econ. feasibilities Ebasco Svcs., Inc., 1960-63, dir. pers. mgmt. cons. dept., 1970-77; regional mgr., orgn. and pers. mgmt. svcs. EBS Mgmt. Cons., 1963-65, nat. dir. orgn. and pers. mgmt. svcs., 1965-70; pres., bd. dirs. Reggio and Assocs., Inc., 1977—; mng. dir. Pay Data Svc., 1977—. Bd. dirs. Pay Data Svcs., Chgo. Contbr. papers to profl. publs. With U.S. Army, 1953-55. Named Solco Cultural Soc. fellow, Rochester, N.Y., 1948. Mem. Am. Compensation Assn., Am. Mgmt. Assn., Chgo. Compensation Assn., Soc. Human Resources Profls., Soc. Human Resources Mgmt., Human Resources Mgmt. Assn. Chgo., Western Soc. Engrs. E-mail: reggio-associates.com. Office: Reggio and Assocs Inc 4365 Lawn Ave Western Springs IL 60558-1465

REGIER, CHARLES E. music educator; b. Newton, Kans., July 23, 1942; s. Walter Henry and Ruby Fern Regier; m. Diann Carol Regier, June 30, 1963; children: Christopher, Charla. Diploma in Bible, Grace Coll. of Bible, 1963; BA in Music Edn., Southwestern Okla. State U., 1965, MA in Music Edn., 1974. Music tchr. Corn (Okla.) Bible Acad., 1965—, pub. rels., 1993—2002, supt., 2000—02. Music dir. 1st Mennonite Ch., Clinton, Okla., 1963—2002. Named Choral Dir. of Yr., Western Okla. Choral Dirs., 1991; named to Hall of Fame, Okla. Music Educators Assn., 2002. Republican. Avocations: grandchildren, golf, yard work. Home: 308 N Reimer Corn OK 73024 Office: Corn Bible Acad 208 N Reimer Corn OK 73024

REGINALD, ROBERT, administrator, writer, university librarian; b. Fukuoka, Kyushu, Japan, Feb. 11, 1948; came to U.S., 1949; s. Roy Walter and Betty Jane (Kapel) Burgess; m. Mary Alice Wickizer, Oct. 15, 1976; step children: Richard Albert Rogers, (Mary) Louise Reynnells. AB (honors) cum laude, Gonzaga U., 1969; MS in Libr. Sci., U. So. Calif., L.A., 1970. Periodicals libr. Calif. State U., San Bernardino, 1970-78, 80-81, asst. bibliographer, 1976-83, chief cataloger with rank of prof., 1984-1994, head tech. services and collection development, 1994—; editor Newcastle Pub. Co., North Hollywood, Calif., 1970-94; pub. The Borgo Press, San Bernardino, 1975-99; owner Millefleurs Info. Svcs., 2000—. As author, editor or pub. directly or indirectly involved in publ. over 1200 vols.; author 92 books including: Contemporary Science Fiction Authors, 1975, Science Fiction and Fanatasy Literature, 2 vols., 1979 (Book of Yr. Choice mag. 1980), Science Fiction and Fantasy Awards, 1981, (with Jeffrey M. Elliot) If J.F.K. Had Lived, 1982, (with Kevin Hancer) The Paperback Price Guide No. 2, 1982, (with T.E. Dikty) The Work of Julian May, 1985, (with J. Elliot) The Work of George Zebrowski, 1986, (with J. Elliot and Mary Burgess) The Arms Control, Disarmament and Military Security Dictionary, 1989, Codex Derynianus, 1998, Katydid and Other Critters, 2001; outside reader: Anatomy of Wonder, 1981, Horror Literature: A Critical Guide, 1989, Fantasy Literature: A Critical Guide, 1989; adv. editor (with others) Science Fiction, 62 books, 1975, Supernatural & Occult Fiction, 63 books, 1976, Lost Race and Adult Fantasy Fiction, 69 books, 1978, others; pub., co-editor: Science Fiction & Fantasy Book Rev., 12 nos., 1979-80; cons. editor: Survey of Modern Fantasy Literature, 5 vols., 1983; editor LTF Newletter, Calif. Faculty Assn., 1987-89, also numerous monographic series; author numerous articles, revs., pubs.' catalogues, state documents; designer, prodn. mgr. over 100 pub. vols. Recipient Meritorious Performance and Profl. Promise award Calif. State U., San Bernardino, 1987; U. So. Calif., fellow, 1969-70. Mem. AAUP, NEA, Calif. Tchrs. Assn., Calif. Faculty Assn. (libr. task force 1987-91, 94—), Sci. Fiction Writers Am., Horror Writers Am., Mystery Writers Am., Sci. Fiction Rsch. Assn., Ky. Hist. Soc., Blue Earth County Hist. Soc., Upper Cumberland Valley Hist. Soc., Geneal. Soc., Internat PEN West. Democrat. Avocations: genealogical and historical research, films, travel. Office: Millefleurs PO Box 2845 San Bernardino CA 92406-2845 also: Calif State Univ Pfau Libr 5500 University Pkwy San Bernardino CA 92407-2318

REGIS, NINA, librarian, educator; b. Corinth, Miss., Oct. 19, 1928; d. W.C. and Mary Isabelle (Rushing) Hanner; m. George Regis, Sept. 5, 1949 (dec. Jan. 6, 1990); 1 child, Simonne Marie. BA, Bridgewater (Mass.) State U., 1971, MEd, 1975; MALS, U. South Fla., 1981. Cert. libr., tchr., Fla., Mass. Geneal. libr., asst. rschr. to curator New Bedford (Mass.) Pub. Libr., 1963-71; assoc. libr. New England Hist. Geneal. Soc., Boston, 1972-73; media specialist, libr. Brevard County Schs., Port Malabar Elem. Sch., Palm Bay, Fla., 1978-90; libr., faculty Brevard C.C., 1990-96, Melbourne, Fla., 1996—. Developer and organizer libraries, 1968, 80, 91—. Mem. ALA, Fla. Assn. C.C.s, Libr. Assn. of Brevard County, Phi Kappa Phi, Beta Phi Mu. Avocations: creative writing, genealogical research. Office: Brevard C C Melbourne Campus Libr 3865 N Wickham Rd Melbourne FL 32935-2310

REGNELL, BARBARA CARAMELLA, retired media educator; b. Paterson, N.J., May 5, 1935; d. William Joseph and Mafalda Erminia (Benedetto) Caramella; m. Joseph C. Tirre, July 12, 1958 (div. June 1977); children: Conrad J., William C.; m. John Albin Regnell, Apr. 2, 1983. BS, Syracuse U., 1957, MA, 1966; postgrad., Washington U., St. Louis, 1972. Editor, continuity dir. Sta. WWBZ-AM, Vineland, N.J., 1958; dir. publicity Conti Adv., Ridgewood, 1958; copywriter Sta. KCNY, San Marcos, Tex., 1959; tchr. Henninger High Sch., Syracuse, N.Y., 1966-67; instr. Belleville (Ill.) Area Jr. Coll., 1968; from instr. to assoc. prof. mass comm. So. Ill. U., Edwardsville, 1967-97, chmn. mass communications, 1985-95, prof. emerita, 1997—; comms. cons., 1997—. Trainer Nat. Iranian Radio, TV, Tehran, Iran, 1974-75; comms. cons., 1997—. Mem. NATAS (Silver Cir., mem. bd. govs. St. Louis chpt., 2d v.p., pres. 2002—), Mo. Osteoporosis Found. (pub. rels. com.), Delta Sigma Rho, Alpha Chi Omega. Republican. Home: 6 Hawthorne Ct Saint Louis MO 63122-4512

REGN FRAHER, BONNIE, special education educator; BA, U. Calif., Santa Cruz, 1978; EdS, Rutgers U., 1982, MA, 1983. Cert. tchr. of the handicapped, cert. elem. tchr. Tchr. Search Day Program, Wanamassa, N.J., 1978-87; v.p. Fin-Addict Charters, Wall, 1987-93; v.p., dir. fin. William Cook Custom Homes, 1987-95; v.p. Archtl. Woodworking, 1993-95; tchr. Elmcrest Hosp., 1996; daycare owner Fraher Acad., West Hartford, Conn., 1996—. Mem. Autism Soc. Am., Long Branch Ski Club. Avocation: writing (short story pub.).

REGNIER, JAMES, state supreme court justice; b. Aurora, Ill., July 22, 1944; m. Linda Regnier; 3 children. BS, Marquette U., 1966; JD, U. Ill., 1973. Judicial Fellow ACTL, Internat. Soc. Barristers; completed atty. mediator tng., Atty.-Mediator Tng. Inst., Dallas, 1993. Lawyer pvt. practice, Rochelle, Ill., 1973-78; co-founder, ptnr. Regnier, Lewis and Boland, Great Falls, Mont., 1979-91; lawyer pvt. practice, Missoula, 1991-97; justice Mont. Supreme Ct., Helena, 1997—. Appt. Mont. Supreme Ct. Commn. on Civil Jury Instrn.; appt. lawyer-rep. to 9th Cir. Judicial Confs., 1987, 88, 89, chair Mont. lawyer delegation, 1989; lectr. U. Mont. Sch. Law, numerous continuing legal edn. seminars. Contbr. Mont. Pattern Jury Instrns. for Civil Cases, 1985. Co-founder Mont. chpt. Am. Bd. Trial Advocates, 1989—, pres. Officer USN, Vietnam. Office: Montana Supreme Ct Justice Bldg 215 N Sanders St Helena MT 59601-4522 also: PO Box 203001 Helena MT 59620-3001*

RÉGNIER, MARC CHARLES, lawyer, corporate executive; b. Rockland, Ont., Can., Apr. 24, 1939; s. Lucien and Joséphine (Mattar) R.; m. Claudette Picard, July 29, 1989; 1 child, Mathieu. BA, U. Ottawa, Ont., 1960, LLB, 1964. Bar: Que. 1969. Spl. asst. combines br. Dept. Justice, Ottawa, 1960-66; sollicitor, sec. Celanese Can. Ltd., Montréal, Que., Can., 1966-72; sec., legal counsel Microsystems Internat., 1972-75; sr. group counsel, sec. No. Telecom Ltd., 1974-75; sr. v.p., gen. counsel Avenor Inc. (formerly Can. Pacific Forest Products Ltd.), 1976-98, Bowater Pulp and Paper Can. Inc., Montréal, 1998—2001. Bd. dirs. CARE Can., Festival de Theatre des Ameriques, City of Trois-Rivieres Port Authority. Mem. Can. Bar Assn., Que. Bar Assn., Law Soc. Upper Can., Assn. Can. Gen. Counsel (pres. 1987-88), Club St.-Denis. Avocations: music, travel, fishing.

REGNIER, RICHARD ADRIAN, lawyer; b. Portland, Oreg., Aug. 23, 1931; s. Augustus Jerome and Marietta (Howland) R.; m. Maria Teresa Arguindegui, Oct. 12, 1957; children: Richard Adrian Jr., Lisa Marina, Augustus Jerome II, Teresa Lynn; m. Georgianna Pennington, Aug. 5, 1993. Student, Harvard U., 1949-50; BS, U.S. Mil. Acad., 1955; LLB, U. Calif., Berkeley, 1962. Bar: Calif. 1963, U.S. Dist. Ct. (so. dist.) Calif. 1963, U.S. Supreme Ct. 1968. Commd. 2d lt. USAF, 1955, advanced through grades to capt., res., 1959; dep. dist. atty. Ventura County, Calif., 1963-65; assoc. Ferguson, Regnier & Paterson, Oxnard, 1965-68, ptnr., 1968-90; pvt. practice, 1990—. Instr. criminal law and evidence Ventura County Jr. Coll. and Ventura County Sheriff's Acad., 1963-65; judge pro tem Superior Ct. Ventura County, 1971—. Speaker Right to Life League So. Calif., Ventura County, 1973—; campaign chmn. MacIntyre for Assessor, Ventura County, 1986; pres. Oxnard Coll. Found., 1994—; bd. advisors Red Cloud Indian Sch. Named Extraordinary Minister of Holy Eucharist, Archbishop of Los Angeles, Ventura, 1971—. Mem. ABA, Am. Bd. Trial Advocates, Calif. Bar Assn. (group ins. com. 1973-76, com. bar examine site rev. team), Ventura County Bar Assn. (exec. com. 1987-89), Assn. Trial Lawyers Am., Consumer Attys. Calif. (recognition of experience certs. various areas), Ventura County Trial Lawyers Assn. (pres. 1971, 86, lectr. trial law), Am. Judicature Soc., Ventura County Legal Aid Assn. (pres. 1968), Am. Arbitration Assn. (arbitrator 1966—), Nat. Bd. Trial Adv. (diplomate, cert.), Ventura Inns of Ct., Saticoy Country Club (pres. 1992). Lodges: Rotary (pres. 1982-83, Paul Harris fellow 1986), K.C. Republican. Avocations: golf, running, weight lifting, skiing. Office: Law Offices Richard Regnier 301 N A St Oxnard CA 93030-4901

REGOPOULOS, EFSTATHIOS A. real estate developer, consultant; b. Chgo., Dec. 28, 1942; s. Angelo Stathey and Despina (Pappas) R.; m. Elaine Bacos, Aug. 17, 1969; children: Dana, Evan, Georgina, Stacie. BS in Phys. Edn., U. Ill., 1969; AA in Real Estate, Real Estate Inst., 1975. Lic. real estate broker, Ill.; cert. property mgr., 1980. Developer numerous urban and suburban real estate devels. incluidng residential and comml. properties; ownr ERA, Chgo., 1978-80, R Realty, 1971-72. Mem. Nat. Assn. Realtors, Ill. Assn. Realtors, Inst. of Real Estate Mgmt., Chgo. chpt. Real Estate Mgmt. Greek Orthodox. Office: The Rego Group Ltd 920 Livingston Ln Barrington IL 60010-6435

REGUEIRO-REN, ALICIA, biomedical researcher; b. Madrid, Oct. 31, 1967; came to U.S., Jan. 1995. d. Joaquin Regueiro and Alicia Miguelez; m. Rex. X.-F. Ren, Dec. 27, 1995. BSc, U. La Laguna, Santa Cruz de Tenerife, Spain, 1990, PhD, 1994. Fulbright postdoctoral fellow Columbia U., N.Y.C., 1995-98; rsch. investigator I Bristol Myers Squibb, NJ, 1998—99, rsch. investigator II Conn., 1999—2001, sr. rsch. investigator I, biomed. investigator, 2001—. Contbr. articles to profl. jours.; patentee in field. Mem. AAAS, Am. Chem. Soc., Sigma Xi. Roman Catholic. Avocations: traveling, reading. Home: 69 Greenview Ter Middletown CT 06457-8738 Office: Bristol Myers Squibb 5 Research Pkwy Wallingford CT 06492-1951 Fax: 203-677-7202. E-mail: alicia.regueiroren@bms.com.

REGULA, RALPH, congressman, lawyer; b. Beach City, Ohio, Dec. 3, 1924; s. O.F. and Orpha (Walter) R.; m. Mary Rogusky, Aug. 5, 1950; children: Martha, David, Richard. BA, Mt. Union Coll., 1948, LLD, 1981; LLB, William McKinley Sch. Law, 1952; LLD, Malone Coll., 1976. Bar: Ohio 1952. Sch. adminstr. Stark County Bd. Edn., 1948-55; practiced law Navarre, 1952—; mem. Ohio Ho. of Reps., 1965-66, Ohio Senate, 1967-72, U.S. Congress from 16th Ohio dist., 1973—; vice chmn. appropriations com., chmn. subcom. depts. Labor, HHS, Edn.; ptnr. Regula Bros. Mem. Pres.'s Commn. on Fin. Structures and Regulation, 1970-71. Mem. Ohio Bd. Edn., 1960-64; hon. mem. adv. bd. Walsh Coll., Canton, Ohio; Trustee Mt. Union Coll., Alliance, Ohio, Stark County Hist. Soc., Stark County Wilderness Soc. With USNR, 1944-46. Recipient Community Service award Navarre Kiwanis Club, 1963; Meritorious Service in Conservation award Canton Audubon Soc., 1965; Ohio Conservation award Gov. James Rhodes, 1969; named Outstanding Young Man of Yr. Canton Jr. C. of C., 1957, Legis. Conservationist of Yr. Ohio League Sportsmen, 1969 Republican. Episcopalian. Office: US Ho of Reps 2306 Rayburn House Off Bldg Washington DC 20515-3516*

REH, THOMAS EDWARD, radiologist, educator; b. St. Louis, Sept. 12, 1943; s. Edward Paul and Ceil Anne (Golden) R.; m. Benedette Texada Gieselman, June 22, 1968; children: Matthew J., Benedette T., Elizabeth W. BA, St. Louis U., 1965, MD, 1969. Diplomate Am. Bd. Radiology, Nat. Bd. Med. Examiners. Intern St. John's Mercy Med. Ctr., St. Louis, 1969-70; resident St. Louis VA Hosp., 1970-73; fellow in vascular radiology Beth Israel Hosp., Boston, 1973-74; radiologist St. Mary's Health Ctr., St. Louis, 1974—, chmn. dept. radiology, 1986—; clin. asst. prof. radiology St. Louis U. Sch. Medicine, 1978-98, clin. prof. radiology, 1998—; clin. assoc. prof. radiology, 1989—. Fellow Am. Coll. Radiology; mem. AMA, Radiol. Soc. N.Am., St. Louis Met. Med. Soc., Alpha Omega Alpha, Alpha Sigma Nu, Delta Sigma Phi. Republican. Roman Catholic. Clubs: St. Louis, Confrerie des Chevaliers du Tastevin. Home: 9850 Waterbury Dr Saint Louis MO 63124-1046 Office: Bellevue Radiology Inc 4 Sunnen Bus Park Saint Louis MO 63143

REHA, ROSE KRIVISKY, retired business educator; b. N.Y.C., Dec. 17, 1920; d. Boris and Freda (Gerstein) Krivisky; m. Rudolph John Reha, Apr. 11, 1941; children; Irene Gale, Phyllis. BS in Bus. and Music Edn., Ind. State U., 1965; MA in Bus. and Psychology, U. Minn., 1967, PhD in Ednl. Psychology and Counseling, 1971. With U.S. and State Civil Svc., 1941-63; tchr. pub. schs., Minn., 1965-66; teaching assoc., instr. U. Minn., Mpls., 1966-68, 68-85; prof. coll. bus. St. Cloud (Minn.) State U., 1968-85, prof. emeritus, 1985—, chmn. bus. edn. & office adminstrn. dept., 1982-83. Advisor Small Bus. Inst., 1972-85, SBA, 1972-85; ct. advocate for women in distress St. Cloud Women's Shelter, 1986-89; adj. prof. profl. and bus. comm. Fla. Atlantic U., Boca Raton, Fla., 1989-90; substitute tchr. Broward County, 1990—; tutor (reading) Lauderdale, Fla., 1990-92; moderator, counselor Posnack Jewish Cmty. Ctr., Davie, Fla.; lectr. in com. Soref Jewish Cmty. Ctr. Continuing Edn. for sr. groups, Sunrise, Fla., 1997—; cons., lectr. in field; small bus. cons. Small Bus. Inst. Coll. Bus. St. Cloud St. U. Minn. Reviewer of bus. comm. and consumer edn. textbooks. Contbr. articles to profl. jours. Camp dir. Girl Scouts U.S., 1960-62; active various cmty. fund drives; sec., mem. relicensure rev. Com. Minn. Bd. Teaching Continuing Edn., 1984-85. Recipient Achievement award St. Cloud State U., 1985, St. Cloud State U. Rsch. and Faculty Improvement grantee, 1973, 78, 83. Mem. Am. Vocat. Assn. (cert.), Am. Counseling Assn. (cert.), Am. Mental Health Counselors Assn. (cert.), Minn. Econ. Assn., Minn. Women of Higher Edn., NEA, Minn. Edn. Assn. (pres. women's caucus 1981-83, award 1983), St. Cloud U. Faculty Assembly (pres. 1975-76), St. Cloud State U. Grad. Coun. (chmn. 1983-85), Fifty-five-plus Sr. Group (moderator North Broward, Ft. Lauderdale chpts. 1994—), Pi Omega Pi (sponsor St. Cloud State U. chpt. 1982-85), Phi Chi Theta, Delta Pi Epsilon, Delta Kappa Gamma. Jewish. Home: Apt 465 3671 Environ Blvd Fort Lauderdale FL 33319-4221 Office: Coll Bus St Cloud State U Saint Cloud MN 56301

REHAK, JAMES RICHARD, orthodontist; b. Chgo., Jan. 2, 1938; s. James Joseph and Lydia Ann (Thomas) R.; m. Joann Marie Tabbert, Oct. 15, 1969; 1 child, Suzanne Terese. BS, U. Ill., 1960, DDS cum laude, 1962, MS, 1967, cert. in orthodontics, 1965. Pvt. practice dentistry, Chgo., 1962-63; pvt. practice orthodontics Chgo., Arlington Heights, Ill., Cape Coral, Naples, Fla. Asst. prof. U. Ill. Coll. Dentistry, 1966-68. Pres. bd. trustees St. Ann Sch. Foun.; chmn. bd. dirs. St. John Neumann H.s.; organizer, dir. 1st Nat. Bank, Naples; trustee Catholic Cultural Ctr., Washington. Kellogg Found. fellow, 1958. Fellow Royal Soc. Health; mem. ADA, Ill. Dental Assn., Chgo. Dental Soc., Fla. Dental Assn., West Coast Dental Soc., Collier County Dental Assn., Am. Assn. Orthodontists, Am. Assn. Lingual Orthodontists, Fedn. Dentaire Internationale, Psi Omega, Omicron Kappa Upsilon. Office: 5100 Tamiami Trl N Ste 101 Naples FL 34103-2810

REHBEIN, EDWARD ANDREW, minister, geologist, consultant; b. Portland, Oreg., Aug. 13, 1947; s. Edward Louis and Marjorie Ann (Simshaw) R; m. Phyllis Jean Boyer, June 23, 1973; children: Matthew Louis, Angela Mae. BS in Geology, Calif. Inst. Tech., 1969. Geologist U.S. Forest Svc., Elkins, W.Va., 1972-74, U.S. Geol. Survey, Billings, Mont., 1974-76; coal geologist W.Va. Geologic Survey, Morgantown, 1977; cons. Morgantown, 1978; geologist Allied Corp., Beckley, W.Va., 1979; sr. exploration geologist Kerr-McGee Corp., Beckley, 1980-82, regional mgr. exploration, Reno, Nev., 1983-85; exploration geologist, Oklahoma City, 1985-88; assoc. min. Ch. of Christ, Beckley, W.Va., 1989-90, min., 1990—; pres. M&R Computer Sales and Svc., Inc., Beckley, W.Va., 1989-90. Author: Remembering God's Word, 1991; contbr. articles to profl. jours. and mags. Mem. Am. Assn. Petroleum Geologists. Club: Shotokan Karate Am. Office: N Beckley Ch of Christ PO Box 951 Beckley WV 25802-0951 *So God created man in his own image. (Genesis 1:27). Search the Scriptures, find the full meaning of this, and your life will never be the same.*

REHBERG, DENNIS R. congressman; b. Billings, Mont., Oct. 5, 1955; m. Janice; 1 child. Student, Mont. State U., Wash. State U. Rancher and businessman; legis. aide, 1977; fin. dir. Congl. Campaigns, 1980-82; Mont. state rep. Dist. 88, 1985-89; lt. gov. Mont., 1991-96; mem. U.S. Congress from Mont. at large, Washington, 2001—; mem. agr. com., resources com., transp. and infrastructure com. Office: US Ho Reps 516 Cannon Ho Office Bldg Washington DC 20515*

REHBOCK, RICHARD ALEXANDER, lawyer; b. New Haven, Sept. 12, 1946; s. Morton J. and Evelyn (Norris) R.; m. Nanette DiFalco, June 5, 1997; 1 stepchild: Gregory. BA, Fairleigh Dickinson U., 1968; JD, St. John's U., 1973. Bar: N.Y. 1974, U.S. Dist. Ct. (ea. and so. dists.) N.Y. 1974, U.S. Ct. Appeals (2d cir.) 1977, U.S. Ct. Appeals (3d cir.) 1996, U.S. Supreme Ct. 1978, U.S. Dist. Ct. (we. dist.) N.Y. 1983, Fla. 1987. Atty. criminal divsn. Legal Aid Soc., N.Y.C., 1973-77; staff atty. U.S. Dist. Ct. N.Y. Legal Aid Soc., Bklyn., 1977-79; ptnr. Rehbock, Fishman & Kudisch, Kew Gardens, N.Y., 1979-83; pvt. practice law N.Y.C., 1983—. Staff sgt. U.S. Army, 1969-70, Vietnam. Fellow Am. Bd. Criminal Lawyers; mem. Criminal Ct. Bar Assn. (bd. dirs. Queens County chpt.), Am. Trial Lawyers Assn., Nat. Assn. Criminal Def. Attys. (vice chmn legis. com.), Nat. Assn. Trial Attys., Fed. Bar Coun., N.Y. State Bar Assn., Queens Bar Assn., N.Y. County Lawyers Assn., N.Y. State Assn. Criminal Def. Attys. (chair fed. legis com.), Fla. Bar Assn. Home and Office: 1 Maple Run Dr Jericho NY 11753-2827 E-mail: rrehbock@msn.com.

REHG, KENNETH LEE, linguistics educator; b. East St. Louis, Ill., Nov. 21, 1939; s. Theophil Albert and Kathryn Louise (George) R.; 1 child, Laura Le'olani. BA, U. Ill., 1962; MA, So. Ill. U., 1965; PhD, U. Hawaii, 1986. Tng. officer Internat. Ctr. for Lang. Studies, Washington, 1966-67; lang. officer U.S. Peace Corp, Saipan, Micronesia, 1967-70; asst. rschr. social sci. rsch. inst. U. Hawaii, Honolulu, 1974-83, assoc. prof., 1984—. Cons. Micronesian govt., 1973-76, 97, 2000, Samoa Dept. Edn., Pago Pago, 1978, U.S. Geol. Survey, Menlo Park, Calif., 1979-81, Japan Nat. Mus. Ethnology, Osaka, 1986; participant Fulbright-Hays Study Group, Ea. Indonesia, 1991. Author: (novels) Ponapean Reference Grammar, 1981; co-author Kitail Lokaiahn Pohnpei, 1969, Ponapean-English Dictionary, 1979; co-editor: (mag.) Issues in Austronesian Morphology. Rsch. fellow U. Hawaii, 1981-82; recipient Excellence in Teaching award Hawaii Tchrs. ESL, 1984, Mortar Bd., 1990, Presdl. Citation for meritorious tchg., 1996. Mem. Linguistic Soc. Am., Linguistic Soc. Hawaii. Office: U Hawaii Dept Linguistics Moore Hall 569 1890 E West Rd Honolulu HI 96822-2318 E-mail: rehg@hawaii.edu.

REHKOP, JOHN, retired air force officer; b. Warrensburg, Mo., Sept. 3, 1949; s. Elmer L. and Mary A. (Baldwin) R.; m. Lynnette L. Rehkop, Aug. 7, 1971; children: Laurin K., Kara L. BS in Math., Ctrl. Mo. State U., 1971; MA in Bus. Adminstrn./Mgmt., N. Mex. Highlands U., 1979. Enlisted 2d lt. USAF, 1971, advanced through grades to col., 1994; test pilot 1550th Aircrew Tng. and Test Wing, Kirtland AFB, N.Mex., 1981-83; test pilot/rotary wing divsn. chief Spl. Missions Operational Test and Evaluation Ctr., Hurlburt Field, Fla., 1983-86; comdr. Detachment 3, 37th Aerospace Rescue and Recovery Squadron, Grand Forks AFB, N.D., 1986-89, 41st Air Rescue Squadron, Patrick AFB, Fla., 1989-91; vice comdr. USAF Airlift Ctr., Pope AFB, N.C., 1991-94; dir., test and evaluation Hdqs. Air Mobility Command, Scott AFB, Ill., 1994—2002; ret. USAF, 2002. Air Force Assn., Ret. Officers Assn., Soc. Exptl. Test Pilots (assoc. mem.), Sigma Phi Epsilon. E-mail: rehkop@accessus.net.

REHM, LEO FRANK, civil engineer; b. Milw., Jan. 8, 1916; s. Joseph V. and Theresa (Binder) R.; m. Irene R. Kegel, Aug. 24, 1940; children: Judith Ann LeDoux, Cecelia C. Nelson. B.C.E., Marquette U., 1938. Civil engr. Consoer, Townsend & Quinlan, Chgo., 1938-43; asso. Consoer Townsend & Assocs. (Cons. Engrs.), 1946-53, gen. partner, 1953-74, mng. partner, 1974-76; pres. PRC Consoer Townsend, Chgo., 1976-83, pres. emeritus, 1983-85; v.p. PRC Engring., Inc., 1976-85. Chmn. bd. Environ. Engring., Inc., 1976-83, Consoer Townsend Harris Internat., Inc., 1976-83; dir., v.p. Planning Research Corp., 1976-80; Mem. planning and adv. bd. Village of River Forest (Ill.), 1964-76; mem. exec. senate Marquette U., Milw., 1978— ; mem., chmn. adv. council Marquette U. (Coll. Engring.), 1976-89. Mem. bldg. bd. appeals Village of River Forest, Ill., 1977-87, pres.'s adv. council Rosary Coll., River Forest, 1986-91, Exec. Svc. Corps Chgo. With U.S. Army, 1943-46. Recipient Disting. Engring. Alumnus award Marquette U. Coll. Engring., 1975; Alumnus of Yr. award Marquette U., 1983 Mem. Am. Public Works Assn., Am. Water Resources Assn., Am. Water Works Assn., Water Environ. Fedn., Inter-Am. Assn. San. Engring., NSPE, Western Soc. Engrs., Ill. State C. of C. (bd. dirs. 1981-85), VFW, KC, Country Club of Naples. Roman Catholic.

REHMAN, SAIFUR, business executive, consultant; b. Lahore, Pakistan, Sept. 9, 1965; s. Mohammad Makhdoom, Naseem Akhtar; m. Sana Rehman. Master of Science, University of Baltimore, Baltimore, Maryland, USA,

1994—95; Bachelor of Science in Business Administration, Central Missouri State University, Warrensburg, Missouri, USA, 1991—93. Chairman & CEO WebBiz Inc., Palo Alto, CA, 2001—Pres; Director KPMG Consulting Inc., Mountain View, 2000—01; Manager Midwest Consulting Group, Kansas City, MO, 1999—2000; Senior Associate PricewaterhouseCoopers, Fairfax, VA, 1997—99; Analyst Andersen Consulting (Accenture), Washington, 1996—97. Mem.: West Valley Flying Club, Delta Sigma Pi, American Society for Quality (ASQ), Data Processing Management Association (DPMA), Society for Information Management (SIM), Project Management Institute (PMI). Office: WebBiz Inc. P.O. Box 61034 Palo Alto CA 94306 Business E-Mail: saif_rehman@hotmail.com.

REHMUS, CHARLES MARTIN, law educator, arbitrator; b. Ann Arbor, Mich., June 27, 1926; s. Paul A. and Amy D. (Martin) R.; m. Carolyn Brown, Dec. 21, 1948 (div. July 1982); children— Paul, James, Jon, David; m. Laura Carlson, Sept. 4, 1982 AB, Kenyon Coll., 1947; MA, Stanford U., 1951, PhD, 1955. Commr. Fed. Mediation and Conciliation Service, San Francisco, 1952-58; staff dir. Presdl. R.R. Commn., Washington, 1959-61; prof. polit. sci. U. Mich., Ann Arbor, 1962-80, dir. Inst. Labor and Indsl. Relations, 1962-76; chmn. Mich. Employment Relations Commn., Detroit, 1976-80; dean N.Y. State Sch. Indsl. and Labor Relations, Cornell U., Ithaca, 1980-86; prof. law U. San Diego, 1988-97. Author: Final-Offer Arbitration, 1975, The Railway Labor Act at Fifty, 1977, Labor and American Politics, 1967, rev. edit., 1978, The National Mediation Board, 1984, Emergency Strikes Revisited, 1990. Chmn. 4 Presdl. emergency bds. at various times. Served to lt. USNR, 1943-45; PTO Mem. Internat. Inst. Labor Studies (bd. govs. 1984-92), Indsl. Rels. Rsch. Assn. (exec. bd. 1984-88), Nat. Acad. Arbitrators (bd. govs. 1979-82, v.p. 1993-95).

REHNQUIST, JANET, federal agency administrator; Grad., U. Va. Assoc. counsel to the pres., 1990—93; asst. U.S. atty. Ea. Dist. Va.; inspector gen. Dept. HHS, Washington, 2001—. Counsel U.S. Senate Permanent Subcom. on Investigations. Office: Dept HHS Inspector Gen 330 Independence Ave SW Washington DC 20201*

REHNQUIST, WILLIAM HUBBS, United States supreme court chief justice; b. Milw., Oct. 1, 1924; s. William Benjamin and Margery (Peck) Rehnquist; m. Natalie Cornell, Aug. 29, 1953; children: James, Janet, Nancy. BA, MA, Stanford U., 1948; MA, Harvard U., 1949; LLB, Stanford U., 1952. Bar: Ariz. Law clk. to former justice Robert H. Jackson, U.S. Supreme Ct., 1952-53; with Evans, Kitchel & Jenckes, Phoenix, 1953-55; mem. Ragan & Rehnquist, 1956-57; ptnr. Cunningham, Carson & Messenger, 1957-60, Powers & Rehnquist, Phoenix, 1960-69; asst. atty.-gen. office of legal counsel Dept. of Justice, Washington, 1969-71; assoc. justice U.S. Supreme Ct., 1971-1986, chief justice, 1986—. Mem. Nat. Conf. Commrs. Uniform State Laws, 1963—69. Author: The Supreme Court: How It Was, How It Is, 1987, Grand Inquests: The Historic Impeachments of Justice Samuel Chase and President Andrew Johnson, 1992, All the Laws But One, 1999; contbr. articles to profl. jours. With USAAF, 1943—46. Mem.: Nat. Conf. Lawyers and Realtors, State Bar Ariz., Am. Maricopa County Bar Assn., Fed. Bar Assn., Order of Coif, Phi Delta Phi, Phi Beta Kappa. Lutheran. Office: Supreme Ct US 1 1st St NE Washington DC 20543-0001

REHNS, MARSHA LEE, magazine editor, writer; b. Balt., Dec. 23, 1946; d. Fred and Ruth (Lieber) R.; m. Walter Richard Arnheim, Sept. 5, 1971; children: Ethan, Phillip. BS, U. Pitts., 1967; MPhil, Yale, 1970. Editor Sci. Med. Pub., N.Y.C., 1972-75; editor Haymarket Pub., London, 1975-76; mng. editor Harcourt Brace Jovanovich, N.Y.C., 1977-79; editor Sta. WGBH-TV, Boston, 1979-80; columnist Weightwatchers Mag., N.Y.C., 1979-81; editor Am. Baby, 1981—; cons. Cradle Pub., 1990-94; writer Kids Discover, 1991—, Nat. Mus. Natural History, 1994—; editor Educating Our Children, N.Y.C., 1996; writer U.S. Geol. Surv., Reston, 1999, Newark Mus., 1999—. Co-author: Seeds of Change: Learning from the Garden, 2000, Brain Attack, 2001. Docent Nat. Mus. Natural History, Washington, 1990—. Home: 10712 Barn Wood Ln Potomac MD 20854-1326

REHO, JAMES HUGHES, religious studies educator; b. New York, Ny, Apr. 12, 1969; s. George Z. and Barbara M. Reho; m. Carolanne C. Reho, Nov. 9, 1996. PhD, Princeton U., Princeton, New Jersey, 2000, MA, 1996; BS, Wagner Coll., Staten Island, New York, 1994; BA, St. John's U., Queens, New York, 1990. Post-doctoral rschr. Los Alamos Nat. Lab., Los Alamos, N.Mex., 2000—01; educator East Carolina U., Greenville, NC, 2001—. Contbr. articles to profl. jours. Ministering to aids patients Bellevue Hosp., New York, NY, 1989—90; religious educator St. John the Bapt. Parish, 1988—89; educator and care provider Queens Lighthouse for the Blind, Queens, 1987—88. Mem.: NSTA, Am. Phys. Soc., Am. Chem. Soc., AAAS. Avocations: poetry, yoga, swimming, travel, music.

REHORN, LOIS M(ARIE) (LOIS MARIE SMITH), nursing administrator; b. Larned, Kans., Apr. 15, 1919; d. Charles and Ethel L. (Canaday) Williamson; m. C. Howard Smith, Feb. 15, 1946 (dec. Aug. 1980); 1 child, Cynthia A. Huddleston; m. Harlan W. Rehorn, Aug. 25, 1981. RN, Bethany Hosp. Sch. Nursing, Kansas City, Kans., 1943; BS, Ft. Hays Kans. State U., Hays, 1968, MS, 1970. RN, N.Mex.; lic. pvt. pilot. Office nurse, surg. asst. Dr. John H. Luke, Kansas City, Kans., 1943-47; supr. nursing unit Larned (Kans.) State Hosp., 1949-68, dir. nursing edn., 1968-71, dir. nursing, 1972-81, ret., 1981. Recipient Order of the Blue Key, 1942-43; named Nurse of Yr. DNA-4, 1986. Mem. Am. Nurses Assn., Kans. Nurses Assn. (dist. treas.), N.Mex. Nurses Assn. (dist. pres. 1982-86, dist. bd. dirs. 1986-88). Avocation: flying (pilot). Home: 1436 Brentwood Dr Clovis NM 88101-4602 *Keep within you a place where dreams may grow. The fountain of understanding is the willingness to listen.*

REHR, HELEN, social worker; b. N.Y.C., Dec. 16, 1919; d. Philip and Rose (Stern) R. BA, CUNY, 1940, DS (hon.) , 1995; MS, Columbia U., 1943, DSW, 1970. Social worker, asst. dir. Sydenham Hosp., N.Y.C., 1943-45; supr. Grasslands Hosp., Valhalla, N.Y., 1945-47; asst. prof. medicine NYU Bellevue Med. Ctr., N.Y.C., 1947-51; med. soc. cons. Dept. Health, Maternal & Child Health, 1951-52; assoc. dir. Mt. Sinai Med. Ctr., 1954—70, dir., 1971—89, Edith S. Baerwald prof. cmty. medicine, 1971—89, prof. cmty. med. emerita, 1998—. Dir. Israel/Australia Leadership Project, 1986—; vis. prof. U. Flinders, U. Melbourne, Australia, 1990, Ben Gurion U., Israel, 1991; Kenneth Pray vis. prof. U. Pa., Phila., 1979-80; cons. Mt. Sinai, 1986—. Author, editor books, jour. and articles in field; mem. edit. bd. Social Work in Health Care, Health and Social Work. Bd. dirs. N.Y. Found., Ctr. for Study of Social Work Practice/Columbia U., Joint Commn. on Accreditation of Hosps.; mem. adv. bd. scholarship and welfare fund Hunter Coll. Named Disting. Practitioner, Nat. Acad. Practitioners; named to Hunter Coll. Hall of Fame, Columbia U. Sch. of Social Work Hall of Fame; recipient Knee-Wittman Lifetime Achievement award. Avocations: gardening. Home: 27 W 96th St # 6C New York NY 10025-6515 Office: Mt Sinai Med Ctr 1 Gustave L Levy Pl New York NY 10029-6500

REHR, PAULA BERNICE BELDOCK, writer; b. Bklyn., Apr. 29, 1946; d. Leo Beldock and Blanche Forman Beldock Sharpe; m. Marc Albert Rehr, July 7, 1968; children: Lorin Sara, Scott Ethan. BA in English Edn., U. Md., 1968; MA in Psychology, Hood Coll., 1975. Cert. secondary edn. and adminstrn., Md. Tchr. Montgomery County Pub. Schs., Md., 1968-82, tchr. specialist acad. skills, 1982-85; TV prodr., instrnl. TV specialist Montgomery County Pub. Schs. Cable TV MCPS-TV, 1985-2000; owner, prodr., freelance writer Co. B. Prodns., N. Potomac, Md., 1999—. Adj. prof. Am. U., Washington, 2000—. Author: Why is Everyone Growing Up and I'm Still in the 8th Grade?, 1976; editor: Directory of U.S. Minority Organizations, 1974; prodr.(writer, prodr.): (documentary video) Voices of Antietam, 1998 (Emmy nomination, 98, Cine Golden Eagle award , 98), Ghosts of Cedar Creek, 1999 (Emmy nomination for Best Dir., 2000). Bd. dirs. Fredericktowne Players, Frederick, Md., 1976; mem. Harbor City Music Co.; bd. dirs. Sweet Adelines Internat., Baltimore, Md., 1997-99; mem. Capital Hill Chorale, 2000—; campaigner Montgomery County Edn. Assn., 1990; vol. NIH Friends of Clin. Ctr., Bethesda, Md., 2000—. Fellow in visual arts Montgomery County Arts Coun., 1998. Mem. Internat. TV Assn. (D.C. chpt.), Nat. Assn. TV Arts and Scis. Avocations: singing, a cappella quartet, community theatre, traveling. Office: Co B Prodns 14723 Maine Cove Ter North Potomac MD 20878 E-mail: Companybee@aol.com.

REIBACK, EARL MARTIN, artist; b. Bklyn., May 30, 1948; s. Sidney Marshall and Beatrice (Rubeinstein) R.; m. Elizabeth M. Meneses, Feb. 24, 1993. BA in English, BS in Engring. Physics, Lehigh U., 1963; MS in Nuclear Engring., MIT, 1967. Lectr. in field. One-man shows include Howard Wise Gallery, N.Y.C., 1965, 66, 68, 69, 70, Met. Mus. Art, N.Y.C., 1967, Chapman Kelley Gallery, Dallas, 1969, Moos Gallery, Montreal, Can., 1969, 70, Waddell Gallery, N.Y.C., 1972, 73, Colibri Gallery, San Juan, P.R., 1974, Esther Robles Gallery, L.A., 1975, 82, Elec. Gallery, Toronto, Can., 1971, 76, 84, Whitney Mus. of Am. Art: TV as a Creative Medium, 1994, O.K. Harris Gallery, N.Y.C., 1995, Cite des arts et des nouvelles techs. de Montreal, 1996, Images du Future, Montreal, 1996, San Jose Mus. of Art: Show Am. Art in the Age of Technology, 1997-98, Long Beach (Calif.) Mus. Art, 1997; represented in permanent collections Whitney Mus. Am. Art, Mus. Modern Art, Phila. Mus. Art, Newark Mus., Flint Inst. Art, Balt. Mus. Art, Milw. Art Ctr., Phoenix Art Mus., Krannert Art Mus., New Orleans Mus. Art, Portland Mus. Art, La Jolla Mus., Long Beach Mus. Contemporary Art, Aldrich Mus. Contemporary Art, Worcester Mus., Wichita Art Mus., Mus. Art, Carnegie Inst., Musee de Art Contemporian, Montreal, Art Mus. Windsor, Can., Lannan Found.Mus., Walker Art Ctr., Art Mus. South Tex., Franklin Inst., U.S. Cultural Ctr., Tel Aviv, Taft Mus., Alexandria Jus., Huntsville Mus. Art, Lawton Gallery, Mus. N.C. Home: 20 E 9th St Apt 80 New York NY 10003-5944 E-mail: eriback@nyc.rr.com.

REIBEL, KURT, physicist, educator; b. Vienna, Austria, May 23, 1926; came to U.S., 1938; s. Michael and Regina (Pak) R.; m. Eleanor Elvira Mannino, June 10, 1954; children— Leah, Michael, David BA, Temple U., Phila., 1954; MS, U. Pa., Phila., 1956, PhD, 1959. Jr. research assoc. in physics Brookhaven Nat. Lab., 1957-59; research assoc. U. Pa., Phila., 1959-61; asst. prof. Ohio State U., Columbus, 1961-64, assoc. prof., 1964-70, prof. physics, 1970-92, prof. emeritus, 1992—. Vis. scientist CERN, Geneva, Switzerland, 1968-69, 75-76 Author research papers on nuclear and elementary particle physics NSF fellow, 1954-56 Mem. Am. Phys. Soc., AAUP, Fedn. Am. Scientists, Union Concerned Scientists, Sigma Xi Jewish. Office: Ohio State U Dept Physics 174 W 18th Ave Columbus OH 43210-1106

REIBER, GREGORY DUANE, forensic pathologist; b. Loma Linda, Calif., May 25, 1955; s. Clifford D. and Anna M. (Field) R.; m. Faustina Mae Davis, Feb. 10, 1980; children: Jenessa Anne, Zachary Duane. BS magna cum laude, Andrews U., Berrien Springs, Mich., 1977; MD, Loma Linda (Calif.) U., 1981. Diplomate Am. Bd. Pathology. Resident in pathology Loma Linda U. Med. Ctr., 1981-85; fellow in forensic pathology Root Pathology Lab., San Bernardino, Calif., 1985-86, assoc. pathologist, 1986-90, No. Calif. Forensic Pathology, Sacramento, 1990—2001; dir. autopsy svcs. U. Calif., Davis, 2002—. Asst. clin. prof. pathology Loma Linda U. Sch. Medicine, 1987-90, U. Calif., Davis, 1990—, assoc. clin. prof. pathology, 2002-; program dir., forensic pathology fellowship NCFP/U. Calif. Davis, 1994—; apptd. Calif. SIDS Autopsy Protocol Com. Contbr. articles to profl. jours. Fellow Am. Soc. Clin. Pathologists, Am. Coll. Forensic Examiners; mem. Am. Bd. Forensic Examiners, AMA, Internat. Wound Ballistics Assn., Nat. Assn. Med. Examiners, Am. Acad. Forensic Scis., Calif. Med. Assn., Sacramento-El Dorado Med. Soc., Alpha Omega Alpha. Republican. Seventh-day Adventist. Avocations: early music, biking, photography, tropical fish. Office: U Calif Davis Med Ctr Dept Pathology 4400 V Street Sacramento CA 95817

REIBLE, DANNY DAVID, environmental chemical engineer, educator; b. Rantoul, Ill., Dec. 21, 1954; s. George Anthony and Mavis Otilla (Prause) R.; m. Susanne Cecilia Schulte, Mar. 17, 1979; children: Kristin Nicole, Monica Lynn. BS, Lamar U., 1977; MS, Calif. Inst. Tech., 1979, PhD, 1982. Registered profl. engr., La. Asst. prof. La. State U., Baton Rouge, 1981-86, assoc. prof., 1986-92, prof. chem. engring., 1992—, Chevron prof. chem. engring., 1998—, dir. Hazardous Substance Rsch. Ctr., 1995—; Shell prof. environ. engring. U. Sydney, Australia, 1993-95. Vis. rschr. U.S. Army Engr. Waterways Experiment Sta., Vicksburg, Miss., 1990; sr. visitor Cambridge (Eng.) U., 1992; cons. in field. Author: Fundamentals of Environmental Engineering, 1999, Diffusion Models of Environmental Transport, 2000; contbr. articles to profl. publs. Environ. Sci. and Engring. fellow AAAS, 1987. Mem. AIChE (exec. bd. 1990-95, mem. nat. programming com., chair Baton Rouge sect. 2000, L.K. Cecil award 2001), Am. Chem. Soc., Am. Geophys. Union, Am. Soc. Engring. Edn. (New Engring. Educator Excellence award 1985), Coms. Nat. Rsch. Coun., Sigma Xi. Achievements include identification and evaluation of new mechanisms for contaminant release in the environment; further quantitative modeling of fate and transport contaminants in environmental systems. Avocations: sailing, computers, wines, jogging, diving. Home: 2112 Oakcliff Dr Baton Rouge LA 70810-1856 Office: La State U HSRC/S&SW 3418 Ceba Baton Rouge LA 70803-0001

REICE, SYLVIE, columnist, editor, author; b. N.Y.C. d. Samuel and Dora (Weinstock) Wolshine; m. Albert Reice, July 15, 1962; children: Milo, Naomi, Seth, Andrew, Richard. BA cum laude, CUNY; postgrad., New Sch. for Social Rsch., N.Y.C. Mng. editor Co-ed mag. Scholastic Publs., N.Y.C., 1955-59; editor-in-chief Ingenue mag. Dell Pub. Co., 1959-67; columnist The Swinging Set, Pubs. Hall Syndicate, 1965-70; sr. editor McCalls mag., N.Y.C., 1967-71; editor-in-chief Family Health mag., 1971-74; exec. editor Newspaper books Chgo. Tribune-N.Y. News Syndicate, 1975-76; sr. editor Grosset & Dunlap Books, 1976-79; columnist United Features Syndicate, 1980—. Freelance writer, 1946—; adj. prof. mag. journalism SUNY-Stony Brook, 1970. Author: (short story collections) For Girls Only, 1957, Season of Love, 1962, (novel) Now or Never, 1994; columnist Adventures in Art, Prime Times, 1998—; contbr. articles to various publs., including McCalls, Health, Seventeen, Ladies Home Jour. Guest editor Taproot mag. for elder citizens, L.I., N.Y., 1986-87. Recipient Penney Missouri award for best article of yr., 1970, award for best short story Bur. of Intercultural Edn., 1952. Mem. PEN, Poetry Soc. Am., Newswomens Club N.Y. (v.p. 1984-94, pres. 1983-84), Phi Beta Kappa. Home and Office: 401 E 81st St New York NY 10028-5811 E-mail: sylvierite@aol.com.

REICH, ABRAHAM CHARLES, lawyer; b. Waterbury, Conn., Apr. 17, 1949; s. Samuel and Esther (Gurvitz) R.; m. Sherri Engelman, Aug. 15, 1971; children: Spencer, Alexander. BA, U. Conn., 1971; JD, Temple U., 1974. Bar: Pa. 1974, U.S. Supreme Ct. 1979. Assoc. Fox, Rothschild, O'Brien & Frankel, Phila., 1974-81, ptnr., 1981—, mng. ptnr., 2001—. Chair lawyers adv. com. Third Cir. Ct. Appeals, 1998. Fellow Am. Coll. Trial Lawyers; mem. ABA (ho. of dels. 1997-2002), Phila. Bar Assn. (chair profl. responsibility com. 1983-84, chair bench-bar com. 1985, chair profl. guidance com. 1987-88, bd. govs. 1987-89, chair bd. govs. 1989, chancellor 1995, del ABA 1996-2000). Home: 2224 Mount Vernon St Philadelphia PA 19130-3115 Office: Fox Rothschild O'Brien Frankel 2000 Market St Ste 10 Philadelphia PA 19103-3231 E-mail: areich@frof.com.

REICH, ALAN ANDERSON, executive; b. Pearl River, N.Y., Jan. 1, 1930; s. Oswald David and Alma Carolyn (Anderson) R.; m. Gay Ann Forsythe, Dec. 19, 1954; children: James, Jeffrey, Andrew, Elizabeth. BA, Dartmouth Coll., 1952; diploma in Slavic Studies, Oxford U., 1953; MA, Russian Inst., Middlebury Coll., 1953; MBA, Harvard U., 1959; LLD (hon.), Gallaudet Coll., 1981, Dartmouth Coll., 1992. Exec. Polaroid Corp., Cambridge, Mass., 1960-70; dep. asst. sec. ednl. and cultural affairs Dept. State, Washington, 1970-75; spl. asst. to sec. HEW, 1976-77; dep. asst. sec. commerce, dir. Bur. East-West Trade, Dept. Commerce, Washington, 1977-78; pres. U.S. Coun. for Internat. Yr. of Disabled Persons, 1978-81, Nat. Orgn. Disability, Washington, 1982—, Bimillennium Found., 1982—, Disability 2000 CEO coun., 1991—. Co-editor: Russian Proverbs, 1998. Chmn. Sudbury (Mass.) Community United Fund, 1962, 66; mem. U.S. del. WHO Gen. Assembly, 1970; pres. Nat. Paraplegia Found.; chmn. bd. dirs. Paralysis Cure Research Found., bd. dirs. of the Healing Community, chmn. People-to-people Com. for Handicapped; Impact Found., 1986—; chmn. World Com. on Disability, 1985—. Served to 1st lt. inf. AUS, 1953-57. Named to U.S. Army Inf. OCS Hall of Fame, 1994; recipient Sevier award for svc. to handicapped, 1994. Mem. Paralyzed Vets. Washington Inst. Fgn. Affairs, Am., Cosmos Club, Achilles Club (London), Beta Theta Pi. Republican. Methodist. Home: 6017 Copely Ln Mc Lean VA 22101-2507 Office: Nat Orgn on Disability 910 16th St NW Ste 600 Washington DC 20006-2916

REICH, ALLAN J. lawyer; b. Chgo., July 9, 1948; s. H. Robert and Sonya (Minsky) R.; m. Lynne Susan Roth, May 23, 1971; children: Allison, Marissa, Scott. BA, Cornell U., 1970; JD cum laude, U. Mich., 1973. Bar: Ill. 1973, U.S. Dist. Ct. (no. dist.) Ill. 1973. Ptnr. McDermott, Will & Emery, Chgo., 1973-93; vice chmn. D'Ancona & Pflaum LLC, 1993—. Trustee Oakmark Family of Mutual Funds, 1994—. V.p., mem. exec. com. Coun. for Jewish Elderly, 1989—97; mem. men's coun. Mus. Contemporary Art, Chgo., 1988—89; mem. Chgo. exec. bd. Am. Jewish Com., 1989—, nat. bd. govs.; mem. met. Chgo. bd. Am. Heart Assn.; bd. dirs. Young Men's Jewish Coun., Chgo., 1974—84, Coun. for Jewish Elderly, 1986—97. Fellow: Am. Bar Found.; mem.: ABA, Chgo. Bar Assn., Execs. Club Chgo., Econ. Club Chgo., Northmoor Country Club (Highland Park, Ill.), Standard Club (Chgo.). Home: 936 Skokie Ridge Dr Glencoe IL 60022-1434 Office: D'Ancona & Pflaum LLC 111 E Wacker Dr Chicago IL 60601-3713 E-mail: areich@dancona.com.

REICH, BERNARD, political science educator; b. Bklyn., Dec. 5, 1941; s. Moe and Rosalyn (Hartglass) R.; m. Madelyn Sue Ingber, June 16, 1963; children— Barry, Norman, Michael, Jennifer BA cum laude with spl. honors, CCNY, 1961; MA, U. Va., 1963, PhD, 1964. Asst. prof. polit. sci. and internat. affairs George Washington U., Washington, 1964-70, assoc. prof., 1970-76, prof., 1976—, chmn. dept. polit. sci., 1976-82, 88-91. Vis. prof. U. Va., 1969, 94, Sch. Advanced Internat. Studies Johns Hopkins U., 1978-80; vis. rsch. assoc. Tel Aviv U., 1971-72. Author: Quest for Peace: United States-Israel Relations and the Arab-Israeli Conflict, 1977, The U.S. and Israel: Influence in the Special Relationship, 1984, Israel: Land of Tradition and Conflict, 1985, 93, Historical Dictionary of Israel, 1992, Securing the Covenant: United States-Israel Relations After the Cold War, 1995; co-editor, co-author: Government and Politics of the Middle East and North Africa, 1980, 86, 95, 2002 Israel Faces the Future, 1986, The Powers in the Middle East, 1987, Israeli National Security Policy: Political Actors and Perspectives, 1988, Political Leaders of the Contemporary Middle East and North Africa: A Biographical Dictionary, 1990, Israeli Politics in the 1990's Key Domestic and Foreign Policy Factors, 1991, Arab-Israeli Conflict and Conciliation: A Documentary History, 1995, An Historical Encyclopedia of the Arab-Israeli Conflict, 1996; editor, co-author: Handbook of Political Science Research on the Middle East and North Africa, 1998; co-author: United States Foreign Policy and the Middle East/North Africa: A Bibliography of Twentieth-Century Research, 1990, Asian States' Relations with the Middle East and North Africa: A Bibliography, 1950-93, 94, U.S. Foreign Relations with the Middle East and North Africa: A Bibliography, 1994, U.S. Foreign Relations with the Middle East and North Africa: A Bibliography, 1998, 99, Political Dictionary of Israel, 2000; mem. adv. bd. editors Middle East Jour., 1977—, Jour. Israel Affairs, 1994—, Terrorism, 1987-93, Fgn. Svc. Jour., 1987-90; contbr. articles to profl. jours. Bd. govs. Middle East Inst. Fulbright research scholar, UAR, 1965; NSF postdoctoral fellow, 1971-72 Mem. Internat. Inst. Strategic Studies, Middle East Studies Assn., Phi Beta Kappa Home: 13800 Turnmore Rd Silver Spring MD 20906-2134 Office: George Washington U Dept Polit Sci Washington DC 20052-0001 E-mail: breich@gwu.edu.

REICH, BERNARD, retired telecommunications engineer; b. N.Y.C., Jan. 7, 1926; s. Adolph and Rose (Gluck) R.; m. Sylvia Greenberg, June 15, 1947; children: Robin Reich Murphy, Richard. BS in Physics, CCNY, 1948; postgrad., Rutgers U., 1954. Electronic engr., supervisory electronic engr. U.S. Army Electronics R & D Command, Ft. Monmouth, N.J., 1948-81; unit mgr. Semcor, Farmingdale, 1981-88; telecommunications engr. Telos Corp., Shrewsbury, 1988-99, retired, 1999. Chmn. spl. working group on semicondrs. and microelectronics NATO, Brussels, 1959-80, chmn. group experts on electronic parts, 1972-80; adv. editor Microelectronics and Reliability, 1970—. Contbr. over 100 articles to tech. jours.; patentee in field. Mem. Juvenile Conf. Com., Ocean Twp., N.J., 1964—; pres. Manor at Wayside Condominium Assn., Ocean Twp., 1990-91. Sgt. U.S. Army, 1945-46, ETO. Recipient decoration for meritorious civilian svc. U.S. Army Electronics R & D Command, 1981. Fellow IEEE (chartered,), IEE (Eng.). Avocations: walking, grandparenting. Home: 45 Gimbel Pl Ocean NJ 07712-2565

REICH, DAVID LEE, library director; b. Orlando, Fla., Nov. 25, 1930; s. P.F. and Opal Katherine (Wood) Reichelderfer; m. Kathleen Johanna Weichel, Aug. 2, 1954 (div. Sept. 1964); 1 son, Robert Weichel. PhB magna cum laude, U. Detroit, 1961; AM in LS, U. Mich., 1963. Tchr. English Jefferson Davis Jr. Sch., San Antonio, 1961-62; dir. engring. library Radiation Inc., Melbourne, Fla., 1963-64; asst. to dir. libraries Miami-Dade Jr. Coll., Miami, 1964-65; dir. learning resources Monroe County C.C., Monroe, Mich., 1965-68; dep. dir. Dallas Pub. Library, 1968-73; dep. chief librarian Chgo. Pub. Library, 1973-74, commr., 1975-78; dir. Bd. Libr. Commrs., Commonwealth of Mass., Boston, 1978-80; exec. sec. New Eng. Libr. Bd., Augusta, Maine, 1980-82, vice chmn., 1979-80; dir. Lakeland (Fla.) Pub. Libr., 1983-99, ret., 1999; exec. sec. Soc. Fla. Archivists, 1999—2001, ret., 2001. Libr. cons. Macomb County C.C., Warren, Mich., 1967; chmn. adv. com. to libr. tech. asst. program El Centro Coll., Dallas, 1969-71; mem. inter-task working group Goals for Dallas, 1968-70, mem. Dallas Area Libr. planning coun., 1970-73; mem. adv. coun. dept. libr. sci. No. Ill. U., 1975-78; v.p., pres.-elect Tampa Bay Libr. Consortium, 1985-86, pres., 1986-87. Co-author: The Public Library in Non-traditional Education, 1974; editor The Villas II News, 1999—; contbr. articles to library jours. Bd. dirs. The Villas II Homeowners Assn., 1994-96, 98-2001; steering com. Friends of Tampa Bay Libr. Consortium, 2000—. Sgt. U.S. Army, 1952-55. Recipient Disting. Alumnus award U. Mich., 1978; William B. Calkins Found. scholar Orlando, 1963; Carnegie L.S. Endowment scholar, 1963. Mem. ALA (coun.-at-large 1968-72, 75-79), S.E. Libr. Assn., Fla. Libr. Assn. (sec.-treas. coll. and spl. librs. divsn. 1965, steering com. mcpl. librs. caucus 1983-84, chmn. 1984-85, exec. bd. 1984-87), Soc. Fla. Archivists (exec. bd. 1994-96, sec. 1996-97, exec. sec. 1999-2001, treas. 2000-01), Fla. Pub. Libr. Assn. (pres. 1987-88, exec. bd. 1988-89, 94-95, pres. emeritus 1996-98, editor newsletter 1992-93, 96-97, chmn. libr. adminstrn. divsn. 1992, friends and trustees divsn. 1993, 95), Alumni Assn. U. Mich. (pres. Libr. Sch. alumni 1973). Home: 3929 Old Road 37 Villa 134 Lakeland FL 33813-1053 E-mail: dreich@tampabay.rr.com.

REICH, HARVEY STEVEN, critical care physician; b. N.Y.C., Feb. 2, 1954; BA, Rutgers U., 1975; MD, N.J. Med. Sch., 1981. Diplomate Am. Bd. Internal Medicine, Am. Bd. Critical Care Medicine. Intern Berkshire Med. Ctr., Pittsfield, Mass., 1981-82, resident, 1982-85; fellow U. Pitts., 1985-87, dir. critical care medicine Magee Womens Hosp., 1987-94; dir. critical care medicine Rutland (Vt.) Regional Med. Ctr., 1994—; clin. assoc. prof. med. U. Vt. Coll. Medicine, Burlington, Vt., 199—. Cons. The Jacob D. Fuschberg Law Firm, N.Y.C., 1992—, Wingate Russotti & Shapiro, N.Y.C., 1994—; med. dir. Park Street Healthshare, Rutland, 1999—. Reviewer (abstracts) Society of Critical Care Medicine, 1988—, (manuscript) Chest, 1997—; contbr. articles to profl. jours. Fellow ACP, Am. Coll. Chest Physicians; mem. Soc. Critical Care Medicine (elecs. comm. com., exec. coun. New Eng. chpt. 1995—), Phi Beta Kappa. Fax: 802-747-6207. E-mail: Hreich@rrmc.org.

REICH, HERB, editor; b. N.Y.C. s. Herman S. and Hattie (Davis) R.; m. Gerri Toog, Aug. 7, 1960; children: Amanda Suri, Elizabeth Jo. BA, Bklyn. Coll., 1950; MA, Bklyn. Coll. and Kings County Hosp., 1951; postgrad., Columbia U., 1951-54. Author sketches and lyrics Tamiment Revues (Pa.), 1951; staff writer NBC-TV, N.Y.C. and Los Angeles, 1955-57; research coordinator Inst. for Motivational Research, Croton-on-Hudson, N.Y., 1958-59; research dir. Scientist and Engr. Technol. Inst., N.Y.C., 1960-64; mng. editor SETI Pubs. Inc., 1961-64; sr. editor Odyssey Press, 1964-65; editorial dir. Profl. and Tech. Programs Inc., 1966-72; dir. Behavioral Sci. Book Service, 1966-72; dir. behavioral scis. program Basic Books Inc., 1973-79; editor intersci. div. John Wiley & Sons Inc., 1979-87, sr. editor profl. and trade divsn., 1987-95; pres. H&G Reich, Publ., Hastings Hdsn., N.Y., 1980—. Publ., rsch., advt. and polit. cons.; rschr., statistician, rsch. cons. Am. Found. for Blind, Pepsi Cola Co., Nowland and Co., Comms. and Media Rsch. Svcs.; freelance TV writer. Mng. editor: Odyssey Science Library Ency. of Engring., Signs and Symbols, 1965, Dictionary of Physics and Mathematics Abbreviations, Signs and Symbols, 1965, Dictionary of Electronics Abbreviations, Signs and Symbols, 1965, Dictionary of Computers and Control Systems Abbreviations, Signs and Symbols, 1965; contbr. Random House Dictionary of the English Language, 1967, rev. edit., 1987, The Greatest Revue Sketches, 1982, Ency. of Psychology, 2d edit., 1994; TV writer: Broadway Open House, 1951, Milton Berle Texaco Star Theatre, 1952, All-Star Revue, 1952, Mel Torme Show, 1952, Red Buttons Show, 1954, Summer Colgate Show, 1954,

Jerry Lester Show, 1954, Jan Murray Time, 1955, Wayne and Schuster Hour, 1957. Co-founder, vice chmn. Mt. Vernon United for Better Edn., N.Y., 1970-73; mem. Westchester County Democratic Com., 1972-76; exec. com. Mt. Vernon Dem. City Com., 1973-76; mem. supt.'s adv. com. Hastings Schs., Hastings-on-Hudson, N.Y., 1981-82. Recipient Gold award of excellence for radio advt. Advt. Club of Westchester, 1980; recipient Gold and Bronze awards of excellence for radio advt. Advt. Club of Westchester, 1981 Mem. AAAS, APA, Alpha Phi Omega. Office: PO Box 38 Hastings On Hudson NY 10706 E-mail: hgreich@aol.com.

REICH, HOWARD LEONARD, journalist; b. Chgo., Apr. 19, 1954; s. Robert and Sonia Reich; m. Pamela Rae Becker. MB, Northwestern U., 1977. Arts critic Chgo. Tribune, 1983—. Author: Van Cliburn, 1993. Recipient Excellence in Journalism award, Chgo. Assn. Black Journalists, 1996, Peter Lisagor award, Soc. Profl. Journalists, 1998, 1999, Deems Taylor award, ASCAP, 1999. Office: Chgo Tribune 435 N Michigan Ave Chicago IL 60611 Office Fax: 312-222-0236. Business E-Mail: hreich@tribune.com.

REICH, KENNETH IRVIN, journalist; b. Los Angeles, Mar. 7, 1938; s. Herman and Ruth Alberta (Nussbaum) R.; children: Kathleen, David. BA, Dartmouth Coll., 1960; MA (Woodrow Wilson fellow), U. Calif., Berkeley, 1962. With UPI, Sacramento, 1962-63, Life mag., 1963-65; with Los Angeles Times, 1965—, polit. writer, 1972-77, 1984 Olympics writer, 1977-84, investigative reporter ins. law, ins. politics & fin. sports, 1985-92. Covering earthquakes, volcanoes, and other issues relating to geology, 1987—; columnist of consumer affairs, 1998-2001; lectr. in field. Author: Making it Happen, Peter Ueberroth and the 1984 Olympics, 1985; contbr. articles to mags. Meml. chmn. Dartmouth Class of 1960, 1993-95, class sec. 1995—. Daniel Webster Nat. Honor scholar Dartmouth Coll., 1956-60 Office: LA Times 202 W 1st St Los Angeles CA 90012 E-mail: ken.reich@latimes.com.

REICH, LARRY SAM, lawyer; b. Bklyn., Sept. 24, 1946; s. Sidney and Regina (Brown) R.; m. Patricia S. Neustein, Aug. 18, 1968; children: Ilysa Jill, Shari Beth. BA, Hofstra U., 1969; JD, Bklyn. Law Sch., 1973. Bar: N.Y. 1974, U.S. Dist. Ct. (so. and ea. dists.) N.Y. 1974, U.S. Ct. Appeals (2d cir.) 1974, U.S. Supreme Ct. 1980. Assoc. S. Edward Orenstein PC, N.Y.C., 1973-78; ptnr. Herzfeld & Rubin PC, 1978-98, Blank Rome Tenzer Greenblatt, LLP, N.Y.C., 1999—. Arbitrator U.S. Dist. Ct. for Ea. Dist. N.Y., Bklyn., 1986—. Mem. ABA, N.Y. State Bar Assn. (chmn. com. on supreme cts. 1986-89, chmn. com. on jud. adminstrn. 1989-92, com. jud. adminstrn. 1989-94), N.Y. County Bar Assn., Nassau County Bar Assn., Assn. Trial Lawyers Am., N.Y. State Trial Lawyers Assn. Avocations: running, rowing, biking, reading. Office: Blank Rome Tenzer Greenblatt LLP The Chrysler Bldg New York NY 10174

REICH, LAURENCE, lawyer; b. Jersey City, Jan. 22, 1931; s. Victor and Miriam (Gross) R.; m. Doris Rita Diamond, Oct. 21, 1965. BA, U. Chgo., 1951, JD, 1953. Bar: N.J. 1954, N.Y. 1982, U.S. Dist. Ct. N.J. 1954, U.S. ct. appeals (3rd cir.) 1958, U.S. Supreme ct. 1963, U.S. Tax Ct. 1971, U.S. Dist. Ct. (so. dist.) N.Y. 1982, U.S. Ct. Appeals (2nd cir.) 1987. Mem. firm Carpenter, Bennett & MOrrissey, Newark, 1957-63, ptnr., 1963-69, sr. ptnr., 1969—. Mem. Bur. Nat. Affairs Tax Adv. bd., 1972—; lectr. NYU Inst. Fed. Taxation, Tulane Tax Inst., Ark. Tax Inst., Fairleigh Dickinson U. Tax Inst., Seton Hall Tax Inst., N.J. Inst. Continuing Legal Edn., Internat. Bus. Conf., Mid-Atlantic Estate Planing Conf. Author: N.J. Corporation Law and Practice; contbr. articles to profl. jours. With U.S. Army, 1955-57. Fellow Am. Coll. Tax Counsel, Am. Bar Found.; mem. ABA (com. chmn. sect. taxation 1972-74, 85-86, mem. coun. 1991-94), N.J. Bar Assn. (chmn. taxation sect. 1975-76), Assn. Fed. Bar State N.J. (v.p. 1982-94, bd. trustees 1994-99), Essex County Bar Assn. Office: 3 Gateway Ctr Newark NJ 07102-4079 E-mail: lr@carpben.com.

REICH, MANUEL DAVID, psychiatrist; b. N.Y.C., July 16, 1956; s. Eugene and Gertrude R. BA, Brandeis U., 1978; DO, N.Y. Coll. Osteo. Medicine, 1982. Cert. adult and child psychiatry. Med. dir. Elmhurst (N.Y.) Hosp. Ctr., 1991-94, U. Pitts., 1994-96, Psychiat. Assn. for Consultation and Therapy, Pitts., 1996—. Office: PACT # B106 401 Shady Ave Apt B106 Pittsburgh PA 15206-4458

REICH, MERRILL DRURY, intelligence consultant, writer; b. Washington, Aug. 28, 1930; s. Merrill Dale Reich and Evelyn Merle Wright; m. Georgia Ann Ewing, Aug. 28, 1953; 1 child, Alexandra Therese. BA in History, Govt., Rollins Coll., 1954; postgrad., U. Vienna, 1954-55, Naval War Coll., 1973-74; MA in Mgmt., Cen. Mich. U., 1981. Commd. ensign USN, 1956, advanced through grades to capt., ret., 1982; dir. systems mgmt. BDM Corp., Columbia, Md., 1982-92; cons. Crytec, Inc., 1992-95. Fulbright scholar, 1954-55. Mem. SAR, Nat. Trust for Hist. Preservation, U.S. Naval Inst., Naval War Coll. Found., Assn. Former Intelligence Officers, Navy Cryptologic Vets. Assn., Fulbright Assn., New Eng. Hist. Geneal. Soc., Omicron Delta Kappa, Pi Gamma Mu, Phi Kappa Tau. Avocations: genealogy, lapidary, antiques, swimming, sailing. Home: 841 Patuxent Run Cir Odenton MD 21113 E-mail: mreich@rocsoft.net.

REICH, MICHAEL, economics educator; b. Poland, Oct. 18, 1945; came to U.S., 1949; s. Melvin and Betty (Mandelbaum) R.; children: Rachel, Gabriel. BA, Swarthmore Coll., 1966; PhD, Harvard U., 1974. Asst. prof. Boston U., 1971-74, U. Calif., Berkeley, 1974-81, acting assoc. prof., 1981-82, assoc. prof., 1982-89, prof., 1989—. Rsch. dir. Nat. Ctr. for the Workplace, 1993—. Author: Segmented Work, Divided Workers, 1982, Racial Inequality, 1981, The Capitalist System, 1986, Social Structures of Accumulation, 1994, Work and Pay in the U.S. and Japan, 1997; editor: Indsl. Rels. Jour., 1986-94; contbr. articles to profl. jours. Mem. Am. Econ. Assn., Indsl. Rels. Rsch. Assn., Phi Beta Kappa, Sigma Xi. Office: Dept of Econs U Calif 611 Evans Hl Berkeley CA 94720-0001

REICH, MICHAEL IRA, obstetrician/gynecologist; b. N.Y.C., Mar. 31, 1951; s. Mark and Esther (Friedman) R.; m. Ann Bennett Terry, Apr. 27, 1991; children: Hannah Gallogley, Thomas Felix BS in Physics, Cooper Union, 1972; MD, Albert Einstein Coll., 1976. Diplomate Am. Bd. Ob/gyn. Intern N.Y. Med. Coll., N.Y.C., 1976-77; resident in ob/gyn. U. Cin., 1978-81; pvt. practice Salem (Mass.) Women's Health Assocs.; staff North Shore Med. Ctr., Salem. Vol. physician to no. Nigeria World Health Mission, Allison Park, Pa., 1996—98, Allison Park, 2000—02. Fellow Am. Coll. Ob-gyn., Am. Soc. Reproductive Medicine. Jewish. Office: 400 Highland Ave Salem MA 01970-7003 E-mail: terreich@massmed.org.

REICH, MICHAEL JAMES, musician, composer; b. Johnstown, Pa., Apr. 6, 1959; s. Philip Beachy and Thelma Mae Reich; m. Susan Diane Lamberson-Blackburn, July 4, 1998. Diploma, Columbia Broadcasting Inst., Pitts., 1981. Banker Citizens Nat. Bank, Meyersdale, Pa., 1977—80; broadcaster various stas., 1981—84; leather craftsman Pa., 1984—89; singer, songwriter. Composer: (music album) Pushing Hard to the Shore, 1989, Before I Let It Go, 2000, Live for Today, 2002. Coun. mem. Meyersdale Borough Coun., 1997—98. Recipient Songwriting award, Billboard Mag., 1990. Mem.: ASCAP (Popular Songwriting award), Elks (exalted ruler 1993—95). Roman Catholic. Avocations: gardening, fishing, writing. Home: 697 Shaffer Mt Rd Cairnbrook PA 15924 Personal E-mail: beachsongs77@aol.com.

REICH, NATHANIEL EDWIN, physician, poet, artist, educator, explorer; b. N.Y.C., May 19, 1907; s. Alexander and Betty (Feigenbaum) R.; m. Joan Finkel, May 22, 1943; children: Andrew, Matthew. BS, NYU, 1927; student, Marquette U. Coll. Medicine, 1927-29; MD, Rush Med. Coll., U. Chgo., 1932. Diplomate Am. Bd. Internal Medicine. Intern, resident pathologist City Hosp., N.Y.C., 1931-33; emeritus attending physician Kingsbrook Jewish Med. Center Hosp.; vis. physician Kings County Hosp., Bklyn.; attending physician State U. Hosp.; faculty SUNY Downstate Med. Center, 1938—, asso. clin. prof. medicine, 1952-74, clin. prof., 1974-77, emeritus prof., 1977—. Vis. prof. San Marcos U. Coll. Medicine, Lima, Peru, 1968, U. Afghanistan, 1970, U. Indonesia, 1972, U. Sri Lanka, 1975; asst. attending physician N.Y. Postgrad. Hosp., Columbia U., 1940; cons. Dept. H and HS; cardiac cons. U.S. R.R. Retirement Bd., 1965—; program cons. Acad. Family Physicians, 1973, N.Y. State Disability Determinations; lectr. univs., Rome, Moscow, Rijeka, Haiti, Jerusalem, Cairo, Athens, Bangkok, Bucharest, Manila, Lisbon, Beijing, Shanghai, Romania, Taiwan, Madras, Dakar, Senegal, Durban, Witwatersrand, Capetown, Natal, Lima, Buenos Aires, Rio de Janeiro, Quito; 1st Am. physician invited to lecture in USSR, 1956; lectr. univs. U. Madras (India), 1969, Spain, 1971, Auckland, N.Z., Sydney, Australia, Senegal, Portugal; lectr. Japan Med. Assn., Philippine Heart Assn., Royal Thai Air Force Med. Svc., China Med. Assn., Shanghai, 1978, Nat. Taiwan U., Taipei, 1978, Beijing Cardiac Inst., 1986; chmn. internat. cardiology sect. Congress Chest Diseases, Cologne, Germany, 1956; impartial specialist U.S. Fed. Employees; cons. N.Y. State Bur. Disability Determinations, N.Y.C., Office Voc. Rehab., Dept. Health and Human Svcs., 1965—; chief med. examiner SSS, 1942-44 (Presdl. commendation). One-man shows include L.I. U., 1961, NYU Loeb Ctr., 1962, 72, 74, Greer Gallery, 1962, 64, St. Charles, La., 1964, Nyack, N.Y., 1986, Prospect Park Ctrl. Art Show, 1966, Art Inst. Boston, 1970, 76, George Wiener Gallery, 1972; exhibited in group shows at Little Studio, 1952, Mus. Modern Art, Paris, 1970, Bodley Gallery, 1965, 69, Nyack, N.Y., 1987, others; represented in permanent collections at Huntington Hartford collection N.Y. Cultural Ctr., 1969, Washington County Mus. of Fine Arts, Hagerstown, md.; author 3 textbooks on cardiology; author chpts. in 3 encys.; author: A Renaissance Man at Large; author: (collected poems) Reflections, 1993, (essays) The Facts of Life, 1999. Served from 1st lt. to maj. M.C., AUS, 1944-47. Recipient St. Gaudens award, 1923, 1st prize Art Assn. AMA, 1948, 1st prize Art Assn. Literary Soc., 1949, Disting. Achievement award Boys' H.S. Alumni Assn., 1988, Am. Poetry Assn. Hon. mention World of Poetry, 1990; named Best New Poets of 1989, 94, 95; named Internat. Man of Yr. in Medicine, 2000-2001. Fellow ACP, Royal Soc. Medicine (London), Am. Coll. Cardiology, Am. Coll. Angiology (med. honor award 1956, 59), Am. Coll. Legal Medicine (founder), Am. Coll. Chest Physicians (chmn. exhibits com. 1961, cardiovascular rehab. com. 1965, coronary disease com. 1968, pres. N.Y. state chpt. 1970); mem. N.Y. State Med. Soc. (vice chmn. space med. sect. 1967, 75, chmn. chest sect. 1972), Internat. Soc. Internal Medicine, World Med. Assn., Am. Heart Assn. (coun. on thrombosis), N.Y. Heart Assn., N.Y. Cardiol. Soc. (exec. bd., pres.), Explorers Club (5 explorations described in jour. 1966—, Internat. Man of Yr. for Medicine 1999-2000), Temple Club (v.p.), Doctors Club Bklyn. (vice chmn. bd. govs.), Circumnavigators. Home: 1620 Avenue I Brooklyn NY 11230-3050

REICH, OTTO JUAN, political analyst, business consultant; b. Havana, Cuba, Oct. 16, 1945; came to U.S., 1960; s. Walter and Graciela Maria (Fleites) R.; m. Connie Lynn Dillinger, Apr. 19, 1975; children: Adrienne Michelle, Natalie Lauren BA, U. N.C., Chapel Hill, 1966; MA, Georgetown U., 1973; grad., Officers Candidate Sch., U.S. Army, 1967. Civil affairs officer U.S. Army, Panama, 1967-69; staff asst. U.S. Ho. Reps., Washington, 1970-71; v.p. Cormorant Enterprises, Miami, Fla., 1972-73; internat. rep. Fla. Dept. Commerce, Coral Gables, 1973-75; community devel. coordinator City of Miami, Fla., 1975-76; dir. Washington ops. Council of the Americas, 1976-81; asst. adminstr. U.S. AID, Washington, 1981-83; spl. adv. for pub. diplomacy to sec. state with rank of ambassador U.S. Dept. State, 1983-86; ambassador to Venezuela, Caracas, 1986-89; sr. assoc. Ctr. for Strategic and Internat. Studies, Washington, 1989—. Ptnr. Brock Group, 1990—; mem. alt. U.S. rep. UN Human Rights Commn., Geneva, 1991-92. Lst lt. U.S. Army, 1966-69. Decorated Order of Liberator grand cordon class (Venezuela); recipient Superior Honor award U.S. State Dept., 1986-89, 91, Exemplary Svc. award U.S. State Dept., 1988. Mem. Coun. Am. Ambs., Nat. Leadership Coun. (vice chmn.), Ctr. for Strategic and Internat. Studies. Office: Ctr for Strategic & Intl Studies 1800 K St NW Ste 400 Washington DC 20006-2202*

REICH, PAULA JUDY, nursing educator; b. Troy, N.Y., Jan. 27, 1942; d. Samuel and Dora (Luskin) Bendick; m. Lawrence W. Reich, Nov. 1, 1964; children: Ronna, Heather, Sheara. AAS in Nursing, Queens Coll., 1961; BSN, St. John's U., Queens, N.Y., 1964; MS in Curriculum and Instrn., SUNY, Albany, 1975; MS in Nursing, Adelphi U., 1982. RN, N.Y. Staff nurse obstetrics Flushing Hosp., Queens, 1962-63; staff nurse ob/gyn. Queens Gen. Hosp., 1963-64; sr. staff nurse pediatrics Mt. Sinai Hosp., N.Y.C., 1964-65; supr. ob-gyn. Nassau Hosp., Mineola, N.Y., 1965-67; staff nurse obstetrics St. Peters Hosp., Albany, 1968-73; dir. Tri Cities Childbirth Instrn., 1973-78; mem. faculty dept. nursing Adelphi U., Garden City, N.Y., 1978-79, SUNY, Farmingdale, 1978—. Clin. instr. Albany Jr. Coll., 1977-78; cons. maternal/child continuing edn. Adelphi U., 1984; dir. nursing continuing edn. SUNY, Farmingdale, 1985-91, dir. LPN/ADN nursing ract, 1990-94. V.p. bd. dirs. Suffolk Network Adolescent Pregnancy, Suffolk County, N.Y., 1985-90. Mem. Suffolk Perinatal Coalition. Avocations: sailing, travel, reading. Office: SUNY Farmingdale Dept Nursing Rt 110 Melville NY 11735

REICH, PETER LESTER, legal educator, legal and historical consultant; b. L.A., Mar. 20, 1955; s. Jack Edward and Lillian (Lerner) R.; m. Alisa Schulweis, Sept. 8, 1985; children: Gabriel, Eli. BA in History, UCLA, 1976, PhD in History, 1991; JD, U. Calif., Berkeley, 1985. Bar: Calif. 1985, U.S. Dist. Ct. (ctrl. dist.) Calif. 1986. Rsch. atty. Calif. Ct. Appeal, Ventura, 1985-86; assoc. Parker, Milliken et al, L.A., 1986-88; asst. prof. law Whittier Law Sch., 1988-91, assoc. prof. law, 1991-93, prof. law Costa Mesa, Calif., 1993—. Vis. prof. of history U. Calif., Irvine, 1999—2002. Author: Mexico's Hidden Revolution, 1995; mem. editl. bd. Western Legal History, 1995—; contbr. articles to profl. jours. Recipient Hubert Herring Meml. award Pacific Coast Coun. on Latin Am. Studies, 1991, Ray A. Billington award Western History Assn., 1995; Fulbright-Hays fellow, 1979-80; Rocky Mountain Mineral Law Found. rsch. grantee, 1993, 95, 99; Huntington Libr. fellow Andrew Mellon Found., 1997. Mem. Am. Soc. for Legal History, Assn. Am. Law Scs. (sec.-treas. immigration sect., exec. bd. legal history sect.), Calif. Supreme Ct. Hist. Soc. Democrat. Jewish. Avocations: sea kayaking, hiking, ice skating. Office: Whittier Law Sch 3333 Harbor Blvd Costa Mesa CA 92626-1501

REICH, RICHARD ALLEN, energy company executive; b. Rhinelander, Wis., Mar. 12, 1962; s. John E. and Alma Louise (Post) R. BBA, U. Wis., 1984; MBA, NYU, 1989. CPA, Okla. Staff acct., cons. Deloitte, Haskins and Sells, N.Y.C., 1984-86; fin. analyst Salomon Bros., Inc., 1986-89; treasury mgr. Citibank-U.S. Card Products Group, 1989-92; with Bankers Trust Corp., 1992-93; v.p., dir. risk mgmt. Nikko Securities Internat., Inc., 1993-95, CDC Capital, Inc., N.Y.C., 1995-99; dir. risk mgmt. and control OGE Energy Corp., Oklahoma City, 1999—. Investment mgr. Wis. Eastern Scholarship Fund, 1996-2001. Mem. AICPA, Okla. State Soc. CPA, Okla. Soc. Security Analysts, Assn. Investment Mgmt. & Rsch., U. Wis. Alumni Assn. N.Y. (sec. 1989-91, v.p. 1991-92, pres. 1992-95). Avocations: golf, skiing. Home: 12300 E 2nd St Arcadia OK 73007-8103 Office: OGE Energy Corp Ste 408 515 Central Park Dr Oklahoma City OK 73105-1704

REICH, ROBERT SIGMUND, landscape architect; b. N.Y.C., Mar. 22, 1913; s. Ulysses S. and Adele G. R.; m. Helen Elizabeth Adams, May, 1945; children: Barbara, Betsy, Bob, Bill. BS, Cornell U., 1934, PhD, 1941; postgrad., U. So. Calif., 1951. Instr. landscape design Cornell U., 1936-39, 40-41; instr. landscape design U. Conn., 1939-40; Inst. Land Design La. State U., 1941-46, asst. prof. landscape architecture, 1946-49, asso. prof., 1949-60, prof., 1960—, Alumni prof., 1967—, head dept. landscape architecture, 1964-79, dir. Sch. Landscape Architecture, 1979-83; prof. Landscape Architecture, 1992—. Instr. Shrivenham (Eng.) Am. U., 1946, Biarritz (France) Am. U., 1947; vis. lectr. Tulane U., 1958-67; judge, instr. Nat. Council Garden Clubs, 1956— ; mem. task force on parks, recreation and tourism Goals for La. Program; mem. com. to establish Chicot State Park Arboretum, Ville Plate, La., 1964, mem. steering com., 1964-75; examiner La. Bd. Examination for Landscape Architects, 1957-77 Co-author: Landscape and You, 1953. Mem. com. to establish City/Parish Beautification Commn., 1961-82; mem. area and facilities com. Baton Rouge Recreation and Pk. Commn., 1957-83; bd. dirs. Hubbard Edn. Trust, Weston, Mass., 1967—; adv. com. Friends of Frederick Law Olmsted Papers, 1983-95. With U.S. Army, 1942-45; in charge alter arrangements U. United Meth. Ch., 1945—. Recipient Tchg. award of merit Gamma Sigma Delta, 1963, Baton Rouge Green Individual Honor award, 1996. Fellow Am. Soc. Landscape Architects (trustee 1968-71, 83-86, 3d v.p. 1971-73, Medal 1992); mem. AIA (hon.), S.W. Park and Recreation Tng. Inst. (dir. 1975-77, award of merit 1968), Phi Kappa Phi, Pi Alpha xi, Omicron Delta Kappa, Sigma Lambda Alpha. Home: 333 E Boyd Dr Baton Rouge LA 70808-4507 Office: La State U Sch Landscape Architecture Coll Design Bldg Baton Rouge LA 70803-0001

REICH, ROSE MARIE, retired art educator; b. Milw., Dec. 24, 1937; d. Valentine John and Mary Jane (Grochowski) Kosmatka; m. Kenneth Pierce Reich, July 13, 1968; 1 stepson, Lance Pierce. BA, Milw. Downer Coll., 1959; MA, U. Wyo., 1967. Art tchr. Oconomowoc (Wis.) Area Schs., 1959-93, ret., 1993. Mem. Oconomowoc Edn. Assn., NEA (life), Wis. Edn. Assn., AAUW (v.p. membership 1989—), Delta Kappa Gamma (past pres.), Oconomowoc Woman's Club. Roman Catholic. Avocations: Newfoundland dogs, needlework, designing stationery, Polish paper cutting, restoring old church statues and mannequins. Home: 3717 N Golden Lake Rd Oconomowoc WI 53066-4104

REICH, STANLEY BENJAMIN, radiologist, medical educator; b. N.Y.C., Feb. 20, 1921; s. Harry Max Reich and Bessie Bangel; m. Adele Axelrod, Dec. 15, 1944; children: Linda, James, Judi. AB, Cornell U., 1941; MD, NYU, 1944. Diplomate Am. Bd. Radiology, Am. Bd. Nuclear Medicine. Intern Bellevue Hosp., N.Y.C., 1944-45, resident in radiology, 1946-49; asst. prof. NYU/Bellevue Hosp., 1949-50; clin. prof. radiology U. Calif., San Francisco, 1952-72, 77—; prof. radiology U. Colo., Denver, 1972-77, U. Calif. Davis, Sacramento, 1977—; chief radiology No. Calif. VA Clinics, Martinez, 1979-98. Contbr. articles to profl. jours. Pres. Concordia-Argonaut Club, San Francisco, 1963-65; cons. Travis AFB, Fairfield, Calif., 1977—, Exec. Svc. Corps., San Francisco, 1997—. Lt. (sr.) USN, 1944-47, 50-52. Fellow Am. Coll. Radiology; mem. Am. Soc. Thoracic Radiology (sec. 1967), Am. Radium Soc. Avocations: travel, photography. Home: 2 Abbott Way Piedmont CA 94618-2610 E-mail: asreich@worldnet.att.net.

REICH, STEPHEN, psychologist; b. N.Y.C., May 24, 1939; s. Arnold and Helen (Rosen) R.; m. E. Laura Hausmann, May 15, 1988; 1 child, Joseph Stephen. BA, Columbia U., 1960, JD, MBA, Columbia U., 1963; MA, Fordham U., 1970, PhD, 1972. Bar: N.Y. Assoc. Herman Odell, N.Y.C., 1964-65; asst. atty. gen. N.Y. State Atty. Gen., 1965-68; USPHS fellow, 1968-71; fellow Cornell Univ. Med. Coll., N.Y.C., 1971-72, from instr. to asst. prof., 1972—; cons. psychologist Consolidated Edison Co., 1978-97; pvt. practice, 1978—. Mem. APA, Assn. Bar City of N.Y., N.Y. State Psychol. Assn. Office: 141 E 55th St New York NY 10022-4030

REICH, STEVE, composer; b. N.Y.C., Oct. 3, 1936; m. Beryl Korot; children: Ezra, Michael. Studies in percussion with Roland Kohloff, 1950-53; BA in Philosophy with honors, Cornell U., 1957; studies in composition with Hall Overton, 1957-58; studies with Bergsma and Persichetti, Julliard Sch. Music, 1958-61; MA in Music, Mills Coll., 1963; studies in drumming, Inst. for African Studies, U. Ghana, 1970; student, Am. Soc. for Ea. Arts, Seattle and Berkeley, 1973, 74, Cantillation of Hebrew Scriptures, N.Y.C. and Jerusalem, 1976-77; D (hon.), Calif. Inst. Arts, 2000. Organized ensemble Steve Reich and Musicians, 1966; performed throughout the world, 1971—; recs. with various cos. including Columbia Records, Disques Shandar, Hungaraton, Angel, ECM, Deutsche Grammophon, Nonesuch, Phillips, Virgin Classics, Argo. Regents lectr. U. Calif., Berkeley, 2000. Composer, performer: (albums) Come Out, 1967, It's Gonna Rain, 1969, Violin Phase, 1969, Four Organs, 1970, Phase Patterns, 1970, Drumming, 1971, Four Organs, 1973, Six Pianos, 1973, Music for Mallet Instruments, Voices, and Organ, 1973, Music for Eighteen Musicians, 1978 (Grammy award 1999), Octet, 1980, Music for a Large Ensemble, 1980,Tehillim, 1982, The Desert Music, 1984, Sextet, 1986, Six Marimbas, 1986, Electric Counterpoint, 1987, Different Trains, 1988 (Grammy award 1989), The Four Sections, 1987, The Cave, 1994, City Life, 1995, Proverb, 1996,Triple Quartet, 1999, others; recordings include (10 CD boxed set) Steve Reich Works: 1965-1995; composer: Vermont Counterpoint, Variations for Winds, Strings and Keyboards, Eight Lines for Chamber Orchestra, Piano Phase, Clapping Music, Pendulum Music, Music for Pieces of Wood, Nagoya Marimbas, other works performed by major orchs. and ensembles; commd. to compose for Holland Festival, 1978, Radio Frankfurt, 1979, San Francisco Symphony, 1980, Rothko Chapel, 1981, West German Radio, Cologne, 1984, Fromm Music Found., 1985, Richard Stoltzman, 1985, Bklyn. Acad. Music, 1987, Kronos Quartet, 1988, St. Louis Sympnony, 1987, The Cave commd. by Vienna Festival, Holland Festival, Festival d'Automne à Paris, Theatre de la Monnaie, Brussels, Hebbel Theatre, Berlin, South Bank Centre/Serious Speakout, London and the Brooklyn Acad. Music, Next Wave Festival, 1993; 4-concert retrospective Lincoln Ctr. Festival, N.Y.C., 1999, video opera (with Beryl Korot) Three Tales, commd. by Vienna Festival Barbican Ctr., London, SPoleto Festival, Bklyn. Acad. Music, Music Strassbourg, Hebbel Theater, Berlin. Recipient Koussevitzky Found. award, 1981, Schuman prize Columbia U., 2000; named Composer of Yr., Musical Am., 2000; Rockefeller Found. grantee 1975, 78, 81, 90, Nat. Endowment for the Arts grantee, 1974, 76, 91, N.Y. State Council on the Arts grantee, 1974; Guggenheim fellow, 1978, Montgomery fellow Dartmouth Coll., 2000; elected to Am. Acad. Arts and Letters, 1994, Bauerische Akademie der Schönen Künst, 1995; named Commr. dans l'Ordre des Arts et des Lettres, 1999. Office: c/o Boosey & Hawkes Inc 35 E 21st St New York NY 10010-6212

REICHARDT, PAUL BERNARD, provost, chemistry educator; b. St. Louis, Aug. 15, 1943; s. Bernard George and Elaine Charlotte (Schmudde) R.; m. Cordelia Morris Hufnagel, Apr. 27, 1968; children: Laura, Rebecca, Daniel. BS, Davidson Coll., 1965; PhD in Organic Chemistry, U. Wis., 1969. Post-doctoral rsch. assoc. Yale U., New Haven, 1969-71, instr., 1971; asst. prof. Ohio State U., Columbus, 1971-72; asst. prof. chemistry U. Alaska, Fairbanks, 1972-75, assoc. prof. chemistry, 1975-81, prof. chemistry, 1981—, dean coll. natural scis., 1991-96, dean coll. sci., engring. & math., 1996-98, provost, 1998—. Head dept. chemistry U. Alaska, Fairbanks, 1978-82, 88-90, interim dean coll. natural scis., 1990-91, interim provost, 1993-94; interim dir. U. Alaska Mus., 1992-93; mem. Gov.'s Sci. & Engring. Adv. Com., 1986-90, Alaska 2000 Sci. Standards Com., 1992-93. Contbr. articles to profl. jours., chpts. to books and monographs. Named one of Outstanding Young Men of Am., Jaycees, 1980; recipient Inspirational Tchr. award U. Alaska at Fairbanks Alumni Assn., 1982. Mem. AAAS, Am. Chem. Soc., Phi Beta Kappa, Sigma Xi (pres. local chpt. 1994-95), Phi Kappa Phi. Presbyterian. Avocations: fishing, camping, hiking. Office: U Alaska Office Provost Signers Hall Fairbanks AK 99775-7580 E-mail: fnpbr@uaf.edu.

REICHART, STUART RICHARD, lawyer; b. N.Y.C., Nov. 18, 1924; s. Stanley and Rae (Wein) R.; m. Joan Feirtag, Mar. 28, 1981. LLB, Bklyn. Law Sch., 1948; LLM, NYU, 1951. Bar: N.Y. 1949, D.C. 1971, U.S. Supreme Ct. Adminstrv. judge Armed Services Bd. Contract Appeals, Washington, 1966-72; asst. gen. counsel for procurement USAF, 1972-75, dep. gen. counsel, 1975-78, gen. counsel, 1978-81; of counsel Fried, Frank, Harris, Shriver & Jacobson, 1982-90; ind. cons., 1991—. Instr. govt. procurement Ohio State U., U. Dayton, U. Md., 1960-70. Contbr. legal articles on govt. procurement to profl. jours. Served with AUS, 1942-45; served to col. USAF, 1951-71. Decorated Legion of Merit, D.F.C., Air medal with silver oak leaf cluster, Purple Heart; recipient Disting. Civilian Service medals Dept. Air Force, 1979, Dept. Def., 1982, Stuart R. Reichart award USAF, 1982. Mem. Masons. Avocations: bridge, tennis, golf. Home and Office: 16873 C Isle of Palms Dr Delray Beach FL 33484-7008

REICHBACH, GUSTIN LEWIS, state supreme court justice; b. Bklyn., Oct. 9, 1946; s. Herman and Lee (Klein) R.; m. Ellen Meyers, Oct. 24, 1984; 1 child, Hope Isadora. BA in Polit. Sci. with high honors, SUNY, Buffalo, 1967; JD, Columbia U., 1970. Bar: N.Y. 1972, U.S. Dist. Ct. (ea. and so. dists.) N.Y. 1972, Calif. 1975, U.S. Dist. Ct. (ea. and no. dists.) Calif. 1975, U.S. Supreme Ct. 1984. Pvt. practice, N.Y., 1972-90, Calif., 1975-90; judge Civil Ct. City of N.Y., Bklyn., 1991-98; justice Supreme Ct. N.Y., 1990—91. Counsel to commr. Calif. Agrl. Labor Rels. Bd., Sacramento, 1975-76. Co-author: The Bust Book, 1970, Litigating Electronic Surveillance Claims in Criminal Cases, 1977. Recipient David Michael award N.Y. State Bar Assn., 1992. Mem. Phi Beta Kappa. Office: Supreme Ct State NY 120 Schermerhorn St Brooklyn NY 11201-5108

REICHBLUM, AUDREY ROSENTHAL, public relations executive; b. Pitts., June 28, 1935; d. Emanuel Nathan and Willa (Handmacher) Rosenthal; m. M. Charles Reichblum, Jan. 25, 1956; children: Robert Nathan, William Mark. Student, Bennington Coll., 1952-53; BS, Carnegie Mellon U., 1956. Founder, creator, chmn. Pitts. Children's Mus., 1970-73; mag. writer Pitts. Mag., 1978; dir. pub. rels. Pitts. Pub. Theater, 1978-79; pres. arPR audrey reichblum PUB. RELS. inc., Pitts., 1980—, arpr, inc., 1996-99. Pub. rels. cons., bd. mem. Pitts. Planned Parenthood, 1980-84, United Jewish Fedn., Bus. and Profl. Women, Pitts., 1980-85, Pitts. City Theater, 1985-94, Pa. Coun. on Aging, 1996—; chmn. Villa de Marillac Nursing, 1999, Vincencian

Collaborative Svcs. Bd. Recipient Gold Cindy award Info. Film Producers Am., 1982, award of excellence Internat. Assn. Bus. Communicators, Pitts., 1986, Matrix award for Three Rivers Arts Festival, Lifetime Achievement award NAWBO-YWCA, Y-Tribute to Women in Comms. award, 1998. Mem. Pub. Rels. Soc. Am. (accredited; award of merit 1983, G. Victor Barkman award for excellence 1984, 1st place award Race For The Cure), Women in Comm. (Matrix-sales promotion award 1987), Nat. Assn. Women Bus. Owners (Life Time Achievement award 1995). Office: 1420 Centre Ave Ste 2216 Pittsburgh PA 15219-3536

REICHE, FRANK PERLEY, lawyer, former federal commissioner; b. Hartford, Conn., May 8, 1929; s. Karl Augustus and LaFetra (Perley) R.; m. Janet Taylor, Sept. 26, 1953; children: Cynthia Reiche Schumacker, Dean S. AB, Williams Coll., 1951; LLB, Columbia U., 1959; MA, George Washington U., 1959; LLM in Taxation, NYU, 1966. Bar: N.J. 1960, D.C. 1981. Assoc. Stryker, Tams & Dill, Newark, 1959-61, Smith, Stratton, Wise & Heher, Princeton, N.J., 1962-64, ptnr., 1964-79; commr. Fed. Election Commn., Washington, 1979-85, chmn., 1982; ptnr. Katzenbach, Gildea & Rudner, Lawrenceville, N.J., 1986-93; pvt. practice law Princeton, 1993-97; of counsel Schragger, Lavine & Nagy, West Trenton, 1997-2000, Archer & Greiner, Princeton, 2001—. Trustee Westminster Choir Coll., Princeton, 1974-86, Ctr. Theol. Inquiry, Princeton, 1991-97, Wells Coll., Aurora, N.Y., 1994—; mem. planned giving com. Williams Coll., Williamstown, Mass., 1973-87, nat. chmn. planned giving, 1983-87. Lt. USN, 1952-56. Mem. ABA, D.C. Bar Assn., N.J. Bar Assn., Am. Coll. Trust and Estate Counsel (N.J. state chair 1995-2000, bd. regents 2001—). Clubs: Washington Golf and Country, Capitol Hill. Republican. Presbyterian.

REICHEK, JESSE, artist; b. Bklyn., Aug. 16, 1916; s. Morris and Celia (Bernstein) R.; m. Laure Guyot, May 16, 1950; children— Jonathan, Joshua. Student, Inst. Design, Chgo., 1941-42; diploma, Academie Julian, Paris, 1951. Instr. dept. architecture U. Mich., Ann Arbor, 1946-47; prof. Inst. Design Ill. Inst. Tech., Chgo., 1951-53; prof. dept. architecture U. Calif., Berkeley, 1953-87, prof. emeritus, 1987—. Cons. Nat. Design Inst. Ford Found. project, Ahmedabad, India, 1963, San Francisco Redevel. Agy. Embarcadero Center, 1966—; lectr. Nat. Inst. Architects, Rome, 1960, U. Florence, 1960, U. Naples, 1960, Israel Inst. Tech., 1960, Greek Architects Soc., Athens, 1960, U. Belgrade, 1960, MIT, 1965, U. N.Mex., 1964, Am. Cultural Center, Paris, 1960, 64, Gujarat Inst. Engrs. and Architects, 1963, U. Colo., 1961, Harvard, 1962, U. Minn., 1962, U. Coll. London, 1967, Inst. Contemporary Arts, London, 1967, Ecole Nationale des Beaux-Ats, 1967; artist in residence Tamarind Lithography Workshop, 1966, Am. Acad. in Rome, 1971-72; research prof. Creative Arts Inst. U. Calif., 1966-67; artist in residence IBM Los Angeles Sci. Center, 1970-71 Exhibited one man shows at, Galerie Cahiers d'Art Paris, 1951, 59, 68, U. Calif. at Berkeley, 1954, Betty Parsons Gallery, N.Y.C., 1958, 59, 63, 65, 67, 69, 70, Molton Gallery, London, 1962, Am. Culture Center, Florence, Italy, 1962, Bennington Coll., 1963, U. N.Mex., 1966, U. So. Calif., 1967, Axiom Gallery, London, 1968, Yoseido Gallery, Tokyo, 1968, Los Angeles County Mus. Art, 1971; exhibited in group shows, Bklyn. Mus., 1959, Mus. Modern Art, N.Y.C., 1962, 65, 69, Knox-Albright Art Gallery, 1962, Art Inst. Chgo., 1963, Cin. Art Mus., 1966, Balt. Art Mus., 1966, Yale Art Gallery, 1967, Grand Palais, Paris, 1970, Nat. Mus. Art, Santiago, Chile, 1970, art and tech. exhibit, Los Angeles County Mus. Art, 1971, Maeght Found., St. Paul de Vence, France, 1971, Mus. Modern Art, Paris, 1971; represented in permanent collections, Mus. Modern Art, Art Inst. Chgo., Bibliotheque Nationale, Paris, Victoria & Albert Mus., London, Los Angeles County Art Mus., Grunwald Graphic Arts Found., U. Calif. at Los Angeles, San Diego Mus. Art, Amon Carter Mus., Fort Worth; Author: Jesse Reichek-Dessins, 1960, La Monte de la Nuit, 1961, Fontis, 1961, Etcetera, 1965, Le Bulletin Des Baux, 1972; e.g., 1976. Served to capt. C.E. AUS, 1942-46. Home: 5925 Red Hill Rd Petaluma CA 94952-9437

REICHEK, MORTON ARTHUR, retired magazine editor, writer; b. N.Y.C., Nov. 2, 1924; s. Meyer and Katherine (Rabinowitz) R.; m. Sybil Green, June 13, 1953; children: Amy, Marjorie (dec.), James. BS, NYU, 1948; postgrad., Am. U., 1948-50. Press officer, editor U.S. Fish & Wildlife Svc., Washington, 1948-49, U.S. Br. Labor Statistics, Washington, 1949-51, U.S. Nat. Prodn. Authority, Washington, 1951-52; Washington corr. McGraw-Hill Mags., 1952-63, Newhouse Newspapers, 1963-65; assoc. editor Forbes, N.Y.C., 1965-66, Bus. WeeK, N.Y.C., 1966-76, sr. editor, writer, 1978-88; dir. editorial svcs. Gulf & Western. Industries, Inc., 1976-78. U.S. rep. NATO journalist program U.S. Dept. State, France, 1957; adj. lectr. Columbia U. Graduate Sch. Journalism, N.Y.C., 1981. Contbr. articles to N.Y. Times Mag., New Republic, others. Staff sgt. U.S. Army, 1943-46, China-Burma-India. Journalist fellow Carnegie-Mellon U. Grad. Sch. Indsl. Adminstrn., 1979; grantee NEH, 1980. Avocations: tennis, computers, music. Home: 1 Worchester Dr Concordia Jamesburg NJ 08831-4723 also: The Cascades 6975 Lismore Ave Boynton Beach FL 33437-6441 E-mail: iankev@att.net.

REICHEL, AARON ISRAEL, lawyer, rabbi, editor; b. N.Y.C., Jan. 30, 1950; s. Oscar Asher and Josephine Hannah (Goldstein) R. BA, Yeshiva U., 1971, MA, 1974; JD, Fordham U., 1976. Bar: N.J. 1977, N.Y. 1978; ordained rabbi, 1975. Atty. editor Securities Regulation Prentice-Hall, Englewood Cliffs, N.J., 1977-78, editor, founder govt. disclosure service Paramus, 1978-82, atty. editor fed. taxation, 1982-89; tech. editor Warren, Gorham & Lamont, Practical Acct., N.Y.C., 1989-90; assoc. Firm A. Edward Major, 1990-91, Firm Allen L. Rothenberg, N.Y.C., 1991-93; pvt. practice, 1993—. Author: The Maverick Rabbi, 1984, 2d edit. 1986, Back to the Past for Inspiration for the Future—West Side Institutional Synagogue Jubilee 1937-87, 1987; co-author (manual) Style and Usage, 1984; contbr. The 1986 Jewish Directory and Almanac, 1986, The 1987-88 Jewish Almanac, 1988; contbg. editor Complete Guide to the Tax Reform Act of 1986, Prentice-Hall's Explanation of the Tax Reform Act of 1986, 1986, Prentice Hall's Complete Guide to the Tax Law of 1987, 1988, Prentice Hall's Explanation of the Technical & Miscellaneous Revenue Act of 1988, 1988, Guide to Equal Employment Practices, 1997; contbr. articles to profl. jours. Bd. dirs. Union Orthodox Jewish Congregations Am., N.Y.C., 1973-74, Harry and Jane Fischel Found., N.Y.C., 1977—, West Side Instl. Synagogue, 1987-98, Amalgamated Dwellings, Inc., 1992-96; nat. pres. YAVNEH, N.Y.C., 1973-74; mem. youth commn. Am. Jewish Congress, N.Y.C., 1973-76. Mem. ABA, N.Y. State Bar Assn. (various coms.), N.Y. County Lawyers Assn. (various coms.), Am. Soc. Access Profls. (founder, 1st chmn. N.Y. chpt.), Nat. Jewish Commn. on Law and Pub. Affairs (family law com.), Yeshiva U. Alumni Assn. (exec. com. 1971-87, editor-in-chief Bull. 1974-78). Avocations: writing, baseball, tennis, compiling proverbs. Home: 83-28 Abingdon Rd Kew Gardens NY 11415-1714

REICHEL, WALTER EMIL, advertising executive; b. Irvington, N.J., Dec. 12, 1935; s. Walter Edwin and Flora Maria (Pfister) R.; m. Priscilla Tedesco, Feb. 1, 1969; 1 son, Bradley Joseph. BA, Columbia U., 1959; MA., NYU, 1971, M Philosophy, 1989, postgrad., 1989—. With Benton & Bowles, N.Y.C., 1959-67, v.p., 1965-67, assoc. media dir., 1965-67; with Ted Bates & Co., Inc. N.Y.C., 1967-87; sr. v.p. Ted Bates & Co., Inc., 1973-82, exec. dir. media and programs, 1974-82, exec. v.p., 1982-87, dir.; cons., 1987-91; mng. ptnr. A.S. Link Inc., N.Y.C., 1991-2000; sr. v.p., dir. client svcs. KSL Media, 2000—01. Mem. Advt. Rsch. Found. Home and Office: 449 1/2 Henry St Brooklyn NY 11231-3011 E-mail: aslreichel@aol.com.

REICHENBACH, DENNIS DALE, physician, pathology educator; b. Billings, Mont., Sept. 14, 1933; s. Ernest A. and Lilli (Stockland) R.; m. Jean Karen Hickey, Feb. 27, 1960; children: Stephen, Laura. BS in Basic Med. Sci., U. Wash., 1955, MD, 1958. Intern King County (Wash.) Hosp., Seattle, 1958-59; resident in pathology U. Wash., 1959-63, asst. prof. pathology, 1966-70, assoc. prof., 1970-75, prof., 1975—. Dir. pathology residency program, U. Wash., 1981-88; pathologist in chief Harvorview Med. Ctr., Seattle, 1982—. Contbr. articles to profl. jours. Served with USPHS, 1963-65. Mem. Am. Assn. Pathologists (cert.), Soc. Cardiovascular Pathologists, King County Med. Assn. Home: 6548 49th Ave NE Seattle WA 98115-7733 Office: Harborview Med Ctr 325 9th Ave Seattle WA 98104-2420

REICHENBACH, ROY EARL, engineering executive; b. Columbus Grove, Ohio, July 29, 1932; s. William Walter and Sibyl Louella (Cooley) R.; m. Iwona Jolanta Madrowska, Aug. 24, 1985; children: Paulina Maria, Ilona Claudia, Anthony William. BME summa cum laude, MS, Ohio State U., 1956; PhD, Calif. Inst. Tech., 1960. Assoc. prof. aeronautics Naval Postgrad. Sch., 1962-68; ballistic missile propulsion mgr. TRW, Inc., L.A., 1968-69; sr. rsch. staff Inst. for Def. Analysis, Arlington, Va., 1969-75; asst. for engrng. tech. Office Sec. of Navy, Washington, 1979-80; mgr. aircraft safety divsn. FAA, Atlantic City, 1980-82, mgr. aircraft safety, security and airport R&D divsn. Washington, 1982-86, mgr. sci. and tech. divsn., 1986-88; head aero. and engrng. sci. European Rsch. Office, London, 1975-79, 88-98; sr. rsch. scientist dept. aerospace engrng. U. Md., College Park, 1998—2001; with Rand Cons., 2001—. Cons. Aerospace Corp., L.A., 1965-68, pvt. cons., 2001—. Contbr. articles to profl. jours. 1st lt. USAF, 1960-62. Recipient Disting. Alumnus award Ohio State U., 1980. Fellow AIAA (assoc. editor 1975-80, pub. com. 1980-88, Svc. Citation 1978); mem. Internat. Combustion Inst., Aircraft Owners and Pilots Assn. Avocations: flight instructing, skiing, walking, sports cars. Home: 1405 Colleen Ln Mc Lean VA 22101-3105 E-mail: rernasa@aol.com.

REICHER, ROBERT NATHAN, consulting firm executive; b. N.Y.C., June 9, 1944; s. Arthur M. and Eleanor G. R.; m. Suzanne P. Carter, Sept. 7, 1969; children— R. Michael, S. Christina. B.S., UCLA, 1966; M.B.A., U. So. Calif., 1967. Account exec. Foote, Cone & Belding, Newport Beach, Calif., 1967-69; mktg. dir. Litton Industries, Newport Beach, 1969-70; mktg. research dir. Leadership Homes, Newport Beach, 1970-73; pres. Reicher Corp., Newport Beach, 1973-83; dir. Orange County ops. The Goodkin Group, Newport Beach, 1983-85; mgr. Deloitte, Haskins & Sells, Costa Mesa, Calif., 1985—. Mem. Hoag Meml. Hosp. 552 Club, Urban Land Inst.; v.p. Newport Beach Improvement Assn., 1980; bd. dirs. Newport Mesa Schs. Found. Mem. Nat. Assn. Realtors, Urban Land Inst., Bldg. Industry Assn., Calif. Assn. Realtors. Club: Balboa Bay (Newport Beach).

REICHERT, DAVID, lawyer; b. Cin., Nov. 23, 1929; s. Victor E. and Louise F. Reichert; m. Marilyn Frankel, May 31, 1959; children— James G., Steven F., William M. BA, Bowling Green State U., 1951; JD, U. Cin., 1954. Bar: Ohio 1954, U.S. Supreme Ct. 1963. Ptnr. firm Porter, Wright, Morris & Arthur, formerly sr. ptnr. Reichert, Strauss & Reed and predecessors, Cin. Dir. numerous corps. Monthly columnist: Scrap Age mag, 1966-74; bd. editors: U. Cin. Law Rev, 1953-54. Pres. brotherhood Rockdale Temple, Cin., 1960-61, temple treas., 1973-75, v.p., 1975-79, pres., 1979-81; mem. Amberley Village Planning Commn. & Zoning Bd. Appeals, 1972-79, Ohio Solid Waste Adv. Group, 1974; treas. Contemporary Arts Ctr., Cin., 1973-75, pres., 1976-77, trustee, 1982-88; trustee Cin. Art Mus., 1978-93, v.p., 1992-93, chmn. vis. com. for contemporary art, 1990-92; trustee Jewish Publ. Soc., 1980-86, Cin. Sculpture Coun., 1984-87; mem. acquisitions com. Miami U. Art Mus., 1982-85. Mem. Cin. Print and Drawing Cir. (pres. 1974-76), The Literary Club (sec. 1988-91, v.p. 1991-92, pres. 1992-93), Losantiville Country Club (bd. govs. 1985-92, sec. 1986-90, pres. 1990-92), ISRI 20th Century Club (hon. 1998), Omicron Delta Kappa, Sigma Tau Delta, Phi Delta Phi, Zeta Beta Tau. Office: Porter Wright Morris & Arthur 250 E 5th St Ste 2200 Cincinnati OH 45202-5177

REICHERT, LEO EDMUND, JR. biochemist, endocrinologist; b. N.Y.C., Jan. 9, 1932; s. Leo and Anne (Holsten) R.; m. Gerda Sihler, July 20, 1957; children: Leo, Christine, Linda, Andrew. BS, Manhattan Coll., N.Y.C., 1955; PhD, Loyola U., Chgo., 1960. Asst. prof. biochemistry Emory U. Med. Sch., Atlanta, 1960-66, assoc. prof., 1966-72, prof., 1972-79; prof., chmn. dept. biochemistry Albany (N.Y.) Med. Coll., 1979-88, prof. biochemistry and molecular biology, 1988-99; dir. Tucker Endocrine Rsch. Inst., Atlanta, 2000—. Dir. human and animal hormone isolation and distbn. program (NIH), Emory U. Med. Sch., 1960-75; mem. med. adv. bd. Nat. Pituitary Agy., 1971-74; com. on glycoprotein hormones Nat. Hormone and Pituitary Program, 1968-86; mem. reproductive biology study sect. NIH, 1971-75; mem. adv. panel on cellular physiology NSF, 1983-86, divsn. of integrative and neuro biology, 1992; mem. WHO Expert Adv. Panel on Biol. Standardization, 1984—, Nat. Bd. Med. Examiners, Part I, 1989-91. Mem. editl. bd. Endocrinology, 1967-75, Molecular and Cellular Endocrinology, 1977-83, 90-94, Biology of Reproduction, 1968-70, 86-90, Andrology, 1983-86, Molecular Andrology, 1989-99; contbr. more than 275 articles to profl. jours.; patentee in field. Served with USMC, 1950-53. List among 75 endocrinologists, 1000 scientists most cited, 1965-78. Mem.: AAAS, Soc. for Study of Reprodn., Andrology Soc. (coun. 1983—87), Endocrine Soc. (ethics adv. com. 2000—01, Ayerst award 1970), Am. Soc. Biol. Chemists. Home: 1974 Mountain Creek Dr Stone Mountain GA 30087-1018 E-mail: lerjr@aol.com.

REICHERT, MARLENE JOY, secondary school educator, writer; b. Davao City, Philippines, Nov. 29, 1957; d. Jacob and Lois Marie Bouw; m. David Julius Reichert, June 13, 1981 (June 23, 1991). BA in English, Nyack Coll., 1980; postgrad., St. Thomas Aquinas, 1988; MA in Writing, Manhattanville Coll., 1997. Cert. tchr., N.Y., N.J. Tchr. St. Anne's Sch., Yonkers, N.Y., 1988-89; substitute tchr. Rockland County Pub. Schs., 1989-91; tchr. BOCES Night High Schs., West Nyack, NY, 1989-92, John Peter Tetard Middle Sch. 143, Bronx, 1991—2000, literacy staff developer, 2000—. Tchr. Achieving Success, 1992—94, Project Success, 1997—99. Contbr. short stories to lit. mags. Democrat. Episcopalian. Avocation: gardening. Home: 114 Depot Pl Nyack NY 10960-4426 Office: John Peter Tetard Mid Sch 120 W 231st St Bronx NY 10463-5905

REICHGOTT JUNGE, EMBER D. former state senator, lawyer, writer, broadcast analyst , small business owner; b. Detroit, Aug. 22, 1953; d. Norbert Arnold and Diane (Pincich) Reichgott; m. Michael Junge. BA summa cum laude, St. Olaf Coll., Minn., 1974; JD, Duke U., 1977; MBA, U. St. Thomas, 1991. Bar: Minn. 1977, D.C. 1978. Assoc. Larkin, Hoffman, Daly & Lindgren, Bloomington, Minn., 1977-84; counsel Control Data Corp., 1984-86; ptnr. The Gen. Counsel, Ltd., 1987—; mem. Minn. State Senate, 1983-2000, chmn. legis. com. on econ. status of women, 1984-86, vice chmn. senate edn. com., 1987-88, senate majority whip, 1990-94, chmn. property tax divsn. senate tax com., 1991-92, chmn. senate judiciary com., 1993-94, senate asst. majority leader, 1995-2000, chmn. spl. subcom. on ethical conduct; pres. Video on Wings, video to web co., Mpls., 2000—. Dem. endorsed candidate Minn. Atty. Gen., 1998; instr. polit. sci. St. Olaf Coll., Northfield, Minn., 1993; bd. dirs. Citizens Ind. Bank, St. Louis Park, Minn. Host cable TV monthly series Legis. Report, 1985-92. State co-chair Clinton/Gore Presdl. Campaign, Minn. Dem. Farmer-Labor Party, 1992, 1996; del. Nat. Dem. Conv., 1984, 1992, 1996; trustee, bd. dirs. N.W. YMCA, New Hope, Minn., 1983—88, Unaited Way Mpls., 1989—, Greater Mpls. ARC, 1988, chair, 2001—02. Recipient Woman of Yr. award North Hennepin Bus. and Profl. Women, 1983, award for contbn. to human svcs. Minn. Social Svcs. Assn., 1983, Clean Air award Minn. Lung Assn., 1988, Disting. Svc. award Mpls. Jaycees, 1984, Minn. Dept. Human Rights award, 1989, Myra Bradwell award Minn. Women Lawyers, 1993, Disting. Alumnae award Lake Conf. Schs., 1993, Disting. Alumnae award St. Olaf Coll., 1998, awards for leadership Am. Lung Assn, 1999, Am. Heart Assn., 1997, Everyday Hero award Up with People, 1995, Unsung Hero award United Way of Mpls., 1999, 1st recipient of award named in her honor for prevention of sexual assault, 2000; charter inductee Robbinsdale H.S. Hall of Fame, 2000; author of Minn. charter sch. law, winner of "2000 Innovations in Am. Govt. award. given by Harvard U. and Ford Found., others; named one of ten Outstanding Young Minnesotans, Minn. Jaycees, 1984, Policy Advocate of Yr., NAWBO, 1988, Woman of Achievement, Twin West C. of C., 1989, Marvelous Minn. Woman, 1993; youngest woman ever elected to Minn. Senate, 1983. Mem. Minn. Bar Assn. (bd. govs. 1992-96, Pro Bono Publico Atty. award 1990), Hennepin County Bar Assn., Corp. Counsel Assn. (v.p. 1989-96). Home: 7701 48th Ave N Minneapolis MN 55428-4515 Fax: 763-536-1447. E-mail: emberrj@msn.com.

REICHL, RUTH MOLLY, editor; b. N.Y.C., Jan. 16, 1948; d. Ernst and Miriam and (Brudno) R.; m. Douglas Wilder Hollis, Sept. 5, 1970 (div. 1985); m. Michael Singer, 1985; 1 child, Nicholas Singer. BA, U. Mich., 1968, MA in History of Art, 1970. Chef, owner The Swallow Restaurant, Berkeley, Calif., 1973-77; food writer, editor New West mag., San Francisco, 1978-84; editor restaurant column L.A. Times, 1984-93, food editor, 1990-93; restaurant critic N.Y. Times, 1993-99; editor-in-chief Gourmet Mag., 1999—. Author: Mmmm: A Feastiary, 1972, The Contest Book, 1977, Tender at the Bone: Growing Up at the Table, 1998, Comfort Me with Apples: More Adventures at the Table, 2001; editor: Endless Feasts: Sixty Years of Writing from Gourmet, 2002, Modern Library Food Series, 2000—. Office: 4 Times Sq New York NY 10036-6518 E-mail: ruth.reichl@gourmet.com.

REICHLEY, A. JAMES, political scientist; b. St. Clair, Pa., Mar. 3, 1929; s. Grant G. and Mary (Thompson) R.; m. Mary Donohue, Apr. 15, 1961; children: Douglas G., Richard J., Susan M. BA, U. Pa., 1950; MA, Harvard U., 1956. Reporter Pottsville (Pa.) Republican, 1957-61; legis. asst. Senator Kenneth Keating, Washington, 1961-62; legis. sec. Gov. William Scranton, Harrisburg, Pa., 1962-67; polit. editor Fortune, N.Y.C., 1967-76; spl. asst. Pres. Gerald Ford, Washington, 1976; sr. fellow Brookings Instn., 1977-91, Georgetown U., Washington, 1992—. Author: Conservatives in an Age of Change, 1981, Religion in American Public Life, 1985 (Benchmark award 1986), rev. edit., 2002, The Life of the Parties, 1992, rev. edit., 2000, The Values Connection, 2001, Faith in Politics, 2002; also others; editor: Elections American Style, 1987; author articles. Served with U.S. Army, 1951-53. Congl. fellow, 1959. Mem. Am. Polit. Sci. Assn., Cosmos Club. Republican. Presbyterian. Home: 11912 Gregerscroft Rd Potomac MD 20854-2145 Office: Georgetown U 3600 N St NW Washington DC 20007-2670 E-mail: j.reichley@worldnet.att.net.

REICHLIN, SEYMOUR, physician, educator; b. N.Y.C., May 31, 1924; s. Henry and Celia (Rosen) R.; m. Elinor Thurman Dameshek, June 24, 1951; children: Seth David, Douglas James, Ann Elise. Student, CCNY, 1940-41; AB, Antioch Coll., 1945; MD, Washington U., St. Louis, 1948; PhD, U. London, 1954. Intern N.Y. Hosp., 1948-49; asst. resident Barnes Hosp., St. Louis, 1949-50, N.Y. Hosp., 1950-51; chief resident Barnes Hosp., 1951-52; research fellow physiology dept. Maudsley Hosp., London, Eng., 1952-54; instr. psychiatry Washington U., 1954-55, asst. prof. psychiatry and medicine, 1955-60; asso. prof. medicine U. Rochester, 1960-66, prof., 1966-69; prof., head dept. med. and pediatric spltys. Sch. Medicine U. Conn., 1969-71, prof., head dept. physiology, 1971-72; prof. medicine Tufts U., 1972-97, prof. emeritus, 1997—; rsch. prof. U. Ariz., 1994-2000. Sr. physician New Eng. Med. Ctr., 1972-93, sr. endocrinologist, 1993-96; mem. endocrinology study sect. NIH, 1966-70; mem. adv. panel FDA, 1977-79; mem. coun. Nat. Inst. Kidney, Diabetes, Digestive Diseases, 1987-90. Mem. editl. bd. Endocrinology, 1969-74, New Eng. Jour. Medicine, 1976-79, Jour. Psychoneuroendocrinology, 1979-83, Brain, Behavior and Immunity, 1990—; contbr. articles to profl. jours., also monographs. Bd. dirs. Founds. Fund, New Haven, 1968-70; med. adv. bd. Med. Found., Boston, adv. bd. MacArthur Found., 1988. Served with AUS, 1943-44. Commonwealth Fund fellow, 1952-54, Lowell M. Palmer fellow, 1954-56. Master ACP; fellow AAAS, Am. Acad. Arts and Scis.; mem. Ctrl. Soc. Clin. Rsch., Am. Soc. Clin. Investigation, Assn. Am. Physicians, Am. Physiol. Soc., Endocrine Soc. (Eli Lilly award 1972, pres. 1975-76), Brit. Soc. Endocrinology, Am. Psychosomatic Soc., Am. Thyroid Assn., Internat. Brain Orgn., Assn. for Rsch. in Nervous and Mental Disease (pres. 1976), Pituitary Soc. (pres. 1994-95), Alpha Omega Alpha. Home: X-9 Ranch 6480 South Upper Valley Rd Vail AZ 85641 E-mail: reichlin@dakotacom.net.

REICHMAN, JOSEPH HARRY, plastic surgeon; b. Phila., May 8, 1947; s. Leonard and Adelaide (Feinstein) R.; children: Andrew, Jeffrey. BA, LaSalle Coll., 1969; MD, Hahnemann Med. Coll., 1973. Diplomate Am. Bd. Surgery, Am. Bd. Plastic Surgery, Am. Bd. Quality Assurance and Utilization Rev. Physicians. Intern Hosp. Univ. Pa., 1973-74, resident in surgery, 1974-79, resident in plastic surgery, 1979-81; v.p. med. affairs Virtua-West Jersey Health Sys., Marlton, NJ. Mem. AMA (alt. del. 1996—), Camden County Med. Soc. (pres. 1996), Med. Soc. N.J. (vice-spkr. ho. of dels. 2001—). Office: One Carnie Blvd Kirkwood Voorhees NJ 08043

REICHMAN, LEE BRODERSOHN, physician; b. N.Y.C., June 25, 1938; s. Theodore and Elinore (Brodersohn) R.; m. Rose Ehrinpreis, Oct. 9, 1965; children: Daniel Mark, Deborah Gar. AB, Oberlin Coll., 1960; MD, NYU, 1964; MPH, Johns Hopkins U., 1971. Intern Bellevue Hosp., I Med. Divsn., N.Y.C., 1964-65, resident, 1967-68, Harlem Hosp. Ctr., N.Y.C., 1968-69, fellow in pulmonary medicine, 1969-70; dir. Bur. Tb, Bur. Chronic Disease, N.Y.C. Health Dept., 1971-73, asst. commr. health, 1973-74; assoc. prof. medicine U. Medicine and Dentistry N.J. Med. Sch., Newark, 1974-78; prof. medicine N.J. Med. Sch., 1978—, prof. preventive medicine, cmty. health, 1993—; dir. pulmonary div. U. Medicine and Dentistry N.J.-N.J. Med. Sch. Univ. Hosp., 1974-92; founding exec. dir. N.J. Med. Sch. Nat. Tuberculosis Ctr., 1993—. Cons. CDC, Atlanta, 1970—; prin. investigator pulmonary complications of HIV infection NHLBI, 1987—95; prin. investigator Motel Tb CDC, 1993—, prin. investigator Nat. Tb Trials Consortium, 1994—99, mem. adv. coun. for eleimination of Tb, 2002—. Editor: Tuberculosis--A Comprehensive International Approach, 2d edit., 2000; author: Time Bomb--The Global Epidemic of Multi-Drug Resistant Tuberculosis, 2002; contbr. articles to profl. jours. Bd. dirs. Art Ctr. No. N.J., 1979-86; chmn. N.J. Commn. on Smoking of Health, 1986-87; mem. N.J. TB Adv. Coun., 1976—, chmn. 1991—; chair Nat. Coalition for Elemination of Tuberculosis, 1992—; mem. N.J. Clean Air Coun., 1987. With USPHS, 1965-67. Recipient Nat. Heart Lung and Blood Inst., Pulmonary Acad. career award, 1975-80, Preventive Pulmonary Acad. career award, 1987-92, Tb Acad. career award, 1993—, 1st prize trade categories Am. Med. Writers Assn., 2002. Fellow ACP, Am. Coll. Chest Physicians (gov. 1984-90, pres. N.J. chpt. 1982-84, Simon Rodbard Meml. lectr. 2000), Acad. Medicine of N.J.; mem. Am. Thoracic Soc. (hon. life), Internat. Union Against Tb and Lung Disease (exec. com. 1982-92, vice chair exec. com. 1989-91, N.Am. Region Disting. Svc. award 2001), Am. Lung Assn. (hon. life, nat. bd. dirs. 1980-94, pres. elect 1991-92, pres. 1992-93, past pres. 1993-94, Will Ross medalist 1999), N.J. Thoracic Soc. (pres. 1982-84), Am. Lung Assn. N.J. (hon. life, bd. dirs. 1976—, pres. 1984-86). Office: PO Box 1709 225 Warren St Newark NJ 07103-1709

REICHMAN, NANCI SATIN, oil company owner; b. Tulsa, July 7, 1939; d. Jack Harold and Tybie Mary (Davis) Satin; m. Louis Reichman, Dec. 25, 1960 (dec. Feb. 1972); children: David Michael, Jill Satin; life ptnr. Phillip M. Citrin. Student, Sarah Lawrence Coll., Bronxville, N.Y., 1957-59; cert. Jungian psychology, C.G. Jung Inst., Evanston, Ill., 1988. Fashion model Miss Jackson's, Tulsa, 1969-70; pres. LIR Investments, 1972-78; pres., dir. devel. Tymar Oil Co., Tulsa and Santa Fe, N.Mex., 1990—; owner ind. oil prodn. Chgo., 1972—. Audio tape lectr for various workshops. Pres. C.G. Jung Inst., Evanston, Ill., 1980-81, 81-82, 84-85, also mem. adv. bd.; v.p. Tulsa Jr. Philharm., 1968; sec. Tulsa Ballet, 1968; mem. Women's Forum N.Mex., 1996—; bd. dirs. Found. Santa Fe Cmty. Coll., 1995—. Avocations: poetry writing, travel, reading, philanthropy. Home: 1104 Piedra Rondo Santa Fe NM 87501-8856

REICHMANIS, ELSA, chemist; b. Melbourne, Victoria, Australia, Dec. 9, 1953; came to U.S., 1962; d. Peteris and Nina (Meiers) R.; m. Francis Joseph Purcell, June 2, 1979; children: Patrick William, Elizabeth Anne, Edward Andrew, Thomas Alexander. BS in Chemistry, Syracuse U., 1972, PhD in Chemistry, 1975. Postdoctoral intern Syracuse (N.Y.) U., 1975-76, Chaim Weizmann rsch. fellow, 1976-78; mem. tech. staff AT&T Bell Labs., Murray Hill, N.J., 1978-84, supr. radiation sensitive materials and applications, 1984-94, head organic and polymer materials, 1994-95; head polymer and organic materials Lucent Techs., Bell Labs., New Providence, NJ, 1996—2000, dir. materials rsch., 2001—. Mem. panel on advanced materials. Japanese Tech. Evaluation Prog., NSF, Washington, 1986, mem. com. to survey materials. rsch. opportunities and needs for electronic industry, Nat. Rsch. Coun., 1986, Nat. Materials Adv. Bd., 1993-98, U.S. Nat. Com. for Internat. Union for Pure and Applied Chemistry, 1996—. Editor: The Effects of Radiation on High Tech Polymers, 1989, Polymers in Microlithography, 1989, Irradiation of Polymer Materials, 1993, Microelectronics Technology: Polymers for Advanced Imaging and Packaging, 1995, Micro and Nano Patterning Polymers, 1998; patentee in field; assoc. editor Chemistry of Materials, 1996—; contbr. numerous articles to profl. jours. Recipient Soc. of Women Engrs. Achievement award, 1993, Engrng. Materials award ASM, 1996, Arents Pioneer medal Syracuse U., 2001. Fellow: AAAS; mem.: IEEE, Soc. Women Engrs., Am. Phys. Soc., Soc. for Photo-optical Engrs., Soc. Chem. Industry (Perkin medal 2001), Am. Chem. Soc. (mem.-at-large 1986—90, sec. 1991—92, polymer materials sci. and engrng. divsn. 1991—, vice chair 1993, chair-elect 1994, chair 1995, pres.-elect 2002, award in applied polymer sci. 1999), Nat. Acad. Engrng. (elected mem.). Avocations: music, reading, needlepoint.

REICHMANN, PÉTER IVÁN, mathematician; b. Budapest, Hungary, Feb. 10, 1942; came to U.S., 1959; s. Rezsö Rudolf and Margit (Grünberger) R. BSEE, Ill. Inst. Tech., 1967, MS in Math., 1973, PhD in Math., 1986. Elec. engr. Zenith Military and Motorola Comm. and Govt. divsns., various cities,

1967—69; instr. math. and elec. engring. depts. Chgo. Tech. Coll., 1973—74; asst. prof. of math. Cath. U. Am., Washington, 1987—89; ind. distbr. Brain Garden Co., American Fork, Utah, 2001—. Grantee NASA, 1982. Achievements include research on the introduction of a novel geometry for individual cell for negative Poisson's ratio foam and computing its volume. Home and Office: 1305 Coloma Way Roseville CA 95661-4604 Fax: 916-773-2318. E-mail: pireichmann@hotmail.com., pireichmann@msn.com.

REICHMANN, SUSAN HELENE, psychotherapist; b. L.A., May 30, 1959; d. Joseph Reichmann and Beatrice Breslaw; m. Michael Dennis Lee, Jan. 1, 1999; children: Mason Nathaniel Reichmann Lee, Gregory Dennis Reichmann Lee. BA in Psychology, BA in French Lit., U. Calif., Berkeley, 1984; MA in Marital and Family Therapy, Loyola Marymount U., 1992; student, Calif. Inst. Arts, 1983-84, Mus. Fine Arts, Boston, 1983-84. Lic. marriage and family therapist, Calif.; registered art therapist, Am. Art Therapy Assn. Art therapist Haven House Shelter, Pasadena, Calif., 1997-98; art therapy cons. Helping Our Mobile Elderly, Venice, 1997-98, Children's Hosp. of L.A., Hollywood, 1999; dir. HIV-AIDS project Open Paths Counseling Ctr., L.A., 1995—98; clinical supr., project coord. youth and family violence project Campion Counseling Ctr., Ocean Park Cmty. Ctr., Santa Monica, Calif., 1998—. Media spokesperson for Here2listen.com., San Mateo, 1999—. Assoc. producer (film) The Golem, 1994; sponsored artist "A Cmty. of Angels, LA, 2001; freelance writer, poet. Vol. Napa State Hosp., St. Anne Hosp., Paris, UCLA Hosp., Free Arts Clnic, Amigos de las Ams.; leader children's workshop Windows Between Worlds, Venice, Calif., 1998-2001; provider Mental Health Network, 2001-. Scholar Squaw Valley (Calif.) Cmty. of Writers, 1998. Mem. Am. Art Therapy Assn. (clin.), Calif. Assn. Marriage and Family Therapists, So. Calif. Art Therapy Assn., Loyola Marymount Grad. Art Therapy Assn., Psi Chi. Democrat. Avocations: painting, writing, travel. Office: 3331 Ocean Park Blvd #103 Santa Monica CA 90405 E-mail: artpsych@aol.com.

REICHOW, CRAIG ALLEN, national security policy analyst; b. Toledo, July 19, 1950; s. Gordon Walter and Elinor Velma (Button) Reichow; m. Jill Michelle Collins, Apr. 28, 1973; children: Collin, Greer. Bachelors degree, U. Minn., 1973; Masters degree, Webster U., St Louis, Mo., 1981. Sr. emergency analyst Argonne Nat. Lab., Washington, 1994—98; sr. nat. security policy analyst ANSER, Inc., Arlington, Va., 1998. Asst. coun. commr., leader Nat. Capital Area coun. Boy Scouts Am., 2002. Maj. USAF, 1973—93. Mem.: Alpha Phi Omega (life; chpt. pres. U. Minn. 1969—70, Disting. Svc. award 1973), Sommers Alumni Assn. (life; sr. wilderness guide 1967—72). Office: ANSER 2900 S Quincy Arlington VA 22206 Office Fax: 703-416-3329. Business E-Mail: craig.reichow@anser.org.

REICHTER, BARBARA F(AST), interior designing company executive; b. Haviland, Ohio, July 23, 1935; d. William Clayton and Marie (Stiebeling) Fast; m. Richard A. Reichter, Feb. 16, 1957; children: Bradley A., Lizabeth R. BS in Edn., Otterbein Coll., 1957; cert., N.Y. Sch. Interior Design, 1977. Tchr., Edwards AFB, Calif., 1957-59, Dayton, Ohio, 1959-60; founder Barbara Reichter Interiors, N. Andover, Mass., 1977-78; pres., chmn., founder Andover Interior Designs, 1978—. Participant Lawrence Gen. Hosp. Showhouse, 1982, Ladies of Merrimack Tour of Homes, 1983-87, 88—, Boston Jr. League Showhouse, 1986, N. Shore Jewish Community Ctr. Showhouse, 1988, 90. Contbr. articles to profl. jours. Mem. The Hay Scales Exch., Inc., N. Andover, 1970—; mem. adv. bd. N. Andover Community Ctr., 1970-77. Mem. ASID, Greater Lawrence C. of C., YWCA Women's Network Assn., N. Andover Country Club (golf com. 1978-82). Republican. Avocations: golfing, traveling, gardening. Home: 1 Coolidge Rd Andover MA 01810-1706 Office: Andover Interior Designs 63 Park St Andover MA 01810-3662

REICHWEIN, JEFFREY CHARLES, archaeologist; b. Cleve., June 10, 1950; s. Gordon Charlton and Grace Leonarda (Tesmer) R.; m. Jean Mabel Brainard, Sept. 16, 1985; 1 child, Juliet Jean Brainard-Reichwein; 1 child from previous marriage, Alyssa L. BA, Ohio U., 1972; MA in Anthropology, Miami U., Oxford, Ohio, 1975; PhD in Anthropology, Ohio State U., 1988. Lectr. Cuyahoga C.C., Parma, Ohio, 1975-83, archaeology field/sch. dir., 1976; grad. tchg. assoc. Ohio State U., Columbus, 1981-86; archaeologist State of Ohio, Dept. Natural Resources, 1986—. Adminstrv. asst. ACLU, Cleve., 1978-79; tribal archaeologist Colville Confederated Tribes, Nespelem, Wash., 1979-81, consulting archaeologist, 1982—; vis. instr. Kenyon Coll., Gambier, Ohio, 1986. Author: Emergence of Native American Nationalism in the Columbia Plateau, 1990. Mem. coll. scholarship com. Am. Fedn. State, County and Mcpl. Employees, Columbus, 1995—. Instrnl. Improvement grantee Cuyahoga C.C., Cleve., 1976, Phillips Fund grantee Am. Philos. Soc., Phila., 1984. Mem. ACLU, Ohio Archaeol. Coun. (trustee 1997—), Phi Kappa Phi. Avocations: hiking, canoeing, movies, golf. Office: Divsn Mineral Resources Mgmt Ohio Dept Natural Resources Bldg H-3 Fountain Sq Columbus OH 43224

REICIN, RONALD IAN, lawyer; b. Chgo., Dec. 11, 1942; s. Frank Edward and Abranita (Rome) R.; m. Alyta Friedland, May 23, 1965; children: Eric, Kael. BBA, U. Mich., 1964, MBA, JD cum laude, U. Mich., 1967. Bar: Ill. 1967, U.S. Tax Ct. 1967; CPA, Ill. Mem. staff Price Waterhouse & Co., Chgo., 1966; ptnr. Jenner & Block, 1967—. Bd. dirs. Nat. Kidney Found., Ill., 1978—, v.p., 1992-95, pres., 1995-98; bd. dirs. Ruth Page Found., 1985—, 1990—; bd. dirs. Scoliosis Assn. Chgo., 1981-90, Kohl Children's Mus., 1991-95, River North Chgo. Dance Co., 1999—. Mem.: Chgo. Mortgage Attys. Assn., Chgo. Bar Assn., ABA, Lawyers (Chgo.), Exec., Beta Alpha Psi, Beta Gamma Sigma, Phi Kappa Phi. Office: Jenner & Block LLC 1 E Ibm Plz Fl 38 Chicago IL 60611-3586 E-mail: rreicin@jenner.com.

REID, ALLISTON KING, psychology educator, researcher; m. Leonor G. Reid; children: Rebecca, Caroline. BS, Wofford Coll., 1975; PhD, Duke U., 1981. Assoc. prof. psychology Nat. Autonomous U. of Mex., Mexico City, 1981-84; prof. computer sci. Ea. Oreg. U., La Grande, 1985-91, prof. psychology, 1991-96; prof., chmn. dept. psychology Wofford Coll., Spartanburg, S.C., 1996—. Editl. bd. Jour. of the Exptl. Analysis of Behavior, 1995-97; contbr. articles to profl. jours. Mem. Am. Psychol. Assn., Am. Psychol. Soc., Assn. for Behavior Analysis, Soc. for the Quantitative Analysis of Behavior, Sigm Xi. Office: Wofford Coll Dept Psychology 429 N Church St Spartanburg SC 29303-3612 E-mail: Reidak@wofford.edu.

REID, ANDY, professional football coach; b. Los Angeles, Mar. 19, 1958; Asst. coach U. Mo., Columbia, 1988-91, Green Bay Packers, 1992-99; head coach Philadelphia Eagles, 2000—. Office: Philadelphia Eagles 3501 S Broad St Philadelphia PA 19148-5298*

REID, ANNA LOUISE, nurse anesthetist; b. McKeesport, Pa., Dec. 21, 1930; d. Earl Francis and Anna Amelia (Treese) R. Diploma, Kings Daus Hosp. Sch. Nursing, 1951; cert., Fairmont Gen. Hosp. Sch. Anesthesia, 1964. Cert. nurse anesthetist. Staff nurse Charlestown Hosp., Ranson, W.Va., 1951-53; head nurse, supr. Kings Daus. Hosp., Martinsburg, 1953-62; staff obstetrics nurse W.Va. U. Hosp., Morgantown, 1962; staff anesthetist St. Vincent Pallotti Hosp., 1964-70, Orange Meml. Hosp., Orlando, Fla., 1970-71, Duke U. Hosp., Durham, N.C., 1971-72, Sentara Hampton (Va.) Gen. Hosp., 1972-94; nurse Anesthesia Assocs. of Hampton (Va.) Ltd., 1994-95, ret., 1995. Mem. ANA, Am. Assn. Nurse Anesthetists Republican. Roman Catholic. Avocations: fishing, archeology, reading. Home: 33 Bainbridge Ave Hampton VA 23663-2301

REID, ANTHONY JOHN STANHOPE, historian, educator; b. Wellington, New Zealand, June 19, 1939; arrived in Australia, 1970; s. John Stanhope and Doris Aileen (Priestley) R.; m. Helen Margaret Gray, Aug. 31, 1963; children: Katharine Mary, Daniel James. BA, Victoria U. Wellington, New Zealand, 1960, MA with honors, 1961; PhD, Cambridge U., U.K., 1965. Lectr. U. Malaya, Kuala Lumpur, Malaysia, 1965-70; fellow Australian Nat. U., Canberra, 1970-74, sr. fellow, 1974-88, prof. S.E. Asian history, 1988-99; prof. history and dir. Ctr. for S.E. Asian Studies UCLA, 1999—; dir. Asia Rsch. Inst. Nat. U. Singapore, 2002—. Vis. assoc. prof. Yale U., New Haven, Conn., 1973-74; sr. specialist Social Sci. Rsch. Tng. Ctr., Ujung Pundang, Indonesia, 1980-87. Author: The Contest for North Sumatra, 1969, The Indonesian National Revolution, 1974, The Blood of the People, 1979, Southeast Asia in the Age of Commerce, vol. I, 1988, vol. II, 1993, Charting the Shape of Early Modern Southeast Asia, 1999; editor 15 books; contbr. over 100 articles to profl. jours. Fellow Australian Acad. Humanities (internat. sec. 1990-92); mem. Asian Studies Assn. Australia (founding convenor 1975-76, pres. 1996-98). Roman Catholic. Office: Asia Rsch Inst Nat Univ Singapore Singapore 117570 Singapore

REID, BELMONT MERVYN, brokerage house executive; b. San Jose, Calif., May 17, 1927; s. C. Belmont and Mary Irene (Kilfoyl) R.; m. Evangeline Joan Rogers, June 1, 1952. BS in Engring., San Jose State U., 1950, postgrad. Pres. Lifetime Realty Corp., San Jose, 1969—77, Lifetime Fin. Planning Corp., San Jose, 1967—77; founder, chmn. bd. Belmont Reid & Co., Inc., 1960—77; pres. JOBEL Fin. Inc., Carson City, Nev., 1980—; pres., chmn. bd. Data-West Systems, Inc., 1984—85. Chmn. Carson City Debt. Mgmt. Commn., 1986—99; mem. Carson City Charter Rev. Com., 1986—91, chmn., 1988—91; rural county chmn. Nev. Rep. Cen. Com., 1984—88; County chmn. Carson City Rep. Cen. Com., 1982—85, treas., 1979—81; Carson City Coun. No. 347, Navy League of U.S., 1987—. With USN, 1945—46, with USN, 1951—55. Decorated Air medals. Mem.: Carson City C. of C. (pres. 1986—87, bd. dir. 1982—88), Mcpl. Securities Rulemaking Bd., Nat. Assn. Securities Dealers, Rotary (chpt. sec. 1983—84, 1986—87, pres. 1988—89, Paul Harris fellow), Capital Club of Carson City. Home: 610 E Bonanza Dr Carson City NV 89706 Office: 711 E Washington St Carson City NV 89701-4063

REID, BENJAMINE, lawyer; b. Concord, N.C., Jan. 11, 1950; s. Fred Herndon and Frances Barnhardt Reid; m. Jennie Lou Divine, Dec. 19, 1970; children: Elisabeth Divine, Margaret Hethcox, Benjamine Joseph. AB, U. N.C., 1971; JD cum laude, U. Ga., 1974. Bar: Fla., Ga., U.S. Ct. Appeals (3rd, 5th and 11th cirs.), U.S. Supreme Ct. Atty., shareholder Kimbrell & Hamann, Miami, Fla., 1974-90; shareholder Popham Haik, 1990-97, Carlton Fields, Miami, 1997—, bd. dirs., mem. exec. com. Bd. dirs. Product Liability Adv. Coun., Washington. Sr. editor U. Ga. Law Rev.; contbr. articles to profl. jours. Vice-chair, exec. com. mem. Greater Miami Chamber; pres. Dade Pub. Edn. Fund; chair Leadership Miami; mem. standing com., exec. bd., vice chancellor Episcopal Diocese of S.E. Fla.; mem. vestry, sr. warden St. Philip's Episcopal Ch.; mem. nat. devel. coun. U. N.C.; founder, bd. dirs., pres. Fla. Internat. U. Coun. of 100; mem. bd. visitors U. N.C.; mem. WLRN Cir. of Friends. Fellow Am. Bar Found.; mem. ABA (coun./com. chair sect. litigation), U. N.C. Gen. Alumni Assn. (bd. dirs.), Phi Kappa Phi. Democrat. Avocations: golf, history, travel.

REID, CHARLES ADAMS, III, lawyer; b. Plainfield, N.J., Apr. 21, 1947; s. Charles Adams Jr. and Gertrude C. (Egan) R.; m. Teresa Keenan, May 11, 1974. BA, Colgate U., 1969; JD, Columbia U., 1974. Bar: N.Y. 1974, U.S. Dist. Ct. (ea. and so. dists.) N.Y. 1975, U.S. Dist. Ct. N.J. 1976, U.S. Ct. Appeals (3d cir.) 1983, U.S. Ct. Appeals (fed. cir.) 1989, U.S. Ct. Appeals (2d cir.) 1991. Law clk. to hon. John R. Bartels U.S. Dist. Ct. (ea. dist.) N.Y., Bklyn., 1974-75; assoc. Coudert Bros., N.Y.C., 1975-77, Shanley & Fisher, Newark, 1977-82, ptnr. Newark and Morristown, N.J., 1983-99, Drinker Biddle & Shanley LLP, Florham Park, 1999—. Mem. planning bd. Peapack-Gladstone, N.J., 1984-88, chmn., 1987-88; bd. dirs. Morris Ctr. YMCA, Cedar Knolls, N.J., 1986-93. Served with U.S. Army, 1970-72, Vietnam. Mem. ABA (litigation sect.), N.J. Bar Assn., Morris County Bar Assn., Essex County Bar Assn., Park Avenue Club (Florham Park). Home: PO Box 716 Gladstone NJ 07934 Office: Drinker Biddle & Shanley LLP 500 Campus Dr Florham Park NJ 07932-1047

REID, CHARLES PHILLIP PATRICK, academic administrator, researcher, educator; b. Columbia, Mo., Jan. 8, 1940; s. Charles Henry and Fern Elnora (Chorlton) R.; m. Miriam Davis, July 17, 1961; children: Clayton Patrick, Miriam. BSF, U. Mo., 1961; MF, Duke U., 1966, PhD, 1968. Asst. prof. dept. forest and wood scis. Colo. State U., Ft. Collins, 1969-73, assoc. prof. dept. forest and wood scis., 1973-77, prof. dept. forest and wood scis., 1977-86; prof., chmn. dept. forestry U. Fla., Gainesville, 1986-92, interim dir. Sch. Forest Resources and Conservation, 1991-92; prof., dir. Sch. Renewable Natural Resources U. Ariz., Tucson, 1992—. Vis. faculty mem. dept. botany Sheffield (Eng.) U., fall 1973; vis. scientist div. of soils Commonwealth Sci. and Indsl. Rsch. Orgn., Glen Osmond, South Australia, 1976-77; sr. Fulbright fellow dept. microbiology U. Innsbruck, Austria, 1985-86; chmn. working group on root physiology and symbiosis Internat. Union Forestry Rsch. Orgns., 1984-88. Contbr. articles to profl. jours. Co-pres. Barton Elem. Parent Tchr. Orgn., Ft. Collins, 1979-80; bd. dirs. Vol. Clearing House, Ft. Collins, 1974-76, Fla. 4-H Found., Gainesville, 1988-89. Lt. (j.g.) USNR, 1961-64, comdr. USNR, ret. Mem. AAAS, Ecol. Soc. Am., Soc. Am. Foresters (nat. program chair 1996), Nat. Assn. Profl. Forestry Schs. and Colls. (exec. com. 1994—, pres. elect 2000-2001, pres. 2002-), Sertoma (treas., bd. dirs. Ft. Collins chpt. 1972-75), Nat. Coalition for Sustaining Ams. Nonfed. Forests (chmn. 1999-2001), Nat. Assn. State Univ. Land Grant Colls. (exec. com. 2000—, bd. natural resources), Rotary. Republican. Episcopalian. Office: U Ariz Sch Renewable Natural Resources Bioscience East Tucson AZ 85721-0001

REID, CLAUDE G. engineer, consultant; b. Columbia, Sc, July 10, 1964; s. Claude G. Reid, Sr. and Nancy Reid; m. Jill Reid, June 4, 1992; children: Angela, Claude Reid, III. BS Mech. Engring., SC State U., Orangeburg, South Carolina, 1987. Computer cons. SC Dept. of Mental Health, Columbia, SC, 1996—; engr. Am. Koyo Corperation, Orangeburg, 1989—90; pres. Innovative Creations & C.G. Reid, Inc., Columbia, 1987—. Mem.: Prince Hall Mason (tiler 1993—94). Baptist. Achievements include patents pending for Ice Master. Avocations: fishing, singing, basketball, swimming, camping. Home: 1511 Craven St Columbia SC 29203

REID, CLEMENT MICHAEL, composer, educator, musician; b. N.Y.C., July 24, 1955; s. Eugene Gordon and Dorothy Gaffney Reid; 1 child Tracey. MusB, Eastman Sch. Music, 1977; MusM, U. So. Calif., 1980. Tchr. piano, string instruments West Coast Music Studios, Tacoma, 1981—; instr. music theory St. Martin's Coll., Lacey, 1984—85; accompanist Tacoma (Wash.) City Ballet, 1989—94; music coord., instr. McChord AFB Youth Ctr., Tacoma, 1994—; instr. composition Pacific Lutheran U., 2002—; dir. CNY Pubs., Tacoma, 1996—. Vis. lectr. Music Tchrs. Nat. Assn., Stephen F. Austin U., Pacific Luth. U., Nacogdoces, Tex., and Tacoma, 1983—2001; panelist Artist Trust Found., Seattle, 1991—94; v.p. Washington Composers Forum, Seattle, 1990—97. Composer: (orchestral, chamber orch. and wind ensemble works) Northwest Fanfare, 2001, Stillness, 1997, Landscape, Theater Piece #3, Narrative, The Far Field, Three Greek Songs, Camden Conversations, First Year Performance, Steps. Named Wash. State Composer of Yr., Music Tchrs. Nat. Assn., 1999; grantee project grantee, King County Arts Commn., 1990, artist initiative grantee, Tacoma Arts Commn., 2001. Mem.: ASCAP (writer mem., yearly awards 1987—), Tacoma New Music (bd. dirs. 2000—), Wash. State Music Tchrs. Assn. (bd. dirs. 1999—2001, treas. 1999—2001). Avocations: woodworking, furniture construction. Home: 12414 28th Ave E Tacoma WA 98445 Office: CNY Pubs PO Box 4401 Tacoma WA 98438

REID, CONSTANCE, writer; b. St. Louis, Jan. 3, 1918; d. Ralph Bowers and Helen Marie (Hall) Bowman; m. Neil Dan Reid, June 23, 1950; children: Julia Emma, Stewart Bowman. AB, San Diego State Coll., Calif., 1938; MEd, U. Calif., Berkeley, 1949. H.s. tchr. San Diego City schs., Calif., 1939-48, Jr. Coll. tchr., 1949-50; writer freelance, 1950—. Author: Slacks and Calluses, 1944, 1999, From Zero to Infinity, 1956, 1991, Introduction to Higher Mathematics for the General Reader, 1959, A Long Way from Euclid, 1963, Hilbert, 1970, 1996, Courant in Goettingen and New York, 1976, (as Courant) 1996, Neyman--from life, 1982, (as Neyman) 1997, The Search for E.T. Bell, also known as John Taine, 1993, JULIA, a life in mathematics, 1996, co-author: International Mathematical Congresses/An Illustrated History 1893-1986, 1986, More Mathematical People, 1990; spkr. in field. Democrat. Avocations: contemporary art, film, reading, education.

REID, DANA MARIE, lawyer; b. Seattle, Mar. 16, 1966; d. Donald James and Linda Marie Reid. BA in History, Whitman Coll., Walla Walla, Wash., 1989; JD, Willamette U., Salem, Oreg., 1993; LLM in Taxation, U. Wash., 1997. Bar: Wash., U.S. Dist. Ct. (we. and ea. dist.) Wash. Asst. atty. gen. Wash. State Atty. Gen.'s Office, Olympia, 1994-96; assoc. Egger Betts Austin Ahrens & Treacy, Bellevue, Wash., 1997-98, Treacy Law Group, Bellevue, 1998-2000, Montgomery, Purdue, Blankinship & Austin PLLC, Seattle, 2000—. Bd. dirs. Overlake Svc. League, Bellevue, 1997-99; v.p. Wash. Women Lawyers Found., 1997-99; mem. Seattle Works, 1996—; mem. Nat. Com. on Planned Giving, 1997—, Wash. Planned Giving Coun., 1997—. Mem.: ABA (taxation sect.), Wash. Women Lawyers (Pres.'s award 1997, State Bd. Mem. of Yr. 1997), Wash. Bar Assn. (taxation sect., real property, probate and trust sect.). Avocations: tennis, golf, running, cooking, the arts. Office: Montgomery Purdue Blankinship & Austin PLLC 701 5th Ave Ste 5800 Seattle WA 98104-7096

REID, DANIEL JAMES, public relations executive; b. Grand Rapids, Mich., Sept. 7, 1960; s. Robert Alexander and Janette Helen (Hickey) R.; m. Meredith Christine Ryan, Apr. 30, 1994; children: Ryan Paul, Katherine Baxter. BA, Mich. State U., 1983. Sr. account exec. Burson-Marsteller, Chgo., 1983-88; group dir. Ogilvy & Mather, 1988-90; sr. ptnr. FRB/BSMG Worldwide (subs. True North Comms.), 1990-98; sr. nat. mng. ptnr. BSMG Worldwide, 1998-2000, pres. fin. svcs., 2000—; exec. v.p. Weber Shandwick Worldwide, 2001—. Contbr. articles to profl. publs. and newspapers. Bd. dirs. Opportunity, Inc., Chgo., LEC Ltd. Mem. Union League Club Chgo. Republican. Roman Catholic. Office: Weber Shandwick 676 St Clair Chicago IL 60611

REID, DAVID G. lawyer; b. N.Y.C., Oct. 28, 1948; s. Donald D. and Charlotte A. (Marois) R. BA, McGill U., Montreal, 1970; JD, Boston U., 1973. Bar: Vt. 1973, U.S. Dist. Ct. Vt. 1973, Mass. 1977, U.S. Supreme Ct. 1978, U.S. Ct. Appeals (2d cir.) 1978, U.S. Dist. Ct. Mass. 1991. Pub. defender Orleans, Caledonia, Essex counties, St. Johnsbury, Vt., 1973-75, Bennington (Vt.) County, 1975-79, Windham County, Brattleboro, Vt., 1979-89; ptnr. Reid & Rodgers, 1989—. Office: Reid & Rodgers 47 Williston St Brattleboro VT 05301-3202 E-mail: drj@sover.net.

REID, DONNA JOYCE, small business owner; b. Springfield, Tenn., June 25, 1954; d. Leonard Earl Reid and Joyce (Robertson) Kirby; m. Kenneth Bruce Sadler, June 26, 1976 (div. Apr. 1980); m. John Christopher Moulton, Oct. 18, 1987 (div. Dec. 1992); m. Peter Leatherland, Apr. 3, 1993. Student, Austin Peay State U., Clarksville, Tenn., 1972-75. Show writer, producer WTVF-TV (CBS affiliate), Nashville, 1977-83, promotion producer, 1983-85, on-air promotion mgr., 1985-86; gen. mgr. Steadi-Film Corp., 1986-90; co-owner Options Internat., 1990—. Big sister Buddies of Nashville, 1981-87. Named to Honorable Order of Ky. Cols. John Y. Brown, Gov., 1980; recipient Significant Svc. award ARC, 1982, Clara Barton Communications award, 1983. Mem. NAFE, Nat. Assn. TV Arts and Scis., Nat. Film Inst., Nat. Assn. Broadcasters, Internat. Platform Assn., Am. Soc. Prevention of Cruelty to Animals, Humane Soc. U.S. Methodist. Avocations: reading, outdoor sports, travel. Office: Options Internat Inc 913 18th Ave S Nashville TN 37212-2102

REID, EDWARD SNOVER , III, lawyer; b. Detroit, Mar. 24, 1930; s. Edward S. Jr. and Margaret (Overington) Reid; m. Carroll Grylls, Dec. 30, 1953; children: Carroll Reid Highet, Richard Gerveys, Jane Reid McTigue, Margaret Reid Boyer. BA, Yale U., 1951; LL.B. magna cum laude (Sheldon fellow), Harvard U., 1956. Bar: Mich. 1957, N.Y. 1958, D.C. 1982, Gaikokuho jimu-bengoshi, Tokyo 1991-96. Asso. Davis, Polk & Wardwell, N.Y.C., 1957-64, partner, 1964-95, sr. counsel, 1996—; dir. Gen. Mills, Inc., 1974-89. Mem. N.Y.C. Bd. Higher Edn., 1971—73; trustee Bklyn. Inst. Arts and Scis., 1966—93, chmn., 1974—79; trustee Bklyn. Mus. Art, 1973—93, 1994—; bd. dirs. Bklyn. Bot. Garden Corp., 1977—92, 1996—, Bargemusic Ltd., 1990—93. Lt. USMC, 1951—53. Mem. ABA, N.Y. State Bar Assn., Assn. of Bar of City of N.Y., Am. Law Inst., Internat. Bar Assn., Heights Casino Club, Rembrandt Club, Century Assn. Club, Yale Club, Quoque Beach Club, Shinnecock Yacht Club, Quoque Field Club. Home: PO Box 39 Quogue NY 11959-0039 Office: Davis Polk & Wardwell 450 Lexington Ave New York NY 10017-3982 E-mail: ereid@dpw.com.

REID, GARY J. management consultant; b. Artesia, Calif., Sept. 29, 1948; s. Fred M. and Marjorie June Reid; m. Judith E. Payne, July 6, 1974; children: Alison Payne, Katherine Payne. BA Philosophy, Stanford U., 1970; MCP City Planning, Harvard U., 1976, PhD Urban Planning, 1985. Postdoc. fellow Carnegie Mellon U., Pitts., 1988—89; asst. prof. U. So. Calif., L.A., 1985—90, assoc. prof., 1990—93; cons. The World Bank, Washington, 1990—93, pub. sector mgmt. specialist, 1991—93, sr. pub. sector mgmt. specialist, 1998—2001, lead pub. sector mgmt. specialist, 2001—. Cons. Contmet Rsch. Corp., Belmont, Mass., 1976—78, L.A. 2000, 1987—88. Contbr. chapters to books; mem. editl. bd. (jours.) Pub. Admin. Rev., 1985—87, jour. referee, 1984—90. Recipient Harry Scoville award, Am. Soc. Pub. Admintrn., 1989. Avocations: classical guitarist, bicycling, runner, cross country skiing. Office: The World Bank 1818 H St NW Washington DC 20433 Business E-Mail: greid@worldbank.org.

REID, GEORGE KELL, biology educator, researcher, author; b. Fitzgerald, Ga., Mar. 23, 1918; s. George Kell and Pauline (Bowles) R.; m. Eugénie Louise Chazal, July 23, 1949 (div. Dec. 1978); children: George Philip (dec.), Deborah Louise. BS, Presbyn. Coll., Clinton, S.C., 1940; MS, U. Fla., 1949, PhD, 1952. Instr. U. Fla., Gainesville, 1949-52; asst. prof. Coll. William and Mary, Williamsburg, Va., 1952-53, Tex. A&M U., College Station, 1953-56, Rutgers U., New Brunswick, N.J., 1956-60; prof. Eckerd Coll., St. Petersburg, Fla., 1960-83, prof. emeritus, 1983—; pvt. practice cons., writer Boca Raton, 1988—. Rsch. scientist Va. Inst. Marine Sci., Gloucester, 1953; rsch. biologist Tex. Game and Fish. Commn., Rockport, 1954-56; cons. in field, 1955—. Author: Ecology of Cedar Key Fishes, 1954, Ecology of Inland Waters and Estuaries, 1961, (co-author) rev. edit., 1976, Pond Life, 1967, rev. edit., 1987, Ecology of Intertidal Zones, 1967; co-author: Bioscience, 1967; contbr. articles to profl. jours. and popular periodicals. Mem. City Environ. Com., St. Petersburg, 1975. 1st lt. U.S. Army, 1942-46. Recipient numerous grants NIH, NSF, Explorers Club, others, 1953—. Fellow AAAS; mem. Am. Soc. Limnology and Oceanography, Am. Inst. Biol. Scis., Fla. Acad. Sci. (pres. 1963-64), Ecol. Soc. Am. (chmn. aquatic ecology sec. 1964-66), Sigma Xi, Phi Sigma, Chi Beta Phi, Sigma Chi. Presbyterian. Achievements include pioneering in fish community ecology research in Gulf of Mexico localities; research in population dynamics in mangrove ecosystems, Wetland utilization, early literature on natural history of Florida. Home: 1056 Sanctuary Cove Dr North Palm Beach FL 33410-4534

REID, GERALDINE WOLD (GERALDINE REID SKJERVOLD), artist; b. Apr. 11, 1944; d. Alden Elroy and Verna (Kocinski) Wold BA in Fine Art, Calif. State U., Sacramento, 1972, MFA, 1975; postgrad., Ind. U. - Purdue U. Instr. dental aux. edn. U. Minn., 1966-70, anthropol. rsch. asst., 1976-78; mng. editor Nat. Arts Guide, Chgo., 1978-80; freelance artist Chgo., 1981-94; pres. Chgo. Art Emerging Inc., 1983-85; graphic artist Reid Design & Illustration, Chgo., 1981-94; dir. show coordination Circle Fine Art, 1981. Instr. comm. art and design Alexandria Tech. Coll., Minn., 1994—; seminar lectr., 1977, 86; lectr., art and math. Dept. Math. U. Ill., 1987-88; guest lectr. women's art history AAUW, Alexandria, 1997. One-woman shows include Artists' Coop. Gallery, Santa Fe, 1976, Artlink, Ft. Wayne, Ind., 1979, 84—, D.E.O. Fine Arts, Inc., Chgo., 1982-83, Union League Gallery, Chgo., 1989, Brodsky Gallery, 1993, Second Floor Gallery, Cen. Square, Glenwood, Minn., 1999, Ann Bickle Heritage House, Glenwood, 2000; group exhbns. include Crocker Art Mus., Sacramento, 1975, Ft. Wayne Mus. Art, 1978, Artists Guild Chgo., 1982, Charles A. Wustum Mus., Racine, Wis., 1983, Limelight, Chgo., 1986, 87, 88, Neville-Sargent Gallery, 1986, 87, Beacon Street Hull House Gallery, 1988, McDonalds Corp., Chgo., 1988, Prairie Ave. Gallery, Chgo., 1990, Peace Mus., Chgo., 1990, Hyde Park Art Ctr., Chgo., 1990, Lettuce Entertain You Enterprises, Inc., 1990, Olive Tree Gallery, Daley Coll., Chgo., 1991, Crown Ctr. Gallery, Loyola U., Chgo., 1992, Agora Syndicate, Inc., 1992, Kieffer-Nolde/TIC, 1992, Flora '92, 1992, Chgo. Botanic Garden, 1992, Open Spectrum, David Adler Cultural Ctr., 1994, August House Studio, Chgo., 1994—, Upper West Gallery, Alexandria Tech. Coll., Minn., 1995, Plains Art Mus., Fargo, N.D., 1997, Regional Art Exhibit, New York Mills, Minn., 1997, Runestone Mus., Alexandria, 1997-98, Art on the Plains, 3d Ann. Regional Exhbn., Plains Art Mus., Fargo, 31st Ann. Fergus Falls Cmty. Coll. Invitational Art Show, Fergus Falls, Minn., 2002, Pope County Artists Exhibit, Lake Region Arts Coun. Gallery, Fergus Falls, Minn., 2002; contbr. artwork to 2 ann. 1994 calendars. Mem. N.Y. Mills Cultural Ctr., Mpls. Art Inst., Am. Inst. Graphic Arts, Mpls. Inst. Arts. E-mail: gerrir@alx.tec.mn.us.

REID, GINGER MEREDITH, school counselor, educator; b. Atlanta, Dec. 5, 1969; d. Ronald Davis Balser and Temme Barkin-Leeds; m. Wayne Dale Reid, II, Aug. 12, 1995. BA in Psychology, Emory U., 1993; MEd in Sch. Counseling, Ga. State U., 1995. Cert. sch. counselor, Ga. Summer day camp counselor Frog Hollow Day Camp, Atlanta, 1988-91; tchr., counselor Haverty

Hollow Pre-Sch. Enrichment Program, 1991-92, 93-96; rsch. asst. Emory Univ., 1992-93; sch. counselor Dacula (Ga.) Mid. Sch., 1996—. Mem. Ga. Sch. Counselors Assn., Ga. Assn. Play Therapy, Ga. Sch. Age Care Assn., Phi Bet Kappa, Psi Chi. Jewish. Avocations: jogging, weight lifting, aerobics, hiking, scuba diving. Home: 1363 Cartecay Dr NE Atlanta GA 30319-3401

REID, HARRY, senator; b. Searchlight, Nev., Dec. 2, 1939; s. Harry and Inez Reid; m. Landra Joy Gould; children— Lana, Rory, Leif, Josh, Key AS, Southern Utah State U., 1959; LLD (hon.), U. So. Utah, 1984; BA, Utah State U., 1961; JD, George Washington U., 1964. Senator from Nev. U.S. Senate, Washington, 1986—, asst. dem. leader. Mem. appropriations, ethics/environment & pub. works, Indian affairs coms.; ranking mem. environ. pub. works.*

REID, INEZ SMITH, lawyer, educator; b. New Orleans, Apr. 7, 1937; d. Sidney Randall Dickerson and Beatrice Virginia (Bundy) Smith. BA, Tufts U., 1959; LLB, Yale U., 1962; MA, UCLA, 1963; PhD, Columbia U., 1968. Bar: Calif. 1963, N.Y. 1972, D.C. 1980. Assoc. prof. Barnard Coll. Columbia U., N.Y.C., 1972-76; gen. counsel youth divsn. State of N.Y., 1976-77; dep. gen. counsel HEW, Washington, 1977-79; inspector gen. EPA, 1979-81; chief legis. and opinions, dep. corp. counsel Office of Corp. Counsel, 1981-83; corp. counsel D.C., 1983-85; counsel Laxalt, Washington, Perito & Dubuc, Washington, 1986-90, ptnr., 1990-91; counsel Graham & James, 1991-93, Lewis, White & Clay, P.C., 1994-95; assoc. judge D.C. Ct. Appeals, 1995—. William J. Maier, Jr. vis. prof. law W.Va. U. Coll. Law, Morgantown, 1985-86. Contbr. articles to profl. jours. and publs. Bd. dirs. Homeland Ministries bd. United Ch. of Christ, N.Y.C., 1978—83, vice chmn., 1981—83; chmn. bd. govs. Antioch Law Sch., Washington, 1979—81; chmn. bd. trustees Antioch U., Yellow Springs, Ohio, 1981—82; trustee Tufts U., Medford, Mass., 1988—98, trustee emeritus, 1999—; trustee Lancaster (Pa.) Sem., 1988—2001; bd. govs. D.C. Sch. Law, 1990—96, chmn., 1991—95. Recipient Emily Gregory award Barnard Coll., 1976, Arthur Morgan award Antioch U., 1982, Service award United Ch. of Christ, 1983, Disting. Service (Profl. Life) award Tufts U. Alumni Assn., 1988. Office: DC Ct Appeals 500 Indiana Ave NW Fl 6 Washington DC 20001-2138

REID, JACKSON BROCK, psychologist, educator; b. Honea Path, S.C., Sept. 18, 1921; s. Alexander Mack and Ann Orr (Brock) R.; m. Avis Boykin Long, Jan. 12, 1947; step-children: Jules Heywood Long, Barbara Banning Long. BS, The Citadel, 1942; postgrad., Ariz. State Coll., Flagstaff, 1948; PhD, UCLA, 1951, postgrad., summer 1951. Cert., lic. psychologist, Tex. Asst. prof. ednl. psychology U. Tex., Austin, 1951-55, assoc. prof., 1955-59, prof., 1959-93, prof. emeritus, 1993—, assoc. dean for grad. studies in edn., 1965-73; coordinator ESEA programs U.S. Office Edn., 1969—, chmn. dept. ednl. psychology, 1972-84. Cons. in field. Served to capt. U.S. Army, 1942-47. Office Edn. grantee, 1966-73 Fellow Am. Psychol. Assn. (exptl. and ednl. divs.); mem. AAAS, Am. Ednl. Research Assn., Interam. Soc. Psychology, AAUP, Southwestern Psychol. Assn. (sec.-treas. 1965-66, pres. 1967-68), Tex. Psychol. Assn., Ret. Officers Assn., Nat. Psoriasis Found., ACLU, Common Cause, Fund for Peace, Planned Parenthood of Am., Sigma Xi. Clubs: U. Tex. Faculty Center; Lighthouse Resort and Club (Sanibel Island, Fla.). Achievements include research, publs. in learning theory, behavioral effects of radiation and drugs, child and adolescent behavior, programmed instn., computer-assisted instrn. Home: 3801 Westlake Dr Austin TX 78746-1617 Office: U Tex Dept Ednl Psychology Austin TX 78712 *The principal goal in my career has been to preserve psychology as an academic discipline devoted to objective inquiry into the etiology of behavior on the basis of logically directed empirical investigation as opposed to rationalistic - mystical - doctrinaire approaches.*

REID, JAMES DOLAN, mathematics educator, researcher; b. Augusta, Ga., June 24, 1930; s. Richard and Katherine (O'Leary) R.; m. Anne Carmody Donohue, Jan. 7, 1959; children: James Jr., Margaret, Gerald. BS, Fordham Coll., 1952, MA, 1954; PhD, U. Wash., 1960; MA (hon.), Wesleyan U., 1972. Asst. prof. Syracuse (N.Y.) U., 1960-61, 1963-65, assoc. prof., 1965-69; research assoc. Yale U., New Haven, 1961-62; asst. prof. Amherst (Mass.) Coll., 1962-63; assoc. prof. math. Wesleyan U., Middletown, Conn., 1969-70, prof., 1970—, chmn. math. dept., 1970-73, 85-88, prof. math., 1980—. Vis. prof. U. Würzburg, Fed. Republic Germany, 1989. Contbr. numerous articles on algebra (Abelian groups) to profl. jours. Mem. Bd. Edn., Regional Sch. Dist. #17, 1983-87. With USN, 1954-56. Mem. Am. Math. Soc., Irish Math. Soc., Math. Assn. of Am. Home: 159 Green Hill Rd Killingworth CT 06419-2218 Office: Wesleyan U Dept Math Middletown CT 06459-0001 E-mail: jreid@wesleyan.edu.

REID, JAMES SIMS, JR. former automobile parts manufacturer; b. Cleve., Jan. 15, 1926; s. James Sims and Felice (Crowl) R.; m. Donna Smith, Sept. 2, 1950; children: Sally, Susan, Anne (dec.), Jeanne. AB cum laude, Harvard U., 1948, JD, 1951. Bar: Mich., Ohio 1951. Pvt. practice law, Detroit, 1951-52, Cleve., 1953-56; with Standard Products Co., 1956-99, dir., 1959, pres., 1962-89, chmn., chief exec. officer, 1989-99; ret., 1999. Trustee John Carroll U., 1967—, chmn., 1987-91, Musical Arts Assn. of Cleve. Orch., 1973—. Office: Hanna Bldg Ste 545 1422 Euclid Ave Cleveland OH 44115-1901

REID, JANET WARNER, biologist consultant; b. Boston, Oct. 18, 1944; d. Clarence Steffens and Elizabeth Tyler (Lancaster) Warner; m. Willis Alton Reid Jr., Apr. 24, 1966; children: Blake Dietrich, Alexander Nathan. BS, Duke U., 1966; MS, N.C. State U., 1971, PhD, 1978. Prof. U. Brasilia, Brazil, 1981-82; sr. postdoctoral fellow Nat. Mus. Natural History, Smithsonian Instn., Washington, 1988-89, rsch. assoc. dept. invertebrate zoology, 1986—2001; rsch. assoc. dept. rsch. Va. Mus. Natural History, Martinsville, Va., 2001—02; pvt. practice biol. cons. Bethesda, Md., 1982—2001, Martinsville, Va., 2001—. Contbr. articles to profl. jours. Fellow Washington Acad. Scis.; mem. World Assn. Copepodologists (founding mem., mem. local organizing com. 1993 congress, gen. sec. 1993-96, v.p. 1999-2002), The Crustacean Soc., Biol. Soc. Washington (coun. 1990-92, 96—, pres.-elect 1992-94, pres. 1994-96), Sociedade Brasileira de Limnologia, Societas Internationalis Limnologiae, Sociedade Brasileira de Carcinologia, Sociedade Brasileira de Zoologia, Helminthological Soc. Washington (co-editor Comparative Parasitology 1998-2001).

REID, JEAN MARGO, retired lawyer; b. Lockport, N.Y., Aug. 31, 1945; m. Richard P. Brief, Jan. 12, 1980; 1 child, Kristin Reid Brief. BA, Wells Coll., 1967; JD, Harvard U., 1970. Atty. Nat. Housing and Econ. Devel. Law Project, Berkeley, Calif., 1970—72; counsel CEDC, Inc., Hempstead, NY, 1972—76, Am. Women's Econ. Devel. Corp., N.Y.C., 1977—79; asst. prof. NYU, 1981—88; atty. Sanford C. Bernstein & Co Inc, 1988—92, assoc. counsel, 1992—96, gen. counsel, 1997—2000; ret., 2000. Personal E-mail: reidjeanmango@juno.com.

REID, JOAN EVANGELINE, lawyer, stockbroker; b. Mich., Apr. 22, 1932; d. August W. and Evangeline R. (Brozeau) Rogers; m. Belmont M. Reid. AA in Bus., San Jose State U., 1951; JD, McGeorge Sch. Law, 1989. Bar: Nev.; lic. realtor, life, disability and annuity ins. Officer, dir. Lifetime Fin. Planning Corp., San Jose, Calif., 1967-77, Lifetime Realty Corp., San Jose, 1967-77; co-founder, officer, dir. Belmont Reid & Co., Inc., 1960-77; officer, corp. counsel, dir. JOBEL Fin. Inc., Carson City, Nev., 1980—. Past sec., treas. Nev. Fedn. Rep. Women; charter pres. Santa Clara Valley Rep. Women Federated; past v.p. Carson City Rep. Women's Club; past pres. Soroptimist Internat. of Carson City. Paul Harris fellow Rotary. Mem. First Jud. Dist. Bar Assn., State Bar Nev., No. Nev. Women Lawyers Assn., Carson City C. of C., Soroptimist Internat. of Carson City (past pres., sec.).

REID, JOHN PHILLIP, law educator; b. Weehawken, N.J., May 17, 1930; s. Thomas Francis and Teresa Elizabeth (Murphy) R. BSS., Georgetown U., 1952; LL.B., Harvard U., 1955; MA, U. N.H., 1957; J.S.D., NYU, 1962. Bar: N.H. 1955. Law clk. U.S. Dist. Ct. N.H., 1956; instr. NYU, N.Y.C., 1960-62, asst. prof. law, 1962-64, assoc. prof., 1964-65, prof. Sch. Law, 1966—. Author: Chief Justice: The Judicial World of Charles Doe, 1967, A Law of Blood: The Primitive Law of the Cherokee Nation, 1970, In a Defiant Stance, 1977, In a Rebellious Spirit, 1979, Law for the Elephant: Property and Social Behavior on the Overland Trail, 1980, In Defiance of the Law, 1981, Constitutional History of the American Revolution: The Authority of Rights, 1986, Constitutional History of the American Revolution: The Authority to Tax, 1987, The Concept of Liberty in the Age of the American Revolution, 1988, The Concept of Representation in the Age of the American Revolution, 1989, Constitutional History of the American Revolution: The Authority to Legislate, 1991, Constitutional History of the American Revolution: The Authority of Law, 1993, Policing the Elephant: Crime, Punishment, and Social Behavior on the Overland Trail, 1997, Patterns of Vengeance: Crosscultural Homicide in the North American Fur Trade, 1999, Contested Empire: Peter Skene Ogden and the Snake River Expeditions, 2002. Fellow Guggenheim Found., 1980, Huntington Library-NEH, 1980, 84; hon. fellow Am. Soc. Legal History, 1986. Fellow Am. Acad. Arts and Scis. Republican. Roman Catholic. Office: NYU Law Sch 40 Washington Sq S New York NY 10012-1099 E-mail: john.reid@nyu.edu.

REID, JOHN MITCHELL (JACK REID), biomedical engineer, researcher, consultant; b. Mpls., June 8, 1926; s. Robert Sherman and Meryl (Mitchell) R.; m. Virginia Montgomery, Dec. 31, 1949 (div.); children: Donald, Kathryn, Richard; m. Shadi Wang, June 30, 1983. BS, U. Minn., 1950, MS, 1957; PhD, U. Pa., 1965. Engring. assoc. U. Minn., Mpls., 1950-54; rsch. engr. St. Barnabas Hosp., 1954-57; assoc. U. Pa., Phila., 1957-66; rsch. asst. prof. U. Wash., Seattle, 1966-72; rsch. engr. Providence Hosp., 1972-74; dir. bioengring. Inst. of Applied Physiology & Medicine, 1973-81; Calhoun prof. Drexel U., Phila., 1981-94, prof. emeritus, rsch. prof., 1994—. Adj. prof. radiology Thomas Jefferson Med. Sch., Phila., 1982—; affiliate prof. U. Washington, 1995—; cons. Inst. Applied Physiology and Medicine, Seattle. Contbr. numerous articles to profl. jours.; 5 U.S. patents on devel. of ultrasonic med. imaging. Scoutmaster Boy Scouts Am., Mpls., 1955-57, Phila., 1960-65, cub and scoutmaster, Seattle, 1965-70. With USN, 1950-52, World War II. Recipient Pioneer award Soc. of Vascular Technologists, 1994; grantee NIH. Fellow IEEE, Am. Inst. Ultrasound in Medicine (bd. govs., Pioneer award), Acoustical Soc. Am., Engring. in Medicine and Biology Soc. (Lifetime Achievement award 1993), Am. Inst. Med. and Biol. Engrs.; mem. World Fedn. Ultrasound in Medicine and Biology (hon.). Home: 16711 254th Ave SE Issaquah WA 98027-6973 also: Inst Applied Physiology and Medicine 701 16th Ave Seattle WA 98122-4525 E-mail: jmreid@u.washington.edu.

REID, JOSEPH BROWNING, retired architect; b. Flint Hill, Va., June 24, 1924; s. Charles Garrison and Grace Pearl (Bradley) R.; m. Maria Aida Amadounian, July 5, 1957; children: Charles, Avedis, Robert. Student, U. Va., 1948; BS in Forestry with highest honors, N.C. State U., 1952; postgrad., Columbia U., 1955; cert. in architecture, Cooper Union, 1960. Registered architect, N.Y., Va., Md., Pa., D.C.; cert. Nat. Coun. Archtl. Registration Bds.; lic. interior designer, D.C. Staff architect Charles Luckman & Assocs., N.Y.C., 1956-63; sr. architect Clive Entwistle & Assocs., 1963-64; sr. assoc. Perkins & Will, Washington, 1964-74; v.p. John Carl Warnecke FAIA, 1974-82; founding ptnr. Kemnitzer Reid & Haffler, 1982-89; prin. Einhorn Yaffee Prescott, 1989-98; cons. McLean, Va., 1998—. Advis0r interior design program Marymount Coll., 1982-85; profl. coord. off-campus work program for architecture students Va. Poly. Inst., 1975-81; lectr. No. Va. C.C.; a juror for residential awards Washingtonian mag., 1986; advisor, organizer archtl. awards program Washington Mayor's Award Program. With Mcht. Marine, 1942-47. Recipient Disting. Svc. cert. USO, Washington, 1976, Presdl. Design award Nat. Endowment for Arts, 1987, Hist. Preservation Honor award, 1988, Design award Washington Metro chpt. Am. Soc. Interior Designers, 1989, 2 awards GSA, 1992; Hilda Johnson Cox scholar N.C. State U., 1950. Mem. AIA (sr. dir. Washington Met. chpt. 1979-80, treas. 1981-82, sec. 1982-83, v.p. 1983-84, pres. 1984-85, cert. of deep appreciation 1984, cert. of appreciation 1984, Centennial medal Washington chpt. 1998), Constrn. Specifications Inst. (bd. dirs. 1979-81, 91-92, citation for disting. svc. 1982, nat. honor awards 1992), Soc. Archtl. Adminstrs. (co-founder Washington chpt.), Phi Eta Sigma, Alpha Zeta, Xi Sigma Pi, Alpha Sigma Pi. Democrat. Methodist. Avocations: surf fishing, Greek history, travel in Greece. E-mail: mariareid@mindspring.com.

REID, JOSEPH WILLIAM, consultant; b. Gainesville, Ga., Apr. 23, 1955; s. William Lowell and Barbara Ann (Trowbridge) R.; m. Elizabeth Chara Sudduth, July 12, 1986; children: Patrick Bennett, Alexandra Mackenzie. BBA in Acctg., U. Ga., 1977. CPA, Ga. Staff acct. KPMG, Atlanta, 1977-81, mgr., 1981-83, sr. mgr., 1983-88, ptnr., 1988—. Active Atlanta Alliance on Devel. Disabilities, bd. dirs., former treas., mem. fin. com., 1990—; mem. adv. coun. Salvation Army Adult Rehab. Ctr., 1998—. Mem. Am. Inst. CPAs, Ga. Soc. CPAs. Avocations: tennis, golf, hiking, water sports. Home: 575 Leather Hinge Trl Roswell GA 30075-4184 Office: KPMG LLP 303 Peachtree St NE Ste 2000 Atlanta GA 30308-3261

REID, JUSTUS WEBB, lawyer; b. Fairfield, Iowa, June 11, 1943; m. Phyllis C. Horne, June 11, 1966; children: Heather, Jebb, Erica, Payton. BA, Fla. State U., 1965; JD, U. Fla., 1968. Bar: Fla. 1968. Assoc. Fisher, Prior, Pruitt, West Palm Beach, Fla., 1968-71, Cone, Wagner, Nugent, West Palm Beach, 1971-74, Howell, Kirby, et al, West Palm Beach, 1974-79; ptnr. Magill Sevier & Reid, West Palm Beach and Miami, 1979-85, Reid Ricca & Rigell, West Palm Beach, 1985-93, Reid Metzger & Assocs., West Palm Beach, 1993—. Bd. dirs. Boys and Girls Clubs, West Palm Beach, 1996—. Named one of Best Lawyers in Am. Mem. U.S. Polo Assn. Avocation: polo. Home: PO Box 2926 West Palm Beach FL 33402 Office: Reid Metzger 250 S Australian Ave West Palm Beach FL 33401-5018 E-mail: JReid@ReidMetzger.com.

REID, KATHERINE LOUISE, artist, educator, author; b. Port Arthur, Tex., Mar. 25, 1941; d. Clifton Commodore and Helen Ross (Moore) Reid. BA, Baylor U., 1963; postgrad. in design and illustration, Kans. City Art Inst., 1964; MEd, U. Houston, 1973; cert. supervision, U. Houston-Clear Lake City, 1980; postgrad., San Jacinto Coll., 1982. Litho reprodn. artist Hallmark Cards, Kansas City, Mo., 1963-64; tchr. art high sch. Pasadena (Tex.) Ind. Sch. Dist., 1964-77, supr. art, gifted and talented and photography, 1977-85, supr. art and photography InterAct, 1985-90, instrnl. specialist, 1990-2000, photography and art, 1990-93, instrnl. specialist in art and spl. programs, 1993-96, rsch. planning, data disaggregation, 1996-2000; internet tchr. recruiter, 2001—02; mural artist Old Car Barn, Edna, Tex., 2000—. 4 MAT learning styles trainer DuPont Leadership Devel. Process Trainer, Selective Rsch., Inst., tchr. perceiver specialist, performance quality sys. trainer, coop. learning trainer, outcome based edn. trainer, integrated unit devel. and authentic assessment trainer The Greater Gulf Coast Adminstr. Assessment Project, Assessor, 1990-2000; head crafts, asst. dir., dir. summer, winter discovery program-ski camp Cheley Colo. Camps, Denver, Estes Park, 1967-75; mem. awards com. John Austin Cheley Found., 1990-92; staff artist, media workshop Tex. Edn. Agy., Austin, summer, 1961; art enrichment tchr. Port Arthur Ind. Sch. Dist. (Tex.), summer, 1961; head crafts Camp Waluta, Silsbee, Tex., summer, 1960; mem. Tex. Edn. Agy., Art Leadership Inst., 1989, 90, Tracking Rsch. Com., 1991, Core Strategic Planning Team, 1992-2000, Outcome Based Edn. Dist. Planning Com., 1991-92, Quality Sys. Improvement Team, 1991-92, Outcome Based Edn. Com. Exit Outcomes, 1991; Region IV data disk trainer, 1998-2000, target teach coord., 1993-2000, multiple intelligence trainer, 1997-2000, data disaggregation trainer, 1997-2000, supt.'s rsch. com., 1999. Author: Through Their Eyes, 1989; inventor, patentee Pet Car Seat, U.S.A. and Can. Mem. Friends of Fine Arts-Baylor U., Waco, Tex., 1981—; mem. Scholastic Art awards Regional Bd., Houston, 1978-84, Tex. Edn. Agy.; bd. dirs. Houston Coun. Student Art Awards, Inc., 1984-90. Named Outstanding Secondary Educator of Am., 1975, Tex. Art Educator of Yr., 1985. Mem. ASCD, Tex. ASCD, Tex. Art Edn. Assn. (rep. editor newsletter 1982-85, chmn. supervision divsn. 1982-83, v.p. membership 1978-80, chmn. pub. info. com., regional chmn. youth art month 1980-82; regional chmn. membership com. 1976-78, pres. elect 1986, sec. 1991-93), Tex. Alliance for Arts Edn. (bd. vice chmn. 1984-86, treas. 1988-90), Nat. Art Edn. Assn. (conv. com. 1977, 85), Tex. Assn. Sch. Adminstrs., Houston Art Edn. Assn. (sec. 1969), Tex. Ret. Tchrs. Assn. (Dist. IV historian 2001-03), Pasadena Area Ret. Sch. Employees (parliamentarian 2002--), Delta Kappa Gamma (2d v.p. 1984-86, pres. 2002--). Baptist. E-mial. Home: 106 Ravenhead Dr Houston TX 77034-1520 E-mail: artist@oldcarbarn.com., klreid@mail.esc4.com.

REID, LANGHORNE, III, merchant banker; b. Dallas, Apr. 3, 1950; s. Langhorne Jr. and Mary Anne (Beasley) R.; m. Sally Wolf, Dec. 26, 1972 (div. Aug. 1977); m. Eve Catherine Murphy, Sept. 6, 1986 (div. 1996); 1 child, Claire Hart Reid; m. Vera Anderson Reid, 1999. BA in Psychology, U. Tex., 1972, JD, 1975; MBA, U. Pa., 1977. Bar: Tex. 1975. V.p. Dillon, Read & Co., Inc., N.Y.C., 1977-82; mng. dir. Drexel Burnham Lambert Inc., 1982-87; co-dir. mergers and acquisitions Paine Webber Group, 1987-89; ptnr. Gordon Investment Inc., 1989-93; pres. Beacon Advisors, Inc., Dallas, 1993-99. Bd. dirs. Windmill Holdings; pres. Partnership Svcs., 1992-93; chmn. Cedco Sys., Inc., 1997—, Amtex Holdings, Inc., 1996—, Garland Broadcast Investors, Inc., 1997—, Poges SA, 2002-. Trustee, treas. Animal Med. Ctr., N.Y.C., 1981—; trustee St. Mark's Sch. of Tex., 2002-. Mem. Tex. Bar Assn. Home: 4109 Windsor Pkwy Dallas TX 75205-1670 Office: Arcady Capital Inc Ste 330 100 Highland Park Village Dallas TX 75205-2726

REID, LISA RAE, program director; b. New Castle, Ind., Aug. 15, 1962; d. Ray and Sarah Catherine (Russ) Caudill; m. James Kenneth Reid; 1 child, Jeremy Kenneth. BS, Troy State U., 1985, MS in Counseling and Human Devel., 1995. Cert. tchr. Tchr. Socastee Middle Sch., Myrtle Beach, S.C., 1985-87; daycare dir. Ea. Hills Bapt. Ch., Montgomery, Ala., 1987; edn. supr. Coun. on Substance Abuse, 1988-92; program dir. info. and referral ministry Perry Hill United Meth. Ch., 1992—. Youth dirs. coord. Montgomery (Ala.) United Meth. Dist., 1993—, young adult coord., 1994—, dist. presenter, 1995. Creator, editor The Beacon. Sec. Mental Health Assn., Montgomery, 1993-95, operation Santa Claus chairperson, 1993-95. Mem. ACA, Ala. Counseling Assn., Am. Christian Counseling Assn., Assn. Marriage and Family Counselors. Republican. Avocations: writing, cooking. Office: Perry Hill United Meth Ch 910 Perry Hill Rd Montgomery AL 36109-4520

REID, LORENE FRANCES, middle school educator; b. St. Louis, May 28, 1946; d. Frank Bernard and Marcella Marie (Froechtenigt) Niemeyer; m. Patrick Joseph Reid, Aug. 11, 1967; 1 child, Christina Marie. BA in Spanish, Maryville U., 1968; MED in Secondary Edn., U. Mo., St. Louis, 1990; PhD in Edn., St. Louis U., 1995; MA in English, Southeast Mo. State U., 1996. Cert. Spanish, social studies, ESL tchr., reading specialist K-12, Mo.; cert. early adolescence/English lang. arts Nat. Bd. for Profl. Tchg. Stds. Spanish tchr. Rosary H.S., Spanish Lake, Mo., 1968-69, Taylor Sch., Clayton, 1969-70, Roosevelt H.S., St. Louis, 1988-89, Cleve. Jr. Naval Acad., St. Louis, 1989-90, Thomas Dunn Meml. Adult Edn., St. Louis, 1992-95; social studies tchr. St. Luke's Sch., Richmond Heights, Mo., 1981-88; ESL tchr. Grant Mid. Sch., St. Louis, 1990-92, Fanning Mid. Sch., St. Louis, 1992-98; tchr. leader Mid. Sch. Initiative, 1998-99; Schs. for Thought coord. MEGA Magnet Cluster, St. Louis, 1999-2000; psychol. examiner Student Support Svcs.—Gifted and Talented, 2000—. Tutor Sylvan Learning Ctr., Crestwood, Mo., 1990-92; mem. St. Louis Edn. Leadership Inst., 1994-97. Mem. Cmty. Leadership Program for Tchrs., St. Louis, 1993-94. Recipient Emerson Electric Excellence in Teaching award, 1994; named Tchr. of Yr., St. Louis Pub. Schs., 1994-95; named as one of 60 tchrs. recognized by Disney Channel Salutes the Am. Tchr., 1995-96. Mem. ASCD, Tchrs. English to Spkrs. of Other Langs., Nat. Coun. Tchrs. English, Midam. Tchs. English to Spkrs. of Other Langs., Internat. Reading Assn., Nat. Assn. Sch. Psychologists, Phi Delta Kappa. Home: 4400 Lindell Blvd Apt 9A Saint Louis MO 63108-2418 E-mail: lorenereid@aol.com.

REID, LYNNE MCARTHUR, pathologist; b. Melbourne, Australia, Nov. 12, 1923; d. Robert Muir and Violet Annie (McArthur) R. MD, U. Melbourne, 1946; MA (hon.), Harvard U., 1976. Reader in exptl. pathology London U., 1964-67, prof. exptl. pathology, 1967-76; dean Cardiothoracic Inst., 1973-76; pathologist-in-chief Children's Hosp., Boston, 1976-89, pathologist-in-chief emeritus, 1990—; S. Burt Wolbach Disting. prof. pathology Harvard Med. Sch., 2001—. Fellow Royal Coll. Physicians (U.K.), Royal Australian Coll. Physicians, Royal Coll. Pathologists, Royal Coll. Radiologists (hon.), Royal Soc. Medicine, Royal Inst. Gt. Britain, Pathol. Soc. Gt. Britain and Ireland, Thoracic Soc., Assn. Clin. Pathologists, Brit. Thoracic Soc., Fleischner Soc., Can. Thoracic Soc., Neonatal Soc., Am. Thoracic Soc., Am. Soc. Pathologists, Fedn. Am. Socs. Exptl. Biology. Office: 300 Longwood Ave Boston MA 02115-5724

REID, MARGARET KATHLEEN, literature educator; b. Syracuse, N.Y., Dec. 23, 1963; d. James Dolan and Anne (Donohue) R. AB cum laude, Holy Cross Coll., 1986; AM in English and Am. Lit., Harvard U., 1988, PhD in English and Am. Lit., 1996. Harper postdoctoral fellow in humanities U. Chgo., 1995-97; asst. prof. English Marquette U., 1997—. Dissertation grantee Mellon Found., 1992. Mem. MLA, Am. Studies Assn. Office: Marquette U Dept English Coughlin Hall PO Box 1881 Milwaukee WI 53201-1881

REID, MARILYN JOANNE, state legislator, lawyer; b. Chgo., Aug. 14, 1941; d. Kermit and Newell Azile (Hahn) N.; m. M. David Reid, Nov. 26, 1966 (div. Mar. 1983); children: David, Nelson. Student, Miami U., Oxford, Ohio, 1959-61; BA, U. Ill, 1963; JD, Ohio No. U., 1966. Bar: Ohio 1966, Ark. 1967, U.S. Dist. Ct. 1967. Trust adminstr. First Nat. Bank, Dayton, Ohio, 1966-67; assoc. Sloan & Ragsdale, Little Rock, 1967-69; ptnr. Reid and Reid, Dayton, 1969-76, Reid & Buckwalter, Dayton, 1975—; mem. Ohio Ho. of Reps., 1993-98. Mem. health ins. and HMO's com., chmn. ins. com., vets. com., pub. utilities com. Mem. Ohio adv. bd. U.S. Commn. Civil Rights; chmn., treas. various polit. campaigns, 1975—; trustee Friends Libr. Beavercreek (Ohio); bd. dirs. Beavercreek YMCA, 1985-88; active Mt. Zion United Ch. of Christ; chmn. Greene County Rep. Party. Mem. ABA, Ohio Bar Assn., Greene County Bar Assn., Beavercreek C. of C. (pres. 1986-87), Dayton Panhellenic Assn. (pres. 1982), Altrusa (v.p. Greene County 1978-79, pres. 1979-80), Lions (pres. Beavercreek 1975), Greene County Rep. Party (chmn.), Rotary, Kappa Beta Pi, Gamma Phi Beta (v.p. 1974-75). Mem. Ch. Christ. Avocations: tennis, skiing, boating, bridge. Office: Reid & Buckwalter 3866 Indian Ripple Rd Dayton OH 45440-3448

REID, MARY WALLACE, retired secondary education educator; b. Charlotte, N.C., Oct. 21, 1922; d. Isaac and Mamie Maude (Torrence) Wallace; m. James Samuel Reid, Feb. 13, 1946; 1 child, Virginia Anne. BA, Johnson C. Smith U., 1945; MEd, Temple U., 1970, Secondary Adminstrn. cert., 1982, EdD, 1983. Cert. English, secondary adminstr., French, reading, lang. arts tchr., Pa. Tchr. English, lang. arts, reading Sch. Dist. Phila.; ret., 1988. Title I reading coord., 1976-82; mem. pupil progress com.; past assn. student govt., mem. PFT Bldg. com. Mem. Internat. Reading Assn., Nat. Coun. Tchrs. of English. Home: 1704 Stenton Ave Philadelphia PA 19141-1433

REID, MICHELLE MARIE BRADY, government official; b. Manhasset, N.Y., May 1, 1973; d. James William and Mary Elizabeth (Hogue) B.; married Stephen Norman Reid, Aug. 14, 1999. BBA, Hofstra U., 1995. From customer svc. rep. to credits & adjustments supervisor Decorators Walk, Plainview, N.Y., 1988-96; benefit authorizer SSA, Jamaica, 1996-99, social ins. specialist, 1999—. Mem. NAFE, Golden Key. Avocations: sports, music, reading. Office: Social Security Adminstrn 1 Jamaica Center Plz Ste 1 Jamaica NY 11432-3898 Home: 143 Broadway Bethpage NY 11714-4922 E-mail: michelle814@aol.com.

REID, NANCI GLICK, health care professional; b. Brookline, Mass., Sept. 22, 1941; d. Robert Louis and Esther (Shostack) Green; m. Ronald Jay Coleman, July 5, 1962 (div. Sept. 1969); 1 child, Lori Sue; m. Alan Marshall Glick, Jan. 12, 1976 (div. Oct. 1978); 1 child, Staci Alison; m. Raymond Augustus Reid, Feb. 15, 1985. AS, Garland Jr. Coll., Boston, 1960; student, Harvard U. Extension, 1961, 64, 65; BS, Northeastern U., 1983, postgrad., 1989—, Ecole Superieure de Commerce, Reims, France, 1990-91; MBA, Northeastern U., 1991. Cert. clin. lab. sci., clin. lab. specialist in cytogenetics. Rsch. technician Children's Hosp., Boston, 1961-63; sr. rsch. technician, med. technician New England Med. Ctr., 1963-65, 67-69; cytogeneticist supr. Carney Hosp., 1969-84; instr. medicine Med. Sch. Tufts U., 1969-86; systems analyst Cognos/Coulter Corp., Waltham, Mass., 1976-77; med. technologist Milton (Mass.) Hosp, 1978-83, Mass. Eye and Ear, Boston, 1983-84; lab. mgr. Harvard Cmty. Health Plan, Braintree, Mass., 1985-88, chairperson com. continuing edn. Boston, 1986-88; quality control mgr. Oncolab Inc., 1988-90; supr. Park Med. Lab., Inc., 1990-91; clin. lab. adminstrn. Dept. Health and Hosp. Mattapan, Boston, 1991-93; labo. coord. New England regional newborn screening program State Lab. Inst., Jamaica Plain, Mass., 1993-95. Presenter in field. Contbr. articles to profl. jours. Vol. human body discovery space program Mus. Sci., 1990; adv. bd. trustees Jordan Hosp., 1993—. Mem. Assn. Cytogenetic Technologists (pres. 1976-78), Am. Soc. Med. Tech. (lectr.), Mass. Ski Club (supr. 1989-99), Plymouth Yacht Club, Pythian Sisters Club (sec., editor 1966-67), Sigma Epsilon Rho (pres. 1994-96, v.p. 1987-88, former treas.). Republican. Jewish. Avocations: sailing, lobstering, game fishing, growing cranberries, photography. Home: 10 Woodbine Dr Plymouth MA 02360-3525 E-mail: cranberrycottage@adelphia.net.

REID, ORIEN, medical association administrator; BA, Clark Coll., Atlanta. MSW. Chmn., bd. dirs. Alzheimer's Assn.'s Nat. Bd. Dirs., 2002—; broadcast journalist Phila. Former mem. bd. govs. Nat. Acad. Television Arts and Scis.; former pres. Phila. Consumer Coun. Recipient Best Investigative Reporting, Phila. Press Assn., Excellence in Journalism award, Inst. Food Technologists. Office: Alzheimers Assn 919 N Michigan Ave Ste 1100 Chicago IL 60611-1676*

REID, ROBERT LELON, retired mechanical engineering educator, dean; b. Detroit, May 20, 1942; s. Lelon Reid and Verna Beulah (Custer) Menkes; m. Judy Elaine Nestell, July 21, 1962; children: Robert James, Bonnie Kay, Matthew Lelon. ASE, Mott C.C., Flint, Mich., 1961; BChemE, U. Mich., 1963; MME, So. Meth. U., 1966, PhDME, 1969. Registered profl. engr., Tenn., Tex., Wis. Asst. rsch. engr. Atlantic Richfield Co., Dallas, 1964-65; assoc. staff engr. Linde Div., Union Carbide Corp., Tonawanda, N.Y., 1966-68; from asst. to assoc. prof. U. Tenn., Knoxville, 1969-75; assoc. prof. Cleve. State U., 1975-77; from assoc. to full prof. U. Tenn., Knoxville, 1977-82; prof., chmn. U. Tex., El Paso, 1982-87; dean Coll. Engring., Marquette U., Milw., 1987-98, prof. mech. engring., 1998-2001; dean emeritus, 2001. Summer prof. NASA Marshall Space Ctr., Huntsville, Ala., 1970, EXXON Prodn. Rsch., Houston, 1972, 73, NASA Lewis Space Ctr., Cleve., 1986; cons. Oak Ridge Nat. Lab., 1974-75, TVA, 1978, 79, State of Calif., Sacramento, 1985, Tex. Higher Edn. Coordinating Bd., Austin, 1987. Contbr. articles 100 articles on heat transfer and solar energy. Grantee NSF, DOE, TVA, NASA, DOI, 1976-87; named Engr. of Yr. Engring. Socs. El Paso, 1986. Fellow ASME (Centennial medallion 1980, chmn. cryogenics com. 1977-81, chmn. solar energy divsn. 1983-84, chmn. Rio Grande sect. 1985-87, John Yellott award, 1997, Dedicated Svc. award 1998); mem. ASHRAE, Engrs. and Scientists Milw. (bd. dirs. 1988-93, v.p. 1989-90, pres. 1991-92), Wis. Assn. Rsch. Mgmt. (pres. 1996-97). Lutheran. Avocations: travel, classic car restoration.

REID, ROBERT ALFRED, physician; b. Milan, Italy, June 8, 1939; BA in English Lit., U. Colo., 1961, MD, 1965. Intern U. Colo. Med. Ctr., 1965-66, resident, 1968-71; dir. med. affairs Santa Barbara (Calif.) Cottage Hosp., 1992—. Mem. AMA, Am. Coll. Ob-gyn., Calif. Med. Assn. (pres. 1998). Office: Cottage Health Sys PO Box 689 Pueblo at Bath St Santa Barbara CA 93102 E-mail: rreid@sbch.org.

REID, ROBERT C. lawyer; b. Ft. Pierce, Fla., Apr. 4, 1951; s. George H. and Caroline (Paul) R.; m. Marian M. Reid, May 19, 1979; stepchildren: Jessica, Matthew, Adam Morgan. BA, Memphis State U., 1973, JD, 1976; LLM in Taxation, U. Fla., 1985. Bar: Tenn. 1976, Fla. 1989. State coordinator Tenn. Assn. Legal Svcs. and Legal Aid Projects, Nashville, 1976-77; sole practice, 1977-84; tax counsel, v.p., asst. corp. counsel Corroon & Black Benefits, Inc., 1977-84; tax atty. Baker, Worthington, Crossley, Stansberry & Woolf, 1985-89; mem. Bryant, Miller and Olive, Tallahassee, 1989—. Contbr. articles to law jours. Bd. dirs. Coordinating Counsel for Community Concerns, Nashville, 1979, pres., 1980. Mem. Fla. Bar Assn., Nat. Assn. Bond Lawyers. Democrat. Avocations: photography, scuba diving. Office: Bryant Miller and Olive 201 S Monroe St Ste 500 Tallahassee FL 32301-1879 E-mail: bobreid@bmolaw.com.

REID, ROBERT CLARK, chemical engineering educator; b. Denver, June 11, 1924; s. Frank B. and Florence (Seerley) R.; m. Anna Marie Murphy, Aug. 26, 1950; children: Donald M., Ann Christine. Student, Colo. Sch. Mines, 1946-48; BS, Purdue U., 1950, MS, 1951; ScD, MIT, 1954. Prof. chem. engring. MIT, Cambridge, from 1954, now prof. emeritus chem. engring.; Olaf A. Hougen prof. chem. engring. U. Wis., 1980-81. Author: (with J.M. Prausnitz and B.E. Poling) Properties of Gases and Liquids, 1966, 4th edit., 1987, (with M. Ohara) Modeling Crystal Growth Rates from Solution, 1973, (with M. Modell) Thermodynamics and Its Applications, 1974, 2d edit., 1983; Contbr. articles to profl. jours. Recipient Warren K. Lewis award, 1976; Chem. Engring. award Am. Soc. Engring. Edn., 1977; research fellow Harvard U., 1963-64 Mem. Am. Inst. Chem. Engrs. (Ann. lectr. 1967, council 1969-71, editor jour. 1970-76, Founders award 1986), Nat. Acad. Engring., Blue Key, Sigma Alpha Epsilon, Tau Beta Pi. Home: 22 Burroughs Rd Lexington MA 02420-1908 Office: MIT 66-409 Cambridge MA 02139

REID, ROBERT H. engineering consultant; b. Pitts., Oct. 8, 1960; s. Clarence George and Mary Kathryn (Haines) R.; m. Paula Ann Groetzinger, May 21, 1988; children: Timothy, Ashley. BS, U. Pitts., 1983; MS, Ill. Inst. Tech., 1985; PhD, Carnegie Mellon U., 2002. Cert. profl. engrs. Engr. Sargent & Lundy Engrs., Chgo., 1983-85, Baker Engrs., Beaver, Pa., 1985-90; mgr. Sen. Engring., Pitts., 1990-92; owner, cons. Robert H. Reid P.E., 1989—. Pres. RHR Cons. Engrs.; adj. prof., Carnegie Mellon U., 2001—. Bd. dirs. Deer Valley YMCA Camp, Fort Hill, Pa., 1990—, treas., 1995-96, chmn. bd. dirs., 1997-98. Engring. Alumni Assn. fellow, 1983. Mem. Am. Soc. Civil Engrs., Tau Beta Pi, Chi Epsilon (editor 1982-83). Republican. Home: 10524 Meinert Rd Wexford PA 15090-9564 Office: 10524 Meinert Rd Wexford PA 15090-9564 Fax: 724-940-2341.

REID, ROBERT JOHN, architect; b. La Jolla, Calif., Oct. 24, 1947; s. Robert Osborne and Marjorie Ada (Ferry) R.; m. Pamela Ann Theberge, July 31, 1971 (div. 1996); children: Kimberlee Erin, Wesley George; m. Christina Margaret Erickson, Dec. 7, 1996; 1 child, Katherine Frances. BArch, U. Tex., 1975. Registered arch., Tex., Ind., Ariz.; registered interior designer, Tex. Designer Fluor Engring., Houston, 1975-77; sr. project mgr. MRW Archs., 1977-81; project arch. Sikes Jennings Kelly, 1981-84; assoc. PBR Archs., 1984; v.p. Hellmuth, Obata & Kassabaum, 1985—. Author pamphlet. Spkr. Office of Mayor-Econ. Redevel., Houston, 1982, IFMA Conf., Austin, Tex., 1999. Served with USN, 1966-71. Mem. AIA, Tex. Soc. Archs. Home: 914 Oakland Ct Sugar Land TX 77478-2674 Office: Hellmuth Obata & Kassabaum 2800 Post Oak Blvd Ste 3700 Houston TX 77056-6119 E-mail: robert.reid@hok.com.

REID, ROBERT OSBORNE, oceanographer; b. Milford, Conn., Aug. 24, 1921; married, 1947; 6 children. BE, U. So. Calif., 1946; MS, U. Calif., 1948; DSc, Old Dominion U., 1988. Asst. Scripps Inst. U. Calif., 1946-47, oceanographer Scripps Inst., 1948-51; asst. prof. to assoc. prof. oceanography & meteorology Tex. A&M U., College Station, 1951-59, emeritus disting. prof. oceanography, 1987—. Cons. U.S. Army Corps Engrs., 1965-78, Hydraulic Divsn., Waterways Exptl. Sta., Vicksburg, Va., 1975—; mem. ad hoc panel Computing Resources & Facilities Ocean Circulation Modeling, Nat Acad. Sci., 1979-80, com. Coastal Flooding, 1980-84, U.S. Nat. Com. Internat. Union Geodynamics & Geophys., 1980-84, Storm Surge Program Rev. Bd., NOAA, 1981-83, subcom. Nat. Marine Bd., Nat. Acad. Sci., 1986-88, Coastal Engring. Rsch. Bd., U.S. Army Corps Engrs., 1988-92. Assoc. editor Jour. Geophys. Rsch., 1961-73, Jour Marine Rsch., 1961-73, 83-85; contbr. numerous articles to profl. tech. publs. Fellow Am. Meteorol. Soc. (editor-in-chief Jour. Phys. Oceanography 1970-80, Spl. award 1975), Am. Geophys. Union; mem. NAE (elected), Internat. Assn. Hydraulic Rsch., Sigma Xi. Office: Tex A&M U Dept Oceanography College Station TX 77843-0001

REID, RORY, former political organization administrator; b. Alexandria, Va., 1963; BA Internat. Rels., Spanish; JD, Brigham Young U. Sr. v.p., gen. counsel Lady Luck Gaming Corp., Nev.; state chmn. Nev. Dem. Party, 1999—; ptnr. Lionel Sawyer & Collins, 2002—. Mem. Dem. Nat. Com. 1999—; nominee Clark County Commr. Address: 1700 Bank Am Plz 300 S Fourth St Las Vegas NV 89101 Office: Nev Dem Party 1785 E Sahara Ave Ste 496 Las Vegas NV 89104-3712 also: 3790 Paradise Rd Ste 130 Las Vegas NV 89109-4648*

REID, ROSEMARY ANNE, insurance agent; b. Portland, Maine, June 15, 1951; d. Kenneth Bruce and Mary (Hollywood) R.; m. Ronald E. Walls, May 7, 1977 (div. Mar. 1986); children: Rachel A., Tate A. BS in Edn., U. South Maine, Portland, 1973. V.p. ins. Gruntal and Co., Inc., Portland, 1987-91; pvt. practice, 1973—. Mem. Cape Elizabeth Town Coun., 1990, 95-99; mem. Cape Elizabeth Sch. Bd., 1991-94, fin. chair, 1992-93. Recipient 10 Yrs. Nat. Quality, 10 Yrs. Nat. Sale Achievement award, 1979-89, Nat. Assn. of Life Underwriters, 1974—, Am. Hometown Leadership award WalMart, 1998. Mem. Million Dollar Round Table (life and qualifying mem., Top of Table 1984, 86), South Maine Assn. Life Underwriters (bd. dirs. 1985-91, officer 1987-91, pres. 1989-90, regional v.p., pub. svc. chair, others), Life Underwriter Tng. Coun. (chair 1986-87), Maine Assn. Life Underwriters (bd. dirs. 1988-92, v.p. 1991-92, pres. elect 1992). Roman Catholic. Avocations: skiing, swimming, biking. Office: PO Box 927 Portland ME 04104-0927

REID, SHARON LEA, educational facilitator; b. Wheeler, Tex., Apr. 24, 1949; d. George S. and Arvazine (Deering) Robinson; m. Thomas Michael Reid, July 9, 1989. BS, McMurry Coll., 1970; MEd, Tarleton State U., 1979. Cert. tchr., edn. adminstr., supr., Tex. Tchr. Fleming Elem. Sch., San Antonio, 1971-72, Peebles Elem. Sch., Killeen, 1972-84, Sugar Loaf Elem. Sch., Killeen, 1984-85, facilitator, 1985-98, campus instructional specialist Tex., 1998-99, Duncan Elem. Sch., Fort Hood, 1999—; emotional intelligence trainer Killeen ISD, 1999—. Trainer/dist. Marilyn Burns Problem Solving, Killeen, 1982-85, trainer/campus 4 MAT Lesson Design/Excel, Inc., Killeen, 1994-2000. Mem. Heights Concert Band, Harker Heights, Tex. Recipient music scholarship McMurry Coll., Abilene, Tex., 1968. Mem. ASCD, Nat. Read Across Am. Com., Tex. Elem. Prins. and Suprs. Assn., Tex. State Tchrs. Assn., Internat. Reading Assn., Tex. State Reading Assn., Bell County Reading Assn., Phi Delta Kappa. Avocations: instrumental music, bowling, sewing, cross-stitch. Office: Duncan Elem Sch 52400 Muskogee Dr Fort Hood TX 76544-1099

REID, S.W. English educator; b. Neptune, N.J., Nov. 24, 1943; s. Sidney Webb and Mary Cook (Bennett) R.; m. Judith Wright, Aug. 22, 1969; 1 child, Laura. BA, Duke U., 1965; MA, U. Va., 1966, PhD, 1972. Grad. tchg. fellow U. Va., Charlottesville, 1968-70; asst. prof. English, Kent (Ohio) State U., 1970-75, assoc. prof., 1975-84, prof., 1984—, dir. Inst. Bibliography and Editing, 1985—. Vis. fellow Clare Hall, Cambridge (Eng.) U., 1992-93, life mem., 1993—. Textual editor Bicentennial Edition of Charles Brockden Brown, 6 vols., 1977-87; editor-in-chief: (Cambridge edits. of Joseph Conrad) The Secret Agent, 1990, Almayer's Folly, 1994. NDEA fellow U. Va., 1965-68; Rsch. grantee NEH, 1977-84. Office: Kent State University Inst Bibliography-Editing 1118 Library Kent OH 44242-0001

REID, TED W. (TED WARREN REID), ophthalmology educator; b. Cayuga, Ind., Sept. 26, 1939; s. Edward W. and Ruth Ida Reid; m. nancy Charlene Greve, Jan. 27, 1961; children: Wayne, Wendy. BA, Occidental Coll., 1961; MS, U. Ariz., 1963; PhD, UCLA, 1967. Assoc. prof. Yale U. Sch. Medicine, New Haven, 1970-84; prof. U. Calif., Davis, 1984-90, Tex. Tech U. Health Scis. Ctr., Lubbock, 1990—; chmn. Selenium Techs. Inc., 1995—. Bd. dirs. Entrepreneurial Family Bus. Inst., Western Eye Rsch. Conf. Guest mem. editl. bd. Investigative Opthamology and Visual Sci., 1997—. Jules Stein Professorship Yale U., 1975. Mem. Assn. Rsch. Vision and Ophthalmology (program planner 1990-93). Avocation: barber shop quartet singing. Office: Tex Tech U Health Scis Ctr 4th St Lubbock TX 79430-0001 Fax: 806-743-2471.

REID, WILLIAM JAMES, social work educator; b. Detroit, Nov. 14, 1928; s. James Macknight and Sophie Amelia (Schneider) R.; m. Anne E. Fortune, May 22, 1988; children by previous marriage: Valerie, Steven. BA, U. Mich., 1950, MSW, 1952; DSW, Columbia U., 1963. Caseworker-in-charge Family Service of Westchester, Mt. Kisco, N.Y., 1956-59; asst. prof. social work U. Chgo., 1962-65, prof., 1968-75, George Herbert Jones prof., 1975-80; prof. Sch. Social Welfare, SUNY, Albany, 1980-98, disting. prof., 1998—. Dir. Center for Social Casework Rsch., Cmty. Svc. Soc., N.Y.C., 1965-68. Author: Brief and Extended Casework, 1969, Task-Centered Casework, 1972, Task-Centered Practice, 1977, The Task-Centered System, 1978, Models of Family Treatment, 1981, Research in Social Work, 1981, 3d edit., 1999, Family Problem Solving, 1985, The Role-Sharing Marriage, 1986, Advances in Clinical Social Work Research, 1990, Task Strategies, 1992, Qualitative Research in Social Work, 1994, Generalist Practice: A Task-Centered Approach, 1994, The Task Planner, 2000, Science and Social Work, 2001. With U.S. Army, 1952-56. Recipient excellence in rsch. award Nat. Assn. Social Workers, 1990, Disting. Svc. award Soc. for Social Work and Rsch. Mem. Phi Beta Kappa. Office: 135 Western Ave Albany NY 12203-1011 E-mail: wreid@albany.edu.

REID, WILLIAM JAMES, mining executive; b. Cowdenbeath, Scotland, Jan. 18, 1941; arrived in U.S., 1968; s. William and Sheila (Davidson) Reid; m. Thelma Rear, Sept. 27, 1969; children: Judith, Robert. Nat. cert. Mining Engring, Ashington County Tech. Coll., Northumberland, Eng., 1961. Student apprentice Brit. Coal, England, 1958-63; sales engr. Huwood Ltd., England, 1964-68; mining engr. Huwood-Irwin Co., Irwin, Pa., 1968-71, mgr. mining sales, 1971-74, gen. sales mgr., 1974-77, v.p., 1977-79; internat. sales dir. Huwood Ltd., England, 1979-81; exec. v.p. Am. Longwall Mining Corp., Abingdon, Va., 1981-83, pres., 1983-95, Am. Longwall Face Conveyors Inc., Abingdon, 1993-95, Internat. Longwall Cons., Abingdon, 1996-98, Internat. Entertainment Assocs., 1996-98; v.p. mktg. Long Airdox Co., Blacksburg, Va., 1998-99; pres. Eimco LLC, Bluefield, W.Va., 1999-2001, Internat. Longwall Cons., Bluefield, 2001—. Apptd. to Nat. Coal Coun. by Sec. Energy, 1994—; dir. Va. Coal Coun., 1994—. Mng. editor: Coal Leader, 2001—. Trustee Sullins Acad., Bristol, Va., 1984. Recipient Overseas medal, Brit. Instn. Mining Engrs., 1992. Mem.: AIME (treas. 1978), Nat. Mining Assn. (bd. govs. mfrs. divsn. 1991—96, 1999—2001), N. Eng. Inst. Mining and Mech. Engrs. (assoc.), Greater Irwin Area C. of C. (bd. dirs. 1977). Presbyterian. Avocations: travel, tennis, wine tasting. Home: 9 Yorkshire Middlebrook Bristol TN 37620-2953 Office: Internat Longwall Cons 106 Tamarack St Bluefield WV 24701-4573 E-mail: billreid@netscope.net.

REID, WILLIE HENRY, engineering executive; b. Cordele, Ga., Oct. 15, 1950; s. Sim and Mattie Rawls Reid; m. Myrtice Berry Reid, Dec. 31, 1981 (div. Feb. 1993); m. Velma Ray Reid. AA in Engring. Tech., CC of Air Force, 1982; BS in Bus. Mgmt., U. Md., 1981. Engring. asst. Contract Mgmt., Kunsan Air Base, Republic of Korea, 1984—85, HQSAC Comm. Planning, Offott AFB, Nebr., 1985—89; chief quality assurance evaluation Engring. Contact Mgmt., Ankara Air Sta., Turkey, 1989—92; engr. tech. support Wright Labs., Wright-Patterson AFB, Ohio, 1992—93; substitute tchr. Dougherty County Schs., Albany, Ga., 1994; contract mgr. Albany Housing Authority, 1994—97; projects supr. dept. engring. City of Albany, 1997—. Total quality mgmt. rep. Wright Labs., Dayton, 1991—92; mem. diversity com. Albany Housing Authority, 1995—97. Mem. Friday father's mentoring program Magnolia Elem. Sch., Albany, 2000—01; active Dougherty 2000 Dougherty County Schs., 1998—99; mem. YMCA, 1994—2001. Master sgt. USAF. Mem.: ASPA (ASU chpt., del. to Thailand and Vietnam People to People Amb. program 2001), Am. Mil. Engrs., Nat. Mgmt. Assn., Miami Valley Literacy Coun. (EASL instr. Vietnam), Indian Creek Residential Assn. (treas. 2001), Air Force Sgts. Assn. (life). Democrat. Baptist. Avocations: tennis, racquetball, table tennis, motorcycling, minor home remodeling projects. Home: 645 Longbow Dr Albany GA 31707-8976 Office: City of Albany Engring Dept 1900 N Monroe St Albany GA 31702

REID, WILMA KATHLEEN, direct marketing agency owner; b. Victory, N.Y., Aug. 24, 1940; d. Sewell Webster and Loretto Margaret (Maroney) R. AB, LeMoyne Coll., 1962; MA, Catholic U., 1964. Instr. Immaculata Coll. Women, Washington, 1963-64; fund raiser Nat. Coun. Catholic Men, 1965-68; promotion mgr. Herder & Herder Publ. Co., N.Y.C., 1968-70; circulation dir. Scholastic, Inc., 1970-83; owner Reid Resources, 1983—. Seminar speaker Direct Mktg. to Schs., N.Y., 1984, N.Y. Venture Group, N.Y., 1990. Recipient Copywriting award, DMA, 1998, Assn. Edn. Publs., 2001. Democrat. Avocation: photography. Office: Reid Resources 245 E 24th St New York NY 10010-3821 E-mail: wkreid@aol.com.

REIDA-ALLEN, PAMELA ANNE, healthcare consultant and administrator; b. Fitchburg, Mass., June 8, 1944; d. Alvah Michael Reida and Sirkka Margaret (Anttila) Kao; m. Dennis Alan Joaquin, 1967 (div. 1973); children: Joshua, Amy, Sebastian; m. Yahya Radazar, Oct. 1983 (dec. Sept. 1987); m. Loyall C. Allen. BA in English, Philosophy, Calif. State U., Los Angeles, 1966; RN diploma with honors, Leominster (Mass.) Hosp., 1976; BS in Nursing cum laude, Fitchburg (Mass.) State Coll., 1982; MS magna cum laude, Lesley Coll., 1986. Substitute tchr. Fitchburg Pub. Schs., 1966-67; social worker N.Y.C. Dept. Social Services, N.Y.C., 1967-68; news correspondent The Lowell (Mass.) Sun, 1969-71; nurse lab., delivery Leominster Hosp., 1976—77; inservice coordinator Birchwood Manor Nursing Home, Fitchburg, 1977, asst. dir. nursing, 1977-78, dir. nursing, 1978-80, Naukeag Hosp., Ashburnham, Mass., 1980-84; asst. dir. nursing Beech Hill Hosp., Dublin, 1984-87, dir nursing, 1987-90, chair utilization rev. com., 1985-95; clin. coord. Hospice of Cape Cod, Yarmouthport, Mass., 1995—. Mem. adv. council allied health majors Mass. Regional Vocat. Sch., Fitchburg, Mass., 1977-84; with Area Speakers Bur., Fitchburg, 1980-84, vice chair Quality Assurance Program, 1988; cons. Quality Healthcare Resources, Inc. subs. Joint Commn. on Accreditation of Hosps., 1988—, Joint Commn. on Accreditation of Healthcare Orgns., Chgo., 1988-95. Vol. Family Planning, Fitchburg, 1981-82; del. Intercity Mgmt. Council, Fitchburg, 1980-84; clin. coord. Hospice Cape Cod, 1995—. Mem. NAFE, Tri-City Nursing Home Assn. (pres. 1978-80), Nat. Nurses Assn., N.H. Nurses Assn. (program com. 1985—), Greater Fitchburg C. of C., N.H. Orgn. Exec. Nurses, N.H. Quality Assurance Assn. Avocations: reading, writing, gardening, knitting, swimming. Office: Hospice of Cape Cod 962 Route 6A Yarmouth Port MA 02675-2125

REIDENBACH, FAITH E. medical educator, writer; b. Columbus, Ohio, May 10, 1960; d. William J. and Joann Raudebaugh Reidenbach; life ptnr. Beverly A. Caley, 1986. BA, Ohio State U., 1980. Editor ASM Internat., Cleveland, Ohio, 1983—86; writer & editor Anadem Pub., Columbus, 1984—92; from med. journalist to exec. med. editor Reuters Health News, N.Y.C., 1997—99, exec. med. editor, 1999—2001; pvt. practice Caley-Reidenbach Cons. LLP, Ashland, Ohio, 2001—. Contbr. articles to newsletters (Publ. Excellence award, 1996), book, ; pub.: internat. newsletter Women's Recovery Network, 1990— (Ruth Ellis Meml. award, 2000). Reading tutor Columbus Literacy Coun., Columbus, 1984—86; trustee, sec. of bd. Women's Outreach for Women, 1987—90, Women's Cmty. Found., Cleve., 1994—97; mem. adv. bd. Lesbian Health News, Columbus. Mem.: Nat. Assn. of Sci. Writers, Assn. of Health Care Journalists, Am. Med. Writers Assn., Phi Beta Kappa. Office: Caley-Reidenbach Consulting LLP PO Box 946 Ashland OH 44805 Office Fax: 419-207-1518. E-mail: faithreidenbach@aol.com.

REIDENBAUGH, LOWELL HENRY, retired sports editor; b. Lititz, Pa., Sept. 7, 1919; s. Harry Martin and Marian Marie (Nies) R.; m. Ruth Elizabeth Cameron, Nov. 23, 1944; children: Karen Lee (Mrs. William Rogers), Kathy Jean (Mrs. William J. Schuchman). AB, Elizabethtown (Pa.) Coll., 1941. Gen. reporter Lancaster (Pa.) Intelligencer Jour., 1941-42; sports writer Phila. Inquirer, 1944-47; mem. staff The Sporting News, St. Louis, 1947-89, mng. editor, 1962-79, sr. editor, 1980-83, corp. editor, 1983-89. Author: National League History, 1976, The Super Bowl Book, 1981, Cooperstown, Where Baseball's Legends Live, 1983, Take Me Out to the Ballpark, 1983, The Sporting News, First 100 Years, 1985, The 50 Greatest Games, 1986, History 33d Va. Infantry Regiment, CSA, 1987, 25 Greatest Pennant Races, 1987, 25 Greatest Teams, 1988, History 27th Va. Infantry Regiment, CSA, 1993, The Battle of Kernstown, 1997. Served with AUS, 1942-43.

REIDENBERG, JOEL R. law educator; AB in Govt., Dartmouth, 1983; JD, Columbia U., 1986; Diplôme d'études approfondies dr.int.eco., U. Paris-Sorbonne, 1987. Bar: N.Y. 1986, D.C. 1988. Friedmann fellow PROMETHEE, Paris, 1986-87; assoc. Debevoise & Plimpton, Washington, 1987-90; prof. law Fordham U. Sch. Law, N.Y.C., 1990—, dir. grad. program, 1998—2001. Cons. FTC, Washington, 1997-99; expert advisor European Commn., Luxembourg, 1993-96, Brussels, 1997-98. Co-author: Data Privacy Law, 1996, Online Services and Data Protection and Privacy: Regulatory Responses, 1998; contbr. articles to profl. jours. Mem. Assn. Am. Law Schs. (chair sect. law and computers 1997, chair sect. defamation and privacy 1998). Fax: 212-636-6899.

REIDENBERG, JUNE WILSON, editor; b. Phila. d. Mark and Anne Wilson. BA, U. Pa., 1958, MA, 1967. Internat. trade specialist, project mgr. divsn. internat. commerce Dept. Commerce State of N.Y., N.Y.C., 1984-85; mng. editor Clin. Pharmacology and Therapeutics, 1985—2001, dir. internat. med. librs. program, 1986—. Co-chair internat. workshop Improving Peer Rev., 2002; mem. instnl. rev. bd. Rockefeller U., 2002—. Author's editor: Renal Function and Drug Action, 1970; author: South of Siena, 2002; corr. editor East European Med. Jour., 1992-99; contbr. articles to profl. publs. Bd. dirs. Lower Merion (Pa.) Human Rels. Coun., 1968-74; mem. LWV, 1975—; lectr. civic orgns., 1970—. Recipient Elliot award for Distinguished Svc., Am. Soc. Clin. Pharmacology and Therapeutics, 1999, Recognition award, ASCAT, 2002, Outstanding Svc. award, 2002. Mem. Internat. Fedn. Sci. Editors (session chairperson 1993), Coun. Scis. Editors (editors coun. task force 2001—), Coun. Biology Editors (presenter workshop 1991, task force 1996, nominating com. 1997), Pi Sigma Alpha.

REIDENBERG, LOUIS MORTON, lawyer; b. Phila., Dec. 1, 1939; s. Bernard and Beatrice (Rauer) R.; children: Daniel J., Jeffrey B. BBA, U. Miami, Fla., 1961; JD, U. Minn., 1965. Bar: Minn. 1965. Law clk. Minn. Supreme Ct., St. Paul, 1965-66; assoc. Katz, Burstein & Galbraith, Mpls., 1966-70; ptnr. Burstein & Reidenberg, 1970-71; pvt. practice, 1971-78, 81-83; ptnr. Reidenberg & Eagon, 1978-81, Reidenberg & Jaycox, Bloomington, Minn., 1983-85, Reidenberg & Ormond, Mpls., 1985-87; pvt. practice, 1988-91; ptnr. Reidenberg & Arrigoni, 1991—. Lectr. Minn. Continuing Legal Edn., 1976, 75, 76, 77, 83, 86, Minn. Inst. Legal Edn., 1987. Mem. Am. Acad. Matrimonial Lawyers, Minn. State Bar Assn. (mem. family law com.), Hennepin County Bar Assn. (family law com. 1971-83). Office: Ste 160 1811 Weir Dr Saint Paul MN 55125-2291

REIDENBERG, MARCUS MILTON, physician, educator; b. Phila., Jan. 3, 1934; s. Leon and Adeline Reidenberg; m. June Wilson, July 14, 1957; children: Bruce, Joel, Julie. Student, Cornell U., 1951-54; MD, Temple U., 1958. Diplomate Am. Bd. Internal Medicine. Intern Community Gen. Hosp., Reading, Pa., 1958-59; resident Temple U. Hosp., Phila., 1962-65; from instr. to assoc. prof. Temple U. Med. Sch., 1962-75; assoc. prof. Cornell U. Med. Coll., N.Y.C., 1975-76, prof. pharmacology, head div. clin. pharmacology, 1976—, prof. medicine, 1980—, acting assoc. dean, 1981-82, asst. dean, 1998—; attending physician N.Y. Hosp., 1980—. Vis. physician Rockefeller U. Hosp., N.Y.C., 1980—; mem. project adv. group FDA, Rockville, Md., 1977-82; vice chmn. Joint Commn. on Prescription Drug Use, Washington, 1977-80; mem. study sect. NIH, Bethesda, Md., 1980-86; del. U.S. Pharmacopeal Conv., 1975-80. Author: Renal Function and Drug Action, 1971; editor various books; editor Clin. Pharmacology and Therapeutics, 1985-2001; contbr. articles to profl. jours. Served to lt. M.C., USNR, 1960-62. Recipient Research Career Devel. award NIH, 1970, Julius Sturmer award Phila. Coll. Pharmacy and Sci., 1982. Fellow ACP; mem. Am. Soc. Clin. Investigations, Assn. Am. Physicians, Am. Soc. Clin. Pharmacology and Therapeutics (pres. 1984-85, Rawls Palmer award 1981), Am. Soc. Pharmacology and Exptl. Therapeutics (award 1983, Harry Gold award 1999), Internat. Union Pharmacology (vice chmn. sect. clin. pharmacology 1984-87, chmn. 1987-89). Office: Cornell U Med Coll Dept Clin Pharmacology 1300 York Ave New York NY 10021-4805

REIDER, MARTHA CRAWFORD, industrial immunologist; b. Red Bank, N.J., Apr. 29, 1954; d. Harry Edward and Ernestine (Bird) Crawford; m. Michael John Reider, Sept. 22, 1979. BA in Biol. Scis., Ohio No. U., 1976; MS in Human Resources Devel., Kennedy-Western U., 1997, postgrad., 1997—. Product devel. scientist E.I. DuPont de Nemours and Co., Newark, 1976-82, supr. animal facility, 1982-84, rsch. immunologist, 1984-87, mfg. process scientist, 1987-89, quality assurance supr. testing and release, 1989-90; co-founder Strategic Diagnostics Inc., 1990—, v.p. human resources, quality assurance, 1990—; co-founder Strategic BioSolutions, 1991—, pres., 2000—01. Mem. product quality com., mem. customer focus group, human resources com.; facilitator for multiple pers. tng. programs. Contbr. articles to profl. conf. procs. Water safety and CPR/first aid trainer/instr. ARC, 1977—, bd. dirs. Del. br., Wilmington; instr. aquatics YMCA Del., Newark, 1988—. Mem.: ASTD, World at Work (cert. benefits prof.), Am. Mgmt. Assn., Soc. Human Resources Mgmt. (cert. sr. prof. human resources), Am. Soc. Quality (cert. quality auditor), Beta Beta Beta. Methodist. Avocations: Private pilot,American sign language, teaching swimming, CPR and first aid. Office: Strategic Diagnostics Inc 128 Sandy Dr Newark DE 19713-1147

REIDER, RICHARD GARY, geographer, educator; b. Denver, Feb. 7, 1941; s. Alexander and Natalie Alice (Frick) R. BA, Colo. State Coll., 1963, MA, 1965; PhD, U. Nebr., 1971. Instr. geography Indiana U. of Pa., 1965-66, U. Wyo., Laramie, 1969-71, asst. prof. geography, 1971-77, assoc. prof. geography, 1977-83, prof. geography, 1983—. Cons. Smithsonian Inst., Washington, 1975-77, Office Wyo. Archaeologist, Laramie, 1975—, dept. anthropology U. Wyo., Laramie, 1975—, various firms, Wyo., 1977—. Contbg. author: The

Agate Basin Site, 1982, The Horner Site, 1987; contbr. articles to profl. jours. NSF grantee, 1975-76, Smithsonian grantee, 1975-77, 79. Mem. Assn. Am. Geographers, Geol. Soc. Am., Am. Quaternary Assn., Plains Anthrop. Soc., Sigma Xi.

REIDINGER, RUSSELL FREDERICK, JR. fish and wildlife scientist; b. Reading, Pa., June 19, 1945; BS, Albright Coll., 1967; PhD in Zoology, U. Ariz., 1972. Asst. prof. biology Augustana Coll., 1971-74; rsch. physiologist The Philippines, 1974-78; asst. mem., wildlife biologist Monell Chem. Senses Ctr., 1978-86; dir. Denver Wildlife Rsch. Ctr. U.S. Dept. Agr., Denver, 1987-93; dir. Ctr. Excellence Wildlife Mgmt. Lincoln U., Jefferson City, Mo., 1993—. Vis. prof. dept. zoology U. Philippines, 1975-78; cons. Bangladesh Agr. Rsch. Coun., USAID, 1977, Ministry Agrl. Devel. & Agrarian Reform, Nicaragua, 1981, CID, Uganda, 1996. Mem. Am. Soc. Mammalogists, Wildlife Soc., Nat. Animal Damage Control Assn. Office: Lincoln U Dept Ag Nat & Home Econ Jefferson City MO 65102-0029

REID-MERRITT, PATRICIA ANN, social worker, educator, author, performing artist; b. Phila., Oct. 31, 1950; d. Curtis McDonald Reid and Etrulia Lucille Chapel; m. Ronald C. Bookhart, May 23, 1970 (div.); children: Christina, Brahim; m. William T. Merritt, Jul. 25, 1992; children: Jeffrey, Gregory. BA, Cabrini Coll., 1973; M in Social Work, Temple U., 1975; PhD in Social Work, U. Pa., 1984. Cert. in sch. social work, African-centered social work; cert. Dunham Technique. Psychiat. social worker Phila. Gen. Hosp., 1975-76; prof. Richard Stockton Coll., Pomona, N.J., 1976—. Founder, artistic dir. Afro-One Dance Drama and Drum Theatre, Inc. Recipient NAACP Freedom award, Outstanding Alumni Achievement award Cabrini Coll., Outstanding Alumni Achievement award Temple U. Mem. Nat. Assn. Black Social Workers (bd. dirs.), Nat. Coun. Black Studies (bd. dirs.), Assn. Black Women in Higher Edn., Coun. on Social Work Edn., Assn. Women in Social Work. Avocations: reading, dancing, gardening, cooking. Home: 2 Rosewood Ter Hamilton NJ 08620-9516 E-mail: patreidmer@aol.com.

REIDY, CAROLYN KROLL, publisher; b. Washington, May 2, 1949; d. Henry August and Mildred Josephine (Mencke) Kroll; m. Stephen Kroll Reidy, Dec. 28, 1974. BA, Middlebury Coll., 1971; MA, Ind. U., 1974, PhD, 1982. Various positions to mgr. subs. rights Random House, Inc., N.Y.C., 1975-83, assoc. pub., 1987-88; dir. subs. rights William Morrow & Co., 1983-85; v.p., assoc. pub. Vintage Books, 1985-87, pub., 1987-88, Anchor Books, Doubleday & Co., N.Y.C., 1988; pres., pub. Avon Books, 1988-92; pres., pub. trade div. Simon & Schuster, 1992—2001, pres. adult publ. divsn., 2001—. Bd. dirs. NAMES Project, 1994—98, Literacy Partners, Inc., 2000—, Nat. Book Found., 2001—. Mem. Women's Media Group, Pubs. Lunch Club. Office: Simon & Schuster 1230 Avenue Of The Americas Fl Concl New York NY 10020-1586 E-mail: carolyn.reidy@simonandschuster.com.

REIDY, DAVID A. philosophy educator; b. Chgo., Sept. 11, 1962; s. David Anthony and Cecelia Ann (Bernbrock) R.; m. Kathy Jean Saunders, July 7, 1990; children: Kiyoko Cecelia, Kame Benjamin. BA, DePauw U., Greencastle, Ind., 1984; JD, Ind. U., 1987; PhD, U. Kans., 1997. Bar: Ind. 1985. Atty. Berry Brown & Mills, Bloomington, Ind., 1988-90; lectr. law Ind. U., Bloomington and Indpls., 1987-90, vis. asst. prof. philosophy Indpls., 1997-2000; asst. prof. philosophy U. Tenn., Knoxville, 2000—. Contbr. articles to profl. jours. Mem. Bloomington Human Rights Commn., 1998-2000, chair, 2000; union organizer Kans. Assn. of Profl. Employees/Am. Fedn. Tchrs., Lawrence, 1991-96. Recipient James Wilbur prize Am. Soc. for Value Inquiry, 1995, Dean's Grad. Award in Western Civilization, U. Kans., 1996; U. Kans. dissertation fellow, 1995. Mem. Am. Philos. Assn., N.Am. Soc. for Social Philosophy, Am. Polit. Sci. Assn., Am. Soc. for Polit. and Legal Philosophy, Internat. Soc. for Social Philosophy and Philosophy of Law. Office: Univ of Tennessee Dept Philosophy 801 McClung Twr Knoxville TN 37996

REIDY, RICHARD ROBERT, publishing company executive; b. Patchogue, N.Y., May 9, 1947; s. Joseph Robert and Irene (Jennings) R.; m. Carolyn Alyce Armstrong, Mar. 21, 1970; children: Dawn Patricia, Shawn Patrick, Christopher Keith. Student, Suffolk County Community Coll., 1966-68, L.I. Tech. Sch., 1969-70, Scottsdale Community Coll., 1983-84, 85-86. Lic. real estate agt., Ariz. Restaurant owner Reidy's, Patchogue, 1973-77; design draftsman Sverdrop & Parcel, Tempe, Ariz., 1978-79, Sullivan & Masson, Phoenix, 1979-81; pres. Success Pub. Co., Scottsdale, 1983—90; with U.S. Postal Dept., 1980—; owner Success Properties LLC, 2000—. Editor, owner, pub.: Who's Who in Arizona, 1984-85, 89-90, Success Properties LLC, 2000-. Chief Scottsdale YMCA, 1983-84; eucharistic minister St. Daniel the Prophet Cath. Ch., Scottsdale, 1985—; mem. World Wide Marriage Encounter, 1986—; pres. Coronado High Sch. Band Boosters, 1988-89. Mem. Scottsdale C. of C., Phoenix Better Bus. Bur. Office: Success Pub Co PO Box 3431 Scottsdale AZ 85271-3431

REIDY, THOMAS ANTHONY, lawyer; b. Bronx, N.Y., Sept. 30, 1952; s. John Alexander and Elinor Ann (Tracey) R.; m. Victoria Mary Moxham, Mar. 12, 1977; children: J. Benjamin, Jacob T., Thomas A. II. BA with honors, Lehigh U., 1974; JD, U. Va., 1978. Bar: Ohio 1978, U.S. Dist. Ct. (so. dist.) Ohio 1980. Assoc. Moritz, McClure, Hughes, Kerscher & Price, Columbus, Ohio, 1978-80, Porter, Wright, Morris & Arthur, Columbus, 1980-87, ptnr., 1987-92; v.p. human resources and employment counsel The Longaberger Co., Dresden, Ohio, 1993-94, gen. counsel, 1994—. Mem.: Direct Selling Assn. (chmn. ethics and self-regulation com. 2001—). Office: Longaberger Co PO Box 3400 Newark OH 43058-3400

REIDY, THOMAS MICHAEL, financial executive; b. Elmira, N.Y., Dec. 22, 1951; s. Bernard Thomas and Betty Pauline Reidy; m. Rosemarie Stella, June 12, 1982; 1 child, Carla. AS, Corning C.C., 1971; BA, St. John Fisher Coll., 1973. Cert. fin. planner. Exec. br. dir. YMCA, Rochester, N.Y., 1975-84; fin. planner IDS/Am. Express, 1984-86; pres., CEO TMR Adv. Group, 1986-95; divsn. mgr. Waddall & Reed, 1995-98; pres. Morgan & Alexander Ltd., 1998—. Pres. CPA/Bus. Forum, Rochester, 1988-80. Author: (tng. manual) The NOW Client System, 1996, The True Wealth Revolution, 1999, Quality Life Management System, 1999. Recipient Outstanding Young Man Am. Jaycees, 1979. Mem. Rotary Club, C. of C. Profl. Sales Soc. (bd. dirs. 1988-89). Home: 24 Columbine Cir Fairport NY 14450-9362

REIF, DAVID (FRANK DAVID REIF), artist, educator; b. Cin., Dec. 14, 1941; s. Carl A. and Rachel L. (Clifton) R.; m. Ilona Jekabsons, July 30, 1966; 1 child, Megan Elizabeth. BFA, Art Inst. Chgo., 1968; MFA, Yale U., 1970. Asst. prof. art U. Wyo., Laramie, 1970-74, assoc. prof., 1974-81, prof., 1981—; assoc. prof. U. Mich., Ann Arbor, 1980-81; acting head dept. art U. Wyo., Laramie, 1986-87. Selection cons. Ucross Found. Residency Program, Wyo., 1983—; exhibit juror Artwest Nat., Jackson, Wyo., 1986; panelist Colo. State U., Ft. Collins, 1981; lectr. U. Mich., 1980; apptd. Wyo. Arts Coun., 1993-96; vis. artist lectr. Colo. State U., 1996; vis. artist Colo. State U., Ft. Collins, 1996; 3-D juror, art exhbn. Colo. State Fair, Pueblo, 2001. One-man shows include U. Wyo. Art Mus., 1993, Dorsky Galleries, N.Y.C., 1980, No. Ariz. U., 1977, 87, U. Mich., 1980, 81, One West Ctr. Contemporary Art, Ft. Collins, 1991, West Wyo. C.C., Rock Springs, 1999; exhibited in group shows at First, Second and Third Wyo. Biennial Tour, 1984-88, U.S. Olympics Art Exhbn., L.A., 1984, Miss. Mus. Art and NEA Tour, 1981-83, L.A. Invitational Sculpture Tour Exhbn., 1991-92, Nicolaysen Art Mus., Casper, Wyo., 1994. Apptd. chair Wyo. Arts Coun., 1995-96. With USAR, 1963-69. Recipient F.D. Pardee award Yale U., 1970; Best Sculpture award Joslyn Art Mus. Omaha, 1978; grantee Nat. Endowment Arts, 1978-79, Wyo. Basic Rsch., 1983-84, 86-87; Tchg. Excellence grantee U. Wyo., 1996-97. Mem. Coll. Art Assn., Internat. Sculpture Ctr. Democrat. Home: 3340 Aspen Ln Laramie WY 82070-5702 Office: U Wyo Dept Art PO Box 3138 Laramie WY 82071-3138

REIF, JOHN HENRY, computer science educator; b. Madison, Wis., Aug. 4, 1951; s. Arnold and Jane (Chess) R.; m. Jane Anderson; children: Katie, Emily. BS in Applied Math. and Computer Sci., Tufts U., 1973; MS in Applied Math., Harvard U., 1975, PhD in Applied Math., 1977. Rsch. asst. Harvard U., Cambridge, Mass., 1975-77; rsch. assoc. U. Rochester, N.Y., 1977-78, asst. prof. computer sci. dept., 1978-79, Harvard U., Cambridge, 1979-83, assoc. prof., 1983-86; prof. computer sci. dept. Duke U., Durham, N.C., 1986—; pres. RSIC, Inc., 1987—, Eagle Eye, Inc., 1998—. Cons. IBM Watson Rsch. Inst., Yorktown Heights, N.Y., 1983-84, Thinking Machines, Inc., Cambridge, Mass., 1985—, NASA Goddard Space Flight Ctr., Geenbelt, Md., 1985—, Microelectronics Ctr. N.C., Research Triangle, 1986-88. Editor: VLSI Algorithms and Architectures, 1986, Synthesis of Parallel Algorithms, 1993, Algorithm Derivation and Transformation, 1993; patentee in field. Fellow IEEE, Inst. of Combinatorics, Assn. for Computing Machinery; mem. Am. Math. Assn., Soc. for Indsl. and Applied Math. Office: Duke U Dept Computer Sci Box 90129 Durham NC 27708-0129

REIF, LOUIS RAYMOND, lawyer, utilities executive; b. Buffalo, July 4, 1923; s. John Dennis and Sadie (Wilkenson) R.; m. Nancy C. Heuer, Apr. 12, 1958; children: Tracey Lynn, Christopher Louis. Student, Mich. State U., 1941-42, The Citadel, 1943; AB, U. Buffalo, 1948; JD, U. Mich., 1951. Bar: N.Y. 1953. Pvt. practice, Chgo., 1951-52, Buffalo, 1953—; atty. Continental Ill. Nat. Bank, Chgo., 1951-52; from atty. to sr. v.p. Iroquois Gas Corp., Buffalo, 1952-71, pres., 1971—, also bd. dirs.; from v.p. to pres., CEO Nat. Fuel Gas Co., N.Y.C., 1960-87, chmn., CEO, 1988—; asst. to chmn. Del. North Cos., Buffalo, 1988, COO, 1989—, also bd. dirs., 1989. Chmn. Bio-Quest Inc., Houston, 1996; bd. dirs. Goldome Bank; chmn. N.Y. Gas Group, 1973—; chmn. 17th World Gas Conf., Internat. Gas Union, 1986-88. Pres., dir. Buffalo Better Bus. Bur., 1970; trustee SUNY-Buffalo Found. Served with C.E. AUS, 1943-46, ETO. Mem. ABA, N.Y. Bar Assn., Fed. Power Bar Assn., Erie County Bar Assn., Barrister Soc., Am. Gas Assn. (chmn. dir. 1984-85, Disting. Svc. award 1986), Nat. Alliance Businessmen (dir., chmn. 1967-68), Buffalo C. of C. (dir. 1973—), chmn. nat. affairs com. 1969—), Buffalo Club (bd. dirs. 1988, pres. 1991-92), Phi Alpha Delta. Office: Biokeys Pharmaceuticals, Inc. 9948 Hibert St., Ste. 100 San Diego CA 92131

REIFF, A.E. writer, artist; b. Phila., July 25, 1941; s. Jacob Howard and Beatrice Blanche Reiff; m. Patricia Carlson, Nov. 2, 1951; children: Elizabeth, Aeyrie, Andrew. BS, Drexel U., 1964; MA, U. Iowa, 1966; PhD, U. Tex., 1975. Curator, supr. Exptl. Drug and Herb Garden Coll. Pharmacy, U. Tex., Austin, 1977-81; assoc. prof. English Bishop Coll., Dallas, 1981-86; editor Red Rose, 1989-91. Author: A Calendar of Poems, 1974, Planet 3: Help Send This Book into Space, 1985. Home: 2532 N Foote Dr Phoenix AZ 85008

REIFF, DANIEL D. art history educator; b. Potsdam, N.Y., Aug. 17, 1941; s. Henry and Ione Drake Reiff; m. Janet Madej Reiff, June 28, 1975; children: Nicholas Andrew, Michael Christopher. BA, Harvard U., 1963, MA, 1964, PhD, 1970. Instr. art history Baylor U., Waco, Tex., 1964-65, 66-67; acting asst. sec. U.S. Commn. Fine Arts, Washington, 1969-70; asst. prof. art history SUNY, Fredonia, 1970-72, assoc. prof. art history, 1972-77, prof. art history, 1977—. Author: Washington Architecture, 1791-1861, 1971, Architecture in Fredonia, 1811-1972, 1972, Small Georgian Houses in England and Virginia, 1986, Architecture in Fredonia, New York, 1811-1997, 1997, Houses from Books...1738-1950, 2000; contbr. articles to profl. jours. Pres. Fredonia Preservation Soc., 1995-98. Recipient Archtl. Heritage award Preservation League of N.Y. State, Albany, 1986, Ruth Emery award Victorian Soc. in Am., Phila., 1999, Hist. Preservation Book prize Ctr. for Hist. Preservation, Mary Washington Coll., 2001; grantee Graham Found. for Advanced Studies in Fine Arts, Chgo., 1991; fellow Rotary Internat., Evanston, Ill., 1965-66, NEH, 1985. Mem. Soc. Archtl. Historians, Coll. Art Assn., Nat. Trust Historic Preservation, Preservation League of N.Y. State, Fredonia Preservation Soc., Inc. (pres. 1995-98), Nature Conservancy. Avocations: photography, canoeing, hiking, camping, travel. Office: Visual Arts Dept SUNY Coll at Fredonia Fredonia NY 14063

REIFF, JAMES STANLEY, osteopathic physician, addictions, psychiatric, surgeon; b. Mar. 17, 1935; s. Nathan Edgar and Freda Matilda (Imhoff) R.; m. Sharon Ann Kraybill, June 9, 1956 (div. April 1970); children: Gregory James, James Stanley II, Cynthia Diane, Jeffery Cameron. BA in Chemistry, Goshen Coll., 1957; DO, Chgo. Coll. Osteo Medicine, 1961. Biochemist Miles/Ames Pharm. Co., Elkhart, Ind., 1955-57; pvt. practice Mich. City, 1962-69; addictions physician Oaklawn Psychiat. Ctr., Elkhart, 1974-84; med. dir. Life Recovery Ctr., 1987-90, Substance Abuse Coun., St. Joe County, Mich., 1990-95, Am. Plasma Mgmt., Inc., various, Mich., Ind, 1991-97; mem. staff Cmty. Mental Health Svcs., St. Joe County, 1993-97. Bd. dirs. Home for Runaway Kids - Victory House, Elkhart, Ind., 1974-76, 12 Step House Meth. Ch.-Halfway House, Elkhart, 1974-77; bd. dirs., treas. Caldwell Home Corp.-Social Rehab. Ctr. for Alcoholism, Elkhart, 1984-87; bd. dirs. Hope House, Jonesville, Mich. Organist First Presbyn. Ch., Sturgis, Mich., 1993-97. Mem. AMA, Am. Osteopathic Assn., Am. Soc. Addiction Medicine (com. on addiction medicine in correctional facilities 1993—), Mich. State Med. Soc., St. Joe County Med. Soc. Avocations: organ and piano playing. Home and Office: 1301 E Congress St Sturgis MI 49091-9181

REIFF, PATRICIA HOFER, space physicist, educator; b. Oklahoma City, Mar. 14, 1950; d. William Henry and Maxine Ruth (Hoffer) R.; m. Thomas Westfall Hill, July 4, 1976; children: Andrea Hofer Hill, Adam Reiff Hill, Amelia Reiff Hill. Student, Wellesley Coll., 1967-68; BS, Okla. State U., 1971; MS, Rice U., 1974, PhD, 1975. Cert. secondary tchr., Okla., Tex. Resident rsch. assoc. Marshall Space Flight Ctr., Huntsville, Ala., 1975-76; rsch. assoc. space physics and astronomy dept. Rice U., Houston, 1975, asst. prof. space physics and astronomy dept., 1978-81, asst. chmn. space physics and astronomy dept., 1979-85, assoc. rsch. sci., 1981-87, sr. rsch. scientist, 1987-90. Adj. asst. prof. Rice U., 1976-78, disting. faculty fellow, 1990-92, prof. 1992—, chmn. dept. space physics and astronomy, 1996-99, dir. Rice Space Inst., 1999—; vice chair Coun. on Instns., 2000—; mem. sci. team Atmosphere Explorer Mission, Dynamics Explorer Mission; co-investigator Global Geospace Sci. Mission, ESA/Cluster Mission, IMAGE Mission; prin. investigator The Public Connection NASA, Mus. Tchg. Planet Earth; cons. Houston Mus. Natural Sci., 1986—; adv. com. on atmospheric scis. NSF, Washington, 1988-92; mem. stategic implementation study panel NASA, Washington, 1989-91; mem. space sci. adv. com. NASA, 1993-98, mem. space sta. utilization subcom., 1995-98; mem. adv. com. Los Alamos Non-Proliferation Divsn., 1998—; univ. rep. U. Space Rsch. Assn., Washington, 1993—; exec. com. George Observatory, Houston, 1989-92, others. Designer Cockrell Sundial/Solar Telescope, 1989; editor EOS (sci. newspaper), 1986-89; contbr. articles to profl. jours. Trustee, Citizens' Environ. Coalition, Houston, 1978-98, pres. 1980-85, adv. com. 1998—; mem. air quality com. Houston/Galveston Area Coun., 1980-83, Green Ribbon Com., City of Houston, 1981-83; active coms. Macedonia United Meth. Ch., 1988—. Named rsch. fellow NAS/NRC., 1975, an Outstanding Young Woman Am., 1977, '80, to Houston's Women on the Move, 1990; NASA grantee 1993, 94, 95, 98, 99; recipient NASA Group Achievement award. Fellow Am. Geophys. Union (fin. com. 1980-82, editor search com. 1992, pub. edn. com.); mem. Cosmos Club, Wellesley Club, Internat. Union of Geodesy and Geophysics (del. 1975, 81, 83, 89, 91, 93, 95, chair working group 2F, 1991-95). Avocations: organic gardening, beef ranching, scouting. Office: Rice U Dept Physics and Astronomy 6100 S Main St Houston TX 77251 E-mail: reiff@rice.edu.

REIFFEL, JAMES, cardiologist, educator; b. N.Y.C., Sept. 20, 1943; s. Martin Lawrence and Roslyn (Siskind) R.; m. Bonnie Geffen, Mar. 18, 1967; children: Gabrielle, Jamie. BA, Duke U., 1965; MD, Columbia U., 1969. Diplomate NASPE, Am. Bd. Internal Medicine, subsplty. bd. Cardiovascular Disease, subsplty. bd. Clin. Cardiovascular Electrophysiology; cert. Nat. Bd. Examiners. Intern Presbyn. Hosp., N.Y.C., 1969-70, resident, 1970-72, asst. physician, 1974-76, asst. attending physician, 1976-80, assoc. attending physician, 1980-88, attending physician, 1988—, assoc. dir. electrophysiology lab., 1979-91; dir. electrophysiology programs Coll. Physicians & Surgeons, Columbia U., 1991-99, dir. electrocardiography lab., 1999—, assoc. in clin. medicine, 1974-76, asst. prof. clin. medicine, 1976-80, assoc. prof. clin. medicine, 1980-88, prof. clin. medicine, 1988—. Author numerous abstracts, sci. papers; contbr. articles to profl. jours. With USAR, 1970-76. Cardiology fellow Presbyn. Hosp., 1972-74. Fellow ACP, Am. Heart Assn., Coun. Clin. Cardiology, Am. Coll. Cardiology, N.Y. Cardiol. Soc.; mem. N.Y. Heart Assn., Med. Soc. County of N.Y., Med. Soc. State of N.Y., Am. Fedn. Clin. Rsch., Cardiac Electrophysiologic Soc., N.Am. Soc. Pacing & Electrophysiology. Office: 161 Ft Washington Ave New York NY 10032-3713

REIFFEL, LEONARD, physicist, medical physicist, scientific consultant; b. Chgo., Sept. 30, 1927; s. Carl and Sophie (Miller) R.; m. Judith Eve Blumenthal, 1952 (div. 1962); children— Evan Carl, David Lee; m. Nancy L. Jeffers, 1971. B.Sc., Ill. Inst. Tech., 1947, M.Sc., 1948, PhD, 1953. Physicist Perkin-Elmer Corp., Conn., 1948; engring. physicist U. Chgo. Inst. Nuclear Studies, 1948-49; with Ill. Inst. Tech. Research Inst., Chgo., 1949-65, dir. physics research, 1956-63, v.p., 1963-65; cons. to Apollo program NASA Hdqrs., 1965-70; pvt. practice cons., 1970—; tech. dir. manned space flight expts. bd. NASA, 1966-68; chmn. bd. Instructional Dynamics, Inc., 1966-81, Interand Corp., 1969-91, Telestrator Industries, Inc., 1970-73; sci. editor Sta. WBBM-CBS radio, Chgo.; sci. cons./commentator WBBM-TV, 1971-72; host Backyard Safari, 1971-73; sci. feature broadcaster WEEI-CBS radio, Boston, 1965-75; syndicated newspaper columnist World Book Ency. Sci. Service, Inc. (later Universal Sci. News, Inc.), 1966-72, Los Angeles Times Syndicate, 1972-76; sci. cons. CBS Network, 1967-71; chmn., CEO Exelar Corp., Chgo., 1991—; chmn. bd., pres., CEO Ameraine Corp., 1992-95; bd. overseers Armour Coll., bd. advisors engrng. dept. Ill. Inst. Tech., 1995—, 98—; founder, chmn. Luxelar Corp., 2001—. Cons. Korean Govt. on establishment atomic energy rsch. program; mem. adv. com. isotope and radiation devel. AEC; com. rsch. reactors NAS, 1958-64; cons. U.S. Army, 1976—. Author: (book) The Contaminant, 1979; author numerous sci. papers; patentee in field. Bd. dirs. Student Competitions on Relevant Engring. Named Outstanding Young Man of Year Chgo. Jr. C. of C., 1954, 61; recipient Merit award Chgo. Tech. Socs., 1968; Peabody award for radio edn., 1968; IR-100 award for inventing Telestrator CBS Chalkboard, 1970; award for coverage space events Aviation Writers Assn., 1971; IR-100 award for invention underwater diver communications system, 1972, IR-100 award for DISCON video teleconferencing systems, 1985, Third Annual High Tech Entrepreneur award, 1986, IR-100 award for invention Audiografix, 1973; Disting. Alumni Achievement award Ill. Inst. Tech., 1974, named to Hall of Fame IIT, 1984. Fellow Am. Phys. Soc.; mem. AAAS, Chgo. Literary Club, Sigma Xi, Tau Beta Pi, Eta Kappa Nu. Achievements include being responsible for world's 1st indsl. nuclear reactor, 1956. Home: 602 W Deming Pl Chicago IL 60614-2618 E-mail: lreiffel@aol.com.

REIFFEL, ROBERT SISKIND, plastic surgeon; b. N.Y.C., June 1, 1946; s. Martin Lawrence and Roslyn Anita (Siskind) R.; m. Suzanne Mara Temkin, June 19, 1977; children: Lauren Kate, Alyssa Julie. BA, Yale U., 1968; MD, Columbia U., 1972. Diplomate Am. Bd. Plastic Surgery, Am. Bd. Surgery, added qualifications in surgery of hand. Intern in gen. surgery Roosevelt Hosp., N.Y.C., 1972-73, resident in gen. surgery, 1973-77; resident in plastic surgery NYU Med. Ctr., 1977-79, fellow in hand surgery, 1979-80; pvt. practice plastic and reconstructive surgery White Plains, N.Y., 1980—. Attending physician White Plains Hosp., chief plastic surgery sect. Contbr. articles to profl. publs. Recipient Best Original Photographic Exhibit award Greater N.Y. Orchid Show, 1993, 1st prize resident's night, sect. plastic surgery N.Y. Acad. Medicine and N.Y. Regional Surgery, 1979. Fellow ACS; mem. Med. Soc. State of N.Y., N.Y. Regional Soc. Plastic and Reconstructive Surgery, N.Y. Soc. for Surgery of the Hand, Westchester County Med. Soc., Am. Burn Assn., Am. Soc. for Surgery of the Hand, Am. Soc. Plastic and Reconstructive Surgeons (1st prize sr. classification scholarship contest of ednl. found. 1980). Avocations: golf, tennis, photography. Office: 12 Greenridge Ave White Plains NY 10605-1238 E-mail: r.reiffel@verizon.net.

REIFMAN, STEVEN MICHAEL, elementary school educator; s. Leonard H. and Estherly Reifman. BA in Sociology, U. Va., 1992; Master's in Edn., UCLA, 1994; Master's in Ednl. Adminstrn., Calif. State U., Northridge, 2001. Cert. profl. clear multiple subject credential with a CLAD emphasis. Classroom tchr. Loyola Village Sch., L.A., 1994—96, Roosevelt Sch., Santa Monica, 1996—98, 2000—, Curtis Sch., L.A., 1999—2000. Continuing edn. instr. UCLA Ext., 1996—; ednl. cons. Anderson Sch., Lawndale, Calif., 1998—99, YouTHink, L.A., 1998—99; mid. sch. athletic coach Brentwood Sch., L.A., 1992—98. Author: (book) How To Be An Effective Teacher, 1996, The Eight Keys to Classroom Quality. Women's maccabiah volleyball co-chmn. U.S. Com. Sports for Israel, Phila., 2000—01. Avocations: sports, music, reading, writing. Office: Roosevelt Sch 801 Montana Ave Santa Monica CA 90403 Personal E-mail: SReifman@aol.com.

REIG, JUNE WILSON, writer, director, producer; b. Schenectady, N.Y., June 1, 1933; d. Wallace John and Lillian Lucy (Gay) Wilson; m. Robert Maxwell, Nov. 26, 1969. BA summa cum laude, N.Y. State U., 1954; MA in Dramatic Arts, NYU, 1962. Instr. NYU, 1962-67; producer, dir. NYU Theater, 1963-67; dir.-prodr., writer news and pub. affairs NBC TV Network, N.Y.C., 1963-67; dir., writer, prodr. divsn. entertainment NBC-TV Network, 1967-73; pres. Bunny/Chord Prodns., 1972-97. Author: Diary of the Boy King Tut-Ankh-Amen, 1978; writer, dir. (TV spl.) Stuart Little, 1966 (Peabody award Prix Jeunesse); writer (TV spl.) The Reluctant Dragon, 1968 (Brotherhood award), (music spls.) The Heart of Christmas, 1965, An Afternoon at Tanglewood (Peabody award); writer, dir., producer (TV spls.) Rabbit Hill, 1966 (ALA award) Bill Cosby As I See It, 1970 (Ohio State award) A Day With Bill Cosby, 1971, Jennifer & Me, 1972; (TV daily series) Watch Your Child - The Me Too Show, 1973 (Action for Children's TV Achievement award); prodr., writer (TV spl.) Little Women, the ballet, 1976, Tut, the Boy King, 1978 (Peabody award); films in permanent collection of Mus. Broadcasting, N.Y.C. Recipient Prix Jeunesse, 1966, Christopher award, 1970, Emmy award nomination, 1966, 76. Mem. Writers Guild Am., Dirs. Guild Am., Nat. Acad. TV Arts and Scis., NYU Alumni Assn., Internat. Soc. Animal Rights, Friends of Animals, Audubon Soc., Alan Devoe Bird Club. Clubs: Alan Devoe Bird (Old Chatham, N.Y.). Avocations: photography, music, animals. Office: c/o Allen H Arrow Esq 111 W 57th St Ste 1405 New York NY 10019-2211 *Whether I am working on a teleplay or book, I write about things I believe children are interested in: feelings, aspirations, caring, animals, loving. As I see it, too much of the fare for young people gives them a distorted view of how much violence there is in the world, and I want to counteract that impression. I want to write about things that create a sense of worth, warm security, and an absence of unnecessary anxiety. When I do write about the darker things that happen in life, it is to help the young person understand himself and the world a little better.*

REIGEL, TIMOTHY JOHN, accountant; b. Harrisburg, Pa., Jan. 16, 1962; s. Jacqueline Reigel. BS in Acctg., Mt. St. Mary's Coll., 1984. Cert. software mgr. Cost acct. Harley Davidson Motor Co., York, Pa., 1984-85; fin. analyst Pa. Housing and Fin. Agy., Harrisburg, 1985-88; managerial acct. Harrisburg Hosp., 1988-89; mgr. fiscal ops. Pa. Health Care Cost Containment Coun., Harrisburg, 1990—. Cons. Reigel & Assoc., Harrisburg, 1990—. Home: PO Box 10411 Harrisburg PA 17105-0411 Office: Pa Health Care Cost Containment Coun 225 Market St Ste 400 Harrisburg PA 17101-2126

REIGHTLER, KENNETH S., JR. astronaut, military officer; b. Patuxent River, Md., Mar. 24, 1951; s. Kenneth S. and Mrs. Reightler; m. Maureen Ellen McHenry; 2 children. BS in Aerospace Engring., USN Acad., Annapolis, 1973; MS in Aeronautical Engring., U.S. Naval Postgrad. Sch., Monterey, Calif. , 1984; MS in Systems Mgmt., USC, 1984. Commd ensign USN, Annapolis, 1973, advanced through grades to Capt.; mission commdr., patrol plane commdr. USN Patrol Squadron 16, Jacksonville, Fla., 1974—78; student pilot USN Test Pilot Sch., Patuxent River , Md., 1978; test pilot Naval Air Test Ctr., 1979—80, instr. test pilots, 1980—81; comm. officer, carrier on bd. delivery pilot USN, USS Dwight Eisenhower, 1981—83; student Naval Post Grad. Sch., Monterey, Calif., 1983—84; chief flight instr. U.S. Naval Test Pilot Sch., 1985—87; sstronaut NASA Johnson Space Ctr., Houston, 1987—. Recipient Mac Short award in Aviation, U.S. Naval Acad., 1973, 2 Space flight medals, NASA, World Altitude Record for Class P aero-spacecraft. Mem.: Soc. Exptl. Test Pilots, Nat. Aeronautic Assn., Assn. Space Explorers, U.S. Naval Acad. Alumni Assn. Achievements include over 4700 hours flying time in 60 different types of aircraft, 2 space flights, 327 hours in space. Avocations: camping, sailing, wind surfing. Office: Astronaut Office/CB Johnson Space Ctr Houston TX 77058

REIGROD, ROBERT HULL, manufacturing executive; b. N.Y.C., Mar. 26, 1941; s. David and Beatrice (Simon) R.; children: Sandra, Donald. BA in Anthropology, Calif. State U., Long Beach, 1973. With Brother Internat. Corp., Irvine, Calif., 1970-77, gen. mgr. west region, 1977-82, v.p., 1982-86, dir., sr. v.p. N.J., 1986—; pres. Brother Internat. de Mexico, S.A. de C.V., 1992—, Brother Internat. do Brasil, Sao Paulo, 1999—. Trustee Leukemia Soc. Am., 1982-84; bd. dirs. Irvine Children's Fund, 1988-90. Mem. Japan Soc. South Fla. (dir. 1994—, trustee). Office: Brother Internat Corp Alameda Nothmann 354 01216000 Sao Paulo Brazil

REIGSTAD, RUTH ELAINE, lay worker, retired physical therapy consultant; b. Mpls., Apr. 26, 1923; d. Olin Spencer and Amanda Sophia (Fjelstad) R. BA, St. Olaf Coll., Northfield, Minn., 1945; cert., U. Minn., 1947. Lic. phys.

therapist, Wash. Phys. therapist Crippled Childrens's Sch., Jamestown, N.D., 1948-52; phys. therapist, clin. instr. Shriners Hosp., U. Minn., Mpls., 1955-58; phys. therapist Rehab. Center, Albuquerque, 1958-60, Brit. Nat. Health Svc., London; phys. therapy cons. Wash. State Health Dept., Olympia, 1961-73, cons., 1961-74; lay worker Good Shepherd Luth. Ch., 1972-75; mem. various coms. Christ Luth. Ch., Tacoma, 1980—. Vol. Children Health Svcs. and Pub. Health of Wash. 1974—; bd. dirs. Morningside Rehab. Orgn., Olympia, Wash., PAVE rehab. orgn. Bd. dirs. Wash. State Phys. Therapy Assn., 1965-68; mem. communiversity planning com. Pierce County Assoc. Ministries. With USCG, 1943-45. Recipient Fellowship award Nat. Easter Seal Soc. Chgo. 1949; Scholarship award US Pub. Health Service Wash. 1962-64. Mem. Am. Phys. Therapy Assn. (life), Am. Pub. Health Assn., Am. Acad. Religion, Luth. Brotherhood Fraternity and Benevolent Orgn. (bd. dirs. Pierce County), Air Force Assn. (exec. coun. Pierce County, 1985—). Mem. Evang. Luth. Ch. Am. Avocations: volunteer work, travel, gardening, public speaking, creative writing. Home: 10420 Gravelly Lake Dr Tacoma WA 98499

REIK, RITA ANN FITZPATRICK, pathologist; b. Cleve., Mar. 9, 1951; d. Charles Robert Sr. and Rita Mae (Wilke) Fitzpatrick; m. Curtis A. Reik, Oct. 19, 1974. BA in Chemistry, Fla. Internat. U., 1985; MD, U. Miami, 1989. Diplomate Am. Bd. Anatomic and Clinical Pathology, Am. Bd. Pathology in Transfusion Medicine. Resident in pathology Jackson Meml. Hosp., Miami, Fla., 1989-95; mem. faculty dept. pathology U. Miami Sch. Medicine, 1995-97; attending physician transfusion med. svcs. U. Miami/Jackson Meml. Hosp., 1996-97; dir. stem cell processing and graft engring. lab. U. Miami Sch. Medicine/Jackson Meml. Hosp., 1996-97; assoc. med. dir. Cmty. Blood Ctr., Dayton, Ohio, 1997-99; dir. sci. svc., med. dir. Cmty. Tissue Svc., 1997-99; faculty Wright State U., 1997-99; sr. cons. Ctr. Cellular therapy, chief med. officer NW ARC, Portland, Oreg., 1999—. Dir. lab. svcs. Jackson U. Maternity Ctr., Miami; dir. lab. svcs. North Dade Amb. Care Ctr., 1996-97. Fellow Coll. Am. Pathologists; mem. AMA, NOW, U. Miami Med. Women (pres. 1988-89), Am. Soc. Clin. Pathologists, Alpha Omega Alpha, Phi Kappa Phi. Achievements include research in bone marrow and stem cell transplantation and transfusion medicine, AIDS. Avocations: painting, raising Japanese Koi, gardening. Office: ARC Pacific NW Blood Svcs 3131 N Vancouver Ave Portland OR 97227-1560 Home: 3680 Swtowle Ave Gresham OR 97080

REILEY, ROBERT, lawyer, educator; b. Pottsville, Pa. s. Edmund Anthony and Evelyn Burke Reiley; m. Elizabeth L. Reiley, Oct. 18, 1986; children: Samuel, Audrey, Benjamin, Daniel. BA, DeSales U., 1983; JD, Ohio No. U., 1991; LLM, George Washington U., 1996. Bar: Pa. 1991, U.S. Supreme Ct. 1996. Atty. Dept. Environ Protection, Harrisburg, Pa., 1998—, U.S. EPA, Washington, 1993-98, Pub. Defenders office, Towanda, Pa., 1991-93. Adj. prof. Alvernia Coll., Reading, Pa., 1998—, USDA, Washington, 1996-98. Contbr. articles to profl. jours. Vol. U.S. Peace Corps., The Philippines, 1985-87; coord. St. Ambrose Ch., Schulykill Haven, Pa., 2000—. Mem. Pa. Bar Assn. (pro bono lawyer 1999-2001). Roman Catholic. Avocations: reading, writing, sports. Home: 144 Fork Mountain Rd Auburn PA 17922 Office: Pa Dept Environ Protection Market St Harrisburg PA 17105

REILEY, T. PHILLIP, consultant; b. Ft. Lewis, Wash., May 5, 1950; s. Thomas Phillip and Anne Marie (Russick) R. BSc in Biophysics, Pa. State U., 1973; postgrad. in Bus. Adminstrn., Rutgers U.; MBA, NYU, 1991. Cert. prodn. and inventory mgmt., cert. integrated resource mgmt. Inventory supr. Leland Tube Co., South Plainfield, N.J., 1973-76; prodn. inventory control supr. Bomar Crystal Co., Middlesex, 1976-79; prodn. control mgr. Codi Semicondr. Inc., Linden, 1979-81; mfg. systems analyst Western Union Info. Systems, Mahwah, 1981-85; bus. analyst Nabisco Brands Biscuit Div., Parsippany, 1985-91, sr. systems analyst, 1991-94, tech. advisor, 1994-97; applications cons. SAP America, 1997—. Mem. Am. Prodn. and Inventory Control Soc. (past chmn. ednl. com. Raritan Valley chpt.), N.Y. Acad. Scis., Mensa, Coun. Logistics Mgmt., Am. Inst. Mgmt. Accts. Republican. Home: 56 Charter Club Dr Piscataway NJ 00854-3114 Office: SAP America 300 Interpace Pkwy Parsippany NJ 07054-1100 E-mail: phillip.reiley@sap.com., preiley@world.std.com.

REILING, HENRY BERNARD, business educator; b. Richmond, Ky., Feb. 5, 1938; s. Henry Bernard and Lucille Frances (Fowler) R.; m. Carol-Lina Maria Schuetz, June 4, 1962; children: Christina Lucille Reiling Breiter, Maria Hays, Carol-Lena Alexis, Reiling Lessans. BA, Northwestern U., 1960; MBA, Harvard U., 1962; JD, Columbia U., 1965. Bar: N.Y. 1965. Mem. faculty Columbia U. Bus. Sch., 1965-76, prof., 1974-76; vis. prof. Stanford U. Bus. Sch., 1974-75; vis. asso. prof. Harvard U. Bus. Sch., 1972-73, prof., 1976—, Eli Goldston prof. bus. adminstrn., 1978—. Contbr. bus. and law jours. Trustee Riverside Ch., N.Y.C., 1976-77; mem. bd. advisors Northwestern U. Coll. Arts and Scis., 1989—, alumni regents, 1997—. Recipient Alumnus Merit award, Northwestern U., 1996, Svc. award, 2002. Mem. ABA, N.Y. Bar Assn., Bar Assn. City N.Y., Am. Fin. Assn., Fin. Mgmt. Assn., Nat. Tax Assn., Tax Inst. Am., Union Club (N.Y.C.), Beta Gamma Sigma (hon.). Home: 28 Meriam St Lexington MA 02420-3618 Office: Harvard U Bus Sch Boston MA 02163

REILING, LOIS MAE, librarian; b. St. Paul, May 10, 1938; d. James and Louise (Jamtoos) Kenney; m. Paul Reiling, Sept. 9, 1961; children: Mary Jo, Amy, Molli. BS, U. Ariz., 1980, Master's, 1984. Flight attendant Delta Airlines, L.A., 1958-61. Composer, prodr. (CD) Jazz Mass Traditional, 1997. Mem. ALA, AAUW, Tucson Jazz Soc., Music Therapy Assn., Jazz Educators Internat. Assn. Jazz Educators. Avocations: skiing, music. Office: 492 N Alvernon Way Tucson AZ 85711-1922

REILLEY, DENNEN, research agency administrator, educator; b. Greenwich, Conn., Mar. 1, 1937; s. Philip Francis and Florence Rita (Junkersfield) R.; m. Margaret Randall, Dougherty, Dec. 26, 1976; children: Philip F., Christopher J., Diane L., Elizabeth S., Katherine M. BSS, Fairfield U., 1959; MEd, U. Hartford, 1965; postgrad., U. Conn., 1965-70, CAGS, 1970. Tchr. New Britain (Conn.) Pub. Schs., 1960-65; tchr., adminstr. West Hartford (Conn.) Pub. Schs., 1965-69, 72-73; mem. faculty Central Conn. State Coll., New Britain, 1969-72; dir. field svcs. Edn. Devel. Ctr., Newton, Mass., 1973-82; sr. assoc., CEO Applied Rsch. Assocs., Sharon, 1980—. Adj. faculty U. Wyo., U. Minn.; cons. Am. Humane Assn., Edn. Devel. Ctr. Author: Training Program for Animal Care and Control Professionals, Sources: A Resource Guide to Funding Assistance for Parenting Programs, Education for Parenthood Conference Report; the Tri-State Parenting Collaborative, (with Jan Mokros) Summary of Exploring Childhood Evaluation Findings, The Animal Welfare Board of Directors, Total Quality Management: Implications for Animal Care and Control Professionals, Management Perspectives for Animal Care and Control Professionals, Board Perspectives for Nonprofit Organizations, Long Range Planning for Nonprofit Organizations; contbr. articles to profl. jours. Mem. New Britain Rep. town com., 1961-65; conductor mgmt. seminars nationally Not-for-profit orgns., 1982—. Recipient Rosemary Ames award Am. Humane Assn., 1983. Mem. Nat. Coun. Social Studies (conv. spkr. 1963-79, curriculum com. 1974-77, field svcs. bd. 1977-80), Conn. Coun. Social Studies (pres. 1965-66), NEA (life), ASCD, Am. Humane Assn., HSUS (conv. spkr. 1980-94, cons. 1994—). Office: 57 Brook Rd Sharon MA 02067-1415

REILLEY, JAMES CLARK, artist, cartoonist, small business owner; b. Detroit, Nov. 4, 1919; s. James Aloyisus and Lillian May (Cole) R.; m. Beatrice C. Clemente, May 10, 1952; children: James A. (dec.), Anthony Francis, Beatrice Anita. Grad., Art Inst. of Pitts., 1948. Artist Banner Advt., Phila., 1948-49; layout artist Lit Bros. Dept. Store, 1949; comic book illustrator John Prentice, Long Island, N.Y., 1950; artist DuPont Co., Wilmington, Del., 1950-59; artist/owner Jim Reilley Studio, 1959-94; ret. Sgt. USAAF, 1942-45. Inducted to Penns Grove H.S. Personal Achievement Hall of Fame, 1996. Roman Catholic. Avocations: fishing, music, sports. Home: 110 N Broad St Penns Grove NJ 08069-1269

REILLY, CHARLES EDMUND, JR. communications company executive; b. Phila., Nov. 4, 1928; s. Charles Edmund Sr. and Kathryn (McHugh) R.; m. Joan Emily Hunter; children by previous marriage: Lynn, Susan, Kathryn, Charles III. BS in Bus., St. Joseph's U., Phila., 1950; postgrad., U. Pa., 1955; MA in Liberal Studies, Villanova U., 2000. Sales rep. Stuart Pharms., Phila., 1954-56; rep. east coast TV Guide Mag., Radnor, 1956-64; asst. to v.p., dir. corp. relations Young & Rubicam Inc., N.Y.C., 1964-66; exec. dir. Nat. Cath. Office for Radio-TV, 1966-71; exec. v.p. Patrick Carr Assocs., 1971-72; corp. exec. J. Walter Thompson, 1972-74; v.p. Ogilvy and Mather, 1975-76; founder In-Person Communications Inc., 1976—. Cons. Pontifical Commn. Social Communications, Vatican City, Italy, 1968-71; adj. assoc. prof. St. John's U., N.Y.C., 1971-72; mem. vis. com. Loyola U., New Orleans, 1987—. Author: (book) You Speak..They Listen, 1984, You and A Life of Reilly, 1987, Special Delivery, 1998, Korea 1950-1953--The War That Never Was, 2000, others; newspaper columnist Suburban and Wayne, 1991—93, Main Line Life, 1994—. Lt. col. Valley Forge Mil. Coll., 1995—. 1st lt. U.S. Army, 1950—53. Inducted into Hall of Fame, The Inf. Sch., Ft. Benning, Ga., 1996. Mem.: Merion Cricket (Haverford, Pa.); Princeton (N.Y.C.); Union League (Phila.); St. David's Golf Club (Wayne, Pa.). Republican. E-mail: crinperson@aol.com.

REILLY, CHARLES JAMES, lawyer, educator, accountant; b. Pawtucket, R.I., Oct. 10, 1950; s. Thomas Joseph and Florence Marie (McKenna) R.; m. Barbara Bouffard, Aug. 7, 1971; children: Kristen, Elizabeth. BSBA, Providence Coll., 1972; JD, Suffolk U., 1979. Bar: R.I. 1979, U.S. Dist. Ct. R.I. 1979, U.S. Ct. Appeals (1st cir.) 1979, U.S. Supreme Ct. 1984, U.S. Ct. Claims, 1985; CPA, R.I. Agt. IRS, Providence, 1972-75; appellate conferee U.S. Dept. Treasury, Boston, 1976-81; ptnr. Arcaro & Reilly, Providence, 1981-91, Reilly Law Assocs., Providence, 1991—. Assoc. prof. Grad. MST program Bryant Coll., Smithfield, R.I., 1983—. Mem. AICPA, R.I. Soc. CPAs, ABA, R.I. Bar Assn. (chair tax sect. 1996-2000). Clubs: R.I. Country. Democrat. Roman Catholic. Avocation: golf. Office: Reilly Law Assocs 1040 Turks Head Bldg Providence RI 02903 E-mail: reillylaw1@aol.com.

REILLY, CHRISTOPHER PATRICK, governor, artist; b. Osaka, Japan, Nov. 4, 1955; arrived in U.S., 1957; s. Philip J. and Dolores F. Reilly; m. Paula M. Reilly, Mar. 17, 1984; children: Patrick, Philip, Joseph. AA in Fire Tech., Sierra Coll., Rocklin, Calif., 2000; Cert. in Fire Tech., Am. River Coll., Sacramento, Calif., 1980. Cert. fire officer Calif., EMT. Seasonal fire fighter N.Y.P. ranger unit Calif. Dept. Forestry and Fire Protection, Auburn, Calif., 1974—79; fire fighter Citrus Hts. Fire Dist., 1980—84; fire fighter/EMT-1A Tiburon Fire Dist., 1984—90, Sacramento Met. Fire Dist., 1990—. Safety com. mem. Sacramento County Fire Dist., Rancho Cordova, Calif., 1992—2000. Author: Firefighter - Red Chrome Knight, 1998. Recipient Commendations, Calif. State Legis., Okla. Gov. Mem.: Internat. Assn. Firefighters. Avocations: painting, landscape deisgn. Mailing: 5326 Humboldt Dr Rocklin CA 95765

REILLY, CONOR DESMOND, lawyer; b. Kansas City, Mo., Feb. 12, 1952; s. Desmond M. and Patricia (Carton) R.; m. Margaret M. Cannella, June 8, 1975; children: Katherine C., Michael C. BS, MIT, 1972; JD cum laude, Harvard U., 1975. Bar: N.Y. 1976, U.S. Dist. Ct. (ea. and so. dists.) N.Y. 1976, U.S. Ct. Appeals (2d. cir.) 1977, U.S. Dist. Ct. (D.C. cir.) 1979, U.S. Dist. Ct. (no. dist.) Calif. 1981, U.S. Dist. Ct. (cen. dist.) Calif. 1982. Law clk. to judge U.S. Dist. Ct. (ea. dist.), Bklyn., 1975-76; assoc. Cravath, Swaine & Moore, N.Y.C., 1976-77, Coudert Bros., N.Y.C., 1977-83, LeBoeuf, Lamb, Leiby & MacRae, N.Y.C., 1983-84, ptnr., 1985-88, Gibson, Dunn & Crutcher, N.Y.C., 1988—. Vice-chmn Memorex-Telex N.V., 1988-90; chmn. bd. dirs. Acorn Products Inc., 1996-99. Editor Harvard U. Law Rev., 1973-74. Hearing officer N.Y.C. Bd. Edn., 1977-79; elected mem. Millburn Twp. Bd. Edn., 1987-92. Mem. ABA, Am. Arbitration Assn. (arbitrator). Democrat. Avocation: tennis. Home: 62 Joanna Way Short Hills NJ 07078-3241 Office: Gibson Dunn & Crutcher 200 Park Ave Fl 47 New York NY 10166-0193

REILLY, DANIEL PATRICK, bishop; b. Providence, May 12, 1928; s. Francis E. and Mary (Burns) R. Student, Our Lady of Providence Sem., 1943-48, Grand Seminaire, St. Brieuc, France, 1948-53, Harvard U., 1954-55, Boston Coll., 1955-56; D (hon.), Providence Coll., St. Michael's Coll., Holy Apostles Coll. and Sem., Salve Regina Coll., Our Lady of Providence Coll., Sacred Heart U., Assumption Coll., 1995, Anna Maria Coll., 1995, Holy Cross Coll., 1996. Ordained priest Roman Catholic Ch., 1953; asst. pastor Cathedral Saints Peter and Paul, Providence, 1953-54; asst. chancellor Diocese of Providence, 1954-56, sec. to bishop, 1956-64, chancellor, 1964-72, adminstr., 1971-72, vicar gen., 1972-75; became monsignor, 1964; consecrated bishop, 1975; bishop of Norwich, Conn., 1975-94; installed bishop of Worcester, Mass., 1994—; Conn. state chaplain K.C., 1976-94; Episcopal moderator Nat. Cath. Cemetery Corp., 1977-87. Ad hoc mem. to aid ch. in Ea. Europe NCCB/U.S. Cath. Conf., adminstrv. com. mem., 1976-86, 92—; pro-life com. mem. NCCB, 1989-92, chmn. 10th anniversary peace pastoral com., 1992-93, chmn. internat. policy com., 1993; mem. Priestly Life and Ministry Commn., 1991-94; past pres. New Eng. Consultation Ch. Leaders; drafting com. mem. U.S. Cath. Conf. Pastoral Letter on Peace, 1983, mem. com. on coms.; active Holy See Pontifical Coun.-Cor Unum, 1984-89. Trustee Cath. Mut. Relief Soc., Omaha, 1979—, St. John's Sem., Brighton, Mass., 1987—, Am. Coll., Louvain, Belgium, St. Mary's Sem., Balt.; bd. dirs. United Way Southeastern Conn., 1976-94, Conn. Drug and Adv. Coun., 1978-80; chmn. bd. Cath. Relief Svcs., 1978-86; mem. fin. and budget com. U.S. Cath. Conf., 1985-87; chancellor Holy Apostles Coll. and Sem., Cromwell, Conn., 1982-94; pres. Conn. Interfaith Housing, 1975-94; cons. Pontifical Coun. Justice and Peace, 1995. Mem. Rotary, K. of C. (R.I. state chaplain 1964-75). Home: 2 High Ridge Rd Worcester MA 01602-1432 *If you would make a true success of your life for time and for eternity, never forget that it will be achieved by your willingness to make countless efforts that will be known only to God.*

REILLY, DAVID HENRY, university dean; b. Paterson, N.J., Nov. 7, 1936; s. David Henry and Ethel Taylor (Alt) R.; m. Jean Lockwood, July 2, 1960; children— David Scott, Chris Robert, Sandra Jean. BA, U. Vt., 1959; Ed.M., Rutgers U., 1962, Ed.D., 1965. Diplomate: Am. Bd. Profl. Psychology. Remedial reading instr. Drake Sch. of N.J. Neuro-Psychiat. Inst., Princeton, 1959-62, jr. fellow psychol. services at inst., summer 1962-63; research asst. N.J. Bur. Research Neurology and Psychiatry; also sch. psychologist Woodbridge (N.J.) sch. system, 1962-63; clin. psychologist, then research asso. N.J. Bur. Research Neurology and Psychiatry, 1963-64, 65; sch. and research psychologist Woodbridge sch. system, 1964-65; post doctoral fellow clin. child psychology Devereux Found., Devon, Pa., 1965-66; mem. faculty U. N.C., Chapel Hill, 1966-74, prof. psychology, 1974—, chmn. dept. sch. psychology program, 1966-74; dean U. N.C. (Sch. Edn.), Greensboro, 1974-86; dean Coll. of Grad. and Profl. Studies The Citadel, Charleston, 1992—. Mem. N.C. Bd. Examiners Practicing Psychologists, 1973—, treas., 1975, chmn., 1976 Contbr. articles to profl. jours. Research grantee NIMH, 1963; Fulbright Vis. scholar Republic of Cyprus, 1986-87, USSR, 1990. Fellow APA; mem. Am. Acad. Sch. Psychology (pres.-elect 1996-97, pres. 1997-98), Southeastern Psychol. Assn., N.C. Psychol. Assn. (pres. 1980-81), N.C. Assn. Coll. Tchr. Edn. (pres. 1981), N.C. Sch. Psychology Assn. (pres. 1976-77), S.C. Grad. Deans Assn. (pres. 1998-99). Home: 8644 Timbermarsh Ln North Charleston SC 29420 E-mail: skipreilly@knology.net.

REILLY, EDWARD FRANCIS, JR. federal agency administrator, former state senator; b. Leavenworth, Kans., Mar. 24, 1937; s. Edward F. and Marian C. (Sullivan) R. BA, U. Kans., 1961. V.P. Reilly & Sons, Inc., Leavenworth, 1967-92; pres. Yllier Lake Estates, Inc., Easton, Kans., 1965-89; mem. Kans. Ho. of Reps., 1963-64, Kans. State Senate, 1964-92, asst. majority leader, 1977-80, vice-chmn. govtl. orgn., chmn. ins. subcom., chmn. fed. and state affairs com.; chmn. U.S. parole comn. U.S. Dept. Justice, Chevy Chase, Md. Chmn. U.S. Parole Commn. Mem. Nat. Commn. on Accreditation of Law Enforcement Agys.; chmn. U.S. Parole Commn. Dept. of Justice, Md., 1992—; commr. ex offioio U.S. Sentencing Commn., Washington; del. to Rep. Nat. Conv., Miami Beach, Fla., 1968; chmn. Leavenworth County Radio Free Europe Fund, 1972; bd. dirs. St. John's Hosp., Leavenworth, 1970-79, sec.; bd. dirs. Leavenworth Assn. for Handicapped, 1968-69, ARC, Leavenworth chpt., Kans. Blue Cross/Blue Shield, 1969-72; apptd. by Pres. Reagan Nat. Hwy. Safety Adv. Com.; active Trinity Nat. Leadership Roundtable, Cath. Campaign Am., Kans. Adv. Bd. Juvenile Offenders, Nat. Com. Cmty. Corrections. Recipient Cmty. Leaders of Am., 1971, 85, 86, Hallpac Pub. Svc. award, 1988, Am. Police Hall of Fame award, 1990, Good Samaritan award Order of Michael the Arch Angel Police Legion, 1990, Commendation award mayor and city commn. of Leavenworth, Kans., 1990, Carnegie Hero Fund Commn. award and medallion, 1991, Silver Angel award Kans. Cath. Conf., 1992; named Outstanding Young Men Am., 1965-76. Mem. Nat. Inst. Corrections (adv. bd.), Advisory Bd., Dept. of Philosophy, Catholic Univ. of America, Am. Paroling Authorities Internat., Am. Correctional Assn., Am. Probation and Paroling Assn., Leavenworth C. of C. (hon. dir. 1970-73), No. Assn. Chiefs Police, Assn. U.S. Army (Henry Leavenworth award 1960), Kansas City (Kans.) C. of C., Leavenworth Hist. Soc. (dir. 1968-73), John Carroll Soc., Native Sons of Kansas City, Ancient Order of Hibernians, U.S. Supreme Ct. Hist. Soc., Kiwanis (dir. 1969-70, Connelly award 1991, Legion of Honor award 1996), K.C., Elks, Eagles, Order of Malta, Equestrian Order Holy Sepulchre Jerusalem, Sacred Military Constantinian Order of Saint George. Republican. Roman Catholic.

REILLY, EDWARD ARTHUR, lawyer; b. N.Y.C., Dec. 17, 1943; s. Edward Arthur and Anna Marguerite (Sautter) R.; children: M. Teresa, Edward A. AB, Princeton U., 1965; JD, Duke U., 1968. Bar: N.Y. 1969, N.C. 1971, Fla. 1979, Conn. 1983. Asst. dean law sch. Duke U., 1970-72; assoc. Shearman & Sterling, N.Y.C., 1972-80, ptnr., 1980-87, Harlow, Reilly, Derr & Stark, Research Triangle Park, N.C., 1988-90; counsel Morris & McVeigh, N.Y.C., 1991-93, ptnr., 1993—. Pres. Am. Friends of Paris Opera and Ballet, Inc.; sec. The Camille and Henry Dreyfus Found., Inc.; sec. The Owen Cheatham Found. Decorated Chevalier de l'Ordre des Arts et des Lettres, French Govt.-Ministry of Culture and Comm., 1992. Fellow Am. Coll. Trust & Estate Counsel; mem. N.Y. State Bar Assn., Fla. Bar Assn., Conn. Bar Assn. Episcopalian. Office: Morris & McVeigh 767 3rd Ave New York NY 10017-2023 Home: 5 Old Field Pl Norwalk CT 06853-1116

REILLY, FRANCIS X. lawyer, consultant; b. Westborough, Mass., Sept. 18, 1916; s. Francis Xavier and Blanche Marie (Marshall) R.; m. Beverly E. Blackwell, Oct. 7, 1941 (dec. July 1982); children: Martha J. Reilly Hinchman, John F. AB, Dartmouth Coll., 1938; JD, Harvard U., 1941. Bar: Mass. 1941, Ill. 1954. Atty., treas. Wilson & Co., Inc., Chgo., 1963-67; v.p. LTV Corp., Dallas, 1967-70; v.p., treas. B. F. Goodrich Co., Akron, Ohio, 1970-73, Katy Industries, INc., Elgin, 1973-76; gen. counsel, v.p. Rollins Burdick Hunter, Chgo., 1976-84; pvt. practice law and cons. Barrington, Ill., 1984-99. Lt. comdr. USNR, 1943-46. Mem. ABA, U. Club of Chgo. Address: The King Home 1555 Oak Ave Apt 202 Evanston IL 60201-4233

REILLY, FRANK KELLY, business educator; b. Chgo., Dec. 30, 1935; s. Clarence Raymond and Mary Josephine (Ruckrigel) R.; m. Therese Adele Bourke, Aug. 2, 1958; children: Frank Kelly III, Clarence Raymond II, Therese B., Edgar B. BBA, U. Notre Dame, 1957; MBA, Northwestern U., 1961, U. Chgo., 1964, PhD, 1968; LLD (hon.), St. Michael's Coll., 1991. CFA. Trader Goldman Sachs & Co., Chgo., 1958-59; security analyst Tech. Fund, 1959-62; asst. prof. U. Kans., Lawrence, 1965-68, assoc. prof., 1968-72; prof. bus., assoc. dir. divsn. bus. and econ. rsch. U. Wyo., Laramie, 1972-75; prof. fin. U. Ill., Champaign-Urbana, 1975-81; Bernard J. Hank prof. U. Notre Dame, Ind., 1981—, dean Coll. Bus. Adminstrn., 1981-87. Bd. dirs., chmn. Brinson Funds, Assn. Investment Mgmt. and Rsch.; past chmn. Inst. Chartered Fin. Analysts; past chmn. bd. dirs. NIBCO Corp.; bd. dirs. Internat. Bd. CFPs, Discover Bank, Ft. Dearborn Income Securities, Battery Park High Yield Fund., Morgan Stanley Dean Witter Trust Fed. Savs. Bank (FSB). Author: Investment Analysis and Portfolio Management, 1979, 6th edit., 2000, Investments, 1982, 5th edit., 1999; co-editor: Ethics and the Investment Industry, 1989; editor: Readings and Issues in Investments, 1975, High Yield Bonds: Analysis and Risk Assessment, 1990; assoc. editor Fin. Mgmt., 1977-82, Quar. Rev. Econs. and Bus, 1979-87, Fin. Rev., 1979-87, 92—, Jour. Fin. Edn., 1981—, Jour. Applied Bus. Rsch., 1986—, Fin. Svcs. Rev., 1989-96, Internat. Rev. Econs. and Fin., 1992—, European Jour. Fin., 1994—. Arthur J. Schmidt Found. fellow, 1962-65; U. Chgo. fellow, 1963-65; recipient faculty award U. Notre Dame, 1999. Fellow Fin. Mgmt. Assn. (pres. 1983-84, chmn. 1985-91, bd. dirs.); mem. Midwest Bus. Adminstrn. Assn. (pres. 1974-75), Am. Fin. Assn., Western Fin. Assn. (exec. com. 1973-75), Ea. Fin. Assn. (exec. com. 1979-84, pres. 1982-83), Midwest Fin. Assn. (pres. 1993-94), Fin. Analysts Fedn., Acad. Fin. Svcs. (pres. 1990-91), Inst. Chartered Fin. Analysts (coun. of examiners, rsch. and edn. com., edn. steering com., C. Stewart Sheppard award 1991), Internat. Assoc. Fin. Planners (ednl. resource com., bd. dirs.), Assn. of Investment Mgmt. and Rsch. (Daniel J. Forrestal III Leadership award for profl. ethics 2001), Investments Analysts Soc. Chgo. (bd. dirs. 1988-89), Beta Gamma Sigma. Roman Catholic. Office: U Notre Dame Mendoza Coll Bus Notre Dame IN 46556-5646 E-mail: reilly.1@nd.edu. *Any success I have enjoyed is due to the talents God has given me and my belief that I have an obligation to maximize the output from those talents by hard work, while never forgetting that my family comes first because they have always provided me with the love and support necessary for success and happiness.*

REILLY, GEORGE, lawyer; b. Waukegan, Ill., Nov. 29, 1934; s. James M. and Hilda Clara (Van Heirseele) R.; m. Dadee Bruce, Dec. 23, 1957; children: Laurene Beth, Theresa Ann. BA, Ill. Coll., 1956; MS, S.D. State U., 1958; JD, U. Minn., 1964. Bar: Minn. 1964, U.S. Dist. Ct. Minn. 1964, U.S. Ct. Appeals (8th cir.) 1965. Assoc. Leonard, Street and Deinard, Mpls., 1964-70, ptnr., 1973-82, mng. ptnr., 1983-91, ptnr., chair of bus. divsn., 1991-96; chief dep. atty. gen. State of Minn., St. Paul, 1971-72. Chief counsel Minn. Housing and Fin. Agy., St. Paul, 1972-80. Campaign chair Spannaus for Atty. Gen. com., 1974, 78, Spannaus for Gov., 1982. Mem. ABA, Minn. State Bar Assn., Citizens League, Variety Childrens Assn. (bd. dirs.). Democrat. Avocations: travel, sports. Office: Leonard Street & Deinard 150 S 5th St Ste 2300 Minneapolis MN 55402-4238

REILLY, JILL MARLENE, school system administrator; b. Chgo., Jan. 27, 1951; d. Jack Louis and Leah M. Cappels; m. Patrick Duane Reilly, May 29, 1971; children: Elizabeth Brama, Joseph, Heather. BA in English, U. Cin., 1974; MA in Curriculum, U. Minn., 1985; D in Edn. Leadership, U. St. Thomas, St. Paul, 1992. Co-ptnr. Featherstone-Reilly Ednl. Cons., Apple Valley, Minn., 1984-95; mentor program coord. Intermediate Sch. Dist. # 917, 1985-93; sr. cons. Honeywell, Inc., Mpls., 1993-95; adj. asst. prof. St. Mary's U., 1994—; pres. Acad. Holy Angels, Richfield, 1995—. Author: Mentorship: The Essential Guide for Schools and Business, 1992; co-author: College Comes Sooner Than You Think, 1987. Bd. dirs. guidance div. Nat. Assn. Gifted Children, Mpls., 1988-93; bd. dirs., chair elect Minn. Coun. Gifted and Talented, Mpls., 1991-94. Office: Acad Holy Angels 6600 Nicollet Ave Richfield MN 55423 E-mail: jreilly@ahastars.org.

REILLY, JOAN RITA, nurse practitioner, educator, school nurse; b. Evanston, Ill., Apr. 3, 1947; d. Thomas A. and Elmira E. (McCauley) R. BSN, U. Mich., 1969; MSN, U. Colo., Denver, 1972, postgrad., 1974, 85. Pediatric nurse cons. U. Colo. John F. Kennedy Child Devel. Ctr., Denver, 1972-74; pediatric nurse practitioner U. Chgo., Wyler Hosp., 1975-77; sch. nurse spl. edn. Chgo. Pub. Schs., 1977-86, sch. nurse coord. spl. svcs., 1986-89; sch. nurse, nurse practitioner Chgo. (Ill.) Pub. Schs., 1989—. Adj. prof. U. Ill., 1981—; seminar dir., Chgo., 1981—. Contbr. articles to profl. jours.; contbr. to profl. books. Bd. dirs. Family and Children's AIDS Network. Angel scholar, 1969; recipient Shirley Titus award, 1972; named Sch. Nurse of Yr., Chgo. Pub. Schs., 1995-96. Mem. ANA, Ill. Nurses Assn., Sch. Nurses Assn., Interdivisional Coun. Nurse Practitioners, Sigma Theta Tau, Delta Kappa Gamma. Home: 615 W Deming Pl Apt 202 Chicago IL 60614-2606 Office: Lincoln Elem Sch 615 W Kemper Pl Chicago IL 60614-3376 E-mail: jr2001@hotmail.com.

REILLY, JOHN B. lawyer; b. Bangor, Maine, Sept. 12, 1947; s. Louis J. and Evelyn I. (Lindsay) R.; children: Carolyn, Bridget. BA, U. R.I., 1970; JD cum laude, Suffolk U., 1976. Bar: R.I. 1976, Mass. 1985, U.S. Dist. Ct. R.I. 1976, U.S. Dist. Ct. Mass. 1985, U.S. Dist. Ct. Conn. 1995, U.S. Claims Ct. 1980, U.S. Ct. Appeals (1st and 2d cirs.) 1984, U.S. Ct. Appeals (3d cir.) 1985, U.S. Supreme Ct. 1983; cert. fraud examiner. Sole practice, Providence, 1976-81, Warwick, R.I., 1981-83; sr. ptnr. John Reilly & Assocs. and predecessor firms, 1984-89, Reilly & Nikolyszyn, LLP, Warwick, 2000—. Mem. Gov.'s Automobile Ins. Task Force, 1992-93. Mem. ABA, R.I. Bar Assn., Def. Rsch. Inst., R.I. Assn. Auth Theft and Arson Investigators (sec. 1995-96, pres. 1997—), Trucking Ind. Def. Assn., Pi Sigma Alpha, Phi Kappa Psi. Home: 80 Paterson Ave Warwick RI 02886-9110 Office: John Reilly & Assocs 300 Centerville Rd Warwick RI 02886-0200 E-mail: jrasoc@gis.net.

REILLY, JOHN MARSDEN, English language educator; b. Pitts., Feb. 18, 1933; s. John Francis and Virginia (Marsden) R.; m. Joyce Jane Whisler, July 16, 1952; children: John David, Bridget Ann, Michael Timothy; m. Janet Louise Potter, June 17, 1995. BA with high honors, W.Va. U., 1954; MA, Washington U., 1963, PhD, 1967. Instr. Wash. U., St. Louis, 1960-61; asst. prof. U. P.R., Rio Piedras, 1961-63, SUNY, Albany, 1963-70, assoc. prof., 1970-83, prof. dept. English, 1983-94; grad. prof., dir. grad. studies Howard

U., Washington, 1994—. Chief negotiator United Univ. Professions, 1981-94, pres., 1987-93 ; bd. advisors St. James Editorial, London, 1971-80, Melus, 1987-94, African Am. Rev., 1986—, Obsidian II, 1985-90; coord. preparing future faculty Howard U., 2000—. Editor: Twentieth-Century Crime and Mystery Writers, 1980, 2d edit., 1985, Richard Wright: The Critical Reception, 1978, Tony Hillerman, 1996, Oxford Companion to Crime and Mystery Writing, 1999, Larry McMurtry, 2000; contbr. articles to profl. jours. Recipient Eugene V. Debs award Dem. Socialists of Am., 1983, George Dove award Popular Culture Assn., Johnetta Davis Svc. to Grad. Students award Howard U., 1999, Fund for Acad. Exellence awards, 1997, 99; Woodrow Wilson fellow, 1955, Humanist fellow NEH, 1970; Danforth Tchrs. grantee, 1966-67, disting. Contbns. to Ethnic Lit. Studies Melus, 1987. Fellow Phi Beta Kappa; mem. Soc. for Study of Multi-Ethnic Lit. U.S. (chmn. 1982-84), MLA (mem. del. assembly 2001—), Am. Fedn. Tchrs., Coll. Lang. Assn., Mystery Writers Am. (Edgar Allan Poe award 1981). Democrat. Avocations: hiking, cooking, travel writing. Home: 10 Overlook Dr Oneonta NY 13820-4635 Office: Howard U English Dept Washington DC 20059-0001 E-mail: jreilly@fac.howard.edu.

REILLY, LAURA KATHERINE, pharmaceutical company executive; b. Bronx, N.Y., Aug. 18, 1957; d. Michael F. and Winfred K. (Lynch) R. BS, Molloy Coll., 1979; MBA, NYU, 1993. Pediatric antiemetic rsch. nurse Meml. Sloan Kettering Cancer Ctr., N.Y.C., 1979-84; med. sales rep. Pennwalt Pharms., Rochester, N.Y., 1984-86; asst. securities analyst Morgan Stanley & Co. Inc., N.Y.C., 1986-89; rsch. nurse Meml. Sloan Kettering Cancer Ctr., 1989-93; acct. supr.-oncology Integrated Comm., Inc., Parsippany, N.J., 1993, account supr., 1993-96; v.p., group acct. supr. NCI Pharma, Princeton, 1996—. Mem. Assn. Pediatric Oncology Nurses, Oncology Nursing Soc., Sigma Theta Tau (chpt. pres. 1979-80). Home: 8350 Boulevard E North Bergen NJ 07047-6048

REILLY, LINDA M. surgeon; b. Pitts., Mar. 5, 1949; d. John Joseph and Marguerite (Lancaster) R. BA, Trinity Coll., 1970; MD, Georgetown U., 1976. Diplomate Am. Bd. Surgeons, Am. Bd. Vascular Surgeons, Critical Care Surgeons. Intern Johns Hopkins U., 1976-77, resident in surgery, 1977-82; fellow in vascular surgery U. Calif., San Francisco, 1982-85, asst. prof. dept. surgery, 1985-91, assoc. prof., 1991-98, prof., 1998—. Contbr. 59 articles to profl. jours., chpts to 23 books. Mem. San Francisco Surg. Soc. (exec. coun. 1992-96), No. Calif. Vascular Soc. (exec. coun. 1993-96), Soc. for Vascular Surgery. Avocation: running. Office: Vascular Surgery M488 505 Parnassus Ave San Francisco CA 94143-0001

REILLY, MICHAEL ATLEE, financial company executive, venture capital investor; b. Ft. Worth, Dec. 10, 1948; s. Thomas William and Alma Margaret (Cox) R.; m. Beverly Ann Yates, Dec. 27, 1974; children: Atlee Michael, Asher Yates, Anson Marcus, Austin Thomas, Axton Carter. BA, U. Tex., 1971. Ptnr. Michael A. Reilly Co., Dallas, 1971; pres., CEO Ryan Cos., Arlington, 1980—90, Reilly Bros., Arlington, 1990—. Trustee Childrens Trust Fund State of Tex; vice chmn. Troy Aikman Found. Mem.: Urban Land Inst. Office: Reilly Bros Property Co 1000 Ballpark Way Ste 304 Arlington TX 76011-5169

REILLY, NANCY (ANNE CAUFIELD REILLY), painter; b. Bryn Mawr, Pa., Mar. 29, 1927; d. Ralph Caulfield and Claire Helena (Roesch) Goodman; m. Donald Elliott Reilly, May 14, 1949; children: Kevin Caulfield, William Stockbridge, Peter Elliott. Studies with Samuel E. Brown, Westport, Conn., 1955-63; studies with Mimi Jennewein, Larchmont, N.Y., 1964-65. Demonstrator, lectr. in portrait painting Bridgeport (Conn.) Art League, Milford (Conn.) Art League, Pen and Brush Club, New Haven, Conn. Classic Arts Assn., Allied Artists Am., Kent (Conn.) Art Assn., SCAN, Newtown, Conn. Exhibited in group shows at Nat. Acad. Design, N.Y.C., 1964, 65, 69, 70, Nat. Acad. Arts and Letters, N.Y.C., 1971, Wadsworth Antheum, Hartford, Conn., 1966, 72, Stamford (Conn.) Mus., 1965, Mus. Sci. and Industry, Bridgeport, 1972, Salmagundi Club, N.Y.C., Nat. Arts Club, N.Y.C., Butler Inst. Am. Art, Youngstown, Ohio, 2001, New Britain Mus. Am. Art, New Britain, Conn., 2001; included in slide collections Smithsonian Instn., Washington, U. Conn. Health Ctr., Farmington. Vol. artist rehab. unit Norwalk Hosp., 1984-95. Recipient Gold medal for oil painting Catherine Lorillard Wolfe Art Club, 1965, Silver medal for oil painting Nat. Arts Club, 1969, Bronze medal for oil painting Hudson Valley Art Assn., 1981, George Height award for portrait, 1969, Blanche Farr award 1971, Best in Show Kent Art Assn., 1991, J.D. Altobello Meml. award Conn. Pastel Soc., 1995. Fellow Am. Artists Profl. League; mem. Allied Artists Am. (hon., bd. dirs. 1991-99, Jane Peterson award for portrait 1971), Nat. Arts Club (Bruce Stevenson award for portrait 1971, 88, 91), Pastel Soc. Am., Hudson Valley Art Assn. (Thora M. Jensen award 1989), Kent Art Assn. (Gordon C. Aymar award for oil 1993, Mabel Rowe Aiken award for oil 1995, Frances B. Townley award for portrait 1998, 99), New Haven Paint and Clay Club (Merit award 1992, 97), Acad. Artists Assn. Springfield, Artists' Fellowship N.Y. Home: 9 Marilane Westport CT 06880-1008

REILLY, PATRICK JOHN, nonprofit executive; b. Phila., Nov. 30, 1969; s. John Michael and Mary Kay R.; m. Rosario Tuason, Aug. 30, 1997; children: Ian Patrick, Joseph Maximilian. BA, Fordham U., 1991; MPA, Am. U., 1993. Comms. cons. Nat. Conf. of Cath., Washington, 1991-93; program analyst U.S. Dept. Edn., 1993-95; exec. dir. Citizens for Ednl. Freedom, Arlington, 1995-97; editor, rsch. assoc. Capital Rsch. Ctr., Washington, 1997-2001; founder Cardinal Newman Soc. for Preservation of Cath. Higher Edn., Falls Church, Va., 1993, exec. dir., 1993-96, 99-01, chmn., bd. dirs., 1996-98, pres., 2001—; sr. rsch. fellow Capital Rsch. Ctr., Washington, 2001—; pres. Non-Profit Consulting, Manassas, Va., 2001—. Editor (newsletter) Found. Watch, 1997-2001, Orgn. Trends, 1997-2001. Mem. Brent Soc. (bd. dirs. 2000—), Fellowship of Cath. Schs., Soc. of Cath. Social Scientists. Republican. Roman Catholic. Office: Cardinal Newman Soc Preservation Cath Higher Edn 207 Park Ave Ste B-2 Falls Church VA 22046

REILLY, ROBERT FREDERICK, valuation consultant; b. N.Y.C., Oct. 3, 1953; s. James J. and Marie (Griebel) K.; m. Janet H. Steiner, Apr. 16, 1975; children: Ashley Lauren, Brandon Christopher, Cameron Courtney. BA in Econs., Columbia U., 1975, MBA in Fin., 1976. CPA, Ohio, Ill.; cert. mgmt. acct., CFA; cert. real estate appraiser; cert. review appraiser; cert. gen. appraiser Ill., Va., Utah, Oreg., N.Y.; cert. bus. appraiser; accredited bus. valuator. Sr. cons. Booz, Allen & Hamilton, Cin., 1975-76; dir. corp. planning Huffy Corp., Dayton, Ohio, 1976-81; v.p. Arthur D. Little Valuation, Inc., Chgo., 1981-85; ptnr., nat. dir. of valution svcs. Deloitte & Touche, 1985-91; mng. dir. Willamette Mgmt. Assocs., 1991—. Adj. prof. accounting U. Dayton Grad. Sch. Bus., 1977-81; adj. prof. fin. econs., Elmhurst (Ill.) Coll., 1982-87; adj. prof. fin. Ill. Inst. Tech. Grad. Sch. Bus., Chgo., 1985-91; adj. prof. taxation U. Chgo. Grad. Sch. Bus., 1985-87. Co-author: Valuing Small Businesses and Professional Practices, 1993, 4th edit., 2000, Business Valuation Video Course, 1993, Valuing a Business, 1995, 4th edit., 2000, Valuing Accounting Practices, 1997, Valuing Professional Practices--A Practitioner's Approach, 1997, Valuing Intangible Assets, 1998, Handbook of Advanced Business Valuation, 1999; editor, columnist Small Bus. Taxation, 1989-90, Bus. Valuation Rev., 1989-90, Jour. of Real Estate Acctg. and Taxation, 1991-93, Ohio CPA Jour., 1984-86, 91—, Jour. Property Taxation Mgmt., 1993—, Jour. Am. Bankruptcy Inst., 1993—; co-editor: Financial Valuation-Valuation of Business and Business Interests, 1997; contbr. more than 200 articles to profl. jours. Mem. AICPA, Am. Soc. Appraisers (mem. bd. examiners 1985-89), Nat. Assn. Real Estate Appraisers, Inst. Bus. Appraisers (life), Inst. Cert. Mgmt. Accts. (chpt. dir. 1976—), Inst. Property Taxation, Ill. Soc. CPAs, Ohio Soc. CPAs (chpt. dir. 1978-81), Accreditation Coun. Accountancy (accredited in fed. income taxation), Bus. Valuation Assn., Chgo. Soc. Investment Analysts, Inst. CFAs, Am. Bankruptcy Inst., Am. Econ. Assn., Nat. Assn. Bus. Economists, Appraisal Inst. Home: 310 Algonquin Rd Barrington IL 60010-6109 Office: 8600 W Bryn Mawr Ave Chicago IL 60631-3579

REILLY, ROBERT JOSEPH, counselor; b. Spokane, Wash., Mar. 7, 1936; s. John Francis and Vivian Helen (White) R.; m. Joan Steiner, June 20, 1960; children: Sean Michael, Patrick Joseph, Bridget Colleen. BA in Psychology, Seattle U., 1985; postgrad., Infantry Officer Candidate Sch, Ft. Benning, 1960, EOAC, Ft. Belvoir, 1968, Leadership Inst. Seattle/City U., 1991-92. Ordained Congl. Ch. Practical Theology, 1992. Enlisted U.S. Army, 1953, advanced through grades to maj., 1981, ret., 1981, with Korea, 1961-62, Vietnam, 1966-67, 69-70; counseling supr. Schick Shadel Hosp., Seattle, 1984-89; dir. Canyon Counseling, Puyallup, Wash., 1987-92, 95—; social worker Wash. State Employee Adv. Svc., Olympia, 1992-99. V.p. Nat. Bd. for Hypnotherapy and Hypnotic Anaesthesiology, 1991-97, pres. Wash. chpt. 1991-94; exec. v.p. Coll. Therapeutic Hypnosis, Puyallup, 1989-94; mem. adj. faculty Pierce Coll., Tacoma, 1991-92; mem. Wash. State Chem. Dependency Counselor Cert. Bd., sec., 1995—. Pres. Irish Cultural Club, Tacoma, 1983-85, 93-94; sec. Tacoma chpt. Ret. Officers Assn., 1983-87, pres., 1993-96, bd. dirs., 1982-97; bd. dirs. Tacoma Mus. Playhouse Theater Co., 1997-2000, adv. bd., 2000—; adv. bd. Friends of the Ctrl. Highlands, Vietnam, 1999—. Decorated Vietnamese Cross of Gallantry with silver star, Bronze Star with oak leaf cluster, Meritorious Svc. medal, Army Commendation medal with 2 oak leaf clusters; named Profl. of Yr. Chem. Dependency Profls. Wash., 1994. Mem. Nat. Bd. Hypnotherapy and Hypnotic Anesthesiology (v.p. 1991-97, Mem of Yr. 1994, pres. Wash. chpt. 1991-94), Nat. Guild Hypnotists, Nat. Assn. Alcohol and Drug Abuse Counselors (mem. del. Russia & Czech Rep. 1996), Am. Congress Hypnotist Examiners, Nat. Assn. Tobacco Addiction Counselors, Army Engr. Assn., Nat. 4th Inf. Divsn. Assn. (sec.-treas. N.W. chpt. 1993—), The Ret. Officers Assn., The Ret. Enlisted Assn. (pres. Wehatchee chpt. 2001-02), Assn. for Addiction Profls., Washington West Home Owners Assn. (pres. 2001-02), La Soc. des Quarante Hommes et Huit Chevaux (Aumonier 2001--). Avocations: volksmarching, symphony music, theater.

REILLY, THOMAS, humanities educator; b. Hollymount, Mayo, Ireland, Dec. 16, 1941; arrived in Eng., 1967; s. Patrick and Josephine (Sheridan) R.; m. Feb. 22, 1977; children: Anna, Siobhān. BA, U. Coll. Dublin, Ireland, 1967; MSc, Royal Free Hosp., London, 1971; PhD, Liverpool (Erg.) Poly., 1975; M.I. Biology, Inst. Biology, London, 1977; DSc, JMU, 1998; F.I. Biology, Liverpool John Moores U., 1999; Doctor Honoris Causa, Vrije U., Brussels, 2001. Clerical officer Dublin Corp., 1960-65; tchr., athletic coach Govt. of Cameroun, 1968-70; technician Med. Rsch. Coun., London, 1971; rsch. asst. Liverpool Poly., 1972-75, lectr., then prin. lectr., reader, 1975-88, prof. sports sci., 1988—; dir. sch. Human Scis. Liverpool John Moores U., 1991-95, dir. grad. sch., 1995—, dir. Rsch. Inst. Space and Exercise Scis., 1997—. Vis. prof. Tsukuba (Japan) U., 1977; vis. coach Nigerian Sports Coun., 1976; vis. rsch. assoc. U. Calif. Berkeley, 1980; invited spkr. 2d World Congress on Sci. and Football, The Netherlands, 1991, 3d World Congress on Sci. and Football, Cardiff, 1995; contbd. consensus statement on nutrition for soccer F.I.F.A., Zürich, 1994. Editor: Sports Fitness and Sports Issues, 1981, Physiology of Sports, 1990, Science and Football, 1988, Science and Football II, 1993, Science and Soccer, 1996, Biological Rhythms and Exercise, 1997, Science and Football III, 1997, The Clinical Pharmacology of Sport and Exercise, 1997, Science and Football IV, 2001, Advances in Sport, Leisure and Ergonomics, 2001; editor Jour. Sports Sci., 1983-96. Organizer Hollymount Internat. Rd. Race, Mayo, Ireland, 1976—; coord. acclimation strategy Brit. Olympic Assn., London, 1993—, chair exercise physiology steering group, 1992—. Fellow Ergonomics Soc., 1990. Mem. Brit. Assn. Sport and Exercise Sci. (chmn. 1994-96), Internat. Steering Group on Sci. and Football (chmn. 1987—), European Coll. Sport Sci. (founder), pres. World Commn. of Sci. and Sports, 2000—. Roman Catholic. Avocations: soccer, Gaelic football, running, squash, orienteering. Office: Liverpool John Moores U Rodney Ho 70 Mount Pleasant Liverpool L3 5UX England E-mail: t.p.reilly@livjm.ac.uk.

REILLY, THOMAS F. state attorney general; b. Springfield, Mass. m. Ruth Reilly; 3 children. BA, Am. Internat. Coll., 1964; JD, Boston Coll., 1970. Atty. Civil Rights divsn. Atty. Gen.'s Office; dist. atty. Middlesex County Dist. Atty. Office, 1991—99; atty. gen. State of Mass., Springfield, 1999—. Founder The Cmty. Based Justice Program. Office: One Ashburton Pl Boston MA 02108-1698 also: 436 Dwight St Springfield MA 01103 also: One Exchange Place Worcester MA 01608*

REILLY, TRACY LYNN, language professional/educator, English; b. Alton, Ill., June 10, 1959; d. Jerry John and Deanne Jean (McDonald) Lavick; m. James Edward Harte, July 26, 1980 (div. Dec. 12, 1988); 1 child, Kateland Jean; m. Kenneth Patrick Reilly, Nov. 26, 1994; 1 child, Joseph Patrick. BA in English Lit. cum laude, U. S.Fla., 1981; MA in English Lit., St. Louis U., 1989. Cert. tchr., Fla. Tchr. English, dept. chair Mary Help of Christian Sch., Tampa, Fla., 1981-85; instr. English St. Louis U., 1988-89, Hillsborough C.C., Tampa, Brandon, Fla., 1989-92, St. Petersburg (Fla.) Jr. Coll., 1989—; sr. English tchr. Admiral Farragut Acad., St. Petersburg, 1992—; tchr. English for fgn. students ELS Ednl. Svcs. Eckerd Coll., 1997; English dept. chmn. Admiral Farragut, 1999. Coord. beginning tchrs. program Mary Help of Christians, Tampa, 1982; selection com. Pinellas County Mid. Sch. and Speech Contest, St. Petersburg, 1992-93, 97-98; bd. dirs. Admiral Farragut Discipline Bd., St. Petersburg. Author: (essay) Quincy Coll. Stylus, 1979; co-author, dir.: (play) Farragut Christmas, 1995, Taming of Shrew, 1996, The Mousetrap, 1998, Grease, 1999; stage mgr. Fiddler on the Roof, 2002. Vol. John Anderson Presdl. Campaign, Tampa, St. Petersburg, 1980; dir. Park St. Neighborhood Assn., 2000. Ill. State scholar, 1977, Acad. scholar Quincy Coll., 1977, St. Louis U., 1988. Mem. Nat. Coun. Tchrs. English, Fla. Fiction Writers Assn., Nat. Cath. Educators Assn., Sigma Tau Delta. Avocations: drama, writing, gardening. Office: Admiral Farragut Naval Acad 501 Park St N Saint Petersburg FL 33710-6743

REILLY, WILLIAM FRANCIS, media company executive; b. N.Y.C., June 8, 1938; s. William F. and Genevieve Reilly; m. Ellen Chapman, Nov. 19, 1966; children: Anthony Chapman and Jane Wasey (twins). AB cum laude, U. Notre Dame, 1959; MBA, Harvard U., 1964. Mgr. fin. analysis W.R. Grace & Co., N.Y.C., 1964-67, asst. to pres., 1969-71, CEO Bekaert Textile Divsn., 1971-74; pres., CEO Herman's World of Sporting Goods, Carteret, N.J., 1974-77; v.p., pres. W.R. Grace and Co., 1978; pres., CEO Home Ctr. Div., 1979-80; pres. Macmillan, Inc., N.Y.C., 1980-90; chmn., CEO Primedia Corp., 1990-2000; founder, chmn., CEO Aurelian Comm., 2000—. Dir. FMC Corp., Chgo., Barnes & Noble.com; trustee U. Notre Dame, South Bend, Ind., WNET, Channel 13, N.Y.C. 1st lt. U.S. Army, 1959-61. Home: 7 Sutton Sq New York NY 10022-2407 Office: Aurelian Comm LLC 375 Park Ave New York NY 10152

REILLY, WILLIAM THOMAS, lawyer; b. Passaic, N.J., Feb. 25, 1949; s. Thomas Edwin and Edna May (Dorritie) R.; m. Sheila Mary Brogan, Aug. 1, 1981; children: Kathleen Anne, Brendan Thomas, Timothy John. BS, Boston Coll., 1971; JD, Harvard U., 1974. Bar: N.J. 1974, U.S. Dist. Ct. N.J. 1974, U.S. Supreme Ct. 1979, U.S. Ct. Appeals (3rd cir.) 1984, U.S. Ct. Claims, 1996, U.S. Ct. Appeals (fed. cir.) 1997. Assoc. McCarter & English LLP, Newark, 1974-81, ptnr., 1982—. Trustee United Hosps. Med. Ctr., Newark, 1983-89, One-to-One/N.J., Inc., 1990-97, chmn., 1993-97. Mem. ABA, N.J. State Bar Assn., Harvard Law Sch. Assn., Eastward Ho Country Club. Avocation: golf. Home: 302 Kensington Dr Ridgewood NJ 07450-1822 Office: McCarter & English LLP Four Gateway Ctr 100 Mulberry St Newark NJ 07102-4004

REIM, RUTHANN, career and personal counselor, corporate trainer; b. Fresno, Calif., Oct. 4, 1943; d. F. Wayne and Charlene Marie (Young) Howd; m. Terry D., Nov. 29, 1963; children: Tracey, Brandon. BA in Sociology, San Jose State U., 1966; MA Guidance & Counseling, Pacific Luth. U., 1984. Cert. counselor, nat. Tchr., elem. sch. Dupont Sch. Dist., Tacoma, 1966-67, Prince Georges Sch. Dist., Lanham, Md., 1967-68, Franklin Pierce sch. Dist., Tacoma, 1968-70; owner Rainbow Glassworks, 1973-76, Creative Womanlife, Tacoma, 1976-78; dir., counselor Individual Devel. Ctr., 1984-88; pres. Career Mgmt. Inst., 1989—. Adj. faculty mem. dept. edn. Pacific Luth. U., 1980-84. Author: (career booklet) Career Change Made Easy, 1990; artist 5' round stained glass window "Dogwood", 1980. Trainer Jr. League Tacoma, 1977-79. Mem. Rotary (1st woman pres. 1991-92, bd. dirs. 1988-97), Phi Kappa Phi. Avocation: photography. Office: Career Mgmt Inst 8404 27th St W University Place WA 98466-2723 E-mail: careermi@nwrain.com.

REIMAN, DONALD HENRY, English language educator; b. Erie, Pa., May 17, 1934; s. Henry Ward and Mildred Abbie (Pearce) R.; m. Mary Warner, 1958 (div. 1974); 1 child, Laurel Elizabeth Reiman Henneman; m. Hélène Liebman Dworzan, Oct. 3, 1975. AB, Coll. of Wooster, 1956, Litt.D., 1981; MA, U. Ill., 1957, PhD, 1960. Instr. English, Duke U., Durham, N.C., 1960-62, asst. prof., 1962-64; assoc. prof. U. Wis., Milw., 1964-65; adj. assoc. prof. grad. program in English CUNY, 1967-68; adj. prof. Columbia U., N.Y.C., 1969-70, sr. rsch. assoc. in English, 1970-73; vis. prof. St. John's U., Jamaica, N.Y., 1974-75; editor Shelley and His Circle, Carl H. Pforzheimer Library, N.Y.C., 1965-86, N.Y. Pub. Libr., 1986-92; with Carl & Lily Pforzheimer Found., 1992—. Vis. lectr. U. Ill., 1963; vis. prof. U. Wash., Seattle, 1981, NYU, 1992; Lyell reader in bibliography Oxford U., 1988-89; adj. prof. English U. Del., 1992—; cons. Harvard U. Press, Yale U. Press, Princeton U. Press, Johns Hopkins U. Press, Garland Pub. Inc., W.W. Norton, Oxford U. Press, others. Author: Shelley's The Triumph of Life, A Critical Study, 1965, 2d edit., 1979, Percy Bysshe Shelley, 1969, 2d edit., 1990, (with D.D. Fischer) Byron on the Continent, 1974, English Romantic Poetry, 1800-1835, 1979, Romantic Texts and Contexts, 1987, Intervals of Inspiration: The Skeptical Tradition and the Psychology of Romanticism, 1988, The Study of Modern Manuscripts, 1993; editor: Shelley and His Circle, Vols. V-VI, 1973, Vols. VII-VIII, 1986, IX-X, 2002, The Romantics Reviewed: Contemporary Reviews of English Romantic Writers, 9 vols., 1972, (with S.B. Powers) Shelley's Poetry and Prose: A Norton Critical Edition, 1977, (with Neil Fraistat) 2nd rev. edit., 2002, The Romantic Context: Poetry, 128 vols., 1976-79, (with M.C. Jaye and B.T. Bennett) The Evidence of the Imagination, 1978; gen. editor: Manuscripts of the Younger Romantics, 1985-98; I The Esdaile Notebook: A Facsimile, 1985, II The Mask of Anarchy: Facsimiles, 1985, III Hellas, 1985, V The Harvard Shelley Poetic Manuscripts, 1991; (with M. O'Neill) VIII Fair-Copy Manuscripts of Shelley's Poems, 1997; editor-in-chief: The Bodleian Shelley Manuscripts, 1986-99, I Peter Bell The Third and the Triumph of Life, 1986, VII Shelley's Last Notebook and Other MSS, 1990, (with M.J. Neth) XVI The Hellas Notebook, 1994, The Complete Poetry of Percy Bysshe Shelley Vol. I (with N. Fraistat), 2000; mem. editl. com. adv. bd. Keats-Shelley Jour., 1968-73, Milton and the Romantics, 1975-80, Studies in Romanticism, 1977—, Romanticism Past and Present, 1980-86, Text, 1981—, Nineteenth-Century Literature, 1986—, Nineteenth-Century Contexts, 1987-90; co-founder, editor (with others) Romantic Cirs. Website; contbr. articles to encyclopedias, books and profl. jours. Active Common Cause. Am. Coun. Learned Socs. fellow, 1963-64, Wesleyan Ctr. Advanced Studies fellow, 1963-64, NEH fellow, 1978; grantee Am. Coun. Learned Socs., 1961, NEH, 1983—. Mem. AAUP, MLA (life), Modern Humanities Rsch. Assn. (life), Wordsworth-Coleridge Assn. Am. (founder), Byron Soc. (Am. com. 1973—, treas. 1999—), Keats-Shelley Assn. Am. (bd. dirs., treas. 1973-91, v.p. 1991—, Disting. Scholar award 1987), Bibliog. Soc. Am., Soc. Textual Scholarship (exec. com. 1981-93), Charles Lamb Soc., Assn. Documentary Editing, N.Am. Soc. Study of Romanticism. Democrat. Presbyterian. Office: NY Pub Libr Fifth Ave at 42nd St Rm 226 New York NY 10018 E-mail: dhreiman@udel.edu.

REIMANN, BERNHARD ERWIN FERDINAND, retired biologist; b. Berlin, Germany, May 30, 1922; s. Philip Berhard Ferdinand and Margarete (Kutzleb) Reimann; m. Beate Eleonore Hedwig, Sept. 1, 1949; 1 child Joachim Oscar Ferdinand. Grad., Paulsen Oberschule, 1941; lic. med. technologist, Berlin, 1949; D in Botany, Zoology, Geology, Freie U., Berlin, 1959. Supr. electo microscopy facility Scripps Inst. Oceanography, La Jolla, Calif., 1961—67; chief electron microscopy dept. pathology and area lab. svcs. William Beaumont Army Med. Ctr., El Paso, Tex., 1967—87; ret. Assoc. prof. biology dept. N.Mex. State U., Las Cruces, 1967—87; assoc. grad. faculty U. Tex., El Paso, 1968—69; assoc. clin. prof. dept. pathology Tex. Tech. U., El Paso, 1980—87. Contbr. articles to profl. jours. Vol. environ. adviser liquid waste disposal problems Village of Capitan N.Mex. and Lincoln County, 1988—. With German Afir Force, 1941—47. Named Civil Servant of Yr., Fed. Bus. Assn., 1981; recipient Comdrs. Civilian Svc. award, William Beaumont Army Med. Ctr., 1987, Recognition for Outstanding Svc. award, 41 Legis., 2d Session, State N.Mex., 1994. Fellow: AAAS; mem.: Microscopy Soc. Am. (emeritus). Democrat. Avocations: history of electron microscopy, photography, history. Home: 115 E Lobo Rd Capitan NM 88316

REIMANN, HELGA LUISE, sociologist; b. Berlin, Germany, July 6, 1937; d. Hans and Renata (Von Radinger) Feick; m. Horst Reimann, July 30, 1963 (dec. Oct. 1994). Dipl.rer.pol., U. Heidelberg (Germany), 1962, DrPhil., 1966; DrHabil., U. Augsburg, 1974. Asst. prof. U. Heidelberg, 1962-70; asst. prof., dir. gen. studies U. Augsburg, 1970-74, privatdozent in sociology, 1976-80, prof. sociology, 1980-2000, ret., 2000; interim prof. U. Würzburg (Germany), 1975-76. Guest prof. U. Pitts., 1968, 98, U. Salzburg (Austria), 1998. Author: Globalisierung, 2002; editor: Weltkultur und Weltgesellschaft, 1997; co-editor: Sizilien, 1985, Das Alter, 3d edit., 1994; watercolor exhbns. in Germany, Malta, Italy. Mem.: Internat. Sociol. Assn., Free German Soc. for Scis. and Arts (hon.), Rotary, Order of Merit Malta. Achievements include developments in international and transnational communication and globalization. Avocations: watercolors, biking. Home: Cuvilliésstr 10 81679 Munich Bavaria Germany Fax: 49 (0) 89 99 88 7941. E-mail: Prof.Helga.Reimann@T-Online.de.

REIMER, CHARLES WILSON, curator, consultant; b. Indpls., May 14, 1923; s. Charles Louis Reimer and Cora Morton-May Wilson; m. Reba Marjorie Fines, Jan. 2, 1944 (div. June 1976); children: Bruce W., Kurt L.; m. Jacquelyn Gayle White, Nov. 13, 1976; children: Laura E., Emilie G. BA, Butler U., 1946, MA, 1948; PhD, Mich. State U., 1952. Instr. Butler U., Indpls., 1946-48, DePauw U., Greencastle, Ind., 1950-51, Mich. State U., East Lansing, 1951-52; from asst. curator to curator Acad. Nat. Scis., Phila., 1952-91, curator proprius, 1991—. Adj. prof. Drexel U., Phila., 1965-72; vis. prof. Iowa Lakeside Lab., Milford, Iowa, 1966-90, Jinan U., Guangzhow, China, 1983, U. Concepcion, Chile, 1984. Co-author: Diatoms of the U.S. vol. I, 1966, vol. II, 1975. With U.S. Army, 1942-45. Decorated Purple Heart; recipient Spl. Recognition award Biennial N.Am. Diatom Symposium, 1993. Mem. Phycol. Soc. Am., Ind. Acad. Sci., Sigma Xi. Avocations: fishing, chess. Home: 458 Woodcrest Ln Media PA 19063-4835 Office: Acad Natural Scis 19th & The Parkway Philadelphia PA 19103

REIMER, JENNIFER ANN, computer scientist; b. Dubuque, Iowa, Feb. 8, 1969; d. Michael Arthur and Carol Ann Reimer. BA in Computer Sci., BA in Psychology, U. Iowa, 1993. Rsch. asst. U. Iowa, Iowa City, 1992-93, computer scientist, 1992-94; case mgr. Mental Health Ctr., Topeka, 1994-96; software engr., database adminstr. Divsn. Info. Resources, 1996-99; computer analyst, database adminstr. Maximus, McLean, Va., 1999-2000; computer programmer, database adminstr. U. Kans, Lawrence, 2000; software engr. Kans. Dept. Human Resources, Topeka, 2000—01, JPL/NASA, Pasadena, Calif., 2001—. Cons., graphic designer NBC Affiliate, Topeka, 1995; bus. owner Child and Adolescent Family Svcs., Topeka, 1996-97. Contbr. to profl. jours. Grantee NSF, 2000. Mem. Internat. Webmasters Assn. Roman Catholic. Avocations: basketball, football, golf, scuba diving, engineering/designing. E-mail: mickey2869#hotmail.com. Home: 1711 N Grismer #29 Burbank CA 91504 Office: JPL/NASA 4880 Oak Grove Dr Pasadena CA 91109

REIMERS, FERNANDO MIGUEL, education educator; b. Caracas, Venezuela, Dec. 20, 1958; m. Eleonora Villegas-Reimers; children: Tomas, Pablo. EdD, Harvard U., 1988. Edn. specialist Harvard Inst. for Internat. Devel., Cambridge, 1988—97; sr. edn. specialist World Bank, Washington, 1996—97; assoc. prof. Harvard U., Cambridge, Mass., 1998—. Author: (book) Unequal Schools, Unequal Chances, 2001, Informed Dialogue, 1997, Hope or Despair. Primary Education in Pakistan. Office: Harvard U Sch Edn Gutman 461 Appian Way Cambridge MA 02138 Personal E-mail: Fernando_Reimers@harvard.edu. Business E-Mail: fernando_reimers@harvard.edu.

REIMERS, ROBERT STOLLT, III, health sciences educator, consultant; b. June 9, 1943; BA, Cornell Coll., 1966; MA, U. Tex., 1968; PhD, Vanderbilt U., 1973. Rsch. scientist process tech. sect. Battelle Columbus Labs., Columbus, Ohio, 1973-75; prof. Sch. Pub. Health & Tropical Medicine Tulane U., New Orleans, 1975—. Home: 4705 Clearview Pkwy Metairie LA 70006-2311 Office: Tulane U Med Ctr Sch Pub Health/Tropical Med 1501 Canal St New Orleans LA 70112-2817 Fax: 504-584-1726. E-mail: rreimers@mailhost.tcs.tulane.edu.

REIN, BERT WALTER, lawyer; b. Bklyn., Feb. 7, 1941; s. Moe and Florence (Fishman) R.; m. Jennifer Christine Bulson, July 11, 1966 (dec. Mar. 1989); children: Joanna, Benjamin, Samantha; m. Barbara Jean Kahn, Oct. 18, 1992. BA, Amherst Coll., 1961; LLB, Harvard U., 1964. Bar: D.C. 1965, U.S. Dist. Ct. D.C. 1965, U.S. Ct. Appeals (D.C. cir.) 1968, U.S. Ct. Appeals (2d cir.) 1973, U.S. Ct. Appeals (8th cir.) 1974, U.S. Ct. Appeals (4th cir.) 1976,

U.S. Ct. Appeals (11th cir.) 1982, U.S. Supreme Ct. 1982. Law ck. to Justice John M. Harlan U.S. Supreme Ct., Washington, 1966-67; assoc. Kirkland & Ellis, 1967-69, ptnr., 1973-83; spl. asst. U.S. Dept. State, 1969-70, dep. asst. sec., 1970-73; ptnr. Wiley, Rein & Fielding, 1983—. Bd. dirs., chmn. govt. and regulation affairs com. U.S. C. of C., 1986-90; bd. dirs. Nat. Chamber Litigation Ctr.; advisor Reagan Dept. Justice Transition, Washington, 1980; mem. adv. com. U.S. Sentencing Commn., 1988-89; edn. gen. counsel Comty. Learning and Info. Network, 1992—. Contbr. articles to profl. publs. Mem. Capitol Area adv. bd. Salvation Army. Capt. USAR, 1964-68. Mem. ABA, Am. Law Inst., Internat. Trade Commn. Trial Lawyers Assn. (pres. 1990-91), Internat. Aviation Club. Republican. Jewish. Home: 6423 Shadow Rd Chevy Chase MD 20815-6613 Office: Wiley Rein & Fielding 1776 K St NW Washington DC 20006-2304 E-mail: brein@wrf.com.

REIN, CATHERINE AMELIA, insurance executive, lawyer; b. Lebanon, Pa., Feb. 7, 1943; d. John and Esther (Scott) Shultz. BA summa cum laude, Pa. State U., 1965; JD magna cum laude, NYU ., 1968. Bar: N.Y. 1968, U.S. Supreme Ct. 1971. Assoc. Dewey, Ballantine, Bushby, Palmer & Wood, N.Y.C., 1968-74; with Continental Group, Stamford, Conn., 1974-85, sec., sr. atty., 1976-77, v.p., gen. counsel, 1980-85; sec., asst. gen. counsel Continental Diversified Ops., 1978-80; v.p. human resources Met. Life Ins. Co., N.Y.C., 1985-88, sr. v.p. human resources, 1988-89, exec. v.p. corp. and profl. svcs. dept., from 1989, sr. exec., v.p. bus. svcs. group and corp. svcs., 1998-99; pres, CEO Met. Life Auto and Home, Warwick, R.I., 1999—. Bd. dirs Bank of NY., First Energy Corp., Corning Inc. Trustee emeritus NYU Sch. Law Found. Mem. ABA, Assn. of Bar of City of N.Y. Episcopalian. Avocations: decorating, restoration, cooking. Home: 21 E 22nd St Apt 8B New York NY 10010-5335 Office: Met Life Ins Co 1 Madison Ave New York NY 10010-3603

REIN, MICHAEL FRANK, physician, medical educator; b. Washington, Jan. 17, 1943; s. Charles Robert and Norma (Spitalny) R.; m. Marjorie Ann Johnson, Feb. 24, 1968; children: Andrew Charles, Allen Jeffrey. BA, Harvard Coll., 1965; MD, Harvard Medical Sch., 1969. Residency in medicine Mt. Sinai Hosp., N.Y.C., 1969-71, Univ. Va. Hosp., Charlottesville, Va., 1971-72, fellow in infectious disease, 1972-73; chief clin. rsch. sect. venereal disease control div. Ctr. for Disease Control, Atlanta, 1973-75; asst. prof. medicine Univ. Va., Charlottesville, 1975-80, assoc. prof. medicine, 1980-89, prof. medicine, 1989—. Chair coun. med. edn. U. Va. Sch. Medicine, 1995-99, assoc. chair undergrad. med. edn. dept. internal medicine, 1997—. Editor: Teaching Atlas of Sexually Transmitted Diseases, 1996; contbr. over 32 articles to profl. jours. Fellow Am. Coll. Physicians, Infectious Disease Soc. Am.; mem. Am. Venereal Disease Assn. (pres. 1980-81). Jewish. Avocations: amateur radio. Home: 109 Sturbridge Rd Charlottesville VA 22901-2113 Office: Univ Va Health Scis Ctr PO Box 592 Charlottesville VA 22902-0592

REIN, STANLEY MICHAEL, lawyer; b. St. Paul, Apr. 15, 1946; s. Clayton George Rein and Rose Gertrude (Mintz) Brown; m. Linda. R. Arnold; children: Gabriel Todd, Leah Suzanne. BA, U. Minn., 1968; JD cum laude, Harvard U., 1973. Bar: Minn. 1973, U.S. Tax Ct. 1973. Assoc. Dorsey & Whitney, LLP, Mpls., 1973-78; ptnr. Dorsey & Whitney LLP, 1979—. Mem. planned giving adv. coun. ARC Mpls. chpt., 1986, 88, planned giving adv. com. Minn. Pub. Radio, 1988-89; bd. dirs. South Metro Airport Action Council, Mpls., 1986, 87. With U.S. Army, 1968-70, Vietnam. Named in Best Lawyers in Am. Fellow Am. Coll. of Trust and Estate Counsel; mem. Minn. Bar Assn. (probate and trust law sect.), Hennepin County Bar Assn. (probate and trust law sect.), Phi Beta Kappa. Jewish. Avocations: reading, travel. Office: Dorsey & Whitney LLP 50 S 6th St Ste 1500 Minneapolis MN 55402-1498 E-mail: rein.stan@dorseylaw.com.

REINA, CHARLES RICCA, orthopedic surgeon; b. N.Y.C., May 27, 1949; s. Vincent F. and Mildred (Ricca) R.; m. Mary E. Walpole, Mar. 5, 1977; children: Christopher Robert, Patricia Carmel. AS, CUNY, 1968, BS in Chemistry, 1970; MD, N.Y. Med. Coll., 1974. Diplomate Am. Bd. Orthopedic Surgery, Am. Bd. Individual Med. Evaluation. Intern St. Vincents Hosp., N.Y.C., 1974-75, resident in surgery, 1975-76, resident in orthopedic surgery, 1976-79; asst. prof. orthopedic surgery Hahneman Med. U., Phila., 1983—; pvt. practice. Cons. pediatric orthopedist, State of N.J., Clinton, 1982—; attending surgeon Easton (Pa.) Hosp., 1982—, Warren Hosp., Phillipsburg, N.J., 1982—; vis. prof. biomechanics Albert Nerkin Sch. Engring., Cooper Union Coll., N.Y.C.; instr. anatomy Allentown Coll. St. Francis de Sales. Named. UNICO Man of Yr., UNICO Nat., Pottsville, Pa., 1980. Fellow ACS, Am. Coll. Orthopedic Surgeons; mem. Pa. Med. Soc., Conn. Med. Soc., LeHigh Valley Orthopedic Soc. Roman Catholic. Avocations: teaching, reading, political observation.

REINALDA, DAVID ANTHONY, elementary education educator; b. Lynwood, Calif., May 17, 1966; s. Robert Aarlen and Marie Antoinette (Presicci) R. AA, Riverside (Calif.) City Coll., 1989; BA, Calif. State U., San Bernardino, 1992; cert. elem. tchr., U. Calif., Riverside, 1994. Instrnl. aide Jurupa Unified Sch. Dist., Riverside, 1985, 89-93, substitute tchr., 1993—; day care worker Our Lady of Perpetual Help, 1988-89; substitute tchr. Riverside Unified Sch. Dist., 1996—; adult edn. tchr. Jurupa Unified Sch. Dist., 1999—. Vol. aide Jurupa Unified Sch. Dist., 1989-91; home tutor, 1987-89. Author: ABC, What's at School for Me, 1997; author children's stories Stone Soup, 1981. Little League coach, Riverside, 1980-82, scorekeeper, 1982-84; Sunday sch. tchr., supr. Hope Cmty. Ch., Riverside, 1988-98. Winner 1st pl. Lions Club speech contest, 1984; named Christian Youth of Yr. Kiwanis Club, 1985, Outstanding Young Man Am., 1992, 96. Mem. Phi Lambda Omega. Democrat. Mem. Christian Reformed Ch. Avocations: bowling, dancing, writing, acting.

REINARZ, ALICE G. academic administrator; b. Austin, Oct. 25, 1945; d. Earl H. and June Pearl (Knape) Goodwin; m. Ronald B. Reinarz, Aug. 23, 1969 (dec. Aug. 1982); children: David Allen Dean, Lisa Christine. BA, U. Tex., 1967, PhD, 1972. Instr. U. Tex., Austin, 1974-78, lectr., 1978-90, sr. lectr., 1990-97; dir. U. Mich., Ann Arbor, 1997—. Cons. U. Tex., Arlington, 1995-97, Tex. A&M, Galveston, 1996, U. Tex., San Antonio, 2000, Tex. A&M U., College Station, 2001, Bowling Green State U., 2002; adj. prof. U. Mich., 1998—. Author: (with others) Encyclopedia of Microbiology, 1998, Academic Advising: A Comprehensive Handbook, 2000; editor: Teaching Through Academic Advising, 1995, Beyond Teaching to Mentoring, 2000. Active Leadership Tex., Austin, 1996, Leadership Am., Washington, 1997. Mem. Am. Soc. Virology, Am. Soc. Microbiology (nat. undergrad. edn. task force 1993-95, Carski Found. Disting. Teaching award 1990), Nat. Acad. Advising Assn., Alpha Epsilon Delta, Phi Eta Sigma, Alpha Lamda Delta. Home: 2732 Maitland Dr Ann Arbor MI 48105-1565 Office: U Mich LSA Advising Ctr 1255 Angell Hall Ann Arbor MI 48109 E-mail: areinarz@umich.edu.

REINBOLT, DONNA MCNULTY, lawyer; b. N.Y.C., Apr. 16, 1961; d. Robert Joseph and Hannah Theresa McNulty; m. Paul Christian Reinbolt; children: Robert, Jake. BA, SUNY, Albany, 1983; JD, Western New Eng. U., 1986. Bar: Conn. 1987, N.Y. 1988, Pa. 1993; lic. real estate broker, N.Y. Assoc. Gallagher and Gallagher, Garden City, N.Y., 1986-87, Bachner Tally, N.Y.C., 1987-88, Wagner Davis and Gold, N.Y.C., 1988-92; assoc. legal counsel Zamagias Properties, Pitts., 1992-95, dir. ops., legal counsel, 1995-98. Bd. dirs. County Fair Air Conditioning Corp., Westbury, N.Y., 1986—, 360 E 72d St. Owners Corp., 1990-92. Mem. Allegheny County Bar Assn. (coun. mem. real estate sect. 1993-97, treas. 1997-98), Am. Women Lawyers of London. Avocations: travel, writing, reading, golf. Home: 2019 Diamond Springs Dr Houston TX 77077-1934

REINECKE, MANFRED G. chemistry educator; b. Milw., May 19, 1935; s. Fritz Wilhelm and Erna (Rittmeyer) R.; m. Marlene Zwisler, June 15, 1957; children: Kurt, Kryn, Claire. BS in Chemistry, U. Wis., 1956; PhD in Organic Chemistry, U. Calif., 1960. Asst. prof. U. Calif., Riverside, 1959-64, Tex. Christian U., Ft. Worth, 1964-68, assoc. prof., 1968-73; vis. prof. U. Tubingen, Fed. Republic of Germany, 1971-72; prof. Tex. Christian U., Ft. Worth, 1973—; vis. prof. U. British Columbia, Vancouver, Can., 1987. Chmn. health professions adv. com. Tex. Christian U., 1974-91; mem. sci. adv. bd. Univera Pharm., Inc., 1996-2002; cons. in field. Contbr. more than 80 articles on natural product, organic chemistry and chem. edn. to profl. jours. Recipient W.T. Doherty award Ft. Worth, Dallas sect. Am. Chem. Soc., 1984; NSF Tchg.fellow, 1971-72, NAS fellow, 1979, 90. Mem. Am. Chem. Soc. (chmn. Ft. Worth, Dallas sect. 1976), So. Assn. Advisors Health Professions (bd. dirs. 1986-89), Alpha Epsilon Delta (dir. SW region 1985-2002). Office: Tex Christian Univ Dept of Chemistry PO Box 298860 Fort Worth TX 76129-0001 E-mail: m.reinecke@tcu.edu.

REINECKE, ROBERT DALE, ophthalmologist; b. Ft. Scott, Kans., Mar. 26, 1929; s. George Alfred and Bessie Irene (Newell) R.; m. Mary Jeannetta Portwood, Oct. 5, 1952; 1 child, Karen Denise. OD, Ill. Coll. Optometry, 1951; AB, U. Kans., 1955, MD, 1959. Diplomate: Am. Bd. Ophthalmology. Research fellow ophthalmology Harvard U. Med. Sch., 1957, 58; intern U. Kans. Med. Center, 1959-60; resident in ophthalmology Mass. Eye and Ear Infirmary, Boston, 1961-63, asst. in ophthalmology, 1963-69; asst. prof. ophthalmology Harvard U. Med. Sch., 1967-69; mem. faculty Albany (N.Y.) Med. Sch., 1970-81, prof. ophthalmology, 1970-81, chmn. dept., 1970-81; prof. ophthalmology Jefferson Med. Coll., Phila., 1981—, chmn. dept., 1981-85; ophthalmologist-in-chief Wills Eye Hosp., 1981-85, dir. Foerderer Eye Movement Ctr., 1985—. Bd. dirs. Conrad Berens Internat. Eye Film Library, 1970-80; exec. com. N.Y. State Bd. Medicine, 1978-80, chmn., 1980-81; com. vision NRC, 1976-81, chmn., 1979-80; Alumni lectr. Georgetown U. Med. Sch., 1970; Proctor lectr. U. Calif. Med. Sch., San Francisco, 1977; Schoenberg lectr. N.Y. Acad. Medicine, 1979; Spaeth lectr. Coll. Physicians, 1982; Bajandas lectr., 1989. Contbr. numerous articles to med. jours. USPHS summer fellow, 1956, 58; Fight for Sight fellow, summers 1957, 60; recipient Senior Honor award Am. Acad. Ophthalmology, 1986. Fellow Am. Acad. Ophthalmology (sec. govt. rels. 1980-86, pres. 1989); mem. ACS, AMA, Am. Bd. Ophthalmology (bd. dirs. 1984-87), Assn. Rsch. Vision and Ophthalmology (trustee sect. on eye movements, strabismus and amblyopia 1986-91), Am. Acad. Ophthalmology (sec. for program 1986-87), Pa. Med. Soc., N.Y. State Ophthal. Assn., Am. Assn. Pediatric Ophthalmology (pres. 1975-76), Phila. County Med. Soc. (chmn. med. econ. com. 1994-95, pres. 1998-99), Pa. Acad. Ophthalmology (pres. 1991), Pa. Med. Soc., Coll. Physicians, Ophthalmic Club of Phila. Office: Wills Eye Hosp 9th And Walnut St Philadelphia PA 19107-5599 E-mail: rdreineck1@aol.com.

REINECKE, WILLIAM T. conductor, educator; b. New Rochelle, N.Y., Oct. 12, 1959; s. Betty Baltz and Ralph James Reinecke. BS, Lebanon Valley Coll., 1980; M in Music Edn., U. S.C., 1986. Profl. edn. cert. Va. Dir. bands Fieldale-Collinsville (Va.) HS, 1980—84, asst. wrestling coach, 1982—84; dir. bands Apopka (Fla.) HS, 1986—. Guest dir. Orange County Pub. Schs. Honor Jazz Band, Orlando, Fla., 2001. Conductor: Boyertown Alumni Marching Unit Spring Concert, 2002. Mem.: Fla. Bandmasters Assn. (dist. sec. 2000—01, mem. adjudication com. 2001, guest dir. dist. 19 jazz band 1999, dist. chmn.). Home: 517 Oakcrest St Altamonte Springs FL 32714 Office: Apopka HS 555 W Martin St Apopka FL 32712 Office Fax: 407-814-6130. E-mail: reinecw@ocps.net.

REINEMUND, JOHN ADAM, geologist, geoscience consultant; b. Muscatine, Iowa, Jan. 14, 1919; s. Julius Adam and Eve Elizabeth (Nelson) R.; m. Ruth Ramona Rees, Nov. 29, 1943. BA, Augustana Coll., 1940; postgrad studies, U. Chgo., 1940-42, 50; LHD (hon.), Augustana Coll., 1952. Jr. geologist U.S. Geol. Survey, Washington, 1942-44, geologist eastern coal investigations, 1946-53, regional supr. fuels br. Denver, 1953-56, chief aid project Quetta, Pakistan, 1956-63, chief office of Int. Geology Reston, Va., 1964-84, scientist emeritus, 1984—; exec. dir. Circum-Pacific Coun. Energy & Mineral Resources, Houston, 1984—. Treas. Internat. Union of Geol. Scis., Ottawa, Can., 1980-84; mem. internat. geol. correlation program Bd. Internat. Union Geol. Scis. and UNESCO, Paris, 1974-80 Author: (books) Geology of the Deep River Coal Field, 1949, Geologic Controls of Lead and Zinc Deposits, Goodsprings Nev., 1952, Geology of the Macha-ri Coal Fields, Korea, 1957. With U.S. Army, 1945, 46. Avocations: gardening, cycling. Home: 945 Oakwood Ln Myrtle Beach SC 29572-5749

REINEMUND, STEVEN S. food products executive; b. Queens, N.Y., Apr. 6, 1948; s. Ott and Dora (Kramer) R.; m. Gail Timbers, Dec. 14, 1974; children: Steven S. Jr., Jonathan Craig. BS in Naval Sci., U.S. Naval Acad., 1970; MBA, U. Va., 1978. Commd. 2d lt. USMC, 1970, advanced through grades to capt., 1974, resigned, 1975; mktg. rep. IBM Corp., 1975-76; v.p., gen. mgr. Marriott-Roy Rogers, 1978-84; sr. v.p., field operator Pizza Hut, Inc., Wichita, Kans., 1984-86, exec. v.p., 1986, pres., CEO, 1986—92, Frito-Lay N.Am., 1992—96; chmn., CEO Frito-Lay, 1996—99; pres., COO PepsiCo, 1999—2001, chmn., CEO, 2001—. Bd. dirs. Bank IV, Wichita. Sec., treas. bd. dirs. U. Va., Darden Sch. Alumni Assn. Named one of Outstanding Young Men Am. Mem. Wichita Area C. of C. (bd. dirs.). Republican. Presbyterian. Avocations: tennis, running. Office: PepsiCo 700 Anderson Hill Rd Purchase NY 10577*

REINER, JOHN, cartoonist; b. N.Y.C., Nov. 9, 1956; s. Allen and Mildred Reiner. BA, SUNY, Stony Brook, 1978. Freelance illustrator Joe Simon, Editor, Stony Brook, 1974-80, Marvel Comics Group, N.Y.C., 1978-84, Mort Drucker, Woodbury, N.Y., 1984-87, Bill Hoest/Wm. Hoest Enterprises, Lloyd Neck, 1985—. Freelance illustrator for various mags., newspaper, advt. agys., also others, 1978—. Cartoonist syndicated daily comic strips Lockhorns, 1986—, Agatha Crumm, 1986-96, What A Guy!, 1986-96; cartoons appear in Parade mag., 1986—. Mem. Nat. Cartoonists Soc. (nat. rep. 1985-87, Best Gag Cartoonist awad 1994), Graphic Artists Guild. Avocation: bibliophile. Office: Wm Hoest Enterprises 27 Watch Way Huntington NY 11743-9707 E-mail: wmhoest@aol.com.

REINER, LEONA HUDAK, consultant, attorney; b. Cleve., Apr. 07; d. Stephen and Anna (Ilko) Hudak; 1 child, Eric. BA, Case Western Res. U.; MA in Libr. Sci., MA in Spanish, U. Wis.; JD, LLM, Cleve. State U., 1971; LLM, Yale U., 1987, D in Jusrisprudential Law, 1991. Bar: Pa. 1973. Pres. Reiner Assocs., New Haven, 1971—, Ctr. for Jud. Accountability, New Haven, 1994—. Author: (book) Early American Women Printers & Publishers, 1978, Lehrnfreiheit: Freedom to Learn, 1991; contbr. articles to profl. jours. Sterling fellow Yale Law Sch., 1981-83, 87-91; Regent's Scholar U. Wis. Mem. Internat. Soc. Needlecrafts (pres.), Phi Beta Kappa, Beta Phi Mu. Avocation: collecting embroidered and needlepoint artwork. Home and Office: 65 Judwin Ave New Haven CT 06515-2312

REINER, MARGOT ELLEN, political scientist, educator; b. N.Y.C., Aug. 16, 1944; d. Elkan and Grace (Leed) R. Student, May O'Donnell-Gertrude Schurr Sch. of Dance, 1955-59; AB in Polit. Sci., Rutgers U., 1965; student, Fgn. Svc. Inst., Washington, Ateneo Sch. Law, Manila, Philippines, 1972-74. Cert. adult educator, Calif., lic. for coll. studies, Calif. Rsch. aide Woodrow Wilson Sch. Internat. Studies, Princeton U., 1965; staff U.S. Ho. of Reps., 1965-66; joined Fgn. Svc., Dept. State, 1966; adminstrv., immigrant visa officer Buenos Aires, 1966-67; consular officer Am. Svcs., Lima, Peru, 1967-69; personnel officer Saigon, Vietnam, 1969-70; consular, personnel officer Manila, Philippines, 1970-75; country desk officer, edn. officer Bur. Cultural, Ednl. Affairs, Washington, 1975-76; mem. staff U.S. delegation U.N., N.Y.C., 1976; adminstrv. officer, spl. asst. to dir. nat. commn. Internat. Women's Yr., Washington, 1977-78; analyst info., computer syss., 1978-79; examiner, aide spl. com., 1979-81; liaison with Ednl. Testing Svc., 1980-81; country personnel officer Brasilia, Brazil, 1981-82; lectr., cons. Unified Sch. Dist., Beverly Hills, Calif., 1984—; lectr. Emeritus Coll. Santa Monica, 1988—. Creator, publ. (poster) Dear Mr. President, 1985; group shows include Greenwich Village Art Show, N.Y.C., Malibu (Calif.) Arts Festival, 1983. Named Outstanding Educator Kiwanis Club, 1989. Mem. Hadassah (hon.), Pi Sigma Alpha. Avocations: photography, writing, research of current events, swimming, bicycling. Office: Beverly Hills Unified Sch Dist Adult Edn 255 S Lasky Dr Beverly Hills CA 90212-3644

REINER, MARK ALLEN, surgeon, educator; b. N.Y.C., Jan. 12, 1949; married; two children. BS, NYU, 1969; MD summa cum laude, SUNY-Downstate, 1974. Diplomate Am. Bd. Surgery. Resident gen. and vascular surgery Mt. Sinai Med. Ctr., N.Y.C., 1974-78, chief resident, 1978-79, clin. asst., 1979—. Sect. chief laparascopic surgery Bronx Vets. Hosp.; attending physician Doctors Hosp., 1982; clin. instr. Mt. Sinai Sch. Medicine Dept. Surgery. Recipient Arthur H. Aufses Sr. award, 1979. Mem.: SAGES, ACS, AMA, N.Y. Surg. Soc., N.Y. Laparoscopy Club, N.Y. Met. Breast Group, N.Y. Acad. Scis., N.Y. Soc. Surgeons, N.Y. State Med. Soc., Am. Geriatric Soc. Home: 1010 5th Ave New York NY 10028-0130 E-mail: surgctr@aol.com.

REINERT, JAMES A. entomology educator; b. Enid, Okla., Jan. 26, 1944; s. Andrew J. and Emma Reinert; m. Anita Irwin; children: Travis J., Gina N., Mindy K., Melanie B., Gregory W., Teresa J. BS, Okla. State U., 1966; MS, Clemson U., 1968, PhD, 1970. Asst. state entomologist U. Md., College Park, 1970; asst. prof. entomology to prof. entomology Ft. Lauderdale Rsch. and Edn. Ctr., U. Fla., 1970-84; resident dir., prof. entomology Rsch. and Ext. Ctr., Tex. A&M U. Sys., Dallas, 1984-94; prof. entomology Tex. A&M Univ. System, 1994—. Contbr. articles. NDEA fellow, 1968; recipient Porter Henegar Meml. award., So. Nurserymen's Assn., 1982. Mem. Inter-Turfgrass Soc., Entomol. Soc. Am. (S.W. br. sec./treas. 1998, pres.-elect 1999, pres. 2000), Fla. Entomol. Soc. (v.p. 1983, pres. 1984, Entomologist of Yr. 1985), Fla. State Hort. Soc. (v.p. 1982), S.C. Entomol. Soc., Rsch. Ctr. Adminstrs. Soc. (v.p. 1994, state rep. 1991-92, sec. 1993), Dallas Agr. Club (bd. dirs. 1989, v.p. 1990, pres. 1991). Roman Catholic. Home: 3805 Covinton Ln Plano TX 75023-7731 Office: Tex A&M Univ Rsch and Ext Ctr 17360 Coit Rd Dallas TX 75252-6599 E-mail: j-reinert@tamu.edu.

REINERT, NORBERT FREDERICK, patent lawyer, retired chemical company executive; b. Hamilton, Ohio, Apr. 12, 1928; s. Fred F. and Jennie A. R.; m. Ida Elizabeth Barickman, Jan. 26, 1956; children: Matthew W., Paul H. B.Ch.E., Ohio State U., 1951; LL.B., Cleve.-Marshall Law Sch., 1959. Bar: Ohio 1959, D.C. 1961. Patent agt. Standard of Ohio, Cleve., 1957-59, patent lawyer, 1959-60, E.I. duPont de Nemours & Co., Wilmington, Del., 1960-91, dir. investor relations, 1981-84, mng. counsel, 1985-91; v.p., gen. counsel Endo Labs, Inc. subs. DuPont, Garden City, N.Y., 1971-73, exec. v.p., 1973-77, pres., 1977-81; pvt. practice patent law, 1991—. Served with Chem. Corps AUS, 1955-56. Mem. Am. Patent Law Assn., Tau Beta Pi. Republican. Roman Catholic. Home: PO Box 311 Mendenhall PA 19357-0311

REINERTSEN, GLORIA MAY, elementary education educator; b. Neptune, N.J., Jan. 28, 1951; d. George Henry and Gloria E. Bennett; m. Bernard Christian Reinertsen, June 17, 1972; children: Erik, Alicia. BA in Elem. Edn., Newark State Coll., Union, N.J., 1973; MA in Reading, Kean Coll., Union, N.J., 1987. Cert. tchr. PreK-12, reading specialist, reading tchr. K-12, English tchr. K-12, supr., N.J. Vol. tchrs. aide, Middletown, N.J., 1972; preshcool aide Morganville Sch., Marlboro Twp., 1973; mem. unit task force for right to read Morganville & Central Schs., 1975, intern for learning, 1976, 1st grade tchr., 1973-76; full time sub Title I reading tchr. Central Sch., 1979; tutor Kean Coll. Reading Clin., Union, 1986-87; 1st grade tchr. M.F. Atchison Sch., Tinton Falls, 1987-91, reading specialist, alternative reading tchr., 1991—, basic skills tchr., 1991—. Mem. staff devel. coun., lang. arts curriculum com., elem. sch. consortium, strategic planning com. Tinton Falls Schs. Bldg. goals planning com. Read Across Am. com. Recipient Celebrate Literacy award Internat. Reading Assn., 2000. Mem. ASCD, Internat. Reading Assn., N.J. Reading Assn., Monmouth County Reading Coun. (rec. sec. 1995-96, treas. 1996-97, v.p. 1997-98, pres. elect 1998-99, pres. 1999-2000), Tinton Falls Edn. Assn., N.J. Edn. Assn., Tinton Falls PTA, Little Silver PTO. Methodist. Avocations: crafts, computers, gardening, reading. E-mail: greinertsen@tfs.k12.nj.us.

REINERTSEN, NORMAN, retired aircraft systems company executive; b. Bklyn., Mar. 27, 1934; s. Berthin and Malene Katherine (Dahl) R.; m. Elizabeth T. O'Shea, Aug. 30, 1958; children: Michael, Christopher, Katherine. BEE, CCNY, 1960; postgrad., Harvard U., 1982. Registered profl. engr., Calif. Various positions Grumman Aerospace Corp., 1960-75; gen. mgr. Grumman Aerospace Corp. (Great River ops.), 1975-77; v.p. automotive Grumman Allied Industries, Melville, N.Y., 1977-83, sr. v.p. vehicle div., 1983-94; sr. v.p. Olson Bodies, Inc., 1977-79; exec. v.p. Grumman Flexible, Delaware, Ohio, 1979-82; pres. Grumman Olson, Mellville, 1983-85; sr. v.p. Vehicle div. Grumman Allied, 1985-87; v.p. quality ops. Grumman Aircraft Sys. div. Northrop Grumman, 1987-94; ret., 1994. With U.S. Army, 1955-57. Mem. Air Force Assn., Northport Yacht Club. Home: 7 Oleander Dr Northport NY 11768-3438

REINERTSON, JAMES WAYNE, retired pediatrician; b. Des Moines, Jan. 25, 1927; s. A. Jennings and Bonnie V. (Wald) R.; m. Beverly E. Sampson, June 6, 1958; children: Mark W., Merilee Reinertson Torres. BA, Luther Coll., 1948; MS in Pub. Health, U. N.C., 1949; MD, U. Iowa, 1959. Diplomate Am. Bd. Pediatrics. Rsch. asst. in parasitology U. Iowa Med. Coll., Iowa City, 1954-59; intern Mercy Hosp., Cedar Rapids, Iowa, 1959-60; resident pediatrics Raymond Blank Hosp., Des Moines, 1960-62; assoc. rsch. parasitologist Parke Davis & Co., Detroit; pvt. practice Cedar Rapids, Iowa, 1962-99; ret. Vice chmn. Iowa Pediat. Soc., 1964—66; pres. med. staff St. Lukes Hosp., Cedar Rapids, 1979; mem. staff Mercy Hosp.; instr. Cedar Rapids Med. Edn. Program; bd. Luther Coll. Alumni Coun., 1988—97. Bd. dirs. Linn County Assn. Retarded Citizens, 1972-78; commr. Iowa Substance Abuse Commn., Des Moines, 1984, chmn., 1988-90; profl. divsn. chmn. United Way, Iowa, 1967-68. Wyeth Pediatric fellow, 1960-62. Mem. AMA, Am. Acad. Pediatrics, Iowa Med. Soc. Lutheran.

REINFELDS, JURIS, computer engineering educator; b. Riga, Latvia, Apr. 1, 1936; came to U.S., 1989; s. Nikolais Janis and Irma (Kaulins) R.; m. Lauma Petersons, Sept. 15, 1962; children: Peteris Maris, Ivars Valdis, Martins Nikolais. BSc, U. Adelaide, Australia, 1959; PhD, U. Adelaide, 1963; postdoctoral work, ICI. Postdoctoral fellow U. Edinburgh, Scotland, 1961-64; postdoctoral rsch. fellow U. Adelaide, Australia, 1964-65; NSF postdoctoral rsch. assoc. NASA, Huntsville, Ala., 1965-66; asst. prof. computer sci. U. Ga., Athens, 1966-72; vis. scientist CERN, Geneva, 1972-75; found. prof. computer sci. U. Wollongong NSW, Australia, 1975-89; prof. computer engring. N.Mex. State U., Las Cruces, 1989—. Cons. Australian Internat. Devel. Program, Hat Yai, Thailand, 1983-91, Los Banos, Philippines, 1983-90. Mem. IEEE Computer Soc., Assn. for Computer Machinery, Australian Computer Soc., Las Cruces Rotary Club. Avocations: skiing, hiking. E-mail: juris@nmsu.edu.

REING, ALVIN BARRY, special education educator, psychologist; b. Bklyn., July 10, 1930; s. Louis B. and Sylvia (Weinstein) Reing; m. Barbara R. Reing, Aug. 18, 1957 (dec. June 1992); children: Lynne Laufer, Sheryl Abramson, Naomi, Phyllis Klein; m. Marjorie J. Wortis, Aug. 15, 1998 (dec. May 2001). BA, CUNY, Bklyn., 1952; MA, CUNY, 1955; PhD, NYU, 1969; certs. guidance and sch. psychology, Yeshiva U., 1962. Lic. psychologist, N.Y.; tchr., counselor. Borough guidance coord. Bd. Edn., Bklyn.; prof. edn. CUNY; pvt. practice. Text author; contbr. articles to profl. jours. Rsch. dir. Corinthian Med. and Health Svcs. Orgn. Fellow Am. Assn. Mental Retardation; mem. APA, NYSPA, CEC, PBK. Home: 579 Johnston Ter Staten Island NY 10309-3954

REINGANUM, MARC RICHARD, finance educator; b. Chgo., June 17, 1953; s. Carrol Harrison Jr. and Maurine Judith (Scheckman) R.; m. Jennifer Freidel, Aug. 22, 1978 (div. 1987); m. Alison Fox, May 13, 1989; children: Daniel Louis, Michael Issac, Margaret Elizabeth, Claire Alexandra. AB, Oberlin Coll., 1975; MBA, U. Chgo., 1977, PhD, 1979. Asst. prof. U. So. Calif., 1979-82, assoc. prof., 1982-87; vis. assoc. prof. fin. U. Chgo., 1985-86; Phillips prof. fin., dir. fin. markets inst. U. Iowa, Iowa City, 1987-95; Mary Jo Vaughn Raucher chair of investments, dir. Fin. Markets Inst., 1995—; chairperson dept. fin. So. Meth. U., 1995-2000. Mem. investments com., bd. trustees So. Meth. U. Contbr. articles, revs. to profl. publs.; mem. editorial bd. various jours. in field. Coach soccer YMCA, 1995-99; coach chess club East Dallas Cmty. Sch., Iowa City Montessori Bd., 1992-95, Huer Sch.; mem. fin. com. Tex. Internat. Theatrical Arts Soc., 1998—. Bank Am. Rsch. scholar, 1984-87. Mem. Am. Fin. Assn., Western Fin. Assn., United Way Bd., Iowa City Community Sch. Dist. Found., Phi Beta Kappa, Beta Gamma Sigma. Home: 3901 Bryn Mawr Dr Dallas TX 75225-7030 Office: SMU Cox School of Business Dallas TX 75230 E-mail: mreingan@mail.cox.smu.edu.

REINGLASS, MICHELLE ANNETTE, lawyer; b. L.A., Dec. 9, 1954; d. Darwin and Shirley (Steiner) R. Student, U. Calif., Irvine, 1972-75; BSL, Western State U., 1977; JD, Western State U., Coll. Law, 1978. Bar: Calif. 1979, U.S. Dist. Ct. (ctrl. dist.) Calif. 1979, U.S. Ct. Appeals (9th cir.) 1981, U.S. Dist. Ct. (so. dist.) Calif. 1990. Pvt. practice employee litig., Laguna Hills, Calif., 1979—. Instr. Calif. Continuing Edn. of Bar, 1990—, Western State Coll., 1991, Rutter Group, 1994—; chmn. magistrate selection com. U.S. Dist. Ct. (ctrl. dist.) Calif., L.A., 1991, 93, 94, 95, mem. commn., 1997; lectr. in field. Contbr. articles to profl. jours. Pres. Child or Parental Emergency Svcs., Santa Ana, Calif., 1982-92; bd. dirs. Pub. Law Ctr., Santa Ana,

Coalition for Justice, Working Wardrobes; mem. exec. com. CHOC Follies. Recipient Jurisprudence award Anti-Defamation League, 1997; named to Hall of Fame, Western State U., 1993; named one of Best Lawyers, Bestlawyers.com, 2001, one of Top 100 Most INfluential Lawyers in Calif., L.A. Daily Jour., 2001. Mem. State Bar Calif., Orange County Bar Assn. (del. to state conv. 1980-94, bd. dirs. 1983-94, chmn. bus. litigation sect. 1989, sec. 1990, treas. 1991, pres.-elect 1992, pres. 1993), Orange County Trial Lawyers Assn. (bd. dirs. 1987-89, Bus. Trial Lawyer of Yr. award 1995), Orange County Women Lawyers (Lawyer of Yr. award 1996), Vols. in Parole (chmn. adv. com. 1990-91), Peter Elliot Inns Ct. (master), Am. Bd. of Trial Advocates. Avocations: distance running, skiing. Office: 23161 Mill Creek Dr Ste 170 Laguna Hills CA 92653-1650 E-mail: michelle@reinglasslaw.com.

REINGOLD, DAVID AMI, sociologist, educator; b. Chgo., Oct. 30, 1968; s. Haim and Badonna Reingold. BA in Sociology and Social Welfare, U. Wis., 1990; MA in Sociology, U. Chgo., 1992, PhD in Sociology, 1996. Asst. prof. Ind. U., Bloomington, 1997—; dir. rsch. and policy devel. Corp. for Nat. and Cmty. Svc., Washington, 2002—. Rsch. assoc. Ctr. for the Study of Urban Inequality, Chgo., 1990—94; program assoc. Govs. Task Force on Human Svcs. Reform, Chgo., 1993; rsch. assoc. Dept. Children and Family Svcs., Chgo., 1996; field assoc. Rockefeller Inst. Govt., Albany, NY, 1996—98. Contbr. articles to profl. jours. Mem. famliy self sufficiency com. Bloomington Housing Authority, 1997—, chmn. family self-sufficiency com., 1998—; housing commr. Bloomington Housing Authority Bd., 1999—, vice chmn., 2000—. Fellow fellwship on race, poverty and social policy, NSF/U. Chgo., 1992—96; grantee rsch. grantee, Ind. Family Social Svcs. Adminstrn., The Joyce Found., Ind. Twp. Assn., 1998—2000, The Joyce Found., 2001—02; scholar Century scholar, U. Chgo., 1990—92. Mem.: Assn. for Pub. Policy Analysis and Mgmt., Urban Affairs Assn., Am. Sociol. Assn. Office: Corp for Nat and Cmty Svc 1201 New York Ave Fl 8 Washington DC 20525

REINGOLD, JANET ROSE, corporate communications specialist; b. Nov. 1, 1949; BS, Washington U., St. Louis, 1971; MA, Am. U., 1982. Acting dep. adminstr. U.S. Dept. Labor, Washington, 1983-85; pres. Reingold Inc., 1985—. Clients include nat. assns., state govts., fed. agys., cities, sch. sys., corps., univs., and philanthropic founds.; mgr. V.P.'s Task Force on Youth Employment, editor Employment and Tng. Report of Pres. Contbr. to articles in N.Y. Times, Time Mag., Newsweek, BusinessWeek and Nation's Bus.; written for 4 U.S. pres., 2 v.p., 9 cabinet secs. Office: Reingold Inc 1415 Elliot PL NW Washington DC 20007

REINHARD, CHRISTOPHER JOHN, merchant banking, venture capital executive; b. Bridgeport, Conn., Nov. 11, 1953; s. Warren John and Marian Louise (Dutter) R.; m. Maureen Francis, Sept. 24, 1977; 1 child, Griffin John. BS, Babson Coll., 1976, MBA, 1977. Sr. fin. analyst Gen. Motors Corp., Detroit and N.Y.C., 1977-81; asst. sec. Wheelabrator-Frye Inc., N.H., 1981-83; asst. sec., asst. treas. The Signal Cos., Inc., La Jolla, Calif., 1983-86; mng. dir., v.p. The Henley Group, Inc., 1986-90; mng. dir. Fisher Sci. Group, Inc., 1986-90; mng. dir., v.p. Wheelabrator Tech. Inc., Henley Mfg. Corp., 1987-90; founder, pres. Colony Group Inc., Rancho Santa Fe, 1990—, Reinhard Assocs., Rancho Santa Fe, 1990-95; founder, v.p., CFO Advanced Access, Inc., San Diego, 1995-97. Pres. Direct Feedback, Inc., 1990, Dairy Queen Ventures, 1990-94, Winsor Sport Fencing, 1993—; founder, pres. and COO, Collateral Therapeutics Inc., 1995—; gen. ptnr. Cabrillo Ventures, 1995—; founder, pres. ihumon, 2000—. Mem. Boston Athenaeum, N.Y. Athletic Club, San Diego Polo Club, Rancho Santa Fe Polo Club, Duquesne Club. Office: Collateral Therapeutics 11622 El Camino Real San Diego CA 92130-2049

REINHARD, JAMES RICHARD, retired judge; b. Pollock, Mo., July 7, 1929; s. Virgil and Meltha (Anspach) R.; m. Shari L. Horton, Dec. 30, 1958; 1 child, James K. Student, N.E. Mo. State U., 1947-50; AB, U. Mo., 1951, JD, 1953. Bar: Mo. 1953. Prosecuting atty. Sullivan County, Mo., 1955-57; prosecuting atty. Monroe County, 1959-65; spl. asst. atty. gen. State of Mo., 1967-68; judge 10th Jud. Circuit, 1973-77, Mo. Ct. Appeals (ea. dist.), St. Louis, 1977-97, chief judge, 1984-85; pvt. practice Milan, 1955-57, Paris, 1957-73. Bd. regents N.E. Mo. State U. (now Truman State U.), Kirksville, 1965-73, pres., 1967-73, now mem. found. bd.; trustee State Hist. Soc. Mo. Sgt. U.S. Army, 1953-55. Mem. ABA, 10th Jud. Bar Assn. (pres. 1972), Mo. Bar Assn. (bd. govs. 1965-69), Met. Bar Assn. St. Louis, Lawyers Assn. St. Louis, Mo. Bd. Cert. Ct. Reporter Examiner (vice chmn. 1988-90), Mo. Press-Bar Commn., Judicial Fin. Commn. (chmn. 1990-94). Home: 5 Hamlin Heights Dr Hannibal MO 63401-1903

REINHARD, SISTER MARY MARTHE, educational organization administrator; b. McKeesport, Pa., Aug. 29, 1929; d. Regis C. and Leona (Reese) R. AB, Notre Dame Coll.; MA, U. Notre Dame. Asst. prin. Regina H.S., Cleve., 1960-62, prin., 1963—65, Notre Dame Acad., Chardon, 1965-72; pres. Notre Dame Coll. of Ohio, Cleve., 1973-88; dir. devel. Sisters of Notre Dame Ednl. Ctr., Chardon, 1989—. Trustee, mem. exec. com. NCCJ, Cleve., 1987; mem. coun. Geagua United Way Svcs., 1990—97, vice chair fund raising, 1991—94, 1995—97; mem. adv. bd. Kent State U., Geauga campus, 1991—94; trustee Leadership Geauga, 1995—96; sec. Notre Dame Edn. Assn., 1990—98, pres., 1998—2001; mem. adv. bd. Regina H.S.; mem. distbn. com. McGinty Family Found., 1989—. Recipient Humanitarian award Cleve. chpt. NCCJ, 1990; named one of 100 most influential women in Cleve., Women's City Club, 1982, one of 79 most interesting people in Cleve., The Cleve. Mag., 1979; named Cleve. United Way Vol. of Yr., 1997, Woman of Yr., Notre Dame Coll. Ohio, 1989; elected to Hall of Excellence, Ohio Found. of Ind. Colls., 1996. Roman Catholic. Home and Office: 13000 Auburn Rd Chardon OH 44024-9331 E-mail: mreinhard@ndec.org.

REINHARD, PHILIP G. federal judge; b. LaSalle, Ill., Jan. 12, 1941; s. Godfrey and Ruth R.; married Virginia Reinhard; children: Bruce, Brian, David, Philip. BA, U. Ill., Champaign, 1962, JD, 1964. Asst. state atty. Winnebago County, 1964-67; atty. Hyer, Gill & Brown, 1967-68; state atty. Winnebago County, 1968-76; judge 17th Jud. Cir., 1976-80, Appellate Ct., 1980-92, U.S. Dist. Ct. (no. dist.) Ill., 1992—2001. Mem. security, space and facilities com. U.S. Jud. Conf. Mem. Am. Acad. Jud. Edn., Winnebago County Bar Assn. Office: US Courthouse 211 S Court St Rockford IL 61101-1219

REINHARD, STEVEN IRA, lawyer; b. Schenectady, N.Y., June 9, 1961; s. Arnold and Lenore (Bluthe) R.; m. Susan Marie Parham, June 15, 1986; children: Laura Suzanne, Samuel Jacob. BSBA, U. N.C., Chapel Hill, 1982, JD, 1985. Bar: N.C. 1985, U.S. Dist. Ct. (ea. dist.) N.C. 1985, U.S. Dist. Ct. (mid. dist.) N.C. 1989. Assoc. Graham & James, Raleigh, N.C., 1985-93, Johnson, Mercer, Hearn & Vinegar, PLLC, Raleigh, 1994-97, Ragsdale Liggett, PLLC, Raleigh, 1997-2000; assoc. gen. counsel Spectrasite Comm., Inc., Cary, 2000—. Mem. N.C. Bar Assn. (chair real property sect. 1998-99), Wake County Real Property Lawyers Assn. (pres. 1994-95). Office: Spectrasite Comm Inc Ste 4000 100 Regency Forest Dr Cary NC 27511 E-mail: steve.reinhard@spectrasite.com.

REINHARDT, JOHN EDWARD, former international affairs specialist; b. Glade Spring, Va., Mar. 8, 1920; s. Edward Vinton and Alice (Miller) R.; m. Carolyn Lillian Daves, Sept. 2, 1947; children: Sharman W. Reinhardt Lancefield, Alice N., Carolyn C. Reinhardt Fenstermaker. AB, Knoxville Coll., 1939; MS, U. Wis., 1947, PhD, 1950. Prof. English Va. State Coll., Petersburg, 1950-56; cultural affairs officer USIS, Manila, 1956-58; dir. Am. Cultural Ctr., Kyoto, Japan, 1958-63; cultural attache USIS, Tehran, Iran, 1963-66; dep. asst. dir. Office East Asia and Pacific, USIA, Washington, 1966-68, 70-71, asst. dir. Office for Africa, 1968-70; ambassador to Nigeria, 1971-75; asst. sec. state for pub. affairs, 1975-77; dir. USIA, Washington, 1977-78, U.S. Internat. Communication Agy., Washington, 1978-81; acting dir. Smithsonian Mus. African Art, 1981-83; asst. sec. for history and art Smithsonian Instn., 1983-84, dir. directorate internat. activities, 1984-87; prof. polit. sci. U. Vt., Burlington, 1987-90, prof. emeritus, 1990—. Served as officer AUS, 1942-46. Mem. MLA, Am. Fgn. Svc. Assn. (v.p. 1969-71). Clubs: Cosmos. Methodist. E-mail: jreinhdt@erols.com.

REINHARDT, JOHN W. dean, educator, researcher, consultant; BA Biology, Ill. Wesleyan U. , 1971; DDS, Loyola U., 1975; MS Operative Dentistry, U. Iowa, 1979; MPH Health Svcs. Rsch., Harvard U., 1988. Diplomate Am. Bd. Operative Dentistry . With U.S. Dental Army Dental Corps; prof. U. Iowa Coll. Dentistry; head dept. operative dentistry U. Iowa Coll. Dentistry, 1988; dean U. Nebr. Coll. Dentistry , 2000—. Tchr., rschr. in field; cons. NIH, ADA, U.S. Navy, Am. Dental Edn. Assn., CODE, OKY, IADR. Contbr. articles to profl. pubs. , scientific papers, chapters to books. Recipient several small grants. Mem.: NIDCR Children's Amalgam Trial Data and Safety Monitoring Bd., Acad. Operative Dentistry (past pres. 1997, chmn. bd. dirs. foundersa fund 2000—, past chmn. ADEA sect. operative dentistry 2001, chmn. 1997—). Office: 40th and Holdrege Sts Box 830740 Lincoln NE 68583*

REINHARDT, LINDA KAY, minister; b. Glen Ridge, N.J., Apr. 4, 1950; d. Irving Raymond and Margaret Louise (Mills) Vanderberg; m. Robert Richard Reinhardt, Feb. 16, 1969. B of Liberal Studies summa cum laude, St. Edward's U., 1991; MDiv, Austin Presbyn. Theol. Sem., 1996. Cert. spiritual counselor; ordained to Presbyn. Ch. 1996; commd. Stephen's min. Payroll tax specialist Great So. Life, Houston, 1980-82; comptr. Cayman Constrn., 1981-83; owner, acct. Reinhardt Acctg. Firm, 1984-93; pastor, dir. The Jeremiah Project, Canyon Lake, Tex., 1994—; restoring creation enabler Mission Presbytery, PC (USA), 1998—. Resource cons. Mission Presbytery, Tex., 1994—; workshop facilitator environtl. theology, 1996—. Editor (newsletter) I Am Jeremiah, 1994—; contbr. articles to profl. publs. Bd. dirs. Tri-Living Cmty. Austin, 1989-91, The Dispossessed Project, 1998—; vol. in parks Fort Davis Nat. Hist. Site, 1986-87; vol. Children's Ctr. for Austin, 1989-91; spokesperson, advocate rights of disabled people, 1969—; worship leader RBJ Retirement Ctr., Austin, 1992-93; worship organizer Brown Schs., Austin, 1991-93. Recipient The Spragens award in Christian Edn., 1996. Mem. Assn. of Civil Litigants (advisor-com. on status of women 1996—), Presbyn. Clergywomen, Friends of the Fort (life), Presbyn. Health, Edn. and Welfare Assn., Christian Environ. Assn., Evangel. Environ. Network, Soc. of the Green Cross. Avocations: environmental concerns, writing, reading, cross stiching. Home and Office: The Jeremiah Project 222 Soft Wind Canyon Lake TX 78133-2414

REINHARDT, UWE ERNST, economist, educator; b. Osnabrueck, Germany, Sept. 24, 1937; came to U.S., 1964; s. Wilhelm and Edeltraut (Kehne) R.; m. Tsung-mei Cheng, May 25, 1968; children— Dirk, Kara, Mark B.Comm. in Econs. with honors, U. Sask., Saskatoon, Can., 1964; MA in Econs., Yale U., 1965, M.Ph. in Econs., 1967, PhD, 1970; DSc (hon.), Med. Coll. of Pa., 1987, CUNY, 1994, SUNY, 1998. Asst. prof. econs. and pub. affairs Princeton (N.J.) U., 1968-74, assoc. prof., 1974-79, prof., 1979—, James Madison prof. polit. economy, prof. econs., 1984—. Bd. dirs. McAllister Holdings; trustee Tchrs. Ins. and Annuity Assn., 1978-93, H&Q Health Fund; cons. Urban Inst., Washington, 1971-75, HEW, 1974—, HHS, Math., Inc., Princeton, 1970-80, AT&T, Basking Ridge, N.J., 1976-82, Nat. Westminster Bank USA, N.Y.C., 1979—, mem. Nat. Leadership Commn. Health Care, 1986—; mem. spl. adv. bd. VA, 1981-85; mem. U.S. Physicians' Payment Rev. Commn., U.S. Congress, 1986—; pres. Assn. for Health Svcs. Rsch., 1989-90, Found. Health Svcs. Rsch., 1990-91; mem. bd. advisors Nat. Inst. Healthcare Mgmt., 1993—, Pew Health Professions Commn., 1997—; mem. Coun. Econ. Impact Health Reform, 1994—; mem. external adv. panel health and nutrition World Bank, 1997—; chair coordinating com. Commonwealth Fund Internat. Program Health Policy, 1998—; commr. Kaiser Commn. Medicaid and Uninsured; trustee Duke U. Health Sys., Triad Hosps., Inc., Medcast/WebMD. Author: Physician Productivity and the Demand for Health Manpower, 1975; mem. editorial bd. Health Affairs, 1982—, New Eng. Jour. Medicine, 1989-92, Health Mgmt. Quar., Health Policy and Edn., Milbank Meml. Quar., Jour. AMA, 1991—; assoc. editor Jour. Health Econs., 1980-85, mem. editorial bd., 1981-83; contbr. articles to profl. jours. Bd. dirs. Nat. Acad. Aging, 1993—. Mem. Nat. Inst. Health Care Mgmt., Inst. Medicine Nat. Acad. Scis. (gov. council 1979-82) Office: Princeton U Woodrow Wilson Sch Prof of Economics & Public Affairs 412 Robertson Hl Princeton NJ 08544-0001

REINHARDT, WILLIAM PARKER, chemical physicist, educator; b. San Francisco, May 22, 1942; s. William Oscar and Elizabeth Ellen (Parker) R.; m. Katrina Hawley Currens, Mar. 14, 1979; children: James William, Alexander Hawley. BS in Basic Chemistry, U. Calif., Berkeley, 1964; AM in Chemistry, Harvard U., 1966, PhD in Chem. Physics, 1968; MA (hon.), U. Pa., 1985. Instr. chemistry Harvard U., 1967-69, asst. prof. chemistry, 1969-72, assoc. prof., 1972-74; prof. U. Colo., Boulder, 1974-84, chmn. dept. chemistry, 1977-80; prof. chemistry U. Pa., Phila., 1984-91, chmn. dept., 1985-88, D. Michael Crow prof., 1987-91; prof. chemistry U.Wash., Seattle, 1991—, assoc. chmn. undergrad. program, 1993-96. Adj. prof. physics U. Wash., Seattle, 1998—; vis. fellow Joint Inst. for Lab. Astrophysics of Nat. Bur. Stds. and U. Colo., 1972, 74, fellow, 1974-84; dir. Telluride Summer Rsch. Ctr., 1986-89, treas., 1989-93; com. on atomic, molecular and optical scis. NRC, 1988-90; vis. scientist Nat. Inst. Stds. and Tech., summers 1993—; vis. prof. chemistry U. Melbourne, Australia, 1997, Harvard U., 1998, Davidson Lctr., u. Kansas, 2000. Mem. editl. bd. Phys. Rev. A., 1979-81, Chem. Physics, 1985-94, Jour. Chem. Physics, 1987-89, Jour. Physics B. (U.K.), 1992—, Internat. Jour. Quantum Chemistry, 1994—; rschr. theoretical chem. physics, theoretical atomic and molecular physics for numerous publs. Recipient Camille and Henry Dreyfus Tchr. Scholar award, 1972; Alfred P. Sloan fellow, 1972; J.S. Guggenheim Meml. fellow, 1978; Coun. on Rsch. and Creative Work faculty fellow, 1978; Wilsmore fellow U. Melbourne (Australia), 1997; J.W. Fulbright sr. scholar, Australia, 1997. Fellow AAAS, Am. Phys. Soc., Phi Beta Kappa; mem. Am. Chem. Soc., Sigma Xi (nat. lectr. 1980-82), Phi Lambda Upsilon (Fresenius award 1977). Office: U Wash Dept Chemistry PO Box 351700 Seattle WA 98195-1700 E-mail: rein@chem.washington.edu.

REINHART, ANNE CHRISTINE, special education educator, consultant; b. Detroit, Mar. 9, 1950; m. Charles Reinhart; children: Kim Meredith, Ted Justin. BS, Ea. Mich. U., 1972; MA, U. Detroit, 1977. Cert. spl. edn., Mich. Spl. edn. tchr. for emotionally impaired State of Mich. Hosp., Pontiac, Berkley (Mich.) Sch. Dist, 1976—. Co-chair ASSET (support group for gifted and talented students), Birmingham, Mich., 1996-98; com. mem. Mich. Dept. of Edn., Office of Spl. Edn. Mem. Kappa Delta Pi. Avocations: writing, tutoring, visiting other sch. sites in country. Home: 25925 Romany Way Franklin MI 48025-1909

REINHART, KELLEE CONNELY, journalist; b. Kearney, Nebr., Dec. 15, 1951; d. Vaughn Eugene and Mary Jo (Mullen) Connely; m. Stephen Wayne Reinhart, June 15, 1974; children: Keegan Connely, Channing Mullen. BA, U. Ala., 1972, MS, 1974. Advt. copywriter Stas. WTBC-AM, WUOA-FM, 1970-72; asst. mgr. Ala. Press Assn., 1972-74; asst. to the editor Antique Monthly mag., 1974-75, mng. editor, 1975-77; editorial dir. Antique Monthly and Horizons mags., 1977-89; dir. univ. rels. U. Ala. System, Tuscaloosa, 1989—. Editor: Wild Birds of America: The Art of Basil Ede, 1991, Centennial Memories, Millennial Hopes, 2000. Bd. dirs. Ala. Humanities Found., Ala. Writers Forum, pres., 1999—. Recipient Druids Arts award, 1995. Mem. Soc. Profl. Journalists, Am. Soc. Mag. Editors, Newcomen Soc. U.S., Art Table, Ala. Writers Forum (pres. 1999-2001), XXXI/U. Ala. Women's Hon. Soc. Office: 401 Queen City Ave Tuscaloosa AL 35401-1551 E-mail: kreinhar@uasystem.ua.edu.

REINHART, MARY ANN, medical board executive; b. Jackson, Mich., Aug. 14, 1942; d. Herbert Martin and Josephine Marie (Keyes) Conway; m. David Lee Reinhart, Dec. 28, 1963; children: Stephen Paul, Michael David. MA, Mich. State U., 1983, PhD, 1985. Rsch. asst. Mich. State U., East Lansing, 1979-82, 85, teaching asst. dept psychology, 1982-84, asst. prof. Office Med. Edn. R&D, Coll. Human Medicine, 1985-88; assoc. exec. dir. Am. Bd. Emergency Medicine, 1988-95, dep. exec. dir., 1995-2000, exec. dir., 2000—. Cons. Am. Bd. Emergency Medicine, 1985—88; chairperson collegewide evaluation com. Coll. Human Medicine, Mich. State U., East Lansing, 1985—88; adj. asst. prof. Office Med. Edn. R&D, Coll. Human Medicine, 1988—2000. Reviewer Annals of Emergency Medicine, 1987-95, Acad. Emergency Medicine, 1995-99. Bd. dirs. Neahtawanta Rsch. and Edn. Ctr., Traverse City, Mich., 1991—. Mem. APA (divsn. indsl./orgnl. psychology, health psychology), Phi Kappa Phi. Achievements include application of chart stimulated recall method of assessment in a national medical recertification examination; development and implementation of national longitudinal study of emergency medicine residents and emergency physicians. Office: Am Bd Emergency Medicine 3000 Coolidge Rd East Lansing MI 48823-6319

REINHART, PETER SARGENT, corporate executive, lawyer; b. Mineola, N.Y., May 17, 1950; s. Charles Woodham and Martha Way (Sargent) R.; m. Susan Stockwell, Aug. 29, 1970 (div. Jan. 1976); 1 child, Amy Lynn; m. Gale McElroy, Oct. 16, 1976 (div. May 1985); 1 child, James Gharrett; m. Carol O. Gaffney, Jan. 4, 1992 (div. Jan. 2001). BA, Franklin and Marshall Coll., 1971; JD, Rutgers U., 1975. Bar: N.J. 1975. Atty. Pillsbury and Russell, Atlantic Highlands, N.J., 1975-78; corp. counsel K. Hovnanian Enterprises, Inc., Red Bank, 1978-81, sr. v.p., gen. counsel, 1981—; also bd. dirs. Pres. Inst. Multi-Family Housing, Plainsboro, N.J., 1989-90. Trustee, mem. editorial bd. Housing N.J. mag., 1991—. Trustee Community Assns. Inst., Arlington, Va., pres. N.J. chpt., 1988; trustee Assn. for Children of N.J., Newark, 1988-93, Keep Middlesex Moving, New Brunswick, 1990-93, Bayshore Cmty. Hosp., Holmdel, N.J., 1992—, v.p., 1995, chmn., 1997; pres. Greater Red Bank Jaycees, 1978-79, Atlantic Highlands Rep. Club, 1978; v.p. Monmouth coun. Boy Scouts Am., Oakhurst, N.J., 1987-94, pres., 1994-95; v.p. Garden State Games, Edison, N.J., 1991-94; mem. Coun. Affordable Housing, Trenton, N.J., 1993—. Named to Community Assns. Inst. Hall of Fame, 1988; named Jaycee of Yr. Greater Red Bank Jaycees, 1977. Mem. N.J. State Bar Assn., N.J. Shore Builders Assn. (pres. 1989-90, Builder of Yr. 1987, Hall of Fame 1991), Nat. Assn. Indsl. and Office Parks (bd. dirs. 1990-92), N.J. Builders Assn. (v.p. 1992-94, pres. 1995-96, Builder of Yr. award 1995, Shore Athletic Club (Oakhurst), Ea. Monmouth C. of C. (trustee 1992-98, Vol. of Yr. 1995). Avocations: road racing, marathon running, golf. Office: Hovnanian Enterprises Inc PO Box 500 10 Hwy 35 Red Bank NJ 07701-5902

REINHART, RICHARD PAUL, lawyer; b. Cleve., Sept. 1, 1954; s. Richard A. and Carole F. (Kaspar) R.; m. Debra Rae Hitchcock, June 20, 1976; children: Geoffrey, Richelle Marie. BA with honors, Rollins Coll., 1976; JD with distinction, Emory U., 1979. Bar: Ga. 1979, Fla. 1980. Ptnr. Morris, Manning & Martin, Atlanta, 1979-89; officer McMillen Reinhart and Voght, P.A., Orlando, Fla., 1989—, also bd. dirs. Mem. ABA, ATLA, Fla. Bar Assn., Ga. Bar Assn., Orange County Bar Assn., Acad. Fla. Trial Lawyers, Order of Coif, Omicron Delta Kappa. Office: McMillen Reinhart and Voght PA PA 111 N Orange Ave Ste 1450 Orlando FL 32801-4641 E-mail: reinhart@floridamalpractice.com.

REINHART, RODERICK LESTER, non-profit organization consultant; b. Portland, Oreg., Oct. 8, 1950; s. William Steiwer and Huia Mary Reinhart. BS, Oreg. State U., 1974, MA, 1978. Campaign dir. Corp. Coun. for Arts, Seattle, 1984-90; devel. mgr. Seattle Art Mus., 1990-95; gen. mgr. Lever Reinhart & Assocs., Mexico City, 1996-97; dir. devel. Sharp Health Care Found., San Diego, 1997-2000; v.p. Alford Group, Chgo., 2000—. Instr. Calif. State U., San Marcos, Calif., 1997—2000, U. Claif., Dan Diego, Calif., 2001—. Co-author study on youth leadership, 1999. Grad. LEAD San Diego, 1998-99; v.p. bd. dirs. N.W. AIDS Found., 1989-95. Recipient Fulbright lectureship J. William Fulbright Fgn. Scholarship Bd., 1995-96. Mem. Assn. Fundraising Profls. (pres.-elect San Diego chpt. 1997—, chmn. internat. devel. com. 2002). Democrat. Avocations: gardening, photography, cooking. Home: 3005 Thorn St Apt 2 San Diego CA 92104-4665 Office: Alford Group 3963 Lamont St San Diego CA 92109-6132

REINHART, WALTER JOSEF, educator; b. N.Y.C., Oct. 9, 1943; s. Julius J. and Augusta M. R.; children: Aaron, Kyle, Richard, Sadie. A of Engring. with honors, Bridgeport Engring. Inst., 1967; BSAE, BSME, Okla. State U., 1969, MBA, 1971; PhD in Fin., U. N.C., 1977. Mgmt. trainee IBM, Armonk, N.Y., 1964-66; engr. Pitney Bowes, Stanford, Conn., 1967-68; supr. Corning Glass, Muskogee, Okla., 1969-70; cons. Theodore Barry & Assocs., L.A., 1971-72; instr. Duke U., Durham, N.C., 1974-75; asst. prof. Va. Tech., Blacksburg, 1975-78; assoc. prof. Fla. State U., Tallahassee, 1978-84, Loyola Coll., Balt., 1984—. Prin. Reinhart & Assocs., Hunt Valley, Md., 1971—; vis. prof. Assumption U., Bangkok, Thailand, 1994, 95. Author: Portfolio Management Theory and Application, 1997; contbr. articles to profl. jours. Organizer Top of Fla., Tallahassee, 1981-84; leader Boy Scouts Am., Balt., 1984-97. English Speaking Union fellow, Oxford, England, 1989; named Vol. of Yr., Tallahassee, 1984. Mem. Am. Fin. Assn., Am. Inst. Decision Scis., Fla. Econs. Club, Fla. Govt. Fin. Officers Assn., So. Fin. Assn. (v.p. 1997-98, bd. dirs. 2000-02), Engring. Soc. Balt. (life), Fin. Mgmt. Assn., Ea. Fin. Assn. (v.p. 2001-02), BPO Elks, Tallahassee C. of C., Beta Gamma Sigma. Office: Loyola Coll 4501 N Charles St Baltimore MD 21210-2601 E-mail: Reinhart@Loyola.edu.

REINHARZ, JEHUDA, academic administrator, history educator; b. Haifa, Israel, Aug. 1, 1944; came to U.S., 1961; s. Fred and Anita (Weigler) R.; m. Shulamit Rothschild, Nov. 26, 1967; children— Yael, Naomi BS, Columbia U., 1967; BRE, Jewish Theol. Sem., 1967; MA, Harvard U., 1968; PhD, Brandeis U., 1972; LHD (hon.) , Hebrew Union Coll., 1995; DHL, Jewish Theol. Soc. Am., 1996, Fairfield U., 1999. Prof. modern Jewish history U. Mich., Ann Arbor, 1972—82; Richard Koret prof. modern Jewish history Brandeis U., Waltham, Mass., 1982—, dir. Tauber Inst. Study of European Jewry, 1984—94; provost, sr. v.p. for acad. affairs Brandeis U., 1992—94; pres. Brandeis U., 1994—. Mem. internat. acad. bd. Annenberg Rsch. Inst., 1986-90; bd. dirs. Yad Chaim Weizmann, 1990-2000, Internat. Editl. Bd. Pardès, 1996—; pres. Israel Prize, 1990, Akiba award, Am.-Jewish Com., 1996. Author: Fatherland or Promised Land: The Dilemma of the German Jew 1893-1914, 1975, Chaim Weizmann: The Making of a Zionist Leader, 1985 (Present Tense Literary award 1985, Kenneth B. Smilen Literary award 1985, Nat. Jewish Book award 1986, Shazar prize in history Israel, 1988), (in Hebrew) Hashomer Hazair in Germany, 1931-39, 1989, Chaim Weizmann: The Making of a Statesman, 1993 (Nat. Jewish Book award 1994); also numerous articles in French, German, Hebrew and English; co-author: Zionism and the Creation of a New Society, 1998, 2d edit., 2000, The Era of Political Zionism, 2000; gen. editor: Studies in Jewish History, 1984, European Jewish History, 1985; co-editor: The Jew in the Modern World, 1980, 2d edit. 1995, Mystics, Philosophers and Politicians, 1982, Israel in the Middle East 1948-83, 1984, The Jewish Response to German Culture, 1985, The Jews of Poland Between Two World Wars, 1989, The Impact of Western Nationalisms, 1992, Zionism and Religion, Hebrew edit., 1994, Essential Papers on Zionism, 1996; editor: The Letters and Papers of Chaim Weizmann, 1918-20, 1977, Dokumente zur Geschichte des deutschen Zionismus, 1882-1933, 1981, Living with Antisemitism, 1987. Bd. govs. United Israel Appeal/Jewish Agy., 1994, 2000; bd. dirs., mem. exec. com. Am. Joint Distbn. Com., 1994; mem. acad. com. U.S. Holocaust Mus., 1990—, mem. com. on conscience nat. adv. forum, 1996—; mem. Presdl. Adv. Commn. on Holocaust Assets in U.S., 1998-2000; mem. Commn. on Israel-Diaspora Rels., 1996-97; trustee Am. Hebrew Acad., Greensboro, N.C., 2000—. Recipient Akiba award, Am. Jewish Com., 1996. Fellow Leo Baeck Inst., Royal Hist. Soc., Am. Acad. Jewish Rsch., Am. Acad. Arts and Scis.; mem. Yad Vashem Soc. (adv. bd. 1983), Nat. Coun. Shazar Ctr., Assn. for Jewish Studies (sec. 1986-88, treas./sec., 1988-94), Coun. on Fgn. Rels. Home: 66 Beaumont Ave Newton MA 02460-2331 Office: Office Of The Pres 415 South St # Ms100 Waltham MA 02453-2728 E-mail: jreinharz@brandeis.edu.*

REINHERZ, HELEN ZARSKY, social services educator; b. Boston, Aug. 4, 1923; d. Zachary and Anna (Cohen) Zarsky; m. Samuel E. Reinherz, Aug. 29, 1943; 1 son, Ellis. AB magna cum laude, Wheaton Coll., 1944; MS, Simmons Coll., 1946; S.M., Harvard U., 1962, Sc.D., 1965. Social worker Newton Family Service, Mass., 1946-49, Mass. Gen. Hosp., Boston, 1949-51; supr. psychiat. social work State Hosp., Waltham, Mass., 1958-61; faculty mem. Simmons Coll., Boston, 1965—, prof. methods rsch., 1972—, dir. research Sch. Social Work, 1968-93, dir. PhD program, 1993-96. Prin. investigator Identifying Children at Risk, 1976—84, Adaption in Adolescence, 1987—93, Early Adulthood Rsch. Project, 1993—97, Simms Longitudinal Study, 1998, Study Adolescent Drug Abuse, 1971—73; rsch. cons. Dept. Mental Health, 1970—80; chmn. Gov.'s Adv. Coun. on Mental Health and Retardation, 1972; mem. adv. com. Mental Health Manpower fo Fed. Govt., 1980—82. Author (with H. Wechler, D. Dobbins): Social Work Research in the Human Services, 1976; author: (with M. Heywood, J. Camp) A Community Response to Drug Abuse, 1976; cons., assoc. editor: Jour. Prevention, 1980—91, mem. fed. adv. com.: Rsch. in Prevention Rev., 1984—87, editl. bd.: Jour. Early Adolescence, cons. editor: NASW Jour.; contbr. articles to profl. jours. Recipient Maida H. Solomon award Simmons Coll. Alumni, 1961; NIH tng. fellow, 1961-65; Grant Found. grantee, 1963; Med. Found. grantee, 1967-69; NIMH grantee, 1975-84, 87—. Fellow Am. Orthopsychiat. Assn.; mem. Acad. Cert. Social Workers, Am. Pub. Health Assn., Council Social Work Edn., Harvard Sch. Pub. Health Alumni Assn. (sec.-treas. 1965-68), Phi Beta Kappa, Delta Omega. Home: 17 Corey Rd Malden MA 02148-1116 Office: Simmons Sch Social Work 51 Commonwealth Ave Boston MA 02116-2348 E-mail:

helen.reinherz@simmons.edu. *As a teacher and researcher my efforts have been directed towards encouraging students to formulate the right questions about human problems as a first step to understanding and change.*

REINHOLD, ALLEN KURT, graphic design educator; b. Salt Lake City, Feb. 21, 1936; s. Eric Kurt and Lillian (Hansen) R.; m. Irene Laura Rawlings, May 4, 1962; children: Cindy Anne, David, Alyce, Bryce, Eugene Patrick. BA, Brigham Young U., 1961, MA, 1962. Cert. secondary and post secondary tech. and indsl., Utah, color cons. Freelance artist Allen Reinhold Art & Design Studio, American Fork, Utah, 1962—; tchr. art Emery County High Sch., Castle Dale, 1962-63; graphic artist Brigham Young U., 1954-56, 63-66; prodn. artist Evans Advt. Agy., Salt Lake City, 1968; dir. ednl. media Olympus High Sch., 1966-68; art dir. Telelecture Utah div. Family Svcs., 1968-69; art instr. Utah Tech. Coll., 1969-85; prof. graphic design Salt Lake Community Coll., 1985-96, prof. emeritus, 1996—. Advisor, coach Vocat. Indsl. Clubs of Am., Salt Lake City, 1978-91. Illustrator: Book of Mormon Stories, 5 vols., 1971-76; exhibited in group shows at Salt Lake Art Festival, 1982, Pageant of the Arts, Am. Fork, 1980-89. Active Boy Scouts Am., American Fork, 1975-90; bd. dirs. art Am. Fork City, 1976-80; team mem. Utah State Bd. for Vocat. Edn. Accreditation, Salt Lake City, 1990; mem. Art Rsch. in Europe, summer 1995. Fellow Delta Phi Kappa (historian 1961-62), Salt Lake Community Coll. Faculty Senate. Republican. Mem. Lds Ch. Avocations: horses, boating, fishing, hunting, gardening. Home: 590 N 200 E American Fork UT 84003-1711 E-mail: reinholdart@aol.com.

REINHORN, ANDREI M. civil structural engineering educator, consultant; b. Bucharest, Romania, Oct. 23, 1945; s. Moritz A. and Dina (Rosenfeld) Reinhorn; m. Tova A. Waldman, Oct. 15, 1968; children: Michal, Gad. BSc, Technion - Israel Inst. Tech., Haifa, 1968, DSc, 1978. Registered profl. engr., N.Y., Israel. Structural engr. Milstein & Singer, Cons. Engrs., Tel Aviv, 1972-73, Haifa, 1973-79, Buffalo, 1980-85, Reinhorn Consulting Engrs., 1990—; vis. asst. prof. U. Buffalo, 1979-81, asst. prof., 1981-86, assoc. prof., 1986-90, prof., 1990—2002; chmn. dept. civil engring. SUNY, Buffalo, 1996-99, eminent prof., 2002—. Contbr. . Pres. W.E.S.T. Age Group Swim Club, Buffalo, 1985. Capt. Israel Def. Force, 1968—72. Grantee rsch., NSF, 1983—84, 1986—95, 1994—. Fellow: ASCE (faculty advisor 1981—83, bd. dirs. 1986—96, pres. Buffalo sect. 1993—94, Outstanding Svc. award 1982, 1983); mem.: N.Y. State Profl. Engring. Assn. (assoc. editor 2002—, Engring. Educator of Yr. award 1991, Hist. Achievement award 1995, Engr. of Yr. 2002), Nat. Ctr. for Earthquake Engring. Rsch. (Outstanding Achievement award L.A. Tall Bldg. Coun. 1995), Earthquake Engring. Rsch. Inst., Am. Concrete Ins. Achievements include invention of press brake deflection compensation structure, automatic diagnostic sys. for elec. cir. breakers; patents for. Avocation: Avocations: photography, skiing, bicycling, scuba diving. Home: 12 Troy View Ln Buffalo NY 14221-3522 Office: SUNY Buffalo Civil Struct/Environ Engrg 231 Ketter Hall Buffalo NY 14260-4300 E-mail: reinhorn@buffalo.edu.

REINHOUDT, JOHANNES FEIKE, pharmaceutical industry executive; b. Kamperland, Zeeland, The Netherlands, Nov. 24, 1962; s. Isaak and Atje (Van Netten) R.; m. Miep Apolonia Huige, Oct. 28, 1983; 1 child, Jurgen Raymond. Student nursing, Sch. voor Verpleegkundigen, The Netherlands, 1984; Nurse Anesthetist, Acad. Hosp. Leiden, The Netherlands, 1987. RN, RN anesthetist. Nurse trainee Found. Oosterschelde Hosps., Goes, The Netherland, 1980-85; nurse anesthetist trainee Acad. Hosp. Leiden (The Netherlands), 1985-88; rsch. nurse Pharma Bio-Rsch. Internat., Zuidlaren, The Netherlands, 1988; product specialist Rhône-Poulenc Pharma B.V., Amstelveen, The Netherlands, 1988-89; clin. rsch. assoc., clin. rsch. assoc.-mgr. Rhône-Poulenc Rorer B.V., The Netherlands, 1989-92; area rsch. cons. Medinet, Breda, The Netherlands, 1992-93; mgr. affiliate liaison, coordination Rhône-Poulenc Rorer SA, Antony, France, 1993-96, sr. mgr. world-wide affiliate liaison and coordination France, 1996-97, sr. mgr. world-wide clin. devel. ops., 1997—. Initiator Good Clin. Practice platform, The Netherlands, 1991-92. Mem. Drug Info. Assn., Assn. Clin. Rsch. Profls. Avocations: reading, cycling, swimming, windsurfing, fishing. Address: 62 Longview Cir Berwyn PA 19312-2501

REINIKE, IRMA, writer, fine artist, poet, lyricist; b. White Harbor, Long Beach, Miss., Oct. 20, 1927; d. Chester Henry and Edna Claire (Latille) R.; children: Harvey Franklin Linn Shows Jr., George David Shows, Thelma Jewell Shows Hoffman. Student, St. Mary's Dominican Coll.; grad., North Light Art Sch., Cin., 1996, 97, 99. Freelance writer, student Famous Writer's Sch., Westport, Conn., 1965—69; freelance writer New Orleans, Long Beach, Miss. Author: Mystery, 1940—41, Long Beach Movie Personality, 1949, Miss Long Beach, 1973, 1989, 1990, My Beach, Thelma, 1991, (poetry) My Lady of Medjugorje, 1987—88, Irma Reinike Poetry-Book 1, 2000—01, I Love My Flag, 2000, other poems; columnist Round the Town, Long Beach, Miss., 1963—66, (radio-TV paper) The Illustrated Press, Irma Reinike's Personality Parade, New Orleans, 1950's; composer: (songs) See You Tomorrow, 1995—96, Days of Love, 1997, The Blue of Your Eyes, 1997, others, (stage play) Ethel Chichester, Peg O' My Heart, Kaye Hamilton, Stage Door, 1949, Song, Dance Dixieland Minstrel and Variety Artists, 1950—51, Charity Performer, Le Petit Theatre de Vieux Carre' Sunday Salon, 1996, Destruction by Hurricane Camille, Times Picayune, 1970; artist Introduction Camille Book-Hurricane, 1969, exhibited artworks books, St. Thomas, 1992, 2 oil/acrylic paintings, St. Thomas Ch., 1970, artist, fine arts and mixed media. Mem. Nat. Rep. Senatorial Com., 1994-97; mem. Nat. Republican Congl. Com., 2000; mem. La. Libr. Found., New Orleans Friends of Pub. Libr., 1994-96; charter mem. World War II Monument Meml., Washington. Honored Author, La. Libr. Assn., 1994, 96, La. State Librarian, 1995, Friends Fest New Orleans Pub. Libr., 1994-96, Patron Le Petit Theatre de Vieux Carre, 1996. Mem. Long Beach Hist. Soc. Republican. Roman Catholic. Avocations: fine arts, songwriting, poetry, lyricist. Home: 105 D'Evereux Dr Slidell LA 70461

REINING, LAWRENCE ROBERT, library director; b. Honesdale, Pa., Mar. 4, 1956; s. William Jacob and Lois Jean (Longrod) R.; m. Deborah Joy Harrell, Aug. 20, 1988; 1 child, Christopher Robert. BS in Chemistry, Houghton (N.Y.) Coll., 1978; MS in Inorganic Chemistry, Purdue U., 1982; MA in Libr. Info. Sci., No. Ill. U., 1992. Chemistry instr. Wheaton (Ill.) Coll., 1985-88, archives asst., 1989-90, cataloger (libr.), 1990-93, asst. head tech. svcs., 1993-94, head tech. svcs., libr., 1994-96; chemistry instr. North Ctrl. Coll., Naperville, Ill., 1989; dir. libr. svcs. Asbury Coll., Wilmore, Ky., 1996—. Author book revs. The Christian Librarian, 1999—. Pres. Wilmore Book Club, 2000. Named Outstanding Tchg. Ass., U. Ill.-Chgo., 1983, Purdue U., 1980. Mem. Assn. of Christian Librs. (fin. adv. bd. 2000—, chair liberal arts sect. 1997-2000), Ky. Libr. Assn., Am. Sci. Affiliation, Assn. of Ind. Ky. Colls. and Univs. (exec. com. Libr. Dirs. Group 2000—), Coun. for Christian Colls. and Univs. (exec. com. Libr. Dirs. Group 1999—), Phi Lambda Upsilon. Republican. Methodist. Avocations: reading, fishing, travel, simulation strategic gaming. Office: Asbury College Kinlaw Libr 1 Macklem Dr Wilmore KY 40390 Home: 108 Franklin Ct Nicholasville KY 40356-9045 E-mail: larry.reining@asbury.edu.

REINING, PRISCILLA COPELAND, anthropologist; b. Chgo., Mar. 11, 1923; d. Kenneth Bayard and Mary Elsie (Weser) Copeland; m. Conrad Copeland Reining, June 26, 1944 (dec. Oct. 1984); children: Robert Cushman, Anne Elizabeth, Conrad Copeland Schilling. AB, U. Chgo., 1945, AM, 1949, PhD, 1967. Lectr. U. Minn., Mpls., 1956-60, Howard U., Washington, 1960-65; rsch. assoc. Cath. U. Am., 1966-68; assoc. Smithsonian Instn., 1966, 68, 70; cons. The World Bank, 1972, USAID, 1973, AAAS, Washington, 1971-73, project dir., 1974-81, program dir., 1982-90; vis. prof. African Studies U. Fla., Gainesville, 1994—. Mem. bd. on sci. and tech. for internat. devel. NAS, Washington, 1976-80; mem. arid ecosys. interation Internat. Geosphere/Biosphere Program, Boulder, 1989—; mem. adv. bd. Population and Environ., N.Y.C., 1990—; bd. dirs. Renewable Natural Resources Found., Bethesda, Md., 1991—, Pub. Interest mem. Renewable Natural Resources Found. (RNRF) bd., 1999.; mem. U.S. del. UN Conf. on Desertification, Nairobi, Kenya, 1977. Author: Challenging Desertification, 1980; author, editor: Village Women, 1977; editor: Village Viability, 1980, Resource Inventory, 1984. Mem. Peace Commn. Washington Cathedral, 1986-91. Grantee NIMH, 1966, NSF, 1967, Nat. Geographic Soc. Com. for Rsch. and Exploration, 1994 Fellow AAAS (sec. 1978-89), Am. Anthrop. Assn. (task force on AIDS, task force on environ., Disting. Svc. award 1990), African Studies Assn. (bd. dirs. 1978-80); mem. Anthrop. Soc. Washington (pres. 1976-77), Soc. Women Geographers (triennial presenter 1996); chairperson planning com. renewable natural resources found. Congress, 1998. Home: 3601 Rittenhouse St NW Washington DC 20015-2413

REININGHAUS, RUTH, retired artist; b. N.Y.C., Oct. 4, 1922; d. Emil William and Pauline Rosa (Lazarik) R.; m. George H. Morales, Feb. 20, 1944; children: George James, Robert Charles; m. Allan Joseph Smith, May 28, 1960. Student, Hunter Coll., NYU, Nat. Acad. Sch. of Design, 1960-61, Frank Reilly Sch. of Art, 1963, Art Students League, 1964, 68; studied oil painting, with Robert Beverly Hale and Robert Philips, with Morton Roberts and Frank Reilly, Robert Maione, with Rudy Colao. Instr. art Banker's Trust, N.Y.C., 1971-77, 79-99, Kittredge Club for Women, N.Y.C., 1967-77. Exhibited in group shows at Berkshire Art Mus., 1970s, Hammer Galleries, Inc., N.Y.C., 1974, Far Gallery, N.Y.C., 1974, Mufalli Gallery, N.Y. and Fla., 1983-90, Pen and Brush Club, 1985—, Petrucci Gallery, Saugerties, N.Y., 1988-94, Pastel Soc. Am., 1988—, John Lane Gallery, Rhinebeck, N.Y., 1992-97, Regianni Gallery, N.Y.C., 1994, Catherine Lorillard Wolfe Club, Salmagundi Club, Allied Artists Am., Heidi Newhoff Gallery, N.Y.C., Hudson Valley Art Assn., Knickerbocker Artists, N.Y.C., Pen & Brush Club Inc., Pastel Soc. Am., Heritage Mus. Recipient 3d prize in Oils, Murray Hill Art Show, 1966, 68; Washington Sq. Outdoor Art Exhibit scholar Nat. Acad., 1960, Frank Reilly Sch. Art, 1963, NYU, 1968, Talens award, 1963, Robert Lehman award, 1968, Baker Brush award, 1969, Salmagund scholar, 1969; subject NBC TV show You Are an Artist, 1950s. Fellow: Hudson Valley Art Assn. (Claude Parson's Meml. award 1970), Am. Artists Profl. League (Claude Parsons Meml. award 1974, 2d prize oils 1992, 3d prize pastel 1993, Pres. award 1994); mem.: Coun. Am. Artists, Soc. West Coast (award 1997), Knickerbocker Artists (Flora B. Giffuni PSA Pres.' award 1990), Oil Pastel Assn. (Pen and Brush award 1987, Strathmore award 1989, Pen and Brush award 1990, Salmagundi Club award 1991), Allied Artists Am. (assoc.), Washington Sq. Outdoor Art Assn. (bd. dirs. 1983—90), Nat. Arts Club (Reciprocal) Artists Fellowship, Soc. Illustrators (hon. 1983—87), Pastel Soc. Am. (bd. dirs. 1988—90, J. Giffuni purchase award 1988, Pastel Soc. of West Coast award 1997), Salmagundi Club N.Y (pres. 1983—87, curator 1989—97, Philip Isenberg award 1974, Hon. mention 1983, 1984, Salmagundi Club prize 1985, Franklin B. Williams Fund prize 1987, Tom Picard award 1987, Mortimer E. Freehof award 1988, John N. Lewis award 1988, Philip Isenberg award 1989, Salmagundi Club Medal of Honor 1989, John N. Lewis award 1989, Philip Isenberg award 1990, Helen S. Coes award 1990, Samuel T. Shaw award 1990, Thomas Moran award 1990, Alice B. McReynolds award 1991, Hon. mention 1991, Salmagundi award 1991, Alphaeus Cole Meml. award 1991, Philip Isenberg award 1992, 1995, Hon. mention 1996, Harry Ballinger Meml. award 2000, 2001, Philip Isenberg award 2001), Pen and Brush Club (Helen Slotman award 1986, OPA Internat. award 1987, Gene Alden Walker award 1988, hon. mention 1991, Pen and Brush Solo award 1992, Margaret Sussman award 1996, 1998, Merit award 2000), Catharine Lorillard Wolfe Art Club (bd. dirs. 1987—, Anna Hyatt Huntington award 1978, Pastel award 1992, Hon. mention 1991, 1st prize 2001), Alpha Delta Pi. Lutheran. Avocations: travel, technical illustration, oil, pastel and watercolor painting, collecting antique music boxes and watches. Home: 222 E 93rd St Apt 26A New York NY 10128-3758

REINIS, MARIA SKERLAVAY, pathologist; b. Buenos Aires, Aug. 27, 1931; came to U.S., 1965; m. Joseph G. Reinis, Mar. 18, 1969. B of Biol. Sci., Liceo Nat., Buenos Aires, 1955; DM, U. Buenos Aires, 1962. Diplomate Am. Bd. Pathology. Rsch. asst. dept. path. chemistry U. Buenos Aires Sch. Pharmacy and Biochemistry, 1962-64; from med. fellow to rsch. fellow Margaret Sanger Rsch. Bur., N.Y.C., 1965-67, rsch. assoc., 1969; intern French Hosp., 1968; resident in pathology NYU Sch. Medicine, 1970-73; fellow in pathology State U. Hosp., Bklyn., 1974-75; asst. dir. lab., asst. attending pathologist Roosevelt Hosp., N.Y.C., 1975-78; dir. dept. pathology and clin. lab., dir. transfusion svc. Victory Meml. Hosp., Bklyn., 1979—. Immunohematology staff Beth Israel Med. Ctr. Blood Bank, N.Y.C., 1976-78; asst. clin. prof. pathology Coll. Physicians & Surgeons/Columbia U., N.Y.C., 1975-78, vis. pathologist, 1978-79; chief examiner N.Y.C. Dept. Health Bur. Lab., 1984—, cons., 1987—; bd. examiners, adv. com. to commr. health City N.Y., 1986—, family living, sex edn. adv. com. mem., bd. edn., 1987-91; Am. del. N.Y. State Internat. Med. Program, 1990; asst. clin. prof. pathology NYU Med. Ctr., N.Y.C., 1980—; lectr. in field. Contbr. articles to profl. jours. Am. Cancer Soc. grantee, N.Y.C., 1988; recipient Civic award for disting. community svc. Dyker Heights Civic Assn., 1984, Community Svc. award Victory Meml. Hosp., 1986, Pathology Continuing Med. Edn. award, 1994. Fellow Coll. Am. Pathologists; mem. AMA (Physicians Recognition award 1994), Am. Soc. Cytology, Am. Cancer Soc. (chair pub. edn. com. Bay Ridge unit 1984—, exec. com. mem., profl. edn. com. mem., chair pap smear com. N.Y.C. 1987-88, pub. edn. com. mem., bd. dirs., exec. com. mem., award 1989), Med. Soc. State N.Y., Coun. Hosp. Blood Bank Dirs. Greater N.Y. (co-chair edn. com. 1990—), Med. Soc. Bay Ridge, Med. Club Bklyn.

REINITZER, SIGRID FRIEDRUN, librarian, educator; b. Graz, Styria, Austria, Feb. 11, 1941; d. Gernot and Edith (Mayer) R. PhD, U. Graz, 1968. Information systems specialist U. Graz, Austria, 1978-88, leader EDP dept. Austria, 1978-88, deputy libr. Austria, 1984-88; dir. U. Libr. Graz, 1989—. Lectr. U. Graz Inst. Anorganic Chemistry, 1973-99. Editor: Bibliotheken bauen und fuehren, 1983, Die Universitätsbibliothek Graz, eine Bibliothek im Wandel, Bibliothekskooperation: Möglichkeit u. Grenzen, 1989. Fellow Ligue des Biblioth+250ques Europ+248ennes de Rechetche, European Libr. Automation Group, Vereingung Österr. Bibliothekare (v.p. 1992—, pres. 1998—), Internat. Fedn. U. Women Austria-Styria (dep. pres. 1968-92), Deutscher Verein Bibliothekare. Office: U Libr Graz Universitatsplatz 3 8010 Graz Styria Austria

REINIUS, MICHELE REED, executive recruiter; b. San Diego, Jan. 17, 1948; d. Wallace Alvin Reed and Dorothy Louise Austin; m. Robin Patric Reinius, Aug. 4, 1990; 1 child, Joselyn Ann Andrews. Supr. Asosa Personnel, Tucson, 1981-83; recruiter TAD Tech., 1983-85; co-cowner Migar Personnel, 1985-90; mgr. Temps by Encore, 1990-2000; pres. Ariz. Recruiting Source, 2000—. Democrat. Jewish. Avocations: reading, swimming. Office: Ariz Recruiting Source 7483 E Broadway Tucson AZ 85710

REINKE, DORIS MARIE, retired elementary education educator; b. Racine, Wis., Jan. 12, 1922; d. Otto William Reinke and Louise Amelia Goehring. BS, U. Wis., Milw., 1943; MS, U. Wis., Whitewater, 1967. Tchr. kindergarten Elkhorn (Wis.) Area Sch. Sys., 1943-69, bldg. prin., 1968-70, summer sch. dir., 1974-75, grade 2 tchr., 1970-84, primary dept. chmn., 1971-84, administrv. asst., supervising tchr., 1957-83, student tchr., 1984, ret., 1984; oriented experience tchr. Program Area Sch. Sys., Elkhorn, 1966. Pres. Elkhorn Edn. Assn., 1949-50; rep. dist. State Kindergarten Conf., Oshkosh, Wis., 1966; participant early edn. conf. State Early Edn. Conf., Eagle River, Wis., 1968; tchr. Covenant Harbor Elderhostel, 1997, 98. Contbr. weekly newspaper column, ; author: Doris' Corner newsletter Walworth County Geneal. Soc., 1992—; author: (with Charlotte and William Gates) Guide to Beckwith's History of Walworth County, 2000; contbr. weekly newspaper column. RSVP Vol. Food Pantry, Elkhorn, 1985—2002; chmn. sch. centennial, 1987; mem. Elkhorn Hist. Preservation Com., 1991—; archivist Sugar Creek Luth. Ch., 1992—; choir mem. Luth. Ch., 1995—2001; chmn. Sesquicentennial com., 1997—; dir. Webster House Mus., 1991—; mem. Walworth County Sesquicentennial Com., 1997—98; mem. sesquicentennial com. Walworth County Fair, 1998—; del. dist. constn. conv. Evang. Luth. Ch. Am., Beloit, Wis., 1987; com. mem. Luth. Ch., Elkhorn, 1987; bd. dirs. Food Pantry, 1985—88, 1995—. Recipient Wis. Edn. Research, West Bend, Wis., 1966, Outstanding Elem. Tchrs., Wash., 1973, Wis. Dept. Edn., Madison, 1980, Local History award State Hist. Soc. Wis., 1993, Outstanding Sr. Citizen award Walworth County Fair, 1999, Cmty. Svc. award, Masons, 2000. Mem.: Walworth County Ret. Tchrs. Assn. (v.p. 1988, pres. 1991), Nat. Ret. Tchrs. Assn., Walworth County Geneal. Soc. (bd. dirs. 1991—92), Walworth County Hist. Soc. (treas. 1985—89, v.p. 1990—91, pres. 1991—96, v.p. 1999—2000, pres. 2000—02), Elkhorn Women's Club (sec. 1999—2000), Alpha Delta Kappa (state pres. 1968—70, 1976—78, chpt. pres. 2002). Avocations: reading, baseball, bird watching, traveling. Home: 516 N Wisconsin St Elkhorn WI 53121-1119

REINKE, RALPH LOUIS, retired academic administrator; b. Elmhurst, Ill., June 22, 1927; s. Louis Fred and Malinda Marie (Beckmann) R.; m. Lois Hermine Borneman, Aug. 28, 1948 (dec. Mar. 1984); children: Janice Reinke Eisenloeffell, Stephan, Sharon Reinke Holaway; m. Carole Louise Rediehs, June 14, 1986 Student, U. Ill., 1945—46; BS, Concordia U., River Forest, Ill., 1949; MA, Northwestern U., 1952; postgrad., U. Chgo., 1956—63; LittD, Concordia Sem., 1972. Prin. St. John Elem. Sch., Houston, 1949-56; assoc. prof. psychology and edn. Concordia U., River Forest, 1956-68; pres., chief exec. officer Concordia Pub. House, St. Louis, 1968-86; pres. Concordia U., Seward, Nebr., 1986—90; ret., 1990. Author: Christian Spelling Series, 2d edit, 1971. Mem. sch. bd. selecting com., Oak Park, Ill., 1965-67, chmn. lit. commn. Mo. Synod Luth. Ch., 1967-69; bd. dirs. Concordia U., 1992—, chair, 1999-2002. With USNR, 1944-46. Mem. Protestant Ch. Owned Pubs. Assn. (dir. 1969-84, pres. 1982-84), St. Louis Printing Assn. (bd. dirs. 1975-77), Am. Assn. Indsl. Mgmt. (bd. dirs. 1981-85), Assn. Ind. Colls. and Univs. of Nebr. (pres. 1988-89), Luth. Edn. Assn. (pres. 1967-69), Rotary, Phi Delta Kappa. Lutheran. E-mail: rlreinke@aol.com. *Life is a most precious and finite gift of God to man. Those who would lead must make a commitment to devote their full energies and intellects to the improvement of the quality of life of their fellowmen. In the highest sense, leadership is the integrity to heed the quiet voice of conscience from within in the quest of that quality.*

REINKE, STEFAN MICHAEL, lawyer; b. Concord, Calif., May 7, 1958; s. Albert Richard and Patricia Eleanor (Stefan) R.; m. Lisa Elaine Williams, June 7, 1997. AA, Bakersfield Coll., 1978; AB, U. So. Calif., 1981; JD, U. Calif., Davis, 1984. Bar: Hawaii 1984, U.S. Dist. Ct. Hawaii 1984, U.S. Ct. Appeals (9th and Fed. cirs.) 1985. Assoc. Carlsmith, Wichman, Case, Mukai & Ichiki, Honolulu, 1984-86; dir. Lyons, Brandt, Cook & Hiramatsu, 1986—. Lectr. Windward C.C., 1995-98; lawyer rep. 9th Cir. Jud. Conf., 1995; lawyer rep. Jud. Conf. for the U.S. Dist. Ct. Hawaii, 1996-98, 2002--. Bd. dirs. Hawaii Ctrs. for Ind. Living, Honolulu, 1985-91, Prevent Child Abuse Hawaii, 1995—, v.p., 1999-2000, pres., 2000-2001; ofcl. U.S. Cycling Fedn. Mem. ABA, FBA (pres. Hawaii chpt. 1994-96, 98-99), Hawaii Bar Assn. (mem. jud. adminstrn. com.), Am. Arbitration Assn. (arbitrator and mediator), Def. Rsch. Inst., Hawaii State Cycling Assn. (bd. dirs. 1998-2001), Phi Beta Kappa, Phi Alpha Delta. Office: Lyons Brandt Cook & Hiramatsu 841 Bishop St Ste 1800 Honolulu HI 96813-3992 E-mail: sreinke@usa.net.

REINKE, WILLIAM JOHN, lawyer; b. South Bend, Ind., Aug. 7, 1930; s. William August and Eva Marie (Hein) R.; m. Sue Carol Colvin, 1951 (div. 1988); children: Sally Sue Taelman, William A., Andrew J.; m. Elizabeth Beck Lockwood, 1991. AB cum laude, Wabash Coll., 1952; JD, U. Chgo., 1955. Bar: Ind. 1955. Assoc. Barnes & Thornburg and predecessors, South Bend, Ind., 1957-61, ptnr., 1961-96, of counsel, 1996—; former chmn. compensation com.; former mem. mgmt. com. Trustee Stanley Clark Sch., 1969-80, pres., 1977-80; mem. adv. bd. Salvation Army, 1973—, pres., 1990-92; bd. dirs. NABE Mich. chpt., 1990-94, pres. 1993-94, Isaac Walton League, 1970-81, United Way, 1979-81; pres. South Bend Round Table, 1963-65; trustee First Meth. Ch., 1976-70. Served with U.S. Army, 1955-57. Recipient Outstanding Local Pres. award Ind. Jaycees, 1960-61, Boss of Yr. award, 1979, South Bend Outstanding Young Man award, 1961. Mem. ABA, Ind. State Bar Assn., St. Joseph County Bar Assn., Ind. Bar Found. (patron fellow), Am. Judicature Soc., Ind. Soc. Chgo., Summit Club (past gov., founders com.), Rotary (bd. dirs. 1970-73, 94-97). Home: 51795 Waterton Square Cir Granger IN 46530-8317 Office: Barnes & Thornburg 1st Source Bank Ctr 100 N Michigan St Ste 600 South Bend IN 46601-1632

REINKER, KENT ALAN, orthopedist, surgeon, educator; b. Cleve., July 15, 1943; s. Arthur George and Barbara Phyllis (Parks) R.; m. Melode Sue Gifford, Dec. 21, 1968 (div. 2001); children: Matthew, Daniel, Lisa. BS, Yale U., 1965; MD, Case Western Res., 1970. Diplomate Am. Bd. Orthop. Commd. 2d lt. U.S. Army, 1969, advanced through grades to col., 1985—89; chief orthop. Moncrief Army Hosp., Columbia, S.C., 1975-78; staff orthop. Tripler Army Med. Ctr., Honolulu, 1978-82, chief orthop., 1983-89; chief of staff Shriners Hosp., 1989—2001; prof. orthopaedics U. Tex., San Antonio, 2001—. Bd. dirs. United Cerebral Palsy, Honolulu. Co-author: Pediatric Orthopedic Secrets Etiology of Scolosis, 2000; contbr. articles to profl. jours. Bd. dirs. Ctrl. Union Ch., Honolulu, 1998—, chmn., 1999-2000. Named Hon. Amb. Guam Govt., 1995, Disting. Alumnus, Lakewood (Ohio) H.S., 1998. Mem.: Hawaii Orthop. Assn., Pan Pacific Surg. Assn. (bd. dirs. 1982—2001, chmn. 1996—98), Western Orthop. Assn. (2d v.p. 2000—, 1st v.p. 2001—02), Pediat. Orthop. Soc. N.Am., Scoliosis Rsch. Soc., Am. Acad. Pediat., Am. Acad. Orthop. Surgeons. Office: U Tex Health Sci Ctr 7703 Floyd Curl Dr MC 7774 San Antonio TX 78229-3900 E-mail: reinkerk@gte.net.

REINKER, NANCY COOKE, artist; b. Owensboro, Ky., July 6, 1936; d. Billie Clayton and Barbara Jane (Mitchell) Cooke; m. Dale Bruce Reinker, Sept. 29, 1956; children: Shahn Elizabeth, Laura Beth, Karen Christian. Student, Kent State U., 1954-55, Cleve. Art Inst., 1956-57; studied sculpture with, Stanley Bleifeld, 1979-80; student, Silvermine Sch. of Art, 1988-89. Owner Nettle Creek Shops of Westport and Cos Cob, Conn., 1974-86, Cross River Design Studio, 1986-89. One-woman shows include Hayes Gallery, 1992, Silvermine Guild Arts Ctr., Art Place, 1993, 1995, 1998, 2000, Westport Art Ctr., 1994, Farrell II Gallery, 1998; works in traveling exhbn. Nat. Assn. Women Artists, Inc., 1996—98, Erector Square Gallery, New Haven, Conn., numerous nat. and internat. exhbns.; sculpture UN, N.Y.C., Rebuilding Torn Societies, 1999; juried and invited shows, Katonah Mus. Art, 2001, Conn. Graphic Arts Ctr., 2001, 52d Art of the Northeast, 2001, Reflections, Norwalk C.C., 2002; Represented in permanent collections , Housatonic C.C. Chmn. Commn. for The Arts, Weston, Conn., 1993-94, Art Bridge-U.S.-Japan, 2000, Gallery Irohani, Sakai City, Japan; pres. Inst. for Visual Artists, New Canaan, Conn., 1992-93; v.p., pres. Art Place Gallery, Southport, Conn., 1991-92, treas., 1998—. Named to 1992 Cir. of Excellence, Soc. Nat. Art Patrons, 1992; recipient 1st prize Spectrum, 1992, 93, 94. Mem. ASID (assoc.), Silvermine Guild of Artists (trustee 1994-99), New Haven Paint and Clay (Merit award 1993, purchase award for permanent collection 1997), Nat. Assn. Women Artists, Conn. Women Artists (Painting award 1991), Greenwich Art Soc. (Randolph Chitwood award 1994), Women's Caucus for Art, Chi Omega. Home: 87 Valley Forge Rd Weston CT 06883-1913 E-mail: ncrtist@aol.com.

REINKING, ANN H. actress, dancer; b. Seattle, Nov. 10, 1950; d. Walter Floyd and Francis Holmes (Harrison) R.; m. Larry Small, 1970; m. Herbert A. Allen; Aug. 25, 1982; (stepchildren): Leslie, Christie, Herbert, Charlie. Student public schs. Guest tchr. NYU, Duke U., Durham, N.C., Rutgers, N.J., Harvard, Cambridge, Mass.; choreographer Pal Joey, Goodman Theater, Chgo., 1988. Broadway appearances include Coco, 1970, Wild and Wonderful, 1972, Pippin, 1973, Over Here, 1974, Goodtime Charlie, 1975, Chicago, 1977, A Chorus Line, 1976, Dancin', 1978, Sweet Charity, 1986-87; TV appearances include Ellery Queen, Doug Henning: Magic on Broadway, 1982, Parade of Stars, 1983, American Treasury, 1985, Salute to Jules Styne, Broadway Salutes Washington, An Introduction to the Dance Gala of the Stars; film appearances include Movie, Movie, 1978, All That Jazz, 1979-80, Annie, 1982, Micki and Maude, 1984; play Ann Reinking ... Music Moves Me, 1984; choreography: Chicago, 1996 (Tony award 1997), Annie Get Your Gun, 1999 (Tony award 1999). Recipient Clarence Derwent award, 1974, Outer Critics Circle award, 1974, Theatre World award, 1974, Dance Educators Am. award, 1979, Harkness Dance award, 1979, two Tony award nominations, Tony award for Choregraphy, 1997; Ford Found. scholar, 1964-66; Robert Joffery scholar, 1967; Harkness scholar; Nat. Dance Educators award. Mem. Actors Equity, AFTRA, Stage Actors Guild. Avocations: horseback riding, skiing, swimming, hiking. also: Steps Contemporary & Classical Dance 2121 Broadway Fl 3 New York NY 10023-1786*

REINL, HARRY CHARLES, economist; b. Muttersdorf, Suden, Germany, Nov. 13, 1932; came to US, 1946; s. Carl and Angela (Plass) R. BS, Fordham U., 1953; MA, George Washington U., 1968; Cert. Career English, USDA Grad. Sch., Washington, 1966; D of Humanistics, London Inst. Applied Rsch., 1992; PhD, Brownell U., 1993. Head market rsch. Timex Mfg., Waterbury, Conn., 1955-58; jr. observer Sperry-Rand Corp., N.Y.C., 1958-62; labor economist manpower adminstrn. U.S. Dept. Labor, Washington, 1962-68; labor economist Office Personnel Mgmt. U.S. Civil Svc. Commn., 1968—. Mgr. N.Y. br. Willmark Svc., N.Y.C., 1971; prof. rsch. Haute Ecole Rsch. Alliance Universelle pour la Paix par la Connaissance, Paris, 1992; rsch. bd. advs. Am. Biograph. Inst., Raleigh, N.C., 1991; mem. adv. coun. Internat. Biograph. Ctr., Cambridge, Eng., 1992. Author: (on microfilm) The Story of My Life, 1984 With neurology testing VA Med. Ctr., Washington, 1989—; mem. choir Internat. Biograph Ctr., 1981, 82; life mem. Rep. Nat. Com.,

Washington, 1979—; mem. Rep. Nat. Senatorial Com., Washington, 1990. Fellow AA, 1988—; recipient John Edgar Hoover Meml. award Police Assn., 1983, HIR Citation of Leadership Rep. Nat. Conv., 1996, Medal of Freedom Rep. Nat. Senatorial Inner Cir., 1999; decorated knight templar Bur. Internat., 1993. Mem. N.Y. Acad. Scis., Family Immigration History Ctr. Ellis Island, Collegiate Network, Inc. (hon. sponsor), George Mason U. Mercatus Ctr. (contbr.). Republican. Mem. Lds Ch. Home: 2425 Mount Vernon Ave Alexandria VA 22301-1347

REINLEITNER, KATHERINE MINDLIN, psychologist, foundation administrator; b. Scarsdale, N.Y., May 10, 1948; m. Theodore B. Day, Aug. 25, 1968 (div. Sept. 1980); children: Eleanor Day, T. Eugene Day, Jennifer Day, David Day; m. Lee A. Reinleitner, Sept. 15, 1990; children: Mark A., Paul H. BA, Barnard Coll., 1967; MA, Columbia U., 1968; PhD, U. Wash., 1974. Diplomate Am. Bd. Psychopharmacology and Forensic Psychology, Am. Bd. Psychology. Intern Astor Home for Children, Reinbeck, NY; psychologist Children's Hosp., Seattle, 1974-83; pvt. practice, Mercer Island, Bellevue, 1976-2000; pvt. practice Bainbridge Island, 1983—2000; adminstr. The Mindlin Found., Bellevue, 1994—. Gov.'s coun. on abuse and neglect State of Wash., Olympia, 1978-80; bd. dirs. Prescribing Psychologists Register, 1996—, curriculum com., 1996—. Author childrens books; author: What To Do After You've Seen the Zoo, 1983. Tng. fellowship IV, VA, 1970-71, 73-74, NIMH, 1969-70. Mem. AAAS, Internat. Coll. of Prescribing Psychologists. Office: The Mindlin Found 146 128th Ave NE Bellevue WA 98005 E-mail: drkathyday@aol.com.

REINMUTH, OSCAR MACNAUGHTON, physician, educator; b. Lincoln, Nebr., Oct. 23, 1927; s. Oscar William and Catharine Anne (MacNaughton) R.; m. Patricia Dixon, June 19, 1951 (div. Jan. 1977); children— David Dixon, Diane MacNaughton, Douglas Stewart; m. Audrey Longridge Holland, June 26, 1980. BS, U. Tex., Austin, 1948; MD (F.B. Hanes research fellow 1950-51), Duke U., 1952. Intern Duke Hosp., 1952-53; asst. resident in medicine Yale U. Med. Ctr., 1953-54, NIH research trainee, 1954-55; asst. resident in neurology Boston City Hosp., 1955-56, chief resident, teaching fellow in neurology Harvard U. Neurol. unit, 1956-57; NIH spl. trainee, clin. asst. Nat. Hosp., London, 1957-58; from asst. prof. to prof. neurology U. Miami (Fla.) Med. Sch., 1958-77; prof. neurology and behavioral neuroscience, chmn. dept. U. Pitts. Med. Sch., 1977-93, prof. emeritus, 1994—; prof. neurology U. Ariz. Coll. Medicine, Tucson, 1993—. Mem. research tng. com. A, B, and C NIH, 1966-73 Served with AUS, 1946-47. Recipient Mosby award, 1952. Fellow ACP, Am. Acad. Neurology (1st v.p. 1973-76), Am. Neurol. Assn. (1st v.p. 1977-78, 2d v.p. 1976-77), Am. Heart Assn. (fellow stroke coun., vice chmn. 1978-79, chmn. 1980-82, editor publs. 1975-78, editor-in-chief Stroke jour. 1987-91, Award of Merit 1992). Home: 5545 N Entrada Quince Tucson AZ 85718-4709 Office: U Med Ctr Dept Neurology 1501 N Campbell Ave Tucson AZ 85724-0001 E-mail: oreinmuth@aol.com.

REINOEHL, RICHARD LOUIS, artist, scholar, martial artist; b. Omaha, Oct. 11, 1944; s. Louis Lawrence and Frances Margaret (Robinson) R.; 1 child, Joy Margaret Iroff-Reinoehl. BS in Sociology, Portland State U., 1970; MSW, U. Minn., Duluth, 1977; postgrad., Cornell U., 1984-88. Acting dir. Vanguard Group Homes, Virginia, Minn., 1976-77; dir. Minn. Chippewa Tribe Group Home, Duluth, 1978, Human Devel. Consortium, Minn., N.Y., Ohio, 1978—. Faculty Social Work Program U. Wis., Superior, 1981-84; adv. bd. Computers in Social Svcs. Network, 1982-85; mem. Com. on Internat. Social Welfare Edn., 1982-86, Am. Evaluation Assn., 1986-89; affiliate scholar Oberlin Coll., 1991—. Editor: Computer Literacy in Human Services Education, 1990, Computer Literacy in Human Services, 1990, Men of Achievement, 16th edit., 1993; mem. editorial bd. Computers in Human Svcs., 1983-96, 99, Jour. Technology in Human Scis., 1999—; assoc. editor book rev., 1996-99; contbr. numerous articles to profl. jours. Mem. Legis. Task Force Regional Alcoholism Bd., 1972-73, Assn. Drug Abuse, Prevention and Treatment, 1973-74, Minn. Pub. Health Assn., 1976-78, Minn. Social Svc. Assn., 1976-83, Wis. Coun. Social Work Edn., 1983-84, N.Y. State Coun. Family Rels., 1986-89, Nat. Coun. Family Rels., 1986-89; exec. bd. Duluth Community Action Program, 1982-83; Dem. precinct chair, Portland, Oreg., 1972-74; precinct vice-chair Dem. Farmer-Labor Party, Duluth, 1979-81, chair, 1981-83, 2d vice-chair exec. bd., 1981-83; mem. Zoning Appeals Bd., New Russia Twp., Ohio, 1996—; mem. art edn. com. Fireland Assn. Visual Arts, 1996-99; mem. land use planning com. New Russia Twp., Ohio, 1998—; chair Lorain County Comprehensive Plan Growth Mgmt. Com., 1999—; mem. Smart Devel. Coalition of Lorain County, 1998—, Lorain County Multi-Modal Transp. Planning Steering Com., 2000—, airport subcom., 2000—, roadways sub-com., 2000—, transit subcom., 2000—, info. tech. sub-com., 2000—. Mem. NASW (exec. com., chair program com. Arrowhead Region Minn. chpt., 1980-81, co-chair task force on computers in social work, 1981-82), Acad. Cert. Social Workers, Cornell U. Sailing Club (pres. 1990). Avocations: canoeing, antique Volkswagens, wilderness hiking. Office: Human Devel Consortium Inc 46180 Butternut Ridge Rd Oberlin OH 44074-9778 E-mail: richard.reinoehl@oberlin.edu. *It's noteworthy that the most sought-after items in a society cannot be bought or sold. Included are wisdom, respect, generosity, truthfulness, and the love of family and friends.*

REINS, RALPH ERICH, automotive components supply company executive; b. Detroit, Sept. 18, 1940; s. Erich John and Florence (Franz) R.; m. Victoria Louise Kolts, Sept. 14, 1963; children— Ann Marie, Christine Louise BSI.E., U. Mich., 1963. Asst. supt. Chevrolet Motor div., Gen. Motors Corp., Detroit, 1963-72; v.p., pres. hwy. product ops. Rockwell Internat., Troy, Mich., 1972-85; sr. v.p. ITT Corp., Bloomfield Hills, 1985-89; chmn. of the bd., pres., chief exec. officer Mack Trucks, Inc., Allentown, Pa., 1989-90; pres. United Tech. Automotive, Dearborn, Mich., 1990-91; exec. v.p., pres. automotive sector Allied Signal Corp., 1991-94; pres., CEO Envirotest Sys. Corp., Phoenix, 1995-96, A.P. Parts Internat., Toledo, 1996-98; chmn., CEO Reins Enterprises, 1998—; pres., CEO Qualitor, Inc., 1999—. Bd. dirs. Rofin-Sinar Corp., Weirton Steel Corp. Mem. Soc. Automotive Engrs., Bloomfield Hills Country Club, Desert Mountain C.C. Republican. Avocations: golf; hunting; fishing. Home: 10801 E Happy Valley Rd Scottsdale AZ 85255-8171

REINSCH, NELSON LAMAR, JR. business educator; b. Lubbock, Tex., Feb. 5, 1947; s. N.L. and Ruth Reinsch; m. Janet Weatherford, May 27, 1969; children: Karl, Paul. BA, BSBA, Abilene (Tex.) Christian U., 1969; MA, Ctrl. Mich. U., 1970; PhD, U. Kans., 1973. Asst. prof. Western Ill. U., Macomb, 1973-77, Okla. State U., Stillwater, 1977-80, assoc. prof., 1980-84; prof. Abilene Christian U., 1984-92; assoc. prof. Georgetown U., Washington, 1992-2000, prof., 2000—. Editor Jour. of Bus. Comm., 1988-92. Fellow Assn. for Bus. Comm. (outstanding rschr. 1994), Acad. of Mgmt., Internat. Comm. Assn., Nat. Comm. Assn. Office: McDonough Sch of Bus Georgetown U Washington DC 20057

REINSCH, WILLIAM ALAN, association executive, educator; b. Evanston, Ill., Jan. 15, 1946; s. Bert and Kathleen (Penn) R.; m. Susan Polley Reinsch, Jan. 3, 1970; children: Andrew, Christian. BA, Johns Hopkins U., 1968; MA in Internat. Rels., Johns Hopkins U.-Sch. Advanced Internat. Studies, 1969. Legis. asst. Congressman Gilbert Gude, Washington, 1973-76, Congressman Richard Ottinger, Washington, 1976; chief legis. asst. Senator John Heinz, 1977-91; legis. asst. Senator John D. Rockefeller IV, 1991-93; cons., under sec. for export adminstrn. Dept. Commerce, 1994-2001; pres. Nat. Fgn. Trade Coun., 2001—. Tchr. Landon Sch., Bethesda, Md., 1968-73; adj. assoc. prof. U. Md. U. Coll. Grad. Sch. Mgmt. and Tech., College Park, Md., 1990—; acting staff dir. Environmental Study Conf. U.S. Ho. Reps., 1976. Contbr. articles to profl. jours. Pres. St. Mark Elderly Housing Corp., Rockville, Md. Mem. Phi Beta Kappa, Omicron Delta Kappa, Alpha Delta Phi. Democrat. Presbyterian. Office: Nat Fgn Trade Coun 1625 K St NW Ste 200 Washington DC 20006 E-mail: breinsch@nftc.org.

REINSCHMIDT, KENNETH FRANK, engineering and construction executive, educator; b. Cin., Mar. 26, 1938; s. Christian Edward and Martha Marie (Kellerman) R.; m. Marlene Faye Taub, Dec. 16, 1967. BSCE, MIT, 1960, MSCE, 1962, PhD in Engring., 1965. Assoc. prof. civil engring. MIT, Cambridge, 1965-75; sr. v.p. Stone & Webster Engring. Corp., Boston, 1975-93, also bd. dirs.; pres. Stone & Webster Advanced Systems Devel. Svcs., 1988-96; bd. dirs. Stone & Webster Advanced Tech. Applications Inc., N.Y.C., 1990-94; sr. v.p. Stone & Webster, Inc., 1993-96; ind. cons., 1996—2001; prof. civil engring., J.L. Frank/Marathon Ashland Petroleum LLP chair in engring. project mgmt. Tex. A&M U., College Station, 2001—; J.L. Frank/Marathon Ashland Petroleum LLC chair in engring. project mgmt. Tex. A & M U., 2001—. Chmn. com. on oversight of Ctr. for Bldg. Tech., Nat. Inst. Standards and Tech., Gaithersburg, Md., 1986-89; adj. prof. civil engring. Tex. A&M U., College Station, 1997-98, vis. prof., 1998-99; chmn. com. to assess policies and procedures of Dept. Energy to design, manage and procure environ. restoration, waste mgmt. and other constrn. projects NRC, 1998-99, Nat. Rsch. coun. com. on oversight and assessment U.S. Dept. Energy Project Mgmt., 2000—. Author: Stress: A User's Manual, 1963; editor: Systems Building, 1974; contbr. numerous articles to profl. jours. Capt. U.S. Army, 1966-67. Decorated Legion of Merit; NSF fellow, 1962. Fellow AAAS; mem. NAE, ASCE, INFORMS. Office: Tex A&M U Dept Civil Engring CE/TTI Bldg Rm 702A 3136 TAMU College Station TX 77843-3136 Office Fax: 979-845-6554. E-mail: kreinschmidt@civilmail.tamu.edu.

REINSDORF, JERRY MICHAEL, professional sports teams executive, real estate executive, lawyer, accountant; b. Bklyn., Feb. 25, 1936; s. Max and Marion (Smith) Reinsdorf; m. Martyl F. Rifkin, Dec. 29, 1956; children: David Jason, Susan Janeen, Michael Andrew, Jonathan Milton. BA, George Washington U., 1957; JD, Northwestern U., 1960. Bar: D.C., Ill. 1960; CPA, Ill.; cert. specialist real estate securities, rev. appraiser; registered mortgage underwriter. Atty. staff regional counsel IRS, Chgo., 1960-64; assoc. law firm Chapman & Cutler, 1964-68; ptnr. Altman, Kurlander & Weiss, 1968-74; of counsel firm Katten, Muchin, Gitles, Zavis, Pearl & Galler, 1974-79; gen. ptnr. Carlyle Real Estate Ltd. Partnerships, 1971, 72; chmn. bd. Balcor Co., 1973-87; mng. ptnr. TBC Films, 1975-83; chmn. Chgo. White Sox, 1981—, Chgo. Bulls Basketball Team, 1985—; ptnr. Bojer Fin., 1987—. Lectr. John Marshall Law Sch., 1966-68; former bd. dirs. Shearson Lehman Bros., Inc., Project Academus of DePaul U., Chgo., Sports Immortals Mus., 1987-89, Com. Commemorate U.S. Constn., 1987; bd. dirs. La Salle Nat. Bank, La Salle Nat. Corp.; bd. overseers Inst. for Civil Justice, 1996-98; lectr. in real estate, sports and taxation. Author: (with L. Herbert Schneider) Uses of Life Insurance in Qualified Employee Benefit Plans, 1970. Co-chmn. Ill. Profls. for Senator Ralph Smith, 1970; mem. Chgo. region bd. Anti-Defamation League, 1986-2001; mem., trustee Ill. Inst. Tech., 1991-96; mem. Ill. Commn. on African-Am. Males, 1992—; bd. dirs. Chgo. Youth Success Found., 1992—, Corp. for Supportive Housing, 1995—; nat. trustee Northwestern U., 1993—; bd. govs. Hugh O'Brian Youth Found.; mem. internat. adv. bd. Barrow Neurol. Found., 1996-97; Chgo. Baseball Cancer Charities, 1994, 98; bd. trustees Equity Office Properties, 1997—. Recipient Hallmark award Chgo. Baseball Cancer Charities, 1986, Corp. Superstar award Ill. chpt. Cystic Fibrosis Found., 1988, Sportsman of Yr. award, 1994, Chicagoan of Yr. award Chgo. Park Dist., 1990, Kellogg Excellence award, 1991, Cmty. Hero award Interfaith Organizing Project, 1991, Operation Push Bridgebuilder award, 1992, Alumni Merit award Northwestern U., 1992, Ellis Island Medal of Honor award Nat. Ethnic Coalition of Orgns., 1993, Lifetime Achievement award March of Dimes, 1994, Hallmark Hall of Fame Civic award Ind. Sports Charities, 1994, Am. Spirit award USAF, 1995, Alpha Epsilon Pi Arthur and Simiteich Outstanding Alumnus award, 1995, Order of Lincoln, 1997, Mayor's medal Hon., 1997, Bklyn. Businessman of Yr., 1997; inductee B'nai B'rith Nat. Jewish Am. Sports Hall of Fame, 1994, Chgo. Sports Hall of Fame, 1997, Guardian of Children award Jewish Coun. for Youth Svc., 1998. Mem.: FBA, ABA, Nat. Assn. Rev. Appraisers and Mortgage Underwriters, Nat. Sports Lawyers Assn., Chgo. Bar Assn., Ill. Bar Assn., Northwestern U. Law Sch. Alumni Assn. (bd. dirs.), Order of Coif, Comml. Club Chgo., Omega Tau Rho. Office: Chgo White Sox 333 W 35th St Chicago IL 60616-3651

REINSMA, HAROLD LAWRENCE, design consultant, engineer; b. Slayton, Minn., Sept. 6, 1928; s. Frank and Ida M. (Zabel) R.; m. Julia A. Tusek, Oct. 18, 1958; children: Frank, Michael, Diane. Student, Macalester Coll., 1948-50; BCE, U. Minn., 1953. Registered profl. engr., Ill. Cons. engr. GM Orr Engring. Co., Mpls., 1953-54; rsch. test engr. Caterpillar Tractor Co., Peoria, Ill., 1955-58, rsch. design engr., 1958-71, rsch. project engr., 1971-73, rsch. supervising engr., 1973-76, rsch. staff engr., 1976-91; design cons. Dunlap, 1991—. Achievements include 44 patents including 1st viable sealed and lubricated track, fundamental to success of a new generation of large high performance elevated sprocket tractors, also sealed maintenance-free linkage and large diameter high speed pressure balanced oil cooled brake wheel seals for mining trucks, all used in abrasive environments. Avocations: skiing, cycling, hiking, gardening. Home and Office: 13600 Lucerne Dr Dunlap IL 61525-9619

REINSTEIN, JOEL, lawyer; b. N.Y.C., July 23, 1946; s. Louis and Ruth Shukovsky; children: Lesli, Louis, Mindy. BSE, U. Pa., 1968; JD cum laude, U. Fla., 1971; LLM in Taxation, NYU, 1974. Bar: Fla. 1971, U.S. Tax Ct. 1973, U.S. Dist. Ct. (so. dist.) Fla. 1976. Atty., office of chief counsel IRS, 1971-74; ptnr. Capp, Reinstein, Kopelowitz and Atlas, P.A., Ft. Lauderdale, Fla., 1975-85; dir., ptnr. Greenberg, Traurig, Hoffman, Lipoff, Rosen & Quentel, P.A., 1985-92; gen. counsel Internat. Magnetic Imaging, Inc., Boca Raton, Fla., 1992-94; prin. Law Offices of Joel Reinstein, 1993—. Lectr. Advanced Pension Planning, Am. Soc. C.L.U.s; lectr. in field. Mem. editl. bd. U. Fla. Law Rev. 1970-71; contbr. articles to profl. jours. Mem. Fla. Bar Assn. (tax sect.), ABA (tax sect.), Order of Coif, Phi Kappa Phi, Phi Delta Pi. Office: 925 S Federal Hwy Ste 325 Boca Raton FL 33432

REINTHALER, RICHARD WALTER, lawyer; b. N.Y.C., Feb. 27, 1949; s. Walter F. and Maureen C. (Tully) R.; m. Mary E. Maloney, Aug. 8, 1970; children: Brian, Scott, Amy. BA in Govt. magna cum laude, U. Notre Dame, 1970, JD summa cum laude, 1973. Bar: N.Y. 1974, U.S. Dist. Ct. (so. and ea. dists.) N.Y. 1974, U.S. Ct. Appeals (2d cir.) 1974, U.S. Ct. Appeals (9th cir.) 1976, U.S. Ct. Appeals (5th cir.) 1978, U.S. Ct. Appeals (11th cir.) 1981, U.S. Supreme Ct. 1977. Assoc. White & Case, N.Y.C., 1973-81, ptnr., 1981-95, Dewey Ballantine LLP, N.Y.C., 1995—. Mem. adv. group U.S. Dist. Ct. (ea. dist.) N.Y., 1992—, chairperson subgroup on ethics, 1993—. Contbr. articles to profl. jours. Served to 1st lt. U.S. Army, 1974. Fellow Am. Bar Found.; mem. ABA (2d cir. chmn. discovery com. 1982-87, program coord. 1986, ann. meeting litigation sect., vice chmn. com. on fed. procedure 1988-89, co-chmn. com. on profl. responsibility 1989-92, vice chmn. securities litigation com. 1993-94, vice chair Hong Kong meeting 1995, co-chair energy litigation com. 1996-97, co-chair antitrust litigation com. 1997-2000, mem. Ethics 2000 task force 1999-2000), N.Y. State Bar Assn., Assn. of Bar of City of N.Y. (mem. com. to enhance diversity in the profession 1990-95, mem. Orison S. Marden Meml. Lectrs. com. 1994-2000, chair 1997-2000, spl. com. on mergers, acquisitions and corp. control contests 1995-2002), Scarsdale Golf Club (Hartsdale, N.Y., bd. govs. 1994—, pres. 2002--), Capital Hill Club (Washington). Republican. Roman Catholic. Avocations: golf, tennis. Office: Dewey Ballantine LLP 1301 Avenue Of The Americas New York NY 10019-6022

REINTZEL, WARREN ANDREW, trust company executive; b. Phila., Jan. 4, 1945; s. Warren H. and Lorna (Geibel) R.; m. Susan Rodgers, Dec. 20, 1969; children: Lisa S., Kurt W. BA with high honors, U. Del., 1967; MA in History, Rutgers U., 1968; JD, U. Pa., 1971. Trust adminstrn. trainee First Pa. Bank, Phila., 1971, trust adminstr., 1972-73, trust officer, 1973-79, sr. trust officer, 1979-81; v.p. Provident Nat. Bank, 1981-86; v.p., head trust adminstrn. dept. Glenmede Trust Co., 1986—, sr. v.p., 1994—. Trustee Wanamaker Inst., Phila., 1986—, 1st v.p., 1995-2000, pres., 2000-; trustee Meml. Fund, Luth. Ch. of our Saviour, Haddonfield, N.J., 1989-2000, Haddonfield Hist. Soc., 1997—, Haddonfield Cmty. Found., 1998-. Mem. Phila. Bar Assn., Phila. Fin. Assn. (treas. bd. trustees 1987-89), Phila. Estate Planning Coun. (trustee 1991, sec. 1994-95, treas. 1995-96, v.p. 1996-97, pres. 1997-98), Corp. Fiduciaries Assn. Phila. (mem. personal trust com. 1986-89, pres. 1996-98), Phi Beta Kappa. Republican. Office: Glenmede Trust Co 1650 Market St Ste 1200 Philadelphia PA 19103-7391

REIS, ARTHUR HENRY, JR. university administrator; b. Chgo., Nov. 6, 1946; s. Arthur Henry and Ardell Louise (Tholotowsky) R.; m. Karen Wessell, Aug. 22, 1970 (div. Apr. 1992); children: Sally Wessell, Rodger Henry; m. Debra-Ann Sowul, Sept. 12, 1992. BA in Chemistry and Physics, Cornell Coll., 1968; MA in Chemistry, Harvard U., 1969, PhD in Chemistry, 1972. Staff chemist Argonne (Ill.) Nat. Lab., 1974-79; adminstr., faculty dept. chemistry Brandeis U., Waltham, Mass., 1979-82, dir. sci. resources and planning, 1982-86, assoc. dean resources and planning, 1986-89, project dir. Nat. Ctr. Complex Systems, 1987-95, assoc. provost, 1989-91, 92—, acting provost, dean of faculty, 1991-92, assoc. v.p. devel., 1994—. Dir. Sat. morning student/tchr. programs, 1983-89, dir. summer rsch. apprentice program, 1983-89, pres. cabinet, 1986—; lectr. chemistry and forensic sci., 1998—. Author: (with others) Neutron Scattering, 1976, Molecular Metals, 1979, Solid State Chemistry: A Contemporary Overview, 1980, Extended Linear Chain Compounds, 1982; author numerous abstracts; contbr. articles to profl. jours. Adminstrv. bd. chmn. United Meth. Ch., Wellesley, Mass., 1984-91; marshal Project Bread Walk for Hunger, Boston, 1995-2000. 1st Lt. USAF, 1972-74. Mem. AAU, Am. Chem. Soc. (mem. inorganic divsn. and solid-state subdivsn.), Am. Crystallographic Soc., Nat. Coun. Univ. Rsch. Adminstrs., Coun. Chem. Rsch., Soc. Rsch. Adminstrs., Coun. Fed. Rels. Home: 28 Williams St Arlington MA 02476-5624 Office: Mail Stop 134 415 South St Waltham MA 02453-2728 E-mail: reis@brandeis.edu.

REIS, DON, publishing executive; b. N.Y.C., Nov. 19, 1927; m. Barbara Weinberg, 1949; children: Robert, Richard. AB, Princeton U., 1947; MA, NYU, 1955. Rsch. editor Bantam Books, 1952-55, edn. editor, 1955-66; editor-in-chief Washington Square Press Divsn. Simon & Schuster, 1966-68; v.p., editorial dir. Ednl. Directions Inc., Westport, Conn., 1968-85; mng. editor Barron's Ednl. Series, 1985-87; gen. and ednl. editor Barron's, 1987-93, sr. cons. editor, 1993-99; editorial dir. Reis Assocs., Forest Hills, N.Y., 1993—. Author (with A. Butman and D. Sohn) Paperback Books in the Schools, 1962; editor The Collected Essays of Aldous Huxley, 1958. Home and Office: 57 Summer St Forest Hills NY 11375-6035 E-mail: reis@wordnet.att.net, donjreis@yahoo.com.

REIS, ERNANE D. surgeon, researcher; b. Campo Grande, Brazil, Mar. 16, 1961; came to the U.S., 1988; s. Daniel and Thereza Reis; m. Katharina Jeker, 1994. MD, U. Fed. do Rio de Janeiro, 1984. Resident Hosp. Clementino Fraga Filno, Rio de Janeiro, 1985-87; cons. Ambulatory Surgery Ctr. Hosp. Israelita Albert Sabin, 1986-87; rsch. fellow Mt. Sinai Med. Ctr., N.Y.C., 1988-90; intern, resident, chief resident dept. surgery Mt. Sinai Sch. Medicine, 1990-95; asst. prof. Mount Sinai Sch. Medicine, 1997—; staff physician, rschr. Lausanne (Switzerland) U. Med. Sch., 1995-97; dir. Vascular Microsurgery Lab. Mount Sinai Sch. Medicine, N.Y.C., 1998—. Named Young Investigator award Merck & Co., Inc., 1999. Fellow ACS (assoc.); mem. Swiss Surg. Soc., N.Y. Acad. Scis., Alpha Omega Alpha. Office: Mount Sinai Sch Medicine Box 1259 1 Gustave L Levy Pl New York NY 10029-6500

REIS, HAROLD F. lawyer; b. N.Y.C., July 22, 1916; s. Bernard and Rose (Frank) R.; m. Ruthanne Abram, June 11, 1951; children: Alan B., Kate Reis Grogan, Deborah Reis Kennedy. BS, CCNY, 1937; LLB, Columbia U., 1940. Bar: N.Y. 1941, D.C. 1953. With Dept. Justice, Washington, 1942-67, 1st asst. Office of Legal Counsel, 1960-63, exec. asst. to Atty. Gen., 1963-67; pvt. practice, Washington, 1967-83; ptnr. Newman Holtzinger, P.C., Washington, 1983-95; sr. advisor Morgan, Lewis & Bockius, Washington, 1995—. Recipient Rockefeller Pub. Svc. award in law, legislation and adminstrn., 1964. Mem. ABA, D.C. Bar Assn., Cosmos Club (Washington). Office: 7800 M St NW Washington DC 20036

REIS, JEAN STEVENSON, administrative secretary; b. Wilburton, Okla., Nov. 30, 1914; d. Robert Emory and Ada (Ross) Stevenson; m. George William Reis, June 24, 1939 (dec. 1980). BA, U. Tex., El Paso, 1934; MA, So. Meth. U., 1935; postgrad., U. Chgo., 1937-38, U. Wash., 1948-49. Tchr. El Paso H.S., 1935-39; safety engr., trainer Safety and Security Divsn., Office of Chief Ordnance, Chgo., 1942-45; tchr. Lovenberg Jr. H.S., Galveston, Tex., 1946; parish sec. Trinity Parish Episcopal Ch., Seattle, 1950-65; adminstrv. sec., asst. Office Resident Bishop, United Meth. Ch., 1965-94. Observer Africa U. installation, Mutare, Zimbabwe, 1994; com. on legislation for 1996 gen. conf. Hist. Soc. of United Meth. Ch. Recipient Bishop's award, 1980. Mem. AAUW, Beta Beta Beta. Home: 9310 42nd Ave NE Seattle WA 98115-3814

REISBERG, BARRY, geropsychiatrist, neuropsychopharmacologist; b. Bklyn., Dec. 3, 1947; s. Harry and Claire (Cohen) R.; m. Rosalie DePaola, Feb. 23, 1974 (dec. Oct. 1975); m. Nancy A. Minich, May 7, 1988. BA, CUNY, Bklyn., 1968; MD, N.Y. Med. Coll., 1972. Diplomate Am. Bd. Psychiatry and Neurology, Am. Bd. Geriatric Psychiatry. Intern N.Y. Med. Coll./Met. Hosp., N.Y.C., 1972-75, resident in psychiatry, 1972-75; fellow dept. psychiatry Middlesex Hosp. Med. Sch. U. London, 1975; staff psychiatrist Franklin D. Roosevelt VA Hosp., Montrose, N.Y., 1975-78; staff psychiatrist Neuropsychopharmacology Rsch. Unit NYU Med. Ctr., N.Y.C., 1978-80, clin. dir. Aging and Dementia Rsch. Ctr., 1978—. Adj. prof. Ctr. for Studies in Aging McGill U., Montreal, Que., 1993—; clin. instr. dept. psychiatry N.Y. Med. Coll., Valhalla, 1975—78; asst. prof. NYU Sch. Medicine, N.Y.C., 1978—84, assoc. prof., 1984—90, prof., 1990—; rsch. collaborator, vis. clinician Brookhaven Nat. Labs., Upton, NY, 1979—90; dir. clin. core NIMH Clin. Rsch. Ctr., 1989—93, Nat. Inst. Aging Alzheimer's Disease Ctr., 1990—; dir. Zachary and Elizabeth M. Fisher Alzheimer's Disease Edn. and Resources Program NYU Sch. Medicine, 1995—; med. and sci. adv. bd. Alzheimer's Assn., Chgo., 1993—97; med. and sci. panel Alzheimer's Disease Internat., 1997—; cons. psychiatrist N.Y. VA Hosp., 1980—89; chmn. work group WHO, Copenhagen, 1984; mem. aging sect. NIH, 1986—90; vis. prof. Palmerston North Postgrad. Med. Soc., New Zealand, 1991; rsch. adv. bd. WHO Project on Alzheimer's Disease, 1995. Author: Brain Failure, 1981; editor: Alzheimer's Disease, 1983; editor: (with others) Diagnosis and Treatment of Senile Dementia, 1989; guest editor Drug Devel. Rsch., Internat. Psychogeriat., mem. editl. bd. Jour. Am. Aging Assn., 1985—, Alzheimer's Disease and Associated Disorders, 1985—, Jour. Geriat. Psychiatry and Neurology, 1986—, Am. Jour. Alzheimer's Disease, 1986—, Internat. Psychogeriat., 1989—96, Am. Jour. Geriat. Psychiatry, 1992—, Integrative Psychiatry, 1994—, Rsch. and Practice in Alzheimer's Disease, 1999—; contbr. over 200 articles to med. and sci. jours. Fellow NSF, 1963, Coun. on Internat. Ednl. Exch.-Japan Soc., Tokyo, 1968; grantee NIH, 1979-81, 82-85, 87-01, 90-95, 92-95, NIMH, 1983-85, Adminstrn. on Aging, 1998—. Mem. Internat. Psychogeriat. Assn. (bd. dirs. 1985-93, treas. 1993-95, pres.-elect 1995-97,pres. 1997-99), Am. Aging Assn. (bd. dirs. 1990-92), Alzheimer's and Related Disorders Soc. India (hon.), Am. Assn. Geriat. Psychiatry (sec. 1991-92, bd. dirs. 1992-96), Am. Coll. Neuropsychopharmacology. Achievements include patents for treatment for memory impairment; method for assessment of dementia; system for diagnosis and staging of dementia; staging of dementia severity by joint function examination; method for diagnosis of incontinence of corticocerebral origin by neurologic examination; method and apparatus employing motor measures for early diagnosis and staging of dementia. Office: NYU Sch Medicine Aging and Dementia Rsch Ctr 550 1st Ave New York NY 10016-6402 E-mail: barry.reisberg@med.nyu.edu. *Our studies have demonstrated that Alzheimer's disease (AD) recapitulates normal human development inversely in terms of cognition, functioning, neurologic reflexes and in other ways. These findings, which we have termed retrogenesis, have profound implications. Retrogenesis appears to represent a new mechanism of disease; retrogenesis implies that a better understanding of AD can improve understanding of normal human development and behavior and vice versa.*

REISCH, MICHAEL STEWART, social work educator; b. N.Y.C., Mar. 4, 1948; s. Joseph and Charlotte (Rosenberg) R.; m. Amy Jane Lewis, May 21, 1972; children: Jennifer, Nikki. BA in History with highest honors, NYU, 1968; PhD in History with distinction, SUNY, Binghamton, 1975; MSW with honors, CUNY, 1979. Youth worker Washington-Heights-Inwood YM-YWHA, N.Y.C., 1965-66; editor, columnist Heights Daily News, Bronx, N.Y., 1966-68; rsch./teaching asst. SUNY, Binghamton, 1970-72; unit dir., program cons. Child Study Assn.-Wel Met, Inc., N.Y.C., 1970-72; asst. dir. youth div. Mosholu-Montefiore Community Ctr., Bronx, 1972-73; project dir. Silberman Found./N.Y. Assn. Deans, N.Y.C., 1973-74; asst. dean Sch. Social Welfare, asst. prof. SUNY, Stony Brook, 1974-79; asst. prof., then assoc. prof. Sch. Social Work U. Md., Balt., 1979-86; dir. Sch. Social Work, prof. social work/pub. adminstrn. San Francisco State U., 1986-95; prof. social work U. Pa., Phila., 1995-99, U. Mich., Ann Arbor, 1999—. Cons. and spkr. in field. Co-author: From Charity to Enterprise, 1989 (Social Sci. Book of Month), Social Work in the 21st Century, 1997, The Road Not Taken, 2001; editor, author various books in field; contbr. articles to profl. publs., chpts. in books. Cons. to numerous local, state, and fed. polit. campaigns, 1971—; mem. Gov.'s Adv. Coun. Human Resources, Md., 1983-86; pres. Welfare Advs., Md., 1983-86; campaign mgr. Rep. Barbara Mikulski, Balt., 1982; bd. dirs. Coleman Advs. for Children and Youth, 1987-95, San Francisco Internat. Program, 1987-95, Calif. Social Work Edn. Ctr., 1991-95, Ctr. for S.E. Asian

Refugee Resettlement, 1992-95, Am. Jewish Congress, N. Calif., 1994-95, Coun. Internat. Programs, 1995, Phila. Citizens for Children and Youth, 1997-99; chair Children's Budget Task Force City of San Francisco, 1989-92; mem. Mayor's Adv. Coun. on Drug Abuse, San Francisco, 1988-91; mem. steering com. Poverty Action Alliance, 1993-95; mem. adv. com. Montreal Consortium for Human Rights Advocacy, 1995—. Woodrow Wilson Found. fellow, 1972-73. Mem. NASW (del. 1990-92, 94-96, chair peace and justice com. 1992-97), Coun. on Social Work Edn. (com. on status of women 1989-92, bd. dirs. 1993-97, chair commn. on ednl. policy 1994-97), Am. Hist. Assn., Social Welfare Action Alliance, Soc. for Social Work Rsch., Assn. for Advancement of Social Work with Groups, Assn. Cmty. Orgns. and Social Adminstrn. Avocations: travel, hiking, cooking, swimming, creative writing. E-mail: mreisch@umich.edu.

REISER, BRIAN SYDNEY, economist, statistician; b. Bklyn., Feb. 28, 1937; s. Eugene N. and Ruth (Cohen) R. BA, Syracuse U., 1961; postgrad. Am. U., 1962, U.S. Dept. Agr. Grad. Sch., 1963. Econ. statistician Bur. of Census, Washington, 1962-69, 1979-88; economist, econ. statistician IRS, Washington, 1969-79; econ. cons., 1988—; exec. sec. Soc. Govt. Economists, 1980-81, adv. com., 1982, dir., 1984-85. Vice pres. Springfield Stamp Club, Va., 1982. Mem. Am. Econ. Assn., Am. Topical Assn., Am. Philatelic Soc., Am. Numismatic Assn., Am. Polit. Items Collectors, Masons, Shriners. Home and Office: 7505 Democracy Blvd Apt 439 Bethesda MD 20817-1284

REISER, MORTON FRANCIS, psychiatrist, educator; b. Cin., Aug. 22, 1919; s. Sigmund and Mary (Roth) R.; m. Lynn B. Whisnant, Dec. 19, 1976; children: David E., Barbara, Linda. BS, U. Cin., 1940, MD, 1943; grad., N.Y. Psychoanalytic Inst., 1960. Diplomate Am. Bd. Psychiatry and Neurology. Intern King's County Hosp., Bklyn., 1944; resident Cin. Gen. Hosp., 1944-49; practice medicine, specializing in psychiatry Cin., 1947-52, Washington, 1954-55, N.Y.C., 1955-69; mem. faculty Cin. Gen. Hosp., also U. Cin. Coll. Medicine, 1949-52, Washington Sch. Psychiatry, 1953-55; faculty Albert Einstein Coll. Medicine, Yeshiva U., N.Y.C., 1955-69, prof. psychiatry, 1958-69, dir. research dept. psychiatry, 1958-65; chief div. psychiatry Montefiore Hosp. and Med. Center, N.Y.C., 1965-69; chmn. dept. psychiatry Yale Med. Sch., 1969—, prof., 1969-78, chmn. dept., 1969-86, Charles B.G. Murphy prof., 1978-86, Albert E. Kent prof., 1986-90, Albert E. Kent prof. emeritus, 1990—. Cons. Walter Reed Army Inst. Research, 1957-58, WHO, 1963; mem. clin. program projects rev. com. NIMH, 1970— , chmn., 1973-74. Author: (with H. Leigh) The Patient: Biological, Psychological, and Social Dimensions of Medical Practice, 1980, Mind, Brain, Body: Toward a Convergence of Psychoanalysis and Neurobiology, 1984; (with H. Leigh) The Patient, 3d edit., 1992; Memory in Mind and Brain: What Dream Imagery Reveals, 1990; editor: American Handbook of Psychiatry, vol. IV, 1975; editor in chief Psychosomatic Medicine, 1962-72; mem. editorial bd. AMA Archives of Gen. Psychiatry, 1961-71, (with H. Leigh) Psychiatry Medicine and Primary Care, 1978; contbr. articles to profl. jours. and books. Fellow Am. Coll. Psychiatrists, Am. Psychiat. Assn. (Seymour Vestermark award 1986); mem. Am. Soc. Clin. Investigation, Am. Psychosomatic Soc. (pres. 1960-61), Am. Fedn. Clin. Research, Am. Assn. Chairmen Depts. Psychiatry (exec. com. 1971— , pres. 1975-76), Acad. Behavioral Medicine Research (exec. council 1978), Am. Psychoanalytic Assn. (pres.-elect 1980-82, pres. 1982-84), Internat. Psycho-Analytical Assn., Assn. Psychophysiol. Study of Sleep, Internat. Coll. Psychosomatic Medicine (pres. 1975), Psychiat. Research Soc., A. Graeme Mitchell Undergrad. Pediatric Soc., Benjamin Rush Soc., Rapaport-Klein Study Group, World Psychiat. Assn. (organizing com. sect. psychosomatic medicine 1967), Sigma Xi, Phi Eta Sigma, Pi Kappa Epsilon, Alpha Omega Alpha. Home: 200 Todd St Hamden CT 06518-1511

REISERT, CHARLES EDWARD, JR. real estate executive; b. New Albany, Ind., Apr. 5, 1941; s. Charles Edward Sr. and Jane. W. (Willcox) R.; m. Mary Lynn Nunemacher, Nov. 9, 1963; children: Perry G., Heidi L. BS in Edn., Ind. U., 1963, MA, 1968. Tchr. Ind. Pub. Schs., 1963-67; mgr. Ind. Bell Tel. Co., Indpls., 1967-70; trust officer Ind. Nat. Bank, 1970-72; ptnr. R.F.R. Prodns. Inc., Zionsville; dir. Wichita (Kans.) Art Assn., 1972-73; realtor Century 21 Reisert & Assocs., Jeffersonville, Ind., 1973—. Mem. Ind. Real Estate Commn., 1982-90, chmn., 1990; past pres. Clark County Youth Shelter; bd. dirs., past pres. United Way Clark County; bd. dirs. New Hope, Inc., Haven House, Inc., Sagamore of Wabash; mem. Leadership So. Ind., Leadership Louisville, Clark County Redevel. Commn.; trustee, pres. Jeffersonville Twp. Pub. Libr.; past bd. dirs. Ctr. for Women and Families; trustee Clark Meml. Hosp. Found. Recipient Pinnacle award, Sales Mgmt. and Mktg. Assn. of Louisville. Mem. So. Ind. Realtors Assn., (past pres., Realtor of Yr., Realtor Hall of Fame 1998) Nat. Assn. Realtors, Ind. Assn. Realtor, Realtors Nat. Mktg. Inst., So. Ind. C. of C. (past bd. dirs., Profl. of Yr. 1990), Rotary (past pres., Paul Harris fellow). Roman Catholic. Home: 14 Abby Chase Jeffersonville IN 47130-9762 Office: Century 21 Reisert & Assocs 1302 E 10th St Jeffersonville IN 47130-4299 E-mail: charleyre@aol.com.

REISFIELD, DEREK R. business executive; b. N.Y.C., 1963; BA, Wesleyan U., 1985; MA, U. So. Calif., 1986. Analyst Times Mirror Corp., N.Y.C., 1987; rsch. analyst, jr. assoc., assoc. McKinsey & Co., 1987-91, engagement mgr., 1991-92, Stockholm, 1992-93, sr. engagement mgr., 1994, N.Y.C., 1995; ptnr. Mitchell Madison Group, 1995-96; dir. strategic mgmt. Westinghouse Elec. Corp./CBS Entertainment Group, 1996-97; v.p. bus. devel. CBS Corp., 1997-98; pres. CBS New Media Group, 1998-99; vice chmn., exec. v.p. Luminant Worldwide Corp., 1999-2000; mng. prin., co-founder i-hatch Ventures, LLC, 1999—; chmn. bd. dirs. Yack.com, Inc., 1999-2001; vice chmn., bd. dirs. Sky Auction.com, 2000—01. Chmn. bd. Marketwatch.Com, LLC, 1998-99. Office: i-hatch Ventures LLC 450 E 52d St New York NY 10022 E-mail: dr@i-hatch.com.

REISIN, EFRAIN, nephrologist, researcher, educator; b. Cordoba, Argentina, Feb. 25, 1943; came to U.S., 1979; s. Maximo and Elisa Reisin; m. Ilana Hershkovitz, Sept. 6, 1971; children: Eyal, Thalia Alexis. MD, Nat. U., Cordoba, 1966. Intern internal medicine Nat. U. Cordoba-Clinicas Hosp., 1966; resident Jimenes Diaz Found., Madrid, 1966-68, Chaim Sheba Med. Ctr., Tel Hashomer, Israel, 1968-71, fellow in nephrology Israel, 1971-74, staff physician nephrology Israel, 1974-77; rsch. fellow in hypertension Health Sci. Ctr., Winnipeg, Man., Can., 1977-78; vis. scientist in hypertension Nat. Health Welfare Can., 1978-79; Ochsner vis. scientist in hypertension Ochsner Found. Hosp., New Orleans, 1979-82; from asst. prof. to assoc. prof. medicine La. State U., 1982-89, prof. medicine, 1985—, chief sect. nephrology, 1999—. Panelist Consensus Conf., NIH, Bethesda, Md., 1991. Author over 100 articles and book chpts. on hypertension and nephrology; conducted 1st research study documenting positive effects of weight reduction in treatment of hypertension, 1978 (citation classic Inst. Sci. Info. 1988). 1st lt. Israel Army, 1971-72. Grantee Nat. Health and Welfare Can., 1978-79, Am. Heart Assn., 1980-81, also several pharm. cos., 1984—. Fellow ACP, Am. Coun. High Blood Pressure Rsch., Am. Heart Fund, Am. Coll. Clin. Pharmacology (counselor south ctrl. regional chpt. 1991-92), Am. Fedn. Clin. Rsch., So. Soc. for Clin. Investigation; mem. Internat. Soc. Nephrology, Internat. Soc. Hypertension, Am. Soc. Nephrology, Am. Soc. Hypertension, Coun. Nephrology, Am. Heart Assn., Inter-Am. Soc. Hypertension, Orleans Parish Med. Soc. Avocations: tennis, reading, movies. Office: La State U Sch Medicine 1542 Tulane Ave New Orleans LA 70112-2825

REISINGER, BARON OF INNERY RONALD BUSCH (BARON OF INNERYNE), bank executive; b. N.Y.C., Jan. 4, 1943; s. Walter Chalmers and Osa-Lisa Bernadotte (Pearson) Reisinger; m. Carolyn Gall, Dec. 17, 1989; children: Christopher, Hope Sullivan, Abigail, William, Timothy. BA, Fairleigh-Dickinson U., 1967; MA, PhD, Montgomery U., 1973. Registered rep., Nat. Assn. Securities Dealers. Pres., CEO The Reisinger Corp. LLC, Grand Haven, Mich., 1990—. Advisor The Kingdom of Biffeche, Biffeche City, 1965—97; v.p. Central Highland Park Assn., Grand Haven, Mich., 1971—2002. Decorated knight Grand Cross Order of the Great White Leopard The Kingdom of Biffeche, knight Grand Cross Order of the Palm, knight Grand Cross of The Military Order the Sword of St. Michael, knight G.C. of the Most Illustrious Order of the Raven, knight Grand Crescent the Order of the Crescent, knight Grand Cross of the Order of The Elephant, knight of Saint Germain Scotland's House of Stuart, knight Grand Cross and Grand Prior for N.Am. the Order of The Holy Trinity Ukraine, comdr. the Military and Hospitaller Order of St. Lazarus of Jerusalem Duc de Brissac. Mem.: Celtic Soc., Monarchist League, Traveler's Century Club, Circumnavigators Club, Carlouel Yacht Club, Royal Yacht Club of Biffeche, Bayou Club, Atlanta Polo Club, Spring Lake Country Club, St. Louis Country Club, Kyles of Bute Angling Club (hon.), Convention of the Baronage of Scotland (life). Home: 9441 Beachberry Pl Pinellas Park FL 33782 Office: The Barony of Inneryne Ascog Castle Argylle Tighnabruaich PA21 2BY Scotland Home Fax: 727-541-4337. Personal E-mail: rreisin1@tampabay.rr.com.

REISLER, HELEN BARBARA, public relations and publicity consultant; b. N.Y.C., June 21; d. George and Elizabeth Lois (Schultz) Gottesman; m. Melvin Reisler, June 5, 1955; children: Susan O'Brien, Karen Reisler, Keith James. BS in Edn., NYU, 1954; MS in Edn. and Reading, L.I. U., 1978. Elem. tchr., N.Y.C., 1954-78; instr. grad. sch., adj. lectr. L.I. U., Bklyn., 1978; acct. exec. N.Y. Yellow Pages, Inc., N.Y.C., 1979, personnel mgr., 1979, adminstrv. dir., 1980-83, v.p. personnel, 1983-84, v.p. adminstrn./personnel, 1984-85, also dir.; staff specialist sales and market support Southwestern Bell Publs., 1985-88; N.Y. mgr. pub. rels. and recruitment N.Y. Yellow Pages/Mast Advt. and Publs., Inc. of Southwe. Bell, 1988; cons. human resources devel. and product promotion, 1989—. Recruiter N.E. Region, N.Y. area cmty. rels. rep.; moderator weekly cable TV show New York Business Forum, N.Y.C., 1983-85. Profiled in various bus. publs. Mem. adv. com. New York Rotary 911 Disaster Fund , 2001—02; founder, coord. 911 New York Rotary Adoption, 2001—02; creator 9/11 Disaster Relief Fund, N.Y. Rotary Found.; bd. dirs. Partk Slope Geriatric Ctr., 2002—. Named Ptnr. in Edn., N.Y.C. Bd. Edn., 1984, Golden Poets Award. Mem. Internat. Assn. Sales Profls. (bd. dirs. 1993, 94), UN Assn., Sales Execs. Club N.Y. (bd. dirs., reception, membership and mem. rels. coms., chmn. youth edn., v.p. 1987-88, chmn. internal com. 1989), Execs. Assn. Greater N.Y. (chmn. com. Sec. Day), Heritage Hills Country Club Westchester (bd. dirs. 2000—), Sales Exec. Club (v.p.), N.Y. Rotary (chmn. environ. com. N.Y. chpt. 1991—, bd. liaison to pub. rels. and membership coms. 1994—, interviewering com. to select ambassadorial scholarship candidates 1993-2001, mentor to Japanese ambassadorial scholars, 1992-93, divsn. chmn. cmty. svcs., chmn. pub. rels. com., bd. liaison, 1996-2001, 1st woman officer elected to bd. dirs. N.Y. chpt., Paul Harris fellow 1992, 2001, co-chmn. advt. com. chmn. pub. rels. Rotary Club N.Y. 1996—, Gift of Life coord. 1998—, elected 2d v.p. bd. dirs. 1998—, 1st v.p. bd. dirs. 1999—, pres.-elect 2000, 1st woman pres. 2001, chair bd. dirs. 2001-, prodr. New York Rotary Cable TV Series, exec. prodr. Gift of Life--A Child's Story, apptd. media liason to N.Y., Rotary Internat. 1998—, Gift of Life bd. dirs. 1999—, creator 911 disaster fund 2001-2002, chmn. publicity and pub. rels. 2002-, pub. rels. award), Dutch Treat Club. Office: 47 Plaza St W Brooklyn NY 11217-3905 E-mail: helenb.reisler@aol.com.

REISMAN, BERNARD, theology educator; b. N.Y.C., July 15, 1926; s. Herman and Esther Sarah (Kavesh) R.; m. Elaine Betty Sokol, Aug. 26, 1951; children: Joel Ira, Sharon Fay, Eric K., Robin Sue. B in Social Sci, CCNY, 1949; M in Social Sci. and Adminstrn., Western Res. U., 1951; LHD, Hebrew Coll., Boston, 1995; DHL (hon.), Gratz Coll., Phila., 1995; PhD, Brandeis U., 1970. Agy. dir. Jewish Cmty. Ctr., Chgo., 1951-67; prof. Brandeis U., Waltham, Mass., 1969—, dir. Hornstein program in Jewish communal svc., 1971-93, Klutznick prof. contemporary Jewish studies, 1993-99, emeritus, 1999—, dir. Adult Learning Inst., 1998—2001. Lectr. in field; vis. prof. Baerwald Sch. Social Work, Hebrew U., Jerusalem, 1978, Ctr. Jewish Edn. in Diaspora, 1978; sr. cons. Josephtal Found., Jerusalem, 1978; cons. European coun. Am. Joint Distbn. Com., 1978, Inst. for Jewish Life, N.Y.C., 1972-76; rsch. assoc. on future of religion Nat. Coun. Chs., 1972-73; Arnulf Pins meml. lectr. Hebrew U., Jerusalem, 1983, 84. Author: Reform Is a Verb, 1972, The Jewish Experiential Book: Quest for Jewish Identity, 1978, The Chavurah: A Contemporary Jewish Experience, 1977. Marshal Sklare Awd. Assoc. Soc. Scientific Study Contemporary Jewry, 1998; Brandeis U. honors: Bernard Reisman Grad. Student Lounge, 2001, Bernard Reisman Fund, 2001. Mem. Conf. Jewish Communal Svc., Nat. Jewish Family Ctr., Am. Jewish Com. (1st chmn. acad. adv. com. 1979-82, 75th Anniversary award 1981), Am. Jewish Hist. Soc. (acad. coun. 1979—), Assn. for Jewish Studies. Home: 28 Fairway Dr Newton MA 02465-1713 Office: Brandeis Univ Adult Learning Inst MS 085 Waltham MA 02454-9110 Fax: (781) 736-2122. E-mail: bali@brandeis.edu.

REISMAN, GARRETT E. astronaut; b. Morristown, NJ, Feb. 10, 1968; s. Robert and Sheila Reisman. BS in Econs., BSME and Applied Math., U. Pa., 1991; MSME, Calif. Inst. Tech., 1992, PhDME, 1997. Cert. flight instr. FAA. Spacecraft guidance, navigation and control engr., divsn. space and tech. TRW, Redondo Beach, Calif., 1996—98; astronaut, mission specialist candidate NASA, Johnson Space Ctr., 1998—. Achievements include discovery of the presence of shock waves in unsteady cloud cavitation. Avocations: flying, skiing, snowboarding, rock climbing, mountaineering. Office: Astronaut Office/CB NASA Johnson Space Ctr Houston TX 77058*

REISMAN, JASON ERIC, lawyer; b. Atlanta, Feb. 15, 1969; s. Stuart Ronald and Donna Faye Reisman; m. Suzanne Gail Barrett, Dec. 31, 1994. BS in Econs. summa cum laude, U. Pa., 1991; JD cum laude, Georgetown U., 1994. Bar: Pa. 1994, N.J. 1994, U.S. Dist. Ct. (ea. dist.) Pa. 1994, U.S. Dist. Ct. N.J. 1994, U.S. Ct. Appeals (8th cir.) 1998, U.S. Ct. Appeals (3d cir.) 1999. Lawyer Obermayer Rebmann Maxwell & Hippel LLP, Phila., 1994—. Vol. lawyer Homeless Advocacy Project, Phila., 1994—; vol. basketball coach Ridley Jr. ABA, Ridley Park, Pa., 1995-99; vol. co-leader Explorers Program, Phila., 1997-98. Mem. ABA, Pa. Bar Assn., Phila. Bar Assn. Democrat. Jewish. Avocations: sports, family, coaching kids. Office: Obermayer Rebmann Maxwell & Hippel LLP One Penn Ctr 19th Fl 1617 Jfk Blvd Ste 1950 Philadelphia PA 19103-1895

REISMAN, RICHARD S. publisher; b. Spring Valley, N.Y., Nov. 6, 1953; s. Herbert and Phyllis Sharon (Hendler) R.; children: Marisa, Kimberly. BA, SUNY, Binghamton, 1975; JD, George Washington U., 1978; MBA, UCLA, 1985. Assoc. McCandless & Barrett, Washington, 1978-80, Donahue, Gallagher, Thomas & Woods, Oakland, Calif., 1980-83; mgr. corp. strategy Times Mirror, L.A., 1985-87; dir. mktg. L.A. Times/Orange County Edit., Costa Mesa, Calif., 1987-90; pub. Orange County Bus. Jour., Irvine, 1990—. Bd. dirs. Employers Group, 1996—; adv. bd. Orange County Com. for the Arts, 1993—; mem. exec. fellows Chapman U., 1998—; bd. dirs. Orange County Bus. Coun., 1995—; bd. dirs., memberhsip chair , Calif. Coast chpt. YPO; chief exec. roundtable U. Calif., Irvine, 1995—. R.C. Baker Found. fellow UCLA Sch. Mgmt., 1984. Mem. Partnership 2010 (bd. dirs. 1992—). Avocations: tennis, reading, pub. affairs. Office: Orange County Bus Jour 2600 Michelson Dr Ste 170 Irvine CA 92612-6595 E-mail: Reisman@ocbj.com.

REISMAN, ROBERT E. physician, educator; b. Buffalo, Nov. 1, 1932; s. Harry S and Jessie (Goldberg) Reisman; m. Rena Estry, Sept. 5, 1954; children: Jeanne, Linda, Nancy, David. MD, SUNY-Buffalo, 1956; Dr.h.c., U. Montpellier (France), 1982. Diplomate (bd dirs 1984-86) Am Bd Internal Med, (bd dirs 1981-86, chmn 1985, mem residency rev comt allergy and immunology 1988-93, chmn 1990-91 Am Bd Allergy and Clin Immunology. Intern Buffalo Gen. Hosp., 1956-57, resident in medicine, 1957-59; practice medicine specializing in allergy and clin. immunology Buffalo, 1961—; clin. prof. pediatrics and medicine SUNY, 1978—. Co-dir Allergy Research Lab Buffalo Gen Hosp, 1970—90; mem panel allergenic extracts Bur Biologists FDA. With U.S. Army, 1968—69. Master: ACP; fellow: Am Acad Allergy (pres 1980—81). Home: 113 Carriage Cir Buffalo NY 14221-2163 Office: 295 Essjay Rd Williamsville NY 14221-8216 also: 85 High St Buffalo NY 14203-1149

REISMAN, ROSEMARY MOODY CANFIELD, writer, humanities educator; b. Des Moines, Nov. 18, 1927; d. V. Alton and Lois Gloria (Slee) Moody; m. Michael Ellison Canfield, Sept. 6, 1952 (div. May 1961); children: Michael, John Charles, Celia Catherine, Christopher James; m. Maurice Reisman, May 10, 1986 (dec. 1990). BA in English, U. Minn., 1949, MA in English, 1952; PhD in English, La. State U., 1971. Reporter Ames Tribune, summer 1944; writer, actor Sta. WOI Pub. Radio, Ames, Iowa, 1944-48; dir., writer children's plays Sta. KASI, 1949; tchg. asst. U. Minn., 1949-52; writer Sta. WOI-TV, Ames, summer 1952; writer, show host Sta. WDGY, Mpls., 1952-54; instr. La. State U., 1961-69, NDEA fellow, 1969-71; asst. prof. English Troy (Ala.) State U., 1971-80, assoc. prof., 1980-90, chairperson dept. English, 1985-90, prof., 1990-94. Mem. honors coun. Troy State U., 1985-94, mem. honors faculty, 1986-94, mem. acad. coun., 1989-92, mem. faculty adv. coun., 1990-92, Rhodes scholar instnl. rep., 1987-91; adj. prof. Charleston So. U., 1996-99, vis. prof., 1999—; coord. sr. honors seminar Coll. of Charleston, 1996-98; writer, cons. Baton Rouge State Times—Morning Adv., 1963-70; prodr., writer Perspectives project films Ala. ETV, 1977-80; chairperson conf. sessions South Ctrl. Soc. for 18th-Century Studies, 1988, Southeastern Am. Soc. for 18th Century Studies, 1991, 93; chairperson workshop Ala. Coun. Tchrs. of English, fall 1987; grant writer, project dir. Ala. Humanities Found., 1980, 89, asst. project dir. summer grad. course, 1990, presenter various instns., 1985-94; grant writer, project dir. Ala. Pub. Libr. Sys., 1977-80; lectr., presenter various pub. librs. for Auburn Ctr. for Arts and Humanities, 1989-97; presenter numerous lectures and lectr. series, various instns., 1970—. Author: Perspectives: The Alabama Heritage, 1978; co-author: Contemporary Southern Women Fiction Writers, 1994, Southern Men Fiction Writers, 1998; chairperson editl. adv. bd. Ala. Lit. Rev., 1986-94; mem. editl. bd. Biog. Guide to Ala. Lit., 1985—; guest editor spl. issue Ala. English 7, spring 1995; contbr. essays, articles and revs. to lit. publs. Baldwin County Humanities scholar Ala. Humanities Found., 1983, 84; finalist Ingalls award for Outstanding Tchg., 1991. Mem.: AAUW (past br. pres., mem. steering com.), NEA, Thomas Cooper Soc. (bd. dirs. 2001—), English Spkg. Union (bd. dirs. Charleston 1997—98, pres. 1998—2002, Sourcelist spkr. 1999—2000), Troy State U. Edn. Assn. (pres. 1990—93), Ala. Edn. Assn., Assn. Coll. English Tchrs. of Ala., Assn. Depts. of English (state pres. 1986—88), South Atlantic MLA, Gamma Beta Phi (nat. pres. 1978—79, cert. of merit 1979), Phi Beta Kappa (del. to nat. triennial coun. 1991, alt. 1994, pres. Low Country Assn. 1996—98, del. 1997, bd. dirs. 1998—2001, alt. del. 2000, past pres. S.E. Ala. assn.). Episcopalian. Home and Office: 121 Innisbrook Bnd Summerville SC 29483-5084

REISMAN, TERRY MILTON, obstetrician, gynecologist; b. West Palm Beach, Fla., 1940; MD, U. Miami, 1967. Diplomate Am. bd. of ObGyn. Intern Jackson Meml. Hosp., Miami, 1967-68, resident in ob-gyn., 1968-69, 71-73; pvt. practice, 1973—. Fellow ACOG; mem. So. Med. Assn., Fla. Ob-Gyn. Soc., Miami Ob-Gyn. Soc. E-amil. Home and Office: 9595 N Kendall Dr S-103 Miami FL 33176-1979 E-mail: treisman@bellsouth.net.

REISMAN, WILLIAM M. lawyer, educator; b. 1939; LL.B., Hebrew U., 1963; LL.M., Yale U., 1964, J.S.D., 1965. Bar: Conn. 1964. Assoc. prof. Yale U. Law Sch., New Haven, 1969-72, prof., 1972-82, Hohfeld prof. jurisprudence, 1982-98, McDougal prof. internat. law, 1998—. Mem. Inter-Am. Commn. on Human Rights, 1990—95, chmn., 1994—95; vice-chmn. Policy Scis. Ctr., Inc., 1992—; assoc. Inst. Droit Internat., 1999; pres. Arbitration Tribunal Bank for Internat. Settlements, 2001—; mem. Eritrea-Ethiopia Boundary Commn., 2001—; pres. Anglo-Irish OSPAR Convention Tribunal, 2001—. Author: Nullity and Revision, 1971, Art of the Possible: Diplomatic Alternatives in Middle East, 1970, Puerto Rico and the International Process, 1974, Folded Lies: Bribery, Crusades and Reforms, 1979, (with Weston) Toward World Order and Human Dignity, 1976, (with McDougal) International Law in Contemporary Perspective, 1981, (with McDougal) International Law Essays, 1981, (with McDougal) Power and Policy in Quest of Law: Essays in Honor of Eugene V. Rostow, 1985, (with Schreiber) Jurisprudence: Understanding and Shaping Law, 1986, (with Willard) International Incidents: The Law that Counts in World Politics, 1988, (with James E. Baker) Regulating Covert Action: Practices, Contexts and Policies of Covert Coercion Abroad in International and American Laqw, 1991, Systems of Control in International Adjudication and Arbitration: Breakdown and Repair, 1992, (with Westerman) Straight Baselines in International Maritime Boundary Delimitation, 1992, (with C. Antoniou) The Laws of War, 1994, The Supervisory Jurisdiction of the International Court of Justice: International Arbitration and International Adjudication, 1997, (with Craig W. Park and J. Paulsson) International Commercial Arbitration: Cases, Materials and Notes on the Resolution of International Business Disputes, 1997, Law in Brief Encounters, 1999, Jurisdiction in International Law, 1999; editor-in-chief Am. Jour. Internat. Law, 1998—. Fulbright grantee, 1966-67 Mem. Fgn. Policy Assn. (bd. dirs. 1997—), Coun. Fgn. Rels., Order of Bahrain (First Class). Office: Yale U Law Sch PO Box 208215 New Haven CT 06520-8215 Fax: 203-432-7247. E-mail: michael.reisman@yale.edu.

REISMANN, HERBERT, engineer, educator; b. Vienna, Austria, Jan. 26, 1926; s. Henrik and Olga (Pokorny) R.; m. Edith Falber, Aug. 14, 1952; children— Sandra Jean, Barbara Anne. BS in Aero. Engring., Ill. Inst. Tech., 1947, MS, 1949; PhD in Engring., U. Colo., 1962. Project engr. Convair, Ft. Worth, 1951-53; prin. structures engr. Republic Aviation Corp., Hicksville, N.Y., 1954-56; chief engr. systems analysis, chief solid mechanics Martin Marietta Corp., 1957-64; prof., dir. aerospace engring. SUNY, Buffalo, 1964—. Cons. NASA, Bell Aero Systems Corp. Co-author: Elastokinetics, 1974, Elasticity, 1980; author: Elastic Plates, 1988; contbr. articles to profl. jours. Assoc. fellow AIAA (award best tech. paper 1962, oustanding aerospace achievement award 1987); mem. ASME, Internat. Assn. Bridge and Structural Engring., AAUP, Sigma Xi, Tau Beta Pi. Home: 71 Chaumont Dr Buffalo NY 14221-3511 Office: SUNY-Buffalo 605 Furnas Hall Buffalo NY 14260-4200 E-mail: herreis@msn.com.

REISNER, ELENA MACKAY, retired educational administrator; b. Inverness, Scotland, June 1, 1922; came to U.S., 1932; d. John Alexander and Jane Logan (Wells) Mackay; m. Sherwood Hartman Reisner, June 1, 1946 (dec. 1990); children: Ruth Reisner Brock, James Sherwood. BA, Wellesley Coll., 1944; MA, Columbia U., 1945. Tchr. St. Margaret's Sch., Waterbury, Conn., 1945-46; missionary tchr. Presbyn. Ch. U.S.A., Mexico City, 1946-50; instr. Tex. A&I U., Kingsville, 1960-65; tchr. Presbyn. Pan Am. Sch., 1957-80, interim pres., 1990-91, asst. to pres., 1991-95; ret., 1995. Founder Amistad Vol. Coun., Kingsville, 1984; vol. Plano Children's Med. Clinic; past pres. Laurel Home Extension Club; chmn. Mission Presbytery's Hispanic Ministries Coun., Presbyn. Ch. U.S.A., 1993, 94, 95; elder Presbyn. Ch., 1976—. Named One of 10 Outstanding Women in Kingsville History, Zonta Club, 1975; recipient lifetime svc. award Kingsville C. of C., Bell-MacKay prize for mission Presbyns. for Renewal-Presbyn. Gen. Assembly, 1994. Mem. AAUW (pres. 1977-79), Presbyn. Women (hon. life, pres. 1985-87), Phi Beta Kappa, Delta Kappa Gamma (hon.). Democrat. Avocations: reading, baking. Home: 5401 Independence Pkwy Apt 406 Plano TX 75023-5434

REISNER, MILTON, psychiatrist, psychoanalyst; b. N.Y.C., Jan. 30, 1934; s. Maximillian and Dora Reisner; m. Linda Ellis, Mar. 3, 1959 (div. 1975); children: Margaret Ann, Amanda Lee. BA, NYU, 1954; MD, Downstate Med. Ctr., 1958. Diplomate Am. Bd. Forensic Examiners, Nat. Bd. Med. Examiners, Am. Bd. Forensic Medicine, N.Y. State Bd. Psychiat. Examiners. Resident in psychiatry Kings County Hosp., Bklyn., 1959-62; sr. psychiatrist Manhattan VA Hosp., N.Y.C., 1962-66; assoc. dir. psychiatry Westchester Community Mental Health Bd., White Plains, N.Y., 1966-69; dir. psychiatry Westchester Mental Health Bd., 1969-74; pvt. practice N.Y.C., 1976—. Cons. Cath. Charities, N.Y.C., 1965-66, H.I.P., N.Y.C., 1973-74, NYU Med. Ctr., 1963-68. Contbr. articles to profl. jours. Lt. j.g. USPHS, 1958-59. Fellow Am. Soc. Psychoanalytic Physicians; mem. Am. Assn. Psychoanalytic Physicians (pres. 1985-86, 87-88, Plaque 1988), Nat. Arts Club, Phi Beta Kappa. Achievements include research in mirroring as a technique for treating delusions. Office: 200 E 84th St New York NY 10028-2906

REISS, ALVIN HERBERT, writer, consultant; b. Bklyn., June 15, 1930; s. Samuel D. R. and Anne H. (Elowsky) Lieberman; m. Ellen A. Komoroff, Aug. 26, 1956; children: Steven, Robert, Michael. BA, U. Wis., 1952, MA, 1953. Editor Arts Mgmt., N.Y.C., 1962—; dir. Related Arts Counsellors, 1962—, Profl. Arts Mgmt. Inst., N.Y.C., 1971—; columnist Fund Raising Mgmt., Garden City, N.Y., 1985—. Dir. arts mgmt. program Marymount Manhattan Coll., 1988—, Adelphi U., 1978-85; vis. prof. Phila. Coll. of Arts, 1986-87; cons./lectr. arts and entertainment orgns. U.S. and overseas, 1962—; vis. fellow The Am. U., 1995-96; lectr., program cons. Columbia Coll. Chgo., 2000—. Author: Cash In!, 1986, Arts Management Reader, 1979, Culture & Company, 1972, Arts Management Handbook, 1970. Arts Management, A Guide to Finding Funds and Winning Audiences, 1992, Don't Just Applaud, Send Money, 1995; CPR for Nonprofits, 2000; contbr. articles various mags.; songwriter, 1962—. With U.S. Army, 1953-55. Recipient Disting. Svc. award, Internat. Soc. Performing Arts Adminstrs., 1986, Internat. Mgmt. Club award, Mgmt. Club of Asian Bus. League, 1989. Mem. Am. Soc. Journalists and Authors (v.p. 1980-81), Music Critics Assn., Authors Guild, Periwinkle Prodns. (bd. dirs.). E-mail: skipreiss@aol.com.

REISS, DALE ANNE, accounting executive, investment company executive; b. Sept. 3, 1947; d. Max and Nan (Hart) R.; m. Jerome L. King, Mar. 5, 1978; children: Matthew Reiss, Mitchell, Stacey King. BS, Ill. Inst. Tech., 1967; MBA, U. Chgo., 1970. CPA, Fla., Ill., Mich., Mo. Cost acct. First Nat. Bank, Chgo., 1967; asst. contr. City Colls. of Chgo., 1967-71; dir. fin. Chgo. Dept. Pub. Works, 1971-73; prin. Arthur Young & Co., Chgo., 1973-80; sr. v.p., contr. Urban Investment & Devel. Co., 1980-85; mng. ptnr. Ernst & Young LLP, 1985-98, Ernst & Young, N.Y.C., 1998-99; global industry leader of real estate, hospitality and constrn. Ernst & Young LLP, 1999—. Bd. dirs. Ill. Inst. Tech., Urban Land Inst.; adv. bd. Kellogg Real Estate, Northwestern U., U. Chgo. Grad. Sch. of Bus. Mem. AICPA, Fin. Execs. Inst., Chgo. Network (bd. dirs.), Econ. of Chgo. Club, Met. Club, Chgo. Yacht Club, N.Y. Athletic Club. Office: Ernst & Young Ste 1600 5 Times Sq New York NY 10036-6530 Office Fax: 212-773-4986. E-mail: dale.reiss@ey.com.

REISS, GEORGE RUSSELL, JR. physician; b. Phila., Dec. 25, 1928; s. G. Russell Sr. and Mary Ellen (Brogan) R.; m. Rosemarie Theresa Curcillo, Sept. 19, 1959; children: Mary Elizabeth, Stephanie, G. Russell III, Charlene. BA, LaSalle U., 1953; MD, Temple U., 1957. Diplomate Am. Bd. Pediatrics. Intern Misericordia Hosp., Phila., 1957-58; resident pediatrics St. Christopher Hosp. for Children, 1958-60; pvt. practice Glenside, Pa., 1960—. With USCG, 1946-49. Mem. Montgomery County Med. Soc., Pa. Med. Soc., Am. Acad. Pediatrics, AMA, Am. Assn. Pro-Life Pediatricians. Roman Catholic. Office: 2220 Mount Carmel Ave Glenside PA 19038-4610

REISS, HOWARD, chemistry educator; b. N.Y.C., Apr. 5, 1922; s. Isidor and Jean (Goldstein) R.; m. Phyllis Kohn, July 25, 1945; children: Gloria, Steven. AB in Chemistry, NYU, 1943; PhD in Chemistry, Columbia U., 1949. With Manhattan Project, 1944-46; instr., then asst. prof. chemistry Boston U., 1949-51; with Ctrl. Rsch. Lab., Celanese Corp. Am., 1951-52, Edgar C. Bain Lab. Fundamental Rsch., U.S. Steel Corp., 1957, Bell Telephone Labs., 1952-60; asso. dir., then dir. rsch. div. Atomics Internat., div. N.Am. Aviation, Inc., 1960-62; dir. N.Am. Aviation Sci. Ctr., 1962-67, v.p. co., 1963-67; v.p. rsch. aerospace systems group N.Am. Rockwell Corp., 1967-68; vis. lectr. chemistry U. Calif. at Berkeley, summer 1957; vis. prof. chemistry UCLA, 1961, 62, 64, 67, prof., 1968-91, prof. emeritus, 1991—; vis. prof. U. Louis Pasteur, Strasbourg, France, 1986, U. Pa., 1989; vis. fellow Victoria U., Wellington, New Zealand, 1989. Vis. fellow Princeton (N.J.) Materials Inst., 1996; cons. to chem.-physics program USAF Cambridge Rsch. Labs., 1950-52; chmn. editor Procs. Internat. Conf. Nucleation and Interfacial Phenomena, Boston; mem. USAF Office Sci. Rsch. Physics and Chemistry Rsch. Evaluation Groups, 1966—, Oak Ridge Nat. Lab. Reactor Chemistry Adv. Com., 1966-68; adv. com. math. and phys. scis. NSF, 1970-72, ARPA Materials Rsch. Coun., 1968—; chmn. site rev. com. NRC Associateships Program, Naval Rsch. Lab., 1989. Author: Methods of Thermodynamics, 1965; author articles; editor in field.; editor: Progress in Solid State Chemistry, 1962-71, Jour. Statis. Physics, 1968-75, Jour. Colloid Interface Sci; mem. editorial adv. bd. Internat. Jour. Physics and Chemistry of Solids, 1955, Progress in Solid State Chemistry, 1962-73, Jour. Solid State Chemistry, 1969, Jour. Phys. Chemistry, 1970-73, Ency. of Solid State, 1970, Jour. Nonmetals, 1971—, Jour. Colloid and Interface Sci., 1976-79, Langmuir, 1985—. Guggenheim Meml. fellow, 1978; Howard Reiss chair in chemistry and biochemistry established named in his honor, UCLA, 1999. Fellow AAAS, Am. Phys. Soc. (exec. com. div. chem. physics 1966-69); mem. NAS, Am. Chem. Soc. (chmn. phys. chemistry sect. N.J. sect. 1957, Richard C. Tolman medal 1973, Kendall award in colloid and surface chemistry 1980, J.H. Hildebrand award in theoretical and exptl. phys. chemistry of liquids 1991, Van Arkel hon. chair in chemistry U. Leiden, The Netherlands, 1994), Am. Assn. for Aerosol Rsch. (David Sinclair award 1997), Phi Beta Kappa, Sigma Xi, Phi Lambda Upsilon. Office: U Calif Dept Chemistry And Biochemis Los Angeles CA 90095-0001

REISS, IRA LEONARD, retired sociology educator, writer; b. N.Y.C., Dec. 8, 1925; s. Philip and Dorothy (Jacobs) R.; m. Harriet Marilyn Eisman, Sept. 4, 1955; children: David, Pamela, Joel. BS cum laude, Syracuse U., 1949; MA, Pa. State U., 1951, PhD, 1953. Instr. in sociology Bowdoin Coll., Brunswick, Maine, 1953-55; asst. prof. sociology Coll. William and Mary, Williamsburg, Va., 1955-59; asst. prof. Bard Coll., Annandale-0n-Hudson, N.Y., 1959-61; assoc. to full prof. U. Iowa, Iowa City, 1961-69; prof. U. Minn., Mpls., 1969-96, prof. emeritus, 1996—. Rsch. evaluator U.S. Dept. Edn. and Nat. Inst. Child Health and Human Devel., Washington, 1966-78; rsch. dir. Family Study Ctr., U. Minn., 1969-74; ednl. advisor Kimberly-Clark Corp., Neenah, Wis., 1971-75; chair planning com. and bd. dirs. Inst. for Child, Adolescent Sexual Health, 1992-93; lectr. at 200 univs., 150 profl. mtgs., 100 civic groups, 1953-96; vis. prof. Uppsala Univ., Sweden, 1975-76. Author: Premarital Sexual Standards in America, 1960, The Social Context of Premarital Sexual Permissiveness, 1967, Family Systems in America , 1971, 4th edit., 1988, Journey into Sexuality: An Exploratory Voyage, 1986, An End to Shame: Shaping Our Next Sexual Revolution, 1990, Solving America's Sexual Crises, 1997, At the Dawn of the Sexual Revolution: Reflections on a Dialogue, 2002; editor: 3 textbooks; contbr. over 150 papers to jours. and textbooks in field. Mem. ACLU, 1948—, Planned Parenthood, 1960—, Nat. Abortion Rights Action League 1975—, Amnesty Internat., 1984—. With U.S. Army, 1944-46, ETO. Mem. Midwest Sociol. Soc. (pres. 1971-72), Am. Sociol. Assn. (chair family sect. 1975-76), Nat. Coun. on Family Rels. (pres. 1979-80, Reuben Hill award 1980, E.W. Burgess award 1984), Polish Acad. Sexual Sci. (hon., Internat. Sexual Sci. award 1989), Soc. for Sci. Study Sex (pres. 1980-81, Disting. Sci. Achievement award 1982, Alfred Kinsey award 1990), Internat. Acad. Sex Rsch. (pres. 1984-85), Am. Assn. Sex Educators, Counselors and Therapists (leadership award 1993). Democrat. Jewish. Avocation: good conversations with family and friends. Home: 5932 Medicine Lake Rd Minneapolis MN 55422-3328 E-mail: Reiss001@atlas.socsi.umn.edu.

REISS, JAMES, poet, English educator, editor; b. N.Y.C., July 11, 1941; s. Joseph Ronald and Cecilia Bee Reiss; m. Barbara Eve Klevs, June 21, 1964 (div. June 1995); children: Heather, Crystal. BA, U. Chgo., 1963, MA, 1964. Tchg. asst. English U. Calif., Davis, 1964-65; instr. English Miami U., Oxford, Ohio, 1965-69, asst. prof. English, 1969-73, assoc. prof. English, 1973-81, prof. English, 1981—; editor Miami U. Press, 1992—. Vis. assoc. prof. English Queens Coll./CUNY, 1975-76; admissions com. jury mem. Dorland Mountain Arts Colony, Temecula, Calif., 1994—. Author: (poetry) The Breathers, 1974, Express, 1983 (Nancy Dasher Book award Coll. English Assn. of Ohio 1984), The Parable of Fire, 1996, Ten Thousand Good Mornings, 2001; contbr. poetry to books, textbooks, profl. jours.; co-editor: Self-Interviews: James Dickey, 1970. Recipient 1st prize Acad. Am. Poets, U. Chgo., 1960, 62, Borestone Mountain Poetry awards, 1974, Creative Artists Pub. Svc. award N.Y. State Coun. on the Arts, 1975-76, 78-79, 1st prize Big Apple Poetry award, 1977, Critics' Choice award Miami U. press, 1995, Pushcart prize, 1996, Discovery award Poetry Ctr. 92d St. Y, N.Y.C., 1974; Bread Loaf fellow Breadloaf Writers Conf., Middlebury, Vt., 1975, fellow MacDowell Colony, Peterborough, N.H., 1970, 74, 76, 77, Writing fellow (poetry) NEA, Washington, 1974-75, N.Y. Found. for the Arts, 1987-88, fellow Dorland Mountain Arts Colony, 1991, 93, 99; Individual Artists grantee Ohio Arts Coun., 1980, 81. Mem. PEN, Poetry Soc. Am. (Consuelo Ford award 1974, Lucille Medwick award 1989), Associated Writing Programs. Office: Miami U English Dept 326 Bachelor Hall Oxford OH 45056 E-mail: reissja@muohio.edu.

REISS, JOHN BARLOW, lawyer; b. London, Aug. 29, 1939; came to U.S., 1963; s. James Martin and Margaret Joan (Ping) R.; m. Mary Jean Maudsley, Aug. 6, 1967 (div. 1978); m. Kathleen Strouse, Aug. 2, 1979; 1 child, Juliette Blanche. BA with honors, Exeter U., Devon, Eng., 1961; AM, Washington U., St. Louis, 1966, PhD, 1971; JD, Temple U., 1977. Bar: Pa. 1977, N.J. 1977, U.S. Dist. Ct. N.J. 1977, D.C. 1980, U.S. Supreme Ct. 1981, U.S. Dist. Ct. D.C. 1982. Economist Commonwealth Econ. Com., London, 1962-63; asst. prof. Allegheny Coll., Meadville, Pa., 1967-71; assoc. prof. Stockton State Coll., Pomona, N.J., 1971-75; asst. health commr. State of N.J., Trenton, 1975-79; dir. office of health regulation U.S. Dept. HHS, Washington, 1979-81; assoc. Baker & Hostetler, 1981-82, Dechert Price & Rhoads, Phila., 1982-86, ptnr., 1986-93, asst. chair health law group, 1984-91, chmn. health law group, 1991-93; ptnr. Saul Ewing LLP, 1993—, chmn. health law dept., 1995—. Mem. editl. bd. Topics in Hosp. Law, 1985-86, Hosp. Legal Forms Manual, 1985—, Jour. Health Care Tech., 1984-86; contbr. Hosp. Contracts Manual, 1983—; contbr. articles to profl. jours., chpts. to books. Bd. dirs. Gateway Sch. Little Children, Phila., 1986-99; bd. dirs. ECRI, Plymouth Meeting, Pa., 1994—, chmn. bd., 2001—; mem. bd. vestry All Saints Ch., Wynnewood, Pa., 1993, 96-2001. Pub. Health Svc. fellow, 1979-81, English Speaking Union fellow, 1963-66, Econ. Devel. Adminstr. fellow Washington U., 1966-67. Mem. Nat. Health Lawyers Assn., Phila. Bar Assn., Brit. Am. C. of C. of Greater Phila. (bd. dirs. 1991), Union League of Phila., Univ. Barge Club, Brit. Officers Club of Phila. Avocations: gardening, house restoring, reading, sculling. Home: 415 Wister Rd Wynnewood PA 19096-1808 Office: Saul Ewing LLP 3800 Centre Sq W Philadelphia PA 19102 E-mail: jreiss@saul.com.

REISS, PAUL JACOB, college president; b. Lake Placid, N.Y., Aug. 10, 1930; s. Julian J. and Daisy M. (Smith) R.; m. Rosemary A. Donohue, June 25, 1955; children: Catherine, Paul, Gregory, Mark, Julia, David, Steven, Martha, John. BS, Holy Cross Coll., 1952; MA, Fordham U., 1954; PhD, Harvard U., 1960; LHD (hon.), Showa U., 1994; LLD (hon.), Middlebury Coll., 1996. Tutor Harvard U., 1954-57; instr., asst. prof. Marquette U., 1957-63, chmn. dept. sociology, 1961-63; asso. prof. sociology Fordham U., Bronx, N.Y., 1963-75, prof., 1976-85, chmn. dept. sociology and anthropology, 1964-68; dean Fordham U. (Liberal Arts Coll.), 1968-69, v.p. acad. affairs, 1969-75, exec. v.p., 1975-85; pres. St. Michael's Coll., Colchester, Vt., 1985-96, pres. emeritus, 1996—. Editor: Sociological Analysis: A Journal in the Sociology of Religion, 1961-68; contbr. articles to profl. jours. Chmn. bd. dir. Julian Reiss Found., Lake Placid, N.Y.; trustee Wadhams Hall Sem. Coll.; bd. dirs. Lake Placid Sinfonietta; treas. Greater Burlington Indsl. Commn., Nat. Assn. Ind. Colls. and Univs., Assn. Cath. Colls. and Univs. Fellow Am. Sociol. Assn.; mem. Assn. for Sociology of Religion (pres.), Assn. Vt. Ind. Colls. (pres.), Vt. Higher Edn. Coun. (pres.), Vt. Bus. Roundtable, Vt. World Trade Office (chmn.). Democrat. Roman Catholic. Home: 10 Forest Brook Rd Lake Placid NY 12946

REISS, STEVEN, psychology educator; b. N.Y.C., Apr. 10, 1947; s. Benjamin A. and Margaret (Schmidt) R.; m. Maggi B. Reiss, Sept. 4, 1971; children: Michael, Ben AB magna cum laude, Dartmouth Coll., 1964; PhD in Psychology, Yale U., 1972. Registered psychologist, Ill. Prof. psychology U. Ill.-Chgo., 1972-91; prof. psychology and psychiatry Ohio State U., Columbus, 1991—, dir. Nisonger Ctr., 1991—. Dir. ISDD Mental Health Clinic, Chgo., 1980-91. Author: Who Am I: The 16 Basic Desires, 2000; editor: Psychophropic Medications, 1998; author psychol. tests: Reiss Screen, 1988, Anxiety Sensitivity Index, 1986. ARC Rsch. awardee, 1991, NADD Career awardee, 1998. Fellow APA, Am. Assn. Mental Retardation (bd. dirs. 1987, Svc. award 1987). Office: Ohio State Univ 1581 Dodd Dr Columbus OH 43210-1267 E-mail: reiss.7@osu.edu.

REISS, STEVEN ALAN, lawyer, law educator; b. N.Y.C., Dec. 18, 1951; s. Louis and Ruth (Harrow) R.; m. Mary A. Mattingly; children: Alexandra Mattingly Reiss, Tyler Brennan Reiss. BA, Vassar Coll., 1973; JD, Stanford (Calif.) U., 1976. Bar: N.Y., D.C., Calif. Law clk. to John Minor Wisdom U.S. Ct. Appeals for 5th Cir., New Orleans, 1976-77; law clk. to justice William J. Brennan U.S Supreme Ct., Washington, 1977-78; assoc. Miller, Cassidy, Larroca & Lewin, 1978-80; vis. prof. Georgetown U. Law Ctr., 1981; asst. prof. Law Sch., NYU, 1981-83, assoc. prof., 1984-87, prof., 1987-91; ptnr. Weil, Gotshal & Manges, N.Y.C., 1990—. Editor-in-chief White Collar Crime Reporter, 1987-91, contbg. editor, 1991—. Trustee Vassar Coll. Poughkeepsie, N.Y., 1978-82; bd. dirs. NYU Cmty. Fund, 1984-87, Concert Artists Guild, 1991-94, Lyrics Chamber Music Soc., 2000—; gen. counsel Brennan Ctr. for Justice, 1996—; bd. trustees Vols. of Legal Svcs. Mem. N.Y. State Bar Assn., D.C. Bar Assn., Calif. Bar Assn., Assn. of Bar of City of N.Y. (fed. legis. com. 1981-87), 2d Jud. Conf. (reporter 1984—). Home: 25 E 86th St New York NY 10028-0553 Office: Weil Gotshal & Manges 767 5th Ave Fl Conc1 New York NY 10153-0119 E-mail: steven.riess@weil.com.

REISS, SUSAN MARIE, editor, writer; b. Washington, Sept. 14, 1963; m. Paul L. Roney Jr., May 25, 1991. BA in English Lit., U. Va., 1985; MA in English, George Mason U., 1989. Editorial asst. Water Pollution Control Fedn., Alexandria, Va., 1985-87; freelance writer, editor Arlington, 1987-90; staff writer George Mason U., Fairfax, 1988-90, Optical Soc. Am., Washington, 1990-91, news editor, 1991-93, mng. editor, 1993-96; freelance writer, editor Arlington, 1996—. Newsletter editor: Arlington County Tennis Assn., 1990-91; contbr. articles to profl. jours. and mags. Mem. Nat. Press Club, Washington Ind. Writers, D.C. Sci. Writers Assn., N.Y. Acad. Scis., Sigma Tau Delta (founding mem. U. Va. chpt.). Avocations: tennis, piano, cross-country skiing. Home and Office: 6814 30th Rd N Arlington VA 22213-1602

REISTER, RAYMOND ALEX, retired lawyer; b. Sioux City, Iowa, Dec. 22, 1929; s. Harold William and Anne (Eberhardt) R.; m. Ruth Elizabeth Alkema, Oct. 7, 1967 AB, Harvard U., 1952, LLB, 1955. Bar: N.Y. 1956, Minn. 1960. Assoc. Paul, Weiss, Rifkind, Wharton & Garrison, N.Y.C., 1955-56; ptnr. Dorsey & Whitney LLP, Mpls., 1959-92; ret., 1993. Instr. U. Minn. Extension Divsn., 1964-66. Editor (with Larry W. Johnson): Minnesota Probate Administration, 1968. Trustee Mpls. Soc. Fine Arts, 1981-87; mem. exec. coun. Minn. Hist. Soc., 1984—; bd. dirs. Mpls. Athenaeum, 1992—, pres., 1998-2001; bd. dirs. Minn. Humanities Commn., 1997—. 1st lt. U.S. Army, 1956-59. Mem. Am. Coll. Trust and Estate Counsel (regent 1980-86), Minn. Bar Assn., Hennepin County Bar Assn. Home: 93 Groveland Ter Minneapolis MN 55403-1142 Office: Dorsey & Whitney 220 S 6th St Minneapolis MN 55402-1498

REISTER, RUTH ALKEMA, lawyer, business executive; b. Grand Rapids, Mich., May 30, 1936; d. Henry and Lena (Land) Alkema; m. Raymond A. Reister, Oct. 7, 1967. BA, U. Mich., 1958, JD, 1964; grad. Program in Bus. Adminstrn., Harvard U., 1959, postgrad. Program in Mgmt. Devel., 1976. Bar: Minn., Mich. 1964, U.S. Supreme Ct. 1976. Trust officer Northwestern Nat. Bank, Mpls., 1964-70; asst. counsel, asst. v.p., sec. Fed. Res. Bank, 1970-81; asst. sec., bd. govs. Fed. Res. System, 1977; dep. under sec. U.S. Dept. Agr., Washington, 1981-83; pres. First Bank Systems Agrl. Credit Corp., Mpls., 1983-84; pres. Groveland Corp., 1986—; dir. Herman Miller, Inc., Zealand, Mich., 1984—. Bd. dirs. United Way, ARC, Jones Harrison Home, Mpls.; bd. dirs., chair Gustavus Adolfus Coll.; chmn. Jones-Harrison Found. Mem. Harvard Bus. Sch. Club Minn., Minn. Women's Econ. Round Table (pres. 1980-81).

REITAN, DANIEL KINSETH, electrical and computer engineering educator; b. Duluth, Minn., Aug. 13, 1921; s. Conrad Ulfred and Joy Elizabeth R.; m. Marian Anne Stemme, July 18, 1946; children: Debra Leah, Danielle Karen. BSEE, N.D. State U., 1946; MSEE, U. Wis., 1949, PhD, 1952. Registered profl. engr., Wis. Control engr. Gen. Electric Co., Schenectady, N.Y., 1946-48; transmission line engr. Gen. Telephone Co., Madison, Wis., 1949-50; mem. faculty Coll. Engring. U. Wis., 1952-85, prof. elec. and computer engring., 1962-85; cons. Energy Industries, 1985-95; dir. power systems simulation lab. Coll. Engring. U. Wis., 1968-84, also dir. wind power research Energy Ctr. Cons. Nat. Inst. Sci. and Tech. (formerly U.S. Nat. Bur. Standards). Author: Interstellar Space Travel at Near Light Speed, 1995, The Visual Appearance of Relativistically Moving Objects, 1999; contbr. articles to profl. jours.; patentee in field. Served with U.S. Army, World War II. Recipient Outstanding Tchr. award Polygon Engring. Council., Gov.'s citation for service to State of Wis. Fellow IEEE (Centennial medal and cert. for outstanding achievement 1984, Centennial medal and cert. dept. ECE U. Wis., 1991, IEE power Engring., Computer Control Indsl. Applications and Edn. Soc.), Conf. Internat. des Grand Reseaux Electriques a Haute Tension, Am. Soc. Engring. Edn., Wis. Acad. Scis., Am. Wind Energy Assn., Sigma Xi, Tau Delta Pi, Tau Beta Pi, Eta Kappa Nu, Kappa Eta Kappa. Lutheran. *I believe that in one's career professionalism and perseverance are key factors in success. In one's personal life, the family should be the center, but not the circumference, about which all activities revolve.*

REITAN, PAUL HARTMAN, geologist, educator; b. Kanawha, Iowa, Aug. 18, 1928; s. John Olsen and Anna (Meldahl) R.; m. Reidun Engebretsen, Sept. 28, 1962; children: Kirsten Berit, Eric Hartmann. AB (Salisbury fellow), U. Chgo., 1953; PhD (Fulbright fellow), U. Oslo, Norway, 1959. Instr. U. Ill., Chgo., 1955; geologist U.S. Geol. Survey, 1953-56; state geologist Geol. Survey of Norway, 1956-60; asst. prof. mineralogy Stanford U., 1960-66; mem. faculty SUNY, Buffalo, 1966-98, prof. dept. geology emeritus, dean, 1975-79. Cons. U. Calif.-Davis, Am. Geol. Inst.; guest scientist Centre for Geol. Sci., Acad. Sci., Warsaw, Poland, Geol. Survey Prague, Czechoslovakia., Geol. Survey, Norway, Nat. Geophys. Rsch. Inst. and Geol. Survey, India Author: (with Davis and Pestrong) Geology, 1976; contbr. articles to profl. jours. Served with U.S. Army, 1946-49. NATO sr. fellow in sci., 1972; G. Unger Vetlesen fellow, 1973; Fulbright sr. lectr., India, 1986; Norwegian Marshall Fund grantee, 1986, 93. Fellow Geol. Soc. Am., Mineral. Soc. Am., Soc. Econ. Geology, Geol. Soc. India; mem. AAAS, Internat. Assn. Geochemistry and Cosmochemistry, Royal Norwegian Soc. Scis. and Letters (fgn.), Norsk Geologisk Forening (life), Sigma Xi. Home: 120 Walton Dr Buffalo NY 14226-4556 Office: U Buffalo Dept Geology Buffalo NY 14260-6030 E-mail: preitan@eng.buffalo.edu.

REITAN, RALPH MELDAHL, clinical neuropsychologist, former educator; b. Beresford, S.D., Aug. 29, 1922; s. John O. and Anna (Meldahl) R.; m. Lucille Ann Kirsch (dec. July 1985); children: Ellen, Jon, Ann, Richard, Erik. BA, Ctrl. YMCA Coll., Chgo., 1944; PhD, U. Chgo., 1950. Cert. in clin. psychology and clin. neuropsychology Am. Bd. Profl. Psychology. Instr. U. Chgo., 1948-51; asst. prof. Roosevelt U., Chgo., 1950-51; from asst. prof. to prof. Ind. U. Med. Sch., Indpls., 1951-70; prof. U. Wash., Seattle, 1970-77, U. Ariz., Tucson, 1977-86; pres. Reitan Neuropsychology Labs., 1981—. Cons. NIH, Bethesda, Md., 1960-71, VA, Washington, 1955-84, NASA, Washington, 1964-66. Author: Traumatic Brain Injury, 1985, Neuropsychological Evaluation of Older Children, 1992, The Halstead-Reitan Psychological Test Battery, 1993, Detection of Malingering and Invalid Test Results, 1998, Mild Head Injury: Intellectual, Cognitive and Emotional Consequences, 2000, also 15 others; contbr. articles to profl. jours. Trustee Easter Seal Rsch. Found., Chgo., 1974-83. With U.S. Army, 1942-43. Fellow APA, Nat. Acad. Neuropsychology; mem. Am. Neurol. Assn., Am. Acad. Neurology (affiliate), Coalition Clin. Neuropsychology Practitioners, Reitan Soc. Avocations: walking, bird watching. Home: 4831 N Via Serenidad Tucson AZ 85718-5715 Office: Reitan Neuropsychology Labs PO Box 66080 Tucson AZ 85728-6080 E-mail: reitanlab@aol.com.

REITEMEIER, RICHARD JOSEPH, physician; b. Pueblo, Colo., Jan. 2, 1923; s. Paul John and Ethel Regina (McCarthy) Reitemeier; m. Patricia Claire Mulligan, July 21, 1951; children: Mary Louise, Paul, Joseph, Susan, Robert, Patrick, Daniel. AB, U. Denver, 1944; MD, U. Colo., 1946; MS in Internal Medicine, U. Minn., 1954. Diplomate Am. Bd. Internal Medicine . Intern Corwin Hosp., Pueblo, 1946—47; resident Henry Ford Hosp., Detroit, 1949—50, Mayo Found., Rochester, Minn., 1950—53; cons. internal medicine and gastroenterology Mayo Clinic, 1954—87; chmn. dept. internal medicine Mayo Clinic (Mayo Clinic and Mayo Med. Sch.), 1967—74, prof., 1971—; bd. govs. Mayo Clinic, 1970—74. Gov. Am. Bd. Internal Medicine , 1971—79, chmn., 1978—79, rep. to Federated Council Internal Medicine , 1977—80, 1983—84, accreditation council grad. med. edn. , 1979—85, chmn., 1982—83; governing bd. Am. Bd. Med. Specialties, 1983—86; sci. and med. dir. Ludwig Inst. Cancer Rsch., 1987—88; cons. Kaiser Family Med. Found., 1989—90; med. dir. Phoenix Alliance Inc., 1990—93. Author (with C.G. Moertel): Advanced Gastrointestinal Cancer, Clinical Management and Chemotherapy, 1969; contbr. articles to profl. jours. Trustee Mayo Found., 1970—74, St. Mary's Hosp., Rochester, 1976—82. With U.S. Army, 1947—49. Recipient Alumni award, U. Colo. Sch. Medicine, Irving Cutter award, Phi Rho Sigma, 1986, Disting. Alumnus award, Mayo Found., 1997. Master: ACP (regent 1979—82, gov. for Minn. 1975—79, pres. 1983—84, Alfred Stengel Meml. award 1990); fellow: AMA, Nat. Bd. Med. Examiners (treas. 1987—89), Am. Assn. Study Liver Disease, Am. Assn. Cancer Rsch., Inst. Medicine, Coun. Med. Splty. Socs., Am. Soc. Clin. Oncology, Am. Fedn. Clin. Rsch., Am. Clin. and Climatol. Assn., Am. Gastroenterol. Assn.; mem.: Alpha Omega Alpha. Republican. Roman Catholic. Home: 707 12th Ave SW Rochester MN 55902-2027 Office: 200 1st Ave SW Rochester MN 55902-3129

REITER, ALLEN GARY, lawyer; b. Bronx, N.Y., Jan. 6, 1950; s. Leo and Anna (Lenchis) R.; m. Karen Kozac, Sept. 16, 1979. BA, SUNY, Albany, 1972; JD, U. Pa., 1975. Bar: N.Y. 1976, U.S. Dist. Ct. (so. dist.) N.Y. 1977, U.S. Dist. Ct. (ea. dist.) N.Y. 1980, U.S. Supreme Ct. 1983, U.S. Ct. Appeals (2d cir.) 1988. Asst. dist. atty. N.Y. County, N.Y.C., 1975-79; assoc. Skadden, Arps, Slate, Meagher & Flom, 1979-85; ptnr. Schonwald, Schaffzin & Mullman, 1985-89, Siller & Wilk LLP, N.Y.C., 1989-98, Cooperman, Levitt, Winikoff, Lester & Newman, N.Y.C., 1998—2000, Sonnenschein Nath & Rosenthal, N.Y.C., 2000—. Mem. Assn. of Bar of City of N.Y. Democrat. Jewish. Home: 1 Washington Sq Larchmont NY 10538-1517 Office: Sonnenschein Nath & Rosenthal 1221 Avenue of the Americas New York NY 10020

REITER, DAVID G. music educator, musician; b. Cleve., Mar. 15, 1959; s. Edward Arthur and Dorothy Ann Reiter; m. Ruth Ann Romanski, Aug. 13, 1982; children: Matthew, Brian, Sarah. B in Music Edn., U. Wis., Eau Claire, 1982; M in Music Edn., Wichita State U., 1992. Cert. instrumental tchr. 5-12 Mo. Dir. instrumental music Hill-Murray HS, St. Paul, 1983—84, Colby (Kans.) HS, 1985—91, Highland (Kans.) CC, 1992—97, Mound City (Mo.) HS, 1997—. Founder, prin. trumpet Sunflower Brass Quintet, Colby, 1985—91, Del. Valley Brass, Highland, 1992—. Author: Beginning Brass, 1986. Mem.: Internat. Trumpet Guild, Mo. Broadcasters Assn., Mo. Educators Nat. Conf. Home: PO Box 252 Highland KS 66035 Office: Mound City R-2 Sch 708 Nebraska St Mound City MO 64470 E-mail: d_reiter@yahoo.com.

REITER, GLENN MITCHELL, lawyer; b. N.Y.C., Feb. 1, 1951; s. Bernard Leon and Helene (Edson) R.; m. Marilyn Beckhorn, Sept. 5, 1976; children: Benjamin, Diana, Julie. BA, Yale U., 1973, JD, 1976. Bar: N.J. 1976, Pa. 1977, D.C. 1978, N.Y. 1979. Law clk. to judge U.S. Ct. Appeals, Phila., 1976-77; assoc. Schnader, Harrison, Segal & Lewis, 1977-78, Simpson Thacher & Bartlett, N.Y.C., 1978-84, ptnr., 1984—, resident ptnr. London, 1986-90. Mem. Phi Beta Kappa.

REITER, HOWARD LEE, political scientist, educator; b. Hanover, Pa., Sept. 29, 1945; s. Harry and Sally (Hayden) R.; m. Laura Rosen, June 28, 1972. BA, Cornell U., 1967; AM, Harvard U., 1969, PhD, 1975. Instr. U. Notre Dame, Ind., 1972-74; prof. U. Conn., Storrs, 1974—. Lectr. U.S. Info. Agy., Europe and Asia; cons. CBS News, N.Y.C., 1980. Author: Selecting the President, 1985 (Choice Mag. award 1986-87), Parties and Elections, 1987, 93; mem. editorial bd. Polity, 1980-92. Recipient Pi Sigma Alpha award N.E. Polit. Sci. Assn., 1975; Fulbright scholar, 1987, Uppsala chair Am. Studies, Sweden, 2001-2002. Mem. Phi Beta Kappa. Office: U Conn PO Box U24 Storrs Mansfield CT 06269-1024

REITER, JOSEPH HENRY, lawyer, retired judge; b. Phila., Mar. 21, 1929; s. Nicholas and Barbara (Hellmann) Reiter; m. Beverlee A. Bearman, Nov. 8, 1993. AB, Temple U., 1950, LLB, 1953. Bar: D.C. 1953, Pa. 1954. Atty. advisor U.S. Army, 1955—61; asst. U.S. atty. Ea. Dist. Pa., 1961—63, asst. U.S. atty. in charge of civil div., 1963—69; chief organized crime and racketeering strike force Western N.Y. State U.S. Dept. Justice, 1969—70, sr. trial atty. tax divsn., 1970—72, regional dir. office of drug abuse law enforcement, 1972—73; dep. atty. gen., dir. Drug Law Enforcement Office of Pa., 1973—77; ptnr. Stassen, Kostos and Mason, Phila., 1978—85, Kostos Reiter & Lamer, 1985—89; judge Armed Svcs. Bd. of Contract Appeals, Falls Church, Va., 1989—95; of counsel Kostos & Lamer, Phila., 1995—. Mem. adv. com. Joint State Commn. on Procurement; lectr. in field. Contbr. articles to profl. jours. Mem. Citizens Crime Commn. Pa. With U.S. Army, 1953—55. Recipient Meritorious Svc. award, U.S. Atty. Gen. Clark, 1967, Spl. Commendation, Asst. U.S. Atty. Gen. Tax Divsn., 1969, Outstanding Performance award, U.S. Atty. Gen. Richardson, 1973. Mem.: ABA, Phila. Bar Assn., D.C. Bar Assn., Fed. Bar Assn., Pan Am. Assn. Phila., Vesper Club, Am. Legion. Office: Kostos & Lamer 1608 Walnut St Ste 1300 Philadelphia PA 19103-5407

REITER, MICHAEL A. lawyer, educator; b. Pitts., Nov. 15, 1941; BS, U. Wis., 1963, MS, 1964, JD, 1967, PhD, 1969. Bar: Wis. 1967, Ill. 1975, U.S. Supreme Ct. 1975. Ptnr. Holleb & Coff, Chgo., 1987-99, Duane Morris LLC, Chgo., 1999—. Adj. prof. law Northwestern U., Chgo., 1977—99; mem. faculty Nat. Inst. Trial Advocacy, 1980—. Office: Duane Morris LLC 227 W Monroe St Ste 3400 Chicago IL 60606-5098

REITER, MITCHELL FOREST, orthopaedic spine surgeon; b. West Orange, N.J., Mar. 13, 1968; s. Norman Arthur and Diane Reiter; m. Patricia Mangelli. BS, U. Miami, 1988, MD, 1992. Diplomate Am. Bd. Orthopaedic Surgery. Resident in orthopaedics Jackson Meml. Hosp., Miami, Fla., 1992-97; fellow in spine surgery Emory U. Hosp., Atlanta, 1997-98; asst. prof. spine surgery N.J. Med. Sch., Newark, 1998—. Mem. resident rsch. com. N.J. Med.

Sch., Newark, 1998—, ambulatory care com., 1998—; instr. orthopaedics Emory U. Sch. Medicine, Atlanta, 1997-98. Author: (book chpts.) Oxford Textbook of Surgery, 1998, Orthopaedic Knowledge Update 6, 1998. Mem. AMA, N.J. Orthopaedic Soc., Alpha Omega Alpha. Jewish. Avocations: running, boating, volleyball, hiking. Office: North Jersey Orthopaedic Inst Ste 1200 90 Berges St Newark NJ 07052 E-mail: reiter_mf@umdnj.edu.

REITER, ROBERT EDWARD, banker; b. Kansas City, Mo., Dec. 27, 1943; s. Robert Vincent and Helen Margaret (Petrus) R.; m. Mary J. Darby, June 20, 1964; children: Mollie K., Jennifer M., Ellen R., Robert E. Jr. BA, Rockhurst Coll., 1964; JD, St. Louis U., 1967; LLM, U. Mo., Kansas City, 1969. Bar: Mo. 1967. Assoc. atty. Burke, Jackson & Millin, Kansas City, 1967-69; personal trust adminstr. City Nat. Bank and Trust Co., 1969-71; estate planning officer United Mo. Bank of Kansas City, 1971-73, v.p., 1973-80, sr. v.p., 1980-85; exec. v.p. UMB Bank, N.A., 1985—. Pres., corp. bd. Seton Ctr., Kansas City, 1992-95. Contbr. articles to profl. jours. Bd. of Counselors St. Joseph Health Ctr., Kansas City, 1977-85; pres. St. Joseph Health Ctr. Adv. Coun., Kansas City, 1985-86; treas., bd. trustees Endowment Trust Fund for Cath. Edn., 1989—; bd. regents Rockhurst U., 1999—, mem. planned giving coun., 1999—. Grantee St. Louis U. Sch. of Law, 1964-67. Mem. Mo. Bar Assn., Kansas City Bar Assn. (chmn. employee benefits com. 1989-90), Employee Benefit Inst. (adv. bd. 1986—, chmn. 1989), Inst. Cert. Bankers (cert. retirement svcs. profl. 1995—), Estate Planning Soc. Kansas City (pres. 1985-86), Serra Club of Kansas City (v.p. 1987-89). Home: 1024 W 70th St Kansas City MO 64113-2004 Office: UMB Bank NA 1010 Grand Blvd PO Box 419692 Kansas City MO 64141-6692

REITER, STANLEY, economist, educator; b. N.Y.C., Apr. 26, 1925; s. Frank and Fanny (Rosenberg) R.; m. Nina Sarah Breger, June 13, 1944; children: Carla Frances, Frank Joseph. AB, Queens Coll., 1947; MA, U. Chgo., 1950, PhD, 1955. Rsch. assoc. Cowles Commn., U. Chgo., 1948-50; mem. faculty Stanford U., 1950-54, Purdue U., 1954-67; prof. econs. and math. Northwestern U., 1967—, now Morrison prof. econs. and math. Coll. Arts and Scis., Morrison prof. managerial econs. and decision scis. Kellogg Sch. Mgmt. Dir. Ctr. for Math. Studies in Econs. and Mgmt. Sci.; cons. in field. Trustee Roycemore Sch., Evanston, Ill., 1969-71, treas., 1970-71. Served with inf. AUS, 1943-45. Decorated Purple Heart. Fellow Econometric Soc., AAAS; mem. Soc. Indsl. and Applied Math., Inst. Mgmt. Scis., Ops. Rsch. Soc. Am., Am. Math. Soc., Math. Assn. Am., Am. Acad. of Arts and Scis. Home: 2138 Orrington Ave Evanston IL 60201-2914 Office: Northwestern U Ctr for Math Studies 2001 Sheridan Rd Evanston IL 60208-0814 E-mail: s-reiter@northwestern.edu.

REITH, CARL JOSEPH, apparel industry executive; b. Peoria, Ill., Jan. 11, 1914; s. Joseph and May (Kolb) R.; m. Jennie S. Habbinga, Apr. 3, 1936; 1 child, Joyce Elaine. Grad. high sch. Office staff sales Peoria Creamery Co., Ill., 1932; with Kroger Co., 1934-60, successively asst. br. acct., office mgr., acct.; adminstr., coord. tng. and mgmt. devel. programing Kroger Co. (Gen. Offices), Cin.; gen. merchandising mgr. Kroger Co. (St. Louis br.), 1946-50; br. mgr. Kroger Co., Indpls., 1950-55, div. v.p. Cin., 1955-57, regional v.p., 1957-60; pres., chief exec. officer Colonial Stores, Inc., 1960-67; bd. dir., pres. Oxford Industries, 1967-78, now dir. Adv. bd. Salvation Army, Atlanta.; bd. dirs. Atlanta Coll. Art; trustee Robert Woodruff Art Ctr. Mem. Indiana Chain Store Council (pres., v.p. 1951-55), Ind. C. of C. (bd. 1954-55), Indpls. C. of C. (bd. 1950), Ga. C. of C. (indsl. devel. council), Atlanta C. of C. (v.p., bd. dir. 1964-67), Augusta (Ga.) Nat. Golf Club, Piedmont Driving Club, Capital City Club, Peachtree Golf Club, Masons, Shriners, Rotary. Home: 3747 Peachtree Rd NE Apt 1708 Atlanta GA 30319-1376 Office: Oxford Industries Inc 222 Piedmont Ave NE Atlanta GA 30308-3391

REITMAN, JERRY IRVING, advertising agency executive; b. Phila., Jan. 9, 1938; s. Benjamin and Ruth (Eisenberg) R.; m. Monica Birgitta Hall, Oct. 27, 1968; children: Jennifer Sharon, Sarah Beth. BS in Fin., Pa. State U., 1961. Exec. v.p., CEO Brit. Pubs., N.Y.C. and London, 1965-69; pres., pub. Acad. Media, Sherman Oaks, Calif., 1969-73; v.p. Pubs. Clearing House, Port Washington, N.Y., 1973-78; exec. v.p. Ogilvy & Mather, N.Y.C., 1978-81; with Scali, McCabe, Sloves, Inc., 1981-86; pres. Scali, McCabe, Sloves Direct; chmn. bd. dirs. The Reitman Group, 1986-87; exec. v.p. The Leo Burnett Co., Chgo., 1986-96; pres., CEO, vice chair Internat. Data Response Corp., 1996—. Dir. Scandinavian Airlines Sys. Pub./Distbn. Svcs.; mem. adv. bd. Ill. Dept. Trade and Tourism, 1988—; internat. awards chmn., bd. dirs. John Caples Internat., 1989—; mem. Internat. Direct Mktg. Symposium, Zürich, Switzerland. Author: A Common Sense Approach to Small Business, 1968, Beyond 2000: The Future of Direct Marketing, 1994; contbr. articles to profl. jours. Trustee Locust Valley Libr. Assn., N.Y., 1982—; exec. com. mem. Pub. Hall of Fame, 1987—; bd. govs. Children's Miracle Network, 1992—, vice chmn., chmn. bd. govs., 1998—, 1999-2001; bd. dirs. Children's Meml. Found. Telethon, The Direct Mktg. Ednl. Found., exec, dir., 1996—. Anderson scholar, 1960; recipient Key to City, New Orleans, 1959, Silver Apple award N.Y. Direct Mktg. Club, 1989, Ed Mayer award Ednl. Found., 1996, Charles S. Downs award, 1997. Fellow Psychiat. Re-Edn. Assn.; mem. Am. Mktg. Assn. (at-large mem., 2000, bd. dirs.), Direct Mktg. Assn. (bd. mem. ethics com. 1984), Creative Guild (dir. 1984), Internat. Direct Mktg. Assn. (bd. dirs. 1981-82), Publ. Hall of Fame (exec. com. 1988—), Direct Mktg. Club N.Y. (pres. 1983-84), Beta Gamma Sigma, Delta Sigma Pi. Avocations: tennis; old car restoration; classical woodworking. Home and Office: Callahan Group LLC 2204 N Leavitt St Chicago IL 60647-3204 E-mail: jireitman@aol.com.

REITMAN, ROBERT STANLEY, business consultant, nonprofit agency advisor; b. Fairmont, W.Va., Nov. 18, 1933; s. Isadore and Freda A. (Layman) R.; m. Sylvia K. Golden, Dec. 24, 1955; children: Scott Alan, Alayne Louise. BS in Acctg., W.Va. U., 1955; JD, Case Western Res. U., 1958. Bar: Ohio 1958. Mem. firm Burke, Haber & Berick, Cleve., 1958-60, ptnr., 1960-68; exec. v.p., vice chmn. Tranzonic Cos. (formerly AAV Cos.), Pepper Pike, Ohio, 1968-70, pres., vice-chmn., 1970-73, chief exec. officer, pres., vice chmn., 1973-82, pres., chmn., CEO, 1982-98, chmn. emeritus, bd. dirs., 1998—; prin. Riverbend Advisors, 1998—. Mem. bus. adv. com. Mandel Ctr. for non-profit Orgn. Case We. Res. U., 1995-99, vis. com. Weatherhead Sch. of Bus., 1995—, vis. com. Sch. of Law, 1998—, chmn. Dean's Nat. Adv. Com., Sch. of Law, 1997-98; mem. pvt. banking adv. bd. Key Bank, N.A., 1997-. Mem. Rep. fin. com., Cuyahoga County, 1968-78; mem. Com. for Econ. Growth for Israel, Cleve., 1977-80, pres., 1978-80; mem. adv. coun. Cleve. Mus. Nat. History, 1982-85, Cleve. Opera, 1977—; del. Coun. of Jewish Fedns., N.Y.C., 1981-97; gen. co-chmn. Jewish Welfare Fund, Cleve., 1975-78, 81-85, gen. vice chmn., 1985-89, gen. chmn., 1989-91; sect. and div. chmn., team capt. United Way Svcs., 1974-97, mem. del. assembly, 1976-85, trustee, 1977-83, 84-90, 91—, v.p., 1985-88, chmn. nominating. com., 1988-90, campaign chmn., 1993, chair fund raising planning com., 1994-97, chair bd. trustees, 1997-2000, life trustee, 2000—; mem. employment com. Jewish Vocat. Svc., Cleve., 1974-83; bd. dirs. Capital for Israel, Inc., N.Y.C., 1986-87; nat. vice chmn. United Jewish Appeal, 1987-92, nat. allocations chmn., 1987-90, trustee, 1988-94, chair retirement fund com., 1994-97; trustee B'nai B'rith Hillel Found., 1975-81, Cleve. Jewish News, 1976-79, Ideastream Ednl. TV Sta. WVIZ, Cleve., 1976-99, vice chmn. 1986-90, chmn. bd., 1990-97, immediate past chair, 1997-99, chair emeritus, 1999—; trustee, pres. Bus. Volunteerism Coun., 1994-96, chmn. 1996-97; trustee Jewish Cmty. Fedn. Cleve., 1983-98, 1999—, treas., 1991-94, v.p., 1995-97, Jewish Edn. Ctr. of Cleve., 1993-96, Cleve. Zool. Soc., 1972—, pres., 1979-87, chmn., 1987-92, chmn. emeritus, 1992—, chmn. JDC-Brookdale Inst. of Gerontology and Human Devel. (Israel), 1995; trustee Am. Jewish Joint Distbn. Com., 1988-96, 97—, United Israel Appeal, 1987-94, Mt. Sinai Med. Ctr., Cleve., 1976-96, chmn., 1982-85; trustee Cleve. State U. Devel. Found., 1988-89, Greater Cleve. Roundtable, 1991—; trustee The Wilds, 1995-99, adv. bd., 1999—, trustee, The Mt. Sinai Health Care Foundation, 1995—, vice chair 1998-2001, chair, 2001—; trustee Univ. Hosps. Health Sys. and Univ. Hosps. Cleve., 1999—; trustee, chair Heather Hill, Inc., 2001—. Mem. The 50 Club Cleve., Case We. Res. Univ. Sch. of Law Soc. Benchers, Am. Kennel Club (regional del. 1960-75), We. Res. Kennel Club (officer, trustee 1959-75), Beechmont Club (fin. com. 1972-80, house com. 1974), Pepper Pike Club, Union Club, Carambola Golf Club, Masons, Zeta Beta Tau, Tau Epsilon Rho. Avocations: golf, swimming, pure-bred dogs. Office: Riverbend Advisors 2087 Chagrin River Rd Gates Mills OH 44040-9740 E-mail: rsrform@megsinet.net.

REITMAN, SANFORD, radiologist; b. Newark, June 12, 1933; BS, Allegheny Coll., U. Pa., 1954; MS in Physiology and Biochemistry, Rutgers U., 1955; MD, U. Ala., 1959. Diplomate Am. Bd. Radiology. Rsch. fellow neuroanatomy Nat. Found., 1956-57; intern radiology Naval Hosp., Phila., 1959-60; resident radiology San Diego Naval Hosp., 1961-64; med. dir. radiology Harris Hosp. NW, Fort Worth; assoc. prof. biomed. engrng. U. Tex.; physician group practice Radiology Assocs. Tarrant County, Fort Worth. Chief resident therapy and diagnosis, Regional Naval Med. Ctr., San Diego; chief of radiology Newport Naval Hosp., 1975-85; sr. cons. interventional radiology Meml. Hosp., R.I.; chmn. radiology Arlington Meml. Hosp., 1973-87, Harris Southwest Hosp., 1987-96. State bd. dirs. Am. Cancer Soc., 1972-74, dist. dir. 1972, pres. county chpt. 1970-71. NIH fellow, 1957-58. Fellow Royal Soc. Health; mem. Am. Coll. Radiology, Assn. Mil. Surgeons of the U.S., Am. Nuc. Soc., Biomed. Engrng. Soc., Royal Coll. Surgeons (faculty radiologist), Radiol. Soc. N.Am., Am. Assn. Univ. Profs., Tex. Med. Assn., Tex. Radiol. Soc., New Eng. Roentgen Ray Soc., Ala. Acad. Sci. E-mail: srbinthardunthat.aol.com. Office: Hidden Creek Ranch 2208 Farmer Rd Weatherford TX 76087-6964

REITSEMA, HAROLD JAMES, aerospace engineer; b. Kalamazoo, Jan. 19, 1948; s. Robert Harold and Bernice Jean (Hoogsteen) R.; m. Mary Jo Gunnink, Aug. 6, 1970; children: Ellen Celeste, Laurie Jean. BA, Calvin Coll., 1972; PhD, N.Mex. State U., 1977. Rsch. assoc. U. Ariz., Tucson, 1977-79, sr. rsch. assoc., 1979-82, vis. scientist, 1987—; sr. mem. tech. staff Ball Aerospace, Boulder, Colo., 1982-85, prin. systems engr., 1985-88, program mgr., 1988-89, staff cons., 1989-96, dir., 1996—. Cons. Aerospace Tech., 1987—. Contbr. articles to Astrophys. Jour., Aston. Jour., Nature, Sci., Icarus. Bd. dirs. EE Barnard Obs., Golden, Colo., 1984-91. Fellow AIAA (assoc., tech. com. chair 1991, Engr. of Yr. Colo. region 1990); mem. Am. Astron. Soc. (planetary sci. com. 1991-94), Internat. Astron. Union. Achievements include discovery of Larissa, fifth satellite of Neptune; co-discovery of Telesto, seventeenth satellite of Saturn; patents for Optically-coupled Shaft Angle Encoder. Home: 4795 Hancock Dr Boulder CO 80303-1103 Office: Ball Aerospace 1600 Commerce St Boulder CO 80301-2734 E-mail: hreitsema@ball.com.

REITZ, BRUCE ARNOLD, cardiac surgeon, educator; b. Seattle, Sept. 14, 1944; BS, Stanford U., 1966; MD, Yale U., 1970. Diplomate: Am. Bd. Surgery, Am. Bd. Thoracic Surgery. Intern Johns Hopkins Hosp., Balt., 1970-71, cardiac surgeon-in-charge, 1982-92; resident Stanford U. Hosp., (Calif.), 1971-72, 74-78; clin. assoc. Nat. Heart Lung Blood Inst., NIH, Bethesda, Md., 1972-74; asst. prof. Stanford U. Sch. Medicine, 1977-81, assoc. prof., 1981-82; prof. surgery Johns Hopkins U. Sch. Medicine, Balt., 1982-92; prof., chmn. Sch Medicine Stanford (Calif.) U., 1992—. Developer heart-lung transplant technique, 1981. Office: Stanford U Sch Medicine Dept Cardiothoracic Surgery Stanford CA 94305-5407 E-mail: breitz@stanford.edu.

REITZ, CURTIS RANDALL, lawyer, educator; b. Reading, Pa. s. Lester S. and Magdalene A. (Crouse) R.; m. Virginia R. Patterson, Dec. 19, 1953 (div.); children— Kevin R., Joanne E., Whitney A.; m. Judith N. Renzulli, Sept. 18, 1983 BA, U. Pa., 1951, LL.B., 1956. Bar: Pa. 1957, U.S. Supreme Ct. 1959. Law clk. to Chief Justice Earl Warren U.S. Supreme Ct., 1956-57; mem. faculty law U. Pa., Phila., 1957—, asst. prof. law, 1957-60, assoc. prof., 1960-63, prof., 1963—, provost, v.p., 1970-71, Algernon Sydney Biddle prof. law, 1985—. Trustee Internat. House Ctr. Phila.; bd. mgrs. Glen Mills Schs., Pa. Served to 1st lt. U.S. Army, 1951-53 Life Mem. Am. Law Inst., Mem., Nat. Conf. Commrs. on Uniform State Laws, Order of Coif Office: U Pa Law Sch 3400 Chestnut St Philadelphia PA 19104-6204 E-mail: creitz@law.upenn.edu.

REITZ, DANA FAITH, choreographer, dancer, visual artist; b. Rochester, N.Y., Oct. 19, 1948; d. Harold Lewis and Neva (Miesen) R. BS, U. Mich., Ann Arbor, 1970; MFA, Bennington (Vt.) Coll., 1994. Artistic dir., owner dance co. Field Papers, Inc. , N.Y.C., 1983—; mem. faculty Bennington Coll., 1994—. Tchg. resident including Dance Umbrella, British Isles, 1983, The Kitchen Ctr., N.Y.C., 1993, Internat. Summer Sch. Dance, Tokyo, 1993, Berlin Hebbel Theater, 1994, Phila. Dance Projects/Arts Bank, 1995, Contredanse, Brussels, 1995, UCLA, 1996, Jacob's Pillow, Lee, Mass., 1997, 99. Dancer Twyla Tharp & Dancers, 1970—71, Laura Dean & Dance Co., 1972, (soloist) Robert Wilson/Philip Glass opera Einstein on the Beach, 1976, (1st solo concert), 1973, (many tours including) Festival d'Automne, Paris, 1979—, Bklyn. Acad. Music, 1983, Incontri Internazionali di Rovereto, 1987, Holland Fest, 1988, Spoleto Fest USA, 1988, PepsiCo Summerfare Fest, 1989, Japanese Asia Dance Event, 1993, Fest d'Avignon, 1993, choreographer (of works including) Phrase Collection, 1978, Steps, 1979, Quintet Project, 1981, Field Papers, 1983, with James Turrell Severe Clear, 1985, Circumstantial Evidence, 1987, Suspect Terrain, 1989, Lichttontanz, 1991, with Jennifer Tipton, Sara Rudner Necessary Weather, 1994, with David Finn Private Collection, 1995, for Mikhail Baryshnikov Unspoken Territory, 1995, Shoreline, 1996, for Baryshnikov and Bando Tamasaburo Cantata for Two, 1998, Gestures for Edwin, 1998, Cadences for Cunningham and Cage, 2000; drawing exhbns., exhibitions include Walker Art Ctr., Mpls., 1981, Paula Cooper Gallery, N.Y.C., 1982, Pyramid Art Ctr., Rochester, N.Y., 1987, Atlantic Ctr. for Arts, New Smyrna Beach, Fla., 1990, Musées de Marseille, France, 1991—93; film and video works (with David Gearey) Airwaves, Once Again, 1974, Footage, 1975, (with Eric Bogosian) Two Sides: A Solo Dance Duet, 1978, (in Rudy Burckhardt's) Have You Seen A Moose-Wayward Women, 1990—93. Named Disting. Alumna in Residence, U. Mich., 1995, Viola Farber Artist-in-Residence, Sarah Lawrence Coll., 2001; recipient New York Dance and Performance award, 1985, 1987; fellow, Creative Artists Pub. Svc. Program, 1977, Creative Artists Pub. Svc. Program, 1982, NEA, 1980, 1982, 1984, 1988—90, 1992—93, 1994—95, John Simon Guggenheim Meml. Found., 1983. Office: Field Papers Inc care Roulette 228 W Broadway New York NY 10013

REITZ, DOUGLAS JOHN FRANK, airline captain, computer consultant; b. Salisbury, Rhodesia, May 7, 1955; came to U.S., 1980; s. Francis Charles Deneys and Zeta Ann (Runham) R.; m. Judy Ann White, Mar. 31, 1978 (div. May 1996); l child, David Douglas; m. Gala Judith Ruzic, Dec. 12, 1998. Dir. ops. Aviex Jet, Inc., Houston, 1980-84; capt. Am. Airlines, Dallas, 1984—; pres. The Reitz Cos., Inc., 1999—. Computer cons., 1983—. Flight lt. Rhodesian Air Force, 1973-80. Recipient Sword of Honor, Rhodesian Air Force, 1974. Mem. Allied Pilots Assn. Home: 5630 18th Ave NW Naples FL 34119-1222

REITZ, H(OWARD) WESLEY, construction company executive; b. Bellefonte, Pa., Apr. 17, 1947; s. Myron Wesley and Isabel (Jodon) R.; m. Carol Frances Stamm, Nov. 27, 1965; children: Brian Wesley, Douglas Myron, Karen Lea. BSCE, Pa. State U., 1969; MBA, U. Phoenix, 1996. Registered profl. engr., Pa., Va., W.Va. Survey and quality control technician The Lane Constrn. Co., Meriden, Conn., 1966-67, job engr., 1968-72, asst. supt., 1973-74, supt., 1975-83, asst. dist. mgr., 1984, dist. mgr., 1985—. Mem. ASCE, NRA, SAR, Am. Concrete Inst., Northumberland County Hist. Soc., Berks County Hist. Soc., Dubors Area Hist. Soc., Moose. Republican. Avocations: hunting, fishing, archery. Home: 1828 Walnut Grove Dr State College PA 16801-8440 Office: The Lane Constrn Corp 965 E Main St Meriden CT 06450-6004 E-mail: hwreitz@psualum.com.

REITZ, JOANNE BELLAM, health information executive; b. Rochester, N.Y., Dec. 26, 1950; d. Ernest Wilson and Anne (Hasenhnor) Bellam; 1 child, Stephen Ernest Reitz. AS in Applied Scis., Monroe C.C., 1971; BS in Bus. Mgmt. and Econs., Health Care Adminstrn., SUNY, Rochester, 1993. Registered health info. technician, info. adminstr. Med. records technician Genesee Meml. Hosp., Batavia, N.Y., 1971-76, St. Jerome Hosp., Batavia, 1976-79; dir. med. records and health info. mgmt. LeRoy (N.Y.) Village Green Nursing Home, 1979-94; health info. mgr., 1995; cons. health info., med. records Scottsville, N.Y., 1996—. Cons. Livingston County Skilled Nursing Home, Geneseo, N.Y., 1987—, Norloch Nursing Home, Rochester, 1991—, Brae Loche Nursing Home, Rochester, 1991—, LivingstonCounty Health Related Facility, Mt. Morris, N.Y., 1992—, Rochester Rehab. Ctr., 1995—; instr. Bryant and Stratton Coll. for Med. Programs, Highlands Living Ctr., 1996-97, neonatal ICU U. Rochester, Strong Meml. Hosp., 1997—; code and compliance officer Anthony L. Jordan Health Corp., 2000— Mem. Am. Health Info. Mgmt. Assn., N.Y. State Health Info. Mgmt. Assn., Rochester Health Info. Mgmt. Assn., greater Rochester chpt. Assn. Records Mgrs. and Adminstrs. Home and Office: 949 Scotts Mumford Rd Scottsville NY 14546

REITZ, MARY ELLEN, pathologist, health facility administrator; b. Dayton, Ohio, Dec. 19, 1952; d. Philip Lewis and Joanne (Tonder) R.; m. Duane David Wilkey, May 15, 1982; children: Deirdre Wilkey, Andrew Wilkey. BA magna cum laude, Mt. Holyoke Coll., 1975; MD, SUNY, Buffalo, 1981. Resident in pathology NYU Med. Ctr./Belluve-Manhattan VA Med. Ctr., N.Y.C., 1981-85; fellow N.Y. Blood Ctr., 1985-86; assoc. pathologist St. Vincent Health Ctr., Erie, Pa., 1986—; med. dir. Cmty. Blood Bank of Erie, 1986—, Associated Clin. Labs., 1999—. Co-contbr. articles to Jour. Clin. Ultrasound, N.Y. State Jour. Medicine. Fellow Coll. Am. Pathologists; mem. Am. Assn. Blood Banks, Am. Soc. Clin. Pathologists. Office: St Vincent Health Ctr 232 W 25th St Erie PA 16544-0001

REIVER, JULIUS, mechanical engineer; b. Wilmington, Del., Sept. 25, 1916; s. Hyman and Ethel R.; m. Iona Peterson, June, 11, 1941; children: Daniel (dec.), Alan Theodore, Joanna, Betsy. BME, Univ. Del., 1938. Engr. E.I. DuPont Co., Wilmington, Del., 1939-42; pres. Hyman Reiver & Co., 1946-78; ret. Author: U.S. Large Cents 1843-1857, 1981, U.S. Half-Dimes 1794-1837, 1984, U.S. Half-Dollars 1836-1839, 1988, U.S. Quarter Dollars, 1987, The U.S. Early Silver Dollar 1793-1803, 1999 (Nat. Literary Guild award of Extraordinary merit 1999). Lt. Col. U.S. Army, 1942-45. Decorated Bronze Star U.S. Army, 1944, Cert. of Merit, 1944. Mem. Optimist Club (Man of Yr. 1986), Citizens Commemorative Coin Adv. Com., Floor Covering Assn. of Greater Phila. (pres. 1975), Nat. Floor Covering Assn. (v.p. 1976). Avocations: coin collecting, classic & antique automobiles, cameras, photography. Home: 1802 Forrest Rd Wilmington DE 19810-4319

REIZNER, GEORGE TERRY, medical educator; b. Sept. 9, 1954; BS, U. mich., 1976; MD, George Washington U., 1980. Asst. prof. U. Wis., Madison, 1986-91, assoc. prof., 1991-97, prof., 1997—, vice-chair dermatology, 2002—. Office: One South Park 7th Flr Madison WI 53715

REJAI, MOSTAFA, political science educator; b. Tehran, Iran, Mar. 11, 1931; came to U.S., 1954; s. Taghi and Forough (Lashgari) R. AA, Pasadena City Coll., 1957; BA, Calif. State U., L.A., 1959, MS, 1961; PhD, UCLA, 1964. Teaching fellow UCLA, 1963-64; asst. prof. polit. sci. Miami U., Oxford, Ohio, 1964-67, assoc. prof., 1967-70, prof., 1970-83, Disting. prof., 1983—. Vis. scholar Ctr. for Internat. Affairs, Harvard U., 1972, Hoover Instn. on War, Revolution and Peace, Stanford U., 1973, Inst. Internat. Studies, Iran, 1974-75; vis. prof. Western Coll., Oxford, 1971, 72. Author: World Military Leaders: A Collective and Comparative Analysis, 1996, The Strategy of Political Revolution, 1973, The Comparative Study of Revolutionary Strategy, 1977, Comparative Political Ideologies, 1984; (with Kay Phillips) Leaders of Revolution, 1979, World Revolutionary Leaders, 1983, Loyalists and Revolutionaries: Political Leaders Compared, 1988, Political Ideologies: A Comparative Approach, 1991, 2d edit., 1995, Demythogizing an Elite: American Presidents in Empirical, Comparative, and Historical Perspectives, 1993, World Military Leaders: A Collective and Comparative Analysis, 1996, Leaders and Leadership: An Appraisal of Theory and Research, 1997, The Young George Washington in Psychobiographical Perspective, 2000, Concepts of Leadership in Western Political Thought, 2002; editor, contbr.: Democracy: The Contemporary Theories, 1967, Decline of Ideology?, 1971; editor: Mao Tse-Tung on Revolution and War, 1969, rev. edit., 1970; assoc. editor Jour. Polit. and Mil. Sociology, 1973—; contbr. articles to profl. jours., book chpts. Recipient Outstanding Teaching award Miami U., 1970. Mem. Am. Polit. Sci. Assn. (polit. psychology sect.), Am. Sociol. Assn. (polit. soc. sect.), Internat. Polit. Sci. Assn., Internat. Soc. Polit. Psychology, Internat. Studies Assn., Inter-Univ. Seminar on Armed Forces and Soc., Conf. for Study Polit. Thought, Midwest Polit. Sci. Assn., So. Polit. Sci. Assn., Western Polit. Sci. Assn., Pi Gamma Mu, Pi Sigma Alpha. Office: Miami U Dept of Political Science Oxford OH 45056

REJENT, MARIAN MAGDALEN, retired pediatrician; b. Toledo, Aug. 12, 1920; d. Casimir Stanley and Magdalen (Szymanowski) R. BS, Mary Manse Coll., 1943; MD, Marquette U., 1946; MPH, U. Mich., 1960. Diplomate Am. Bd. Pediatrics. Intern St. Vincent Med. Ctr., Toledo, 1946-47; resident communicable diseases City Hosp., Cleve., 1947-48; resident pediatrics Childrens Hosp., Akron, Ohio, 1948-50; pvt. practice Toledo, 1950-54; chief div. maternal child health Toledo Bd. Health, 1953-64; dir. pediatrics Maumee Valley Hosp., Toledo, 1964-69; assoc. prof. pediatrics Med. Coll. Ohio, 1969-76; med. dir. State Crippled Childrens Program, Columbus, Ohio, 1976-78; attendant pediatrician St. Vincent Med. Ctr., Toledo, 1978-80, 87-99; chief pediatric svcs. Wake County Health Dept., Raleigh, N.C., 1980-87; ret. clin. prof. pediatrics Med. Coll. Ohio, 1998; ret., 1999. Exec. com. March of Dimes, 1988-92. Mem. AMA, APHA, Am. Acad. Pediatrics, Am. Med. Women's Assn., Ohio PHA, Ohio State Med. Assn., NW Ohio Pediatric Assn., Acad. Medicine Toledo, Alpha Omega Alpha. Republican. Roman Catholic. Avocations: travel, photography, painting. Home: The Woodlands Apt #401 4030 Indian Rd Toledo OH 43606

REJINO, MONA, music educator, composer; b. Haskell, Tex., Feb. 4, 1959; m. Huey Miller Bledsoe and Patsy Ruth Smith; m. Richard Rejino, Dec. 18, 1982; children: Margaret, Adam. MusB, West Tex. State U., 1981; MusM, North Tex. State U., 1983. Group piano instr. Dallas Ind. Sch. Dist., 1982-84; staff pianist Old San Francisco Steakhouse, Dallas, 1982-92; piano instr. Rejino Piano Studio, 1983—. Co-author, composer Hal Leonard Student Piano Libr., 1996—; co-arranger Popular Piano Solos, Books 3 and 4, 1997, Christmas Piano Solos, Books 1-4, 1997, God Bless America and Other Patriotic Piano Solos, Books 1-5, 2001, More Popular Piano Solos, Books 1-5, 2002, Traditional Hymns, Books 1-5, 2002; featured composer in Hal Leonard Showcase Solos Series, 2000-02; contbr. to Clavier's Keys Piano Music mag., Keyboard Companion mag., In Touch newsletter. Mem. Music Tchrs. Nat. Assn., Tex. Music Tchrs. Assn., Carrollton Music Tchrs. Assn. (pres. 1989, v.p. 1998—, Tchr. of Yr. 1987-88). Home: 2515 Willowdale Dr Carrollton TX 75006-2032

REJMAN, DIANE LOUISE, business analyst; b. Hartford, Conn., Jan. 14, 1956; d. Louis P. and Genevieve (Walukevich) R. BS in Aviation Adminstrn., Embry Riddle Aero. U., 1980; MBA in Internat. Mgmt., Thunderbird Am. Grad. Sch. Internat. Mgmt., 1991; cert. in cross cultural negotiation, Western Internat. Univ., 1994. Lic. ins. agt. Calif., Series 7 lic., Series 66 Lic. Indsl. engr./planner Hamilton Aviation, Tucson, 1980-82; indsl. engr. assoc. Gates Learjet, 1984; tech. writer, FAA coord. Dee Howard Co., San Antonio, 1984-86; indsl. engr. McDonnell Douglas Helicopter Systems, Mesa, Ariz., 1986-88; systems analyst McDonnell Douglas Helicopter Sys., 1988-95; sr. aerospace industry market rsch. analyst Frost & Sullivan, Mountain View, Calif., 1995-97; mfg. sys. applications analyst Ross Systems, Redwood City, 1997-2000; sr. bus. analyst Charitable Way, San Carlos, 2000; video spokesperson Andiron Technologies, Inc., 2001—; fin. advisor Am. Express Fin. Svcs., 2001—. Bd. dirs. McDonnell Douglas Helicopter Sys. Employee Community Fund., adminstr. 1992-95. Author: (reports) World Commercial Avionics Market, 1996, World Airport Ground Equipment Markets, 1996, World Air Traffic Control Equipment Markets, 1997. Mem. City of Mesa Leadership Tng. Class of 1995. With U.S. Army, 1977-80. Avocations: dancing, photography, travel, reading, music. Home: 146 Mission Dr Palo Alto CA 94303-2751 E-mail: dianere@global.t-bird.edu.

REKAS, EDWARD PAUL, professional society administrator; b. Phila., June 7, 1947; s. John Harry and Catherine Cecilia (Brennan) Rekas; m. Bonilyn Twila Knapp, June 19, 1976; children: Melissa Ann, James Brennan. BSc in Chemistry, Villanova U., 1969; MBA in Fin., Loyala Coll., 1977. Chemist E.I. du Pont & Co., Phila., 1969—71, Glidden-Durkee R&D, Strongsville, Ohio, 1972—73; sales rep. W.R. Grace & Co., 1974—79, mktg. mgr. Balt., 1980—86; dept. head Am. Chemical Soc., Washington, 1987—95; dir. pub. FASEB, 1996—99; comptroller, CFO Fedn. Am. Soc. for Exptl. Biology, Bethesda, Md., 1999—. Mem.: AAAS, Am. Soc. Assn. Exec. Achievements include patents for silica aerosol as dentifrice abrasive, Can., 1985. Office: Federation American Soc for Experimental Biology 9650 Rockville Pike Bethesda MD 20814 Fax: 301-634-7143. E-mail: erekas@faseb.org.

REKATE, ALBERT C. physician; b. Buffalo, June 12, 1916; s. Gustave E. and Fannie (Hummell) R.; m. Elizabeth Foster, June 12 1943 (dec. 1985); 1 child, Suzanne (Mrs. R. Willis Post); m. Linda Ann Holt, Aug. 1, 1992. MD, U. Buffalo, 1940. Diplomate Am. Bd. Internal Medicine. Intern E.J. Meyer Meml. Hosp., Buffalo, 1940-41, med. resident, 1941-44; asst. prof. medicine SUNY-Buffalo, 1954-61, assoc. prof., 1961-65, prof., 1965-86, prof. emeritus, 1986—; dir. rehab. medicine SUNY, Buffalo, 1965-72, acting dean Sch. Health Related Professions, 1965-66, assoc. dean, 1966-74, acting chmn. dept. rehab. medicine, 1972-75; assoc. dir. medicine E.J. Meyer Meml. Hosp., 1957-63, head dept. rehab. medicine, 1964-69, dir. primary rehab. center, 1965-69, acting head cardiology, 1966-69, dir., 1970-72. Bd. dirs. Buffalo Hearing and Speech Ctr., 1973-99; mem. adv. bd. Coastal Empire Mental Health Ctr., S.C., 1980-81, bd. dirs., 1981-93; mem. dean's adv. coun. SUNY-Buffalo Sch. Medicine and Biomed. Scis., 1995—, med. emeritus faculty group steering com., 2000—. Contbr. articles to profl. jours. Served with M.C. AUS, World War II. Mem. Am. Heart Assn., Western N.Y. Heart Assn. (pres. 1954-55), Assn. Am. Med. Colls., N.Y. State Heart Assembly, N.Y. Acad. Scis., Med. Union (pres. 1974-75), Buffalo Acad. Medicine (pres. 1969-70), Erie County Med. Soc., Med. Alumni Assn. U. Buffalo (pres. 1960-61), Beaufort-Jasper Mental Health Assn. (dir. 1980-86). Home: PO Box 3164 Hilton Head Island SC 29928-0164 Office: 462 Grider St Buffalo NY 14215-3021 E-mail: lre1832886@aol.com.

REKAU, RICHARD ROBERT, architect; b. June 6, 1936; s. Robert Richard and Charlotte (Ryan) Rekau Altier; m. Carolyn Pritchett, Dec. 20, 1962; 1 child, Ryan Richard. BArch, BS, Ga. Tech. Inst., 1965. Registered arch., Ga., N.C., Ala., Fla., Md., S.C., Tenn.; cert. Nat. Coun. Archtl. Registration Bds. Project mgr. John Portman & Assocs., Atlanta, 1970-76; assoc. Herndon & Harris, 1976-77; v.p. Devel. Contractors, Inc., 1979-81; pres. Richard R. Rekau, Arch., P.C., 1977—. Pres. Rekau Properties, 1984—. Prin. works include Lanier Plaza, Gainesville, Ga. Corp. Plaza N.W., Atlanta, Pkwy. Village, Macon, Ga., Carrollton (Ga.) Crossroads Shopping Ctr., Tuxedo Park, Atlanta, Griffin (Ga.) Mall, Festival Ctr. Hilton Head, Perimeter Village, Atlanta, Tuxedo Park, Carrollton Crossroads, Festival Ctr. Indigo Run, Hilton Head, S.C., Park Centre Commons, Ocala, Fla., The Desoto, Savannah, Ga, Tenenbaum Residence, Kronowitz Residence, Savannah; two residential works featured in Savannah Tour of Homes. Mem. AIA, Am. Solar Energy Soc., Hist. Preservation Found. N.C., Nat. Trust Hist. Preservation, Ga. Tech. Alumni Assn., Ga. Canoeing Assn. Home: 1771 Beverly Woods Ct Atlanta GA 30341-1418 Office: Ste 1240 1000 Abernathy Rd NE Atlanta GA 30328-5653 E-mail: rekauarch@aol.com.

REKTORIK-SPRINKLE, PATRICIA JEAN, Latin language educator; b. Robstown, Tex., Feb. 19, 1941; d. Julius and Elizabeth Lollie (Ermis) Rektorik; m. Edgar Eugene Sprinkle, June 22, 1963; children: Julie Anne, Mark. BA in English and Latin, Our Lady of the Lake Coll., San Antonio, 1963, MA, 1967; doctoral student, Tex. A&M U., 1968-74, U. North Tex., 1987—. Cert. secondary tchr., Tex. Latin and English tchr. Ysleta Independent Sch. Dist., El Paso, Tex., 1963-64, El Paso Independent Sch. Dist., 1964-65; instr. Our Lady of the Lake Coll., 1965-66; rhetoric and composition instr. Tex. A&M U., College Station, 1968-69, 72-74, Harford Community Coll., Bel Aire, Md., 1970-71; Latin tchr. Denton (Tex.) Pub. Schs., 1974—2002. Mem. residents adv. com. Tex. Acad. Math. and Sci., Denton, 1987-88; chmn. Latin reading competition Nat. Jr. Classical League, Miami, Ohio, 1988-93; mem. methodology com. Am. Classical League, 1993-95; dir. Tex. State Jr. Classical League Conv., 1996, 2001; presenter workshops in field; mem. Tex. State Textbook Adv. Com., 1989-90. Costume designer Denton Cmty. Theater, 1984; choir dir. Immaculate Conception Ch., Denton, 1985-87; chmn. costume competition Tex. State Jr. Classical League, 1987—, exec. bd. sponsor, 1981—. Arthur Patch McKinlay scholar, 1986, 91. Mem. Am. Classical Assn., Classical Assn. of the Mid-West and South, Metroplex Classics Assn. (constl. adv. com. 1988), Classics Assn. Southwestern U.S. (pres. 1987-88), Tex. Classics Assn. (historian 2000—), Tex. Fgn. Lang. Assn. (chmn. hon. mem. 1988-89, chmn. local arrangements 1977). Roman Catholic. Office: Billy Ryan High Sch 5101 E Mckinney St Denton TX 76208-4630

RELDAN, ROBERT RONALD, law educator, psychological consultant, poet; b. Bklyn., June 2, 1942; s. William and Marie (Garis) R.; m. Judith Feldman, Nov. 7, 1971 (div. June 1979); 1 child, Edward. BS, Fairleigh Dickinson U., 1965; MS (hon.), Park Coll., 1975; JD, LaSalle U., St. Louis, 1988. Sales mgr. Pistilli Ford, Oradell, N.J., 1967-69; owner Triple "R" Co., Tenafly, 1969-75; dir. Legal Ltd., Trenton, 1975—. Author of poetry. Facilitator in Alternative to Violence program, Trenton. Served with USN, 1965-67. Mem. Nat. Lawyers Guild, Toastmasters Internat. (v.p. Trenton chpt. 1987-88), Am. Entrepreneurs Assn., Aircraft Owners and Pilots Assn. Avocations: flying, skydiving, scuba diving, poetry. Office: ACSU 557463 Bag R Rahway NJ 07065

RELIAS, JOHN ALEXIS, lawyer; b. Chgo., Apr. 2, 1946; s. Alexis John and Marie Helen (Metos) R.; m. Linda Ann Pontious, Nov. 27, 1971; children: Anne, Alexandra. BA, Northwestern U., Evanston, 1968; LLB, Northwestern U., Chgo., 1972. Bar: Ill., 1972, U.S. Dist. Ct. (no. dist.) Ill. 1972, U.S. Ct. Appeals (9th cir.) 1981, U.S. Ct. Appeals (7th cir.) 1983, U.S. Supreme Ct. 1997. Assoc. Vedder, Price, Kaufman & Kammholz, Chgo., 1972-78, ptnr., 1979-94, Franczek, Sullivan, Mann, Crement, Hein & Relias, Chgo., 1994—. Mem. bd. edn. Wilmette (Ill.) Sch. Dist. 39, 1989-97, 2001—, pres., 1992-93, 1995-96. Mem. Nat. Assn. Sch. Attys., Ill. Assn. Sch. Attys., Order of the Coif, Phi Beta Kappa. Greek Orthodox. Home: 2500 Kenilworth Ave Wilmette IL 60091-1337 Office: Franczek Sulian Mann Crement Hein & Relias 300 S Wacker Dr Chicago IL 60606-6680

RELIGA, JAMES PAUL, software engineer; b. Berwyn, Ill., Sept. 11, 1953; s. John James and Stella Gertrude (Pavlis) R.; m. Peggy Lee Partlow, Mar. 15, 1982. BA in Physics, U. Calif., Irvine, 1975. Sci. programming specialist Lockheed Missiles and Space Co., Sunnyvale, Calif., 1983, sr. rsch. engr., 1983-85, rsch. specialist, 1985-94; software cons., 1994-99; sr. engr. ADAC Labs., 2000—. Avocation: ballroom dancing.

RELIN, LEONARD, lawyer; b. Rochester, N.Y., Nov. 8, 1936; s. Benjamin W. and Bernice L. Relin; 1 child, David S. BS in Econ., U. Pa., 1957; JD, Albany Law Sch., 1961. Assoc. Lacy, Katzen, Green & Jones, Rochester, 1962-63; pvt. practice, 1963—. Guest lectr. Simon Sch. Bus., U. Rochester, 1990-99. Sgt. USAFR, 1960-65. Named for Best of TV, Bank Mktg. Assn., 1987, for Best of Print Media, Bank Mktg. Assn., 1990. Mem. Monroe County Bar Assn., N.Y. State Bar Assn., N.Y. State Trial Lawyers Assn., U. Pa. Alumni Assn. (pres. western N.Y. chpt. 1979, past pres.). Republican. Jewish. Avocations: boating, travel, tennis. Home: 227 Thackery Rd Rochester NY 14610-3360 Office: 1 Main St E Rochester NY 14614-1807

RELKIN, MICHELE WESTON, artist; b. L.A., Jan. 17, 1946; d. Ruben and Vivian (Demerer) Weston; m. Stephen Relkin, July 18, 1982; 1 child, Gregory Aaron. Student, Santa Monica Coll. Curator, co-founder Gallery 9, Thousand Oaks, Calif., 1994—. Art instr. for children and adults; artist in residence Walnut Canyon Elem. Sch., Moorpark, Calif. Represented in permanent collections Nat. Archives , Washington, William J. Clinton Presdl. Libr., Ark. Recipient Printmaking award Moorpark Coll., 1992. Mem. Nat. Assn. Women Artists, Thousand Oaks Art Assn. (program dir. 1990—, Art awards), Santa Barbara Printmakers Soc. Avocations: walking, pets, nature, teaching children's art. Home: 1944 Woodside Dr Thousand Oaks CA 91362-1265

RELL, M. JODI, lieutenant governor; b. Norfolk, Va. m. Lou Rell; children: Meredith, Michael. Student, Old Dominion U., Western Conn. State U.; LLD (hon.) , Univ. of Hartford, 2001. Mem., dep. minority leader Conn. Ho. Reps., 1984-94; lt. gov. State of Conn., 1995—. Past vice chmn. Brookfield Rep. Town Com., appt. chair of the Hartford Econ. Devel. Adv. Group, (HEDAG), 1998 ; trustee YMCA Western Conn; played a key role in raising funds for the Conn. Firefighters Meml.; estab. the Lt. Gov.'s Comm. on State Mandate Reform, Lt. Gov.'s Conn. Treasures award. Recipient of the Leadership award, Nat. Order of Women Legislators (NOWL), Impact award, Conn. Tech. Coun., 2001, First Kids 2001 Policy Leadership award, Conn. Voices for Children. Mem. Nat. Order Women Legislators (past nat. pres., former v.p., treas., corr. sec.), Women Execs. in State Govt., Brookfield Rep. Women's Club (past pres.), Brookfield Bus. and Profl. Women's Club, Prison and Jail Overcrowding comm., Governor's Law Enforcement Coun., Yale Corp., State Finance Advisory Com. Address: 125 Long Meadow Hill Rd Brookfield CT 06804-1339 Office: Office Lt Governor State Capitol Rm 304 Hartford CT 06106 E-mail: ltgovernor.rell@po.state.ct.us.*

RELLE, ATTILA TIBOR, dentist, geriodontist; b. Columbus, Ohio, Aug. 31, 1959; s. Ferenc Matyas and Trudi (Tubach) Relle; m. Kim Ann McDonald, Apr. 26, 1986; 1 child Ilona. DDS, Case We. Res. U., 1985; BS, Ohio State U., 1985, postgrad., 1985-88, 93, Wright State U. Sch. Medicine, 1988-93. Dentist Mobile Care Corp., Dublin, 1985; assoc. dentist Richard P. Deeds, DDS and Assocs., Columbus, 1985-86; dentist Family Dental and Denture Ctr. II, Dayton, Ohio, 1986-87; geriodontist Midwest Mobile Dental Care, Inc., Hamilton, 1988-91, Mobile Dental Care, Inc., Hamilton, 1991-92; dentist/owner Attila T. Relle, DDS and Assocs., Columbus, 1985—, Attila T. Relle, DDS & Assocs., Hilliard, 1995—; dentist Jerry Owens, D.D.S. and Assocs., Lancaster, Ohio, 1989-92; state dir. Ohio Residentcare dental geriatric program Meridian Svc. Care Corp. of Ohio, 1992-94, dentist/geriodontist, 1992-94. Co-chmn. Ohio Dental Careers Day, Columbus, 1980—81; regional dir. Midwest Mobile Dental Care, Inc., 1988—89; mem. adv. com. N.Am. Health Corp., 1989—92; sci. judge Ohio Acad. Sci., Delaware, 1985—92. Mem.: Civitan Internat. (pres. Ea. Columbus club 1986—87). Presbyterian. Avocations: tennis, skiing, soccer, ice skating, flying. Home: 5203 Carifa Ct Hilliard OH 43026-9589 Office: Attila T Relle DDS & Assocs 5203 Carifa Ct Hilliard OH 43026-9589 also: 4984A Scioto Darby Rd Ste 100 Hilliard OH 43026-1550 Business E-Mail: relle.core@core.com.

RELLE, FERENC MATYAS, chemist; b. Gyor, Hungary, June 13, 1922; came to U.S., 1951, naturalized, 1956; s. Ferenc and Elizabeth (Netratics) R.; m. Gertrud B. Tubach, Oct. 9, 1946; children: Ferenc, Ava, Attila. BSChemE, MS, Jozsef Nador Poly. U., Budapest, Hungary, 1944. Lab. mgr. Karl Kohn Ltd. Co., Landshut, Germany, 1947-48; resettlement officer Internat. Refugee Orgn., Munich, 1948-51; chemist Farm Bur. Coop. Assn., Columbus, Ohio, 1951-56; indsl. engr. N.Am. Aviation, Inc., 1956-57; rsch. chemist Keever Starch Co., 1957-65, Ross Labs. divsn. Abbott Labs., Columbus, 1965-70, rsch. scientist, 1970-89; cons. in field. Chmn. Columbus and Ctrl. Ohio UNWeek, 1963; pres. Berwick Manor Civic Assn., 1968; trustee Stelios Stelson Found., 1968-69; deacon Brookwood Presbyn. Ch., 1963-65, 92-93, trustee, 1990-91. Decorated knight St. Stanislaus Order. Mem. Am. Chem. Soc. (alt. councilor 1973, chmn. long range planning com. Columbus sect. 1972-76, 78-80), Am. Assn. Cereal Chemists (chmn. Cin. sect. 1974-75), Ohio Acad. Sci., Arpad Acad. (gold medl mem.), Internat. Tech. Inst. (adv. dir. 1977-82), Nat. Intercollegiate Soccer Ofcls. Assn., Am. Hungarian Assn., Hungrian Cultural Assn. (pres. 1978-81), Ohio Soccer Ofcls. Assn., Columbus Mannerchor, Germania Singing and Sport Soc., Civitans (gov. Ohio dist. 1970-71, dist. treas. 1982-83, pres. Ea. Columbus 1963-64, 72-73, gen. sec. for Hungary 1991-92, Ea. European growth mgr. 1993-94, amb. at large 1994—, established 1st Civitan club in Hungary 1991, Ukrina 1992, Solvakia 1994, Internat. Gov. of Yr. awardd 1971, Internat. Honor Key 1992, master club builder award 1992, various other awards), World Fedn. Hungarian Engrs. Home and Office: 3487 Roswell Dr Columbus OH 43227-3560

RELMAN, ARNOLD SEYMOUR, physician, educator, editor; b. N.Y.C., June 17, 1923; s. Simon and Rose (Mallach) Relman; m. Harriet Morse Vitkin, June 26, 1953; children: David Arnold, John Peter, Margaret Rose. AB, Cornell U., 1943; MD, Columbia U., 1946; LLD (hon.) , U. Pa.; ScD (hon.) , Med. Coll. Wis., Union U., Med. Coll. Ohio, CUNY; DMSc (hon.) , Brown U.; DLH (hon.) , SUNY; LittD (hon.) , Temple U. Diplomate Am. Bd. Internal Medicine. House officer New Haven Hosp., Yale, 1946—49; NRC fellow Evans Meml., Mass. Meml. hosps., 1949—50; practice medicine, specializing in internal medicine Boston, 1950—68, Phila., 1968—77; asst. prof., prof. medicine Boston U. Sch. Medicine, 1950—68; dir. Boston U. Med. Services, Boston City Hosp., 1967—68; prof. medicine, chmn. dept. medicine U. Pa.; chief med. services Hosp. of U. Pa., 1968—77; editor New Eng. Jour. Medicine, Boston, 1977—91, editor emeritus, 1991—; sr. physician Brigham and Women's Hosp., 1977—; prof. medicine and social medicine Harvard Med. Sch., 1977—93, prof. medicine and social medicine emeritus, 1993—95, prof. emeritus, 1995—. Cons. NIH, USPHS; mem. bd. registration in medicine Commonwealth of Mass., 1995—. Editor: Jour. Clin. Investigation, 1962—67; editor: (with F.J. Ingelfinger and M. Finland) Controversy in Internal Medicine, Vol. 1, 1966, Controversy in Internal Medicine, Vol. 2, 1974; contbr. articles to profl. jours. Trustee Columbia U., 1990—96; bd. dirs. Hastings Ctr., 1981—83. Recipient Columbia Alumni Gold medal, 1980, Disting. Svc. award, Am. Coll. Cardiology, 1987, McGovern award, Cosmos Club Washington, 1991, John Peters award, Am. Soc. Nephrology, 1992. Master: ACP (John Phillips medal 1985); fellow: Am. Acad. Arts and Scis.; mem.: AMA, Am. Fedn. Clin. Rsch. (past pres.), Am. Soc. Clin. Investigation (past pres.), Inst. of Medicine of NAS (coun. 1979—82), Mass. Med. Soc., Am. Physiol. Soc., Assn. Am. Physicians (coun., pres. 1983—84, Kober medal 1993), Alpha Omega Alpha, Phi Beta Kappa (senator 1991—98). Office: Brigham and Women's Hosp Dept of Medicine 181 Longwood Ave Fl 5 Boston MA 02115-5804

RELWANI, NIRMAL MURLIDHAR (NICK RELWANI), mechanical engineer; b. Bombay, Aug. 9, 1954; came to the U.S., 1976; m. Prema Vasandani; children: Karuna, Daksh. BS in Mech. Engring., U. Baroda, 1976; student, U. Nebr., 1977-78; MS in Mech. Engring., U. Wis., Milw., 1980. Registered profl engr., Wis., Ill. Rsch. asst. dept. mech. engring. U. Nebr., Lincoln, 1978; design engr. Allis Chalmers Corp., Milw., 1978-80; engring. cons. Bombay, 1980-86; assoc. engr. IIT Rsch. Inst., Chgo., 1986; mech. engr. Gen. Energy Corp., Oak Park, Ill., 1987-89, Arrowhead Environ. Control, Chgo., 1989-90; environ. engr. Ill. Dept. Pub. Health, Bellwood, 1990-92; sr. environ. protection engr. field ops. sect. bur. air Ill. EPA, Maywood, 1992—. Recipient Cert. of appreciation Ill. EPA, 1993, 94. Mem. ASME, ASHRAE (energy conservation award 1991), Assn. Energy Engrs. (sr.). Home: 1806 Marne Rd (River Bend) Bolingbrook IL 60490-4589

RELYEA, CARL MILLER, hydrologist; b. Claverack, N.Y., Dec. 29, 1912; s. Charles Miller Croswell and Edna (Pulver) R.; m. Harriet Watson, Sept. 6, 1946 (dec. Nov. 1982); children: Richard, Deborah, Cornelia. AB, Columbia U., 1935; MA, Columbia U., 1938; postgrad., MIT, 1943. Organist, choirmaster Morrow Meml. Ch., Maplewood, N.J., 1937-41; meteorologist Air Corps, Pan Am., Weather Bur., Bermuda, 1946-48, Weather Bur., JFK Internat. Airport, N.Y., 1948-50; hydrologist Ohio River Forecast Ctr., Cin., 1950-65, hydrologist-in-charge, 1965-77; ret., 1977; dep. dir. Hamilton County Emergency Mgmt. Agy., Cin., 1979-2000. Contbr. articles to profl. jours. Organist Highland United Meth. Ch., Fort Thomas, Ky., 1962-99, now organist emeritus; clk. of vestry Grace Episcopal Ch., Cin. Capt. U.S. Army Air Corps, 1943-46. Recipient Pub. Svc. cert. Hamilton County Disaster Coun., Cin., 1990. Mem. Ret. Engrs. and Scientists Cin. (chmn. 1984-86), N.Y. Acad. Scis., Columbia U. Club N.Y., Downtown Kiwanis Club. Republican. Avocations: travel, music, organist, home maintenance. Home: 1346 Teakwood Ave Cincinnati OH 45224-2126 Office: Vol Hamilton County Emergency Mgmt Agy 2377 Civic Center Dr Cincinnati OH 45231-1305

RELYEA, HAROLD CLARENCE, political scientist; b. Oneida, N.Y., Apr. 5, 1944; s. Clyde Frederick and Pauline Elizabeth R.; children: Jennifer L., Stephen F. AB, Drew U., 1966; PhD, American U., 1971. Specialist in Am. nat. govt. Congrl. Rsch. Svc. Libr. Congress, Washington, 1971—. Author: A Brief History of Emergency Powers in the United States, 1974, The Evolution and Organization of the Federal Intelligence Function: A Brief Overview 1776-1975, 1988, Silencing Silence: National Security Controls and Scientific Communication, 1994; co-author: Presidential Staffing--A Brief Overview, 1978, United States Government Information: Policies and Sources, 2002; editor, contbg. author: The Presidency and Information Policy, 1981, Striking a Balance: National Security and Scientific Freedom, 1985, The Executive Office of the President, 1997; co-editor, contbg. author: Freedom of Information Trends in the Information Age, 1983, United States Government Information Policies: Views and Perspectives, 1989; invited contbr. The Moral Authority of Government, 2000; bd. editors Presdl. Studies Quarterly, 1979-99, Govt. Publs. Rev., 1981-83, Transnational Data Report, 1982-89, Jour. Media Law and Practice, 1982-95, Govt. Info. Quarterly, 1984—; contbr. articles to profl. jours. Named Expert on U.S. Freedom Info. Act, The Economist of London, 1981; recipient Exec. Bd. award for superior pub. svc. Am. Soc. Access Profls., 1983, The Best of 1983 award for essay selection Libr. Lit. 14, 1984, Blue Pencil award Nat. Assn. Govt. Communicators, 1984; named to Freedom of Info. Act Hall of Fame, Freedom Forum, 1996. Mem. Pi Sigma Alpha. Office: Libr Congress CRS 101 Independence Ave SE Washington DC 20540-7470

REMAKUS, BERNARD LEO, physician, medical journalist, author, educator; b. Wilkes-Barre, Pa., Oct. 28, 1948; s. Leo W. and Adel Bertha (Macho) R.; m. Charlotte M. Amorebello, Aug. 17, 1974; children: Christopher B., Alexandra T., Matthew B. BS, King's Coll., 1970; MEd, E. Stroudsburg State Coll., 1972; MD, Temple U., 1978. Diplomate Nat. Bd. Med. Examiners, Am. Bd. Internal Medicine. Resident Abington Meml. Hosp., 1978-81; pvt. practice Hallstead, Pa., 1981—; instr. SUNY, Binghamton, N.Y., 1981—. Chief of staff, dir. emergency medicine, chmn. ethics com. Barnes-Kasson County Hosp., Susquehanna, Pa.; med. journalist Internal Medicine World Report, Old Bridge, N.J., 1991—; lectr. Discovery Internat., Deerfield, Ill., 1994—; spkr. in field. Author: The Malpractice Epidemic, 1990, Cassidy's Solution, 1995; mem. editl. adv. panel Internal Medicine World Report, 1998—; pub. 221 East Pub.; contbr. over 200 articles to profl. jours. Coach varsity baseball Blue Ridge H.S.; athletic scout Coll. Prospects of Am. Recipient Physicians Recognition award AMA, 1981, 84, 87, 90, 93, 96, 99. Roman Catholic. Office: Rd 2 PO Box 367 Hallstead PA 18822-0367

REMBAR, JAMES CARLSON, psychologist; b. N.Y.C., May 4, 1949; s. Charles Isaiah and Billie Ann (Olsson) R.; m. Jill Bailin, June 4, 1988; 1 child, Lilianna. BA, Sarah Lawrence Coll., 1972; MA, U. Mich., 1976, PhD, 1978. Lic. psychologist, psychoanalyst, N.Y. Clin. psychologist U. Mich. Med. Ctr., Ann Arbor, 1978-80; instr. psychology in psychiatry N.Y. Hosp. Cornell U. Med. Coll., White Plains, 1980-84, clin. asst. prof., 1984—2002, coord. child and adolescent psychology Westchester div., 1982-87; pvt. practice clin. psychologist Irvington, White Plains, N.Y., 1981—. Mem. faculty Westchester Ctr. for Study of Psychoanalysis and Psychotherapy, 1989—, dir. continuing edn., 1992-95, dir. child and adolescent psychotherapy tng. program, 1998—; cons. Andrus Children's Home, Yonkers, N.Y., 1987-97. Contbr. articles to profl. jours., chpt. in book. Mem. N.Y. State Psychol. Assn., Westchester County Psychol. Assn., Psychoanalytic Assn. Westchester Ctr. Avocations: tennis, music. Home and Office: 9 Sunnyside Pl Irvington NY 10533-1300 Office: 510 N Broadway White Plains NY 10603-3217

REMBE, TONI, lawyer, director; b. Seattle, Apr. 23, 1936; d. Armin and Doris (McVay) R.; m. Arthur Rock, July 19, 1975. Cert. in French Studies, U. Geneva, 1956; LL.B., U. Wash., 1960; LLM in Taxation, NYU, 1961. Bar: N.Y., Wash., Calif. Assoc. Chadbourne, Parke, Whiteside & Wolff, N.Y.C., 1961-63, Pillsbury, Madison & Sutro, San Francisco, 1964-71, ptnr., 1971—. Bd dirs. Aegon N.V., The Netherlands, Potlatch Corp., Spokane, Wash., SBC Comms., Inc., San Antonio. Pres. VanLobenSels/RembeRock Charitable Found., San Francisco; trustee Am. Conservatory Theatre, San Francisco. Fellow Am. Bar Found.; mem. ABA, Am. Judicature Soc., State Bar Calif., Bar Assn. San Francisco, Commonwealth Club of Calif. Office: Pillsbury Winthrop LLP 50 Fremont St San Francisco CA 94105-2230

REMBOLD, KRISTEN STABY, writer; b. Wurtzburg, Germany, Dec. 4, 1957; d. Richard Carl and Joan Behrens Staby; m. Christopher Mark Rembold, June 30, 1979; children: Karen, Ingrid. BS in Journalism, Northwestern U., 1979. From asst. editor to mng. editor Cahners Pub. Co., Chgo., 1979-81, contbg. editor, 1981-83; copy editor IRIS: A Jour. About Women, Charlottesville, Va., 1986-87, editor, 1988-91, fiction editor, 1991-97. Bd. dirs. Piedmont Coun. for Arts, Charlottesville. Author: (novel) Felicity, 1994, (poetry) Coming into this World, 1992; author of poems. Recipient 1st Novel award Mid-List Press, Mpls., 1993; Va. Ctr. Creative Arts fellow, 1991, 93.

REMBUSCH, JOSEPH JOHN, psychologist, management consulting company executive; b. Joliet, Ill., June 29, 1939; s. Joseph Earl and Agnes Cecilia (Heinen) R. AA, Joliet Jr. Coll., 1959; BS in Psychology, U. Ill., 1962; MA in Teaching, Rockford (Ill.) Coll., 1970; postgrad., No. Ill. U., 1961-66, 70-73, Western Colo. U., 1973-75. Registered psychologist, Ill. Sci. tchr. Crete-Monee Sch. Dist., Crete, Ill., 1963-64; clin. caseworker Ill. State Sch. Boys, St. Charles, 1964-65; dir. guidance Hiawatha Unit Dist. #426, Kirkland, Ill., 1966-69; registrar Kishwaukee Community Coll., Malta, 1969-81; spl. rep., dist. mgr., regional mgr. George S. May Internat., Park Ridge, 1982-86, 89-01, divisional sales mgr., 1986-89, coord. client svcs., 2001—02, maj. account exec., 2002—. Pvt. practice psychology DeKalb, Ill., 1971-80; cons. psychologist Ill. Div. Vocat. Rehab., DeKalb, 1971-79. Mem. Illini Great Dane Club, Delta Upsilon, Phi Delta Kappa. Republican. Roman Catholic. Home: 3499 Regent Dr Palatine IL 60067-4744

REMELIUS, ROGER MARTIN, broadcasting and licensing executive; b. Belleville, Ill., June 17, 1948; s. Elmer A. and Marie (Hoercher) R.; 1 child, Royce Freeman. Asst. buyer May Co., St. Louis, 1970-71; pub. rels. account exec. C.A. Grinde & Assocs., San Francisco, 1975-78; mktg. dir. Marlboro Limousine Svc., Beverly Hills, Calif., 1978-80; sr. exec. licensing Broadcast Music Inc., Hollywood, 1980—. Appeared in (films) Speed, Independence Day; (TV) Murphy Brown, Dr. Quinn Medicine Woman, Lois and Clark. Second term com. mem. for Pres. William J. Clinton, 1996-2000. Staff sgt. USAFR, 1968-74. Mem. Screen Actors Guild, Am. Film Inst. (music cons. 1988-90), Hollywood C. of C. (entertainment industry coun. 1988-90). Avocations: golf, bowling, billiards, tennis, writing.

REMEN, RACHEL NAOMI, pediatrician, psycho-oncologist; b. N.Y.C., Feb. 8, 1938; d. Isidore J. and Gladys Sara Remen. MD, Cornell U., 1962; PhD in Psychology (hon.), Calif. Inst. Integral Studies, San Francisco, 1996; PhD in Humane Letters (hon.), John F. Kennedy U., 1999; MA (hon.) , Spertus Inst. Jewish Studies, Chgo., 2000. Intern N.Y. Hosp., N.Y.C., 1962-63, resident, 1963-65; fellow Stanford U. Sch. Medicine, Palo Alto, Calif., 1965-67; asst. prof. pediat. Stanford U., 1967-74, assoc. dir. pediat. clinic, 1974-77; clin. prof. family and cmty. medicine U. Calif. Sch. Medicine, San Francisco, 1996—; med. dir. Commonweal Cancer Help Program, Bolinas, Calif., 1985—; psycho-oncologist pvt. practice, 1981—; founding dir. Inst. Study of Health & Illness, 1992—. Author: Kitchen Table Wisdom, 1996, My Grandfather's Blessings, 2000; editor: (poetry book) Wounded Healers, 1995. Fellow Am. Acad. Pediats. Office: Commonweal PO Box 316 Bolinas CA 94924-0316

REMER, DONALD SHERWOOD, engineering educator, economist, consultant; b. Detroit, Feb. 16, 1943; s. Nathan and Harriet R.; m. Louise Collen, Dec. 21, 1969; children: Tanya, Candace, Miles. BS, U. Mich., 1965; MS, Calif. Inst. Tech., 1966, PhD, 1970. Registered profl. engr., Calif., Mich., La. Tech. service engr., chem. raw materials div. coordinator, sr. running plan coordinator, task team mgr. Exxon, Baton Rouge, 1970-75; assoc. prof. engring. Harvey Mudd Coll., Claremont, Calif., 1975-79, prof., 1980—, Oliver C. Field prof. engring., dir. Energy Inst., 1981-83; cons., mem. tech. staff, mgr. planning analysis Jet Propulsion Lab., Calif. Inst. Tech., 1976-98; co-founder, ptnr. Claremont Cons. Group, 1979—; mem. adv. council Nat. Energy Found., N.Y.C., 1981-85. Mem. Inst. Mgmt. Cons., 1988—89; presenter short courses Calif. Inst. Indsl. Rels. Ctr., 1994—2001; Lyceum spkr. St. Jude Med., 2001; presenter short courses UCLA engring. & mgmt. program, 1994—. Case study editor Am. Soc. Engring. Edn., Inst. Indsl. Engrs., Engring. Economist, 1977-89; mem. editorial bd. Jour. Engring. Costs and Prodn. Econs., 1985-91, Internat. Jour. Prodn. Econs., 1992—; contbr. articles to profl. jours. Shelter mgr. ARC, Baton Rouge, 1965-70. Recipient Outstanding Chem. Engr. award U. Mich., 1965, First Place Pub. Relations award Am. Inst. Chem. Engring., 1975, Outstanding Alumni Fund Achievement award Calif. Inst. Tech., 1976, Outstanding Young Man of Am. award, 1976, NASA award, 1983, Best Paper of the Year in Jour. Parametrics, Internat. Soc. Parametric Analysts, 1991-92, Centennial award certificate Am. Soc. Engring. Edn., 1993; named Outstanding Research Seminar Speaker Occidental Research Corp., 1976. Mem. Am. Soc. Engring. Mgmt. (bd. dirs. 1981-83), Toastmasters Club (pres. Claremont-Pomona chpt. 1978).

REMETTA, JANET, pharmaceutical company executive, veterinarian; b. Camden, N.J., July 11, 1952; d. John Matthew and Marie Stella (Klemaszewski) R.; m. Neal Robert Frank, Oct. 19, 1974. BA, Trenton State Coll., 1974; MSW, Rutgers U., 1975; postgrad., Delaware Valley Coll., 1977-79; VMD, U. Pa., 1985. Lic. vet. medicine, Pa., N.J. Program specialist N.J. Dept. Health, Trenton, 1975-77, labor/mgmt. cons., 1977-79, supervising program specialist, 1979-81; clin. vet. Emerson Vet. Clinic, Buckingham, Pa., 1985-86, Ewing

Vet. Hosp., Trenton, 1986-88; mgr. issues mgmt. Sandoz Pharm. Corp., East Hanover, N.J., 1988-90, assoc. dir. issues mgmt., 1990-91, dir. issues mgmt., 1992, dept. head sci. and external affairs, 1992-93, exec. dir. site ops., 1993-95; exec. dir. internat. pub. policy Rhône-Poulenc Rorer Pharms., Collegeville, Pa., 1995-97, v.p. world-wide health safety and environ. ops., 1997—. Mem. policy and legis. com. N.J. Chem. Industry Coun., Trenton, 1988-92, chairperson-biotech. com., 1989-91; legis. com. N.J. Bus. and Industry Assn., Trenton, 1988-92; apptd. mem. N.J. Commn. on Smoking and Health, 1991-92; exec. chairperson N.J. Lung Assn., 1994; mem. bus. adv. bd. Women in Govt., 1994—; mem. steering com. Ctr. for the Am. woman, 1995; bd. dirs. YWCA, 1994-95; grad. Leadership Am., 1999. Recipient Tribute to Women in Industry award, 1992. Mem. AVMA, European Women's Mgmt. Devel. Network, Pa. Vet. Med. Assn. (legis. com. 1990—, long range planning com. 1995), Am. Mgmt. Assn., Am. Lung Assn. (exec. chairperson 1994), Assn. Indsl. Vets. Healthcare Businesswomen's Assn., N.J. Health Products Coun. (chairperson elect 1989-91, chairperson 1991-93), Nat. Pharm. Coun. (pub. affairs com. 1988-91, sci. affairs com. 1989-90), Pharm. Rsch. and Mfrs. Assn. (govt. affairs com. 1989-93, internat. com. 1995, exec. com. internat. sect. 1995-97, econ. policy task force 1995-97), Greater Valley Forge Rhodesian Ridge Back Club (founding mem.), Internat. Pharm. Aerosol Consortium (corp. rep. 1996, chair exec. com. 1996-99), Internat. Bus. Coun. (corp. rep. 1996-97). Home: 379 Sweet Briar Rd Perkasie PA 18944-3868 E-mail: nrfjr@concentric.net.

REMICK, FORREST JEROME, JR. former university official; b. Lock Haven, Pa., Mar. 16, 1931; s. Forrest Jerome Sr. and Ruth Betsy (Saiers) R.; m. Grace Louise Grove, June 7, 1953; children: Beth Ann Remick Gillio, Eric Forrest. BSME, Pa. State U., 1955, MSME, 1958, PhD in ME, 1963; diploma, Oak Ridge (Tenn.) Sch. Reactor Tech., 1956. Engr. Bell Telephone Labs., Whippany, N.J., 1955-56; dir. nuclear reactor facility Pa. State U., University Park, 1959-65, dir. Inst. Sci. Engring., 1967-79, acting dir. Ctr. Air Environ. Studies, 1976-78, dir. intercoll. research programs, 1979-85, asst. v.p. research, grad. studies, 1979-84, assoc. v.p. research, 1985-89; dir. Curtiss Wright Nuclear Research Lab., Quehanna, Pa., 1960-65; chief tng. sect. dept. tech. assistance IAEA, Vienna, Austria, 1965-67. Mem. Nat. Nuclear Accrediting Bd., Inst. Nuclear Power Ops., Atlanta, mem. adv. coun., 1995—; mem. Sci. Adv. Com. Idaho Nat. Engring. Lab., Idaho Falls, 1984-89, Reactor Safety Adv. Com., Savannah River Lab., Aiken, S.C., 1986-89, chmn., 1989; mem. Adv. Com. on Reactor Safeguards, Washington, 1982, vice chmn., 1987-88, chmn., 1989; commr. U.S. Nuclear Regulatory Commn., 1989-94, cons., 1994—; bd. dirs. Pub. Svc. Enterprise Group, Pub. Svc. Electric and Gas; mem. adv. bd. Applied Rsch. Lab., Pa. State U., 1994—. Served to sgt. U.S. Army, 1951-52. Named Outstanding Engring. Alumnus, Pa. State U., 1993; recipient Thomas P. Hamrick award for contbns. to tng. of nuclear facility pers., 1995. Fellow Am. Nuclear Soc. (bd. dirs. 1995—, meml. lectr. award 1971, disting. speaker award 1983); mem. ASME, Am. Soc. Engring. Edn., Nuclear Accrediting Bd. Republican. Lutheran. Home and Office: Canterbury Crossing 439 Brandywine Crossing State College PA 16801-7984

REMINE, WILLIAM HERVEY, JR. surgeon; b. Richmond, Va., Oct. 11, 1918; s. William Hervey and Mabel Inez (Walthall) ReM.; m. Doris Irene Grumbacher, June 9, 1943; children: William H., Stephen Gordon, Walter James, Gary Craig. BS in Biology, U. Richmond, 1940, D.Sc. (hon.), 1965; MD, Med. Coll. Va., Richmond, 1943; MS in Surgery, U. Minn., Mpls., 1952. Diplomate Am. Bd. Surgery. Intern Doctor's Hosp., Washington, 1944; fellow in surgery Mayo Clinic, Rochester, Minn., 1944-45, 47-52; instr. surgery Mayo Grad. Sch. Medicine, 1954-59, asst. prof. surgery, 1959-65, assoc. prof. surgery, 1965-70, prof. surgery, 1970-83, prof. surgery emeritus, 1983—. Surg. cons. to surgeon gen. U.S. Army, 1965-75; surg. lectr., USSR, 1987, 89, Japan, 1988, 90, Egypt, 1990; lectr. Soviet-Am. seminars, USSR, 1987, 89. Sr. author: Cancer of the Stomach, 1964, Manual of Upper Gastro-intestinal Surgery, 1985; editor: Problems in General Surgery, Surgery of the Biliary Tract, 1986; mem. editorial bd. Rev. Surgery, 1965-75, Jour. Lancet, 1968-77; contbr. 200 articles to profl. jours. Served to capt. U.S. Army, 1945-47 Recipient St. Francis surg. award St. Francis Hosp., Pitts., 1976, Disting. Svc. award Alumni Council, U. Richmond, 1976, Dist. Alumnus award Mayo Found., 2000. Mem. ACS, AAAS, Am. Assn. History of Medicine, AMA, Am. Med. Writers Assn., Am. Soc. Colon and Rectal Surgeons, Soc. Surgery Alimentary Tract (v.p. 1983-84), Am. Surg. Assn., Assn. Mil. Surgeons U.S., Internat. Soc. Surgery, Digestive Disease Found., Priestley Soc. (pres. 1968-69), Central Assn. Physicians and Dentists (pres. 1972-73), Central Surg. Assn., Soc. Med. Cons. Armed Forces, Mayo Clinic Surg. Soc. (chmn. 1964-66), Soc. Head and Neck Surgeons, Soc. Surg. Oncology, So. Surg. Assn., Western Surg. Assn. (pres. 1979-80), Minn. State Med. Assn., Minn. Surg. Soc. (pres. 1966-67), Zumbro Valley Med. Soc., Sigma Xi; hon. mem. Colombian Coll. Surgeons, St. Paul Surg. Soc., Flint Surg. Soc., Venezuelan Surg. Soc., Colombian Soc. Gastroenterology, Dallas So. Clin. Soc., Ga. Surg. Soc., Soc. Postgrad. Surgeons Los Angeles County, Japanese Surg. Soc., Argentine Surg. Digestive Soc., Bassanese Surg. Assn. (Italy), Tex. Surg. Soc., Omicron Delta Kappa, Alpha Omega Alpha, Beta Beta Beta, Kappa Sigma. Methodist. Avocations: hunting, fishing, golf, photography, boating, music. Home: Sawgrass Players Club 8212 Seven Mile Dr Ponte Vedra Beach FL 32082-3129

REMINGER, RICHARD THOMAS, lawyer, artist; b. Cleve., Apr. 3, 1931; s. Edwin Carl and Theresa Henrietta (Bookmyer) Reminger; m. Billie Carmen Greer, June 26, 1954; children: Susan Greer, Patricia Allison, Richard Thomas. AB, Case-Western Res. U., 1953; JD, Cleve. State U., 1957. Bar: Ohio 1957, Pa. 1978, U.S. Supreme Ct. 1961. Pers. and safety dir. Motor Express, Inc., Cleve., 1954-58; mng. ptnr. Reminger & Reminger Co., L.P.A., 1958-90. Mem. nat. claims coun. adv. bd. Comml. Union Assurance Co., 1980—90; lectr. transp. law Fenn Coll., 1960—62; lectr. bus. law Case Western Res. U., 1962—64; lectr. products liability U. Wirtschaft at Schloss Gracht, Erfstadt-Liblar, Germany, 1990—91, Bar Assn. City of Hamburg, Germany, 1990; mem. faculty Nat. Inst. Trial Advocacy, 1992. Trustee Cerebral Palsy Assn., 1984—87, Cleve. Zool. Soc., Andrew Sch., 1984—96, Meridia Huron Hosp., Cleve., 1978—96, Cleve. Sch. Blind, 1987—88, Intracoastal Health Sys., Palm Beach, Fla., 1992—2000; mem. joint com. Cleve. Acad. Medicine-Greater Cleve. Bar Assn.; v.p. Cleve. Zool. Soc. With AC USNR, 1950—58. Mem.: FBA, ABA (profl. responsiblity com. 1977—90, com. law and medicine), Palm Beach County Bar Assn., Internat. Ins. Law Soc., 8th Jud. Bar Assn. (life Ohio dist.), Am. Coll. Law and Medicine, Maritime Law Assn., Def. Rsch. Inst., Am. Judicature Soc., Ohio Assn. Civil Trial Attys., Soc. Ohio Hosp. Attys., Am. Soc. Hosp. Attys., Cleve. Assn. Civil Trial Attys., Transp. Lawyers Assn., Cleve. Bar Assn. (prof. liability com. 1977—90, chmn. med. legal com. 1978—79), Pa. Bar Assn., Ohio Bar Assn. (coun. dels. 1987—90, internat. law com. 1990—91), Internat. Bar Assn., Fedn. Ins. and Corp. Counsel, Internat. Soc. Marine Painters (profl. mem., v.p.), Oil Painters Am., Soc. Four Arts, Cleve.-Marshall Law Alumni Assn. (hon. trustee 1980—), Univ. Club (N.Y.C.), Salmagundi Club (N.Y.C.), Rolling Rock Club (Pa.), Kirtland Country Club (Cleve.), Everglades Club (Fla.), Lost Tree Club (Fla., bd. govs. 1991—94), Hermit Club (pres. 1973—75), Union Club, Mayfield Country Club (pres. 1980—82), Case Res. Athletic Club (life). E-mail: monhegan1@aol.com.

REMINGTON, DEBORAH WILLIAMS, artist; b. Haddonfield, N.J., June 25, 1935; d. Malcolm Van Dyke and Hazel Irwin (Stewart) R. BFA, San Francisco Art Inst., 1957. Adj. prof. art Cooper Union, N.Y.C., 1973-97, NYU, 1994—98. One-woman shows include Dilexi Gallery, San Francisco, 1962, 63, 65, San Francisco Mus. Art, 1964, Bykert Gallery, N.Y.C., 1967, 69, 72, 74, Galerie Darthea Speyer, Paris, 1968, 71, 73, 92, Pyramid Gallery, Washington DC, 1973, 76, zola-Leiberman Gallery, Chgo., 1976, Hamilton Gallery, N.Y.C., 1977, Portland (Oreg.) Ctr. for Visual Arts, 1977, Michael Berger Gallery, Pitts., 1979, Mary Ryan Gallery, N.Y.C., 1982, Ramon Osuna Gallery, Washington D.C., 1983, Newport Harbor Art Mus., 1983, Oakland (Calif.) Mus., 1984, Jack Shainman Gallery, N.Y.C., 1987, Shoshana Wayne Gallery, L.A., 1988, Mitchell Algus Gallery, N.Y.C., 2001; group shows include Whitney Mus. Am. Art, N.Y.C., 1965, 67, 72, San Francisco Mus. Art, 1956, 60, 61, 63, 64, 65, Lausanne Mus., Switz., 1966, Fondation Maeght, St. Paul de Vence, France, 1968, Smithsonial Inst., Washington, D.C., 1968, Art. Inst., Chgo., 1974, Inst. Contemporary Art, Boston, 1975, Nat. Gallery Modern Art, Lisbon, Portugal, 1981, Toledo Mus. Art, 1975, The 6 Gallery, 1954-57, Natsoulas Gallery, Davis, Calif., 1990, 1st Trienalle des Ameriques Maubeuge, France, 1993, Tamarind Inst. Retrospective, 2000, Worcester (Mass.) Art Mus., 2001, San Jose (Calif.) Mus. Art, 2002, numerous others; represented in permanent collections Whitney Mus. Am. Art, Nat. Mus. Am. Art, Washington, Art Inst., Chgo., Centre d'Art et de Culture Georges Pompidou, Paris, Carnegie Mus., Pitts. Recipient Hassam and Speicher Purchase award Am. Acad. and Inst. Arts and Letters, 1988; NEA fellow, 1979-80; Tamarind Inst. fellow, 1973; Guggenheim fellow, 1984; Pollock-Krasner Found. grantee, 1999. Mem. Nat. Acad. Design. Home: 309 W Broadway New York NY 10013-5325 *Be aware of yourself, aware of what makes you distinctive from others, and make those individual characteristics part of your work, whatever that may be. Read philosophy. Develop your own. This gives you ballast when the pendulum swings too far in one direction.*

REMINGTON, MARY, artist, author; b. Kansas City, Mo., Jan. 15, 1930; d. Edwin Jennings and Mary Pauline (Remington) Anderson; m. Robert Alan Smith, Dec. 14, 1957 (div. 1978); 1 child, Susanah Mara Smith. BA, Ottawa (Kans.) U., 1951; postgrad., U. Kans., 1951, Kansas City Art Inst. Artist animation dept. Walt Disney Prodns., Burbank, Calif., 1954-58; pvt. cartoonist, 1977-92; humor and cartooning tchr. Mira Costa Coll. Extension course, 1992; tchr. So. Oreg. U., 1993. Freelance cartoonist, caricaturist, Calif., Oreg. Author: Long Ago Elf, 1968, Crocodiles Have Big Teeth All Day, 1970; artist: paintings of landscapes, protraits, still lifes exhibited nationally. Mem. Grants Pass Art Museum. Avocations: theology, interior design, reading, history, politics. Studio: 1002 NW Lawnridge Ave Grants Pass OR 97526-1106

REMINGTON, PAUL JAMES, mechanical engineer, educator; b. Plainfield, N.J., Mar. 19, 1943; s. Elmer Joseph and Genevieve Leona (Kehoe) R.; m. Lynne Louise Harris, Aug. 21, 1965; children: Christopher, Alexander. BSME, MSME, MIT, 1966, PhD, 1970. Prin. engr. BBN Techs. (Verizon Comm.), Cambridge, Mass., 1969—; adj. prof. mech. engring. Boston U., 1995. Vis. lectr. Tufts U., Medford, Mass., 1979; vis. scientist Tech. U. Berlin, 1990; organizer 3rd Internat. Workshop on Rlwy. and Tracked Transit System Noise, 1981. Contbr. chpts. to: Handbook of Machine Design, 1986, Transportation Noise Reference Book, 1987, Encyclopedia of Acoustics, 1997, Noise and Vibration from High Speed Trains, 2001, also articles to profl. publs. Recipient Cert. of Recognition, NASA, 1976, Excellence in Presentation award Soc. Automotive Engrs., 1984. Fellow Acoustical Soc. Am. (assoc. editor jour. 1982-2001, nominee Biennial award 1977); mem. ASME, Tau Beta Pi, Pi Tau Sigma (pres. 1964-65). Achievements include development of basic understanding of rolling noise generation, development of approaches for controlling wheel/rail noise from trains; 3 patents in field. Avocations: hiking, downhill and cross-country skiing, tennis, cabinet making. Office: BBN Technologies 10 Moulton St Cambridge MA 02138-1119 E-mail: premington@bbn.com.

REMINGTON, THOMAS FREDERICK, political science educator; b. Pitts., Dec. 11, 1948; s. Thomas Frederick and Frances (Hartwell) R.; m. Nancy Roth, June 16, 1974; 1 child, Alexander Frederick. BA, Oberlin Coll., 1970; MA, Yale U., 1974, PhD, 1978. Asst. prof. polit. sci. Emory U., 1978-84, assoc. prof., 1984-89, prof., 1989—. Author: Building Socialism in Bolshevik Russia, 1984, Truth of Authority, 1988, Politics in Russia, 1999; co-author: The Politics of Institutional Choice: Formation of the Russian State Duma, 2000. Mem. Nat. Coun. for Eurasian and East European Rsch. (bd. dirs. 1998—). Home: 1002 Clifton Rd NE Atlanta GA 30307-1228 Office: Emory U Dept Polit Sci Atlanta GA 30322 Fax: 404-727-4586. E-mail: polstfr@emory.edu.

REMINICK, MARSHAL SCOTT, intensivist, pulmonologist; b. N.Y.C., Dec. 26, 1954; s. Arnold Jerome and Mildred (Rosenow) R.; m. Jennifer Marguerite Isaac, Aug. 11, 1983; children: Drew, Lorne, Kyle. BS, BA, Syracuse U., 1976; MD, St. George's U., 1982. Diplomate Am. Bd. Internal Medicine, Am. Bd. Pulmonary Medicine, Am. Bd. Critical Care Medicine. Med. dir. respiratory care L.I. Coll. Hosp., Bklyn., 1988-97; chief of pulmonary Bklyn. Hosp. Ctr., 1997—. Fellow Am. Coll. of Chest Physicians; mem. Am. Thoracic Soc., Soc. of Critical Care Medicine, Nat. Assn. of Med. Dirs. of Respiratory Care. Avocations: husband/father, computer science, photography, reading. Office: The Bklyn Hosp Ctr 121 Dekalb Ave Brooklyn NY 11201-5425

REMLEY, R. DIRK, English educator, consultant; b. Cleve., July 27, 1964; s. Roland E. and Anna Marie Remley. BA, Bowling Green State U., 1986, MA, 1988. Lectr. Kent (Ohio) State U., 1990—; prin. Strategic Market Consulting Group, Ravenna, Ohio, 1994—. Author: The Red Notebook, 1998, Snapshots of Americana, 1999, In Transit, 1999; contbr. articles to profl. jours. Lector Immaculate Conception Ch., Ravenna, 1997—; vol. Meals on Wheels, Chagrin Falls, Ohio, 1996-97; mem. com. Playhouse Square Ptnrs., Cleve., 1992-96. Mem. MLA, Dante Soc. Am. Office: Kent State U Dept English Kent OH 44242-0001

REMMEN, LAWRENCE P. city planner; b. Detroit Lakes, Minn., Oct. 21, 1958; s. Palmer H. and Lois D. (Brown) R.; m. Kellie R. Newton, June 21, 1980; children: Grant Newton, Cole Nicolai. BA in Geography and City Planning, Moorhead State U., 1981; M in Cmty. and Regional Planning, N.D. State U., 1983. Planning asst. City of Moorhead, 1980-83, cmty. devel. planner, 1983, planning dir., 1983-86; planning cons. Detroit Lakes, Minn., 1986-89; cmty. devel. dir. City of Henning, 1989-90, City of Detroit Lakes, 1990—. Planning cons. Detroit Lakes, 1986-89; exec. dir. Becker Lakes Indsl. Devel. Corp., Detroit Lakes, 1990—. Den leader Boy Scouts of Am., Detroit Lakes, 1997—; ch. coun. First Luth. Ch., 1997—; pres. Geography Club, Moorhead State U., 1980-81. Mem. Am. Inst. Cert. Planners (Nat. Outstanding Planning Student award 1983), Am. Planning Assn., Minn. Planning Assn., Econ. Devel. Assn. of Minn., Mid-Am. Econ. Devel. Coun., Urban Land Inst. Republican. Lutheran. Avocations: music, history, refinishing antiques, snow sculpture, sailing. Office: City of Detroit Lakes 1025 Roosevelt Ave Detroit Lakes MN 56501-3637 Home: 1228 Summit Ave Detroit Lakes MN 56501-3802

REMNICK, DAVID J. journalist, editor; b. Hackensack, N.J., Oct. 29, 1958; s. Edward C. and Barbara (Seigel) R.; m. Esther B. Fein; children: Alexander, Noah, Natasha. AB, Princeton U., 1981. Reporter The Washington Post, 1982-91; staff writer The New Yorker, N.Y.C., 1992—, editor, 1998—. Vis. fellow Coun. Fgn. Rels., N.Y.C., 1992-94. Author: Lenin's Tomb: The Last Days of the Soviet Empire, 1993 (Pulitzer Prize for gen. non-fiction 1994, George Polk award 1994), Resurrection, 1997, The Devil Problem, 1997, King of the World, 1998. Recipient Livingston award, 1991, Helen Bernstein award N.Y. Pub. Libr., 1994. Office: The New Yorker 4 Times Sq New York NY 10036-6561

REMY, RAY, management and public affairs consultant; b. San Francisco, June 17, 1937; s. Lucien Albert and Josephine Ann R.; m. Sandra Phyllis Shortridge, Jan. 19, 1963; children: Kimber Lynn Remy Edwards, Erin Christine Petrossi. AB, Claremont McKenna Coll., 1959; MPA, U. Calif., Berkeley, 1963. Adminstrv. intern Berkeley City Mgr.'s Office, 1961-62; asst. to dir. League Calif. Cities, L.A., 1962-69; exec. dir. So. Calif. Assn. Govts., 1969-76; dep. mayor City of L.A., 1976-84; pres. L.A. Area C. of C., 1984-97; exec. dir. State of Calif. Employment Devel. Dept., 1997-99; pres. RR Cons., 1999—. Mem. L.A. County Transp. Commn., L.A., 1976—92; Calif. Trust for the Environment, 1976—; trustee Claremont (Calif.) McKenna Coll., 1989—; mem. bd. govs. Rose Inst. State and Local Govt., 1990—; chair Calif. Goods Movement Com., Sacramento, 1992—94; nat. pres. Am. Soc. Pub. Adminstrn., Washington, 1980; mem. adv. bd. U. So. Calif. Sch. Pub. Policy and Devel. Sgt. U.S. Army, 1960—66. Recipient Don Stone award for Intergovtl. Mgmt., Bowron award U. So. Calif., 1984, Am. Soc. Pub. Adminstrn., 1982, Earl Warren award Am. Soc. Pub. Adminstrn., 1986, Disting. Alumni of Yr. award Claremont McKenna Coll., 1992. Fellow Newcomen Soc.; mem. Nat. Acad. for Pub. Adminstrn., Calif. Assn. for Ind. Colls. (mem. exec. com. 1995—), Calif. Club, Flintridge Golf Club. Avocations: tennis, golf, reading, teaching. Home: 1621 Oak St South Pasadena CA 91030-4714

REN, CHUNG-LI, engineer; b. Chefoo, China, June 1, 1931; came to U.S., 1955; s. Shantsai and Fooching (Wang) R.; m. Rosalie Fen Lo, Aug. 4, 1962; children: Eric W., Caroline W. BSEE, Taiwan Coll. Engring., 1953; MSEE, U. Notre Dame, 1957; PhD in Electro Physics, Polytech Inst. Bklyn., 1964. Teaching asst. U. Notre Dame, South Bend, Ind., 1956-57; grad. asst., sr. lectr. Polytech Inst. Bklyn., Microwave Rsch. Inst., 1959-65; disting. mem. tech. staff AT&T Bell Labs., North Andover, Mass., 1965-90; lead engr. Mitre Corp., Advanced Satellite Terminals and Tech., Bedford, 1990-95; microwave cons., 1996—. Chmn. tech. session Asia-Pacific Microwave Conf., Taiwan, 1993; spkr. and panelist in field. Patentee in field; contbr. articles to profl. jours. Rsch. fellow Polytech Inst. Bklyn., 1957-59. Mem. IEEE (sr., mem. review bd. 1982—,), Sigma Xi. Avocations: tennis, soccer, classical music, landscape design.

REN, HONG-WEN, physicist, materials scientist; b. Jinan, Shandong, China, Oct. 25, 1964; came to the U.S., 1999—; s. Yun-Qing and Fa-Ying (Yao) R.; m. Yan Zhao, Aug. 16, 1987; 1 child, Kuo. BSc, Shandong U., Jinan, China, 1984, MSc, 1987, PhD, 1990. Lectr. Shandong U., 1990-92, assoc. prof., 1993-94; postdoctoral fellow U. Tokyo, 1994-96; rsch. scientist Japan Sci. and Tech. Corp., Tsukuba, 1996-99; sr. rsch. scientist Space Vacuum Epitaxy Ctr., U. Houston, 1999-2000, Applied Optoelectronics Inc., 2000—. Contbr. articles to profl. jours. Japan Soc. for Promotion of Sci. postdoctoral fellow, 1994-96. Mem. AAAS, Am. Phys. Soc., Sigma Xi. Office: Applied Optoelectronics Inc 13111 Jess Pirtle Blvd Sugar Land TX 77478 Fax: 281-295-1888. E-mail: hwren@ao-inc.com.

REN, JIAN-FANG, echocardiologist, medical educator; b. Shanghai, Feb. 27, 1937; came to U.S., 1982; s. Dao-Yuan and De-Xin (Sun) R.; m. He Tong, Jan. 13, 1963; 1 child, Kenna. MD, Zhe-Jiang Med. U., Hangzhou, China, 1960. Cert. Am. Registry Diagnostic Cardiac Sonographer. Rsch. dr. Inst. Ocupl. Hygiene, Beijing, 1963-72; attending dr. Beijing Rlwy. Gen. Hosp., 1972-81; sr. investigator Likoff Cardiovasc. Inst. Hahnemann U., Phila., 1982-84; chief physician, dir. diagnostic ultrasound divsn. Beijing Rlwy. Gen. Hosp., 1984-88; prof. medicine Shanghai Rlwy. Med. Coll., 1985-88; prof., faculty cardiology fellow Third Tchg. Hosp., Beijing Med. U., 1988; rsch. prof. medicine Likoff Cardiovasc. Inst. Hahnemann U., Phila., 1988-92; dir. ultrasound rsch., adj. prof. medicine Phila. Heart Inst., Presbyn. Med. Ctr., U. Pa., 1993-95; rsch. prof. medicine Hahnemann divsn. Allegheny U. Hosps., Phila., 1996-98; rsch. assoc. exptl. and clin. electrophysiology labs. Hosp. U. Pa., 1999—2001, sr. rsch. investigator, 2002—. Adv. prof. medicine Nanjing (China) Rlwy. Med. Coll., 1985-88. Author: (book chpts.) Practical Cardiology, 1993, Doppler Echocardiography, 1993; contbr. articles to profl. jours. including Chinese Jour. Cardiology, Am. Heart Jour., Jour. Am. Coll. Cardiology, Am. Jour. Cardiology, Circulation, Echocardiography, PACE, Ultrasound in Medicine and Biology, Jour. Cardiovas. Electrophysiology. Recipient Pioneer award World Fedn. Ultrasound in Medicine and Biology and Am. Inst. Ultrasound in Medicine, 1988. Fellow Am. Coll. Cardiology; Internat. Cardiac Doppler Soc. (bd. dirs. 1986-91), Soc. Ultrasound in Medicine of Chinese Med. Assn. (pres. 1986-91), Asian Fedn. Socs. for Ultrasound in Medicine and Biology (councillor, v.p., pres. 1985-93). Achievements include advanced research on diagnostic ultrasound cardiovascular diseases; recent contributions to development of intracardiac catheter echocardiography. Office: Cardiac Electrophysiology Rsch Lab Divsn Cardio Med MSRL Bldg Presbyn Med Ctr 39th & Market Sts Philadelphia PA 19104 E-mail: jfren@mail.med.upenn.edu.

REN, JIYU, library director; b. Pingyuan County, Shandong, China, Apr. 15, 1916; s. Zijiu and Guofang (Song) R.; m. Zhong Yun Feng, Sept. 15, 1946; children: Ren Yuan, Ren Zhong. Student, Beijing U., 1934-37; BA, Southwest Union U., Kun Ming, China, 1938; MA, Southwest Union U., 1939-42. Lectr. philosophy dept. Southwest Union U., 1946-49; assoc. prof. philosophy dept. Beijing U., 1949-56, prof. philosophy dept., 1956-64; dir. Inst. for World Religion Study Chinese Acad. Social Scis., Beijing, 1964-87; dir. Nat. Libr. of China, 1987—. Author: Re-Explanation of Philosophy, 1981; editor: History of Chinese Philosophy, vols. 1-4, 1963-79 (Nat. Excellent Textbook spl. prize 1987), Chinese History of Buddhism, Vols. 1-3, 1984, The Complete Collections of Buddhism, Vols. 106 (Zhung Hwa Da Zangjing), 1984-93, History of Chinese Taoism, 1990, Religion Dictionary, 1981, (100 books) The Historical Knowledge of Chinese Culture Series, 1998; co-editor: Abstracts of Classical Works of Daoism, 1991, Selected Essays of Ren Jiyu, 1991, Ren Jiyu's Essays on Philosophy and Religion, 1996, Relations Between God and Man, 1998, Great Religion Dictionary, 1998, Great Buddhism Dictionary, 2002; mem. editl. bd. Chinese Ency., philosophy vol., 1987. Rep. Nat. People's Congress 1980, 84, 88, 92. Mem. Chinese Religion Soc. (dir.), Chinese Soc. Philosophy History (pres.), Chinese Libr. Soc. (dir.), Chinese Inst. of Tibetan Buddhists. Mem. Communist Party of China. Home: Sanlihe Rd 100045 Beijing China Office: Nat Libr of China 39 Baishiqiao Rd 100081 Beijing China

REN, XING JIAN, physician; b. Shanghai, China, June 27, 1961; s. Yun Feng Ren and Xin Yi Zhang; m. Bei Xie, June 27, 1990; 1 child, Oriana Leigh. MD, Shanghai First Med. Coll., 1984. Diplomate internal medicine and geriatric medicine Am. Bd. Internal Medicine. Resident in surgery Shanghai Ruhui Hosp., China, 1984-85; resident Ft. Wayne (Ind.) Med. Edn. Program, 1993-94; resident, intern in medicine Loyola U. of Chgo., Maywood, Ill., 1994-97; fellow in medicine Harvard Med. Sch., Boston, 1997-99; staff physician Scripps Clinic Found., La Jolla, Calif., 1999—. Co-author: Virology, 1986; contbr. articles to profl. jours. Fellow Harvard Med. Sch., 1998; recipient 1st prize Nat. Med. Student Competition for Knowledge of Med. Lit., 1983, grad. student scholarship U. N.C., Chapel Hill, scholarship Carolina Biotechnolgoy Ctr., others. Mem. AMA, Mass. Med. Soc., Am. Geriatrics Soc., Fell. Am. Coll. Physician.

RENARD, DEBORAH ELAINE, psychologist, counselor; b. Memphis, May 18, 1956; BA, Kalamazoo Coll., 1982; MA, Western Mich. U., 1994, PhD, 2001. Lic. profl. counselor, Mich.; lic. ltd. psychologist, Mich. Mem. staff Cmty. Mental Health Ctrs., Kalamazoo, 1978-93; group home coord. Residential Opportunities, Inc., 1983-93; intern in psychology cmty. mental health bd. Clinton, Eaton, Ingham Counties, Mich., 1997-98; pvt. practice, 1998—; asst. prof. dept. ednl. psychology U. Wis., Milw., 2001—. Instr. Kalamazoo Valley C.C., 1997, Western Mich. U., 1998-01, Eastern Mich. U., 1999; counselor Univ. Substance Abuse Clinic, Kalamazoo, 2000-01. Active HIV Prevention Planning group, Mich., 1995-01; vol. ARC Disaster Mental Health Svcs., 2000-. Mem. APA, ACA, Mich. Counseling Assn., Mich. League Handweavers, Weaver's Guild Kalamazoo, Phi Kappa Phi. Avocations: weaving, bead work, gardening. E-mail: renard@uwm.edu.

RENARD, KENNETH GEORGE, retired civil engineer; b. Sturgeon Bay, Wis., May 5, 1934; s. Harry Henry and Margaret (Buechner) R.; m. Virginia Rae Heibel, Sept 8, 1956; children: Kenlynn T., Craig G., Andrew T. BCE, U. Wis., 1957, MCE, 1959; PhD in Civil Engring., U. Ariz., 1972. Registered profl. civil engr., Ariz. Hydraulic engr. Agrl. Rsch. Svc., USDA, Madison, Wis., 1957-59, resident engr. Tombstone, Ariz., 1959-64, rsch. hydraulic engr. Tucson, 1964-72, rsch. leader, 1972-87, rsch. hydraulic engr., 1987-95, collaborator, 1995—; ret. Adj. prof. agrl. and biosys. engring. U. Ariz., Tucson, 1990—. Contbr. articles to profl. jours. Fellow ASCE (pres. Ariz. sect. 1981, exec. com. irrigation and drainage divsn. 1987-94, chair 1990, mgmt. group D 1991-96, editor Jour. Irrigation and Drainage Engring. 1983-85, John C. Park award 1987, Arid Lands Hydraulic Engr. award 1992), Soil Conservation Soc. Am. (pres. Ariz. sect. 1975, Conservationist of Yr. 1983), Am. Geophys. Union; mem. Lions (pres. Tombstone chpt. 1963). Roman Catholic. Home: 4822 E Paseo Del Bac Tucson AZ 85718-6708 Office: USDA Agrl Rsch Svc 2000 E Allen Rd Tucson AZ 85719-1596

RENARD, MEREDITH ANNE, marketing and advertising professional; b. Newark, Apr. 12, 1952; d. W. Edward and Lois E. (Velthoven) Young; m. Robert W. Renard, Nov. 11, 1995. BA, Caldwell Coll., 1974. Advt., pub. rels. asst. Congoleum Corp., Lawrenceville, NJ, 1974-77; account mgr. Saatchi & Saatchi Compton, N.Y.C., 1977-82; dir. advt., sales promotion Singer Sewing Co., Edison, N.J., 1982-86, dir. product mktg., 1986-88, dir. nat. accounts, 1988-90; sr. mktg. rep. Walt Disney World Co., Lake Buena Vista, Fla., 1990-91; div. mktg. rep. Vista Advt., Walt Disney World Co., 1991-92; mgr. advt. Walt Disney World Co., 1992-94, mgr. Fla. tourist mktg., 1994-97; mgr. spl. events Disney Cruise Vacations, Celebration, 1997—; mgr. ops. integration Disney Cruise Line, 2000—02, dir. programming and ops., 2002—, dir. youth activities & ops. integration, 2002—. Contbr. articles to profl. jours. Vol. North Brunswick Dem. Orgn., 1985—87; pub. rels. mgr. Cultural Arts Com., North Brunswick, 1986—87; props chair Adult Drama Group, 1986—87; mem. mktg. com. Vol. Ctr. Ctrl. Fla., 1993—94. Mem.: Ctrl. Fla. Direct Mktg. Assn. (bd. dirs. 1990—92), Fla. Direct Mktg. Assn. Episcopalian. Avocations: cross stitch, reading. Office: Disney Cruise Vacations 210 Celebration Pl Ste 400 Celebration FL 34747-4978

RENARD, PAUL STEVEN, music educator; b. N.Y.C., May 5, 1934; s. Joseph Maurice and Elsie (Wolpow) R. Student, Miami (Fla.) Conservatory, 1947-48, Sch. of Am. Music, 1950-51; cert., Ida Elkan Sch. of Music, 1958. Staff concert organist Hammond Organ Co., N.Y.C., 1950-74; staff organist various TV stas., 1952-61, King Records and Riverside Records, N.Y.C., 1955-64; staff organist, ednl. dir. Lyon-Healy Music Co., Chgo., 1962-72; founder, dir. Paul Renard's Music Dynamics, 1972—. Cons. in field. Co-inventor first electric piano, Wurlitzer Mus. Instruments Co., 1953-54; author (software) Paul Renard's Music Dynamics, 1999; author numerous piano and organ texts; contbr. articles tor profl. jours. Office: 203 N Wabash Ave Ste 1510 Chicago IL 60601-2415

RENAUD, BERNADETTE MARIE ELISE, author; b. Ascot Corner, Que., Can., Apr. 18, 1945; d. Albert and Aline (Audet) R. Diploma, Présentation de Marie, Granby, Que., 1962-64. Librarian asst. Schs. of Waterloo, Que., 1964-67, tchr. primary schs., 1967-70; adminstrv. sec. Assn. Medi-Tech-Sci., Montreal, Que., 1972-76. Author: Emilie La Baignoire A Pattes, 1976 (Can. Coun. Children's Lit. prize, 1976, Assn. Advancement of Scis. and Technics of Documentation award, 1976), Le Chat de l'Oratoire, 1978, Emilie la baignoire á pattes album, 1978, La maison tête de pioche, 1979, La révolte de ala courte pointe, 1979, La dépression de l'ordinateur, 1981, Une boîte Magique Très Embêtante, 1981, La grande question de Tomatelle, 1982, Comment on fait un livre?, 1983, The Cat in the Cathedral, 1983, The Computer Revolts, 1984, (book and movie) Bach et Bottine, 1986 (awards for movie, 19 awards across the world, transl. ino 8 langs., subtitled into 18 langs.), Bach and Broccoli, 1986, Quand l'accent devient grave, 1989, (novels) Une Homme Comme Tant d'Autres, tome 1 1992, tome, III, 1994, Gala des Arts du Bas-Richelieu (QC) (short movie for Nat. Film Bd. Can.); dir., coord.: Ecrire pour la jeunesse, 1990, dir., coord.: La quête de Kurweena, 1997, dir., coord.: CD Le petit violon muet, 1997, dir., coord.: Héritiers de l'éternité, 1998, dir., coord.: Les Funambules D'un Temps Nouveau, 2001; author: short stories, adaptations of 8 children's classics.

RENAUD, BERTRAND M. economist, consultant; b. Argentat, Correze, France, Dec. 28, 1939; arrived in U.S., 1963; s. Pierre Georges Renaud, Jeanne Emerentienne Magnin; m. Young-Key Kim-Renaud; 1 child Nicole-Kyonguan. Engr., INA, Paris, 1962; MS, U. Calif., Berkeley, 1964, PhD, 1966. Asst. prof. U. Hawaii, Honolulu, 1968—75, prof., 1975—76; economist World Bank, Washington, 1976—80, prin. economist, 1983—93, advisor fin. devel., 1993—; head urban affairs divsn. OECD, Paris, 1980—82. Vis. prof., lectr. and fellow Seoul Nat. U., Republic of Korea, 1970, Republic of Korea, 78, MIT, Cambridge, Mass., 1990, U. Hong Kong, 1989, 96, 97; adv. bd. Internat. Union of Housing Fin., London and Chgo., 1995—2001; cons. in field; adj. prof. Korea Devel. Inst., Seoul, 1999—; internat. expert in devel. of fin. systems. Author: National Urbanization, 1980—81, Hawaii Economy, 1969, Hong Kong, 1997, Asia Crisis and Real Estate, 2002. With French Army, 1967—68. Recipient Donald Robertson Meml. award, Urban Studies Bd., U. Glasgow, 1995. Mem.: IUHF, MBA, KAEA, Am. Econ. Assn., Urban Land Inst., AAAS.

RENAUD, PAULA MARIE, researcher; b. Annapolis, Md., Dec. 16, 1963; d. Frederick Albert and Sarah Marie (Chrobak) Renaud; married; 1 child Forest Gabriel. AS, Northwest Coll., Powell, Wyo., 1987; BS, U. Wyo., 2001. Receptionist Buffalo Bill Hist. Ctr., Cody, Wyo., 1983—85; gallery owner Raven's Nest Gallery, Greybull, 1987—89; art salesperson Harry Jackson Studio, Cody, 1990—92; tutor coord. Learning Skills Ctr., Powell, Wyo., 1992—99, adminstrv. asst., 1992—99; archival maintenance State Hist. Preservation Office, Laramie, 2001; rsch. asst. dept. anthropology U. Wyo., 2001—. Presenter in field. Contbr. . Mem. Rocky Mountain Activists, Laramie, 2000—01. Recipient Outstanding Student Paper award, Plains Anthropologist, 2000, Local Soroptomist award, Park County, Wyo., 1997; grantee Arts and Sci. Rsch. grantee, U. Wyo., 2000, McNair Scholars Rsch. grantee, 2000; scholar Paul Crissman scholar, 2001—02, Ronnie Bathrick Meml. scholar, 2001—02, George Frison scholar, 2001—02, Seibold Meml. scholar, 1999—2001, John Christopher Meml. scholar, 1999—2000, forensic scholar, Northwest Coll., 1989, theater scholar, 1988, 1989. Mem.: Nat. Assn. Student Anthropologists, Am. Anthropol. Assn., Am. Soc. for Ethnohistory, Smithsonian Instn. (assoc.), Phi Kappa Phi. Avocations: organic gardening, primitive skills, figure drawing, pottery, theater. Home: 610 S 5th Laramie WY 82070 Office: U Wyo Dept Anthropology PO Box 3431 Ivinson St Laramie WY 82070 Home Fax: 307-766-2473 . E-mail: prenaud@uwyo.edu.

RENAUD, ROBERT (EDWIN RENAUD), college administrator; b. Westmount, Que., Can., Dec. 31, 1952; came to the U.S., 1994; naturalized, 2002; s. Lawrence Joseph and Caroline (Elie) R.; m. Martha Jane Carnegie, Sept. 12, 1987 (div. Jan. 1990); m. Jennifer Stairs, Aug. 7, 1993. AB, Vassar Coll., 1976; MLS, U. Toronto, Ont., Can., 1980. Cataloger McGill U., Montreal, Que., 1976-78; sys. analyst U. Toronto, 1980-84; mgr. sys. Met. Toronto Libr., 1984-90; dep. CEO Markham (Can.) Pub. Libr., 1990-94; dept. head U. Ariz. Libr., Tucson, 1994-98; assoc. dean, information svcs. Conn. Coll., New London, 1998—2001; asoc. dean Dickinson Coll., Carlisle, Pa., 2001—. Contbr. chpt. to book and articles to profl. jours. Scholar Vassar Coll., Poughkeepsie, N.Y., 1973-76; Grad. fellow U. Toronto, 1978-80; Resident fellow Massey Coll.-U. Toronto, 1978-80. Roman Catholic. Avocations: tennis, running, downhill skiing. Office: Waidner-Spahr Libr Box 1773 Carlisle PA 17013

RENBAUM, BARRY JEFFREY, lawyer; b. Balt., Feb. 26, 1948; s. David and Leah (Cohen) R.; m. Carol Barbash, June 22, 1980. BS magna cum laude, Rider U., 1970; postgrad., NYU, 1973; JD, Georgetown U., 1973. Bar: Md. 1973, U.S. Dist. Ct. (Md.), 1998. Jud. clk. to Hon. John C. Eldridge, Md. Ct. Appeals, 1974-75; asst. pub. defender State of Md., 1975-79; exec. v.p., gen. counsel Custom Savs. Bank, Tmple Fin. Co., Balt., 1980-91; pvt. practice Glyndon, Md., 1991—. Mem. ATLA, Md. Bar Assn., Alpha Epsilon Zeta. Office: Brydonwood Glyndon MD 21071-0326 E-mail: brydonwoods@cs.com.

RENBERG, MICHAEL LOREN, lawyer; b. San Francisco, Apr. 9, 1962; s. Charles and Margaret Renberg; m. Shelley Maher, Oct. 19, 1991; children: Kristen, Kyle, Brian, Lauren. BA, UCLA, 1985; JD, U. San Francisco, 1988. Bar: Calif. 1988. Law clk. U.S. Dist. Ct. (ea. dist.) Calif., Fresno, 1988-89; assoc. Adams, Duque & Hazeltine, L.A., 1989-94; ptnr. Parichan, Renberg, Crossman & Harvey, Fresno, 1994—. Mem. Woodward Park Rotary (pres. Fresno 2000-2001). Avocations: basketball, golf. Office: Parichan Renberg Et Al 2350 W Shaw Ave Ste 130 Fresno CA 93711-3400 E-mail: mrenberg@msn.com.

RENCH, STEPHEN CHARLES, lawyer; b. Coffeyville, Kans., Oct. 11, 1930; s. Stephen and Gladys Mae (Carpenter) R.; m. Loraine Pennock, Oct. 11, 1966. BA in Econs., U. Kans., 1952; JD, Georgetown U., 1959. Bar: Colo. 1959, U.S. Dist. Ct. Colo. 1959, U.S. Ct. Appeals (10th cir.) 1961, U.S. Supreme Ct. 1979. Law clk to judge U.S. Ct. Appeals (10th cir.), Denver, 1959; law clk. to chief judge U.S. Dist. Ct. Colo., 1960-61; assoc. Tippit and Haskell, 1961-63; clk. Probate Ct., 1964-65; dep. state pub. defender, 1966-74; tng. dir. Colo. State Pub. Defender System, 1974-77, tng. dir. as ind. contractor tng. seminars, 1980-82; pvt. practice, 1977—. Mem. permanent lecturing faculty for summer sessions and seminars Nat. Coll. Criminal Def., Houston, 1974— , course dir., 1977; instr. trial tactics and strategy, evidence courses U. Denver Law Sch., 1979-91; lectr. in field throughout U.S. Author: Fingertip Law for Colorado Public Defenders, 1975, Strategy for Colorado Public Defenders, 1979, The Rench Book, Trial Tactics and Strategy, 1990, Courtbook, 1982, monthly columnist Trade Secrets of a Trial Lawyer, Washington Memo, 1977-78; contbr. articles to profl. jours. 1st lt. USAF, 1952-56. Mem. ABA, Colo. Trial Lawyers Assn., Colo. Criminal Def. Bar, Nat. Assn. Criminal Def. Lawyers, Nat. Legal Aid and Defenders Assn., Nat. Practice Inst., Assn. Trial Lawyers Am., Denver Bar Assn., Colo. Bar Assn. Office: 580 S Franklin St Denver CO 80209-4502

RENCIS, JOSEPH JOHN, engineering educator, mechanical and civil engineer; b. Denville, N.J., May 19, 1958; s. Joseph John and Leila Jean (Colin) R.; m. Minerva Vasquez, Sept. 14, 1991; 1 child, Christina. AAS in Archtl. & Bldg. Constrn. Engring., Milw. (Wis.) Sch. Engring., 1978, BS in Archtl. & Bldg. Constrn. Engring., 1980; MS in Theoretical & Applied Mechanics, Northwestern U., 1982; PhD in Engring. Mechanics, Case Western Res. U., 1985. Registered profl. engr., Mass. Engring. technician U.S. Army Armament Rsch., Devel. and Engring. Ctr., Picatinny Arsenal, N.J., summer 1979; instr., grader dept. archtl. & bldg. constrn. engring. tech. Milw. (Wis.) Sch. Engring., 1979-80; rsch. asst. dept. civil engring. Northwestern U., Evanston, Ill., 1980-81; rsch. and tchg. asst. dept. civil engring. Case Western Res. U., Cleve., 1982-85; grad. student rschr. Flight Dynamics Lab. Wright-Patterson AFB, Dayton, Ohio, summer 1984; instr. engring. tech. dept. Cuyahoga C.C., Cleve., 1984; asst. prof. mech. engring. dept. Worcester (Mass.) Poly. Inst., 1985-90, assoc. prof. mech. engring. dept., 1990-2000, assoc. prof., Russel M. Searle disting. instr. mech. engring, 1994-95, Russel M. Searle disting. instr. mech. engring., 1994-95, prof. mech. engring., 2000—. Engring. cons. Brooks Sci., Inc., Cambridge, Mass., 1986-89; ASEE-NASA faculty fellow NASA-Lewis Rsch. Ctr., Cleve., summers 1989, 90; rsch. assoc. Phillips Lab., Geophysics Directorate, Space Sys. Tech. br., Hanscom AFB, Mass., summer 1991; mem. adv. bd. for engring. tech. Sussex County Vocat. Tech. H.S., Sparta, N.J., 1994—; mem. adv. bd. Sussex County Engring. and Design Acad., 1997—. Mem. editl. bd. Boundary Elements Commn., 1989—, Engring. Analysis with Boundary Elements, 1993—; asssoc. editor Advances in Boundary Elements, 1996—; contbr. articles to profl. jours. Recipient Class of 1980 Outstanding Alumni award Milw. (Wis.) Sch. Engring., 1990, Citizen of the Yr. award West Boylston (Mass.) Sch. Sys., 1992; Walter P. Murphy fellow Northwestern U., Evanston, 1980-81; Wessex Inst. of Great Britian fellow, 2000. Fellow ASME (sec. Ctrl. Mass. sect. 1988-89, vice-chair 1989-90, chair 1990-92), Wessex Inst. of Gt. Britain; mem. ASCE (structural divsn. com. on electronic computation, subcom. on personal computers and work stas. 1986-91), Internat. Soc. for Boundary Elements (sci. steering com. 1989—), Am. Soc. Engring. Edn. (chair mechanics divsn. 1999-2000), Am. Acad. Mechanics, Internat. Assn. for Boundary Element Methods, Pi Tau Sigma, Tau Omega Mu. Roman Catholic. Achievements include pioneering work on error estimation and self-adaptive mesh refinement technique for Boundary Element Method; research on iterative/direct equation solving strategies for Boundary Element Method. Home: 2 Keep Ave Paxton MA 01612-1038 Office: Worcester Poly Inst Mech Engring Dept 100 Institute Rd Worcester MA 01609-2247

RENDA, DOMINIC PHILLIP, airline executive; b. Steubenville, Ohio, Dec. 25, 1913; s. Joseph J. and Catherine (Roberta) R.; m. Delores E. Noland, July 12, 1980; children: Dominique Patricia, Dominic Phillip, Patrick Blake. BS in Bus. Adminstrn; JD, Ohio State U., 1938. Bar: Ohio 1938. Practice law, Steubenville, 1938-41; adminstrv. asst. to mem. Congress, 1941-42; with Western Air Lines, Inc., Los Angeles, 1946-68, asst. sec., 1947, v.p. legal, 1954-65, sr. v.p. legal, corp. sec., 1958-68; pres. Air Micronesia, Inc., Los Angeles, 1968-73; sr. v.p. internat. and pub. affairs Continental Air Lines, Inc., 1968-73; exec. v.p., dir., mem. exec. com. Western Air Lines, 1973-76, pres., mem. exec. and nominating coms., 1976-81, chief exec. officer, mem. mgmt. resources and compensation com., 1979-81, chmn. bd., 1981, emeritus chmn., 1982-85. Dir. Bank of Montreal, Calif.; Mem. bus. adminstrn. adv. council Coll. Adminstrv. Sci., Ohio State U., 1974-82; bd. councilors Sch. Internat. Relations, U. So. Calif., 1967-82 Trustee Peace Found., Ponape, Caroline Islands, 1976-84; chmn. devel. com. Marymount High Sch., 1977-82. Served to lt. comdr. USNR, 1942-46. Mem. Calif., Ohio state bars, ABA, Los Angeles County Bar Assn. (past trustee), Calif. C. of C. (dir.), Phi Alpha Delta (pres. Los Angeles 1965-66) Clubs: Los Angeles Chancery (pres. 1966-67), Morningside Country Club, Rancho Mirage.

RENDA, PATRICK BLAKE, investment company executive; b. Santa Monica, Calif., July 19, 1968; s. Dominic P. and Patricia Renda; m. Karen Suzanne Krieger, Nov. 28, 1998. BA, U. So. Calif., 1991. Prodn. mgr. NBC, Burbank, Calif., 1991-93; paralegal Fragomen, Del Rey, Bernsen & Loewy, Palo Alto, 1994-96; v.p., investment officer J&W Seligman & Co., 1996—. Named among Best of Buyside 2000, Instl. Investor Mag. Mem.: Balboa Bay Club. Republican. Roman Catholic. Avocations: athletics, music, travel. Office: J&W Seligman & Co 101 University Ave Palo Alto CA 94301-1622 Fax: 650-330-1015. E-mail: rendap@jwseligman.com.

RENDA, ROSA A. special education educator; b. Jamaica, N.Y., Nov. 03; d. Liborio and Josephine (Finamore) Lombardo; m. Philip F. Renda, Mar. 30, 1980; children: Felicia-Anne, Philip Jr. BA, Molloy Coll., 1971; MEd, St. John's U., Jamaica, N.Y., 1973; postgrad., L.I. U., 1977. Tchr., asst. prin. St. Rose of Lima, Massapequa, N.Y., 1967-73, Acad. of St. Joseph, Brentwood, 1973-79; tchr. Sewanhaka H.S., Floral Park, 1979-81, Queen of the Rosary Acad., Amityville, 1981-86, Blessed Trinity, Ocala, Fla., 1987-93, math. coord., 1993-94; S.E.D. tchr. Emerald Ctr., 1994; tchr./children's supr. for the emotionally/mentally disturbed Marion Citrus Mental Health, 1994-96; tchr. for autistic children Maplewood Sch., 1996-97; tchr. math. Lake Weir H.S., 1997-99; pres. North Marion Mid. Sch. for Emotionally Handicapped, Citra, Fla., 1999—2001. Author: Teaching Metrics, 1975. Vol. Nassau County Rep. Club, Hempstead, N.Y., 1974-76. Mem. ASCD, NEA, Nat. Coun. Tchrs. Math., Nat. Cath. Edn. Assn., Marion Edn. Assn., Nassau/Suffolk Math. Tchrs., Women of the Moose, Columbiettes, K.C. Aux. Roman Catholic. Avocations: reading, swimming, gourmet cooking. E-mail: twofar85@aol.com.

RENDAL, CAMILLE LYNN, artist; BFA, Otis Parsons Sch. Design, L.A., 1981; MFA, N.Mex. State U., 1996. Art educator, dept. chmn. Crossroads Sch. for the Arts & Scis., Santa Monica, Calif., 1981-88; profl. artist L.A., 1984—; art prof. N.Mex. State U., Las Cruces, 1993-96; art prof., gallery dir. Columbia Basin Coll., Pasco, Wash., 1998-2000; prof. sculpture Ctrl. Mich. U., Mt. Pleasant, 2000—; prof. art Roger Williams U., 2002—. Artist posters; created commemorative postage stamp Halley's Comet, 1985. Recipient Kay Neilsen Young Talent award, L.A. County Museum of Art, 1980, Cert. for Inspired Teaching, Nat. Found. for Advancement in Arts, N.Y.C., 1989; scholarship Parsons Sch. Design, L.A., 1980, 81. Mem. Rosicrucian Order.

RENDELL, EDWARD GENE, mayor, lawyer; b. N.Y.C., Jan. 5, 1944; s. Jesse T. and Emma (Sloat) R.; m. Marjorie Osterlund, July 10, 1971; 1 son, Jesse Thompson. BA in Polit. Sci., U. Pa., 1965; JD, Villanova U., 1968. Bar: Pa. 1968, U.S. Supreme Ct. 1981. Asst. dist. atty., chief homicide unit Office Dist. Atty., Phila., 1968-74; dep. spl. prosecutor, 1976; dist. atty., 1978-86; mayor City of Phila., 1992—2000. Gen. chmn. Dem. Nat. Com., 1999—2000. 2d lt. USAR, 1968—74. Recipient Man of Yr. award VFW, 1980, Am. Cancer League, 1981, Disting. Pub. Svc. award Pa. County Detectives Assn., 1981. Mem. ABA, Pa. Dist. Attys. Assn. (legis. chmn. 1979—), Phila. Bar Assn., B'nai B'rith, United Jewish Orgns., Jewish War Vets. Office: 1735 Market St Fl 51 Philadelphia PA 19103-7501

RENDELL, KENNETH WILLIAM, rare and historical documents dealer, consultant; b. Boston, May 12, 1943; s. Harry H. and Pauline (Walsh) R.; m. Diana J. Angelo, June 3, 1967 (div. 1985); children: Jeffrey H., Jason J. (dec.); m. Shirley L. McNerney, July 14, 1985; 1 child, Julia Louise. Student, Boston U., 1961-63. Pres. Kingston Galleries, Inc., Somerville, Mass., 1960-67, Kenneth W. Rendell, Inc., Newton, 1967—, Kenneth W. Rendell, Ltd., London, 1970—, Kenneth W. Rendell Gallery, Inc., N.Y.C., Tokyo, 1985—. Bd. dirs. John Wilson Autographs Ltd., London, 1961-75, Charles Ede Gallery Ltd., London, 1976-92; chmn. New England Antiquarian Booksellers Assn., 1975-77; pres. Internat. League Autograph and Manuscript Dealers, 1975-77; cons. numerous univ. librs., govtl. and media orgns. 0uthor: The Fundamentals of Autograph Collecting, 1976, Tax Appraisals of Manuscript Collections, 1983, Changing Concepts of Value and Rarity, 1985, The Hitler Diaries: Bad Forgeries But a Great Hoax, 1986, The Mormon Conman, Forger and Killer, 1987, Other People's Mail: 30 Years As a Dealer in Historical Documents, 1988, The One Hundred Americans Who Have Made America What it is Today, 1989, The Detection of Forged Historical Letters and Documents, 1990, With Weapons and Wits: Propaganda and Psychological Warfare in World War II, 1991, Forging History: The Detection of Fake Historical Letters and Documents, 1994, History Comes to Life, !995; co-editor: Autographs and Manuscripts: A Collector's Manual, 1978 (Outstanding Reference Book award ALA); contbr. numerous articles in field to mags. and profl. jours. Trustee D-Day Mus., New Orleans, 1998, Youth Enrichment Svcs., Boston, 1998, William J. Donovan Meml., N.Y., 1998. Recipient Dept. Justice award, 1991. Fellow Manuscript Soc. (bd. dirs. 1968-74, pres. 1972-74); mem. Assn. Internat. de Bibliophilie Paris, Art and Antique Dealers League Am., Inc., Grolier Club, Union League Club, Army and Navy Club, Am. Antiquarian Soc., Bohemian Club (San Francisco), Appalachian Mountain Club (trustee 2000). Avocation: ski racing. Office: Kenneth W Rendell Inc 46 Eliot St Natick MA 01760-6042 also: 989 Madison Ave New York NY 10021-1825

RENDELL, MARJORIE O. federal judge; m. Edward G. Rendell. BA, U. Pa., 1969; postgrad., Georgetown U., 1970—71; JD, Villanova U., 1973; LLD (hon.) , Phila. Coll. Textile and Sci., 1992. Ptnr. Duane, Morris & Heckscher, Phila., 1972—93; judge U.S. Dist. Ct. (ea. dist.) Pa., 1994—97, U.S. Ct. Appeals (3d cir.), Phila., 1997—. Asst. to dir. ann. giving Dept. Devel. U. Pa., 1973—78; mem. adv. bd. Chestnut Hill Nat. Bank/East Falls Adv. Bd.; mem. alternative dispute resolution com. mediation divsn. Ea. Dist. Pa. Bankruptcy Conf.; active Acad. Vocal Arts, Market St. East Improvement Assn., Pa.'s Campaign for Choice, Phila. Friends Outward Bound; vice chair Ave. of Arts, Inc.; vice chair bd. trustees Vis. Nurse Assn. Greater Phila. Mem.: ABA, Phila. Bar Found. (bd. dirs.), Phila. Bar Assn. (bd. dirs. young lawyers sect. 1973—78), Pa. Bar Assn., Am. Bankruptcy Inst., Internat. Women's Forum, Forum Exec. Women, Phi Beta Kappa. Office: US Courthouse 601 Market St Rm 21613 Philadelphia PA 19106-1715*

RENDER, JOHN CLIFFORD, lawyer; b. Logansport, Ind., Aug. 16, 1943; s. John Clifford and Joan Helen (O'Connor) R.; m. Mary Jane Allison, Aug. 12, 1967 (div. Apr. 1975); children: Allison A. Render Porter, Meredith M.; m. Diane Lois Dougherty, July 30, 1976. BS, Butler U., 1966; JD, Ind. U., 1971. Tchr. English Indpls. Pub. Schs., 1966-69; dir. of planning Ind. Hosp. Assn., Indpls., 1969-71; atty., dir. Hall, Render, Killian, Heath & Lyman, P.C., 1971—. Gen. counsel Ind. Hosp. and Health Assn., Indpls., 1982—; adj. faculty health law Ind. U. Named Sagamore of Wabash, Gov. State of Ind., 1989. Mem. Columbia Club, Skyline Club, Indpls. Athletic Club. Avocations: golf, traveling, reading. Office: Hall Render Killian Heath & Lyman # 2000 One American Sq Indianapolis IN 46282 E-mail: jrender@hrkhl.com.

RENDIN, ROBERT WINTER, environmental health officer; b. Jamaica, N.Y., Oct. 21, 1949; s. Anthony and Gertrude Helen (Winter) R.; m. Janet Elizabeth Meyer, Apr. 8, 1972; children: Cheryl, Valerie, Scott. BS, Rutgers U., 1971; MS in Environ. Health, E. Tenn. State U., 1974; postgrad., U.S. Marine Corps Command & Staff Coll., 1985-86, Tulane U., 1994-95. Commd. lt. (j.g.) USN, 1974, advanced through grades to comdr.; environ. health officer U.S. Naval Hosp., San Diego, 1988, chief preventive medicine Taipei, Taiwan, 1976-78, chief occupational and preventive medicine Great Lakes, Ill., 1978-81; environ. health officer U.S. Navy Atlantic Fleet, Norfolk, Va., 1981-84; chief environ. health svc. Navy Environ. & Preventive Medicine Unit, Virginia Beach, 1984-85; med. planner 1st Marine Force Svc. Support Group, Camp Pendleton, Calif., 1986-87, 4th Marine Div., New Orleans, 1987-90; exec. officer Naval Biodynamics Lab., 1990-92, comdg. officer, 1992-95; dep. dir. preventive medicine and health promotion Navy Environ. Health Ctr., Norfolk, Va., 1995-96, dir. Preventive Medicine, 1996—. Contbr. articles to profl. jours. Decorated Navy Commendation award (2), Meritorious Svc. medal (2); recipient Combined Svc. Hon. award Republic of China, 1977. Mem. U.S. Naval Inst., Nat. Environ. Health Assn. (registered sanitarian), Uniformed Svcs. Environ. Health Assn., Phi Kappa Phi. Lutheran. Home: 646 Edgwood Arch Chesapeake VA 23322-5835 Office: Navy Environ Health Ctr 2510 Walmer Ave Norfolk VA 23513-2601 E-mail: andiamo@series2000.com., rwrendin@mar.med.navy.mil.

RENDL-MARCUS, MILDRED, artist, economist; b. May 30, 1928; d. Julius and Agnes (Hokr) Rendl; m. Edward Marcus, Aug. 10, 1956. BS, NYU, 1948, MBA, 1950; PhD, Radcliffe Coll., 1954. Economist GE, 1953-56, Bigelow-Sanford Carpet Co., Inc., 1956-58; instr. econs. Hunter Coll. CUNY, 1959-60, Columbia U., 1960-61, rschr., 1961-63; sr. economist Nat. Indsl. Conf. Bd., 1963-66; asst. prof. Pace Coll., 1964-66; assoc. prof. Borough of Manhattan C. C. CUNY, 1966-71, prof., 1972-85. Lectr. econs. CCNY, 1953-58; vis. prof. Fla. Internat. U., 1986; bd. dirs. N.Y.C. Coun. on Econ. Edn.; cons. in field. Exhibited group shows at in New Canaan Art Show, 1982-85, Am. Soc. Bus. and Behavioral Scis., 1990-96, New Cannan Soc. for Arts Ann., 1983, 85, New Canaan Arts, 1985, Silvermine Galleries, 1986, Stamford Art Assn., 1987, Phoenix Gallery, 1988, N.Y.C., Parkview Point Gallery, 1982-89, Miami Beach, Fla., 1982-89, Art Complex, New Canaan, Miami Beach, 1985—, Lever House, N.Y.C., 1990, Cork Gallery, Lincoln Ctr., N.Y.C., 1990, Women's Caucus for Art, San Antonio, 1990, Artist's Equity, Broome St. Gallery, N.Y.C., 1991, Greater Hartford Architecture Conservancy, 1991, N.H. Arts Ctr., 1997, Just Originals Art Web, Albuquerque, 1999, Ward-Nasse Gallery, N.Y.C., 2000—, Liliana Fine Art Gallery, Lenox, Mass., 2002; author (with E. Marcus) Investment and Development of Tropical Africa, 1959, International Trade and Finance, 1965, Monetary and Banking Theory, 1965, Economics, 1969, Economic Progress and the Developing World, 1970, Economics, 1978, Fine Art with Many Equilibrium Prices, 1995; editor Women in the Arts Found. Newsletter, 1986-92; contbr. articles to profl. jours. Founder Rendl Fund for Slavic Art, Mus. of Modern Art, N.Y.C., 1999—, Harvard U. Art Mus. Fund for Slavic Art, Cambridge, 2000—, Harvard Mus. Natural History, Peabody Mus. Archeology and Ethnology, Rendl Fund for the Conservation of Slavic Artifacts, 2000—, Rendl Fund for the Conservation of the Ware Collection of Blaschka Glass Models of Plants, 2001—; mem. mus. coun. Harvard Mus. Natural History, 2001—. Recipient Merit award Manhattan Arts Internat., 1998, Excellence award 1998, Artist Showcase award Manhattan Arts Internat., 1999; Dean Bernice Brown Cronkhite fellow Radcliffe Coll., 1950-51, Anne Radcliffe Econ. Rsch. Sub-Sahara Africa fellow, 1958-59; fellow Gerontol. Assn. Mem. AAUW, Internat. Schumpeter Econs. Soc. (founding), Met. Econ. Assns. (sec. 1954-56), Indsl. Rels. Rsch. Assn., Women's Econ. Roundtable (program planning com.), N.Y.C. Women in Arts, Allied Social Sci. Assn. (artist 1994), NYU Grad. Sch. Bus. Adminstrn. Alumni (sec. 1956-58), Radcliffe Club, Women's City Club (art and landmarks com.). Office: Art Complex PO Box 814 New Canaan CT 06840-0814 also: 205 E Harmon Ave Las Vegas NV 89109

RENDON, MARIO IVAN, psychiatrist; b. Medellin, Antioquia, Colombia, May 9, 1938; came to U.S., 1966; s. Jairo and Melania (Cardona) R.; m. Diane Cristine Courchesne, Oct. 4, 1969; children: Adan, Renata. MD, U. Antioquia, 1963. Diplomate Am. Bd. Psychiatry and Neurology, Am. Bd. Child Psychiatry. Intern Hosp. St. Vicente De Paul, Medellin, 1962-63; med. dr. Hosp. Urrao and Andes, 1963-66; resident in psychiatry Fairfield Hills Hosp., Newtown, Conn., 1966-67; resident, fellow in child psychiatry Bellevue Hosp., N.Y.C., 1967-70, faculty, 1970-79; clin. dir. Leake and Watts Children's Home, Yonkers, N.Y., 1979-89; dir. bilingual-bi-cultural Hispanic svc. Bronx Mcpl. Hosp. Ctr., N.Y.C., 1989-90; dir. dept. psychiatry Lincoln Hosp., 1990-97; vis. prof. social medicine AECOM Montefiore, 1981-86; dir. psychiat. ambulatory svcs. Woodhull Hosp., Bklyn., 1998—2001; vice chmn. dept. psychiatry Bronx (N.Y.)-Lebanon Hosp. Ctr., 2001—. Clin. assoc. prof. psychiatry NYU Med. Ctr., 1982-89, AECOM, 1989—; prof. clin. psychiatry N.Y. Med. Coll., 1989-97. Editor Am. Jour. of Psychoanalysis, 1984-91. Fellow Am. Acad. Psychoanalysis; mem. Am. Inst. for Psychoanalysis (dean 2000—), Assn. for Advancement of Psychoanalysis (pres. 1979-81). Home: 333 E 30th St Apt 8L New York NY 10016-6472 Office: 320 E 54th St New York NY 10022-5030 E-mail: mrendon@pol.net.

RENDU, JEAN-MICHEL MARIE, mining executive; b. Tunis, Tunisia, Feb. 25, 1944; s. Paul C. and Solange M. (Krebs) R.; m. Karla M. Meyer, Aug. 18, 1973; children: Yannick P., Mikaël P. Ingénieur des Mines, Ecole des Mines St. Etienne, France, 1966; MS, Columbia U., 1968, D. Engring. Sci., 1971. Mgr. ops. rsch. Anglovaal, Johannesburg, Republic of South Africa, 1972-76; assoc. prof. U. Wis., Madison, 1976-79; assoc. Golder Assocs., Denver, 1979-84; dir. tech. and sci. systems Newmont Mining Corp., Danbury, Conn., 1984-88; v.p. Newmont Gold Co., Denver, 1988-93, Newmont Mining Corp., Denver, 1993-2001; ind. cons., 2001—. Author: An Introduction to Geostatistical Methods of Mineral Evaluation, 1978, 81; contbr. tech. papers to profl. jours. Fellow South African Inst. of Mining and Metallurgy (corr. mem. of coun.), Australasian Inst. Mining and Metallurgy; mem. NAE, Soc. Mining, Metallurgy and Exploration (bd. dirs. 1998—, Jackling award 1994, Pres.'s citation 1993), Sigma Xi. Roman Catholic. Fax: 720-493-8464. E-mail: JMRendu@aol.com.

RENÉ, NICHOLE See SANDS, MARTHA

RENEAU, MARVIN BRYAN, military officer, business educator; b. Wharton, Tex., Jan. 22, 1939; s. Marvin Cecil Reneau and Bessie Marie (Petrash) Ward; m. Doris Faye Martin, Jan. 2, 1957; children: Terran Bryan, Kevin Troy,

Shannon Lyn. BS, U. Tampa, Fla., 1971; MS, Am. Tech. U., U. Cen. Tex., 1978; MA, Webster Coll., 1979, PhD (hon.), 1996. Commd. 2d lt. U.S. Army, 1964; advanced through grade to col. USAR, 1990; co. comdr., armor U.S. Army, Vietnam, 1968, engring. ops. mgr. Tex., chief, tng. support div., 1989, sr. tng. analyst Tex. Cons. U.S. Army C.E., Ft. Worth, 1978—, Army Rsch. Inst., Boise, Idaho, 1987—, Army Tng. Bd., Ft. Monroe, Va., 1987—; asst. prof. bus. Incarnate Word Coll., San Antonio. Author: Beneath the Canopy, 1978, And Where the Rockets Can't Reach, 1993; contbr. articles to profl. jours. Mem. Army Mut. Aid Fund, Arlington, Va., 1968; acad. advisor Incarnate Word Coll., San Antonio, 1981; vol. counselor DAV, San Antonio, 1980; referral agt. United Way, San Antonio, 1988. Comdr. USAR. Decorated Bronze Star, Purple Heart, 3 Meritorious medals, 2 Air medals (1 for valor), 3 Army Commendation medals, Army Achievement medal, Conbar Infantryman badge, Rep. of Vietnam Cross of Gallantry with palm, Legion of Merit, commd. admiral in Tex. Navy; names to Hon. Order Ky. Cols. Mem. Am. Mktg. Assn., ASTD, Assn. U.S. Army, Mil. Order of Purple Heart, NSW Leagues, Fed. Mgrs. Assn., S.W. Mktg. Assn., Res. Officer Assn., Orders and Medals Rsch. of Great Britain, 34th Armor Regiment (disting. mem.), Berlin U.S. Mil. Vets. Assn., 2d Bn. 34th Armor Assn., 25th Inf. Divsn. Assn., Alpha Kappa Psi (sponsor). Methodist. Avocations: researching and collecting historical artifacts. Home: PO Box 39292 San Antonio TX 78218-1292

RENEE, LISABETH MARY, art educator, artist, galley director; b. Bklyn., July 28, 1952; d. Lino P. and Elizabeth M. (Dines) Rivano; m. John S. Witanowski, May 15, 1982. Student, U. Puget Sound, 1972-74; BA in Art, SUNY, Buffalo, 1977; MFA, L.I. U., 1982; EdD, U. Ctrl. Fla., 1996. Cert. art tchr., Fla. Adj. faculty L.I. U., Greenvale, N.Y., 1980-82, Rollins Coll., Winter Park, Fla., 1982; art tchr. Phyllis Wheatley Elem. Sch., Apopka, 1983-85, McCoy Elem. Sch., Orlando, 1985-86, Lake Howell H.S., Winter Park, 1986-93; adj. faculty U. Ctrl. Fla., 1994-95, vis. instr., coord. art edn., 1995-96; gallery dir., prof. West Campus Valencia (Fla.) C.C., 1996-98; owner, designer Nartique, 2002—; dir. Renée Studios, Casselberry, Fla. Adj. faculty Valencia C.C., 1995-96; dir. So. Artists Registry, Winter Park, 1984-87; cons. Fla. Dept. Edn., 1989-90, mem. curriculum writing team for arts edn. program; mem. com. Fla. Bd. Edn. Task Force for Subject Area Subtest of Fla. Tech. Cert. Exam.; visual arts dir. Very Spl. Arts Ctr. Fla. Fest, 1996; presenter at profl. confs. Author: The Phenomenological Significance of Aesthetic Communion, 1996, Co-operative Art, 1991; editor: Children and the Arts in Florida, 1990. Visual arts dir. Very Spl. Arts Ctrl. Fla. Festival, 1995; mem. local Sch. Adv. Coun., Winter Park, 1992. Grantee Found. for Advancement of Cmty. Throught Schs., 1991, Divsn. Blind Svcs. Invision, 1995, Tangelo Park Project, 1995; ACE scholar Arts Leadership Inst., 1993-96; recipient Tchr. Merit award Walt Disney World Co., 1990. Mem. NEA, ASCD, Nat. Art Edn. Assn., Fla. Art Edn. Assn. (regional rep. 1989-94), Seminole County Art Edn. Assn., Coll. Art Assn., Caucus on Social Theory and Art Edn., Women's Caucus for Art, Phi Kappa Phi, Kappa Delta Pi. Home and Office: Nartique Renée Studios 20 Cobblestone Ct Casselberry FL 32707-5410 Office: Nartique Renée Studios at Anclote Harbors Marina 523 Anclote Rd Slip 10 Tarpon Springs FL 34689-6702

RENEHAN, EDWARD JOHN, writer; b. N.Y.C., Aug. 7, 1956; s. Edward John Renehan and Joan Margaret Salvesen; m. Christa Elizabeth Bartkovick, Aug. 24, 1985; children: William James, Katherine Eleanor. BA in Polit. Sci., SUNY, New Paltz, 1980. Author: (books) John Burroughs: An American Naturalist, 1992, The Secret Six: The True Tale of the Men Who Conspired with John Brown, 1995, The Lion's Pride: Theodore Roosevelt and His Family in Peace and War, 1998, The Kennedys at War, 2002. Dir. So. R.I. Conservation Dist., Warwick, 2000-2003. Mem. Am. Irish Hist. Soc., Theodore Roosevelt Assn. (trustee 2000-2003), Hudson River Sloop Clearwater, Inc. (dir. 1976-80), West Bay Yacht Club, Boston Atheneaum, Pi Sigma Alpha. Avocations: hiking, mountain climbing, sailing. Office: Chris Calhoun/Sterling Lord Literistic 65 Bleecker St New York NY 10012

RENEHAN, ROBERT FRANCIS XAVIER, Greek and Latin educator; b. Boston, Apr. 25, 1935; s. Francis Xavier and Ethel Mary (Sullivan) R.; m. Joan Lee Axtell-Damerow, Sept. 9, 1966; children— Martin, Sharon, Stephen, Judith, John. AB, Boston Coll., Chestnut Hill, Mass., 1956; A.M., Harvard, 1958, PhD, 1963. Instr. Greek and Latin U. Calif. at Berkeley, 1963-64; instr. Harvard U., 1964-65; asst. prof. Boston Coll., 1966-69, assoc. prof., 1969-71, prof., 1971-77, chmn. dept. classical studies, 1969-77; prof. Greek and Latin U. Calif. at Santa Barbara, 1976—, chmn. dept., 1984-88, 93-200. Author: Greek Textual Criticism, 1969, Leo Medicus, 1969, Greek Lexicographical Notes, 1975, 2d series, 1982, Studies in Greek Texts, 1975; assoc. editor Classical Philology, 1976—, Am. Jour. Philology, 1987-95; sr. mem. editl. bd. Classical Antiquity, 1980-87, Revised Supplement to Liddell-Scott-Jones Greek-English Lexicon, 1987-96; contbr. articles to profl. jours. Nat. Endowment for Humanities Sr. fellow, 1972-73 Mem. Am. Philol. Assn., Soc. for Ancient Medicine. Office: U Calif Dept Classics Santa Barbara CA 93106 E-mail: renehan@classics.ucsb.edu.

RENEK, NAVA, writer, educator; b. Nyack, Ny, Feb. 12, 1960; d. Morris and Ethel Renek; m. Paul Robert Sweet, Jan. 30, 1991; children: Evan Sweet. MFA, Bklyn Coll., Brooklyn, New York, 1989; BA, Clark U., Worcester, Massachusetts, 1982. Lectr. Bklyn Coll., Brooklyn, NY, 1987—2001, ednl. coord., 1991—2000, interim dir., 2000—01, counselor, 2001—, grant writer, 2001—. Cons. Bklyn Coll. Women's Ctr., Brooklyn, NY, 2001—02; vol. cons. After-School Com., Brooklyn, NY, 2000—02. Author: (short stories) Window of Tears, Find a Penny - The Brooklyn Rail, (novels) Spiritland. Recipient Cmty. Svc. Award, Rsch. Found. LUNY, 1998, 2000. Home: 633A Baltic Street Brooklyn NY 11217

RENEKER, MAXINE HOHMAN, librarian; b. Chgo., Dec. 2, 1942; d. Roy Max and Helen Anna Christina (Anacker) Hohman; m. David Lee Reneker, June 20, 1964 (dec. Dec. 1979); children: Sarah Roeder, Amy Johannah, Benjamin Congdon. BA, Carleton Coll., 1964; MA, U. Chgo., 1970; DLS, Columbia U., 1992. Asst. reference libr. U. Chgo. Libraries, 1965-66; classics libr. U. Chgo. Libr., 1967-70, asst. head acquisitions, 1970-71, personnel libr., 1971-73; personnel/bus. libr. U. Colo. Libr., Boulder, 1978-80; asst. dir. sci. and engring. div. Columbia U., N.Y.C., 1981-85; assoc. dean of univ. librs. for pub. svcs. Ariz. State U. Libr., Tempe, 1985-89; dir. instrnl. and rsch. svcs. Stanford (Calif.) Univ. Librs., 1989-90; assoc. provost for libr. and info. resources Naval Postgrad. Sch., Monterey, Calif., 1993—. Acad. libr. mgmt. intern Coun. on Libr. Resources, 1980-81; chmn. univ. librs. sect. Assn. Coll. and Rsch. Librs., 1989-90. Contbr. articles to profl. jours. Rsch. grantee Coun. on Library Resources, Columbia U., 1970-71, fellow, 1990-92. Mem. ALA, Am. Soc. Info. Sci., Sherlockian Scion Soc., Phi Beta Kappa, Beta Phi Mu. Home: 740 Dry Creek Rd Monterey CA 93940-4208 Office: Naval Postgrad Sch Dudley Knox Libr 411 Dyer Rd Monterey CA 93943-5198 E-mail: mreneker@nps.navy.mil.

RENETZKY, ALVIN, publisher; b. Bklyn., Aug. 2, 1940; s. Sam and Anna (Preiser) R.; m. Phyllis Ann (div.); 1 child, Davida; m. Cheryl Linden. PhD, U. Southern Calif., 1966. Publisher Academic Media, Los Angeles, 1967-70, Ready Reference Press, Santa Monica, Calif., 1974—. Editor: Directory of Career Resources for Women, 1980, Directory of Career Resources for Minorities, 1981, Career Employment Opportunities Directory, 1985, Directory of Internships; exec. prodr.: (video series) Guidance Club for Kids, 1992, Guidance Club for Teens, 1993, 94, Guidance Club for Women, 1994, Guidance Club for Parents, 1994, Career Club, 1994. Office: Ready Reference Press PO Box 5879 Santa Monica CA 90409-5879

RENFREW, ANDREW COLIN (LORD RENFREW OF KAIMSTHORN), archaeologist, academic administrator; b. July 25, 1937; s. Archibald and Helena Douglas (Savage) R.; m. Jane Margaret Ewbank, Apr. 21, 1965; children: Helena Margaret, Alban Robert, Magnus Archibald. BA, St. John's Coll., Cambridge U., 1962, MA, 1964, PhD, 1965, ScD, 1976. Lectr. archaeology U. Sheffield, 1965-72; prof. U. Southampton, 1972-81; Disney prof. archaeology Cambridge U., 1981—. Vis. lectr. UCLA, 1967; fellow St. John's Coll., 1981-86; master Jesus Coll., Cambridge, 1986-97, fellow, 1997—; George Grant McCurdy lectr. Harvard U., 1977; Patten lectr. Ind. U., 1982; field excavations in Saliagos, 1961-64, Sitagroi, 1968-70, Quanterness, Orkney, 1972-74, Phylakopi, Melos, 1974-76. Author (with J. D. Evans): Excavations at Saliagos Near Antiparos, 1968 in Orkney, 1979; author: Problems in European Prehistory, 1979; author: (with J. M. Wagstaff) An Island Polity, 1982; author: Approaches to Social Archaeology, 1984, The Prehistory of Orkney, 1985, The Archaeology of Cult, 1985, Archaeology and Language, 1987; author: (with G. Daniel) The Idea of Prehistory, 1988; author: The Cycladic Spirit, 1991; author: (with P. Bahn) Archaeology, 1991; author: Loot, Legitimacy and Ownership: The Ethical Crisis in Archaeology, 2000, Figuring It Out, 2003; editor: The Explanation of Culture Change, 1973, British Prehistory, 1974, Transformations: Mathematical Approaches to Culture Change, 1979, Theory and Explanation in Archaeology, 1982; presenter (TV films) The Tree That Put the Clock Back, 1970, Islands Out of Time, 1973, Orkney Underground, 1974, Aphrodite's Other Island, 1977, Bronze Age Blast Off, 1978, Lost Kings of the Desert, 1980, The Emperor's Immortal Army, 1981, City of the Dead, 1982, Who Built Stonehenge, 1986. Trustee Brit. Mus., 1991-2001. With RAF, 1956-58. Recipient Rivers Meml. medal Royal Anthrop. Inst., 1979, Huxley Meml. medal, 1991; named Fgn. Assoc. NAS, 1996; elevated to peerage, 1991. Fellow Brit. Acad., Soc. Antiquaries London; mem. Athenaeum. Office: Dept Archaeology Downing St Cambridge CB2 3DZ England also: House of Lords London SW1A 0PW England

RENFREW, CHARLES BYRON, lawyer; b. Detroit, Oct. 31, 1928; s. Charles Warren and Louise (McGuire) R.; m. Susan Wheelock, June 28, 1952 (div. June 1984); children: Taylor Allison Ingham, Charles Robin, Todd Wheelock, James Bartlett; m. Barbara Jones Orser, Oct. 6, 1984; 5 stepchildren. AB, Princeton U., 1952; JD, U. Mich., 1956. Bar: Calif. 1956. Assoc. Pillsbury, Madison & Sutro, San Francisco, 1956-65, ptnr., 1965-72, 81-82; U.S. dist. judge No. Dist. Calif., 1972-80; dep. atty. gen. U.S. Washington, 1980-81; instr. U. Calif. Boalt Hall Sch. Law, 1977-80; v.p. law Chevron Corp. (formerly Standard Oil Co. Calif.), San Francisco, 1983-93, also bd. dirs.; ptnr. LeBoeuf, Lamb, Greene & McRae, 1994-97; pvt. practice, 1998—. Mem. exec. com. 9th Cir. Jud. Conf., 1976-78, congl. liaison com. 9th Cir. Jud. Council, 1976-79, spl. com. to propose standards for admission to practice in fed. cts. U.S. Jud. Conf., 1976-79; chmn. spl. com. to study problems of discovery Fed. Jud. Ctr., 1978-79; mem. council on role of cts. U.S. Dept. Justice, 1978-83; mem. jud. panel Ctr. for Pub. Resources, 1981—; head U.S. del. to 6th UN Congress on Prevention of Crime and Treatment of Offenders, 1980; co-chmn. San Francisco Lawyers Com. for Urban Affairs, 1971-72, mem., 1983—; bd. dirs. Internat. Hospitality Ctr., 1961-74, pres., 1967-70; mem. adv. bd. Internat. Comparative Law Ctr., Southwestern Legal Found., 1983-93; trustee World Affairs Council No. Calif., 1984-87, 94—, Nat. Jud. Coll., 1985-91, Grace Cathedral, 1986-89. Contbr. articles to profl. jours. Bd. fellow Claremont U., 1986-94; bd. dirs. San Francisco Symphony Found., 1964-80, pres., 1971-72; bd. dirs. Coun. Civic Unity, 1962-73, pres., 1971-72; bd. dirs. Opportunity Through Ownership, 1969-72, Marin County Day Sch., 1972-74, No. Calif. Svc. League, 1975-76, Am. Petroleum Inst., 1984—, Nat. Crime Prevention Coun., 1982—; alumni trustee Princeton U., 1976-80; mem. vis. com. u. chgo. Law Sch., 1977-79, u.Mich. Law Sch., 1977-81; bd. visitors J. Reuben Clark Law Sch., Brigham Young U., 1981-83, Stanford Law Sch., 1983-86; trustee Town Sch. for Boys, 1972-80,pres. 1975-80; gov. San Fransciso Symphony Assn., 1974—; mem. nat. adv. bd. Ctr. for Nat. Policy, 1982—; bd. dirs. Nat. Coun. Crime and Deliquency, 1981-82,NAACP Legal Def. and Edn. Fund, 1982—; parish chancellor St. Luke's Episcopal Ch., 1968-71, sr. warden, 1974-76; mem. exec. coun. San Francisco Deanery, 1969-70; mem. diocesan coun. Episcopal Diocese of Calif., 1970; chmn. Diocesan Conv., 1977, 78, 79. Served with USN, 1946-48, 1st lt. U.S. Army, 1952-53. Fellow Am. Bar Found.; mem. ABA (coun. mem. sect. antitrust law 19778-82, vice c hmn. sect. antitrust law 1982-83), San Francisco Bar Assn. (past bd. dirs.), Assn. Gen. Counsel, State Bar Calif., Am. Judicature Soc., Am. Coll. Trial Lawyers (pres. 1995-96), Am. Law Inst., Coun. Fgn. Rels., Order of Coif, Phi Beta Kappa, Phi Delta Phi. Office: 710 Sansome St San Francisco CA 94111-1704

RENFREW, MALCOLM MACKENZIE, chemist, educator; b. Spokane, Wash., Oct. 12, 1910; s. Earl Edgar and Elsie Pauline (MacKenzie) R.; m. Carol Joy Campbell, June 26, 1938. BS, U. Idaho, 1932, MS, 1934, D.Sc., 1976; PhD, U. Minn., 1938. Asst. physics U. Idaho, 1932-33, Asst. chemistry, 1933-35, U. Minn., 1935-37, duPont fellow, 1937-38; research chemist plastics dept. duPont Co., 1938-44, supr. process devel., 1944-46, supr. product devel., 1946-49; head chem. research dept., research labs. Gen. Mills, Inc., 1949-52, dir. chem. research, 1952-53, dir. chem. research and devel., 1953-54; dir. research and devel. Spencer Kellogg & Sons, Inc., 1954-58; phys. sci. div. head, prof. chemistry U. Idaho, 1959-73, prof., 1973-76, emeritus, 1976—; dir. U. Idaho (Coll. Chem. Cons. Service), 1969-76. On leave as sr. staff asso. Adv. Council Coll. Chemistry, Stanford, 1967-68; mem. materials adv. bd. Nat. Acad. Scis.; exec. v.p. Idaho Research Found., 1977-78, patent dir., 1978-88. Editor: Safety in the Chemical Laboratory, Vol. IV, 1981, (with Peter Ashbrook), Safe Laboratories: Principles and Practices for Design and Remodeling, 1991; safety editor: Jour. Chem. Edn, 1977-91; Contbr. to tech. and trade publs. on plastics, coatings, safety, chem. edn. Recipient Excellence in Teaching award Chem. Mfrs. Assn., 1977, Outstanding Achievement award U. Minn., 1977; named to U. Idaho Hall of Fame, 1977, Idaho Hall of Fame, 1996. Fellow AAAS, Am. Inst. Chemists; mem. Am. Chem. Soc. (councilor 1948, 59, 67-89 , chmn. paint varnish and plastics div. 1949, chmn. chem. mktg. and econs. div. 1958-59, chmn. chem. health and safety div. 1982, James Flack Norris award 1976, Chem. Health and Safety award 1985, Mosher award 1986), Am. Inst. Chem. Engrs., Soc. Chem. Industry, Phi Beta Kappa, Sigma Xi, Phi Kappa Phi, Sigma Pi Sigma, Phi Gamma Delta (disting. Fiji 1986). Presbyterian. Home: 1271 Walenta Dr Moscow ID 83843-2426 Office: U Idaho Coll Letters and Sci Dept Chem PO Box 442343 Moscow ID 83844-2343

RENFRO, BRAD, actor; b. Knoxville, Tenn., July 25, 1982; Actor: (films) The Client, 1994, The Cure, 1995, Tom and Huck, 1995, Sleepers, 1996, Telling Lies in America, 1997, Apt Pupil, 1998, 2 Little, 2 Late, 2000, Skipped Parts, 2000, Hershcel Hopper: New York Rabbit, 2000, Delilah, 2000, Happy Campers, 2001, Tart, 2001, Bully, 2001, Ghost World, 2001, Deuces Wild, 2002, American Girl, 2002, (voice): (TV series) Hercules, 1998; (assoc. prodr.): Bully, 2001. Office: c/o United Talent Agy 9560 Wilshire Blvd Fl 5 Beverly Hills CA 90212-2400

RENFROE, AUBREY VANCE, think-tank executive; b. Jackson, Miss., Feb. 25, 1948; s. Foster Aubrey and Eleanor Pauline (Roberts) R.; m. Anita Louise Boyle, Aug. 31, 1969; children: Audra Lynn Renfroe Campbell, Aubrey Nicholas. BA in Religion, La. Coll., 1969; M in Gen. Studis, Ark. State U., 1977; postgrad., So. Bapt. Theol. Sem., 1977-79; MA in Internat. Rels., Salve Regina U., 1985; MA in Nat. Security, Naval War Coll., 1991; EdD, George Washington U., 2002. Commd. 2d lt. USAF, 1970, advanced through grades to col., 1988, comml. pilot, instr., evaluator, 1970-99, ret., 1996, sr. advisor dir. plans hdqrs., 1988-89; dir. ops. and programs Air Nat. Guard USA, 1989-92; sr. advisor to Supreme Allied Comdr. Europe U.S. European Command, Stuttgart, Germany, 1992-94; dir. internat. affairs Nat. Guard Bur., Washington, 1994-96; sr. assoc. George Washington U., 1996-2000; pres., CEO Renfroe & Assocs. Internat., Millersville, Pa., 1997—. Cons. Dept. of Def., Washington, 1997-98, Moscow Sch. for Polit. Studies, 1999. Author: Works, 1997; contbr. chpts. to books and articles to profl. jours. Decorated Legion of Merit, Pres. of the U.S., Washington, 1996; named Disting. Alumni, La. Coll., Pineville, 1994. Mem. Capital City Club Montgomery Ala. Republican. Presbyterian. Avocation: golf. Office: Renfroe & Assocs Internat 605 Crestgate Pl Millersville PA 17551-2113 E-mail: vancerenfroe@va.gwu.edu.

RENFROE, JACKIE LOUISE, interior consultant; b. Dalton, Ga., Jan. 23, 1944; d. James Turner and Helen Beatrice (Jergian) Phillips; m. Donnie Renfroe, July 23, 1961; children: Donna, Tracy, Karen. Student pub. schs., Dalton, Interior cons. Aero Drapery, Dalton, 1972-78, Decorating Den, Dalton, 1978-80, Fashion, Inc., Dalton, 1980—. Vice pres. PTA, Dawnville Elem. Sch., 1972, pres., 1973-75; bd. dirs. Cherokee Estate, Dalton, 1978-82; mem. adv. bd. Dawnville Elem. Sch., 1978-82, Dalton Retail Trade Commn., 1984—; mem. Small Bus. Council Bd., 1984—. Mem. Dalton C. of C., LWV (dir. 1980-85). Democrat. Mormon. Home: Beaverdale Rd 2056 Dawnville Rd NE Dalton GA 30721-5028

RENFROW, JAY ROYCE, lawyer; b. Canon City, Colo., Feb. 19, 1943; s. J.F. and Fern W. Renfrow; m. Evelyn Lee Renfrow, July 25, 1964; children: Seadon T., Stephanie J. BS in Bus., U. Colo., 1964, JD, 1969. Bar: Colo. 1969, U.S. Dist. Ct. Colo. 1969, U.S. Ct. Appeals (10th cir.) 1970, U.S. Supreme Ct. 1970. Pres. J. Royce Renfrow, P.C., Colorado Springs, Colo., 1969-96, Speedway Gas and Oil Co., Colorado Springs, 1969—, Wine Corp. of N.Am., Colorado Springs, 1982-88; v.p., gen. counsel MedLogic Global Corp., 1991-92; sec., gen. counsel InnterCircle Group, Inc., 1996-97; mgr. J. Royce Renfrow PLLC, Mt. Crested Butte, Colo., 1997-98, Renfrow & Frazier PLLC, Mt. Crested Butte, 1998-2000; pvt. practice J. Royce Renfrow PLLC, 2000—. Patentee in field. Bd. dirs. ARC, Colorado Springs, 1970-94, Colo. Opera Festival, Colorado Springs, 1990-96. Mem. Winter Night Club. Avocations: skiing, backpacking, astronomy, food and wine, hunting. Office: J Royce Renfrow PLLC PO Box 608 Crested Butte CO 81224 E-mail: cblaw@rmi.net.

RENFROW, PATRICIA ANNE, secondary education educator; b. Oakland, Calif., Dec. 29, 1951; d. Joseph Montez and Suzanne Leona (Anglada) Galindo; m. Victor E. Renfrow, May 10, 1975; children: Mary Suzanne, Alicia Mariane. BA in Polit. Sci., Calif. State U., Chico, 1973. Spl. edn. instrnl. asst. Vintage H.S., Napa, Calif., 1987-91; instr. ESL Napa Valley Adult Sch., 1992, instr. H.S. diploma program for teen parents, 1992-98, sch. to career liaison, 1994-96, coord. cmty. mentor program, 1996; Cal Works student advisor Napa Valley Coll., 1998—. Teen parent task force Napa Valley Adult Sch., 1992-98, Apple Pie subcom. for pregnancy prevention, 1996—; mem. Calif. Alliance Concerned with Sch. Age Parents, Sacramento, 1992-97. Active Vintage Music Boosters, Vintage H.S., Napa, 1993-97; youth counselor First Unith Meth. Ch., Napa, 1994-96. Named Most Caring Woman, Napa Valley Commn. on the Status of Women, 1995. Mem. AAUW (v.p. membership 1996—). Democrat. Avocations: fitness, reading, collecting Disneyania. Office: Napa Valley Coll 2277 Napa Vallejo Hwy Napa CA 94558-6236

RENGARAJAN, SEMBIAM RAJAGOPAL, electrical engineering educator, researcher, consultant; b. Mannargudi, Tamil Nadu, India, Dec. 12, 1948; came to U.S., 1980; s. Srinivasan and Rajalakshmi (Renganathan) Rajagopalan; m. Kalyani Srinivasan, June 24, 1982; children: Michelle, Sophie. BE with honors, U. Madras, India, 1971; MTech, Indian Inst. Tech., Kharagpur, 1974; PhD in Elec. Engring., U. N.B., Fredericton, Can., 1980. Tech. staff Jet Propulsion Lab., Pasadena, Calif., 1983-84; asst. prof. elec. engring. Calif. State U., Northridge, 1980-83, assoc. prof., 1984-87, prof., 1987—. Vis. rschr. UCLA, 1984-93, vis. prof., 1987-88; vis. prof. U. de Santiago de Compastela, Spain, 1996, U. Pretoria, South Africa, 1997, Tech. U. Denmark, 1999; cons. Hughes Aircraft Co., Canoga Park, Calif., 1982-87, NASA-Jet Propulsion Lab., Pasadena, 1987-90, 92-94, 96—, Ericsson Radar Electronics, Sweden, 1990-92, Martin Mariette, 1995-96; guest rschr. Chalmers U., Sweden, 1990, UN Devel. Program, 1993, Rome Lab., USAF, summer 1995, Naval Rsch. Lab., Washington, summer 1995, guest prof. Technical U. Denmark, 1999. Contbr. articles to profl. jours. Recipient Outstanding Faculty award Calif. State U., Northridge, 1985, Disting. Engring. Educator or Yr. award Engrs. Coun., L.A., 1995, Meritorious Performance and Profl. Promise award, 1986, 88, Merit award San Fernando Valley Engrs., Coun., 1989, Cert. of Recognition NASA, 1991-92; Nat. Merit scholar Govt. India, 1965-71. Fellow Inst. Advancement Engrs., IEEE (L.A. chpt. sec., treas. antennas and propagation soc. 1981-82, vice-chmn. 1982-83, chmn. 1983-84), Internat. Union Radio Sci. (U.S. nat. com.), The Electromagnetics Acad. Avocations: swimming, camping, jogging, tennis. Office: Calif State U 18111 Nordhoff St Northridge CA 91330-0001 *Personal philosophy: I wish to contribute to the society through my work in science and technology.*

RENICK, KYLE, artistic director; b. St. Louis, Apr. 24, 1948; s. Mark Allen and Annabelle (Myers) R. BA magna cum laude, Tufts U., 1970. Sr. fund acct. New Eng. Mchts. Nat. Bank, Boston, 1970-73; fund acct. Fidelity Mgmt. and Rsch. Corp., 1973; bus. mgr. Am. Pl. Theatre, N.Y.C., 1973-78; producing dir. WPA Theatre, 1977-82, artistic dir., 1982—; pres. WPA Prodns., Inc., 1987—. Trustee Alliance of Resident Theatres-N.Y., 1982-92; cons. N.Y. State Council on Arts, 1982-85, Nat. Endowment for Arts, 1986. Producer Steel Magnolias, 1987, The Lady in Question, 1989; contbr. articles to profl. publs. Recipient spl. award for outstanding achievement Drama Desk Assn., 1983. Mem.: Neue Bachgesellschaft, Nev. Hist. Soc., Film Music Soc., Wildlife Conservation Soc., The Packard Club, Phi Beta Kappa. Avocations: early music, record collecting, ghost town photography. Home: 2 Bethune St Apt 4B New York NY 10014-1862 Office: WPA Theatre 159 W 25th St # 301 New York NY 10001-7203 E-mail: wpatheatre@msn.com.

RENKA, ROBERT JOSEPH, computer science educator, consultant; b. Summit, N.J., Dec. 28, 1947; s. John and Elizabeth (Pierce) R. BA in Computer Sci., BS in Math., U. Tex., 1976, MA in Math., 1979, PhD in Computer Sci., 1981. Numerical analyst Oak Ridge (Tenn.) Nat. Lab., 1981-84; asst. prof. computer sci. U. North Tex., Denton, 1984-89, assoc. prof. computer sci., 1989-99, prof. computer sci., 1999—. Cons. in scientific computing. Contbr. articles to profl. jours. With USN, 1967-69, Vietnam. Rsch. grantee U. North Tex., 1984-89, NSF, 1990-93, Nat. Security Agy., 1999—. Mem. Assn. for Computing Machinery (algorithms editor 1988-94, editor-in-chief 1989-94), Soc. Indsl. and Applied Math. Avocations: racquetball, rock climbing. Home: 1700 Kendolph Dr Denton TX 76205-6931 Office: U North Tex Dept Computer Scis PO Box 311366 Denton TX 76203-1366

RENKENS, MADELINE A. lawyer; BA, U. Rochester, N.Y., 1973; MLS, Queens Coll., 1974; JD cum laude, Fordham U., 1979. Bar: N.Y. 1980, Conn. 1981, Wash. 1984, Alaska 1986, U.S. Dist. Ct. Alaska, U.S. Dist. Ct. (so. dist.) N.Y., U.S. Dist. Ct. (we. dist.) Wash., U.S. Ct. Appeals (9th cir.), U.S. Supreme Ct. Tchr., library media specialist Southampton (N.Y.) Pub. Schs., 1974-76; law clk. U.S. Dept. Justice, 1978-79, trial atty. anti-trust div., 1979-82; assoc. Willkie Farr & Gallagher, N.Y.C., 1982-84, Barokas & Martin, Seattle, 1984-87; pvt. practice, Snohomish, Wash., 1988—. Mem. St. James Cathedral Choir, Snohomish County Hist. Soc. Mem. Washington Women Lawyers. Home and Office: 329 Ave C Snohomish WA 98290-2732

RENKIS, ALAN ILMARS, plastics formulating company executive; b. Preili, Latvia, Apr. 16, 1938; came to U.S., 1950; naturalized, 1958. s. Joseph and Malvine (Sturitis) R.; m. Inara Balodis, July 15, 1961; children: Martin Alan, Laura Alise. BSChemE, Pa. State U., 1960. Staff product devel. and tech. svc. divsn. Diamond Alkali Co., Painesville, Ohio, 1960-63; tech. dir. G.S. Plastics Co., Cleve., 1963; founder, pres. Thermoclad Co., Erie, Pa., 1963—, Riverside, Calif., 1972-80, Ocala, Fla., 1985—. Developer comml. PVC resins for formulating fluidized bed and electrostatic coating powders; formulations and compounding techniques. Mem. World Pres. Orgn., Soc. Plastic Engrs., Soc. Mfg. Engrs., Am. Latvian Assn., Erie Yacht Club, Kahkwa Club, Aviation Club, Sigma Pi, Fraternitas Met. Home: 214 Crystal Point Dr Erie PA 16505 Office: Thermoclad Co 361 W 11th St Erie PA 16501-1797 E-mail: arenkis@thermoclad.com.

RENNE, JANICE LYNN, interior designer; b. Los Angeles, July 16, 1952; d. George Joseph and Dolly Minni (Neubaurer) R.; m. William Lee Kile, Dec. 6, 1975 (div. Sept. 1983); m. James Alan Steffen, May 31, 1998. BA, Sweet Briar Coll., 1974; AA, Interior Designers Inst., 1985. Lic. gen. contractor, Calif.; cert. interior designer, Calif. Coun. for Interior Design Certification. Exec. trainee Bullock's, Santa Ana, Calif., 1974, Pub. Fin., Inc., Huntington Beach, 1975; bookkeeper William L. Kile DDS, Inc., Santa Barbara, 1979-81, Nelson & Hamilton, Inc., Santa Barbara, 1981-82; interior designer Ultimate Designs, Irvine, Calif., 1984-85, sr. designer, 1985-86; draftsperson JBI Inc., Long Beach, 1984-85; prin. designer Janice Renne Interior Designs, Newport Beach, 1986-92, Costa Mesa, 1992—, Janice Renne Design, Costa Mesa, 1998-2000; instr. AutoCad Brooks Coll., Long Beach, 2000—; prin. designer Janice Renne Design, Santa Ana, Calif., 2000—. Space planner Design Pak II, Newport Beach, 1987-88; State of Calif. rep. task force for developing self-cert. process for Calif. interior designers, Internat. Soc. Interior Design, 1991. Created utility room design for Easter Seals Design House, 1985; weekly radio show host on restaurant design, 1986; work published in Orange County mag. and L.A. Times., 1988. Fund agt. Sweet Briar Coll. Class of '74, 1979-84, webmaster, 1999—. Recipient scholarship Calif. Inst. Applied Design, Newport Beach, 1984. Mem. AIA (allied), Internat. Soc. Interior Designers (grad. assoc. designer butler's pantry, assoc. designer Design House powder room 1988, asst. editor Orange County chpt. 1988-89, chpt. Quar. Newsletter, chpt. gen. bd. 1991-92, chmn. licensing com. 1991-92, bd. dirs. 1991-92), Color Assn. U.S., Constrn. Specifications Inst., Nat. Exec. Women in Hospitality, Calif. Legis. Conf. in Interior Design (gen. bd. 1991-92, v.p. comm. 1992-93), Orange County and Newport Beach Letip Internat. (sec. 1987, 89-90, treas. 1991, pres. 1993), Internat. Interior Design Assn. (city ctr. dir. 1998, 99, bd. rep. Expo 1998, 99), Internt. Coun. Bldg. Ofcls., Building

Ofcls. Assn., Tall Club Internat. (editor 1998-99, 1999-2000, tall topics editor, 1999, merit award 1998), Tall Club Orange County (exec. v.p. 1995, co-editor High Life 1995-96, editor 1995-2000, Miss Congeniality award 1994, rec. sec. 1996-97, del. to conv. 1996, del. Tall Club Internat. Conv. 1996). Republican. Lutheran. Avocations: skiing, tennis, biking, photography, ballroom dancing competition. Office: 12611 Vista Panorama Santa Ana CA 92705-1312 E-mail: Janice@janicerennedesign.com.

RENNEBERGER, RAYMOND CECIL, real estate professional; b. Washington, July 19, 1932; s. Raymond cecil and Virginia Hall (Cologne) R.; m. Linda Carolyn Conover, Nov. 19, 1966; children: Deborah Lynn Weller, Martin Scott Snyder. BA, U. Md., 1957. Sales assoc. 3M Co., Washington, 1957-60, sales supr. San Francisco, 1960-65, dist. sales mgr., 1965-71; v.p. and gen. mgr. Ingels, Co., Colorado Springs, 1971-87; ptnr., owner, broker Fidelity Real Estate, 1987—. Chmn. E.D.C. com. C. of C., Colorado Springs, 1991-96; v.p. Nat. Microfilm Assn., San Francisco, 1970-71; co-chmn. Olympathon, Nat. Olympic Com., 1979. Sgt.-at-arms Rep. Nat. Conv., San Francisco, 1964. With U.S. Army, 1953-56. Mem. Broadmoor Golf Club, El Paso Club, Garden of Gods Club, Sigma Phi Epsilon. Republican. Methodist. Avocations: golf, fishing. Home: 720 Count Pourtales Dr Colorado Springs CO 80906-4208

RENNELS, MARSHALL LEIGH, neuroanatomist, biomedical scientist, educator; b. Marshall, Mo., Mar. 2, 1939; s. Ivory P. and Alfrieda S. Rennels; m. Margaret Ann Baker, Dec. 28, 1971. BS, Ea. Ill. U., 1961; MA, U. Tex., Galveston, 1964, PhD, 1966. Asst. prof. anatomy U. Md., Balt., 1966-71, assoc. prof., 1971-79, prof., 1979—, dir. MD/PhD program, 1989-97. Contbr. articles to sci. jours. Mem. AAAS, Am. Assn. Anatomists, Soc. Neurosci., Soc. Cerebral Blood Flow and Metabolism. Office: Dept Anatomy & Neurobiology Sch Medicine Univ Md Sch Medicine Baltimore MD 21201

RENNER, ANDREW IHOR, surgeon; b. Buenos Aires, Aug. 1, 1951; came to U.S., 1956; s. Vladimir and Emelia R.; m. Cristina Sasyk, Apr. 17, 1982. MD, Albert Einstein Coll. Medicine, 1975. Diplomate Am. Bd. Surgery. Pvt. practice gen. surgery, Burbank, Calif. Chmn. dept. surgery St. Joseph Hosp., Burbank, 1995-97. Fellow ACS, Internat. Coll. Surgeons; mem. Am. Soc. Gen. Surgeons, L.A. Surg. Soc. Office: 2701 W Alameda Ave Ste 300 Burbank CA 91505-4408 Fax: 818-843-5283.

RENNER, GLENN DELMAR, agricultural products executive; b. Greeneville, Tenn., Nov. 18, 1925; s. Charles Dana and Lula Lucille (Hilton) R.; m. Gladys June Brooks, June 30, 1945; children: Glenna June, Joan Phyllis. BA, Tusculum Coll., 1948; MS, U. Tenn., 1950. Sales trainee Parks Belk Co., Greeneville, 1946-47; tchr., coach Greene County Schs., 1947-48; tchr. City of Greeneville Schs., 1950-54; salesman personal insurance co., Greeneville, 1954-76; real estate owner, pres. Brook Glen Farm Supply, Inc., 1976-98, ret., 1998; farmer, 1998—. Rep. Tenn. Legis., Greeneville, 1965-66; elected commr. Greene County, 1990, 94. Mem. Greeneville Bd. Realtors (bd. dirs., pres. 1964, 71), Greeneville C. of C. (pres. 1986), Kiwanis (pres. Greeneville chpt. 1989—), Shriners (v.p. 1989, pres. 1991). Republican. Methodist. Avocation: hunting. Home: 104 Reed Ave Greeneville TN 37743-4529

RENNER, JOHN ARTHUR, psychiatrist; b. Youngstown, Ohio, Oct. 8, 1938; s. John Arthur and Margaret (Hartman) R. BA, Yale U., 1960; MD, Case-Western Res., 1964. Diplomate Am. Bd. Psychiatry and Neurology and Addiction Psychiatry. Med. intern Tufts-New Eng. Med. Ctr., Boston, 1964-65, psychiatric resident, 1965-68; dir. alcohol and drug program Mass. Gen. Hosp., 1970-76; dir. city drug program Dept. Health and Hosps., 1976-79; chief alcohol program VA Outpatient Clinic, 1979-88, asst. chief psychiatry svc., 1988-94, chief substance abuse treatment program, 1988—; assoc. chief psychiatry svc., 1994—. Clin. instr. in psychiatry Harvard Med. Sch., Boston, 1976—; assoc. prof. psychiatry Boston U. Sch. Medicine, 1976—; asst. clin. prof. psychiatry Tufts U. Sch. Medicine, Boston, 1986—; tng. faculty divsn. on addictions Harvard Med. Sch., 1987—. Contbg. author: Treatment Choices in Alcoholism and Substance Abuse, 1990, Handbook of Chemical Dependence, 1991, MGH Handbook of General Hospital Psychiatry, 1991, Psychiatry Update and Board Preparation, 2000. Bd. dirs. Project Turnabout, Inc., Hingham, Mass., 1970-92, Spectrum Health Sys., Marlboro, Mass., 1992—; acting chmn. Drug Rehab. Adv. Bd., Commonwealth Mass., 1978-79. Lt. comdr. USNR, 1968-70, Vietnam. Recipient Nyswander-Dole award Nat. Methadone Conf., 1992. Fellow APA; mem. Mass. Psychiat. Soc. (chmn. addictions com. 1990—), Am. Acad. Health (sec. bd. trustees 1989—). Office: VA Outpatient Clinic 251 Causeway St Boston MA 02114-2104

RENNER, JOHN ROBERT, lawyer; b. Cleve., July 10, 1964; s. John William and Gail Medora (Eaton) R. AB, Dartmouth Coll., 1986; JD, U. Calif. Berkeley, 1990. Bar: Calif. 1990, U.S. Dist. Ct. (no. dist.) Calif. 1990, (cen. dist.) Calif. 1992, U.S. Ct. Appeals (9th cir.) 1990, U.S. Dist. Ct. (so. dist.) Calif. 1997. Law clk. Hon. Oliver W. Wanger U.S. Dist. Ct. Ea. Dist., Fresno, Calif., 1991; dep. atty. gen. Calif. Dept. Justice, L.A., 1991-95; assoc. Coudert Bros. LLP, 1995—. Republican. E-mial. Office: Coudert Brothers LLP 333 S Hope St 23d Fl Los Angeles CA 90071 E-mail: rrenner@coudert.com.

RENNER, MARGUERITE, history educator; b. San Antonio, Oct. 17, 1947; d. Robert Nelson and Paula Irene (Hess) R.; m. Robert Nelson; children: Tom, Chet. BA, U. Pitts., 1969, MA, 1971, PhD, 1981. Asst. prof. history Stephens Coll., Columbia, Mo., 1980-81, U. Tex., El Paso, 1983-84, U. Utah, Salt Lake City, 1984-85, Calif. State U., Northridge, 1985-89; prof. history Glendale (Calif.) Coll., 1989—. Pres. Western Assn. Women Historians, 1992-94, UN Assn., Pasadena, 1999, Dem. Club, Pasadena, 1989-91; mem. Commn. on Status of Women, Pasadena, 1988-95, Huntington Women's Studies Seminar, San Marion, Calif., 1992-96. Named to Daus. of Honor, Phila. H.S. for Girls, 2000. Mem. Am. Hist. Assn., Coord. Coun. for Women in History (exec. dir. 1994-97). Avocations: gardening, carpentry, animal care. Office: Glendale Coll 1500 N Verdugo Rd Glendale CA 91208

RENNER, RICHARD ROY, education educator, educator; b. Gettysburg, Pa., Aug. 22, 1927; s. Roy David and Gertrude E. (Enck) R.; m. Elisabeth Jean Wood, Dec. 20, 1958; children: Lisanne, Russell, Randall. AB in Econs., Dickinson Coll., 1950; MA in Interam. Affairs, U. N.Mex., 1953; PhD in History and Philosophy of Edn., U. Tex., 1956. Social sci. instr. Sullins Coll., Bristol, Va., 1952-54; coord. Guatemalan tchg. project U. Tex., Austin, 1954; program officer Internat. Divsn. Dept. Edn., Washington, 1957-58; dir. L.Am. edn. divsn. Pa. State U., University Park, 1959-63, social sci. coord., asst. prof., 1963-65; from assoc. prof. to prof. foundations of edn. U. Fla., Gainesville, 1965—. Vis. lectr. Flinders U., Adelaide, Australia, 1970, Innsbruck U. of New Orleans, Austria, 1980; lectr. U.S. Info. Agy., Caribbean and L.Am., 1983; guest lectr. Dept. State-Govt. Turkey, Ankara, 1988; observer, cons. U. Fla., Utrecht, The Netherlands, 1990. Author: Education for a New Colombia, 1971; contbr. articles to profl. jours. Chmn. Unitarian Fellowship, Gainesville, 1972. Fulbright grantee, 1970, 77, 84. Mem. Am. Ednl. Studies Assn., United Fac. Fla. (founding group 1972-95), Comparative Edn. Soc. Home: 2713 NW 30th Ter Gainesville FL 32605-2724 Office: U Fla 1420 Norman Hall Gainesville FL 32611-2053

RENNER, ROBERT GEORGE, federal judge; b. Nevis, Minn., Apr. 2, 1923; s. Henry J. and Beatrice M. (Fuller) R.; m. Catherine L. Clark, Nov. 12, 1949; children: Robert, Anne, Richard, David. BA, St. John's U., Collegeville, Minn., 1947; JD, Georgetown U., 1949. Bar: Minn. 1949. Pvt. practice, Walker, 1949-69; U.S. atty. Dist. of Minn., 1969-77, U.S. magistrate, 1977-80, U.S. dist. judge, 1980-92, assumed sr. status, 1992—. Mem. Minn. Ho. of Reps., 1957-69. Served with AUS, 1943-46. Mem. FBA. Roman Catholic. Office: US Dist Ct 748 US Courthouse 316 Robert St N Saint Paul MN 55101-1495

RENNERFELDT, EARL RONALD, state legislator, farmer, rancher; b. Epping, N.D., July 10, 1938; s. Carl John and Margaret E. (Long) R.; m. Lois Ann Thune, Sept. 12, 1959; children: Charysse Renee, Carter Ryan. Student, NDSSS, Wahpeton, N.D., 1958. Farmer/rancher, Williston, N.D.; mem. N.D. Ho. of Reps., Bismarck, 1991—, chmn. nat. resources com. Bd. dirs. Am. State Bank. Mem. Lake Sacajawea Planning Bd., Williston, 1992; mem. Am. Legis. Exch. Coun., 1991-92; mem. adv. bd. N.D. State U. Exptl. Sta.; bd. dirs. Mercy Med. Found., 1990-96. With U.S. Army, 1962-64. Recipient Harvest Bowl award N.D. State U., 1988; named Outstanding Young Farmer C. of C., 1972. Mem.: ND Durum Growers, Williston C. of C. (agrl. com., energy com.), Elks, Moose, Am. Legion. Republican. Mem. Evangelical Free Ch. Avocations: antiques, golf. Home and Office: 1704 Rose Ln Williston ND 58801-4362

RENNERT, OWEN MURRAY, physician, educator; b. N.Y.C., Aug. 8, 1938; s. David Rennert and Frieda (Weinsteiner) Sommer; m. Sandra Serota, Mar. 22, 1964; children: Laura, Rachel, Ian. BS, BA, U. Chgo., 1957, MD, 1961, MS in Biochemistry, 1963. Diplomate Am. Bd. Pediatrics, Am. Bd. Genetics, Am. Bd. Med. Genetics. Assoc. prof. pediatrics U. Fla., Gainesville, 1968-71, prof. pediatrics and biochemistry, 1971-78; prof. biochemistry, prof. and head dept. pediatrics U. Okla., Oklahoma City, 1977-88; chief pediatrics service and head genetics, endocrinology and metabolics Okla. Children's Mem. Hosp., 1977-88; prof., chmn. dept. pediatrics Georgetown U. Sch. Medicine, Washington, 1988-98, prof. emeritus, 1998—2000; spl. asst. to dir. ctr. rsch. mothers and children Nat. Inst. Child Health Human Devel., NIH, Bethesda, Md., 1998-2000, sci. dir. divsn. intramural rsch., 2000—. Co-author: Metabolism of Trace Metals in Man: Developmental Biology and Genetic Implications (2 vols.), 1983; assoc. editor: Molecular Clinical Medicine, 1999—; contbr. articles to profl. jours. Bd. dirs. Children's Med. Research, Oklahoma City, 1984-88. Served to sr. surgeon USPHS, 1964-66. Named Clin. Scientist of Yr., Am. Assn. Clin. Scientists, 1978. Mem. Am. Pediatric Soc., Am. Acad. Pediatrics, Soc. Pediatric Research, Am. Coll. Clin. Nutrition, Biochem. Soc., Am. Soc. Molecular Biology and Biochemistry, Am. Coll. Med. Genetics, Am. Soc. Human Genetics. Office: NICHD/NIH Divsn Intramural Rsch 2425 Rm 2A46 31 Center Dr Bldg 31 Bethesda MD 20892-0001 E-mail: or5H@nih.gov.

RENNIE, MILBREY TOWER, television news producer; b. Milw., Aug. 19, 1946; d. William Roxburgh and Jean (Tower) R.; m. David Hendrickson Taylor, Jr., Sept. 15, 1973; children: Rennie, Milbrey. BA, Vassar Coll., 1968. Caseworker Sen. Charles Percy, Washington, 1968-69; campaign asst. to Re-elect Mayor John Lindsay, N.Y.C., 1969; rschr. ABC News, Washington, 1970-71; reporter, prodr. NPACT (PBS), 1971-75; exec. prodr. CBS News, N.Y.C., 1976—. Trustee Vassar Coll., Poughkeepsie, N.Y., 1989—, Miss Porter's Sch., Farmington, Conn., 1976-81, 93—, Nightingale Bamford Sch., 1994—; dir. OTR Lecture Series, FPA, N.Y.C., 1990—; mem. Counkilon Fgn. Rels. Luce scholar Henry Luce Found., Manila, 1975-76. Avocation: tennis. Office: CBS News Weekend News/Sunday News 524 W 57th St New York NY 10019-2924

RENNIE, PAUL STEVEN, research scientist; b. Toronto, Ont., Can., Feb. 9, 1946; m. Carol Andrews, 1968; 1 child, Ian. BSc, U. Western Ont., 1969; PhD in Biochemistry, U. Alta., 1973. Rsch. assoc. U. Alta., 1975-76, asst. prof. medicine, 1976-79, assoc. prof., 1979; rsch. scientist B.C. Cancer Agy., 1979-92, dir. rsch., 1992-97; prof. surgery U. B.C., 1986—, dir. prostate rsch. lab., 1998—. Med. Rsch. Coun. rsch. fellow Imperial Cancer Rsch. Fund, 1973-75; rsch. scholar Nat. Cancer Inst. Can., 1976-79. Mem. Can. Soc. Clin. Investigation, Biochem. Soc., Endocrine Soc. Achievements include research on biochemical control of growth in androgen responsive organs and neoplasms; genetic markers in prostate cancer. Office: Prostate Ctr Jack Bell Rsch Ctr 2660 Oak St Vancouver BC Canada V6H 3Z6 E-mail: prennie@interchange.ubc.ca.

RENNINGER, JOHN SNOWDEN, lawyer; b. Phila., Oct. 10, 1924; s. Francis X. and Mary R. Renninger; m. Katharine Steele, Nov. 17, 1951; children: Ann, Molly, Sarah, Patrick. BA, U. Pa., 1948, LLB, 1951. Bar: Pa. 1951; lic. pvt. pilot. Law clk. Ct. of Common Pleas, Phila., 1951-52; atty. Atlantic Refining Co., 1952-55; assoc. Ross & Smith, Doylestown, Pa., 1955-58; ptnr. Ross, Smith & Renninger, 1958-68, Pepper, Hamilton & Sheetz, Phila., 1968-72, Renninger & Kupits, Doylestown, 1972—, Renninger, Spear & Myers, Doylestown, 1987-94. Bd. dirs., counsel Bucks Beautiful, Doylestown; pres., bd. dirs. The Pennsbury Soc., Morrisville, Pa., 1963—; bd. dirs. Pearl S. Buck Internat.; bd. dirs., chmn. Washington Crossing Re-enactors. Mem. Pa. Ho. of Reps., Harrisburg, 1964-76. Sgt. USAF, 1943-46, PTO. Mem. ABA, Pa. Bar Assn., Phila. Bar Assn., Bucks County Bar Assn. (sec.), Lawyer Pilots Bar Assn. (bd. dirs. 1990-94), Law Rev. Republican. Episcopalian. Avocation: flying. Office: 301 S State St Newtown PA 18940-1997 E-mail: JRennin5/96@aol.com.

RENNINGER, MARY KAREN, librarian; b. Pitts., Apr. 30, 1945; d. Jack Burnell and Jane (Hammerly) Gunderman; m. Norman Christian Renninger, Sept. 3, 1965 (div. 1980); 1 child, David Christian. BA, U. Md., 1969, MA, 1972, M.L.S., 1975. Tchr. English West Carteret High Sch., Morehead City, N.C., 1969-70; instr. in English U. Md., College Park, 1970-72; head network services Nat. Libr. Svc., Libr. of Congress, Washington, 1974-78, asst. for network support, 1978-80; mem. fed. women's program com. Libr. of Congress, 1978-80; chief libr. divsn. Dept. Vets. Affairs, 1980-90; chief serial and govt. publs. divsn. Libr. of Congress, 1991—, mem. fed. libr. com., 1980-90, mem. exec. adv. bd., 1985-90. Mem. USBE pers. subcom., 1982-84; bd. regents Nat. Libr. of Medicine, 1986-90, mem. outreach panel, 1988-89; fed. libr. task force for 1990 White House Conf. on Librs., 1986-90; liaison to The White House Conf. Med. Libr. Assn., 1989-90. Recipient Meritorious Svc. award Libr. of Congress, 1974, Spl. Achievement award, 1976, Performance award VA, ann. 1982-89, Adminstr.'s Commendation, 1985, Spl. Contbn. award, 1986. Mem. ALA (Govt. Documents Roundtable), Libr. Tech. Assn., Med. Libr. Assn. (govt. rels. com. 1985—), D.C. Libr. Assn., Soc. Applied Learning Tech., Med. Interactive Videodisc Consortium, Govt. Documents Roundtable, Knowledge Utilization Soc., Nat. Multimedia Assn. Am., U.S. Tennis Assn., Phi Beta Kappa, Alpha Lambda Delta, Beta Phi Mu. Home: 840 College Pky Rockville MD 20850-1931 Office: Libr of Congress Ser and Govt Pub Divsn Lm 133 Washington DC 20540-0001

RENNIX, PAUL DONLEY, accountant; b. East Liverpool, Ohio, June 8, 1956; s. Donley and Katherine (Allison) R. BSBA, W.Va. U., 1978, MBA, 1979. CPA, Ohio. Internal auditor Am. Elec. Power, Canton, Ohio, 1979-85, sr. acctg. policy and rsch. acct. Columbus, 1985-98; dir. corp. acctg. AEP Conoco Energy Mgmt., Houston, 1998; sr. fin. analyst Am. Elec. Power, Columbus, Ohio, 1998-2000; mgr. acctg. and fin. svcs. AEP Pro Serv, 2000—. Dir. Rennix Corp., Newell, W.Va., 1985—. Republican. Home: 434 Old Village Rd Columbus OH 43228-1374 Office: AEP Pro Serv 1 Riverside Plz Columbus OH 43215-2355

RENO, JANET, former attorney general; b. Miami, Fla., July 21, 1938; d. Henry and Jane (Wood) R. AB in Chemistry, Cornell U., 1960; LL.B., Harvard U., 1963. Bar: Fla. 1963. Assoc. Brigham & Brigham, 1963-67; ptnr. Lewis & Reno, 1967-71; staff dir. judiciary com. Fla. Ho. of Reps., Tallahassee, 1971-72; cons. Fla. Senate Criminal Justice Com. for Revision Fla.'s Criminal Code, spring 1973; adminstrv. asst. state atty. 11th Jud. Circuit Fla., Miami, 1973-76, state atty., 1978-93; ptnr. Steel Hector and Davis, 1976-78; U.S. atty. gen. Dept. Justice, Washington, 1993-2001. Mem. jud. nominating commn. 11th Jud. Circuit Fla., 1976-78; chmn. Fla. Gov.'s Council for Prosecution Organized Crime, 1979-80. Recipient Women First award YWCA, 1993. National Women's Hall of Fame, 2000. Mem. ABA (Inst. Jud. Adminstrn. Juvenile Justice Standards Commn. 1973-76), Am. Law Inst., Am. Judicature Soc. (Herbert Harley award 1981), Dade County Bar Assn., Fla. Pros. Atty.'s Assn. (pres. 1984-86). Democrat.*

RENO, JOHN F. foundation administrator; b. Peoria, Ill., June 15, 1939; s. John Henkle and Alice Hanna (Findley) R.; m. Suzanne McKnight, Apr. 18, 1964; children: David, Anne. AB, Dartmouth Coll., 1961; MBA, Northwestern U., 1963. Ptnr. G.H. Walker & Co., Boston, 1968-74; divsn. pres. Dynatech Cryomedical Co., Burlington, Mass., 1974-79; corp. v.p. Dynatech Corp., 1979-82, group v.p., 1982-87, pres., COO, 1987-93, pres., CEO, 1993-99, chmn., 1996-99, Reno Family Found., Winchester, Mass., 1999—. Bd. dirs. Millipre Corp., Bedford, Mass. Trustee, chmn. Boston Mus. of Sci., 1992—; bd. dirs. CEOs for Fundamental Change in Edn., Cambridge, Mass.; dir. WGBH Pub. TV, 1999— Named Entrepreneur of Yr., Inc. mag., 1995. Avocations: oil painting, writing. Office: Reno Family Found 63 Shore Rd Ste 33 Winchester MA 01890-2828

RENO, JOSEPH HARRY, retired orthopedic surgeon; b. Allentown, Pa., Mar. 5, 1915; s. Harvey Luther and Olive May (Wilson) R.; m. Maude Olivia Mutchler, June 27, 1942; children: Joseph David, Sally Jo, Diana Jane, Deborah Marion. Student, Temple U., 1934-37, MD, 1941. Intern. Chester (Pa.) Hosp., 1941-42; resident Tex. Scottish Rite Hosp. for Crippled Children, Dallas, 1942-43, 44-45, Robert Packer Hosp., Sayre, Pa., 1943-44; assoc. Homer Stryker, M.D., Kalamazoo, 1945-46; pvt. practice Bethlehem, Pa., 1946-71, Flagstaff, Ariz., 1971-93; team physician Lehigh U., Bethlehem, 1946-70, No. Ariz. U., Flagstaff, 1971-77, Ariz. State U., Tempe, 1977-84. Chief surg. staff Flagstaff Hosp., 1975. Contbr. articles to profl. jours.; prodr. surg. films for Am. Acad. Ortho. Surgeons and others, 1952-70. Pres. Coconino County Easter Seal Soc., 1973; bd. dirs., med. advisor Ariz. Easter Seal Soc., 1974-84. Recipient Pioneer award Ariz. Med. Assn., 1981, Cert. of Appreciation, Pa. Dept. Health Crippled Children's Div., 1971; Dr. Joseph Reno Sports Medicine award named in honor, No. Ariz. State U. and Blue Cross Blue Shield, 1986. Fellow Am. Acad. Ortho. Surgeons, Am. Assn. for Surgery of Trauma, Am. Coll. Sports Med., Am. Coll. Surgeons (chmn. Lehigh Valley subcom. on trauma 1954-66, Ea. Pa. chpt. pres. 1969); mem. NRA, Am. Bd. Ortho. Surgery (cert., diplomate 1948), Coconino County Med. Soc. (pres. 1976), Western Ortho. Assn., Babcock Surg. Soc., Mason, Phi Chi, Alpha Tau Omega. Home: 405 Jacks Canyon Rd Apt 105 Sedona AZ 86351-9222

RENO, OTTIE WAYNE, former judge; b. Pike County, Ohio, Apr. 7, 1929; s. Eli Enos and Arbannah Belle (Jones) Reno; m. Janet Gay McCann, May 22, 1947; children: Jennifer Lynn, Lorna Victoria, Ottie Wayne II. A in Bus. Adminstrn., Franklin U., 1949; LLB, Franklin Law Sch., 1953; JD, Capital U., 1966; grad. Coll. Juvenile Justice, U. Nev., 1973. Bar: Ohio 1953. Practiced in Pike County; recorder Pike County, 1957-73, common pleas judge probate and juvenile divsn., 1973-79. Author: Story of Horseshoes, 1963, Pitching Championship Horseshoes, 1971; ; author: The American Directory of Horseshoe Pitching, 1983, Ohio vs. Smith, Murder, 1990, Reno and Apsaalooka Survive Custer, 1996. Del. Dem. Nat. Conv., 1972, 1996; mem. Camp Creek precinct Dem. Ctrl. Com., 1956—72, 1983—90, 1999—; sec. Pike County Dem. Exec. Com., 1971—72, 1988—90; mem. Ohio Dem. Ctrl. Com., 1969—70; Dem. candidate 6th Ohio dist. U.S. Ho. of Reps., 1966; Dem. candidate 88th Ohio dist. Ohio Ho. of Reps., 1992; pres. Scioto Valley Local Sch. Dist., 1962—66. Named to Nat. Horseshoe Pitchers Hall of Fame, 1978; recipient Disting. Svc. award, Ohio Youth Commn., 1974, 6 Outstanding Jud. Svc. awards, Ohio Supreme Ct., 17 times Ala. horseshoe pitching champion. Mem.: Pike County Bar Assn., Nat. Coun.Juvenile Ct. Judges, Ohio Bar Assn., Am. Legion. Mem. Ch. Of Christ In Christian Union. Home: 148 Reno Rd Lucasville OH 45648-9580

RENO, ROGER, lawyer; b. Rockford, Ill., May 16, 1924; s. Guy B. and Hazel (Kinnear) R.; m. Janice Marie Odelius, May 17, 1952; children: Susan Marie, Sheri Jan Reno-Rudolph, Michael Guy. Student, Kenyon Coll., 1943-44, Yale U., 1944, U. Wis., 1946; AB, Carleton Coll., 1947; LL.B., Yale U., 1950. Bar: Ill. 1950. Practiced in Rockford, 1950; assoc. firm Reno, Zahm, Folgate, Lindberg & Powell, 1950-56, partner, 1956-84, of counsel, 1984—. Chmn. Amcore Fin. Inc., 1982-95; atty. Rockford Bd. Edn., 1955-64. Past pres., bd. dirs. Childrens Home Rockford; trustee Swedish-Am. Hosp. Assn., 1967-77, Keith Country Day Sch. Served to 1st lt. USAAF, 1943-46. Mem. ABA, Ill. Bar Assn., Winnebago County Bar Assn. (pres. 1979-80) Clubs: Forest Hills Country (Rockford). Republican. Methodist. Home: 2515 Chickadee Trl Rockford IL 61107 Office: Reno Zahm Folgate Lindberg & Powell Amcore Fin Plaza Rockford IL 61104 Fax: 815-961-7723.

RENO, RUSSELL RONALD, JR. lawyer; b. Gary, Ind., Nov. 28, 1933; s. Russell Ronald Sr. and Katherine Narcissus (White) R.; m. Mary Ellen Klock, Jan. 30, 1956; children: Mary Hall, Russell III, William, Elizabeth. AB, Haverford Coll., 1954; JD, U. Pa., 1957. Bar: Md. 1957, D.C. 1983. Assoc. Venable, Baetjer & Howard, Balt., 1958-66, ptnr., 1966—; asst. atty. gen. State of Md., 1962-64. Author: Maryland Real Estate Law-Practice, 1983. Bd. dirs. Balt. Choral Arts Soc., 1966—; trustee Goucher Coll., Balt., 1978—; chancellor Episcopal Diocese of Md., Balt., 1985—; bd. mgrs. Haverford Coll., 1990-2002. Fellow Am. Bar Found., Md. Bar Found.; mem. ABA, Md. State Bar Assn., Am. Coll. Real Estate Lawyers, Hamilton St. Club, Wednesday Law Club. Home: 706 W Joppa Rd Baltimore MD 21204-3810 Office: Venable Baetjer & Howard 2 Hopkins Plz Ste 2100 Baltimore MD 21201-2982 E-mail: rrreno@venable.com.

RENO, THOMAS RICHARD, education educator; b. Canton, Ohio, Nov. 16, 1939; s. Edward Clement and Lucille Karolyn (White) R.; m. Jacquelyn Ruth Venters, children: Lucy Van Andel, Frances Rasmus, Matt, Mike Beals. BS, Ariz. State U., 1962, MA, 1965; PhD, Mich. State U., 1971. Tchr. Coolidge (Ariz.) Pub. Schs., 1961-62; vol. Peace Corps, Teheran, Iran, 1962-64; dir. Navajo Demonstration Sch., Rough Rock, Ariz., 1965-69; adminstrv. asst. Roosevelt Sch. Dist., Phoenix, 1969-71; supt. Apache Junction (Ariz.) Schs., 1971-75, Yuma (Ariz.) Pub. Schs., 1975-77; assoc. state supt. Ariz. Dept. Edn., Phoenix, 1977-85; prof. No. Ariz. U., Flagstaff, 1985—.

RENOUF, ANNE, technology commercialization financier; b. N.Y.C., Apr. 3, 1937; Diploma, Emma Willard Sch., 1954; student, Inst. World Affairs, 1957; AB magna cum laude, honors in Anthropology, Columbia U., 1959; MA, Yale U., 1962, PhD, 1966; JD with honors, Am. U., 1978; postgrad., Duke U. Asst. prof. U. N.C., Chapel Hill, 1966-71; sr. profl. cons. U.S. Govt., Washington, 1972-75; pvt. practice fin. cons., 1976—; vis. assoc. prof. George Washington U. Sch. Bus. Adminstrn., 1983-84; gen. ptnr., v.p. Tech. Mgmt. Corp., Montgomeryville, Pa., 1986-88; chmn. Pivot, Inc., 1988—; founding prin. SaraTech Fin. Inc., 1990-92; sr. v.p., head internat. bus. Hectron Inc., Washington, 1992-93. Founding dir., chmn. bd., CFO/bd. treas. Initiatives in Industry, Inc., 1996—; corp. dir.; dir. fin. devel. Ctr. for Space and Advanced Tech., 1990; cons. The Brookings Instn., Washington, 1966, U.S. Dept. State, Washington, 1967, World Bank, 1992—; mem. Pres.'s Commn. Grad. Edn., 1967-68, Nat. Chamber Found. Task Force on Space Commercialization, Washington, 1983-86; vis. scholar Carnegie Endowment for Internat. Peace, N.Y.C., 1968-69; fellow U.S. Dept. State, EUR/RPE, 1967; northeastern dir. Va. Advanced Tech. Assn., 1984-88; fin. and tech. spkr.; mem. Coun. on Competitiveness, 1998—, Tech. Coun. Washington, 1998—; mem. Greater Washington Bd. Trade, The Potomac Conf., 1999—; mem. The World Bank, The Global Devel. Network, 1998—. Contbr. articles on tech. commercialization and fin. to profl. jours. Co-chair, charter mem. U.S./China Capital Cities Coun., Washington, 1985-95; advisor Greater Washington D.C. Bd. Trade, 1985-86, Internat. Red Cross, 1987-90; mem. Mayor's Adv. Coun. on Trade and Investment, 1987-91; mem. adv. coun. Ctr. for Internat. Bus. Edn. U. Alaska, Fairbanks, 1990-91, co-chmn. World Trade Day, 1989; bd. dirs. Nat. Symphony Orch., 1990-99, Greater Washington Met. Boys and Girls Clubs, 1992-2000; dir. Initiatives in Industry, Inc., 1996—. Woodrow Wilson fellow, 1958, Bushnell fellow, Yale U., 1964, Hon. Officer-Faculty fellow U.S. Dept. State, 1967; recipient citation Washington D.C. Mayor's Office, 1986. Fellow Washington Acad. Scis.; mem. Am. Soc. Internat. Law, Internat. Forum U.S. C. of C., Internat. Energy Seminar-Johns Hopkins Sch. for Advanced Internat. Study, Corcoran Gallery of Art (nat. coun.), Washington Internat. Trade Assn., Assn. for Corp. Growth, Phi Beta Kappa.

RENOUF, EDDA, artist; b. Mexico City, June 17, 1943; d. Edward and Catharine (Smith) R.; m. Alain Middleton, Sept. 20, 1977; 1 child, Mélisande. BA, Sarah Lawrence Coll., 1965; M.F.A., Columbia U., 1971. One-woman shows include Yvon Lambert Gallery, Paris, 1972, 1974, 1976, 1978, 1980, 1982, 1984, 1993, Konrad Fischer Gallery, Düsseldorf, Germany, 1974, 1979, Blum-Helman Gallery, N.Y.C., 1978, 1980, 1982, 1985, 1987, 1989, U. Mich. Mus. Art, 1995, Elisabeth Kaufmann Gallery, Basel, Switzerland, 1994, 1996, Galerie Sollertis, Toulouse, France, 1994, 1996, 1998, Staatliche Kunsthalle Karlsruhe, Germany, 1997, Galerie Hubert Winter, Vienna, Austria, 1998, Galerie Liesbeth Lips, Rotterdam, 1998, 2001, Helman Gallery, N.Y.C., 2001—02, Joseph Helman Gallery, 2002, exhibited in group shows at Mus. Modern Art, N.Y.C., 1973, 1990, 1998, Stedelijk Mus., Amsterdam, 1974, 8th Paris Biennale, 1973, Whitney Mus. Am. Art, N.Y.C., 1979, 1985, Centre Georges Pompidou, Paris, 1979, 2002, Met. Mus. Art, N.Y.C., 1982, Serpentine Gallery, 1984, Galerie Denise René, Paris, 1985, The Tel Aviv Mus., 1986, 1998, Mus. Fridericianum, Kassel, Germany, 1988, Mus. d'Art Moderne de Lille, France, 1992, Bibliothèque Nationale, Paris, 1992, Nat. Gallery Art, Washington, 1993—94, Harvard U. Straus Gallery, 1996, Yokohama (Japan) Mus. Art, 1998, Yale U. Art Gallery, 1998, Cabinet des Estampes et des Dessins, Liege, Belgium, 1999, Brit. Mus., 2000, Corcoran Gallery, Washington, 2001, Represented in permanent collections Mus. Modern Art, Whitney Mus. Am. Art, Met. Mus. Art, Centre Georges Pompidou, Paris, Chgo. Art Inst., Mus. of Contemporary Art, Chgo., Phila. Art Mus., Yale U. Art Gallery,

Neuberger Mus., Australian Nat. Gallery, Cin. Mus. Art, St. Louis Art Mus., Tel Aviv Mus., La. Mus., Denmark, Walker Art Ctr., Washington, BibliotequeNationale Paris, Brit. Mus., London, Bklyn. Mus. Am. Art, Dallas Mus. Fine Art, Detroit Mus. Art, Mus. Contemporary Art, L.A., High Mus., Atlanta, Corcoran Gallery, Washington, Staatliche Kunsthalle, Karlsruhe, Nat. Gallery Art, Washington, Kunstmuseum Winterthur, Switzerland. Nat. Endowment Arts grantee, 1976-77, Pollock-Krasner Found. Inc. grantee, 1990-91, Ctr. Nat. Arts Plastiques grantee, 1996. Address: 26 Juniper Meadow Rd Washington CT 06794

RENOUF, HAROLD AUGUSTUS, business consultant, retired; b. Sandy Point, Nfld., Can., June 15, 1917; s. John Robert and Louisa Maud (LeRoux) R.; m. Janet Dorothy Munro, June 16, 1942; children: Janet Dorothy, Ann Louise Petley-Jones, John Robert, Susan Elizabeth Thompson. B.Commerce, Dalhousie U., 1938, LL.D. (hon.), 1981. N.S.C.A., Halifax, 1942 C.M.A., 1950. With H.R. Doane and Co., Halifax, N.S., Can., 1938-75, ptnr. Can., 1942-75, ptnr. in charge New Glasgow, Can., 1947-62, ptnr. in charge mgmt. svcs. Halifax, 1963-67, chmn., 1967-75; bd. dirs. Associated Acctg. Firms Internat., N.Y.C., 1967-75; commr. Anti-Inflation Bd., Ottawa, Ont., 1975-77, chmn., 1977-79, Petroleum Monitoring Agy., Ottawa, 1980-82, VIA Rail Can. Inc., Montreal, Que., 1982-85; pres. Fundy Industries Ltd., Halifax, 1990-94; ret., 1996. Cons. to N.S. Provincial Mcpl. Fact-Finding Com., 1967-70; pres. Can. Inst. Chartered Accts., 1974-75. Contbr. articles to profl. publs. Chmn. adv. commn. Dalhousie U. Grad. Sch. Bus. Adminstrn., 1978-86; past dir. Can. Inst. Child Health. Decorated Queen's medal, 1977, officer Order of Can., 1979; recipient Commemorative medal for 125th anniversary of Can. Confederation, 1992; named to Acctg. Hall of Fame St. Mary's Univ., N.S., 1993. Fellow Inst. Chartered Accts. N.S. (pres. 1948); mem. Can. Inst. Chartered Accts. (pres. 1974-75), Can. Tax Found. (gov. 1969-71), Soc. Mgmt. Accts. N.S., Dalhousie U. Alumni Assn. (hon. chmn. 1987-89), Halifax Club, Saraguay Club (treas. 1972-75), Waegwaltic Club. Liberal. Mem. United Ch. Can. Avocations: boating, fishing. Home: 6369 Coburg Rd Apt 1605 Halifax NS Canada B3H 4J7

RENOUX, ANDRÉ, physicist, educator; b. Courbevoie, France, Oct. 27, 1937; s. Robert and Jeanne (Noël) R.; divorced; children: Vincent, Nathalie. Lic. Sci., Faculty Scis. Paris, 1958, Dr 3rd cycle, 1961, Drs, 1965. Asst. Faculty Scis., Paris, 1959-61, master asst., 1961-66; prof. faculty of scis. U. Tunis, Tunisia, 1966—69, U. Brest, France, 1969-80; prof. U. Paris, 1980—, dir. lab. phys. aérosols et transfert des contaminations, 1980—, dir. DESS (3d cycle) sci. des aerosols-génie de l'Aérocontamination, 1983—. Gen. conf. chmn. European Aerosol Conf., Blois, France, 1994; del. Internat. Coun. for Engring. and Tech., UNESCO, 2000—. Author: (with D. Boulaud, Lavoisier, Ed.) Les Aérosols, Physique et Métrologie, 1998; mem. editl. bd. Idojaras, 1979—, Pollution Atmospherique, 1979—, Aerosol Sci. & Tech., 1992-2000, Revue Salles Propres, 2000—; contbr. over 300 articles to profl. jours. Gen. sec. Syndicat d'initiative, Brest, 1973-77; mem. Cons. Com. Univs., France, 1973-77. Mem. AAAS, N.Y. Acad. Scis., Com. Regional Anti-Pollution Brest (pres. 1973-80), Soc. France for Nuclear Energy idFNE (pres. 1987-91), Am. Assn. Aerosol Rsch., Gesellschaft Aerosolforschung, Hungarian Meteorol. soc. (hon.), French Aerosol. Rsch. Assn. (pres. 1983-2000, hon. pres. 2000—), European Aerosol Assembly (co-founder, pres. 1998-2000), Office Professionnel de qualification des Entreprises de l'Ultrapropreté (pres. 1995—), Chevalier des Dames du vin et de la Table, Ordre de l'Echarpe. Avocations: tennis, opera, photography. Home: 11 Sq de L'eau Vive 94000 Créteil France Office: U Paris XII Lab Phys Aerosols Ave Gal de Gaulle 94000 Creteil France E-mail: renoux@univ-paris12.fr.

RENSHAW, AMANDA FRANCES, retired physicist, nuclear engineer; b. Wheelwright, Ky., Dec. 10, 1934; d. Taft and Mamie Nell (Russell) Wilson; divorced; children: Linda, Michael, Billy. BS in Physics, Antioch Coll., 1972; MS in Physics, U. Tenn., 1982, MS in Nuclear Engring., 1991. Rsch. asst. U. Mich., Ann Arbor, 1970-71; teaching asst. Antioch Coll., Yellow Springs, Ohio, 1971-72; physicist GE, Schenectady, N.Y., 1972-74, Union Carbide Corp., Oak Ridge, Tenn., 1974-79; rsch. assoc. Oak Ridge Nat. Lab., 1979-91, mgr. strategic planning, 1991-92, liaison for environ. scis., 1993-96; ret., 1996. Asst. to counselor for sci. and tech. Am. Embassy, Moscow, 1990; asst. to dir. nat. acid precipitation assessment program Office of Pres. U.S., 1993-94. Contbr. articles to profl. jours. Mem. AAUW, Am. Women in Sci., Am. Nuclear Soc. (Oak Ridge chpt.), Soc. Black Physicists. Avocations: reading, travelling. Home: 1850 Cherokee Bluff Dr Knoxville TN 37920-2215

RENSHAW, JOHN HUBERT, retired secondary education educator; b. Hazleton, Pa., July 9, 1936; s. Charles William and Mary (Drobeck) R.; m. Dorothy Sharon Montgomery, June 20, 1964; children: John Michael, Rebecca Lynn. BS in Edn., East Stroudsburg State U., 1961; MA in History, U. Del., 1965. Cert. tchr., Del. 10th and 12th grade social studies tchr. Pocomoke City (Md.) High Sch., 1961-64; 7th and 8th grade social studies tchr. Forwood Jr. High Sch., Wilmington, Del., 1965-78; 8th grade U.S. govt. and U.S. history tchr. Springer Jr. High Sch., 1978-81; 8th grade U.S. history tchr. Hanby Middle Sch., 1981-96, ret., 1996. Audiovisual dir., equipment maintenenace Hanby Jr. High Sch. and Brandywine Sch. Dist., 1981-94; curriculum leader social studies dept. Hanby Jr. High Sch., 1988—, chmn. social studies dept., 1994—; coach baseball, girl's softball teams Forwood Jr. High Sch., 1973-78, Springer Jr. High Sch., 1979-81, Hanby High Sch., 1982-86. Cpl. USMC, 1954-57. Mem. Nat. Coun. Social Studies, Del. Edn. Assn., Brandywine and New Castle County Edn. Assn. (rep. 1978-81). Republican. Methodist. Avocations: jogging, reading, mind-body readings and projects, baseball card collecting, sports watching and participation. Home: 2506 Bona Rd Wilmington DE 19810-2220 E-mail: emrjhr@aol.com.

RENSINK, JACQUELINE BIDDIX, secondary school educator; b. Spruce Pine, N.C., May 17, 1954; d. Joe and Virginia Dare (Glenn) Biddix; m. Michael Lynn Rensink, Apr. 2, 1988; 1 child, Sarah Jane Buchanan. MusB, Appalachian State U., 1976, MA, 1983, specialist in mid. grades edn., 1990. Cert. level A music, N.C., level G middle grades edn., N.C. Band dir. Mitchell County Sch. System, Bakersville, N.C., 1977, tchr., 1981—. Mem. supt. adv. coun. Mitchell County Sch. System, 1986-88, site-based mgmt. team Harris Mid. Sch., Spruce Pine, 1992-93; student-tchr. supr. Harris Mid. Sch., 1988, 89, 90; coord. World Day Festival Harris Mid. Sch, 1988—. Organist Cen. Bapt. Ch., Spruce Pine, 1990—; bd. dirs. Winterstar-Fairway Assn., Burnsville, N.C., 1992-93. Named Tchr. of Yr., Harris Mid. Sch., 1992, 94. Mem. NEA, Nat. Coun. Social Studies, N.C. Assn. Educators (treas. 1987-88, 91-92, assn. rep. 1992-93), N.C./Nat. Geographic Alliance, N.C. Coun. Social Studies, Delta Kappa Gamma. Republican. Baptist. Avocations: reading, hiking, piano. Home: 1175 Highway 80 S Burnsville NC 28714-9738 Office: Harris Middle Sch 231 Harris St Spruce Pine NC 28777-3119

RENSLOW, CHARLES G. entrepreneur; b. Chgo., Aug. 26, 1929; Degree, Wright U., Northwestern U. Pub. Kris Studio, 1950—79; owner GoldCoast Leather Bar, 1958—93; pub. Gay Life Newspaper, 1979—85; prodr. Internat. Mr. Leather, Inc., 1979—; owner Chgo. Eagle Leather Bar, 1997—. Pres. Leather Archives and Mus., 1994—. Charter mem. City Chgo. Gay/Lesbian Hall of Fame , 1991; participant Internat. Gay/Lesbian Assn. Conf. , Austria, 1989; mem. Nat. Gay Task Force , 1981—88; founder Am. Found. AIDS Rsch., 2002—; mem. Nat. Trust Historic Preservation , 2002—; Nat. Orgn. Women, 2002—; mem. Dem. Nat. Com., 2002—; mem. adv. bd. (O'Brien) 43d Ward Dem. Party; mem. adv. bd. (Orbach) 46th Ward Dem. Party; organizer Second Harvest, 1st Dist. Wide Masonic Food Dr., 1997, Masonic Children's Home, Franzen Circus fundraiser, 1995; charitable fundraiser Gay Rights Nat. Lobby , 1979—85. Named Humanitarian of Yr., 1977, Pantheon Bus. Person of Yr., Leather Jour., 1996, Leather Man of Century, 2000; named to Hall of Fame, Gay Chgo. mag., 1982; recipient Chgo. Gay/lEsbian CC, Cmty. Svc. award, 1997, Lodge Builder's award, Hesperia Masonic Lodge AF & AM, 1999. Home: 4535 N Beacon Chicago IL 60640 Office: Renslow Family Enter 5015 N Clark St Chicago IL 60640 Fax: (773) 878-5184. E-mail: renslow@chicagonettech.com.

RENSON, JEAN FELIX, retired psychiatry educator; b. Liège, Belgium, Nov. 9, 1930; came to U.S., 1960; s. Louis and Laurence (Crahai) R.; m. Gisèle Bouillenne, Sept. 8, 1956; children: Marc, Dominique, Jean-Luc. MD, U. Liege, 1959; PhD in Biochemistry, George Washington U., 1971. Diplomate Am. Bd. Psychiatry. Asst. prof. U. Liège, 1957-60; rsch. fellow U. Liege, 1966-72; clin. assoc. prof. dept. psychiatry U. Calif., San Francisco, 1978—; ret. 1994. Vis. asst. prof. Stanford U., Palo Alto, Calif., 1972-77. Assoc. editor: Fundamentals of Biochemical Pharmacology, 1971. NIH fellow, 1960-66. Avocations: neurosciences, music. E-mail: grenson@attbi.com.

RENT, CLYDA STOKES, academic administrator; b. Jacksonville, Fla., Mar. 1, 1942; d. Clyde Parker Stokes Sr. and Edna Mae (Edwards) Shuemake; m. George Seymour Rent, Aug. 12, 1966; 1 child, Cason Rent Lynley. BA, Fla. State U., 1964, MA, 1966, PhD, 1968; LHD (hon.), Judson Coll., 1993. Asst. prof. Western Carolina U., Cullowhee, N.C., 1968-70, Queens Coll., Charlotte, 1972-74, dept. chair, 1974-78, dean Grad. Sch. and New Coll., 1979-84, v.p. for Grad. Sch. and New Coll., 1984-85, v.p. acad. affairs, 1985-87, v.p. cmty. affairs, 1987-89; pres. Miss. U. for Women, Columbus, 1989—. Bd. dirs. Nat. Women's Hall of Fame; cons. Coll. Eb. N.Y.C., 1983-89; sci. cons. N.C. Alcohol Rsch. Authority, Chapel Hill, 1976-89; bd. mem. So. Growth Policies Bd., 1992-94; adv. bd. Nat. Women's Hall of Fame, Trustmark Nat. Bank, 1991-97; rotating chair Miss. Instns. Higher Learning Pres. Coun., 1990-91; commn. govtl. rels. Am. Coun. Edn., 1990-93; mem. adv. bd. Entergy/Miss., 1994-97, Freedom Forum 1st Amendment Ctr., 1996-2001; mem. Miss. adv. bd. Trustmark Nat. Bank, 1991-97; mem. Mary Baker Eddy Adv. Group, 2000—; mem. Rhodes Scholar selection com. of Miss., 1996-98; mem. Free Sprit Awards selection com., 1996—; mem. ACE Commn. on Women in Higher Edn., 1999—. Mem. editl. bd. Planning for Higher Education, 1995; contbr. articles to profl. jours.; speeches pub. in Vital Speeches; mem. editl. bds. acad. jours. Trustee N.C. Performing Arts Ctr., Charlotte, 1988-89, Charlotte County Day Sch., 1987-89; bd. visitors Johnson C. Smith U., Charlotte, 1985-89; exec. com. bd. dirs. United Way Allocations and Rev., Charlotte, 1982-88; bd. advisors Charlotte Mecklenburg Hosp. Authority, 1985-89; bd. dirs. Jr. Achievement, Charlotte, 1983-89, Miss. Humanities Coun., Miss. Inst. Arts and Letters, Miss. Symphony, Miss. Econ. Coun.; chair Leadership Miss. and Collegiate Miss.; chmn. bd. dirs. Charlotte/Mecklenburg Arts and Sci. Coun., 1987-88; Danforth assoc. Danforth Found., St. Louis, 1976-88, Leadership Am., 1989; mem. golden triangle adv. bd. Bapt. Meml. Hosp., 1999—; pres. So. Univs. Conf., 1994-95; mem. commn. govt. rels. Am. Coun. Edn., 1990-93; mem. alumni bd. First United Meth. Ch., 1996—. Recipient Grad. Made Good award Fla. State U., 1990, medal of excellence Miss. U. for Women, 1995, Women Who Make a Difference award IWF, 2000; named Prof. of Yr., Queens Coll., 1979, One of 10 Most Admired Women Mgrs. in Am., Working Women mag., 1993, One of 1000 Women of the 90's, Mirabella mag., 1994; Ford Found. grantee, 1981; Paul Harris fellow, 1992; OWHE fellow, 1999—. Mem. Am. Assn. State Colls. and Univs. (bd. dirs. 1994-96, 99), Sociol. Soc., So. Assn. Colls. and Schs. (mem. commn. on colls. 1996-98), N.C. Assn. Colls. and Univs. (exec. com. 1988-89), N.C. Assn. Acad. Officers (sec.-treas. 1987-88), Soc. Internat. Bus. Fellows, Miss. Assn. Colls. (pres. 1992), Newcomen Soc. U.S., Internat. Women's Forum, Univ. Club, Rotary. Achievements include 1st female pres. of Miss. U. for Women (1st pub. coll. for women in Am.). Office: Miss State U Social Scis Rsch Ctr PO Box 5287 Mississippi State MS 39762

RENTELN, ALISON DUNDES, political science educator; b. Bloomington, Ind., Jan. 9, 1960; d. Alan and Carolyn (Browne) Dundes; m. Paul Alexander Renteln, June 9, 1985; children: David Alexander, Michael Alan. BA in History and Lit. cum laude, Harvard U., 1981; postgrad., London Sch. Econs., 1981-82; M of Jurisprudence, U. Calif., Berkeley, 1985, PhD in Jurisprudence and Social Policy, 1987; JD, U. So. Calif., 1991. Acting dir., vis. lectr. law and soc. U. Calif., Santa Barbara, 1986-87; asst. prof. polit. sci. U. So. Calif., L.A., 1987-93, assoc. prof. polit. sci., 1993—, acting dir. Unruh Inst. Pol., 1995-96, vice-chair dept. polit. sci., 1995—2002. Vis. prof. Sch. Law, U. Calif., Berkeley, 1996-97; vis. prof. dept. polit. sci. Stanford U., 1997; lectr. Calif. State Judges Assn., Nat. Assn. Women Judges, UN Assn., Nat. Assn. Fgn. Student Affairs, L.A. Refugee Forum, Calif. Assn. of Adminstrn. of Justice Educators Delinquency Control Inst.; others; coord. Contemporary Issues in Law and Pub. Policy lectr. series Pasadena Sr. Citizens Ctr.; participant Hearing of U.S. Adv. Bd. on Child Abuse and Neglect. Author: International Human Rights: Universalism Versus Relativism, 1990; co-editor: (with Alan Dundes) Folk Law: Essays on the Theory and Practice of Lex Non Scripta, 1994; reviewer: Am. Anthropologist, Am. Jour. Comparative Law, Am. Jour. Polit. Sci., Human Rights Quar., Jour. of Peace Rsch., others; contbr. numerous articles to profl. publs. Named Mentor of Distinction, Women's Caucus for Polit. Sci., 1993; Soroptomist Internat. Founder fellow, 1986; grantee Mark De Wolfe Howe Fund for rsch. in civil rights, civil liberties, and legal history Harvard U., 1985, Faculty Rsch. and Innovation Fund, 1988, Irvine Found. for diversity course devel., 1991, Faculty Fund for innovative tchg., 1993, Zumberge Faculty Rsch. and Innovation Fund, 1994. Mem. Am. Polit. Sci. Assn., Law and Soc. Assn., Commn. on Folk Law and Legal Pluralism, Am. Soc. Internat. Law, Internat. Law Assn. Office: U So Calif Dept Polit Sci Vkc 327 Los Angeles CA 90089-0044

RENTER, LOIS IRENE HUTSON, librarian; b. Lowden, Iowa, Oct. 23, 1929; d. Thomas E. and Lulu Mae (Barlean) Hutson; m. Karl A. Renter, Jan. 3, 1948; children: Susan Elizabeth, Rebecca Jean, Karl Geoffrey. BA cum laude, Cornell Coll., 1965; MA, U. Iowa, 1968. Tchr. Spanish Mt. Vernon High Sch., 1965-67; head libr. Am. Coll. Testing Program, Iowa City, 1968-89, ret., 1989. Vis. instr. U. Iowa Sch. Library Sci., 1972-82. Mem. Phi Beta Kappa. Methodist. Home: 1308 Brendel Hill Dr NW Cedar Rapids IA 52405-1566 E-mail: KLRenter1308@mchsi.com.

RENTERIA, JUANA, community health educator; b. Celaya, Mex., Apr. 26, 1972; d. Raul and Elisa (Rojas) R. BS in Health Info. Mgmt., U. Ill., Chgo., 1995; MPH, UCLA, 1997. Registered records adminstr. Rsch. asst. U. Ill., Urbana-Champaign, 1992, U.S. EPA, Chgo., 1994; adminstrv. intern U. Ill. Hosp., 1995; adminstrv. analyst purchasing dept. Evanston (Ill.) Hosp. Corp., 1995; rsch. asst. UCLA Jonsson Comprehensive Cancer Ctr., L.A., 1995-97; rsch. asst. dept. cmty. health UCLA, 1997—; sr. health educator L.A. County Dept. Health Svcs., 1998—. Mem. APHA, Am. Health Info. Assn. Democrat. Roman Catholic. Avocations: cooking, travel, dancing, reading, crafts. Home: 10340 Larry Lyn Dr Whittier CA 90603 Office: Whittier Health Ctr 7643 S Painter Ave Whittier CA 90602 E-mail: jrenteri@dhs.co.la.la.us.

RENTOUMIS, ANN MASTROIANNI, psychotherapist; b. New Haven, Apr. 27, 1928; d. Luigi Mastroianni and Marion Dallas; m. George Rentoumis, June 27, 1959; children: Michael, Mary, Anne. BA in Psychology, Vassar Coll., 1949; postgrad., Boston U. Med. Sch., 1949-50; MS in Social Work, Columbia U., 1952. Diplomate Am. Bd. Social Work, Am. Psychotherapy Assn.; lic. cert. social worker; lic. marriage and family therapist. Child and adolescent therapist Bklyn. Psychiat., 1952-55; family therapist Community Svc. Soc., N.Y.C., 1955-58; psychotherapist Bleuler Psychotherapy Ctr., L.I., N.Y., 1958-60, Adolescent Psychiat. Clinic, Tex. Children's Hosp., Houston, 1975-76; pvt. practice, 1976-77, Lauderdale Psychiat. Group, Ft. Lauderdale, Fla., 1978-90, Pompano Beach, 1990-93, Ft. Lauderdale, 1993—. Bd. dirs. Envirodyne, Inc. Pres. Pine Crest Sch. Mothers Club, 1985-86; v.p. Opera Soc., 1987-88, bd. mem., 1998—, parliamentarian 2000—; bd. govs., v.p. exec. bd. Fla. Philharm Orch., 1988-91, bd. dirs., 1990—; pres. Ft. Lauderdale Philharm. Soc., 1988-90. Recipient Golden Rule award J.C. Penney Co., 1990; named Woman of Yr., Am. Cancer Soc., 1989, Woman of Style and Substance, Ft. Lauderdale Philharm. Soc., 1998. Fellow Am. Psychotherapy Assn., Am. Orthopsychiat. Assn.; mem. Am. Assn. Marriage and Family Therapists, Am. Group Therapy Assn., Harbor Beach Surf Club (v.p. 1986-90). Avocations: piano, tennis, swimming. Home: 2200 S Ocean Ln Ph 6 Fort Lauderdale FL 33316-3836 Office: 1326 SE 3d Ave Fort Lauderdale FL 33316-1260

RENTSCHLER, CARL THOMAS, real estate executive, consultant; s. Franklin K. Rentschler and Della Diana Bucks; m. Madelynne Layden, Aug. 8, 1946; children: Patricia, Laron, Deborah. BS in Indsl. Edn., Pa. State U., 1942. Mem. Alaska Territorial Legis., Juneau, 1952; active in organization of First Fed. Savings and Loan, Anchorage, 1955, Anchorage Real Estate Multiple Listing Svc., 1955, Alaska Mutual Savings Bank, Anchorage, 1960. Capt. Army Air Corps, 1944-47. Republican. Baptist. Avocations: golfing, traveling, hunting, fishing. Home: 2901 Mccollie Ave Anchorage AK 99517-1223 Office: Rentschler Ins Agy 440 Eagle St Anchorage AK 99501-2631 E-mail: madcarl2@alaska.net.

RENWICK, EDWARD S. lawyer; b. L.A., May 10, 1934; AB, Stanford U., 1956, LLB, 1958. Bar: Calif. 1959, U.S. Dist. Ct. (cen. dist.) Calif. 1959, U.S. Ct. Appeals (9th cir.) 1963, U.S. Dist. Ct. (so. dist.) Calif. 1973, U.S. Dist. Ct. (no. dist.) Calif. 1977, U.S. Dist. Ct. (ea. dist.) Calif. 1981, U.S. Supreme Ct. 1985. Ptnr. Hanna and Morton LLP, L.A. Mem., bd. vis. Stanford Law Sch., 1967-69; mem. environ. and natural resources adv. bd. Stanford Law Sch. Bd. dirs. Calif. Supreme Ct. Hist. Soc. Fellow Am. Coll. Trial Lawyers, Am. Bar Found.; mem. ABA (mem. sect. on litigation, antitrust law, bus. law, chmn. sect. of nat. resources, energy and environ. law 1987-88, mem. at large coord. group energy law 1989-92, sect. rep. coord. group energy law 1995-97, Calif. del. legal com., interstate oil compact com.), Calif. Arboretum Assn. (trustee 1986-92), L.A. County Bar Assn. (chmn. natural resources law sect. 1974-75), The State Bar of Calif., Chancery Club (pres. 1992-93), Phi Delta Phi. Office: Hanna and Morton LLP 444 S Flower St Ste 1500 Los Angeles CA 90071-2922 E-mail: erenwick@hanmor.com.

RENWICK, J. ALAN, chemist, ecologist; b. Dundee, Scotland, May 7, 1936; arrived in U.S., 1960; s. Charles Renwick, Davina (Young) Alexander; m. Anne Marie Doyle, Apr. 23, 1983; children: Katherine, Fiona. Higher Nat. Cert., Dundee Tech. Coll., Scotland, 1960; MS in Chemistry, CCNY, 1964; PhD, U. Göttingen, Germany, 1970. Rsch. asst. Boyce Thompson Inst., Yonkers, NY, 1960—66, asst. chemist, 1966—73, assoc. chemist, 1973—83, chemist Ithaca, 1983—2001, chem. ecologist emeritus, 2001—. Adj. prof. entomology Cornell U., Ithaca, 1987—; guest prof. U. Freiburg, Germany, 1975. Contbr. over 130 articles to profl. jours., 23 chpts. to books. Recipient Silverstein-Simeone award for outstanding rsch. in chem. ecology, 1999. Mem.: Internat. Soc. of Chem. Ecology, Entomol. Soc. Am., Am. Chem. Soc. Office: Boyce Thompson Inst Tower Rd Ithaca NY 14853

RENYI, JUDITH A. foundation administrator; b. Phila., July 31, 1947; d. Eric and Liselotte Feyertag; children: Jessica, Quentin, Hodgson. AB, U. Pa., 1968, PhD, 1973; MA, Warwick U., 1972. Sponsored programs assoc. NYU, N.Y.C., 1979-80, asst. dean, 1980-83, fellow humanities coun., 1983-84; exec. dir. Paths/Prism, 1984-89, Collaboratives Humanities and Arts Tchg., Phila., 1989-94, NEA Found., Washington, 1994—. Bd. dirs. Grantmakers for Edn., other adv. bds. and commns. Author: Going Public, 1993; contbr. articles to profl. jours. Bd. dirs., founder Richard H. DeLone Meml. Scholarship, Phila., 1991, A.H. Scouten Meml. Book Fund, Phila., 1997. Recipient of numerous grants from founds. and pub. agencies. Mem. Coun. on Founds., Washington Regional Assn. Grantmakers, Univ. Club. Avocations: avid amateur cellist, chamber music.

RENYI, THOMAS A. bank executive; b. 1946; BA, Rutgers U., 1967, MBA, 1968. With The Bank of N.Y., Inc., 1971—; pres., COO, dir. parent holding co., 1992—; vice chmn., dir. The Bank of N.Y., Inc., 1992-98, chmn., CEO, 1998—. With U.S. Army, 1968-70.*

RENZETTI, ATTILIO DAVID, JR. physician; b. N.Y.C., Nov. 11, 1920; s. Attilio and Anna (Accardi) R.; m. Mabel Lucille Woodruff, May 24, 1947; children: Patricia Ann, Laurence, Pamela Sorensen, David. AB, Columbia Coll., 1941, MD, 1944. Diplomate: Am. Bd. Internal Medicine (chmn. subsplty. bd. pulmonary disease 1970-72). Intern, resident Bellevue Hosp., N.Y.C., 1944-45, 47-49, 51-52, fellow cardiopulmonary physiology, 1949-51; asst. prof. medicine U. Utah, 1952-53, State U. N.Y., Syracuse, 1953-57; assoc. prof. SUNY, 1957-60; asst. prof. Johns Hopkins U., 1960-61; assoc. prof. U. Md., 1960-61, U. Utah, Salt Lake City, 1961-67, prof., 1967-90, emeritus, 1990—. Editorial bd.: Am. Rev. Respiratory Disease, 1964-67; Contbr. articles to med. jours. Pres. Utah TB and Health Assn., 1965-66; bd. dirs. Am. Lung Assn., 1965-74, 78-81. With M.C. AUS, 1945-47. Mem. Am. Thoracic Soc. (pres. 1975-76) Home and Office: 1801 London Plane Rd Salt Lake City UT 84124-3531

RENZETTI, PHYLLIS JEAN, retired technical editor; b. Kingman, Ind., Feb. 3, 1925; d. Claude and Helen (Duchene) A.; divorced; 1 child, Jeanne. BA, Wheaton (Ill.) Coll., 1947; MA, Columbia U., 1950; PhD, Ind. U., 1961. Tchr. Wheaton Coll., 1948-49; tech. editor U.S. Geol. Survey, Reston, Va., Menlo Park, Calif., 1963-94, ret., 1994. Mem. AAAS, Paleontological Soc. Home: 3266 Hanover Dr Lafayette IN 47909-3852

RENZI, MICHAEL PAUL, b. Perth Amboy, Nj, Feb. 21, 1964; s. Michael Francis and Ruth Renzi; m. Teresa Marie Kimmet, June 7, 1986; children: Kristen Michaela, Lauren Alexandra, Paul Michael. Bachelor, Bowling Green State U., Bowling Green, Ohio, 1983—86. Bachelors of Music Ohio, 1986. Dir. of bands Cedarville H.S., Cedarville, Ohio, 1986—90, Bishop Watterson, Columbus, 1990—. Mem.: Music Educators Nat. Conv., Ohio Music Educators Assn., Phi Mu Alpha (treas. 1985—86). Home: 786 Erin Street Lewis Center OH 43035 Office: Bishop Watterson High School 99 E Cooke Road Columbus OH 43214 Personal E-mail: mptmrenzi@cs.com.

REOCK, ERNEST C., JR. retired government services educator, academic director; b. Belleville, N.J., Oct. 13, 1924; s. Ernest C. and Helen Rutan (Evans) R.; m. Jeanne Elizabeth Thomason, Jan. 25, 1953; children: Michael, Thomas, Kathleen. BS, Swarthmore Coll., 1945; AB, Rutgers U., 1948, MA, 1950, PhD, 1959. Rsch. assoc. bur. govt. rsch. Rutgers U., New Brunswick, N.J., 1950-59, asst. prof., dir., 1960-63, assoc. prof., dir., 1963-68, prof., dir., 1968-92. Cons. N.J. Constnl. Conv., New Brunswick, 1966, N.J. State and Local Revenue and Expenditure Commns., 1986-88, N.J. State Apportionment Commn., 1981, 91, 2001. Author: Handbook for New Jersey Assessors, 1962, School Budget Caps in New Jersey, 1981 (Govtl. Rsch. Assn. award 1983); editor: New Jersey Legislative District Data Book, 1972-92. Chmn. Middlesex County Charter Study Commn., New Brunswick, 1973-74; cons. various mcpl. charter commns., 1965-97. Lt. USN, 1943-46, 51-53. Recipient Gov.'s award for Pub. Svc., 1997. Mem. Am. Soc. Pub. Adminstrn. (Pub. Adminstr. of Yr. 1982), Am. Ednl. Fin. Assn. Avocations: sailing, swimming. Home: 7 Kendall Rd Kendall Park NJ 08824-1010 Office: Rutgers U Ctr Govt Svcs 33 Livingston Ave New Brunswick NJ 08901-1900

REPA, EDWARD WILLIAM, waste management association executive, hydrologist; b. Pitts., May 17, 1953; s. Edward V. Repa and Mary Alice (Crusan) Betsch; m. Deborah Helen Zak, May 14, 1976; children: Edward J., Erica T., Julia S. BS, Baldwin-Wallace Coll., 1975; MS, W.Va. U., 1977, PhD, 1981. Mgr. natural resources divsn. Underground Techs. Devel., Inc., Alexandria, Va., 1979-82; mgr. groundwater sect. Sci. Applications Internat. Corp., McLean, 1982-86; dir. environ. programs Environ. Industry Assn., Washington, 1986—. Author: Leachate Plume Management, 1985; contbg. author: Handbook of Solid Waste Management, 1994; editl. advisor Waste Age, 1986—; mem. editl. adv. bd. Environ. Geology, 1993—. Scoutmaster troop 688 Boy Scouts Am., Fairfax Sta., Va., 1992—. Mem. Nat. Ground Water Assn., Potomac River Smallmouth Bass Assn. Avocations: freshwater fishing, camping. Home: 9689 S Run Oaks Dr Fairfax Station VA 22039-2623 Office: Environ Industry Assn 4301 Connecticut Ave NW Ste 300 Washington DC 20008-2304 E-mail: erepa@erols.com., erepa@envasns.org.

REPASKY, MARK EDWARD, oil and gas company executive; b. Mueyguez, P.R., Sept. 7, 1956; s. Robert E. and Pauline M. (Kinney) R.; m. Ivy D. Wilde, June 3, 1978. BS in Petroleum Engring., U. Wyo., 1978. Registered profl. engr., Colo. Engr. No. Natural Gas Co., Tulsa, 1978-80; petroleum engr. Nortex Oil and Gas Co., Denver, 1980-84; sr. petroleum engr. Tex. Oil and Gas Co., 1984-87, mgr. project Dallas, 1987-88; v.p. Panda Resources, Inc., Tulsa, 1988-93; pres. Marker Petroleum, Inc., 1993—. Patentee in field. Richardson Trust scholar, 1974-77. Mem. Soc. Petroleum Engrs., Nat. Soc. Profl. Engrs., Nat. Gas Men's Assn. Avocations: sailing, skiing, reading, photography, golf. Home: 8086 S Yale Ave # 195 Tulsa OK 74136-9003 Office: Marker Petroleum Inc 5727 S Lewis Ave Ste 700 Tulsa OK 74105-7148 E-mail: mrepasky@bluegrassenergy.com.

REPETTI, ANAMARIA, healthcare foundation executive; b. Pasadena, Calif., Oct. 8, 1962; d. Francis Joseph Repetti and Dextra Kay Sharples; m. Gregory Rel Schmitt, Oct. 27, 1990; children: Siena Louise, Maximilian Finn Clyde, Wyatt Francis Gregory. AB, U. Calif., Irvine, 1993. Cmty. rels. rep. U. So. Calif. Sch. Medicine, L.A., 1984-85, asst. editor periodicals, 1985-87; pub. rels. mgr. Huntington Meml. Hosp., Pasadena, 1987-90; prin., cons. Repetti Comms., 1990-95; dir. pub. rels. ARC San Gabriel Valley, 1995-96; v.p., exec. dir. Palomar Pomerado Health Found., San Diego, 1996—. Cons. ARC, Pasadena, 1994-95, San Diego County Podiatric Med. Soc., 1997-2000, L.A. Soc. Ophthalmology, 1997—, Rsch. Study Club, 2000—. Mem. AAUW, NAFE, Assn. for Healthcare Philanthropy, Nat. Soc. Fundraising Execs.

Republican. Roman Catholic. Avocations: running, kayaking, painting, horticulture, reading. Office: Palomar Pomerado Health Found 15255 Innovation Dr San Diego CA 92128 E-mail: axr5@pphs.org.

REPHAN, JACK, lawyer; b. Little Rock, Mar. 16, 1932; s. Henry and Mildred (Frank) R.; m. Arlene Clark, June 23, 1957; children: Amy Carol, James Clark. BS in Commerce, 1954; LLB, U. Va., 1959. Bar: Va. 1959, D.C. 1961. Assoc. Kanter & Kanter, Norfolk, Va., 1959-60; law clk. to Judge Sam E. Whitaker, U.S. Ct. Claims, Washington, 1960-62; assoc. Pierson, Ball & Dowd, 1962-64; ptnr. Danzansky, Dickey, Tydings, Quint & Gordon, 1964-77; mem. Braude, Margulies, Sacks & Rephan, 1977-87; ptnr. Porter, Wright, Morris & Arthur, 1987-88, Sadur, Pelland & Rubinstein, Washington, 1988-93; counsel Hofheimer Nusbaum P.C., Norfolk, Va., 1993-00; principal Rephan Lassiter & Warren PLC, 2001—. Mem. nat. panel arbitrators Am. Arbitration Assn., NASD Bd. Arbitrators; lectr. joint com. continuing legal edn. State Bar Va. Contbr. articles to legal jours. Pres. Patrick Henry PTA, Alexandria, Va., 1968-69, Linkhorn Bay Condominium Assn., 2000—; treas. John Adams Mid. Sch. PTA, Alexandria, 1970-71; pres. Seminary Ridge Citizens Assn., 1976-77; Dem. candidate for Alexandria City Com., 1969. 1st lt. AUS, 1955-57. Mem. ABA (chmn. subcom. on procurement of jud. remedies pub. contract sect. 1973-74), Va. Bar Assn. (govt. sect. constrn. law 1979-81, 99—, vice chmn. 1980-81, chmn. 1981-82), D.C. Bar Assn., Assoc. Gen. Contractors, Hampton Roads Utility and Heavy Contractors Assn. (gen. counsel), Cavalier Golf and Yacht Club, Kiwanis (pres. Landmark Club 1969). Jewish. Home: 1276 Laskin Rd Ste 402 Virginia Beach VA 23451-5272 Office: 500 E Main St Ste 830 Norfolk VA 38510-2204 E-mail: jrephan@rephan.com.

REPIK, ALEKSANDR VLADIMIROVICH, molecular biologist; b. Perm, Russia, Sept. 2, 1958; s. Vladimir Iosiphovich and Mariya (Grigorevna) R.; m. Galina Alekseevna, Oct. 9, 1981; children: Dmitriy, Aleksander. MSc in biology, Perm State U., 1981; MSc in Molecular Biology, Moscow State U., 1987; PhD in Biochemistry, Russian Acad. Scis., 1994. Jr. rsch. scientist Perm State U., 1981-83, Russian Acad. Scis. Inst. Ecology & Physiology Microorganism, Perm, 1983-86; rsch. scientist Russian Acad Scis. Inst. Biochem. & Physiology Microorganism, Pushino, 1989-93, 94-97; vis. scientist Inst. Pflanzengenet and Kulturpflanzenforsch, Gatersleben, Germany, 1993; post-doctoral rsch. scientist Loma Linda (Calif.) U., 2000—, U. Mass., Worcester, 2000—. Contbr. articles to sci. and profl. jours. Mem. AAAS, Am. Soc. for Microbiology, Sigma Xi. Russian Orthodox. Avocation: reading. E-mail: Repiale@yahoo.com.

REPKO, LISA, medical/surgical nurse; b. Boston, Oct. 7, 1954; ADN, Regents Coll., Albany, N.Y., 1980, BSN, 1984; MPH, U. Albany, 1995. RN, N.Y. Staff nurse Albany Med. Ctr. Hosp., 1980—.

REPLINGER, JOHN GORDON, architect, retired educator; b. Chgo., Nov. 9, 1923; s. Roy Lodawick and Dorothy Caroline (Thornstrom) R.; m. Dorothy Thiele, June 26, 1945; children: John Gordon Jr., Robert Louis, James Alan. BS in Architecture with highest honors, U. Ill., Urbana, 1949, MS in Architecture, 1952. Registered architect, Ill. Designer-draftsman L. Morgan Yost (Architect), Kenilworth, Ill., 1949-50; instr. U. Ill., 1951-53, asst. prof. architecture, 1953-57, assoc. prof. architecture, 1957-61, prof. architecture, 1961-85, prof. housing research and devel., 1972-85, prof. emeritus, 1985—, assoc. head dept. for acad. affairs, 1970-71; practice architecture Urbana, 1951—. Served as combat pilot USAAF, 1943-45. Decorated Air medal with oak leaf clusters; recipient Sch. medal AIA, 1949, List of Tchrs. Ranked as Excellent by Their Students award U. Ill., 1976, 77, 78, 82, 83; Allerton Am. travelling scholar, 1948. Mem. Nat. Trust Hist. Preservation. Home and Office: 403 Yankee Ridge Ln Urbana IL 61802-7113

REPLOGLE, DAVID ROBERT, publishing company executive; b. Chgo., Feb. 24, 1931; s. Homer Mock and Helen (Fluke) R.; m. Jeanne Lonnquist, Nov. 4, 1954; children: William T., Bruce R., Stewart D., James M., John B. AB, Dartmouth Coll., 1953; postgrad., Princeton U., 1957-58. V.p., gen. mgr. Doubleday & Co., Inc., N.Y.C., 1958-70; pres., chmn. bd. G. & C. Merriam Co., Springfield, Mass., 1970-75; pres. Praeger Publishers, N.Y.C., 1970-75; exec. v.p., dir. Houghton Mifflin Co., Boston, 1975-91; pres. DR&A Inc., Cohasset, Mass., 1992—; pres., publ. Hot House Press. Dir. L.I. Replogle Found., Chgo., 1982—; trustee South Shore Health and Ednl. Found. Served to lt. USNR, 1953-57. Mem. Cohasset Golf Club, Plantation Golf and Country Club. Home: 84 Gammons Rd Cohasset MA 02025-1406 Office: David Replogle & Assocs 760 CJ Cushing Hwy Cohasset MA 02025-2124 E-mail: drreplogle@aol.com.

REPLOGLE, MICHAEL A. civil engineer, urban planner, environmentalist; b. Gt. Lakes, Ill., Dec. 28, 1953; s. Fred W. and Wilma E. (Furhman) R.; m. Linda Frazee Baker, June 6, 1986. BA in Sociology cum laude, BSE in Civil & Urban Engring. cum laude, MSE in Civil & Urban Engring., U. Pa., 1978. USPHS officer U.S. Indian Health Svc., Kayenta, Ariz., 1978; rsch. assoc. Pub. Tech. Inc., Washington, 1979-82; transp. coord. for Montgomery County Nat. Capital Park and Planning Commn., Silver Spring, Md., 1983-92; transp. dir. Environ. Def., Washington, 1992—. Cons. World Bank, U.S. Fed. Hwy. Adminstrn., 1990-92. Author: Bicycles and Public Transportation, 1983, Transportation Conformity and Demand Management, 1993; contbr. articles to profl. jours. Nat. coord., founder, Bikes Not Bombs Campaign, Washington, 1984-89; steering com. Campaign for New Transp. Priorities, Washington, 1989-92. Mem. Inst. for Transp. Devel. Policy (founder, pres. 1985-92, bd. dirs. 1992—). Office: Environ Def 1875 Connecticut Ave NW Washington DC 20009-5728 E-mail: michaelr@environmentaldefense.org.

REPLOGLE, ROBERT LEE, cardiovascular and thoracic surgeon; b. Ottumwa, Iowa, Sept. 30, 1931; s. Ralph Ruby and Edith Dorothy (Swartz) R.; m. Carol A. Heeschen, Aug. 24, 1958; children: Robert E., Jennifer Bremer, Edith Sheffer. MD cum laude, Harvard U., 1960; DSc (hon.), Cornell Coll., 1972. Diplomate Am. Bd. Surgery, Am. Bd. Thoracic Surgery, Am. Bd. Pediat. Surgery. Intern in surgery U. Minn. Hosp., 1960-61; asst. resident in surgery Peter Bent Brigham Hosp., Boston, 1961-63, Mass. Gen. Hosp., Boston, 1965-66; sr. resident in surgery Children's Hosp. Med. Ctr., 1966; asst. in surgery Children's Hosp. Med. Ctr. and Harvard Med. Sch., 1966-67; asst. prof. surgery Pritzker Sch. Medicine U. Chgo., 1967-70, assoc. prof. surgery and head, sect. pediat. surgery, 1970-73, prof. surgery and head, sect. pediat. surgery, 1973-74, prof. surgery and head, sect. cardiac surgery, 1973-80, prof. surgery, sect. cardiac surgery, 1973-90; med. dir. cardiac surgery unit Ingalls Meml. Hosp., 1989-98; chief divsn. cardiac surgery Columbus Hosp., Chgo., 1987-97; pres. CTS Net Inc., 1998—. Vis. prof. Albany Med. Coll., 1974, Dalhousie Sch. of Medicine, Halifax, 1975, Walter Reed Army Med. Ctr., 1978, U. Miami Med. Sch., 1992, Philippine Heart Ctr. for Asia March, 1979, Health Inst. Japan, Tokyo, 1982, Creighton Med. Sch., 1988, Brooke Army Med. Ctr., 1993, U. Heidelberg, 1995, Kerkoff Clinic/Max Planct Inst., Bad Nanheim, Germany, 1995, German Heart Ctr., Munich, 1995, Peter Bent Brigham Hosp. Harvard Med. Sch., 1996; mem. surgery and bioengring. study sect. HHS, NIH, 1979-83; mem. ad hoc adv. com. bypass angioplasty revascularization investigation, NIH, 1993-94; mem. subcom. on quality N.Y. State Dept. Health, 1989-96, mem. subcom. on resources and facilities, 1993—, mem. cardiac adv. com., 1989—; pres. Ctsnet.org, Inc., 1999—. Author: (with others) Microcirculation, Perfusion, and Transplantation of Organs, 1970, The Critically Ill Child, 1972, Surgical Clinics in North America, 1976, Biprosthetic Cardiac Valves, 1979, Year Book of Nuclear Medicine, 1981, among others; mem. editl. bd. Jour. Cardiac Surgery, 1982-99; contbr. more than 125 articles to profl. jours. With USN, 1951-54. Recipient Merit award Philippine Heart ctr. for Asia, Manila, 1985, Friendship award Shanghai Chest Hosp., 1987. Mem. AMA (diagnostic and therapeutic tech. assessment panel 1995—, ho. of dels. 1992—, joint rev. com. on ednl. programs for physicians assts. 1979-84), ACS (com. on allied health pers. 1979-84, chmn. 1983-84, com. on med. motion pictures 1979-85, com. on membership 1988—, residency rev. com. for thoracic surgery of the accreditation com. for grad. med. edn. 1992-95, 96—), Ill. State Med. Soc., Chgo. Med. Soc., Am. Surg. Assn., European Assn. for Cardiothoracic Surgery, Soc. for Acad. Surgery, Am. Heart Assn. (adv. coun. cardiovasc. surgery 1968-71), Soc. Univ. Surgeons, Internat. Cardiovasc. Soc., Societe Internationale de Chirurgie (N.Am. chpt.), Am. Assn. for Thoracic Surgery (del. AMA 1992—, com. on soc. responsibility 1991—), Soc. Thoracic Surgeons (program com. 1978-81, chmn. 1981, com. on medico-legal affairs, chmn. 1985-88, ad hoc fin. adv. com. 1987-89, ad hoc exhibitors adv. com. 1988-89, ad hoc com. on social responsibility 1992-95, ad hoc database liaison com. 1993-94, database liaison com. 1994—, ad hoc com. on physician-specific mortality for cardiac surgery 1993-96, stds. and ethics com. 1984-88, treas. 1986-92, exec. com. 1986—, pres.-elect. 1995-96, pres. 1996-97, rep. to the coun. of med. specialty socs. 1990—, annals of thoracic surgery liaision com. 1992—, com. on grad. edn. in thoracic surgery 1992—, com. on major issues in thoracic surgery 1993, chmn. 1994, 95, pres.-elect coun. med. splty. socs. 1997-98, pres. coun. med. specialty socs. 1998-99), Coun. of Med. Specialty Socs., German Cardiac Surgery Soc. (hon. mem.). Avocations: wine collecting, photography, travel. Address: CTS Net Inc 1160 E 56th St Chicago IL 60637-1541

REPP, ANDREW SCOTT, secondary school educator; b. Plymouth, Ind., July 17, 1970; s. Russell Frederick and Gloria Helen Muriel R.. BS, Bob Jones U., Greenville, S.C., 1994; MS, Va. Poly. Inst. and State U., Blacksburg, 1996, PhD, 1998. Cert. secondary specialist Am. Assn. Christian Schs., 1999. Math. educator Christian Liberty Sch., Kea'au, Hawaii, 1998—. Contbr. articles. Worship leader Kea'au (Hawaii) Bible Ch., 1999—. Mem.: BobJones U. Alumni Assn., Nat. Coun. Tchrs. Maths., Creation Rsch. Soc., Phi Kappa Phi. Avocation: guitar. Home: PO Box 1779 Keaau HI 96749-1779 Office: Christian Liberty Sch 16-675 Milo St Keaau HI 96749-1779

REPP, RONALD STEWART, insurance company executive; b. Phila., Dec. 12, 1944; s. Carl George Jr. and Pauline Francis (Hunley) R.; m. Nancy Elaine Hannigan, Sept. 16, 1967; children: Christopher Robert, Justin Ronald. Grad. high sch., Pitts.; cert., Am. Coll., Bryn Mawr, Pa., 1973, Am. Inst., Malvern, Pa., 1977. CLU, CPCU, assoc. in risk mgmt. Admistr. Liberty Mut. Ins. Group, Pitts., 1963-65, sales rep., 1967-70, sales supr., 1970-72, sales mgr., 1972-78; spl. agt. The Prudential, 1966-67; account exec. Ind. Ins. Svc. Corp., Canton, Ohio, 1978-83, v.p., 1983-90, sr.v.p., 1990—. Mem. adv. bd. dirs. Silver Lake Estates. Contbr. articles to profl. jours. Staff sgt. U.S. Army, 1964-65. Mem. Soc. CPCUs, Soc. CLUs, Ind. Ins. Agts. Assn., Akron City Club (chmn. mem. com. 1992-94), Bay Point Yacht Club, Akron Cruising Club (vice commodore), Silver Lake Country Club. Lutheran. Avocation: sailing (Coast Guard captain, Masters license). Home: 3103 Silver Lake Blvd Silver Lake OH 44224-3130 Office: Ind Ins Svc Corp 200 Market Ave N Ste 100 Canton OH 44702 E-mail: rrepp@schauergroup.com.

REPPER, GEORGE ROBERT, lawyer; b. Topeka, Dec. 22, 1954; s. George Vincent Jr. and Maria Magdalena (Bullert) R.; m. Helen Linda Zeichner, Aug. 23, 1981; children: Brian Lawrence, Kevin Michael, Michelle Suzanne. BS, SUNY, Albany, 1977; JD, Albany Law Sch., 1981. Bar: N.Y. 1982, D.C. 1982, U.S. Patent and Trademark Office 1984, U.S. Ct. Appeals (fed. cir.) 1989. V.p. Rothwell, Figg, Ernst & Manbeck, Washington, also bd. dirs. Contbr. articles to profl. jours. including Patent World. Mem. ABA (patents, trademarks and copyrights sect.), D.C. Bar Assn. (patents, trademarks and copyrights sect.), Am. Intellectual Property Law Assn., Internat. Intellectual Property Assn., Internat. Fedn. Indsl. Property Attys., Intellectual Property Owners, Internat. Trademark Assn. Republican. Office: Rothwell Figg Ernst & Manbeck 1425 K St NW Ste 800 Washington DC 20005

REPPERGER, DANIEL WILLIAM, electrical engineer; b. Charleston, S.C., Nov. 24, 1942; s. Daniel William and Mary (Schurer) R.; m. Frances Sullivan, Jan. 2, 1988; children: Lisa A. Repperger Cornwell, Daniel William III. BSEE, Rensselaer Poly. Inst., 1967, MSEE, 1968; PhD in Elec. Engring., Purdue U., 1973. Registered profl. engr., Ohio. Instr. Purdue U., West Lafayette, Ind., 1968-71, David Ross rsch. fellow, 1971-73; postdoctoral fellow NRC, Washington, 1973-75; electronics engr. Air Force Rsch. Lab., Dayton, Ohio, 1975—; adj. prof. Wright State U., 1984—. Contbr. articles to profl. jours. Author 4 book chpts.; contbr. mroe than 60 articles to profl. jours. Recipient Comdr.s Disting. Paper award Wright Patterson AFB, 1987; named Rsch. Scientist of Yr., Affiliates Coun., 1991; fellow Air Force Rsch. Lab., 2000. Fellow IEEE (assoc. editor Transactions on Control Sys. Tech. 1991—, chmn. Conf. on Control Applications 1992, H. Schuck award 1980, Biomed. Engring. award 1990), Am. Inst. Med. and Biol. Engring.; mem. Dayton IEEE (chmn. Control Sys. Soc. 1994—, chmn. Engring. Medicine and Biology Soc. 1988-93), Sigma Xi. Achievements include 12 patents; 23 Air Force inventions; development of joint Dept. of Def.-VA program to transfer technology from the military uses to help handicapped people. Home: 833 Blossom Heath Rd Dayton OH 45419-1102 Fax: (937) 255-8752. E-mail: D.Repperger@IEEE.ORG.

REPPERT, JAMES EUGENE, mass communications educator; b. Paxton, Ill., Sept. 24, 1958; s. Everett and Berdine Anita (Nelson) R.; m. Rita Jane Glennon, Aug. 1, 1987. Cert., 1st class lic. FCC, Brown Inst., 1977; B Univ. Studies, N.D. State U., 1981; MA, U. Nev., Las Vegas, 1985. Vis. instr. Purdue U. Calumet, Hammond, Ind., 1985-86; instr. Southeastern La. Univ., La., 1986-87, So. Ark. Univ., Magnolia, 1987-93, asst. prof., 1993-2001, assoc. prof., 2001—, dir. broadcast journalism, 1987—; exec. prodr. radio and TV programs, 1987—, audio Webcasts, 1999—; faculty senator, 2000—. Co-anchor WRTL-AM, Rantoul, Ill., 1973-76, KFME-TV (PBS), Fargo, N.D., 1981; assoc. dir. forensics, tchg. asst. U. Nev., Las Vegas, 1983-85; news intern WJLA-TV (ABC), Washington, 1984; textbook reviewer Focal Press, 1994, Wadsworth, 1991, 94, Houghton Mifflin, 1993, 96, Longman, 1999, Harcourt, 2001, Allyn & Bacon, 2001, 02; mem. selection com. MBC Radio Hall of Fame, Chgo., 1994; faculty seminar del. C-SPAN, 1993, 95, Acad. TV Arts and Scis., 1989, Internat. Emmy Nominee Festival, 1999; presenter over 80 nat. confs.; cons. in field. Contbg. author: Video Rating Guide for Libraries, 1990-95, C-SPAN Campaign '96: A Resource Guide for Professors, 1995, College Broadcaster, 1993, The Ency. of Television News, 1998, Resources in Education: ERIC Document Reproduction Service, 1996—; mem. editl. adv. bd. Roxbury Pub., 1990-91, Collegiate Press, 1992-93. Recipient Landmark award Ark. Com. State Lands Office, 1998; named Ky. Comm. Assn. Scholar of Yr., 1997-98; grantee Tangipahoa Parish, Amite, La., 1987, C-SPAN, 1993, 95; Nat. Assn. TV Program Exec. faculty fellow, 1999, Radio and TV News Dirs. Found. faculty fellow, 2002. Mem. Nat. Comm. Assn., So. States Comm. Assn., So. Forensics Assn. (divsn. chair 1998-99), Internat. Radio TV Soc. Found. (faculty seminar del. 1993, 95, 97, 99, 2002, Stephen H. Coltrin award for excellence in comms. edn. 1999), Ark. Broadcast Edn. Assn., Ark. State Comm. Assn., Ky. Comm. Assn. (Tchr. of Yr. 2000-01), Phi Kappa Phi. Home: PO Box 2149 Magnolia AR 71754-7149 Office: So Ark Univ PO Box 9229 Magnolia AR 71754-9229 E-mail: jereppert@saumag.edu., jereppert@usa.net.

REPPERT, RICHARD LEVI, lawyer; b. Phila., Nov. 6, 1948; s. William Downing and Angela R. (Schmid) R.; m. Faith Simpson, Dec. 30, 1972 (div. Aug. 1992); 1 child, Richard Jacob; m. Jeanette T. deHaven, Apr. 10, 1994. BA, Lehigh U., 1970; JD, Villanova U., 1974. Bar: Ohio 1974, U.S. Dist. Ct. (no. dist.) Ohio 1974, Pa. 1993. Assoc. Thompson, Hine and Flory, Cleve., 1974-82, ptnr., 1982-89, Jones, Day, Reavis & Pogue, Cleve., 1989—. Mem. ABA, Am. Coll. Real Estate Lawyers, Nat. Assn. Office and Indsl. Pks., Ohio State Bar Assn., Cleve. Bar Assn., Mortgage Bankers Assn. Greater Cleve. Office: Jones Day Reavis & Pogue North Point 901 Lakeside Ave Cleveland OH 44114-1190 E-mail: rreppert@jonesday.com.

REPPERT, STEVEN MARION, pediatrician, scientist, educator; b. Sioux City, Iowa, Sept. 4, 1946; s. Ray Fred and Norma Grace (Coppock) R.; m. Mary Alice Herman, Dec. 28, 1968; children: Jason Steven, Katherine Mary, Christina Marie. BS, U. Nebr., Lincoln, 1973; MD with distinction, U. Nebr., Omaha, 1973; MA (hon.), Harvard U., 1993. Diplomate Nat. Bd. Med. Examiners. Intern Mass. Gen. Hosp., Boston, 1973-74, resident in pediatrics, 1974-76, asst. in pediatrics, 1979-80, asst. pediatrician, 1980-85, dir .lab devel. chronobiology, 1983-2001, assoc. pediatrician, 1985-2000, pediatrician, 2000-2001. Clin. assoc. NIH, Bethesda, Md., 1976-79; instr. pediatrics Harvard Med. Sch., Boston, 1979-81, asst. prof., 1981-85, assoc. prof., 1985-93, prof., 1993—, Higgins family prof. neurosci., 2001—; vis. scientist Lab. Molecular Neurobiology, Mass. Gen. Hosp., 1989-90; prof., chair dept. neurobiology U. Mass. Med. Sch., 2001—. Editor: Development of Circadian Rhythmicity and Photoperiodism in Mammals, 1989; co-editor: Suprachiasmatic Nucleus: The Mind's Clock, 1991; mem. editl. bd. Neuron, 1997—; contbr. articles to sci. jours., chpt. to books. Mem. adv. com. Charles H. Hood Found., 1993-98. Recipient E. Mead Johnson award, 1989, NIH Merit award, 1992; Regents scholar U. nebr., 1971; Pfizer Labs. Med. scholar, 1971; Charles King Trust rsch. fellow, 1981-83; grantee NIH, 1981—, Nat. Found./March of Dimes, 1981-88. Mem. Am. Pediatric Soc., Am. Physiol. Soc., Am. Soc. for Clin. Investigation, Endocrine Soc., Soc. for Pediatric Rsch., Soc. for Neurosci., Soc. for Rsch. on Biol. Rhythms (adv. com.), Am. Heart Assn. (established investigator 1985-90), Lepidopterists Soc., Cambridge Entomol. Club, Alpha Omega Alpha. Democrat. Office: Mass Gen Hosp 32 Fruit St Boston MA 02114-2620

REPPUCCI, NICHOLAS DICKON, psychologist, educator; b. Boston, May 1, 1941; s. Nicholas Ralph and Bertha Elizabeth (Williams) R.; m. Christine Marlow Onufrock, Sept. 10, 1967; children: Nicholas Jason, Jonathan Dickon, Anna Jin Marlow. BA with honors, U. N.C., 1962; MA, Harvard U., 1964, PhD, 1968. Lectr., rsch. assoc. Harvard U., Cambridge, Mass., 1967-68; from asst. prof. to assoc prof. Yale U., New Haven, 1968-76; prof. psychology U. Va., Charlottesville, 1976—, dir. grad. studies in psychology, 1984-95, 97-98. Originator biennial conf. on community rsch. and action, 1986. Author: (with J. Haugaard) Sexual Abuse of Children, 1988; (with P. Britner and J. Woolard) Preventing Child Abuse and Neglect Through Parent Education, 1997; editor: (with J. Haugaard) Prevention in Community Mental Health Practice; (with E. Mulvey, L. Weithorn and J. Monahan) Mental Health, Law and Children, 1984; assoc. editor Law and Human Behavior, 1986-96, mem. editl. bd., 1996—; mem. editl. bd. Am. Jour. Cmty. Psychology, 1974-83, 88-91; contbr. articles to profl. jours., chpts. in books. Adv. bd. on prevention Va. Dept. Mental Health, Mental Retardation and Substance Abuse Svcs., Richmond, 1986-92. Recipient Disting. Scholar in psychology award Va. Assn. Social Sci., 1991. Fellow APA (chmn. task force on pub. policy 1980-84), Am. Psychol. Soc., Soc. for Cmty. Rsch. and Action (pres. 1986, Disting. Contbn. award in theory and rsch. 1998, Inaugural award for ednl. mentoring 1999), Phi Beta Kappa. Office: U Va Dept Psychology PO Box 400400 Charlottesville VA 22904-4400 E-mail: ndr@virginia.edu.

REPS, DAVID NATHAN, finance educator; b. N.Y.C., July 30, 1926; s. Samuel and Fannie (Ginsberg) R.; m. Helene Shifrin, Aug. 10, 1958; children: Tamara, Aaron, Steven, Jennifer. BSEE, Columbia U., 1948; MSEE, U. Pitts., 1953, PhD, 1966. Elec. utility systems engr. Westinghouse Elec. Corp., Pitts., 1950-63, corp. planner, 1963-67; prin. mgmt. svcs. Ernst & Young, N.Y.C., 1967-75; prof., chmn. bus. econs., fin., pub. policy L.I. Univ., 1975-78; prof. fin. Pace U., Pleasantville, N.Y., 1978—; v.p. Video Frame Store, Inc., N.Y.C., 1983—, The Photoboard Group, N.Y.C., 1989-92; v.p. and treas. Digital Video Photo Imaging, Inc., 1992—. Bd. dirs. The Storyboard Group, Inc., N.Y.C.; exec. v.p. Video Frame Imaging, Inc., N.Y.C., 1994—. Contbr. articles to profl. jours. With USN, 1944-46. Home: 98 Soundview Ave White Plains NY 10606-3617 Office: Pace U Bedford Rd Pleasantville NY 10570

REQUARTH, WILLIAM HENRY, surgeon; b. Charlotte, N.C., Jan. 23, 1913; s. Charles William and Amelia (George) R.; m. Nancy Charlton, 1948 (div. 1966); children— Kurt, Betsy, Jeff, Jan, Tim, Suzanna; m. Connie Harper, 1977. AB, Millikin U., 1934, LLD, 1996; MD, U. Ill., 1938, MS, 1939. Diplomate: Am. Bd. Surgery. Intern St. Luke's Hosp., Chgo., 1938-39; resident Cook County Hosp., 1940-42, 46-48; pvt. practice medicine, specializing in surgery Decatur, Ill., 1950—. Clin. prof. surgery U. Ill. Med. Sch., from 1962, now emeritus; Mem. Chgo. Bd. Trade. Author: Diagnosis of Abdominal Pain, 1953, The Acute Abdomen, 1958; also contbg. author chpts. books. Chmn. trustees Millikin U.; chmn. James Millikin Found.; bd. dirs. Decatur Meml. Hosp. Served to comdr. USNR, 1941-46. Mem. ACS, Cen. Surg. Assn., Western Surg. Assn., Chgo. Surg. Soc., Ill. Surg. Soc. (founder, pres. 1970-71), Am. Soc. Surgery Hand (founder), Am. Soc. Surgery Trauma, Soc. Surgery Alimentary Tract, Warren Cole Soc. (founder), Societe Internationale Chirurgie, Nat. Pilots Assn. (pres. 1960-61), Soaring Soc. Am., Sportsman Pilot Assn. (pres. 1966-67), Aerobatic Club Am., Internat. Aerobatic Club. Home: 1860 S Spitler Dr Decatur IL 62521-4417 Office: 158 W Prairie Ave Decatur IL 62523-1230 E-mail: bilreq@fginet.com.

REQUÉNEZ, EUNICE LOIDA, medical, surgical, and community nurse; b. Tex., Oct. 31, 1938; d. Thomas and Mary (Gonzalez) Requénez; children: Jonathan Warmkessel, Ethan Warmkessel. BSN, Loma Linda U., 1960; diploma in audiometry, Fullerton State Coll., 1965; grad. FNP and physician asst., U. Calif., Davis, 1998. Cert. myofunctional therapist, home nutritionist, home health nurse. Sch. nurse Orange County, Calif., 1965-67, Tahoe Truckee (Calif.) Unified Sch. Dist., Tahoe City, 1988—. Vol. ARC; instr. Basic First Aid/CPR, breast self-exam. facilitator Am. Cancer Soc.; mem. Tahoe Truckee Children's Network. Mem. ANA, Calif. Sch. Nurse Orgn., No. Calif. Sch. Nurse Orgn. (mktg. chmn.), Sigma Theta Tau.

REQUENO, NESTOR DANILO, human services administrator; b. San Salvador, El Salvador, 1964; came to U.S., 1979; s. Humberto Flores and Maria Elodia Requeno; m. Raquel Gonzalez, July 3, 1988. AA in Liberal Arts, East L.A. Coll., 1993; BS in Pub. Adminstrn. summa cum laude, Calif. State U., Dominguez Hills, 1997, MPA, 2000. Real estate and retail entrepreneur, Bell, Calif., 1988-91; social svcs. worker L.A. County Dept. Social Svcs., Rancho Dominguez, 1991-95, job developer, cons. South L.A. County, 1995-98, lead analyst City of Industry, Calif., 1998, strategic planner, 1999—2002; dir. Intergovernmental & Interagency Relations, 2002—, adminstr., 2002—. Cons., mem. adv. bd. Super Job Fair Com., Carson, Calif., 1997-98; exec. dir. Transp. & Human Svc. Exec. Coun., 1999-2001; analyst Dept. Children & Family Svc. Author: Cash Assistance Program for Immigrants Implementation and Resource Guide, 1998 (Spl. Commendation award), speech and written testimony U.S. Ho. of Reps., 1998; author, designer: General Relief Opportunities for Work Program Interactive On-line Policy Manual: A "Killer App": to implement digital strategies and welfare-to-work best-practices for masses of users via L.A. County Info. Web. (Spl. Commendation award). Pub. rels. dir. 7th Day Adventist Spanish Ch., Huntington Park, Calif., 1986, missionary outreach dir., 1987; vol. U.S. Citizenship Action Network, L.A. County, 1996-98, City of L.A. Marathon, 1995-2000. Recipient The Pub. Social Svcs. Partnerships in Excellence award. Mem. Am. Soc. Pub. Adminstrn., L.A. County Hispanic Mgrs. Assn., Am. Inst. Certified Pub. Acct., Pub. Adminstrn. Alumni Soc. (adv. bd. 1997—), Pi Alpha Alpha, Phi Kappa Phi. Avocations: public speaking, volunteerism, fundraising, mentoring, hiking. Office: LA County Dept Pub Social Svcs 12860 Crossroads Pkwy S Los Angeles CA 91746-3411 E-mail: nrequeno@dpss.co.la.ca.us.

RESAT, HALUK, biophysicist, researcher; b. Corum, Turkey, 1964; PhD, SUNY, Stony Brook, New York, 1992—92. Assoc. prof. Koc U., Istanbul, Turkey, 1996—99; sr. rsch. scientist Pacific NW Nat. Lab, Richland, Wash., 1999—. Mem.: Biophysical Soc. Office: Pacific Northwest Nat Lab P.O. Box 999 MS: K1-83 Richland WA 99352 Office Fax: 509-375-6631. Business E-mail: haluk.resat@pnl.gov.

RESCH, CYNTHIA FORTES, secondary education educator; b. Providence, Dec. 9, 1951; d. Alfred Antone and Mabel (Duarte) F.; m. Joseph Bernard Resch III, June 26, 1982; children: Jeffrey, Jason, Steven, Kayla. BA, R.I. Coll., 1974; postgrad., U. Sorbonne, Paris, 1975, U. Valencia, Spain, 1979, Providence Coll., 1981. Cert. secondary edn. tchr., R.I. Tchr. French and Spanish, North Kingstown (R.I.) H.S., 1977—. Mem. North Kingstown Cmty. Chorus, 1996—; advisor North Kingstown H.S. Internat. Club, La Romana, Dominican Republic Mission Project, 2001. Mem. NEA, Am. Assn. Tchrs. Spanish and Portuguese, R.I. Fgn. Lang. Assn. Avocations: cooking, needlecraft, reading, photography, travel, sewing, aerobics. Office: North Kingstown HS 150 Fairway Dr North Kingstown RI 02852-6202

RESCH, JOSEPH ANTHONY, neurologist; b. Milw., Apr. 29, 1914; s. Frank and Elizabeth (Zetsch) R.; m. Rose Catherine Ritz, May 25, 1939; children— Rose, Frank, Catherine. Student, Milw. State Tchrs. Coll., 1931-34; BS, U. Wis., Madison, 1936, MD, 1938. Intern St. Francis Hosp., LaCrosse, Wis., 1938-39; gen. practice medicine Holmen, 1939-40; med. fellow in neurology U. Minn., 1946-48, clin. instr. neurology, 1948-51, clin. asst. prof., 1951-55, clin. assoc. prof., 1955-62, assoc. prof., 1962-65, prof., 1965-84, prof. emeritus, 1984—, head dept. neurology, 1976-82, asst. v.p. health sci., 1970-79, prof. lab. medicine and pathology, 1979-84; practice medicine specializing in neurology Mpls., 1948-62. Contbr. articles and abstracts to profl. jours., chpts. in books. Served to lt. col. M.C. U.S. Army, 1940-46; col. Med. Res. 1946-53. Mem. Hennepin County Med. Soc., Minn. Med. Assn., AMA, Minn. Soc. Neurol. Scis., Am. Acad. Neurology, Am. Neurol. Assn., Am. Assn. Neuropathologists, Am. Clin. Neurophysiol. Soc., Sonoma County Med. Assn., Am. Epilepsy Soc. Home: 8942 Acorn Ln Santa Rosa CA 95409

RESCH, MARY LOUISE, social services administrator; b. David City, Nebr., Oct. 26, 1956; d. Ernest John and Mary Jean (Roelandts) Cermak. BS in Psychology, SUNY, Albany, 1984; MS in Counseling and Edn. with high honors, U. Wis., Platteville, 1986. Enlisted U.S. Army, 1974, advance through ranks to sgt., 1982, bomb disposal tech. Kans., 1977-79, bomb disposal instr. Indian Head, Md., 1979-80, resigned, 1985; instr., intern family advocacy Army Community Svc., U.S. Army, Ft. Belvoir, 1986; sr. counselor, child therapist Community Crisis and Referral Ctr., Inc., Waldorf, Md., 1986-87; adminstr. Walter Reed Army Med. Ctr. USDA Grad. Sch., Washington, 1987-88, contract mgr. Ft. Jackson, S.C., 1988-91; pres. Athena Cons., Columbia, 1991-93; dir. spl. programs Newberry (S.C.) Commn. on Alcohol and Drug Abuse, 1993-95; resource devel. coord. Cities in Schs.-SC, Inc., Columbia, 1995-97; exec. dir. S.C. Ctr. for Family Policy, 1997—2001; pub. rels. dir. Xpress Group, Inc., 2001—. Human svcs. cons., Washington, 1986-87; adj. instr. Coker Coll., Ft. Jackson, 1989-95. Active Govs. Juvenile Justice Adv. Coun., Govs. Substance Abuse Prevention Coun. Mem. S.C. Assn. Prevention Profls. and Advs., State Assn. Crime Prevention Officers, Nat. Contract Mgmt. Assn. (fellow, former pres., mentor). Republican. Lutheran. Avocations: needlepoint, racquetball, reading, bowling, jewelry making. Home: 312 Edgewater Ln West Columbia SC 29169-6957

RESCHER, NICHOLAS, philosopher, educator; b. Hagen, Westphalia, Germany, July 15, 1928; came to U.S., 1938, naturalized, 1944; s. Erwin Hans and Meta Anna (Landau) R.; m. Dorothy Henle, Feb. 10, 1968; children: Mark, Owen, Catherine; 1 child from previous marriage, Elizabeth. BS in Math., Queens Coll., 1949; PhD, Princeton U., 1951; LHD (hon.), Loyola U., Chgo., 1970, Lehigh U., 1993; Dr. honoris causa, U. Córdoba, Argentina, 1992, U. Konstanz, Germany, 1995; DSc (hon.), CUNY, 1999; PhD (hon.), Fern U., Hagen, 2001. Instr. philosophy Princeton (N.J.) U., 1951-52; mathematician RAND Corp., 1954-56; assoc. prof. philosophy Lehigh U., Bethlehem, Pa., 1957-61; univ. prof. philosophy U. Pitts., 1961—, vice chmn. Ctr. for Philosophy of Sci., 1988—. Trustee St. Edmunds Acad., Pitts., 1980-85; nonresident mem. Corpus Christi Coll., Oxford; disting. vis. lectr. Oxford, Salamanca, Munich, Konstanz; cons. in field. Author: The Coherence Theory of Truth, 1973, Methodological Pragmatism, 1977, Scientific Progress, 1978, The Limits of Science, 1985, Luck, 1995, Predicting the Future, 1997, Nature and Understanding, 2000, Philosophical Reasoning, 2001; exec. editor Am. Philos. Quar., 1961—; mem. editl. bd. 15 jours.; contbr. over 250 articles to profl. jours. Sec. gen. Internat. Union History and Philosophy of Sci., UNESCO, 1969-75. With USMC, 1952-54. Recipient Alexander von Humboldt Humanities prize, 1983; fellow Ford Found., 1959-60, Guggenheim Found., 1970-71. Mem. Am. Philos. Assn. (past pres.), Am. Cath. Philos. Assn. (pres.), Royal Asiatic Soc., G.W. Leibniz Soc. Am. (past pres.), C.S. Peirce Soc. (past pres.), Inst. Internat. de Philosophie, Academie Internat. de Philosophie des Scis., Acad. Europaea. Roman Catholic. Avocation: reading history and biography. Home: 5818 Aylesboro Ave Pittsburgh PA 15217-1446 Office: Univ of Pitts Dept Philosophy 1012 Cathedral Pittsburgh PA 15260 E-mail: rescher@pitt.edu.

RESCIGNO, ALDO, pharmacokinetics educator; b. Milan, Italy, Aug. 27, 1924; s. Vincenzo and Celeste R.; m. Luisa Frisia, Sept. 2, 1950; 1 child, Federico. BS, Naval Coll., 1942; MS, U. Fribourg, 1945; PhD, U. Milan, 1948. Prof. physiology U. Minn., Mpls., 1969-78; prof. biomaths. U. Witwatersrand, Johannesburg, South Africa, 1979-81; rsch. collaborator Brookhaven Nat. Lab., Upton, N.Y., 1982-84, Yale U. Sch. Medicine, New Haven, 1982-87; prof. pharmacokinetics U. Parma, Italy, 1987-96. Adj. prof. U. Mass. Med. Ctr., Worcester, 1988-90; vis. scientist Genentech, Inc., San Francisco, 1991-92. Author: Drug and Tracer Kinetics, 1962, 2d edit., 1966; editor: Tracer Kinetics & Physiological Modeling, 1983, Pharmacokinetics, 1988, Cerebral Blood Flow, 1988, New Trends in Pharmacokinetics, 1991. Home: 14767 Square Lake Trail N Stillwater MN 55082-9278 E-mail: rescigno@earthlink.net.

RESCIGNO, RICHARD JOSEPH, editor; b. N.Y.C., Apr. 13, 1946; s. Vincent James and Rose (Sofia) R.; m. Carol Sue Conyne, Apr. 22, 1978; children: Timothy, Daniel. BA in English Lit., Fairleigh Dickinson U., 1967; MS in Journalism, Columbia U., 1968. Reporter The Hudson Dispatch, Union City, N.J., 1967; reporter, copy editor The Bergen Record, Hackensack, 1971-75; reporter, copy editor, asst. city editor Newsday, Melville, N.Y., 1975-81; news editor, asst. mng. editor, mng. editor Barron's, The Dow Jones Bus. and Fin. Weekly, N.Y.C., 1981—, mng. editor, 1987—. With U.S. Army, 1968-70. Avocations: foreign languages, travel, sports. Office: Barron's 200 Liberty St New York NY 10281-1003

RESCORLA, FREDERICK JOHN, pediatric surgeon, educator; b. York, Pa., May 22, 1954; s. Charles Laverne Rescorla and Charlotte Mulder; m. Michelle Daniels, Apr. 12, 1988; children: Andrew John, Grant Daniels. BS, Calvin Coll., 1976; MD, U. Wis., 1981. Resident in gen. surgery Sch. Medicine Ind. U., Indpls., 1981-86, resident in pediats. surgery, 1986-88, asst. prof. surgery, 1988-94, assoc. prof. surgery, 1994-2000, prof. surgery, 2000—. Mem. editl. bd. Jour. Pediat. Surgery, Jour. Surg. Oncology. Fellow ACS, Am. Acad. Pediats.; mem. Am. Assn. Pediat. Surgeons. Office: Pediat Surgery 702 Barnhill Dr Indianapolis IN 46202-5128 E-mail: frescor@iupui.edu.

RESCORLA, ROBERT ARTHUR, psychology educator; b. Pitts, May 9, 1940; s. Arthur R. and Mildred J. (Jenkins) Rescorla; m. Shirley Steele; children: Eric, Michael. BA, Swarthmore Coll., 1962; PhD, U. Pa., 1966; MA, Yale U., 1974. Successively asst. prof., assoc. prof., prof. Yale U., New Haven, 1966—80; prof. psychology U. Pa., Phila., 1981—, James Skinner prof. sci., 1986—2000, Christopher Browne Disting. Prof. psychology, 2000—, dean of coll. Sch. Arts and Scis., 1994—97. Author: Pavlovian Second-Order Conditioning, 1980; editor: Animal Learning and Behavior, 1995—97; contbr. articles to profl. jours. Recipient Ira Abrams Tchg. award, 1999. Mem.: AAAS (pres. sect. J., psychology 1988—89), NAS, APA (pres. divsn. 3 1985), Psychonomic Soc. (mem. governing bd. 1979—85, chmn. publ. bd. 1985—86), Ea. Psychol. Assn. (bd. dirs. 1983—86, pres. 1986—87), Soc. Exptl. Psychologists, Am. Psychol. Soc. Office: U Pa Dept Psychology 3815 Walnut St Philadelphia PA 19104-3604

RESDEN, RONALD EVERETT, medical devices product development engineer; b. Littleton, N.H., Oct. 27, 1944; s. Lawerence A. and Rita Mae (Bowen) R.; m. Dee Kronenburg, Apr. 20, 1974 (div.); children: Philip, Alison; m. Louise Simons, June 18, 1994. Cons. Franklin Mfg. Co., Norwood, Mass., 1984—, Boston Sci. Co., Watertown, 1985—, Via Med, Easton, 1986—, White Marsh Labs., Balt., 1989—, Spectraphos Malmo Sweden, 1991—, Vision Scis. Inc., Natick, Mass., 1991—, Cordis Corp., Miami, Fla., 1993—; cons. Cardiology Catheter Lab. Mass. Hosp. Cardiology, Boston, 1993—; cons. Boston Med. Products, Inc., Westborough, Mass., 1998—. Active MIT Enterprise Forum. Author: Hologram Control Transfer, 1984; inventor, patentee in field. Mem. NRA (life), Soc. Plastics Engrs. (mem. med. plastics and biomaterials mag. rev. bd.), Soc. Mfg. Engrs., Nat. Geog. Soc., Mass. Chiefs of Police Assn., Citizens for Ltd. Taxation. Home and Office: Arrowhead Rsch Inc 25 Arnold Rd Pelham MA 01002-9757 Office: Ron Resden Gunsmith Box 145 3545 Fellows Rd Guildhall VT 05905-0145 Fax: 413-253-9606; 802-328-4451. E-mail: resden@yahoo.com.

RESEK, ROBERT WILLIAM, economist; b. Berwyn, Ill., July 2, 1935; s. Ephraim Frederick and Ruth Elizabeth (Rummele) R.; m. Lois Doll, July 9, 1960; 1 child, Richard Alden. BA, U. Ill., 1957; AM, Harvard U., 1960, PhD, 1961. Vis. scholar MIT, Cambridge, 1967-68; asst. prof. econs. U. Ill., Urbana, 1961-65, assoc. prof., 1965-70, prof., 1970—; dir. Bur. Econ. and Bus. Rsch., 1977-89, acting v.p. for acad. affairs, 1987-89, v.p. for acad. affairs, 1989-94; prof. Inst. Govt. and Pub. Affairs, 1994—. Tchg. fellow Harvard U., 1959-61; vis. prof. U. Colo., 1967, 74, 75, 76, 82, Kyoto (Japan) U., 1976; cons. GM, 1964-66, U.S. Congress Joint Econ. Com., 1978-80, ABA, 1980-82; vis. scholar UCLA, 1994-95; co-dir. Midwest Economy: Issues and Policy, Midwest Govs. Conf., 1981; bd. dirs. Midwest U. Consortium Internat. Activities, v.p., 1991-94; mem. Ill. Gov.'s Econ. Policy Coun., 1999—. Co-author: Environmental Contamination by Lead and Other Heavy Metals—Synthesis and Modeling, 1978, Special Topics in Mathematics for Economists, 1976, A Comparative Cost Study of Staff Panel and Participating Attorney Panel Prepaid Legal Service Plans, 1981, Illinois Higher Education: Building the Economy, Shaping Society, 2000; editor: Illinois Economic Outlook, 1982-87, Illinois Economic Statistics, 1981, Economic Edge, 1996—; co-editor: The Midwest Economy: Issues and Policy, 1982, Frontiers of Business and Economic Research Management, 1983, Illinois Statistical Abstract, 1987. Mem. exec. com. Assn. Univ. bus. and Econ. Rsch., 1977-89, v.p., 1978-82, pres., 1982-83. Woodrow Wilson fellow, 1957; Social Sci. Rsch. Coun. grantee, 1964; NSF fellow, 1967-69, grantee, 1974-77; U.S. Dept. State scholar, Japan, 1976; grantee Ill. Bd. Higher Edn., 1998-99. Mem. Am. Statis. Assn., Econometric Soc., Beta Gamma Sigma, Phi Kappa Phi. Home: 201 E Holmes St Urbana IL 61801-6612 Office: Univ Ill 211 IGPA 1007 W Nevada St Urbana IL 61801-3812 E-mail: r-resek@uiuc.edu.

RESENDE, MARCELO, economist, educator; b. Rio de Janeiro, Aug. 26, 1963; s. Eduardo de Mendonça e Silva and Edna Vieira de Resende. BA in Econs., State U. Rio de Janeiro, 1985, BS in Psychology, 1990; MSc in Econs., Pontifical Cath. U., Rio de Janeiro, 1989; MA in Econs., U. Pa., 1993; DPhil in Econs., Oxford (Eng.) U., 1997. Lectr. Pontifical Cath. U. Rio de Janeiro, 1987-89; asst. prof. econs. State U. Rio de Janeiro, 1990, Fed. U. Rio de Janeiro, 1990-98, assoc. prof., 1998—. Contbr. articles to profl. jours., including Oxford Econ. Papers, Bull. Econs. Rsch., Oxford Bull. Econs. and Stats., Rev. Indsl. Orgns., Info. Econs. and Policy. Scholar Brazilian Ministry Sci. and Tech., 1986-88, rsch. grants, 1998-2001; scholar Brazilian Ministry Edn., 1991-95; rsch. grantee Brazilian Ministry Planning, 1988. Mem. Brazilian Econometric Soc. Avocations: music concerts, movies, sports practice (soccer), Theatre. Office: Fed U Rio de Janeiro Inst Econs Av Pasteur 250 22290-240 Rio de Janeiro Brazil E-mail: mresende@ism.com.br., mresende@ie.ufrj.br.

RESER, ELIZABETH MAY (BETTY RESER), bookkeeper; b. Le Roy, Kans., Sept. 4, 1939; d. William David II and Vera Hazel (Dreyer) Meats; m. William Joseph Reser, Sept. 26, 1958; children: Dee Anna Reser, Donna Sue Reser Larson. Diploma in computer programming, Control Data Inst., St. Louis, 1980; student, Washburn U., 1991. Cert. computer programmer, Mo. Computer programmer Regional Justice Info. Sys., St. Louis, 1980; sec. Shawnee Heights H.S., Tecumseh, Kans., 1973-78, bookkeeper, 1984-90. Treas. Secs. Assn. Shawnee Heights Unified Sch. Dist. 450, 1975-76, 86-87; vol. March of Dimes, Topeka, 1995-2001; mem. bd. trustees Susanna Wesley United Meth. Ch., Topeka, 1992-94, mem. prayer chain, 1993-94. Republican. Avocations: computers, quilting, shopping, crocheting, family activities. Home: 2849 SW Dukeries Rd Topeka KS 66614-4726

RESHOTKO, ELI, aerospace engineer, educator; b. N.Y.C., Nov. 18, 1930; s. Max and Sarah (Kalisky) R.; m. Adina Venit, June 7, 1953; children: Deborah, Naomi, Miriam Ruth. BS, Cooper Union, 1950; MS, Cornell U., 1951; PhD, Calif. Inst. Tech., 1960. Aero. research engr. NASA-Lewis Flight Propulsion Lab., Cleve., 1951-56, head fluid mechanics sect., 1956-57; head high temperature plasma sect. NASA-Lewis Research Center, 1960-61, chief plasma physics br., 1961-64; assoc. prof. engrng. Case Inst. Tech., Cleve., 1964-66, dean, 1986-87; prof. engrng. Case Western Res. U., 1966-88, chmn. dept. fluid thermal and aerospace scis., 1970-76, chmn. dept. mech. and aerospace engrng., 1976-79, Kent H. Smith prof. engrng., 1989-98, Kent H. Smith prof. emeritus, 1999—. Susman vis. prof. dept. aero. engrng. Technion-Israel Inst. Tech., Haifa, Israel, 1969-70; cons. United Technologies Research Ctr., Inst. Def. Analyses, Dynamics Tech. Inc., Micro Craft Tech., Martin-Marietta Corp., Rockwell Internat.; mem. adv. com. fluid dynamics NASA, 1961-64; mem. aero. adv. com. NASA, 1980-87, chmn. adv. subcom. on aerodynamics, 1983-85; chmn. U.S. Boundary Layer Transition Study Group, NASA/USAF, 1970—; U.S. mem. fluid dynamics panel AGARD-NATO, 1981-88; chmn. steering com. Symposium on Engring. Aspects Magneto-hydro-dynamics, 1966, Case-NASA Inst. for Computational Mechanics in Propulsion, 1985-92, USRA/NASA ICASE Sci. Coun., 1992; Joseph Wunsch lectr. Technion-Israel Inst. Tech., 1990. Contbr. articles to tech. jours. Chmn. bd. govs. Cleve. Coll. Jewish Studies, 1981-84; mem. bd. govs. Technion-Israel Inst. Tech., Haifa, Israel, 1999—; mem. NRC Air Force Sci. Tech. bd., 2000—. Guggenheim fellow Calif. Inst. Tech., 1957-59. Fellow ASME, AAAS, AIAA (Fluid and Plasma Dynamics award 1980, Dryden lectr. in rsch. 1994), Am. Phys. Soc. (vice-chmn. divsn. fluid dynamics 1998, chair-elect 1999, chair 2000, Otto Laporte award in fluid dynamics 1999), Am. Acad. Mechanics (pres. 1986-87); mem. NAE, AAUP, Ohio Sci. and Engring. Roundtable, Sigma Xi, Tau Beta Pi, Pi Tau Sigma. Office: Case Western Reserve Univ University Cir Cleveland OH 44106

RESIKA, PAUL, artist; b. N.Y.C., Aug. 15, 1928; Student, Sol Wilson, N.Y.C., 1940-44, Hans Hofmann Sch., 1945-47, Venice, Italy, 1950-53. Adj. prof. art Cooper Union, 1966-78; instr. Art Students League, 1968-69; faculty Skowhagen Sch. Painting and Sculpture, 1973, 76; chmn. M.F.A. program Parsons Sch. Design, 1978-89. One-man shows include George Dix Gallery, N.Y.C., 1948, Peridot Gallery, 1965, 1967, 1968, 1969, 1970, Washburn Gallery, 1971, 1973, Hopkins Ctr. Dartmouth Coll., 1972, Graham Gallery, 1976, 1979, 1981, 1983, 1985, Longpoint Gallery, Provincetown, Mass., 1979, 1981, 1989, 1992, 1995, 25-yr. survey Artists Choice Mus., 1985, Merideth Long Gallery, Houston, 1986, 1997, Walker-Kornbluth Gallery, Fair Lawn, N.J., 1986, Walter Kornbluth Gallery, 1995, 1997, Crane Kalman Gallery, London, 1986, Graham/Modern Gallery, 1987—88, 1990, Salander-O'Reilly Galleries, N.Y.C., 1993, 1994, 1995, Vered Gallery, East Hampton, N.Y., 1995, Gerald Peters Gallery, Santa Fe, 1996, Provincetown Art Assn. and Mus., 1997, Lori Bookstein Gallery, N.Y.C., 1998, 2001, Berta Walker Gallery, Provincetown, 1998, 2001, Lizan Tops Gallery, East Hampton, N.Y., 1998, Salander-O'Reilly Galleries, N.Y.C., 1999, 2001, 2002, Hackett Freedman, San Francisco, 1998, Hackett-Freedman, 1999, 2000, Metta Galleria, Madrid, 2000, Nat. Mus. Am. Art, Washington, Muson-Williams-Proctor Inst. Mus. Art, Utica, N.Y., Represented in permanent collections U. Nebr. Art Gallery, Indpls. Mus. Art, Chase Manhattan Bank, N.Y.C., Neuberger Mus., SUNY, Purchase, U. Wyo., Laramie, Met. Mus. Art, N.Y., Colby Coll., NAD, Owensboro (Ky.) Mus. Art, U. Ariz., William Benton Mus. Art, Hood Mus., Dartmouth Coll., Hanover, N.H., Tucson Mus. Art, Crackow Mus. Art, Poland, Parish Art Mus., Southampton, N.Y., Heckscher Mus., Huntington, N.Y., Mills Coll. Mus., Oakland, Calif., Meml. Art Gallery, Rochester, also pvt. collections. Recipient award Am. Acad. Arts and Letters, 1977; Altman prize NAD, 1982, 91, 97, Obrig prize, 1996; Louis Comfort Tiffany grantee, 1959, Ingram Merrill grantee, 1969; John Simon Guggenheim Meml. fellow, 1984. Mem. NAD, Am. Acad. Arts and Letters. Office: care Salander-O'Reilly Galleries 20 E 79th St New York NY 10021-0106

RESKE, STEVEN DAVID, lawyer, writer; b. Mpls., May 31, 1962; s. Albert Edgar Reske and Florence Mae Altland. BA with distinction, St. Olaf Coll., Northfield, Minn., 1985; JD cum laude, Boston U., 1988. Bar: Ill. 1988, Minn. 1989, D.C. 1998, U.S. Dist. Ct. Minn. 1991, U.S. Ct. Appeals (5th cir.) 1989, (7th and 8th cir.) 1992, (D.C. circuit) 1998, U.S. Supreme Ct. 1993. Intern U.S. Senator Durenberger, Washington, 1981-82, Citizens for Ednl. Freedom, Washington, 1981-82, Abbott-Northwestern Hosp., Mpls., 1984, U.S. Dist. Ct. Judge Magnuson, St. Paul, 1986; summer assoc. Faegre & Benson, Mpls., 1987; assoc. Sidley & Austin, Chgo., 1988; law clk. to Hon. Judge Politz U.S. Ct. Appeals 5th cir., Shreveport, La., 1988-89; pvt. practice, 1989—; writer, 1989—. Contbr. CD Rev., 1993-95, JAZZIZ, 1996—, Skyway News, 1997—, City Pages, 2000—; contbr. articles to profl. jours.; mem. Am. Jour. Law and Medicine, 1986-87, editor, 1987-88; legal editor-at-large Law and Politics, 1998—; columnist Twin Cities Revue, 1998—. Recipient Minn. Super Lawyer award, 1998, Am. Jurisprudence award, 1988; Edward F. Hennessey scholar, 1988, G. Joseph Tauro scholar, 1986. Mem. ABA (antitrust divsn.), Minn. State Bar Assn., Hennepin County Bar Assn., Am. Econ. Assn., Am. Philos. Assn. Office: 3422 Douglas Dr N Crystal MN 55422-2414 E-mail: stevenresk@aol.com.

RESNICK, ALAN NEAL, law educator, lawyer; b. N.Y.C., Dec. 11, 1947; s. Samuel and Mollie Resnick; m. Jill Sherry Hirsh, Aug. 15, 1970; children: Brian, Craig. BS, Rider Coll., 1969; JD, Georgetown U., 1972; LLM, Harvard U., 1974. Bar: N.Y. 1973. Asst. prof. law Hofstra U. Sch. Law, Hempstead, N.Y., 1974-76, assoc. prof. law, 1976-79, assoc. dean, 1979-81, prof. law, 1979—, Benjamin Weintraub disting. prof. bankruptcy law, 1984—. Of counsel, Fried, Frank, Harris, Shriver & Jacobson, N.Y.C., 1989—; reporter, adv. com. on bankruptcy rules of Jud. Conf. U.S., Washington, 1987-99, mem. adv. com., 1999—; faculty, NYU workshop on bankruptcy and bus. reorgn., N.Y.C., 1988—; spkr., Uniform Comml. Code Inst., Washington, 1982-87; frequent spkr. profl. seminars on bankruptcy and comml. law. Author: (with Benjamin Weintraub) Bankruptcy Law Manual, 1st edit., 1980, 2d edit., 1986, 3d edit., 1992, 4th edit., 1996, 5th edit., 2002; editor: Bankruptcy Reform Act of 1978: A Legislative History, 1979, Bankruptcy Practice and Strategy, 1987; editor-in-chief: Collier on Bankruptcy, 2002-; contbr. numerous articles on bankruptcy law to profl. jours. Mem. profl. adv. bd., Children with Learning Disabilities, Hempstead, 1977-80. Fellow Am. Bar Found., Am. Coll. Bankruptcy (scholar-in-residence 1999-); mem. ABA, Am. Law Inst., Nat. Bankruptcy Conf. Office: Hofstra U Sch Law 121 Hofstra U Hempstead NY 11549

RESNICK, ALICE ROBIE, state supreme court justice; b. Erie, Pa., Aug. 21, 1939; d. Adam Joseph and Alice Suzanne (Spizarny) Robie; m. Melvin L. Resnick, Mar. 20, 1970 PhB, Siena Heights Coll., 1961; JD, U. Detroit, 1964. Bar: Ohio 1964, Mich. 1965, U.S. Supreme Ct. 1970. Asst. county prosecutor Lucas County Prosecutor's Office, Toledo, 1964-75, trial atty., 1965-75; judge Toledo Mcpl. Ct., 1976-83, 6th Dist. Ct. Appeals, State of Ohio, Toledo, 1983-88; instr. U. Toledo, 1968-69; justice Ohio Supreme Ct., 1989—. Co-chairperson Ohio State Gender Fairness Task Force. Trustee Siena Heights Coll., Adrian, Mich., 1982— ; organizer Crime Stopper Inc., Toledo, 1981— ; mem. Mayor's Drug Coun.; bd. dirs. Guest House Inc. Mem. ABA, Toledo Bar Assn., Lucas County Bar Assn., Nat. Assn. Women Judges, Am. Judicature Soc., Toledo Women's Bar Assn., Ohio State Women's Bar Assn. (organizer), Toledo Mus. Art, Internat. Inst. Toledo. Roman Catholic. Home: 2407 Edgehill Rd Toledo OH 43615-2321 Office: Supreme Ct Office 30 E Broad St Fl 3 Columbus OH 43215*

RESNICK, DANIEL KAREL, neurosurgeon, spinal surgeon, medical educator; b. Phila., Apr. 3, 1965; married. AB, Princeton U., 1987; MD, U. Pa., 1991; MS, U. Pitts., 1997. Lic. Am. Bd. Neurol. Surgery, Wis., Am. Bd. Neurol. Surgery, Pa. Asst. prof. neurosurgery U. Wis., Madison, 1998—. Cons. Ortho-Vita, Phila., 1999—. Contbr. articles to profl. jours., chpts. to books. Mem. AMA, Am. Assn. Neurol. Surgeons, Congress Neurol. Surgeons (spinal cord injury subcom. AANS/CNS sect. on spine), N.Am. Spine Soc. Office: U Wis K4/834 600 Highland Ave Madison WI 53792

RESNICK, DON, artist; b. N.Y.C., May 19, 1928; s. Reuben David and Helen Ella (Edelson) R.; m. Jeanette Haberstock; children: H. David Alexander, Helen Elizabeth. BA, Hobart Coll., 1949; BS magna cum laude, SUNY, Brockport, 1951; postgrad., New Sch. for Social Rsch., Internat. Acad. Visual Art, Salzburg, Austria; studies with Oskar Kokoschka, Raphael Soyer, Seymour Lipton. With pub. rels. dept. NBC, N.Y.C., 1950-51; tchr. Rockville Centre (N.Y.) Jr. High Sch., 1954-74, chmn. social studies and lang. arts dept., 1962-72; tchr. Waldorf Sch., Garden City, N.Y., 1978-89; represented by Wright Gallery, N.Y.C., Odon Wagner Fine Art, Toronto, Andrea Marquit Fine Art, Boston, F.A.N. Gallery, Phila., River Gallery, Damariscotta, Maine. Exhibited in group shows Corcoran Gallery, Washington, Mus. Fine Art, Roslyn, N.Y., Kraushaar Galleries, Artists' Gallery, Jayne Baum Gallery, David Findlay Jr. Gallery (all N.Y.C.), Art Assn. Newport (R.I.), Adelphi U., Hofstra U., Isis Gallery, Port Washington, N.Y., Gallery North, Setauket, N.Y., Elaine Benson Gallery, Bridgehampton, N.Y., Mus. Fine Arts, Roslyn, Sheldon Meml. Art Gallery, U. Nebr., L.I. Artists Exhbn., Nassau County, Mus. Fine Arts, Roslyn, N.Y., Andrea Marquit Fine Arts, Boston, Portland Mus. Art, Martha Lincol Gallery, Vero Beach, Fla., also others; represented in permanent collections Williams Coll., Dartmouth Coll., Hobart Coll., C.W. Post Coll., Sheldon Meml. Art Gallery, U. Mich. Mus. Art, IBM, Touche Ross, Am. Re-Ins., Price Waterhouse, Nippon Kodo, Currier Gallery Art, Manchester, N.H., Portland (Maine) Mus. Art, Westmoreland Mus. Art, Greensburg, Pa., Nat. Mus. Am., Smithsonian Instn., Washington, Colby Coll. Mus. Art, J.B.S. Speed Mus. Art, Bowdoin Coll. Mus. Art, Fred L. Emerson Gallery, Hamilton Coll., Mus. Art Ft. Lauderdale, Farnsworth Art Mus., Rose Art Mus./Brandeis U., Heckscher Art Mus., Bates Coll. Mus. Art, Kresge Art Mus./Mich. State U., Nat. Archives Am. Art, Am. Capital Resources Inc., Carter Wallace, IBM, Avis Collection, Klett Verlagi, Stuttgart, Germany, Fidelity Investments, Harvest Mgmt.; included in books: The Best of Drawing and Sketching, 1998, The Eye of God, A Life of Oskal Kokoschka, 2000, Poets and Artists Collaborations, 2000, Toward the Light, 2000, Earth, Sea and Sky. 2000. Recipient award Millay Found. for the Arts, 1989, medal of excellence Hobart Coll., 1999. Mem.: Am. Acad. and Inst. of Arts and Letters, Century Assn., Artists Equity, Artists Fellowship. Avocations: music, long distance running. Home: 15 Revere St Rockville Centre NY 11570

RESNICK, DONALD IRA, lawyer; b. Chgo., July 19, 1950; s. Roland S. and Marilyn B. (Weiss) R.; m. Jill Allison White, July 3, 1977; children: Daniel, Allison. BS with high honors, U. Ill., 1972; JD, Harvard U., 1975. Bar: Ill. 1975, U.S. Dist. Ct. (no. dist.) Ill. 1975. Assoc. Arvey, Hodes, Costello & Burman, Chgo., 1975-80, ptnr., 1981-83; sr. ptnr. Nagelberg & Resnick, 1983-89, Levenstein & Resnick, Chgo., 1989-91; chmn. real estate dept. Jenner & Block, 1992—. Bd. dirs. Ill. chpt. Real Estate/Investment Assn., Chgo., 1986—. Mem. ABA, Birchwood (Highland Park, Ill.) Club. Office: Jenner & Block 1 E Ibm Plz Fl 4000 Chicago IL 60611-7603 E-mail: dresnick@jenner.com.

RESNICK, HARVEY, physician; b. Winnipeg, Manitoba, Can., May 12, 1940; came to U.S., 1964; s. Joseph and Leah (Kestenbaum) R.; m. Marcia Harriett David, June 2, 1963; children: Carl, Jodie, Joey. MD, BS in Medicine, U. Manitoba, 1964. Diplomate Am. Bd. Family Practice. Intern Kings County Hosp., Bklyn., 1964-66; emergency rm. physician N.Y.C., 1966; pvt. practice family physician Freeport/Lake Jackson, Tex., 1966—. Bd. trustees Brazosport Cmty. Hosp., Lake Jackson, 1994—. Lt. col. U.S. Army, 1980, Desert Storm, 1990-91. Mem. Am. Acad. Family Practice, Tex. Med. Assn., Brazoria County Med. Assn. Jewish. Avocation: sports. Office: Dr H Resnick Assoc 201 Oak Dr S Lake Jackson TX 77566-5676 E-mail: nresnick@mastnet.net.

RESNICK, JEFFREY LANCE, federal magistrate judge; b. Bklyn., Mar. 5, 1943; s. Bernard and Selma (Monheit) R.; m. Margery O'Connor, May 27, 1990. BA, U. Conn., 1964; LLB, U. Conn., West Hartford, 1967. Bar: Conn. 1967, N.Y. 1968, U.S. V.I. 1968, D.C. 1979, U.S. Ct. Appeals (3d cir.) 1979. Assoc. Office of J.D. Marsh, Christiansted, St. Croix, V.I., 1967-69; asst. atty. gen. Dept. Law, 1969-73; ptnr. James & Resnick, 1973-89; magistrate judge U.S. Dist. Ct. V.I., 1989—. Active V.I. Bridge Team, 1971—. Jewish. Avocations: writing poetry and palindromes. Office: US District Court 3013 East Golden Rock Christiansted VI 00820-4256

RESNICK, MARTIN I. urologist, educator; b. Bklyn., Jan. 12, 1943; s. Daniel and Bertha (Becca) R.; m. Victoria Klein, July 4, 1965; children: Andrew Howard, Jeffrey Scott. BA, Alfred (N.Y.) U., 1964; MD, Bowman Gray Sch. Medicine, Winston-Salem, N.C., 1969; MS, Northwestern U., 1973. Diplomate Am. Bd. Urology. Instr. urology Northwestern U., Chgo., 1974-75, Bowman Gray Sch. Medicine, 1974-77, asst. prof., 1977-79, assoc. prof., 1979-81; prof., chmn. dept. urology Case Western Res. U., Cleve., 1981—, prof. oncology, 1987—. NIH awardee. Mem. Am. Urol. Assn. (pres. 2002—), Am. Bd. Urology (pres. 2002—), Alpha Omega Alpha. Jewish. Avocation: running. Office: 11100 Euclid Ave Cleveland OH 44106-2602

RESNICK, MINNA, artist, educator; b. N.Y.C., Oct. 30, 1946; d. Herbert and Eve (Cohen) Chester; m. Sidney I. Resnick, Aug. 31, 1969; children: Rachel, Nathan. BFA, Univ. of the Arts, 1968; MFA, San Francisco Art Inst., 1974. One-woman shows include Gallery Huntly, Canberra, Australia, 1979, Loveland (Colo.) Mus., 1980, Harrington St. Gallery, Hobart, Tasmania, 1981, Yellowstone Art Ctr., Billings, Mont., 1981, Roeland Gallery, The Hague, The Netherlands, 1981, Boulder (Colo.) Ctr. for Visual Arts, 1983, Corvallis (Oreg.) Art Ctr., 1984, Monterrey (Calif.) Mus. Art, 1987, Cortland (N.Y.) Arts Coun. Gallery, 1988, Purdue U., West Lafayette, Ind., 1994, Kougeas Gallery, East Boston, Mass., 1999, Rathbone Gallery, Sage Colls., Albany, N.Y., 1999, U. of Arts, Phila., 2001, Gallery 72, Omaha, 2002, exhibitions include Br. Internat. Print Biennale, Bradford, England, 1974, New Am. Graphics, Madison, Wis., 1975, Nat. Exhbn. Prints, Washington, 1975, Oakland (Calif.) Mus., 1975, Santa Barbara (Calif.) Mus., 1975, San Jose (Calif.) Mus. Art, 1975, 1977, San Francisco Mus. Art, 1977, The Bklyn. Mus., 1978, Boulder Ctr. for Visual Arts, 1984, Visual Arts Ctr. Alaska, 1984, The Print Club, Phila., 1990, Denver Art Mus., 1993, exhibited in group shows at Laguna Gloria Art Mus., Austin, Tex., 1993, Oklahoma City Art Mus., 1993, Everson Mus., Syracuse, N.Y., 1994, Am. Coun. Arts, N.Y.C., 1995, Sheldon Meml. Art Gall., Lincoln, Nebr., 1998, Lakeview Mus., Peoria, Ill., 1998, collections, , , , , exhibited in group shows at Arnot Art Mus., 2000, Johnson Mus. Art, Ithaca, N.Y., 2001, Knoxville Mus., 2001, Edinboro U., Pa., 2001. NEA fellow, 1980, Western States Arts Found. fellow, 1979, N.Y. Found. Arts fellow, 1991, 95; grantee Upper Catskill Cmty. Coun. Arts, 1996, 97, Saltonsall Found., 1999. Home: 130 Lexington Dr Ithaca NY 14850-1719

RESNICK, MYRON J. retired insurance company executive, lawyer; b. Louisville, July 13, 1931; s. Harry C. and Sybil G. (Glick) R.; m. Alicia M. Ward, Dec. 16, 1967; children— Hugh, Clay, David BS in Econs., U. Pa., 1953; JD, U. Mich., 1956. Various positions Allstate Ins. Co., Northbrook, Ill., 1959-88, sr. v.p., treas. bd. dirs., 1959-95; chmn. bd. Federated Ins. Co. Ltd. (U.K.), Sale, Cheshire, Eng., 1979-81. Dir. Allstate Ins. Co. Ltd. (U.K.), Sale; pres. Allstate Investment Mgmt. Co.; mem. adj. faculty John Marshall Law Sch., Chgo., 1996-98; bd. dirs. Am. Horizon Property & Casualty Ins. Co. Mem. Chgo. exec. com. Anti-Defamation League, 1975—; bd. dirs. Chgo. Urban League, 1987-2001, St. Scholastica High Sch., Chgo., 1977-79; trustee George Williams Coll., Downers Grove, Ill., 1981-93, chmn. bd. trustees, 1991-93; trustee Aurora U., 1993—; bd. advisors Inst. Law and Econs. U. Pa., 1994—. With U.S. Army, 1956-58. Mem. ABA, Chgo. Bar Assn., Ill. Bar Assn., Assn. Life Ins. Counsel, Chgo. Mortgage Attys. Assn. (bd. dirs. 1965-75), Reform Club (London).

RESNICK, OSCAR, neuroscientist; b. Bayonne, N.J., Apr. 27, 1924; s. Samuel and Rebecca (Rubinstein) R.; m. Janice Zelda Ravitz, July 13, 1949; children— Sandra, Scott. A.B., Clark U., Worcester, Mass., 1944; M.A., Harvard U., 1945; Ph.D., Boston U., 1955. Research fellow U. Iowa Med. Sch., 1945-46; instr. St. Petersburg Jr. Coll., 1946-47; research fellow U. Kans., 1947-49; instr. U. Minn., 1949-50; editorial asst. Biol. Abstracts, U. Pa., 1950-51; scientist Nat. Drug Co., Phila., 1951-53, Worcester Found. Exptl. Biology, Shrewsbury, Mass., 1953— ; now sr. scientist, lectr. Boston U., 1961— , Clark U., 1965— ; dir. research Worcester County Rehab. and Detention Ctr., West Boylston, Mass., 1965-76; cons. Medfield State Hosp., Mass., Norwich State Hosp., Conn. Contbr. articles to profl. jours. Mem. mental retardation research com. NIH, 1975-78. NIH grantee, 1957—. Fellow Am. Coll. Neuopsychopharmacology; mem. AAAS, Soc. Biol. Psychiatry, Am. Psychopath. Soc., N.Y. Acad. Sci., Soc. Neurosci., Sigma Xi. Office: Boston U Sch Medicine Ctr Behavioral Dev Mental Retardation 85 E Newton St Roxbury MA 02118-2340 Address: 270 E Douglas Ave El Cajon CA 92020-4514

RESNICK, RHODA BRODOWSKY, psychotherapist; b. Mar. 22, 1930; d. Isador and Rose (Wasserman) Brodowsky; m. Jack H. Resnick, May 21, 1950; children: Steven E., Caryn B. BS, CCNY, 1951; MS, Queens Coll., 1973; postgrad., Hunter Coll. Tchr. N.Y.C. Bd. Edn., 1960—80, guidance counselor, 1980—; psychotherapist L.I. Cons. Ctr., 1973—77; pvt. practice psychotherapy, 1975—. Fellow, L.I. Inst. Mental Health, 1975. Mem.: United Fedn. Tchrs., Am. Pers. and Guidance Assn. Home: 340 E 64th St New York NY 10021-7503 E-mail: krojac@hotmail.com.

RESNICK, ROBERT, physicist, educator; b. Balt., Jan. 11, 1923; s. Abraham and Anna (Dubin) R.; m. Mildred Saltzman, Oct. 14, 1945; children— Trudy, Abby, Regina. AB, Johns Hopkins U., 1943, PhD (Pres.'s Fund scholar 1946-49), 1949. Physicist NACA, Cleve., 1944-46; asst. prof., assoc. prof. physics U. Pitts., 1949-56; assoc. prof., prof. physics Rensselaer Poly. Inst., Troy, N.Y., 1956-93; prof. emeritus, 1993—; chmn. interdisciplinary sci. curriculum Rensselaer Poly. Inst., Troy, N.Y., 1973-88, Edward P. Hamilton Disting. prof. sci., 1975-93; hon. research fellow Harvard U., 1964-65; Fulbright prof. Peru, 1971. Hon. vis. prof. Peoples Republic of China, 1981, 85; mem. Commn. on Coll. Physics, 1960-68; commencement speaker Rensselaer Poly. Inst., 1993; mem. U.S. adv. bd. Quantum Joint USSR/USA sci. mag., 1989-93. Author: A Manual for Laboratory Physics, 1954, (with D. Halliday) Physics, 1960, 3d edit., 1978, 4th edit., 1991, 5th edit., 2000, (with Halliday and Krane) extended version, 1986, 2d edit. extended version, 1991, 3rd edit., 2000, (with Halliday and Krane) Introduction to Special Relativity, 1968, (with R. Eisberg) Notes on Quantum Theory, 1968, Notes on Modern Physics, 1969, Quantum Physics of Atoms, Molecules, Solids, Nuclei and Particles, 1974, 2d edit., 1985, (with D. Halliday) Fundamentals of Physics, 1970, 5th edit., 1996, extended version, 1988, 2d edit., 1993, 3rd edit., 1996, 4th edit., 1999, (with J. Walker and D. Halliday) 6th edit., 2000, (with others) Student Study Guide for Physics, 1970, 6th edit., 2000, Basic Concepts in Relativity and Early Quantum Theory, 1972, 2d edit., 1985, Basic Concepts in Relativity, 1991; author: (with others) Sourcebook for Programmable Calculators, 1978, (with E. Derringh) Solutions to Physics Problems, 1980, 5th edit., 1996, (with K. Brownstein) Tests for Physics, 1987, (with J. Walker and D. Halliday) CD Physics, 1993, 3rd edit., 2000; books translated into numerous fgn. langs; So You Want to Write a Textbook, 1999 (video); mem. adv. bd., project staff: Physical Science for Non-Scientists, 1964-68, pub., 1968; co-dir.: Project Physics Demonstration Experiments, 1962-70; pub. project, 1970, Workshop on Apparatus for College Physics, 1964-65, 66, Videotapes in Physics Instruction, 1975-78; dir. Physics Demonstration and Laboratory Apparatus Workshop, 1960-61; adv. editor: John Wiley & Sons, Inc., 1967-89, Macmillan Pubs., 1990-94. Recipient Disting. Svc. citation Am. Assn. Physics Tchrs., 1967, Hans Christian Oersted medal, 1974, Esso award for outstanding teaching, 1953, Disting. Faculty award Rensselaer Poly. Inst., 1971; named to Hall of Fame, Balt. City Coll., 1989; Robert Resnick Ctr. for Physics established at Rensselaer Poly. Inst., 1993, Robert Resnick Ann. Sci. Lectr. series endowed, 1993. Fellow AAAS, Am. Phys. Soc.; mem. AAUP, Am. Assn. Physics Tchrs. (v.p. 1986, pres.-elect 1987, pres. 1988), Am. Soc. Engring. Edn., Am. Inst. Physics (governing bd. 1987-90, mem. coun. Ctr. for History of Physics 1997—), Philosophic Soc. South Fla. (exec. bd. 1997-2000), Textbook Author Assn. (coun. 1990-93), Phi Beta Kappa, Sigma Xi. Achievements include rsch. publs. in aerodynamics, nuclear physics, atomic physics, upper atmosphere physics, history of physics, physics edn. Home: 23221 L'Ermitage Cir Boca Raton FL 33433-7144

RESNICK, STEPHANIE, lawyer; b. N.Y.C., Nov. 12, 1959; d. Diane Gross. AB, Kenyon Coll., 1981; JD, Villanova U., 1984. Bar: Pa. 1984, N.J. 1984, U.S. Dist Ct. (ea. dist.) Pa. 1984, U.S. Dist Ct. N.J. 1984, N.Y. 1990, U.S. Ct. Appeals (3d cir.) 1993, U.S. Dist. Ct. (so. dist.) N.Y. 1996, U.S. Dist. Ct. (ea. dist.) N.Y. 2001, U.S. Supreme Ct. 1998. Assoc. Cozen and O'Connor, Phila., 1984-87, Fox, Rothschild, O'Brien & Frankel, Phila., 1987-92, ptnr., 1992—. Mem. Vols. for Indigent Program, Phila., 1987-92. Mem.: ABA, Womens Way (vice-chair 2000—02, chmn. bd. dirs. 2002—), N.Y. Bar Assn., N.J. Bar Assn., Phila. Bar Assn. (investigative divsn. Commn. on Jud. Selection and Retention 1988—94, profl. guidance com. 1992—96, profl. responsibility com. 1992—2000, women's rights com. 1993—, Women in the Profession com. 1993—, co-chair 1995—96, Comm. on Jud. Selection and Retention 1995—2001, vice-chair 1996, chair 1997, fed. cts. com. 2000—, vice-chair 2001—02), Pa. Bar Assn. (disciplinary bd. and study com. 1989—91, prof. liability com. 1991—92, commr. on Women in the Profession 1997—99). Home: 233 S 6th St Apt 2306 Philadelphia PA 19106-3756 Office: Fox Rothschild O'Brien & Frankel 2000 Market St Ste 10 Philadelphia PA 19103-3231

RESNIK, DAVID ALAN, manufacturing company executive; b. Providence, June 9, 1956; s. Sol Leon and Esther (Petersohn) R.; m. Susan Winoker, Aug. 12, 1979; children: Joshua Michael, Alissa Joy. BA, U. Pa., 1978, MS, 1979. Gen. mgr. Emblem & Badge, Inc. (merger with Westcalind Corp. 1988), Providence, 1980—, exec. v.p., 1986-87, pres., 1987—, EASTbyNORTH Retail Sys., Providence, 1992—. V.p. Polar Cap Ice, Inc., 1991-95, pres., 1995-97; pres. North Main Industries, Inc. Contbr. articles to profl. jours. Bd. dirs. Jewish Fedn. R.I., 1999—, Bur. Jewish Edn., 1999—, assoc. treas. 2000—, Jewish Family Svc., 1999-02, Jewish Srs. Agy., 1999—; apptd. R.I. Comdr. by Gov. of R.I., 1999. Paul Harris fellow Rotary Internat. numerous years. Mem. Profl. Assn. Diving Instrs. (cert. master scuba diver trainer), Divers Alert Network, Rotary (bd. dirs. Providence 1994-2001, pres. 1999-2000). Jewish. Avocations: microcomputers, tropical fish, photography, scuba diving. Office: Emblem & Badge Inc PO Box 6226 Providence RI 02940-6226 E-mail: dr@recognition.com.

RESNIK, HARVEY LEWIS PAUL, psychiatrist; b. Buffalo, Apr. 6, 1930; s. Samuel andCelia (Greenberg) R.; m. Audrey Ruth Frey, Aug. 30, 1964 (dec. 1993); children: Rebecca Gabrielle, Henry Seth Maccabee, Jessica Ruth. BA magna cum laude, U. Buffalo, 1951; MD, Columbia, 1955; grad., Phila. Psychoanalytic Inst., 1967. Diplomate: Am. Bd. Psychiatry and Neurology. Intern Phila. Gen. Hosp., 1955-56, resident in surgery, 1956-57; resident in psychiatry Jackson Meml. Hosp., Miami, Fla., 1959-61; fellow U. Pa. Hosp., 1961-62, mem. staff, 1962-67; instr. Sch. Medicine, U. Pa., 1962-66; instr. med. hypnosis Sch. Medicine, U. Pa. (Grad. Sch. Medicine), 1963-65; clin. dir. psychiatry E. J. Meyer Meml. Hosp., Buffalo, 1967, dir. psychiatry, 1968; from assoc. prof. to prof. Sch. Medicine, SUNY at Buffalo, Buffalo, 1967—68; prof. Dept. Medicine, SUNY, 1968—70; chief Nat. Center for Studies of Suicide Prevention, NIMH, 1969-74, chief mental health emergencies sect., 1974-76; with Reproductive Biology Rsch. Found., St. Louis, 1971; clin. prof. psychiatryand human behavior Sch. Medicine, George Washington U., 1969—2002, prof. emeritus clin. psychiatry and behavioral scis., 2002—; dir. Human Behavior Found., 1975—; lectr. Sch. Medicine, Johns Hopkins, Balt., 1969-74; adj. lectr. Johns Hopkins U. Sch. Pub. Health, 1981-82. Prof. cmty. health Fed. City Coll., 1971-75; med. dir. Johns Hopkins U. Compulsive Gambling Ctr., 1981-83; med. dir. alcohol and substance abuse program U. Md., College Park, 1986-2000; vis. prof. Katholieke U., Leuven, Belgium, 1986-93; cons. to Sec.-Gen. Ministry of Health, Belgium, 1986-95, NATO fellow, 1986-87; cons. various hosps. and orgns., Medicare, Pa. Blue Shield, 1984-96, Trailblazer Health, 1996-99, Blue Cross/Blue Shield S.C., 1999. Author: Suicidal Behaviors: Diagnosis and Management, 1968, 2d edit., 1994, (with M. E. Wolfgang) Treatment of the Sexual Offender, 1971, Sexual Behaviors: Social, Clinical and Legal Aspects, 1972, (with B. Hathorne) Suicide Prevention in the Seventies, 1973, (with H.L. Ruben) Emergency Psychiatric Care, 1974, (with others) The Prediction of Suicide, 1974, Emergency and Disaster Management, 1976; (with J.T. Mitchell) Emergency Response to Crisis, 1981; Editor: Bull. Suicidology, 1969-74; Contbr. (with others) articles on hypnosis, sexual offenders, marriage and sexual dysfunction treatment, suicide, death and dying, emergency psychiatric care. Mem. Addictions Adv. Bd. Prince Georges County, 1980-85. Served to capt. USAF, 1957-59, ETO-Middle East; capt. USNR; ret. Decorated officer in the Order King Leopold, Belgium, 1990. Fellow Am. Coll. Mental Health Adminstrs. (life), Am. Coll. Psychiatrists (life), Am. Psychiat. Assn. (life); mem. Med-Chi of Md., Prince Georges County Med. Assn. (co-chair joint com. with Bar Assn. 1996—), Washington Psychiatry Soc., Am. Acad. Psychiatry and Law (suicidology com. 1998-2000), Phila. Psychoanalytic Soc., NIH Alumni Assn., Columbia U. Med. Alumni Assn. (bd. dirs. 1993-95), Cosmos Club (Washington), Phi Beta Kappa, Beta Sigma Rho (grand vice warden 1963). Jewish. Office: Univ Profl Ctr 4700 Berwyn House Rd Ste 202 College Park MD 20740-4717

RESNIK, LINDA ILENE, marketing and information executive, publisher, consultant, writer; b. Dallas, Oct. 26, 1950; d. Harold and Reatha (Gordon) R. BJ in Broadcast Journalism, U. Mo., 1971; MA in Journalism, U. North Tex., 1977, MBA in Mktg., 1980. News and documentary producer Sta. KDFW-TV, Dallas, 1971-73; mktg.-info. officer Dallas County C.C. Dist., 1973-79; dir. mktg. The Learning Channel, Washington, 1980-82; dir. Nat. Narrowcast Svc., Pub. Broadcasting Svc., 1982-85; exec. dir. Am. Soc. Info. Sci., 1985-89, White House Conf. on Libr. and Info. Svcs., Washington, 1990-91; cons., 1991—; mng. ptnr. FAQs Press, 1998—. Adv. com. ALA Library/Book Fellows Project; fellow Ctr. for Info. and Comm. Scis., Ball State U.; U.S. exec. com. U. of the World; mktg., tng. and telecomm. cons. to ednl. assns., others Writer and editor college-level study guides; scriptwriter college credit TV courses. Youth activities coordinator YMCA, Dallas, 1975-78; spl. event organizer Am. Cancer Soc., Dallas, 1976-77; com. leader Goals for Dallas, 1978-80; co-chair Friends of the Troup (Tex.) Libr., 1996—; mem. com. Tyler Race for the Cure, 1999. Recipient Best TV Feature Story award AP, Tex., 1973. Mem. Am. Soc. Assn. Execs., Am. Soc. Info. Sci. (pub. bull. 1985-89), Women in Cable, Info. Inst., Am. Mktg. Assn. Avocations: travel, racquet sports, reading, theater. Office: PO Box 130115 Tyler TX 75713-0115 E-mail: LIResnik@FAQsPress.com.

RESNIK, ROBERT, medical educator; b. New Haven, Dec. 7, 1938; s. Nathan Alfred and Elsie (Hershman) R.; m. Lauren Brahms, Oct. 29, 1966; children: Andrew Scott, Jamie Layne. BA, Yale U., 1960; MD, Case Western Res. U., 1965. Intern in internal medicine Mt. Sinai Hosp., Cleve., 1965-66; resident in ob-gyn. Yale U. Sch. Medicine, 1966-70; asst. prof. Sch. Medicine U. Calif., San Diego, 1974-78, assoc. prof., 1978-82, prof. reproductive medicine, 1982—, chmn. dept., 1982-95, dean clin. affairs, 1988-90, dean admissions, 1995—. Cons. Nat. Heart, Lung and Blood Inst. NIH, Washington, 1987; mem. exec. com. Coun. Residency Edn. Ob-Gyn, Washington, 1988-94, residency rev. com., 1988-94. Editor: (textbook) Maternal-Fetal Medicine: Principles and Practice, 1984, 4th edit., 1999; contbr. numerous articles to profl. jours. Major U.S. Army, 1970-72. Rsch. grantee Nat. Found., NIH. Fellow: Royal Coll. Obstet. Gynecologists, N.W. Obstet. Gynecological Soc., Pacific Coast Obstet. and Gynecol. Soc., Am. Coll. Ob-Gyn. (vice chmn. obs. practice com. 1998—2000), New England Osbtet. Gynecological Soc.; mem.: San Diego Gynecol. Soc. (pres. 1982), Am. Gynecologic and Obstet. Soc. (coun.), Perinatal Rsch. Soc. (pres. 1985), Soc. Gynecologic Investigation (coun. 1983—88), Yale Club, Am. Gynecol. Club (sec., treas., pres.-elect). Office: U Calif Sch Medicine 9500 Gilman Dr Dept 0621 La Jolla CA 92093-0621

RESO, ANTHONY, geologist, educator, earth resources economist; b. London, Aug. 10, 1931; arrived in U.S., 1940, naturalized, 1952; AB, Columbia Coll., N.Y.C., 1954; MA, Columbia U., 1955; postgrad., U. Cin., 1956-57; PhD (fellow), Rice U., 1960; postgrad., Grad. Sch. Bus. U. Houston, 1964-68. Instr. geology Queens Coll., Flushing, NY, 1954; geologist Atlantic Richfield Corp., Midland, Tex., 1955-56; asst. prof. geology and curator invertebrate paleontology Pratt Mus., Amherst (Mass.) Coll., 1959-62; staff rsch. geologist Tenneco Oil Co., Houston, 1962-86; geol. mgr. Peak Prodn. Co., 1986—, v.p., 1988—. Cons. in geol. rsch. Tenn. Gas and Oil Co., 1960—61; lectr. U. Houston, 1962—65; vis. prof. Rice U., 1980; mem. bd. advisers Gulf Univs. Rsch. Corp., Galveston, Tex., 1967—75, chmn., Tex., 1968—69. Contbr. articles to profl. jours. Grantee Rsch., Eastman Fund, 1962. Fellow: AAAS, Geol. Soc. Am. (com. investments 1984—95, chmn. 1985—92, budget com. 1993—95, found. trustee 1999—, Rsch. grantee 1958, Disting. Svc. award 1996); mem.: English-Speaking Union U.S. (dir. Houston br. 1978—, v.p. 1982—88, mem. scholarship com. 1988—97, chmn. 1991—97, pres. 1997—98), Houston Geol. Soc. (v.p. 1973—75, pres. 1975—76, chmn. constn. revision com. 1981, Disting. Svc. award 1985), Tex. Acad. Sci., Am. Assn. Petroleum Geologists (life; com. convs. 1977—83, gen. chmn. nat. conv. 1979, chmn. 1980—83, com. investments 1982—88, chmn. com. group ins. 1986—88, treas. 1986—88, found. trustee assoc. 1991, Rsch. grantee 1958, 1959, Disting. Svc. award 1985), Paleontol. Rsch. Instn., SEPM Soc. for Sedimentary Geology (com. investments 1990—, chmn. 1992—95, treas. SEPM Found. 1997—), Paleontol. Soc., Varsity C Club, Beta Theta Pi, Sigma Gamma Epsilon, Sigma Xi. Episcopalian. Home: 1805 Brun St Houston TX 77019-5712 Office: care Peak Prodn Co PO Box 130785 Houston TX 77219-0785 E-mail: aresogeo@swbell.net.

RESOR, STANLEY ROGERS, lawyer; b. N.Y.C., Dec. 5, 1917; s. Stanley Burnet and Helen (Lansdowne) R.; m. Jane Lawler Pillsbury, Apr. 4, 1942 (dec.); children: Stanley R., Charles P., John L., Edmund L., William B., Thomas S., James P.; m. Louise Mead Walker, May 1, 1999. BA, Yale U., 1939, LLB, 1946. Bar: N.Y. 1947. Assoc., then ptnr. firm Debevoise & Plimpton, N.Y.C., 1946-65, 71-73, 79-87, of counsel, 1988-90; undersec. Dept. Army, 1965, sec., 1965-71, ambassador negotiations for Mut. and Balanced Force Reductions in Central Europe, 1973-78; undersec. for policy Dept. Def., 1978-79. Fellow Yale Corp., 1979-86. Served to maj. AUS, 1942-45. Decorated Silver Star, Bronze Star, Purple Heart; recipient George C. Marshall award Assn. U.S. Army, 1974, Sylvanus Thayer award Assn. Graduates of U.S. Mil. Acad., 1984. Mem. ABA, Assn. of Bar of City of N.Y. (chmn. com. internat. arms control and security affairs 1983-86), Atlantic Coun. (bd. dirs.), Arms Control Assn. (chmn. bd.), UN Assn. U.S.A. (nat. coun.), Coun. Fgn. Rels., Lawyers Alliance for World Security (bd. dirs.), Internat. Inst. Strategic Studies. Republican. Episcopalian. Home: 809 Weed St New Canaan CT 06840-4023 Office: # 724 2801 New Mexico Ave NW Apt 724 Washington DC 20007-3934 Home Fax: 966-3965; Office Fax: (202) 337-2306.

RESS, CHARLES WILLIAM, management consultant; b. Columbus, Ohio, Aug. 6, 1933; s. George Leonard and Martha (Lake) R.; m. Virginia M. Beck, Aug. 28, 1954; children: Beverly Beck, Suzanne E., Charles W. Jr., Linda Perrins Foxworth, Jennifer Laurel Brulé. BS, Miami U., 1955; MA in Psychology, Rutgers U., 1969. Buyer The Higbee Co., Cleve., 1956-59; asst. to gen. mdse. mgr. The Halle Bros. Co., 1959-64; research dir. The Associated Mdse. Corp., N.Y.C., 1964-73; v.p. Mgmt. Horizons, Columbus, 1973-76; founder, chmn. bd. C.W. Ress & Assoc., Inc., 1976-90; gen. mgr. Levi Strauss & Co., 1990-94, mgmt. cons., 1994—. Lectr. in field. Author: Future Trends in Retailing, 1983, Trans National Retailing, 1988, Retailing 2000, 1991; contbr. articles to profl. jours. Republican. Avocations: cooking, wine tasting. Office: 3860 Lyon Dr Columbus OH 43220-4907 E-mail: Ressandress@Aol.com.

RESS, PATRICIA COLLEEN, author, freelance writer; b. Sioux City, Iowa, Aug. 7, 1945; d. Charles Francis and Alice Joanna (Krofta) Griffin; m. Lawrence Wright Dec. 13, 1969 (dec.); children: Alice Wendy, Cindy Marie; m. Fred Callsen Ress, Sept. 7, 1979; 1 child, Eric Christopher. BS in Edn., U. S.D., 1967; postgrad. studies in Journalism, U. Iowa, 1968, 69; cert. in lab. sci., Gradwohl Sch. Med. Lab. Tech., St. Louis, 1979; environ. lab. sci., S.E. Comty. Coll., Lincoln, Nebr., 1979. Feature writer, columnist Clay County News-Sun, Sutton, Nebr., 1977—; feature writer, photographer Sun Newspapers, Lincoln, 1977-78; feature writer -strange and unusual column The Nebr. Voice, Lincoln, Omaha, Kearney, 1979-81; reporter, photographer The Walton County Tribune, Monroe, Ga., 1986; feature writer Omaha Met. Update and Midland Bus. Jour., 1990, 91; feature writer, free lance Paragon Publ. Ltd., Bournemouth, Eng., 1992—; editor The Constitutional Liberator, Omaha, 1995—. Mem. St. Louis Theosophical Soc., 1969-72; cons. to Mike Jarmus radio show; instr. pub. course Metro. C.C. Author: Stranger Than Fiction: The True Time-Travel Adventures of Steven L. Gibbs, the Rainman of Time-Travel, 2002, Seven Chilling Things You Should Know About Your Soul, 2002, Travel Tips for Tightwads, 2002; co-author: Strangers In the Heartland, 1998, Armageddon: The Last Alien Battle, 1998; pub.: Amazing Things Catalog; editor: Summary Mag.; pub.: ; contbr. articles. Mem. Dem. Nat. Com. Recipient scholarship Oelwein (Iowa) Daily Register, 1963, Hon. Mention, Sioux City (Iowa) Jour. Ann. photography contest, 1969; Third Pl. medallion Nat. Libr. of Poetry, Owings Mills, Md., 1995. Mem. Oakcrest Inst. Elkhorn, Nebr. (bd. mem. in charge of pub. rels.), Mutual UFO Network of Nebr., PEO Sisterhood. Avocations: playing music, listening to short wave radio, riding horses, cooking, painting. Home and Office: 618 N 172d Ct Omaha NE 68118

RESS, RICHARD JOSEPH, judge; b. Wells, Minn., Oct. 9, 1952; s. Frank C. and Inez L. (Gibbs) R.; m. Melonie A. Stearley, May 25, 1985; 1 child, Courtney Elizabeth. BA, Kans. State U., 1974; JD, Washburn Sch. of Law, 1979. Bar: Kans. 1982, U.S. Dist. Ct. Kans. 1982. Pvt. practice, Colby, Kans., 1982-83; spl. dep. atty. Thomas County Atty., 1983; mcpl. judge City of Colby, 1983—; dist. magistrate judge State of Kans., 1983—; mcpl. judge City of Brewster, Kans., 1992—, City of Rexford, 1997—. Instr. Colby C.C., Colby, 1989—. Mem. Thomas County Bar Assn. (sec./treas. 1982—), Kans. Bar Assn., Kans. Magistrate Judges Assn., Mcpl. Judges Assn. (bd. dirs. Kans. chpt. 1984-95, pres. 1993-94). Roman Catholic. Avocations: hunting, reading military history, cartography. Office: Kans Dist Ct PO Box 805 Colby KS 67701-0805

RESSEGUIE, JAMES LYNN, theology educator; b. Buffalo, Jan. 1, 1945; m. Dianne Laverne Paulson, 1970; children: Timothy, Carin, Jay. AB, U. Calif., Berkeley, 1967; MDiv, Princeton Theol. Sem., 1972; PhD in New Testament, Fuller Theol. Sem., 1978. Ordained minister Presbyn. Ch., 1976. Vol. Peace Corps, Cameroon, 1967-69; asst. prof. Winebrenner Theol. Sem., Findlay, Ohio, 1976-78, assoc. prof. New Testament, 1979-83, J. Russell Bucher prof. New Testament, 1984—, dean acad. and student affairs, registrar, 1990-97, v.p. acad. and student affairs, 1997; Fulbright prof. lit. theory and New Testament U. Iceland, Reykjavik, 1990. Lectr. in field. Author: Revelation Unsealed: A Narrative Critical Approach to John's Apocalypse, 1998, The Strange Gospel: Narrative Design and Point of View in John, 2001; contbr.: Eerdmans Dictionary of the Bible, 2000; contbr. articles to profl. publs., chpts. to books. Trustee Marion Twp., 1991; theologian-in-residence Zoar Luth. Ch., Perrysburg, Ohio, 1996; moderator Dola Presbyn. Ch., Dola, Ohio, 1996-98, Eron Valley Presbyn. Ch., 2002-. Fellow NEH, 1979, 82, 85, 88, 91, Case Method Inst., 1981, Inst. for Ecumenical and Cultural Rsch., 1983, Collidge rsch. fellow, 1987, Fulbright fellow, 1990; named Outstanding Educator, 1990, 97, 2001; recipient Cert. of Appreciation for Peace Corps svc. Mem. Soc. Biblical Lit., Maumee Valley Presbytery. Office: Winebrenner Theol Sem Dept New Testament Findlay OH 45840 E-mail: resseguiej@mail.findlay.edu.

RESSEL, HOWARD ROBERT, civil engineer; b. Rochester, N.Y., May 12, 1962; s. Leonard L. and Susan J. (Morse) R.; m. Amy Joyce Rosenfeld, June 7, 1987. BSCE, SUNY, Buffalo, 1984. Registered profl. engr. Jr. engr. N.Y. State Dept. Transp., Rochester, 1984-85, civil engr. I, 1985-90, civl engr. II, 1990—. Chmn. JCC Ctr. Stage Community Theater, Rochester, 1989-90. Mem. ASCE, N.Y. State Assn. of Transp. Engrs., Jewish Community Ctr. (bd. dirs. 1992-2002). Home: 148 Penhurst St Rochester NY 14619-1520 Office: NY State Dept Transp 1530 Jefferson Rd Rochester NY 14623-3110

RESSETAR, NANCY, foreign language educator; b. Paterson, N.J., Dec. 19, 1947; d. Marino Angelo and Florence Mae (Patterson) DeMattia; m. Michael Ressetar, Jr., Aug. 15, 1981; 1 child, Tatyana Marina. BA, Montclair State U., 1970. Cert. tchr., N.J. Model various agencies, 1953-84; tchr. Spanish Clifton (N.J.) Sch. Sys., 1970—. Sponsor Spanish Club, Clifton, 1981—, Student Leadership, Clifton, 1988—, Travel to Spain, Clifton, 1982-96; campaign worker Dem. Party, Clifton, 1968-72. Recipient Gov.'s award for excellence in tchg. State of N.J., 1996. Mem. NEA, N.J. Edn. Assn., Passaic County Edn. Assn., Clifton Tchrs. Assn. (sec. 1973-75), Fgn. Lang. Tchrs. N.J., Am. Assn. Tchrs. Spanish and Portuguese. Democrat. Lutheran. Avocations: travel, theatre, doll collecting, classic Hollywood, tutoring. Home: 20 Robin Hood Rd Clifton NJ 07013-3112

RESTIVO, JAMES JOHN, JR. lawyer; b. Pitts. s. James J. and Dorothy (Ardolino) R.; m. Gail Sharon Hackenburg, July 11, 1970; 4 children BA in History, U. Pa., 1968; JD, Georgetown U., 1971. Bar: Pa. 1971, U.S. Dist. Ct. (we. and ea. dists.) Pa. 1971, U.S. Ct. Appeals (3d cir.) 1971, U.S. Supreme Ct. 1979. Ptnr. Reed Smith, Pitts., 1979—; head litigation dept. Reed, Smith, Shaw & McClay, 1986-97. Mem. editl. staff Georgetown Law Rev., 1970-71. Bd. dirs. Greater Pitts. C. of C., Rebuilding Together-Greater Pitts., Pitts. Regional Alliance. Fellow Am. Coll. Trial Lawyers; mem. Acad. Trial Lawyers Allegheny County, Allegheny County Bar Assn., Pa. Economy League (Western divsn.), Def. Rsch. Inst. Home: 209 Deer Meadow Dr Pittsburgh PA 15241-2253 Office: Reed Smith 435 6th Ave Ste 2 Pittsburgh PA 15219-1886 E-mail: jrestivo@reedsmith.com.

RESTON, ROCKY RUSSELL, anesthesiologist, engineer, educator; b. Cheyenne, Wyo., Sept. 8, 1962; s. Russell Turrefiel and Beverly Elaine Reston. BSEE, USAF Acad., 1984; PhD, Air Force Inst. Tech., 1993; MD, Uniformed Svcs. U. Health Scis, 1998. Commd. 2d lt. USAF, 1984, advanced through grades to maj., 1999; instrumentation engr. 4484th Test Squadron, Tyndall AFB, Fla., 1984-87; electronics device processing engr. Wright Labs., Wright Patterson AFB, Ohio, 1992-94; resident in internal medicine Wilford Hall Med. Ctr., Lackland AFB, Tex., 1998-99, resident in anesthesiology, 1999—; assoc. prof. tech. and mgmt. U. Md., College Park, 1996—. Presenter in field. Contbr. articles to profl. jours.; patentee in field. Mem. IEEE, USAF Acad. Assn. Grads, Eta Kappa Nu (treas. 1988-89), Tau Beta Pi. Address: 5225 Sideburn Rd Fairfax VA 22032-2641 Office: 59 MDW/MCOA 2200 Bergquist Dr Lackland A F B TX 78236 E-mail: Rocky_R@msn.com.

RESTOUT, DENISE, musician; b. Paris, Nov. 24, 1915; arrived in US, 1941; d. Fernand Emile Jules and Juliette Louise François Restout. Grad., Nat. Conservatoire de Musique, Paris, 1930. Asst., sec. to Wanda Landowska Ecole de Musique Ancienne, St. Leu-La Foret, France, 1935-41, Lakeville, Conn., 1941-59; dir. Landowska Ctr., 1959—. Mem jury, hon patron Int Bach Competitions, 1969—81; lectr in field. Author: (book) Landowska on Music, 1965; contbr. articles, concert revs to mags; musician (soloist): Chamnber Orchestra, 1939; musician: (accompanying harpsicordist) Landowska concert, 1943; musician: (solo harpsicordist) Bach Suites, others; musician: recitals; appeared various radio and TV programs: Voice of America, 1950, appeared various radio and TV programs: Radio-Geneve, 1952, appeared various radio and TV programs: CBS Radio, 1960, appeared various radio and TV programs: , 1985, appeared various radio and TV programs: Conn Pub Radio, 1985, appeared various radio and TV programs: Radio France, 1990, appeared various radio and TV programs: Video TV, 1999; (appeared in documentary film): Visionary; co-prodr.: (several CDs for Pearl and others). Organist St Mary's Ch, Lakeville, 1971—97. Recipient Amicus Poloniae, Poland Mag,

1973, St. Joseph medal, Archdiocese of Hartford, 2002. Mem.: French and Am Musicological Asn, Am Guild Organists, French Guild Organists, Am Fedn Musicians (Woman of the Yr 1996). Republican. Roman Catholic. Avocations: reading, photography. Home and Office: PO Box 313 63 Millerton Rd Lakeville CT 06039-0313

RESTUCCIA, JOSEPH D. healthcare educator; b. Boston, June 28, 1947; s. Joseph P. and Maria C. Restuccia; m. Nancy M. Restuccia, May 23, 1970. BA, Tufts U., 1969; MPH, U. Calif., Berkeley, 1974; DPH, U. Calif., 1977. Prof. health care mgmt. U. Mich., Ann Arbor, 1977—80; prof. health care mgmt. & ops. mgmt. Boston U., Boston, 1980—. Chief scientist Utilization Mgmt. Associates, Wellesley, Mass., 1988—96; adv. bd. Health Care For All, Boston, 1995—, Lombardy Sch. of Health Care Mgmt., Milan, 2002—. Contbr. articles to profl. jours. Grantee, U.S. Dept. Health & Human Svcs., 1983—86, Blue Cross of Mass., 1987—90, R.W. Johnson Fedn., 1988—90, U.S. Dept. Health & Human Svcs., 1992—98. Office: Boston Univ Sch Mgmt 595 Commonwealth Ave Boston MA 02215

RESWICK, JAMES BIGELOW, former government official, rehabilitation engineer, educator; b. Ellwood City, Pa., Apr. 16, 1922; s. Maurice and Katherine (Parker) R.; children: James Bigelow, David Parker (dec.), Pamela Reswick; m. Irmtraud Orthlies Hoelzerkopf, Dec., 27, 1973. SBME, MIT, 1943; SM, Mass. Inst. Tech., 1948, ScD, 1952; DEng (hon.), Rose Poly. Inst., 1968. Asst. prof., then assoc. prof., head machine design and graphics div. MIT, 1948-59; Leonard Case prof. engring., dir. Engring. Design Ctr., Case Western Res. U., 1959-70; prof. biomed. engring. and orthopaedics U. So. Calif., also dir. of rsch. dept. orthopaedics, 1970-80; assoc. dir. tech. Nat. Inst. Handicapped Rsch., U.S. Dept. Edn.; dir. VA Rehab. R & D Evaluation Unit VA Med. Ctr., Washington, 1984-88; dir. rsch. scis. Nat. Inst. on Disability and Rehab. Rsch. U.S. Dept. Edn., 1989-94; ret.; acting dir. Nat. Inst. Disability and Rehab. Rsch., 1989-91. Engring. cons. on automatic control, product devel., automation and bio-med. engring. Mem. com. on prosthetics R & D Nat. Acad. Scis., 1962— ; chmn. design and devel. com.; mem. bd. rev. Army R & D Office, 1965— ; mem. applied physiology and biomed. engring. study sect. NIH, 1972— Author: (with C.K. Taft) Introduction to Dynamic Systems, 1967; also articles.; Editor: (with F.T. Hambrecht) Functional Electrical Stimulation, 1977; series on engring. design, 1963—; patentee in field. Chmn. Mayor's Commn. for Urban Transp., Cleve., 1969. Served to lt. (j.g.) USNR, 1943-46, PTO. Decorated officer Yugoslav Flag with golden wreath medal (Yugoslavia), 1990; recipient Product Engring. Master Designer award, 1969, Isabelle and Leonard H. Goldenson award United Cerebral Palsy Assn., 1973; NSF sr. postdoctoral fellow Imperial Coll., London, 1957. Fellow IEEE, Am. Inst. Med. and Biological Engring. (founder); mem. ASME (honor award for best paper 1956, sr. mem.), Am. Soc. Engring. Edn., Instrument Soc. Am., Biomed. Engring. Soc. (sr. mem., pres. 1973, dir.), Am. Acad. Orthopedic Surgeons (asso.), Inst. Medicine of Nat. Acad. Scis., Nat. Acad. Engring., Internat. Soc. Orthotics and Prosthetics, Orthopaedics Research Soc., Rehab. Engring. Soc. N.Am. (founding pres.), Sigma XI. Home: 1834 Calf Mountain Rd Crozet VA 22932 E-mail: jimreswick@aol.com.

RETALLACK, GREGORY JOHN, geologist, educator; b. Hobart, Australia, Nov. 8, 1951; came to U.S., 1977; s. Kenneth John Retallack and Moira Wynn (Dean) Gollan; m. Diane Alice Johnson, May 31, 1981; children: Nicholas John, Jeremy Douglas. B.A., Macquarie U., Sydney, 1973; B.Sc. with honors, U. New Eng., 1974, Ph.D., 1978. Vis. asst. prof. Northern Ill. U., Dekalb, 1977-78; vis. scholar Ind. U., Bloomington, 1978-81; asst. prof. U. Oreg., Eugene, 1981-86, assoc. prof., 1986-92, prof., 1992—. Author: Geological Excursion Guide to the Sea Cliffs North of Sydney, 1978, Late Eocene and Oligocene Paleosols from Badlands National Park, South Dakota, 1983, Soils of the Past, 1990, Miocene Paleosols and Ape Habitats in Pakistan and Kenya, 1991, Colour Guide to Paleosols, 1997; contbr. numerous articles in field to profl. jours. Grantee NSF, 1979—, Wenner-Gren Found., 1983. Fellow AAAS, Geol. Soc. Am.; mem. Geol. Soc. Australia, Bot. Soc. Am., Paleontol. Soc. (pres. Pacific sect. 1986), Oreg. Acad. Sci. (pres. 1986), Soc. Econ. Paleontologists and Mineralogists, Sigma Xi (pres. U. Oreg. chpt. 1983-84). Home: 2715 Elinor St Eugene OR 97403-2513

RETHEMEYER, ROBERT JOHN, social studies educator; b. St. Louis, Jan. 20, 1948; s. John Henry and Olivia Antonia (Fallbeck) R.; m. Kay Lynn Jones, Aug. 22, 1971; children: Robin Lynn, Rustin John. BS in Edn., Cen. Mo. State Coll., 1970; M in Sch. Adminstrn., Cen. Mo. State U., 1973, EdS in Supt., 1985. Tchr. 7th grade social studies Smith-Hale Jr. H.S., Kansas City, Mo., 1970-78, asst. prin., 1978-80, tchr. 7th and 8th grade social studies, 1980-2000. Chmn. bldg. dept. Cons. Sch. Dist. 1, Kansas City, 1982-2000, alt. sch. com., 1993—, summer sch. prin., 1981-97, summer sch. coord., 1998, ret., 2000; part-time profl. staff Hickman Mills C-1 Sch., 2000—; supr. U. Mo.-Kansas City student tchrs. Mem. NEA, Nat. Coun. for Social Studies, Phi Delta Kappa. Home: 1026 SE Timbercreek Ln Lees Summit MO 64081-3003 Office: Adminstrn Ctr 9000 Old Santa Fe Rd Kansas City MO 64138-3998

RETHORE, BERNARD GABRIEL, retired manufacturing and mining company executive; b. May 22, 1941; s. Francis Joseph and Katharine Eunice (MacDwyer) Rethore; m. Marilyn Irene Watt, Dec. 1, 1962 (div. Apr. 2002); children: Bernard Michael, Tara Jean, Kevin Watt, Alexandra Marie, Rebecca Ann, Christopher Philip, Abigail Lyn. BA, Yale U., 1962; MBA, U. Pa., 1967. Assoc. McKinsey & Co., Inc., Washington, 1967—73, sr. assoc., 1973; v.p., gen. mgr. Greer div. Microdot, Inc., Darien, Conn., 1973—77, v.p. ops. connector group, 1977—78, pres. bus. devel. group, 1978—82, pres. fastening sys. and sealing devices groups, 1982—84; pres. Microdot Industries, 1984—87, pres., CEO, 1988; pres. Microdot Europe Ltd., 1984—88; sr. v.p. Phelps Dodge Corp., Phoenix, 1989—95; group exec. Phelps Dodge Industries, 1989—90, pres., 1990—95; pres., CEO, bd. dirs. BW/IP Internat., Inc., 1995—97, chmn., 1997; CEO, chmn. bd. dirs. Flowserve Corp., 1997—2000, chmn. emeritus, 2000—; chmn. McDyre & Spendley, Ltd., 2000—. Bd. dirs. Maytag Corp., Belden, Inc., Amcast Indsl. Corp., Dover Corp., Walter Industries, Inc.; cons. U.S. Govt., UN; mem. Thunderbird Global Bus. Coun., Am. Grad. Sch. Internat. Mgmt., 1990—, chmn., 1991—94; mem. dean's adv. bd. Wharton Sch. Bus., U. Pa., 1972—80. Elected mem. bd. fin. Town of Westport, Conn., 1986-90; trustee Ballet Ariz., 1989-95, vice chmn., 1991-95; bd. dirs. Boys Hope of Phoenix, 1989-95; trustee Phoenix Country Day Sch., 1992—, Thunderbird, Am. Grad. Sch. Internat. Mgmt., 1994—. Served to Capt., inf., AUS, 1962-65. Decorated Bronze Star. Mem. Nat. Assn. Mfrs. (bd. dirs. 1994-95, 96-99), Yale Club (N.Y.C.), Union League (Chgo.), La Cima (Dallas), Wharton Bus. Sch. Alumni Assn., Nat. Assn. Corp. Dirs. (blue ribbon com. on bd. role in strategic plan 2000), Gainey Ranch Club (Scottsdale, Ariz.). Home: 7010 East Avenida El Alba Paradise Valley AZ 85253 Office: McDyre & Spendley Ltd Ste 300 7702 E Doubletree Ranch Rd Scottsdale AZ 85258 Business E-Mail: brethore@msltd.cc.

RETSON, NICHOLAS PHILIP, lawyer, military officer; b. Appleton, Wis., Oct. 20, 1947; s. Philip Nicholas and Catherine Retson; m. Birgit Maria Abromaitis, Dec. 30, 1977; children: Philip N., Kathryn L., Nicholas Peter. BA in Chemistry, Ripon Coll., 1969; JD, Marquette U., 1972; LLM in Govt. Procurement, George Washington U., 1983. Bar: Wis. 1972, U.S. Dist. Ct. (ea. and we. dists.) Wis. 1972; cert. ct. mediator Va. Commd. 2nd lt. U.S. Army, 1969, advanced through grades to col., 1990-01; ops. officer Trial Def. Svc., Falls Church, Va., 1976-78; prof. contract law Judge Adv. Gen.'s Sch., Charlottesville, 1979-82; trial team chief Office Chief Trial Atty., Falls Church, 1983-86; chief contract law divsn. Hdqrs. U.S. Army Europe, Heidelberg, Germany, 1986-90; chief counsel U.S. Army Test and Evaluation Command, Aberdeen Proving Ground, Md., 1990-93; chief contract law divsn. Office Judge Adv. Gen., Washington, 1993-95; army chief trial atty. U.S. Army Litigation Ctr., Arlington, Va., 1995-00, chief stds. of conduct and profl. responsibility, 2000-01, dep. gen. counsel, def. contract mgmt. agy., 2001—. Fellow Wis. Bar Found.; mem. ABA (vice chair alternative disputes resolution subcom. sect. on pub. contract law 1995—), State Bar Wis. (dir. non resident lawyers divsn. 1980—), Ripon Coll. Alumni Assn. (dir. 1995-2001). Greek Orthodox. Avocations: travel, stocks, scouting. Office: Def Contract Mgmt Agy Office Gen Counsel 6350 Walker Ln Ste 300 Arlington VA 22310-3241

RETTENBERG, ANNE ELIZABETH, social worker; b. Alexandria, Va., Mar. 22, 1964; d. Frank and Sharon Lee (Kalass) R. BA, Earlham Coll., 1985; MSW, NYU, 1991. Cert. social worker, N.Y. Reporter Md. Ind., Waldorf, 1986-87, Potomac News, Woodbridge, Va., 1987-89; reporter, Washington corr. Pace Pubs., N.Y.C., 1989; social worker Samaritan Village, Inc., 1991-92, Ednl. Alliance, N.Y.C., 1992—. Pvt. practice psychotherapy, N.Y.C., 1991—. NYU scholar, 1990. Mem. NASW, Nat. Women's Polit. Caucus, Amnesty Internat. Democrat.

RETTIE, DWIGHT FAY, political science educator, writer; b. New Haven, Mar. 27, 1930; s. James Cardno and Lois (Morris) Rettie; m. Karen Ross, Aug. 4, 1984; children: Stuart, Catherine, Thomas, Jeffery. BA, Yale U., 1952; MA, U. Calif., Berkeley, 1955; cert. leadership tng., George Washington U., 1959; cert. def. mgmt. sys. course, U.S. Naval Postgrad. Sch., 1964. Various positions Dept. of Interior, Washington, 1957-65; program dir. Dept. Housing and Urban Devel., 1965-71; exec. dir. Nat. Recreation and Park Assn., Arlington, Va., 1971-75; exec. Nat. Park Svc., Washington, 1975-81, chief office policy devel., 1981-86; instr. Carteret C.C., Morehead City, N.C., 1995-98; vis. prof. East Carolina U., Greenville, 1998—. Dir. Arlington Telecomm. Inc., Va., 1973-79; cons. Nat. Parks and Conservation Assn., 1995-96. Author: Our National Park System: Caring for America's Greatest Natural and Historic Treasures, 1995. Mem. nat. coun. Boy Scouts Am., 1958-62; chmn. Arlington County Pub. Utilities Commn., 1967-73; mem. U.S. Bd. Geographic Names, Washington, 1981-86; gov. bd. No. Va. Regional Park Authority, Fairfax, Va., 1973-81. Staff sgt. U.S. Army, 1952-54. Democrat. Mem. Unitarian Ch. Avocations: sailing, writing. Home: 415 Hardy Rd Newport NC 28570 E-mail: tarwathie@coastalnet.com.

RETTIG, CAROLYN FAITH, educator; b. Tarentum, Pa., June 30, 1951; d. William and Jennie Annetta (Lear) Ambrose; m. Gary Alan Rettig, July 10, 1985. BS in Edn., Ind. U. Pa., 1973; MA in Student Pers., Slippery Rock U., 1988. Cert. secondary English tchr., Pa. Jr. high tchr., Saxonburg and Butler, Pa., 1974-75; English tchr. Butler Area High Sch., 1975-76; assessor cmty. needs Butler County C.C., Pa., 1977-78; tchr. English Butler Area Sch. Dist., 1978—, speech and debate coach, 1979-84, curriculum writing coord., 1986-87; chmn. English dept. Butler Intermediate High Sch., 1986-88. Coord. fin. aid counselor practicum Butler County C.C., 1988. Pub. high sch. student art and lit. mag., 1988-91. Mem. NEA, Am. Quarter Horse Assn., Nat. Wildlife Fedn., Defenders Wildlife, Pa. State Edn. Assn., Butler Edn. Assn., Nature Conservancy. Democrat. Lutheran. Avocations: reading, swimming, hiking, horseback riding, gardening. Home: 421 Fisher Rd Cabot PA 16023-2111 Office: Butler Intermediate HS 151 Fairground Hill Rd Butler PA 16001-5619

RETTIG, TERRY, veterinarian, wildlife consultant; b. Houston, Jan. 30, 1947; s. William E. and Rose (Munves) R.; m. Helen Rettig, Mar. 12, 1996; 1 child, Bill; children from previous marriage: Michael Thomas, Jennifer Suzanne. BS in Zoology, Duke U., 1969, MAT in Sci., 1970; DVM, U. Ga., 1975. Resident veterinarian, mgr. animal health The Wildlife Preserve, Largo, Md., 1975-76; wildlife veterinarian dept. environ. conservation State of N.Y., Delmar, 1976-77; owner Atlanta Animal Hosp., 1976—2001; CEO Atlanta Svcs., P.C. Quality Home Builders, 1976—, owner, 1976—, Merial Pharmaceuticals Special Projects, 2001—. Sec., dir. Atlanta Pet Supply, Inc., 1983-89; cons. Six Flags Over Ga., Yellow River Game Ranch, Stone Mountain Park Animal Forest, Atlanta Zoo. Author: (with Murray Fowler) Zoo and Wild Animal Medicine (Aardvark award 1978), 1978, 2d edit., 1986 (Order of Kukukifuku award 1986); contbr. articles to profl. jours. Del. Dekalb County Republican Conv., 1983; mem. Roswell United Meth. Ch., Boy Scouts Am., 1954—, mem. troop coun., asst. scoutmaster, scout master, Philmont expedition leader, 1988, 89. Spl. scholar Cambridge U. Coll. Vet. Medicine, 1973-74, Honor Medal with Crossed Palms, 1995. Mem. AVMA, Nat. Assn. Homebuilders, Gerater Atlanta Assn. Homebuilders, Sys. Homebuilders Assn. Ga., Ga. Vet. Med. Assn., Greater Atlanta Vet. Med. Assn., Dekalb Vet. Soc., Acad. Vet. Medicine, Am. Assn. Zoo Veterinarians, Am. Assn. Zool. Parks and Aquaria, Nat. Wildlife Health Found., Nat. Wildlife Assn., Atlanta Zool. Soc., Am. Fedn. Aviculturists, Cousteau Soc., Am. Assn. Avian Veterinarians, Am. Animal Hosp. Assn., Internat. Wildlife Assn., Soc. Aquatic Veterinary Medicine, Am. Buffalo Assn. Methodist. Home and Office: Atlanta Svcs PC 5035 Kimball Bridge Rd Alpharetta GA 30005-5649 E-mail: atlantaservices@attbi.com.

RETZ, WILLIAM ANDREW, retired naval officer; b. Blauvelt, N.Y., June 3, 1940; s. Andrew Macmillan and Katherine (Deyoe) R.; m. Julia Irene Patterson, Sept. 23, 1989; children: Andrew, Gregory, Mark, Alyse Reavis, Mark Rogers. Student, Tex. A&M U., 1957; BS in Mech. Engring., U. N.Mex., 1963; MS, George Washington U., 1970; grad., Naval War Coll., 1972. Commd. ensign USN, 1963, advanced through grades to rear adm., 1991, patrol officer river div. 511 Vietnam, 1968-69, flag sec. to comdr. Amphibious Group Two Va., 1972-74, exec. officer USS Ainsworth, 1974-76, commanding officer USS Stump, 1980-82, commodore Destroyer Squadron 22, 1985-87, dep. for ops. U.S. Cen. Command Tampa, Fla., 1987-90; comdr. Naval Base Pearl Harbor, 1992-94, Naval Surface Group Mid. Pacific, 1992-94; commanded and closed Naval Base Phila., 1994-95; ret. USN, 1995; v.p. govt. svcs. Aramark Corp., Phila., 1996-99; ind. cons., 1999; CEO Nofire Techs., Inc., 2000—. Bd. dirs. Aeptec, Inc. Active Episcopal Ch., Media, Pa.; bd. dirs. Nat. Def. Indsl. Assn., Leadership Inc., Ind. Seaport Mus. Decorated Disting. Svc. medal, Legion of Merit, Def. Disting. Svc. medal, Meritorious Svc. medal, Bronze star. Mem. Surf Navy Assn. (bd. dirs.). Avocations: running, sailing. Office: Nofire Techs Inc 21 Indistrial Dr Upper Saddle River NJ 07458 E-mail: retzw@worldnet.att.net.

RETZER, KENNETH ALBERT, mathematics educator; b. Jacksonville, Ill., Nov. 6, 1933; s. Samuel Stark and Cora Edith (Martin) R.; m. Dorcas Anne Schroeder, Apr. 18, 1953 (dec. Aug. 1990); children: Martin Wayne, Kent Arnold, Sheryl Kaye; m. Wei Dong, Feb. 14, 1991; 1 child, Roger Dong Retzer. AB, Ill. Coll., 1954; MEd, U. Ill., 1957, PhD, 1969. Cert. tchr., Ill., 1954-57; cert. sch. adminstrn., Ill., 1957—. Tchr. Saunemin (Ill.) Twp. High Sch., 1954-58, asst. supt., 1955-58; prof. math. Ill. State U., Normal, 1959-89, Abilene (Tex.) Christian U., 1989—. Asst. chmn. math. dept. Ill. State U., Normal, 1969-71; vis. prof. U. Ga., Athens, 1973, Tex. A&M U., College Station, 1984, U. Hawaii-Maui, Kahului, 1990, 91; cons. Arabian Am. Oil Co., Dhahran, Saudi Arabia, 1984, Ill. State Bd. Edn., Springfield, 1983-88; rsch. fellow U. Western Sydney, Australia, 1993; lectr. Zhejiang U., Hangzhou, China, Northwest Normal U., Lanzhou, China, Gansu Edn. U., Lanzhou, Lanzhou Normal U., Zhangye Normal U., China, summer 1994. Contbr. articles to profl. jours. in the U.S., Can., China. Mem. NEA, AAUP, Nat. Coun. Tchrs. Math., Sch. Sci. and Math. Assn., Math. Assn. Am., Rsch. Coun. on Diagnostic and Prescriptive Math., Ill. Coun. Tchrs. Math. (Max Beberman award 1988), Tex. Coun. Tchrs. Math., Big County Coun. Tchrs. Math., Ill. Assn. Higher Edn., Pi Mu Epsilon, Phi Delta Kappa. Mem. Church of Christ. Avocations: travel, photography, hiking, reading, Christian studies. Home: 31 Rue Maison St Abilene TX 79605-4710 Office: Abilene Christian Univ Math Dept ACU Box 8012 1600 Campus Ct Abilene TX 79601-3701

RETZER, MARY ELIZABETH HELM, retired librarian; b. Balt. d. Francis Leslie C. and Edna (Smith) Helm; m. William Raymond Retzer, June 28, 1945; children: Lesley Elizabeth, April Christine. BA, Western Md. Coll., 1940; MA, Columbia U., 1946; postgrad., George Washington U., 1941, Ind. U., 1952, U. Ill., 1958-59, Ill. State U., 1964-66, Bradley U.; PhD, Western Colo. U., 1972. Faculty Rockville (Md.) Bd. Edn., 1940-47, elem. supr., 1945-47; staff Peoria Pub. Libr., 1957-63, homebound libr., 1961-63; cons., organizer libr. Bergan High Sch., 1964-67; condr. libr. sci. course in reference Bradley U., 1966-83. Libr. Hines Elem. Sch., 1963-66, Roosevelt Jr. H.S., 1966-69; head media ctr. Manual H.S., Peoria, Ill., 1969-83. Instr. water safety courses ARC, 1938-93; pres. Entre Nous, 1949-51; pres. women's bd. Salvation Army, 1952-54; pres. Peoria Nursery Sch. Assn., 1953-54; mem. legis. action com. Ill. Congress PTA, 1955-56; mem. Crippled Children's Adv. Com., Peoria, 1957-60; active various community drives; women's adv. bd. Peoria Jr. Star, 1970-73; vol. Sarasota Internat. Airport, 1990-98. Mem. AAUW (life), NEA, ALA (life), Ill. Edn. Assn. (life), Peoria Edn. Assn. (life), Ill. Libr. Assn., Ill. Valley Librs. Assn. (pres. 1971-72), Ill. Assn. Media in Edn. (cert. com. 1973-80), Ill. Audiovisual Assn., Internat. Platform Assn., Order Ea. Star (life), Ill. State U. Adminstrs. Club, Willowknolls Country Club, Sarasota Yacht Club, Ladies Oriental Shrine. Republican. Presbyterian. Home: Unit 308 435 S Gulfstream Ave Sarasota FL 34236-6705

REUBEN, ADRIAN, clinician, researcher, medical educator; b. London, Mar. 4, 1945; came to U.S., 1979; s. Moss and Hilda Reuben; m. Eleanor Kirk Spicer, Aug. 24, 1981; children: Sara Elizabeth, Aaron Samuel. BSc in Pharmacology, U. Coll., London, 1966; MBBS, U. Coll. Hosp. Med. Sch., 1969. Fell. Royal Coll. of Physicians, 1990. Asst. prof. medicine Yale U. Sch. Medicine, New Haven, 1981-86, assoc. prof. medicine, 1986-93; prof. medicine Med. U. of S.C., Charleston, 1993—. Grantee NIH, 1992-95. Fellow Royal Coll. of Physicians (London); mem. Am. Assn. for Study of Liver Disease, Am. Gastroenterology Assn., Am. Soc. for Transplantation, British Soc. of Gastroenterology, European Assn. of the Study of Liver, Internat. Liver Transplant Soc. Jewish. Avocations: reading, outdoors, music. Office: Med U SC PO Box 250327 96 Jonathan Lucas St Charleston SC 29425 E-mail: reubena@musc.edu.

REUBEN, ALVIN BERNARD, communications and entertainment executive; b. Harrisburg, Pa., Aug. 11, 1940; s. Maurice and Lillian (Katzef) R.; m. Barbara Ann Harrison, Mar. 18, 1968; 1 dau., Mindee Jill. BS in Commerce, Rider U., 1962. Buyer Pomeroy's div. Allied Stores Corp., Harrisburg, 1962-67; sales rep. Random House, Inc., N.Y.C., 1967-74; dir. mktg. Ballantine Books, Inc. (div. Random House), 1974-76; v.p. sales Simon & Schuster, 1976-79, sr. v.p. sales Pocket Books div., 1979-81, sr. v.p. mktg., 1981-82, pres. ref. and promotional pub. group, 1982-83, exec. v.p. electronic pub. div., 1983-85; exec. v.p. Prentice Hall div. Simon & Schuster, 1985-86; sr. v.p. mktg., sales and distbn. Vestron, Inc., 1986-89; sr. v.p. St. Martin's Press, N.Y.C., 1989-91; sr. v.p. sales, mktg. Sony Music Video, 1991-92; sr. v.p. spl. markets Sony Music, 1992-95; sr.v.p. video and interactive sales and distbn. BMG Entertainment, 1995-97; pres. BMG Video, 1997-99. Instr. edn. in pub. program, grad. program SUNY. With USAFR, 1963-69. Mem. Tau Kappa Epsilon. Home and Office: 5 Tyler Ln Bluffton SC 29909-5028 E-mail: alreuben1@aol.com.

REUBEN, DON HAROLD, lawyer; b. Chgo., Sept. 13, 1928; s. Michael B. and Sally (Colucci) R.; m. Evelyn Long, Aug. 27, 1948 (div.); children: Hope Reuben Boland, Michael Barrett, Timothy Don, Jeffrey Long, Howard Ellis; m. Jeannette Hurley Haywood, Dec. 13, 1971; stepchildren: Harris Hurley Haywood, Edward Gregory Haywood. BS, Northwestern U., 1949, JD, 1952. Bar: Ill. 1952, Calif. 1996. With firm Kirkland & Ellis, Chgo., 1952-78, sr. ptnr., until 1978, Reuben & Proctor, Chgo., 1978-86, Isham, Lincoln & Beale, Chgo., 1986-88; sr. counsel Winston & Strawn, 1988-94; of counsel Altheimer & Gray, Chgo., 1994—. Spl. asst. atty. gen. State of Ill., 1963-64, 69, 84; gen. coun. Tribune Co., 1965-88, Chgo. Bears Football Club, 1965-88, Cath. Archdiocese of Chgo., 1975-88; coun. spl. session Ill. Ho. of Reps., 1964, for Ill. treas. for congl., state legis. and jud. reapportionment, 1963; spl. fed. ct. master, 1968-70; dir. Lake Shore Nat. Bank, 1973-93; dir. Heitman Fin., 1993-98; mem. citizens adv. bd. to sheriff County of Cook, 1962-66, mem. jury instrn. com., 1963-68; rules com. Ill. Supreme Ct., 1963-73; past mem. pub. rels. com. Nat. Conf. State Trial Judges; mem. com. study caseflow mgmt. in law div. Cook County Cir. Ct., 1979-88; mem. adv. implementation com. U.S. Dist. Ct. for No. Dist. Ill., 1981-82; mem. Chgo. Better Schs. Com., 1968-69, Chgo. Crime Commn., 1970-80; mem. supervisory panel Fed. Defender Program, 1971-78; gen. counsel Palm Springs Air Mus., 1996—; dir. News-Gazette, Champaign, Ill., 1997-99; lectr. on libel, slander, privacy and freedom of press. Bd. dirs. Lincoln Park Zool. Soc., 1972-84 ; trustee Northwestern U., 1977—; mem. vis. com. U. Chgo. Law Sch., 1976-79; bd. dirs. Blood Bank of the Desert, 1999—, vice-chmn. 2001—; sec., gen. counsel Palm Springs Air Mus., 2000—. Recipient Northwestern U. Law Sch. Alumni Achievement medal, 2002. Fellow Internat. Acad. Trial Lawyers; mem. Ill. Bar Assn., Chgo. Bar Assn. (chmn. subcom. on propriety and regulation of contingent fees com. devel. law 1966-69, subcom. on media liaison 1980-82, mem. com. on profl. info. 1980-82), ABA (standing com. on fed. judiciary 1973-79, standing com. on jud. selection, tenure and compensation 1982-85), Am. Law Inst., Fellow: Am. Bar Found., Am. Coll. Trial Lawyers (Rule 23 com. 1975-82, judiciary com. 1987-91), Am. Arbitration Assn. (nat. panel arbitrators), Calif. Bar Assn., Desert Bar Assn., Tavern Club, Mid-Am. Club, Lawyers Club Chgo., Casino Club, Desert Riders of Palm Springs, Com. of 25 Palm Springs, The Chgo. Club, Springs Club, Phi Eta Sigma, Beta Alpha Psi, Beta Gamma Sigma, Order of Coif. Office: 20 Jill Ter Rancho Mirage CA 92270-2635

REUBEN, GLORIA, actress; b. Toronto, Ont., June 9, 1964; T.V. and movie actress; backup singer and dancer Tina Turner's World Tour. T.V. films include The Day They Came to Arrest the Book, 1986, Shadowhunter, 1993, Dead Air, 1994, Indiscreet, 1998, Sara, 1999, Deep in My Heart, 1999, Little John, 2002; film appearances include Immediate Family, 1989, Johnny's Girl, 1993, Timecop, 1994, Nick of Time, 1995, Macbeth in Manhattan, 1999, Bad Faith, 1999, Happy Here and Now, 2001; T.V. series include ER, 1995-99 (Emmy Best Supporting Actress nominee 1997, 98); T.V. guest appearances in The Flash, 1990, Silk Stalkings, 1991, Homicide: Life on the Street, 1993, others. Recipient SAG Awards, 1998, 99, Q Award, 1997, 98. Office: Gerson Saines Mgmt Ste 2303 250 W 57th St New York NY 10107-2399*

REUBER, GRANT LOUIS, banking insurance company executive; b. Mildmay, Ont., Can., Nov. 23, 1927; s. Jacob Daniel and Gertrude Catherine (Wahl) R.; m. Margaret Louise Julia Summerhayes, Oct. 21, 1951 (dec. Feb. 1998); children: Rebecca, Barbara, Mary. BA, U. Western Ont., 1950; AM, Harvard U., 1954, PhD, 1957; LLD (hon.), Wilfred Laurier U., 1983, Simon Fraser U., 1985, U. Western Ont., 1985, McMaster U., 1994; postgrad., Cambridge U., 1954-55. Mem. research dept. Bank Can., Ottawa, 1950-52; mem. Can. Dept. Finance, 1955-57; asst. prof. econ. U. Western Ont., London, 1957-59, assoc. prof., 1959-62, prof., head dept., 1963-69, 1963-69; mem. bd. govs. U. Western Ont., London, 1974-78, acad. v.p., provost, 1975-78, chancellor, 1988-92; sr. v.p., chief economist Bank of Montreal, Que., Can., 1978-79, exec. v.p., 1980-81, dep. chmn., dep. chief exec. officer, 1981-83, dir., mem. exec. com., 1981-89, pres., chief operating officer, 1983-87, dep. chmn., 1987-89; dep. minister fin. Can., 1979-80; chmn. Can. Deposit Ins. Corp., 1993-99; sr. adv., dir. Sussex Circle, 1999—. Staff mem. Royal Commn. Banking and Fin., Toronto, 1962—63; chmn. Ont. Econ. Coun., 1973—78; cons. Can. Internat. Devel. Agy., 1968—69; hon. rsch. assoc. in econs. Harvard U., 1968—69; cons. devel. ctr. OECD, 1969—73; lectr. U. Chgo. Sch. Bus., 1992—93. Author: Private Foreign Investment in Development, 1973, Canada's Political Economy, 1980; contbr. articles. Bd. dirs. Can. Merit Scholarship Found., 1994—2000; bd. govs. Royal Ont. Mus., 2000—02; pres. Can. Ditchley Found., 1981—. Decorated officer Order of Can. Fellow Royal Soc. Can.

REUM, JAMES MICHAEL, lawyer; b. Oak Park, Ill., Nov. 1, 1946; s. Walter John and Lucy (Bellegay) R. BA cum laude, Harvard U., 1968, JD cum laude, 1972. Bar: N.Y. 1973, D.C. 1974, U.S. Dist. Ct. (so. dist.) N.Y. 1974, Ill. 1979, U.S. Dist. Ct. (no. dist.) Ill. 1982. Assoc. Davis Polk & Wardwell, N.Y.C., 1973-78; assoc. Minority Counsel Com. on Judiciary U.S. Ho. of Reps., Washington, 1974; ptnr. Hopkins & Sutter, Chgo., 1979-93, Winston & Strawn, Chgo., 1994—. Midwest advance rep. Nat. Reagan Bush Com., 1980; nominee commr. Securities and Exchange Comm., Pres. Bush, 1992; mem. G.W. Bush fin. com, 2000. Served to SP4 USAR, 1969-75. Recipient Harvard U. Honorary Nat. Scholarship, 1964-72. Mem. Monte Carlo Country Club (Monaco), Univ. Club (N.Y.C.). Republican. Home: 12 E Scott St Chicago IL 60610-2320 Office: Winston & Strawn 35 W Wacker Dr Ste 4200 Chicago IL 60601-1695 E-mail: jreum@winston.com.

REUPKE, WILLIAM ALBERT, engineer; b. Chgo., Jan. 22, 1940; BA, Northwestern U., Evanston, Ill., 1961; AM, Ind. U., 1967; MS, Ga. Inst. Tech., Atlanta, 1973, PhD, 1977. Gen. physicist NASA, Cleve., 1963-64; staff physicist Aerospace Rsch. Applications Ctr., Bloomington, Ind., 1965-67; rsch. engr. Lockheed Missiles and Space Co., Sunnyvale, Calif., 1967-68; engring. physicist Stanford (Calif.) Linear Accelerator Ctr., 1968-71; staff mem. Los Alamos (N.Mex.) Nat. Lab., 1977-82; sr. engr. Computer Scis. Corp., Lanham-Seabrook, Md., 1983-95, Gen. Scis. Corp., Seabrook, 1996—. Recipient Group Achievement award NASA, 1987, 91, 93, Dr. Robert H. Goddard Hist. Essay award Nat. Space Club, 1991. Fellow Brit. Interplanetary Soc.; mem. AAAS, AIAA (sr.), IEEE, Am. Phys. Soc., Am. Nuclear Soc. Achievements include development of method of adjusting neutron cross sections to improve fit of measured and calculated reaction rates in nuclear fusion integral experiments and application of that method to show that a neutron cross section important for fusion energy production is significantly smaller than was previously believed. Office: Gen Scis Corp 7501 Forbes Blvd Ste 103 Lanham Seabrook MD 20706-6201

REUSCHLEIN, ROBERT WILLIAM, accountant, researcher; b. Madison, Wis., Jan. 8, 1950; s. Earl Vincent and Rosemary (Markham) R. BSEE, U. Wis., 1972; MBA, Oreg. State U., 1977. Surveyor and draftsman Ctrl. Wis. Builders, Madison, 1971-72; estimator Dyson Constrn., 1972; pub. acct. Earl V. Reuschlein & Assocs., 1973-74; mgmt. intern Portland (Oreg.) Gen. Elec., 1976; contr. Doorcraft, Inc., Harrisburg, Oreg., 1977-79; pub. acct. C.F. Rogers CPA, Eugene, 1980; lobbyist Dem. Party of Oreg., Salem, 1981-85; rschr. Earlwal, Ltd., Eugene, 1986-93, acct., pres. Madison, Wis., 1993—. Mem. Citizen Involvement Com., City of Springfield, Oreg., 1979; founding dir. Neighborhood Econ. Devel. Corp., Eugene, 1979-81; dir. Eugene Peace Works, 1991-93; del. Hague Appeals for Peace, 1999; pres. One Hour Cleaners, Inc., 1999—; gen. mgr. Jomblee, Inc., Madison, 1995-96, controller, 1997—, pres., 1998—; instr. peace econs. U. Oreg., 1987, 89; prof. U. of the Air, Radio for Peace Internat., Costa Rica, 1997-98; lectr. Econ. Conversion Conf., Miami, Fla., 1990. Author: Peace Economics, 1986, Strength Through Peace, 1989, Real Economy, 1999; columnist Peace Economics in Oreg. Peace Worker, 1989-97; developer Natural Global Warming Theory, 1991, www-.realeconomy.com website, 1999. Mem. Dem. Exec. Com., Oreg., 1981-87; del. Dem. Nat. Conv., San Francisco, 1984; chmn. 4th Congl. Dist. Dems., Oreg., 1982-87; program dir. Prairie Soc. Unitarian Ch., 1995-97, fin. chair, 1999-2002. Mem. AICPA, Wis. Inst. CPAs, Madison Progressive Inst., World Federalists (pres. local chpt. 2002). Avocations: hiking, politics, lecturing, dancing, biking. Office: Earlwal Ltd 6425 Odana Rd Madison WI 53719-1127 E-mail: earlwal@itis.com.

REUSE, RONALD, real estate developer; b. Cleve., Apr. 5, 1946; s. Lester Reuse and Leona Hopson.; m. Elizabeth Britt. BSBA, Bowling Green (Ohio) State U., 1964. Salesman Liberty Mut. Ins., Cleve., 1969-71; prin. Home Improvement, 1971-73; pres. B.A. Constrn. Co., 1973-75, Namar Demolition, Cleve., 1975-78; owner, chief exec. officer R & H Mgmt., 1978—. Office: 7407 Cedar Ave Cleveland OH 44103-4925

REUSS, MARTIN ALAN, historian; b. Denver, Feb. 25, 1945; s. Stanley Gustav and Ruth Reuss; m. Carolyn Jane Posey, Aug. 7, 1971. BA, Penn. State U., 1966; MA, Duke U., 1968, PhD, 1971. Asst. prof. history Ga. So. Coll., Statesboro, 1971-73, Va. Poly. Inst. and State U., Blacksburg, 1973-75; command historian U.S. Army Logistics Ctr., Ft. Lee, Va., 1977-78; historian U.S. Army Corps Engrs., Washington, 1977-81, sr. historian Alexandria, Va., 1981—. Pres. Soc. for History in the Fed. Govt., Washington, 1988-89, nat. capt. sect. Am Water Resources Assn., Washington, 1993-94. Author: Shaping Environmental Awareness: The United States Army Corps of Engineers Environmental Advisory Board, 1970-1980, 1983, Designing the Bayous: The Control of Water in the Atchafalaya Basin, 1800-1995, 1998; editor: Water Resources Administration in the United States: Policy, Practice and Engineering Issues, 1993; contbr. articles to profl. jours.. Fellow Exch. fellow, Free U. Berlin-Duke U., 1968—69, Dibner Sr. fellow, MIT, 2001—02. Mem. Soc. History of Tech. (mem. adv. coun. 2001—, chair bldg. tech. and civil engring. interest group 1991-95), Am. Soc. Environ. History, Fulbright Alumni Assn., Cosmos Club (Washington). Home: 2911 Seminole Rd Woodbridge VA 22192-1853 Office: US Army Corps Engrs 7701 Telegraph Rd Alexandria VA 22315-3865

REUSS VON PLAUEN XXVI, PRINCE ARCHBISHOP HEINRICH, Metropolitan, nursing, medical-legal consultant, educator; b. Greiz, Plauen, Germany, Feb. 3, 1942; s. Prince Heinrich XXV and Princess Maria (Obrenovic-Brankovic) Reuss von Plauen. BSN, U. der Heiligen Dreifeltigkeit, Fed. Republic Germany, 1968, PhD, STD (hon.), 1974, MD, 1980, LL.D., 1984; BA, San Francisco State U., 1970, MS, 1980; LLD (hon.), South East U., Hong Kong, 1973; MSN, San Jose State U., 1989. Therapist The Counselling Centre, Calif., 1968-74, adminstr., 1972-73; prof. psychiat. medicine, nursing and law Order of St. John, 1974-78; adminstr. Hospice of the Holy Spirit, Calif., 1981-84; prof. nursing and med. ethics and law Order of St. John/U. Heiligen Dreifeltigkeit, Austria, Germany, 1981-84. Nursing-med. cons. Order of St. John of Jerusalem, Calif., Germany, 1964—; chmn. Hospice of the Holy Spirit, Germany, 1974—; rector Holy Trinity Seminary, 1974—; bd. dirs. Hospice of St. John, Denver. Contbr. articles on law, ethics, nursing practices, therapy and theology. Decorated Prince-Grand Master Order St. Thomas the Apostle, Ea. Cath. Order of the Holy Sepulchre, Knight Grand Cross Order Royal Crown Balearica (Spain), Order St. Agatha (Spain), Order of Black Eagle, Order St. Constantine (Greece), Bailiff Grand Cross Knights of the Holy Sepulchre (Germany), Knight Grand Cross of Justice Order St. George (Eng.), Order St. John of Knights of Malta, Grand Prelate Sovereign Hospitaller Order St. John of Knights of Malta. Avocations: fencing, pistol shooting, archery, horseback riding. Address: Eastern Cath Archdiocese (Chaldean-Syrian) PO Box 3337 Daly City CA 94015-0337 *The purpose of the Church is to serve and to love Christ's flock, especially the poor, needy, sick and the dying, in accordance with the Holy Scriptures. The Church must maintain the Apostolic Traditions and Canons of the Historic Church, in order to bring mankind up to God's level, not bring God down to mankind's level.*

REUTER, FRANK THEODORE, history educator; b. Kankakee, Ill., Mar. 18, 1926; s. Frank Theodore and Evelyn Marie (Scott) R.; m. Kathleen Ann Pester, June 16, 1951; children: Mark, Stephen, Christopher, Ann, Katherine. BS, U. Ill., 1950, MA, 1959, PhD, 1960. Instr. West Liberty (W. Va.) State Coll., 1960-62; asst. prof. Texas Christian U., Fort Worth, 1962-66, assoc. prof., 1966-71; prof. history Tex. Christian U., 1971-92; dean Texas Christian U. (Grad. Sch.), 1970-75, chmn. dept. history, 1980-83; prof. emeritus Tex. Christian U., 1992—. Vis. prof. Pázmány Péter Cath. U., Budapest, Hungary. Author: West Liberty State College: The First 125 Years, 1963, Catholic Influence on American Colonial Policies, 1898-1904, 1967, Trials and Triumphs: George Washington's Foreign Policy, 1983; co-author: Injured Honor: The Chesapeake-Leopard Affair, 1996. Served with USNR, 1944-46. U. Durham Rsch. fellow, 1991. Mem. Orgn. Am. Historians, Am. Hist. Assn., Soc. Historians Early Republic, Soc. Historians Am. Fgn. Relations, Phi Beta Kappa, Phi Alpha Theta. Roman Catholic. Home: 3617 Winifred Dr Fort Worth TX 76133-2126 Office: Tex Christian U Dept History Fort Worth TX 76129-0001 E-mail: rfkreuter@aol.com.

REUTER, HELEN HYDE, psychologist; b. McGehee, Ark. d. John Lloyd and Sallie Elizabeth (Holcomb) Hyde; m. George S. Reuter Jr.; children: Don N., M. Allan, K.L. BA, Westmar U., 1968; AM, U. S.D., 1969; PhD, Westgate U., 1976; LHD (hon.), Sioux Empire Coll.; LLD (hon.), St. John U., New Orleans; DD (hon.), Temple Bapt. Coll. Ordained So. Bapt. minister. Post-master U.S. Post Office, College Heights, Ark.; sch. counselor various pub. sch. systems, Mo., Iowa; sch. psychologist Oak Park (Ill.) and River Forest High Sch.; v.p., sec. Internat. Assocs. for Christians, Holden, Mo. Cons. in field. Co-author: One Blood, 1964, 2d edit., 1988, Democracy and Quality Education, 1965, 2d edit., 1986. Named Mother of Yr., City of Monticello, 1960; cited as Psychologist of Yr., Internat. U., Lagos, Nigeria, 1992. Mem. P.E.O. (v.p.), Shakespeare Club (v.p.), Garden Club (v.p.). Democrat. Baptist. Avocations: travel, classical music. Home: 3100 Club Dr Apt 320 Lawrenceville GA 30044

REUTER, JAMES WILLIAM, lawyer; b. Bemidji, Minn., Sept. 30, 1948; s. John Renee and Monica (Dugas) R.; m. Patricia Carol Creelman, Mar. 30, 1968; children: Kristine, Suzanne, Natalee. BA, St. John's U., 1970; JD, William Mitchell Coll. Law, 1974. Bar: Minn. 1974, U.S. Dist. Minn. 1975, U.S. Ct. Appeals (8th cir.) 1985; cert. civil trial specialist. Editor West Pub. Co., St. Paul, 1970-73; assoc. Terpstra & Merrill, Mpls., 1974-77; ptnr. Barna, Guzy, Merrill, Hynes & Giancola, Ltd., 1977-89, Lindquist & Vennum, Mpls., 1989—. Recipient Cert. award Nat. Inst. Trial Advocacy, 1978. Mem. ABA (torts and ins. practice, and civil litigation sects.), ATLA, Minn. Bar Assn. (civil litigation and computer sects.), Hennepin County Bar Assn. (ins. com.), Anoka County Bar Assn. (pres. 1981-82). Avocations: skiing, golf, camping, reading. Office: Lindquist & Vennum 4200 IDS Ctr 80 S 8th St Ste 4200 Minneapolis MN 55402-2274

REUTER, KAREN L. physician, radiologist; b. June 20, 1944; BS, Bucknell U., 1966; MAT, Yale U., 1967; MS, U. Pa., 1971; MD, Tufts U., 1974. Staff radiologist U. Mass. Meml. Med. Ctr., Worcester, 1979—, Ctrl. Mass. Med. Imaging Ctr., Worcester, 1991—. Med. advisor La Leche League New Eng., 1980—. Office: Dept Radiology 55 Lake Ave N Worcester MA 01655-0002

REUTER, LINDA N. corporate design executive; b. Akron, Ohio, Dec. 27, 1947; d. George William Reuter and Charlotte Neal Gray. BS in Design with honors, U. Cin., 1971; MFA in Graphic Design with honors, U. Utah, 1975. Assoc. prof. No. Ill. U., DeKalb, 1975-77; sr. graphic designer Kimberly Clark Corp., Neenah, Wis., 1977-79, mgr. graphic design, 1979-86, mgr. design and prodn., 1986-93, package graphics dir., 1993-98; dir. graphic design Polaroid Corp., Cambridge, Mass., 1998-2001; dir. packaging and brand design Kraft Foods, Glenview, Ill., 2001—. Designs featured in various publs. Design advisor to mayor Future Neenah Devel. Corp., 1982-83. Recipient various awards from design competitions, 1975-2000, 1st award Braun Young Designers Packaging, 1970, Golden award Franklin Typographers Competition, 1970, spl. diploma Icograda Phlips award, Helsinki, Finland, 1985. Mem. Am. Inst. Graphic Arts, Brand Design Assn. Avocations: reading, fitness, nature hiking, cooking, drawing. Office: Kraft Foods 1 Kraft Ct GV 535 Glenview IL 60025 E-mail: linda.reuter@kraft.com.

REUTER, ROBERT CARL, JR. retired engineering scientist; b. Pitts., Apr. 30, 1939; s. Robert Carl and Grace Marie Reuter; m. Victoria Nedanovich, Sept. 10, 1961; children: Linda Marie, Susan Margaret, Paul Benjamin. BS in Engring. Mechanics, U. Ill., 1964, MS in Theoretical and Applied Mechanics, 1965, PhD in Theoretical and Applied Mechanics, 1967. Registered profl. engr., N.Mex. Mem. tech. staff Martin Marietta Corp., Denver, 1967—68, Sandia Nat. Labs., Albuquerque, 1968—79, supr. engring. analysis, 1979—91, mgr. mfg. techs., 1991—99; chief scientist dir. ops. Def. Intelligence Agy., Washington, 2000; ret., 2000. Tech. cons. U.S. Dept. Energy, Washington, 1994—96. Fellow, U.S. Dept. Health, Edn. and Welfare, 1964—67. Lutheran. Avocations: sailing, woodworking, fishing. Home: 6000 Barber Pl NE Albuquerque NM 87109

REUTER, STEWART RALSTON, retired radiologist, lawyer, educator; b. Detroit, Feb. 14, 1934; s. Carl H. and Grace M. R.; m. Marianne Ahfeldt, June 6, 1966. BA, Ohio Wesleyan U., 1955; MD, Case Western Res. U., 1959; JD, U. San Francisco, 1980. Diplomate: Am. Bd. Radiology, Am. Bd. Legal Medicine. Bar: Tex. 1981. Intern U. Calif., San Francisco, 1959-60, resident in radiology, 1960-63; instr. radiology Stanford (Calif.) U., 1963-64; asst. prof. U. Mich., Ann Arbor, 1966-69, prof., 1972-76; assoc. prof. U. Calif., San Diego, 1969-72, prof. San Francisco and Davis, 1976-80; prof., chmn. dept. radiology Health Scis. Ctr., U. Tex., San Antonio, 1980-2001, prof. emeritus, 2001. Co-author: Gastrointestinal Radiology, 3d edit., 1986; mem. editorial bd. Am. Jour. Roentgenology, 1975-91, Iatrogenics, 1990-93; contbr. articles to profl. jours. Picker fellow, 1964-66 Fellow: Soc. Cardiovascular and Interventional Radiologists, Am. Coll. Legal Medicine (pres. 1979, bd. govs. 1985—91, 1992—94, sec. 1994, pres.-elect 1995), Am. Heart Assn., Am. Coll. Radiology (councillor 1996—99, fellow emeritus); mem.: AMA, Soc. Gastrointestinal Radiologists, Tex. Radiol. Assn. (trustee 1989—92, pres. 1994, trustee 1995—98, Gold medal 2000), Am. Roentgen Ray Soc., Assn. Univ. Radiologists, Am. Bd. Legal Medicine, Tex. Bar Assn. Home: 3923 Morgans Creek San Antonio TX 78230-1945 Office: U Tex Health Sci Ctr Dept Radiology 7703 Floyd Curl Dr San Antonio TX 78284-6200 E-mail: reuter@uthscsa.edu.

REUTHER, DAVID LOUIS, children's book publisher, writer; b. Detroit, Nov. 2, 1946; s. Roy Louis and Fania (Sonkin) R.; m. Margaret Alexander Miller, July 21, 1973; children: Katherine Anna, Jacob Alexander. BA with honors, U. Mich., 1968. Tchr. Lewis-Wadhams Sch., Westport, N.Y., 1969-71; asst. dir. Children's Book Council, N.Y.C., 1971-73; editor children's books Macmillan Publishing Co., 1973-76; sr. editor Four Winds Press-Scholastic Inc., 1976-82; sr. v.p., pub. Morrow Jr. Books, 1982-98; co-founder Baseball Ink, Inc., 1986-90; pub. Lothrop Lee & Shepard, N.Y.C., 1996-98, Beech Tree Books, N.Y.C., 1997-98; pres., pub. SeaStar Books, 1999—, North-South Books, N.Y.C., 1999—2002. Chmn., bd. dirs. Children's Book Coun. Author: (with Roy Doty) Fun To Go, A Take-Along Activity Book, 1982, Save-the-Animals Activity Book, 1982, (with John Thorn and Pete Palmer) The Hidden Game of Baseball, 1984, Total Baseball, 1989, The Whole Baseball Catalog, 1990, Total Baseball II, 1991; editor: (with John Thorn) The Armchair Quarterback, 1982, The Armchair Aviator, 1983, The Armchair Mountaineer, 1984, The Armchair Book of Baseball, 1985, The Armchair Angler, 1986, The Armchair Book of Basesball II, 1987, The Armchair Traveler, 1988. Mem.: ALA (cco-hmn. children's book coun. joint com. 2000—), Am. Bookseller Assn. (childrens book coun. joint com. 1990—93), Nat. Sci. Tchrs. Assn. (children's book coun. joint com. 1982—85), Soc. Children's Book Writers, Authors Guild. Home: 271 Central Park W New York NY 10024-3020 E-mail: dreuther@northsouth.com.

REUTHER, RONALD THEODORE, museum director; b. Dec. 29, 1929; s. Frederick and Grace (Roehll) R.; m. Mary B. Howard, 1956; children: Catherine Virginia, Paul Douglas, Jon Frederick, Victoria Grace. BA, U. Calif., 1951, postgrad., 1953, U. Ariz., 1952. Mgr. Micke Grove Zoo, 1957-62; gen. curator Cleve. Zoo, 1958-62; asst. dir., 1964-66; dir. Indpls. Zoo, 1962-64, San Francisco Zoo, 1966-73; pres., exec. dir. Phila. Zoo, 1973-78; dir. corp. devel. Exploratorium, San Francisco, 1980-81; founder We. Aerospace Mus., Oakland, Calif., 1980, exec. dir., 1995-99; field rep. Bell & Howell Edn. Corp./DeVry Inst. Tech., 1983-88; exec. dir. Whale Ctr., Oakland, Calif., 1988-89; edn. cons. Sierra Acad. Aeronautics, 1989-92; lectr. Golden State U., San Francisco, 1992. Co-founder Pt. Reyes Bird Observatory, Calif., 1968-70; v.p. Del. Valley Mus. Coun., 1976-78. Author zoo guidebooks, Wings Over San Francisco Bay, 1997, Mem. exec. com. Greater Phila. Cultural Alliance, 1976-78. 1st lt. USAF, 1953-57; with USARNG, 1958-66; lt. col. USAR, 1966-81, ret. Mem. The Explorers Club (chmn. No. Calif. chpt. 1990-95), Tamalpais Conservation Club (life mem.), Ox-5 Pioneers (bd. govs. Golden Gate chpt. 1996—). E-mail: reuther@itilink.com.

REUTHER, ROSANN WHITE, advertising agency executive; b. Nashville, Nov. 24, 1943; d. Wiley Butler and Mildred Elizabeth (Little) White; m. Peter Martin Reuther, Oct. 3, 1964. Student, George Peabody Coll., 1961-64. Advt. copywriter Sta. WHMA, Anniston, Ala., 1964-65, Bapt. Sunday Sch. Bd., Nashville, 1965-72, Thomas Nelson Pubs., Nashville, 1972-73; account exec. Holder-Kennedy Pub. Rels., 1973-74; pub. rels. dir. T. Nelson, 1974-75; pension adminstr. Wood, Bateman, Nord & Assocs., 1975-76; owner, pres. In-Vision Advt. and Pub. Rels., 1976—. Lectr. Tenn. State U., 1978-79; part-time instr. Nashville State Tech. Inst.; mem. faculty Tenn. Entrepreneur Forum, 1984. Worker Carter for Pres. Campaign, Tenn., 1976; bd. dirs. Nashville Neighborhood Alliance, 1992; pres. Hist. Waverly Place Neighborhood Assn., 1988-89, 98-99. Recipient Paul M. Hinkhous award of excellence in advt., 1974. Mem. Am. Women in Radio and TV (pres. Nashville chpt. 1981-82, dir. dist. B, 1982-83), Nashville Advt. Fedn. (bd. dirs. 1986-88). Baptist. Home: 1908 Elliott Ave Nashville TN 37204-2004 Office: PO Box 41161 Nashville TN 37204-1161 E-mail: rosannr@comcast.net.

REUTHINGER, GEORGEANNE, special education educator; b. Laredo, Tex., Mar. 10, 1952; d. George and Maria Josefina (Elizondo) Ramon; m. David Lawrence Reuthinger, Apr. 5, 1952; 1 child, David L. Jr. AA in Music and Drama, Laredo Jr. Coll., 1972; BS in Speech and Drama Edn., Tex. A&I U., 1974, MS in Edn., 1978; postgrad., Tes. A&M Internat. U. Lic. speech therapist, Tex.; cert. speech therapist, ednl. diagnostician, profl. supervision. Speech and drama tchr. Laredo ISD Martin High Sch., 1974; supr., diagnostician spl. edn. program Laredo ISD Martin H.S., 1992-96, Cigarra H.S., Nixon H.S., 1998—; speech therapist Laredo ISD, 1974-78, ednl. diagnostician, 1978-92; sales assoc. Country Wide Real Estate, Laredo, 1997—; cons. in spl. edn. United Ind. and Laredo Ind. Sch. Dists., 1997-98. Founding mem., lead actress in bilingual theatrical touring co. Tex. A&I U., 1974. Active in fundraising for charities Women's City Club, Boy Scouts Am.; judge UIL Acad. & Fine Arts events, Spl. Olympics. Scholar Art League, 1970, Tex. A&I Alumni, 1972-74; recipient awards U.S. Army, 1973, USO Shows, 1973-74. Mem. Tex. Speech and Hearing Assn. (legis. network 1992-97), Coun. for Exceptional Children (lobbyist 1995, sec. Laredo chpt. 1975), Valley Coun. Adminstrs. and Suprs. in Spl. Edn., ASCD, Tex. Coun. Adminstrs. and Suprs. in Spl. Edn., Delta Kappa Gamma (sec. Alpha Nu chpt. 1977-78). Avocations: directing and acting in theatrical productions, singing in community choirs, Special Olympics volunteering and judging. Home: 206 Granada Dr Laredo TX 78041-2615 Office: Country Wide Real Estate 1303 Calle Del Norte Ste 6 Laredo TX 78041-6041 also: Laredo Ind Sch Dist 1702 Houston St Laredo TX 78040-4906

REUTIMAN, ROBERT WILLIAM, JR. lawyer; b. Mpls., June 4, 1944; s. Robert William and Elsbeth Bertha (Doering) R.; m. Virginia Lee Traxler, June 25, 1983; children: Robert James, Joseph Lee. BA magna cum laude, U. Minn., 1966, JD, 1969. Bar: Minn. 1969, U.S. Ct. Mil. Appeals 1969, U.S. Dist. Ct. Minn. 1973, U.S. Ct. Appeals (8th cir.) 1976, U.S. Tax. Ct. 1979. Mem. Armstrong, Phleger, Reutiman & Vinokour, Ltd., Wayzata, Minn., 1973-76; ptnr. Phleger & Reutiman, 1976-81; pvt. practice, 1981—. Chmn. Spring Pk. Planning Commn., 1978. Capt. U.S. Army, 1969-73. Decorated Army Commendation medal. Mem. ABA, Minn. Bar Assn., Hennepin County Bar Assn., Am. Arbitration Assn. (panel of arbitrators), Phi Beta Kappa. Lutheran. Avocations: fishing, rose growing. Home: 11610 3rd Ave N Plymouth MN 55441-5919 Office: 305 Rice St E Wayzata MN 55391-1615

REUTTER, EBERHARD EDMUND, JR. education and law educator; b. Balt., May 28, 1924; s. Eberhard Edmund and Irene Louise (Loewer) R.; m. Bettie Marie Lytle, Aug. 16, 1947; 1 son, Mark Douglas. BA, Johns Hopkins U., 1944; MA, Columbia U., 1948, PhD, 1950. Dir., Tokyo Army Edn. Program Sch., 1945-47; head math. dept. Barnard Sch., N.Y.C., 1947-49; mem. faculty Tchrs. Coll., Columbia U., 1950—, prof., 1957-96, prof. emeritus, 1996—. Vis. prof. U. Alaska, 1960, 66, U. P.R., 1954, U. So. Calif., 1960; speaker, cons. Coordinator spl. edn. projects NAACP Legal Def. Fund, 1965-68 Author: The School Administrator and Subversive Activities, 1951, Schools and the Law, 5th edit., 1981, (with W.S. Elsbree) Staff Personnel in the Public Schools, 1954, (with R.R. Hamilton) Legal Aspects of School Board Operation, 1958, (with W.S. Elsbree) Principles of Staff Personnel Administration in Public Schools, 1959, (with L.O. Garber) The Yearbook of School Law, 1967, 68, 69, 70, Legal Aspects of Control of Student Activities by Public School Authorities, 1970, The Law of Public Education, 4th edit., 1994, The Courts and Student Conduct, 1975, The Supreme Court's Impact on Public Education, 1982; also articles, chpts. in books. Chmn. citizens adv. com. Emerson (N.J.) Bd. Edn., 1954-57. Served from pvt. to 1st lt. inf. AUS, 1943-46. Recipient Marion A. McGhehey award for outstanding service in field edn. law, 1986. Mem. Nat. Orgn. Legal Problems of Edn. (pres. 1967), AAUP, Am. Assn. Sch. Adminstrs., NEA, Am. Assn. Sch. Personnel Adminstrs., Internat. Personnel Mgmt. Assn., Phi Beta Kappa, Kappa Delta Pi, Phi Delta Kappa. Home: 316 Grand Blvd Emerson NJ 07630-1157 Office: Columbia Univ Tchrs Coll New York NY 10027

REVAK, FRANCIS CHARLES, priest, educator; b. Philadelphia, Pa., Jan. 28, 1914; s. Joseph J. and Emma E. Revak. BA, St. Charles Sem., Overbrook, PA, 1939; ME, Lehigh U., Bethlehem, PA, 1968; MA, St. Charles Sem., Overbrook, PA, 1974. Ordained Catholic Priest Diocese of Phila., 1940. Priest Parish Ministry, 1940—67; theology and lang. educator Allentown Ctrl. Cath. H.S., Allentown, Pa., 1967—2002. Moderator, chaplain Allentown Ctrl. Cath. H.S. Football Team, Allentown, Pa., 1990—90. Roman Catholic. Avocations: spiritual reading, spiritual reading, biking, church and world news. Office: Allentown Central Catholic High School 301 N Fourth Street Allentown PA 18102-3098 Office Fax: 610-437-6760. E-mail: altlcchs@ptd.net.

REVANKAR, NAGESH SUBRAY, economics educator; b. Kumta, India, Aug. 2, 1936; came to U.S., 1963, naturalized, 1974; d. Subray Ganapat and Saraswati Babu Shet; m. Neena Shantaram Rajani Revankar, June 4, 1969; children— Usha, Rajeev. B.A. in Math., U. Poona (India), 1958, M.A. in Stats., 1960; M.A. in Econs., U. Wis., 1965, Ph.D., 1967. Lectr. stats. Vikram U., Ujjain, India, 1960-61; asst. prof. econs. SUNY-Buffalo, Amherst, 1967-72, assoc. prof., 1972-78, prof., 1978— ; cons. migrant farm workers, Western N.Y., 1983, participant Migrant Enumeration Conf., Washington, 1983. Contr. articles to profl. jours. Mem. Am. Econ. Assn., Econometric Soc., Am. Statis. Assn.

REVANKAR, SHRIPAD T. nuclear engineering educator; b. Tadas, India, Aug. 20, 1954; m. Jayashree Shet Revankar, June 12, 1985; children: Pavan, Sachit, Vedang. BS, Karnatak U., Dharwad, India, 1975, MS, 1977; PhD, Karnatak U., 1981; M in Engring., McMaster U., Hamilton, Can., 1983. Vis. rsch. engr. Ont. Hydro industry, Mississuaga, Can., 1982; postdoctoral rsch. engr. Lawrence Berkeley (Calif.) Lab., 1984-87; vis. asst. prof. Purdue U., West Lafayette, Ind., 1987-89, sr. rsch. engr., 1989-97, assoc. prof. nuc. engring., 1997—. Cons., U. Wis., Milw., 1988-92, Korea Atomic Energy Rsch. Inst., Seoul, 1998-2000. Contbr. more than 80 articles to profl. jours. and publs. Mem. ASME, Am. Soc. Engring. Edn., Am. Nuc. Soc. Home: 2719 Henderson St West Lafayette IN 47906 Office: Purdue U 1290 Nuc Engring Bldg West Lafeyette IN 47907 Fax: (765) 494-9570. E-mail: shripad@ecn.purdue.edu., shripad_revankar@hotmail.com.

REVANN, MIRIAM CIRA, programmer; b. Havana, Cuba, Dec. 19, 1959; d. Carlos Francisco Diaz-Silveira and Miriam (Estenger) Northland; m. Thomas Richard Revann, May 14, 1994. BA, U. Miami, Fla., 1981. Jr. programmer IBM, Boca Raton, Fla., 1981-82, assoc. programmer, 1982-84, 92-93, sr. assoc. programmer, 1984-92; programmer SunGard Data Systems (formerly FDP Corp.), Miami, 1993-96, programmer, project leader, 1996—. Roman Catholic. Avocations: reading psychology, photography. Office: Sun-Gard Data Systems 2000 S Dixie Hwy Miami FL 33133-2487

REVEAL, ERNEST IRA, III, lawyer; b. Chgo., Oct. 19, 1948; s. Ernest Ira Jr. and Hazel (Holt) R.; m. Katherine Trennerry, Nov. 24, 1979; children: Genevieve, Adrienne, Danielle. BA, Cornell U., 1970; JD cum laude, U. Mich., 1973. Bar: Minn. 1973, U.S. Dist. Ct. Minn. 1973, U.S. Ct. Appeals (8th cir.) 1974, U.S. Dist. Ct. S.D. 1976, U.S. Ct. Claims 1976, U.S. Ct. Appeals (7th cir.) 1984, U.S. Dist. Ct. (so. dist.) Calif. 1991, U.S. Ct. Appeals (9th cir.) 1991, U.S. Supreme Ct., 1991. Assoc. Robins, Kaplan, Miller & Ciresi, Mpls., 1973—79, ptnr., 1979—2002. Author: Public Sector Labor Law, 1983. Mem. Civl Svc. Commn., St. Paul, Minn., 1976. Mem. ABA, Minn. Bar Assn. (past chair labor law and employment law sect.), Calif. Bar Assn. (exec. com. antitrust and unfair competition sect.), Cornell Club of Minn. (past pres.). Democrat. Presbyterian. Avocations: history, travel. Office: Robins Kaplan Miller & Ciresi 600 Anton Blvd Ste 1600 Costa Mesa CA 92626-7652 E-mail: ernest.reveal@cox.net.

REVEL, JEAN-PAUL, biology educator; b. Strasbourg, France, Dec. 7, 1930; came to U.S., 1953; s. Gaston Benjamin and Suzanne (Neher) R.; m. Helen Ruth Bowser, July 27, 1957 (div. 1986); children: David, Daniel Neher, Steven Robert; m. Galina Avdeeva Moller, Dec. 24, 1986; 1 stepchild, Karen. BS, U. Strasbourg, 1949; PhD, Harvard U., 1957. Rsch. fellow Cornell U. Med. Sch., N.Y.C., 1958-59; from instr. to prof. Harvard Med. Sch., Boston, 1959-71; prof. Calif. Inst. Tech., Pasadena, 1971—, AB Ruddock chair in biology, 1978—, dean of students, 1996—. Mem. sch. advisors bd. Nat. Insts. Aging, Balt., 1977-80; mem. ad hoc adv. biology NSF, Washington, 1982-83; mem. Nat. High Voltage Microscopy Adv. Group, Bethesda, Md., 1983, Nat. Rsch. Resources Adv. Coun., 1986-90. Author: (with E.D. Hay) Fine Structure of Developing Avian Cornea, 1969; editor: Cell Shape and Surface Architecture, 1977, Science of Biological Specimen Preparation, 1986; mem. editl. bd. Jour. Cell Biology, 1969-72, Internat. Rev. Cytology, 1970, Cell and Tissue Rsch., 1979—, Molecular and Cell Biology, 1983-91; editor in chief Jour. Microscopy Soc. Am., 1994-96. Fellow AAAS (leader biol. scis. sect. 1991-92, Gordon conf. cell adhesion); mem. Am. Soc. Cell Biology (pres. 1972-73), Electron Micros. Soc. Am. (pres. 1988, Disting. Scientist award 1993), Soc. Devel. Biology. Avocations: watercolors, photography. Office: Calif Inst Tech # 156-29 Pasadena CA 91125-0001 E-mail: revelj@caltech.edu.

REVELEY, WALTER TAYLOR, III, dean; b. Churchville, Va., Jan. 6, 1943; s. Walter Taylor and Marie (Eason) R.; m. Helen Bond, Dec. 18, 1971; children: Walter Taylor, George Everett Bond, Nelson Martin Eason, Helen Lanier. AB, Princeton U., 1965; JD, U. Va., 1968. Bar: Va. 1970, D.C. 1976. Asst. prof. law U. Ala., 1968-69; law clk. to Justice Brennan U.S. Supreme Ct., Washington, 1969-70; fellow Woodrow Wilson Internat. Ctr. for Scholars, 1972-73; internat. affairs fellow Coun. on Fgn. Rels., N.Y.C., 1972-73; assoc. Hunton & Williams, Richmond, Va., 1970-76, ptnr., 1976-98, mng. ptnr., 1982-91, cons., 1998—; dean William and Mary Law Sch., 1998—. Lectr. Coll. William and Mary Law Sch., 1978-80; cons. in field. Author: War Powers of the President and Congress: Who Holds the Arrows and Olive Branch, 1981; mem. editl. bd. Va. Law Rev., 1966-68; contbr. articles to profl. jours. Trustee Princeton U., 1986-90, 91-2001, Presbyn. Ch. (U.S.A.) Found., 1991-97, Va. Hist. Soc., 1991-96, Union Theol. Sem., 1992-2000, Andrew W. Mellon Found., 1994—, JSTOR, 1995—, Va. Mus. Fine Arts, 1995—, pres.

1996-99, St. Christopher's Sch., 1996-01, Carnegie Endowment for Internat. Peace, 1999—; bd. dirs. Fan Dist. Assn., Richmond, Inc., 1976-80, pres., 1979-80; bd. dirs. Richmond Symphony, 1980-92, pres., 1988-90, pres. symphony coun., 1994-99; bd. dirs. Presbyn. Outlook Found., 1985—, pres., 1992-95; bd. dirs. Va. Mus. Found., 1990-99; elder Grace Covenant Presbyn. Ch.; bd. dirs. New Covenant Trust Co., 1997-99, Va. Found. Humanities, 2001-. Mem. ABA, Va. Bar Assn., D.C. Bar Assn., Am. Bar Found., Va. Bar Found., Princeton Assn. Va. (bd. dirs. 1981—, pres. 1983-85), Va. State Bar (edn. Lawyers sect. bd. govs. 1992—, chmn. 1992-95), Raven Soc., Phi Beta Kappa, Omicron Delta Kappa. Home: 2314 Monument Ave Richmond VA 23220-2604 Office: William and Mary Law Sch PO Box 8795 Williamsburg VA 23187-8795 E-mail: Taylor@wm.edu.

REVELLE, DONALD GENE, manufacturing and health care company executive, consultant; b. Cape Girardeau, Mo., July 16, 1930; s. Lewis W. and Dorothy R.; m. Jo M. Revelle, Aug. 1, 1954; children— Douglas, David, Daniel, Dianne BA, U. Mo., 1952; JD, U. Colo., 1957; grad., Harvard U. Bus. Sch., 1971. Dir. employee relations Westinghouse Corp., Pitts., 1957-65; asst. to v.p. Diebold Corp., 1966; v.p. human resources TRW Corp., Cleve., 1967-84; sr. v.p. human resources Black and Decker Co., Towson, Md., 1984-86; exec. v.p. corp. rels. Montefiore Acad. Med. Ctr., Bronx, 1987-98; pres., CEO Syzygy, Inc., 1998—. Univ. lectr.; cons. Duerba Ship, Blue Cross N.Y., Windsor Hosp., Salvation Army Contbr. articles to profl. jours. Mem. sch. bd. State of N.Y. Lt. USNR, 1952-54 Mem.: ABA (labor law com.), Human Resource Planning Soc., Fed. Bar Assn., Colo. Bar Assn., MBA Assn., Rotary. Methodist. Home and Office: Syzygy Inc 29903 Baywood Ln Wesley Chapel FL 33543-9744

RE VELLE, JACK B(OYER), statistician, consultant; b. Rochester, N.Y., Aug. 2, 1935; s. Mark A. and Myril (Bubes) Re V.; m. Brenda Lorraine Newcombe, Aug. 2, 1968; 1 child, Karen Alyssa. BSChemE, Purdue U., 1957; MS in Indsl. Engring. and Mgmt., Okla. State U., 1965, PhD in Indsl. Engring. and Mgmt., 1970. Commd. 2d lt. USAF, 1957, advanced through grades to major, 1968, resigned, 1968; adminstrv. asst. Gen. Dynamics, Ft. Worth, 1970-71; cons. engr. Denver, 1971-72; chmn. decision scis. U. Nebr., Omaha, 1972-77; dean Chapman U. Sch. Bus. and Mgmt., Orange, Calif., 1977-79; sr. staff engr. McDonnell Douglas Space Systems, Huntington Beach, 1979-81; head mfg. tng. and devel. Hughes Aircraft Co., Fullerton, 1981-82, sr. statistician, 1982-86, corp. mgr. R & D L.A., 1986-88, corp. chief statistician, 1988-93; leader continuous improvement Raytheon Missile Systems Co., Tucson, 1994-97; dir. Ctr. for Process Improvement GenCorp Aerojet, Azusa, Calif., 1998-99; consulting statistician Tustin, 1999—. Bd. examiners Malcolm Baldrige nat. quality award Nat. Inst. Stds. and Tech., U.S. Dept. Commerce, Washington, 1990, 93; judge Ariz. Quality Alliance, Phoenix, 1994-96, Rochester Inst. Tech.-USA Today Quality Cup Competition, 1994-2001, Def. Contract Mgmt. Command-Commdrs. Cup, 1995-2000; cons., presenter, lectr. in field. Author: Safety Training Methods, 1980, 2d edit., 1995, The Two-Day Statistician, 1986, The New Quality Technology, 1988, Policy Deployment, 1993; (with others) Quest for Quality, 1986, Mechanical Engineers Handbook, 1986, 2d edit., 1998, Production Handbook, 1987, Handbook of Occupational Safety and Health, 1987, A Quality Revolution in Manufacturing, 1989, Quality Engineering Handbook, 1991; co-author: Quantitative Methods for Managerial Decisions, 1978, The Executive's Handbook on Quality Function Deployment, 1994, From Concept to Customer, 1995, The Quality Function Deployment Handbook, 1998, What Your Quality Guru Never Told You, 2000, Manufacturing Handbook of Best Practices, 2001; (software) TQM ToolSchool, 1995, QFD/Pathway, 1998. Bd. dirs. Assn. for Quality and Participation, Cin., 1985-86; mem. adv. bd. dept. indsl. and mech. engring. Calif. Poly. State U.-Pomona, 1985-2000; mem. adv. bd. dept. indsl. and sys. engring. Ohio U., Athens, 2000—. Recipient Disting. Econs. Devel. award Soc. Mfg. Engrs., 1990. Fellow Am. Soc. for Quality (co-chair total quality mgmt. com. 1990-92), Inst. Advancement Engring., Inst. Indsl. Engrs. (regional v.p. 1982-84, treas. 1992-93, sr. v.p. 1993-94); mem. Aerospace and Def. Divsn. (dir. 1997-99). Office: The Wizard of Odds A Consulting Statistician Re Velle Solutions LLC 14101 Yorba St Ste 104 Tustin CA 92780-2041 E-mail: cactus_statman@yahoo.com.

REVENS, JOHN COSGROVE, JR. state legislator, lawyer; b. Providence, Jan. 29, 1947; s. John C. and Rita M. (Williams) R.; m. Susan L. Shaw, Aug. 31, 1974; children: Leigh Elizabeth, Marcie Greene, Emily May. AA, C.C. of R.I., 1966; BA, Providence Coll., 1969; JD, Suffolk U., 1973. Bar: R.I. 1973. Mem. R.I. Ho. of Reps., Providence, 1968-74, sec. house steering com., 1971-74; mem. edn. and welfare com. RI Ho. of Reps., 1968—78; pres. Revens, Revens & St. Pierre, Warwick, 1977—; mem. R.I. Senate, Dist. 18, Providence, 1990—. Mem. R.I. Senate, 1974-89, 1991—, mem. jud. and labor coms., 1974, chmn. jud. com., 1980-83, majority whip, 1977-80, Senate majority leader, 1983-89; Senate pres., pro tempore, 1993-95, 2001—; dir. New Eng. Bd. Higher Edn., 1975-83, chmn., 1977-81; chmn. R.I. Children's Code Commn., 1979-83; bd. dirs. C.C. of R.I. Found., Vols. of Warwick Schs., R.I. Acad. Decathlon Assn.; mem. Commn. on Jud. Tenure and Discipline, 1982-84, Family Ct. Bench Bar Com., 1980-82, Women and Infants Hosp. Corp., 1983—; commr. Uniform State Laws, 1982-84. Mem. R.I. Bar Assn., Kent County Bar Assn., Am. Arbitration Assn. (panel of arbitrators 1980—), KC. Democrat. Roman Catholic. Office: 946 Centerville Rd Warwick RI 02886-4398

REVERCOMB, HORACE AUSTIN, III, judge; b. Richmond, Va., Sept. 22, 1948; s. Horace Austin Jr. and Mary Virginia (Kelley) R.; m. Annie S. Anthony, July 10, 1976; children: Brian Austin, Suzanne Melanie. BA, Pembroke State U., 1971; JD, George Mason U., 1977. Bar: Va. 1978. Pvt. practice law, King George, Va., 1978-82; ptnr. Revercomb & Revercomb, 1982-90; judge Gen. Dist. Cts. of 15th Jud. Dist. Va., 1990-99, Cir. Cts. 15th Jud. Cir. Va., 1999—. Mem. Va. Bar Assn. Methodist. Avocation: music. Home: PO Box 216 King George VA 22485-0216

REVERDIN, BERNARD J. lawyer; b. Baden, Switzerland, June 21, 1919; came to U.S., 1948, naturalized, 1954; s. Jean and Germaine Reverdin; m. Marcelle Coicou Reverdin; children: Caroline Reverdin Flanagan, Brigitte, Nathalie. LLB, U. Geneva, 1942; postgrad., Harvard Law Sch., 1949. Bar: Switzerland 1945, N.Y. 1955. Atty., legal asst. Geneva Govt., 1945-48; assoc. Sullivan & Cromwell, N.Y.C., 1949-51; assoc., ptnr. Lovejoy, Wasson & Ashton, 1951-84; ptnr., counsel Hunton & Williams, 1984-88; ptnr. Eaton & Van Winkle, 1988-97, sr. counsel intern, 1998—. Dir. subs. of European corps. Contbr. articles to profl. jours.; lectr. in field V. p., treas., bd. dirs. Friends of Cuttington Coll., Liberia; v.p. LCM Found. on European Affairs Inc. Mem. N.Y. State Bar Assn. (chair com. internat. trust and estate 1988-90), Am. Fgn. Law Assn. (past pres.), Consular Law Soc. (past pres.), Internat. Law Assn., Union Internat. des Avocats, Swiss Soc. N.Y., German Am. Law Assn. Home: 4 Drohan St Huntington NY 11743-1830 Office: Eaton & Van Winkle 3 Park Ave Fl 16 New York NY 10016-5902

REVERE, VIRGINIA LEHR, clinical psychologist; b. Long Branch, N.J. d. Joseph and Essie Lehr; m. Robert B. Revere; children: Elspeth, Andrew, Lisa, Robert Jr. PhB, U. Chgo., 1949, MA, 1959, PhD, 1971. Lic. cons. clin. psychologist, Va. Intern, staff psychologist Ea. Mental Health Reception Ctr., Phila., 1959-61; instr. Trenton (N.J.) State Coll., 1962-63; psychologist Trenton State Hosp., 1964-65, Bucks County Psychiat. Ctr., Phila., 1965-67; assoc. prof. Mansfield (Pa.) State U., 1967-77; clin. rsch. psychologist St. Elizabeth Hosp., Washington, 1977-81, tng. psychology coord., 1981-83, psychologist, 1985-91; child psychologist Cmty. Mental Health Ctr., 1983-85; pvt. practice Alexandria, Va., 1980—. Cons., lectr. in field. Author: Applied Psychology for Criminal Justice Professionals, 1982; contbr. articles to profl. jours. Recipient Group Merit award St. Elizabeth's Hosp., 1983, Community Svc. award D.C. Psychol. Assn., 1978, Outstanding Educator award, 1972; traineeship NIH, USPHS, Chgo., 1963-65; fellow Family Svcs. Assn., 1958-59. Mem. APA, No. Va. Soc. Clin. Psychologists, Va. Acad. Clin. Psychologists. E-mail: rrevere923@aol.com.

REVES, JOSEPH GERALD, dean, anesthesiology educator; b. Charleston, S.C., Aug. 14, 1943; s. George Everett and Frances (Masterson) R.; m. Virginia Cathcart, Jan. 05, 1945; children: Virginia Masterson, Christine Frances, Elizabeth Cathcart. BA, Vanderbilt U., 1965; MD, Medical Coll. S.C., 1969; MS, U. Ala., Birmingham, 1973. Lic. anesthesiologist S.C., Ala., Md., N.C.; Diplomate Am. Coll. Anesthesiology, Am. Bd. Anesthesiology. Rsch. asst., dept. pharmacology Med. Coll. S.C., 1965, 66 (summers); intern U. Ala. Hosp. and Clinics, Birmingham, Ala., 1969-70, resident in anesthesiology, 1970-72; post-doctoral, dept. anesthesia and physiology U. Ala. Med. Sch., 1972; instr., dept anesthesiology U. Ala. Hosp. and Clinics, 1973; dept. tng. staff, anesthesiology Nat. Naval Med. Ctr., Bethesda, Md., 1973-75; clin. instr., dept. anesthesiology George Washington U. Sch. Med., Washington, 1973-75; assoc. prof., dept. anesthesiology U. Ala. Hosp. and Clinics, 1975-78; dir., div. anesthesiology rsch. U. Ala., 1977-84, prof. anesthesiology, 1978-84; clin. anesthesia coord. UAB Cardiac Transplant Program, Birmingham, 1982-84; prof. anesthesiology, dir. cardiothoracic anesthesia Duke U. Med. Ctr., Durham, N.C., 1984-1991; dir., Duke Heart Ctr., Duke Med. Ctr., 1987-97; interim chmn., dept. anesthesiology Duke U. Med. Ctr., 1990-91, prof. and chmn., dept. anesthesiology, 1991—2001; dean, v.p. for medical affairs U. of South Carolina Sch. of Med., 2001—. Cons. Hoffman-LaRoche, Somatogen, Abbott/Oximetric. Contbr. to numerous profl. jours., refereed jours., chpts. in books, published scientific reviews, selected abstracts, editorials, films, audio visual presentations, letters, positions and background papers; author: Acute Revascularization of the Infracted Heart, 1987, Common Problems in Cardiac Anesthesia, 1987, Intravenous Anesthesia and Analgesia, 1988, Anesthesiology Clinics of North America, 1988, Anesthesia, 1990, International Anesthesiology Clinics, 1991; Cardiac Anesthesia, Privileges and Practice, 1994; editor: Anesthesia and Analgesia, 1984—, cardiovascular sect. editor 1991—; editorial bd. Society Cardiovascular Anesthesia Monograph Series (chmn. 1986-89), Current Opinion in Anaesthesia 1987—, American Antec Newsletter 1989—; co-editor in chief: Current Opinion in Anaesthesiology 1990—. Dir. Clairmont Ave Hist. Preservation Com. 1976-78; Am. Heart Assn. (Durham chpt. pres. 1988-90, com. mem. anesthesiology, radiology and surgery rsch. study com. 1988-91). Grantee NIH 1991—, Janssen Pharmaceutica 1991-93, Anaquest 1989-92, Diprivan Ednl. grant ICI Pharmaceuticals Group 1991-92. Fellow Am. Coll. Cardiology; mem. AMA, Durham County Medical Soc., Internat. Soc. on Oxygen Transport to Tissue, N.C. Soc. Anesthesiologist (edn. com. 1992—), N.C. State Medical Soc., Birmingham Vanderbilt Club (bd. dirs. 1975-80, 1st v.p. 1979, pres. 1980), Southern Med. Assn. (chmn. elect. anesthesiology sect. 1976-77, chmn. 1977-78, chmn. 1988-89), Southern Soc. Anesthesiologists (v.p. 1978-79, pres. elect 1979-80, pres. 1980-81), Soc. Cardiovascular Anesthesiologists (pres. 1979-80), Assn. Univ. Anesthetists (elected to mem. 1980), Assn. Cardiac Anesthesiologists (elected to mem. 1982, pres. 1990), Soc. for Neuroleptanalgesia (bd. dirs. 1988), U. Ala. Birmingham Nat. Alumni Soc. (dist. dir., bd. dirs. 1991-93), Internat. Anesthesia Rsch. Soc. (bd. Trustees 1992—), Am. Soc. Anesthesiologists (com. sub-specialty representation 1980—, subcommittee on clin. circulation 1992—, com. geriatric anesthesia 1992—), Sigma Xi, Alpha Omega Alpha. Achievements include research on effects of age on neurologic response to cardiopulmonary bypass; cerebral blood flow and metabolism during cardiac surgery; automated delivery system of intravenous anesthetic drugs; pathophysiology of cardiopulmonary bypass. Office: U of South Carolina Med Sch, PO Box 250617 96 Jonathan Lucas St, Ste 601 Charleston SC 29425*

REVESZ, AKOS GEORGE, physicist; b. Balassagyarmat, Hungary, July 25, 1927; came to U.S., 1959; s. Eugen and Ilona (Rachler) R.; m. Agnes Ernszt, June 1956 (div. May 1973); 1 child, Tom; m. Kinga M. Lutter, Jan. 10, 1975; 1 child, Paul. Diploma in engring., Tech. U., Budapest, Hungary, 1950, PhD, 1968. Rsch. asst. Tech. U., Budapest, 1947-48; rsch. engr. Iron and Steel Rsch. Inst., 1950, Philips, Eindhoven, The Netherlands, 1957-59; rsch. engr., head dept. Tungsram, Budapest, 1951-53, 56; mem. tech. staff RCA Rsch. Labs., Princeton, N.J., 1959-69; sr. scientist Comsat Labs., Clarksburg, Md., 1969-83; ind. cons. Revesz Assocs., Bethesda, 1984—. *Akos Revesz did pioneering work on silicon / silicon-dioxide interface structures that are crucial in microelectronic devices; especially, as related to the non-crystalline structure of the oxide film, hydrogen contamination, and the presence of small excess silicon clusters in the oxide film in some devices. He developed a novel anti-reflection film, which was instrumental for increasing the conversion efficiency of silicon solar cells by 50%. He also discovered the failure mechanism of germanium tunnel diodes, and changed their technology and acceptance criteria; as a result, no more failure has occurred during the 10-year period of their use in communications satellites.* Co-author: Field-Effect Transistors, 1966; editor books in field; contbr. over 150 articles to profl. publs.; patentee in field. Mem. Electrochem. Soc. Avocations: reading, classical music, hiking, swimming. Home and Office: 7910 Park Overlook Dr Bethesda MD 20817-2719

REVESZ, PETER Z. computer science educator; b. Budapest, Mar. 24, 1965; s. Gyorgy and Jolan (Gadanyi) R.; m. Lilla Galy Revesz, Dec. 23, 1995. BS summa cum laude, Tulane U., New Orleans, 1985; MS, Brown U., 1987, PhD, 1991. Postdoctoral fellow U. Toronto, 1991-92; asst. prof. U. Nebr., Lincoln, 1992-98, assoc. prof., 1998—2001, prof., 2001—. Author: Introduction to Constraint Databases, 2002. Rsch. grantee NSF, 1996-99, 96-2000, 01--, Gallup Rsch. Professorship. Mem. AAAS, Assn. Computing Machinery, Sigma Xi. Home: 6930 S 44th St Lincoln NE 68516-5144 Office: Univ Nebr 214 Ferguson Hall Lincoln NE 68588

REVIE, JEAN E. science educator; b. Davenport, Iowa; d. Lloyd E. and Margaret V. Bentley; m. Steven T. Revie, May 26, 1972; children: Jonathan, Brian, Kevin, Alanna, Lindsey, Mikel, Carin. BA, U. Northern Colo., 1970, MA, 1973. Sci. tchr. Banner County H.S., Harrisburg, Nebr., 1970-71; life and earth sci. tchr. Kyrene Jr. H.S., Tempe, Ariz., 1983-85; biology instr. Northland Pioneer Coll., Winslow, 1997-2000, South Mountain C.C., Phoenix, 2000—. Adj. instr. Minot State U., N.D., 1995-97, N.D. State Coll. Sci., Minot AFB, 1994-97; soil conservationist Natural Resource Conservation Svc., Turtle Lake, N.D., 1992-93; mus. aid Theodore Roosevelt Nat. Park, Medora, N.D., 1992. Field exec. Sakakawea Girl Scout Coun., Bismarck, N.D., 1991-92. Recipient Great Ideas scholarship Great Books, 1966, Acad. scholarship U. Northern Colo. 1966-70. Mem. Lds Ch. Avocations: family and nature activities, reading, cross stitch, music. Office: 7050 S 24th St Phoenix AZ 85042-5806 Fax: 602-243-8080. E-mail: jean.revie@smcmail.maricopa.edu.

REVOILE, CHARLES PATRICK, lawyer; b. Jan. 15, 1934; s. Charles Patrick and Olga Lydia (Zecca) R.; m. Sally Cole Gates, Nov. 8, 1963. BA, U. Md., 1957, LLB, 1960. Bar: Md. 1962, U.S. Dist. Ct. Md. 1962, U.S. Supreme Ct. 1970, U.S. Ct. Claims 1976, U.S. Ct. Appeals (fed. cir.) 1982. Legis. counsel Nat. Canners Assn., Washington, 1960-64; asst. counsel Deco Electronics Inc., 1964-67; divsn. counsel Westinghouse Electric, Leesburg, Va., 1967-71; v.p., gen. counsel Stanwick Corp., Arlington, 1971-85; sr. v.p., gen. counsel, sec. CACI Internat. Inc., 1985-92, bd. dirs., 1992—, chmn. compensation com., 1995—, exec. com., 1999—, mem. investor rels. com., 2001—. Mem. regional adv. coun. NASD, 1989-92; lectr., panelist, advisor. Active in Md. Ednl. Found., College Park, 1974-98; assoc. Nat. Symphony Orch., Washington, 1972-93, Smithsonian Instn., 1980-93, M Club Found., 1985-98; lawyer, lobbyist various non-profit orgns., Washington, 1984-98; mem. exec. com. ann. bus. campaign Gallaudet U., 1989-91; chmn. various coms. Kemper Open Championships, 1980-86; exec. com. 1995 USGA Sr. Open, 1997 USGA Open Championships; gen. counsel, mem. exec. com. 1995, 96, 97 Kemper Open Championship. Mem. Md. Bar Assn., Washington Corp. Counsels Assn., Am. Corp. Counsels Assn., Nat. Assn. Corp. Dirs., USGA, Mid. Atlantic Golf Assn. (exec. com. 1989-99, v.p., pres. 1998), Roger Howell Soc. U. Md. Sch. Law (charter), Congl. Country Club (com. chmn. 1966-92, bd. govs. 1987-93, Bethesda, Md.), Avondale Golf Club (Pymble, Australia), Ocean Forest Golf Club (Sea Island, Ga.), Sea Island Club (founder). Home: PO Box 31223 Sea Island GA 31561-1223

REVOR, BARBARA KAY, secondary school educator; b. Mt. Vernon, Ill., June 16, 1948; d. Russell Harold and Mary Alice (Byars) Page; m. Bryan J. Revor, Dec. 19, 1981; children: Rachel, Joshua, Jacob. BA, Okla. Bapt. U., 1971; MS in Edn., Nat. Louis U., 1991. Tchr., chair English dept. North Palos Sch. Dist. 117, Hickory Hills, Ill., 1971—. Author: Immanuel, a collection of poems and inspirational stories, 2002. Mem. Nat. Coun. Tchrs. of English, Ill. Assn. Tchrs. of English, Romance Writers Am., Windy City Romance Writers.

REW, WILLIAM EDMUND, civil engineer; b. Corning, N.Y., Nov. 24, 1923; s. Robert James and Clara (Neal) R.; m. Jean Ella Ohls, Aug. 16, 1947 (dec.); children: Virginia Ann, Robert James, John Edward. BE, Yale U., 1954, M in Engring., 1955. Registered profl. engr., N.Y., Fla., Calif., Ill. Project engr. Texaco & Affiliate, USA and Saudi Arabia, 1955-62; sr. engr. Martin-Marietta Corp., Cape Kennedy, Fla., 1962-63, Chrysler Corp, Cape Kennedy, 1963-65, The Boeing Co., Cape Kennedy, 1965-70; project mgr. Brevard Engring. Co., Cape Canaveral, Fla., 1970-74; city engr. City of Vero Beach (Fla.), 1974-77; resident engr. Post, Buckley, Schuh & Jernigan, Miami, Fla., 1977-85; mgr. Keith & Schnars, P.A., West Palm Beach, 1985-90; pvt. practice consulting Lake Placid, 1990—. Active Dem. Party of Brevard County. 1st lt. U.S. Army, 1942-46, ATO. Scholar of 2d rank Yale U., 1953, grad. scholar, 1955. Fellow ASCE (chmn. Fla. ann conv. 1971, Engr. of Yr. 1974); mem. NSPE, Soc. Am. Mil. Engrs. (bd. dirs. 1982-83), Fla. Engring Soc. (chpt. pres. 1976), Yale Club, Browning Assn. Club. Episcopalian. Avocations: woodworking, reading. Home: 1425 S Washington Blvd NW Lake Placid FL 33852-4031 Fax: 863-465-3921.

REWAK, WILLIAM JOHN, former academic administrator, clergyman; b. Syracuse, N.Y., Dec. 22, 1933; s. William Alexander and Eldora Venetia (Carroll) R. BA, Gonzaga U., 1957, MA in English, 1958; MA in Theology, Regis Coll., Toronto, Ont., Can., 1965; PhD in English, U. Minn., 1970. Joined S.J., 1951, ordained priest Roman Cath. Ch., 1964. Tchr. English Bellarmine Coll. Prep. Sch., 1958-61; asst. prof. English Santa Clara (Calif.) U., 1970-71, pres., 1976-88; rector Jesuit Community, 1971-76; pres. Spring Hill Coll., Mobile, Ala., 1989-97; ret., 1997. Bd. dirs. Gulf Coast Broadcasting Inc., Badger-Stonewall Ins. Co., Marine Environ. Scis. Consortium. Contbr. articles to theol. and critical jours., poetry, short stories to lit. jours. Bd. dirs. Mobile Bay Area Partnership for Youth, Mercy Med. Ctr.; mem. Ala. Ind. Colls., Coun. for Advancement Pvt. Colls. in Ala.; bd. trustees Loyola U. New Orleans. Mem. MLA, Coll. English Assn., Bienville Club. Democrat. Home and Office: Spring Hill Coll Office of Pres 4000 Dauphin St Mobile AL 36608-1780

REWCASTLE, NEILL BARRY, neuropathology educator; b. Sunderland, Eng., Dec. 12, 1931; arrived in Can., 1955; s. William Alexander and Eva (Coapes) R.; m. Eleanor Elizabeth Barton Boyd, Sept. 27, 1958 (dec. Jan. 1999); 4 children. MB, ChB in Medicine cum laude, U. St. Andrews, Scotland, 1955; MA, FRCPC in gen. pathology, U. Toronto, 1962, FRCPC in neuropathology, 1968. Licentiate Med. Coun., Can. Rotating intern U. Vancouver, 1955-56; resident in pathology Shaughnessy Hosp., Vancouver, 1956-57; prof. head divsn. neuropathology U. Toronto, 1969—81, resident in pathology Canada, 1957-60; fellow Med. Rsch. Coun. Can., 1960-64; demonstrator dept. pathology U. Toronto, Canada, 1964-65, lectr., acting head div. neuropathology Canada, 1965—69, assoc. prof. Canada, 1969-70, head div. neuropathology Canada, 1969-81; prof., head dept. pathology U. Calgary, Alta., Can., 1981-91, prof. Can., 1981-2000, prof. emeritus pathology, lab. medicine, clin. neuroscis. Can., 2000—; sr. pathologist Toronto Gen. Hosp. Dir. dept. histopathology Foothills Hosp., Calgary, 1981-91, pathologist, 1981—, cons. neuropathology, 1981—; spl. acad. adv. to dean faculty medicine U. Calgary, 1995-97. Recipient Queen Elizabeth Silver Jubilee medal, 1977. Fellow: Royal Coll. Physicians (cert.); mem. Can. Assn. Neuropathologists (sec. 1965-69, pres. 1976-79).

REX, LONNIE ROYCE, religious organization administrator; b. Caddo, Okla., May 11, 1928; s. Robert Lavern and Lennie Cordy (Gilcrease) R.; m. Betty Louise Sorrells, Apr. 8, 1949; children: Royce DeWayne, Patricia Louise, Debra Kaye. MusB, Oklahoma City U., 1950; DD (hon.), Am. Bible Inst., 1970; LLD (hon.), Wesley Synod, N.Y.C., 1999, Meth. Wesley Synod, Toledo, 1999; LittD, Wesley Synod, 2000. Advt. mgr. Oral Roberts Evang. Assn., Tulsa, 1955-57; bus. mgr. T.L. Osborn Found., 1957-69; gen. mgr. Christian Crusade, 1969-80; sec.-treas. David Livingstone Missionary Found., 1970-80, pres., 1980—. Dep. dir. gen. Internat. Biog. Assn.; bd. dirs. Intra-Ch. Pension Fund, Bethany, Okla.; spkr. internat. confs. Eng., Hungary, Korea, Singapore, Spain, N.Y.C., Congress of Arts and Comms., Oxford U., 1997; invited Pyongyang, North Korea to meet as an NGO with Peace Com. and med. aid, 1996, 97; participant peace conf. Carter Ctr. between North Korea and South Korea, 1997. Author: Never a Child, 1989. Mem. Internat. PHC Loan Fund; bd. dirs. Armand Hammer United World Coll. of Am. West, 1993—; bd. mem. Internat. Humanitarian Centre Russia, Moscow, 2000. Recipient Merit award Korea, 1975, Moran medal Republic of Korea, Humanitarian award Senator Hugh Scott, 1983, Svc. to Mankind award Internat. Biog. Congress, Spain, 1987, Internat. Lions Club award, UN award, medal Gen. Ground Forces USSR, 1990, World Humanitarian Leadership award by M. Susan Savage Mayor of Tulsa, 1998, Roseland Cook Bronze award David Livingstone Found., 1998; knighted in Moscow, 1993; Lonnie Royce Rex Day named in his honor by Gov. Keating of Okla., Jan. 24, 1998. Mem. Knights of Malta (Sword of Svc. 1996), Phi Beta Kappa. Home: 2437 E 73d Pl Tulsa OK 74136-5520 Office: St Matthews Pub Tulsa OK 74136-1010 *In my work among the starving in Ethiopia, I walked into a tent of over 100 mothers, lying on mats, who had given birth during the last three days. It was silent! Morbid silence! That haunting silence lives with me since that moment. I asked why? I was informed the babies did not have the strength to cry. I have given my life to "cry out" for those in need that did not have the strength to "cry".*

REX, WALTER EDWIN, III, humanities educator; b. Bryn Mawr, Pa., Jan. 31, 1927; s. Walter Edwin Jr. and Barbara (Clayton) R. AB, Harvard U., 1950, AM, 1951, PhD, 1956. Instr. Brown U., Providence, 1956-57, Harvard U., Cambridge, Mass., 1957-60; asst. prof. U. Calif., Berkeley, 1960-65, assoc. prof., 1965-72, prof., 1972-92, prof. emeritus, 1992—. Chair James L. Clifford prize com. U. Calif., Berkeley, 1997-98. Author: Essays on Pierre Bayle and Religious Controversy, 1965, The Attraction of the Contrary, 1987, Diderot's Counterpoints, 1998; collaborator multi-vol. book (7 vols.) Inventory of Diderot's Encyclopédie, 1971-72, 89; mem. editl. bd. Eighteenth-Century Studies, 1979-82, 89-92; asst. editor The French Rev., 1981-86. Grantee Humanities Rsch. Inst., 1966-67, 73-74; Pres.'s fellow U. Calif., 1990-91. Mem. MLA, Am. Soc. 18th Century Studies (Clifford lectr. ann. meeting 2000), Soc. Francaise d'étude du 18 siècle, Arts Club (Berkeley), Kosmos Club (Berkeley). Avocation: chamber music. Home: 287 Alvarado Rd Berkeley CA 94705-1512 E-mail: Tedrex@AOL.com.

REXINE, JOHN EFSTRATIOS, JR. museum registrar, artist; b. Hamilton, N.Y., Oct. 3, 1960; s. John Efstratios and Elaine Lavrakas R. BA, Colgate U., 1983. Chief registrar Everson Mus. Art, Syracuse, N.Y., 1985-92; mus. registrar Rose Art Mus. Brandeis U., Waltham, Mass., 1993-2000; registrar List Visual Arts Ctr. MIT, Cambridge, 2000—. Core fellow Glassell Sch. Art Mus. Fine Arts, Houston, 1992-93. Mem. Am. Assn. Mus. (registrar's com. 1985—), Archaeological Inst. Mem. Greek Orthodox Ch. Avocations: contemporary art, archaeology. Home: 118 Myrtle St Fl 2 Waltham MA 02453-0517 Office: MIT List Visual Arts Ctr Cambridge MA 02139 E-mail: rexine@mit.edu.

REXNER, ROMULUS, publishing executive; b. Odessa, Russia, July 16, 1920; came to U.S., 1951; s. Richard Rexner and Nina Norvid; m. Elisabeth Unger, Aug. 22, 1964. BS in Econs. with hons., Univ. London, 1951. Founder, mgr. Pantheon Press, Gen. Enterprises, L.A., 1951-86, Honolulu, 1986—. Author: (book) Planetary Legion, 1961, 4th edit., 2001; pub.: periodical Cosmopolitan Contact, 1962—. Founder Planetary Legion for Peace, 1955. With Brit. Forces WWII. Achievements include patents in field. Office: Pantheon Press Gen Enterprises Planetary Legion PO Box 89300 Honolulu HI 96830-7300 E-mail: rexner@planetary-legion.pl.

REXROAT, VICKI LYNN, occupational child development educator; b. Oklahoma City, June 12, 1957; d. Troy Bill and Opal Pauline (Flinn) Miller; m. David Edward Rexroat, Sept. 6, 1980; children: Jamie Lynn, Amber Donn, Emily Sue. BS, U. of Sci. and Arts, 1991; MS, U. Ctrl. Okla., 1997. Presch. tchr. Caddo-Kiowa Vocat. Sch., Fort Cobb, Okla., 1981-84, child devel. dir., 1984-89, child devel. instr., 1989—. Rep., advisor Child Devel. Assoc., Washington, 1989—; mem. curriculum team Okla. Dept. of Vocat. Edn., Stillwater, Okla., 1991—; adv. bd. Child Care Careers, Oklahoma City, 1992—. Contbr. articles to profl. jours. Co-chair Reach Out, Inc. Homeless Shelter, Anadarko, Okla., 1995—; founder, vol. Caddo County Welfare Vols., 1989—; friends for life mem. Fort Cobb Sr. Citizens, 1990—; mem. Fort Cobb Booster Club, 1989—. Named Friend of Children Okla. Inst. of Child Advocacy, 1993, New Tchr. of Yr. Okla. Vocat. Assn., 1993. Mem. Friends in the Okla. Early Childhood Assn. (pres. 1989—), So. Early Childhood Assn., Okla. Assn. for the Edn. of Young Children, Nat. Assn. for the Edn. of Young

Children, Am. Vocat. Assn. (dist. v.p. 1989—, New Tchr. of Yr. 1994). Democrat. Bapt. Avocations: basketball games, fishing, boating, student organizations. Office: Caddo-Kiowa Vocat Sch North 7th Fort Cobb OK 73038

REXROTH, NANCY LOUISE, photographer; b. Washington, June 27, 1946; d. John Augustus and Florence Bertha (Young) R. B.F.A., Am. U., 1969; M.F.A. in Photography, Ohio U., Athens, 1971. Asst. prof. photography Antioch Coll., Yellow Springs, Ohio, 1977-79, Wright State U., Dayton, 1979-82; dealer Light Gallery, 1995—. Author: Iowa, 1976, The Platinotype, 1977, 1976. Nat. Endowment Arts grantee, 1973; Ohio Arts Council, 1981. Mem. Am. Massage Therapy Assn. Democrat. Home and Office: 2631 Cleinview Ave Cincinnati OH 45206-1810 E-mail: rexnex@cinci.com.

REY, ALIX CHARLES, psychiatrist; b. Port-Au-Prince, Haiti, Nov. 4, 1940; came to U.S., 1965; s. Stenon and Luce (St. Gerard) Rey; m. Phyllis Ann Harris, Oct. 24, 1969; children: David Alix, Marc Christopher. Baccalaureate, St Louis De Gonzague, Port-Au-Prince, 1960; physician and surgeon, Facultad De Medicina, Mex. City, 1968. Resident in psychiatry Med. Coll. Ohio, 1973-75; clin. rsch. assoc. NIMH, Bethesda, Md., 1975-78; sr. rsch. assoc. Hispano Health Ctr. Md. Psychiat. Rsch. Ctr., 1976-78; asst. prof. psychiatry Psychiat. Rsch. Ctr., 1978-81; clin. dir. psychiat. svc. Howard County Gen. Hosp., 1979-85, chmn. dept. psychiatry, 1985-91, 99-01, pres. med. staff, 1989—, chmn. dept. psychiatry, 1999-2001; med. dir. Pressley Ridge Sch., Md., 2000—. Med. dir. Howard Emergency Psychiat. Svc., 1991—. Lt. comdr. USPHS, 1975-81. Fellow Am. Psychiat. Assn.; mem. AMA, Med. and Chirurgical Facility Md., Md. Psychiat. Soc., Soc. Biol. Psychiatry, Black Psychiatrists Am. Roman Catholic. Avocations: swimming, fishing. Office: 10808 Hickory Ridge Rd Columbia MD 21044-3622 E-mail: alixcrey@hotmail.com., reville@aol.com.

REY, MARK E. federal agency administrator; b. Canton, Ohio; BS in Wildlife Mgmt., BS in Forestry, MS in Natural Resources Policy and Adminstrn., U. Mich. Staff asst. bur. land mgmt. U.S. Dept. of Interior's, 1974—75; various positions Am. Paper Inst./Nat. Forest Products Assn. , 1976—84; v.p. pub. forestry programs Nat. Forest Products Assn., 1984—89; exec. dir. Am. Forest Resource Alliance, 1989—92; v.p. forest resources Am. Forest and Paper Assn., 1992—94; staff mem. U.S. Senate Com. on Energy and Natural Resources, 1995—2001; under sec. for natural resources and environ. USDA, Washington, 2001—. Office: USDA Natural Resources and Environ 1400 Independence Ave SW Washington DC 20250 Office Fax: 202-720-4732.

REYBURN, JERRY HERBERT, diplomat, educator; b. Kokomo, Ind. s. Ben Earl and Regina Ruth Reyburn; m. Helene Elaine Baker, Aug. 15, 1958; children: Thomas Allen, Bret Andrew. BS, Purdue U., West Lafayette, Ind., 1957; MS, Purdue U., 1964, PhD, 1974. Staff mem. U.S. Forest Svc. USDA, Gifford Pinchot, Wash., 1954—58; forester watershed Ind. Dept. Conservation, Indpls., 1961—64; agt. Ind.-Purdue Extension, West Lafayette, 1964—66; asst. prof. Pa. State U., 1966—76, assoc. prof., 1976—83; prof., 1983—91; agt. Pa. Extension Svc. Pa. State U., University Park, 1966—91; U.S rep. and tech. diplomat UN Food & Agrl. Orgn., Rome, Ibadin, Nigeria, Kingston, Jamaica, 1991—93; prof. emeritus Pa. State U., 1991—. Appt. U.S. Rep. Coun. of Europe, Strasbourg, 1980—84. Author: (book) Careers in Agriculture , 1984, Hoosier Forester , 1990. Capt. USAF, 1958—61. Recipient Swedish Nat. 4H medal, Swedish Govt., 1986; scholar Fulbright scholarship, U.S. Govt. to nat. Swedish 4-H, Katrine, Stockholm, Sweden, 1986. Mem.: Pa. Extension Agts. Assn. (life), Nat. 4H Extension Agents Assn. (life). Republican. Unitarian Universalist. Avocations: cartooning, golf, travel, writing. Office: Coll Agrl Scis 301 Agr Adminstrn Bldg University Park PA 16802

REYES, ANN MARIE, contractor; b. St. Paul, Aug. 20, 1960; d. Franklin William and Alice Ann Holloway; m. Victor Manuel Reyes, Aug. 9, 1980 (div. Nov. 2000); children: Dawn, Victor, Christopher, Vincent. Independent cons. contractor, Clermont, Fla., 1999—; sec. Exceptional , Orlando, 2000—. Poet:. Cubmaster Cub Scouts, Fla., 1997—98. With USMC, 1979—81. Recipient Editor's Choice award, Internat. Libr. Poetry, 2001. Mem.: Sewcialables. Avocations: writing, crochet, target shooting, exercising at the gym. Office: 10301 US Hwy 27 Unit 92 Clermont FL 34711-8978

REYES, ANNA MARIA, broadcast executive; b. Phoenix, Aug. 21, 1957; d. Perfecto C. and Esperanza (Del Castillo) R. BA in Fin., Ariz. State U., 1983. Radio-Tel. operators permit FCC; notary public, Ariz. Traffic/continuity dir. First Media Corp./KOPA AM and FM, Scottsdale, Ariz., 1978-81, music dir., air talent, 1981-83; bus. mgr., asst. sta. mgr. Cook Inlet Radio Ptnr. KSLX-FM and KOPA-AM, 1983-92; sta. contr., asst. gen. mgr. Jacor/Citicasters KSLX AM/FM, Phoenix, 1992-96; gen. mgr. Jacor Comm. KSLX AM/FM, 1997—. Interviewer KSLX FM/KOPA AM, Scottsdale, 1990. Co-author: INXS Newsletter, 1994. Spokeswoman campaign against radio for men format KSLX FM/KOPA AM, Scottsdale, 1988. Recipient Cert. for Announcing, City of Phoenix-Hello Phoenix, 1985, Bus. Mgr. award Corp. Chain Contest, Phoenix, 1990-92. Mem. AAUW, Am. Women in Radio and TV, Broadcast Cable Fin. Mgmt., Univ. Women London. Democrat. Roman Catholic. Avocations: European travel, ballet, reading, music. Home: 12340 W Elwood St Avondale AZ 85323-9618 Office: KSLX Radio FM/AM 4343 E Camelback Rd Ste 200 Phoenix AZ 85018-8306

REYES, EDWARD, pharmacology educator; b. Albuquerque, May 5, 1944; s. Salvador and Faustina (Gabaldon) R.; m. Shirley Ann Trott, Aug. 15, 1970; children: David Joshua, Elizabeth Ann, Steven Mark. BS in Pharmacy, U. N.Mex., 1968; MS in Pharmacology, U. Colo., 1970, PhD in Pharmacology, 1974. Asst. prof. pharmacy U. Wyo. Sch. of Pharmacy, Laramie, 1974-75; asst. prof. pharmacology Dept. Pharmacology, U. N.Mex., Albuquerque, 1976-85, assoc. prof. pharmacology, 1985-97, assoc. prof. biochemistry and molecular biology, assoc. prof. pharmacy, 1997-2000; dir. minority biomed. rsch. support program U. N.Mex. Sch. of Medicine, 1994-97, co-coord. MBRS program, 1998—; prof. emeritus U. N.Mex., 2000—. Referee Pharmacology Biochemistry Behavior, San Antonio, 1986—; adv. com. mem. NIMH Minority Neuro Sci. Fellowship, Washington, 1991—; cons. alcohol pharmacokinetics and breath alcohol testing. Author: (with others) Alcohol and Drug Abuse Review, 1991; contbr. articles to profl. jours. Scoutmaster Boy Scouts Am., Albuquerque, 1986-94, dist. camping com. chair, 1994—, Silver Beaver, 1996; vis. scientist N.Mex. Acad. Sci., Las Vegas, 1988—; youth preacher Rio Grande Bapt. Ch., Albuquerque, 1980—. Grantee Nat. Inst. of Alcohol Abuse and Alcoholism, NSF. Mem. Rsch. Soc. on Alcoholism, Western Pharmacology Soc., Soc. for Neurosci. (chair minority edn. tng. and profl. adv. 1987-94), Soc. for Advancement of Chicanos and Native Ams. in Sci., UNM/MBRS (co-dir. program). Achievements include rsch. that the in utero adminstration of alcohol produces an increase in liver and brain Y-glutamyl transpeptidase activity; isolated-GTP from brain of rats, in utero adminstration of alcohol lowers GSH in liver and brain.

REYES, FRANCISCO I. reproductive endocrinologist, researcher; b. Mexico City, Jan. 5, 1935; came to U.S., 1980; s. Francisco T. Reyes-Boccaccio and Maria Rodriguez de Reyes; m. Urte Erm, Dec. 21, 1971 (div. 1989); children: Urte, Andrea, Carmen; m. Mary A. Bray, Mar. 21, 1991. B in Biol. Sci., A. von Humboldt Coll., Mexico City, 1952; MD, Univ. Nacional de Mexico, Mexico City, 1959. Diplomate Am. Bd. Obstetrics and Gynecology, sub-bd. Reproductive Endocrinology. Intern Cambridge (Mass.) City Hosp., 1961-62; resident U. Manitoba, Winnipeg, Manitoba, Can., 1967-71; fellow rep. endocrinology Columbia U., N.Y., 1971-72; asst. prof. U. Man., Winnipeg, Can., 1972-78, head div. reproductive endocrinology Can., 1972-80, assoc. prof. Can., 1978-80; prof., dir. reproductive endocrinology SUNY, Bklyn., 1980-91; dir. Fertility and Hormone Ctr. of N.Y., 1991—. Hosp. staffs: Univ. Manitoba Health Svc. Ctr., Winnipeg, 1972-80, Suny Health Svcs. Ctr., 1980-91, Long Island Coll. Hosp., (vol.), 1991—; vis. scientist Primate Rsch. Ctr., N.Mex. State U., Holloman AFB, 1980—. Contbr. articles to profl. jours. Deutscher Akad. Austausthdienst fellow Govt. of Germany, 1959-61; R.S. McLaughlin Found. traveling fellow, Can., 1971-72. Fellow Royal Coll. Physicians and Surgeons Can.; mem. Soc. Can. Investigators in Reprodn. (caucus 1976-78), Am. Fertility Soc., Endocrine Soc., Am. Coll. Obstetricians and Gynecologists, Soc. Gynecologic Investigation, Soc. Reproductive Endocrinologists (founding). Avocations: literature, music, tennis. Office: Fertility/Hormone Ctr NY 161 Atlantic Ave Brooklyn NY 11201-6720

REYES, MARCIA STYGLES, medical technologist; b. Winchester, Mass., July 15, 1950; d. Bernard Francis and Eleanore Cecilia (Nicgorska) Stygles; m. Carlos Reyes, Aug. 5, 1978. BS in Med. Tech., Merrimack Coll., North Andover, Mass., 1972; MS in Health Scis., SUNY, Buffalo, 1977. Sr. med. technologist Symmes Hosp., Arlington, Mass., 1970-73; sr. microbiologist and serologist Mt. Auburn Hosp., Cambridge, 1973-75; asst. prof., clin. coord. Quinnipiac Coll., Hamden, Conn., 1976-81; lab. supr. Canberra Clin. Labs., Meriden, 1981-86, Hill Health Ctr., New Haven, 1984—, clin. lab. mgr., dir., 1995—. Cons. in med. tech. mgmt., allied health edn.; cons. F.Q.H.C. Lab. Devel./Implementation. Mem. adv. bd. to bd. dirs. Sawyer Schs.; mem. adv. bd. New Haven Adult Edn. Programs. Mem. Am. Soc. Clin. Pathologists, Am. Soc. Med. Tech., Conn. Soc. Med. Tech. (Spkr. awards, bd. dirs. 1996—), Am. Soc. Microbiology, Am. Soc. Allied Health Profls. Home: 199 Dover St New Haven CT 06513-4818 E-mail: mreyes@hillhealthcenter.net.

REYES, RAUL GREGORIO, surgeon; b. Tegucigalpa, Morazan, Honduras, June 18, 1928; came to U.S., 1939; s. Julio Gregorio and Mercedes Ofelia (Mazzoni) Reyes-Zelaya; m. Mildred Dane Smith, 1951 (dec. May 1990); children: Tyra, Kimberly; stepchildren: Javier, Christian; m. Blanca Lidia Milla, Apr. 2, 1993. BS, Georgetown U., 1945; MD, George Washington U., 1950. Diplomate Nat. Bd. Med. Examiners, Am. Bd. Surgery. Intern Charity Hosp., New Orleans, 1950-51; resident Emergency Hosp./George Washington U., Washington, 1951, Charity Hosp., New Orleans, 1952-55; chief thoracic surgery San Felipe Hosp., Tegucigalpa, 1955-56; assoc. to ptnr. Browne-McHardy Clinic, New Orleans, 1955-60, 60-73; med. dir. New Orleans Indsl. Clinic, 1956-58; chief of surgery and orthopedics Lallie Kemp Regional Hosp., Independence, La., 1987-89, med. dirs., 1988-89; owner, pres. Raul G. Reyes, A Med. Corp., New Orleans, 1973—. Owner, pres. Internat. Maritime Med. Svcs., New Orleans, 1978—, Catracho Enterprises, New Orleans, 1975—, Phys. Therapy Svcs. of New Orleans, 1975—; faculty La. State Univ. Sch. Medicine, 1953—, others. Inventor in field; contbr. articles to profl. jours. Chmn. Rep. Hispanic Assembly, New Orleans, 1983; pre-cand. Nat. Party, Honduras, 1985; founder Literacy Ctrs. of Honduras, 1991; presdl. candidate Christian Dem. Party of Honduras, 1994. Named to Hon. Consul of Honduras, Hon. Citizen, City of New Orleans. Mem. ACS, AMA, So. Med. Assn., La. State Med. Soc., Orleans Parish Med. Soc., Colegio Medico de Honduras. Roman Catholic. Avocations: tennis, reading, writing, social progs. Office: PO Box 15379 New Orleans LA 70175-5379

REYES, REYNERIS, dancer; Student, Escuela Vocacional de Arte Raúl Sánchez, Pinar del Rio, Cuban Nat. Ballet Sch. Mem. Cuban Nat. Ballet, 1993—99; soloist Royal Winnipeg Ballet, 1999—. Dancer toured U.S., Spain, France, Switzerland and Columbia, 1998—99. Dancer (ballets) Swan Lake, Cuban Nat. Ballet, Cinderella, Giselle, Don Quixote, Coppélia, La Fille Mal Gardée, Les Sylphides, Romeo and Juliet, Royal Winnipeg Ballet, Cherry Pink and Apple Blossom White, Dracula, Butterfly, Giselle. Office: Royal Winnipeg Ballet 380 Graham Ave Winnipeg MB Canada R3C 4K2*

REYES, SILVESTRE, congressman; b. Canutillo, Texas, Nov. 10, 1944; m. Carolina Gaytan; children: Monica, Rebecca, Silvestre Jr. AA, El Paso C. C., 1977; student, U. Tex. Mem. 105th-106th Congress from 16th Tex. Dist., 1997—; asst. regional commr. U.S. Immigration and Naturalization Svc., chief, 1984-95, mem. nat. security and vet. affairs coms.*

REYHNER, JON ALLAN, education educator; b. Fountain Hill, Pa., Apr. 29, 1944; s. Theodore O. and Alice Elizabeth (Cornish) R.; m. Helen Marie Bennett, July 15, 1972; children: Deborah Dawn, Tsosie Dean. BA, U. Calif., Davis, 1966, MA, 1977; MEd, No. Ariz. U., 1973, EdS, 1977; EdD, Mont. State U., 1984. Asst. prin. Navajo (N.Mex.) Pub. Sch., 1975-77; prin. Wallace Sch., Parker, Ariz., 1977-78, Rocky Boy (Mont.) Sch., 1978-80, Heart Butte (Mont.) Sch., 1982-84; chief adminstr. Havasupai Sch., Supai, Ariz., 1984-85; assoc. prof. Mont. State U., Billings, 1986-95; prof. No. Ariz. U., Flagstaff, 1995—. Coord. Indian tchr. tng. program Ea. Mont. Coll., Billings, 1986. Editor: Teaching American Indian Students, 1992, Teaching Indigenous Languages, 1997, Partnership in Education, 1997; co-author: A History of Indian Education, 1989; co-editor: Revitalizing Indigenous Languages, 1999, Learn in Beauty: Indiginous Education for a New Century, 2000, Indigenous Languages Across the Community, 2002. Mem. Am. Ednl. Rsch. Assn., Phi Alpha Theta, Phi Delta Kappa. Home: 1719 W Sunshine Dr Flagstaff AZ 86001-9025 Office: No Ariz U PO Box 5774 Flagstaff AZ 86011-5774

REYMAN, JONATHAN ERIC, archaeologist, anthropologist, researcher; b. Greenwich, Conn., July 31, 1943; s. Solon Aaron and Ethel Jeanette (Pearlman) R.; 1 child, Mika Ranjit Mini. BA, Ind. U., 1965; PhD, So. Ill. U., 1971. Instr. anthropology So. Ill. U., Carbondale, 1969-70, postdoctoral rsch. assoc., 1971-72; asst. prof. anthropology Ill. State U., Normal, 1972-77, assoc. prof., 1977-82, prof., 1982-91; rsch. assoc. in anthropology Ill. State Mus., Springfield, 1993—. Rsch. collaborator Nat. Park Svc., Mesa Verde Nat. Park, Colo., 1975-76; founder, operator Feather Distbn. Project, Springfield, 1982—; vis. prof. anthropology U. Ill., Urbna, 1994, 95; mem. peer rev. panel tchg. with tech. NEH, Washington, 1996. Editor: Rediscovering Our Past: Essays on the History of American Archaeology, 1992, The Gran Chichimeca: Essays on the Archaeology and Ethnohistory of Northern Mesoamerica, 1995; contbr. over 140 articles and revs. to profl. jours., also chpts. to books. NDEA Title IV grad. fellow So. Ill. U., 1966-69; sr. rsch. grantee NSF, 1973-78, 87-88, rsch. grantee Wenner-Gren Found. for Anthrop. Rsch., 1980. Fellow Am. Anthrop. Assn., Soc. Profl. Archeologists (tchg. cert. panel 1989-93, chmn. com. on pub. land use, 1978-79), Soc. for Applied Anthropology (co-chmn. Am. Indian issues com. 1997-2000), Coun. for Mus. Anthropology, Soc. for Am. Archaeology (history of archaeology com. 1987-89), Sigma Xi, Phi Kappa Phi. Avocations: travel, cooking, reading, music, tennis. Home: 2424 Milford Rd Springfield IL 62704-2117 Office: Ill State Mus Rsch and Collections Ctr 1011 E Ash St Springfield IL 62703-3535 E-mail: reyman@museum.state.il.us.

REYMOND, PATRICIA ANN, social worker; b. Meadville, Pa., Feb. 13, 1935; d. James Thomas and Margaret Alice (Ewing) Bulger; m. Ralph Daniel Reymond, Feb. 4, 1961; 1 child, Eric Daniel. BA, Villa Maria Coll., 1957; MSW, Cath. U., 1960. Caseworker House of Good Shepherd, Balt., 1960-61; sch. social worker Balt. Pub. Schs., 1961-69; social worker Travelers Aid Soc., Balt., summers 1962-69; part-time med. social worker St. Francis Hosp. and Med. Ctr., Topeka, 1988-99. Vol. Shawnee County Med. Soc. Aux., Topeka, 1972—, Am. Cancer Soc., Topeka, 1978—81, Stormont-Vail Hosp. Aux., Topeka, 1975—80, Capper Found., Topeka, 1989—91, St. Francis Hosp. and Med. Ctr. Aux., Topeka, 1984—, Meals on Wheels, 1993—; mem. adv. coun. Kans. Children's Svc. League, Topeka, 1989—92. Avocations: travel, reading, tennis. Home: 2816 SW Macvicar Ave Topeka KS 66611-1705

REYNA, BENIGNO G. federal agency administrator; BS in Criminal Justice, U. Tex., Brownsville; grad., FBI Nat. Acad. Joined Brownsville (Tex.) Police Dept., 1976, various positions including comdr. profl. stds. and emergency mgmt. coord., chief of police; mem. Tex. Commn. on Law Enforcement Officer Stds. and Edn., 1997—2000, presiding officer, 2000—01; dir. U.S. Marshals Svc. U.S. Dept. Justice, Arlington, Va., 2001—. Instr. criminal justice U. Tex., Brownsville; regional law enforcement tech. expert Counter Drug Tech. Assessment Ctr., 1998—2001; law enforcement advisor to law enforcement coordinating com. U.S. Attys. Office, So. Dist. Tex. Recipient Disting. Alumnus award, Tex. Southmost Coll., 2002. Mem.: Internat. Assn. Chiefs Police. Office: US Dept Justice-US Marshals Svc Ste 1200 CS3 600 Army Navy Dr Arlington VA 22202-4210*

REYNALDS, JEREMY GRAHAM, rescue mission administrator; b. Bath, Eng., Oct. 19, 1957; came to U.S., 1978; s. Graham John and Ruth (Bowden) R.; m. Sylvia Ellen Page, Apr. 14, 1979; children: Ben, Joshua, Jeremiah, Joel, Josiah. B Univ. Studies, U. N.Mex., 1996, postgrad., 1996—. Founder, exec. dir. His Place, Santa Fe, 1982-86, Joy Junction, Albuquerque, 1986—. Author: Homeless in America, 1994, The Walking Wounded, 1996. Recipient Jefferson award Am. Inst. for Pub. Svc., 1994. Mem. Internat. Union Gospel Missions. Mem. Calvary Chapel. Avocations: his children, reading. Office: Joy Junction PO Box 27693 4500 2d St SW Albuquerque NM 87125

REYNARD, MURIEL JOYCE, lawyer; b. Miami Beach, Fla., May 20, 1945; d. Hyman and Faye (Feinstein) Friedkin; m. Brian Patrick Delaney, Nov. 27, 1983; children: Kelly, Charlotte. BA, SUNY, Stony Brook, 1967, MS, 1973; JD cum laude, Yeshiva U., 1983. Bar: N.Y. 1984, U.S. Dist. Ct. (so. and ea. dists.) N.Y. 1984. Health planner Nassau-Suffolk RMP/CHP, Centereach, N.Y., 1972-74; adminstr. N.Y.C. Health and Hosps. Corp., 1974-75; health planner AFSCME Dist. Coun. 37, N.Y.C., 1975-76; adminstr. Inst. Emergency Medicine Albert Einstein Coll. Medicine, 1977-80; asst. atty. U.S. Atty.'s Office (so. dist.) N.Y., summer 1982; assoc. Skadden, Arps, Slate, Meagher & Flom, 1983-85, Paskus, Gordon & Mandel, N.Y.C., 1985-86; v.p., sr. assoc. counsel The Chase Manhattan Bank, N.A., 1986-96; v.p. assoc. gen. counsel Citicorp Credit Svcs. Inc., 1997—. Notes and comments editor Cardozo Law Rev.; contbr. numerous articles to law jours. Mem. ABA, N.Y.C. Bar Assn., N.Y. State Bar Assn. Office: Citicorp Credit Services Inc One Court Square New York NY 11120

REYNIK, ROBERT JOHN, materials scientist, research and education administrator; b. Bayonne, N.J., Dec. 25, 1932; s. Mary Reynik; m. Georgiana M. Walker, Apr. 12, 1959; children: Michael, Christopher, Jonathan, Katherine, Steven, Kevin. BS in Math. and Physics, U. Detroit, 1956; MSEE, U. Cin., 1960, PhD in Phys. Chemistry, 1963. Cert. substitute tchr. K-12, math, sci. N.J., 2000. Rsch. assoc. Sch. Metall. Engring. U. Pa., Phila., 1963-64, asst. prof., 1964-67; assoc. prof. Drexel U., 1967-70; assoc. dir. engring. materials program NSF, Washington, 1970-71, dir. engring. materials program, 1971-74, dir. metallurgy program, 1974-82, head metallurgy, polymers, ceramics and electronic materials, 1983-90, head office spl. programs in materials, 1990-94, sr. staff scientist divsn. materials rsch. Arlington, Va., 1994-96; exec. sec. and cognizant program dir. US-USSR Internat. Agreement in Sci. and Tech., Washington, 1974-79; NSF liaison rep. Nat. Materials Adv. Bd., 1985-94; math. and phys. sci. directorate coord. Integration of Rsch. and Edn., 1996-97; sr. scientist Office of Sci. and Tech. Infrastructure, 1997-98, sr. staff scientist divsn. materials rsch., 1998-99; cons. in field, 1999—; grantsmanship cons. and 6-state planning advisor, 1999—. Dir. electrometallurgy and materials, corrosion, program US-USSR internat. agreement sci. and tech., 1974-80; mem. First U.S. Metall. Del. People's Republic China, 1978; vis. prof. materials sci. and engring. U. Pa., 1982-83; tech. coord. Sci. & Tech. Ctrs. in Materials Sci. & Engring., 1990-94; co-chair Fed. Coord. Coun. for Sci., Engring. and Tech. joint com. edn. and tng. Office of Sci. and Tech. Policy, 1992-93; co-chair task group edn. and tng. Aeronautics Materials and mfg. Techs. Working Groups Nat. Sci. and Tech. coun., Office of Vice Pres. of U.S., 1994; tech. mgr. rsch. grants mfg. devel. and mfg. Tech. Reinvestment Project, Fed. Govt., 1994-96. Fellow Am. Soc. Materials Internat. (mem.-at-large materials sci. coun. 1990-96, mem.-at-large materials sci. tech. sector coun. 1996—, mem. fed. affairs com. 1996—, mem. golf medal selection com.); mem. AAAS, AIME (chairperson govt. pub. affairs com. 1994-96), Am. Chem. Soc., Am. Phys. Soc., Am. Assn. Engring. Socs. (mem. honors and awards com.), The Metals, Minerals and Materials Soc. (mem. and chmn. many tech. coms.), Materials Rsch. Soc., Sr. Exec. Assn., Sigma Xi (past chpt. pres., exec. counselor), Tau Beta Pi. Fax: 856-428-2186. E-mail: r.reynik@worldnet.att.net.

REYNOLDS, ALBERT BARNETT, nuclear engineer, educator; b. Lebanon, Tenn., Feb. 1, 1931; s. George Lazenby and Marion (Barnett) R.; m. Helen Buck, Sept. 6, 1954; children— Albert Jr., Charlotte, Marion Student, U. of South, 1948-51; S.B. in Physics, MIT, 1953, S.M. in Nuclear Engring., 1955, Sc.D. in Chem. Engring., 1959. Physicist-mgr. Gen. Electric Co., San Jose, Calif., 1959-68; prof. nuclear engring. U. Va., Charlottesville, 1968-96, chmn. dept. nuclear engring. and engring. physics, 1991-92, prof. emeritus, 1996—. Cons. NRC, Washington, 1970-84, U.S. Dept. Energy, 1987-89; fields of rsch. include liquid metal reactor safety, electric cable aging. Author: Bluebells and Nuclear Energy, 1996; co-author: Fast Breeder Reactors, 1981; contbr. numerous articles to profl. jours. Fellow Am. Nuclear Soc. (exec. com. div. nuclear reactor safety 1980-83, chair Va. sect. 1986-87); mem. ASME, IEEE, Am. Soc. Engring. Edn. Sigma Xi, Tau Beta Pi Home: 1502 Holly Rd Charlottesville VA 22901-3132 E-mail: hareyn@aol.com.

REYNOLDS, BENEDICT MICHAEL, surgeon; b. N.Y.C., Sept. 12, 1925; s. Benedict and Delia (Coan) R.; m. Alice Marie Hodnett, May 3, 1952; children: Benedict, John, Ann Marie, Mary Alice, Daniel. Student, Columbia U., 1942-43, U. Rochester, 1943-44; MD, NYU, 1948. Diplomate: Am. Bd. Surgery, Pan Am. Med. Assn. Intern Bellevue Med. Center, N.Y.C., 1948-49, surg. resident, 1951-55; asst. in surgery N.Y. U., N.Y.C., 1953-55; instr. surgery Albert Einstein Coll. Medicine, Bronx, N.Y., 1955-56, asst. prof. surgery, 1956-58, clin. asst. prof., 1958-71, vis. prof. surgery, 1977; prof. surgery N.Y. Med. Coll., N.Y.C., 1971—; practice medicine specializing in surgery Bronx, 1955—; dir. surgery Misericordia Hosp. Med. Center, 1962-83, Fordham Hosp., 1964-76; chmn. dept. surgery Lincoln Hosp., Bronx, 1976-82. Attending surgeon Met. Hosp., N.Y.C., 1972—; cons. Community Gen. Hosp. of Sullivan County, 1972—; dir. dept. surgery N.Y. Westchester Square Med. Ctr., Bronx, 1994—. Contbr. articles in field to med. jours. Served with USN, 1943-45, 49-51. Fellow N.Y. Acad. Medicine, A.C.S.; mem. AMA, N.Y. State Med. Soc., N.Y. Acad. Sci., Soc. Surgery Alimentary Tract, N.Y. and Bklyn. Regional Chpt. on Trauma, Internat. Soc. Lymphology, N.Y. Surg. Soc., Am. Gastroent. Assn. Roman Catholic. Home: 55 Roundtop Rd Yonkers NY 10710-2327 Office: 1578 Williamsbridge Rd Bronx NY 10461-6265

REYNOLDS, BETTY ANN, elementary education educator; b. Plattsburgh, N.Y., Nov. 16, 1942; d. Morton Jay and Thelma Gladys (Baxter) R. BS in Edn., SUNY, Plattsburgh, 1964; MS in Edn., SUNY, Potsdam, 1973. Tchr. 1st grade Ogdensburg (N.Y.) Ctrl. Schs., 1964-65, Massena (N.Y.) Ctrl Schs., 1965-68, 69—; tchr. 2d grade Ft. Richardson (Alaska) On-Base Sch., 1968-69, Ctrl. Schs., Massena, 1969-98—. Mem. N.Y. State Reading Assn. Avocations: reading, cross-county skiing, walking, travel, crafts.

REYNOLDS, BETTY JANE, retired nursing administrator and educator; b. Terre Haute, Ind., Dec. 19, 1926; d. George H. and Mary I. (Lambeth) Defel; m. Alex J. Reynolds (dec.); children: Cindy Carley, Elaine Platt. AAS, Mohawk Valley C.C., Utica, N.Y., 1971; BSN, Syracuse U., 1975; MSN, U. Cin., 1977; EdD, U. Rochester, 1984. RN, N.Y., Ohio, N.C. Instr. Syracuse U., 1977-79; asst. prof. SUNY, Utica, 1979-85; assoc. prof. East Carolina U., Greenville, N.C., 1985-90, U. N.C., Wilmington, 1990-92, assoc. dean, 1992-95; ret., 1995. Surveyor N.C. Commn. on Accreditation of Home Care, Raleigh, 1986-94; cons. for nursing Reynolds Consultation, Stokes, N.C., 1985-98. Author chpt. and articles in field. U. Cin. scholar, 1975-77, U. Rochester fellow, 1982-84. Mem. Nat. League for Nursing, Sigma Theta Tau, Kappa Delta Pi. Avocations: gourmet cooking, quilting, walking, swimming, stained glass. Home: 4454 Oakley Rd Stokes NC 27884-9754

REYNOLDS, BILLIE ILES, financial representative and counselor, former national association executive director; b. Oakland, Calif., Mar. 26, 1929; d. Walter F. and Frances Olive (Blakesley) Iles; m. William V. Reynolds, June 23, 1950; children: Gilbert, Wendy Lee Bryant, Cynthia Lea Waple, Christy Dirren. Registered fin. rep., fin. counselor, pension and retirement specialist, investment advisor. Ptnr. Reynolds Advt. Agy., 1963-70; asst. exec. dir. Nat. Sch. Transp. Assn., Springfield, Va., 1964-76, exec. dir., 1976-83, Ariz. Landscape Contractors Assn., 1984-86. Registered life and health ins. agt. Freelance writer scripts for radio, TV, newspapers, nat. mags., 1953-70; author: Planning is the Key: Basics of Financial Understanding for Beginners, 1984. Methodist. E-mail: azreynolds@juno.com. *Freedom must also be balanced with responsibility...and truth.*

REYNOLDS, CALVIN, management consultant, business educator; b. N.Y.C., Oct. 2, 1928; s. Charles Edward and Edna (Klockgeter) R.; m. Mary Virginia Gregg, May 4, 1985; children from a previous marriage: Dwight, Neal J. BS in Bus., Columbia U., 1952, MS in Bus., 1959. Dir. ops. Europe Uniroyal Internat., Geneva, 1956-67; v.p. Nat. Fgn. Trade Coun., N.Y.C., 1967-74; sr. v.p. Orgn. Resources Counselors, 1975-92, sr. counselor Ossining, N.Y., 1993—; pres. Calvin Reynolds and Assocs., NY, 1993—2001; ret., 2001. Author: Guide to Global Compensation and Benefits, 2001; contbr. articles to profl. jours. Wharton Sch. U. Pa. sr. fellow, 1993-94. Republican. Congregationalist. Avocations: golf, music, reading. Home and Office: Calvin Reynolds & Assocs 52 Underhill Rd Ossining NY 10562-5118 E-mail: reynolds@bestweb.net.

REYNOLDS, CHARLES PATRICK, pediatric oncologist, researcher; b. El Paso, Tex., Aug. 8, 1952; s. Charles Albert and Lallah Elizabeth (Munro) R.; m. Debra Dawn Adams, Feb. 3, 1979; children: Amy Elizabeth, Jennifer Ann. BA in Biology, U. Tex., 1974; MD, U. Tex. Southwestern Med. Sch., Dallas, 1979; PhD, U. Tex., 1979. Lic. Tex., Calif., Ga. Postdoctoral fellow U. Tex.

Southwestern Med. Sch., Dallas, 1979-80; pediatric intern Nat. Naval Med. Ctr., Bethesda, Md., 1980-81; battalion surg. Third Marine Div., Okinawa, Japan, 1981-82; rsch. med. officer Naval Med. Rsch. Inst., Bethesda, 1982-87; asst. prof. UCLA, 1987-89; assoc. prof. U. So. Calif., L.A., 1989-2000, prof., 2000—; head devel. therapeutics sect. divsn. hematology-oncology Children's Hosp. L.A., 1993—; co-dir. develpmental therapeutics program U. So. Calif. Norris Comprehensive Cancer Ctr., 2000—. Dir. Neuroblastoma Marrow Purging Lab. Childrens Cancer Group, L.A., 1988-99; team physician U.S. Shooting Team, 1991—; dir. neuroblastoma purging lab. Children's Oncology Group, L.A., 2000—. Patentee in field; contbr. articles to profl. jours. Mem. 1992 USA Olympic Shooting Team, Barcelona, Spain. Grantee Nat. Cancer Inst. Mem. Am. Soc. Clin. Oncology, Am. Assn. Cancer Rsch., Soc. Analytical Cytology, AAAS, Children's Oncology Group, Internat. Soc. for Pediat. Oncology. Roman Catholic. Avocations: filmmaking, guitar playing. Office: Childrens Hosp LA Divsn Hematology Oncology PO Box 54700 Los Angeles CA 90054-0700

REYNOLDS, CYNTHIA FURLONG, writer, researcher; b. Portland, Maine, Feb. 1953; d. Charles Robert and Elizabeth Leighton Furlong; m. Mark Anthony Reynolds, Sept. 2, 1978; children: Charles L., Benjemin K., Elizabeth H. BA, Coll. William & Mary, Williamsburg, VA, 1975. Journalist Hunterdon County Dem., Flemington, NJ, 1976—80; assoc. dir. comm. & publications Princeton U., Princeton, 1980—82. Dir. comm. & publications U. Tampa, Tampa, Fla., 1982—84; journalist St. Petersburg Times, Saint Petersburg, Fla., 1984—86, Saint Petersburg, 1992—95. Author: (book) Our Hometown America's History as seen through the eyes of a Midwestern Village., (children's book) H is for Hoosier, L is for Lobster, S is for Star., M is for Maple Syrup. Vice chmn. Planning Bd., Flemington, NJ, 1980—82; bd. mem. St. Louis County Heritage & Arts Ctr., Duluth, Minn., 1996—98. Recipient Case Award, Princeton U., 1980, 1981, Best Writing, U. Network Pub., 1982, Addy, Tampe, Fla., Advt. Coun.: U. Tampa Publications, 1984. Mem.: Soc. of Children's Book Writers & Illustrators, Washtenaw County Hist. Soc., Associations Pesonal Historians. Presbyterian. Avocations: travel, cross-country skiing, needlework, needlework. Home: 4216 Corey Circle Ann Arbor MI 48103

REYNOLDS, DAVID G(EORGE), retired physiologist, educator; b. South Chicago Heights, Ill., Nov. 25, 1933; s. Gilbert J. and Louise C. (Roescheisen) R.; m. Carol J. Adams, Nov. 8, 1958 (div. 1981); children: Stephen D., Douglas S.; m. Julia M. Davis, Aug. 26, 1987. BA, Knox Coll., 1955; MS, U. Ill., 1957; PhD, U. Iowa, 1963. Commd. 2d lt. M.C., U.S. Army, 1957, advanced through grades to lt. col., 1971; chief basic scis. Med. Field Sci. Sch., Fort Sam Houston, Tex., 1957-60, 1963-65; chief gastroenterology Walter Reed Army Inst. Research, Washington, 1965-72, dir. surgery, 1972-77; ret., 1977; prof. surgery, dir. surg. research U. Iowa Hosp., Iowa City, 1977-87, U. South Fla., Tampa, 1987-90; prof. surgery, dir. exptl. surgery, dir. divsn. surg. scis. U. Minn., Mpls., 1991-97; ret., 1997. Mem. rev. bd. U. Iowa Med. Ctr. Inst., 1999—. Co-editor: Advances in Shock Research, 1983; others; contbr. numerous articles, chpts., abstracts to profl. publs. Active youth athletics, Iowa City Mem. AAAS, Am. Physiol. Soc., Assn. Acad. Surgery, Shock Soc. (pres. 1986-87), Soc. Exptl. Biology and Medicine. Home: 55 Rita Lyn Ct Iowa City IA 52245-3504 E-mail: jmdanddgr@aol.com.

REYNOLDS, DEBBIE (MARY FRANCES REYNOLDS), actress; b. El Paso, Tex., Apr. 1, 1932; m. Eddie Fisher, Sept. 26, 1955 (div. 1959); children— Carrie, Todd; m. Harry Karl, Nov., 1960 (div. 1973); m. Richard Hamlett (div. May 1996). Active high sch. plays; screen debut Daughter of Rosie O'Grady; motion pictures include: June Bride, 1948, The Daughter of Rosie O'Grady, 1950, Three Little Words, 1950, Two Weeks With Love, 1950, Mr. Imperium, 1951, Singin' in the Rain, 1952, Skirts Ahoy!, 1952, I Love Melvin, 1953, The Affairs of Dobie Gillis, 1953, Give a Girl a Break, 1953, Susan Slept Here, 1954, Athena, 1954, Hit the Deck, 1955, The Tender Trap, 1955, The Catered Affair, 1956, Bundle of Joy, 1956, Tammy and the Bachelor, 1957, This Happy Feeling, 1958, The Mating Game, 1959, Say One for Me, 1959, It Started With a Kiss, 1959, The Gazebo, 1959, The Rat Race, 1960, Pepe, 1960, The Pleasure of His Company, 1961, The Second Time Around, 1961, How the West Was Won, 1962, My Six Loves, 1963, Mary, Mary, 1963, The Unsinkable Molly Brown, 1964, Goodbye Charlie, 1964, The Singing Nun, 1966, Divorce American Style, 1967, How Sweet It Is!, 1968, What's the Matter with Helen?, 1971, Charlotte's Web, (voice only) 1973, That's Entertainment!, 1974, The Bodyguard, 1992, Heaven and Earth, 1993, (with Albert Brooks) Mother, 1996, That's Entertainment III, 1994, In & Out, 1996, In and Out, 1997, Zack and Reba, 1998; star TV program The Debbie Reynolds Show, 1969; star Broadway show Irene, 1973-74, Annie Get Your Gun, Los Angeles, San Francisco, 1977, Woman of the Year, 1984, The Unsinkable Molly Brown, 1989-90 (nat. tour); author: If I Knew Then, 1963, Debbie-My Life, 1988; creator exercise video Do It Debbie's Way, 1984; recurring role (TV series) Will and Grace.. Prin. Debbie Reynolds's Hotel/Casino and Hollywood Motion Picture Mus., Las Vegas, 1993—. Named Miss Burbank, 1948 Office: Debbie Reynolds Studios care Margie Duncan 6514 Lankershim Blvd North Hollywood CA 91606-2409

REYNOLDS, DON WILLIAM, geologist; b. Centerburg, Ohio, Apr. 6, 1926; s. Loren William and Charlotte Lones (Hunt) R.; m. Betty Jeannette Spears, Sept. 4, 1953; children: Don William Jr., Richard Allen (dec.), Brenda Gay. BS, Ohio State U., 1952. Registered profl. geologist, Calif. Mgr. Geochem. Engring., Inc., Midland, Tex., 1950-52; geologist Union Oil Co. Calif., 1953-66, dist. exploration geologist Anchorage, 1966-68, area geologist Bakersfield, Calif., 1968-76, dis. devel. geologist Ventura, 1976-86, dis. devel. geologist mid-continent divsn. Oklahoma City, 1986-89, regional mgr. mid-continent devel., 1989-90, advisor geology, 1990-92. Gen. ptnr. Reynolds Farm, 1979—; sec. ASF Inc., IFP Inc., Austin, 1989—; chmn. bd. Future Petroleum Corp., 1992-98, bd. dirs., 2001—. Pres. Park Stockdale Civic Assn., Bakersfield, 1970, Clearpoint Homeowner's Assn., Ventura, 1980-86; chmn. Kern County Freeway Com. Bakersfield, 1970-73. Served with USAF, 1944-45. Mem. Am. Assn. Petroleum Geologists, West Tex. Geol. Soc. (sec. 1965-66), Kans.-Okla. Oil and Gas Assn. (nomenclature com. 1987-92), San Joaquin Geol. Soc. (treas. 1974-75), Am. Assn. Petroleum Geologists (sec. Pacific sect. 1975-76). Republican. Methodist. Home: 5009 Reynolds Rd Centerburg OH 43011 E-mail: Don_Wm_Reynolds@compuserve.com.

REYNOLDS, DONALD MARTIN, art historian, foundation administrator, educator; b. Kansas City, Mo., Jan. 11, 1931; s. James Martin and Mary Helen (Hughes) R.; m. Nancy Zlobik, June 5, 1970. Student, Amarillo Coll., 1949-51; BA, Assumption Sem., San Antonio, 1955, Columbia U., 1968, MA, 1970, PhD, 1975. Announcer KGNC Radio/TV, Amarillo, Tex., 1949-51; account exec. Monte Rosenwald & Assocs., 1957-59; copy writer, account rep., account supr. J. Walter Thompson, N.Y.C., C.Am., 1959-61; mgr. Ctrl. Am., Young & Rubicam Advt., N.Y.C., Panama, 1961-62; advt. mgr., mktg. dir. Colgate-Palmolive Co. Western Hemisphere Divsn., 1962-64; founder, dir. Image, Internat. Mktg. Agy., N.Y.C., 1964-66; mus. educator in charge Dept. Pub. Edn. Met. Mus. of Art, 1977-79; curator of parks Dept. Parks and Recreation, N.Y.C., 1986-88; founder, coord. Ann. Symposium on Pub. Monuments, 1991—; founder, dir. The Monuments Conservancy, Inc., 1992—. Adj. prof. art history Columbia U., N.Y.C., 1973—; adj. prof. art history Fairfield (Conn.) U., 1981—; adj. asst. prof. art history Hunter Coll., 1972-81; asst. prof. art history Coll. Mt. St. Vincent and Manhattan Coll., 1973-77. Author: The Ideal Sculpture of Hiram Powers, 1977, Manhattan Architecture, 1988, Eng., French edits., The Architecture of New York City: Histories and Views of Important Structures, Sites, and Symbols, 1984, paper, 1988, rev. edit., 1994, Monuments and Masterpieces: Histories and Views of Public Sculpture in New York City, 1988, Nineteenth-Century Art, 1985, also fgn. langs. edits., Nineteenth Century Architecture, 1992, Masters of American Scultpure, the Figurative Tradition from the American Renaissance to the Millennium, 1993; editor, compiler: The Impact of Non-European Civilizations on the Art of the West: Selected Lectures of Rudolf Wittkower, 1989; contbg. author The Macmillan Ency. of Architects, 1982. With U.S. Army, 1955-61. Mem. Nat. Sculpture Soc., Coll. Art Assn., Authors Guild. Office: PO Box 608 New York NY 10003

REYNOLDS, EDWIN WILFRED, JR. retired secondary education educator; b. Englewood, N.J., Mar. 23, 1937; s. Edwin W. and Ellen H. (Hueber) R.; m. Sharon Policastro, Feb. 12, 1983. BA cum laude, Fairleigh Dickinson U., 1961, MAT magna cum laude, 1966; postgrad., NYU, 1964-65, Seton Hall U., 1970-71, Montclair State Coll., 1972-73. Cert. social studies tchr., supr., tchr. psychology, N.J. Supr. installation Western Electric Co., N.Y.C., 1961-65; tchr. social studies Teaneck (N.J.) High Sch., 1965-92, chmn. dept. social studies, 1968-71; supr. social studies Teaneck Secondary Schs., 1971-80, supr. grades K-12, 1980-92, supr. bus. edn. grades 7-12, 1984-92, ret., 1992. Pres. bd. dirs. Global Learning, Inc., 1992-97; sr. state cons. in Holocaust Edn., N.J.; curriculum coord. Ctr. for Holocaust/Genocide Studies, Ramapo Coll.; guest lectr. Kean Coll.; coord. M.A.T. program Fairleigh Dickinson U., 1969-71; mem. planning com. N.E. Regional Social Studies Conf., mem. steering com. Mid-Atlantic Conf.; mem. N.J. Dept. Edn. Social Studies Adv. Com., N.J. Gov.'s Adv. Coun. for Holocaust Edn. in the Pub. Schs.; cons. world history Scott Foresman Pub. Co. Author curriculum devel. and learning guides, 1973-92; co-editor: Holocaust and Genocide: A Search for Conscience. V.p., newsletter editor Pike County Hist. Soc.; elder Presbyn. Ch. U.S. With USN, 1955-57. Recipient Human Rights Award Temple Beth Tikvah, 1985, Brotherhood Award B'nai B'rith No. and Pascack Valleys, 1986, Daniel Roselle Lectr. award Mid. States Coun. for Social Studies, 1988. Mem. ASCD, Nat. Coun. for Social Studies (former bd. dirs.), N.J. Coun. for Social Studies (bd. dirs., past pres.), Greater Bergen County (N.J.) Coun. for Social Studies (bd. dirs., past pres.), Nat. Social Studies Suprs. Assn. (bd. dirs., past pres.), Assn. Ednl. Suprs. (bd. dirs., past pres.), Am. Hist. Assn., Pike County Hist. Soc. (pres. 1998-99), Phi Delta Kappa, Phi Omega Epsilon. Home: PO Box 626 Milford PA 18337-0626

REYNOLDS, ELIZABETH BURSON, social worker; b. Bronx, N.Y., Mar. 23, 1953; d. John and Rose Marie (Russo) Burson; m. Michael P. Reynolds, May 1, 1983; children: Michael, Christopher. AA, Suffolk C.C., 1973; BSW, Adelphi U., 1975, MSW, 1979. Cert. social worker, sch. social worker. Social worker Indsl. Home for the Blind, Bay Shore, N.Y., 1975-80, S. Oaks Psychiat. Hosp., Amityville, NY, 1980-85, Am. Counseling Found., Smithtown, N.Y., 1985-90, Good Samaritan Long Term Home Health Care Program, Bay Shore, 1988-94, Hope Counseling Ctr., Sayville, N.Y., 1989-94, Just Kids Presch. Learning Ctr., Middle Island, 1994—. Part time social worker S. Oaks Psychiat. Hosp., 1992, Skills Unlimited Success Day Program, Bohemian, NY, 1993—94. Mem. NASW (diplomate). Roman Catholic.

REYNOLDS, ELLEN AAKER, pediatric nurse practitioner; b. Sleepy Eye, Minn., Sept. 3, 1957; d. O. A. and M. Helene (Gerhardsen) Aaker; m. Richard C. Reynolds, Jan. 19, 1980; children: Christopher, Brett. BSN magna cum laude, St. Olaf Coll., 1979; MS in Maternal-Child Nursing, U. Maryland, 1985; MSN in Pediatric Nurse Practice, U. Pitts., 2000. Cert. lactation cons., pediatric advanced life support instr.; cert. pediat. nurse practitioner. Clin. nurse Children's Hosp. of the King's Daughters, Norfolk, Va., 1981-82; nurse ICU Jacksonville (Fla.) Children's Hosp., 1982-83; primary nurse critical care float pool Children's Hosp. Nat. Med. Ctr., Washington, 1983-85, clin. nurse, 1985-86; head nurse pediatric ICU U. S. Ala. Med. Ctr., Mobile, 1986-87, pediatric trauma coord., 1987-89, pediatric nursing instr., 1989-90; trauma clin. nurse specialist Children's Hosp. of Pitts., 1990-92, clin. rsch. nurse specialist, 1992-96; clin. instr. pediatrics Duquesne U., 1996-97. Camp nurse Concordia Language Villages, Minn., 1989—; adj. nursing faculty U. Pitts., 1992-98. Contbr. articles to profl. jours. Mem. Nat. Assn. Pediat. Nurse Assocs. and Practitioners, Assn. Camp Nurses (bd. dirs. 1998—), Phi Kappa Phi, Sigma Theta Tau.

REYNOLDS, ERNEST EUGENE, III, lawyer; b. Aug. 5, 1949; s. Ernest Eugene Jr. and Marianne Reba Reynolds; m. Barbara Ann Lovas, Dec. 27, 1973; children: Colleen, Sarah, Katherine. BA in Polit. Sci. with honors, U. Tex. El Paso, El Paso, 1972, MA, 1974; JD with honors, U. Tex., Austin, 1977. Bar: Tex., U.S. Dist. Ct. (ea. dist.) Tex. 1978, U.S. Dist. Ct. (no. dist.) Tex. 1984, U.S. Dist. Ct. (we. dist.) Tex. 1983, U.S. Ct. Appeals (5th cir.) 1987; diplomate Taft Seminar of Govt. Former ptnr. Cantey & Hanger, L.L.P., Ft. Worth; ptnr. Reynolds & Pennington, LLP, 1995—2001, Reynolds & Assocs., Ft. Worth, 2001—. Course dir. Profl. Liability--A Performance Enhancement Course, State Bar of Tex., 1986; mem. Tex. Disciplinary Rules of Profl. Conduct Com., State Bar Tex. Contbr. articles to profl. jours.; editor-in-chief Am. Jour. Criminal Law, 1976-77; former mem. legal rsch. bd. U. Tex. Sch. Law. Bd. dirs. Tex. Girls' Choir, Rep. Forum of Tarrant County, 2001—; co-course dir. The Ultimate Trial Notebook: Masters of Trial, State Bar of Tex., 1993; mem. zoning bd. adjustment City of Colleyville, Tex., 2000—. Recipient Pres.'s award Tex. Young Lawyers Assn., 1983-84. Fellow (charter) Tarrant County Bar Found.; mem. Am. Health Lawyers Assn., Tex. Assn. Def. Counsel (former bd. dirs., chmn. CLE com. 1987-88, punitive damages legis. team 1993-94, chmn. trial acad. 1994), Tarrant County Civil Trial Lawyers Assn. (past pres.), Def. Rsch. Inst., State Bar of Tex. (former vice chmn. CLE, past mem. com. on ct. rules, past mem. administrn. justice com., past mem. citizens and law focused edn. com., task force on practice skills 1987, chmn. CLE planning com. 1999, annual meeting com. 1998-99), Ft. Worth C. of C. (aviation com.), Tarrant County Bar Assn. (Pres.'s Cert. Outstanding Achievement 1999, co-chair law and tech./web page com. 1998-99, past chmn. CLE com., jud. evaluation and polls com. 2000—), Fort Worth Club. Episcopalian. Avocations: reading, travel, art. Office: Reynolds & Associates 933 W Weatherford Ste 210 Fort Worth TX 76102

REYNOLDS, ERNEST WEST, retired physician, educator; b. Bristow, Okla., May 11, 1920; s. Ernest West and Florence (Brown) R. BS, U. Okla., 1942, MD, 1946, MS, 1952. Diplomate: Am. Bd. Internal Medicine. Intern Boston City Hosp., 1946-47; resident Grady Meml. Hosp., Atlanta, 1949-50; practice medicine Tulsa, Okla., 1953-54; prof. medicine U Mich., 1965-72; prof. medicine, dir. cardiology U. Wis., 1972-90, prof. emeritus, 1991—. Dir. Kellogg Found. Comprehensive Coronary Care Project, 1967-72; chmn. NIH Cardiovascular Study Sect. A, 1972-73 Mem. editorial bd.: Am. Heart Jour; Contbr. articles to profl. jours. Served to capt. AUS, 1947-49. Mem. Am. Heart Assn. (fellow coun. clin. cardiology), Ctrl. Soc. Clin. Rsch. Home: 17 Red Maple Trl Madison WI 53717-1515 Office: U Wis 600 Highland Ave Madison WI 53792-0001 E-mail: ewreynolds@prodigy.net. *In the academic environment, research oriented toward the solution of human problems is more productive in career advancement than the pursuit of applications of new technology. In the private sector applied research which solves real problems rather than copies or improves existing technology is met with surprising sales success and few failures.*

REYNOLDS, FRANK EVERETT, religious studies educator; b. Hartford, Conn., Nov. 13, 1930; s. Howard Wesley and Caroline Mills Roys R.; m. Mani Bloch, Mar. 28, 1959 (dec. 1993); children: Roy Howard, Andrew Everett, Roger Frank; m. June Nash, Aug. 16, 1997. Student, Princeton U., 1948-51; BA, Oberlin U., 1952; B.D., Yale Div. Sch., 1955; MA, U. Chgo., 1963, PhD, 1971. Ordained to ministry Am. Baptist Ch., 1955. Program dir. Student Christian Ctr., Bangkok, Thailand, 1956-59; minister to fgn. students U. Chgo. Ecumenical Ministries, 1961-64; instr. U. Chgo., 1967-69, asst. prof. then assoc. prof., 1969-79, prof. history of religions and Buddhist studies, 1979-2001, prof. emeritus, 2001—; dir. Inst. for the Advanced Study of Religions/Martin Marty Ctr., 1991-2001. Tchr. Am. history and lit. Chulalongkorn U., Bangkok, 1956-59; co-dir. Liberal Arts and Study of Religions Project, 1985-90, NEH Sangitiyavasama Transl. Project, 1991-93. Author: (with others) Guide to Buddhist Religion, 1981, Two Wheels of Dhamma, 1971, Religions of the World, 3d edit., 1993; editor, co-translator: 3 Worlds According to King Ruang, 1981; co-editor: The Biographical Process: Studies in the History and Psychology of Religion, 1976, Religious Encounters with Death, 1977, Transitions and Transformations in the History of Religions, 1980, Anthropology and the Study of Religion, 1984, Cosmogony and Ethical Order, 1985, Myth and Philosophy, 1990, Beyond the Classics? Religious Studies and Liberal Education, 1990, Discourse and Practice, 1992, Religion and Practical Reason, 1994, Life of Buddhism, 2000, History of Religion Jour. 1977-2001, Towards a Comparative Philosophy of Religious Series, 1990-95, Religion in History, Society and Culture Series, 2001--; assoc. editor Jour. Religion, 1976—, Jour. Religious Ethics, 1981-2001; mem. editl. bd., History of Religion Jour., 2001—. Chair organizing com. Sawyer Seminar on Religious Law and Constrn. of Identities, 1996-97. Jacob Fox Found. fellow, 1952, Danforth Found. fellow, 1960, 64; sr. rsch. grantee Fulbright Commn., 1973-74, NEH, 1978-79. Mem. Am. Coun. Learned Socs. (com. on history of religions 1985-93), Am. Soc. Study Religion, Am. Acad. Religion (chmn. com. on history of religions 1993-96), Assn. Asian Studies (co-editor monograph series 1978-86, mem. Benda prize com. 1993-96), Internat. Assn. History of Religions, Internat. Assn. Buddhist Studies, Law and Soc. Home: 68 Prospect St Plainfield MA 01070 E-mail: freynold@midway.uchicago.edu.

REYNOLDS, FRANK MILLER, retired government administrator; b. Tulsa, Jan. 8, 1917; s. Frank Miller and Grace (Shields) R.; m. Barbara G. MacWilliams, Dec. 7, 1946; children: Susan G., Ellen M., Frank M. AB, LL.B., U. Okla., 1939; LL.M., George Washington U., 1942; BS, Georgetown Sch. Fgn. Service, 1946. Bar: Okla. 1940. Mem. firm Flippo & Reynolds, Tulsa, 1940; elec. engr. Bur. Ships, Dept. of Navy, 1942-43; with Office Gen. Counsel, Dept. of Navy, 1946; chief negotiator, dep. dir. contract div. Office Naval Research, 1947-54; dep. dir., dir. resources div. Office Asst. Sec. Def., 1954-57; asst. sec. Inst. for Defense Analyses, 1957-61; sec., treas. Logistics Management Inst., Washington, 1961-65, v.p., 1966-76; dir. adminstrv. affairs Uniformed Services U. Health Scis., Bethesda, Md., 1976-78, dir. resource mgmt., 1978-82, exec. sec. bd. regents, 1978-83; dir. patient relations Sibley Meml. Hosp., 1983-84, cons., 1984-87. Professorial lectr. mgmt. research George Washington U. Sch. Engring., 1956— ; cons. Nat. Exec. Service Corps., United Srs. Health Coop., 1984— . Served with radio divsn. Naval Research Lab., 1944-46. Mem. Okla. Bar Assn., Congl. Country Club, Delta Upsilon. Home: 415 Russell Ave Apt 113 Gaithersburg MD 20877-2845 E-mail: frank17r@comeast.net.

REYNOLDS, FREDERICK DELOS, III (RENNY REYNOLDS), event designer; b. St. Louis, June 15, 1947; s. Frederick Delos and Margaret Ray Reynolds. BS in Urban and Regional Planning, U. Wis. Pres. Renny Design for Entertaining, N.Y.C., 1973—. Author: Design for Entertaining-The Art of the Party, 1992. Bd. dirs. U. Pa. Sch. Design, Phila., 1995—, Royal Oak Found., N.Y.C., 1996—, P.S.I.-Mus. Modern Art, N.Y.C., 1989—, Hetrick Martin Inst., N.Y.C., 1989—95, Heritage Conservancy, Doylestown, Pa., 1998—. Recipient Emery award, Hetrick Martin Inst., N.Y.C., awards of achievement, Pa. Hort. Soc., Phila., 1995—2001. Achievements include a 100 acre garden and nursery and 18th century farm in Bucks County, Pa. featured in many national publications. Home: 62 Thompson Mill Rd Newtown PA 18940 Office: Renny Design for Entertaining 505 Park Ave New York NY 10022 Office Fax: 212-593-3549.

REYNOLDS, GENEVA B. special education educator; b. Saginaw, Mich., Nov. 2, 1953; d. Roger and Alrine (Braddock) Rucker; m. Montie Reynolds, Aug. 1, 1981; children: Monte, Marcus. BS, Chgo. State U., 1992, MA in Gen. Adminstrn., 2000. Cert. educable mental handicap and learning disability, social/emotional disturbed. Adminstrv. specialist USAF, 1973-77, command and control specialist, 1977-81; info. supt. USAFR, Chgo., 1981—; head tchr. South Ctrl. Cmty. Svcs., 1986—. SM sgt. USAF, 1973-81, USAFR, 1981—. Mem. Coun. for Exceptional Children, Kappa Delta Pi. Democrat. Baptist. Avocations: reading, computers, going to plays.

REYNOLDS, GEORGE ANTHONY, JR. engineering executive; b. Columbia, S.C., May 5, 1961; s., George Anthony and Flora Mae (La Coste) R.; m. Katherine Alison Albea, Apr. 14, 1984; children: Amanda Kate, William Anthony. BSME, Clemson U., 1983; postgrad., U. Ala., Huntsville, 1985. Design engr. Motorola, Plantation, Fla., 1983-85; sr. engr. Chrysler, Huntsville, Ala., 1985-88; prin. engr. NCR, Liberty, S.C., 1988-91, project leader, 1991-94; mgr. mech. engring. Sensormatic Electronics, Boca Raton, Fla., 1994-96, dir. product engring., 1996-98, dir. active products, 1998-2000, v.p. hard tag and product line engring., 2000—02; v.p. electronic article csurveillance Tyco Internat., 2002—. Mem. editl. quality audit panel Electronic Packaging & Prodn. Mag., N.Y.C., 1992. Advisor Clemson U. Mech. Engring. Endowment Fund; elder, mem. ednl. dir. search com., chair Christian edn. com., nominating com., chair stewardship campaign 1st Presbyn. Ch., Delray Beach, Fla.; pres. Seagate Neighborhood Assn., 1996-97; team mgr. Caloosa Park Girls Fast Pitch Softball Assn. Finalist S. Fla. Up and Comers award, 1997. Mem. ASME, NRA (Legion of Honor), S.E. Pro/Engr. User Group (pres. 1992-93), S. Fla. Clemson Alumni Club, Nature Conservancy, Nat. Wildlife Fedn., Ducks Unltd., Fla. Sheriff's Assn. (life), Fla. Wildlife Fedn., Billfish Found., Tau Beta Pi, Phi Kappa Phi, Alpha Tau Omega (alumni adv. bd. Eta Pi chpt. 1993-94). Republican. Presbyterian. Avocations: tennis, genealogy, hunting, fishing. Home: 944 Brookdale Dr Boynton Beach FL 33435-6101 Office: Sensormatic Electronic Corp 951 Yamato Rd Boca Raton FL 33431-4425

REYNOLDS, GERALD, federal agency administrator; Grad., CUNY York Coll., Boston U. Atty. Schatz & Schatz, Ribicoff & Kotkin, Conn.; legal analyst Ctr. Equal Opportunity; pres. Ctr. New Black Leadership; sr. regulatory counsel Kansas City Power and Light Co.; asst. sec. civil rights Dept. Edn., Washington, 2001—. Mem. editl. bd.: Am. Jour. Law and Medicine. Office: Dept Edn Office Civil Rights 400 Maryland Ave SW Washington DC 20202-1100*

REYNOLDS, GREGORY EDWARD, minister; b. Boston, May 10, 1949; s. Edward John Reynolds, Barbara Ann Ferguson; m. Roberta Ellen Cheney, Mar. 24, 1973; children: Rebekah, Thomas, Christopher. Student, Boston Archtl. Ctr., 1967—70, L'Abri Fellowship, Huemoz, Switzerland, 1971—72; cert., Bible Inst. New Eng., 1972—73; BA magna cum laude, Covenant Coll., 1975; MDiv, Westminster Theol. Sem., Phila., 1979; DMin, Westminster Theol. Sem. Calif., Escondido, 2001. Cert. ordained Presbytery of N.Y. and New Eng., 1980. Archtl. designer Pro Con Constrn., Hooksett, NH, 1993—96; headmaster, instr. Granite State Sch. of Theology and Missions, Manchester, 1997—. Author: The Word is Worth a Thousand Pictures Preaching in the Electronic Age, 2001; book reviewer Conservative Book Club, Harrison, N.Y., 1987—99; contbr. Recipient Home Owner's award, Manchester Hist. Assn., 1997. Mem.: SAR (chaplain N.H. chpt. 1997—), Quill and Scroll Soc., Nat. Honor Soc., Boston Athen[00e6]um. Republican. Avocations: antiquarian book collecting, architectural historic preservation, skiing, mountain climbing, poetry. Home: 827 Chestnut St Manchester NH 03104 Office: Amoskeng Presbyn Ch 95 Brook St Manchester NH 03104

REYNOLDS, H. GERALD, lawyer; b. Alexander City, Ala., July 16, 1940; s. James H. and Melba V. (Scott) R.; m. Mary Alice McGiboney, Sept. 3, 1960; children: Cathy, Gerre, Amy, Richie. BA, Auburn U., 1962; JD, Cumberland Sch. Law, 1965. Bar: Ala. 1965, Fla. 1977. Ptnr. King and Reynolds, Alexander City, 1965-66; sole practice, 1966-71; corp. counsel U.S. Pipe and Foundry, Birmingham, Ala., 1971-72; environ. counsel Jim Walter Corp., Tampa, Fla., 1972-87, Walter Industries Inc., 1988-2000. Judge Ct. Common Pleas, Tallapoosa County, Ala., 1967-68; mem. faculty Alexander City State Jr. Coll., 1966-71; ad hoc instr. Coll. Pub. Health Grad. Sch. U. South Fla., 1988-90. Contbr. articles to profl. jours. Mem. Ala. Constl. Revision Commn., 1970-75; mem. Ala. Dem. Exec. Com., 1970-72. Mem. Fla. Bar Assn. (chmn. environ. and land use law sect. 1981-82, vice chmn. CLE com. 1980-94). Methodist.

REYNOLDS, HAROLD MARK, language educator; b. Oct. 4, 1944; BA, U. Ala., 1967, MA, 1970; DA, Carnegie Mellon U., 1981. Prof. Jefferson Davis C.C., Brewton, Ala., 1968—. Editor: Teaching English in the Two-Year College, 1994—2001. Office: PO Box 958 Brewton AL 36427-0033

REYNOLDS, HARRAH (H.) ROBERT, conductor, artistic director; b. Canton, Ohio, Apr. 10, 1934; BMus in Edn., U. Mich., 1956, MMus in Performance, 1958. Dir. univ. bands, dir. divsn. instrumental studies Sch. Music, U. Mich. Condr. Detroit Chamber Winds and Strings; guest condr., clinician numerous univs. and confs.; lectr., condr. internat. confs. World Assn. of Symphonic Bands and Ensembles, Norway, Belgium, Eng., The Netherlands; master condr., tchr. Europaisches Seminar fur Dirigenten von Blasorchestern, Bundesakademie, Trossingen, Germany, Austrian Wind Band Condrs. Assn.; condr. Royal Danish Band, Copenhagen, Carnegie Hall, Lincoln Ctr., N.Y.C., Orch. Hall, Chgo., Kennedy Ctr., Washington, Powell Symphony Hall, St. Louis, Acad. Music, Phila.; condr. premiers La Scala Opera, Milan, concerts at Maggio Musicale, Florence, Italy, Tonhalle, Zurich, Switzerland, Concergebouw, Amsterdam, The Netherlands; condr. recs. for Koch Internat., Pro Arte, Caprice, Deutsche Grammophon; mem. nat. awards panel ASCAP. Mem. Coll. Band Dirs. Nat. Assn. (past pres.), Big Ten Band Dirs.' Assn. (past pres.). E-mail: hrr@umich.edu.

REYNOLDS, HARRY LINCOLN, physicist, researcher; b. Port Chester, N.Y., Mar. 31, 1925; s. Harry Benson and Lydia (Wilde) R.; m. Katherine Haile, 1950; children: Patricia Reynolds Cabral, Margaret Benson Neufeld. BS, Rensselaer Poly. Inst., 1947; PhD, U. Rochester, 1951. Sr. scientist Oak Ridge Nat. Lab., 1951-55; physicist Lawrence Livermore Nat. Lab., 1955-65; asst. program mgr. NASA Manned Spacecraft Center, Houston, 1965; asso. dir. nuclear test, nuclear design and nuclear explosives programs Lawrence Livermore Nat. Lab., Calif., 1965-80, spl. asst. to dir., 1980-81; dep. asso. dir. advanced concepts Los Alamos Nat. Lab., 1981-85; dir. advanced concepts Rockwell Internat. Corp., Seal Beach, Calif., 1985-94. Cons. in field. Contbr. articles to profl. jours. Trustee Valley Meml. Hosp., Livermore, 1980-81; mem. Army Sci. Bd., 1982-88. Served with U.S. Navy, 1944-46. AEC fellow, 1947-49 Fellow Am. Phys. Soc. Home: 1100 Via Media Lafayette CA 94549-2922

REYNOLDS, HELEN ELIZABETH, management services consultant; b. Minerva, N.Y., Aug. 30, 1925; d. Henry James and Margurite Catherine (Gallagher) McNally; m. Theodore Laurence Reynolds, Feb. 27, 1948; children: Laurence McBride, David Scott, William Herbert. BA, SUNY, Albany, 1967; MA, Union Coll., Schenectady, N.Y., 1971. Grad. Realtors Inst., N.Y. Owner, mgr. Schafer Studio, Schenectady, 1970-73; co-owner, v.p. Reynolds Chalmers Inc., 1971-97; program coord. Schenectady County, 1980-81; adminstr. Wellspring House of Albany, N.Y., 1981-94. Cons., examiner N.Y. State Civil Service, Albany, 1971-81; mem. adv. council SBA, Washington, 1978-80. Mem. planning bd. Town of Niskayuna, N.Y., 1977-81, town councilwoman, 1986-94; co-chair Great N.E. Festival on the Mohawk River, 1989, 90; bd. dir. HAVEN, Schenectady YWCA; mem. N.Y. State Commn. on The Capital Region, 1994-98, Acad. of Women of Achievement, Schenectady, 1994, Libr. of Congress; pres. Photo Arts Group of Charlotte County, 1998—, Buena Vista Property Owners Assn., Port Charlotte, Fla., 1998—. Named Woman Vision, 1986, 87, Today's Woman, 1987, Schenectady YWCA. Mem. Antique and Classic Boat Soc. (bd. dirs. 1974-89, Disting. Svc. award 1979, Founders award 1989), Assn. Adminstrs. Ind. Housing (pres. 1986-88, 92-94), Zonta (pres. 1981-82), Adirondack Mus., Antique Boat Mus., Lake George Antique Boat & Auto Mus. (bd. dirs.), Charlotte Symphony League (bd. dirs.), Union Coll. Alumni Assn., Charlotte Harbor Yacht Club, Charlotte County Art Guild. Avocations: photography, reading, golf, skiing, canoeing. Home and Office: 104 Leland St SW Port Charlotte FL 33952-9131

REYNOLDS, HERBERT HAL, academic administrator; b. Frankston, Tex., Mar. 20, 1930; s. Herbert Joseph and Ava Nell (Taylor) R.; m. Joy Myrla Copeland, June 17, 1950; children: Kevin Hal, Kent Andrew, Rhonda Sheryl. BS, Trinity U., 1952; MS, Baylor U., 1958, PhD, 1961; ScD (hon.) , Seinan Gakuin U., Japan, 1990, Baylor Coll. Dentistry, 1993, Yonok Coll., Thailand, 2000. Entered USAF, 1948, advanced through grades to col., 1966; dir. research (Aeromed. Lab.), Alamogordo, N.Mex., 1961—68; comdr., dir. of plan Air Force Human Resources Lab., San Antonio, 1968; ret., 1968; exec. v.p. Baylor U., Waco, Tex., 1969—81, pres., 1981—95, chancellor, 1995—2000, pres. emeritus, 2000—. Vis. fellow, scholar Cambridge U., 1994-97. Contbr. articles to profl. jours. Mem.: Sigma Xi, Phi Beta Kappa, Omicron Delta Kappa, Alpha Chi. Office: Baylor U Office of Pres Emeritus Waco TX 76798 E-mail: president_emeritus@baylor.edu.

REYNOLDS, HERBERT YOUNG, physician, internist; b. Richmond, Va., Aug. 20, 1939; s. George Audney and Pearle Maupin (Young) R.; m. Anne Browning Leavell, July 11, 1964; children: Nancy, George, William Stuart. BA in English, U. Va., 1961, MD, 1965; MA (hon.), Yale U., 1979. Diplomate Am. Bd. Internal Medicine, Am. Bd. Allergy and Immunology. Intern The N.Y. Hosp., Cornell Med. Ctr., N.Y.C., 1965-66, asst. physician, fellow in medicine, 1966-67; clin. assoc., lab. clin. investigation Nat. Inst. Allergy and Infectious Diseases, NIH, Bethesda, Md., 1967-70, chief clin. assoc. lab. clin. investigation, 1968-69, sr. investigator lab. of clin. investigation, 1971-76; chief resident, instr. medicine U. Hosp. U. Wash., Seattle, 1970-71; assoc. prof. internal medicine, head pulmonary div. Sch. Medicine Yale U., New Haven, 1976-79, prof., 1979—88; J. Lloyd Huck prof. medicine, chmn. dept. Pa. State U.-Milton S. Hershey Med. Ctr., 1988—; assoc. chmn. divsn. medicine Pa. State Geisinger Health Sys., 1997-2000, chief medicine ops. Hershey Med. Ctr. Region, 1997-2000. Exec. com. Coll. Medicine Pa. State U.-Hershey Med. Ctr., 1988—, exec. bd. U. Hosp., 1988—, fin. bd. acad. enrichment fun, 1988-95, dean's adv. com., 1988-97, diversity task force, 1995—, physicians faculty practice plan exec. com. 1996-97, human resources team leader, 2000-; dept. chair rep. Milton S. Hershey Med. Ctr. Bd., 2000-2002; cons. in infectious diseases Nat. Naval Med. Ctr. NIH, Bethesda, 1971-76, clin. rsch. com., 1971-76, chmn., 1974-76, pulmonary disease adv. com. divsn. of lung diseases Nat. Heart, Lung and Blood Inst., 1978-82, sci. counselors bd., 1984-88, data and safety monitoring bd. registry of patients with deficiency of Alpha-1 Antitrypsin, 1989-96. Mem. editl. bd. Lung, 1978—, Am. Jour. Medicine, 1979-89, Jour. Clin. Investigation, 1980-86, Am. Rev. Respiratory Disease, 1980-87, Jour. Applied Physiology, 1981-89, Resident Physician, 1981-95; contbr. over 285 articles to profl. jours. Parent com. Troop 1 Boy Scouts Am., Madison, 1979-82; bd. dirs. Neighborhood Music Sch., Guilford, Conn., 1978-87, Music at Gretna, 1994—; bd. dirs. Harrisburg Symphony, 1996-2000; active All Saints Episc. Ch., Hershey; pulmonary infections com. Cystic Fibrosis Found., Bethesda, 1980-86; mem. coun. sci. advisors Parker B. Francis Found., Kansas City, Kans., 1983-87; internat. com. World Orgn. for Sarcoidosis and other Granulomatous Disorders, 1987-95; bd. dirs., mem. coun. Am. Lung Assn., 1989-93, bd. govs. 1990-93, com. mem., 1990—; coach Guilford Soccer League, 1985-88. Surgeon USPHS, 1967-70. John Edward Nobel fellow, 1961-65; named Outstanding Med. Specialist in USA, Town and Country Mag., 1989, 97, The Best Med. Specialists, Town & Country mag., 1995, One of 400 Best Doctors in U.S. Good Housekeeping Mag., 1991, named in The Best Doctors in Am., 1st edit. 1992-93, 2d edit. 1994-95, 3rd edit. 1997-98, The Best Doctors in Am., N.E., 1st edit., 1996-97. Fellow ACP (coun. subsplty. socs. 1989-00, gov.-elect Pa. eastern region I 1999, gov. Pa. 2000—), Am. Coll. Chest Physicians (program com. 1978-84), Infectious Disease Soc. Am., Coll. Physicians Phila.; mem. Am. Thoracic Soc. (sec.-treas. 1987-88, bd. dirs. 1989-93, v.p. 1988-89, pres. 1992-93), Am. Soc. Clin. Investigation, Assn. Am. Physicians, Am. Assn. Immunologists, Am. Fedn. Clin. Rsch., Am. Clin. and Climatological Soc. (v.p. 2001-02), Interurban Clin. Club (emeritus 1989), Assn. Profs. Medicine, Country Club of Hershey, Farmington Country Club, Raven Soc., Phi Beta Kappa, Alpha Omega Alpha, Omicron Delta Kappa. Republican. Avocations: tennis, violin. Home: 226 E Caracas Ave Hershey PA 17033-1309 Office: Pa State U Milton S Hershey Med Ctr 850 University Dr Hershey PA 17033 E-mail: hreynolds@psu.edu.

REYNOLDS, JAMES, management consultant; b. Detroit, Mar. 22, 1941; s. Richard James and Esther (Nikander) R.; m. Joanne M.J. BA in Econs., NYU, 1965, postgrad., 1965-66. Cons. to pres. Rothrock, Reynolds & Reynolds Inc., N.Y.C., 1966-70; sr. v.p. health, med. div. Booz, Allen & Hamilton, 1970-80; pres. Reynolds & Co. (mgmt. cons.), San Francisco, N.Y.C., Washington, 1981—. Developer value chain analysis in the health field, 1994, Advanced Delivery Systems, 1999; bd. dirs. Booz, Allen & Hamilton, 1977-79; chmn. bd. J.X. Reynolds Fine Arts, Ltd., 1979—; bd. dirs. Health Center Mgmt. Inst.; lectr. Harvard Sch. Pub. Health; faculty mem. Am. Coll. of Healthcare Execs.; bd. dirs. Health Ctr. Mgmt. Inst., Richmond, Va., 1977; mem. health adv. bd. Hunter Coll., 1980—. Editorial bd. Physicians Fin. News. Recipient NYU Founders award, 1965 Mem. Am. Pub. Health Assn., Am. Mgmt. Assn., Assn. Am. Med. Colls., Am. Hosp. Assn., Hosp. Mgmt. Systems Soc., Hosp. Fin. Mgmt. Assn., Asia Soc., China Inst., Phi Beta Kappa, Guggenheim Mus., Mus. Modern Art, Met. Mus. Art, Met. Opera Guild (N.Y.C.) Episcopalian. Home and Office: Reynolds & Co 333 E 51st St New York NY 10022-6702 also: 2500 3 Mile Run Rd Perkasie PA 18944-2020 E-mail: jreynolds@jxreynolds.com.

REYNOLDS, JEAN EDWARDS, publishing executive; b. Saginaw, Mich., Dec. 11, 1941; d. F. Perry and Kathrine (Edwards) R.; m. Cary Wellington, Sept. 10, 1975 (div. 1982); children, Bradley, Abigail, Benjamin; m. Jon Haddon, Nov. 8, 1997. BA, Wells Coll., 1963; postgrad., CCNY, 1965-67. Asst. editor, sr. editor trade book div. Prentice-Hall, Englewood Cliffs, N.J., 1963-66, dir. children's books, 1966-69, McCall Pub. Co., N.Y.C., 1969-71; sr. v.p., editorial dir. Franklin Watts Inc., 1971-75; pres. Pet Projects Inc., Ridgefield, Conn., 1975-81; editor in chief young people's publs. Grolier Inc., Danbury, 1981-89; founder, pub., exec. v.p. The Millbrook Press, Brookfield, 1989—. Bd. dirs. Wellington Leisure Products, Atlanta, Kiper Enterprises, Oswego, N.Y.; chairperson Conn. Ctr. for the Book, 1991-94. Pres. Jewish Fedn. Greater Danbury, 1991—93; bd. dirs. Jewish Home for the Elderly, Fairfield, Conn., 1989—90, 1999, Book Industry Study Group, 1991—98, The Wooster Sch., Danbury, Conn., 1992—, chair headmaster search, 2002—; bd. dirs. Temple Shearith Israel, Ridgefield, 1994—97, chair Kehila campaign, 2002; bd. dirs. The Children's Book Coun., 1996—2000, vice chair, 1997—98, chair, 1998—99. Mem. ALA, Children's Book Coun., Mensa. Jewish. Avocations: skiing, sailing, needlework. Home: 33 Corntassle Rd Danbury CT 06811-3208 Office: The Millbrook Press Inc 2 Old New Milford Rd Brookfield CT 06804-2426

REYNOLDS, JOHN FRANCIS, insurance company executive; b. Escanaba, Mich., Mar. 29, 1921; s. Edward Peter and Lillian (Harris) R.; m. Dorothy Gustafson, May 1, 1946; children— Lois, Margaret, Michael BS, Mich. State U., 1942. Claims and assoc. surety mgr. Hartford Ins. Co., Escanaba, Mich. and Chgo., 1946-55; asst. v.p., bond mgr. Wolverine Ins. Co., Battle Creek, Mich., 1955-64, v.p. underwriting, 1964-69; Midwest zone underwriting mgr. Transamerica Ins. Co. (Wolverine Ins. Co.), 1969-74; pres., gen. mgr. Can. Surety Co. subs. Transamerica Ins. Co., Toronto, Ont., Canada, 1974-75; v.p. midwestern zone mgr. Transamerica Ins. Group, Battle Creek, Mich., 1975-83, pres., chief operating officer Los Angeles, 1983-84, chmn., chief exec. officer, 1984-85; apptd. spl. dep. ins. commr., dep. conservator Cadillac Inc. Co., 1989. Pres. Underwriting Exec. Council Midwest, 1967; dir. Underwriters Adjustment Bur., Toronto, 1974, Underwriters Labs. of Canada, Montreal, 1974; chmn. Mich. Assn. Ins. Cos., Lansing, 1976, Mich. Basic Property Ins. Assn., Detroit, 1973. Commr. City of Battle Creek, 1967-69; dir. Urban League, Battle Creek, 1969, 70, dir. Mich. Ins. Fedn., Lansing, 1975-83. Served to sgt. U.S. Army, 1942-45; New Guinea Roman Catholic. Avocations: golf; fishing. E-mail: jackreynolds@prodigy.net.

REYNOLDS, JOHN HUGHES, IV, research and development executive; b. Rome, Sept. 25, 1940; s. John Hughes and Catherine (Neal) R.; m. Lee Boling Smith, Aug. 18, 1963; 1 child, Alison Lee. BA, Shorter Coll., 1962; MS, Clemson U., 1965, PhD, 1968. Chemist III R.J. Reynolds Tobacco Co., Winston-Salem, N.C., 1968-76, group leader, 1976-80, divsn. mgr., 1980-90, prin. scientist, 1990-96. Contbr. articles to profl. jours.; patentee designs for smoking articles and machines for lab. smoking of cigarettes. NDEA fellow Clemson U., 1962-65. Mem. AAAS, Sigma Xi (pres. Wake Forest U. chpt. 1977-78).

REYNOLDS, JOHN W. federal judge; b. Green Bay, Wis., Apr. 4, 1921; s. John W. and Madge (Flatley) R.; m. Patricia Ann Brody, May 26, 1947 (dec. Dec. 1967); children: Kate M. Reynolds Lindquist, Molly A., James B.; m. Jane Conway, July 31, 1971; children: Jacob F., Thomas J., Frances P., John W. III. PhB, U. Wis., 1946, LLB, 1949. Bar: Wis. 1949. Since practiced in Green Bay; dist. dir. price stblzn., 1951-53; U.S. commr., 1953-58; atty. gen. of Wis., 1958-62; gov. State of Wis., 1963-65; U.S. dist. judge Ea. Dist. Wis., Milwa., 1965-71, chief judge, 1971-86, sr. judge, from 1986. Served with U.S. Army, 1942-46. Mem. State Bar Wis., Am. Law Inst., Fed. Judges Assn., Former Govs. Assn. Died Jan. 6, 2002.

REYNOLDS, JOSEPH PATRICK, chemical engineering educator, consultant; b. N.Y.C., May 19, 1935; s. Patrick Joseph Reynolds and Ann Marie Brady; m. Barbara Geary, Apr. 22, 1974; children: Megan, Marybeth. BA in Chemistry, Cath. U. Am., 1957; PhD in Chem. Engring., Rensselaer Poly. Inst., 1964. Mem. chem. engring. faculty Manhattan Coll., Bronx, N.Y., 1964—, chmn. dept. chem. engring., 1975-83, prof. chem. engring., 1976—. Cons. U.S. Dept. Justice, Washington, 1993-94, 97-00, U.S. EPA, Raleigh, N.C., 1996-97; gen. chmn. 7th Nat. Conf. on Energy and the Environment, Phoenix, 1980. Co-author: Introduction to Hazardous Waste Incineration, 1987, 2d edit., 2000, Hazardous Waste Incineration Calculations and Software, 1991; contbr. over 50 articles to profl. jours. and conf. procs. Mem. AIChE (bd. dirs. local sect. 1997-00), Air and Waste Mgmt. Assn., Sigma Xi (past pres. Manhattan Coll. chpt.). Democrat. Roman Catholic. Avocations: skiing, jogging, travel. Office: Manhattan Coll Chem Engring Dept Manhattan Coll Pkwy Bronx NY 10471 E-mail: joseph.reynolds@manhattan.edu.

REYNOLDS, KAREN JEANNE, musician; b. Baraga, Mich., Mar. 24, 1940; d. Arthur Johannes and Ila Amanda (Björkqvist) Hill; m. Roger Lee Reynolds, Apr. 11, 1964; 1 child, Erika Lynn. MusB, U. Mich., 1962; MA, U. Calif. San Diego, La Jolla, 1975. Instr. flute San Diego State U., 1979-86, The Bishop's Sch., La Jolla, 1989—, Fairbanks Sch. Performing Arts, Rancho Santa Fe, Calif., 1998—. Free-lance performer ONCE Festivals, Ann Arbor, Mich., 1961-63, Am. Wind Ensemble, Pitts., 1962, Am. Students' and Artists' Ctr., Paris, 1963-64, CROSS TALK Media Series, Tokyo, 1967-69, Orchestral Space, Tokyo, 1968, N.H. Music Festival, Plymouth, 1981; artistic coord. CROSS TALK Media Series, Tokyo, 1967-69, The Pacific Ring Festival, La Jolla, 1986; adjudicator solo and ensemble festivals, San Diego, 1980s, San Diego Flute Guild Contest, 1989—; condr. workshops San Diego Civic Youth Orch., 1979, 80, 82, 86; selection jurist Sibelius Acad. Music Festival, Finlandia U., 1999—. Rec. artist Electronic/Instrumental Music, CRI SD 285, Roger Reynolds: All Known All White, Pogus P21025-2. Fulbright scholar, Paris, 1963-64. Mem. Music Tchrs'. Assn., Nat. Flute Assn., Am. Fedn. Musicians, Finlandia Univ. Finnish Coun. in Am., Phi Kappa Phi.

REYNOLDS, LEO THOMAS, electronics company executive; b. Mpls., May 24, 1945; s. Donald Charles and Elizabeth (Graham) R.; m. Betty Gail Herrington, Aug. 8, 1966 (div. 1978); children: William, Nathan; m. Diana Frances Boyd, Feb. 26, 1982 (div. 1990); children: Jeffrey, Daniel; m. Sandra Kay Sonne, Feb. 26, 1994; stepchildren: Troy, Tyler. BSEE, U. Iowa, 1972; postgrad. in bus., Mankato State U., 1972-74. Registered profl. engr., S.D. Mech. draftsman John Deere Co., Dubuque, Iowa, 1970-71; engring. supr. 3M Co., New Ulm, Minn., 1972-76; supt. Litton Microwave, Sioux Falls, S.D., 1976-80; founder, pres., CEO Electronic Systems, Inc., 1980—. Apptd. 21st Century Workforce Commn., 1998. Editor Transit mag., 1972. Bd. dirs., exec. com. Sioux Falls Devel. Found., 1989-97, chmn. bd. dirs., 1996; svc. team chmn. Sioux Exploring Coun., 1992-96; bd.d irs. Vols. Am. S.D. Mem. NSPE, 21st Century Workforce Commn., Surface Mount Tech. Assn., IPC (sec.-treas., bd. dirs.), Sioux Falls C. of C. (leadership trainer). Republican. Avocations: reading, sailing, motorcycling, performing arts. Office: Electronic Systems Inc 600 E 50th St PO Box 5013 Sioux Falls SD 57117-5013

REYNOLDS, LEWIS DAYTON, pastor; b. Charleston, W.Va., July 26, 1937; s. James Shelby and Sybil Catherine (Lanham) R.; m. Ann Kathryn Combs, Aug. 25, 1962; children: John Mark, Daniel Adam. BBA, Marshall U., 1959; BTh, Aurora U., 1961; MDiv, Evang. Theol. Sem., Naperville, Ill., 1962. Ordained to ministry Advent Christian Ch., 1962. Pastor Mendota (Ill.) Advent Christian Ch., Mendota, Ill., 1961-64, Clendenin (W.Va.) Advent Christian Ch., Clendenin, W.Va., 1964-72, New Covenant Fellowship, Penfield, N.Y., 1972-89; gen. overseer Elim Fellowship, Lima, 1989-97; sr. pastor Faith Christian Fellowship, Clarksburg, W.Va., 1997—2002, Charismatic Episcopal Ch. of the Transfiguration, Sterling, Va., 2002—. Mem. Phi Eta Sigma. Republican. E-mail: ldaytonr@aol.com.

REYNOLDS, LLOYD GEORGE, economist, educator; b. Wainwright, Alberta, Can., Dec. 22, 1910; came to U.S., 1934, naturalized, 1940; s. George F. and Dorothy (Carl) R.; m. Mary F. Trackett, June 12, 1937; children: Anne Reynolds Skinner, Priscilla Reynolds Roosevelt, Bruce Lloyd. AB, U. Alberta, 1931, LL.D., 1958; A.M., McGill U., 1933; PhD, Harvard, 1936. Instr. econs. Harvard, 1936-39; asso. polit. economy Johns Hopkins, 1939-41, asso. prof., 1941-45; asso. prof. econs. Yale, 1945-47, prof. econs., 1947-52, Sterling prof. econs., 1952-81, chmn. dept. econs., 1951-59; prof. emeritus, 1981—; dir Econ. Growth Center, 1961-67; vis. fellow All Souls Coll., Oxford, 1967-68. Mem. adv. bd. Pakistan Inst. Devel. Econs., 1965-73; cons. to Social Sci. Research Center, U. P.R., 1951-65; dir. Nat. Bureau Econ. Research, 1958-81; Research dir. labor studies 20th Century Fund, 1940-43; research sec., com. on employment Social Sci. Research Council, 1941-42; co-chmn. appeals com. N.W.L.B., 1943-45; cons. Bur. of Budget, 1945-47; Guggenheim fellow, 1954-55, 1966-67; dir. program in econs. and bus. adminstrn. Ford Found., 1955-57 Author: The British Immigrant in Canada, 1935, Control of Competition in Canada, 1940, Labor and National Defense, 1941, An Index to Trade Union Publications, 1945, Labor Economics and Labor Relations, 1949, The Structure of Labor Markets, 1951, The Evolution of Wage Structure, 1956, Economics: A General Introduction, 1963, Wages, Productivity and Industrialization in Puerto Rico, 1965, The Three Worlds of Economics, 1971, Agriculture in Development Theory, 1975, Image and Reality in Economic Development, 1977, The American Economy in Perspective, 1981, Economic Growth in the Third World, 1850-1980, 1985; contbr. articles to profl. jours. Fellow Am. Acad. Arts and Scis.; mem. Indsl. Rls. Rsch. Assn. (pres. 1955), Am. Econ. Assn. (v.p. 1959, exec. com. 1952-54), Am. Acad. Polit. Sci., Am. Statis. Assn., Phi Beta Kappa. Clubs: Graduates (New Haven) (pres. 1961-64); Harvard (Boston); Century (N.Y.C.); Cosmos (Washington). Home: 4000 Cathedral Ave NW Washington DC 20016-5249 Office: Yale University Economics Dept New Haven CT 06520

REYNOLDS, LOUISE MAXINE KRUSE, retired school nurse; b. Waynesboro, Va., May 28, 1935; d. Emil Herman and Cora Lee (Hammer) Kruse; m. Elbert B. Reynolds Jr., June 13, 1964; children: David Emil, Jane Marie. Diploma, Rockingham Meml. Hosp., 1956; student, Madison Coll., Tex. Tech U. RN, Tex., Va, cert. sch. nurse. Head nurse orthopedic, opthalmology dept. surgery Duke U., Durham, N.C., 1961-62; head nurse surg. fl. Waynesboro (Va.) Hosp., 1962-64; sch. nurse Lubbock (Tex.) Ind. Sch. Dist., 1974-94, ret., 1994. Pres. Vol. Network Luth. Home, Lubbock, Tex., 1996-2000; sec. Luth. Student Coun., Tex. Tech., Lubbock, 1999-2000. Recipient recognition for contbn. to ch. and cmty., Aid Assn. for Luths. Mem. DAR (sec. Nancy Anderson chpt. 2000—), Va. Nurses Assn. (dist. sec., chair), Tex. Assn. Sch. Nurses (sec., treas. dist. 17, program chair 1989 state conv.).

REYNOLDS, MARGARET ANN, minister, educator; b. York, Nebr., Dec. 9, 1920; d. Emmett and Nora Estelle (Jacobs) Osborn; m. John Milton Reynolds, June 27, 1948; children: Matthew Osborn (dec.), Jonathan Mark. BA, U. Nebr., 1942; MA, Columbia U., 1947; MDiv, Union Theol. Sem., 1948. Cert. tchr., Calif.; ordained to ministry Disciples of Christ, 1948. Dir. Christian edn. Plymouth Congl. Ch., Ft. Wayne, Ind., 1942-43; nat. sec. Forerunners Fellowship of Reconciliation, N.Y.C., 1943-45; dir. youth campaign Japan Internat. Christian U., 1949-50; county dir. Retarded and Handicapped Ctr., San Bernardino, Calif., 1966-67; tchr. McKinley Sch., Colton, 1967-78; assoc. min. Laguna Beach, 1979-83; min. emerita Neighborhood Congl. Ch., Claremont, 1983—. Moderator N.J. Assn. Congl. Christian Chs., 1954-56, Kern Assn. United Ch. of Christ, Bakersfield, Calif., 1963-64; bd. dirs. Pacific S.W. Conf. on Christian World Missions, 1989-99; del. Oslo World Christian Youth Conf., N.Y.C., 1946-47; mem. planning com., historian Ea. Assn. United Ch. of Christ, 1995—. Author: Handbook for retarded and Handicapped of San Bernardino County, 1967, Journey in Ministry, 1995, (novels) Peg's charms, 1999. Mem. AAUW, So. Calif. Campanology Club (chaplain 1995—, past pres.), Nat. Mus. Women in Arts (charter), Am. Bell Assn. Internat., McKinley Sch. PTA (life). Democrat. Avocations: reading, painting, collecting bells and eggs, swimming, travel. Home: 627 Leyden Ln # 202 Claremont CA 91711-4236 E-mail: Belleggs@aol.com.

REYNOLDS, MARJORIE LAVERS, nutrition educator; b. Collingwood, Ont., Can., Jan. 10, 1931; d. Henry James and Laura (Wilson) Lavers; m. John Horace Reynolds, Aug. 17, 1963; children: Steven, Mark. BA, U. Toronto, 1953; MS, U. Minn., 1957; PhD, U. Wis., 1964; AS, State Tech. Inst. Knoxville, 1982. Registered dietitian. Rsch. dietitian Mayo Clinic, Rochester, Minn., 1957-59; rsch. dietitian Cleve. Met. Gen. Hosp., 1959-60; rsch. assoc. U. Tenn., Knoxville, 1963-66; instr. Ft. Sanders Sch. Nursing, 1967-76, State Tech. Inst., Knoxville, 1982-88; substitute secondary sch. tchr. Knox County Schs., 1989-93. Contbr. articles to biochem. and nutrition jours.; newsletter editor Juvenile Diabetes Found., Knoxville, 1985-93. Sec. Midway Rehab. Ctr., Knoxville, 1987—2001. Mem.: LWV, Knoxville Dist. Dietetic Assn. (pres. 1971—72, Outstanding Dietitian 1973—74), Tenn. Dietetic Assn. (pres. 1973—74, Outstanding Dietitian 1973—74), Omicron Nu. Democrat. Presbyterian. Avocations: reading, sports. Home: 7112 Stockton Dr Knoxville TN 37909-2534

REYNOLDS, MARK ALLAN, periodontist, educator; s. Jack Kile and Nancy Ann Reynolds; m. Mary Elizabeth Kenney; children: Gregory, Jessica, Patrick. MA, U. Md., Balt., 1982, DDS, 1986, cert., 1995, PhD, 1999. Diplomate Am. Bd. Periodontology. Assoc. prof. U. Md., Balt., 2000—, dir. postdoctoral residency in periodontics, 2001—. Contbr. articles to profl. jours. Recipient Postdoctoral Rsch. award, Am. Coll. Dentists, Md. sect., 1995, Spl. Svc. award, National Inst. on Aging, N.I.H., 1984, Walter Nicolai prize in biomed. gerontology, Am. Aging Assn., 1984. Mem.: ADA, Md. State Dental Assn. (del. 1995—), Am. Assn. Dental Rsch. (counselor 1995—), Am. Acad. Periodontology (Young Investigator fellow 1995), Omicron Kappa Upsilon. Office: U Md Dental Sch 666 W Baltimore St Baltimore MD 21201

REYNOLDS, MARSHALL TRUMAN, printing company executive; b. Logan, W.Va., Feb. 21, 1937; s. Douglas Vernon and Dorothy Lee (Dingess) R.; m. Shirley Ann Earwood, Mar. 24, 1968; children: Jack Marine, Douglas Vernon. Student, Marshall U., 1956-58. Sales mgr. Chapman Printing Co., Huntington, W.Va., 1960-61, gen. mgr., 1961-64, pres., gen. mgr. Huntington, Parkersburg and Charleston, W.Va., Lexington, Ky., 1964—. Chmn. bd. McCorkle Machine & Engring., Huntington, KYOWVA Corrugated Container, Huntington, Stationers, Inc., Huntington, Charleston, Radisson Hotel, Huntington, Huntington Indsl. Corp., Champion Industries Inc., Am. Babbit Bearing Inc.; bd. dirs. Guyan Machinery, Huntington, United Huntington Industries, Persinger Supply Co., Prichard, W.Va., First Guaranty Bank, Hammond, La., Banc One WV Corp., Charleston, W.Va. Bd. dirs. W.Va. Roundtable, Huntington, 1989—, W. Va. Bus. Found., Huntington, 1989—, Boys and Girls Club, Huntington, 1989—, Huntington United Way, 1989—; mem. Gov.'s Task Force on Children, Youth and Families, 1989—; guest lectr. various high schs. on free enterprise. Named Outstanding Small Businessman of Yr., Huntington Jaycees, 1983, Business Man of Yr. Jaycess, 1988. Mem. Huntington C. of C., Western Star Lodge (Guyandotte, W.Va.). Republican. Baptist. Avocation: raising cattle. Home: 1130 13th St Huntington WV 25701-3632 Office: Chapman Printing Co 2450 1st Ave Huntington WV 25703-1218

REYNOLDS, MARY EVELYN LIVERMORE, addiction counselor; b. Williamsport, Pa., May 25, 1949; d. Harry Leroy and Anna Margaret (Dinsmore); children: Terry Joe, Robert Allan, Paul Harry. BA, Lycoming Coll., 1980; DDiv, Religious Sci. Sem., 1993. Ordained minister Religious Sci. Ch.; cert. addictions counselor, cert. forensic counselor, cert. clin. supr. Exec. dir. Freedom Unlimited, Hulmeville, Pa.; dir. drug and alcohol Greater Phila. Psychol. Ctr. Human resource cons. Substitute min. Religious Sci. Ch.; exec. dir. Spiritual Learning Ctr. Home: PO Box 145 Mc Ewensville PA 17749

REYNOLDS, MICHAEL TIMOTHY, lawyer; b. N.Y.C., June 29, 1968; s. Timothy John and Patricia Mary Reynolds. AB in History magna cum laude, Dartmouth Coll., 1990; MPhil in Medieval History, Cambridge (Eng.) U., 1991; JD, Yale U., 1995. Bar: N.Y. 1996, U.S. Dist. Ct. (so. and ea. dists.) N.Y. 1996. Law clk. to Hon. Diarmuid F. O'Scannlain, U.S. Ct. Appeals for 9th Cir., Portland, Oreg., 1995—96; litig. assoc. Cravath, Swaine & Moore, N.Y.C., 1996—. Exec. editor Yale Law Jour., 1994-95. Mem. bd. proprietors The Dartmouth, Inc., Hanover, NH, 2001—. Keasbey Found. scholar Cambridge U., 1990-92. Mem.: Assn. Bar City NY, Phi Beta Kappa. Office: Cravath Swaine & Moore 825 8th Ave Fl 38 New York NY 10019-7475

REYNOLDS, MICHEAL JOHN, accountant; b. Leavenworth, Kans., Oct. 30, 1958; s. David Myron and Elizabeth Ann (Lauer) R. BS in Acctg., U. Kans., 1982; MBA, Rockhurst Coll., 1987. Computer operator Midwest Data Processing, Kansas City, Mo., 1977-79; asst. controller Fixtures Furniture, 1982-86; sr. cost acct. FMC Corp., Lawrence, Kans., 1986-90, sr. internal auditor Chgo., 1990-92; contr. Mid-Am. Plastics, Inc., Gardner, Kans., 1992-93, Reliable Cap and Closure Inc., Olathe, 1994-98, Devine Lighting, Dvsn. Hubbell Lighting, N. Kansas City, 1998-2000; controller Construction Design Inc., 2000—. Mem. MBA Network (treas. 1988-89). Republican. Roman Catholic. Home: 5522 Apache Ct Lenexa KS 66226 Office: Contruction Design Inc 5621 Kansas Ave Kansas City KS 66106 E-mail: mreynold@watkins.dillingham.com.

REYNOLDS, NANCY REMICK, editor, writer; b. San Antonio, July 15, 1938; d. Donald Worthington and Edith (Remick) R.; m. Brian Rushton, June 25, 1983; 1 child, Ehren T. Park. Student, Sch. Am. Ballet, 1951, 53-61, Juilliard Sch. Music, 1957, Martha Graham Sch. Contemporary Dance, N.Y.C., 1959, U. Sorbonne, Paris, 1962; BA in Art History, Columbia U.,

1965; postgrad., Goethe Inst., Prien, 1972, U. Chgo. and Sarah Lawrence Coll., 1974-77. Dancer N.Y.C. Ballet, 1956-61; editor Praeger Pubs., N.Y.C., 1965-71; dir. rsch. book Choreography by George Balanchine: A Catalogue of Works, N.Y., 1979-82 (pub. 1983); dir. rsch. pub. TV spl. Balanchine, N.Y., 1983-84; assoc. editor Internat. Ency. of Dance, (pub. 1998); dir. rsch. The George Balanchine Found., N.Y.C., 1994—. Co-pub. Twentieth-Century Dance in Slides, 1978-93. Author: Repertory in Review: Forty Years of the New York City Ballet, 1977 (De la Torre Bueno prize 1977), The Dance Catalog: A Complete Guide to Today's World of Dance, 1979, co-author: In Performance,1980, Dance Classics, 1991 (rec. for teen age N.Y. Pub Libr.); editor: Movement and Metaphor: Four Centuries of Ballet (Lincoln Kirstein), 1970, Dance as a Theatre Art: Source Readings in Dance History from 1581 to the Present (Selma Jeanne Cohen), 1974, School of Classical Dance (V. Kostrovitskaya and A. Pisarev), 1978; contbr. (book) Ballet: Bias and Belief, "Three Pamphlets Collected" and Other Dance Writings of Lincoln Kirstein, 1983, also numerous articles and revs. to Dancing Times, Ballet News, Playbill, ArtsLine, Dancemag., Town & Country, Connoisseur, N.Y. Times, Ency. Britannica., Ency. of N.Y.C., others. Ford Found. Travel and Study grantee, 1974; Mary Duke Biddle Found. grantee, 1990. Mem. Dance Critics Assn. (pres. 1986-87), Soc. Dance History Scholars, Soc. for Dance Rsch., Am. Soc. for Theatre Rsch., European Assn. Dance Historians, Internat. Fedn. for Theatre Rsch. in affiliation with Societe Internat. des Bibliotheques et Musees des Arts du Spectacle, Phi Beta Kappa. Home: 9 Prospect Park W Brooklyn NY 11215-1758 E-mail: bnr9ppw@pipeline.com.

REYNOLDS, PETER JAMES, physicist; b. N.Y.C., Nov. 19, 1949; s. Rudolph and Lydia Mary (Schanzer) R.; m. Louise Perini, Aug. 7, 1982. AB in Physics, U. Calif., Berkeley, 1971; PhD, MIT, 1979. Rsch. assoc., lectr. Boston U., 1978, asst. rsch. prof., 1979-83; mem. sci. staff Nat. Resource for Computation in Chemistry Lawrence Berkeley Lab., U. Calif., 1980-81, mem. rsch. staff materials and chem. scis. divsn., 1982-88; vis. scientist NEC Fundamental Rsch. Lab., Kawasaki, Japan, 1986; vis. rsch. chemist U. Calif., Berkeley, 1988; adj. assoc. prof. dept. chemistry San Francisco State U., 1988-91; program mgr. Office Naval Rsch., 1988—. Vis. scientist Inst. for Theoretical Physics, Santa Barbara, 1994; rsch. prof. Georgetown U., Washington, 1996—; lectr. and rschr. in field of statis., chem. and computational physics and Monte Carlo Methods; program mgr. atomic and molecular physics, laser cooling, Bose-Einstein condensates, quantum coherence and control, atom lasers, quantum computing. Editor: On Clusters and Clustering: From Atoms to Fractals, 1993; co-author: Monte Carlo Methods in Ab Initio Quantum Chemistry, 1994; contbr. articles to profl. jours., also rev. articles, book chpts. NATO lectr., NSF fellow, 1971-74, IBM fellow, 1975; Lawrence Berkeley Lab. grantee, 1982-83. Fellow Am. Phys. Soc. (chmn. membership com. 1998, nominating com. Divsn. Computational Physics and Forum on Physics and Soc. 1996-97, exec. com. Divsn. Computational Physics 1992-96, 2002—); mem. Materials Rsch. Soc., Optical Soc. Am., N.Y. Acad. Scis., Phi Beta Kappa, Sigma Xi. Office: ONR Phys Scis Divsn 800 N Quincy St Arlington VA 22217-5660 E-mail: pjr@ohm.nrl.navy.mil.

REYNOLDS, RICHARD CLYDE, physician, educator; b. Saugerties, N.Y., Sept. 2, 1929; s. Thomas Watson and Myrtle Edith (Myer) R.; m. Mary Jane Beck, July 7, 1954; children— Karen Sue, Stephanie Ann, Wayne Thomas. BSc, Rutgers U., 1949; MD, Johns Hopkins U., 1953; DSc (hon.), Hahnemann U., 1988, N.Y. Med. Coll., 1992, Uniformed Svcs. U. Health Sci., 1995, U. Medicine and Dentistry N.J., 1997, SUNY Downstate Med. Ctr. Coll. Medicine, 2000. Diplomate Am. Bd. Internal Medicine. Intern Johns Hopkins Hosp., Balt., 1953-54, asst. resident, 1954-55, 57-58, fellow in infectious disease, 1958-59; practice medicine specializing in internal medicine Frederick, Md., 1959-68; mem. faculty U. Fla. Coll. Medicine, 1968-78, prof. medicine, prof., chmn. dept. community health and family medicine, 1970-78; prof. medicine, prof. environ. and community medicine, dean U. Medicine and Dentistry N.J., Robert Wood Johnson Med. Sch., 1978-87; sr. v.p. acad. affairs U. Medicine and Dentistry N.J., 1984-87; exec. v.p. Robert Wood Johnson Found., 1987-96; mem. faculty U. Fla. Coll. Medicine, Gainesville, 1997—. Mem. Liaison Com. on Med. Edn., 1982-87. Co-author: The Health of a Rural County: Perspectives and Problems, 1976, Patient Wishes and Physician Obligations, 1978; co-editor: On Doctoring: Stories, Poems, Essays, 1991, 3d edit., 2001; contbr. articles to med. publs. Sr. asst. surgeon USPHS, 1955-57. Mem. ACP, AMA. Office: U Fla Coll Medicine PO Box 100277 Gainesville FL 32610-0277 E-mail: rreyn63922@aol.com.

REYNOLDS, ROBERT EDGAR, academic administrator, physician; b. Pontiac, Mich., June 3, 1938; s. Arthur James and Jean Lucille (Thompson) R.; m. Barbara Fisher, June 11, 1961 (div. May 1980); children: Jennifer Robin, Lisa Anne; m. Erika Renate Forte, July 25, 1981; children: Timothy William, Julia Renate. BA, Yale U., 1960; MD, Harvard U., 1964; MPH, Johns Hopkins U., 1967, DrPH, 1970. Med. dir. Chonic Disease Hosp., Balt. City Hosps., 1968-70; assoc. prof. medicine and community medicine, assoc. dean Med. Coll. Ga., Augusta, 1970-73; med. dir. br. hosps. Rush Presbyn. St. Lukes Med. Ctr., Chgo., 1973-81, assoc. prof. internal medicine, prof. preventive medicine, 1973-81, med. dir., 1975-81; assoc. dean, assoc. prof. medicine Johns Hopkins U. Sch. Medicine, Balt., 1981-88; sr. assoc. v.p. for health scis., prof. medicine U. Va. Health Sci. Ctr., Charlottesville, 1988-96; prof. health evaluation scis. U. Va., 1995—, dir. divsn. clin. info., 1997—, vice provost for health scis., 1995—99, v.p., chief info. officer, 1999—. Sec.-treas. Med. Adminstrs. Conf., 1979-80, pres., 1981. Served to capt. USAR, 1965-73. Fellow ACP, Am. Coll. Preventive Medicine; mem. AMA, Assn. Am. Med. Colls. (assoc., chmn. group on instnl. planning 1988-89), Found. for Health Svcs. Rsch. (nat. adv. com.), Assn. for Health Svc. Rsch., Nat. Libr. Medicine (biomed. rev. com. 1992-95), Computer-based Patient Record Inst. (bd. dirs. 1992—). Office: U Va 108 Cresap Rd Charlottesville VA 22903-1710 Fax: (804) 924-3579. E-mail: rreynolds@virginia.edu.

REYNOLDS, ROBERT HUGH, lawyer; b. St. Louis, Jan. 3, 1937; s. Leslie A. and Rebecca (McWaters) R.; m. Carol Jemison, Apr. 8, 1961; children: Stephen H., Cynthia C., Laura M. BA, Yale U., 1958; JD, Harvard U., 1964. Assoc. Barnes & Thornburg, Indpls., 1964-70, ptnr., 1970—, chmn. bus. dept., 1983-91; chmn. internat. practice group, 1992—. Co-chmn., editor Comml. Real Estate Financing for Ind. Attys., 1968; vice-chmn., co-editor Advising Ind. Businesses, 1974; chmn., editor Counseling Ltd. Businesses, 1981, The Purchase and Sale of a Business, 1987. Bd. dirs. Crossroads Am. Coun. Boy Scouts Am., v.p., 1971-75, pres., 1987-89; v.p. Area 4 Ctrl. Region Boy Scouts Am., 1989-92, pres., 1992-93, pres. Ctrl. Region, 1993-96, Nat. Exec. Bd., 1993— (Silver Buffalo award); bd. dirs. Family Svc. Assn. Indpls., 1974-81, pres., 1978-80; bd. dirs. Family Svc. Am., 1979-88, Greater Indpls. Fgn. Trade Zone, 1987-2000, Indpls. Conv. and Visitors Assn., 1989-2000, Indpls. Econ. Devel. Corp., 1983-99, Greater Indpls. Progress Com., 1986-2000, exec. com., vice chmn. (Charles L. Whistler award); hon. trustee Children's Mus. Indpls., trustee, 1988-96, chmn., 1992-94; bd. dirs. Indpls. Downtown Inc., chmn., 1996-99; bd. gov. Legacy Fund, 1992—, v.chmn., 2000-; bd. dirs. Noyes Mem. Found., Japan-Am. Soc. Ind., pres., 1994—; vice chmn. TerraLex, 1996— Named Hon. Consul Gen. of Japan, 1999—. Fellow Ind. Bar Found., Indpls. Bar Found.; mem. ABA, Ind. Bar Assn. (chmn. corp., banking and bus. law sect. 1981-82, chmn. internat. sect. 1994-96), Internat. Bar Assn., Indpls. Bar Assn., Greater Indpls. C. of C. (bd. dirs., sec. 2000—), Econ. Club Indpls. (bd. dirs.). Clubs: Univ., Skyline (Indpls.). Lodges: Kiwanis. Republican. Office: Barnes & Thornburg 11 S Meridian St Indianapolis IN 46204-3535 E-mail: rreynolds@btlaw.com.

REYNOLDS, ROBERT JOEL, economist, consultant; b. Indpls., May 13, 1944; s. Joel Burr and Betty (Schimpf) R.; m. Lucinda Margaret Lewis, May 27, 1979; children: Joel, Sarah. BSBA in Fin., Northwestern U., 1965, PhD in Econs., 1970. Asst. prof. econs. U. Idaho, Moscow, 1969-73, assoc. prof., 1973-75; asst. dir, sr. economist econ. policy office Dept. Justice, Washington, 1973-81; sr. economist, v.p. ICF Inc., 1981-87, sr. v.p., 1987-91; exec. v.p., prin. Econsult Corp., 1991-96; chmn., exec. v.p. Econsult of D.C., Inc., 1997; chmn. Competition Econs., Inc., 1997—. Vis. assoc. prof. U. Calif., Berkeley, 1976-77, Cornell U., Ithaca, N.Y., 1981. Reviewer: NSF, Rand Jour. of Econs., Internat. Econ. Rev., Internat. Jour. Indsl. Orgn., Jour. Indsl. Econs., Am. Econ. Rev.; mem. editorial bd. Managerial and Decision Econs.; contbr. numerous papers to profl. jours. Recipient Dow Jones award Wall St. Jour., 1965; AT&T grantee, 1971-72, Brookings Instl. grantee, 1968-69; NDEA fellow, 1965-69. Mem. AAAS, IEEE (computer sect.), SIAM, Am. Math. Assn., Am. Econ. Assn., Econometric Soc., Royal Econ. Soc., Am. Statis. Assn., European Assn. for Rsch. in Indsl. Econs., Soc. for the Promotion of Econ. Theory, Math. Assn. Am. Congregationalist. Home: PO Box 59712 Potomac MD 20859-9712 Office: Competition Econs Inc 4800 Montgomery Ln Bethesda MD 20814

REYNOLDS, ROGER LEE, composer, educator; b. Detroit, July 18, 1934; s. George Arthur and Katherine Adelaide (Butler) R.; m. Karen Jeanne Hill, Apr. 11, 1964; children: Erika Lynn, Wendy Claire. BSE in Physics, U. Mich., 1957, MusB in Music Lit., 1960, MusM in Composition, 1961. Assoc. prof. U. Calif. San Diego, La Jolla, 1969-73, founding dir. Ctr. Music Expt. and Related Rsch., 1972-77, prof., 1973—; George Miller prof. U. Ill., 1971—. Vis. prof. Yale U., New Haven, 1981; sr. rsch. fellow ISAM, Bklyn. Coll., 1985; Valentine prof. Amherst (Mass.) Coll., 1988; Rothschild composer in residence Peabody Conservatory of Music, 1992-93. Author: MIND MODELS: New Forms of Musical Experience, 1975, A Searcher's Path: A Composer's Ways, 1987, A Jostled Silence: Contemporary Japanese Musical Thought, 1992-93, Form and Method: Composing Music, 2002; first Dolby Digital 5.1 DVD release of custom-designed, multichannel classical compositions: WATERSHED, Mode Records, 1998; contbr. numerous articles and revs. to profl. jours. Bd. dirs. Am. Music. Ctr., Meet the Composer, Fromm Found. Harvard U.; mem. bd. govs. Inst. Current World Affairs; co-founder ONCE festivals, 1960. Recipient Koussevitzky Internat. Rec. award, 1970, citation Nat. Inst. Arts and Letters, 1971, NEA awards, 1975, 78, 79, 86, Pulitzer prize for music, 1989; sr. fellow Inst. Studies in Am. Music, 1985, fellow Inst. Current World Affairs, Rockefeller Found., Guggenheim Found.; Fulbright scholar. Office: U Calif San Diego Dept Music 0326 La Jolla CA 92093

REYNOLDS, RONALD, research scientist, educator; b. Chicago Heights, Ill., May 17, 1943; s. James Lonnie and Elsie Gerhardt Reynolds; m. Carla Strohmeyer Reynolds; children: Julie Elizabeth, Suzanne Emilie. BS, U. of Illinoinois, Champaign, IL, 1965; MS, U. of Wis., Madison, WI, 1967, PhD, 1971. Nas-nrc rsch. assoc. Goddard Space Flight Ctr., Greenbelt, Md., 1971—73; rsch. assoc. U. of Wisconsin-Madison, Madison, Wis., 1973—76, asst. scientist, 1976—81, assoc. scientist, 1981—87, sr. scientist physics, 1987—96, prof. of astronomy, 1996—. Grantee Rsch. Grants, NASA, 1974, 2002. Mem.: Internat. Astron. Union, Am. Astron. Soc. Achievements include first to Developed unique high sensitivity spectrometers for astronomy; discovery of Detected and characterized the diffuse ionized component of our galaxy's interstellar hydrogen. Office: Department of Astronomy 475 N Charter Street Madison WI 53706

REYNOLDS, SALLIE BLACKBURN, artist, civic volunteer; b. Kansas City, Mo., Feb. 9, 1940; d. Anton and Sallie Churchill (Blackburn) Zajic; m. Jeffrey Calhoun Loker, Mar. 25, 1959 (div. May 1965); children: Toni Lynne, Michael David, Kathryn Lee Loker Simpson; m. Everett Lee Reynolds, Mar. 29, 1969 (dec. Sept. 1992). Student, William Jewell Coll., 1959, BA magna cum laude, 1977; student, U. Mo., Kansas City, 1966-67, Kansas City Art Inst., 1966-70; Cert., Famous Artists Sch., 1965. Cert. tchr., Mo. From clk. to sec. Hdqrs. Strategic Air Command, Offutt AFB, Omaha, 1960-62; sec., wage and hr. law enforcement asst., wage-hr. divsn. U.S. Dept. of Labor, Kansas City, 1963-68, exec. sec. to regional manpower adminstr., 1968-71, spl. asst. to regional exec. com., 1971-72, mgmt. asst. Office of Regional Dir., 1972-73; from. clk. to sec. air carrier dist. office FAA, 1978-81; from clk. typist to sec. regional personnel officer Bur. of Reclamation, U.S. Dept. of Interior, Boulder City, Nev., 1982-84; editorial asst. div. of planning Bur. of Reclamation, 1984-86; owner, operator B-Bar-L Wandering Star Ranch (registered angus and horses, beefalo, various real estate), Versailles and Stover, Mo., 1989—. Editor newsletter Laurie Fine Art, 1989-90; designer historic landmark plaque Clay County, Mo.; designer hist. painting for annual Dogwood Festival pageants Camden County, Mo., 1994. Ofcl. commr., sec., corr. Clay County (Mo.) Bicentennial Commn., 1974-76; mem. Ozark Brush and Palette, Inc., Camdenton, Mo., 1987—, editor newsletter, 1988-89; v.p., sec., life mem. Clay County Hist. Soc., 1972—, active Nat. Wildlife Fedn. Recipient 1st Pl. award Nat. Soc. DAR Am. Heritage Contest in oil/acrylic painting, 1990, 3d pl., 1991, 1st pl. gold award 1992, 1st pl. award profl. photography Laurie Fine Art Show, 1991, miscellaneous local art show awards, 1988—. Mem. Nat. Soc. DAR (pub. rels. chmn., rec. sec., archives chmn., corr. sec. Niangua chpt. Camdenton 1987—, Eldon Mo. chpt. 1999), Nat. Oil and Acrylic Painters Soc., Phi Epsilon of Phi Beta Kappa, Versailles Saddle Club, Mo. Paint Horse Club (sec. 1998). Presbyterian. Avocations: horses, art, history, cats, needlework, music, photography. Home and Office: B-Bar-L Wandering Star Ranch 23688 S 135 Hwy Stover MO 65078

REYNOLDS, SAMUEL D., JR. metallurgical engineer, consultant; b. Upper Darby, Pa., Dec. 19, 1931; s. Samuel Dornon and Winifred (Rumble) Reynolds; m. Barbara Jean Charles (div. Apr. 1984); children: Elizabeth, William, Alexander, Samuel; m. Angela Corvelli, July 19, 1984. BSMetE, Lehigh U., 1953. Cert. profl. engr. metall. engring., Pa., profl. engr. corrosion engring., Ca. Various engring. positions Westinghouse Electric Corp., Lester, Pa., 1953—77, Tampa, Fla., 1977—80, Orlando, 1986—94; cons. Nickel Devel. Inst., Toronto, Canada, 1996—. Lectr. in field. Contbr. articles to profl. jours. Lt. USNR, 1954—57, lead reactor engr. USNR, 1980—86. Fellow: ASME, Am. Welding Soc., Am. Soc. Metals. Achievements include patents in field. Avocation: music. Home and Office: 1003 Neely St Oviedo FL 32765

REYNOLDS, SCOTT WALTON, academic administrator; b. Summit, N.J., July 15, 1941; s. Clark Leonard and Shirley (Hill) R.; m. Margaret Ann Johnson, July 5, 1969; children: Jane, Amy, David. BA, Trinity Coll., Hartford, Conn., 1963; MBA, Harvard U., 1965. Mng. dir. corp. staff Bankers Trust Co., N.Y.C., 1967-94; asst. to the pres. St. Peter's Coll., Jersey City, 1994-96, Trinity Coll., Hartford, Conn., 1996-98, sec., 1998—. Chmn. fund campaign Montclair (N.J.) ARC, 1974; chmn. bus. and fraternal group Montclair Bicentennial Com., 1976; bd. fellows Trinity Coll., 1982-88, trustee, 1992—, sec., exec. com., 1993—. 1st lt. U.S. Army, 1965-67. Recipient 150th Anniversary award Trinity Coll., 1978, Alumni medal for Excellence, 1988, Pres.' Leadership medal, 1993. Mem. Montclair Jaycees (treas. 1973), Trinity Coll. Alumni Assn. N.Y. (pres. 1972-73) Clubs: Harvard (N.Y.C.). Episcopalian. Office: Trinity Coll Office of Pres 300 Summit St Hartford CT 06106-3100

REYNOLDS, SHARON BARBARA, education educator; b. Cleve., Sept. 30, 1942; d. William Ellsworth O'Brien and Barbara Alice Farquer; 1 child Matthew Alan. BS in Phys. Edn., U. Ariz., 1964; MS in Phys. Edn., So. Ill. U., 1965; MA in Counseling, Tex. Woman's U., 1976, PhD in Edn1. Psychology, 1983. Grad. asst. in phys. edn. So. Ill. U., 1964—65; instr. phys. edn. Northwestern U., Evanston, 1965—67; tchr. Maine East H.S., Des Plaines, 1967—70; field dir. Ariz. Cactus-Pine Girl Scout Coun., Inc., Phoenix, 1970—74; exec. dir. Scottsdale (Ariz.) Girls Club, 1974—76; grad. asst. dept. psychology and philosophy Tex. Woman's U., Denton, 1976—79, programmer, analyst, 1980—82, grad. asst. dept. math., physics and computer sci., 1980—81, adj. instr., 1981—83; systems engr. Electronic Data Systems, Dallas, 1979—80; vis. asst. prof. dept. computer sci. Tex. Christian U., Ft. Worth, 1984—85, prof., 1987—; dir. counseling svcs. St. Andrews Cath. Ch., 1985—87. Cons. U.S. Govt. Office Pers. Mgmt., Dallas, 1985, U.S. Govt. Social Security Office, Ft. Worth, 1985, Gumm Industries, Ft. Worth, 1985, NSF Grant, 1988—89, Tex. Advanced Rsch. Program Grant, 1991, S.W. Med. Found. Mobility Found. Grant, 1991—92, NIH, 1992—94; program evaluation cons. Mus. Sci. and History NSF Grant, 1992—94; session chair Nat. Ednl. Computing Conf., 1988; mem. nat. rev. panel EDUCOM/NCRIPTAL Higher Edn. Software Awards Program, 1989; statis. cons. State of Tex. Block Grant, 1990; presenter in field. Author: Learning is a Verb, 2000; contbr. articles to profl. jours.; reviewer: jours. in field. Grantee, Apple Computer Corp., 1988, NSF, 1992—96, 1993—96, Exxon Edn. Found., 1993—94, 1994—95, 1995—96, Bank of Am., 1997—99. Mem.: Jean Piaget Soc., Am. Ednl. Rsch. Assn. (sec. chair Chaos and Complexity SIG 2001—). Avocations: golf, fly fishing, reading. Office: Tex Christian U PO Box 297900 Fort Worth TX 76129 E-mail: s.reynolds@tcu.edu.

REYNOLDS, STEPHEN CURTIS, hospital administrator; b. Little Rock, May 1, 1946; married. BA, Ark. State U., 1968; MA, Washington U., 1972. Adminstrv. resident Baptist Meml. Health Care System, Memphis, 1971-72, adminstrv. asst., 1972-75, asst. v.p., 1975-80, v.p., 1980-86, sr. v.p., 1986-89, exec. v.p., 1992, Baptist Meml. Hosp., Memphis, 1990-92, pres., 1992—. With Armed Forces, 1968-70. Mem. Tenn. Hosp. Assn. (chmn., 1989-90, bd. dirs. 1986-91). Home: 461 Princeton Wood Cv Memphis TN 38117-1907 Office: Bapt Meml Hosp 350 N Humphreys Blvd Memphis TN 38120*

REYNOLDS, STEPHEN H. insurance consultant; b. Mt. Kisco, N.Y., Nov. 2, 1951; s. Henry C. Reynolds, Lorraine M. Reynolds; m. Kate N. Niver, May 12, 1973; children: Gregory, Christine. B in Engring., SUNY, 1973. Cert. assoc.in risk mgmt. Ins. Industry Am., 1980, assoc.in loss control mgmt. Ins. Industry Am., 1985. Contbr. articles to profl. jours. Youth Leader United Methodist Church, Simsbury, CT, 1997—99. Mem.: Theatre Guild of Simsbury. Methodist. Avocations: writing novels, guitar, acting, singing. Home: 30 Fox Den Rd. West Simsbury CT 06092 Office: Travelers Insurance Co. 300 Windsor St. Hartford CT 06120 Business E-Mail: shreynol@travelers.com.

REYNOLDS, THOMAS M. congressman; b. Sept. 3, 1950; m. Donna Reynolds. Student, Kent (Ohio) State U. Pres. T.M. Reynolds Ins. Agy.; rep. Dist. 147 N.Y. State Assembly, 1988-98, ranking rep. mem. housing com., mem. banking com., mem. corrections com.; mem. U.S. Congress from 27th N.Y. dist., 1999—; mem. rules com., adminstrn. com.; dep. majority whip in Ho. Leadership. Exec. asst. N.Y. State Assemblyman Ronald Tillis; councilman Town of Concord, N.Y.; clk. Erie County Legis.; legis. asst. to minority Rep. leader, 1987. Mem. NRA, Southtowns Walleye Assn., Masons. Address: 10 E Main St Victor NY 14564 Office: Ho of Reps 413 Cannon Hob Washington DC 20515-0001*

REYNOLDS, TOM, communications executive; b. Torrington, Conn., Aug. 20, 1950; s. Theodore Joseph and Lena (Cirillo) Bruttomesso; m. Linda Perlini, May 21, 1977; children: Tricia, Kimberly. Diploma, Leland Powers Sch. Radio, 1970. News and sports dir. Sta. WOWW, Naugatuck, Conn., 1970-72; reporter, anchor Sta. WRCQ, Farmington, 1972-73; sales rep. Sta. WOWW, Waterbury, 1973-74; ops. mgr. Sta. WIOF, 1974-77; gen. mgr. Full of Baloney Corp., 1977-81; sports dir. Sta. WPOP, Hartford, Conn., 1981-83, news dir., 1983-86; comm. dir. YMCA Met. Hartford, 1986-99, v.p. comms. & fund raising, 1999—2002, v.p. devel. svcs., 2002—. Voting mem. Conn. Soc. to Prvent Blindness, Middletown, Conn., 1984—; trustee Martin Luther King Jr. Youth Found., Hartford, 1984-88; trainer YMCA of the U.S.A., Chgo., 1987—. Vol. Boy Scouts Am., Newington, Conn., 1987-88. Mem. Internat. Assn. Bus. Communicators (Bronze Quill 1988, 95-99, 2000, Silver Quill 1997-99, 2000, bd. dirs. Conn. chpt. 1993-94, 98-99, Award of Comm. Excellence 1997, 2001, Bronze Anvil award 1998, Iris award 1999), Pub. Rels. Soc. Am. (Mercyru award 2001, 2002). Roman Catholic. Avocations: sports, reading, golf. Office: Hartford YMCA 160 Jewell St Hartford CT 06103-2006

REYNOLDS, VALRAE, museum curator; b. San Francisco, Dec. 18, 1944; d. Ralph Stanley and Valberta May (Eversole) R.; m. Richard Lee Huffman, Sept. 14, 1974; children: Elizabeth Anne, Margaret Lee. BA in Fine Arts with honors, U. Calif., Davis, 1966; MA, NYU, 1969. Asst. curator Asian collections Newark Mus., 1969-70, curator Asian collections, 1970—. Cons. SITES Exhbn., 1988; adj. prof. art history Columbia U., 1996; lectr., presenter in field. Author: From the Sacred Realm, Treasures of Tibetan Art from the Newark Museum, 1999; editor: Newark Mus. Quar., 1976, Tibetan Jour., 1976, Asia Soc., 1977, Arts of Asia, 1989, Explore Tibet, 1992; contbr. over 36 articles and revs. to profl. jours.; prodr. multimedia prodns. in field. Grantee NEA, NEH, 1972-74, 82-83, 85-86, 88-91, 89-92, 99, J. Paul Getty grantee, 1986, 89-91, Travel grantee Asian Cultural Coun., 1989. Mem. Japan Soc. (art com.). Office: Newark Mus PO Box 540 49 Washington St Newark NJ 07102-3176

REYNOLDS, VERNE, musician, retired music educator; b. July 18, 1926; MusB, U. Cin., 1950; MusM, U. Wis., 1951. Musician Cin. Symphony Orch., 1947-50; instr. U. Wis., Madison, 1950-53; asst. prof. Ind. U., 1954-59; prof. Eastman Sch. Music, U. Rochester, N.Y., 1959-95, prof. emeritus, 1995—. Home and Office: 102 Southern Pkwy Rochester NY 14618-1042

REYNOLDS, WARREN JAY, retired publisher; b. Chgo., Mar. 10, 1918; s. Bradford Jay and Bessie Pearl (Bon Durant) R.; m. Mary Ellen Seaman, June 29, 1940 (dec. Sept. 1995); children: William, Nancy, David, Linda (dec.). BA, DePauw U., 1939. Retail salesman Gen. Foods Corp., Chgo., 1939-41; advt. salesman Capper Publs., 1941-42, 45-47; with Parade Publs., Inc., N.Y.C., 1947—; pub., dir. Parade Publs., Inc. (Parade Mag.), 1967-83; pub. emeritus Parade Publs., Inc., 1983—. Served to lt. comdr. USN, 1942-45. Recipient Alumnus of Yr. award DePauw U., 1968 Mem.: Venice Yacht (Fla.). Republican. Home: 281 Hidden Bay Dr Unit 103 Osprey FL 34229-6606 Office: 711 3rd Ave New York NY 10017-4014

REYNOLDS, WILLIAM ARTHUR, retired physician, educator; b. Havre, Mont., Apr. 20, 1930; s. F. Gordon and Nettie Elizabeth (Porter) R.; m. M. Joanne Flanagan, July 27, 1930; children: Susan Ballinger, Janet, James. BS, U. Mont., 1952; MD, Washington U., St. Louis, 1956; MS, U. Minn., Rochester and Mpls., 1964. Diplomate Am. Bd. Internal Medicine. Intern U. Minn., Mpls., 1956-57; fellow in internal medicine Mayo Clinic Found., Rochester, 1957-59, 61-63; asst. to the staff Mayo Clinic, 1963; staff internist Western Mont. Clinic, Missoula, 1963—2000; from asst. prof. to clin. prof. medicine U. Wash., Seattle, 1974—2000; chief med. officer Invizeon Corp., Missoula, 2001—. Pres. Western Mont. Clinic, 1975; pres. staff St. Patrick Hosp., Missoula, 1974-75, 87-88. Contbr. articles to profl. jours. Vol. health policy fellow U.S. Senator, Washington, 1992; bd. dirs. Action Internat. Medicine Inc., treas., 1992—; bd. dirs. ACP-ASIM Found., Internat. Heart Inst. of Mont., 1996—; adv. bd. Eurasian Med. Edn. Program, 1998—. Recipient Disting. Alumni award U. Mont., 1997. Master: ACP (pres. 1997—98, regent 1990—99, Laureate award Mont. chpt. 1995, Willard O. Thompson traveling fellow 1970); mem.: Am. Soc. Internal Medicine (Mont. pres. 1976, bd. dirs. 1999—), Kiwanis. Methodist. Avocations: fishing, racquetball, travel, hunting. Home: 429 King St Missoula MT 59801-8607 E-mail: r137@mssl.uswest.net.

REYNOLDS, WILLIAM BRADFORD, lawyer; b. Bridgeport, Conn., June 21, 1942; s. William Glasgow and Nancy Bradford (DuPont) R.; m. Marguerite Lynn Morgan, June 27, 1964 (div. Feb. 1987); children: William Bradford Jr., Melissa Morgan, Kristina DuPont, Wendy Riker; m. Clare Alice Conroy, Aug. 29, 1987 (div. June 2000); 1 child, Linda Matisan; m. Barbara Lynn Wooster, July 15, 2000; children: Courtney Enright, Brooke Ashley. BA, Yale U., 1964; LLB, Vanderbilt U., 1967. Bar: N.Y. 1968, D.C. 1973, U.S. Supreme Ct. 1971. Assoc. Sullivan and Cromwell, N.Y.C., 1967-70; asst. to Solicitor Gen. U.S. Dept. Justice, Washington, 1970-73; ptnr. Shaw, Pittman, Potts & Trowbridge, 1973-81; asst. atty. gen. Civil Rights div. U.S. Dept. Justice, 1981-88, counselor to Atty. Gen., 1987-88; ptnr. Ross & Hardies, 1989-91, Dickstein, Shapiro & Morin, 1991-94, Collier, Shannon, Rill & Scott, 1994-2000, Howrey Simon Arnold & White, Washington, 2000—. Chmn. Archtl. Transp. Barriers Compliance Bd., 1982-84. Editor-in-chief Vanderbilt Law Rev., 1966. Disting. scholar Free Congress Found., 1989-93, Disting. fellow Nat. Legal Ctr. for Pub. Interest, Washington, 1989-90. Mem. ABA, Fed. Bar Assn., D.C. Bar Assn., Order of Coif. Republican. Episcopalian. E-mail: reynoldsw@howrey.com.

REYNOLDS, WILLIAM FRANCIS, mathematics educator; b. Boston, Jan. 31, 1930; s. William Leo and Grace Regina (Devlin) R.; m. Pauline Jane Fitzgerald, Aug. 5, 1962; children— Nancy, Jane. AB summa cum laude, Holy Cross Coll., 1950; A.M., Harvard, 1951, PhD, 1954. Instr. Holy Cross Coll., Worcester, Mass., 1954-55; instr. Mass. Inst. Tech., Cambridge, 1955-57; asst. prof. math. Tufts U., Medford, Mass., 1957-60, assoc. prof., 1960-67, prof., 1967-98, Walker prof. math., 1970-98, prof. emeritus, 1998—. Contbr. articles to math. jours. Mem. Am. Math. Soc. Achievements include research on modular and projective representations of finite groups. Home: 3 Preble Gardens Rd Belmont MA 02478-3460 E-mail: wfr@post.harvard.edu.

REYNOLDS, WILLIAM LEROY, lawyer, educator; b. Balt., July 26, 1945; s. Austin Leroy and Doris (Hill) R.; m. Theodora Hoe, Sept. 3, 1966; children: William, Megan, Sarah AB, Dartmouth Coll., 1967; JD, Harvard U., 1970. Bar: Md. 1972, U.S. Supreme Ct. 1975. Clk. to judge U.S. Dist. Ct. Md., 1970-71; asst. prof. law U. Md., 1971-74, assoc. prof., 1974-77, prof., 1977—. Of counsel Piper, Marbury, Rudnick and Wolfe, 1992—; bd. dirs. Md. Jud. Inst. Author: Judicial Process in a Nutshell, 1980, 2d edit., 1991, Understanding the Conflict of Laws, 1984, 2d edit., 1993, Cases and Materials on Conflict of Laws, 1990. Mem. Am. Law Inst., Md. State Bar Assn., Am. Judicature Soc. Clubs: Serjeants' Inn, Wranglers (Balt.); St. Regis Yacht (Paul Smiths, N.Y.), Hamilton St. Office: U Md Sch Law 500 W Baltimore St Baltimore MD 21201-1701

REYNOLDS, WILLIAM STEPHEN, language educator; b. Nashville, Mar. 23, 1951; s. William Calvin and Jean Loraine Reynolds; m. Jennifer Alison, Dec. 10, 1972 (div. June 1990); children: William Nicholas, Timothy James; m. Cheryl Susan Reynolds, June 13, 1998. BA in English, U. Tenn.; MA in English, Western Ky. U. Tchr. English City H.S., Chattanooga, 1975—83, Hendersonville H.S., 1985—, wrestling and tennis coach, 1985—99. Author: (novels) The Murder of Che Guerara, 1983, The Reich Muting, 2002. Office: Hendersonville High Sch 123 Cherokee Rd Hendersonville TN 37075

REYNOLDS, W(YNETKA) ANN, academic administrator, educator; b. Coffeyville, Kans., Nov. 3, 1937; d. John Ethelbert and Glennie (Beanland) King; m. Thomas H. Kirschbaum; children— Rachel Rebecca, Rex King. BS in Biology-Chemistry, Kans. State Tchrs. Coll., Emporia, 1958; MS in Zoology, U. Iowa, Iowa City, 1960, PhD, 1962; DSc (hon.), Ind. State U., Evansville, 1980; LHD (hon.), McKendree Coll., 1984, U. N.C., Charlotte, 1988, U. Judaism, L.A., 1989, U. Nebr., Kearney, 1992; DSc (hon.), Ball State U., Muncie, Ind., 1985, Emporia (Kans.) State U., 1987; PhD (hon.), Fu Jen Cath. U., Republic of China, 1987; LHD (hon.), U. Nebr., Kearney, 1992, Colgate U., 1993; LHD, No. Mich. U., 1995. Asst. prof. biology Ball State U., Muncie, Ind., 1962-65; asst. prof. anatomy U. Ill. Coll. Medicine, Chgo., 1965-68, assoc. prof. anatomy, 1968-73, rsch. prof. ob-gyn, 1973—, prof. anatomy, 1973—, acting assoc. dean acad. affairs Coll. Medicine, 1977, assoc. vice chancellor, dean grad. coll., 1977-79; provost, v.p. for acad. affairs, prof. ob-gyn. and anatomy Ohio State U., Columbus, 1979-82; chancellor Calif. State Univ. system, Long Beach, 1982-90, prof. biology, 1982-90; chancellor CUNY, 1990-97; pres. U. Ala., Birmingham, 1997—2002. Bd. dirs. Abbott Labs., Maytag, Owens-Corning, Humana, Inc., News-Gasette, Champaign, Ill.; clin. prof. ob-gyn. UCLA, 1985-90; mem. Nat. Rsch. Coun. Com. Undergrad Si. Edn., 1993-97; co-chair Fed. Task Force on Women, Minorities and Handicapped in Sci. and Tech., 1987-90, Pacesetter Program Reform for Secondary Sch. Coll. Bd., 1992-96; adv. bd. Congl. Black Caucus Inst. Sci., Space and Tech., 1987-91. Contbr. chpts. to books, articles to profl. jours; assoc. editor Am. Biology Tchr., 1964-67. Active activities involving edn. and the arts; nat. adv. bd. Inst. Am. Indian Arts, 1992-97; bd. dirs. Lincoln Ctr. Inst., 1993—; trustee Internat. Life Scis. Inst.-Nutrition Found., 1987-2001, Southwest Mus. Recipient Disting. Alumni award Kans. State Tchrs. Coll., 1972, Calif. Gov.'s Award for the Arts for an Outstanding Individual in Arts in Edn., 1989, Prize award Cen. Assn. Obstetricians and Gynecologists, 1968; NSF Predoctoral fellow, 1958-62, Woodrow Wilson Hon. fellow, 1958. Fellow ACOG; mem. AAAS, Perinatal Rsch. Soc., Soc. Gynecol. Investigation (sec./treas. 1980-83, pres. 1992-93), Nat. Assn. Systems Heads (pres. 1987-88), Sigma Xi. Office: Ctr for Cmty Outreach Devel Univ Ala 933 19th St S Birmingham AL 35294-2041

REYNOLDSON, WALTER WARD, retired state supreme court chief justice, lawyer; b. St. Edward, Nebr., May 17, 1920; s. Walter Scorer and Mabel Matilda (Sallach) R.; m. Janet Aline Mills, Dec. 24, 1942 (dec. 1986); children: Vicki, Robert; m. Patricia A. Frey, June 3, 1989. BA, State Tchrs. Coll., 1942; JD, U. Iowa, 1948; LLD (hon.), Simpson Coll., 1983, Drake U., 1987. Bar: Iowa 1948. Justice Iowa Supreme Ct., 1971-78, chief justice, 1978-87, sr. judge, 1989-93; of counsel Reynoldson Law Firm, Osceola, Iowa, 1993—. Adj. prof. law Drake U., 1989-93; county atty., Clarke County, Iowa, 1953-57. Contbg. author: Trial Handbook, 1969. Pres. Nat. Ctr. for State Cts., 1984-85; trustee Drake U., 1987-2000. Served with USNR, 1942-46. Recipient Osceola Community Svc. award, 1968 Fellow Am. Bar Found.; mem. Iowa Bar Assn. (chmn. com. on legal edn. and admission to bar 1964-71), Am. Judicature Soc. (bd. dirs. 1983-87, Herbert Harley award 1990), Iowa Acad. Trial Lawyers, Conf. Chief Justices (pres. 1984-85), Am. Coll. Trial Lawyers. Office: Reynoldson Law Firm 200 W Jefferson St Osceola IA 50213-1206

REYNOLDS-SAKOWSKI, DANA RENEE, science educator; b. Centralia, Ill., June 28, 1968; d. David Lavern and Betty Lou (Shelton) Reynolds; m. Jason Bielas Sakowski, Oct. 8, 1994. BS in Edn., U. No. Colo., 1991, MEd in Middle Sch. Edn., 1996. Tchr. life sci. and math. Ken Caryl Mid. Sch., Littleton, Colo., 1991-92; tchr. sci. Moore Mid. Sch., Arvada, 1992-93, tchr. life sci., 1993—. Mem. Nat. Wildlife Fedn., Colo. Assn. Sci. Tchrs., Colo. Biology Tchrs. Assn., Sierra Club, World Wildlife Fund, Nat. Parks and Conservation Assn., Natural Resources Def. Coun., Audubon Soc., Nature Conservancy. Avocations: camping, writing poetry, hiking, singing. Office: Moore Mid Sch 8455 W 88th Ave Arvada CO 80005-1620

REYNOLDS WESTERFELT, DEBRA KAY, education educator, consultant; b. Ashland, Ohio, Sept. 18, 1952; d. John Sample and Lois (Swartz) R.; m. Jobe Westerfelt. AS in Applied Bus., North Cen. Tech. Coll., 1972; BS in Edn., Ashland U., 1975; MA, Ohio State U., 1981, PhD, 1993. Cert. tchr., Ohio. Instr. Huntington (W.Va.) Jr. Coll., 1976-77; tchr. bus. Groveport (Ohio) Madison High Sch., 1977-79; instr. Eastland Vocat. Ctr., Groveport, 1979-81; adult coord. Mansfield (Ohio) City Schs., 1981-83; prof. North Cen. Tech. Coll., Mansfield, 1983-95; assoc. prof. Mt. Vernon (Ohio) Nazarene Coll., 1995-98, prof., 1998—. Cons., spkr. Mansfield City Schs., 1982-83; adj. instr. Ashland U., 1992—; lectr. Wayne Coll./U. Akron, 1998-2002; cons. Mid-Ohio Ednl. Svcs., 1998; prof. fellow Ashland U., 1999—; prof. Marion Tech. Coll., Ohio, 2000—. Crusader Am. Cancer Soc., Mansfield, 1990; vol. Am. Heart Assn., 1993; edn. com. Alzheimer's Assn., 1992-94, 96, 98-99; program dir. Alzheimers Assn., 1999; adv. com. Pioneer JVS; chair faith sharing, liturgist, lay spkr. Ctrl. United Meth. Ch. Recipient Outstanding Tchr. of Yr. award bus. divsn. North Ctrl. Tech. Coll., 1991, 92, Ohio Bus. Tchrs. Assn. scholar, 1993, Outstanding Tchr. of Yr. award Mt. Vernon Nazarene Coll., 1997, 98; Rueble scholar, 1991, 92. Mem. AAUW, Ohio Bus. Tchrs. Assn., Ctrl. Ohio Adult Continuing Edn. Assn., Bus. and Profl. Women's Assn. (chairperson), Delta Pi Epsilon. Avocations: golf, travel, reading. Home: 4600 Deer Creek Dr Wooster OH 44691-7422

REZA, ALI HAJMOHAMMAD, cardiologist; b. Tehran, Iran, Apr. 14, 1957; came to U.S., 1988; s. Tayeh Hajmohammad and Fakhri (Mohajer) R.; m. Elizabeth Gheisari; children: Tara, Arleen. MD, Nat. U. Iran, Tehran, 1982. Diplomate Am. Bd. Internal Medicine, Am. Cardiovasc., Am. Bd. Interventional Cardiology; bd. cert. nuclear cardiology. Rsch. in pathology Rush Med. Sch., Chgo., 1988-89; resident in internal medicine SUNY, Buffalo, 1989-93, fellow in nephrology, 1992-93; fellow in cardiology Tulane U., New Orleans, 1993-96; pvt. practice, Chalmette, 1996—; pvt. practice Oschner Cardiovascular Inst., 2001—. Mem. ACP, AMA, Am. Coll. Cardiology. Moslem. Home: 6340 Eastover Dr New Orleans LA 70128-3622 Office: 800 W Virtue St Chalmette LA 70043-1200

REZAC, DEBRA DOWELL, bilingual educator; b. Modesto, Calif., Feb. 20, 1952; d. Charles Hubert and Peggy Sue (Hittle) Dowell; divorced; children: Aaron Vincent, Amanda Lael; m. Stephan R. Rezac. Cert. tchr., Calif. State U., Fresno, 1986, BS, 1994; M Lang. Devel., Pacific Coll., 1995; cert. reading recovery tchr. leader, Calif. State U., Fresno, 2000. Cert. lang. devel. specialist, Calif., cert. reading recovery tchr., recover tchr. leader; cert. reading specialist Calif. Dept. Edn.; cert. equity trainer, character counts trainer. Bilingual tchr. Selma (Calif.) Unified Sch. Dist., 1986—, mentor tchr. drug prevention edn., 1989-93, mentor tchr. health edn., 1993—, mentor tchr. lang. devel. and early literacy, 1996—, staff developer, 1996-97, tchr. spl. assignment reading recovery tchr., 2000-01. Project Drug Alcohol and Tobacco Edn. coord. Selma Unified Sch. Dist., 1989—, chair Healthy Kids Healty Calif. task force, 1990—, parent educator, 1992—; mem. adv. bd. Gang Task Force, Selma, 1993—; mem. English Lang. Arts Curriculum Com., 1990—, Health Curriculum Com., 1993—; mentor tchr. Early Literacy, 1996-97; mem. coordinating com. Gifted and Talented Edn., 1996, 97-98, mem. adv. bd., 1996; instr. 2nd grade literacy group, mentor tchr. Beginning Tchr. Mentor Program, 1998—, adult literacy/ESL Selma High Adult Sch.; mentor Beginning Tchr. Support Adv., 1998—; mem. CalStat TEACH Learning Support faculty Calif. State U., Fresno, 2000-01. Author: Mostly Magnets, 1990, Supplemental Guide to HLAY 200, 1995, other curriculum materials; coauthor: Gang Curriculum 1993. Mem. El Concilio, Fresno, 1993-94, Fresno Zool. Soc., 1980—, Selma Pub. Edn. Found. Grantee Selma Unified Sch. Dist., 1987, Selma Pub. Edn. Found., 1994, S. USD Pub. Edn. Found., 1996. Mem. NEA, Calif. Tchrs. Assn., Nat. Coun. Tchrs. Edn., C.U.E. Democrat. Methodist. Avocations: snow skiing, snow boarding, ice skating, running, swimming, tennis. Home: 2051 Oak St Selma CA 93662-2443

REZAIAN, MOHAMAD ALI, scientist; b. Fassa, Fars, Iran, July 29, 1945; arrived in Australia, 1983; s. Bozorg Rezaian and Iran Shariati; m. Mitra Iraji, Aug. 3, 1978; children: Pouria, Nimah. BSc, Tehran (Iran) U., 1968, MSc, 1970; PhD, U. Adelaide, Australia, 1975. Asst. prof. Shiraz (Iran) U., 1975-80, chmn. dept. biology, 1978-79, assoc. prof., 1980-83; rsch. fellow U. Adelaide, 1983-85; sr. prin. scientist CSIRO, Adelaide, 1985—. Vis. asst. prof. Purdue U., West Lafayette, Ind., 1979-80. Contbr. articles to profl. jours. Mgr. rural cmty.-assisted water supply project Nat. Devel. Scheme, Shiraz, 1976. Recipient Disting. Student award Ministry of Sci., Iran, 1970. Mem. AAAS, Internat. Soc. for Plant Molecular Biology, Iranian Assn. South Australia (co-founder). Avocations: hiking, woodcraft, community work. Home: 14 Sitters Memorial Dr Burnside SA 5066 Australia Office: CSIRO Divsn Plant Industry GPO Box 350 Adelaide SA 5001 Australia

REZANKA, THOMAS W. lawyer; b. Plainfield, N.J., Mar. 3, 1954; s. William L. and Helen G. Rezanka; m. Karen T. Rezanka, May 21, 1977. BA, Montclair State U., Upper Montclair, N.J., 1976; JD, Stetson U., 1980. Bar: Fla. 1980, U.S. Ct. Appeals (5th and llth cirs.) 1980. Pvt. practice, Palm Harbor, Fla., 1980—. Presenter Joint Conf. on Law and Aging, Washington, 1995-2001. Monthly legal columnist Tropical Breeze, Countryside Cougar, East Lake Eagle, Palm Harbor Panther, Dunedin Highlander, 1995—. Mem. adv. com. Countryside H.S., Clearwater, Fla., 1998-99; bd. dirs. Tampa Bay Area Planned Giving Coun., Clearwater, 2001. Mem. ABA, Nat. Acad. Elder Law Attys., Fla. Bar Assn. (former mem. legis. drafting com. real property, probate and trust law sect., exec. coun. elder law sect. 1995-99, faculty counseling your Fla. client seminar for out-of-state attys. 1999, faculty elder law bd. cert. rev. course 1998, editor The Advocate newsletter 1996-97), Clearwater Bar Assn. (estate planning columnist 1996-97, 2000-01, probate, guardianship and trust practice com.), Pinellas County Estate Planning Coun. (bd. dirs. 1995-99). Office: 2672 West Lake Rd Palm Harbor FL 34684

REZEK, GEOFFREY ROBERT, management consultant; b. Queens, N.Y., Nov. 23, 1941; s. Joseph and Louise (Martin) R.; m. Jacqueline Ann Greenfield, Aug. 23, 1973; children: Christopher Robert, Joseph Paul. BS in Indsl. Mgmt., L.I. U., 1964, MS in Mgmt. Engring., 1966. Cert. purchasing mgr.; cert. fellow prodn. and investment mgmt.; cert. systems integrator; cert. internat. resource mgmt. Indsl. engr. IBM Corp., East Fishkill, N.Y., 1965-67, systems engr. Garden City, 1967-73, mfg. industry specialst, 1973-81, N.Y.C., 1981-83, mfg. industry mktg. Norwalk, Conn., 1983-91; area specialist J.D. Edwards and Co., 1993—2001; cons. G.R. Rezek & Assocs., Darien, 1991-93; pres. G.R. Rezek & Asssocs., LLC, 2001—. With USNG, 1967-73. Mem. Am. Prodn. and Inventory Control Soc. (cert., v.p. bd. dirs. 1973-76, 91-94, internat. conf. 1992, 93), Nat. Assn. Purchasing Mgmt., Assn. for Mfg. Excellence, Inst. Indsl. Engrs. Office: GR Rezek & Assocs LLC 110 Raymond St Ste 19 Darien CT 06820-4926 E-mail: grrezek@optonline.net.

REZENDES, GUY FRANCIS, civil engineer; b. Petersburg, Va., Mar. 20, 1970; s. Francis Anthony and Ann Shirley (Farley) R. BS, U. Mass., North Dartmouth, 1992. Cert. engr.-in-tng., profl. civil engr. Civil engr. III Mass. Hwy. Dept., Taunton, 1992—. Mem. ASCE, Inst. Transp. Engrs. Roman Catholic. Home: 4 Alisha Dr Franklin MA 02038-1207 Office: 10 Park Plz Boston MA 02116

REZIN, ANDREW ANTHONY, academic administrator, educator; b. Cleve., May 25, 1950; s. Andrew Frank and Josephine (Rozinka) R.; m. Michele Elizabeth Rezin, Mar. 31, 1973; children: Jennifer, Jonathan, Jessica, Jordan. BA in Mktg., Kent State U., 1972; MA in Vocat. Edn., Ohio State U., 1993, PhD in Edn., 1998. Dist. mgr. Chrysler Corp., Centerline, Mich., 1976-81; svc. dir. Bob Caldwell Chrysler-Plymouth, Columbus, Ohio, 1981-86; ops. mgr. Spitzer Columbus, 1986-87; svc. dir. David Hobbs BMW, Columbus, 1987-88; svc. mgr. Dennis Pontiac, 1988-93; dept. chair automotive tech. Columbus State C.C., 1993-99, adminstr. automotive and applied tech., 1999—. Adv. bd. Paul C. Hayes Tech. H.S., Grove City, Ohio, 1997—, Northwest Career Ctr., Dublin, Ohio, 1997—; mem. nat. ASSET steering com. Ford Motor Co., Dearborn, Mich., 1996—. Contbr. articles to profl. jours. Chmn. Westerville Baha'i Assembly, Westerville, Ohio, 1995—. Mem. Ohio Coop. Edn. Assn., Phi Kappa Phi, Omicron Tau Theta (past pres.). Office: Columbus State Cmty Coll 550 E Spring St Columbus OH 43215-1722 E-mail: arezin@cscc.edu.

REZNECK, DANIEL ALBERT, lawyer; b. Troy, N.Y., Apr. 26, 1935; s. Samuel and Elizabeth (Fishburne) R.; m. Beverly Ann Macht, Mar. 7, 1971; children: Jonathan Noah, Abigail Rebecca. BA, Harvard U., 1956, JD, 1959. Bar: N.Y. 1959, D.C. 1961. Rsch. asst. Harvard U. Law Sch., Cambridge, Mass., 1959-60; law clk. to Justice William J. Brennan U.S. Supreme Ct., Washington, 1960-61; asst. U.S. atty. Dept. Justice, 1961-64; assoc. Arnold & Porter, 1964-68, ptnr., 1969-95; gen. counsel D.C. Fin. Responsibility and Mgmt. Assistance Authority, 1995—2001, D.C. Office of the Corp. Counsel, 2001—. Adj. prof. law Georgetown U., Washington, 1963—; mem. D.C. Commn. on Jud. Disabilities and Tenure, 1979-86, D.C. Bd. Profl. Responsibility, 1994-2000; trustee D.C. Pub. Defender Svc., 1981-87. Contbr. articles to profl. jours. Named Young Lawyer of Yr. for D.C., 1971 Fellow Am. Coll. Trial Lawyers, Am. Bar Found.; mem. ABA, D.C. Bar (pres. 1975-76, pres. Bar Found. 1994-97), Bar Assn. D.C., Asst. U.S. Attys. Assn., D.C. B'nai Brith. Jewish. Avocations: American history; reading; writing. Home: 2852 Albemarle St NW Washington DC 20008-1036 Office: DC Fin Respons/Mgmt Asst Au 441 4th St NW #570 Washington DC 20001 E-mail: drezneck@pcfra.com.

REZNICK, RICHARD HOWARD, pediatrician; b. Chgo., Oct. 31, 1939; s. Louis and Mae Reznick; m. Barbara Ann Glantz, June 20, 1965; children: Steven L., Alicia T., Scott M., Stacey R. BS, U. Ill., 1961; MD, Loyola U., Chgo., 1965. Diplomate Am. Bd. Pediatrics. Resident in pediat. Michael Reese Hosp., Chgo., 1966-68; pediatrician USAF, Homestead AFB, Fla., 1968-70; pediatrician pvt. practice Winnetka, Ill., 1970-71, Scottsdale, Ariz., 1971—. Pres. med. staff Phoenix Children's Hosp., 1990-93, bd. dirs. 1990-94. Capt. USAF, 1968-70. Fellow Am. Acad. Pediatrics (treas. Ariz. chpt. 1982-84); mem. AMA, Ariz. Med. Assn., Phoenix Pediatric Soc. (treas. 1976-77), Maricopa County Med. Soc. Avocations: aerobics, bicycling, gardening, classical music, collecting stamps. Office: Papago Buttes Pediatric Ctr 8573 E San Alberto Ste E100 Scottsdale AZ 85258-4318

REZNICK, STEVEN MICHAEL, orthopedic surgeon, educator; b. Washington, 1954; 3 children. BS, U. Md., 1975; MD, George Washington U., 1979; MBA, Columbia U., 2000. Diplomate Am. Bd. Orthopedic Surgery. Resident in gen. surgery George Washington U., 1979-81; resident in orthop. surgery U. Mich., Ann Arbor, 1981-84; clin. instr. orthopedic surgery UCLA Sch. Medicine, 1988-94. Sr. aviation med. examiner FAA, 1985-87; talk show host KGIL-Radio, L.A., 1987-90. Mem. Calif. Rep. Party, Calif. Rep. Assembly, bd. dirs. Palm Springs chpt., 1996-98. Fellow Internat. Coll. Surgeons, Am. Coll. Surgeons, Am. Acad. Orthopedic Surgeons, Beta Gamma Sigma Honor Soc. Avocation: commercial pilot. Home: PO Box 101 Somers NY 10589 E-mail: smr50@columbia.edu.

REZNIK, ALAN A. petroleum engineering educator; b. Pitts., Sept. 25, 1939; s. Lawrence S. and Rose R.; m. Marion Bergstein, Sept. 8, 1963; children: Amy Jean, Robert I.S. BS, U. Pitts., 1963, MS, 1964, PhD, 1971. Research scientist Continental Oil Co., Ponca City, Okla., 1964-66; instr. chem. and petroleum engring. dept. U. Pitts., 1966-67; instr. dept. civil engring. Technion-Israel Inst. Tech., Haifa, 1967-68; sr. research assoc. Calgon Corp., Pitts., 1969; engring. supr. U.S. Bur. Mines, Pitts., 1973-75; assoc. prof. chem. and petroleum engring. U. Pitts., 1975— , dir. petroleum engring. program, 1981-92 ; cons. and lectr. in field. Assoc. editor Jour. Petroleum Sci. and Engring., 1986-93 . Contbr. articles to profl. jours. Recipient Continental Oil Co. fellowship, 1961, Socony Mobil Internat. fellowship, 1962, U. Pitts. Outstanding Sr. award, 1963; U.S. Dept. Energy grantee, 1976-78, Gulf Oil Found. grantee, 1979, U.S. Dept. Energy grantee, 1978-79, 80-82, 85-86. Mem. Soc. Petroleum Engrs. of AIME, Am. Chem. Soc. (sec.-treas. 1975-76), Sigma Xi, Sigma Tau, Sigma Gamma Epsilon. Achievements include research in flow in porous media enhanced petroleum recovery and methane production from coals, tensor analysis. Office: U Pitts Chem & Petroleum Engring Dept 1249 Benedum Hall Pittsburgh PA 15261-2212

REZNIK, SANDRA EVE, pathologist; b. Newark, May 2, 1962; d. Frank and Renée Breitbarth; m. Edward Jonathan Reznik, Sept. 6, 1987; children: Samantha Jill, Sabrina Mae. AB, Harvard U., 1984; MD, PhD, Mt. Sinai Sch. Medicine, N.Y.C., 1991. Diplomate Nat. Bd. Med. Examiners. Resident pathology N.Y. Hosp., N.Y.C., 1991-94; fellow dept. pathology Albert Einstein Coll. Medicine, Bronx, 1996-98, asst. prof. pathology, 1998—, asst. prof. dept. ob-gyn., 1999—. Med.-legal expert/cons., Bronx, 1999—. Mentored Clin. Investigator awardee NIH, 1998—. Avocations: ice skating, cooking, travel. Home: 7 Dante St Larchmont NY 10538-1608 Office: Albert Einstein Coll of Medicine Dept Path Forchheimer Bldg 1300 Morris Park Ave Bronx NY 10461-2373 E-mail: sreznik@aecom.yu.edu.

RGORMAN, COLUM ALPHONSUS, endocrinologist; b. Mayobridge, No. Ireland, June 27, 1936; arrived in U.S., 1960; s. James and Mary (McCollum) Gorman; m. Una Elizabeth O'Neill, Feb. 9, 1961; children: Kevin Gorman, Paul Gorman, Fiona Gorman, Michael Gorman. MB, Bch, BAO, Queens U., Belfast, Ireland, 1959; PhD, U. Minn., 1968. Cons. endocrinology Mayo Clinic, Rochester, Minn., 1966—; from asst. prof. to assoc. prof. Mayo Grad. Sch. Medicine, 1971—81, prof., 1981-89; chmn. div. endocrinology Mayo Clinic, 1985-92, bd. govs., 1997-2000, acting chair dept. health scis. rsch., 2000—01. Editor, author: book The Eye and Orbit in Thyroid Disease, 1984. Fellow: ACP; mem.: AAAS, Endocrine Soc., Am. Thyroid Assn. (sec. 1984—88, pres. 1995—96). Republican. Avocations: reading, cross country skiing, auto restoration. Home and Office: 2607 Merrihills Dr Rochester MN 55902-1168

RHAME, HAROLD ELLIS, JR. law educator; b. El Paso, July 3, 1926; s. Harold Ellis and Ethel Clara (Dunagan) R.; m. Joan Williams, Feb. 14, 1955; children: Lucy S., Ann B., Ellis W. AB, Princeton U., 1946; MD, George Washington U., 1950; JD, U. Bridgeport, 1990. Bar: Conn. 1991. Intern Barnes Hosp., St. Louis, 1952; resident NYU-Bellevue Med. Ctr., N.Y.C., 1952-56; pvt. med. practice Bridgeport, Conn., 1956-88; law educator Quinnipac Coll. Law, 1994.

RHATIGAN, RONALD MERLIN, pathologist; b. Iowa City, Feb. 21, 1936; s. Clarence A. and Mabel (Bartlett) R.; m. Alice A. Jones, June 21, 1957 (div. Jan. 1981); children: Jennifer, Ronald G., Douglas; m. Ola M. Griffis, Dec. 5, 1983; children: Claire N., Caleb. BA, U. Iowa, 1958, MD, 1961. Diplomate Am. Bd. Pathology, Am. Bd. Dermatology. Intern in pathology Ind. U., Indpls., 1961-62, resident in pathology, 1962-65; asst. chief pathology Womack Army Hosp., Ft. Bragg, NC, 1965—67; chief of pathology Univ. Med. Ctr., Jacksonville, Fla., 1968-92, med. dir., 1972-88, exec. v.p. med. staff, 1972-88; asst. prof. pathology U. Fla., Gainesville, 1968-72, assoc. prof., 1972-76, prof., 1976-99, prof., staff pathologist, 1992-99; chief dermatopathology Meml. Hosp. Jacksonville, Fla., 1999—. Chmn., founding mem. U. Fla. Self Ins. Trust Fund, 1986-88; bd. trustees Univ. Med. Ctr., 1980-88. Contbr. numerous articles to profl. jours. Bd. dirs. Jacksonville Urban League, 1980-82, Mayor's Select Com. Pub. Safety, Jacksonville, 1984. Capt. M.C. U.S. Army, 1965-67. Recipient Appreciation award for concern and devotion Eartha White Nursing Home, 1987. Fellow Am. Soc. Clin. Pathology, Coll. Am. Pathologists; mem. Internat. Soc. Dermatopathology, Internat. Soc. Gynecologic Pathology, Fla. Soc. Pathology, Fla. Med. Soc., Jacksonville Faculty Practice Assn. (chmn. bd. 1972-88). Democrat. Avocations: running, skiing, fishing, agriculture, reading. Home: 13795 Sawpit Rd Jacksonville FL 32226-1629

RHEA, DONNA KAY, nurse; b. Smithville, Mo., Mar. 31, 1963; d. Ralph Lyle and Donna Faye Allen; m. Terry Allan Rhea, Aug. 28, 1980; children: Jason, Alicia. AAS in Nursing, S.E. Mo. Hosp. Coll. Nursing, 2000. RN, Mo. LPN S.E. Mo. Hosp., Cape Girardeau, Mo., 1994-2000; RN St. Francis Med. Ctr., 2000—. Vol. Camp Daybreak, Cape Girardeau, 1999. Home: 109 Rutherford Dr Jackson MO 63755 Office: St Francis Med Ctr 211 St Francis Dr Cape Girardeau MO 63703-8399

RHEA, JERRY DWAINE, director consumer lending; b. Knoxville, Tenn., Dec. 11, 1950; s. Paul Edward and Pearl (Cornett) R.; m. Lamara Hurt, Aug. 22, 1973; children: Kathryn, Jerry. BS in Acctg., Tenn. Wesleyan Coll., Athens, 1969-73. Corp. credit adminstr. G.E. Capital, Stamford, Conn., 1973-88; exec. v.p., consumer lending officer, dir. Chase Fin., Cleve., 1988-97; exec. v.p. ops. So. Pacific Funding Corp., Lake Oswego, Oreg., 1997-98; pres., COO Financial Partners, Portland, 1998—. Avocations: photography, boating.

RHEA, MARCIA CHANDLER, accountant; b. Columbia, S.C., Apr. 27, 1956; d. Foster Frazier and Virginia Elizabeth (Goude) Chandler; m. Randall W. Rhea, Aug. 23, 1980. AA, Bauder Coll., Atlanta, 1975; BA magna cum laude, Coll. of Charleston, S.C., 1981; postgrad., CPA studies. Cert. tax practice ptnr., notary pub., S.C., CPA, S.C. Writer, prodr. U.S. Army C.E., Charleston, 1984; mng. ptnr. Care/Share Prodns., 1981—; ptnr. Chandler Rhea, CPA, Johns Island, S.C., 1987—. Ins. agt., registered rep. H.D. Vest Investment Securities; screenwriter, agt. Agape Prodns.-Terry Porter-Writer's Guild Am.; media cons., roving reporter Worldfest-Charleston Internat. Film Festival, 1994. Author: Does It Have to Happen Again?, From Hell's Angel to Heaven's Saint; author (screenplays) The Carolina Storyteller (semifinalist Austin Film Festival, 1999, Fade-in Awards winner 2000), The Life Shift, The Geriatric Tour; contbr. articles to mags. and profl. jours.; prodr. various films. Adult tchr. Ashley Rivers Bapt. Ch.; mem. Tri-County Advocates for Women on Bds. and Commns. for S.C. Recipient Outstanding Acad. Achievement award Coll. of Charleston, H.D. Vest Svc. award, 2001. Mem. AICPA, Am. Soc. Notaries, S.C. Assn. CPAs, S.C. Motion Picture TV Assn., Charleston Film Soc. (bd. dirs.), Screenwriters Guild of Charleston (charter), Acctg. Assn., Coll. of Charleston Alumni, Film Soc. Coll. Charleston (bd. dirs.), Charleston Film Soc. (bd. dirs.), Phi Kappa Phi, Phi Mu. Republican. Baptist. Avocation: helping to develop an indigenous film industry in South Carolina. Office: 3226 Maybank Hwy Ste 1 PO Box 508 Johns Island SC 29457-0508 E-mail: mrheaicpa@es.com.

RHEAD, WILLIAM JAMES, biochemical geneticist; b. Feb. 20, 1946; s. Wallace Max and Marie Jeanne (Muller) R.; m. Deborah Elizabeth Sheppard, July 15, 1972 (div. Apr. 1997); children: Paul Joseph, Evan James, Jack; m. Pamela Finberg, Jan. 11, 1998. BA with highest honors, U. Calif., San Diego, 1968, MD, 1974, PhD, 1975; MPh, Yale U., 1969. Diplomate Am. Bd. Human Genetics, Am. Bd. Pediats. Intern and resident in pediats. U. N.C., Chapel Hill, 1975-77; fellow in human genetics and pediats. Yale U. Sch. Medicine, 1977-79; asst. prof. pediats. U. Iowa Coll. Medicine, 1979-84, assoc. prof. pediats., 1984-89, prof. pediats., 1989-2000; prof., sect. chief med. genetics Med. Coll. Wis., Milw., 2000—. Bd. dirs. Assn. for Glycogen Storage Disease, 1984. Recipient Noel Raine award Soc. Study of Inborn Errors of Metabolism, 1983. Fellow Am. Acad. Pediats.; mem. Am. Soc. Human Genetics, Soc. Inherited Metabolic Disease, Soc. Pediat. Rsch., Soc. Study Inborn Errors of Metablism. Democrat. Avocations: bicycling, skiing, travel, gardening. Home: 12605 W Grove Ter Elm Grove WI 53122-1976 Office: Med Coll Wis Med Genetics/Pediats PO Box 1997 Milwaukee WI 53201-1997 Fax: (414) 266-1616. E-mail: wrhead@mcw.edu.

RHEAMS, ANNIE ELIZABETH, education educator; b. Lake Providence, La. d. Curtis Kleinpeter Sr. and Annie Augusta (Webb) Kleinpeter; 1 child, Darryl Jemall Rheams. BA, Grambling (La.) U., 1971; MS, Ala. A&M U., 1975; PhD, U. Wis., Milw., 1989. Cert. tchr. in exceptional edn., adminstrn. Tchr. Ala. A&M U., Normal, 1971-79, adminstr., 1977-79; acad. specialist U. Wis., Milw., 1979-82, Parkside, 1982-84; tchr. diagnostician, adminstr. Milw. Schs., 1984-89; asst. prof. dept. edn. Marquette U., Milw., 1989-96; asst. prin. North Divsn. H.S., 1996—, Marshall H.S., Milw., 1997—, tchr. exceptional edn. cognitively disabled, consumer math., 1999—. Career counselor Madison County Career Counseling Svcs., Huntsville, 1975; adj. prof. Oakwood (Ala.) SDA Coll., 1975-78; tchr. Gateway to Engring. Program, Milw., 1984-88; cons. pub. schs./Wee Care Day Care, Milw., 1992-96; condr. workshops in field. Author: P.A.C.E.: A Thematic Approach to Developing Essential Experiences, 1996. Voter registrar/poll watcher NAACP, Lake Providence, 1966; v.p. Work for Wis., Inc., Milw., 1993-94, Messmer H.S. Bd., Milw., 1990-94; com. chmn. Citizen's Rev. Bd., Milw., 1980-82, Met. Milw. Alliance Black Sch. Educators, 1994-95. Assoc. fellow Ctr. for Great Plains Studies, U. Nebr.-Lincoln, 1995; named Outstanding Tchr. Educator, Am. Assn. for Coll.

Tchr. Educators Directory, 1995. Mem. Zonta Internat., Alpha Kappa Alpha, Phi Delta Kappa. Avocations: tennis, sewing, ceramics, horseback riding, biking. Home: PO Box 90681 Milwaukee WI 53209-0611 Fax: 414-902-8315. E-mail: rheams@mailandnews.com.

RHEAUME, JANA MARIE, mathematician, educator; b. Middlebury, Vt., Sept. 30, 1970; d. Raymond Marcel and Lynda Noyes Rheaume. BS Math, Johnson State Coll., Johnson, VT, 1993; MS Math, Univ. Vt., Burlington, VT, 2002. Math educator, grades 7-12 Missing Info, Missing Info, Vt., 1994—. Mem.: Am. Math. Soc. Avocations: biking, biking, biking, biking, needlework crafts. Home: 76 Hayes Ave South Burlington VT 05403-7249

RHEE, ALBERT, lawyer, author; b. Pa., June 25, 1958; s.S.K. Rhee and B.C. Chun; m. I.Y. Choi, June, 1992. AB, Wabash (Ind.) Coll., 1980; JD, U. So. Calif., 1985; postgrad., Oxford U.; M Jurisprudence, U. Calif., Berkeley, 1990, postgrad., 1990—94. Bar: N.Y. 1986. Fellow Bryn Mawr (Pa.) Coll., 1985-87; instr. U. Calif. Boalt Hall Sch. Law, 1987-95, Columbia U., 1999—. Editor: Patent Law in Korea, 1994, Intellectual Property in Korea, 1995. Recipient Franklin award, 1985, fellowship Bryn Mawr Coll., 1985-87, U. Calif. Berkeley grad. fellowship, 1988-90, Boalt Hall fellowship, 1990-92. Avocations: music, fine arts, zen. E-mail: albersjr@aol.com.

RHEE, YANG HO, radiologist; b. Kunsan, Republic of Korea, Mar. 22, 1943; came to U.S., 1973; s. Young Whan and Ae Wol (Rah) R.; m. Shin Ae Kang; children: Hoyeon, Thomas, Karen. MD, Chonnam Med. Sch., Kwangju, Republic of Korea, 1968. Diplomate Am. Bd. Radiology. Intern Seoul Adventist Hosp., Republic of Korea, 1972-73, Cook County Hosp., Chgo., 1973-74; resident Hines (Ill.) VA Hosp., 1974-77; staff physician Illini Hosp., Silvis, Ill., 1977—, Trinity Med. Ctr., Moline, 1995—. Chmn. bd. trustees Quad City Korean Assn., Ill. and Iowa, 1986-88, v.p., 1980-81; mem. adv. coun. on peaceful unification policy Republic of Korea, 1984-93; chmn. dept. radiology Ilini Hosp., Silvis, Ill., 1988-99. Capt. Korean Army, 1968-72, Korea and Vietnam. Mem. AMA, Am. Coll. Radiology, Radiol. Soc. N.Am., Soc. Nuclear Medicine, Am. Inst. Ultasound in Medicine, Am. Roentgen Ray Soc. Office: 801 Hospital Rd Silvis IL 61282-1804

RHEIN, JOHN HANCOCK WILLING, III, publishing executive; b. Richmond, Va., Aug. 8, 1931; s. John Hancock Willing Jr. and Margaret (Packard) R.; m. Phyllis Betz, June 13, 1953; children: Susan Rhein Dubowski, Deborah B., John Hancock Willing IV. BA, Hobart Coll., 1953. With rsch. dept. Benton & Bowles Advt., N.Y.C., 1957; sales mgmt. asst. to pub. Forbes Mag., 1957-71; sr. v.p., assoc. pub. Fin. Mag., 1971-73, Fin. World Mag., N.Y.C., 1973-81; pres. Nat. Bus. Confs., 1975-81; sr. v.p. dir. sales and mktg. Sat. Rev. Mag., 1980-81, View Mag., N.Y.C., 1980-81; pub. Equities Mag. (formerly OTC Rev.), 1981-93, Emeritus Equities Mag., 1993—; pres., CEO Am. Depository Receipt Assn., 1993—. Pub. ADR Investor & Global Securities Almanac; chmn. bd. W.R. Keegan Corp., Focus the Nat. H.S. News Mag., 1994—; pres. The Investor Intelligence Group, Garden City, N.Y., 1981—; dir. Celebrity Writers, Inc., 2000—; pub. Coiningmoney.com. Office: Investor Intelligence Group 96 10th St Garden City NY 11530-1560

RHEIN, KEVIN DOUGLAS, music educator; b. Massapequa, NY, June 7, 1956; s. Marshall Maclean and Gladys Lorraine Rhein; m. Pamela Anne Kagdis, May 14, 1977; children: Benjamin, Nia, Rebekah. BM in Music Edn., Westminster Choir Coll., 1979. Cert. K-12 music tchr. Maine. Choral dir. Sparks (Nev.) Mid. Sch., 1979—81; gen. music tchr. Messalonskee Sch. Dist., Oakland, Maine, 1981—98; choral dir. Messalonskee H.S., 1998—. Dir. Carnegie Hall Choir, Oakland, Maine, 2000—01. Mem.: ACDA, Music Educators Nat. Conf. Home: RR 2 Box 1535 Belgrade ME 04917 Office: Messalonskee HS 131 Messalonskee High Dr Oakland ME 04963 Personal E-mail: rhein@dialmaine.com.

RHEINISH, ROBERT KENT, university administrator; b. Mt. Vernon, N.Y., Oct. 27, 1934; s. Walter Washington and Doris Elizabeth (Standard) R.; m. Dorothy Ellen Steadman, May 3, 1957 (div. 1976); children: Robert Scott, Joel Nelson; m. Shirley Marie Suter, Aug. 1, 1976. BA, U. South Fla., 1963; MS, Ind. U., 1969, EdD, 1971. Staff engr. Armed Forces Radio & TV Svc., Anchorage, 1960-61; trainee Nat. Park Svc. Tng. Ctr., Grand Canyon, Ariz., 1965; historian Home of F.D.R., Nat. Historic Site, Hyde Park, N.Y., 1964-65, Sagamore Hill Nat. Hist. Site, Oyster Bay, 1965-66; asst. coord. nat. environ. edn. devel. program Dept. of Interior, Washington, 1968; supervisory historian Lincoln Boyhood Nat. Meml., Lincoln City, Ind., 1966-68; dir. learning resources ctr. Whittier (Calif.) Coll., 1971-73; dir. media and learning resources Calif. State U., Long Beach, 1973-88. Chmn. media dirs. The Calif. State Univs., Long Beach, 1975-76; radio announcer Sta. WTCX-FM, St. Petersburg, Fla., 1961-63; co-host with David Horowitz (2 broadcasts) On Campus, Sta. KNBC-TV, L.A., 1972-73; guest lectr. 6th Army Intelligence Sch., Los Alamitos Armed Forces Res. Ctr., 1987; founder Rheino Ltd., 1997. Coord. multi-media program: In Search of Yourself, 1975 (Silver award Internat. Film and TV Festival of N.Y.), The House that Memory Built, 1981 (Cindy award Info. Film Producers of Am.), The Indochinese and Their Cultures, 1985 (Silver award Internat. Film & TV Festival of N.Y.); holder 2 patents. With RCAF, 1954-55, USAF, 1957-61. U.S. Office of Edn. grad. fellow, 1969-71; recipient Learning Resources Ctr. Devel. Fund award Pepsico, Sears, Prentice-Hall, et al. 1973; Nat. Def. Edn. Act grantee, 1974-76. Mem. NRA, VFW, Am. Legion. Republican. Avocations: collecting militaria, boating, political writing. Home: 380 Long Br W Prescott AZ 86303-5306 E-mail: rheino@commspeed.net.

RHEINS, CARL JEFFREY, university administrator, historian, educator; b. Cin., Sept. 17, 1945; s. Joseph Melvin and Gertrude (Mandell) R.; m. Brenda Dale Gevertz, July 8, 1979; children: Jason Gabriel, Jaclyn Gail. BS with distinction, U. Wis., 1967; MA, SUNY, Albany, 1970; PhD, SUNY, Stony Brook, 1978. Lectr. Judaic studies SUNY, Stony Brook, 1974-78, asst. to provost, 1978-80, 81-86; dir. acad. affairs Nat. Found. Jewish Culture, N.Y.C., 1980-81; asst. dean Adelphi U., Garden City, N.Y., 1986-87, assoc. dean, 1987, exec. asst. to pres., 1987-90, dean student life and devel., 1990-92, v.p. student life and devel., 1992-97; v.p. external affairs and comty. rels., 1997—. Bd. dirs. Coalition on Higher Edn., Jewish Community Rels. Coun., N.Y.C. Contbg. author: Yearbook of the Leo Baeck Inst., 1978, 80, 81; co-editor: Jewish Almanac, 1980 (dual main selection Jewish Book Club Am. 1981). Mem. nat. governing coun. Am. Jewish Congress, N.Y.C., 1986-87, 1st v.p. Suffolk County, N.Y., 1985-87; bd. govs. L.I. region Am. Jewish Com., N.Y., 1984-85; judge Nat. Jewish Book Awards, 1993, 94; trustee Adelphi Acad., Bklyn., 1995. Summer fellow NEH, 1987. Mem. Garden City C. of C. (bd. dirs. 1997—), Rotary, Kiwanis, Phi Kappa Phi, Phi Alpha Theta, Alpha Epsilon Pi. Home: 5 Merrimac Ct Dix Hills NY 11746-6011 Office: YIVO Institute 15 W 16th St New York NY 10011-6301

RHEINSTEIN, PETER HOWARD, healthcare company executive, consultant, physician, lawyer; b. Cleve., Sept. 7, 1943; s. Franz Joseph Rheinstein and Hede Henrietta (Neheimer) Rheinstein Lerner; m. Miriam Ruth Weissman, Feb. 22, 1969; 1 child, Jason Edward BA with high honors, Mich. State U., 1963, MS, 1964; MD, Johns Hopkins U., 1967; JD, U. Md., 1973. Bar: Md. 1973, D.C. 1980, U.S. Supreme Ct. 2000; diplomate Am. Bd. Family Practice; cert. added qualifications in geriatric medicine. Intern USPHS Hosp., San Francisco, 1967-68, resident in internal medicine Balt., 1968-70; instr. internal medicine U. Md., 1970-73; med. dir. extended care facilities CHC Corp., 1972-74; dir. drug advt. and labeling divsn. FDA, Rockville, Md., 1974-82, acting dep. dir. Office Drugs, 1982-83, acting dir. Office Drugs, 1983-84, dir. Office Drug Standards, 1984-90, dir. medicine staff Office Health Affairs, 1990-99; sr. v.p. for med. and clin. affairs Cell Works, Inc., Balt., 1999—. Chmn. Com. on Advanced Sci. Edn., 1978-86, Rsch. in Human Subjects Com., 1990-92; adj. prof. forensic medicine George Washington U., 1974-76; WHO cons. on drug regulation Nat. Inst. for Control Pharm. and Biol. Products, China, 1981-90; advisor on essential drugs WHO, 1985-90; FDA del. to U.S. Pharmacopeial Conv., 1985-90, exec. com. for assessment and transfer of tech. NIH, 1990-99, mem. health care fin. adminstrn. tech. adv. com., 1990-98, Nat. Adv. Coun. on Healthcare Policy, Rsch. and Evaluation, 1990-99, Healthy People 2000/2010 Steering Com., 1990-99, CDC and Prevention Task Force on Cmty. Preventive Svcs., 1996-99, Nat. Task Force on CME Industry/Provider Collaboration, 1992—; cons. in legal medicine and regulatory affairs, 1999—. Co-author: (with others) Human Organ Transplantation, 1987; spl. editorial advisor Good Housekeeping Guide to Medicine and Drugs, 1977-80; mem. editorial bd. Legal Aspects Med. Practice, 1981-89, Drug Info. Jour., 1982-86, 91-95; pub. Discovery Medicine, 2001--; contbr. articles to profl. jours. V.p. Intercultural Friends Found., 1998—. Recipient Commendable Svc. award, FDA, 1981, Group award of merit, 1983, 1988, Group Commendable Svc. award, 1989, 1992, 1993, 1995, 1995, 1999, Commr.'s Spl. citation, 1993; grantee NIH Nat. Cancer Inst. SBIR grant, 2001. Fellow Am. Coll. Legal Medicine (bd. govs. 1983-93, treas., chmn. fin. com. 1985-88, 90-91, chmn. publs. com. 1988-93, jud. coun. 1993-95; Pres.'s awards 1985, 86, 89-91, 93), Am. Acad. Family Physicians; mem. Am. Acad. Pharm. Phys. (bd. trustees 1999—, v.p. AMA rels. 1999—), AMA (life; ho. of dels. 2002--), ABA, Drug Info. Assn. (bd. dirs. 1982-90, pres. 1984-85, 88-89, v.p. 1986-87, chmn. ann. meeting 1991, 94, steering com. Ams. 1991—, Outstanding Svc. award 1990), Fed. Bar Assn. (chmn. food and drug com. 1976-79, Disting Svc. award 1977), Med. and Chirurgical Faculty Md., Balt. City Med. Soc., Johns Hopkins Med. and Surg. Assn., APHA, Md. Bar Assn., Math. Assn. Am., Soc. Indsl. and Applied Math., Mensa (life), U. Md. Alumni Assn. (life), Fed. Exec. Inst. Alumni Assn. (life), Johns Hopkins U. Alumni Assn., Mich. State U. Alumni Assn. (life), Mich. State U. Honors Coll. Alumni Assn. (bd. dirs. 1998-2001, pres. 2000-2001), Chartwell Golf and Country Club, Annapolis Yacht Club, Johns Hopkins Club, Delta Theta Phi (life). Avocations: boating, electronics, physical fitness, real estate investments. Home: 620 Holly Ridge Rd Severna Park MD 21146-3520 Office: Cell Works Inc 6200 Seaforth St Baltimore MD 21224-6506 E-mail: phr@jhu.edu, peter@cell-works.com.

RHEINTGEN, LAURA DALE, research center official; b. Takoma Park, Md., July 13, 1962; d. Robert William and Ethel Frances (Snyder) Schiedel. BA in Internat. Studies and German, W.Va. U., 1984; MA in Internat. Affairs, Am. U., 1988. Rsch. asst. Brookings Instn., Washington, 1986; staff cons. Birch & Davis Assocs., Inc., Silver Spring, Md., 1988-89; devel. analyst Ctr. for Strategic and Internat. Studies, Washington, 1989-92, mgr. devel. rsch. and records, 1992-93, asst. dir. devel., 1994-95, dir. found. rels., 1995-97; assoc. dir. devel. Aspen Inst., Washington, 1997-98; devel. assoc. Nat. Acad. Scis., 1998-99, devel. officer, 1999; devel. dir. Am. Inst. Contemporary German Studies, Johns Hopkins U., 1999—. Mem. Women in Internat. Security Studies, German Lang. Soc. Office: Am Inst Contemporary German Studies Johns Hopkins U 1400 16th St NW Ste 420 Washington DC 20036-2216

RHETT, HASKELL EMERY SMITH, educator; b. Evanston, Ill., Aug. 29, 1936; s. Haskell Smith and Eunice Campbell (Emery) R.; m. Roberta Teel Oliver, Sept. 9, 1961 (div. 1973); children: Kathryn Emery, Cecily Coffin; m. Anita Leone, May 30, 1983 (div. 1993); m. Janet Lee Rollings, Nov. 15, 1997. AB, Hamilton Coll., 1958; MA, Cornell U., 1967, PhD, 1968. Asst. to the pres. Hamilton Coll., Clinton, N.Y., 1961-64; rsch. asst. Cornell U., Ithaca, 1964-66; rsch. assoc. U. London, 1966-67; dir. program devel. Ednl. Testing Svc., Princeton, N.J., 1967-73; asst. chancellor N.J. Dept. Higher Edn., Trenton, 1973-85; v.p. The Coll. Bd., N.Y.C., 1985-90; pres. The Woodrow Wilson Nat. Fellowship Found., Princeton, 1990-97, pres. emeritus, 1997—. Author: Going to College in New Jersey, 1978; contbg. author: Government's Role in Supporting College Savings, 1990. Commr. N.J. Pub. Broadcasting Authority, Trenton, 1983-85; mem. Nat. Task Force on Student Aid Problems, Washington, 1974-75; mem. Gov.'s Adv. Panel on Higher Edn. Restructuring, State of N.J., 1994; trustee Dominican U. of Calif., San Rafael, Calif., 1990-99, 2001—, William Alexander Procter Found., 1998—; del. Dem. Nat. Conv., Miami, 1972; sr. warden Trinity Episcopal Ch., Princeton, 1988-92, vestryman, 1979-82, 87-88, 2001—; dep. Gen. Conv., Detroit, 1988, Phoenix, 1991; mem. standing com. Episcopal Diocese of N.J., 1992-97; trustee The Coll. of N.J., 1992-97, vice-chmn., 1995-97, chmn., 1997; trustee Gov. Dummer Acad., Mass., 1993—, Heartland Edn. Comty., Ohio, 1992-97, Forums Inst. for Pub. Policy, N.J., 1999—, treas., 2000—; bd. dirs. Reach the World, Inc., N.Y.C., 1998-2000, Trenton After Sch. Program, 2001—. Nat. Def. fellow U.S. Govt., 1966-67, Eliot-Winant fellow Brit.-Am. Assocs., 1982, Harvard U. fellow, 1985, faculty fellow Wilson Coll., Princeton U., 1993-97. Mem. Nat. Assn. State Scholarship and Grant Programs (pres. 1976-78), Princeton Officers Soc., Springdale Golf Club. Avocations: travel, tennis, golf, sailing, classic automobiles. Home: 80 Province Line Rd Skillman NJ 08558-1102 E-mail: hrhett@rcn.com.

RHETTS, PAUL FISHER, publishing executive; b. Washington, Mar. 26, 1946; s. Charles Edward and Ruth (Fisher) R.; m. JoAnn Rhodes, Aug. 26, 1968 (div. Dec. 1979); children: Joanna Katherine, Alexandra Copeland; m. Barbe J. Awalt, Mar. 13, 1982. BA, Bucknell U., 1968; student Pub. Adminstrn. MS program, U. So. Calif., 1975-77. Pub. affairs producer Sta. WMAL-TV, Washington, 1969-70, Md. Pub. TV, Owings Mills, 1970-73; asst. supt. Balt. City Pub. Schs., 1973-74; publs. cons. Community Coll. Balt., 1975-78; pub. info. officer Howard County Schs., Ellicott City, Md., 1976-86; pres. Laser Pub. and Design, Md. and N.Mex., 1986-95; sr. ptnr. LPD Press, 1995—. Trainer Pagemaker Desktop Pub. Software, 1986-94; mem. adj. faculty Loyola Coll., Balt., 1978-80; bd. dirs. UNM Cancer Ctr., Maxwell Mus. of Anthropology. Author: Finding Out How People Feel, 1984, Charlie Carrillo: Tradition & Soul, 1994; pub. Tradición Revista: The Jour. of Contemporary and Traditional Spanish Colonial Arts and Culture, 1995—, The Regis Santos: Thirty Years of Collecting, 1966-96, 1997, Our Saints Among Us: 400 Years of New Mexican Devotional Art, 1997, Seeds of Struggle: Harvest of Faith, 1998, Portfolio of Spanish Colonial Design in New Mexico, 2001. Mem. exec. bd. Family Life Ctr., Columbia, Md., 1980-86, Humanities Inst., Columbia, 1978-82, Columbia Archives, 1984-86. Recipient award San Francisco Internat. Film Festival, 1971, Broadcasting award Ohio State U., 1972, Community Svc. Merit award So. Ednl. Communications Assn., 1973, Nat. Community Svc. award Corp. for Pub. Broadcasting, 1973, Publ. award of Excellence, 1986. Mem. Nat. Sch. Pub. Rels. Assn. (state coord. 1978-83, pres. Chesapeake chpt. 1981-82, 86-87, exec. bd., 1976-90, chmn. nat. conv. planning com., treas. N.Mex. chpt. 1991-92, Blue Ribbon award 1982, 87, Gold Medallion award 1985-92, Mariner award 1990, Pres. award 1991), Pub. Rels. Soc. Am. (treas. N.Mex. soc. 1991-92, Conquistador award 1991, 93, 94, 95, pres. elect 1993, pres. 1994, Nat. Pres.'s Citation for Leadership 1994), Am. Profl. Graphic Artists Assn., N.Mex. Book Assn., Columbia Bus. Exch., Ednl. Press Assn., Desktop Pub. Assn., C. of C. (bd. dirs.). Democrat. Episcopalian. Home: 925 Salamanca St NW Albuquerque NM 87107-5647 E-mail: info@nmsantos.com.

RHI, SANG-KYU, lawyer, educator; b. Namwon, Cheon-buk, Republic Korea, July 1, 1933; s. Byong-Choon and Pil-Soon (Huh) R.; m. Hyo-Sook Kim, June 4, 1956; children: Eun-Sook, Jihn-u, Eun-Yong, Jihn-Soo. LLB, Chongchy Coll., 1955; LLM, So. Meth. U., 1961; postgrad., Nottingham (Eng.) U., 1966-67; LLD (hon.), Harding U., 1992, Taegoo U., 1999. Legislating officer Office Legislation, Republic Korea, 1961-67; pres. Korea Environ. Law Assn., Seoul, 1977-83; vice min. Ministry Edn., Republic Korea, 1980; lawyer Rhi Law Offices, Seoul, 1981—; prof. Coll. Law Korea U., 1982-96. Rep. Korea Legal Ctr., Seoul, 1989-93. Author: American Administrative Law, 1962, Administrative Law, 1965, Law of Administrative Remedy, 1985, State Liability and Compensation, 1995. 1st Lt. Republic Korea army, 1957-58. Recipient Presdl. commendation Govt. Korea, 1963, Red-Stripe Keunjeong medal, 1971. Mem. Seoul Bar Assn. (chmn. legis. com. 1989-91, Commendation Merit 1990), Korea Bar Assn. (exec. dir. 1991-93, bd. dirs. 1994-96, pres. Tng. Inst. for Lawyers 1997-2001, v.p. 2002-), Inter-Pacific Bar Assn. (mem. coun. 1995-2001, v.p. 2002--), Internat. Bar Assn., Lawasia (mem. coun. 1995-97), Korea Agama Sutra Assn. (hon. pres. 2001-). Avocations: golf, classical music. Home: 2-201 Asia Athletes Apt 86 Jamshil 7-dong Songpa-ku Seoul 138-227 Republic of Korea Office: Rhi Law Offices Ste 1153 KCCI BLDG 45 Namdaemunro 4ka Seoul 100-743 Republic of Korea Fax: 82 2 753 3029. E-mail: rhilaw@netsgo.com.

RHIEW, FRANCIS CHANGNAM, radiologist, physician; b. Korea, Dec. 3, 1938; came to U.S., 1967, naturalized, 1977; s. Byung Kyun and In Sil (Lee) R.; m. Kay Kyungja Chang, June 11, 1967; children: Richard C., Elizabeth. BS, Seoul Nat. U., 1960, MD, 1964. Cert. Am. Bd. Nuclear Medicine. Intern St. Mary's Hosp., Waterbury, Conn., 1967-68; resident in radiology and nuclear medicine L.I.U.-Queens Hosp. Ctr., N.Y., 1968-71; instr. radiology W. Va. U. Sch. Medicine, Morgantown, 1971-73; mem. staff Mercy Hosp. and Moses Taylor Hosp. Scranton, Pa., 1973—; also dir. nuclear medicine; clin. instr. Temple U., 1987—. Pres. Radiol. Consultants, Inc., 1984—, F.C.R. Co. Chmn., CEO Francis and Kay Rhiew Charitable Found. With M.C., Korean Army, 1964-67. Recipient Minister of Health and Welfare award, 1963. Mem. AMA, Soc. Nuclear Medicine, Radiol. Soc. N.Am., Am. Coll. Nuclear Medicine, Am. Coll. Radiology, Am. Inst. Ultra Sound, Country Club Scranton, Pres.'s Club U. Scranton, Elks. Home: 14 Lakeside Dr Clarks Summit PA 18411-9419 Office: 746 Jefferson Ave Scranton PA 18510-1624

RHIM, JOHNG SIK, physician, educator, medical researcher; b. Kwang Ju, Korea, July 24, 1930; came to U.S., 1958; s. Hac Woon and Moo Duc (Choi) R.; m. Mary Margaret Lytle, Aug. 24, 1930; children: Jonathan, Christopher, Peter, Andrew, Michael, Kathleen. MD, Seoul (Korea) Nat. U., 1957. Intern Seoul Nat. U. Hosp., 1958; rsch. fellow Children's Hosp. Rsch. Found., Cin., 1958-60, Baylor U. Coll. Medicine, Houston, 1961; rsch. assoc. Grad. Sch. Pub. Health, U. Pitts., 1962, La. State U. Acad. Medicine, New Orleans, 1962-64; vis. scientist Nat. Inst. Allergy and Infectious Diseases, NIH, Bethesda, Md., 1964-66; project dir. cancer rsch. Microbiol. Assocs., 1966-78; sr. investigator Nat. Cancer Inst., NIH, 1978-98; assoc. dir., prof. surgery Ctr. Prostate Disease Rsch., Uniformed Svcs. U. of the Health Sci., 1999—; rsch. prof. dept. surgery Uniformed Svcs. U. Health Scis., 2000—. Adj. prof. Georgetown U. Med. Ctr., Washington, 1988—. Editor: Neoplastic Transformation in Human Cell Culture, 1991, 1995, 1999; ; mem. editl. bd. Internat. Jour. Oncology; contbr. articles to profl. jours., chpts. to books. Mem. AAAS, AMA, Am. Assn. Cancer Rsch., Am. Soc. Virology, Soc. Exptl. Biology and Medicine, Internat. Assn. Leukemia Rsch. Achievements include patents for in field. Home: 11455 S Glen Rd Potomac MD 20854-1851 Office: CPDR Dept Surgery Uniformed Svcs Univ Health 4301 Jones Bridge Rd Bethesda MD 20814-4712

RHIND, CONSTANCE, economist, educator; b. Chgo., June 14, 1959; d. James Thomas and Laura (Campbell) Rhind. BA, Wellesley Coll., 1981; MSc, London Sch. Econs., 1984; PhD, Boston Coll., 1990. Economist Congl. Budget Office, U.S. Congress, Washington, 1989—. Fundraiser, Wellesley (Mass.) Coll., 1986-91. Mem. Am. Econ. Assn., Soc. Govt. Econs. (treas. 1991-93, v.p. 1993—), Washington Wellesley Club (sec. 1992-93), Washington Wellesley Friends Art (com. mem. 1991—), Alpha Sigma Nu. Home: 4615 N Park Ave Apt 604 Chevy Chase MD 20815-4513 Office: Congl Budget Office Us Congress Washington DC 20515-0001

RHIND, JAMES THOMAS, lawyer; b. Chgo., July 21, 1922; s. John Gray and Eleanor (Bradley) R.; m. Laura Haney Campbell, Apr. 19, 1958; children: Anne Constance, James Campbell, David Scott. Student, Hamilton Coll., 1940-42; AB cum laude, Ohio State U., 1944; LL.B. cum laude, Harvard U., 1950. Bar: Ill. bar 1950. Japanese translator U.S. War Dept., Tokyo, Japan, 1946-47; congl. liaison Fgn. Operations Adminstrn., Washington, 1954; atty. Bell, Boyd & Lloyd, Chgo., 1950-53, 55—, ptnr., 1958-92, of counsel, 1993—. Bd. dirs. Kewaunee Scientific Corp., Statesville, N.C. Commr. Gen. Assembly United Presbyn. Ch., 1963; life trustee Ravinia Festival Assn., Hamilton Coll., Clinton, N.Y., U. Chgo.; Northwestern Univ. Assocs.; chmn. Cook County Young Republican Orgn., 1957; Ill. Young Rep. nat. committeeman, 1957-58; v.p., mem. bd. govs. United Rep. Fund Ill., 1965-84; pres. Ill. Childrens Home and Aid Soc., 1971-73, life trustee; bd. dirs. E.J. Dalton Youth Center, 1966- 69; governing mem. Chgo. Symphony Orch., Chgo.; mem. Ill. Arts Council, 1971-75; mem. exec. com. div. Met. Mission and Ch. Extension Bd., Chgo. Presbytery, 1966-68; trustee Presbyn. Home, W. Clement and Jessie V. Stone Found., U. Chgo. Hosps. Served with M.I. AUS, 1943-46. Mem. ABA, Ill. Bar Assn., Chgo. Bar Assn. (bd. mgrs. 1967-69), Fed. Bar Assns., Chgo. Council on Fgn. Relations, Japan Am. Soc. Chgo., Lawyers Club Chgo., Phi Beta Kappa, Sigma Phi. Clubs: Chicago, Glen View (Ill.), Commercial (Chgo.), Mid-Day Club (Chgo.), Economic (Chgo.). Home: 830 Normandy Ln Glenview IL 60025-3210 Office: Bell Boyd & Lloyd 3 First National Pla 70 W Madison St Ste 3200 Chicago IL 60602-4244 E-mail: jrhind@bellboyd.com.

RHINE, KELLY ANNE, secondary education educator; b. Ft. Ord, Calif., June 9, 1966; d. Edward V. and Sandra J. (Berthiaume) R.; m. Carmine J. Pellicone (div. Dec. 1990). BS in Elem. Edn. and Spl. Edn., St. Thomas Aquinas Coll., Sparkill, N.Y., 1989; MS in Spl. Edn., SUNY, New Paltz, 1995. Part-time tchr. Spanish and French St. Peter's Elem. Sch., Haverstraw, NY, 1987—88; part-time resource rm. tchr. Warwick Valley Schs., Warsick, 1989; tchr. multiply handicapped Assn. for the Help of Retarded Children Presch., Middletown, 1989; resource rm. tchr. Beacon City Schs., 1989—90; spl. educator Fallsburg Ctrl. Schs., 1990—92, West Park Union Free Sch. Dist., 1993—94; presch. home worker, classroom tchr. Western Orange Cty. Head Start, Middletown, NJ, 1994—96; spl. educator rehabilitating teens DAYTOP Village Secondary Sch., Millbrook, NY, 1996—98; spl. educator grades 6, 7, 8 Valley Ctrl. Schs., Montgomery, 1998—. Spl. educator summer sch. incarcerated youth N.Y. State Divsn. Youth, 1993, 95, 96, 99, 2000, 2001, 2002; Adkins life skills educator DAYTOP, Millbrook, 1997-98. Vol. tchr., writer curriculum Latino Coalition of Middletown, 1994-96. Recipient cert. of appreciation Blythdale Children's Hosp., Valhalla, N.Y., 1988, Outstanding Tchr. award N.Y. State Divsn. Youth, 1996, Coun. Svc. award N.Y. State Reading Assn., 2000; selected to participate in People to People, Cuba, 2001, 2002. Mem. ASCD, Nat. Head Start Assn., N.Y. State Spl. Educators (1st v.p. 1999-2001, pres. 2001-2002), N.Y. State Reading Assn. (dir. Hudson Valley Region, chair silent auction 2002, conf. presenter 2001), N.Y. State Unified Tchrs., The Nature Conservancy, Audubon Soc. Am., Ulster County Reading Coun. (v.p. 1998-99, pres. 1999-2000, 2000-2001, 2001-2002, 2002-), Smithsonian Inst., Museum of Natural History, ANYSEED, Assn. of N.Y. Spl. Educators of the Emotionally Disturbed, Theater Devel. Fund Hudson River Clearwater Bardavon Theater. Democrat. Roman Catholic. Home: 734 Sheldon Rd Wallkill NY 12589-3324 E-mail: specialk6966@yahoo.com.

RHINES, MARIE LOUISE, composer, violinist; b. Boston; BA in History and Polit. Sci., Northeastern U.; postgrad., Yale U.; MusM, New Eng. Conservatory, Boston. Dir. chamber music Groton (Mass.) Sch. for Boys; prof. of violin King's Coll. Choir Sch., Cambridge, Eng.; concertmaster, asst. conductor Cape Cod Symphony, Hyannis, Mass.; producer, announcer, founder The Folk Heritage program Nat. Pub. Radio, Sta. WGBH-FM, Boston; guest faculty U. Colo., Boulder; conductor, Mozart Orch. Harvard U., Cambridge, Mass., 1985-86; panelist Mass. Coun. on Art and Humanities, Boston, 1986; pub., pres., founder Sedona (Ariz.) Music Pub. Co., 1988—; composer, guest soloist USAF Concert Band, Southwestern States, 1990—; guest soloist, composer in residence U.S. Command Band of Air Force Res., Warner Robins AFB, Ga., 1991; artist Ariz. Commn. on Arts and Humanities, Phoenix, 1990—; guest solo violin artist Holland Am. Cruise Lines, 1996. Artist-in-residence U. Calif., LaJolla; composer-artist-in-residence State of Tenn., Nashville; guest poet, musician Ariz. Cowboy Poets Gathering, Prescott, 1990-91; mem. violin faculty No. Ariz. U. 1993. Composer, publisher numerous works for solo violin, voice, chamber orchestra, full symphony orch. and opera chorus; solo violin concert appearances at major concert halls and as soloist with symphony orchs. throughout U.S., Can., Europe; numerous radio and TV interviews and documentaries; recording artist, N.Y., Nashville, 1996, RCA Studios. Cmty. Speakers Bureau Lect. Ariz. Humanities Council, 2000-01. Recipient Music Composition award, Artist Found.; Rockefeller grantee Am. Music Ctr. Mem. ASCAP (22 composing and performing awards), Nashville Assn. of Musicians, Meet the Composer. Avocations: mountain climbing, gourmet cooking, gardening, psychology, philosophy. Home and Office: Sedona Music 2255 Corral Rd Sedona AZ 86336-3272

RHINESMITH, STEPHEN HEADLEY, management consultant; b. Mineola, N.Y., Dec. 13, 1942; s. Homer Kern and Winifred Headley (Long) Rhinesmith; m. Kathleen Alys Law, Aug. 28, 1965; children: Christopher Law, Colin Headley. BA (Baker scholar), Wesleyan U., 1965; M in Pub. and Internat. Affairs, (Heinz fellow), U. Pitts., 1966, PhD (NDEA fellow), 1972. Dir. internat. svcs. McBer and Co., Cambridge, Mass., 1969-71; pres. AFS Intercultural Programs, N.Y.C., 1972-80, 87-89, Holland Am. Cruises, N.Y.C., 1980-82, Moran, Stahl, Boyer, N.Y.C., 1982-84, Rhinesmith & Assocs. Inc., Boston, 1984—; ptnr. CDR Internat., 1998—. Named amb., coord. Pres.'s U.S.-Soviet Exch. Initiative, 1986—87; chmn. dept. orgnl. sociology Moscow State U., 1991—96. Author: (book) Bring Home the World: A Management Guide to Community Leaders of International Programs, 1975, 1985, A Manager's Guide to Globalization: Six Skills for Success in a Changing World, 1993, A Manager's Guide to Globalization: Six Skills for Success in a

Changing World, 2d edit., 1996. Mem.: ASTD (chair 1994), Union League (N.Y.C.), Met. Club (Washington). Home and Office: PO Box 1645 West Chatham MA 02669-1645 E-mail: SHRglobal@aol.com.

RHOAD, RICHARD ARTHUR, secondary school educator, writer; b. Tiffin, Ohio, May 7, 1935; s. Cecil Feree and Iva Grace (Spitler) R. BA, Heidelberg U., 1956; MEd, Ohio U., 1957; postgrad., Bowling Green (Ohio) State U., 1958, U. N.Mex., Albuquerque, 1960-63, Rhode Island State U., 1964, DePauw U., 1966, Ohio State, 1991, Roosevelt U., 1991. Tchr. Avon Lake (Ohio) High Sch., 1957-60; thcr. Homewood-Flossmoor (Ill.) High Sch., 1960-66, New Trier High Sch., Winnetka, Ill., 1966-97; retired, 1997. Chmn. math. contest Ill. Coun. Tchrs. of Math., 1978-84. Writer and singer several original math. songs; contbr. articles to profl. jours. Mem. NEA (life), Ill. Edn. Assn., Nat. Coun. Tchrs. of Math. (life), Ill. Coun. Tchrs. of Math., Ohio Coun. Tchrs. of Math. (life), Sch. Sci. and Maths. (life), Phi Delta Kappa (life). Avocations: bridge, sports. Home: 1517 Elmwood Ave Wilmette IL 60091-1652 E-mail: r.rhoad@worldnet.att.net.

RHOADES, DONALD SCOTT, zoo and botanical park curator, biology educator; b. Madison, Wis., Aug. 15, 1950; s. Albert Leonard and Rosemary Agnes (Patterson) R.; m. Beverly Lynn Grey (div.); children: Aaron Douglas, Amy Cherie; m. Cheryl Jean McCulloch, Mar. 21, 1986; children: Ryan Alexander MacDonald, Amelia Lee MacDonald. BS, No. Ariz. U., 1972, MS, 1976; D of Arts, Idaho State U., 1980. Lectr. in biology Idaho State U., Pocatello, 1978; educator San Diego Zoo, 1980-83; curator of edn. Kansas City Zoo, 1983-87; curator edn. Riverbanks Zoo and Garden, Columbia, 1987—; adj. asst. prof. U. S.C., 1992—. Contbr. essays to Riverbanks Mag., 1987—. Mem. exec. bd. Midlands Improving Math. and Sci., Columbia, 1993—; co-founder AMAZE, 1988. Fellow Am. Zoo and Aquarium Assn. (profl., mem. edn. com. 1990-92, studbook keeper for hawk-headed parrot 1993—); mem. Am. Assn. Bot. Gardens and Arboreta, Internat. Assn. Zoo Educators, Explorers Club. Office: Riverbanks Zool Park Bot Garden 500 Wildlife Pkwy Columbia SC 29210-8093 Home: 511 S Chester St Gastonia NC 28052-4021 E-mail: drhoades@riverbanks.org.

RHOADES, JOHN SKYLSTEAD, SR. federal judge; b. 1925; m. Carmel Rhoades; children: Mark, John, Matthew, Peter, Christopher. AB, Stanford U., 1948; JD, U. Calif., San Francisco, 1951. Prosecuting atty. City of San Diego, 1955-56, dep. city atty., 1956-57; pvt. practice San Diego, 1957-60; ptnr. Rhoades, Hollywood & Neil, 1960-85; judge U.S. Dist. Ct. (so. dist.) Calif., 1985—. With USN, 1943-46. Office: US Dist Ct 940 Front St San Diego CA 92101-8994

RHOADES, MARYE FRANCES, paralegal; b. Ft. Defiance, Va., Jan. 29, 1937; d. Silas Caswell Sr. and Mary Ann Frances (James) Rhodes; m. Minter James Rowe, May 1964 (div. 1968); children: Margaret Frances Omar, James Robert Rowe; m. Robert Charles Rhoades Jr., July 25, 1980. Student, Mountain State U., 1956-58, 68, U. Charleston, 1962-63, 74, 89, Antioch U., 1972-73; grad., Mike Tyree Sch. Real Estate, 1984, Evans Coll. Legal Studies, 1990. Educator Nicholas County Sch. Sys., Summersville, W.Va., 1958-61; edit. staff, columnist, staff writer, reporter, photographer Beckley Newspapers Corp., 1962-76; educator Raleigh County Bd. Edn., Beckley, W.Va., 1967-68; exec. editor, columnist Local News Jour., Whitesville, 1976-77; libr. bookmobile, asst. ref. libr., outreach coord. Raleigh County Pub. Libr., Beckley, 1977-78; agt. Combined Ins. Co., Chgo., 1978-79; legal sec., paralegal W.Va. Legal Svcs. Inc., Beckley, 1979-82; paralegal Applachian Rsch and Defense Fund Inc., 1982-83; exec. dir., owner Rhoades and Rowe, 1983-85; paralegal patinet advocate Comty. Health Sys. Inc., 1986-96; pvt. practice, 1996—. Contbr. articles to mags. State bd. dirs., pub. resl. LWV, Beckley; pub. rels., various coms. Raleigh County Dem. Women, Beckley; sec., pub. rels. Orchard Valley Women's Club, Crab Orchard, W.Va.; trustee Fraternal Order Eagles; pub. rels., various coms. Loyal Order Moose, Beckley, Beckley Profl. Bus. Women; com. mem. Nat. Coalition to Save the New River; sales rep. So. U.S. Rep. to U.S. Mil. Acad., West Point, N.Y.; active Am. Legion Aux., Mullens, W.Va. Mem. NEA, Classroom Tchrs. Assn., Nat. Paralegal Assn., Nat. Fedn. Paralegals Assn., Nat. Ind. Paralegals Assn., Nat. Com. Save Soc., Sec. Medicare, Nat. Legal Aid and Def. Assn., Nat. Orgn. Social Security Claimants Reps., State Soc. Sec. Task Force, Nat. Vets. Legal Svcs. Project Inc., W.Va. U. Alumni Assn., Community AIDS Edn. Com., W.Va. Edn. Assn., Am. Disability Repr. Specs. Assn. Democrat. Mem. Ch. of God. Avocations: creative arts and music, walking, NASCAR, doll collecting, writing. Home: PO Box 416 Mac Arthur WV 25873-0416 Office: Benefit Services PO Box 7265 Beckley WV 25801 E-mail: tv65000@aol.com., bnftsvcs@aol.com.

RHOADES, ROBERT WILLIAM, art educator, artist; b. Cleve., Jan. 15, 1948; s. Robert and Nancy Rhoades; m. Bronwyn Ford Rhoades, July 22, 1977; children: Ryan, Chelsea. BA, Duke U., 1970; postgrad., Coll. Arts and Crafts, 1976—78; MFA, U. N.Mex., 1980. Instr. Foothill H.S., Bakersfield, Calif., 1970—76, Calif. H.S., San Ramon, 1976—78; artist, owner Graphflux Design, Oakland, 1976—81; prof., dept. chair Coll. of the Redwoods, Ft. Bragg, 1981—; artist, owenr Creekwood Studios, Mendocino, 1998—. Mem. supt. coun. Kern Union H.S. Dist., Bakersfield, 1975—77; bd. prs., v.p. Mendocino County Artists Coalition, Ukiah, Calif., 1983—85. One-woman shows include , Misa, Japan, 1995, Wilkes Gallery, Mendocino, 1988, Pacific Echo, Philo, Calif., 2000. Youth soccer coach Coast Youth Soccer League, Mendocino, 1986—94; troop leader Boy Scouts Am., 1990—94; bd. pres., mem. Sea Fair Rd. and Water Co., 1989—95. Grantee Dem. Soc. grantee, Kern Union, Bakersfield, 1975, Nat. Endowment for the Arts, Washington, 1988, Edn. Excellence grantee, Coll. of the Redwoods, Ft. Bragg, 1991. Mem.: Fort Bragg Art Ctr., San Francisco Mus. Modern Art, Mendocino Art Ctr. (trustee 1989—92), Coll. Art Assn., Redwood Health Club, Theta Chi (alumnus, v.p. 1967—70). Avocations: skiing, gardening, cooking. Home: 13100 Pomo Ln Mendocino CA 95460 Office: Coll of the Redwoods 1211 Del Mar Dr Fort Bragg CA 95437-5641

RHOADES, RODNEY ALLEN, physiologist, educator; b. Greenville, Ohio, Jan. 5, 1939; s. John H. and Floris L. Rhoades; m. Judith Ann Brown, Aug. 6, 1961; children: Annelisa, Kirsten. BS, Miami U., 1961; MS, 1963; PhD, Ohio State U., 1966. Asst. prof. Pa. State U., State Coll., 1966-72; assoc. prof., 1972-75; rsch. scientist NIH, Bethesda, Md., 1975-76; prof. Ind. U. Sch. Medicine, Indpls., 1976-81, 81—, chmn., 1981—. Dir. Indpls. Ctr. for Advanced Rsch. Author: Physiology, 1984; contbr. articles to profl. jours. Fellow NASA, 1964-66; recipient Rsch. Career Devel. award NIH, 1975-80. Mem. Am. Physiol. Soc, AHA, Am. Thoracic Soc., Biophysics Soc., Sigma Xi. Home: 1768 Spruce Dr Carmel IN 46033-9025 Office: Ind U Sch Medicine 635 Barnhill Dr Indianapolis IN 46202-5126

RHOADS, GEORGE GRANT, medical epidemiologist; b. Phila., Feb. 11, 1940; s. Jonathan Evans and Teresa (Folin) R.; m. Frances Ann Secker, June 5, 1965; children: Thomas C., James E. MD, Harvard U., 1965; MPH, U. Hawaii, 1970. Intern Hosp. of U. Pa., Phila., 1965-66, resident in internal medicine, 1966-68; resident in preventive medicine U. Hawaii Sch. Pub. Health, 1968-71; epidemiologist Japan-Hawaii Cancer Study, Honolulu, 1974-75; assoc. prof. U. Hawaii, 1974-79, chair dept. pub. health sci., 1978-81, dir. gen. preventive medicine, 1978-81, prof. pub. health, 1979-82; chief epidemiology br. Nat. Inst. Child Health and Human Devel./NIH, Bethesda, Md., 1982-89; prof., dir. grad program in pub. health U. Medicine and Dentistry N.J.-Robert Wood Johnson Med. Sch., Piscataway, 1989-2000; assoc. dean UMDNJ Sch. Pub. Health, 2000—. Contbr. more than 160 articles on the epidemiology of non-infectious diseases to profl. jours. Recipient Dirs. award NIH, 1987, EEO award NICHD, 1984. Fellow Am. Coll. Physicians; mem. Am. Epidemiol. Soc. Mem. Soc. Of Friends. Achievements include research on the protective effect of high density Lipoprotein in the blood against development of heart attacks. Office: Environ and Occupl Health Scis Inst 170 Freinghuysen Rd Piscataway NJ 08854

RHOADS, GERALDINE EMELINE, editor, consultant; b. Phila., Jan. 29, 1914; d. Lawrence Dry and Alice Fegley (Rice) R. AB, Bryn Mawr Coll., 1935. Publicity asst. Bryn Mawr (Pa.) Coll., 1935-37; asst. Internat. Students House, Phila., 1937-39; mng. editor The Woman mag., N.Y.C., 1939-42; editor Life Story mag., 1942-45, Today's Woman mag., N.Y.C., 1945-52, Today's Family Mag., N.Y.C., 1952-53; lectr. Columbia U., 1954-56; assoc. editor Readers Digest, 1954-55; producer NBC, 1955-56; assoc. editor Ladies Home Jour., 1956-62, mng. editor, 1962-63; exec. editor McCall's mag., 1963-66; editor Woman's Day mag., 1966-82, editorial dir., 1982-84, Woman's Day Resource Center, 1984-89; v.p. Woman's Day mag., 1972-77, 78-84, CBS Consumer Publs., 1977-84; cons. Woman's Day, N.Y.C., 1989-91. Editorial cons., dir. Nat. Mag. Awards, 1991-94. Author: (with others) Woman's Day Help Book, 1988. Journalism awards com., James Beard Found., 1993—. Recipient award for profl. achievement Diet Workshop Internat., 1977; Elizabeth Cutter Morrow award YWCA Salute to Women in Bus., 1977; Recipient Econ. Equity award Women's Equity Action League, 1982; March of Dimes Women Editor's citation, 1982 Mem. Nat. Press Club (dir.), Fashion Group (bd. govs. 1977-79, 87-88, chmn. bd. govs. 1978-80, treas. bd. govs. 1983-85, bd. dirs. Found. 1980-81), Am. Soc. Mag. Editors (chmn. exec. com. 1971-73), N.Y. Women in Comms. (Matrix award 1975), Advt. Women in N.Y. (bd. govs. 1983-85, 2d v.p. 1985-87, 1st v.p. 1987-89, bd. dirs. 1989-90, Pres.'s award 1987), Women's Forum (bd. dirs. 1985-87), YWCA Acad. Women Achievers, Women's City Club of N.Y. (bd. dirs. 1996—, chair comms.), Literacy Vols. of N.Y.C. (bd. dirs. 1986-93), Turtle Bay Assn. (bd. dirs. 1989-92), Bryn Mawr Coll. Alumni Assn. (bd. dirs. 1989-94), Bryn Mawr Club of N.Y.C. (bd. dirs. 1994-2000). Home: 185 W End Ave Apt 21A New York NY 10023-5548 E-mail: rhoadsge@aol.com.

RHOADS, JAMES BERTON, archivist, former government official, consultant, educator; b. Sioux City, Iowa, Sept. 17, 1928; s. James Harrison and Mary (Keenan) R.; m. S. Angela Handy, Aug. 12, 1947; children: Cynthia Patrice Neven, James Berton, Marcia Marie MacKellar. Student, Southwestern Jr. Coll., 1946-47, Union Coll., Lincoln, Neb., 1947-48; BA, U. Calif.-Berkeley, 1950, MA, 1952; PhD, Am. U., 1965. With GSA-Nat. Archives and Records Service, Washington, 1952-79, asst. archivist for civil archives, 1965, dept. archivist U.S., 1966-68, archivist U.S., 1968-79; chmn. Nat. Archives Trust Fund Bd., 1968-79; chmn. adminstrv. com. Fed. Register, 1968-79; chmn. Nat. Hist. Publs. and Records Comm., 1968-79; mem. Fed. Council on Arts and Humanities, 1970-79; pres. Rhoads Assos. Internat., 1980-84; dir. grad. program in archives and records mgmt. Western Wash. U., Bellingham, 1984-94, prof. history, 1987-94, dir. Ctr. for Pacific N.W. studies, 1994-97; prof. emeritus, 1994—. Trustee Woodrow Wilson Internat. Center for Scholars, 1969-79; v.p. Intergovtl. Coun. UNESCO Info. Program, 1977-79; mem. adv. bd. Wash. State Hist. Records, 1990-97. Recipient Meritorious and Disting. Service awards GSA, 1966, 68, 79 Fellow Soc. Am. Archivists (pres. 1974-75); mem. Internat. Coun. Archives (pres. 1976-79), Am. Antiquarian Soc., Am. Coun. Learned Socs. (com. Soviet-Am. archival coop. 1986-91), Mass. Hist. Soc. (corr.), Wash. State Hist. Soc. (trustee 1986-95), Acad. Cert. Archivists (pres. 1992-94).

RHOADS, LINDA SMITH, editor; b. Harrisburg, Pa., Feb. 22, 1949; d. Charles and Virginia Smith; m. David Brian Rhoads, 1969; children: Charles Gabriel, Julian Cooper. BA in English Lit. with honors, Simmons Coll., 1971; MA in English Lit. with honors, U. Chgo., 1973, postgrad., 1973-76. Copy editor Holbrook Press, Inc., Boston, 1971-72; mng. editor Critical Inquiry U. Chgo. Press, 1974-77, editl. cons. Critical Inquiry, 1977-79; freelance editor, 1978-79; asst. editor New Eng. Quar., 1981-82, assoc. editor, 1982-96, co-editor, 1996—2002, editor, 2002—; edn. coord. Mass. Hist. Soc., 2002—. Tchr. grad. history program Northeastern U., 1995--. Author: Amelia Peabody, A Biographical Sketch, 1998, Lt. Col. Ruby Winslow Linn: Doubling a Life of Service, 2001; editor Traditions and Innovations: Reflections on Northestern University's First Century, 1998. Trustee Paul Revere Meml. Assn., 1994—; fellow Mass. Hist. Soc., 1993—; mem. adv. bd. New England Women's Diaries Project. Mem. Colonial Soc. Mass. (chair outreach). Avocation: social justice activities. Office: Mass Hist Soc 1154 Boylston St Boston MA 02215 E-mail: lrhoads@masshist.org.

RHOADS, MICHAEL DENNIS, sales executive; b. Vinton, Iowa, June 25, 1949; s. Lloyd and Marilyn Mae (Appleton) R.; children: Melissa, Angela, Lori, Alan. BS in Indsl. Edn., Iowa State U., 1973; MBA, York Coll. of Pa., 1984. Order detailer, sales rep. Fisher Controls Inc., Marshalltown, Iowa, 1973-75; inside sales engr. Proconex, King of Prussia, Pa., 1975-79, outside sales engr. York, 1979-85, br. mgr., 1985-87, v.p. process instrumentaion sales King of Prussia, 1987-90, v.p., sales mgr., 1990—, sr. v.p., 1992—. Youth group leader Meth. Ch., Center Square, Pa., 1977-79; instr. Continuing Adult Edn., Marshalltown, 1973-75. With USN, 1968-70, Vietnam. Mem. Instrument Soc. Am. (v.p. 1984-86, pres. 1986-87, Best Sect. Pres. award 1987, Old Shoe award 1990), Am. Legion, VFW. Lutheran. Avocations: woodworking, carpentry, hunting, boating, sailing. Home: 205 Claremont Ln Downingtown PA 19335-1563 Office: Proconex 101 Enterprise Dr Royersford PA 19468 E-mail: mrhoads835@aol.com.

RHOADS, NANCY GLENN, lawyer; b. Washington, Oct. 15, 1957; d. Donald L. and Gerry R. R.; m. Robert A. Koons, June 23, 1984. BA, Gettysburg Coll., 1980; JD, Temple U., 1983. Bar: Pa., U.S. Dist. Ct. (ea. dist.) Pa. 1983. Rsch. asst. Prof. Mikochick, Phila., 1982-83; law clk. Phila. Ct. of Common Pleas, 1983-85; assoc. Post and Schell P.C., Phila., 1985-90, Sheller, Ludwig and Badey, Phila., 1990—. Co-author: Aging and the Aged: Problems, Opportunities, Challenges, 1980. Vol. Spl. Olympics. Mem. ATLA, Pa. Bar Assn., Phi Beta Kappa, Phi Alpha Theta, Pi Delta Epsilon, Eta Sigma Phi. Avocations: classical piano, horticulture, swimming. Home: 401 Audubon Ave Wayne PA 19087-4006 Office: Sheller Ludwig and Badey 1528 Walnut St Philadelphia PA 19102-3604

RHOADS, PAUL KELLY, lawyer; b. La Grange, Ill., Sept. 4, 1940; s. Herbert Graves and Mary Margaret (Gurrie) R.; m. Katheryn Virginia Reissaus, Sept. 14, 1963; children: Elizabeth R. Saline, Katheryn R. Meek, Julia C. BA, Washington & Lee U., 1962; JD, Loyola U., Chgo., 1967. Bar: Ill. 1967, U.S. Dist. Ct. (no. dist.) Ill. 1967, U.S. Tax Ct. 1980. Trust officer 1st Nat. Bank Chgo., 1963-69; with Schiff Hardin & Waite, Chgo., 1969-98, ptnr., 1973-98; sole practitioner Western Springs, Ill., 1999—. Bd. dirs. McKay Enterprises, Chgo. Author: Starting a Private Foundation, 1993, Managing a Private Foundation, 1997; contbr. articles to profl. jours. and chpts. to books. Trustee Ill. Inst. Tech., 1985-95, Western Springs (Ill.) Hist. Soc., 1983-92, Philanthropy Roundtable, Washington, 1992-2000; bd. dirs. Cyrus Tang Scholarship Found., 1984-91; bd. overseers Ill. Inst. Tech. Chgo.-Kent Coll. Law, 1985-95; pres., bd. dirs. Grover Hermann Found., Chgo., 1984—; sec., bd. dirs. Western Springs Svc. Club, 1976-86; sec. Vandivort Properties, Inc., Cape Girardeau, Mo.; mem. adv. com. estate, tax and fin. planning Loyola U., 1986-92; adv. com. Thomas A. Roe Inst. for Econ. Policy Studies, Heritage Found., 1989—. Fellow Am. Coll. Trust and Estate Coun.; mem. Ill. State Bar Assn., Chgo. Bar Assn., Union League Club Chgo., Salt Creek Club (Hinsdale, Ill.) (pres. 1982, bd. dirs. 1981-83), Portage Lake Yacht Club (Onekama, Mich.) (commodore 1988, bd. dirs. 1985-89), Manistee (Mich.) Golf and Country Club. Republican. Avocations: sailing, golf, tennis. Office: 1000 Hillgrove Ave Western Springs IL 60558-1420 E-mail: paulkrhoads@aol.com.

RHOADS, PRESTON MARK, pharmacist, consultant; b. Tucson, Dec. 28, 1957; s. Larry Herman and Juanita Colleen (Pugh) R.; m. Cynthia Lou Wolfer, Mar. 9, 1996; children: James Branden, Candace Lovell. BS in Pharmacy, U. Ariz., 1980. Registered pharmacist, Ariz. Dir. pharmacy Holy Cross Hosp., Nogales, Ariz., 1982-83; poison info. specialist Ariz. Poison and Drug Info. Ctr., Tucson, 1984-86; staff pharmacist Drug Emporium, 1986-89, Walgreens Co., Tucson, 1989-92, Danny's Pharmacy, Tucson, 1993-95; long term care mgr. Sunscript Pharmacy, 1995-96; cons. pharmacist Danny's Sunscript Pharmacy, 1996—, divisional cons. dir., 1999-2000, dir. pharmacy, 2000—. Regional rep. Sunscript Nat. Adv. Panel; mem. profl. adv. com. C.O.A.C.H. Assisted Living Coun., Tucson, 1996—; mem. regional adv. bd. U. Ariz. Coll. Pharmacy; bd. dirs. U. Ariz Alumni Assn., 2000-2002. Contbr. articles to profl. jours. Adv. bd. mem. Serve Our Srs. LLC, Tucson, 1996-97; bd. govs. adv. coun. on aging, 2000—. Gen. resident scholar U. Ariz., 1975-78. Fellow Am. Soc. Cons. Pharmacists; mem. Students Am. Pharm. Assn. (newsletter editor 1977), Rho Chi. Avocations: leathercraft, music, woodworking. E-mail: mark.rhoads.sunh.com. Office: Dannys Sunscript Pharmacy 5395 E Erickson Dr Tucson AZ 85712-2826

RHOADS, STEVEN ERIC, political science educator; b. Abington, Pa., May 12, 1939; s. John Reginald and Barbara Ann (Dugan) R.; m. Diana Cabanis Akers, May 17, 1944; children— Christopher, Nicholas, John. B.A., Princeton U., 1961; M.P.A., Cornell U., 1965, Ph.D., 1972. Mem. staff Office Mgmt. and Budget, Washington, 1965-66; asst. prof. dept. govt. and fgn. affairs U. Va., Charlottesville, 1970-76, assoc. prof., 1977-86, prof. 1986— . Served to lt. (j.g.) USN, 1961-63. Fellow NEH, Inst. Ednl. Affairs, Earhart Found., Bradley Found., Olin Found. Mem. Am. Polit. Sci. Assn., Assn. Pub. Policy and Mgmt. Author: Policy Analysis in the Federal Aviation Administration, 1974; Valuing Life: Public Policy Dilemmas, 1980; The Economist's View of the World: Government, Markets and Public Policy, 1985, Incomparable Worth: Pay Equity Meets the Market, 1993; contbr. articles to profl. publs. Home: 3190 Dundee Rd Earlysville VA 22936-9621 Office: U Va Dept Politics Cabell Hall 232 Charlottesville VA 22903

RHODE, ALFRED SHIMON, business consultant, educator; b. Vienna, Austria, July 31, 1928; came to U.S., 1940, naturalized, 1949; s. Aron and Olga (Schwarz) Rothkirch; m. Phyllis Mazur, Dec. 28, 1959; children: Yael, Tamar, Yvette, Liane. BCE, CUNY, 1950; MEA, George Washington U., 1959; PhD, Am. U., 1973. Registered profl. engr., Md. Engr. Bur. of Reclamation, Sacramento, 1950-52; various engring. positions U.S. Govt., 1954-63; head logistics rsch. Navy Supply Sys. Command, Washington, 1963-68; head support forces, manpower and logistics br. Navy Program Planning Office, 1968-75; sr. v.p. nat. security analysis and warfare support group Info. Spectrum, Inc., Arlington, Va., 1976-89, cons., 1989-92; professorial lectr. George Washington U., Washington, 1969-75; adj. faculty Sch. Mgmt. George Mason U., Fairfax, Va., 1990—; adj. faculty Sch. Bus. Adminstrn. Georgetown U., Washington, 1998—. Exec. dir. Montgomery County Retail Security and Loss Prevention Assn. Contbr. articles to profl. jours. Capt. USAF, 1952-54. Congl. fellow, 1962. Fellow Mil. Ops. Rsch. Soc. (1st v.p., dir.); mem. Inst. Ops. Rsch. and Mgmt. Scis. (chmn. mil. applications sect.), Washington Inst. for Ops. Rsch. and the Mgmt. Scis. Home: 8305 Fox Run Potomac MD 20854-2576 E-mail: arhode@erols.com.

RHODE, EDWARD ALBERT, veterinary medicine educator, veterinary cardiologist; b. Amsterdam, N.Y., July 25, 1926; s. Edward A. and Katherine (Webb) R.; m. Dolores Bangert, 1955; children: David E., Peter R., Paul W., Robert M., Catherine E. DVM, Cornell U., 1947. Diplomate Am. Coll. Veterinary Internal Medicine. Prof. emeritus vet. medicine U. Calif., Davis, 1964—, chmn. dept. vet. medicine, 1968-71; assoc. dean instrn. U. Calif. Sch. Vet. Medicine, 1971-81, dean, 1982-91. Mem. AAAS, Nat. Acad. Practices, Am. Coll. Vet. Internal Medicine, Am. Vet. Medicine Assn., Basic Sci. Coun., Am. Heart Assn., Am. Acad. Vet. Cardiology, Am. Physiol. Soc., Calif. Vet. Medicine Assn. Office: U Calif Sch Vet Med Davis CA 95616

RHODEN, WILLIAM GARY, lawyer; b. Aiken, S.C., June 20, 1955; s. Thomas Gary and Catherine (Moseley) R.; m. Paula Jean Henderson, Aug. 8, 1981. BS in Psychology, U. S.C., Aiken, 1977; JD, U. S.C., 1980. Bar: S.C. 1981, U.S. Dist. Ct. S.C. 1982, U.S. Ct. Appeals (4th cir.) 1985. Lab. asst. psychology dept. U. S.C., Aiken, 1975-77; asst. dir. Greer (S.C.) YMCA, 1977-78; law clk. U.S. Atty. Office, Greer, 1977-78; intern U.S. Justice Dept., Columbia, S.C., 1980-81; staff atty. Office of Atty. Gen. State of S.C., Florence, 1981, asst. atty. gen. Charleston, S.C., 1981-83; asst. solicitor 7th Jud. Cir., Spartanburg, 1984-86; pvt. practice Gaffney, 1986—. Bd. dirs. Cherokee Children's Home, S.C. Peach Festival. Mem. ABA, Cherokee County Bar Assn. (sec.-treas. 1988-96, pres. 1996—), Rotary (Paul Harris fellow), Phi Alpha Delta. Avocations: tennis, golf, racquetball. Office: 221 E Floyd Baker Blvd PO Box 1937 Gaffney SC 29342-1937 Home: 414 Arrowhead Trl Columbus NC 28722-3453

RHODES, ALAN CHARLES, minister; b. Plattsburgh, N.Y., July 25, 1951; s. Charles Oliver and Lillian Mary (Cromie) R.; m. Holly C. Craver, June 14, 1975 (div. June 1987); m. Nancy Lichtenhan, June 18, 1988. BA, Lycoming Coll., Williamsport, Pa., 1973; MDiv, Boston U., 1976; DMin, Bangor (Maine) Theol. Sem., 1997. Ordained to ministry United Meth. Ch. as deacon, 1974, as elder, 1977. Assoc. pastor Shenendehowa United Meth. Ch., Clifton Park, N.Y., 1976-79; pastor Ft. Plain (N.Y.) and Freysbush United Meth. Chs., 1979-83, St. Paul's United Meth. Ch., Castleton-on-Hudson, N.Y., 1983-87, Grace United Meth. Ch., Ravena, 1987-98, North Main St. United Meth. Ch., Gloversville, NY, 1998—2002, Mechanicville (N.Y.) United Meth. Ch., 2002—. Trustee Troy Ann. Conf., 1993—, mem. bd. ordained ministry Troy Conf., 1996—. Founder, former co-chair R.C.S. Task Force Against Domestic Violence; chair Fulton County Domestic Violence Task Force, 1998—2002; mem., v.p. Troy Conf. Adminstrv. Svcs. Com., 2000—, Gloversville Ethics Bd., 2000—02, Gloversville Coun. Chs., 1998—2002. Mem.: Lions Club. Republican. Home: 320 N Main St Gloversville NY 12078-2141 Office: North Main St United Meth Ch 316 N Main St Gloversville NY 12078-2141 E-mail: anrhodes@telenet.net.

RHODES, ALICE GRAHAM, lawyer; b. Phila., June 15, 1941; d. Peter Graham III and Fannie Isadora (Bennett) Graham; m. Charles Milton Rhodes, Oct. 14, 1971 (dv. Apr. 21, 1997); children: Helen, Carla, Shauna. BS, East Stroudsburg U. Pa., 1962; MS, U. Pa., 1966, LLB, 1969, JD, 1970. Bar: N.Y. 1970, U.S. Dist. Ct. (so. and ea. dists.) N.Y. 1971, U.S. Ct. Appeals (2d cir.) 1971, Ky. 1983, U.S. Dist. Ct. (ea. dist.) Ky. 1985. Staff atty. Harlem Assertion Rights, Mobilization for Youth Office Econ. Opportunity, N.Y.C., 1969-70, coord. Cmty. Action Legal Svcs., 1970-72; assoc. dir. in charge of civil representation HUD Model Cities Cmty. Law Offices, 1972-73; resource assoc. Commn. on Edn. & Employment of Women, N.C. Dept. Adminstrn., Raleigh, 1975-76; mgr. policies and procedures Div. for Youth, N.C. Dept. Human Resources, 1976; in-house counsel, petroleum transactional atty. Ashland, Inc. (formerly Ashland Oil, Inc.), 1980-82; mem. core group Ashland, Inc., 1985-87, 88-91; with Ashland City Commn. Human Rights, 1993-99; mem. bd. regents Ea. Ky. U., 1994-2001; exec. bd., chmn. internal affairs com., academic affairs, 1997-98; asst. county atty. family ct. Jefferson County, 1999-2000. Mem. Property Valuation Appeals Commn., 1994; cons. pub. mem. selection and performance stds. review bd. Fgn. Svc., U.S. Dept. State, 1995, Fgn. Agrl. Svc. USDA, 1997; prison program planner, cons. N.Y. City Dept. Corrections, 1971; lectr. N.Y.C. Corrections Acad., Riker's, 1971; lectr. juvenile justice N.C. Law Enforcement Acad., Salemburg, 1976. Mem. usher bd. New Hope Bapt. Ch., Ashland, 1980-94; bd. dirs. YWCA Ashland, 1983-84, Ashland Heritage Pk. Commn., 1983-85; bd. dirs., budget com. United Way, Greenup County, Ky., Boyd County, Ashland, 1988-92; driver Meals on Wheels, 1983-91; vol. Am. Heart Assn., 1982-91; bd. dirs. Our Lady of Bellefonte Hosp. Found. Franciscan Sisters of the Poor, 1996-99, Ky. Health System, 1996-99, Carter G. Woodson Found. 1997, Study Afro-Am. Life and History; mem. adv. com. task force post secondary edn. Gov. of Ky.; bd. dirs. exec. com. Boyd County Dem. Women, 1996-2000; mem. presdl. search com. Ea. Ky. U., 1997-98, Ky. Gov.'s Conf. on Postsecondady Edn., 1999. Recipient Cmty. Svc. award Queens Community Corp., N.Y.C., 1972, Ashland C.C., 1986, Cmty. Svc. award NAACP, Ky.; NSF fellow, 1964, 65, ; faculty friends of Pa. scholar U. Pa., 1966-69, Reginald Heber Smith postgrad. fellow cmty. law, 1969-71; named to Hon. Order of Ky. Cols., 1989. Fellow Ky. Bar Found.; mem. AAUW (bd. dirs. Phila. chpt. 1963-65), Nat. Bar Assn., N.Y. Bar, Ky. Bar Assn. (mem. edn. law, corp. house counsel, workers compensation law sects.), Pilot Club (exec. bd. Ashland 1983), Links, Inc., Penn Club (charter mem. N.Y. chpt.), Assn. Gov. Bds. Colls. and Univs., Jefferson Club, Bellefonte Country Club. Democrat. Avocations: interior decorating, sports, dancing, gourmet cooking, gardening. Home: PO Box 12408 Philadelphia PA 19151

RHODES, ALLEN FRANKLIN, engineering executive; b. Estherville, Iowa, Oct. 3, 1924; m. Carol Haisler, 1962; children: James Fleming, Stephen Haisler. BSME, Villanova U., 1947; ML, U. Houston, 1950. Reg. profl. engr., Tex. Asst. dir. engring. adminstrn. Hughes Tool Co., Houston, 1947-52; pres. McEvoy Co., 1952-63; v.p. engring. & Rsch. Rockwell Mfg. Co., Pitts., 1963-70; v.p. corp. planning & devel. ACF Industries, N.Y.C., 1971-73; pres., CEO McEvoy Oilfield Equipment Co., Houston, 1974-79; exec. v.p., CEO Goldrus Marine Drilling, 1979-82; pres., CEO Warren Oilfield Svc., 1981-82, Anglo Energy, N.Y.C., 1983-86, Gripper Inc., Houston, 1987-90; v.p., CFO Hydrotech Sys. Inc., 1991; cons. Allen F. Rhodes, Bus. Advisor & Consulting Engr., 1991—, Silver Fox Advisors, 1986—; adj. prof. U. Houston, 2001—. Chmn. Com. Dept. Transp. Gas Pipelin Safety Std., 1969-73; dir. Keystone Internat., 1980-97, Triten Corp., 1980—, Rawson-Koenig, 1986-98, S.W. Rsch. Inst., 1989—, Tex. Microsystem, 1989-92, Houston Humane Soc., 1999—; adj. prof. mech. engring. U. Houston, 2001--. Dir. T&B Lehman Animal Shelter, Inc., 2002—. Recipient Charles Russ Richards Meml. award, 1987, Howard Conley medal Am. Nat. Std. Inst., 1980. Fellow ASME (past pres., Robert Henry Thurston award 1978), Inst. Mech. Engrs. (Gt. Britain); mem. Nat. Acad. Engring., Soc. Petroleum Engrs., Am. Petroleum Inst. Home and Office: 8720 Memorial Dr Houston TX 77024-7011

RHODES, ANN L. theatrical producer, investor; b. Ft. Worth, Oct. 17, 1941; d. Jon Knox and Carol Jane (Greene) R. Student, Tex. Christian U., 1960-63. V.p. Rhodes Enterprises Inc., Ft. Worth, 1963-77; owner, mgr. Lucky R Ranch, 1969-97, Ann L. Rhodes Investments, Ft. Worth, 1976—. Pres., chmn. bd. ALR Enterprises, Inc., Ft. Worth, 1977-93; pres. ALR Prodns., Inc., 1993—. Bd. dirs. Tarrant Coun. Alcoholism, 1973-78, hon. bd. dirs., 1978—; bd. dirs. N.W. Tex. Coun., Arthritis Found., 1977-84, Circle Theatre, 1987-94, Arts Coun. of Ft. Worth and Tarrant County, 1991-94; mem. adv. bd. Stage West, 1987—, Hip Pocket Theatre, 1994—; bd. govs. Ft. Worth Theatre, 1989-93; mem. pro-arts bd. Tex. Christian U. Coll. Fine Arts & Comm., 1994; mem. exec. com. Tarrant County Rep. Party, 1964-69; bd. dirs. Live Theatre League Tarrant County, 1993—, Casa Mañana Theatre, 1993—, mem. exec. com., 1995—. Recipient various svc. awards, including Patron of Yr. award Live Theatre League Tarrant County, 1992-93. Office: Ste 908 Ridglea Bank Bldg Fort Worth TX 76116

RHODES, ARTHUR DELANO, benefits administrator; b. Philadelphia, Miss., Nov. 26, 1960; s. A.D. and Mary (McNair) R.; m. Angela Marie Jolly, May 21, 1988. AA, Miss. Delta Jr. Coll., Moorhead, 1980; BA in Polit. Sci., Millsaps Coll., 1982; JD, U. Miss., 1985. Bar: Miss. 1985, U.S. Dist. Ct. (no. and so. dist.) Miss. 1985. Intern asst. dist. atty. Dist. Atty's Office, Hernando, Miss., 1985; counsel Child Support Unit, Dept. of Human Svcs., Brookhaven, 1985-87; assoc. Prewitt & Bradley, Jackson, 1987-88; chief of staff Congressman Mike Parker, Washington, 1988-98; pres., CEO The Benefits Bd., Inc., Cleveland, Tenn., 1999—. Republican. Mem. Ch. of God. Avocations: travel, reading. Home: 2014 Woodchase Way NE Cleveland TN 37311-1461 Office: The Benefits Bd PO Box 4608 Cleveland TN 37320-4608

RHODES, ARTHUR RUSSELL, dermatologist, researcher; b. Phila., Feb. 2, 1943; m. Susan Schotz (div. Aug. 2001); children: Zoe Maura, Maggie Lise. BA Chemistry magna cum laude, Wesleyan U., Middletown, Conn., 1965; MD, Columbia U., 1969; MPH, Harvard U. Diplomate Am. Bd. Internal Med., Am. Bd. Dermatology. Intern in internal med. Columbia Divsn. Harlem Hosp. Ctr., N.Y.C., 1969—70; resident in internal med. Beth Israel Hosp., Boston, 1970—72; resident in dermatology Mass. Gen. Hosp., Harvard Dermatology, 1975—78; chief divsn. dermatology Boston Children's Hosp., 1978—87; dir. ped. dermatology Mass. Gen. Hosp., 1987—89; assoc. prof. dermatology Harvard Med. Sch., 1988—89; prof. dept. dermatology U. Pitts. Sch. Med., 1989—99, Rush Med. Coll., Chgo., 1999—. Contbr. articles to profl. jours. Maj. U.S. Army, 1973—75. Fellow: Am. Bd. Dermatology, Am. Bd. Internal Med.; mem.: Phi Beta Kappa, Sigma Xi. Achievements include development of of methods to assess risk factors for melanoma; helped to define risk factors and potential precursor moles that have a high melanoma risk; defined the pathology and significance of sun-induced freckles in children; development of of methods to grade the pathology of molar melanoma. Avocations: running, photography, skiing, horseback riding, dancing. Office: Rush Med Ctr Dept Dermatology 1653 W Congress Pkwy Kidstan 507 Chicago IL 60612 Office Fax: 312-942-7778.

RHODES, BETTY FLEMING, rehabilitation services professional, nurse; b. Franklin, Pa., Nov. 28, 1920; d. John and Twyla Odella (Callen) Fleming; m. Donald Muir Cain, Dec. 31, 1952 (div.); m. Lee Chester Rhodes, June 23, 1962 (dec. Apr. 1997). RN, Allegheny Gen. Hosp., Pitts., 1942. Lic. phys. therapist, Pa. Phys. therapist Ky. Soc. for Crippled Children, Louisville, 1947-51, St. Anthony Hosp., Louisville, 1953-78. Nurse U.S. Army, 1943-45; capt. Army Nurse Corps, 1951-52. Decorated Bronze Star. Mem. Am. Phys Therapy Assn. (pres. Ky. chpt.). Roman Catholic. Home: Providence Retirement Home 4915 Charleston Rd Apt 210 New Albany IN 47150

RHODES, CARL ANTHONY, engineer; b. Springfield, Ohio, Jan. 9, 1970; s. Carl Anthony and Phyllis Matekunas R.; m. Alexandra Dumas Rhodes, Aug. 28, 1993. BS, Stanford U., 1992; MS, Calif. Inst. Tech., Pasadena, 1995, PhD, 1998. Rsch. asst. Calif. Inst. Technology, Pasadena, 1992-95, ETH-Swiss Federal Inst. Tech., Zurich, 1995-97; engr. RAND, Santa Monica, Calif., 1997—. Mem. AIAA, Am. Inst. Chem. Engring. Avocations: sailing, jogging, aerobics. Office: Rand 1700 Main St Santa Monica CA 90401-3208 E-mail: crhodes@rand.org.

RHODES, DAISY CHUN, writer, researcher, oral historian; b. Kahuku, Hawaii, Nov. 16, 1933; d. Pyung Chan Chun and Shin Ai Park; children: Joseph, Carmella, Thomas Francese. BA in Creative Writing, Eckerd Coll., 1995. Info. specialist Reconstrn. Devel. Corp., Washington, 1970; specialist indigent funding George Washington U. Hosp., 1971-74; mgr. hosp. assistance Alexandria (Va.) Hosp., 1975-79; asst. editor Employee Futures Rsch., Luray, Va., 1980-84; editor Inside Negotiations, Rochester, N.Y., 1985-87, Educators Negotiating Svc., New Port Richey, Fla., 1987-89; novelist, writer, 1989-95; rschr., oral historian Honolulu, 1994; writer Colorado Springs, 1995—; rschr., cons. Donna Ladd, Writer, 1996. Rschr., cons. Donna Ladd, Writer, Colorado Springs, 1996; presenter Asian Studies Conf., Honolulu; presenter scholarly and abstract Korean Picture Brides We. Asian Studies Conf., Boulder, Colo., 1997; lectr. Ctr. for Korean Studies U. Hawaii, 1998. Author: Forever Long-Never End, 1990, Wahaiawa Red Dirt, 1991, At Crossroads of Inspiration, 1993, Shirley Temple Feet, 1993, Remembering the Fallen, 1994, Passages to Paradise: Early Korean Immigrant Narratives from Hawaii, 1998; author: (play) I Know About Olympus, 1993; author: Eye of the Dragon, 1994 (finalist Hemingway 1st Novel Competition, 1994); author: (scholarly and abstract) How Oral History of the First Koreans in America Advances Archival Research, 1996; author: My Father's Voice, Echoes Upon Echoes, 2002. Pres. Colorado Springs Friends of Aquatics, 1997—; bd. dirs. All Souls Unitarian Ch. Recipient Work Study award for profls., Rotary Internat. Found., South Korea, 1998—99. Mem.: Korean Am. Women's Soc. Greater Washington (pres. 1983—84, bd. dirs., Commendation), Korea Soc., Assn. for Asian Studies, West Pasco Kiwanis (pres. 1990—92). Home: 1912 Eastlake Blvd #211 Colorado Springs CO 80910 E-mail: dyschun@msn.com.

RHODES, DAMIAN, professional hockey player; b. St. Paul, May 28, 1969; Goaltender Toronto Maple Leafs, 1990-96, New York Islanders, 1996, Ottawa Senators, 1996-99, Atlanta Thrashers, 1999—. Mem. St. John's Leafs of Am. Hockey League, 1992-93 Avocations: music, golf. Office: Atlanta Thrashers 1 Cnn Ctr NW # 13S Atlanta GA 30303-2762*

RHODES, DEBORAH JANE, internist; b. Swansea, Wales, July 21, 1963; d. Frank and Rosa (Carlson) R.; m. Frederick Savage Groves, May 30, 1992. BA, Harvard Coll., 1986; MD, Cornell U. Med. Coll., 1992. Diplomate Am. Bd. Internal Medicine. Intern Johns Hopkins Hosp., Balt., 1992-93, resident, 1993-95, clin. scholar, 1995-97; cons. Mayo Clin., Rochester, Minn., 1997—; asst. prof. Mayo Med. Sch., 2001—. Office: Mayo Clinic 200 1st St SW Rochester MN 55905-0002

RHODES, DONALD ROBERT, musicologist, retired electrical engineer; b. Detroit, Dec. 31, 1923; s. Donald Eber and Edna Mae (Fulmer) R.; children: Joyce R. Holbert, Jane E., Roger C., Diane R. Herran. BEE, Ohio State U., 1945, MEE, 1948, PhD, 1953. Research assoc. Ohio State U., Columbus, 1945-54; research engr. Cornell Aero. Lab., Buffalo, 1954-57; head basic research dept. Radiation, Inc., Orlando, Fla., 1957-61, sr. scientist Melbourne, 1961-66; Univ. prof. N.C. State U., Raleigh, 1966-94, univ. prof. emeritus, 1994—. Author: Introduction to Monopulse, 1959, 2d edit., 1980, Synthesis of Planar Antenna Sources, 1974, A Reactance Theorem, 1977. Co-founder Central Fla. Community Orch., Winter Park, 1961, pres., 1961-62. Recipient Benjamin G. Lamme medal Ohio State U., 1975; Eminent Engr. award Tau Beta Pi, 1976; named to N.C. State U. Acad. Outstanding Tchrs., 1980 Fellow AAAS, IEEE (John T. Bolljahn award 1963, pres. Antennas and Propagation Soc. 1969); mem. Am. Musicological Soc. Home: Apt 101 625 Centennial Pkwy Raleigh NC 27606-3255 Office: PO Box 7911 Raleigh NC 27695-7911

RHODES, DORIS CHANEY, freelance/self-employed secondary school educator; b. Ft. Worth, Sept. 10, 1942; d. R. C. and Louis (Churchill) Chaney; m. Larry Williams, Jan. 19, 1969 (div. 1975); m. King Rhodes, 1981. BS, Bishop Coll., 1968; MS, Calif. State U., Hayward, 1975. Cert. tchr. Tex., Calif. Tchr. Dallas Ind. Sch., 1968—69, Kansas City (Kans.) Schs., 1969—70; project dir., counsellor Oakland (Calif.) Sch. Dist., 1974—75, tchr., resource, 1970—73, sch. adminstr., 1975—80; owner Opportunities Unltd., Plano, Tex., 1980—. Bd. dirs. Boys and Girls Club, Collin County, Tex., 1998, Goodwill Industries, Oakland, 1978. Recipient Excellence in Field of Bus. award, Dallas Met. Bus. and Profl. Womens Club, 1982. Avocations: reading, writing, art, music, travel. Office: Opportunities Unltd Ste 267-153 1900 Preston Rd Plano TX 75093

RHODES, EDDIE, JR. medical technologist, phlebotomy technician, educator; b. Memphis, Apr. 14, 1955; s. Eddie Sr. and Mabel (Payne) R. AS, Shelby State C.C., Memphis, 1979; BS, Memphis State U., 1981. Cert. med. technologist. Rsch. technologist St. Jude's Children Rsch. Hosp., Memphis, 1980-81; med. lab. asst. Roche Biomedical Lab., Tucker, Ga., 1991-92; med. technologist Damon / MetPath Clin. Lab., Smyrna, 1992-93, ARC, Norcross, 1993-95, Ga. Bapt. Med. Ctr., Atlanta, 1994—; instr. microbiology Atlanta Area Tech., 1995-96, adv. bd. mem., 1995—; blood donor specialist Civitan Regl. Blood Sys., 1996—; med. lab./phlebotomy program coord. W. Ga. Tech., LaGrange, 1996—. Named one of the Outstanding Young Men of Am., Atlanta, 1989. Mem.: Am. Med. Technologists (cert.), Am. Soc. of Phlebotomy Technicians, Am. Soc. Microbiology. Avocations: cycling, basketball, chess. Home: 410 Park Pl Lagrange GA 30240-1747 Office: West Ga Technical 303 Fort Dr Lagrange GA 30240-5901

RHODES, ERIC FOSTER, employee relations consultant, writer; b. Luray, Va., Feb. 5, 1927; s. Wallace Keith and Bertha (Foster) R.; m. Barbara Ellen Henson, Oct. 19, 1946; children: Roxanne Jane, Laurel Lee; m. Lorraine Endresen, July 29, 1972; m. Daisy Chun, May 31, 1980 AA, George Washington U., 1949, AB, 1950, MA, 1952, EdD, 1967. Tchr. high sch., Arlington, Va., 1950-52; counselor Washington Lee High Sch., 1952-53, dir. publs., 1953-54, chmn. dept. English, 1954-55; exec. sec. Arlington Edn. Assn., 1952-53, Montgomery County (Md.) Edn. Assn., Rockville, Md., 1955-57; lectr. edn. George Washington U., Washington, 1955-60, 65-70; salary cons. NEA, 1957-58, asst. dir. membership div., 1958-60; dir. N.Y. regional office, N.Y.C., 1960-64; ednl. cons. Ednl. Rsch. Svcs., White Plains, N.Y., 1964-65; pres. Ednl. Svc. Bur., Inc., Arlington, Va., 1965-72, chmn. bd., 1972-80; pres. Negotiations Consultation Svcs., Inc., 1969-80, Eastern States Advt. Inc., Arlington, 1970-79, EFR Corp., Arlington, 1972-90; exec. dir. Assn. Negotiators and Contract Adminstrs., 1981-89; area coord. U.S. Legal Protection Co., 1989-95; pres. Employee Futures Rsch., Colorado Springs, Colo., 1980—, Waterfront Only Real Estate, New Port Richey, Fla., 1988-92, Inst. for Negotiations Tng., New Port Richey, 1989-95, Asset Protection Co., 1991—; asst. supt. for adminstrn. Brighton Schs., Rochester, N.Y., 1983-88; owner Frederick Foster Galleries, Arlington, 1974-80. Cons. Va. Dept. Community Colls., Richmond, 1965-77; vice chancellor Va. Community Coll. System, 1970-71; employee rels. ofcl. City of Orlando, 1980-83; lectr. edn. Frostburg (Md.) State Coll., 1967 Author: Negotiating Salaries, 41 Ways to Cut Budget Costs, Making Good Things Happen Through Negotiation; editor: Inside Negotiations, Wages and Benefits, Employers' Negotiating Service. Mem. Civil Rights Commn., Franklin Twp., N.J., 1962-64; mem. sr. victim assistance team Colorado Springs Police Dept., 1997—; mem. Franklin Twp. Bd. Edn., 1964-65; mem. adv. bd. Keep Am. Beautiful, 1964-75, nat. chmn., 1968; bd. dirs., v.p. Unitarian-Universalist Ch., Tarpon Springs, Fla., 1990-95, pres., 1994-95; treas. Friends of Aquatics, 2001—. With U.S. Army, 1945-47. Mem. Am. Assn. Sch. Adminstrs., Internat. Assn. Sch. Bus. Officials, NEA, Edn. Press Assn., Nat. Assn. Ednl. Negotiators (exec. dir. 1971-81), Am. Arbitration Assn. (labor arbitrator), Indsl. Rels. Rsch. Assn., United C. of C. of Pasco County (sec., treas. 1989-90, exec. dir. 1990-91), Am. Legion, Fed. Schoolmen's Club, N.Y. Schoolmen's Club, Lions (v.p. N.Y.C. club 1964-65), Kiwanis (pres. West Pasco club 1991-93), Order of St. John of Jerusalem, Phi Delta Kappa (chpt. pres. 1959-60). Home: # 211 1912 Eastlake Blvd Colorado Springs CO 80910 E-mail: dysychun@qwest.net.

RHODES, FRANK HAROLD TREVOR, university president emeritus, geologist; b. Warwickshire, Eng., Oct. 29, 1926; came to U.S., 1968, naturalized, 1976; s. Harold Cecil and Gladys (Ford) R.; m. Rosa Carlson, Aug. 16, 1952; children: Jennifer, Catherine, Penelope, Deborah. BSc, U. Birmingham, 1948, PhD, 1950, DSc (hon.), 1963; LLD (hon.), Wooster Coll., 1976, Nazareth Coll. Rochester, 1979, Skidmore Coll., 1989, U. Mich., 1990, Clemson U., 1991, Dartmouth Coll., 1993, U. Birmingham, U.K., 1999; LHD (hon.), Colgate U., 1980, Johns Hopkins U., 1982, Wagner Coll., 1982, Hope Coll., 1982, Rensselaer Poly Inst., 1982, LeMoyne Coll., 1984, Pace U., 1986, Alaska Pacific U., 1987, Hamilton Coll., 1987, SUNY, 1992, Canisius Coll., 1994, Ithaca Coll., 1995; DSc (hon.), U. Wales, Eng., 1981, Fla. Atlantic U., 1996, Bucknell U., 1985, U. Ill., 1986, Reed Coll., 1988, Elmira Coll., 1989, U. Southampton, U.K., 1989, U. Sydney, Australia, 1995, U. Durham, Eng., 1995, Millsaps Coll., 1996; DLitt (hon.), U. Nev., 1982; EdD (hon.), Ohio State U., 1992; D. Univ. (hon.), U. Stirling, Eng., 1994; LLD (hon.) (hon.) , Fla. Internat. U., 2000. Post-doctoral fellow, Fulbright scholar U. Ill., 1950-51, vis. lectr. geology, summers 1951, 52; lectr. geology U. Durham, 1951-54; asst. prof. U. Ill., 1954-55, assoc. prof., 1955-56; dir. U. Ill. Field Sta., Wyo., 1956; prof. geology, head geology dept. U. Wales, Swansea, 1956-68, dean faculty of sci., 1967-68; prof. geology and mineralogy Coll. Lit., Sci. and Arts, U. Mich., 1968-77, dean, 1971-74, v.p. for acad. affairs, 1974-77; pres., prof. geology Cornell U., Ithaca, N.Y., 1977-95, pres emeritus, 1995—. Gurley lectr. Cornell U., 1960; Bownocker lectr. Ohio State U., 1966; Case lectr. U. Mich., 1976; Jefferson lectr. U. Calif., Berkeley, 1996-98; dir. NSF, Am. Geol. Inst., summer field inst., 1963; Australian vice-chancellors' visitor to Australian univs., 1964; vis. fellow Clare Hall, Cambridge, Summer 1982; Bye fellow Robinson Coll., Cambridge, Summers, 1986, 87; Am. Fulbright Disting. fellow, Kuwait, 1987, scholar in residence, Bellagio study and conf. ctr., 1995. Author: The Evolution of Life, 1962, 2d edit., 1976, Fossils, 1963, Geology, 1972, Evolution, 1974, Language of the Earth, 1981; author numerous articles and monographs on sci. and edn.; editor, contbr.: Successful Fund Raising for Higher Edn., 1997. Trustee Carnegie Found. for Advancement Tchg., 1978-86, vice chmn., 1983-85, chmn. 1985-86; trustee The Freedom Forum, 1983-93, Com. for Econ. Devel., 1984-93; prin. Washington Adv. Group, 1997—; bd. dirs. KMI Continental, Inc., 1979-86, Tompkins County Trust Co., 1984-99, Gen. Electric Co., 1984—, NBC, 1986—, H. John Heinz III Ctr. Sci., Econs. & Environ., 1996-98, Am. Coun. on Edn., 1983-88, vice chair, 1985-86, chair, 1986-88, The Johnson Found., 2000—, The Atlantic Found., 2000—; bd. dirs. Goldman Sachs Found., 2000—; bd. overseers Meml. Sloan-Kettering Cancer Ctr., 1979-91, Koç U., Turkey, 1996—; chmn. adv. bd. Freedom Forum Media Studies Ctr., 1984-93; mem. Nat. Sci. Bd., 1987-98, chair, 1994-96, Internat. Exec. Svc. Corps Coun., 1984-95; v.p. Dyson Charitable Trust, 1996-98; bd. mem. The Johnson Found., 2000—; chair The Atlantic Found., 2000—. Recipient Clark Kerr medal U. Calif., Berkeley, 1995; NSF sr. vis. rsch. fellow, 1965-66; scholar U. Calif., Berkeley, 1995. Fellow Am. Acad. Arts and Scis., Geol. Soc. London (council 1963-66, Bigsby medal 1967); mem. Am. Philos. Soc. (pres. 1999—), Palaeontol. Assn. (v.p. 1963-68), Brit. Assn. Advancement Sci., Geol. Soc. Am., Am. Assn. Petroleum Geologists, Soc. Econ. Paleontologists and Mineralogists, Phi Beta Kappa (hon.) Office: Cornell U Office of President Emeritus 3104 Snee Hall Ithaca NY 14853-1504

RHODES, GENE PAUL, small business owner; b. Houma, La., Feb. 2, 1955; s. Kirby Francis and Jenny (Kraemer) R.; m. Sally Ann Romano, June 7, 1975; children: Chris Michael, Corey Francis, Cade Anthony. AS, Nicholls State U., 1975; cert. in banking, La. State U., 1984, degree in banking, 1987. Sr. computer operator Terrebonne Bank and Trust, Houma, La., 1975-78; mgr. computer ops. First Nat. Bank of Jefferson, Gretna, 1979-80, v.p., mgr. info. systems, 1980-86, v.p. info. systems and ops., 1986-87; v.p. info. systems, ops. and adminstrn. South Savs. and Loan, Slidell, 1987-90; owner Svc. Master Quality Svcs., Houma, 1990—, Automation Cons. La., Houma, 1991-97, Servicemaster Action Cleaning, Baton Rouge, 1995-99. Pres. Greenacres Subdiv. Civic Assn., Bourg, La., 1986-87. Mem. Am. Mgmt. Assn., Bank Adminstrn. Inst., Data Processing Mgmt. Assn. (bd. dirs. New Orleans chpt. 1983-89, pres. chpt. 1987-88). Republican. Roman Catholic. Avocations: sports, bass fishing, reading. Home: 4015 Kerr Dr Bourg LA 70343-3637 Office: PO Box 766 Houma LA 70361-0766

RHODES, GEORGE FREDERICK, JR. lawyer; b. Houston, Nov. 2, 1952; s. George F. and Marion Kathleen Rhodes; m. Bebe Lyn Burns, Nov. 30, 1980; 1 child, Elizabeth Kathleen. BS, U. Tex., 1974; JD, U. Houston, 1991. Bar: Tex. 1991, U.S. Dist. Ct. (all dists.) Tex. 1992. Reporter KTBC-TV, Austin, 1974-76; reporter KHOU-TV, Houston, 1977-79, KTVI-TV, St. Louis, 1979-82; dir. pub. rels. Inn on the Park Four Season Hotel, Houston, 1982-84; editor in chief Houston City Mag., 1984-86; dir. pub. affairs Tex. Children's Hosp., Houston, 1986-88; assoc. Hirsch & Westheimer, P.C., 1991-94, Haynes and Boone, LLP, Houston, 1994-99, Gibson-Gruenert, 1999—. Co-author: Annual Survey of Texas Privacy and Related Claims Against the Media, 1996-98. Pres. The Park People, Houston, 1987-88; bd. dirs. U. Houston Law Alumni Assn., 1994-96. Avocations: reading, traveling. Office: 7707 Fannin St Ste 203 Houston TX 77054-1989 E-mail: frhodes@gibson-gruenert.com.

RHODES, GERALDINE BRYAN, secondary school administrator; b. Asheville, N.C., Dec. 7, 1941; d. Robert Gerald and Myrtle (Bartlett) B.; m. Gayle Dean Rhodes, May 27, 1967; children: Jennifer, Rebecca. BM, So. Meth. U., 1967; MA, Columbia U., 1987, MEd, 1988, postgrad., 1988—. Permanent tchr. cert., N.Y. Music tchr. Dallas Ind. Sch. Dist., 1967-69, Yamaha Music Sch., Poughkeepsie, N.Y., 1971-75, Hudson Valley Philharmonic Music Sch., Poughkeepsie, 1986-88, Poughkeepsie Day Sch., 1987-90, dir. music edn., 1990-92; tchr. fine arts Ctrl. Tex. Coll., Youngsan U.S. Army Base, Seoul, 1992-94; music tchr. Arlington Ctrl Schs, Poughkeepsie, NY, 95—. Tchr., cons. Dutchess Arts Camp, Poughkeepsie, 1986-92, Hollingworth Pre-sch., Columbia U., N.Y.C., 1987-88; tchr., dir. Inter-generation Chorus N.Y. State Coun. Arts, Poughkeepsie, 1988-92. Bd. dirs. Children's Home Poughkeepsie. Mem. Music Educators Nat. Congress, N.Y. State Sch. Music Assn., Am. Orff Schulwerk Assn. Republican. Episcopalian. Office: Arlington Ctrl Schs 120 Dutchess Tpke Poughkeepsie NY 12603-6426

RHODES, JAMES DEVERS, therapist; b. Midland, Tex., Apr. 28, 1955; s. James Ireland and Loys Ruth (McElrath) R.; m. Moira Sheelagh Josephine Fox Elmore, June 21, 1986. BS, Tex. Christian U., 1978; MEd, U. North Tex., 1991. Lic. profl. counselor, Tex.; lic. chem. dependency counselor, Tex.; nat. cert. addictions counselor II.; nat. cert. clin. hypnotherapist; diplomate Am. Acad. Forensic Counselors. Substance abuse technician Tarrant Coun. Mental Health-Mental Retardation, Ft. Worth, 1986; substance abuse counselor CPC Millwood Hosp., Arlington, Tex., 1986-89; family therapist Parkside Lodge-Westgate, Denton, 1989-90; co-dependence therapist, dir. Parkside Outpatient Svcs., Ft. Worth, 1990-91; psychotherapist Behavioral Health Unit La Hacienda Treatment Ctr., Hunt, Tex., 1991-92; pvt. practice Kerrville, 1991—. Peer evaluator Tex. Bd. Alcoholism and Drug Counselors, Austin, 1988—96; cons. Hill Country Crisis Coun., Hill Country Ind. House, Sid Peterson Regional Hosp., Medina Children's Home; ct. cons. 216th Dist. Ct., Kerrville, Tex., 198th Dist. Ct., County Ct.-at-Law; clin. supr. Youth Habitat Tex., 1995—97; adj. psychology faculty San Antonio Jr. Coll., 1995—98; res., chief adminstr. Verde Springs Care Ctr. of Devine, Inc., 1996—99. Author: Adult Recovery Handbook, 1988. Comty. liaison Mid-South Redevel. Assn., Ft. Worth, 1979-83; mem. Fairmount Assn., Ft. Worth, 1979-84; bd. dirs. Mid-South Housing Coop. Study, Ft. Worth, 1983, Hill County Rehab House, 1993-96. Mem.: ACA, Hill Country Counselors Assn. (senator 1999—2002, Counselor of Yr. 2001), Tex. Mental Health Counselors Assn. (treas. 1994—97), Tex. Counseling Assn., Matt Talbot Retreat Movement (sec. 1989—91), Nat. Assn. Eagle Scouts, Rotary (bd. dirs. 2000—01, 2001—02). Episcopalian. Avocations: reading, investing, acting, Beatlemania, traveling. Office: The Comfort Zone Ste 103 448 Sidney Baker South Kerrville TX 78028 E-mail: moja@omniglobal.net.

RHODES, JOHN JACOB, retired lawyer, former congressman; b. Council Grove, Kans., Sept. 18, 1916; s. John Jacob and Gladys Anne (Thomas) R.; m. Mary Elizabeth Harvey, May 24, 1942; children: John Jacob 3d, Thomas H., Elizabeth C. Rhodes Reich, James Scott. BS, Kans. State U., 1938; LLB, Harvard U., 1942. Bar: Kans. 1942, Ariz. 1945, D.C. 1965. Mem. 83d-97th congresses from 1st Dist. Ariz., chmn. Republican policy com. 89th-93d congresses, house minority leader, 1973-81; of counsel Hunton & Williams, Washington, 1985-97; mem. bd. overseers Hoover Instn., 1984-92. Chmn. platform com. Nat. Rep. Conv., 1972, permanent chmn., 1976, 80 Mem. Ariz. Bd. Pub. Welfare, 1951-52. Served with AUS, World War II; Col., ret. Mem. Mesa C. of C. (pres. 1950), SAR, Am. Legion, Ariz. Club, Mesa Golf and Country Club, Capitol Hill Club, Met. Club, Burning Tree Club (Bethesda, Md.), Pinetop Country Club, Masons (33 deg., Grand Cross), KP, Elks, Moose, Rotary, Beta Theta Pi (internat. pres. 1984-87). Republican. Methodist.

RHODES, KARREN, public information officer; b. Calif., 1947; married; two children. Diploma in Journalism, U. Utah, 1984. Journalist, Salt Lake City, 1983—85, UPI, Cheyenne, Wyo., 1985—86, Green River (Wyo.) Star, 1986—88; pub. info. officer Nev. Dept. Employment Security, Carson City, 1989—94, Nev. Dept. Employment, Tng. and Rehab., Carson City, 1994—2002. Past trustee Carson Access TV Found., 1996—2001; e-commerce entrepreneur, founder NueWorld.com, 2000—. Photograph (recipient Best of Nat. Collegiate Photography award 1984). Vol. of Yr. award State of Utah Gov.'s Office, Salt Lake City, 1984. Mem. Soc. Profl. Journalists. Avocations: graphic design, writing, travel. E-mail: nueteam@nueworld.com.

RHODES, KARREN S. personnel director, small business owner; BA, U. Utah, 1984. Journalist UPI, Salt Lake City, 1983—85, Green River Star, Green River, Wyo., 1986—88; pub. info. officer Nev. Dept. Employment Security, Carson City, 1989—94, Nev. Dept. Employment Tng. and Rehab., Carson City, 1994—. Past trustee Carson Access Found., Carson City, 1996—2000. Recipient Vol. of Yr. award, Gov. State of Utah, 1984. Mem.: Soc. Profl. Journalists. Avocations: travel, writing, graphic designing. Office: Nue World PO Box 1489 Dayton NV 89403

RHODES, LAWRENCE, artistic director; b. Mt. Hope, W.Va., Nov. 24, 1939; Studied with Violette Armand. Joined Ballet Russe de Monte Carlo, 1958-60; from dancer to prin. dancer Joffrey Ballet, N.Y.C., 1960-64; prin. dancer Harkness Ballet, 1964-68, dir., prin. dancer, 1968-70; tchr. dance dept. NYU, 1978—, prin. ballet tchr., 1981—, chmn. dance dept., 1981-91; ballet master, choreographer, tchr., artistic dir. Les Grands Ballets Canadiens, Montreal, 1989-99; dir. dance divsn. The Juilliard Sch., 2002—. Guest artist Het Nationale Ballet, Amsterdam, 1970-71, Pa. Ballet, 1971-76, Feld Ballet, N.Y.C., 1973-75; free-lance master ballet tchr., coach. Danced with Makarova, Hayden and Fracci; danced for Butler, Joffrey, Ailey, Lubovitch, Harkarvy, Nault, Van Dantzig and Mac Donald; featured dancer in film A Dancer's Vocabulary, PBS's Dance Am. series, CBS's Camera Three. E-mail: llrhodes@worldnet.att.net.

RHODES, LEE ANN, anesthesiologist; b. Washington, July 18, 1964; MD, U. Md., 1990. Diplomate Am. Bd. Anesthesiology with subspeciality in pain mgmt. Intern Greater Balt. Med. Ctr., 1990-91; resident in anesthesiology Johns Hopkins U. Hosp., Balt., 1991-94, fellow in pain mgmt., 1994-95; dir. pain mgmt. Washington Hosp. Ctr., 1995—. Mem.: Internat. spinal Injection Soc., Alpha Omega Alpha. Office: Washington Hosp Ctr 110 Irving St NW Washington DC 20010-2975

RHODES, MARY, academic administrator; b. Marion, Kans., Jan. 21, 1941; d. John Sword and Patricia Opal Marie (Olson) R. BA, U. Kans., 1964; MA, U. Va., 1970; PhD, Ohio State U., 1981. Rschr. Sen. James Pearson U.S. Senate, Washington, 1965-67; history instr. U. of the Ozarks, Clarksville, Ark., 1967-68; registrar, asst. prof. history Cottey Coll., Nevada, Mo., 1968-80; adminstrv. dir. AAUP, Columbus, Ohio, 1980-83; assoc. registrar Ohio State U., 1983-86; sr. courseware developer DPEC, 1986-88; coll. registrar, dir. student svcs. Cornell U., Ithaca, N.Y., 1989-98, functional analyst, rsch. assoc., 1998-2000; assoc. registrar Oreg. State U., Corvallis, 2000—. Author: Three Episodes in the Posthumous Reputation of Thomas Paine, 1819-1820, 1970, Dried Flowers: History of Women's Culture at Cottey College, 1981. Named Fulbright scholar, 1992. Mem. Assn. for Womens Rights in Devel., Am. Assn. Collegiate Registrars and Admission Officers, Gamma Sigma Delta, Phi Kappa Phi, Phi Alpha Theta. Democrat. Presbyterian. Avocations: travel, outdoor sports, genealogy, golf. Home: 1922 NW Garryanna Pl Corvallis OR 97330-2008 E-mail: mary.rhodes@orst.edu.

RHODES, PETER EDWARD, label company executive; b. Rochester, N.Y., Sept. 25, 1942; s. Robert A. and Anne (Ward) R.; m. Cassandra Durkee, May 26, 1962 (div. Sept. 1991); children: Tamara, Amy, Brian; m. Nancy Lewis, Aug. 16, 2002. BS, Rochester Inst. Tech., 1964, MBA, 1970. With Touche Ross & Co., Rochester, 1962-69, sr. auditor, to 1969; with Xerox Co., Rochester, 1969, Fay's Drug Co., Inc., Liverpool, N.Y., 1970-87, exec. v.p., 1974-87, also dir.; exec. v.p. Syracuse Label Co., Inc., Liverpool, 1987—, also bd. dirs. Dir. Byrne Dairy Inc. Mem.: AICPA, NY State Soc. CPAs, Bellevue Country Club.

RHODES, RHONDA LYNN, business educator; b. Cottonwood, Ariz., Dec. 9, 1951; d. Thomas Pierce and Merry Lynn (Tissaw) R.; m. Randall E. Hanna, May 26, 1978. B in bus. edn., Northern Ariz. Univ., 1973, M in bus. edn., 1977; PhD in bus. adminstrn., Ariz. State Univ., 1983. Bus. tchr. Prescott (Ariz.) H.S., 1973-77; bus. instr. Yavapai Cmty. Coll., Prescott, Ariz., 1977-78; lectr. Calif. State Polytech. Univ., Pomona, Calif., 1978-80; western reg. dir. Wiley Office Systems Seminars Wiley Publ. Co., N.Y., 1980-82; mgr., mktg. dir. Info Ctr., Inc., Prescott, 1982-85; trainer/systems analyst RR Cons., Hermosa Beach, Calif., 1982—. Dir. grad. bus. programs Calif. State Polytech. Univ., 1988-97, prof. tech. and ops. mgmt., 1985—; cons. Calif. Inst. Local Gov., Claremont; adv. bd. Prescott Coll. Co-author: Office Systems, 1990; contbr. articles to profl. jours. Named Rodeo Queen Prescott Frontier Days Rodeo, 1970. Mem. Nat. Assn. Female Execs., Am. Quarter Horse Assn., Golden Key Hon. Soc., Delta Pi Epsilon. Avocations: training Quarter horses, team roping. Office: Calif State Polytech Univ 3801 W Temple Ave Pomona CA 91768-2557 Fax: 520-639-4282. E-mail: rrhodes@csupomona.edu.

RHODES, RICHARD LEE, writer; b. Kansas City, Kans., July 4, 1937; s. Arthur and Georgia Saphronia (Collier) R.; children: Timothy James, Katherine Hampton; m. Ginger Kay Untrif, Oct. 3, 1993. BA cum laude, Yale U., 1959; LHD (hon.), Westminster Coll., Fulton, Mo., 1988. Author: The Inland Ground, 1970, The Last Safari, 1970, The Ungodly, 1973, The Ozarks, 1974, Holy Secrets, 1978, Looking for America, 1979, Sons of Earth, 1981, The Making of the Atomic Bomb, 1987, Farm, 1989, A Hole in the World, 1990, Making Love, 1992, Nuclear Renewal, 1993, How to Write, 1995, Dark Sun, 1995, (with Ginger Rhodes) Trying to Get Some Dignity, 1996, Deadly Feasts, 1997, Visions of Technology, 1998, Why They Kill, 1999, Masters of Death, 2002. Trustee Andrew Drumm Inst., Independence, Mo., 1991. Recipient Nat. Book Critics Cir. award for nonfiction, Nat. Book award for nonfiction, 1987, Pulitzer prize, 1988; Guggenheim fellow, 1974-75, fellow Nat. Endowment for Arts, 1978-79, Ford Found., 1981-83, Sloan Found., 1985, 89, 91, 92, 2002-, MacArthur Found., 1990-91. Office: c/o Janklow & Nesbit Assoc 445 Park Ave New York NY 10022-2606

RHODES, ROBERT CHARLES, cable company executive, consultant; b. Hannibal, Mo., Apr. 8, 1926; s. William Cleveland and Callie Lee (DeLaporte) R.; m. Doris Marie Priest, Oct. 12, 1947; children: Martha Rhodes Figley, Carol Rhodes Tempel, Robert Charles Jr. BA, Drury Coll., 1962. Communications engr. Southwestern Bell Telephone, Springfield, Mo., 1949-65; regional mgr. United Telephone, Pa., 1966-70; dir. mktg. United Transmission, Kansas City, Mo., 1970-72; pres. Met. Cable TV Mgmt., 1972-76, Higginsville, Mo., 1976-82, R.C. Rhodes Investments, Higginsville, 1982—. Del. Nat. Republican Conv., New Orleans, 1988. With Mo. N.G., 1943-44. Mem. Springfield Jr. C. of C. (pres. 1962-67), Mo. Jr. C. of C. (Young Man of Yr. 1963), Nat. Pachyderms (v.p. 1986—), Pachyderm Club (pres. Lafayette County, Mo. chpt. 1981), Shriners. Republican. Methodist. Avocation: study of history. Home and Office: PO Box 504 Higginsville MO 64037-0504 E-mail: dustyr@ctcis.net.

RHODES, ROBERT MILFORD, management consultant; b. Stanley, N.D., June 25, 1931; s. Oliver David Rhodes and Clara Mathilde (Paulson) Coe; previous marriages: Joyce Elaine Pine, Hope Edith Sutherland; children: Susan Elaine Rhodes, Catherine Karen Leigh Rhodes Gillette; m. Rea Lorraine Treco Rhodes, Sept. 1, 1971; stepchildren: Clifton T. Holman, III, Richard Merle Holman. BSEE, Kans. U., 1956; MEE, NYU, 1959. Engr. Sperry Electronic Tube Divsn., Gainesville, Fla., 1956-57; mem. tech. staff Bell Telephone Labs., Murray Hill, N.J., 1957-61; sr. systems engr. GE Computer Dept., Phoenix, 1961-67; mng. assoc. Arthur Young & Co., Washington, 1967-70; chmn., pres. Synthesis Corp., Fernandina Beach, Fla., 1970—. EDP cons. Fla. Info. Resource Commn., Tallahassee, 1978-89; assoc. rsch. dir. Jacksonville Exptl. Health Care Delivery System, Fla., 1972-75; bd. dirs. Synthesis Corp., Fernandina Beach, Fla.; cons. to commr. Cmty. Svcs., DHEW, Washington, 1971; DHEW, Washington, 1969; project mgr. nationwide demonstration program of social and rehabilitative svcs. for computer-based social info. sys. Editor/author: (3 vols.) Evaluation of the Northeast Florida Eight-County Emergency Medical Care Project, 1975; contbr. articles to profl. jours. and mags.; prodr./composer: (record) St. Augustine Memories, 1976. Mem. Econ. Roundtable of Jacksonville, 1990—,X3.3 Data Comm. Control Standardization Com., 1961-67; sec. ISO TC-9, Berlin, 1963. 1st lt. USAF, 1950-53. Mem. IEEE (life), AAAS, Amelia Island Club. Achievements include the co-design and release of the first modem: Data-Phone 202A; part of GE team to design, develop and install first data comm. processor: Datanet 30/Chrysler Corp., 1961. Avocations: sailing, computer programming. Office: Synthesis Corp 2059 Beachwood Rd Fernandina Beach FL 32034-6533

RHODES, SAMUEL, violist, educator; b. Long Beach, N.Y., Feb. 13, 1941; s. Bernard and Martha (Ephraim) R.; m. Hiroko Yajima, Dec. 30, 1968; children— Amy, Harumi. BA, Queen's Coll., CUNY, 1963; M.F.A., Princeton U., 1967; D.F.A. (hon.), Mich. State U., 1984; MusD (hon.), Jacksonville U., 1986, San Francisco Conservatory, 1996. Mem. faculty Juilliard Sch., N.Y.C., 1969—, Mich. State U., East Lansing, 1977-85, SUNY-Purchase, 1982-86; violist Marlboro Festival, 1960-68, 78-81, 91—, Galimir String Quartet, 1961-68, Juilliard String Quartet, 1969—; mem. faculty Tanglewood Music Ctr., 1988—. Office: Juilliard Sch Music Lincoln Ctr New York NY 10023

RHODES, THOMAS WILLARD, lawyer; b. Lynchburg, Va., Mar. 9, 1946; s. Howard W. and Ruth R.; m. Ann Bloodworth, May 31, 1975; children: Mildred Claiborne, Andrew. AB, Davidson (N.C.) Coll., 1968; JD, U. Va., 1971. Bar: Ga. 1971. Assoc. Smith, Gambrell & Russell and predecessor firms, Atlanta, 1971-76, ptnr., 1976—. Dir., pres. Atlanta Vol. Lawyers Found., 1984-89, Fed. Defender Program, Atlanta, 1989-94. Contbr. articles to profl. jours. Capt. USAR, 1971-72. Recipient Heiner award, Atlanta Vol. Lawyers Found., 1989. Fellow Am. Law Inst.; mem. Ga. Bar Assn. (past chmn. antitrust law sect.), ABA. Office: Smith Gambrell & Russell Promenade II 1230 Peachtree St NE Ste 3100 Atlanta GA 30309-3592

RHODES, WILLIAM REGINALD, banker; b. N.Y.C., Aug. 15, 1935; s. Edward R. and Elsie Rhodes; divorced; 1 child, Elizabeth. BA in History, Brown U., 1957. Sr. officer internat. banking group-Latin Am. and Caribbean Citibank, N.A., N.Y.C., 1977-80, sr. corp. officer Latin Am. and Caribbean, 1980-84, chmn. restructuring com., 1984-90, group exec., 1986-90, also chmn. bank adv. coms. for Brazil, Argentina, Peru, and Uruguay, 1982-90, co-chmn. bank adv. com. for Mexico, 1982-90, sr. exec.-internat., 1990-91, vice chmn., 1991—2001, Citigroup, 1999—2001, sr. vice chmn., 2001—. Vice chmn., sr. vice chmn. Inst. Internat. Fin., Met. Mus. Bus. Com.; mem. U.S.-Russia Bus. Coun.; past chmn. adv. com. Export-Import Bank of U.S.; past chmn., U.S. Sect., Venezuela-U.S. Bus. Coun.; founding mem. U.S. Nat. Adv. Coun. to the Internat. Mgmt. Ctr., Budapest; active U.S.-Egyptian Pres. Coun.; bd. dirs. Conoco, Inc., Pvt. Export Funding Corp., ChipCo. Chmn. Northfield-Mt. Hermon Sch.; bd. dirs. N.Y. and Presbyn. Hosp.; bd. overseers of Watson Inst. for Internat. Studies; active Lincoln Ctr. Corporate Leadership Com.; bd. dirs. Africa-Am. Inst.; vice chmn. bd. Nat. Com. on U.S.-China Rels. Decorated comdr. and grand officer Nat. Order of the Southern Cross, Brazil, chevalier Legion of Honor, France, Orden de Mayo, Argentina, officer Order Francisco Miranda 1st and 3rd classes, Order Merito en el Trabajo 1st class, Venezuela, Order of Diplomatic Service, Heung-In medal, Korea, Americas award, 1997; recipient African Bus. Devel. award African Am. Inst., 1998, Banker's Lifetime Achievment award Arab Bankers Assn. N.Am., 1999, Stephen P. Duggan award for Internat. Understanding, Inst. for Internat. Edn., 1999, William I. Spencer award N.Y. Blood Ctr., 1999. Mem. Americas Soc. (chmn. bd. dirs.), Coun. of Ams. (chmn. bd. dirs.), Bankers Assn. for Fgn. Trade (past pres.), Coun. Fgn. Rels., Venezuelan-Am. C. of C. (past pres.), Fgn. Policy Assn. (bd. dirs.). Avocations: reading history, jogging, swimming, archaeology. Office: Citigroup Inc 399 Park Ave New York NY 10043-0001

RHODES, YORKE E(DWARD), organic chemist, educator; b. Elizabeth, N.J., Mar. 25, 1936; s. Yorke Edward and Helen (Pyper) R.; m. Mechthilde Weggenmann, May 24, 1975; children: Yorke Edward III, Christopher A., Matthias Raabe, Timothy A. BS, U. Del., 1957, MS, 1959; PhD, U. Ill., 1963. Chemist Thiokol Chem. Corp., Elkton, Md., 1959; lectr. Yale U., New Haven, 1964-65; asst. prof. chemistry NYU, N.Y.C., 1965-71, assoc. prof., 1971—, asst. dean Coll. Arts and Sci., 1987-89, dir. NYU-Stevens dual degree program in sci. and engring., 1988-2000. Vis. prof. U. Freiburg, Germany, 1972-73, Tech. U. Munich, 1977, Harvard U., 2001; vis. prof. astrophysics U. Grenoble, France, 1987; Humboldt vis. prof. Tech. U. Munich, 1978; Dept. State sci. exch. visitor Zagreb, Yugoslavia, and Prague, Czechoslovakia, 1977. Contbr. articles to sci. jours. Committeeman Englewood Dem. Com., 1968-72. NIH fellow Yale U., 1964-65, NASA summer faculty fellow Jet Propulsion Lab., Pasadena, Calif., 1980, 81; recipient Humboldt award, 1978. Mem.: Planetary Soc., Royal Chem. Soc., Am. Chem. Soc. (vice-chmn. N.Y. sect. 1997, chmn. 1998, councilor 1998—, chair local sect. activities com. 2001), Sigma Xi. Avocations: opera, photography, travel, gardening, railroads. Office: NYU Dept Chemistry 100 Washington Sq E New York NY 10003-6688 E-mail: yorke.rhodes@nyu.edu.

RHODY, RONALD EDWARD, banker, communications executive; b. Frankfort, Ky., Jan. 27, 1932; s. James B. and Mary M. (Clark) R.; m. Patricia Schupp, Apr. 23, 1955; children: Leslie K., Mary M., Virginia K., Ronald C. Student, Georgetown (Ky.) Coll., 1950-52, U. Ky., 1953-55. Pub. rels. dir. Kaiser Aluminum & Chem. Corp., Ravenswood, W.Va., 1959-62, N.Y.C., 1962-67, corp. v.p. Oakland, Calif., 1967-83; sr. v.p. corp comm. Bank of Am. NT&SA, San Francisco, 1983—, exec. v.p., 1992-94; CEO Rhody, Inc., 1994—. Author: The CEO's Playbook, 1999; contbr. articles to profl. jours. Founding chmn. adv. bd. San Francisco Acad.; mem. Global Pub. Affairs Inst., N.Y.C. Named Pub. Rels. Profl. of Yr., Pub. Rels. News, 1981; recipient Hall of Fame award Page Soc., 1997. Mem. Pub. Rels. Soc. Am. (accredited, pres.'s adv. coun. Rex Harlow award), Internat. Assn. Bus. Communicators (Gold Quill award 1980), Pub. Rels. Roundtable San Francisco (mem. bd. govs., awards 1980, 85). Home: 2725 Pontiac Dr Walnut Creek CA 94598-4437 Office: Rhody Inc 2725 Pontiac Dr Walnut Creek CA 94598-4437 E-mail: ron.rhody@att.net.

RHONE, DOUGLAS PIERCE, pathologist, educator; b. Bloomsburg, Pa., Mar. 27, 1940; s. Wilbur Clayton and Marian Faye (Shaffer) R.; m. Leta Daiva Budelskis, Sept. 27, 1969; children: Jennifer Ann, Todd Brader. BS, Ill. Benedictine U., 1965; MD, MS in Pathology, U. Ill., 1969. Diplomate Am. Bd. Pathology. Attending pathologist Ill. Masonic Med. Ctr., Chgo., 1976, chmn. dept. pathology, 1976—, dir. residency pathology, 1976—90; asst. prof. pathology U. Ill. Coll. Medicine, 1976—80, assoc. prof. pathology, 1980—98; prof. pathology, 1998—; dir. residency pathology U. Ill. Met. Hosps., Chgo., 1990—; assoc. dir. med. affairs Ill. Masonic Med. Ctr., 1992—95; pres. Ill. Masonic Med. Ctr. Pathologists, S.C., 1977—, Lab. Cons., Ltd., Chgo., 1977—2001. Contbr. articles to profl. jours. Maj. U.S. Army, 1974-76. Recipient Raymond B. Allen award U. Ill. Coll. Medicine, 1979, 80, 95, 97, 98, 2000, C. Thomas Bombeck award, 1991, 2002. Fellow: Coll. Am. Pathologists, Am. Soc. Clin. Pathologists (Sheard-Sanford Rsch. award 1969); mem.: Ill. Soc. Pathologists, Chgo. Pathology Soc., Alpha Omega Alpha. Roman Catholic. Avocations: antiquities, gardening, oil painting, classical music and opera, Russian history and culture. Home: 222 S Spring Ave La Grange IL 60525-2243 Office: Ill Masonic Med Ctr Dept Pathology 836 W Wellington Ave Chicago IL 60657-9224

RHONE, SYLVIA, recording industry executive; b. Phila., Mar. 11, 1952; d. James and Marie (Christmas) R.; 1 daughter, Quinn. MA, Wharton Sch. Bus. U. Pa., 1974. Dir. nat. black music promotion Atlantic Records, New York, N.Y., 1985-88, Sr. V.P., 1988-91; chair/CEO EastWest Records America, 1991—, Elektra Entertainment, N.Y.C., 1994—. Mem., bd. dirs. Alvin Ailey Am. Dance Theatre, The RIAA, Rock n' Roll Hall of Fame, Jazz at Lincoln Ctr., R&B Found., The Phillips-Van Heusen Corp., Studio Mus. of Harlem; bd. dirs. Nat. Acad. Rec. Arts and Scis. Achievements include became 1st African Am. and first woman chmn. and CEO of a major record co., 1994. Office: Elektra Entertainment 75 Rockefeller Plz New York NY 10019-6908*

RHOTEN, JULIANA THERESA, retired school principal; b. N.Y.C., June 28; d. Julius Joseph and Gladys Maude (Grant) Bastian; B.A., Hunter Coll., 1954; M.S., 1956; Ed.S., U. Wis., Milw., 1977; m. Marion Rhoten, Aug. 7, 1956 (dec.); 1 son, Don Carlos. Tchr. elem. schs., Milw., 1957-65, reading specialist, 1965-71, adminstr., 1971-80; prin. Ninth St. Sch., Milw., 1980-83, Parkview Sch., Milw., 1983-90. Bd. dirs. Eisenhower Ctr., 1994—. Mem. ASCD, Internat. Reading Assn., Nat. Assn. Elem. Sch. Prins., Nat. Coun. Tchrs. English, Adminstrs. and Suprs. Council, Phi Delta Kappa, Alpha Kappa Alpha. Home: 7222 N 99th St Milwaukee WI 53224-3802

RHOTEN, KENNETH D. writer; b. Hammond, Ind., Dec. 28, 1950; s. James Edward and Helen Louise (Wasson) R.; m. Virginia Haynie (div.); m. Linda Robin Damron (div.); m. Josephine Meese (dec.). Grad. H.S., New Carlisle, Ind. Draftsman Hahn, Inc., Evansville, Ind., 1973-75; laborer Inland Steel Works, 1975; draftsman N.W. Ind. Regional Planning Com., Highland, 1975-76; draftsman, artist graphic sys. divsn. Rockwell Internat., Cicero, Ill., 1977-78; designer Roper Outdoor Products (in cooperation with Espo Engring.), Bradley, 1978-79; draftsman Fedders Corp., Effingham, 1982-83. Author, editor: Dark Twist of Fate, 1995, Dark Twist of Fate and Other Works, 1999; author: A Voice From Beyond, 1999, The Complete Works of Kenneth D. Rhoten, 1999; composer pub. songs; patentee automatic brewing apparatus, 1984. Candidate state rep. State of Ill.-Rep. Party, 1986. Achievements include successful redevelopment of the Edison storage cell, and development of new secondary cell. Avocations: classical music, nature study. Home: PO Box 225 Stoy IL 62464-0225

RHOTON, ALBERT LOREN, JR. neurological surgery educator; b. Nov. 18, 1932; s. Albert Loren and Hazel Arnette (Van Cleve) R.; m. Joyce L. Moldenhauer, June 23, 1957; children: Eric L., Albert J., Alice S., Laural A. BS, Ohio State U., 1954; MD cum laude, Washington U., St. Louis, 1959. Diplomate Am. Bd. Neurol. Surgery (bd dirs. 1985-91, vice-chmn. 1991). Intern Columbia Presbyn. Med. Ctr., N.Y.C., 1959; resident in neurol. surgery Barnes Hosp., St. Louis, 1961-65; cons. neurol. surgery Mayo Clinic, Rochester, Minn., 1965-72; chief divsn. neurol. surgery U. Fla., Gainesville, 1972-80, R.D. Keene prof., 1980—, chmn. dept. neurol. surgery, 1980-2000, chmn. emeritus, 2000—. Developer microsurg. tng. ctr.; guest lectr. Neurol. Socs. Switzerland, Japan, Venezuela, France, Colombia, Costa Rica, Uruguay, Korea, Australia, Egypt, Argentina, Hong Kong, U.K., Turkey, Thailand, Latin Am.; invited faculty, guest lectr. Harvard U., Washington U., Emory U., UCLA, U. Calif., San Francisco, Stanford U., U. Miami, U. Okla., U. So. Calif., U. Mich., Northwestern U., U. Chgo., U. Pa., Johns Hopkins U., Ohio State U., Temple U., Duke U., Cornell U., NYU, Mt. Sinai, N.Y.C., U. Cin., Tulane U., Vanderbilt U., U. Minn., U. Md., U. Pa., Albany Med. Coll., Cleve. Clin. Found., St. Louis U., Henry Ford Med. Found., Med. Coll. N.Y., Jefferson Med. Coll., Hahnemann Med. Coll., U. P.R., U. Calif., Irvine, U. Hong Kong, La. State U., U. Ky., U. Louisville, Singapore Nat. U., U. Adalaide, U. Sydney, Walter Reed Army Med. Ctr., Beijing Capital U., China, Sinshu U., Japan, Mt. Sinai Coll. Medicine, Driscoll Found., England; Olivecorona lectr. Stockholm. Author: The Orbit and Sellar Region: Microsurgical Anatomy and Operative Approaches, 1996; contbr. to Millenium issue Neurosurgery, 25th Anniversary issue; designed more than 200 microsurgery instruments; mem. editl. bd. Neurosurgery, Jour. Microsurgery, Surg. Neurology, Jour. Fla. Med. Assn., Am. Jour. Otology, Skull Base Surgery; contbr. numerous articles to profl. jours. Recipient Disting. Faculty award, U. Fla., 1981, Alumni Achievement award, Washington U. Sch. Medicine, 1985, Jones award for outstanding spl. med. exhibit of yr., Am. Assn. med. Illustrators, 1969, Jameison medal, Neurosurg. soc. Australasia, 1997, Outstanding Achievement award, World Congress of Skull Base Surgery, 2000, medal of honor, World Fedn. Neurosurg. Socs., 2001, medal, Neurosurg. Soc. Am., 2001, endowed professorship named in his honor, U. Fla., Lifetime Achievement award, Wall of Fame Honoree, Honorary Alumnus award, 2001, medal of honor, Neurosurg. Soc. of Am., 2001; grantee NIH, VA, Am. Heart Assn. Mem. ACS (bd. govs. 1978-84), AMA (Billings Bronze medal for sci. exhibit 1969), Congress Neurol. Surgeons (pres. 1978, honored guest 1993), Nat. Found. Brain Rsch. (bd. dirs. 1990-94), Nat. Coalition for Rsch. in Neurol. Disorders (bd. dirs. 1990-94), Neurol. Soc. Am. (medal 2001), Internat. Congress Meningiomas (hon. pres. 2000), Neurosurg. Soc. Brazil (hon.), Neurosurg. Soc. Japan (hon.), Neurosurg. Soc. Mex. (hon.), Neurosurg. Soc. Can. (hon.), Neurosurg. Soc. Uruguay (hon.), Neurosurg. Soc. Venezuela (hon.), Neurosurg. Soc. Turkey (hon.), Neurosurg. Soc. Tex. (hon.), Neurosurg. Soc. Okla. (hon.), Neurosurg. Soc. Wis. (hon.), Neurosurg. Soc. Ga. (hon.), Neurosurg. Soc. Rocky Mountain (hon.), Neurosurg. Soc. China (hon.), Neurosurg Soc. Argentina (hon.), Fla. Neurosurg. Soc. (pres. 1978), Am. Assn. Neurol. Surgeons (chmn. vascular sect., treas. 1983-86, v.p. 1987-88, pres. 1989-90, exec. com. 1993, Cushing medal 1998), Soc. Neurol. Surgeons (treas. 1975-81, pres. 1993), So. Neurol. Soc. (v.p. 1976), Alachua County Med. Soc. (exec. com. 1978), Fla. Med. Assn., Am. Surg. Assn., Soc. Univ. Neurosurgeons, Am. Heart Assn. (stroke coun., Outstanding Achievement award 1971), N.Am. Skull Base Soc. (pres. 1993-94, honored guest 2001), Am. Acad. Neurol. Surgery, Acoustic Neuroma Assn. (med. adv. bd. 1983—, chmn. 1992—), Trigeminal Neurol. Assn. (med. advisor bd. 1992—), Internat. Interdisciplinary Congress on Craniofacial and Skull Base Surgery (pres. 1996-97), Internat. Soc. Neurosurg. Tech. and Instrument Invention (pres. 1997—), Japanese Skull Base Soc. (hon. pres. 2000). Home: 2505 NW 22d Ave Gainesville FL 32605-3819 Office: U Fla Shands Hosp Gainesville FL 32610

RHYNE, CHARLES SYLVANUS, lawyer; b. Charlotte, N.C., June 23, 1912; s. Sydneyham S. and Mary (Wilson) R.; m. Sue Cotton, Sept. 16, 1932 (dec. Mar. 1974); children: Mary Margaret, William Sylvanus; m. Sarah P. Hendon, Oct. 2, 1976; children: Sarah Wilson, Elizabeth Parkhill. BA, Duke U., 1934, LLD, 1958; JD, George Washington U., 1937, DCL, 1958; LLD, Loyola U., Calif., 1958, Dickinson Law Sch., 1959, Ohio No. U., 1966, De Paul U., 1968, Centre, 1969, U. Richmond, 1970, Howard U., 1975, Belmont Abbey, 1982. Bar: D.C. 1937. Pvt. practice, Washington; sr. ptnr. Rhyne & Rhyne. Gen. counsel Nat. Inst. Mcpl. Law Officers, 1937-88, of counsel; prof. govt. and aviation law George Washington U., 1948-53; prof. govt. Am. U., 1939-44; gen. counsel Fed. Commn. Jud. and Congl. Salaries, 1953-54; spl. cons. Pres. Eisenhower, 1957-60; Dir. Nat. Savs. & Trust Co., 1941-76, ACCIA Life Ins. Co., 1966-84; Mem. Internat Commn. Rules Judicial Procedures, 1959-61, Pres.'s Comm. on UN, 1969-71; spl. ambassador, personal rep. of Pres. U.S. to UN High Commr. for Refugees, 1971-73 Author: Civil Aeronautics Act, Annotated, 1939, Airports and the Courts, 1944, Aviation Accident Law, 1947, Airport Lease and Concession Agreements, 1948, Cases on Aviation Law, 1950, The Law of Municipal Contracts, 1952, Municipal Law, 1957, International Law, 1971, Renowned Law Givers and Great Law Documents of Humankind, 1975, International Refugee Law, 1976, Law and Judicial Systems of Nations, 1978, Law of Local Government Operations, 1980, (autobiography) Working for Justice in America and Justice in the World, 1996; editor Mcpl. Atty., 1937-88; contbr. articles to profl. jours. Trustee George Washington U., 1957-67, Duke U., 1961-85, now trustee emeritus. Recipient Freedoms Found. award for creation Law Day-U.S.A., 1959; Alumni Achievement award George Washington U., 1960; Nat. Bar Assn. Stradford award, 1962; 1st Whitney M. Young award, 1972; Harris award Rotary, 1974; U.S. Dept. State appreciation award, 1976; Nansen Ring for refugee work, 1976, 1st Peacemaker award Rotary Internat., 1988. Mem. ABA (life mem. ho. dels., pres. 1957-58, chmn. ho. dels. 1956-58, chmn. commn. world peace through law 1958-66, chmn. com. aero. law 1946-48, 51-54, chmn. internat. and comparative law sect. 1948-49, chmn. UN com., chmn. commn. on nat. inst. justice 1972-76, nat. chmn. Jr. Bar Conf. 1944-45, ABA Gold Medal 1966, Advocacy award state and local govt. sect. 1999), D.C. Bar Assn. (pres. 1955-56, Grotius Peace award 1958, Disting. Svc. award, 1975, Heroes in Law award 1999), Inter-Am. Bar Assn. (v.p. 1957-59), Am. Bar Found. (pres. 1957-58, chmn. fellows 1958-59), Internat. Bar (founder patron 1947, v.p. 1957-58), Am. Judicature Soc. (dir. life), Am. Law Inst. (life), Am. Soc. Internat. Law (life), World Peace Through Law Ctr. (pres. 1963-89), World Jurist Assn. (pres. 1989-91, hon. life pres.), Nat. Aero. Assn. (bd. dirs. 1945-47), Washington Bd. Trade, Duke U. Alumni Assn. (chmn. nat. coun. 1955-56, pres. 1959-60), Barristers, Met. Club Washington (life), Nat. Press Club, Congl. Country Club (life), Nat. Lawyers Club (life), Univ. Club, Order of Coif (life), Scribes, Delta Theta Phi (life), Omicron Delta Kappa. Home and Office: 1404 Langley Pl Mc Lean VA 22101-3010

RHYNE, JAMES JENNINGS, condensed matter physicist; b. Oklahoma City, Nov. 14, 1938; s. Jennings Jefferson and Clyde Margaret (Russell) R.; m. Susan Margaret Watson, May 26, 1990; children: Nancy Marie, Edward Paxton. BS in Physics, U. Okla., 1959; MS in Physics, U. Ill., 1961; PhD in Physics, Iowa State U., 1965. Rsch. scientist Naval Ordnance Lab., White Oak, Md., 1965-75; rsch. physicist Nat. Inst. of Stds. and Tech., Gaithersburg, 1975-90; prof. physics U. Mo., Columbia, 1991—, dir. Rsch. Reactor Ctr., 1991-96. Adv. editor Jour. of Magnetism and Mag. Materials, 1990—; editl. bd. Jour. Applied Physics, 1986-89; co-editor procs. Fellow Am. Phys. Soc., Neutron Scattering Soc. Am. (pres. 1999—). Home: 2704 Westbrook Way Columbia MO 65203-5221 Office: U Mo Dept Physics And Astronomy Columbia MO 65211-0001 E-mail: rhynej@missouri.edu.

RHYNE, SIDNEY WHITE, lawyer; b. Charlotte, N.C., Apr. 2, 1931; s. Sidney White and Ruth (Dry) R.; m. Rosemarie Kennedy, July 11, 1959; children: Patricia Ruth, Kendall Sidney, Randall Sylvanus. AB, Roanoke Coll., 1952; LLB, U. Pa., 1955; LLM, Georgetown U., 1961. Bar: Pa. 1955, D.C. 1957, U.S. Supreme Ct. 1959, Md. 1987. Assoc. Rhyne, Mullin, Connor and Rhyne, Washington, 1957-60; mem. Mullin, Rhyne, Emmons and Topel, 1961-97; individual practice law, 1997—. Lectr. law ctr. Georgetown U., Washington, 1964-70. Pres. Legal Aid Soc. of D.C., 1976-78, trustee, 1968-80, pres. coun., 1991—; trustee Luth. Theol. Sem. at Phila., 1988-93, pres. coun., 1993—. With U.S. Army, 1955-57. Prettyman fellow Georgetown U., 1960-61. Fellow Am. Bar Found. (life); mem. ABA (mem. house delegates 1972-73, 75, 76-78, 98-2001), Bar Assn. D.C. (bd. dirs. 1969-73, 92-94, 98-2002, trustee Found., v.p. 1990-91, presdl. award 2000-2001), Fed. Comm. Bar Assn. (mem. exec. com. 1988-96, treas. 1991-92, Disting. Svc. award 1992, pres. 1994-95). Republican. Lutheran. Office: 3250 Arcadia Pl NW Washington DC 20015-2330 E-mail: swrhyne@abanet.org.

RHYNEDANCE, HAROLD DEXTER, JR. lawyer, consultant; b. New Haven, Feb. 13, 1922; s. Harold Dexter and Gladys (Evans) R.; m. Barbara Ann Hall (dec.); 1 child, Harold Dexter III; m. Ruth Cosline Hakanson. BA, Cornell U., 1943, JD, 1949; grad., U.S. Army Command and Gen. Staff Coll., 1961, U.S. Army War Coll., 1970. Bar: N.Y. 1949, D.C. 1956, U.S. Tax Ct. 1950, U.S. Ct. Mil. Appeals 1954, U.S. Supreme Ct. 1954, U.S. Ct. Appeals (D.C. cir.) 1956, (2d cir.) 1963, (3rd cir.) 1965, (4th cir.) 1973, (5th cir.) 1968, (7th cir.) 1973, (9th cir.) 1964, U.S. Temporary Emergency Ct. Appeals 1975, U.S. Dist. Ct. D.C. 1956, U.S. Dist. Ct. (so. and ea. dist.) N.Y. 1963. Pvt. practice, Buffalo, Eggertsville, N.Y., 1949-50; examiner/gen. atty. ICC, Washington, 1950-51; atty.-advisor Subversive Activities Control Bd., 1951-52; trial atty., spl. asst. to atty. gen., asst. U.S. atty. U.S. Dept. Justice, 1953-62; sr. trial atty., asst. gen. counsel, gen. counsel FTC, 1962-73; counsel Howrey & Simon, 1973-76; mng. atty., asst. gen. counsel, corp. counsel Washington Gas Light Co., 1977-87; counsel Conner & Wetterhahn, 1987-90; cons. Fairview, N.C., 1990—. Exec. sec. adv. coun. on rules of practice and procedures FTC; mem. Jud. Conf. (D.C. Cir.), 1967—; chmn. legal and regulatory subcom. Solar Energy Com., Am. Gas Assn., Washington, 1978-84; lectr. George Washington U. Law Ctr., 1974; faculty moderator Def. Strategy Seminar Nat. War Coll., 1973; participant spl. programs Indsl. Coll. of Armed Forces, 1962, 69, Armed Forces Staff Coll., 1964. V.p. bd. dirs. Peninsula Symphony Assn., Palos Verdes Peninsula, Calif., 1989-94; bd. dirs. Help-The-Homeless-Help-Themselves, Inc., Palos Verdes Peninsula, 1991-93. 1st lt. U.S. Army, 1943-46, PTO; col. AUS, 1982—. Mem. ABA, Fed. Bar Assn., D.C. Bar Assn., Bar Assn. of D.C., Washington Met. Area Corp. Counsel Assn. (bd. dirs. 1981-84), Cornell Lawyers Club D.C. (pres. 1959-61), The Selden Soc. (London), Biltmore Forest Country Club (Asheville, N.C.), Montreat (N.C.) Scottish Soc., Ret. Officers Assn., Res. Officers Assn. (life), Mil. Order Carabao, U.S. Army War Coll. Alumni Assn. (life), Leadership Asheville Forum, Downtown Club Asheville (past pres.), Cornell Alumni Assn., Am. Legion (life), Sigma Chi, Phi Delta Phi. Republican. Episcopalian. Home and Office: Eagles View 286 Sugar Hollow Rd Fairview NC 28730-9559

RIACH, DOUGLAS ALEXANDER, retired marketing executive, retired military officer; b. Victoria, B.C., Can., Oct. 8, 1919; came to U.S., 1925, naturalized, 1942; s. Alex and Gladys (Provis) R.; m. Eleanor Montague, Mar. 28, 1942; 1 child, Sandra Jean. BA, UCLA, 1948; postgrad., Fenn Coll., 1959; student, Grad. Sch. Sales Mgmt., 1959-60, Armed Forces Staff Coll., 1968, Indsl. Coll. Armed Forces, 1970-71; DMS, Am. Cornerstone U., 1999. With Gen. Foods Corp., 1948-80; terr. sales mgr. San Francisco, 1962-80; with Food Brokers, 1980-90; exec. v.p. Visual Market Plans Inc., Novato, Calif., 1984-87; terr. mgr. Ibbotson, Berri, DeNola Brokerage, Inc., Emeryville, 1990-96; acct. exec. Sales Max Inc., Richmond, 1996-97; terr. mgr. Kelly Clarke, Inc., Pleasanton, 1997-98, Acosta Sales & Mktg., Pleasanton, 1997-2000; ret., 2000. Capt. inf. AUS, 1941-46, ETO; col. inf. USAR, 1946-79; from comdr. 2nd inf. brigade Calif. State mil. res., 1984-87 to brigadier gen.

(ret.) 1990. Decorated Legion of Merit, Medal of Merit, Commendation medal, Bronze Star with V device and oak leaf cluster, Purple Heart, Combat Infantry Badge, Croix de Guerre avec palme (France and Belgium), Combattant Cross-Vol. (France), Combattant Cross-Soldier (France), Medaille Commemorative de la Liberee (France), Medaille Commemorative Francais, Medaille-War Wounded (France), Medaille Commemorative Belgique, Medaille Reconnoisance (Belgium), Medaille du Vol. (Belgium), Cross of Freedom (Poland), Virtuti Militari- Silver Cross (Poland), Royal Commemorative War Cross (Yugoslavia), knight Order of the Compassionate Heart (internat.), knight Magnus Officialis (GOTJ), Sovereign Mil. Order, Temple of Jerusalem (Knights Templar), CDR Commandery of Calif. (Knights Templar), knight comdr. of grace Sovereign Order of St. John of Jerusalem (knights hospitaller), comdr. Commandery of St. Francis (mil.) San Francisco, Knights Hospitaller), Knight Comdr. Cross with Star (class II), Polonia Restituta (Poland), knight Grand Cross Order St. Stanislaus, comdr. Commandery of San Francisco, Order of St. Stanislas, 1996-97, dep. prior Priory of Calif. Order of St. Stanislas, 1997, prior, 1998-2000, Cross of Justice, Silver Cross of Merit Order of St. Stanislas, 1997, Sword of Honor Order of St. Stanislas 1999; named to U.S. Army Inf. Hall of Fame, 1982. Mem. Long Beach Food Sales Assn. (pres. 1950), Assn. Grocers Mfrs. Reps. (dir. 1955), Am. Security Coun. (nat. adv. bd. 1975—), Res. Officers Assn. (pres. San Francisco Presidio 1974-76, v.p. 1977-82, v.p. dept. Calif. 1979, exec. v.p. 1980, pres. 1981, nat. councilman 1981-82), Nat. Assn. Uniformed Svcs., Exchange Club (v.p. Long Beach 1955), St. Andrews Soc. Queens Club San Francisco, Combat Infantry Assn., Assn. U.S. Army, Am. Legion, Vets. Battle of the Bulge Assn., Assn. Former Intelligence Officers, Presidio Soc., Navy League, Ret. Officers Assn., Mil. Order Purple Heart, DAV, Psychol. Ops. Assn., Nat. Guard Assn. Calif., State Def. Force Assn. Calif., State Guard Assn. of U.S., Internat. Diplomacy Coun. San Francisco, Merchandising Execs. San Francisco (dir. 1970-75, sec. 1976-77, v.p. 1978-79, pres. 1980, bd. dirs. 1981-89), Commonwealth of Club Calif. (nat. def. sect. vice chmn. 1964-66, chmn. 1967-72), Elks, Masons (master, lodge 400, Shrine, Islam temple, 32nd degree Scottish Rite, sojourner chpt. # 277). Republican. Episcopalian. Home: 2112 Estates Dr Fairfield CA 94533-9718

RIAN, DOUGLAS (DOUGLAS RIAN ARNTS), educator, writer, actor; b. Bismarck, N.D., Oct. 21, 1963; s. Allen Vinton Arnts and Mildred Marie Persinger. BA, U. N.D., 1985; MA, U. Chgo., 1991. Rsch. analyst Office of Atty. Gen., Bismarck, 1986-87; rsch. cons. Minn. Ho. of Reps., St. Paul, 1989; instr. Columbia Coll., Chgo., 1991-93; analyst, product support Morningstar, 1992-93; lead instr. ITT, Nashville, 1994-99; adj. instr. Trevecca Nazarene U., 1997-99, Nashville State Tech. Inst., 1998-99; prof. polit. sci. Valencia C.C., Orlando, Fla., 2000—. Rschr. Office of the Gov., Bismarck, 1984, Office of the Tax Commr., Bismarck, 1984-87, Office of Atty. Gen., 1985-86, Office of Minn. State Planning, 1988; owner Riandance Music/BMI. Author: You Say You Want a Revolution, 1995, (songs) Vivid, Scraps, 1999. Precinct chair Ind. Rep. Party, Mpls., 1989, del., 1990. Noyes fellowship U. Chgo., 1990-91; Violet Eastmann scholarship U. N.D., 1984. Mem. Internat. Assn. of Bus. Communicators, Associated Bus. Writers of Am., Pi Sigma Alpha. Avocations: raquetball, music production, horseback riding, hiking.

RIASANOVSKY, NICHOLAS VALENTINE, historian, educator; b. Harbin, China, Dec. 21, 1923; came to U.S., 1938, naturalized, 1943; m. Arlene Ruth Schlegel, Feb. 15, 1955; children— John, Nicholas, Maria. BA, U. Oreg., 1942; AM, Harvard U., 1947; DPhil, Oxford (Eng.) U., 1949. Mem. faculty U. Iowa, 1949-57, U. Calif., Berkeley, 1957—, prof. history, 1961—, Sidney Hellman Ehrman prof. European history, 1969—; trustee Nat. Council Soviet and E. European Research, 1978-82; mem. Kennan Inst. Acad. Council, 1986-89. Vis. research prof. USSR Acad. Scis., Moscow, 1969, Moscow and Leningrad, 1974, 79 Author: Russia and the West in Teaching of the Slavophiles: A Study of Romantic Ideology, 1952, Nicholas I and Official Nationality in Russia, 1825-1855, 1959, A History of Russia, 1963, 6th edit., 1999, The Teaching of Charles Fourier, 1969, A Parting of Ways: Government and the Educated Public in Russia, 1801-1855, 1976, The Image of Peter the Great in Russian History and Thought, 1985, The Emergence of Romanticism, 1992, Collected Writings 1947-94, 1993; co-editor: California Slavic Studies, 1960—; editl. bd. Russian rev., Zarubezhnaia Periodicheskaia Pechat' na Russkom Iazyke, Simvol; contbr. articles to profl. jours. Served to 2d lt. AUS, 1943-46. Decorated Bronze Star; recipient Silver medal Commonwealth Club Calif., 1964; Rhodes scholar, 1947-49; Fulbright grantee, 1954-55, 74, 79; Guggenheim fellow, 1969; sr. fellow Nat. Endowment Humanities, 1975; Fulbright sr. scholar, sr. fellow Ctr. Advanced Studies in Behavioral Scis., 1984-85; sr. fellow Woodrow Wilson Internat. Ctr. for Scholars, 1989-90. Mem. AAAS, Am. Assn. Advancement Slavic Studies (pres. 1973-76, Disting. Contbr. award 1993), Am. Hist. Assn. (award for Scholarly Distinction 1995), Am. Acad. Arts and Scis.

RIAZI, KAMBIZ, civil engineer; b. Teheran, Iran, May 21, 1957; came to U.S., 1974; s. Homayoun Hooshang and Ensieh (Moghiseh) R. B in Archtl. Engring., Pratt Inst., 1981; BCE, CCNY, 1983. Asst. civil engr. Dept. Environ. Protection, N.Y.C., 1983-85; staff engr. various cos., 1985-87; chief inspector Envirodyne Engrs. Inc., 1987-90, office engr., 1990—. Founder, chmn. Am. Soc. Archtl. Engrs., Pratt Inst., 1978-81. Fellow ASCE. Office: Envirodyne Engrs Inc 41 E 42nd St New York NY 10017-5202

RIBA, NETTA EILEEN, retired secondary school educator; b. Bronx, N.Y., Apr. 6, 1944; d. Jack and Anne (Parnes) Browner; m. Benjamin Riba, July 22, 1975; children: Rebecca, Joseph. BS, Queens Coll., 1965, MS, 1968. Cert. tchr., N.Y. Math. tchr. Bayside (N.Y.) H.S., 1965-68, Flushing (N.Y.) H.S., 1968-75, Harry S Truman H.S., Bronx, 1975-95, Christopher Columbus H.S., Bronx, 1996-2001, SUNY Rockland Country C.C., Suffern, 2001—. Vol. guide N.Y. Zool. Soc., Bronx, 1973-75; leader Rockland County Coun. Girl Scouts USA, 1985-88. Mem. Nat. Coun. Tchrs. Math. Jewish. Avocations: animal behavior, sewing. Office: SUNY Rockland County CC 145 College Rd Suffern NY 10901

RIBAC, CATALINO TAGATAC, retired accountant; b. Batac, The Philippines, Apr. 30, 1934; came to U.S., 1969; s. Felixberto and Gerarda (Tagatac) R.; m. Adelaida Obando, Dec. 26, 1964; 1 child, Maria-Elma Ribac-Horton. BS in Acctg., Adamson U., Manila, 1967. CPA, Calif. Janitor Ker & Co., Ltd., Manila, 1957-59, messenger, 1960-61, bill collector, 1961-62, acctg. clk., 1963-64, internal auditor, 1965-69; acct. Belinkoff & Co., L.A., 1969-75; ptnr. Berlinkoff & Co., 1976-2001; ret., 2001. Mem. AICPA, Calif. Soc. CPAs. Republican. Roman Catholic. Avocations: gardening, playing acoustic guitar, travel. Home: 4941 Herperia Ave Encino CA 91316 E-mail: linor34b@netzero.net.

RIBACK, ESTELLE POSNER, independent art historian; b. Bklyn., June 8, 1934; d. Max Jacob and Rose (Rosen) Posner; m. Arnold O. Riback, June 17, 1956; children: Phillip Scott, Stephen Craig, Debra Lyn. BS in Psychology, Tufts U., 1956; MS in Elem. Edn., Hofstra U., 1964; MA in Art History, Inst. Fine Art, NYU, 1981; cert. art appraiser, NYU, 1993. Cert. elem. tchr., N.Y. Tchr. reading improvement Glen Cove (N.Y.) Pub. Schs., from 1964; ptnr., v.p. Artlego, N.Y.C., 1980-83; devel. officer East Harlem Tutorial Program, 1985-86; asst. to dir. devel. Ams. Soc., 1986-89; pres., ptnr. Manley-Riback, Inc., 1989-96; pres. Estelle Riback Fine Arts Inc., 1996-98. Curator Am. Barbizon Art. Author: (monograph) Henry Ward Ranger, 2000 (Best Book in art history Bay Area Ind. Book Pub. Assn. 2001). Pres., bd. dirs. Azzizz Theatre, Inc., Bklyn., 1993-95, chmn. benefit com., 1993-94, chmn. fundraising, 1993-95; former mem. bd. Hebrew Sch. of Congregation Tifereth Israel Bd. Edn., Glen Cove; former chmn. major gifts Suffolk region Hadassah Med. Orgn., former v.p. for fundraising Huntington chpt. Mem.: Nat. Coalition Ind. Scholars, Assn. Historians Am. Art, Assn. Historians of 19th Century, Coll. Art Assn., West End Synagogue, Candlewood Yacht Club, Alpha Xi Delta, Psi Chi. Democrat. Avocations: tennis, sailing, bridge, travel, collecting art and artifacts. Home and Office: 201 E 79th St Apt 19D New York NY 10021-0844

RIBAK, CHARLES ERIC, anatomy educator; b. July 19, 1950; s. Marcus and Adele (Blank) R.; m. Julia Marianne Wendruck, Jan. 2, 1977; children: Marc Aaron, William Michael. BS, SUNY, Albany, 1971; PhD, Boston U., 1975. Assoc. rsch. scientist City of Hope Med. Ctr., Duarte, Calif., 1975-78; from asst. prof. to full prof. U. Calif., Irvine, 1978-90, prof., 1990—. NIH NLS-2 Study Sect., 1989-92. Assoc. editor Jour. Neurocytology, London, 1984-88, Epilepsy Rsch., 1986—, Brain Rsch., 1988—, Jour. Mind and Behavior, 1988—, Anatomy and Embryology, 1992-96, Jour. Hirnforschung, 1993—, Archives of Med. Rsch., 1993—, Epilepsia, 1995—, Hippocampus, 2000—; contbr. over 100 articles on brain rsch. to profl. jours. Recipient Michael prize, 1987, Citation Classic award, 1987, Javits award, 1990; NSF grantee, Washington, 1981-84, 87-91, rsch. grantee NIH, 1979, 83, 86, 90, 99; Klingenstein fellow, 1983. Fellow AAAS; mem. Am. Assn. Anatomists, Soc. Neurosci., Internat. Brain Rsch. Orgn., Cajal Club (pres. 2000-02). Office: U Calif Dept Of Anatomy Neurob Irvine CA 92697-1275 E-mail: ceribak@uci.edu.

RIBALOW, MEIR Z. playwright, educator; b. N.Y.C., Sept. 3, 1948; s. Harold Uriel and Susan (Shuck) R. BA, Princeton U., 1970. Artist-in-residence Fordham U., N.Y.C., 1995—; artistic dir. The Playwrights Project, Healing Springs, N.C., 1998—; project dir. sports website and magic website N.Y.U. Ctr., N.Y.C., 2000—. Author: (plays) Sundance, Raindance, Honey, the Domino Theory, Winner Take All, Irish Coffee, Shrunken Heads; co-author: The Jew in American Sports, Jewish Baseball Stars, Great Jewish Chess Champions; author (children's book series) Gallavants; dir. (plays) Winning Hearts and Minds, The Emperor of Late Night Radio, A Tribute to Jack MacGowran; assoc. dir. (plays) Wedding Band, As You Like It; contrb. poetry to popular mags, articles to newspapers. Bd. dirs. The Creative Coalition, N.Y.C., L.A., Washington, 1989—; coord. internat. arts The Global Forum, N.Y.C., 1991—. Mem. The Players (dir. playwrights workshop 1996—). Home: 431 E 20th St New York NY 10010

RIBARY, URS, neuroscientist, researcher, educator; b. Lucerne, Switzerland, Nov. 24, 1955; came to U.S., 1988; s. Max and Hilde (Brunner) Ribary; m. Evelyne Dahinden, July 11, 1986; 1 child Samantha R. MS, U. Tech., Zurich, Switzerland, 1981, DSc, 1985. Rsch. asst. prof. NYU Med. Ctr., N.Y.C., 1988-93, dir. ctr. for neuromagnetism, 1989—, rsch. assoc. prof., 1993—. Vis. asst. prof. Simon Fraser U., Can., 1986-88. Cons. (Time Life series) The Brain, 1990; contbr. articles to profl. jours. Mem. AAAS, Am. Soc. Neurosci., N.Y. Acad. Scis., European Neurosci. Assn., Soc. Cognitive Neuroscience. Avocations: recreational activities. Achievements include work on using functional brain imaging techniques, especially magneto encephalography (MEG) to study coherent thalamo-cortical activity in humans during normal cognitive processing, and its alterations in neurological and neuropsychiatric patients. Office: Dept Physiology and Neurosci NYU Med Ctr 550 1st Ave New York NY 10016-6402 E-mail: ribaru01@popmail.med.nyu.edu.

RIBBENS, ERIC, plant ecologist, educator; b. Pipestone, Minn., Dec. 19, 1957; s. Dennis Neil and Harriet (Hofstede) Ribbens; d. Barbara Ann Ribbens, July 9, 1983; children: Neltje Siew, Samara Namorik. BS in Natural Resources Mgmt., U. Wis., Green Bay, 1986; MS in Bot., U. Wyo., 1988; PhD in Ecology, U. Conn., 1995. Asst. prof. biology St. John's U., Collegeville, 1994-97, U. Evansville, Ind., 1997-2000, Western Ill. U., Macomb, 2000—. Author: (with others) Growing Pains: Environmentalism, 1999; contbr. articles to profl. jours. including Ecology, Ecol. Monographs, Am. Jour. Bot., Biotropica, among others. Mem. Assn. Tropical Biology, Ecol. Soc. Am. (Best Ecology Paper of Yr. 1997), Am. Bot. Soc., Internat. Vegetation Assn., Ill. Am. Scis., Am. Naturalists Soc. Home: 90 Emmy Rd Macomb IL 61455 Office: Western Ill U 1 University Cir Macomb IL 61455 E-mail: e-ribbens@wiu.edu.

RIBBLE, ANNE HOERNER, communications executive; b. Balt., Oct. 30, 1932; m. John C. Ribble, July 26, 1974. BA, Smith Coll., 1954; MA, Harvard U., 1955. Tech. asst. IBM, N.Y.C., 1958-63, editor Armonk, White Plains, N.Y., 1969-75, mgr. editl. svcs. data processing divsn. White Plains, 1976-77, program adminstr. sys. comm. divsn. N.Y.C., 1977-78, staff tech. edn., fed. sys. divsn. Houston, 1978-80, info. rep., 1980-87; staff info. IBM Fed. Sys. Co., 1988-93; prin. Creative Commn., Houston, 1993—. Mem. allocations com. United Way, Houston, 1989—94; bd. dirs. Stanley Isaacs Cmty. Ctr, N.Y.C., 1968—72, Bayou Bend Docent Orgn., 1999—2001. Mem. Pub. Rels. Soc. Am. (accredited), Internat. Assn. Bus. Communicators (pres. Houston chpt. 1982, cmty. rels. dir. 1989-92, accredited). Home: 6200 Willers Way Houston TX 77057-2808 Office: Creative Commn 6355 Westheimer Rd # 171 Houston TX 77057-5103 E-mail: aribble@houston.rr.com.

RIBBLE, JOHN CHARLES, medical educator; b. Paris, July 26, 1931; s. Elbert Alfred and Dorothy (Pyeatt) R.; m. Anne Blythe Hoerner; 1 stepchild Helen Blythe Strate Kielty. MD, U. Tex., 1955. Diplomate Am. Bd. Internal Medicine. Asst. prof. medicine Cornell U., N.Y.C., 1962-66, assoc. prof. pediatrics, 1966-78, dean, 1974-78, Med. Sch., U. Tex., Houston, 1978-86, dean, 1986-95; vis. scholar The Health Inst. New Eng. Med. Ctr., Boston, 1995-96; prof. medicine U. Tex., Houston, 1996—. Mem. Nat. Adv. Coun. Gen. Med. Scis. NIH, Bethesda, Md., 1988-91. Episcopalian. E-mail. Home: 6200 Willers Way Houston TX 77057-2808 Office: U Tex Med Sch 6431 Fannin St Houston TX 77030-1501 E-mail: jribble@houston.rr.com.

RIBBLE, RONALD GEORGE, retired psychologist, educator, writer; b. West Reading, Pa., May 7, 1937; s. Jeremiah George and Mildred Sarah (Folk) Ribble; m. Catalina Valenzuela Torres, Sept. 30, 1961; children: Christina, Timothy, Kenneth. BSEE cum laude, U. Mo., 1968, MSEE, 1969, MA, 1985, PhD, 1986. Bd. cert. forensic examiner, diplomate Am. Bd. Psychol. Specialities, Am. Coll. Forensic Examiners. Enlisted man USAF, 1956-60, advance through grades to lt. col., 1976; rsch. dir. Coping Resources, Inc., Columbia, Mo., 1986; pres., co-owner Towers and Rushing Ltd. (Pubs., Troubadour 1997—), San Antonio, 1986—; referral devel. Laughlin Pavilion Psychiat. Hosp., Kirksville, Mo., 1987; program dir. Psychiat. Insts. of Am., Iowa Falls, Iowa, 1987-88; lead psychotherapist Gasconade County Counseling Ctr., Hermann, Mo., 1988; sr. lectr. U. Tex., San Antonio, 1989—2002; lectr. Trinity U., 1995-96; assessment clinician Afton Oaks Psychiat. Hosp., 1989-91; ret., 2002. Faculty cons. Edn. Testing Svc., 1997; psychologist Olmos Psychol. Svcs., Inc., San Antonio, 1991—93; vol. assessor Holmgreen Children's Shelter, San Antonio, 1992—93; founder Ruth Bohn Weissman Scholarship in Creative Writing U. Tex., San Antonio, 1994; cosponor Lyric Recovery Festival, Carnegie Hall, 2000; condr. seminars, revs. for maj. publs. Author: (book) Apples, Weeds, and Doggie Poo, 1995, Dont' Eat the Snake!; contbr. essays to psychol. refernce books, poetry to anthologies periodicals, lyrics to popular music; interviewer: celebrities in performing and lit. arts, 1995—, columnist: Feelings, 1993—97; pub. access TV appearances, 1991—. Vol. announcer pub. radio sta., Colombia, 1993; vol. Cath. Family and Children's Svc., San Antonio, 1989—91; chpt. advisor Rational Recovery Program for Alcoholics, 1991—92; mem. Pres. Leadership Cir., 1994—99, 2002; contbg. mem. Dem. Nat. Com., 1983—, Presdl. Congl. Task Force, 1994; del. Boone County (Mo.) Dem. Conv., 1984. Recipient Roberts Meml. prize in Poetry, 1995, Pushcart nominee, 1999—2001. Master: APA; fellow: Am. Coll. Forensic Examiners; mem.: ACLU, AAUP, NEA, Physicians for Social Responsibility (leadership cir.), So. Poverty Law Ctr. (leadership coun. for tchg. tolerance), Poetry Soc. Am., Soc. Profl. Journalists, Interfaith Alliance, Ret. Officers Assn., Air Force Assn., Bexar County Psychol. Assn., Internat. Platform Assn. (Poetry award 1995). Deist. Avocations: running and fitness, poetry, singing, public speaking. Home: 14023 N Hills Village Dr San Antonio TX 78249-2534 Office: U Tex Divsn Behavioral and Cultural Scis San Antonio TX 78249 also: Towers and Rushing Ltd San Antonio TX 78249 E-mail: rribble@utsa.edu., rgribel@stic.net.

RIBEZZO, JOHN STEVEN, business administration educator, accountant; b. Providence, June 25, 1948; s. Frank and Virginia (Gentile) R.; m. Linda Susan Romano, July 14, 1954; children: Jacqueline, Michael. BSBA, Bryant Coll., 1972; MBA, Plymouth State Coll., 1976; MS in Acctg., U. R.I., 1986. CPA, cert. mgmt. acct., cert. internal auditor, cert. fin. mgr. Prof. bus. adminstrn. C.C. of R.I., Warwick, 1978—, chmn. dept. bus. adminstrn.; sole proprietor acct. Cranston, R.I., 1981—. Contbr. articles to profl. jours. Soccer coach Cranston League for Cranston's Future, 1995. Mem. AICPA, Am. Acctg. Assn. (chair two-yr. coll. sect. 1996-98, Lifetime Achievement in Acctg. Edn. award from Two-Yr. Coll. Sect.), R.I. Assn. Acctg. Profs. (pres. 1992-2000), Assn. Collegiate Bus. Schs. and Programs (Northeast region pres. 1997-98), R.I. Soc. CPAs, Inst. Mgmt. Accts. Avocation: golf. Office: CC of RI 400 East Ave Warwick RI 02886-1807

RIBLER, RANDY LOUIS, computer scientist, educator; b. Van Nuys, Calif., Nov. 29, 1957; s. Ronald Irwin and Nancy Elizabeth Ribler; m. Binh-Minh Tran, Apr. 12, 1997. PhD, Va. Tech, 1991. Programmer, analyst Ensco, Inc., Springfield, Va., 1980—83; sr. engr. Westinghouse Electric Corp., Annapolis, Md., 1983—86; software engr. Xenologic, Newark, 1986—88; sr. engr. Star Techs., Inc, Sterling, Va., 1988—92; postdoctoral rsch. assoc. U. Ill., Urbana-Champaign, Ill., 1996—98; asst. prof., program coord. computer sci. Lynchburg (Va.) Coll., 1998—. Home: 1190 Cuddington Ln Forest VA 24551 Office: Lynchburg Coll 1501 Lakeside Dr Lynchburg VA 24501 Business E-Mail: ribler@lynchburg.edu.

RIBNER, HERBERT SPENCER, physicist, educator; b. Seattle, Apr. 9, 1913; s. Joseph Herman and Rose Esther (Goldberg) R.; m. Lelia Carolyn Byrd, Oct. 29, 1949; children— Carol Anne, David Byrd BS, Calif. Inst. Tech., 1935; MS, Washington U., St. Louis, 1937; PhD, Washington U., 1939. From physicist to dir. lab. Brown Geophys. Co., Tex., 1939-40; from physicist to head stability sect. Langley Lab., NACA, Va., 1940-49, cons. to head boundary layer sects. Lewis Lab., 1949-54; research assoc. Inst. aerospace studies U. Toronto, Ont., Can., 1955-56, asst. prof., 1956-57, assoc. prof., 1957-59, prof., 1959-78, prof. emeritus, 1978—. Vis. prof. U. Southampton, 1960-61; staff scientist NASA Langley Research Ctr., 1975-76, disting. rsch. assoc., 1979—; chmn. sonic boom panel Internat. Civil Aviation Orgn., 1969-70; adviser com. on hearing, bioacoustics and mechanics Nat. Acad. Scis., 1972-74 Contbr. over 100 articles to profl. jours. Recipient Can. 125th Commemorative medal, 1993, Pub. Svc. medal NASA, 1994. Fellow AIAA (Aero-Acoustics award 1976, Dryden lectr. 1981), Royal Soc. Can., Am. Phys. Soc., Acoustical Soc. Am., Can. Aero. and Space Inst. (Turnbull lectr. 1968). Office: U Toronto Inst Aerospace Studies 4925 Dufferin St Downsview ON Canada M3H 5T6 E-mail: h.sribner@sympatico.ca.

RIBOTSKY, BRET MICHAEL, podiatric surgeon; b. Miami Beach, Fla., Aug. 9, 1962; s. Marvin Howard and Harriet Diane (Lanzner) R.; m. Mimi Bright, June 12, 1993; children: Robyn Beth, Benjamin Harris. BS, U. South Fla., 1984; DPM, Pa. Coll. Podiatric Medicine, 1989. Diplomate Am. Bd. Podiatric Surgery, Am. Bd. Podiatric Orthops. and Primary Podiatric Medicine. Dir. podiatric surgery Inst. Med. Specialties, Aventura, Fla., 1992; chief of foot surgery Cleveland Clinic Fla., Ft. Lauderdale, 1992-95; pvt. practice Boca Raton, Fla., 1995—. Fellow Am. Coll. Foot and Ankle Surgery, Am. Coll. Foot and Ankle Orthopedics and Medicine (pres., sec.-treas.). Jewish. Avocations: photography, scuba diving, cycling. Office: 880 NW 13th St Ste 1C Boca Raton FL 33486-2342 E-mail: ribotsky@yahoo.com.

RICAPITO, JOSEPH VIRGIL (GIUSEPPE RICAPITO), Spanish and comparative literature educator; b. Giovinazzo, Bari, Italy, Oct. 30, 1933; came to U.S. , 1935; s. Frank and Filomena (Cervone) R.; m. Carolyn Sue Kitchen, Apr. 7, 1958; children: Frank Peyton, Maria Avadna. BA, CUNY, Bklyn., 1955; MA, U. Iowa, 1956; PhD in Romance Langs., U. Calif., L.A., 1966. From instr. to asst. prof. Pomona Coll., Claremont, Calif., 1962-70; from assoc. prof. to prof. Ind. U., Bloomington, Ind., 1970-80; prof. La. State U., Baton Rouge, 1980—, chmn. dept., 1980-85, Joseph Yenni disting. prof. Italian studies, 1999. Author: Bibliografia Razonada y anotada, 1980; editor: La Vida de Laz de Tormes, 1976; translator: Dialogue of Mercury and Charon, 1986, Cervantes's Novelas ejemplares: Between History and Creativity, 1996. Pres. Greater Baton Rouge Am.-Italian Assn., 1984-85. With U.S. Army, 1957-59. Grantee NEH, 1981; named Knight Order of Merit, Republic of Italy, 1988, Knight Order of Queen Isabel, Govt. of Spain, 1990; named Joseph Yenni Meml. Fund Disting. prof., 1999, Disting. Rsch. Master La. State U., 2001. Mem. MLA, Renaissance Soc. Am., Am. Comparative Lit. Assn., Am. Assn. Tchrs. Spanish and Portuguese, Cervantes Soc. Am. Avocations: jogging, photography, films. Office: La State U 209 Prescott Hall Baton Rouge LA 70803-0001 E-mail: ricapito@lsu.edu.

RICARD, THOMAS ARMAND, electrical engineer; b. Waterbury, Conn., Sept. 10, 1954; s. Armand Andrew and Mary Jean (Clark) Ricard; m. Gina Marie Harris, Sept. 10, 1983; children: Bernadette Allison, Amanda Valentine. BSEE, U. Hartford, 1988; MSEE, Syracuse U., 1991. Edison engr. GE, Syracuse, NY, 1988-92; radio frequency/microwave engr. EZ Form Cable Corp., New Haven, 1992—. Mem. Electronic Industry Assn. Working Group on Cable and Connectors, New Haven, 1995—. Mem.: Am. Radio Relay League, Eta Kappa Nu, Tau Beta Pi. Avocations: amateur radio, amateur musician. Home: 186 Peck Ln Cheshire CT 06410-2000 Office: EZ Form Cable Corporation 275 - 285 Welton St Hamden CT 06517 E-mail: tricard@ezform.com.

RICARDO-CAMPBELL, RITA, economist, educator; b. Boston, Mar. 16, 1920; d. David and Elizabeth (Jones) Ricardo; m. Wesley Glenn Campbell, Sept. 15, 1946; children: Barbara Lee, Diane Rita, Nancy Elizabeth BS, Simmons Coll., 1941; MA, Harvard U., 1945, PhD, 1946. Instr. Harvard U., Cambridge, Mass., 1946—48; asst. prof. Tufts U., Medford, 1948—51; labor economist U.S. Wage Stabilization Bd., 1951—53; economist Ways and Means Com. U.S. Ho. of Reps., 1954; economist, 1957—60; prof. San Jose State U., 1960—61; sr. fellow Hoover Instn. on War, Revolution, and Peace, Stanford, Calif., 1968—95, sr. fellow emerita, 1995—. Lectr. health Stanford U. Med. Sch., 1973—78; bd. dirs. Watkins-Johnson Co., Palo Alto, Calif., Gillette Co., Boston; mgmt. bd. Samaritan Med. Ctr., San Jose. Author: Voluntary Health Insurance in the U.S., 1960, Economics of Health and Public Policy, 1971, Food Safety Regulation: Use and Limitations of Cost-Benefit Analysis, 1974, Drug Lag: Federal Government Decision Making, 1976, Social Security: Promise and Reality, 1977, The Economics and Politics of Health, 1982, 1985, Resisting Hostile Takerovers: The Gillette Company, 1997; co-editor: Below-Replacement Fertility in Industrial Societies, 1987, Issues in Contemporary Retirement, 1988; contbr. Commr. Western Interstate Commn. for Higher Edn. Calif., 1967-75, chmn., 1970-71; mem. Pres. Nixon's Adv. Coun. on Status Women, 1969-76; mem. task force on taxation Pres.'s Coun. on Environ. Quality, 1970-72; mem. Pres.'s Com. Health Services Industry, 1971-73, FDA Nat. Adv. Drug Com., 1972-75; mem. Pres. Reagan's Econ. Policy Adv. Bd., 1981-90, Pres. Reagan's Nat. Coun. on Humanities, 1982-89, Pres. Reagan's Nat. Medal of Sci. com., 1988-91, Pres. Bush's Nat. Medal of Sci. com., 1991-94; bd. dirs. Ind. Colls. No. Calif., 1971-87; mem. com. assessment of safety, benefits, risks Citizens Commn. Sci., Law and Food, Rockefeller U., 1973-75; mem. adv. com. Ctr. Health Policy Rsch., Am. Enterprise Inst. Pub. Policy Rsch., Washington, 1974-80; mem. adv. coun. on social security Quadrennial Health and Human Svcs., 1974-75; bd. dirs. Simmons Coll. Corp., Boston, 1975-80; mem. adv. coun. bd. assocs. Stanford Librs., 1975-78; mem. coun. SRI Internat., Menlo Park, Calif., 1977-90. Mem. Am. Econ. Assn., Mont Pelerin Soc. (bd. dirs. 1988-92, v.p. 1992-94), Harvard Grad. Soc. (coun. 1991-94), Phi Beta Kappa. Home: 26915 Alejandro Dr Los Altos Hills CA 94022-1932 Office: Stanford U Hoover Instn Stanford CA 94305-6010

RICART, GLENN, internet executive; b. Wheeling, W.Va., Aug. 1, 1949; s. Donald Glenn and Elizabeth Ricart; m. Patricia M. Guenther, Oct. 26, 1974; children: Brendon Guenther, Genevieve Guenther. BS, Case We. Res. U., 1971, MS in Computing and Info. Scis., 1973; PhD in Computer Sci., U. Md., 1980. Head, DEC-10 systems NIH, Bethesda, Md., 1971-82; prin. investigator SURAnet, College Park, 1984-94; dir., Computer Sci. Ctr. U. Md., 1982-93; asst. vice chancellor U. Md. Sys., Adelphi, 1990-93; program mgr. Def. Advanced Rsch. Projects Agy., Fairfax, Va., 1993-95; sr. v.p., chief tech. officer Novell, Provo, Utah, 1995-99; exec. v.p., chief tech. officer CenterBeam, Santa Clara, Calif., 1999—. Dir. Nat. Assn. State Univs. and Land Grant Colls., Washington, 1993-94, SCO, Inc., Santa Clara, 1996-98, 1st USA Fin. Svcs., Salt Lake City, 1998—, CACI, Inc., Arlington, Va., 1998—. Patentee in field. Ruling elder, 1st Presbyn. Ch., Salt Lake City, 1998-01; asst. scoutmaster, Boy Scouts Am., Salt Lake City, 1995-99, coach Odyssey of the Mind, 1995-99, asst. leader, Girl Scouts USA, Bethesda, 1990-2002 co-chair Blue Ribbon Panel on Netcentricity, 1999-2000. Environ. Health Officer, USPHS, 1971-78, Bethesda. Mem. IEEE Computer Soc., Assn. Computing Machinery, Internet Soc., Tau Beta Pi, Phi Kappa Phi. Presbyterian. Avocation: American Coaster Enthusiasts. Office: CenterBeam 5302 Betsy Ross Dr Santa Clara CA 95054-1101

RICCELLI, RICHARD JOSEPH, advertising agency executive; b. Winchester, Mass., Dec. 7, 1954; s. Carmen Joseph and Arline Muriel (Young) R.; m. Constance Elizabeth McCabe, May 17, 1980 (div. Oct. 1987). BS, Kent State U., 1977. Copywriter Ogilvy & Mather, Inc., N.Y.C., 1978-80; creative supr. Bozell & Jacobs, Inc., Mpls., 1980-81; v.p. Quinn & Johnson, BBDO, Boston, 1982-85; pres. Smith & Jones Inc., Newburyport, Mass., 1985-86; v.p. Mullen, Inc., Prides Crossing, 1986-87; pres. Riccelli Direct, Inc., Boston, 1987—. Recipient Echo award Direct Mktg. Assn., N.Y.C., 1979, 91, Caples award, N.Y.C., 1991, Circulation Direct Mktg. award, 1991, 92, 93, 94, 95, 97, 98, Mag. Pubs. Assn. and Folio Mag., N.Y.C. Home: 32 Claremont Park Boston MA 02118-3002 Office: Riccelli Direct Inc 32 Claremont Park Boston MA 02118-3002

RICCI, DANIEL MICHAEL, protective services official; b. Troy, N.Y., Sept. 23, 1955; s. Anthony Joseph and Dolores Margaret (Poland) R.; m. Joan Frances Fleming, May 14, 1977; children: Brian Matthew, Scott Michael. AA in Criminal Justice, L.A. City Coll., 1978; grad., FBI Nat. Acad. Cert. police instr. N.Y. State Divsn. of Criminal Justice Svcs. Police officer Various Cities, 1979-89; sgt. Stony Point (N.Y.) Police Dept., 1989, adminstrv. sgt., 1989-96, lt., exec. officer, 1996—. Accreditation project mgr. Stony Point Police Dept., 1991—. Dep. mayor Village of Highland Falls, 1993—, trustee, 1993—, vol. counselor Birch Summer Project, Springfield Gardens, N.Y., 1995. Recipient Cert. of Merit N.Y. Sen., 1991, Cert. of Achievement N.Y. State Divsn. Criminal Justice Svcs., 1992. Mem. FBI Nat. Acad. Assn., Mensa, Rockland County Police Benevolent Assn., Stony Point Police Benevolent Assn. Home: 26 South St Highland Falls NY 10928-1421 Office: Stony Point Police Dept 79 Route 210 Stony Point NY 10980-1750

RICCI, MARY JEAN, community health nurse, educator; b. Phila., Apr. 30, 1962; d. Raymond and Mary L. Ricci. BA, Temple U., 1984, BSN, 1986; MS in Nursing, U. Pa., 1988. ACLS instr., BCLS instr. Staff nurse St. Mary Hosp., Phila., adminstrv. supr., 1986-88; asst. DON Paul's Run Life Care Commmunity, 1988-89; asst. prof. Holy Family Coll., 1989—; instr. staff devel. Episc. Hosp., 1988-99; staff devel. Episcopal Hosp. Longterm Care, 1995-98; adminstrv. supr. Episcopal. Hosp., 1998—2001; adminstr. Sacred Heart Hosp., Chester, Cmty. Hosp. Divsn. of Crozier Chester Med. Ctr., Chester, 1991-96; clin. educator Parkview Hosp., 1999; staff devel. educator Northeastern Hosp., 2000—; staff devel. instr. Temple East, 2000—. Mem. Dem. Exec. Com.; Women of the Moose Chairlady Nature Conservancy, Ctr. for Marine Conservation. Mem.: AACN, APHA, Sigma Theta Tau (past chpt. pres., past newsletter editor).

RICCIARDI, CHRISTINE SECOLA, international trade consultant; b. New Haven, Apr. 19, 1963; d. Carl Albert and Marie Rose (Pupello) Secola; m. Carmine C. Ricciardi, Nov. 24, 1990. BA, Fairfield (Conn.) U., 1985. Editl. asst. Conn. Woman Mag., Fairfield, 1984-85; corr. internat. money transfer divsn. Chase Manhattan Bank, N.Y.C., 1985-86; editor employee comm. Port Authority of N.Y. & N.J., 1986-88; internat. trade assn. adminstr. World Trade Ctrs. Assn., Inc., 1988-95, dir. mem. svcs., 1990-95; ind. cons., 1995—. Editor, contbg. author Corporate Comm., 1986-95; contbg. writer newspaper and mag. articles and trade publs., 1988—. Vol. mem. Conn. Spl. Olympics Com., 1981-82; big sister Conn. Big Sister Program, Bridgeport, 1984-85. Recipient Good Citizenship award City of Hamden, Conn., 1981. Mem. Am. Soc. Assn. Execs., Internat. Assn. Bus. Communicators, Alpha Mu Gamma, Nat. Lang. Honor Soc. Avocations: art, theater, skiing, foreign languages.

RICCIARDI, KAREN JANE, interior designer; b. N.Y.C., July 17, 1951; d. John Robert and Lillian (Marchak) R.; BS, U. Conn., 1973. Comml. and residential interior designer; pres. Ricciardi Assocs., Waterford, Conn.; lectr. design U. Conn. Continuing Edn., 1977-78. Bus. and Profl. Women's Assn. Young Career Woman of Yr. nominee, 1979. Mem. Am. Soc. Interior Designers, Southeastern Conn. Women's Network. Office: Ricciardi Assocs 567 Vauxhall Street Ext Waterford CT 06385-4330

RICCIARDI, LOUIS MICHAEL, brokerage house executive; b. Worcester, Mass., 1959; s. Michael Joseph and Mary Theresa Ricciardi; m. Cynthia Anne Booth. BA, Bridgewater State Coll., 1981. Account exec. Shearson/Am. Express, Brockton, Mass., 1981-83; v.p. Thomson McKinnon, Taunton, 1983-87; sr. v.p. Morgan Stanley Dean Witter, 1988—2002, UBS Paine Webber, 2002—. Bd. corporators Bristol County Savs. Bank, Taunton, Mass., 1985—, bd. trustees, 1992—; trustee Taunton Devel. Corp., 1994—, treas. 1995—. Weekly investment columnist, 1983—. Bd. corporators Morton Hosp., Taunton, 1987—, trustee, 1994—; pres. Heart of Taunton (Mass.) Revitalization Corp., 1988-89; trustee Bridgewater (Mass.) State Coll., 1989-99, chmn. 1990-94; trustee Bridgewater Found., 1989—, chmn. 1996—; bd. dirs. Taunton Boys & Girls Club, 1999—. Recipient Rondileau award for Outstanding Profl. Achievement and Cmty. Svc., 1999, Disting. Svc. award Bridgewater State Coll., 2002. Mem. Taunton Area C. of C. (dir. 1988-94, treas. 1993-94), Taunton Rotary Club (Paul Harris fellow 2000, pres. 1991-92), Bridgewater Coll. Alumni Assn. (treas. 1992-95). Avocations: guitar, coin collecting, baseball, community svc., Coca Cola memorabilia. Home: PO Box 228 Taunton MA 02780-0228

RICCIO, FRANK JOSEPH, lawyer, educator; b. Somerville, Mass. BS, Boston Coll., 1973; JD, Suffolk U., 1985; D of Dental Medicine, Boston Coll., 1986. Bar: Mass. 1985, U.S. Dist. Ct. Mass. 1986, U.S. Ct. Appeals (1st cir.) 1986. Dentist, Lowell, Mass., 1977-83, Metheun, 1983-84; assoc. Sugarman & Sugarman, Boston, 1985-87; pvt. practice Braintree, Mass., 1987. Clin. instr. oral medicine Harvard U., Boston, 1995—. Dental extern USPHS, 1976. Mem. Am. Assn. Trial Attys., Nat. Bd. Trial Attys. (cert. civil trial specialist), Mass. Bar Assn., Mass. Acad. Trial Attys., Million Dollar Advocates Forum. Office: Law Offices of Frank J Riccio PC 25 Braintree Hill Park Ste 208 Braintree MA 02184-8702 E-mail: fjriccio@socialaw.com.

RICE, ANNE, writer; b. New Orleans, Oct. 14, 1941; d. Howard and Katherine (Allen) O'Brien; m. Stan Rice, Oct. 14, 1961; children: Michele (dec.), Christopher. Student, Tex. Woman's U., 1959-60; BA, San Francisco State Coll., 1964, MA, 1971. Author: Interview with the Vampire, 1976, The Feast of all Saints, 1980, Cry to Heaven, 1982, The Vampire Lestat, 1985, The Queen of the Damned, 1988, The Mummy or Ramses the Damned, 1989, The Witching Hour, 1990, Tale of the Body Thief, 1992, Lasher, 1993, Taltos, 1994, Memnoch the Devil, 1995, Servant of the Bones, 1996, Violin, 1998, The Vampire Armand, 1998, Pandora: New Tales of the Vampires, 1998, Vittorio the Vampire, 1999, Merrick, 2000, Blood and Gold, 2001; (as A.N. Roquelaure) The Claiming of Sleeping Beauty, 1983, Beauty's Punishment, 1984, Beauty's Release: The Continued Erotic Adventures of Sleeping Beauty, 1985 (as Anne Rampling) Exit to Eden, 1985, Belinda, 1986 ; screenwriter: Interview with a Vampire, 1994. Office: care Alfred A Knopf Inc 201 E 50th St New York NY 10022-7703*

RICE, BARBARA LYNN, stage manager; b. Hartford, Conn., Nov. 9, 1955; d. Joe Roger and Betty Barbara (Baxter) R. BA in Theatre and French, Ind. U., 1978; MFA in Directing, U. Cin., 1982. Freelance stage mgr., N.Y.C.; dir. The Open Eye: New Stagings, 1989; prodn. stage mgr. Belmont Italian-Am. Playhouse, 1994, 95; prodn. assn. Silence, Cunning, Exile, 1995; asst. stage mgr. The Merry Wives of Windsor, 1995. Dir. The Open Eye: New Stagings, N.Y.C., 1989; stage mgr. 20 Years Ago Today, Cin., 1989, Fourscore & 7 Years Ago, Paramus, N.J., 1989-90, Hanging the President, N.Y.C., 1990; prodn. asst. Kiss of the Spiderwoman, Purchase, N.Y., 1990, (off-Broadway) Beau Jest, N.Y.C., 1992, Belmont Italian-Am. Playhouse, N.Y.C., 1994, 95, Transformations, 1997; listings editor Back Stage, 1998. Mem. Actors' Equity Assn., Stage Mgrs. Assn. Presbyterian. Avocations: music, history, art, reading, foreign languages. Home: 412 W 56th St Apt 10 New York NY 10019-3647 E-mail: barbara-rice@webtv.net.

RICE, CANICE TIMOTHY, JR. lawyer; b. St. Louis, Apr. 4, 1950; s. Canice Timothy and Jane Elizabeth (Tobin) R. AB, Holy Cross Coll., 1972; JD, U. Mo., 1976. Bar: Mo. 1976, Ill. 1977, U.S. Dist. Ct. (cen. and so. dists.) Ill. 1977, U.S. Ct. Appeals (7th and 8th cirs.) 1977, U.S. Dist. Ct. (ea. dist.) Mo., US. Ct. Appeals (2d cir.) 1991. Pvt. practice law, St. Louis, 1976—. Mem. ATLA, Bar Assn. Met. St. Louis (chair fed. litigation and practice com. 1996-97, co-chair 1997—), Ill. Bar Assn., Mo. Assn. Trial Attys., Lawyers Assn. Home: 6624 Kingsbury Blvd Saint Louis MO 63130-4605 Office: 319 N 4th St Ste 602 Saint Louis MO 63102

RICE, CHARLES LANE, surgical educator; b. Atlanta, May 22, 1945; s. Marion Jennings and Molly Black (Moore) R.; m. Lynn Carol Inscoe, Dec. 27, 1968 (div. 1976); m. Judith Josephine Bousha, July 9, 1977; children: Aaron Nicholas, Patrick Marion. AB, U. Ga., 1964; MD, Med. Coll. Ga., 1968. Commd. ensign USN, 1966, advanced through grades to comdr., 1976, ret., 1977; intern Bowman Gray Sch. Medicine, Winston-Salem, N.C., 1968-69; resident Nat. Naval Med. Ctr., Bethesda, Md., 1969-73; asst. prof. surgery U. Chgo., 1977-80, assoc. prof. surgery, 1980-84; dir. intensive care unit Michael Reese Hosp., Chgo., 1977-84; prof., vice chmn. dept. surgery U. Wash., Seattle, 1985-92; surgeon-in-chief Harborview Med. Ctr., 1985-92; Dr. Lee Hudson- Robert R. Penn prof., chmn., divsn. gen. surgery U. Tex. Southwestern Med. Ctr., Dallas, 1992-93; prof. surgery U. Ill., Chgo., 1993—, prof. physiology and biophysics, 1996—, vice dean Coll. Medicine, 1994-99, vice chancellor health affairs, 1999—. Robert Wood Johnson Health Policy fellow, 1991-92; legis. asst. to U.S. senator Tom Daschle, 1991-92. Assoc. editor Jour. of Surg. Rsch., 1983-90; contbr. articles to profl. jours. Rep. Accrediting Coun. Grad. Med. Edn., chair elect. Capt. USNR, 1989—. Fellow ACS (gov. 1992-98, vice chmn. com. on trauma 1992-93), Am. Surg. Assn., Am. Assn. for Surgery of Trauma (com. chair 1989-91); mem. Soc. Univ. Surgeons, Am. Physiol. Soc., Shock Soc. (pres. 1991-92). Democrat. Episcopalian. Office: U Ill at Chgo V Chancellor Health Affairs 914 S Wood St Rm 101 Chicago IL 60612-7337

RICE, CHARLES DALE, labor relations specialist, writer; b. Coulterville, Ill., Sept. 6, 1934; s. Eugene Frank and Mildred Elizabeth (Patton) R.; m. Donna JoAnn Schnoeker, Feb. 8, 1958; children: Scott Alan, Stacy Lynn, Sherri Renee. AS, So. Ill. U., 1963. Spray painter Empire Stove Works, Belleville, Ill., 1952-53; top assembler Fisher Body Corp., St. Louis, 1953-62; coal miner Midland Coal Co., Marissa, Ill., 1962-64; surface coal miner Southwestern Ill. Coal Corp., Percy, 1964-74; pres. United Mine Workers Am., 1974-80; supr. human resources Arch of Ill. Coal Corp., 1980-85, mgr. labor rels., 1985-94, labor rels. cons. Ill., 1994-96, ret., 1996. Ret. capt. Steeleville (Ill.) Vol. Fire Dept., 1970-89. Cpl. U.S. Army, 1957-63. Mem. Am. Arbitration Assn., Ill. Labor Reps. Group. Lutheran. Avocations: hunting, fishing, basketball. Office: 1397 Puxico Rd Percy IL 62272-2619 E-mail: DDRice@egytian.net.

RICE, CINDY G. estate planning associate; b. Kansas City, Mo., Mar. 13, 1951; d. Victor Eugene and Treva Irene (Glancy) Hutchison; m. Rex Dale Rice, May 22, 1971; children: Ami Rae, Lori Janelle. BS in English and Psychology cum laude, S.W. Bapt. U., Bolivar, Mo., 1973, Teaching Cert., 1976. Notary pub. Receptionist, office worker S.W. Bapt. U., Bolivar, Mo., 1969-70, libr. asst., 1970-71, student pers. sec., 1973-77, career placement sec., 1981-90, estate planning adminstrv. asst., 1990-92, dir. found. devel., 1992-97, assoc. dir. gift planning, 1997-99, estate planning assoc., pvt. scholarship coord., 1999—. Mem. newsletter com. S.W. Bapt. U., 1993—95, mem. homecoming com., 1993—98, 2002—. Mem. Assn. Fundraising Execs. (sec. 1997, v.p. 1998, pres. 1999), Alpha Chi. Republican. Baptist. Avocations: crafts, walking, family. Office: SW Bapt U 1600 University Ave Bolivar MO 65613-2597

RICE, CLARE I. electronics company executive; b. Rice Lake, Wis., Nov. 3, 1918; s. Chris Nilson and Ingeborg (Haug) R.; m. Virginia M. Bateman; children: Karen Bateman, Carol Rice Brannon, David Alan; m. Barbara Carlson Denniston, 2002. BSEE, U. Wis., 1943; BS in Law, St. Paul Coll. Law, 1950; DEngring, Rose-Hulman Inst. Tech., 1979. Registered profl. engr., Minn., D.C. Supr. aircraft radio engring. Northwest Airlines, Inc., Mpls., 1946-51; staff engr. Aero. Radio, Inc., Washington, 1951-53; aviation sales mgr., gen. mgr. Bendix Avionics Divsn., Balt., 1953-62; pres. Sunbeam Electronics, Inc., Ft. Lauderdale, Fla., 1962-66; v.p. Nova U., 1966-68; asst. v.p., v.p., sr. v.p. Collins Radio Co., pres. Collins Avionics group Rockwell Internat. Corp., Cedar Rapids, Iowa, 1968-83. Dir. Rockwell-Collins Internat., Inc., Dallas. Chmn. United Way, Cedar Rapids, 1973-74; trustee Coe Coll., 1979-83, Hoover Presdl. Libr.; eminent fellow Wisdom Hall of Fame; bd. dirs. St. Luke's Hosp., 1976-82, Mchts. Nat. Bank, 1977-83; chmn. Mcpl. Airport Commn., Cedar Rapids, 1980-84; charter mem. Aviation Hall of Fame; capt. Hon. Dep. Sheriffs Assn., 1987—; pres. Sales and Mktg. Execs. Balt., 1960—, Cmty. Assn. Rancho Bernardo Heights, 1988-91; dir. Rancho Bernardo Cmty. Found. Lt. comdr. USNR, 1943-46. Recipient Disting. Svc. citation U. Wis., 1979, 84; Pioneer award Milw. Sch. Engring., 1981. Sr. mem. IEEE; mem. Iowa Mfrs. Assn. (bd. dirs. 1975-81), Gen. Aviation Mfrs. Assn. (dir. 1970-81, chmn. 1979), U. Wis. Alumni Assn. (chmn. 1981-82, pres. 1980-81, Disting. Svc. award 1984). Clubs: Wings (N.Y.C.); Nat. Aviation (Washington); Rancho Bernardo Heights Country. Lodges: Royal Order of Jesters (dir. 1979). Republican. Presbyterian. Home: 12201 Fairway Pointe San Diego CA 92128-3230

RICE, CONDOLEEZZA, national security advisor; b. Birmingham, Ala., Nov. 14, 1954; BA cum laude, U. Denver, 1974, PhD, 1981; MA, U. Notre Dame. Asst. prof. dept. polit. sci. to assoc. prof. Stanford (Calif.) U., 1981-93, prof., 1993—99, provost, 1993-99; spl. asst. to U.S. President Nat. Security Affairs, Washington, 1989-91; dir. Soviet and East European Affairs; sr. fellow Hoover Inst., Stanford, Calif.; National Security Advisor Nat. Security Council, Washington, 2001—. Cons. ABC News, Washington; mem. spl. advisory panel to comdr. and chief strategic air commd.; mem. gov. ind. advisory redistricting the state of Calif.; mem. U.S. Delegation to 2+4 Talks on German Unification. Author: Uncertain Allegiance; The Soviet Union and the Czechoslovak Army, 1984; co-author (with Alexander Dallin): The Gorbachev Era, 1986; co-author: (with Philip Zelikow) Germany Unified and Europe Transformed, 1995. Recipient Walter J. Gores award, 1984. Mem. Coun. Fgn. Rels. Republican. Office: The White House National Security Council 1600 Pennsylvania Ave Washington DC 20500

RICE, DALE R. education educator; b. New Castle, Pa., Aug. 6, 1948; s. Paul Richard and Charlotte Mae Rice; m. Judy B. Rice, Aug. 6, 1984; children: Brandon Dale, Kristen Leigh, Courtney Alletta; m. Luann Moser Rice, June 10, 1972 (div. Nov. 4, 1983). EdB, Penn State, State College, PA, 1966—70, MEd, 1970—73; PhD, Ohio State, Columbus, OH, 1974—77. Educator Bethel Pk. City Schools, Bethel Park, Pa., 1970—74; rsch. asst. Ohio State U., Columbus, Ohio, 1970—73; lectr. East Carolina U., Greenville, NC, 1977—80; asst. prof. U. of So. Ala., Mobile, Ala., 1980—86; assoc. prof. Auburn U., Auburn, 1986—89; educator Gwinnett County Schools, Lawrenceville County Schools, 1989—. Article reviewer Sch. Sci. & Math Jour., 1980—88; ednl. cons. Ednl. Jour., 1987—89. Author: (book) Life Science, Earth Science, Energy from Fossil Fuels. Avocation: landscaping. Home Fax: 770-339-8201. Personal E-mail: dale8648@aol.com.

RICE, DARREL ALAN, lawyer; b. Denver, Jan. 8, 1947; s. Dale Harvey and Dorothy (Enewold) F.; m. Jeffrey Lynn Taylor, May 31, 1970; children: Ashley, Justin, Chandler. BSIE, U. Ark., 1969; JD, So. Meth. U., 1972. Bar: Tex. 1972. Assoc. Butler & Binion, Houston, 1972-75, Winstead, McGuire, Sechrest & Minick, P.C., Dallas, 1975-78; shareholder Winstead Sechrest & Minick, P.C., 1978—. Trustee 1st Presbyn. Ch. Found., Dallas, 1982-94; adv. dir. Spl. Camps for Spl. Kids, Dallas, 1987-90, bd. dirs., mem. exec. com., 1990—; bd. dirs. Tex. Bus. Law Found., 1989—, Jubilee Park and Cmty. Ctr. Corp.; bd. dirs., mem. exec. com. Dallas CASA, 1989—; bd. dirs. Dallas Opera, 1997—; mem. exec. bd. So. Meth. U. Law Sch., 1991-97. Mem. ABA, Tex. Bar Assn., State Bar Tex. (chmn. legal opinions com. 1989-92, mem. coun. bus. law sect. 1992-94), Dallas Bar Assn., Tex. Assn. Bank Counsel, City Club. Office: Winstead Sechrest & Minick PC Renaissance Tower 1201 Elm St Ste 5400 Dallas TX 75270-2199

RICE, DAVID PRESTON, minister, educator; b. Parkersburg, W.Va., July 7, 1953; s. Ernest Granville Rice and Mary Alice Lee; m. Dorothy Lee Tehas, Sept. 18, 1976; 1 child, Nathan Granville. BS, U. Tex., San Antonio, 1978; M of Divinity, Christian Bible Coll. and Sem., 1993, D of Divinity, 1996. Cert. trainer Evangelist Explosion, Tex. Pastor, ch. planter Benjamin Ave. Bapt. Ch., Grand Rapids, Mich., 1986-88; assoc. pastor Columbia Ave. Bapt. Ch., Pontiac, 1988-90, Bell Shoals Bapt. Ch., Brandon, Fla., 1990-93; sr. pastor Belmont Bapt. Ch., Tampa, 1993-97; assoc. dir. Sunday sch. dept. Fla. Bapt. Conv., Jacksonville, 1997-99; sr. pastor Ancient City Bapt. Ch., Augustine, Fla., 1999—. Nat. ch. growth cons. So. Bapt. Conv., Nashville, 1991—. Author: (implementation strategy) FAITH Sunday School Evangelism Strategy, 1998. Sgt. 1st class U.S. Army, 1972-85, Vietnam. Mem. So. Bapt. Religious Educators Assn., Fla. Bapt. Religious Educators. Southern Baptist Convention. Avocations: golf, horticulture, collecting miniature lighthouses. Office: Ancient City Bapt Ch 27 Sevilla St Saint Augustine FL 32084-3550

RICE, DONALD BLESSING R. business executive, former secretary of air force; b. Frederick, Md., June 4, 1939; s. Donald Blessing and Mary Celia (Santangelo) R.; m. Susan Fitzgerald, Aug. 25, 1962; children: Donald Blessing III, Joseph John, Matthew Fitzgerald. BSChemE, U. Notre Dame, 1961, DEng (hon.), 1975; MS in Indsl. Adminstrn., Purdue U., 1962, PhD in Mgmt. and Econs., 1965, D. Mgmt. (hon.), 1985; LLD (hon.), Pepperdine U., 1989; LHD (hon.), West Coast U., 1993; D in Pub. Policy (hon.), Rand Grad. Sch., 1995. Dir. cost analysis Office Sec. Def., Washington, 1967-69, dep. asst. sec. def. resource analysis, 1969-70; asst. dir. Office Mgmt. and Budget, Exec. Office Pres., 1970-72; pres., CEO The Rand Corp., Calif., 1972-89; sec. USAF, 1989-93; pres., COO Teledyne, Inc., L.A., 1993-96; chmn., pres., CEO Agensys, Inc., Santa Monica, Calif., 1996—. Bd. dirs. Vulcan Materials Co., Wells Fargo & Co., Pilkington Aerospace, Unocal Corp., Amgen Inc.; chmn., bd. dirs. Scios Inc.; mem. nat. adv. com. oceans and atmosphere Dept. Commerce, 1972-75; mem. Nat. Sci. Bd., 1974-86; adv. council Coll. Engring., U. Notre Dame, 1974-88; chmn. Nat. Commn. Supplies and Shortages, 1975-77; mem. adv. panel Office Tech. Assessment, 1976-79; mem. Def. Sci. Bd., 1977-83, sr. cons., 1984-88; dir. for sec. def. and Pres. Def. Resource Mgmt. Study, 1977-79; mem. U.S. Commn. Nat. Security/21st Century, 1998-2001; trustee RAND, 2001—, chmn. grad. sch. bd. govs., 1999—. Author articles. Served to capt. AUS, 1965-67. Recipient Sec. Def. Meritorious Civilian Service medal, 1970, Def. Exceptional Civilian Svc. medal, 1993, Forrestal award, 1992; Ford Found. fellow, 1962-65 Fellow AAAS, Nat. Acad. of Pub. Adminstrn.; mem. Inst. Mgmt. Scis. (past pres.), Tau Beta Pi. Office: Agensys Inc 1545 17th St Santa Monica CA 90404 E-mail: drice@agensys.com.

RICE, DONALD SANDS, lawyer, entrepreneur; b. Bronxville, N.Y., Mar. 25, 1940; s. Anton Henry and Lydia Phipps (Sands) R.; m. Edgenie Higgins, Aug. 27, 1966; children: Alice Higgins, Edgenie Reynolds. AB magna cum laude, Harvard U., 1961, LLB/JD cum laude, 1964; LLM in Taxation, NYU, 1965. Bar: N.Y. 1964, U.S. Ct. Claims 1965, U.S. Supreme Ct. 1981. Law clk. to judge U.S. Ct. Claims, 1965-67; assoc. Barrett, Smith, Schapiro & Simon, N.Y.C., 1967-71; ptnr. Barrett, Smith, Schapiro, Simon & Armstrong, 1971-86; vice chmn. bd. The Bowery Savs. Bank, 1986-88; ptnr. Chadbourne & Parke, 1988-96; mng. dir. and prin. Ravitch Rice & Co. LLC, 1996—; ptnr. Rice & Ravitch LLP, 1996—. Bd. dirs. B-Line, LLC, CertCo, Inc.; lectr. Nat. Assn. Real Estate Investment Trusts, Bank Adminstrs. Inst., Bank Tax Inst., 1971-86; chmn., bd. dirs. Corp. of Yaddo, 1986—; co-chmn. Soviet-Am. Banking Law Working Group, 1991-96; v.p., treas., bd. dirs. Soviet Bus. and Comml. Law Edn. Found., 1991-96; vol. lectr. Fin. Svcs. Vol. Corps Mongolian Bank Tng. Program, 1993, Georgetown Internat. Law Inst., NYU Sch. Continuing Edn., Russian Trade Fair-U.S. Dept. Commerce, 1994; mem. nat. com. Am. fgn. policy study group dels. to China, Taiwan, 1996, 2000, 01, Roundtable on U.S.-China Policy and Cross-Strait Rels., 1996—; mem. real estate adv. bd. to N.Y. State Comptr., 1987-93; bd. advisors Am.-Russian Investment Forum, 1999—. Trustee Nat. Com. Am. Fgn. Policy, 1994—, sr. v.p., 1996—; trustee Marimed Found., 1984—97, Chapin Sch., 1980—91, v.p., 1989—91; trustee The Hackley Sch., 1974—81, St. Philip's Episcopal Ch., Mattapoisett, Mass., 1987—; pres. Quadequina Co./Mattapoisett Casino, 2001—; bd. dirs. African Med. Rsch. Found., 1978—. Mem. ABA, Coun. Fgn. Rels., N.Y. State Bar Assn., Assn. of the Bar of the City of N.Y., Century Assn., Harvard Club N.Y., N.Y. Yacht Club. Home: 1120 Fifth Ave New York NY 10128-0144 Office: Ravitch Rice & Co LLC 610 5th Ave Rm 420 New York NY 10020-2403 E-mail: ravricellc@aol.com.

RICE, DONNA S. educational administrator; b. Tulsa; d. Grady and Mildred Steed; m. Donald Rice, Aug. 3, 1956 (dec. Jan. 1990); children: Michael, Donna E., Nadine. BA in Linguistics, SUNY, Buffalo, 1971, MA in Linguistics, 1973, PhD in Comms., 1985. LPN, N.Y. Asst. dir. English Lang. Inst. SUNY at Buffalo, 1980-85, assoc. dir. edn. opportunity ctr., 1985-86, staff assoc. office of the pres., 1986-87, dir. ednl. opportunity ctr., 1987-90, assoc. vice provost spl. programs, 1990-91, assoc. v.p. spl. programs, 1991-93, assoc. v.p. student affairs, 1993—. Bd. dirs. N.Y.-Pa. region ARC, 1996—; dir.-in-residence English Lang. Inst. SUNY, Beijing, 1981, chair SUNY Com. Promotion of Tolerance and Diversity, Buffalo, 1993—. Contbr. articles to profl. jours. Bd. dirs. King Urban Ctr., 1998—; scholarship com. Humboldt Pkwy. Bapt. Ch., 1985—; mem. policy adv. bd. Bethel Head Start, 1994-98; bd. dirs. Neighborhood Info. Ctr., 1984-97, Leadership Buffalo, 1989—. Recipient Cmty. Svc. award Neighborhood Info. Ctr., 1997, Outstanding Cmty. Svc. award County of Erie, 1990, Leadership award Great Lakes Bapt. Assn., 1989. Mem. Ptnrs. of Am. (life), Am. Assn. Univ. Adminstrs. (bd. dirs. 1987—), Am. Assn. Higher Edn., Nat. Assn. Student Pers. Adminstrs., Delta Sigma Theta. Democrat. Baptist. Avocations: reading, choir, cooking. Home: 84 Guilford St Buffalo NY 14212-1134 Office: SUNY Student Affairs 545 Capen Hall Buffalo NY 14260-1600 E-mail: drice@buffalo.edu.

RICE, DOROTHY PECHMAN (MRS. JOHN DONALD RICE), medical economist; b. Bklyn., June 11, 1922; d. Gershon and Lena (Schiff) Pechman; m. John Donald Rice, Apr. 3, 1943; children: Kenneth D., Donald B., Thomas H. Student, Bklyn. Coll., 1938—39; BA, U. Wis., 1941; DSc (hon.) , Coll. Medicine and Dentistry N.J., 1979. With hosp., and med. facilities USPHS, Washington, 1960—61; med. econs. studies Social Security Adminstrn., 1962—63; health econs. br. Community Health Svc., USPHS, 1964—65; chief health ins. rsch. br. Social Security Adminstrn., 1966—72, dep. asst. commr. for rsch. and statistics, 1972—75; dir. Nat. Ctr. for Health Stats., Rockville, Md., 1976—82; prof. Inst. Health & Aging U. Calif., San Francisco, 1982—94, prof. emeritus, 1994—. Developer, mgr. nationwide health info. svcs.; expert on aging, health care costs, disability, and cost-of-illness. Contbr. articles to profl. jours. Recipient Social Security Adminstrn. citation, 1968, Disting. Svc. medal, HEW, 1974, Jack C. Massey Found. award, 1978, UCSF medal, 2002. Fellow: Am. Statis. Assn.; mem.: LWV, APHA (domestic award for excellence 1978, Sedgwick Meml. medal 1988), Assn. Health Svc. Rsch. (President's award 1988), Inst. Medicine. Home: 13895 Campus Dr Oakland CA 94605-3831 Office: U Calif Sch Nursing Calif San Francisco CA 94143-0646

RICE, DURWIN DAN, artist, art dealer; b. Slayton, Minn., Dec. 8, 1954; s. Durwin Russell Rice and Mabel Bernadine Baer. BA in English, U. Mo., 1979. Ptnr. Advt. Preston-Rice, Inc., Kansas City, Mo., 1980-85; fine art dealer N.Y.C., 1985—; owner Durwin Rice Designs, 1989—. Product designer N.Y. Pub. Libr., The Pierpont Morgan Libr., The Cooper-Hewitt Nat. Design Mus. Author: New Decoupage, 1998; appeared on Today Show, 1999, The Christopher Lowell Show, 1999, others; contbr. articles to profl. jours. Landmark restoration St. Paul's Meml. Ch. Rectory, S.I., 1995-99. Mem. Nat. Guild Decoupeurs (keynote spkr.). Avocations: garden design, historic restoration. Office: Durwin Rice Designs 1501 NW 18th St Blue Springs MO 64015-6414 E-mail: durwinrice@aol.com.

RICE, EARLE, JR. (EARLE WILMONT RICE JR.), writer; b. Lynn, Mass., Oct. 21, 1928; s. Earle Wilmont and Grace Elizabeth (Nottingham) Rice; m. Georgia Joy Black Wood, Nov. 1, 1958; children: Ellen Jean, Earle Wilmont, III. Student, Sch. Practical Art, Boston, 1947, San Jose (Calif.) City Coll., 1959, Foothill Coll., Los Altos, Calif., 1971. Product engr. ISS/Sperry Univac, Cupertino, Calif., 1973-74; sr. design specialist GTE/Sylvania, Mountain View, 1974; sr. design checker Westinghouse Corp., Sunnyvale, 1974; tech. writer Nuclear Svcs. Corp., Campbell, 1974; lead checker, tech. writer ESL, Inc., Sunnyvale, 1975; sr. E/M designer Finnigan Corp., 1975-76, Advanced Devices Labs., Inc., Santa Clara, Calif., 1976, Argosys., Inc., Palo Alto, 1976; equipment designer Raytheon Co., Goleta, 1976-78; sr. staff specialist Vitro Labs./Automation Ind., Oxnard, 1978-79; engring. drawing checker Gen. Dynamics, San Diego, 1979, 87-89; sr. E/M designer GE Co., Lompoc, Calif., 1980; sr. field engr. Martin Marietta Corp., Vandenberg AFB, 1980-84; engring. pub. specialist Lockheed Austin Divsn., Austin, Tex., 1984-85; design engr. Sundstrand Turbomach, San Diego, 1985-87; sr. design engr. ROHR, INC., Chula Vista, 1989-93. Author (fiction) Tiger, Lion, Hawk, 1977, The Animals, 1979, Fear on Ice, 1981, More Than Macho, 1981, Death Angel, 1981, The Gringo Dies at Dawn, 1993, (chpt.) The Secret of the Barking Dog Bayou, 1993 (Second Pl. award Fla. Freelance Writers Assn.), White Sun and Blue Sky, 1994 (Third Place award Fla. Freelance Writers Assn.), So Long, Slimeball!, 1994, (non-fiction) The Cuban Revolution, 1995, The Battle of Britain, 1996, The Battle of Midway, 1996, The Inchon Invasion, 1996, The Battle of Belleau Wood, 1996, The Attack on Pearl Harbor, 1996, The Tet Offensive, 1996, The Nuremberg Trials, 1996, The Salem Witch Trials, 1996, The O.J. Simpson Trial, 1996, The Final Solution, 1997, Nazi War criminals, 1997, The Battle of the Little Bighorn, 1997, Life Among the Great Plains Indians, 1997, Life During the Crusades, 1997, Life During the Middle Ages, 1998, Kamikazes, 1999, The Third Reich, 2000, The Bombing of Pearl Harbor, 2000, The Cold War, 2000, Strategic Battles in Europe, 2000,

Sir Francis Drake, 2002, Normandy, 2002, First Battle of the Marne, 2002, Gettysburg, 2002, The Tonkin Gulf Affair, 2002; adaptor: Cracula, 1995, All Quiet on the Western Front, 1995, The Grapes of Wrath, 1996; contbr. articles to mags. With USMC, 1948-57. Mem. U.S. Naval Inst., Soc. Children's Book Writers and Illustrators, League WW I Aviation Historians, Cross & Cockade Internat., Air Force Assn. Republican. Avocations: reading, spectator sports. Home and Office: 2648 Bonita Vista Dr PO Box 2131 Julian CA 92036-2131 E-mail: ericejr@julian-ca.com.

RICE, EDMUND BURKE, trade association executive; b. Cambridge, Mass., Feb. 19, 1949; s. Edmund Townsend and Catherine Burke Rice; m. Rosemarie Sweeney, Feb. 23, 1978; 1 child, Jonathan Field. BA, Colgate U., 1971. Congl. staff U.S. rep. Margaret Heckler, Washington, 1971-76; with Am. Hosp. Assn., 1976-83, v.p., 1983-87; v.p. Washington office New Eng. Health Cons., Inc., 1987; legis. dir. U.S. rep. Toby Roth, 1988-90; profl. staff House Internat. Rels. Com., 1990-97; pres. Coalition for Employment Through Exports, 1997—. Mem. citizens' bd. Providence Hosp., Washington, 1985-90. With N.G./Res., U.S. Army, 1970-76. Named Outstanding Young Man of Am., U.S. Jaycees, 1977. Office: Coalition for Employment through Exports # 810 1100 Connecticut Ave NW Ste 810 Washington DC 20036-4145 E-mail: edmundr@worldnet.att.net.

RICE, EDWARD EARL, former government official, author; b. Saginaw, Mich., Feb. 6, 1909; s. William Edward and Katherine Marie (Meyer) R.; m. Mary June Kellogg, Oct. 26, 1942. Student, U. Wis., 1926-28; BS, U. Ill., 1930, postgrad., 1934-35, U. Mex., 1931, Coll. Chinese Studies, also pvt. tutors, Beijing, 1935-37. Joined Fgn. Svc., Dept. State, 1935; lang. attache Beijing, 1935-37; vice consul Canton, China, 1938-40; consul Foochow, China, 1940-42; 2d sec. Am. Embassy, Chungking, China, 1942-45; asst. chief div. Chinese affairs Dept. State, 1946-48, asst. chief div. Philippine affairs, 1948-49; 1st sec., consul Am. Embassy, Manila, 1949-51; consul gen. Stuttgart, Fed. Republic Germany, 1952-56; fgn. svc. insp. Dept. State, 1956-58, dep. dir. pers., 1959, mem. plicy planning coun., 1959-61, dep. asst. sec. of state for Far Ea. affairs, 1962-63; consul gen., min. Hong Kong, 1964-67; diplomat in residence with rank of prof. U. Calif., Berkeley, 1968-69, rsch. assoc. Ctr. for Chinese Studies, 1969—. Vis. prof. Marquette U., 1973; advisor U.S. del. 3d, 4th and 5th sessions Econ. Commn. for Asia Far East, 1948-49. Author: Mao's Way, 1972, Wars of the Third Kind, 1988. Recipient Gold medal for non-fiction Commonwealth Club, 1973. Mem. Beta Gamma Sigma. Home: 1819 Lagoon View Dr Belvedere Tiburon CA 94920-1807

RICE, EMILY JOY, retired secondary school and adult educator; b. Terrell, Tex., Aug. 30, 1928; d. Martin Alexander Joy Jr. and Susan Martha (Helen) Ruth Joy; m. LeRoy Noonon Rice Jr., May 30, 1951; children: Edna Anne Rice-Padhi, Margaret Elizabeth (dec.). BS, Tex. Woman's U.; postgrad., U. Tex., Tex. A&I U. Tchr. adult Bible studies First United Meth. Ch., Harlingen and Austin, Tex., Bellaire United Meth. Ch., Houston; instr. Austin C.C., 1982-90; tchr. Austin Ind. Sch. Dist., 1982-92; writer, lectr. Vol. Meth. Hosp., Houston; mem. scholarship com. U. Tex. Mem. Current Study Club Houston (pres. 2000-2002), Tex. Woman's Univ. Nat. Alumnae Assn. (pres. 2001-2002), Delta Kappa Gamma. Home: 5220 Weslayan St # 201 Houston TX 77005-1095 E-mail: emilyjrice@aol.com.

RICE, FRANCES MAE, physician; b. Oakland, Calif., Apr. 19, 1931; d. George Henry and Clara Evelyn (Youngman) Rice. AB cum laude, U. Calif., Berkeley, 1953, MPH in Epidemiology, 1964; MD, U. Calif., San Francisco, 1957. Intern U. Calif. Hosp., San Francisco, 1957-58; pediatric resident U. Calif., 1959-61; pediatric and family physician HMO, Hanford, Calif., 1974-75; clin. pediatrician Kern County Health Dept., Bakersfield, 1975-76; physician Kern Med. Group, Inc., 1976-83; pvt. practice Shafter, Calif., 1983-89; physician Kern County Health Dept., Bakersfield, 1989, Mercy Medicenter, Bakersfield, 1990-91, K.C.E.O.C. Family Health Clinic, Bakersfield, 1993-98, Berkeley Women's Health Ctr., 1999—. USPHS fellow, 1963-64. Fellow Royal Soc. Medicine; mem. N.Y. Acad. Sci. Avocation: music. Home: 3528 Wilson Ave Oakland CA 94602-2927

RICE, FUHRMAN D. (RUNT RICE), retired paper company executive; b. June 12, 1927; s. Robert Fulton and Carie Ann (Whitaker) R.; m. Marie Mayben, 1967; 1 child, Kathleen Ann. Forest ranger Ala. Forestry Commn., Marshall County, 1951-74; procurement agent Paperboard Divsn. Mead Corp., Stevenson, Ala., 1974-91. Pres. Grant Conservation Club, 1964-73; chmn. Marshall County Rep. Exec. Com., Ala., 1995-99; bd. dirs. Ala. Wildlife Fedn., 1961-77 (Conservationist of Yr. 1970); mem. Boy Scouts of Am. (Dist. Scouters award 1964, Silver Beaver award 1974); v.p. soc. Ala. Retirees, Guntersville, 1999, Alder Springs Cmty. Assn., Marshall County, 1999. Home: 5050 Hustleville Rd Albertville AL 35951-4747 E-mail: runt@hiwaay.net.

RICE, GARY D. software engineer, consultant; b. Bentonville, Ark., July 16, 1951; s. Dale H. and Dorothy A. Rice; m. Denise A. Smith, Dec. 22, 1974; children: Corey, Casey, Stephen. BSIE, U. Ark., Fayetteville, 1973, MSIE, 1975. Indsl. engr. Standard Register Co., Fayetteville, 1976-77; head data processing Winamac divsn. NI Industries, 1979-84; systems analyst U. Ark., 1984-85; sr. sys. analyst Masco Industries ATD, Novi, Mich., 1985-88; mgr. applications devel. Douglas & Lomason Co., Farmington Hills, 1989-98, Neumenon, Inc., Livonia, 1998-2000; dir. devel. Freedom Techs., Brighton, 2000—. Cons. Gary Rice Consulting, Brighton, Mich., 2001—. Republican. Evangelical Presbyterian. Home: 4142 Nancy Dr Brighton MI 48114 E-mail: garydrice@hotmail.com.

RICE, GARY RUSSELL, special education educator; b. Franklin, Pa., Oct. 11, 1951; s. Robert Russell and Della Elizabeth Rice. Grad. cum laude, Cleve. State U., 1973. Cert. polit. sci. tchr., learning disabilities, behavioral disorders, Ohio. Substitute tchr. Lakewood, Rocky River, Westlake (Ohio) Schs., 1973-77; instr. West Side Inst. Tech., Cleve., 1977-78; spl. edn. tchr. Parma (Ohio) City Sch. Dist., 1978—. Learning disabilities tutor, Lakewood, 1974-75; guitar conservator Rock and Roll Hall of Fame and Mus., Cleve. Asst. scoutmaster, leader Boy Scouts Am., Cleve.; former Sunday sch. tchr. local chs., Lakewood; spkr. to various groups on Exceptional Children, the Holocaust and Native Americans; charter mem. U.S. Holocaust Meml. Mus. Recipient Outstanding Spl. Educator award Parma PTA Spl. Edn. com., 1985, Thanks to Tchrs. award Sta. TV-8 WJW, Cleve., 1994, dist. award of merit Boy Scouts Am., 1997. Mem. Parma Edn. Assn., Cleve. Fedn. Musicians, DeMolay (active Legion of Honor 1996), Masons, Shriners. Avocations: music, photography.

RICE, GEORGE LAWRENCE, III (LARRY RICE), lawyer; b. Jackson, Tenn., Sept. 24, 1951; s. George Lawrence Jr. and Judith W. (Pierce) R.; m. Joy Gaia, Sept. 14, 1974; children: George Lawrence IV (Nick), Amy Colleen. Student, Oxford U., 1972-73; BA with honors, Rhodes Coll., 1974; JD, U. Memphis, 1976, Nat. Coll. Advocacy, ATLA, 1978. Bar: Tenn. 1977, U.S. Supreme Ct. 1980; cert. family law trial advocate Nat. Bd. Trial Advocacy, family law specialist, Tenn. Assoc. Rice, Rice, Smith, Admundsen & Jewell LLPC, 1976-81, ptnr., 1981—, acting sr. ptnr., 1995. Cert. family law trial advocate NBTA and Family Law Specialist by Tenn. Author: Divorce Practice in Tenn., 1987, 2d edit., 1987, Family Law, 1988, Winning for Your Client, 1988, Divorce Practice A to Z, 1989, Divorce Lawyer's Handbook, 1989, (video) Divorce: What You Need to Know When it Happens to You, 1990, Rice's Divorce Practice Manual, 1990, Child Custody in Tennessee, 1992, Divorce Trial, Tribulations, Tactics and Triumphs, 1993, The Complete Guide to Divorce Practice, 1993, 2d edit., 1998, Divorce Practice Made Easier, 1993, Divorce Practice, 1994, Visual Persuasion, AIDS 1996 Clients, Prenuptial Agreements, 1996, The Ethical Effective Lawyer: Divorce and Personal Injury, 1996, In Pursuit of the Perfect Personal Injury Practice, 1997, Wiley Family Law Update, Discovery Supplement, 1997, Tennessee Evidence Workshop Handbook, 1997, Hot Topics in Family Law, 1997, Child Custody and Visitation in Tennessee, 1998, Larry Rice on Divorce: How to Run an Efficient and Effective Divorce Practice and Improve Client Satisfaction, 1998, Client Communications, 1998, Post Nuptial Agreement A Proposal for Consideration, 1998, Larry Rice of Divorce, 1998; mem. bd. editors Matrimonial Strategist, 1995-99, Hunt, Hide Shoot--a Guide to Paintball, 1996; contbr. articles to profl. jours. Founding chmn. Student Legal Assistance Program, 1975; active Supreme Ct. Child Support Guidelines Commn., 1989, Family Law Revision Commn., 1990—91, 1998—; mem. Timberwolves Paintball Team, 1988—2000; exec. com. Rhodes Coll. Red and Black Soc., 1999—, chmn., 2001—; treas. Rocky Mountain Elk Found., Memphis, 2001. Named one of Best Lawyers in Am., 1993, 94; recipient Excellence in Edn. award PESI, 1997; Outstanding intern supr. Rhodes Coll., Mentor award, 1997-98, award Amicus Curi Family Laws Sect. Wilson-Wilson, 1997-98. Mem. ABA (conv. lectr. 1993, 94, 98, 99, 01), ATLA, Tenn. Bar Assn. (chmn., co-founder family law sect. 1987-88), Memphis Bar Assn. (founding chmn. family law sect.), Tenn. Trial Lawyers Assn. Office: Rice Rice Smith et al 275 Jefferson Memphis TN 38103-2251 E-mail: home@ricelaw.com, lrice@ricelaw.com.

RICE, J. ANDREW, management consultant, tree farmer; b. Cleveland, Tex., July 24, 1953; s. Jakie Andrew and Neva (Richardson) R.; m. Susan Elaine Black, July 29, 1977; children: Faith Ann, Joy Elizabeth, Jakie Weldon, Luke Andrew. BA in Psychology cum laude, Baylor U., 1975; MA in Pub. Mgmt., U. Houston, 1979. Tchr. Tarkington Ind. Sch. Dist., Cleveland, Tex., 1975-76, La Marque (Tex.) Ind. Sch. Dist., 1976-77; jobs coord. Galveston (Tex.) County, 1977-78; adminstrv. asst. City of La Marque, 1978-80; cons. Community Mgmt. Svcs., Houston, 1980-82; owner, cons. Pub. Mgmt., Cleveland, 1982-92; pres. Pub. Mgmt., Inc., Cleve., 1992—. Min. of music Rural Shade Bapt. Ch.; pres. Tarkington Comty. Devel. Assn.; pres. Rice Richardson Found.; mem. Liberty County Hist. Soc. Mem. World Future Soc., Tex. Forestry Assn., Cleveland C. of C. (bd. dirs.), Omicron Delta Kappa. Office: Pub Mgmt PO Box 1827 Cleveland TX 77328-1827

RICE, JAMES PHILIP, surgeon; b. Richland, Wash., Dec. 2, 1956; s. James Edward and Elizabeth Agnus (O'Leary) R. BS, Wash. State U., 1979; MD, St. Louis U., 1983. Diplomate Am. Bd. Surgery. Commd. officer USN, 1983, advanced through grades to capt., 2000; intern in gen. surgery Nat. Naval Med. Ctr., Bethesda, Md., 1983-84, resident gen. surgery, 1985-89; med. dept. head USS Nassau, 1984-85; staff surg. privileges Naval Hosp., Jacksonville, 1989-90; ship's surgeon USS Saratoga, 1989-90; staff surgeon Naval Hosp. Bremerton, 1991-93, head dept. surgery, 1992-93; staff surgeon Naval Hosp. Jacksonville, 1993—2001, asst. dept. head, 1995-97, head dept. surgery, 1997-99; ships surgeon USS John F. Kennedy, 1999-2000; head, staff surgeon Naval Hosp. Bremerton, 2001—. Adj. asst. prof. Uniformed Svcs. U. of the Health Scis., 1995—; Surface Warfare Med. Dept. officer, 1997—; chmn. breast cancer working group Naval Hosp., 1998-2000. Fellow ACS; mem. Assn. Mil. Surgeons U.S., Bethesda Surg. Soc., St. Louis U. Sch. Medicine Alumni Assn., Phi Chi. Avocations: tennis, guitar, cycling. Office: US Naval Hosp Dept Surgery HP01 Boone Rd Bremerton WA 98312 E-mail: ricej@pnw.med.navy.mil., jprice06@earthlink.net.

RICE, JERRY LEE, professional football player; b. Starkville, Miss., Oct. 13, 1962; m. Jackie Rice; children, Jaqui, Jerry Jr. Student, Miss. State Valley U. Football player San Francisco 49ers, 1985—2000; Sports Illustrated Player of the Year, 1986, 90; NFL MVP, 1987; AP/NFL/Sports Illustrated Offensive Player of the Year, 1993; football player Oakland Raiders, 2001—. MVP in Blue-Gray Game. Named MVP, Super Bowl XXIII, 1989, Sporting News NFL Player of Yr., 1987, 90; named to Sporting News Coll. All-Am. team, 1984, Sporting News All-Pro team, 1986-92, Pro Bowl team, 1986-96, 95, Pro Bowl MVP, 1995. Achievements include being a holder of NFL career records for most touchdown receptions (131), most touchdowns (139); most consecutive games with one or more touchdowns (13), 1987; NFL single-season record for most touchdown receptions (22), 1987; shares NFL single-game record for most touchdown receptions (5), 1990. Office: Oakland Raiders 1220 Harbor Bay Pkwy Alameda CA 94502*

RICE, JERRY MERCER, biochemist; b. Washington, Oct. 3, 1940; s. John Earle Rice and Leona (Mercer) Greiner; m. Mary Jane Janocha, Jan. 10, 1978; children: Stacey Lynn, Stephen Mark. BA, Wesleyan U., 1962; PhD, Harvard U., 1966. Commd. officer USPHS, 1966, ret., 1996; rsch. scientist Nat Cancer Inst., Bethesda, Md., 1966-81, chief Lab. of Comparative Carcinogenesis Frederick, 1981-94, 96, assoc. dir. Frederick Cancer Rsch. and Devel. Ctr., 1994-95, acting dir. divsn. cancer etiology, 1994-95, ret., 1996; sr. scientist WHO, 1996—; chief unit of carcinogen identification and evaln. Internat. Agy. for Rsch. on Cancer, Lyons, France, 1996—. Editor: Perinatal Carcinogenesis, 1979; co-editor: Organ and Species Specificity in Chemical Carcinogenesis, 1983, Perinatal and Multigeneration Carcinogenesis, 1989; contbr. rsch. articles and revs. in mechanisms of chem. carcinogenesis to profl. jours.; dir. IARC monographs on the evaluation of carcinogenic risks to humans. Mem. Am. Soc. Microbiology, Soc. Toxicology, European Assn. Cancer Rsch., Am. Assn. Cancer Rsch., Internat. Soc. Differentiation, Phi Beta Kappa, Sigma Xi. Avocation: viticulture. Home: 3213 Coquelin Ter Bethesda MD 20815-4840 Office: Internat Agy Rsch Cancer 150 Cours Albert Thomas 69372 Lyon Cedex 08 France E-mail: rice@iarc.fr.

RICE, JIM, state supreme court justice; b. Ramore Air Force Base, Ont., Canada, Nov. 15, 1957; (parents Am. citizens); BA in Polit. Sci., Mont. State U., 1979; JD U. Mont., 1982. Pub. defender Lewis and Clark County; ptnr. Jackson & Rice, Helena, Mont., 1985—2001; assoc. justice Mont. Supreme Ct., 2001—. Mem. Mont. Ho. Reps., 1989—95, ho. majority whip, 1993. Office: Justice Bldg Rm 323 PO Box 203003 Helena MT 59620-3003*

RICE, JOHN THOMAS, architecture educator; b. New London, Conn., Feb. 4, 1931; s. Clarence Benjamin and Emily (Gudal) R. BS in Engring., U. Conn., 1952; MSME, Newark Coll. Engring., 1954; D.Sc. in Engring., Columbia U., 1962. Registered profl. engr., N.Y. Test equipment designer propeller div. Curitss-Wright Corp., Caldwell, N.J., 1952-54; stress analyst Wright Aeronautical div. Curtiss-Wright Corp., Woodridge, 1954-59; chief structural mechanics Gen. Dynamics/Electric Boat, Groton, Conn., 1962-64; asst. prof. mech. engring. Pratt Inst., Bklyn., 1964-66, assoc. prof., 1966-74, prof., 1974—, chmn. dept. mech. engring., 1981-90. Mem. ASME (chmn. mech. engring. dept. heads com. region II 1987-89, chmn. profl. devel. region II 1989-93, mem. exec. com. met. sect. 1990—, vice chmn. 1991-92, chmn. 1992-93, sec. region II 1993-96, treas. met. sect. 1999—), Pi Tau Sigma, Tau Beta Pi. Office: Pratt Inst Dept of Architecture 200 Willoughby Ave Brooklyn NY 11205-3899

RICE, JON RICHARD, managed care administrator, physician; b. Grand Forks, N.D., July 10, 1946; s. Harry Frazer and Marian (Lund) R.; m. Roberta Jane Lindbergh, June 7, 1969; children: Kristen, Jennifer. BA, U. N.D., 1969, BS, 1970; MD, U. Tex., San Antonio, 1972; MS in Health Adminstrn., U. Colo., 1991. Intern U.S. Naval Hosp., San Diego, 1972-73; resident U. N.D. Sch. Medicine, Minot, 1975-77; physician Valley Med., Grand Forks, 1977-93; state health officer N.D. Dept. Health, Bismarck, 1993-97; dir. managed care Blue Cross Blue Shield of N.D., Fargo, 1997—. Contbg. author: Pilots, Personality and Performance. Lt. USN, 1972-75. Recipient Outstanding Vol. award Dakota Heart Assn., 1989, YMCA, 1992, Outstanding Health Care Provider Grand Forks C. of C., 1992, Award of Excellence N.D. Hosp. Assn., 1995. Mem. AMA, Am. Acad. Family Physicians, Am. Coll. Physician Execs., Alpha Omega Alpha. bus. Office: Blue Cross Blue Shield ND 4510 13th Ave S Fargo ND 58121-0002 E-mail: jon_rice_1999@yahoo.com., jon.rice@noridian.com.

RICE, JOSEPH ALBERT, banker; b. Cranford, N.J., Oct. 11, 1924; s. Louis A. and Elizabeth J. (Michael) R.; m. Katharine Wolfe, Sept. 11, 1948; children: Walter, Carol, Philip, Alan. B in Aero. Engring., Rensselaer Poly. Inst., 1948; M in Indsl. Engring., NYU, 1952, MA, 1968. With Grumman Aircraft Engring. Corp., 1948-53; with IBM, N.Y.C., 1953-65, mgr. ops., real estate, constrn. divsns., 1963-65; dep. group exec. N.Am. comml. telecomm. group, pres. telecomm. divsn. ITT, 1965-67; sr. v.p. Irving Trust Co., 1967-69, exec. v.p., 1969-72, sr. exec. v.p., 1972-73, vice chmn., 1973-74, pres., 1974-83, chmn., 1984-88. Exec. v.p. Irving Bank Corp., 1971-74, vice chmn., 1974-75, pres., 1975-83, chmn. bd., CEO, 1984-88. Chmn., trustee John Simon Guggenheim Meml. Found.; trustee Blanton-Peale Inst., vice chmn., trustee Hist. Hudson Valley. Mem. Coun. Fgn. Rels., N.Y. Acad. Scis., Univ. Club, Links, Sky Club.

RICE, JOSEPH LEE, III, lawyer; b. Bklyn., Feb. 24, 1932; s. Joseph Lee Jr. and Frances (Plunkett) R.; m. Franci Blassberg, Jan. 4, 1992; children: Kimberley, Daniel, Lee Ann. BA, Williams Coll., Williamstown, Mass., 1954; LLB, Harvard U., 1960. Assoc. Sullivan & Cromwell, N.Y.C., 1960-66; v.p. Laird Inc., 1966-68, McDonnell & Co., N.Y.C., 1968-69; founding ptnr. Gibbons, Green & Rice, 1969-78; founder, chmn. Clayton, Dubilier & Rice, Inc., 1978—. Trustee, Williams Coll., 1988—. Lt. USMC, 1954-57. Mem. Maidstone Club, The Links Club, River Club. Office: Clayton Dubilier & Rice Inc 375 Park Ave New York NY 10152-0002 E-mail: jrice@cdr-inc.com.

RICE, JOY KATHARINE, psychologist, educational policy studies and women's studies educator; b. Oak Park, Ill., Mar. 26, 1939; d. Joseph Theodore and Margaret Sophia (Bednarik) Straka; m. David Gordon Rice, Sept. 1, 1962; children: Scott Alan, Andrew David. B.F.A. with high honors, U. Ill., Urbana, 1960; MS, U. Wis., Madison, 1962, MS, 1964, PhD, 1967. Lic. clin. psychologist. USPHS predoctoral fellow dept. psychiatry Med. Sch. U. Wis., Madison, 1964-65, asst. dir. Counseling Ctr., 1966-74, dir. Office Continuing Edn. Svcs., 1972-78, prof. ednl. policy studies and women's studies, 1974-95, clin. prof. psychiatry, 1995—; pvt. practice psychology Psychiat. Svcs., S.C., 1967—. Mem. State Wis. Ednl. Approval Bd., Madison, 1972-73; mem. Adult Edn. Commn., U.S. Office Career Edn., Washington, 1978 Author: Living Through Divorce, A Developmental Approach to Divorce Therapy, 1985, 2d edit., 1989; edit. bd. Lifelong Learning, 1979-86; cons. editor Psychology of Women Quar., 1986-88, assoc. editor, 1989-94; cons. editor Handbook of Adult and Continuing Education, 1989, Encyclopedia of Women and Gender, 2001; contbr. articles to profl. jours. Knapp fellow U. Wis.-Madison, 1960-62, teaching fellow, 1962-63; recipient Disting. Achievement award Ednl. Press Assn. Am., 1992. Fellow APA (exec. bd. psychology of women divsn. 1994—, internat. psychology divsn. 1998—, chair internat. com. for women 2000-02), Disting. Leadership award 2000-02; mem. Nat. Assn. Women in Edn. (editl. bd. jour. 1984-88, cons. editor Initiatives 1988-91), Internat. Coun. Psychologists, Am. Assn. Continuing and Adult Edn. (meritorious svc. award 1978-80, 82), TEMPO Internat. (bd. dirs., sec. 2000-02), Big Bros. Big Sisters of Dane County (pres. 2002, bd. dirs. 2001), Wis. Psychol. Assn., Phi Delta Kappa. Avocations: interior design, collecting art, gardening, travel. Home: 4230 Waban Hl Madison WI 53711-3711 Office: 2727 Marshall Ct Madison WI 53705-2255 E-mail: jkrice@facstaff.wisc.edu.

RICE, KATHY STRICKLAND, city manager; b. Concord, Ga., Aug. 12, 1947; d. Roger Head and Patricia (Paynter) Strickland; m. C. Matthew Rice, Apr. 12, 1970; children: C. Michael, Adam P., Timothy Burt. BSA, U. Ga., 1970, MPA, 1983. Edn. coord. Action, Inc., Athens, Ga., 1974-78, program dir., 1978-80; pers. dir. Clarke County, 1980-82; planner, rschr. E. Cen. Fla., Orlando, Fla., 1982-83; city mgr. Lake Mary, 1983-86, Gulfport, 1986-89; dep. asst. city mgr. Clearwater, 1989-91, deputy city mgr., 1991-98; city mgr. Waco, Tex., 1998—. Adj. instr. U. South Fla. Grad. Sch. Pub. Adminstrn., 1990-98; bd. dirs., v.p. Neighberly Sr. Svcs., 1994-98. Pres. Citizens Against Spouse Abuse, St. Petersburg, Fla., 1989; bd. dirs. St. Petersburg Unitarian Universalist Ch., 1986-90; mem. adv. bd. Exec. Fellows Program, Tampa, 1989; mem. Govs.'s Adv. Com. on Unemployment, 1989—; bd. dirs. Palm Shores Retirement Ctrs., 1992-95; mem. adv. task force U. Fla. Pub. Adminstrn. Dept., 1991-98; mem. Leadership Pinellas, 1993, Leadership Am., 1995; treas. Clearwater/St. Petersburg Film Commn., 1993-98; bd. dirs. Jazz Holiday Found., 1988-96; mem. mgmt. com. Nat. Estuary Program; trustee Fla. Orch., 1993-96; mem. Waco Policy Bd., MPO, 2000-, Waco Health Dept. Bd., 2000-, Waco AB Loan Com., 1999-. Mem. Fla. City and County Mgrs., Texas City Mgrs. Assn., Assn., Internat. City Mgrs. Assn., Internat. Pers. Mgmt. Assn., Fla. Pub. Pers. Assn., Am. Soc. for Pub. Adminstrn. (pres. Gulf Coast chpt. 1992-93), Fla. Pub. Employee and Labor Rels. Assn., Inst. Govt. Steering Com., Leadership Am., Waco C. of C. (bd. dirs. 1998—). Democrat. Avocations: sailing, reading, creative basketry. Home: 2709 Cedar Point Dr Waco TX 76710-1605 Office: City of Waco PO Box 2570 Waco TX 76702-2570 E-mail: KathyR@Ci.waco.tx.us.

RICE, KENNER CRALLE, medicinal chemist; b. Rocky Mount, Va., May 14, 1940; s. Kenner Cralle Jr. and Annie Grace R. Rice. BS, Va. Mil. Inst., 1961; PhD, Ga. Inst. Tech., 1966. Sr. scientist Ciba-Geigy Corp., Summit, 1969—72; sr. staff fellow NIH, Bethesda, Md., 1972—76, rsch. chemist, 1977—86; chief sect. drug design and synthesis Nat. Inst. Diabetes, Digestive and Kidney Diseases, 1987—88; chief lab. medicinal chemistry NIDDK, NIH, 1989—. Adj. prof. pharmacology U. Md., Balt., 1985—; mem. Fed. Sr. Exec. Svc., Bethesda, 1989—98, Fed. Sr. Biomed. Rsch. Svc., 1998—; affiliate prof. Va. Commonwealth U., Richmond, 1995—; vis. prof. pharmacology U. Ill., Peoria, 1995—; adj. prof. medicinal chemistry Comprehensive Drug Rsch. Ctr. U. Miami, 1995—. Author (with others): Pharmacology Reviews, 1987; editor: NIDA Research Monograph 96, 1990; contbr. Capt. U.S. Army, 1966—68. Recipient Internat. Sato Meml. award, Japanese Pharm. Soc., 1983, Rsch. Achievement award, Am. Pharm. Assn., 1987, Hillebrand prize, Chem. Soc. Washington, 1986, Divsn. Medicinal Chemistry award, Am. Chem. Soc., 1996, Rsch. Achievement award, Am. Assn. Pharm. Scientists, 1998, Chem. Pioneer award, Am. Inst. Chemists, 2000, Nathan B. Eddy award, Coll. Problems of Drug Dependence, 2001. Fellow: Coll. on Problems of Drug Dependence (bd. dirs. 1988—92, 1997—2001); mem.: Am. Coll. Neuropsychopharmacology, Cosmos Club. Achievements include 36 patents in organic chemical synthesis and pharmacology of drugs of abuse; development of NIH opiate total synthesis as first practical synthesis of opium alkaloids as narcotics and narcotic antagonists. Office: NIH NIDDK Lab Medicinal Chemistry Bldg 8 Rm B1-23 Bethesda MD 20892

RICE, KENNETH LLOYD, environmental services executive, educator; b. St. Paul, June 17, 1937; m. Elizabeth Lyman VanKat, May 11, 1963 (dec. 1992); children: Anne Louise, Ken neth L. Jr., Elizabeth Ellen, Stephen James. BBA, U. Wis., 1959; postgrad., N.Y. Inst. Finance, 1960-64; completed 71st Advanced Mgmt. Program, Harvard U., 1975. Trainee, asst. br. mgr. JW Sparks & Co., St. Paul, 1959-64, mgr. corp. fin., 1964-70; mgr. corp. finance The Milw. Co., 1969-70; dir. finance Cedar Riverside Assocs. Inc., Mpls., 1970-71; prin. Kenneth L. Rice & Assocs., St. Paul, 1971-88; investment banking chmn., CEO Allegro Tech. Corp., 1988-92; prof. mgmt. and environ. econs. Budapest (Hungary) U. Econs. Scis., from 1992; chmn., edtl. bd. New Horizons Magazine, Hungary, from 1995. Minn. del. World Trade Ctrs. Assn., Budapest, Hungary, 1987; dir. Hungarian U.S. Fulbright, 1995-97. Founder Chimera Theatre, St. Paul, 1969; pres. Liberty Pla. Non-Profit Housing Project, St. Paul, 1975-77; judge Leadership Fellows Bush Found., St. Paul, 1985-90; co-chmn. Parents Fund, Macalester Coll., St. Paul, 1985-87; Hungary hon. rep. State of Minn. Trade Office, 1992-99. Bush Leadership fellow, 1974. Mem. Harvard Bus. Club Minn.(local bd. dirs. 1978-83), Harvard Club of Hungary (v.p. 1994—), Am. C. of C. in Hungary (dir. 1995-97, v.p. 1997), Masons, KT, Shriners. Home: Budapest, Hungary. Died May 24, 2001.

RICE, LESTER, electronics company executive; b. Detroit, Feb. 23, 1927; s. Carvel Lester and Irene R.; m. Barbara Helen Winston, June 27, 1957; children— Scott W., Jody I., Jeffrey C., Judy A., Timothy D. BSE.E., U. Mich., 1951. Gen. sales mgr. Westinghouse Semicondr. Div., Youngwood, Pa., 1951-68; pres. Airco Speer Elec. div. Airco Inc., Bradford, 1968-80; vice chmn., dir. KOA Speer Electronics, Inc., 1980-98; chmn. KOA Europe GMBH, 1998—. Bd. dirs. DeFond No. Am. Inc.; chmn. bd. Lester Rice, Inc., Bradford, 1980—. Adv. bd. U. Pitts. With USN, 1945-46. Mem. IEEE, Electronics Industries Assn. (bd. govs.), Am. Legion, Masons. Republican. Home: 2 Vista Avenue Ext Bradford PA 16701-2759 Office: PO Box 547 Bradford PA 16701-0547

RICE, LINDA ANGEL, music educator; b. New Philadelphia, Ohio, July 23, 1939; d. Leonard Leroy and Anna Mary (Fackler) Angel; m. James Kinsey Rice, June 9, 1963; children: Deborah Lynn, Diane Rice Sequra. BS in Music Edn., Muskingum Coll., 1961. Organist, choir dir., Ohio, 1957-63; organist Calif., 1963-70; tchr. music Jr. High and Elem. Schs., Ohio, 1962-63, Elem. Sch., Calif., 1963-67; organist Albuquerque, 1970—; pvt. practice pvt. practice, 1970—; founder Albuquerque Girl Choir, 1991—. Pres. N.Mex. Symphony Chorus, Albuquerque, 1991-92, bd. dirs., 1991-95, pres., 1988-89. Mem. Am. Choral Condrs. Guild, Am. Guild Organists (exec. bd. 1967), Sigma Alpha Iota. Avocations: knitting, travel, gardening. Home: 12428 Chelwood Trl NE Albuquerque NM 87112-4628 Office: Albuquerque Girl Choir PO Box 23037 Albuquerque NM 87192-1037

RICE, LOIS DICKSON, former computer company executive; b. Portland, Maine, Feb. 28, 1933; d. David A. and Mary D. Dickson; m. Alfred B. Fitt, Jan. 7, 1978 (dec. 1992); children: Susan, John Rice. AB magna cum laude, Radcliffe Coll., 1954; postgrad. (Woodrow Wilson fellow), Columbia U., 1954-55; LLD (hon.) , Brown U., 1981, Bowdoin Coll., 1984. Dir. counseling services Nat. Scholarship Service and Fund for Negro Students, N.Y.C., 1955-59; with The Coll. Bd., N.Y.C. and Washington, 1959-81, v.p. Washington, 1973-81; sr. v.p. govt. affairs, bd. dirs. Control Data Corp., 1981-91. Guest scholar The Brookings Inst., Washington, 1991—; bd. dirs. McGraw Hill, Inc., Internat. Multifoods, UNUM/Provident Corp.; overseer Tuck Sch. Mgmt.

Dartmouth Coll., 1990—94; mem. Pres.'s Fgn. Intelligence Adv. Bd., 1993—2001; trustee George Washington U., 1992—98, co-chair Mgmt. Leadership for Tomorrow, 1994—; trustee CNA Corp. Pub. Agenda Found., Harry Frank Guggenheim Found. Contbr. articles on edn. to profl. publs.; editor: Student Loans: Problems and Policy Alternatives, 1977. Mem. adv. bd. to dir. NSF, 1981—89, chair, 1986—89; mem. Gov.'s Commn. on Future of Postssecondary Edn. in N.Y. State, 1976—77, Carnegie Coun. on Higher Edn., 1975—80; trustee Radcliffe Coll., 1969—75, Stephens Coll., Mo., 1976—78, Beauvoir Sch., Washington, 1970—76, Children's TV Workshop, 1970—73; bd. dirs. Potomac Inst., 1977—92, German Marshall Fund, 1984—94, Joint Ctr. Polit. and Econ. Studies, 1991—94, Reading is Fundamental, 1991—. Recipient Disting. Service award HEW, 1977 Mem. Cosmos Club, Phi Beta Kappa. Episcopalian. Home: 2332 Massachusetts Ave NW Washington DC 20008 Office: The Brookings Instn 1775 Massachusetts Ave NW Washington DC 20036-2103

RICE, MARVIN ELWOOD, dentist; b. Mexico, Mo., Nov. 18, 1951; s. Marvin Everett and Una Belle (Hogan) R.; m. Elizabeth Kay Pearl, Mar. 3, 1977; children: Nicole Josephine, Megan Elizabeth, Laura Ellen, Marvin Elliott. BS in Biology, Cen. Mo. State U., 1975; med. asst., Coll. Med. and Dental Assts., 1976; MBA, Cen. Mo. State U., 1978; DDS, U. Mo., 1982. Gen. practice dentistry, Mexico, Mo., 1982—. Commr. TIF commn. City of Mex., 1995. Bd. dirs. Mo. Dental Found., 1992-99; mem. Cmty. Betterment Com., Mexico, 1984-92, PTA, Mexico, 1986; mem. state legis. com. Mo. Sch. Bd. Assn., 1989-97, regional exec. com., 1989, pres., 1995-97, bd. dirs., 1995-97; mem. fed. rels. network Nat. Sch. Bd. Assn., 1992-97; bd. dirs. Mexico Sch. Bd., 1987-2000, v.p. 1989-91, 97-98, treas., 1999-2000, v.p. Choir Boosters, 1999-2000, co-pres. 1999-2000; co-pres. McMillian PTA, Mexico Dixie Gray Band, 1997-98; chmn. Christian edn. com., Sunday Sch. tchr., deacon First Presbyn. Ch., elder, 1999—. Recipient Resolution for Dedicated Svc. for Pub. Edn., Mo. Senate, 1987-2000. Fellow Am. Coll. Dentists, Internat. Coll. Dentists; mem. ADA (Mo. del. 1988-92), Mo. Dental Assn. (comms. com. 1983-88, peer rev. com. 1987—, coun. dental health 1987, alt. to ho. of dels. 1983-86, del. 1987-88, chmn. peer rev. com. 1989-90, chmn. use tax com. 1990-91, sec. treas. 1992-99, bd. dirs. 1992-99, found. bd. 1994-99, Disting. Svc. award 1999), Columbia Dental Soc., Cen. Dental Soc. (v.p., pres.-elect 1987-88, pres. 1988-89), Mo. Dental Mgmt. Svcs. (bd. dirs. 1995—, treas.), Mo. Dental Ins. Svcs. (bd. dirs. 1993—, sec.-treas. 1999—), Mexico Area C. of C. (chmn. edn. com. 1995, 96, 97-98), Kiwanis (treas. Mex. 1983, v.p. 1984, pres. 1986—, Disting. Svc. award 1993), Sigma Tau Gamma (Outstanding Alumnus 1977, bd. dirs., treas. 1983-89). Republican. Avocations: gardening, art, canoeing, fishing, drummer Ultrasound Group. Home: 11340 Audrain Road 9907 Mexico MO 65265-7213 Office: 703 Medical Park Dr Mexico MO 65265-3727

RICE, MARY ESTHER, biologist; b. Washington, Aug. 3, 1926; d. Daniel Gibbons and Florence Catharine (Pyles) R. AB, Drew U., 1947; MA, Oberlin Coll., 1949; PhD, U. Wash., 1966. Instr. biology Drew U., Madison, N.J., 1949-50; rsch. assoc. Columbia U., N.Y.C., 1950-53; rsch. asst. NIH, Bethesda, Md., 1953-61; curator invertebrate zoology and dir. Smithsonian Marine Sta., Smithsonian Instn., Washington, 1966—. Mem. adv. panel on systematic biology NSF, Washington, 1977-78; mem. com. on marine invertebrates Nat. Acad. Sci., 1976-81; mem. overseers com. on biology Harvard U., Cambridge, Mass., 1982-88. Assoc. editor Jour. Morphology, Ann Arbor, Mich., 1985-91, Invertebrate Biology, 1995—; editor: (with M. Todorovic) Biology of Sipuncula and Echiura, 1975, 2nd vol., 1976, (with F.S. Chia) Settlement and Metamorphosis of Marine Invertebrate Larvae, 1978, (with F.W. Harrison) Microscopic Anatomy of Invertebrates, Vol. 12, 1993; contbr. articles to profl. jours. Recipient Drew U. Alumni Achievement award in sci., 1980. Fellow AAAS; mem. Am. Soc. Zoologists (pres. 1979), Am. Microscopical Soc. (pres. 1999), Phi Beta Kappa. Office: Smithsonian Marine Sta 701 Seaway Dr Fort Pierce FL 34949-3140

RICE, MATTHEW SHAWN, music educator, educator; b. Natrona Heights, Pa., May 23, 1974; s. Nancy Arlene Ray Munson and Woodrow Harry Rice, Jr., Emil Arthur Munson (Stepfather). BS in Music Edn., Indiana U. of Pa, 1997; M Music Edn., U. NC, Greensboro, 2002. Music tchr. Pub. Schs. of Robeson County, Lumberton, NC, 1997—98; elem. music tchr. Charlotte (NC)-Mecklenburg Schs, 1998—2000; band tchr. Hickory Pub. Schools, Hickory, 2000—02, Person County Pub. Schools, Roxboro, 2002—. High risk intervention technician Carolina Behavioral Svcs, Lumberton, 1997—98. Mem.: NEA, NC Music Educators Assn., NC Assn. of Educators, Music Educators Nat. Conf. Democrat. Methodist. Avocations: travel, roller coasters, music, outdoor activities. Home: 305 Woodlawn Ave Roxboro NC 27573 Office: Person County Public Schs Roxboro NC 27573 Personal E-mail: fugalmess@hotmail.com.

RICE, MELVA GENE, retired education educator; b. Celeste, Tex., July 24, 1918; d. Lilbum Miller and Mary Ruth (Green) Powell; m. Clarence Prather Rice, Feb. 6, 1944; 1 child, Anna Rice Cleary. BS, East Tex. U., 1955, MEd, 1958. Cert. elem. tchr. Elem. tchr. Tidwell Ind. Sch., Greenville, Tex., 1938-39; prin. Merrick Ind. Sch., 1942-44, Ctr. Pt. Ind. Sch., Greenville, 1944-45; office mgr. S.H. Kress and Co., 1945-55; tchr. Greenville Ind. Schs., 1955-84; adj. prof. Tex. A&M U., Commerce, 1985-95; ret., 1995. Dir., instr. summer enrichment Greenville Ind. Sch., 1961-63; supr. student tchrs. East Tex. State U., 1985-95. Soliciter silent auction Hunt County Mus., Greenville, 1991; bd. dirs. YMCA, Greenville, 1987-88; bell ringer, register Salvation Army, Greenville, 1980—; fund collector Am. Heart Assn., 1980-98; lifetime mem. Travis Elem. Sch. PTA, Greenville, 1983—. Fellow Ret. Tchrs. Assn., Tex. State Tchrs. Assn., Nat. Educators; mem. Delta Kappa Gamma (pres. 1964-66, auditor). Democrat. Baptist. Avocations: reading, working with children, travel, music, gardening. Home: 525 S Anaheim Hills Rd Anaheim CA 92807-4721 Office: Greenville Ind Sch Dist 3504 King St Greenville TX 75401-5103 also: Tex A&M U Ctr Edn Field Experiences Commerce TX 75429

RICE, MICHELLE ANGELINA, community health nurse; b. Akron, Ohio, Dec. 30, 1958; d. William Radford Rice and Carmelie Jordan; 1 child, Marcel Joseph. BSN, Mt. St. Mary's Coll., L.A., 1981; MPH, Columbia U., 2000. RN; cert. in neonatal intensive care. Charge nurse Daniel Freeman Hosp., L.A., 1981-82; mem. staff relief Nursing Svc. Internat., 1982-87; traveling nurse PICU, NICU Trav Corp., Nurse Am., Cross Country, Star Med, Ohio, Calif., N.Y., Fla., N.C., Washington, 1987-91; NICU staff nurse St. Luke's/Roosevelt Hosp., N.Y.C., 1991-96, cmty. health nurse, 1996—. Instr. U.S. Army Res., 1988-99. Avocations: skiing, tennis, roller blading, swimming, scuba. Home: 301 Cathedral Pkwy Apt 5B New York NY 10026-4060 E-mail: babypalm1@aol.com.

RICE, NANCY MARIE, nursing consultant; b. Murphy, N.C., Aug. 3, 1940; d. Berlon and Elizabeth Beryl (Ammons) Lovingood; m. Lewis T. Rice, Jan. 23, 1976; 1 child, Elizabeth Robertson Flowers. Diploma, Grady Meml. Hosp., Atlanta, 1961; BA, U. West Fla., Pensacola, 1973; MS, Fla. State U., Tallahassee, 1979. Cert. cmty. health nurse, nursing administr.; diplomate Am. Bd. Quality Assurance and Utilization Review Physicians. Staff nurse Riegel Community Hosp., Trion, Ga., 1961; pub. health nurse Escambia County Health Unit, Pensacola, 1962-63, Santa Rosa County Health Unit, Milton, Fla., 1963-73; pub. health nursing supr. I Leon County Health Unit, Tallahassee, 1973-77; pub. health nurse Broward County Health Unit, Ft. Lauderdale, 1977-78; nursing cons. social and econ. svcs. Tallahassee, 1978-79; HMO program specialist social and econ. scvs. program office DHRS Dist. X, Ft. Lauderdale, 1979; pub. health nurse, supr. II Sarasota (Fla.) County Health Unit, 1979-81; health program specialist health program office DHRS Dist X, Ft. Lauderdale, Fla., 1981-83; nursing cons. Dept. Labor, Div. Workers' Compensation, Tallahassee, 1983—. Recipient Cert. of Svc. State of Fla., 10 yr., 20 yr., 25 yrs., 30 yrs., 35 yrs.Cert. of Appreciation, 1976, Leon County-Tallahassee Community Action Program. Mem. Am. Nurses Assn., Fla. Nurses Assn., Eta Sigma Gamma. Home: PO Box 13731 Tallahassee FL 32317-3731

RICE, PATRICIA OPPENHEIM LEVIN, special education educator, consultant; b. Detroit, Apr. 5, 1932; d. Royal A. and Elsa (Freeman) Oppenheim; m. Charles L. Levin, Feb. 21, 1956 (div. Dec. 1981); children: Arthur David, Amy Ragen, Fredrick Stuart; m. Howard T. Rice, Dec. 16, 1990 (div. Apr. 1994). AB in History, U. Mich., 1954, PhD, 1981; MEd, Marygrove Coll., 1973. Cert. elem. tchr., Mich. Tchr. reading and learning disabled, cons., Detroit Pub. Schs., 1967-76; coord. spl. edn., Marygrove Coll., 1976-86; adj. prof. Oakland U., 1987-90, U. Miami, 1989-95; edn. curriculum cons. Lady Elizabeth Sch., Jávea (Alicante) Spain, 1988-91; v.p. Machpelah Cemetary Bd., Ferndale, Mich., 1978-87, co-pres., 1987—; adv. bd. Eton Acad., Birmingham, Mich., 1991-93; workshop presenter Dade City Schs., 1992-97; presenter in field. Mem. Mich. regional bd. ORT, 1965-68; mil. affairs and youth svcs. S.E. Mich. chpt. ARC Bd., 1973-79; v.p. exec. bd. Women's Aux. Children's Hosp. Mich., 1968-73; bd. dirs. women's com. United Cmty. Svcs., 1968-73; judge Dade County Schs. for Tchr. Grants, 1996-2000; bd. dirs. Detroit Grand Opera Assn., 1970-75; com. chair morning of music benefits Detroit Symphony Orch.; torch drive area chmn. United Found., 1967-70; benefactor Fla. Grand Opera, 1990-2000, guild exec. bd., 1992-, v.p., 1998-99, co-pres. 2000-02, chair, found. bd. dirs., 2000-01; guild exec. bd. Miami City Ballet, 1996-2000, Choreographers Cir., 1990-; chair Lincoln Rd. Walk, 1996, co-chair All Star Luncheon, 1996, Ball Com., 1992; active Diabetes Rsch. Inst. & Found. Love & Hope Com., Fla. Concert Assn. Cresendo Soc., 1993-97, Villa Maria Angel, 1996—, v.p. angel bd. 1998—, found. bd. dirs. 2000-. Mem. NAACP (life), Navy League, Greater Miami Social Register, Citizens Interested in the Arts (charter, grant chair, exec. bd. 1997—), Williams Island Club, Turnberry Isle Golf Club (signature), Miami Shores Country Club, Surf Club, Phi Delta Kappa, Pi Lambda Theta. E-mail: oceania32@msn.com.

RICE, PATRICIA JANE, journalist; b. St. Louis, Oct. 20, 1942; d. Canice T. and Jane Elizabeth Tobin) R. BA, Maryville Coll., 1964; postgrad., St. Louis U., 1965, 66. Copywriter Wohl Co., St. Louis, 1964-67; free-lance journalist Paris, 1967; copywriter D'Arcy Adut. Co., St. Louis, 1968; feature writer, columnist St. Louis Post, 1969-94, religion writer, 1994—. Moderator Rutgers U./Eagleton Ctr. Women in Politics Conf., 1980, 82, 84; lectr. in field. Author: City House, 1968, The Eclectic Shopper, 1973; co-author: In the Running: The New Political Woman, 1981. V.p. The St. Louis Forum, 1997—; bd. dirs. Leadership St. Louis, 1985-90. Recipient Quest award Mo. Press Women's, 1998; Knight Ctr. fellow, U. Md., College Park, 1996. Mem. Journalism Found. Met. St. Louis (pres. 1984-91), St. Louis Newspaper Guild (treas. 1977-87), Soc. Profl. Journalists. Avocations: gardening, skiing. Office: St Louis Post 900 N Tucker Blvd Saint Louis MO 63101-1069

RICE, PAUL JACKSON, lawyer, educator; b. East St. Louis, Ill., July 15, 1938; s. Ray Jackson and Mary Margaret (Campbell) R.; m. Carole Jeanne Valentine, June 6, 1959; children: Rebecca Jeanne Ross, Melissa Ann Hansen, Paul Jackson Jr. BA, U. Mo., 1960, JD, 1962; LLM, Northwestern U., 1970; student, Command and Gen. Staff Coll., 1974-75, Army War Coll., 1982-83. Bar: Mo. 1962, Ill. 1969, U.S. Dist. Ct. (no. dist.) Ill. 1970, U.S. Supreme Ct. 1972, U.S. Ct. Appeals (D.C. cir.) 1991, D.C. 1993, U.S. Dist. Ct. (D.C.) 2000. Commd. 1st lt. U.S. Army, 1962, advanced through grades to col., 1980; asst. judge advocate 4th Armored Div., Goeppingen, Fed. Republc Germany, 1966-69; dep. staff judge advocate 1st Cavalry Div., Republic Vietnam, 1970-71; inst., prof. The Judge Adv. Gen. Sch., Charlottesville, Va., 1971-74, commdt., dean, 1985-88; br. chief Gen. Law Br., Pentagon, 1975-78; chief adminstrv. law div. Office Judge Adv. Gen., Pentagon, Washington, 1978-79; staff judge adv. 1st Inf. Div., Ft. Riley, Kans., 1979-82, V Corps U.S. Army, Frankfurt, Fed. Republic Germany, 1983-85, USACAC, Ft. Leavenworth, Kans., 1989-90; faculty Indsl. Coll. Armed Forces, 1988-89; chief counsel Nat. Hwy. Traffic Safety Adminstrn., Washington, 1990-93; ptnr. Arent Fox Kintner Plotkin & Kahn, 1993—. Contbr. articles to profl. jours. Granted Legal Svc. award State of Hessen, Weisbaden, Fed. Republic Germany, 1985, Cert. Merit U. Mo. Alumni Assn., 1987. Mem. ABA, Mo. Bar Assn., Ctr. For Law and Nat. Security, U. Va. Sch. Law (1985-89), Lion Tamers, Phi Delta Phi. Methodist. Avocations: writing, reading, sports. Home: 7835 Vervain Ct Springfield VA 22152-3107 Office: Arent Fox Kintner Plotkin & Kahn 150 Connecticut Ave NW Washington DC 20036-5339 E-mail: ricepj@arentfox.com.

RICE, PETER J. pharmacologist, pharmacist; b. Bronx, Apr. 4, 1953; s. Joseph X. and Elaine M. R.; m. Sandra Etson; children: Tamar M., Huckle B., Daniel P., Emily M. BS in Pharmacy, Northeastern U., Boston, 1976; PhD in Pharmacy (Pharmacology), Ohio State U., 1983; PharmD, U. Ky., 2000. Cert. pharmacist, Mass., Ohio, W.Va., Tenn. Rsch. technician Lab. Neuropharmacology Mass. Gen. Hosp., Boston, 1975-77; sr. rsch. asst. dept. pharmacology Harvard Med. Sch., 1977-78; postdoctoral rsch. assoc. dept. pharmacology and toxicology W.Va. U., Morgantown, 1983-86; asst. prof. pharmacology East Tenn. State U., Johnson City, 1986-93, assoc. prof. pharmacology, 1993—. Pharmacy continuing edn. coord. East Tenn. State U., Johnson City, 1990—, clin. faculty obgyn., 1996—, clin. faculty nursing, 1997—; dir. biomolecular interaction analysis facility, 1998—. Recipient Advanced Predoctoral fellowship Pharm. Mfrs. Assn. Found., 1980-82, Postdoctoral Nat. Rsch. Svc. award NIH, 1983-85, Pharmacist of the yr. award 1st Dist. Pharm. Assn., 1992, 99. Mem. Am. Soc. Pharmacology and Experimental Therapeutics. Avocation: amateur radio. Home: 212 Peachtree St Johnson City TN 37604-4430 Office: East Tenn State U PO BOx 70577 Johnson City TN 37614-1708 Fax: 423-439-8773. E-mail: rice@etsu.edu.

RICE, REGINA KELLY, marketing executive; b. Yonkers, N.Y., July 11, 1955; d. Howard Adrian and Lucy Virginia (Butler) Kelly; m. Mark Christopher Rice, Sept. 11, 1981; children: Amanda Kelly, Jaime Brannen. BS in Community Nutrition, Cornell U., 1978. Account exec. J. Walter Thompson Co., N.Y.C., 1978-79; sr. account exec. Ketchum, MacLeod & Grove, 1979-80; supr. Burson Marstellar, Hong Kong, 1981-83; v.p., dep. dir. food and beverage unit, creative dir. N.Y. office Hill and Knowlton, N.Y.C., 1983-91; mktg. cons. Rice & Rohr, 1991-93; sr. v.p., dir. consumer mktg. practice Manning, Selvage & Lee, 1993-97, sr. v.p. global tng. dir., 1999—; chief inspiration officer, dir. corp. devel. Internat. Pub. Rels. Assn., 1999-2001. Writer Fast and Healthy Mag., 1991-2000. Mem. Pub. Rels. Soc. Am. Roman Catholic. Avocation: provence pottery. Home: 3635 Patrick Henry Pl Agoura Hills CA 91301-3636 Office: Pondel Wilkinson/MS&L 12100 Wilshire Blvd Ste 400 Los Angeles CA 90025 E-mail: Kelly.Rice@MSLPR.com.

RICE, RICHARD CAMPBELL, retired state official, retired army officer; b. Atchison, Kans., Dec. 11, 1933; s. Olive Campbell and Ruby Thelma (Rose) R.; m. Donna Marie Lincoln, Aug. 4, 1956; children: Robert Alden, Holly Elizabeth. BS in History, Kans. State Univ., 1955; MA in Social Studies, Eastern Mich. Univ., 1965; grad., U.S. Army Command and Gen. Staff Coll., 1968, U.S. Army War Coll., 1977; attended, FBI Nat. Exec. Inst., 1990; grad. prog. for sr. execs., state and local govt., Harvard Univ., 1985. Commd. 2nd lt. U.S. Army, 1955; advanced through grades to col., 1976; with Joints Chief of Staff, Washington, 1975-76; fac. U.S. Army War Coll., Carlisle Barracks, PA, 1977-79; chief of staff Hdqrs. 3rd ROTC Region, Ft. Riley, KS, 1982-83; ret., 1983; dir. Mo. State Emerg. Mgmt. Agy., Jefferson City, 1983-85, Mo. Dept. Pub. Safety, Jefferson City, 1985-93. Trustee Mo. State Employees Retirement System, 1990-93; bd. visitors Nat. Emerg. Mgmt. Inst., 1991-92. Grad. Leadership, Mo., 1991; mem. Coordinating Coun. Health Edn., Mo.'s Chldrn. and Adolescents, Mo. Jail and Prison Overcrowding Task Force, Gov.'s Domestic Violence Task Force, Gov.'s Commn. on Crime, Gov.'s Adv. Coun. on Driving While Intoxicated, Mo. Children's Svcs. Commn., Blur Ribbon Commn. on Svcs. to Youth, Campaign to Protect Our Children; mem. policy com. Mo. Youth Initiative; chmn. Gov.'s Cabinet Coun. for Justice Adminstrn., Mo. Statistical Analysis Ctr. adv. bd., adv. bd. Mo. Criminal Hist. Records; bd. dirs. Mo. Law Enforcement Meml. Found., Gt. Rivers coun. Boy Scouts Am. (James E. West fellow), 1993—; bd. dirs. Mid-Mo. chpt. Alzheimer's Assn., 2002--; peer rev. cons. Nat. Inst. of Justice; chmn. Alliance for Uniform Hazmat Transp. Procedures, 1991-93. Decorated Legion of Merit, Bronze Star (3), Meritorious Svc. Medal (4), Air medal (2), Joint Svc. Commendation medal, Army Commendation medal (2); Republic of Vietnam Cross of Gallantry with Silver Star; recipient Conspicuous Svc. medal State of Mo., Silver Beaver award Boy Scouts Am.; James E. West fellow. Mem. Nat. Eagle Scout Assn., ASsn. U.S. Army, Soc. First Div., Am. Legion, VFW, Disabled Am. Vets., AMVETS, Mil. Order of World Wars, Nat. Soc., Sons Am. revolution, The Retired Ofcrs. Assn., Nat. Criminal Justice Assn. (bd. dirs. 1987-93), Rotary (Paul Harris fell.), St. Andrews Soc., Theta Xi. Republican. Avocation: sailing. E-mal. E-mail: rrice54864@aol.com.

RICE, RICHARD LEE, retired architect; b. Raleigh, N.C., May 4, 1919; s. Robert Edward Lee and Grace Lucille (Betts) R.; m. Cora Belle Stegall, Apr. 12, 1946; children— Richard Lee, Westwood Carter, David Sinclair. BS in Archtl. Engring., N.C. State U., 1941; grad., U.S. Army Command and Gen. Staff Coll., 1961. Assoc. Cooper-Shumaker, Architects, Raleigh, 1946-47; prin. Richard L. Rice, Architects, 1947-48; assoc. Cooper, Haskins & Rice and predecessor firm, 1948-52, ptnr., 1953-54, Haskins & Rice, Architects, Raleigh, 1954-85; prin. Haskins, Rice, Savage & Pearce, Architects, 1985-91, pres., 1985-91. V.p. N.C. Design Found., 1973; pres. N.C. Archtl. Found., 1975; mem. Raleigh Arts Commn., 1978-82, Raleigh Hist. Properties Commn., 1990-92, Raleigh Hist. Dists. Commn., 1991-92. Archtl. works include renovations, Raleigh Meml. Auditorium, 1964, 78, 91 (SE Regional AIA award of merit 1964), Auditorium, 4 high schs. and 13 elem. schs., Raleigh Civic Ctr., stack addition Wilson Libr. U. N.C., Chapel Hill, 1977, Reidsville, N.C. Jr. High Sch.; assoc. architect Raleigh Radisson Hotel, 1980, One Hanover Sq. Office Bldg., 1985, Two Hannover Sq. Office Bldg., 1990, additions and renovations to Raleigh Meml. Auditorium, 1989, 3 indsl. plants, 7 bldgs., Wake Tech. C.C., 50 chs. Pre.s Wake County (N.C.) Hist. Soc., 1973-74; mem. N.C. Gov.'s Com. for Facilities for Physically Handicapped, 1970-73; arbitrator Am. Arbitration Assn. With inf. and C.E. U.S. Army, 1941-46, ETO; col. USAR; ret. Decorated Silver Star.; Legion of Merit; Bronze Star; Purple Heart. Fellow AIA (pres. N.C. chpt. 1970, Disting. Svc. award N.C. chpt. 1975); mem. Raleigh Council Architects (pres. 1950), Nat. Trust for Hist. Preservation, N.C. State Art Soc., Ret. Officers Assn. U.S. (pres. Triangle chpt. 1983), N.C. State U. Gen. Alumni Assn. (pres., chmn. bd. 1960-61, pres. Class 1941, 1986-91), Carolina Country Club, Lions, Torch Club (pres. 1982-83), Phi Eta Sigma, Phi Kappa Phi. Democrat. Baptist.

RICE, RICK BLACKBURN, computer programmer, systems analyst; b. Louisville, Sept. 17, 1954; s. Blackburn M. and Alice Jane (Walker) R.; m. Peijuan Miao, June 23, 1989; children: Richard J., Franklin W. BA in Psychology, U. Mich., 1978; MS in Computer Systems Mgmt., U. Md., 1997. Mem. computing staff Hughes Aircraft Co., El Segundo, Calif., 1980-84; programmer, analyst Candle Corp., L.A., 1984-86; sr. programmer, analyst Computer Assocs., 1986-88; fgn. expert Shaanxi Inst. Fin. and Econs., Xi'an, People's Republic of China, 1989-90; sr. programmer, analyst Disclosure, Inc., Bethesda, Md., 1988-96; info. sys. specialist IBM, Gaithersburg, 1996—97; sr. programmer analyst Sci. Applications Internat. Corp., Falls Church, Va., 1998—. Avocations: sinology. Home: 7610 Maple Ave Apt 302 Takoma Park MD 20912-5523 Office: SAIC 6565 Arlington Blvd Falls Church VA 22042

RICE, ROBERT ARMSTRONG, geographer; b. Raleigh, N.C., Feb. 4, 1952; s. John Carl and Elisabeth Evans Rice; 1 child Anika. BA, U. N.C., 1974; Master's degree, U. Mich., 1982; Doctorate, U. Calif., Berkeley, 1990. Geographer, policy rschr. Smithsonian Instn., Washington, 1995—; prof., rschr. U. del Valle, Guatemala City, Guatemala, 1993—95. Grantee rsch./tchg. grantee, Fulbright Found., 1984—86, 1991, 1994—95. Mem.: Am. Assn. Geographers, Specialty Coffee Assn. Am. (mem. environment com. 1995—2002). Office: Smithsonian Migratory Bird Ctr National Zool Park Washington DC 20008 Business E-Mail: rarice@igc.org.

RICE, ROBERT ARNOT, school administrator; b. San Francisco, Apr. 4, 1911; s. Abraham Lincoln and Mary Eugenia (Arnot) R.; m. Frances Von Dorsten, Aug. 15, 1936 (dec. sept. 1986); m. Esther Pauline Railton, July 11, 1989. BA, U. Calif., Berkeley, 1934, MA, 1947; postgrad., Columbia U., 1948. Various ednl. positions, 1935-61; supr. sci. and math. Berkeley Unified Sch. Dist., 1961-64; adminstr. NSF Summer Insts. for Sci. Tchr., U. Calif., Berkeley, 1957-65; dir. On Target Sch., Berkeley Unified Sch. Dist., 1971-73; coord. pub. programs Lawrence Hall of Sci., 1964-70; work experience edn. coord. Berkeley Unified Sch. Dist., 1973-75; exec. dir. Calif. Sci. Tchr. Assn., 1964-90; dir. No. Calif.-Western Nev. Jr. Sci. and Humanities Symposium, 1962-93. Cons. Berkley Unified Sch. Dist., 1964-70; bd. dirs. San Francisco Bay Area Sci. Fair, 1960—; mem. steering com. Chem. Study, 1960-75; coord. Industry Initiatives for Sci. and Math. Edn. Program, 1985-86; dir. Industry Initiatives for Sci. and Math. Edn. Acad., 1987; mem. Internat. Sci. and Engring. Fair Coun., Sci. Svc., Inc., 1959-68; dir. 18th Internat. Sci. and Engring. Fair, San Francisco, 1967; exec. dir. San Francisco Bay Area Sci. Fair, 1954-59; resource cons. Calif. Farm Bur. Fedn.-Youth Power Conf., Asilomar, 1966; judging chair Nat. Jr. Sci. and Humanities Symposium, 1993-97. Contbr. articles to profl. publs. Bd. dirs. Calif. Heart Assn., 1966-71, Alameda County Heart Assn., 1966-71; mem. Cen. Calif. Sci. Com., 1965-70; mem. rsch. com. Alameda County TB and Health Assn., 1965-69, mem. adv. com., 1965-69. Recipient Benjamin Ide Wheeler medal, 1985, San Francisco Bay Area Sci. Fair award of honor Calif. Acad. Sci., 1970, Armed Forces Chem. Assn. award for outstanding chemistry tchr. in San Francisco Bay Area, 1965, Robert Rice award No. Calif JSHS Competition, 1996; named to Berkeley H.S. Hall of Fame, 1994. Mem. NEA, Nat. Sci. Tchrs. Assn. (pres. 1960-61, region VIII dir. 1955-57, Calif. state dir. 1949-56, mem. chemistry com. 1956-60, Disting. Svc. to Sci. Edn. award 1986), No. Calif. Com. on Problem Solving in Sci., Calif. Sci. Tchrs. Assn. (pres. no. sect. 1949-50, Disting. Svc. to Sci. Tchg. award 1981, Lifetime Achievement award 1999), Calif. Tchrs. Assn., N.C. Sci. Specialists, Berkeley Kiwanis Club, Phi Delta Kappa (pres. Lambda chpt. 1942-43). Office: U Calif Berkeley Lawrence Hall Of Sci Berkeley CA 94720-0001

RICE, ROBERTA G. retired surgeon; b. Le Center, Minn., May 29, 1917; MD, U. Minn., 1944. Diplomate Am. Bd. Surgery. Intern U. Ill. Rsch. Edn. Hosps., Chgo., 1943-44; resident in pathology U. Minn., Mpls., 1944-45; resident in surgery Mayo Found., Rochester, 1945-49. Fellow Am. Coll. Surgeons; mem. AMA. E-mail: rgrice@buncombe.main.nc.us.

RICE, RONALD JAMES, hospital administrator; b. Springfield, Mo., Feb. 5, 1944; s. Glen Elwood and Alice Jeanett (Robinson) R. BSBA, Cen. Mo. State U., 1966, MABA, 1969, Specialist, 1972. Lic. nursing home adminstr.; lic. risk mgr. Unit mgr. Bapt. Med. Ctr., Kansas City, Mo., 1970-71; dir. unit mgmt. Ind. Health Ctr., Independence, 1971-72; adminstrv. officer Meth. Hosp., Jacksonville, Fla., 1972-73, dir. personnel, 1973-74; assoc. adminstr. Humana Hosp. Orange Park (Fla.), 1974-77; adminstr. Cathedral Rehab. Hosp., Jacksonville, 1977-79, Marion County Gen. Hosp., Hamilton, Ala., 1979-80, Nassau Gen. Hosp., Fernandina Beach, Fla., 1980-85, Reception Med. Ctr., Lake Butler, 1985-91; regional adminstr. health svcs. Dept. Corrections, Gainesville, 1991—. Cons. Clay Meml. Hosp., Green Cove Springs, Fla., 1976-77, Allied Health Care, Jacksonville, 1989. Mem. Polit. Action Com., Fla. Hosp. Assn., 1990, Coun. on Crime and Delinquency, Gainesville, 1990, Human Resources Com., Orlando, 1991; active Orange Park Presbyn. Ch. With U.S. Army, 1967-69. Decorated Army Commendation medal. Fellow Am. Coll. Health Care Execs.; mem. Am. acad. Med. Adminstrs., Am. Coll. Health Care Adminstrs., Am. Soc. Personnel Adminstrs., Fla. Hosp. Assn., Rotary (pres. 1984-86). Democrat. Avocations: boating, auto collecting model, antique juke box collecting, reading. Home: 1744 Horton Dr Orange Park FL 32073-2757

RICE, ROSS R(ICHARD), political science educator; b. Shenandoah, Iowa, Jan. 13, 1922; s. Bird O. and Della (Goodner) R.; m. Marie Puzach, Mar. 20, 1948; children: Marilyn, Roxanne, Valerie, Laurie. Student, Creighton U., 1939-41, U. No. Iowa, 1941-42; MA, U. Chgo., 1949, PhD, 1956. Elem. sch. tchr., 1941-42; Instr. Ariz. State U., Tempe, 1950-53, asst. prof., 1953-57, assoc. prof., 1957-60, prof. polit. sci., 1960-89, prof. emeritus, 1989—. Vis. prof. U. Calif., Santa Barbara, 1962-63. Author: Extremist Politics, 1964, An Annotated Bibliography of Arizona Politics and Government, 1976, Carl Hayden: Builder of the American West, 1994; contbr. numerous articles to scholarly publs. Mem. council, mayor City of Tempe, 1958-62. With Air Corps U.S. Army, 1942-45. NEH grantee, 1972. Mem. Tempe Hist. Soc. (pres. 1971-73), Am. Polit. Sci. Assn., Western Polit. Sci. Assn. Democrat. Home: Unit C-131 2625 E Southern Ave Tempe AZ 85282-7636 also: 2625 E Southern Ave Unit C131 Tempe AZ 85282-7636

RICE, SHARON JEAN, secondary school educator; b. L'Anse, Mich., Feb. 6, 1947; d. Albert George and Beatrice Jeanette Roy; m. Thomas E. Rice, Aug. 23, 1969; 1 child Scott Thomas. BA in Secondary Edn., We. Mich. U., 1969; mid. sch. endorsement, Ctrl. Mich. U., 1976. Cert. reproductive health Mich. Dept. Edn., 1996, crisis prevention Mich. Dept. Edn., 1999. Substitute tchr. pub. schs., Greenville and Stanton, Mich., 1969—76; adult edn. tchr. Ctrl. Montcalm Pub. Sch., Stanton, 1976—83, alternative edn. tchr., 1983—96, H.O. Steele H.S., Fenwick, 1996—2001, Montcalm Area Ind. Sch. Dist. Career Acad., Sidney, 2001—. Tchr. sch. improvement team, Stanton,

1994—96; graduation spkr. H.O. Steele H.S. Career Acad., 1997—. Mem.: Mich. Ednl. Assn., Greenville Women's Bowling Assn. (league officer, dir. 1989—), Sheridan Women's Bowling Assn. (pres. 1990—2002, sec.-treas. 1976—99, Hall of Fame). Roman Catholic. Office: Career Acad MACC 1550 Sidney Rd Sidney MI 48885

RICE, STAN, JR. poet, painter, English language educator; b. Dallas, Nov. 7, 1942; s. Stanley Travis and Margaret Nolia (Cruse) R.; m. Anne O'Brien, Oct. 14, 1961; children: Michele (dec.), Christopher. BA, San Francisco State U., 1963, MA, 1965. Asst. prof. San Francisco State U., 1965-71, assoc. prof., 1971-76, prof. English and creative writing, 1977-88, asst. dir. Poetry Ctr., 1964-72, chmn. dept. creative writing, 1980-88, ret. Author: Some Lamb, 1975, Whiteboy, 1976 (Edgar Allen Poe award Acad. Am. Poets 1977), Body of Work, 1983, Singing Yet: New and Selected Poems, 1992, Fear Itself, 1995, Paintings—Stan Rice, 1997, The Radiance of Pigs, 1999, Red to the Rind, 2002; one-man show of paintings Gallerie Simone Stern, New Orleans, La., 1992. Nat. Endowment Arts grantee, 1966, writing fellow, 1972; recipient Joseph Henry Jackson award San Francisco Found., 1968

RICE, STANLEY ARTHUR, biology educator; b. Cushing, Okla., May 30, 1957; s. Arthur John and Nina Irene (Hicks) R.; m. Althea Lisette Clarkston, June 9, 1984; 1 child, Anita. BA, U. Calif., Santa Barbara, 1979; PhD, U. Ill., 1987. Vis. teaching specialist Univ. Ill., Urbana, 1986-87; asst. prof. The King's Coll., Briarcliff Manor, N.Y., 1987-90; vis. faculty Sarah Lawrence Coll., Bronxville, 1989-90; asst. prof. Huntington (Ind.) Coll., 1990-93, S.W. State U., Marshall, Minn., 1993-98, S.E. Okla. State U., Durant, Okla., 1998—. Vis. faculty mem. Wheaton (Ill.) Coll. Sci. Sta., 1993—, Taylor U., Upland, Ind., 1993. Contbr. articles to Am. Biol. Tchr., Oecologia, Perspectives on Sci. and Christian Faith, Creation/Evolution. Predoctoral fellowship NSF, Univ. Ill., 1980. Mem. Ecol. Soc. Am., British Ecol. Soc., Bot. Soc. Am., Am. Sci. Affiliation, Am. Biol. Tchrs. Office: Dept Biol Sci SE Okla State Univ Durant OK 74701 E-mail: srice@sosu.edu.

RICE, STEPHEN GARY, medical educator, sports medicine physician; b. Bklyn., Dec. 21, 1945; s. Abraham S. and Anne (Shelling) R.; m. Hilary Jo Turett, May 10, 1987; children: Adam, Bryan. AB, Columbia Coll., 1967; MD, PhD, NYU, 1974; MPH, U. Wash., 1983. Diplomate in pediatrics and sports medicine Am. Bd. Pediatrics. Intern, resident Children's Hosp. & U. Wash., Seattle, 1974-77; faculty mem. sports medicine U. Wash., 1977-96; program dir. primary care sports medicine fellowship Jersey Shore Med. Ctr., Neptune, N.J., 1996—; clin. assoc. prof. pediat. Robert Wood Johnson Med. Sch. U. Medicine and Dentistry N.J., New Brunswick, 1999—. Developer, dir. Athletic Health Care Sys., 1978—; cons. in field. Author: Athletic Health Care System, 1988. Team physician U. Wash., 1977-81. Fellow Am. Acad. Pediat. (chmn. sports medicine com. N.J. chpt. 1999—, chmn. govt. affairs com. N.J. chpt. 2000—, sec.-editor N.J. chap. 2002—), Am. Coll. Sports Medicine (sec. Greater N.Y. regional chpt. 1997—); mem. Am. Alliance Health, Phys. Edn., Recreation and Dance, Nat. Strength and Conditioning Assn., Am. Med. Soc. Sports Medicine, Med. Soc. N.J. Avocations: sports, cooking, gardening, Gilbert & Sullivan, chess. Home: 6 Wildflower Ct Manalapan NJ 07726-2861 Office: Jersey Shore Med Ctr Dept Pediatrics PO Box 397 Neptune NJ 07754-0397 E-mail: srice@meridianhealth.com.

RICE, STEVEN DALE, electronics educator; b. Valparaiso, Ind., Aug. 11, 1947; s. Lloyd Dale and Mary Helen (Breen) R.; m. Reyanna Danti, Mar. 4, 1972; children: Joshua, Breanna. AAS, Valparaiso Tech. Inst., 1969; BS Health Sci., Ball State U., 1973; BSEE, Valparaiso Tech. Inst., 1973; MS in Vocat. Edn., No. Mont. Coll., 1991. Electronics technician Heavy Mil. Electronic Systems GE, Syracuse, N.Y., 1969-70; electronics technician Ball State U., Muncie, Ind., 1974-75; with electronic sales Tandy Corp., Valparaiso, 1976-77; electronics technician Missoula (Mont.) Community Hosp., 1977-84; instr. electronics Missoula Coll. Tech. U. Montana-Missoula, 1984-88; chmn. dept. electronics Coll. of Tech. U. Mont., Missoula, 1988—. Book reviewer Merrill Pub., 1988—, Delmar, McGraw Hill. Bd. dirs. Victor (Mont.) Sch. Bd., 1989-99 (ret.), chmn. bd., 1992-95. Mem. IEEE, Instrument Soc. Am., Mont. Fedn. Tchrs. Office: Coll Tech U Mont 909 South Ave W Missoula MT 59801-7910 E-mail: sdrice@selway.umt.edu.

RICE, STUART ALAN, chemist, educator; b. N.Y.C., Jan. 6, 1932; s. Harry L. and Helen (Rayfield) Rice; m. Marian Ruth Coopersmith, June 1, 1952 (dec. June 1994); children: Barbara, Janet; m. Ruth O'Brien, Sept. 27, 1997; 1 child David Lawrence. BS, Bklyn. Coll., 1952; MA, Harvard, 1954, PhD, 1955. Jr. fellow Harvard, 1955—57; faculty U. Chgo., 1957—60, prof. chemistry, 1960—69, Louis Block prof. phys. scis., 1969—77, chmn. dept. chemistry, 1971—76, Frank P. Hixon disting. service prof., 1977—, dean phys. scis. div., 1981—95, dir. Inst. Study Metals, 1981—95; Newton-Abraham prof. Oxford (Eng.) U., 1999—. Mem. Nat. Sci. Bd., 1980—86. Author: Polyelectrolyte Solutions, 1961, Statistical Mechanics of Simple Liquids, 1965, Physical Chemistry, 1980, 2d edit., 2000, Optical Control of Molecular Dynamics, 2000; contbr. articles to profl. jours. Named Falk-Plautt lectr., Columbia U., 1964, Riley lectr., Notre Dame U., 1964, U. lectr. chemistry, U. Western Ont., 1970, Seaver lectr., U. Soc. Calif, 1972, Noyes lectr., U. Tex., 1975, Foster lectr., SUNY, 1976, Frank T. Gucker lectr., Ind. U., 1976, Fairchild lectr., Calif. Inst. Tech., 1979, Baker lectr., Cornell U., 1985—86, Centenary lectr., Royal Soc. Chemistry, 1986—87, Nat. lectr., Phi Beta Kappa, 1994—95; recipient Centennial medal, Harvard U., 1997, Nat. Medal of Sci., 1999, Hirschfelder award for Theoretical Chemistry, 2002; fellow, Guggenheim, 1960—61, Sr. Postdoctoral fellow, NSF, 1965—66, USPHS Spl. Postdoctoral fellow, U. Copenhagen, 1970—71. Fellow: Am. Philos. Soc.; mem.: AAAS, Danish Acad. Sci. and Letters, N.Y. Acad. Scis. (A. Cressy Morrison prize 1955), Faraday Soc. (Marlowe medal 1963), Am. Phys. Soc., Am. Acad. Sci., Nat. Acad. Sci., Am. Chem. Soc. (Pure Chemistry award 1963, Leo Hendrik Baekland award 1971, Peter Debye award 1985, Hildebrand award 1987).

RICE, SUE ANN, dean, industrial and organizational psychologist; b. Ponca City, Okla., Sept. 17, 1934; d. Alfred and Helen (Revard) R. BS in Edn., U. Okla., 1956; MA, Cath. U., 1979, PhD, 1988. Ensign USN, 1956, advanced through grades to comdr., 1973; ednl. svcs. officer 9th Naval Dist., Great Lakes, Ill., 1956-58; adminstr., asst. staff, comdr. in-chief Pacific Fleet, Honolulu, 1958-61; head edn. div. Naval Air Sta., Lemoore, Calif., 1961-63; instr., acad. dir. Women Officers' Sch., Newport, R.I., 1963-66; head. tng. div. Naval Command Systems Support Activity, Washington, 1966-70; head, ops. support sec., comdr.-in-chief Lant, Norfolk, Va., 1970-74; sr. U.S. rep. NATO, subgroup 5 orgn. JCS, Washington, 1974-77; ret. USN, 1977; head vocation office Archdiocese of Washington, 1977-78; cons. Notre Dame Inst., Arlington, Va., 1989-97, dean of students, 1990-95. Lectr. Cath. U. Am., Washington, 1983-84; bd. dirs. Villa Cortona Apostolic Ctr., Bethesda, 1984-94. Tech. reviewer Personnel Administration, 1964; editor (newsletter) Vocation News, 1978. Conoco scholarship Continental Oil Co., 1952-56; recipient Meritorious Svc. medal Pres. of U.S., 1977, rsch. grant Cath. U., Sigma Xi, 1986. Mem.: U.S. Conf. Secular Insts. (vocation com.), Lay Women's Assn. (internat. v.p., internat. mem. fin. com., nat. v.p.), Cath. War Vets. (nat. membership task force com., nat. youth act com., vets. affairs com.), Gamma Phi Beta, Kappa Delta Pi. Roman Catholic. Avocations: travel, music, gardening, woodworking.

RICE, WALLACE WILLIAM, secondary education educator; b. Basin, Wyo., May 3, 1936; s. William Peace Jr. and Emma Anna (Wahl) R.; m. Rozella Peterson, June 23, 1962 (div. 1998); children: Steven C., Kevin E. BS in Geology, U. Wyo., 1959, MS in Natural Sci., 1967. Oil well logger Anders Well Logging, Fort Collins, Colo., 1959-61; office mgr. Wyo. Hwy Dept., Cheyenne, Wyo., 1962; adminstrv. asst. Sch. Dist. #1, 1962-63; sci. tchr. Johnson H.S., 1963-65; earth sci. tchr. Ctrl. H.S., 1966-96; ret., 1996. Athletic ticket mgr. Ctrl. H.S., Cheyenne, 1968-96, asst. wrestling coach, 1962-63, 67—. Sec.-treas. Laramie County Rheumatic Fever Prevention Soc., Cheyenne, 1962—; leader Boy Scouts Am.; v.p. Trinity Luth. Ch., 1978-79, King of Glory Luth. Ch., 1989-91. With USNG, 1954-62. Recipient Silver Beaver award Boy Scouts Am., 1985, Commr. award, 1988, Dist. award of Merit, 1994, Founder's award Order of Arrow, 1996. Mem. Nat. Sci. Tchr. Assn. (regional meeting dir. 1972), Wyo. Math. Sci. Assn., Am. Fedn. Tchrs. (pres. 1978-79, 82, sec. 1982-96). Home: 222 E 2nd Ave Cheyenne WY 82001-1406

RICE, WALTER HERBERT, federal judge; b. Pitts., May 27, 1937; s. Harry D. and Elizabeth L. (Braemer) R.; m. Bonnie Rice; children: Michael, Hilary, Harry, Courtney Elizabeth. BA, Northwestern U., 1958; JD, MBA, Columbia U., 1962; LLD (hon.), U. Dayton, 1991; DHL (hon.), Wright State U., 2000. Bar: Ohio 1963. Asst. county prosecutor, Montgomery County, Ohio, 1964-66; assoc. Gallon & Miller, Dayton, 1966-69; 1st asst. Montgomery County Prosecutor's Office, 1969; judge Dayton Mcpl. Ct., 1970-71, Montgomery County Ct. Common Pleas, 1971-80, U.S. Dist. Ct. (so. dist.) Ohio, 1980-95, chief judge, 1996—. Adj. prof. U. Dayton Law Sch., 1976— , bd. visitors, 1976— ; chmn. Montgomery County Supervisory Council on Crime and Deliquency, 1972-74; vice chmn. bd. dirs. Pretrial Release, Inc., 1975-79 Author papers in field. Pres. Dayton Area Coun. on Alcoholism and Drug Abuse, 1971-73; chmn. bd. trustees Stillwater Health Ctr., Dayton, 1976-79, Family Svc. Assn. Dayton, 1978-80; chmn. RTA in 2000 Com., 2003 Com. Designed To Bring Nat. Park to Dayton To Honor Wright Bros. and Birth of Aviation; chmn. Martin Luther King Jr. Meml. Com., Dayton Aviation Heritage Commn.; trustee Montgomery County Vol. Lawyers Project, Miami Valley Cultural Alliance, Barbara Jordan Com. Racial Justice; co-chmn., Dayton Dialogue on Race Rels.; former bd. mem. Sinclair C.C., U.S. Air & Trade Show. Recipient Excellent Jud. Service award Ohio Supreme Ct., 1976, 77, Outstanding Jud. Service award, 1973, 74, 76, Man of Yr. award Disting. Service Awards Council, Dayton, 1977, Outstanding Jurist in Ohio award Ohio Acad. Trial Lawyers, 1986, Pub. Ofcl. of Yr. award Ohio region of Nat. Assn. Social Workers, 1992, Humanitarian award NCCJ, 1993, City Mgr.'s Cmty. Svc. award City of Dayton, 1994, Paul Laurence Dunbar Humanitarian award, 1996, Pres.' award NAACP, 1996, greater Dayton Peace Bridge (civil rights) Hall of Fame, Mark of Excellence award Nat. Forum Black Pub. Adminstrs., 2001. Mem. Dayton Bar Assn., Fed. Judges Assn., Carl D. Kessler Inn of Ct. (founder, former chmn.).

RICE, WILLIAM PHIPPS, investment counselor; b. Bronxville, N.Y., Mar. 27, 1944; s. Anton Henry Jr. and Lydia Phipps (Sands) R.; m. Lynn Lucas Rice, May 21, 1972; children: William Phipps Jr., Paige Sands Rice. BA cum laude, Kenyon Coll., 1966. Analyst Spencer Trask & Co., N.Y.C., 1960-67; v.p., portfolio mgr. Endowment Mgmt. and Rsch. Corp., Boston, 1969-77, Ft. Hill Investors Mgmt. Corp., Boston, 1977-83; pres., founder Anchor Capital Advisors Inc., 1983—, Anchor/Russell Capital Advisors, Boston, 1989—. Trustee Mass. Bible Soc., Boston, 1985-89; trustee of donations Episcopal Ch. Diocese of Mass., Boston, 1989—; trustee Albert O. Wilson Found., Inc., 1998—. With U.S. Army, 1967-69. Mem. Assn. for Investment Mgmt. and Rsch., Assn. Investment Mgmt. Sales Execs., Boston Security Analysts Soc., Boston C. of C., N.Y. Yacht Club, Duxbury Yacht Club, Ocean Reef Club, Boston Coll. Club, Down Town Club. Avocations: skiing, boating, woodworking. Home: PO Box 1599 Duxbury MA 02331-1599 Office: Anchor Capital Advisors Inc 1 Post Office Sq Boston MA 02109-2106

RICE, WILLIAM CRAIG, writing and humanities educator; b. Washington, May 4, 1955; s. Frank Aydelotte and Ann Craig (Sutton) R.; m. Carolina Agravante Reyes, May 10, 1986. BA, U. Va., 1975, MA, 1979; MFA, U. Mich., 1988, PhD, 1991. Instr. Webb Sch., Bell Buckle, Tenn., 1975-76, Temple U., Phila., 1982-86; lectr. U. Pa., 1982-83; asst. prof. Fairfield (Conn.) U., 1991-92; preceptor Harvard U., Cambridge, Mass., 1992—. Mem. Com. on Pub. Doublespeak, 1991-94; dir. writing program Tyler Sch. Art, 1985-86. Author: Public Discourse and Academic Inquiry, 1996; contbr. short stories, essays, poetry, and articles to profl. publs. Recipient Hopwood award, 1987; Henry A. Parker Meml. fellow, 1987, L. D. Goodrich fellow, 1988, Claude R. Lambe fellow Inst. for Humane Studies, 1990-91, Salvatori fellow Heritage Found., 1995. Mem. MLA, Associated Writing Programs, Nat. Coun. Tchrs. of English. Avocations: nature study, fine and decorative arts, boxing. Office: Harvard U Expository Writing Program Cambridge MA 02138

RICE, WILLIAM EDWARD, newspaper columnist; b. Albany, N.Y., July 26, 1938; s. Harry Edward, Jr. and Elizabeth (Lally) R.; m. Carol Timmon, June 3, 1978 (div.); m. Jill Van Cleave, Aug. 20, 1983. BA in History, U. Va., 1960; MS with honors, Columbia U., 1963. Reporter, editorial writer, critic Washington Post, 1963-69; student LeCordon Bleu, Paris, 1969-70; dir. L'Ecole de Cuisine, Bethesda, Md., 1971-72; freelance writer, restaurant critic Washingtonian Mag., 1971-72; exec. food editor Washington Post, 1972-80; editor-in-chief Food and Wine Mag., N.Y.C., 1980-85; food and wine columnist Chgo. Tribune, 1986—. Dining In columnist Gentlemen's Quarterly, 1987-89; chmn. restaurant awards com.James Beard Found., 1993-. Author: Feasts of Wine and Food, 1986, Steak Lovers Cookbook, 1997; editor: (with others) Where to Eat in America, 1978, 2d edit., 1980, 3d edit., 1987. Served with USN, 1960-62. Recipient Vesta award as outstanding newspaper food editor, 1979, Ordre du Merite Agricole (France), 1983 Home: 655 W Buena Ave Chicago IL 60613-2201 Office: Chgo Tribune Co Po Box 25340 435 N Michigan Ave Chicago IL 60611-4066 E-mail: wrice@tribune.com.

RICE, WINSTON EDWARD, lawyer; b. Shreveport, La., Feb. 22, 1946; s. Winston Churchill and Margaret (Coughlin) R.; m. Barbara Reily Gay, Apr. 16, 1977; 1 child, Andrew Hynes; children by previous marriage: Winston Hobson, Christian MacTaggart. Student, Centenary Coll. La., 1967; JD, La. State U., 1971. Bar: La. 1971, Colo. 1990, Tex. 1992. Cons. geologist, Gulfport, Miss., 1968-70; ptnr. Phelps, Dunbar, New Orleans, 1971-88; sr. ptnr. Rice, Fowler, Houston, Miami, Fla., London and Bogota, 1988-2000; gen. mgr. Winston Edw. Rice LLC, Covington, La., 2000—. Instr. law La. State U., Baton Rouge, 1970-71. Assoc. editor La. Law Rev., 1970-71. Mem.: Trucking Industry Def. Assn., Ctr. Transp. Law and Policy, Soc. Ins. Trainers and Educators, Assn. Average Adjusters (U.K.), Assn. Average Adjusters U.S., Maritime Law Assn. U.S. (chmn. subcom. on offshore exploration and devel. 1985—88, vice chmn. com. internat. law of the sea 1988—91, chmn. 1991—95, membership sec. 1998—2002), Com. Maritime Internat. (titulary mem.), Fedn. Ins. and Corp. Counsel, La. Assn. Def. Counsel, New Orleans Assn. Def. Counsel, Can. Transp. Lawyers Assn., New Orleans Bar Assn., Tex. State Bar, Colo. State Bar Assn., La. Bar Assn., Coral Beach and Tennis Club, Stratford Club, Mariners Club (treas. 1974—75, 1978—79, sec. 1975—76, v.p. 1976—77, pres. 1977—78), Boston Club, Kappa Alpha, Phi Kappa Phi, Phi Delta Phi, Order of Coif. Republican. Episcopalian. Office: 328 N Columbia St Covington LA 70433-2918

RICH, ADRIENNE, writer; b. Balt., May 16, 1929; d. Arnold Rice and Helen Elizabeth (Jones) R.; m. Alfred H. Conrad (dec. 1970); children: David, Paul, Jacob. AB, Radcliffe Coll., 1951; LittD (hon.), Wheaton Coll., 1967, Smith Coll., 1979, Brandeis U., 1987, Coll. Wooster, Ohio, 1988, CCNY, Harvard U., 1990, Swarthmore Coll., 1992. Tchr. workshop YM-WHA Poetry Ctr., N.Y.C., 1966-67; vis. lectr. Swarthmore Coll., 1967-69; adj. prof. writing divsn. Columbia U., 1967-69; lectr. CCNY, 1968-70, instr., 1970-71, asst. prof. English, 1971-72, 74-75; Fannie Hurst vis. prof. creative lit. Brandeis U., 1972-73; prof. English Douglass Coll., Rutgers U., 1976-79; Clark lectr., disting. vis. prof. Scripps Coll., 1983-84; A.D. White prof.-at-large Cornell U., 1981-87; disting. vis. prof. San Jose State U., 1984-85; prof. English and feminist studies Stanford U., 1986-93. Marjorie Kovler vis. lectr. U. Chgo., 1989. Author: (poetry) Collected Early Poems, 1950-1970, 1993, Diving into the Wreck, 1973, The Dream of a Common Language, 1978, A Wild Patience Has Taken Me This Far, 1981, Your Native Land, Your Life, 1986, Time's Power, 1989, An Atlas of the Difficult World, 1991, Dark Fields of the Republic, 1995, Midnight Salvage, 1999, Fox, 2001, The Fact of a Doorframe: Selected Poems 1950-2001, 2002; (prose) Of Woman Born: Motherhood as Experience and Institution, 1976, 10th anniversary edit., 1986, On Lies, Secrets and Silence, 1979, Blood, Bread and Poetry, 1986, What Is Found There: Notebooks on Poetry and Politics, 1993, Arts of the Possible: Essays and Conversations, 2001. Mem. nat. adv. bd. Nat. Writers Union, Rosenberg Fund for Children. Recipient Yale Series of Younger Poets award, 1951, Nat. Inst. Arts and letters award in poetry, 1961, Eunice Tietjens Meml. prize, 1968, Shelley Meml. award, 1971, Nat. Book award, 1974, Fund for Human Dignity award Nat. Gay Task Force, 1981, Ruth Lilly Poetry prize, 1986, Brandeis U. Creative Arts medal for Poetry, 1987, Nat. Poetry Assn. award, 1989, Elmer Holmes Bobst award arts and letters NYU, 1989, MacArthur fellowship, 1994-99, Dorothea Tanning award Acad. Am. Poets, 1996, others; chancellor Acad. Am. Poets, 1999-2001, Lannan Found. Lifetime Achievement award, 1999, others. Mem. PEN, Nat. Writers Union. Office: care W W Norton Co 500 5th Ave New York NY 10110-0002

RICH, ALAN, music critic, editor, author; b. Boston, June 17, 1924; s. Edward and Helen (Hirshberg) R. AB, Harvard, 1945; MA, U. Calif-Berkeley, 1952. Alfred Hertz Meml. Traveling fellow in music, Vienna, Austria, 1952-53; asst. music critic Boston Herald, 1944-45, N.Y. Sun, 1947-48; contbr. Am. Record Guide, 1947-61, Saturday Rev., 1952-53, Mus. Am., 1955-61, Mus. Quar., 1957-58; tchr. music U. Calif. at Berkeley, 1950-58; program and music dir. Pacifica Found., FM radio, 1953-61; asst. music critic N.Y. Times, 1961-63; chief music critic, editor N.Y. Herald Tribune, 1963-66; music critic, editor N.Y. World Jour. Tribune, 1966-67; contbg. editor Time mag., 1967-68; music and drama critic, arts editor N.Y. mag., 1968-81, contbg. editor, 1981-83; music critic, arts editor Calif. (formerly New West mag.), 1979-83, contbg. editor, 1983-85; gen. editor Newsweek mag., N.Y.C., 1983-87; music critic L.A. Herald Examiner, 1987-89, L.A. Daily News, 1989-92, L.A. Weekly, 1992—. Tchr. New Sch. for Social Rsch., 1972-75, 77-79, U. So. Calif. Sch. Journalism, 1980-82, Calif. Inst. Art, 1982-94, UCLA, 1990-91; artist-in-residence Davis Ctr. for Performing Arts CUNY, 1975-76. Author: Careers and Opportunities in Music, 1964, Music: Mirror of the Arts, 1969, Listeners Guides to Classical Music, Opera, Jazz, 3 vols., 1980, The Lincoln Center Story, 1984, Play-by-Play: Bach, Mozart, Beethoven, Tchaikovsky, 4 vols., 1995, American Pioneers, 1995; author: (interactive CD-ROM computer programs): Schubert's Trout Quintet, 1991, So I've Heard: Bach and Before, 1992, So I've Heard: The Classical Ideal, 1993, So I've Heard: Beethoven and Beyond, 1993; contbr. articles to entertainment mags. Recipient Deems Taylor award ASCAP, 1970, 73, 74 Mem. Music Critics Circle N.Y. (sec. 1961-63, chmn. 1963-64), N.Y. Drama Critics Circle, Am. Theatre Critics Assn., Music Critics Assn., PEN. Home: 2925 Greenfield Ave Los Angeles CA 90064-4019 E-mail: KV467@mediaone.net.

RICH, ALBERT CLARK, solar energy manufacturing executive; b. Wolfeboro, N.H., Feb. 8, 1950; s. Nelson Barnard and Alberta Louise (Pigon) R.; m. Patricia Ann Murphy, July 16, 1973 (div. Aug. 1975); m. Susan Maura McGee, Jan. 26, 1985; children: Ashley, Katherine, Clark, Thomas. BA in Polit. Sci. and Research Processes, Principia Coll., 1979; cert., Solar Energy Research Inst., Golden, Colo., 1981. Owner Antique Classic Auto Restoration, Ft. Lauderdale, Fla., 1975-77, AC-Rich & Sun, Herndon, Va., 1979—; pres., CEO AnuPower Corp. Founder., pres. Am. Solar Network Ltd., 1989—; pres. Suncorps Inc., Watertown, Mass., 1980-82, Cambridge Alt. Power Co., 1982-83; dist. mgr. Sears/Am. Solar King, Herndon, 1983-85; bd dirs. Monegon Solar, Washington br., 1984; cons. NEEIC, Boston, 1982; chmn. Sec. Energy, Boston, 1983; speaker New Eng. Solar Energy Assn. MIT, Cambridge and Boston, 1983; chmn. solar thermal div. New Eng. Solar Energy Assn., Bay chpt., Boston, 1982-83; contractor White House Pagent of Peace Exhibit. Developer heat cell, heliophase, solar storage tank; inventor, patentee Solar "Skylite" water heater, "Fireball 2001", "Megamatt." Organizer Earth Day, Boston, 1982-83, Sec. of Energy, Boston, 1983, founder ACR Solar Internat., 1997, SolarRoof.com, 1998. Mem. Sacramento Solar Energy Industries Assn. (DOE energy innovation award 1992, DOE energy related inventions program grantee 1994). Avocations: automobile restoration, squash, woodcraft. Four patents granted, including Modular Firebar 2001 solar system, Megamat solar system, 1999. Home and Office: ACR Solar Internat 5840 Gibbons Dr Carmichael CA 95608-6903

RICH, ALEXANDER, molecular biologist, educator; b. Hartford, Conn., Nov. 15, 1924; s. Max and Bella (Shub) R.; m. Jane Erving King, July 5, 1952; children: Benjamin, Josiah, Rebecca, Jessica. AB magna cum laude in Biochem. Scis, Harvard U., 1947, MD cum laude, 1949; Dr. (hon.), Fed. U. Rio de Janeiro, 1981; PhD honoris causa, Weizmann Inst. Sci., Rehovot, Israel, 1992; DSc (hon.), Eidgenössische Technische Hochschule, Zurich, Switzerland, 1993, Freie U., Berlin, 1996. Rsch. fellow Gates and Crellin Labs., Calif. Inst. Tech., Pasadena, 1949-54; chief sect. phys. chemistry NIMH, Bethesda, Md., 1954-58; vis. scientist Cavendish Lab., Cambridge (Eng.) U., 1955-56; assoc. prof. biophysics MIT, Cambridge, 1958-61, prof. biohpysics, 1961—, William Thompson Sedgwick prof. biophysics, 1974—. Mem. AAAS (coun. mem. 1967-71); com. career devel. awards NIH, 1964-67, postdoctoral fellowship bd., 1955-58; mem. com. exobiology space sci. bd. NAS, 1964-65, adv. bd., acad. forum, 1975-82, nominating com., 1980, exec. com. of council, 1985-88; mem. U.S. nat. com. Internat. Orgn. Pure Applied Biophysics, 1965-67; vis. com. biology dept. Yale U., 1963, Weizmann Inst. Sci., 1965-66, co-chmn. sci. and adv. com. 1987-91; life scis. com. NASA, 1970-75, lunar planetary missions bd., 1968-70; biology team Viking Mars Mission, 1969-80; mem. corp. Marine Biol. Lab., Woods Hole, Mass., 1965-77, 87—; sci. rev. com. Howard Hughes Med. Inst., Miami, Fla., 1978-90; vis. com. biology div. Oak Ridge Nat. Lab., 1972-76; chmn. com. on USSR and Ea. Europe Exch. Bd. NAS, 1973-76; mem. Internat. Rsch. and Exchs. Bd. Am. Coun. Learned Socs., N.Y.C., 1973-76, panel judges N.Y. Acad. Sci. ann. book award for children's sci. books, N.Y.C., 1973-90; chmn. nominating com. Am. Acad. Arts and Sci., 1974-77; sci. adv. bd. Stanford Synchrotron Radiation Project, 1976-80, Mass. Gen. Hosp., Boston, 1978-83; mem. U.S. Nat. Sci. Bd., 1976-82; bd. govs. Weizmann Inst. Sci., 1976—; rsch. com. Med. Found., Boston, 1976-80; mem. U.S.-USSR Joint Commn. on Sci. and Tech., Dept. State, Washington, 1977-82; sr. cons. Office of Sci. and Tech. Policy, Exec. Office of Pres., Washington, 1977-81; mem. council Pugwash Confs. on Sci. and World Affairs, Geneva, 1977-82; chmn. basic rsch. com. Nat. Sci. Bd., Washington, 1978-82; mem. U.S. Nat. Com. for Internat. Union for Pure and Applied Biophysics, NAS, 1979-83; bd. dirs. Med. Found., Boston, 1981-90; vis. com. divsn. med. sci. Harvard U., 1981-87; mem. govt.-univ.-industry rsch. round table, 1984-87; chmn. sci. adv. com. dept. molecular biology Mass. Gen. Hosp., Boston, 1983-87; governing bd. NRC, 1985-88; nat. adv. com. Pew Scholars program Pew Meml. Trust, 1986-88; com. on USSR and Eastern Europe Nat. Rsch. Council, Washington, 1986-92; external adv. com. Ctr. for Human Genome Studies, Los Alamos Nat. Lab., N.Mex., 1989-97, Nat. Critical Techs. Panel, Office of Sci. & Tech. Policy, Exec. Office of Pres., Washington, 1990-91; vis. com. NASA Ctr. Exobiology, La Jolla, Calif., 1992-95; vis. prof. Coll. France, Paris, 1987. Editor: (with Norman Davidson) Structural Chemistry and Molecular Biology, 1968; mem. editl. bd. Biophys. Jour., 1961-63, Currents Modern Biology, 1966-72, Science, 1963-69, Analytical Biochemistry, 1969-81, Bio-Systems, 1973-86, Molecular Biology Reports, 1974-85, Procs. NAS, 1973-78, Jour. Molecular and Applied Genetics, 1980-84, DNA, 1981-89, EMBO Jour., 1988-90, Jour. Biotech., 1987—, Genomics, 1987—, Proteins, Structure, Function and Genetics, 1986-91, Jour. Molecular Evolution, 1983—, Springer Series on Molecular Biology, 1980-88; mem. editl. adv. bd. Jour. Molecular Biology, 1959-66, Accounts of Chemical Research, 1980-82, Jour. Biomolecular Structure and Dynamics, 1983—, PAABS Revista, 1972-77, Biopolymers, 1963-74, Jour. of Molecular Evolution, 1983-94, others; contbr. over 500 articles to profl. jours. With USN, 1943-46. Fairchild disting. scholar Calif. Inst. Tech., Pasadena, 1976; recipient Skylab Achievement award NASA, 1974, Theodore von Karmin award Viking Mars Mission, 1976, Presdl. award N.Y. Acad. Scis., 1977, Jabotinsky medal Jabotinsky Found., 1980, James R. Killian Faculty Achievement award MIT, 1980, Lewis S. Rosenstiel Basic Biomed. Rsch. award Brandeis U., 1983, Nat. medal Sci. NSF, 1995, Merck award Am. Soc. Biochemistry and Molecular Biology, Washington, 1998, Bower award Franklin Inst., 2000, Proctor prize Sigma Xi, 2001, Passano award, Passano Found., 2002; NRC fellow, 1949-51; Guggenheim Found. fellow, 1963; mem. Pontifical Acad. Scis. The Vatican, 1978. Fellow AAAS; mem. NAS (chmn. biotech., program, com. on scholarly comm. with China 1986-93, exec. com. 1985-88, com. on sci. comm. and nat. security 1982), Am. Chem. Soc. (exec. com. divsn. biol. chemistry 1962, Linus Pauling award 1995), Biophys. Soc. (coun. 1960-69), Am. Soc. Biol. Chemists, Am. Crystallographic Soc., Internat. Soc. for Study of Origin of Life (fgn.), French Acad. Scis., Russian Acad. Scis. (fgn., Lomonosov Large Gold medal 2002), European Molecular Biology Orgn. (assoc.), Japanese Biochem. Soc. (hon.), Physicians for Social Responsibility (nat. adv. bd. 1983—), Am. Philos. Soc., Inst. of Medicine (sr.), Phi Beta Kappa, Alpha Omega Alpha. Office: MIT Dept Biology 77 Mass Ave Rm 68-233 Cambridge MA 02139-4307

RICH, ANDREA LOUISE, museum administrator; BA, UCLA, 1965, MA, 1966, PhD, 1968. Asst. prof. comms. studies UCLA, L.A., 1976, asst. dir. office learning resources, 1976, acting dir. Media Ctr., 1977, dir. office of instructional devel., 1978-80, asst. vice chancellor office of instructional devel., 1980-86, asst. exec. vice chancellor, 1986-87, vice chancellor acad.

adminstrn., 1987-91, exec. vice chancellor, 1991-95; pres., CEO L.A. County Mus. of Art, L.A., 1995—, pres., dir. Office: L A County Mus Art 5905 Wilshire Blvd Los Angeles CA 90036-4597*

RICH, BEN ARTHUR, lawyer, educator; b. Springfield, Ill., Mar. 27, 1947; s. Ben Morris and Betty Lorraine (Ingalls) R.; m. Caroline Rose Castle, Oct. 4, 1984 (div. Nov. 1988); m. Kathleen Mills, Aug. 17, 1991. Student, U. St. Andrews, Scotland, 1967-68; BA, DePauw U., 1969; JD, Washington U., 1973; PhD, U. Colo., 1995. Bar: Ill. 1973, N.C. 1975, Colo. 1984. Rsch. assoc. U. Ill. Coll. Law, Urbana, 1973-74; staff atty. Nat. Assn. Attys. Gen., Raleigh, N.C., 1974-76; prin. Hollowell, Silverstein, Rich & Brady, 1976-80; dep. commr. N.C. Indsl. Commn., 1980-81; counsel N.C. Meml. Hosp., Chapel Hill, 1981-84; assoc. univ. counsel U. Colo. Health Scis. Ctr., Denver, 1984-86; gen. counsel U. Colo., Boulder, 1986-89, spl. counsel to the regents, 1989-90; asst. clin. prof. U. Colo. Sch. Medicine, 1992-94; asst. prof. U. Colo. Health Scis. Ctr., 1995-99, asst. dir. program in healthcare ethics, humanities and law, 1995-99; assoc. prof. bioethics program U. Calif.-Davis Med. Ctr., Sacramento, 2000—. Asst. prof. attendent U. Colo. Sch. Medicine, 1986-91, adj. instr. Sch. Law, 1988-95, adj. prof., 1996—; vis. assoc. prof., 1990-91; lectr. U. Denver Coll. Law; vis. prof. U. Calif. Davis Sch. Law. Author: (book) Strange Bedfellows: How Medical Jurisprudence Has Influenced Medical Ethics and Medical Practice, 2001; contbr. articles to jours., chpts. to books. Mem. Am. Coll. Legal Medicine (assoc.-in-law 1987), Am. Philos. Assn., Am. Soc. Bioethics and Humanities, Am. Soc. Law, Medicine and Ethics (health law tchrs. sect.), Toastmasters Internat. (pres. Raleigh chpt. 1978). Unitarian Universalist. Avocations: sailing, jogging, tennis. Home: 4905 Ridgeline Ln Fair Oaks CA 95628-6585 Office: U Calif Davis Med Ctr Bioethics Program 4150 V St Ste 2400 Sacramento CA 95817

RICH, CLAYTON, retired university official and educator; b. N.Y.C., May 21, 1924; s. Clayton Eugene and Leonore (Elliot) R.; m. Mary Bell Hodgkinson, Dec. 19, 1953 (div. May 1974); 1 son, Clayton Greig; m. Rosalind Morgan-Jones, Apr. 6, 1987. Grad., Putney Sch., 1942; student, Swarthmore Coll., 1942-44; MD, Cornell U., 1948. Diplomate Am. Bd. Internal Medicine. Intern Albany (N.Y.) Hosp., 1948-49, asst. resident, 1950-51; research asst. Cornell U. Med. Coll., 1949-50; asst. Rockefeller U., 1953-58, asst. prof., 1958-60; asst. prof. medicine U. Wash. Sch. Medicine, 1960-62, assoc. prof., 1962-67, prof., 1967-71, assoc. dean, 1968-71; chief radioisotope service VA Hosp., Seattle, 1960-70, assoc. chief staff, 1962-71, chief staff, 1968-70; v.p. med. affairs, dean Sch. Medicine; prof. medicine Stanford U., 1971-79, Carl and Elizabeth Naumann prof., 1977-79; chief staff Stanford U. Hosp., 1971-77, chief exec. officer, 1977-79. Sr. scholar Inst. Medicine, Nat. Acad. Sci., Washington, 1979-80; Mem. gen. medicine B study sect. NIH, 1969-73, chmn., 1972-73; mem. spl. med. adv. group VA, 1977-81; provost U. Okla. Health Scis. Ctr., Oklahoma City, 1980-92—, v.p. for health scis., 1983-92; also exec. dean, prof. U. Okla. Coll. Medicine, 1980-83, emeritus Regents prof. and provost U. Okla., 1993—. Editorial bd.: Calcified Tissue Research, 1966-72, Clin. Orthopedics, 1967-72, Jour. Clin. Endocrinology and Metabolism, 1971-72; Contbr. numerous articles to med. jours. Bd. dirs. Children's Hosp. at Stanford, Stanford U. Hosp., 1974-79; chmn. Gordon Research Conf. Chemistry, Physiology and Structure of Bones and Teeth, 1967; bd. dirs. Okla. Med. Research Found.; bd. dirs. Leadership Oklahoma City, 1981-92, v.p., 1985-92; bd. dirs. Okla. Blood Inst., 1982-92, Oklahoma City chpt. ARC, 1983-92. Lt. USNR, 1951-53. Fellow ACP, AAAS; mem. Assn. Am. Physicians, Western Assn. Physicians, Am. Soc. Mineral and Bone Research (adv. bd. 1977-80), Am. Soc. Clin. Investigation, Assn. Am. Med. Colls. (exec. council 1975-79), Inst. of Medicine, Western Soc. Clin. Research (v.p. 1967-68), Endocrine Soc., Assn. Acad. Health Ctrs. (bd. dirs. 1984-88, chmn. 1987-88), Sigma Xi, Alpha Omega Alpha. Office: 13450 64th Ter NE Kirkland WA 98034-1656 E-mail: claytrich@aol.com.

RICH, CYNTHIA GAY, elementary education educator; b. Jamestown, N.Y., Feb. 16, 1945; d. Alpheus T. and Gloria (Adler) Gable; m. David G. Rich, Aug. 26, 1967. BA in Elem. Edn., SUNY, Fredonia, 1967, MS in Elem. Edn. and Remedial Reading, 1971; EdD in Elem. Edn., Gifted and Talented Edn., Remedial Reading and Early Childhood, SUNY, Buffalo, 1989. Cert. tchr. elem., remedial reading, N.Y. Tchr. Ft. Carson (Colo.) Sch., 1967-68, Frewsburg (N.Y.) Cen. Sch., 1968-2000; ret., 2000. Presenter in field; cheerleading advisor Frewsburg (N.Y.) Cen. Sch., 1977-79; coun. for Spl. Edn., 1990-2000, student adv. bd., 1990-2000, chmn. early literacy com., 1998-2000, Reading coun., 1991-2000. Vol. Am. Cancer Soc., Am. Heart Assn., Mental Health Assn.; mem. Parent, Student and Tchr. Assn., 1968-2000, Chautauqua County Humane Soc., 1990—; mem. ednl. commn. First United Meth. Ch., Jamestown, N.Y., mem. parish commn., also Altar Guild, United Meth. Women; patron Little Theater of Jamestown, 1968—. Mem. AAUW (rec. sec., chairperson numerous programs, conv. del., v.p. 1994—), Bus. and Profl. Women (chairperson New Careerist), Internat. Reading Assn. (presenter New Orleans conf. 1989, Phila. conf. 1986), Green Thumb Garden Club, Order Ea. Star, Shriners Aux., Consistory Aux., Soc. for Prevention Cruelty Animals, Kiwanis (Disting. Kiwanian 1989-92, pres. 1991-93, Disting. Pres. Southwestern N.Y. 1991-92), Kiwanis Wives (pres.), Phi Delta Kappa (life, rec. sec., historian 1980—, Educator of Yr. 1988, Researcher of Yr. 1988).

RICH, DANIEL HULBERT, chemistry educator; b. Fairmont, Minn., Dec. 12, 1942; married, 1964; 2 children. BS, U. Minn., 1964; PhD in Organic Chemistry, Cornell U., 1968. Rsch. assoc. organic chemist Cornell U., 1968; rsch. chemist Dow Chem. Co., 1968-69; rsch. assoc., organic chemist Stanford U., 1969-70; asst. prof. pharm. chemistry U. Wis., Madison, 1970-75, assoc. prof., 1975-81, prof. dept. medical chemistry, 1981—, prof. dept. organic chemistry, 1988—, Ralph F. Hirschmann prof. medicinal and organic chemistry, 1994—. Cons. biorganic natural product study sect., NIH, 1981-85, chmn., 1985. Recipient H.I. Romnes award, 1980, Vincent du Vigneaud award, 1990, Hitchings award for innovative methods in drug design, 1992, Alexander von Humboldt award, 1993, E. Volwiler award Am. Assn. Colls. Pharmacy, 1995; fellow NIH, 1968. Fellow AAAS, Am. Chem. Soc. (Ralph F. Hirschmann award in peptide chemistry 1993, divsn. medicinal chemistry award 1991, A.C. Cope scholar 1999), Am. Assn. Pharm. Sci. (rsch. achievement award 1992), Am. Assn. Coll. Pharmacy (Volwiler award 1995). Am. Peptide Soc. (R.B. Merrifield award 1999). Achievements include research in synthesis in peptides and hormones, inhibition of peptide receptors and proteases, characterization, synthesis and mechanisms of action of peptide natural products. Office: U Wis Dept Med Chemistry 7109 Rennebohm Hall 777 Highland Ave Madison WI 53705-2222

RICH, DAVID BARRY, financial executive, accountant, entertainer; b. Bronx, N.Y., July 3, 1952; s. Steven and Gizella (Kornfeld) R.; m. Biverly Hayag, Dec. 6, 1995; 1 child, Suzanne Stephanie. BS in Health Adminstrn., Ithaca Coll., 1976; postgrad. in acctg., Bryant and Stratton Coll., Buffalo, 1977. Office mgr. Rubin Gorewitz, CPA, N.Y.C., 1977-78; auditor State of Ariz., Phoenix, 1979-83; internal auditor City of Phoenix, 1983-84; sales use tax auditor City of Mesa (Ariz.), 1984-98. Pres. Clovis Acctg. Inc., Mesa, 1980-94; rep. H.D. Vest Investment Inc., Irving, Tex., 1984-94; owner D.B. Rich Enterprises Import/Export, Chandler, 1992—; stage name Barry Rich, Stand-up Comedy, 1994—. Treas., bd. dirs. Missing Mutts Inc., Tempe, Ariz., 1986-88. With USAF, 1971-76. Fellow Nat. Assn. Tax Preparers; mem. Toastmasters (treas. Mesa 1986-87), Phi Beta Kappa. E-mail: mmem2@yahoo.com. *The world is one big neighborhood and we are all neighbors. If we will survive as a planet we must work together as friends. We must treat all people as our equals.*

RICH, DONNA BONEM, fundraising consultant; b. N.Y.C., N.Y., Feb. 13, 1942; d. Morton and Margaret (Spott) Cohn; Franklin S. Bonem, Aug. 9, 1964 (div. 1972); children: Julia, Jane; m. Martin E. Rich, Oct. 15, 1978. BA magna cum laude, U. R.I., 1963; MSW, Hunter Coll., 1976. Assoc. dir. devel. Henry St. Settlement, N.Y.C., 1978-80, dir. devel., 1980-82; asst. exec. dir. Lenox Hill Neighborhood House, 1982-86; regional dir. devel. Brandeis U., 1986-89; pres. Rich Assocs., 1989—. Chmn. Fund Raising Day in N.Y., 1986-87; instr. The New Sch., N.Y.C., 1995—. Bd. dirs. NSFRE Found. Mem. Nat. Soc. Fundraising Execs. (cert., nominating com., exec. com., pres. greater N.Y. chpt. 1990-91, bd. dirs. greater N.Y. chpt. 1984—), Hunter Coll. Alumni Assn. (bd. dirs. 1986-90). Democrat. Jewish. Home: 90 Riverside Dr 8C New York NY 10024 Office: Rich Assocs 2112 Broadway Ste 205 New York NY 10023 E-mail: donna@richassociates.com.

RICH, DOROTHY KOVITZ, educational administrator, author; BA in Journalism and Psychology, Wayne U.; MA, Columbia U.; EdD, Catholic U. Founder, pres. The Home and Sch. Inst., Inc., Washington, 1964—. Adv. coun. Nat. Health Edn. Consortium; adv. com. Ctr. for Workplace Prep. and Quality Edn., U.S. C. of C.; mem. readiness to learn task force U.S. Dept. Edn., urban edn. team Coun. Gt. City Schs.; legislative nat. initiatives including work on Family/Sch. Partnership Act, 1989, Improving America's Edn. Act, 1994; formulator New Partnerships for Student Achievement program, 1987; creator MegaSkills Edn. Ctr. The Home and Sch. Inst. Inc., 1990; designer MegaSkills Leader Tng. for Parent Workshops, 1988, MegaSkills Essentials for the Classroom, 1991, Learning and Working program for sch.-to-work initiatives, 1996, Career Megaskills, 1999, New MegaSkills Bond Tchr./Parent Partnership, 1994, Career MegaSkills materials and tng., 1998, Adult MegaSkills for Profl. Growth, 1999, MegaSkills Behavior Mgmt. Kit and MegaSkills Menebooks, 2002; developer NEA/MegaSkills nat. mentor tng. initiative, 2000—, MegaSkills for the Job, 2002. Author: MegaSkills in School in Life: The Best Gift You Can Give Your Child, 1988, rev. edit., 1992, What Do We Say? What Do We Do? Vital Solutions for Children's Educationsl Success, 1997, MegaSkills, 3d edit., 1997, 12 tng. books, MegaSkills: Building Children's Achievement for the Information Age, new and expanced edit., 1998; TV appearances include The Learning Channel, NBC Today Show, Good Morning Am.; subject of videos nat. ednl. programs in Thailand and China: Families and Schools: Teaming for Success, Survival Guide for Today's Parents. Recipient Am. Woman Leader award, Citation U.S. Dept. Edn., Nat. Gov.'s Assn., Alumni Achievement award in edn. Cath. U., 1992, Golden Apple award for MegaSkills Tchrs. Coll., Columbia U., 1996; grantee John D. and Catherine T. MacArthur Found.; named Washingtonian of Yr. Mem. Nat. Press Club. Office: MegaSkills Edn Ctr Home and Sch Inst Inc 1500 Massachusetts Ave NW Washington DC 20005-1821 E-mail: edstaff@megaskill.hsi.

RICH, ELIZABETH MARIE, nursing educator; b. Bklyn., Nov. 20, 1949; d. Oren Edward and Catherine (Raffaele) R. ADN, Grossmont Coll., El Cajon, Calif., 1983; BSN, U. Phoenix, 1988; MS, Nat. U., San Diego, 1991. Cert. pub. health nurse, gerontol. nurse. ICU-CCU staff nurse Villa View, San Diego, 1983-85, AMI Valley Hosp., El Cajon, 1985-86; nurse Nursing Registries, 1986-87; charge nurse, supr. nights Beverly Manor Convalescent Home, Escondido, Calif., 1987-88, dir. staff devel., 1988-90; DON, nurse educator cons. Vista Del Mar Care Ctr., San Diego, 1990; instr. vocat. nursing Maric Coll. Med. Careers, Vista, Calif., 1991—, curriculum coord., placement coord., 1992-94. Faculty St. John's U., Springfield, La., 1995—, instr. on-line courses, 1999. Mem. Calif. Vocat. Nurse Educators. Home: 872 Venice Gln Escondido CA 92026-3165 E-mail: lizrich@lizreducationalconsulting.com., whitewolfspirit2@aol.com.

RICH, FRANK HART, journalist, author; b. Washington, June 2, 1949; s. Frank Hart Rich and Helene Bernice (Aaronson) Fisher; m. Alexandra Rachelle Witchel, 1991; children from previous marriage: Nathaniel Howard, Simon Hart. BA in Am. History and Lit. with honors, Harvard U., 1971. Co-editor Richmond (Va.) Mercury, 1972-73; sr. editor, film critic New Times mag., N.Y.C., 1973-75; film critic N.Y. Post, 1975-77; film and TV critic Time mag., 1977-80; chief drama critic N.Y. Times, 1980-93; columnist N.Y. Times Sunday Mag., 1993; Op-Ed columnist N.Y. Times, 1994—. Author: (with others) The Theatre Art of Boris Aronson, 1987, Hot Seat: Theater Criticism for the New York Times 1980-93, 1998, Ghost Light, 2000. Assoc. fellow Jonathan Edwards Coll., Yale U., 1998—. Office: The NY Times 229 W 43rd St New York NY 10036-3959

RICH, GEORG, economist, bank executive; b. Schaffhausen, Switzerland, Nov. 11, 1939; s. Arthur Georg Rich and Elisabeth Schneider; m. Ruth Beatrice Bischhausen, 1980; children: Daphne, Clemens. Lic.oec.publ., U. Zurich, Switzerland, 1962; PhD in Econs., Brown U., 1969. Asst. prof., then assoc. prof. Carleton U., Ottawa, Ont., Can., 1967-78, chmn. dept. econs. Can., 1972-74; postdoctoral fellow Yale U., New Haven, 1974; economist, head rsch. Swiss Nat. Bank, Zurich, 1977-85, chief economist, 1985—. Vis. prof. Grad. Inst. Internat. Studies, Geneva, 1975; vis. scholar Grad. Sch. Indsl. Adminstrn., Carnegie Mellon U., Pitts., 1989; lectr. U. Zurich, 1978-95, U. Bern, Switzerland, 1980-81. Author monograph: The Cross of Gold. Money and the Canadian Business Cycle, 1867-1913, 1988; contbr. articles to profl. jours. Mem. Swiss Soc. for Stats. and Econs. (pres. 1999—2002), Am. Econs. Assn., Can. Econs. Assn., German Econs. Soc. Avocation: hiking. Home: Parkweg 7 CH 5000 Aarau Switzerland Fax: 41-62-8236916. E-mail: g-rich@richcons.ch.

RICH, JOHN MARTIN, humanities educator, researcher; b. Tuscaloosa, Ala., Dec. 14, 1931; s. Emanuel Morris and Bertha (Rose) R.; m. Martha Elaine Schur, June 6, 1955 (div. June 1966); children— Jeffrey Brian, Suzanne Elon; m. Joyce Ann Stegemoller, Aug. 28, 1967 (div. Mar. 1985); m. Audrey Faye Arnold, Aug. 1, 1987. BA, U. Ala., 1954, MA, 1955; PhD, Ohio State U., 1958. Grad. asst. Ohio State U., Columbus, 1955, asst. instr. edn., 1956-58; asst. prof. edn. U. Tenn.-Martin, 1958-60; assoc. prof. edn. Coll. SUNY-Oneonta, 1960-61; from asst. prof. to assoc. prof. Iowa State U., Ames, 1961-66; assoc. prof. social and philos. studies U. Ky., Lexington, 1966-69; prof. cultural founds. edn. U. Tex., Austin, 1969-96, prof. emeritus, 1996—, chmn. dept. cultural founds. edn., 1969-75. Vis. lectr. Nat. Kaohsiung (Taiwan) Normal U., 1993. Author: (books) Education and Human Values, 1968, Humanistic Foundations of Education, 1971, Portuguese translation, 1975, Korean translation, 1985, Challenge and Response, 1974, New Directions in Educational Policy, 1974, Discipline and Authority in School and Family, 1982, Professional Ethics in Education, 1984, Innovative School Discipline, 1985, Foundations of Education, 1992; co-author: Theories of Moral Development, 1985 (named an Outstanding Book of 1985-86 Choice mag.), 2d edit., 1994, Korean translation, 1999, Helping and Intervention, 1988, Competition in Education, 1992, The Success Ethic, Education, and the American Dream, 1996, Korean translation, 1998; editor: Readings in the Philosophy of Education, 1966, 2d edit., 1972, Conflict and Decision, 1972, Innovations in Education, 6th edit., 1992; co-editor, editl. adv. bd. Ednl. Studies, 1970-74, 77-80, 89-91; bd. contbg. editors Rev. Edn., 1977-85; editl. bd. Focus on Learning, 1980-84, Educational Foundations, 1985-91; bd. cons. Jour. Rsch. and Devel. in Edn., 1982-96, Ednl. Theory, 1991-95; contbr. articles to profl. jours., U.S., Can., Eng., Australia. Recipient Faculty Research Assignment award Univ. Research Inst., Austin, Tex., 1983-84; vis. scholar U. London, 1977; Univ. Research Inst. grantee, 1981-82, 84-85 Mem. North Central Philosophy of Edn. Soc. (pres. 1966-67), Ohio Valley Philosophy of Edn. Soc. (pres. 1967-68), Philosophy of Edn. Soc. (exec. bd. 1967-68, 80-82, Cert. Significant Svc.), Am. Ednl. Studies Assn. (exec. council 1972-74, pres. 1975-76) Home: 1801 Lavaca St Apt 8M Austin TX 78701-1312 Office: U Tex Edn Bldg 406 Austin TX 78712

RICH, JOSEPH DAVID, psychiatrist; b. Springfield, Mo., Apr. 22, 1939; s. William Daniel and Madge Lucile (Clark) R.; m. Judith Ann Briggs, Aug. 19, 1961; children: Joseph Curtis, David William, Scott Thomas. BA in Chemistry, S.W. Mo. State Coll., 1961; MD, U. Minn., 1965. Diplomate Am. Bd. Psychiatry and Neurology, Am. Bd. Forensic Examiners, Am. Bd. Forensic Medicine; lic. physician, Mont. Intern San Diego County (Calif.) Gen. Hosp., 1965-66; lt., gen. med. officer USN, Guam, 1966-68; resident in gen. psychiatry U. Kans. Med. Ctr., Kansas City, 1968-71; pvt. practice Billings, Mont., 1971—2001; med. dir. psychiatric unit Deaconess Med. Ctr., 1974-79, 85-88; med. dir. Deaconess Psychiat. Ctr., 1998—2001, Deaconess Behavioral Health Clinic, Billings, 1992—2001; med. dir. psychiat. svcs. Deaconess Billings Clinic, 1995—2001; pvt. practice forensic psychiatry, 2001—. Chief resident dept. psychiatry U. Kans., 1970-71; pres. med. staff Deaconess Med. Ctr., 1982; psychiat. cons. South Ctrl. Mont. Regional Mental Health Ctr., Billings, 1976-87, Indian Health Svc. PHS Hosp., Crow Agy., Mont., 1984-87, dept. spl. edn. Billings Pub. Schs., 1985-87. Mem. med. exec. com. No. Rockies Cancer Ctr., Billings, 1993—; med. dir. Yellowstone Boys and Girls Ranch, Billings, 1977-87 Fellow Am. Psychiat. Assn., Am. Coll. Forensic Examiners; mem. AMA, Mont. Psychiat. Assn. (pres. 1985, 96, sec. 1987, 88, legis. rep. 1986-96, Gladys V. Holmes award 1994), Mont. Med. Assn., Yellowstone Valley Med. Soc., Am. Acad. Psychiatry and the Law. Office: PO Box 21406 Billings MT 59104 E-mail: jdrich@yahoo.com.

RICH, JOSEPH JOHN, accountant; b. Detroit, Sept. 5, 1944; s. John H. and Edna R. (Swallow) R.; m. Carolyn A. Atkinson, Nov. 3, 1962 (div. Dec. 19, 1983); children: Marcella, Loren; m. Darlene E. Kornfehl, Aug. 2, 1985 (div. Sept. 20, 2000). A in Ins. Law, Am. Edn. Inst., 1974; A of Commerce, Alpena Community Coll., 1975. Accredited bus. acct. Pres. Tax Svcs., Inc., Portland, Mich., 1965—; claim specialist State Farm Ins., Marshall, 1966-80; owner Someplace Else Travel Ctr., Portland, 1990—2002, The Expresso Experience, 1995-2001, Benefit Mgmt. Corp., Portland, 1996—. Author: Insurance Guide for Theatres, 1977, Accounting for Non-Profit Theatres, 1976. Chmn. Ionia (Mich.) County Commn., 1986-90. Named one of Outstanding Young Men in Am., 1981. Mem. Portland Civic Club, Ind. Accts. Assn. of Mich., Comdrs. Club of Lansing. Republican. Avocations: theatre, travel. Office: Tax Svcs Inc 200 W Bridge St Portland MI 48875-1153 E-mail: JoeRich@voyager.net.

RICH, JOSEPH WILLIAM, engineering educator, consultant; b. New Orleans, Aug. 6, 1937; s. William Edward and Hortense Maud (Martinez) R.; m. Beatrice Mae Jewell, July 9, 1960; children: Grant Jewell, Anne Elizabeth. BSME, Carnegie Inst. Tech., 1959; MAE, U. Va., 1961; M.A., Princeton U., 1963, PhD, 1965. Aero. engr. Calspan Corp., Buffalo, 1965-71, prin. engr., 1971-82, mgr. laser physics and chemistry program, 1982-86; adj. prof. elec. engring. SUNY-Buffalo, 1983-86; vis. prof. mech. engring. Carnegie-Mellon U., Pitts., 1985; prof. mech. engring. Ohio State U., 1986—, Ralph W. Kurtz prof. mech. engring, 1996—. Contbr. articles to profl. jours. Patentee in field. Mem. Com. on Ednl. Goals, East Aurora (N.Y.) pub. schs., 1982-83. Panelist Joint U.S.-Japan Seminar on Molecular Energy Transfer, U.S. Nat. Acad. Scis., 1976; Guggenheim Found. fellow, 1961-65, Fulbright sr. fellow Ecole Centrale Paris, 1988. Fellow AIAA (assoc.); mem. Am. Phys. soc., AAAS, Sigma Xi. Democrat. Office: Ohio State U Dept Mech Engring 206 W 18th Ave Columbus OH 43210-1189

RICH, KENNETH MALCOLM, executive search and management consultant; b. Newark, Aug. 17, 1946; s. Lucien Ludwell and Grace (Hardy) R.; m. Sandra Ann Arrington; children: Stephen Montgomery, Khristine Nicole. AB in Chemistry, Lafayette Coll., 1967; MBA in Fin., Mktg., U. Chgo., 1969; cert. in acctg., NYU, 1979. Assoc., corp. fin. Kuhn, Loeb & Co., N.Y.C., 1969-73; spl. asst. to asst. sec. policy, devel. and rsch. HUD, Washington, 1973-74; mng. dir. fgn. investments The Dornbush Co., Atlanta, 1974; resident v.p. Citibank, N.A., N.Y.C., Athens and Dubai, U.A.E., 1975-78; mng., cons. divsn. Peat, Marwick, Mitchell & Co., N.Y.C., 1978-80; mng., strategic planning Gen. Elec. Credit Corp., Stamford, Conn., 1981-83; ptnr. Ray & Berndtson, Inc., N.Y.C., 1983—, also bd. dirs.; mktg. com. Paul R. Ray & Co., Inc., 1985-88, chmn. fin. svcs. practice com., 1989-92, fin. svcs. practice com., 1989—, chmn. investment com., 1995-96, stk. com., bd. dirs. practice group, compensation com., 1989-96, 98—, chmn. nominating com. of the bd., 2000—. Trustee Lafayette Coll., Easton, Pa., 1970-75. Chief umpire Ridgefield (Conn.) Little League, 1980-89; mem. Lafayette Leadership Coun., 1993-96; bd. dirs. Juvenile Diabetes Found. Internat., 1993-99, exec. com., 1995-96, chmn. nominating com., 1995-97, long range planning com., 1995, nominating com., 1993-99. Standard Oil of N.J. fellow U. Chgo., 1967-69; named one of N.Am.'s top exec. recruiters The New Career Makers (by John Sibbald), 1994. Mem. Assn. Exec. Search Cons. (bd. dirs. 1994-97, chair regional affairs com. 1995-97). Presbyterian. Avocations: reading, music, cross training. Home: 67 St Johns Rd Ridgefield CT 06877-5524 Office: Ray & Berndtson Inc 245 Park Ave New York NY 10171-0002 *At the end of the day, all anyone really has is his integrity. That is why I place such a high value on honesty, sincerity, empathy, and generosity. But unless you have a sense of humor, no one will ever notice your other virtues.*

RICH, LAWRENCE, Spanish language educator; b. Hong Kong, Aug. 6, 1951; s. Stanley and Doris (Logeman) R.; m. Celia Maria Escudero Espadas, June 27, 1989; 1 child, Ruben Salgado Escudero. BM, Peabody Inst./Johns Hopkins U., 1978, MM, 1981; cert. TESOL, Am. U., 1987; MA, NYU, Madrid, 1988; PhD, U. Md., 1995. Cert. in TESOL. Instr. music Pa. State U., State College, 1980-81; tchr. English, Thamesis, S.A., Madrid, 1981-86, ELS Internat. Taiwan Lang. Sch., Taipei, 1987; instr. English, Montgomery Coll., Rockville, Md., 1989; tchg. asst. U. Md., College Park, 1989-94; instr. Spanish, Univ. Coll., 1991, 93, 94, St. Mary's Coll. of Md., St. Mary's City, 1995-96, asst. prof., 1995-2001. Assoc. prof. No. Va. C.C., 2001—. Author: The Narrative of Antonio Muñoz Molina, 1999; contbr. articles to Dactylus, Romance Langs. Ann., Ariel, La Corónica, Revista canadiense de estudios hispánicos Hispania. Recipient scholarship and grant. Mem. MLA, Am. Assn. Tchrs. Spanish and Portuguese, Twentieth Century Spanish Assn. Am. Office: No Va Cmty Coll Divsn Humanities & Social Scis Alexandria VA 22311 E-mail: lrich@nvcc.vcc.edu.

RICH, LESLEY MOSHER, artist; b. Chgo., May 12, 1944; d. Robert Gollnick and Lillian Schmelzle; m. Keith Rich, July 6, 1995. Student, U. Ill., 1962-66, Inst. Allende, San Miguel de Allende, Mex., 1976-78. Cons., artist Med. Imaging Sys., Chgo., 1990-93; art instr., 1993—. One-woman shows include Palette & Chisel, Chgo., 1995 (Best Show of Yr. 1995), Gallery North, New Buffalo, Mich., 1995, 98, Birchstone, Egg Harbor, Wis., 1996, 1997; exhibited in group show at China Art Mus., Beijing, 1996. Artist At for Inner City, Chgo., 1988-89, Arusha (Tanzania) Women's Devel. Ctr., 1996. Recipient award of excellence Oil Painters of Am., 1994, Wichita Art Mus., 1994, Arts for Parks, 1996, 98, Am. Impressionist Soc., 2001, Hilton Head Nat., 2002. Mem. Palette & Chisel (Harriet Bitterly award 1994, award of excellence 1994), Am. Artists Profl. League, Pacific Art League, Allied Artists, Alla Prima Internat. Home: 4225 Park Blvd Palo Alto CA 94306-4144 E-mail: llrich@netzero.net.

RICH, LINVIL GENE, civil engineering educator; b. Pana, Ill., Mar. 10, 1921; s. Orville Cadell and Lillian Muriel (Watkins) R.; m. Peggy Jane Burton, June 17, 1944; children: Linvil Burton, Graham Watkins; m. Martha Darby George, Feb. 20, 2000. BS in Civil Engring, Va. Poly. Inst., 1947, MS in San. Engring, 1948, PhD in Biochemistry, 1951. Registered profl. engr., Va., Ill., S.C. Asso. prof. civil engring. Va. Poly. Inst., 1951-55; prof. civil engring. Ill. Inst. Tech., 1956-60; head dept. civil engring. Clemson (S.C.) U., 1960-61, dean engring., 1961-72, prof. environ. systems engring., 1972-82, Disting. Alumni prof., 1982-87, prof. emeritus, 1987—. Cons. U.S. Army, EPA. Author: Unit Operations of Sanitary Engineering, 1961, Unit Processes of Sanitary Engineering, 1963, Environmental Systems Engineering, 1973, Low Maintenance, Mechanically Simple Wastewater Treatment Systems, 1980, High Performance Aerated Lagoons, 2000. Fellow ASCE; mem. Am. Acad. Environ. Engrs. (diplomate), Am. Soc. Engring. Edn. Water Pollution Control Fedn., Sigma Xi, Chi Epsilon, Tau Beta Pi, Phi Kappa Phi, Phi Sigma, Phi Lambda Upsilon. Home: 117 Victoria Cir Anderson SC 29621-4058

RICH, MICHAEL JOSEPH, lawyer; b. N.Y.C., June 19, 1945; s. Jessee and Phyllis (Sternfeld) R.; m. Linda Christine Kubis, July 19, 1969; children: David lawrence, Lisa Diane. BA, Gettysburg Coll., 1967; JD, Am. U., 1972. Bar: Del. 1973, U.S. Dist. Ct. Del. 1973, U.S. Supreme Ct., 1976, Pa., 1981. Law clk. Del. Supreme Ct., Georgetown, 1972-73; assoc. Tunnell & Raysor, 1973-76; ptnr. Dunlap, Holland & Rich, P.A., 1976-80; gen. counsel Pearlette Fashions, Inc., Lebanon, Pa., 1981-83; assoc. Morris, Nichols, Arsht & Tunnell, Georgetown, 1983-86; ptnr., 1987-91, Twilley, Street, Rich Braverman & Hindman, P.A., Dover, Del., 1991-95; state solicitor, 1995-2001; dep. atty. gen., 2001—. Mem. Bd. Bar Examiners, Del., 1986-97, chmn., 1996-97;minority counsel Del. Ho. of Reps., Dover, 1977-79; mem. Del. Gov's Magistrate Commn., 1980, 83-86; sec. Del. Gov's. Jud. Nominating Commn., 1986-89. Bd. dirs. People's Place II, Inc., Milford, Del., 1973-77; pres. Bi-COunty United Way, Inc., Milford, 1977-78; mem. Partnership Greater Milford Commn., 1987-89, Friends Milford Library. Served to 1st lt. U.S. Army, 1967-69, Vietnam. Dean's fellow Am. U., 1971-72. Mem. ABA, Am. Judicature Soc., Del. Bar Assn. (pres. 1990-91), Sussex County Bar Assn. (pres. 1987-89). Republican. E-mail: mrich@deins.state.de.us.

RICH, MICHAEL DAVID, research corporation executive, lawyer; b. L.A., Jan. 23, 1953; s. Ben Robert and Faye (Mayer) R.; m. Debra Paige Granfield, Jan. 12, 1980; children: Matthew, William. AB, U. Calif., Berkeley, 1973; JD, UCLA, 1976. Bar: Calif., 1976. Extern law clk. to judge U.S. Dist. Ct., Boston, 1975; staff mem. RAND, Santa Monica, Calif., 1976-85, dir. resource mgmt. program, 1980-85, dep. v.p., 1986, v.p. nat. security rsch. and dir. Nat. Def. Rsch. Inst., 1986-93, sr. v.p., 1993-95, exec. v.p., 1995—. Chmn. bd. dirs. Coun. for Aid to Edn., 1996—; mem. governing coun. Internat. Inst. Strategic Studies. Author numerous classified and unclassified reports and articles. Bd. dirs. WISE Sr. Svcs.; mem. bd. councillors UCLA Found., 2000—; chmn. fin. oversight com., Santa Monica-Malibu Unified Sch. Dist., 2000—; mem. acad.

adv. bd. Fathom, 2000—; bd. advisers Santa Monica-UCLA Med. Ctr. Mem. Council Fgn. Relations. Office: RAND PO Box 2138 1700 Main St Santa Monica CA 90401-3297 E-mail: mrich@rand.org.

RICH, NORMAN MINNER, surgeon; b. Ray, Ariz., Jan. 13, 1934; s. George and Leona LuVerne Minner R.; m. Ann Lois Rich, June 20, 1959; children: Suzanne, Alison, David, Bethany. BA, Stanford U., 1956, MD, 1960, Cath. U., Santiago, Chile, 1977; MD (honoris causa), Mayab U., 2000. Diplomate Am. Bd. Surgery; cert. ATLS instr., med. care of catastrophes. Rotating intern Tripler Gen. Hosp., Honolulu, 1960-61; gen. surgery resident Letterman Gen. Hosp., San Francisco, 1961-65; chief surg. svc. 2d Surg. Hosp., Fort Bragg, N.C., and Rep. of Vietnam, 1965-66; chief vascular surgery svc. Walter Reed Army Med. Ctr., Washington, 1967-78, dir., vascular fellowship program, 1967-78; vascular rsch. coord. Armed Forces Inst. of Pathology, Edgewood Arsenal, Md., 1966-76; cons. in vascular surgery The Surgeon Gen. of the Army, Washington, 1970-82; chmn. dept. of surgery USUHS, Bethesda, Md., 1977—, prof. surgery, 1976—, mil. medicine, 1983—. Leonard Heaton and David Packard Prof., 1999; lectr. in field worldwide, including Scudder Oration/Am. Coll. Surgeons, Mitchiner Meml. Lectr./Royal Army Med. Coll.; cons. to nat. and internat. activities and mem. govt./specialty socs. Author/co-author books in field, including: (with Frank C. Spencer) Vascular Trauma, 1978; mem. 10 editl. bds. jours. in field. Decorated Legion of Merit, Bronze Star, Meritorious Svc. award, Vietnam medals, Medaille D'Honneur, France, others; recipient J.E. Wallace Sterling Lifetime Alumni Achievement award Stanford Med. Alumni Assn., 1999. Fellow Am. Coll. Surgeons, Am. Surg. Assn.; mem. Am. Assn. for the Surgery for Trauma, Am. Soc. for Vascular Surgery, Apothecaries of London, Am. Venous Forum, Assn. Acad. Surgery, Mexican Acad. Surg., French Surg. Assn., Chesapeake Vascular Soc., Ea. Vascular Soc., Halsted Soc., Hellenic Surg. Soc., Internat. Soc. for Cardio-vascular Surgery, Soc. of Univ. Surgeons, Soc. for Vascular Surgery, So. Assn. for Vascular Surgery, So. Surg. Assn., Royal Belgian Soc. of Surgery (assoc.), Royal Australian Coll. Surgeons (vascular sect.), Alpha Omega Alpha, numerous others. E-mail: nrich@usuhs.mil.

RICH, PHILIP DEWEY, publishing executive; b. Nashua, N.H., Feb. 1, 1940; s. John Parker and Olive Frances (Hussey) R.; m. Leslie Ann Burke, June 14, 1974 (div. 1982). AB magna cum laude, Harvard U., 1961; MA, NYU, 1962; postgrad., Princeton U., 1962. Editor Houghton Mifflin Co., Boston, 1964-73; asst. mng. editor UpCountry Mag. Berkshire Eagle, Pittsfield, Mass., 1976-77; editor Book Creations Inc., Canaan, N.Y., 1977-80, editor-in-chief, 1980-91, v.p., exec. editor, 1991-92; cons. editor Berkshire Ho. Publs., Lee, Mass., 1992-93, mng. editor, 1993-96, mng. editor and prodn. editor, 1996-99, editl. dir., prodn. dir., 1999—. Office: Berkshire House Pubs 480 Pleasant St Ste 5 Lee MA 01238-9265 E-mail: prich@bcn.net., philipr@berkshirehouse.com.

RICH, ROBERT WAYNE, cartoonist; b. Escanaba, MI, Nov. 10, 1953; s. John James Rich, Francis Pauline Rich; m. Gloria Ann Heitz; children: Robert. None, Ohio University, Athens, Ohio, 1972—74, Sinclair Community College, Dayton, Ohio, 1974—76. Editorial Cartoonist (freelance) New Haven Register, New Haven, 2001—; Editorial cartoonist/art director Connecticut Post, Bridgeport, 1992—2001; Staff artist Knoxville Journal, Knoxville, TN, 1991—91; Editorial Cartoonist New Haven Register, New Haven, 1983—90; Staff artist Knoxville News-Sentinel, Knoxville, TN, 1980—83. Mem.: National Cartoonist Society, Association of American Editorial Cartoonists. Roman Catholic. Avocation: Painting, sailing, running, naval history.

RICH, R(OBERT) BRUCE, lawyer; b. N.Y.C., Oct. 28, 1949; s. John J. and Sylvia (Berkenblit) R.; m. Melissa Jo Saxe; children— Megan, Alexander. A.B., Dartmouth Coll., 1970; J.D., U. Pa., 1973. Bar: N.Y. 1974, U.S. Dist. Ct. (so. and ea. dists.) N.Y. 1974, U.S. Ct. Appeals (2d cir.) 1980, U.S. Supreme Ct. 1980, U.S. Ct. Appeals (D.C. cir.) 1985. Assoc. firm Weil, Gotshal & Manges, N.Y.C., 1973-81, ptnr., 1981—. Contbg. author: Cultivating the Wasteland: Can Cable Put the Vision Back in TV?, 1983, The International Libel Handbook, 1995. Contbr. articles to profl. jours.; co-editor: Business and Legal Guide to Online-Internet Law, 1997. Mem. ABA (antitrust law sect., forum com. on communications law), Assn. Bar City N.Y. (com. on trade regulation 1982-85, communications law com. 1985-88), Phi Beta Kappa. Office: Weil Gotshal & Manges 767 5th Ave Fl Concl New York NY 10153-0119

RICH, ROBERT EDWARD, lawyer; b. Corbin, Ky., Feb. 4, 1944; s. Edward Bluch and Marjorie Brooks (Wentworth) R.; m. Janet Sue Shearer, May 14, 1966; children: Susan M., Christopher R., David E., Sarah M. AB, U. Ky., 1966; JD, Harvard U., 1969. Bar: Ohio 1970. Jud. clk. U.S. Ct. Appeals for 6th Cir., Louisville, 1969-70; assoc. Taft, Stettinius & Hollister, Cin., 1970, ptnr., 1978—. Pres. Lighthouse Youth Svcs., Inc., Cin., 1985, YMCA, Frankfort, Ky., 2001, Ctr. for Hope, Inc., Mt. Health, Ohio, 1991, Cin. Bar Found., 1991. Mem. ABA, Cin. Bar Assn. Republican. Presbyterian. Home: 215 Hilltop Ln Wyoming OH 45215-4121 Office: 1800 US Bank Tower 425 Walnut St Cincinnati OH 45202-3923

RICH, ROBERT F. law and political science educator; married; 3 children. BA in Govt. with honors, Oberlin Coll., 1971; student, Free U. of Berlin, 1971-72; MA in Polit. Scis., U. Chgo., 1973, PhD in Polit. Scis., 1975. Project dir., asst. rsch. scientist Ctr. for Rsch. on Utilization Sci. Knowledge, Inst. Social Rsch., U. Mich., lectr. dept. polit. sci., 1975-76; asst. prof. politics and pub. affairs Princeton U., 1976-82, coord. domestic and urban policy field Woodrow Wilson Sch., 1976-82; assoc. prof. polit. sci., pub. policy and mgmt. Sch. Urban and Pub. Affairs, Carnegie-Mellon U., 1982-86; prof. polit. sci. law, health resources mgmt., medical humanities and social svcs., community health, prof. Inst. Environ. Studies U. Ill., Urbana, 1986—, dir. Inst. Govt. and Publ. Affairs, 1986-97, acting head med. humanities and social scis. program Urbana-Champaign, 1988-90, prof. law and polit. sci., health resources mgmt., 1996—, prof. law; fellow Johns Hopkins U. Ctr. for Study of Am. Govt., Washington, 1993-95. Cons. U.S. Dept. Health and Human Svcs., Carnegie-Mellon U., 1986—, MacArthur Found., NIMH, 1988-89, Food, Drug and Law Inst., HHS, 1989, Am. Career Soc., 1996-97; disting. lectr. German Marshall Fund, Hamburg, Germany, 1997. Author: Social Science Information and Public Policy Making: The Interaction Between Bureaucratic Politics and the Use of Survey Data, 1981; co-author: Government Information Management: A Counter-Report of the Commission on Federal Paperwork, 1980; editor: Translating Evaluation into Policy, 1979, The Knowledge Cycle, 1981, Knowledge, Creation, Diffusion, Utilization, 1979-88, 88-91; co-editor: Competitive Approaches to Health Policy Reform, 1993, Health Policy, Federalism and the Role of the American States, 1996; assoc. editor Society, 1984-88, Evaluation Rev., 1985-89; mem. editl. bd. Policy Studies Rev. Series, 1980-83, Evaluation and Change, 1979-82, Law and Human Behavior, 1983-87; contbr. articles to profl. jours., book chpts. Recipient Emil Limbach Teaching award Carnegie-Mellon U., Sch. Urban and Pub. Affairs, 1985; fellow German Acad. Exch. Program, Fed. Republic Germany, 1971-72, Nat. Opinion Rsch. Ctr. fellow, 1972-73, German Govt. fellow, 1974, Russel Sage Found. Rsch. fellow, 1974-75; vis. scholar Hastings Ctr. for Society, Ethics and Life Scis., 1982. Mem. APA (task force on victims of crime and violence 1982-84), Soc. for Traumatic Stress Studies (bd. dirs. 1980—), World Fedn. for Mental Health (chmn. com. on mental health needs of victims 1985—, vice chmn. 1981-83, Robert F. Rich rsch. ann. award established in his honor, sci. com. on mental health needs of victims 1983), Howard R. Davis Soc. for Knowledge Utilization and Planned Change (pres. 1986-89), Polit. Sci. 400, Policy Studies Assn. (Aaron Wildausky award 1994), Phi Beta Kappa, Sigma Xi, Phi Kappa Phi. Office: U Ill Inst Govt & Pub Affairs 1007 W Nevada St # 204 Urbana IL 61801-3812 also: 815 W Van Buren St Chicago IL 60607-3506

RICH, ROBERT REGIER, immunology educator, physician; b. Newton, Kans., Mar. 7, 1941; s. Eldon Stahly and Margaret Joy (Regier) R.; m. Susan Jepsen Solliday, Mar. 22, 1974; children from previous marriage: Kenneth Eldon, Cathryn Louise. AB, Oberlin Coll., 1962; MD, U. Kans., 1966. Diplomate Am. Bd. Internal Medicine (bd. dirs. 1990-93), Am. Bd. Allergy and Immunology (bd. dirs. 1987-93, chmn. 1991); cert. spl. qualification Diagnostic Lab. Immunology. Intern, resident in internal medicine U. Wash., Seattle, 1966-68; clin. asso., chief clin. asso., sr. staff fellow NIH, Bethesda, Md., 1968-71; research asso. Harvard Med. Sch., Boston, 1971-73; asst. in medicine Peter Bent Brigham Hosp., 1972-73; asst. prof., assoc. prof. microbiology, immunology and internal medicine Baylor Coll. Medicine, Houston, 1973-78, prof., 1978-95, Disting. Svc. prof., 1995—, head immunology sect., 1978-98, chief clin. immunology, 1979-91, v.p., dean rsch., 1990-98; exec. assoc. dean, prof. medicine & microbiology/immunology Emory U. Sch. Medicine, 1998—. Investigator Howard Hughes Med. Inst., Bethesda, Md., 1977-91; mem. immunobiology study sect. NIH, 1977-81; mem. transplantation biology and immunology com. Nat. Inst. Allergy and Infectious Disease, 1982-86, chmn., 1984-86; mem. nat. ctr. grants com. Arthritis Found., 1983-86, chmn., 1984-86, nat. rsch. com., 1984-89, chmn., 1986-89, ho. of dels., 1985-91, Blue Ribbon com. on rsch. 2000-01; mem. rsch. adv. com. Nat. Multiple Sclerosis Soc., 1989-94, chmn., 1993-94; adv. panel on rsch. Assn. Am. Med. Coll., 1990—, shared responsibility advocacy com., 1997-98; chmn. ctrs. working group Nat. Inst. Arthritis Musculoskeletal Skin Diseases, 1996-97; mem. nat. human rsch. protections adv. com., dept. health and human svcs., 2000—. Assoc. editor: Jour. Immunology, 1978-82, sect. editor, 1991-96, deputy editor, 1997-2002, editor-in-chief, 2003--; assoc. editor: Jour. Infectious Diseases, 1984-88; adv. editor: Jour. Exptl. Medicine, 1980-84; mem. editl. bd. Jour. Clin. Immunology, 1989-96, Clin. and Exptl. Immunology, 1995—; editor-in-chief Clin. Immunology: Principles and Practice, 1996, 2d edit., 2001; contbr. articles to profl. jours. Served with USPHS, 1968-70. Recipient Research Career Devel. award NIH, 1975-77, Merit award NIH, 1987. Fellow ACP, Am. Acad. Allergy, Asthma, and Immunology (chmn. basic and clin. immunology interest sect. 1992-93, chmn. profl. edn. coun. 1996-98, v.p. 2001-2002), Infectious Diseases Soc. Am.; mem. AMA, AAAS, Am. Bd. Internal Medicine (diplomate, bd. dirs. 1990-93), Am. Bd. Allergy and Immunology (diplomate, bd. dirs. 1987-93), Assn. Am. Physicians, Am. Soc. Clin. Investigation, Am. Assn. Immunologists (chmn. pub. affairs com. 1994-2000, Disting. Svc. award 1999), Am. Assn. Investigative Pathology, Am. Soc. Microbiologists, Am. Fedn. Med. Rsch., Am. Clin. Climatological Assn. (councillor 2001-), Fedn. of Am. Socs. for Exptl. Biology (bd. dirs. 1998—, pres. 2001-02), Clin. Immunology Soc. (coun. 1990-96, pres. 1995), Alpha Omega Alpha, Sigma Xi. Office: Emory U Sch Medicine 1440 Clifton Rd NE Atlanta GA 30322-1053 E-mail: rrich@medadm.emory.edu.

RICH, ROBERT STEPHEN, lawyer; b. N.Y.C., Apr. 30, 1938; s. Maurice H. and Natalie (Priess) R.; m. Myra N. Lakoff, May 31, 1964; children: David, Rebecca, Sarah. AB, Cornell U., 1959; JD, Yale U., 1963. Bar: N.Y. 1964, Colo. 1973, U.S. Tax Ct. 1966, U.S. Supreme Ct. 1967, U.S. Ct. Claims 1968, U.S. Dist. Ct. (so. dist.) N.Y. 1965, U.S. Dist. Ct. (ea. dist.) N.Y. 1965, U.S. Dist. Ct. Colo. 1980, U.S. Ct. Appeals (10th cir.) 1978; conseil juridique, Paris, 1968. Assoc. Shearman & Sterling, N.Y.C., Paris, London, 1963-72; ptnr. Davis, Graham & Stubbs, Denver, 1973—. Adj. faculty U. Denver Law Sch., 1977—; mem. adv. bd. U. Denver Ann. Tax Inst., 1985—, global bus. and culture divsn., U. Denver, 1992—, Denver World Affairs Coun., 1993—, Coll. Arts & Scis., U. Colo., Denver, 2000—; mem. Colo. Internat. Trade Coun., 1985—; mem. Rocky Mt. Dist. Export Coun., U.S. Dept. Commerce, 1993—; tax adv. com. U.S. Senator Hank Brown; bd. dirs. Clos du Val Wine Co. Ltd., Danskin Cattle Co., Ouray Ranch, Areti Wines, Ltd., Taltarni Vineyards, Christy Sports, others. Author treatises on internat. taxation; contbr. articles to profl. jours. Bd. dirs. Copper Valley Assn.; actor, musician N.Y. Shakespeare Festival, 1960; sponsor Am. Tax Policy Inst., 1991—; adv. bd. Denver World Affairs Coun., 1993—; pres. So. Boulder Park Ecol. Assn., 1999—; sec. Bhutan Found.; bd. dirs. Alliance Francaise, 1977—, Denver Internat. Film Festival, 1978—79; trustee, sec. Denver Art Mus., 1982—; dir. Anschutz Family Found.; adv. bd. U. Colo. Coll. Arts and Sci., Denver, 2000—; pres., dir. Ouray Ranch, Granby, 2001—. Capt. U.S. Army, 1959—60. Fellow Am. Coll. Tax. Coun. (bd. regents 10th cir. 1992—), Soc. Fellows Aspen Inst.; mem. ABA, Internat. Bar Assn., Colo. Bar Assn., N.Y. State Bar Assn., Assn. Bar City of N.Y., Asia-Pacific Lawyers Assn., Union Internat. des Avocats, Internat. Fiscal Assn. (pres. Rocky Mt. br. 1992—, U.S. regional v.p. 1988—), Japan-Am. Soc. Colo. (bd. dirs. 1989—, pres. 1991-93), Confrerie des Chavaliers du Tastevin, Rocky Mt. Wine and Food Soc., Meadowood Club, Denver Club, Mile High Club, Cactus Club Denver, Yale Club, Denver Tennis Club. Office: Cherry Creek Sta PO Box 61429 Denver CO 80206-8429 also: Antelope Co 555 17th St Ste 2400 Denver CO 80202-3941 E-mail: robertrich@aya.yale.edu.

RICH, RUTHANNE, musician, educator; b. Salisbury, N.C., Dec. 20, 1941; d. Arthur Lowndes and Helen (Wall) R. MusB, Fla. State U., 1963; MusM, Peabody Conservatory of Music, 1964; diplôme de Virtuosité, Schola Cantorum, Paris, 1966; MusD, U. Rochester, 1973. Piano soloist various symphony orchs., 1957—, Europe, 1964—; artist-in-residence Mercer U., Macon, Ga., 1966-68; asst. prof. Lawrence U., Appleton, Wis., 1968-69; assoc. prof. Valdosta State U., Ga., 1971-73; prof. piano Kansas City (Mo.) Conservatory Music, 1974—2002, prof. emerita; piano soloist Asia, 1977—. Contbr. articles to profl. jours. Del. Edgar Snow Found., China, 1981, 84, Sister City, Macon, Ga.; with Kaohsiung, Taiwan, 1979. Recipient First Prize Nat. Biennial Contest Nat. Fedn. Music Clubs, 1961, Nat. Marie Morrissey Keith award Nat. Fedn. Music Clubs, 1962; Fulbright scholar, 1964-65; Hariett Hale Woolley Grant Found. des Etats-Unis, 1965-66. Mem. Music Tchrs. Nat. Assn., Mo. Music Tchrs. Assn. (v.p. 1975-78), Internat. Guild of Piano Tchrs. (Gold medal for Best Rec.). Avocations: karate, environmental issues. Home: 6537 Valley Rd Kansas City MO 64113-1822

RICH, S. JUDITH, public relations executive; b. Chgo., Apr. 14; d. Irwin M. and Sarah I. (Sandock) R. BA, U. Ill., 1960. Staff writer, reporter Economist Newspapers, Chgo., 1960-61; asst. dir. pub. rels. and communications Coun. Profit Sharing Industries, 1961-62; dir. advt. and pub. rels. Chgo. Indsl. Dist., 1962-63; account exec., account supr., v.p., sr. v.p., exec. v.p. and nat. creative dir. Edelman Pub. Rels. Worldwide, Chgo., 1963-85; exec. v.p., dir. Ketchum Pub. Rels. Worldwide, 1985-89, exec. v.p., exec. creative dir. USA, 1990-97, exec. v.p., chief creative officer worldwide, 1998—2001; pres. Rich Rels. A Creativity Consultancy, 2002—. Frequent spkr. on creativity and brainstorming; workshop facilitator. Contbr. articles to popular mags. Mem. pub. rels. adv. bd. U. Chgo. Grad Sch. Bus., Roosevelt U., Chgo., DePaul U., Chgo., Gov.'s State U. Recipient Pub. Rels. All-Star award for Creativity, Inside PR mag., 1999. Mem. Pub. Rels. Soc. Am. (Silver Anvil award, judge Silver Anvil awards), Counselors Acad. of Pub. Rels. Soc. Am. (exec. bd.), Chgo. Publicity Club (8 Golden Trumpet awards). Avocations: theatre, swimming, cycling, racquetball. Office: Rich Rels A Creative Consultancy Ste 2603 2500 N Lakeview Ave Chicago IL 60614-1846

RICH, SHARON LEE, financial planner; b. Houston, Sept. 7, 1956; d. Hershel Maurice and Hilda R.; children: Mariah, Sophie. BA, Cornell U., 1977; MAT, U. Chgo., 1978; diploma in fin. planning, Boston U., 1985; EdD, Harvard U., 1986. Registered investment advisor, Mass. High sch. tchr. Clear Lake High Sch., Houston, 1978-80; rschr. Harvard U., Cambridge, Mass., 1981-86; fin. planner, pres. Womoney, Belmont, 1984—. Instr. Cambridge Ctr. for Adult Edn. Co-author: The Challenges of Wealth, 1988; co-editor: Women's Experience and Education, 1985. Conf. organizer Haymarket People's Fund, Jamaica Plain, Mass., 1988—; spkr. Pub. Edn. Svcs., Boston, 1984—; organizer, mem. The Consortium, 1991—; referral for battered women B'nai Brith Women's Connection Card, 1991—95; co-founder Pride Planners LLP; treas. Beth El Temple Ctr., Belmont, 1999—2001, trustee, 1999—, chair social action com., budget com.; bd. dirs. Boston Women's Fund, 1988—90. Named One of Ams. Top Fin. Advisors, Worth Mag., 1994, 96. Mem.: Nat. Assn. Personal Fin. Advisors, Fin. Planners Assn. Avocations: parenting. Office: Womoney 76 Townsend Rd Belmont MA 02478-3435

RICH, THOMAS PAUL, engineering educator, administrator; b. Pitts., Nov. 18, 1943; s. Paul Felix and Jean M. (Ritter) R.; m. Mary Lou Colver, Aug. 5, 1967; children: Wendy Jean Rich Stetson, Thomas Wesley Rich. BSME, Carnegie Mellon U., Pitts., 1965; MSME, Lehigh U., Bethlehem, Pa., 1967, PhD in Mech. Engring., 1969. Engr. Peoples Natural Gas Co., Gibsonia, Pa., 1963, Blaw Knox Co., Pitts., 1964; rsch. mech. engr. Army Materials & Mechanics Rsch. Ctr., Watertown, Mass., 1970-73, 75-78; vis. prof. U. Southampton, 1974; assoc. prof. Mech. Engring. Dept. Tex. A&M U., College Station, 1978-81, Bucknell U., Lewisburg, Pa., 1982-86, dean engring., 1986-97, prof., 1986—. Mem. adv. bd. Ben Franklin Partnership, Pa., 1985-97, Pa. Small Bus. Devel. Ctrs., 1989-97; mem. Assn. Engring. Colls. Pa., 1986-97, pres., 1989-90; presenter in field. Editor: (book) Case Histories in Fatigue and Fracture Mechanics, 1986. Sponsor pre-coll. engring. activities for high sch. students Jr. Engring. Tech. Soc., 1989-97. Capt. U.S. Army, 1970-71. Recipient Wm. Spraragen award Am. Welding Soc., 1971; 12 external rsch. grants from fed., state and pvt. sources. Mem. ASME, Am. Soc. Engring. Edn., Am. Acad. Mechanics, Sigma Xi, Tau Beta Pi. Presbyterian. Avocations: hiking, camping, sports memorabilia, history of technology. Office: Coll Engring Bucknell U Lewisburg PA 17837

RICH, WALTER GEORGE, railroad transportation executive; b. Oneonta, N.Y., Jan. 9, 1946; s. George C. and Dorretta (Gregg) R.; m. Karine Schmook, July 14, 1990; children: Derik, Stephanie. BA, Syracuse (N.Y.) U., 1968, JD, 1971. Gen. mgr. Delaware Otsego Corp., Oneonta, 1966-68, v.p., gen. mgr., 1968-71, chmn., pres., CEO Cooperstown, N.Y., 1971—, N.Y. Susquehanna & Western Rwy., Cooperstown, NY, 1980—. Bd. dir. Delaware Otsego Corp., Cooperstown, Security Mut. Life Ins. Co. of N.Y., Energy East Corp.; chmn. bd. dir. Am. Shortline and Regional R.R. Assn.; mem. N.Y. Pub. Transp. Safety Bd., 1993—. Commr. of elections Delaware County, 1971-78; trustee Glimmerglass Opera, Cooperstown, 1986—; mem. N.Y. Gov. George Pataki's transition team, 1994; bd. dirs. N.Y. Bus. Devel. Corp., 1995—. Mem. Nat. Rwy. Hist. Soc., Eastern Gen. Mgrs. Assn. (pres. 1985, sec.-treas. 1986—), Lexington Group in Transp., N.Y. Athletic Club (N.Y.C.), Ft. Orange Club (Albany), Union League Club (Phila.). Episcopalian. Republican. Office: NY Susquehanna & Western Rwy 1 Railroad Ave Cooperstown NY 13326-1110 E-mail: wrich@nysw.com.

RICH, WILLIS FRANK, JR. banker; b. Ft. Dodge, Iowa, July 26, 1919; s. Willis Frank and Agnes Reed (Paterson) R.; m. Jo Ann Rockwell, Apr. 12, 1947; children: Ronald Rockwell, Roxanne, Andrew Paterson. BA, Princeton U., 1941. Credit analyst Northwestern Nat. Bank, Mpls., 1947-52, asst. cashier, 1952-55, asst. v.p., 1955, v.p., 1955-57; pres. N.W. Nat. Bank, Bloomington-Richfield, Minn., 1952-58, v.p., cashier, 1957-60, v.p. div. A, 1960-68, sr. v.p. nat. and internat. divs., 1968-73, exec. v.p., 1973-81, vice chmn. bd. dirs., chief credit officer, 1981-84; fin. cons., 1984—. Dir. Advance Acceptance Corp., 1985-2000. Pres. Viking coun. Boy Scouts Am., 1970-71, trustee found., 1971-86; mem. exec. bd. Minn. Cmty. Rsch. Coun., 1969-77; dir. Minn. Zoo, 1987-95; trustee St. Martin's Found., 1986-90; vestry mem. St. Martin's-By-The-Lake Ch. With AUS, 1941-46. Decorated Bronze Star. Mem. Robert Morris Assocs. (nat. pres. 1977-78), Mpls. Suburban Gyro Club. Clubs: Woodhill, Swan Lake Country. Episcopalian. Home: 378 Waycliffe Dr N Wayzata MN 55391-1390

RICHARD, ALISON FETTES, anthropology educator; b. Great Britain, Mar. 1, 1948; BA, Cambridge U., 1969; PhD, London U., 1973. Asst. prof. anthropology Yale U., New Haven, 1972-76, assoc.prof. anthropology, 1976-85, prof. anthropology, 1985—, provost prof., 1994—, Franklin Muzzy Crosby prof., 1998—. Dir. Yale Peabody Mus. Natural History, 1990-94. Bd. dirs. Yale-New Haven Health Svcs., 1994—, World Wildlife Fund, 1995—. Mem. Am. Primatological Soc., Am. Assn. Phys. Anthropologists, Am. Anthrop. Assn., Brit. Ecol. Soc., Primate Soc. Gt. Britain, Zool. Soc. London, Cambridge Philosophical Soc. Office: Office of the Provost Yale U New Haven CT 06520-8118

RICHARD, CHAVA WOLPERT, artist; b. Frankfurt, Germany, Feb. 26, 1933; arrived in Palestine, 1934; came to U.S., 1958; d. Ludwig Y. and Else (Ahrens) Wolpert; m. Henry A. Richard, 1959 (dec. Jan. 1971). Student, Bezalel Acad. Arts and Crafts, Jerusalem, 1954-56. Artist-in-residence The Jewish Mus., N.Y.C., 1958—88. Painter, designer/creator of contemporary style ceremonial Judaica such as candelabra, Passover sets, Torah ornaments in enamel, silver, other metals; represented in 10 mus. collections in U.S., Australia, Europe, Israel. Pvt. Israeli Army, 1953, 1951. Recipient 2 Merit awards Interfaith Forum on Religion, Art and Arch., 1980, 83, Jurors' Choice award Liturgical Art Guild, 1991, Best in Judaica award Liturgical Art Guild, 1997. Mem. Judaic Art Guild, Liturgical Art Guild. Avocation: reflexology. Studio: PO Box 750 783 Forest Hills Sta Forest Hills NY 11375

RICHARD, CONNIE LEON, education director; b. Chattanooga, Aug. 25, 1948; s. Elmer and Jean (Croon) R.; m. Janice Jackson, Aug. 15, 1970; children: Johari, Maisha. BA in Elem. Edn., Coll. Santa Fe, 1970; MA in Edn. Adminstrn. and Supervision, Seton Hall U., 1978. Cert. elem. tchr., edn. adminstr. and supervision, N.J. Tchr. Newark Bd. Edn., 1970-74, sch. coord., 1974-80, ctrl. coord., 1980-81, supr., 1981-84, dir., 1984—. Mem. N.J. Minority Groups Caucus, 1973-80; exec. bd. Newark Tchrs. Assn., Newark, 1977-80. Recipient edn. awards Essex County Civic Club, 1986, Phi Delta Kappa Sorority, 1991, Benedetto Croce Soc., 1991; Appreciation award Newark Guidance Counselors, 1989. Mem. Nat. Assn. Fed. Program Adminstrs., Nat. Coalition of Title I/Chpt. I Parents, N.J. Edn. Assn. (minority caucus 1973-80), N.J. Assn. Fed. Program Adminstrs., N.J. Congress of Parents and Tchrs., City Assn. Sch. Adminstrs. Avocations: camping, weight lifting. Home: 27 Howard St Irvington NJ 07111-3508

RICHARD, DAVID DEAN, publishing executive; b. Bloomington, Ind., Dec. 24, 1955; s. Elwood Eugene and Betty Jean (Lashley) R. BS, Ill. State U., Normal, 1978. Tech. writer Jewel Food Stores, Melrose Park, Ill., 1978-82; programmer, analyst The Ofcl. Airline Guides, Oak Brook, 1982-89; mgr. retail store The Fruitful Yield Corp., Glendale Heights, 1989-92, also bd. dirs.; brokerage mgr., import mgr. Health Co. Internat., 1992-96; mng. editorial publ. Vital Health Publishing, Bloomingdale, Ill., 1996—. Author: Gathering the Wind, 1993, A Seed, 1995, Stevia Rebaudiana, 1996, Anoint Yourself With Oil For Radiant Health, 1997, My Whole Foods ABC's, 1997; editor Taste Life: The Organic Choice, 1998. Democrat. Avocations: writing, music, poetry, singing, photography. Office: Vital Health Publishing PO Box 152 Ridgefield CT 06877 E-mail: vitalhealth@compuserve.com.

RICHARD, EDWARD H. manufacturing company executive, former municipal government official; b. Mar. 15, 1937; s. Henry and Ida Richard. BA, Antioch Coll., 1959. Pres., chmn., bd. dirs. Magnetics Internat. Inc., Maple Heights, Ohio, 1967-86; exec. v.p. Stearns Magnetics S.A., Brussels, Belgium, 1974-77; prin. Edward H. Richard & Assocs., Cleve., 1967-96; pres., treas. David Round & Son, Inc. Chmn. Cleve. dist. adv. council Small Bus. Adminstrn., 1975-79; former mem. nat. adv. council Dept. Treasury; cons. and advisor in field; del. world trade fairs. Former trustee Regional Econ. Devel. Coun., Met. Cleve. Jobs. Coun., Cleve. Devel. Found., Cleve. BBB; former trustee Hiram House, Antioch U., former treas., 1972-77; N.E. Ohio Regional Sewer Dist., Greater Cleve. Domed Stadium Corp., Greater Cleve. Conv. and Visitor Bur.; former trustee, vice-chmn. Cleve. Ctr. Econ. Edn.; former pres. Bratenahl Condominium Assn.; mem., chmn. fin. com. Bratenahl Bd. Edn., 1971-75; mem., bd. trustees, treas., chair fin. com. La Jolla Playhouse; chair bd. Mainly Mozart Festival, 1998—' mem. fin. com. San Diego Mus Art.

RICHARD, ELAINE, educational therapist; b. N.Y.C., Apr. 24, 1930; d. Jacob Michael and Mildred (Levenstein) Simon; m. Jack Richard, Apr. 11, 1954; children: Mark Steven, Susan Richard Weiller. BA, St. Lawrence U., 1950; MA, Columbia U., 1981. Cert. spl. edn. tchr., N.Y. Psychiat. social worker Ralph S. Banay, M.D., N.Y.C., 1950-54, 61-66; asst. to headmaster Dalton Sch., 1967-70; asst. to prin. Horace Mann Elem. Sch., 1970-72; dir. admissions Calhoun Sch., 1972-80; ednl. cons. Ethical Culture Schs., 1980-81; pvt. practice as ednl. therapist, 1981—. Bd. dirs. Ind. Schs. Admissions Assn. Greater N.Y., 1974-80. Creator "bright ideas" learning games for children, 2000. Mem. Internat. Reading Assn., Nat. Coun. Tchrs. Math., Assn. for Children with Learning Disabilities, N.Y. Orton-Dyslexia Soc. Avocations: theater, golf, travel. Home and Office: 501 E 79th St New York NY 10021-0735

RICHARD, GERALD LAWRENCE, retired soil scientist; b. Brush, Colo., Oct. 26, 1931; s. Donald Lehman and Gladys Lucile (Eikenbary) R.; m. Phyllis Darlene Hansen, Dec. 28, 1952; children: Donald Lawrence, Dale Kendall, Lori Ann Fosmire, Julie Lynn Young. BS in Agronomy, Colo. State U., 1956. Soil scientist Soil Conservation Svc., Wheatland, Wyo., 1957, Torrington and Cheyenne, 1959-65, work unit conservationist Laramie, 1965, area soil scientist Bellefonte, Pa., 1965-71, asst. state soil scientist Spokane, Wash., 1971-78; sr. soil scientist Soil Conservation Svc./U.S. Agy. for Internat. Devel., Lashkar Gah, Afghanistan, 1978-79, soil scientist/land use interpreter Kathmandu, Nepal, 1979-80; dep. co-mgr./soil scientist Soil Conservation Svc./Western Carolina U., 1980-82, team leader resource conservation project, 1982-85; state soil scientist Soil Conservation Svc., Boise, Idaho, 1985-89; cons. soil scientist Spokane, 1989—2001; ret., 2001—. Contbr. articles to profl. publs. 1st lt. U.S. Army, 1957-59. Mem. Am. Soc. of Agronomy, Soil

Sci. Soc. Am., Soil and Water Conservation Soc. (pres. keystone chpt. Pa. 1971), Washington Soc. of Profl. Soil Scientists. Methodist. Avocations: woodworking, fishing, travel. Home: 2709 S Post St Spokane WA 99203-1877

RICHARD, JACK, retired internist, medical association administrator; b. N.Y.C., May 24, 1929; s. Henry and Ida (Witkin) R.; m. Elaine Simon, Apr. 11, 1954; children: Mark S., Susan Richard Weiller. BA, Cornell U., 1950, MD, 1953. Diplomate in internal medicine, endocrinology and metabolism Am. Bd. Internal Medicine. Intern, resident in internal medicine N.Y. Hosp., N.Y.C., 1953-60; pvt. practice, 1960—2002; clin. prof. medicine Weill Med. Coll., Cornell U., 1987—; attending physician N.Y. Hosp., 1987—; med. coord. N.Y. State Dept. Health, New Rochelle, N.Y., 1994—. Mem. med. bd. N.Y. Hosp., 1975-79; mem. bd. overseers Cornell Med. Coll., 1996-99. Contbr. chpts. to books, articles to profl. jours. Mem. adv. bd. Cornell's Adult U., Ithaca, N.Y., 1990-97. Fellow Am. Coll. Endocrinology; mem. AMA, ACP/Am. Soc. Internal Medicine, Med. Soc. State N.Y., New York County Med. Soc. (bd. dirs.), Endocrine Soc., Am. Assn. Clin. Endocrinologists, Phi Beta Kappa, Alpha Omega Alpha. Avocations: tennis, skiing, photography, travel.

RICHARD, JAMES THOMAS, retired psychologist, educator; b. Phila., Dec. 18, 1937; s. Elwood and Anna F. (McCall) R.; m. Ruth Mary D. Guiniven, May 5, 1962; children: Marianne, James Jr., Susan, Barbara, Jeannine. BA, LaSalle U., 1960; EdM, Temple U., 1963, EdD, 1968. Lic. psychologist, Pa. Tchr., counselor Cardinal Dougherty H.S., Phila., 1960-62; dir. student affairs Temple U. C.C., 1962-67; prof. psychology Bucks County C.C., Newtown, 1967-2000; ret., 2000; prof. emeritus, 2000—. Pres., psychologist Newtown Psychol. Ctr., 1972—. Author: Not Too High, Not Too Low: Stress Management for Professional Baseball Players and Their Fans, 1991. Sgt. Pa. Nat. Guard, 1956-65. Fellow Pa. Psychol. Assn., Phila. Soc. Clin. Psychologists; ; mem. APA. Roman Catholic. Avocations: golf, photography, finance. Office: Newtown Psychol Ctr 660 Newtown Yardley Rd Ste 102 Newtown PA 18940-1759

RICHARD, NORMAN BERNARD, allergist; b. Perth Ambey, N.J., Mar. 16, 1926; children from previous marriage; Susan, Kenneth, Douglas, Barbara; m. Rachel D. Richard, July 12, 1981; 1 child, Jennifer. Student, Cornell U., 1946; MD, SUNY, 1950. Diplomate Am. Bd. Allergy and Immunology. Intern U. Pa. Grad. Hosp., Phila., 1951-52; resident Children's Hosp. Buffalo, 1953, fellow in allergy, 1954; pvt. practice Buffalo, 1954—. Clin. asst. prof. SUNY, Buffalo. Author: (jour.) Allergy, 1956. With USN, 1944-45. Fellow Am. Acad. Allergy and Immunology, Am. Coll. Allergy and Immunology, Am. Assn. Cert. Allergists; mem. Buffalo Allergy Soc. (past pres.). Avocations: tennis, traveling. Office: 1077 Delaware Rd Buffalo NY 14223-1056

RICHARD, PATRICIA ANTOINETTE, physician, dentist, inventor, author; b. Bridgeport, Conn., June 15, 1950; d. Mr. and Mrs. Richard. DMD, U. Conn., 1976; MD, Hahnemann U., 1980. Cert. sr. FAA med. examiner; cert. advanced clin. fellow Internat. Acad. Med. Acupuncture. Intern in internal medicine St. Vincents Med. Ctr., Bridgeport, Conn., 1980-81; resident in surgery U. Med. and Dentistry, Rutgers U., Camden, N.J., 1983-84; resident in internal medicine U. Hosp., Jacksonville, Fla., 1984-85; sr. resident in internal medicine Hartford (Conn.) Hosp., 1985-86; emergency medicine physician St. Francis Hosp., Hartford, 1985-87, U. Conn.-John Dempsey Hosp., Farmington, 1986-88, Bristol (Conn.) Hosp., 1986-87; pvt. practice in medicine, dentistry, acupuncture Fairfield, Conn., 1987—; biotech. R&D cons., 1987—. Mem. medico-legal com. Fairfield County Med. Assn., 1994—, Fairfield County Ctr. for Trauma and Internal Medicine, Temporomandibular Joint Disorders, Aviation Medicine and Biotech., R&D, 1993—. Author: Neurology for Attorneys, 1997; contbg. author: Pain Management: A Practical Guide for Clinicians, 1998, Reducing Pharmacological Medications with Medical Acupuncture; contbr. chpts. to book. Mem. Rep. Senatorial Inner Cir., Washington, 1992; perpetual mem. Franciscan Benefactors Assn., Mt. Vernon, N.Y., 1994; mem. Lourdes Prayer League, Shrine of Our Lady of Snows, Belleville, Ill., 1995. Recipient Rep. Presidential award Bd. of Govs.-Rep. Presidential Task Force, 1994. Fellow Internat. Acad. of Med. Acupuncture (cert.); mem. AIAA, AMA, ADA, Aerospace Med. Assn., Am. Bd. Forensic Examiners. Achievements include 4 patents in fields of hematology, metabolism, endocrinology, pharmacology and orthopedics. Office: PO Box 702 1735 Post Rd Fairfield CT 06824-0702

RICHARD, RAE LINDA, nurse practitioner, vascular access specialist; b. Bridgeport, Conn., Sept. 27, 1952; d. Normand and Rafaela (Medina Pavone) R. RN, BS, Point Loma Coll., San Diego, 1976; MSN, U. San Diego, 1998. Bd. cert. adult nurse practitioner, bd. cert. acute care nurse practitioner ANCC, RN 1st asst. Staff and rotating charge nurse in telemetry Scripps Meml. Hosp., La Jolla, Calif., 1976-80, intravenous therapist, 1981-82, coord. intravenous therapy dept., 1982-94, vascular access nurse clinician, 1994-99, Scripps Meml. Hosp., Green Hosp Scripps Clinic, 1996; nurse practitioner, vascular access specialist LaJolla Vascular and Surgery General, La Jolla, 1999—. Mem. nurse cons. bd. Abbott Labs., 1989-90. Mem.: AACN, Am. Coll. Nurse Practitioners, Calif. Coalition of Nurse Practitioners, Intravenous Nurse Soc. (cert. RN intravenous), Nat. Venous Access Network, Sigma Theta Tau (Zeta Mu chpt.). Office: 9850 Genesee Ave Ste 560 La Jolla CA 92037-1229 E-mail: raelrichard@aol.com.

RICHARD, ROBERT CARTER, psychologist; b. Waterloo, Iowa, Apr. 4, 1938; s. Quentin Leroy and Adeline Pauline (Halverson) R.; m. Shirley Ruth Jones, Aug. 25, 1962 (div. Mar. 1999); children: David, John; m. Jacqueline J. Mendes, Feb. 19, 2000. BA Wheaton (Ill.) Coll., 1960; BD, Fuller Theol. Sem., 1963, PhD, 1973; STM, Andover Newton Theol. Sch., 1964. Ordained to ministry Am. Bapt. Conv., 1963; lic. psychologist, Calif. Pastor Peninsula Bapt. Ch., Gig Harbor, Wash., 1965-68; marriage and family counselor Glendale (Calif.) Family Svc., 1970-71; psychol. asst. Oakland and Pleasant Hill, Calif., 1972-71; psychologist Rafa Counseling Ctr., Pleasant HIll, 1974—. Mem. faculty John f. Kennedy U., Orinda, Calif., 1975-78; adj. faculty mem. New Coll., Berkeley, Calif, 1986; co-founder, bd. dirs. New Directions Counseling Ctr., 1974-81; rschr. assertiveness tng., lay counselor tng., psychotherapy and religious experience, treatment of adults abused as children. Author: (with Deacon Anderson) The Way Back: A Christian's Journey to Mental Wholeness, 1989; contbr. articles to profl. publs. Recipient Integration of Psychology and Theology award, 1973. Mem.: APA, Christian Assn. Psychol. Studies, Contra Costa Psychol. Assn. (past pres.), Calif. Psychol. Assn. Republican. Baptist. Office: Rafa Counseling Ctr 101 Gregory Ln Ste 33 Pleasant Hill CA 94523-4915 E-mail: robertcrichard@cs.com.

RICHARD, ROBERT MAX, cardiologist; b. Harmon, Okla., Sept. 11, 1926; s. Rolla Roy and Edith Belle (Drake) R.; m. Betty Ann Heavin, Aug. 14, 1948; 1 child, Robert Max. PhD in biochemistry, U. Wis., 1952; MD, U. Okla., 1961; postgrad., U. So. Calif., 1962-67. Physician specialist in internal medicine L.A. County, 1967-90, Motion Picture and TV Hosp., Woodland Hills, Calif., 1967-69; cardiology specialist Rancho Los Amigos Hosp.-U. So. Calif., Downey, 1969-72; assoc. prof. medicine, sect. cardiology U. So. Calif., L.A., 1973-90; cardiology specialist, dir. So. Calif. Heart Inst., Newport Beach, Laguna Beach, Calif., 1991—; staff cardiologist U. So. Calif. Diagnostic Ctr., Norris Cancer Hosp.-U. So. Calif., Doheny Eye Inst.-U. So. Calif., Univ. Hosp.-U. So. Calif. Author: Electrocardiography, 1980, Electrocardiology-Vector Cardiology, 1999, Holtre Monitoring and Exercise Stress Testing, 2001. With USN, 1945-46. Fellow Am. Coll. Cardiology (Outstanding Young Cardiologist 1975, Honoree plaque Dr. George Griffith Meml. Libr. 1975, Heart House Outstanding Cardiology 50th Anniversary 1999); mem. AMA (Master of Profession award 1993), AHA, Am. Soc. Internal Medicine, Oil Prodr. Soc. Okla., Phi Kappa Phi, Phi Lambda Upsilon, Sigma Xi. Republican. Presbyterian. Office: 522 Emerald Bay Laguna Beach CA 92651-1270

RICHARD, ST. CLAIR SMITH, editor; b. Newton, Iowa, Nov. 16, 1910; d. William Walter and Nelle Grace (Van Dusseldorp) Smith; m. George Charles Richard, Dec. 3, 1933; children: Thomas, Randall, D. du Chane. BS, Columbia U., 1933. Mng. ptnr. Halo House, Larchmont, N.Y., 1946—; journalism instr. Good Counsel Coll., White Plains, 1961-64; pub. rels. dir. Westchester Libr. Sys., Mt. Vernon, 1966-71; pub. info. officer Westchester Med. Ctr., Valhalla, 1974-76; editor Sound View News, Larchmont, 1986—. Author: Women in Public Service, 1964. Press sec. Rep. State Com., Albany, 1964-65; mem. pub. rels. com. Westchester Dem. Com., White Plains, 1972-74; campaign dir. Dems., White Plains, 1972-74, Mt. Vernon, 1960, Reps., Mamaroneck, N.Y., 1955-56; active ARC, Mt. Vernon, 1936; exec. dir. Mcpl. Ofcls. Westchester, 1969-89. Mem. Woman's Club of Mamaroneck (v.p. 1998—), Westchester County Fedn. Woman's Club (pres. 1987-89), Delta Gamma. Episcopalian. Home and Office: 60 The Blvd New Rochelle NY 10801-2813

RICHARD, SUSAN MATHIS, communications executive, screenwriter; b. Detroit, June 21, 1949; d. Robert Louis and Maybelle Ann (Kromm) Engel; m. Paul Carl Mathis, May 12, 1973 (div. 1982); m. Robert Stephen Richard, Oct. 26, 1985. BA, U. Mich., 1971. Cert. tchr., Mich. Tchr. Carl Brablec High Sch., Roseville, Mich., 1971-73; anchorperson, producer Sta. WNCC-Cable TV, East Lansing, 1973-76; press asst. Ford-Dole Presdl. Campaign, Washington, 1976; TV and radio reporter Cox Communications, 1977-81; dep. dir. media rels. White House, 1981-84, spl. asst. to Pres., dir. media rels., 1985-87; mgr. pub. rels. Walt Disney World, Lake Buena Vista, Fla., 1987-88; v.p. industry communications Nat. Cable TV Assn., Washington, 1989; dep. assoc. adminstr. for pub. affairs NASA, 1990-93; v.p. Dittus Comm., 1998-2000; mgr. press rels. INTEL, 2000—. Mem. exec. com. Radio-TV Corrs. Galleries, Washington, 1978-81. Dir. promotions Action for Children's TV, East Lansing, 1975; mem. Strategic Planning Adv. Coun. of the Orange County (Fla.) Pub. Schs., 1988; communications dir. Bush-Quayle Fla. Campaign, 1988. Named Outstanding Young Working Woman, Lansing C. of C., 1975, Outstanding Working Woman, Washington Woman mag., 1985. Mem. AAUW (bd. dirs. Lansing chpt. 1974), Am. Soc. Assn. Execs. (Pub. Rels. trophy 1994), Radio-TV News Dirs. Assn., Fla. Youth and Family Svcs. Network (bd. dirs. 1988), Acad. TV Arts and Scis. (pub. rels. com. 1989), Women in Aerospace, Women in Wireless, Women in Film and Video, Washington Women in Pub. Rels., U. Mich. Alumni Assn. (bd. dirs. 1983-85), Gamma Phi Beta Alumnae Assn. Episcopalian.

RICHARD, TIMOTHY C. journalist, editor; b. Detroit, Nov. 5, 1935; s. Clemens L. and Eleanore A. Richard; m. Nancy A. Jeschke, June 10, 1961. BA, U. Mich., 1957, MBA, 1959; AA (hon.), Schoolcraft Coll., 1980, Oakland C.C., Bloomfield, Mich., 1988. Asst. news editor The Herald-Press, St. Joseph, Mich., 1961-62; reporter, bus. editor Kalamazoo Gazette, 1962-67; editor, state capitol corr. HomeTown Comm. Corp., Livonia, Mich., 1967-99; corr. Manistee (Mich.) News Advocate, 1999—. Editor: Making Healthy Tomorrows, 1993, Awake to Nature, 1994. Regional amb. S.E. Mich. Coun. of Govts., 1988. Recipient Wade McCree Jr. award for advancement of justice State Bar of Mich., 1995; named George Pierrot Journalist of Yr., Wayne State U., Detroit, 1997; inducted to Mich. Journalism Hall of Fame, East Lansing, 1998. Mem. Soc. Profl. Journalists (freedom of info chair metro Detroit chpt. 1988-99). Avocation: dog performance competition. Home: 6362 Potter Rd Bear Lake MI 49614 E-mail: trichard@bearlake-net.com.

RICHARD, ZACHARY, singer, songwriter, poet; b. Lafayette, La. s. Eddie Joseph and Marie Pauline (Boudreaux) R. BA summa cum laude, Tulane U., New Orleans, 1972. Singer/songwriter: Bayou des Mysteres, 1976, Mardi Gras, 1977, Migration, 1978, Allons Danser, 1979, Live in Montreal, 1980. Vent D'Eté, 1981, Zack Attack, 1984, Looking Back, 1986, Zack's Bon Ton, 1988, Mardi Gras Mambo, 1989, Women in the Room, 1990, Snake Bite Love, 1992, Cap Enragé, 1996 (Double Platinum Recording Inst. Assn. Am. Can. 1997), Travailler C'est Trop Dur, 1999, Coeur Fidele, 2000 (cert. Gold); innovator Cajun and Zydeco musical styles; author: (poetry) Voyage de Nuit, 1988, Faire Récolte, 1997; author: Feu, 2001, (children's book) Conte Cajun, 1999; prodr., narrator, mus. supr. (TV documentary) Against the Tide, The Story of the Cajun People of Louisiana; co-prodr. Contre vents, contre marees, portrait du peuple Cajun. Decorated Officier de l'Ordre Des Arts et Lettres de la République Français; recipient Cert. Gold Album for Migration, L'industrie Canadienne de l'enregistrement, 1978, Cert. Gold 45 L'Arbre est dans ses feuilles, 1978, Prix de la jeune Chanson Française, Ministre de la Culture de France, 1980, Prix Miroir Festival D'été de Québec, 1996, Prix Champlain Littéraire, 1999, Disquaire du Quebec, Felix, Assn. Disquaire du Quebec, 1997, 1998, 1999, Prix du Publique, Sept Iles, 2000, Chanson de l'Annee award, Cajun French Music Assn., 2002. Mem. L'Ordre Français d'Amérique. Avocations: painting, swimming, kyudo, tea ceremony, ornithology. Home: PO Box 1378 Scott LA 70583-0305

RICHARDS, ALETA WILLIAMS, marketing and quality professional; b. Pitts., Nov. 16, 1965; d. John Quincy and Sara Ann (Dorman) Williams; m. Frank D. Richards III, Nov. 16, 1982; 1 child, Cassandra Nicolle. BSBA, U. Pitts., 1990, MBA, 1998. Asst. to exec. directory Allegheny County Pvt. Industry Coun., Pitts., 1984-90; co-owner Richards Properties, 1991-93; tech. mktg. rep. II Miles, Inc., 1990-94, bus. champion Miles re-engring. project, 1995; cons. AWR Comm., 1994-97; mgr. continuous improvement Bayer Corp., 1996-99, leader Chlor- Alkali Mgmt. Team, 1999, bus. group mgr. Chlor-Alkali/Acids Bus. Group, 2000—01, sr. mgr. strategic planning, 2001—. Spkr. employment Salem (W.Va.)-Teikyo U., 1991-92. Author, editor: (reference book) Funding Resources Guide, 1989. Bd. dirs. Ptnrs. in Self-Sufficiency, Pitts., 1986-90. Recipient Mayor's Recognition award City of Pitts., 1990. Mem.: NAFE, The Chlorine Inst., Am. soc. Quality, River City Elite Track Club (treas. 1995—98, v.p. 2000). Home: PO Box 2816 Pittsburgh PA 15230-2816 E-mail: aleta-w.richards.b@bayer.com.

RICHARDS, ANN, actress, poet; b. Sydney; came to U.S., 1942; d. Mortimer Delaforce and Marion Bradshaw (Dive) Richards; m. Edmond J. Angelo, Feb. 4, 1949 (dec. Mar. 1983); children: Christopher E., Mark R., Juliet M.; m. Paul M. Kramer, Feb. 14, 1987 (dec. Aug. 1996). Student, Stotts Coll., 1936-37, Studio Sch. of Drama, 1936-38. Actress Cinesound Studio, Australia, 1936-42, Metro-Goldwyn Mayer, 1942-45, Hall Wallis-Paramount, 1945-47, R.K.O., 1947, Eagle-Lion Studios, 1947-48, Edmond Angelo Prodns., 1953, Anthony Buckley Prodns., Australia, 1995. Poetry reader with Robert Pinsky's nat. program Lib. of Congress Bicentennial Project, 1999. Author: The Grieving Senses, 1971, Odyssey for Edmond, 1996, New Poems-Old Themes, 1997; contbr. poetry to anthology Poetry From the Art, 1999; actress films including An American Romance, Love Letters, The Searching Wind, Badman's Territory, Sorry, Wrong Number, Lost Honeymoon, Breakdown, Don't Call Me Girlie, Celluloid Heroes, 1994-95; appearances TV program, film, and tape maker Australia, Time Life Assocs., 1977. Vice pres. Tchr. Remembe-rance Day Found., 1952—; internat. chmn. Apple of Gold Edn. awards, 1953—. Recipient meritorious svc. citation Govs. of Great Britain, U.S., New Zealand, Australia, 1939-46, Star Pattern award Inst. Profl. Direction, 1951, Cert. of Appreciation award Literacy is Reading Program, 1997, Edward Dean Mus., 1996. Mem. AAUW, Nat. Mus. Women in Arts, San Gorgonio Poets Soc., San Gorgonio Artists Soc., Zeta Phi Eta (v.p. nat. coun. 1970-73).

RICHARDS, ANN WILLIS, former governor; b. Lakeview, Tex., Sept. 1, 1933; d. Cecil and Ona Willis; children: Cecile, Daniel, Clark, Ellen. BA, Baylor U., 1954; postgrad., U. Tex., 1954-55. Cert. tchr. Tex. Tchr. Austin Ind. Sch. Dist., Tex.; mgr. Sarah Weddington Campaign, Austin, 1972, adminstrv. asst., 1973-74; county commr. Travis County, 1976-82; treas. State of Tex., 1983-91, gov., 1991-95; sr. advisor Verner, Liipfert, Bernhard, McPherson & Hand, Austin, 1995—; with Pub. Strategies Inc., 2001—. Chair Dem. Nat. Conv. 1992; Austin Transp. Study, Tex., 1977-82, Capital Indsl. Devel. Corp., Austin, Tex., 1980-81, Spl. Commn. Delivery Human Services in Tex., 1979-81; Dem. com. Southern Governor's Assn. Travis County Dem. com. Author (with Peter Knobler): Straight From the Heart, 1989. Com. mem. strategic planning Dem. Nat. Com., 1983; keynote speaker Dem. Nat. Conv., 1988. Named Woman of Yr. Tex. Women's Polit. Caucus, 1981, 83. Mem. Nat. Govs. Assn. Office: Public Strategies Inc 98 San Jacinto Ste 900 Austin TX 78701

RICHARDS, BERNARD, investment company executive; b. N.Y.C., July 12, 1927; s. Charles and Sadie (Rubin) R.; m. Arlene Kaye, Dec. 23, 1948; children: Carol Leslie, Patricia Ellen, Lori Gale. BBA, Baruch Coll., 1949. CPA, N.Y. Acct. Eisner & Lubin, N.Y.C., 1949-53, S.D. Leidesdorf, N.Y.C., 1953-56; from controller to treas. to v.p. fin. to pres. Slattery Group Inc., 1956-87; pres. Slattery Investors Corp., 1988—; chmn. bd. dirs. Slattery Assocs., Inc., 1968-87. Trustee Temple Sinai, Roslyn, N.Y., 1987-89; bd. dirs. Variety Boys Club, Queens, N.Y., 1972-96; bd. dirs. N.Y.C. Indsl. Devel. Bd., 1973-76; bd. dirs. Baruch Coll. Fund, N.Y.C., 1975—, pres., 1996-98, Man Yr., 1972. Recipient Heavy Constrn. award United Jewish Appeal, 1980, Pres.'s medal Baruch Coll., 1989; named Oustanding Alumnus of Yr. Baruch Coll., 1979, Man of Yr. United Jewish Appeal, 1980, March of Dimes, 1983; Wood fellow Baruch Coll., 1979. Mem. AICPA, N.Y. State Soc. CPAs, Moles, Beavers (bd. dirs. 1982-96), Shelter Rock Tennis Club. Republican. Jewish. Avocations: tennis, travel, cycling, swimming, hiking. Home: 18 Applegreen Dr Old Westbury NY 11568-1203 Office: Slattery Investors Corp 1 Hollow Ln Ste 311 New Hyde Park NY 11042-1215

RICHARDS, CARMELEETE A. computer training executive, network administrator, consultant; b. Springport, Ind., Feb. 8, 1948; d. Gordon K. and Virginia Christine (New) Brown; 1 child, Annasheril. AA in Elem. Edn., No. Okla. Coll., 1969; BS in Edn., Southwestern State Coll., Weatherford, Okla., 1971; postgrad., Ashland (Ohio) Coll., 1981—; postgrad. in Edn., U. Phoenix, 1994—. Cert. tchr., Ohio. 6th grade tchr., Scott City, Kans., 1971; salesperson, customer svc. Jafra Cosmetics, 1979-81; br. asst. mgr. Barclays Am. Fin., Columbus, 1981-84; tng. mgr., ednl. dir. Computer Depot, Ohio, 1984-85; corp. trainer, exec. sales Litel Telecommunications, Worthington, 1985-87; communications cons. Telemarketing Communications of Columbus, 1988-89; corp. computer tng. O/E Learning, Troy, Mich., 1989-98; corp. computer trainer ETOP Cols., Ohio, 1989—; dist. asst. network adminstr. Bexley Sch. Dist., 1998-99. Pres. PTA, 1981-82. Recipient Outstanding Participation award Dorothy Carnegie Pub. Speaking; winner Ms. Ohio Beauties of Am. Pageant, 1991. Mem. NAFE, Am. Soc. for Tng. and Devel., Columbus Computer Soc., Kappa Delta Pi. Baptist. Avocations: western square dancing, bowling, boating, reading, hiking.

RICHARDS, CAROL ANN RUBRIGHT, editor, columnist; b. Buffalo, Sept. 24, 1944; d. Jesse Bailey and Emma Amanda (Fisher) Rubright; m. Clay F. Richards, Aug. 12, 1967; children: Elizabeth Amanda, Rebecca Diana. BA, Syracuse U., 1966. Reporter Rochester (N.Y.) Times-Union, 1966; legis. corr. Gannett News Svc., Albany, N.Y., 1967-73, White House corr. Washington, 1974-76, regional/nat. editor, 1979-84; founding editor USA Today, Arlington, Va., 1982, mem. editl. bd., 1985-87; dep. editor editl. page Newsday, Melville, N.Y., 1987—. Pres. Washington Press Club, 1981-82; trustee Northport Hist. Soc. Mem. Nat. Press Club. Home: 352 Scudder Ave Northport NY 11768-3021 Office: Newsday 235 Pinelawn Rd Melville NY 11747-4250

RICHARDS, CHARLES FRANKLIN, JR. lawyer; b. Evergreen Park, Ill., Jan. 30, 1949; s. Charles Franklin and Mary Corinne (Joyce) R.; m. Maureen Patricia Duffy, June 17, 1972 (div. Mar. 1989); m. Deborah Ann Murphy, May 20, 1991; children: Patrick, Corrine, Meghan, Shannon, Nicole. BA, St. Mary's of Minn., 1971; JD, U. Ill., 1974. Bar: Minn. 1974, U.S. Dist. Ct. Minn. 1974, Ariz. 1985, U.S. Dist. Ct. Ariz. 1985, U.S. Ct. Appeals (9th cir.) 1985; cert. civil trial adv. Nat. Bd. Trial Advocacy. Asst. city atty. City of Rochester, Minn., 1974-76; assoc., then ptnr. O'Brien, Ehrick, Wolf, Deaner & Downing, Rochester, 1976-85; assoc., shareholder Gallagher & Kennedy, PA, Phoenix, 1985-94; pvt. practice, 1994—. Judge pro tem Ariz. Ct. Appeals, 1994. Contbr. articles to legal publs. Bd. dirs. St. Mary's Hosp., Rochester, 1983-85; del. Dem. Nat. Conv., San Francisco, 1984. Mem. ABA, ATLA, State Bar Ariz. (exec. coun. trial practice sect. 1994-99, mem. civil jury instrns. com. 1994-2000, co-editor Trial Practice Newsletter 1990-99), Minn. Bar Assn. Roman Catholic. Avocations: golf, bicycling, hiking, reading, astronomy. Office: 1202 E Missouri Ste 150 Phoenix AZ 85014 E-mail: cfr@rlopc.com.

RICHARDS, CONSTANCE ELLEN, nursing school administrator, consultant; b. Exeter, N.H., June 21, 1941; d. Edward Nowell and Mary Isabel (Bean) R. BSN, U. Cin., 1971, MA in Pub. Adminstrn., MS in Comprehensive Health Planning, U. Cin., 1973. RN, Mass. Nurse ICU/Opening CCU Syracuse (N.Y.) Meml. Hosp., 1964; instr. ICU and CCU Crouse-Irving Meml. Hosp., Syracuse, 1967-72; instr. cardiovascular, orthopedic and surg. The Christ Hosp., Cin., 1973-78; instr. med.-surg. nursing Md. Gen. Hosp., Balt., 1978-80; night supr. Manor Care Ruxton, Towson, 1980-82; adult health svcs. mgr. Exeter Vis. Nurses Assn., 1982-83; dir. insvc. edn. Bethany Hosp., Framingham, Mass., 1983-85; assoc. prof. nursing Mass. Bay C.C., 1985-86; instr. insvc. edn. Brockton-West Roxbury (Mass.) VA Hosp., 1986-87; staff nurse Charles River Hosp., Wellesley, Mass., 1987-88; night supr. Blair House, Milford, 1988-89; staff nurse psychogeriatrics Worcester State Hosp., 1989-90; with Agys. Internat. Health Talent Tree, Olsten Health Care Svcs., 1990-92; with indsl. svcs. program, CNA tng. program Northampton State Hosp., 1992; nursing asst., state tester ARC, 1992-93; pres. Caring Hands, Inc., 1993—; DON Excel Health Svcs., Inc., 1993—. Instr. LPN evening program Greater Lowell Regional Vocat. Tech. Sch., 1992-94; adv. bd. Excel Health Svcs., Tewksbury, Mass., 1993-94; pres. Splitap Arts, Lowell, Mass., 1993-94. Author: Freddie the Foot, 1982. Mem. Lowell Hist. Soc., 1994, Women's Network, Lowell, 1994, Crime Watch Group Edn. Component, Lowell, 1994. Recipient academic honors. Mem. ANA, Mass. Nurses Assn., Nat. League Nurses. Democrat. Roman Catholic. Avocations: writing, poetry, minature dollhouses, painting, church group. Home: 130 South St Apt 57 Lowell MA 01852-3382

RICHARDS, DARRIE HEWITT, investment company executive; b. Washington, May 31, 1921; s. George Jacob and Esmee (MacMahon) R.; m. Patricia Louise Moses, Jan. 1, 1947; children: Hilary Wade, Craig Hewitt, Lynn Cotter. Student, Brown U., 1937-39; BS, U.S. Mil. Acad., 1943; MS, Princeton U., 1949. Commd. 2d lt. U.S. Army, 1943, advanced through grades to maj. gen., 1970; mem. Army Gen. Staff Logistics, 1962-66; brigade comdr., logistics staff officer Europe, 1966-68; comdr. Qui Nhon (Vietnam) Support Command, 1968-69, Western Area Mil. Traffic Mgmt. Command, 1969-70; asst. dep. chief staff for logistics Dept. Army, 1970-73; dep. dir. Def. Logistics Agy., 1973-74, ret., 1974; v.p. Capital Resources Inc., Washington, 1974-75; asso. Devel. Resources, Inc., Alexandria, Va., 1975-79; pres. the Montgomery Corp., 1976-84; mng. gen. ptnr. Craighill Co., 1980—; pres., chmn. Montgomery Group, Inc., 1987—. Author publs. on devel allied strategy in World War II, also nat. transp. policy. Decorated D.S.M. with oak leaf cluster, Legion of Merit with 3 oak leaf clusters, Bronze Star, Air medal with 3 oak leaf clusters; Order Chung Mu (Republic of Korea); Disting. Svc. Order; Honor medal 1st class (Vietnam). Mem. Def. Mgmt. Assn. (v.p. 1973-74), Am. Def. Preparedness Assn. (nat. council 1974-76), Assn. U.S. Army (pres. Heidelburg chpt. 1967-68), alumni assns. U.S. Mil Acad., Princeton U., Brown U. Episcopalian. Home: Apt 709 1250 S Washington St Alexandria VA 22314-4455 Office: 300 Montgomery St # 200 Alexandria VA 22314-1516

RICHARDS, DAVID ALAN, lawyer; b. Dayton, Ohio, Sept. 21, 1945; s. Charles Vernon and Betty Ann (Macher) R.; m. Marianne Catherine Del Monaco, June 26, 1971; children: Christopher, Courtney. BA summa cum laude, Yale U., 1967, JD, 1972; MA, Cambridge (Eng.) U., 1969. Bar: N.Y. 1973. Assoc. Paul, Weiss, Rifkind, Wharton & Garrison, N.Y.C., 1972-77, Coudert Bros., N.Y.C., 1977-80, ptnr., 1981-82; ptnr., head real estate group Sidley & Austin, 1983-2000; ptnr. McCarter & English, 2001—, mng. ptnr. N.Y. office, 2002—. Gov. Anglo-Am. Real Property Inst. U.S./U.K., 1983-88, chair, 1993; mem. Chgo. Title N.Y. Realty Adv. Bd., 1992—. Co-editor: Kipling and His First Publisher, 2001; contbr. articles to profl. jours. Trustee Scarsdale Pub. Libr., 1984-89, pres., 1988-89; co-chair N.Y. Lawyers for Clinton/Gore, 1996. Fellow Am. Bar Found.; mem. ABA (real property, probate and trust sect., coun. 1982-88, chair 1991-92), Am. Coll. Real Estate Lawyers (gov. 1987-93), Assn. of Bar of City of N.Y. (real property com. 1978-80, 84-87), Kipling Soc. (N.Am. rep.), Shenorock Shore Club (Rye, N.Y.), The Grolier Club (N.Y.C.), Yale Club (N.Y.C.). Democrat. Home: 18 Forest Ln Scarsdale NY 10583-6464 Office: McCarter & English 300 Park Ave Fl 18 New York NY 10022 E-mail: darichards21@aol.com., drichards@mccarter.com.

RICHARDS, DAVID CHRISTOPHER, small business owner, organist; b. Pitts., July 11, 1954; s. Earl Ralph and Dorothy Fay Richards; m. Karen Jean Richards, Oct. 10, 1992; 1 child, Geena Marie. B in Ch. Music, Cin. Bible Coll., 1976; postgrad., Duquesen U., 1977, 78. Apprentice William Mellor - Organ Builder, Castle Shannon, Pa., 1973, Virgal Jonson - Organ Builder, Mt. Lebanon, 1974-75, Halo-Prellwitz Organ Co., Pitts., 1977-79; organist Mt. Nebo (Pa.) Presbyn. Ch., 1976-77, 2d United Presbyn. Ch., Wilkenburg, Pa., 1977-80, Riverview United Presbyn. Ch., Pitts., 1980-93; proprietor Allegheny Pipe Organ Co., Valencia, Pa., 1980—. Mem. Am. Guild Organists, Am. Inst. Organ Builders. Avocations: landscaping, woodworking. Office: Allegheny Pipe Organ Co 338 Glade Mill Rd Valencia PA 16059

RICHARDS, DAVID GLEYRE, German language educator; b. July 27, 1935; s. Oliver L. and Lilian Marie (Powell) R.; m. Annegret Horn, Sept. 3, 1959 (div. 1992); 1 child, Stephanie Suzanne; m. Friederike Hensler, Oct. 11, 1997. BA, U. Utah, 1960; MA, 1961; PhD, U. Calif.-Berkeley, 1968. Asst.

prof. German SUNY, Buffalo, 1968-74; assoc. prof., 1974-84; prof., 1984-99; prof. emeritus, 1999—. Author: Georg Buchners Woyzeck, 1975, George Buchner and the Birth of the Modern Drama, 1976, The Hero's Quest for the Self: An Archetypal Approach to Hesse's Demian and other Novels, 1987; editor: (with H. Schulte) Crisis and Culture in Post-Enlightenment Germany: Essays in Honor of Peter Heller, 1993, Exploring the Divided Self: Hermann Hesse's Steppenwolf and its Critics, 1996, Georg Buchner's Woyzeck: A History of Its Criticism, 2001. SUNY grantee, 1973; NEH grantee, 1977-78, Fulbright Commn. grantee, 1980. Rsch. Found. of SUNY fellow, 1982. Democrat. Avocation: photography. E-mail: dgrich1@cs.com.

RICHARDS, EARL FREDERICK, electrical engineer, educator; b. Detroit, Mar. 11, 1923; s. Earl Frederick Richards and Esther Branning; m. Marjorie Phyllis Holt, Jan. 12, 1946; 2 children. BSEE, Wayne State U., 1951; MSEE, Mo. Sch. of Mines and Metallurgy, Rolla, 1961; PhD, U. Mo., 1971. Registered engr., Mo. , Mich. Elec. engr. Electronic Control Corp., Detroit, 1951—52, Pa. Salt Mfg. Co., Wyandotte, 1952—53; chief elec. engr. Revere Copper and Brass, Detroit, 1954—58; prof. elec. engring. U. Mo.-Rolla, 1958—92, prof. emeritus, 1992—. Cons. numerous cos., including Eagle-Picher Technologies, Basic Rsch. Corp., Tempel Steel Co., CR Magnetics, Inc., Black & Decker, others. Author: (book) Handbook of Small Electric Motors, 2000; contbr. articles. With Office of strategic Svcs. U.S. Army, 1942—46. Named to Hall of Fame, Sml. Motors Mfrs. Assn., 1995. Mem.: Eta Kappa nu, Sigma Xi. Avocation: antiques, woodworking, reading.

RICHARDS, EDWARD JOSEPH, physician; b. Stanton, Tex. s. Cutter and Nellie (Abu Raslan) R.; m. Norma Jeanne Hamady, Nov. 23, 1957; children: Mark Edward, Andrea Lynn, Laura Jean. BS, U. Md., 1949; MD, U. Iowa, 1955. Intern D.C. Gen. Hosp., Washington, 1955-56; pvt. practice Silver Spring, Md., 1956—. With U.S. Army, 1944-47. Mem. D.C. Acad. Family Physicians (pres.), Montgomery Med. Soc. Avocations: golf, travel. Office: Primary Care of Silver Spring 10301 Georgia Ave Ste 203 Silver Spring MD 20902-5020

RICHARDS, FREDERIC MIDDLEBROOK, biochemist, educator; b. N.Y.C., Aug. 19, 1925; s. George and Marianna Richards; m. Heidi Clarke, 1948 (div. 1955); children: Sarah, Ruth Gray; m. Sarah Wheatland, 1959; 1 child, George Huntington. BS, MIT, 1948; PhD, Harvard U., 1952; DSc (hon.), U. New Haven, 1982. Rsch. fellow in phys. chemistry Harvard Med. Sch., Cambridge, Mass., 1952-53; NRC postdoctoral fellow Carlsberg Lab., Denmark, 1954; NSF fellow Cambridge U., Eng., 1955; asst. prof. biochemistry Yale U., New Haven, 1955-59, assoc. prof., 1959-62, prof., 1963-89, Henry Ford II prof. molecular biophysics, 1967-89, Sterling prof. molecular biophysics, 1989-91, Sterling prof. emeritus, 1991—, chmn. dept. molecular biology and biophysics, 1963-67, chmn. dept. molecular biophysics and biochemistry, 1969-73. Dir. Jane Coffin Childs Meml. Fund Med. Rsch., 1976-91, bd. dirs., 1997—; mem. Nat. Adv. Rsch. & Resources Coun., 1983-87; mem. corp. Woods Hole Oceanographic Inst., 1977-83, 84-90; mem. bd. advisors Whitney Marine Lab., 1979-84, Purdue U. Magnetic Resonance Lab., 1980-84, Biology divsn. Argonne Nat. Lab., 1982-84, Brookhaven Nat. Lab., Nat. Synchrotron Light Source; mem. sci. adv. bd. structural biology Howard Hughes Med. Inst., 1988-89, adv. bd., 1989-92; mem. sci. adv. bd. Donaghue Found. Med. Rsch., 1991-92, external adv. bd. U. Ill. Beckman Inst., 1994-99. Mem. editorial bd. Jour. Biol. Chemistry, 1963-69, 82-84, Jour. Molecular Biology, 1973-75, Advances in Protein Chemistry, 1963—; contbr. articles on protein and enzyme chemistry to profl. jours. Sgt. U.S. Army, 1944-46. Recipient Pfizer-Paul Lewis award in enzyme chemistry, 1965, Kai Linderstrom-Lang prize in protein chemistry, 1978, Sci. medal State of Conn., 1995; Guggenheim fellow, 1967-68. Fellow AAAS, Am. Acad. Arts and Scis. (mem. coun. 1998—); mem. NAS, Am. Philos. Soc., Am. Soc. Biochemistry and Molecular Biology (Merck award 1988), Protein Soc. (Stein and Moore award 1988), Internat. Union Pure and Applied Biophysics (mem. coun. 1975-81), Am. Soc. Biol. Chemists (pres. 1979-80), Biophys. Soc. (pres. 1972-73), Am. Chem. Soc., Am. Crystallographic Assn., Conn. Acad. Sci. and Engring. Avocations: sailing, hiking trail maintenance. Home: 69 Andrews Rd Guilford CT 06437-3715 Office: Yale U Dept Molecular Biophysics PO Box 208114 New Haven CT 06520-8114

RICHARDS, FREDERICK FRANCIS, JR. manufacturing company executive; b. Payette, Idaho, Jan. 28, 1936; s. Frederick Francis and Dorothy Lucille (Taylor) R.; m. DeAnne Aden, Aug. 10, 1958; children: Frederick Francis III, Craig, Jeffrey. BS in Indsl. Engring., So. Meth. U., 1959; MBA, Harvard U., 1961. Indsl. engr. Collins Radio Inc., 1955-59; rsch. asst. Harvard U., 1961-62; fin. analyst H.F. Linder & William T. Golden, N.Y.C., 1962-65; pres. Adrich Corp. and subs., Dallas, 1965—; exec. v.p. FSE Corp., Plano, 1990—91; pres. Resource Locators Inc., Dallas, 1992—. Exec. v.p. FSE Corp., Plano, Tex., 1991-92; v.p. and prin. Capital Alliance Corp., Dallas, 1985-91; v.p. GTex., Inc., Dallas, 1986-87; pres. Work Lite Dist., Dallas, 1990-95, AR Assocs., internat. mgmt. cons., Dallas, 1972—; dir. Dallas Pub. Inc., 1982-84, Aden-Richards Inc., 1979—. Author papers in field; bus. columnist. Mem. ASTM, Am. Inst. Indsl. Engrs. (sr.), Airplane Owners and Pilots Assn., Am. Soc. Indsl. Security, Internat. Assn. Chiefs Police, Nat. Pilots Assn., Exptl. Aircraft Assn., Harvard Club (N.Y.C.), The Tech. Club of Dallas. Home and Office: 3 Cumberland Pl Richardson TX 75080-4926 E-mail: ffr@adrich.com.

RICHARDS, GALE LEE, communication educator; b. Long Run, W.Va., July 31, 1918; s. Robert Amaziah and Edna Jane (Scott) R.; m. Barbara Lee Neely, Apr. 19, 1944; children: Robin Lee, Wendell Scott, Jeffrey Marshall. BA (Pixley scholar), U. Akron, O., 1940; MA (C.S. Knight Meml. scholar), U. Ia., 1942, PhD, 1950. Instr. speech U. Akron, 1941-42; asst. prof. speech Drake U., 1947-48; asst. prof. English U. Nev., 1948-52; asst. prof. speech U. Wash., 1952-58; assoc. prof. speech U. So. Calif., 1958-65; prof. communication Ariz. State U., Tempe, 1965—, chmn. dept. speech and theatre, 1965-73. Pub. relations cons. Red Feather campaign United Fund, Los Angeles, 1955-58; mgmt. and tng. cons. various profl. and comml. orgns., 1955— Cons. editor: Western Speech, 1957-61, 62-65, 69-72, Jour. of Communication, 1961-67; Contbr. articles profl. jours. Bd. dirs. Phoenix Little Theatre. Served to lt. USNR, 1942-45, PTO. Recipient Distinguished Alumni award Radio Sta. WSUI, 1942 Mem. We. States Communication Assn. (adminstrv. coun., legis. coun., chair commn. on Am. Parliamentary procedure, 1988, emeritus 1991), Internat. Communication Assn. (adminstrv. coun.), Am. Inst. Parliamentarians, Western States Communication Assn. (2d v.p. 1956, 71, pres. Execs. club 1975, Disting. Svc. award 1989), Ariz. Communication and Drama Assn. (pres. 1967, editor jour. 1984-87), Blue Key, Phi Kappa Phi, Delta Sigma Rho. Democrat. Presbyterian. Home: 614 E Bishop Dr Tempe AZ 85282-2325 E-mail: galeri@imap3.asu.edu.

RICHARDS, GEORGE ALVAREZ, psychiatrist, educator; b. La Paz, Bolivia, May 11, 1934; came to U.S., 1952; s. John Joseph and Matilde (Alvarez) R.; m. LaClaire Lissetta Jones, July 26, 1958; children: Leslie Rosario Richards-Yellen, Lia Mercedes Richards Palmiter. BA, Hastings Coll., 1957; MD, U. Autonoma Guadalajara, Jalisco, Mex., 1970. Lic. physician, S.D. Lang. asst. Hastings (Nebr.) Coll., 1953-57; nursing asst. Hastings State Hosp., 1952-57; tchr. lang. and sci. Knoxville (Iowa) Pub. Sch., 1960-65; rotating intern Regina (Sask., Can.) Gen. Hosp., 1970-71; gen. med. officer Dept. Vets. Affairs, Knoxville, 1974; resident psychiatrist Mental Health Inst., Cherokee, Iowa, 1974-77; acting chief, adminstrv. chief, staff psychiatrist Royal C. Johnson Vets. Meml. Hosp., Sioux Falls, S.D., 1977—; asst. prof. psychiatry U. S.D. Sch. Medicine, 1977—. Mem. planning and health coms. Multi-Cultural Ctr., Sioux Falls, 1996—; mem. NAACP, Sioux Falls, 1980—. Recipient Exemplary Psychiatrist award Nat. Alliance for Mentally Ill, 1996—. Fellow Interam. Coll. Physicians and Surgeons; mem. AMA (Hispanic Physicians), Am. Psychiat. Assn. (Nancy C. A. Roeske, MD, Cert. of Excellence 1998), S.D. State Med. Assn., S.D. Psychiat. Assn., 7th Dist. Med. Assn. Avocations: languages, mentoring, music, reading, jogging. Office: Royal C Johnson Vets Meml Hosp 2501 W 22d St Sioux Falls SD 57117

RICHARDS, GERALD THOMAS, lawyer, consultant, educator, writer; b. Monrovia, Calif., Mar. 17, 1933; s. Louis Jacquelyn Richards and Inez Vivian (Richardson) Hall; children: Patricia M. Richards Grauf, Laura J., Dag Hammarskjold; m. Mary Lou Richards, Dec. 27, 1986. BS magna cum laude, Lafayette Coll., 1957; MS, Purdue U., 1963; JD, Golden Gate U., 1976. Bar: Calif. 1976, U.S. Dist. Ct. (no. dist.) Calif. 1977, U.S. Patent Office 1981, U.S. Ct. Appeals (9th cir.) 1984, U.S. Supreme Ct. 1984. From computational physicist to asst. lab. counsel Lawrence Livermore Nat. Lab., Calif., 1967—84, asst. lab. counsel, 1984—93; sole practice Livermore, 1976-78, Oceanside, 1994-97; emeritus atty. pro bono participant Calif. State Bar, 1998—; staff atty. Contra Costa Sr. Legal Svcs., Concord, 1998—. Constrn. law instr. Contrs. State License Schs., Van Nuys, Calif., 1998; mem. exec. com., policy advisor Fed. Lab. Consortium for Tech. Transfer, 1980-88; panelist, del. White House Conf. on Productivity, Washington, 1983; del. Nat. Conf. on Tech. and Aging, Wingspread, Wis., 1981. Commr. Housing Authority, City of Livermore, 1977, vice chairperson, 1978, chairperson, 1979; pres. Housing Choices, Inc., Livermore, 1980-84; bd. dirs. Valley Vol. Ctr., Pleasanton, Calif., 1983, pres., 1984-86; mem. staff Calif. Boys' State Am. Legion, 1996—. Served to maj. U.S. Army, 1959-67. Recipient Engring. award GE, 1956. Mem. ABA, Calif. State Bar (conv. alt. del. 1990-92, del. 2000, mem. com. on sr. lawyers 2002—), Alameda County Bar Assn., Contra Costa County Bar Assn., Ea. Alameda County Bar Assn. (sec. 1978, bd. dirs. 1991-92, chair lawyers referral com. 1992-93), Santa Barbara County Bar Assn., San Diego County Bar Assn., Bar Assn. No. San Diego County, San Francisco Bar Assn., Phi Beta Kappa, Tau Beta Pi, Sigma Pi Sigma. Home: 2505 Whitetail Dr Antioch CA 94531-7744 E-mail: hesiodsplace@yahoo.com.

RICHARDS, HERBERT EAST, minister emeritus, commentator; b. Hazleton, Pa. s. Herbert E. and Mabel Richards; m. Lois Marcey, Jan. 1, 1942; children: Herbert Charles, Marcey Lynn, Robyn Lois, Fredrick East, Mark Allen. AB, Dickinson Coll., 1941; BD, Drew U., 1944; MA, Columbia, 1944; DD, Coll. of Idaho, 1953; postgrad., Union Theol. Sem., 1941-48, Bucknell U., 1943-44. Accredited news reporter Nat. Assn. Broadcasters. Ordained to ministry Methodist Ch., 1944; pastor in Boiling Springs, Pa., 1937-40, West Chester, 1940-41, Basking Ridge, N.J., 1941-47; mem. faculty Drew U. and Theol. Sem., 1944-51, assoc. prof. homiletics and Christian criticism, chmn. dept., asst. dean, 1947-51; spl. lectr. religion Howard U., 1947; minister 1st Meth. Cathedral, Boise, Idaho, 1951-69, 1st United Meth. Ch., Eugene, Oreg., 1969-78, Tabor Heights United Meth. Ch., Portland, 1978-86, minister emeritus, 1986—. Weekly radio broadcaster Sta. KBOI, Sta. KIDO, 1941— ; weekly TV broadcaster CBS, 1945— , ABC, 1969— , NBC, 1973; pres. Inspiration, Inc., TV Found., 1965— , TV Ecology, 1973; producer Life TV series ABC, 1974-85, PBS TV, 1968-85, also BBC, Eng., Suise Romande, Geneva; chmn. Idaho bd. ministerial tng. Meth. Conf., 1954-60, TV, Radio and Film Commn., 1954-62, Oreg. Coun. Public Broadcasting, 1973; del. Idaho Conf. Meth. Gen. Conf., 1956, Jurisdictional Conf., 1956, World Meth. Coun., 1957, 81, World Meth. Conf., 1981, mem. Gen. Conf., 1956-60, Jurisdictional Conf., 1956, 60; meml. chaplain Idaho Supreme Ct., 1960; chaplain Idaho Senate, 1960-68; mem. Task Force on TV and Ch., 1983 Author: In Time of Need, 1986, Faith and the Pursuit of Healing, 1996; contbr. articles to religious publs.; composer: oratorios Prophet Unwilling, 1966, Meet Martin Luther, 1968, Dear Jesus Boy, 1973. Mem. Commn. on Centennial Celebration for Idaho, 1962-63; committeeman Boy Scouts Am.; bd. dirs. Eugene chpt. ARC, 1954-73; trustee Willamette U., Cascade Manor Homes; adv. bd. Medic-Alert Found. Recipient Alumni citation in religious edn. Dickinson Coll., 1948, Golden Plate award Am. Acad. Achievement, 1965, Jason Lee Mass Media TV award, 1983, Disting. Citizen award Idaho Statesman Newspaper, 1964, Disting. Alumnus award Drew U., 1965, disting. Eagle award Boy Scouts Am. ; named Clergyman of Yr., Religious Heritage Am., 1964. Mem. AAUP, CAP (chaplain Idaho wing, lt. col.), Am. Acad. Achievement (bd. govs. 1967—), Am. Found. Religion and Psychiatry (charter gov.), Idaho Found. Medicine and Biology (charter), Greater Boise Ministerial Assn. (pres.), Eugene Ministerial Assn. (pres. 1978), Masons (33 degree, editor Pike's Peak Albert That Is), Shriners, Elks, Rotary (editor Key and Cog, pres. dist. 510 Pioneer Club), Kappa Sigma (Grand Master of Beta Pi). Home: 10172 SE 99th Dr Portland OR 97266-7227 Office: Tabor Heights United Meth Ch 6161 SE Stark St Portland OR 97215-1935 *When a person presses his face against the window pane of life, he becomes as a child waiting for his father's return; simple, trusting and infinitely wiser. In our present time of growth/conflict, such a face-pressing is essential to get us safely from where we are to where we ought to be.*

RICHARDS, HUGH TAYLOR, physics educator; b. Baca County, Colo., Nov. 7, 1918; s. Dean Willard and Kate Bell (Taylor) R.; m. Mildred Elizabeth Paddock, Feb. 11, 1944; children: David Taylor, Thomas Martin, John Willard, Margaret Paddock, Elizabeth Nicholls, Robert Dean. BA, Park Coll., 1939; MA, Rice U., 1940, PhD, 1942. Research assoc. Rice U., Houston, 1942; scientist U. Minn., Mpls., 1942-43, U. Calif. Sci. Labs., Los Alamos, N.Mex., 1943-46; research assoc. U. Wis., Madison, 1946-47, mem. faculty, 1947-52, prof., 1952-88, prof. emeritus, 1988—, physics dept. chairperson, 1960-63, 66-69, 85-88. Assoc. dean Coll. Letters and Sci., U. Wis, 1963-66. Author: Through Los Alamos 1945: Memoirs of a Nuclear Physicist, 1993; contbr. articles to profl. jours. Fellow Am. Phys. Soc.; mem. Am. Assn. Physics Tchrs. Unitarian-Universalist. Achievements include neutron measurements first A-Bomb test; fission neutron (and other) spectra by new photo-emulsion techniques; mock fission neutron source; spherical electrostatic analyzer for precise reaction energy measurements; negative ion sources for accelerators (He ALPHATROSS, SNICS); accurate proton, deuteron, and alpha particle scattering and reaction cross sections; systematics mirror nuclei; isospin violations in nuclear reactions. Home: 1320 12th Ave E Apt # 115 Menomonie WI 54751

RICHARDS, JACQUELINE, artist, curator; b. Chgo., July 25, 1930; d. Harris Nathan Turner and Henrietta Sheade; m. Seymour Richards, Dec. 22, 1949 (div. Dec. 1973); children: Robin, Philip. BS in Cmty. Health, Ga. State U., 1978; postgrad. in art history, U. Chgo., 1949—50; postgrad. in art theory and design, The New Bauhaus, Chgo., 1947—49. Registered dietitian Am. Dietetic Assn., lic. State of Ga. Clin. dietitian Griffin-Spalding Hosp., Griffin, Ga., 1980—86, R.T. Jones Hosp., Canton, 1986—88; artist, painter Atlanta, 1988—; curator, 2000—. Illustrator Raymond Lowey Designs an Automobile for Studebaker, 1950, one-woman shows include Art Inst. Chgo., 1952—, Fulton County Libr., Atlanta, 2002—, exhibited in group shows at Am. Fedn. Arts, 1952—59, House of Color, 2001—; artist, curator Atlanta Bur. Cultural Affairs, 2002. Achievements include development of hypoallergenic skin cream for cancer patients. Avocation: Avocations: building model automobiles, birding. Home: 479 E Paces Ferry Rd NE Apt 210 Atlanta GA 30305-3308

RICHARDS, JAMES CARLTON, microbiologist, business executive; b. Storm Lake, Iowa, Aug. 19, 1947; s. Jack M. and June G. Richards; m. Lois Ruth Rebbe, July 22, 1974 (div. Sept. 1986); 1 child, Kimberly Ann; m. Susan M. Wos, Aug. 27, 1988; children: Derek Anthony, Kristin Marie. BS in Microbiology, U. Ill., 1970; PhD in Microbiology, So. Ill. U., 1977. Postdoctoral fellow Pa. State U. Med. Ctr., Hershey, Pa., 1977-79; sr. scientist E.I. duPont de Nemours, Wilmington, Del., 1979-85; program mgr. Amoco, Naperville, Ill., 1985-86; dir. bus. Gene-Trak Systems, Framingham, Mass., 1986-90; mng. dir. Carlton BioVenture Ptnrs., Sudbury, 1990—; pres., CEO, bd. dirs. Symbollon Corp., Framingham, 1991-95, IntelliGene, Ltd., Sudbury, 1995-2000, Jerusalem, Israel, 1995-2000; pres., CEO, chmn. bd. dirs. Edgelight Bioscis., Inc., Sudbury, Mass., 2000—. Invited lectr. on genetic analysis and advances in gene amplification and detection 4th ann. Advances in Gene Amplification and Selection Conf. Cambridge Healthtech Inst., McLean, Va., 1996. Contbr. chpt. to books, articles to sci. jours.; patentee in field. Deacon, chair capitol fund dr. United Ch. of Christ, Framingham, 1988—. Mem. AAAS, Am. Soc. for Microbiology, Am. Chem. Soc., Inst. Food Technologists, N.Y. Acad. Scis., Clin. Ligand Soc., Ill. Alumni Assn., Sigma Xi, Theta Xi. Avocations: golf, travel, jogging, gardening, skiing. Home and Office: 44 Codman Dr Sudbury MA 01776-1745 E-mail: intelli@tiac.net., jrichards@edgeLightbiosciences.com.

RICHARDS, JAMES WILLIAM, electromechanical engineer; b. Portland, Oreg., Oct. 24, 1921; s. Jarvis William and Thelma Helen (Eoff) R.; m. Violet Victor Ray, Oct. 9, 1946; children: Betty, Sandra, Diane, William Student, Nat. Tech. Sch., 1942, Nat. Radio Inst., 1948, Internat. Corr. Sch., 1955; AA, Pierce Coll., 1968. Mgr. Western Design, Santa Barbara, Calif., 1948-55; sr. engr. Bendix Corp., North Hollywood, 1955-66; v.p. Talley Corp., Newbury Park, 1966-75, dir. engring., 1982-87; pvt. practice electromech. engr., Eugene, Oreg., 1975-82, 87-89; pres. Western Design, 1990—. Mem. Masons. Republican. Baptist. Avocation: travel. Home: PO Box 5498 Eugene OR 97405-0498 Office: Western Design PO Box 5549 Eugene OR 97405-0549 E-mail: westrndesn@aol.com.

RICHARDS, JANE AILEEN, family nurse practitioner; b. Oakland, Calif., Oct. 19, 1948; d. John Donald and Mary Dolores (Peters) R. BSN, U. San Francisco, 1970; MSN, San Jose State U., 1976, FNP, 1995. RN; cert. FNP. Staff nurse ICU Mills Meml. Hosp., San Mateo, Calif., 1970-73, asst. head nurse ICU, 1973-76, edn. specialist, 1976-80, mgr. acute rehab. ctr., 1980-83; case mgr. J.R. Assocs., 1983-95; nurse cons. Calif. State Dept. Corps., 1989-97; FNP Seneca Hosp. Dist., Lake Almanor Clinic, Chester, Calif., 1995—. Pres. United Cerebral Palsy Assn., Mt. View, Calif., 1979-85, 93-94, bd. dirs. nat. chpt. 1983-91. Mem. Rotary, Sigma Theta Tau (Alpha Gamma chpt.), PEO (chpt. BO-Calif., pres. 1999—). Republican. Avocations: golf, camping, hiking, gardening. Home: PO Box 408 Willow Creek CA 95573 Office: Willow Creek Family Health Clin PO Box 726 Willow Creek CA 95573

RICHARDS, JAY CLAUDE, commercial photographer, news service executive, historian; b. Glen Ridge, N.J., Apr. 6, 1954; s. Jacob Tilghman and Joan Louise (Walsh) Richards. Student, Tenn. Wesleyan Coll., Athens, 1972-73. Various positions armed security work, 1973-75; reporter, photographer Press Publs.: The News, Belvidere, N.J., 1977-98; pres. J.C. Richards Assocs., Harmony Twp., 1980—; owner Poor Richards' Brit. Gun Shop, 1976—; freelance ct. reporter The Morning Call, Allentown, Pa., 1986—; reporter The Knowlton News, 1998—2002. Photography judge Warren County 4-H, Belvidere, 1990—; press officer Warren County Office Emergency Mgmt, Belvidere, 1989—98; news corresp WRNJ-News, 1991—, NJN Pubs, The News, 2001—02. Author: (book) Penn, Patriots and the Pequest: The History of Pre-Victorian Belvidere, 1716-1845, 1995, Flames Along the Delaware, 1996 (NJ Frontier Guard's Book Award, 1997), Bugles, Battles and Belvidere: Warren County, N.J. in the Civil War, 1997, Officers and Men of Warren County, N.J. in the Civil War, 1998, More Bugles, Battles and Belvidere: Warren County, N.J. in the Civil War Letters to Home, 1999, Following the Hand of Franklin: Warren County, N.J. and the Search for the North Pole, 2000; contbr. art work. Mem Hazardous Materials Adv Coun, Warren County, NJ, Joint Emergency Mgmt Coun, Belvidere/White Township, Warren County Arts Adv Coun, Warren County War Mem Comt, 1997—98; trustee Warren County War Mem Corp, 1999—; consult Harmony NJ Hist Preservation Comn, 2000—; mem Warren County Purple Heart Monument Construction Comt, 2000. Named Hon Mem, Boy Scout Troop 141, Belvidere, 1993; recipient Oustanding Community Serv Award, Am Legion Post 131, 1994. Mem.: Nat Indian Wars Asn, Oxford NJ Hist Soc, US Naval Inst, Sr Army Res Comdrs Asn, Res Officers Asn US, Soc Profl Journalists, Nat Press Photographers Asn, Sigma Delta Chi. Episcopalian. Avocations: collecting Richards of Sheffield pocket knives and tools, gourmet cooking, gardening, herbal medicine. Home and Office: 3110 Belvidere Rd Phillipsburg NJ 08865-9515 E-mail: jayrichards@enter.net.

RICHARDS, JODY, state legislator, journalism educator, small business owner; b. Columbia, Ky., Feb. 20, 1939; m. Neva Richards; 1 child, Roger. BA in English, Ky. Wesleyan Coll., Owensboro; MA in Journalism, U. Mo., 1962. Mem. faculty in journalism Western Ky. U., from 1962; owner Superior Books, Bowling Green, Ky.; mem. Ky. Ho. of Reps., 1976—, speaker, 1995—; vice chair So. Legislative Conf., 1998—. Mem. adv. bd. dirs. Republic Savs. Bank. Pres. bd. dirs. So. Ky. Fair; bd. dirs. Bowling Green Girls Club, United Way, Warren County (Ky.) Drug Abuse Task Force. Recipient Disting. Svc. award Nat. Art Edn. Assn., 1992. Mem. Bowling Green C. of C., Bowling Green Noon Rotary Club. Office: Ky Ho of Reps State Capitol Frankfort KY 40601

RICHARDS, JOHN DALE, sociology and philosophy educator, counselor; b. South Charleston, W.Va., July 31, 1958; s. Guy Edward and Margaret Jane (Gray) R.; m. Susan Lynn McCallister, June 23, 1990. BA, W.Va. State Coll., 1978; MA, Ohio U., 1982, 88. Lic. profl. counselor, W.Va. Bd. Examiners in Counseling; lic. cert. social worker, W.Va. Bd. Social Work Examiners. Family counselor Family Svc. Kanawha Valley, Charleston, W.Va., 1988-93; pvt. practice family counselor South Charleston, 1991-93; asst. prof. W.Va. State Coll., Institute, 1993—. Cons. Gov.'s Cabinet on Families and Children, Charleston, 1995, Human Resource Mgmt. Co., Charleston, 1995. Author: Coping with Grief, 1995, (poetry) Uncreated Light, 1995; co-author; The Family Education Experience, 1995. Pres. bd. dirs. Dreikurs Family Edn. Ctr., Charleston, 1995—; mem. adv. bd. Glenwood Family Resource Ctr., Charleston, 1995—. Recipient Dr. W.E.B. Dubois award Alpha Kappa Delta, 1995. Mem. Am. Sociol. Assn., W.Va. Soc. Adlerian Psychology (pres. 1995-96, Dr. Manford A. Sonstegard award 1995), W.Va. Sociol. Assn. (v.p. 1995-96), Masons. Democrat. Avocations: writing music, writing poetry, collecting rocks, woodworking, archaeology. Home: 1211 Strawberry Rd Saint Albans WV 25177-3357

RICHARDS, JOHN RAY, emergency physician, educator; BA, U. Calif., Berkeley, 1989; MD, U. Calif., Davis, 1993. Cert. Am. Bd. Emergency Medicine. Prof. U. Calif.-Davis Sch. Medicine, 1996—. Author: (book) Management of Office Emergencies, 1999; contbr. articles to profl. jours. Recipient Outstanding Rsch. award Am. Fedn. for Clin. Rsch., 1991; rsch. fellow Alpha Omega Alpha, 1991. Fellow Am. Acad. Emergency Medicine; mem. Soc. Acad. Emergency Medicine (Excellence in Emergency Medicine award 1993). Office: Emergency Medicine 2315 Stockton Blvd Sacramento CA 95817-2201 Fax: (916) 734-7950. E-mail: jrrichards@ucdavis.edu.

RICHARDS, JOSEPH EDWARD, artist; b. Des Moines, Oct. 10, 1921; s. Earl L. and Ivanore M. (Shelledy) R.; m. Elizabeth Anne Morrow, Mar. 23, 1943. Student, Am. Acad. Art, Chgo., 1946-49, Pa. Acad. Fine Arts, 1950-52. Exhbns. include: Butler Inst. Am. Art, Youngstown, Ohio, 1976, 77, 78, 81, 2001, Tex. Fine Arts Assn./Laguna Gloria Art Mus., Austin, Tex., 1977, NAD, N.Y.C., 1978, Silvermine Guild Artists, New Canaan, Conn., 1978, 79, Pa. Acad. Fine Arts, Phila., 1978, 80, 94, Va. Mus., Richmond, 1979, O.K. Harris Gallery, N.Y.C., 1982, 89, 92, 94, 1998-2002, O.K. Harris West Gallery, Scottsdale, Ariz., 1981, 82, Robert Kidd Galleries, Birmingham, Mich. 1984, Soghor, Leonard & Assocs. Gallery, N.Y.C., 1985, O.K. Harris South, Miami, Fla., 1986, Butler Inst. Am. Art, Youngstown, 1987, Tortue Gallery, Santa Monica, Calif., 1988, Art Expo, Tokyo, 1990, Art Now Gallery, Gothenburg, Sweden, 1990, Louis Stern Gallery, Beverly Hills, Calif., 1991, Bobbitt Visual Arts Ctr., Albion (Mich.) Coll., 1991, Survey of Am. Realism, Seoul, Korea, 1996, OK Harris, N.Y.C., 1998; represented in pvt. and corp. collections in U.S., Can., Europe. Recipient Disting. Artists award Va. Mus. Fine Art, 1979. Fellow Pa. Acad. Fine Arts. Home: PO Box 374 Hillsdale NY 12529-0374

RICHARDS, LACLAIRE LISSETTA JONES (MRS. GEORGE A. RICHARDS), social worker; b. Pine Bluff, Ark. d. Artie William and Geraldine (Adams) Jones; m. George Alvarez Richards, July 26, 1958; children: Leslie Rosario, Lia Mercedes. BA, Nat. Coll. Christian Workers, 1953; MSW, U. Kans., 1956; postgrad, Columbia U., 1960. Diplomate Clin. Social Work, Am. Bd. of Examiners in Clin. Social Work, Nat. Assn. Social Workers; cert. gerontologist. Psychiat., supr., tchg., cmty. orgn., adminstrv., cons. Hastings Regional Ctr., Ingleside, Nebr., 1956-60; supr., cons., adminstrv. VA Hosp., Knoxville, Iowa, 1960-74; field instr. for grad. students U. Mo., 1969-74, 78-90, com. chmn., 1969-70; sr. social worker Mental Health Inst., Cherokee, Iowa, 1974-77; adj. asst. prof. dept. social behavior U. S.D., 1974-77, instr. dept. psychiat., 1988-96, Augustina Coll., 1981-86; outpatient social worker VA Med. and Regional Office Ctr., Sioux Falls, S.D., 1978-96, med., surg. and intensive care social worker, 1992-96, 1990-92, sur. and intermediate care social worker, 1992-96, EEO counselor. EEO counselor. Mem. Knoxville Juvenile adv. com., 1963-65, 68-70, sec., 1965-66, chmn., 1966-68; sec. Urban Renewal Citizens' adv. com., Knoxville, 1966-68; mem. United Meth. Ch. task force Expt. Styles Ministry and Leadership, 1973-74, mem. adult choir, mem. ch. and society com.; counselor Knoxville Youth Line program; sec. exec. com. Vis. Nurse Assn., 1979-80; canvasser cmty. fund drs., Knoxville; mem. Cherokee Civil Rights Commn.; bd. dirs., pub. rels., mem. devel. and program devel. cons. YWCA, 1983-85; bd. dirs. Family Svc. Agy., 1989-90, Food Svcs. Ctr., Inc., 1992-96, mem. S.D. Symphonic Choir, 1991—; mem. Youth-At-Risk Task Force and Multicultural Ctr. Advocate; deaconness 1st Evang. Free Ch., 1999—. Named S.D. Social Worker of Yr., 1983. Mem.

NAACP (chmn. edn. com. 1983-85), AAUW (sec. Hastings chpt. 1958-60), Nat. Assn. Social Workers (co-chmn. Nebr. chpt. profl. standards com. 1958-59), Acad. Cert. Social Workers, S.D. Assn. Social Workers (chmn. minority affairs com., v.p. S.E. region 1980, pres. 1980-82, exec. com. 1985-84, mem. social policy and action com.), Nebr. Assn. Social Workers (chmn. 1958-59), Seventh Dist. S.D. Med. Soc. Aux., Coalition on Aging., Nat. Assn. Social Workers (qualified clin. social worker 1991—), Methodist (Sunday Sch. tchr. adult divsn.; mem. commn. on edn.; mem. Core com. for adult edn.; mem. Adult Choir; mem. Social Concerns Work Area). Mem. 1st Evangelical Free Ch. (deaconness 1999—). Home: 1701 E Ponderosa Dr Sioux Falls SD 57103-5019

RICHARDS, LEONARD MARTIN, investment executive, consultant; b. Phila., June 4, 1935; s. Leonard Martin and Marion Clara (Lang) R.; m. Phyllis Janelle Mowrey, Aug. 26, 1961 (div. Aug. 1978); children: Lisa, David Reed. BS, Pa. State U., 1957; MBA, U. Pa., 1963; MTh, Universal Sem., 1996, ThD, 2000. Asst. to sr. ptnr. Van Cleef, Jordan & Wood, N.Y.C., 1963-68; v.p., portfolio mgr. Bernstein-Macaulay, Inc., 1968-72; ptnr. G. H. Walker, Laird Co., 1972-74; v.p., trust officer, mgr. instnl. funds group Republic Bank N.A., Dallas, 1974-77; v.p., sr. investment officer, mem. exec. com. Variable Annuity Life Ins. Co., Houston, 1977-88; v.p., sr. investment officer Am. Gen. Series Portfolio Co., 1985-88; pres. L.M. Richards & Co., Houston, 1982—, also bd. dirs.; pres. Capital Instnl. Svcs., Inc., Dallas, 1990-99, also bd. dirs.; mem. adv. bd. Trinity Life Ctr., Houston, 1996-2000, also bd. dirs. Pres., bd. dirs. San Dollar, Inc., Houston, 1985—96; trustee Post Oak Sch., 1997—99, Universal Sem., 1997—2000, pres., 2001—; bd. dirs. Houston Chorale, 1988—90. Capt. U.S. Army, 1957—65. Mem. Assn. Investment Mgmt. and Rsch., Houston Soc. Fin. Analysts. Republican. Avocations: skiing, travel, scuba. Home: 9023 Briar Forest Dr Houston TX 77024-7220 Office: LM Richards & Co 4600 Post Oak Place Dr Ste 301 Houston TX 77027-9727 E-mail: lrichards1@qwest.net.

RICHARDS, LLOYD GEORGE, theatrical director, university administrator; b. Toronto, Ont., Can. came to U.S., 1923; s. Albert George and Rose Isabelle (Coote) R.; m. Barbara Davenport, Oct. 11, 1957; children: Scott, Thomas. Grad., Wayne U., 1944. Head actor tng. NYU Sch. Arts, N.Y.C., 1966-72; artistic dir. Nat. Playwrights Conf., Eugene O'Neill Meml. Theatre Ctr., Waterford, Conn., 1969—; prof. theatre and cinema Hunter Coll., N.Y.C., 1972-79; dean Yale U. Sch. Drama, New Haven, 1979-91; artistic dir Yale Repertory Theatre, 1979-91. Prof. emeritus Sch. Drama, 1991—; artistic dir. Yale Repertory Theater, 1979-91; pres. Theater Devel. Fund; head actor tng. Sch. Arts NYU, 1966-72; lectr., cons. in field; bd. dirs. Theatre Comm. Group, U.S. Bicentennial World Theatre Festival; mem. various profl. adv. groups, task forces; mem. playwrights selection com. Rockefeller Found.; mem. new Am. plays program com. Ford Found.; mem. com. on profl. theater tng. Nat. Endowment Arts. Actor on radio, TV and theater, 1943—; including Broadway plays The Egghead, 1957, Freight, 1956; disc jockey, Detroit; dir. for: radio, TV, film and theater, including Broadway plays A Raisin in the Sun, 1958, The Long Dream, 1960, The Moon Besieged, 1962, I Had a Ball, 1964, The Yearling, 1966, Paul Robeson, 1977-78, Ma Rainey's Black Bottom, 1984, Fences, 1987 (Tony award 1987), Joe Turner's Come and Gone, 1986, The Piano Lesson, 1990, Two Trains Running, 1992, 7 Guitars, 1996; and TV prodns. include: segment of Roots: The Next Generation, 1979, Bill Moyers' Jour, 1979, Robeson, 1979, Hallmark Piano Lesson 95. Served with USAAF, 1943-44. Recipient Pioneer award Audience Devel. Co., 1986-87, Frederick Douglas award, 1986-87, Golden Plate award, 1987, Nat. Medal of Arts, 1993, Mr. Abbott award, 1996; Hoffman Eminent scholar Fla. State U., 1997. Mem. Soc. Stage Dirs. and Choreographers (pres.), Actors Equity Assn., AFTRA, Dirs. Guild Am. Office: 18 W 95th St New York NY 10025-6708

RICHARDS, LYNN, company training executive, consultant; b. Kansas City, Mo., Sept. 2, 1949; d. Robert A. and Betty (Arnold) Nelson. BS in Edn., U. Kans., 1971; MA in Edn., San Diego State U., 1979. Prin. staff ORI, Inc., Silver Spring, Md., 1980-81; sr. corp. trainer Amerada Hess Corp., Woodbridge, N.J., 1981-83; tng. and devel. mgr. Kimberly-Clark Corp., Beech Island, S.C., 1983-85; orgn. devel. mgr. M&M Mars, Hackettstown, N.J., 1985-89; corp. tng. and devel. mgr. Rohr, Inc., Chula Vista, Calif., 1989-93; customer edn. mgr. ComputerVision, Corp., San Diego, 1993-95; leadership devel. cons. Children's Hosp., 1995-97; learning tech. cons. Hewlett-Packard Co., 1997-98, site learning ctr. mgr., 1998-99; dir. edn. svcs. N.Am. Peregrine Sys., 1999—2001. Cons. in field. Contbr. articles to profl. mags. Mem.: Internat. Soc. Productivity Improvement (chmn. awards com. 1988, presdl. citations, achievement awards).

RICHARDS, MARIA LYNN, music educator; b. Madison, Wis., Feb. 3, 1968; d. Vernon Joseph Sr. and Billie Jean (Tucker) Weisensel; m. Todd David Richards, Nov. 27, 1993. MusB, U. Wis., Whitewater, 1991. Cert. gen. music K-12, instrumental music K-12, vocal music 6-12, Wis. Limited term employment music educator Lodi (Wis.) Sch. Dist., 1992; music educator Mayville (Wis.) Sch. Dist., 1992—. Vocalist, saxophonist, aux. percussionist J. Harrison B. Band, Fond du Lac, Wis., 1994—; French hornist Paragon Brass Quintet, Mayville, Wis., 1993—. Mem. Music Educators Nat. Conf., Wis. Youth Band Dirs. Assn. Roman Catholic. Avocations: toy collector, homemaker. Office: Mayville Sch Dist 500 N Clark St Mayville WI 53050-1055

RICHARDS, MARK ANDREW, signal processing research engineer; b. Ft. Worth, Jan. 20, 1952; s. William George and Winnifred (Adams) R.; m. Theresa Charlene Speake, June 6, 1974; children: Jessica Speake, Benjamin Speake. BSEE, Ga. Inst. Technology, 1974; MSEE, Stanford U., 1976; PhD, Ga. Inst. Technology, 1982. Rsch. engr. Ga. Tech Rsch. Inst., Atlanta, 1982-85; sr. scientist Lockheed-Ga. Co., Marietta, 1985-88; from sr. rsch. engr. to prin. rsch. engr. Ga. Tech Rsch. Inst., Atlanta, 1988—, fellow, 1997—, chief radar sys. divsn., 1999—. Adj. prof. Ga. Inst. Tech., 1989—; program mgr. U.S. Def. Advanced Rsch. Projects Agy., Arlington, Va., 1993-95. Editor: Rapid Prototyping of Application-Specific Signal Processors, 1997; contbr. chpts. to books and articles to profl. jours. Mem. IEEE (sr., chmn. Atlanta sect. 1988-89, assoc. editor Signal Processing Transactions 1989-93, assoc. editor Image Processing Trans. 2000—). Avocation: tennis. E-mail: mark.richards@ece.gatech.edu.

RICHARDS, MARTA ALISON, lawyer; b. Mar. 15, 1952; d. Howard Jay and Mary Dean (Nix) Richards; m. Richard Peter Massony, June 16, 1979 (div. Apr. 1988); 1 child, Richard Peter Massony Jr. Student, Vassar Coll., 1969-70; AB cum laude, Princeton U., 1973; JD, George Washington U., 1976. Bar: La. 1976, U.S. Dist. Ct. (ea. dist.) La. 1976, U.S. Ct. Appeals (5th cir.) 1981, U.S. Supreme Ct. 1988, U.S. Dist. Ct. (mid. dist.) La. 1991. Assoc. Phelps, Dunbar, Marks, Claverie & Sims, New Orleans, 1976-77; assoc. counsel Hibernia Nat. Bank, 1978; assoc. Singer, Hutner, Levine, Seeman & Stuart, 1978-80, Jones, Walker, Waechter, Poltevent, Carrere & Denegre, New Orleans, 1980-84; ptnr. Mmahat, Duffy & Richards, 1984, Montgomery, Barnett, Brown, Read, Hammond & Mintz, 1984-86, Montgomery, Richards & Ballin, 1986-89, Gelpi, Sullivan, Carroll and Laborde, 1989; gen. counsel Maison Blanche Inc., Baton Rouge, 1990-92, La. State Bond Commn., 1992-97; pvt. practice, cons., 1998—. Lectr. paralegal inst. U. New Orleans, 1984-89, adj. prof., 1989. Contbr. articles to legal jours. Treas. alumni coun. Princeton U., 1979-81. Mem. ABA, La. State Bar Assn., New Orleans Bar Assn., Baton Rouge Bar Assn., Nat. Assn. Bond Lawyers, Princeton Alumni Assn. New Orleans (pres. 1982-86), Princeton Alumni Assn. Baton Rouge (pres. 2002-). Episcopalian. Home and Office: 4075 S Ramsey Dr Baton Rouge LA 70808-1653

RICHARDS, MARTY GROVER, university foundation director; b. Spartanburg, S.C., July 14, 1962; s. Joseph Defoe and Anne Ellen (Chastain) R. BA, Wofford Coll., 1984; MA, Ohio State U., 1986. Chmn. dept. polit. sci. Spartanburg Meth. Coll., 1987-89; assoc. prof. U. S.C., Spartanburg, 1989-92; campaign mgr. Hartnett for U.S. Senate, Greenville, S.C., 1992-94; found. dir. Spartanburg Tech. Coll., 1994—. Pres.-elect Spartanburg Music Guild, 1997, pres., 1998; bd. dirs. Spartanburg Little Theater, 1995—, pres., 1999-2001; bd. dirs. Arts Partnership Greater Spartanburg, 1998-2001, Mobile Meals of Spartanburg, 1986-94, Habitat for Humanity, 1988-92, Team Spartanburg, Spartanburg C. of C., 2000—, Ballet Spartanburg, 2001—; publicity chmn. A Dickens of a Christmas Festival, Spartanburg, 1997-00, chmn. 2001—, Bill Drake Christmas Music Festival, Spartanburg, 1996—, Spartanburg County Tennis Assn., 1987-95; bd. dirs. Team Spartanburg, Greater Spartanburg C. of C., 2000—, Ballet Spartanburg, 2001—; com. mem. Arts in Edn. Arts Partnership of Greater Spartanburg. Mem. S.C. Nat. Soc. Fund Raising Execs. (pres. Piedmont chpt. 1997-98). Presbyterian. Avocations: tennis, music, theater, reading, Ohio state sports. Office: Spartanburg Tech Coll Found PO Box 4386 Spartanburg SC 29305-4386 E-mail: richardsm@spt.tec.sc.us.

RICHARDS, MAURICE, lawyer; b. Tremonton, Utah, Apr. 16, 1922; s. Bernard M. and Lula (Winchester) R.; m. Sophie Reed, Sept. 6, 1944 (div. Sept. 1977); children: Sheree, Reed, Brett, Tina, Jeff. AA, Weber Coll., 1942; BA, BL, U. Utah, 1950, JD, 1967; postgrad., Yale U., 1951. Bar: Utah 1951. Atty. City of Clinton and North Ogden, Utah, 1950, Weber County, Ogden, 1951-63, commr., 1965-68, pub. defender, chief trial atty., 1972-86; ptnr. Richards, Caine & Allen, 1953—. Served to capt. U.S. Army, 1943-47; as col. Utah State Guard. Capt. Air Corps U.S. Army, 1943—47, col. Utah State Guard. Decorated D.F.C., Air medal with three bronze oak leaf clusters. Democrat. Mem. Lds Ch. Home: 6160 Wasatch Dr Ogden UT 84403 Office: Richards Caine & Allen 2568 Washington Blvd Ste 6 Ogden UT 84401-3114

RICHARDS, MORRIS DICK, social work administrator, psychotherapist, educator; b. L.A., Aug. 20, 1939; s. Morris Dick Richards and Annette Fox Briggs, Lynn Rich Briggs (Stepfather); m. Leslie Sondra Lefkowitz, Mar. 22, 1975. BA cum laude, Claremont Men's Coll., 1962; MA, U. Chgo., 1964; MPA, U. So. Calif., 1965; LLB, La Salle Ext. U., 1971; MS in Hygiene, PhD in Social Work, U. Pitts., 1973; MBA, Chapman Coll., 1987. LCSW, lic. marriage family therapist. Asst. dep. dir. children and youth services Orange County (Calif.) Dept. Mental Health, 1973-77; gen. mgr., indsl. therapist Paragon West, Anaheim, Calif., 1977-83; acting dir. alcohol and drug program Horizon Health Corp., Newport Beach, 1983-84; editor, pub. relations rep., sr. social worker Orange County Social Services Agy., 1983-85; staff analyst Environ. Mgmt. Agy., Orange County, 1985-90; exec. asst. to dir. planning Orange County, 1990-92; staff analyst Orange County Social Svc. Agy., 1992-95; ret., 1995; part-time health care contract adminstr., staff analyst, 1996-97; part-time staff analyst Mgmt. Svcs., 1997-2001; clin. social worker County of Orange Drug Abuse and Alcohol Svcs., 2001—02; clin. social worker dual diagnosis program Healthcare Agy., Orange County, Calif., 2002—. Adj. clin. prof. Chapman Coll., Orange, Calif., 1974-85; instr. Calif. Grad. Inst., 1988-93; instr. U. Phoenix, 1992-95; instr. Calif. State U., Fullerton, 1997-2000; supervising child welfare worker, program analyst, head child welfare worker, exec. asst. L.A. County Pub. Social Svcs., 1967-71; psychiat. clin. specialist Jewish Big Bros., L.A. County, 1964-67; med. social work cons. Whittier (Calif.) Presbyn. Hosp., 1973-76; pvt. practice psychotherapy, Tustin, Calif., 1975-77. Editor newsletter Orange County Adv., 1984-85, Planning Perspective, 1990-91, Broadmoor Cmty. News, 1992-93; contbr. articles to profl. jours. Past bd. dirs. Orange County chpt. Am. Jewish Com., 1982-88, Broadmore Cmty. Assn., Anaheim Hills, Calif., 1981-83, sec., 1990-94, treas., 1998-2001; mem. Orange County Mental Health Adv. Bd., 1981-88, sec., bd. dirs.; mem. bd. dirs. Orange County Mental Health Assn., 1988-91, Orange County Assn. Retarded Citizens, 1999—; mem. Juvenile Diversion Task Force of Orange County, 1977. Served with USAR, 1958-64. Fellow U. Chgo., 1962, NIMH, 1962, 72; Haynes scholar U. So. Calif. Sch. Pub. Adminstrn., 1964; grantee Faulk Program in Urban Mental Health, U. Pitts., 1973. Mem. NASW (mental health liaison, v.p. local chpt. 1975-88, Social Worker of Yr. award Orange County chpt. 1987), Acad. Cert. Social Workers (lic. clin. social worker and marriage and family therapist), Registry Clin. Social Workers (past diplomate in clin. social work), Orange County Mental Health Assn. (past sec.). Avocations: karate (black belt), tennis, basketball.

RICHARDS, NORMAN BLANCHARD, lawyer; b. Melrose, Mass., May 27, 1924; s. Henry Edward and Annie Jane (Blanchard) R.; m. Diane Maionchi, July 9, 1977; children— Terri, Jeffrey. BS, Bowdoin Coll., 1945; JD, Stanford U., 1951. Bar: Calif. bar 1951. Mem. firm McCutchen Doyle Brown & Enersen, San Francisco, 1951—, partner, 1960—. Mem. faculty Tulane Admiralty Law Inst., Hastings Coll. Advocacy. Bd. visitors Stanford Law Sch. With USN, 1943-46. Fellow Am. Coll. Trial Lawyers; mem. ABA, Calif. State Bar, San Francisco Bar ASsn., Maritime Law Assn. U.S. Home: 85 Platt Ave Sausalito CA 94965-1897 Office: Bingham McCutchen 3 Embarcadero Ctr San Francisco CA 94111-4003

RICHARDS, PATRICIA JONES, artist, poet; b. Pomona, Calif., Nov. 20; d. Earle Feurte Jones and Florence Frable Slawson; m. Addison Whitaker Richards, May 1, 1950 (dec. Mar. 1964). BA, Pomona Coll., 1944; cert. nursery sch. tchr., Scripps Coll., 1944. Acquistions libr. Calif. State Polytechnic U., Pomona, 1979-85. Author: Self-Expression-Poems and Watercolors, 1996, "Old Friends" Through Sun and Showers, 1997, Pensativo-Poems and Watercolors (Golden Leaves award 1996-97, 99-2000), 2000; composer, pianist Jazz CD, To a Woven Fitness, 2001.

RICHARDS, PAUL A. retired lawyer; b. Oakland, Calif., May 27, 1927; s. Donnell C. and Theresa (Pasquale) R.; m. Ann Morgans, May 20, 1948 (dec. 1984); 1 child: Paul M.; m. Elise Hall, Dec. 6, 1996. Practiced law, Reno, from 1953; settlement judge settle conf. program Supreme Ct. State of Nev., 1998-2000; ret., 2000.

RICHARDS, PAUL GRANSTON, geophysics educator, seismologist; b. Cirencester, Eng., Mar. 31, 1943; came to U.S., 1965; s. Albert George and Kathleen Margaret (Harding) R.; m. Jody Margaret Porterfield, June 1, 1968; children: Mark, Jessica, Gillian. BA, Cambridge (Eng.) U., 1965; MS, Calif. Inst. Tech., Pasadena, 1966, PhD, 1970. Prof. geol. scis. Columbia U., N.Y.C., 1971—, chmn. dept. geol. scis., 1980-83. Co-author: Quantitative Seismology, 2 vols., 1980, 2nd edit., 2002. Guggenheim Found. fellow, 1977-78, MacArthur Found. fellow, 1981-86. Fellow Royal Astron. Soc.; mem. Am. Geophys. Union (Macelwane award 1976), Coun. Fgn. Rels. Episcopalian. Office: Lamont-Doherty Earth OBS Palisades NY 10964 E-mail: richards@ldeo.columbia.edu.

RICHARDS, PAUL LINFORD, physics educator, researcher; b. Ithaca, N.Y., June 4, 1934; s. Lorenzo Adolph and Zilla (Linford) R.; m. Audrey Jarratt , Aug. 24, 1965; children: Elizabeth Anne, Mary-Ann. AB, Harvard U., 1956; PhD, U. Calif., Berkeley, 1960. Postdoctoral fellow U. Cambridge (Eng.), 1959-60; mem. tech. staff Bell Telephone Labs., Murray Hill, N.J., 1960-66; prof. physics U. Calif., Berkeley, 1966—. Faculty sr. scientist Lawrence Berkeley Lab., 1966-2001; advisor NASA, 1975-92, 98—; hon. prof. Miller Inst. Rsch. in Phys. Scis., Berkeley, 1969-70, 87-88, 2001; vis. prof. Ecole Normale Superieure, Paris, 1984, 92; vis. astronomer Paris Obs., 1984. Contbr. over 300 articles to profl. jours. Guggenheim Meml. Found. fellow, Cambridge, Eng., 1973-74; named Calif. Scientist of Yr. Mus. Sci., L.A., 1981; recipient sr. scientist award Alexander von Humboldt Found., Stuttgart, Fed. Republic Germany, 1982, Button medal, 1997; Berkeley Faculty Rsch. lectr. 1991. Mem. NAS; fellow Am. Phys. Soc. (Isakson prize 2000), Am. Acad. Arts and Scis. Avocations: vineyardist, wine making.

RICHARDS, RICHARD N. astronaut, military officer; b. Key West, Fla., Aug. 24, 1946; s. Marjorie Richards; m. Lois Hollabaugh. BS in Chem. Engring., U. Mo., Columbia, 1969; MS in Aero. Systems, U. W. Fla., 1970. Commd. ensign USN, 1969, advanced throught grades to capt., naval pilot, 1970—71, USN Fighter Squadron 103, Carrier USS America Atlantic and Mediterranean patrol, 1972—76; student pilot Navel Test Pilot Sch., Patuxent River, Md., 1976—77; project test pilot automatic carrier landing systems USN., 1977—80; astronaut NASA, Houston, 1981—. Mem.: Soc. Exptl. Test Pilots, Tau Beta Pi, Lambda Chi Alpha. Office: Space Shuttle Program Office Johnson Space Ctr Houston TX 77058

RICHARDS, RILEY HARRY, insurance company executive; b. North Judson, Ind., Oct. 6, 1912; s. Harry J. and Chestie (Johnson) R.; m. Eloise Quinn Smith, May 4, 1940; children: Roy, Lynne. AB, U. Calif., Berkeley, 1934; MBA, Harvard U., 1937. Chartered fin. analyst. Fin. analyst Savs. Bank Trust Co. N.Y.C., 1937-40, SEC, Washington, Phila., 1940-45; accountant U.S. Steel Corp., Pitts., 1945-47; with Equitable Life Ins. Co. Iowa, Des Moines, 1947-77, v.p. finance, 1961-73, v.p., sec., treas., 1973-76, sr. v.p., sec.-treas., 1976-77; dir., mem. exec. com. Equitable of Iowa Cos., 1977-84. Pres. Westminster House, Inc., 1989-96; dir. F.M. Hubbell Sons & Co., 1977-85. Mem. Des Moines Plan and Zoning Commn., 1959-70, chmn., 1968-69; mem. bd. pensions U.P. Ch. in U.S.A., 1960-72, chmn. finance com., 1963-72; trustee United Presbyn. Found., 1979-87, vice chmn., 1981-83, chmn., 1983-87; bd. regents Life Officers Investment Seminar, 1969-70; trustee Thompson Trust, 1976— , Frederick M. Hubbell Estate, 1977-85. Mem. Am. Coun. Life Ins. (chmn. fin. sect. 1970), Iowa Soc. Fin. Analysts (pres. 1965-67), Sigma Alpha Epsilon. Clubs: Des Moines. Lodges: Masons, Rotary. Republican. Home: 2909 Woodland Ave Apt 310 Des Moines IA 50312-3863

RICHARDS, RUTH, psychiatrist, educational psychologist; b. Lincoln, Nebr. d. Dexter N. and Ruth (Fulton) R. BS with honors, Stanford U., 1965; MA, U. Calif., Berkeley, 1969, PhD, 1971; MD, Harvard Med. Sch., Boston, 1980. Diplomate Am. Bd. Psychiatry and Neurology; lic. psychologist, Mass.; cert. secondary edn. educator in physics, math, art, Calif. Asst. prof. ednl. psychology Boston U. Sch. Edn., 1971-75; lectr. in psychology dept. psychiatry Harvard Med. Sch., Boston, 1978—, fellow, instr., asst. clin. prof. psychiatry, 1981-94; assoc. attending psychiatrist, various appointments McLean Hosp., Belmont, Mass., 1978—, rsch. affiliate; assoc. clin. prof. U. Calif., San Francisco, 1994—; prof. psychology Saybrook Grad. Sch., 1995—, faculty co-chair, 1996-98; chair Consciousness and Spirituality, 1999-2000. Mem. exec. adv. bd. Ency. of Creativity, 1996-99; adv. bd. Manic-Depressive Illness Found., 1989—. Mem. editl. bd. Creativity Rsch. Jour., 1992—, Jour. Humanistic Psychology, 1996—; co-editor: Eminent Creativity, Everyday Creativity and Health, 1997; contbr. numerous articles to profl. jours. and chpts. to books. Mem. adv. panel biol. application program, Office of Technol. Assessment, U.S. Congress, 1987-88; dir. women's leadership project in adult edn., Boston U., 1974-75, others. Sr. asst. surgeon USPHS, 1980-81. Mem. APA, Soc. Chaos Theory in Psychology and the Life Scis. Avocations: visual art, creative writing, photography, physics.

RICHARDS, SUSAN LYNNE, library director; b. Franklin, Pa., Dec. 4, 1956; d. L. Burton and Phyllis D. (Ditzenberger) R.; m. Rex C. Myers, Jan. 10, 1987; stepchildren: Gary Myers, Laura Myers Wight. AB, Grove City Coll., 1978; MA in History, Clarion U., 1980; MLS, Kent State U., 1982; PhD, U. N.H., 2002. Profl. libr. Tech. svcs. libr. Morningside Coll., Sioux City, Iowa, 1983-85; head serials dept. Briggs Libr. S.D. State U., Brookings, 1986-88, head acquisitions dept. Briggs Libr., 1988-91; asst. dir. librs. U. Vt., Burlington, 1992-95; dir. libr. svcs. Western State Coll., Gunnison, Colo., 1995-99; univ. libr. Lawrence U., Appleton, Wis., 1999—. Editor VLA News, Vt. Libr. Assn., 1992-94, Book Marks, S.D. Libr. Assn., 1989-91; gov. bd. dirs. Pathfinder Libr. Sys., Colo.; mem. Vt. Newspaper Project Adv. Bd., 1994-95. Contbr. articles to profl. jours. and mags. Mem. Cmty. Band Bd., Brookings, 1991, City Planning Commn., Brookings, 1989-91, City Historic Preservation Com., Gunnison, 1998-99; judge Nat. History Day, S.D. a nd Iowa, 1984, 85, 88. Grantee NEH, 1984. Mem.: ALA (com. mem. 1987—), AAUW (local and state officer 1990), Wis. Libr. Assn., Mountain Plains Libr. Assn. (com. chair 1990, 1991), Beta Phi Mu, Phi Alpha Theta. Avocations: cross country skiing, hiking. Office: Lawrence U Seeley G Mudd Library Appleton WI 54912

RICHARDS, SUSAN R. management consultant; b. Madison, Ind., Aug. 30, 1948; d. Chester Burns and Martha (Mefford) Goins; m. Kim E. Richards, Sept. 6, 1967 (div. 1969); 1 child, Natalie S. Richards. Student, Ind. U.-Purdue U., Indpls., 1970-72. Co-owner, pres. Baker Bros. Sales & Rentals, Indpls., 1976-87; owner, chmn. Party Concepts, 1982-87; asst. dir., adminstr. L.A. Land Co., 1989-90; mgmt. cons. to small bus. cos., Malibu, Woodland Hills, Calif., 1990—. Inner city boys basketball coach, Indpls., 1977; tchr. Profl. Women Entrepreneurs, Indpls., 1980-81, Indpls. chpt. Exec. Women's Network, 1983; mem. Tri Valley Spl. Olympics, 1992—. Mem. Actors and Others for Animals. Republican. Roman Catholic. Avocations: tennis, polo.

RICHARDS, SUZANNE V. lawyer; b. Columbia, S.C., Sept. 7, 1927; d. Raymond E. and Elise C. (Gray) R. AB, George Washington U., 1948, JD with distinction, 1957, LLM, 1959. Bar: D.C. 1958. Sole practice, Washington, 1974—. Lectr. in family and probate law; mem. D.C. Jud. Conf., 1975—2002. Bd. dirs. Coun. for Ct. Excellence. Recipient John Bell Larner award George Washington U., 1958; named Woman Lawyer of Yr., Women's Bar Assn. D.C., 1977. Mem. ABA (ho. of dels. 1988-90), Bar Assn. D.C. (pres. 1989-90), Women's Bar Assn. (pres. 1977-78), Trial Lawyers Assn. of D.C. (bd. govs. 1978-82, 85-2001, treas. 1982-85), D.C. Bar, Fed. Bar Assn. Home: 530 N St SW Washington DC 20024-4546 Office: PO Box 65466 Washington DC 20035-5466

RICHARDS, THOMAS H. lawyer, arbitrator; b. Exeter, N.H., May 29, 1942; s. Frank F. and Ella (Higgins) R.; m. Barbara M. Blackmer, Mar. 23, 1975; children: Daniel, Matthew. BA cum laude, U. N.H., 1964; JD, NYU, 1967. Bar: N.H. 1967, U.S. Dist. Ct. N.H., U.S. Ct. Appeals (1st cir., D.C. cir.) 1987. Assoc. to v.p. Sheehan Phinney Bass & Green, Manchester, N.H., 1967-68, 70-99, ret., 1999, of counsel. Mem. N.H. Jud. Coun., Concord, 1988-90; mem. long range planning com. N.H. Supreme Ct., 1989-90, mem. profl. conduct com., 1989-90. Capt. 25th inf. divsn., U.S. Army, 1968-69. Root-Tilden fellow. Fellow Am. Bar Found., Am. Coll. Trial Lawyers, Internat. Soc. Barristers, N.H. Bar Found. (chmn. 1991-92); mem. Manchester Bar Assn. (bd. govs. 1975-80), New Eng. Bar Assn. (bd. govs. 1989-92), N.H. Bar Assn. (bd. govs. 1985-87, pres. 1989-90), Nat. Conf. Bar Pres., Phi Beta Kappa. Avocations: carpentry, collecting and restoring antique tools. Home: 164 Browns Hill Rd Sunapee NH 03782 Office: Sheehan Phinney Bass & Green 1000 Elm St Manchester NH 03101-1801

RICHARDS, TODD LYNN, radiologist; b. Salt Lake City, Apr. 10, 1955; s. Wilford Lynn and Claire Maughan Richards, Beatrice Richards (Stepmother); m. Alicia Wilson; children: Anne, Kimberly, Eve, Theresa, Juliet, Carolyn. PhD, U. Calif., Berkeley, 1985. Prof. radiology U. Wash., Seattle, 1985—. Reviewer NIH, Bethesda, 2001—. Author: (book) Brain Literacy for Educators and Psychologists, 2002, (clin. trials) Trials to Test New Treatments for Multiple Sclerosis, 2002; contbr. Grantee, NIH, 1987—99. Mem.: Am. Acad. Clin. Neurophysiology. Achievements include patents for magnetic resonance neuography; research in neuroscience, neuroimaging, dyslexia, MR spectroscopy, functional MRI; invention of automatic detection of brain lesions on MRI images. Office: U Wash 1959 NE Pacific Seattle WA 98195 Office Fax: 206-543-3495. Business E-Mail: toddr@u.washington.edu.

RICHARDS, VINCENT PHILIP HASLEWOOD, retired librarian; b. Sutton Bonington, Nottinghamshire, Eng., Aug. 1, 1933; emigrated to Can., 1956, naturalized, 1961; s. Philip Haslewood and Alice Hilda (Moore) R.; m. Ann Beardshall, Apr. 3, 1961; children: Mark, Christopher, Erika. A.L.A., Ealing Coll., London, 1954; B.L.S. with distinction, U. Okla., 1966. Cert. profl. librarian, B.C. Joined Third Order Mt. Carmel, Roman Catholic Ch., 1976; with Brentford and Chiswick Pub. Libraries, London, 1949-56; asst. librarian B.C. (Can.) Pub. Library Commn., Dawson Creek, 1956-57; asst. dir. Fraser Valley Regional Library, Abbotsford, B.C., 1957-67; chief librarian Red Deer (Alta., Can.) Coll., 1967-77; dir. libraries Edmonton (Alta.) Pub. Library, 1977-89; libr. and book industry cons. Victoria, Can., 1990—. Pres. Faculty Assn. Red Deer Coll., 1971-72, bd. govs., 1972-73 Contbr. articles to profl. jours., 1954— . Vice pres. Jeunesses Musicales, Red Deer, 1969-70; bd. dirs. Red Deer TV Authority, 1975-76, Alta. Found. Lit. Arts, 1984-86. Served with Royal Army Ednl. Corps, 1951-53. Home and Office: 105 1049 Costin Ave Victoria BC Canada V9B 2T4 E-mail: varichards@pacificcoast.net. *Dedication to public service, in spite of its frustrating aspects, diversity of experience, people and places, and the avoidance of overspecialization are great contributors to an enjoyable working life.*

RICHARDS, WALTER DUBOIS, artist, illustrator; b. Penfield, Ohio, Sept. 18, 1907; s. Ralph DuBois and Ruby Mildred (Smith) R.; m. Glenora Case, June 20, 1931; children: Timothy, Henry Tracy. Grad., Cleve. Sch. Art, 1930. With Sundblom Studios, Chgo., 1930-31, Tranquillini Studios, Cleve., 1931-36, Charles E. Cooper Studios, N.Y.C., 1936-50; freelance artist, 1950—. Executed paintings and illustrations for leading indsl. corps., nat. mags.; designed: U.S. postage stamps including Frederick Douglas 25 cent stamp; block of 4 stamps on beautification of Am.; Am. bald eagle-Mus. Natural History with commemorative; Cape Hatteras Nat. Parks Centennial block of four stamps; Paul Lawrence Dunbar Am. Poets commemorative; block of 4 stamps on Am. trees, 1978, blocks of 4 stamps on Am. architecture, 1979-82; co-designer anti-pollution block of four stamps; James Hoban stamp, 1981, Timberline Lodge 50th Anniversary U.S. commemorative stamp, 1987; exhibited, Cleve. Mus. Art, Art Inst., Chgo., Met. Mus., N.Y.C., Pa. Acad. Fine Arts, Bklyn. Mus., N.A.D., Whitney Mus., 200 Years Watercolor Painting, Met. Mus., 1966, 200 Years Am. Illustration, N.Y. Hist. Soc., 1976; represented in permanent collection, Whitney Mus., New Britain Mus. Am. Art, Cleve. Mus.

Art, William A. Farnsworth Library and Art Mus., West Point Mus., Worcester (Mass.) Art Mus., Yale U. Art Gallery-New Haven, Conn., Smithsonian, Washington, D.C. Bd. dirs. Rowayton Art Center, Historic New Orleans Collection, 1989. Recipient highest award in lithography Cleve. Mus. Art, ann. 1935-38; Spl. Honor USAF, 1964; ann. Environ. Improvement award, 1983; named to Rocky River (Ohio) High Sch. Hall of Fame, 1991. Mem. Am. Watercolor Soc. (2d v.p. 1965-67), Conn. Watercolor Soc., NAD, Soc. of Illustrators, Fairfield Watercolor Group (pres., founder), Westport Artists. Address: 87 Oak St New Canaan CT 06840-5840

RICHARDS, WESLEY JON, newscaster, writer, producer; b. N.Y.C., Apr. 9, 1942; s. Mark and Pearl R. Richards; m. Carole A. Louis, June 8, 1962; children: Wesley, Julie, Lynn, Charles. Student, Hofstra U., 1959-62; MA, Antioch U., 1990. Radio personality Sta. WFYI, Mineola, N.Y., 1965, Sta. WGBB, Freeport, 1966-70; editor AP, N.Y.C., 1971-74; radio personality Sta. WHLI, Hempstead, N.Y., 1974-76, Sta. WRFM, N.Y.C., 1976-86; broadcaster NBC Radio Network, 1987-89; newscaster Sta. WYNY, 1989-90, Sta. WOR, N.Y.C., 1990-92; writer, prodr. NBC News, 1992—, 1992—. Freelance entertainer, 1955—; correspondent ABC Radio Network, N.Y.C., 1975, 90. Writer numerous essays, poems and songs, 1960—. Mem. AFTRA, Writers Guild Am., Broadcast Pioneers, Nat. Assn. Broadcast Employees and Technicians.

RICHARDS, WINSTON ASHTON, mathematics educator, statistician; b. Chaguanas, Trinidad and Tobago, Mar. 7, 1935; s. Edward Ivan and Leanora Fidelcia Richards; m. Kathleen Marie Hoolihan, Apr. 4, 1964; children: Ashton, Winston, Marie, Michael, Bridgette, Mary, Patricia, Edward. BS, Marquette U., 1959, MS, 1961; MA, U. Western Ont., Can., 1966, PhD, 1970. Asst. prof. math. and stats. Pa. State U.-Harrisburg, Middletown, 1969-72, assoc. prof. math. and stats., 1972—. Fellow Inst. Statisticians, Am. Statis. Assn. Home: 2100 Chestnut St Harrisburg PA 17104-1333 Office: Pa State U-Harrisburg 777 W Harrisburg Pike Middletown PA 17057-4846

RICHARDS-BARNARD, SANDRA L. control systems engineer, computer graphics consultant; b. Houston, Oct. 18, 1948; d. Earl Douglas and Joleta (Phillips) Lively; m. Daniel R. Barnard (dec.); children: Jamie Raquel Richards, Laurie Joanna Richards Nichols, Micah Waverly Barnard. Student, San Jacinto Coll., 1966-68; BS in Chemistry and Math., Sam Houston State U., 1970; MBA, Houston Bapt. U., 1987; post-Baccalaureate, U. St. Thomas, 2000, 01, Tex. A&M U., 2000. INTEL cert. Chemist Sorbotec, Inc., Houston, 1971-72, Champion Papers, Inc., Pasadena, Tex., 1974-75, Core Labs., Inc., Houston, 1981-82; account rep. Foxboro Co., 1982-88; sr. control systems engring. technologist SIP (Parsons) Engring. Inc., 1989-90; sr. control sys. engr., control sys. supr. Bechtel, 1990-93; moon rock chemist at Lunar Receiving Lab. Johnson Space Ctr., Brown & Root-Northrup, Houston, 1970-71; salesman Tex. Real Estate Commn., 1972—; staff chem. cons. HL&P Reliant Energy, 1993-95; owner Richards & Assocs., Houston, 1995—. Tchr. bus. comm. and info. sys. Pasadena Ind. Sch. Dist., 1999—; mem. Act for Eight Community TV, Cousteau Soc. Charter mem. Nat./State Leadership Tng. Inst. on Gifted and Talented, Ventura, Calif., 1979—; mem. Houston Mus. Natural Sci., Houston Contemporary Arts Mus.; ann. rep. Nat. Engrs. Week, Bechtel, sci. fair judge. Sam Houston State U. undergrad. rsch. fellow in organic chemistry, 1969-70; grantee Job Shadowing, 2000; recipient Pedagogy award PISD, 2000. Mem. Soc. Women Engrs., Nat. Assn. Corrosion Engrs., Am. Chem. Soc., Instrument Soc. Am. (sr., bd. dirs. standards and practices com. 1987, standards and practices com. liaison), Nat. Mus. for Women in the Arts (charter), Christian Women's Club. E-mail: s4andra@yahoo.com.

RICHARDSON, ALBERT EDWARD, chemistry educator, consultant, researcher; b. Lovelock, Nev., Feb. 4, 1929; s. James Harold and Mary Lorraine Richardson; m. Shirley Arlene Richardson, June 10, 1959 (dec. Apr. 1997); children: Anne Ikard, John (dec.), Stephen; stepchildren: Corinne Jameson, Elisabeth Anderson, David Beckman, Margaret Chambers. BS in Chemistry, U. Nev., 1950; PhD, Iowa State U., 1956. Accredited profl. chemist Am. Inst. Chemists. Rsch. chemist Ames (Iowa) Lab. of the Atomic Energy Commn., 1950—55; asst. prof. chemistry N.Mex. State U., Las Cruces, 1955—60, radiation safety officer, 1957—75, assoc. prof. chemistry, 1960—91, assoc. prof. emeritus, 1991—. Vis. scientist N.Mex. secondary schs., 1960—91; vis. prof. chemistry Adams State Coll., Alamosa, Colo., 1963; summer rschr. Ames Lab. Atomic Energy Commn., 1964, Lawrence Livermore (Calif.) Nat. Lab., 1979; cons. White Sands (N.Mex.) Missile Range, 1965—71, contractor, 1973—74, chemist, 1981—82, 1984—92; vis. staff mem. Los Alamos (N.Mex.) Nat. Labs., 1975—80; summer faculty Sandia Nat. Lab., Albuquerque, 1983; owner, mgr. Timberline Bed and Breakfast, Cedaredge, Colo., 1992—98. Contbr. articles to profl. jours. Bus. mgr. Coll. Cmty. Chorus, Las Cruces, 1956—57; pres. U. Park Toastmaster's Club, 1961; dir. Southwestern N.Mex. Regional Sci. Fair, 1967—68; vol. reading aide to elem. schs., 2000—. Rsch. grantee NASA, 1966, Equipment grantee Atomic Energy Commn., 1968; postdoctoral rsch. fellow Atomic Energy Commn., 1968-69. Mem. Am. Chem. Soc. (chmn. so. N.Mex. sect. 1962, chmn. Rio Grande Valley sect. 1977), Sigma Xi, Phi Kappa Phi (pres. N.Mex. State U. chpt. 1972-73), Phi Lambda Upsilon, Sigma Pi Sigma. Democrat. Avocations: photography, collecting coins and CD's, traveling, gardening, cultural activities. Home: 1185 Villita Loop Las Cruces NM 88007 E-mail: aerinlc@earthlink.net.

RICHARDSON, ALFONSO AUSTIN, accountant, financial services executive; b. St. Nicholas, Aruba, W.I., Feb. 29, 1932; came to U.S., 1951; s. Ashley A. and Elvia H. Richardson; m. Florence C. St. Hilaire, Sept. 7, 1957; children: Paula, Kathy, Peter, Steven, Edward, Vernon. BS, L.I. U., 1959. Cert. internat. financier. V.p., treas. Node 4 Assocs., Inc., Bklyn., 1970-71; asst. contr. Kings County Hosp. Ctr., 1971-74; owner Richardson Mgmt. Assoc., 1971—; contr. Kings County Hosp. Ctr., Bklyn., 1974-79; contr., CFO Harlem Hosp. Ctr., N.Y.C., 1979-95; CFO L.B.J. Health Complex, Inc., Bklyn., 1996-98; pres., CEO Accudata Sys. Svcs., Inc., N.Y.C., 1997—. Contbr. articles to profl. publs. Dir., treas. Bklyn. Local Econ. Devel. Corp., 1965-70, L.B.J. Health Complex, Inc., Bklyn., 1991-96; mem. Pub. Citizens. Sgt. U.S. Army, 1952-55. Mem. Healthcare Fin. Mgmt. Assn. (Follmer Bronze Merit award 1996), Nat. Soc. Accts., Ind. Assn. Accts. Bklyn., Caribbean Am. C. of C., Oxford Club, VFW, Disabled Am. Vets., Contrs. Orgn. (past pres.), Internat. Assn. Fin. Planning, Internat. Soc. Financiers. Avocations: bowling, scrabble, philately, numismatics, cycling. Home: 704 Empire Blvd Brooklyn NY 11213-5309 Office: Accudata Sys Svcs Inc Empire State Bldg Ste 4200 New York NY 10118

RICHARDSON, ALMA SUSAN, consultant; b. West Helena, Ark., Nov. 25, 1951; d. Alvin Young and Dorothy (Scott) Blue; m. Ernest R. Richardson, Dec. 28, 1974 (div. Oct. 1988); 1 child, Candace Ray. BS, Jackson State U., 1972. Sec., libr. asst., adminstrv. asst. AT&T, Atlanta and Washington, 1973-95; cons. KRA Corp., Silver Spring, Md., 1995—; rschr. U. Mich., Ann Arbor, 1996. Election judge Rep. Party, Landover, Md., 1996; mem. Akosua Visions Global Ministries, 1996—; mentor Nicholas Orem Mid. Sch., 1994-95; founder FGO-For Girls Only Program Series, 1996. Mem. Nat. Mus. for Women in Arts, Network Enhancement Self-Esteem. Avocations: reading, traveling, cooking, people watching, teaching. Home and Office: 6201 Springhill Dr Apt 103 Greenbelt MD 20770-5318

RICHARDSON, ANN BISHOP, foundation executive, lawyer; b. New Rochelle, N.Y., Dec. 15, 1940; d. Erwin Julius and Mary Frances (Stuart) Heilemann; children: Timothy William, Lynn Patricia, Melanie Elizabeth. BA summa cum laude, Georgetown U., 1977; JD, George Washington U., 1984; cert., Oxford (Eng.) U., 1986. Bar: Md. 1988, D.C. 1989. Student counselor Amideast, Beirut, 1967-68, program specialist, 1970-73; adminstrv. asst. UN Devel. Program, Yaounde, Cameroon, 1968-70; adminstrv. mgr. Antioch Sch. Law, Washington, 1977-79; chief adminstrv. officer for internat. ops. Peace Corps, 1980-84; dir. adminstrn. and fin. African Devel. Found., 1984-87; atty. Karr and McLain, 1987-92; v.p., gen. counsel Time Dollar, Inc., 1992-98; adj. prof. law D.C. Sch. Law, 1994-98, prof., acad. dean, 1998—. Bd. dirs. Bur. Rehab., Inc. Active Neighbors, Inc., Washington, 1976—, Time Dollar, Inc. Recipient Spl. Achievement award Peace Corps, 1981, 82, African Devel. Found., 1986. Mem. ABA, ACLU, D.C. Bar Assn., Am. Women Univ. Grads., Soc. for Internat. Devel., Phi Beta Kappa. Office: DC Sch Law 4200 Connecticut Ave NW Washington DC 20008-1122

RICHARDSON, ARLINE ANNETTE, accountant, comptroller; b. N.Y.C., Aug. 20, 1939; d. Charles Sidney and Kathleen Gertrude (Sinclair) Hunt; m. David Edward Richardson, Sept. 13, 1958; children: Valerie-Jayne, LaVerne. AA, Bronx (N.Y.) C.C., 1976; BBA, CUNY, 1979, MPA, 1984. Mgr. patient accounts Jewish Home and Hosp. for Aged, N.Y.C., 1960-80; chief bookkeeper Edwin Gould Svcs. for Children, 1980-81; staff acct. N.Y. Hosp., 1981-84; mgr. Met. Transp. Authority, 1984-92; compt. The Computer Lab., Morrisville, N.C., 1993—. Substitute tchr. Vance County Schs., 1998-2000; instr. Vance-Granville C.C., 1999—. Vol. cmty. tax aide, N.Y.C., 1979-83; tutor Henderson (N.C.) Mid. Sch., 1993-95; vol. Maria Parham Hosp., 1993-99, mem. ethics com., 1996—; mem. Henderson-Vance County Human Rels. Commn., 1996—; mem. Henderson Zoning Bd. Adjustment, 1996—; active Leadership Vance, 1996. Recipient Mitchell-Titus award, 1979. Mem. Am. Assn. Ret. Persons (assoc. dist. coord., instr. tax-aide program North Ctrl. N.C. 1993-99, dist. coord.), Henderson Bus. and Profl. Women's Club, (v.p.), Beta Gamma Sigma, Phi Theta Kappa (Mitchell-Titus award 1979). Home: 1614 Peace St Henderson NC 27536-3549 Office: The Computer Lab 2700 Gateway Centre Blvd Morrisville NC 27560-9137

RICHARDSON, ARTEMAS P(ARTRIDGE), retired landscape architect; b. Phila., May 24, 1918; s. Eugene Stanley and Jessica (Ripple) R.; m. Frederica McAfee, Sept. 2, 1945; children: Steven, David, Ann, Vida, Stanley. BA in Fine Arts, Williams Coll., 1940; student, Pa. State U., 1940-42; BS in Landscape Architecture, Iowa State U., 1947. Registered landscape architect, Conn., Fla., Md., Mass., Miss., N.Y., Ohio, R.I., Tenn. Asst. landscape architect McCloud & Scatchard, Lilitz, Pa., 1947-48, Olmsted Bros., Brookline, Mass., 1949-50, ptnr., 1950-61, Olmsted Assocs., Brookline, 1961-64, pres, treas., 1964-80; owner The Olmsted Office, Fremont, N.H., 1980-2000; ret. Lectr. Harvard U., Cambridge, 1961; mem., chair Bd. Registration Landscape Architects, Mass., 1968-77. Illustrator: Trees for Every Purpose, 1980. Mem., chair Planning Bd., Needham, Mass., 1956-62, Conservation Commn., Fremont, 1982-2000, chair, 1984-2000; mem. N.H. Gov.'s Task Force on Community Trees, Concord, 1989-91; mem., chair Exeter River Local Adv. Com., 1995-2001. Lt. USNR, 1942-46, ETO. Named Outstanding Mcpl. Vol., N.H. Mcpl. Assn., 1993. Fellow Am. Soc. Landscape Architects, Boston Soc. Landscape Architects (pres. 1952-56); mem. N.H. Landscape Assn. (bd. dirs. 1984-87), Granite State Landscape Architects (vice chair 1990-91), Herb Soc. Am. (life), Scarab, Rotary (pres. local club 1965-66, dist. trustee 1968-69, dist. gov. 1970-71, bd. dirs. R.I. 1978-80), Delta Phi, Tau Sigma Delta, Pi Gamma Alpha. Avocations: photography, woodworking, gardening. Home: Langdon Pl 17 Hampton Rd Apt 106 Exeter NH 03833-4822 E-mail: aprich@ttlc.net.

RICHARDSON, ARTHUR WILHELM, lawyer; b. Glendale, Calif., Apr. 3, 1963; s. Douglas Fielding and Leni (Tempelaar-Lietz) R.; m. Noriko Satake, Nov. 14, 1998. AB, Occidental Coll., 1985; student, London Sch. Econs., 1983; JD, Harvard U., 1988. Bar: Calif. 1989. Assoc. Morgan, Lewis and Bockius, L.A., 1988-90; staff lawyer U.S. SEC, 1990-92, br. chief, 1992-96, sr. counsel, 1996—2001. Mem. ABA, Calif. Bar Assn., L.A. County Bar Assn., Harvard/Radcliffe Club So. Calif., Town Hall Calif., L.A. World Affairs Coun., Sierra Club, Phi Beta Kappa. Presbyterian. Home: 2328 Mallard Ln #6 Beavercreek OH 45431

RICHARDSON, A(RTHUR) LESLIE, former medical group consultant; b. Feb. 21, 1910; came to U.S., 1930, naturalized, 1937; s. John William and Emily Lilian (Wilkins) R.; m. B. Kathleen Sargent, Oct. 15, 1937. Student spl. courses, U. So. Calif., 1933-35. Mgr. Tower Theater, L.A., 1931-33; acct. Felix-Krueper Co., 1933-35; indsl. engr. Pettengill, Inc., 1935-57; purchasing agt. Gen. Petroleum Corp., 1937-46; adminstr. Beaver Med. Clinic, Redlands, Calif., 1946-72, exec. cons., 1972-75, 85; sec.-treas. Fern Properties, Inc., 1955-75, Redelco, Inc., Redlands, 1960-67; pres. Buinco, Inc., 1956-65; vice-chmn. Redlands adv. bd. Bank of Am., 1973-80; exec. cons. Med. Adminstrs. Calif., 1975-83. Pres. Redlands Area Cmty. Chest, 1953; vol. exec. Internat. Exec. Svc. Corps, Jakarta, 1977, Singapore, 1979; mem. San Bernardino County (Calif.) Grand Jury, 1952-53; bd. dirs. Beaver Med. Clinic Found., Redlands, 1961-2000, sec.-treas., 1961-74, pres., 1974-75, chmn. bd. dirs., 1992-2000. Lt. Med. Adminstrv. Corps, AUS, 1942-45. Recipient Redlands Civic award Elks, 1953. Fellow Am. Coll. Med. Practice Execs. (life, disting. fellow 1980, pres. 1965-66, dir.); mem. Med. Group Mgmt. Assn. (hon. life; mem. nat. long range planning com. 1963-68, pres. western sect. 1960), Kiwanis (pres. 1951), Masons. Episcopalian. Home: 1 Verlie Dr Redlands CA 92373-6943

RICHARDSON, BARBARA HULL, state legislator, social worker; b. Danville, Pa., Sept. 30, 1922; d. Robert Alonzo and Clara Lucille (Woodruff) H.; widowed; children: Barbara Follansbee, Lawrence, Christine, Lovel Pratt. BA, Bryn Mawr Coll., 1944; MSW, Smith Coll. School for Social Work, 1973. Social worker child and family svcs. divsn. children and youth svcs. HHS, Keene, N.H., 1969-71, adminstr. child and family svcs. Concord, 1975-88, supr. policy writers, 1988-91; mem. N.H. Ho. Reps., 1992—. Trustee Meeting Sch., 1980—; bd. dirs. Cheshire Housing Trust, 1986-93, pres., 1993—; adv. bd. Casey Family Svcs. N.H., 1990—; vol. Hospice Monadnock Region, 1991—; mem. community coun. Luth. Social Svcs. New England, 1993—; bd. dirs. Keene Day Care Ctr. Democrat. Home: 101 Morgan Rd Richmond NH 03470-4909 Office: NH Ho of Reps State Capitol Concord NH 03301

RICHARDSON, BARBARA KATHRYN, social worker; b. Magnet Cove, Ark., Nov. 28, 1936; d. Fred Lee and Lillian Catherine (Adkins) R. BA, Mary Hardin-Baylor U., 1961; MSW, Washington U., St. Louis, 1965. Cert. social worker. Sec., Dyke Bros., Little Rock, 1953-55; legal sec. Donalson, Bullard & Kucera, Dallas, 1955-57; pub. welfare worker Henderson County Pub. Welfare, Hendersonville, N.C., 1961-62; child welfare worker Tex. Dept. Pub. Welfare, Belton, 1962-63, adoption worker, Tyler, 1965-66, asst. dir. child welfare, Houston, 1966-69; dir. adoptions Hope Cottage Children's Bur., Dallas, 1970-74; dir. emergency-crisis unit Dallas County Mental Health-Mental Retardation, 1974-76; ednl. contract specialist, continuing edn. bur. Tex. Dept. Human Services, 1977-81, project developer Office Research, Demonstration and Eval., 1981-88, wellness specialist Personnel div., 1988-89; program devel. specialist Family Health Resources and Childrens Protective Svcs., 1989-90; owner Barkrich, Ltd., 1990—. Dem. precinct del., Dallas, 1972. Mem. Nat. Assn. Social Workers (state dir. 1974-75), Acad. Cert. Social Workers, Council on Social Work Edn. (ho. of dels. 1980-82), Gov.'s Club (charter mem. 1992). Home and Office: Barkrich Ltd 506 E 54th St Austin TX 78751-1305

RICHARDSON, BETTY H. lawyer, former prosecutor; b. Oct. 3, 1953; BA, U. Idaho, 1976; JD, Hastings Coll. Law, 1982. Staff aid U.S. Senator Frank Church, 1976-77; teaching asst. Hastings Coll. Law, 1980-82, tchg. asst., 1980-82; legal rsch. asst. criminal divsn. San Francisco Superior Ct., 1982-84; jud. law clk. Chamber of Idaho Supreme Ct. Justice Robert C. Huntley Jr., 1984-86; atty. U.S. Dept. Justice, Boise, Idaho, 1993-2001, Richardson & O'Leary, Eagle, 2001—. Instr. Boise State U., 1987, 89; mem. U.S. Atty. Gen.'s Adv. Com. subcoms. on environ., civil rights and native Am. issues, others; mem. hon. adv. bd. for Crime Victims Amendment in Idaho, 1994; mem. Dist. of Idaho Judges and Lawyer Reps. com., gender fairness com., Civil Justice Reform Act com. and criminal adv. com. Mem. Idaho Indsl. Commn., 1991-93, chmn., 1993; mem. adv. bd. Family and Workplace Consortium; mem. Assistance League of Boise. Recipient Harold E. Hughes Exceptional Svc. award Nat. Rural Inst. on Alcohol and Drug Abuse, 1999; Tony Patino fellow Hastings Coll. Law, 1982. Mem. Idaho Bar Assn. (governing coun. govt. and pub. sectors lawyers sect., Pro Bono Svc. award 1988—), Idaho Pros. Attys. Assn., Assistance league of Boise, YMCA. Office: Richardson & O'Leary 99 E State St Eagle ID 83616 also: 5796 N Dalspring Boise ID 83713

RICHARDSON, CAMPBELL, retired lawyer; b. Woodland, Calif., June 18, 1930; s. George Arthur and Mary (Hall) R.; m. Patricia Packwood, Sept. 3, 1957 (dec. Oct. 1971); children: Catherine, Sarah, Thomas; m. Carol Tamblyn, June 1975 (div. Dec. 1977); m. Susan J. Lienhart, May 3, 1980; 1 child, Laura. AB, Dartmouth Coll., 1952; JD, NYU, 1955. Bar: Oreg. 1955, U.S. Dist. Ct. Oreg. 1957. Ptnr. Stoel Rives LLP, Portland, 1964-2000; ret., 2000—. Co-author: Contemporary Trust and Will Forms for Oregon Attorneys and for Idaho Attorneys; contbr. articles to profl. jours. Mem. Portland/Metro Govt. Boundary Commn., 1976; mem. Oreg. Adv. Com. to U.S. Commn. on Civil Rights, 1976-84; bd. dirs. Ctr. for Urban Edn., Portland, 1980-84, Dorchester Conf., Inc., 1982, Oreg. Zoo Found., 1993—; chmn. planned giving com. St. Vincent Med. Found., 1988-98; mem. planned giving coun. Oreg. Health Scis. Found., 1994—; trustee Met. Family Svc. Found., 1990-98; bd. dirs. Elders in Action, Portland, 2000—. Served with U.S. Army, 1955-57. Mem. ABA, Oreg. Bar Assn., Multnomah County Bar Assn., Estate Planning Coun. Portland (pres. 1978), Am. Coll. Trust and Estate Counsel, City Club, Multnomah Athletic Club (Portland). Republican. Home: 1500 SW 5th Ave Unit 1701 Portland OR 97201-5430 Office: Stoel Rives LLP 900 SW 5th Ave Ste 2300 Portland OR 97204-1229 E-mail: crichardson@stoel.com.

RICHARDSON, CARL COLLEY, JR. thoroughbred farm owner; b. Inverness, Fla., Sept. 14, 1941; s. Carl Colley and Margaret (Barnes) Richardson; m. Linda Lou Dale, June 6, 1965; children: Heather Anne, Holly Anne. BA, Cen. Mo. State U., 1965. Spl. agt. U.S. Secret Svc., Washington, 1965-66; ins. agt. Coll. Life Ins. Co., Warrensburg, Mo., 1966-67; salesman Skelly Oil Co., Kansas City, 1967; numerous sales and mgmt. positions Mobil Oil Co., nationwide, 1967-76; mgr. co. ops. Amerada Hess Corp., Woodbridge, NJ, 1976-77; v.p., corp. officer Cheker Oil Co., Chgo., 1977-79; dir. mktg. and planning Suburban Propane Gas Corp. divsn. Quantum Chem. Corp., Whippany, NJ, 1979-80, area v.p., 1980-86, group v.p. western ops., 1986-89, sr. group v.p. suburban propane ops., 1989-90; mem. mgmt. com. Quantum Chem. Corp., 1989-93, sr. v.p. ops. and sales suburban propane and petrolane, 1990-93; owner, mgr. Richardson & Assocs., Abingdon, Va., 1994-96; owner Goose Creek Farm/Registered Thoroughbreds, Bristol, 1996—. Mem.: Morris County Indsl. Rec. Assn., Nat. L.P. Gas Assn., Am. Gas Assn., Order of De Molay, Order of Ky., Theta Chi. Republican. Baptist. Avocations: golf, bass fishing, deer hunting. Home: 11080 Goose Creek Rd Bristol VA 24202-3130

RICHARDSON, CHARLES CLIFTON, biochemist, educator; b. Wilson, N.C., May 7, 1935; s. Barney Clifton and Florence Elizabeth (Barefoot) R.; m. Ute Ingrid Hanssum, July 29, 1961; children: Thomas Clifton, Matthew Wilfrid BSM., Duke U., 1959, MD, 1960; A.M. (hon.), Harvard U., 1967. Intern dept. medicine Duke U., Durham, N.C., 1960-61; postdoctoral fellow dept. biochemistry Stanford U. Med. Sch., Calif., 1961-63; asst. prof. biol. chemistry Harvard Med. Sch., Boston, 1964-67, assoc. prof., 1967-69, prof. biol. chemistry, 1969—, chmn. dept. biol. chemistry, 1978-87, Edward S. Wood prof., 1979—. Mem. physiol. chemistry study sect. NIH, 1970-74; mem. Fachbeirat of Max-Planck Inst. für Moleculare Genetik, Berlin, Fed. Republic Germany, 1980-89; mem. sci. adv. com. U. S. Biochem. Corp., Cleve., 1983-93, Genetics Inst., Cambridge, Mass., 1986-99, NYCOMED-Amersham, U.K., 1998-2000; mem. Nat. Bd. Med. Examiners, 1973-76; mem. nucleic acids and protein adv. com., Am. Cancer Soc. Inst., 1975-78; mem. vis. com. Boston Biomed. Rsch. Found., 1985—; assoc. Helicon Found., San Diego, 1983-2000; mem. sci. adv. bd. Amersham Life Sci. Inc., 1994-98. Editor: Ann. Rev. Biochemistry (assoc. editor 1973-82), 1983—; mem. editorial bd. Jour. Biol. Chemistry, 1968-73, 84-88, Jour. Molecular Biology, 1976-79 Recipient Career Devel. award NIH, 1967-76, Merit award, 1986. Fellow Am. Acad. Arts and Scis., Inst. of Medicine; mem. Nat. Acad. Scis., Am. Chem. Soc. (Eli Lilly Co. biol. chem. award 1968), Am. Soc. Biol. Chemists (mem. nominating com. 1974-75, 1983-84), Am. Cancer Soc. (coun. for rsch. and clin. investigation 1989-92), Am. Soc. Biochemistry and Molecular Biology (Merck award in biochemistry and molecular biology 1996). E-mail: ccr@hms.harvard.edu.

RICHARDSON, CHARLES MARSH, electrical engineer, educator; b. Leominster, Mass., May 24, 1925; s. James Putnam and Sarah Belle (Marsh) R.; m. Mildred Ann Crowley, Nov. 19, 1949 (dec.); children: Charles Michael, James Dana. BSEE, Worcester Poly. Inst., 1945; MS in Edn., C.W. Post, Greenvale, N.Y., 1975; postgrad., C.W. Post, 1975-78. Registered profl. engr.; cert. elem. tchr., secondary math., physics, gen. sci., spl. edn. Engr. magnetron devel. Raytheon Mfg. Co., Waltham, Mass., 1945-51; engr., standards Sperry Gyroscope Co., Great Neck, N.Y., 1951-53; sales engr. G. Curtis Engel & Assoc., Ridgewood, N.J., 1953-54; sr. engr. Sperry Corp., Great Neck, N.Y., 1954-70; owner, dir. Learning Foundations, Hauppauge, 1970-86; sr. engr. Sperry (Unisys) Corp., Great Neck, 1983-89. Adj. prof. spl. edn. and reading C.W. Post Coll., 1979-81; pres. Ednl. Enginig., South Setauket, N.Y.; founder, exec. dir. The Literacy Coun.; founder ASTOR Literacy Program. Patentee in field; contbr. articles to profl. jours. Mem. Internat. Dyslexia Assn., Balt. Recipient Award for Outstanding Contbns. to Edn. N.Y. State Soc. Profl. Engrs., 1993 and Engrs. Joint Com. of L.I., 1996, Disting. Leadership award L.I. Bus. News, 1998. Mem. IEEE (pre-coll. edn. com., Long Island assn. edn. com.). Avocations: music, writing, sailing, bridge. Home: Ste 5152 1 Jefferson Ferry Dr South Setauket NY 11720-4724 E-mail: cmr1234@aol.com.

RICHARDSON, DANA ROLAND, video producer; b. Mason City, Iowa, Jan. 11, 1945; s. Dana Roland Richardson and Louise Marion (Duke) Sarles; m. Sandra Anderson, June 12, 1966; children: Patricia Nan, Dana Roland, Jr. BS, UCLA, 1966, MBA, 1967. CPA, Calif., N.Y. Staff acct. Arthur Young, L.A., 1967-72, mgr., 1972-76, prin. N.Y.C., 1976-78; ptnr. Ernst & Young, 1978-94, Dream Street Prodns., New Canaan, Conn., 1994—. Author: A Manager's Guide to Computer Timesharing, 1975, Audit and Control of Information Systems, 1987. Staff sgt. Reserves USANG, 1967-73. Recipient Nat. Videographer award, 1998, 99, Telly award, 1999; named one of Techology 100 Top 100 Achievers in Technology in Am., Technology Mag., 1982. Mem. AICPA, Calif. Soc. CPA's. Republican. Episcopalian. Avocations: boating, fishing, music, videography, multimedia. Office: Dream St Prodns PO Box 73 New Canaan CT 06840-0073

RICHARDSON, DANIEL RALPH, lawyer; b. Pasadena, Calif., Jan. 18, 1945; s. Ralph Claude and Rosemary Clare (Lowery) R.; m. Virginia Ann Lorton, Sept. 4, 1965; children: Brian Daniel, Neil Ryan. BS, Colo. State U., 1969; MBA, St. Mary's Coll. of Calif., 1977; JD, JFK U., 1992. Bar: Calif. Systems engr. Electronic Data Systems, San Francisco, 1972-73; programmer/analyst Wells Fargo Bank, 1973-74; systems analyst Crown-Zellerbach Corp., 1974; programming mgr. Calif. Dental Svc., 1974-75, Fairchild Camera and Inst., Mountain View, Calif., 1975-77; sr. systems analyst Bechtel Corp., San Francisco, 1977; pres. Richardson Software Cons., Inc., 1977-99; pvt. practice, 1993—. Instr. data processing Diablo Valley Coll., Concord, Calif., 1979-80. Author: (book) System Development Life Cycle, 1976, (computer software) The Richardson Automated Agent, 1985. Asst. scoutmaster Boy Scouts Am., Clayton, Calif., 1983-91; soccer coach Am. Youth Soccer League, Clayton, 1978-83. 1st lt. USAF, 1966-72. Mem. ABA, State Bar Calif., Computer Law Assn. Avocations: travel, reading, writing. Office: 870 Market St Ste 400 San Francisco CA 94102-3010

RICHARDSON, DAVID B. writer, journalist; b. Maplewood, N.J., July 13, 1916; s. Percy Bacon and Elizabeth (Jones) R.; m. Ruth Cummings (dec.); children: Hilary C., Julia R. Neilson, Francesca Richardson-Allen; m. Anne Phelan Werner, Oct. 8, 1994. BA, Ind. U., 1940; Edward R. Murrow Postgrad. Press fellow, Princeton U., 1953-54. Sports reporter Daily Courier, Orange, N.J., 1934-36; mng. editor, editor-in-chief Ind. Daily Student, 1939-40; editl. staff N.Y. Herald Tribune, N.Y.C., 1940-41; combat corr. Yank, The Army Weekly, New Guinea, Burma, 1942-45; corr. Time mag., India, 1945-46, Germany, 1947-50, U.K., 1950-52, Mideast, 1952-53, Mex., 1954-56; assoc. editor U.S. News & World Report, Washington, 1956-59, bur. chief S.Am., 1959-64, chief domestic news burs., 1964-73, chief European corr. Rome, 1974-81, chief nat. corr. Washington, 1981-82; freelance writer, 1983—. Ernie Pyle lectr. Ind. U., 1958; lectr. WWII in Burma. Contbr. to books The Best From Yank, 1945, Yank, the GI Story of the War, 1947. V.p., bd. dirs. Iona Sr. Svcs., 1993-96, steering com. Citizens Adv. Coun. Sr. Svcs., 1996-99; pres., bd. dirs. Greenbriar Condo., Washington, 1984-87; comms. adviser Samaritan Ministry, 1989-96. Sgt. U.S. Army, 1941-45, PTO, CBI. Decorated Legion of Merit, Bronze Star; recipient Valor medal Nat. Headliners Club, Disting. Alumni Svc. award Ind. U.; Cmty. Hero torchbearer Olympic Torch Relay, 1996. Mem. Coun. Fgn. Rels., Washington Inst. Fgn. Affairs, Soc. Profl. Journalists (com. concerned journalists), Merrill's Marauders Assn. (mil. liaison officer 1995—), Burma Star Assn., Internat. Combat Camera Assn., Cosmos Club. Episcopalian. Home and Office: 4201 Cathedral Ave NW Apt 1014E Washington DC 20016-4976

RICHARDSON, DAVID WALTHALL, cardiologist, educator, consultant; b. Nanking, China, Mar. 22, 1925; s. Donald William and Virginia (McIlwaine) R.; m. Frances Lee Wingfield, June 12, 1948; children: Donald, Sarah, David.

BS, Davidson Coll., 1947; MD, Harvard U., 1951. Diplomate Am. Bd. Internal Medicine, Am. Bd. Cardiology. Intern, resident Yale New Haven Hosp., 1951-53; resident, fellow Med. Coll. Va., Richmond, 1953-56, assoc. prof. to prof. medicine, 1962-95, prof. emeritus, 1995—. Chmn. divsn. cardiology, 1972-87; interim chmn. dept. medicine, 1973-74; chief cardiology, assoc. chief staff for rsch. VA Hosp., Richmond, 1956-61, dir. cardiology tng. program, 1990-95; vis. scientist Oxford U., Eng., 1961-62; vis. prof. U. Milan, Italy, 1972-73. Contbr. articles to profl. jours. Moderator Hanover Presybery, Presbyn. Ch. U.S., Richmond, 1970; chmn. events com., NHLBI Cardiac Arrhythmia Suppression Trial, 1983-92, NHLBI Anti-Arrhythmics versus Implantable Defibrillators Trial, 1993-97. Served with USN, 1944-46. Fellow Am. Coll. Cardiology (gov. VA 1970-72), Am. Heart Assn. (coun. clin. cardiology and high blood pressure rsch.); mem. Am. Soc. Clin. Investigaiton, Am. Clin. and Climatol. Assn. Home: 5501 Queensbury Rd Richmond VA 23226-2121 E-mail: davidwrl@attbi.com.

RICHARDSON, DENNIS JAMES, biologist, educator; b. Conway, Ark., Jan. 1, 1963; s. James William Richardson and Rita Jean Brown Collums; m. Kristen Elizabeth Henn, Sept. 23, 1994; children: Katherine Rose, Marjorie Anne, Emma Louise. BS, Ark. Tech. U., 1988; MS, U. Ctrl. Ark., 1990; PhD, U. Nebr., 1995. Instr. U. Ctrl. Ark., Conway, 1995-96; asst. prof. Quinnipiac U., Hamden, Conn., 1996—. Contbr. articles to profl. jours. Mem. Am. Soc. Parasitologists, Am. Soc. Tropical Hygiene & Medicine, Southwestern Assn. Parasitologists, New Eng. Assn. Parasitology, Helminthological Soc. Wash. (pres. 2000-01), Sigma Xi. Avocation: 19th century natural listings text. Office: Quinnipiac U Box B8 275 Mount Carmel Ave Hamden CT 06518 E-mail: Dennis.Richardson@quinnipiac.edu.

RICHARDSON, DENNIS MICHAEL, lawyer, educator; b. L.A., July 30, 1949; s. Ralph Lee and Eva Catherine (McGuire) R.; 1 child from previous marriage, Scott Randol; m. Catherine Jean Coyl, July 27, 1973; children: Jennifer Eve, Valerie Jean, Rachel Catherine, Nicole Marie, Mary Rose, Marie Christina, Laura Michelle, Alyssa Rose. BA, Brigham Young U., 1976, JD, 1979. Bar: Oreg. 1979. Owner Dennis Richardson & Assocs., P.C., Central Point, Oreg., 1979—; pvt. practice law, 1979—; CEO IMPEX U.S. Corp., 1999—. Guest lectr. in field. Contbr. articles to profl. jours. Bd. dirs. Oreg. Lung Assn., 1980, Shakespearean Festival, Ashland, 1981, Jackson County Legal Services, 1982; chmn. GOP Oreg. 2d. Congl. Dist., 1996-2000, treas. GOP Oreg. Exec. Com., 1999—; councilman Ctrl. Point City, 2001—. Served as helicopter pilot U.S. Army, 1969-71, Vietnam. Decorated Vietnamese Cross Gallantry. Republican. Office: Dennis Richardson & Assocs PC 55 S 5th St Central Point OR 97502-2474 E-mail: dennis@law.com.

RICHARDSON, DENNISE MARIE, physician assistant; b. Patuxent River, Md., July 16, 1944; d. Hershel Elroy and Suzanne Marie (Ahern) R.; m. Richard Harold Browne, Aug. 10, 1970. BS, Lamar U., 1966, U. Tex., 1995; MS, Okla. State U., 1970, PhD, 1973. Cert. physician asst. Rsch. technician MD Anderson Hosp., Houston, 1967-68; fellow U. Tex., Dallas, 1974-75, rsch. assoc., 1978-93; rsch. immunologist Wadley Insts., 1975-76; physician asst. Lakewood Med. Ctr., 1996-97, Lewis Group, Dallas, 1997-98; pediat. physician asst. George Monroe, MD, 1998—. Fellow Am. Assn. Physician Assts.; mem. People to People Internat., Tex. Acad. Physician Assts., Alzheimer Assn. (group leader), Dallas Com. Fgn. Visitors, Dallas Camera Club (sec.), Beta Beta Beta, Phi Sigma. Republican. Avocations: photography, canoeing, writing. Home: 12045 Inwood Rd Dallas TX 75244-8016

RICHARDSON, DON RAMON, communication educator; b. Malta, Ohio, Aug. 7, 1938; s. Russell Curtis Richardson and Wanda (Ashton) Brown; m. Janet Lynn Davis, July 18, 1980; children: Roger, Keith, Scott. BA, Auburn (Ala.) U., 1961; MA, Ohio U., 1963, PhD, 1964. Asst. prof. U. Ga., Athens, 1964-66, Auburn U., 1966-69, chmn. arts and scis. Ala., 1969-72, assoc. grad. dean Auburn, 1972-86, head dept. communication, 1986-91; chair dept. pub. communication Sam Houston State U., Huntsville, Tex., 1991—2002. Cons. Union Camp Paper Co., Prattville, Ala., Ala. State Mental Hosp., Tuscaloosa, U.S. Agrl. Stabilization and Conservation Svc., Montgomery, others. Editor: Conversations with Carter, 1998; contbr. articles to profl. jours. Avocations: tennis, bridge, flying, chess. Home: 740 Fm 980 Huntsville TX 77320-7407 Office: Sam Houston State U Sch Pub Communication Huntsville TX 77341 E-mail: scm_drr@shsu.edu.

RICHARDSON, DONALD CHARLES, engineer, consultant; b. Glendale, Calif., June 6, 1937; s. George Robert and Margaret Josephine (Bichholz) R. BA in Sci., Calif. State U., 1965; MS in Engring., Queens U., 1981, MEd, 1983; PhD, Clarkson U., 1988. Sr. engr. Control Data Corp., Toronto, Ont., Can., 1972-75; tchr. Algonquin Coll., Kingston, Can., 1975-79; assoc. prof. Royal Mil. Coll. Can., Can., 1982-84; instr. Clarkson U., Potsdam, N.Y., 1988; superconductor cons., 1989; mgr. tech. support Multiflow Computer, Inc., 1988; mem. tstaff Fla. Inst. Tech., 1999. Author of engring. papers. Lt. comdr. USN, 1964-69, Vietnam. Electrochem. Soc. fellow, 1984. Mem. Am. Soc. Engring. Edn., Mensa, Fraternal Order of Seals, Sigma Xi.

RICHARDSON, DONALD EDWARD, neurosurgery educator; b. Vicksburg, Miss., Oct. 5, 1931; s. Edward K. and Ina Mae (Cooper) R.; children: Donna Richardson Boas, Scott, David, W. Jeffrey, Cooper E.H. BS in Chemistry, Millsaps Coll., 1953; MD, Tulane U., 1957. Diplomate Am. Bd. Neurol. Surgery. Intern in surgery Charity Hosp., New Orleans, 1957-58, resident in neurosurgery, 1961-62, Ochsner Found. Hosp., New Orleans, 1958-60, VA Hosp., New Orleans, 1960-61; instr. Dept. Neurosurgery, Tulane U., 1962-64, asst. prof., 1964-67, assoc. prof., 1967-74, prof., chmn., 1980—, adj. prof. dept. biomed. engring., 1984—; clin. assoc. prof. dept. neurosurgery La. State U., 1974-80. Dir. Pain Treatment Ctr. Hotel Dieu Hosp., New Orleans, 1978-93, mem.-at-large exec. com., 1978-84, chmn. spl. procedures com., 1984-93; chief neurosurgery sect. Charity Hosp. La. New Orleans, 1980—, VA Hosp. New Orleans, 1980—; mem. neurosurgery staff, Toure Infirmary, So. Bapt. Hosp., Pendelton Meml. Meth. Hosp., St. Jude Med. Ctr.; chmn. Neurosurgery dept. Tulane U. Med. Ctr. Hosp., 1980—, oper. rm. and exec. coms., 1980—; lectr. in field. Contbr. articles to profl. jours. Fellow ACS; mem. AAAS, Am. Assn. Neurol. Surgeons, AMA, Am. Pain Soc., Am. Soc. for Stereotactic and Functional Neurosurgery, Assn. for Acad. Surgery, Congress Neurol. Surgeons, Internat. Assn. for Study Pain, Internat. Neurosurg. Soc., La. Neurol. Soc. (pres. 1979), La. State Med. Soc., Neuroelectric Soc., N.Y. Acad. Sci., Orleans Parish Med. Soc., Research Soc. Neurol. Surgeons, Royal Soc. Medicine, Soc. for Neurosci., So. Med. Assn., So. Neurosurg. Assn., Oscar Creek Surg. Soc., Midwest Pain Soc., Can. Neurosurg. Soc., Am. Acad. Pain Medicine, Alton Ochsner Med. Found. Soc., Soc. Neurol. Surgeons, La. Med. Rev. Found., Am. Acad. Clin. Neurophysiology, Alpha Omega Alpha. Lodges: Rotary. Avocations: skiing, travel, collecting art. Office: Tulane U Sch of Medicine Dept of Neurosurgery 1430 Tulane Ave New Orleans LA 70112-2699

RICHARDSON, DONN CHARLES, business and marketing educator; b. Indpls., Mar. 3, 1940; s. George Covey and Edythe Francis (Chesterfield) R.; m. Carolyn Jean Hassan, Nov. 8, 1969; children: Bradley George, Jason Arthur, Christopher Charles. BA in Journalism and Polit. Sci., Butler U., 1962; MA in Mass Comm., Ohio State U., 1969. Staff editor Cin. Bell Mag. Cin. (Ohio) Bell, 1969-73; mgmt. newsletter editor, spl. projects mgr. US West Comms., Denver, 1973-76, Colo. pub. rels. and outreach dir. Boulder, 1976-84, Colo. employee comm. mgr., 1984-85, market mgr. market planning, 1986-88, fed. govt. market mgr. Englewood, Colo., 1989-94; pres. Richardson Info. Resources, Boulder, 1994—. Cons. Northglenn (Colo.) Recreation Ctr., 1982; presenter, spk. in field. Author, pub.: The Quick Consultant's Guide to Public Speaking; contbr. articles to profl. jours. Pres. Shannon Estates Homeowners Assn., Boulder, 1978-80; pub. rels. dir. Boulder (Colo.) Mental Health Ctr. Benefit, 1980; publicity dir. FC Boulder (Colo.) Soccer Club, 1991-94. Capt. USAF, 1963-69. Mem. Internat. Assn. Bus. Communicators (dist. profl. devel. chair 1982-84, chpt. v.p. 1985, internat. pub. rels. chair 1985-86, regional conf. program chair 1996, accredited bus. communicator), Pub. Rels. Soc. Am. (accreditation judge 1989, accredited pub. rels. profl.). Avocations: youth recreation coaching, traveling. Home: 1212 Cavan St Boulder CO 80303-1602

RICHARDSON, EARL WILSON, elementary education educator, retired; b. Emporia, Kans., June 4, 1942; s. Clarence Earl and Dorothy Ann (Draper) R.; m. Mariann Hirsig, July 31, 1965; 1 child, Rachelle Ranae. BS in Elem. Edn., Emporia (Kans.) State U., 1964; MED in Elem. Edn., U. Wyo., 1971. Tchr. 5th-6th grades Alta Vista Elem. Sch., Cheyenne, Wyo., 1964-68, eco-lab. and sci. tchr. 5th-6th grades, 1972-74, 83-84; tchr. 5th-6th grades Bain Elem. Sch., 1968-97, ret., 1997. Recipient Presdl. award NSF, 1990. Mem. NEA, Wyo. Edn. Assn., Wyo. Sci. Tchrs. Assn. (Excellence in Sci. Teaching award 1984), Phi Delta Kappa. Home: 708 Arapaho St Cheyenne WY 82009-4216

RICHARDSON, ELIZABETH HALL, retired ecologist; b. Waltham, Mass., June 5, 1937; d. Livingston and Elizabeth (Blodgett) Hall; m. (div.); children: Elisabeth F. Richardson, Anne K. Richardson. AB, Radcliffe Coll., 1959; MPA, U. So. Calif., 1975; MBA, U. Denver, 1986. Asst. biology tchr. Presbyn. Ladies Coll., Pymble, NSW, Australia, 1959; tchr. drama Middlesex Sch., Concord, Mass., 1961-62; adminstrv. asst. Gov. Richard D. Lamm, Denver, 1975-76; coord. govt. affairs Rocky Mountain Energy Co., Lakewood, 1977-79; exec. dir. Thorne Ecol. Inst., Boulder, 1981-82; rsch. asst. Boettcher & Co., Denver, 1988-89; land protection specialist Colo. Open Lands, Lakewood, 1991—2002. Sec. Colo. Coalition of Land Trusts, Golden, 1992—. Sec. Simon's Rock Coll. of Bard, 1989—. Mem. ASPA, Rocky Mountain Women's Inst. (chair 1982-97). Democrat. Home: 2400 S Jackson St Denver CO 80210-5637

RICHARDSON, EMILIE WHITE, manufacturing company executive, investment company executive, lecturer; b. Chattanooga, July 08; d. Emmett and Mildred Evelyn (Harbin) White; 1 child Julie Richardson Milunic. BA, Wheaton Coll., 1951. With Christy Mfg. Co., Inc., Fayetteville, N.C., Ft. Lauderdale, Fla., 1952—, sec., 1956-66, v.p., 1967-74, exec. v.p., 1975-79, pres., CEO, 1980—. V.p. E. White Investment Co., 1968-83, pres., 1983— ; cons. Aerostatic Industries, 1979— ; v.p. Gannon Corp., 1981— ; cons. govt. contacts and offshore mfg., 1981— ; lectr., spkr. in field. V.p. pub. rels. Ft. Lauderdale Symphony Soc., 1974-76, v.p. membership, 1976-77, adv. bd., 1978—; active Atlantic Found., Ft. Lauderdale Mus. Art, Beaux Arts, Freedoms Found.; mem. East Broward Women's Rep. Club, 1968—, Americanism chmn., 1971-72. Mem. Internat. Platform Assn., Nat. Spkrs. Assn., Fla. Spkrs. Assn., Toastmasters, Coral Ridge Yacht Club. Methodist. Home: 1531 NE 51st St Fort Lauderdale FL 33334-5709 Office: 3311 Fort Bragg Rd Fayetteville NC 28303-4763 E-mail: emilier@mindspring.com.

RICHARDSON, ERNEST RAY (ROCKY RICHARDSON), housing program supervisor; b. Dermott, Ark., Sept. 5, 1932; s. Louis Jr. and Leila Mae (Purdom) R.; m. Deloris Cobb, Mar. 25, 1955 (div. Apr. 1964); children: Victor Ray, Rodney Lynn, Regenia Ann; stepchildren, Denise Nelson, Darrin Hicks; m. Doretha Tolbert, Apr. 1964 (div. June 1978); m. Shirley Ann Johnson, June 8, 1978; 1 child, Kimberly Ann; stepchildren: Janet, Kay, and Jerome Pate. BA in Bus. Adminstrn., Franklin U., 1975; AA in Real Estate, Parkland Coll., 1980; postgrad., Lewis U., 1980-83; grad., Intergovtl. Mgmt. Tng., 1993, Leadership Modesto, 1996. Cert. real estate broker, Ill. Dir. edn. & tng. Champaign County Opportunities Industrialization Ctr., Champaign, Ill., 1968-70, exec. dir., pers. dir., 1970-73; fin. specialist City of Urbana, 1975-79, City of Joliet, 1979-82, dir. neighborhood svcs. divsn., 1982-87; exec. pers. dir. Aurora (Ill.) Housing Authority, 1987-89; housing program supr. City of Modesto, Calif., 1989—. Mem. adv. bd. Ctrl. Valley Opportunities Ctr., Inc. Modesto, 1992-96, bd. dirs., 1996-98; vice chmn. mgmt. devel. com., City of Modesto, 1993-94, mem. mgmts. continuous improvement com., 1995, 96; alt. Stanislaus County Civil Grand Jury, 1996-97, mem., rec. sec., 1997-98; mem. nat. funds allocation rev. com. Opportunities Industrialization Ctr., 1971-72. Sgt. USAF, 1951-67. Mem. nat. Assn. Real Estate Appraisers (pres.-elect Ill. chpt. 1984-85, pres. Ill. chpt. 1985-86, Ill. chpt. Mem. of the Yr., 1988), Am. Legion, Modesto Kiwanis Club. Avocations: income tax business and real estate appraisal, walking, reading, travel. Home: 309 Yuba Ridge Ln Modesto CA 95354-3369 Office: City of Modesto Ofc Housing/Neighborhoods PO Box 642 Modesto CA 95353-0642

RICHARDSON, EVERETT VERN, hydraulic engineer, educator, administrator, consultant; b. Scottsbluff, Nebr., Jan. 5, 1924; s. Thomas Otis and Jean Marie (Everett) R.; m. Billie Ann Kleckner, June 23, 1948; children: Gail Lee, Thomas Everett, Jerry Ray BS, Colo. State U., 1949, MS, 1960, PhD, 1965. Registered profl. engr., Colo. Hydraulic engr. U.S. Geol. Survey, Wyo., 1949-52, hydraulic engr. Iowa, 1953-56, rsch. hydraulic engr. Colo., 1956-63, project chief, 1963-68; prof. civil engring., adminstr. engring. rsch. ctr. Colo. State U., 1968-82, prof. in charge of hydraulic program, 1982-88, prof. civil engring., 1988-94, prof. emeritus, 1994—, dir. hydraulic lab. engring. rsch. ctr., 1982-88, dir. Egypt water use project, 1977-84, dir. Egypt irrigation improvement project, 1985-90; dir. Egypt Water Rsch. Ctr. Egypt Water Rsch. Ctr. Project, 1988-89; sr. assoc. Ayers Assocs. Inc. (formerly Resource Cons./Engrs., Inc.), Colo., 1989-93, Ayres Assocs., Ft. Collins, 1994—. Dir. Consortium for Internat. Devel., Tucson, Ariz., 1972-87; developer stream stability and scour at hwy. bridges course for State Dept. Transps. for NHI, FHWA; investigator for NTSB of 1987 I-90 bridge failure, N.Y., 1997, railroad bridge failure, Ariz., CALTRAN of 1995 I-5 bridge failure; cons. in field; lectr. in field. Sr. author: Highways in the River Environment, Fed. Hwy. Adminstrn., 1975, 90, 2001, Evaluating Scour at Bridges, Fed. Hwy. Adminstrn., 1991, 93, 95, 2001; contbr. to Engring. and Civil Engring. Handbook, 1995, Handbook of Fluid Dynamics and Fluid Machinery, 1996, Water Resources-Environmental Planning, Management, and Development, 1996; contbr. articles to profl. jours., chpts. in books. Mem. Ft. Collins Water Bd., 1969-84; mem. N.Y. State Bridge Safety Assurance Task Force, 1988-91. Decorated Bronze Star, Purple Heart; Combat Infantry Badge, U.S. Govt. fellow MIT, 1962-63. Fellow ASCE (J.S. Stevens award 1961, chair task com., bridge scour rsch. 1990-96, vice chair 1997—, hydraulics divsn. task com. excellence award, 1993, Hans Albert Einstein award 1996, editor Compendium of Stream Stability and Scour Papers, 1991-98); mem. Internat. Congress for Irrigation and Drainage (bd. dirs.), Sigma Xi, Chi Epsilon, Sigma Tau. Home: 824 Gregory Rd Fort Collins CO 80524-1504 Office: Ayres Assocs PO Box 270460 Fort Collins CO 80527-0460

RICHARDSON, GARY BURLEIGH, lawyer; b. Windsor, Vt., Oct. 16, 1944; s. Dwight Bailey and Lucy B. Richardson; m. Katrina Copeland, Oct. 8, 1966; children: Justin C., Sarah B. BA, Middlebury Coll., 1967; JD, Boston Coll. Law Sch., 1970. Atty. Upton & Hatfield, LLP, Concord, NH, 1970—75; ptnr. Upton, Sanders & Smith, N.H., 1976—. Chair N.H. Ballot Law Com., Concord, 1991—, Hopkinton (N.H.) Zoning Bd., 1975-87, Hopkinton Planning Bd., 1988-92; bd. dirs. Biddeford Pool Improvement Assn., 1999—, New Vision Teen Ctr., 1999—. Mem. N.H. Trial Lawyers Assn. (pres. 1990-91), Am. Bd. Trial Advs. Avocations: golf, tennis, sailing, skiing. Office: Upton Hatfield LLP 10 Centre St Concord NH 03301-6302 E-mail: Grichardson@Upton-Hatfield.com.

RICHARDSON, HERBERT HEATH, mechanical engineer, educator, institute director; b. Lynn, Mass., Sept. 24, 1930; s. Walter Blake and Isabel Emily (Heath) R.; m. Barbara Ellsworth, Oct. 6, 1973. SB, SM with honors, MIT, 1955, ScD, 1958. Registered profl. engr., Mass., Tex. Research asst., research engr. Dynamic Analysis and Control Lab. MIT, 1953-57, instr. Dept. Mech. Engring., 1957-58, mem. faculty, 1958-84, prof. mech. engring., 1968-85, head dept., 1974-82, assoc. dean engring., 1982-84; Disting. prof. engring. Tex. A&M U., 1984—; Regents prof. Tex. A&M U. System, College Station, 1993—; dean, vice chancellor engring. Tex. A&M U. Sys., 1984-85; dep. chancellor, dean, dir. Tex. Engring. Expt. Sta. Tex. A&M U., 1985-91; chancellor Tex. A&M U. System, College Station, 1991-93, assoc. vice chancellor engring., 1993—, assoc. dean engring., 1993—; dir. Tex. Trans. Inst., Tex. A&M Univ. Sys., 1993—. With Ballistics Rsch. Lab. Abderdeen Proving Ground, Md., 1958; chief scientist U.S. Dept. Transp., 1970-72; bd. dirs. Foster-Miller Inc., Mass., Ten X Inc., Tex. Utilities Co.; chmn. adv. com. for engring. NSF, 1987-89, adv. com. basic energy scis. U.S. Dept. Energy, 1987-91. Author: Introduction to System Dynamics, 1971; contbr. articles to profl. publs. Trustee S.W. Rsch. Inst. Officer U.S. Army, 1968. Recipient medal Am. Ordnance Assn., 1953, Gold medal Pi Tau Sigma, 1963, Meritorious Service award and medal Dept. Transp., 1972. Fellow AAAS, ASME (Moody award fluid engring. divsn. 1970, Centennial medallion 1983, Rufus Oldenberger medal 1984, Meritorious Svc. medal 1986, Disting. Svc. award 1986, hon. mem. 1987); mem. NAS (assoc.), NAE (coun. 1986-92, com. on engring. edn.), Am. Soc. Engring. Edn. (Disting. Svc. medal 1993, Lamme award 1997), N.Y. Acad. Sci., Inst. Transp. Engrs., Nat. Rsch. Coun. (gov. bd. 1986-92, chmn. transp. rsch. bd. 1988-89), Nat. Acads. (nat. assoc., life), Sigma Xi, Tau Beta Pi. Office: Tex A&M U Sys MS 3135 College Station TX 77843-0001

RICHARDSON, IAN WILLIAM, actor; b. Edinburgh, Scotland, Apr. 7, 1934; s. John and Margaret R.; m. Maroussia Frank, Feb. 2, 1961; children: Jeremy, Miles. Diploma in Acting and Teaching, Royal Scottish Acad. Music and Drama, D in Drama, 1999. Actor Royal Shakespeare Co., Stratford on Avon and London, 1960-75, Shaw Festival Theatre, Niagara, Ont., Can., 1977. Appeared in plays including My Fair Lady, Broadway, 1976-77, The Miser, 1995, The Magistrate, 1997-98, The Seven Ages of Man, The Hollow Crown, 1999; films and TV plays include Tinker, Tailor, Soldier, Spy, Private Shulz, The Sign of Four, The Hound of the Baskervilles, Phantom of the Opera, 1990, The Gravy Train, 1990, House of Cards, 1991, The Gravy Train Goes East, 1991, To Play the King, 1993, Foreign Affairs Remember, Savage Play, 1994, The Final Cut, 1995; films include Brazil, Whoops!, Apocalypse, The Fourth Protocol, Cry Freedom, The Fifth Province, 1996, Dark City, 1998, From Hell, 2000; TV programs includes Star Quality, Porterhouse Blue, The Winslow Boy, 1989, An Ungentlemanly Act, 1992, Catherine the Great (miniseries), 1994, Gormenghast, 1999, (miniseries) Magician's House, 1999, Murder Rooms, 1999, Murder Rooms II, 2000, Strange, BBC TV, 2001; author prefaces to Shakespearean works. Recipient CBE award, 1989, BAFTA award, 1991, award Royal TV Soc., 1991. Fellow Royal Scottish Acad. Music and Drama; mem. Brit. Actors Equity, Actors Equity, Screen Actors Guild, Garrick Club (London), Players Club (N.Y.C.). Office: care London Mgmt 2-4 Noel St London W14 3RB England

RICHARDSON, JAMES DAVID, surgeon; b. Morehead, Ky., 1945; MD, U. Ky., 1970. Diplomate Am. Bd. Surgeons, Am. Bd. Vascular Surgery, Am. Bd. Thoracic Surgery, Am. Bd. SCC. Intern U. Ky. Med. Ctr., Lexington, 1970, resident, 1971-72, U. Tex., San Antonio, 1972-76; surgeon Norton Kosair Children's Hosp., Louisville, 1977—; prof. surgery U. Louisville, 1979—; pres. Am. Bd. Surgery, 1998-99. Fellow ACS; mem. AMA, Am. Assn. Surgery of Trauma, SSAT, Alpha Omega Alpha. Office: U Louisville Dept Surgery 550 S Jackson St Louisville KY 40202-1622

RICHARDSON, JAMES SOMMERFIELD, real estate company executive; b. Hialeah, Fla., Jan. 27, 1941; s. William Summerfield Richardson and Mary Lee McCorvey; m. Eileen Patricia McKeon, May 7, 1961; children: Amie Patricia Calderon, Patricia Kelly, Erin Theresa Cappelluti. BA, U. Miami, Coral Gables, Fla., 1965. Cert. real estate broker Ga., Fla., Ala., registered prin. SEC, NASD. Pres. James S. Richardson & Associates, Inc., Coral Springs, Fla., 1977—90; pvt. practice real estate developer Sautee Nacoochee, Ga., 1996—. Registered prin. Lord, Abbett & Co., N.Y.C., 1976—78. Author: (book) Paine in the Ass: A Patriot's View of the System, 1997, (website) netdirectory.com, 1995, wildmustang.org, 2000. Rep. candidate Ho. Reps. State of Fla., Coral Springs, 1972. Mem.: Coral Springs JayCees, Coral Springs C. of C. Office: James S Richardson Real Estate 2134 Asbestos Rd Sautee Nacoochee GA 30571

RICHARDSON, JASPER EDGAR, nuclear physicist; b. Memphis, Nov. 8, 1922; s. Jasper Edgar and Katherine Cecil (Copp) R.; m. Nellie Carolyn Harwell, May 30, 1947; children: Ann Helen, Janet Katherine, Susan Carolyn, Patricia Lynn, Ellen Claire. BS in Physics, Yale U., 1944; MA in Physics, Rice U., 1948, PhD in Physics, 1950. Instr. physics U. Miss., Oxford, 1946-47; asst. prof. Auburn (Ala.) U., 1950-51; AEC fellow Oak Ridge (Tenn.) Inst. Nuc. Studies, 1951-53; physicist U. Tex. M. D. Anderson Hosp., Houston, 1953-55; rsch. physicist Shell Bellaire Rsch. Ctr., 1955-69; sr. engr. Shell Oil Co., Midland, Tex., 1969-74, staff engr. Houston, 1974-86; ret. Patentee in electronics, oil discovery, measurement; contbr. articles to profl. jours. With USN, 1944-46, Guam. Mem. Am. Phys. Soc., Soc. Petroleum Engrs. Episcopalian.

RICHARDSON, JAY, lawyer; b. Vernal, Utah, June 24, 1957; s. Harold H. and Norma (Anderson) R.; 1 child, Bryce Cameron. BS, Brigham Young U., 1979; JD, Willamette U., 1982. Bar: Oreg. 1982; CPA, Oreg.; CMA. Sr. tax. specialist Peat Marwick Mitchell, Portland, Oreg., 1982-85; assoc. Zalutsky, Klarquist and Johnson, P.C., 1985-88; tax mgr. Coopers & Lybrand, 1988-91; mgr. N.W. group Price Waterhouse, 1991-92; ind. benefits cons., 1993—. Vice chmn. Northwest Tax Inst., Portland, 1988. Contbr. articles to profl. jours. and The Oregonian. Mem. planning com. Oreg. Mus. Sci. and Industry, 1985-88. Mem. ABA, AICPA, Oreg. Soc. CPAs (chmn. joint atty. com. 1996—), Nat. Assn. Accts. Republican. Avocations: astronomy, sociobiology, photography, running, golf. Home and Office: 7100 SW Windemere Loop Portland OR 97225-6168

RICHARDSON, JEAN BROOKS, artist, printmaker; b. Hollis, Okla., Feb. 10, 1940; d. E. Whitson and Mildred E. (Redus) Brooks; m. Ronald A. Richardson, Dec. 29, 1961 (div. 1974); children: Andrea Lynn, Karen Kathleen, Brooks Allen; m. Laurence D. Lucas, Aug. 11, 1977. BFA, Wesleyan Coll., Macon,Ga., 1961. Instr. various mus., Oklahoma City, 1971—. Subject of (book) Plains Myths and Other Tales, 1988; subject of articles to profl. jours.; one-woman shows include Enthios Gallery, Santa Fe, 1984, John Szoke Gallery, N.Y.C., 1985, Cogswell Gallery, Vail, Colo., 1986, Robertson Gallery, Beverly Hills, Calif., 1987, Kirkpatrick Ctr. Mus., Oklahoma City, 1988, Four Winds Gallery, Sydney, Australia, 1988, Beth O'Donnell Gallery, Aspen, Colo., 1990, Harrington Galleries, Vancouver, B.C., Can., 1990, Merrill Chase Galleries, Washington, 1991, Lucas Gallery, Telluride, Colo., 1995, Kirkpatrick Galleries, Oklahoma City, Okla., 1997, JR Fine Arts, Scottsdale, Ariz., 1998, Pickard Galleries, Oklahoma City, 1998; represented in permanent collections Oklahoma State Art Collection, Oklahoma City, Minn. Mus. Art, Okla. State Capitol. Mem. Nat. Women in the Arts, Okla. Art Ctr., Individual Artists of Okla., Visual Arts Assn. Democrat. Presbyterian. Avocations: tennis, cinema. Studio: 1106 NW 50th St Oklahoma City OK 73118-4402

RICHARDSON, JENNIFER JANE GOODE, musician, social worker, psychotherapist, author; b. LaGrange, Ga., Sept. 3, 1951; d. Thomas Earle and Jane (Mitcham) Williams; m Larry Allen Goode, March 17, 1973 (div. 1980); m. Alan Wayne Richardson, Oct. 5, 1985. B.Mus., Ga. State U., 1973, M.Mus., 1977; MSW, U. Ga., 1981. Lic. clin. social worker, music tchr., cert. cognitive behavior therapist, Ga. Mus. therapist Peachtree-Parkwood Hosp., Atlanta, 1977-80; intern psychotherapy Jewish Family Services, 1981; psychiatric social worker West Paces Ferry Hosp., 1982; rehab. counselor Shepherd Spinal Ctr., 1983-85; pvt. practice psychotherapy Ctr. For Psychiatry, Smyrna, Ga., 1985-87, Brawner Psych. Inst., Smyrna, 1985-87, Phoenix, 1987-88, Ctr. for Cognitive Therapy, 1987-91; pvt. practice Phoenix Psychol. Assocs., 1991-98. Alto singer Oakhurst Choir, Decatur, Ga., 1969-80, Third Ave. Consort, Decatur, 1978-84, Atlanta Bach Choir, 1983-84, Atlanta Vocal Consort, 1984-88, All Saints Episcopal Ch. Choir, Atlanta, 1983—; alto tenor Master Arts Sacred Singers, Atlanta, 1985—; flutist Prevailing Winds Quintet, Atlanta, 1978-80, Atlanta-Emory Orch., 1986—, Wind and Wood Chamber Players, 1991—; ptnr. Richardson and Assocs., Atlanta, 1985—; mem. Phoenix Trio, 1996. Editor: (lit. mag.) Kudzu Revue, 1981—; contbr. article to book: J.S. Bach, 1984; feature writer Bond Community Star, Atlanta, 1979—(Community Service award 1987); author: Diary of Abuse; Diary of Healing, 1996, Holy Dirt, 2000. Mem. Appalachian Trail Conf., Harpers Ferry W.Va., 1969-79, Candler Park Neighborhood Assn., Atlanta, 1973—. Recipient John Philip Sousa award Druid Hills Band, 1969. Mem. Acad. Cert. Social Workers, Ga. Soc. Clin. Social Workers, Am. Fed. Musicians. Clubs: Caution. Democrat. Episcopalian. Avocations: painting, writing, hiking, gardening, reading. Office: Edgewood 620 Clifton Rd NE Atlanta GA 30307-1710

RICHARDSON, JOEL GLENN, lawyer; b. Houston, Jan. 25, 1955; s. Joseph Gerald and June (Sneddon) R. BA in Am. Studies, Southwestern U., Georgetown, Tex., 1976; JD, Regent U., Virginia Beach, Va., 1987, South Tex. Coll. Law, Houston, 1988. Bar: Tex. 1989, U.S. Ct. Appeals (5th cir.) 1991, U.S. Supreme Ct. 1991. Pvt. practice, San Antonio. With USMCR, 1978-79; with USNR, 1979-90. Mem. State Bar Tex. Office: PO Box 780254 San Antonio TX 78278-0254

RICHARDSON, JOHN, retired international relations executive; b. Boston, Feb. 4, 1921; s. John and Hope (Hemenway) R.; m. Thelma Ingram, Jan. 19, 1945; children: Eva Teleki, Teren de Cossy, Hope Gravelly, Catherine Munch, Hetty L. AB, Harvard U., 1943, JD, 1949. Bar: N.Y. 1949. Assoc. Sullivan & Cromwell, N.Y.C., 1949-55; with Paine, Webber, Jackson & Curtis, 1955-69, gen. ptnr., 1958-61, ltd. ptnr., 1961-69; pres., chief exec. officer Free Europe, Inc. (Radio Free Europe), 1961-68; asst. sec. for ednl. and cultural affairs Dept. State, 1969-77, also acting asst. sec. state for pub. affairs, 1971-73; exec. dir. for social policy Ctr. for Strategic and Internat. Studies; research prof.

internat. communication Sch. Fgn. Service, Georgetown U., Washington, 1977-78; pres., chief exec. officer Youth for Understanding, Inc., 1978-86, bd. dirs., 1986-98; counselor U.S. Inst. of Peace, 1987-90. Spl. advisor Aspen Inst. Humanistic Studies, 1977-80 Founder Polish Med. Aid Project, 1957—61; co-founder, chmn. bd. Am. Com. to Aid Poland, 1989—95; pres. Internat. Rescue Com., 1960—61, bd. dirs., 1958—61, 1978—; chmn. Am. Coun. for UN U., 1977—87, Consortium for Internat. Citizens Exch., 1980—84, Delphi Internat., 1995—99, bd. dirs., 1991—2001; chmn. Nat. Endowment for Democracy, 1984—88, 1991—92, bd. dirs., 1984—92, chmn. emeritus, 1992—; bd. dirs. Freedom House, 1963—69, pres., 1977—84; mem. Coun. Fgn. Rels., 1957—; Citizens Commn. on S.E. Asian Refugees, 1978—85; bd. dirs. Fgn. Policy Assn., 1958—68, 1977—86, Japan-U.S. Friendship Commn., 1976—77; chmn. N.Y.C. Met. Mission United Ch. of Christ, 1966—69; bd. dirs. Kennedy Ctr. for the Performing Arts, 1970—77, Inter-Am. Found., 1970—77, East-West Ctr., 1975—77, Am. Forum for Global Edn., 1977—, Social Sci. Found., U. Denver, 1992—, World Learning, 2001—, Meridian House Internat., 1978—83, Atlantic Coun. U.S., 1982—84, Fgn. Student Svc. Coun., 1978—82, Coun. for Advancement of Citizenship, 1991—96, Coun. for Cmty. of Democracies, 1996—, pres., 1999—2001, pres. emeritus, 2001—. With USAR, WWII. Decorated Bronze Star with v device, Japan Order of the Sacred Treasure, Gold and Silver Star; Germany Order of Merit, Commdr.'s Cross, Poland Order of Merit, Knight Cross. Home: 9707 Old Georgetown Rd Apt 1104 Bethesda MD 20814-1746

RICHARDSON, JOHN CARROLL, lawyer, tax legislative consultant; b. Mobile, Ala., May 3, 1932; s. Robert Felder and Louise (Simmons) R.; m. Cicely Tomlinson, July 27, 1961; children: Nancy Louise, Robert Felder III, Leslie. BA, Tulane U., 1954; LLB cum laude, Harvard U., 1960. Bar: Colo. 1960, N.Y. 1965, D.C. 1972. Assoc. Holland & Hart, Denver, 1960-64; legal v.p. Hoover Worldwide Corp., N.Y.C., 1964-69; v.p., gen. counsel Continental Investment Corp., Boston, 1969; dep. tax legis. counsel U.S. Dept. Treasury, Washington, 1970-71, tax legis. counsel, 1972-73; ptnr. Brown, Wood, Ivey, Mitchell & Petty, N.Y.C., 1973-79, LeBoeuf, Lamb, Leiby & MacRae, N.Y.C., 1979-88, Morgan, Lewis & Bockius, N.Y.C., 1988-93; ret., 1993. Tax legis. cons., Orford, N.H., 1993—; adj. prof. Law Sch. Fordham U., 1990-94. Served to lt. comdr. USN, 1954-57 Mem. ABA (chmn. com. adminstrv. practice tax sect. 1984-86), N.Y. State Bar Assn. (exec. com. tax sect. 1975-84), D.C. Bar Assn., Am. Coll. Tax Counsel, N.Y. Athletic Club, Royal Automobile Club.

RICHARDSON, JOHN DAVID, retired protective services official; b. Baltimore, Md., Jan. 25, 1942; s. Horace Lemuel and Pauline Elizabeth Richardson; m. Glenda Faye Richardson, June 28, 1963; children: Kelley Faye Hodges, John David Richardson, II. BA, Florence State U., Florence, Alabama, 1976. Cert. Law Enforcement Ala. Police Acad., 1965. Draftman Engrng. Dept., Florence, Ala., 1963—64; patrolman Florence Police Dept., 1965—73; investigator Lauderdale County Sheriff's Dept., 1973—94. Coord. Fellowship Christian Law Enforcement, Shoals, Ala., 1986—2002; chaplain Fraternal Order of Police, 2001—02. Methodist. Avocations: reading, fishing, traveling, ministering. Home: 3050 County Road 112 Florence AL 35633 Personal E-mail: jgrich@hiwaay.net.

RICHARDSON, JOHN EDMON, marketing educator; b. Whittier, Calif., Oct. 22, 1942; s. John Edmon and Mildred Alice (Miller) R.; m. Dianne Elaine Ewald, July 15, 1967; 1 child, Sara Beth. BS, Calif. State U., Long Beach, 1964; MBA, U. So. Calif., 1966; MDiv, Fuller Theol. Sem., 1969, D of Ministry, 1981. Prof. mktg. Sch. Bus. and Mgmt. Pepperdine U., Malibu, Calif., 1969—. Author: (leader's guides) Caring Enough to Confront, 1984, The Measure of a Man, 1985; editor: Ann. Editions: Marketing, 1987—, Bus. Ethics, 1990—. Mem. Am. Mgmt. Assn., Soc. Bus. Ethics, Christian Writers Guild, Fuller Sem. Alumni Cabinet (pres. 1982-85), Am. Mktg. Assn., Beta Gamma Sigma. Avocations: fishing, woodworking, golf, photography. Office: Pepperdine U Sch Bus and Mgmt 400 Corporate Pointe Fl 4 Culver City CA 90230-7627

RICHARDSON, JOHN MACLAREN, JR. clergyman; b. Plainfield, N.J., Nov. 6, 1942; s. John MacLaren and Lucy Lenox (Baker) R.; m. Sharon Rae Kellogg, June 20, 1964; children: Elizabeth R. Updike, John M. III, James Kellogg. AA, George Washington U., 1965, BA, 1969; MA, Grace Theol. Sem., 1993. Bus. mgr. ComMission, Inc., Harrisonburg, Va., 1983-84; cons. in human resources/edn., 1980-88; prin. The Norman A. Whitesel Christian Sch., Mt. Crawford, Va., 1988-90; supt., founding mem. Blue Ridge Christian Sch., Bridgewater, 1990-99; encounter dir. Wingfield Ministries, Harrisonburg, 1999—. Bd. dirs. Trinity Christian Sch., Mt. Crawford, Va., 1985-88; v.p., bd. dirs. Valley Haven Inc., Harrisonburg, Va., 2001—. Elder Grace Covenant Ch., Harrisonburg, 1988—92, 1997—98. Decorated Nat. Def. medal, USN, 1964, Navy Good Conduct medal, USN, 1966, Armed Forces Reserve medal, USN, 1976. Mem.: Ret. Officers Assn., Officers Christian Fellowship, Naval Res. Assn., Rotary Internat. Republican. Home: 301 Broad St Bridgewater VA 22812-1719 Office: Wingfield Ministries Inc 2389 Grace Chapel Rd Harrisonburg VA 22801-4523 E-mail: richardsonjack@msn.com. *I am convinced that a worldview which is not based upon the unchanging truth of the Holy Bible is, at best, irrelevant and, at worst, entirely misleading and without legitimate foundation.*

RICHARDSON, JOHN VINSON, JR. library and information science educator; b. Columbus, Ohio, Dec. 27, 1949; s. John Vinson Sr. and Hope Irene (Smith) R.; m. Nancy Lee Brown, Aug. 22, 1971. BA, Ohio State U., 1971; MLS, Peabody Coll., 1972; PhD, Ind. U., 1978. Asst. prof. UCLA, 1978-83, assoc. prof., 1983-98, editor The Libr. Quar., 1994—, prof., 1998—. Faculty coord. UCLA-St. Petersburg State Acad. of Culture Exch. Program, 1996—; fellow advanced rsch. Inst. U. Ill., 1991; pres. Info. Transfer, Inglewood, Calif., 1988—; mem. editl. bd. Ref. Svcs. Rev., Ann Arbor, Mich., 1991—, Jour. Govt. Info., Oxford, Eng., 1975—, Index to Current Urban Documents, Westport, Conn., 1987—, U. Calif. Press Catalogues and Bibliographies series, 1994-97; vis. fellow Charles Stuart U. NSW Australia, 1990; vis. scholar ALISE Russia Project, St. Petersburg and Moscow, 1996; vis. disting. scholar OCLC Inc., Dublin, Ohio, 1996-97; presidential scholar, Libr. Sys. & Svcs., LLC, 2002; chmn. Calif. Pacific Ann. Conf. Com. on Archives and History, 1992-96; Henderson lectr. U. N.C., Chapel Hill, 1997; mem. UCLA Privilege and Tenure, 1999-2000, chair, 2000-2002. Author: Spirit of Inquiry, 1982, Gospel of Scholarship, 1992, Knowledge-based Systems for General Reference Work, 1995, Understanding Reference Transactions, 2002. Mem. UCLA Grad. Coun., 1992-96, chair, 1995-96; mem. U. Calif. systemwide coord. com. on grad. affairs, 1993-96; pres. Wesley Found., L.A., 1981-87; lay del. Cal-Pac Conf. United Meth. Ch., 1985, 86, 92-96, chair conf. commn. on archives and history, 1992—96. Rsch. grantee Coun. on Libr. Resources, 1985, 90, Assn. Libr. and Info. Sci. Educators rsch. grantee, 1984, 87, 98, Online Computer Libr. Ctr. Libr. and Info. Sci. rsch. grantee, 1999; Harold Lancour scholar Beta Phi Mu, 1986, 99, Kaliper Sr. scholar U. Mich., 1998-99, Presdl. scholar Libr. Systems and Svcs. LLC, 2002; recipient Louise Maxwell award Ind. U. Alumni Assn., 1995. Mem. ALA (Justin Winsor prize 1990, Ref. and Adult Svcs. divsn. Outstanding Paper award 1992), AAAS, Assn. Libr. and Info. Sci. Educators (rsch. paper prize 1986, 91, rsch. grants 1984, 87, 98), Am. Soc. for Info. Sci. (Best Info. Sci. book 1995), Am. Assn. Adv. Slavic Studies, Sigma Xi. Democrat. Avocations: wine tasting,reading, fgn. travel, lilac point Siamese. Office: UCLA GSE&IS DIS Campus Box 951520 Los Angeles CA 90095-1520 E-mail: jrichard@ucla.edu. *By our common action, we can bend the flow of history.*

RICHARDSON, JOSEPH BLANCET, former biology educator, educational facilities planning consultant; b. Louisville, Nov. 12, 1936; s. Orla Coburn and Alma (Mason) R. m. Mary Irene Murphy, Dec. 27, 1960; children: Pamela, Joseph Blancet Jr., John, Karen BSCE, The Citadel, 1958; BA in Zoology with high honors, Rutgers U., 1973, PhD in Zoology, 1979; MS in Anatomy, N.Y. Med. Coll., 1975; Grad. Cert. in Work Life Ministry, Immaculate Conception Sem., 2001. Ordained deacon Roman Catholic Ch., 1995. Design engr. Ky. Hwy. Dept., 1958-59; tech. rep. Shell Oil Co., Balt., 1968-72; asst. prof. biology Ramapo Coll., Mahwah, N.J., 1976-80, from program coord. for biology to dir. campus planning, 1979-86; pres. Richardson Recreational Svcs., Inc., Kinnelon, 1981-88, Waterworld Assocs., Inc., Kinnelon, 1986—. Dir. recreational water testing programs Kinnelon Environ. Commn., 1977—82; trustee Kinnelon Bd. Edn., 1989—94; pres. Morris County Ednl. Svcs. Commn., 1991—92; deacon Our Lady of Mt. Carmel Roman Cath. Ch., Boonton, NJ, 2001; coord. Work Life Ministry, Diocese of Paterson, 1997—; bd. dirs. St. Ephrem Found., Inc., 1998—. Capt. U.S. Army, 1959—68, Vietnam. Mem. N.J. Sch. Bds. Assn., N.J. Assn. Sch. Bus. Adminstrs., N.J. Assn. Sch. Bus. Ofcls., Soc. Am. Mil. Engrs. (treas. N.J. post 1988-90), The Citadel Alumni Assn., Rutgers U. Alumni Assn., N.Y. Med. Coll. Alumni Assn., N.Y. Acad. Sci., Coun. Ednl. Facility Planners, Sigma Xi. Republican. Home and Office: 65 Fayson Lake Rd Kinnelon NJ 07405-3129 E-mail: whitehall@msn.com.

RICHARDSON, JOSEPH HILL, physician, medical educator; b. Rensselaer, Ind., June 16, 1928; s. William Clark and Vera (Hill) R.; m. Joan Grace Meininger, July 8, 1950; children: Lois N., Ellen M., James K. MS in Medicine, Northwestern U., 1950, MD, 1953. Diplomate Am. Bd. Internal Medicine. Intern U.S. Naval Hosp., Great Lakes, Ill., 1953-54; physician internal medicine, hematology pvt. practice, Marion, Ind., 1959-67, Ft. Wayne, 1967—. Assoc. clin. prof. medicine, Ind. U. Sch. Medicine, 1993—; med. dir. The Med. Protective Co., Ft. Wayne, 1995-2001. Contbr. articles to profl. jours. Fellow in medicine Cleve. Clinic, 1956-59. Fellow ACP, AAAS; mem. AMA, Masons. Home and Office: 8726 Fortuna Way Fort Wayne IN 46815-5725

RICHARDSON, K. SCOTT, sales executive; b. Laurens, Iowa, Nov. 3, 1951; s. Kenneth and Lanore R.; m. Theresa Ann Fitzsimmons, Aug. 31, 1974; children: Seth Ian, Aaron Paul, Evan Scott, Claire Elizabeth, Anna Christine. BS in Radiologic Tech., Creighton U., Omaha, 1974; MS, U. Nebr., Omaha, 1976. Spl. procedures tech. Med. Coll. Va., Richmond, 1974-75; chief spl. procedure tech. St. Vincent Hosp., Sioux City, Iowa, 1975; inservice coordinator to radiology mgr. Nebr. Meth. Hosp., Omaha, 1975-78; sales rep. to sr. sales rep. Philips Med. Systems, Inc., 1978-81; adminstrv. dir. radiology The Meth. Hosp., Houston, 1981-83; reg. mgr. R.P. Kincheloe Co., Dallas, 1983-84, mgr. sales and svc., 1984-87, v.p. sales and svc., 1987-98, sr. v.p. sales and svc., 1998—; COO Perkins Electronics, Dallas, 2000—. Bd. dirs. Strategic Med. Svcs., Inc., Strategic Med. Svcs. San Antonio, SMS Acquisition #1. Eucharistic min., svc. min., lector, tchr. continuing Cath. edn., mem. fin. com., chmn. bldg. steering com. St. Philips Ch.; T-ball coord. Braeburn Little League, 1989—; coach YMCA Indoor Soccer League, 1987—, Highland Village Area Baseball and Softball Assn., 1998—; mgr. Lewisville Baseball Assn., 1990—, team sponsor, 1990—, bd. dirs., commr., 1992—; active ARC, Glenshire Soccer Club, Braeburn Valley West Swim Team; chmn. City of Highland Village Parks and Recreation Bd.; mem. City of Highland Village Tree Bd., Highland Village Cmty. Ctr. Com.; bd. dirs. Louisville Baseball Assn. Mem. Am. Registry Radiologic Technologists, Iowa Soc. Radiologic Technologists, Assn. Univ. Radiology Technologists, Tex. Soc. Radiologic Technologists. Republican. Roman Catholic. Avocations: fishing, travel, swimming, golf, basketball, collecting wine. Home: 2415 Silverthorne Ct Highland Village TX 75077-3109

RICHARDSON, LAUREL WALUM, sociology educator; b. Chgo., July 15, 1938; d. Tyrrell Alexander and Rose (Foreman) R.; m. Herb Walum, Dec. 27, 1959 (div. 1972); children: Benjamin, Joshua; m. Ernest Lockridge, Dec. 12, 1981. AB, U. Chgo., 1955, BA, 1956; PhD, U. Colo., 1963. Asst. prof. Calif. State U., Los Angeles, 1962-64; postdoctoral fellow Sch. Medicine Ohio State U., Columbus, 1964-65, asst. prof. sociology, 1970-75, assoc. prof., 1975-79; prof. sociology Sch. Medicine Ohio State U., 1979—, prof. cultural studies, edn. policy and leadership; asst. prof. sociology Denison U., Granville, Ohio, 1965-69. Mem. editorial bd. Jour. Contemporary Ethnography, Symbolic Interaction, Gender & Soc., Qualitative Sociology, The Sociol. Quar. Author: Dynamics of Sex and Gender, 1977, 3d edit. 1988, The New Other Woman, 1985, Die Neve Andere, 1987, A Nova Outra Mulher, 1987, Writing Strategies: Reaching Diverse Audiences, 1990, Gender and University Teaching: A Negotiated Difference, 1995; editor: Feminist Frontiers, 1983, 5th edit., 2000, Fields of Play Constructing an Academic Life, 1997 (Charles H. Cooley award for best sociology book 1998); assoc. editor Symbolic Interaction; author more than 100 rsch. articles and papers. Ford Found. fellow, 1954-56; NSF dissertation fellow, 1960-62; post doctoral fellow Vocat. Rehab., Columbus, 1964; grantee Ohio Dept. Health, 1986-87, Nat. Inst. Edn., 1981-82, NIMH, 1972-74, NSF, 1963-64, NEH, 1992; recipient Disting. Affirmative Action award Ohio State U., 1983, Feminist Mentor award, 1998. Mem. Am. Sociol. Assn. (com. on coms. 1980-81, com. on pub. info. 1987—), North Ctrl. Sociol. Assn. (pres. 1986-87), Sociologists for Women in Soc. (coun. mem. 1978-80), Ctrl. Ohio Sociologists for Women in Soc. (past pres.), Women's Poetry Workshop, Soc. for Study of Symbolic Interaction (publs. com.). Avocations: hiking, poetry. Office: Ohio State Univ Dept of Sociology 190 N Oval Mall Columbus OH 43210-1328 E-mail: Richardson.9@osu.edu.

RICHARDSON, LAWRENCE, JR. Latin language educator, archeologist; b. Altoona, Pa., Dec. 2, 1920; widower. BA, Yale U., 1942, PhD in Classics, 1952. Instr. classics Yale U., New Haven, 1946-47, instr. to assoc. prof., 1955-66; prof. Duke U., Durham, N.C., 1966-78, James B. Duke prof. Latin, 1978-91, prof. emeritus, 1991—. Field archeologist Am. Acad. Rome, 1952-55, Mellon prof., 1980-81; mem. Inst. Advanced Study, 1967-68. Author: Pompeii: An Architectural History, 1988, A New Topographical Dictionary of Ancient Rome, 1992, A Catalog of Identifiable Figure Painters of Ancient Pompeii, Herculaneum and Stabiae, 2000; contbr. articles to profl. jours. Guggenheim fellow, 1958-59; Am. Council Learned Socs. fellow, 1967-68, 72-73; NEH fellow, 1979-80 Mem. German Archeol. Inst. (corr.), Am. Philol. Assn., Archeol. Inst. Am. Office: Duke U West Campus Dept Classical Studies Durham NC 27708 E-mail: classics@duke.edu.

RICHARDSON, LEATRICE JOY, artist; b. N.Y.C., Dec. 26, 1940; d. Sidney and Ottilia (Moldovan) Mayer; m. Robert John Richardson, Aug. 7, 1965; children: Todd Harper, Tiffany Jill. Student, Chouinard Art Inst., L.A., 1960-65. Oup shows and exhbns. include: Akron Soc. of Artists, 1998, Houston Watercolor Soc., 1994, 97, 98, 99, La. Watercolor Soc., 1996, Midwest Watercolor Soc., 1993, 95, 97, 98, 99, Miss. Watercolor Soc., 1994, Nat. Assn. Women Artists, N.Y.C., Northwest Watercolor Soc., 1994, 95, San Diego Watercolor Soc., 1995, Taos Nat. Exhbn. of Watercolor II, 1996, Watercolor USA, 1996, Western Colo. Watercolor Soc., 1995, Western Fedn. of Watercolor Socs., 1996, others; publs. include People in Watercolor, 1996, Best of Watercolor: Painting Color, 1997. Recipient 2d award Houston Watercolor Soc., 1997, Jack Richeson & Co. Merit award Midwest Watercolor Soc., 1995, Art Study Club award Miss. Watercolor Soc., 1994, Northwest Watercolor Soc., Margaret Malloy Merit award, 1994, San Diego Watercolor award Watercolor West, 1992, Svoir Faire, Lana Paper Merchandise award 1992, Winsor Newton Merchandise award 1994. Mem. Watercolor West (signature), Midwest Watercolor Soc. (signature), Women Painters West (signature), Nat. Assn. Women Artists. Avocations: film, animation. Home: 3540 Ridgeford Dr Westlake Village CA 91361-4820

RICHARDSON, MARGARET MILNER, accounting firm executive, lawyer; b. Waco, Tex., May 14, 1943; d. James W. and Margaret Wiebusch Milner; m. John L. Richardson, July 22, 1967; 1 child, Margaret Lawrence. AB in Polit. Sci., Vassar Coll., 1965; JD with honors, George Washington U., 1968. Bar: Va. 1968, D.C. 1968, U.S. Dist. Ct. D.C. 1968, U.S. Ct. Appeals (4th, 5th, D.C. and Fed. cirs.) 1968, U.S. Claims Ct. 1969, U.S. Tax Ct. 1970, U.S. Supreme Ct. 1971. Clk. U.S. Ct. Claims, Washington; with Office Chief Counsel IRS, 1969-77; with Sutherland, Asbill and Brennan, 1977-80, ptnr., 1980-93; commr. IRS, 1993-97; ptnr. Ernst & Young, 1997—. Mem. commr.'s adv. group IRS, 1988-90, chair, 1990; bd. advisors George Washington Law Sch.; mem. D.C. Bar Commn. on Multidisciplinary Practice, Presdl. Commn. on Holocaust Assets. Contbr. articles to profl. jours. Assisted Clinton 1992 primary and gen. election campaign; served as team leader Justice Dept./Civil Rights Cluster during Presdl. Transition; mem. bd. Nat. Mus. Women in Arts, Mayor's Transition Team, 1998, Women's Campaign Fund, Nat. Cathedral Sch., Hosp. for Sick Children; bd. trustees Eurasia Found. Mem. ABA, D.C. Bar Assn. (tax sect.), Va. State Bar, Fed. Bar Assn. (com. taxation), Fin. Women's Assn. N.Y., Washington Women's Forum, Internat. Alliance, U.S. Russia Bus. Coun., Woodrow Wilson Ctr. Avocations: travel, antiques, needlepoint, gardening. Office: 1225 Connecticut Ave NW Washington DC 20036-2604

RICHARDSON, MARK A. otolaryngologist; b. Cleve., Sept. 22, 1949; MD, Med. U. S.C., 1975. Diplomate Am. Bd. Otolaryngology. Intern U. South Fla., Tampa, 1975-76; resident in otolaryngology Med. U. Hosp., Charleston, S.C., 1976-79; fellow in pediatric otolaryngology Children's Hosp. Med. Ctr., Cin., 1979-80, mem. staff Seattle, 1980-94; prof. U. Wash., 1980-94; prof. dept. otolaryngology/head and neck surgery Johns Hopkins U., Balt., 1995-2001; prof. and chmn. dept. otolaryngology/head and neck surgery Oreg. Health Scis. U., Portland, 2001—. Fellow ACS, Am. Soc. Head and Neck Surgery; mem. Am. Acad. Otolaryngology/Hea dnd Neck Surgery, Am. Acad. Pediatrics, Am. Broncho-Esophogeal Assn. Office: Oreg Health Scis U Dept Oto/Head and Neck Surg 3181 Sam Jackson Park Rd Portland OR 92201-3098

RICHARDSON, MAURINE JANET, reading educator; b. Portland, Maine, May 17, 1944; d. Maurice Joseph and Rena (Prevost) Vaillancourt; m. James Alexander Richardson, Apr. 30, 1966. AA, Palm Beach Jr. Coll., Lake Worth, Fla., 1964; BA, Fla. Atlantic U., 1966; MEd, U. Ark., 1979, EdD, 1981. Tchr. Pewamo-Westphalia Sch. Dist., Pewamo, Mich., 1967-69, River Valley Sch. Dist., Three Oaks, 1974-76; asst. prof. tchr. edn. Bethel Coll., McKenzie, Tenn., 1981-88; asst. prof. reading edn. U. Tenn., Martin, 1988-89, U. S.D., Vermillion, 1989—. Author: Directed Reading, Writing, and Art Activity, 1990, Imagery Format, 1987. Mem. adv. bd. Area 7 Spl. Olympics, Martin, 1988-89. Named Duchess of Paducah City of Paducah, Ky., 1987. Mem. Internat. Reading Assn., Nat. Coun. Tchrs. English, S.D. Reading Coun. (chair studies and rsch.), Vermillion Valley Reading Coun. (pres. 1992-93), Epsilon Sigma Alpha, Delta Kappa Gamma, Phi Delta Kappa. Avocations: reading, traveling, sailing, stamp collecting. Home: 902 Ridgecrest Dr Vermillion SD 57069-3531 Office: U SD 414 E Clark St Vermillion SD 57069-2307

RICHARDSON, MIRANDA, actress; b. Lancashire, Eng., Mar. 3, 1958; Studied, Drama Program Bristol. Stage performances include Moving, stage performances include All My Sons, Who's Afraid of Virginia Woolf, The Life of Einstein, A Lie of the Mind, Edmond, Insignificance, Aunt Dan & Lemon, The Changeling, Mountain Language, Educating Rita, The Maids, The Designated Mourner, Ella Jenks; actor(TV appearances): The Hard Word, Sorrel and Son, A Woman of Substance, Underworld, Death of the Heart, The Scold's Bridle, 1998, Merlin, 1998, Alice, 1999, : (TV series) Black Adder II & III, Sweet as You Are; (TV miniseries) Die Kinder, The James Bond Story, 1999, (voice): The Miracle Maker, 2000, : (films) Dance with a Stranger, 1985, The Innocent, 1986, Empire of the Sun, 1987, Eat the Rich, 1987, Twisted Obsession, 1990, The Bachelor, 1991, Enchanted April, 1992 (Golden Globe award), Damage, 1992 (B.A.F.T.A. award for Best Supporting Actress), The Crying Game, 1992 (B.A.F.T.A. award for best supporting actress), Fatherland, HBO, 1994 (Golden Globe award), Tom & Viv, 1994 (Acad. award nominee for best actress, 1995), La Nuit et Le Moment, 1994, Kansas City, 1996, The Evening Star, 1996, Swann, 1996, Saint-Ex, 1997, The Apostle, 1997, The Designated Mourner, 1997, All for Love, 1998, Jacob Two Two and the Hooded Fang, 1998, Sleepy Hollow, 1999, Blackadder Back and Forth, 1999, Get Carter, 2000, Spider, 2001, The Hours, 2001, Rage on Placid Lake, 2002, The Lost Prince, 2002, Chicken Run, 2000, Snow White , 2000, On Placid Lake , 2002, The Actors, 2002. Address: c/o Harriet Robinson 76 Oxford St London W1D 1BS England

RICHARDSON, PAMELA F. federal agency administrator; BS in Aeronautical and Astronautical Engring., MS in Fluid Mechanics, Ohio State U. Aerospace engr. NASA Langley Rsch. Ctr., 1975—82, aeronautics engr., 1982—85, with Nat. Aerospace Plane Program, 1985—90; various positions in program mgmt. and program assessment integration NASA Hdqrs. Office: NASA Hdqrs Mail Code Q 300 E St SW Washington DC 20546

RICHARDSON, PATRICIA JEAN, librarian; b. Walla Walla, Wash., Jan. 31, 1943; d. Francis and Melba Lorraine (Bryant) Hagel; m. Henry Vokes-MacKey Richardson, May 7, 1965 (div. July 1992); children: Shasha L., Kathrine E., Frances du Bruyeres, John E. du Bruyeres; m. Michael E. Ovens, Nov. 1, 1999. AA, Yakima Valley Coll., Yakima, Wash., 1963; BA in English, U. Wash., 1966, MLS, 1994. Cert. libr., Wash. Libr.'s asst. Yakima Valley Regional Libr., Yakima, 1956-63, Microsoft, Redmond, Wash., 1993-94; libr. asst. children's dept. Walla Walla Pub. Libr., 1984-92; libr. for children's svcs. King County Libr. Sys., Seattle, 1993—. Mem. ALA, AAUW (membership chmn. 1971, scholar Walla Walla chpt. 1992), Pacific N.W. Libr. Assn., Wash. Libr. Assn., bd. mem. CAYAS, 1998—. Episcopalian. Avocations: gardening, reading, hiking, collecting.

RICHARDSON, PATRICK WILLIAM, lawyer; b. Huntsville, Ala., Oct. 5, 1925; s. Schuyler Harris and Suzane Agnes (Smith) R.; m. Martha Alice Holliman, Dec. 23, 1949; m. Mary McAlpine Moore, Oct. 9, 1970; children: Schuyler Harris, III, James Holiman. BS, U. Ala., 1946, JD, 1948, LLD (hon.), 1976. Bar: Ala. 1948, U.S. Ct. Appeals (5th cir.) 1955, U.S. Supreme Ct. 1957, U.S. Ct. Appeals (11th cir.) 1981. Ptnr. Bell Richardson LLP, Huntsville, 1948—; dep. atty. gen. State of Ala., 1996—. Spl. cir. solicitor 23d Cir. Ala., 1951. Bd. dirs. U. Ala. Huntsville Found., 1962—, pres., 1962-74. Fellow Am. Coll. Trial Lawyers; mem. ABA, Ala. State Bar (pres. 1969-70), Huntsville-Madison County Bar Assn. (pres. 1966-67), Ala. Law Inst. (council), Am. Coll. Mortgage Attys. (regent 1975-77), Rotary. Republican. Methodist. Office: 116 Jefferson St S Huntsville AL 35801-4818 E-mail: pwr@bellrich.com.

RICHARDSON, RALPH HERMAN, lawyer; b. Detroit, Oct. 12, 1935; s. Ralph Onazime and Lucinda Ollie (Fluence) R.; m. Arvie Y., June 1, 1956 (div. 1961); children: Cassandra, Tanya, Arvie Lynn; m. Julia A., Sept. 16, 1962 (div. 1982); children: Traci, Theron. BA, Wayne State U., 1964, JD, 1970. Bar: Mich., U.S. Ct. Appeals (6th cir.), Supreme Ct. U.S., 1970. Postal transp. clk. U.S. P. O., Detroit, 1954-56; clk. pub. aid worker City Detroit, 1956-65; sr. labor relations rep. Ford Motor Co., Ypsilanti, Mich., 1965-70, wage admins., 1966, labor relations rep., 1967; atty. Brown Grier, Richardson P.C., Detroit, 1970-71; atty Richardson, Grier P.C., 1971-73; ptnr. Stone, Richardson P.C., 1973—. Bd. dirs. Legal Aid, Defender Assn. Detroit, 1985-86; apptd. hon. spl. agt. Office of Investigations, Office Inspector gen., U.S. Printing Office, 1997. Mem. bd. dirs. YMCA Fisher Branch; Boy Scouts Am.; apptd. to Bd. Appeals for Hosp. Bed Reduction by Gov. State of Mich., 1982, apptd. Spl. Asst. Atty. Gen., by Frank J. Kelley, Atty Gen. for the State Mich., May 23, 1984, apptd. to Task Oriented Com. to review the issue in-home child care by Detroit City Council Mem., Maryann Mahaffey. With U.S. Army, 1964. Mem. NAACP (life), Am. Arbitration Assn., Legal Aid Defender Assn., Mich. State Bar Fellows, Optimists, Masons, Shriners (imperial legal advisor, gen. counsel 1994-2002, Right Eminent Grand Comdr. of the Knights Templar, State of Mich. 1997—), Phi Alpha Delta, Kappa Alpha Psi. Democrat. Office: Stone Richardson PC 2910 E Jefferson Ave Detroit MI 48207-4208 Fax: 313-393-6701. E-mail: aretwo@msn.com.

RICHARDSON, RICHARD JUDSON, retired political science educator; b. Poplar Bluff, Mo., Feb. 16, 1935; s. Jewell Judson and Naomi Fern (Watson) R.; m. Sammie Sue Cullum, Dec. 29, 1961; children: Jon Mark, Anna Cecile, Ellen Elizabeth, Megan Leigh. BS, Harding Coll., 1957; cert., U. Dublin, 1958; MA, Tulane U., 1961, PhD, 1967. Instr. Tulane U., 1962—65; 67asst. prof. polit. sci. Western Mich. U., Kalamazoo, 1965, assoc. prof., 1967—69; vis. assoc. prof. U. Hawaii, 1967—68; from assoc. prof. to v.p. acad. affairs U. N.C., Chapel Hill, 1969—91, assoc. v.p. acad. affairs univ. gen. adminstrn., 1991—92. Adj. prof. Duke U., Durham, 1972-74; provost, vice chancellor acad. affairs U. N.C., 1995-2000; cons. in field. Author: (with Kenneth Vines) The Politics of Federal Courts, 1971, (with Darlene Walker) People and the Police, 1973, (with Marian Irish, James Prothro) The Politics of American Democracy, 1981. Del. County Dem. Conv., 1972, 83; vice chmn. Dem. Party Precinct, 1983-85; chmn. bldg. fund YMCA, 1976; chmn. Carolina Challenge for endowment U. N.C., Chapel Hill, 1979-80; chmn. U. N.C. Bicentennial Observance, 1991-94; chmn. United Way, 1983, pres., 1985; pres. PTA County Coun., 1984. Recipient Edward S. Corwin award Am. Polit. Sci. Assn., 1967, Tanner Disting. Teaching award U. N.C., 1972, Univ. award for Outstanding Teaching, 1981, Thomas Jefferson award, 1987, James Johnston Disting. Tchg. award, 1993, Alumni Faculty Disting. Svc. award, 1994, Disting. Eagle Scout award Boy Scouts Am., 1998, Laura Thomas award, 1999, C. Knox Massey award, 2000, Disting. Svc. medal U. N.C. Alumni Assn., 2001; named life regent Boy Scouts Am., 1998; Edgar Stern fellow, 1959-61; NEH grantee, 1970. Mem. N.C. Polit. Sci. Assn. (pres. 1978-79), Am. Polit. Sci. Assn., So. Polit. Sci. Assn., ACLU (bd. dirs. local chpt. 1985-88, state bd. dirs. 1988-89), Order of Janus, Order of the Long Leaf Pine, Order of Golden Fleece, Order of the Grail. Home: 234 Terrells Creek Ln Pittsboro NC 27312-5145

RICHARDSON, ROBERT ALLEN, retired lawyer, educator; b. Cleve., Feb. 15, 1939; s. Allen B. and Margaret C. (Thomas) R.; m. Carolyn Eck Richardson, Dec. 9, 1968. BA, Ohio Wesleyan U., 1961; LLB, Harvard U., 1964. Bar: Ohio 1964, Hawaii 1990. Ptnr. Caffee, Halter & Griswold, Cleve., 1968-89; counsel Mancini, Rowland & Welch (formerly Case & Lynch), Maui, Hawaii, 1990—2001; lectr., affirmative action officer, atty., exec. com. Maui (Hawaii) C.C., 1989—2001; ret., 2001. Chmn. gov. fin. dept., chmn. cmty. svc. com., mem. oper. com. Caffee, Halter & Griswold; past lectr. Sch. Law Cleve. State U.; counsel Maui C. of C., Kahului, 1994-98. Pres. trustee Big Bros., Big Sisters of Maui, 1990-94; v.p., trustee, pres. Ka Hole A Ke Ole Homeless Resource Ctr., 1990—; trustee Maui Acad. Performing Arts, 1990-97, Maul Counseling Svc., 1990-96, Kapalua Music Festival, Friends of Children Advocate Ctr., Legal Aid Soc. Hawaii, pres., 1998-88; v.p., trustee, chmn. devel. com. Cleve. Playhouse, 1984-89; trustee, mem. exec. com., program chmn. Cleve. Coun. World Affairs, 1970-89; past model UN chmn. Cleve. Com. on Fgn. Rels.; trustee, mem. exec. com., budget chmn. Neighborhood Ctrs. Assn., 1980-89; trustee Maui Symphony, 1995-98, v.p., 1999—. Recipient T.S. Shinn award Maui C. of C., 2000. Mem. Rotary Club of Maui, Maui Country Club, Roufant Club (adv.), Cleve. Skating Club. Home: 1365 Lower Kula Rd Kula HI 96790-9724

RICHARDSON, ROBERT CARLETON, engineering consultant; b. Grand Junction, Colo., Mar. 17, 1925; s. Carleton O. and Mabel Grace (Davy) Richardson; m. Ruby Lucille Morrison, Jan. 11, 1947 (dec.); children: Robert James, Lorie Dianne Richardson Dismont. Student, U. Colo., Boulder, 1943-44, U. Calif., Berkeley, 1946-47, I.C.S., Scranton, Pa., 1947-50, Calif. State U., Long Beach, 1983, John F. Kennedy U., Martinez, Calif., 1967. Chief engr., gen. mgr. Gilmore Fabricators, Oakland, Calif., 1948-56; nat. sales mgr. Gilmore Steel Contrs., 1957-72; v.p. engring. R&D Davis Walker Corp., L.A., 1972-86; tech. dir. Ivy Steel divsn. MMI, Houston, 1986-93; engring. cons. R.C. Richardson & Assocs., Sun Lakes, Ariz., 1993—. Engring. instr. Calif. State U., Long Beach, 1983—85; pres. Nat. Concrete Industry Bd., San Francisco, 1984; chmn. bd. Wire Reinforcement Inst., Findlay, Ohio, 1978, Findlay, 82; bd. dirs. ASCC, 1982—84. Author: (book) New Developments with Structural WWR in Zones of High Seismicity, 1999; co-author: Manual of Standard Practice, 1988—90, Structural Detailing Manual, 1990—94. With USMC, 1943—45. Named Boss of the Yr., Women in Constrn., Oakland, 1964, 1965, Eminent Fellow, Wisdom Hall of Fame, 2000; recipient Outstanding Achievement award, Wire Reinforcement Inst., 1993. Fellow: Am. Concrete Inst. Internat.; mem.: ASTM, China Marine Assn., Marine Corps. Assn., Bldg. Seismic Safety Coun., Alliance for Concrete Codes and Standards, Earthquake Engring. Rsch. Inst., Marines Meml. Assn., Structural Engrs. Assn. Calif., Nat. Coun. Structural Engrs. Assns., ASCE/Fed. Emergency Mgmt. Agy. Republican. Achievements include research in on high strength steel reinforcement under seismic loadings; on fatigue of wire reinforcement under dynamic loads; on crack behavior of shear reinforcement in concrete beams and girders. Avocations: swimming, walking, golf, fishing, hunting. Home and Office: 2800 N Central Ave Ste 1000 Phoenix AZ 85004 Fax: 480-895-2870. E-mail: RCRAssoc@att.net.

RICHARDSON, ROBERT COLEMAN, physics educator, researcher; b. Washington, June 26, 1937; s. Robert Franklin and Lois (Price) R.; m. Betty Marilyn McCarthy, Sept. 2, 1962; children: Jennifer, Pamela. BS in Physics, Va. Poly. Inst. and State U., 1958, MS, 1960; PhD in Physics, Duke U., 1966. Research assoc. Cornell U., Ithaca, NY, 1966-67, asst. prof., 1968-71, assoc. prof., 1972-74, prof., 1975—97, Floyd R. Newman prof. of physics & vice provost for research, 1998—. Chmn. Internat. Union Pure and Applied Physics Commn. (C-5), 1981-84; mem. bd. assessment Nat. Bur. Standards, 1983—. Mem. editorial bd. Jour. of Low Temperature Physics, 1984—. Served to 2d lt. U.S. Army, 1959-60. Guggenheim fellow 1975, 83; recipient Simon Meml. prize Brit. Phys. Soc., 1976; co-recipient Nobel prize in physics, 1996. Fellow AAAS, Am. Phys. Soc. (Oliver E. Buckley prize 1981), Am. Philosophical Soc, 2001-; mem. Nat. Acad. Scis, Internat. Space Station Mgmt. and Cost Evaluation Task Force, NASA, 2001-. Avocations: photography, gardening. Office: Cornell Univ Office of Vice Provost for Research 314 Day Hall Ithaca NY 14853*

RICHARDSON, ROBERT DALE, JR. English language educator; b. Milw., June 14, 1934; s. Robert Dale and Lucy Baldwin (Marsh) R.; m. Elizabeth Hall, Nov. 7, 1959 (div. 1987); m. Annie Dillard, Dec. 10, 1988; children: Elisabeth, Anne, Rosy. AB magna cum laude in English, Harvard U., 1956, PhD in English Lit., 1961. Instr. English Harvard U., Cambridge, Mass., 1961-63; asst. prof. English U. Denver, 1963-68, assoc. prof., 1968-72, prof., 1972-87, Lawrence C. Phipps prof. humanities, 1979-82, chmn. dept., 1968-73, pres. Univ. senate, 1972-73, assoc. dean grad. studies, 1975-76; prof. English, U. Colo., Boulder, 1987; vis. prof. letters Wesleyan U., Middletown, Conn., 1989-94. Vis. prof. Harvard U., summer 1976, CUNY, 1978, Sichuan U., 1983; vis. fellow Huntington Libr., 1973-74; vis. instr. Yale U., 1988; bd. dirs. David R. Godine Pub. Author: Literature and Film, 1969, Henry Thoreau: A Life of the Mind, 1986 (Melcher award, 1986), Emerson: The Mind on Fire, 1995 (Parkman prize, 1995, Melcher award, 1995, Washington Irving award, 1995), Myth and Literature in the American Renaissance, 1978; author: (with Burton Feldman) The Rise of Modern Mythology 1680-1860, 1972; author: (with Allen Mandelbaum) Three Centuries of American Poetry, 1999. Trustee Meadville-Lombard Theol. Sch., 1981-87. Guggenheim fellow, 1990; recipient Acad. award in lit. Am. Acad. of Arts and Letters, 1998. Fellow Nat. Humanities Ctr.; mem. Soc. Am. Hist., Soc. Eighteenth Century Studies, Melville Soc., Author's Guild, Thoreau Soc., Emerson Soc., Assn. Lit. Scholars and Critics. Democrat. Unitarian Universalist. E-mail: rrchardson@aol.com.

RICHARDSON, ROBERT EDWARD, data processing analyst; b. Ann Arbor, Mich., Dec. 13, 1955; s. Stanley G. and Frances A. (Raes) R.; m. Pamela Lee Blewer. BBA, U. Iowa, 1978. Rsch. group mgr. Sears, Roebuck & Co., Des Moines, 1978-79; data processing mgmt. trainee Armstrong Dept. Store, Cedar Rapids, Iowa, 1979-81; level II programmer analyst City of Cedar Rapids, 1981-84; sr. programmer analyst Life Investors, Cedar Rapids, 1984-88; systems software programmer II, Wang system adminstr. AEGON USA Inc. (formerly Life Investors), 1988-91; Wang system adminstr. AEGON USA, Inc., 1991-92, tech. analyst, 1992-94, sys. software programmer, 1994-96, sys. software programmer III, 1996-2000, sr. sys. engr., 2000—. Fellow Mgmt. Inst. (life), Office Mgmt. Assn. (life); mem. Alpha Kappa Psi (pres. Hawkeye State Alumni chpt. 1987-88, editor pub. directory 1989-97, bd. dirs. north ctrl. region 1988-90, Alumni Disting. Svc. award 1981). Avocation: personal computers. Home: 6901 Bowman Ln NE Cedar Rapids IA 52402-1577 Office: AEGON USA Inc Mail Stop 9000 4333 Edgewood Rd NE Cedar Rapids IA 52499-9000 E-mail: planet1577@yahoo.com.

RICHARDSON, ROBERT JAY, investment company executive; b. Honolulu, Aug. 8, 1958; s. Edward Adams and Dorothy Jane (Smith) R.; m. Carol Ann Zippi, Sept. 4, 1982; children: Tedd Adams, Bobbie Phyllis. BS in Bus. Adminstrn., U. Fla., 1980. Cert. fund specialist. Credit analyst Royal Trust Bank, Miami, Fla., 1981, comml. lending officer, 1981-82; mktg. coord. First Capital Cos., Coral Gables, Fla., 1982-83, mktg. dir., 1983-84; dir. mktg. Charter Fin. Group, Houston, 1984-86; regional v.p. Integrated Resources, Inc., 1986-89, MFS Fin. Svcs., Houston, 1990-93; v.p. Dreyfus Corp., 1993-95, Franklin/Templeton Group, San Mateo, Calif., 1995—. Mem. Internat. Assn. for Fin. Planning, Inst. Cert. Fund Specialists. Home: 10719 Marsha Ln Houston TX 77024-3122

RICHARDSON, ROBERT JOHN, producer, director animation; b. Chgo., Dec. 1, 1942; s. Andrew John Harper and Lillian Joan (Cazzell) R.; m. Leatrice Joy Mayer; children: Todd Harper, Tiffany Jill. BA, Calif. Inst. of the Arts, 1965. Asst. animator Walt Disney Prodns., Burbank, Calif., 1965-67; dir., animator Depatie Freleng Films, Van Nuys, 1967-80; producer, dir. Marvel Prodns. Ltd., 1980-90; producer Walt Disney TV Animation, North Hollywood, Calif., 1990-92, Film Roman, 1992-93; supervising producer Marvel Films Animation, 1993-97; pres. Snazz-Wah Entertainment, Inc., 1998—; prodr., dir. Columbia TriStar TV, 1998—; dir. Porchlight Entertainment, 2002—. Producer (animated TV show) Jim Henson's Muppet Babies, 1984-90 (Emmy awards 1985, 86, 87, 88, The Humanitas prize 1985), Emmy nominee, 1989, (65 episodes) Spider Man, 1995 (Golden Reel award 1995). Nom. Image award, Access Media award 1995. Mem. Acad. TV Arts and Scis. Avocations: drawing, painting, gardening. Fax: 818-879-8449. E-mail: richardsonatsnazzwah@earthlink.net.

RICHARDSON, R(OSS) FRED(ERICK), insurance executive; b. Renfrew, Ont., Can., Feb. 4, 1928; came to U.S., 1980; s. Garfield Newton and Grace Mary (MacLean) R.; m. Betty Blanche Betts, Feb. 4, 1972; children by previous marriage— Sheri Joan, Robert John, Paul Frederick. BA in Math. and Physics with honors, Queens U., 1950. Actuarial asst. Empire Life Ins. Co., Kingston, Ont., Can., 1950-55; sec. Maritime Life Ins. Co., Halifax, N.S., Can., 1955-59, dir. sales Can., 1959-65, chief exec. officer Can., 1967-72; mng. dir., chief exec. officer Abbey Life Ins. Co., U.K., 1972-80; group gen. mgr. Hartford Europe Group, 1975-80; sr. v.p., dir. worldwide life ins. ops. Hartford Ins. Group, Conn., 1980-83, dir. worldwide life ins. ops., 1983-88; pres., COO, Hartford Life Cos., 1983-88; pvt. ins. cons., Boca Raton, Fla., 1988; pres., CEO, Crown Life Ins. Co., 1988-93; cons. INSCE, Boca Raton, 1993—. Fellow Soc. Actuaries, Can. Inst. Actuaries. Home and Office: 300 SE 5th Ave Apt 1090 Boca Raton FL 33432-6093 E-mail: rfredbetty1@aol.com.

RICHARDSON, ROY, management consultant; b. Chgo., Mar. 22, 1931; s. John George and Margaret Beattie (Henderson) Richardson; m. Mary C. Westphal, May 16, 1970; children: Beth Barnett, Jessica Eubanks, Adam, Roman, Alexis. BA in Psychology, Macalester Coll., 1952; MA in Labor and Indsl. Relations, U. Ill., 1953; PhD in Indsl. Relations, U. Minn., 1969. With Honeywell, Inc., Mpls., 1956-70, corp. manpower mgr., 1967-70; mgr. manpower devel. and tng. Internat. Harvester, Chgo., 1970-73; dir. pers. U. Minn., 1973—75; v.p. human resources Onan Corp., Mpls., 1975-82, Graco Corp., Mpls., 1982-84, v.p. human resources and corp. devel., 1985-91; v.p. Human Resources and Quality Mgmt. Sys., 1992-94; pres. Integrated Mgmt. Sys., 1994—. Pres. Pers. Surveys, Inc., Mpls., 1978-80; dir., chmn. exec. com. Kotz Grad. Sch. Mgmt., St. Paul, 1984-90; adj. prof. U. St. Thomas, Mpls. Author: Fair Pay and Work, 1971. V.p. Mpls. Urban League, 1962-64. Recipient Disting. Citizens award City of Mpls., 1964. Mem. U. Minn. Indsl. Rels. Alumni Soc. (dir. 1979-85, pres. 1981), Am. Soc. Quality. Clubs: Ford's Colony Country. Republican. Episcopalian. E-mail: roypiper@erols.com.

RICHARDSON, SCOTT WILLIAM, asset management executive; b. St. Louis, July 19, 1963; s. Sherwood William and Dian (Dempsey) R. BS in Mktg., Southwest Mo. State U., 1985. With Edward D. Jones, St. Louis, 1985-87; v.p. asset mgmt. SunAm., Dallas, 1987-93, Goldman Sachs, Chgo., 1993-95; v.p. Jackson Nat. Life, 1994—, sr. v.p. Creator, author tng. tape Success with Seminars, 1990-91. Vol. Chgo. Cares, 1993-94; team in tng. Leukemia Soc., 1999. Republican. Avocations: golf, triathalons and tng., reading. Office: Jackson Nat 900 Circle 75 Parkway St 1750 Atlanta GA 30339 Address: 4515 Crestwicke Pointe NE Atlanta GA 30319-1084

RICHARDSON, STEPHEN GILES, biotechnology company executive; b. Mpls., Sept. 17, 1951; s. Richard Giles and Constance Bernice (Krieg) R. BA cum laude, Wartburg Coll., 1972; MS, U. Iowa, 1974, PhD, 1981; postdoctoral, Duke U., 1982-84. Cert. project mgmt. profl. Ter. mgr. Wyeth Labs., Phila., 1974-76; rsch. asst. U. Iowa, Iowa City, 1976-82; rsch. assoc. Duke, Durham, N.C., 1982-84; scientist Becton Dickinson Rsch. Ctr., Research Triangle Park, 1984-86; devel. group leader Dade Diagnostics divsn. Baxter Healthcare, Miami, Fla., 1986; rsch. group leader Organon Teknika Corp divsn., Akzo Nobel N.V, Durham, N.C., 1987-89, R & D sect. head, internat. R & D area mgr., 1989-90, program mgr., 1990-94, assoc. dir., head product devel., 1994-96, project mgmt. dir., microbiology bus. area R & D NC, 1997—2001; program dir. global mktg. and strategic devel. BioMerieux, Inc., 2001—. Contbr. articles to profl. jours.; patentee in field; bd. readers IVD Technology Mag. Co-founder Libertarian Party Minn., Mpls., 1972, del. nat. conv., 1998; exec. sec. Iowa Coun. to Repeal Conscription, Waterloo, 1971. Mem. Am. Soc. for Microbiology, Am. Chem. Soc., Am. Assn. for Clin. Chemistry, Royal Soc. Chemistry (U.K.), N.Y. Acad. Scis., Electronic Frontier Found., Sigma Xi. Achievements include discovery of transient neutral heteroaryl radicals as viable organic synthetic intermediates, such as, to halopurine nucleosides; MDA-180 hemostasis analyzer system, BacT/ALERT 3D blood culture system. Home: PO Box 17284 Chapel Hill NC 27516-7284 Office: BioMerieux Inc 100 Rodolphe St Durham NC 27712-9402

RICHARDSON, THADDEUS MAURICE, funeral director; b. Amite, La., June 21, 1965; s. Samuel Richardson, Dorothy (Johnson) Richardson. FSC, Commonwealth Coll., 1985; GSC, So. U., 1986; NC, Southeaster La. U., 1997. Dir. Richardson Funeral Home, Hammond, La., 1985—. Author: How To Get the Strong Man in Marriage, 2000. Bd. dirs. La. State Bd. Funeral Dirs., New Orleans; city coun. bd. State of La., Baton Rouge, 1996—2000; v.p. L.M.A.B.C., 1998—2000; pres. L.E.T.A., Greensburg, 1995—96, P.D.A., Amite, 2000—; bd. dirs. Health Care, Independence, La., S.E.F.A., Covington, R.F.C., Amite. Mem.: Progressive Citizens (pres. 2001, Star award 2002), Mt. Nebo Grand Lodge (Master 1994). Democrat. Avocations: farming, fishing, football, hunting, racing. Home: 411 E Palmetto St Amite LA 70422 Office: Richardson Funeral Home 1601 W Thomas St Hammond LA 70404

RICHARDSON, THOMAS ANDREW, business executive, educator; b. Providence, Aug. 31, 1955; s. Edward Ferris and Olive Elizabeth (Lynaugh) R.; m. Patricia Ann Mundie, Dec. 30, 1982; children: Michael Edward, Lauren Elizabeth, Kristen Mundie. AS in Oceanography, Fla. Inst. Tech., 1977, BS in Environ. Sci., 1979, MBA, 1985; Doctoral Candidate, Nova Southeastern U., 1998—. Asst. prof., div. head sch. marine and environ. tech. Fla. Inst. Tech., Jensen Beach, 1979-85; tng. mgr. PADI Internat., Santa Ana, Calif., 1985-88, dir. tng. and edn., 1988-90, sr. v.p., 1991—; v.p. Capital Investment Ventures Corp., 1991—. Dir. lakefront City of Evanston, Ill., 1980-82; bd. dirs. CIVCO, Project AWARE Found., Santa Ana; pres. DSAT Inc., Santa Ana, 1989—; guest faculty Duke Med. Sch. continuing edn., Durham, N.C., 1992. Editor in chief: Open Water Diver Manual, 1988, Rescue Diver Manual, 1988, Divemaster Manual, 1990, Undersea Journal, 1987, Adventures in Diving; Open Water Diving video, Adventures in Diving video, Peak Performance video; contbr. articles to profl. jours. CPR and first aid instr. Martin County Sch. Dist., Stuart, Fla., 1982-83. Recipient Diver of Yr. award Divers Alert Network/Rolex, Inc., 1992, Craig Hoffman Meml. award for diving safety, Undersea and Hyerbaric Med. Soc., 2000; scholar Nova Southeastern U., 1998. Mem. Am. Mgmt. Assn., Am. Soc. Training and Devel., Am. Soc. Assn. Exec., Undersea and Hyperbaric Med. Soc., South Pacific Undersea Med. Soc., Sierra Club, Nat. Audubon Soc., Emergency Med. Planning Inc., Am. Acad. Underwater Scis., Nat. Assn. Search and Rescue, PADI Diving Soc. (pres. 1998—). Avocations: photography, music, woodworking, family activities, scuba diving. E-mail: drewr@padi.com.

RICHARDSON, THOMAS HAMPTON, design consulting engineer; b. St. Louis, Nov. 25, 1941; s. Claude Hampton and Pearl Lily (Burks) R.; m. Lois Louise Atteberry June 8, 1963; children: Shelley Ann, David Hampton, Stephanie Lynn. BTEE, Wash. U., St. Louis, 1974. Registered profl. engr., Mo., Ill., Ind., Kans., Iowa, Fla., Ky., Miss. Elec. project designer Fruco Engrs. Inc., St. Louis, 1967-68; mgr., mech./elec. engr. MBA Engrs. Inc., 1968-74, Kenneth Balk and Assoc., St. Louis, 1974-76; instr. elec. engring. Wash. U., 1976; v.p., chief engr. John F. Steffen Assoc., 1976-79; prin. ptnr. Keeler, Webb and Richardson, 1979-94; pres./owner The Richardson Engring. Group, 1979—. Contbr. articles to profl. jours. Recipient Internat. Lgt. Des. award Illuminating Engr. Soc. St. Louis 1985, Edwin F. Guth award of Merit Illuminating Engr. Soc. N.Am. 1986. Mem. NSPE, ASHRAE, Illuminating Engring. Soc. (past pres.), Soc. for Mktg. Profl. Svcs. (v.p.), Mo. Soc. Profl. Engrs. (govt. rels. com.), Engr's Club St Louis, Nat. Fire Protection Assn., Green Turtle Bay Yacht Club, Grand Lake Yacht Club, Ky. Lake Club, U.S. Coast Guard Aux. (divsn. vice capt.). Avocations: sailing, flying, horses, photography. Office: The Richardson Engring 7227 Devonshire Ave Saint Louis MO 63119-3419

RICHARDSON, TIA MARIA, civil engineer, educator; b. Charleroi, Pa. d. Raymond Charles and Elida (Visca) Como; children: Elida, Elisa, Malia Rae. BSCE, W.Va. U., 1984, MSCE, 1996. Registered profl. engr. W.Va. Hwy. insp. Pa. Turnpike Commn., Greensburgh, 1983; project engr. Dick Corp., Pitts., 1984-86, Ackenneil Engrs., Pitts., 1986-95; engring. scientist dept. civil and environ. engring. W.Va. U., Morgantown, 1995—. Asst. prof. Fairmont (W.Va.) State Coll., 1995—. Active Girl Scouts U.S.A., Morgantown, 1996—. Mem. ASCE, Student Club (treas. no. br., W.Va. faculty advisor). Democrat. Roman Catholic. Avocations: certified aerobics instructor, camping, singing, cooking. Home: 569 Wisconsin St Morgantown WV 26501-3987 Office: Fairmont State Coll Tech Divsn 1201 Locust Ave Fairmont WV 26554-2451 E-mail: Tia@Adelphia.net .

RICHARDSON, TOM (EDWARD THOMPSON RICHARDSON), artist; b. Upper Darby, Pa., Aug. 12, 1948; s. Edward Thompson and Elizabeth Catherine (Fredericks) R.; m. Margaret Reed Colvin, July 1, 1972; 1 child, Edward Thompson III. BFA, U. Pa., 1974, MFA, 1975. Scenic artist San Francisco Opera Assn., 1979-84, San Francisco Ballet Assn., 1982-84; scenic designer music dept. Stanford U., Calif., 1980-84; scenic designer San Jose (Calif.) Opera Assn., 1985; lead scenic artist FM Prodns., Brisbane, Calif., 1984-87, artist-in-charge, 1987-93. (Scenic artist): (films) James and the Giant Peach; Down Periscope; Phenomenon; A Smile Like Yours; Rainmaker; Flubber; What Dreams May Come; The Horse Whisperer; Mumford; Bicentennial Man; Invisible Circus; A Woman on Top; Boys and Girls; Bartleby; Sweet November; Forty Days and Forty Nights; High Crimes; The Matrix Reloaded; Revolutions; (TV series) Nash Bridges; Partners. Mem. Internat. Alliance Theatrical Stage Employees (Bay area bus. rep. 1984-88, Bay area field rep. 2000—, pres. 1998—). Home: 87 Roosevelt Cir Palo Alto CA 94306-4219

RICHARDSON, VANESSA, education educator; b. Camp Lejeune, N.C., Aug. 31, 1960; d. Matthew and Margaret Ethel (Cox) R. Cert. in traffic mgmt., U.S. Army Transp. Sch., Ft. Eustis, Va., 1985; BS in Urban and Regional Planning, East Carolina U., 1988; MS in Safety and Driver Edn., N.C. Agrl. and Tech. State U., 1990, MS in Reading Edn., 1992; PhD, U. N.C., Greensboro, 1998. Cert. G grad. level tchr., N.C. Planning intern Pitt County Econ. Devel. Commn., Greenville, N.C., summer 1987; grad. intern in transp. planning City of Greensboro, 1989; transp. adminstrn. mgmt. clk. USMCR, Greensboro, 1985-90; planning/grants coord. City of Fayetteville, N.C., 1990-91; rsch. asst. Sch. Bus. and Econs. N.C. Agrl. and Tech. State U., Greensboro, 1988, grad. asst. Sch. Tech., 1989-90, tutor coord., 1991-92, instr. Upward Bound program, 1992-93, instr., tech. assoc., 1992-94; grad. tchg. asst. U. N.C., 1993-97; cmty. rels. coord. Sch. Tech., N.C. A&T State U, 1997—. Co-author: New Teacher Handbook for Trade and Industrial Educators, 1993, Research on Teaming: Insights from Selected Studies; also author articles. Vol. Greater Greensboro Cities in Schs., 1991-92; coord. Fayetteville Area Sys. Transit campaign United Way. With USMCR. Mem. NEA, ASCD, N.C. Assn. Educators, Internat. Reading Assn., Soc. Tech. Comm., Assn. Grad. Students (v.p.), Am. Planning Assn., N.C. Pub. Transp. Assn., N.C. Driver and Traffic Safety Edn. Assn., Gamma Theta Upsilon, Epsilon Pi Tau, Delta Nu Alpha. Avocations: physical fitness, health, travel. Home: 1504 Cedar Ln Kinston NC 28501-5844

RICHARDSON, WALTER JOHN, architect; b. Long Beach, Calif., Nov. 14, 1926; s. Walter Francis and Ava Elizabeth (Brown) R.; m. Marilyn Joyce Brown, June 26, 1949 (div. 1982); children: Mark Steven, Glenn Stewart; m. Mary Sue Sutton, Dec. 4, 1982. Student, UCLA, 1944-45, Long Beach City Coll., 1946; BA, U. Calif., Berkeley, 1950. Registered architect, Ala., Ariz., Calif., Colo., Fla., Hawaii, Ill., Kans., Md., Mass., Nev., N.J., N.Y., Okla., Oreg., Tex., Utah, Vt., Va., Wash. Draftsman Wurster, Bernardi, Emmons, San Francisco, 1950-51, Skidmore, Owings & Merrill, San Francisco, 1951; designer Hugh Gibbs Architect, Long Beach, 1952-58; ptnr. Thomas & Richardson Architects, Long Beach, Costa Mesa, 1958-70; pres. Walter Richardson Assocs. Architects, Newport Beach, Calif., 1970-74; chmn. bd. Richardson, Nagy, Martin Architects and Planners, 1974—. Co-author: The Architect and the Shelter Industry, 1975. Chmn. Planning Commn., City of Orange, Calif., 1967-68. With USAF, 1945. Recipient over 200 Gold Nugget Design awards Pacific Coast Builders Conf., San Francisco, 1969-96, 12 Builders Choice Design awards Builder Mag.; named Architect of Yr. Profl. Builder mag., 1986. Fellow AIA (pres. Orange County chpt. 1970, chmn. nat. housing com. 1976, 7 design awards); mem. Nat. Assn. Home Builders, Nat. Coun. Archtl. Registration Bds., Urban Land Inst., Alpha Tau Omega. Republican. Avocations: photography, downhill skiing, travel. Office: RNM Archs Planners 4611 Teller Ave Ste 100 Newport Beach CA 92660-2104

RICHARDSON, WANDA LOUISE GIBSON, nurse; b. Dallas; d. Ralph Harrison Gibson and Letha Lee Thompson; children: James L. (dec.), Bruce S., Judith Richardson Prueitt, Janai Richardson Buentello. Lic. vocat. nurse, Dallas Vocat. Sch., 1960; ADN, Dallas/El Centro Coll., 1981; student, U. Dallas, Irving, 1978. RN, Tex. Staff nurse RHD Hosp., Dallas, 1981; head nurse physicians office, Irving, 1960—80; sr. nurse family practice residency program St. Paul Hosp./U. Tex. Southwestern Med. Sch., Dallas, 1984—97; nurse case mgr. Medicaid waiver primary home care Vis. Nurses Assn., 1997—98, 1998—, cmty. based alternative long term care dept.; cmty. health nurse; case mgr. Visiting Nurses Assn.; health promotions coord. Vis. Nurse Assn., 2002—. Sys. operator Health Profls. Forum and New Age Living Forum. Contbg. columnist Lake Cities Sun News; contbr. poems to anthologies. Vol. tutor Literacy Program, Denton, Tex.; founding mem., mem. choir Cornerstone Bapt. Ch., Plano, 1990; mem. Friends of Libr. of Denton; vol. Big Sisters/Big Bros., Denton; vol. probate ct. visitor Denton County; tour guide Elm Fork Edn. Ctr., U. North Tex.; mem. Ret. Sr. Vol. Program. Named one of Notable Women Tex., 1984; recipient Golden Poet award World Poetry, 1991, 92. Mem. Cercle Internat. le Recherches Culturelles et Spirituelles Inc. (charter, officer local chpt.), Nurse Healers Profl. Assn., Dallas Archeol. Soc., Denton J.S. Bach Soc., Dallas Inst. Culture and Humanities, Isthmus Inst. Mailing: PO Box 308 Lake Dallas TX 75065-0308 E-mail: 112020.3101@compuserve.com.

RICHARDSON, WILLIAM WIGHTMAN, III, personnel and employee benefits consultant; b. Phila., May 15, 1928; s. William Wightman Jr. and Ruth (Mathers) R.; m. Elizabeth Fritz Rich (div. June 1979); children: William Wightman IV, Brenda Fritz. BA, U. Md., 1954. Commd. 2d lt. USAF, 1951, advanced through grades to capt., 1955; dir. pers. Kinney Nat. Svc. Co., N.Y.C., 1964-67; mgr. human resource sys. Bristol-Myers Co., 1968-75; dir. employee info. The Coastal Co., Houston, 1976-78; mgr. employee benefits Valero Energy Corp., San Antonio, 1979-90, ret., 1990; cons. on pers. and employee benefits and pers. automation Houston, 1991—; ptnr. Creature Crafts, Bellaire, 1993—. Maj. USAFR ret. Republican. Episcopalian. Home and Office: 4815 Mayfair St Bellaire TX 77401-2313

RICHARDSON, WILLIAM WINFREE, III, lawyer; b. Williamsburg, Va., Aug. 12, 1939; s. William Winfree Jr. and Ellen Blanche (Johnson) R.; m. Constance Diane Niver (div. July 1985); children: Christine Marie, Kenneth Erik. BA, Coll. William and Mary, 1963, Bachelor of Civil Law, 1966, JD, 1967. Bar: Va. 1968. Pvt. practice, Providence Forge, Va., 1968—; commr. accounts New Kent Cir. Ct., 1968—2000, atty. correctional field unit, 1968—; asst. commr. accounts Charles City Cir. Ct., 1970—2000. Bd. dirs. C.H. Evelyn Piling Co. Inc., Providence Forge. Advisor Selective Svc. System, New Kent County, Va., 1972. Internat. Order Kings Daus. and Sons scholar, 1957. Mem. Williamsburg Bar Assn., Colonial Bar Assn., Sigma Pi. Avocations: hist. restoration, collecting antiques. Home: Chelsea Plantation West Point VA 23181 Office: PO Box 127 Providence Forge VA 23140-0127

RICHARDSON-MELECH, JOYCE SUZANNE, music educator, singer; b. Perth Amboy, N.J., Nov. 15, 1957; d. Herbert Nathaniel and Fannie Elaine (Franklin) Richardson; m. Gerald Melech, July 28, 1990. MusB, Westminster Choir Coll., 1979, MusM, 1981; postgrad., Rutgers U., 1999—. Cert. music tchr., N.J. Musical play dir. Perth Amboy H.S., 1989-92, asst. band dir., 1984-94; music tchr. Perth Amboy Bd. Edn., 1981—, gifted and talented music tchr., 1992-96; vocal soloist N.Y.C. Vocal soloist N.Y. Philharm. and Westminster Symphonic Choir, 1977, United Moravian Ch., N.Y.C., 1980-81, Ctrl. Jersey Concert Orch., Perth Amboy, 1994-96; mezzo-soprano soloist in The Messiah, John Hus Moravian ch., Bklyn., 1998; master tchrs. collaborative with N.J. Symphony Orch., 2000—01 (award for Excellence in teaching N.J. Symphony Orchestra, 2000). Co-author: Teacher's Resource Book, 2000, 2001. Participant Perth Amboy Adult Cmty. Theatre, 1983. Mem. NAACP, Am. Fedn. Tchrs., Am. Fedn. Musicians (local 204-373), Music Educators Nat. Conf., Internat. Platform Assn., Am. Mus. Natural History (assoc.), Alliance for Arts Edn. N.J., Ctrl. Jersey Music Educators, N.J. Music Educators Assn., Alpha Phi Omega. Democrat. Mem. African Meth. Episcopal

Zion Ch. Avocations: needlepoint, cross-stitch, knitting, sewing, crocheting. Home: 148 Carson Ct Somerset NJ 08873-4790 Office: Samuel Shull Sch 380 Hall Ave Perth Amboy NJ 08861-3205 E-mail: joyrichardson@paps.net.

RICHART, DOUGLAS STEPHEN, chemist; b. Harrisburg, Pa., June 6, 1931; s. Howard Winans and Muriel M. Richart; m. Joan J. Lombardo, Apr. 19, 1986; children: Deborah, Sandra, Stephen, Catherine. BS in Chemistry, Franklin and Marshall Coll., Lancaster, Pa., 1954. Rsch. chemist Union Carbide Corp., Bound Brook, N.J., 1954-60; group leader R&D, Polymer Corp., Reading, Pa., 1960-65, mgr. R&D coatings, 1965-86; mgr. R&D chem. divsn. Morton Internat. Powder Coating, 1986-89, sr. scientist, 1989-94; pres. coating powder cons. D.S. Richart Assocs., 1994—. Author in field; patentee powder coatings. Mem. AAAS, Am. Chem. Soc., Soc. Plastics Engrs., Nat. Assn. Corrosion Engrs., The Powder Coating Inst. Republican. Office: 6 Golfview Ln Reading PA 19606-9597 E-mail: dsrichart@aol.com.

RICHBART, CAROLYN MAE, mathematics educator; b. Catskill, N.Y., Aug. 12, 1945; d. George R. and Frances (Reynolds) Eden; m. Lynn A. Richbart, Aug. 15, 1987. BS, SUNY, Geneseo, 1967, MEd, 1982; PhD, U. Albany, 1992. Cert. math. tchr., elem. tchr., N.Y. Tchr. Wolcott St. Sch., Le Roy, N.Y., 1967-69; math. tchr. Le Roy Cen. High Sch., 1969-72, Attica (N.Y.) Mid. Sch., 1978-84; assoc. prof. Genesee C.C., Batavia, N.Y., 1984-87; grad. asst. U. Albany, 1987-90; asst. prof. Russell Sage Coll., Troy, N.Y., 1990-92, SUNY, New Paltz, 1992-97; assoc. in math. edn. N.Y. State Edn. Dept., 1997-2000; adj. prof. Charleston So. U., 2001—. Project dir. grades kindergarten through 8, 1994-97, N.Y. State Math Mentor Network, 1999-2000; facilitator Network of Urban Math. Edn. Leaders. Contbr. articles to profl. jours. Mem. Nat. Coun. Tchrs. Math. (speaker), Assn. Math. Tchrs. N.Y. State (rec. sec. 1988-89, corr. sec. 1991-92, pres. 1995-96, chair workshop 1992, chair program 1989, chair Wyoming County sect. 1985-88), N.Y. State Assn. Two-Yr. Colls. (exec. bd. 1986-90, legis. chair 1986-89, curriculum chair 1989-90). Home and Office: 2419 Racquet Club Dr Johns Island SC 29455

RICHBURG, BILLY KEITH, healthcare manager, consultant, entrepreneur; b. Memphis, Dec. 16, 1946; s. Byron C. and Marjorie Mae (Draper) R.; children: Gretchen, Jeremy; m. Paula Anita Mason, July 27, 1990. BA, U. Alaska, Anchorage, 1974; MS in Health Care Adminstrn., Trinity U., San Antonio, 1978. Diplomate Am. Coll. of Healthcare Execs. Exec. dir. Med. Park Hosp. (Am. Med. Internat.), Hope, Ark., 1979-84; asst. adminstr. Columbia (Mo.) Regional Hosp. (Am. Med. Internat.), 1984-85, v.p., CFO, 1985-96; exec. dir. VNA Ctrl. Mo., Columbia, 1996-98; gen. mgr. Coram Healthcare, Earth City, Mo., 1999-2000; CFO HP3 Rsch. Inst., Bethlehem, Pa., 2000-01; dir. govt. programs and compliance IMACS, Inc., Dallas, 2001—. Founder The Borealis Group, LLC. With USAF, 1969-76. Fellow Healthcare Fin. Mgmt. Assn.; mem. Mensa. Episcopalian. Avocations: motorcycles, on-line computing.

RICHBURG, SHIRLEY, business owner, operator; BA, U. Md., 1978; M of Bus. and Pub. Adminstrn., Southeastern U., 1985. Tax practitioner, real estate broker, publisher, merchandiser, Balt. Office: 4810 Norwood Ave Baltimore MD 21207-6839

RICHE, ROBERT SAVERY, writer; b. Pittsfield, Mass., Sept. 23, 1925; s. Leon Louis Riche and Ruth Alden Savery Riche; m. Frances Schmidt, Feb. 21, 1964; children: Pierre, Michele Justine Riche Schuster. BA, Yale U., 1947. Author: (novels) What Are We Doing in Latin America?, 1990, Poppy and Me, (plays) Malcolm X:Message from the Grassroots, 1966, (murals) The Stag at Eve, 1989 (Stanley Drama award, 1989); author: (with Lawrence Bauman) Ten Most Troublesome Teen-age Problems, 1998; contbr. articles. Recipient, Rockefeller Found., 1972, Conn. Found. for Arts, 1976, Stanley Drama award, SI Coll., 1989; grantee, NEA, 1975; scholar Breadloaf Writers Conf. scholar, Middlebury Coll., 1961. Mem.: Nat. Writers Union, Writers Guild Am., Dramatists Guild, Authors League. Home: 45 New St Ridgefield CT 06877 Home Fax: 203-431-3248; Office Fax: 203-431-3248. Personal E-mail: richriter@aol.com.

RICHE, WENDY, television producer; b. N.Y.C., Jan. 8, 1945; d. Elliot and Janice (Fantel) Fields; m. Alan Riche, Dec. 4, 1966; children: Tim, Peter. Student, Syracuse U. Sec. ABC, 1973, program coord. Late Night Programs, 1974, assoc. prodr. In Concert series and specials, 1974; developer, prodr. Levenback/Riche and Wittman/Riche Prodn. Co., 1975-78; prodr. Universal TV, 1978-86; exec. prodr. ABC Entertainment, 1986-89; sr. v.p. prodr. Fox Broadcast Co., 1989-91; exec. prodr. Gen. Hosp. ABC-TV, 1992-99, exec. prodr. Port Charles, 1997-00. Prodr. (movies of the week) Who Will Love My Children? (8 Emmy award nominations), Madame X, I Saw What You Did, Friendships, Secrets, and Lies, Deadly Care; exec. prodr. (ABC pilot) Never Again, (movies for TV, dir. programming ABC Entertainment) God Bless the Child, David (Emmy award nomination), My Name is Bill W (Emmy award winner), Women of Brewster Place, Unspeakable Acts, Our Sons, Fight for Life, (exec. producer daytime drama) General Hosp. (Emmy award for outstanding drama series 1994/95, 95/96, 96/97, 97/98, 98/99, 99/2000), (after school spl.) Positive: A Journey Into Aids (3 Emmy award nominations). Recipient Soap Opera Update Editors award, 1993, Pub. Svc. award Nat. Kidney Found., 1994, Soap Opera Hall of Fame, 1994, 96, Nancy Susan Reynolds award, 1994, 95, 96, Chair's award Am. Cancer Soc., 1994/95, 15th Media Access award, 1995, Imagen award, 1996, Komen award, 1996, Ryan White Youth Svc. award, 1996, Daytime TV Mag. Readers Poll award for best show, 1996/97, Soap Opera Digest award for Gen. Hosp. favorite show, 1997, 98, 99, 2000, Media Access Michael Landon award, 1997. Mem. Writes Guild Am., Producers Guild Am.

RICHELSON, PAUL WILLIAM, curator; b. Montpelier, Idaho, Sept. 27, 1939; s. Paul Newton and June (Quayle) R. BA, Yale U., 1961; MFA, Princeton U., 1967, PhD, 1974. Asst. prof. Lawrence U., Appleton, Wis., 1970-77, U. Denver, 1977-84; asst. dir., curator Trisolini Gallery of Ohio U., Athens, 1984-87; chief curator Grand Rapids (Mich.) Mus., 1987-91; curator of Am. art Mobile Mus. Art, Mobile, Ala., 1991-97, asst. dir., chief curator, 1997—. Author: (book) Studies in the Personal Imagery Collection of 20th Prints Ohio University, 1985, (catalogue) The Golden Age 19th Century Prints by David Roberts, 1988, Lee Loring: A Southern Sophisticate, 1992, Modernism and American Painting of the 1930s, 1993, ThirtySomething, 1994, Alabama Impact: Contemporary Artists with Alabama Ties, 1995, Louise Lyons Heustis (1865-1951): A Retrospective, 1995, The French Connection: Jean Simon Chaudron Returns To Mobile, 1996, John Roderick Dempster MacKenzie (1865-1941): A Retrospective, 1997, Celebrating the Creative Spirit, 1998, Contemporary Southeastern Furniture, 1998. Lt. (j.g.) USN, 1961-63. Recipient Elizabeth B. Gould Rsch. award Mobile Hist. Devel. Commn., 1997; Fulbright-Hays fellow to Italy, 1967-69; Mus. Purchase Plan grantee Nat. Endowment for the Arts, 1991; grantee Mus. Loan Network, 2002. Mem. Southeastern Museums Conf. Home: 6427 Grelot Rd Apt 405 Mobile AL 36695-2630 Office: Mobile Museum of Art 4850 Museum Dr Mobile AL 36608-1917 Fax: 251-208-5201. E-mail: prichelson@mobilemuseumofart.com.

RICHENBURG, ROBERT BARTLETT, artist, retired art educator; b. Boston, July 14, 1917; s. Frederick Henry and Spray (Bartlett) R.; m. Libby Chic Peltyn, Nov. 11, 1942 (dec. 1977); 1 child, Ronald P.; m. Margaret Kerr, Feb. 9, 1980; stepchildren: William Blakeley Kerr, David Garrett Kerr, Margaret Frances Kerr. Student, Boston U., George Washington U., Corcoran Sch. Art, Art Students League N.Y., Ozenfant Sch. Fine Arts, Hans Hofmann Sch. Art. Tchr. painting Schrivenham Am. U., Eng., 1945; instr. Coll. City N.Y., 1947-52, Cooper Union, 1954-55; instr., dir. Bklyn.-Queens Central YMCA, 1947-51; instr. NYU, 1960-61, Pratt Inst., Bklyn., 1951-64; assoc. prof. art Cornell U., Ithaca, N.Y., 1964-67; prof. art Hunter Coll., N.Y.C., 1967-70, Aruba (Netherlands Antiles) Research Center, 1970, Ithaca Coll., 1970-83, mem. council on arts. Panelist in field. One-man shows include Hendler Gallery, Phila., N.Y. Artists Gallery, Tibor DeNagy Gallery, Hansa Gallery, N.Y., Dwan Gallery, Los Angeles, Santa Barbara Mus. (Calif.), Dayton Art Inst., Dana Arts Center Colgate U., Ithaca Coll. Mus. Art, Grad. Sch. Bus. Cornell U., Rose Art Mus., Brandeis U., U. Art Gallery, Staller Ctr., SUNY Stonybrook, Pollock-Krasner House and Study Ctr., East Hampton, N.Y., Arlene Bujese Gallery, East Hampton, Guild Hall Mus., East Hampton, MB Modern Gallery, N.Y., 2001, Thomas McCormick Gallery, Chgo., 2002, others; exhibited in group shows at Mus. Modern Art, Solomon Guggenheim Mus., N.Y.C., Chrysler Art Mus., Yale Art Gallery, Whitney Mus., N.Y.C., Univ. Art Mus., Austin, Tex., Balt. Mus., Cocoran Mus. Art, Washington, Bklyn. Mus., Knox Albright Mus., Buffalo, Larry Aldrich Mus., Seattle Art Mus., Boston Mus. Fine Arts, others; represented in permanent collections Mus. Modern Art, Whitney Mus., Hirschorn Mus., Inst. Valenciano de Arte Moderno, Valencia, Spain, Phila. Mus. Art, Pasadena Mus. Fine Art, U. Art Mus. U. Calif.-Berkeley, U. Tex. Art Mus., Austin, Zimmerli Art Mus. Rutgers U., Rose Art Mus. Brandeis U., Coll. William and Mary, Chrysler Mus. Art, Hofstra U. Mus., Johnson Mus. Cornell U., Ithaca Coll. Mus., Parrish Mus. Art, Southampton, Guild Hall Mus., East Hampton, Heckscher Mus. Art, Huntington, N.Y., others. Served with AUS, 1942-45. Mem. Am. Assn. U. Profs., Coll. Art Assn., Internat. Platform Assn., Art Students League N.Y. (life) Clubs: (N.Y.C.).

RICHENS, MURIEL WHITTAKER, marriage and family therapist, educator; b. Prineville, Oreg. d. John Reginald and Victoria Cecilia (Pascale) Whittaker; children: Karen, John, Candice, Stephanie, Rebecca. BS, Oreg. State U.; MA, San Francisco State U., 1962; postgrad., U. Calif., Berkeley, 1967-69, U. Birmingham, Eng., 1973, U. Soria, Spain, 1981. Lic. sch. adminstr., tchr. 7-12, pupil pers. specialist, Calif.; lic. marriage and family therapist, Calif. Tchr. Springfield (Oreg.) High Sch.; instr. San Francisco State U.; instr., counselor Coll. San Mateo, Calif., San Mateo High Sch. Dist., 1963-86; therapist AIDS Health Project U. Calif., San Francisco, 1988—; marriage and family therapist, pvt. practice San Mateo. Guest West German-European Acad. seminar, Berlin, 1975. Lifeguard, ARC. Postgrad. student Ctr. for Human Communications, Los Gatos, Calif., 1974, U. P.R., 1977, U. Guadalajara (Mex.), 1978, U. Durango (Mex.), 1980, U. Guanajuato (Mex.) 1982. Mem. U. Calif. Berkeley Alumni Assn., Am. Contract Bridge League (Diamond Life Master, cert. instr., cert. dir.), Women in Comm., Computer-Using Educators, Commonwealth Club, Pi Lambda Theta, Delta Pi Epsilon. Republican. Roman Catholic. Home and Office: 847 N Humboldt St Condo 309 San Mateo CA 94401-1451

RICHER, MIRIAM R. clinical social worker; b. Mason City, Iowa, Aug. 27, 1939; d. Samuel and Madelyn (Joseph) R. BA, U. Miami, Coral Gables, Fla., 1961; teaching cert., U. Calif., Berkeley, 1964, MSW, 1969. Lic. clin. social worker, Fla. Social worker State of Fla., Miami, 1961-62, City, County of San Francisco, 1962-63, Contra Costa County, Martinez, Calif., 1965-69; clin. social worker Jewish Family Svc., Miami, 1972-74, East Ark. Regional Mental Health Ctr., Helena, 1974-76; counselor Daytona Beach Community Coll., Daytona, 1984-85; clin. social worker Children's Home Soc., Dayton Beach, Fla., 1986—. Pvt. practice, 1988—. Mem. Acad. Cert. Social Workers

RICHERSON, HAL BATES, physician, internist, allergist, immunologist, educator; b. Phoenix, Feb. 16, 1929; s. George Edward and Eva Louise (Steere) R.; m. Julia Suzanne Bradley (dec. 1996), Sept. 5, 1953; children: Anne, George, Miriam, Julia, Susan. BS with distinction, U. Ariz., 1950; MD, Northwestern U., 1954. Diplomate Am. Bd. Internal Medicine, Am. Bd. Allergy and Immunology, Bd. Diagnostic Lab. Immunology; lic. physician, Ariz., Iowa. Intern Kansas City (Mo.) Gen. Hosp., 1954-55; resident in pathology St. Luke's Hosp., Kansas City, 1955-56; trainee in neuropsychiatry Brooke Army Hosp., San Antonio, 1956; resident in medicine U. Iowa Hosps., Iowa City, 1961-64, fellow in allergy and immunology, 1964-66; fellow in immunology Mass. Gen. Hosp., Boston, 1968-69; instr. internal medicine U. Iowa Coll. Medicine, Iowa City, 1964-66, asst. prof., 1966-70, assoc. prof., 1970-74, prof., 1974-98, prof. emeritus, 1998—; acting dir. divsn. allergy/applied immunology U. Iowa Hosps. and Clinics, 1970-72, dir. allergy and clin. immunology sect., 1972-78, dir. divsn. allergy and immunology, 1978-91; gen. practice, asst. to Gen. Surgeon Ukiah, Calif., 1958; gen. practice medicine Holbrook, Ariz., 1958-61. Vis. lectr. medicine Harvard U. Sch. Medicine, Boston, 1968-69; vis. prof., rsch. scientist U. London and Brompton Hosp., 1984; prin. investigator Nat. Heart, Lung and Blood Inst., 1971-94, mem. pulmonary diseases adv. com., 1983-87; prin. investigator Nat. Inst. Allergy and Infectious Diseases, 1983-94; dir. Nat. Inst. Allergy and Infectious Diseases' Asthma and Allergic Diseases Ctr., U. Iowa, 1983-94; mem. VA Merit Rev. Bd. in Respiration, 1981-84; mem. com. NIH Gen. Clin. Rsch. Ctrs., 1989-93; mem. rev. reserve NIH, 1993-98; mem. bd. sci. advisors Merck Inst., 1990-94; presenter lectures, seminars, continuing edn. courses; mem. numerous univ., coll. and hosp. coms., 1970—; cons. Merck Manual, 1982, 87, 92, 96-97. Contbr. numerous articles and revs. to profl. jours., chpts. to books; reviewer Sci., Jour. Immunology, Jour. Allergy and Clin. Immunology, Am. Rev. Respiratory Disease, New Eng. Jour. Medicine, Ann. Internal Medicine. Served to capt. U.S. Army, 1956-58. NIH fellow 1968-69. Fellow ACP (Laureate award 1996), Am. Acad. Allergy Asthma & Immunology (Disting. Clinician award 1998); mem. AMA (mem. residency and rev. com. for allergy and immunology; mem. accreditation coun. for grad. med. edn. 1980-85, vice-chmn. 1984-85), AAAS, Iowa Med. Soc., Iowa Thoracic Soc. (chmn. program com. 1964-65, 69-71, pres. 1972-73, mem. exec. com. 1972-74), Am. Thoracic Soc. (bd. dirs. 1981-82, councilor assembly on allergy and immunology 1980-81, mem. nominating com. 1988-90), Iowa Clin. Med. Soc., Am. Fedn. Clin. Rsch., Am. Assn. Immunologists, Ctrl. Soc. Clin. Rsch. (chmn. sect. on allergy-immunology 1980-81, mem. coun. 1981-84), Alpha Omega Alpha. Avocations: reading, trombonist, swimming, scuba diving. Home: 331 Lucon Dr Iowa City IA 52246-3300 Office: U Iowa Health Care Dept Internal Medicine 200 Hawkins Dr Iowa City IA 52242-1009 E-mail: richersonh@mchsi.com., hal-richerson@uiowa.edu.

RICHERT, HARVEY MILLER, II, ophthalmologist; b. Weatherford, Okla., Aug. 25, 1948; s. Harvey Miller and Catherine Cornelia (Ryan) R.; m. Diana Dee Sisney, Nov. 23, 1966; children: Ronald Lance, Rachelle Lea. BS, Southwestern Okla. State U., 1970; MD, U. Okla., Oklahoma City, 1974. Intern St. Anthony Hosp., Oklahoma City, 1974-75; resident in ophthalmology Tulane U., New Orleans, 1975-78; physician Tucker & Walker Ophthalmology Assocs., Abilene, Tex., 1978-80; ptnr. Tucker, Walker & Richert, 1980-86; pvt. practice, 1986—. Med. dir. Lions Eye Bank, Abilene, 1979—; head opthalmology sect. Humana Hosp., 1984-90, Hendrick Med. Ctr., 1984-92. V.p. Chisholm Trail coun. Boy Scouts Am., 1984-89, 92-96, dist. chmn., 1990-92, asst. scoutmaster, 1982-85, scoutmaster, 1985-88, nat. coun. rep., 1997—. Recipient Scoutmaster of Merit award, Silver Beaver award, Dist. award of Merit, Boy Scouts Am., 1988. Fellow Am. Acad. Ophthalmology, Castroviejo Soc. (assoc.); mem. AMA, Tex. Ophthal. Assn., Tex. Med. Assn., Lions (founders club). Republican. Baptist. Avocations: backpacking, snow skiing, tennis, camping. Home: 15 Glen Abbey St Abilene TX 79606-5023 Office: 1750 Pine St Abilene TX 79601-3044

RICHERT, JOHN ROLIN, neuroimmunologist, educator; b. Boston, June 9, 1945; s. Daniel Arnold and Esther (Beamer) Richert; m. Nancy Dembeck, July 5, 1969. BA, Cornell U., 1966; MD, U. Rochester, 1970. Diplomate Am. Bd. Med. Examiners, Am. Bd. Psychiatry and Neurology. Intern, resident in medicine Strong Meml. Hosp. U. Rochester, N.Y., 1970-72; resident in neurology Mayo Clinic, Rochester, Minn., 1974-77; fellow Nat. Multiple Sclerosis Soc. NIH, Bethesda, Md., 1977-80; rsch. asst. prof. neurology Georgetown U. Med. Ctr., Washington, 1980-83, asst. prof. neurology, 1983-89, assoc. prof. neurology, 1989-93, prof. neurology, 1993—, prof., chair dept. microbiology and immunology, 1997—. Mem. physician adv. bd. Biogen Inc., Cambridge, Mass., 1994-2000; cons. Immunex, Inc., Seattle, 1998-2000; bd. dirs. Georgetown U. Hosp., Washington. Mem. editl. bd.: NeuroRx. Mem. immunol. scis. study sect. NIH, 1989, mem. mental health AIDS and immunology rsch. study sect., 1992, mem. neurol. disorders program project com., 1997. Maj. USAF, 1972-74. Fellow Am. Acad. Neurology; mem. Internat. Soc. Neuroimmunology, Nat. Multiple Sclerosis Soc. (med. adv. bd. 1988-91, 93-96, profl. adv. com. 1988—, sci. peer rev. com. 1993-98), Am. Neurol. Assn., Am. Assn. Immunologists, Assn. Med. Sch. Microbiology and Immunology Chairs. Avocations: tennis, golf, skiing. Office: Georgetown U Med Ctr 3900 Reservoir Rd NW Washington DC 20007

RICHERT, PAUL, law educator; b. Elwood, Ind., Aug. 31, 1948; m. Catherine George Stanton, June 24, 1972; children: John, William. AB, U. Ill.-Urbana, 1970, MS, 1971; JD, Tulane U., 1977. Bar: Ohio 1977. Asst. law librarian U. Akron, 1977-78, law librarian, asst. prof. law, 1978-83, assoc. prof., 1983-87, prof. law, 1987—. Cons. to cts. Editor: Ohio Appellate Decision on Fiche, 1981; indexer Publs. Clearing House Bull., vols. 1-4. Mem. United Chs. of Christ. With U.S. Army, 1971-74. Mem. Am. Assn. Law Librs., Akron Bar Assn., ABA. Home: 2030 Ganyard Rd Akron OH 44313-6050 Office: U Akron Sch of Law Libr 150 University Ave Akron OH 44325-2902

RICHES, KENNETH WILLIAM, nuclear regulatory engineering manager; b. Long Beach, Calif., Oct. 23, 1962; s. William Murray Riches and Carlene Katherine (Simmons) Anderson; children: Benjamin William Bancroft Riches, Jennifer Ella Noel Riches; m. Beth Anne Riches, Nov. 19, 2002. BSEE, U. Ill., 1984; MS in Engring. Mgmt., Santa Clara U., 1989. Registered profl. engr., Calif., Ill. Engr. Detroit Edison Co., Monroe, Mich., 1995-97, Pacific Gas & Electric Co., San Luis Obispo, Calif., 1984-95, elec. engr., 1988—; prin. K.W. Riches & Assocs., Arroyo Grande, 1988—; owner The Peaberry Coffee Pub, 1991-92, Riches to Rags, Clown Alley, 1995—; engr. Detroit Edison Co., Monroe, Mich., 1995-97; proj. mgr. Sargent and Lundy LLC., Chgo., 1997-99. Mem. Rep. Nat. Com., 1986—; active Corp. Action in Pub. Schs., San Francisco, 1987, 88, World Wildlife Fund. Univs. Rsch. Assn. scholar, 1980. Mem. NSPE, IEEE (chpt. chmn. 1986-87, sect. dir. 1988-90), Am. Nuclear Soc., Power Engring. Soc. of IEEE (mem. nat. chpts. coun. 1988-92), Pacific Coast Engring. Assn., Nature Conservancy, Order of DeMolay (master counselor Paul Revere chpt. 1979), Eagle Alliance. Methodist. Avocations: golf, skiing, reading, travel. Home: 62430 Locust Rd Lot 205 South Bend IN 46614 Office: Am Electric Power 500 Circle Drive Buchanan MI 49107 E-mail: kwriches@aep.com.

RICHESON, HUGH ANTHONY, JR. lawyer; b. Aberdeen, Md., Apr. 22, 1947; s. Hugh Anthony Sr. and Mary Evelyn (Burford) R.; m. Melissa Anne Baum, Apr. 4, 1970; children: Hugh Anthony III, Heidi E., Holly K., Hagin G., Herald Joshua. BBA, U. Richmond, 1969; JD, U. Fla., 1973; student, St. Catherine's Coll., Oxford U., Eng., summer 1973. Bar: Fla. 1974, U.S. Dist. Ct. (mid. dist.) Fla. 1975, U.S. Supreme Ct. 1992. Assoc. Bryant, Dickens, Rumph, Franson & Miller, Jacksonville, Fla., 1974-76, ptnr., 1977; sole practice Orange Park, 1977-82; ptnr. Smith, Hallowes & Richeson, 1982-83; sole practice Palm Harbor, Fla., 1984-98; of counsel Carey & Leisure, Clearwater, 1998—. Author: Legally Yours, 2002. Pres. Full Gospel Bus. Men's Fellowship Internat., Orange Park, 1983-84, Palm Harbor, 1985-92, field rep., 1987—. Mem. Fla. Coun. Bar Assn. Pres. (life), Christian Legal Soc., Gideons Internat., Phi Delta Phi. Republican. Methodist.

RICHEY, CLARENCE BENTLEY, agricultural engineering educator; b. Winnipeg, Manitoba, Can., Dec. 28, 1910; (parents Am. citizens); s. Raus Spears and Emily Cornelia (Bentley) R.; m. Marguerite Anne Jannusch, Dec. 27, 1936; children: David Volkman, Stephen Bentley. BS in Agrl. Engring., Iowa State U., 1933; BS in Mech. Engring., Purdue U., 1939. Registered agrl. engr., Calif. Instr. agrl. engring. Purdue U., West Lafayette, Ind., 1936-41; asst. prof. dept. agrl. engring. Ohio State U., Columbus, 1941-43; head devel., engr. Electric Wheel Co., Quincy, Ill., 1943-46; project engr. Harry Ferguson, Inc., Detroit, 1946-47; sr. project engr. Dearborn Motors Corp., 1947-54; supt., chief rsch. engr. Ford Tractor Divsn., Birmingham, Mich., 1954-62; chief engr. Fowler (Calif.) divsn. Massey-Ferguson Ltd., 1964-69, product mgmt. engr. Ont., Can., 1970-71; assoc. prof. agrl. engring. Purdue U., West Lafayette, 1971-76, prof. emeritus, 1976—. Farm equipment cons. Ford Found., Allahabad, India, 1963. Author: (autobiography) Fifty Years of Engineering Farm Equipment, 1989; editor-in-chief: Agricultural Engineer's Handbook, 1961; contbr. bulls. and articles to profl. jours. Fellow Am. Soc. Agrl. Engrs. (Cyrus Hall McCormick Gold medal 1977); mem. Lafayette Kiwanis. Achievements include patent for farm equipment; holder or co-holder of 79 patents. Home: 3055 Hunting Valley Dr Ann Arbor MI 48104-2842

RICHEY, KENT RAMON, lawyer; b. Churubusco, Ind., Jan. 9, 1960; m. Robin Kamen, Sept. 23, 1989; children: Jacob, Henry. BA, MA, Northwestern U., 1982; JD, Harvard U., 1986. Bar: N.Y. 1987. Law clk. to Judge Walter Mansfield U.S. Ct. Appeals (2d cir.), N.Y.C., 1986-87; assoc. Cravath, Swaine & Moore, 1987—97; gen. counsel Allegro Resorts Corp., 1997-99, The Peabody Group, N.Y.C., 2000-01, Cravath, Swaine & Moore, N.Y.C., 2001—. Mem. ABA. Office: Cravath Swaine & Moore Worldwide Plaza 825 8th Ave New York NY 10019 E-mail: krichey@cravath.com.

RICHEY, RUSSELL E. university dean; b. Asheville, N.C., Oct. 19, 1941; m. Merle Bradley Umstead, Aug. 28, 1965; children: William McMurry, Elizabeth Umstead. BA with with high honors, Wesleyan U., 1963; BD, Union Theol. Sem., 1966; MA, Princeton U., 1968, PhD, 1970. From instr. to prof. ch. history Drew U., 1969-86, asst. to pres., 1978-81; assoc. dean acad. programs Duke U., 1986-2000, rsch. prof. ch. history Div. Sch., 1986-92, prof. ch. history, 1992-2000; dean Candler Sch. Theology Emory U., Atlanta, 2000—. Mem. editl. adv. bd. Quar. Rev., Christian History, Jour. So. Religion, Ch. History, editor, 2000; pres. Wesley Wks. Editl. Project. Co-editor: American Civil Religion, 1974, 2d edit., 1990, Rethinking Methodist History, 1985, Perspectives on American Methodism: Interpretive Essays, 1993, The People(s) Called Methodist: Forms and Reforms of Their Life, 1998, Doctrines and Discipline, 1999; editor, co-author: Denominationalism, 1977, Ecumenical and Interreligious Perspectives: Globalizaion in Theological Education, 1992; co-author, co-editor: Reimagining Denominationalism, 1994; author: Early American Methodism, 1991, The Methodist Conference in America: A History, 1996; co-author: The Methodists, 1998, The Methodist Experience in America, 2000; co-author, primary co-editor: Questions for the Twenty-First Century Church, 1999. Mem. Am. Soc. Ch. History (mem. coun. 1976-78, 95-97), Am. Acad. Religion, Hist. Soc. United Meth. Ch., Wesleyan Theol. Soc. Home: 1198 Oakdale Rd Atlanta GA 30307 Office: Emory U Candler Sch. Theology Atlanta GA 30322

RICHGELS, GLEN WILLIAM, mathematics educator; b. Madison, Wis., Aug. 5, 1949; s. Marion Urban and Eudelma Rosena (Bomkamp) R.; m. Sharon Rae Hart, Aug. 14, 1976; children: Amber Rae, Erin Ellen, Erik Glen. BA, U. Wis., 1971, MA, 1976, PhD. Cert. tchr. math./computer sci. Tchr. math. Woodstock (Ill.) Cmty. H.S., 1973-76; tchr. math. and computer sci. Beloit (Wis.) Pub. Schs., 1976-82, Baraboo (Wis.) Pub. Schs., 1982-93; prof. math. Bemidji (Minn.) State U., 1993—, also dir. summer math. insts. Computer cons. Custom Data Svcs., Baraboo, 1984—. Author: Individualized Planning Program, 1990. Named Regional Basketball Coach of Yr., Wis. Basketball Coaches Assn., 1984, Basketball MVP, U. Wis.-Madison, 1971. Mem. Nat. Coun. Tchrs. Math., Math. Assn. Am., Wis. Math. Coun. Avocations: computer programming, fishing, basketball, football. E-mail: grichgels@bemidjistate.edu.

RICHIE, JEROME PAUL, surgeon, educator; b. San Antonio, 1944; MD, U. Tex., 1969. Surg. intern UCLA, 1969—70, resident in gen. surgery, 1970—71, resident in urology, 1971—75, lectr. surg. urology, 1974—75; asst. clin. prof. U. Calif., San Diego, 1975—77; asst. prof. urology Harvard U., 1977—80, assoc. prof., 1980—86, prof., 1986—, Elliott C. Cutler prof. surgery, 1987—, chmn. program in urology, 1987—. Chief urol. Brigham and Women's Hosp., Boston, 1977—; cons. Dana Farber Cancer Ctr., Boston, 1977—. Lt. comdr. M.C. USN, 1975—77. Mem.: ACS, Am. Surg. Assn., Am. Soc. (Clin.) Oncology, Assn. Acad. Surgery, Am. Urol. Assn., Am. Assn. Gerito-Urinary Surgeons. Office: Brigham & Womens Hosp 45 Francis St # 3 Boston MA 02115-6105 E-mail: jrichie@parnters.org.

RICHIE, ROBERT DOUGLAS, foundation administrator; b. Washington, Sept. 25, 1962; s. David Arthur and Catherine Richie; m. Cynthia R. Terrell, Apr. 6, 1964; children: Savanna, Lucas, Rebecca. BA, Haverford Coll., 1987. Media rels. profl. Christic Inst., Washington, 1987-89; rschr. Jolene Unsoeld for Congress, Olympia, Wash., 1990-92; exec. dir. Ctr. for Voting and Democracy, Washington & Takoma Park, Md., 1992—. Coord., newsletter editor S.P.E.E.C.H., Olympia, Wash., 1990—91; mem. adv. bd. Democracy 2000, N.Y.C., 1999—. Co-author: (book) Reflecting All of Us, 1999, Whose Vote Counts, 2001; contbr. articles to profl. jours.; mem. editl. adv. bd.: Representation, 1997—. Office: Ctr for Voting and Democracy 6930 Carroll Ave Ste 610 Takoma Park MD 20912-4466 E-mail: rr@fairvote.org.

RICHIE, RODNEY CHARLES, critical care and pulmonary medicine physician; b. Big Springs, Tex., Aug. 17, 1946; s. Howard Mouzon and Gloria (Hollingshead) R.; m. Sara Lee Dilley, July 13, 1968; children: Megan Kathryn, Paul Nathan. BA in Chemistry, So. Meth. U., 1968; MD cum laude, Baylor Coll., 1972. Diplomate in Internal Medicine, Pulmonary, Crit. Care and Ins. Medicine. Resident in medicine Baylor Affiliated Hosps., Houston, 1973-75, chief med. resident, 1975, fellow in pulmonary medicine, 1976-77; pvt. practice, pres. Waco (Tex.) Lung Assocs., 1977—. Med. dir. Tex. Life Ins., Waco, 1985—, Cmty. Hospice of Waco, 1996—, EMSI, Waco, Tex., 1997—. Chmn. med. staff Hillcrest Bapt. Med. Ctr., Waco, 1993; chmn. bd. dirs. GH Pape Found., Waco, 1993. Fellow Am. Coll. Chest Physicians; mem. ACP,

AMA, Am. Acad. Internal Medicine (del. to AMA), Am. Thoracic Soc., Tex. Club Internists. Episcopalian. Avocations: snow skiing, writing, reading. Home: 3509 Lake Heights Dr Waco TX 76708-1005 Office: Waco Med Group 2911 Herring Ave Ste 212 Waco TX 76708-3244

RICHKIN, BARRY ELLIOTT, financial services executive; b. N.Y.C., Apr. 14, 1944; s. Harry and Celia (Goldberg) R. BA, Bklyn. Coll., 1964. CLU, cert. in personal fin. planning, NASD. Auditor First Nat. Bank of N.Y., N.Y.C., 1968-70; sr. supr. ABC, 1970-73; account rep. Met. Life Ins. co., Atlanta, 1973-74; rep. Mixon-Baker Fin. Svcs., 1974-78; owner Barry Richkin Fin. Svcs., 1978—. Owner Barry Richkin Philatelics, Atlanta, 1991—; cons., owner Benefit Group, Atlanta, 1989—; cons., pres., bd. dirs. Am. Health Network, Atlanta, 1982-97. Author: Guide to Preferred Provider Organizations, 1986. Mem. Am. Soc. CLU and ChFC, Am. Philatelic Soc., Am. Ind. Bus. Assn. (pres. bd. dirs. 1997—), Manuscript Soc., U.S. Postal Hist. Soc., Conn. Hist. Soc. Avocations: manuscripts, philatelics, jogging. Office: Barry Richkin Fin Svcs PO Box 957315 Duluth GA 30095-9522 E-mail: benefitsaiba@msn.com.

RICHLAND, LISA, library director; b. N.Y.C., July 28, 1945; d. W. Bernard and Pauline Richland; m. Daniel Philip Maciejak, May 28, 1965 (div. Dec. 1992); 1 child, Rafael Luke Maciejak; m. Bruce Edward Saul. BS in Mgmt., Syracuse U., 1985; MLS, U. Ky., 1989. Alumni dir. Bklyn. Friends Sch., 1971-81; libr. dir. Floyd Meml. Libr., Greenport, N.Y., 1989—. Mem. shared decision making com. Shelter Island Sch., 1994-97, budget rev. com., 1992-93; exec. bd. Cmty. Action of Southold Town, Inc., Greenport, N.Y., 1994-2000; mem. standing com. on arts and culture Village of Greenport, 1996—. Dewey fellow N.Y. Libr. Assn., 1994. Mem. ALA, Pub. Libr. Dirs. Assn. Suffolk County (exec. bd. 1990-92, treas. 1992-95), Pub. Libr. Assn. Office: Floyd Meml Libr 539 1st St Greenport NY 11944-1399 E-mail: lrichlan@suffolk.lib.ny.us.

RICHLEN, SCOTT LANE, federal government program administrator; b. Ames, Iowa, July 23, 1949; s. Ellsworth Mark and Betty Jane (Wegner) R.; m. Deborah Lou Dick, Feb. 6, 1971; children: Mindy Lou, Gwendolyn Anne. BSME, Mont. State U., 1972; M.Engring. in Mech. Engring., U. Idaho, 1982; grad. exec. potential program, Office Pers. Mgmt., 1995. Assoc. engr. Thiokol Chem. Corp., Brigham City, Utah, 1973-75; rsch. engr. EG&G Idaho, Inc., Idaho Falls, 1975-79, sr. program specialist, 1979-84; program mgr. indsl. heat pumps U.S. Dept. Energy, Washington, 1984-87, program mgr. advanced heat exchangers, 1984-94, program mgr. continuous fiber ceramic composites, 1990-95, team leader steel industry R&D, 1995-99, integrated delivery sys. devel. team, 1998-99, dir. Office Indsl. Techs., 2000—. Lectr. profl. extension U. Wis., Madison, 1982-83. Author: (reference text) ASM, Engineered Materials, 1992, Ceramics Information Analysis Center/American Ceramic Society Handbook on Continuous Fiber Reinforced Ceramic Matrix Composites, 1993; editor (conf. procs.) Industrial Heat Exchangers, 1985; inventor, patentee corrosive resistant heat exchanger. Vol. Martha's Table, Washington, 1986—; v.p. Aid Assn for Lutherans, Br. 2792, Annandale, Va., 1988-92. Mem. Precision Aerobatics Model Pilots Assn., No. Va. Control-line Assn. (pres. 1987-89, 91-92, 2000—), Mont. State Soc. Mont. State U. Alumni Assn. (life). Avocations: woodworking, martial arts, control-line model airplanes, gardening, readings in psychology, history and law. Office: US Dept Energy 1000 Independence Ave SW Washington DC 20585-0001

RICHMAN, ALAN, magazine editor; b. Bronx, N.Y., Nov. 12, 1939; s. Louis and Sonia (Carity) R.; m. Kelli Shor, June 21, 1964; children: Lincoln Seth Shor, Matthew Mackenzie Shor. BA, Hunter Coll., 1960. Reporter Leader-Observer, N.Y.C., 1960-61; asst. editor Modern Tire Dealer, 1962-64; assoc. editor ASTA Travel News, 1964-65; pub. rels. rep. M.J. Jacobs, Inc., 1965-66; mng. editor Modern Floor Coverings, 1966-68; editor Bank Systems & Equipment, 1968-79, Health Care Product News, N.Y.C., 1976; from assoc. pub. to pub. Bank Systems & Equipment, 1969-79; editorial dir. Nat. Jeweler, 1979-81; editor Health Foods Bus.; editorial dir. Army/Navy Store and Outdoor Merchandiser, 1981-88, The Pet Dealer, 1983-88; editor Cabinet Mfg. and Fabricating KBC Publs., 1988-94. Program dir. Cabinet Mfg. Fair, 1989-94; adj. faculty NYU, 1989—, Brookdale C.C., 1992—, Bergen County C.C., 1994—. Exec. editor: Kitchen and Bath Design News, 1992-93; editor-in-chief Wood Digest, PTN Pub. Co., 1992-94; editor: Whole Foods, 1994—; author: Czechoslovakia in Pictures, 1969, A Book on the Chair, 1968. With AUS, 1961-62. Recipient Jesse H. Neal certificate merit Am. Bus. Press, 1973. Mem. Internat. Platform Assn.

RICHMAN, ANTHONY E. textile rental industry association executive; b. Dec. 13, 1941; s. Irving M. and Helen V. (Muchnic) R.; Judy Harriet Richman, Dec. 19, 1964; children: Lisa Michele, Jennifer Beth. BS, U. So. Calif., 1964. With Reliable Textile Rental Svcs., L.A., 1964—; svc. mgr., 1969; sales and svc. mgr., 1970-73; plant mgr., 1973-75; gen. mgr., bd. dirs., 1975-78; v.p., sec.-treas., 1975-82; exec. v.p., CEO, 1982-84; pres., CEO, 1984—. Bd. dirs. Guild for Children, 1979—, Valley Guild for Cystic Fibrosis, 1974—, Cystic Fibrosis Found. of L.A. and Orange Counties, 1989—; pres. Textile Rental/Svc. Assn. Am., 1993-95; exec. dir. Western Textile Svcs. Assn., Studio City, Calif., 1996—. Office: Western Textile Svcs Assn 12444 Ventura Blvd Ste 204 Studio City CA 91604-2409

RICHMAN, ARLEEN, professional society administrator; b. N.Y.C., Jan. 1, 1941; d. Abraham Friedel and Judith Anne Hecht; m. Sheldon B. Richman, May 26, 1970. AAS, Hofstra Coll., 1960; BBA in Acctg. summa cum laude, Adelphi U., 1969, postgrad., 1969-71. Women's page editor AP, N.Y.C., 1960-69; adminstrv. positions various assns., Washington, 1976-80; mng. editor Trips Travels, 1980-83; comm. mgr. Appropriate Tech. Internat., 1984-90; grants adminstr. Coun. for Internat. Devel., 1990-93; dir. comm. and spl. projects U.S. Parachute Assn., Alexandria, Va., 1993-97; mgr. spl. projects Nat. Soc. Accts., 1997—; editor Nat. Pub. Acct., 2001—. Cons. various UN Devel. Program and AID projects, 1986-93; cons., editor, writer Com. on Internat. Liaison for Agr., Puebla, Mexico, 1988-90. Author: Opening the Marketplace to Small Enterprise, 1990; editor: High Impact Case Studies, 1989, (jour.) The Profl., 1995-97; contbr. numerous articles to newspapers and jours. Com. mem. local homeowners assn., Alexandria, 1984—; vol. friend Mental Health Assn., Alexandria, 1992—; vol. mentor Alexandria Jail, 1998—. Recipient Keep Am. Beautiful award Keep Am. Beautiful Fedn., Washington, 1966, Point of Light award Compeer, Alexandria, 1998, 2000. Mem. Am. Soc. Assn. Execs. Jewish. Avocations: tennis, birdwatching. Home: 2741 Carter Farm Ct Alexandria VA 22306-3242 Office: Nat Soc Accts 1010 N Fairfax St Alexandria VA 22314-1504 E-mail: arichman@nsacct.org.

RICHMAN, ARTHUR SHERMAN, sports association executive; b. N.Y.C., Mar. 21, 1926; s. Samuel Abraham and Clara (Ganbarg) R.; m. Martha Landgrebe, Nov. 9, 1979. Student, Bklyn. Coll., 1942-44. Baseball writer, columnist N.Y. Mirror, N.Y.C., 1943-63; acct. exec. Grey Pub. Rels., 1963-65; dir. promotions, pub. rels., traveling sec., spl. asst. to gen. mgr. N.Y. Mets, Flushing, 1965-89; sr. v.p. N.Y. Yankees, Bronx, 1989—. Contbr. articles to profl. and popular jours. Leader baseball groups USO/U.S. Dept. Def., Vietnam, Thailand, Japan, Korea, Philippines, Guam, Hawaii and Greenland, 1965-74 Recipient Ben Epstein Good Guy award N.Y. Baseball Writers, 1983, Long and Meritorious Svc. award Major League Baseball Scouts, 1984, Good Guy award N.Y. Press Photographers, 1988, George Sisler Long and Meritorious Svc. award St. Louis Browns Hist. Soc., 1996, Long Meritorious Svc. award N.Y. Baseball Writers Am., 1999; inductee Bklyn. Coll. Athletic Hall of Fame, 1984, St. Louis Browns Baseball Media Hall of Fame, 1986, Nat. Jewish Am. Sports Hall of Fame, 1996. Mem. Assn. Profl. Baseball Players Am. (v.p. 1986—). Jewish. Office: NY Yankees Yankee Stadium E 161st St & River Ave Bronx NY 10451

RICHMAN, DAVID PAUL, neurologist, educator, researcher; b. Boston, June 9, 1943; s. Harry S. and Anne (Goodkin) R.; m. Carol Mae von Bastian, Aug. 31, 1969; children: Sarah Ann, Jacob Charles. AB, Princeton U., 1965; MD, Johns Hopkins U., 1969. Diplomate Am. Bd. Psychiatry and Neurology. Intern, then asst. resident in medicine Albert Einstein Coll. Medicine, N.Y.C., 1969-71; resident in neurology Mass. Gen. Hosp., Boston, 1971-73, chief resident, 1973-74; instr. neurology Harvard U. Med. Sch., 1975-76; assoc. prof. neurology U. Chgo., 1976-80, assoc. prof., 1981-85, prof., 1985-91, Straus prof. neurol. Scis., 1988-91; prof. neurology U. Calif., Davis, 1991—, chmn. dept., 1991-97. Mem. com. Nat. Inst. Aging, NIH, 1984-85, mem. immunogical scis. study sect., 1986-90. Mem. AAAS, Am. Assn. Immunologists, Am. Acad. Neurology, Am. Neurol. Assn., Phi Beta Kappa, Sigma Xi. Office: U Calif Davis Dept Neurology 1515 Newton Ct Davis CA 95616-4859

RICHMAN, DOUGLAS DANIEL, medical virologist, educator, internist; b. N.Y.C., Feb. 15, 1943; s. Daniel Powell and Louise Kohnstamm (Woolf) R.; m. Eva Acquino, June 21, 1965; children: Sara, Matthew. AB cum laude, Dartmouth Coll., 1965; MD, Stanford U., 1970. Diplomate, Am. Bd. Internal Medicine, diplomate Am. Bd. Infectious Diseases; diplomate Am. Bd. Med. Examiners. Intern Stanford (Calif.) Med. Sch., 1970-71, resident, 1971-72; rsch. assoc. LID/NIAID NIH, Bethesda, Md., 1972-75; fellow Beth Israel and Children's Hosps., Harvard Med. Ctr., Boston, 1975-76; asst. prof. depts. pathology and medicine U. Calif., San Diego, 1976-82, assoc. prof., 1982-88, prof., 1988—. Vis. prof. Hubei Med. Coll., Wuhan, People's Republic of China, 1987, Tokyo Med. and Dental U., Kumamoto U. Sch. Medicine, Inst. for Virus Rsch. at Kyoto U., St. Marianna U., Tokyo, Inst. Med. Rsch., Tokyo, Fukishima Prefecture Med. Sch., Japan, 1990; mem. U. Calif. President's Cancer Rsch. Coord. Com., 1984-89, NIH AIDS Rsch. Review Com., 1987-90; cons. FDA Ctr. for Drugs and Biologics, 1986-89; pubs. com. Infectious Disease Soc. Am., 1987-90, and other national committees; dir. U. Calif.-San Diego Ctr. for AIDS Rsch., AIDS Rsch. Inst. Contbr. more than 450 articles to profl. jours. including , ; co-editor: Clin. Virology, —; mem. editl. bd.: Antimicrobial Agts. and Chemotherapy , 1987—, mem. editl. bd.: Jour. of AIDS, 1988—, mem. editl. bd.: Antiviral Agts., 1988—, mem. editl. bd.: AIDS, 1990—, mem. editl. bd.: AIDS Alert, 1990—, mem. editl. bd.: Antiviral Drug Resistance, 1996—, mem. editl. bd.: Virology, 1997—, mem. editl. bd.: others. Recipient Lowell Rantz award in infectious diseases, 1970, AMA Physicians Recgonition award, 1976, 79, 82, 85, 88, John Simon Guggenheim fellowship, 1984, Visiting Fellowship, Clare Hall, U. Cambridge, 1984-85. Fellow: ACP, AAAS, Western Assn. Physicians, Am. Assn. Physicians, Infectious Diseases Soc. Am.; mem.: VA Soc. for Physicians in Infectious Diseases, Internat. AIDS Soc., Internat. Soc. Antiviral Rsch., Soc. for Gen. Microbiology, Am. Venereal Disease Assn., Am. Soc. for Virology, Pan Am. Group for Rapid Viral Diagnosis, Am. Fedn. for Clin. Rsch., Am. Soc. for Microbiology. Office: U Calif San Diego Dept Pathology & Medicine 9500 Gilman Dr La Jolla CA 92093-0679

RICHMAN, ERIC I. pharmaceutical executive; BS in Biomed. Sci., Sophie Davis Sch. Biomed. Edn. CUNY Med. Sch.; MBA, Am. Grad. Sch. Internat. Mgmt. Dir. internat. commercialization MedImmune; v.p. corp. devel. MaxCyte. Office: MaxCyte 9640 Med Ctr Dr Rockville MD 20850*

RICHMAN, GERTRUDE GROSS (MRS. BERNARD RICHMAN), civic worker; b. N.Y.C., May 16, 1908; d. Samuel and Sarah Yetta (Seltzer) Gross; B.S., Tchrs. Coll. Columbia U., 1948, M.A., 1949; m. Bernard Richman, Apr. 5, 1930; children— David, Susan. Vol. worker Hackensack Hosp., 1948-70; mem. bd. dirs. YM-YWHA, Bergen County, N.J., 1950-75, bd. mem. emeritus, 1975— ; chmn. Leonia Friends of Bergen County Mental Health Consultation Center, 1959; founder, hon. pres. Bergen County Serv-A-Com., affiliated with women orgns. Div. Nat. Jewish Welfare Bd.; v.p. N.J. sect. Nat. Jewish Welfare Bd., 1964-71; hon. trustee women's div. Bergen County United Jewish Community; mem. adv. council Bergen County Office on Aging, 1968-83, reappointed, 1984—; mem. Hackensack Bd. Edn., 1946-51; mem. pub. relations com. Leonia Pub. Schs., 1957-58; N.J. del. White House Conf. on Aging, 1971; trustee Mary McLeod Bethune Scholarship Fund; v.p. Bergen County nat. women's com. Brandeis U., 1966-67. Recipient citation Nat. Council Jewish Women and YWCA in Bergen County, 1962; citation Nat. Jewish Welfare Bd., 1964, Harry S. Feller award N.J. Region, 1965; 14th Ann. Good Scout award Bergen council Boy Scouts Am., 1977; Woman Vol. of Distinction, Bergen County council Girl Scouts, 1979; Human Relations award Bergen County sect. Nat. Council Negro Women, 1982; recipient Gov.'s award, 1988, Cert. of Commendation County Exec. and the Bergen County Bd. of Chosen Freeholders, 1989; honored at testimonial United Jewish Community Bergen County, 1987; Senior Advocate award Divsn. on Aging, 1993; honoree Temple Beth El, 1997. Mem. Kappa Delta Pi.

RICHMAN, HAROLD ALAN, social welfare policy educator; b. Chgo., May 15, 1937; s. Leon H. and Rebecca (Klieman) R.; m. Marlene M. Forland, Apr. 25, 1965; children: Andrew, Robert. AB, Harvard U., 1959; MA, U. Chgo., 1961, PhD, 1969. Asst. prof., dir. Ctr. for Study Welfare Policy, Sch. Social Svc., U. Chgo., 1967-69, dean, prof. social welfare policy, 1969-78, Hermon Dunlap Smith prof., 1978—, dir. of ctr., 1978-81, dir. Children's Policy Rsch. Project, 1978-84, dir. Chapin Hall Ctr. for Children, 1985—2002, faculty assoc. Chapin Hall Ctr. for Children, 2002—, chmn. univ. com. on pub. policy studies, 1974-77. Chmn. Univ. Lab. Schs., 1985-88; cons. to gov. State of Ill., Edna McConnell Clark Found., 1984-95, Lilly Endowment, 1987-90, Ford Found., 1987-89; co-chair Aspen roundtable on comprehensive cmty. initiatives, 1993—. Chmn. editorial bd. Social Svcs. Rev., 1970-79; contbr. articles to profl. jours. Bd. dirs. Chgo. Com. Fgn. and Domestic Policy, 1969-78, S.E. Chgo. Commn., 1970—, Jewish Fedn. Met. Chgo., 1970-75, Ill. Facilities Fund, 1989-94, Welfare Coun. Met. Chgo., 1970-72, Erikson Inst. Early Childhood Edn., 1972-79, Nat. Urban Coalition, 1975-86, Family Focus, 1980-89, Jewish Coun. Urban Affairs, 1982-87, Ctr. for Study Social Policy, 1983-92, Nat. Family Resource Coalition, 1990-93, Pub./Pvt. Ventures, 1992-98, Benton Found., 1994—; bd. dirs. Israel Ctr. on Children, chmn., 1995—; bd. dirs. Jordan Children's Rsch. Ctr., 2001—, Michael Reese Health Trust, 2002—, U. Capetown Childen's Inst. Capt. USPHS, 1961-63. White House fellow, Washington, 1965-66; recipient Disting. Svc. citation U.S. Dept. Health, Edn. & Welfare, 1970, Quantrell award U. Chgo., 1990. Mem. White House Fellows Assn. (v.p. 1976-77), Am. Pub. Welfare Assn. (bd. dirs. 1989-92). Home: 5715 S Dorchester Ave Chicago IL 60637-1726 Office: U Chgo Chapin Hall Ctr for Children 1313 E 60th St Chicago IL 60637-2830

RICHMAN, IRWIN, history educator, author, consultant, lecturer; b. Bklyn., Jan. 1, 1937; s. Alexander and Bertha (Schwebel) R.; m. M. Susan Steigerwalt, May 23, 1970; children: Alexander Eugene, Joshua Solomon. AA, George Washington U., 1956, BA in History, 1957; MA in History, U. Pa., 1958, PhD in History, 1965. Various positions Pa. Hist. and Mus. Commn., Harrisburg, 1961-68; curator sci., industry and tech. William Penn Meml. Mus. (now State Mus. Pa.), 1965-68; prof. Am. studies and history Pa. State U., 1968—, past chmn. grad. program in Am. studies. Archtl. hist. cons. Nat. Park Svc., U.S. Army C.E., City of Harrisburg, Heritage Ctr. Mus. Lancaster County; lectr. continuing edn. program Longwood Gardens, Kennett Square, Pa., 1994-97; presenter numerous confs., including Am. Studies Assn., Am. Folklore Assn., Am. Aesthetics Assn., Catskill Inst.; Commonwealth spkr. Pa. Humanities Coun., 1996—; spkr. in field. Author: Historial Manuscript Depositories in Pennsylvania, 1965, Penn Pictures, 1966, The Brightest Ornament, 1967, Pennsylvania's Architecture, 1968, rev. edit., 1997, Pennsylvania's Decorative Arts in the Age of Handcraft, 1978, reprint, 1995, Pennsylvania's Painters, 1983, Borcht Belt Bungalows: Memories of Catskill Summers, 1998, The Catskills in Vintage Postcards, 1999, Pa. German Arts, 2001, Sullivan County: Borscht Belt, 2001, The Hudson River: From New York City to Albany, also others; contbr. over 170 articles and revs. to profl. jours. Past vice chmn. Pa. Hist. Preservation Bd.; lectr. numerous groups, including Allentown Art Mus., Bradford County (Pa.) Med. Soc., Bucks County Hist. Soc., Pa., Cumberland County Hist. Soc., Pa., Ebenezer Maxwell Mansion Soc., Landis Valley Assocs., Dauphin County Hist. Soc.; past coun. mem. Pa. Hist. Assn.; treas. Catskill Inst.; pres. parents leadership coun. Bard Coll., 1994—. Mem. Soc. Archtl. Historians (conf. presenter), Nat. Trust for Hist. Preservation. Office: Pa State U Sch Humanities Middletown PA 17057

RICHMAN, JOEL ESER, lawyer, mediator, arbitrator; b. Brockton, Mass., Feb. 17, 1947; s. Nathan and Ruth Miriam (Bick) R.; m. Elaine R. Thompson, Aug. 21, 1987; children: Shawn Jonah, Jesse Ray, Eva Rose. BA in Psychology, Grinnell Coll., 1969; JD, Boston U., 1975. Bar: Mass. 1975, U.S. Dist. Ct. Mass. 1977, U.S. Supreme Ct. 1980, U.S. Ct. Appeals (1st cir.) 1982, Hawaii 1985, U.S. Dist. Ct. Hawaii 1987. Law clk. Richman & Perenyi, Brockton, Mass., 1973-75, atty., 1975-77; pvt. practice pvt. practice, Provincetown, 1977-82, Paia, Hawaii, 1985—. Arbitrator Am. Arbitration Assn., Paia, 1992—, mediator, 1994—. Pres. Jewish Congregation Maui (Hawaii), 1989-97, bd. dirs., 1984-89; bd. dirs. Pacific Primate Ctr., 1991, pres., 1994. Mem. Haiku Cmty. Assn. (dir. 1998, pres. 2000-), Kalama Band Boosters (pres. 2001-). Avocations: windsurfing, youth soccer, T'ai Chi. Office: PO Box 791539 Paia HI 96779-0046 E-mail: jer@haikulaw.com.

RICHMAN, JOSEPH HERBERT, retired public health services official; b. Balt., Aug. 13, 1941; s. Samuel and Beatrice R. BS, Howard U., 1962, MD, 1966; MPH, Johns Hopkins U., 1974. Intern Maimonides Med. Ctr., Bklyn., 1966-67; resident in pediat. Sinai Hosp. of Balt., 1967-69; chief sch. health P.G. Health Dept. of Md., Cheverly, Md., 1972-75; dir. area health svcs. Montgomery County Health Dept., Bethesda, 1975-82; county chief pub. health physician State of Del., Dover, 1982-99; ret., 1999. Capt. USAF, 1969—71. Fellow Am. Acad. Pediatrics (emeritus), Am. Coll. Preventive Medicine; mem. AMA, Masons, Phi Beta Kappa. Democrat. Jewish. Avocations: golf, photography. Home: 4485 Sedgwick St NW Washington DC 20016-2713 E-mail: joefortsedgwick@aol.com.

RICHMAN, MARC HERBERT, forensic engineer, educator; b. Boston, Oct. 14, 1936; s. Samuel and Janet (Gordon) R.; m. Ann Raeshel Yoffa, Aug. 31, 1963 BS, MIT, 1957, ScD, 1963; MA, Brown U., 1967. Registered profl. engr., Conn., Mass., R.I.; cert. forensic examiner. Cons. engr., 1957—; engr. shipbldg. div. Bethlehem Steel Corp., Quincy, Mass., 1957; instr. metallurgy MIT, Cambridge, 1957-60, research asst. dept. metallurgy, 1960-63; instr. metallurgy div. univ. extension Commonwealth of Mass., 1958-62; asst. prof. engring. Brown U., Providence, 1963-67, assoc. prof., 1967-70, prof., 1970-98, dir. central electron microscopy facility Materials Research program, 1971-86, dir. undergrad. program in engring., 1991-98; prof. emeritus, 1998—; pres. Ednl. Aids of Newton Inc., Providence, 1968-71, Marc H. Richman Inc., Providence, 1981—. Guest scientist Franklin Inst., Phila., 1959; vis. prof. U. R.I., Kingston, 1970-71; biophysicist dept. medicine Miriam Hosp., Providence, 1974-87; biogengr. dept. orthopaedics R.I. Hosp., 1979-93; prof. emeritus Brown U., Providence, 1998—. Author: Introduction to Science of Metals, 1967; also articles; editor Soviet Physics: Crystallography, 1970-94; mem. editorial adv. bd. Materials Characterization, 1970—; mem. editorial adv. bd. Jour. Forensic Engring., 1985-88. Maj. Ordnance Corps, U.S. Army, 1963. Served to maj. Ordnance Corps, U.S. Army, 1963 Recipient Engr. of Yr. award R.I. Soc. Profl. Engrs., 1993. Fellow Nat. Acad. Forensic Engrs. (cert.), Am. Coll. Forensic Examiners (cert.), Am. Inst. Chemists, Inst. Materials (U.K.); mem. ASCE, AIME, NSPE, ASEE (Outstanding Young Faculty award 1969), NAFE (bd. cert. diplomate in forensic engring.), Am. Acad. Forensic Scis., Am. Soc. Metals (sec.-treas. 1965-68, chmn. R.I. chpt. 1968-69, Albert Sauveur Meml. award 1968, 69), Providence Engring. Soc. (pres. 1991-92, Freeman award for engring. achievement 1989), B'nai B'rith, Sigma Xi, Tau Beta Pi. Home: 291 Cole Ave Providence RI 02906-3452 Office: One Richmond Sq Providence RI 02906 E-mail: MHRichman@aol.com.

RICHMAN, MARTIN FRANKLIN, lawyer; b. Newark, Feb. 23, 1930; s. Samuel L. and Betty E. (Goldstein) R.; stepson Doris (Bloom) R.; m. Florence E. Reif, May 6, 1962; children— Judith, Andrew. BA magna cum laude, St. Lawrence U., 1950; LL.B. magna cum laude, Harvard U., 1953. Bar: N.Y. 1953. Law clk. to Judge Calvert Magruder and Chief Justice Earl Warren, 1955-57; assoc., mem. firm Lord Day & Lord, Barrett Smith (and predecessors), N.Y.C., 1957-66, 69-94; of counsel Kirkpatrick & Lockhart, LLP, 1994—; dep. asst. atty. gen. Office Legal Counsel, Dept. Justice, Washington, 1966-69. Public mem. Adminstrv. Conf. U.S., 1970-76; bd. dirs. Community Action for Legal Services, 1977-80 Trustee St. Lawrence U., 1979-95, trustee emeritus, 1995—, vice chmn. bd., 1988-95; bd. dirs. Friends of Law Libr. of Congress, 1992-99. Recipient Alumni citation St. Lawrence U., 1972 Fellow Am. Bar Found., N.Y. Bar Found.; mem. ABA (chmn. sect. adminstrv. law 1983-84), N.Y. State Bar Assn. (ho. of dels. 1981-84), Assn. of Bar of City of N.Y. (sec. and mem. exec. com. 1976-79, chmn. com. fed. legislation 1972-75, com. lawyer's pro bono obligations 1977-81), Am. Law Inst. Office: Kirkpatrick & Lockhart LLP 599 Lexington Ave New York NY 10022-6030 E-mail: mrichman@kl.com.

RICHMAN, PAUL, semiconductor industry executive, educator; b. N.Y.C., Nov. 17, 1942; s. Harry and Molly (Armel) Richman; m. Ellen Margaret Kleiman, July 3, 1966; children: Lee Stuart, Alyson Michelle, Daniel Noah. BSEE, MIT, 1963; MSEE, Columbia U., 1964. V.p. R & D Standard Microsystems Corp., Hauppauge, N.Y., 1971-76, pres., 1976-81, pres., chief exec. officer, 1981-83, pres., chmn. bd., chief exec. officer, 1983-2000; co-founder Toyo Microsystems Corp., Tokyo, 1987—. Pres Consortium Technology Licensing Ltd, Nissequogue, NY, 1994—99, chmn bd dirs, CEO, 1999—; vis prof elec eng SUNY, Stony Brook, 1976—85; mem vis comt elec eng and computer sci dept MIT, 1996—; adj. prof. elec. engring. CUNY, 1973—75. Author: (book) Characteristics and Operation of MOS Field Effect Devices, 1967, MOS Field Effect Transistors and Integrated Circuits, 1974. Named one of 30 Most Important Contributors in the World to Devel Integrated Circuit Technology, Elec Eng Times/Elec Buyer's News/VLSI Sys Design, 1988; recipient Ann Award Achievement in Electronics, Electronics Mag, 1978. Fellow: IEEE (Award for Outstanding Technical Achievement 1980, Third Millennium Medal 2000). Achievements include invention of COPLAMOS technology. E-mail: paul.richman@smsc.com.

RICHMAN, PETER, electronics executive; b. N.Y.C., Nov. 7, 1927; s. Emil H. and Janet (Seidler) R.; m. Vivian Hoffman, July 29, 1951; children: Meredith, Jeremy. BS, MIT, 1946; MS, NYU, 1953. Asst. chief engr. Reeves Instrument Corp., Garden City, N.Y., 1948-58; chief engr. Epsco, Inc., Cambridge, Mass., 1959-60; v.p., co-founder Rotek Instrument Corp., Watertown, 1960-64; v.p. Weston-Rotek, Lexington, 1964-67; cons. electronics engr., 1967—. Bd. dirs. Thermo Voltek Corp, Thermo Sentron Corp.; founder, pres. KeyTek Instrument Corp., 1975-93; mem. NRC/NAS/Nat. Acad. Engring. Evaluation Panel for electricity divsn. Nat. Bur. Standards; mem. sci. adv. groups for several indsl. and sci. orgns. Patentee in precision electronic instrumentation; pioneer in precision dc and audio-frequency measurements, surge electrostatic discharge generation and electrostatic discharge measurements; author: The Insider's Guide to Growing a Small Business, 1996; contbr. articles to profl. jours. Mem. bd. overseers Boston Mus. Sci. Fellow IEEE; mem. Electromagnetics Acad., Instrument Soc. Am. (sr.), Sigma Xi, Tau Beta Pi.

RICHMAN, PETER MARK, actor, painter, writer, producer; b. Phila., Apr. 16, 1927; s. Benjamin and Yetta Dora (Peck) R.; m. Theodora Helen Landess, May 10, 1953; children: Howard Bennett, Kelly Allyn, Lucas Dion, Orien, Roger Lloyd. BS in Pharmacy, U. of the Scis., 1951; student of Lee Strasberg, N.Y.C., 1952-54; mem., Actors' Studio, N.Y.C., 1954—. Registered pharmacist, Pa., N.Y. Appeared in little theater, Phila., 1946-51, on stage radio and in live TV, Phila., N.Y.C., and Los Angeles, 1948-65, including Have I Got a Girl for You (pre-Broadway tryout), Biltmore Theater, L.A., 1962, The Deputy, Ctr. Theater Group, L.A., 1965; appeared at Grove Theater, Nuangola, Pa., 1952, Westchester Playhouse, 1953, Drury Lane, Chicago, 1957, Strand, N.J., 1957, Capri, 1959, Ogonquit (Maine) Playhouse, 1955-62, Matunuck, R.I., 1955, Falmouth, Mass., 1953-55, Westport, Conn., 1955, Harrison, Maine, 1962, Dennis, Mass., 1955-62, Phila. Playhouse in the Park, 1962-63; Broadway plays include End as a Man, 1953, Hatful of Rain,Broadway and Nat. Tour, 1956-57, Masquerade, 1959; off-Broadway plays include End as a Man, 1953, The Dybbuk, 1954, The Zoo Story (400 performances), 1960-61; Rainmaker, Private Lives, Angel Street, Arms and the Man, Rose Tattoo, Liliom, Funny Girl, Owl and the Pussycat, Hold Me, Equus, Night of the Iguana, Blithe Spirit, Twelve Angry Men, Henry Fonda Theatre, L.A., 1985, Babes in Toyland, Calif. Mus. Theater, 1988, Ray Bradbury's Next in Line, L.A., 1992, and numerous others; writer, performer (one man show) 4 Faces, L.A., 1995, N.Y.C., 1996, The Actors Studio, N.Y.C., 1996, and others; motion pictures include Friendly Persuasion, 1956, The Strange One, 1956, Black Orchid, 1958, The Dark Intruder, 1965, Agent for HARM, 1965, For Singles Only, 1967, Judgement Day (formerly The Third Hand), 1988, Friday the 13th, Part 8 (Jason Takes Manhattan), 1989, Naked Gun 2 1/2 (The Smell of Fear), 1991, Pool Hall Junkies, 2001; prodr., writer, actor 4 Faces (film), 2000; appeared on TV series as Nick Cain in Cain's Hundred, 1961-62, as David in David Chapter III for CBC, 1966, as Duke Page in series Longstreet, 1971-72, as Reverend Snow in series Three's Company, 1978-79, as Andrew Laird in series Dynasty, 1981-84, as Channing Capwell in series Santa Barbara, 1984, voice of God series Heroes of the Bible, 1979, voice of the Phantom in animated series Defenders of the Earth, 1986, as Madros in Berlin series My Secret Summer (formerly Mystery of the Keys), 1991; guest star over 500 TV shows, including Hotel, Dallas, Hart to Hart, Fantasy Island, Murder She Wrote, Nothing Sacred, Three's Company, Knight Rider, Star Trek: The Next Generation, Matlock, Beverly Hills 90210, others; starred in TV movies House on Greenapple Road, 1968, McCloud, 1969, Yuma, 1970, Nightmare at 43

Hillcrest (Wide World of Entertainment), 1974, Mallory, 1975, The Islander, 1978, Greatest Heroes of the Bible, 1979, Blind Ambition, 1979, The PSI Factor, 1981, Dynasty, 1981, Dempsey, 1983, City Killer, 1984, Bonanza, The Next Generation, 1988; one-man shows (paintings) Am. Masters Gallery, L.A., 1967, Orlando Gallery, L.A., 1966, McKenzie Gallery, L.A., 1969, 73, Hopkins Gallery, L.A., 1971, Goldfield Gallery, L.A., 1979, Galerie des Stars, L.A., 1988, Crocker Mus., Sacramento, Calif., 1967, Parkhurst Gallery, Seal Beach, Calif., 1991, 1996 March thru July, inaugural exhibition of the Henley Gallery Chapman U., Orange, Calif. (a 30 yr. retrospective, A life in Art); group shows include Bednarz Gallery, L.A., 1968, Dohan Gallery, L.A., 1966, Celebrity Art Exhibits, 55-city tour, 1964-65; represented in permanent collections U.S. and abroad; playwright: Heavy, Heavy What Hangs Over? , 1971, a Medal for Murray, 1991 4 Faces, 1995 (Prism award nominee 2002); dir. plays Apple of His Eye, 1954, Glass Menagerie, 1954; author: (novels) Hollander's Deal, 2000, (stories) The Rebirth of Ira Masters, 2001; featured in book Actor as Artists, 1992, Guide to Artists in Southern California, 1994. Trustee Motion Picture and TV Fund. Served with USN, 1945-46. Recipient silver medallion Motion Picture TV Fund, 1990, Sybil Brand Humanitarian award Jeffrey Found., 1990, Spl. award, 1997, Drama-Logue critics performance award for 4 Faces, 1996, Golden Halo Eagle award, So. Calif. Motion Picture Coun., 1997. Mem. SAG, AFTRA, Actors Equity Assn., Assn. Can. TV and Radio Artists, Acad. Motion Picture Arts and Scis., Acad. TV Arts and Scis. Office: c/o Spencer Kazarian Assoc 11365 Ventura Blvd PO Box 7403 Studio City CA 91604 also: 4 Faces Prodns Office 19528 Ventura Blvd Ste 385 Tarzana CA 91356 E-mail: pmri@petermarkrichman.com. *I have always been grateful to be able to work in more than one medium. In a way they are all related, each solidifying and nurturing the other. I have a strong belief in God...and spiritual values. This, along with my marriage, children, and family life, has helped me enormously to express my own individuality as an artist.*

RICHMAN, STEPHEN ERIK, lawyer; b. Austin, Tex., Mar. 10, 1945; s. Allen A. and Erika (Zimmerman) R.; m. Frances Ellen Sharpe, Aug. 29, 1971; children: Joshua Eric, Wendy Michelle. BA magna cum laude, Amherst Coll., 1967; JD cum laude, Harvard U., 1970. Bar: Wis. 1972. Assoc. Webster Sheffield, N.Y.C., 1970-72, Quarles & Brady, Milw., 1972-78, ptnr., 1978—. Pres. Milw. Youth Symphony Orch., 1985-87, Milw. Jewish Fedn., 1996-98; chmn. Milw. Symphony Orch., 2000-2002; bd. dirs. Jewish Cmty. Found., Milw., 1992—. Mem. ABA, Nat. Assn. Bond Lawyers, State Bar Wis., Phi Beta Kappa. Home: 709 E Carlisle Ave Milwaukee WI 53217-4835 Office: Quarles & Brady 411 E Wisconsin Ave Ste 2550 Milwaukee WI 53202-4497

RICHMAN, STEPHEN I. lawyer; b. Washington, Pa., Mar. 26, 1933; m. Audrey May Gefsky. BS, Northwestern U., 1954; JD, U. Pa., 1957. Bar: Pa. 1958, U.S. Dist. Ct. (we. dist.) Pa. With McCune Greenlee & Richman, 1960-63, Greenlee Richman Derrico & Posa, 1963-84, ptnr. Richman, Smith Law Firm, P.A., Washington, 1985—; bd. dirs. Three Rivers Bank; lectr. U. South Fla. Sch. Medicine, Mine Safe Internat. Chamber of Mines of Western Australia, W.Va. U. Med. Ctr. Grand Rounds, Am. Coll. Chest Physicians, Pa. Thoracic Soc., Am. Thoracic Soc., The Energy Bur., Coll. of Am. Pathologists, Allegheny County Health Dept., APHA, Internat. Assn. Ind. Accident Bds. and Commns., Indsl. Health Found., Nat. Coun. Self-Insurers Assn., Am. Iron and Steel Inst., Can. Thoracic Soc., I.L.O./N.I.O.S.H., Univs. Associated for Rsch. and Edn. in Pathology, Am. Ceramics Soc., Nat. Sand Assn.; mem. adv. com. U.S. Dist. Ct. Western Dist. Pa., 1994—; lectr. in field. Author: Meaning of Impairment and Disability, Chest, 1980, Legal Aspects for the Pathologist, in Pathology of Occupational and Environmental Lung Disease, 1988, A Review of the Medical and Legal Definitions of Related Impairment and Disability, Report to the Department of Labor and the Congress, 1986, Medicolegal Aspects of Asbestos for Pathologists, Arch. Pathology and Laboratory Medicine, 1983, Legal Aspects of Occupational and Environmental Disease, Human Pathology, 1993, Impairment and Disability in Pneunoconiosis, State of the Art Reviews in Occupational Medicine-The Mining Industry, 1993, other publs. and articles; author House Bills 2103 and 885 co-author Act 44 and 57 amending Pa. Workmen's Compensation Act. Mem. legal com. Indsl. Health Found., Pitts.; bd. dirs. Pitts. Opera Soc., 1994—, Pitts. Jewish Fedn., 1994-97; dir. Jewish Family and Children's Svc., Pitts., 1995—. Mem. ABA (former vice chair workers compensation and employers liability law com., toxic and hazardous substance and environ. law com., lectr.), ATLA, Pa. Bar Assn. (former mem. coun. of worker's compensation sect., lectr., contbg. author bar assn. quarterly 1992, 93), Pa. Chamber Bus. and Industry (workers' compensation com., chmn. subcom. on legis. drafting, lectr.). Home: 820 E Beau St Washington PA 15301-2906 Office: Washington Trust Bldg Ste 200 Washington PA 15301

RICHMOND, ALICE ELENOR, lawyer; b. N.Y.C. d. Louis A. and Estelle (Muraskin) R.; m. David L. Rosenbloom, July 26, 1981; 1 child, Elizabeth Lara. BA magna cum laude, Cornell U., 1968; JD, Harvard U., 1972; student, Owners and Pres.'s Mgmt. Program Harvard U., 2001; DLH (hon.), North Adams State U., 1987. Bar: Mass. 1973, U.S. Dist. Ct. Mass. 1975, U.S. Ct. Appeals (1st cir.) 1982, U.S. Supreme Ct. 1985. Law clk. to justices Superior Ct., Boston, 1972-73; asst. dist. atty. Office of Dist. Atty., 1973-76; spl. asst. atty. gen. Office of Atty. Gen., 1975-77; asst. prof. New Eng. Sch. of Law, 1976-78; assoc. Lappin, Rosen, 1978-81; ptnr. Hemenway & Barnes, 1982-92, Deutsch, Williams, Boston, 1993-95, Richmond, Pauly & Ault, Boston, 1996—. Asst. team leader, faculty Trial Advocacy Course, 1978—82; examiner Mass. Bd. Bar Examiners, Boston, 1983—; trustee Mass. Continuing Legal Edn., Inc., Boston, 1985—96, Boston, 1998—; treas. Nat. Conf. Bar Examiners, 1995—, sec., 2001—02; v.p., bd. dirs. Am. Bar Ins., Inc., 1996—. Author (2 chpts.) Rape Crisis Intervention Handbook, 1976; contbr. articles to profl. jours. Bd. of overseers Handel & Haydn Soc., Boston, 1985-94, mem. bd. govs. Handel & Haydn Soc., 1994—, v.p., 1996—; mem. Pres. Adv. Com. on the Arts, 1995-99; mem. Boston 2000 Millenium Commn., 1997-98; sec., dir. Boston 2000, Inc., 1998-2001; mem., pres. Coun. of Cornell Women, Cornell U. Coun.; trustee Red Auerbach Youth Found., Fund for Justice and Edn.; mem. adv. bd. Cen. and Ea. European Law Initiative. Named one of Outstanding Young Leaders Boston Jaycees, 1982; Sloan Found. Urban fellow, N.Y.C., 1969 Fellow Am. Coll. Trial Lawyers; mem. ABA (ho. of dels. 1980—, vice chmn. com. on rules and calendar 1986-88, bd. govs. 2002-), Am. Law Inst., Mass. Bar Assn. (pres. 1986-87), Mass. Bar Found. (pres. 1988-91), NOW, Legal Def. and Edn. Fund (trustee 1995—, sec. 1998—), Latin Am. Legal Initiatives Coun., Internat. Judicial Acad., Harvard Club, Boston Club. Office: Richmond Pauly & Ault One Beacon St Boston MA 02108

RICHMOND, ALLEN MARTIN, speech pathologist, educator; b. N.Y.C., July 24, 1936; m. Deborah Moll (dec.). BS, SUNY, Geneseo, 1958; MEd, Pa. State U., 1961; PhD, Ohio U., 1965. Instr. N.Y. State Pub. Schs., 1958-60, Penn. Rehab. Ctr., 1960-62, Buffalo Hearing and Speech Ctr., 1969-88; clin. instr. dept. otolaryngology SUNY Med. Sch., 1980—; speech pathologist dept. otolaryngology SUNY, Buffalo, 1989—. Vis. prof. U. Md., 1968; adj. asst. prof. comm. disorders dept., 1989—; mem. staff Sisters of Charity Hosp.; advisor New Voice Club of Niagara Frontier, Buffalo, 1980—2000; cons. Bry-Lin Hosp, Buffalo, 1989—95, W.B. Saunders Co., 1988—; adj. asst. prof. SUNY, Fredonia. Contbg. author: An Atlas of Head and Neck Surgery. Participant Very Spl. Arts, Niagara, 1990—. Mem. Am. Speech-Lang.-Hearing Assn. Avocations: running, baseball, reading, travel. Home: 423 Walton Dr Cheektowaga NY 14225-1005 Office: Sisters Hosp Head and Neck Ctr 2157 Main St Buffalo NY 14214-2692

RICHMOND, ANGIE ANNA ALICE MURRAY, government official; b. Thibodaux, La., July 6, 1949; d. Edward Justin Paul and Anna Angelina (Himmler) Hebert; m. Daniel William Richmond Jr., July 24, 1993; children: Thomas Joseph Murray, Anthony Michael Murray, Daniel William Richmond III. Speedwriting cert., Sawyer Secretarial Sch., 1974. Customer svc. staff European Exch. System, Ramstein, Fed. Republic Germany, 1967-68; buyer, expeditor Thurow Electronics, Tampa, Fla., 1968-70; quotation clk. Thomas & Betts Co., Elizabeth, N.J., 1970-75; cost acct., girl Friday Fulton Shirt Co., 1975-76; office sec. Rapides Parish Police Jury, Alexandria, La., 1977-81, parish sec., 1981—; sec. Rapides Parish Stormwater Mgmt. and Drainage Dist., 1983—. Recipient Journalism award Noncommd. Officers Wives Club, 1967. Mem. Am. Soc. Notaries, Sec.-Treas. Orgn. La. (past pres.), VFW Aux. Democrat. Roman Catholic. Avocations: reading, handicrafts. Home: PO Box 187 Elmer LA 71424-0187 Office: Rapides Parish Police Jury PO Box 1150 Alexandria LA 71309-1150

RICHMOND, ANTHONY HENRY, sociologist, emeritus educator; b. Ilford, Essex, Eng., June 8, 1925; s. Henry James and Ellen Bertha (Hankin) R.; m. Freda Williams, Mar. 29, 1952; 1 dau., Glenys Catriona Richmond Troth. BSc in Econs., London Sch. Econs., 1949; MA, U. Liverpool (Eng.), 1951; PhD, U. London, 1965. Rsch. officer U. Liverpool, 1949-51; lectr. dept. social study U. Edinburgh, Scotland, 1952-63; reader in sociology Bristol (Eng.) Coll. Sci. and Tech., 1963-65; prof. sociology York U., Toronto, Ont., Can., 1965-89, prof. emeritus, sr. scholar, 1989—; dir. York U. (Inst. Behavioral Rsch.), 1979-82. Social rsch. cons.; vis. prof. Australian Nat. U., Canberra, 1971, 77, St. Antony's Coll., Oxford, Eng., 1984-85. Author: Colour Prejudice in Britain, 1954, 2d edit., 1971, The Colour Problem: A Study of Racial Relations in Britain, Africa and the West Indies, 1955, rev. edit., 1961, Post-War Immigrants in Canada, 1967, (with others) Immigrant Integration and Urban Renewal in Toronto, 1973, Migration and Race Relations in an English City, 1973, (with W. E. Kalbach) Factors in the Adjustment of Immigrants and Their Descendants, 1980, Immigration and Ethnic Conflict, 1988, Caribbean Immigrants: A Demoeconomic Analysis, 1989, Global Apartheid: Refugees, Racism and the New World Order, 1994; editor: Readings in Race and Ethnic Relations, 1972, (with D. Kubat) Internal Migration: The New World and the Third World, 1976; contbr. chpts. to books, articles to profl. jours. Recipient research grants and scholarships. Fellow Royal Soc. Can.; mem. Can. Sociology and Anthropology Assn. (Outstanding Contbrn. award 2001), Can. Population Soc. Mem. Soc. Of Friends. Avocations: classical music, photography. E-mail: richmond@yorku.ca.

RICHMOND, BRANFORD J. radiologist, educator; b. Cleve., Feb. 6, 1949; s. Robert and Lillian Richmond; m. Margaret Ann Richmond, July 10, 1970; children: Heather, Christopher, Matthew. BS in Biology, Cleve. State U., 1974, MS in Biology, 1976; MD, Case Western Res. U., 1981. Diplomate Am. Bd. Radiology (examiner). Clin. instr. U. Calif., San Francisco, 1985; clin. assoc. Cleve. Clinic, 1985, staff bone and joint radiology, 1985-88, head sect. muskuloskeletal, 1988—; assoc. prof. Ohio State U., Columbus, 1999—. Cons. Merck & Co., Inc. Co-author: Newborn Respiratory Care, 1979, Diagnostic Radiology, 1986, Lumbar Spine Surgery: Indications, Techniques, Failures, and Alternatives, 2d edit., 1988, Magnetic Resonance Imaging, 1988, Neonatal Respiratory Care, 2d edit., 1988, Helical/Spiral CT, 1994; contbr. articles to profl. jours. Mem. Internat. Soc. Clin. Densitometry (cert., mem. sci. advisor panel, mem. edn. com.), Bone Club Soc., Cleve. Radiol. Soc. Home: 1122 Forest Rd Lakewood OH 44107 Office: Cleve Clinic Found 9500 Euclid Ave Cleveland OH 44195 E-mail: richmob@ccf.org.

RICHMOND, DAVID WALKER, lawyer; b. Silver Hill, W.Va., Apr. 20, 1914; s. David Walker and Louise (Finlaw) R.; m. Gladys Evelyn Mallard, Dec. 19, 1936; children: David Walker, Nancy L. LL.B., George Washington U., 1937. Bar: D.C. 1936, Ill. 1946, Md. 1950. Partner firm Miller & Chevalier, Washington. Lectr. fed. taxation. Contbr. to profl. jours. Served from ensign to lt. comdr. USNR, 1942-46. Decorated Bronze Star; recipient Disting. Alumni Achievement award George Washington U., 1976 Fellow Am. Bar Found., Am. Coll. Tax Counsel; mem. ABA (chmn. taxation sect. 1955-57, ho. of dels. 1958-60), Am. Law Inst., Lawyers' Club of Washington, Union League (Chgo.), Masons. Republican. Methodist. Home: 7979 S Tamiami Trl Apt 359 Sarasota FL 34231-6819 Office: 655 15th St NW Washington DC 20005-5701

RICHMOND, DONNA, speech-language pathologist; b. Huntington, W.Va., Aug. 19, 1961; d. Joseph Roy and Marie (Cunningham) Wright; m. David Lawrence Richmond, Nov. 3,1990; children: Jonathan Andrew, Lydia Brooke. BA in Speech-Lang. Pathology, Marshall U., 1983, MA in Comm. Disorders, 1992; postgrad., U. Ky., 1996-98. Lic. in speech pathology, N.C., Ky.; cert. clin. competence, 1994. Speech therapist, itinerant Greenup County Bd. Edn., Greenup, Ky., 1983-84; speech pathologist Lawrence County Bd. Edn., Louisa, 1984-94; speech pathologist, floater NOVA, Gallipolis, Ohio, 1993-94; speech pathologist Boyd County Bd. Edn., Ashland, Ky., 1994-98; co-lead speech pathologist Orange County Bd. Edn., Hillsborough, N.C., 1998—. Univ. practicum supr. U. N.C., Chapel Hill. Mem. N.C. Speech-Lang. Assn., Ky. Speech-Lang. Assn., Am. Speech-Lang.-Hearing Assn., Coun. for Exceptional Children (profl.). Avocations: reading, crafts. Home: 7 Chartwell Ct Durham NC 27703-3739 Office: Central Elem 139 Hayes St Hillsborough NC 27278

RICHMOND, EERO, composer, music librarian; b. Tacoma, Jan. 5, 1938; s. Orin August and Esther Maija (Johnson) R. BA in Music, U. Wash., 1961, MLS, 1966. Music libr. N.Y.C. Pub. Libr., 1966-68, head music cataloger, 1969-80; dir. info. svcs. Am. Music Ctr., N.Y.C., 1982-93, head music cataloger, 1994-95, coord. info. svcs., 1995-99. Pianist Slavic Arts Ensemble, N.Y.C., 1985—, Inoue Chamber Ensemble, N.Y.C., 1993—. Composer musical works performed throughout U.S., Europe, South Am., Japan; contbr. articles to profl. jours. Mem. ASCAP, Internat. Soc. for Contemporary Music (v.p. 1986-90), Sibelius Soc. (v.p. 1985—), Phi Mu Alpha Sinfonia, Beta Phi Mu. Democrat. Lutheran. Avocations: travel (especially Berlin), reading. Home: 152 Kent St Brooklyn NY 11222-2142

RICHMOND, ELIZABETH LEAH, interior design and planning firm executive; b. Val D'Or, Que., Can. Aug. 16, 1951; came to U.S., 1979; d. James and Christina J. (Toscani) Dent; m. Richard E. Richmond, Dec. 18, 1971 (div. Aug. 1978); m. Terry Lee Coffin, Mar. 3, 1984. Cert. in Interior Design, Humber Coll., Toronto, Ont., Can., 1974. Space planner IMCO, Toronto, 1974-76; cons. Can. Govt., Toronto, 1976-77; designer PAJ, Toronto, 1977-79; project mgr. EPR, San Francisco, 1979-80, Dodson & Henry, San Diego, 1980-81; owner, operator Facilities Planning Assn., San Diego, 1981—; mem. exec. com. Interior Designers Can. Toronto, 1977-79. Bldg. design and interiors pub. in profl. jours. Asst. Renaissance Fair, San Diego, 1982. Mem. San Diego C. of C., Inst. Bus. Designers. Republican. Baptist. Avocations: swimming; sailing; riding; biking; reading.

RICHMOND, ERNEST LEON, research engineer, consultant; b. Catskill, N.Y., Sept. 11, 1914; s. Leon J. and Beulah B. (Garling) R.; m. Constance R. Vroom, Oct. 9, 1943. B of Mech. Engring. cum laude, Clarkson U., 1942; postgrad., N.J. Inst. Tech., 1950-60, Rutgers U., 1950-60. Registered profl. engr., N.J. Test engr. Mack Trucks, Inc., Plainfield, N.J., 1936-45; from asst chief to chief engr. Worthington Corp., Plainfield Works, 1945-58; rsch. engr. Ethicon, Inc. (div. Johnson & Johnson), Somerville, N.J., 1958-75, ret., 1975; consulting engr. Dunellen, 1975—. Seminar speaker Worthington Corp. Speakers' Bur., Plainfield, 1950-58. Author design papers; patentee in field. Vol. United Fund, Plainfield, 1940-50, Cancer Fund, Plainfield, 1940-50, Heart Fund, Plainfield, 1940-50; coach YMCA Ch. Basketball League, Plainfield, 1960-65, chmn. exec. com., 1964-65. Mem. ASME, NSPE, Am. Electroplaters and Surface Finishers Soc. Republican. Presbyterian. Avocations: civil war history, golf, working with young people. Office: PO Box 314 Dunellen NJ 08812-0314

RICHMOND, GAIL LEVIN, law educator; b. Gary, Ind., Jan. 9, 1946; d. Herbert Irving and Sylvia Esther (Given) Levin; children: Henry, Amy. AB, U. Mich., 1966, MBA, 1967; JD, Duke U., 1971. Bar: Ohio 1971, U.S. Claims Ct. 1986, U.S. Ct. Mil. Appeals, 1994; CPA, Ill. Acct. Arthur Andersen & Co., Chgo., 1967-68; assoc. Jones, Day, Cleve., 1971-72; asst. prof. Capital U. Law Sch., Columbus, Ohio, 1972-73, U. N.C. Law Sch., Chapel Hill, 1973-78; vis. asst. prof. U. Tex. Law Sch., Austin, 1977-78, Nova U. Law Ctr., Ft. Lauderdale, Fla., 1979-80, assoc. prof., 1980-81, assoc. prof., assoc. dean, 1981-85, prof., assoc. dean., 1985-93, 95—, prof., acting dean, 1993-95. Author: Federal Tax Research, 6th edit., 2002; co-author: Tax Planning for Lifetime and Testamentary Dispositions, 1997; contbr. articles to profl. jours. Pres. Greater Ft. Lauderdale Tax Coun., 1987-88; chair audit com. Assn. Am. Law Schs., 1992; trustee Law Sch. Admission Coun., 1994-99, chair audit com., 1991-93, chair svcs. and programs com., 1997-99. Mem. ABA (chair commn. on individual income, tax sect. 2001-03), Am. Assn. Atty.-CPAs (dir. Fla. chpt. 1992-98), Assn. Am. Law Schs. (mem. audit com. 1990-92, chair sect. adminstrn. of law schs. 1996, pres. S.E. chpt. 1993-94, 2002-03, sec. S.E. chpt. 1995-2002), Broward County Women Lawyers Assn. Democrat. Jewish. Avocation: reading. Office: Nova Southeastern U Shepard Broad Law Ctr 3305 College Ave Fort Lauderdale FL 33314-7721

RICHMOND, HAROLD NICHOLAS, lawyer; b. Elizabeth, N.J., Apr. 5, 1935; s. Benjamin I. and Eleanor (Turbowitz) R.; m. Elaine Zemel, June 16, 1957 (div. Nov. 1972); children: Bonnie J. Ross, Michele Weinfeld; m. Marilyn A. Wenrich, Aug. 26, 1973; children: Eric L., Kacy L. BA, Tulane U., 1957; LLB, NYU, 1961, LLM in Taxation, 1965. Estate tax examiner IRS, Newark, 1963-65; tax mgr. Puder & Puder/Touche Ross & Co., CPAs, 1965-73; ptnr. Sodowick Richmond & Crecca, 1973-84; prin. Harold N. Richmond, West Orange, N.J., 1984-86; ptnr. Wallerstein Hauptman & Richmond, 1986-91, Hauptman & Richmond, West Orange, 1992—. With U.S. Army, 1959-60. Mem. ABA (tax sect. closely held bus. com., real property and probate sect.), N.J. Bar Assn. (tax, real property and probate sects.), Essex County Bar Assn. (chmn. tax com. 1989, real property and probate sect.). Avocations: running, tennis. Office: Hauptman & Richmond 100 Executive Dr Ste 330 West Orange NJ 07052-3309

RICHMOND, JAMES ELLIS, retired restaurant company executive; b. Chgo., Feb. 16, 1938; s. Kenneth E. and Irene M. (Anderson) R.; m. Karen Ann Ryder, Oct. 6, 1956; children: Scott, Brian, Ann, Susan. BBA, Case Western Res. U., 1960. CPA, Ohio. Sr. auditor Ernst & Ernst, Cleve., 1960-64; treas. Cook United, Inc., 1964-75, Fairmont Foods Co., Houston, 1975-80, v.p. ops., 1980-82; v.p., treas. U-tote-M, Inc., 1982-84; mktg. exec. Circle K Convenience Stores, 1984-86; v.p. Consol. Products, Inc., Indpls., 1986-2000; ret. Lutheran. Home: 331 Wild Turkey Blvd Boerne TX 78006- E-mail: jrichm5540@aol.com.

RICHMOND, JONATHAN Y. public health administration officer; b. Norwalk, Conn., Feb. 10, 1941; BA in Zoology, U. Conn., 1962, MS in Genetics, 1964; PhD in Genetics, Hahnemann U., 1967. Post-doctoral resident rsch. fellow Plum Island Animal Disease Ctr., Greenport, N.Y., 1967-69; rsch. microbiologist Plum Island Animal Disease Ctr., USDA, ARS, 1969-79; biol. safety officer Plum Island Animal Disease Ctr., USDA, 1979-83; chief safety ops. sect. Occupl. Safety and Health br., Divsn. Safety NIH, Bethesda, Md., 1983-90; dir. WHO Collaborating Ctr. Applied Biosafety and Tng., Ctrs. for Disease Control, Atlanta, 1990—, Office Health and Safety, Ctrs. for Disease Control and Prevention, Atlanta, 1990—. Mem. planning com. ann. NIH Rsch. Safety Symposia, 1983—84, 1988; chairperson Ctrs. for Disease Control Nat. Symposium on Biosafety, 1992, 94, 96, 98, 2000, 02; coord. Pub. Health Merit Badge Sem., 1993, 95; internat. cons. lab. desing project, San Juan, PR, 1993—; internat. cons. Project RETRO-CI, Abidjan, Ivory Coast, Africa, 1994—, Kemri, Kenya, 1996—, Plasma-derived Hepatitis B Vaccine Project, Bulandshar, Uttar Pradesh, India, 1994, Viral Diagnostic Lab., Toronto, 1995. Editor: Biosafety in Microbiological and Biomedical Laboratories, 4th edit., 1999, Primary Containment of Biohazards: Selection and Use of Biological Safety Cabinets, 2d edit., 2001, Designing a Modern Microbiol./Biomed. Lab., 1998, Anthology of Biosafety Vols. I, II, III, IV, V; contbr. articles to profl. jours. Fellow: Am. Acad. Microbiology; mem.: Am. Soc. Microbiology (coord. biosafety workshops 1986—, mem. lab. safety com. 1993—), Am. Biol. Safety Assn. (steering com. 1979—81, pres. 1986—87, exec. coun. 1985—88, ann. cong. chairperson 1988, pres. Chesapeake Area chpt. 1989—90, Everett Hanal Jr. Meml. award 1995, Arnold G. Wedum Disting. Achievement award 1999). Office: Office of Health & Safety CDC & Prevention Bldg 14 Rm 126 1600 Clifton Rd NE Atlanta GA 30329-4018

RICHMOND, JULIUS BENJAMIN, retired physician, health policy educator emeritus; b. Chgo., Sept. 26, 1916; s. Jacob and Anna (Dayno) Richmond; m. Rhee Chidekel, June 3, 1937 (dec. Oct. 9, 1985); children: Barry J., Charles Allen; m. Jean Rabow, Jan. 11, 1987; 1 child Dale Keith (dec.). BS, U. Ill., 1937, MS, MD, 1939; DSc (hon.) , Ind. U., 1978, Rush-Presbyn.-St. Luke Med. Ctr., 1978, U. Ill., 1979, Georgetown U., 1980, SUNY, Syracuse, 1986, U. Ariz., 1991; DMS (hon.) , Med. Coll. Pa., 1980; D in Pub. Svc. (hon.) , Nat. Coll. Edn., Evanston, Ill., 1980; DHL (hon.) , Tufts U., 1986; DMS (hon.) , Yale U., 1999; DEd (hon.) , Wheelock Coll., 2000, Harvard U., 2002. Intern Cook County Hosp., Chgo., 1939—41, resident, 1941—42, 1946, Mcpl. Contagious Disease Hosp., Chgo., 1941; faculty U. Ill. Med. Sch., 1946—53, prof. pediat., 1950—53; dir. Inst. Juvenile Rsch., 1952—53; prof., chmn. dept. pediatrics Coll. Medicine, SUNY at Syracuse, 1953—65, dean med. faculty, chmn. dept. pediatrics, 1965—70; prof. child psychiatry and human devel., prof., chmn. dept. preventive and social medicine Harvard Med. Sch., 1971—77, prof. health policy, 1981—88, dir. divsn. health policy rsch. and edn., 1983—88, prof. health policy emeritus, 1988—; also faculty Harvard Sch. Pub. Health. Psychiatrist-in-chief Children's Hosp. Med. Ctr., Boston, 1971—77, adv. on child health policy, 1981—; dir. Judge Baker Children's Ctr., Boston, 1971—77; asst. sec. health and surgeon gen. HHS, 1977—81; mem. Pres.'s Commn. on Mental Health, 1977. Author: Pediatric Diagnosis, 1962, Currents in American Medicine, 1969. Nat. dir. Project Head Start; dir. Office Health Affairs, OEO, 1965—66. Flight surgeon U.S. Army Air Force, 1942—46. Recipient Agnes Bruce Greig Sch. award, 1966, Parents Mag. award, 1966, Disting. Svc. award, Office Econ. Opportunity, 1967, Family Health Mag. award, 1977, Myrdal award, Assn. for Evaluation Rsch., 1977, award for disting. sci. contbn., Soc. for Rsch. in Child Devel., 1979, Dolly Madison award, Inst. on Clin. Infants Programs, 1979, Pub. Health Disting. Svc. award, HEW, 1980, Illini Achievement award, U. Ill. Alumni Assn., 1982, Cmty. Svc. awrad, Health Planning Coun. Greater Boston, 1985, Lemuel Shattuck award, Mass. Pub. Health Assn., 1985, 1st Ann. Ronald McDonald Children's Charities award for Outstanding Contbns. to Child Health and Welfare, 1986, David E. Rogers award, Assn. Am. Med. Colls., 1997, A.L. Ellis award, Children's Home Soc. Fla., 1997, John Stearns award, N.Y. Acad. Medicine, 1999. Fellow: Am. Psychiat. Assn. (disting.), Am. Orthopsychiat. Assn. (Ittleson award 1994); mem.: APHA (Martha May Eliot award 1970, Sedgwick medal 1992), AMA (AMA-ERF award in health edn. 1988), Am. Psychosomatic Soc., Soc. Pediatric Rsch., Am. Acad. Child Psychiatry (hon.), New Eng. Coun. Child Psychiatry (assoc.), Am. Acad. Pediat. (C. Anderson Aldrich award 1966, ann. award sect. on cmty. pediat. 1977, Outstanding Contbn. award sect. cmty. pediat. 1978, Job Lewis Smith award 2000), Am. Pediatric Soc. (John Howland award 1990), Inst. Medicine of NAS (1st ann. Gustav O. Lienhard award 1986, McDermott medal 2022), Phi Eta Sigma, Alpha Omega Alpha, Sigma Xi.

RICHMOND, MARDELL C. family nurse practitioner; b. San Francisco, Feb. 7, 1951; d. Ian Ferguson and Louise Eleanor (Kohler) Hardie. BSN, Dominican Coll., 1987; MSN, Seattle Pacific U., 1993. Nurse Wilcox Hosp., Lihue, Hawaii, 1987-88, Merritt Hosp., Oakland, Calif., 1988-89, Mt. Diablo Hosp., Concord, 1988-89, Auburn (Wash.) Gen. Hosp., 1989-90, Port Angeles (Wash.) Clinic, 1990-97; family nurse practitioner Clinicare, Port Angeles, 1997—2001; family nurse practitioner, emergency dept. Olympic Med. Ctr., 2001—. Mem. Sigma Theta Tau. Avocations: hiking, gardening, astronomy. Home: PO Box 1772 Port Angeles WA 98362-0093

RICHMOND, MARILYN SUSAN, lawyer; b. Bethesda, Md., Oct. 19, 1949; d. Carl Hutchins Jr. and Elizabeth Adeline (Saeger) R. BA with honors, U. Fla., 1971; JD, Georgetown U., 1974. Bar: Md. 1974, D.C. 1975. Atty. Office of Gen. Counsel, FTC, Washington, 1974-77, antitrust atty. Bur. of Competition, 1977-81; counsel, consumer subcom. of com. on commerce, sci. and transp. U.S. Senate, 1981-85; assoc. Heron, Burchette, Ruckert & Rothwell, 1985-87, ptnr., 1987-90; dep. asst. sec. for govtl. affairs U.S. Dept. Transp., 1990-91, acting asst. sec. for govtl. affairs, 1991-92; cons. Raffaelli, Spees, Springer & Smith, 1993-94; asst. exec. dir. govt. rels. APA Practice Orgn., 1995—. Lectr. Brookings Instn. Ctr. for Pub. Policy Edn., Washington, 1985-88. Active Lawyers for Bush-Quayle, Washington, 1988. Mem. ABA (antitrust, adminstrv. law sect., vice chair transp. industry com. antitrust sect. 1992-99). Republican. Methodist. Avocations: horseback riding, tennis. Home: Apt 601 2725 Connecticut Ave NW Washington DC 20008-5305

RICHMOND, MITCHELL JAMES, professional basketball player; b. Ft. Lauderdale, Fla., June 30, 1965; M. Juli Richmond; children: Phillip Mitchell, Jerin Mikell. Bachelor in Social Sci., Kansas State U., 1988. Guard Golden State Warriors, 1988-91, Sacramento Kings, 1991-98, Washington Wizards, Washington DC, 1998—2001; player L.A. Lakers, El Segundo, Calif., 2002—. Hon. bd. dirs. NCPCA (Spl. Friend award); established Solid As A Rock Scholarship Found., Ft. Lauderdale, 1992. Selected Rookie of the Yr., 1989, Rookie of the Month 3 times, Dec., Jan., March; named NBA Player of the Week, Mar. 25, 1991; selected to NBA All-Star Team, 1993, 94, 95. Avocations: bowling, video games. Office: 555 N Nash St El Segundo CA 90245*

RICHMOND, RAY S(AM), journalist; b. Whittier, Calif., Oct. 19, 1957; s. Henry and Terri C. (Epstein) R.; m. Beth Lyn Trachman, Oct. 2, 1983 (div. Feb. 1993); children: Joshua Adam, Gabrielle Reneé; m. Heidi Merle Lieberman, May 28, 1994; 1 child, Dylan Jake. B, Calif. State U., Northridge, 1980. Feature writer L.A. Daily News, Woodland Hills, Calif., 1978-85; segment prodr. Merv Griffin Show, Hollywood, 1985-86; television writer L.A. Herald Examiner, 1986-87; television critic Orange County Reigster, Santa Ana, Calif., 1987-92, L.A. Daily News, 1992-96; television reporter Daily Variety, L.A., 1996—. Co-author: Unofficial Olympic Guide, 1984; editor: The Simpsons: A Complete Guide to our Favorite Family, 1997. Vol. AIDS Project L.A., 1993-94. Mem. Television Critics Assn. Democrat. Jewish. Avocations: exercise, reading, family, television, travel. Home: 1010 Hammond St Apt 302 West Hollywood CA 90069-3851 Office: Daily Variety 5700 Wilshire Blvd Ste 120 Los Angeles CA 90036-5804

RICHMOND, RICHARD THOMAS, journalist; b. Parma, Ohio, May 16, 1933; s. Arthur James and Frances Marie (Visosky) R.; m. Charlotte Jean Schwoebel, Dec. 19, 1933; children: Kris Elaine, Leigh Alison, Paul Evan. AB, Washington U., St. Louis, 1961. Bur. mgr. UPI News Pictures, St. Louis, 1957-62; from asst. picture editor to editor color sect. Post-Dispatch, 1962-80, columnist Clayton, 1971—2001, editor calendar sect. St. Louis, 1983-94, asst. entertainment editor, 1995-96, prodn. coord. Get Out Mag., 1996-2000; v.p. Golden Royal Enterprises, 1976-78; pres. Oroquest Press, 1977-80; dir. U.S. Mortgage & Investment Corp., Hilton Head Island, N.C., 1977-81; pres. Magalar Mining, Texarkana, Ark., 1979-83. Co-author: Treasure Under Your Feet, 1974, In the Wake of the Golden Galleons, 1976, Diabetes: The Facts That Will Let You Regain Control of Your Life, 1986; editor: You Can Be Rich By Thursday, 1997, Male Homemaker's Handbook, 1997. Avocation: undersea treasure hunting. Home: 307 Lebanon Ave Belleville IL 62220-4126

RICHMOND, ROCSAN, television and video producer, director, publicist, actress, inventor, teacher; b. Chgo., Jan. 30; d. Alphonso and Annie Lou (Combest) R.; divorced; 1 child, Tina S. Student, Wilson Jr. Coll., 1963, 2d City Theatre, Chgo., 1969, Alice Liddel Theatre, 1970; cert. fingerprint classifier, L.A. City Coll., 1996. Lic. 3d class radio/tel. operator FCC. Vegetarian editor Aware mag., Chgo., 1977-78; investigative reporter, film critic Chgo. Metro News, 1975-81; prodr., talk show host Sta. WSSD, Chgo., 1980-81; dir. pub. rels. IRMCO Corp., 1981-82; pub. rels. agt., newsletter editor Hollywood (Calif.) Reporter newspaper, 1985-86; exec. producer Donald Descendent's Prodns., Hollywood, 1983—; exec. prodr. Future News, TV show, 1983-86; pres. Richmond Estates; tchr. TV prodn. Profl. Bus. Acad., Hollywood, 1998—. Founder, dir. Richmond Acad. Etiquette, 2000—; fingerprint identification classifier. Inventor invisible drapery tieback. Jehovah'S Witness. Office: PO Box 665 Los Angeles CA 90078-0665 E-mail: rocsanr@yahoo.com.

RICHMOND, RONALD LEROY, aerospace engineer; b. L.A., Aug. 16, 1931; s. William Paul and Martha Emelia (Anderson) R.; m. Mary Louise Gates, Jan. 2, 1955; children: Pandora Deanne Richmond Perry, Steven Lee. BSME, U. Calif., Berkeley, 1952; MS in Aero. Engring., Calif. Inst. Tech., 1953, PhD in Aero. Engring., 1957. Aerodynamicist Lockheed Aircraft Co., Burbank, Calif., 1952-54; teaching/rsch. asst. Calif. Inst. Tech., Pasadena, 1952-57; asst. group leader aero. performance Douglas Aircraft Co., Long Beach, Calif., 1957-59; chief engr. adv. devel. Ford Aerospace, Newport Beach, 1959-87; adj. assoc. prof. Sch. Engring., U. Calif., Irvine, 1987-88; dir. engring. Brunswick Def., Costa Mesa, Calif., 1988-94. Aerodynamics cons. Douglas Aircraft, 1956-57, Shelby-Am. (Ford) Auto., L.A., 1960-62; subgroup leader NATO Indsl. Adv. Group #16, Brussels, Belgium, 1984-86. Res. dep. Orange County Sheriff's Dept., 1976—. Calif. Inst. Tech. Rsch. assistantship, 1953, 54, 55, 56, 57, teaching asst., 1955, 56, 57, grantee, 1955, 56, 57. Assoc. fellow AIAA (Orange County sect. chmn. 1989-90); mem. Western States Assn. Sheriff's Air squadrons (comdr. 1987-88), Skylarks of So. Calif. (pres., chmn. bd. 1987-88). Republican. Achievements include experimentally proved that skin friction force on long, slender cylinders was several times that on flat plates, at Mach 5.8 for both laminar and turbulent boundary layers. Home: 1307 Seacrest Dr Corona Del Mar CA 92625-1227

RICHMOND, ROSALIND, clinical social worker; b. Boston, May 18, 1938; d. Leonard J. and Esther (Greenberg) R. BS, MS, Simmons Coll. Clin. social worker MGH, Boston, 1962-65, VA Hosp., Livermore, Calif., 1966-67, San Francisco, 1967—. Lic. examiner Bd. Behavioral Scis., Sacramento, 1982; chmn. patient edn. com. San Francisco Hosp., 1983-87, social work student supr. psychiat. emergency room; co-organizer psychiatric AIDS program, 1989—; co-leader substance abuse AIDS group, 1995. Recipient Dir's. Commendation, San Francisco Hosp., 1982, 83, 85, 91. Mem. Nat. Assn. Social Workers (cert.), Simmons Coll. Alumnae Assn. (v.p. 1972-73, pres. 1973-74). Democrat. Jewish. Home: 1 Summerhill Way San Rafael CA 94903-3813 Office: VA Med Ctr 4150 Clement St San Francisco CA 94121-1598

RICHMOND, SAMUEL BERNARD, management educator; b. Boston, Oct. 14, 1919; s. David E. and Freda (Braman) R.; m. Evelyn Ruth Kravitz, Nov. 26, 1944; children: Phyllis Gail, Douglas Emerson, Clifford Owen. AB cum laude, Harvard U., 1940; MBA, Columbia U., 1948, PhD, 1951. Mem. faculty Columbia U., 1946-76, assoc. prof., 1957-60, prof. econ. and statistics, 1960-76; assoc. dean Grad. Sch. Bus. Columbia U., 1971-72, acting dean, 1972-73; dean prof. mgmt. Owen Grad. Sch. Mgmt. Vanderbilt U., Nashville, 1976-86, Ralph Owen prof. mgmt., 1984-88, Ralph Owen prof. mgmt. emeritus, dean emeritus, 1988—, adj. prof., 1988-96. Vis. prof. U. Sherbrooke, Que., 1967, U. Buenos Aires, Argentina, 1964, 65, Case Inst. Tech., Cleve., 1958-59, Fordham U., N.Y.C., 1952-53; dir. IMS Internat. Inc., N.Y.C., 1978-88, 1st Am. Corp., Nashville, 1981-86, Winners Corp., Nashville, 1983-89, Corbin Ltd., N.Y.C., 1970-85, Ingram Industries Inc., Nashville, 1981-92; cons. to maj. comml., ednl., profl. and govtl. orgns. Author: Operations Research for Management Decisions, 1968, Statistical Analysis, 1957, 2d edit., 1964, 3d edit., 1997, Regulation and Competition in Air Transportation, 1961; talk show host Nashville Bus. Edit., WDCN-TV, 1984-86. Trustee Ramapo Coll., N.J., 1975-76; bd. dirs. Jewish Fedn. Nashville and Middle Tenn., Temple Ohabai Shalom, Nashville; trustee Endowment Fund Jewish Fedn. Nashville and Middle Tenn. 1st lt. USAAF, 1943-45. Recipient Honor award CAB, 1971, Alumni award for outstanding svc. Grad. Sch. Bus., Columbia U., 1973 Mem. Am. Statis. Assn. (chmn. adv. com. rsch. to CAB 1966-74, dir. 1965-67), Am. Econ. Assn., Inst. Mgmt. Sci., Ops. Rsch. Soc. Am., Beta Gamma Sigma. Home: 5404 Camelot Rd Brentwood TN 37027-4113 Office: Vanderbilt U Owen Grad Sch Mgmt Nashville TN 37203 E-mail: samuel.b.richmond@vanderbilt.edu.

RICHSTONE, BEVERLY JUNE, psychologist, writer; b. N.Y.C., N.Y., June 8, 1952; d. Max and Rosalyn Richstone. BA summa cum laude, Queens Coll., 1975; MEd, U. Miami, 1978; PsyD, Nova U., 1982. Lic. clin. psychologist. Clin. fellow Harvard Med. Sch., 1982-83; staff psychologist Met. State Hosp., Waltham, Mass., 1983-85; asst. attending psychologist McLean Hosp., Belmont, 1983-84; asst. psychologist Cambridge Hosp./N. Charles Mental Health Rsch./Tng. Found., Cambridge, 1984-85; assoc. dir. Coastal Geriatric Svcs., Hingham, 1985-86, Alpha Geriatric Svcs., Hingham, 1986-87; freelance writer Hudson, Mass. Instr. psychology Harvard Med. Sch., Boston, 1983-84; consulting psychologist Coastal Geriatric Svcs., Hingham, 1985. Author: From Harvard to Humility, 2000; contbg. author: The New Our Bodies, Ourselves, 1992, Our Bodies, Ourselves For The New Century, 1998. Cmty. advisor Mass. Office Disability, Boston, 1992—. Mem. APA, Phi Beta Kappa.

RICHT, JUERGEN ALBRECHT, veterinarian; b. Pforzheim, Germany, Nov. 15, 1958; s. Albrecht Johannes and Rosemarie Johanna (Zundel) R.; m. Cheryl Lynn Johnson, Dec. 29, 1992; children: Elisabeth Marie, Alexander Richard William, Christopher Johannes. BS in Agr., U. Hohenheim, Stuttgart, Germany, 1980; DVM, U. Munich, Germany, 1985; PhD in Immunology/Virology, U. Giessen, Germany, 1988. Fellow Deutsche Forschungsgemeinschaft Johns Hopkins U., Balt., 1989-91; project leader German Rsch. Found., Giessen, Hessen, Germany, 1991-93, Justus-Liebig U./German Rsch. Found., Giessen, 1993-2001; vet. med. officer NADC-ARS-USDA, Ames, Iowa, 2001—. Contbr. articles to profl. jours.; patentee in field. Recipient Förderpreis der DGHM Deutschen Gesellschaft Hygiene and Microbiology, 1992, Franz Vogt Preis Justus-Liebig U., Giessen, 1993. Mem. AAAS, Am. Soc. Virology, Gesellschaft Virologie. Avocations: music (vocal, piano), concerts, travel, skiing. Office: Nat Animal Disease Ctr 2300 Dayton Ave Ames IA 50010

RICHTER, BURTON, physicist; b. N.Y.C., Mar. 22, 1931; s. Abraham and Fanny (Pollack) Richter; m. Laurose Becker, July 1, 1960; children: Elizabeth, Matthew. BS, MIT, 1952, PhD, 1956. Research assoc. Stanford U., 1956—60, asst. prof. physics, 1960—63, assoc. prof., 1963—67, prof., 1967—, Paul Pigott prof. phys. sci., 1980—, tech. dir. Linear Accelerator Ctr., 1982—84, dir. Linear Accelerator Ctr., 1984—99; dir. emeritus, 1999—. Cons. NSF; sec. Energy Adv. Bd.; bd. dirs. Varian Med. Systems, Litel Instruments; Loeb lectr. Harvard U., 1974; DeShalit lectr. Weizmann Inst., 1975; pres. Internat. Union of Pure and Applied Physics, 1997. Contbr. over 300 articles to profl. publs. Recipient E.O. Lawrence medal, Dept. Energy, 1976, Nobel prize in Physics, 1976. Fellow: AAAS, Am. Phys. Soc. (pres. 1994); mem.: NAS, 1977, Am. Acad. Arts and Scis.(fellow, 1989). Achievements include research in elementary particle physics. Office: Stanford Linear Accel Ctr Mail Stop 80 Stanford CA 94305*

RICHTER, DONALD PAUL, lawyer; b. New Britain, Conn., Feb. 15, 1924; s. Paul John and Helen (Racoske) R.; m. Jane Frances Gumpright, Aug. 10, 1946; children: Christopher Dean, Cynthia Louise. AB, Bates Coll., 1947; LL.B., Yale U., 1950. Bar: N.Y. 1951, Conn. 1953. Assoc. Winthrop, Stimson, Putnam & Roberts, N.Y.C., 1950-52; ptnr. Murtha, Cullina, Richter and Pinney, Hartford, Conn., 1954-94; counsel Murtha Cullina LLP, 1994—. Trustee Bates Coll., 1962-94, Manchester (Conn.) Meml. Hosp., 1963-94, Hartford Sem., 1973-85; trustee Suffield Acad., 1974—, pres., 1982-89; bd. dirs. Met. YMCA Greater Hartford, 1970-94, pres., 1976-81, trustee, 1994—; mem. nat. coun. YMCA, 1978-82; bd. dirs. Church Homes, 1967-81; trustee, v.p., Silver Bay Assn., 1971-96. With USNR, 1943-46. Fellow Am. Coll. Trust and Estate Counsel; mem. ABA, Conn. Bar Assn., Univ. Club, Hartford Club, 20th Century Club, Rotary (Paul Harris fellow 1996), Phi Beta Kappa, Delta Sigma Rho. Congregationalist. Home: 140 Boulder Rd Manchester CT 06040-4508 Office: Murtha Cullina LLP City Place I 185 Asylum St & 29th St Hartford CT 06103-3469

RICHTER, HARVENA, retired english literature and creative writing teacher, writer; b. Reading, Pa., Mar. 13, 1919; d. Conrad Michael and Harvena Maria (Achenbach) R. BA, U. N.Mex., 1938; MA, NYU, 1955, PhD, 1967. Advt. copyrighter Saks 5th Ave., N.Y.C., 1942-43, R.H. Macy, N.Y.C., 1944-46; copy chief Elizabeth Arden, 1946-47; advt. dir. I. Miller, 1947-48; European corr. various newspapers, 1948-49; lectr. NYU, N.Y.C., 1952-66, U. N.Mex., 1969-89. Author: The Human Shore, 1959, Virginai Woolf: The Inward Voyage, 1970, Virginia Woolf: The Inward Voyage, 1970, Writing to Survive: The Private Notebooks of Conrad Richter, 1988, The Yaddo Elegies and Other Poems, 1995, Green Girls, Poems Early and Late, 1996, The Innocent Island, 1999, The Golden Fountains, 2001, Frozen Light, the Crystal Poems, 2002, The Golden Fountains, Sources of Energy and Life, 2002; contbr. poetry to The New Yorker, Chelsea, New Letters, others; short stories to Sat. Eve. Post, New Am., Blue Mesa Rev.; essays to Atlantic, Modern Fiction Studies, U.S. Monitor, others. AAUW fellow, 1964-65; grantee Yaddo, 1963-64, MacDowell Colony, 1965-66, Wurlitzer Found., Taos, N.Mex., 1968, 73-75, Va. Ctr. for Creative Arts, 1983, 85, Ragdale Found., 1990.. Mem. Author's Guild, Virginia Woolf Soc., Kappa Kappa Gamma. Avocation: gardening. Home and Office: 1932 Candelaria Rd NW Albuquerque NM 87107

RICHTER, HENRY ANDREW, electrical engineer; b. Lancaster, Mass., Dec. 27, 1930; s. Benjamin David and Agnes Ellis (Kilgour) R. Cert., Franklin Tech. Inst., 1953; AEE, Worcester Jr. Coll., 1957. Technician Gen. Electric Co., Lynn, Mass., 1957-58; asst. engr. Raytheon Co., Wayland, 1958-63, assoc. engr. Waltham, 1963-69, engr., 1969—. Pres. Lancaster Social Svc. Assn., 1977—; chmn. Lancaster Bd. Selectmen, 1984-90; treas. Town of Lancaster, 1993—; sustaining mem. Rep. Nat. Com., 1987—; trustee Clinton Hosp. Assn., 1986-90; bd. dirs. Clinton Home for Aged People, 1983—. Served with U.S. Army, 1953-55. Mem. Am. Legion (color guard 1983—, comdr. post 96 2000—). Congregationalist. Avocations: working with youths, boating, horticulture, reading, current events. Home: Neck Rd Lancaster MA 01523-2235

RICHTER, LISA SHERRILL, lawyer; b. Moon Twp., Pa., Aug. 3, 1969; d. Larrymore and Kay Johnson Sherrill; m. Timothy J. Richter, Oct. 17, 1998. BA with honors, U. Tenn., 1990, JD, 1994. Bar: Tenn. 1994, U.S. Dist. Ct. (mid. dist.) Tenn. 1995. Assoc. Larry D. Wilks, Springfield, Tenn., 1994—. Named Bus. Woman of the Yr., Robertson County Career Women, 2000. Mem. Tenn. Bar Assn. (bd. dirs. young lawyers div. 1994—), Robertson County Bar Assn. (pres. 2000—). Democrat. Methodist. Avocation: football. Office: Larry D Wilks Law Office 509 W Court Sq Springfield TN 37172-2413

RICHTER, MICHAEL THOMAS, professional hockey player; b. Phila., Sept. 22, 1966; Student, U. Wisconsin. With N.Y. Rangers, 1985—. Goalie U.S. Nat. Team, 1987-88, U.S. Olympic Team, 1987-88. Recipient WCHA Rookie of the Yr. award, 1985-86; named MVP, All-Star Game, 1994. Played in NHL All-Star Game, 1992-93, Stanley Cup Championship, 1994. Office: NY Rangers 2 Penn Plz New York NY 10121-0101*

RICHTER, PETER CHRISTIAN, lawyer; b. Opava, Czechoslovakia, June 13, 1944; came to U.S., 1951; s. Hanus and Alzbeta (Kindlarova) R.; m. Leslie Diane Rousseau, Nov. 25, 1967; children: Timothy Jason, Lindsey Berta. BS, U. Oreg., 1967, JD, 1971. Bar: Oreg. 1971, U.S. Dist. Ct. 1972, U.S. Ct. Appeals (9th cir.) 1972, U.S. Supreme Ct. 1983. Assoc. Veatch, Lovett & Stiner, Portland, Oreg., 1971-73; ptnr. Miller Nash LLP, 1978—. Adj. prof. law trial advocacy Northwestern Sch. of Law, Lewis and Clark Coll., Portland, 1986—; pro tempore judge Multnomah County Cir. Ct., Portland, 1985—. Oreg. State Bar Trial Advocacy Seminars, 1988—; trial advocacy coll. planner, instr. Oreg. State Bar, 1998—. Author: (handbook) Oregon State Bar, 1987, 88, 89; co-author: (chpt. in book) Oregon State Bar Damage Manual, 1985, 90; editor, program planner Sales: The Oregon Experience, 1989. Trustee, bd. dirs. Parry Ctr. for Children, Portland, 1990; former bd. dir. Boy Scouts of Am., Columbia Pacific Coun., Portland, Nat. Conf. Christians and Jews, Portland, 1983; bd. advisers Pacific Crest Outward Bound, 2000. With Oreg. Army N.G., 1967-75. Recipient Cert. of Appreciation Northwestern Sch. of Law, 1990; named one of ten Best Litigators in Oreg, Nat. Bar Jour. Fellow Am. Bar Found.; mem. ABA (trial techniques com.), Fed. Bar Assn. (Oreg. chpt.), Am. Bd. Trial Advocates (advocate), Internat. Assn. of Def. Counsel, Oreg. Bar Assn. (lectr. trial advocacy seminars 1988—, mem. jud. adminstn. com, bus. lit. sec. exec. comm.), Multnomah Bar Assn. (former bd dirs.), Oreg. Assn. Def. Counsel (cert. of appreciation 1987, 89) Inns of Ct., Multnomah Athletic Club (trustee, pres.), Arlington Club. Avocations: squash, tennis, skiing, golf, reading, motorcycling riding. Office: Miller Nash LLP 111 SW 5th Ave Ste 3500 Portland OR 97204-3699 E-mail: richter@millernash.com.

RICHTER, RICHARD PAUL, academic administrator; b. Bryn Mawr, Pa., Mar. 6, 1931; s. Manuel DeWitt and Emma Margaret (Theilacker) R.; m. Margot Denithorne, Sept. 5, 1953; children: Karen Lee, Kurt Richard. BA, Ursinus Coll., 1953, LLD (hon.), 1976; MA, U. Pa., 1957; cert., Inst. Ednl. Mgmt., Harvard U., 1974; DHL (hon.), Tohoku Gakuin U., Sendai, Japan, 1986, Muhlenberg Coll., 1989. Editor Provident Mut. Life Ins. Co., Phila., 1956-58; supr. employee communications Phila. Gas Works divsn. UGI Corp., 1958-65; alumni dir. Ursinus Coll., Collegeville, Pa., 1965-67, asst. to pres., 1967-69, v.p. adminstrv. affairs, 1969-76, pres., 1976-94; pres. emeritus, 1995—; instr. in English Ursinus Coll., Collegeville, Pa., 1965-73, asst. prof. English, 1973-86, prof. of coll. Collegeville, 1986-94. Chmn. Commn. for Ind. Colls. and U. Pa., 1984, Found. for Ind. Colls. of Pa., Harrisburg, 1985; past chmn. Coun. for Higher Edn. United Ch. of Christ. Contbr. articles, poems to various publs. Recipient Gold Quill award Am. Assn. Indsl. Editors, 1964, Lindback award for excellence in tchg. Ursinus Coll., 1973, Silver Beaver award Boy Scouts Am., 1985, Muhlenberg Leadership award Hist. Soc. Trappe, Pa., 1994, Francis J. Michelini award for outstanding svc. Assn. Ind. Colls. and Univs. of Pa., 1996, Arthur V. Ciervo award Coll. and Univ. Pub. Rels. Assn. of Pa., 1996. Mem. Pa. Assn. Colls. and Univs. (bd. dirs.), Phi Beta Kappa. Home: 236 6th Ave Collegeville PA 19426-2510 Office: Ursinus Coll PO Box 1000 Collegeville PA 19426-1000 E-mail: rrichter@ursinus.edu.

RICHTER, TOBIN MARAIS, lawyer; b. Washington, Dec. 31, 1944; s. Vivian Craig and Leora Chapelle (Aultman) R.; m. Elizabeth Mills Dunlop, July 11, 1970; children: Ian, Lauren. B in City Planning, U. Va., 1967, JD, 1973. Bar: Ill. 1973, U.S. Dist. Ct. (no. dist.) Ill. 1973, U.S. Ct. Fed. Claims, 1976, U.S. Ct. Appeals (7th cir.) 1977, U.S. Supreme Ct. 1979, U.S. Dist. Ct. (ea. dist.) Wis. 1987. Assoc. Ross & Hardies, Chgo., 1973-80, ptnr., 1981-84, Spindell, Kemp & Kimball, Chgo., 1984-89; pvt. practice, 1989—. Adj. instr. U. Wis., Osh Kosh, 1976; ct. apptd. arbitrator Cir. Ct. Cook County, 1991—; chancellor Seabury-Western Theol. Sem., 1998-2001. Co-author: Federal Land Use Regulation, 1977; contbr. articles to profl. jours. Legal counsel 44th Ward Community Zoning Bd., Chgo., 1980; v.p., Aux. Bd. Chgo. Architecture Found., 1983; pres., bd. dirs. Landmarks Preservation Council Ill., Chgo., 1986; v.p., bd. dirs. Counseling Ctr. of Lakeview, 1997—. 1st lt. U.S. Army, 1968-70, Vietnam. Mem. ABA, Chgo. Bar Assn., Soc. Am. Mil. Engrs. (v.p. 1980, 84, 86), Econ. Club (Chgo.). Avocations: tennis, pottery, genealogy. Office: 53 W Jackson Blvd Ste 560 Chicago IL 60604-3667 E-mail: tmrichter@corecomm.net.

RICHTER, WILLIAM, JR. technical management consulting executive; b. Bklyn., Aug. 20, 1934; s. William and Emma (Zehender) R.; m. Eleanor E. Wharton, Nov. 1956; children; Mike S., John E., Kathryn L. AAS, N.Y. C.C., 1956; BSEE, NYU, 1957; MBA, U. Ala., 1970. Program mgr., group engr. Walleye, GPS, Mil Systems, Titan, Gemini Martin Marietta, Denver, 1960-67, program mgr. Skylab Huntsville, Ala., 1967-75, from dir. mil. space systems, program dir. space station, mgr. system integration .MX to program mgr. Manned Manuvering Unit Denver, 1975-89; mgr. program devel., space and launch sys. SCI Sys. Inc., Huntsville, 1989-96; pres. Guest Assocs. Inc., 1996—. Assoc. prof. Met. State U., Denver, 1964-67. Mem. sch. bd. Cherry Creek, Colo., 1976. Recipient Collier trophy, 1982, Group Achievement award NASA, 1987, Pub. Svc. Group Achievement medal NASA, 1988. Mem. AIAA (sr.), Am. Soc. Quality Control (pres. 1963-65), Am. Def. Preparedness Assn., Armed Forces Comms. and Electronics Assn. Avocations: skiing, flying. Home: 1715 Drake Ave SE Huntsville AL 35802-1042 Office: PO Box 1000 Mail Stop 206 8600 S Memorial Pkwy Huntsville AL 35802-3031

RICHTER, WILLIAM LOUIS, university administrator; b. Covina, Calif., Apr. 9, 1939; s. Louis Ernest and Gwendolyn Marguerite (Hughes) R.; m. Linda Kay Clark, Aug. 29, 1964; children: Mark William, Robert Clark. BA, Willamette U., 1961; MA, U. Chgo., 1963, PhD, 1968. Instr. Ill. Inst. Tech., Chgo., 1964, U. Hawaii, Honolulu, 1964-66; asst. prof. Kans. State U., Manhattan, 1966-73, assoc. prof., 1973-81, prof., 1981—, dept. head, 1984-93, asst. provost, 1991-96, assoc. provost for internat. programs, 1996—2002. Vis. Fulbright lectr. Panjab U., Chandigarh, India, 1969-70; faculty rsch. fellow Am. Inst. Indian Studies, New Delhi, India, 1972-73, 1985; faculty rsch. fellow Am. Inst. Pakistan Studies, Lahore, Pakistan, 1976-77; cons. USAID, NDI, 1990—. Co-editor: (books) The Landon Lectures, 1987, Combating Corruption/Encouraging Ethics, 1990. Mem. Rotary (Rotarian of Yr., 1993). Home: 2383 Grandview Ter Manhattan KS 66502-3729 Office: Kans State U Dept Polit Sci 226 Waters Hall Manhattan KS 66506-4030 E-mail: wrichter@ksu.edu.

RICHTERS, ARNIS, medical educator, researcher; b. Sauka, Latvia, Sept. 23, 1928; arrived in U.S., 1950; s. Arturs and Alma Richters; m. Valda Zalmans, June 2, 1951; 1 child. BS, U. Ariz., 1957, MS, 1959; PhD, U. So. Calif., L.A., 1967. Instr. pathology U. So. Calif., L.A., 1968—70, asst. prof. pathology, 1970—75, assoc. prof. pathology, 1975—91, prof. pathology, 1991—. Cons. U. Latvia, Riga, 1994—; mem. breast cancer task force NCI, Bethesda, Md., 1972—75; Fulbright sci. and environ. rschr. Fulbright Assn., Washington, 1995—. Author: (films) The Embattled Cell, 1968 (Gold medal, 1968); contbr. Cpl. U.S. Army, 1951—53. Scholar Fulbright scholar, CIES, Washington, 1994. Mem.: So. Calif. Soc. Electron Microscopy (pres. 1984—85), Tissue Culture Assn. (pres. Calif. br. 1978—79). Avocations: golf, cooking, photography. Home: 2205 Tall Pine Dr Duarte CA 91010 Office: Univ of Southern Calif 1840 N Soto St EDM-130 Los Angeles CA 90089

RICHTMAN, JACK, French language educator; b. N.Y.C., Mar. 15, 1927; s. Fred and Rose (Blumenfeld) R. BA, Bklyn. Coll., 1959; MA, Columbia U., 1961, PhD, 1969. Prof. French studies SUNY, Albany, 1962-95, prof. emeritus, 1995—. Assoc. dean Coll. of Humanities SUNY, Albany, 1992-94. Author: Adrienne Lecouvreur: The Actress and the Age, 1971; contbr. articles to profl. jours. Fulbright fellow Fulbright Commn., 1961-62. Mem. MLA (editor Lesbian and Gay Studies Newsletter, 1999—), Les Amis de Jean Ccteau (Am. corr. 2002--). Home: 484 W 43d St Apt 44G New York NY 10036

RICKABAUGH, VICKI, horse farm owner, dressage instructor; b. Phila., June 22, 1951; d. William C. and Marilyn Kirschner; m. Charles David Rickabaugh Jr., Sept. 15, 1973; children: Gloria, George, Peggy, Marc. AA, Brookdale C.C., 1981; BS in Edn., Monmouth U., 1972. RN, N.J., state cert. EMT, N.J.; cert. elem. tchr., N.J. Owner, instr. Blue Spruce Horse Farm Dressage Ctr., Jackson, N.J., 1972—; dep. mayor Jackson Twp. (N.J.) Com., 1996, 99, mayor, 1997-98; owner, instr. Blue Spruce Farm Dressage Ctr. Founder, dressage advisor East Coast Regional Dressage Assn., Medford, N.J., 1993—; lectr. in field. Author: (book) Horse Riding for Beginners, 1985; author: (lecture series) Trace and Equine Circle of Needs, 1982—; contbr. articles on dressage and horses to East Coast Regional Dressage Assn. newsletter, 1994—. Bd. dirs. Jackson Twp. Bd. of Edn., 1991-94, v.p., 1992; Rep. committeewoman Ocean County (N.J.) Rep. Orgn., 1995—; committeewoman Jackson Twp. Com., 1996; founder, mem. Jackson Coun. for Arts, 1998—, Tourism and Bus. Coun., Jackson, 1997-99; EMT Jackson Twp. 1st Aid Squad, 1989-95; mem. Jackson Twp. Mcpl. Alliance for Prevention of Alcohol and Drug Abuse, 1995-99. Recipient Proclamation to Mayor Rickabaugh, N.J. Gov. Christine Todd Whitman, N.J. Exec. Dept., Trenton, 1997, Senate and Gen. Assembly Joint Legis. Resolution for disting. svc. State of N.J., 1997, Svc. award Jackson Coun. for Arts, 1998. Mem. Am. Horse Show Assn. (life), U.S. Dressage Fedn. ("L" judge), Ea. States Dressage and Combined Tng. Assn. (life), Pathfinders (founder). Republican. Avocations: horses, tennis, sailing. Home: 5 Stanley Pl Jackson NJ 08527-4454 Fax: 732-833-0255. E-mail: v.rickabaugh@usa.net.

RICKARD, DAVID LAWRENCE, fundraising consultant; b. Logansport, Ind., Apr. 7, 1939; s. Thomas Oden Rickard, Catherine Opal Rickard; m. Judith Safly Stanley; children: Michael , Kenneth. BA, DePauw U., 1961; MPA, Harvard U., 1972. Mem. staff Fed. Aviation Adminstrn., Washington, 1961—72, planning & appraisal specialist Burlington, Mass., 1972—83; sr. policy analyst Ark. Advocates for Children & Families, Little Rock, 1988—94; spl. asst. to the dir. Ark. Dept. Human Svcs., 1994—98; cons., 1998—. Author: (study) Jet Aircraft Departure Procedures for Boston Logan Airport, 1978, Recruitment and Retention of Health Care Professionals in Rural Areas, 2001. Dir.& pres. Ctrl. Ark. Libr. Sys., Little Rock, 1993—; mem. Ark/. Commn. on Ethics Legis., 1984—85; pres. Unitarian Universalist Ch. of Little Rock, 1999—2000; chmn. Arkansas Coalition to Abolish the Death Penalty, 1985—; bd.d ir. ACLU, Ark. Affiliate, 1987—99; bd. dir. American Civil Liberties Union, Arkansas Affiliate, 1987—, Ark. Coalition to Abolish the Death Penalty, 1985—. Recipient Disting. Svc. award, ACLU, Ark. affiliate, 1999; scholar Proctor & Gamble scholar, DePauw U., 1957—61, Edn. for Pub. Mgmt. scholar, U. S. Civil Svc. Commn., 1971—72. Unitarian Universalist. Avocations: tennis, fishing, reading.

RICKARD, DENNIS CLARK, sheriff, educator; b. Butler, Pa., Dec. 15, 1948; s. Dean Clark and D'Lauris Mae (Jones) R.; m. Elaine Kay Harbison, Nov. 6, 1982; children: Kellie Jean, David Harbison. Student, U. Pitts., 1966-68; BA, Slippery Rock U., 1971, MEd, 1973. Cert. mcpl. police instr., Pa. Probation officer Butler (Pa.) County, 1971-77; exec. sec., treas. The Benefit Fund, New Castle, Pa., 1977-92; instr. Ind. U. of Pa., Indiana, 1971—, Butler County C.C., 1977—; sheriff County of Butler, 1982—. Mem. Saxonburg Vol. Fire Co.; bd. dirs. United Way, 1987-83, county campaign chair, 1987. Mem. ACSO, Nat. Sheriffs Assn. (bd. dirs. 2001—), Butler County Law Enforcement Officers Assn. (past pres.), Pa. Sheriffs Assn. (sec.-treas. 1995—), Ducks Unltd., Ruffed Grouse Soc., Waterfowl USA, Masons (33 deg.), Butler City Hunting and Fishing Club, Moose, Elks, Lambda Chi Alpha, Psi Chi. Republican. Methodist. Avocations: golf, bowling, coaching. Home: PO Box 1825 Butler PA 16003-1825 Office: Sheriffs Office PO Box 1208 Butler PA 16003-1208

RICKARD, MARGARET LYNN, library and grants consultant, former library director; b. Detroit, July 31, 1944; d. Frank Mathias and Betty Louise (Lee) Sieger; m. Cyriac Thannikary, Nov. 13, 1965 (div. Feb. 1973); 1 child, Luke Anthony; m. Marcos T. Perez, Mar. 1973 (dec. Oct. 1973); m. Lui Gotti, Dec. 23, 1984 (dec. Aug. 1997); m. William A. Rickard, Aug. 22, 1998. AB, U. Detroit, 1968; MLS, Pratt Inst., 1969; postgrad., NYU, 1976-77. Cert. libr., N.Y. Sr. libr. Queens Pub. Libr., Jamaica, N.Y., 1969-77; libr. dir. El Centro (Calif.) Pub. Libr., 1977-99; ret., 1999. County libr./cons. Imperial County Free Libr., 1993-99; vice chmn., chmn. Serra Coop. Libr. Sys., San Diego, 1980-82; libr. cons., 1998—. Pres. Hist. Site Found., El Centro, 1988-99, 92, sec., 1989, trustee, 1989-99, v.p., 1991-92; fin. sec. St. Elizabeth Luth. Ch., El Centro, 1988; mem. Downtown El Centro Assn., mem. arches bus. improvement dist.; active numerous civic coms., fundraising events; mem. comm. and arts task force Imperial County Arts Coun.; coord. arts and culture com. City of El Centro Strategic Plan. Title IIB fellow Pratt Inst., 1968-69. Mem. ALA, AAUW (v.p. El Centro 1988), Calif. Libr. Assn., Calif. County Librs. Assn., El Centro C. of C., Toastmasters, Soroptimist Internat. of El Centro (v.p. El Centro 1978, corr. sec. 1990-91, 1st v.p. 1991-92, pres. 1992-93, 2d v.p. 1995-96, 98-99, recording sec. 1997-98, life mem.), Women of Moose (sr. regent El Centro 1988-89, ednl. advancement chmn. 1999-2000). Democrat. Lutheran. Home and Office: 6169 Terrace Dr PO Box 232 Pollock Pines CA 95726

RICKARD, RUTH DAVID, retired history and political science educator; b. Fed. Republic Germany, Feb. 20, 1926; came to U.S., 1940; d. Carl and Alice (Koch) David; m. Robert M. Yaffe, Oct. 1949 (dec. 1959); children: David, Steven; m. Norman G. Rickard, June 1968 (dec. 1988); 1 stepson, Douglas. BS cum laude, Northwestern U., 1947, MA, 1948. Law editor Commerce Clearing House, Chgo., 1948; instr. history U. Ill., 1949-51, instr. extension program Waukegan, 1960-67; instr. history Waukegan Schs., 1960-69; original faculty, prof. western civilization, polit. sci. Coll. of Lake County, Grayslake, Ill., 1969-92. Mem. Inter-Univ. Seminar on Armed Forces and Soc.; mem. Hospitality Info. Svc. for Diplomatic Residents and Families affiliate Meridian Internat. Ctr.; spkr. in field. Author: History of College of Lake County, 1987 (honored by city of Waukegan 1987), (poem) I Lost My Wings, 1989, Au Revoir from Emeritusdom, 1993, Where are the Safety Zones, 1994; contbg. author: History of National Press Club: Reliable Sources, 1997; contbr. articles to profl. jours. Mem. Econ. Devel. Com., Waukegan, 1992-93; working with homeless through Samaritans of Greater Washington area, 2000—. Scholar Freedoms Found. Am. Legion, Valley Forge, Pa., 1967. Mem. AAUW (pres. Waukegan chpt. 1955-57, scholarship named for her 1985, program co-chair McLean chpt. 1997-2000), LWV (charter, v.p. Waukegan chpt.), Nat. Press Club D.C., Northwestern U. Alumni Washington (bd. dirs.). Avocations: writing, travel, lecturing, reading, theater.

RICKARDS, CHERYL ANN, counselor, minister, educator; b. Englewood, N.J., Aug. 24, 1952; d. Harry Robert Jones and Marion Cousins; m. Robert Richard Rickards, Dec. 31, 1977; children: Jordan Bennett, Wesley Clayton, Gabriel Harrison. AD, Middlesex Coll., 1975; diploma, Liberty Bible Inst., 1990; BS, Liberty U., 1990, MA in Counseling, 1993; PhD in Theocentric Counseling, LaSalle U., 1994; MA in Religion, Liberty U., 1997, MDiv, 2001. Ordained min. World Christian Ch., 1995. Intern JFK Ctr. for Drugs & Alcohol Prevention & Treatment, Avanel, N.J., 1992-93; pvt. practice pvt. practice, Milltown, 1993—; acad. dean Sonshine Bible Coll., 2002—. Dir. Lighthouse Counseling Ctr.; adj. prof. LaSalle U. Contbr. articles to profl. jours. Rep. candidate N.J. Gen. Assembly, 1989. Mem. ACA, Am. Assn. Christian Counselors, Assn. for Religious & Value Issues Counseling, Assn. for Addictions & Offender Counselors, N.J. Horsemen's Benevolent Assn., MENSA. Avocation: cross cultural evangelism, aviation (commercial pilot). Home: 10 Lake Dr North Brunswick NJ 08902-4826 Office: Lighthouse Counseling PO Box 188 196 Riva Ave Milltown NJ 08850-2150

RICKEL, ANNETTE URSO, psychology and psychiatry researcher, educator; b. Phila. d. Ralph Francis and Marguerite (Calcaterra) Urso; 1 child, John Ralph Rickel. BA, Mich. State U., 1963; MA, U. Mich., 1965, PhD, 1972, MD, 1972. Lic. psychologist, Mich. Faculty early childhood edn. Merrill-Palmer Inst., Detroit, 1967-69; adj. faculty U. Mich., Ann Arbor, 1969-75; asst. dir. N.E. Guidance Ctr., Detroit, 1972-75; asst. prof. psychology Wayne State U., 1975-81; vis. assoc. prof. Columbia U., N.Y.C., 1982-83; assoc. prof. psychology Wayne State U., 1981-87, asst. provost, 1989-91, prof. psychology, 1987-95; Am. Coun. on Edn. fellow Princeton and Rutgers Univs., 1990-91. AAAS and APA Congl. Sci. fellow on Senate Fin. Subcom. on Health and Pres.'s Nat. Health Care Reform Task Force, 1992—93; dir. mental health and devel. Nat. Com. for Quality Asurance, Washington, 1995—96; clin. prof. dept. psychiatry Georgetown U., Washington, 1995—2000; program officer The Rockefeller Found., 2000—. Cons. editor Jour. of Cmty. Psychology, Jour. Primary Prevention; co-author: Social and Psychological Problems of Women, 1984, Preventing Maladjustment..., 1987; author: Teenage Pregnancy and Parenting, 1989, Keeping Children From Harm's Way, 1997, Understanding Managed Care, 2000; contbr. articles to profl. jours Mem. Pres.'s Task Force on Nat. Health Care Reform, 1993; bd. dirs. Children's Ctr. of Wayne County, Mich., The Epilepsy Ctr. of Mich., Reading is Fundamental, Nat. Symphony Orch., The Kellogg Found., 1996-97, The John D. and Catherine T. MacArthur Found., 1998-99. Grantee NIMH, 1976-86, Eloise and Richard Webber Found., 1977-80, McGregor Fund, 1977-78, 82, David M. Whitney Fund, 1982, Katherine Tuck Fund, 1985-90, NIH, 2000; recipient Career Devel. Chair award, 1985-86. Fellow APA (div. pres. 1984-85); mem. Internat. Women's Forum, Soc. for Rsch. in Child Devel., Soc. for Rsch. in Child and Adolescent Psychopathology, Internat. Assn. of Applied Psychologists, Sigma Xi, Psi Chi. Roman Catholic. E-mail: arickel@rbf.org.

RICKELS, KARL, psychiatrist, physician, educator; b. Wilhelmshaven, Germany, Aug. 17, 1924; came to U.S., 1954, naturalized, 1960; s. Karl E. and Stephanie (Roehrhoff) R.; m. Rosalind Wilson, June 27, 1964; children: Laurence Arthur, PhD, Stephen W., Michael R. MD, U. Muenster, 1951. Intern Dortmund (Germany) City Hosp., 1951-52; postgrad. tng. U. Erlangen, U. Frankfurt, City Hosp. Kassel, 1952-54; resident in psychiatry Mental Health Inst., Cherokee, Iowa, 1954-55, Hosp. U. Pa., Phila., 1955-57; from instr. to assoc. prof. U. Pa., 1957-69, prof. psychiatry, 1969—, prof. pharmacology, 1976-98, Stuart and Emily B.H. Mudd prof. human behavior, 1977—, chief mood and anxiety disorders program, 1964—, chmn. com. on studies involving human beings, 1985-98. Chief psychiatry Phila. Gen. Hosp., 1975-77. Editor, author 8 books; contbr. over 540 articles to profl. pubs. Fellow Am. Coll. Neuropsychopharmacology (charter), Am. Soc. Clin. Psychopharmacology, Am. Psychiat. Assn., Coll. Physicians Phila., Collegium Internat. Neuro-Psychopharmacologicum; mem. Psychiat. Rsch. Soc., European Coll. Neuropsychopharmacology (corr.). Home: 1324 Youngsford Rd Gladwyne PA 19035 Office: U Pa Dept Psychiatry Ste 670 3535 Market St Philadelphia PA 19104-3515 E-mail: krickels@mail.med.upenn.edu.

RICKER, RICHARD EDMOND, metallurgical scientist; b. Newport News, Va., Feb. 26, 1952; s. Harry Hamlin and Edith Elizabeth (Slayton) R.; m. Winifred Lou Vinson, June 20, 1975; children: Carrie Elizabeth, Jacob Edmond. BS in Materials Engring., N.C. State U., 1975; PhD in Materials Engring., Rensselaer Poly. Inst., 1983. Engr. trainee NASA Marshal Space Flight Ctr., Huntsville, Ala., 1973-75; sr. engr. The Babcock and Wilcox Co. Inc., Lynchburg, Va., 1977-79; asst. prof. U. Notre Dame, Ind., 1984-86; metallurgist Nat. Inst. Standards and Tech., Gaithersburg, Md., 1986-90, group leader, 1990—. Co-editor: Environmental Effects on Advanced Materials, 1991; bd. review Jour. Metall. Transactions; contbr. articles to profl. jours. Recipient Bronze medal U.S. Dept. Commerce, 1991. Mem. AAAS, ASM Internat. (treas.-chmn. local chpt. 1988-93), The Metallurg. Soc. AIME, Electrochem. Soc., Nat. Assn. Corrosion Engrs., Sigma Xi, Alpha Sigma Mu (trustee 1987-89). Achievements include research in the mechanism of accelerated fatigue failure of aluminum aircraft alloys, the effect of ordering on the electrochemical behavior of intermetallics; discovery of intermetallic alloys susceptible to stress corrosion cracking, a brittle film's ability to induce cleavage in a ductile substrate; electrochemical synthesis of quantum dot arrays, influence of nanostructural multilayer films of fatigue crack initiation. Office: Nat Inst Standards & Tech 100 Bureau Dr MS 8553 Gaithersburg MD 20899-0001 Home: 12809 Talley Ln Gaithersburg MD 20878-6108 E-mail: richard.richer@nist.gov.

RICKERD, DONALD SHERIDAN, foundation executive; b. Smiths Falls, Ont., Can., Nov. 8, 1931; s. Harry M. and Evaline Mildred (Sheridan) R.; m. Julie Rekai, Dec. 14, 1968; 1 child, Christopher. Student, St. Andrews U., Scotland, 1951-52; BA, Queen's U., Can., 1953; LLD, Queen's U., 1985; BA (Rotary Found. fellow), Balliol Coll., Oxford U., Eng., 1955; MA, Oxford U., Eng., 1963; DCL, Mount Allison U., Can., 1985; LLD, Trent U., Can., 1986; LLB, York U., Can., 1991. Bar: Ont. 1959; apptd. Queen's Counsel, 1978. Assoc. Fasken & Calvin, Toronto, 1957-61; registrar, lectr. history, asst. prof. law Faculty of Adminstrv. Studies York U., 1961-68; pres. Donner Can. Found., 1968-89, W.H. Donner Found., Inc., N.Y.C., 1971-87, Max Bell Found., Toronto, 1989-97, Zavikon Found., 1997—. Chmn. bd. dirs. Draeger Can. Ltd.; former bd. dirs. ICWI Found., Kingston, Jamaica; acting dir. Asian bus. studies program Toronto-York U. Ctr. Asian-Pacific Studies. Former chmn. Coun. Ont. Coll. Art., Toronto; past chmn. Ctrl. Hosp., 1993—96; mem. Royal Commn. concerning activities Royal Can. Mounted Police, 1977—81; former bd. govs. Upper Can. Coll., Toronto; trustee, vice chmn. bd. trustees Queens U., 1989—2001; former mem. bd. regents Mt. Allison U.; former chair, pres. Wellesley Ctrl. Health Corp., Toronto. Decorated Order of Can. Mem.: Bd. Trade Met. Toronto (pres.), U. Club Toronto. E-mail: drickerd@yorku.ca.

RICKERS, CARSTEN, physician; b. Lingen, Germany, Oct. 6, 1964; s. Erich and Helga (Haempel) R.; m. Hedwig Silies, July 12, 1996; children: Eva Sophia, Karla Maria. MD, U. Muenster, Germany, 1993. Resident in adult cardiology U. Hosp. Eppendorf, Hamburg, Germany, 1993-96, resident in pediatric cardiology Germany, 1997-2000, physician Germany, 2000—. Contbr. articles to profl. jours. Rsch. grantee German Rsch. Soc., 2000—; Cardiovasc. Rsch. fellow U. Minn., Mpls., 2000—. Mem. German Soc. Cardiology, German Soc. Pediatric Cardiology, Soc. Cardiovasc. Magnetic Resonance, Am. Heart Assn. (coun. cardiosasc. disease in the young). Roman Catholic. Avocations: skiing, swimming, soccer. Home: Lehmweg 31 A 20251 Hamburg Germany Office: Univ Hosp Eppendorf Martinistrasse 52 20246 Hamburg Germany also: U Minn MRS-Rsch Radiology MMC 292 420 Delaware St SE Minneapolis MN 55455 E-mail: ricke023@tc.umn.edu.

RICKERSHAUSER, PAUL ERIC, human resources specialist; b. Newark, Nov. 14, 1957; s. Carl Rickershauser and Edna Wright; m. Anita M. Essig, Sept. 24, 1983; children: Lisa, Katie. BA, Rutgers U., 1980, MS, 1985. Cert. SPHR, SHRM. Human rels. mgr. RH Macy, N.Y.C., 1980-86, Rexham Corp., Charlotte, N.C., 1986-88; v.p. benefits, compensation and assoc. rels. United Stationers, DesPlaines, Ill., 1988—. Avocations: sailing, traveling. Office: United Stationers 2200 E Golf Rd Des Plaines IL 60016-1257 E-mail: perickershauser@hotmail.com, prickershauser@ussco.com.

RICKERT, EDWIN WEIMER, investment consultant; b. Connersville, Ind., June 17, 1914; s. Edwin and Grace (Weimer) R.; m. Ruth Alma Fulcher, July 9, 1942; children: Jean Adelia, Wendy Grace, Allen. AB, Columbia U., 1936. Security analyst, economist Mackubin, Legg & Co., Balt., 1936-40; indsl. analyst Office of Prodn. Mgmt., Washington, 1940-41; supr. commodity econ. rsch. Standard Brands, Inc., N.Y.C., 1946-53; with Brundage Story & Rose, 1953-2000, ptnr., 1966-83, sr. investment cons., 1984-2000; ret., 2000. Trustee Columbia U. Press, 1977-96, trustee emeritus, 1996—; bd. visitors Columbia Coll., N.Y.C., 1986-92. Served to capt. U.S. Army, 1941-46; ret. lt. col. Res. Mem. N.Y. Soc. Security Analysts, India House (N.Y.C.), Grachur Club (Balt.). Republican. Presbyterian. Home: Apt 232 14905 Bothell-Everett Hwy Mill Creek WA 98012-5323

RICKERT, JONATHAN BRADLEY, retired foreign service officer; b. Washington, July 23, 1937; s. Van Dusen and Margaret Eleanor (Bradley) R.; m. Ulla Gerd Margareta Granstrand, June 20, 1969; children: Ulla Margaret, Jonathan Bernt. AB cum laude, Princeton U, 1959; diploma Russian lang., U.S. Army Lang. Sch., 1962; student, Harvard U., 1976-77; MA, George Washington U., 1982. Rotational jr. officer Exec. Sec. State Dept., 1963-65; consular officer Embassy, London, 1965-66, staff aide to amb., political officer Moscow, 1966-68; exchanges officer Office Soviet and Eastern European Exchanges State Dept., 1969-70, with Romanian Lang. Tng. FSI, 1971; consular officer Embassy Bucharest, 1971-73, polit. officer, 1973-74; spl. asst. to U.S. Rep. U.S. Delegation MBFR, Vienna, 1974-76; polit./labor officer Embassy Port of Spain, 1977-80; desk officer Trinidad, Guyana, Suriname, acting dep. dir. Office Caribbean Affairs State Dept., 1980-82, desk officer Romania, Office Eastern European and Yugoslav Affairs, 1982-84, with Bulgarian Lang. Tng., 1984-85; dep. chief mission Embassy Sofia, 1985-88; chief European Assignments divsn. State Dept., 1988-90; legis. asst. to Sen Bob Packwood, 1990-91; dep. chief mission Embassy Bucharest, 1991-95; dir. Office of N. Cen. European Affairs State Dept., 1995-98, sr. advisor coord. Ea. European Assistance, 1998; bd. dirs. Project on Ethnic Rels., Princeton, N.J., 1999. With U.S. Army, 1961-62. Mem. Am. Fgn. Svc. Assn. Episcopalian. E-mail: rickertjb@state.gov.

RICKERT, ROBERT RICHARD, pathologist, educator; b. Harrisburg, Pa., Oct. 19, 1936; s. Alton G. and Henrietta (Gey) R.; m. Sonja Murray Hansen, Aug. 26, 1961; children: Kristin, Robin, Anne. AB, U. Mich., 1958; MD, John Hopkins U., 1962. Diplomat Am. Bd. of Pathology. Intern Yale-New Haven (Conn.) Med. Ctr., 1962-63, resident in internal medicine, 1963-64, 66-67; rsch. assoc. Atomic Bomb Casulty Commn., Hiroshima, Japan, 1964-66; asst. prof. pathology Yale U. Sch. Med., New Haven, 1968-70; attending pathologist Yale New Haven Med. Ctr., 1968-70; dir. surg. pathology U. Med. and Dentistry N.J.-N.J. Med. Sch., Newark, 1970-73, assoc. prof. pathology, 1970-73; clin. prof. pathology U. of Med. and Dentistry N.J.-N.J. Med. Sch., 1985—; co-chmn. dept. pathology St. Barnabas Med. Ctr., Livingston, N.J., 1973-2000, chmn. dept. pathology, 2000—. Adj. assoc. prof. pathology Columbia U. Coll. Physicians & Surgeons, N.Y.C., 1974-89. Contbr. chpts. to med. textbooks and articles to profl. jours. Chmn. med. com. Am. Cancer Soc., N.J., 1989-91, v.p. 1991-93, pres. elect 1993-94, pres. 1995-97 (Physician of Yr., N.J. Divsn., 1998), chief med. spokesperson, bd. dirs. Ea. divsn., 1998-2000. Fellow Coll. Am. Pathologists (vice-chmn., internat. regional commr. commn. on lab. accreditation, Pathologist of Yr. 2001), Am. Soc. Clin. Pathologists, U.S.-Can. Acad. Pathology; mem. AMA, N.J. Soc. Pathologists (pres. 1980-82), Gastrointestinal Pathology Soc. (pres. 1988-89), Med. Soc. N.J., Acad. Medicine N.J. (trustee 1988—, treas. 1994-95, v.p. 1995-97, pres. 1998), Am. Soc. Cytopathology, Short Hills Club, Phi Beta Kappa, Alpha Omega Alpha. Republican. Congregationalist. Avocations: antiques, wine collecting, art. Office: St Barnabas Med Ctr Dept Pathology Livingston NJ 07039

RICKERT, RONALD DEAN, music educator; b. Columbus, Nebr., Aug. 22, 1956; s. Marvin Wilbur and Laverna Ruth Rickert; m. Susan Marie Dudley, July 28, 1979; children: Benjamin, Robert, Samuel. AA, Platte Coll., Columbus,NE, 1976; BA, Doane Coll., Crete, NE, 1979. Band dir. Sutton Pub. Schools, Sutton, Nebr., 1980—87, Aurora Pub. Schools, Aurora, 1987—88, Fillmore Ctrl. Schools, Geneva, 1988—. Dir. Fillmore County Cmty. Band, Geneva, 1988; treas. Geneva Arts Coun., 1990—96. Recipient Geneva Jaycees Outstanding Educator, Geneva Jaycees, 1991, Donald A Lentz Outstanding Bandmaster, NSBA, 2002. Mem.: Nebr. Music Educators Nat. Conf., Nebr. State Band Directors Assn. (sec. 1999—2001). Avocations: fishing, golf, cross stitching. Home: 800 N 9th Geneva NE 68361 Office: Fillmore Central Schools 1410 L St Geneva NE 68361 Office Fax: 402-759-4038. Personal E-mail: rrickert@esu6.org.

RICKETSON, GEORGE MANNING, III, retired surgeon; b. Atlanta, 1937; MD, U. Fla., 1966. Diplomate Am. Bd. Surgery. Intern Behtesda Naval Hosp, Md., 1966-67; resident in surgery USN Hosp., Portsmouth, Va., 1967-71; pvt. practice Sacred Heart Hosp., Pensacola, Fla.; pvt. practice, group partnership McMahon Ricketson Stockamp; ret., 2001. Fellow ACS; mem. AMA, Southeastern Surg. Congress, So. Med. Assn. Office: McMahon Ricketson Stockamp 5147 N 9th Ave Ste 303 Pensacola FL 32504-8700 also: 5014 Barranca Lora Pensacola FL 32514-7910

RICKETT, CAROLYN KAYE MASTER, artist, criminologist; b. Ft. Worth, Apr. 24, 1941; d. Lester Buford and Dorothy Minerva (Whittington) Master; m. David Franklin Rickett, May 3, 1981; 1 child Julia Beth Allen. BFA, Tex. Christian U., 1993; MFA, Tex. Woman's U., 1997; M in Criminology, U. Tex., Arlington, 2001; postgrad. U. Tex., Arlington, 2002—. Artist, owner StarMaster Graphic Design and Fine Art, Ft. Worth, 1988—; represented by Downstairs Gallery, Dallas, Kincannon Fine Arts Gallery. Presenter in field. Represented in permanent collections Jasper Mus., Nat. Women's Caucus Arts Archives, also pvt. collections, one-woman shows include Jasper Mus., Alta., Can., 1994, Downstairs Gallery, Jasper, 1994, Del Bello Gallery, Toronto, Ont., Can., 1996, exhibitions include Tex. Christian U., Ft. Worth, 1991, Greater Denton Coun. Arts., Tex., 1994—96, Tex. Christian U., 1995, 1997, UN 4th Conf. Women, Beijing, 1995, Bass Mus., Miami Broward C.C., Davie, Fla., 1996, San Jacinto Coll., Houston, 1996, Aisling Studio, Durango, Colo, 1996, U. Tex., Arlington, 1998, World Trade Ctr., Dallas, 1998, (traveling show) Beijing and Beyong , N.Y., 1998—2000, others. Grantee, Tex. Christian U., 1990—93; scholar, 1991—93, Ray and Bertha Lakey Meml., 1994—96. Mem.: Am. Soc. Crime, Tex. Art Educators Assn., Nat. Trust for Historic Preservation, Mus. Women in Arts, Am. Soc. Criminology, Am. Criminal Justice Scis., Phi Alpha Alpha. Home: 5816 Broadway Ave Fort Worth TX 76117-3305

RICKETTS, MARIJANE GNEGY, poet; b. Mountain Lake Park, Md., July 16, 1925; d. Clyde Columbus Gnegy and Zelda Adeline Stemple; m. Aubrey Eugene Ricketts, Apr. 9, 1950; children: Kenneth, Jennifer Riffer. BA, W.Va. Wesleyan Coll., 1947. Sec. to the adminstrv. asst. Landon Sch. for Boys, Bethesda, Md., 1961—62; sec. to the prin. Montgomery County Pub. Schs., Bethesda/Rockville, 1962—87. Pres. and editor The Writers' League of Wash., Washington, 1989—92; nat. contest poetry judge Nat. League of Am. Pen Women, Washington, 2000—00; poetry programs chairwoman Women's Cmty. Club of Kensington, Kensington, Md., 1997—2000; poet for 50th yr. class reunion Alumni, W.Va. Wesleyan Coll., Buchannon, W.Va., 1997—97; leader, md. poet laureate program Md. Humanities Coun., Annapolis, Md., 2000—00. Author: (book of poetry) Is it the Onions Making Life Pungent?, 1985; editor: (poetry anthology) The Poets of Ellicott Street, 1989; editor: (and publisher) (writer's league 75th year anthology) A Diamond Anthology of Prose and Poetry, 1992. Prodr. poetry programs Montgomery County Pub. Libr., Kensington, Md., 1997—98; prodr., Christmas readings Women's Cmty. Club, 1997—2000. Recipient Grand Prize First Ann. Lit. award, Byline Mag., 1986, First Prize for Poetry, D.C. Commn. on the Arts, 1992, First Prize Poetry, Md. Fedn. Women's Clubs, 1997, Grand Prize, Gen. Fedn. Women's Clubs, 1997, First Prize for Poetry, Writer's League of Wash., 1999, 2000. Mem.: Live Poets Soc., The Poets Ellicott St. (pres. 1990—91), The Writers' Ctr., Writer's League Wash. (archivist 1992—2001). Methodist. Avocations: choir, concerts, museums, gardening, collecting art prints. Home: 10203 Clearbrook Pl Kensington MD 20895-4121 Personal E-mail: marijane@ioip.com.

RICKETTS, SONDRA LOU, librarian; b. McFall, Mo., Aug. 4, 1941; d. Jewell E. and Daisie Glenn (Weller) Rainey; m. Rex Errol Ricketts, June 14, 1964; children: Chad Errol, Trina Rae, Neysa Carrie. BS, U. Mo., 1963—. Cert. tchr., Mo. Libr. East Ladue Jr. High Sch., Ladue, Mo., 1963-65; adminstrv. asst. Jacksonville (Ill.) Pub. Libr., 1965; reference libr. Ill. Coll., Jacksonville, 1965-66; cataloger Stephens Coll., Columbia, Mo., 1966-69; libr. Clark (Mo.) Elem. Sch., 1981-95, Middle Grove Elem. Sch., 1996—. Sun. sch. tchr. Presbyn. Ch., Columbia, 1977-84; mem. Hallsville (Mo.) Sch. bond com., 1980; cmty. leader Hallsville 4-H, 1980-82, mem. state com., Columbia, 1985, project leader Hallsville 4-H, 1980-85, 94-2000; bd. dirs. 4-H Found., Columbia, 1991—, sec., 1997-2000; mem. Boone County 4-H Auction com., 1994-2000; mem. ways and means com., hallsville PTA, 1980, publicity com., 1981; co-chmn. Hallsville H.S. All Night Sr. party, 1985, 90. Conf. honoree AIJCA, 1991. Mem. Am. Internat. Charolais Assn., Mo. Assn. of Sch. Librs., Mid.-Mo. Regional Assn. Sch. Librs., Mo. Univ. Alumnae Assn., Boone County Alumnae Assn., Alpha Chi Omega Alumni Assn., U. Mo. Jefferson Club, Pi Lambda Theta. Avocations: crafts, swimming, reading. E-mail: sondra14800@yahoo.com.

RICKETTS, VIRGINIA LEE, historian, researcher; b. Jamestown, Kans., Jan. 12, 1925; d. Roy Earl Eastman and Alma Anna Hunter; m. Clair Keith Ricketts, June 3, 1944; children: Keith Alan, Dennis Lee, Donald Gene. Grad. H.S., Filer, Idaho. Clk. dist. ct., auditor, recorder Jerome County, Idaho, 1972-79; pvt. practice historian, rschr. Jerome, 1979—. Mem. Idaho State Hist. Records Adv. Bd., Boise, 1976-2002; pres. Idaho Assn. Recorders and Clks., 1977-78; cons. Idaho State Supreme Ct., Boise, 1979-81; tour dir., instr. Coll. So. Idaho, Twin Falls, 1984-97; mem. Bur. Land Mgmt. Adv. Bd., Shoshone, Idaho, 1989-95, Upper Snake River Ecosystem Adv. Bd., Idaho, 1995-98; Internat. Toastmistress communicator, 1988; lectr. in field. Author: The History of the North Side-The First 75 Years, 1982, Greater Twin Falls Historical Guide, 1988, A History of the Middle Snake River, 1996, Then and Now in Southern Idaho, 1998. Organizer Friends St. Stricker Ranch, Inc., Twin Falls, 1984. Recipient Cert. of Commendation, Am. Assn. for State and Local History, 1984, Cert. of Resolution of Appreciation, Idaho State Bd. Edn., 1998; named Idaho Disting. Citizen, Idaho Statesmen, 1988, Centennial Citizen, Citizens of Jerome County Idaho, 1990. Mem. Idaho State Hist. Soc. (trustee 1987-99, chairperson bd. trustees 1991-98), Oreg. Calif. Trails Assn. (organizer Idaho chpt. 1984, treas. Idaho chpt. 1985-99), Jerome County Hist. Soc., Inc. (co-organizer 1984, former pres., curator 1985-2001), Idaho Assn. of Mus. (Outstanding Svc. award 1998), Soroptimist Internat. of Am. (Woman of Distinction 1999), PEO (chpt. E Idaho, historian 1987-98). Republican. Presbyterian. Avocations: needlework, gardening, sports, family activities. Home: 516 E 300 S Jerome ID 83338-6747

RICKEY, HORACE B., JR. retired engineer; b. New Orleans, July 2, 1924; s. Horace Bushnell Rickey and Marjorie Bouvier; m. Jewel Katherine Seybold, Aug. 15, 1947 (dec. Dec. 1984); children; Sharon Jewel, Marjorie Anna, Priscilla Gail; m. Maude Elizabeth Dudley, Nov. 30, 1985 (div. Apr. 1995). BSCE, U. Wyo., 1947, BS in Archtl. Engring., 1948. Registered profl. engr., La.; lic. profl. surveyor, realtor, ins. agt., La. Treas., CAO Horace B. Rickey Constrn. Co., Lafayette, La., 1948-67; profl. engr. Horace B. Rockey Jr. PE, 1948-89; pres. S.W. Materials, 1956-78, S.W. Homes, Lafayette, 1963-78, Buck Enterprises, Albuquerque, 1978-86; real estate agt. Lafayette, 1986-92; dir. pub. works City of Lafayette, 1992; project engr. Lafayette Consol. Govt., 1993-98; ret., 1998. V.p. Union Fed. S&L, Lafayette, 1960-85; sec., treas., CAO Motor Logdes of Lafayette, 1966-86; operating dir. Computers for Bus. Mgmt., Lafayette, 1970-86; pres., CAO Buck Enterprises Motel, Albuquerque, 1978-86. Scoutmaster, cubmaster Boy Scouts Am., New Orleans, 1942-43; v.p. Bayou coun. Girl Scouts U.S., Lafayette, 1961-65, pres., 1965-69; bd. dirs. Hunter-Jumper Assn., La., 1971, Southwestern La. Inst. Assn., Lafayette, 1969-72, Salvation Army, Lafayette, 1960-62; chmn. constrn. divsn. United Fund, Lafayette, 1968, campaign chmn., 1969, pres., 1970; bd. dirs. Lafayette C. of C., 1960-62, 69-71, v.p., 1961; chmn. Citizen's Adv. Com. for City and Parish, Lafayette, 1960-62; chmn. Rep. Parish Exec. Com., Lafayette, 1953-65; sec. Rep. State Ctrl. Com., La., 1955-65; deacon First Presbyn. Ch., Lafayette, 1958-62, ruling elder, 1962-74. Sgt. AUS, 1943-46, ETO. Decorated Bronze Star; recipient Thanks Badge, Bayou coun. Girl Scouts U.S., 1969, Outstanding Svcs. to Arts award La. Arts Coun., 1971, Expert Tapiestier award Acadian Weavers, 1978. Avocations: flat loom weaving, goblin tapestry weaving, genealogy. Home: 211 N Williams Dr Lafayette LA 70506

RICKIN, SHEILA ANNE, personnel professional; b. N.Y.C., Oct. 13, 1945; d. Louis and Ethel (Schmukler) Bernstein; BA, CCNY, 1966; postgrad. NYU; MBA, Pace U., 1988. Rsch. asst. pre-baccalureate program CCNY, 1966-68; placement counselor Elaine Revell, Inc., N.Y.C., 1968; adminstr. assoc. to CEO Parenthood Fedn. of Am., N.Y.C., 1969-74; pers. mgr. Family Circle Mag./N.Y. Times Mag. Group, 1974-87; sr. human resources rep., Drexel Burnham Lambert, 1987-88; asst. v.p., dir. pers. and adminstrn. Oppenheimer Mgmt. Corp. div. Mass Mut. Ins. Co., 1989-93; assoc. human resources mgr. AVSC Internat., N.Y.C., 1994-96; cons. human resources, 1993-96; dir. human resources WNYC Found., 1996-97; mgr. human resources C&S Sys./N.Y. Times Co., N.Y.C., 1997—. Mem. APHA, ASTD (security industry group 1987-93), Am. Compensation Assn., Human Resources Soc., Soc. Human Resources Mgmt. (employee rels./diversity com.), Internat. Found. Benefits, Am. Mgmt. Assn., N.Y. Human Resources Planners, N.Y. Pers. Mgrs. Assn. (program com.), Mag. Pubs. Assn. (pers. com. 1978-87). Office: C&S Sys/NY Times Co 47-25 34th St New York NY 11101

RICKLEFS, DALE LYNNE, library director; b. Chgo., July 29, 1953; d. Glenn Harley and Eleanor Clara Rogers; children: Reyhan. BA, Ill. Wesleyan U., 1974; MLS, U. Tex., 1977. Libr. Radian Corp., Austin, Tex., 1975—80; libr. dir. City of Round Rock, Round Rock, 1980—. Mem. ex officio Friends

Round Rock Pub. Libr., Round Rock, 1983—, Round Rock Pub. Libr. Found., Round Rock, 1991—. Pres. Round Rock Rotary Club, Round Rock, 2000—01, Bus. and Profl. Women's Club, Round Rock, 1983—84; mem. bd. dirs. United Way Greater Williamson Co., 1999—2002, Round Rock Cmty. Choir, Round Rock, 1998—2002; pres. Folk Art Soc. of Round Rock, 2000—01; boy scout dist. cub trainer Boy Scouts of Am. Tomahawk Dist., Austin-Georgetown, Tex., 1991—92. Recipient Dist. Cubscouter of Yr., Boy Scouts Am. Tomahawk Dist., Texas, 1992. Mem.: ALA, Texas Mun. League Libr. Dir.'s Divsn. (pres. 1988—89), Tex. Libr. Assn. (chmn. dist. 3 1984—85). Avocations: quilting, machine embroidery, old house renovations, painting. Office: City Round Rock Pub Libr 216 E Main St Round Rock TX 78664 Office Fax: 512-218-7061. Business E-Mail: dale@round-rock.tx.us.*

RICKLEFS, ROGER ULRICH, retired newspaper editor; b. San Rafael, Calif., July 26, 1940; s. Robert U. and Marian (Markarian) R. BA, Harvard U., 1961. With Wall Street Jour., 1964—, Paris bur. chief, 1983-86, nat. corr., 1986-89, dep. news editor, 1989-90, enterprise editor, 1990-97, Can. editor, 1997-2001; ret., 2001. Editor: The Mind of Robert Louis Stevenson, 1963. 1st lt. U.S. Army, 1962-64. E-mail: ricklefs@att.net.

RICKLES, DONALD JAY, comedian, actor; b. L.I., N.Y., May 8, 1926; s. Max S. and Etta (Feldman) R.; m. Barbara Sklar, Mar. 14, 1965; children: Mindy Beth, Lawrence Corey. Grad., Am. Acad. Dramatic Arts, N.Y.C. Appeared in TV shows The Don Rickles Show, 1971-72, C.P.O. Sharkey, 1976-77, Foul-Ups, Bleeps and Blunders, 1984, Daddy Dearest, 1993; appeared in movies Run Silent, Run Deep, 1958, The Rat Race, 1960, Kelly's Heroes, 1992, Casino, 1995, Toy Story, 1995, Quest for Camelot, 1998, Toy Story 2, 1999, others; appeared as comedian at Stardust Hotel, Las Vegas, Nev., Harrah's Club, Reno and Lake Tahoe, Nev., Tropicana Hotel, Atlantic City, numerous other nightclubs; numerous appearances TV variety shows; rec. albums include Don Rickles Speaks and Hello Dummy. Served with USN, 1943-45. Named Entertainer of Yr., Friars Club, 1974; awarded star on Hollywood Walk of Fame, 2000. Jewish. Office: care Shefrin Co 808 S Ridgeley Dr Los Angeles CA 90036-4727

RICKLIN, ELAINE PAULA, artist, educator; b. Bklyn., Sept. 10, 1940; d. Louis Nathan and Sylvia (Oppenheim) Wank; m. Richard Ricklin, Nov. 1, 1959; children: Audrey Ellen, Roseanne, Peter Jason. BA in Edn., Bklyn. Coll./CUNY, 1962; BA in Fine Art, Met. State Coll., Denver, 1982. Art instr. C.C. of Denver, 1981-84; tchr. art Denver Mus. Natural History, 1987; art instr. Arapahoe C.C., Littleton, Colo., 1988-92; art tchr. for people with AIDS Spark Gallery, Denver, 1993; art tchr. Denver Art Mus., 1985-87, 93; art workshop instr. City Arts on tour-Artreach, Denver, 1994-95; art instr. Curtis Arts & Humanities Ctr., Greenwood Village, 1994—2002, Arvada (Colo.) Ctr. for the Arts, 1988-99; artist-in-residence Denver Pub. Schs./Artreach, 1996—. Juror for nat. art exhibit Spark Gallery, 1995; curator art exhibit of 25 artists U. So. Colo., Pueblo, 1995; lectr. Denver Art Mus., 1993; vis. artist Red Rocks C.C., Golden, Colo., 1991. (hand colored photo permanent collections) Nat. Mus. Women in Arts , (prin. in permanent collection) Tulsa City-County Libr. Sys., (2 person shows) Spark Gallery, Denver, 1986—2001, The Nat. Mus. Women in the Arts, Washington, 1991, UN 4th World Conf. on Women, Beijing, 1995, Denver Art Mus., 1993, 1996, 1998, 1999, 2001, Loveland (Colo.) Mus., 1994, Dana Art Gallery, Wellesley, Mass., 1996, Western N.Mex. U. Gallery , Silver City, 1996, ARC Gallery , Chgo., 1997, Fremont Ctr. Arts , Canon City, Colo., 1997, Arvada (Colo.) Ctr. for Arts, 1997, Balt. Mus. Contemporary Art , 2001, (exhibitions) Decker Libr., Denver, Lights & Fibers Gallery, Portland, The Lincoln Ctr., Ft. Collins, Colo., Auraria Libr. Gallery, Denver;Exhibited in group shows at Mus. Modern Art, N.Y.C., 2002. Recipient First Prize Art award Calcasieu Arts and Humanities Coun., Lake Charles, La., 1987, Spl. Photography award Colo. State Fair Art Exhibit, 1985, 86, 87. Mem. Women's Caucus for Art. Democrat. Jewish. Avocations: dancing (ballet and tap), collecting antiques, reading. Home: 4012 S Wabash St Denver CO 80237-1754

RICKS, CECIL EDWARD, architect; b. Coffeyville, Kans., Nov. 19, 1955; s. Cecil and Pearlie Mae R.; m. Deborah Louise, Jan. 1, 1980; children: Tiffany, Grahamn. AAS, Coffeyville C.C., 1975; Diploma in Drafting Tech., Sekan Tech. Sch., Coffeyville, 1975; BArch, Kans. State U., 1980. Lic. arch., Okla. Intern arch. Architecture Unltd., Coffeyville, 1973-79, McKinley Archs., Tulsa, Okla., 1980-81; arch. assoc. Chadsey Archs., 1981-86; arch. ptnr. Matrix Arch. Engrs. Planners, 1986—. Mem. elec. examiners and appeals bd. City of Tulsa, 1998—. Prin. works include historic renovation Severs Hotel, Muskogee, Okla., 1987, designer Vater's Showroom, Tulsa1991, designer, arch. sports complex Strezhevoy (Siberia) Sports Complex, 1993, designer, arch. USPS Process/Distbn. Ctr., Tulsa, 1998, Schusterman Ctr. U. Okla., Tulsa, 2000. Asst. scoutmaster troop 1 Boy Scouts Am., Tulsa, 1995—. Placed 1st Okla. Excellence in Design competition for Vater's Office Sys. ASID, 1991. Mem.: AIA (bd. dirs. ea. Okla. 2002, chair pubs. com. ea. Okla., chair ea. Okla. newsletter team). Avocations: electronics, music, fitness, camping, information technology. Office: Matrix Archs Engrs Planners Inc 624 S Boston Ave Tulsa OK 74119-1225 E-mail:携cericks@matrixae.com.

RICKS, DAVID ARTEL, business educator, editor; b. Washington, July 21, 1942; s. Artel and Focha (Black) R. BS, Brigham Young U., 1966; MBA, Ind. U., 1968, PhD, 1970. Asst. prof. Ohio State U., 1970-75, assoc. prof., 1975-81; prof. internat. bus. U. S.C., Columbia, 1981-92; v.p. acad. affairs Thunderbird-the Am. Grad. Sch. Internat. mgmt., 1992-94, disting. prof., 1992-99, U. Mo., St. Louis, 1999—. Author books, articles in field, including Directory of Foreign Manufactures in the U.S. (Best Reference Book 1974 ALA, 1975); editor Kent Pub. Co., Boston, 1978—; editor-in-chief Jour. of Internat. Bus. Studies, 1984-92, Jour. Internat. Mgmt., 1994-97. Mem. Acad. internat. bus. (treas. 1981-82), Acad. Mgmt. (chmn. internat. divsn. 1988-89). Home: 7445 Byron Pl Clayton MO 63105-2967 Office: 8001 Natural Bridge Rd Saint Louis MO 63121-4401

RICKS, DAVID JOEL, consumer products executive, consultant; b. Rexburg, Idaho, Dec. 18, 1953; s. Rudger Vernon and Laura Louise R.; m. Nelly Ricks, Sept. 18, 1981. BS, Brigham Young U., 1978, MBA, 1983. Mgr. Record with the Hits, Salt Lake City, 1986-87; supr. Fidelity Investments, 1987-88; dir. tech. svcs. Desert King Corp., Chula Vista, Calif., 1988-89, Coronado Natural Oils, Chula Vista, 1989-93; con. DR Enterprises, 1993-95; sr. v.p. Superior Natural Oils, Inc., Tucson, 1996-98; cons. D.R. Cons., Rexburg, Ill., 1998—. Bd. dirs. Vinegar Inst., Atlanta; cons. Spectrum Organic Products Inc., Petaluma, Calif., 1998—, Nembus Publs., Vancouver, Can., 1998—. Author: Bailey's Book on Industrial Oils and Salts, 1998, (mag.) Cosmetics and Toiletries, 1991; inventor in field. Mem. N.Y. Acad. Scis. Avocations: music, fishing, writing, golfing. Office: DR Cons PO Box 828 Rexburg ID 83440 E-mail: dricks@nstep.net.

RICKS, JOHN ADDISON, history educator; b. Charlotte, N.C., Aug. 18, 1939; s. John Addison II and Mamye Snow (Turner) R.; m. Nancy Elaine Ricks, Apr. 23 1966; children: Elizabeth Anne, John Addison IV. BA, Davidson Coll., 1961; MA, Tulane U., 1963; PhD, U. N.C., 1974. Instr. history Montreat (N.C.) - Anderson Coll., 1966-68; from instr. to prof. Valdosta (Ga.) State U., 1968-88; prof. history, chmn. social sci. edn., bus. adminstrn. div. Mid. Ga. Coll., Cochran, 1988—. Contbr. articles to jours., newspapers. Pres. Friends of the Libr., Cochran, 1989-90; clk. of session, elder First Presbyn. Ch., Eastman, 1990-93; scoutmaster Boy Scouts Am., Valdosta, 1982-84; mem. Valdosta Bd. Edn., 1976-80. 1st lt. U.S. Army, 1963-65. Fulbright Found. grantee, 1997. Mem. So. Assn. Colls. and Schs. (mem. vis. team 1990), So. Assn. Secondary Schs. and Colls. (mem. vis. team 1979), Ga. Assn. Historians (pres. 1994-95), Cochran C. of C., Rotary (pres. 1993-94, Rotarian of Yr. 1997, Paul Harris fellow 2001), Kiwanis (treas. 1980-82, Kiwanian of Yr. 1979). Democrat. Presbyterian. Avocations: piano, weightlifting, Nordic Track exercise, reading, chess. Home: 712 Beech St Cochran GA 31014 Office: Mid Ga Coll 1100 Second St Cochran GA 31014 E-mail: jricks@warrior.mgc.peachnet.edu.

RICKS, JOHN PAUL, management consultant; b. Greenwood, Miss., Mar. 1, 1955; s. James Vernon and Myrdice Mae (Bailey) R. AA, Miss. Delta Jr. Coll., 1975; BSBA, Delta State U., 1978. Ptnr. Rick's Motor Svc., Greenwood, Miss., 1960-81; v.p. MMR Enterprises, Ltd., 1981-83; pres. Creative Concepts, 1983—. Mktg. cons. MMR Enterprises Ltd., Greenwood, 1985-88. Sustaining mem. Rep. Nat. Com., Washington, 1975-83. With Miss. N.G., 1990—. Mem. Am. Mktg. Assn., Beta Alpha Scholars Soc., Phi Theta Kappa, Delta Mu Delta, Phi Kappa Phi. Republican. Baptist. Avocations: backpacking, photography, antique car restoration. Home and Office: Creative Concepts PO Box 44 Greenwood MS 38935-0044

RICKS, JOYCIA CAMILLA, complaints manager, lawyer; b. Atlanta, Feb. 17, 1949; d. George Palmer and Johnnie Mae (Ricks) Redd. BBA, Albany State Coll., 1971; MS, Ga. State U., 1977; JD, Woodrow Wilson Coll. Law, Atlanta, 1979, LLM, 1987. Bar: Ga. 1979, U.S. Dist. Ct. (no. dist.) Ga. 1979, U.S. Ct. Appeals (5th cir.) 1979. Acctg. clk. Gulf Oil Corp., Atlanta, 1971; clk. EEOC, 1971-73, paralegal specialist, 1973-79, investigator, 1979-91, supervisory investigator, 1992-2000, complaints mgr., 2000—; gen. counsel Albany State Coll. Alumni Assn., 1986-90. Mem. NAACP, Atlanta, 1983—. Recipient Presdl. citation award Equal Opportunity in Higher Edn., Washington, 1981, Spl. Achievement award EEOC, Atlanta, 1982-84, 86-89, Employee of Yr., Atlanta Dist. Office, 1997. Mem. ABA, Atlanta Bar Assn., Ga. Assn. Black Women Attys., Albany State Coll. Alumni Assn. (pres. Atlanta chpt. 1983-85, gen. counsel 1986-90), ATLA, Ga. State U. Alumni Assn., Woodrow Wilson Coll. Law Alumni Assn., Women of the Ch. Presbyn. (hon. life), Am. Bus. Women's Assn. (Woman of Yr., Tara chpt. 1985, 91), Spreading Oak Cmty. Club. Democrat. Presbyterian. E-mial. Office: CDC/OEEO Mail Stop D-20 1600 Clifton Rd Atlanta GA 30333 E-mail: JRicks@cdc.gov.

RICKS, MARY F(RANCES), archaeologist, anthropologist, consultant; b. Portland, Oreg., July 6, 1939; d. Leo and Frances Helen (Corcoran) Samuel; m. Robert Stanley Ricks, Jan. 7, 1961; children: Michael Stanley, Allen Gilbert. BA, Whitman Coll., 1961; MA, Portland State U., 1977, MPA, 1981, PhD, 1995. Asst. to dir. auxiliary services Portland State U., 1975-79, instnl. researcher, 1979-85, dir. instnl. research and planning, 1985-97, rsch. assoc. prof., 1994-97, rsch. assoc. prof. emerita, 1997—. Presenter in field. Contbr. articles to profl. jours. Vol. archeologist BLM-USDI, Lakeview, Oreg., 1975—. Fellow Soc. Applied Anthropology; mem. Soc. Am. Archaeology, Pacific N.W. Assn. Instnl. Rsch. and Planning (pres. 1990-91), Assn. Oreg. Archaeologists (v.p. 1988-90), Assn. Instl. Rsch., Sigma Xi. Home: 8106 SW 187th Ave Beaverton OR 97007-5697 E-mail: ricksm@pdx.edu.

RICKS, RICHARD, information technology executive; married; 2 children. Various positions with opers., quality, customer svc., tech. product line mgmt. and installation Nortel Networks, 1979, v.p. global opers, info. svcs., chief info. officer Canada. Mem. various profl. coms.; bd. dirs. various cos.; lectr. in field. Office: Nortel Networks 8200 Dixie Rd Brampton ON Canada L6T 5P6*

RICKS, RICHARD KENNETH, retired thoracic surgeon; b. St. Augustine, Fla., Sept. 19, 1933; s. Claude Lee and Thelma Cecilia Ricks; m. Kathryn Elaine Ricks, Dec. 28, 1990 (div.); children: Jeffrey Mark, Richard Scott, Stephen Bret, Carol Gaye. BA, Vanderbilt U., 1954; MD, Baylor U., 1958. Diplomate Am. Bd. Surgery, Am. Bd. Thoracic Surgery. Pvt. practice thoracic and cardiovascular surgery, Houston, 1966—2000; asst. prof. surgery Baylor Coll. Medicine, 1966—2000; chief surgery Meml. Hosp. S.W., 1972—73, 1977—78, asst. chief thoracic surgery, 1979, 1997—2000. Capt Med. Corps. U.S. Army, 1965—66. Fellow: ACS. Methodist. Avocations: hunting, fishing, golf. Home: 95 N Windsail Pl Spring TX 77381

RICKS, ROBERT MICHAEL, software engineer, educator; b. Chester, Pa., Mar. 22, 1950; s. Thomas Eugene and Lucille (Manning) R. AA in Lang. Arts, Allan Hancock Community Coll., 1983; BS in Computer Sci., Nat. U., 1987, MS in Software Engring., 1988. Sr. console operator Penn Cen. Transp. Co., Phila., 1968-75; data editor RCA, Kwajalein, Mich., 1975-78; programmer, analyst Logicon, San Diego, 1978-77; system engr. Singer-Link, Sunnyvale, Calif., 1979-82; system analyst ITT/Fed. Electric, Vanderberg AFB, 1982-83; sr. sci. analyst Northrop ASD, Pico Rivera, 1983-85; sr. software engr. Jet Propulsion Lab., Pasadena, 1985-89; sr. engr. CTA, Ridgecrest, 1989-90, Unisys, Camarillo, 1990—. Mem. Presdl. Task Force, Vanderberg AFB, 1981. With U.S. Army, 1970-73. Republican. Baptist. Avocations: flying, teaching, cub scouts. Office: Unisys 5151 Camino Ruiz Camarillo CA 93012-8625

RICOTTA, JOHN JOSEPH, vascular surgeon, educator; b. Buffalo, Sept. 13, 1949; s. Joseph J. and Joan (Tarantino) R.; m. Gloria DeSantis, July 25, 1970; children: Joseph, Genna, Lise. BA, Yale Coll., 1969; MD, Johns Hopkins U., 1973. Diplomate Am. Bd. Surgery. Intern, resident Johns Hopkins Hosp., 1973-79; instr. surgery Johns Hopkins U., Balt., 1979-80; asst. prof. surgery U. Rochester, N.Y., 1980-85, assoc. prof. surgery, 1985-88; prof. surgery, dir. vascular surgery SUNY, Buffalo, 1988-97, prof., chmn. dept. surgery Stony Brook, 1997—. Fellow ACS; mem. Soc. Vascular Surgery, Internat. Soc. Cardiovascular Surgery, Soc. Univ. Surgeons, Ctrl. Surg. Assn., Ea. Vascular Soc. (recorder 1992—, sec. 1996—, pres. 2001), Soc. Clin. Vascular Surgery (pres. 2000), Am. Surg. Assn. Office: U Med Ctr Hsc T 19 Rm 020 Stony Brook NY 11794-0001 E-mail: Ricotta@surg.som.sunysb.edu.

RIDDER, LINDA GAYLE, librarian; b. Chgo., Apr. 17, 1949; d. Gale Eugene and Yvonne Lucille (Marcotte) A.; m. George Larry Ridder, Mar. 29, 1970; 1 child, Michael Eric. BA English, St. Mary's U., 1971; MS Libr. Sci., Our Lady of the Lake U., 1977. Cert. media specialist; profl. libr.; provisional cert. secondary English and social studies, Tex. Tchr. fourth grade St. Thomas More Cath. Sch., San Antonio, 1971-72; tchr. English/dept. coord. Sam Rayburn Mid. Sch., 1972-77; libr. media specialist Gregorio Esparza Elem., 1977-85, H.B. Zachry Mid. Sch., San Antonio, 1985—. Mem. Sch. Leadership Team, 1985—, Sch. Adv. Team, 1994—, recording sec.; mem. Northside Dist. Comm. Network Com., 1996—, Zachry Tech. Task Force Com., 1996—. Author Middle School Integrated Curriculum Guide of Library Skills, 1991; dir. accreditation reports, 1979, 84. Mem. St. Luke's Cath. Ch., San Antonio, 1975—. Mem. Nat. Reading Assn., Tex. Libr. Assn., Phi Delta Kappa. Home: 4607 Lightning Ln San Antonio TX 78238-2907 Office: HB Zachry Mid Sch 9410 Timber Path San Antonio TX 78250-4921

RIDDER, PAUL ANTHONY, newspaper executive; b. Duluth, Minn., Sept. 22, 1940; s. Bernard H. and Jane (Delano) R.; m. Constance Louise Meach, Nov. 6, 1960; children: Katherine Lee Pennoyer, Linda Jane, Susan Delano Cobb, Paul Anthony, Jr. BA in Econs., U. Mich., 1962. With Aberdeen (S.D.) Am. News, 1962-63; With Pasadena (Calif.) Star News, 1963-64; with San Jose (Calif.) Mercury News, 1964-86, bus. mgr., 1968-75, gen. mgr., 1975-77, pub., 1977-86, pres., 1979-86, Knight-Ridder Newspaper Div., Miami, Fla., 1986—; pres., chmn., CEO Knight-Ridder, 1989—, also bd. dirs. Bd. dirs. Seattle Times, Knight-Ridder, Inc., Newspaper First. Bd. dirs. United Way; mem. adv. bd. Ctr. for Econ. Policy Devel. Stanford U., U. Mich.; mem. pres.' adv. bd. U. Mich. Named Calif. Pub. of Yr., 1983, Newspaper Exec. of Yr., Ad Week, 1991. Mem. Fla. C. of C. (bd. dirs., coun. of 100), Cypress Point Club, Indian Creek Club, Pine Valley Golf Club.*

RIDDERHEIM, MARY MARGARET, psychotherapist; b. Chillicothe, Ohio, Mar. 13, 1946; d. Marion Othello and Esther Marie (Justice) Park; m. Denson Coy Pate, Jr., Dec. 19, 1965 (dec. Mar., 1990); children: Elizabeth Jewel, Mary Kathryn, Melissa Fay; m. David Sigfreid Ridderheim, Jr., Oct 19, 1991; stepchildren: Cheryl, Carla, Katie, Kris, David, Joe. BS in Psychology, W. Tex. A&M, Canyon, 1988; MS in Psychology, St. Francis Coll., Fort Wayne, Ind., 1991; postgrad studies in Psychology, Adler Sch. Profl. Psychology, Chgo., 1992-96. Lic. mental health counselor, Fort Wayne, Ind., 1996—; therapist Barry and Barry, 1996-98; ind. contractor therapist Luth. Social Svcs., 1998—. Program dir. After Sch. Activities Forest Hills Sch. Dist., Cin., 1972-74, New Richmond Exempted Sch. Dist., 1973-75; initiator Young Authors Program, New Richmond Sch. Dist., 1976; outpatient svcs. counselor Charter Beacon Hosp., Fort Wayne, 1994-95. Mem. APA, Am. Counseling Assn., Am. Assn. Christian Counselors, Stepfamily Assn. Am. (pres. Ind. chpt.), Ind. Counselors Assn., Ind. Counselor Assn. Alcohol and Drug Abuse, No. Am. Soc. Adlerian Psychology. Home: 12117 Chesterbrook Ct Fort Wayne IN 46845-1965 Office: Luth Social Svcs of Indiana Barry & Barry Counseling 330 Madison St Fort Wayne IN 46802-3126

RIDDERING, DONALD LEE, retired language educator, historian; b. Marysville, Mich., Feb. 28, 1922; s. Albert A. and Blanche Hannah (Kirk) R.; m. Ali Anna Drijver, Dec. 19, 1950; children: Hannah, Emily, Julia, Martha. BA, Ea. Mich. U., 1943; postgrad., U. Amsterdam (The Netherlands), 1949—50, U. Poitiers, France, 1950—51; MA, Columbia U., 1952. Cert. tchr., Mich. Tchr. Latin, counselor Garden City (Mich.) H.S., 1952-55; tchr. Latin dept., head fgn. langs. Cooley H.S., Detroit, 1955-86; tchr. Latin Wayne State U., 1975-86, ret., 1986. Pres. Mich. Classical Conf., 1963, 67, Fgn. Lang. Assn., Mich., 1974-76; leader Experiment in Internat. Living, Putney, Vt., 1954, 60. Author: History of Salem, 8 monographs, 1989-91. Supr. Salem (Mich.) Twp., 1993-96; treas. South Lyon (Mich.) Sch. Bd., 1960-62; mem. Historic Dist. Commn., Washtenaw County, Mich., 1993—. Lt. (jg) USNR, 1943-46. Fulbright grantee, U. Amsterdam, 1949-50, summer study grantee U.S. Govt., Am. Acad. Rome, 1962; recipient Barbara Ort-Smith award Mich. Fgn. Lang. Assn., 2000. Mem. Hist. Soc. (Salem, Mich., pres. 1991—). Democrat. Avocations: local history, Dutch-American topics, historic preservation, nature preservation. Home: PO Box 75228 Salem MI 48175-0228

RIDDICK, ANDREA CELESTINE, accountant; b. Bklyn., Jan. 9, 1963; d. Cicero and Shirley Temple (Magee) R. BBA in Acctg., Bernard M. Baruch Coll., 1986. Profl. tax preparer. Acctg. intern Victoreen Inc., Carle Place, N.Y., 1985-86; acct. Pinkerton's Inc., Manhattan, 1986-88; tax acct. Fleischman & Co., CPAs, 1988-89; acct. Am. Internat. Group/Fin. Products, 1989, Fed. Aviation Adminstrn./John F. Kennedy Internat. Airport, Queens, N.Y., 1989—. Acct. Neighborhood Housing Svcs., Inc., Queens, 1992—. Mem. 145th St. Neighborhood Block Assn., Queens, 1980—, Square Deal Civic Assn., Queens, 1991—. Recipient Bernard M. Baruch Incentive award Bernard M. Baruch Coll., Manhattan, 1981-82. Mem. N.Y. State Assn. CPA Candidates, Baruch Coll. Alumni Assn., Fed. Women's Prog. Democrat. Avocations: computer programming, reading, tennis, karate, tutor for young children in reading and math. Home: 11457 145th St Jamaica NY 11436-1140

RIDDICK, DANIEL HOWISON, obstetrics and gynecology educator, priest; b. Lynchburg, Va., Dec. 12, 1941; s. Joseph Henry and Nancy Eloise (Gordon) R.; m. Louisa McIntosh Spruill, June 9, 1963; children: Ellen, Daniel. BA, Duke U., 1963, MD, 1967, PhD in Physiology, 1969. Diplomate Am. Bd. Ob-Gyn, Am. Bd. Reproductive Endocrinology; ordained priest Episc. Ch., 1969. Asst. prof. physiology Duke U., Durham, N.C., 1973-74; asst. prof. ob-gyn U. Conn. Sch. Medicine, Farmington, 1974-76, dir. reproductive endocrinology and infertility, 1974-85, assoc. prof. ob-gyn, 1976-81, prof. ob-gyn, 1981-85; prof., chmn. ob-gyn dept. U. Vt., Burlington, 1985-97, assoc. dean grad. med. edn., 1987-88. Editor: Reproductive Endocrinology in Clinical Practice, 1987; editor: (with others) Pathology of Infertility, 1987. Mem. ACOG, Am. Fertility Soc. (pres. 1992-93), Am. Gynecol. and Obstet. Soc. Avocation: sheep-raising. Home: 680 Mayo Rd Huntington VT 05462-9410 Office: Fletcher Allen Health Care Dept of Obstetrics & Gynecology 111 Colchester Ave Burlington VT 05401-1416

RIDDICK, FRANK ADAMS, JR. physician, medical association administrator; b. Memphis, June 14, 1929; s. Frank Adams and Falba (Crawford) Riddick; m. Mary Belle Alston, June 15, 1952; children: Laura Elizabeth Dufresne, Frank Adams III, John Alston. BA cum laude, Vanderbilt U., 1951, MD, 1954. Diplomate Am. Bd. Internal Medicine. Intern Barnes Hosp., St. Louis, 1954—55, resident in medicine, 1957—60; fellow in metabolic diseases Washington U., 1960—61; staff Ochsner Clinic (Ochsner Found. Hosp.), New Orleans, 1961—, head sect. endocrinology and metabolic disease, 1976—83, asst. med. dir., 1968—72, assoc. med. dir., 1972—75, med. dir., 1975—92; CEO Alton Ochsner Med. Found., New Orleans, 1992—2001; CEO emeritus Ochsner Clinic Found., 2001—. Bd. govs. Am. Bd. Internal Medicine, 1973—80; clin. prof. Tulane U., New Orleans, 1977—; trustee Alton Ochsner Med. Found., 1973—, CEO, 1991—; chmn. bd. Ochsner Health Plan, 1983—92; pres. Orleans Svc. Corp., 1976—80, South La. Med. Assocs., New Orleans, 1978—; dir. Brent House Corp., New Orleans, 1980—; chmn. Accreditation Coun. on Grad. Med. Edn., 1986—87, v.p. nat. resident matching program, 1986—90, mem. accreditation coun. on med. edn., 1988—90. Bd. govs. Isidore Newman Sch., New Orleans, 1987—93; trustee St. Martin's Protestant Episc. Sch., Metairie, 1970—84. Recipient Tchg. award, Alton Ochsner Med. Found., 1969, Disting. Alumnus award, Castle Heights Mil. Acad., 1979, Physician Exec. award, Am. Coll. Med. Group Adminstrs., 1984, Disting. Alumnus award, Vanderbilt U. Sch. Medicine, 1988. Master: ACP; fellow: Am. Coll. Physician Execs. (pres. 1987—88); mem.: NAS Inst. Medicine, AMA (ho. dels. 1971—92, chmn. coun. on med. edn. 1983—85, coun. on jud. and ethical affairs 1995—2002, chair 2001—02), Am. Group Practice Assn. (pres. 1992—94), Soc. Med. Adminstrs. (pres. 1995—), Am. Diabetes Assn., Endocrine Soc., Am. Soc. Internal Medicine (trustee 1970—76, Disting. Internist award), Cosmos Club, New Orleans Country Club, Boston Club. Home: 1923 Octavia St New Orleans LA 70115-5651 Office: Ochsner Clinic 1516 Jefferson Hwy New Orleans LA 70121-2429

RIDDICK, JOSEPH ROBERT, health analyst, columnist; b. Suffolk, Va., Feb. 1, 1952; s. Joseph Robert and Lillian Barber Riddick; children: Lucy, Andrew. BS, Barton Coll., 1975; MBA, Averett U., 1998; postgrad., Va. Commonwealth U., 1998—. Program adminstr. Ea. Va. Med. Sch., Norfolk, 1992-98; faculty rschr. Va. Commonwealth U., Richmond, 1998-2000; sr. health analyst Va. Dept. Juvenile Justice, 2000—; owner Joseph Robert Riddick and Assocs., 2000—. Cons. Va. Dept. Health, Richmond, 1992-99, Ea. Va. HIV Care Consortium, Norfolk, 1999. Cofounder Camp Wakonda, Norfolk, 1995; pres. AIDS Legal Svcs. in Ea. Va., Virginia Beach, 1996-98; mem. Suffolk Leadership Acad., 2000. Mem. Am. Soc. Pub. Adminstrn., Nat. Trust for Hist. Preservation, Assn. for Preservation of Va. Antiquities, Pi Alpha Alpha. Episcopalian. Avocations: antiques, reading. Home: PO Box 773 Nellysford VA 22958 Office: Va Dept Juvenile Justice 700 E Franklin St PO Box 1110 Richmond VA 23219 E-mail: jrmcr@msn.com.

RIDDICK, WINSTON WADE, SR. lawyer; b. Crowley, La., Feb. 11, 1941; s. Hebert Hobson and Elizabeth (Wade) R.; m. Patricia Ann Turner, Dec. 25, 1961;1 child, Winston Wade. BA, U. Southwestern La., 1962; MA, U. N.C., 1963; PhD, Columbia U., 1965; JD, La. State U., 1973. Bar: La. 1974, U.S. Dist. Ct. (so., mid. and we. dists.) La., U.S. Ct. Appeals (5th cir.), U.S. Supreme Court. Asst. prof. gov., dir. Inst. Gov. Research, La. State U., Baton Rouge, 1966-67; dir. La. Higher Edn. Facilities Commn., 1967-72; exec. asst. state supt. La. Dept. Edn., 1972-73; law ptnr. Riddick & Riddick, 1973—; asst. commnr., gen. counsel La. Dept. Agr., 1981-82. Cons. Riddick & Assoc., Baton Rouge, 1973—; part-time law faculty mem. So. Univ. Law Ctr., Baton Rouge, 1974-95; assoc. prof., 1995-99, prof. law, 1999—, exec. asst. atty. gen. State of La., 1987-91. Spl. asst. to Gov. John J. McKeithen on Nat. Ctr. for Edn. in Politics Fellowship, 1966-67; state campaign mgr. Gillis W. Long for Gov., Baton Rouge, 1971; mem. East Baton Rouge Parish Dem. Exec. Com., 1981-84. Mem. La. Trial Lawyers Assn. (bd. govs. 1978-80), real estate investor and property mgr., 1975—. Presbyterian. Office: Riddick & Riddick 1563 Oakley Dr Baton Rouge LA 70806-8622 E-mail: wriddick@sus.edu.

RIDDLE, CHARLES ADDISON, III, state legislator, lawyer; b. Marksville, La., June 8, 1955; s. Charles Addison Jr. and Alma Rita (Gremillion) R.; m. Margaret Susan Noone, Mar. 24, 1978; children: Charles Addison IV, John H., Michael J. BA, La. State U., 1976, JD, 1980. Bar: La. 1980, U.S. Dist. Ct. (mid. and we. dists.) La. 1983, U.S. Ct. Appeals (5th cir.) 1988, U.S. Supreme Ct. 1991, U.S. Ct. Vets. Appeals 1994. Assoc. Riddle & Bennett, Marksville, 1980; pvt. practice, 1981—; mem. La. Ho. of Reps., Baton Rouge, 1992—; reelected La. House of Reps., 1995-99, 1999—. Elected La. State Dem. Cen. com., Avoyelles Parish, 1983-87, Parish Exec. Demo. Com. 1987-91. Mem. Avoyelles Bar Assn. (pres. 1987-88), Bunkie Rotary (bd. dirs.), Marksville Lions, Marksville C. of C. (pres. 1988-92). Office: PO Box 608 208 E Mark St Marksville LA 71351-2416 E-mail: criddle777@aol.com.

RIDDLE, DON RAMON, lawyer; b. Abilene, Tex., Dec. 28, 1937; s. Glen Boyce and Pauline (Price) R.; m. Jenny Lu Brunton, Apr. 27, 1963; children: Stacy, Todd. BA, Baylor U., 1960; LLB cum laude, U. Houston, 1966. Bar: Tex. (State Bar) 1966, Tex. (U.S. Dist. Ct. (so. dist.)) 1966, Tex. Bd. legal specialization (Bd. cert. Personal Injury Trial Law). Assoc. Brown Kronzer Abraham Watkins & Steely, Houston, 1966-69, ptnr., 1969-74, Riddle, Murphrey, O'Quinn & Cannon, Houston, 1974-79; prin. Riddle & Assocs., 1979-94; ptnr. Riddle & Baumgartner, 1994—. Mem. Tex. State Bar grievance Com., Houston, 1975-78. Sgt. USMC, 1960-66. Mem. Tex. Trial Lawyers Assn. (dir. 1971-73). Office: Riddle & Baumgartner 5625 Fm 1960 Rd W # 210 Houston TX 77069-3804

RIDDLE, EARL WALDO, retired church official, small business owner; b. St. Joseph, Mo., Jan. 29, 1920; s. Roderick Edwin and Nannie Myrtle (Albertson) R.; m. Etta Kathryn McGauhey, Aug. 23, 1942; children: Martha Anne Riddle Moretty, Mary Janet Riddle Switzer, David Earl. AS, Mo. Western Coll., 1940; AB, U. Kans., 1942; MDiv, Boston U., 1945, postgrad.,

1946-50; D Ministry, San Francisco Theol. Sem., 1976. Ordained to ministry United Meth. Ch. as elder, 1945; cert. leader in sex edn. for youth. Assoc. pastor College Ave. Meth. Ch., West Somerville, Mass., 1946-50; dir. Wesley Found. Oreg. State U., Corvallis, 1950-54; pastor Forest Grove (Oreg.) Meth. Ch., 1954-60; sr. pastor lst Meth. Ch., Twin Falls, Idaho, 1960-65, Caldwell, 1965-68; coun. dir. Oreg.-Idaho Conf., United Meth. Ch., Portland, Oreg., 1968-85; owner, operator Riddle Enterprises, 1968—; dir. youth work Morgan Meml. Ch. All Nations, Boston, 1942-45. Cons. on fin. and ministerial tax; ptnr. Riddle Engring. Co.; dir. Stewardship Enterprises; mem. Nat. United Meth. Assn. Communicators, 1954—; exec. dir. local com. Gen. Conf., United Meth. Ch., Portland, 1976, mem. Gen. Conf., 1964, 66,68, 70, Western Juridsictional Conf., 1964, 68, Gen. Bd. Edn., 1966-72; mem. Interbd. Com. on Missionary Edn., 1968-72; mem. exec. com. Conf. Program Dirs. Assn., 1968-72, Conf. Officers Assn., 1973-76; pres. Nat. Assn. Conf. Coun. Dirs., 1982-84, Nat. Assn. Stewardship Leaders, 1983-84; conf. sec. Oreg.-Idaho Ann. Conf., 1985-88; chmn. com. on correlation and edit. revision The Gen. Conf. of United Meth. Ch., 1988-2000. Editor: History of National Association of Conference Council Directors, 1974, Oreg.-Idaho Conf. jour., 1985-88, Tax Talk for Ministers, 1976-90; chmn. com. on correlation and editorial revision The Discipline, 1988, 92, 96; contbr. numerous articles to profl. jours. Coun. officer, scoutmaster Boy Scouts Am., 1942-45, 60-65, 68-76; exec. sec. Oreg.-Idaho United Meth. Found., 1970-85; bd. dirs., chmn. Forest Grove Union High Sch., 1955-60; mem. Oreg. Gov.'s Com. on Sexual Preference, 1976-78; mem. human rsch. com. Oreg. Health Scis. U., 1974—; bd. dirs. Planned Parenthood Assn., 1984-89, Samaritan Counseling Ctr., 1985-88; mem. fin. devel. com. Ecumenical Ministries Oreg., 1970-86, mem. Edn. Commn., 1970-85; mem. clergy com. on Oreg. Health Decisions, 1983-85; mem. health edn. curriculum development com. Oreg. Dept. Edn., 1985-88. Chaplain USNR, 1945-46. Recipient plaques and awards Boy Scouts Am., Exceptional Svc. Jason Lee award for excellence in communications, 1977, Exceptional Svc. award Parents and Friends of Lesbians and Gays, 1986, civil liberties award ACLU, 1989, spl. svc. award for Russian refugee work, 1990, Spl. Mission award United Meth. Women, 1998, Life Saver award Family Homeless Shelter, 1998. Home: 12705 SE River Rd Apt 312N Portland OR 97222-9777 E-mail: earl.riddle@worldnet.att.net., riddlee@ohsu.edu. *It is my hope that the world would be a better place because I traveled here.*

RIDDLE, JARED MATTHEW, language educator, actor; b. Gary, Ind., July 3, 1969; adopted s. Lee Jay and Sandie Lee Jewett; s. Gerald Ellis and Wava Marie Riddle; life ptnr. Brian Michael Stevens, Aug. 15, 1998. BA, Ind. U., 1994; postgrad. in engring., Purdue U. Pineapple picker Maui (Hawaii) Pineapple Co., 1985; shoe salesman Kaplan Shoe, Merrillville, Ind., 1987-88; missionary LDS Ch., Tampa, Fla., 1988-90; artistic dir. Bulldog Enterprises, Hobart, Ind., 1994-96; adj. faculty Ivy Tech. State Coll., East Chicago, 1996-2000, full time faculty, 2000—. Actor Joseph and the Amazing Technicolor Dreamcoat, 1995, 2001, Jesus Christ Superstar, 1996, 2001, 2002, Elvis the Musical, 1999, Little Shop of Horrors, 1998, Brigadoon, 1999. Mem. Nat. Coun. Tchrs. English, Alpha Psi Omega (pres. 1993-94, Outstanding Sr. in Theatre 1994). Democrat. Unitarian-Universalist. Avocations: Shakespeare, movies, theories of Follcah & Deleuze. Office: Ivy Tech State Coll 410 E Columbus Dr East Chicago IN 46312 E-mail: naoslives@aol.com., jriddle@ivy.tech.edu.

RIDDLE, MARK ALAN, child psychiatrist; b. Huntingburg, Ind., Feb. 18, 1948; s. James G. and Louise (Burgdorf) R.; m. Clarine Carol Nardi, Aug. 15, 1971; children: Carl, Julia. BA, Ind. U., 1970, MS, 1973, MD, 1977. Intern in pediatrics Ind. U. Med. Ctr., Indpls., 1977-78; resident in psychiatry Sch. Medicine Yale U., New Haven, 1978-81; fellow in child psychiatry Yale Child Study Ctr., 1981-83; asst. prof. child psychiatry Sch. Medicine Yale U., 1983-89, assoc. prof. child psychiatry, 1989-93; dir. divsn. child and adolescent psychiatry Johns Hopkins Med. Inst., 1993—. Mem. pediatrics panel U.S. Pharmacopea, 1995-2000. Assoc. editor Jour. Child and Adolescent Psychopharmacology, 1992—; editor Pediatric Psychopharmacology I & II, 1995; contbr. over 100 articles to profl. jours. Mem. med. com. Tourette Syndrome Assn., 1989-98. Mem. Am. Acad. Child and Adolescent Psychiatry (coun. mem. 1999—). E-mail: mriddle@jhmi.edu.

RIDDLE, MARNITA MARIE, medical nurse; b. Dubuque, Iowa, Mar. 18, 1962; d. Cletus Arthur and Monica Agnes (Decker) Thielen; m. Michael Eugene Riddle, June 15, 1991. BSN, U. Iowa, 1984; MSN, St. Louis U., 1994. ACLS, BLS. Staff nurse U. Iowa Hosp., Iowa City, 1984-87, Traveling Nurses, 1987-88; supr. cardiovasc. unit Morristown (N.J.) Meml. Hosp., 1988-90; mgr. cardiovasc. unit Deaconess Med. Ctr., St. Louis, 1990-92; clin. nurse cardiovasc. unit St. Louis U. Health Ctr., 1992-95; clin. nurse Heart Inst., St. Joseph's Hosp. Atlanta, 1995—, dir. Heart and Vascular Ctr. and Stroke Ctr., 1997-99, dir. neurosci. ctr. and stroke ctr., 1999-2000; nurse clinician St. Luke's Hosp., St. Louis, 2001—02; nurse clinician/researcher law firm, 2001—. Mem. ANA, AACN (cert.), Am. Assn. Neurosci. Nurses, Nat. Stroke Assn., Am. Heart Assn., Assn. Clin. Rsch. Profsl., Sigma Theta Tau.

RIDDLE, MICHAEL LEE, lawyer; b. Oct. 7, 1946; s. Joy Lee and Francis Irene (Brandes) R.; m. Suzan Ellen Shaw, May 25, 1969 (div.); m. Carol Jackson, Aug. 13, 1977; 1 child, Robert Andrew. BA, Tex. Tech U., 1969, JD with honors, 1972. Bar: Tex. 1972, U.S. Dist. Ct. (no. dist.) Tex. 1972, U.S. Ct. Appeals (5th cir.) Tex. 1972. Assoc. Geary Brice Barron & Stahl, Dallas, 1972-75; ptnr. Baker Glast Riddle Tuttle & Elliott, 1975-80; ptnr., mng. ptnr. Middleburg, Riddle & Gianna, 1980—; chmn., CEO MRG Document Techs., 2000—. Bd. dirs. Dallas Opera. Bd. dirs. U.S.A. Film Festival, pres., 1984-86, North Tex. Pub. Broadcasting, 1992-97; chmn., bd. dirs. Provident Bancorp Tex., 1987-90. Mem. ABA, Tex. Bar Assn., Dallas Bar Assn., Coll. of State Bar of Tex., Lakewood Country Club, Crescent Club. Democrat. Lutheran. Office: 717 N Harwood Ste 2400 Dallas TX 75201 E-mail: mriddle@midrid.com.

RIDDLE, STURGIS LEE, minister; b. Stephenville, Tex., May 26, 1909; s. Lee and Linda (McKinney) R.; m. Elisabeth Pope Sloan, Oct. 14, 1939. BA magna cum laude, Stanford U., 1931; student, Gen. Theol. Sem., N.Y.C., 1931-32; B.D. cum laude, Episcopal Theol. Sch., Cambridge, Mass., 1934; D.D., Seabury Western Theol. Sem., Evanston, Ill., 1957. Ordained deacon P.E. Ch., 1934, priest, 1935; Episcopal chaplain U. Calif., 1934-37; instr. church Div. Sch. of Pacific, 1934-37; rector Caroline Ch., Setauket, L.I., 1937-40; asst. minister St. Thomas Ch., N.Y.C., 1940-46; rector St. James Ch., Florence, Italy, 1947-49; dean Am. Cathedral of Holy Trinity, Paris, France, 1949-74, dean emeritus, 1974—. Exchange preacher Trinity Ch., N.Y.C., 1956-57, 62, St. Bartholomew's Ch., N.Y.C., 1958, 63, 73, St. John's Cathedral, Denver, 1959, Grace Cathedral, San Francisco, 1960, Nat. Cathedral, Washington, 1961, Trinity Ch. Boston, 1964, St. Andrew's Cathedral, Honolulu, 1965, St. John's Ch., Washington, 1966, 67, 68, 70, 73, St. Thomas' Ch., N.Y., 1968, 73, St. Paul's Cathedral, Boston, 1969; clerical dep. Europe to Gen. Conv. P.E. Ch., 1949-60, 64, 70 Author: One Hundred Years, 1950; contbg. Author: We Believe in Prayer, 1958, That Day with God, 1965. Hon. gov. Am. Hosp. in Paris; fellow Morgan Library, N.Y.C., trustee bd. fgn. parishes; chmn. Friends of the Am. Cathedral in Paris. Decorated Legion of Honor France; grand cross and grand prelate Sovereign Order St. John of Jerusalem Knights of Malta; grand cross Ordre du Milice de Jesus Christ; Patriarchal Order Mt. Athos. Mem. Nat. Inst. Social Sci., Am. Soc. French Legion of Honor, Phi Beta Kappa. Clubs: Union, University, Pilgrims, Spouting Rock Beach Assn. Home: 870 5th Ave New York NY 10021-4953

RIDDLE, VERYL LEE, lawyer; b. Campbell, Mo., Dec. 6, 1921; s. Elvis Lloyd and Etter Whitehead (Wood) R.; m. Mary J. Riggs, Jan. 15, 1941 (div. 1967); children— Kay, Jo, Janet, Veryl Lee, Jr.; m. Janet Lewis, Nov. 24, 1985. Student, Southeast Mo. U., 1939-41; student, U. Buffalo, 1942, 45-46; JD, Washington U., St. Louis, 1948. Bar: Mo. 1948, U.S. Dist. Ct. (ea. and we. dists.) Mo. 1949, U.S. Ct. Appeals (8th cir.) 1949, U.S. Supreme Ct. 1969, U.S. Ct. Appeals (7th cir.) 1970, U.S. Ct. Appeals (5th cir.) 1974, U.S. Ct. Appeals (3d cir.) 1975. Agt. U.S. Dept. Justice, N.Y., Ohio, Tex., Mex., 1942-43; U.S. atty. Eastern Dist. Mo. Dept. Justice, St. Louis, 1967-69; ptnr. Riddle, Baker & O'Herin, Malden, Mo., 1948-67; sr. ptnr. Bryan Cave, St. Louis, 1969—. Pros. atty. Dunklin County, Mo., 1950-53; chmn. merit selection panel for U.S. Magistrate, St. Louis, 1983-84 Del., Nat. Democratic Conv., Chgo., 1956, Los Angeles, 1960. With U.S. Army, 1943-45, European Theatre, Military Intelligence. Recipient Disting. Alumni award Washington U. Sch. Law, 1993. Fellow Am. Coll. Trial Lawyers, Internat. Acad. Trial Lawyers; mem. Acad. Mo. Squires. Clubs: Bellerive Country, Noonday, Round Table (St. Louis). Baptist. Office: Bryan Cave 211 N Broadway Saint Louis MO 63102-2733

RIDDLE, WESLEY ALLEN, army officer, writer; b. Houston, Apr. 19, 1961; s. Walter Abige Riddle and Gloria Texane (Longnecker) Riddle-Roe; m. Maria Aida Albesa, Dec. 21, 1985; stepchildren: Catalina Louise Oates, Danilo Albesa Calabia. BS cum laud, U.S. Mil. Acad., 1983; MPhil in Modern History with distinction, Oxford (Eng.) U., 1993. Commd. U.S. Army, 1983, advanced through grades to lt. col., 2000, platoon leader, battery exec. officer 1-62 ADA (C/V) Hawaii, 1984-87; asst. S-3 Plans, S-4 and Battery Comdr. 2-43 ADA (Patriot) Hanau, Germany, 1988-91; battery comdr. B/2-43 ADA Gulf War SWA, 1991; asst. prof. history U.S. Mil. Acad., West Point, N.Y., 1993-96; Theater Missile Def. evaluation officer Air Def. Directorate Operational Test and Evaluation Command, Alexandria, Va., 1996-98; exec. officer 2-6 ADA, Ft. Bliss, Tex., 1998-99; chief AD br., requirements divsn. DCD, 1999-2000; air def. readiness br. chief (OMC-K) USASATMO, Ft. Bragg, N.C., 2000—. Chmn. Am. Civility Project, 1996-99. Mem. adv. bd. The Social Critic mag., 1996-99; U.S. corr. Fragments Mag., 1998—; contbr. chpts. to books; columnist Belton Jour., 2000—. Founder, pres. Northbrook Teenage Reps., Houston, 1975-79; youth advisor State of Tex. to Citizens for the Republic, 1978-79; page, Rep. Nat. Conv., Kansas City, Mo., 1976. Decorated Bronze Star; Salvatori fellow Heritage Found., Washington, 1996-99; Nat. Humanities Inst. fellow, 1997—. Mem. VFW, Am. Legion, Mil. Order of Saint Barbara, Phi Kappa Phi, Phi Alpha Theta. Republican. Christian Scientist. Avocations: music, poetry, weightlifting, running, water sports.

RIDDLE-DVORAK, BARBARA SHAUN, writer; b. N.Y.C., Jan. 9, 1944; d. Robert Horatio Riddle and Mary-Madeleine Lanphier; m. Michael J. Dennis; 1 child, Laramie Dennis; m. Ivo Dvorak, June 30, 1984. BA, Reed Coll., 1964; PhD in Biochemistry, Brandeis U., 1970. Sr. editor dept. neurosurgery U. Calif., San Francisco, 1974-78, founding editor health scis. quar. MOBIUS, 1978-86; freelance writer, editor. Author: (novel) The Girl Pretending to Read Rilke, 2000. Woodrow Wilson Fellow Reed Coll., 1964. Mem. Amnesty Internat. Mem. Green Party. Avocations: fiction, theater, films, 1920s American pottery, furniture, painting. Home: PO Box 460414 San Francisco CA 94146 E-mail: barbdvorak@earthlink.net.

RIDDOCH, HILDA JOHNSON, accountant; b. Salt Lake City, July 25, 1923; d. John and Ivy Alma (Wallis) Johnson; m. Leland Asa Riddoch, Nov. 22, 1942 (dec.); children: Ivy Lee (dec.), Leland Mark. Vocal student, Ben Henry Smith, Seattle; student, Art Instrn. Schs. Sales clk., marking room and sec. dist. office Sears, Seattle, 1940-42; with billing dept., receptionist C.M. Lovsted & Co., Inc., 1942-51; acct., exec. sec. Viking Equipment Co., Inc., 1951-54; acct., office mgr. Charles Waynor Collection Agy., 1955-57, Argus Mag., Seattle, 1962-67; acct. Law Offices Krutch, Lindell, Donnelly, Dempsey & Lageschulte, 1967-72, Law Offices Sindell, Haley, Estep, et al, Seattle, 1972-77; co-founder, acct. Bus. Svc., Inc. and Diversified Design & Mktg., Fed. Way, Auburn & Orting, Wash., 1975-96; co-founder L & H Advt. and Distbg. Co., Wash., 1992-96. Sec.-treas., dir. Jim Evans Realty Inc., Seattle, 1973-87; agt. Wise Island Water Co., P.U.D., Wise Island, B.C., 1973-88, Estate Executrix, Seattle, 1987-96; exec. sec., acct. Cougar Mountain Assn. Ltd. Partnership, 1964-78. Author: Ticking Time on a Metronome, 1989-90, Beloved Miss Ivy, 1996-97, Siegfield, Earth Angel; writer, dir. hist. video Presidents of Relief Society Thru Ages; writer epic poetry; writer, dir. teenager activation video, 1984; pub., editor Extended Family Newsletter, 1983-96. Dir. speech and drama LDS Ch., 1983-88; ward pres. young women's orgn.; mem. ward and stake choirs, 1963-85; stake genealogy libr., Fed. Way, 1983-85; ward and stake newsletter editor various areas, West Seattle, Seattle, Renton, Auburn, Wash., 1950-90; 1st counselor in presidency, tchr. various courses Ladies' Relief Soc. Orgn., 1965-96; co-dir., organizer 1st Silver Saints Group, 1990-92; interviewer LDS Ch. Employment Svcs., 1992-93; co-resident mgr. Mountain View Estates, Orting, Wash., 1994-96. Recipient Letter of Recognition Howard W. Hunter, Pres. LDS Ch. Mem. NAFE. Avocations: needlework, oil painting, writing, singing, speech and drama. Home: Mountain Falls Apts II 1277 S Woodruff #103 Idaho Falls ID 83404

RIDE, SALLY KRISTEN, physics educator, scientist, former astronaut; b. L.A., May 26, 1951; d. Dale Burdell and Carol Joyce (Anderson) R.; m. Steven Alan Hawley, July 26, 1982 (div.). BA in English, BS in Physics, Stanford U., 1973, PhD in Physics, 1978. Teaching asst. Stanford U., Palo Alto, Calif., researcher dept. physics; astronaut candidate, trainee NASA, 1978-79, astronaut, 1979-87, on-orbit capsule communicator STS-2 mission Johnson Space Ctr., on-orbit capsule communicator STS-3 mission, mission specialist STS-7, 1983, mission specialist STS-41G, 1984; sci. fellow Stanford (Calif.) U., 1987-89; dir. Calif. Space Inst. of U. Calif. San Diego, La Jolla, 1989-96, pres. space com., 1999-2000; prof. Physics U. Calif. San Diego, 1989—; pres., CEO Imaginary Lines, Inc. Mem. Presdl. Commn. on Space Shuttle, 1986, Presdl. Com. of Advisors on Sci. and Tech., 1994—; pres., CEO Imaginary Lines, 2001—. Author: (with Susan Okie) To Space and Back, 1986, (with T.O'Shaughnessy) Voyager: An Adventure to the Edge of the Solar System, 1992, The Third Planet: Exploring the Earth From Space, 1994, The Mystery of Mars, 1999. Office: U Calif San Diego Calif Space Inst 0426 La Jolla CA 92093-0426

RIDEN, MICHAEL DAVID, nuclear engineer; b. Maryville, Tenn., July 2, 1947; s. William Walter and Grace Ella (Elrod) R.; m. Perry Dene Thyberg, Mar. 28, 1970; children: Chad Michael, Kirk David, Eric Wesley. Cert. nuclear weapons specialist, Lowry Tng. Ctr., Denver, 1968; cert. nuclear weapons technician, Gen. Electric Co. Tng. Program, King of Prussia, Pa., 1969; BS, U. Tenn., Knoxville, 1974. Cert. regional judge, Duck Town, Tenn., 1995. Asst. engr. Duke Power Co. Oconee Nuclear Sta., Seneca, S.C., 1974-78; reactor insp. Nuclear Regulatory Commn., Glen Ellyn, Ill., 1978-79; gen. mgr. Chgo. Barra Corp. Am., Inc., Wheaton, 1979-82; reg. mgr. Watpro, Inc., Orland Park, 1982-83; pres. ETs, Glen Ellyn, 1983-87; engring. assurance engr. TVA Watts Bar Nuc. Plant, Spring City, Tenn., 1987-88, Sequoyah Nuc. Plant, Soddy-Daisy, 1988-89; supervising engr. United Energy Svcs. Corp., Palo Verde Nuc. Power Plant, Wintersburg, Ariz., 1989-90; nuc. engr. Sigma Sci. Browns Ferry Nuc. Plant, Athens, Ala., 1990-93; lead auditor SECORE Svcs. Inc., Trans-Alaska Pipeline, Anchorage, 1994; plant ops. and betterment I&C cons. engr. Raytheon Engrs. and Constructors Inc. TVA Watts Bar Nuclear, Spring City, Tenn., 1994-95; cons. nuc. engr. Sci. Applications Internat. Corp. TVA Sequoyah Nuclear Plant, Soddy-Daisy, 1995-96; sports staff mem. Atlanta com. Olympic Games, Cherokee Nat. Forest, 1996; cons. nuc. engring. environ. qualification Cooper Nuc. Station, Brownville, Nebr., 1996-97; sys. engring. mentor Duke Engring. & Svc. Resources, Inc., Two Rivers, Wis., 1997-98; maintenance commitment project mgr. Cook Nuc. Plant Cook Nuc. Plant, Duke Engring. & Svcs. Resources, Inc., Sun Tech. Svcs., Inc. and S&L, Bridgman, Mich., 1998-2001; mng. dir. Ednl. Tng. Svcs., Riceville, Tenn., 2000—; elec. supt. Newberg, Perini, Stone and Webster, Braceville, Ill., 2001—02. Re-entry system evaluation team mem. minuteman III missile USAF, Minot, N.D., 1969-71. Deacon Presbyn. Ch. U.S., Seneca, 1976-77; lay spkr. United Meth. Ch. Holston Conf., 1991-2001.. Sgt. USAF, 1967-71. Recipient Outstanding Achievement in Poetry During the 20th Century award Internat. Libr. of Poetry, 2000. Mem. Am. Nuclear Soc. Sovereign American.

RIDENOUR, AMY MORITZ, research center administrator; b. Pitts., Nov. 9, 1959; d. Karl Berkoben and Carol Lee (Riley) M. B or Econs., U. Md., 1981. Exec. dir. Nat. Ctr. for Pub. Policy Rsch., Washington, 1982-88, trustee, 1986—; pres. The Nat. Ctr. for Pub. Policy Research, 1988—; formerly host Scoop!, Nat. Empowerment Television; nationally syndicated columnist UPI and Knight-Ridder Tribune, 1998—. Chmn. Liberty Inst., Washngton. Assoc. pub. Cath. Study Coun. Bull.; editor Nat. Policy Watch Jour., Liberation Bull.; exec. editor Liberty Letter; contbr. articles to Policy Rev. and other profl. jours. Regional coord. Reagan-Bush Nat. Campaign, Washington, 1980; bd. dirs., v.p. Internat. Youth Yr. Commn. for U.S., 1985; chmn. Md. Fedn. Coll. Rep. Clubs, 1978-80. Mem. Accuracy in Academia (adv. bd.). Lutheran. Avocations: skiing, books, history. Office: Nat Ctr for Pub Policy Rsch 777 N Capitol St NE Ste 803 Washington DC 20002-4294

RIDEOUT, EDNA BAKER, artist; b. Billings, Mont., Sept. 29, 1918; d. Frederick Hubbard and Edna Beers (Baker) Ballou; m. Horton Burbank Rideout, May 26, 1951; children: Douglas Burbank Rideout, Nancy Penelope Rideout, Thomas Ballou Rideout. BA, U. Wash., 1940, MA, 1949. Cert. secondary tchr., Wash. Art editor Croftonian Crofton House Sch., Vancouver, B.C., Can., 1935-36; art tchr. Neah Bay (Wash.) High Sch., 1940-41, Winlock (Wash.) High Sch., 1942-44, Seattle Pub. Schs., 1945-47, 49-51, Fish and Wildlife Svc. Pribilof Islands, St. George Island, Alaska, 1951-53; dir. Visual Art Sch., Edmonds, Wash., 1972-74; sec. Gallery North, 1974-76; artist, 1953—. Watercolors included in nat. juried exhbns., 8 juried mem. and regional exhbns., 36 nat. juried shows in 7 yrs., invitational exhbns. sponsored by Bellevue, Wash. Art Mus., North West Water Color Soc., Arts Olympia; works included in In Harmony with Nature, 1990, Seattle Asian Art Mus. Kado Shows, 1998, 99; 2 ink drawings used as cover designs for Alaska Timber Econ. Studies texts. Recipient Masterfield award Fla. Soc. Exptl. Artists, 2 purchase awards Watercolor U.S.A., Ajomari/Arches/Rives award Watermedia Mont., 1st pl. award Artstravaganza Nat., 3rd pl. award Navarro Coun. of Arts, Judge's Spl. award North Coast Collage Soc. Mem. Nat. Collage Soc. (sec. 1994), Women Painters of Wash. (program dir. 1992-93), North West Watercolor Soc. (asst. program dir. 1989-91), Soc. Exptl. Artists Fla., Pa. Watercolor Soc., North West Collage Soc. (sec. 1995—), East Side Assn. Fine Arts, Gallery North (hon.), Planetary Soc. Avocations: photography, hiking, observing nature, studying outer space. Home: 18616 92nd Ave NE Bothell WA 98011-2207

RIDEOUT, PATRICIA IRENE, operatic, oratorio and concert singer; b. St. John, N.B., Can., Mar. 16, 1931; d. Eric Aubrey and Florence May (Chase) R.; m. Rolf Edmund Dissmann, Sept. 3, 1955 (dec. 1975); m. Leonard R. Rosenberg, May 25, 1987. Ed., U. Toronto Opera Sch., Royal Conservatory Music, 1952-55. Tchr. voice Queen's U., Kingston, Ont., 1980-86, Royal Conservatory Music, Toronto, 1980-91. Singer Can. Opera Co., Toronto, 1954-85; leading roles in operas, Stratford, Ont., Vancouver, B.C., Guelph, Ont., 1956-85, CBC, 1958-90. Mem. Actors Equity Assn., Assn. Radio and TV Artists, Toronto Heliconian Club. Unitarian Universalist.

RIDEOUT, WALTER BATES, English educator; b. Lee, Maine, Oct. 21, 1917; s. Walter John and Helen Ruth (Brickett) R.; m. Jeanette Lee Drisko, Aug. 2, 1947; children: Linda Carolyn, Richard Bates, David John. AB, Colby Coll., 1938; MA, Harvard U., 1939, PhD, 1950. Teaching fellow English Harvard U., 1946-49, asst. prof., summer 1954, prof., summer 1969; from instr. to assoc. prof. English Northwestern U., Evanston, Ill., 1949-63, dir. program Bell System execs., 1957-58, 59-61; prof. English U. Wis., Madison, 1963—, Harry Hayden Clark prof. English, 1972—, chmn. dept., 1965-68, sr. vis. prof. Inst. Research in Humanities, 1968-69. Vis. prof. U. Hawaii, summer 1977; Disting. lectr. English Kyoto Am. Studies Summer Seminar, Kyoto, Japan, 1981 Author: The Radical Novel in the United States, 1900-1954, 1956; editor: (with Howard Mumford Jones) Letters of Sherwood Anderson, 1953, (with James K. Robinson) A College Book of Modern Verse, 1958, A College Book of Modern Fiction, 1961, The Experience of Prose, 1960, I. Donnelly-Caesar's Column, 1960, (with G.W. Allen and J.K. Robinson) American Poetry, 1965, Sherwood Anderson: Collection of Critical Essays, 1974. Recipient MidAm. award Soc. for Study of Midwestern Lit., Mich. State U., 1983, Outstanding Educator award, 1993; fellow Newberry Libr., 1951, Guggenheim fellow, 1957; Fulbright grantee to Kyoto, 1981. Mem. ACLU, MLA (mem. nat. exec. council 1970-73), Phi Beta Kappa. Home: Brookline Apts 7707 N Brookline Dr Apt 220 Madison WI 53719-3532 Office: Dept English U Wis 600 N Park St Madison WI 53706-1403

RIDER, ALAN JAMES, career counselor; b. Unionville, Mich., Mar. 8, 1948; s. Kenneth and Hannah Rider; m. Karen Letke; children: Mark, David. BA, Valparaiso U., 1970; Mdiv, Gettysburg Luth. Sem., 1977; MA in Counseling, Ea. Ky. U., 2000. Dir. Luth. Field Svc., Frankfurt, Germany, 1986-92; pastor Evang. Luth. Ch. in Am., 1977—; lead career advisor Bernard Haldane Assocs., Lexington, Ky., 1995—. Mem. ACA, Ky. Counseling Assn., Nat. Career Devel Assn. (cert. master career devel. profl.). Office: Bernard Haldane Assocs 330 E Main St Ste 200 Lexington KY 40507 E-mail: arider@bernardhaldane.com.

RIDER, BRIAN CLAYTON, lawyer; b. San Antonio, Oct. 8, 1948; s. Ralph W. and Emmie Rider; m. Patsy Anne Ruppert, Dec. 27, 1970; children: Christopher, David, James, Andrew. BA, Rice U., 1969; JD, U. Tex., 1972. Bar: Tex. 1972. Assoc. then ptnr. Dow, Cogburn & Friedman, Houston, 1972-83; ptnr. Brown, McCarroll & Oaks Hartline, Austin, Tex., 1983-96. Adj. prof. law U. Tex., 1997—. Contbr. articles to profl. jours.; lectr. in field. Mem. Am. Coll. Real Estate Lawyers, Travis County Bar Assn. (bd. dirs. 1986-88, chmn. Travis County real estate sect. 1986-88), State Bar of Tex. (coun. real estate and probate sect. 1992-96), Tex. Coll. Real Estate Lawyers (chair 1999—). Home: 2906 Hatley Dr Austin TX 78746-4613 Office: 1300 S Mopac Austin TX 78746 E-mail: brider@ccsi.com., brider@lumbermensinv.com.

RIDER, GREGORY ASHFORD, investment company executive; b. Douglas, Wyo., Nov. 16, 1949; s. Keith Shumway and Margaret Elizabeth (Markle) R.; m. Katherine Elizabeth Winn, June 24, 1979; 1 child, Elizabeth Winn. BS, Georgetown U., 1972; MBA, Harvard U., 1979. Mktg. specialist Marshall Internat., Chgo., 1972-77; asst. to chmn. McLean Securities, N.Y.C., 1978-81; dir. corp. devel. SHV N.Am. Corp., Cin., 1981-83; gen. ptnr. Criterion Investments, Houston, 1983-85; pres. Ocean Ventures Mgmt., Inc., N.Y.C. and L.A., 1986-93; mng. dir. Ocean Capital Corp., L.A., 1991-93, Smith New Ct., N.Y.C., 1993-95; dir. Merrill Lynch, 1996-97; sr. mgr., dir. Bear Stearns & Co., Inc., 1997-99; pvt.investor, investment advisor Greenwich, Conn., 1999—. Mem. Circumnavigators Found. (pres. 1994-99, Global Rsch. fellow 1971), Harvard Club (N.Y.C.), Greenwich Country Club. Episcopalian.

RIDER, JOHN ALLEN, II, business educator, paralegal; b. Gage, Okla., Mar. 11, 1928; s. George Henry Rider and Laurenna Agnes Meek; m. Audrey Claudine Baker, July 16, 1961; children: Michelle Renee Rider Brown, John Allen III. BS, Northwestern Okla. State U., 1952; MA, U. Wyoming, 1956; EdD, U. Nebr., 1966; postgrad., U. Ky. Cert. profl. tchr., Tenn., Iowa. Court reporter, stenographer USN, 1946-48; dep. ct. clk., ct. reporter Ellis County, Okla., 1948-49; tchr. bus. Rozel (Kans.) Rural High Sch., 1952-53, Norwich (Kans.) High Sch., 1953-54, Bluff City (Kans.) High Sch., 1954-56; instr. Black Hills State Coll., Spearfish, S.D., 1956-58; tchr. bus. Balboa (C.Z.) High Sch., 1958-60; instr. Northwestern Coll., Orange City, Iowa, 1958-60, chair divsn. edn., 1962-64; asst. prof. Northwestern State Coll., Alva, Okla., 1962-63; teaching asst. U. Nebr., Lincoln, 1963-64; head bus. edn. program, assoc. prof. U. N.Mex., Albuquerque, 1966-70; prof. West Tex. State U., Canyon, 1970-74; chair prof. occupational edn. divsn. Coffeyville (Kans.) Community Jr., 1974-75; assoc. prof. East Tenn. State U., Johnson City, 1975-94, coord. bus. edn. program, 1985-94; ret., 1994. Cons. various bus.; bd. dirs. Enid Literacy Coun., 1996-98, also tutor. Active Johnson City Literacy Coun., v.p./tutor trainer, 1978-80; relief worker, registrar Mid-Am.. yearly meeting Friends Ch., Wichita, 1981; cons. yearly meeting N.C. Soc. Friends, 1987; vol. Circle of Love Hospice, 1998-2001. Recipient Meritorious award West Tex. Bus. Tchr., 1970-74, Outstanding Edn. Grad. award Northwestern Okla. State U. Alumni Assn., 1995; named Tchr. of Yr., Dist. 16 Tex. Bus. Edn. Assn., 1973. Mem. NEA (life), Assn. for Career and Tech. Edn. (life), Nat. Bus Edn., Nat. Assn. Tchr. Edn. (life, bus. and office edn.), Tex. State Edn. Assn., Tenn. Bus. Edn. Assn. (treas., pres.-elect, pres., past pres., Educator of Yr. 1986), So. Bus. Edn., Kiwanis (Johnson City exec. bd. 1975-80, 92), Am. Legion (King's Mt. post), SAR (former sec., pres. Panhandle-Plains chpt., Tex. soc.), Holt County (Mo.) Hist. Soc. (charter, life), Lions Club (Pioneer-Pleasant Vale 1997-98). Republican. Avocations: genealogy, history, photography. Home: 3002 N Grant St Enid OK 73703-1686 E-mail: jrider@intercorp.com.

RIDER, JOSEPH KUNTZMAN, information systems specialist; b. Sewickley, Pa., Feb. 28, 1939; s. Joseph Weber and Evelyn Margaret (Kuntzman) R.; m. Sharon Pearl Allison, Dec. 26, 1967 (div. Mar. 1993); 1 child, Kendra Allison. BA, Rice U., 1961; postgrad., So. Ill. U., 1961-62; MFA, U. Tex., 1964. Resident designer Ft. Wayne (Ind.) Civic Theatre, 1965-66; guest designer U. Victoria, B.C., Can., 1966; assoc. prof. Sam Houston State Coll., Huntsville, Tex., 1966-67; carpenter, upholsterer Feller Scenery Studios, N.Y.C., 1967-70; design asst. Broadway designers, 1967-74; pres., CEO Theatrical Catalysts, Inc., 1969-72, Telesette, Inc., N.Y.C., 1972-74; fiscal affairs mgr. N.Y.C. Dept. Transp., 1974-80, info. svcs. mgr., 1980-87; v.p. Dreman Value Advisors, N.Y.C., 1987-98; founder, prin. Rider Group Info.

Sys. Cons., 1998—. Founding v.p. West 71st St. Assn., N.Y.C., 1969-78; pres. Ansonia Dems., N.Y.C., 1975-79; chair, pres. Westside Cmty. Recycling Corp., N.Y.C., 1975-81; jud. del. N.Y.C., 1981-84; pres. 404 West 48th St. Housing Devel. Corp., 1984—; lay reader and treas. St. Clement's Episcopal Ch., Manhattan. Avocations: jazz, writing. Home: 404 W 48th St New York NY 10036-1209 E-mail: wrangler3@mindspring.com.

RIDER, KATHERINE LOVETA THOMPSON, clinical social worker; b. Roswell, N.Mex., Apr. 18, 1945; d. Donald and Setta Loveta (Jones) Thompson; m. Kent Morrison Rider, June 8, 1968; children: Tracy Lyn, Courtney Elizabeth, Kelley Michelle. BA, U. Tex., 1967, MSSW, 1969. Lic. master social worker, advanced clin. practitioner, Tex.; cert. group psychotherapist. Social worker adult mental health staff Austin-Travis County Mental Health-Mental Retardation Ctr., 1969-77; cons. Model Cities Project, Austin, Tex., 1971-72, cmty. orgn. specialist alcohol-related svcs., 1974-76; clin. field faculty Sch. Social Work, U. Tex., 1977-81; pvt. practice social work, 1977—. Clin. staff mental health dept. Austin Regional Clinic, 1982—84; mem. homemaker svcs. bd. Child and Family Svc. Austin, 1970—75; adj. prof. St. Edward's U., 1983—91; adj. faculty Sch. Social Work U. Tex., Austin, 1999—. Pres. L.L. Campbell Elem. Sch. PTA, 1984—86; mem. Austin Family Mediation Assn. Bd., 1985—87; pres. Brykerwoods Elem. Sch. PTA, 1987—88, Austin H.S., 1988—89; v.p., trustee Austin Ind. Sch. Dist., 1992—94, pres., 1994—2002; adminstrv. v.p. Austin City Coun. PTAs, 1986—88, pres., 1991—92; mem. Austin Travis County MHMR Bd., 1989—99, First Bapt. Day Sch. Bd., Austin, 1980—82. Mem.: NASW (dir. Tex. chpt. 1980—84), Tex. Soc. Clin. Social Work (chair govtl. affairs 2000—), Tau Beta Sigma. Baptist. Home: 3221 Clearview Dr Austin TX 78703-2753 Office: 3724 Jefferson St Ste 206 Austin TX 78731-6221

RIDER, KATHLEEN MARY, dietitian; b. Bronx, N.Y., Mar. 21, 1953; d. William Anthony and Elizabeth Catherine (Gavin) Browne; m. David York Rider, Oct. 15, 1983; children: Kathleen M., Colleen M., David Y., Elizabeth A., Erin M. AAS, Maria Coll., 1976; BS, Empire State Coll., 1978; M of Profl. Studies, SUNY, New Paltz, 1982; cert. alternative & complimentary health, Marist Coll., 1999. Cert. dietitian/nutritionist, N.Y.; cert. diabetes educator, Nat. Cert. Bd. Diabetes Educators. Food svc. dir./dietitian Lovely Hill Nursing Home, Pawling, N.Y., 1979-81; adminstrv. dietitian Hudson River Psychiat. Ctr., Poughkeepsie, 1981-82; cmty. svc. dietitian Wassaic (N.Y.) Developmental Ctr., 1982-83; ind. cons. dietitian, 1981—. Cons. Hudson Haven Health Care Ctr., Bapt. Home, Hospice Inc., Greystone Inc., New Paltz Nursing Home, Assn. for Retarded Citizens, Dutchess Ulster and Orange Counties, Home Care, Alcohol Rehab. Ctr., United Cerebral Palsy, various other orgns.; advisor Mid Hudson Food Svc. Mgrs. Assn., Poughkeepsie, N.Y. State Cancer Pain Inst., N.Y.C. Vol. nutrition educator area parochial schs., Dutchess County, 1996; instr. religious edn. St. Peter's Ch., Poughkeepsie, 1981-84; team mem. engaged encounter Cath. Engaged Encounter, Dutchess County, 1986-89. Soroptomist scholar, Schenectady, N.Y., 1976. Fellow Am. Dietetic Assn. (registered, mem. cons. dietitian practice group, mem. diabetes educator practice group, del. 1999, Flora Wishart Davies Meml. award for Outstanding Caregiver 1994, Outstanding Svc. award); mem. Am. Assn. Diabetes Educators, N.Y. State Dietetic Assn. (state profl. recruitment coord. 1976—, scholar 1976), Mid Hudson Dietetic Assn. (pres. 1992-94). Democrat. Home and Office: 13 Edna Dr Hyde Park NY 12538-2939

RIDER, PAUL EDWARD, physicist, educator; b. Des Moines, June 22, 1965; s. Paul Edward and Carole Catherine (Teresavich) R.; m. Angela Merici Gude, July 16, 1994. BS, U. Iowa, 1987; MS in Physics, U. Minn., 1989, PhD in Physics, 1995. Instr. physics Grand View Coll., Des Moines, 1995—. Rschr. U. Minn., Mpls., 1995—. Mem. Meteoritical Soc., Iowa Acad. Sci., Phi Beta Kappa. Democrat. Avocations: reading, basketball, music.

RIDER, SUSAN MARIE, musician; b. Manhattan, Kans., May 27, 1967; d. Paul Edward and Carole Teresavich Rider. MusB, U. No. Iowa, 1989; MusM, Ind. U., 1991, MusD, 2000. 2nd/3rd trumpet Columbus (Ind.) Philharm., 1995-96; 3rd trumpet Owensboro (Ky.) Symphony, 1995-96; mem. trumpet sect. Spoleto Festival USA Orch., Charleston, SC, 1996; trumpet New World Symphony, 1997; co-prin. trumpet Midland (Tex.)/Odessa Symphony, 1996-97; mem. cornet/trumpet sect. The Pres. Own U.S. Marine Band, Washington, 1997—. Trumpet instr. Purdue U., West Lafayette, Ind., 1996; pvt. cornet/trumpet instr. Ector County Ind. Sch. Dist., Odessa, Tex., 1996-97; mem. adv. bd. U. No. Iowa Sch. Music, Cedar Falls, 1997—. Co-editor Internat. Women's Brass Conf. Newsletter; contbr. articles to profl. jours. Staff sgt. USMC, 1997—. Recipient Citizenship award Iowa Bar Assn., 1985; Merchant scholar U. No. Iowa, 1993-95. Mem.: Internat. Trumpet Guild, Internat. Women's Brass Conf., Sigma Alpha Iota, Pi Kappa Lambda.

RIDER, WILLIAM JACKSON, research scientist; b. Spokane, Wash., Sept. 5, 1963; s. Frank and Carol Rider; m. Felicia Forbes; children: Rachel, Jackson. PhD, U. N.Mex., 1992. Scientist Los Alamos (N.Mex.) Nat. Lab., 1989—. Office: Los Alamos Nat Lab MS D413 Los Alamos NM 87544 Business E-Mail: wjr@lanl.gov.

RIDGE, MARTIN, historian, educator; b. Chgo., May 7, 1923; s. John and Ann (Lew) R.; m. Marcella Jane VerHoef, Mar. 17, 1948; children: John Andrew, Judith Lee, Curtis Cordell, Wallace Karsten. AB, Chgo. State U., 1943; AM, Northwestern U., 1949, PhD, 1951. Asst. prof. history Westminster Coll., New Wilmington, Pa., 1951-55; from asst. prof. to prof. San Diego State Coll., 1955-66; prof. history Ind. U., Bloomington, 1966-79, Calif. Inst. Tech., 1980-95; prof. emeritus, 1995. Vis. prof. UCLA, summer 1963, Northwestern U., summer 1959; editor Jour. Am. History, 1966-77; sr. research assoc. Huntington Library, 1977— ; bd. dirs. Calif. Hist. Landmarks Commn., 1954-64; cons. in field; Tanner lectr. Mormon Hist. Assn., 1991; Whitsett Meml. lectr., Calif. State U., 1992. Author: (book) Ignatius Donnelly: Portrait of a Politician, 1962, Ignatius Donnelly: Portrait of a Politician, 2d edit., 1991, The New Bilingualism: An American Dilemma, 1981, Frederick Jackson Turner: Wisconsin's Historian of the Frontier, 1986, My Life East and West, 1994; co-author: California Work and Workers, 1963, The American Adventure, 1964, America's Frontier Story, 1969, Liberty and Union, 1973, American History after 1865, 1981, Westward Expansion, 1982, Westward Expansion, 6th edit., 2001; editor: Children of Ol'Man River, 1988, Westward Journeys, 1989, History, Frontier and Section, 1993, The American West: The Reader, 1999. Served with U.S. Maritime Service, 1943-45. William Randolph Hearst fellow, 1950; fellow Social Sci. Research Council, 1952; fellow Guggenheim Found., 1965; fellow Am. Council Learned Socs., 1960; Newberry fellow, 1964; Huntington fellow, 1974; Annenberg scholar U. So. Calif., 1979-80; recipient Best Book award Phi Alpha Theta, 1963, Gilberto Espinos prize N.Mex. Historical Review, 1989, Ray Allan Billington prize Western History Assn., 1991. Mem. Am. Hist. Assn. (v.p. Pacific Coast br. 1994, pres. 1995, Best Book award 1963), Orgn. Am. Historians, Western History Assn. (v.p. 1985-86, pres. 1986-87), So. History Assn., Agrl. History Soc., Social Sci. History Soc., Hist. Soc. So. Calif. (pres. 1994-99). Democrat. E-mial. E-mail: mridge@huntington.org.

RIDGE, THOMAS JOSEPH, federal agency administrator, former governor, former congressman; b. Munhall, Pa., Aug. 26, 1945; m. Michele Moore, 1979, children, Lesley & Tommy. BA, Harvard U., 1967; JD, Dickinson Sch. Law, Carlisle, Pa., 1972. Bar: Pa. 1972. Pvt. practice, Erie, Pa., 1972-82; asst. dist. atty., 1979-82; mem. 98th-103rd Congresses from Pa. 21st dist., Washington, 1983-1995; mem. Banking, Fin., Urban Affairs com., subcoms. Econ. Growth and Credit Formation, Housing and Community Devel., Veteran's Affairs com.; gov. State of Pa., 1995—2001; dir. Homeland Security, Washington, 2001—. Mem. banking, fin., urban affairs com., subcoms. econ. growth and credit formation, housing and cmty. devel., vets. affairs com.; subcom. Hosps. and Healthcare, Oversight and Investigation, Post Office and Civil Svc., com., subcom. Census and Population, Civil Svc. With U.S. Army, 1968-70, Vietnam. Office: Office of Homeland Security 3801 Nebraska Ave., N.W. Washington DC 20016*

RIDGEWAY, DOMINIC CHARLES, advocate; b. Balt., Nov. 19, 1974; s. Bearnard Anore Ridgeway and Denise Ethelyn Hughes. Grad.(hon.) , Williams Bear Sch., 1994. CEO, founder United Cerebral Palsy Advocacy, Balt., 1991—, Leaders for Independence, Balt., 1998—. Mem. Ptnrs. in Policy Making, Annapolis, Md., 1998—. Active The Arc Md., Annapolis, 1998—2002. Baptist. Avocations: travel, swimming. Home: 3845 Brownhill Rd Randallstown MD 21133 Office: United Cerebal Palsy 1660 Sulphur Spring Rd Baltimore MD 21227 Personal E-mail: sarahprize@yahoo.com.

RIDGEWAY, JAMES FOWLER, journalist; b. Auburn, N.Y., Nov. 1, 1936; s. George L. and Florence (Fowler) Ridgeway; m. Patricia Carol Dodge, Nov. 1966; 1 child David Andrew. AB, Princeton U., 1959. Assoc. editor New Republic, Washington, 1962-68, contbg. editor, 1968-70; editor Hard Times, 1968-70, Elements, 1974-78; assoc. editor Ramparts, 1970-75; assoc. fellow Inst. for Policy Studies, 1973-77; mem. Pub. Resource Center, 1977—; staff writer Village Voice, 1973—. Author: (book) The Closed Corporation, 1969, Politics of Ecology, 1970, The Last Play, 1973, New Energy, 1975; author: (with Alexander Cockburn) Smoke, 1978; author: Political Ecology, 1979, Energy-Efficient Community Planning, 1979, Who Owns the Earth, 1980, Powering Civilization, 1983, Blood in the Face, 1991, The March to War, 1991; author: (with Jean Casella) To Cast a Cold Eye, 1991; author: The Haiti Files, 1994; author: (with Jasmika Udovicki) Yugoslavia's Ethnic Nightmare, 1995; author: (with Sylvia Plachy) Red Light, 1996; author: (with Jeffrey St. Clair) Environmental Bad Guys, 1999; author: (with Kevin Rafferty, Fran K. Kerandren) Who Wants to Be President; (prodr., dir. (with Anne Bohlen, Kevin Rafferty): (films) Blood in the Face, 1990; (prodr., dir. (with Kevin Rafferty) Feed, 1992; (cons. prodr.) Awful Truth, 1999. With N.G. U.S. Army, 1959. Home: 3103 Macomb St NW Washington DC 20008-3325 E-mail: jridgew@yahoo.com.

RIDGLEY, THOMAS BRENNAN, lawyer; b. Columbus, Ohio, Apr. 29, 1940; s. Arthur G. and Elizabeth (Tracy) R.;); children: Elizabeth, Jennifer, Kathryn; m. Lisa Lester, Nov. 27, 1999 BA, Princeton (N.J.) U., 1962; JD with honors, U. Mich., 1965. Bar: Pa. 1965, Ohio 1968, U.S. Dist. Ct. (so. and no. dists.) Ohio, U.S. Dist. Ct. (ea. dist.) Pa., U.S. Ct. Appeals (6th, 3d and 10th cirs.), U.S. Supreme Ct. Assoc. Dechert, Price and Rhoades, Phila., 1965-67; ptnr. Vorys, Sater, Seymour and Pease, Columbus, 1967—. Author: Interstate Conflicts and Cooperation, 1986, (with others) Fending Off Corporate Raiders, 1987. Bd. dirs., mem. exec. com. United Way of Franklin County, Columbus, 1986-98; bd. dirs. Cmty. Shelter Bd., 1992-98, pres. 1997-98; bd. dirs. Columbus Bar Found., 1992-99, pres., 1998. Fellow Am. Coll. Trial Lawyers. Office: Vorys Sater Seymour & Pease 52 E Gay St Columbus OH 43215-3161

RIDGWAY, JAMES MASTIN, government official; b. Sedalia, Mo., Mar. 14, 1917; s. Amelius Biddle and Maude Anna (Brandt) R.; m. Lillian Belle Shaneyfelt, May 25, 1941; children: Duressa, Richard (dec.), Cheryl. BSBA, U. Mo., 1939, MA, 1940; PhD, U. Chgo., 1953. Tchr. High Schs., Mo., Kans., 1940-44, prin. Mo., 1944-45; instr. Southwest & Ctrl. Mo. State U., Springfield, Warrensburg, 1945-47; chmn. dept. edn. Carroll Coll., Waukesha, Wis., 1949-55; instr. dept. head Nat. Civil Def. Coll., Battle Creek, Mich., 1955-62, dir., 1958-62; deputy asst. dir. tng. & edn. Office Civil Def., Def. Civil Preparedness Agy., Washington, 1963-73; edn. advisor OCPA/DOD and FEMA, 1973-80. Cons. in field. Contbr. articles to profl. jours. Mem. Am. Civil Def. Assn., Am. Strategic Def. Assn., Internat. Assn. Emergency Mgrs. Avocation: stamp collecting.

RIDGWAY, MARCELLA DAVIES, veterinarian; b. Sewickley, Pa., Dec. 24, 1957; d. Willis Eugene and Martha Ann (Davies) R. BS, Pa. State U., 1979; VMD, U. Pa., 1983; MS, U. Ill., 1997. Diplomate Am. Coll. Veterinary Internal Medicine. Intern U. Ill., Urbana, 1983-84, resident in small animal internal medicine, 1984-87; small animal vet. Vet. Cons. Svcs., Savoy, Ill., 1987-97; clin. asst. prof. small animal vet. medicine U. Ill., Urbana, 1997—. Contbr. articles to profl. jours. Mem. Am. Vet. Med. Assn., Acad. Vet. Clinicians, Ea. Ill. Vet. Med. Assn. (pres. 2000-2001), Heartland Pathways (bd. dirs.), Savoy Prairie Soc. (pres. 1989—), Grand Prairie Friends (bd. dirs. 1993-96), Sangamon Valley Conservancy (bd. dirs. 1995—). Avocations: prairie conservation activities, hiking, sketching, canine collectibles. Home: 194 Paddock Dr E Savoy IL 61874-9663 Office: U Ill Vet Med Teaching Hosp 1008 W Hazelwood Dr Urbana IL 61802-4714

RIDGWAY, ROZANNE LEJEANNE, retired diplomat, executive; b. St. Paul, Aug. 22, 1935; d. H. Clay and Ethel Rozanne (Cote) R.; m. Theodore E. Deming. BA, Hamline U., 1957, LLD (hon.), 1978; hon. degree, U. Helsinki, George Washington U., Elizabethtown Coll., Coll. of William and Mary, Hood Coll., Albright Coll., The Citadel. Career diplomat U.S. Fgn. Svc., 1957-89, amb. at large for oceans and fisheries, 1975-77; amb. to Finland, 1977-80; counselor of Dept. State, 1980-81, spl. asst. to sec. state, 1981, amb. to German Dem. Republic East Berlin, 1982-85, asst. sec. state Europe and Can., 1985-89; pres. Atlantic Coun. U.S., 1989-92, co-chmn., 1993-96; chmn. Baltic-Am. Enterprise Fund, Washington, 1994—. Bd. dirs. 3M Corp., Emerson Electric Co., The Boeing Corp., Sara Lee Corp., Manpower, Inc., Nat. Geog. Soc., New Perspective Fund. Trustee Hamline U.; bd. dirs. Ptnrs. for Democratic Change, Brookings Instn., Ctr. for Naval Analyses, George C. Marshall Found. Recipient Profl. awards Dept. State, Presdl. Disting. Performance award, Joseph C. Wilson internat. rels. achievement award, 1982, Sharansky award Union Couns. Soviet Jewry, 1989, Grand Cross of the Order of the Lion, Finland, 1989; named Person of Yr., Nat. Fisheries Inst., 1977, Knight Comdr. of the Order of Merit, Fed. Republic Germany, 1989, U.S. Presdl. Citizens Achievement medal, 1989; Inducted into Nat. Women's Hall of Fame, 1998. Fellow Nat. Acad. Pub. Adminstrn.; mem. Am. Acad. Diplomacy, Met. Club, Army-Navy Country Club. Fax: 703 527-3862.

RIDINGS, DOROTHY SATTES, association executive; b. Charleston, W.Va., Sept. 26, 1939; d. Frederick L. and Katharine E. (Backus) Sattes; m. Donald Jerome Ridings, Sept. 8, 1962 (dec. June 1997); children: Donald Jerome Jr., Matthew Lyle. Student, Randolph-Macon Woman's Coll., 1957-59; BSJ, Northwestern U., 1961; MA, U. N.C., 1968; D.Pub. Svc. (hon.), U. Louisville, 1985; LHD (hon.), Spalding U., 1986; LLD (hon.), U. Charleston, 1999. Reporter Charlotte Observer, N.C., 1961-66; instr. U. N.C. Sch. Journalism, 1966-68; freelance writer Louisville, 1968-77; news editor Ky. Bus. Ledger, 1977-80, editor, 1980-83; communications cons., editor, 1983-86; mgmt. assoc. Knight-Ridder Inc., Charlotte, N.C., 1986-88; pres., pub. The Bradenton (Fla.) Herald, 1988-96; pres., CEO, Coun. on Founds., Washington, 1996—. Adj. prof. U. Louisville, 1982-83; v.p. Nat. Mcpl. League, 1985-86; bd. dirs. com. on Constl. Sys., Nat. Com. Against Discrimination in Housing, 1982-87, Com. for Study of Am. Electorate, 1982—; bd. dirs. Ind. Sector, 1983-88, 92-97; mem. exec. com. Leadership Conf. Civil Rights, 1982-86; mem. Accrediting Coun. on Edn. in Journalism and Mass Comm., 2000—. Pres. LWV U.S., 1982-86, 1st v.p., 1980-82, human resources dir., 1976-80, chair edn. fund, 1982-86, 1st vice chair, 1980-82, trustee, 1976-80, pres. Louisville/Jefferson County, 1974-76, bd. dirs., 1969-76; chmn., bd. dirs. Nat. Civic League, 2000—; trustee Louisville Presbyn. Theol. Sem., 1992—, chmn., 2000—; trustee Ford Found., 1989-96, Manatee C.C., 1992-96; bd. dirs. Benton Found., 1989-96, Fla. Press Assn., 1994-96, Leadership Ky., 1984-87, Leadership Louisville, 1983-86, Louisville YWCA, 1978-80, Jr. League Louisville, 1972-74; mem. ABA Accreditation Com., 1987-93, Gov.'s Coun. Ednl. Reform, 1984-85; chair Prichard Com. Acad. Excellence, 1985-86; mem. Gov.'s Commn. Full Equality, 1982-83; mem. state adv. coun. U.S. Commn. Civil Rights, 1975-79; mem. steering com. Task Force for Peaceful Desegregation, 1974-75; elder 2d Presbyn. Ch., 1972-75, 78-81; mem. adv. coun. on ch. and soc. United Presbyn. Ch. in U.S., 1978-84; mem. bd. visitors U. N.C., 1993-96; mem. Nat. Commn. on Presdl. Debates, 1997—. Recipient Northwestern U. award of merit, 1994, Disting. Alumna award U. N.C., 1995, Leadership award Nat. Assn. Cmty. Leadership Orgns., 1986, Alumnae Achievement award Randolph-Macon Woman's Coll., 1985, Disting. Citizen award Nat. Mcpl. League, 1983; inducted into Northwestern U. Medill Sch. Journalism Hall of Fame, 1996, U. N.C. Journalism Hall of Fame, 1997. Mem. ABA (coun. on legal edn. and admissions to the bar 1997—). Office: Council on Foundations 1828 L St NW Washington DC 20036-5104

RIDINGS, SUSAN ELIZABETH, social worker; b. Bethlehem, Pa., July 6, 1949; d. Charles Frederick Schmidt and Eleanor Martin Jenico; m. Edward Haslam Ridings, Aug. 28, 1971; children: Alexis Katherine, Adam Edward. BSW, Pa. State U., 1971. Caseworker Pa. Dept. Welfare, Phila., 1973-78; bus. mgr. Vallemont Surg. Assocs., Lewistown, Pa., 1987—. Pres. bd. dirs. Cmty. Counseling Ctr., Lewistown, 1986-88, Mifflin County Children and Youth Svcs., Lewistown, 1990—; bd. dirs. Mifflin-Juniata Assn. of the Blind, Lewistown, 1987-91, v.p., 1994—; pres.-elect Lewistown Hosp. Aux., 1989, pres., 1991-93, pres., 1996—; bd. dirs. Mifflin County 2000, 1995, chmn. Goal 8 Com.; mem. Mifflin County Sch. Dist. steering com.; rec. sec. P.A.H.A., 1994—; legis. chairperson State P.A.H.A., 1994—; trustee Mifflin County Libr. Assn., 1988-91, Lewistown Hosp., 1991—; co-founder Teen Parenting Program, Lewistown, 1985; mem. Lewistown Hosp. Found.; founding mem. Teen Pregnancy Coalition, 1995. Mem. AAUW (programming v.p. 1994-96, Outstanding Woman 1985), Pa. Assn. Hosp. Auxs. (chair ctrl. regional legis., record exec. ctrl. region, legis. chair state bd.), Alpha Omicron Pi. Avocations: reading, gardening, needlework, playing piano. Home: 1 Pine Ln Lewistown PA 17044-2626 Office: Vallemont Surgical Assocs 310 Electric Ave Ste 230 Lewistown PA 17044-1369

RIDLEN, LILLIAN MAY HEIGLE, public relations, sales and marketing executive, writer, inventor; b. New Orleans, Nov. 15, 1946; d. Joseph Manuel and Lillian Mae (Theriot) H.; m. Larry Vinson Ridlen, Dec. 28, 1968; children: Larry V. Jr., Kenneth C., Jennifer C. Degree in Nursing, Orleans Parish Sch. Practical Nursing, 1969. Nurse So. Bapt. Hosp., New Orleans, 1970-72; pres. Sunshine & Co., LaPlace, La., 1983-86, The Gift Gallery, LaPlace, 1984-85; v.p. La. Bartending Inst., Kenner, Baton Rouge and New Orleans, 1986-87, dir., 1987-89; pub. rels. officer, sales and mktg. dir. Universal Fast Foods of LaPlace, Chalmette and Marrero, 1989—; nurse St. Charles Manor Nursing Ctr., 1989—. Owner, pres. Ton-Lil Pub. Co., LaPlace, 1990—, Who Dunit and Co./Hair Salon and Gifts, LaPlace, 1996-97; owner Rosary & Jewelry Crafts by Lillian, LaPlace, La., 1997—. Author: A Sampling of Southern Cooking, 1985, A Home Study Course in Bartending, 1989; co-author: Songs of the Wind, 1995; composer, lyricist songs; lyricist Tony's Song for artist Wayne Presley; inventor Santa's Snack Pack; author poetry pub. in anthologies, 1996; contbr. Best Poems of 1998, contbr. poems in field, 1999. Organizer Mothers for Safe Edn. St. John the Bapt. Parish, La., 1984. Poetry selected for inclusion in world record effort by Internat. Soc. of Poets, 1994; recipient Poet Editors Choice Outstanding Achievement in Poetry award Nat. Libr. Poetry Editors, 1995, 2000, 01; nominated for Poet of Yr. award Internat. Soc. Poets, 1995-2001; elected to Poetry Hall of Fame, 1997. Mem. NAFE, Internat. Soc. Poets, Acad. Am. Poets. Democrat. Roman Catholic. Achievements include having a poem presented to the United Nations, 1992.

RIDLEN, SAMUEL FRANKLIN, agriculture educator; b. Marion, Ill., Apr. 24, 1916; s. Will and Leoma Josephine (Sneed) R.; m. Helen Louise Camp, Apr. 17, 1946; children: Judith Elaine, Barbara Jo, Mark Ellis. BS, U. Ill., 1940; MS, Mich. State U., 1957. Agr. instr. Westville (Ill.) Twp. High Sch., 1940-43; gen. mgr. Honegger Breeder Hatchery, Forrest, Ill., 1953-56; assoc. prof. poultry sci. U. Conn., Storrs, 1957-58; from asst. prof. to prof. poultry extension U. Ill., Urbana-Champaign, 1946-86, prof. emeritus poultry extension, 1986—, asst. head dept. animal scis., 1978-86. Author: An Idea and An Ideal-Nabor House Fraternity 1939-1989, 1989; poultry editorial cons. Successful Farming, Wonderful World Ency., 1960; poultry editor Am. Farm Youth, 1949-53, Ill. Feed Folks, 1949-53. Founding mem., charter mem. Nabor House Frat. Recipient Superior Svc. award U.S. Dept. Agr., 1982, Paul A. Funk Recognition award Coll. Agr., U. Ill., 1983, numerous others. Fellow Poultry Sci. Assn.; mem. World's Poultry Sci. Assn., Ill. State Turkey Growers Assn., Ill. Poultry Industry Coun., Ill Egg Market Devel. Coun. (adv. mem.), Ill. Animal Industry Coun., Coun. for Agr. Sci. and Tech., Ill. Alumni Assn. (life), DAV (life), Alpha Tau Alpha, Epsilon Sigma Phi, Gamma Sigma Delta (pres. 1982-83). Home: 1901 Lakeside Dr # C Champaign IL 61821-5997

RIDLEY, BRIAN WARD, physics educator, researcher; b. Sunderland, N. Umbria, Eng., June 10, 1929; came to US, 1964; s. Charles Norman and Bernice Dorothy R.; m. Elizabeth Cicely Ridley, June 24, 1954 (div. June 1976); children: Katharine Ann, Elizabeth Sarah, Charles Aidan, James Edward; m. Julia Penelope Gibbs, Mar. 3, 2001. MA, U. Cambridge (Eng.), 1951; PhD, 1956. Grad. researcher Cavendish Lab. Cambridge U., 1951-54; coll. fellow Magdalene Coll., Cambridge, 1952-54; Harwell fellow U.K. Atomic Energy Assn., 1954-57; prin. scientist group leader Rutherford Lab., Didcot, Berkshire, Eng., 1957-64; vis. prof. dept. physics U. Colo., Boulder, 1964-67; prof., 1968-94; prof. emeritus, 1994—; chair Nuclear Physics Lab. dept. physics, 1970-74. Contbr. articles to profl. jours.; inventor positive ion detector (The Ridley Detector); designer, developer cyclotron. Grantee US Dept. Energy, 1970-73, Tektronix, Inc., U. Colo. Coun. Creative Works, 1985, Tektronix, Inc., 1986. Mem. Am. Phys. Soc., Am. Assn. Physics Tchrs., AAAS, Amnesty Internat. (life), Sierra Club (life), Consumer Union, Union Concerned Scientists. Home: 93 Camino Bosque Boulder CO 80302-8735 E-mail: bwridley@earthlink.net.

RIDLEY, CAROLYN FLUDD, social studies educator; b. Nashville, Jan. 21, 1942; d. Quitman Daniel and Glennora Elizabeth (Cannon) F.; m. Raymond Bennett, June 23, 1962 (div. 1984); 1 child, Karen Elizabeth Bennett Moore; m. Cornelius Theodore Ridley, July 16, 1988; stepchildren: Constance Maria Ridley Smith, William Keith. BA, CUNY, 1973; MEd, Tenn. State U., 1985. Cert. tchr., prin., Tenn., N.Y. Tchr. N.Y.C. Bd. Edn., 1973-75, Dickson (Tenn.) County Bd. Edn., 1976-77, Hickman County Bd. Edn., Centerville, Tenn., 1977-86, Met. Nashville Bd. Edn., 1986—. Dir. Hickman County Career Day, 1982-83; bd. dirs. Assn. Retarded Citizens, Centerville, 1982-86; adv. com. Hickman County Bicentennial Com., Centerville, 1984-86, initiator commemorative quilt; participant NEH lectr. Author: A Black History of Hickman County, 1985. Campaign worker Met. Nashville Bd. Edn., 1991; campaigner Met. Nashville Edn., Assn., 1992; attendant Dem. Socialization Meeting, Nashville, 1992; participant Nat. Endowment for the Humanities Summer Inst. Furman U., Greenville, Tenn., 1995. Grantee Mid. Tenn. State U., Murfreesboro, 1990, Tenn. State U., Nashville, 1992; James R. Stokeley Inst. fellow U. Tenn., 1993; participant NEH Summer Inst. at Furman U., Greenville, Tenn., 1995; named Tchr. of Yr., 1997. Fellow Taft Inst. (cert. 1992, tchr. of yr. 1997); mem. AAUW, NEA, NASA Space Inst. (cert. 1990), Smithsonian Instn., Internat. Platform Assn., Nat. Historic Preservation Soc., Nat. Geographic Soc., Nat. Coun. Social Studies, Internat. Platform Assn., Holocaust Meml. Mus. (charter mem.). Democrat. Mem. Ch. of Christ. Avocations: travel, reading, music, studying quilting folk art. Home: 4348 Setters Rd Nashville TN 37218-1839 Office: Haynes Mid Sch 510 W Trinity Ln Nashville TN 37207-4944

RIDLEY, CLARENCE HAVERTY, lawyer; b. Atlanta, June 3, 1942; s. Frank Morris Jr. and Clare (Haverty) R.; m. Eleanor Horsey, Aug. 22, 1969; children: Augusta Morgan, Clare Haverty. BA, Yale U., 1964; MBA, Harvard U., 1966; JD, U. Va., 1971. Bar: Ga. 1971. Assoc. King & Spalding, Atlanta, 1971-77, ptnr., 1977—. Bd. dirs. Haverty Furniture Cos., Inc., mem. exec. com., 1992—, vice chmn. bd. dirs., 1996—. Author: Computer Software Agreements, 1987, 2d edit., 1993; exec. editor Va. Law Rev., 1970-71. Chmn. St. Joseph's Hosp. Found., Atlanta, 1986-89; trustee St. Joseph's Health Svcs., 1987—, chmn. fin. com., 1992-96, vice chmn. bd. trustees, 1996—. Roman Catholic. Home: 2982 Habersham Rd NW Atlanta GA 30305-2854 Office: Haverty Furniture Companies Inc 866 Peachtree St NW Atlanta GA 30308

RIDLEY, KEITH ALEXANDER, IV, funeral director; b. Petersburg, Va., Jan. 7, 1968; s. Janice Ridley Harkins. BA, U. D.C., 1987; MBA, Am. U., 1992. Funeral svc. asst. James M. Wilkerson Funeral Establishment, Va., 1977-89; pres., gen. mgr. Ridley Funeral Establishment, Washingtno, 1991—. Bd. dirs. Kate B. Moorefield Scholarship, 1993—, Moorefield Found., 1993—, Greater S.W. Hosp., Washington, 1995—; vice chmn. Dem. Bus. Coun. Mem. NAACP, Alpha Phi Alpha, Pi Sigma Eta. Democrat. Baptist. Avocations: reading, travel, classical studies, history, writing. Office: Ridley Funeral Establishment Inc 131 Mississippi Ave SE Washington DC 20032-6162 E-mail: KRidleyiv@netscape.net.

RIDLEY, MARION BERTON, otolaryngologist/facial plastic surgeon, medical educator; b. Whitwell, Tenn., Nov. 14, 1956; s. Billy Joe and Bonnie Lynn (Cagle) R. BA magna cum laude, U. Tenn., Chattanooga, 1978; MD, U. Tenn., Memphis, 1982. Diplomate Am. Bd. Otolaryngology, Am. Bd. Facial Plastic and Reconstructive Surgery. Intern and resident U. Tenn. Hosps., Memphis, 1982-84; resident Johns Hopkins Hosp., Balt., 1984-87, instr., 1987-88; fellow U. Mich., Ann Arbor, 1988-89; asst. prof. surgery U. South Fla., Tampa, 1989-96, assoc. prof., 1996—; chief otolaryngology sect. James A. Haley VA Hosp.; med. staff HLEE Moffitt Cancer Ctr. and Rsch. Inst., Tampa Gen. Hosp. Author: (chpt.) Facial Plastic and Reconstructive Surgery, 1991, Medical Clinics of North America, 1993, Otolaryngology Head and Neck Surgery, 1994, The Larynx, 1995, Best Practices in Oncology Management: Focus on Swallowing and Communication Disorders, 1998; contbr.

articles to profl. jours. Fellow Am. Acad. Otolaryngology/Head and Neck Surgery, Am. Acad. Facial Plastic and Reconstructive Surgery, Am. Coll. Surgeons, Am. Head and Neck Soc., Am. Bronchoesophagologic Assn.; mem. AMA, Johns Hopkins Med. and Surg. Assn., Fla. Soc. Otolaryngology/Head and Neck Surgery (pres. 1996-97). Democrat. Episcopalian. Avocation: choral music. Office: Univ South Florida Dept Otolaryngology 12901 Bruce B Downs Blvd MDC73 Tampa FL 33612 Fax: 813-974-7314. E-mail: ridleymb@moffitt.usf.edu.

RIDLEY, STANLEY EUGENE, clinical psychologist, consultant; b. Atlanta, Aug. 9, 1950; s. Young Walter and Bessie M. (Jones) R.; children: Mark B., Jason. BA in French and Human Rels., Domincan Coll., 1972; MS in Clin.-Cmty. Psychology, Howard U., 1975, PhD in Clin. Psychology, 1981. Lic. psychologist. Clin. instr. child devel. and psychiatry George Washington U. Med. Sch., Washington, 1981-89; dir. clin. psychology grad. program Howard U., 1984-90; clin. psychologist, cons. Ridley and Assocs., Washington and Lanham, Md., 1983—; grad. assoc. prof. psychology Howard U., Washington, 1987-91; rsch. cons. Hogan and Hartson Attys. at Law, 1988-90; assessment, tng. and rsch. cons. Carter Goble Assocs. Inc., 1988-92; dir. mental health unit Correctional Med. Svcs., Arlington, Va., 1994-97; sr. assoc. tng. and orgn. Resolution Dynamics Inc., Washington, 1994—. Vis. assoc. prof. George Mason U., Fairfax, Va., 1992-94; cons. St. Luke Inst., Suitland, Md., 1991-94; cons., trainer Nuclear Regulatory Commn., Rockville, Md., 1995—. IRS, Washington, 1995—; distbr. Carlson Learning Co., Mpls., 1996—. Author (book chpt.) Ethnic Minority, 1991; contbr. articles to profl. jours. Bus. champion Archbishop Carroll H.S., Washington, 1996-99; mem. mental health adv. bd. D.C. Pub. Schs. Head Start, 1997—. Mem. APA, ASTD, Am. Coll. Forensic Examiners, Orgn. Devel. Network, Am. Bd. Psychol. Spltys., Soc. Indsl. and Orgnl. Psychology, Beta Kappa Chi, Alpha Mu Gamma. Avocations: roller skating, tennis, bowling, golf, developing quotable sayings. Home and Office: Ridley & Assocs 4360 Varnum Pl NE Washington DC 20017-2101

RIDLOFF, RICHARD, real estate investment advisor, lawyer, consultant; b. N.Y.C., July 18, 1948; s. Sol and Daisey (Metz) R.; m. Caren Sara Berger, Mar. 27, 1977; children: Michael Joshua, Daniel Joseph. BA cum laude, Queens Coll., 1969; JD, Cornell U., 1972. Bar: N.Y. 1973. Assoc. counsel MONY, N.Y.C., 1972-79; sr. v.p., gen. counsel, sec. MONY Real Estate Investors, 1979-85; v.p. investments MONY Fin. Svcs., 1985-87; pres. MONY Realty Ptnrs. Inc., Glen Point, N.J., 1985-91; v.p. for investment mgmt. MONY Real Estate Investment Mgmt., N.Y.C., 1988-91; exec. v.p. Tibor Pivko and Co., Clifton, N.J., 1991-94; pres., dir. Growth & Income Inc., 1993-94; spl. projects dir. Kimco Realty Corp., 1995-96; pres. The Richardson Co., 1996—. Mem. adv. commn. on real property ins. to Calif. Sen. Com. on Ins. Claims and Corps., 1986-92; adv. com. N.Y. chpt. Nat. Assn. Corp. Real Estate Execs., 1990. Author: A Practical Guide to Construction Lending, 1985; editor Real Estate Financing Newsletter, 1980-85 ; contbr. articles to profl. jours. Mem. secondary sch. interviewing com. Cornell U., Ithaca, NY, 1981—; treas. Lansman Housing Corp., 2000—02; chmn. fed. legis. com. Nat. Assn. Real Estate Investment Trusts; trustee Jericho Jewish Ctr., 2002—. Mem.: Oakwood-Princeton Park Civic Assn., N.Y. Bar Assn., Alpha Epsilon Pi, Pi Sigma Alpha, Omicron Delta Epsilon. E-mail: ricar77@hotmail.com.

RIDLON, MARGARET AGNES, retired social worker; b. Pittsburg, Kans., Feb. 27, 1923; d. Evan Anthony and Agnes Jessie (Staib) Naylor. BA, BS, Pittsburg State U., 1943; MS in Social Work (fellowship 1969-71, univ. grantee 1971), U. Tenn., 1971. Diplomate Clin. Social Work; lic. cert. social worker; children: Evan Anthony, William Frank, II. Med. supr. Ark. Social Svcs., 1967-71, utilization rev. supr., 1971-73; social work supr. Ark. State Hosp., Little Rock, 1973-76; counselor supr. Ark. Mental Retardation Dept., 1976-81; client and family support dir. S.E. Ark. Human Devel. Ctr., Warren, 1981-87, dir., Arkadelphia Human Devel. Ctr., 1987-88, ret., 1988; cons. counselor Lions World Svcs for the Blind, 1989—. Mem. Ark. Comprehensive Health Planning Commn., 1972-76, Environ. Barriers Council, 1977-87; field instr. U. Ark. Sch. Social Work; bd. dirs. North Central Ark. Mental Health, 1974-76. Mem. Am. Assn. Mental Deficiency (chmn. social work Ark. 1979-85), Am. Assn. Ret. Persons, Nat. Assn. Social Workers, Acad. Cert. Social Workers, Sigma Delta Chi, Alpha Sigma Alpha. Democrat. Methodist. Home: 212 Indianhead Dr North Little Rock AR 72120-3607

RIDNER, MELANIE MARIE, writer, composer; b. Dayton, Apr. 18, 1957; d. George Glenn and Lou Gray (Shifflett) R.; m. Johhny Edward Ridner (div. Apr. 20, 1986); children: GinayMarion Gray Clark, Dawn Renee' Clark. paralegal, civil litigation, computer, Profl. Career Devel. Inst., 1996. Author: (poetry) Romantic Feelings, 1999 (Internat. Libr. Poetry, 1995), (poetry book) Tears On My Shoulder, 2001 (award, 1996), (poetry) Romantic Feelings 2, 1999 (award, 1996); composer: Love Like This, 2001, PennyHeartbreaker, 2001; contbr. poetry to anthologies (awards, 2002); , composer 40 songs. Mem.: Broadcasting Music Inc. (writer 1999—2002), Internat. Libr. Poetry (poet 1995—2002), Modern Poetry Assn. (assoc.). Methodist. Home: Lot 44 2318 Hamilton Eaton Rd Hamilton OH 45011 Personal E-mail: CyrillCovesongs@aol.com.

RIDOLFI, PATRICK MURPHY, music educator, tenor; b. San Francisco, July 29, 1954; s. Joseph Oreste Ridolfi and Lillian Ruth Scott; m. Margie Gayatin, May 22, 1993; children: Justin Robert; m. Barbara Ridolfi, Sept. 20, 1980 (dec. Nov. 6, 1989); children: Joseph Patrick. BA, U. of Calif. at Santa Barbara, Santa Barbara, CA, 1977; BM, Calif. State U. at Northridge, Northridge, CA, 1987. Elem. tchr. LA Unified Sch. Dist., Los Angeles, Calif., 1991—95; free-lance operatic tenor LA Opera, LA Master Chorale, Long Beach Opera, Roger Wagner Chorale, 1981—; elem. music tchr. LA Unified Sch. Dist., 1995—. Grantee ELSA Grant, Fed. Arts Grant, 1999, 2000. Mem.: UTLA, MENC. Avocations: swimming, snorkeling, travel.

RIDPATH, JAMES S. retired sales executive; b. Haxton, Colo., Nov. 12, 1921; s. Mike and May Ridpath; m. Helen C. DiPietranio, Sept. 7, 1955; 1 child Mary Ridpath Raver. Student, U. Nebr., Delaware County C.C., Media, Pa. Sales agt., sales mgr., agt. dir., educator ins. industry, Drexel Hill, Pa. Tchr. children the game of marbles NMCA, Drexel Hill. Author: The Wonderful World of Marbles, 1995. Petty officer USN, 1940—46. Mem.: Masons. Home: 1250 Harbor Towne Dr Myrtle Beach SC 29577

RIEBER, JESSE ALVIN, psychotherapist; b. N.Y.C., Mar. 18, 1945; s. Jesse Paul and Edith Thyra (Marion) R.; m. Marnie Dianne Campbell, Dec. 11, 1971; children: Kahlil Jason, Jennifer Edith. BA, Syracuse U., 1968; MA, U. Man., Winnipeg, Can., 1974, M City Planning, 1981; MA in Clin. Mental Health Counseling, Lesley Coll., 1994. Psychotherapist in pvt. practice, Centerville and New Bedford, Mass. Dep. for Moldova to Internat. Parliament for Safety and Peace, UN. Mem. Maison Internationale des Intellectuels. Buddhist. Avocations: sailing, creative writing, boat designing. Office: 836 Strawberry Hill Rd Centerville MA 02632-2561 also: 222 Union St Ste 203 New Bedford MA 02740 E-mail: jesmarn@aol.com., jarieber@aol.com.

RIEBER, ROBERT W. psychology educator, linguistics educator; BS, Pa. State U., 1954; MEd, Temple U., 1955; PhD in Psycho-Linguistics, Univ. Coll./U. London, 1971. From assoc. prof. to prof. psychology John Jay Coll./CUNY, 1972—; lectr. Columbia U. Phys. and Surg. Editor: Language Development and Aphasia in Children, 1980, Mind and Body: Past, Present, and Future, 1980, Psychology, Language, and Thought: Essays on the Theory and History of Psycholinguistics, 1980, Advances in Forensic Psychology and Psychiatry, Vol. 1, 1984, Vol. 2, 1987, Psychology of War and Peace: Image of the Enemy, 1991, The Psychopathology of Language and Thought, 1994, Manufacturing Social Distress, 1997, Psychology: Theoretical-Historical Perspectives, 2d edit., 1998, Wilhelm Wendt in History: The Making of A Scientific Psychology, 2001; co-editor various books in field; founding editor: Communication Disorders, 1967-92, Jour. Psycholinguistic Rsch., 1972—, Jour. of Social Distress and Homelessness, 1993—, others. Fellow APA, AAAS, N.Y. Acad. Scis., Am. Anthropol. Assn., Am. Psychol. Assn. Office: CUNY John Jay Coll Criminal Justice 445 W 59th St New York NY 10019-1104

RIECHERS, ROGER NEIL, urologist, surgeon; b. N.Y.C., May 18, 1942; s. Francis Riechers and Lethea Marion Helsel. AB, Columbia Coll., 1964; MD, NYU, 1968. Diplomate Am. Bd. Urology. Urologist Mt. Kisco (N.Y.) Med. Group, 1975—, Northern Westchester (N.Y.) Hosp., 1975-99, Mt. Kisco (N.Y.) Med. Group, 1996-99. Cons. MRI Am., N.Y.C., Lexus Nexus, Greenwich, Conn. Capt. U.S. Army. Fellow ACS; mem. AMA, Alpha Omega Alpha. Office: Mt Kisco Med Group 90 S Bedford Rd Mount Kisco NY 10549-3412

RIECK, ALBERT CHARLES, chemist; b. Norristown, Pa., Sept. 27, 1951; s. Albert F. Rieck and Kathryn Kulp; m. Barbara Jo White, Sept. 4, 1982; children: Marie Kathryn, Albert John. BA in Chemistry, Temple U., 1973. Chemist Phila. Resins Co., Montgomeryville, Pa., 1973-78; sr. chemist Rohm & Haas Co., Spring House, 1979—. Tchr. North Penn Regional CCD Program, 1981-87; treas. North Penn Area Dem. Com., 1988-94, 1st vice chair, 1994-98; chmn. Lansdale Dem. Com., 1991—; candidate Dem. State Rep., Pa., 1994, 98; 2d vice chair Montgomery County Dem. Com., 1994-98; den leader Cub Scouts Pack 414, 1995-99, asst. cubmaster, 1996-99, asst. scoutmaster trooop 303, 1999-2000, scoutmaster, 2000—; active Lansdate Borough Coun., 1988-95. Recipient Eagle Scout award, 1967. Roman Catholic. Avocations: American history, golf, photography. Home: 521 Perkiomen Ave Lansdale PA 19446-3430 Office: Rohm & Haas Co Spring House Tech Ctr 727 Norristown Rd Spring House PA 19477 Personal E-mail: alrieck@aol.com. Business E-Mail: arieck@rohmhaas.com.

RIECK, JANET RAE, special education educator; b. Atchison, Kans., Oct. 24, 1948; d. Clinton Everett and Bernice Marie (Schreurs) Wendland; m. Arthur Wyman Hand, Mar. 1970 (div. Feb. 1977); m. Doyle Elmer Rieck, Sept. 21, 1986. B in Music Edn., Otterbein Coll., 1970; MA, U. No. Colo., 1980; MS, No. Ill. U., 1989. Cert. tchr. Nebr. Music tchr. Blanchester (Ohio) Schs., 1970-74; tchr. aide N.Mex. Sch. for Visually Handicapped, Alamogordo, 1976-78; tchr. visually impaired Edn. Svc. Unit 7, Columbus, Nebr., 1979—. Piano tchr., Cin., 1975-76, Alamogordo, 1976-78. Mem. NEA, Coun. Exceptional Children, Assn. for Edn. and Rehab. of Blind and Visually Impaired (Nebr. pres. elect 1990-92, pres. 1992-94, cert. orientation and mobility specialist). Lutheran. Avocations: piano, sewing, horseback riding, swimming. Office: Ednl Svc Unit 7 2657 44th Ave Columbus NE 68601-8537

RIECK, WILLIAM ALBERT, secondary school educator and administrator, professor; b. Hackensack, N.J., Jan. 15, 1942; s. William Emanual and Grace Adeline (Bormann) R.; m. Judith Ann Klindt, Apr. 18, 1965; children: Melissa, William Albert Jr. BA, Jersey City State Coll., 1963; MA, Montclair (N.J.) State Coll., 1966; DEd, Loyola U., Chgo., 1976. Asst. prof. Trenton (N.J.) State Coll., 1966-69; area mgr. Dupont Chem., Chgo., 1969-72; chemistry tchr. Lockport (Ill.) High Sch., 1972-74; asst. prin. Oak Forrest (Ill.) High Sch., 1974-75; prin. Evanston (Ill.) Twp. High Sch., 1975-76, Rock Island (Ill.) High Sch., 1975-77, Fallsburg (N.Y.) High Sch., 1977-80, Hicksville (N.Y.) High Sch., 1980-90, Nottingham High Sch., Trenton, 1982-90; prof. edn./dir. tchr. cadet corps U. Louisville, Lafayette, 1991—; prof., dir. grad. studies edn. U. La., 1991—. Contbr. articles to profl. jours. Mem. Hamilton (N.J.) Say No to Drugs Com., 1987—, Hamilton Citizens for Edn., 1989—; advisor DeMolay chpt., Hamilton Sq., N.J., 1987—; trustee First Presbyn. Ch., Levittown, N.Y., 1981-84. Recipient Disting. Alumnu award Jersey City State Coll., 1983, Citation, N.J. Gen. Assembly, 1983, Cert. of Appreciation, N.Y. Congress Parents and Tchrs., 1982; NSF grantee, 1968, 1994-95. Mem. Nat. Assn. Secondary Sch. Prins. (Svc. award 1989), N.J. Prins. and Suprs. Assn. (exec. coun. 1985—, Svc. award 1989), Assn. for Supervision and Curriculum Devel., Mercer County Prins. and Suprs. Assn. (sec. 1988—), Masons, Shriners (youth com. chmn. 1975-80). Presbyterian. Home: 108 Shadowbrush Bnd Lafayette LA 70506-7852 Office: U La Foster Hall 221 PO Box 42051 Lafayette LA 70504-0001 E-mail: wrieck@louisiana.edu.

RIECKEN, HENRY WILLIAM, psychologist, research director; b. Bklyn., Nov. 11, 1917; s. Henry William and Lilian Antoinette (Nieber) R.; m. Frances Ruth Manson, Aug. 7, 1955; children— Mary Susan, Gilson, Anne AB, Harvard U., 1939, PhD, 1950. Social sci. analyst Dept. Agr., 1941-46; lectr. social psychology, research assoc. clin. psychology Harvard U., 1949-54; assoc. prof. then prof., sr. mem. lab. research social relations U. Minn., 1954-58; program dir. social sci. research NSF, Washington, 1958-59; head Office Social Sci., 1959-60, asst. dir. social scis., 1960-64, assoc. dir. sci. edn., 1964-66; v.p. Social Sci. Research Council, N.Y.C., 1966-69, pres., 1969-71; prof. behavioral scis. U. Pa., Phila., 1972-85, prof. emeritus, 1985—; assoc. dir. for planning Nat. Library Medicine, Bethesda, Md., 1985-87. Fellow Ctr. Advanced Study Behavioral Scis., Stanford, Calif., 1971-72; Paterson Meml. lectr. U. Minn., 1970; Jensen lectr. Duke U., 1973; mem. adv. com. to dir. NIH, 1966-70, chmn. internat. ctrs. com., 1968-73; pres. Am. Psychol. Found., 1971-73; vice chmn., chmn. com. nat. needs for biomed. and behavioral rsch. pers. NRC, 1975-80; report rev. com. Nat. Acad. Scis., 1982-99; adj. prof. psychiatry U. Tex. Med. Br., 1988—. Author: The Volunteer Work Camp, 1952, When Prophecy Fails, 1956, Social Experimentation, 1974, Experimental Testing of Public Policy, 1976; contbr. articles to profl. jours. Bd. dirs. Found. Child Devel. (formerly Assn. Aid Crippled Children), N.Y., 1962-2002; trustee W.T. Grant Found., N.Y., 1979-96. Served with USAAC, 1943-45 Fellow Am. Psychol. Assn. (Harold M. Hildreth award 1971), Am. Acad. Arts and Scis.; mem. Am. Assn. Pub. Opinion Research, Sociol. Research Assn. (pres. 1966), Nat. Acad. Scis., Inst. Medicine. Clubs: Harvard (N.Y.C.); Cosmos (Washington).

RIED, TESSA, environmentalist; b. Berlin, Oct. 19, 1935; came to U.S., 1936; d. Werner Wilhelm and Ruth (Heinitz) Jaeger; m. Robert Samuel Byck, May 4, 1963 (div. July 1974); children: Carl Werner, Gillian, Lucas Julian; m. Horace John Ried, Jan. 1, 1978. BA, Radcliffe Coll., 1956; MA, Yale U., 1957. Asst. dir. Meridian House Found., Stamford, Conn., 1977-81, sec. bd. dirs., 1976-77; publishing dir. Taxwise Giving, Old Greenwich, 1981-84; asst. dir Gateway Cmtys., Inc., Stamford, 1985-90, pres. bd. dirs., 1982-84; dir. tng. and pub. info. Vol. Ctr. of S.W. Fairfield County, 1990-99. Mem. Coalition for Basic Human Rights, 1994-2001; bd. dirs. Environ. Coun. Stamford, 1999-2002. Author: Why WE Need YOU, 1992, Where Is Tomorrow?, 1994. Vol. EMT Stamford Ambulance Corps, 1972-73; organizer Save Our Swans, 1990, Nat. Youth Svc. Day, 1991-99; founder Rippowam Neighbors, 1996; lic. vol. wildlife rehabilitator State of Conn., 2000—. Pilot program grantee Corp. Nat. and Cmty. Svc., 1992-95. Mem. Phi Beta Kappa. Avocations: social issues and environmental advocacy, linguistics, landscaping. Home: 101 Maltbie Ave Stamford CT 06902-1109

RIEDEBURG, THEODORE, management consultant, consultant; b. Milw., June 7, 1912; s. Theodore and Elva Pauline (Wolf) R.; m. Margaret Anna Louise Oertel, Dec. 24, 1937 (dec.); children: Theodore, Charles Howard; m. Ruth Jones Keith, May 3, 1980. BS, Marquette U., 1934, MS, 1936. Dist. sales mgr. Philip Morris & Co., 1937-42; asst. mgr. fumigants dept. Dow Chem. Co., Midland, Mich., 1942-45; sales mgr. agrichems. Westvaco Chem., N.Y.C., 1945-50; mng. dir. Theodore Riedeburg Assocs., 1950-80; ind. forensic chemist-pesticides St. Simons Island, Ga., 1980—. Contbr. articles to profl. jours. Pres. Citizens League White Plains, N.Y., 1962; chmn. St. Simons Island Beautification Coun., 1995-97; mem. St. Simons Land Trust, Glynn Environ. Coalition, Residents United Planning Action. Fellow Soc. Profl. Mgmt. Cons. (past pres.); mem. Am. Arbitration Assn., Nat. Bur. Profl. Mgmt. Cons. (exec. adv. bd. 1989-2001) Home: 136 Heritage Dr # B1 Saint Simons GA 31522-2023 Office: PO Box 21158 Saint Simons GA 31522-0658

RIEDEL, ALAN ELLIS, retired manufacturing company executive, lawyer; b. Bellaire, Ohio, June 28, 1930; s. Emil George and Alberta (Shafer) R.; m. Ruby P. Tignor, June 21, 1953; children: Ralph A., Amy L., John T. AB magna cum laude, Ohio U., 1952, LLD (hon.), 1994; JD, Case Western Res. U., 1955; grad., Advanced Mgmt. Program, Harvard, 1971. Bar: Ohio 1955, Tex. 1968. Assoc. Squire, Sanders & Dempsey, Cleve., 1955-60; from gen. counsel to sec. Cooper Industries Inc. (formerly Cooper Bessemer Co.), Mt. Vernon, Ohio, 1960-68; from sec. to v.p. indsl. rels. Cooper Industries Inc., 1963-73; from sr. v.p. adminstrn. to vice chmn. Cooper Industries, Inc., Houston, 1973-94. Dir. Factory Mut. Ins., 1999-2000; bd. dirs. Belden Inc., St. Louis, 1993-2000, Gardner Denver Inc., Quincy, Ill., 1994-2000, chmn. bd. dirs., 1994-98; of counsel Squire, Sanders & Dempsey, Houston, 1994—. Past chmn. bd. dirs. Jr. Achievement of S.E. Tex.; trustee, past chmn. bd. trustees Ohio U. Endowment Found. Mem. Order of Coif, Phi Beta Kappa, Omicron Delta Kappa, Delta Tau Delta. Home: 803 Creek Wood Way Houston TX 77024-3023 E-mail: aeriedel@swbell.net.

RIEDEL, BERNARD EDWARD, retired pharmaceutical sciences educator; b. Provost, Alta., Can., Sept. 25, 1919; s. Martin and Naomi E. (Klingaman) R.; m. Julia C. McClurg, Mar. 5, 1944 (dec. Mar. 1992); children: Gail Lynne, Dwain Edward, Barry Robert; m. Della Williams, Sept. 2, 2000. BS in Pharmacy, U. Alta., Edmonton, 1943, MS in Pharmacology, 1949; PhD in Biochemistry, U. Western Ont., 1953; DSc (hon.), U. Alta., 1990. Lectr., asst. prof. Faculty of Pharmacy U. Alta., Edmonton, 1946-49, asst. prof. then assoc. prof., 1953-58, prof., 1959-67, exec. asst. to v.p., 1961-67; dean, prof. Faculty Pharm. Scis. U. B.C., Vancouver, 1967-84, coordinator Health Scis. Centre, 1977-84. Mem. sci. adv. com. Health Rsch. Found. of B.C., 1991-95. Contbr. numerous articles on pharmacology to profl. jours. Elder Ryerson United Ch.; mem. exec. bd. Boy Scouts Can., Edmonton Region, Alta.; mem. Cancer Control Agy. of B.C., trustee 1979-86, v.p., 1984, pres. 1985-86; bd. dirs. B.C. Lung Assn., 1988-2000, v.p., 1989, pres., 1990-91; chmn., bd. dirs. B.C. Organ Transplant Soc., 1986-89, hon. bd. dirs., 2000. Wing comdr. RCAF, 1943-46, 49-67. Decorated mem. Order of Can.; recipient Gold medal in Pharmacy, 1943; Centennial medal, 1967, 75th Anniversary medal U. B.C., 1990; Can Forces decoration, 1965; Commemorative medal for 125th Anniversary of the Confedn. of Can., 1992, Spl. Svcs. award Assn. Faculties of Pharmacy of Can., 2001. Mem. Alta. Pharm. Assn. (hon. life), Can. Pharm. Assn. (hon. life), Assn. of Faculties of Pharmacy of Can. (hon. life, chmn. 1959, 69, special svc. award 2001), Can. Biochem. Soc., Pharmacol. Soc. Can., Can. Assn. of Univ. Tchrs., Can. Soc. Hosp. Pharmacists, B.C. Coll. Pharmacists (hon. life), U. B.C. Profs. Emeriti Divsn. Alumni Assn. (pres. 1993-95). Home: 8394 Angus Dr Vancouver BC Canada V6P 5L2 E-mail: briedel@interchange.ubc.ca.

RIEDHAMMER, THOMAS MARTIN, pharmaceutical executive; b. Buffalo, Mar. 18, 1948; s. Harold M. and Marjorie P. (Walsh) R.; m. Evelyn M. Albano, July 25, 1970; children: Michael, Marcus, Tanya. BA, SUNY, Buffalo, 1970; PhD, SUNY, 1975. Dir. rsch. and devel. Bausch and Lomb, Inc., Rochester, NY, 1975-84, pres. global pharm., 1992—2000; v.p. Paco Rsch. Corp., Lakewood, N.J., 1984-86, pres., 1986—91; COO Presby Corp., Dallas, 2001—02. Contbr. articles to profl. jours. Former mem. Prevent Blindness Am., Jr. Achievement Internat.; bd. dirs. Prevent Blindness Fla., Sjogrens Syndrome Found. Home: 309 Hidden Lake Dr Brandon FL 33511-8126

RIEDI, RUDOLF HERMANN, mathematics researcher; b. St. Gallen, Switzerland, June 18, 1961; s. Hermann Albiez and Martha Zellweger. MSc, Swiss Fed. Inst. Tech., Zurich, 1986, MEd, 1987, DSc in Math., 1993. Rsch. asst. ETH Zurich, 1987-93; postdoctoral assoc. Yale U., New Haven, 1993-95, Nat. Rsch. Inst. France, Le Chesnay, 1995-97; faculty fellow Rice U., Houston, 1997—. Contbr. articles to profl. jours. Grantee, Nat. Found. Sci., Switzerland, 1993, rsch. grantee, Ctr. Internat. Etudiants & Stagiares, 1996, NSF, 1999, 2001, Def. Advanced Rsch. Projects Agy., 2000, Dept. of Energy, 2001. Mem. Swiss Math. Assn., Am. Math. Soc. Avocations: skiing, basketball, photography. Office: Rice U Dept ECE 380 6100 Main St Houston TX 77005-1892 E-mail: riedi@rice.edu.

RIEDINGER, EDWARD ANTHONY (TED RIEDINGER), international educator, Brazilianist; b. Cin., Mar. 26, 1944; s. Charles Anthony and Ida Gertrude (Winter) R. Student, Latin Sch. Indpls., 1962; BA cum laude, Butler U., 1967; MA, U. Chgo., 1969, PhD, 1978; MLIS, U. Calif., Berkeley, 1989; postgrad., Harvard U., 1969, U. Oxford, 1970, U. Cambridge, 1986. Pvt. sec. to ex-pres. Brazil Juscelino Kubitschek, 1972-76; asst. prof. Pontifical Cath. U., Rio de Janeiro, 1976-77, U. Ams., Puebla, Mex., 1978; ednl. adv. officer Fulbright Commn. U.S. Consulate, Rio de Janeiro, 1979-88; founder Overseas Ednl. Advisers Profl. Edn. Group Nat. Assn. for Fgn. Student Affairs, 1985, Latin Am. rep., 1988; acting bibliographer L.Am., Spain, Portugal U. Calif., Berkeley, 1990; lectr. Brazilian history San Francisco State U., 1990; bibliographer Latin Am., assoc. prof. univ. librs. Dept. History Ohio State U., 1991—. Mem. organizing exec. com. Brazilian Studies Assn., 1993, sec., 1994-96; founder, adminstr. Overseas Ednl. Advisers Profl. Net, 1992-95; cons. on Brazil and internatl ednl. advising for U.S. and internat. orgns. and agys. Author: Brief View of American Literature, 1976, Como Se Faz Um Presidente, a Campanha de J.K., 1988, Proceedings of 1st BRASA conf., 1994, Proceedings of 2d BRASA conf., 1995, Turned on Advising, 1995, Where in the World to Learn, 1995, Training Modules for Overseas Educational Advisers, 1997; contbr. numerous articles to profl. and scholarly jours. and reference books; mem. editl. bd. Phi Beta Delta Internat. Rev., 1992-96, Manguinhos, 1994—. Ford Found. fellow, 1968-72; travel grantee NEH, 1992, OSU/Tinker Found. field rsch. grantee 1992, 96; Fulbright-Hays scholar, 1996; recipient commendations Brazilian Army Corps of Engrs., 1982, U.S. Info. Svc., 1984, Brazilian War Coll., 1985, Fulbright Commn., 1988, U.S. amb. to Brazil, 1988, Berkeley City Commons, 1990, Instituto Brasil-Estados Unidos, Rio de Janeiro, 1995, Brasa, 1997. Office: Ohio State U Librs Office Lat Am Bibliography 1858 Neil Ave Rm 312 Columbus OH 43210-1225

RIEDL, JOHN ORTH, university dean; b. Milw., Dec. 9, 1937; s. John O. and Clare C. (Quirk) R.; m. Mary Lucille Priestap, Feb. 4, 1961; children: John T., Ann E., James W., Steven E., Daniel J. BS in Math. magna cum laude, Marquette U., Milw., 1958; MS in Math., U. Notre Dame, 1960, PhD in Math., 1963; postgrad., Northwestern U., 1963. Asst. prof. math. Ohio State U., Columbus, 1966-70, assoc. prof., 1970—, asst. dean Coll. Math. and Phys. Sci., 1969-74, assoc. dean, 1974-87, acting dean, 1984-86, spl. asst. to provost, 1987, dean, dir. Mansfield (Ohio) Campus, 1987—, exec. dean regional campus, 1988—. Panelist sci. edn. NSF, 1980-91; cons. Ohio Dept. Edn., 1989, Ohio bd. regents subsidy cons., 1991, 95, 97, 99, 2001. Pres., v.p. exec. com. Univ. Cmty. Assn., Columbus, 1970-78; mem. edn. commn. St. Peter's Schs., Mansfield, 1989-95; trustee Rehab. Svc. N. Ctrl. Ohio, Mansfield, 1990-99, v.p., 1993-94, pres., 1995-97; pres. Ohio Assn. Regional Campuses, 1993-94; co-chair capital campaign St. Peter's Schs., 1998. NSF grad. fellow, 1960, 61, 62; recipient Faculty Svc. award Nat. U. Continuing Edn. Assn., 1988, Creative Programming award, 1988. Mem. Math. Assn. Am. (chair com. on minicourse 1981-87), Downs Am. Chestnut Found. of Ohio (bd. dirs. 2001--), Rotary Internat. (bd. dirs., pres.-elect, pres.) C. of C. (bd. dirs.). Democrat. Roman Catholic. Avocations: fishing, woodworking, handball, gardening. Home: 745 Clifton Blvd Mansfield OH 44907-2284 Office: Ohio State U 1680 University Dr Mansfield OH 44906-1547 E-mail: riedl.1@osu.edu.

RIEDLING, ANN MARLOW, multi-media specialist, educator; b. New Albany, Ind., July 26, 1952; d. Floyd Guy and Martha Riddle; m. Russell Edward Riedling, Aug. 4, 1982; 1 child Marlow. BS, Ind. U., 1973; MEd, U. Ga., 1975; EdD, U. Louisville, 1996. Cert. sch. libr. media specialist P-12, elem. edn. Libr. media specialist New Albany/Floyd County Schs., 1984—94, Jefferson County Pub. Schs., Louisville, 1994—96; assoc. prof., chair sch. libr. media dept. Spalding U., 1996—. Author: (book) Reference Skills for the School Library Media Specialist, 2000 (Fulbright scholar, 1999), Catalog It! A Guide to Cataloging School Library Materials, 2002 (Metroversity award Tchg., 2000), Learning to Learn, Helping Teachers Teach, Essentials of Information Literacy; contbr. Mem.: Fulbright Fellows. Roman Catholic. Avocations: reading, swimming, travel. Home: 1328 Tycoon Way Louisville KY 40213 Office: Spalding U 851 S 4th St Louisville KY 40203 Home Fax: 502-585-7123; Office Fax: 502-585-7123. Personal E-mail: ariedling@directvinternet.com. Business E-Mail: ariedling@spalding.edu.

RIEDLINGER, STEPHEN C. federal judge; b. 1950; BA, La. State U., 1971, JD, 1977. Bar: La. 1977, U.S. Dist. Ct. (ea. dist.) La. 1979, U.S. Dist. Ct. (mid. dist.) 1978, U.S. Ct. Appeals (5th cir.) 1983. Law clk. U.S. Dist. Ct. La., 1977-78; pvt. practice Baton Rouge, 1978-86; magistrate judge U.S. Dist. Ct. (mid. dist.) La., 1986—. With USNR, 1971-77. Office: Russell B Long Fed Bldg & Courthouse 777 Florida St Ste 260 Baton Rouge LA 70801-1717 Fax: 225-389-3501. 225-389-3585.

RIEDTHALER, WILLIAM ALLEN, risk management professional; b. Cleve., May 13, 1948; s. Robert Wilbert and Jean Margaret (Trojanowski) R.; m. Janet Louise Clark, Nov. 10, 1973; children: Jennifer Margaret, Valerie Gretchen. AS in Law Enforcement, Cuyahoga C.C., 1968; BA in Pub. Safety Adminstrn., BA in Criminal Justice Studies, Kent State, 1974; EMBA in Healthcare, Baldwin-Wallace Coll., 2000. Cert. instr. and peace officer; cert. tchr., Ohio, Fla., Tex., Mich. Police cadet Cleve. Police Dept., 1967-69, patrolman, 1969-74, detective, 1974-81, sgt. police, 1981-84; assoc. security advisor Cleve. Electric Illuminating Co., 1984-87, investigator, 1987-90; security advisor Centerior Energy Corp., Cleve., 1990-93, supr. claims

Independence, 1993-96, mgr. risk mgmt., 1996-98; dir. spl. risk programs N.Am. Benefits Network, INc., Rocky River, Ohio, 1998—. Instr. gambling and vice Case Western Res. U., Cleve., 1979-90, Cleve. Police Acad., 1974—, Ohio Peace Officers Tng. Acad., 1976—, Cuyahoga County Sheriffs Officers Acad., Cleve., 1981—, Shaker Heights (Ohio) Police Acad., 1990—. Author: An Enforcement Guide to Carnival Games Gambling and Fraud, 1981, An Enforcement Guide to Monetary Operated Gambling Devices or Slot Machines, 2002; contbr. articles to profl. jours. Spl. dep. sheriff Cuyahoga County Sheriff's Office, Cleve., 1985—; trustee Cleve. Crime Clinic, 1999—; bd. govs. Nat. Healthcare Antifraud Assn., 1999—. Recipient Patrolman of Yr. award Cleve. Exchange Club, 1979. Mem. Am. Soc. Indsl. Security, Met. Crime Bur. (v.p. 1992-93, pres. 1994-95), German Am. Police Assn., Fraternal Order of Police, Cleve. Claims Assn. Republican. Avocations: photography, scuba diving, boating, aircraft piloting, hiking. Home: 7992 Vesta Ave Northfield OH 44067-2048 Office: North Am Benefits Network Inc 19800 Detroit Rd Rocky River OH 44116-1816 E-mail: breidthaler@nabn.com., wreidthaler@enforcementguide.com.

RIEDY, MARK JOSEPH, finance educator; b. Aurora, Ill., July 9, 1942; s. Paul Bernard and Kathryn Veronica R.; m. Erin Jeanne Lynch, Aug. 29, 1964; children: Jennifer Erin, John Mark. BA in Econs. maxima cum laude, Loras Coll., 1964; MBA, Washington U., St. Louis, 1966; PhD, U. Mich., 1971. Asst. prof. bus. adminstrn. U. Colo., Boulder, 1969-71; sr. staff economist Council of Econ. Advisers, Washington, 1971-72; spl. asst. to chmn. Fed. Home Loan Bank Bd., 1972; v.p., dir. research PMI Investment Corp., San Francisco, 1973; v.p., chief economist Fed. Home Loan Bank of San Francisco, 1973-77; exec. v.p., chief operating officer Mortgage Bankers Assn. of Am., Washington, 1978-84; pres., chief operating officer Fed. Nat. Mortgage Assn., 1985-86, cons., 1986-87; pres., chief operating officer J.E. Robert Cos., Alexandria, Va., 1987-88; pres., chief exec. officer Nat. Coun. Community Bankers, Washington, 1988-92, also bd. dirs.; Ernest W. Hahn prof. real estate fin. U. San Diego, 1993—, dir. Real Estate Inst. Mem. adv. coun. Credit Rsch. Ctr., Purdue U., 1981-82, Trellion Techs., 2000--; bd. dirs. Fed. Nat. Mortgage Assn., Am. Residential Mortgage Corp., Continental Savs. Bank, AccuBanc Mortgage Corp., Pan Pacific Retail Properties, Inc., Am. Residential Investment Trust, Noble Broadcast Group, Drayton Ins. Cos., Perpetual Savs. Bank, Ctr. for Fin. Studies, TeoMedia, Inc.; bd. dirs., chmn. bd. Neighborhood Bancorp; mem. San Diego Mayor's Renaissance Commn. Chmn. St. Vincent De Paul Village; bd. dirs. Lambda Alpha Internat.; mem. bd. govs. San Diego Regional Policy Inst. Woodrow Wilson scholar, 1964; Nat. Def. scholar, 1964-66; U.S. Steel Found. fellow, 1966-68; Robert G. Rodkey Found. fellow, 1966-69; Earhart Found. fellow, 1968-69 Mem. Am. Econ. Assn., Am. Fin. Assn., Nat. Assn. Bus. Economists, Am. Soc. Assn. Execs., Urban Land Inst. Office: U San Diego Sch Bus Adminstrn 5998 Alcala Park San Diego CA 92110-2492 Business E-Mail: mriedy@sandiego.edu.

RIEFLER, DONALD BROWN, financial consultant; b. Washington, Nov. 10, 1927; s. Winfield W. and Dorothy (Brown) R.; m. Patricia Hawley, Oct. 12, 1957; children: Duncan, Linda, Barbara. BA, Amherst Coll., 1949. With J.P. Morgan & Co. Inc., N.Y.C., 1952-91; v.p. Morgan Guaranty Trust Co. of N.Y., 1962-68, sr. v.p., 1968-77, chmn. sources and uses of funds com., 1977—88, chmn. market risk com., 1989—91; fin. mkts. cons., 1991—. With U.S. Army, 1950-52. Mem. John's Island Club, Riomar Country Club, Cordillera Club. Home: 512 Bay Dr Vero Beach FL 32963-2107

RIEFLER, ROGER FRANK, economics educator; b. Freeport, N.Y., Sept. 16, 1940; s. Frank W. and Madeline C. (Engelke) R.; m. Carolyn J. Kelsey, Sept. 1, 1962. BA, Bowdoin Coll., 1962; MA, U. Washington, 1965, PhD, 1966. Economist Dept. of Def., Washington, 1966-68; asst. prof. economics U. Pitts., Pitts., 1968-73; assoc. prof. economics U. Nebr., Lincoln, Nebr., 1973-77, prof. of economics, 1977—. Cons. Westingham Corp., Pitts., 1969-70, Jack Faucett Assocs., Silver Springs, Md., 1969-76, LTV Inc., Dallas, 1970-71, Resource Economics and Mgmt. Analysts, Lincoln, 1983—. Contbr. articles to jours. Capt. U.S. Army, 1966-68. Mem. Mid-Continent Regional Sci. Assn. (pres. 1984-85), Regional Sci. Assn., Am. Economic Assn., Canadian Regional Sci. Assn., Economic History Assn. Democrat. Lutheran. Home: 3221 Weaver Ln Lincoln NE 68506-6135 Office: Dept of Economics U of Nebraska Lincoln NE 68588

RIEGEL, BYRON WILLIAM, ophthalmologist; b. Evanston, Ill., Jan. 19, 1938; s. Byron and Belle Mae (Huot) Riegel; m. Marilyn Hills, May 18, 1968; children: Marc William, Ryan Marie, Andrea Elizabeth. BS, Stanford U., 1960; MD, Cornell U., 1964. Diplomate Am Bd Ophthalmology, Nat Bd Med Examiners. Intern King County Hosp., Seattle, 1964-65; asst. resident in surgery U. Wash., 1965; resident in ophthalmology U. Fla., Visalia, Calif., 1968-71; pvt. practice medicine specializing in ophthalmology Sierra Eye Med. Group, Inc., 1972—. Mem staff Kaweah Delta Dist Hosp, chief staff, 1978—79, bd dirs, asst secy, 1983—90; mem staff St Agnes Hosp, Fresno, Calif.; asst med dir Sierra Ambulatory Surg Ctr, Visalia, Calif., 2000—. Flight surgeon USN, 1966—68. Co-recipient Fight-for-Sight Citation for rsch. in retinal dystrophy, 1970. Fellow: ACS, Am. Acad. Ophthalmology; mem.: Phacoemulsification and Cataract Methodology Soc, Internat. Pacoemulsification and Cataract Methodology, Am. Soc. Cataract and Refractive Surgery, Calif. Acad. Ophthalmology (v.p. 3d party liaison 1994—96, dir. 1996—98), Tulare County Med Asn, Calif. Med. Assn. (del. 1978—79), Rotary (Visalia). Roman Catholic. Home: 3027 Keogh Ct Visalia CA 93291-4228 Office: 2830 W Main St Visalia CA 93291-4300 E-mail: briegel@sierraeye.com.

RIEGEL, KURT WETHERHOLD, environmental protection executive; b. Lexington, Va., Feb. 28, 1939; s. Oscar Wetherhold and Jane Cordelia (Butterworth) R.; children: Tatiana Suzanne, Samuel Brent Oscar, Eden Sonja Jane. BA, Johns Hopkins U., 1961; PhD, U. Md., 1966; PMD, Harvard U., 1977. Asst. prof. astronomy UCLA, 1966-74; prof. astronomy U. Calif. Extension, Los Angeles, 1968-74; mgr. energy conservation program Fed. Energy Adminstrn., Washington, 1974-75; chief tech. and consumer products energy conservation Dept. Energy, 1975-78, dir. consumer products div., conservation and solar energy, 1978-79; assoc. dir. environ. engring. and tech. EPA, 1979-82; head Astronomy Ctrs. NSF, 1982-89; dir. Environ. Protection Office USN, 1989-94, dir. environ. tech., 1994—2001. Adj. prof. George Washington U., 1995, Johns Hopkins U., 2001—; vis. prof. Washington & Lee U., 1993; cons. Aerospace Corp., El Segundo, Calif., 1967-70, Rand Corp., Santa Monica, Calif., 1973-74; vis. fellow U. Leiden, Netherlands, 1972-73; mem. Casualty Council Underwriters Labs., Nat. Radio Astron. Observatory Users Com., 1968-74; chair gov.'s environ. edn. adv. com. Colls. & Univs., Va., 2000-01. Contbr. articles to profl. jours. Mem. AAAS, Am. Phys. Soc., Sierra Club, Audubon Soc., Internat. Radio Sci. Union, Am. Astron. Soc., Internat. Astron. Union, Assn. of Scientists and Engrs. Home: 171 Gulchleigh Ln Glasgow VA 24555-2266 E-mail: riegel.kurt@apl.jhu.edu.

RIEGER, DONNA MARIE, critical care nurse, educator, consultant; b. St. Louis, May 5, 1957; d. Elvern E. and Eleanore E. (Zimmerer) R. BSN, St. Louis U., 1979. Cert. BLS affiliate faculty, Mo., ACLS affiliate/regional faculty, Mo., BLS, ACLS Am. Heart Assn. Critical care nurse St. Anthony's Med. Ctr., St. Louis, 1979-86, Barnes Hosp., St. Louis, 1986-88; nursing edn. specialist, profl. devel. cons. BJC Health Care, 1988—. Mem. ACLS regional com., BLS/ACLS regional faculty Am. Heart Assn., St. Louis, 1988—, chair ACLS regional com., 1991-95, mem. ACLS state com., 1993-98, del. to bd., 1991-93; adj. faculty Barnes Coll.; chair critical care curriculum devel., orgn. and profl. devel. cons. BJC Health Care merger, 1994—. Mem. AACN (edn. com. St. Louis chpt. 1991-93), Barnes Coll. Nursing Honor Soc., Sigma Theta Tau. Roman Catholic. Avocations: music, nature hikes, bicycling, reading, roller skating. Home: 418 Autumn Peak Dr Fenton MO 63026-3962 Office: Profl Devel Svc Excellence BJC Health System 4353 Clayton Ave Saint Louis MO 63110-1621 E-mail: DMR8750@bjcmail.carenet.org.

RIEGER, ELAINE JUNE, retired nursing administrator; b. Lebanon, Pa., June 7, 1937; d. Frank and Florence (Hitz) Plasterer; m. Jere LeFever Longenecker, Sept. 13, 1958 (div. 1968); children: Julie Lyn Porto, Jere Lee Longenecker; m. Bernhard Rieger, Oct. 12, 1971. Nursing diploma, Coatesville (Pa.) Hosp. Sch. of Nursing, 1958; BA, U. Redlands, 1976; MS in Healthcare Mgmt., Calif. State U., L.A., 1984. Cert. nursing adminstr., gerontol. nurse. From staff nurse to clin. supr. to dir. of nurses St. Johns Regional Med. Ctr., Oxnard, Calif., 1966-86; dir. of nurses Motion Picture and TV Hosp., Woodland Hills, 1987-89; with Care West, Nothridge-Reseda, 1989-90; dist. nurse mgr. Hillhaven Corp., Newbury Park, 1990-91; quality mgmt. nursing cons. Beverly Enterprises, Memphis, 1991-95; DON Beverly Manor Rehab. and Nursing Ctr., Van Nuys, Calif., 1996-98; Utilization rev. specialist Blue Cross of Calif., Camarillo, 1998-2000. Home: 1817 Shady Brook Dr Thousand Oaks CA 91362-1335 Office: Blue Cross Calif 5151 Camino Ruiz Ste A Camarillo CA 93012-8648

RIEGER, JOERG, theology studies educator; M.Div., Theologisches Seminar der Evangelisch-methodistischen Kirche, Reutlingen, Germany, 1989; Th.M., Duke U., 1990, PhD, 1994. Ordained min. United Meth. Ch., 1997. Assoc. prof. systematic theology Perkins Sch. Theology So. Meth. U., Dallas, 1994—. Author: (books) God and the Excluded: Visions and Blindspots in Contemporary Theology, 2001, Remember the Poor: The Challenge to Theology in the Twenty-First Century, 1998; editor: Liberating the Future: God, Mammon, and Theology, 1998, Theology from the Belly of the Whale: A Frederick Herzog Reader, 1999. Named H.O.P.E. Prof. (Honored on Prof. Excellence), So. Meth. U., 1999. Mem.: Am. Acad. Religion (Jr. Scholar of Yr. award S.W. Commn. on Religious Studies 1997). Office: Perkins Sch. Theology So Meth Univ Dallas TX 75275-0133 Office Fax: 214-768-1042. Business E-Mail: jrieger@mail.smu.edu.

RIEGER, MITCHELL SHERIDAN, lawyer; b. Chgo., Sept. 5, 1922; s. Louis and Evelyn (Sampson) R.; m. Rena White Abelmann, May 17, 1949 (div. 1957); 1 child, Karen Gross Cooper; m. Nancy Horner, May 30, 1961 (div. 1972); stepchildren: Jill Levi, Linda Hanan, Susan Perlstein, James Geoffrey Felsenthal; m. Pearl Handelsman, June 10, 1973; stepchildren: Steven Newman, Mary Ann Malarkey, Nancy Halbeck. *Wife, Pearl H. Rieger, born in Chicago (1928), received a B.A. degree in Speech and Language Pathology from the University of Michigan (1948) and an M.A. degree in Educational Psychology from the University of Chicago (1974). Since then she has been in private practice as a psychoeducational diagnostician. In January, 1997 she became a consultant at the Rush Neurobehavioral Center, Skokie, Illinois. In 1997, the Center established the Pearl H. Rieger award to honor a pioneer in the field of neurobehavioral disorders in children. On November 13, 1997 Pearl Rieger became the first recipient of the award named after her.* AB, Northwestern U., 1944; JD, Harvard U., 1949. Bar: Ill. 1950, U.S. Dist. Ct. (no. dist.) Ill. 1950, U.S. Supreme Ct. 1953, U.S. Ct. Mil. Appeals 1953, U.S. Ct. Appeals (7th cir.) 1954. Legal asst. Rieger & Rieger, Chgo., 1949-50, assoc., 1950-54; asst. U.S. atty. No. Dist Ill., 1954-60, 1st asst., 1958-60; assoc. gen. counsel SEC, Washington, 1960-61; ptnr. Schiff Hardin & Waite, Chgo., 1961—, sr. counsel, 1998—. Instr. John Marshall Law Sch. Chgo., 1952-54. *Notable cases: before federal court juries (Chicago) for U.S. convictions in 1st vote fraud trial (U.S. v Louis Nathan, 1955), and last income tax evasion trial involving post WWII sale of new automobiles for unreported amounts exceeding price control (U.S. v. Leonard Bernard, 1959); for SEC first judicial opinion interpreting SEC's then Statement of Policy about literature used in mutual fund shares sales (Boruski v. SEC, U.S. Court Appeals, 2nd Circuit, 1961); successfully represented 35 investment banking firms in one of 1st class action jury trials involving legality of initial public offering (Bisgeier v. Fotomat Corp., (federal court, San Diego, 1976).* Contbr. articles to profl. jours. Active Chgo. Crime Commn., bd. dirs., 1998—; pres. Park View Home for Aged, 1969-71; Rep. precinct committeeman, Highland Park, Ill., 1964-68; bd. dirs. Spertus Mus. Judaica, 1987-91, vis. com., 1991—. Served to lt. (j.g.) USNR, 1943-46, PTO. Fellow Am. Coll. Trial Lawyers; mem. ABA, FBA (pres. Chgo. chpt. 1959-60, nat. v.p. 1960-61), Chgo. Bar Assn., Ill. Bar Assn., Am. Judicature Soc., 7th Circuit Bar Assn., Standard Club, Lawyers Club Chgo., Vail Racquet Club, Phi Beta Kappa. Jewish. Avocations: photography, skiing, sailing. Home: 4950 S Chicago Beach Dr Chicago IL 60615-3207 Office: Schiff Hardin & Waite 6600 Sears Tower Chicago IL 60606 E-mail: mrieger@schiffhardin.com, msheridanr@aol.com.

RIEGER, PEARL BEVERLY, psychoeducational diagnostician, consultant; b. Chgo., Feb. 8, 1928; d. Meyer and Anne (Goldkin) Handelsman; m. Edward Arthur Newman, Oct. 30, 1949 Idiv. Dec. 1971); children: Steven B., Mary Ann Malarkey, Nancy L. Halbeck; m. Mitchell Sheridan Rieger, June 10, 1973. BA in Speech and Lang. Pathology, U. Mich., 1948; MA in Ednl. Psychology, U. Chgo., 1974. Speech therapist Michael Reese Hosp. and Med. Ctr., Chgo., 1948-51; cons. psychoednl. diagnostician Ancona Montessori Sch., U. Chgo. Lab. Schs., 1974-77, Near North Montessori Sch., Harris Sch., 1974-77; cons. to Office of Provost U. Chgo., 1994—; rsch. assoc., cons. Rush Neurobehavioral Ctr., Skokie, Ill., 1997—; psychoednl. diagnostician in pvt. practice, Chgo., 1974—. Mem. women's bd. dirs. Jewish Fedn. Met. Chgo., 1952-60, Jewish Cmty. Ctrs., Chgo., 1955-61, Michael Reese Hosp., Chgo., 1955-69; v.p. bd. govs. U. Chgo. Lab. schs., 1966-69, 74-75; trustee, 1966-95, life trustee Inst. for Psychoanalysis, Chgo., 1995—; mem. women's bd. U. Chgo., 1984—. Mem. APA (assoc.), Am. Speech-Lang.-Hearing Assn., Profls. in Learning Disabilities, Internat. Orton Dyslexia Soc., Coun. for Exceptional Children, Internat. Reading Assn., Assn. for Children with Learning Disabilities, Quadrangle Club, Standard Club, Pi Lambda Theta, Zeta Phi Eta.. Jewish. Avocations: skiing, classical music, reading. Home: 1440 N Lake Shore Dr Chicago IL 60610 Office: 567 W Hawthorne Pl Chicago IL 60657 E-mail: prlrieger@aol.com.

RIEGERT, ROBERT ADOLF, law educator, consultant; b. Cin., Apr. 21, 1923; s. Adolf and Hulda (Basler) R.; m. Roswitha Victoria Bigalke, Oct. 28, 1966; children: Christine Rose, Douglas Louis. BS, U. Cin., 1948; LLB cum laude, Harvard U., 1953; Doctoris Juris Utriusque magna cum laude, U. Heidelberg, Germany, 1966; postgrad., U. Mich., Harvard U., Yale U., MIT. Bar: D.C. 1953, Cts. Allied High Commn. Germany 1954. Mem. Harvard Legal Aid Bur., 1952-53; sole practice Heidelberg, 1954-63; vis. assoc. prof. So. Meth. U. Law Sch., Dallas, 1967-71; prof. law Cumberland Law Sch., Samford U., Birmingham, Ala., 1971-97, prof. emeritus, 1997—; dir. Cumberland Summer Law Program, Heidelberg, 1981-94. Disting. vis. prof. Salmon P. Chase Coll. Law, 1983-84. Author: (With Robert Braucher) Introduction to Commercial Transactions, 1977, Documents of Title, 1978; contbr. articles to profl. jours. Served to 1st lt. USAAF, 1943-46 Grantee Dana Fund for Internat. and Comparative Law, 1979; grantee Am. Bar Found., 1966-67; German Acad. Exchange, 1953-55, mem. Harvard Legal Aid Bur., Salmon P. Chase Coll. law scholar, 1950; Pres.'s scholar U. Cin., 1941 Mem. ABA (com. on new payment systems), Internat. Acad. Comml. and Consumer Law, Am. Law Inst., Ala. Law Inst. (coun.), Assn. Am. Law Schs. (sect. internat. legal exchs., subcom. on com. laws), German Comparative Law Assn., Acad. Soc. German Supreme Cts., Army-Navy Club (Washington). Office: Samford U Cumberland Law Sch Birmingham AL 35229-0001

RIEGLE, ROBERT M. art dealer, retired architect; b. Sedan, Kans., Nov. 11, 1924; s. Ellis Warren and Marian Edith Riegle; m. Lucille Elaine Kuykendall, Aug. 16, 1947. Student, El Dorado (Kans.) Jr. Coll., 1942, Tex. A&M U., 1943; BSArch, U. Kans., 1950. Registered arch. Kans. Arch. Glenn E. Benedick, Arch., Wichita, Kans., 1950—75, Planning Devel. Svc., Wichita, 1975—77; art dealer Wichita Gallery Fine Art, 1977—2001. Treas. Civic Enterprises Found., Wichita, 1985—2001; bd. dirs. Downtown Wichita Assn., 1990—99, Orpheum Theatre, Wichita, 1995—2001, Am. Heart Assn., Wichita, 1984—90, Wichita Transit Authority, 1990—96, Wichita Hist. Mus., 1998—2001. 2d lt. USAF, 1950—53. Republican. Avocations: travel, photography, gardening, museums, military history. Office: Wichita Gallery Fine Art 100 N Broadway Wichita KS 67202

RIEGLER, GUENTER, federal agency administrator; m. Sandra Riegler; 2 children. Degree, Vienna Inst. Tech., 1964; PhD, U. Md., 1969. Postdoctoral fellow Calif. Inst. Tech., 1969—71; group supr. space sci. group Bendix Aerospace, 1971—75; mem. tech. staff Jet Propulsion Lab., 1975—87; detailee from Jet Propulsion Lab. NASA, Washington, 1987—95, chief scientist rsch. divsn. Office Space Sci., 1995—99, exec. dir. sci. Office Space Sci., 1999—. Office: NASA Hdqrs Mail Code S 300 E St SW Washington DC 20546

RIEGSECKER, MARVIN DEAN, pharmacist, state senator; b. Goshen, Ind., July 5, 1937; s. Levi and Mayme (Kauffman) R.; m. Norma Jane Shrock, Aug. 3, 1958; children: Steven Scott, Michael Dean. BA in Pharmacy, U. Colo., 1967. Pharmacist Parkside Pharmacy, Goshen, Ind., 1967-73; pharmacist, mgr. Hooks Drugs, Inc., 1973-94; coroner Elkhart County, 1977-84; mem. Ind. Senate from 12th dist., Indpls., 1988—; pharmacist Walgreens, Goshen, 1994-96, Meijer, Goshen, 1998—. Bus. affairs cons. Goshen Health Sys., 1997-98. Rep. commr. Elkhart County, 1985-88; bd. commrs. pres., 1987-88; past adv. bd. dirs. Oaklawn Hosp.; past chmn. Michiana Area Coun. of Govts. Mem. Ind. Pharm. Assn. Republican. Mennonite. Avocation: jogging. Home: 1814 Kentfield Way Goshen IN 46526-5610 Office: Ind Senate Statehouse 200 W Washington St Indianapolis IN 46204-2728

RIEHECKY, JANET ELLEN, writer; b. Waukegan, Ill., Mar. 5, 1953; d. Roland Wayne and Patricia Helen (Anderson) Polsgrove; m. John Jay Riehecky, Aug. 2, 1975; 1 child, Patrick William. BA summa cum laude, Ill. Wesleyan U., 1975; MA in Comm., Ill. State U., 1978; MA in English, Northwestern U., 1983. Tchr. English Blue Mound (Ill.) H.S., 1977-80, West Chicago (Ill.) H.S., 1984-86; editor Child's World Pub. Co., Elgin, Ill., 1987-90; freelance writer, 1990—. Author: Dinosaur series, 24 vols., 1988, UFOs, 1989, Saving the Forests, 1990, Irish Americans, 1995, The Mystery of the Missing Money, 1996, The Mystery of the UFO, 1996, Stegosaurus, 1998, Triceratops, 1998, Tyrannosaurus, 1998, Velociroptor, 1998, A Ticket to China, 1999, Greece, Sweden, 2000, George Lucas, 2001, The Emancipation Proclamation, 2002, The Osage Nation, 2002, The Cree Nation, 2002, Indonesia, 2002. Nat. dir. Kids Love a Mystery, 1999—. Recipient Summit award for best children's nonfiction Soc. Midland Authors, 1988. Mem. Soc. Am. Magicians, Soc. Children's Book Writers and Illustrators, Mystery Writers of Am. (midwest bd. dirs. 2000—), Sisters in Crime, Phi Kappa Phi. Democrat. Baptist. Avocations: reading, hiking, dinosaur hunting.

RIEHL, JANE ELLEN, education educator; b. New Albany, Ind., Oct. 17, 1942; d. Henry Gabbart Jr. and Mary Elizabeth (McGraw) Willham; m. Richard Emil Riehl, June 15, 1968; 1 child, Mary Ellen. BA in Elem. Edn., U. Evansville, 1964; MS, Ind. U., Bloomington, 1966; postgrad., Spalding U., 1979, Ind. U. S.E., New Albany, 1991-93. Cert. 1-8 and kindergarten tchr., Ind.; lic. profl. kindergarten tchr., Ind. Elem. tchr. Clarksville (Ind.) Cmty. Sch., 1964-68, 70-75, 81-82, tchr. kindergarten, 1975-81; elem. tchr. Chapelwood Sch. Wayne Twp., Indpls., 1968-70; lectr. edn. Ind. U. S.E., 1988-97, dir. tchg. and rsch. project, 1990-91, 92-93, dir. field and career placement, cert./lic. advisor, 1998, coord. elem./spl. edn. field & career placement & license advisor, 1998—. Cons. Riehl Assocs., Jeffersonville, Ind., 1995—. Co-author: An Integrated Language Arts Teacher Education Program, 1990, The Reading Professor, 1992, Multimedia: HyperStudio and Language Education, 1996, Technology: Hypermedia and Communications, 1997, others; author procs. Parent vol. Girl Scouts U.S.A., Jeffersonville, 1988-95; mem. adminstrv. bd. Wall Street United Meth. Ch., Jeffersonville, 1993-95; mem. women's health adv. coun. Clark Meml. Hosp., Jeffersonville, 1995—; bd. dirs. Clark Meml. Hosp. Found., vice chair, 1999, chair 2000; team mem. People to People Citizen Amb. Program, 1993, 95, 96; chair internat. bylaws Altrusa Internat., Inc., 2001—. Named Young Career Woman of Yr. Bus. and Profl. Women New Albany and Dist. 13 Ind., 1966; tchg. and rsch. grantee Ind. U. S.E., 1990, 94, 95, 96, 97, 2000; recipient Disting. Tchg. award Ind. U. S.E., 1997, Tchg. Excellence Recognition award, 1997. Mem. Nat. Coun. Tchrs. English, Profs. Reading Tchr. Edn., Ind. State Med. Assn. Alliance (v.p. so. area 1999-2000), Clark County Med. Soc. Alliance (pres.-elect 1997-98, pres. 1998-99), Altrusa Internat. Inc. (internat. bd. 1993-95, dist. gov. 1993-95, svc. award 1995), Phi Delta Kappa (v.p. 1991-92, pres. 1997—, svc. award 1991), Kappa Kappa Kappa (pres. Jeffersonville 1975-76, 90-91, Outstanding Mem. award 1987). Avocations: travel, reading, crafts, decorating. Home: 1610 Fox Run Trl Jeffersonville IN 47130-8204 Office: Ind U SE 4201 Grant Line Rd New Albany IN 47150-2158

RIEHLE, B. HUDSON, trade association executive; b. Cin., Sept. 10, 1953; s. Robert Arthur Riehle and Lois W. Hudson; m. Eileen Patricia Betit, Aug. 2, 1986; children: B. Hudson, Jr., Bradley Patrick. BA, Skidmore Coll., 1975; MBA, U. Pa., 1986. Rsch. cons. Avmark, Inc., Washington, 1976-78; rsch. analyst Airline Pilots Assn., 1978-81, supr. econ. analysis, 1981-84; rsch. mgr. Nat. Restaurant Assn., 1986-91, sr. rsch. mgr., 1991-95, dir. rsch., 1995-97, sr. dir. rsch., 1997-99, v.p. rsch. & info. svcs., 1999-2000, sr. v.p. rsch. and info. svcs., 2000—. Editor: Comml. Airline Fleets, 1976-78, Restaurant Industry Ops. Report, 1986—; contbr. to Airline Pilot, 1978-84, Restaurants USA, 1986—. Mem., bd. dirs., 1st v.p. Fairlington Meadows, Arlington, 1990-92. Mem. Alexandria Convention and Visitors Assn. (vice chmn. bd. govs. 2001—). Avocations: geology, cross country skiing, photography. Home: 2431 Davis Ave Alexandria VA 22302-3209 Office: Nat Restaurant Assn 1200 17th St NW Ste 700 Washington DC 20036-3006

RIEHLE, ROBERT ARTHUR, JR. medical director, surgeon; b. San Diego, Oct. 24, 1947; s. Robert Arthur and Lois (Wulfkoetter) R.; children: Christopher, Kyra. BA, Yale U., 1969; MD, Columbia U., 1973. Intern Columbia Presbyn. Hosp., 1973-74, resident, 1974-77, N.Y. Hosp., Cornell, N.Y.C., 1977-80, assoc. prof. surgery, 1980-90; med. dir. Albany (N.Y.) Meml. Hosp., 1990-94, Blue Shield Northeastern N.Y., Albany, 1994-97, Prudential Healthcare, Charlotte, N.C., 1997-98, Cigna Healthcare, Charlotte, NC, 1998-2000; chief med. officer Spartanburg Regional Healthcare Sys., 2000—. E-mail: rriehle@srhs.com.

RIEHM, SARAH LAWRENCE, writer, arts administrator; b. Iowa City, Sept. 8, 1952; d. Stuart Parker and Elizabeth Jane (Munson) Lawrence; m. Charles Curtis Riehm, May 18, 1974; children: Andrew, Amanda, Jennie Frances. BGS, U. Iowa, 1974; MA in Internat. Fin., U. Tex., 1981. Mgr., adminstr. IBM, Cedar Rapids, Iowa, 1974-75; program mgr. Rockwell Internat., Dallas, 1975-80; mgr. internat. tax Peat, Marwick, Mitchell, Hong Kong, 1981-82; writer, playwright, 1981—; exec. dir. Playwright's Project, Dallas, 1992-94, Tex. Composers Forum, Dallas, 1995-96; faculty mem. U. Tex., 1996-97; dir. ops. Chestnut Petroleum, 2002—. Bd. dirs. Radio for Peace Internat.; lectr. So. Meth. U., 1999—; prin., owner peacebeginswithme.com, 2001—. Playwright: Liberty-A Drama in Two Acts, 1994 (So. Playwrights award 1994), The King & Me, 1994, The Chute, 2000; author: Entrepreneurship: Building the American Dream, 1993, 50 Great Businesses for Teens, 1997. Founder Playwrights Project; chair Dallas 10,000, 1995; commr. Richardson Arts Commn., 1998—. Mem. NOW, Handgun Control, Amnesty Internat. Democrat. Presbyterian. Avocations: pipe organ, composer, racquetball, skiing, travel. E-mail: slriehm@buz.net.

RIEKE, RONALD ALFRED, computer company executive; b. Rugby, N.D., Aug. 16, 1951; s. Lawrence Allen Rieke and Emma Marie (Lord) Cooper; m. Madelyn E. Owens, May 2, 1987; children: Ronald Alexander, Sara Emma, Ren William. AS, N.D. State U., 1971; BS, U. N.D., 1973; MA, Webster U., St. Louis, 1976. Operator Lystads, Inc., Kansas City, Kans., 1972-74; sales rep. Parke-Davis Co., St. Louis, 1974-76; with bio-med. engring. and sales Gen. Electric Corp., Tulsa, 1976-78; mgr., sales engr. Digital Equipment Corp., Houston, 1978-85; pres. R.A.R.E. Systems, Inc., 1985—. Bd. dirs. TechSmith Corp., Dallas, Cam-Eng, Inc., Houston, Title Techs., Houston. Mem. Houston Fine Arts Council, 1988. Mem. Am. Mgmt. Assn., Digital Dealer Assn., Digital Equipment Soc. Republican. Mem. Christian Ch. (Ch. of Christ). Avocation: karate, computer technology. Office: RARE Systems Inc 1500 W Sam Houston Pkwy N Houston TX 77043-3113

RIEKE, WILLIAM OLIVER, foundation director, medical educator, former university president; b. Odessa, Wash., Apr. 26, 1931; s. Henry William and Hutoka S. (Smith) R.; m. Joanne Elynor Schief, Aug. 22, 1954; children: Susan Ruth, Stephen Harold, Marcus Henry. BA summa cum laude, Pacific Luth. U., 1953; MD with honors, U. Wash., 1958. Instr. anatomy U. Wash. Sch. Medicine, Seattle, 1958, asst. prof., 1961-64, adminstrv. officer, 1963-66, assoc. prof., 1964-66; prof., head dept. anatomy Coll. Medicine U. Iowa, Iowa City, 1966-71; dean protem Coll. Medicine U. Iowa (Coll. Medicine), 1969-70, chmn. exec. com., 1969-70; vice chancellor for health affairs, prof. anatomy U. Kans. Med. Center, Kansas City, 1971-73, exec. vice chancellor, prof. anatomy, 1973-75; affiliate prof. biol. structure U. Wash. Sch. Medicine, Seattle, 1975-96; pres. Pacific Lutheran U., Parkland, Wash., 1975-92; pres. emeritus, 1992—; exec. dir. Ben B. Cheney Found., 1992—. Mem. interdisciplinary gen. basic sci. test com. Nat. Bd. Med. Examiners, 1968-72, chmn. anatomy test com., 1972-75, mem. at large, 1975-79; spl. cons. NIH, 1970-72; mem. adv. com. Inst. Medicine, Nat. Acad. Scis., 1974-76; mem. Commn. on Colls., NW Assn. Schs. and Colls., 1979-84 Editor: Procs. 3d Am. Assn. Leucocyte Culture Conf, 1969; editorial bd.: Am. Jour. Anatomy, 1968-71. Bd. dirs. Luth. Ednl. Council N. Am., 1980-83, pres., 1982-83; chmn. Wash. Friends Higher Edn., 1983-91. Named one of Most Effective Coll. or Univ. Pres., Bowling Green State U. Rsch. Study, 1986, Disting. Alumnus Pacific Luth. U., 1970,

Disting. Alumnus Pi Kappa Delta, 1977, Disting. Alumnus U. of Washington Med. Alumni, 1989; decorated Knight First Class Royal Norwegian Order of Merit, 1989; named to Cashmere H.S. Wall of Fame, 1995. Lutheran (mem. ch. council 1967-70). Home: 13905 18th Ave S Tacoma WA 98444-1006 Office: Ben B Cheney Found 1201 Pacific Ave Ste 1600 Tacoma WA 98402-4379 E-mail: cheneyfndn@aol.com.

RIEKELS, LYNDA MARIE, materials engineer; b. Detroit, Oct. 4, 1949; d. Carl Herman and Shirley Jean (Page) Piethe; m. Bruce Warren Riekels, Mar. 27, 1971; children: Ryan, Robyn. BS in Geology cum laude, Mich. Tech. U., 1971; MS in Geology, U. Ill. Chgo., 1973; PhD of Materials and Sci. Engring., Northwestern U., 1979. Engr., rsch. engr.,sr. rsch. engr. Inland Steel Co., East Chicago, Ind., 1973-82; pres. Geomet Tech., Longview, Tex., 1982-84; dir. R&D, v.p. tech. ops., v.p. quality and tech. Lone Star (Tex.) Steel, 1984-89; from sr. rsch. engr. to engring. cons. Mobil R&D Co., Dallas, 1989-95; group mgr. materials and corrosion Mobil Tech. Co., 1995-98; tech. mgr. Mobil de Venezuela, Caracas, 1998-99; sr. engr. cons. Mobil Tech. Co., 2000-01; sr. bus. cons. IPA, Chgo., 2001—02; v.p. bus. devel. Delfasco, Inc., 2002—. Mem. adv. bd. North Tex. Rsch. Inst., Dallas, 1993-96. Patentee in field; contbr. articles to profl. jours. Mem. Am. Soc. Metals, Nat. Assn. Corrosion Engrs., Am. Soc. Quality Control, Soc. Petroleum Engrs., The Metals Soc., Am. Assn. Iron and Steel Engrs., Phi Kappa Phi, Tau Beta Pi (hon.), Alpha Sigma Mu (hon.). Avocations: painting, drawing, rock collecting, sailing, gardening. Home: 3403 Raintree Dr Flower Mound TX 75022-6314 E-mail: lriekels@mindspring.com.

RIEKENBERG, WARREN GLENN, civil engineer; b. Topeka, Aug. 3, 1936; s. Lorenz J. and Vergie Weese (Ingraham) R.; m. Carol Lee Alberts, May 15, 1971; children: Eric Karl, Lee Ann Marie. BSCE, U. Kans., Lawrence, 1959. Registered profl. engr., Ill., Kans., Iowa. Civil engr. State Hwy. Commn. Kans., Topeka, 1959, 61-63, Consoer, Townsend and Assocs., Chgo., 1970-78, Clark, Dietz and Assocs., Chgo., 1978-82, Metcalf and Eddy, Inc., Arlington Heights, Ill. and Des Moines, 1982-92, Iowa Dept. Natural Resources, Des Moines, 1992-95, City of Des Moines, 1995—. Maj. U.S. Army, 1959-61, 63-70, Vietnam. Decorated Bronze Star. Mem. ASCE, NRA. Home: 3209 Melanie Dr Des Moines IA 50322-6851 Office: City Des Moines Wastewater Reclamation Fac 3000 Vandalia Rd Des Moines IA 50317-1346

RIEL, MARK M, music educator; b. Erie, Pa., Nov. 5, 1973; s. Katherine A and Ronald R Riel; m. Meagan L Beichner, July 14, 2001. BS in Music Edn., Slippery Rock U., Slippery Rock, PA, 1993—98. Dir. of bands Pender H.S., Burgaw, NC, 2000—02; music/choral tchr. Littlefield Mid. Sch., Lumberton, 1998—2000. Recipient Tchr. of the Week - WGNI Radio - 11/2000. Mem.: NC Music Educators Assn., NC Band Masters Assn., Phi Mu Alpha Sinfonia of Am. (life). Home: 1512 Setter Lane Wilmington NC 28411

RIEL, STEVEN JOSEPH, librarian; b. Palmer, Mass., Dec. 31, 1959; s. Alfred Joseph Riel and Joan Constance Jolly. AB, Georgetown U., 1981; MLS, Simmons Coll., 1987. Head copy cataloging Harvard Univ. Libr., Cambridge, Mass., 1987-89, serials cataloger, 1993-96, sr. serials cataloger, 1996-99, tech. svcs. libr., 1999—2001, preservation cataloger, projects mgr., 2001—; cataloger Amherst (Mass.) Coll. Libr., 1990-93. Author: How to Dream, 1992; contbg. author: Lives in Translation, 1990, Boyhood, Growing Up Male, 1993, Liberating Minds, 1997; poetry editor RFD, 1987-95. Mem. organizing com. Mass. Men's Gathering, Cambridge, 1989. Mass. Cultural Coun. grantee, 1992. Mem. ALA, Assn. Coll. Rsch. Librs. (co-chair 2000-2002, subject bibliographic access com., sci. tech. sect.), Assn. New England Poetry Club, Phi Beta Kappa, Phi Beta Mu. Avocation: tennis. Office: Weissman Preservation Ctr Holyoke Ctr 821 Cambridge MA 02138

RIELLY, JOHN EDWARD, educational association administrator; b. Rapid City, S.D., Dec. 28, 1932; s. Thomas J. and Mary A. (Dowd) R.; m. Elizabeth Downs, Dec. 28, 1957 (marriage annulled 1976); children: Mary Ellen, Catherine Ann, Thomas Patrick, John Downs; m. Irene Diedrich, Aug. 1, 1987. BA, St. John's U., Collegeville, Minn., 1954; postgrad. (Fulbright scholar), London Sch. Econs. and Polit. Sci., 1955-56; PhD, Harvard U., 1961. Faculty dept. govt. Harvard U., 1958-61; with Alliance for Progress programs Dept. State, Washington, 1961-62; fgn. policy asst. to Sen. then Vice Pres. Hubert Humphrey, 1963-69; cons. office European and internat. affairs Ford Found., N.Y.C., 1969-70; sr. fellow Overseas Devel. Council, Washington, 1970-71; exec. dir. Chgo. Council on Fgn. Relations, 1971-74, pres., 1974—2001; vis. fellow Sidley & Austin, Chgo., 2001—. Adj. prof., Northwestern U., 2001—; cons. NSC; mem. adv. bd. Grad. Sch. Arts and Scis., Harvard U.; bd. dirs. Am. Coun. on Germany, Nat. Com. on U.S.-China Rels., China Coun. of Asia Soc., Am. Ditchley Found., Trilateral Commn., commn. on U.S.-Brazilian Rels.; past pres. Nat. Coun. Comty. World Affairs Orgns. Contbr. articles to profl. jours.; editor: American Public Opinion and U.S. Foreign Policy, 1975, 2d edit., 1979, 83, 87, 91, 95, 99; editl. bd. Fgn. Policy Quar., 1974—. Former trustee St. John's U. Recipient Legion d'Honneur, France, Distinguished Service Cross, Germany, Commendatore of the Italian Republic, Bernardo O'Higgins Award, Chile, The Golden Decoration, Austria, European Friendship Award, European Union, Order of Leopold (Belgium). Mem. Am. Polit. Sci. Assn., Council on Fgn. Relations, N.Y.C. Home: 2021 Kenilworth Ave Wilmette IL 60091-1519 Office: Sidley & Austin One First National Plz Chicago IL 60603

RIELY, JOHN CABELL, English educator, art historian, consultant; b. Phila., Aug. 27, 1945; s. James Evans and Marianne Augusta (Gateson) R.; m. Elizabeth Dumesnil Gawthrop, Aug. 23, 1969 (separated 2001); children: Christopher Cabell, Andrew Carrington. AB, Harvard Coll., 1967; MA, U. Pa., 1968, PhD, 1971. Assoc. rsch. editor Yale Edn. of Horace Walpole's Correspondence, New Haven, 1971-79; lectr. English Yale U., 1973-77; asst. prof. English Columbia U., N.Y.C., 1979-80; vis. prof. English U. Minn., Mpls., 1980-81; from asst. to assoc. prof. English Boston U., 1981—. Author: The Age of Horace Walpole in Caricature, 1973, Rowlandson Drawings from the Paul Mellon Collection, 1977, Henry William Bunbury (1750-1811), 1983; co-author: Gainsborough and Rowlandson, 1990; editor: Horace Walpole's Misc Corresp, 3 vols., 1980; cons.-reviewer Choice, 1983-92; mem. adv. bd. The Age of Johnson AMS Press, 1987-90, Studies in 18th-Century Culture Johns Hopkins Univ. Press, 1986—; contbr. articles to profl. jours; curator several internat. exhbns. Fellow Am. Coun. Learned Socs., 1972, Huntington Libr., 1973, Yale Ctr. for Brit. Art, 1982-83, Swann Found. for Caricature and Cartoon, 1984, NEH, 1988-89, Boston Pub. Libr., 1995-96. Fellow Soc. Antiquaries London, Royal Soc. Arts; mem. Commanderie de Bordeaux Boston (prévot), Boston Athenaeum, The Johnsonians (U.S.), The Johnson Club (U.K.), Walpole Soc. (U.K.), St. Botolph Club, Club of Odd Vols. (v.p. 1995-96), Signet Soc. Harvard U., Elizabethan Club Yale U. Democrat. Episcopalian. Avocations: reading, book and art collecting, wine and food, mountain climbing, racquet sports. Home: Hammond Gardens 33 Hammond Pond Pkwy Chestnut Hill MA 02467 Office: Boston Univ Dept English 236 Bay State Rd Boston MA 02215-1403 E-mail: jriely@attbi.com.

RIEMENSCHNEIDER, ALBERT LOUIS, retired engineering educator; b. Cody, Nebr., May 18, 1936; s. Albert L. and Agnes E. (Schilling) R.; m. Norma Mae Geisler, June 24, 1962 (dec.); children: Richard L., David F., Barbara J.; m. Sandra Ann Pryor, Feb. 14, 1998. BSEE, S.D. Sch. Mines and Tech., 1959, MSEE, 1962; PhD, U. Wyo., 1969. Registered profl. engr., S.D. Engr. Sperry Utah Corp., Salt Lake City, 1959-60; design engr. Dakota Steel & Supply Co., Rapid City, S.D., 1960-61; instr. U. Wyo., Laramie, 1961-67; chief engr. Dunham Assocs., Rapid City, 1974-80; grad. tchg. asst. S.D. Sch. Mines and Tech., 1961-62, asst. prof., 1967-73, assoc. prof., 1973-74, 80-84, prof., dept. head, 1983-95, prof., 1995-98, prof. emeritus, 1998—. Cons. ALR Engring., RE/SPEC, Inc., Rapid City, 1987—, HC Galloways, Black Hawk, S.D., 1999—. Mem. IEEE, NSPE, Am. Soc. Engring. Edn., Elks. Democrat. Episcopalian. Avocations: electronics, computers, hunting, fishing. Home and Office: ALR Engring 1204 Cheyenne Ave Alliance NE 69301-2529

RIEMER, NEAL, political scientist; b. Freehold, N.J., Aug. 25, 1922; s. Elick Jacob and Elizabeth (Krupnick) R.; m. Ruby Riemer, Sept. 15, 1946; children: David Raphael, Jeremiah Michael, Seth Daniel. BA, Clark U., Worcester, Mass., 1943; MA, Harvard U., 1947, PhD, 1949. Instr. to prof. Pa. State U., State College, 1948—64; prof. U. Wis., Milw., 1964—72; Andrew V. Stout prof. polit. philosophy Drew U., Madison, NJ, 1976—92, prof. emeritus, 1992—2002. Author: The Revival of Democratic Theory, 1962, The Democratic Experiment, 1967, The Future of the Democratic Revolution: Toward a More Prophetic Politics, 1984, James Madison: Creating the American Constitution, 1986, Karl Marx and Prophetic Politics, 1987, Creative Breakthroughs in Politics, 1996; co-author: World Affairs: Problems and Prospects, 1958, The New World of Politics, 1983, 4th edit., 1997; editor, co-author: New Thinking and Developments in International Politics: Opportunities and Dangers, 1991, Let Justice Roll: The Prophetic Challenge in Religion, Politics and Society, 1996, Protection Against Genocide: Mission Impossible?, 2000. Del. Dem. Nat. Conv., Chgo., 1968; bd. dirs. ACLU, Madison, Wis., 1964-69. With USAAF, 1943-45; ETO. Recipient Disting. Vis. Honors Profl., U. Ctrl. Fla., 1996; Rockefeller fellow in polit. philosophy, 1958-59, Fulbright fellow, U. Innsbruck, Austria, 1961-62, NEH fellow, summer 1977, Wallach fellow Inst. for World Order, 1980. Mem. Am. Polit. Sci. Assn. Jewish. Avocation: swimming. Home: Green Village, NJ. Died Oct. 13, 2001.

RIEMKE, RICHARD ALLAN, mechanical engineer; b. Vallejo, Calif., Oct. 11, 1944; s. Allan Frederick and Frances Jewell (O'Brien) R. BA in Physiology, U. Calif., Berkeley, 1967, MA in Physiology, 1971, PhD in Engring. Sci., 1977. Postdoctoral fellow U. So. Calif., Los Angeles, 1977-78; rsch. engr. Del Mar Avionics, Irvine, Calif., 1979; staff fellow NIH, Bethesda, Md., 1980; cons. engr. Idaho Nat. Engring. and Environ. Lab., Idaho Falls, 1980—. Served with U.S. Army Res. 1969-75. Mem. AAAS, ANS, Am. Soc. Mech. Engrs., Biomed. Engring. Soc., Soc. Computer Simulation, Soc. Math. Biology, Soc. Engring. Sci., Order of Golden Bear, Alpha Sigma Phi. Republican. Roman Catholic. Avocations: swimming, surfing. Home: 1727 Grandview Dr # 4 Idaho Falls ID 83402-5016 Office: Bechtel BWXT Idaho Idaho Nat Engring Envir Lab Idaho Falls ID 83415-3890

RIENDEAU, THERESA FRANCES, rehabilitation nurse; b. Revere, Mass., June 12, 1953; d. Samuel and Eleanor M. (Rizzo) Spinazzola; m. Armand D. Riendeau, Dec. 31, 1994; children: James, Richard, Mark Russo. Diploma, New Eng. Bapt. Hosp. Sch., Boston, 1975. Reiki practioner. Charge nurse VA Med. Ctr., West Roxbury, Mass., 1975-80; asst. nurse mgr. Braintree (Mass.) Hosp., 1981-90; supr. nursing Randolph (Mass.) Crossings Nursing Ctr., 1990—93; utilization rev. coord., home health aide/homemaker educator Alternative Care Med. Svcs., Salem, NH, 1990—98; rehab. nurse Vis. Nurse Assocs. Inc., Dedham, Mass., 1993—94, VNA Homecare, Andover, 1994—95; unit mgr., restorative coord., staff developer Greenery Extended Care Ctr., North Andover, 1998—2001; clin. practice leader Spaulding Rehab. Hosp., Boston, 2001—. Mem. Assn. Rehab. Nurses. Home: 35 Wheeler St Dracut MA 01826-4219 Office: 125 Nashua St Boston MA 02114 E-mail: tfrrncrrn@aol.com.

RIENDL, ROBIN WENDY, financial advisor; b. Madison, Wis., Feb. 8, 1966; d. Jim McCaslin and Dean Naomi Brown; m. Paul Alex Riendl, Feb. 4, 1994. B in Natural Resources Mgmt., U. Alaska, Fairbanks, 1988; MBA, U. Alaska, 1991. Field investigator Harding Lawson Assocs., Anchorage, 1988—89; rsch. asst. U. Alaska, Fairbanks, 1989; planner Fairbanks N. Star Borough, 1989—90; forestry tech. Environ. Rsch. Inst., 1989—90; environ. analyst State of Alaska Dept. Transportation, Anchorage, 1992—96; financial advisor Morgan Stanley, 1996—. Mem. U. Alaska, Fairbanks Alumni Assn., 1983—; vol. instr. Tudor Cmty. Schs., Anchorage, 1996—. Recipient Outstanding Young Woman of Am., 1997. Avocations: martial arts, skiing, horseshowing. Office: Morgan Stanley 3601 C St Ste 140 Anchorage AK 99503-5925 Fax: 907-561-0243.

RIENNER, LYNNE CAROL, publishing executive; b. Pitts., Aug. 3, 1945; d. David and Molly (Rice) R. BA, U. Pa., 1967. Exec. v.p., assoc. publisher, editorial dir. Westview Press Inc., Boulder, Colo., 1975-84; pub., owner Lynne Rienner Pub. Inc., 1984—. Pub. cons. various orgns.; lectr. U. Denver Pub. Inst., 1981-84, 93—; panelist nat. meetings Bd. dirs. Boulder Breast Cancer Coalition, 1993-95. Mem. Assn. Am. Pubs. (bd. dirs. 1992-96, 99—, exec. coun. of profl. and scholarly pub. divsn. 1996—). Office: Lynne Rienner Pub Inc 1800 30th St Ste 314 Boulder CO 80301-1026

RIEPE, DALE MAURICE, philosopher, writer, illustrator, educator, Asian art dealer; b. Tacoma, June 22, 1918; s. Rol and Martha (Johnson) R.; m. Charleine Williams, 1948; children: Kathrine Leigh Riepe Herschlag, Dorothy Lorraine. BA, U. Wash., 1944; MA, U. Mich., 1946, PhD, 1954; postgrad. (Rockefeller-Watamull-McInerny fellow), U. Hawaii, Banaras and Madras, India, Tokyo and Waseda, Japan, 1949; diploma, Universidad de la Habana, 1997. Instr. philosophy Carleton Coll., 1948-51; asst. prof. U. S.D., 1952-54; assoc. prof. U. N.D., 1954-59, prof., 1959-62, chmn. dept., 1954-62; prof., chmn. C.W. Post Coll., 1962-63; prof. philosophy SUNY, Buffalo, 1963—; chmn. dept. social scis., assoc. dean SUNY Grad. Sch., 1964—. Instr. marine electricity Naval Tng. Program, Seattle, 1943-45; mem. nat. screening bd. South Asia, Fulbright Selection, 1968-70, Asia, 1970-72; chmn. Fulbright Selection Com. for Asia, 1972, 82; vis. Fulbright lectr. Tokyo U., 1957-58; vis. lectr. Western Wash. U., 1961, Delhi U., 1967; exchange lectr. U. Man., 1955, Moscow State U., 1979, Beijing Higher Edn. Inst., 1984; docent Albright-Knox Art Gallery; cons. Ctr. for Sci., Tech. and Devel., Council of Sci. adn Indsl. Rsch., Govt. India, 1978—, Inst. Fang Studies, 1987—, Can. Ednl. Coun.; del. Cuban-N.Am. Philosophy Conf., Cuban Inst. Social Sci., 1982, Fang Centennial, Taiwan Nat. U., Taipeh, 1987, Hungarian-Am. Philos. Conf., Budapest, 1988; sports columnist The Town Crier; vis. scholar Andhra U., 1996; lectr. NSF, 1960, Alfred U., Delhi U., Bangalore U., Budapest U., Fla. State U., Linfield Coll., Parma U., Sanskrit Coll., Calcutta, Moscow Acad. Sci., Moscow Acad. Oriental Studies. Author: The Naturalistic Tradition in Indian Thought, 1961, The Philosophy of India and its Impact on American Thought, 1970, Indian Philosophy Since Independence, 1979, The Owl Flies by Day, 1979, Asian Philosophy Today, 1981, Objectivity and Subjectivism in the Philosophy of Science, 1985, Philosophy and Revolutionary Theory, 1986, also articles in field.; editor: Phenomenology and Natural Existence, 1973, Philosophy and Political Economy; co-editor: The Structure of Philosophy, 1966, Contributions of American Sankritists in the Spread of Indian Philosophy in the United States, 1967, Radical Currents in Contemporary Philosophy, 1970, Reflections on Revolution, 1971, Philosophy at the Barricade, 1971, Contemporary East European Philosophy, 1971, Essays in East-West Dialogue, 1973, Explorations in Philosophy and Society, 1978; illustrator The Quick and the Dead, 1948; editorial com. Chinese Studies in History, 1970—, Chinese Studies in Philosophy, 1970—; publs. bd. Conf. for Asian Affairs; Editor various series.; editl. bd. Philos. Currents and Revolutionary World, 1972-86, Soviet Studies in Philosophy, 1979-87, Marxist Dimensions, 1987—, Active ACLU; mem. com. overseers Chung-an U., Korea; bd. dirs. Evergreen Coll. Cmty. Orgn., 1988—; bd. dirs. Friends of Evergreen Coll. Libr., 1992—; active Henry Gallery, Frye Gallery, Palm Springs Desert Mus., Seattle Art Mus., Phila. Mus. Art; mem. Capital Mus. and Art Soc., Wash. State Hist. Soc.; mem. libr. bd. Evergreen Coll.; founder Ars Asiatica. Fulbright scholar India, 1951-52; Fulbright lectr. U. Tokyo, 1957-58; U. Mich. fellow, 1945-48, Carnegie Corp. fellow Asian Studies, 1960-61, Am. Inst. Indian Studies Rsch. fellow, 1966-67; grantee 4th East-West Philosophers Conf., 1964, Penrose fund Am. Philos. Soc., 1963; SUNY Research Found., 1965-67, 69, 72-73, Bulgarian Acad. Sci., 1975, London Sch. Oriental and African Studies, 1971. Fellow Royal Asiatic Soc., Far Eastern Inst. (Tokyo); mem. AAAS, Internat. Hegel-Vereinigung, Conf. Asian Affairs (sec. 1995), Am. Oriental Soc., Am. Philos. Soc., Indian Inst. Psychology, Philosophy and Psychical Rsch. (hon. adviser), Soc. for Am. Philosophy (chmn. 1960), Am. Inst. Indian Studies (trustee 1965-66), Soc. for Creative Ethics (sec.), Am. Archaeol. Soc., Am. Assn. Asian Studies, Am. Math. Soc., Am. Aesthetics Soc., Internat. Soc. Aesthetics, Am. Soc. Comparative and Asian Philosophy, N.Y. Acad. Scis., Asiatic Soc. (Calcutta), Soc. for Philos. Study Dialectical Materialism (founding sec.-treas. 1962—), Soc. for Philos. Study Marxism (publs. sec. 1973-86), Union Am. and Japanese Profls. Against Nuclear Omnicide (treas. U.S. sec. 1978—), Internat. House of Japan, Internat. Philosophers for Prevention Nuclear Omnicide, United Univ. Profs. of SUNY-Buffalo (v.p.), Kokusai Bunka Shinkokai, N.Y. Acad. Scis., Union Concerned Scientists, Nat. Geog. Soc., Olympia Philosophy Club (co-founder 1988—), Alpha Pi Zeta. Office: SUNY 605 Baldy Hall Buffalo NY 14260-1000

RIEPE, JAMES SELLERS, investment company executive; b. Bryn Mawr, Pa., June 25, 1943; s. Henry Brunt and Marjorie (Sellers) R.; m. Gail Nelms Petty, Sept. 14, 1968; children: Christina, James, Jr. BS, Wharton Sch., U. Pa., 1965, MBA, 1967. Mem. audit staff Coopers & Lybrand, C.P.A.s, Phila., 1967-69; asst. to pres. Wellington Mgmt. Co., 1969-72, v.p., 1972-75; exec. v.p. Vanguard Group, Inc., Valley Forge, Pa., 1975-82, dir., 1979-82; mng. dir., mem. mgmt. com. T. Rowe Price Assocs., Inc., Balt., 1982—; pres. T. Rowe Price Investment Services, 1982—; chmn. TRP Trust Co., 1982—, TRP Retirement Plan Svcs., 1982—; dir. Rhône-Poulenc Rorer. Bd. dirs. Balt. Equitable Soc. Trustee, former chmn. Balt. Mus. Art; trustee U. Pa., mem. exec. com., mem. exec. com. health sys.; pres. Gilman Sch., 1994—. Mem. NASD (gov.), Investment Co. Inst. (gov.), Greenspring Valley Hunt Club, Caves Valley Golf Club. Office: T Rowe Price Assocs Inc 100 E Pratt St Fl 4 Baltimore MD 21202-1090

RIER, DAVID ALAN, sociologist, educator; b. N.Y.C., Oct. 30, 1962; s. Stanley and Alice I. (Richmond) R.; m. Vida Freedman, June 19, 1986; children: Rivka, Pinchas, Moshe, Tzvi, Miriam Chava. AB, Columbia U., 1984, MA, 1989, MPhil, 1990, PhD, 1995. Teaching asst. Columbia U., N.Y.C., 1987, grad. rsch. asst., 1988-89, Mt. Sinai Sch. Medicine, N.Y.C., 1989-91, asst. rsch. scientist, 1991-92, rsch. analyst, 1992-95; lectr. (asst. prof.) Bar-Ilan U., Ramat-Gan, Israel, 1995—, chair, grad. program med. sociology Israel, 2000—. Adj. instr. NYU, 1991, New Sch. for Social Rsch., 1991, Columbia U., 1992. Contbr. articles to profl. jours. Recipient Jack Elinson Sociomedical Scis. award, 1990, Columbia U. Sch. Pub. Health Alumni award, 1990, Elise Boulding Student Paper award Am. Sociol. Assn. Sect. on Peace and War, 1993, NSF Dissertation improvement, 1992-94, Marisa de Castro Benton Dissertation prize, Columbia U., 1995; citation for excellence, Israel Def. Force Med. Corps, Army Health Br., 1997. Fellow Inter-Univ. Seminar on Armed Forces and Soc.; mem. APHA, Am. Sociol. Assn. (Eliot Freidson Outstanding Rsch. prize 2001), Soc. for Social Studies of Sci. Office: Bar-Ilan U Dept Sociology & Anthropology Grad Program Med Sociology Ramat-Gan 52900 Israel E-mail: rierda@mail.biu.ac.il.

RIERSON, ROBERT LEAK, retired broadcasting executive, television writer; b. Walnut Cove, N.C., Sept. 5, 1927; s. Sanders C. and Anna (Cox) R.; m. Barbara Eugenia McLeod, Sept. 23, 1950 (dec. Feb. 1988); children: Barbara Elaine, Richard Troy; m. Rosemary L. McCampbell, Apr. 20, 1997. Student, Duke U., 1945-46, Davidson Coll., 1946-47; BS in Speech cum laude, Northwestern U., 1948. Program dir., program ops. mgr. WBT Radio and WBTV, Charlotte, N.C., 1948-66; program mgr. WJBK-TV, Detroit, 1966-69, WTOP-TV, Washington, 1969-71; dir. broadcasting WCBS-TV, N.Y.C., 1971-73; pres. Rierson Broadcast Consultants, 1973-75; program exec. Grey Advt., 1975-77; v.p., dir. programming Dancer-Fitzgerald-Sample, 1977-80; exec. producer Corinthian Prodns., 1980-82; dir. news programming CNN TV, Atlanta, 1982-96; ret., 1996. Producer-creator TV show ABCs of Democracy, 1965; producer, writer TV show George Washington's Mt. Vernon, 1970; creator, writer TV series 24 Days of Christmas, 1978, 21 Days of America, 1979. Bd. dirs. Mich. Coun. Chs., Detroit, 1968-69, ARC, Charlotte, 1960-62; 1st v.p. Charlotte Oratorio Singers, 1960-66. Lt. USNR, 1952-54. Recipient Edn. award Charlotte Jr. Woman's Club, 1961, George Washington Honor medal Freedoms Found., 1970; named Young Man of Yr., 1960. Mem. Nat. Assn. Radio-TV Program Execs. (charter mem., bd. dirs. 1964—), Radio-TV News Dirs. Assn., Order of Long Leaf Pine (hon. N.C. award). Republican. Mem. Moravian Episcopal Ch. Avocations: reading, travel, movies. Home: 31 S Cherrywood Ln Pisgah Forest NC 28768-9543

RIES, BARBARA ELLEN, alcohol and drug abuse services professional; d. Laurence B. and Genieveve Ries. AAS in Human Svcs., Coll. of DuPage, Glen Ellyn, Ill., 1973; BA in Social Work, U. Ill., Springfield, 1978; postgrad., U. Mo., 1987-88, U. Tex., Arlington, 1991—. Cert. social therapist, criminal justice counselor-master addiction counselor; nat., internat. cert. alcohol and drug counselor; lic. social worker, Ohio. Counselor Ray Graham Assn. for Handicapped, Addison, Ill., 1975-76; child abuse counselor Ill. Dept. Children and Family Svcs., Springfield, 1977-78; alcoholism counselor non-med. detoxification program S.H.A.R.E., Villa Park, Ill., 1978-80; outpatient therapist Ingalls Meml. Hosp., Harvey, 1980-83; dir. aftercare Lifeline Program, Chgo., 1984-85; case mgr. Lifecenter Program, Kansas City, Mo., 1985-87; counselor, acting clin. coord. Lakeside Hosp., 1988-89; program mgr., dir. chem. recovery programs Two Rivers Psychiat. Hosp., 1989-90; dir. day program and chem. dependency program SW Hosp./Citadel, Dallas, 1990—; dir. Flexcare program Dallas Meml. Hosp., 1990-91; pvt. practice Columbus, Ohio, 1991—; program coord. Advanced Clin. Svcs., Federal Way, 1992-94. Recovery svc. adminstr. Orient Correctional Insts., 1996-2002, London Correctional Insts., 2002--; spkr. in field. Recipient commendation Ingalls Hosp., 1983. Mem.: ACA, NASW, Nat. Assn. for Advanced Relapse Prevention Counselors, Nat. Assn. Drug and Alcohol Counselors (cert., NCAC II, Ohio alcohol and drug cert. III-E, master addiction counselor), Am. Correctional Assn., Nat. Assn. Forensic Counselors (cert. criminal justice specialist). Avocations: exercise, reading, listening to music, writing.

RIES, CHARLES WILLIAM, lawyer; b. Mankato, Minn., June 1, 1952; s. William Charles and Margaret Theresa Ries; m. Carol Jean Kaduce; children: Ryan Charles, Thalia Anne, William John Michael. BS in Acctg. cum laude, Mankato State Coll., 1974; JD cum laude, William Mitchell Coll. Law, 1981. Bar: Minn. 1981, U.S. Dist. Ct. Minn. 1981, U.S. Ct. Appeals (8th cir.) 1990; CPA, Minn. Law clk. Lamm, Lamm & Nelson, Mankato, 1979, Farrish, Johnson & Maschka, PLLP, Mankato, 1979-81, assoc., 1981-84, ptnr., 1984-99, Maschka, Riedy & Ries, PLLP, Mankato, 1999—. Staff sgt. U.S. Army, 1970-76. Mem. Minn. State Bar Assn. (bankruptcy sect., pres. 1994-95), Madison Lake Am. Legion (adjutant), Mankato Area Girls Fastpitch Assn. (dir., pres. 1996-97). Roman Catholic. Office: Maschka Riedy & Ries PLLP PO Box 7 Mankato MN 56002-0007

RIES, EDWARD RICHARD, petroleum geologist, consultant; b. Freeman, S.D., Sept. 18, 1918; s. August and Mary F. (Graber) R.; m. Amelia D. Capshaw, Jan. 24, 1949 (div. Oct. 1956); children: Rosemary Melinda, Victoria Elise; m. Maria Wipfler, June 12m 1964. AB magna cum laude, U. S.D., 1941; MS, U. Okla., 1943, PhD, 1951; postgrad., Harvard U., 1946-47, Harvard, 1946-47. Asst. geologist Geol. Survey S.D., White River area, 1941; geophys. interpreter Robert Ray Inc., Western Okla., Okla., 1942; jr. geologist Carter Oil Co., Mont., Wyo. 1943-44; geologist Standard Vacuum Oil Co., Mont., Wyo., Colo., India, 1944-49, sr. geologist Asam, Tripura, Bangladesh, India, 1951-53; sr. regional geologist N.Y. Standard Vacuum Petroleum, Maatschappij, N.Y., Indonesia, 1953-59, geol. advisor Far East and Africa White Plains, 1959-62, Oceania, Mobile Petroleum Co., N.Y.C., 1962-65; geol. advisor Europe, Far East Mobil Oil Corp., 1965-71, sr. regional explorationist Far East, Australia, New Zealand, 1971-73, sr. regional explorationist Asia-Pacific, Dallas, 1973-76, sr. geol. advisor Rsch. Geology, 1976-79; assoc. geol. advisor Geology-Geophysics, Dallas, 1979-82; sr. geol. cons., 1982-83. Ind. internat. petroleum geol. cons. Europe, Africa, Sino-Soviet and S.E. Asia, 1986—; grad. asst., teaching fellow U. Okla., 1941-43, Harvard, 1946-47. Contbr. numerous domestic and internat. proprietary and pub. hydrocarbon generation and reserve evaluations, reports and profl. papers. With AUS, 1944-46. Warden-Humble fellow, U. Okla., 1951. Mem. AAAS, Am. Inst. Econ. Rsch., Am. Assn. Petroleum Geologists (assoc. editor 1978-83, 50 Yr. Mem. Svc. award 1993), Geol. Soc. Am., Am. Geol. Inst., Nat. Wildlife Fedn., Nat. Audubon Soc., N.Y. Acad. Sci., Soc. Exploration Geophysicists, Wilderness Soc., Am. Legion, Harvard Club (Dallas), Phi Beta Kappa, Sigma Xi, Sigma Gamma Epsilon. Republican. Mennonite. Home and Office: 6009 Royal Crest Dr Dallas TX 75230-3434

RIES, MARTIN, artist, educator; b. Washington, Dec. 26, 1926; s. Martin Frank and Kathryn (Stretch) R.; m. Dianys d'Arcy Frobisher, June 8, 1953; children: d'Arcy, Von, Gannett, Nicole. BFA, Am. U., 1950; MA in Art History, postgrad. in mus. adminstrn., Hunter Coll., 1968. Asst. dir. pub. rels. Nat. Congl. Com., Washington, 1951; asst. dir. Hudson River Mus., 1957-67; advisor Westchester Cultural Ctr., 1965-66; curator instnl. art exhibits, prof. art L.I. U., Bklyn., 1967-94; juror Fulbright art scholarships Inst. Internat. Edn., UN, 1998. One-man shows include Atelier Gallery, N.Y.C., 1968, Paul Gallery, Tokyo, 1968, Atelier Terre d'Ocre, France, 1973, Unicorn Gallery, Soho, N.Y., 1976, Ganesh Gallery, Lenox, Mass., 1978, Belanthi Gallery, Bklyn., 1984, Stamford (Conn.) Mus., 1987, Raja Idris Gallery, Melbourne, Australia, 1989, Robb St. Gallery, Bairnsdale, Australia, 1989, Salena Gallery, L.I. U., 1996, 2/20 Gallery, N.Y.C., exhibited in group shows at Smithsonian Inst., 1952, Mus. of Modern Art, N.Y.C., 1956, SUNY-Albany, 1967, Casa de la Cultura Ecuatoriana in Cuayaquil, Ecuador, 1979, Hammer Gallery, N.Y.C., 1980, Muestra Internacional de Obra Grafica, Spain, 1982, Aaron Berman Gallery, N.Y.C., 1983, Kenkeleba Gallery, 1985, Inst. of Contemporary Art, London, 1988, Williamsburg Art & Hist. Ctr., Bklyn., retrospective; U.S.

editor : Irony & Rude Questions, art editor: art editor Greenwich Village News, 1976—77, contbg. editor: Arts Mag., 1974—75; contbr. ;one-man shows include Karpeles Mus., Newburgh, N.Y., 2002. With Intelligence and Reconnaissance, U.S. Army, 1945-46. Mem. Artists Representing Environ. Art (bd. dirs.), Assn. Internationale des Critiques d'Art (Am. sect.), Am. Soc. Contemporary Artists, Nat. Writer's Union. Home: 36 Livingston Rd Scarsdale NY 10583-6845 E-mail: ries@erols.com.

RIES, WILLIAM CAMPBELL, lawyer; b. Pitts., Apr. 8, 1948; s. F. William and Dorothy (Campbell) R.; m. Mallory Burns, Oct. 26, 1968; children: William Sheehan, Sean David. AB, Cath. U. Am., 1970; JD, Duquesne U., 1974; cert. Grad. Sch. Indsl. Adminstrn., Carnegie Mellon U., 1980. Bar: Pa. 1974, U.S. Dist. Ct. (we. dist.) Pa. 1974, U.S. Supreme Ct. 1979. Atty., then mng. counsel trust and investment svc. Mellon Bank, N.A., Pitts., 1974-90; ptnr. Dickie, McCamey and Chilcote, 1990-98; mem. Sweeney, Metz, Fox, McGrann & Schermer, LLC, 1998-2001; shareholder Tucker Arensberg, 2001—. Mem. adv. com. decedents' estates and trust law Pa. Joint State Govt. Commn., 1981—; adj. prof. Duquesne U., 1984—. Author: The Regulation of Investment Management and Fiduciary Services West, 1997. Pres. McCandless Twp. Civic Assn., Pitts., 1981—, McCandless Town Coun., chair pub. safety com., vice chair fin com.; sec. McCandless Indsl. Devel. Auth.; liaison McCandless zoning hearing bd. Fellow Am. Bar Found.; mem. ABA (chmn. fiduciary svcs. subcom.), Pa. Bar Assn., Allegheny County Bar Assn., Pitts. Estate Planning Coun., Am. Bankers Assn. (co-chmn. nat. conf. lawyers and corp. fiduciaries, chmn. trust counsel com.), Pa. Bankers Assn. (trust com., trust legis. com.), Rivers Club, Treesdale Golf and Country Club. Republican. Avocations: golf, sailing, cross-country skiing, fitness. Home: 9602 Fawn Ln Allison Park PA 15101-1737 E-mail: wries@tuckerlaw.com.

RIESCO, ARMANDO, II, management consultant, educator; b. Cuba, May 21, 1943; s. Armando Riesco Puyol and Bertha Cartaya Gutierrez; m. Blanca Rosa Farinas Torres, Dec. 16, 1972; children: Natascha Beatrice, Armando, Alejandro Jose. Student U. Bridgeport, 1960-61; BS in Indsl. Engring. magna cum laude, U. Fla., 1965, MS in Indsl. Engring., 1967, PhD in Indsl. and Systems Engring. and Ops. Research, 1970. Prof. indsl. engring. U. P.R., Mayaguez, 1970-79; pres. Sistema Inc., Guaynabo, P.R., 1979— ; vis. prof. indsl. and systems engring. U. Fla., Gainesville, 1976-77; sr. cons., co-founder Mgmt. Systems Design and Analysis, 1974-79; pvt. practice cons., 1967-74, corps. including Citibank, Electronic Data Systems, IBM, Pfizer Corp., Fed. Savs. Bank P.R., First Fed. Savs. Bank, govt. agys. including NASA, govts. P.R., Costa Rica, Dominican Republic, Jamaica; chmn., dir. organizational meetings profl. orgns.; lectr. in field. OAS fellow, 1968-70. Mem. Inst. Indsl. Engrs., Ops. Research Soc. Am., Inst. Mgmt. Scis., Phi Kappa Phi, Alpha Pi Mu (past regional v.p.), Sigma Xi, Tau Beta Pi. Roman Catholic. Contbr. sci. papers to profl. confs. and publs.

RIESELBACH, ALLEN NEWMAN, lawyer; b. Milw., June 2, 1931; s. Allen Saxe and Renee (Newman) R.; m. Patricia Fried, May 27, 1956; children: Anne, William. AB, Harvard U., 1953, LLB, 1956. Bar: Wis. 1956, Fla. 1971, Colo. 1986. Shareholder Reinhart, Boerner, Van Deuren, Norris & Rieselbach, S.C., Milw., 1959-99, sr. counsel, 1999—. Gov. Am. Coll. Real Estate Lawyers, 1989-92. Editor: Wisconsin Condominium Law, 1980. Mem. exec. bd. Milw. County Boy Scouts, 1975-92, 99—; bd. dirs. Milw. Repertory Theater, 1984-90; pres. Milw. Symphony Orch., 1995-98, mem. exec. com., 1992—. Mem. Rotary. Avocations: sailing, biking. Office: Reinhart Boerner Van Deuren Norris & Rieselbach 1000 N Water St Ste 2100 Milwaukee WI 53202-3197 E-mail: arieselb@reinhartlaw.com.

RIESELMAN, DEBORAH SUE, editor; b. Cin., Jan. 15, 1953; d. Robert Henry and Gail Dixon (Cato) R.; div. Apr. 1995; 1 child, Charles R. Hamilton. Student, U. Ky., U. Aberdeen, Scotland, U. Cin. News editor Dixie News, Florence, Ky., 1974-79; mng. editor Recorder Newspapers, Burlington, 1979-84, Christian Music Place, Close to Home Website, 1996-97; editor, asst. dir. U. Cin., 1984—. Writing instr. U. Cin.; editl. judge Internat. Assn. Bus. Communicators, 1992-99, Cath. Press Assn., 2001. Editor, author (mag. and newsletter) Horizons, 1988— (49 awards Cin. Editors Assn. 1988-2000, 23 awards Internat. Assn. Bus. Communicators 1992-2001, Gold medal Coun. Advancement and Support of Edn. 1998); contbg. author: Mentors, Models and Mothers, 1997. Pub. chmn. 2 state senatorial races, Ky., 1980s; site coord., pub. rels. dir. NAMES Project AIDS Meml. Quilt, Cin., Covington, Ky., Lexington, Ky., Washington, 1989-98; interpreter and storyteller Cin. Hist. Soc., 1996—; bd. dirs. Women of Evang. Luth. Ch., Ind.-Ky. Synod, 1999—. Named Outstanding Citizen of Erlanger, Erlanger (Ky.) City Coun., 1982, one of Outstanding Young Women of Am., 1985. Mem. Internat. Assn. Bus. Communicators (Bronze Quill judge 1995—), Cin. Editors Assn. (various membership committees 1988—), U. Cin. Assn. Women Adminstrs. (former bd. dirs.), Kappa Kappa Kappa. Lutheran. Avocations: clogging instructor (recipient several clogging awards), mountain dulcimer performer, lay leader in Evangelical Lutheran Church Am. Fax: 513-556-3237. E-mail: Deb.Rieselman@UC.edu.

RIESENBERGER, JOHN RICHARD, pharmaceutical company executive; b. N.Y.C., Sept. 25, 1948; s. Richard Raymond and Marie Teresa (Long) R.; m. Patricia Ann Casey, Nov. 23, 1974; children: Christine, Jennifer. BS in Econs. and Bus., Hofstra U., 1970, MBA in Mgmt., 1975; cert. internat. sr. mgmt. program, Harvard U., 1989. Customer svc. supr. Chase Manhattan Bank, 1970-72; gen. sales rep. various regions Upjohn Co., Bklyn., 1972-75, sales rep., sales mgr. various locations, N.Y., 1976-81, profl. tng. and devel. officer Kalamazoo, 1981-83, dir. Chgo. sales area, 1983-87; v.p., group mgr. Upjohn Co. of Can., Toronto, Ont., 1987-89; exec. dir., worldwide med. scis. liaison Upjohn Co., Kalamazoo, 1989-92, exec. dir. worldwide strategic mktg., 1992-95; exec. dir. corp. info. tech. Pharmacia & Upjohn, Inc., 1995, v.p. bus. info., 1996-97; v.p. global bus. mgmt. Pharmacia & Upjohn Inc., Bridgewater, N.J., 1998-99; pharm. cons., 1999—; exec.-in-residence Mich. State U., 2000—; pres. Consilium Ptnrs. Inc., 2000—; exec. v.p. Shaw Sci. Ptnrs., Atlanta, 2000—. Chmn. industry adv. bd. dirs. SEI Ctr. Advanced Studies in Mgmt., Wharton Sch., U. Pa.; mem. Global Adv. bd. Am. Mktg. Assn., 1999; mem. edtl. review bd. Jour. Internat. Mktg.; Ciber adv. bd. Mich. State U. Author: (with Robert T. Moran) The Global Challenge: Building the New Worldwide Enterprise, 1994, Global Business Strategies for the Year 2000, 1995. Mem. ciber adv. bd. Mich. State U. Mem. Am. Mgmt. Assn., Am. Mktg. Assn., Strategic Mgmt. Soc., Pharm. Rsch. Mfrs. Am. (chmn. mktg. practices com.), The Planning Fom, Internat. Soc. for Strategic Planning and Mgmt., Harvard Bus. Sch. Club, Pharm. Bus. Intelligence and Rsch. Group, European Pharm. Market Rsch. Assn., Harvard Bus. Sch. Health Industry Alumni Assn. Avocation: golf. Home: 42 Independence Dr Basking Ridge NJ 07920-3815

RIESER, JOHN PAUL, lawyer; b. Homestead, PA, Sept. 24, 1956; BA with distinction, Northwestern U., 1978; cert., Pushkin Inst., Moscow, 1978; JD cum laude, Harvard U., 1981. Bar: Ohio 1981, Fla. 1998, U.S. Dist. Ct. (so. dist.) Ohio 1981, U.S. Ct. Appeals (6th cir.) 1982, U.S. Tax Ct. 1991, U.S. Dist. Ct. (so. dist.) Fla. 2000, U.S. Ct. Appeals (11th cir.) 2000. Assoc. Estabrook, Finn & McKee, Dayton, Ohio, 1981-83; sole practice, 1983-85; ptnr. Rieser & Marx, Ohio, 1985—, Fla., 1998—. Lectr. bus. law Sinclair Community Coll., Dayton, 1984—, other orgns.; mem. rules com. for so. dist. Ohio, U.S. Bankruptcy Ct. Editor Harvard Internat. Law Jour., 1979-81; contbr. articles to newspapers and profl. jours. Arbitrator Montgomery County (Ohio) Arbitration Panels, 1983—; trustee Chpt. 7 Bankruptcy, 1989—; participant Vol. Lawyer Project. Mem. ABA, ATLA, Am. Bankruptcy Law Forum (trustee), Nat. Assn. Bankruptcy Trustees, Ohio Bar Assn., Fla. Bar, Palm Beach County Bar Assn., Dayton Bar Assn., Harvard U. Alumni Assn. Office: Rieser & Marx Ste 800 West Tower 777 S Flagler Dr West Palm Beach FL 33401 E-mail: jprieser@aol.com.

RIESER, JOSEPH A., JR. lawyer; b. Pitts., Aug. 28, 1947; s. Joseph Alexander and Ruth Margaret (Piper) R.; m. Susan Jean Irving, Feb. 28, 1976; 1 child, Alexander H.I. AB, Princeton U., 1969; JD, MPP, Harvard U., 1974. Bar: Pa. 1974, D.C. 1976, U.S. Supreme Ct. 1979. Assoc. Reed Smith LLP, Pitts. and Washington, 1974-82, ptnr. Washington, 1983—. Mem. D.C. Office of Tax and Revenue Adv. Group, 1997-2001. Chmn. nat. alumni assn. Kennedy Sch. Govt., Cambridge, Mass., 1979-82; bd. dirs. Harvard U. Alumni Assn., 1982-84; gen. counsel 1984 Dem. Nat. Conv., Washington, 1983-84; gen. counsel Nat. Dem. Party, Washington, 1985-89; spl. counsel Clinton/Gore '92, Inc.; mem. Clinton-Gore 1992 Presdl. Transition Team. Mem. D.C. Bar (chmn. bus. related taxes com. 1989-92, tax policy steering com., chmn. D.C. Bar Nat. Fed. Tax Inst. 1991, 92, 2000, chmn. state and local taxes com. 1994-97, tax section steering com. 1997—, co-chair tax sect. 1998-2001), Ctr. for Nat. Policy Bd. Advisors, Harvard-Yale-Princeton Pitts. Club, Cosmos Club. Presbyterian. Home: 3517 Davis St NW Washington DC 20007-1426 Office: Reed Smith & McClay 1301 K St NW Washington DC 20005-3317

RIESS, GORDON SANDERSON, management consultant; b. Thessaloniki, Greece, Feb. 25, 1928; came to U.S., 1932; s. Lewis William and Dorothy Onward (Sanderson) R.; m. Priscilla Rich, June 2, 1951; children: Mark C., Kimberly A., Blake G. AB with highest honors, Whitman Coll., 1949; MBA cum laude, Harvard U., 1951. Cert. mgmt. cons.; registered profl. cons.; accredited profl. cons. With Ford Internat. Div., N.Y.C., 1951-53; asst. fin. mgr. Ford Motor Co., Mid. East, Alexandria, Egypt, 1953-57; gen. sales mgr. Ford Motor Co., Rome, Italy, 1957-60; regional fin. mgr. Ford Motor Co., Scandinavia, Copenhagen, Denmark, 1960-62; gen. mgr. Ford Motor Co., European, Brussels, Belgium, 1962-67; v.p. Internat. Paper Co., Zurich, Switzerland, 1967-71; exec. v.p. Cinema Internat. Corp., London, 1971-75; chmn., pres. Stewart-Riess Labs. Inc., Tarzana, Calif., 1976-83; pres., CEO Intercontinental Enterprises Ltd., Beverly Hills, 1983—. Chmn. Vis. Nurse Found., L.A., 1985-87; bd. dirs., chmn. Vis. Nurse Assn., L.A., 1976-97; bd. dirs. Beverly Found., Pasadena, Calif., 1990-97; vice-chmn. of bd. Witman Coll., Walla Walla, Wash., 1985-96. Author: Confessions of a Corporate Centurion--Tales of International Adventures, 2000, From Communism to Capitalism, 2001; inventor/patentee pre-fillable hypodermic syringe. Chmn. Inter-Community Sch. Zurich, 1968-71; trustee Am. Sch. London, 1972-75; vice chmn. Krafterliner Mfgs. Assn., Zurich, 1968-71; bd. dirs. Vols. in Tech. Assistance, Arlington, Va., 1986-93; bd. overseers Muhlenberg Coll., 1993—; internat. bd. Czechoslovak Mgmt. Ctr., 1992—. Sgt. U.S. Army, 1946-47. R.H. Macy scholar, Harvard Bus. Sch., 1949. Mem. Am. Assn. Profl. Cons., Am. Cons. League, Asia Acad. Mgmt., Hollywood Radio & Television Soc., Inst. Mgmt. Cons., Lic. Execs. Soc. Avocations: skiing, scuba diving. Office: Intercontinental Ent Ltd # 3194 256 S Robertson Blvd Beverly Hills CA 90211-2898 E-mail: gsr@mindspring.com.

RIESSER, GREGOR HANS, arbitrage investment advisor; b. Riga, Latvia, Apr. 13, 1925; came to U.S., 1948; s. Hans Edward and Gilda (Von Scherf) R.; m. Joanna Gray (dec. Aug. 1991); children: Cindy Laughlin, William Riesser; m. Edith Naparst, Dec. 19, 1992 (dec. July 1997); stepchildren: Nicole Monacelli, Harold Naparst; m. Marjory Patterson, Oct. 27, 2002; stepchildren: Bruce , Laura, Elisa, T. Graham, Cynthia Quinn. MS in Chemistry, U. Geneva, 1949; PhD, U. Calif., Berkeley, 1952. Rsch. chemist Shell Chem. Co., Houston, 1952-70, catalysis bus. ctr., 1970-73; sr. staff chemist Shell Devel. Co., 1973-84. Spkr. on long-term options, scores and primes, arbitrages, dual funds and the stock market; mem. bd. arbitrators NASD. Featured in Forbes, Houston Post, Houston Chronicle. Mem. Am. Assn. Individual Investors, Houston Investment Assn. (Guru award, dir. 1990—), Am. Chem. Soc. Unitarian Universalist. Home and Office: 2309 A Nantucket Dr Houston TX 77057-2974 E-mail: griesser@houston.rr.com.

RIESZ, PETER CHARLES, marketing educator, consultant; b. Orange, N.J., Apr. 30, 1937; s. Kolman and Ellen (Wachs) R.; m. Elizabeth Strider Dunkman, Dec. 28, 1968; children— Sarah Kathleen BS, Rutgers Coll., 1958; MBA, Columbia U., 1963, PhD, 1971. From asst. prof. to assoc. prof. U. Iowa, Iowa City, 1968-80, prof. mktg., 1980—, chmn. dept. mktg., 1981-87, Williams prof. tchg., 1994-97. Vis. prof. Boston U., 1974-75, Duke U., Durham, N.C., 1984-85; cons. in field. Contbr. articles to profl. jours. Recipient Teaching Excellence award HON Industries, 1989; named MBA Prof. of Yr., 1990; Old Gold fellow U. Iowa, 1972. Mem. Am. Chem. Soc., Am. Mktg. Assn. Democrat. Presbyterian. Avocations: photography. Home: 2411 Tudor Dr Iowa City IA 52245-3638 Office: U Iowa Dept Mktg Coll Bus Adminstrn Iowa City IA 52242 E-mail: peter-riesz@uiowa.edu.

RIESZ, WANDA WALLACE, educational administrator, educational consultant; b. Lafayette, Ind., July 13, 1942; d. George Murdock and Byrdena Maude (McDill) Wallace; m. William H. Riesz, July 28, 1963 (div. 1972); children: James W. (Jay) (dec.), Nicole Elies. Student, Purdue U., 1960-61, U. Md., Madrid, 1962; AB in Spanish, Ind. U., 1962, BS in Edn., 1963, MS in Edn., 1965, D in Cultural Studies, 1972; cert., U. Madrid, 1962; student, Berlitz Lang. Sch., Freiburg, Germany, 1966, Internat. U. Menendez Pelayo, Santander, Spain, 1967, Alliance Francaise, Paris, 1967. Lic. superintendent adminstr. K-12, tchr. Spanish K-9, elem. tchr., Ind.; lic. K-12 elem. sch., Spanish K-12, Va.; lic. real estate sales, broker, Ind. Tchr. elem. sch., French Fairfax (Va.) County Schs., 1963-65; dir. GED drop-out program U.S. Army, Kaiserslautern, Germany, 1965-66; assoc. prof. SUNY, Stony Brook, 1968-70; lectr. sch. edn. Ind. U., Purdue U., Columbus, Bloomington, Ind., 1970-78; founder, prin. Pub. Alternative H.S., Bloomington, 1970-80; legis. aide Ind. Ho. of Reps., Indpls., 1988-96, edn. policy analyst, family & social svcs. specialist, 1996-97. Cons. edn., legis., polit., drunk driving, vets.' affairs Hampton Inst.,Appalachia, Cleve., Lexington, Ky., L.A., Cleveland, Tenn., Grand Rapids, Mich., 1970—; grant writer Fed. Law Enforcement Agy., Ind., Washington, 1970—; dir. alternative edn. programs Indpls. Pub. Schs., 1997—; spkr. in field. Contbr. articles to profl. jours.; co-developer: (video and board game) Peer Supervision, 1976. Rep. Ind. Baccalaureate Edn. Sys. Trust Ind. Ho. of Reps. Dem. Caucus; cons. Vietnam and Korean War Meml. Commn., 1990—, Goals 2000, 1990—, U.S. Sec. Edn., 1990—, Coalition Essential Schs., 1990—; bd. dirs. Luggage for Foster Kids, State of Ind., 1990—, Middle Way Shelter for Battered Women, Bloomington, 1984, State Juvenile Justice Task Force, 1982, Big Brothers/Big Sisters; bd. dirs., pres. Jay Riesz Found. to Prevent Drunk Driving, Women for Better Govt., Greater Indpls., 1994-96; legis. liaison State Mothers Against Drunk Driving; vol. Habitat for Humanity, Indpls., 1995; pres. Dem. Woman's Club, 1994—; founding mem. Ind. Victims of Violent Crimes, 1995—; elected del. Ind. Dem. State Conv., 1988, 92, 96; mem. youth adv. bd., New Directions Com. St. Paul's Episc. Ch., 1994—; pres. Ind. State Alternative Learning Options, Ind. Sagamore of the Wabash, 1997. Named Ky. Col., 1995; recipient State POW/MIA award DAV, Spl. Merit Recognition award State of Ind. Dept. Vets. Affairs, 1995, Spl. Legis. award Mothers Against Drunk Driving, State of Ind., 1990, Outstanding Cmty. award Indpsl. Boys and Girls' Club, 1998. Mem. Edn. Commn. of the States, NOW, Indpls. Athletic Club, Culver Mil. Acad. Club (Indpls.), Am. Legion Aux. (life), Metro. Indpls. Bd. Realtors, Studebaker Drivers Club, Mustang Owners Club, Maxinkuckee Yacht Club, Inpls. Ski Club, Phi Sigma Iota (treas. 1972), Pi Lambda Theta (sec. 1971), Psi Iota Xi. Avocations: swimming, skiing, vintage cars. Office: Indpls Pub Schs Edn Svc Ctr 501E Indianapolis IN 46204 Home: 9804 Gulfstream Dr Fishers IN 46038-9726

RIETSCHEL, ROBERT LOUIS, dermatologist; b. New Orleans, Oct. 9, 1946; s. Frederick Arnt and Estelle Marie (Fleckinger) R.; m. Connie Joanne Dent, Sept. 3, 1966; children: Eric, Penny. BA, North Tex. State U., 1968; MD, U. Tex., Galveston, 1972. Diplomate Am. Bd. Dermatology. Intern Letterman Army Med. Ctr., San Francisco, 1972-73, dermatology rschr., 1973-74; resident in dermatology Brooke Army Med. Ctr., San Antonio, 1974-77, staff dermatologist, 1977-79; assoc. prof. dermatology Emory U. Sch. Medicine, Atlanta, 1981-85, acting chmn. dept. dermatology, 1984-85; assoc. chmn. dept. dermatology Ochsner Clinic, New Orleans, 1985-88, chmn. dept. dermatology, 1988—2001. Contbr. articles to profl jours. Cubmaster Boy Scouts Am., Decatur, Ga., 1983-84. Maj. U.S. Army, 1971-79. NIOSH grant, 1981-84. Fellow Am. Acad. Dermatology, Soc. for Investigative Dermatology; mem. Am. Dermatol. Assn., N.Am. Contact Dermatitis Group (sec. 1985-93), Am. Contact Dermatitis Soc. (sec. 1989-93, pres. 1993-95). Republican. Lutheran. Avocation: sailing. Office: Ochsner Clinic 2005 Veterans Blvd Metairie LA 70005

RIFAI, HISHAM K. political scientist, consultant; b. Aleppo, Syria, Aug. 11, 1931; came to U.S., 1955; s. Omar Besim and Samir Rifai; m. Branka Koljensic, June 1, 1968; 1 child, Maja. JD, Damascus U., Syria, 1952; postgrad., Columbia U., 1956-58. Translator UN, N.Y.C., 1956-57, polit. officer, 1957-68, sect. chief, 1968-78, dir., 1978-84, exec. sec. Vienna, 1984-88; sr. fellow UN Inst. for Tng. and Rsch., N.Y.C., 1989-94; vis. prof. Ga. State U., Atlanta, 1992-93; sr. cons. Inter-Univ. Assocs., N.Y.C., 1994—. Lectr., prof. L.I. U., N.Y.C., 1995-96. Vice pres. Francophone Cultural Assn. UN, 1994—; mem. Problems of Peace Seminars, Columbia U., 1994—, Ralph Bunche Inst., CUNY, 19956. Avocation: violin playing.

RIFE, ELIZABETH, musician, music educator; b. Zebulon, Ga., Feb. 23, 1938; d. Jack and Ouida Dorothy (Walker) Bridges; m. Robert M. Hill, June 25, 1959 (div.); 1 child, Dorothy Hill Bremer; m. C. David Rife, Feb. 15, 1986. BS in Music Edn., Ga. State Coll. and U., 1959; postgrad., Ga. State U., 1976-81, Vanderbilt U., 1977-79. Music tchr. , Marietta, Ga., 1959—; choir master, organist Holy Trinity Luth. Ch., 1966-79. Pres., chmn. bd. Assist, Inc., Marietta, 1982-84. Guest columnist Marietta Daily Jour., 1980-84, Horizons mag., 1997. Dir. WSB-TV Call for Action, Atlanta, 1980—82; spkr. Foster Children Program, Marietta, 1980—83, United Way, 1982—83; sec. bd. dirs. Help for Hispanics, 2002; conducted seminars, workshops on hunger ch. and civic groups, Atlanta, 1981—; mem. steering com. Presbyn. Answer to Hunger, 1991—. Mem. Music Tchrs. Nat. Assn., Music Educators Nat. Assn., Ga. Music Educators Conf. (adjudicator piano competition 1967—), Cobb County Music Tchrs. Assn., Sigma Alpha Iota. Presbyterian. Avocations: running, reading, travel, fashion consulting, tutoring. Home: 1296 Poplar Pointe SE Smyrna GA 30082-2213

RIFE, JOHN MERLE, JR. retired educator, pilot; b. Bloomington, Ind., Apr. 5, 1925; s. John Merle and Ruth Ramsey Rife; m. Wanda Petty, Mar. 28, 1958; children: John Albert, Roseann Pennings. BA, Muskingum Coll., 1950; MA, Ohio State U., 1952, PhD, 1964. Flight instr. NAS, Pensacola, Fla., 1946; tchr. Oak Harbor (Ohio) H.S., 1953-55; prof. Ind. U. of Pa., 1958-94, dean social scis., 1976; comml. pilot Ind. Airways, 1964-72. Contbr. articles to profl. publs. Bd. dirs. Muskingum Coll., 1990-2000. With USNR, 1942-46. Rsch. grant Ind. U. of Pa., 1964, 84. Mem. Mack Found. (bd. dirs.). Democrat. Presbyterian. Avocations: photography, flying. Home: 450 Health Camp Rd Indiana PA 15701-8997

RIFENBURGH, RICHARD PHILIP, investment company executive; b. Syracuse, N.Y., Mar. 3, 1932; s. Russell D. and Edna (MacKenzie) R.; m. Doris Anita Hohn, June 24, 1950; children: David, Susan, Robert. Student, Wayne State U. With Mohawk Data Scis. Corp., Herkimer, N.Y., 1964-74, pres., 1970-74, chmn., 1974, Moval Mgmt. Corp., Herkimer, 1968—; CEO, GCA Corp., Andover, Mass., 1986-87; gen. ptnr. Hambrecht and Quist Venture Ptnrs., 1987-90; chmn. Miniscribe Corp., Longmont, Colo., 1988-91, Ironstone Group Inc., 1988-91, St. G Crystal Ltd., Jeannette, Pa., 1985—; vice-chmn. Paradise Music and Entertainment Inc., 2001. Bd. dirs. Verance Corp.; chmn. Tristar Corp., 1992—2002. With USAF, 1951-55. Address: Moval Mgmt Corp PMB 133 2637 E Atlantic Blvd Pompano Beach FL 33062-4939 E-mail: dickrif@aol.com.

RIFFE, DELMAR RAY, engineer; b. Mabscott, W.Va., Mar. 6, 1930; BSME, Va. Polytech. Inst., 1953; MSME, Va. Polytechnic Inst., 1957. Various engrng. positions to cons. engr. Copeland Corp., Sidney, Ohio, 1988—92; chief engr. R&D Amerigold Compressor Corp., Cullman, Ala., 1990—95; cons. engr. UN, Beaver, W.Va., 1995—. Patentee (patents) 19 patents in field; contbr. articles. Cpl. U.S. Army, 1954—56. Mem.: Internat. Legion of Intelligence, Mensa. Republican. Avocation: long distance running, triathlete (completed Boston Marathon and Hawaiian Iron Man World Championship Triathlon twice).

RIFKIN, BARRY, dean, educator, researcher; DDS, PhD. Dir. grad. program oral biology, prof., head Divsn. Basic Scis. NYU Coll. Dentistry; dean SUNY, Stony Brook, 1999—. Rschr. in field. Sr. editor The Biology and Physiology of the Osteoclast ; mem. editl. bd.: Jour. Dental Rsch. Office: Rockland Hall Stony Brook NY 11794*

RIFKIN, GARY D. physician, educator; b. N.Y.C., Feb. 24, 1946; s. Ira and Ruth (Mann) R.; m. Thelma Freeman, Nov. 22, 1969; children: Jay, Scott, Lori. BA, Rutgers U., 1967; MD, Albert Einstein Coll. Medicine, 1971. Diplomate Am. Bd. Infectious Diseases, Am. Bd. Internal Medicine. Physician epidemiologist St. Anthony Med. Ctr., Rockford, Ill., 1981—; cons. Rockford Infectious Disease Cons., 1981—; assoc. prof. of medicine U. Ill. Coll. Medicine, 1983—, acting chmn. dept. medicine, 2001—. Pres. Rockford Infectious Disease Cons., 1981—. Pres. No. Ill. AIDS Resource Ctr., Rockford, 1989-2000; chmn. Mayors Task Force on Harm Reduction, Rockford, 1995-96; v.p. No. Ill. HIV/MDS Network, Rockford, 2000-01. Maj. U.S. Army, 1973-75. Fellow ACP, Infectious Diseases Soc. Am. Avocations: tennis, reading. Office: Univ Ill Coll Medicine 1601 Parkview Ave Rockford IL 61107-1822 also: Rockford Infectious Disease Consultants 129 Phelps Rockford IL 61108 E-mail: grifkin@uic.edu.

RIFKIN, JOSEPH S. political and business consultant; b. Port Jervis, N.Y., Dec. 6, 1960; s. Robert P. and Marlene Rifkin; 1 child, Jack. BA in Labor Rels., SUNY, Buffalo, 1983, JD, 1986. Bar: N.J. 1987. COO, Marine Equipment Functions, Port Jervis, 1989-91; polit. and bus. cons. JSR Cons., 1988—. Chmn. Port Jervis Bicentennial of Costn. Com., 1986-87; pres. Port Jervis Coun. for Arts, 1995-2000, Arts Coun. Orange County, Middletown, N.Y. 2000-01. Mem. Port Jervis Country Club (bd. govs. 1999-2002). Democrat. Avocations: wine and jazz enthusiast, drummer, golf. Office: JSR Cons PO Box 101 Port Jervis NY 12771 E-mail: jrifkin@citlink.net.

RIFKIN, SANDRA ANDERSON, interior designer; b. Bismarck, N.D., May 22, 1938; d. Ervin William and Marguerite C. Anderson; student St. Mary's Hall, Faribault, Minn., 1957, Bergman Art Inst., Denver, 1959; m. Robert C. Rifkin, Oct. 24, 1971; 1 dau., Terri Lin. Owner, Design Studio, Denver, 1967-71, Design Assos., Denver, 1971— . Designs include Turn of the Century Restaurant, The Lady and the Dove Restaurant, Lyle Alzado's Restaurant, Juliano's Restaurant, Reflections Disco, Miss Rosy Bottoms Disco and Restaurant, The Parlour Disco, The Charley Horse Saloon, The Proof of the Pudding, also various pvt. residences. Office: 7300 E Hampden Ave Denver CO 80231-4802

RIFKIND, ARLEEN B. physician, researcher; b. N.Y.C., June 29, 1938; d. Michael C. and Regina (Gottlieb) Brenner; m. Robert S. Rifkind, Dec. 24, 1961; children: Amy, Nina. BA, Bryn Mawr Coll., 1960; MD, NYU, 1964. Intern Bellevue Hosp., N.Y.C., 1964-65, resident, 1965; clin. assoc. Endocrine br. Nat. Cancer Inst., 1965-68; rsch. assoc., asst. resident physician Rockefeller U., 1968-71; asst. prof. medicine Cornell U. Med. Coll., N.Y.C., 1971-82, assoc. prof. medicine, 1983—, asst. prof. pharmacology, 1973-78, assoc. prof., 1978-82, prof., 1983—, chmn. Gen. Faculty Coun., 1984-86. Mem. Nat. Inst. Environ. Health Scis. Rev. Com., 1981-85, chmn., 1985-86; mem. toxicology study sect. NIH, 1989-91, chmn., 1991-93; bd. sci. counselors USPHS Agy. for Toxic Substances and Disease Registry, 1991-95; adv. com. FDA, Spl. Studies Relating to the Possible Long-Term Health Effects of Phenoxy Herbicides and Contaminents, 1995-99; external adv. bd. Environ. Health Scis. Ctr., Wayne State U., 1999—. Assoc. editor Drug Metabolism and Disposition, 1997—; mem. editl. bd. Toxicology and Applied Pharmacology, 1996-2002, Biochem. Pharmacology, 1996—; contbr. articles to profl. jours. Chair Friends of the Libr., Jewish Theol. Sem. Am., 1984-86; trustee Dalton Sch., 1986-92; mem. Environ. Health and Safety Coun., Am. Health Found., 1990—; bd. govs. Am. Jewish Com., 1999—; bd. dirs. N.Y. chpt. Am. Jewish Com., 2001-. Recipient Andrew W. Mellon Tchr.-Scientist award, 1976-78; USPHS spl. fellow, 1968-72. Mem. AAAS, Internat. Soc. Study Xenobiotics, Am. Soc. Clin. Investigation, Am. Soc. Pharmacology and Exptl. Therapeutics, Endocrine Soc., Soc. Toxicology. Office: Cornell U Med Coll Dept Pharmacology 1300 York Ave New York NY 10021-4805 E-mail: arifkind@med.cornell.edu.

RIFKIND, RICHARD ALLEN, physician; b. N.Y.C., Oct. 26, 1930; s. Simon H. and Adele (Singer) R.; B.S., Yale U., 1951; M.D., Columbia U., 1955; m. Carole Lewis, June 24, 1956; children— Barbara, Nancy. Intern. Presbyn. Hosp. N.Y.C., 1955-56, resident, 1957-61, dir. hematology, 1972-81; asst. prof. dept. medicine Columbia U., 1963-67, asso. prof., 1967-70, prof., 1970-81; dir. comprehensive Cancer Center, 1980-81, chmn. dept. genetics, 1980-81; dir. Grad. Sch. Meml. Sloan-Kettering Cancer Center, N.Y.C., 1981-2000, chmn. Sloan-Kettering Inst., 1983—2000, chmn. emeritus, 2000-. Served to capt. M.C., USAF, 1957-59. Diplomate Am. Bd. Internal Medicine. Mem. Am. Soc. Clin. Investigation, Am. Assn. Physicians, Am. Soc. Hematology. Democrat. Jewish. Contbr. articles in field.

RIFKIND, ROBERT S(INGER), lawyer; b. N.Y.C., Aug. 31, 1936; s. Simon H. and Adele (Singer) R.; m. Arleen Brenner, Dec. 24, 1961; children: Amy, Nina. BA, Yale U., 1958; JD, Harvard U., 1961; LHD (hon.), Jewish Theol. Sem. Am., 1998. Bar: N.Y. 1961, U.S. Supreme Ct. 1965. Asst. to solicitor gen. Dept. Justice, 1965-68; assoc. firm Cravath, Swaine & Moore, N.Y.C., 1962-65, 68-70, ptnr., 1971—2001, sr. counsel, 2002—. Trustee Dalton Sch., N.Y.C., 1975-83, hon. trustee, 1983—, pres., 1977-79; trustee Brandeis U., 1998—, The Loomis Inst., 1987-95, Citizens Budget Commn.; bd. dirs. Charles H. Revson Found., 1991—, chmn., 1997—; bd. dirs. Jewish Theol. Sem. Am., 1983—, Jerusalem Found., 1998--, Leo Baeck Inst., 1999—, Benjamin N. Cardozo Sch. Law, 1984-89; pres. Am. Jewish Com., 1994-98; chmn., adminstr. coun., Jacob Blaustein Inst. Advancement of Human Rights. Fellow Am. Coll. Trial Lawyers, Am. Bar Found.; mem. ABA, Coun. Fgn. Rels., Am. Law Inst., Assn. of Bar of City of N.Y., Phi Beta Kappa. Democrat. Office: Cravath Swaine & Moore Worldwide Pla 825 8th Ave Fl 38 New York NY 10019-7475

RIFMAN, EILEEN, music educator; b. Bklyn., June 10, 1944; m. Samuel Sholom Rifman, Aug. 12, 1972; children: Edward, Aimee. MusB, Manhattan Sch. Music, 1966, M Music Edn., 1967; MusM, Ind. U., 1970; cert., Fontainebleau, France, 1967. Music specialist N.Y.C. Pub. Sch. System, 1966-67; instr. Long Beach (Calif.) City Coll., 1970-72, Immaculate Heart Coll., Hollywood, Calif., 1971-74, U. Judaism, Hollywood, 1973-74; co-coord. Community Sch. Performing Arts, L.A., 1974-82, instr., 1973-83; pvt. piano tchr. Manhattan Beach, Calif., 1963—; tchr. gifted and talented edn. program GATE, 1990-91. Tchr. Etz Jacob Hebrew Acad., L.A., 1991-95, Ohr Eliyahu Acad., Culver City, 1995-96; peer counselor Beach Cities Health Dist., 1997—. Performer Pratt Inst., Clinton Hill Symphony, N.Y.C., 1962, Sta. WNYC-FM, 1964. Chair Cultural Arts Com., Manhattan Beach, 1985-86; bd. dirs. Hermosa Beach (Calif.) Community Ctr., 1990-91. Mem. Nat. Fedn. Music Clubs (adjudicator 1970). Home: 1700 Lynngrove Dr Manhattan Beach CA 90266-4242 E-mail: eileenrifman@hotmail.com.

RIGAS, ANTHONY LEON, university department director; b. Andros, Greece, May 3, 1931; s. Leon Anthony and Katina (Sarris) R.; m. Harriett B. Rigas, Feb. 14, 1959 (dec. 1989); 1 child, Marc Leonard; m. Mary Dunham, Dec. 29, 1990. BSEE, U. Kans., 1958, MSEE, 1962; postgrad., Stanford U., 1965; PhD in Engring., U. Beverly Hills, 1978. Elec. engr. Naval Missile Ctr., Point Mugu, Calif., 1958-61; engring. analyst Mpls. Honeywell Co., 1962; instr. elec. engring. U. Kans., Lawrence, 1962-63; sr. rsch. engr. aerospace systems Lockheed Missile and Space Co., Sunnyvale, Calif., 1963-65, Dalmo-Victor Co., Belmont, 1965-66; asst. prof. elec. engring. San Jose (Calif.) State U., 1963-65; asst. prof., assoc. prof., then prof. elec. engring. U. Idaho, Moscow, 1966-84, dir. instrnl. media svcs., 1983-84; prof. elec. and computer engring. Naval Postgrad. Sch., Monterey, Calif., 1984-87; dir. engring. lifelong edn. Mich. State U., East Lansing, 1987-92; prof. elec. engring., dir. engring outreach emeritus U. Idaho, 1994—. Presenter at profl. confs.; prof. elec. engring., dir. engring. outreach emeritus U. Idaho, 1994—. Contbr. to profl. publs. Grantee NSF, 1971-75, 71-76, 1979-82, HEW, 1979-80, Kellogg Found., 1977-80. Fellow IEEE; mem. Am. Soc. Engring. Edn., Nat. Soc. Profl. Engrs., Nat. Univ. Continuing Edn. Assn., Sigma Xi, Sigma Tau, Tau Beta Pi. Home: 300 Hidden Harbor Ln Sandpoint ID 83864-7488

RIGBY, KENNETH, lawyer; b. Shreveport, La., Oct. 20, 1925; s. Samuel and Mary Elizabeth (Fearnhead) Rigby; m. Jacqueline Carol Brandon, June 8, 1951; children: Brenda, Wayne, Glen. BS magna cum laude, La. State U., 1950, JD, 1951. Bar: La. 1951, U.S. Ct. Appeals (5th cir.) 1966, U.S. Supreme Ct. 1971, U.S. Tax Ct. 1981, U.S. Ct. Appeals (11th cir.) 1982. Ptnr. Love, Rigby, Dehan & McDaniel, 1951—. Adj. prof. La. State U. Law Ctr., 1990—; mem. marriage-persons com. La. Law Inst., 1981—, mem. coun., 1988—; mem. La. Supreme Ct. Jud. Coun., 1999—2001. Contbr. articles to profl. jours. Sec. mandatory CLE com. La. Supreme Ct., 1987—95. With USAF, 1943—46. Fellow: Am. Coll. Trial Lawyers, Am. Acad. Matrimonial Lawyers; mem.: ABA, Shreveport Bar Assn. (pres. 1973—74), La. State Bar Assn. (chmn. com. CLE 1974—75, chmn. family law sect. 1981—82, bd. govs. 1986—88). Office: Beaird Tower 330 Marshall St Ste 1400 Shreveport LA 71101-3018 E-mail: charli@prysm.net.

RIGBY, PAUL CRISPIN, artist, cartoonist; b. Melbourne, Australia, Oct. 25, 1924; came to U.S., 1977; s. James Samuel and Violet Irene (Wood) R.; m. Marlene Anne Cockburn, Nov. 16, 1956; children: Nicole, Pia, Peter, Paul, Danielle. Student, Brighton Tech. Sch., Australia, Art Schs., Victoria, Victoria Nat. Gallery, Australia. Free lance artist, 1940-42; illustrator West Australian News, Ltd., 1948-52; editorial cartoonist Daily News Australia, 1952-69; daily cartoonist London Sun and News of the World, 1969-74; editorial cartoonist New York Post, 1977—84, 1993—2000, New York Daily News, 1984-93. Illustrator numerous books; represented in exhbns. of painting in, Australia, Europe and U.S.A.; Contbr. work to numerous publs., U.S., Europe, Asia. With Royal Australian Air Force, 1942-46. Decorated Order of Australia, knight comdr. Order of St. John, Knights of Malta; recipient Walkley award Australia, 1960, 61, 63, 66, 69; N.Y. Press Club award for art, 1981, 83, Page One award for excellence in journalism Newspaper Guild, 1982, 83, 84, 85. Mem.: Rolls Royce Owners, Royal Freshwater Bay Yacht; Friars (N.Y.C.), Players (N.Y.C.). Mem. Ch. Of Eng. Home: 119 Monterey Point Dr Palm Beach Gardens FL 33418 E-mail: rigbyateastend@aol.com.

RIGBY, PERRY GARDNER, medical center administrator, educator, former university dean, physician; b. East Liverpool, Ohio, July 1, 1932; s. Perry Lawrence and Lucille Ellen (Orin) R.; m. Joan E. Worthington, June 16, 1957; children: Martha, Peter, Thomas, Matthew. BS summa cum laude, Mt. Union Coll., 1953, D.Sc. hon., 1976; MD, Western Res. U., 1957. Diplomate: Am. Bd. Internal Medicine. Intern in medicine U. Va. Hosp., Charlottesville, 1957-58, asst. resident in medicine, 1958-60; research fellow in hematology Mass. Meml. Hosp., Boston, 1960-62; clin. asst. in medicine Boston City Hosp., 1961-62; research assoc. in medicine Mass. Meml. Hosp., Boston U. Med. Ctr., 1961-62; asst. prof. internal medicine and anatomy U. Nebr., Omaha, 1964-66, assoc. prof. internal medicine and anatomy, 1966-69, prof. internal medicine, 1969-78, prof. anatomy, 1969-74, prof. med. edn., 1973-74, head sect. hematology Eugene C. Eppley Inst. for Research in Cancer and Allied Diseases, 1964-68, dir. hematology div., 1968-74, asst. dean for curriculum Coll. Medicine, 1971-72, assoc. dean for acad. affairs, 1972-74, dir. office ednl. services, 1972-74, acting assoc. dean for allied health professions, 1973-74, vice chmn. dept. med. and ednl. adminstrn., 1974, dean, 1974-78, chmn. dept. med. and ednl. adminstrn., 1974; prof. internal medicine La. State U., Shreveport, 1978—, assoc. dean acad. affairs Sch. Medicine, 1978-81, acting dean, 1981-82, dean, 1982-85, chancellor, 1985-94, dir. Health Care Systems, 1994—, mem. clin. bd. Univ. Hosp., 1978-94, chmn. clin. bd., 1981-85, program dir. biomed. research support grant program, 1980-81; chmn. dean's com. VA Hosp., 1978-85; mem. courtesy staff Immanuel Med. Ctr.; bd. dirs. Health Planning Council of Midlands, Omaha, 1976-78; cons. WHO, Kabul, Afghanistan, 1976. Bd. dirs. Fontenelle Forest, Omaha, 1976-78; bd. dirs. River Cities High Tech. Group, Shreveport, 1982-85. Served as capt. M.C. U.S. Army, 1962-64. Markle scholar, 1965 Fellow ACP; mem. Am. Fedn. Clin. Research (councillor 1971), AMA (del.), Am. Soc. Hematology, N.Y. Acad. Scis., Am. Assn. Med. Colls. (council of deans of Midwest-Gt. Plains 1974-78, chmn. Midwest-Gt. Plains 1976), Am. Assn. Cancer Research, AAAS, Am. Heart Assn., Central Soc. Clin. Research, Internat. Soc. Hematology, Health Edn. Media Assn., Am. Assn. Physicians' Assts., So. Soc. Clin. Investigation, Shreveport C. of C. (dir. 1982-85), Sigma Xi, Alpha Omega Alpha, Phi Rho Sigma Office: La State U Med Ctr Resource Ctr 433 Bolivar St New Orleans LA 70112-2223

RIGDON, DAVID TEDRICK, air force officer, geneticist, director; b. Laurel, Miss., Jan. 27, 1948; s. James T. and Marie T. (Taylor) R.; m. Elizabeth Sue Jones, June 1, 1973; children: Angela Denise, Michael David. BS in Biology, U. Ala., 1970; MD cum laude, U. Miss., 1975. Diplomate Am. Bd. Pediats., Am. Bd. Med. Genetics. Commd. USAF, 1975, advanced through grades to col., 1991; intern in pediats. USAF Med. Ctr., Keesler AFB, Miss., 1975-76, resident in pediats., 1976-78; fellow in med. genetics U. Ala., Birmingham, 1978-80; med. geneticist USAF Med. Genetics Ctr., Keesler AFB, 1980-85, dir. Air Force Med. Genetics Ctr., 1985—. Cons. Surgeon Gen. USAF, Miss. State Dept. Health; clin. asst. prof. pediats. Uniformed Svcs. Univ. of Health Scis., F. Edward Herbert Sch. Medicine, Bethesda, Md. Contbr. articles to profl. jours. Recipient Physician's Recognition award AMA, 1978, 81, 84, 87, 90, 93, 96, 99. Fellow Am. Acad. Pediats.; mem. Am. Soc. Human Genetics, So. Genetics Group, Alpha Omega Alpha. Republican. Methodist. Avocations: boating, fishing. E-mail: david.rigdon@keesler.af.mil.

RIGDON, JAY ALDEN, lawyer; b. Syracuse, Ind., Apr. 7, 1960; s. Jay A. and Elsie B. R.; m. Brenda Jo Rhodes, Nov. 17, 1984; children: Jay, Chelsea, Isaac. BA in Polit. Sci and Econs., George Washington U., 1981; JD, Ind. U., 1984. Bar: Ind. 1984. Ptnr. Rockhill, Pinnick LLP, Warsaw, 1984—. Mem. Ind. Domestic Violence Coun., Indpls., 1990-96; pres., bd. dirs. Kosciusko County United Way, Warsaw, 1992-96; v.p. Bd. Aviation Commrs. Mem. ABA, Ind. Bar Assn. Democrat. Episcopalian. Office: Rockhill Pinnick 105 E Main St Warsaw IN 46580-2742

RIGG, CHARLES ANDREW, pediatrician; b. Hamilton, Vic., Australia, Oct. 18, 1926; came to U.S., 1963; s. Arthur Oscar and Mary Eileen (Wingrove) R. B in Medicine, Surgery with honors, Sydney U., 1951. Registrar, professorial unit Children's Hosp., Sydney, Australia, 1954-56; registrar pediat. unit St. Mary's Hosp. Med. Sch., London, 1956, 58; from sr. resident to chief resident Children's Hosp., Boston, 1957, fellow in adolescent medicine, 1963-64, staff adolescent medicine, 1964-65, chief dept. adolescent medicine Washington, 1967-80; asst. prof. pediat. Georgetown U. Med. Sch., 1965-67; from asst. prof. to assoc. prof. child health George Washington U. Med. Sch., 1967-80; chief dept. adolescent medicine Boston City Hosp., 1981-83; assoc. prof. pediatrics Sch. Medicine Boston U., 1981-83; med. dir. Outer Cape Health, Provincetown, Mass., 1983-88; pediatrician, med. dir. Medicenter Five, Harwich, 1988-95, pediatrician, 1995-97, May Ctr. Child Devel., Chatham, 1990—, Harwich Town Pub. Sch. System, 1997—. Cons. Nat. Naval Med. Ctr., Bethesda, Md., 1973-80, Walter Reed Army Med. Ctr., Washington, 1973-80; courtesy staff medicine Children's Hosp., Boston, 1983—; vis. prof. Philippine Pediat. Soc., 1978, 9th Congress of the Brazilian Med. Assn., 1979, 16th Internat. Congress of Pediat., Barcelona, 1980. Editor: Adolescent Medicine Present and Future Concepts, 1980; contbr. articles to profl. jours. Mem. Mus. Fine Arts, Boston, Folger Shakespeare Libr., Washington, Nat. Trust for Hist. Preservation, Nat. Trust Australia, Tasmania, Royal Oak Soc. Maj. M.C. Royal Australian Army, 1951-60; lt. col. USAR, 1985-91. Model Tng. Program in Adolescent Medicine grant Maternal and Child Health Svcs.-U.S. Govt., 1967-80, Comprehensive Health Svcs. Adolescent Ctr. grant Mass. Dept. Pub. Health, 1981-83. Fellow: Royal Australasian Coll. Physicians, Am. Headache Soc., Royal Soc. Medicine, Am. Acad. Pediatrics (life); mem.: Soc. Adolescent Medicine (charter, treas., chmn., legis. com.), City Tavern Club (Washington), Royal Sydney Golf Club. Episcopalian. Avocations: historic preservation, gardening, theater, music, walking. Office: Pediatrics/Adol Medicine PO Box 401 940 Main St South Harwich MA 02661

RIGG, DAME DIANA, actress; b. Doncaster, Yorkshire, Eng., July 20, 1938; d. Louis and Beryl (Helliwell) R.; m. Menahem Gueffen, July 6, 1973 (div. Sept. 1976); m. Archibald Hugh Stirling, Mar. 25, 1981 (div. Apr. 1993); 1 child, Rachael Atlanta. Grad., Fulneck Girls' Sch., Pudsey, Yorkshire; student, Royal Acad. Dramatic Art, London; D (hon.), Stirling U., Eng., 1988, Leeds U., 1992, Southbank U., 1996. Prof. of theater studies Oxford U., 1998—. Stage debut as Natella Abashwilli in The Caucasian Chalk Circle, Theatre Royal, York, Eng., 1957; joined Royal Shakespeare Co., Stratford-on-Avon, 1959, debut as Andromache in Troilus and Cressida, 1960; London debut as Philippe Trincant in The Devils, London, 1961; numerous repertory appearances; joined Nat. Theatre, 1972; appeared in Jumpers, Macbeth, 1972, The Misanthrope, 1973, Pygmalion, 1974, Phaedra Britannica, 1975, Night and Day, 1978, Colette, 1982, Heartbreak House, 1983, Little Eyolf, 1985, Antony and Cleopatra, 1985, Wildlife, 1986, Follies, 1987, Love Letters, 1990, All for Love, 1991, Putting It Together, 1992, Berlin Bertie, 1992, Medea, 1992 (Tony award, Broadway prod., 1994, Eve. Standard award, Variety Club award), Mother Courage and Her Children, 1995, Who's Afraid of Virginia Wolf, 1996, Humble Boy, 2001; film appearances include A Midsummer Night's Dream, The Assassination Bureau, On Her Majesty's Secret Service, Julius Caesar, The Hospital, Theatre of Blood, A Little Night Music, The Great Muppet Caper, Evil Under the Sun, A Good Man in Africa, Parting Shots, 1998; co-starred as Emma Peel in Brit. TV series The Avengers, 1965-67; star TV series Diana, 1973-74; numerous TV movies including This House of Brede, 1975, Hedda Gabler, 1981, Little Eyolf, 1982, Witness for the Prosecution, 1982, King Lear, 1983, Bleak House, 1984, A Hazard of Hearts, 1987, Worst Witch, 1987, Unexplained Laughter, 1989, Mother Love (Broadcasting Guild Award, BAFTA), 1989, Genghis Cohn, 1994, Zoya, 1995, The Haunting of Helen Walker, 1995, Moll Flanders, 1996, Samson and Delilah, 1996, Rebecca, 1997 (Emmy award, 1997); host PBS series Mystery, 1989—, Mrs. Bradley Mysteries, 1999—, In the Beginning, 2000, The American, 2000, Victoria & Albert, 2001; author: No Turn Unstoned, 1982, U.S. edit., 1983, So To The Land, 1994. Decorated comdr. Brit. Empire; created dame, 1994; recipient Tony award nomination as best actress in Abelard and Heloise and The Misanthrope; Plays and Players award for Phaedra Britannica and Night and Day; Variety Club Gt. Britain award for best actress for Evil Under the Sun; Brit. Acad. Film and TV Arts award for best TV actress in Mother Love, 1989, Award for Women in TV & Film, 2001. Mem. United Brit. Artists (co-founder, dir. 1982—). Address: c/o Lionel Larner Ltd 119 W 57th St New York NY 10019-2303*

RIGG, RICHARD LEE, church musician, composer, music educator; b. Newport, RI, Feb. 17, 1961; s. James and Joan R.; m. Christann Marie Rehak; children: Michael, Mary Catherine. BS in Secondary Edn., Old Dominion U., Norfolk, Va., 1988. Strings/orch. tchr. Norfolk (Va.) Pub. Schs., 1988—2001, harp instr., 1990—2001; orchestral and choral dir. Va. Beach (Va.) Mid. Sch., 2001—. Assoc. music dir. St. Andrew's Episcopal Ch., Norfolk, 2001—. Composer: (composition for string orchestra) Fiddler's Fancy, 1995, Fiddler's Fancy, Too, 1996, Symphony No. I (in 3 movements), 1998. Mem.: Am. Fedn. of Musicians, Music Educators Nat. Conf. Home: 817 Buck St Chesapeake VA 23323 Office: Va Beach Mid Sch 500 25th St Virginia Beach VA 23451 Personal E-mail: rrigg@iol18.com. E-mail: rrigg@vbcps.k12.va.

RIGGLE, PATRICIA CAROL, science educator; b. Gallipolis, Ohio, May 28, 1965; d. Pat and Freadith Fay Price; m. Richard Allan Riggle; children: Darlene Ritter, James Ritter, Lauren Ritter. BS, U. Rio Grande, 1989. Sub. tchr. Gallia County Local Schs., Gallipolis, Ohio, 1989—92, Gallipolis City Schs., Gallipolis, 1989—92; tchr. Wellston City Sch., Wellston, 1992—; child care provider Rio Grande Child Devel. Ctr., Rio Grande, 1992—93. Vol. asst. dir. drama club Wellston H.S., Wellston, Ohio, 1998—; career assessment adv. com. Gallia-Jackson-Vinton Joint Vocats. Sch. Dist., Rio Grande, Ohio, 2001—. Youth Sunday sch. tchr. Okey Chapel, Scottown, Ohio, 1985—2000. Mem.: NEA, Wellston Tchrs. Assn., Ohio Edn. Assn. Avocations: camping, travel, crafts. Home: 4767 Hannan Trace Rd Patriot OH 45658*

RIGGS, ANNA CLAIRE, metals company executive; b. Danville, Ind., Jan. 22, 1944; d. Leland Wesley and Mary Alice (Miller) Cox; m. Michael Ross Riggs, Dec. 10, 1983; 1 child, Matthew. BS in Edn., Ind. U., 1966. Credit tng. and promotion mgr. L.S. Ayres, Indpls., 1966-74; cons., credit dept., 1984; credit ops. mgr. Burdine's, Miami, Fla., 1974-77; br. mgr. Centaur Metals, Indpls., 1977-85; regional mgr. Cooper & Brass Sales, 1985—. Louisville, 1989—. Chairperson vision com., co-chair lay leadership com., lay leader United Meth. Ch., Danville, Ind. Mem. NAFE, Am. Jersey Cattle Club (exec. com., All Am. 1991, 95, 2002), Ind. Jersey Cattle Club. Avocations: traveling, reading. Home: 576 N 200 W Danville IN 46122 Office: Copper & Brass Sales 530 Northfield Dr Brownsburg IN 46112-2111 E-mail: ariggs@thyssenmx.com.

RIGGS, ARTHUR JORDY, retired lawyer; b. Nyack, N.Y., Apr. 3, 1916; s. Oscar H. and Adele (Jordy) R.; m. Virginia Holloway, Oct. 15, 1942 (dec.); children: Arthur James (dec.), Emily Adele Riggs Freeman, Keith Holloway, George Bennett; m. Priscilla McCormack, Jan. 16, 1993. AB, Princeton U., 1937; LLB, Harvard U., 1940. Bar: Mass. 1940, Tex. 1943; cert. specialist in labor law. Assoc. Warner, Stackpole, Stetson & Bradlee, Boston, 1940-41; staff mem. Solicitors Office U.S. Dept. Labor, Washington, Dallas, 1941-42; mem. Johnson, Bromberg, Leeds & Riggs, Dallas, 1949-81; of counsel Geary & Spencer, 1981-91. Mem. ABA, State Bar Tex., Phi Beta Kappa. Avocations: Maya archeology, history, photography. Home and Office: 2110 Antibes Dr Carrollton TX 75006-4326 E-mail: ariggs9@home.com.

RIGGS, CLAUDESTA LAVERN, professional storyteller; b. Wilmington, N.C., May 7, 1957; d. Sylvester Stephen and Frances Claudia Riggs. BS in Telecomms., Mid. Tenn. State U., 1980. Profl. storyteller/sml. bus. entrepreneur. Vol. TC Thompson Children's Hosp., Sunday sch. Avocations: writing, reading, singing. Home and Office: 115 Woodlawn Dr Chattanooga TN 37411 Home Fax: 423-698-6801; Office Fax: 423-698-6801. Personal E-mail: Lavernscreations@aol.com. Business E-Mail: Lavernscreations@aol.com.

RIGGS, DONALD EUGENE, librarian, university official; b. Middlebourne, W.Va., May 11, 1942; m. Jane Vasbinder, Sept. 25, 1964; children: Janna Jennifer, Krista Dyonis. BA, Glenville State Coll., 1964; MA, W.Va. U., 1966; MLS, U. Pitts., 1968; EdD, Va. Poly. Inst. and State U., 1975. Head librarian, tchr. sci. Warwood (W.Va.) High Sch., 1964-65; head librarian, audiovisual dir. Wheeling (W.Va.) High Sch., 1965-67; sci. and econs. librarian California State Coll. of Pa., 1968-70; dir. library and learning center Bluefield State Coll., 1970-72; dir. libraries and media services Bluefield State Coll., Concord Coll., Greenbrier Community Coll., and So. campus W.Va. Coll. of Grad. Studies, 1972-76; dir. libraries U. Colo., Denver, Met. State Coll., and Community Col. of Denver— Auraria Campus, 1976-79; univ. librarian Ariz. State U., 1979-88, dean univ. libraries, 1988-90; prof. info. and libr. sci., dean univ. libr. U. Mich., Ann Arbor, 1991-97; prof., v.p. for info. svcs., univ. libr. Nova Southeastern U., Ft. Lauderdale, Fla., 1997—. Adj. prof. Calif. State Coll., 1968-70, W.Va. U., 1970-72, U. Colo., 1977-79, U. Ariz., 1985, Emporia State U., 1996—, U. South Fla., 1997—; fed. rels. coord. Am. and W.Va. Libr. Assns., 1970-75; chmn. bd. dirs. Ctrl. Colo. Libr. Sys., 1976-79; chmn. Colo. Coun. Acad. Librs., 1977-78; mem. exec. bd. Colo. Alliance Rsch. Librs., 1978-79; cons. to librs.; fgn. assignments in Xi'an, China, 1988, Guadalajara, Mex., 1990, Budapest, Hungary, 1991, 95, Hong Kong, 1992, 94, San Juan, P.R., 1993, Melbourne, Australia, 1994, Eupatory, Republic Crimea, Ukraine, 1995, London, 1996, Prague, Czech Republic, 1996, Beijing, China, 1996, 98, Pretoria, South Africa, 1996, others; del. Users Coun. Online Computer Libr. Ctr., Dublin, Ohio, 1987-91, pres.-elect, 1990-91, chair artificial intelligence and expert systems nat. group, 1987-88; bd. govs. Rsch. Librs. Group, Inc., Mountain View, Calif., 1991-92; vice chmn. mgmt. com. William L. Clements Libr., 1991-97. Editor: W.Va. Librs., 1973-75, Libr. Hi Tech, 1993-96, Coll. & Rsch. Librs., 1996-2002; founding editor: Libr. Adminstrn. and Mgmt., 1987-89; assoc. editor: Southeastern Libr., 1973-75; contbg. editor: Libraries in the Political Process, 1980, Options for the 80's, 1982, Library and Information Technology: At the Crossroads, 1984; contbg. author, editor: Library Leadership: Visualizing the Future, 1982; author: Strategic Planning for Library Managers, 1984, (with Helen Gothberg) Time Management in Academic Libraries, 1986, (with Gordon Sabine) Libraries in the 90's: What the Leaders Expect, 1988, Creativity, Innovation and Entrepreneurship in Libraries, 1989, Library Communication: The Language of Leadership, 1991, (with Rao Aluri) Expert Systems in Libraries, 1990, Cultural Diversity in Libraries, 1994; editl. bd. Am. Librs., 1987-89, Jour. Libr. Adminstrn., 1987-97, Coll. and Rsch. Librs., 1990-96, Coll. and Rsch. Librs. News, 1996-2002. Trustee Mesa (Ariz.) Pub. Library, 1980-86, chmn., 1985-86; mem. Ariz. State Library Adv. Council, 1981-84; bd. dirs. Documentation Abstracts, Inc., 1986-90. Recipient Alumnus of Yr. award Glenville State Coll., 1992; named Outstanding Young Educator, Ohio County Schs., 1966; Coun. on Libr. Resources grantee, 1985; sr. fellow UCLA, 1989. Mem. ALA (councilor-at-large 1982-86, 89-93, chmn. coun.'s resolutions com. 1985-86, pub. com. 1988-92, Hugh Atkinson award 1991), Ariz. Libr. Assn. (pres. coll. and univ. divsn. 1981-82, pres. 1983-84, Spl. Svc. award 1986, Disting. Svc. award 1990), Colo. Libr. Assn. (pres. 1978-79), W.Va. Libr. Assn. (pres. 1975-76), Assn. Coll. and Rsch. Librs. (pres. Tri-State chpt. 1972-74, pres. Ariz. chpt. 1981-82), So. Libr. Assn. (chmn. coll. and univ. sect. 1982-83), Assn. Rsch. Librs. (100th meeting planning com. 1982, mgmt. of rsch. libr. resources com. 1990-93, rsch. collections com. 1993-96), AMIGOS Bibliograph Coun. (trustee 1986-90, chmn. bd. trustees 1988-89), Libr. Adminstrn. and Mgmt. Assn. (bd. dirs. 1987-89, pres.-elect 1993-94, pres. 1994-95), Libr. Info. and Tech. Assn. (bd. dirs. 1989-93), Ctr. for Rsch. Librs. (councilor 1979-97), Mountain Plains Libr. Assn. (bd. dirs. 1987-90, pres.-elect 1990-91), S.E. Fla. Libr. Info. Network (exec. com., bd. dirs. 1997—, pres. 1998-99), Beta Phi Mu, Chi Beta Phi, Phi Delta Kappa, Phi Kappa Phi. Office: Nova Southeastern U Libr Rsch & Info Tech Ctr Ray Ferrero Jr Blvd Fort Lauderdale FL 33314-7721 E-mail: driggs@nova.edu.

RIGGS, FRED WARREN, political science educator; b. Kuling, China, July 3, 1917; (parents Am. citizens); s. Charles H. and Grace (Frederick) R.; m. Clara-Louise Mather, June 5, 1943; children: Gwendolyn, Ronald (dec.). Student, U. Nanking, China, 1934-35; BA, U. Ill., 1938; MA, Fletcher Sch. Law and Diplomacy, 1941; PhD, Columbia U., 1948. Lectr. CUNY, 1947-48; rsch. assoc. Fgn. Policy Assn., 1948-51; asst. dir. Pub. Adminstrn. Clearing House, N.Y.C., 1951-55; Arthur F. Bentley prof. govt. Ind. U., 1956-67; dir. Social Sci. Rsch. Inst. U. Hawaii, 1970-73, prof. polit. sci., 1967-87, prof. emeritus, 1987—. Vis. asst. prof. Yale U., 1955-56; vis. lectr. Nat. Officials Tng. Inst., Korea, 1956; vis. prof. U. Philippines, 1958-59, MIT, 1965-66, CUNY, 1974-75; vis. scholar Inst. Soc. Studies, The Hague, 1972; sr. specialist East-West Ctr. U. Hawaii, 1962-63. Author: Pressures on Congress: A Study of the Repeal of Chinese Exclusion, 1950, reprinted, 1973, Formosa under Chinese Nationalist Rule, 1952, reprinted, 1972, The Ecology of Public Administration, 1961 (pub. in Portuguese, 1964), Administration in Developing Countries: The Theory of Prismatic Society, 1964 (pub. in Korean, 1966, Portuguese, 1968), Thailand: The Modernization of a Bureaucratic Polity, 1966, Organization Theory and International Development, 1969, Administrative Reform and Political Responsiveness: A Theory of Dynamic Balancing, 1971, Prismatic Society Revisited, 1973 (pub. in Korean, 1987), Applied Prismatics, 1978, (with Daya Krishna) Development Debate, 1987; author: (with others) Contemporary Political Systems: Classifications and Typologies, 1990, Handbook of Comparative and Development Public Administration, 1991, Terminology: Applications in Interdisciplinary Communication, 1993, Parliamentary vs. Presidential Government, 1993, Public Administration in the Global Village, 1994, Comparing Nations: Concepts, Strategies, Substance, 1994, Handbook of Bureaucracy, 1994, Standardizing and Harmonizing Terminology, 1995, Korea in the Era of Post-Development and Globalization, 1996,Designs for Democratic Stability, 1997, Modernity and Bureaucracy, 1997, Presidentialism vs. Parliamentarism, 1998, Public Administration in America, 1998, The Modernity of Ethnic Identity and Conflict, 1998, Impeachment vs. Harassment, 1999; Ethnic Diversity, Nationalism and Constitutional Democracy, 2000, The Para-Modern Context of Ethnic Nationalism, 2000, Globalization, Ethnic Diversity and Nationalism, 2002; co-author, editor: Frontiers of Development Administration, 1971, Tower of Babel: On the Definition and Analysis of Concepts in the Social Sciences, 1975. Dir. INTERCOCTA project Internat. Social Sci. Coun., 1970-93; chair UNESCO com. INTERCONCEPT project, 1977-79; chair Comm. on Conceptual and Terminological Analysis (COCTA), Internat. Polit. Sci. Assn., Internat. Sociol. Assn. and Internat. Social Sci. Coun., 1973-79; co-chair N.AM. roundtable on cooperation Social Sci. Info. Mpls., 1979; chair lexicographic terminology com. Dictionary Soc. N.Am., 1983-86; co-chair Com. on Viable Constitutionalism (COVICO), 1993—. Decorated Order of White Elephant, King of Thailand, 1986; fellow com. comparative politics Social Sci. Rsch. Coun., 1957-58, Ctr. Advanced Study in Behavioral Scis., 1966-67; honoree Eastern Regional Orgn. Pub. Adminstrn. Conf., 1983. Mem. Am. Soc. for Pub. Adminstrn. (chair comparative adminstrn. group 1960-71, Dwight Waldo award 1991), Am. Polit. Sci. Assn., Internat. Studies Assn. (chair comparative interdisciplinary studies sect. 1970-74, v.p. 1970-71, co-chair ethnicity, nationalism and migration sect. 1994-95), Internat. Polit. Sci. Assn., Internat. Sociol. Assn., Assn. Asian Studies (chair com. rsch. materials S.E. Asia 1969-73), Soc. for Comparative Rsch. (co-founder 1994—). Home: 3920 Lurline Dr Honolulu HI 96816-4006 Office: U Hawaii Political Science Dept 2424 Maile Way Honolulu HI 96822-2223 E-mail: fredr@hawaii.edu.

RIGGS, HENRY EARLE, academic administrator, engineering management educator; b. Chgo., Feb. 25, 1935; s. Joseph Agnew and Gretchen (Walser) Riggs; m. Gayle Carson, May 17, 1958; children: Elizabeth, Peter, Catharine. BS, Stanford U., 1957; MBA, Harvard U., 1960. Indsl. economist SRI Internat., Menlo Park, Calif., 1960—63; v.p. Icore Industries, Sunnyvale, 1963—67, pres., 1967—70; v.p. fin. Measurex Corp., Cupertino, 1970—74; prof. engring. mgmt. Stanford U., 1974—88, Ford prof., 1986—88, Ford prof. emeritus, 1990, v.p. for devel., 1983—88; pres. Harvey Mudd Coll., Claremont, 1988—97, pres. emeritus, 1997; pres. Keck Grad. Inst., 1997—. Bd. dirs. Capital Rsch. Group. Author: Accounting: A Survey, 1981, Managing High-Tech Companies, 1983, Financial and Cost Analysis, 1994; contbr. articles to profl. jours. Recipient Gores Tchg. award, Stanford U., 1980;

scholar Baker scholar, Harvard Bus. Sch., 1959. Mem.: Stanford U. Alumni Assn. (bd. dirs. 1990—94, chmn. 1993), Twilight Club, Sunset Club, Calif. Club, Tau Beta Pi, Phi Beta Kappa. Congregationalist. Office: Keck Grad Inst 535 Watson Dr Claremont CA 91711-4817 E-mail: henry_riggs@kgi.edu.

RIGGS, JACK TIMOTHY, lt governor, emergency physician; b. Coeur d'Alene, Idaho, Oct. 1, 1954; m. Rachel, children, Shannon, Peter, Jennifer. BS summa cum laude, U. Idaho, 1976; MD, U. Wash., 1980. Diplomate Am. Bd. Emergency Medicine. Intern Deaconess Med. Ctr., Spokane, Wash., 1980-81; mem. Idaho Senate, Dist. 4, Boise, 1996-2000; owner North Idaho Immediate Car Ctrs., 1985—; lt. gov. State of Idaho, 2001—. Fellow Am. Coll. Emergency Physicians; mem. AMA, Am. Coll. Physician Execs., Idaho Med. Assn., Am. Coll. Occupl. and Environ. Medicine. Address: 1701 Lincoln Way Coeur D Alene ID 83814-2537 Office: Office of Lt Gov State Capitol PO Box 83720 Boise ID 83720-3720

RIGGS, KENNETH ALLAN, music educator; b. Seattle, Mar. 8, 1969; s. Donald William and Maria Ann Riggs; m. Kristina Elise Schupp, Aug. 1, 1992; children: Natalie Grace, Jeremy William. BA, Ctrl. Wash. U., 1992, MA, 1996. Tchr. Tahoma Sch. Dist., Maple Valley, Wash., 1996—; chair music dept. Tahoma H.S., 1999—. Music dir. Faith Luth. Ch., Redmond, Wash., 1996—. Composer: (choral piece) Snow, 2001 (Editor's Choice award), O Sacrum Convivium, 1998. Lutheran. Avocations: reading, singing.

RIGGS, LEW, foundation executive; b. Indpls., Apr. 1, 1937; s. Frank Lloyd Riggs and Marie Loretta (Shaner) Ellis; m. Christine Marie Stiemke, Dec. 2, 2000. BS in Bus. Adminstrn., U. Ariz., 1961, EdD, 1976; MBA, George Washington U., 1964. Mktg. adminstr. TRW Systems, L.A., 1964-67; assn. exec. Electric League Ariz., Phoenix, 1967-68; pub. affairs adminstr. Ariz. Regional Med. program Coll. of Medicine, U. Ariz., Tucson, 1968-73; dir. community affairs Tucson Med. Ctr., 1973-82; dir. pub. rels. Good Samaritan Med. Ctr., Phoenix, 1982-85; pres. The Lew Riggs Co., 1985-88; chief exec. officer Tucson Osteo. Med. Found., Tucson, 1988—. Adj. prof. U. Ariz. Coll. Edn., Tucson, mem. internat. adv. bd., 1996-99, pres., 2000—; cons. to hosps. and physicians in group practice nationally; presenter in field. Editor: Public Relations Handbook, 1982; co-author booklets; contbr. articles to profl. jours. Chmn. pub. rels. Nat. Arthritis Found., Atlanta, 1985-87; participant Ariz. Strategic Planning and Econ. Devel., 1991-92. Lt. col. USAFR, 1987. Recipient IABC gold quill award, Silver Anvil award Pub. Rels. Soc. Am., Golden Mike award Am. Legion Aux., MacEachern citation Acad. Hosp. Pub. Rels., Pres.'s citation Pub. Rels. Soc. Mem. Pub. Rels. Soc. Am. (trustee 1999—), Nat. Assn. Osteo. Founds. (pres. 1991-93), Student Osteo. Med. Assn. (found. bd. dirs. 1990—), Soc. Assn. Execs. (bd. dirs. 1995—), Rotary. Republican. Presbyterian. Home: 4566 E Camino De Oro Tucson AZ 85718-4475 Office: Tucson Osteo Med Found 4280 N Campbell Ave Ste 200 Tucson AZ 85718-6594 E-mail: lriggs@tomf.org.

RIGGS, LORRIN ANDREWS, psychologist, educator; b. Harput, Turkey, June 11, 1912; parents Am. citizens; s. Ernest Wilson and Alice (Shepard) R.; m. Doris Robinson, 1937 (dec.); children: Douglas Rikert, Dwight Alan; m. Caroline Cressman, 1994. AB, Dartmouth Coll., 1933; MA, Clark U., 1934, PhD, 1936. NRC fellow biol. scis. U. Pa., 1936-37; instr. U. Vt., 1937-38, 39-41; with Brown U., 1938-39, 41—, from asst. to assoc. prof., 1938-51, prof., 1951—, L. Herbert Ballou prof., 1960-68, E.J. Marston Univ. prof., 1968-77, prof. emeritus, 1977—; Guggenheim fellow U. Cambridge, 1971-72. Author sci. articles on vision, physiol. psychology. Recipient Kenneth Craik award Cambridge U., 1979, Prentice medal Am. Acad. Optometry, 1973 Mem. AAAS (chmn., v.p. sect. 1 1964), APA (div. pres. 1962-63, Disting. Sci. Contn. award 1974), Eastern Psychol. Assn. (pres. 1975-76), Optical Soc. Am. (Tillyer medal 1969, Ives medal 1982), Nat. Acad. Scis., Am. Physiol. Soc., Internat. Brain Rsch. Orgn., Soc. for Neurosci., Soc. Exptl. Psychologists (Howard Crosby Warren medal 1957), Assn. Rsch. in Vision and Ophthalmology (pres. 1977, Friedenwald award 1966), Am. Acad. Arts and Scis., Am. Psychol. Soc. (William James fellow 1989), Sigma Xi (chpt. pres. 1962-64). Home: Kendal at Hanover # 104 80 Lyme Rd Hanover NH 03755-1225 E-mail: clriggs@bigplanet.com.

RIGGS, M. DAVID, lawyer, rancher; b. Nov. 29, 1937; s. James Ray and Thelma Beatrice (Fisher) R.; m. Dora Arleen Hoppes, Dec. 31, 1959; children: Lisa René, Michael Eric, Jennifer Lee, Andrea Lynn, Aaron David. BA, Phillips U., Enid, Okla., 1959; MA, Okla. U., 1962; JD, Tulsa U., 1968. Bar: Okla. 1969, U.S. Dist. Ct. (no., we. and ea. dists.) Okla. Mem. Okla. Ho. of Reps., Oklahoma City, 197-84, Okla. Senate, Oklahoma City, 1985—88; founder, shareholder Riggs, Abney, Neal, Turpen, Orbison and Lewis, Tulsa, Oklahoma City, Muskogee, Denver, 1972—. Democrat. Avocation: farming/ranching. Home: HC 67 Box 798 Skiatook OK 74070-9140 Office: Riggs Abney 502 W 6th St Tulsa OK 74119-1016

RIGGS, MICHAEL DAVID, writer, editor; b. Frankfort, Ky., Apr. 30, 1951; s. Homer David and Helen Marion (Webber) R.; m. Elizabeth Susan Borman, Apr. 24, 1983; children: David B., William B. AB, Washington U., 1973. Chief trader Thomte & Co., Boston, 1975-77; tech. writer Saddlebrook Corp., Cambridge, Mass., 1977-79; assoc. editor Mini-Micro Systems Mag., Boston, 1979-80; editor High Fidelity Mag., N.Y.C., 1980-89; exec. editor Stereo Review Mag., 1989-95; editor-in-chief Audio Mag., 1995-2000; ind. technology writer, editor, cons. Westfield, N.J., 2000—. Editor: Sound & Vision Mag., AOL edit., 2002—; author: Understanding Audio and Video, 1989. Mem. Audio Engring. Soc., Boston Audio Soc. E-mail: michael@riggsnet.com.

RIGGS, R. WILLIAM, state supreme court judge; Grad., Portland State U., 1961; JD, U. Oreg., 1968. Atty. Willner Bennett & Leonard, 1968—78; judge circuit ct. 4th Jud. Dist., 1978—88; judge Oreg. Ct. of Appeals, 1988—98, Oreg. Supreme Ct., 1998—. Active mem. Cmty. Law Project; founder Integra Corp. Capt. USNR. Office: Supreme Ct Bldg 1163 State St Salem OR 97310-0260 E-mail: r.william.riggs@ojd.state.or.us.

RIGGS, ROBERT DALE, plant pathology and nematology educator, researcher; b. Pocahontas, Ark., June 15, 1932; s. Rosa MacDowell and Grace (Million) R.; m. Jennie Lee Willis, June 6, 1954; children: Rebecca Dawn, Deborah Lee, Robert Dale Jr., James Michael. BS in Agr., U. Ark., 1954, MS in Plant Pathology, 1956; PhD in Plant Pathology, N.C. State U., 1958. Grad. asst. U. Ark., Fayetteville, 1954-55, asst. prof., 1958-62, assoc. prof., 1962-68, prof., 1968-92, univ. prof., 1992—; grad. asst. N.C. State U., Raleigh, 1955-58. Chair of faculty Coll. Agrl., Food and Life Scis., 1999. Editor: Nematology in the Southern United States, 1982; co-editor: Biology and Management of the Soybean Cyst Nematode, 1992; contbr. articles to profl. jours.; inventor fungal control of nematodes. Recipient John W. White award Coll. Agr. and Home Econs., 1989, Honor award for Rsch. in Environ. Protection USDA, 1994, Outstanding Rschr. award Ark. Agrl. Extension Specialists, 2000, Spitze Land Grant Univ. Faculty award, 2001, Meritorious Svc. award United Soybean Bd., 2002. Fellow Soc. of Nematologists (v.p. 1991-92, pres.-elect 1992-93, pres. 1993-94, editor-in-chief jour. 1987-90), Am. Phytopath. Soc. (Outstanding plant pathologist in so. region 1994); mem. So. Soybean Disease Workers (Disting. Svc. award 1987), U. Ark. Alumni Assn. (Dist. Faculty Achievement award 1993), Wash. Helm. Soc., Orgn. of Nematologists of Tropical Am., Sigma Xi, Gamma Sigma Delta. Democrat. Baptist. Home: 1840 Woolsey Ave Fayetteville AR 72703-2557 Office: U Ark 217 Plant Sci Fayetteville AR 72701 E-mail: rdriggs@mail.uark.edu.

RIGGS, RORY B. pharmaceutical executive; b. Orange, N.J., May 5, 1953; d. Thomas Jeffries and Virginia (Griggs) R. BA, Middlebury Coll.; MBA, Columbia U. Mng. dir. PaineWebber, Inc.; CEO RF&P Corp.; mng. dir. Pharma Ptnrs. LLC; pres. Biomatrix Inc., Ridgefield, N.J., 1995—. Bd. dirs. Biomatrix, Inc. 1990—; bd. mem. Fibrogen Corp., Spartan Corp., Pharma Ptnrs, LLC. Mem. Young Pres. Orgn. Office: Biomatrix Inc 65 Railroad Ave Ste 3 Ridgefield NJ 07657-2176

RIGGS, SCOTT, race car driver; Racecar driver PPC Racing. Named champion, So. Nat. Speedway; recipient 5th pl., NASCAR Craftsman Truck Series, 2001. Office: PPC Racing Team 177 Knob Hill Rd Mooresville NC 28117*

RIGGS, SONYA WOICINSKI, elementary school educator; b. Newhall, Calif., Oct. 9, 1935; d. Jack Lewis Woicinski and Mittie Mozelle (Bennett) Gillett; m. Eugene Garland Riggs, Dec. 21, 1956; children: Georgia Ann, Madeline Sue, Dana Eugene. BS in Elem. Edn., U. Tex., 1970; MEd in Reading Edn., S.W. Tex. State U., 1980. Cert. elem. tchr., Tex.; cert. reading specialist K-12. Sec. state govts., Nebr./Tex., 1955-57; piano instr. Elgin, Tex., 1961-66; tchr. 1st grade Elgin Elem. Sch., 1967-69, tchr. Music 3rd/4th grades, 1971-72, tchr. 4th grade, 1972-73; pres. El Tesoro internacionale, 1973-74; sec. region office Planned Parenthood/World Population, Austin, 1975-76; tchr. 8th-12th grades Giddings (Tex.) State Sch., 1976-78; tchr. 4th/5th grades Thorndale (Tex.) Ind. Sch. Dist., 1979-80; tchr. remedial reading Brazosport Ind. Sch. Dist., Freeport, Tex., 1980-81; tchr. 6th grade reading and chpt. I Bastrop (Tex.) Mid. Sch., 1981-94, Bastrop Intermediate, 1994-99. Developer Enrichment Ctr., Bastrop Intermediate, 1995—2000, Cedar Creek Elem. Enrichment, 2000—01; mem. 12th ann. Highlights Found. Writers Workshop at Chautauqua Instn., NY, 1996; adj. instr. reading Austin C.C., 2000—; puppy cons. Contbr. articles to Shih Tzu Reporter, 1993 French Bulldog Ann., French Bullytin, Boston Quar., Golden Retriever World; contbr. poetry to anthologies Garden of Life, 1996, Best Poems of 1996, Of Sunshine and Daydreams, 1996, A View from Afar, 1997. Mem. Elgin Band Boosters, 1970-83, sec., 1976. Mem. Assn. Tex. Profl. Educators (campus rep. 1996-97, state del. 1997, sec. 1997-98), Austin Kennel Club (bd. dirs. 1990-91, 95-97, sec. 1996-97), Am. Shih Tzu Club (edn. and rescue com. mem. south ctrl. regional hearing com.), French Bulldog Club Am. (rescue com.), Mission City Ring Stewards Assn., Internat. Soc. Poets, Tex. Writers League, Greater Austin Doberman Pinscher Club. Avocations: exhibiting dogs to Am. Kennel Club confirmation and obedience championships, writing poetry, playing piano, painting, drawing.

RIGGSBY, DUTCHIE SELLERS, education educator; b. Montgomery, Ala., Oct. 26, 1940; d. Malcolm Sellers and Marcelia Sellers Dickman; m. Ernest Duward Riggsby, Aug. 25, 1962; 1 child Lyn. BS, Troy (Ala.) State Coll., 1962, MS, 1965; postgrad., George Peabody Coll., 1963; EdD, Auburn U., 1972. Cert. tchr., Ala., Ga.; cert. libr., Ga. Tchr. Montgomery Pub. Schs., 1962-63, Troy City Schs., 1963-67; instr. Auburn (Ala.) U., 1968-69; asst. prof. Columbus (Ga.) Coll., 1972-77, assoc. prof., 1978-83, prof., 1983—; coord. Instrnl. Tech. Sch. Edn., 1996-97; program coord. Ednl. Founds., 2001—. Vis. prof. U. P.R., Rio Piedras, 1972—73; leader various workshops, 1989, 1993—; sorfware reviewer NSTA; chmn. publicity Ga. Ednl. Tech. Conf., 1997—, bd. dirs., 1998—; bridal cons. Hist. Moments, Inc., 1998—2001, v.p., 1998—2001; chair scholarship com. Ga. Ednl. Consortium, 1999—. Contbr. more than 90 articles on state, regional, nat., and internat. programs to profl. jours., 1968—. Active Internal Aerospace Edn. CAP, Maxwell AFB, 1980-90; dir. Air and Space Camp for Kids, 1990-98. Recipient STAR Tchr. award NSTA, 1968; named to Lee H.S. Hall of Fame, Montgomery, 1997. Mem. Assn. for Ednl. Comms. and Tech. (non-periodical publs. com. 1994-99, awards com. 1994-96, chair meml. awards com. 1996-99), Nat. Congress on Aviation and Space Edn. (dir. spl. promotions 1986-90), World Aerospace Edn. Orgn. (v.p. for the Ams. 1996-98, pres. for the Ams. 1998—, pres. 1999—), Ga. Assn. Instrnl. Tech. (bd. dirs. 1982-84), Phi Delta Kappa (pres. Chattahochee Valley chpt. 1986-87, Svc. award 1989, Svc. Key award 1993). Baptist. Avocations: photography, mining for gemstones. Office: Columbus State U Coll Edn 4225 University Ave Columbus GA 31907-5679 E-mail: riggsby_dutchie@colstate.edu.

RIGGSBY, ERNEST DUWARD, science educator, educational development executive; b. Nashville, June 12, 1925; s. James Thomas and Anna Pearl (Turner) R.; m. Dutchie Sellers, Aug. 25, 1964; 1 child, Lyn-Dee. BS, Tenn. Polytech. Inst., 1948; BA, George Peabody Coll. Tchrs., 1952, BA, 1953, MA, 1956, EdS, 1961, EdD, 1964. Vis. grad. prof. U. P.R., Rio Piedras, George Peabody Coll., 1963-64; prof. Auburn (Ala.) U., Troy (Ala.) State U., Columbus (Ga.) Coll.; pres. Ednl. Developers, Inc., Columbus, Ga. Vis. grad. prof. George Peabody Coll., 1963-64; vis. lectr. Fla. Inst. Tech., summers 1967-77. Contbr. articles to profl. jours. Col., USAF, 1944-85. Named to Aerospace Crown Cir., 1984; elected to Aerospace Edn. Hall of Fame, 1982. Fellow AAAS; mem. Nat. Sci. Tchrs. Assn., World Aerospace Edn. Assn. (v.p. for the Ams.). Office: Columbus State U Columbus GA 31907-5645

RIGHTER, ANNE ROBINSON, clinical social worker, psychotherapist; b. N.Y.C., July 5, 1939; d. Hamilton and Elizabeth Parker (Case) Robinson; m. James Volney Righter, June 22, 1962; children: Eliot Day Righter Ramos, Mark Hamilton Righter. BA in Sociology summa cum laude, U. New Haven, 1974; M of Social Work, U. Conn., 1976; postgrad., Yale U., 1976-77. Lic. ind. clin. social worker, Mass.; cert. Acad. of Cert. Social Workers. Clin. instr. social work Child Psychiatry Unit-Yale U., New Haven, 1977-80; staff social worker Yale Univ. Child Study Ctr.; clin. instr., field work supr. Simmons Sch. of Social Work, Boston, 1981-82; clin. social worker, chief court clinics Mass. Mental Health Ctr., 1981-82; clin. social worker Ctr. for Counseling Family Svc. Assn., 1982-84; chief social worker Ctr. for Therapy, Boston Children's Svc., 1983-86; pvt. practice, 1982-95. Bd. dirs., officer Planned Parenthood Greater New Haven, 1967-75, Affiliated Children's Svcs., Brookline-Lexington, Mass., 1981-85, Island Health Project, Inc., Fishers Island, N.Y., 1991—, Trinity Hospice, Brookline, Mass., 1998—, Rutland Corner House, Inc., Brookline, 1982-96, pres. 1984-91; bd. dirs. Health Care Dimensions, 1996—. Vestry mem. St. Johns Ch., Fishers Island, 1990—; bd. visitors Walnut Hill Sch. Performing Arts, Natick, Mass., 1995—; bd. overseers New Eng. Conservatory, Boston, 1995—. Mem. Nat. Assn. Social Workers, Nat. Registry Health Care Providers in Clin. Social Work, Mass. Acad. Clin. Social Workers, Tuesday Club, Tavern Club. Democrat. Episcopalian. Avocations: musical theatre, singing, creative writing. Home and Office: 68 Beacon St Boston MA 02108-3422

RIGHTER, WALTER CAMERON, bishop; b. Phila., Oct. 23, 1923; s. Richard and Dorothy Mae (Bottomley) R.; m. Nancy Ruth DeGroot, Aug. 22, 1992; children: Richard, Rebecca. *Walter is a ninth generation descendent of Peter Righter, one of the earliest German settlers in the Philadelphia, Pa Area. He is also a descendent of Abraham Tunis, head of one of the original 13 families from Krefled , Germany invited by William Penn to join him in settling his colony. They settled (And Founded) Germantown. Now a part at Philadelphia. In the city there is a street named for the family. In the suburb of lower Merion two roads (Righter's Ferry and Righter Mill) are named for the family. Fellow descendents include Author, Astrologers, inventors, lawyers; veteran's scientist- a creative gene runs through all nine generations. Walter's brother, Richard, is an active architect in the Pittsburgh, Pa, Area.* BA, U. Pitts., 1948; MDiv, Berkeley Div. Sch., New Haven, 1951, DD, 1972; DCL, Iowa Wesleyan U., 1982; DD, Seabury Western Sem., 1984. Ordained priest Episcopal Ch., 1951, consecrated bishop, 1972; lay missioner St. Michael's Ch., Rector, Pa., 1947-48; priest-in-charge All Saints Ch., Aliquippa, 1951-54, St. Luke's, Georgetown, 1952-54; rector Ch. of Good Shepherd, Nashua, N.H., 1954-71; bishop Diocese of Iowa, Des Moines, 1972-89; asst. bishop Dio. of Newark, 1989-91; interim rector St. Elizabeth's, Ridgewood, N.J., 1991; assisting bishop Diocese of Mass., 2000—. Mem. exec. coun. Protestant Episcopal Ch. U.S.A., 1979-85; spl. adv. NH Cursillo, 1994-96. *Walter is a retired Episcopal Bishop with more than 50 years as an ordained person. During that time he has stood quietly but firmly, for justice for all persons. As Bishop he was a leader in the move to ordain women, in liturgical reform and in inclusively, for gay and lesbian persons. He pioneered the use of marketing research and techniques preparatory to using advertising to produce church growth. Six years after his retirement he became the second Bishop in the History of the Episcopal Church to be charged with heresy. He had ordained a partnered gay man. The case was dismissed after the church court determined no "core" Doctrine or Christian teaching, had been violated.* Author: A Pilgrim's Way, 1998. Mem. N.H. com. White House Conf. on Youth, 1962, Regional Crime Commn., Hillsboro County, N.H., 1969-71; trustee Nashua Libr., 1968-71, Seabury Western Sem., 1986-89; founding trustee The Morris Fund, Des Moines; planning com. Town of Alstead, N.H., 1993-96. Fellow Coll. Preachers, Washington Cathedral. E-mail: WCRighter@aol.com.

RIGHTS, GRAHAM HENRY, retired minister; b. Winston-Salem, N.C., Jan. 14, 1935; s. Douglas LeTell and Cecil Leona (Burton) R.; m. Sybil Critz Strupe, Sept. 7, 1963; children: Susan Elizabeth, John Graham. BA, U. N.C., 1956; BD, Yale U., 1959; postgrad., Moravian Theol. Sem., 1959-60, DHL (hon.), 1997; postgrad., U. Edinburgh, Scotland, 1965-66; DD (hon.), Wofford Coll., 1989. Ordained to ministry Moravian Ch., 1960. Pastor Union Ch., Managua, Nicaragua, 1960-63, Managua Moravian Ch., 1960-65, Mayodan (N.C.) Moravian Ch., 1966-72, Messiah Moravian Ch., Winston-Salem, 1972-81; exec. dir. Bd. World Mission Moravian Ch., Bethlehem, Pa., 1981-83, pres. exec. bd. so. province Winston-Salem, 1983-95, pres. exec. bd. world-wide, 1991-94; pastor First Moravian Ch., Greensboro, N.C., 1995-2000; ret. Bd. dirs. Crisis Control Ministry, Forsyth County, 1976—, Ecumenical Inst., 1995—, Moravian Ch. Found., 1988—, Moravian Music Found., 1996—, Comenius Comm., Inc., 1998—. Mem. N.C. Soc. Mayflower Descendants (elder 2000—). Home: 553 Steeple View Ct Winston Salem NC 27101-5850

RIGNEY, JANE, copy editor, writer; b. Flushing, N.Y., Dec. 4, 1948; d. William John and Janet (Teesink) R. BA in English, U. Ill., 1972. Dance critic, night copy desk chief N.Y. Tribune, N.Y.C., 1983-85; copy editor TIME Mag., 1988—. Pub. rels. cons. The Juilliard Sch., N.Y.C., 1977-82; freelance writer Dance Mag., 1982—, Am. Banker, 1988-95, freelance copy editor, 1988-95, N.Y. Daily News, N.Y.C., 1984-90; freelance editor, writer Am. Health, N.Y.C., 1990-93. Editor: Dance Horizons, 1978-85. Freedom writer Amnesty Internat., N.Y.C., 1980—; vol. spl. projects Sch. Am. Ballet, N.Y.C., 1988—. Mem.: NY Press Club, Editl. Freelancers Assn., The Newspaper Guild, Women in Comm., U. Ill. Alumni Club NY. Democrat. Roman Catholic. Avocations: swimming, crocheting, reading, traveling, theater. Office: TIME Mag Time & Life Bldg 1271 Ave of Americas New York NY 10020 E-mail: jrigney0264@aol.com.

RIGNEY, THOMAS GREGORY, music educator, musician; b. Meadowbrook, Pa., Feb. 10, 1969; s. Thomas George and Mary Eileen Rigney. BA, Pa. State U., 1992; MusM in Orchestral Conducting, U. Houston, 1994. Grad. fellow U. Houston, 1992—94, grad. fellow/tchr., 1998—2001; dir. of instrumental music Bishop McDevitt H.S., Wyncote, Pa., 2001—. Asst. condr. Independence Sinfonia Chamber Orch., Wyncote, 1995—98, Old York Rd. Symphony Orch., Abington, Pa., 1996—98; guest condr./music dir. Bux-Mont Chamber Orch., Ambler, Pa., 2000—; asst. condr. Old York Rd. Symphony Orch., Abington, 2001—. Recipient Instrumental Music scholarship, Pa. State U. Sch. of Music, 1987—92, Moores Sch. of Music, U. Houston, 1992—94, Moores Sch. of Music, U. Houston, 1998—2001. Mem.: Pa. Music Educators Assn., Phi Mu Alpha Sinfonia, Omicron Delta Kappa, Phi Sigma Theta. Roman Catholic. Avocations: tennis, coins, film history, cooking, antiques. Home: 515 Highland Ave Jenkintown PA 19046-2249 Personal E-mail: condbass@hotmail.com.

RIGO, SANDRA LUISA, literature educator; b. Bklyn., Jan. 31, 1962; d. Felipé Rigo, Verna Angelica (Mongerard) Rigo; m. Tyrone Cecil Joseph, Jan. 30, 1998; children: Tyrone Christen Adam Joseph, Keenan David Joseph. BA magna cum laude, L.I. U., 1989, MA mmagna cum laudeagna cum laude, 1991. Prof. English L.I. U., Bklyn., 1989—96, Mercy Coll., Bklyn., 1997—98; tchr. English N.Y.C. Bd. Edn., 1998—. Author: Voices In a Dream, 1991, Exposure, 2002, The Mango Tree, 2002. Democrat. Avocations: writing, travel, creating gift baskets. Home: 387 Marlborough Rd Brooklyn NY 11226

RIGOLOSI, ELAINE LA MONICA, lawyer, educator, consultant; b. Astoria, N.Y., Oct. 12, 1944; d. Richard Anthony La Monica and Caroline La Monica; m. Robert Salvatore Rigolosi, June 15, 1997. BS, Columbia Union Coll., Takoma Park, Md., 1964; MN, U. Fla., 1967; EdD, U. Mass., 1975; JD, Benjamin N. Cardozo Sch. Law, N.Y.C., 1993. Bar: N.J. 1994, N.Y. 1994, D.C. 1995; RN, N.Y. Chair dept. nursing edn. Tchrs. Coll., Columbia U., N.Y.C., 1988-91, prof. nursing edn., 1982-96, acting chair dept. nursing edn., 1994-96, prof. dept. orgn. and leadership, 1996—, dir. Inst. Rsch. in Nursing, 1981—; health care mgmt. cons. in pvt. practice, 1974—. Bd. dirs. Hooper Holmes, Inc., Basking Ridge, N.J., 1989—; cons. Delaware Valley Transplant Program, Phila., 1998, U. Tenn. Coll. Pharmacy, Memphis, 1995-98. Author: The Nursing Process: A Humanistic Approach, 1979 (Am. Jour. Nursing Book of Yr. 1979), Management in Health Care, 1994. Dept. HHS grantee, 1977-80, 80-83. Fellow Am. Acad. Nursing; mem. ABA, Assn. Bar City N.Y. (com. on health law 1994-97), Am. Health Lawyers Assn., Am. Assn. Nurse Attys., Am. Coll. Legal Medicine, Sigma Theta Tau. Avocations: tennis, skiing, needlepoint, interior design. Home: 158 Summit Dr Paramus NJ 07652-1312 Office: Tchrs Coll Columbia U 525 W 120th St New York NY 10027-6625

RIGOR, BRADLEY GLENN, lawyer; b. Cheyenne Wells, Colo., Aug. 9, 1955; s. Glenn E. and Lelia (Teed) R.; m. Twyla G. Helweg, Sept. 4, 1983; children: Camille, Brent, Tiffany, Lauren. BS in Mktg., Ft. Hays State U., 1977; JD, Washburn U., 1980. Bar: Kans. 1980, U.S. Dist. Kans., 1980, U.S. Tax Ct. 1981, U.S. Ct. Appeals (10th cir.) 1982, U.S. Supreme Ct. 1986, Colo. 1990, Tex. 1991, U.S. Dist. Ct. Colo. 1991, Mo. 1993, Fla. 1998; cert. trust and fin. advisor Inst. Cert. Bankers; cert. fin. planner. Ptnr. Zuspann & Rigor, Goodland, Kans., 1980-82; city atty., 1981-82; asst. county atty. Wallace County, Sharon Springs, Kans., 1982-84, county atty., 1984; city atty., 1983-84; judge Mcpl. Ct., Goodland, 1988-93; ptnr. Fairbanks, Rigor & Irvin, P.A., 1982-93; v.p., mgr. personal trusts Merc. Bank, St. Joseph, Mo., 1993-96; sr. v.p., mgr., personal trust adminstr. SunTrust Bank, Naples, Fla., 1996-98; ptnr. Bond Schoeneck & King P.A., 1998—. Mem. Estate Planning Coun., Naples. Mem. Kans. Bar Assn., Tex. Bar Assn., Mo. Bar Assn., Colo. Bar Assn., Fla. Bar Assn., Collier County Bar Assn. (trust and estates sect.). Republican. Baptist. Office: Ste 250 4001 Tamiami Trl N Naples FL 34103-3555 E-mail: rigorb@bsk.com.

RIGOUTSOS, ISIDORE, computer scientist; b. Athens, Greece, Feb. 6, 1963; came to U.S., 1985; s. Ioannis and Fragkiska Rigoutsos. BS magna cum laude, Nat. U. Athens, 1984; MS, U. Rochester, 1987, NYU, 1989, PhD, 1992. Computational biology rschr. IBM Corp., Yorktown Heights, N.Y., 1992—. Vis. lectr. dept. chem. engring. MIT, 2000, 2001, 2002; adj. prof. dept. computer sci. Courant Inst. Math. Scis., NYU, 2000. Patentee in field. Fellow Fulbright Found., 1985-90. Mem. AAAS, IEEE, IEEE Computer Soc., Internat. Soc. for Computational Biology. Roman Catholic. Avocation: photography, fishing, drawing. Office: IBM TJW Rsch Ctr PO Box 218 Yorktown Heights NY 10598-0218

RIGSBEE, DAVID E. poet, educator; b. Durham, N.C., Apr. 1, 1949; s. Earl Hickman and Geneva (Odom) R.; m. Doris Francine Low, Oct. 7, 1978 (div. July 1984); m. Jill Bullitt, July 28, 1995; 1 child, Makaiya. BA, U. N.C., Chapel Hill, 1971; MA, Johns Hopkins U., 1972, Hollins Coll., 1991; PhD, U. Va., 1995. English instr. Hamilton Coll., Clinton, N.Y., 1972-76, U. N.C., Greensboro, 1978-82, La. State U., Baton Rouge, 1982-86, Va. Tech., Blacksburg, 1987-92; prof. English, chair dept. langs. and lit. Mount Olive (N.C.) Coll., 1995—. Vis. assoc. prof. St. Andrews Coll., Laurinburg, N.C., 1986-87; vis. prof., dir. creative writing Hamilton Coll., Clinton, N.Y., 1992-95; dir. St. Andrews Press, Laurinburg, 1986-87; cons. Ardis Pubs., Ann Arbor, Mich., 1974-77. Author: (poetry) A Skeptic's Notebook: Longer Poems, 1997, The Dissolving Island, 1999, Scenes on an Obelisk, 2000, David Rigsbee's Greatest Hits: 1975-2000; co-editor: Invited Guest: An Anthology of Twentieth Century Southern Poetry, 2001; (criticism) Styles of Ruin: Joseph Brodsky and the Postmodernist Elegy, 1999, (nonfiction) Trailers, 1996. Fellow NEH, 1999, creative Writing fellow NEA, 1985, Artist's fellow Va. Commn. on the Arts, 1993; Am. Acad. in Rome vis. fellow, 1999; recipient prize Acad. Am. Poets, 1992, Vachel Lindsey Poetry prize Willow Springs Lit. mag., 1994. Mem. MLA, Poetry Soc. Am. Democrat. Episcopalian. Avocations: opera, art, photography. Home: 315 Oakwood Ave Raleigh NC 27601-1062 Office: Mount Olive Coll 634 Henderson St Mount Olive NC 28365-1263

RIGSBEE, STEPHEN REESE, risk management executive; b. Durham, N.C., Mar. 11, 1956; s. William Alton and Shirley (Morgan) R.; m. Lisa Lou Sloan, Dec. 10, 1992; 1 child, Henry Morgan. AB, Duke U., 1978; AM in Econs., U. Chgo., 1982, MBA, 1984. With Allstate Life Ins. Co., Northbrook, Ill., 1978-81; sr. v.p., dir. rsch. GNP Fin., Chgo., 1984-87; pres. Quantitative Risk Mgmt. Group, 1987—. Co-author: Handbook of Mortgage Backed Securities, 1988, Asset/Liability Management, 1991, 96; contbr. articles to profl. jours. Mem. Chgo. Coun. on Fgn. Rels. Mem. Am. Fin. Assn., Beta Gamma Sigma. Republican. Home: 2314 N Lincoln Park W Fl 7 Chicago IL 60614-3455 Office: Quantitative Risk Mgmt Group 181 W Madison St Fl 49 Chicago IL 60602-4510

RIGSBY, LINDA FLORY, lawyer; b. Topeka, Dec. 16, 1946; d. Alden E. and Lolita M. Flory; m. Michael L. Rigsby, Aug. 14, 1963; children: Michael L. Jr., Elisabeth A. MusB, Va. Commonwealth U., 1969; JD, U. Richmond, 1981. Bar: Va. 1981, D.C. 1988. Assoc. McGuire, Woods, Battle & Boothe, Richmond, Va., 1981-85; dep. gen. counsel and corp. sec. Crestar Fin. Corp.,

1985-99, gen. counsel, 1999-2000; mng. atty. Sun Trust Banks Inc., 2000—. Recipient Disting. Svc. award U. Richmond, 1987; named Vol. of Yr. U. Richmond, 1986, Woman of Achievement, Met. Richmond Women's Bar, 1995. Mem. Va. Bar Assn. (exec. com. 1993-96), Richmond Bar Assn. (bd. dirs. 1992-95), Va. Bankers Assn. (chair legal affairs 1992-95), U. Richmond Estate Planning Coun. (chmn. 1990-92). Roman Catholic. Avocations: music, gardening. Home: 163 W Square Pl Richmond VA 23233-6157 Office: SunTrust Bank 919 E Main St Richmond VA 23219-4625

RIGTRUP, KENNETH, state judge, arbitrator, mediator; b. Burley, Idaho, Mar. 13, 1936; s. Robert Peter and Bessie Viola (Price) R.; m. Susanne Joan Remund, May 15, 1964; children: Mark Robert, Michael James, Scott Kenneth, Melissa Ann, Jennifer Marie. BS in Acctg., U. Utah, 1960, JD, 1962. Bar: Utah 1962; U.S. Dist. Ct. Utah, 1962. Clk. Utah Supreme Ct., Salt Lake City, 1962; ptnr. Rigtrup & Hadley, 1962-68; pvt. practice, 1968-72; admin. law judge Indsl. Commn., 1972-77; mem. Pub. Svc. Commn., 1977-80; judge 3d Dist. Ct., 1980-97; active sr. judge Utah Cts., 1997—. Chmn. Bd. Sr. Judges, 1998-99; mem. adv. com. on rules of juvenile procedure Utah Supreme Ct., Salt Lake City, 1993-95. Copy and rsch. editor Utah Law Rev., 1961-62. Chmn. Utah White House Conf. on Handicapped Individuals, Salt Lake City, 1976—77; mem. Citizens Evaluation and Selection Com. to Rev. Pvt. Non-profit Orgn. Applications for Urban Mass Transit Authority Grants, 1975—77; dir., chair Utah Assistive Tech. Found., 1991—; mem. Utah Gov.'s Com. on Employment of Handicapped, 1976—80, vice chmn. and acting chmn., 1977—80. Recipient Disting. Svc. award Utah Rehab. Counseling Assn., Salt Lake City, 1976-77; Nat. Citation award Nat. Rehab. counseling Assn., 1977; Maurice Warshaw Golden Key award, Utah Gov.'s Com. on Employment of Handicapped, 1975. Mem. ABA, ATLA, Utah Bar Assn. (exec. com. family sect. 1980-90, lawyers helping lawyers com., alt. dispute resolution com.), Nat. Ass. Regulatory Utility Commns. (water com. 1977-78, gas com. 1978-80), Am. Judicature Soc., Utah Coun. on Conflicts Resolution. Republican. Mem. Lds Ch. Home: 1961 Millbrook Rd Salt Lake City UT 84106-3853 Office: Arbitration/Mediation Svcs 3098 Highland Dr Ste 399 Salt Lake City UT 84106-6004

RIHANI, SARMAD ALBERT (SAM RIHANI), civil engineer; b. Beirut, Lebanon, Feb. 22, 1954; s. John Albert and Loreen Salim (Schoucair) R.; m. Ina Lee Hand, July 12, 1975; children: Cedar, Paul, Michael. BSCE, Oreg. State U., 1977. Registered profl. engr., D.C., Va., Mo., Oreg., Calif. Designer Butler Mfg. Co., Kansas City, Mo., 1977-79; applications analyst United Computing Systems, Overland Park, Kans., 1979-80; mgmt. info. systems supr. Zamil Steel Bldgs. Co., Saudi Arabia, 1980-81, sr. structural engr. Saudi Arabia, 1981-82, design mgr. Saudi Arabia, 1982-84, engring. mgr. Saudi Arabia, 1984-87, bldg. products mgr. Saudi Arabia, 1987-89; gen. mgr. multistory bldg. system Butler Mfg. Co., Kansas City, Mo., 1989-91; v.p. project mgmt. and engring. Beaman Corp., Greensboro, N.C., 1991-92, bd. dirs.; divsn. svc. mgr. Varco-Pruden Bldgs., Little Rock, 1992-94; mng. dir. Options For Sr. America Corp., Rockville, Md., 1994—. Bd. dirs. Engrs. Coun., Saudi Arabia, 1988-89. Am. Field Svc. scholar, 1970. Mem. ASCE (pres. Saudi Arabia 1988, bd. dirs. 1989, appreciation award 1989), Nat. Soc. Profl. Engrs., Am. Lebanese League (bd. dirs. 1990), Tau Beta Pi. Republican. Roman Catholic. Avocations: personal computers, reading, tennis, skiing.

RIIKONEN, CHARLENE BOOTHE, international health administrator; b. Washington, June 10, 1942; d. John Edward and Frances Elizabeth (Jett) Boothe; m. Esko Riikonen, 1989; children: Cynthia Lee, Anthony John, Jennifer Elizabeth. AA with high honors, Howard C.C., 1977; BA magna cum laude, U. Md., 1979. Asst. dir. univ. rels., alumni dir. U. Md., Catonsville, 1977-81, assoc. dir. univ. rels. and devel. College Park, 1982-83; sr. devel. officer Internat. Ctr. Diarrhoeal Disease Rsch., Dhaka, Bangladesh, 1984-86; exec. v.p. Child Health Found. (formerly Internat. Child Health Found.), Columbia, Md., 1985-97; pres. Cera Products, LL., Jessup, 1997—, mng. dir., CEO. Cons. to organize symposium oral rehydration therapy Nat. Coun. Internat. Health, Washington, 1987; organizer internat. symposium on food-based oral rehydration therapy Aga Khan U., Pakistan, 1989; organizer consensus conf. cereal-based oral rehydration therapy, Columbia, Md., 1993. Author: (tng. manual) Prevention and Treatment of Childhood Diarrhea with Oral Rehydration Therapy, Nutrition and Breastfeeding, 1992; editor procs. Oral Rehydration Therapy Symposia, 1987, 89, 93, 94; editor Child Health News, 1993—; contbr. articles to profl. jours. Pub. affairs chmn. United Way, Washington Capital Area, Prince Georges County, 1981-83; v.p. Waterfowl Assn.; pres. Windstream Assn., 1988-89; v.p. Waterfowl Terrace Assn., 1994—; mem. pub. rels. com. Md., Del. Cable TV Assn., Balt., 1981-83. Mem. APHA (internat. maternal-child health com.), AAUW, Nat. Coun. Internat. Health Assn., U. Md. Balt. County Alumni Assn. (bd. dirs. 1979-83), Women's Internat. Pub. Health Network. Clubs: Columbia Assn. Athletic (Md.) (capt. women's traveling racquetball team 1979-83). Democrat. Avocations: racquetball, windsurfing, skiing, oil painting. Fax: 410-792-8671. E-mail: criikonen@ceralyte.com.

RIIPI, LINDA RUTH, biology educator; b. Hancock, Mich., June 19, 1952; d. Jacob and Linda Edna Maria (Lindgren) Karinen; m. Matthew William Riipi, Oct. 4, 1975; 1 child, Erin Elizabeth. BS in Med. Technology with honors, Mich. State U., 1974; MA in Biology, No. Mich. U., 1983; PhD in Biol. Scis., Mich. Technol. U., 1991. Cert. clin. lab. scientist. Med. technologist William Beaumont Hosp., Royal Oak, Mich., 1975; med. technologist, supr. E.W. Sparrow Hosp., Lansing, 1976-78; med. technologist Marquette (Mich.) Gen. Hosp., 1979; instr. No. Mich. U., Marquette, 1979-83, asst. prof. biology, 1983-88, assoc. prof., 1988-92, prof., 1992—. Coord. clin. edn. No. Mich. U., Marquette, 1995—; bd. dirs. Med. Tech. Internship Matching Program, East Lansing, Mich., 1985-87. Doctoral fellow Mich. Technol. U., Houghton, 1989-91; No. Mich. U. rsch. grantee, 1992; recipient Merit award No. Mich. U., 1985, 86, 92, Disting. Faculty award Mich. Assn. Governing Bds., 1993. Mem. AAAS, AAUP (No. Mich. U. exec. com. 1999—), Am. Soc. Clin. Pathology (cert.), Am. Soc. Microbiology, Am. Soc. Med. Technologists (coord 1980-81, pres.-elect 1983-84, pres. 1984-85, past pres. 1985-86), Am. Soc. for Clin. Lab Sci. (bd. dirs. 1985-89, 92-93, 95-96), Mich. Soc. for Clin. Lab. Scis. (bd. dirs. 1995—), Nat. Accrediting Agy. Clin. Lab. Scis. (program reviewer 1996—), Marquette Pub. Schs. Edn. Found. (bd. dirs. 1996—), Phi Kappa Phi, Beta Beta Beta, Sigma Xi. Lutheran. Avocations: piano, golf, cross-country skiing. Office: No Mich U Coll Nursing and Allied Health Scis Marquette MI 49855 E-mail: lriipi@nmu.edu.

RIKER, WALTER F., JR. pharmacologist, physician; b. N.Y.C., Mar. 8, 1916; s. Walter F. and Eleanore Louise (Scafard) R.; m. Virginia Helene Jaeger, Nov. 28, 1941; children: Donald K., Walter F., Wayne S. BS, Columbia U., 1939; MD, Cornell U., 1943; D.Sc. (hon.), Med. Coll. Ohio, 1980. Instr. pharmacology Cornell U. Med. Coll., N.Y.C., 1944-47, instr. medicine, 1945-46, asst. prof. pharmacology, 1947-50, assoc. prof., 1950-56, prof., chmn. dept. pharmacology, 1956-83, Revlon chair pharmacology and toxicology, 1980-83, prof. emeritus, 1983—. Mem. study sect. NIH, 1956-63, 65-68; mem. Nat. Inst. Gen. Med. Scis. Council., 1963-64, Nat. Inst. Environ. Health Scis. Council, 1971-75, Pres.'s Sci. Adv. Com. on Toxicology, 1964-65; vis. prof. pharmacology U. Kans. Med. Coll., 1953; mem. Unitarian Service Med. Exchange Program, Japan, 1956; mem. sci. adv. com. Pharm. Mfrs.'s Assn. Found., 1966-87; adj. mem. Roche Inst. Molecular Biology, 1972-80; med. advisor on drugs Nat. Football League, 1973-84; adv. com. Irma T. Hirschl Found., N.Y.C., 1973—; bd. sci. advisors Sterling Drug, 1973-76; dir. Richardson-Vicks Inc., 1979-85. Recipient Teaching award Cornell U. Med. Coll., 1968, 78, citation Pharm. Mfrs.'s Assn. Found., 1972, 87, Award of Distinction Cornell U. Med. Coll. Alumni Assn., 1981, Maurice R. Greenberg Svc. award N.Y. Hosp./Cornell U. Med. Ctr., 1990; Sterling Drug vis. professorship established in honor at Cornell U. Med. Coll., 1979; named Hon. Fellow, Am. Coll. Clin. Pharmacology, 1987. Fellow AAAS, N.Y. Acad. Medicine, Harvey Soc.; mem. Am. Soc. Pharmacology and Exptl. Therapeutics (chmn. membership com. 1956-59, councillor 1959-62, bd. publs. trustees 1962-64, chmn. bd. publs. trustees 1964-70, chmn. com. ednl. and profl. affairs 1972-74, John Jacob Abel award 1951, Publs. citation 1970, Torald Sollman award 1986, Oscar B. Hunter award 1990), Japanese Pharmacology Soc., Am. Soc. Clin. Pharmacology and Therapeutics, N.Y. Acad. Scis., Sigma Xi, Alpha Omega Alpha.

RIKER, WILLIAM KAY, pharmacologist, educator; b. N.Y.C., Aug. 31, 1925; s. Walter Franklin and Eleanore Louise (Scafard) R.; m. Carmela Louise DePamphilis, Dec. 21, 1947 (dec. 1981); children: Eleanor Louise, Gainor, Victoria; m. Leena Mela, Aug. 13, 1983. BA, Columbia U., 1949; MD, Cornell U., 1953. Intern 2d Cornell med. div., Bellevue Hosp., 1953-54; practice medicine, specializing in pharmacology Phila., 1954-69, Portland, Oreg., 1969—. Instr., asst. prof. dept. pharmacology U. Pa. Sch. Medicine, 1954-61; spl. fellow dept. physiology U. Utah Sch. Medicine, 1961-64; assoc. prof., prof., chmn. dept. pharmacology Woman's Med. Coll., Phila., 1964-69; prof., chmn. dept. pharmacology U. Oreg. Sch. Medicine, U. Oreg. Health Scis. Center, 1969-91, prof., 1991-98, prof. emeritus, 1998—, asst. dean. for admissions, 1986-89; mem. neurol. disorders program project com. NIH, 1975-79. Editor: Jour. Pharmacology and Exptl. Therapeutics, 1969-72; contbr. articles to biomed. jours. Served with USNR, 1943-46. Recipient Christian R. and Mary F. Lindback Found. award for disting. teaching, 1968; Pa. Plan scholar, 1957-61; Nat. Inst. Neurol. Diseases and Blindness spl. fellow, 1961-64; USPHS-NIH research grantee, 1958-83 Mem. Am. Soc. Pharmacology and Exptl. Therapeutics (sec.-treas. 1978-81, pres. 1985-86), Western Pharmacol. Soc. (pres. 1976), Japanese Pharmacol. Soc., Assn. Med. Sch. Pharmacologists (sec. 1976-78), Epilepsy Assn. Am., Pharm. Mfrs. Assn. Found. (chmn. pharmacology-morphology adv. com., sci. adv. com. 1976-92), Cosmos Club.

RIKLEEN, SANDER A. lawyer; b. N.Y.C., Jan. 2, 1953; s. Alexander Sander and Rebecca F. Rikleen; m. Lauren Stiller, May 25, 1975; children: Alex, Ilyse. BA, Clark U., 1973; JD, Boston Coll., 1976. Bar: Mass. 1977, U.S. Dist. Ct. Mass. 1977, U.S. Ct. Appeals (1st cir.) 1977, U.S. Supreme Ct. 1985, U.S. Dist. Ct. Appeals (D.C. cir.) 1985, U.S. Tax Ct. 1990, U.S. Dist. Ct. (D.C.) Dist. 1994. Assoc. Rich, May, Bilodgau & Flaherty, Boston, 1976-82, ptnr., 1983-91, Widett, Slater & Goldman, Boston, 1991-92, Hutchins, Wheeler & Dittmar, Boston, 1992—. Adj. faculty New Eng. Sch. Law, Boston, 1977-85. Bd. dirs. Temple shir Tikva, Wayland, Mass., 1987— Office: Hutchins Wheeler & Dittmar 101 Federal St Boston MA 02110-1817

RIKLI, DONALD CARL, lawyer, deceased; b. Highland, Ill., June 16, 1927; s. Carl and Gertrude Louise (Stoecklin) R.; m. Joan Tate, Oct. 10, 1953; children: Kristine, David. AB, Ill. Coll., 1951; JD, U. Ill., 1953. Bar: Ill. 1953, U.S. Dist. Ct. (so. dist.) Ill. 1961, U.S. Ct. Appeals (7th cir.) 1968, U.S. Supreme Ct. 1974. Pvt. practice law, Highland, 1953-97. Atty. City of Highland, 1956-59; lectr. in field. Author: The Illinois Probate System, 1974, 75, 77, 78; bd. editors Illinois Real Property I, 1966, 71, Lawyers World, 1970-72, Law Notes, 1981-83, The Compleat Lawyer, 1985-87; contbr. over 60 articles to profl. jours. Mem. consistory United Ch. of Christ, 1960-62, 93-95. With U.S. Army, 1945-47. Fellow Am. Coll. Trust and Estate Counsel, Ill. Bar Found., Am. Bar Found.; mem. ABA (sec. chairperson gen. practice sect. 1990-91, Ho. of Dels. 1991-93, mem. coun. gen. practice sect. 1981-93, Sole Practitioner of Yr. 1990, posthumous Donald C. Rikli Solo Lifetime Achievement award gen. practice, solo practice and small firms sect.), Ill. Bar Assn. (chmn. Bill of Rights com. 1967-68, coun. estate planning probate and trust sect. 1976-81, sec. 1980-81), Madison County Bar Assn. (pres. 1966-67), Am. Acad. Estate Planning Attys. (bd. govs. 1994-95). Address: PO Box 366 Edwardsville IL 62025-0366

RIKON, MICHAEL, lawyer; b. Bklyn., Feb. 2, 1945; s. Charles and Ruth (Shapiro) R.; m. Leslie Sharon Rein, Feb. 11, 1968; children: Carrie Rachel, Joshua Howard. BS, N.Y. Inst. Tech., 1966; JD, Bklyn. Law Sch., 1969; LLM, NYU, 1974. Bar: N.Y. 1970, U.S. Dist. Ct. (so. and ea. dists.) N.Y. 1971, U.S. Ct. Appeals (2d cir.) 1972, U.S. Supreme Ct. 1973, U.S. Ct. Appeals (5th and 11th cirs.) 1981. Asst. corp. counsel City of N.Y., 1969-73; law clk. N.Y. State Ct. Claims, 1973-80; ptnr. Rudick and rikon, P.C., N.Y.C., 1980-88; pvt. practice, 1988-94; ptnr. Goldstein, Goldstein and Rikon, P.C., 1994—. Contbr. articles to profl. jours. Pres. Village Greens Residents Assn., 1978-79; chmn. bd. Arden Heights Jewish Ctr., Staten Island, N.Y., 1976-77; pres. North Shore Repub. Club., 1977; mem. cmty. bd. Staten Island Borough Pres., 1977. Fellow Am. Bar Found.; mem. ABA (chair com. Condemnation) ATLA, TLPJ Found., N.Y. State Bar Assn. (spl. com. of condemnation law), Suffolk County Bar Assn., N.Y. County lawyers Assn. (chair Condemnation com.), Assn. Bar of City of N.Y. (condemnation com.), Mt. Vernon Bar Assn. Republican. Jewish. Avocations: collecting stamps, photography, collecting miniature soldiers. Home: 133 Avondale Rd Ridgewood NJ 07450-1301 Office: 80 Pine St New York NY 10005-1702

RIKOSKI, RICHARD ANTHONY, engineering executive, electrical engineer; b. Kingston, Pa., Aug. 13, 1941; s. Stanley George and Nellie (Gober) R.; m. Giannina Batchelor Petrullo, Dec. 18, 1971 (div. 1979); children: Richard James, Jennifer Anne; m. Carol Loestbron. BEE, U. Detroit, 1964; MSEE, Carnegie Inst. Tech., 1965; PhD, Carnegie-Mellon U., 1968; postdoctoral fellow, Case-Western Res. U./NASA, 1971. Registered profl. engr., Ill., Mass., Pa. Engr. 1st communication satellite systems Internat. Tel. & Tel., Nutley, N.J., 1961-64; engr. Titan II ICBM program Gen. Motors, Milw., 1964; trainee NASA, 1964-67; instr. Carnegie-Mellon U., Pitts., 1966-68; asst. prof. U. Pa., Phila., 1968-74; assoc. prof., dir. hybrid microelectronics lab., chmn. ednl. TV com. IIT, Chgo., 1974-80, chmn. ednl. TV com., 1974-80; rsch. engr. nuclear effects ITT Rsch. Inst., 1974-75; pres. Tech. Analysis Corp., 1980—. Engr. color TV colorimetry Hazeltine Rsch., Chgo., 1969; engr. Metroliner rail car/roadbed ride quality dynamics analysis U.S. Dept. Transp., ENSCO, Inc., Springfield, Va., 1970; pres. Tech. Analysis Corp., Chgo., 1978-91; contractor analysis of color TV receiver safety hazards U.S. Consumer Product Safety Commn., 1977, analysis heating effect in aluminum wire Beverly Hills Supper Club Fire, Covington, Ky., 1978; engr. GFCI patent infringement study 3M Corp., St. Paul, 1979-81; elec. systems analyst Coca-Cola Corp., Atlanta, 1983-91; fire investigator McDonald's Corp., Oak Brook, Ill., 1987-90; engring. analyst telephone switching ctrs. ATT, Chgo., 1990-91; expert witness numerous other govtl. and corp. procs.; evaluator Accreditation bd. Engring. and Tech., 2000—. Author: Hybrid Microelectronic Circuits, 1973; editor: Hybrid Microelectronic Technology, 1973; contbr. articles to profl. jours. Officer Planning Commn., Beverly Shores, Ind., 1987-93, trustee town coun., 1992—, police liason 1993-96, dir. emergency mgmt., 1998, coun. pres., 1999-2000; mem. Chgo. Coun. Fgn. Rels., USAF SAC Comdrs. Disting.is. Program; adv. coun. Nat. Park Svc. Ind. Dunes Nat. Lake Shore, 1993—. NASA fellow, 1964-67, 70. Mem. IEEE (sr. ednl. activities bd. N.Y.C. 1970-74, USAB career devel. com. 1972-74, editor Soundings 1973-75, Cassette Colloquia 1973-74, del. Popov Soc. Tech. Exch. USSR, mgr. Dial Access Tech. Edn. program 1972), Assn. for Media Based Continuing Engring. Edn. (bd. dirs.), Nat. Fire Protection Assn., Sigma Xi, Tau Beta Pi, Eta Kappa Nu. Republican. Avocations: sailing, travel. Home: One E Lakefront Dr Beverly Shores IN 46301-0444 Office: Tech Analysis Corp 1032 W Diversey Pkwy Chicago IL 60614-1317 E-mail: rikoski@technicalanalysiscorp.com.

RIKVOLD, PER ARNE, physics researcher and educator; b. Hadsel, Norway, Oct. 4, 1948; came to U.S., 1980; s. Per and Inger-Johanne (Corneliussen) R.; m. Paulette Alice Bond, Apr. 10, 1993. BS, U. Oslo, 1971, MS in Physics, 1976; cert. Japanese lang., Osaka (Japan) U. Fgn. Studies, 1977; PhD in Physics, Temple U., 1983. Rsch. assoc. dept. physics U. Oslo, 1978-81; rsch. assoc. dept. mech. engring. SUNY, Stony Brook, N.Y., 1983-85; sr. rsch. chemist ARCO Chem. Co., Newtown Square, Pa., 1985-87; assoc. prof. physics Fla. State U., Tallahassee, 1987-92, prof. physics, 1992—. Vis. scientist Kyushu U., Fukuoka, Japan, 1979, U. Geneva, Switzerland, 1981-82, Inst. Solid State Physics, Jülich, Germany, 1982; vis. rschr. IBM, Bergen, Norway, 1987, 88, U. Colo., Boulder, 1997, U. Tex., Austin, 1999; cons. Pony Industries, Malvern, Pa., 1987; vis. scholar Temple U., Phila., 1986-87, Tohwa Inst. Sci., Japan, 1991, Kyushu (Japan) U., 1991, Kyoto (Japan) U., 1993, 96, 98, 2001, McGill U., Montreal, Que., Can., 1995. Contbr. numerous articles to profl. jours. and books. Rsch. grantee Petroleum Rsch. Fund, 1988-91, NSF, 1991—; grad. rsch. fellow Japanese Ministry Edn., 1976-78, Norwegian Rsch. coun., 1981-83, Japan Found. Ctr. for Global Partnership Sci. fellow, 1996. Fellow Am. Phys. Soc.; mem. AAAS, Materials Rsch. Soc., Electrochem. Soc., Norwegian Phys. Soc., European Phys. Soc., Sigma Xi. Democrat. Achievements include theoretical and computational research in statistical and condensed-matter physics and complex-systems theory, with applications to materials science, electrochemistry and engineering. Office: Fla State U Physics Dept Tallahassee FL 32306 E-mail: rikvold@csit.fsu.edu.

RILEY, ANTHONY DALE, lawyer; b. Sheffield, Ala., Mar. 31, 1964; s. Dan Richard and Virginia (Harris) R.; m. Jennifer Leah Misner, Mar. 12, 1988; children: Elizabeth Anne, Sarah Katherine, Emma Caroline. BA, U. Ala., 1985, JD, 1988. Bar: Ala. 1989, U.S. Dist. Ct. (no. dist.) Ala. 1990. Sole practice, Tuscumbia, Ala., 1989-93, Muscle Shoals, 1993—. Treas. Shoals Republican Club, Florence, Ala., 1994-2000, Muscle Shoals Civil Svc. Bd., 1997-2000, chmn. 1998-2000; mem. State Rep. Exec. Com., 2002—. Mem. Colbert County Bar Assn. (v.p. 1996-98, pres. 1999-2000). Avocations: politics, fishing. Office: 1705 Gusmus Ave Muscle Shoals AL 35661-2459

RILEY, ANTHONY WILLIAM, German language and literature educator; b. Radcliffe-on-Trent, Eng., July 23, 1929; s. Cyril Frederick and Winifred Mary (White) R.; m. Maria Theresia Walter, July 16, 1955; children: Christopher, Katherine, Angela. BA with honors, U. Manchester, Eng., 1952; DrPhil, U. Tübingen, Germany, 1958. Lectr. U. Tübingen, 1957-59, 60-62; asst. lectr. Queen Mary Coll., U. London, Eng., 1959-60; asst. prof. German lang. and lit. Queen's U., Kingston, Ont., Can., 1962-65, asso. prof., 1965-68, prof., 1968-92, emeritus prof. Ont., Can., 1993—, head dept. German lang. and lit., 1967-76, acting head dept., 1979-80, 86-87. Vis. prof. U. Munich, 1996. Author: Elisabeth Langgässer Bibliographie mit Nachlassbericht, 1970; also articles on Elisabeth Langgässer, Alfred Döblin, Thomas Mann, Herman Hesse, Frederick Philip Grove, Joseph Wittig, Cordelia Edvardson; co-editor: The Master Mason's House (F.P. Grove), 1976, Echoes and Influences of German Romanticism, 1987, Muse and Reason, The Relation of Arts and Sciences 1650-1850, 1994; co-translator, co-editor: Fanny Essler, 2 vols. (Grove), 1984; editor: Der Oberst und der Dichter/Die Pilgerin Aetheria (Alfred Döblin), 1978, Der unsterbliche Mensch/Der Kampf mit dem Engel (Alfred Döblin), 1980, Jagende Rosse/Der schwarze Vorhang (Alfred Döblin), 1981, Wadzeks Kampf mit der Dampfturbine (Alfred Döblin), Kleine Schriften I (1902-1921) (Döblin), 1985, Kleine Schriften II (1922-24) (Döblin), 1990, Schicksalsreise (Döblin), 1993, Kleine Schriften III (1925-33), 1999. Served with Brit. Army, 1947-49. Summer fellow Weil Inst. for Studies in Religion and the Humanities, Cin., 1965; Can. Council Leave fellow, 1969-70, 76-77, 83-84 Fellow Royal Soc. Can. (sec. acad. humanities and social scis. 1992-95, editor 1995-98); mem. Can. Assn. Univ. Tchrs. German (v.p. 1973-75, pres. 1975-76, Hermann Boeschenstein medal 1987, prize for Excellence in Rsch. 1983, Konrad Adenauer rsch. award Alexander von Humboldt Found. 1989, Humboldt rsch. grant 1999), Deutsche Schillergesellschaft, Internat. Alfred Döblin-Gesellschaft (v.p. 1984-95), Internat. Assn. for German Studies, Elisabeth Langgässer-Gesellschaft (Darmstadt). Home: 108 Queen Mary Rd Kingston ON Canada K7M 2A5 E-mail: rileyaw@post.queensu.ca.

RILEY, ARCH WILSON, JR. lawyer; b. Wheeling, W.Va., Jan. 15, 1957; s. Arch W. Sr. and Mary List (Paull) R.; m. Sally Ann Goodspeed, Aug. 9, 1980; children: Ann Jerome, Sarah Paull. BA in French and Econs., Tufts U., 1979; JD, W.Va. U., 1982. Bar: W.Va. 1982, U.S. Dist. Ct. (no. and so. dists.) W.Va. 1982. Assoc. Riley & Yahn, Wheeling, 1982, Riley & Broadwater, Wheeling, 1982-83; ptnr. Riley & Riley, L.C., 1983-92, Bailey, Riley, Buch & Harman, L.C., Wheeling, 1993—. Bd. dirs. Wheeling Health Right, Inc.; mem. nat. coun. W.Va. U. Coll. Law. Pres. Upper Ohio Valley Crisis Hotline Inc., Wheeling, 1987-88; chmn. Human Rights Commn., Wheeling, 1985; committeeman Ohio County Dem. Execs., Wheeling, 1984-88; mem. Planning Commn., City of Wheeling, 2001—, mem. zoning com., 2002—; bd. dirs., pres. Northwood Health Sys., Inc., Wheeling, 1988-89; bd. dirs. Ohio Valley ARC, Wheeling, 1988; del. 1988 Dem. Nat. Conv. Mem. Am. Bankruptcy Inst., Am. Health Lawyers Assn., W.Va. State Bar (bankruptcy law com., mental health law com.), W.Va. Bar Assn., W.Va. Bankruptcy Bar Assn. (founding mem. no. dist.), Ohio County Bar Assn. (sec. 1983-84), Wheeling C. of C., Wheeling Country Club. Presbyterian. Office: Bailey Riley Buch & Harman PO Box 631 Wheeling WV 26003-0081 E-mail: arileyjr@brbhlaw.com.

RILEY, BARBARA POLK, retired librarian; b. Roselle, N.J., Nov. 21, 1928; d. Charles Carrington and Olive Bond P.; AB, Howard U., 1950; BS, N.J. Coll. Women, 1951; MS, Columbia U., 1955; m. George Emerson Riley, Feb. 23, 1957 (dec.); children: George E., Glenn C., Karen O.; m. William I. Scott, Oct. 6, 1990 (div. 1998). Asst. librarian, Fla. A&M U., 1951-53; with Morgan State Coll., 1955; with Dept. Def., 1955-57, S.C. State Coll., 1957-59, U.Wis., 1958-59; asst. librarian Atlanta U., 1960-68; asst. dir. Union County Anti Poverty Council, 1968; librarian Union County Tech. Inst., Scotch Plains, N.J., 1968-82, Plainfield campus Union County Coll., 1982-95; ret., 1995. Mem. Roselle Bd. Edn., 1976-78; bd. dirs. Union County Anti Poverty Council, 1969-72; mem. Roselle Human Relations Commn., 1971-73, Plainfield Sci. Center, 1974-76, Union County Psychiat. Clinic, 1980-83, Pinewood Sr. Citizens Council, 1981-85; bd. dirs. Project, Women of N.J, 1985-93, Pinewood Sr. Citizen Housing, 1981-85, Black Women's History Conf., 1985-92, pres., 1989-91. Mem. N.J. Library Assn., Council Library Tech., ALA (Black caucas), N.J. Coalition of 100 Black Women, African Am. Women's Polit. Caucus, N.J. Black Librarians Network (bd. dirs.), Links, Inc. (North Jersey chpt.), Black Women's History Conf., Alpha Kappa Alpha. Mem. A.M.E. Ch. Club: Just-A-Mere Lit. Home: 114 E 7th Ave Roselle NJ 07203-2028

RILEY, BENJAMIN KNEELAND, lawyer; b. Pompton Plains, N.J., June 3, 1957; s. Christopher Sibley and Katharine Louise (Piper) R.; m. Janet Welch McCormick, Sept. 15, 1984; children: Keith McCormick, Jamin McCormick. AB, Dartmouth Coll., 1979; JD, U. Calif., Berkeley, 1983. Bar: Calif. 1983, U.S. Dist. Ct. (no. dist.) Calif. 1983, U.S. Ct. Appeals (9th cir.) 1983, U.S. Dist. Ct. (ea. dist.) Calif. 1985, U.S. Dist. Ct. (cen. dist.) Calif. 1987. Assoc. McCutchen, Doyle, Brown & Enerson, San Francisco, 1983-84; ptnr. Cooley Godward LLP, 1984—. Lectr. Boalt Hall Sch. Law, 1989; mem. San Francisco Legal Svcs. Clinic, 1983—; mem. adv. bd. Berkeley Ctr. for Law and Tech., 1998—. Assoc. editor Calif. Law Rev. Spl. asst. dist. atty., San Francisco, 1988; chair, commr. Orinda Pks. & Recreation Commn., 1992-97; mem. City Orinda Task Force, Heart of Orinda Commn., Gateway and Cmty. Ctr. Renovation, 1990-97; bd. dirs. Children's Garden, 1987-92; v.p., mem. Orinda Assn., chmn. Orinda's 4th of July celebration, planning com. Orinda Union Sch. Dist., 1998. Mem.: ABA, Assn. Bus. Trial Lawyers (bd. govs. No. Calif. chpt. 2001—, editor: Assn. Bus. Trial Lawyers No. Calif. Report), San Francisco Bar Assn., Calif. Bar Assn. Democrat. Office: Cooley Godward 1 Maritime Plz Fl 20 San Francisco CA 94111-3510 E-mail: briley@cooley.com.

RILEY, BETTY STANLEY, material manager; b. McRae, Calif., Oct. 4, 1963; d. Crawford Willie and Mary Etta (Dupree) Stanley; m. Arthur Riley Jr., Oct. 1, 1988; 1 child, Jasmine Ciara. ABA, Mid. Ga. Coll., 1983; BBA, Ga. Southwestern Coll., 1985; MBA, Ga. Coll. and State U., 1996. Cert. program mgr.; cert. acquisition logistician. Prodn. mgr. Warner Robins Air Logistics Ctr., Robins AFB, Ga., 1986-88, material mgr., 1988—. Mem. NAFE. Democrat. Baptist. Avocations: tennis, biking, reading.

RILEY, CAROLE A. music educator, religious institute director; b. Pitts. d. Ralph and Emly (Stewart) Lacey; m. Walter Joseph Meserve, June 18, 1981. Student, Carlow Coll., 1959-61, Royal Conservatory, Montreal, Ont., Can., 1966-67; BS in Music Edn., Duquesne U., 1968, MusM, 1972, MA in Formative Leadership, 1978, PhD in Formative Spirituality, 1983; cert. in pastoral counseling, Pitts. Pastoral Inst., 1972-74; studies with Gregory Sebok, Adirondack Inst., 1972; postgrad., U. Pitts., 1978, Slippery Rock U., 1984. Joined Congregation Divine Providence, Roman Cath. Ch., 1959; cert. tchr., Pa. Staff, spiritual dir. Cenacle Retreat House, Pitts. and Charleston (W.Va.), 1972—2000; prof. Duquesne U., Pitts., 1972—, prof. piano, 1982—; asst. dean Duquesne U. Sch. Music, 1982-85; exec. dir. Inst. Formative Spirituality Duquesne U.; wxec. dir. W.Va. Inst. Spirituality, 2000—. Adj. prof. U. Charleston, Parkersburg, W.Va., 1983-88, St. Mary Coll., Moraga, Calif., 1983, U. San Diego, 1984, 86; lectr. in Thailand, Korea, Germany, Australia, Brazil, 8 countries in Africa. Fellow Am. Assn. Pastoral Counselors; mem. Coll. Theology Soc., Coll. Music Soc., Music Tchrs. Nat. Assn., Pa. Music Tchrs. Assn., Pitts. Piano Tchrs., Soc. for Sci. Study of Religion, Religious Rsch. Assn. Avocations: sewing, walking, cooking. Home: 700 Forbes Ave Ste 214 Pittsburgh PA 15219-4722 Office: Duquesne U 600 Forbes Ave Pittsburgh PA 15219-3002 E-mail: rileyc@duq.edu.

RILEY, CARROLL LAVERN, anthropology educator; b. Summersville, Mo., Apr. 18, 1923; s. Benjamin F. and Minnie B. (Smith) R.; m. Brent Robinson Locke, Mar. 25, 1948; children: Benjamin Locke, Victoria Smith Evans, Cynthia Winningham AB, U. N.Mex., 1948, PhD, 1952; MA, UCLA, 1950. Instr. U. Colo., Boulder, 1953-54; asst. prof. U. N.C., Chapel Hill, 1954-55, So. Ill. U., Carbondale, 1955-60, assoc. prof., 1960-67, prof., 1967-86, Disting. prof., 1986-87, Disting. prof. emeritus, 1987—, chmn. dept., 1979-82, dir. mus., 1972-74; rsch. assoc. lab. anthropology Mus. N.Mex., 1987—. Rsch. collaborator Smithsonian Instn., 1988—; adj. prof. N.Mex. Highlands U., 1989—. Author: The Origins of Civilization, 1969, The Frontier People, 1982, expanded edit., 1987, Rio del Norte, 1995, Bandelier, 1996, The Kachina and Cross, 1999; editor: American Historical Anthropology, 1967, Man Across the Sea, 1971, Southwestern Journals of Adolph F. Bandelier, 4 vols., 1966, 70, 75, 84, Across the Chichimec Sea, 1978, A Zuni Life, 1998, The Casas Grandes World, 1999, others; contbr. numerous articles to profl. jours. Served in USAAF, 1942-45 Decorated 4 battle stars; grantee Social Sci. Research Council, NIH, Am. Philos. Soc., Am. Council Learned Socs., NEH, others Home and Office: 1106 6th St Las Vegas NM 87701 E-mail: criley@newmexico.com.

RILEY, CHARLES JOHN, JR. aerospace engineer; b. N.Y.C., Nov. 15, 1951; s. Charles John and Alvina Marie R.; m. Kiyomi Tanaka, Jan. 7, 1977; 1 child, Tanya. BS in Liberal Studies, SUNY, Albany, 1991; MEd, U. West Fla., 1997. Cert. FAA airline transport pilot, cert. naval aviator, cert. aircraft carrier qualified C-1A trader, cert. navy flight instr., cert. navy carrier transport plane comdr., cert. aircraft carrier qualified E-2C hawkeye, cert. aircraft carrier qualified C-2A greyhound. Commd. ensign USN, 1973, advanced through grades to lt. comdr.; instrnl. developer, aviation subject matter expert AmerInd Inc., Pensacola, Fla., 1994-97; rsch. asst. U. West Fla., 1997-98; sr. instrnl. designer Advanced Sys. Tech., 1998-2000, SI Internat. WPI, Rockville, Md., 2000—. Cons. U. West Fla. Office Cmty. Learning, Pensacola, 1998-2001. Treas. Woodham H.S. Band Boosters, Pensacola, 1994-96. Decorated 2 Navy Commendation medals, Navy Achievement medal. Mem. Monumental City Fife and Drum Corps, Md. Cold Fusion Users Group, Co. Fifers and Drummers, Boy Scouts Am. (life scout). Avocations: drumming, golf.

RILEY, CHRISTOPHER SIBLEY, museum supervisor; b. Pitts., Feb. 5, 1926; s. Lester Leake and Eleanor Harriet (Sibley) Riley; m. Katharine Louise Piper, Oct. 28, 1950; children: Katharine Pulnam, Christopher Andrew, Benjamin Keeland. Student, Sampson Coll., 1946—47; BA, Amherst Coll., 1950. Artist, puppeteer Kingsland-Then Suzari Marionettes, N.Y.C., 1950—52; chief film libr. CBS-TV-News, 1950—58; tech. writer Curtiss-Wright & Pratt & Whitney, Patterson, NJ, 1958—65, Hartford, Conn., 1958—65; writer, translator Olivetti-Underwood, 1965—67; reporter Hartford Times Courant, 1967—82; mus. asst. Conn. Hist. Commn., 1979—; prprietor, narrator, sculptor C.S. Riley Co., North Granby, 1967—. Selectman Town of Granby, 1961—65; founder, sec. Friends of New Gate Prison, East Granby, 1982—; town chmn. Dem. Town Com., Granby, 1960—62. Seaman U.S. Maritime Svc., 1944—46, ETO. Named Man of Yr., Conn. Toruism Coun., 1968; recipient citation for outstanding work, Conn. Hist. Commn., 1968. Democrat. Achievements include patents for sound film editing machine with speech compressor. Avocation: studying history and art. Home: 152 East St North Granby CT 06060 Office: Old New Gate Prison & Coppermine 115 New Gate Rd East Granby CT 06026

RILEY, DAVID RICHARD, management consultant, retired military officer; b. Spokane, Wash., Mar. 28, 1940; s. Lee James and Louise Elizabeth (Duncan) R.; m. Anna Maria Formigoni, July 6, 1963; children: David Scott, Michelle Andrea. BS in Naval Sci., USN Acad., 1963; MS in Applied Math., USN Post Grad. Sch., 1972; postgrad., Armed Forces Staff Coll., 1975. Navy ops. mgmt. specialist, Navy aerospace engring. specialist, Navy material specialist, Navy weapon sys. mgmt. specialist. Ensign USN, 1963, advanced through grades to capt., 1984, antisubmarine warfare/antisubmarine rocket officer Fla., 1963-65, pilot trainee Pensacola, 1965-67, designated naval pilot San Diego, 1967, with antisubmarine/antiair warfare, 1967-74, maintenace officer, 1976-78, officer in charge Nerra Naples, Italy, 1978-81; exec. officer Naval Aviation Depot, Alameda, Calif., 1981-84, comdg. officer Pensacola, 1987-90; aviation depot program mgr. Navairsyscom Hdqrs., Washington, 1984-87; ret., 1990; cons. bus. planning and organizational devel., internat. commerce Chula Vista, Calif., 1990-94; pres., COO Speco Corp., Springfield, Ohio, 1994-95; pres. David Riley Assocs., Inc., 1998—. Mem. Turnaround Mgmt. Assn., Assn. Naval Aviation, Ret. Officers Assn., Am. Legion, Naval Helicopter Assn. Republican. Presbyterian. Avocation: golf. Home and Office: David Riley Assocs Inc 115 Eastwick Ct Dayton OH 45440-3647 E-mail: dra2000@worldnet.att.net.

RILEY, DAWN C. educational philosopher, researcher; b. Rochester, N.Y., Mar. 18, 1954; d. John Joseph Jr. and June Carol (Cleveland) R. BA in Edn., Polit. Sci., SUNY, 1976; MEd, in Special Edn., summa cum laude, U. Ariz., 1980; PhD, Univ. Calif., Berkeley, 1994. Cert. multiple subject credential (K-Coll.), specialist credential (K-12), Calif., coun. of educators for deaf; elem. permanent credential, N.Y. Elem. sch. tchr., 4th grade Escola Americana do Rio de Janeiro, Brazil, 1975; pvt. practice, comml. artist Rochester, 1972-80; elem. tchr. Rochester City Sch. Dist., 1976-78; rsch. asst., summer vestibule program The Nat. Tech. Inst. for Deaf, 1976-79; tchr. English, 7th-12th grades The Calif. Sch. for Deaf, 1980-94; rsch. asst. to Dr. Richard J. Morris The Univ. Ariz., 1978-80; rsch. asst., Calif. new tchr. support project The Far West Lab. for Ednl. R & D., San Francisco, 1989; chair high sch. English dept. The Calif. Sch. for Deaf, 1990-96; prin. Calif. Sch. for the Deaf, Fremont, 1996-97; asst. prof. edn. founds. So. Ill. U., 1998—. Coord. & devel. Practical Lang. in Applied Settings Program, 1981-82; chair Computer Curriculum Com., 1982-84, Critical and Creative Thinking Skills Com., 1983-84; coord. Gifted and Talented Program, 1983— Recipient Kate Navin O'Neill Grad. scholar Univ. of Calif., Berkeley, 1989; University fellow, 1978-80, Evelyn Lois Corey fellow, 1990; Recipient Sustained Superior Accomplishment award Calif. Dept. Edn., 1991. Mem. AAUW, Nat. Coun. Tchrs. English, Far Western Philosophy of Edn. Soc., Am. Ednl. Rsch. Assn., Am. Assn. Colls. for Tchr. Edn., Philosophy of Edn. Soc., John Dewey Soc., Soc. Profs. Edn. (bd. dirs. 2001—)m Phi Beta Kappa (Berkeley chpt.). Home: 1205 Oakland Ave Edwardsville IL 62025-2452 Office: So Ill U Dept Edn Leadership And Foun Edwardsville IL 62026-0001

RILEY, FRANCENA, nurse, retired non-commissioned officer; b. New Smyrna Beach, Fla., May 5, 1957; d. Willard Harrell and Jacqueline Delores (Griffen) R. 1 child, Daniel Albert Cross (dec.). AA, U. Md., Heidelberg, Fed. Republic Germany, 1987; BS, Upper Iowa U., 1994; MA in Edn., Ctrl. Mich. U., 2001. Enlisted U.S. Army, 1980, advanced through grades to sgt. 1st class, 1991, expert field med. badge, parachutist; practical nurse emergency room Keller Army Hosp., West Point, N.Y., 1981; bn. tng. noncommd. officer 34th Med. Bn., Ft. Benning, Ga., 1988-89, practical nurse 2d Mobile Army Surg. Hosp., 1989-91; wardmaster intensive care unit #1 2d MASH, 1990-91; practical nurse pediatric ward Walter Reed Army Med. Ctr., Washington, 1982-84; practical nurse, then nursing supr. 913th Med. Detachment, Kaiserslautern, Fed. Republic Germany, 1984-86; wardmaster surgery clinic Army Regional Med. Ctr., Landstuhl, Fed. Republic Germany, 1987; with 2D MASH 44th med. brigade operation desert shield U.S. Army, Saudi Arabia, 1990-91; ops. non-commd. officer 2d MASH, 1991-92; wardmaster newborn nursery USA MEDDAC, Ft. Polk, La., 1992-94; wardmaster med. surg. unit US-AMEDDAC, 1994-95; ret., 1995; distbn. clk. USPS, Atlanta, 1995-2000; anesthesia nurse Northside Hosp., 2002—. Maintenance support clk. USPS, Atlanta; adj. instr. Ga. Perimeter Coll., Clarkston, Ga., 2001—. Mem. handbell choir, sr. usher bd. hist. com. Ebenezer Bapt. Ch., Atlanta. Recipient med. badge U.S. Army, 1991. Baptist. Avocations: bicycling, plate collecting, visiting zoos and nature parks. Home: 8773 Valley Lakes Ct Union City GA 30291-6011 E-mail: honedoo2000@yahoo.com.

RILEY, HARRIS DEWITT, JR. pediatrician, medical educator; b. Clarksdale, Miss., Nov. 12, 1924; s. Harris DeWitt and Louise (Allen) R.; m. Margaret Barry, Sept. 16, 1950; children: Steven Allen, Mark Barry, Margaret Ruth. BA, Vanderbilt U., 1945, MD, 1948. Intern Balt. City Hosps., Johns Hopkins Hosp., 1948-49; resident in pediatrics Babies and Children's Hosp., Case Western Res. U., Cleve., 1949-50, Vanderbilt U. Hosp., 1950-51; instr., fellow in pediatrics and infectious diseases Vanderbilt U. Med. Sch., 1953-57; prof. pediatrics, chmn. dept. U. Okla. Med. Sch., 1958—; med. dir. Children's Meml. Hosp., 1972—; disting. prof. pediatrics U. Okla., 1976; prof. pediatrics Vanderbilt U. Sch. of Medicine, Nashville, 1991—. Served as capt. M.C. USAF, 1951-53. Office: Vanderbilt Children Hosp Vanderbilt U Med Ctr Nashville TN 37232-0001 E-mail: harris.riley@mcmail.vanderbilt.edu.

RILEY, HENRY CHARLES, banker; b. Newton, Mass., Mar. 23, 1932; s. Charles Matthew and Marion Anna (Armstrong) R.; m. Patricia Ann Buchanan, Mar. 3, 1962; children: Lauren Elizabeth, Carolyn Ann, Julie Louise. AB, Yale U., 1954; MBA, Boston Coll., 1965. With BayBank Harvard Trust Co., Cambridge, Mass., 1958-89, treas., sec., 1967-70, v.p., treas., 1970-72, sr. v.p., sec., 1972-82, exec. v.p., 1982-87; mng. dir. community banking BayBank Systems Inc., Waltham, Mass., 1987-90; exec. v.p., dir. community banking BayBank Boston, 1990-92; exec. v.p. BayBank Systems, Inc., Waltham, 1992-97. Mem. pvt. banking adv. com. Fleet Boston, Sarasota, Fla., 2000—. Trustee, treas. Longy Sch. Music, 1970-92; bd. dirs. Richard Warren Surg. Rsch. and Ednl. Fund Inc., 1984—; bd. dirs., pres. Cambridge Econ. Devel. Corp., 1982-87; corporator, past asst. treas. Mt. Auburn Hosp.; past mem. exec. bd. Gettysburg Coll. Parents Assn.; past treas. St. John's Episcopal Ch., sr. warden, Westwood, Mass., 1982-85; mem. St. Paul's Cathedral chpt., Boston, 1990-93. With USNR, 1956-57. Mem. Am. Bankers Assn. (chmn. 1991-92, exec. com. br. adminstrv. divsn. 1992, chmn. nat. retail banking conf. 1990), Nat. Br. Adminstrs. Roundtable, Boston Coll. Sch. Mgmt. Alumni Assn. (past dir., pres.), Harvard Sq. Bus. Assn. (past dir.), Cambridge C. of C. (past dir., past treas., v.p. 1975-87), Rotary (club dir. 1976-80, pres. 1979-80), Yale Club (Boston, Sarasota, Fla.), Harvard Club (Boston), Dennis Yacht Club (mem. bd. govs., treas. 1993-94), The Meadows Country Club (Sarasota, Fla.), Ivy League Club (Sarasota, Fla.). Episcopalian. Home: 33 York Way Westwood MA 02090-2633 also: PO Box 1192 240 New Boston Rd Dennis MA 02638-2121 also: 5284 Huntingwood Ct Sarasota FL 34235-5600

RILEY, JACK, actor, writer; b. Cleve., Dec. 30, 1935; s. John A. and Agnes C. (Corrigan) R.; m. Ginger Lawrence, May 18, 1975; children: Jamie, Bryan. BS in English, John Carroll U., 1961. Mem.: Rolling Along of 1960, Dept. Army Travelling Show; co-host: Baxter & Riley, Sta.-WERE, Cleve., 1961-65; numerous TV appearances, including: as Mr. Carlin on Bob Newhart Show, CBS-TV, 1972-78; Occasional Wife, 1966, Mary Tyler Moore, 1972, Barney Miller, 1979, Diff'rent Strokes, 1979, Hart to Hart, 1980, Love Boat, 1984, Night Court, 1985-91, St. Elsewhere, 1986, Evening Shade, 1992, Family Matters, 1993, Married with Children, 1994, Coach, 1996, The Drew Carey Show, 1996, Seinfeld, 1997, Working, 1998, numerous appearances on Tonight Show with Jay Leno, 1997-99; appeared in feature films including Catch-22, 1969, McCabe and Mrs. Miller, 1970, Long Goodbye, 1972, Calif. Split, 1974, World's Greatest Lover, 1978, High Anxiety, 1978, Butch and Sundance: The Early Years, 1979, History of the World, Part I, 1981, Frances, 1983, To Be or Not To Be, 1983, Finders Keepers, 1984, Spaceballs, 1987, Rented Lips, 1987, Gleaming the Cube, 1988, C.H.U.D. II, 1988, The Player, 1992, T-Rex, 1995, (voice) The Rugrat's Movie, 1998, Boogie Nights, 1997; plays West Coast premier of Small Craft Warnings, 1975, Los Angeles revival of 12 Angry Men, 1985, Zeitgeist, 1990, House of Blue Leaves, at Cleve. Playhouse and tour Ea. Europe, 1993, The Odd Couple, Beck Ctr., Cleve., 1999, Do I Hear a Waltz? at Pasadena playhouse, 2001; TV writer: Don Rickles Show, 1968, Mort Sahl Show, 19667; writer commls. for, Blore & Richman Inc., Los Angeles, 1966-84; numerous radio commls. and TV voice-overs, Rugrats (cartoon series), 1993. Served with U.S. Army, 1958-61. Mem. Screen Actors Guild, Actor's Equity, AFTRA, Writers Guild Am., Acad. Motion Picture Arts and Scis., Acad. TV Arts and Scis. Office: c/o Ho Reps 400 S Beverly Dr Beverly Hills CA 90212-4424

RILEY, JOHN FREDERICK, lawyer; b. Salisbury, N.C., Oct. 18, 1938; s. John Horace and Beatrice (Williams) R.; m. Jan Colby, June 20, 1965; children: John Michael, Jennifer Lynn, Julia Grace. BA, Wake Forest U., 1960; JD, U. N.C., 1967. Bar: N.C. 1967. Law clk. to presiding justice N.C. Supreme Ct., Raleigh, 1967-68; assoc. Leroy, Wells, Shaw & Hornthal, Elizabeth City, N.C., 1968-70; ptnr. Leroy, Wells, Shaw, Hornthal & Riley, 1970-85, Hornthal, Riley, Ellis & Maland, Elizabeth City, 1985-2001, of counsel, 2001—. Chmn. adv. bd. Salvation Army, Elizabeth City, 1976-77; trustee Elizabeth City State U., 1981-86. Hankins scholar Wake Forest U., Winston-Salem, N.C., 1956. Mem. ABA, N.C. Bar Assn. (bd. dirs. real property sect. 1979-83), N.C. Land Title Assn., Elizabeth City Bar Assn. (pres. 1973-74), 1st Jud. Dist. Bar Assn. (pres. 1985-86), Rotary, Pine Lakes Country. Democrat. Methodist. Avocations: golf, tennis, boating. Home: 101 Inlet Dr Elizabeth City NC 27909-3225 Office: Hornthal Riley Ellis & Maland 301 E Main St # 220 Elizabeth City NC 27909-4425 E-mail: friley@hrem.com.

RILEY, JUDITH MERKLE, writer, educator; b. Brunswick, Maine, Jan. 14, 1942; d. Theodore Charles and Helen Antonia Merkle; m. W. Parkes Riley (div.); children: Elizabeth, Marlow. BA, U. Calif., Berkeley, 1962, PhD, 1974; MA, Harvard U., 1964. Intelligence analyst Dept. of Def., Washington, 1965—66; tchg. asst., acting instr., lectr. U. Calif., Berkeley, 1967—70; vis. asst. prof., asst. prof. U. Oreg., Eugene, 1971—82; assoc. prof. Claremont (Calif.) McKenna Coll./Claremont Grad. Sch., 1982—. Author: (non-fiction) Management and Ideology, 1980, (novels) A Vision of Light, 1989, In Pursuit of the Green Lion, 1990, The Oracle Glass, 1993, The Water-Devil , 1995, The Serpent Garden, 1997, The Master of All Desires, 1999 (Libr. Jour. 100 Best of 1999). Recipient Career Achievement award, Romantic Times, 1999. Fellow: Brit. Inst. Homeopathy (Di Hom 1998); mem.: Am. Soc. Pub. Adminstrn., Am. Polit. Sci. Assn., Novelists, Inc., Pen USA West, Nat. Ctr. Homeopathy, Phi Beta Kappa. Democrat. Episcopalian. Avocations: homeopathy, painting, choral singing. Office: Claremont McKenna Coll Dept Govt 850 Columbia Ave Claremont CA 91711 E-mail: jmerkle@mckenna.edu.

RILEY, KENNETH JEROME, athletic director; b. Bartow, Fla., Aug. 6, 1947; m. Barbara Moore, May 3, 1969; children: Kimberly, Kenneth II, Kenisha. BS in Health, Physical Edn. & Recreation, Fla. A&M U., 1969; MS in Ednl. Administrn. Suprv., U. North Fla. Cornerback Cin. Bengals, 1969-84; asst. coach Green Bay (Wis.) Packers, 1984-85; football coach Fla. A&M U., Tallahassee, 1986-93, dir. athletics, 1994—. Mem. NFL's Player's Coun. Named to Fla. A&M U. Sports Hall Fame, Tallahassee Sports Hall Fame, Fla. Sports Hall Fame, Bartow County Sports Hall Fame, Polk County Sports Hall Fame. Avocations: fishing, reading. Office: Fla A&M U Martin Luther King Jr Blvd Tallahassee FL 32307

RILEY, MARY JANE, computer scientist; b. Raleigh, N.C., May 26, 1946; d. Charles William and Geraldine Lucile (Adams) Hampton; m. William Walter Schubert, Dec. 30, 1967 (div. June 1979); children: Kristen, Stephen, Betsy, Kathryn; stepchildren: Lee, Scott; m. Jim Riley, Oct. 17, 1998. BA in Math., Park Coll., 1967. Cert. IBM project mgr. Programmer U. Mo. Med. Ctr., Columbia, 1968-72, City and County of Denver, 1979-80; sr. sys. programmer Citicorp Person to Person, Denver, 1980-82; sys. support rep. Software AG, NA, 1982-83; prin. info. sysm. specialist Idaho Nat. Engring. Lab., EG&G, Idaho Falls, 1983-89; adv. svcs. specialist IBM Profl. Svcs., Albuquerque, 1989-91; field mgr. IBM Svc., Boulder, Colo., 1991-93; project mgr. IBM Global Svcs., Denver, 1993-99; exec. project mgr. IBM Global Svcs. Healthcare, 1999—. Presenter career workshop for girls No. Colo. U., Greeley, 1993. Leader Girl Scout Am., Pocatello, Idaho, Columbia, Mo., 1969-79, Idaho Falls, 1986-89, cluster leader, Rigby, Idaho, 1988-89; active Albuquerque Civic Chorus, 1990-91, Luth. Ch. Coun., 1994-96; bd. dirs. LWV, Pocatello, 1977-79, 84-85, pres., 1978-79; bd. dirs. Luth. Ch. Women, Pocatello, 1978-79; youth advisor Luth. Ch., Idaho Falls, 1984-89; tchr. Sunday sch. local ch., Albuquerque, 1990-91; youth com. chair local ch., Boulder, Colo., 1994-96; tchr. 7th and 8th grade Sunday sch., 1993-96, mem. ch. choir, 1995-96; mem. Denver Art Mus., Denver Nat. History Mus. Mem. AAUW. Episcopalian. Avocations: youth work, reading, choir, photography, skiing. E-mail: mjriley.us.ibm.com. Home: 6581 S Cook Way Littleton CO 80121-3605

RILEY, MATILDA WHITE (MRS. JOHN W. RILEY JR.), retired sociologist; b. Boston, Apr. 19, 1911; d. Percival and Mary (Cliff) White; m. John Winchell Riley, Jr., June 19, 1931; children: John Winchell III, Lucy Ellen Riley Sallick. BA, Radcliffe Coll., 1931, MA, 1937, DSc (hon.), 1994; DSc, Bowdoin Coll., 1972; LHD (hon.), Rutgers U., 1983, SUNY, Albany, 1997. Rsch. asst. Harvard U., Cambridge, Mass., 1932; v.p. Market Rsch. Co. Am., 1938-49; chief cons. economist WPB, 1941; rsch. specialist Rutgers U., 1950, prof., 1951-73, dir. sociology lab., chmn. dept. sociology and anthropology, 1959-73, emeritus prof., 1973—; Daniel B. Fayerweather prof. polit. econ. and sociology Bowdoin Coll., Brunswick, Maine, 1974-78, prof. emeritus, 1978—, hon. rsch. prof. Assoc. dir. Nat. Inst. on Aging, 1979-91, sr. social scientist, 1991-98, scientist emeritus, Nat. Inst. of Health, 1998—; mem. faculty Harvard U., summer 1955; staff assoc., dir. aging and society Russell Sage Found., 1964-73, staff sociologist, 1974-77; chmn. com. on life course Social Sci. Rsch. Coun., 1977-80; sr. rsch. assoc. Ctr. for Social Scis., Columbia U., 1978-80; adv. bd. Carnegie Aging Soc. Project, 1985-87; mem. Commn. on Coll. Retirement, 1982-86; vis. prof. NYU, 1954-61; cons. Nat. Coun. on Aging, Acad. Ednl. Devel.; mem. study group NIH, 1971-79, Social Sci. Rsch. Coun. Com. on Middle Years, 1973-77; chmn. NIH Task Force on Health and Behavior, 1986-91; cons. WHO, 1987—; Winkelman lectr. U. Mich., 1984, Selo lectr. U. No. Calif., 1987, Boettner lectr. Am. Coll., 1990, Claude Pepper lectr. Fla. State U., 1993, Disting. lectr. Southwestern Social Scis. Assn., 1990, U. N.C., 1997; Standing lectr. SUNY, 1992, Inaugural lectr. Cornell U., 1992; lectr. Internat. Inst. of Sociology, Plenary, 1993, Inter-Univ. Consortium Pol. and Social Rsch., U. Mich., 1993, Duke U., 1993; adv. bd. Internat. Encyclopedia of the Social and Behavioral Sciences, 2000. Author: (with P. White) Gliding and Soaring, (with Riley and Toby) Sociological Studies in Scale Analysis, 1954, Sociological Research, vols. I, II, 1964, (with others) Aging and Society, vol. I, 1968, vol. II, 1969, vol. III, 1972, (with Nelson) Sociological Observation, 1974, Aging from Birth to Death: Interdisciplinary Perspectives, 1979, (with Merton) Sociological Traditions from Generation to Generation, 1980, (with Abeles and Teitelbaum) Aging from Birth to Death: Sociotemporal Perspectives, 1982, (with Hess and Bond) Aging in Society, 1983; editor: (with M. Ory and D. Zablotsky) AIDS in an Aging Society: What We Need to Know, 1989; co-editor: Perspectives in Behavioral Medicine: The Aging Dimension, 1987, (with J. W. Riley) The Quality of Aging, 1989, The Annuals, 1989; mem. editl. com. Ann. Rev. Sociology, 1978-81, Social Change and the Life Course, vol. 1, Social Structures and Human Lives, (with B. Huber and B. Hess) Sociological Lives, vol. II, 1988, (with R. Kahn and Anne Foner) Structural Lag, 1994; contbr. chpts. to books, articles to profl. jours. Former trustee The Big Sisters Assn. Recipient Lindback Rsch. award Rutgers U., 1970, Social Sci. award Andrus Gerontology Ctr., U. So. Calif., 1972, Radcliffe Alumnae award, 1982, Commonwealth award 1984, Kesten Lecture award U. So. Calif., 1987, Sci. Achievement award Washington Acad. Scis., 1989, Disting. Sci. award, 1989, Disting. Creative award Gerontol. Soc. Am., 1990, Presdl. Meritorious award, 1990, Stuart Rice award D.C. Columbia Sociol. Soc., 1992, Kent award Gerontol. Soc. Am., 1992; fellow Advanced Study in Behaviorial Scis., 1978; Matilda White Riley award in rsch. and methodology established in her honor Rutgers U., 1977; Matilda White Riley prize established Bowdoin Coll., 1987; Matilda White Riley House dedicated Bowdoin Coll., 1996. Fellow AAAS (chmn. sect. on social and econ. scis. 1977-78); mem. NAS, Inst. Medicine of NAS (sr.), Acad. Behavioral Medicine Rsch., Am. Sociol. Assn. (exec. officer 1949-60, v.p. 1973-74, pres. 1986, 91, chmn. sect. on sociology of aging 1989, Disting. Scholar in Aging 1988, Career award 1992), Am. Assn. Public Opinion Rsch. (sec.-treas. 1949-51, Disting. Svc. award 1983), Eastern Sociol. Soc. (v.p. 1968-69, pres. 1977-78, Disting. Career award 1986), Soc. for Study Social Biology (bd. dirs. 1986-92), Am. Acad. Arts and Scis., D.C. Sociol. Soc. (co-pres. 1983-84), Sociol. Rsch. Assn., Internat. Orgn. Study Human Devel., Am. Philos. Soc. (membership lectr. 1987), Phi Beta Kappa, Phi Beta Kappa Assocs. Home: 22 Monument Ln Brunswick ME 04011-8106 Office: Bowdoin Coll Brunswick ME 04011 E-mail: rileym@suscom-maine.net.

RILEY, NANCY MAE, retired vocational home economics educator; b. Grand Forks, N.D., May 1, 1939; d. Kenneth Wesley and Jeanne Margaret Olive (Hill) R. BS in Edn., Miami U., 1961; postgrad., Ohio U., 1964-69; MA, Marietta Coll., 1989. Cert. high sch. tchr. Tchr. home econs. Malta-McConnelsville (Ohio) High Sch., 1961-67; tchr. home econs. Waterford (Ohio) High Sch., 1968-92. Advisor Malta-McConnelsville Future Homemakers, 1961-66, Waterford Future Homemakers Am., 1968-92; advisor to state officer Ohio Future Homemakers Am., McConnelsville, 1963, Waterford, 1976. Leader Girl Scouts Am., McConnelsville, 1962-66, camp counselor, 1962-76; fair judge Waterford Cmty. Fair, Waterford, 1970-85. Mem.: DAR, NEA, Ohio Vocat. Assn. (life), Ohio Edn. Assn. (life) (del. 1979), Am. Vocat. Assn. (life), Ohio Geneal. Soc., Daus. War of 1812 (pres. 1991—, state sec. 1995—97, state 2d v.p. 2001—), Daus. Union Vets. (del. 1992—, tent pres. 1993—98, dist. pres. 1996, Ohio Dept. pres. 1999), White Shrine of Jerusalem (worthy high priestess 1979—81, 1983), Order Eastern Star (worthy matron 1967—68, dep. grand matron 1978). Republican. Baptist. Avocations: ceramics, genealogy, camping, reading, handcrafts. Home: PO Box 137 Waterford OH 45786-0137

RILEY, PATRICK JAMES, professional basketball coach; b. Rome, Mar. 20, 1945; s. Leon R.; m. Chris Riley; children: James Patrick, Elisabeth. Grad., U. Ky., 1967. Guard San Diego Rockets, 1967-70, L.A. Lakers, 1970-75, asst. coach, 1979-81, head coach, 1981-90, N.Y. Knicks, 1991-95; guard Phoenix Suns, 1975-76; broadcaster L.A. Lakers games Sta. KLAC and Sta. KHJ-TV, 1977-79, NBC Sports, 1990-91; player NBA Championship Team, 1972, coach, 1982, 85, 87, 88; head coach Miami (Fla.) Heat, 1995—. Author: The Winner Within: A Life Plan for Team Players, 1993. Named NBA Coach of Yr., 1990, 93, 97 Achievements include being a holder of NBA record most playoff wins (137). Office: Miami Heat SunTrust Int'l Ctr 601 Biscayne Blvd Miami FL 33132-1801*

RILEY, RICHARD WILSON, lawyer, federal official; b. Greenville, S.C., Jan. 2, 1933; s. Edward Patterson and Martha Elizabeth (Dixon) Riley; m. Ann Osteen Yarborough, Aug. 23, 1957; children: Richard Wilson, Anne Y., Hubert D., Theodore D. BA, Furman U., 1954; JD, U. S.C., 1959. Bar: S.C. 1960. Ptnr. Riley & Riley, Greenville, 1959—78, Nelson, Mullins, Riley & Scarborough, Greenville and Columbia, 1987—93, Greenville, 2001—; gov. State of S.C., 1979—87; sec. U.S. Dept. Edn., Washington, 1993—2001; disting. univ. prof. U. S.C., Columbia, 2001—. Spl. asst. to subcom. U.S. Senate Jud. Com., 1960; mem. S.C. Ho. of Reps., 1963—66, S.C. Senate senate form Greenville-Laurens Dist., 1966—76. Lt. (j.g.) USNR, 1954—56. Recipient Dist. Svc. award, Coun. Chief State Sch. Officers, 1994, James Bryant Conant award, Edn. Comm. of the States, 1995, T.H. Bell award for outstanding edn. advocacy, Com. for Edn. Funding, 1996, Dist. Svc. award, Am. Coun. on Edn., 1998. Mem.: Greenville Bar Assn., S.C. Bar Assn., Furman U. Alumni Assn. (pres. 1968—69), Rotary, Phi Beta Kappa. Office: Nelson Mullins Riley & Scarborough Poinsett Plaza Ste 900 104 S Main St Greenville SC 29601 E-mail: rwr@nmrs.com.

RILEY, RICHARD HAYDN, anaesthetist, researcher; b. Perth, W. Aus., Australia, Nov. 11, 1955; s. Bertram Leon and Lyle Emily (Rees) R.; m. Vera Josefine Fisch, Mar. 13, 1982; children: Benjamin Aaron, Matthew Joel. MB, BS, U. of Western Australia, Perth, 1980. Diplomate Am. Bd. Anesthesiologists. Staff anaesthetist Royal Perth (Australia) Hosp., 1988—. Dir. Acute Pain Svc., Royal Perth Hosp., 1994-95. Contbr. articles to profl. jours. Fellow: Australian and New Zealand Coll. Anaesthetists, Am. Coll. Anesthesiologists; mem.: Australian Med. Assn., Australian Soc. Anesthetists, Am. Soc. Anesthesiologists. Anglican. Avocations: music appreciation, Japanese language. Office: Royal Perth Hosp Box X2213 Perth WA 6001 Australia E-mail: richard@pobox.com.

RILEY, ROBERT, congressman, entrepreneur, cattleman; b. Ala. m. Patsy Adams; children: Rob, Jenice, Minda, Krisalyn. Degree in bus. administrn., U. Ala. Past poultry and egg bus. co-owner, Ala.; past owner automobile dealership; owner trucking co.; past owner grocery store and local pharmacy; mem. Ho. of Reps. from 3d Ala. dist., 1996—, asst. whip, mem. house armed svcs. com., mem. house banking and fin. svcs. com., mem. house agr. com., house-senate conference on FY 1998 Def. Authorization bill, 1997, mem. ho. agrl. com. Past chmn. fin. com. Clay County Hosp.; mem. First Baptist Ch., men's Sunday sch. tchr., past chmn. bd. trustees. Mem. Masons, Shriners, Jaycees (past pres. Ashland chpt.). Office: 322 Cannon Ho Office Bldg Washington DC 20515-0001

RILEY, ROBERT BARTLETT, landscape architect; b. Chgo., Jan. 28, 1931; s. Robert James and Ruth (Collins) R.; m. Nancy Rebecca Mills, Oct. 5, 1956; children: Rebecca Hill, Kimber Bartlett. PhB, U. Chgo., 1949; BArch, MIT, 1954. Chief designer Kea, Shaw, Grimm & Crichton, Hyattsville, Md., 1959-64; prin. partner Robert B. Riley (A.I.A.), Albuquerque, 1964-70;

campus planner, asso. prof. architecture, dir. Center Environ. Research and Devel., U. N.Mex., 1966-70; prof. landscape architecture and architecture U. Ill., Urbana-Champaign, 1970—, head dept. landscape architecture, 1970-85, dir. PhD program, 1999—; vis. prof. Harvard U., 1996-97; prof. emeritus, dir. joint PhD program U. Ill., 1997—. Sr. fellow landscape architecture studies Dumbarton Oaks/Harvard U., 1992—, chmn. fellows, 1996—; mem. rev. panel landscape architects Fed. Civil Service-Nat. Endowment Arts. Assoc. editor Landscape mag., 1967-70; editor Landscape Jour., 1987—. Served with USAF, 1954-58. Nell Norris fellow U. Melbourne, Australia, 1977; project fellow Nat. Endowment Arts, 1985 Fellow Am. Soc. Landscape Architects (Nat. Honor award 1979); mem. Coun. of Educators in Landscape Architecture, pres. 1984-85, chmn. bd. dirs. 1985-86, Outstanding Educator award 1992, Pres.'s award 1994, chmn. editl. adv. bd. Landscape Architecture 1996-99), AIA (Design award Md. 1962, N.Mex. 1968, Environ. Svc. award N.Mex. 1970), Environ. Design Rsch. Assn. (chmn. bd. 1990-91), Phi Beta Epsilon. Unitarian Universalist. Office: Univ Ill 101 Temple Buell Hall 611 E Lorado Taft Dr Champaign IL 61820-6921 Home: 407 E George Huff Dr Urbana IL 61801-6703

RILEY, ROBERT SHEAN, Colonel, United States Army, retired, writer, publisher; b. West Point, Ky., Oct. 16, 1929; s. Niram Brooks and Nan Estelle (Shean) R.; m. Matsuko Uechi, Mar. 24, 1955; children: Elizabeth Mae, Robert Jr. BS in Engring., U.S. Mil. Acad., 1952; MPA, U. Okla., 1974; M in Internat. Affairs, Columbia U., 1975. Commd. 2d lt. U.S. Army, 1952, advanced through grades to col., ret., 1978; writer, pub. Lawton, Okla., 1978—. Author: History of Shumate Family, 1992, Our European Origins, 1992, History O'Ferrall-Shaen Family, 1994, History of Ditto Families, 1996, The Colonial Riley Families of the Tidewater Frontier, 1999. Decorated Bronze Star medals (3OLC), Air medal, Joint Svc. Commendation medal, Meritorious Svc. medal (1OLC), Army Commendation medal, Korean and Vietnamese War Campaign medals. Mem. Mil. Order of the World Wars, West Point Soc. Texhoma Chapter. Methodist.

RILEY, RONALD JIM, industrial engineer, consultant; b. Flint, Mich., June 10, 1950; s. Jack Robert and Rose Alice (Millard) R.; m. Laura Jean Gill, June 23, 1979; children: Meghan Kathleen, Caitlin Rose. Student, C.S. Mott C.C., Flint, 1969-70. Asst. mgr., salesman Howat Electronics, Flint, 1968-70; proprietor Customtronics, 1970-74; engr. med. equipment Werby Labs., 1974-76; plant engr. Cara Corp., Detroit, 1976-78; indsl. controls engr. Atlas Techs., Fenton, Mich., 1978-84; engr., mgr. J.N. Fauver Co. subs. Sun Oil, Madison Heights, 1984-90; inventor Riley & Assocs. Inc., Grand Blanc, 1990—. Founder, exec. dir. InventorEd, Inc., 1996—. Contbr. articles to profl. jours.; patentee in field. Mem. ACLU, Union of Concerned Scientists, Action on Smoking and Health, Pub. Citizen, Profl. Inventors Alliance (pres. 1996-2001), Alliance for Am. Innovation Inc. (pres. adv. bd. 1996-), Intellectual Property Creators (adv. bd. 1995-2000), Student Coalition for Handling Intellectual Property. Avocations: horticulture, carpentry, solar and renewable energy, education. Office: Riley & Assocs 1323 W Cook Rd Grand Blanc MI 48439-9364 E-mail: rjriley@rjriley.com.

RILEY, SARAH ANNE, information scientist; b. Balt., Oct. 23, 1946; d. Eugene John and Carroll Morley (Young) R. BA, Mt. St. Agnes Coll., 1968. Asst. registrar Loyola Coll., Balt., 1968-70; lab. scientist Med. Sch. U. Md., 1970-75; retail store mgr. Fabri-Ctrs. Am., Beechwood, Ohio, 1975-79; info. sci. tech. McCormick & Co., Inc., Hunt Valley, Md., 1979-82, assoc. info. sci., 1982-85, info. scientist, 1985-87. Mem. bd. trustees Mercy High Sch., Balt., 1983-89. Mem. Md. Online Users Group (sec. 1982-84, chmn. 1985-87), Spl. Libraries Assn., Am. Soc. Microbiology, Mercy High Sch. Alumnae Assn. (chmn. 1981-84). Republican. Roman Catholic. Office: McCormick & Co Inc 10 Loveton Cir Sparks MD 21152-1502

RILEY, SCOTT C. lawyer; b. Bklyn., Oct. 5, 1959; s. William 42A. and Kathleen (Howe) R.; m. Kathleen D. O'Connor, Oct. 6, 1984; children: Matthew, Brendan. BA, Seton Hall U., South Orange, N.J., 1981; JD, Seton Hall U., Newark, 1984. Bar: N.J. 1985, U.S. Dist. Ct. N.J. 1985. Assoc. Dwyer, Connell & Lisbona, Montclair, N.J., 1985-87; assoc. gen. counsel, v.p. Consolidated Ins. Group, Wilmington, Del., 1987-91; counsel Cigna Ins. Group, Phila., 1991-94; assoc. gen. counsel KWELM Cos., N.Y.C., 1994-98, head U.S. legal ops., 1998—; head U.S. ops. KMSIS Ltd., 1998—. Mem. ABA (com. on environ. ins. coverage), Fedn. of Ins. and Corp. Counsel, Excess and Surplus Lines Claims Assn., N.J. State Bar Assn., Profl. Liability Underwriting Soc. Office: KWELM Companies 599 Lexington Ave New York NY 10022-6030

RILEY, TERRY ZENE, biologist, researcher; b. Onawa, Iowa, July 27, 1949; s. Zene LaVerne Riley and Mary Kathleen Thompson; m. Nancy Louise Derey, June 4, 1994; children: Jason Matthew, Samantha Michele Derey, Anna Louise Derey-Wilson; m. Monica Joan McGlothlin, May 3, 1968 (div. Dec. 30, 1988); children: Jason Matthew, Samantha Michelle. BS, Kans. State U., Manhattan, KS, 1976; MS, N.Mex State U., Las Cruces, NM, 1978, Ohio State U., Columbus, OH, 1987, PhD, 1989. Upland rsch. biologist Iowa Dept. Natural Resources, Chariton, Iowa, 1989—94; field rep. Wildlife Mgmt. Inst., 1994—97, Aberdeen, SD, 1997—99, dir. conservation Washington, 1999—. Sgt. e-4 U.S. Air Force, 1967—71, Vietnam. R-Consevative. Methodist. Avocations: hunting, fishing, flying. Office: 1101 14th Street NW Suite 801 Washington DC 20005

RILEY, THOMAS JOSEPH, anthropologist, educational administrator; b. Portland, Maine, Nov. 2, 1943; s. Joseph Gerard and Virginia C. (Cunningham) R.; m. Karma Jean Ibsen, July 10, 1967 (div. 1985); children: Kirsten, Katharine, Erin; m. Carol Ann, Nov. 21, 1989; 1 child, Julia Wade. BA, Boston Coll., 1965; MA, U. Hawaii, 1970, PhD, 1973. Asst. prof. NYU, 1972-74; from asst. prof. to prof. anthropology U. Ill., Urbana, 1974-96, assoc. dean Grad. Coll., 1983-86, head dept. anthropology, 1986-93, chmn. univ. senate coun., 1995-96; dean Coll. Arts, Humanities/Social Scis., prof. anthropology N.D. State U., Fargo, 1996—; dir. N.D. Inst. for Regional Studies, 1996—. Acad. adv. bd. SALT Ctr., Portland, 1980-96. Co-author: Prehistoric Agriculture, 1972; mem. editl. bd. Ency. of World Cultures, 1993-96, Ency. of Cultural Anthropology, 1994-95, Encyclopedia of World Prehistory, 1996-2001; contbr. over 100 articles to profl. jours. Chmn. bd. Devel. Svcs. Ctr., Champaign, 1986-89, Human Rels. Area Files at Yale U., 1995-96, v.p. 1996; sec. bd. C-U Independence, Champaign, 1987-96; bd. dirs. Disabled Citizens Found., Champaign, 1988-96, Ill. Assn. Retarded Citizens, Chgo., 1988-94, Champaign County Mental Health Bd., 1993-96, Prairie Pub. Broadcasting, 1999—, Plains N.D. State Hist. Soc. Found., 2001—, Ill. State Hist. Sites Adv. Coun., 1986-89, United Way Cass-Clay, 2001—, Plains Art Mus., Fargo, vice chair, 2001—. NSF fellow, 1978-79; NSF grant, 1978-99. Mem. AAAS, Am. Assn. State and Local History, Am. Anthropology Assn., Ill. Archeol. Survey, Soc. Am. Archaeology, Soc. Archeol. Scis. (treas. 1982-83), Sigma Xi (chpt. v.p. 1987-88, chpt. pres. 1988-91). Roman Catholic. Home: 1108 42nd Ave N Fargo ND 58102-5318 also: 155 Beach Ave Kennebunk ME 04043-7625 Office: ND State U 221 Minard Hall Fargo ND 58105 E-mail: thomas.riley@ndsu.nodak.edu.

RILEY, TOM JOSEPH, lawyer; b. Cedar Rapids, Iowa, Jan. 9, 1929; s. Joseph Wendell and Edna (Kyle) R.; m. Nancy Evans, Jan. 21, 1952; children: Pamela Chang, Peter, Lisa Thirnbeck, Martha Brown, Sara Riley, Heather Mescher. BA, U. Iowa, 1950, JD, 1952. Bar: Iowa 1952, U.S. Dist. Ct. (no. dist.) Iowa 1952, U.S. Ct. Appeals (8th cir.) 1960, U.S. Supreme Ct. 1966. Assoc. Simmons, Perrine, Allbright & Ellwood, Cedar Rapids, 1952-60, ptnr., 1960-80; pres. Tom Riley Law Firm, P.C., 1980—. Adj. prof. trial advocacy Coll. Law, U. Iowa, Iowa City, 1979. Author: Proving Punitive Damages, 1981, The Price of a Life, 1986, Trial Handbook for Iowa Lawyers (Civil), 1997, Iowa Practice: Civil Litigation Handbook, 2000-01. Mem. Iowa Ho. of Reps., 1960-64, Iowa Senate, 1965-74. First lt. USAF, 1952-54. Named Outstanding Freshman Legislator, Des Moines Press and Radio Club, 1961. Fellow Iowa Acad. Trial Lawyers (bd. govs. 1982-91); mem. Iowa Trial Lawyers Assn. (bd. govs. 2000 —2002), Cedar Rapids Country Club, U. Athletic Club, Iowa City, Des Moines Club, Masons. Republican. Presbyterian. Avocations: tennis, sailing, downhill skiing. Home: 5300 Lakeside Rd Rural Route Marion IA 52302 Office: 4040 1st Ave NE Cedar Rapids IA 52402-3143

RILEY, WILLIAM, corporate executive, writer, conservationist; b. Indpls., June 30, 1931; s. Leo Michael and Edna (Wilhelm) R.; m. Laura Etz, Apr. 20, 1957. AB, U. Notre Dame, 1952; LLB, Yale U., 1955. V.p., dir., chmn. Ivy Corp., Atlanta, 1960-80; CEO, chmn. Moore-Handley, Inc., Birmingham, Ala., 1981—. Bd. dirs. Fabco-Air, Inc., Gainesville, Fla. Author: (with Laura Riley) Guide to the National Wildlife Refuges, 1979 (Pulitzer prize nominee), 2d edit., 1993, Lifetime Conservation award Nat. Audubon Soc., 2000. Trustee The Raptor Trust, Basking Ridge, N.J., 1980-2000; bd. dirs. Nat. Wildlife Refuge Assn., Potomac, Md., 1985-94, Hawk Mountain Sanctuary Assn., Kempton, Pa., 1989-98, Nat. Audubon Soc., N.Y.C., 1990-94; chmn. exec. com. Everglades Fdn., 1997—. With U.S. Army, 1957-58. Recipient Conservationist of Yr. award Everglades Coalition, 2001. Mem.: Explorers Club of N.Y.C., Met. Club of N.Y.C. Office: 767 Fifth Ave 44th Floor New York NY 10153

RILEY, WILLIAM JAY, federal judge; b. Lincoln, Nebr., Mar. 11, 1947; s. Don Paul and Marian Frances (Munn) R.; m. Norma Jean Mason, Dec. 27, 1965; children: Brian, Kevin, Erin. BA, U. Nebr., 1969, JD with distinction, 1972. Bar: Nebr. 1972, U.S. Dist. Ct. Nebr. 1972, U.S. Ct. Appeals (8th cir.) 1974; cert. civil trial specialist Nat. Bd. Trial Advocacy. Law clk. U.S. Ct. Appeals (8th cir.), Omaha, 1972-73; assoc. Fitzgerald, Schorr Law Firm, P.C., LLO, 1973-79; shareholder Fitzgerald, Schorr Law Firm, 1979—2001; US Circuit Judge 8th Circuit Ct. Appeals , 2001—. Adj. prof. trial practice Creighton U. Coll. Law, Omaha, 1991—; chmn. fed. practice com. Fed. Ct., 1992-94. Scoutmaster Boy Scouts Am., Omaha, 1979—89, scout membership chair Mid. Am. coun., 1995—98, trustee, 2001—. Recipient Silver Beaver award Boy Scouts Am., 1991. Fellow Am. Coll. Trial Lawyers (chair state com. 1997-99), Nebr. State Bar Found.; mem. Am. Bd. Trial Advs. (Nebr. chpt. pres. 2000), Nebr. State Bar Assn. (chmn. ethics com. 1996-98, ho. of dels. 1998—), Omaha Bar Assn. (treas. 1997-98, pres. 2000-01), Robert M. Spire Inns of Ct. (master 1994—, counselor 1997-98), Order of Coif, Phi Beta Kappa. Republican. Methodist. Avocations: reading, hiking, cycling. Office: Roman L Hruska US Courthouse 111 S 18th Plaza Ste 4179 Omaha NE 68102-1322

RILEY, WILLIAM JOHN, neurologist; b. Seattle, Oct. 24, 1930; s. William John and Virginia (McCarthy) R.; m. Joan Marie Weismann, 1956 (div. 1976); children: Sean, Kevan, Megan, Janeen, Michael; m. Margit Mary, 1976; children: Britta, Shane, Timothy. MS in Anatomy, U. Chgo., 1958, MD, 1960; PhD, U. Minn., 1965. Intern Mpls. Gen. Hosp., 1961-62; resident U. Minn. Hosps., 1962-65; asst. chief neurology Mpls. Gen. Hosp., 1965-69; chief neurology St. Luke's Episcopal Hosp., Houston, 1970-85; pres., CEO Tex. Neurol. Clinic Assn., 1969—. Staff sgt. USAF, 1951-55. Recipient Disting. Tchg. award Minn. Med. Found., Mpls., 1969. Fellow: ACP, Tex. Neurol. Soc. (pres. 2002—), Am. Acad. Neurology; mem.: Alpha Omega Alpha, AMA, Tex. Med. Assn. (pres. 9th dist. 1991), Sigma Xi. Roman Catholic. Avocation: ranching. Office: Tex Neurol Clinic Assn 41126 SE Freeway # 1210 Houston TX 77027-7306

RILL, JAMES FRANKLIN, lawyer; b. Evanston, Ill., Mar. 4, 1933; s. John Columbus and Frances Eleanor (Hill) R.; m. Mary Elizabeth Laws, June 14, 1957; children: James Franklin, Roderick M. AB cum laude, Dartmouth Coll., 1954; LLB, Harvard, 1959. Bar: D.C. bar 1959. Legis. asst. Congressman James P. S. Devereux, Washington, 1952; pvt. practice, 1959-89; assoc. Steadman, Collier & Shannon, 1959-63; ptnr. Collier, Shannon & Rill, 1963-69, Collier, Shannon, Rill & Scott, 1969-89; asst. atty. gen., antitrust div. U.S. Dept. Justice, Washington, 1989-92; ptnr. Collier, Shannon, Rill & Scott, 1992-2000; co-chair internat. competition policy adv. com. U.S. Dept. Justice, 1997-2000; ptnr. Howrey Simon Arnold & White, Washington, 2000—. Pub. mem. Adminstrv. Conf. of U.S., 1992-94; coun. prin. Coun. for Excellence in Govt.; mem., advisor panel Office of Tech. Assessment of Multinat. Firms and U.S. Tech. Base. Contbr. articles to profl. jours. Trustee emeritus Bullis Sch., Potomac, Md. Served to 1st lt. arty. AUS, 1954-56. Fellow: Am. Bar Found.; mem.: ABA (antitrust law sect., past chmn.), DC Bar Assn., Loudoun Valley Club, Met. Club, Phi Delta Theta. Home: 7305 Masters Dr Potomac MD 20854-3850 Office: Howrey Simon Arnold & White, LLP Rm 621 1299 Pennsylvania Ave NW Washington DC 20004-2402

RILLA, DONALD ROBERT, social services administrator; b. Feb. 6, 1941; AS, Berkshire Community Coll., Pittsfield, Mass., 1964; BA, U. Mass., 1967; MSW, U. Conn., 1974. LCSW Lic. clin. social worker Conn., diplomate Am. Bd. Clin. Social Work, cert. in drugs and alchohol Conn., Lic. Alcohol & Drug Counselor. Social worker Children and Youth Svcs., New Haven, 1967-73, Branford (Conn.) Counseling Ctr., 1973-74; psychiatric social worker Whiting Forensic Inst., Middletown, Conn., 1974-79; psychiatric social worker supr. Cts. Diagnostic Clinic, Hartford, 1979-87; dir. Bridgeport (Conn.) Ct. Clinic, 1987-97; owner Forensic & Behavioral Assocs., Fairfield, Conn., 1997—2000; psychiat. social worker supr. Liberation, Meridian and Guenster, Stamford, 1998-2000; dir. drug ct. LMG, Inc., Bridgeport, 2000—01; clin. coord. Coastal Behavioral Healthcare CSU, 2001—. Cons. Bridgeport Mental Health Ctr., 1990-97; with Family Resource Assocs., Stratford, Conn., 1994-97; credentialing priviledges Yale U. Sch. of Medicine, New Haven, 1997—; presenter at profl. confs. Contbr. articles to profl. jours. Chair Town-Bus Safety Commn., North Haven, 1975; mem. Mental Health Assn. Conn., New Haven, 1968-75; chair, mem. New Haven Halfway House, 1969-73. With USN, 1958-62. Mem. NASW, Nat. Assn. Alcoholism Drug Abuse Counselors, Nat. Assn. Drug Ct. Profls., Nat. Orgn. Forensic Social Work (founding mem. 1983—, chair ethics com. 1985-93, treas. 1994-95, pres.- elect 1995, pres. 1996), Acad. Cert. Social Workers, Acad. Forensic Social Workers (diplomate, chmn. bd. dirs.), Lions Club (pres. 2000). Avocations: photography, sports, volunteering, Spl. Olympics. Home: PO Box 51743 Sarasota FL 34232-0314 Office: Costal Recovery Ctrs Inc Crisis Stabilization Unit 1451 10th St Sarasota FL 34236

RILLING, DAVID CARL, surgeon; b. Phila., Oct. 10, 1940; s. Carl Adam and Elizabeth Barbara (Young) R.; m. Karina Sturman, Mar. 25, 1972; children: Jonathan David, Alexander Valentine, Claudia Carla. BS with honors in Biology, Dickinson Coll., Carlisle, pa., 1962; MD, Hahnemann U., 1966. Diplomate Am. Bd. Surgery. Intern Hosp. of U. Pa., Phila., 1966-67; resident Abington (Pa.) Meml. Hosp., 1967-68, 70-73; surgeon Pennridge Surg Assocs., Sellersville, Pa., 1973—. Active staff Grand View Hosp., Sellersville, Pa., chmn. dept. surgery, 1985-89, pres. med. staff, 1995. Lt. col. U.S. Army, 1968-70, Vietnam, USARMC. Decorated Bronze Star medal, Nat. Def. Svc. medal, Vietnam Svc. medal. Fellow Am. Coll. Surgeons; mem. AMA, Soc. Clin. Vascular Surgery, Pa. Med. Soc., Bucks County Med. Soc., Vietnam Vascular Registry. Avocations: paleontology, tennis, skiing. Office: Pennridge Surg Assocs 670 Lawn Ave Sellersville PA 18960-1571

RILLING, JOHN ROBERT, history educator; b. Wausau, Wis., Apr. 28, 1932; s. John Peter and Esther Laura (Wittig) R.; m. Joanne Marilyn McCrory, Dec. 21, 1953; children: Geoffrey Alan, Andrew Peter. BA summa cum laude, U. Minn., 1953; AM, Harvard U., 1957, PhD, 1959. Asst. prof. history U. Richmond, Va., 1959-62, assoc. prof. history, 1962-68, prof. history, 1968-99, prof. English history emeritus, 1999—, chmn. dept. history, 1977-83, Westhampton Coll., 1965-71. Pres. Faculty Senate of Va., 1975-77. Contbr. articles to profl. jours. Elder, Ginter Park Presbyn. Ch., 1973-83. Served with U.S. Army, 1953-55. Recipient U. Richmond Disting. Educator award, 1975, 76, 77, 80, 87, Prof. of Yr. finalist Coun. for Advancement and Support of Edn., 1981. Woodrow Wilson fellow, 1955-59; Harvard U. travelling fellow, 1958; Coolidge fellow, 1955-56; Folger Libr. fellow, 1960. Mem. Am. Hist. Assn., Econ. History Soc., Agecroft Assn. (bd. dirs.), Conf. Brit. Studies, Phi Beta Kappa, Omicron Delta Kappa (Prof. of Yr. 1995). Avocations: hiking, bicycling, enology. Home: 1507 Wilmington Ave Richmond VA 23227-4429 Office: U Richmond Dept History Richmond VA 23173 Business E-Mail: jrilling@richmond.edu.

RIMA, INGRID HAHNE, economics educator; b. Fed. Republic of Germany; d. Max F. and Hertha G. (Grunsfeld) Hahne; m. Philip W. Rima; children: David, Eric. BA with honors, CUNY, 1945; MA, U. Pa., 1946, PhD, 1951. Prof. econs. Temple U., Phila., 1967—. Author: Development of Economic Analysis, 1967, 6th edit., 2000, Labor Markets Wages and Employment, 1981, The Joan Robinson Legacy, 1991, The Political Economy of Global Restructuring, Vol. I, Production and Organization, Vol. II, Trade and Finance, 1993, Measurement, Quantification and Economic Analysis, 1994, Labor Markets in a Global Economy, 1996. Fulbright Disting. Lectr. Lingnan U., China, 2000. Fellow Ea. Econ. Assn.; mem. Am. Econ. Assn., History of Econs. Soc. (pres. 1993-4), Phi Beta Kappa. Office: Temple U Broad & Montgomery Ave Philadelphia PA 19122

RIMBACH, EVANGELINE LOIS, retired music educator; b. Portland, Oreg., June 28, 1932; d. Raymond Walter and Viola Clara (Gaebler) Rimbach. BA, Valparaiso (Ind.) U., 1954; MMus, Eastman Sch. Music, Rochester, N.Y., 1956; PhD, Eastman Sch. Music, 1967; student, Pacific Luth. U., Parkland, Wash., 1950-52. Vocal music instr. Goodwin Jr. High Sch., Redwood City, Calif., 1956-57; music instr. Calif. Concordia Coll., Oakland, 1957-62; prof. music Concordia U., River Forest, Ill., 1964-97, chmn. dept., 1989-97; ret., 1997. Contbg. editor: Church Music, 1965—80; editor: (book) Johann Kuhnau: Magnificat, 1980, (cantata) Johann Kuhnau: Lobe den Herrn, 1993; contbr. (essays) Hymnal Supplement '98 Handbook, Keywords in Ch. Music, 2002; contbr. articles to profl. jours. Bd. dirs. Civic Symphony of Oak Park-River Forest, 1974-80, concert com. chmn., 1976-78, prog. annotator, 1976-80; mem. choir Grace Luth. Ch., River Forest, 1964-97. AAUW postdoctoral fellow, 1969-70; DAAD grantee, Munich, 1980; recipient Rose of Honor award, Sigma Alpha Iota, 1987. Mem. Am. Musicol. Soc., Assn. Luth. Ch. Musicians (editor newsletter 1998—), Luth. Edn. Assn., Sigma Alpha Iota (Rose of Dedication award 1997). Republican. Lutheran. Avocations: travel, cooking, needlework. Home: Apt L-206 12121 Admiralty Way Everett WA 98204-7507 Fax: 425-265-0837. E-mail: rimbachtwo@earthlink.net.

RIMEL, LINDA JUNE, writer; b. Seattle, June 4, 1952; d. Ira Wesley Rimel and Mary Mackinlay (Weir) R. BA in Gen. Humanities, U. Oreg., 1977; postgrad., Willamette U., 1977-79. Rschr., writer, Eugene, Oreg., 1979-84; English instr. U. Great Falls, Great Falls, Mont., 1988-90; asst. libr., acting libr. dir. Columbus Health Scis. Libr., 1990-92; writer, rschr., editor, tchr., 1984—97; writer, editor, tutor Seattle, 1997—2001, Eugene, Oreg., 2001—. Exhibited quilts in Gallery 16, Great Falls, 1985; workshop instr. D.A. Davidson & Co., Great Falls, 1990; staff writer Merit System Index and Digest, 1979; author: Quicker Quilts, 1985, (play) Treasure This House, 1989; contbr. books revs., humor to popular publs.; lyricist, librettist The Ms. Seattle Skyline Contest, 1990, Anybody but Liza, 1996; librettist (ballets) Thumbelina, 1996, The Trial, 1997; songs include Five Poems by Linda Rimel, Roses and Sweet Peas, A Mixed Metaphor of Love, Alarm Clock, This January Morning, How Did We Catch Her?, 1997—, Silent Fall the Silos, 1997, The More I Think About You, 1997, Alleluia: Word Made Flesh to Word Returns, 1998, You Say It's Over, 1998, We Know What We Want, 1998, Ask Me Now, 1999, Simple Simon Says, 2000, When I Become a Ms., 2001, There Is Peace, 2001; contbr. drama and book revs., features, humor to profl., popular publs. Costume builder, wardrobe mistress Eugene (Oreg.) Ballet, Eugene Opera, 1980-82; machine quilting instr. Paris Gibson Sq. Mus. of Art, Great Falls, 1984-86; tutor Native Am. Program, Great Falls, 1987-89; publicity chair Cascade County chpt. '89ers Mont. Statehood Centennial, 1988; program annotator, performer mus. theater U. Great Falls, 1992-93; active Urgent Action Network of Amnesty Internat., 1987—; bd. dirs. Sister Cities-Great Falls-Sharia, Russia Com., 1997. Mem. ASCAP, Dramatists Guild (assoc.), Internat. Alliance Women in Music, Falls Quilt Guild (bd. dirs., program chair 1992-94, publicity chair 1992-93). Avocations: quilting, music. Home: 3150 University St Eugene OR 97405-4242 E-mail: rhymeswithprimal@juno.com.

RIMEL, REBECCA WEBSTER, foundation executive; BS, U. Va., 1973; MBA, James Madison U., 1983. Head nurse, emergency dept. U. Va. Hosp., Charlottesville, 1973-74, coord. med. out-patient dept., 1974-75, nurse practitioner dept. neurosurgery, 1975-77, instr. in neurosurgery, 1975-80, asst. prof., 1981-83; program mgr. health Pew Charitable Trusts, Phila., 1983-84; asst. v.p. Glenmede Trust Co., Pew Charitable Trusts, 1984-85; v.p. for programs Pew Charitable Trusts, 1985-88, exec. dir., 1988-94, pres., 1994—. Mem. Coun. on Founds., Washington; prin. investigator dept. neurosurgery U. Va., 1981—83; adv. com. Boxing U.S. Olympics , 1983—86; adv. coun. Nat. Inst. of Neurol. Disorders and Strokes, 1988—91, bd. dirs., Thomas Jefferson Meml. Found., Deutsche Banc Flag Investors Fund. Contbr. . Recipient Disting. Nursing Alumni award, U. Va., 1988; fellow Kellogg Nat. fellow, 1992. Mem.: APHA, ANA, Va. State Nurses Assn. (membership and credentials com. 1982—86), Emergency Dept. Nurses Assn., Am. Assn. Neurosurg. Nurses, Am. Acad. Nursing.

RIMER, BARBARA K. health facility administrator, educator; b. Wilkes Barre, Pa., Jan. 14, 1949; married. BA in English, U. Mich., 1970, MPH in Med. Care Adminstrn. and Health Edn., 1973; PhD in Health Edn., Johns Hopkins Sch. of Hygiene and Public Health, 1981. Instr. Wayne State U. Sch. Medicine, Detroit, 1973-75; program dir. Nat. Cancer Inst., Bethesda, Md., 1975-77; intervention coord. Johns Hopkins Oncology Ctr., Balt., 1977-79; rsch. assoc. Johns Hopkins Sch. Hygiene and Public Health, 1977-79; sr. health educator Fox Chase Cancer Ctr., Phila., 1981-87, dir. health comms. rsch., 1981-87, dir. behavioral rsch., 1987-91, dir. population sci. for behavioral rsch., 1990-91; dir. cancer prevention, detection and ctrl. rsch. Duke Comprehensive Cancer Ctr., Durham, NC, 1991-97; sr. fellow Aging Ctr. Duke U. Med. Ctr., 1991-97, assoc. prof. in cmty. and family medicine, 1991-93, prof. cmty. and family medicine, 1993-97; acting dep. dir. Duke Comprehensive Cancer Ctr., 1995-96; dir. cancer ctrl. and population scis. Nat. Cancer Inst., Rockville, Md., 1997—. Adj. assoc. prof. dept. health behavior and health edn. U. N.C. Sch. of Public Health, Chapel Hill, NC, 1992-97; adj. mem. Fox Chase Cancer Ctr., Phila., 1992-97; preceptor, lectr. Temple U., 1983-91; guest lectr. Duke U. Med. Ctr., 1991-97, U. N.C. Sch. Public Health, 1991-93; Judith P. Schlager vis. prof. Dana-Farber Cancer Inst., 1995; disting. vis. lectr. Harvard U., 1998; mem. institutional review bd. Fox Chase Cancer Ctr., 1983-88, vice chair, 1988-91; proposal review, site visitor Nat. Cancer Inst., 1985-95; chairperson tech. advisory com. Am. Lung Assn., 1987; external advisory com. Vermont Regional Cancer Ctr., 1988-89; advisory com. Brown U., U. R.I. Cancer Prevention Rsch. unit, 1988-95; mem. Am. Assn. Retired Persons task force on smoking, 1989-91, Health Promotion adv. bd. Wesley Found., 1990-91, program com. annual mtg. Am. Soc. Preventive Oncology, 1990-93, chair, 1993 mtg., expert adv. com. AMC Cancer Rsch. Ctr./Ctrs. for Disease Ctrl. Coop. Agreement, 1991, adult edn. subcom. and tobacco materials review group Am. Cancer Soc., 1991; mem. Nat. Task Force on Breast Cancer Ctrl. Am. Cancer Soc., 1992, chair Nat. and State (NC) Task Force on Breast Cancer Ctrl., 1992; mem. Pub. Edn. subcom. on Adult Edn. Am. Cancer Soc., 1992; mem. adv. bd. Office of Cancer Comms., NCI, 1992; mem. Clin. Cancer com. Duke U. Med. Ctr., 1992-95; mem. Cancer Ctrs.' Support com. NCI, 1993-94, Recruitment and Adherence com. Office of Women's Health NIH, 1993, Report com. Internat. Workshop on Screening for breast cancer NCI, 1993, Detection and Treatment subcom. on Breast Cancer Am. Cancer Soc., 1993, 94, Nominating com. Soc. Behavioral Medicine, 1993-96, adv. com. on cancer coordination and ctrl. State of NC, 1993-97; invited participant and com. chair Frontiers of Behavioral Medicine mtg., Chantilly, Va., 1993; invited co-chair Sec. Shalala's Mtg. to develop nat. strategic plan for breast cancer, Bethesda, Md., 1993; chair, mem. Nat. Cancer Adv. Bd. (presdl. appointment), 1994-97; bd. dirs. Am. Family Life Assurance Corp., 1995—; fellowship selection com. Am. Assn. Cancer Rsch., 1996; mem. exec. com. Acad. Behavioral Medicine Rsch., 1998, Charles S. Mott Selection com. of Gen. Motors Cancer Rsch. Found., 1999, Inst. Medicine com. effective health comm. and behavior change strategies for diverse populations, 2000. Editor: special cancer issue Health Education Research, 1998-89; editl. bd. Health Education Quarterly, 1985-87, guest editl. bd. 1983; editl. bd. Jour. of Compliance in Health Care, 1989-90, Health Edn. Rsch., 1990-98, Cancer Prevention, Epidemiology and Biomarkers, 1990—, Patient Edn. and Counseling, 1994—, Breast Diseases, 1998—, Cancer Causes and Control, 1998—, Effective Clin. Practice, 2000—; assoc. editor: Preventive Medicine, 1990—; reviewer Am. Jour. Preventive Medicine, Am. Jour. Public Health, Annals of Internal Medicine, Health Edn. Quarterly, Health Services Research, Jour. of Am. Med. Assn., Jour. Nat. Cancer Inst., Milbank Quarterly, Women's Health, 1986—; contbr. numerous articles, papers to profl. pubs. Fellow Johns Hopkins Sch. of Hygiene and Public Health, 1979-81, Soc. of Behavioral Medicine, 1997; recipient Mayhew Derryberry award Am. Public Health Assn., 1992, Best Visual Presentation of Session award Soc. of Behavioral Medicine, San Diego, 1995, Citation award Soc. Behavioral Medicine, 1996, Disting. Achievement award Am. Soc. Preventive Oncology, 1997, Herbert J. Block Leadership award Ohio State U., 1997, John P.

McGovern award in Health Promotion U. Tex. Sch. Public Health, 1999. Office: Nat Cancer Inst DCCPS Rm 6134 6130 Executive Blvd Exec Plz N Rockville MD 20852 Fax: 301-594-6787. E-mail: barbara.rimer@nih.gov.*

RIMER, JOHN THOMAS, foreign language educator, academic administrator, writer, translator; b. Pitts., Mar. 2, 1933; s. John T. and Naomi (Bowser) R.; m. Laurence E. Mus., Apr. 18, 1964; children: John, Mark. BA, Princeton U., 1954; MA, Columbia U., 1969, PhD, 1971. Asst. cultural officer USIA, Laos, Japan; then dir. Am. Cultural Ctr. Kobe, Japan, 1958-67; assoc. prof., then prof. Japanese lang. and lit. Washington U., St. Louis, 1973-83, chmn. dept. Chinese and Japanese, 1973-83; chief Asian div. Library of Congress, Washington, 1983-86; chmn. Hebrew and East Asian langs. and lits. U. Maryland, College Park, 1986-91; chmn. East Asian langs. and lits. U. Pitts., 1991—. Mem. Am. adv. bd. Japan Found., 1984— Author: Toward a Modern Japanese Theatre, 1974, Traditions in Modern Japanese Fiction, 1978; translator: stories Mori Ogai, 2 vols., 1977, Mask and Sword: Two Plays for the Contemporary Japanese Theatre, 1980, On the No Drama, 1983, Pilgrimages, 1988, A Reader's Guide to Japanese Literature, 1988; editor: Multiple Meanings, 1987; editor, contbr.: Culture and Identity, Japanese Intellectuals during the Interwar Years, 1990, Shisendo, 1991, Youth and Other Stories by Mori Ogai, 1994, Kyoto Encounters, 1995, A Hidden Fire: Russian and Japanese Cultural Encounters, 1868-1929, 1995, The Blue-eyed Tarôkaja: Essays by Donald Keene, 1996, Nara Encounters, 1997, The Voyage of Japanese Theatre: Theatre Criticism of Senda Akihiko, 1997, Poems to Sing: The Wakan Rôeishû, 1997, (with Marlene J. Mayo) War, Occupation, and Creativity: Japan and East Asia 1920-1960, 2001. Served with U.S. Army, 1955-58. NEH fellow France, 1976-77; NEH grantee, 1979-81; recipient Order of the Sacred Treasure award Japanese Govt., 1997. Mem. Social Sci. Research Council (joint com. on Japan studies 1979-83) Episcopalian. E-mail: rimer+@pitt.gov. Home: 1400 N Negley Ave Pittsburgh PA 15206-1118 Office: U Pitts Dept East Asian Langs and Lits 1501 CL Pittsburgh PA 15260

RIMLAND, LISA PHILLIP, writer, composer, lyricist, artist; b. Stamford, Conn., Mar. 27, 1954; d. Maurice Louis and Eva (Kreiz) R. BA, U. Conn., 1978. Owner Ph Rimland Press, Storrs, Conn., 1991—. Composer numerous songs, including Your Heart or Mine, 1990, Drive Me Crazy, 1991, Send Me an Angel, 1992; author: The Candida Manual: Candida Overgrowth and the Quest for Human Wellness, 1999, Voices From the Farm, 1999, Machronomarker Observations Conducted During the First Three Months of the Life of a Cloned Heifer Dairy Calf, 2000, An Evaluation of Machronomarker Observations, 2001; contbr. articles, poems, essays to profl. jours. Vol. dairy barn U. Conn., 1992—, vol. photographer Morgan horse facility, 1982-91. Recipient DAR award, 1969, Soc. Women Engrs. award, 1971, Editor's Choice award Nat. Libr. Poetry, 1995, 96; Nat. Merit scholar, 1972. Mem. ASCAP. Avocations: film and drama, art, poetry, athletics, Morgan horses. Home: PO Box 408 Storrs Mansfield CT 06268-0408

RIMLER, ANITA A. secretary of state; Campaign aide, legis. asst. former Del. Rob James, 1975; asst. Atty. Gen. Mary Sue Terry, 1985—91; dir. fin. ops. Terry for Gov. campaign, 1993, Robb for Senate campaign , 1994, Warner's U.S. Senate campaign , 1996; sr. advisor, dir. fin. ops. Warner for Gov. campaign; Sec. of State State of Va., 2002—. Office: Office Sec Commonwealth 830 E Main St 14th Fl Richmond VA 23219 Fax: 804-371-0017. Business E-Mail: socmail@gov.state.va.us.*

RIMOIN, DAVID LAWRENCE, physician, geneticist; b. Montreal, Nov. 9, 1936; s. Michael and Fay (Lecker) Rimoin; m. Mary Ann Singleton, 1962 (div. 1979); 1 child Anne ; m. Ann Piilani Garber, July 27, 1980; children: Michael, Lauren. BSc, McGill U., Montreal, 1957, MSc, MD, CM, 1961; PhD, Johns Hopkins U., 1967; LHD (hon.), Finch U., 1997. Asst. prof. medicine, pediat. Washington U., St. Louis, 1967—70; assoc. prof. UCLA, 1970—73, prof., 1973—, chief med. genetics, Harbor-UCLA Med. Ctr., 1970—86; dir. dept. pediat., dir. Med. Genetics and Birth Defects Ctr., 1986—; Steven Spielberg chmn. pediat. Cedars-Sinai Med. Ctr., L.A., 1989—. Chmn. coun. Med. Genetics Orgn., 1993. Co-author: Principles and Practice of Medical Genetics, 1983, 1990, 1996, 2002; contbr. articles, chapters to books. Recipient E. Mead Johnson award, Am. Acad. Pediat., 1976, Col. Harland Saunders award, March of Dimes, 1997, Pioneer in Medicine award, Cedars Sinai Med. Ctr., 2001. Fellow: Am. Coll. Med. Genetics Found. (pres. 1999—), Am. Coll. Med. Genetics (pres. 1990—98, pres. 1991—96, bd. dirs. 1996—2000), AAAS, ACP; mem.: Inst. of Medicine, Assn. Am. Physicians, Am. Pediat. Soc., Am. Soc. Human Genetics (pres. 1984), Am. Bd. Med. Genetics (pres. 1979—83,), Western Soc. Pediat. Rsch. (pres. 1995, Ross Outstanding Young Investigator award 1976), Western Soc. Clin. Rsch. (pres. 1978,), Am. Fedn. Clin. Rsch. (sec.-treas. 1972—75), Johns Hopkins Soc. Scholars. Office: Cedars Sinai Med Ctr 8700 Beverly Blvd Los Angeles CA 90048-1865 E-mail: david.rimoin@cshs.org.

RIMPEL, AUGUSTE EUGENE, JR. management and technical consulting executive; b. St. Thomas, V.I., Aug. 25, 1939; s. Auguste Eugene and Leah Eudora (Harris) R. B.A. magna cum laude, Inter-Am. U. P.R., 1957; M.S. in Ch.E., M.I.T., 1961; Ph.D., Carnegie Inst. Tech., 1964; M.B.A., Columbia U., 1964-65; m. Maria Czernetski, Sept. 23, 1966; children: Nicole, Christopher. Research chem. engr. Am. Cyanamid Co., Stamford, Conn., 1961-62; with Arthur D. Little, Inc., Cambridge, Mass., 1965-75, sr. staff mem., 1973-75; commr. of commerce, spl. advisor to gov. for econ. affairs Govt. U.S. V.I., St. Thomas, 1975-78; mem. corp. spl. staff Arthur D. Little, Inc., Cambridge, 1978-81, also v.p. Arthur D. Little Internat., Inc.; v.p. Booz-Allen and Hamilton, Inc., 1981-83; v.p., ptnr., Price Waterhouse, 1983-98, ptnr. Price Waterhouse Coopers, 1998—. sr. partner Boston Global Partners, 2001-; Bd. dirs. Caribbean/Lat. Am. Action, 1979-; chair, bd. dirs. U. V.I., 1997—; mem. subcoms. on internat. econ. devel. U.S. C. of C., 1980-83; bd. dirs. travel adv. bd. U.S. Dept. Commerce, 1977-78; pres. Caribbean Tourism Assn., 1977-78; bd. dirs., mem. exec. com. Caribbean Tourism Research Center, 1976-78. Mem. Am. Inst. Chem. Engrs., Am. Chem. Soc., Am. Inst. Chemists, Soc. Internat. Devel., Sigma Xi. Office: Ste 400 283 Franklin St Boston MA 02103-1195 E-mail: ARIMPEL@AOL.COM.

RIMROTT, FRIEDRICH PAUL JOHANNES, engineer, educator; b. Halle, Germany, Aug. 4, 1927; emigrated to Can., 1952; s. Hans and Margarete (Hofmeister) R.; m. Doreen McConnell, Apr. 7, 1955; children: Karla, Robert, Kira, Elizabeth-Ann. Dipl. Ing., U. Karlsruhe, Germany, 1951; MASc, U. Toronto, Ont., Can., 1955; PhD, Pa. State U., 1958; Dr Ing., Tech. U., Darmstadt, Germany, 1961; P.Eng., Ontario Prov., 1954; C.Eng., U.K., 1987; D.Eng. (hon.), U. Victoria, 1992; DSc (hon.), St. Petersburg State U., 1996; Dr.Ing. (hon.), Otto-von-Guericke-U., Magdeburg, 1997. Asst. prof. engring. mechanics Pa. State U., 1958-60; mem. faculty dept. mech. engring. U. Toronto, 1960—, assoc. prof., 1962-67, prof., 1967-93, prof. emeritus, 1993—. Vis. prof. Tech. U. Vienna, Austria, 1969-70, 86, Tech. U. Hanover, Germany, 1970, U. Bochum, Germany, 1971, U. Wuppertal, Germany, 1987, 89, U. Lanzhou, People's Republic of China, 1989, Otto-von-Guericke-U. Magdeburg, 1992, 93, 94, 95, 96, 97; mng. dir. German Lang. Sch. (Metro Toronto) Inc., 1967-91; pres. 15th Internat. Congress Theoretical and Applied Mechanics, 1980; pres. CSME Mech. Engring. Forum, 1990. Author: Introductory Attitude Dynamics, 1988, Introductory Orbit Dynamics, 1989, (with K.Y. Yeh) Orbital Mechanics Introduction, Chinese edit., 1993, (with B. Tabarrok) Variational Methods and Complementary Formulations in Dynamics, 1994, (with Yongxi Yu) Satellite Gyrodynamics, Chinese edit., 1996; editor: (with J. Schwaighofer) Mechanics of the Solid State, 1968, (with L.E. Jones) Proceedings CANCAM 67, 1968, (with J.T. Pindera, H.H.E. Leipholz, D.E. Grierson) Experimental Mechanics in Research and Development, 1973, (with W. Eichenlaub) Was Du ererbt, 1978, (with B. Tabarrok) Theoretical and Applied Mechanics, 1980. Mem. Can. Council on Multiculturalism, 1972-79. NRC postdoctoral fellow, 1959, Alexander von Humboldt sr. fellow, 1962, NRC sr. rsch. fellow, 1969-70; recipient Can. Congress Applied Mechanics award, 1989, Alexander von Humboldt Rsch. prize, 1993. Fellow ASME, Instn. Mech. Engrs., Engring. Inst. Can., Can. Soc. Mech. Engring. (pres. 1974-75), Can. Aero. and Space Inst.; mem. Can. Congress Applied Mechanics (ctrl. com., chmn. congress com. 1967, 69, 71, 77), Can. Metric Assn. (pres. 1971-72), Soc. German Engrs. (Germany), Soc. for Applied Math. and Mechanics (Germany) (dir. 1971-79). Home: RR 2 Comp 54 Minden ON Canada K0M 2K0 Office: Dept Mech and Idust Engring U Toronto Toronto ON Canada M5S 3G8 E-mail: frimrott@halhinet.on.ca.

RIMSAY, REBEKAH, ballerina; b. Ft. Collins, Colo. Student, Nat. Ballet Sch., Toronto, Ont., Can. Mem. Nat. Ballet Can., Toronto, 1990—98, first soloist, 1998—. Dancer (ballets) Onegin, Swan Lake, Washington Square, The Fairy's Kiss, Jewels, Forgotten Land, the weight of absence, one hundred word for snow, Terra Firma, Musings, Cruel World, The Four Seasons. Office: Walter Carsen Ctr for Nat Ballet Can 470 Queens Quay W Toronto ON Canada M5V 3K4 Office Fax: 416-345-8323.*

RIMSZA, SKIP, mayor; b. Chgo. m. Kim Gill; children: Brian, Jenny, Alexander, Taylor, Nicole. Mem. Phoenix City Coun., 1990-94; vice mayor City of Phoenix, 1993, mayor, 1994—. Former pres. Bd. Realtors. Mem. several cmty. bds. Office: Office Mayor 200 W Washington St Fl 11 Phoenix AZ 85003-1611*

RINAKER, SAMUEL MAYO, JR. retired utilities executive; b. Chgo., Sept. 29, 1922; s. Samuel Mayo and Marjorie (Horton) R.; m. Alice Benthey, Dec. 17, 1949 (div. 1974); children: Elizabeth Cherry, Samuel M. III, Laura Frazier, Mary Clark. Student, UCLA, 1941-42. Farmer, Nebr. and Ill., 1946-49; exec. sec. to atty. gen. Olympia, Wash., 1949-52; news dir. Sta. KTNT-TV, Tacoma, 1952-57, Sta. KIRO-TV, Seattle, 1957-60; assoc. news dir., news anchor Sta. KGTV, San Diego, 1960-75; dir. pub. policy San Diego Gas & Electric Co., 1976-84. Bd. dirs. 1st Nat. Bank, Beatrice, Neb., 1976-93. Maj. U.S. Army Air Corps, 1942-46, ETO. Mem. Rotary (bd. dirs. 1965-67), La Jolla Beach Tennis Club. Republican. Presbyterian. Avocations: golf. Home: 5935 Rutgers Rd La Jolla CA 92037-7834 E-mail: smr11@san.rr.com.

RINALDI, ROBERT R., JR. artist, photographer, publisher; b. Conn. BFA, SUNY, Purchase, 1987; MFA, Md. Inst. Coll. Art, Balt., 1989. Art dir. N-News Mag., Stamford, 1989-94, Chelsea, Vt., 1994-98, pub. Stamford, 1999—; prodn. designer Fred Collins Studio, 1991-95; owner, artist Rinaldi Works, Topsham, Vt., 1993—; new products mgr. Visual Departures, Riverside, Conn., 1996-98; pub. N-News Mag., 1999—. Vis. Artist grantee Vt. Studio Ctr., Johnson, 1997.

RINALDO, PETER MERRITT, publishing executive; b. Evanston, Ill., June 21, 1922; s. Philip Sidney and Harriet Huntington (Beach) R.; m. Dorothy Hastings Warren, July 20, 1946; children: David, Marjory, John. BA, Bowdoin Coll., 1943; BS, MIT, 1944, MS, 1947. Chem. engr. Dewey & Almy Chem. Co., Cambridge, Mass., 1947-54; v.p. overseas chem. divsn. W.R. Grace & Co., 1954-65, v.p. indsl. chem. group N.Y.C., 1965-77, v.p. gen. indsl. prodn. group, 1977-82; pres. Dorpete Press, Briarcliff Manor, N.Y., 1982—. Chmn. bd. Flexible Steel Lacing Co., Downers Grove, Ill., 1984-96; cons. Nat. Exec. Svc. Corps., N.Y.C., 1982-85. Author: The Five-day Week End, 1989, Unnecessary Wars?, 1993, Marrying the Natives, 1996, The Great Reindeer Caper, 1997, Nature, Nurture, and Chance, 1998, Atheists, Agnostics, and Deists in America, 2000. Pres. Briarcliff Vol. Fire Dept., Briarcliff Manor, N.Y. 1983-85; pres. bd. trustees Ossinining (N.Y.) Pub. Libr., 1990-92. Lt. USN, 1944-46. Mem. Am. Chem. Soc., Am. Inst. Chem. Engineers. Avocations: hiking, canoeing, nordic skiing. Home: 543 Scarborough Rd Briarcliff Manor NY 10510-2019 E-mail: dorpete@bestweb.net., books@dorpete.com.

RINAMAN, JAMES CURTIS, JR. lawyer; b. Miami, Fla., Feb. 8, 1935; s. James Curtis and Ruth Marie (Rader) R.; m. Gloria Margaret Kaspar; children: James, Mark, Christine, Karen BA, U. Fla., 1955, JD, 1960. Bar: Fla. 1960, U.S. Dist. Ct. (so. dist.) Fla. 1960, U.S. Ct. Appeals (5th cir.) 1960, U.S. Supreme Ct. 1963, U.S. Dist. Ct. (mid. dist.) Fla. 1967, U.S. Dist. Ct. (no. dist.) Fla. 1981, U.S. Ct. Appeals (11th cir.) 1981, U.S. Ct. Claims 1991, U.S. Ct. Mil. Appeals 1994; cert. civil trial lawyer Fla. Bar. With Marks, Gray, Conroy & Gibbs, P.A., Jacksonville, Fla., 1960—. Gen. counsel Fla. Bd. Architecture, 1965-79, City of Jacksonville, 1970-71, Jacksonville C. of C., 1973-76, 90; adj. prof. Coll. Architecture, U. Fla., 1975-90; dir. gen. The Southern Acad. Letters, Arts and Scis., 1997—. Pres. Jacksonville Cmty. Coun. Inc., 1985. Leadership Jacksonville, Inc., 1987; mem. Jacksonville Transp. Authority, 1971-80, Jacksonville Base Realignment and Closure Commn., 1993-95. Jacksonville Cecil Field Devel. Commn., 1994-96; chmn. N.E. Fla. chpt. ARC, 1996. With U.S. Army, 1955-57, Fla. NG, 1957-92. ret. brig. gen., 1992. Named to U. Fla. Hall of Fame. Fellow Am. Coll. Trial Lawyers, Am. Bar Found., Fla. Bar Found. (bd. dirs. 1982-87, 88, Disting. Svc. award 1983, 86, Medal of Honor 1988); mem. ABA (ho. of dels. 1982-86), Jacksonville Bar Assn. (pres. 1972-73, Lawyer of Yr. 1994), The Fla. Bar (pres. 1982-83), Def. Rsch. Inst. (so. regional v.p. 1980-83, bd. dirs. 1976-78, 83-87), Am. Judicature Soc. (Herbert Harley award 1987), Fla. Coun. Bar Pres. (Outstanding Past Pres. award 1989), Lawyers for Civil Justice (pres. 1989-91, chmn. bd. dirs. 1991-94), Vol. Lawyers Resource Ctr. of Fla., (pres. 1984-89, chmn. bd. dirs. 1989-93), So. Conf. of Bar, Nat. Conf. of Bar, Assn. Def. Trial Attys. (internat. pres. 1976-77), Internat. Assn. Def. Counsel, Jacksonville Assn. Def. Counsel, Fla. Defense Lawyers Assn. (pres. 1973), Fla. C. of C., Jacksonville C. of C. (chmn. 1994), Meninak Civic Club (pres. 1986), Jacksonville Commodores League, The Army War Coll. Alumni Assn. (life), Fla. Blue Key, San. Jose Country Club, River Club, Phi Gamma Delta (bd. trustees edn. found. 1995—), Phi Alpha Delta. Republican. Methodist. Office: Marks Gray Conroy & Gibbs 1200 Riverplace Blvd Ste 800 Jacksonville FL 32207-1805 also: PO Box 447 Jacksonville FL 32201-0447 E-mail: jrinaman@marksgray.com.

RINCK, JAMES RICHARD, lawyer; b. Grand Rapids, Mich., Mar. 6, 1958; s. Richard John and Ann Louise (Weening) R; m. Lorelei Landheer, Apr. 30, 1988. BA, Calvin Coll., 1975-79; JD, U. Ill., 1979-82. Bar: Mich. 1982, U.S. Dist. Ct. (we. dist.) Mich. 1982. Asst. prosecutor Muskegon County, Muskegon, Mich., 1983-84; sole practice Grand Rapids, 1984—. Deacon Westminster Presbyn. Ch., 1985-89, mem. pastoral search com., 1989-90; mem. exec bd. Kent County Dems., 1984-2001; mem. exec. bd. Mich. Young Dems., 1986-88, candidate Mich. State Senate, 1990; state asst. atty. gen., 1990-99; mem. Bd. Edn. of Grand Rapids, 1993—; bd. dirs. Grand Rapids Downtown Devel. Authority, 1995-2001. Mem. Mich. Bar Assn. (workers' compensation and negligence sects. 1987—, criminal law sect. 1983—), Grand Rapids Bar Assn., Nat. Orgn. Social Security Claimants Reps. (sustaining). Avocations: reading, sports, cooking. Home: 2353 Swensberg Ave NE Grand Rapids MI 49505-4066 Office: 1108 McKay Twr 146 Monroe Center St NW Grand Rapids MI 49503-2833

RINCÓN-MORA, GABRIEL ALFONSO, electrical engineer, educator; b. Caracas, Distrito Federal, Venezuela, Jan. 30, 1972; arrived in U.S., 1983; s. Gilberto Rincón, Gladys Maria Rincón. BSEE, Fla. Internat. U., 1992; MSEE, Ga. Inst. Tech., 1994, PhD in Elec. Engring., 1996. Sr. integrated cir. designer, mem. group tech. staff. Tex. Instruments, Dallas, 1994—. Dir. Ga. Tech. Analog Consortium, 2002—; prof. Ga. Inst. Tech., Atlanta, 1999—. Author: (Textbook) Voltage References, 2001, (book) Short Stories and Poems to Boot!, 2001, short stories; contbr. articles to profl. jours. Active in minority issues Ga. Inst. Tech., Atlanta. Named one of The 100 Most Influential Hispanics, Hispanic Bus. Mag., 2000; named to Coun. Outstanding Young Engring. Alumni, Ga. Inst. Tech., 2000; recipient Profiled on the cover of La Fuente, 2000, Featured on EE Times & Planet Analog, Electrical Engring. Trade Mag., 2000, Charles E. Perry Visionary award, Fla. Internat. U., 2000, State Calif. Commendation cert., Lt. Gov. Cruz M. Bustamante, 2001, featured in Intow, Atlanta, 2002, Profiled in and on cover of Nuevo Impacto, 2002. Mem.: IEEE (sr.), Soc. Profl. Hispanic Engrs. (Nat. Hispanic in Tech. award 2000). Achievements include patents for integrated circuits; patents pending for integrated circuits; design of chips for cellular phones, laptops, etc. Office: Ga Inst Tech 777 Atlantic Dr Atlanta GA 30332-0250 Business E-Mail: rincon-mora@ece.gatech.edu.

RINDE, JOHN JACQUES, internist; b. Przemysl, Poland, Jan. 3, 1935; came to U.S., 1952; s. Maurice and Stella (Klein) R.; m. Toni Igel, June 21, 1959; children: Debbie Ann, Barbara Gail. BS, MIT, 1957, MS, 1958, MME, 1959; MSEE, Poly. Inst. Bklyn., 1965; MD, U. Ark., 1975. Cert. profl. engr.; diplomate Am. Bd. Internal Medicine. Sr. engr. Sperry Gyroscope Co., Great Neck, N.Y., 1959-67, 70-71; v.p. Olson Assocs. Inc., Huntington, 1967-69; sr. engr. Hydrosystems, Inc., Farmingdale, 1969-70; physician Clearwater, Fla., 1978—. NSF fellow, 1958. Fellow ACP; mem. Am. Soc. Internal Medicine, Fla. Med. Assn., Pinellas County Med. Soc. (bd. govs. 1989-92). Avocations: tennis, skiing, photography, swimming. Office: 1305 S Fort Harrison Ave Clearwater FL 33756-3301

RINDER, HERBERT ROY, retired electrical engineer; b. Chgo., Feb. 19, 1928; s. Emanuel and Sadelle (Schwartz) R.; children: Lawrence, Kenneth, Gregg. BSEE, U. Ill., 1950. Registered profl. engr., Ill. Engr. Admiral Corp., Chgo., 1952-54; field engr. Motorola, 1954-58; engr. U.S. Dept. Energy, 1958-82, engr. in charge PSR divsn., 1980-82; ret., 1982. Author: New Testament, Fact or Fiction, 1984, Quest for Truth and Fulfillment, 1995, Human Psyche/Nature Man, 1996, The Human Mind/Relationship to Freud's Systems, 1996, Einstein's Mistake?, 1998, Nature of Gravity, 1999, Summary New Testament Books, 1999, Universal Energy, 2000, Federal Reserve Monetary Policy, 2001. Cpl. U.S. Army, 1950-52. Mem. Internat. Brotherhood Magicians. Avocations: golf, bicycling, bowling, tennis.

RINDFUSS, RONALD RICHARD, sociology educator; b. Buffalo, Dec. 11, 1946; married Aug. 1968; 2 children. BA, Fordham U., 1968; PhD, Princeton U., 1974. Rsch. asst. Nat. Fertility Study, Office Population Rsch., Princeton U., 1971-73; rsch. assoc. Ctr. Demography and Ecology U. Wis., Madison, 1973-76; asst. prof. sociology U. N.C., Chapel Hill, 1976-79, assoc. prof., 1979-84, prof. sociology, 1984-2000, Robert Paul Ziff Disting. prof., 2000—; dir. Carolina Population Ctr., Chapel Hill, 1992-97. Cons. in field Contbr. numerous articles to profl. jours.; assoc. editor Social Forces, 1976—; cons. editor Am. Jour. Sociology, 1977-80; contbg. editor Sociol Biology, 1974; referee for numerous jours. Recipient NIH traineeship, 1968—71, 1st place Erdas award for best sci. paper on remote sensing, 2000. Fellow: AAAS (mem. nominating com. sect. K 2001—); mem.: Sociol. Rsch. Assn., Coun. on Family Rsch., So. Sociol. Soc., So. Regional Demographic Group, Nat. Coun. on Family Rels., Internat. Union for Sci. Study Population, Population Assn. Am. (pres. 1991, Mindel C. Sheps award com. 1990, bd. dirs. 1984—87), Am. Sociol. Assn. (chmn. sociology of population sect. 1989—90, publs. com. 1983—84). Office: Carolina Population Ctr CB # 8120 University Sq 123 W Franklin St Chapel Hill NC 27516-2524 E-mail: Ron_Rindfuss@unc.edu.

RINDONE, JOSEPH PATRICK, clinical pharmacist, educator; b. Santa Fe, Oct. 4, 1954; s. Guido Salvatore and Elizabeth Ann (Murphy) R.; m. Diane Marie Rollins, June 11, 1991; children: Jacqueline, Alexandra. BS, U. Nebr., 1977; PharmD, Creighton U., 1978. Lic. pharmacist, Nebr., Calif. Staff pharmacist Bergan Mercy Hosp., Omaha, 1978, Phoenix (Ariz.) VA Med. Ctr., 1978-81, clin. resident, 1981; clin. pharmacist Tucson VA Med. Ctr., 1982-93; assoc. prof. U. Ariz., Tucson, 1982—; clin. pharmacist Prescott (Ariz.) VA Med. Ctr., 1993—, rsch. coord., 1994—. Author: Therapeutic Monitoring of Antibiotics, 1991; contbr. articles to Arch. Internal Medicine, Pharmacotherapy, Clin. Therapeutics, Am. Jour. Cardiology, Am. Jour. Therapeutics, Chest, West Jour. Medicine, Am. Jour. Health Sys. Pharm., Jour. AMA. Regents scholar U. Nebr., 1976. Mem. Ariz. Soc. Hosp. Pharmacists. Avocations: sports, photography, bridge, astronomy. E-mail: JosephRindone@med.va.gov.

RINEHART, ALICE DAY DUFFY, retired education educator; b. Hartford, Conn., Mar. 2, 1919; d. Ward Everett and Louise Van Ness (Day) Duffy; m. Robert Lloyd Rinehart, 1946 (dec. Apr. 1964); children: Ward E., Janice D. Rinehart Freund, Bradford R. BA, Smith Coll., 1940; MEd, Lehigh U., 1965, EdD, 1969. Cert. social studies tchr., Mass.; cert. history and govt. tchr., Pa. Tchr. social studies, guidance counselor Amherst (Mass.) H.S., 1940-46; sec. Child Psychology Clinic Stanford U., Palo Alto, Calif., 1946-47; supr. intern tchrs. Lehigh U. Grad. Sch. Edn., Bethlehem, Pa., 1964-84, asst. to and dir. tchr. intern program, ednl. placement dir., 1965-84, prof. sociology of edn., 1965-84, mem. Lehigh U. grad. com., 1978-83; instr. sociology of edn. summer sch. DeSales U. Sch. Nursing (formerly Allentown Coll. Sch. Nursing), Center Valley, 1986. Grad. com. Lehigh U., Bethlehem, 1978-93. Author: Mortals in the Immortal Profession, 1983, One Woman Determined to Make a Difference, 2001; co-author: Early Retirement-Promises and Pitfalls, 1992, Country School Memories, 1999; contbr. articles, chpts., and book revs. to profl. pubs. Pres. PTA, Lanark Elem. Sch., Center Valley, 1957-59, PTA, So. Lehigh H.S., Center Valley, 1962-63; chmn. edn. study group AAUW, Allentown, Pa., 1956-58; mem. Lehigh County Area Agy. on Aging Adv. Com., Allentown, 1988-96.

RINEHART, HARRY ELMER, retired sales executive; b. Monessen, Pa., Nov. 9, 1921; s. Harry F. and Stella (Shirey) R.; m. Janet M. Herschell, Mar. 19, 1949 (dec. Feb. 1986); children: Donna C., Ellen L., Scott M. BBA, U. Miami, 1943; MBA, Harvard U., 1948. Salesman Nat. Gypsum Co., Buffalo, 1949-53, asst. dist. mgr. Jacksonville, Fla., 1953-62, dist. sales mgr., 1962-86; exec. dir. Exec. Service Corps N.E. Fla. Chmn. bd. dirs. Hospice of Meth. Hosp., Jacksonville. Elder, clk. of session South Jacksonville Presbyn. Ch., 1987—. Capt. USNR, PTO, Korea. Mem. U. Miami Alumni Assn. (chmn. 1987, Outstanding Svc. award 1986), Rotary (pres. South Jacksonville chpt. 1984), San Jose Country Club, Jacksonville Quarterback Club (dir.), The Champions Club, Am. Legion (post 0088), Sigma Chi (life), Alpha Phi Omega (life). Republican. Presbyterian. Avocations: golf, collecting coins. Home and Office: 6848 La Loma Dr Jacksonville FL 32217-2612

RINEHART, JAMES FORREST, educator; b. Kansas City, Mo., Dec. 1, 1950; s. Kenneth Perry and Eleanor Louise (Lane) R.; m. Betty Keller, Feb. 3, 1973; children: Erica Christine, Andrew James. BA, U. Fla., 1972; M of Social Sci., Syracuse U., 1991, PhD, 1993. Vis. prof. internat. rels. U. Tenn., Chattanooga, 1993-95; dir., prof. grad. program in internat. rels. U.S. Army John F. Kennedy Spl. Warfare Sch. Troy State U., 1995—, lectr. regional studies program, 1996—. Author: Revolution and the Millennium: China, Mexico and Iran, 1997; contbr. articles to profl. jours. Mem. Coun. on Peace Rsch. in History, 1992-94; founding mem. Mediation Svcs. Task Force for Chattanooga, 1991-95; active Program on Analysis and Resolution of Conflict, Syracuse U., 1991-93; bd. dirs. Ulster Project Chattanooga, 1993-94. Capt. USAR, 1972-80. Recipient Cert. of Achievement U.S. Army JFK Spl. Warfare Ctr. and Sch., 1996. Mem. Am. Polit. Sci. Assn., Internat. Studies Assn, Soc. for Scientific Study of Religion, Internat. Soc. Polit. Psychology, Am. Radio Relay League, Pinewild Country Club, Phi Gamma Delta, Fla. Blue Key Soc. Democrat. Presbyterian. Home: 201 Hampton Ave Troy AL 36081-4045

RINELLA, BARBARA, book dramatist; b. Rochester, Minn., Aug. 18, 1943; d. George Donald and Agnes Dorothy (van Oostenbrugge) Albers; m. Richard Anthony Rinella, Mar. 22, 1969; children: Richard A. Jr., Anne Albers. AB, Duke U., 1965; MA, U. Mich., 1966. Asst. editor Putman Pub. Co., Chgo., 1966, 67; English tchr. Needham (Mass.) H.S., 1966-67, New Trier H.S., Northfield, Ill., 1967-73; rschr. Mademoiselle mag., Chgo., 1973-78; book reviewer, dramatist Chgo. area, 1979—. Developer creative writing program Joseph Sears Sch., Kenilworth, Ill., 1979-90; guidebook editor Lincoln Park Zoo, Chgo., 1970-75. Mem. drama dept. adv. bd. Duke U., Durham, N.C., 1994-97, mem. alumni governing bd., 1995-99, chmn. alumni admissions coun., 1994—, interviewer, 1979—; mem. sch. bd. New Trier H.S., 1993-97; vol. United Way/Crusade of Mercy, Chgo., 1979-90, chmn. spl. gifts, 1979-80; coach Wilmette (Ill.) Girls Softball, 1988-89; coach, commn., Kenilworth Little League Baseball, 1982-83; vol. Joseph Sears Sch., 1979-90; troop leader, mem. adv. com. local coun. Boy Scouts Am.; variety show coord. local coun. Girl Scouts U.S.A.; chmn. Upward Bound tutoring project, Chgo., 1975; mem. Guild Bd. Lyric Opera, 1974-81; benefit chmn. Mental Health Assn. Chgo., 1982. Recipient Outstanding Vol. award, Duke U., 1988, Woman of Distinction in the Arts award, Girl Scouts U.S., 1997, Best Lectr. rating, Crystal Cruises, 1998—, Breast Cancer Heroine award, BMW Ultimate Drive for the Cure, 1999. Avocations: tennis, paddle tennis, travel, reading, writing.

RINER, RONALD NATHAN, cardiologist, business consultant; b. Mar. 7, 1949; AB, Princeton U., 1970; MD, Cornell U., N.Y.C., 1974. Diplomate Am. Bd. Internal Medicine, Am. Bd. Cardiovasc. Disease. Resident in internal medicine N.Y. Hosp., Meml. Sloan-Kettering, Hosp. for Spl. Surgery, 1974-76; resident in cardiology Mayo Grad. Sch. Medicine, Rochester, Minn., 1976-79; chmn. dept. internal medicine St. Mary's Health Ctr., St. Louis, 1980-82, program dir. internal medicine, 1979-82; pvt. practice, 1979-95. Asst. prof. medicine, Washington U. Med. Ctr., 1985-88, pres. Riner Group, Inc., 1980—, Riner Heart Group, Inc., 1980-95; sr. sci. advisor pharm. divsn. BioMed Sys., St. Louis, 1984-95; prof. St. Louis U.; corp. dir. quality affairs SSM Health Care Sys. 1989-91; chmn. Mo. State Med. Assn. Commn. on Med. Econs., 3rd Party Medicine and Govt. Rels., 1990-92; v.p. clin. svcs. Daus. Charity Nat. Health Sys., 1991-95; bd. dirs. Alleghany Health Sys., Tampa, Fla., 1991-96, chmn. bd. dirs., 1994-96; bd. dirs. Horizon/CMS Healthcare, 1996-98, Seton Inst. for Internat. Devel., San Francisco, 1995-97.

Bd. dirs. Seton Inst. for Internat. Devel., San Francisco, 1995-97; bd. dirs. Liferate Sys., Inc., 1997-99; bd. dirs. Assn. for Corp. Growth, 1998-2001, Mathew Dickey Acad., St. Louis, Mo., 1998-2001. Editor practice mgmt. and econs. sect. Jour. Invasive Cardiology, 1996—. Fellow Inst. for Advanced Study in Internat. Bus., Washington U., 1991. Fellow ACP, Am. Coll. Cardiology, Am. Acad. Med. Dirs.; mem. AAAS, N.Y. Acad. Scis. (life), Mo. Soc. Internal Medicine (coun.), Gov. Rel. Com., Am. Acad. Physician Execs., Mayo Alumni Assns., Am. Cons. League, Am. Mgmt. Assn., Cornell U. Alumni Assn., Princeton Alumni Assn., Princeton U. Club (bd. dirs. 2000—). Office: The Riner Group Inc 1034 S Brentwood Blvd Ste 1640 Saint Louis MO 63117-1216

RINES, JOHN RANDOLPH, investment banker; b. Balt., Aug. 3, 1947; s. John William and Betty (Singer) R.; m. Peggy J. Daugaard, Sept. 19, 1969 (dec. 1978); m. Katherine M. Duff, Nov. 29, 1980; children: Jacqueline D., Eleanor W. BS in Econs., Colo. State U., 1970; MBA, U. Va., 1977. With GM, 1970-75, 77—, fin. analyst, 1977-78, dir. product programs, 1978-80, asst. to pres., 1980-81, gen. dir. fin., 1981-82, exec. dir. Sao Paulo, Brazil, 1982-84, dir. fin. Buick/Oldsmobile/Cadillac group Flint, Mich., 1984-85, gen. mgr. motors holding div. and GM auction Detroit, 1985-91, gen. mgr. parts ops., 1991—; pres. GM Acceptance Corp., 1992-97; exec. v.p. Citicorp, Global Markets, 1997-2000; ptnr. Carday.com., N.Y.C., 2000—; pres. Sand Bros. Ltd., 2001—. Trustee Arts Found. Mich., Detroit. Mem. Grosse Pointe (Mich.) Club, Old Club (Harsen's Island), Birmingham Athletic Club. Office: Sands Bros 90 Park Ave New York NY 10016 E-mail: jrines@sandsbros.com

RINES, ROBERT HARVEY, lawyer, inventor, educator, composer; b. Boston, Aug. 30, 1922; s. David and Lucy (Sandberg) R.; m. Carol Williamson, Dec. 29, 1972 (dec. 1993); 1 son, Justice Christopher; children by previous marriage: Robert Louis, Suzi Kay Ann; m. Joanne Hayes, June 2, 1996; 1 stepchild, Laura Ellen Hayes. BS in Physics, MIT, 1942; JD, Georgetown U., 1947; PhD, Nat. Chiao Tung U., 1972; DJ, New Eng. Coll. Law, 1974; DSc, Notre Dame Coll., 1994. Bar: Mass. 1947, D.C. 1947, N.H. 1974, Va. 1983, U.S. Supreme Ct., FCC, Tax Ct., U.S. and Can. patent offices; Registered profl. engr., Mass. Asst. examiner U.S. Patent Office, 1946; partner Rines & Rines, Boston, 1947—; pres., founder, chmn. emeritus Franklin Pierce Law Center, 1973-97. Bd. dirs. Megapulse, Inc., Nat. Inventors Hall of Fame Found., 1997-99, Lord Corp., pres. Jura Corp., 1997—, New England Fish Farming Enterprises-D.E. Salmon Inc., 1983-99, Acad. Applied Sci.-Project Orbis Bangladesh and Singapore Opthamology Programs, Sportsmans Handbook, Beltronics Inc., Seagull Technology, Inc., Albavision Ltd., Promotion of Am. Chinese Tech., Knox Mt. Licensors Inc., Ctr. Broadcasting Corp. of N.H., Accelerated Genomics Inc.; Gordon McKay lectr. patent law Harvard, 1956-58; lectr. inventions and innovation Mass. Inst. Tech., 1962—; Mem. commerce tech. adv. bd. Dept. Commerce, 1963-67, mem. nat. inventors council, 1963-67, 81—; mem. N.H. Gov.'s Crime Study Com., 1976-78; trustee Mass. Eye and Ear Infirmary, 2001—. Author: A Study of Current World-Wide Sources of Electronic and Other Invention and Innovation; Computer Jurisprudence: Create or Perish--The Case for Patents and Inventions; patentee in field of radar and sonar, fish farming and plant nutrients; composer of music for onn and off broadway prodns. including, Drums Under the Windows (S. O'Casy, P. Shyre), Different, Long Voyage Home, Whitman Portrait, Blasts and Bravos (H.L. Menken), Hizzoner the Mayor (Emmy winning tv prodn.), 1-800-Save Me and Friendly Acquaintances (Jack Betts), and Lincoln Ctr. Bailet of Rines, Life at MIT suite. Campaign chmn. United Fund, Belmont Mass., 1960; mem. adv. bd. Harvard-Mass. Inst. Tech. Biomed. Engring. Center, 1976-80; bd. dirs. Allor Found. 2d lt. to capt. AUS, 1942-46, Brevet Col., 1994, U.S. Army Signal Corps. Silver Order of Mercury (inducted Wall of Fame, Ft. Gordon, GA, 1994). Named to Nat. Inventors Hall of Fame, 1994; recipient Inventions Citation Pres. Carter and U.S. Dept. Commerce, 1980, N.H. High Tech. Entrepreneur award, 1989, Beyond Peace award, 1989, Bangladesh (N.Am.) Disting. Svc. award, 1990, 96; recipient Robert H. Rines Bldg. dedication at Franklin Pierce Law Ctr., 1993; MIT Distance Learning Ctr. Bldg. dedication, 1997. Fellow Internat. Soc. Cryptozoology; mem. IEEE (sr.), AAAS, ABA, Acad. Applied Sci. (pres., founder, Medal of Honor 1989), Am. Patent Law Assn., Sci. Rsch. Soc. Am., Aircraft Owners and Pilots Assn., Nat. Acad. Engring. (patent com. 1969-80, cons. to exec. officer 1979-80), Explorers Club, Harvard Club, Torquay Co. Theatrical Prodns., Chemists Club, MIT Faculty Club, Nat. Lawyers Club, Capitol Hill Club, Highland Club, Commonwealth Club, Sigma Xi. Unitarian Universalist. Home: 13 Spaulding St Concord NH 03301-2571

RINEY, ALVIN RAYNARD, educational consultant; b. St. Louis, Jan. 23, 1956; s. Printon Louis Patrick and Hortense Loretta (Marshall) Riney; children: Alvin Raynard, Nathan Gerald Patrick, Ryan Wesley. Student, Rockhurst Coll., Kansas City, 1974—76, Mo. Bapt. Coll., 1995, Jefferson Coll., Hillsboro, Mo., 1994—95, U. Mo., St. Louis. Mailroom clk. Ligouri Pubs., Libouri, Mo., 1976—78; with Dow Chem. Co., Pevely, 1978—80; patrolman 1st class/cpl. Mo. State Hwy. Patrol, Jefferson City, 1980—92; patrolman Crystal City Police Dept., Mo., 1993—94; paraprofl., tchr. aid Spl. Svcs. Co-op, Hillsboro, 1996—97, Crystal City Sch. Dist., 1997—. Jr. high basketball coach Crystal City Elem. Sch., 1997—. Co-chmn. Giving Something Back to the Cmty., Festus, Mo., 1999—; councilman Ward 1 City of Crystal City, 1998—2000. Mem.: NEA (Ednl. Support Profl. of the Yr., Mo. chpt. 2000—01). Avocations: reading, writing. Home: 4300 Arrow Tree #K Saint Louis MO 63128 Office: Crystal City Elem Sch 600 Mississippi Ave Crystal City MO 63019

RINEY, HAL PATRICK, advertising executive; b. Seattle, July 17, 1932; s. Hal Patrick and Inez Marie R.; children: Benjamin Kennedy, Samantha Elizabeth. BA, U. Wash., Seattle, 1954. From art dir./writer to v.p., creative dir. BBDO, Inc., San Francisco, 1956-72; exec. v.p., creative dir. Botsford Ketchum, 1972-76; sr. v.p., mng. dir., creative dir. Ogilvy & Mather, 1976-81; exec. v.p. Ogilvy & Mather West, 1981-86; chmn., CEO, Hal Riney & Ptnrs., Inc., San Francisco, 1986-98; chmn. emeritus Publicis & Hal Riney, 1998—. Recipient 5 Lion d'Or du Cannes awards, 19 Clio awards, 15 Addy awards, Grand Prix du Cannes; named to Creative Hall of Fame, Advt. Hall of Fame. Mem. Am. Assn. Advt. Agys., San Francisco Soc. Communicating Arts, Wild Goose Club. Home: 3022 Washington St San Francisco CA 94115 Office: Publicis & Hal Riney 2001 The Embarcadero San Francisco CA 94133-5200

RING, ALICE RUTH BISHOP, retired physician; b. Ft. Collins, Oct. 11, 1931; d. Ernest Otto and Mary Frances Bishop Ring; m. Wallace Harold Ring, July 26, 1956 (div. 1969); children: Rebecca, Eric, Mark; m. Robert Charles Diefenbach, Sept. 10, 1977. BS, Colo. State U., 1953; MD, U. Colo., 1956; MPH, U. Calif., Berkeley, 1971. Diplomate Am. Bd. Preventive Medicine. Physician cons. Utah State Divsn. Health, Salt Lake City, 1960—65; med. dir., project head start Salt Lake City Cmty. Action Program, 1965—70; resident Utah State Divsn. Health, 1969—71; asst. assoc. regional health dir. USPHS, San Francisco, 1971—75, med. cons. Atlanta, 1975—77, dir. primary care, 1977—84; dir. divsn. diabetes control Ctrs. Disease Control, 1984—88; dir. WHO Collabor Ctr., 1986—91; dir. preventive medicine residency Ctrs. Disease Control, 1988—93; exec. dir. Am. Bd. Preventive Medicine, 1993—98. Trustee Am. Bd. Preventive Medicine, 1990—92; lectr. Emory U. Sch. Pub. Health, 1988—94; bd. dirs. Redwood Coast Med. Svcs., v.p., 1994—; mem. adv. com. Shamli Hospice, Gualala, Calif., Sonoma County Area Agy. on Aging, Santa Rosa, Calif. Co-author: Clinical Diabetes, 1991; author: History of the American Board of Preventive Medicine, 2002. Bd. dirs. Diabetes Assn. Atlanta, 1985—90. Fellow: Am. Coll. Preventive Medicine (bd. dirs. 1990—94, Spl. Recognition award 1998); mem.: AMA (grad. med. edn. adv. com. 1993—97), Am. Acad. Pediat., Assn. Tchrs. Preventive Medicine. Office: PO Box 364 Gualala CA 95445-0364 E-mail: ard@mcn.org.

RING, ALVIN MANUEL, pathologist, educator; b. Detroit, Mar. 17, 1933; s. Julius and Helen (Krolik) R.; m. Cynthia Joan Jacobson, Sept. 29, 1963; children— Jeffrey, Melinda, Heather. BS, Wayne State U., 1954; MD, U. Mich., 1958. Intern Mt. Carmel Hosp., Detroit, 1958-59; resident in pathology Michael Reese Hosp., Chgo., 1960-62; asst. pathologist Kings County Hosp., Bklyn., 1962-63; assoc. pathologist El Camino Hosp., Mountain View, Calif., 1963-65; chief pathologist, dir. labs. St. Elizabeth's Hosp., Chgo., 1965-72, Holy Cross Hosp., Chgo., 1972-87, Silver Cross Hosp., Joliet, Ill., 1990—. Instr. SUNY, 1962-63, Stanford U., 1963-65; asst. prof. pathology U. Ill., Chgo., 1966-69, assoc. prof., 1969-78, prof., 1978—; adj. clin. prof. No. Ill. U., 1981-87; adj. prof. med. edn. U. Ill. Coll. Medicine, 1988—; chmn. histotech. Nat. Accrediting Agy. for Clin. Lab Scis., 1977-81; mem. spl. adv. com. Health Manpower, 1966-71; pres. Spear Computer Users Group, 1981-82; mem. adv. com. Mid-Am. chpt. ARC, 1979-85; pres. Pathology and Lab Cons., Inc., 1985—; adj. prof., med. dir. Med. Tech., Moraine Valley C.C., 1994—; originator, coord. pathology, med. decision-making courses Nat. Ctr. for Advanced Med. Edn., 1981—, others; co-coord. computer courses Midwest Clin. Conf., 2000—. Author: Laboratory Correlation Manual, 1968, 82, 86, Laboratory Assistant Examination Review Book, 1971, Review Book in Pathology, Anatomic, 1986, Review Book in Pathology, Clinical, 1986; mem. editorial bd. Lab. Medicine, 1975-87; contbr. articles to med. jours. Fellow Coll. Am. Pathology (insp. 1973—, ins. com. 2002-), Am. Soc. Clin. Pathology; mem. AMA, Ill. Med. Soc., Chgo. Med. Soc. (alt. councilor 1980-85, mem. adv. com. on health care delivery), Ill. Pathol. Soc. (trustee 1997—), Chgo. Pathol. Soc. (censor 1980-88, exec. com. 1985-89, program. com. 1987—), Am. Assn. Blood Banks, Assn. Brain Tumor Rsch. (cons.), Exec. Svc. Corps (exec. cons. 1988—), Phi Lambda Kappa (chpt. pres.). Home: 100 Graymoor Ln Olympia Fields IL 60461-1213 Office: Silver Cross Hosp 1200 Maple Rd Joliet IL 60432-1497

RING, GERALD J. real estate developer, insurance executive; b. Madison, Wis., Oct. 6, 1928; s. John George and Mabel Sarah (Rau) R.; m. Armella Marie Dohm, Aug. 20, 1949; children: Michael J., James J., Joseph W. Student public schs., Madison. With Sub-Zero Freezer Co., Madison, 1948-70, mfr.'s rep., 1954-70; founder, pres. Parkwood Hills Corp., Madison, from 1965, Park Towne Devel. Corp., Madison, from 1969, Ring Devel. Co., 1992—. Bd. dirs. CUNA Mut. Ins. Soc., CUNA Mut. Ins. Group, CUNA Mut. Investment Corp., CUDIS Ins. Soc., all Madison, 1968-98, exec. com., 1973-83, chmn. bd., 1979-81; bd. dirs. CUMIS Ins. Soc., mem. exec. com., 1973-83, chmn. bd., 1977-79; bd. dirs. CMCI Corp., mem. exec. com., 1974-83, chmn. bd., 1981-83; treas. CUNADATA Corp., 1974-81; bd. dirs. Wis. Credit Union League, 1958-79, pres., 1965-67; mem. Wis. Credit Union Rev. Bd., 1967-83, chmn., 1973-76, 82-83; bd. dirs. CUNA Credit Union Nat. Assn., Inc., 1964-81, League Life Ins. Co., League Gen. Ins. Co., Southfield, Mich., CUNA Mut. Fin. Svcs. Corp., Century Ins. Co. Am., Waverly., Iowa. Chmn. Greater Madison C. of C., 1980, bd. dirs., 1976-89, v.p. econ. devel., 1983-85, v.p. govtl. affairs, 1985-89, mem. capital fund raising com., 1983—, chmn. 1983-86; mem. Mayor's Emergency Housing Com., 1984-85; chmn. fin. com. St. Patrick's Congregation, 1983-89; bd. dirs. Cath. Charities of Madison, 1995—, pres., 1996-99; bd. dirs. Future Madison Housing Fund, 1997—. Served with USMC, 1951-53. Mem. Aircraft Owners and Pilots Assn. Lodges: Rotary. (bd. dirs. 1981-83). Roman Catholic. Home: 607 Farwell Dr Madison WI 53704-6029 Office: 402 S Gammon Rd Madison WI 53719-1002

RING, HERBERT EVERETT, management executive; b. Norwich, Conn., Dec. 19, 1925; s. Herbert Everett and Catherine (Riordan) R.; m. Marilyn Elizabeth Dursin, May 21, 1955 (dec. Jan. 1994); children: Nancy Marie, Herbert Everett. BA, Ind. No. U., 1971, MBA, 1973; AMP, Harvard U., 1981. V.p. ops. Ogden Foods, Inc., Toledo, 1963-74, sr. v.p. Boston, 1974-75; v.p. concessions SportSvc. Corp., Buffalo, 1976-78, sr. v.p., 1978-80, pres., 1980-83, bd. dir.; pres. Universal Mgmt. Concept Counseling, Sylvania, Ohio, 1983—; prin. Hysen Group II, Livonia, Mich., 1991-95. Counselor L.A. Olympic Concessions Food Svc., 1984, Phila. Meml. Stadium, 1985, Del. North Cos. Internat. London Eng., 1985-86, Chgo. Stadium Corp., 1989-92, Buffalo Sabres N.Y., 1992, Fine Host Inc. Greenwich Ct., 1993, Delaware North of Australia Ltd., 1994, Temp DNC Health Support Ltd., Wellington, New Zealand, 1995, Fanfare Enterprises, 1997, Geneva Lakes Kennel Club, Delavan, Wis., 1997, St. Francis Health Care Ctr., Greenspring, Ohio, 1998, Detroit Opera House, 2000; bd. dirs. Greenfield Restaurant Co., Inc., Letheby and Christopher Ltd., Reading, Berkshire, Eng., Air Terminal Svcs., Inc., The Aud Club, Inc., Bluegrass Turf Svc., Inc., Concession Suppliers, Inc., Cosel Drive-In Theatre, Inc., G&H Sports Concessions, Inc., Hazel Park Parking, Inc. Mem. Toledo Mus. Art., 1985-92. Sgt. Air Corps U.S. Army, 1944-46, ETO, USAF, 1950-51. Mem. Internat. Assn. of Auditorium Mgrs., N.W. Ohio Restaurant Assn. (bd. dirs. 1990-93), Am. Culinary Fedn. Inc., Harvard Bus. Club (Detroit). Roman Catholic. Home and Office: 5540 Radcliffe Rd Sylvania OH 43560-3740

RING, JAMES EDWARD PATRICK, mortgage banking consulting executive; b. Washington, Feb. 12, 1940; s. Edward Patrick and Eleanor Elizabeth R.; m. Kathleen Murphy, Aug. 10, 1979; children: Christopher James, Daniel Edward Patrick. Student, Holy Cross Coll., Worcester, Md., 1958-59; BSEE, U.S. Naval Acad., 1963; MBA in Fin., Wharton Sch. Bus., U. Pa., 1972. Lic. securities broker, comml. pilot. Fin. analyst Exec. Office of the President, Washington, 1972-74; sr. budget analyst Bd. Govs. Fed. Res. System, 1974-77; dir. fin. planning Fed. Home Loan Mortgage Ins., 1977-83; dir. mktg. Ticor Mortgage Ins., Falls Church, Va., 1983-84, G.E. Mortgage Ins., Mc Lean, 1985-86; sr. v.p. First Chesapeake Mortgage, Beltsville, Md., 1986-88; v.p. G.E. Capital Mortgage Corp., McLean, 1988-94; cons. Mortgage Dynamics, 1994—2001; sr. mortgage analyst Fed. Housing Fin. Bd., 2001—. Mem. fin. coun. Blessed Sacrament Cath. Cmty., Alexandria, 1996—; vol. Big. Bros. Am., Washington, 1973-81; pres. U.S. Naval Acad. Class of 1963 Found., 1983-2000. Lt. USN, 1963-69. Mem. Wharton Club (Washington), U.S. Naval Acad. Alumni Assn., Army-Navy Country Club. Republican. Roman Catholic. Home: 1716 Stonebridge Rd Alexandria VA 22304-1039 Office: 1777 F St NW Washington DC 20006

RING, JAMES WALTER, physics educator; b. Worcester, N.Y., Feb. 24, 1929; s. Carlyle Conwell and Lois (Tooley) R.; m. Agnes Elizabeth Muir, July 18, 1959; 1 son, Andrew James. AB, Hamilton Coll., 1951; PhD (Root fellow), U. Rochester, 1958. Asst. prof. physics Hamilton Coll., Clinton, N.Y., 1957-62, assoc. prof., 1962-69, prof., 1969—, Winslow prof., 1975—, chmn. dept. physics, 1968-80, 87-88, 91-92, radiation safety Officer, 1964-84, engring. liaison officer, 1969—. Attached physicist Atomic Energy Rsch. Establishment, Harwell, Eng., 1965-66; vis. physicist Phys. Chemistry Lab., Oxford (Eng.) U., 1973; vis. fellow Ctr. for Energy and Environ. Studies, Princeton U., 1981; vis. scientist Lab. for Heating and Air Conditioning, Danish Tech. U., Copenhagen, 1987. Contbr. articles to profl. jours. and books in physics, chemistry, solar energy, environ. sci., health physics, archaeology, and engring. Recipient prize Acad. Edn./Devel., 1980; NSF grantee, 1959-66; NSF sci. faculty fellow, 1965-66 Mem. AAUP (chpt. pres. 1987-92), Am. Phys. Soc., Am. Assn. Physics Tchrs., Phi Beta Kappa, Sigma Xi. Achievements include solar house design and testing; indoor air studies in radon dangers and thermal comfort; study of the use of solar energy by the Romans during the Roman Empire; analysis of experimental evidence for the validity of continuous spontaneous localization theory as an alternative to standard quantum mechanics; detection of Pb210 gamma radiation to establish geochronology for sediment core samples taken in antarctic peninsula bay and straits; to study global warming. Office: Hamilton Coll Dept Physics Clinton NY 13323

RING, K(ARIN) ELISABETH, physician assistant, paramedic; b. Falun, Dalarna, Sweden, Jan. 26, 1954; came to U.S., 1975; d. Stig Anders Yngve and May Ingegärd (Arvidson) Ihlar; m. Bruce L. Ring; children from previous marriage: Rachel, David, Sarah. RN, Sjosköterskeskola, Falun, 1977; cert. physician asst., U. N.D., 1993. RN, Minn. Staff nurse Ada (Minn.) Mcpl. Hosp., 1979-83; ho. supr., staff nurse Riverview Hosp., Crookston, Minn., 1983-92; physician asst. Altru, 1993—; adj. faculty U. N.D., Grand Forks, 1993—. Instr. Pineto Prairie Coop. Ctr., Red Lake Falls, Minn., 1979—80; clin. nursing instr., Northland C.C., Thief River Falls, Minn.; paramedic County EMS, 1988—2001. Mem. sr. choir Concordia Luth. Ch., Fertile, Minn., 1993—99, mem. ch. coun., mem. worship com., 1997—2000. Named Outstanding Young Women of Am., 1988. Fellow: Minn. Acad. Physician Assts., Am. Assn. Physician Assts.; mem.: Christian Med. Dental Assn. Office: Altru 400 S Minnesota St Crookston MN 56716-1808

RING, LATIFA SEFIANE, computer scientist, consultant; b. Azrou, Morocco, Dec. 23, 1955; d. Zahra; m. Stephen Edward Ring, July 21, 1980; children: Richard, Lisa. Student, Bryn Mawr Coll., 1974—75; BS in Biology, N.E. Mo. State U., Kirksville, 1979. Pres. The Software Pros, Houston, 1985—88; computer sales cons. Valcom Computer Svcs., 1989—92; IS cons. Meml. Health Care Systems, 1992—95; network cons. Electronic Data Systems, 1996—. Mem.: NAFE, Minority / Women Owned Bus.Assn.

RING, MICHAEL WILSON, lawyer; b. Phoenix, Feb. 14, 1943; s. Clifton A. and Leona (Wilson) R. BA, U Wash., 1964; JD, U. Calif., Berkeley, 1968. Bar: Calif. 1969. Assoc. Sheppard, Mullin, Richter & Hampton, L.A., 1968-76, ptnr., 1976-87, Mayer, Brown & Platt, L.A., 1987-92, Sonnenschein Nath & Rosenthal, L.A., 1992—. Mem. ABA, L.A. County Bar Assn., Am. Coll. Real Estate Lawyers, Urban Land Inst. (assoc.), Internat. Coun. Shopping Ctrs. (assoc.). Home: 3658 Mountain View Ave Los Angeles CA 90066-3129 Office: Sonnenschein Nath & Rosenthal 601 S Figueroa St Ste 1500 Los Angeles CA 90017-5720 E-mail: mwr@sonnenschein.com.

RING, NANCY GAIL, writer, artist; b. Irvington, N.J., Dec. 24, 1956; d. Frank and Dorothy (Kasoff) R.; m. Eric Mark Kaplan, Aug. 1, 1993. Student, Sch. of Mus. of Fine Arts, Boston, 1975-76; BFA, Syracuse U., 1978. Food history columnist Newark Star Ledger, feature food article contbr., 1998—. Author, illustrator: Walking on Walnuts, 1996; art exhibited Women Figure, 1990. Recipient Drawing award Barbara Chase Burke, 1978; fellow Mid-Atlantic Arts Found., 1988, N.Y. Found. for Arts, 1987, Montalvo Ctr. for Arts, 1987. Avocations: baking, cooking, exercise, traveling, reading.

RING, RENEE ETHELINE, lawyer; b. Frankfurt, Germany, May 29, 1950; arrived in U.S., 1950; d. Vincent Martin and Etheline Bergetta (Schoolmeesters) R.; m. Paul J. Zofnass, June 24, 1982; Jessica Renee, Rebecca Anne. BA, Catholic U. Am., 1972; JD, U. Va., 1976. Bar: N.Y. 1977. Assoc. Whitman & Ransom, N.Y.C., 1976-83, Carro, Spanbock, Fass, Geller, Kaster & Cuiffo, N.Y.C., 1983-86, ptnr., 1986, Finley Kumble Wagner et. al., N.Y.C., 1987; of counsel Kaye, Scholer, Fierman, Hays & Handler, 1988; ptnr. Kaye, Scholer, Fierman, Hays & Handler, LLP, 1989-97, Hunton & Williams, N.Y.C., 1997—2002. Mem. exec. com. Lawyers for Clinton, Washington, 1991-92; team capt. Clinton Transition Team, Washington, 1992-93; mem. Nat. Lawyers Coun. Dem. Nat. Com., 1993-98; trustee The Clinton Legal Expense Trust, 1998—; mem. Alumni Coun. U. Va. Sch. of Law, 1997—, 2d v.p., 2000-2001, 1st v.p., 2001—; trustee The Spence Sch, 2001-2002. Mem. ABA, N.Y. Women's Bar Assn. Democrat. Roman Catholic. Office: Hunton & Williams 200 Park Ave Rm 4400 New York NY 10166-0091 E-mail: rring@hunton.com.

RING, RONALD HERMAN, lawyer; b. Flint, Mich., Nov. 30, 1938; s. Herman and Lydia (Miller) R.; m. Joan Kay Whitener, Aug. 5, 1966. AB, U. Mich., 1961, LLB, 1964. Bar: Mich. 1964, U.S. Dist. Ct. (ea. dist.) Mich. 1966. Assoc. Beagle, Benton & Hicks, Flint, 1964-69; ptnr. Beagle & Ring, 1970-80, Beagle, Ring & Beagle, Flint, 1980-85, Ring, Beagle & Busch, Flint, 1985-93, Ronald H. Ring, P.C., Flint, 1993-95; pvt. practice, 1991—. Mem. meml. com. Crossroads Village, Flint, 1981; pres. Family Service Agy., Genesee County, Mich., 1986. Mem. ABA, Assn. Trial Lawyers Am., Mich. Bar Assn. (delivery of legal service com. 1986, med. malpractice panel 1986), Genesee County Bar Assn. (pres. 1980-81, bd. dirs. 1979-82, cir. ct. mediation panel 1986). Clubs: Ostego Ski (Gaylord, Mich.). Avocations: skiing, sailing. Office: 7993 Bussa Ln Rapid City MI 49676-9203 E-mail: ronhring@cs.com.

RING, VICTORIA ALEXANDRA, small business owner; b. Columbus, Ohio, July 5, 1958; d. James H. and Barbara C. (Wise) R. BA, East Tenn. State U., 1984; MA, Columbus Bus. U., 1986; AS paralegal studies, Ashworth Coll., 2002. Typesetter, designer Battelle Meml. Inst., Columbus, Ohio, 1986-88; owner YouOnLine.Net/Graphics, Bristol, Tenn., 1988—, The Lawyer asst., 2001—. Instr. Ohio State U., Columbus, 1990—91; creator, designer Grape-Vine News, 1992—94; spkr. at seminars and workshops in field; Internet instr. www.victoriaring .com Eastland Vocat. Sch. and Ohio State U., 1995—2000. Author: Word Perfect Just For Fun, 1991, (book/video) How To Design Your Own Web Site With Netscape, 1996, How to Sell Your Products on the Internet, 1998, Business Advice for Beginners, More Business Advice for Beginners, Web Designers Workbook Beginners Series, 101 Things You Need to Know before You File Bankruptcy, 2001, Internet Training Video Series, 2002; contbr. Avocations: computer graphic design, web page design and site design, reading, photography. Address: Ste 123 1601 W Fifth Ave Columbus OH 43212-2307 E-mail: victoria@lawyerassistant.com.

RINGEL, DEAN, lawyer; b. N.Y.C., Dec. 12, 1947; m. Ronnie Sussman, Aug. 24, 1969; children: Marion, Alicia. BA, Columbia Coll., 1967; JD, Yale U., 1971. Bar: N.Y. 1972, U.S. Ct. Appeals (6th cir.) 1972, U.S. Ct. Appeals (2d and D.C. cirs.) 1974, U.S. Supreme Ct. 1976, U.S. Ct. Appeals (10th cir.) 1982, U.S. Ct. Appeals (11th cir.) 1997, U.S. Ct. Appeals (9th cir.) 2000. Law clk. to Judge Anthony J. Celebrezze U.S. Ct. Appeals (6th cir.), 1971-72; assoc. Cahill Gordon & Reindel, N.Y.C., 1972-79; ptnr. Cahill, Gordon & Reindel, 1979—. Mem.: ABA (vice chmn. com. on freedom of speech and press 1978—79), Pub. Edn. Assn. (trustee, sec. 1997—2000, trustee CEI-PEA 2000—), Assn. Bar City NY (commn. comm., fed. litigation, antitrust and trade regulation), NY State Bar (chmn. antitrust litigation com., sect. comml. and fed. litigation 1994—96, co-chmn. fed. judiciary com. 1997—2001, co-chair newsgathering com. Libel Def. Resource Ctr. 2001—, media law com.). Office: Cahill Gordon & Reindel 80 Pine St 17th Fl New York NY 10005-1790

RINGEL, ROBERT LEWIS, university administrator; b. N.Y.C., Jan. 27, 1937; s. Benjamin Seymour and Beatrice (Salis) R.; m. Estelle Neuman, Jan. 18, 1959; children— Stuart Alan, Mark Joseph. BA, Bklyn. Coll., 1959; MS, Purdue U., 1960, PhD, 1962. cert. speech pathologist. Rsch. scientist, laryngeal rsch. lab. Ctr. Health Scis., UCLA, 1962-64; asst. prof. communication disorders U. Wis., 1964-66; from mem. faculty to provost Purdue U., 1966—91, provost, 1991—. Vis. prof. Inst. Neurology and Nat. Hosps. Coll. Speech Scis., U. London, 1985; cons. NIH, NEH, Bur. Edn. Handicapped of U.S. Office Edn.; bd. dirs. Indpls. Ctr. for Advanced Rsch., 1988-92; hon. prof. Coll. of Computer Scis. and Mgmt., Rzeszów, Poland, 2000—; bd. dir., faculty adv. Hillel Found. Purdue U., 2000-. Author sci. articles; contbr. to monographs and textbooks; cons. editor Chapman & Hall, London. Bd. dirs. Lafayette Home Hosp., 1978-87, Lafayette Symphony Orch., 1983-85. Recipient Research Career Devel. award Nat. Inst. Dental Research, 1967-70, Award for highest merit for sci. article Jour. Speech and Hearing Research, 1979, Disting. Alumnus award Bklyn. Coll., 1985; Para-Rabbi fellow Hebrew Union Coll., 2001—. Fellow Am. Speech and Hearing Assn. (v.p. Found. 1990—, honors 1998); mem. AAUP, Nat. Assn. State Univs. and Land Grant Colls. (exec. com. 1988-91, rsch. policy and grad. edn., exec. com. coun. on acad. affairs 1991—, com. on instnl. coop., exec. com. provosts instn. coop. com. 1991—), Sigma Xi (v.p. 1986—). Office: Purdue Univ Audiology & Speech Sci 1353 Heavilon Hall G-12B West Lafayette IN 47907-1353 Home: 208 Rosebank Ln West Lafayette IN 47906-8613

RINGEN, CATHERINE OLESON, linguistics educator; b. Bklyn., June 3, 1943; d. Prince Eric and Geneva Muriel (Leigh) Oleson; m. Jon David Ringen, Nov. 22, 1969; children: Kai Mathias, Whitney Leigh. Student, Cornell U., 1961-63; BA, Indiana U., 1970, MA, 1972, PhD, 1975. Vis. lectr. U. Minn., Mpls., 1973-74; asst. prof. U. Iowa, Iowa City, 1975-79, assoc. prof., 1980-87, prof., 1988—, chair linguistics, 1987-93. Author: Vowel Harmony: Theoretical Implications, 1988; co-editor Nordic Jour. Linguistics, 2001—; contbr. articles to profl. jours. Sr. Fulbright prof. Trondheim, Norway, 1980, Poznan, Poland, 1994-95. Mem. AAAS, Linguistic Soc. Am., Nordic Assn. Linguists, Phi Beta Kappa. Office: U Iowa Dept Linguistics Iowa City IA 52242 E-mail: catherine-ringen@uiowa.edu.

RINGER, DARRELL WAYNE (DAN RINGER), lawyer; b. Elizabeth, N.J., Apr. 14, 1948; s. Darrell Wayne and Elva (Brown) R.; m. Rebecca Ruth Bonner, Feb. 23, 1979; children: Daniel Benjamin, Darren Wayne. BS in Physics, W.Va. U., 1971; MBA, U. N.D., 1975; JD, W.Va. U., 1978. Bar: W.Va. 1978, U.S. Dist. Ct. (no. and so. dists.) W.Va. 1978. Assoc. Jones, Williams, West & Jones, Clarksburg, W.Va., 1978-80, Moreland & Ringer, Morgantown, 1980-83, Reeder, Shuman, Ringer & Wiley, Morgantown, 1983-91, Ringer Law Offices, Morgantown, 1991—2001, Ringr & Sal, PLLC, Morgantown, 2002—. 1st asst. prosecutor Monongalia County, W.Va., 1985-87; host W.Va. Pub. TV, PBS Pub. Affairs Programming, 1991—. Bd. dirs. Monongalia County (W.Va.) Mental Health Assn., Morgantown, 1981-83; mem. W.Va. U. Animal Care and Use Com., 1985—. Capt. USAF, 1971-75. Named W.Va. Bar Found. Lawyer Citizen of Yr., 1996. Mem. ABA (named Sole Practitioner of Yr., 2000), ATLA, W.Va. State Bar (pres. 1999-2000), Monongalia County Bar Assn. (sec. 1980-92, pres. 2001), W.Va. Trial Lawyers

Assn. (bd. govs. 1982-91, Pres.'s award 2001). Democrat. Avocation: amateur radio. Home: 18 W Front St Morgantown WV 26501-4507 Office: 823 Fairmont Rd Morgantown WV 26501-3812

RINGER, JAMES MILTON, lawyer; b. Orlando, Fla., July 9, 1943; s. Robert T. and Jessie M. (Rowe) R.; m. Jaquelyn Hope, Apr. 10, 1965; children— Carolyn Hope, James Matthew AB, Ohio U., 1965; JD, Cornell U., 1968. Bar: N.Y. 1968, U.S. Dist. Ct. (no. dist.) N.Y. 1968, U.S. Dist. Ct. (so. and ea. dists.) N.Y. 1972, U.S. Ct. Appeals (2d cir.) 1972, U.S. Ct. Claims 1976, U.S. Dist. Ct. (we. dist.) N.Y. 1978, U.S. Ct. Appeals (4th cir.) 1981, U.S. Ct. Appeals (9th cir.) 1983. Assoc. Clifford Chance Rogers & Wells, LLP, N.Y.C., 1968-78, ptnr., 1978—. Instr. bus. law U. Alaska, 1970-71 Editor Cornell Law Rev., 1967-68 Served to lt. JAGC, USNR, 1969-72 Republican. Episcopalian. Office: Clifford Chance Rogers & Wells LLP 200 Park Ave Fl 8E New York NY 10166-0899

RINGER, JENNIFER, dancer; b. New Bern, N.C. m. James Fayette, July 2000. Student, Wash. Sch. Ballet, Sch. Am. Ballet; BA in English, Fordham U., 1997. Apprentice N.Y.C. Ballet, 1989—90, mem. corps de ballet, 1990—95, soloist, 1995—2000, prin., 2000—. Dancer (ballets) Brahms-Schoenberg Quartet, Divertimento No. 15, A Midsummer Nights Dream, The Nutcracker, Gershwin Concerto, Mozart Serenade, The Sleeping Beauty, Swan Lake, Tributary, I Have My Own Room, Correlazione, 1994, Prism, 2000, Appalachia Waltz, 2000, Morgen, Huoah, The Beethoven Seventh. Office: NYC Ballet NY State Theatre 20 Lincoln Ctr Plz New York NY 10023-6913*

RINGER, KEITH WILLIAM, state education professional, consultant; b. Columbia, S.C., Feb. 7, 1962; s. Thomas Edward and Louanna (Parrott) R.; m. Mary Smith, Aug. 22, 1987; children: Christopher, AnnaMarie. BA, Newberry (S.C.) Coll., 1984; MPA, U. S.C., 1987. Ops. mgr. S.C. Dept. Edn., Columbia, 1984-87, bus. mgr., 1987-92, education assoc., 1992—. Adj. instr. Newberry Coll., 1991—. Vol. Easter Seals Soc., Columbia, 1976-83, Coop. Ministry, Columbia, 1999—, Children's Hosp., Columbia, 2000—. Recipient Susy P. Rattray State Svc. award Easter Seals Soc., 1980, Golden Pencil award Coop. Ministry, 1998, 99; named Outstanding Young Man in Am., 1985, 86, 88. Mem. S.C. State Employees Assn., S.C. Sch. Bus. Officials Assn., Tau Kappa Epsilon (life). Baptist. Avocations: sports, outdoors. Home: 224 Steeple Dr Columbia SC 29229 Office: SC Dept Edn 1429 Senate St Columbia SC 29201

RINGERWOLE, JOAN MAE, music educator, recitalist; b. Grand Rapids, Mich., Aug. 6, 1943; d. Alvin and Lula (Artz) R. AB, Calvin Coll., 1965; MM, Eastman Sch. Music, 1967; DMA, U. Iowa, 1979. Prof. music Dordt Coll., Sioux Center, Iowa, 1967-72, 75—. Author: Bibliography of Organ Music on the Psalter Hymnal and Rejoice in the Lord, 1989; recordings include Dedicatory Organ Recital, Psalms and Hymns, Spiritual Songs. Mem. Am. Guild Organists (sec. we. Iowa chpt. 1990-92, dean 1984, 85), Hymn Soc. Am., Organ Hist. Soc., Music Tchrs. Nat. Assn., Iowa Fedn. Music Clubs, Sioux County Concert Assn. (bd. dirs.). Republican. Avocations: travel, bowling. Home: 1362 4th Ave SE Sioux Center IA 51250-2907 Office: Dordt Coll Dept Music 498 4th Ave NE Dept Music Sioux Center IA 51250-1606 E-mail: jringer@dordt.edu.

RINGGOLD, FAITH, artist; b. N.Y.C., Oct. 8, 1930; BS, CCNY, 1955, MA, 1959; DFA (hon.), Moore Coll. Art, Phila., 1986, Coll. Wooster, Ohio, 1987, Mass. Coll. Art, Boston, 1991, CCNY of CUNY, 1991, Russell Sage Coll., Troy, N.Y., 1996, Parsons Sch. Design, 1996; DSc (hon.), Brockport (N.Y.) State U., 1992, Calif. Coll. Arts and Crafts, Oakland, 1993; DHL (hon.), Malloy Coll., 1997. Art tchr. N.Y. Pub. Schs., 1955-73; lectr. Bank St. Coll. Grad. Sch., N.Y.C., 1970-80; prof. art U. Calif., San Diego, 1984—. Solo exhbns. include Spectrum Gallery, N.Y.C., 1967, 70 10 year retrospective, Studio Mus. in Harlem, N.Y.C., 1984, Bernice Steinbaum Gallerym N.Y.C., 1987-88, Balt. Mus., Deland (Fla.) Mus., Faith Ringgold 25 Yr. Survey Fine Arts Mus. L.I., Hempstead, 1990-93, Textile Mus., Washington, 1993, Children's Mus. of Manhattan, N.Y.C., 1993-95, Hewlett-Woodmere Pub. Libr., Hewlett, N.Y., 1993-94, St. Louis Art Mus., 1994, Athenaeum, La Jolla, Calif., 1995, A.C.A. Gallery, N.Y.C., 1995, 98, Ind. U. of Pa., 1995, Bowling Green State U., Ind., 1996, New Mus. Contemporary Art, N.Y.C., 1998; exhibited in group shows at Harlem Cultural Coun., N.Y.C., 1996, Meml. Exhibit for MLK, Mus. Modern Art N.Y.C., 1968, Chase Manhattan Bank Collection, Martha Jackson Gallery, N.Y.C., 1970, Am. Women Artists, Gedok, Kunstalle, Hamburg, Ger., 1972, Jubliee, Boston Mus. Fine Arts, 1975, Major Contemporary Women Artists, Suzanne Gross Gallery, Phila., 1984, Committed to Print Mus. Modern Art, N.Y.C., 1988, The Art of Black Am. in Japan, Terada Warehouse, Tokyo, Made in the USA, Art in the 50s and 60s U. Calif. Berkeley Art Mus., Craft Today Poetry of the Physical, Am. Craft Mus., N.Y.C., Portraits and Homage to Mothers Heckscher Mus. Huntington, 1987, N.J. State Mus., Trenton, 1992-94, Fukui Fine Art Mus., Fuki, Japan, 1992, Takushima Modern Art Mus., Japan, 1993, Otani Meml. Art Mus., Japan, 1993, Salina Art Atr., Kans., 1993, Bruce Watkins Ctr. Kansas City, Mo., 1993, Barton County C.C., Great Bend, Kans., 1993, Del. State Coll. Arts Ctr. Gallery, Dover, 1993-94, Roswell Mus. and Art Ctr., N.Mex., 1994, Aknaton Gallery, Cairo, Alexandria, Egypt, Exit Art, N.Y.C., 1994, New Mus. Contemporary Art, N.Y.C., 1996, Spellman Coll. Mus., Atlanta, 1996, Whitney Mus., N.Y.C., 1996, Centre Georges Pompidou, Paris, 1997, Mus. Art, Ft. Lauderdale, Fla., 1997, N.J. Ctr. Arts, Summit, N.J., 1997, Trout Gallery Dickenson Coll., Carlisle, Pa., numerous others; represented in collections at Chase Manhattan Bank, N.Y.C., Philip Morris Collection, N.Y.C., Children's Mus., Bklyn., Newark Mus., The Women's House of Detention, Rikers Island, N.Y., The Studio Mus., N.Y.C., High Mus., Atlanta, Guggenheim Mus., Met. Mus. Art, Boston Mus. Fine Arts, MOMA, AARP, Washington, Am. Craft Mus., N.Y.C., Clark Mus., Williamstown, Mass., ARCO Chem., Phila., Coca-Cola, Atlanta, Ft. Wayne Mus. Fine Art, Ind., Harold Washington Libr. Ctr., Chgo., Lang Comm. Corp., Coll., Phila. Mus. Art, Pub. Art Pub. Schs., P.S. 22, Bklyn., Spenser Mus. Lawr., Kans., St. Louis Mus. Art, Balt. Mus., Nat. Mus., Washington, Woman's Mus., Washington, Eugenio Maria de Hostos C.C., N.Y.C., MTA 125th St. IRT subway sta. installation, N.Y.C., numerous others; author: Tar Beach, 1991, Aunt Harriet's Underground Railroad in the Sky, 1992 (Picture Book award 1993, Best Children's Book of Yr. 1993), Dinner at Aunt Connie's House, 1993 (Reading Magic award 1993), We Flew Over the Bridge: Memoirs of Faith Ringgold, 1995, Talking to Faith Ringgold, 1995, Bonjour Lonnie, 1996, My Dream of Martin Luther King, Jr., 1996, The Invisible Princess, 1999, If a Bus Could Talk: The Story of Rosa Parks, 1999, Counting to Tar Beach, 1999, Cassie's Colorful Day with Daddy, 1999, Cassie's Word Quilt, 2000; contbr. articles to profl. jours. Recipient AAUW travel award to Africa, 1976; John Simon Guggenheim Meml. Found. Fellowship (painting), 1987, N.Y. Found. for Arts award (painting), 1988, Nat. Endowment Arts award (sculpture), 1978, (painting) 1989, La Napoule Found. award (painting in So. of France), 1990, Video and Software award Calif. children's book, 1991, Parent's Choice Gold award, 1991, Artist award Studio Mus., Harlem, 1991, Artist of Yr. award Sch. Art League N.Y., 1991, Coretta Scott King award for illustration, 1992, Dist. Artist award Nat. Coun. Art Adminstrs., 1992, award, 1993, Arts Internat. award (travel to Morocco), 1992, Honors award for outstanding achievement in the visual arts Woman's Caucus Arts, N.Y., 1994, Towsend Harris medal City Coll. Alumni Assn., 1995, N.J. Artist of Yr. award N.J. Ctr. Visual Arts, 1997, 31st NAACP Image award, 1999. Home: PO Box 429 Englewood NJ 07631-0429 Office: ACA Gallery 529 W 20th St Fl 5 New York NY 10011-2800 E-mail: any1canfly@aol.com.

RINGLE, BRETT ADELBERT, lawyer, petroleum company executive; b. Berkeley, Calif., Mar. 17, 1951; s. Forrest A. and Elizabeth V. (Darnall) R.; m. Sue Kinslow, May 26, 1973. BA, U. Tex., 1973, JD, 1976. Bar: Tex. 1976, U.S. Dist. Ct. (no. dist.) Tex. 1976, U.S. Supreme Ct. 1980, U.S. Ct. Appeals (5th cir.) 1984. Ptnr. Shank, Irwin & Conant, Dallas, 1976-86, Jones, Day, Reavis & Pogue, Dallas, 1986-96; v.p. Hunt Petroleum Corp., 1996—. Adj. prof. law So. Meth. U., Dallas, 1983. Author: (with J.W. Moore and H.I. Bendix) Moore's Federal Practice, 2d edit., Vol. 12, 1980, Vol. 13, 1981, (with J.W. Moore) Vol. 1A, 1982, Vol. 1A Part 2, 1989. Mem. Dallas Bar Assn. Home: 3514 Gillon Ave Dallas TX 75205-3220 Office: Hunt Petroleum Corp 5000 Thanksgiving Tower 1601 Elm St Dallas TX 75201 E-mail: bar@huntpetroleum.com.

RINGLEE, ROBERT JAMES, consulting engineering executive; b. Sacramento, Apr. 23, 1926; s. Francis and Marie N. R.; m. Helen Laura Carleton, Aug. 27, 1949; children— Sarah N., Jane C., Robert K. BSEE, U. Wash., 1946, MSEE, 1948; PhD in Mechanics, Rensselaer Poly. Inst., 1964. Registered profl. engr., N.Y. With advanced engrng. program Gen. Electric Co., 1948-51, advanced devel. engr., power transformer dept., 1951-55, supr. power transformer design, 1955-60, sr. analytical engr., 1960-65, mgr. system and equipment reliability, 1965-69; prin. engr. dir. Power Technologies, Inc., Schenectady, 1969-86, prin cons., 1986-93; TAG assoc. Power Techs., Inc., 1993-94, assoc. cons., 1994-98. Contbr. articles to profl. publs.; patentee in field. Mem. Schalmont Bd. Edn., 1966-70, pres., 1968-69. Served with USNR, 1944-46. Recipient Managerial award Gen. Electric Co., 1953 Fellow IEEE (3 prize paper awards), AAAS; mem. Internat. Conf. on High Voltage Power Systems (expert advisor, Attwood Assoc.), Adirondack Mountain Club (pres. 1990-93, acting exec. dir. 1994). Democrat. Unitarian Universalist. Home and Office: 315 Juniper Dr Schenectady NY 12306-1705 E-mail: ringlee@banet.net.

RINGLER, JEROME LAWRENCE, lawyer; b. Detroit, Dec. 26, 1948; BA, Mich. State U., 1970; JD, U. San Francisco, 1974. Bar: Calif. 1974, U.S. Ct. Appeals (9th cir.) 1974, U.S. Dist. Ct. (no. dist.) Calif. 1974, U.S. Dist. Ct. (ctrl. dist.) Calif. 1975, U.S. Dist. Ct. (so. dist.) Calif. 1981. Assoc. Parker, Stansbury et al, L.A., 1974-76, Fogel, Feldman, Ostrov, Ringler & Klevens, Santa Monica, Calif., 1976-80, ptnr., 1980—. Arbitrator L.A. Superior Ct. Arbitration Program, 1980-85. Named Verdictum Juris Trial Lawyer of Yr., 1996. Mem. ATLA, ABA, State Bar Calif., L.A. County Bar Assn. (litigation sect., exec. com. 1994—), L.A. Trial Lawyers Assn. (bd. govs. 1981—, treas. 1988, sec. 1989, v.p. 1990, pres.-elect 1991, pres. 1992, Trial Lawyer of the Yr. 1987), Calif. Trial Lawyers Assn., Internat. Acad. Trial Lawyers, Am. Bd. Trial Advs. (assoc. 1988, adv. 1991), Inns of Ct. (master). Avocations: skiing, tennis. Office: Fogel Feldman Ostrov Ringler & Klevens 1620 26th St # 100S Santa Monica CA 90404-4013

RINGLER, LENORE, educational psychologist, educator; d. Albert Haendel and Ida (Brafstein) Haendel; 1 son., Adam. BA, Bklyn. Coll.; MA, Queens Coll., 1954; PhD, NYU, 1965. Tchr., then reading specialist N.Y.C. Bd. Edn.; prof. NYU, N.Y.C., 1965-98, prof. emerita, 1998—, chmn. dept. ednl. psychology, 1974-79. Ednl. cons. Psychol. Corp., Council on Interracial Books for Children, N.Y.C. Bd. Edn. Author: Skills Monitoring System-Reading, 1977, A Language-Thinking Approach to Reading, 1984; author reading series for Holt Rhinehart & Winston, 1989; contbr. articles to profl. jours. Mem. Citizens Com. for Children; mem. Commn. on Reading Nat. Acad. Edn., 1983-85 Grantee U.S. Office Edn., 1968-69, Newspapers in Edn., 1990. Mem. APA, Am. Ednl. Rsch. Assn., Internat. Reading Assn. (past pres. Manhattan coun.), Nat. Reading Conf. (v.p. 1982-84, pres. 1984-85), Pi Lambda Theta (rsch. fellow 1963-64), Kappa Delta Pi. E-mail: lenore.ringler@nyu.edu.

RINGO, BETTY PENFOLD, hypnotherapist; b. Wheaton, Ill., Apr. 26, 1924; d. Alexander Derby and Vega Thelma (Friborg) Penfold; children: Susan K. Paul, Robert B., Richard G., Peter A. ADN, Purdue U., 1982, BLS, 1985. RN Ind.; lic. hypnotherapist, neurolinguistic practitioner, Reiki master. Medication nurse Meml. Hosp., Michigan City, Ind., 1982-83; pvt. practice in reflexology, 1981—; pvt. practice in hypnotherapy, reiki, reflexology and healing touch, 1985—; pvt. practice massage therapy, 1998. Design human engrng. I facilitator AIDS Support Group, 1990-92. Mem. AAUW (pres. 1988-89, v.p., program chair 1986-88, 90-92). Lutheran.

RINGOLD, JOEL, internist; b. Phila., May 3, 1937; s. Isadore and Hannah Ringold; m. Harriett Lee Emdur, Dec. 5, 1964; children: Michael, Steven, Daniel. BA, Temple U., 1958, MD, 1962. Diplomate Am. Bd. Internal Medicine, Am. Bd. Endocrinology, Diabetes and Metabolism. Pvt. practice, Chester, Pa., 1968-71; staff physician So. Calif. Permanente Med. Group, Harbor City, Calif., 1971-80; pvt. practice Torrance, 1980—. Dir. Diabetes Treatment Ctr., Little Co. of Mary Hosp., Torrance, 1990-94; asst. prof. medicine UCLA, 1972-96, assoc. prof., 2000; tchg. staff Harbor/UCLA Med. Ctr., Torrance; adv. bd. So. Calif. Regional Occpl. Ctr., Torrance. Lt. comdr. USPHS, 1963-65. Fellow Am. Coll. Endocrinology; mem. ACP-ASIM, Endocrine Soc., Am. Diabetes Assn., Am. Assn. Clin. Endocrinologists, Alpha Omega Alpha. Avocations: hiking, gardening, cross-country skiing, violin, piano. Office: 3500 Lomita Blvd Ste 305 Torrance CA 90505-5019

RINGQUIST, EVAN JOHN, political science educator; b. Mpls., Aug. 6, 1962; s. Earl James and Georgia Lois Marie Ringquist; m. Laurie Ann Ringquist, Aug. 21, 1991; children: Rachel Marie, Hannah Grace. BA, Moorhead (Minn.) State U., 1984; MA, U. Wis., 1986, PhD, 1990, MS, 1996. Prof. polit. sci. Tex. Tech. U., Lubbock, 1990-93, Fla. State U., Tallahassee, 1993—2001, Ind. U., Bloomington, 2002—. Cons. Dade County Human Svcs. Coalition, Miami, Fla., 1998-99, Wis. SAVE Commn., Madison, 1994, Nat. Pk. Svc., Key Largo, Fla., 1997, NSF, Washington, 1997, 99, 2000. Author: Environmental Protection at the State Level, 1993, Contemporary Regulatory Policy, 2000. Adv. bd. Legal Environ. Assistance Found., Tallahassee, 1995—; mem. rsch. adv. bd. Sierra Club, Washington, 1997. Mem. Am. Polit. Sci. Assn., Midwest Polit. Sci. Assn. (sect. head), So. Polit. Sci. Assn., Western Polit. Sci. Assn., Southwestern Polit. Sci. Assn. (v.p.), Policy Studies Orgn. (editl. bd.). Democrat. Lutheran. Avocations: fishing, camping, reading, woodworking, hiking. Office: Ind U Sch Pub and Environ Affairs 1315 E 10th St Bloomington IN 47405 Business E-Mail: eringqui@indiana.edu.

RINGQUIST, LYNN ANNE, micrographics company executive; b. Panama City, Fla., June 12, 1952; d. George Willard and Juanita Anne (Vinson) Thomas; m. Ronald Scott Nelson, Sept. 5, 1970 (div. Mar. 1978); children: Faith Nichole, Jason Jay; m. Eric James Ringquist, Sept. 19, 1993 (div. Apr. 2000). Student, Fullerton (Calif.) Jr. Coll., 1970-71, Mpls. Coll. Art & Design, 1987-93. Microfilm technician Microfilming Services, Corona, Calif., 1970-71, Blue Cross/Blue Shield, Eagan, Minn., 1972-73, customer service rep., 1973-76; regional sales rep. MicroD Internat., Burnsville, 1974-83, gen. sales mgr., 1983-85, v.p., 1985-98, pres., 1998—. Bd. dirs. Neoteric Arts, Inc., Burnsville, 1983—; creator LA Beeds, 1994; distbr. Rexall Showcase Internat., 1995. Mem. Assn. Info. and Image Mgmt. Avocations: painting, drawing, bartending, trap shooting, jewelry making. Home: 14901 Judicial Rd Burnsville MN 55306 Office: MicroD Internat 14901 Judicial Rd Burnsville MN 55306

RINI, ALICE GERTRUDE, law educator, lawyer, nursing educator; b. N.Y.C. d. John W. and Jacqueline F. (Dilworth) Anderson; m. Leonard Paul Rini; children: Alice Marie, Paul William, Anthony John. BS, Adelphi U., 1961, MS, 1966; postgrad., St. John's U., 1975-79; JD, No. Ky. U., 1988. Bar: Ky. 1989. Prof. nursing Nassau C.C., Garden City, N.Y., 1966-79; chair dept. nursing No. Ky. U., Highland Heights, 1980-87, assoc. prof. nursing, 1980—2000, adj. prof. nursing, 2000—; of counsel Wasson, Braden, Heeter & King, Newport, N.Y., 1996-97. Adj. prof. law No. Ky. U., Highland Heights, 1987-95; cons. long term care agys., 1999--. Author: (with others) Core Curriculum Gerontology Nursing, 1995, 2d edit., 2000, Core Curriculum Advanced Nursing Practice, 1998, Nursing Documentation: Legal Focus Across Practice Settings, 1998, Care of the Older Adult with Cancer, 2000, Core Concepts in Advanced Practice Nursing, 2001; contbr. articles to profl. jours. Bd. dirs. Brighton Ctr., Newport, Ky., 1983-89; mem. adv. bd. Inst. for Health Freedom, Washington. Mem. Am. Assn. Nurse Attys. (bd. dirs. 1989-92), Nat. Gerontology Nurses Assn. (mem. editl. bd. 1996—), No. Ky. Bar Assn. (sect. officer 1989-97, health law com. officer 1992-97), Sigma Theta Tau (nominating com. 1991, rsch. com. 1997-99). Home: PO Box 176 Alexandria KY 41001-0176 E-mail: alicegr@fuse.net., rini@nku.edu.

RINI, WILLIAM ANTHONY, communications company executive, multimedia engineer; b. L.A., Sept. 14, 1967; s. William Leonard and Vonnie Lou (Stark) R. Student, Calif. State U., Northridge, L.A. Valley Coll. Registered rep. gen. securities series 7. Investment exec. Smith Barney, Beverly Hills, Calif., 1991-93, Paine Webber, Santa Monica, 1993, Cowles Sabol, Encino, 1993-94; pres. The Syndicate, Santa Monica, 1994—; dir. programming Digital Planet, Culver City, 1995-97; sr. prodr. Lightspeed Media/Asylum Inc., 1997-98; dir. devel. eToys, Santa Monica, 1998—. Contbr. articles to profl. jours. With U.S. Army, 1987-90. Roman Catholic.

RINK, LAWRENCE DONALD, cardiologist; b. Indpls., Oct. 14, 1940; s. Joe Donald and Mary Ellen (Rand) R.; m. Eleanor Jane Zimmerly, Aug. 10, 1963; children: Scott, Virginia. BS, DePauw U., 1962; MD, Ind. U., 1966. Diplomate Am. Bd. Internal Medicine, Am. Bd. Cardiology, Critical Care Medicine. Clin. asst. prof. Ind. U. Med. Sch., Indpls., 1973-79, clin. assoc. prof., 1979-85, clin. prof. medicine, 1985—; cardiologist IMA, Inc., Bloomington, Ind., 1974-95; pres., CEO Internal Medicine Assocs., 1994—; dir. cardiac rehab. Bloomington Hosp., 1976—, dir. cardiology, 1983—; CEO, chmn. bd. dirs. IMA Inc., 1995—. Physician Ind. U. Basketball Team, 1979—; dir. med. edn. Bloomington Hosp., 1976—; med. dir. Track and Field Pan Am. Games, 1987; U.S. Olympic Physician Olympic Sports Festival, 1989, World Univ. Games, 1990, Olympic Games, Barcelona, 1992, World Univ. Games, Fukuoka, Japan, 1995, Korea, 1997, Majorca, Spain, 1999; N.Am. continent rep. Fed. Internat. Student Univ. Sports. Bd. dirs. J.O. Ritchie Soc., Ind. U. Med. Sch. Bd. dirs., dean's coun. Ind. U. Med. Sch., 1992—. Recipient Quality of Life award Major Bloomington, 1978; named Most Outstanding Flight Surgeon, USN, 1968, Most Outstanding Alumnus, Ind. U. Med. Sch., 1998. Fellow Am. Coll. Cardiology, Am. Heart Assn., Am. Soc. Critical Care, Am. Coll. Sports Medicine; mem. AMA, Ind. U. Med. Alumnae Assn. (pres. 1986-87, exec. alumna coun.). Avocations: reading, writing, golf, tennis. Office: IMA Inc 550 Landmark Ave Bloomington IN 47403

RINK, RICHARD CARLOS, pediatric urologist, educator; b. Indpls., June 24, 1952; s. J. Don and Mary Ellen Rink; m. Kanda Rink, May 31, 1975; children: Richard Andrew, Stephanie Morgan. BA, Western Ky. U., 1974; MD, Ind. U., 1978. Diplomate Am. Bd. Urology. Resident in gen. surgery Emory U. Sch. Medicine, Atlanta, 1978-80; resident in urology Ind. U. Sch. Medicine, Indpls., 1980-84; pediat. urology fellowship Harvard U. Sch. Medicine, Boston, 1984-85; pediat. urologist Ind. U. Med. Ctr., Indpls., 1985-89, chief pediat. urology, prof. pediat. urology, 1989—. Contbr. articles to profl. jours. Fellow Am. Acad. Pediat. (bd. dirs. 1998), Am. Coll. Surgeons; mem. Soc. Pediat. Urology, Am. Assn. Pediat. Urologists (pres. 1996), Soc. Genitourinary Reconstructive Surgeons (bd. dirs., pres. 1999—), European Soc. Pediat. Urologists, Am. Urologic Assn. (North Ctrl. sect. exec. com. 1998—). Avocations: golf, skiing, basketball. Office: Riley Hosp for Children # 1739 702 Barnhill Dr # 1739 Indianapolis IN 46202-5128

RINK, WESLEY WINFRED, retired banker; b. Hickory, N.C., June 14, 1922; s. Dewey Lee and Mabel E. (Yount) R.; m. Patricia A. Jones, Aug. 19, 2000; children from previous marriage: Rebecca S., Christopher L. BS in Accountancy, U. Ill., 1947, MS, 1948. Acct., Glidden Co., Chgo., 1948-58; adminstrv. mgr. Central Soya Co., 1958-65; v.p., comptroller State Nat. Bank, Evanston, Ill., 1965-71; exec. v.p., dir. Pioneer Trust & Savs. Bank, Chgo., 1971-76; corp. v.p. Exchange Bancorp., Inc., Tampa, 1977-82; sr. v.p. NCNB Nat. Bank Fla., 1982-86; fin cons. Temple Terrace, Fla., 1986-2001; ret., 2001. Served to capt. USAAF, 1942-46. Home: 11402 Robles Del Rio Pl Temple Terrace FL 33617-3819

RINKENBERGER, RICHARD KRUG, physical scientist, geologist, consultant; b. Gridley, Ill., May 15, 1933; s. Burl E. and Olive J. (Krug) R.; m. Marilyn Ruth Ratliff, Feb. 19, 1960; children: Janice L., Ginger R., Rebekah P. BA in Geology, U. Colo., 1959. Dir. prospecting Grubstake Assn., Sask., Can., 1958-59; engr. Martin-Marietta Aerospace Co., Denver, 1960-75; geologist U.S. Geol. Survey, 1975; geologist remote sensing U.S. Mine Safety and Health Adminstrn., 1975-79; pres., exploration geologist Banner Set, Ltd., 1980-84; pres., cons. geologist R.K. Rinkenberger & Assocs., Aurora, Colo., 1979-87; phys. scientist U.S. Dept. Energy, Germantown, Md., 1987-97; cons. geologist, rsch. geologist Denver, Rockville, 1988—. Educator prospecting Denver Sch. Prospecting, 1968-71, U. Colo., Denver, Boulder, 1970-75; rsch. geochemist Heritage Chem. Co., Englewood, 1984-86; prospecting researcher, gold and silver prospector R.K. Rinkenberger & Assocs., 1965—. Contbr. articles to profl. publs. Mem. parent adv. bd, supt. of schs. Westminster, Colo., 1982-83. Grantee Saskatchewan (Can.) Dept. Mineral Resources, 1958, 59, U.S. Geol. Survey (remote sensing), 1978. Mem. Denver Mining Club, Sigma Gamma Epsilon. Mem. Ch. of the Nazarene. Achievements include geological theory and experimentation, research on animal and plant killing mechanisms responsible for dinosaur extinction and other mass plant and animal extinctions. Office: 12183 Monaco Dr Brighton CO 80602-9603

RINKER, H. BRUCE, ecologist; b. Winchester, Va., May 17, 1955; BS, Va. Tech, 1979; postgrad., Antioch New Eng. Grad. Sch., 1999—. Biology educator Langley Sch., McLean, Va., 1979—87; sci. dept. chmn., dire. forest canopy walkway Millbrook (N.Y.) Sch., 1987—2000; dir. rsch. and conservation Marie Selby Bot. Gardens, Sarasota, Fla., 2000—. Sci. instr. Smithsonian Instn., Washington, 1979—87; co-dir., treas. Internat. Student Rsch., Inc., McLean, 1986—90; rschr. Radeau des Cimes, Montpellier, 1991—96; editl. bd. Marie Selby Botanical Gardens, Sarasota, 2000—, BioScience Productions, Inc., Nokomis, 2000—; rsch. bd. dirs. Amazon Conservatory for Tropical Studies, Iquitos, Peru, 2001—. Contbr. articles. Bd. dirs. Childrens Environ. Trust Found., Zeeland, 1996—2000. Recipient Best of the Hudson Valley, Hudson Valley Mag., 1996, Outstanding Biology Tchr., Nat. Assn. Biology Tchrs., 1997. Fellow: Switzer Found. (Environ. fellow 2000—), The Explorers Club (Nat. fellow 1998—); mem.: Assn. Tropical Biology, Orgn. Tropical Studies, Soc. Conservation Biology, Am. Soc. Plant Taxonomists, Fla. Acad. Sci., N.Y. Acad. Sci., Aldo Leopold Soc. Roman Catholic. Avocations: travel, hiking, photography, antiquarian books. Office: Marie Selby Botanical Gardens 811 S Palm Ave Sarasota FL 34236 Office Fax: 941-951-1474. Business E-Mail: brinker@selby.org .

RINKER, MARIANNE MARIE, rehabilitation nurse; b. Milford, Del., Aug. 5, 1960; d. James Warren and Ann Marie (Vissman) Graham. LPN, Parkview Hosp., Nashville, 1982; BSN, Vanderbilt U., Nashville, 1988. CRRN. Staff nurse West Side Hosp., Nashville, 1982-85; primary nurse Vanderbilt Med. Ctr., 1986-89; head trauma coord. Georgetown Pinnacle Rehab., Louisville, 1989-91; clin. mgr. rehab. svcs. Alliant Health Svcs., 1991-92; dir. rehab. nursing Healthsouth Med. Ctr., Richmond, Va., 1992-94; program cons. Rehabcare Group, Inc., St. Louis, 1994-98, dir. clin. edn., 1998—. Facilitator Ky. Head Injury Assn., Louisville, 1989-91; surveyor Commn. on Accreditation of Rehab. Facilities, 1997—. Counselor cmty. educator Vanderbilt AIDS Project, Nashville, 1987-88. Mem. Assn. Rehab. Nurses (adminstrv. mgmt. group 1994—). Avocations: music, literature, swimming, running.

RINKER, RUBY STEWART, foundation administrator; b. Dayton, Ohio, June 11, 1936; d. Encle Stewart and Addie (Hamilton) Stewart-Smith; children: William Bertram Klawonn, Elizabeth Lynn Dennis, William Stewart-Bradley Klawonn. Human relations counselor Palm Beach County Sch. System, West Palm Beach, Fla., 1974-84; adminstrv. asst. Bohmfalk Estate, Palm Beach, Fla., N.Y.C, Newport, R.I., 1984—; pres., CEO Ruby S. Rinker Co., Inc., Palm Beach. Hon. counselor U.S. Naval Acad., U.S. Air Force Acad.; mem. exec. bd. Intercoastal Health Care Sys. Trustee Bohmfalk Charitable Found., Crystal Cathedral Ministries; bd. dirs. Crystal Cathedral Ministries Internat. Bd., Vatican Mus.; mem. adv. bd. Drug Free Am. Mem. Phi Delta Kappa. Home: 561 Island Dr Palm Beach FL 33480-4746 Office: 225 Peruvian Ave Palm Beach FL 33480-4672

RINNAN, BARBARA GUY, retired non-profit organization executive; b. Oak Park, Ill., Dec. 18, 1929; d. Harry Lee and Anna Sophia (Gard) Guy; m. Carl Hagen Bergersen, Sept. 6, 1952 (div. May 1970); children: Laura Marie Bergersen, Paul Andrew Bergersen; m. Robert Malcolm Rinnan, June 3, 1972 (dec. Apr. 1998). BS magna cum laude, U. Ill., 1952. Med. technologist Westlake Cmty. Hosp., Melrose Park, Ill., 1952-54, Dr. Howard M. Sheaff, Oak Park, 1954-56; underwriter Prudential, L.A., 1956-59; comms. dir. Chgo. Sunday Evening Club, 1979-88; midwest rep. Ctr. U.S.-U.S.S.R. Initiatives, San Francisco, 1984-88; founder, pres. Midwest Ctr. Citizen Initiatives, Oak Park, 1988-96. Adv. bd. Caretakers of the Environ. Internat., Wilmette, Ill., 1992-96; sch. bd. mem. Oak Park Pub. Sch. Dist. 97, 1978-81. Democrat. Lutheran. Avocations: reading, writing, community volunteering, collecting Russian artifacts, Chicago Symphony Orchestra. Home: 221 N Kenilworth Ave Apt 510 Oak Park IL 60302-2053

RINNE, AUSTIN DEAN, retired insurance company executive; b. Aug. 14, 1919; s. Hermann Henry and Marie (Knudsen) R.; m. Martha Jo Runyan, Dec. 29, 1941; children: Erik Knudsen, Barbara Jane Rivera. Student, Ind. U., 1938-40; grad. ins. mktg., Purdue U., 1947. Spl. agt. Northwestern Mut. Life, Indpls., 1946-56, dist. agt., 1956-58, gen. agt. Dallas, 1958-84, gen. agt.

emeritus, 1984—. Chmn. bd. dirs. Comm. and Mgmt. Assocs., Ann Arbor, Mich. Bd. dirs., v.p. English Speaking Union, Dallas, 1972, Dallas Opera, 1984—, Indianapolis Philarmonic Orch., 2001— (hon.), Taca Bd., Dallas Cultural Arts Assn. Capt. USAF, 1941-45, ETO. Decorated Purple Heart, Air Medal with cluster, POW medal, Presdl. unit citation Happy Warriors WWII Combat pilots, 8th Air Force Assn., 1995; recipient Trail Boss award S.W. Gen. Agts. and Mgrs. Assn., 1993. Mem. Dallas Estate Planning Coun. (pres. 1965-66), Dallas Assn. Life Underwriters (bd. dirs. 1960-63, Hall of Fame 1989), Million Dollar Roundtable (life), Dallas Knife and Fork (pres., bd. dirs. 1986—), Mil. Order World Wars, English-Speaking Union (dir., v.p. Dallas chpt. 1972—), Dallas Coun. on World Affairs, Dallas Sales and Mktg. Execs. (bd. dirs. 1970-73), Am. Legion Dallas (comdr. met. post 1967), VFW, Sertoma (pres. Dallas chpt. 1967-68, mem. found. bd. 1975—, Sertoman of Yr. 1990), Phi Kappa Psi Alumni Assn. (pres. 1951-52), Ind. U. Alumni Assn. (pres. Dallas/Ft. Worth 1968-69), Phi Kappa Psi (exec. coun. 1972-76, endowment bd. 1989—, Dallas sales and mktg. chpt. bd. 1969-72), Park City Club, Dallas Country Club, Northshore Club. Republican. Methodist. Home: 4311 Bordeaux Ave Dallas TX 75205-3719 Office: 3102 Oak Lawn Ave Ste 650 Dallas TX 75219-6400 Fax: (214) 521-4760.

RINSCH, MARYANN ELIZABETH, occupational therapist; b. L.A., Aug. 8, 1939; d. Harry William and Thora Analine (Langlie) Hitchcock; m. Charles Emil Rinsch, June 18, 1964; children: Christopher, Daniel, Carl. BS, U. Minn., 1961. Registered occupational therapist, Calif. Staff occupational therapist Hastings (Minn.) State Hosp., 1961-62, Neuropsychiat. Inst., L.A., 1962-64; staff and sr. occupational therapist Calif. Children's Svcs., 1964-66, head occupational therapist, 1966-68; researcher A. Jean Ayres, U. So. Calif., 1968-69; pvt. practice neurodevel. and sensory integraton Tarzana, Calif., 1969-74; pediat. occupational therapist neurodevel. & sensory integration St. Johns Hosp., Santa Monica, 1991-95; pvt. practice, cons. Santa Monica-Malibu Unified Sch. Dist., 1994-2001; pvt. practice, 2001—. Mem. alliance bd. Natural History Mus., L.A. County, 1983—, pres., 1998-99; cub scouts den mother Boy Souts Am., Sherman Oaks, Calif., 1986-88, advancement chair Boy Scout Troop 474, 1989-92; mem. Vol. League San Fernando Valley, Van Nuys, Calif., 1985-93; trustee Viewpoint Sch., Calabasas, Calif., 1987-90, Valley Women's Ctr., 1990-91. Mem. Am. Occupational Therapy Assn., Calif. Occupational Therapy Assn. Home: 19849 Greenbriar Dr Tarzana CA 91356-5428

RINSKY, JOEL CHARLES, lawyer; b. Bklyn., Jan. 29, 1938; s. Irving C. and Elsie (Millman) R.; m. Judith L. Lynn, Jan. 26, 1963; children: Heidi M., Heather S., Jason W. BS, Rutgers U., 1961, LLB, 1962, JD, 1968. Bar: N.J. 1963, U.S. Dist. Ct. N.J. 1963, U.S. Supreme Ct. 1967, U.S. Ct. Appeals (3d cir.) 1986; cert. civil trial atty., N.J. Pvt. practice, Livingston, N.J., 1964-97; sr. ptnr. Rinsky & Marley L.L.C., 1997-98; of counsel Gonzalez and Weichert P.C., 1999—. Committeeman Millburn-Short Hills (N.J.) Dem. Com., 1982-97, vice chmn., 1983-87; trustee Student Loan Fund, Millburn, 1983-91. Fellow Am. Acad. Matrimonial Lawyers; mem. N.J. Bar Assn., Essex County Bar Assn. (exec. com. sect. family law). Jewish. Avocations: tennis, chess, golf, piano. Home: 87 Sullivan Dr West Orange NJ 07052-2262 Office: 127 E Mount Pleasant Ave Livingston NJ 07039-3005 E-mail: Rinsky3@aol.com.

RINSKY, JUDITH SUE LYNN, foundation administrator, educator consultant; b. Sept. 12, 1941; d. Allan A. and Sophie (Schwartz) Lynn; m. Joel C. Rinsky, Jan. 29, 1963; children: Heidi Mae Schnapp, Heather Star Maxon, Jason Wayne. BA in Home Econs., Montclair State U., 1963. Notary pub., N.J. Tchr. home econs. Florence Ave. Sch., Irvington, N.J., 1963-66; substitute tchr. Millburn-Short Hills Sch. System, Millburn Twp., 1978-82, 90-98, sr. citizen coord., 1982-87; respite care coord. Essex County Divsn. on Aging, East Orange, 1988-90; pvt. practice educator Short Hills, NJ, 1990—98; tchr. basic skills Millburn (N.J.) H.S., 1998—. Bd. mem. adv. com. gerontology Seton Hall U., 1984—90; coord. Mayor's Adv. Bd. Sr. Citizens, Millburn-Short Hills, 1982—87; home instrn. Millburn-Short Hills Sch. Sys., 1997—98; tchr. adv. Millburn H.S. Interart Club, 2000—. Pres. Deerfield Sch. PTA, 1979-80, Millburn H.S. PTA, 1983-85; co-chmn. dinner dance Charles T. King Student Loan Fund, 1981; active Handicapped Access Study Com., 1983-85; bd. dirs. Coun. on Health and Human Svcs., 1985-90, 94-97; acting dir. B'nai Israel Nursery Sch., 1994. Mem. Lake Naomi Assn. (chmn. sailing com. 1981), N.J. Home Econs. Assn., Am. Home Econs. Assn., Rotary (hon. mem., pres. Millburn-Short Hills club 1992-93, bd. dirs. 1992-2000, advisor Millburn interact club 1987-98, 2000—, chmn. internat. interact dist. 7470 1993-95, advisor 1995-98). Home and Office: 87 Sullivan Dr West Orange NJ 07052-2262 E-mail: jsr_07041@yahoo.com., rinsky@millburn.org.

RINSLAND, ROLAND DELANO, retired university official; b. Apr. 11, 1933; s. Charles henry and Lottie Rinsland. AB with distinction, Va. State U.; AM, profl. diploma, EdD, Columbia U. Asst. to dean of men Va. State Coll., Petersburg; asst. purchasing agt. Glyco Products Co., Inc., N.Y.C.; asst. office registrar Tchrs. Coll. Columbia U., tchr. cert. advisor, registrar, 1966-71, asst. dean student affairs, registrar, dir. doctoral studies, 1971-95; ret., 1995. Mem. Tchrs. Coll. Devel. Coun.; rep., presenter degrees Tchrs. Coll., Japan, 1989, 91, 93, 94. 1st lt. AUS, 1954-56. Mem. AAAS, NEA (Leah B. Sykes award for life mem.), Am. Coll. Pers. Assn., Nat. Soc. Study Edn., Am. Ednl. Rsch. Assn., Assn. Collegiate Registrars and Admission Officers (inter-assn. rep. to state edn. depts. tchr. cert. 1973-74, mem. com. orgn. and adminstrn. registrars activities 1973, 74-76), Assn. Records Execs. and Adminstrs. (charter mem., by-laws and program chmn. 1969), Am. Acad. Polit. and Social Sci., Am. Assn. Higher Edn., Assn. Instl. Rsch., Internat. Assn. Applied Psychology, Soc. Applied Anthropology, Am. Assn. Counseling and Devel., Assn. Study Higher Edn., Mid. States Assn. Collegiate Registrars and Officers of Admission., N.Y. State Pers. and Guidance Assn., N.Y. Acad. Scis., Scabbard and Blade, Kappa Phi Kappa, Kappa Delta Pi.

RINTA, CHRISTINE EVELYN, nurse, air force officer; b. Geneva, Oct. 4, 1952; d. Arvi Alexander and Catharina Maria (Steenbergen) R. BSN, Kent State U., 1974; MSN, Case Western Res. U., 1979. CNOR. Staff nurse oper. room Euclid (Ohio) Gen. Hosp., 1974-76, oper. room charge nurse, 1977-79; commd. 1st lt. USAF, 1979, advanced through grades to lt. col.; staff nurse oper. room Air Force Regional Hosp., Sheppard AFB, Tex., 1979-82; staff nurse oper. room, asst. oper. room supr. Regional Med. Ctr. Clark, Clark Air Base, Philippines, 1982-83; chief, nurse recruiting br. 3513th Air Force Recruiting Squadron, North Syracuse, N.Y., 1983-87; nurse supr. surg. svcs. 432d Med. Group, Misawa Air Base, Japan, 1987-89; course supr., instr. oper. room nursing courses 3793d Nursing Tng. Squadron, Keesler Med. Ctr., Keesler AFB, Miss., 1989-92; asst. dir., then dir. oper. room and ctrl. sterile supply Keesler Med. Ctr., 1992-93; comdr., enlisted clin. courses flight 383d Tng. Squadron, Sheppard AFB, Tex., 1993-94; comdr., officer clin. courses flight 383rd Tng. Squadron, 1994-95; comdr. enlisted courses flight 383rd Tng. Squadron, 1995-96; ops. officer, oper. room svcs. 74th Med. Ops. Squdron, Wright-Patterson AFB, Ohio, 1996-2000; ret., 2000. Decorated Air Force Commendation medal, Air Force Achievement medal, Meritorious Svc. medal. Mem. ANA, Ohio Nurses Assn., Assn. Operating Rm. Nurses, Air Force Assn., Sigma Theta Tau. Home: 3110 Cymar Dr Beavercreek OH 45434-6355

RINTAMAKI, JOHN M. automotive executive; BBA, U. Mich., 1964, JD, 1967. Bar: Mich. 1968, Pa. 1973. Sr. atty. internat. Ford Motor Co., 1978-84, assoc. counsel corp. and financings, 1984-86, asst. sec., assoc. counsel, 1986-92, sec., asst. gen. counsel, 1993-98, v.p., gen. counsel, sec., 1999-00, chief staff, 2000—. Office: Ford Motor Co One American Rd Dearborn MI 48126-1899

RINTELMAN, DONALD BRIAN, lawyer; b. Madison, Wis., May 25, 1955; s. Donald Carl Rintelman and Eugenie Elizabeth Kroll; m. Ann Marie Gall, Aug. 2, 1980; children: Katherine Ann, Brian James. BA, U. Wis., 1976; JD, U. Mich., 1980. Bar: Wis. 1980, U.S. Dist. Ct. (ea. dist.) Wis. 1980, U.S. Dist. Ct. (we. dist.) Wis. 1984. Assoc. Whyte & Hirschboeck, S.C., Milw., 1980-86, shareholder, 1986—; mng. dir. Whyte Hirschboeck Dudek, S.C., 1994—. Chmn. comml. practice group Am. Law Firm Assn. Internat., L.A., 1998-2001. Bd. dirs. Ozaukee County United Way Allocations, Mequon, Wis., 1986-88; treas. Cedarburg (Wis.) Cmty. Scholarship Fund, 1991-93; coun. pres. Advent Luth. Ch., Cedarburg, 1996-97, Greater Cedarburg Cmty. Found., Inc., 2002—. Fellow Am. Coll. Investment Counsel; mem. ABA, Wis. Bar Assn., Milw. Bar Assn. Republican. Avocations: travel, golf, enjoying children's soccer, swimming. Home: N108W7365 Balfour St Cedarburg WI 53012-3248 Office: Whyte Hirschboeck Dudek SC 111 E Wisconsin Ave Ste 2100 Milwaukee WI 53202-4861

RINTOUL, DAVID SKINNER, lawyer; b. Westport, Conn., July 11, 1961; s. Stephen Rich and Eve Clark (Green) R.; m. Judy Mae Duncan, Aug. 7, 1988; children: Emily Grace, Maxwell Duncan. BA, Johns Hopkins U., 1983; JD with high honors, U. Conn., Hartford, 1986. Bar: Ill. 1986, Conn. 1989, U.S. Dist. Ct. (no. dist.) Ill. 1987, U.S. Dist. Ct. Conn. 1989, U.S. Ct. Appeals (2d cir.) 1997. Atty. Schwartz & Freeman, Chgo., 1986-89, Levin & D'Agostino, Hartford, Conn., 1989-91; ptnr. Rintoul & Rintoul, Glastonbury, 1991-2001, Brown, Paindiris & Scott, Glastonbury, 2001—. Mem. Nat. Employment Lawyers Assn., Conn. Employment Lawyers Assn. (bd. dirs. 1996—). Democrat. Episcopalian. Avocations: bicyle racing, skiing. Home: 73 Hunter Ln Glastonbury CT 06033-1440 Office: Brown Paindiris & Scott 2252 Main St Glastonbury CT 06033 E-mail: drintoul@bpslawyers.com.

RIOLA, PETER W. bishop, dean; b. Bklyn., May 16, 1936; s. William R. and Sara Hewitt Riola; m. Martha Stacy Riola, Aug. 9, 1984; children: Peter W. Riola, Jr., Mari Frances Partyka. PhD in Philosophy, Coll. Philosophy, Kansas City, Mo., 1975; DBA/MBA, Pacific U., 1979; PhD in Bibl. Studies, Evang. Theol. Sem., Dixon, Mo., 1988; ThD in Theology, Laud Hall Seminary, 1998; DD, St. Marus Seminary, Patterson, La., 1996. Diplomate, bd. cert. Christian Coll. Chaplains. Dir. mktg. Burlington No. Railroad, Ft. Worth, 1954—92; v.p., dean Minn. Grad. Sch. Theology, Mpls., 1995—; bishop Communion Evang. Episcopal Chs., Diocese Minn., 1996—; chaplain, ethicist Hospice of the Twin Cities, Mpls., 1996—; chaplain Park River Estates Care Ctr., Coon Rapids, 2002—. Dir. edn. Delta Nu Alpha Transp. Soc., 1960—92; fellow U. Minn. Grad. Sch., Mpls., 1980—90. Author: Socrates, Plato and Aristotle, 1995, The Sanctity of Life, 1998, Anglican Church History, 2000. Commr. City of Bloomington, Minn., 1975—80, City St. Francis, 2000—. Capt. USAF, 2001—. Named Man of the Yr., Delta Nu Alpha, 1979; recipient Sir George Williams award, Walter Hervey Coll., N.Y.C., 1956. Fellow: Oxford Found., Grad. Theol. Found., Oxford Soc. Scholars. Anglican. Avocations: whale watching, opera, travel. Home: 23198 Jivaro St NW Saint Francis MN 55070

RIOPELLE, ARTHUR JEAN, psychologist; b. Thorp, Wis., Apr. 22, 1920; s. Wilfred Gaspar and Ann Marie (Schroeder) R.; m. Mary Jane Astell, May 2, 1942; children— Mary Ann, James Michael, Jean Elizabeth. BS, U. Wis., 1941, MS, 1948, PhD, 1950. Asst. prof., then assoc. prof. Emory U., 1950-57; dir. psychology div. U.S. Army Med. Research Lab., Ft. Knox, Ky., 1957-59; dir. Yerkes Labs. Primate Biology, Orange Park, Fla., 1959-62, Delta Regional Primate Research Ctr., Covington, La., 1962-71; prof. psychology La. State U., Baton Rouge, 1972—, Boyd prof., 1977-89, Boyd prof. emeritus, 1989—. Mem. NRC panel on manganese, Com. on Med. and Biol. Effects of Environ. Pollutants Editor Jour. Gen. Psychology, 1978-95; asst. editor Animal Behavior, 1962-65; cons. editor Jour. Genetic Psychology and Genetic Psychology Monograph, 1978-95; contbr. chpts. to books. La. Bd. Examiners of Psychologists, 1972-75; mem. panel on Air Force tng. Nat. Acad. Sci.-NRC, 1955-56; primate research study sect. Am. Inst. Biol. Scis.-NASA, 1959-63; chmn. sub-com. on man Lunar Receiving Lab. Study, 1970-71; chmn. U.S.-Japan Conf. Primate Research, 1963-64; chmn. sub-com. primate standards Inst. Lab. Animal Resources, NRC, 1964-69. Served with USAAF, 1942-46, ETO. Mem. Am. Psychol. Assn., Am. Physiol. Soc., So. Soc. Philosophy and Psychology, Internat. Primatological Soc., AAAS, Psychonomic Soc., Southeastern Psychol. Assn., Sigma Xi, Phi Kappa Phi, Sigma Chi. Home: 9710 Highland Rd Baton Rouge LA 70810-4031 Office: La State U Dept Psychology Baton Rouge LA 70803-0001

RIORDAN, BRIDGET GUERNSEY, educational administrator; b. Gary, Ind., Oct. 4, 1957; d. Marcus Jean Guernsey and Edna June Richardson; m. Michael P. Riordan, Oct. 14, 1995; 1 child, Colleen Bridget. BS, Ball State U., 1979; MEd, U. Cin., 1984; PhD, U. Pitts., 1991. Nat. collegiate field adviser Alpha Chi Omega Fraternity, Indpls., 1979-80; coord. Greek affairs U. Cin., 1980-83; asst. dir. student activities U. Pitts., 1983-92; asst. dean for campus life Emory U., Atlanta, 1992-96, asst. to sr. v.p. for campus life, 1996—. Cons. various colls., 1990—; spkr. various colls. and civic orgns., 1985—. Recipient Outstanding Advisor award N.E. Intrafraternity Conf., 1989; advisor fellow Order of Omega, 1989. Mem. Nat. Assn. Student Pers. Advisors, Assn. Fraternity Advisors (pres. 1989, Disting. Svc. award 1995), Omicron Delta Kappa, Alpha Chi Omega (chpt. pres. 1978-79). Roman Catholic. Home: 2626 Shetland Dr Decatur GA 30033-2943 Office: Emory U Drawer PP Atlanta GA 30322

RIORDAN, CORNELIUS, sociology educator, writer, consultant; b. Worcester, Mass., May 29, 1940; s. Cornelius H. and Mary J. Riordan; m. Arline K. Riordan; children: Julie, Kate. BS in Edn., Fitchburg (Mass.) State Coll., 1962; MA in Sociology, Clark U., 1970; PhD in Sociology, Syracuse (N.Y.) U., 1975. Prof. sociology Providence Coll., 1972—; postdoctoral fellow The Johns Hopkins U., Balt., 1979-81. Cons. Childreach, USA, Warwick, R.I., 1993-98, Regional Lab. at Brown U., Providence, 1997-98, NSF, 2000—; expert witness cases involving single-sex schooling, 1989-2000. Author: Girls and Boys in School: Together or Separate, 1990, Equality and Achievement, 1997; contbr. articles to profl. jours. Vol. U.S. Peace Corps, Kerman, Iran, 1963-65; dir. Encampment for Citizenship, N.Y.C., 1965-69. Mem. Am. Sociol. Assn. (coun. 1990-92), Am. Ednl. Rsch. Assn. (grantee 1992-93, 2000—). Office: Dept Sociology Providence Coll River & Eaton Sts Providence RI 02918

RIORDAN, GEORGE NICKERSON, investment banker; b. Patchogue, N.Y., May 16, 1933; s. E. Arthur and Constance E. (Whelden) R.; m. Ann Wiggins, Jan. 4, 1958; children— Susan M., Peter G. BS, Cornell U., 1955; MBA, Harvard U., 1960. Vice-pres. Lehman Bros., N.Y.C., 1960-71; mng. dir. Blyth Eastman Paine Webber, Los Angeles and N.Y.C., 1971-81, Prudential-Bache Securities, Los Angeles, 1981-88, Bear Stearns & Co., Inc., L.A., 1988-89, Dean Witter Reynolds Inc., 1989-91. Chmn. bd. MSC Software, Inc., 1997-99; bd. dirs. MSC Software, Inc., L.A. Served to capt. USAF, 1955-57 Mem. Calif. Club, Quoque Field Club (L.I., N.Y.), Athenaeum Club, Valley Hunt Club (Pasadena, Calif.). Office: 815 Colorado Blvd Ste 104 Los Angeles CA 90041-1720 E-mail: george.riordan@mscsoftware.com.

RIORDAN, JAMES QUENTIN, retired company executive; b. Bklyn., June 17, 1927; s. James A. and Ruth M. (Boomer) R.; m. Gloria H. Carlson, June 23, 1951; children: Harris, Susan, James, Ruth. BA, Bklyn. Coll., 1945; LLB, Columbia U., 1949. Bar: N.Y. 1951, U.S. Supreme Ct 1954. Atty. Winthrop, Stimson, Putnam & Roberts, N.Y.C., 1949-51; mem. staff Ways and Means sub-com., Washington, 1951-52; atty. tax div. Justice Dept., 1952-55; atty. Chadbourne, Parke, Whiteside & Wolff, N.Y.C., 1955-57; various positions to vice chmn., chief fin. officer Mobil Corp., 1957-89; pres. Bekaert Corp., 1989-92; chmn. Quentin Ptnrs. Co., 1996—. Bd. dirs. The Houston Exploration Co., Tri-Continental Corp. and other J & W Seligman mut. funds. Bd. dirs. Com. Econ. Devel., Tax Foun., Inc.; trustee Bklyn. Mus. Mem. Rembrandt Club (N.Y.C.), Blind Brook Club, Sailfish Point (Fla.), Stockbridge Club. Office: 60 E 42nd St New York NY 10165-0799

RIORDAN, MICHAEL C. hospital administrator; b. N.J., 1959; BA in liberal arts and English, Columbia U., 1980, MA in edn. and psychology, 1981; M in health sys., Ga. Inst. Tech., 1986. Various positions Crawford Long Hosp., Atlanta; COO Emory U. Hosp. Sys., 1995—2000; exec. v.p. and COO U. Chgo. Hosps. and Health Sys., 2000—01, pres. and CEO, 2001—. With USMC, 1981—85. Office: U Chgo Hosps and Health Sys 5841 S Maryland Ave Chicago IL 60637*

RIORDAN, RICHARD J. former mayor, lawyer; b. Flushing, N.Y., 1930; m. Eugenia Riordan; 6 children (2 dec.); m. Jill Riordan; m. Nancy Daly Riordan; 3 children. Attended, U. Calif., Santa Clara; grad., Princeton U., 1952; JD, U. Mich., 1956. With O'Melveny & Myers, L.A.; owner, operator Original Pantry Cafe; founder Total Pharmaceutical Care, Tetra Tech; atty. Riordan & McKinzie, 1970—; mayor L.A., 1993—2001. Co-founder LEARN, 1991; sponsor Writing to Read computer labs Riordan Found.; active Eastside Boys and Girls Club. Lt. U.S. Army, Korea. Address: 300 S Grand Ave Ste 29 Los Angeles CA 90071-3109 Office: Los Angeles City Hall 200 N Main St Rm 800 Los Angeles CA 90012*

RIOS, EVELYN DEERWESTER, columnist, musician, artist, writer; b. Payne, Ohio, June 25, 1916; d. Jay Russell and Flossie Edith (Fell) Deerwester; m. Edwin Tietjen Rios, Sept. 19, 1942 (dec. Feb. 1987); children: Jane Evelyn, Linda Sue Rios Stahlman. BA with honors, San Jose State U., 1964, MA, 1968. Cert. elem., secondary tchr., Calif. Lectr. in music San Jose State U., 1969-75; bilingual cons., then assoc. editor Ednl. Factors, Inc., San Jose, 1969-76, mgr. field research, 1977-78; writer, editor Calif. MediCorps Program, 1978-85; contbg. editor, illustrator The Community Family Mag., Wimberly, Tex., 1983-85; columnist The Springer, Dripping Springs, 1985-90. Author, illustrator, health instr. textbooks elem. schs., 1980-82. Author: The Best of It Seems To Me. Choir dir. Bethel Luth. Ch., Cupertino, Calif., 1965-66, Bethel Luth. Ch., 1968-83; dir. music St. Aban's Ch., Bogota Colombia; organist Holy Spirit Episcopal Ch., Dripping Springs, Tex., 1987-94; music dir. Cambrian Park (Calif.) Meth. Ch., 1961-64; chmn. Dripping Springs Planning and Zoning Commn., 1991-93. Mem. AAUW, Am. Guild Organists (dean 1963-64), Phi Kappa Phi (pres. San Jose chpt. 1973-74). Episcopalian. Avocations: weaving, stitching, painting. Home and Office: 5700 Maya Ln Atascadero CA 93422-2552

RIOS, JO MARIE, political science educator; b. San Antonio; d. Joseph and Guadalupe S. Rios MA, St. Mary's U., San Antonio, 1989, U. Okla., 1994, PhD in Polit. Sci., 1995. Asst. prof. pub. adminstrn. U. Ctrl. Fla., Orlando, 1996-99; asst. prof. polit. sci. and pub. adminstrn. Tex. A&M U., Corpus Christi, 1999—. Vis. instr. pub. adminstrn. U. Tex., San Antonio, 1995-96. Mem. Am. Soc. Pub. Adminstrs., Am. Polit. Sci. Assn., Southwest Polit. Sci. Assn., Policy Studies Orgn., Pi Alpha Alpha. Home: 7130 Everhart # 35 Corpus Christi TX 78413 Office: Tex A&M U 6300 Ocean Dr Corpus Christi TX 78412 Fax: 361-825-6098. E-mail: jo.m.rios@att.net., jrios@falcon.tamucc.edu.

RIOUX, PATRICE, medical research company executive; b. Neuilly, France, Feb. 17, 1951; MD, Paris U., 1976, PhD, 1978. Rschr. French Nat. Inst. Health and Med. Rsch., France, 1975-95; assoc. med. dir. Biogen, France, 1995-98; dir. clin. pharm.-genetics Variagenics, Inc., Cambridge, Mass., 1998-99; dir. clin. affairs Arrow Internat., Walpole, 1999-2000; v.p. med. rsch. Repligen Corp., Needham, 2000—. Med. dir. Group for Pharmacol. Rsch., France, 1990-95. Author (med. software) Expert Sys. Mem. Faculty Pharm. Medicine, Royal Coll. Physicians (London), Internat. Assn. for Study of Pain, French Pharmacol. Soc. Avocation: rowing club. Office: Repligen Corp 117 4th Ave Needham MA 02494 E-mail: prioux@usa.net., prioux@repligen.com.

RIOUX, PIERRE AUGUST, psychiatrist; b. Hartford, Conn., Sept. 2, 1953; s. Berchmans and Mary (Sauter) R. BA, Concordia Coll., 1975; MD, U. N.D., 1981. Diplomate Am. Bd. Psychiatry and Neurology. Intern U. Mich., 1981-82, resident, 1982-85; asst. prof. dept. psychiatry Emory U., Atlanta, 1985-86; attending physician VA Med. Ctr., 1985-86; staff physician UniMed Med. Ctr., Minot, N.D., 1986-87, med. dir. adult partial hospitalization program, 1988-98, dir. behavioral health svcs., 1990—2001; med. dir. North Ctrl. Human Svc. Ctr., 1987-98; med. dir. stress unit Austin Med. Ctr., 2001—. Cons. North Ctrl. Human Svc. Ctr., 1986—2001; mem. chem. dependency unit UniMed Med. Ctr, 1986—; mem. adv. bd. UniMed Med. Ctr., 1998—2001; clin. asst. prof. neurosci. U. N.D. Sch. Medicine, 1986—96; mem. family practice residence adv. bd. com. U. N.D., 1987—95; physician advisor N.D. Health Care Rev., Inc., 1987—2001; dir. psychiat. svcs. Dakota Boys Ranch, Minot, 1990—94; med. dir. Rural Mental Health Consortium, 1999—2001. Recipient Nat. Alliance for the Mentally Ill Exemplary Psychiatrist award, 1993. Fellow Am. Coll. Forensic Examiners (life); mem. AMA, Am. Psychiat. Assn. (pres. N.D. dist. br. 1993-96, dep. rep. area IV coun. 1993—, bd. mem. psychiat. svcs. achievement awards bd. 1996-97, chmn. 1998, fellowship award 1996), Assn. Am. Physicians and Surgeons, Am. Soc. Clin. Psychopharmacology, N.D. Psychiat. Assn. (dist. br. exec. coun. 1997—), N.D. Med. Assn. (mem. commn. on socio-economic affairs), Internat. Soc. for Philos. Enquiry (diplomate), The Nat. Assn. of Established Families in Am. (adv. coun. 2000). Avocation: art. Office: PO Box 188 Austin MN 55912-0188

RIPA, LOUIS WILLIAM, dentist, educator; b. Summit, N.J., Dec. 24, 1936; s. Louis and Anne (DeTrolio) R.; m. Irene Arabolos, June 25, 1960; children: Christine, Michael, John, Karyn. Student, U. Chgo., 1956; DDS, Georgetown U., 1960; MS, U. Rochester, 1966; MA, SUNY, 1994, 99. Diplomate Am. Acad. Pediatric Dentistry. Asst. prof. U. Ala. Sch. Dentistry, Birmingham, 1966-67; rsch. assoc., chair gen. dentistry Eastman Dental Ctr., Rochester, 1967-70; assoc. prof. U. Rochester, 1967-70; chair dept. pediatric dentistry Eastman Dental Ctr., 1970-73; prof., chair dept. childrens dentistry SUNY, Stony Brook, 1973-94, assoc. dean, 1976-77, disting. prof., 1992—. Cons. Nat. Inst. Dental Rsch., Washington, Colgate-Palmolive Co., Piscataway, N.J.; prin. investigator numerous clin. studies dental therapeutic agts.; chmn. coun. faculties Am. Assn. Dental Schs., Washington, 1980-81. Co-author: Oral Hygiene in Oral Health, 1977, Management of Dental Behavior in Children, 1979, Fluoride in Preventive Dentistry, 1983; contbr. 14 other dental textbooks. Lt. USNR, 1960-62. Recipient Cmty. Dentistry Meritorious award ADA, Chgo., 1981, N.Y. State/United Univ. Profls. Excellence award, 1990. Mem. Internat. Assn. Dental Rsch. (pres. cariology group 1984-85, Hatton award 1965, Disting. Scientist award 1987). Avocation: painting military miniatures. Office: SUNY at Stony Brook Sch Dental Medicine Dept Childrens Dentistry Stony Brook NY 11794-0001

RIPKEN, CALVIN EDWIN, JR. (CAL RIPKEN), professional baseball player; b. Havre de Grace, Md., Aug. 24, 1960; Player minor league teams, Bluefield, Miami, Charlotte, Rochester, 1978-81; player Balt. Orioles, 1978—. Recipient Rookie of Yr. award Internat. League, 1981, Rookie of Yr. award Baseball Writers Assn., Am. League, 1982, Silver Slugger award, 1983-86, 89, 91, 93-94, Gold Glove award, 1991-92; named Am. League Rookie of the Yr., The Sporting News, 1982, Player of the Yr., 1983, 91, Am. League MVP, 1983, 91, Major League Player of Yr., Sportsman of the Year, (1995) The Sporting News, 1983, 91; named to Am. League All-Star Team, 1983-96. Achievements include being a holder of the major league record for consecutive games played; broke Lou Gehrig's record of 2131 consecutive games played, 1995; maj. league record home runs by shortstop; highest single season fielding percentage (.996), 1990; most consecutive errorless games at shortstop (95). Office: care Balt Orioles Oriole Pk at Camden Yards 333 W Camden St Baltimore MD 21201-2435

RIPLEY, ALEXANDRA BRAID, author; b. Charleston, S.C., Jan. 8, 1934; m. Leonard Ripley, 1958 (div. 1963); m. John Graham, 1981 (div. 2002); children Elizabeth, Merrill. BA in Russian, Vassar Coll., 1955. Former tour guide, travel agent, underwear buyer; former manuscript reader, publicity director N.Y.C. Author: Charleston, 1981, On Leaving Charleston, 1984, The Time Returns: A Novel of Friends and Mortal Enemies in Fifteenth Century Florence, 1985, New Orleans Legacy, 1987, Scarlett: The Sequel to Margaret Mitchell's Gone With the Wind, 1991, From Fields of Gold, 1994, A Love Divine, 1996.

RIPLEY, BRENT A. music educator; b. Gettysburgh, Pa., Dec. 22, 1971; s. Rosemary Persons and Charles Edward Ripley; m. Angela Marie Ripley, Nov. 18, 1995; children: Bethany Paige, Adam Jonah. BA, West Liberty State Coll., West Liberty, WV, 1990—94. Music educator Eaton City Schools, Eaton, Ohio, 1994—95, Stratford Publick Schools, Stratford, NH, 1995—97, Harrison Hills City Sch. Dist., Codiz, Ohio, 1998—. Dir. Jewett United Meth. Ch. Choir, Jewett, Ohio, 2001—; asst. play dir. Harrison Ctrl. H.S., Cadiz, Ohio, 2001—. Mem.: Ohio Music Educators Assn. Independent. Methodist. Avocations: skiing, singing.

RIPLEY, STUART MCKINNON, real estate consultant; b. July 28, 1930; s. Rob Roy and Nina Pearl (Young) R.; m. Marilyn Haerr MacDiarmid, Dec. 28, 1964; children: Jill, Bruce, Kent. BA, U. Redlands, 1952; MBA, U. Calif., Berkeley, 1959. V.p., dir. J.H. Hedrick & Co., Santa Barbara/San Diego, 1958-63; v.p. mktg. Cavanaugh Devel. Co., San Gabriel, Calif., 1963-65; v.p. mktg. dir. Calabasas Park, Bechtel Corp., Calabasas, 1967-69; v.p. mktg. Avco Cmty. Developers, Inc., La Jolla, 1969-74; mktg. dir. U.S. Home Corp., Fla. Divsn., Clearwater, 1974-75; pres., dir. Howard's Camper Country, Inc., National City, Calif., 1975-77; v.p., mktg. dir. Valcas Internat. Corp., San Diego, 1976-77, pres., 1977-79, Stuart M. Ripley, Inc., 1977-79, Sunview Realty, Inc., a Watt Industries Co., Santa Monica, Calif., 1979-80; owner Everett Stunz Co., Ltd., La Jolla, 1981—. Exec. v.p. Harriman-Ripley Co.,

Fallbrook, Calif.; avocado/floraculture rancher, subdivider, Fallbrook, 1978—; lectr. UCLA, 1961; pres. Century 21 Coastal, Century 21 Bajamar, Baja California, Mex., 1994-97. Comdr. USNR, 1952-55, ret. U. Redlands fellow, 1960—. Mem. Nat. Assn. Homebuilders, Sales and Mktg. Coun., Sales and Mktg. Execs., Elks, Pi Chi. Republican. Episcopalian. Home: 2085 Via Jadeta La Jolla CA 92037-6905 Office: 7624 Girard Ave La Jolla CA 92037-4420

RIPPE, LYNN E. contract administrator; b. Superior, Nebr., Dec. 27, 1947; children: Douglas E., Christopher C. BA in Econs., Kansas State U., 1969; MBA, So. Ill. U., Edwardsville, 1977. Contract specialist, contracting officer Naval Constrn. Bn. Ctr., Port Hueneme, Calif., 1989-93; sr. contract adminstr. U. Calif. Lawrence Livermore (Calif.) Nat. Lab., 1993-98; computing scis. subcontracts mgr. U. Calif. Lawrence Berkeley Nat. Lab., 1998—. Mem. Nat. Contract Mgmt. Assn. (v.p. Tri Valley chpt. 1995-96, pres. 1996-97, nat. dir. 1997-98, 2000-01). Republican. Roman Catholic. Home: 3478 FM 1670 Belton TX 76513 Office: U Calif Lawrence Berkeley Nat Lab M-50B One Cyclotron Rd Berkeley CA 94720 E-mail: lerippe@nersc.gov.

RIPPEL, HARRY CONRAD, mechanical engineer, consultant; b. Phila., Feb. 19, 1926; s. Philip and Emma (Metzger) R.; m. Dorothy Ann Tartala, Nov. 20, 1948; children— Linda Jean, Richard Peter. B.M.E., Drexel U., Phila., 1952, MS, 1957. Registered profl. engr., Pa. With Franklin Research Center, div. Franklin Inst., Phila., 1952-87, Inst. fellow, 1978—; cons. in tribology, 1987—; resident consultant Rotor Bearing Tech. & Software Inc., 1987—. Mem. Com. on Sci. and the Arts, Franklin Inst., Phila. Author manuals and articles in field. Chalice bearer, layreader St. James Episcopal Ch., Phila.; bd. dirs. Turbo Rsch. Found. With AUS, WWII, ETO. Decorated Bronze Star. Fellow ASME, Soc. Tribologists and Lubrication Engrs.; mem. Sigma Xi, Pi Tau Sigma. Home: 1434 Sharon Park Dr Sharon Hill PA 19079-2218 Office: Rotor Bearing Tech & Software Inc 1040 W Bridge St Phoenixville PA 19460-4291 E-mail: hrippel@RBTS.com.

RIPPER, RITA JO (JODY RIPPER), strategic planner, researcher; b. Goldfield, Iowa, May 8, 1950; d. Carl Phillip and Lucille Mae (Stewart) Ripper. BA, U. Iowa, 1972; MBA, NYU, 1978. Fin. and credit specialist Control Data Corp., Mpls., 1974-78; regional mgr. Raytheon Corp., Irvine, Calif., 1978-83; v.p. Caljo Corp., Des Moines, 1980-84; asst. v.p. Bank of Am., San Francisco, 1984-88; pres. The Northhaven Co., 1988—, The Boardroom Adv. Group, San Francisco, 1990-93; v.p. project mgr. Imperial Bank, 1998-99. Am. United. Vol. Cancer, Heart, Lung Assns., Edina, N.Y.C., Calif., 1974-78, 84—. Mem. Amnesty Internat., Ams. United for Separation of Ch. and State, ACLU, Peoples for the Am. Way, Internat. Mktg. Assn., World Trade Ctr. Assn., Acctg. Soc. (pres. 1975-76), World Trade Club, Intertel, Mensa, Beta Alpha Psi (chmn. 1977-78), Phi Gamma Nu (v.p. 1971-72), Corinthian Yacht Club. Presbyterian. E-mail: jodyripper@aol.com.

RIPPERT, ERIC THEODORE, oral and maxillofacial surgeon; b. Ft. Devens, Mass., Feb. 22, 1942; s. Jacob Kopf and Kathleen (Faughan) R.; m. Mary Ellen Dormer, Nov. 25, 1965; children: Thomas, Kathleen. AB, Holy Cross Coll., 1964; DMD, U. Pa., 1968. Diplomate Am. Bd. Oral and Maxillofacial Surgery. Intern Phila. Gen. Hosp., 1968-69, resident, 1973-76; dental officer U.S. Navy, 1965-95; asst. prof. oral and maxillofacial surgery U. Nebr., Lincoln, 1996-99; asst. prof. U. Pitts., 1999-2000; assoc. prof. Med. Coll. Va., Richmond, 2000—. Clin. asst. prof. Med. Coll. Va., Richmond, 1979-81; adj. assoc. prof. Temple U., Phila., 1984-87; asst. prof. U. Calif., San Francisco, 1991-93. Fellow Am. Assn. Oral and Maxillofacial Surgeons, Internat. Coll. Dentists; mem. Varsity Club Coll. Holy Cross, Delta Sigma Delta. Republican. Roman Catholic. Avocations: tennis, skiing, speech and dialogue, writing. Office: Dept Oral and Maxillofacial Surg Med Coll Va PO Box 980338 Richmond VA 23298 E-mail: etrippert@aol.com.

RIPPETEAU, BRUCE ESTES, archaeologist, administrator; BA, U. Nebr., 1968; MA, U. Ariz., 1970; PhD, Case Western Res. U., 1973. Faculty SUNY, Oneonta, 1973-76; state archaeologist State Mus. Colo., Denver, 1976-80; v.p. archaeology svcs. A.C. Nielsen subs. Powers Elevation, 1980-83; pres., owner The Rippeteau Co., 1974-84; dir. S.C. Inst. Archaeology and Anthropology, U. S.C., Columbia, 1984—, rsch. prof., 1984—. Mem. adv. coun. Pub. Lands Inst., Natural Resources Def. Coun., 1979—; mem. com. on engring. responsibility Am. Soc. Civil Engrs., 1979-93; spkr. in field; adj. prof. U. Denver, 1976-80, U. Colo., 1977-80. Editor-in-chief Southwestern Lore, 1976-78; contbg. editor Am. Archaeology, 1981-90; contbr. numerous articles to profl. pubis. Mem. Hist. Commn. Bd., Historic Camden, S.C., 1984—; founding mem. S.C. Quincentennial Commn., Palmetto Trust for Hist. Preservation, 1990-98; pres. Crimestoppers of the Midlands, 1993; mem. adv. bd. S.C. Heritage Trust, 1984-2000, chmn. 1990-92; mem. Richland County Airport Commn., 1997—, vice chmn., 2000—. Fellow AAAS; mem. Soc. Am. Archaeology (sec. 1992-95, chair bylaws com. 1997—, Presdl. Citation award 1995), Soc. Profl. Archaeologists, Loblolly Soc., Nature Conservancy, Archaeology Soc. S.C. (bd. dirs. 1984-2000, pres. 2001-2002, Outstanding Svc. award 1989, 99), Explorers Club (pres. Greater Piedmont chpt. 1991-92), Rotary (bd. dirs. Columbia 1998-2001), Sigma Xi. Office: U SC SC Inst Archaeology 1321 Pendleton St Columbia SC 29201-3715 Fax: 803-254-1338. E-mail: rippeteau@sc.edu.

RIPPETEAU, DARREL DOWNING, retired architect; b. Clay Center, Nebr., Jan. 14, 1917; s. Claude LaVerne and Eva (Downing) R.; m. Donna Doris Hiatt, Jan. 8, 1939 (dec. 1988); children: Bruce Estes, Darrel Downing, Jane Upson Heffron; m. Joyce Spencer, May 18, 1991. BA in Architecture, U. Nebr., 1941. Staff architect FHA, Omaha, 1941-42; project mgr., mng. ptnr. Sargent-Webster-Crenshaw & Folley, Archs. and Engrs., Watertown, Buffalo, Syracuse, N.Y., Burlington, Vt, Bangor, Maine, 1946-81; treas., dir. Empire Forest System, Albany, N.Y., 1984-89; ret., 1990. Bd. dirs. Archtl. Corp. Atlanta, Key Bank No. N.Y., Watertown, Assn. Island Recreational Corp.; commr. N.Y. State Coun. Architecture, 1975-85; mem. N.Y. State Forest Practice Bd., 1980-2000, chmn., 1994-98; nat. adv. bd. mem. Remington Art Mus., Ogdensburg, N.Y., 1983-95. Prin. works include Justice Bldg, Albany, N.Y. State Office Bldg Watertown, Toomey Abbott Towers Syracuse, State U. N.Y. Cortland, U.S. P.O. Facility Syracuse. Mem. nat. fin. com. Rep. Party, 1971-73; bd. trustees The Antique Boat Mus., Clayton, N.Y., 1973-99, Glenn Curtiss Mus., Hammondsport, N.Y. Maj. U.S. Army, 1942-46; lt. col. Corps of Engrs. retired, 1977. Recipient North Country citation St. Lawrence U., Canton, N.Y., 1971; Sears-Roebuck scholar, 1936-37; U. Nebr. Dept. Architecture grantee, 1940-41; Nebr. master U. Nebr., 1971; Disting. Alumni award Coll. of Architecture Alumni Assn., U. Nebr., 1996. Fellow AIA (nat. dir. 1969-73, trustee AIA Found. 1970-73); mem. Greater Watertown C. of C. (past pres.), N.Y. State Assn. Indsl. Devel. Agys. (past v.p.), N.Y. State Assn. Architects (pres. 1968-69, polit. action com. 1980-98, James Kideney award 1987), Bldg. Rsch. Inst., Res. Officers Assn. (past pres.), Am. Tree Farm Assn., Jefferson County Hist. Soc. (dir. 1974-78), OX-5 Aviation Pioneers (chpt. pres.), Assn. U.S. Army (chpt. pres. 1985-86). Republican. Presbyterian. Home: 1011 NW 3rd Ave Delray Beach FL 33444-2938

RIPPLE, KENNETH FRANCIS, federal judge; b. Pitts., May 19, 1943; s. Raymond John and Rita (Holden) Ripple; m. Mary Andrea DeWeese, July 27, 1968; children: Gregory, Raymond, Christopher. AB, Fordham U., 1965; JD, U. Va., 1968; LLM, George Washington U., 1972, LLD (hon.), 1992. Bar: Va. 1968, N.Y. 1969, U.S. Supreme Ct. 1972, U.S. Supreme Ct. 1972, D.C. 1976, Ind. 1984, U.S. Ct. Appeals (7th cir.), U.S. Ct. Mil. Appeals, U.S. Dist. Ct. (no. dist.) Ind. Atty. IBM Corp., Armonk, NY, 1968; legal officer U.S. Supreme Ct., Washington, 1972—73, spl. asst. to chief justice Warren E. Burger, 1973—77; prof. law U. Notre Dame, 1977—; judge U.S. Ct. Appeals (7th cir.), South Bend, 1985—. Reporter Appellate Rules Com., Washington, 1978—85; commn. on mil. justice U.S. Dept. Def., Washington, 1984—85; cons. Supreme Ct. Ala., 1983, Calif. Bd. Bar Examiners, 1981, Anglo-Am. Jud. Exch., 1977; adv. com. Bill of Rights to Bicentennial Constn. Commn., 1989; adv. com. on appellate rules Jud. Conf. U.S., 1985—90, chmn., 1990—93; chmn. adv. com. on appellate judge edn. Fed. Jud. Ctr., 1996—. Author: Constitutional Litigation, 1984. With JAGC USN, 1968—72. Mem.: ABA, Am. Law Inst., Phi Beta Kappa. Office: US Ct of Appeals 208 US Courthouse 204 S Main St South Bend IN 46601-2122 also: Fed Bldg 219 S Dearborn St Ste 2660 Chicago IL 60604-1803

RIPPLE, ROCHELLE POYOUROW, educational administrator, educator; b. N.Y.C., Apr. 23, 1936; d. Gerald G. and Hortense (Philips) Bernheimer; m. Julian D. Ripple, Mar. 15, 1985; children: Mitchell, Jill, David. AAS, Fashion Inst. Tech., 1955, Pace U., BPS, 1974; MEd, Temple U., 1977, EdD, 1990. Cert. tchr. handicapped, Pa.; cert. prin., sch. supt., Wyo. Fashion designer Skampalon, Inc., N.Y.C., 1955-60; tchr. fashion design Pleasantville (N.Y.) Cottage Sch., 1969-74; spl. edn. tchr. Horsham Clinic, Ambler and Phila., Pa., 1974-78; fed. project dir. Montgomery County Intermediate Unit, Norristown, 1978-80; exec. dir. N.E. Wyo. Bd. Coop. Ednl. Svcs., Gillette, Wyo., 1980-86; tchg. assoc. Temple U., Phila., 1986-88; dir. vocat.-tech. edn. Ulster County BOCES, New Paltz, 1988-90; prof. ednl. adminstrn. Columbus (Ga.) State U., 1990—. Contbr. articles to profl. jours. Pres. Yorktown (N.Y.) Cmty. Rels. Coun., 1967-70; mem. adv. bd. Sheridan (Wyo.) Coll. Pace U. Trustee scholar, 1973; named Woman of Yr., Beta Sigma Phi, 1982. Mem. LWV, ASCD, Coun. for Exceptional Children, Am. Assn. Sch. Adminstrs., Assn. Retarded Citizens, Assn. Severely Handicapped, Phi Delta Kappa. Home: 612 Rudgate Rd Columbus GA 31904-2927 Office: Columbus State Univ Dept Edn Columbus GA 31907-5645

RIPPLEY, LAVERN J. German language and literature educator, real estate developer; b. Waumandee, Wis., Mar. 2, 1935; s. Louis George and Johanna Helen (Rucinski) R.; m. Barbara Jean Rippley, Aug 20, 1960; children: John Francis, Larissa Rippley Tadavarthy. BA, BS, U. Wis., River Falls, 1958; MA, Kent State U., 1961; PhD, Ohio State U., 1965. H.s. tchr. Pub. Schs., River Falls, Wis., 1958-60; asst. prof. Ohio Wesleyan U., Delaware, Ohio, 1964-67; prof. German St. Olaf Coll., Northfield, Minn., 1967—. Author: (books) Of German Ways, 1970, Russian-German Settlements in the U.S., 1974, The German Americans, 1976, 2d revised edit. 1984; The Immigrant Experience in Wisconsin, 1985, The German Bohemians, 1995, Noble Women, Restless Men, 1996. Mem. sch. bd. Northfield, Minn., 1975-79. Sgt. AUS, 1957-63. E-mai. Home: 909 Ivanhoe Dr Northfield MN 55057-3215 Office: Saint Olaf Coll 1520 Saint Olaf Ave Northfield MN 55057-1574 E-mail: rippleyl@stolaf.edu.

RIPPLINGER, GEORGE RAYMOND, JR. lawyer; b. East St. Louis, Ill., Apr. 19, 1945; s. George Raymond and Virginia Lee (Toupnot) R. AB, U. Ill., 1967, JD, 1970. Bar: Ill. 1970, U.S. Dist. Ct. (so. dist.) Ill. 1970, U.S. Ct. Appeals (7th cir.) 1970, U.S. Dist. Ct. (cen. dist.) Ill. 1972, U.S. Tax Ct. 1971, U.S. Claims Ct. 1973, U.S. Ct. Mil. Appeals 1985, U.S. Supreme Ct. 1973, U.S. Ct. Internat. Trade 1973, U.S. Dist. Ct. (ea. dist.) Mo. 1977, U.S. Ct. Appeals (8th cir.) 1977. Assoc. Meyer & Meyer, Belleville and Greenville, Ill., 1970-72; assoc. Meyer & Kaucher, Belleville and Highland, 1972-73; sole practice Belleville, 1974; ptnr. Ripplinger & Walsh, Clayton, Mo., 1974-76, Ripplinger, Dixon & Johnston, Belleville, Ill., St. Louis, Scott AFB, and Bellvue, Neb., 1976-94; prin. George Ripplinger & Assoc., Belleville, Ill., 1994—. Bd. visitors Coll. of Law U. Ill., 1979-86, pres., 1983-84; chmn. Southwestern Ill. chpt. ACLU, 1971-74, 76-80; mem. exec. com. Sierra Club, 1981-85. Col. USAR, 1970-2001. Fellow Am. Bar Found., Ill. Bar Found. (bd. dirs. 1988—, treas. 1998—); mem. ABA (ho. of dels. 1989-93, 95-99, chmn. workers compensation com. 1985-88, divsn. dir. 1988-89, 95-99, mem. coun. 1989-93, 99—, sec. 1999-2000, vice-chair 2000-2001, chair 2001-02, gen. practice/solo and small firm sect.), ATLA, Lawyers Trust Fund Ill. (bd. dirs. 1988-94), Ill. Bar Assn. (bd. govs. 1981-83, 87-93, sec. 1991-92), St. Clair County Bar Assn., Met. St. Louis Bar Assn., Mo. Bar Assn., Ill. Trial Lawyers Assn. (bd. advs. 1993—), Land of Lincoln Legal Assistance Found. (bd. dirs. 1982-88, vice chmn. 1987-88), Res. Officers Assn. Democrat. Office: George Ripplinger & Assoc 2215 W Main St Belleville IL 62226-6668 E-mail: george@ripplingerlaw.com.

RIPPO, OLGA ALICIA, art director; b. Brighton, Mass., Jan. 25, 1923; Student, Boston Trade Sch./Art, 1937—39. Fashion sketch artist, Detroit, 1939—40; boilermaker U.S. Naval Shipyard, Boston, 1941—44; comms. prof. Nat. Weather Bur., San Bruno, Calif., 1946—51; art prodn. supr. Seal Beach Jour., Seal Beach, 1963—74; graphic artist News Enterprise, Los Alamitos, 1974—85; catalog prodn. prof. Clifford Rsch. and Devel., Huntington Beach, 1974—88. Entrepreneur OAR Entepprises, Los Alamitos, Calif., 2001—. Author: (novels) (children's story) My Life as a Dime, 1995; contbr. articles. Home: 11456 Harrisburg Rd Los Alamitos CA 90720

RIPPON-LOVETT, DODIE, social worker; b. Herndon, Pa., Aug. 27, 1949; d. Robert Claude and Clara Irene Crousore; m. Thomas R. Rippon; children: F. Norman Rippon, Jason Aaron Rippon; m. Rick Lovett, July 4, 1998. BA in English and Theatre, Bucknell U., 1982; student in history and theatre, Univ. Coll., Oxford, Eng., 1981. Artist in residence Ctrl. Pa. Sch. Assn., Lebanon, 1977—78; real estate agt. Caldwell Banker, Camphill, 1985—87; social worker Children and Youth, Montaeu County, 1990—95, Aging Office Dauphin County, Elizabethville, Pa., 1995—. Playwright: ; editor: T.A.P., 1977—; (founder): Metamorphasis Improv Theatre, 1978; performer: Bloomburgs Ensemble, 1990—. Vol. Susquehanna Svc. Dogs; pres. Valley Players, 1990—92. Mem.: ASPCA, Best Friends, Sierra Club, Northcumberland County Hist. Soc. (life). Democrat. Lutheran. Avocation: Civil Ware reenactment. Home: Box 296 Herndon PA 17830 Office: Dauphin County Office Aging Clearfield St Elizabethville PA 17023

RIPPY, FRANCES MARGUERITE MAYHEW, English language educator; b. Ft. Worth, Sept. 16, 1929; d. Henry Grady and Marguerite Christine (O'Neill) Mayhew; m. Noble Merrill Rippy, Aug. 29, 1955 (dec. Sept. 1980); children: Felix O'Neill, Conrad Mayhew, Marguerite Hailey. BA, Tex. Christian U., 1949; MA, Vanderbilt U., 1951, PhD, 1957; postgrad., U. London, 1952-53. Instr. Tex. Christian U., 1953-55; instr. to asst. prof. Lamar State U., 1955-59; asst. prof. English Ball State U., Muncie, Ind., 1959-64; assoc. prof. English, Ball State U., 1964-68, prof., 1968—, dir. grad. studies in English, 1966-87; editor Ball State U. Forum, 1960-89. Vis. asst. prof. Sam Houston State U., 1957; vis. lectr., prof. U. P.R., summers 1959, 60, 61; exch. prof. Westminster Coll., Oxford, Eng., 1988; cons.-evaluator North Cen. Assn. Colls. and Schs., 1973—, commn.-at-large, 1987-91; cons.-evaluator New Eng. Assn. Schs. and Colls., 1983. Author: Matthew Prior, 1986; contbr. articles to profl. jours., encys., ref. guides, chpts. to anthology; contbr. to Dictionary of Literary Biography. Recipient McClintock award, 1966; Danforth grantee, 1964, Ball State U. Rsch. grantee, 1960, 62, 70, 73, 76, 87, 88, 89, 90, 92, 93, 95, 96, 98, Lilly Libr. Rsch., 1978; Fulbright scholar U. London, 1952-53; recipient Outstanding Faculty award Ball State U., 1992, Ind. Coll. Tchr./Scholar of 1994, Ind. Coll. English Assn., 1994. Mem. MLA, AAUP, Coll. English Assn, Nat. Coun. Tchrs. English, Am. Soc. 18th Century Studies, Am. Fedn. Tchrs., Ind. Coll. English Assn. (pres. 1984-85) Johnson Soc. Midwest (sec. 1961-62). Home: 1205 S Main St Georgetown TX 78626-6726 *I have found all of the worlds which the above biographical paragraph touches upon— familial, academic, literary— lively and stimulating and thoroughly satisfying. Each world demands a great deal and offers a great deal in return.*

RIQUELME, EVA, management consultant; b. Santiago, Chile, Aug. 30, 1972; came to U.S., 1976; d. Orlando and Gloria Riquelme. BA in English and Spanish, U. Calif., Irvine, 1995; M Pub. Affairs, U. Tex., Austin, 1998. Rsch. assoc. FCC, Washington, 1997, Tex. Lower Income Housing Info. Svc., Austin, 1997-98; cons. Accenture, 1998—. Vol. Jr. Achievement, Austin, 1999, United Way, Austin, 1999-2001. Democrat. Avocations: cooking, reading, swimming, music, travel. E-mail: eva.riquelme@accenture.com.

RIS, HANS, zoologist, educator; b. Bern, Switzerland, June 15, 1914; came to U.S., 1938, naturalized, 1945; s. August and Martha (Egger) R.; m. Hania Wislicka, Dec. 26, 1947 (div. 1971); children: Christopher Robert, Annette Margo; m. Theron Caldwell, July 14, 1980. Diploma high sch. teaching, U. Bern, 1936; PhD, Columbia, 1942. Lectr. zoology Columbia U., 1942; Seessel fellow in zoology Yale U., 1942; instr. biology Johns Hopkins U., 1942-44; asst. Rockefeller Inst., N.Y.C., 1944-46, assoc., 1946-49; assoc. prof. zoology U. Wis., Madison, 1949-53, prof., 1953-84, prof. emeritus, 1984—. Hon. prof. Peking U., Beijing, 1995—. Fellow AAAS, Am. Acad. Arts and Scis.; mem. Nat. Acad. Scis., Electron Microscopy Soc. Am. (Disting. Investigator award 1983), Am. Soc. for Cell Biology (E.B. Wilson award 1993). Achievements include research on mechanisms of nuclear division, chromosome structure, nuclear envelope, cell ultrastructure, electron microscopy. Office: U Wis Zoology Rsch 1117 W Johnson St Madison WI 53706-1705 E-mail: hris@facstaff.wisc.edu.

RIS, HOWARD CLINTON, JR. nonprofit public policy organization administrator; b. Rockville Centre, N.Y. BA in Math., Duke U., 1970, postgrad., 1972; M Landscape Architecture, SUNY, Syracuse, 1974. Sr. assoc. Roy Mann Assocs., Inc., Cambridge, Mass., 1974-76; sr. planner Mass. Office Coastal Zone Mgmt., Boston, 1976-78; program mgr. New Eng. River Basins Commn., 1980-81; dep. dir. Union Concerned Scientists, Inc., Cambridge, 1981-84, exec. dir., 1984—2001, pres., 2001—. Founding dir. Profls. Coalition for Nuclear Arms Control, Internat. Network Engrs. and Scientists for Global Responsibility. Mem. Energy and Transp. Task Force, Pres. Clinton's Coun. on Sustainable Devel.; mem. adv. bd. Inst. for Transp. Studies U. Calif., Davis; bd. dirs. Keystone Ctr. Mem. Environ. Media Assn. (adv. bd.). Office: 2 Brattle Sq Cambridge MA 02138-3742

RISCH, JAMES E. lawyer, state legislator; b. Milw., May 3, 1943; s. Elroy A. and Helen B. (Levi) R.; m. Vicki L. Choborda, June 8, 1968; children— James E., Jason S., Jordan D. BS in Forestry, U. Idaho, 1965, JD, 1968. Dep. pros. atty. Ada County, Idaho, 1968-69, chief dep. pros. atty., 1969-70, pros. atty., 1971-75; mem. Idaho Senate, Dist. 18, Boise, 1974-88, 95—; majority leader Idaho Senate, 1977-82, 97—, pres. pro tem, 1983-88, asst. majority leader, 1996; ind. counsel to Gov. of Idaho, 1996; ptnr. Risch Goss & Insinger, Boise, Idaho, 1975—. Prof. law Boise State U., 1972-75. Bd. dirs. Nat. Dist. Attys. Assn., 1973,, Idaho Co., 1992-94; chmn. bd. dris. Am. Trailer Mfg. Co., 1995—; pres. Idaho Prosecuting Attys., 1970-74; chmn. George Bush Presdl. Campaign, Idaho, 1988; gen. counsel Idaho Rep. Party, 1991—. Mem. ABA, Idaho Bar Assn., Boise Bar Assn., Ducks Unlimited, Nat. Rifle Assn., Nat. Cattlemans Assn., Idaho Cattlemans Assn., Am. Angus Assn., Idaho Angus Assn., Am. Legis. Exch. Coun., Boise Valley Angus Assn., Phi Delta Theta, Xi Sigma Pi Republican. Roman Catholic. Avocations: hunting, fishing, skiing. Home: 5400 S Cole Rd Boise ID 83709-6401 Office: Risch Goss & Insinger 407 W Jefferson St Boise ID 83702-6012

RISCH, NEIL J. geneticist, statistican; b. L.A., Feb. 25, 1951; s. Frank and Sonya Risch. BS, Calif. Tech. Inst., Pasadena, 1972; MS, U. Ill., 1974; PhD, UCLA, 1979; MA (hon.), Yale U., 1993. Asst. prof. Columbia U., N.Y.C., 1981-84, Yale U., New Haven, 1984-87, assoc. prof., 1987-92, prof., 1992-95, Stanford (Calif.) U., 1995—. Scientific adv. bd. Distonia Med. Rsch. Found., Chgo., 1997—. Glaxo-Wellcome, Inc., Research Triangle, N.C., 1998—, Genaissance Pharm., New Haven, 1998—. Contbr. articles to profl. jours. Recipient Rsch. Career Devel. award NIH, 1982, Mental Health Fund Rsch. award, 1987. Mem. AAAS, Am. Soc. of Human Genetics, Biometrics Soc. Office: Dept Genetics Stanford U Sch Medicine Stanford CA 94305-5120

RISCH, VICTOR RENÈ, radiation oncologist, researcher, educator; b. Vienna, Austria, Aug. 9, 1951; came to U.S., 1966; s. Grant and Elly Risch; m. Mary Jane Shelhamer, June 3, 1972; children: Laura Renee, Grant Frederick, Martin Joseph. BS in Chemistry, Lehigh U., 1972, MS in Chemistry, 1974, PhD in Chemistry, 1975; MD, Hahnemann U., 1980. Instr. radiation oncology Hahnemann U., Phila., 1974-80; resident in internal medicine Thomas Jefferson U., 1980-83; fellow in med. oncology Johns Hopkins U., Balt., 1983-84, asst. oncology, 1984-87, asst. prof. radiation oncology, 1987-88; pvt. practice Lehigh Valley Hosp., Allentown, Pa., 1988—; clin. asst. prof. radiation oncology Hahnemann U., 1989-94; chmn. radiation oncology Lehigh Valley Hosp., 1991—. Assoc. chair, assoc. prof. clin. radiology Pa. State U. Sch. Medicine, Hershey, 1994-99; chair, prof. clin. radiology, 1999—. Contbr. articles to profl. jours. Mem. Hon. Order of Ky. Cols., 1987—. Recipient Jane Stuart prize Hahnemann U., 1980 and UpJohn Achievement award, 1980. Mem. Am. Soc. for Therapeutic Radiology and Oncology, Am. Soc. Clin. Oncology, Am. Coll. Radiation Oncology, Am. Coll. Physician Execs. Achievements include only faculty member in history of Johns Hopkins to attend both in medical and radiation oncology concurrently; built critically acclaimed radiation oncology department and cancer center at Lehigh Valley Hosp. Avocations: science fiction, gardening, reading, epicurean food and drink. Office: Lehigh Valley Hosp Morgan Cancer Ctr PO Box 689 Allentown PA 18105-1556

RISDEN, NANCY DIKA, mathematics educator; b. Englewood, N.J., Sept. 14, 1948; d. John and Dorothy Louise (Eisberg) Macris; m. Dennis Richard Risden, Apr. 6, 1974; children: Jeannine, Steven, David. BS, Ursinus Coll., Collegeville, Pa., 1970; MA, Montclair State Coll., Upper Montclair, N.J., 1976. Cert. postgrad. prof. tchr. secondary math., Va., N.J. Tchr. math. West Essex Regional Mid. Sch., North Caldwell, N.J., 1970-71, South Jr. H.S., Bloomfield, 1971-79; substitute tchr. Oldham County Mid. Sch., Oldham County, Ky., 1981-82; instr. math. Watterson Coll., Louisville, 1984; tchr. math. Duke U. Hosp. Sch., Durham, N.C., 1988-90; substitute tchr. York County Pub. Schs., Yorktown, Va., 1991-93; tchr. math. Tabb Mid. Sch., 1993—. Treas. Mangum Primary Sch. PTA, Durham County, 1988-89; cookie chmn. Girl Scouts U.S., Durham County, 1989; den leader cub scouts Boy Scouts Am., Durham County, 1988-91, com. chairperson pack 104, Yorktown, Va., 1991-95, advancement chair Troop 201, 1994-2002. Mem. NEA, Va. Edn. Assn., York County Edn. Assn., Nat. Coun. Tchrs. Math., Va. Mid. Sch. Assn., Order Ea. Star N.J. (Worth Matron 1975-76, Grand Adah 1976-77). Presbyterian. Avocations: needlework, church choir. Home: 113 Daphne Dr Yorktown VA 23692-3220 Office: Tabb Middle School 300 Yorktown Rd Yorktown VA 23693-3504

RISDON, MICHAEL PAUL, manufacturing executive; b. Hamburg, Iowa, Feb. 24, 1946; s. Paul A. and Vesta Mae (Melton) R.; m. Ann Lorraine Grandowski, June 4, 1966; children: Anita Ann, Carter Paul. BS, Iowa State U., 1967, U. Ky., 1968; MBA, U. Pitts., 1971. Sr. acct. Ernst & Young, Indpls., 1971-75; audit supr. Ashland (Ky.) Oil, Inc., 1975-77; v.p. fin. and sys. Diesel ReCon Co., Memphis, 1982-86; budget analyst Cummins Engine Co., Columbus, Ind., 1969-70, mgr. corp. audit, 1977-78, dir. corp. and EDP audit, 1978-82, dir. fin. and planning power sys. group, 1987-88; v.p. Cummins Power Generation, 1989; v.p. fin., CFO Metal Powder Products Co., Inc., Indpls., 1989-99; pres. MPM LLC, Carmel, Ind., 1998-99; sr. exec. v.p. The Cumbernauld Group, 1999—; exec. v.p., chief adminstrv. officer PiezoTech, LLC, Indpls., 1999—. V.p. Columbus Child Care Ctr., 1981-82; vol. Big Sisters Ctrl. Ind., 1994-98. Mem. AICPA, Ind. CPA Soc., Metal Powder Industry Fedn. (fin. com. 1991-98, chmn. 1994-98), APMI Internat., Fin. Execs. Internat. (sec. 1997-98, v.p. 1998, pres. 1999), Inst. Mgmt. Accts. (nat. bd. dirs. 1981-87, v.p. 1985), Kiwanis (v.p. Columbus 1981). Roman Catholic. Avocation: bicycling, hiking, spectator sports, motor sports. Office: The Cumbernauld Group 9801 Fall Creek Rd # 404 Indianapolis IN 46256-4802

RISHEL, JAMES BURTON, manufacturing executive, director; b. Omaha, Apr. 27, 1920; s. James Blaine and Elizabeth Helen (Kerr) R.; m. Alice Jane Snyder, June 30, 1945; children: James Richard, Sara Jane Rishel Fields. BSME, U. Nebr., 1946. Profl. engr., Ohio. Pres. Corp. Equipment Co., Cin., 1962-82; chmn. bd. Systecon Inc., 1982-2000; cons. Pumping Solutions LLC, 2000—. Author: The Water Management Manual, HVAC Pump Handbook, 1996, Water Pumps and Pumping Systems, 2002; patentee hydraulic systems; contbr. numerous articles to profl. jours. Capt. USAF, 1942-46, 51-52. Fellow ASHRAE. Avocations: philanthropy, walking. Home: 7570 Thumbelina Ln Cincinnati OH 45242-4937 E-mail: jbrishel@fuse.net.

RISHEL, KENN CHARLES, school superintendent; b. Utica, N.Y., Nov. 19, 1946; s. Lester and Lois (Keehle) R.; m. Leslie Ann Syposs, Dec. 30, 1967; children: Samantha D., Andrea L. BS, SUNY, Oneonta, 1968; MS in Edn., SUNY, Cortland, 1973, Cert. Advanced Study/Adminstrn., 1985. Elem. tchr. Holland Patent (N.Y.) Ctrl. Sch., 1968-81, math coord., 1977-81; cons. CIMS program Oneida/Madison BOCES, New Hartford, N.Y., 1977-81; asst. supt. for bus. Carthage (N.Y.) Ctrl. Sch., 1981-87, supt., 1987-96; supervising adminstrn., CEO Carthage Area Hosp., 1994-98; cons. Sch. Constrn. & Collective Bargaining Radio Broadcaster, Lowille, N.Y., 1998-99; supt. S.A.U. #30, Laconia, NH, 1999—2001. Esxcelsior examiner N.Y. State Award for Quality, Albany, 1992-94; adj. prof. SUNY-Oswego, Watertown, 1994, SUNY, Oneonta, 2001-02; notary pub., N.Y. State. Author: Be True to Your School-Reality and the School Superintendency. Recipient Pathfinder award NYSAWA, 1995. Mem. N.Y. Coun. Sch. Supts. (mem. ethics com. 1991-95, Black River Coun. Sch. Supts., Am. Assn. Sch. Adminstrs., Assn. U.S. Army, Rotary (v.p., pres. 1981-86), Lions, Elks. Bus. Home: 1006 Trackside Dr Marcy NY 13403 E-mail: mgtcon1@aol.com.

RISHEL, RICHARD CLINTON, retired banker; b. Oreland, Pa., June 7, 1943; S. Herbert Beale and Evelyn (Lauer) R.; m. Carol Staub, Apr. 3, 1965; children: Christian Daniel, Peter James. BA, Pa. State U., 1965; postgrad., Drexel Inst. Tech., 1965-66. Credit analyst 1st Pa. Banking & Trust Co., Phila., 1965-69; comml. lending officer Nat. Bank of Chester County, West Chester,

Pa., 1969; asst. v.p. Continental Bank of Norristown, 1969-70, sec., 1970-71, v.p., 1971-73, sr. v.p., chief fin. officer, 1973-75, exec. v.p., chief fin. officer, 1975-81, vice chmn., 1981-83, pres., chief adminstrv. officer, 1984-89, also dir.; pres., chief exec. officer Continental Bank, Continental Bancorp, 1990-92; vice chmn. bd. Continental Bank, 1981-84; pres. parent co. Continental Bancorp., 1981-92; dir. Barnett Inst. U. North Fla., 1993-94; sec. of banking Commonwealth of Pa., 1995-99; ret., 1999.

RISI, LOUIS JAMES , JR. business executive; b. Highland Park, Ill., July 2, 1937; s. Louis J. and Ann E. Risi; m. Mary Jean Anson, Jan. 15, 1958; children: Steven, Janet, Andrew. BS, Bradley U., 1958; MBA, U. Chgo. Pres. and CEO, bd. dirs., mem. exec. com. Norin Corp., Miami, Fla., 1969-81; exec. com. dir. Maple Leaf Mills Ltd., Toronto, Can., 1970-81, Corp. Foods, Inc., 1970-81; chmn. bd. dirs. Louis Sherry, Inc., 1976-81; chmn. bd., chief exec. officer Nat. Investors Fire & Casualty Co., 1975-77; exec. com. dir. Investors Equity Life Ins. Co. of Hawaii, 1970-75; pres., dir. The Abbey, Lake Geneva, 1970-75; exec. com., dir. Upper Lakes Shipping, Ltd., Toronto, Can., 1970-76; pres., dir. The Pioneer, Lake Oshkosh, 1971-76; exec. com., dir. Port Weller and St. Lawrence Dry Dock, Ltd., St. Catharines, Can., 1971-76; pres., dir. Homosassa Springs, Fla., 1971-78, Ivan Tors Films Inc., Culver City, Calif., 1971-78, Ivan Tors Studios Inc., Miami, Fla., 1976-80; exec. com. dir. Midland Nat. Bank, 1976-80; pres., dir. Norris Grain Co., 1980-82; chmn. bd., CEO CTC Corp., 1981-83. Exec. com., dir. Nat. Investors Life Ins. Co., 1970-77; chmn. bd., CEO Enginenuity.com, Inc.; chmn. bd., pres. Victory Industries, Inc.; chmn. bd. dirs. Red Wing Co., Oklawaha Farms, Inc., Assured Security Co.; dir. Breckinridge Group; exec. v.p., bd. dirs. Detroit Red Wings Hockey Club, Inc., 1976-82; bd. govs. Nat. Hockey League, 1976-82; bd. dirs. Chgo. Rock Island and Pacific R.R., dir. exec. com., Bankmgrs. Corp.; exec. com., bd. dirs. Afriair Corp., 1972-79; exec. com., bd. dirs. Peter Bowden Drilling Ltd.; U.S. rep. Grain negotiations with USSR; U.S. rep. Feedstuffs negotiations with China; mem. adv. coun. Am. Stock Exch.; mem. Agrl. Processors Liaison com. FTC; mem. adv. bd. Nat. Millers Assn.; exec. v.p., bd. dirs. Adirondack Red Wings Hockey Club, Inc., 1976-82, Ft. Worth Red Wings Hockey Club, Inc., 1975-78; bd. govs. Internat. Hockey League, 1978-82, Am. Hockey League, 1975-79; dir. TBA Entertainment, Inc.; pres., chmn. bd. dirs. Kinnard Body Works, Inc., 1970-73; exec. com., bd. dirs. Southeastern Airlines, Inc., 1972-78. Trustee Fairchild Tropical Garden, Miami, Fla. Lt. comdr. USN, 1959-66. Mem. Ocean Reef Yacht Club (Key Largo, Fla.), Santa Rosa (Calif.) Country Club, Riviera Country Club (Coral Gables, Fla.), Coral Reef Yacht Club (Miami, Fla.), Anabelle's Club (London), St. James Club (London). Home: 10915 Lakeside Dr Coral Gables FL 33156-4209 Office: 9200 S Dadeland Blvd Miami FL 33156-2715 also: 4535 E Elwood St Phoenix AZ 85040-1981

RISIN, JACK See BUTCHER, JACK ROBERT

RISINGER, C. FREDERICK, social studies educator; b. Paducah, Ky., July 15, 1939; s. Charles Morris and Mary Neal (Barfield) R.; m. Margaret M. Marker, July 4, 1994; children: Donna Lyne, Alyson, Laura, John. BS in Edn., So. Ill. U., 1961; MA in History, No. Ill. U., 1968. Newscaster, disc jockey WMOK Radio, Metropolis, Ill., 1955-61; tchr., adminstr., coach Lake Park H.S., Roselle, 1962-73; coord. sch. social studies Ind. U., Bloomington, 1973-86, assoc. dir. social studies devel. ctr., 1986-90, dir. nat. clearinghouse for U.S.-Japan studies, 1990—, assoc. dir. tchr. edn., 1995-97, dir. profl. devel., sch. svcs. and summer sessions, 1997—. Mem. adv. bd. Learning Mag., Boston, 1988—; pres. Nat. Coun. for the Social Studies, 1990-91. Co-author: America! America!, 1974, America's Past and Promise. 1997, Creating America, 2000; editor jour. News and Notes on the Social Sciences, 1973-86. Pres. Social Studies Suprs. Assn., Washington, 1985-86; exec. dir. Ind. Coun. for Social Studies, Bloomington, 1975-87. Recipient numerous pub. and pvt. ednl. grants; named Tchr. of Yr. DuPage County Edn. Assn., 1973. Mem. ASCD, Nat. Coun. for Social Studies, Ind. Assn. Historians, Phi Delta Kappa. Democrat. Home: 7039 E State Rd 45 # E Bloomington IN 47408-9580 E-mail: risinger@indiana.edu.

RISINGER, FRED OWEN, pharmacologist; b. Shreveport, Aug. 12, 1954; s. Reggie and Margaret Risinger; m. Deborah Christman; children: Stewart, Lynn. BS, La. State U., 1978; MS, PhD, U. of La., 1987. Postdoctoral fellow Oreg. Health Sciences U., Portland, 1988—91, asst. prof., 1991—2002; assoc. prof. Idaho State U., Pocatello, 2002—. Grantee, Alcoholic Beverage Med. Rsch. Found., 1995, NIH, 1993—95. Mem.: Rsch. Soc. on Alcoholism, Soc. Neurosci., APA (assoc.), Psi Chi, Rho Chi, Omicron Delta Kappa. Avocation: reading, cooking, camping. Home: 11780 SW Ebberts Ct Beaverton OR 97008 Office: Department of Pharmaceutical Sciences CollPharmacy Idaho State Univ. Pocatello ID 83209

RISK, ROBERT TERENCE, printer, publisher; b. N.Y.C., June 25, 1943; s. Robert C. and Reta M. (Bragg) R. BA, SUNY, Buffalo, 1965; MA in Tchg., Oberlin Coll., 1972. Proprietor Typographeum, Francestown, N.H., 1975—. Author: Why Potocki?, 1981, Erhard Ratdolt, Master Printer, 1982, Four Private Presses, 1993, Typographeum, 1997. Avocations: gardening, European cinema, book collecting, building stone walls. Home and Office: 246 Bennington Rd Francestown NH 03043-3007

RISKE, WILLIAM KENNETH, producer, cultural services consultant; b. Lamont, Alta., Can., May 9, 1949; s. Norman Elmer and Clara Jeanette (Krause) R.; m. Barbara Elizabeth Malcolm, Apr. 28, 1973; children: Elizabeth Nicola, William Norman Malcolm. BFA, U. Alta., 1969. Stage mgr. Royal Winnipeg Ballet, Man., Can., 1971-73, prodn. stage mgr., 1973-76, prodn. mgr., 1976-77, assoc. gen. mgr., 1978-79, gen. mgr., 1979-92, cultural svcs. cons., 1992—; assoc. prodr., gen. mgr. Cirque Du Soleil-Mystère, 1994-96; gen. mgr. Cirque du Soleil U.S., Inc., 1996—. Mem. Assn. Cultural Execs. Home: 227 Deer Crossing Way Henderson NV 89012-2289 E-mail: wriske@vegas.cirquedusolek.com.

RISKEN, JARED CLEVELAND, physician; b. Oakland, Calif., Dec. 13, 1947; s. Maurice Forrest and Virginia (Cleveland) R.; m. Gloria Leona Hanger, Jan. 11, 1969; children: Douglas Jared, Sarah Julianne. BA in Anthropology and Biology, Loma Linda U., 1973; MD, Am. U., 1979. Resident in family practice Luth. Med. Ctr., St. Louis, 1980-81; med. dir. Alpha Therapeutics, 1981-85; indsl. medicine-safety engr. Torno America, Cortez, Colo., 1989-91, OJB Engring., Apple Valley, Calif., 1990-92; with U. Ill. Sch. Medicine, Champaign, 1992—. Active cmty. and ch. activities. Mem. Am. Profl. Practice Assn., Nat. Assn. Residents and Interns, Physicians for Social Responsibility, Christian Med. Dental Soc. Office: 2617 Willoughby Rd Champaign IL 61822-7567 E-mail: jrisken@uiuc.edu.

RISKOWSKI, GERALD LEE, engineering educator; b. Loup City, Nebr., Feb. 26, 1952; s. Stanley George and Rose Marie (Eurek) R.; m. Janet Ann Riskowski, June 19, 1976; 1 child, Ryan Lee. BS in Agrl. Engring., U. Nebr., 1974, MS in Agrl. Engring., 1976; PhD in Agrl. Engring., Iowa State U., 1986. Registered profl. engr., Ill., Iowa, Wis. Design engr. Lesters Bldgs., Lester Prairie, Minn., 1976-77; product engr. Wick Bldg. Systems, Mazomanie, Wis., 1977-80; instr. Iowa State U., Ames, 1980-86; prof. dept. agrl. engring. U. Ill., Urbana, 1986—. Swine facilities cons. Am. Tech. Products, Savoy, Ill., 1997—; pres. Internat. Air Technologies, Savoy, 1994—. Author: Designing Facilities for Pesticide and Fertilizer Containment, 1991 (Am. Soc. Agrl. Engrs. Blue Ribbon 1992); editor: Swine Housing and Equipment Handbook, 1983 (Am. Soc. Agrl. Engrs. Blue Ribbon 1984), Livestock Waste Facilities, 1985, Farm Buildings Wiring Handbook, 1986 (Am. Soc. Agrl. Engrs. Blue Ribbon 1987). Named to Rural Builders Hall of Fame, 1998. Mem. ASHRAE (TC.2 Handbook chair 1993-2000), Am. Soc. Agrl. Engrs. (S&E program chair, stds. chair, Henry Giese award 2001). Office: Tex A&M U 2117 TAMU College Station TX 77843-2117 E-mail: riskowski@tamu.edu.

RISLEY, GREGORY BYRON, furniture company executive, interior designer; b. Vincennes, Ind., Feb. 2, 1949; s. Jack Byron and Elizabeth Louise (Rockwell) R.; children: Christopher Byron, Timothy Neal. BS, Oakland City (Ind.) Coll., 1973; postgrad., Butler U., 1973-74, Oxford Worcester Coll. Pres. Risley Furniture & Design, Bicknell, Ind., 1974—, Risley Enterprises Inc., Bicknell, 1979—. Co-author: Preview IV The Home Furnishings Store. Pres. Better Bicknell Club, 1971; coach Pee Wee League, Bicknell, 1975-77; leader cub pack Boy Scouts Am., Bicknell, 1977; chmn. Queen Pageant, Bicknell, 1978-85. Mem. Nat. Home Furnishings Assn. (chmn. nat. execs. 1978-80), Am. Contract Bridge League (life master, unit sec. 1986-88, v.p. 1989, pres. 1991-92, bd. dirs. unit 193, 1993-95), Bicknell Mchts. Assn., Interior Design Soc. (outstanding rm. design award 1980), Knox County Assn. Retarded Citizens, French Club, Masons, Scottish Rite, Old Town Players (charter), Elks (past exalted ruler Bicknell 1976-77). Avocations: bridge, golf, reading. Office: 114 S Main St Bicknell IN 47512-2626

RISLEY, ROD ALAN, education association executive; b. Hutchinson, Kans., Oct. 17, 1954; s. Ralph Edward and Patricia Ann (Gaulding) R. AA, San Jacinto Coll., 1975; BBA, Sam Houston State U., 1982; AA (hon.), Austin (Tex.) Community Coll., 1991; MBA, Millsap Coll., 1995; PhD (hon.), Highpoint U., 1996, Mt. Ida Coll., 1996. Dir. alumni affairs Phi Theta Kappa, 1976-82; assoc. dir. Phi Theta Kappa Internat. Hdqrs., Jackson, Miss., 1982-85, exec. dir., 1985—. Grant reviewer NSF, C.C. Humanities Assn., NEH; mem. adv. bd. Horne CPA Group. Judge Truman Scholarship Found., 1993, 94, Coca-Cola Scholars Found., 2001-02. Named one of Outstanding Young Men Am., 1982, 83, 84, 85, 86, 87, 88, 89, Top Bus. Leaders Miss., 1994, Disting. Alumnus, San Jacinto Coll., 1997; Mid South Found. C.C. fellow, 2001. Mem. Assn. Coll. Honor Soc. (stds. and definitions com.), Am. Assn. of Cmty. Colls. (commr. coun. for acad., student and cmty. devel., grant reviewer, disting. alumnus award 1996), Phi Theta Kappa (sec., pub. jour.). Episcopalian. Office: Phi Theta Kappa Soc PO Box 13729 Jackson MS 39236-3729

RISLEY, TODD ROBERT, psychologist, educator; b. Palmer, Alaska, Sept. 8, 1937; s. Robert and Eva Lou (Todd) R.; 1 child, Todd Michael; m. Cheryl Thomas, Mar. 30, 1996. AB with distinction in Psychology, San Diego State Coll., 1960; MS, U. Wash., 1963, PhD, 1966. Asst. prof. psychology Fla. State U., Tallahassee, 1964-65; research assoc. Bur. Child Research, U. Kans., Lawrence, 1965-77, sr. scientist, 1977—, asst. prof. dept. human devel., 1967-69, assoc. prof., 1969-73, prof., 1973-84; prof. psychology U. Alaska, Anchorage, 1982—. Pres. Ctr. for Applied Behavior Analysis, 1970-82; dir. Johnny Cake Child Study Ctr., Mansfield, Ark., 1973-74; vis. prof. U. Auckland (N.Z.), 1978; acting dir. Western Carolina Ctr., Morgantown, N.C., 1981; dir. Alaska Div. Mental Health and Devel. Disabilities, 1988-91; cons. in field to numerous orgns. and instns. Co-author: The Infant Center, 1977, Shopping with Children: Advice for parents, 1978, The Toddler Center, 1979, Meaningful Differences, 1995, The Social World of Children, 1999; editor: Jour. Applied Behavior Analysis, 1971-74; mng. editor: Behavior Therapy, The Behavior Therapist, Behavioral Asessment, 1977-80; assoc. editor: Jour. Positive Behavior Support, 1998--; mem. editl. bds. of numerous profl. jours.; contbr. revs. and numerous articles. Co-chmn. Fla. task force on use of behavioral procedures in state programs for retarded, 1974— ; mem. resident abuse investigating com. div. retardation Fla. Dept. Health and Rehab. Services, 1972— ; mem. adv. com. Social Research Inst., U. Utah, 1977— ; mem. Alaska Gov.'s Council on Handicapped and Gifted, 1983-88, NIH Mental Retardation Research Com., 1987-88, Alaska Mental Health Bd., 1988. Grantee NIMH, 1971-72, 72-73; rsch. grantee Nat. Ctr. Health Services, 1976-79; grantee Nat. Inst. Edn., 1973, NIH, 1967-86; grantee U.S. Dept. Edn., 1997-2002. Fellow APA (coun. of reps. 1982-85, pres. div. 25, 1989, Edgar Doll award 2000), Am. Psychol. Soc.; mem. AAAS, Am. Assn. Mental Deficiency (Rsch. award 2000), Assn. Advancement of Behavior Therapy (dir. 1975-80, pres. 1976-77, chmn. profl. rev. com. 1977—, series editor Readings in Behavior Therapy 1977—), Soc. Behavioral Medicine, Assn. Behavior Analysis, Sigma Xi. E-mail: risley@alaska.net.

RISMAN, MICHAEL, lawyer, business executive, securities company executive; b. Everett, Mass., Apr. 2, 1938; s. Morris Charles and Doris (Rosenbaum) R.; m. Rebecca R. Fuchs, Mar. 23, 1974; 1 stepchild, Ian Carlton Murray; children: Matthew Craig, Deborah Gayle, Jared Evan. BA, U. Mich., 1960; LLB, Georgetown U., 1964. Bar: D.C. 1964. Staff mem. Democratic Nat. Com., Washington, 1964; atty. U.S. Fgn. Claims Settlement Commn., 1964-66, SEC, Washington, 1966-67; counsel Seaboard Planning Corp., Beverly Hills, Calif., 1967-72, pres., 1970-72; v.p. Seaboard Corp., 1970-72; sec. B.C. Morton Realty Trust, 1967-71; with Arlington Investments Corp., Santa Monica, Calif., 1979-86; founder The Quincey Group, 1986; owner, pres. Armstrong Kitchens, San Francisco, 1988-90; sr. v.p. AFC Am. Housing Corp., L.A., Calif., 1991-97; mng. dir. Hollingsworth & Lord, 1997—. Bd. dir. Competitive Capital Fund, Income Fund Boston, Inc., Admiralty Fund. Home: 1133 Centinela Ave Santa Monica CA 90403-2316

RISOM, JENS, furniture designer, manufacturing executive; b. Copenhagen, May 8, 1916; came to U.S., 1939; naturalized, 1944; s. Sven J. and Inger Risom; m. Iben Haderup, Dec. 12, 1939 (dec. Jan. 1977); children: Helen Ann, Peggy Ann, Thomas Christian, Sven Christian; m. Henny Panduro, May 12, 1979. Student, Krebs, Denmark, 1922-27, St. Annae, 1927-32, Niels Brock Bus. Coll., 1932-34, Sch. for Arts and Indust., Denmark, 1935-38. With design and decorating divsn. Nordiska Kompanet, Stockholm, Inge Westin, Stockholm, 1934-35, Ernst Kühn, Arch., Copenhagen and N.Y.C., 1937-38; with Dan Cooper, Inc., N.Y., 1939-41; freelance furniture designer, 1941-46; founder, pres. Jens Risom Design Inc., 1946-71; pres. Jens Risom Design, Inc. (became subs. Dictaphone Corp. 1971); v.p. Dictaphone Corp., 1971-73; pres. Design Control, New Canaan, Conn., 1973—. Cons. design, mktg., space planning. Trustee RISD, New Canaan Libr., Indsl. Design Soc. Am. With U.S. Army, 1943-45, ETO. Decorated Cross of Dannebrog (Denmark); recipient awards Archtl. League, Am. Inst. Internat. Design, Lifetime Achievement award Bklyn. Mus. Art, 1994, numerous Danish and Am. design awards. Home and Office: 24 Parade Hill Ln New Canaan CT 06840-4119 also: PO Box 596 Block Island RI 02807-0596 Fax: (203) 966-6144.

RISS, ERIC, psychologist; m. Miriam Barbara Schoen, July 22, 1956; children: Arthur, Suzanne, Wendy. BA, Bklyn. Coll., 1950; PhD, NYU, 1958. Diplomate Am. Bd. Psychotherapy. Pvt. practice psychotherapy, family therapy and marriage counseling, N.Y.C., 1952; sr. psychologist N.Y.C. Diagnostic Ctr., 1954-57; with Marriage and Family Life Inst., N.Y.C., 1956-92, cons., 1956-58, dir. pub. edn., 1960-73, chmn. bd. dirs., 1961-73, dir., 1973-92; mem. attending staff, supr. psychotherapy and family therapy Payne Whitney Psychiat. Clinic, N.Y. Hosp., N.Y.C., 1971-78; clin. instr. psychology and psychiatry Cornell U. Med. Coll., 1971-72, clin. asst. prof., 1973-78; dir. Inst. for Exploration of Marriage, 1976-84; chief psychologist Artists, Writers and Performers Psychotherapy Ctr., 1978-92. Sr. psychologist N.Y.C. Diagnostic Center, 1954-57; with Marriage and Family Life Inst., N.Y.C., 1956-92; cons., 1956-58, dir. pub. edn., 1960-73, chmn. bd. dirs., 1961-73, dir., 1973-92; mem. attending staff, supr. psychotherapy and family therapy Payne Whitney Psychiat. Clinic, N.Y. Hosp., N.Y.C., 1971-78; clin. instr. psychology and psychiatry Cornell U. Med. Coll., 1971-72, clin. asst. prof., 1973-78; dir. Inst. for Exploration of Marriage, 1976-84; chief psychologist Artists, Writers and Performers Psychotherapy Center, 1978-92; lectr. Bklyn. Coll., 1955-62; cons. Fordham Hosp., 1956-68; psychotherapist N.Y. Neuropsychiat. Center, 1958-60; psychotherapist Community Guidance Service, N.Y.C., 1958-61; founder, head Natural Psychotherapy Internat., 1999—; webmaster www.naturalpsychotherapy.com. Contbr. numerous articles to profl. jours. Mem. APA, N.Y. State Psychol. Assn. (chair colleague assistance program 2000—), Am. Acad. Psychotherapy, N.Y. State Marriage, Family and Child Counseling Assn. (pres. 1971-72), Acad. Family Psychology. Office: 174 E 73rd St New York NY 10021-4352 E-mail: eriss@naturalpsychotherapy.com, eriss@npsy.com.

RISS, MURRAY, photographer, educator; b. Stryj, Poland, Feb. 6, 1940; came to U.S., 1951, naturalized, 1958; s. Elias and Dora (Feit) R.; m. Karen Mason; children: Shanna, Adya. Student, CCNY, 1958-63; BA, Cooper Union, 1966; M.F.A., R.I. Sch. Design, 1968. Prof., chmn. dept photography Memphis Acad. Arts, 1969-84; lectr. film and photography Southwestern U., Memphis, 1972-82; artist-in-residence U. Syracuse, N.Y., 1980, U. Haifa, Israel, 1976 One man shows include Art Inst., Chgo, 1971, Mpls. Inst. Fine Arts, 1971, U. Rochester, N.Y., 1975, Photographers Gallery, London, 1977, Afterimage Gallery, Dallas, 1979, Visual Studies Workshop, Rochester, 1980, Hampshire (Mass.) Coll., 1981, Loomis Inst., Conn., 1984; group shows include Mus. Modern Art, N.Y.C., 1970, 71, New Orleans Mus. Art, 1975, Nexus Gallery, Atlanta, 1981, Askew Nixon Gallery; touring show So. Arts Fedn., 1985-86; conceived, organized, dir. Southern Eye, Southern Mind, A Photographic Inquiry, Memphis, 1981; illustrator: History of Memphis Architecture until 1900, 1983, Guide to Mud Island, 1989; curator, dir. Emerging Southern Photographers, Memphis Coll. Art Gallery, 1992, Memphis Brooks Mus. Art, 1994. Nat. Endowment for Arts fellow, 1979 Mem. Soc. Photographic Edn. Home: 1306 Harbert Ave Memphis TN 38104-4514 Office: Murray Riss Photography 516 S Main St Memphis TN 38103-4443 E-mail: mur3435ris@aol.com. *Had I designed the events and outcomes of my life I would not have done as well as my fate has done for me.*

RISS, RICHARD MICHAEL, research economist, church history educator; b. Rochester, N.Y., May 22, 1952; s. Walter and Barbara Ann (Johnson) R.; m. Kathryn Janet Grieser, Mar. 3, 1979. BA, U. Rochester, 1974; MCS, Regent Coll., Vancouver, B.C., Can., 1979; MA, Trinity Evang. Div. Sch., Deerfield, Ill., 1988; MPhil, Drew U., 2002. Instr. ch. history Christian Life Coll., Mt. Prospect, Ill., 1980-83; data base mgr. Systems and Mgmt. Infor. Svcs. 1st Chgo. Corp., 1980-85; rsch. assoc. to chief economist Prudential Securities, N.Y.C., 1988-91, C.J. Lawrence/Deutsche Bank Securities Corp., N.Y.C., 1991-96; asst. prof. ch. history Somerset Christian Coll. , 1989—. Author: The Evidence for the Resurrection of Jesus Christ, 1977, Latter Rain, 1987, A Survey of Twentieth Century Revival Movements in North America, 1988, A History of the Worldwide Awakening, 1992-95, 1995, A Defense of the Revival, 1996, Images of Revival, 1997; also articles to Zondervan Dictionary of Pentecostal and Charismatic Movements, Ency. Hanoverian Eng. and The Library of Christian Worship. Mem. Soc. for Pentecostal Studies, Conf. on Faith and History, Evang. Theol. Soc., Soc. Christian Philosophers, Am. Soc. Ch. History, Wesleyan Theol. Soc. Avocation: playing violin. Home: 290 River Rd Apt M-1 Piscataway NJ 08854-7516

RISS, ROBERT BAILEY, real estate investor; b. Salida, Colo., May 27, 1927; s. Richard Roland and Louise (Roberts) R.; married; children: Edward Stayton, G. Leslie, Laura Bailey, Juliana Warren. BSBA, U. Kans., 1949. Pres. Riss Internat. Corp., Kansas City, Mo., 1950-80, chmn. bd., 1964-86; founder, chmn. bd., pres. Republic Industries, Inc., 1969-86; chmn. bd. Grandview Bank and Trust Co., 1969-86, Commonwealth Gen. Ins. Co., 1986-93. Chmn. bd. dirs., exec. com. Heart of Am. Fire and Casualty Co.; chmn. bd. dirs. Comml. Equipment Co. Vice chmn. bd. trustees Kansas U. Endowment Assn., 1980-89. Recipient Silver Beaver award Kansas City Area coun. Boy Scouts Am., 1972; Disting. Svc. citation U. Kans., 1976; Fred Ellsworth medal U. Kans., 1979; named Most Outstanding Young Man in Mo. U.S. Jr. C. of C., 1956 Mem. Kans. U. Alumni Assn. (nat. pres. 1969-70), Sigma Nu. Episcopalian.

RISSANEN, JORMA JOHANNES, computer scientist; b. Pielisjarvi, Finland, Oct. 20, 1932; came to the U.S., 1964; m. Riitta T. Åberg, Nov. 6, 1956; children: Juhani, Natasha. PhD, Finland Inst. Tech., 1960. Assoc. editor: Jour. Control and Info.; contbr. articles to profl. jours.; patentee in field:. Recipient Outstanding Innovation award, IBM Rsch. divsn., 1980, Best Paper award, Automatica, 1982, Infithy Group, 1986. Fellow: IEEE (info. theory soc.), Helsinki Inst. Info. Tech. Home: 140 Teresita Way Los Gatos CA 95032-6517

RISSE, GUENTER BERNHARD, physician, historian, educator; b. Buenos Aires, Argentina, Apr. 28, 1932; s. Francisco B. and Kaete A. R.; m. Alexandra G. Paradzinski, Oct. 14, 1961; children— Heidi, Monica, Alisa. MD, U. Buenos Aires, 1958; PhD, U. Chgo., 1971. Intern Mercy Hosp., Buffalo, 1958-59; resident in medicine Henry Ford Hosp., Detroit, 1960-61, Mt. Carmel Hosp., Columbus, Ohio, 1962-63; asst. dept. medicine U. Chgo., 1963-67; asst. prof. dept. history of medicine U. Minn., 1969-71; asso. prof. dept. history of medicine and dept. history of sci. U. Wis., Madison, 1971-76, prof., 1976-85, chmn. dept. history of medicine, 1971-77; prof. dept. history health scis. U. Calif., San Francisco, 1985-99, prof. dept. anthropology, history and social medicine, 1999-2001, prof. emeritus, 2001—. Dept. chair, 1985-99; mem. project com. Ctr. for Photog. Images in Medicine and Health Care. Author: Paleopathology of Ancient Egypt, 1964, Hospital Life in Enlightenment Scotland, 1986, Mending Bodies—Saving Souls: A History of Hospitals, 1999; editor: Modern China and Traditional Chinese Medicine, 1973, History of Physiology, 1973, Medicine Without Doctors, 1977, AIDS and the Historian, 1991, Culture, Knowledge and Healing, Historical Perspectives of Homeopathic Medicine in Europe and North America, 1998; mem. editl. bd. Jour. History of Medicine, 1971-74, 90-93, Clio Medica, 1973-88, Bull. History of Medicine, 1980-94, Medizinhistorisches Jour., 1981—, Med. History, 1989-95, NTM Internat. Jour. of History, Ethics, Medicine, 1992—, History of Philos. Life Scis., 1993—, Asclepio, 1995—, Health and History, 1998—. Served with Argentine Armed Forces, 1955. Recipient NIH grants, 1971-73, 82-84, WHO grant, 1979, named Logan Campbell Disting. Lectr., New Zealand, 1994, Karl Sudhoff Meml. Lectr., Germany, 2000. Mem. Am. Assn. History of Medicine (pres. 1988-90, William H. Welch medal 1988), History Sci. Soc., Deutsche Gesellschaft fur Geschichte der Medizin, European Assn. History of Medicine and Health, Internat. Network for History of Pub. Health, Mex. Soc. History and Philosophy of Medicine, Peruvian Assn. Med. Ethnology and History, Brit. Soc. for Social History of Medicine, Argentine Ateneo de Historia de la Medicina, AIDS History Group (co-chair 1988-94), Internat. Network for History of Hosps. (convenor 1995—), Bay Area Med. Hist. Club (pres. 1994-96). Home: 933 NW Richmond Beach Rd Seattle WA 98177-3219 E-mail: profgrisse@home.com.

RISSER, ARTHUR CRANE, JR. zoo administrator; b. July 8, 1938; s. Arthur Crane and Mary Winn (Stevenson) R.; children: Michelle W., Stephen C., Michael R. BA, Grinnell Coll., Iowa, 1960; MA, U. Ariz., Tucson, 1963; PhD, U. Calif., Davis, 1970. Mus. technician Smithsonian Instn., Washington, 1963-64; rsch. assoc. Sch. Medicine U. Md., Balt., 1964-65; grad. teaching asst. U. Calif., Davis, 1965-70; asst. prof. biology U. Nev., Reno, 1970-74; asst. curator birds Zool. Soc., San Diego, 1974-76, curator birds, 1976-81, gen. curator birds, 1981-86; gen. mgr. San Diego Zoo, 1986—. Co-chmn. Calif. Condor Working Group on Captive Breeding and Reintroduction, 1983-85; mem. Calif. Condor Recovery Team, 1984-86; bd. dirs. Internat. Found. Conservation Birds, 1979-88, Rsch. and Conservation Found. of Papua New Guinea, 1991—. Treas. Planned Parenthood, Reno, 1972; bd. dirs. Chinese Hist. Soc. Greater San Diego & Baja, Calif., 1995-99. Fellow Am. Assn. Zool. Parks and Aquariums. Office: San Diego Zoo PO Box 120551 San Diego CA 92112-0551 E-mail: arisser@sandiegozoo.org.

RISSER, FRED A. state legislator; b. Madison, Wis., May 5, 1927; married; 3 children. BA, U. Oreg., LLB, 1952. Bar: Wis. Sole practice, Madison, 1952—; mem. Wis. Senate from 26th dist., 1962—; asst. minority leader Wis. State Senate, 1965-67, minority leader, 1967-75, pres. pro tem, 1975-79, pres., 1979-93, asst. minority leader, 1993-96, pres., 1996—. Mem. Wis. State Assembley, 1956-62; del. Democratic Conv., 1960, 64; presdl. elector-chmn. Wis. Electoral Coll., 1964; vice chmn. Bldg. Commn., Wis. also: 5008 Risser Rd Madison WI 53705-1365 Office: Madison Office, State Capitol Rm. 220 South, PO Box 7882 Madison WI 53707-7882 E-mail: sen.risser@legis.state.wi.us.*

RISSER, JAMES VAULX, JR. journalist, educator; b. Lincoln, Nebr., May 8, 1938; s. James Vaulx and Ella Caroline (Schacht) R.; m. Sandra Elizabeth Laaker, June 10, 1961; children: David James, John Daniel. BA, U. Nebr., 1959, cert. in journalism, 1964; JD, U. San Francisco, 1962. Bar: Nebr. 1962. Pvt. practice law, Lincoln, 1962-64; reporter Des Moines Register and Tribune, 1964-85, Washington corr., 1969-85, bur. chief, 1976-85; dir. John S. Knight fellowships for profl. journalists, prof. communication Stanford U., 1985-2000. Lectr. Wells Coll., 1981; mem. com. on agrl. edn. in secondary schs. Nat. Acad. Scis., 1985-88. Trustee Reuter Found., 1989-2000, Am. Conservatory Theater, 2000—; mem. Pulitzer Prize Bd., 1990-99; mem. journalism adv. com. Knight Found., 2000—. Profl. Journalism fellow Stanford U., 1973-74; recipient award for disting. reporting public affairs Am. Polit. Sci. Assn., 1969; Thomas L. Stokes award for environ. reporting Washington Journalism Center, 1971, 79; Pulitzer prize for nat. reporting, 1976, 79; Worth Bingham Found. prize for investigative reporting, 1976; Raymond Clapper Meml. Assn. award for Washington reporting, 1976, 78; Edward J. Meeman award for Conservation Reporting, 1985. Mem. Soc. Environ. Journalists, Soc. Profl. Journalists (Disting. Svc. award 1976), Investigative Reporters and Editors Assn., Com. Concerned Journalists, Gridiron Club. Clubs: Gridiron. Home: 1111 Bay St # 404 San Francisco CA 94123 E-mail: jimrisser@earthlink.net.

RISSER, PAUL GILLAN, academic administrator, botanist; b. Blackwell, Okla., Sept. 14, 1939; s. Paul Crane and Jean (McCluskey) R.; children: David, Mark, Stephen, Scott. BA, Grinnell Coll., 1961; MS in Botany, U. Wis., 1965, PhD in Botany and Soils, 1967. From asst. prof. to prof. botany U. Okla., 1967-81, also asst. dir. biol. sta., chmn. dept. botany and microbiology,

1977-81; dir. Okla. Biol. Survey, 1971-77; chief Ill. Natural History Survey, 1981-86; program dir., ecosystem studies NSF; provost and v.p. acad. affairs U. N.Mex., 1989-92; former pres. Miami U., Oxford, Ohio; pres. Oreg. State U., 1996—. Author: (with Kathy Cornelison) Man and the Biosphere, 1979, (with others) The True Prairie Ecosystem, 1981; research, numerous publs. in field. Trustee Pioneer Multi-County Library Bd. Mem. Am. Acad. Arts and Scis., Ecol. Soc. Am. (pres.), Brit. Ecol. Soc., Soc. Range Mgmt., Southwestern Assn. Naturalists (pres.), Am. Inst. Biol. Sci. (pres.), Torrey Bot. Club. Presbyterian. Office: Oregon State U Kerr Adminstrn Bldg Office of the Pres Corvallis OR 97331-8507*

RISSMAN, BURTON RICHARD, lawyer; b. Chgo., Nov. 13, 1927; s. Louis and Eva (Lyons) R.; m. Francine Greenberg, June 15, 1952; children: Lawrence E., Thomas W., Michael P. BS, U. Ill., 1947, JD, 1951; LLM, NYU, 1952. Bar: Ill. 1951, U.S. Dist. Ct. (no. dist.) Ill. 1954, U.S. Ct. Appeals (7th cir.) 1978, U.S. Supreme Ct. 1982. Assoc. Schiff, Hardin & Waite, Chgo., 1953-59, ptnr., 1959—, mem. mgmt. com., 1984-92, chmn. mgmt. com., 1986-90. Mem. faculty Practicing Law Inst. Bd. editor U. Ill. Law Forum, 1949-51; contbr. articles to profl. jours. 1st lt. JAGC USAF, 1952—53. Food Law fellow, 1951. Mem. ABA, Ill. Bar Assn., Chgo. Bar Assn., Chgo. Coun. Lawyers, Met. Club, Carlton Club. Office: Schiff Hardin & Waite 6600 Sears Tower Chicago IL 60606-6473

RISTAU, MARK MOODY, lawyer, petroleum consultant; b. Warren, Pa., Mar. 21, 1944; s. Harold J. and Eleanor K. (Moody) R. BA, Pa. Mil. Coll., 1966; BA, Widner Coll., 1966; JD, Case Western Res. U., 1969. Bar: Pa. 1970, D.C. 1972, U.S. Supreme Ct. 1973, N.Y. 1982. Pvt. practice, Warren, 1970-85, Warren and Vancouver, B.C., Can., 1976-85, Jamestown, N.Y., 1982-85, sr. ptnr. Ristau & McKeirnan, Warren, 1986—; sr. dir. Pa. Allied Oil Producers, 1972-78, atty. for Pa. Field Producers, 1981-85; ptnr. SAR Devel., 1984-91, Slagle Almendinger & Ristau, 1983-89; dir. Try-M Fin. Co., 1978-81; counsel United Refining Co., Pennbank, Enchanced Oil Recovery, Consol. Services, 1982-84; chmn. bd. Comml. Service Corp., U.S. interim trustee, 1979-88, bankruptcy trustee, 1988-98; CEO, Silicon Electro-physics Corp., Inc., 1988-91, Phoenix Materials Corp., Inc., 1988-91, chmn. bd. dirs. Warren Industries, Inc., 1991-94; bd. dirs. Petrex, Inc., A & A Metal Fabricating; U.S. counsel Brazilian Promotions, Inc. of Brazilian Govt., 1981-85; v.p. Daytona Apts., Inc., Daytona Beach, Fla.; sec. Daytona Devel. League. Mem. Warren County Bd. Pub. Assistance, 1970-71, chmn., 1971-72; mem. Broward County (Fla.) Devel. League, 1981-83; mem. Fla. Profl. Recruitment Assn., 1980-83. Recipient Tate Meml. award, 1981; Sambas award, 1981. Mem. Assn. Trial Lawyers Am., Am. Arbitration Assn., Warren County Bar Assn. (past pres.). Clubs: Eagles (hon. life); Ipanema (Brazil); Conewango (Warren). Contbr. articles on law to profl. jours.; case reporter Legal Intelligencer, 1972-79. Home and Office: 203 W 3d Ave Warren PA 16365-2331

RISTER, GENE ARNOLD, humanities educator; b. Merkel, Tex., Apr. 18, 1943; s. Jettie William and Mary Evelyn (Scott) R.; m. Janet Kathleen Ledermann, Jan. 21, 1967. BA summa cum laude, McMurry U., 1965; MA, Tex. Christian U., 1966; PhD, U. Wis., 1972; postgrad., U. Ariz., 1990, No. Ariz. U., 1990. Prof., divsn. chmn. McMurry U., Abilene, Tex., 1970-81, East Ctrl. U., Ada, Okla., 1981-83; prof. dept. humanities, divsn. chmn. Maricopa C.C., Phoenix, 1983—. Adj. prof. No. Ariz. U., Phoenix, 1994—; del. Nat. Inst. Higher Edn. for Mex.-Ams., Albuquerque, 1975. Book reviewer Tex. Rev., 1985; illustrator Tex. Rev. and Tex. Anthology, 1979-82; contbr. articles to profl. jours.; contbr. poetry to Galleon, Originals, Quetzal, Rectangle, Sam Houston Lit. Rev., Tex. Anthology, Tex. Rev., Works by Abilene Writers, Canticles: Sound and Sight, 2002, The 2002 32nd Street Arts Festival, Paradise Valley Coll., Phoenix, Ariz. Regional cons. Human Rels. Coun., Midland; moderator, dir. West Tex. Coun. Govts.; mem. Tex. Com. for Humanities and Pub. Policy, 1975-81; ECU rep. Intertribal Coun., Five Nations, Sulphur, Okla., 1981; co-sponsor Tex. Reading Cir. Consortium of Univs., 1977-79. Recipient Faculty Recognition award Consortium for C.C. Devel., 1996; named Innovator of the Yr. Maricopa CCD/League for Innovation, 1988, Outstanding Faculty Employee award Maricopa C.C. Dist., 1985, 89, 92; NDEA Title VI fellow, 1965-67, Am. Grad. Sch. Internat. Mgmt. fellow, 1995, East-West Ctr. fellow, 1994, Japan Found. fellow, 1995; U.S. Dept. Edn. Title VIA grantee, 1996-98. Mem. C.C. Humanities Assn. (Ariz. state rep. to nat. bd. 1992). Democrat. Baptist. Avocations: archaeology, art and art history, cinema, music, travel. Home: 14407 N 60th St Scottsdale AZ 85254-5540 Office: Paradise Valley Community Coll 18401 N 32nd St Phoenix AZ 85032-1210 E-mail: gene.rister@pvmail.maricopa.edu.

RISTER, ROBERT STEPHEN, author, medical jouranlist; b. Taylor, Tex., Apr. 16, 1955; s. Raymond Howard and Rosemary (Radford) R. BA, Baylor U., 1978; MBA, U. Tex., 1985. Author: Japanese Herbal Medicine: The Healing Art of Kampo, 1999, Healing without Medication, 2002; assoc. editor: The Complete German Commission E Monographs: Therapeutic Guide to Herbal Medicine, 1999 (Doolly award 1999). E-mail: robertsrister@jump.net.

RISTICH, MIODRAG, psychiatrist; b. Belgrade, Yugoslavia, July 19, 1938; came to U.S., 1967; s. Teodosije and Gordana (Isailovic) Ristic; m. Yvonne Muriel Cunliffe, May 6, 1967; children: Katharine Alexandra, Elizabeth Victoria. MD, U. Belgrade, 1962. Diplomate Am. Bd. Psychiatry and Neurology. Resident in psychiatry Manhattan Psychiat. Ctr., NYU, 1980-83; med. dir. Cambridge (Minn.) State Hosp., 1967-72; dir. Willowbrook State Sch., Staten Island, N.Y., 1972-74; med. dir. DeWitt Rehab. and Nursing Ctr., N.Y.C., 1976—; clin. asst. prof. psychiatry NYU Med. Sch., 1996—. Pvt. practice psychiatry, N.Y.C., 1973—. Mem. AMA, Am. Psychiat. Assn., Am. Assn. for Geriatric Psychiatry, Royal Coll. Psychiatrists. Republican. Avocation: tennis. Home: 37 Sunrise Ln Upper Saddle River NJ 07458-1631 Office: 201 E 79th St Apt 7J New York NY 10021-0833 E-mail: mristich@yahoo.com.

RISTOW, BRUNNO, plastic surgeon; b. Brusque, Brazil, Oct. 18, 1940; came to U.S., 1967, naturalized, 1981; s. Arno and Ally Odette (von Buettner) R.; student Coll. Sinodal, Brazil, 1956-57, Coll. Julio de Castilhos, Brazil, 1957-58; M.D. magna cum laude, U. Brazil, 1966; m. Urannia Carrasquilla Gutierrez, Nov. 10, 1979; children by previous marriage: Christian Kilian, Trevor Roland. Intern in surgery Hosp. dos Estrangeiros, Rio de Janeiro, Brazil, 1965, Hospital Estadual Miguel Couto, Brazil, 1965-66, Instituto Aposentadoria Pensão Comerciarios Hosp. for Gen. Surgery, 1966; resident in plastic and reconstructive surgery, Dr. Ivo Pitanguy Hosp. Santa Casa de Misericordia, Rio de Janeiro, 1967; fellow Inst. of Reconstructive Plastic Surgery, N.Y. U. Med. Center, N.Y.C., 1967-68, jr. resident, 1971-72, sr. and chief resident, 1972-73; practice medicine specializing in plastic surgery, Rio de Janeiro, 1967, N.Y.C., 1968-73, San Francisco, 1973—; asst. surgeon N.Y. Hosp., Cornell Med. Center, N.Y.C., 1968-71; clin. instr. surgery N.Y. U. Sch. of Medicine, 1972-73; chmn. plastic and reconstructive surgery div. Presbyn. Hosp., Pacific Med. Center, San Francisco, 1974-92, chmn. emeritus, 1992—. Served with M.C., Brazilian Army Res., 1959-60. Decorated knight Venerable Order of St. Hubertus; Knight Order St. John of Jerusalem; fellow in surgery Cornell Med. Sch., 1968-71; diplomate Am. Bd. Plastic and Reconstructive Surgery. Fellow A.C.S., Internat. Coll. Surgeons; mem. Am. Soc. Aesthetic Plastic Surgery (chmn. edn.), Am. Soc. Plastic and Reconstructive Surgeons, Internat. Soc. Aesthetic Plastic Surgeons, Calif. Soc. Plastic Surgeons, AMA (Physician's Recognition award 1971-83), Calif. Med. Assn., San Francisco Med. Assn. Republican. Mem. Evang. Lutheran Ch. Club: San Francisco Olympic. Contbg. author: Cancer of the Hand, 1975, Current Therapy in Plastic and Reconstructive Surgery, 1988, Male Aesthetic Surgery, 1989, How They Do It: Procedures in Plastic and Reconstructive Surgery, 1990, Middle Crus: The Missing Link in Alar Cartilage Anatomy, 1991, Surgical Technology International, 1992, Aesthetic Plastic Surgery, 1993, Mastery of Surgery: Plastic and Reconstructive Surgery, 1993; Reoperative Aesthetic Plastic Surgery of the Face and Breast, 1994, 95; contbr. articles on plastic surgery to profl. publs. E-mail: ristow@worldnet.att.net. Office: Calif Pacific Med Ctr 2100 Webster St San Francisco CA 94115-2373

RISTOW, GAIL ROSS, art educator, paralegal, children's rights advocate; b. Carmel, Calif., Oct. 18, 1949; d. Kenneth E. and Lula Mae (Craft) Ross; m. Steven Craig Ristow, Sept. 15, 1971. BS in Biochemistry, Calif. Polytech State U., San Luis Obispo, 1972; MEd, Ariz. State U., 1980. Cert. tchr., Calif. Asst. instr. Calif. State Polytech U., Pomona, 1972; grad. asst. Calif. Polytech State U., 1973-74; tchr. Mt. Carmel High Sch., L.A., 1974-76, Cartwright Sch. Dist., Phoenix, 1976-80; pres., owner Handmade With Love, Bay City, Tex., 1984-88; tchr. art Aiken, S.C., 1989-96. Tchr. Community Edn., Bay City, 1986-88, Palacios, Tex., 1987. Sec. Chukker Creek Homeowners, Aiken, S.C., 1989-96; mem. S.C. Foster Care Rev. Bd., 1991-96; vol. tchr. elem. schs., Korea. Mem. AAUW, Am. Chem. Soc., Nat. Soc. Tole and Decorative Painters, Aiken Newcomer's Club (sec. 1989-91), Aiken Lioness Club (pres. 1991-94), Alpha Delta Kappa (v.p. 1986-87). Avocations: painting, woodworking, sewing, reading, children's rights advocacy. Home: PO Box 5441 Kennewick WA 99336-5441

RISTOW, GEORGE EDWARD, neurologist, educator; b. Albion, Mich., Dec. 15, 1943; s. George Julius and Margaret (Beattie) R.; 1 child, George Andrew Martin. BA, Albion Coll., 1965; DO, Coll. Osteo. Medicine/Surgery, Des Moines, 1969. Diplomate Am. Bd. Psychiatry and Neurology. Intern Garden City Hosp., 1969-70; resident Wayne State U., 1970-74; fellow U. Newcastle Upon Tyne, 1974-75; asst. prof. dept. neurology Wayne State U., Detroit, 1975-77; assoc. prof. Mich. State U., East Lansing, 1977-83, prof., 1983-84, 95—, prof., chmn., 1984-95, prof. emeritus, 2001—. Fellow Am. Acad. Neurology, Royal Soc. Medicine; mem. AMA, Am. Osteo. Assn., Pan Am. Med. Assn., World Fedn. Neurology, Am. Coll. Neuropsychiatrists (sr.). Home: 2070 Riverwood Dr Okemos MI 48864-2814 E-mail: ristoowge@aol.com.

RITACCO, PATSY RICHARD, sales executive; b. Newark, Aug. 27, 1956; s. Michael Patsy and Adelaide (Caruso) R.; m. Linda La Falce, Nov. 5, 1978; children: Michael A., Patsy Richard Jr. B of History, William Paterson Coll., 1978. Notary pub., N.J., 1990—. Tchr. Belleville (N.J.) High Sch., 1978-82; bd. pneumatics Robert Tool, Saddle Brook, N.J., 1983-94; dist. sales mgr. Standard Abrasives, Simi Valley, Calif., 1994—. Concert promotion dir. for edn. groups of 50s and 60s, Brooklyn Bridge, Coasters, 1980—; v.p. Unico Nat., Nutley, 2000—; guest lectr. in field. Contbr. poetry to anthologies, including Best Poets of 2001; contbg. writer Italian Tribune. Fellow Christ Ch. Sch. Bd., bldgs. & grounds publ rels., 1985-88; assoc. mem. Mus. Natural History; scholar bd. Unico Nat., Nutley, N.J., 1995—, treas., 1998-99. Recipient Editor's Choice award "Riddle of the Rose" Internat. Libr. of Poetry, Color of Heart, 2000; inclusion in Greatest Poets and Poems of the 20th Century., 1999, Poetry's Elite: The Best Poets of 2000, 2001, Unican of the year award, Nutley chpt. Unico Nat., 2002. Mem. Soc. Engrs. (contbg.), Platers Assn. (contbg.), Am. Softball Assn. (assoc.), Internat. Soc. Poets. Roman Catholic. Avocations: reading, cooking, music, sports. Home: 45 Edgar Pl Nutley NJ 07110-1747 Office: Standard Abrasives 4201 Guardian St Simi Valley CA 93063-3372 E-mail: patsrr@aol.com., pritacco@standardabrasives.com.

RITCH, HERALD LAVERN, finance company executive; b. Los Angeles, Feb. 13, 1951; s. Herald Lester and Caroline (Lillevold) R.; m. Linda Suzanne Lundberg, June 11, 1972; children: Eleanor Loring, Seth Alden. BA in Econs., Stanford U., 1973; MBA, U. Pa., 1975. Assoc. Dean Witter Reynolds Inc., N.Y.C., 1975-79, v.p., 1979-82, mng. dir., mgr. merger and acquisition dept., 1982-83; v.p. Kidder, Peabody & Co Inc., 1983-86, mng. dir., 1987-88; gen. ptnr. Freeman Spogli & Co., 1988-90; managing dir. Donaldson Lufkin & Jenrette, 1991-94, mng. dir. and dir. mergers and acquisitions, 1994-2000; mng. dir., co-head global mergers and acquisitions Salomon Smith Barney Inc., 2000—. Contbr. articles to profl. jours. Pres. The Greenwich ARC Found., Inc.; elder 1st Presbyn. Ch., Greenwich. Mem. Stanwich Club, Met. Club. Avocations: tennis, skiing, reading. Office: Salomon Smith Barney Inc 25th Fl 388 Greenwich St New York NY 10013 E-mail: herald.ritch@ssmb.com .

RITCH, KATHLEEN, diversified company executive; b. Harbor Beach, Mich., Jan. 23, 1943; d. Eunice (Spry) R. BA, Mich. State U., 1965; student, Katharine Gibbs Sch., 1965-66. Exec. sec., adminstrv. asst. to pres. Katy Industries, Inc., N.Y.C., 1969-70; exec. sec., adminstrv. asst. to chmn. Kobrand Corp., 1970-72; adminstrv. to chmn. and pres. Ogden Corp., 1972-74, asst. sec., adminstr. office svcs., asst. to chmn., 1974-81, corp. sec., adminsr. office svcs., 1981-84, v.p., corp. sec., adminstr. office svcs., 1984-92, v.p. corp. sec., 1992-2000; freelance executive NYC, 2000—. Co-owner Unell Mfg. Co., Port Hope, Mich., 1966-87. Bd. dir. Young Concert Artists, Inc. Mem. Am. Soc. Corp. Secs. Home: 500 E 77th St New York NY 10162-0025

RITCH, ROBERT HARRY, ophthalmologist, educator; b. New Haven, May 14, 1942; s. Edward Lewis and Minerva (Grosberg) R. BA cum laude (hon. scholar), Harvard U., 1965, MA (NSF fellow), 1967; postgrad. (Harvard traveling fellow), Rice U., 1967-68; MD, Albert Einstein Coll. Medicine, 1972. Diplomate Am. Bd. Ophthalmology, Am. Bd. Laser Surgery. Intern St. Vincent's Med. Ctr., N.Y.C., 1972-73; resident in ophthalmology Mt. Sinai Sch. Medicine, 1973-75, chief resident, 1975-76, Heed Ophthalmic Found. fellow, 1976-77, NIH-Nat. Rsch. Svc. fellow, 1976-78, asst. clin. ophthalmologist, 1976-77, instr., 1977-78, asst. prof., 1978-80, assoc. prof., 1980-82; attending ophthalmologist Beth Israel Med. Ctr., 1978—. Cons. ophthalmologist VA Hosp., Bronx, 1978-82, Manhattan Eye, Ear & Throat Hosp., 1989—; dir. glaucoma svc. Elmhurst Hosp., 1978-82, acting dir. dept. ophthalmology, 1979-82, chief glaucoma svc. N.Y. Eye and Ear Infirmary, N.Y.C., 1983—, surgeon dir., 1991—; prof. clin. ophthalmology N.Y. Med. Coll., Valhalla, 1983—; Arthur Bedell Meml. lectr. Wills Eye Hosp., Phila., 1995; John Edwin Brown Meml. lectr. Ohio State U., Columbus, 1996; Schoenburg Meml. lectr. Ill. Eye and Ear Infirmary, Chgo., 1996; Schlaegel lectr. U. Ind., Indpls., 1996; Gerasimos Frenimopoulos Meml. lectr. Duke U., 1997, Joseph M. Bryan Meml. lectr., 1997; Roger P. Mason Meml. lectr. Howard U., 1997; Abraham S. Ticho lectr., Jerusalem, 1998; Anagnostakis-Trantus lectr., Athens, 1998; Sanford Gifford Meml. lectr., Chgo., 1998, Annie Wong lectr. Chinese U., Hong Kong, 1999, Arthur Lim lectr., Hong Kong, 2001, Am. Glaucoma Soc. Subspecialty Day lectr., Am. Acad. Ophthalmology, New Orleans, 2001; cons. Sukhumvit Hosp., Bangkok, Thailand, 1994—; pres. Internat. Eye Cons., Ltd., 1995—, N.Y. Glaucoma Rsch. Inst., 1996; adj. sr. scientist Singapore Eye Rsch. Inst., 1997; mem. adv. bd. Doctor-to-Doctor, Berkeley, Calif., 1995—; sec., treas., chmn. sci. adv. bd. Glaucoma Found., 1984—, med. dir. Children's Right to Sight, prin. investigator Collaborative Initial Glaucoma Treatment Study, 1993—; mem. adv. bd. Sturge-Weber Found., 1996: mem. glaucoma adv. com. Nat. Soc. to Prevent Blindness, 1986—; organizing chmn. Bangkok Ophthal. Cong., 1985-93, Optic Nerve Rescue & Restoration Think Tank, N.Y., 1994-2001, First Internat. Think Tank on Exfoliation Syndrome, New York, 1999, Myanmar Internat. Ophthal. Cong., 1997, 99; internat. sci. com. Internat. Cong. of Ophthalmology, Sydney, Australia, 2002; sci. organizing com. mem. 4th Internat. Glaucoma Cong., Barcelona, Spain, 2003; external assessor U. Malaya, 1988-96; cons. Tun Hussein Onn Nat. Eye Hosp., Kuala Lumpur, Malaysia, 1996—. Author: (with M.B. Shields) The Secondary Glaucomas, 1982; (with M.B. Shields and T. Krupin) the Glaucomas, 1988, 2d edit., 1996, (with R. Caronia) Classic Papers in Glaucoma, 2000; spl. sect. editor Jour. Glaucoma, 1991-98; mem. editl. bd. Sightsaving, 1981-86, Ophthalmic Laser Therapy, 1984-88, Ophthalmic Resident, 1992-95, Ophthalmic Surgery and Lasers, 1995—, Microsurgery, 1994—, Ophthalmology Times, 1996-2001, Jour. Glaucoma, 1998—, Internat. Glaucoma Rev., 1999—; contbg. editor Ophthalmic Practice, 1993—; contbr. to films on laser therapy, over 800 articles and abstracts in field. Bd. dirs. Dooley Found./Intermed. U.S.A., 1991—, UN, Southeastern Nigeria Eye Care Outreach Coll. Med. Scis. U. Calabar, Nigeria, 1996—; vol. Devel. Coun., 1991-93; chmn. bd. dirs. I-Med. Devel Corp., 1991-94; sci. adv. bd. Singapore Eye Rsch. Inst. Recipient Acad. Investigator award NIH, 1978-81, Disting. Svc. award Internat. Ctr. N.Y. 1981, Exec. Dirs. award, 1985, Founders award Nat. Exhibits by Blind Artists, 1985, Gold medal of Merit and Honor Greek Glaucoma Soc., 1998, Ophthalmology Times Achievement in Ophthalmology award, 1998, Louis Rudin award for rsch. in glaucoma, 1999, Jesse H. Neal award for editl. achievement, 2000; spl. honoree Helen Keller Found., 2000, spl. honoree Glaucoma Found, 2000; comdr. Grace Sovereign Order of Orthodox knights Hospitaller of St. John of Jerusalem. Fellow Am. Acad. Ophthalmology (edn. distbn. subcom. 1994-97, book/jour. link subcom. 1994-97, distbn. adv. subcom. 1997-2000, chmn. subcom., 2001—, Honor award, 1985, sr. honor award 1995), Heed Ophthalmic Found. (ophthalmologist of Yr. award 1996), Am. Ophthalmol. Soc., N.Y. Acad. Medicine, Royal Coll. Ophthalmologists (U.K.), ACS, Internat. Coll. Surgeons, Am. Soc. Laser Surg. Medicine (chmn. ophthalmology sect. 1991-92, moderator and program chmn. joint sci. symposium on glaucoma 1991), N.Y. Acad. Medicine (sec. sect. on ophthalmology 1991-92, chmn. 1993-94, Charles May Meml. Lectr. 1991); mem. AMA, AAAS, N.Y. State Med. Soc., N.Y. County Med. soc., Assn. Rsch. in Vision and Ophthalmoogy (program com., glaucoma sect. 1991-93, program chmn. 1993-94), Am. Assn. Ophthalmology, Ophthal. Soc. U.K., Internat. Assn. Ocular surgeons, Internat. Congress Ophthalmology (glaucoma com. 1994—), N.Y. Intra-Ocular Lens Implant Soc., Manhattan Ophthal. Soc., Internat. Soc. Eye Rsch., Soc. Clin. Trials, Pan-Pacific Anterior Segment Soc. (v.p. 1985-88), N.Y. Acad. Sci., Ophthalmic Laser Surg. Soc. (sec.-treas. 1982-98, pres. 1998—), N.Y. Soc. Clin. Ophthalmology (rec. sec. 1988-90, program chmn. 1990-91, pres. 1991-92), N.Y. Glaucoma Rsch. Inst. (pres. 1996—), Am. Soc. Cell Biology, Am. Telemed Assn., Internat. Soc. On-Line Ophthalmologists (mem. orgn. com., chmn. glaucoma sect. 1995—), Internat. Fedn. Cell Biologists, Philippine Soc. Ophthalmology (hon.), Thailand Ophthal. Soc. (hon.), Italian Assn. for Study of Glaucoma (hon.), La.-Miss. Ophthal. and Otolarygol. Soc. (hon.), Can. Implant Soc. (hon), program chmn. East Coast Glaucoma Sumposium, New York, 2000. Home: 455 E 57th St # 14D New York NY 10022-3065 Office: NY Eye and Ear Infirmary 310 E 14th St New York NY 10003-4201 E-mail: ritchmd@earthlink.net.

RITCHEY, KENNETH WILLIAM, administrator; b. Washington, June 7, 1947; s. Conrad Monroe and Katherine Costance (Sheris) R.; m. Nancy Jayne Kirk, Aug. 22, 1970; children: Kirk Damon, Erin Kathryn (dec. Apr. 1988). BS in Edn., Shippensburg U., 1969; MEd in Spl. Edn., U. Va., 1972; MS in Ednl. Adminstrn., U. Dayton, 1980; grad. sr. execs. in state & local govt. program, Harvard U., 1992. Spl. edn. tchr. Shippensburg (Pa.) Area Sch. Dist., 1969-71; head cross country and track coach Shippensburg U., 1970-74; master tchr., coord. work experience program Lincoln Intermediate Unit, New Oxford, Pa., 1971-76; adult edn. tchr. Franklin County Prison, Chambersburg, 1972-76; asst. supt. mgmt. svcs. Montgomery County Bd. Mental Retardation & Devel. Disabilities, Dayton, Ohio, 1977-83, supt. bd., 1983-99; dir. Ohio Dept. Mental Retardation and Devel. Disabilities, Columbus, 1999—; mem. Gov.'s Cabinet. Mem. part-time faculty edn. dept. U. Dayton, 1983-97; mem., vice-chair cmty. and mil. adv. com. ARC, 1986-95, needs and priorities com. Human Svcs. Levy Coun., 1982-84, 87-99; trustee Ohio Polit. Action Com., Brighter Tomorrow Found., 1990-2000, County Corp., 1992-98, Leadership Dayton, 1991. Former editor statewide newsletter for tchrs. and profls. in Work Experience. Vol. mem. cmty. and agys. resources coun. United Way, 1986—98; v.p. HelpLink Bd., pres.; mem. Gov.'s Vision Com., Ill., 1997—2000; bd. dirs. Ohio Pub. Images, Inc., past pres. Mem.: Nat. Assn. State Dirs. Developmental Disabilities Svcs. (mem. nat. policy work group 2002), Supts. Assn. (exec. com.), Ohio Supts. County Bds. Mental Retardation (v.p., pres.), Am. Assn. Mental Retardation, Phi Beta Kappa. Democrat. Methodist. Home: 7660 Turtle Creek Dr Dayton OH 45414-1756 Office: 1810 Sullivant Ave Columbus OH 43222-1055 E-mail: k1ritchey@aol.com.

RITCHEY, PATRICK WILLIAM, lawyer; b. Pitts., July 9, 1949; s. Joseph Frank and Patricia Ann (Giovengo) R. BA, Haverford Coll., 1971; JD, Yale U., 1974. Bar: U.S. Dist. Ct. (we. dist.) Pa. 1974, U.S. Ct. Appeals (3d. cir.) 1976, U.S. Supreme Ct. 1980, U.S. Ct. Appeals (4th cir.) 1981, U.S. Ct. Appeals (6th cir.) 1982, U.S. Dist. Ct. (ea. dist.) Wis. 1987, U.S. Ct. Appeals (7th cir.) 1991, U.S. Ct. Appeals (D.C. cir.) 1993, U.S. Ct. Appeals (8th cir.) 1993. Assoc. Reed Smith Shaw & McClay, Pitts., 1974-82, ptnr., 1982—. Mem. Pitts. Personnel Assn., Pitts., 1982—, U.S. Dist. Ct. Rules Task Force, Pitts., 1988. Bd. dirs. Pitts. Opera. Mem. Fed. Bar Assn. (labor and employment sect.), Allegheny County Bar Assn. (labor law and fed. ct. sects.), Harvard-Yale-Princeton Club, Duquesne Club. Office: Reed Smith LLP James H Reed Bldg 435 6th Ave Ste 2 Pittsburgh PA 15219-1886

RITCHEY, PAUL ANDREW, accountant; b. Zanesville, Ohio, July 24, 1950; s. Leonard E. and Emma Elizabeth (Geolz) R.; m. Molly McGee. Student, Ohio U., 1970; BS, Ohio State U., 1972; postgrad., Leadership Acad., Ohio U., 1988; M in Taxation, Capital U., 1997. CPA, Ohio. Dir. fin. Mt. St. Mary Hosp., Nelsonville, Ohio, 1972-74; acct. Good Samaritan Med. Ctr., Zanesville, 1974-76; staff assoc. Lynch, Tucker & Assocs., CPAs, 1976-80; mng. ptnr. Ritchey and Assocs., CPAs, 1980-90; ptnr. Norman Jones Enlow & Co., CPA's, 1990—. Mem. acct. curriculum com. Muskingum Area Tech. Coll; mem. various coms.; mem. fin. com. Bishop Rosecrans High Sch.; coach Little League Baseball; past pres. St. Nicholas Elem. Sch. Bd.; Eucharistic minister St. Nicholas Ch. Mem. AICPA, Ohio Soc. CPAs, Sml. Bus. Devel. Ctr., Zanesville Area C. of C., Aircraft Owners Pilots Assn., Zanesville Country Club, Rotary, KC. Republican. Avocations: private pilot, traveling, skiing, sailing. E-mail: pritchey@nje.com.

RITCHEY, THOMAS IRVING, non-profit organizations consultant; b. Natrona Heights, Pa., July 5, 1951; s. Lawrence L. Ritchey and Emily Jean (Irving) Ritchey Mosberger; m. Cynthia Lynn Boyd, July 4, 1981; children: David, Sarah. BS, Westminster Coll., New Wilmington, Pa., 1973; MA, Bowling Green State U., 1974; postgrad., Pa. State U. Cert. fund-raising exec. Assoc. dean students Wake Forest U., Winston-Salem, N.C., 1974-76; exec. dir. alumni Westminster Coll., 1976-82; dir. devel. Rhodes Coll., Memphis, 1982-85, Pa. State U., State College, Pa., 1985-89; pres. UPMC Shadyside Hosp. Found., Pitts., 1989-91; v.p. Pitts. Symphony Soc., 1991-93; mng. ptnr. Richland Ptnrs., 1996—; sr. exec. dir. devel. U. Pitts., 2001—. Trustee Saltworks Theatre Co., Pitts., 1993-99; vice chair Family Guidance, Inc., Pitts., 1993-99; pres., bd. dirs. Pine-Richland Baseball Assn.; trustee Pine-Richland Youth Ctr., 1999-2002; bd. dirs. AF Bd., Westminster Coll. With USNR, 1970-73. Named Outstanding Young Men Am.; Fed. Policy Seminar grantee, 1983; Paul Harris fellow. Faculty mem. Templeton Inst.; mem. Rich-Mar Rotary (bd. dirs.), Duquesne Club, Kappa Mu Epsilon, Omicron Delta Kappa. Republican. Presbyterian. Avocations: reading, volunteer services, basketball official, hunting. Home: 5129 Karrington Dr Gibsonia PA 15044-6007 Office: 249 Benedum Hall Pittsburgh PA 15261 Fax: (724) 449-9666.

RITCHIE, ALEXANDER BUCHAN, lawyer; b. Detroit, Apr. 19, 1923; s. Alexander Stevenson and Margaret (May) R.; m. Sheila Spellacy, June 1998; 1 child, Barbara Ritchie Drolshagen. BA, Wayne State U., 1947, JD, 1949. Bar: Mich. 1949. Pvt. practice, Detroit, 1949-52, 84—; asst. gen. counsel, asst. v.p. Maccabees Mutual Life Ins. Co., 1952-65, v.p., sec., gen. counsel Southfield, Mich., 1977-84; sec., house counsel Wayne Nat. Life Ins. Co., Detroit, 1966-67; ptnr. Fenton, Nederlander, Dodge & Ritchie, 1967-77. Spl. asst. atty. gen. State Mich., 1974-77. Bd. mem. Detroit Bd. Edn., 1971-77, Detroit Ctrl. Bd. Edn., 1971-73; bd. Police Commrs., Detroit, 1974-77; bd. dirs. Doctor's Hosp., Detroit, 1974-89. With U.S. Army, 1943-46. Recipient Key to the City of Detroit, Mayor Coleman Young, 1977. Mem. Mich. State Bar Assn. Avocations: reading, golf, theatre, gourmet. Home: 29255 Laurel Woods Dr Apt 201 Southfield MI 48034-4647

RITCHIE, ANNE, educational administrator; b. Grants Pass, Oreg., July 1, 1944; d. William Riley Jr. and Allie Brown (Clark) R.; m. Charles James Cooper, Sept. 4, 1968 (div. 1985); children: Holly Anne, Wendy Nicole. BA in Edn. with honors, Calif. State U., Sacramento, 1981. Cert. elem. tchr., Calif. CEO El Rancho Schs., Inc., Carmichael, Calif., 1981—. Citizen amb. del. People to People Internat., Russia, Lithuania, Hungary, 1993, China, 1994. Active Crocker Art Mus.; mem. Rep. Senatorial Inner Circle, Washington, 1999. Mem. AAUW, Nat. Assn. Edn. for Young Children, Profl. Assn. Childhood Educators, Nat. Child Care Assn. Episcopalian. Avocations: traveling, skiing, reading.

RITCHIE, DANIEL LEE, academic administrator; b. Springfield, Ill., Sept. 19, 1931; s. Daniel Felix and Jessie Dee (Binney) R. BA, Harvard U., 1954, MBA, 1956. Exec. v.p. MCA, Inc., Los Angeles, 1967-70; pres. Archon Pure Products Co., 1970-73; exec. v.p. Westinghouse Electric Corp., Pitts., 1975-78; pres. corp. staff and strategic planning Westinghouse Broadcasting Co., 1978-79, pres., chief exec. officer, 1979-81, chmn., chief exec. officer, Westinghouse Broadcasting & Cable, Inc., 1981-87; owner Rancho Cielo, Montecito, Calif., 1977—; chancellor U. Denver, 1989—. With U.S. Army, 1956-58. Office: U Denver Office of Chancellor University Park Denver CO 80208-0001 E-mail: dritchie@du.edu.*

RITCHIE, ELISAVIETTA, poet, educator; b. Kansas City, Mo., June 29; d. George Leonidovich and Jessie Downing Artamonoff; m. Clyde Henri Farnsworth; children: Lyelle Kirk, Elspeth Cameron, Alexander George. Diploma Mention Tres Bien, Sorbonne, U. Paris; BA in French, Russian and English, U. Calif., Berkeley; postgrad., Cornell U., Georgetown U.; MA in

French Lit., Am. U.; student, The Writer's Ctr. Writer, poet, editor, transl., small press pub., pub. rels. profl., tchr. creative writing; pres., now v.p. for fiction Washington Writers' Pub. House. Part-time lectr., then grad. tchg. fellow Am. U., 1968—76. Author: In Haste I Write You This Note: Stories and Half-Stories, 2000 (Washington Writer's Pub. House premiere fiction competition, 2000), (poetry) The Arc of the Storm, 1998, Elegy for the Other Woman: New and Selected Poems, 1996, (novella in verse) Wild Garlic: The Journal of Maria X., 1995, (poetry) A Wound-Up Cat and Other Bedtime Stories, 1993, Flying Time: Stories and Half-Stories, 1982, 1986 (includes 4 PEN Syndicated Fiction winners), (poetry) The Problem with Eden, 1985 (Poetry Soc. of Ga. competition winner, 1985), Raking the Snow, 1982 (Washington Writer's Pub. House competition winner, 1981), Moving to Larger Quarters, 1977, A Sheath of Dreams and Other Games, 1976, Tightening the Circle Over Eel Country, 1974 (Gt. Lakes Colls. Assn.'s New Writer's Prize for Best First Book of Poetry, 1975), (novella in verse) Timbot, 1970; creator, editor: anthologies The Dolphin's Arc: Endangered Creatures of the Sea, 1986, creator, editor: anthologies Finding the Name, 1983; contbr. Vol. various pro bono activities. Recipient ann. Poetry Soc. of Am. awards, 1973, 1975; fellow several fellowships, Va. Ctr. for Creative Arts, 1980; grantee 4 grants, D.C. Commn. for Arts, 1970. Mem.: Writer's Ctr. (instr.). Avocations: tennis, sailing, wildlife conservation. Home: 3207 Macomb St NW Washington DC 20008-3327

RITCHIE, FRAN A. interior designer; b. Seminole, Tex., Nov. 23, 1940; d. Homer C. and Margret A. (Simmons) Kyle; m. Byron D. Ritchie, Dec. 23, 1959. Grad. Seminole High School; interior design student LaSalle Extension U., Chgo., 1967. Designer and sales staff Miller-Waldrop Furniture, Hobbs, N.Mex., 1967— , mgr., buyer, 1976— ; buyer, part-owner Eileen's Bed, Bath, and Kitchen, Hobbs, 1976—; co-owner Chapperal Racing Farm, 1985; leader seminars and high school programs on design. Recipient Woman of Yr. award Am. Bus. Women's Assn., 1970. Mem. Am. Soc. Interior Design (assoc.), Am. Bus. Women's Assn., Hobbs C. of C. (bd. dirs. 1983-86—, pres.1987-88, chairperson southeastern chambers legis. tour), Beta Sigma Phi. Home: 620 E Luna Dr Hobbs NM 88240-4016 Office: 100 W Bender Blvd Hobbs NM 88240-2232

RITCHIE, GARRY HARLAN, television broadcast executive; b. Earling, W.Va., Aug. 18, 1938; s. Edgar Harlan and Elsie Pearl (Meador) R.; m. Nancy Lee Gladwell, June 14, 1958; children: Arthur Harlan, Michael Lee. Student, U. Charleston, 1956-60; student, Baldwin-Wallace Coll., 1965; BA, Thomas Edison State Coll., 1979. Engr., reporter Sta. WTIP Radio, Charleston, W.Va., 1956—60; sta. mgr. Sta. WRON Radio, Ronceverte, 1960—63; reporter, newscaster Stas. WDOK AM & FM Radio, Cleve., 1963—65, Sta. WHK AM & FM Radio, Cleve., 1965—67; reporter, assignment editor Scripps-Howard Broadcasting Co., Sta. WEWS-TV, 1967—69, from news dir. to sta. mgr., 1969—82; cable news mgr. corp. office Scripps-Howard Broadcasting Co., Westport, Conn., 1982—83; asst. gen. mgr. Scripps-Howard Broadcasting Co., Sta. WCPO-TV, Cin., 1983—84; v.p., gen. mgr. Diversified Communications, Sta. WCJB-TV, Gainesville, Fla., 1984—86, Diversified Communications, Sta. WYOU-TV, Scranton, Pa., 1986—91; pres. broadcast divsn. Diversified Communications, Portland, Maine, 1991—93; v.p., gen. mgr. Gateway Comms., Inc., Sta. WOWK-TV, Huntington, W.Va., 1993—96, v.p. community affairs, 1996—99; pres. Mus. Radio and Tech., 2000—02. Bd. dirs. Hippodrome Theatre, Gainesville, 1985-86, Vol. Ctr. Alachua County, Gainesville, 1985-86, Crimetrac Gainesville, Fla., 1985-86, Police Adv. Commn., Gainesville, 1985-86, Barnett Bank Alachua County, Gainesville, 1986, Scranton chpt. ARC, 1988-91, Better Bus. Bur. N.E. Pa., Scranton, 1988-91, United Way Lackawanna County, Scranton, 1989-91, Cabell Huntington (W.Va.) Hosp. Found., 1995—; bd. dirs., v.p. Girls Club Alachua County, Gainesville, 1985-86; mem. adv. bd. Scranton Area Found., 1989-91; trustee Keystone Jr. Coll. Laplume, Pa., 1991-92; trustee Huntington Mus. of Art, 1996-99, v.p., 1998-99, gen. chmn. ann. fund campaign, 1998; trustee Tri-State Amateur Radio Assn., Huntington, 1998—, v.p., 1999-2000, pres., 2000-02. Recipient 5 Emmy awards Cleve. chpt. NATAS, 1973-80, Mel Burka Outstanding Broadcaster of W.Va. award, W.Va. Assn. Broadcasters, 1999. Mem. Nat. Assn. Broadcasters, Nat. Assn. TV Programming Execs., W.Va. Broadcasters Assn. (bd. dirs. 1995-99), Pa. Assn. Broadcasters (bd. dirs. 1989-91), Greater Scranton C. of C. (bd. dirs. 1987-90), Downtown Scranton Bus. Ass. (bd. dirs. 1989-91), Rotary (Scranton, bd. dirs. 1989-91), Rotary (Huntington, Wva.), Huntington Area C. of C. (bd. dirs. 1995-99, vice-chmn. 1996-98). Republican. Methodist. Avocations: ham radio, astronomy, computers, reading. Home and Office: 19 Pinecrest Dr Huntington WV 25705-3439 E-mail: W8oi@aol.com.

RITCHIE, J. MURDOCH, pharmacologist, educator; b. Aberdeen, Scotland, June 10, 1925; came to U.S., 1956; s. Alexander Farquharson and Agnes Jane (Bremner) R.; m. Brenda Rachel Bigland; children: Alasdair J., A. Jocelyn. BSc, Aberdeen (Scotland) U., 1944, U. Coll. London, 1949, PhD, 1952, DSc, 1960; MA, Yale U., 1968; DSc, Aberdeen U., 1987. Lectr. physiology U. Coll. London, 1949-51; sci. staff Nat. Inst. Med. Rsch., London, 1951-55; asst. prof. to prof. Albert Einstein Coll. Medicine, N.Y.C., 1954-63, prof. pharmacology, 1963-68; prof. and chmn. pharmacology Yale U., New Haven, 1968-74, dir. biol. scis., 1975-78, prof. pharmacology, 1968—. Contbr. articles to profl. jours.; editor sci. books and jours. Fellow Royal Soc., Univ. Coll. London, Inst. Physics London. Home: 47 Deepwood Dr Hamden CT 06517-3414 Office: Yale Univ Sch Medicine 333 Cedar St New Haven CT 06510-3206 E-mail: murdoch.ritchie@yale.edu.

RITCHIE, ROBERT OLIVER, materials science educator; b. Plymouth, Devon, U.K., Jan. 2, 1948; came to U.S., 1974; s. Kenneth Ian and Kathleen Joyce (Sims) R.; m. Connie Olesen (div. 1978); 1 child, James Oliver; m. HaiYing Song, 1991. BA with honors, U. Cambridge, Eng., 1969, MA, PhD, 1973, ScD, 1990. Cert. engr., U.K. Goldsmith's rsch. fellow Churchill Coll. U. Cambridge, 1972-74; Miller fellow in basic rsch. sci. U. Calif., Berkeley, 1974-76; assoc. prof. mech. engring. MIT, Cambridge, 1977-81; prof. U. Calif., Berkeley, 1981—; dep. dir. Materials Scis. Divsn. Lawrence Berkeley Nat. Lab., Cambridge, 1990-94, dir. Ctr. for Advanced Materials, 1987-95, head Structural Materials Dept., Materials Scis. Divsn., 1995—. Cons. Alcan, Allison, Applied Materials, Boeing, Chevron, Exxon, GE, GM, Grumman, Guidant, Instron, Northrop, Rockwell, Westinghouse, Baxter, Carbomedics, Med. Inc., Shiley, St. Jude Med.; Van Horn Disting. lectr. Case Western U., 1997. Editor 12 books; contbr. more than 400 articles to profl. jours. Recipient Curtis W. McGraw Rsch. award Am. Soc. Engring. Educators, 1987, Rosenhain medal Inst. Materials London, 1992, G.R. Irwin medal ASTM, 1985, Mathewson gold medal TMS-AME, 1985, Van Horn Disting. Lectr. award Case Western Res. U., 1997; named one of Top 100 Scientists, Sci. Digest mag., 1984. Fellow: Royal Acad. Engring. London, Internat. Congress on Fracture (pres. 1997—2001), Inst. Materials (London), Am. Soc. Metals Internat.; mem.: NAE, ASME, Minerals, Materials and Metals Soc. (Mathewson Gold medal 1985, Disting. Structural Materials Scientist/Engr. award 1996), Materials Rsch. Soc., Am. Soc. Materials. Avocations: skiing, antiques, orchids, tennis. Home: 590 Grizzly Peak Blvd Berkeley CA 94708-1238 Office: U Calif Dept Materials Sci and Engring Berkeley CA 94720-1760 E-mail: RORitchie@LBL.gov.

RITCHIE, STEVEN JOHN, foundation administrator, fundraising consultant; b. Salem, Oreg., Aug. 23, 1951; s. John Allen and Hilda Rose (Speasl) R.; m. Susan Katherine Murray, Nov. 17, 1979; children: Shea, Emma, Steven. BS, Western Oreg. State U., 1974. Dir. Lents Edn. Ctr., Portland, Oreg., 1978-83; devel. dir. Portland Art Mus., 1983-86; exec. dir. Benedictine Found. of Oreg., Mt. Angel, 1986—. Co-owner Inquiry Consulting, Silverton, Oreg., 1993—. Editor (jour.) Developments, 1993-95. Mem. budget com. Silverton Elem. Sch. Dist., 1993—. Recipient Willamette Valley Devel. Officers Leadership award, Portland, 1994, Outstanding Capital Campaign award Willamette Valley Devel. Officers Assn., 1997, Coach of Yr. award Boys Cross Country Tri-River Conf., 1998. Mem. Lions Club (pres. 1990-91), C. of C. (bd. mem. 1988-91). Democrat. Roman Catholic.

RITCHIE, WALLACE PARKS, JR. surgeon, educator; b. St. Paul, Nov. 4, 1935; s. Wallace Parks and Alice Ransome (Otis) R.; m. Barbara Carey Jewell, Aug. 10, 1960; children: Stephanie, David, Jessica. BA, Yale U., 1957; MD, Johns Hopkins U., 1961; PhD, U. Minn., 1971. Diplomate Am. Bd. Surgery. Intern, resident in surgery Yale U., New Haven, 1961-63; resident in surgery U. Minn. Hosps., Mpls., 1963-69, instr. in surgery, 1969-70; from asst. prof. to prof. surgery U. Va. Sch. Medicine, Charlottesville, 1973-83; prof., chmn. dept. surgery Temple U. Sch. Medicine, Phila., 1983-93; exec. dir. Am. Bd. Surgery, 1994—2002. Editor textbook: Essentials of Surgery, 1994; contbr. over 160 sci. articles to profl. jours. Lt. col. Med. Corps U.S. Army, 1970-73. USPHS grantee, 1974-85. Office: Am Bd Surgery Inc 1617 John F Kennedy Blvd Philadelphia PA 19103-1821

RITCHIN, BARBARA SUE, educational administrator, consultant; b. N.Y.C., Mar. 7, 1940; d. Harry and Miriam Rosalyn (Schoenberg) R. BS in Spl. Edn., SUNY, Buffalo, 1961; MS in Ednl. Guidance, CCNY, 1969; diploma in ednl. supervision-adminstrn., Fordham U., 1982, PhD in Urban Edn., 1990; postgrad., Harvard U., 1991, 96. Cert. tchr., spl. edn. tchr., counselor, adminstr., N.Y. Tchr. spl. edn. East Elem. Sch., Long Beach, N.Y., 1962-68; asst. prof. N.Y.C. Community Coll., Bklyn., 1970-76; ednl. cons. N.Y.C., 1976-92; dir. bus. programs N.Y.C. Tech. Coll., Bklyn., 1981-87; exec. dir. continuing edn. programs Queens Coll. CUNY, Flushing, N.Y., 1988—. Bd. dirs. Foresight Sch., S.I., N.Y., 1986-92; cons. N.Y. Telephone Co., N.Y.C., 1988-92; chair subcom. on community outreach Queens Coll. Presdl. Com. on Multiculturalism. Co-author: Teachers Learn Metrics, 1981. Pres. bd. dirs. Greenwich Village Orch., 1991; mem. admissions and rules mem. 401 E. 74 Corp., N.Y.C., 1990-92, sec. bd. dirs., 1997—. Named Disting. Woman of Yr. Queens Women's Ctr., 1989. Mem. Continuing Edn. Assn. N.Y. (pres. 1995-96, regional chair 1990-91, membership chair 1988-90), UN Assn. N.Y. (bd. dirs.), Assn. Continuing Higher Edn. (sec.-treas. 1991-92), Phi Delta Kappa, Kappa Delta Pi. Avocations: collecting Depression glass, British detective novels, needlepoint, quilting. Office: Queens Coll CUNY 65-30 Kissena Blvd Flushing NY 11367-1575

RITCHINGS, FRANCES ANNE, priest; b. Balt., June 26, 1946; d. Edward Peyton and Frances Evangeline (Beegle) R. BA in Edn., English, Salisbury (Md.) State U., 1968; MA in English, U. Va., 1970; MS in Libr. Sci., Cath. U., Washington, 1975; MDiv, Episc. Div. Sch., Cambridge, Mass., 1987. Ordained priest, 1988. Instr. Germanna C.C., Locust Grove, Va., 1970-74; ref. libr. Libr. of Congress, Washington, 1975-79, supervisory libr., congl. rsch., 1979-84; assoc. rector St. Stephen's Ch., Providence, 1987-89, St. Thomas Ch., Ft. Washington, Pa., 1989-93; founding pastor Ch. of the Holy Spirit, Harleysville, 1993—2001; CEO, Bear Resources, LLC , 2002—. Chair, Liturgical Commission of Diocese of Penn., 1998-2001. Painter icon, 1994—; contbr. poems to Windchimes, 2000. Recipient Salmon Wheaton prize Episc. Div. Sch., 1987; DuPont fellow, 1970, S.S.U. Achievement Key, 1967, 68. Mem. Soc. of St. Margaret (assoc.), Fellowship of St. John the Evangelist (assoc.), Network of Bibl. Storytellers, Assn. of Anglican Musicians, Associated Parishes, Ecclesiol. Soc., Assn. of Diocesean Liturgy and Music Commns., Beta Phi Mu, Phi Alpha Theta, Alpha Psi Omega. Office: Church of the Holy Spirit PO Box 575 Harleysville PA 19438-0575

RITER, BRUCE DOUGLAS, lawyer; b. Harvey, Ill., Dec. 20, 1949; s. Russell and Kathryn Nina (Boller) R.; m. Gudrun Weinheimer, May 12, 1978; children: Christina Marianna, Andreas Karl. BEE, So. Ill. U., 1972; JD, Northwestern U., 1975. Bar: U.S. Patent and Trademark Office 1974, Md. 1975, U.S. Ct. Appeals (D.C. cir.) 1977, Va. 1979, U.S. Supreme Ct. 1980, Calif. 1987. Assoc. Beall & Jeffery, Bethesda, Md., 1975-78, Schwartz, Jeffery, Schwaab, Mack, Blumenthal & Koch, P.C., Alexandria, Va., 1979, ptnr., 1980; patent counsel Schlumberger Drilling and Prodn. Services N.Am., Sugarland, Tex., 1980-82, Schlumberger Wireline Atlantic, Clamart, France, 1982-85, Schlumberger Computer Aided Systems, Sunnyvale, Calif., 1985-88; of counsel Ware & Freidenrich, P.C., Palo Alto, 1988; pvt. practice Los Altos, 1988—. Stipendary, patent, copyright and competition law Max Planck Inst., Munich, 1978. Grantee, Max. Planck Inst. Mem. ABA (patent, trademark and copyright com.), IEEE, Am. Intellectual Property Law Assn. Clubs: Commonwealth (San Francisco). Avocations: skiing, aviation, languages. Office: 101 1st St PMB 208 Los Altos CA 94022-2750 E-mail: briter@mindspring.com.

RITHER, ALAN CRAIG, lawyer; b. Mpls., May 14, 1947; s. Clifford Lawrence and Martha (Kirstine) R.; m. Kathy Lorene Richardson, Sept. 12, 1969; children: David, Sara. BA in Polit. Sci., U. Wash., 1969, JD, 1972. Bar: Wash. 1973, U.S. Dist. Ct. (ea. dist.) Wash. 1976. Sr. atty. Battelle, Pacific N.W. divsn., Richland, Wash., 1973—. Chmn. Export Control Coord. Orgn., 1994-95. V.p. Radiant Light Broadcasting, Richland, 1989—. Major, USAFR. Fellow Nat. Contract Mgmt. Assn. (cert.); mem. Wash. State Bar Assn. (chmn. internat. practice sect. 1995-96). Mem. Assemblies of God. Avocations: bowhunting, astronomy, camping. Office: Battelle Pacific Northwest Divsn 902 Battelle Blvd Richland WA 99352-1793

RITT, ROGER MERRILL, lawyer; b. N.Y.C., Mar. 26, 1950; m. Mimi Santini, Aug. 25, 1974; children: Evan Samuel, David Martin. BA, U. Pa., 1972; JD, Boston U., 1975, LLM, 1976. Bar: Mass. 1977, Pa. 1975, U.S. Tax Ct. Sr. ptnr. Hale and Dorr, Boston, 1984—. Adj. prof. grad. tax program Boston U., 1979-92; panelist Am. Law Inst., Mass. Continuing Legal Edn., World Trade Inst., NYU Inst. on Fed. Taxation; mem. exec. com. Fed. Tax Inst. New Eng. Treas. Found. for Tax Edn. Mem. ABA (tax sect.), Boston Bar Assn. Office: Hale and Dorr 60 State St Boston MA 02109-1816

RITTENHOUSE, ELLEN CARYLL, social worker; b. Everest, Kans., Oct. 30, 1941; d. Elmer Andrew and H. Inez (Limbo) Knudson; m. Donald Wade, July 23, 1970; children: Karen J., Kristi J., Kalli J. AA, Highland (Kans.) Jr. Coll., 1961; BS, Dana Coll., Blair, Nebr., 1963; MS in Social Work, U. Mo., 1965. Cert. social worker; lic. social worker, Minn. Social worker Kans. Neurol. Inst., Topeka, 1965-66, Topeka State Hosp. O.P.C., 1966-69, Ft. Logan Mental Health Ctr., Denver, 1969-70, Arapahoe Mental Health Ctr., Aurora, 1970-71; exec. dir. Jackson-Grand Mental Health Ctr., Granby, 1971-72; social worker Lakeland Mental Health Ctr., Fergus Falls, Minn., 1978-81, Moorhead, 1982-91; social worker Hope Unit St. Francis Med. Ctr. and Nursing Home, Breckenridge, 1991—; owner Rittenhouse Industries, Kent, 1996—. Mem. adj. faculty U. N.D. Med. Sch., Fargo, 1988—93. Great Books leader Breckenridge (Minn.) Elem. Sch., 1982, 1983; mem. adv. com. Gull Harbor Group Home, Moorhead, 1989—91. Fellow NASW. Home: PO Box 7 Kent MN 56553-0007 Office: St Francis Med Ctr And Nursing Home Breckenridge MN 56520

RITTER, ALEXANDER, ballet dancer; b. Ottawa, Can. Studied, Nat. Ballet Sch., Can. Dancer Nat. Ballet Can., Am. Ballet Theatre; mem. corps de ballet N.Y.C. Ballet, 1992—95, soloist, 1995—. Dancer (ballets) Agon, Haieff Divertimento, The Nutcracker, La Sonnambula, Symphony in Three Movements, La Valse, The Cage, The Concert, Dances at a Gathering, Fanfare, The Goldberg Variations, Interplay, 2 & 3 Part Inventions, Jazz, The Sleeping Beauty, Symphonic Dances, prin. roles Pastoral Dances, Martin's Mozart Piano Concerto, Dvorak Bagatelles, Huoah, Viola Alone, Episodes & Sarcasms. Office: NYC Ballet NY State Theatre 20 Lincoln Plz New York NY 10023-6913*

RITTER, ALFRED FRANCIS, JR. retired communications executive; b. Norfolk, Va., Dec. 31, 1946; s. Alfred Francis Ritter and Lucile Grey Woodward; m. Caroline Buchanan O'Keefe, Aug. 10, 1968; children: Alfred F. III, Caroline O'Donnell. BA, Coll. of William and Mary, 1968. CPA Va. Staff acct. Goodman & Co. CPAs, Norfolk, Va., 1971-76; corp. contr. Landmark Comm., 1976-78, v.p., contr., 1978, v.p. fin., 1978, TeleCable Corp., Norfolk, 1983-89, exec. v.p., 1989-96, Landmark Comm., Inc., Norfolk, 1996—2001; ret., 2001. Trustee Norfolk Acad., 1991—, pres. bd. trustees, 1998—. Lt. USN, 1968—71. Mem.: Bayville Golf Club (pres. 1995—98). Episcopalian.

RITTER, ANN L. lawyer; b. N.Y.C., May 20, 1933; d. Joseph and Grace (Goodman) R. BA, Hunter Coll., 1954; JD, N.Y. Law Sch., 1970; postgrad. Law Sch., NYU, 1971-72. Bar: N.Y. 1971, U.S. Ct. Appeals (2d cir.) 1975, U.S. Supreme Ct. 1975. Writer, 1954-70; editor, 1955-66; tchr., 1966-70; atty. Am. Soc. Composers, Authors and Pubs., N.Y.C., 1971-72, Greater N.Y. Ins. Co., N.Y.C., 1973-74; sr. ptnr. Brenhouse & Ritter, 1974-78; sole practice, 1978—. Editor N.Y. Immigration News, 1975-76. Mem. ABA, Am. Immigration Lawyers Assn. (treas. 1983-84, sec. 1984-85, vice-chair 1985-86, chair 1986-87, chair program com. 1989-90, chair spkrs. bur. 1989-90, chair media liaison 1989-90), N.Y. State Bar Assn., N.Y. County Lawyers Assn., Assn. Trial Lawyers Am., N.Y. State Trial Lawyers Assn., N.Y.C. Bar Assn., Watergate East Assn. (v.p., asst. treas. 1990—). Democrat. Jewish. Home: 47 E 87th St New York NY 10128-1005 Office: 420 Madison Ave Rm 1200 New York NY 10017-1171

RITTER, DALE WILLIAM, obstetrician, gynecologist; b. Jersey Shore, Pa., June 17, 1919; s. Lyman W. and Weltha B. (Packard) Ritter; m. Winnie Mae Bryant, Nov. 13, 1976; children: Eric, Lyman, Michael, Gwendolyn, Daniel. AB, UCLA, 1942; MD, U. So. Calif., 1946. Diplomate Am. Bd. Obstetrics and Gynecology. Intern Los Angeles County Hosp., L.A., 1945-46, resident, 1948-52, admitting room resident, 1948-52; pvt. practice Chico, Calif., 1952-98; founder, mem. staff, past chmn. bd. dirs. Chico Cmty. Meml. Hosp. Guest lectr. Chico State Coll., 1956—; mem. staff Enole Hosp., Chico, 1952—, Glenn Gen. Hosp., Willows, Calif., 1953-98, Gridley Meml. Hosp., Calif., 1953-80; spl. cons. obs. Calif. Dept. Pub. Health, No. Calif., 1958-70. Contbr. articles to med. and archeol. jours. Bd. dirs. No. dist. Children's Home Soc., Chico, 1954-70. Served with AUS, 1943-45, M.C., AUS, 1946-48. Recipient Pro-Life award Calif. KC; Paul Harris fellow Rotary Internat., 1989. Fellow ACS, Am. Coll. Ob-Gyn; mem. AMA, AAAS, Calif. Med. Assn., Internat. Soc. Hypnosis, Am. Soc. Clin. Hypnosis, Am. Fertility Soc., Pacific Coast Fertility Soc., Assn. Am. Physicians and Surgeons, Pvt. Drs. of Am., Butte-Glenn County Med. Soc. (past pres.), Am. Cancer Soc. (former bd. dirs. Butte County), Christian Med. Soc., Am. Assn. Pro-life Obstetricians and Gynecologists, Butte-Glenn County Tumor Bd., Anthrop. Assn. Am., Archaeol. Inst. Am., Soc. Calif. Archaeology, Oreg. Archaeology Soc., Archeol. Survey Assn., Southwestern Anthrop. Soc., Am. Rock Art Rsch. Assn. (Pioneer award), Calif. Hist. Soc., Calif. Oreg. Trails Assn., Australian Rock Art Rsch. Assn., Internat. Assn. for Study of Prehistoric and Ethnologic Religions, Fretted Instrument Guild Am. (dir. Banjo Kats 'n Jammers), North Valley Banjo Band, Am. Philatelic Soc., Am. Horse Coun., Peruvian Paso Horse Registry of N.Am., Assn. Owners Breeders Peruvian Paso Horses, Gideon Soc., Am. Legion, Phi Chi, Lambda Sigma, Zeta Beta Sigma, Rotary (Paul Harris fellow). Republican. Home: PMB 156 975 East Ave Chico CA 95926-1308

RITTER, DANIEL BENJAMIN, lawyer; b. Wilmington, Del., Apr. 6, 1937; s. David Moore and Bernice Elizabeth (Carlson) R.; m. Shirley F. Sether, Jan. 29, 1971 (dec. Jan. 1998); 1 child, Roxane Elise. AB with honors, U. Chgo., 1957; LLB, U. Wash., 1963. Bar: Wash. 1963, U.S. Dist. Ct. (we. dist.) Wash. 1963, U.S. Tax Ct. 1965, U.S. Ct. Appeals (9th cir.) 1963. Assoc. Davis, Wright Tremaine (formerly Davis, Wright and Jones), 1963-69, ptnr., 1969—. Lectr. Bar Rev. Assocs. Wash., Seattle, 1964-86; chmn. internat. dept. Davis, Wright and Jones, Seattle, 1984-85, chmn. banking dept., 1986-89. Casenote editor U. Wash. Law Rev., 1962-63; contbg. author: Washington Commercial Law Desk Book, 1982, rev. edit., 1987, Washington Community Property Desk Book, 1977. Trustee Cathedral Assoc., Seattle, 1980-86; legal counsel Wash. State Reps., Bellevue, 1983-92; bd. dirs. U. Chgo. Club Puget Sound, Seattle, 1982—, pres., 1984-86; bd. dirs. Am. Lung Assn. Wash., Seattle, 1983-92; mem. vis. com. U. Wash. Law Sch., 1984-88; trustee U. Wash. Law Sch. Found., 1989-92; chmn. alumni rels. coun. U. Chgo., 1986-88; mem. statute law com. State of Wash., 1978-87; bd. dirs. Seattle Camerata, 1991-93; bd. dirs. Early Music Guild, Seattle, 1993-96. Mem. ABA (bus. law sect.), Wash. State Bar Assn. (chmn. bus. law sect. 1988-89, uniform comml. code com. 1980—, chmn. 1980-86, chmn. internat. law com. 1979-81, judicial recommendations com. 1991-93), Seattle-King County Bar Assn. (chmn. internat. and comparative law sect. 1980-82), Rainier Club, Order of Coif. Republican. Lutheran. Avocation: reading, theater, early music. Home: 907 Warren Ave N Apt 202 Seattle WA 98109-5635 Office: Davis Wright Tremaine 2600 Century Sq 1501 4th Ave Seattle WA 98101-1688

RITTER, ELISE DAWN, therapist, clinical social worker, writer; b. Balt., Aug. 14, 1952; d. Nelson Fred and Marjorie Jean (Corke) Ritter; m. Philip Anthony Gibson, Apr. 7, 1979 (div. Feb. 1990); 1 child, Christopher Ritter Gibson; m. Victor Wayne Clough, Jr., Mar. 3, 1990; stepchildren: Wesley T., Lindsay, Sharon. Student, Austro-Am. Inst., Vienna, Austria, 1973; BS, U. Kans., 1974; M Psychiatric Social Work, Va. Commonwealth U., 1998. LCSW. Rschr. impeachment inquiry staff U.S. Ho. of Reps., Washington, 1974; rschr. APA, 1975; editor prodn. The New Republic Mag., 1976-77; copy editor Time-Life Books, Alexandria, Va., 1977-79, assoc. editor, 1979-83, adminstrv. editor, 1983-87, asst. dir. editl. resources, 1988-90; dir. editl. resources Time Warner, Time-Life Books, 1990-94; pvt. practice therapist, 2000—. With Arlingtonians Ministering to Emergency Needs-AMEN, 1995; vol. Mental Health Program, Visiting Nurse Assn., 1996, Women's Ctr., Vienna, Va., 1997-99, PsychologyNetwork.com, 2000—, DiscoveryHealth-.com, 2002-.

RITTER, GUY FRANKLIN, structural engineer; b. Detroit, Feb. 9, 1933; s. Guy Franklin and Ethel (Reed) R.; m. Peggy Anne Maloy, Sept. 20, 1954; children: Constance Elaine, Margaret Anne, Sallie Reed. BS in Architecture, Ga. Inst. Tech., 1954, B Arch. Engring., 1955; MS in Bldg. Engring., MIT, 1956. Registered profl. engr., Ga., Fla., S.C., N.C., Ala., Tenn. Structural detailer I.E. Morris Assocs., Atlanta, 1955-56; structural engr. Morris, Boehmig & Tindel, 1956-58; dist. structural engr. Portland Cement Assn., 1958-61; sr. structural engr. Lindsey Tucker Ritter, Albany, Ga., 1961-74; v.p. Lindsey & Ritter, Inc., 1974-79; pres., CEO Lindsey & Ritter, 1979-98; cons., chief structural engr. Lindsey & Ritter, Inc., 1998-2000; structural cons. engr. G.F. Ritter P.E., Clayton, Ga., 2000—. Mem. Ga. Bd. Registration for Engrs. and Land Surveyors, 2000—. Mem. Ga. Industrialized Bldgs. adv. com., 1990-95; dir. Structural Engrs. Risk Mgmt. Coun., 1989-92. Recipient Value Engr. award GSA, 1974. Mem. ASCE, NSPE, Coalition of Am. Structural Engrs. (nat. vice chmn. 1995-96), Am. Cons. Engrs. Coun., Am. Concrete Inst. (Spl. Structure award-bridge 1994), Prestressed Concrete Inst., Rotary (local pres. 1983-84, Paul Harris fellow 1997). Republican. Presbyterian. Avocations: gardening, reading, bridge. Office: GF Ritter PE 108 Post Oak St Clayton GA 30525-5638 E-mail: gfritter@alltel.net.

RITTER, JACK CHARLES, mathematician, computer graphics designer; b. Hokkaido, Sopporo, Japan, Apr. 4, 1948; arrived in U.S., 1949; s. James William Ritter and Maureen Ruth Gutenkunst; m. Barrie Jane Jacobs, Sept. 5, 1973. Student, Princeton U., 1966—68; BA in Philosophy, U. Wis., 1970, MS in Computer Sci., 1973. Software engr. Nat. Cash Register, San Diego, 1974—79; video game designer Atari Games, Sunnyvale, 1981—83; 2D graphics engr. Versatec-Xerox, Santa Clara, 1984—88; 3D programmer-artist Sho Graphics, Mountain View, 1989—93; 3D hardware mktg. nVidia, Sunnyvale, 1995—96; PC video game programmer Accolade Games, San Jose, 1997—2000. Ecstacy graphics game engine designer Accolade, San Jose, 1998; lead designer stereoscopic video game sys. Cinematronics Corp., 1980. Author: Graphics Gems, Vol. 1 & 2, 1990, (software image synthesizer) Rat Racer, 1985. Mem. Homicide Rsch. Working Group, Chgo., 2000—; vol. City of Racchi, Sacred Valley, Peru, 2000—01. Mem.: Computer Game Developers, The Manly Club. Achievements include design of prototype for computer controlled electronic dog trainer. Avocations: skydiving, website development, artificial intelligence, writing. E-mail: jack@you2peru.com.

RITTER, JEFF, business administration educator; b. Bronx, N.Y., July 24, 1961; s. Michael and Harriet Ritter. BBA, Baruch Coll., 1984; MBA, L.I. Univ., 1992; postgrad., Nova Southeastern U., 1998—. With Strategic Consultings, Inc., Palm Beach, Fla., 1998-2000; adj. prof. bus. U. Phoenix, Ft. Lauderdale, 1998—. Home and Office: 398 E Coral Trace Cir Delray Beach FL 33445 E-mail: jri6581102@cs.com.

RITTER, JEFFREY BLAKE, lawyer, consultant; b. Iowa City, Sept. 13, 1954; s. Charles Clifford and Patricia Ann (Wise) R.; children: Jordan, Chelsea. BA, MA, Ohio State U., 1976; JD, Duke U., 1979. Bar: Ky. 1979, D.C. 1980, Ohio 1983. Assoc. Barnett & Alagia, Louisville, 1979-82, Schwartz, Kelm, Warren & Rubenstein, Columbus, Ohio, 1982-90; of counsel Vorys, Sater, Seymour & Pease, 1991-94; U.S. legal adviser for facilitation UN Working Party, Geneva, 1990-96; dir. ECLIPS, Columbus, 1994-98, Document Authentication Sys., Inc., Balt., 1998-99; counsel Kirkpatrick & Lockhart, Washington, 1999-2000, ptnr., 2000—. Chair Adv. Group on Internat. Trade, Columbus, 1990. Mem. ABA (chair sect. of bus. law com. on cyberspace law, 1995-98, reporter, subcom. on scope of uniform comml. code 1990-91). Democrat. Avocations: cycling, jazz, poetry. Office: 1800 Massachusetts Ave NW Washington DC 20036-1806 E-mail: jritter@kl.com-office.

RITTER, MADELIENE, practical nurse, surgical technologist; b. Camden, N.J., Feb. 11, 1954; m. James W. Ritter; children: Sebastián O'Neill, Sergio O'Neill. Degree in practical nursing, Ocean County Vocat. Tech. Sch., 1975. Cert. surgical technologist; lic. practical nurse. Staff nurse Cmty. Meml. Hosp., Toms River, NJ, 1975—77, staff nurse/pacu, 1979—85; office nurse Stafford Orthopedics, Manahawkin, 1985—98; oper. rm. nurse Cmty. Med. Ctr., Toms River, 1998—2000, So. Ocean County Hosp., Manahawkin, 1999—, 1999—. Mem. Am. Cancer Soc. Relay for Life, Manahawkin, NJ, 2001, co-captain, NJ. Leader Ocean County Girl Scouts, Toms River, NJ, 1982—98; lifetime mem. Girl Scouts of Am.; mem. Barnegat First Aid Squad, Barnegat, NJ; co-leader internat. travel Switzerland/Mex. troops Ocean County Girl Scout Coun., Toms River. Mem.: Assn. Surg. Technologists, Nat. Assn. Practical Nurse Edn. and Svc.*

RITTER, MARY CATHERINE, research scientist; b. Mpls., May 10, 1943; d. George Michael and Lorraine Marie (Schwappach) R. BS, Coll. St. Francis, Joliet, Ill., 1965; MS, U. Minn., 1969, PhD, 1971. Postdoctoral rsch. fellow U. Chgo., 1971-75, rsch. assoc., 1975-77, rsch. assoc., instr., 1977-79, rsch. assoc., asst. prof., 1980; instr. endocrinology Rush-Presbyn.-St. Luke's Med. Ctr., Chgo., 1985—95. Home: 1700 E 56th St Apt 3007 Chicago IL 60637-5095 Office: Rush Presbyn-St Lukes Md Ct Sect Digestive Diseases 1653 W Congress Pkwy Chicago IL 60612-3833

RITTER, MARY L. interior decorator; b. Glencoe, Ill. children: Caroline Victoria, Mark Henry. BA, Stanford U.; postgrad., N.Y. Sch. Interior Design. Cert. interior designer. Interior decorator, N.Y.C., 1951-56; model, 1951-56; editl. scout numerous shelter mags. & advt. agys., 1951-56, San Francisco, 1956-63; interior decorator, 1956—; model home decorator Joseph Eichler Corp., 1958. Cons. Earl W. Smith Devel. Corp., 1958-60, Draper Shopping Ctrs., Inc., 1959-61; adj. prof. interior design adult edn. divsn. Redwood City (Calif.) Dept. Recreation 1968, West Valley C.C., 1976-78, Can. Coll., 1977—; rep. sculptor Richard Lippold, 1983—, Peter Lobollo, 1985—; decor designer San Francisco City Hall, Opus I, Symphony Ball, 1984. Contbr. articles to profl. mags. Bd. dirs. Children's Home Soc. Calif., 1966, sec. bd. dirs., 1968; chmn. internat. social svcs. spl. event WAIF, 1976, v.p. spl. events, 1969; chmn. benefit March of Dimes, 1979; bd. dirs. San Francisco Host. Com., 1979, host com. mem., 1984, chmn. dinner honoring mayor and consuls gen., 1979; mem. mayor's sister city del. to Abidjan, Cote d'Ivoire, 1997, to Paris, 1996; mem. Child Abuse Prevention Soc. Recipient Cert. Merit World Disting. Svc. Field Interior Design, London, 1968, Gold medal Pro-Am Ski Races, Sun Valley, Idaho, 1971; named as model room designer Children's Home Soc. Decorator Showhouse, 1968, San Mateo County Jr. Mus. Aux. Decorator Showcase, 1972. Mem. Stanford U. Alumni Assn., Calif. Palace Legion of Honor, San Francisco Mus. Art, Am. Soc. Interior Designers (bd. dirs. 1983-84), Patrons of Art of Vatican Mus., Friends Les Vieilles Maisons Francaises. Home and Office: 349 Selby Ln Atherton CA 94027-3932

RITTER, ROBERT FORCIER, lawyer; b. St. Louis, Apr. 7, 1943; s. Tom Marshall and Jane Elizabeth (Forcier) R.; m. Karen Gray, Dec. 28, 1966; children: Allison Gray Campione, Laura Thompson Capstick, Elisabeth Forcier Schoenecker. BA, U. Kans., 1965; JD, St. Louis U., 1968. Bar: Mo. 1968, U.S. Dist. Ct. (ea. and we. dists.) Mo. 1968. U.S. Ct. Mil. Appeals 1972, U.S. Supreme Ct. 1972, U.S. Ct. Appeals (8th cir.) 1980, U.S. Dist. Ct. (so. dist.) Ill. 1982. Assoc. Gray & Sommers, St. Louis, 1968-71; ptnr. Gray Ritter & Graham, P.C., 1974—; chmn., pres. Gray & Ritter, 1983—. Bd. dirs. Marine Bank and Trust Co.; adv. com. 22d cir. Supreme Ct., 1985-92; mem. Supreme Ct. com. civil jury instrns., 1988—, U.S. Dist. Ct. adv. com., 1993-95; lectr. Contbr. articles to profl. jours. Bd. dirs. Cystic Fibrosis Found., Gateway chpt., pres., 1991. Capt. USAR, 1968-74. Recipient Law Week award Bur. Nat. Affairs, 1968, award of merit Nat. Conf. Met. Cts., 1995. Fellow Internat. Soc. Barristers (bd. govs. 1994—), Am. Coll. Trial Lawyers, Internat. Acad. Trial Lawyers; mem. ABA, Am. Judicature Soc., Assn. Trial Lawyers Am., Am. Bd. Trial Advocates (advocate), Bar Assn. Met. St. Louis (chmn. trial sect. 1978-79, exec. com. 1980-82, award merit 1976, award achievement 1982, chmn. bench bar conf. 1983), Mo. Bar Assn. (coun. practice and procedure com. 1972—, coun. tort law com. 1982—, bd. govs. 1984-91, fin. com. 1984-91), Mo. Bar Found. (outstanding trial lawyer award 1978), Lawyers Assn. St. Louis (exec. com. 1976-81, pres. 1977-78), Mo. Assn. Trial Attys. (bd. govs. 1984—), Noonday Club, Bellerive Country Club, John's Island Club (bd. dirs. 1998—), Racquet Club (bd. govs. 1988-93, pres. 1991-92), Red Stick Golf Club (founding mem.), Roaring Fork Club (founding mem.), Windsor Club. Presbyterian. Office: Gray Ritter & Graham PC 701 Market St Fl 8 Saint Louis MO 63101-1850 E-mail: ritter@grgpc.com.

RITTER, ROBERT THORNTON, lawyer; b. N.Y.C., Nov. 4, 1956; s. Robert J. and Barbara W. (Foust) R.; m. Rebecca L. Grubbs, July 25, 1981; children: Sarah, Luke, Robert R. BA, Duke U., 1979; JD, Washington U., 1984. Bar: Mo., 1984, U.S. Dist. Ct. (ea. dist.) Mo., 1985. Assoc. William Brown, Atty. at Law, Bridgeton, Mo., 1984-85, Kopsky & Vouga, Chesterfield, 1986; pvt. practice Clayton, 1987-89; ptnr. Ritter & Gusdorf, 1990-96; mem. Ritter & Gusdorf L.C., 1997—2002; ptnr. Belze Jones, P.C., 2002—. Treas. Campaign Election of State Rep. Steve Moore, 1988; coach Little League Baseball; head coach Christian H.S. Baseball. Mem.: St. Louis Assn. Christian Attys., Bar Assn. Met. St. Louis, Mo. Bar Assn. Republican. Avocation: tennis. Office: Belze Jones PC 7777 Bonhomme Ste 1710 Clayton MO 63105

RITTER, SANDRA HELEN, psychology educator; b. Kingston, Pa., Dec. 31, 1947; d. Earl Jean and Lois Mae (Hartley) R.; stepfather Harry R. Smith; m. Billy Lee Ferguson, May 23, 1995; children: Christopher Andrew Hawkins, Alexander Cameron Hawkins (dec.); stepchildren: William Lee Ferguson, Ann Ferguson Bishop. BSME, Villanova U., 1969; MBA, Ctrl. Mich. U., 1981; MEd in Counseling, U. N.C., Greensboro, 1994, PhD in Counseling, 2000. Nat. cert. counselor; lic. profl. counselor, N.C. Engr. Automation Industries, Silver Spring, Md., 1974-83; sr. engr. Naval Sea Sys. Command, Alexandria, Va., 1983-85; ptnr. Clemmons (N.C.) Primary Care, 1987-91; owner, proprietor Serendipity Resource Ctr., Clemmons, 1985-91; mental health asst. Charter Hosp., Greensboro, N.C., 1992-94; pvt. practice, 1994—2001; asst. prof. dept. psychology, counseling and edn. Troy State Univ. , Troy, Ala., 2001—. Co-author: Assessment in Counseling and Therapy, 1995; sr. author: Leadership Development on a Shoestring, 1995; mem. editl. bd. Jour. Addictions and Offenders Counselors, 1995-97. Vol. hospice, Winston-Salem, N.C., 1990-92; vol. counselor The Listening Post, Greensboro, 1993-94; vol. Southeastern Regional Vision for Edn., 1999—; mem. worship com. Unitarian Universalist Fellowship, Greensboro, 1993-95, svc. leader coord., 1994-95. Mem. ACA (mem. adv. coun. 1996-98), Assn. for Adult Devel. and Aging (Midlife chair 1996-97), Internat. Assn. Addictions and Offenders Counselors (chair addictions com. 1993-96, mem. accreditation com. 1995-96, pres. 1997-99), Am. Mental Health Counselors Assn., Assn. for Counseling Edn. and Supervision (Outstanding Doctoral Student 1995), C.G. Jung Soc., N.C. Assn. for Adult Devel. and Aging (pres. 1995-96), N.C. Assn. for Specialists in Group Work (pres. 1996-97), N.C. Counseling Assn. (co-chair spl. task force 1995-96, treas. 1995-96, exec. coun. 1994—, chair strategic planning com. 1996-97, pres.-elect 1997-98, pres. 1998-99), Chi Sigma Iota (fellow, mem. Upsilon Nu Chi chpt., treas. 1993-94, awards chair 1993-96, pres.-elect 1994-95, pres. 1995-96, Internat. Outstanding Master's Student 1994). Avocations: reading, volunteer work, duplicate bridge, travel, breeding Persian cats. Office: Troy St Univ Psychology Dept McCartha Hall Troy AL 36082

RITTER, THOMAS NEAL, clinical neuropsychologist; b. Newport, Ark., Sept. 23, 1948; s. Thomas Albert and Sammy Elizabeth (Bowie) R.; m. Ana Maria Trevino. BA, Hendrix Coll., 1970; MA, U. Ark., 1974, PhD, 1978. Lic. psychologist Ark. Pres. Profl. Studies Inst., Phoenix, 1979-83; clin. dir. Cmty. Counseling Svc., Hot Springs, Ark., 1983-88, New Medico Rehab. Ctr., Folsom, La., 1988-90; dir. Pain & Rehab. Ctr., Chalmette, 1990-91; dir. psychol. svc. Northwest Ark. Rehab. Hosp., Fayetteville, 1991-92; pvt. practice clin. neuropsychology Springdale, Ark., 1992—; owner AutoQual USA N.C., 2000—. Owner The Entrepreneur's Source, 1999—. Mem. APA. Office: 2116 Township Fayetteville AR 72703

RITTER, TIMOTHY MACTARY, physics educator; b. Morristown, N.J., Nov. 3, 1964; s. Paul Revere and Dorothy L. (Fuss) R.; 1 child, Blayne Z.; m. Marie A. Amero, Mar. 9, 2000. BS, SUNY, Buffalo, 1989, MA, 1996, PhD, 1997. Rsch. asst. SUNY, Buffalo, 1989-96, lectr., 1993-94; assoc. prof. U. N.C., Pembroke, 1996—. Faculty fellow NASA, Huntsville, Ala., 1997-99. Lt USNR, 1998—. Mem. Am. Phys. Soc., N.C. Sci. Tchrs. Assn., Am. Assn. Physics Tchrs., N.c. Acad. Sci., Res. Officers Assn.

RITTER, WILLIAM FREDERICK, civil and agricultural engineering educator; b. Stratford, Ont., Can., Mar. 25, 1942; came to U.S., 1966. s. John Louis and Norma Willehmine (Foerster) R.; m. Carol-Anne Gertrude Turner, June 25, 1966; children: John WIlliam, Amy Lynn. BSA, U. Guelph, Ont., 1965; BAS, U. Toronto, 1966; MS, Iowa State U., 1968, PhD, 1971. Rsch. assoc. Iowa State U., Ames, 1966-71; asst. prof. U. Del., Newark, 1971-77, assoc. prof., 1977-82, prof., 1982—, dept. chair, 1992—; owner Ritter Engring., Elkton, Md., 1984—. Sr. engr. Environ. Cons. Internat., Rehoboth Beach, Del., 1991-94. Editor: Irrigation and Drainage Conf. Procs., 1991; contbr. more than 230 articles to profl. jours. and tech. reports. Pres. Newark Day Nursery, 1984-86. Recipient Superior Achievement award U.S. EPA, Phila., 1979; Salzberg fellow U. Del., 1987. Fellow Am. Soc. Agrl. Engrs. (Young Engr. of Yr. 1981, Country Side Engring. award 1988); mem. ASCE (Outstanding Svc. award 1993), Am. Water Works Engrs. Assn., Water Environment Fedn. Lutheran. Home: 63 Papermill Rd Elkton MD 21921-3518 Office: U Del Newark DE 19717

RITTERBUSCH, DALE E. English educator; b. Waukesha, Wis., Jan. 12, 1946; s. Karl Walter Ritterbusch and Dorothy Ethel (Schultz) Holmes; m. Patricia Ellen Oppitz, Nov. 28, 1981; 1 child, Kerry. AB in Ethno-poetics, U. Pa., 1972, AM in Am. Civilization, 1975; MFA in Creative Writing, Bowling Green State U., 1985. Tchg. asst. U. Pa., Phila., 1973-74; vis. lectr. C.C. of Phila., 1975-79; tchg. fellow Bowling Green State U., 1983-85; lectr. I U. Wis.-Whitewater, 1985-88, lectr. II, 1988-93, asst. prof., 1993-96, assoc. prof. English, 1997—, chair h.s. creative writing festival, 1989—. Author: Lessons Learned, 1995 (Posner award 1996); poetry pub. various anthologies and mags. including Carrying the Darkness, From Both Sides Now, Viet Nam War GEneration Jour., Aethlon, The Vietnam War in American Stories, Songs, and Poems, Wis. Rev., Wis. Acad. Rev., Am. Poetry Mo., Rattle, War, Literature and the Arts, Vietnam War Generation Journal, Line Drives: 100 Contemporary Baseball Poems. 1st lt. U.S. Army, 1966-69. Wis. Arts Bd. fellow, 1997. Mem. Wis. Fellowship of Poets, Coun. for Wis. Writers, Popular Culture Assn., Sport Lit. Assn., Blue Key. Avocation: wilderness canoeing. Office: Univ of Wisconsin 800 W Main St Whitewater WI 53190-1705

RITTERHOFF, C(HARLES) WILLIAM, retired steel company executive; b. Balt., Nov. 1, 1921; s. Ernest F. and Anna M. (Luerssen) R.; m. Margery A. McKenney, June 24, 1944 (dec. May 1987); children: Leslie, William, James; m. Marita C. Halsey, Feb. 20. 1988. BS in Mech. Engring, Mass. Inst. Tech., 1947; grad., Advanced Mgmt. Program, Harvard, 1973. Asst. engr. mech. dept., then various supervisory positions Bethlehem Steel Co., Sparrows Point, Md., 1948-57; asst. supt. Sparrows Point plate mills, 1957-60, asst. chief engr. plant engring. dept., 1960-63; asst. chief engr. Burns Harbor project, 1963, asst. gen. mgr., 1963-67; gen. mgr. Burns Harbor plant, 1967-70; v.p. manufactured products and West Coast steel plants, 1970-71, v.p. steel operations-prodn., 1971-74, dir., 1974-82, exec. v.p., 1974-77, vice chmn., 1977-80, exec. v.p. steel ops., 1980-82. Served to 1st lt. U.S. Army, 1943-46. Mem. NAM (past bd. dirs.), Am. Iron and Steel Inst., Assn. Iron and Steel Engrs., Hwy. Users Fedn. (past bd. dirs.), Moorings Club, Bridgehampton Club (N.Y.). Home: 150 Anchor Dr Vero Beach FL 32963-2957

RITTERSKAMP, DOUGLAS DOLVIN, lawyer; b. St. Louis, July 7, 1948; s. James Johnstone Jr. and Linn M. (Dolvin) R.; m. Linda S. Vansant, Mar. 23, 1974; 1 child, Tammy. AB, Washington U., 1970, JD, 1973; LLM in Taxation, NYU, 1978. Bar: N.Y. 1974, Mo. 1979. Assoc. Patterson, Belknap, Webb & Tyler, N.Y.C., 1974-78; jr. ptnr. Bryan Cave LLP (and predecessors), St. Louis, 1978-82; ptnr. Bryan Cave LLP, 1983—. Trustee Scottish Rite Clinic for Childhood Lang. Disorders of St. Louis, Inc., 1987-97, St. Louis Mission and Ch. Ext. Soc., United Meth. Ch., 1987-97, Mo. United Meth. Found., 1994—, pres., 2000—; trustee The Coll. Sch., 1995-2001. Capt. USAR, 1970-79, active duty tng., 1973. Mem. ABA (employee benefits com. sect. taxation 1987-91, 96—), Bar Assn. Met. St. Louis (steering com. employee benefits 1989—), Masons (32d degree, knight comdr. ct. of honor), Shriners. Methodist. Home: 5223 Sutherland Ave Saint Louis MO 63109-2338

RITTLE, VALERIE ANN, pharmacist; b. Lebanon, Pa., July 21, 1959; d. James Lynn and Elizabeth Ann (Schaeffer) R. BS in Pharmacy, Phila. Coll. Pharmacy/Sci., 1982. Registered pharmacist, Pa. Staff pharmacist Good Samaritan Hosp., Lebanon, Pa., 1982-84, Harrisburg (Pa.) Hosp., 1984-95, VA Med. Ctr., Lebanon, 1995-96, Hanover (Pa.) Gen. Hosp., 1996-97, Pinnacle Health Systems, Harrisburg, 1997-2000, lead pharmacist, 2000—. Mem. therapeutic drug utilization rev. com. Pharm. Assistance and Care for Elderly Program for Pa., Harrisburg, 1990-95. Mem. staff parish rels. com. Zion United Meth. Ch., Myerstown, Pa., 1996-99. Mem. Am. Soc. Hosp. Pharmacists, Am. Pharm. Assn., Pa. Soc. of Hosp. Pharmacists. Republican. Methodist. Avocations: ice hockey fan, music, photography. Office: Pinnacle Health System Hosp 111 S Front St Harrisburg PA 17101-2099 E-mail: v.rittle@pinnaclehealth.org.

RITTMAYER, MARK CALVIN, global systems consultant; b. Camden, N.J., June 2, 1958; s. Calvin Carl and Jane (Foehl) R.; m. Anne-Dorothee Muller, Mar. 28, 1986; children: Julian, Joana, Jonathan. BS in Acctg. and Fin., Lehigh U., 1980. CPA,Calif.; CISA, CIA, SAP cons. Mgr. Coopers & Lybrand LLP, L.A., 1988-91; pres. Imago Interactive, Napa, Calif., 1991-94; sr. program mgr., prin. cons. Price Waterhouse LLC, Phila., 1995-98; dir. wireless web solutions WaveBend LLC, San Francisco, 1998—. Mem. CMP Adv. Bd., San Francisco. Mem. Calif. Soc. CPA's, Bay Club San Francisco. Avocations: squash, investing. Home: 107 Farmington Rd Cherry Hill NJ 08034-3310 Office: 4745 Dejertuista Las Vegas NV 89121 E-mail: mrittmayer@aol.com., mark@squashplus.com.

RITTMER, ELAINE HENEKE, library media specialist; b. Maquoketa, Iowa, Feb. 4, 1931; d. Herman John and Clara (Luett) Heneke; m. Sheldon Lowell Rittmer, June 11, 1950; children: Kenneth, Lynnette, Robyn (dec.), infant son (dec.). BA, Marycrest Coll., 1973; MS, Western Ill. U., 1980. Permanent teaching cert. K-14, Iowa; cert. libr. media specialist K-14, Iowa. Sch. libr. Calamus-Wheatland (Iowa) Community Schs., 1970-74; high sch. libr. media specialist, libr. coord. Camanche (Iowa) Community Sch., 1974-96; legis. asst. State Capitol, Des Moines, 1997—. Ind. tech. cons., 1988—. Mem. Iowa Edn. Media Assn., Iowa State Edn. Assn., Camanche Edn. Assn., Camanche Cmty. Schs. Tech. Com., Media Tech. Cons. Republican. Avocations: reading, walking, education, political activities, technology developments. Home: 3539 230th St De Witt IA 52742-9208 E-mail: shelaine@netins.net.

RITVO, ELIZABETH ANN, lawyer; b. Washington, July 14, 1951; d. Martin and Zelma Ritvo; m. Robert G. Kunzendorf, June 5, 1971; children: Jennifer, Rebecca. AB, Yale Coll., 1973; JD, U. Va., 1976. Bar: Va. 1976, D.C. 1978, U.S. Dist. Ct. D.C. 1978, Mass. 1980, U.S. Ct. Appeals (D.C. cir.), U.S. Dist. Ct. Mass. 1980, U.S. Ct. Appeals (1st cir.) 1980, U.S. Supreme Ct. 1987. Staff atty. U.S. Dept. Transp., Washington, 1976—77; assoc. Kirlin Campbell & Keating, 1977—79, Brown Rudnick Freed & Gesmer, Boston, 1980—84; ptnr. Brown Rudnick Berlack Israels, 1985—. Mem. Women's Bar Found. (trustee 1994-99, pres. 1998-99). Office: Brown Rudnick Berlack Israels One Financial Ctr Boston MA 02111 E-mail: eritvo@brbilaw.com.

RITVO, ROGER ALAN, vice chancellor, health management-policy educator; b. Cambridge, Mass., Aug. 12, 1944; s. Meyer and Miriam R.S. (Meyers) R.; m. Lynn Lieberman; children: Roberta, Eric. BA, Western Res. U., 1967; MBA, George Washington U., 1970; PhD, Case Western Res. U., 1976. Asst. adminstr. N.Y. Mental Health System, 1968-70; asst. prof., asst. dean Sch. Applied Social Scis. Case Western Res. U., Cleve., 1976-79, assoc. prof., 1981-83; assoc. prof., founding dir. Grad. Program in Health Adminstrn. Cleve. State U., 1983-87; prof. health mgmt. and policy, dean Sch. Health and Human Svcs. U. N.H., Durham, 1987-97; sr. health policy analyst to sec. DHHS, Washington, 1980-81; vice chancellor acad. and student affairs Auburn U. Montgomery, Ala., 1997—. Vis. rsch. scholar WHO, Copenhagen, 1978; vis. prof. Am. U., Washington, 1980-81, U. W.I., 1993; chair Ala. Coun. Chief Acad. Officers, 1998-2000; vis. scholar U. Sheffield, Eng., 1985; cons. to numerous orgns. on profit and non-profit strategic planning. Editor, author 5 books, including Managing in the Age of Change, 1994, Improving Governing Board Effectiveness, 1996, Sisters in Sorrow Voices of Care in the Holocaust, 1998; mem. cmty. editl. bd. Montgomery Advertiser newspaper, 1999; contbr. articles to profl. jours. Trustee Hosp. Sisters of Charity, Cleve., 1980-85, Greater Seacoast United Way, 1991-93; chmn. health care adv. com. Ohio Senate, 1983-85; bd. mem. Fairmount Temple, Beachwood, Ohio, 1980-85; trustee Leadership Seacoast, 1991-93, bd. dirs., 1992-95; bd. dirs. N.H. chpt. United Way, 1992-95, Higher Edn. Leadership Partnership, 1998-2000. Recipient Outstanding Adminstr. award, 1982, Cert. of Merit U. N.H. Pres.'s Commn. on Women, 1994; Govt. fellow Am. Coun. Edn., 1980-81. Mem. Nat. Tng. Labs. Inst. (bd. dirs. 1981-85, 92-96), Cert. Cons. Internat., Jewish Philatelic, Hist. Soc. N.Y.C. Avocations: collecting flat irons and masks, philatelist, white water rafting. Office: Auburn U Montgomery 7300 University Dr Montgomery AL 36117-3596

RITVO, SAMUEL, psychoanalyst, researcher, educator; b. New Haven, Nov. 4, 1917; s. Jacob Ritvo and Fannie Mellman; m. Lucille Bernstein, Sept. 7, 1941; children: Jonathan I., David Z., Rachel Z. AB, Harvard U., 1938; MD, Yale U., 1942. Diplomate Am. Bd. Psychiatry & Neurology, Am. Bd. Child Psychiatry. Intern in pediats. U. Minn. Hosps., 1942-43; resident in pediats. Babies Hosp., Columbia-Presbyn. Med. Ctr., 1943-44; resident N.Y. State Psychiat. Inst., 1944-47; clin. prof. psychiatry Yale Child Study Ctr., New Haven, 1963—. Freud Meml. lectr. N.Y. Psychoanalytic Soc., 1981, Psychoanalytic Assn. N.Y., 1985, Yale U., 1994. Mem. Am. Psychoanalytic Assn. (pres. 1968-69), Internat. Psychoanalytic Assn. (v.p. 1969-71), Assn. Child Psychoanalysis (pre. 1978-80). Democrat. Jewish. Home: 1221 Racebrook Rd Woodbridge CT 06525-1822 Office: Yale Child Study Ctr 230 S Frontage Rd New Haven CT 06519-1124 E-mail: samuel.ritvo@yale.edu.

RITZ, ESTHER LEAH, civic worker, volunteer, investor; b. Buhl, Minn., May 16, 1918; d. Matthew Abram and Jeanette Florence (Lewis) Medalie; m. Maurice Ritz, Apr. 8, 1945 (dec. 1977); children— David Lewis, Peter Bruce BA summa cum laude, U. Minn, 1940, postgrad., 1940-41, Duke U., 1941-42. Adminstrv. analyst, economist Office of Price Adminstrn., N.Y., Washington and Chgo., 1942-46. Pres., Nat. Jewish Welfare Bd., 1982-86; v.p. Council of Jewish Fedns., 1981-84; pres. World Conf. Jewish Community Ctrs., 1981-86; bd. dirs. Am. Jewish Joint Distbn. Com., 1977-93, bd. dirs. (hon. life mem.) Joint Distbn. Com., 1994; trustee United Jewish Appeal, 1982-87; vice-chmn. bd. dirs. Jerusalem Ctr. Pub. Affairs, 1984—; bd. dirs. Wurzweiler Sch. Social Work Yeshiva U., 1984-89, HIAS, 1983-86; mem. Jewish Agy., bd. govs., 1988-92; bd. dirs. Legal Aid Soc., Milw. County, 1983-85; mem. Community Issues Forum, Milw.; vice chmn. bd. United Way Greater Milw., 1977-81; pres. Florence G. Heller Jewish Welfare Bd. Research Ctr., 1979-83; pres. Mental Health Planning Council of Milw. County, 1976-79; vice chmn large city budgeting conf. Coun. of Jewish Fedns., 1976-82; pres. Jewish Community Ctr. Milw., 1966-71; pres. Milw. Jewish Fedn., 1978-81; bd. dirs. Shalom Hartman Inst., Jerusalem, 1989—; bd. dirs.; mem. exec. com., policy com. Nat. Jewish Dem. Coun., 1991—, vice-chmn. bd. dirs., 1994-96; bd. dirs. Nat. Jewish Ctr. for Learning and Leadership, 1988-92, Ams. Peace Now, 1989—, vice-chmn. bd. dirs., 1995-96, Coun. Initiatives Jewish Edn., 1990-99, Friends of Labor Israel (steering com. 1988-94, chair 1988-90); bd. vis. Ctr. for Jewish Studies U. Wis., Madison, 1994—; bd. dirs. Inst. Wis. Future, 1996—. Named to Women's Hall of Fame YWCA, 1979, Mentor of Yr., Tempo, 2002; recipient Cmty. Svc. award Wis. Region NCCJ, 1977, William C. Frye award Milw. Found., 1984, Telesis award Alverno Coll., Milw., 1984, Hannah G. Solomon award. Nat. Coun. Jewish Women, ProUrbe award Mt. Mary Coll., Evan P. Helfer award Milw. chpt. Nat. Soc. of Fund Raising Execs., 1994, Margaret Miller award Planned Parenthood of Wis., 1994, Cmty. Builders award JCC Assoc., 1996, Isaiah award Americans for Peace Now, 1997; Comty. Activist award, U.S. Postal Svc., 2001, Mentor of Yr. award Milw. chpt. Tempo, 2002. Mem. LWV, NAACP, NOW, Hadassah, Na'amat, Common Cause, Nat. Women's Polit. Caucus, Nat. Coun. Jewish Women, Planned Parenthood. Democrat. Avocations: music, bridge, art collecting. Home: 626 E Kilbourn Ave Milwaukee WI 53202-3241

RITZ, GERRY, member of parliament; Mem. House of Commons, Ottawa, Canada. Can. Alliance Caucus. Office: House of Commons Ottawa ON K1A 0A6 Canada Address: 1322-100th St North Battleford SK S9A 0V8 Canada Office Fax: 613-996-8472., 306-445-0207. E-mail: ritz.g@parl.gc.ca., ritz@canadianalliance.ca.

RITZ, JOHN MICHAEL, education educator; b. Latrobe, Pa., Oct. 31, 1948; s. John Edward and Catharine May (Mills) R.; m. Sally Louise Ward, July 18, 1970; 1 child, Molly. BS, Purdue U., 1970; MS, U. Wis., Stout, 1974; EdD, W.Va. U., 1977. Tech. tchr. Nova High Sch., Ft. Lauderdale, Fla., 1970-72; faculty asst. U. Wis.-Stout, Menomonie, 1973-74; tng. assoc. W.Va. U., Morgantown, 1974-77; prof., chmn. Old Dominion U., Norfolk, Va., 1977—. Bd. dirs. Tidewater Tech. Assocs., Virginia Beach, Va. Author: Exploring Communication, 1996, 4th edit., 2002, Exploring Production Systems, 1990. With U.S. Army, 1971-73, Fed. Republic of Germany. Recipient Tonelson award Old Dominion U., 1982. Mem. Internat. Tech. Edn. Assn. (bd. dirs. 2000—, Disting. Tech. Educator 1986, Meritorious Svc. award 1990, Acad. Fellows award, 1997), Coun. on Tech. Tchr. Edn. (treas. 1981-85, pres. 1996-2000, Tech. Tchr. Educator of Yr. 1993), Va. Tech. Edn. Assn. (pres. 1983), Acad. of Scholars, Tech. Found. Am. (Honor Roll 2000). Avocations: salt water fishing, writing. Office: Old Dominion U 4600 Hampton Blvd Norfolk VA 23529

RITZ, STEPHEN MARK, financial advisor, lawyer; b. Midland, Mich., Aug. 23, 1962; s. Alvin H. and Patricia M. (Padway) R. BA, Northwestern U., 1985; JD, Ind. U., 1989. Bar: Ill. 1990, U.S. Dist. Ct. (no. dist.) Ill. 1990, Ind. 1996. Atty. Chapman & Cutler, Chgo., 1990-93; pres., CEO S.M. Ritz and Co., Inc., Indpls., 1994-97; CEO Newport Pension Mgmt. LLC, 1997—. Dir. Indsl. Logistics, Inc., Indpls., 1994-96. Mem. ABA, Inst. CFPs, Registry CFPs, Internat. Assn. Fin. Planners. Office: Newport Pension Mgmt 12360 Pebblepointe Pass Carmel IN 46033-9683

RIVARA, FREDERICK PETER, pediatrician, educator; b. Far Rockaway, N.Y., May 17, 1949; s. Frederick P. and Mary Lillian (Caparelli) R.; m. J'May Bertrand, May 17, 1975; children: Matthew, Maggie. BA, Holy Cross Coll., 1970; MD, U. Pa., 1974; MPH, U. Wash., 1980. Diplomate Am. Bd. Pediatrics. Intern Children's Hosp. and Med. Ctr., Boston, 1974-75, resident, 1975-76, Seattle, 1978-80; RWJ clin. scholar U. Wash., 1978-80, assoc. prof. pediatrics, 1984-89, prof. pediatrics, head divsn. gen. pediatrics, 1990—; mem. staff Nat. Health Svc. Corps, Hazard, Ky., 1976-78; asst. prof. pediatrics U. Tenn., Memphis, 1981-84. Editor Archives of Pedatrics and Adolescent Medicine. Fellow Am. Acad. Pediatrics; mem. Ambulatory Pediatrics Assn., Internat. Assn. Child, Adolescent and Injury Prevention (pres. 1993-2000). Office: Harborview Med Ctr 325 9th Ave PO Box 359960 Seattle WA 98195-9960

RIVAS-VAZQUEZ, ANA VICTORIA, federal official; b. Miami, Fla., Aug. 25, 1963; d. Rafael A. and Ana (Albarran) R. BA in Govt., Georgetown U., 1985, MA in Latin Am. Studies, 1987. Staffer Times of the Americas, Washington, 1987-88; press aide Dukakis-Bentsen Campaign Hdqrs., Boston, 1988; assignment editor Univision, Miami, 1989; news prodr. Sta. WLTV-Channel 23, 1990-92; elections prodr. Univison News, 1992; asst. press sec. White House Press Office, Washington, 1993-96; dep. press sec. Clinton-Gore Campaign Hdqrs., 1996. Avocations: movies, travel. Office: White House Press Office 1600 Pennsylvania Ave NW Washington DC 20500-0004

RIVELLI, WILLIAM RAYMOND ALLAN, photographer; b. Providence, May 10, 1935; s. William and Virginia C. (Capece) R.; m. Margaret A. Cronin, June 2, 1963 (dec. 1973); children: William Dante, Sarah Kerry; m. Cynthia Jean Lepore, Sept. 7, 1974; 1 child, Taylor Elia. BA in Philosophy, Brown U., 1957. Asst. to photographer Nina Leen Life Mag., N.Y.C., 1959-60, asst. to photographer Ralph Steiner, 1960-61; photographer Rivelli Photography, 1959—; instr. Sch. Visual Arts, 1991—. Instr. Cape Cod Photo Workshops, 1999—. Subject/photographer profile and portfolio Communication Arts, 1982; dir. photography, photographer multi-media slide presentation Naked Chambers, 1987; photographer: Christmas in New York, 1997; chosen contbr.: American Photography, 1990, Graphis Photo, 1994, Communication Arts Photography Ann., 1995, 2001, Graphis Fine Art Photography, 1995; artist, photographer exhbn. Cathedral Portfolio, 1988-92; exhibited in groups shows Art Dirs. Club Exhbns., N.Y., N.J., Mass., Can., 1976-99, Advt. Photographers Awards Ann. Exhbn., 1988-91, 95, CUNY, 1995; pvt. collections Citibank, J.P.

Morgan Getty Mus., Internat. Mus. Photography. Recipient Cert. of Excellence award Art Dirs. Club, 1976-82, Creativity Cert. of Excellence award Art. Dir. Mag., 1976-77, 80, Ann. Report Photography award Mead Corp., 1974, Outstanding Achievement award Champion Internat., 1995. Mem. Am. Soc. Media Photographers (nat. bd. dirs. 1987-89, chosen contbr. Kodak Traveling Exhbn. 1986-87, 89), Indsl. Photographers Assn. (bd. dirs. 1979-80). Home and Office: 303 Park Ave S Apt 508 New York NY 10010-3625

RIVENBARK, JAN MEREDITH, management consultant; b. Spartanburg, S.C., Feb. 22, 1950; s. George Meredith and Audrey Isabel (Frady) R.; m. Barbara N. Newton, Sept. 25, 1976; children: Abigail, Justin, Patrick. BS in Math., Duke U., 1972; postgrad., Ga. State U., 1980. Mgmt. trainee Citizens & So. Nat. Bank, Atlanta, 1972, br. mgr., 1974, employee rels. mgr., 1975-77, v.p. compensaton, benefits, payroll and data mgmt., 1977-80; mgr. pers. 1st Tenn. Bank, Memphis, 1980-81; dir. compensation and benefits Hanes group Consol. Foods Corp. (now Sara Lee Corp.), Winston-Salem, N.C., 1981-83, exec. dir. compensation and benefits Chgo., 1983-84; exec. dir. internat. staff Sara Lee Corp., 1985, exec. dir. corp. planning, 1985-87, sr. v.p. PYA/Monarch divsn. Greenville, S.C., 1987-89; pres. JP Foodsvc., Hanover, Md., 1989-92; COO PCA Internat., Inc., Charlotte, N.C., 1992-97; pres., COO Starboard Inc., 1997-2000; pres. Fresher-than-Fresh, Inc., 1998-2000; pres., CEO The Rivenbark Group, 2000—. Mem. Alpha Tau Omega. Republican. Home: 4107 Foxcroft Rd Charlotte NC 28211-3760 Office: 831 E Morehead St Ste 360 Charlotte NC 28202 E-mail: jan@rivenbark.com.

RIVER, GEORGE LAMBERT, hematologist, oncologist; b. Oak Park, Ill., June 5, 1932; s. Louis Philip and Mary Elizabeth (Lambert) R.; m. Renee DeVere Kaplan, Sept. 5, 1953 (div. May 1972); children: Gregory, Geoffrey, Catherine, Linda, Robert (dec.), David; m. Judith Ann Stav, Sept. 30, 1973; 1 child, John Thomas Wendorf. BA, U. Chgo., 1952; MD, Loyola U. Med. Sch., 1956. Intern, resident Cook County Hosp., Chgo., 1956-59, fellow in hematology, 1959-60; capt. USAF, San Antonio, 1960-62; staff Marshfield (Wis.) Clinic, 1962-71; head hematology St. Elizabeth's Hosp., Youngstown, Ohio, 1971-74; internal medicine Dr. William Stone, Atlanta, 1974-76; physician Internal Medicine Assocs., Davenport, Iowa, 1976-92, Dubuque (Iowa) Internal Medicine, 1992-96; dir. Cancer Ctr. Freeman Hosp., Joplin, Mo., 1996—. Dir. cancer ctr. St. Luke's Hosp., Davenport, 1989-92, Finley Hosp., Dubuque, 1992-96. Fellow Am. Coll. Physicians; mem. Am. Soc. Hematology, Am. Soc. Clin. Oncology. Republican. Roman Catholic. Avocations: travel, photography, medical legal testimony. Home: 1527 Point Kirby Ave Las Vegas NV 89123-0313 Office: Freeman Cancer Ctr 3415 McIntosh Cir Joplin MO 64804-3649 Fax: 417-347-4064. E-mail: glrivermd@dnamail.com.

RIVERA, ANGEL LUIS, chemical engineer; b. Bayamon, P.R., Oct. 7, 1950; s. Luis and Felicita (Lopez) R.; m. Marta V. Rivera, Mar. 21, 1975; children: Luis E., Mayra Lynn, Carlos A. BAChemE, U. P.R., Mayaquez, 1974, MS in Nuclear Enginrg., 1976; PhD in Environ. Enginrg., Northwestern U., Evanston, Il., 1981; MBA, U. Tenn., 1986. Devel. engr. Oak Ridge (Tenn.) Nat. Lab., 1980-84, group leader, 1984-86, project mgr., 1986-89, program mgr., 1990—. Contbr. articles to profl. jours. and publs. Mem. Am. Chem. Soc., Am. Inst. Chem. Engrs., Am. Assn. Cost Engrs., Am. Mgmt. Assn., IEEE Computer Soc., Tau Beta Pi. Home: 107 Garnet Ln Oak Ridge TN 37830-5601 Office: Bechtel Jacobs Co E Tenn Tech Pk PO Box 2003 Oak Ridge TN 37831-2003

RIVERA, BEATRIZ, writer, educator; b. Havana, Sept. 27, 1957; came to US, 1960; d. Mario Lorenzo and Aida (Rufin) R.; m. Denis Beneich, Oct., 1986 (div. Sept. 1987); m. Charles S.C. Barnes, June 21, 1988; children: Nigel Barnes, Rebecca Barnes. DEUG, Paris IV Sorbonne, 1975, Lic., 1977, Master, 1979; DEA, Paris III Sorbonne, 1996; PhD, CUNY, 2002. Newspaper corr. The Daily Freeman, Kingston, N.Y.; reporter The Jersey Jour., Jersey City; corr. The Poughkeepsie (N.Y.) Jour. Adj. lectr. Fordham U., N.Y.C., 1997—, Borough Manhattan C.C., N.Y.C., Dutchess County C.C.; tchr. Poughkeepsie Day Sch., 2001—02. Author: African Passions and Other Stories, 1995, Midnight Sandwiches at the Mariposa Express, 1997, Playing with Light, 2000. Home: 105 Upper Whitfield Rd Accord NY 12404-5936

RIVERA, CHITA (CONCHITA DEL RIVERO), actress, singer, dancer; b. Washington, Jan. 23, 1933; d. Pedro Julio Figuerva del Rivero; m. Anthony Mordente. Student, Am. Sch. Ballet, N.Y.C. Broadway debut: Call Me Madam, 1952; appeared on stage in: Guys and Dolls, Can-Can, Seventh Heaven, Mister Wonderful, West Side Story, Father's Day, Bye Bye Birdie, Three Penny Opera, Flower Drum Song, Zorba, Sweet Charity, Born Yesterday, Jacques Brel is Alive and Well and Living in Paris, Sondheim-A Musical Tribute, Kiss Me Kate, Ivanhoe, Chicago, Bring Back Birdie, Merlin, Jerry's Girls, 1985, The Rink, 1984 (Tony award 1984), Can-Can, 1988, Kiss of the Spider Woman (Tony award, Best Actress in a musical), 1993; performs in cabarets and nightclubs around world; starred in: film Sweet Charity, 1969; numerous TV appearances include Kojak and the Marcus Nelson Murders, 1973, The New Dick Van Dyke Show, 1973-74, Kennedy Ctr. Tonight-Broadway to Washington!, Pippin, 1982, The Mayflower Madam, 1987, Sammy Davis Jr.'s 60th Birthday Celebration, 1990, Ira Gershwin at 100: A Celebration at Carnegie Hall, 1997, Venecia, 2001, Anything Goes, 2000, The Visit, 2001. Recipient Best Actress, Outer Critics Circle award, 1993, Drama League award, Spider Woman, 1993, Ellis Island Medal of Honor, 2000, Best Leading Actress in a Musical, Tony award. Mem. AFTRA, SAG, Actors Equity Assn. Office: William Morris Agy c/o Samuel Liff 1325 Ave of the Ams New York NY 10019

RIVERA, GEORGE, field investigator, security consultant; b. N.Y.C., Nov. 29, 1959; s. George Franco Rivera and Sara (Diaz) Perez; m. Linda Marie Donnelly, Apr. 12, 1986. AS, Mt. San Antonio Coll., 1994; BS, U. La Verne, 1996. Cert. in risk mgmt., Calif.; cert. fraud examiner. EMT Arcadia-Monrovia Amb. Svc., Monrovia, Calif., 1979-81; dep. sheriff Los Angeles County Sheriff's Dept., L.A., 1981-94; legal investigator Miramar Rsch. Group, Alta Loma, Calif., 1994—. Cons. Rex Gutierrez for Congress Com., Rancho Cucamonga, Calif., 1995-96; labor rep. Assn. L.A. Dep. Sheriff's, L.A., 1982-94. Mem. Am. Soc. for Indsl. Security, Calif. Assn. Lic. Investigators, Assn. Cert. Fraud Examiners. Republican. Roman Catholic. Avocations: boating, water sports. Office: Kaiser Permanente Investigations Unit 94 S Los Robles Ave Ste 320 Pasadena CA 91101-2433

RIVERA, GERALDO, television personality, journalist; b. N.Y.C., July 4, 1943; s. Cruz Allen and Lillian (Friedman) R.; m. Sheri Rivera (div. 1984); m. C.C. Dyer, 1987 (div. 2002); children: Gabriel, Cruz, Isabella, Simone. BS, U. Ariz., 1965; JD, Bklyn. Law Sch., 1969; postgrad., U. Pa., 1969, Sch. Journalism, Columbia U., 1970. Bar: N.Y. 1970. Mem. anti-poverty neighborhood law firms Harlem Assertion of Rights and Community Action for Legal Svcs., N.Y.C., 1968-70; with Eyewitness News, WABC-TV, 1970-75; reporter Good Morning America program ABC-TV, 1973-76, corr., host Good Night America program, 1975-77, corr., sr. producer 20/20 Newsmag., 1978-85; host syndicated talk show The Geraldo Rivera show, N.Y.C., 1987-98; host investigative show on cable CNBC Rivera Live, 1994—2001; host nightly news show on cable CNBC Upfront Tonight, NJ, 1998—2000; spl. corr. Fox News Channel, 2001—; host weekend show on cable War Zone, At Large with Geraldo Rivera; contbr. Fox newsmag. The Pulse. Author: Willowbrook, 1972, Island of Contrasts, 1974, Miguel, 1972, A Special Kind of Courage, 1976, Exposing Myself, 1991; host numerous syndicated TV spls.; film appearances: The Bonfire of the Vanities, 1990; television movie: Perry Mason: The Case of the Reckless Romeo. Recipient 7 Emmy awards, Peabody award, Kennedy Journalism award, 1973, 75, numerous others; named Broadcaster of Yr. N.Y. State AP, 1971, 72, 74; Smith fellow U. Pa., 1969. Jewish. Office: Fox News Channel 1211 Ave of Ams New York NY 10036

RIVERA, JOSE DE JESUS, lawyer; b. Zacatecas, Mex., 1950; m. Nina Rivera; 5 children. BA, No. Ariz. U.; JD, Ariz. State U. Atty. civil rights divsn. Dept. of Justice, 1976—77; asst. U.S. atty. Dist. Ariz., 1977—81; with Langerman, Begam, Lewis and Marks, 1981—84; ptnr. Rivera, Scales and Kizer, 1984—98; atty. City of El Mirage, U.S. Atty., Dist. of Ariz., 1998—2001; with Haralson, Miller, Pitt & McAnally PLC, Phoenix, 2001—. Vice-chair adv. com. civil rights Atty. Gen. Ariz. dist., 1998-2001, adv. com. native Am. issues, domestic terrorism subcom., 1998-2001, chair subcom. no Mem. com. Los Abogados; bd. dirs. Inst. for Cmty. Initiatives, 1996-98; coach Little League. With N.G. Mem. Ariz. State Bar. (bd. govs. 1995-98, bd. officer, sec. treas. 1996, 2d v.p. 1997-98, exec. dir. search com. 1996-97, chair appointments com. 1997-98), Hispanic Bar Assn., Los Abogados Bar Assn. (bd. dirs. 1981-83). Democrat. Avocation: reading. Office: Haralson Miller Pitt & McAnally PLC 3003 N Central Ave Ste 1400 Phoenix AZ 85012 E-mail: jrivera@hmpmlaw.com.

RIVERA, OSCAR R. lawyer, corporate executive; b. Havana, Cuba, Dec. 8, 1956; s. Alcibiades R. and Marian (Fernandez) R.; children: Peter, Taylor. BBA, U. Miami, 1978; JD, Georgetown U., 1981. Bar: Fla. 1981, U.S. Dist. Ct. (so. dist.) Fla. 1982, U.S. Tax Ct. 1982. Assoc. Corrigan. Zelman & Bander P.A., Miami, Fla., 1981-83; ptnr. Siegfried, Rivera, Lerner De La Torre & Sobel P.A., 1984—. Adj. prof. law U. Miami, 1987—. Asst. mgr. campaign to elect Michael O'Donovan, Miami, 1976; mem. youth adv. bd., Miami, 1975-78, youth planning council Dade County, Miami, 1975-78. Mem. ABA, Cuban Am. Bar Assn., Internat. Coun. Shopping Ctrs. (pres. Fla. polit. action com., v.p. Fla. govtl. affairs com., state dir. Fla.), Little Havana Kiwanis, Orange Key, Omicron Delta Kappa, Phi Kappa Phi. Avocations: photography, skiing.

RIVERA, RHONDA RAE, lawyer, labor artibrator; b. Phila., Mar. 9, 1938; d. Preston Robert and Katherine Lowe (MacSorley) Rieley; 1 child, Robert Preston. BA cum laude, Douglass Coll., 1959; MPA, Syracuse U., 1960; JD magna cum laude, Wayne State U., 1967; cert. in urban econs., MIT, 1972. Bar: Mich. 1968, Ohio 1976, Ariz. 1995, N.Mex., 2002, U.S. Dist. Ct. (so. dist.) Hio 1977, Ariz. 1995. Asst. prof. law Ohio State U. Law Sch., Columbus, 1976-78, assoc. prof. law, 1978-81, prof. law, 1982-95, prof. emeritus, 1995, assoc. dean, 1982-86, dir. 2d Yr. Legal Writing Program, 1983-87. Vis. prof. law, U. Ariz., 1995-99. Author: (with D.J. Whaley) Problems and Materials on Sales, 1983; contbr. articles and revs. to legal and bus. jours. Mem. fin. com. LWV, 1971-74; lay reader St. Stephen's Episcopal Ch., Columbus, 1976-95, mem. Ctrl. Ohio Diocesan Coun., 1980-81, chancery judge So. diocese Ohio, 1982-90; active Boy Scouts Am., 1976-80, Columbus Com. for Battered Women, 1979-80; pres. Stonewall Union, Columbus, 1983-84, bd. dirs. and clk., 1981-88; founder Integrity Ctrl. Ohio, 1983; bd. dirs,. Ohio Women Ind., 1980-82, treas., 1981-82; bd. dirs., Franklin County Legal Aid Soc., Columbus, 1983-85. Recipient Susan B. Anthony award Woman Law Students Assn. U. Mich., 1976, Evelyn Hooker Rsch. award Gay Acad. Union, 1984, Dir.'s award Ohio Dept. Health for AIDS work, 1988, Woman of Achievement award YWCA, 1989. Mem. ABA (mem. adv. bd. sect. individual rights and responsibilities 1979-80), ACLU, FMCS (labor arbitrator 1986-), VSPS (labor arbitrator), AFPWU (labor arbitrator), Am. Arbitration Assn. (labor arbitrator 1990-), Nat. Acad. Arbitrators (labor arbitrator 1990-), NOW (Legal Achievement award Legal Def. and Edn. fund 1986, Uppity Woman of Yr. Ann Arbor chpt. 1975), AAUP, Am. Assn. Law Schs. (chmn. women in legal edn. sect. 1979-80, mem. sect. exec. com. 1980-82, chmn. gay and lesbian legal issues sect. 1982-83), Soc. Am. Law Tchrs. (mem. exec. com. of bd. govs. 1979-81, mem. bd. govs. 1978-95, pres. 1984-86), Nat. Lawyers Guild, Ohio Human Rights Bar Assn. (founder 1988, pres. 1989-91, bd. trustees 1991-95). Home and Office: 10218 Prescott Ct NW Albuquerque NM 87114-4519 E-mail: rrivera38@comcast.net.

RIVERA, RICHARD EDWIN, restaurant chain executive; b. Jan. 6, 1947; m. Leslie Suzanne Pliner, Nov. 18, 1984. BA, Washington & Lee U., 1968. Credit analyst Nat. Bank Commerce, Dallas, 1970-71; from mgmt. trainee to exec. v.p., dir. Steak and Ale Restaurants of Am., 1971-80; pres. restaurant div. El Chico Corp., 1980-82; exec. v.p., chief operating officer T.J. Applebee's and Taco Villa Mexican Restaurant, Dallas, 1982-87; exec. v.p. ops. TGI Friday's Inc., 1987-88, pres., chief exec. officer, 1988-94; pres., CEO RARE Hosp. Internat., Inc., Atlanta, 1994-97; Chart House Enterprises, Inc., 1997; pres. Red Lobster Restaurants, Orlando, Fla., 1997—. Office: Red Lobster PO Box 593330 Orlando FL 32859-3330 Home: 10940 Emerald Chase Dr Orlando FL 32836-5854 E-mail: drivera@redlobster.com.

RIVERA, RUTH ELLEN, special services director; b. Auburn, N.Y., Aug. 1, 1944; d. Robert James and Edna Louise (Lawrence) Stebbins; m. Edward L. Malec, Sept. 2, 1967 (div. Oct. 1977); children: Edward L., Amy Beth; m. Carlos A. Rivera, July 18, 1999. B, Houghton (N.Y.) Coll., 1966; student, Ohio U., 1966-67; M, Montclair State Coll., 1970; EdD, Nova Southeastern U., 1999. Tchr. Newark Pub. Schs., N.J., 1967-69; social worker Passaic County Bd. Soc. Svcs., Paterson, 1970-72, Boonton Pub. Schs., 1979-88; dir. spl. edn. Sch. Union 44, Sabattus, Maine, 1988-90; dir. spl. svcs. Kinnelon Pub. Schs., N.J., 1990-93, Linden (N.J.) Pub. Schs., 1993—. Women's ministry Jacksonville Chapel, Lincoln Park, N.J. Mem. ASCD, N.J. Dept. Edn. Prof. Svcs. Coun., N.J. Assn. Sch. Social Workers (v.p. 1985-87, pres. 1987-88), N.J. Assn. for Pupil Svcs. Adminstrs., N.J. Prins. and Suprs. Assn., N.E. Coalition of Ednl. Leaders, Union County Assn. of Dirs. of Spl. Svcs., Morris County Assn. Dirs. Spl. Edn., Knnelon Women's Svc. Orgn. Avocations: reading, music. Home: 35 Cliff Trl Kinnelon NJ 07405-3107 Office: Bloomfield Pub Schs 155 Broad St Bloomfield NJ 07003-2638

RIVERA, WALTER, lawyer; b. N.Y.C., Jan. 18, 1955; s. Marcelino and Ana Maria (Reyes) R. BA, Columbia U., 1976; JD, U. Pa., 1979. Bar: N.Y. 1980. Law clk. to cen. legal research staff N.Y. State Ct. Appeals, Albany, 1979-81; asst. atty. gen. State of N.Y., N.Y.C., 1981-85; sole practice, 1985-88; shareholder Rivera & Muniz, P.C., 1988-93, Law Offices of Walter Rivera P.C., 1994-97; ptnr. Rivera, Hunter, Colon & Dobshinsky, LLP, N.Y.C., 1998—. Chmn. Third World Lawyers Caucus, N.Y. State Atty. Gen.'s Office, N.Y.C., 1984; arbitrator City Ct. N.Y.C., 1985. Bd. dirs. Andrew Glover Youth Program. Mem. ABA, Puerto Rican Bar Assn., Nat. Hispanic Bar Assn., N.Y. State Bar Assn., Assn. Bar City N.Y. (past chmn. com. on small law firm mgmt.), Sch. of Visual Arts (bd. dirs.). Avocations: golf, travel. Home: 19 Orchard Ln Elmsford NY 10523 Office: Rivera Hunter Colon & Dohshinsky LLP 61 Broadway Rm 1030 New York NY 10006-2701 E-mail: wrivera@rhcdlaw.com.

RIVERA-DOMINGUEZ, ALBERTO, mathematics educator, mechanical engineer; b. Vega Baja, P.R., June 17, 1958; s. Angel Rivera-Delgado and Concepcion Dominguez-Suarez; m. Elli Reyes-Grote, Jan. 6, 1985; 1 child, Albert Vincent Rivera-Reyes. BSME magna cum laude, U. P.R., 1981; MSME, La. Tech. U., 1990. Engr. Boeing Comml. A/P Co., Seattle, 1981-82; lectr. U. P.R., Mayaguez, P.R., 1983-84, asst. to the assoc. dean of engring., 1984; tchg. asst. La. Tech. U., Ruston, 1985-86; mech. engr. U.S. Army, Fort Buchannan/San Juan, P.R., 1987-90, USN/AFWTF, Ceiba, 1990-91; gen. engr. USN - NUWC, Newport, R.I., 1991-95; engr. Breeze-Eastern, Union, NJ, 1995—2001; tchr. h.s. math, 2001—. Lectr. U. P.R., 1983-84. Contbr. articles to profl. jours. Recipient tuition award MIT, Cambridge, Mass., 1982-84, Panam. Surety Assn. scholarship La. Tech. U., Ruston, 1986. Mem. ASME, NSPE, Am. Soc. for Composites, NJ Edn. Assn., Colegio de Ingenieros Y Agrimensores de P.R. Achievements include rsch. on viscoelastic characterization of composite materials; theoretical rsch. findings include: coestablished the prin. of virtual equilibrium state of viscoelasticity; devel. a generalized predictive creep response formulation suitable for composite materials; developed algorithm and techniques for reliability prediction of assembled products; developed finite-difference modeling to simulate the performance of mechanically-assembled products. Avocations: baseball, basketball, soccer, coaching, writing. Home: PO Box 868 Matawan NJ 07747-1370

RIVERA-GARZA, CRISTINA, historian, educator, writer; b. Matamoros, Mex., Oct. 1, 1964; arrived in U.S., 1989; d. Antonio Rivera-Peña and Hilda Garza-Bermea; 1 child Matias R. De Hoyos. BA in Sociology, Autonomous U. Mex., 1987; MA in History, U. Houston, 1993, PhD in Latin Am. History, 1995. Asst. prof. DePauw U., Greencastle, Ind., 1995—99; assoc. prof. San Diego State U., San Diego, 1997—. Author: No One Will See Me Weeping, 2000 (IHPAC award, 2000); contbr. articles to profl. jours. Recipient Best Book award, Internat. Book Fair Guadalajera, 2001, J. Vicente Meio Nat. award, Veracruz Cultural Inst., 2001; grantee, NIH, 2001—02. Office: San Diego State Univ History Dept 5500 Campanile Dr San Diego CA 92182

RIVERA-MARTINEZ, SOCORRO, retired educator, assistant principal; b. Mayagüez, P.R., Apr. 19, 1942; d. Sotero R. and Rafaela Martinez; m. Carmelo Torres, Dec. 26, 1965; 1 child, Yolivette. AEd., Catholic U., 1963, BA in Elem. Edn., 1980. Cert. tchr., mentor tchr. Tchr. 1-6 grades P.R. Dept. Edn., Mayagüez, 1962-93; auxilliary administr. Colegio San Agustin, Cabo Rojo, P.R., 1993-94, asst. principal, 1994-98. Tchr. in charge Rio Hondo Sch. Mayagüez, 1964-70, 73-93, gifted children club, 1990-91, dir.'s resource for tng., 1985-93; math and sci. counselor Rio Hondo, Sch., Castillo Sch., 1971-93. Co-leader troop 384 Girl Scouts Am., Rio Hondo Sch., Mayagüez, P.R., 1975-79; vol. leader Catholic Ch. Summer camp, Cabo Rojo, P.R., 1990-92. Recipient Presidential award Excellence in Sci. and Math. Tchg. The White House, 1993, State award Excellence in Math. Nat. Coun. Math. Tchrs., 1993, Excellence in Math. award Dept. Edn., 1993; named Tchr. of the Year Dept. Edn., 1975, 82. Mem. Educadores Puertorriqueños en Acción, Coun. Elem. Sci. Internat., Coun. Presidential Awardees. Roman Catholic. Avocations: reading, poetry, writing, wire craft, gardening. Home: L22 Calle 3 Borinquen Cabo Rojo PR 00623-3324 Office: Colegio San Agustin Cabo Rojo PR 00623

RIVERA PEREZ, EFRAIN E. state official; b. Mayaguez, P.R. , July 15, 1951; s. Efrain Padilla Creek and Irene Perez Camacho; m. Border Mariluz; 1 child Mariela Mariluz. B in Adminstrn. of Cos. , U. Enclosure Mayaguez, 1971; JD, Pontifica Cath. U. Ponce Sch. Right, Ponce, P.R. , 1975. Gov. State of P.R., PR, 1983; judge adminstr. Dist. Ct. Judicial Region Mayaguez, judge sub-adminstr.; judge pres. Supreme Ct. Puerto Rico; lawyer Offices in City Mayaguez, 1985—92; chmn. U. Enclosure Mayaguez U. P.R., 1986—92; adviser judicial subjects, dir. office judicial appts.; dir. office of commn. Judicial Reformation; temp. sec. justice, 1993; judge of Appeals Ct. Cir. Appeals, 1995—2000; assoc. justice Supreme Ct. of P.R. , PR, 2000—; justice Supreme Ct. State of P.R., 2000—. Office: PO Box 902 2392 San Juan PR 00902-2392*

RIVERA-REYES, GLADYS M. (GLADYS DALTON), retired stenographer, court reporter; b. Carthage, Ill., Dec. 7, 1909; d. Carl Olaf and Anna Mathilda Sundstrom; m. Henry Gerry Dalton, Oct. 15, 1937 (dec.); 1 child Denny Carlanne Dalton Fritsche ; m. Ramon Luis Rivera-Reyes, July 1, 1969 (dec.). Student, Kans. U., 1928—29; BS, tchr.'s cert., Northwestern U., 1931. Head cashier Chgo. World's Fair, 1933—34; entertainer, pianist, accordianist, singer, actress Chgo. Fedn. Musicians, 1934—37; civilian gen. ct. martial reporter USAF, 1944—46; stenotype conv. reporter, 1949—89; entertainer Denver Musicians Assn., 1952—61, 1989. Contbr. poetry to anthologies. Mem.: Nat. Ct. Reporters Assn. (life), Denver Musicians Assn. (life), Chgo. Fedn. Musicians (life). Avocations: poetry, oil painting, singing, piano. Home: Legacy Ctr 1335 Bauer Ln Canon City CO 81212

RIVERA-SINCLAIR, ELSA, psychologist, consultant, researcher; b. Lima, Peru, Dec. 2, 1927; came to U.S. 1954; d. Jorge Maximo Rivera Bodero and Hortencia Resurreccion Vega Alvarado; m. Walter Ward Sinclair, Oct. 30, 1957; children: Harold Anthony, Thomas Edgar (dec.), Ian Paul. AA in Gen. Edn., Montgomery Coll., Takoma Park, Md., 1976; BA in Psychology, U. Md.-College Park, 1979; MA in Clin. Psychoolgy, U. Md.-Balti. County, 1982; PhD in Counseling Psychology, U. Md.-College Park, 1988. Diplomate Am. Bd. Psychological Specialties, 1998. Psychology intern Spring Grove Hosp., Catonsville, Md., 1980-81, Veterans Administrn. Med. Ctr., Washington, 1985-86; clin. psychologist PHS evaluation facility/inpatient care St. Elizabeths Hosp. Immigration/Naturalization, 1989; clin. psychologist acute care St. Elizabeths Hosp., 1989; clin. psychologist North Cmty. Mental Health Ctr., 1996—. Bd. mem. Mayor of Dist. Ct. Columbia Multicultural Task Force, 1992-94,CMHS, Dept. Human Svcs. Contbr. article to profl. jour. Recipient APA fellowship Am. Psychological Assn., 1982; Vol. award Andromeda Transcultural Hispano Mental Health Ctr., 1998. Mem. APA, Am. Coll. Forensic Examiners, Md. Psychol. Assn., Nat. Hispanic Psychol. Assn., D.C. Psychol. Assn., Phi Kappa Phi. Avocations: traveling, oil painting, reading, poetry, classic music. Home: 116 Fleetwood Ter Silver Spring MD 20910 Office: St Elizabeth Hosp N Cmty Mntl Hlth Ctr 1125 Spring Rd NW Washington DC 20010-1421 E-mail: universe@erols.com.

RIVERA-URRUTIA, BEATRIZ DALILA, psychology and rehabilitation counseling educator; b. Bayamón, P.R., Jan. 16, 1951; d. José and Carmen B. (Urrutia) Rivera; m. Julio C. Ribera, July 1, 1978; 1 child Alejandra B. Ribera. BA, U. P.R., 1972, MA, 1975; PhD, Temple U., 1982. Cert. rehab. counselor Commn. Rehab. Counselor Cert., lic. pscyhologist P.R. Staff pscyhologist Learning Plus, Inc., Phila., 1979-80; cons. Hispanic Mental Health Inst., 1981-82; staff psychologist J.F. Kennedy Community Mental Health Ctr., 1982-83; prof. U. P.R., Rio Piedras, 1983—. Cons. Jewish Employment & Vocat. Svcs., Phila., 1980; staff psychologist San Juan VA Hosp., Rio Piedras, 1990—; coord. grad. program Rehab Counseling Grad. Sch., 2000—. Contbr. articles to profl. jours. Vol. Parroquia San Juan Apóstol y Evangelista, Caguas, PR, 1988—90, ARC, San Juan, 1990. Grantee Faculty Instnl. Rsch., U. P.R., 1986—87. Mem.: P.R. Lic. Bd. Psychologists (pres. ethics com. 1991—92), P.R. Psychol. Assn. (bd. editors jour. 1984—89, bd. dirs. 1989—91). Avocations: walking, theater. Home and Office: PO Box 22724 San Juan PR 00931-2724 E-mail: ribera@prtc.net.

RIVERO, ALBERT J. English educator; b. Aug. 2, 1953; s. Albert I. and Angela Esther Rivero; m. Lisa M. Furrey, July 8, 1989; 1 child, Albert H. AB summa cum laude, Princeton U., 1975; MA, U. Va., 1977, PhD, 1982. Asst. prof. Marquette U., 1982-90, assoc. prof., 1990-98, prof., 1998—, dir. honors program, 1998-2001. Acting chmn. dept. English Marquette U., 1996, hiring com. dept. English, 1994, 95, 97, dir. undergrad. studies, 1993-97, dean's adv. coun., 1996, 1998-2001, mem. acad. area budget com., 1996, mem. advising com. Coll. Arts and Scis., 1993-95, curriculum com. Coll. Arts and Scis., 1993-95, Fulbright campus com., 1993-95, tchr. preparation com., 1993-94, sabbatical rev. com., 1993-96, chmn., 1994-96, exec. com., 1987, 90-91, 93-97, Marquette univ. honors com., 1990-93, pre-majors and majors advisor, 1982—. Author: The Plays of Henry Fielding: A Critical Study of His Dramatic Career, 1989; author, editor: New Essays on Samuel Richardson, 1996; Augustan Subjects, 1997, Critical Essays on Henry Fielding, 1998; editor: Jonathan Swift Gulliver's Travels, 2001; editor, contbr. books and articles to profl. jours. Rsch. fellowship Am. Philos. Soc., 1996, Clark Libr., 1986, Am. Coun. of Learned Socs., 1985, Exxon Edn. Found. fellowship Newberry Libr., 1985, Fulbright scholarship U. London, 1975-76; NEH sr. fellow for univ. tchrs., 2000-01. Mem. MLA, Johnson Soc. of the Ctrl. Region (pres. 1995-96), Am. Soc. for 18th Century Studies, Assn. of Literary Scholars and Critics, East-Ctrl. Am. Soc. for 18th Century Studies, Midwestern Am. Soc. for 18th Century Studies, The Johnsonians. Office: Dept of English Marquette U PO Box 1881 Milwaukee WI 53201-1881

RIVERO, ANDRIA, education educator; b. Alacranes, Matanzas, Cuba, Feb. 04; came to the U.S., 1956; d. Javier and Juana Maria Rivero; m. Hermann E. Diehl (div. Dec. 1983); children: Hermann J., Karina J. BS, Fla. Internat. U., 1974; MS, Nova U., 1981. Elem. tchr. St. Patrick Cath. Sch., Miami Beach, Fla., 1979-81; instr., dean instrn. Ft. Lauderdale Coll., Miami, 1981-84; prof., disability svcs. advisor St. Thomas U., 1984-99; assoc. dean acad. Internat. Fine Arts Coll., 1999—. Edn. specialist Accrediting Commn. for Colls. and Tech. Career Schs., 1993—; adv. bd. Tech. Career Inst., Miami, 1997-2000; adj. prof. Miami Dade C.C., 2000—, Fla. Internat. U., 2000—. Mem. safety com. City of Miami Beach, 1995-97. Roman Catholic. E-mail: arivero@bellsouth.net.

RIVERO, MAGDA, counselor; b. Big Lake, Tex., Nov. 4, 1975; d. Mario and Maria Esther Rivero. BA with honors, Angelo State U., 1997, MS in Counseling Psychology, 2001. House mgr. Inst. Cognitive Devel., San Angelo, Tex., 1996-97; vol. coord. Adult Literacy Coun. of Concho Valley, 1997-2000; co-therapist, temp. lic. profl. counselor New Directions, 2000—. Acad. scholar Angelo State U., 1994-99. Mem. Psi Chi. Home: 3509 Ridge Crest Ln San Angelo TX 76904 E-mail: magdarr@aol.com.

RIVERS, ALMA FAYE, secondary education educator; b. Marion, N.C., Oct. 13, 1949; d. Arthur Henry and Lena (Deyton) Letterman; m. Charles Edwin Rivers, June 29, 1980. BA, Mars Hill Coll., 1971; MEd, W. Ga. Coll., 1978. Tchr., choral dir. W. Fannin H.S., Blue Ridge, Ga., 1971-76, W. Fannin Jr. H.S., Blue Ridge, 1976-80; tchr. Truett-McConnell Coll., Young Harris, Ga., 1975-76, 78-80, Sprayberry H.S., Marietta, 1980—. Student tchr. supr. State of Ga., 1988—, tchr. mentoring program, 1990—; tchr., cons. Kennesaw (Ga.) State U., 1995—; presenter workshops, confs., and confs. on 19th century women's lit. and multiculture lit. Mem. Standing Peachtree NA, Atlanta, 1994—; vol. PGA Tournament. NEH fellow, 1995. Mem. Nat. Coun. Tchrs. English, Ga. Coun. Tchrs. English, Thomas Wolfe Soc., Cooking Club of Am.,

Alpha Delta Kappa. Methodist. Avocations: golfing, piano, literature, traveling, book collecting. Home: 1711 Fernleaf Cir NW Atlanta GA 30318-1417 Office: Sprayberry High Sch 2525 Sandy Plains Rd Marietta GA 30066-5799

RIVERS, DONALD LEE, marketing professional; b. Sioux City, Iowa, Feb. 10, 1943; s. Thomas Harvey and Helen Catherine (Brenner) R.; m. Robin Dee Magee, Jan. 7, 1968 (div.); m. Beverly Doss, Oct. 13, 1979 (div.); m. Diane Dankenbring, Oct. 1, 1994. BS, Drake U., 1966; MA, U. Iowa, 1968. Sales rep. Holt, Rinehart & Winston, Inc., Mpls., 1969-72, editor N.Y.C., 1973-76; sales rep. Rand McNally & Co., Tampa, Fla., 1972-73; editor William C. Brown Co., Dubuque, Iowa, 1976-78; sales mgr. nat. accounts Better Homes & Gardens Books, Meredith Corp., Des Moines, 1978-85, dir. nat. accounts, 1985-87; dir. of nat. accounts XLM Co., 1988-89; v.p. sales Steelworks, Des Moines, 1989-94; v.p. sales and mktg. Enviro Industries, 1994-95; mktg. cons. Rivers & Assocs., Ankeny, Iowa, 1995—. Mem. Kappa Delta Pi. Republican. Avocation: biking. Home and Office: 2918 NW 5th St Ankeny IA 50021-1048 E-mail: driverslabels@att.net.

RIVERS, GLENN ANTON (DOC RIVERS), professional basketball coach, former basketball player; b. Maywood, Ill., Oct. 13, 1961; m. Kris Rivers, 1987. Student, Marquette U., 1980-83. Player Atlanta Hawks, 1983-91, Los Angeles Clippers, 1991-92, New York Knicks, 1992-94, San Antonio Spurs, 1994-96; sports analyst Turner Sports, 1996-1999; head coach Orlando Magic, 1999-. Mem. NBA All-Star Team, 1988; recipient Coach of Yr. award, 1999-2000. Office: Orlando Magic 2 Magic Pl 8701 Maitland Summit Blvd Orlando FL 32810-5915*

RIVERS, JULIE ELAINE, concert pianist, composer, recording industry executive; b. Ft. Worth; d. Theodore and Astrid (Ojerholm) Moberg; m. James C. Rivers (div.); children: David Aaron, James Arthur. MusB magna cum laude, U. North Tex., 1966. Concert pianist, 1960—; rec. artist, 1994—; pres. EarthStar Recs./Pubns., Topeka, 1996—. Premier Season com. Topeka Performing Arts Ctr., 1990. Rec. albums include Tidings of Joy, 1995, Spinning Gold: The Piano Music of Eugenie Rocherolle, 1995; pianist, composer: One Starry Night, 1996, The Kiss of the Sun, 1998, Romancing the Piano, 1998, Christmastide, 1999. Recipient Disting. Guest Artist award Zonta Internat., Topeka, 1989; fellow in composition Kans. Arts Commn., 1998. Mem. ASCAP (award 1997-2002), Kans. Music Tchrs. Assn. (composition chmn. 1993-95), Topeka Music Tchrs. Assn. (pres. 1973-74), Northeast Kans. Music. Tchrs. Assn. (pres. 1994-95), Nat. League Am. Pen Women (Nat. Composition award 1992, 98, 2002), Nat. Guild Piano Tchrs., Nonosa Honor Soc., Mortar Bd. Office: EarthStar Rec/Pubns PO Box 4462 Topeka KS 66604-0462 E-mail: julie@earthstarrecordings.com.

RIVERS, KENNETH JAY, retired judicial administrator, consultant; b. N.Y.C., Feb. 13, 1938; s. Alexander Maximillian and Albertina Ray (Gay) R.; m. Leah B. Files, Sept. 21, 1957 (div.); children: Londa Denise, Nancy Laura, Terrie Ruth, Kenneth J. Jr. AAS in Criminal Justice, BS in Criminal Justice, St. Francis Coll., Bklyn., 1978; MPA, L.I. Univ., 1981. Correction officer N.Y.C. Dept. Correction, 1965-69; ct. officer N.Y. State Unified Ct. System, N.Y.C., 1969-71, asst. ct. clk., 1971-73, sr. ct. clk., 1973-85, assoc. ct. clk., 1985-88, prin. ct. clk., 1988-90, dep. chief clk., 1991-93; ret., 1993. Tng. instr. N.Y. State Unified Ct. System, N.Y.C., 1985—, pers. assessor, 1985—; lectr. John Jay Coll. NYU, N.Y.C., 1987. Author: Juvenile Crime Survey, 1982, New York State Jury Selection, 1984. Bd. dirs. Parkway Consumers Med. Coun., Bklyn., 1983—, Cen. Bklyn. Tenant's Rights, 1988—. Recipient Leadership award Tribune Soc., N.Y. State Cts., 1987, Svc. award, 1988, Cert. of Merit award Fedn. Afro-Am. Civil Svc. Orgns., 1987. Mem. ASPA, Internat. Pers. Mgmt. Assn., Acad. Polit. Sci., Conf. Minority Pub. Adminstrs., Masons. Democrat. Methodist. Avocation: jazz musician. E-mail: kchiefclerk@aol.com.

RIVERS, LORETTA J. film producer, film director, consultant; b. Stafford Springs, Conn., Sept. 7, 1955; d. Everett Joseph and Jean Petrone Rivers. BA Anthropology and Archaeology, U. Conn., 1978, postgrad., 1988—94, Ctrl. Conn. State U., 1995—96. Mus. tchr., interpreter Old Sturbridge Village, Sturbridge, Mass., 1979—82, 1988; curator edn., asst. dir. Jefferson County Hist. Soc., Watertown, NY, 1983—85; curator edn. Lutz Children's Mus., Manchester, Conn., 1987—88; archives cons. CIGNA Corp., Hartford, 1988—91; archives asst. Dept. Hist. Manuscripts Archives, Storrs, 1992—94; exec. dir., founder Lojeri Prodns., Inc., East Hartford, 1996—. Archaeological rschr. Marc Banks, Archaeologist, Simsbury, Conn., 1999—2000; pub. access vol. Cox Comms. , Manchester, Conn., 1995—; programming internship CPTV/Channel 24, Hartford, 1996, WGBY/Channel 57, Springfield, Mass., 1995; field crew Mich. State U., East Lansing, Mich., 1979; rsch., lab and field asst. Pub. Archaeology Survey Team, Storrs, Conn., 1977—86. (prodr., dir.): (documentaries) Wadsworth Atheneum Mus. Art, 1995 (1st place, 1996); prodr., dir. (documentaries) Mus. Insider, 1995—97; (prodr., dir.): (documentaries) Lutz Children's Mus., 1997 (3rd place, 1997); prodr., dir. (documentaries) Huntington House, 1997 (Honorable mention, 1997), mem. editl. bd., contbg. editor (newsletter) Archaeology and Education, 1989—92; contbr. articles to profl. jours. Conn. History Day judge Conn. Hist. Soc., Hartford, 2001—, Conn. History Day tchr. workshop, 2001; design com. mem. Rockville (Conn.) Downtown Assn., 2001—. Recipient award, Connecticare, 1998, Gaylord Hosp., 2000, Am. Savings Bank Found., 2001, George and Grace Long Found., 2001. Mem.: Conn. League History Orgns., Bay State Hist. League, Conn. League History Orgns., New England Mus. Assn. Avocations: music, cultural events, travel. Home and Office: Lojeri Prodns Inc PO Box 280304 50 Chapman Pl Studio 209 East Hartford CT 06128 Office Fax: 860-291-0180. Business E-Mail: lrivers@lojeriproductions.org.

RIVERS, LYNN N. congresswoman; b. Augres, Mich., Dec. 19, 1956; 2 children. BA, U. Mich., 1987; JD, Wayne State U., 1992. Mem. sch. bd. City of Ann Arbor, Mich., 1984-92; mem. Mich. House of Reps., 1992-94, U.S. Congress from 13th Mich. dist., 1994—; mem. edn. and workforce com., sci. com., 1994. Office: US House Reps 1724 Longworth Bldg Washington DC 20515-2213

RIVERS, PATRICK A. education educator, researcher; b. Oct. 18, 1958; s. Cosmas and Amma Rivers; m. Mary Alice Patton, May 3, 1983; 1 child Patrick Cosmas. PhD, U. Ala., 1997; MBA in Fin., Investment, & Banking, U. Wis., Madison, 1988; cert., Maguire Energy Inst., 2000. Faculty devel. fellow U. Ala., Birmingham, 1993—97; rsch. fellow RAND Corp., Santa Monica, Calif., 1997—98; clin. prof. U. Ariz., Tucson, 1998—; prof. Ariz. State U., Tempe, 1998—. Recipient Nat. Rsch. Svc. award, Agy. for Health Rch. and Quality, 1997—98; scholar Most Published scholar, U. Ala., 1996—97. Fellow: Am. Coll. Health Care Execs.; mem.: Strategic Mgmt. Soc., Acad. Mgmt. Home: 491 E Krista Way Tempe AZ 85284 Office: Ariz State Univ PO Box 874506 Tempe AZ 85287-4506 Office Fax: 480-965-6654. Business E-Mail: patrick.rivers@asu.edu.

RIVERS, RICHARD ROBINSON, lawyer; b. Dallas, June 9, 1942; s. Stewart Robinson and Madge (Fiske) R.; children : Laura Ellen, Jonathan Stewart. BA, Tulane U., 1964; JD, Cath. U. of Am., 1974. Bar: D.C. 1974. Writer Bauerlein, Inc., New Orleans, 1965-68; staff asst. Office of House Majority Whip, Washington, 1968-70, Office of House Majority Leader, Washington, 1971-73; internat. trade counsel Com. on Fin. U.S. Senate, 1973-77; gen. counsel Office Spl. Trade Rep., 1977-79; ptnr. Akin, Gump, Strauss, Hauer & Feld, 1979-96. Instr. Dalian (Peoples Republic of China) Inst. Tech., 1986. Trustee Am. Indian Coll. Fund. Mem. ABA, D.C. Bar Assn., Coun. Fgn. Rels., Met. Club of City of Washington. Democrat. Episcopalian. Home: 1600 Avon Pl NW Washington DC 20007-2910

RIVERS, THEODORE JOHN, paralegal, educator; b. Rochester, N.Y., Nov. 12, 1944; s. Gordon Richard and Mary Elizabeth (Baart) R. BA, Marquette U., 1967; MA, Fordham U., 1969, PhD, 1973. Litigation paralegal Paul, Weiss, Rifkind, Wharton & Garrison, 1976-84, Cowan, Liebowitz & Latman, 1984-87, Morgan, Lewis & Bockius, 1987-92, Pfizer, Inc., 1992-96, Baer, Marks & Upham, 1997; tchr. N.Y.C. Pub. Schs., 1999—. Contbr. articles to profl. jours., chpts. to books; author four books in history and philosophy. Recipient award Inst. Medieval & Renaissance Studies, Duke U., 1974. Mem. Medieval Acad. Am. Home: 115-31 Union Tpke Forest Hills NY 11375-6057

RIVERS, VIRGINIA, physiologist, educator, photographer; b. Tacoma, Sept. 22, 1944; d. Lloyd and Josephine Claire Rivers; life ptnr. Scott Huber. MS, San Diego (Calif.) State U., 1982. Instr. Southwestern CC, San Deigo, Calif., 1980—84; prof. Truckee Meadows CC, Reno, 1985—. Pres. Human Anatomy and Physiology Soc., 1990—91. Grantee EPSCoR Grant, NSF, 1994, 1995, 1996, 1998. Avocations: cooking, gardening, photography. Office: Truckee Meadows C C 7000 Dandini Blvd Reno NV 89512 E-mail: vrivers@tmcc.edu.

RIVERS, WILGA MARIE, foreign language educator; b. Melbourne, Australia, Apr. 13, 1919; came to U.S., 1970; d. Harry and Nina Diamond (Burston) R. Diploma in edn. U. Melbourne, 1940, BA with honours, 1939, MA, 1948; Licence es L., U. Montpellier, France, 1952; PhD, U. Ill., 1962; MA (hon.), Harvard U., 1974; D Langs. (hon.), Middlebury Coll., 1989. High sch. tchr., Victoria, Australia, 1940-48; asst. in English lang. France, 1949-52; tchr. prep. schs., 1953-58; asst. prof. French No. Ill. U., DeKalb, 1963-64; assoc. prof. Monash U., Australia, 1964-69; vis. prof. Columbia U., 1970-71; prof. French U. Ill., Urbana-Champaign, 1971-74; prof. Romance langs. and lit., coord. lang. instrn. Harvard U., 1974-89, prof. emerita, 1989—. Cons. NEH, Ford Found., Rockefeller Found., others; lectr 44 countries and throughout U.S.; mem. adv. bd. Modern Lang. Ctr., Ont. Inst. for Studies in Edn., Nat. Fgn. Lang. Ctr., Lang. Acquire Rsch. Ctr., San Diego. Author: The Psychologist and the Foreign-Language Teacher, 1964, Teaching Foreign-Language Skills, 1968, 2d edit., 1981, Speaking in Many Tongues, 1972, 3d edit., 1983, A Practical Guide to the Teaching of French, 1975, 2d edit., 1988, Opportunities for Careers in Foreign Languages, 1993; co-author: A Practical Guide to the Teaching of German, 1975, 2d edit., 1988, A Practical Guide to the Teaching of Spanish, 1976, 2d edit., 1988, A Practical Guide to the Teaching of English as a Second or Foreign Language, 1978, Communicating Naturally in a Second Language, 1983, Teaching Hebrew: A Practical Guide, 1989, others; editor, contbr. Interactive Language Teaching, 1978, Teaching Languages in College: Curriculum and Content, 1992; writing translated into 10 langs.; edtl. bd. Studies in Second Language Acquisition, Applied Linguistics, Language Learning, Mosaic, System; adv. com. Can. Modern Lang. Rev.; contbr. articles to profl. jours. Recipient Nat. Disting. Fgn. Lang. Leadership award N.Y. State Assn. Fgn. Lang. Tchrs., 1974. Decorated Chevalier des Palmes Académiques, 1995; recipient Disting. Alumni award U. Ill., 1999. Mem. MLA, Am. Assn. Applied Linguistics (charter pres.), Am. Coun. on Teaching Fgn. Langs. (Florence Steiner award 1977, Anthony Papalia award 1988), Mass. Fgn. Lang. Assn. (Disting. Svc. award 1983), Tchrs. of English to Speakers of other Langs., Am. Assn. Tchrs. French, Linguistic Soc. Am., Am. Assn. Univ. Suprs. and Coords. Fgn. Lang. Programs Northeast Conf. (Nelson Brooks award 1983), Internat. Assn. Applied Psycholinguistics (v.p. 1983-89), Japan Assn. Coll. English Tchrs. (hon.), Am. Assn. Tchrs. German (hon.), Internat. Assn. Lang. Labs. (hon.). Episcopalian. Home and Office: 84 Garfield St Watertown MA 02472-4916

RIVERS, WILLIAM PATRICK, language policy researcher, consultant; b. Munich, Apr. 26, 1969; came to U.S., 1971; s. William John and Ann Daly Rivers; life ptnr. Netania Zagorski. BA, BS in Aerospace Engring., U. Md., 1992, MA, 1993; postgrad., Bryn Mawr Coll., 2001. Rsch. assoc. Nat. Fgn. Lang. Ctr., Washington, 1997-99, assoc. in lang. policy, 1999—. Cons. various ednl. exch. orgns. Co-author: Language and National Security in the 21st Century, 2000. Bd. dirs. Nat. Mus. Lang., College Park, Md., 1998-2000. Mem. ASTM, Am. Coun. Tchrs. Russian, Am. Assn. Tchrs. of Slavic and East European Langs., Am. Assn. Advancement of Slavic Studies, Ctrl. Eurasian Studies Soc., Am. Coun. on Tchg. of Fgn. Langs., Am. Assn. Applied Linguistics. Office: Nat Fgn Lang Ctr Ste 1000 1029 Vermont Ave NW Washington DC 20005 Fax: (202) 637-9244. E-mail: wrivers@nflc.org.

RIVERS BAKER, DAWN, writer, publisher, consultant; b. Phila., Apr. 3, 1959; d. David Dean and Gwendolyn Regina Rivers; m. Aubrey B. Baker III, Mar. 21, 1984; children: A. David, Regina, Kimberly, Richard. Student, Princeton U., 1977-1979, Columbia U., 1980-1981. Editor-in-chief WAHMPRENEUR News Mag., Sidney, N.Y., 1999—; owner, CEO, Wahmpreneur Pub., Inc., 2000—. Small bus. cons. Career-Intelligence.com., Rowayton, Conn., 2000—. Author: (novel) The Rise of the Phoenix, 1999. Mem. NAFE, Soc. Profl. Journalists, Online News Assn. Office: Wahmpreneur Pub Inc PO Box 41 Sidney NY 13838 E-mail: editor@wahmpreneur.com., dawn@wahmpreneur.com.

RIVES, JACK L. military officer; BA in Polit. Sci., U. Ga., 1974, JD, 1976; postgrad., Squadron Officer Sch., 1982, Air Command and Staff Coll., 1983, Nat. Security Mgmt., 1985, Naval War Coll., 1993. Commd. 2d lt. USAF, 1974, advanced through grades to maj. gen., 2002; asst. staff judge advocate Griffiss AFB, NY, 1977; area def. counsel, 1977—78; dep. staff judge advocate Kunsan AB, Republic of Korea, 1978—79; asst. staff judge advocate Hellenikon AB, Greece, 1979—81; cir. def. counsel Pacific Cir., Clark AB, Philippines, 1981—83; judge advocate air staff tng. officer The Pentagon, Washington, 1983—84; staff judge advocate Plattsburgh AFB, NY, 1984—86; chief officer br., judge advocate profl. devel. divsn. Office of Judge Advocate Gen., Washington, 1986—90; appellate judge USAF Ct. Mil. Rev., Bolling AFB, 1990—93; dep. legal counsel Chmn. Joint Chiefs of Staff, Washington, 1993—95; commandant Air Force Judge Advocate Gen. Sch., Maxwell AFB, Ala., 1995—98; chief AF Exec. Issues Team Office of Sec. of Air Force, Washington, 1998—2000; staff judge advocate Hdqrs. Air Combat Command, Langley AFB, Va., 2000—02; dep. judge advocate gen. Hdqrs. USAF, Washington, 2002—. Decorated Legion of Merit with oak leaf cluster. Office: USAF Pentagon Washington DC 20330

RIVES, STANLEY GENE, university president emeritus; b. Decatur, Ill., Sept. 27, 1930; s. James A. and Frances (Bunker) R.; m. Sandra Lou Belt, Dec. 28, 1957; children: Jacqueline Ann, Joseph Alan. BS, Ill. State U., 1952, MS, 1955; PhD, Northwestern U., 1963; EdD (hon.), Lincoln Coll., 1998. Instr. W.Va. U., 1955-56, Northwestern U., 1956-58; prof. Ill. State U., Normal, 1958-80, Am. Council on Edn. Fellows Program, 1969-70, assoc. dean faculties, 1970-72, dean undergrad. instrn., 1972-80, assoc. provost, 1976-80, acting provost, 1979-80; provost, v.p. acad. affairs, prof. Eastern Ill. U., Charleston, 1981-83, pres., 1983-92, pres. emeritus, 1992—. Vis. prof. U. Hawaii, 1963-64 Author: (with Donald Klopf) Individual Speaking Contests: Preparation for Participation, 1967, (with Gene Budig) Academic Quicksand: Trends and Issues in Higher Education, 1973, (with others) Academic Innovation: Faculty and Instructional Development at Illinois State University, 1979, The Fundamentals of Oral Interpretation, 1981; contbr. articles to profl. jours. Bd. dirs. Ill. State Univs. Retirement System, 1992—, treas., 1995-2001, pres., 2001—; Ea. Ill. Univ. Found., 1993-98, also pres., 1996-98, East Ctrl. Ill. Devel. Corp., 1983-92, Charleston Area Econ. Devel. Found., 1986-92, Coles Together, 1988-92; mem. pres. commn. NCAA, 1986-91; trustee Nat. Debate Tournament, 1967-75. With U.S. Army, 1952-54. Recipient Alumni Achievement award Ill. State U., 1998, Co. of Edn. Hall of Fame. Mem. Am. Assn. State Colls. and Univs., Ill. State C. of C. (bd. dirs. 1990-92), Charleston C. of C. (bd. dirs. 1985-88), Theta Alpha Phi, Phi Kappa Delta, Pu Gamma Mu, Alpha Phi Omega, Alpha Zeta, Sigma Phi Epsilon (hon.). Home: 2231 Andover Pl Charleston IL 61920-3807 E-mail: srives@mcleodusa.net.

RIVET, DIANA WITTMER, lawyer, developer; b. Auburn, N.Y., Apr. 28, 1931; d. George Wittmer and Anne (Jenkins) Wittmer Hauswirth; m. Paul Henry Rivet, Oct. 24, 1952; children: Gail, Robin, Leslie, Heather, Clayton, Eric. BA, Keuka Coll., 1951; JD, Bklyn. Law Sch., 1956. Bar: N.Y. 1956, U.S. Dist. Ct. (ea. and so. dists.) N.Y. 1975; cert. organic NOFA, 2001. Sole practice, Orangeburg, NY, 1957—2000; farmer Danny's Backyard Organic Farm, 2000—. County atty. Rockland County (N.Y.), 1974-77; asst. to legis. chmn. Rockland County, 1978-79; counsel, adminstr. Indsl. Devel. Agy., Rockland County, 1980-91, Rockland Econ. Devel. Corp., 1981-90; counsel, exec. dir. Pvt. IndustryCoun. Rockland county, 1980-90; pres., CEO Environ. Mgmt. Ltd., Orangeburg, 1980-98; mem. air mgmt. adv. com. N.Y. State Dept. Environ. Conservation 1984-92, Orangetown Planning Bd., 1993-2000, master plan com., 2000—. Pres. Rockland County coun. Girl Scouts U.S., 1981-84; chmn. Rockland County United Way, 1996-97, mem. campaign com., 1983-84, 88-89, 93, sec., 1997-99, bd. dirs., 1988-94, 95—; mem. Leadership Rockland, 1991-94. Recipient Cmty. Svc. award Keuka Coll., 1965, Disting. Svc. award Town of Orangetown, 1970, Disting. Svc. award Rockland County, 1989, Econ. Devel. award Rockland Econ. Devel. Corp., 1990; named Businessperson of Yr. Jour. News, Rockland County, 1982. Mem. ABA, N.Y. State Bar Assn. (mcpl. law sect. exec. com. 1976-83, environ. law sect. exec. com. 1974-86), Rockland County Bar Assn. (chair environ. law com. 1994-96), Rockland Bus. Assn. (bd. dirs. 1981-97, small bus. adv. com. 1998, gov. affairs com. 1998—), Rockland Computer Users' Group (bd. dirs. 1998-99). Democrat. Mem. Religious Soc. of Friends. Home: 1 Lester Dr Orangeburg NY 10962-2316 E-mail: danny@ucs.net.

RIVETTE, FRANCIS ROBERT, lawyer; b. Syracuse, N.Y., May 1, 1952; s. Francis Patrick and Barbara Parker (Smith) R.; m. Judith A. La Manna, 1993. BA, Allegheny Coll., 1974; JD, Syracuse U., 1977. Bar: N.Y. 1978, D.C. 1980, U.S. Dist. Ct. (no. dist.) N.Y. 1978, U.S. Supreme Ct. 1993. Ptnr. Rivette & Rivette P.C., Syracuse, 1978—; corp. counsel Nicom Techs., Inc., 1995-2000. Corp. counsel Fangand Enterprises Ltd., 1978—. Mem. ATLA, N.Y. State Trial Lawyers Assn., Syracuse Corvette Club (pres. 1985-86), Sportscar Vintage Racing Assn., Nat. Corvette Restorers Soc. (nat. judge, 1985, 88, 95, 97), Historic Sportscar Racing Ltd., Phi Delta Phi, Phi Gamma Mu. Republican. Home: 200 Old Liverpool Rd Liverpool NY 13088-6354 Office: Rivette & Rivette PC 224 Harrison St Ste 306 Syracuse NY 13202-3067 E-mail: holymoly@accucom.net.

RIVETTE, GERARD BERTRAM, manufacturing company executive; b. Syracuse, N.Y., May 18, 1932; s. George Francis and Helen (McCarthy) R.; m. Patricia Anne Yates, June 20, 1953; children: Kevin Gerard, Brian Yates. AB, Syracuse U., 1954; postgrad., U. Buffalo, 1957-59, Rutgers U., 1962-65; DHL, Monterey Inst. Intl. Studies, 1998. Owner-mgr. Rivette Sales and Svc., Syracuse, 1950-54; sales rep. Sperry-Rand, Inc., Elmira, N.Y., 1954-55; with Hewitt-Robins Inc., Buffalo, 1955-62, mgr. conveyor equipment sales Passaic, N.J., 1962-65; pres. Hewitt-Robins (Can.) Ltd., Montreal, 1965-69, also dir.; Can. regional mgr. Hewitt-Robins Inc., 1965-69; pres. Conergics Corp., Kansas City, Kans., 1970-86, Mid-West Conveyer Co., 1970-86, Alpine Metals Co., Salt Lake City, Con Cal Corp., Orange, Calif.; chmn. bd. Versa Corp., Mt. Sterling, Ohio, 1972-86, Baker Erection Co., Kansas City, Mo., 1971-86, Arrowhead Conveyer Corp., Oshkosh, Wis., 1979-86, Conveyer Sales and Mfg., Seattle, 1983-86; chmn. bd., pres. Conveyer Corp. Am., Ft. Worth, 1978-86, Mayfran Internat. Inc., Cleve., 1984-86, Mayfran Limburg B.V., The Netherlands, 1984-86, Guardian Resources Ltd., Palo Alto, Calif., 1982—; chmn. bd. Jeffrey Chain Co., Morristown, Tenn., 1985-96, Whitney Chain Corp., Morristown, 1985-96; chmn. bd., pres. Guardian Resources Ltd., Redwood City, 1966-91, Jeffrey Chain Can. Inc., Toronto, 1987-96; chmn. bd. Intelligent Software Internat. Inc., Redwood City, 1985-96, Tsubakimoto Mayfran, Osaka, Japan, 1984-86, Greaves Midwest Engring. Ltd., Bangalore, India, 1977-86. Bd. dirs. Jeffrey Chain Can., Toronto. Trustee U. Kansas City, 1983-95, Midwest Rsch., Inst., 1983-93; bd. dirs. Monterey Inst. Internat. Studies, 1989—. Office: PO Box 205 Pebble Beach CA 93953-0205

RIVIN, ARTHUR UDELL, medical educator; b. Sioux City, Iowa, June 30, 1923; s. Hyman and Bella (Woolf) R.; m. Frieda Riekes; children: Kenneth, Carol, Laurie. BS, U. Nebr., 1943, MD, 1946. Diplomate Am. Bd. Internal Medicine. Intern Michael Reese Hosp., Chgo., 1946-47; resident VA Wadsworth Hosp., L.A., 1949-51; clin. instr. medicine UCLA, 1952-56, asst. clin. prof. medicine, 1956-66, assoc. clin. prof. medicine, 1967-76, clin. prof. medicine, 1976—. Chmn. UniHealth Am. Bioethics Com., 1994-96, Santa Monica/West L.A. Clin. Rsch. Coop., 1992-96, Ctr. for Humane and Ethical Med. Care, founder, chmn.; lectr. in field. Contbr. articles to profl. jours. Pres. Calif. Health Decisions, L.A., 1987-92, bd. dirs., 1991-94. Cardiology fellow UCLA, 1952, Nat. Endowment Humanities fellow, Washington, 1977. Fellow Am. Coll. Physicians, Am. Coll. Cardiology; mem. AMA, Am. Heart Assn., L.A. Med. Assn., L.A. Heart Assn., Assn. Hosp. Med. Educators, Phi Beta Kappa, Alpha Omega Alpha. Office: 11980 San Vicente Blvd Los Angeles CA 90049-5012 also: Santa Monica UCLA Hosp 1250 16th St Santa Monica CA 90404-1249 E-mail: arivin@mednet.ucla.edu.

RIVKIN, EVGENY J. musician, educator; b. Nizhny Novgorod, Russia, Jan. 30, 1956; s. Yuliy A. Rivkin and Rayisa I. Rivkina; m. Liana K. Embovica, Mar. 18, 1978; 1 child Robert. DM, Moscow Conservatory, 1982. Prof. piano Latvian Acad. of Music, Riga, Latvia, 1988—95, U. Ga., Athens, 1995—. Recipient prize, All- Union Pianist Competition, USSR, 1997, 6th Internat. Tchaikovsky Competition, 1978, Bavarian Radio Internat. Competition, 1985, L. MacMahon Internat.. Competition, 1998. Mem.: Music Tchrs. Nat. Assn. Home: 210 Spalding Cir Athens GA 30605 Office: 250 River Rd Athens GA 30602-1521 Office Fax: 706-542-2287. Business E-Mail: erivkin@arches.uga.edu.

RIVKIN, STEVEN ROBERT, lawyer; b. Boston, Jan. 11, 1937; s. Bernard Morris and Ruth (Lasker) R.; m. Mary Stimpson Seckinger, Aug. 17, 1975; children: Caroline Seckinger Carlson, Robert Edward Seckinger, Sarah Edith Rivkin, Jesse Stimpson Rivkin. AB, Harvard U., 1958, LLB, 1962. Bar: Mass. 1963, D.C. 1967, Md. 1992, U.S. Supreme Ct. 1968. Analyst Weapons Systems Evaluation Group, Washington, 1958-59; tech. asst. for legal affairs White House Staff and Exec. Office of Pres., 1961-65; assoc. Foley Hoag & Eliot, Boston, 1965-67; counsel Fisher Sharlitt & Gelband, Washington, 1967—68; counsel, ptnr. Nicholson & Carter, 1971-75; ptnr. Rivkin & Lewis, 1982-83; pvt. practice, 1968-70, 75-81, 83—. Vis. fellow Progressive Policy Inst. of Dem. Leadership Coun., Washington, 1992; counsel Sloan Commn. on Cable Comms., N.Y.C., 1970-71. Author, editor 5 books; contbr. articles to profl. jours., mags. and newspapers. With USAR, 1962-67. Recipient Travel and Study award Ford Found., 1970. Democrat. Jewish. Home and Office: 8013 Maple Ridge Rd Bethesda MD 20814-1307 Fax: 202-628-7630. E-mail: srrivkin@msn.com.

RIVKIND, PERRY ABBOT, federal railroad agency administrator; b. Boston, Jan. 22, 1930; s. Samuel Alexander and Mae Edna (Polisnor) R.; m. Dolores Russo; children: Robert Douglas, Valerie Jean; m. Kathleen Marie Lysher, Aug. 14, 1989. AA, Miami (Fla.) Community Coll., 1963; BA, Fla. State U., 1965; MA, Fla. Atlantic U., 1966; postgrad., Nat. War Coll., Washington, 1981. Comml. charter pilot, 1956-58; police officer Met. Police Dept., Miami, 1958-61; chief investigator Dade County State Atty. Office, 1961-67; prof., dir. dept. Cen. Piedmont Coll., Charlotte, N.C., 1967-68; asst. dir. Fed. Bur. Narcotics, Washington, 1968-74; asst. adminstr. Law Enforcement Assistance Adminstrn., 1974-81; assoc. commr. U.S. Immigration and Naturalization Svc., 1981-84, dist. dir. Miami, 1984-88; safety mgr. Miami Herald Pub. Co., 1988-89; dep. adminstr. Fed. R.R. Adminstrn., Washington, 1989—. Chmn. com. on tng. Pres.'s Coun. on Drug Abuse, Washington, 1971-74, chmn. com. on rsch. Working Group on Terrorism Nat. Security Coun., Washington, 1978-81. With U.S. Army, 1951-53. Perry A. Rivkind Day established in his honor City of Miami/Dade County/City of Miami Beach, 1985-89. Republican. Avocations: boating, hunting, fishing, motorcycling, camping.

RIVLIN, BENJAMIN, political science educator; b. Bklyn., July 10, 1921; s. Moses and Esther (Ribnick) R.; m. Leanne Green, July 9, 1957; 1 child, Marc Alexander. BA, Bklyn. Coll., 1942; MA, Harvard U., 1947, PhD, 1949. With OSS, 1943-45; teaching fellow Harvard U., 1948; mem. trusteeship dept. UN Secretariat, 1948, 50, 52; research assoc. Hoover Commn., 1948; mem. faculty Bklyn. Coll. of CUNY, 1949-75, prof. polit. sci., 1962-70, chmn. dept., 1966-70; mem. Grad. Sch. faculty CUNY, 1970-85, exec. officer polit. sci. Ph.D. program, 1970-75, dean research and univ. programs Grad. Sch. and Univ. Center, 1975-78, prof. emeritus, 1985—, dir. Ralph Bunche Inst. on UN, 1984—91, dir. emeritus, 1991—. Vis. lectr. Johns Hopkins Sch. Advanced Internat. Studies, 1956; vis. prof. African and Middle East Insts., Columbia U., 1963-68; co-chair RalphBunche Centenary Commemoration com., 2001—. Author: The United Nations and The Italian Colonies, 1950, Self-Determination and Dependent Areas, 1955, (with J.S. Szyliowicz) The Contemporary Middle East: Tradition and Innovation, 1965, Ralph Bunche: The Man and His Times, 1990, (with Leon Gordenker) The Challenging Role of the UN Secretary-General, 1993; also articles. Served with AUS, 1942-45. Grantee Social Sci. Research Council, 1951, 54, 64; Fulbright scholar France and N. Africa, 1956-57 Fellow Middle East Studies Assn.; mem. Internat. Studies Assn. (pres. Middle Atlantic region 1978-80), Am. Polit. Sci. Assn., Acad. Coun. on UN System (vice chair 1990-91). Office: CUNY Grad Ctr 365 5th Ave New York NY 10016-4334 E-mail: brivlin@gc.cuny.edu.

RIVLIN, RACHEL, lawyer; b. Bangor, Maine, Sept. 1, 1945; d. Lawrence and A. Sara (Rich) Lait. BA, U. Maine, 1965; MA, U. Louisville, 1968; JD, Boston Coll., 1977. Bar: Mass. 1977, U.S. Dist. Ct. Mass. 1978, U.s. Ct. Appeals (1st cir.) 1983, U.S. Supreme Ct. 1985. Audiologist Boston City

Hosp., 1969-72; dir. audiology Beth Israel Hosp., 1972-74; atty. Legal Sys. Devel., 1977-78, Liberty Mut. Ins., Boston, 1978-82; counsel, sec. Lexington Ins. Co., 1982-85, v.p., assoc. gen. counsel, sec., 1985—. Mem. civil rights com. Anti-Defamation League, Boston, 1982—; bd. dirs. DanceArt, Inc., 1985—92. Mem.: ABA (vice chmn. 1980—81, com. pub. regulation of ins. 1980—, vice chmn. pub. rels. 1981—84, excess surplus lines and reins com. 1983—, internat. ins. law com. 1983—, chmn. elect 1984—85, chmn. 1985—86, nat. inst. insurer insolvency 1986, vice chmn. 1986—87, chair-elect 1987—88, ann. meeting arrangements chmn. TIPS 1988, nat. inst. reins collections and insolvency 1988, chmn. 1988—89, nat. inst. insurer insolvency 1989, sr. vice chmn. 1989—90, vice chmn. 1997—, task force ins. and corp. counsel interests and involvement 1999—), Boston Bar Assn. (chmn. membership com. 1978—83, coun., 1983-86 2002—, chmn. corp. counsel com. 1987, steering com. corp. bus. law and fin. sect. 1987—89, edn. com. 1987—89, chmn. ins. law com. 1987—90, nominating com. 1988, dinner dance com. 1989, edn. com. 1990—91, chmn. ins. com. 1990—, ethics com. 1993—, dinner dance com. 1994, comprehensive revision Mass. corp. law 2000—, multi-disciplinary practice task force 2000—02, coun. 2002—), Boston Coll. Law Sch. Alumni Assn. (ann. fund com. 1981—89, coun. 1983—87, chmn. telethon com. 1989—94, nominating com. 1990, search com. for dean 1993, search com. for law sch. fund dir. 1993, leadership gifts exec. com. 1994—98, search com. for dir. instl. advancement 1995, reunion com. 2002, Father James Malley award 1996). Home: 122 Lincoln St Newton MA 02461-1528 Office: Lexington Ins Co 200 State St Ste 12 Boston MA 02109-2605

RIVLIN, RONALD SAMUEL, mathematics educator emeritus; b. London, May 6, 1915; came to U.S., 1952, naturalized, 1955; s. Raoul and Bertha (Aronsohn) R.; m. Violet Larusso, June 16, 1948; 1 son, John Michael. BA, St. John's Coll., Cambridge U., 1937, MA, 1939, ScD, 1952; D.Sc. h.c., Nat. U. Ireland, 1980, Nottingham U., 1980, Tulane U., 1982; Dr. h.c., Sch. Tech. U. Thessaloniki, 1984. Rsch. physicist GE, Eng., 1937-42; sci. officer Telecom. Rsch. Establishment, Ministry Aircraft Prodn., Eng., 1942-44; rsch. physicist, head phys. rsch., supt. rsch. Brit. Rubber Prodrs. Rsch. Assn., 1944-52; head rsch. group Davy-Faraday Lab., Royal Instn., London, 1948-52; cons. Naval Rsch. Lab., Washington, 1952-53; prof. applied math. Brown U., 1953-63, L. Herbert Ballou U. prof., 1963-67, prof. applied math. and engring sci., 1963-67, chmn. divsn. applied math., 1958-63; professeur associé U. Paris, 1966-67; Centennial Univ. prof., dir. Ctr. for Application of Math. Lehigh U., Bethlehem, Pa., 1967-80, prof. emeritus, 1980—, adj. Univ. prof., 1980-88. Co-chmn. Internat. Congress Rheology, 1963; Russell Severance Springer vis. prof. U. Calif.-Berkeley, 1977; fellow Inst. Advanced Study, Berlin, 1984-85; Disting. vis. prof. U. Del., 1985-86. Contbr. articles profl. publs.; mem. editorial com. Jour. Rational Mechanics and Analysis, 1952-57, Archive for Rational Mechanics and Analysis, 1957-72, Jour. Math. Physics, 1960, Jour. Applied Physics, 1960-63, Acta Rheologica Acta, 1963-2000, Internat. Jour. Biorheology, 1972-74, Mechanics Research Communications, 1974-2002, Jour. Non-Newtonian Fluid Mechanics, 1975-2001, Meccanica, 1975-94, Internat. Jour. Solids and Structures, 1990-95, Zietschrift für Angewandte Mathematik und Mechanik, 1992—; collected papers pub., 1996. Recipient Panetti prize, 1975, von Humboldt Sr. award, 1981, Charles Goodyear medal Am. Chem. Soc., 1992, von Karman medal ASCE, 1993; Guggenheim fellow, 1961-62. Fellow ASME (mem. exec. com. applied mechanics divsn. 1975-80, vice-chmn. and sec. 1978-79, chmn. 1979-80, Timoshenko Medal 1987), Acad. Mechanics, Am. Phys. Soc.; mem. NAE, Soc. Natural Philosophy (chmn. 1963-64), Am. Acad. Arts and Scis., Inst. Physics (gov. 1974-76), Soc. Rheology (exec. com. 1957-59, 71-77, Bingham medal 1958, v.p. 1971-73, pres. 1973-75, nat. com. theoretical and applied mechanics 1973-82, chmn. 1976-78, vice chmn. 1978-80), Internat. Union Theoretical and Applied Mechanics (gen. assembly 1975-82, chmn. U.S. del. 1978), Coun. Sci. Pres. (sec.-treas. 1975, exec. bd. 1975-77), Mex. Soc. Rheology (hon.), Accademia Nazionale dei Lincei (fgn.), Royal Irish Acad. (hon.). Home: 1604 Merryweather Dr Bethlehem PA 18015-5249 E-mail: rsrivlin@aol.com.

RIVNER, MICHAEL HARVEY, neurologist; b. Bklyn., Sept. 26, 1950; s. Norman and Carol (Simson) R.; m. Roberta Fran Gottlieb, Aug. 13, 1972; children: Asher, Joshua, Peter, Harold. BA, Duke U., 1972; MD, Emory U., 1978. Diplomate Am. Bd. Psychiatry and Neurology, added qualifications in clin. neurophysiology; diplomate Am. Bd. Electrodiagnostic Medicine. Intern, resident in neurology Med. Coll. Ga., Augusta, 1978-82, from fellow to prof. neurology, 1982—. Cons. neurology Eisenhower Med. Hosp., Ft. Gordon, Ga., 1982—, VA Med. Ctr., Augusta, 1982—. V.p., campaign chmn. Augusta Jewish Fedn., 1994, pres., 1995-97; treas. CSRA Swim League, Augusta, 1993-97; treas. Augusta Jewish C.C. Fellow Am. Acad. Neurology (computer com. 2000—, publs. com. 2001); mem. Am. Assn. Electrodiagnostic Medicine (equipment com. 1984-87, tng. program com. 1989-92, edn. com. 1992-97, chmn. edn. com. 1994-97, chmn. media com. 1999-2000), Southeastern Neuromuscular Group (pres. 1996—). Avocations: computer programming, bicycling. Office: Med Coll Ga EMG Lab Augusta GA 30912 E-mail: mrivner@neuro.mcg.edu.

RIX, ROBERT ALVIN, JR. retired neurosurgeon; b. Grimes County, Tex., Nov. 8, 1917; s. Robert Alvin Sr. and Amy Hunter Rix.; m. Marjorie Bozeman, Dec. 11, 1939 (dec. Dec. 1974); children: Judith Carolyn Rix Jones, Robert Michael; m. Patricia H. Botkin, Nov. 21, 1975. BA, Tex. A&M U., Commerce, 1937; MD, U. Tex. Med. Br., Galveston, 1941. Diplomate Am. Bd. Neurol. Surgery, 1950. Intern Univ. Hosp., Oklahoma City, 1941-43, resident in neurosurgery, 1947-48, Barnes Hosp., St. Louis, 1943-44, 46-47; pvt. practice specializing in neurosurgery Drs. Wilkins, Herrmann and Rix, Oklahoma City, 1948-66; pvt. practice neurosurgeon, neurologist, 1966-93; mem. faculty Okla. U. Health Scis. Ctr., 1948-92, clin. prof. emeritus, 1992—. Mem. med. staff St. Anthony Hosp., Oklahoma City, 1948-93, Bapt. Integris Hosp., Oklahoma City, 1959-93, Univ. Hosps., Oklahoma City, 1948-92, Mercy Hosp., Oklahoma City, 1948-91, Presbyn. Hosp., Oklahoma City, 1948-91. Contbr. articles to profl. jours. Lt. Med. Corps U.S. Navy, 1944-46, PTO. Mem. AMA, Okla. State Med. Assn., So. Neuro-Surg. Assn., Okla. Neurol. Soc. (pres. 1971-72), Rocky Mountain Neurosurgery Soc. (v.p. 1975-76), Oklahoma City Acad. Medicine (sec. 1987, pres. 1988). Episcopalian. Avocation: gardening. Home: 608 NW 42d St Oklahoma City OK 73118-7004

RIZEL, PAUL JONAS, small business owner; b. Brockton, Mass., July 22, 1957; s. Richard Roy and Theresa (Venslauskas) R. BA in Psychology, U. Mass., Boston, 1979; student, Wentworth Inst. Tech., Boston, 1985-86, Peterson Sch. Steam Engring., Woburn/Westwood, Mass., 1992. Lic. in oil heating, refrigeration, boiler operation/maintenance, grade 4 drinking water treatment, grade 7 waste water treatment. Locksmith Able Locksmiths, Canton, Mass., 1982-83; founder, owner Friday Locksmiths, West Bridgewater, 1983—; plumbing and heating cons. Brockton area, 1986-92; founder, owner Prospect Heating, West Bridgewater, 1992—. Mem. People for the Am. Way, 1985—, ACLU, 1986—, Halt and Common Cause, 1988—, Pub. Citizen, 1990&, others. Served with U.S. Army, 1979-82. Mem. Artists-Blacksmiths Assn. N.Am., Nat. Safeman's Orgn., Assoc. Locksmiths Am., Nat. Locksmith Assn., Am. Water Works Assn. and Water Environment Fed. Avocations: blacksmithing, machinist work, travel, collecting Civil War equipment, electrical experimentation.

RIZER, FRANKLIN MORRIS, physician, otolaryngologist; b. Gallipolis, Ohio, Aug. 13, 1953; s. Franklin Morris and Wanda Mae (Potts) R.; m. Maria Nicolette Guglielmi, Feb. 8, 1986. BS cum laude, Ohio State U., 1975; MD, U. Cin., 1979; M in Med. Mgmt., Tulane U., 1997; MBA, Youngstown State U., 1998. Diplomate Am. Bd. Otolaryngology. Intern U. Calif., Davis, 1979-80; resident U. Wash., Seattle, 1980-81, Ea. Va. U. Coll. of Medicine, Norfolk, 1981-84; fellow House Ear Inst., 1984-87; chief otology St. Joseph's Riverside Hosp., Warren, Ohio, 1989—; assoc. prof. Ea. Va. Coll. of Medicine, Norfolk, 1987—, Northeastern Ohio U. Coll. of Medicine, Rootstown, 1987—, Ohio State U., Columbus, 1995—. Fellowship dir. Warren Otologic Group, Warren, 1991—. Contbr. articles to profl. jours. Trustee Makoning Valley Macintosh Users Group, Warren, 1989-92; active Leadership Warren, 1989; chmn., bd. dirs. Humility of Mary Integrated Delivery Network, 1995—. With USAF, 1971-73. Fellow Am. Acad. Otolaryngology; mem. Am. Acad. Facial Plastics, Am. Coll. Physician Execs., Am. Laryngological, rhinological and Otological Soc., Soc. of Wilderness Medicine, Undersea and Hyperbaric Med. Soc., Delta Mu Delta, Phi Kappa Phi. United Methodist. Avocations: scuba diving, bicycling, camping, gardening. Home: 469 Country Club Dr NE Warren OH 44484-4616 Office: Warren Otologic Group 3893 E Market St Ste 2 Warren OH 44484-4791

RIZK, MYSOON, art historian, artist, educator; b. Damascus, Syria, Feb. 4, 1961; came to the U.S., 1963; d. Samir Habib and Jalilah Rizk. BA in Studio Arts, Oberlin Coll., 1983; BS in Archl. Studies with honors, U. Ill., 1987, AM, 1994, PhD in Art History, 1997. Cataloging asst. Watson Libr., Met. Mus. Art, N.Y.C., 1988; sr. art editor Publ. Svcs., Champaign, Ill., 1988-89; editl. asst., copywriter Wolfram Rsch., Inc., 1989-90; rsch. asst. art history program U. Ill., Champaign-Urbana, 1991-94; gallery asst. Gracie Mansion Gallery, N.Y.C., 1994-95; dir., founder The Centuries Gallery, Bklyn., 1995; gallery asst., rschr. PPOW Gallery, N.Y.C., 1994-96; archivist Estate of David Wojnarowicz, 1994-96; asst. prof. art history and humanities Milw. Inst. Art and Design, 1997—. Grad. tchg. asst. U. Ill., Champaign-Urbana, 1990-91, grad. tchg. asst. art history program, 1993; mus. intern Inst. València (Spain) d'Art Modern Julio González, 1993; presenter and cons. in field. Contbr. articles to profl. jours. Mem. Coll. Art Assn., Midwest Art History Soc., Phi Kappa Phi. Democrat.

RIZOWY, CARLOS GUILLERMO, lawyer, educator, political analyst; b. Sarandi Grande, Uruguay, Mar. 5, 1949; came to U.S., 1973, naturalized, 1981; s. Gerszon and Eva (Visnia) R.; m. Charlotte Gordon, Mar. 14, 1976; children: Brian Isaac, Yael Deborah, Michal Evie. BA, Hebrew U., Jerusalem, 1971; MA, U. Chgo., 1975, PhD, 1981; JD, Chgo. Kent Coll. Law, Ill. Inst. Tech., 1983. Bar: Ill. 1983, U.S. Dist. Ct. (no. dist.) Ill. 1983, U.S. Ct. Appeals (7th cir.) 1983. Asst. prof. polit. sci. Roosevelt U., Chgo., 1982-89, chmn. dept. polit. sci., 1983-86, dir. internat. studies program, 1986-89; mng. ptnr. Ray, Rizowy & Fleischer, 1983-90; ptnr. corp. law dept. Gottlieb and Schwartz, 1990-92; ptnr. Levenfeld, Eisenberg, Janger, Glassberg, Samotny & Halper, 1993-94; of counsel Sonnenschein, Nath & Rosenthal, 1994—. Dir. Midwest Am. Friends of Hebrew U., 1997—; hon. consul of Uruguay, Chgo., 1994—; adj. assoc. prof. Spertus Coll. Judaica, Chgo., 1984—; weekly polit. analyst on Middle East, internat. law and fgn. policy, resource specialist Sta. WBEZ Pub. Radio and BBC Latin Am.; mem. panel of arbitrators of Mediation and Arbitration Ctr., Internat. Arbitration Ct. for Mercosur Bolsa de Comercio, Uruguay, 1999—. Author: Avoiding Premises Liability Suits by Improving Security, 1991, Middle East Security: Five Areas to Watch, 1997. V.p., resource specialist to exec. com. Orgn. Children of Holocaust Survivors, Chgo., 1982; pres. Assn. Children Holocaust Survivors, 1986-91; pres. bd. dirs. Soviet Jewry Legal Advocacy Ctr., 1986-88; rsch. com. Nat. Strategy Forum, bd. dirs. UN Assn. U.S., 1985-89; mem. cmty. rels. com. Jewish Fedn. Met. Chgo., 1983-84; mem. adv. bd., chmn. internat. affairs commn. Am. Jewish Congress, Chgo., 1983-85, chmn. subcom. for Israel, 1986-88; mem. Nat. Spkrs. Bur. United Jewish Appeal, Nat. Spkrs. Bur. Devel. Corp. for Israel; mem. adv. bd. Chgo. Action for Soviet Jewry, 1983-85; bd. dirs. Am. Friends of Hebrew U., Chgo., 1984-86, Florence Heller Jewish Cmty. Ctr., 1986-88, Soviet Jewry Legal Advocacy Ctr., 1986-88; mem. human rights com. Anti-Defamation League, 1986, bd. dirs., 1989—; bd. dirs. Bd. Jewish Edn., 1989-91, Hispanic Coalition for Jobs, 1991-94; chmn. univ. educators divsn. Jewish United Fund, 1988-90; mem. consular corp. adv. bd. Internat. Vis. Ctr. Chgo., 1995—, com. fgn. affairs Chgo. Coun. Fgn. Rels., 1994—. Scholar Hebrew U., 1967-72, U. Chgo., 1972-78, Hillman Found., 1978, Peter Volid Found., 1980; recipient Globalist award Heritage Internat. Trade Assn., 1997. Mem. ATLA, ABA (chmn. bus. com. 1993-95), Assn. Ibero-Am. Consuls of Chgo., Ill. State Bar Assn., Chgo. Bar Assn. (internat. trade com.), Latin Am. Bar Assn., Nat. Hispanic Bar Assn., Am. Immigration Lawyers Assn., Am. Polit. Sci. Assn., Am. Judicature Soc., Exec. Club Chgo., Internat. Platform Assn., Wexner Heritage Found., Am. Forum, Latin Am. C. of C. (bd. dirs. 1991—, gen. counsel 1992—), Anshe Emet Congregation, Masons. Office: Sonnenschein Nath & Rosenthal 8000 Sears Tower Chicago IL 60606

RIZZETTA, CAROLYN TERESA, musical instrument, sound recording entrepreneur; b. Chgo., June 22, 1942; d. Frank Thomas and Teresa Margaret (Sylvester) Peter; m. Samuel Charles Rizzetta, Apr. 23, 1966. Student, Art Inst. Chgo., 1961-63; BA, Rosary Coll., 1964, MLS, 1965. Reference librarian Art Dept. Chgo. Pub. Library, 1965; freelance illustrator Macmillan Pub. Co., N.Y.C., 1966; registrar, cataloger Kalamazoo (Mich.) Pub. Mus., 1967; asst. librarian Def. Nuclear Agy., Washington, 1968-69; serials cataloger Library of Congress, 1970-73, with intern, 1971-72; head of serials U. Va., Charlottesville, 1974-77; musical instrument maker Valley Head, W.Va., 1978-83; bus. mgr. Rizzetta Music, Inwood, 1984—. Illustrator Invertebrate Zoology, 1969. Mem. Am. Craft Council, Guild of Am. Luthiers. Avocations: photography, gardening, hiking. Home and Office: Rizzetta Music PO Box 530 Inwood WV 25428-0530

RIZZI, JOSEPH VITO, banker; b. Berwyn, Ill., Dec. 5, 1949; s. Joseph and Mary Catherine (Mancini) R.; m. Candace Kunz, June 24, 1972; children: Jennifer, Joseph, Sammantha. BS in Commerce summa cum laude, DePaul U., 1971; MBA, U. Chgo., 1973; JD magna cum laude, U. Notre Dame, 1976. Bar: Ill. 1976. Law clk. to judge U.S. Dist. Ct. (no. dist.) Ill., 1976-77; exec. v.p. T.B.R. Enterprises, Inc., Downers Grove, Ill., 1977-83; sr. v.p. ABN AMRO, Amsterdam, The Netherlands, 1983—. Mem. Delta Epsilon Sigma. Roman Catholic. Home: 287 Bartram Rd Riverside IL 60546-1886 Office: ABNAMRO Bank New York NY Netherlands E-mail: Joe.Rizzi@abnamro.com.

RIZZI, TERESA MARIE, speech and language pathologist; b. Denver, Aug. 8, 1964; d. Theophilus Marcus and Maudie Marie (Pitts) R. BA in Speech Pathology, BA in Spanish, U. Denver, 1986; MS in Speech Pathology, Vanderbilt U., 1988. Pediatric speech-lang. pathologist Rose Med. Ctr., Denver, 1988-90; pvt. practice, 1990—; Spanish tchr. Temple Emanual, 1992-95; owner, operator Niños De Colo., Talk of The Town Speech-Lang. Pathologists. Spanish tutor and interpreter, Denver, 1988—; bilingual pediatric speech-lang. pathologist The Children's Hosp., Denver, 1994-98, United Cerebral Palsy Assn., 1998-99; presenter in field. G'arin grantee Ctrl. Agy. Jewish Edn., 1993, grantee U. No. Colo. Grad. Sch., 1994. Mem. Am. Speech-Lang.-Hearing Assn. (Continuing Edn. award 1991), Colo. Speech-Lang.-Hearing Assn., Internat. Assn. Orofacial Myology, Phi Sigma Iota. Avocations: computers, chess. Office: Talk of Town Speech Lang Pathologists 1805 S Bellaire St Ste 217 Denver CO 80222-4313 E-mail: duquesahuera@earthlink.net.

RIZZO, DONALD CHARLES, biology educator; b. Boston, June 10, 1945; s. Michael S. and Rita F. (Ward) R. BA, Boston State Coll., 1968; MS, Cornell U., 1970, PhD, 1973. Rsch. asst. Dept. Entomology Cornell U., Ithaca, N.Y., 1968-73; instr. Siena Heights Coll., Adrian, Mich., 1973-74; asst. prof. Marygrove Coll., Detroit, 1974-78, assoc. prof., 1978-95, prof., 1995—, head biology dept., 1974—, unit head math. and sci., 1975—, project dir. Minority Instns. Sci. Improvement program grants, 1983-85, 85-87. Mem. Am. Inst. Biolog. Sci., Nat. Assn. Sci. Tchrs., AAUP, Mich. Depression Glas Soc. (chmn. book com. 1985—). Democrat. Roman Catholic. Home: 41 Cambridge Blvd Pleasant Ridge MI 48069-1104

RIZZO, FRANK ALBERT, physician; b. Detroit, June 7, 1936; MD, U. Mich., 1960. Diplomate Am. Bd. Neurology. Intern Harper Hosp., Detroit, 1960-61; resident Henry Ford Hosp., 1963-65; resident in neurology Mt. Sinai Hosp., N.Y.C., 1965-68, fellow in neurology, 1968-70; chief divsn. neurology Jersey City Med. Ctr., 1969-81; pvt. practice N.Y.C., 1971—. Asst. clin. prof., attending neurologist Mt. Sinai Sch. Medicine, N.Y.C., 1971—, chmn. med. records com., 1991-93; attending neurologist Beth Israel Med. Ctr., N.Y.C., 1971—. Lt. USNR, 1961-63. Mem. AMA, AAAS, Am. Acad. Neurology, Med. Soc. N.Y., Tinnitus Soc. Office: 1155 Park Ave New York NY 10128-1209

RIZZO, GARY EDWARD, college dean; b. Erie, Pa., Mar. 28, 1944; s. Carl Joseph and Marie Grace (Manuele) R.; children: Brian, Gary, Thomas. BS, Gannon U., Erie, Pa., 1967; MS, Case Western Res. U., Cleve., 1969; PhD, U. Pitts., 1974. Nat. cert. counselor. Counselor Cuyahoga C.C., Cleve., 1969-71, Westmoreland County C.C., Youngwood, Pa., 1972-82; dir. counseling Montgomery C.C., Blue Bell, 1982-84, assoc. dean lifelong learning, 1984-89, assoc. acad. dean, 1989—. Cons. in field. Chairperson, bd. dirs. Harmony Theater, 1997—; ednl. rep. Montgomery County Fire Academy, 1994—. Am. Coun. on Edn. fellow, 1984-85; named Outstanding Faculty Mem., Westmoreland Community Coll., Greensburg, Pa., 1974. Fellow Am. Coun. on Edn.; mem. Pa. Coll. Personnel Assn. (bd. dirs. 1984-88, Outstanding Contbr. 1988), Am. Coll. Personnel Assn., Montgomery County Counselors Assn. (cons.), Pa. Counseling Assn. (dir. Outstanding Counseling Ctr. 1982). Avocations: skiing, camping, travel, model trains. Home: 705 Karens Ct North Wales PA 19454-2039 Office: Montgomery County CC 340 Dekalb Pike Blue Bell PA 19422-1412

RIZZO, JAMES GERARD, lawyer; b. Hartford, Conn., Nov. 6, 1962; s. Thomas Dignan and Jean Kathryn (Foley) R.; m. Patricia Marie Conrad, Oct. 5, 1996; children: Madeleine Patrice, Abigail Rose, Peter James. AB, Georgetown U., 1984; JD, Fordham U., 1990. Bar: Conn. 1990, N.Y. 1991, U.S. Dist. Ct. (ea. and so. dists.) N.Y. 1991, D.C. 1996, U.S. Supreme Ct. 1998. Assoc. Bower & Gardner, N.Y.C., 1990-93, Mudge, Rose, Guthrie, Alexander & Ferdon, N.Y.C., 1993-94, O'Melveny & Myers LLP, N.Y.C., 1994-97; ptnr. Carr Goodson Warner, Washington, 1997-2000, McDermott, Will & Emery, Washington, 2000—. Hon. usher St. Patrick's Cathedral, N.Y.C., 1984—; v.p. St. Joseph's Parish Coun., Bronxville, N.Y., 1988-90. Mem. Bar Assn. D.C., Soc. of the Friendly Sons of St. Patrick, John Carroll Soc., Lowes Island Club, Sea Island Club. Republican. Roman Catholic. Office: McDermott Will & Emery 600 13th St NW Washington DC 20005

RIZZO, RONALD STEPHEN, lawyer; b. Kenosha, Wis., July 15, 1941; s. Frank Emmanuel and Rosalie (Lo Cicero); children: Ronald Stephen Jr., Michael Robert. BA, St. Norbert Coll., 1963; JD, Georgetown U., 1965, LLM in Taxation, 1966. Bar: Wis. 1965, Calif. 1967, Ill. 1999. Assoc. Kindel & Anderson, L.A., 1966-71, ptnr., 1971-86, Jones, Day, Reavis & Pogue, L.A., 1986-93, Chgo., 1993—. Bd. dirs. Guy LoCicero & Son Inc., Kenosha, Wis. Contbg. editor ERISA Litigation Reporter, 1994-99; mem. internat. adv. editl. bd. Jour. Pensions Mgmt. and Mktg. Schulte zur Hausen fellow Inst. Internat. and Fgn. Trade Law, Georgetown U., 1966. Fellow Am. Coll. Tax Counsel, Am. Coll. Employee Benefits Counsel (charter); mem. ABA (chmn. com. on employee benefits sect. on taxation 1988-89, vice chair com. on govt. submissions 1995-99), Los Angeles County Bar Assn. (chmn. com. on employee benefits sect. on taxation 1977-79, exec. com. 1977-78, 90-92), State Bar Calif. (co-chmn. com. on employee benefits sect. on taxation 1980), West Pension Conf. (steering com. L.A. chpt. 1980-83). Avocations: reading, golf, travel. Home: # 19C 1040 N Lake Shore Dr Chicago IL 60611-6164 Office: Jones Day Reavis & Pogue 77 W Wacker Ste 3500 Chicago IL 60601-1692 E-mail: rsrizzo@jonesday.com.

RIZZO, THOMAS DIGNAN, orthopedic surgeon; b. N.Y.C., May 25, 1931; s. Peter-Cyrus and Rose Ann (Dignan) R.; m. Jean Foley; children: Thomas D. Jr., Peter F., James G., Kathryn Anne Marie, William J., Francis V. BS cum laude, Georgetown U., 1958, MD cum laude, 1956. Diplomate Am. Bd. Orthopedic Surgery, Nat. Bd. Med. Examiners. Intern Georgetown U. Med. Ctr., Washington, 1956-57; asst. resident surgeon St. Vincent's Hosp., N.Y.C., 1957-58; resident in orthopedic surgery Hosp. for Spl. Surgery, 1958-59, fellow in orthopedic surgery, 1961-62; resident fellow in orthopedic surgery Newington Hosp. for Crippled Children, Conn., 1962; pvt. practice Bronxville, N.Y., 1962—. Clin. cons. orthopedic surgery N.Y. State Dept. Health, 1965; assoc. dir. orthopedics Lawrence Hosp., Bronxville, 1970-79, attending staff, 1963—; asst. attending St. John's Riverside Hosp., Yonkers, N.Y., 1963-74, sr. attending surgeon, 1974-87, dir. dept. orthopedic surgery, 1975-86, courtesy staff, 1987-96; assoc. attending Dobbs Ferry Hosp., 1970-73, cons. staff, 1973—; asst. attending Hosp. for Spl. Surgery, N.Y.C., 1963, Doctors Hosp., 1973-80; asst. attending surgeon N.Y. Hosp., 1981-83. Mem. adv. bd. Bapt. Home for Aged; trustee Fordham Prep. Sch., 1987-93; mem. Westchester Health Planning Coun., 1983-96, sec., 1988-89; bd. dirs. Hudson Valley Health Sys. Agy., 1988-96; bd. visitors Georgetown U. Med. Ctr., 1997—. Fellow ACS, Am. Acad. Orthopedic Surgeons, N.Y. Acad. of Medicine, Westchester Acad. Medicine (bd. trustees 1968—), Am. Orthopedic Foot and Ankle Soc.; mem. AMA, N.Y. State Med. Soc. (county del. 1975-87), Westchester County Med. Soc. (bd. dirs. 1968—, pres. 1975-76), Irish Am. Orthopedic Soc., N.Y. State Soc. Orthopedic Surgeons, Ea. Orthopedic Assn., Georgetown U. Alumni Assn. (bd. govs. 1970-73, chpt. pres. 1970-72), KC, Knight of Malta, Knight of Holy Sepulchre, Lotos Club (N.Y.C.), Sea Island (Ga.) Club (founder), Lawrence Beach Club (Atlantic Beach, N.Y.), Alpha Omega Alpha. Home: Cottage 349 Cook PO Box 31229 Sea Island GA 31561-1229 Office: 77 Pondfield Rd Bronxville NY 10708-3809 Fax: 914-634-6025.

RIZZO, WILLIAM OBER, lawyer; b. Boston, Aug. 19, 1948; s. Nicholas Daniel and Edith Katherine (Kepler) R.; m. Susan J. Parker, May 17, 1984; 1 child, Aura E.P. AB, Lawrence U., 1970; JD, Columbia U., 1973. Bar: Mass. 1974, U.S. Dist. Ct. (fed. dist.) Mass. 1975. Law clk. to Hon. Irving R. Kaufman U.S. Ct. Appeals (2nd cir.), N.Y., 1973; assoc. Ropes & Gray, Boston, 1974-81; ptnr. McDermott & Rizzo, 1981-90, Kirkpatrick & Lockhart, Boston, 1990-96, Cherwin, Theise, Adelson & Loria, LLP, Boston, 1996—. Bd. dirs. Lawrence U. Alumni Assn., 1980-86, Beacon Hill Civic Assn., 1977-91, chmn. zoning and licensing com., 1977-84, pres., 1984-86, chmn. bd. dirs., 1986-88; trustee Thompson Island Edn. Ctr., 1981-95; chmn. Boston Groundwater Trust, 1986-91; mem. Beacon Hill Archtl. Commn., 1991-93, Brookline Preservation Commn., 1999—, Boston Preservation Alliance, 2000—, Brookline Zoning Commn., 2001—. Avocations: reading, Italian opera, collecting prints and antiques, tennis. Office: Cherwin Theise Adelson & Loria LLP One Internat Pl 11th Fl Boston MA 02110 E-mail: WRizzo@ctallaw.com.

RIZZUTO, LEANDRO PETER, consumer products company executive; b. N.Y.C., Apr. 10, 1938; s. Julian and Josephine (Rizzo) Rizzuto; children: Leandro P. Rizzuto Jr., Denis, Rita. Student, St. Johns U. Pres., chmn. bd. Conair Corp., Edison, N.J., 1959—. Bd. dirs. St. Jude's Children's Hosp., Memphis. Named Humanitarian of Yr., Cabrini Hosp., 1985; recipient Man of Yr. award, Boys Town of Italy, 1980, Achievement award, Italian Legions of Merit, 1983; fellow faculty, U. Bridgeport, 1984. Mem.: Columbus Club N.Y.C. Roman Catholic. Office: Conair Corp 1 Cummings Point Rd Stamford CT 06902-7901

RO, JAE YUN, pathologist; b. Seoul, Korea, Oct. 7, 1945; s. Kyeung-Yong and Soon Ie (Ha) R.; m. Jung-sil Cho, Oct. 23, 1972; 1 child, Bobby W. MD, Yonsei U. Sch. of Medicine, Seoul, Korea, 1969, MS, 1971, PhD, 1974. Diplomate Am. Bd. Pathology in Anatomic and Clin. Pathology; Korean Bd. Pathology in Anatomic Pathology; MD, Ohio, Tex., Ind. Resident dept. pathology Yonsei U., Seoul, Korea, 1969-73; chief dept. pathology Korean Army Hosp., Korea, 1973-76; instr. dept. pathology Yonsei U., 1976-78, asst. prof. dept. pathology, 1978-80; resident in anat. and clin. pathology Inst. Pathology Case Western Res. U., Cleve., 1980-84; fellow in pathology U. Tex./M.D. Anderson Cancer Ctr., Houston, 1984-85, asst. prof., 1987-89, assoc. prof., 1989-92, prof., 1992—. Author: Atlas of Surgical Pathology of the Male Reproductive Tract, 1997; mem. editorial bd. Internat. Jour. Surg. Pathology, 1993—, Advances in Anatomic Pathology, 1994—; guest editor Seminars in Diagnostic Pathology, 1988; contbr. over 300 articles to profl. jours., numerous abstracts to profl. publs., and numerous chpts. to books. Bd. dirs. Youth Meml. Mission Fund, Houston, 1990—. Maj. Korean Army, 1973-76. Named Top Honor Student, Yonsei U., 1969, Tchr. of Yr. M.D. Anderson Cancer Ctr., 1992, 94, 95, 96; grantee NIH, 1988-92, 91-95, 93-96. Mem. AMA, Am. Soc. Clin. Pathologists (chmn. short courses 1993—), Ohio Med. Assn., Coll. Am. Pathologists, Houston Soc. Pathologists (co-chmn. spring seminar 1991), Cleve. Soc. Pathologists, Internat. Acad. Pathology, Korean Soc. Pathology (chmn. short course 1994), Arthur Purdy Stout Soc. Surg. Pathologists. Baptist. Avocations: reading, golf. Address: 4702 Dickson St Houston TX 77007-7305

ROACH, DAVID GILES, computing administrator; b. Wisner, La., Oct. 26, 1948; s. David and Annie Laura (Hanks) R.; m. Vivian Viola Curry, July 23, 1967. BS in Math., U. La., 1970; MSc in Math. and Geology, U. Miss., 1975. Grad. teaching asst. computer ctr. U. La., Monroe, 1970-72; grad. asst. computer ctr. U. Miss., University, 1972, user svcs. mgr., 1973-74, asst. dir. user svcs., 1974-78; assoc. dir. computer ctr. Office Computing & Info. Systems, 1978-88; dep. dir. Office of Info. Tech., 1988-98; dir. Miss. Ctr. for Supercomputing Rsch., 1998—. Apptd. mem. Miss. Info. Tech. Svcs. Bd., 1994—, chmn. 1997-98, 99-00; chmn. Miss. Higher Edn. Rsch. Network Policy and Planning Com., 1992-94; chmn. bd. dirs. DEC Computer User Soc. S.E. U.S., 1977-78; voting rep. IBM Share, 1981—, CDC Users Group,

1987-90, Amdahl Users Group, 1986-98, Cray Users Group, 1991—. Contbr. article to profl. jour. Planning com. mem. Oxford (Miss.)/Lafayette County Sequicentennial, 1987; bd. dirs. Oxford/Lafayette County United Way, 1987-90; sustaining mem. Yocona Area Coun. Boy Scouts Am., 1981—. Mem. Assn. Computing Machinery, Spl. Interest Group on Univ. and Coll. Computing Svcs., Miss. Hist. Soc., Oxford Lions (pres. 1986-87, Lion of Yr. 1986-87, Svc. award 1992-93). Methodist. Avocations: college football, fishing, Miss./La. history, genealogy.. Home: PO Box 2241 University MS 38677-2241 Office: Office Info Tech Miss Ctr Supercomputing Rsc 303 Powers Hall University MS 38677-1848 E-mail: ccdavid@olemiss.edu.

ROACH, ELEANOR MARIE, elementary education educator; b. Indpls., Nov. 30, 1932; d. Armand Dunnington and Ruth (Holman) R. BS in Art Edn., Ind. U., 1954; MS in Elem. Edn., Butler U., 1966. Cert. life K-12 art tchr., K-8 gen. elem. tchr., Ind. Tchr. art Wayne Twp. Pub. Schs., Indpls., 1954-57; freelance artist, 1957-60; artist, libr. designer Remington Rand, Indpls., 1960-61; elem. tchr. Indpls. Pub. Schs., 1962-70, tchr. academically talented, 1970-92, upper elem. tchr., 1992-94. Content cons. Macmillan-McGraw Hill, N.Y.C., 1989-90, 1996; cons. Ind. State Mus., Indpls., 1988, 92. Photographer textbook Indiana, 1990. Former set designer Footlite Mus., Indpls.; stage mgr. Christian Theol. Sem. Repetory Theatre, Indpls., 1979-75. Recipient 1st place for ceramics Ind. State Fair, 1953, 2d place, 1954. Mem. NEA, Ind. Tchrs. Assn., Indpls. Edn. Assn., Ind. Coun. for Social Studies, Washington County Ind. Hist. Soc., Rush County Heritage, Inc., Nature Conservancy, Ind. Audubon Soc., Ind. Hist. Soc.. Morgan County (Ind.) Master Gardeners Club. Democrat. Roman Catholic. Avocations: writing poetry, gardening, visiting historical sites and museums, arts and crafts, music. Home and Office: PO Box 278 Brooklyn IN 46111-0278

ROACH, JAMES CLARK, government official; b. Charleston, W. Va., Sept. 29, 1943; m. Susan Roelke Roach, June 27, 1970; children: Edward J., Andrew A. BA in Social Studies and History, W. Va. Wesleyan Coll., 1965; MA in Am. History, W. Va. U. Historian Harpers Ferry (W. Va.) Nat. Hist. Pk., 1967-68, 70-72; chief interpretation resource mgmt. Ft. Frederica Nat. Monument, St. Simons Island, Ga., 1972-74; asst. chief interpretation visitor svcs. Colonial Nat. Hist. Pk., Yorktown, Va., asst. chief interpretation, visitor svc. Jamestown; chief interpretation visitor svcs. Gettysburg (Pa.) Nat. Mil. Pk., Eisenhower Nat. Hist. Site, 1981-94; site mgr. Eisenhower Nat. Hist. Site, 1995—2001; sch.-to-work coord. Adams County Bus. Edn. Partnership, Gettysburg, Pa., 2001—. Sec. Gettysburg Peace Celebration Commn. Inc. (former bd. dirs.). With U.S. Army, 1968-70, Vietnam. Recipient Freeman Tilden award Mid-Atlantic Region Interpreter of Yr., 1984, Ea. Superior Performance award Nat. Park and Monument Assn., 1985, Spl. Events award GETT Travel Coun. award, 1986, 87. Mem. Assn. Nat. Pk. Rangers, Lincoln Fellowship Pa. (sec., past pres.), Adams County Torch Club (past pres.), Rotary (bd. dirs. Gettysburg club). Lutheran. Avocations: gardening, reading, fishing, stamp collecting. Home: 84 Knoxlyn Orrtanna Rd Gettysburg PA 17325-7215 Office: Adams County Bus Edn Partnership 18 Carlisle St Ste 203 Gettysburg PA 17325

ROACH, JAMES ROBERT, retired political science educator; b. Rock Rapids, Iowa, Aug. 25, 1922; s. Paul Ramsey and Doris (Kline) R. BA, U. Iowa, 1943; AM, Harvard U., 1948, PhD, 1950. Mem. faculty, adminstrn. U. Tex., Austin, 1949—, prof. govt., 1965-95, prof. emeritus, 1995—, dir. spl. programs, 1965-69, vice provost, dean interdisciplinary programs, 1971-72, dean divsn. gen. and comparative studies, 1972-74; counselor for cultural affairs Am. embassy, New Delhi, 1974-78. Fulbright vis. lectr. polit. sci. Rajasthan U., India, 1961-62; mem. Bd. Fgn. Scholarships, 1965-74, chmn., 1969-71; mem. U.S. Commn. for UNESCO, 1966-69. With USNR, 1943-46. Fulbright rsch. grantee, Australia, 1951-52, Ford Found. fgn. fellow, India, 1956-57. Mem. Assn. Asian Studies, Phi Beta Kappa, Kappa Tau Alpha, Sigma Delta Chi, Phi Kappa Psi. Democrat. Congregationalist. Home: 8604 Dorotha Ct Austin TX 78759-8113 Office: U Tex Dept Govt Austin TX 78712-1087

ROACH, JOHN D. building products company executive; b. West Palm Beach, Fla., Dec. 3, 1943; s. Benjamin Browning and Margaret (York) R.; m. Pam Flebbe, Dec. 29, 1967 (div. Aug. 1981); children: Vanessa, Alexandra; m. Elizabeth Louise Phillips, Aug. 28, 1982; children: Bruce Phillips, Bryce Phillips, Brian Phillips. BS in Indsl. Mgmt., MIT, 1965; MBA, Stanford U., 1967. Dir. mgmt. acctg. and info. systems Ventura div. Northrop Corp., Thousand Oaks, Calif., 1967-70; co-founder, mgr. Northrop Venture Capital, Century City, 1970-71; v.p., dir. Boston Consulting Group, Boston and Menlo Park, Calif., 1971-80; v.p., world-wide strategic mgmt. practice mng. officer Booz, Allen, Hamilton, San Francisco, 1980-82; Houston, 1982-83; vice chmn., mng. dir. Braxton Assocs., 1983-87; sr. v.p., chief fin. officer Manville Corp., Denver, 1987-88, exec. v.p. ops., 1988-91; pres. Manville Bldg. Products Group, 1988-90, Manville Mining and Minerals Group, Denver, 1990-91, Celite Corp., Denver, 1990-91; chmn., pres., chief exec. officer Fibreboard Corp., Dallas, 1991-97; chmn., pres., CEO Stonegate Resources, 1997—2001, Builders FirstSource, Inc., Dallas, 1998—2001; chmn., CEO Stonegate Internat., 2001—, PMI Group, Kaiser Aluminum. Bd. dirs. Kaiser Aluminum, 2002—, NCI Bldg. Systems, PMI Group, 1995—, Am. Stock Exch., Thompson PBE, Magma Power, Fibreboard Corp., Builders First Source. Author: Strategic Management Handbook, 1983. Bd. dirs. Opera Colo., Denver, 1987-91, Bay Area Coun., San Francisco, 1991-96, Dallas Symphony, 1996—, mem. exec. com., 1996—; bd. trustees Alta Bates Med. Ctr.; mem. exec. com. San Francisco Opera Assn. Mem.: MIT Alumni Club, Stanford Grad. Sch. Bus. Club, Dallas Country Club, Cordillera Country Club (Colo.), Beaver Creek (Colo.) Country Club, Red Sky Golf Club (Wolcott, Colo.), Preston Trail Golf Club (Dallas), Cherry Hills Country Club (Englewood, Colo.). Avocations: skiing, hunting, golf. Home: 4278 Bordeaux Ave Dallas TX 75205-3718 Office: Stonegate Internat 100 Crescent Ct 7th Fl Dallas TX 75201

ROACH, JOHN HANDEE, JR. bank executive, investment banker, financial service executive; b. N.Y.C., Oct. 24, 1941; s. John Hendee and Julia (Casey) R.; m. Joan Hayden Muchmore, Sept. 23, 1972; children: Hayden, Cameron, John, Lauriston, Schuyler. BA, Washington and Jefferson Coll., 1964; postgrad., Aspen Inst., 1987, Harvard U., 1989. With Chem. Bank, N.Y.C., 1968-71, sr. v.p. corp. bank, 1972-87, mng. dir. corp. fin., 1987-92; ret., 1992; sr. mng. dir., vice chmn. The Geneva Cos., N.Y.C., 1992-94; sr. mng. dir., client mgmt. and mktg. Am. Internat. Group, 1994-97; sr. mng. dir. Reliance Nat., 1998-99, JP Morgan Pvt. Bank, Greenwich, Conn., 2000—01. Bd. dirs. Strategic Capital Resources Inc., Boca Raton, Fla. Capt. U.S. Army, 1964-66. Mem. Round Hill Club. Republican. Roman Catholic. E-mamil. Home: 16 Oakwood Ln Greenwich CT 06830-3909 E-mail: jhr.jr@att.net.

ROACH, JOHN ROBERT, retired archbishop; b. Prior Lake, Minn., July 31, 1921; s. Simon J. and Mary (Regan) R. BA, St. Paul Sem., 1946; MA, U. Minn., 1957; L.H.D. (hon.), Gustavus Adolphus Coll., St. Mary's Coll., St. Xavier U., Villanova U., U. St. Thomas, Coll. of St. Catherine. Ordained priest Roman Catholic Ch., 1946; instr. St. Thomas Acad., 1946-50, headmaster, 1951-68; named domestic prelate, 1966; rector St. John Vianney Sem., 1968-71; aux. bishop St. Paul and Mpls., 1971; consecrated bishop, 1971; pastor St. Charles Borromeo Ch., Mpls., 1971-73, St. Cecilia Ch., St. Paul, 1973-75; archbishop of, 1975-95. Appointed vicar for parishes, 1971, vicar for clergy, 1972— ; Episc. moderator Nat. Apostolate for Mentally Retarded, 1974; Mem. Priests Senate, 1968-72; pres. Priests Senate and Presbytery, 1970; chmn. Com. on Accreditation Pvt. Schs. in Minn., 1952-57; mem. adv. com. Coll. Entrance Exam. Bd., 1964; Episc. mem. Bishops and Pres.'s Com.; chmn. Bishops Com. to Oversee Implementation of the Call to Action Program, 1979-80; chmn. priestly formation com.; mem. Cath. Charity Bd. Trustee St. Paul Sem. Sch. Div., 1971-75, chmn., 1975-95; trustee Cath. U. Am., 1978-81, Coll. St. Catherine, 1975-95; chmn. bd. trustees St. Thomas Acad., U. St. Thomas, St. John Vianney Sem.; v.p. Nat. Conf. Cath. Bishops, 1977-80, pres., 1980-83, chmn. ad hoc com. on call to action, 1977; chair internat. policy com. U.S. Catholic Conf., 1990-93. Mem. Am. Coun. Edn. (del. 1963-65), Minn. Cath. Edn. Assn. (past pres.), Assn. Mil. Colls. and Schs. U.S. (past pres.), North Cen. Assn. Colls. and Secondary Schs., Nat. Conf. Cath. Bishops (adminstrv. com., priestly formation com., chmn. vocations com., priorities and plans com., com. on sexual abuse), U.S. Cath. Conf. (com. on social devel. and world peace 1990-93, priorities and plans com.), Nat. Cath. Edn. Assn. (chmn. bd. dirs.), Nat. Cath. Rural Life Conf. (past chmn. task force on food and agr. 1987-89). Address: Chancery Office 226 Summit Ave Saint Paul MN 55102-2121

ROACH, JOHN VINSON, II, retail company executive; b. Stamford, Tex., Nov. 22, 1938; s. John V. and Agnes M. (Hanson) R.; m. Barbara Jean Wiggin, Mar. 31, 1960; children: Amy, Lori. BA in Physics and Math., Tex. Christian U., 1961, MBA, 1965. V.p. Radio Shack, 1972-75, Radio Shack Mfg., 1975-78; exec. v.p. Radio Shack, 1978-80; gen. mgr. data processing Tandy Corp., Ft. Worth, 1967-73, pres., from 1980, CEO, from 1981, chmn., 1982-99. Chmn. bd. Justin Ind., 1999—2001. Bd. dirs. Van Cliburn Found.; chmn. bd. Tex. Christian U. Mem. Ft. Worth Club, City Club, Colonial Country Club. Office: River Crest Country Club 400 Throck Morton Ste 480 Fort Worth TX 76102-2819

ROACH, JON GILBERT, lawyer; b. Knoxville, Tenn., June 17, 1944; s. Walter Davis and Lena Rose (Chapman) R.; m. Mintha Marie Evans, Oct. 22, 1977; children: Jon G., II, Evan Graham. BS, U. Tenn., 1967, JD, 1969. Bar: Tenn. 1970, D.C. 1981, U.S. Ct. Appeals (6th cir.). Assoc. Stone & Bozeman, Knoxville, 1970—71; pvt. practice, 1971—75; delinquent tax atty. Sevier County, 1971—76; city atty., dir. of law City of Knoxville, 1976-83; ptnr. Peck, Shaffer & Williams, Knoxville, 1983-90, Watson, Hollow & Reeves, PLC, Knoxville, 1990—2002, Watson & Hollow, P.L.C., Knoxville, 2002—. City atty. City of Plainview, 1999—, City of Maynardville, 2000—; faculty Knoxville Bus. Coll., 1973-74; mem. Tenn. Commn. on Continuing Legal Edn. and Specialization of Tenn. Supreme Ct., 1995-2000. Mem. bd., Bapt. Health Sys. Found. Mem. ABA, Tenn. Bar Assn. (mem. ho. of dels.), Knoxville Bar Assn., D.C. Bar Assn., Kiwanis (East Knoxville). Democrat. Baptist. Office: Watson & Hollow PLC PO Box 131 1700 First Tennessee Plz Knoxville TN 37921-2639 Home: 722 Cheowa Cir Knoxville TN 37919-6676

ROACH, MARGOT RUTH, retired biophysicist, educator; b. Moncton, N.B., Can., Dec. 24, 1934; d. Robert Dickson and Katherine (McMillan) R.; m. Franklyn St. Aubyn House, Dec. 20, 1994 (wid. Feb. 2000). B.Sc. in Math. and Physics with honors, U. N.B., Fredericton, Can., 1955; MD, C.M. cum laude, McGill U., Montreal, Can., 1959; PhD in Biophysics, U. Western Ont., Can., 1963; D.Sc. (hon.), U. N.B., St. John, Can., 1981. Jr. intern Victoria Hosp., London, Can., 1959-60, fellow in cardiology Can., 1962-63, asst. resident in medicine Can., 1963-64, Toronto Gen. Hosp., 1964-65; mem. faculty, dept. biophysics U. Western Ont., London, Can., 1965—, head dept. biophysics Can., 1970-78, prof. Can., 1971-98, asst. prof. medicine Can., 1965-72, assoc. prof. Can., 1972-78, prof. Can., 1978-98, prof. emeritus Biophysics & Med. Can., 1998. Mem. staff dept. medicine Victoria Hosp., 1967-72, U. Hosp., London, 1972-98; Commonwealth vis. sci., dept. applied math. theoretical physics Cambridge U., 1975; vis. sci. Bioengring. Inst., Chonqing U., People's Republic of China, 1991; mem. bioengring. grants com. Med. Rsch. Coun. Can., 1993-96; cons. and lectr. in field. Active civic orgns. and coms. including Univ. Rsch. Coun., 1976-79; mem. interview bd. London Conf. of United Ch., 1967-90; steward United Ch. Can., 1967-73, elder, 1973-82, chair unified bd.; chmn. stewardship devel. com. Colborne St. United Ch., 1990-93; Tatamagouche pastoral charge United Ch. of Can., 2001-. Recipient A. Wilmer Duff prize in physics U. N.B., 1955, Cushing prize in pediatrics, 1959, Ciba Found. award for research in aging, 1959, Teaching award Faculty of Medicine U. Western Ont., 1990, Dean's award, 1997, Women of Distinction award YWCA, 1997; Med. Research Council fellow U. Western Ont., 1960-62, Arthur Guyton award Internat. Soc. Cardiovascular Medicine and Sci., 1997; numerous other fellowships and grants in medicine. Fellow Royal Coll. Physicians (Can.), Am. Coll. Cardiology (Young Investigator's award 1963); mem. Can. Physiol. Soc., Can. Cardiovascular Soc. (off council), Can. Clin. Investigation Soc. (council 1980-84), Can. Biophys. Soc., Can. Soc. Internal Medicine. Address: RR #1 Tatamagouche NS Canada B0K 1V0 E-mail: mroach@north.nsis.com.

ROACH, RALPH LEE, human services and rehabilitation consultant; b. Silver Spring, Md., Mar. 27, 1957; s. William A. and Mary B. (Collins) R.; m. Susan Diane Schirmacher, Aug. 17, 1985. BA, Messiah Coll., 1982; MS, Shippensburg U., 1985; postgrad., Kennedy-We. U., 1992—. Cert. rehab. counselor. Inventory controller Messiah Coll., Grantham, Pa., 1977-85; therapist, crisis interviewer Stevens Mental Health, Carlisle, 1983-86; psychotherapist, teenline counselor Holy Spirit Cmty. Mental Health Inst., Camp Hill, 1986—; presentor, cons. Lebanon (Pa.) Valley Coll., 1986; vocat. tng. mgr. Ctr. for Indsl. Tng., Mechanicsburg, Pa., 1985-87; program mgr. living unltd. program U. Hosp. Rehab./Children Pa. U. Hosp. Milton S. Hershey Med. Ctr., Hershey, 1987-92; corp. officer, clin. dir. Avalon Affiliates Rehab. Consultants, Inc. (now MRW, Inc.), Duncannon, 1993-95, MRW, Inc., 1995-97; behavior specialist and mobile therapist United Staffing Svcs./Edgewater Psychiat. Ctr., 1998-99; teenline counselor Holy Spirti Hosp./E. Pennsboro H.S., Camp Hill, Pa., 1999—. Faculty instr. dept. psychology Elizabethtown Coll., 1987; presenter at profl. confs. Edn. dir. Cumberland Valley Ch., Dillsburg, Pa., 1980-83; presentor Gov.'s Com. on Handicapped, Harrisburg, Pa., 1986; presentor various state/nat. confs. on vocat. rehab., Harrisburg, 1986—. Mem. ACA, Am. Acad. Rehab. Medicine, Pa. Specialists in Group Work, Pa. Crisis Intervention Assn., Pa. Assn. Rehab. Facilities, Keystone State Head Injury Found. Presbyterian. Avocations: boating, fishing, black powder hunting, gardening, Civil War history and curio collecting. Home: 901 Rupp Ave Apt 2 Camp Hill PA 17011-6656 Office: Holy Spirit Hosp 503 N 21st St Camp Hill PA 17011-2288 E-mail: rroach@057yahoo.com.

ROACH, THOMAS ADAIR, lawyer, mediator, arbitrator; b. Akron, Ohio, May 1, 1929; s. Edward Thomas and Mayme Bernice (Turner) R.; m. Sally Jane Bennett, July 11, 1953; children: Thomas, David, James, Dorothy, Steven, Patrick. AB, U. Mich., 1951, JD with distinction, 1953. Bar: Mich. 1953. Assoc. McClintock, Fulton, Donovan & Waterman (and successor firms), Detroit, 1956-62, ptnr., 1962-87; counsel Bodman, Longley & Dahling, Detroit and Ann Arbor, Mich., 1988-90, ptnr. Detroit and Ann Arbor, Mich., 1990-2000, sr. lawyer, 2001—. Bd. dirs. Ferndale Labs, Inc., Canterbury Health Care, Inc. Contbr. articles to profl. jours. Vice chmn. 14th Congl. Dist. Democratic Orgn., 1971-75; chmn. platform and resolution com. Mich. Dem. Party, 1971-74, treas., 1975-87; permanent chmn. Dem. State Conv., 1976; mem. platform com. and drafting subcom. Dem. Nat. Conv., 1972, mem. rules com., 1980, alt. del., 1984; bd. regents U. Mich., 1975-90; bd. dirs. Mich. Tech. Coun., 1983-92, vice chmn. 1984-86, south-ctrl. region 1992-95; pres. 9th Dist. Res. Policy Bd. 1976-77; nat. chmn. Ann. Giving, U., Mich., 1987-97; mem. history and traditions com. U. Mich., 1998—; mem. Mich. Higher Edn. Assistance Authority, Mich. Higher Edn. Student Loan Authority, 1990-94, bd. dirs. Legal Counsel, 1999—, Great Sauk Trail Coun. Boy Scouts Am., 1993—; bd. dirs. Wolverine Coun. Boy Scouts Am., 1991-93; officer Compensation Commn. Pittsfield Twp., 1991-93. Served to capt. USCGR, 1953-56; res. group comdr., 1974-77. Mem. ABA, Fed. Bar Assn., Mich. Bar Assn. (chmn. constrn. law com. 1983-85), Detroit Bar Assn., Washtenaw County Bar Assn., Res. Officers Assn., Order of Coif (Disting. Alumni Achievement award, Spirit of Mich. award, Disting. Citizen of Yr., Washington Ct.), Thomas M. Cooley Club, U. Mich. Club (gov. 1970-74), U. Mich. Alumni Assn. (bd. dirs. 1991-94, 95—, pres. 1995-97, pres. Emeritus Club 2001-02), Rotary Club of Ann Arbor (bd. dirs. 1991-96, pres. 1994-95, chair Dist. Permanent Fund 1999-2001), Sigma Alpha Iota. Anglican. Home: 11825 Durston St Pinckney MI 48169-9502 Office: Bodman Longley & Dahling 110 Miller Ave Ste 300 Ann Arbor MI 48104-1339 E-mail: thomasa.roach@worldnet.att.net.

ROACH, WESLEY LINVILLE, lawyer, insurance executive; b. Norlina, N.C., Oct. 8, 1931; s. Joseph Franklin and Florence G. (Sink) R.; m. Mary Jon Gerald, Aug. 13, 1955; children: Gerald, Mary Virginia. BS, Wake Forest U., 1953, JD, 1955. Bar: N.C. 1955. With Pilot Life Ins. Co., Greensboro, N.C., 1958-66, also bd. dirs.; sr. v.p., gen. counsel Jefferson-Pilot Life Ins. Co., 1986-88; sec. Great Ea. Lif. Ins. Co., 1975-85; of counsel Smith, Anderson, Blount, Dorsett, Mitchell & Jernigan, Attys. at Law, Raleigh, N.C., 1988—. Former chmn. bd. dirs. N.C. Life and Accident and Health Ins. Guaranty Assn., Va. Life, Accident and Health Guaranty Assn., S.C. Life, Accident and Health Guaranty Assn.; sec. JP Investment Mgmt. Co., Jefferson-Pilot Equity Sales, Inc., Spl. Services Agy., Inc., 1974-84; mem. exec. com., bd. dirs. N.C. Ins. Edn. Found., 1978—; trustee In-Home Care, Inc., 1999—, chmn., 2001. Mem. fin. com. Greensboro United Fund, 1964-65; mem. fin. com. Greensboro 1st Bapt. Ch., 1963-66, 83-86, chmn., 1983-85, chmn. bd. deacons, 1974-76, 80-81; nat. chmn. alumni coun. coll. fund Wake Forest U., 1971-76, pres. nat. alumni coun., 1975-76, trustee univ., 1978-82, emeritus trustee, 1999—; trustee So. Bapt. Theol. Sem., Louisville, 1973-84; trustee Bapt. Retirement Homes N.C., Inc., 1992-2000, chmn., 1993-94, emeritus trustee, 2001-; trustee In Home Care, Inc., 1997—, chmn., 2001. With USNR, 1955-58. Mem. ABA, N.C. Bar Assn., Raleigh Bar Assn., Assn. Life Ins. Counsel (bd. govs. 1984-88), Greensboro C. of C. (chmn. nat. legis. com. 1973—), Nat. Orgn. Life Guaranty Assn. (bd. dirs. 1982-87). Democrat. Home: PO Box 1690 601 Selma Rd Wendell NC 27591-8648 Office: 2500 First Union Capitol Ctr PO Box 2611 Raleigh NC 27602-2611

ROACH, WILLIAM RUSSELL, training and education executive; b. Bedford, Ind., 1940; s. George H. and Beatrice M. (Schoenlaub) R.; m. Margaret R. Balogh, 1961 (div. 1994); children: Kathleen L., Keith W. BS in Fin. and Acctg., UCLA, 1961. CPA, Calif. Internal auditor Hughes Aircraft Corp., L.A., 1962; sr. acct. Haskins & Sells, 1962-66; asst. to group v.p., asst. corp. contr. Lear Siegler, Inc., Santa Monica, Calif., 1966-71; exec. v.p., corp. sec., dir. Optimum Sys. Inc., Santa Clara, 1972-79; pres., dir. Banking Sys. Inc. subs. Optimum Sys. Inc., Dallas, 1976-79, BancSystems, Inc., Santa Clara, 1976-79, DMA/Optimum Honolulu, 1978-79; v.p. URS Corp., San Mateo, Calif., 1979-81; pres. URS Internat., Inc., 1980-81; pres., CEO, dir. Advanced Sys., Inc., 1981-88. Pres., CEO, dir. Applied Learning Internat., Inc. (formed from merger of Advanced Systems, Inc. and Deltak Training Corp.), Naperville, Ill., 1981-88; sr. v.p., bd. dirs. Nat. Edn. Corp. (parent co. Applied Learning Internat.), Irvine, Calif., 1988-89; chmn. bd., CEO Plato Learning Inc. (former known as TRO Learning Inc. (acquisition and edn. group Control Data Corp.), Hoffman Estates, Ill., 1989-2000; guest speaker numerous industry related funtions including Rep. Platform Com., 1988. Mem. AICPA, Calif. Soc. CPAs, Biltmore Country Club, Marco Island Yacht and Sailing Club, Theta Delta Chi. E-mail: wrroach@plato.com.

ROACHE, PATRICK MICHAEL, JR. management consultant; b. Elizabeth, N.J., Oct. 8, 1946; s. Patrick Michael and Rose Marie (Remite) R. BS, St. Peter's Coll., 1969. Adminstrv. aide to a state assemblyman N.J. Assembly, N.J., 1969-71; supr. acctg. Dept. Pub. Works Newark, Newark, 1971-78, asst. to dir. pub. works, 1978-79, mgr. div. motors, 1979-84; mgmt. specialist Dept. Gen. Svcs., 1985-86, 2002; pvt. practice as mgmt. and fin. cons. Brick, N.J., 1986—. Mem. Lions (treas. 1983-86, pres. 1988-89). Republican. Roman Catholic. Home and Office: 170 Binnacle Rd Brick NJ 08723-6704 E-mail: proache@hotmail.com., proache@haywardnet.com.

ROACH-REEVES, CATHARYN PETITT, librarian, educator; b. Houston, Sept. 25, 1950; d. Robert Duane and Nelma Belle Petitt; m. Paul Alton Roach, Aug. 21, 1971 (div. Aug. 1982); m. Gary L. Reeves, Nov. 27, 1991. BS in Elem. Edn., Dallas Bapt. Coll., 1974; MLS, North Tex. State U., 1976; PhD in Libr. Sci., U. North Tex., 1989. Cert. elem. tchr., Tex.; cert. libr., Tex. Tchr., libr. White Hall Sch., Cedar Hill, Tex., 1976-78; libr. Patton Elem. Sch., Dallas, 1978-83, Macmillan Elem. Sch., Dallas, 1981-82, George Washington Carver Elem. Sch., Dallas, 1982-86, Arlington Pk. Elem. Sch., Dallas, 1982-86, W.L. Cabell Elem. Sch., Dallas, 1986-90, Dan D. Rogers Elem. Sch., Dallas, 1990—. Presenter various workshops; cons. (video) In Search of a Libr. Adventure, 1995. Author: Teaching Library Skills in Grades K-6, 1993; co-editor Libr. Media Program Handbook, 1991. Troop leader Girl Scouts AM., 1982-88, coun. trainer, 1987-88; instr. Dallas Mus. Natural History, Summer Ednl. Program, 1984-87; hon. life mem. PTA, 1990, 93. Recipient Green Angel award Girl Scouts USA, 1985. Mem. Tex. Libr. Assn., Tex. Assn. Sch. Librs., Dallas Assn. Sch. Librs. (v.p., pres. elect. 1991-92, pres. 1992-93, Elem. Libr. of Yr. 1992-93, Positive Parents of Dallas Libr. Apple award 1992-93), Delta Kappa Gamma, Alpha Chi, Lambda Sigma Alpha, Phi Lambda Theta. Republican. Avocations: rubber stamp art, doll collecting, cake/cookie decorating, needlework, collecting Beatrix Potter and Laura Ingalls Wilder books and memorabilia. Home: 10106 Deermont Trl Dallas TX 75243-2523 Office: Dan D Rogers Elem Sch 5314 Abrams Rd Dallas TX 75214-2001

ROADARMEL, STANLEY BRUCE, civilian military employee; b. Albion, N.Y., May 5, 1937; s. Kenneth A. and Catherine Louise (Bobel) R.; m. Carole Ann Hayes, Nov. 26, 1959; children: Karen Marie, Oscar Pacific, Ann Catherine, William Hayes. Student, Purdue U., 1956-58; BA, Syracuse U., 1962; postgrad., Golden Gate U., 1976-78; grad., Squadron Officer Sch., 1965, Air Command Staff Coll., 1974-76, Indsl. Coll. Armed Forces, 1976. Commd. 2d lt. USAF, 1962, advanced through grades to maj.; adminstrv., security and recruiting ops. officer Air Tng. Command, Tex. and W.Va., 1962-69; chief field maintenance Titan II ICBM Strategic Air Command, Davis Monthan AFB, Ariz., 1969-71, chief 3901st Titan II maintenance evaluation team Vandenberg AFB, Calif., 1971-74, logistics staff officer, 1974-77, contract specialist, 1977-82, U.S. Air Forces Europe, Adana, Turkey, 1980-81; ret. USAF, 1982; launch complex constrn. contract negotiator, adminstr. NASA/USAF Space Shuttle Program, Lompoc, Calif., 1983-89, USAF Titan IV Space Booster, Vandenberg AFB, 1991-92; constrn. and maj. svcs. contract negotiator, adminstr. 30th Contracting Squadron USAF Space Command, 1992-2001; ret. active fed. svc., 2001—. With Ctrl. Coast Profls., Mut. Profl. Counseling/Placement, Santa Maria, Calif., 1990-91. Author manual: Man Lifting Crane Operations, 1976 (Air Force Commendation award 1977); revision officer Air Force Manual 66-1 Maintenance Management, 1976 (Air Force Commendation award 1977); contbr. Strategic Air Command Manual 66-12 ICBM Maintenance Mgmt. Spkr. World Orgn. Ovulation Method, Calif., 1987—; pro life advocate, activist Am. Life League, Nat. Right to Life, 1980—; vol. Rep. Party, 1992—; marriage preparation instr. Cath. Archdiocese of L.A., Santa Maria, Calif., 1995—. Mem. NRA, Nat. Contract Mgmt. Assn., Air Force Assn. (life), Ret. Officers Assn. (life), Assn. Air Force Missileers (life), Am. Legion, Couple to Couple League. Avocations: aviation, music, marksmanship, travel, literature. Home and Office: 4532 Glines Ave Santa Maria CA 93455-4313 E-mail: csroadarmel@earthlink.net.

ROADEN, ARLISS LLOYD, retired higher education executive director, former university president; b. Bark Camp, Ky., Sept. 27, 1930; s. Johnie Samuel and Ethel Nora (Killian) R.; m. Mary Etta Mitchell, Sept. 1, 1951; children: Janice Arletta Roaden Skelton, Sharon Kay Roaden Vogt. Grad., Cumberland Coll., 1949; AB, Carson Newman Coll., 1951; MS, U. Tenn., 1958, EdD, 1961; PhD (hon.), Cumberland Coll., 1986; DLitt (hon.), Tusculum Coll., 1992. With Oak Ridge Inst. Nuclear Studies, 1957-59, Auburn U., 1961-62; mem. faculty Ohio State U., 1962-74, prof. edn., 1967-74, acting dean Coll. Edn., 1968-70, vice provost for research, dean Grad. Sch., 1970-74; pres. Tenn. Tech. U., 1974-85, pres. emeritus, 1985—; dir. Tenn. Higher Edn. Commn., Nashville, 1985-95, exec. dir. emeritus, 1995—. Summer vis. prof. Marshall U., 1961, U. So. Calif., 1964, Ind. U., 1967; cons. ednl. instns., 1961—; pres. Tenn. Coll. Assn., 1978; chmn. sci. and tech. com. Am. Assn. State Colls. and Univs., 1980; chmn. task force on program and instl. assessment State Higher Edn. Exec. Officers', 1987, pres. 1993-94, chmn. coun. postsecondary accreditation liaison com., 1986-88, exec. com., 1988-95, pres. elect 1992-93; mem. exec. bd. trustees Southern Assn. Colls. and Schs., 1986—, chair communications com., 1990—, mem. task force, 1990—; mem. Southern Regional Edn. Bd., 1985—, chmn. procedures com. for reviewing bylaw changes and revisions, 1988-89; mem. exec. com., state rep., treas., chair Internal Audit Com., 1990-91, Edn. Commn. States, 1987-90; mem. Tenn. Econ. Cabinet Coun., 1988—, chmn.m 1988-91, bd. dirs. 1988—, Fgn. Lang. Inst.; treas., chair Internal Audit Com., 1990-91; mem. Performance Standards in Vocat.-Tech. Edn. Working Group, U.S. Dept. Edn., 1990. Co-author: The Research Assistantship: Recommendations for Colleges and Universities, 1975; editor: Problems of School Men in Depressed Urban Areas, 1967; contbr. articles to profl. jours. State chmn. Tenn. Cancer Soc. Crusade, 1986-88, bd. dirs., 1987—; mem. exec. bd., commr. Mid. Tenn. coun. Boy Scouts Am., 1987-88, mem. nat. coun., 1988—, chmn. scouts membership rels. com.; mem. Phi Delta Kappa Found., 1965—, past chmn. bd. govs., mem. futures and diamond jubilee coms., 1989—; chmn. Blue Ribbon Com. To Respond to Edn. Goals, 1990; bd. dirs. Nat. Project 714, 1986—, pres.-elect, 1987-88, chmn., 1988-89; pres. alumni assn. bd. Cumberland Coll., 1987-88, chmn. devel. bd., 1994—; adult Sunday sch. tchr. Woodmont Bapt. Ch., chmn. pers. com. , 1989—, chmn. deacons, ch. moderator, 1998-99. With U.S. Army, 1951-53. Research grantee Phi Delta Kappa Internat., 1968; named Distinguished Alumnus Cumberland Coll.,

1970; recipient Distinguished Alumni and Faculty Centennial medallion Coll. Edn., 1970, Distinguished Service award Council Grad. Students, 1974; both Ohio State U.; recipient Silver Beaver award Boy Scouts Am., Rotarian of Yr., 1984; Eagle Scout honoree Middle Tenn. Coun. Boy Scouts Am., 1989, others. Fellow Oxford Soc. Scholars; mem. AAAS, Am. Assn. Higher Edn., Acad. Polit. and Social Scis., Am. Ednl. Rsch. Assn. (chmn. publs. com. 1979-80), Nat. Soc. Study Edn., Nat. Assn. State Colls. and Land Grant Univs.,, Lions (bd. dirs. Nashville 1988-90, pres. 1991-92, zone chmn. 1992-93, dist. gov. 1996), Rotary (bd. dirs.), Order of Lion and Eagle, Phi Kappa Phi, Phi Delta Kappa (Disting. Svc. award Ohio State U. chpt. 1974), Kappa Phi Kappa, Kappa Delta Pi. Baptist.

ROADES, JOHN LESLIE, lawyer; b. El Campo, Tex., Mar. 29, 1951; s. Ora E. and Carolyn Elizabeth (Roten) R.; m. Therese Carol Pavlas, Mar. 20, 1982; children: Leslie Carol, Elizabeth Ann. AA, Wharton (Tex.) Coll., 1971; BBA, U. Tex., 1973, JD, 1975. Bar: Tex. 1976. Assoc. Manske and Hajovsky, El Campo, Tex., 1976-77; county atty. Wharton County, 1981-83; dist. atty. 23rd Jud. Dist., Wharton and Matagorda counties, 1983-84; pvt. practice law Wharton, 1977—. Chmn. Wharton County Dem. Party, 1978-79, 91-95, state exec. com., 1981-82; state pres. Young Dems., 1981-82; U.S. del. Am. Coun. Young Polit. Leaders, 1981. Mem. Tex. Bar Assn. (coun. mem. gen., solo and small firm sect., 1995—, sec./treas. 2000-01, chair elect 2001—, local bar svcs. com. 1990-95), Wharton County Bar Assn. (pres. 1989-90), Lions (v.p. 1992-94, pres. 1994-95). Methodist. Office: 1201 N Alabama Rd PO Box 1219 Wharton TX 77488-1219 E-mail: roadesjo@intertex.net.

ROADS, CURTIS, music educator, composer; b. Cleve., May 9, 1951; BA summa cum laude, U. Calif., San Diego, 1977; PhD, U. Paris, 1999. Editor, assoc. editor Computer Music Jour., MIT Press, Cambridge, Mass., 1978-2000; rsch. assoc. MIT, 1980-87; lectr. Harvard U., 1989, U. Paris 8, 1994-95; dir. pedagogy Les Ateliers UPIC, Paris, 1993-96; prof. U. Calif., Santa Barbara, 1996—, assoc. prof. media arts and tech., 2002—. Vis. prof. Oberlin (Ohio) Conservatory, 1991. Author: Foundations of Computer Music, 1985, The Music Machine, 1987, The Computer Music Tutorial, 1996, Field electronic music, 1981, Clang-Tint, 1994, Half-life, 1999, Tenth Vortex, 2000, Eleventh Vortex, 2001, Sculptor, 2002; inventor creatovox synthesizer. Office: U Calif Media Arts and Tech Santa Barbara CA 93106 E-mail: clang@create.ucsb.edu.

ROAF, WILLIAM LAYTON, professional football player; b. Pine Bluff, Ark., Apr. 18, 1970; s. Clifton George and Andree Yvonne (Layton) R. Left offensive tackle New Orleans Saints, 1993—2001; tackle Kansas City Chiefs, 2002—. Named All-American, Sports Writers, 1993, finalist Outland Trophy, Sports Writers, 1993; named to All-Rookie Team, Football News, 1994, Pro-Bowl Alt., 1994. Episcopal. Achievements include being named to Dr. Z's All-Pro team, 1994. Office: One Arrowhead Dr Kansas City MO 64129*

ROALES, ROBERT R. natural science educator; b. N.Y.C., July 17, 1944; s. John and Gertrude (Buxo) R.; m. Francoise A. Galland, Nov. 29, 1969; 1 child, Nicole. BS, Iona Coll., 1966; MS, NYU, 1969, PhD, 1973. Asst. prof. Ind. U.-Kokomo, 1974-79, assoc. prof., 1979—, coordinator natural sci., 1981-87, chairperson dept. biol. and physical scis., 1987—, coord. allied health scis., 1987-91, asst. dean. Sch. Allied Health Scis., Sch. Medicine, 1992—, acting dean of arts and sci., 1990. Contbr. articles to profl. jours. Mem. AAAS, Nat. Assn. Advisors for Health Professions, Am. Fisheries Soc., Am. Inst. Biol. Sci., Am. Soc. Ichthyologists and Herpetologists, N.Y. Acad. Scis., Sigma Xi. Avocations: photography, gardening. Home: 1001 N Hickory Ln Kokomo IN 46901-6420 Office: Ind U 2300 S Washington St PO Box 9003 Kokomo IN 46904-9003

ROAN, FORREST CALVIN, JR. lawyer; b. Waco, Tex., Dec. 18, 1944; s. Forrest Calvin and Lucille Elizabeth (McKinney) R.; m. Vickie Joan Howard, Feb. 15, 1969 (div. Dec. 1983); children: Amy Katherine, Jennifer Louise; m. Leslie D. Hampton Roan, Jan. 2, 1999. BBA, U. Tex., Austin, 1973, JD, 1976. Bar: Tex. 1976, U.S. Dist. Ct. (we. dist.) Tex. 1977, U.S. Dist. Ct. (so. dist.) Tex. 1998, U.S. Ct. Appeals (5th cir.) 1977, U.S. Supreme Ct. 1979, U.S. Ct. Appeals (11th cir.) 1981, U.S. Ct. Appeals (fed. cir.) 1998, U.S. Ct. Internat. Trade, 1998. Prin. Roan & Assocs., Austin, 1969-71; counsel, com. dir. Tex. Ho. of Reps., 1972-75; assoc. Heath, Davis & McCalla, Austin, 1975-78; prin. Roan & Gullahorn, P.C., 1978-85, Roan & Autrey (formerly Roan & Simpson), P.C., 1986-99; sr. ptnr. Cantey, Hanger, Roan & Autrey, 1999—. Bd. dirs. Lawyers Credit Union, chmn., 1982-83; bd. dirs. pub. law sect. State Bar Tex., 1980-84; dir. Am. Bankers Gen. Agy.; mem. chancellor's coun. U. Tex. With Tex. Army N.G., 1966-74. Fellow Tex. Bar Found.; mem. ABA, Tex. Assn. Def. Counsel, Tex. Assn. Bank Counsel, Def. Rsch. Inst., Travis County Bar Assn., Tex.-Mexico Bar Assn., Knights of the Symphony (vice chancellor 1997—), Tex. Lyceum Assn. (v.p., bd. dirs. 1980-87), Austin C. of C., Austin Club, Headliners Club, Masons, Shriners (Parsons Masonic master 1976-77). Methodist. Office: Cantey Hanger Roan & Autrey 200 Wells Fargo Bank Tower 400 W 15th St Austin TX 78701-1600 E-mail: froan@canteyhanger.com.

ROANE, DAVID JAMES, JR. information technology auditor; b. Petersburg, Va., Nov. 11, 1960; s. David James Roane, Sr. and Anne (Vest) Savage; m. Bonnie L. Dear, Dec. 3, 1983; two children. BS, Va. Commonwealth U., 1984. CPA, Va.; cert. info. systems auditor. Audit intern Continental Fin. Services Co., Richmond, Va., 1983-84, staff auditor, 1984-85; EDP auditor Life Ins. Co. of Va., 1985-86, Fort James Corp., Richmond, Va., 1986-88, sr. EDP auditor, 1990-2000; technologies group specialist Mgmt. Info. Systems, 1989-90; info. tech. audit cons. Ft. James Corp./Ga. Pacific, 2000-01; info. tech. audit supr. The Pittston Co., Richmond, Va., 2001—. Treas. Civic Assn., Chester, Va., 1985-91; chmn. fin. com. Matoaca United Meth. Ch., 1990-92, 1997-98, chmn. adminstrv. bd., 1993-95. Methodist. Avocation: micro computers. Home: 3148 Talleywood Ln Chester VA 23831-7036 E-mail: djroane@hotmail.com.

ROARK, BARBARA ANN, librarian; b. Evanston, Ill., July 24, 1958; d. Edward B. and Ann H. Rowe; m. Paul E. Roark, Sept. 18, 1982; children: Sarah, John. BA in History, U. Ky., 1981, MLS, 1982. Dir. Hopkins County Madisonville (Ky.) Pub. Libr., 1983-85; ops. mgr. Wurzburg Inc., Nashville, 1985-91; dir. Spies Pub. Libr., Menominee, Mich., 1991-98, Franklin (Wis.) Pub. Libr., 1998—. V.p. adv. coun. Mid-Peninsula Libr. Coop., Mich., 1993-95, sec. adv. coun., 1991-93; chair tech. adv. com. Milwaukee County Federated Libr. Sys., 2001—. Grant writer Title II, 1994, Title I, 1995. Treas. Franklin Area Jr. Woman's Club. Recipient Cert. of Excellence Libr. of Mich., 1995, Cert. of Appreciation Menominee Area C. of C., 1998. Mem. ALA, Wis. Libr. Assn. (pers. and profl. concerns com. 1999—, Muriel Fuller award 2002), Spies Pub. Libr. Found., PEO, Order Ea. Star, U. Ky. Alumni Assn., Franklin Area Jr. Women's Club (treas. 1999—), Kiwanis (pres. Milw. suburban S.W. chpt. 2002—), Zeta Tau Alpha. Methodist. Avocations: golf, reading, cross stitching, travel. Office: Franklin Public Library 9151 W Loomis Rd Franklin WI 53132-9630 E-mail: barbara.roark@mcfls.org.

ROARK, ROBERT CAMERON, insurance broker; b. San Diego, Jan. 11, 1931; s. Alfred T. and Virginia J. Roark; m. Lois J. Maynard, July 19, 1952; children: Cynthia, Susan, Kellie, Robert. BA, San Diego State U., 1954. Life underwriter Mass. Mut. Life, San Diego, 1955-57; supr. John Hancock Mut., 1957-59; gen. agt., mgr. Am. Mut. Life Ins., 1959-65; regional v.p. Northwestern Life Ins., Seattle, 1965-68; broker, owner Roark Ins., San Juan Capistrano, Calif., 1968—. Author: Good News Letter, 1991—. Divsn. capt. USCG Aux., 1990, flotilla comdr., 1987, vice capt., 1989, publs. officer, 1997. Mem. Mission Hills Homeowners Assn. (pres. 1970-73, bd. mem. 1991-92), Lions Internat. (zone chmn. 1972, club pres. 1971).

ROATH, STEPHEN D. retired pharmaceutical company executive; b. 1941; With Long's Drug Stores Corp., 1964—, exec. v.p. store ops., 1988-91, pres., CEO, 1991—2001. Office: c/o Longs Drug Stores Corp 141 N Civic Dr Walnut Creek CA 94596-3858*

ROAZEN, PAUL, writer; b. Boston, Aug. 14, 1936; s. Julius and Anna (Lebow) R.; divorced; children: Jules, Daniel. BA, Harvard U., 1958, PhD, 1965. Instr. dept. govt. Harvard U., Cambridge, Mass., 1965-68, asst. prof., 1968-71; assoc. prof. social and polit. sci. York U., Toronto, Ont., Can., 1971-74, prof. Can., 1974-95; ret., 1995. Author: Freud: Political and Social Thought, 1968, Brother Animal: The Story of Freud and Tausk, 1969, Freud and His Followers, 1975, Erik H. Erikson, 1976, Helene Deutsch, 1985, Encountering Freud: The Politics and Histories of Psychoanalysis, 1990, Meeting Freud's Family, 1993, How Freud Worked: First-Hand Accounts of Patients, 1995, Canada's King: An Essay in Political Psychology, 1998, The Historiography of Psychoanalysis, 2001, Political Theory and the Psychology of the Unconscious, 2000, Oedinus in Britain: Edward Glover and the Struggle Over Klein, 2000. Fellow Royal Soc. Can.; mem. Phi Beta Kappa. Home: 73 Prince St Cambridge MA 02139-4413

ROAZZI, VINCENT MICHAEL, marketing professional; b. June 6, 1949; s. John Michael and Rose Mary Roazzi; m. Marlene Sciame, Oct. 20, 1973; children: Daria, Jessica, Vincent, Dana, Victoria. BA in Econs., Bklyn. Coll., 1972. Various positions various Wall St. firms, N.Y.C., 1969-73; bus. investor, buyer, 1973-89; area mktg. dir. Cornerstone Mktg., Dallas, 1989-97; exec. dir. mktg., devel. Alliance for Affordable Svcs., Washington, 1997—. Author: The Spirituality of Success, 1999; contbr. Wealth mag. Pres. Red Fox Farm Homeowners Assn., Solebury, Pa., 1998. With USMC, 1969-71. Recipient national acknowledgement award Nat. Assn. Bus. Leaders, 1999. Mem. Inst. of Noetic Scis., Rosicrucians. Roman Catholic. Avocations: reading, writing, public speaking, coin collecting, intellectual challenges. Home and Office: 21 Red Fox Dr New Hope PA 18938-9664 E-mail: vinny@spiritualityofsuccess.com.

ROBAKIS, NIKOLAOS K. medical educator; b. Finikounda, Messinia, Greece, Dec. 4, 1945; came to U.S., 1974; s. Konstantinos G. and Efstathia A. (Koutris) R.; m. Davida Ellen Scharf, June 4, 1974; children: Thalia, Daphne, Efstathia. Diploma, U. Thessaloniki, Greece, 1971; MA, NYU, N.Y.C., 1976, PhD, 1979. Tchg. fellow NYU, N.Y.C., 1974-79; postdoctoral fellow Roche Inst. Molecular Biology, Nutley, N.J., 1979-82; rsch. fellow Hoffman-LaRoche, Inc., 1982-83; sr. rsch. mem. N.Y. Inst. Basic Rsch., S.I., 1983-87; assoc. prof. Mt. Sinai Sch. Medicine, NYU, N.Y.C., 1987-93, prof. dept. psychiatry and neurobiology, 1993—. Rsch. advisor Merck Sharp and Dohme, 1992-93, Bristol-Myers Squibb Co., Wallingford, Conn., 1991-93; advisor Am. Fedn. on Aging, N.Y.C., 1999, Internat. Symposium on Alzheimer's Disease, 1994—. Contbr. numerous sci. articles to profl. publs. Pres. Greek Dem. Assn., N.Y.C.-Boston, 1985. Recipient McKnight Neurosci. award McKnight Neurosci. Inc., 1988, Zenith award Alzheimer's Assn., 1994, Disting. Scientist award Hellenic Med. Assn., 1997; named Endowed Prof., Mt. Sinai Sch. Medicine, NYU, 1994. Office: Mount Sinai Sch of Medicine One Gustave Levy Pl New York NY 10029

ROBALINO, BENJAMIN DAVID, cardiologist; b. Peru, Jan. 7, 1957; MD, Cayetano Heredia U., 1982. Diplomate Am. Bd. Internal Medicine, Cardiovascular Disease, Interventional Cardiology. Intern, resident Jackson Meml. Hosp.-U. Miami, Fla., 1983-86; fellow cardiology Cleve. Clinic Found., 1986-91; chief cardiologist McAllen (Tex.) Med. Ctr., 1994-95; dir. cath. lab. Mc Allen Heart Hosp., 1998—; cardiologist McAllen, 1991—. Cardiologist Rio Grande (Tex.) Regional Hosp., Mission (Tex.) Hosp., Edinburg (Tex.) Hosp., McAllen Heart Hosp., Knapp (Tex.) Med. Ctr. Mem. AMC, AMA, Am. Coll. Cardiology, Tex. Med. Assn., Tex. Med. Found., Soc. for Cardiac Angiography and Interventions. Office: 500 E Ridge Rd Ste 101 Mcallen TX 78503-1508 E-mail: bdrobalino@hotmail.com.

ROBARDS, BOURNE ROGERS, elementary education educator; b. Milw., Jan. 5, 1950; s. William Simpson and Janet (Cross) R.; m. Martha Jane Snider, Oct. 29, 1977; children: Jonathan Matthew, Sara Elizabeth. BS, U. Mo., 1971; MAT, Webster U., St. Louis, 1989. Cert. elem. tchr., Mo. Classroom tchr. 4th and 6th grades Hazelwood Sch. Dist., Florissant, Mo., 1971-73; classroom tchr. 4th grade Jennings (Mo.) Sch. Dist., 1986—. Troop leader Boy Scouts Am., St. Louis, 1972-73; ch. leader St. Mark's Episcopal Ch., St. Louis, 1977—. Mem. Omicron Delta Kappa. Avocations: travel, reading, swimming, bicycling, music, photography. Home: 6320 Monterey Dr Saint Louis MO 63123-1510 Office: Northview Elem Sch Jennings Sch Dist 8920 Cozens Ave Jennings MO 63136-3996

ROBB, BRUCE, former insurance company executive; b. Norman, Okla., July 28, 1919; m. Betty Jane Sharrar, May 6, 1950; children: Elizabeth (dec.), Bruce. BS, U.S. Naval Acad., 1941; MBA, Columbia U., 1949. Security analyst Clark, Dodge & Co., Inc., N.Y.C., 1948-52, 53-62; asst. treas. SAFECO Corp., Seattle, 1962-66, v.p., treas., 1966-72, sr. v.p., treas., 1972-84. Mem. Wash. State Fin. Adv. Com., 1970-80; mem. investment com. Diocese of Olympia, 1964-94. Mem. Sand Point Country Club, Beta Gamma Sigma. Home: 6307 NE 57th St Seattle WA 98105-2011

ROBB, CAROLE, artist; b. Port-Glasgow, Scotland, Aug. 25, 1943; U.S. resident, 1984; d. William Fraser and Christina (McKechnie) R.; m. Dennis Nicholas, 1964 (div. 1974); m. Terence Horsley, 1974 (div. 1984); 1 child, Robb Horsley. BA in Painting/Drawing, Glasgow Sch. of Art, 1965; MFA in Painting, U. Reading, Eng., 1979. Vis. artist Royal Coll. Art, London, Slade Sch. Fine Art, London, Camberwell Sch. of Art, London, U. Va., Charlottesville, Bard Coll., Annandale-on-Hudson, N.Y., Am. U., Washington, Am. U., Rome, Nat. Acad. Sch. of Fine Art, N.Y.C., N.Y. Acad., N.Y.C., Cleve. Art Inst., CUNY, N.Y.C.; mem. faculty N.Y. Studio Sch. Drawing, Painting and Sculpture, N.Y.C., 1988—. One-person shows include Collectors Gallery, London, 1966, 70, Air Gallery, London, 1981, Forum Gallery, N.Y.C., 1982, 83, 86, 88, 89, 96, South London Art Gallery and Mus., London, 1983, Galleria C'a d'Oro, Rome, 1996, 2000, J.T. Fassbinder Gallery, Berlin, 2001; exhibited in group shows Inst. of Contemporary Arts, London, 1981, The 1980's, Met. Mus. Art, N.Y.C., 1988, The Artists Mus., Washington, 2000, Am. U., Rome, 2001, J.T. Fassbinder Gallery, Berlin, 2001; represented in pub. collections Met. Mus. Art, N.Y.C., Tate Gallery, London; represented by Forum Gallery, N.Y.C. Recipient Prix de Rome for painting Rome Scholarship Com., 1979, Maj. award for painting Greater London Arts Assn., 1979; Fulbright scholar, U.S., 1980. Fellow Accademia Britannica (Rome scholar 1979—). Avocations: t'ai chi, traveling in Italy. Home: 308 Mott St Apt 1B New York NY 10012-2815 E-mail: carolerobbNY@aol.com.

ROBB, CHARLES SPITTAL, former senator, governor, lawyer, educator; b. Phoenix, June 26, 1939; s. James Spittal and Francis Howard (Wooley) R.; m. Lynda Bird Johnson, Dec. 9, 1967; children: Lucinda Desha, Catherine Lewis, Jennifer Wickliffe. BBA, U. Wis., 1961; JD, U. Va., 1973. Bar: Va. 1973, U.S. Supreme Ct. 1976. Law clk. to Hon. John D. Butzner 4th U.S. Ct. Appeals, 1973—74; atty. Williams & Connolly, 1974-77; lt. gov. State of Va., 1978—82, gov., 1982—86; ptnr. Hunton & Williams, 1986—88; U.S. Senator from Va., 1989—2001; disting. prof. law and pub. policy George Mason U., 2001—. Former mem. armed svcs. com., intelligence com., senate Dem. policy com., senate Dem. tech. and comm. com., subcom. on readiness, subcom. on seapower, subcom. on strategic forces Com. on Fin., subcom. on internat. trade, subcom. on social security and family policy, subcom. on taxation and IRS oversight Select Com. on Intelligence, Joint Econ. Com., Dem. Policy Com.; chmn. Nat. Conf. Lt. Govs., 1979-80, Am. Coun. Young Polit. Leaders Dels. to Peoples Republif of China, 1979, edn. Commn. of the States, 1985; vis. prof. pub. affairs George Mason U., spring 1987. Chmn. Jobs for Am.'s Grads. Inc., 1985-90, Dem. Leadership Coun., 1986-88; gov. Atlantic Inst. for Internat. Affairs, 1987. With USMC 1961-70. Active duty USMC, 1961—70. Decorated Bronze Star, Vietnam Service medal with 4 Stars; Vietnamese Cross of Gallantry with Silver Star; recipient Raven award, 1973, Seven Soc. award U. Va. Mem. ABA, Va. Bar Assn., So. Govs. Assn. (chmn.), Dem. Govs. Assn. (chmn.), Coalition for Dem. Majority, Res. Officers Assn., USMC Res. Officers Assn., U.Fa. La. Alumni Assn. (bd. dirs. 1974-85), Am. Legion, Raven Soc., Navy League U.S., Coun. on Fgn. Rels., Omicron Delta Kappa. Episcopalian. Office: George Mason U Sch Law 3301 N Fairfax Dr Rm 415 Arlington VA 22201-4498

ROBB, GEOFFREY LAWRENCE, plastic surgeon; b. El Paso, Tex., May 28, 1946; s. Giles Anthony and Mary Jo (Lawrence) R.; m. Cathy Jean Cross, May 31, 1974; children: Tiffany, Kimberly, Courtney, Carly, Melaney, Mary. BS, U. Miami, 1969, MD, 1974. Diplomate Am. Bd. Otolaryngology. Commd. ensign USNR, 1970-92; advanced through grades to capt., 1989; resident in otalaryngology, mem. staff US Naval Hosp., San Diego, 1974-79, otolaryngologist Orlando, Fla., 1979-83; plastic surgeon USN Sponsorship at U. Pitts., 1983-85, microvascular surgeon, 1985; plastic surgeon U.S. Naval Hosp., Portsmouth, Va., 1985-88; ret., 1992; chief plastic surgery U.S. Naval Hosp., Portsmouth, Va, 1988-92; vice chmn. plastic surgery M.D. Anderson Cancer Ctr., Houston, 1992-97, chmn. plastic surgery, 1997—, dep. chmn. divsn. surgery, 1994—, dir. postgrad. med. edn., 1992—, med. dir. plastic surgery clinic, 1992—, assoc. med. dir. skin cancer ctr., 1996. Contbg. author: Reconstructive Plastic Surgery for Cancer, 1995, Endoscopic Plastic Surgery, 1995, Advanced Skin Cancer of Head and Neck, 1995; contbr. articles to profl. jours. Fellow ACS, Am. Soc. Plastic Reconstructive Surgeons, Am. Soc. Reconstructive Microsurgeons, Am. Assn. Plastic Surgeons; mem. Internat. Soc. Reconstructive Microsurgery, Tex. Soc. Plastic Surgeons, Houston Soc. Plastic Surgeons, KC. Avocations: physical fitness, weight lifting, tennis, running. Office: MD Anderson Cancer Ctr 1515 Holcombe Blvd # 443 Houston TX 77030-4009 E-mail: grobb@mdanderson.org.

ROBB, JAMES ALEXANDER, lawyer; b. Huntingdon, Que., Can., May 3, 1930; s. Alexander George and Irma Mary (Martin) R.; m. Katherine Ann Teare, June 26, 1960; children: Laura, John, Andrew. BA, McGill U., 1951, B.C.L., 1954; postgrad., U. Montreal, 1961-63. Bar: Que. 1955, queen's counsel 1970. Lectr. comml. law and taxation Sir George Williams U., 1958-60; ptnr. Stikeman Elliott and predecessor firm Stikeman, Elliott, Tamaki, Mercier & Robb, Montreal, 1967—. Bd. dirs. Robapharm (Can.), Inc., Itochu Can. Ltd., Majorich Investments Inc., YKK Can. Inc., NGK Spark Plugs Can. Ltd., TESSAG KSH Ltd., KSH Constrn. Inc., Vancana Inc.; chmn. Hi-Alta Capital Inc.; pres. Que-Japan Bus. Forum, 1993-95. Mem. Protestant Sch. Bd. Greater Montreal, 1971-75; chmn. bd. trustees Martlet Found., 1967-69; v.p. Que. Liberal Party, 1976-79; mem. adv. com. McGill Ctr. for Study of Regulated Industries; bd. dirs. Montreal Mus. Fine Arts, 1987-90; bd. govs. McGill U., 1991-95. Mem.: Consumers Assn. Can. (past chmn. regulated industries program), Bar Que. (chmn. multidisciplinary com. 1998—2001), McGill Alumni Assn. (pres. 1996—98), Hillside Tennis Club, Royal Montreal Curling Club (pres. 1999—2000), Kanawaki Golf Club (Que.), Univ. Club, Can. Club Montreal (pres. 1990—91). Home: 9 Renfrew Ave Westmount QC Canada H3Y 2X3 Office: 1155 Renè Lèvesque Blvd W Ste 4000 Montreal QC Canada H3B 3V2 E-mail: jrobb@mtl.stikeman.com.

ROBB, JAMES ARTHUR, surgical pathologist; b. Pueblo, Colo., Nov. 13, 1938; s. William Arthur and Mary Ann (Hutchinson) R.; m. Carla May Felte, June 16, 1962; 4 children. BA, U. Colo., 1960, postgrad., 1960-61, MD, 1965. Diplomate Am. Bd. Anat. and Clin. Pathology, Am. Bd. Dermatopathology, Am. Bd. Cytopathology. Intern then resident in anatomic pathology Yale U., New Haven, 1965-68; research assoc. NIH, Bethesda, Md., 1969-71; asst. prof. pathology U. Calif., San Diego, 1971-75, assoc. prof., 1975-78; staff pathologist Scripps Clinic, La Jolla, Calif., 1978-81, vice chmn. pathology, 1981-90; assoc. dir. pathology, dept. pathology Cedars Med. Ctr., Miami, 1990—, dir., anatomic & molecular pathology, 1990—. Assoc. adj. prof. U. Calif., San Diego, 1978-84, adj. prof., 1984-90. Contbr. articles to profl. jours. Treas. San Diego Jr. Theatre, 1981. Served with USPHS, 1962-80. Grantee NIH, Am. Cancer Soc. Mem. AMA, AAAS, Am. Soc. Cell Biology, Am. Assn. Pathologists, Fla. Med. Assn., South Fla. Soc. Pathology, Dade County Med. Assn., Internat. Soc. Dermatopathology, Internat. Acad. Cytology, Am. Soc. Dermatopathology, Internat. Acad. Pathology, Am. Soc. Virology, Alpha Omega Alpha, Sigma Tau, Sigma Pi Sigma. Office: Cedars Med Ctr Dept Pathology 1400 NW 12th Ave Miami FL 33136-1003

ROBB, JAMES WILLIS, Romance languages educator; b. Jamaica, N.Y., June 27, 1918; s. Stewart Everts and Clara Johanna (Mohrmann) R.; m. Cecilia Uribe-Noguera, 1972. Student, Inst. de Touraine, Sorbonne, 1937-38; BA cum laude, Colgate U., 1939; postgrad., U. Nacional de Mex., 1948; MA, Middlebury Coll., 1950; PhD, Cath. U. Am., 1958. Instr. romance langs. Norwich U., 1946-50; from asst. prof. to prof. romance langs. George Washington U., Washington, 1950-88, prof. emeritus, 1988—. Corr. mem. Academia Mexicana de la Lengua, 1998. Author: El Estilo de Alfonso Reyes, 1965, 78, Repertorio Bibliográfico de Alfonso Reyes, 1974, Prosa y Poesía de Alfonso Reyes, 1975, 84, Estudios sobre Alfonso Reyes, 1976, Por los Caminos de Alfonso Reyes, 1981, Imágenes de América en Alfonso Reyes y en Germán Arciniegas, 1990, Más Páginas Sobre Alfonso Reyes, 1996-97; contbr. articles to profl. jours. With USNR, 1942-44, Brazil, 1944-46, PTO. Recipient Alfonso Reyes Internat. Lit. prize, 1978; Lit. Diploma of Merit, State of Nuevo León and City of Monterrey, Mex., 1979; OAS grantee, 1964; Am. Philos. Soc. grantee, 1977 Mem. MLA, Internat. Assn. Ibero-Am. Lit., Am. Assn. Tchrs. Spanish and Portuguese, Assn. Colombianistas, Phi Beta Kappa. Office: George Washington U Romance Langs Dept Washington DC 20052-0001

ROBB, JOHN WESLEY, religion educator; b. Los Angeles, Dec. 1, 1919; s. Edgar Milton and Alta (Boger) R.; m. Ethel Edna Tosh, June 13, 1942; children: Lydia Joan Robb Durbin, Judith Nadine Robb Eggerman. AB, Greenville Coll., 1941; Th.M., U. So. Calif., 1945, PhD, 1952; L.H.D., Hebrew Union Coll.-Jewish Inst. Religion, 1977. Asst. prof. philosophy and religion Dickinson Coll., Pa., 1948-51; fellow Fund for Advancement Edn., 1951-52; asso. prof. U. So. Calif., L.A., 1954-62, chmn. dept. religion, 1954-67, assoc. dean humanities Coll. Letters, Arts and Scis., 1963-68, Leonard K. Firestone prof., 1974-75, prof., 1962-87, prof. emeritus, 1987—, prof. Sch. Medicine, 1981-87; coun. mem. Inst. of Lab. Animal Resources Nat. Acad. Scis. Nat. Rsch. Coun., 1986-93. Vis. disting. prof. USAF Med. Ctr., Wilford Hall, Tex., 1985; mem. rev. com. NIH Guide for the Care and Use of Lab. Animals, NRC, NAS, 1993-96; advisor/tutor Med. Quality Assurance Commn., Dept. Health, State of Wash., 1994-2001; mem. ethics com. Swedish Med. Ctr., N.W. Hosp., Seattle, 1992-2002; adj. prof. bioethics Sch. Medicine, U. So. Calif., 1989-91, adj. prof. emeritus, 1991—. Author: Inquiry Into Faith, 1960; co-editor: Readings in Religious Philosophy; The Reverent Skeptic, 1979. Served as lt. (j.g.) USNR, 1945-47; to lt. 1952-54. Recipient award for excellence in tchg. U. So. Calif., 1960, 74, Dart award for acad. innovation, 1970, Raubenheimer Disting. Faculty award divsn. humanities, 1980, Robert Fenton Craig award Blue Key, 1980, Outstanding Faculty award Student Senate, 1981, Disting. Emeritus award, 1995, Educator of Yr. award Swedish Med. Ctr., Providence, Seattle, 2002. Fellow Soc. for Values in Higher Edn.; mem. Am. Acad. Religion (v.p. 1966, pres. 1967), Am. Philos. Assn., AAUP (v.p. Calif. Conf. 1977, pres. 1978-79), Phi Beta Kappa (hon.), Phi Kappa Phi, Phi Chi Phi. United Methodist. Home: 8001 Sand Point Way NE Apt C35 Seattle WA 98115-6356

ROBB, KIMBERLY KAY, cardiovascular nurse, nursing administrator, medical-surgical nurse, infant immunization nurse; b. Princeton, Ind., Nov. 18, 1963; d. Carl Eugene and Cherry Johnetta (Lewis) R. AD, Ind. Vocat. Tech. Sch., 1990. Cert. IV and TB nurse; cert. CPR; cert. ACLS, peripheral inserted ctrl. catheter nurse; cert. advanced trauma mgmt. Staff nurse Holiday Manor Nursing Home, Princeton, Ind., 1990-91, Gibson Gen. Hosp., Princeton, 1991-2000, Gibson County Health Dept., 1994-98; relief supr. Gibson Gen. Hosp., Princeton, Ind., 1995-97, evening nursing supr., 1997-2000; cardiovascular ICU nurse Deaconess Hosp., Evansville, 2000—. Mem.: AACN (Greater Evansville chpt.). Baptist. Avocations: bowling, reading. Home: 429 W Glendale St Princeton IN 47670-1221 E-mail: KimberlyRobb@Deaconess.com.

ROBB, LYNDA JOHNSON, writer; b. Washington, Mar. 19, 1944; d. Lyndon Baines and Claudia Alta (Taylor) Johnson; m. Charles Spittal Robb, Dec. 9, 1967; children: Lucinda Desha, Catherine Lewis, Jennifer Wickliffe. BA with honors, U. Tex., 1966. Writer McCall's Mag., 1966-68; contbg. editor Ladies Home Jour., 1968-80; lectr., bd. dirs. Reading Is Fundamental, 1968—, Lyndon B. Johnson Family Found., 1969-95; nat. chair Reading is Fundamental, 1996. Past mem. Va. State Coun. on Infant Mortality, Va. Maternal & Child Health Coun.; mem. Nat. Commn. to Prevent Infant Mortality, 1987-93; chmn. Pres.'s Adv. Com. for Women, 1979-81; chmn. bd. dirs. Nat. Home Libr. Found., Ford Theatre; chmn. Va. Women's Cultural History Project, 1982-85; chmn. Reading is Fundamental, 1996—. Mem. Zeta Tau Alpha. Office: Reading is Fundamental Ste 400 1825 Connecticut Ave NW Washington DC 20009-5708

ROBB, NATHANIEL HEYWARD, JR. retired remote sensing company executive; b. Columbia, S.C., Sept. 10, 1942; s. Nathaniel Heyward Robb and Dorothy Claiborne (Cabell) Dortch; m. Louise Taber Rivers, Sept. 26, 1964; children: Elizabeth R. Graff, Nathaniel Heyward III, Catherine Pease. BSBA, The Citadel, 1964; grad. Realtors Inst., U. N.C., 1972; grad., Command and Gen. Staff Coll. Pres. Robb Realty, Raleigh, N.C., 1972-95; adj. gen. State of N.C., 1989-93; dep. comdr. in chief U.S. Atlantic Command, 1993-96; v.p. Ariel Images, Inc. and Spin-2 Digital Imagery, Raleigh, 1996—2002. Exec.

sec. Gov.'s Adv. Commn. Mil. Affairs, 1985-89; mem. Raleigh Bd. Realtors, 1975-85; dir. state property office N.C. Dept. Adminstrn., 1975-77; asst. sec. N.C. Dept. Crime Crontrol and Safety, Raleigh, 1985-89; bd. dirs. Aerial Images, Inc., Raleigh. Dir. Mordecai Sq. Hist. Soc.; mem. Raleigh Hist. Dists. Commn., 1973-78; dir., v.p. Raleigh Hist. Properties Commn., 1973-78; mem. Gov.'s Mgmt. Coun., Raleigh, 1985-89, Gov.'s Waste Mgmt. Bd., 1985-89; mem. Gov.'s Drug Cabinet, 1988-89; life mem. Nat. Rep. Com., 1970—; pres., founding mem. Raleigh Comml. Listing Svc., 1975-85. Maj. gen. inf., U.S. Army N.G., 1964-70, Vietnam; N.C. N.G., 1970-96. Decorated D.S.M., D.S.S.M., N.C. D.S.M. with one device, Legion of Merit, Bronze Star with v device and one oak leaf cluster, Meritorious Svc. medal; Nat. Def. medal with star, USAR Components Achievement medal with four oak leaf clusters; Republic Vietnam Cross of Gallantry with bronze and silver stars and palm, other mil. awards; recipient Disting. Milit. Grad. award The Citadel, Humanitarian Svc. medal, Legion de Lafayette of Hist. Socs. of Militia and N.G. Mem. N.G. Assn. U.S., N.C. N.G. Assn., 2500 Club, The Citadel Alumni Assn. (N.C. dir.). Episcopalian. Avocations: skiing, pistol shooting. Home: 2209 Atlantic Ave Sullivans Island SC 29482 E-mail: robbn2@aol.com.

ROBB, WALTER LEE, retired electric company executive, management company executive; b. Harrisburg, Pa., Apr. 25, 1928; s. George A. and Ruth (Scantlin) R.; m. Anne Gruver, Feb. 27, 1954; children: Richard, Steven, Lindsey. BS, Pa. State U., 1948; MS, U. Ill., 1950, PhD, 1951; DEng (hon.), Milw. Sch. Engring., 1994, Worcester Poly. Inst., 1988. With GE, 1951-93, mgr. R & D dept. silicone products N.Y., 1966-68, venture mgr. med. devel. ops. Schenectady, 1968-71, sr. v.p., group exec. med. sys. group Milw., 1973-86, sr. v.p. corp. R & D Schenectady, 1986-93; pres. Vantage Mgmt., N.Y., 1993—. Bd. dirs. Celgene Corp., Mech. Tech., Inc., Plug Power; chmn. Capital Dist. Sports, Inc. Recipient Nat. Tech. medal, 1993, Indsl. Rsch. Inst. medal, 1994. Mem. NAE, Am. Philos. Soc. Achievements include patentee in field of membranes and gas separation; research in diagnostic imaging equipment. Home: 1358 Ruffner Rd Niskayuna NY 12309-2500 Office: Vantage Mgmt 3000 Troy-Schenectady Rd Schenectady NY 12309-1643 E-mail: waltrobb@albany.net.

ROBBA, WILLIAM A. research scientist, consultant; b. N.Y.C., Dec. 28, 1923; s. William Hugh and Charlotte Gisela Robba; m. Nancy Belinda DeHarte, Feb. 23, 1944 (div. Feb. 1974); children: Suzanne, Bonnie, Harte, Brady, Mallory. BSc, Fordham Coll., 1950; MSc, Tex. A&M U., 1951; cert. nuclear engring., Oakridge Sch. Reactor Tech., 1952. Nuclear physicist Convair, Ft. Worth, 1953-54, Brookhaven Nat. Lab., Upton, N.Y., 1954-55, mgr. advanced concepts group, 1959-62; mgr. nuclear group Raytheon Corp., Waltham, Mass., 1955-59; v.p. rsch. Pfizer, Inc., N.Y.C., 1962-72; tech. cons., Boulder, Colo., 1973—. Rep. U.S. AEC, to Euratom, Brussels, 1959. Fellow AIAA (assoc.), ASME (life). Republican. Roman Catholic. Avocations: reading, chess, hiking, model making, woodworking. Home: 1670 S Cherryvale Rd Boulder CO 80303-9703 Office: Tech Cons PO Box 3374 Boulder CO 80307-3374

ROBBINS, ALLEN BISHOP, physics educator; b. New Brunswick, N.J., Mar. 31, 1930; s. William Rei and Helen Grace (Bishop) R.; m. Shirley Mae Gernert, June 14, 1952 (div. 1978); children: Catherine Jean, Marilyn Elizabeth, Carol Ann, Melanie Barbara; m. Alice Harriet Ayars, Jan. 1, 1979. Student, Oberlin Coll., 1948-49; BS, Rutgers U., 1952; MS, Yale U., 1953, PhD, 1956. Research fellow U. Birmingham (Eng.), 1957-58, lectr., 1960-61; instr. physics Rutgers U., New Brunswick, N.J., 1956-57, asst. prof. physics, 1957-60, assoc. prof., 1960-68, prof., 1968-97, prof. emeritus, 1997—, chmn. dept. physics and astronomy, 1979-95. Contbr. articles on nuclear physics to profl. jours. Recipient Lindbach Christian and Mary F. Lindbach Found., Rutgers U., 1975 Fellow Am. Phys. Soc.; mem. Am. Assn. Physics Tchrs., AAAS, Phi Beta Kappa, Sigma Xi Office: Rutgers U Dept Physics and Astronomy 136 Frelinghuysen Rd Piscataway NJ 08854-8019 E-mail: robbins@physics.rutgers.edu.

ROBBINS, ANNE FRANCIS See REAGAN, NANCY DAVIS

ROBBINS, ARTHUR M. retired aerospace engineer; b. N.Y.C., Dec. 16, 1928; s. Albert R. and Rebecca L. Robbins; m. Donna Dale Coates, Mar. 15, 1958 (dec. June 1987); children: Janice, Linda, William, Mark. BSME, NYU, 1949; MEE, Pa. Inst. Tech., 1955. Registered profl. engr., Pa. Sect. mgr. Am. Electronic Labs., Lansdale, Pa., 1953-77; v.p. Antenna Corp. Am., Harleysville, 1977-82; engring. mgr. Teledyne Microetics, San Diego, 1982-87; pres. UnLtd, 1987-98; ret., 1998. Author: Thoughts of an Unrepentant Liberal, 1995, (essays) Defrocking Religious Fundamentalism, 1998; patentee angular RF connector. Sgt. U.S. Army, 1951-53. Mem. ACLU, Americans United for Separation of Church and State, Freethinker Soc. of San Diego, Am. Humanist Assn., Hemlock Soc. Avocations: cosmology, anthropology, world travel. Home: 4070 Kansas St Apt 307 San Diego CA 92104-2546

ROBBINS, AUDREY, county official; b. Chgo., Mar. 1, 1932; d. Philip I. and Manya Lehr; children: Dana Merfeld, Cindy Buss. BA, DePaul U., 1993. Mfrs. rep. Museum Reprodns. - Marwall Industries, N.Y.C., 1969—79; asst. to chief counsel Arthur Andersen & Co., Chgo., 1979—98; mem. staff Office of Chief Judge, Cook County Cir. Ct., 1999—. Author: Goldblatt's Galloping Gourmets, 1974 (Tribune award, 74). Vol. intensive care infants Northwestern Meml. Hosp., Chgo., 1979—80; vol. Art Inst. Chgo., 1984—86; touring docent Terra Mus. Am. Art, 1999—; bd. dirs., sec., pres. Nathan & Francis Goldblatt Soc. for Cancer Rsch., 1955—83. Mem.: Golden Key (life). Avocations: art history, watercolors, cooking. Home: 910 N Lake Shore Dr # 718 Chicago IL 60611 Office: Cir Ct Cook County 50 W Washington Chicago IL 60602

ROBBINS, CARRIE F(ISHBEIN), costume designer, educator; b. Balt., Feb. 7, 1943; d. Sidney W. and Bettye A. (Berman) Fishbein; m. Richard D. Robbins, Feb. 15, 1969. BS, BA, Pa. State U., 1964; MFA, Yale Drama Sch., 1967. Over 27 Broadway shows, N.Y.C., 1968-2001, A Class Act at the Ambassador Theatre, 2001— (Off-Broadway), Grease (Tony nomination best costumes), Over Here (Tony nomination Best Costumes), Secret Affairs of Mildred Wilde, Yentl, Cyrano, Iceman Cometh, Octette Bridge Club, Look to the Lillies, Sweet Bird of Youth, Agnes of God, Boys of Winder, The First, Frankenstein, Shadow Box, San Francisco Opera, 1980, L.A. Opera, 1999, Houston Grand Opera, 2002, Opera Co. of Boston, 1975, 76, 86, 89, Hamburg State Opera (W.Ger.), 1979, Washington Opera Soc., 1975, many shows designed for the following including N.Y. Shakespeare Festival, Jules Irving's Lincoln Ctr. Repertory Theatre, Tyrone Guthrie Theatre, Mpls. (including Hamlet, Julius Ceasar and Three Penny Opera) , various shows Mark Taper Forum, L.A. (including The Tempest with Anthony Hopkins, Fashion Inst. Tech. Surface Design award, Flea in Her Ear Dramalogue Critics award), other various regional theatres U.S. (including Williamstown), Chelsea Theatre Ctr., Bklyn., John Houseman's City Ctr. Acting Co., Juilliard Sch., N.Y.C, WNET and cable TV, many Off-Broadway Theatres, N.Y.C., including High Infidelity starring Morgan Fairchild, Promenade Theatre, It's Only a Play starring John Davidson, Big Potato (new play by Arthur Laurents), Women's Project's Exact Center of the Universe starring Frances Sternhagen, Two-Headed, Westport Country Playhouse Bench's in the Sun starring Tim Conway, Arclite Theatre Tennessee Williams Remembered with Eli Wallach and Anne Jackson, Paper Mill Playhouse Rags, designer sets and costumes for new play by Ed Dixon; tchr. Henry Le Tang Profl. Sch. Tap Dance, 1989-91; vis. guest lectr. on costume design U. Ill., UCLA, Oberlin Coll., Penn State U., others; master tchr. costume design NYU, 30 yrs.; costume designer Saturday Night Live-NBC, 1985-86, The Rita Show (CBS pilot), (feature film) In the Spirit (with Elaine May and Peter Falk), 1987; designer apparel for staff and special events of Rainbow Room, Rockefeller Ctr., 1987-97, Aurora Grill, 1988, Empress Ct., Caesar's Palace, Las Vegas, 1988, Windows on the World Restaurant Complex, 1996 (Image of the Yr. award Nat. Assn. Uniform Mfrs. and Distbrs. 1997); recent regional theatre includes Berkshire Theatre, Mass., Toys in the Attic (directed by John Tillinger), Fla. Stage It's Only a Play (by Terrance McNally). Solo exhibit art work, Cen. Falls Gallery, N.Y.C., 1980; participant group exhbns. Cooper Hewitt Mus., Pa. State U., Wright-Hepburn Gallery, N.Y.C., Scottsdale, Ariz., Cen. Falls Gallery, 1983; illustrations and calligraphy pub. ann. calendar Soc. of Scribes competition, also Ms. mag.; work chosen to hang in juried show Salmagundi Club (Fine Arts Soc.), 1983, 84; original costume work photographed in books; Costume Design, 1983, Fabric Painting and Dying for the Theatre, 1982; original drawing reproduced Time-Life Series: The Ency. of Collectibles; profiled in Costume Design-Techniques of Modern Masters, 1996, Contemporary Designers, 1990, 97; designer loft conversions, comml. lobby space, studios, numerous others; contbr. articles to Theatre Crafts International, contbr. to profl. jours. Named Disting. Alumna, Pa. State U., 1979; recipient Antoinette Perry nominations for Best Costumes for a Broadway Show, 1971-72, 73-74, Drama Desk award, Am. Theatre Wing, N.Y.C., 1971, 72, Maharam award for design, Joseph Maharam Found., N.Y.C., 1975, nomination, 1984, Juror's Choice award for surface design, Fashion Inst. of Tech., 1980, Dramalogue Critics' award for Outstanding Achievement in Theatre Costume Design, L.A., 1982, Silver Medal, 6th Triennial of Theatre Design, Novisad, Yugoslavia, 1981, Diplome L'Honneur, 1990, Audelco nomination, 1990, Henry Hewes nomination, 1999, League N.Y. Theatres, N.Y.C., 1971-72, 73-74. Mem. League Profl. Theatre Tng. Programs (steering com.), League Profl. Theatre Women (bd. dirs. 2001—), Graphic Artists Guild, Soc. Scribes, Am. Soc. Interior Designers, United Scenic Artists Local 829; adv. com. The Costume Collection of Theatre Devel. Fund. Home and Office: 11 W 30th St 15th Fl New York NY 10001 E-mail: crobb10001@aol.com.

ROBBINS, CORNELIUS (CORNELIUS VAN VORSE), educational administration educator; b. Wilmington, Del., Nov. 2, 1931; s. Cornelius V. and Irene (Tatman) R.; m. Janet Porter, Aug. 1953; children: Eva Robbins Burke, Susan Robbins, Laurel Robbins, Melissa Robbins Beegle. BA in Polit. Sci, U. Del., 1953, MEd in Social Scis, 1961; EdD in Ednl. Adminstrn, U. Pa., 1964. Asst. mgr. Robbins & Clark Hardware, 1953-57; mem. faculty U. Del., 1957-58; tchr. Marshallton (Del.) Sch. Dist., 1958-60, Mt. Pleasant (Del.) Sch. Dist., 1960-62; asst. to dir. sch. study councils U. Pa., 1962-64; dean instrn. Ocean County Coll., 1965-67; dean of coll. C/C. of Delaware County, Pa., 1967-69; sr. assoc., coll. div. dir. McManis Assocs., Washington, 1969-70; pres. Genesee C.C., 1970-75; assoc. chancellor for community colls. SUNY, 1975-85; acting pres. Potsdam State Coll. (N.Y.), 1982-83; pres. Cobleskill (N.Y.) Coll. Agr. & Tech., 1985-92; prof. edn. adminstrn. SUNY, Albany, N.Y., 1992—. Cons. Middle States Assn. Colls.; area liaison officer U.S. Mil. Acad., 1971-75; chmn. SUNY West Pres.'s Council and mem. Chancellor's Council, 1973-91. Contbr. articles to profl. publs. Served with U.S. Army, 1954-56; maj. USAR ret. Recipient Outstanding Educator's award N.Y. State Assn. Jr. Colls., 1975, Disting. Svc. award Faculty Coun. Community Colls., 1988. Mem. Am. Assn. Higher Edn., State Dirs. of Community Colls. Assn., Phi Delta Kappa. Office: SUNY Albany Ed 329 Albany NY 12222-0001 E-mail: crobbins@uamail.albany.edu.

ROBBINS, DARRYL ANDREW, pediatrician; b. Modesto, Calif., Sept. 16, 1945; s. Jerome and Grace (Bass) R.; m. Harriette Lee Eisenberg, June 12, 1971; children: Jennifer Lynn, Julie Ellen, Allison Beth. BS, Dickinson Coll., 1967; DO, Phila. Coll. Osteo. Medicine, 1971. Diplomate Am. Bd. Pediat. Intern Doctor's Hosp., Columbus, Ohio, 1971-72; resident in pediatrics Children's Hosp. Med. Ctr., Cin., 1972-75; practice medicine specializing in pediatrics Columbus, 1975—. Vice-chmn. Diocesan Child Guidance Ctr., Columbus, 1986; genetics svcs. adv. com. Ohio Dept. Health, 1978-86; pres. med. staff Columbus Children's Hosp., 1996. Trustee Columbus Children's Hosp., 2001, Children's Practicing Pediatricians, Columbus, bd. dirs., 1998—, pres., 2001—, bd. dirs., 1991—94. Recipient Samuel Dalinsky Meml. award for Outstanding Graduating Resident Cin. Children's Hosp., 1975; named Pediatrician of Yr., Columbus Children's Hosp., 1982, 90. Fellow Am. Acad. Pediatrics; mem. Cen. Ohio Pediatric Soc. (pres. elect 1988, pres. 1989-90). Jewish. Home: 953 Old Farm Rd Columbus OH 43213-2674 Office: 453 Waterbury Ct Gahanna OH 43230-5309

ROBBINS, DAVID BARCLAY, writer, educator; b. Ann Arbor, Mich., Nov. 23, 1951; s. Ronald George and Beverly Barclay Robbins; m. Nancy Marie Nadeau; children: Philip, Matthew, Jonathan, Derrick. BS, Mich. State U., 1973; MSc, U. Calgary, Alta., Can., 1976. Rsch. asst. U. Mich., Ann Arbor, 1976—79, Traverse Group, Ann Arbor, 1979—81; tech. writer Margaux Sys., 1983—86; product info. specialist Unisys, Plymouth, 1986—. Adj. prof. Lawrence Technol. U., Southfield, Mich., 2001—; mem. adj. faculty Unisys U., Blue Bell, Pa., 2000—01. Contbr. articles to profl. jours. and confs. Vol. Boy Scouts Am., Ann Arbor, 1990—97. Mem.: Soc. Tec. Comm. (3 Disting. awards Regional Competitions 1996—2001, Excellence awards (2) for Video Internat. Level 2000). Republican. Evangelical Presbyterian. Avocations: theology, skiing, camping, video production. Home: 1393 Rue Deauville Ypsilanti MI 48198 Office: Unisys Corp 41100 Plymouth Rd Plymouth MI 48170

ROBBINS, DENNIS ALAN, health services executive, educator; b. Detroit, Dec. 2, 1945; s. Max and Fay (Eisenberg) R.; m. Lora Ann Affinito, Dec. 30, 1969; children: Diana, Lynne. PhD, U. North Tex., 1970; MPhil, U. Okla., 1972; PhD with high distinction, Boston Coll., 1974; MPH, Harvard U., 1980; postgrad., U. Miss., 1981-83. Tchg. asst. U. Okla., Norman, 1971-72; asst. prof. U. N.C., Wilmington, 1975-79; assoc. prof. U. Miss., Oxford, 1981-83; assoc. prof., dir. grad. program health adminstrn. Salve Regina Coll., Newport, R.I., 1983—; pres. Integrated Decisions, Ethics, Alternatives, and Solutions, Farmington Hills, Westmont, Mich., Ill., 1983—; assoc. prof. dept. medicine Loyola Strich Sch. Medicine, Maywood, Ill., 1991—. Adj. assoc. prof. medicine Loyola U. Med. Ctr., Maywood, Ill., 1994; pres., prof. NCNM, Portland, Oreg.; mem. editl. bd., columnist Managed Health Care Mag. Legal and Ethical Issues; tchg. fellow Boston Coll., Chestnut Hill, Mass., 1972-74; fellow interfaculty program med. ethics Harvard Schs. Medicine and Pub. Health, Boston, 1979-80; adj. asst. prof. internal medicine Wayne State U. and Affiliated Hosps., Detroit, 1985-89; clin. ethicist VA Med. Ctr., Allen Park, 1985-89; dir. med. ethics med. ICU, surg. ICU, CCU, pulmonary and oncology units Sinai Hosp.; cons., spkr. in field; presenter, participant seminars in field; mem. Joint Commn. for Accreditation Healthcare Orgns., Alternative Medicine Inc., Highland Park, Ill.; mem. adv. bd. Managed Healthcare mag., Humana and Golden Springs, Northport, Fla.; v.p. for industry devel. Cardiobeat.com, Scottsdale, Ariz., 1999—; cons. Healthcare Dimensions, Tempe, Ariz. Author: Ethical Issues in Biomedicine and Related Areas, 1978, Ethical Dimensions of Clinical Medicine, 1981, Legal & Ethical Issues in Cancer Care, 1983, Ethical and Legal Issues in Home Care and Long Term Care: Challenges and Solutions, 1996, Integrating Managed Care and Ethics: Transforming Challenges into Positive Outcomes, 1998, Managed Care on Trial: Recapturing Trust, Integrity and Accountability in Healthcare, 1998, Putting Healthcare Promises into Practice: Strategic Innovations, 2000, Weaving Wellness and Alternative Medicine into the Mainstream: Ethics, Promise, Controversy, 2001; contbr. chpts. to books and articles to profl. jours.; interviewed by Dateline, Healthcare Channel et al. Organizer The Boston Hospice, Cambridge, 1980; exec. v.p. Hospice Lower Cape Fear, Wilmington, N.C., 1978. Nat. Fund Med. Edn. fellow Harvard Interfaculty Program Med. Ethics; subject of numerous jour. articles. Jewish. Avocations: water sports, travel, sculpture. Fax: (630) 663-0017. E-mail: DrDRobbins@aol.com.

ROBBINS, DONALD KENNETH, real estate investment advisor, consultant; b. Portland, Oreg., Sept. 21, 1928; s. Joseph and Anna Mae (Dexter) R.; m. Helen Virginia Holder (div. 1974); children: Beverly, Roland, Sandra, Debra, Roxanne; m. Barbara Ann Rabel, Mar. 10, 1976; children: Gia, Lisa. BS in Engring., U.S.. Naval Acad., 1950; AA in Real Estate, Mt. Hood C.C., Gresham, Oreg., 1968. Cert. real estate cons., review appraiser, mortgage underwriter. Enlisted USN, 1945, commn. ensign, 1950, advanced through grades to lt. (j.g.), 1953, resigned, 1955; founder Realty Exch., Portland, 1955—. Real estate broker Realty Exch., Portland, 1970-86; registered rep. Omega Securities, Portland, 1973; registered prin. Real Estate Securities Exch. Co., Portland, 1983; exec. dir. Better Housing Trustcorp, Portland, 1988-93; cons. in field; bd. dirs. Realty Factors, Inc., REO Properties, Ltd., Estate Liquidators, Inc., Realty Remodeling Contractors Inc., Realty Trustcorp, Project 2000, Eagles' Co., Eagles Net. Com., Inc., Genesis Group, LLC; exec. mgr. Eagles' Investment Club, LLC, Portland, 1994—, ATM Ventures, LLC, 1996-99, OpportunityPlace, LLC, 1997—, MoneyPlace, LLC, 1997—, AngelInvestor.net, LLC, 1997—, CyberVentures, LLC, 1997—, Eagles Mint, LLC, 1998—; State of Oreg. System of Higher Edn. accredited instr. U. Oreg., Eugene. Author, editor (newsletter) Investors' Clinic, 1970—; author DPP Study Outline (NASD), 1980; editor (newsletter) Eagles' Edge, 1995—; editor, pub. (electronic mag.) Eagles Network, 1995—; contbr. articles to Update newsletter, 1980-82. Mem. legis. coun. Oreg. Assn. Realtors, Salem, 1982-85; bd. dirs. Oreg. Housing Now!, Portland, 1990-92, Third Sector, Portland, 1991-92; regional v.p. for 5 Western states Real Estate Securities and Syndication Inst. of the Nat. Assn. Realtors, Chgo., 1981. Mem. Nat. Assn. Securities Dealers, Oreg. Mortgage Brokers Assn., Royal Rosarians of Portland, Oreg., Eagles' Network. Home and Office: 10285 NW Flotoma Dr Portland OR 97229-6218 E-mail: drobbins@eagles-network.com., email@donaldrobbins.com., drobbins@moneyplace.com.

ROBBINS, DOREN GURSTEIN, poet, educator, artist; b. L.A., Aug. 20, 1949; s. Ralph and Florence R.; m. Linda Drand Mazak Janakos; 1 child, Samantha. MFA, U. Iowa, 1993. Instr. English Umpqua C.C., Roseburg, Oreg., 1993-95, Linfield Coll., McMinnville, 1994-95; instr. creative writing U. Iowa, Iowa City, 1991-93; English instr. East Los Angels Coll., Monterey Park, Calif., 1997—; instr. creative writing, poetry U. Calif., L.A., 1996-99; English instr. Santa Monica (Calif.) Coll., 1998—; instr. advanced creative wiritng Mount Saint Mary's Coll., L.A., 2001—. Author: (poetry) Driving Face Down, 2001 (Blue Lynx prize 2001), The Donkey's Tale, 1998 (The Villon prize 1998), Sympathetic Manifesto, 1988 (Emma Goldman award 1988), Seducation of the Groom, 1982, Dignity in Naples and North Hollywood, 1996. Poet, artist Salvadoran Med. Relief Fund, Salinas, Calif., 1984-85; poet-activist Ctrl. Am. Refugee Com., L.A., 1984-86; poetry organizer Amnesty Internat., L.A., 1980. Recipient Anna Davidson Roseberg award Judah Magnes Mus., Commendation prize Chester H. Jones Found., 1993, 96, 97; poetry fellowship Oreg. Literary Arts, L.A. County Mus. of Art, 1999, The Loft Found., 1985. Jewish. Avocations: contemplation, travel, walking. E-mail: 310-822-2748. Home: 4161 Alla Rd Los Angeles CA 90066 Office: Foothill Coll care Lang Arts 12345 El Monte Rd Los Altos Hills CA 94022-4599 E-mail: pantagruli@aol.com.

ROBBINS, DOROTHY ANN, foreign language educator; b. Little Rock, Mar. 17, 1947; d. W.E. and Ina (Spencer) R. BA in Sociology, U. Ark., 1971; cert., U. Heidelberg, Germany, 1975; PhD, U. Frankfurt, Germany, 1981. Cert. state translator, Germany. Lectr. U. Heidelberg, 1977; head English dept. European Bus. Sch., Germany, 1978-80; dir. Inst. German Studies, Minn., 1985-87; asst. prof., then assoc. prof. fgn. lang. Ctrl. Mo. State U., Warrensburg, 1988-99, prof., 1999—. Am. liaison Tolstoy Inst. Fgn. Langs., Moscow, 1983—; faculty advisor Alpha Mu Gamma, 1998—. Author: (introduction) Collected Works of L. S. Vygotsky, Vygotsky's Psychology-Philosophy: A Metaphor for Language Theory and Learning, 2001, L.S. Vygotsky's and A.A. Leontiev's Russian Educational Semiotics and Psycholinguistics: Applications for Second Language Theory, 2001, Voices with Vygotskian Non-Classical Psychology: Past, Present and Future, 2001; contbr. articles to profl. jours. Fulbright-Hays Travel fellow to Russia, 1994, sr. level Fulbright fellow to Moscow, 1999. Mem. Internat. Vygotsky Soc. (co-founder exec. com., Western coord. ZPD summer conf., Russia, 2000), Am. Assn. Applied Linguistics, Phi Beta Delta (campus pres. 1994-95). Avocations: travel to Russia, Russian language and literature, writing prose, trips to the sea, candlelight meals. Office: Ctrl Mo State U Martin 236 Warrensburg MO 64093 E-mail: robbins@cmsu1.cmsu.edu.

ROBBINS, DOROTHY ANN, librarian; b. Altha, Fla., Dec. 2, 1939; d. Robert C. and Pauline Johnson; m. Richard N. Robbins, Jan. 16, 1960; children: Cynthia R. Peacock, Pamela T., LeAnne M. Lusk. AA, Gulf Coast C.C., Panama City, 1959. With Bay County Pub. Libr., Panama City, Fla., 1959—, libr. clk., bookmobile clk., br. mgr., circulation supr., literacy dir., pub. svcs. supr. Adv. bd. Literacy Vols. of Bay County, Panama City, 1982-99; troop leader Girl Scouts of the Apalachee Bend, Panama City, 1972-75. Mem. Greater Panama City Dog Fanciers (sec. 1988-99), S.E. Bullmastiff Assn. (b. dirs., pres. 1991-99), Am. Bullmastiff Assn., United Daus. of the Confederacy. Democrat. Baptist. Avocations: showing bullmastiffs, reading, antiques, crafts, gardening. Home: 435 S Palo Alto Ave Panama City FL 32401-3954 Office: Bay County Pub Libr 25 W Government St Panama City FL 32401-2743

ROBBINS, EDWIN, lawyer, business executive; b. N.Y.C., Dec. 30, 1931; s. Abraham and Lena (Cohen) R.; m. Beverly C. Leonard, July 29, 1956; children: Clifton Scott, Alison Robbins Gould, Brian Devin. AB, Columbia U., 1953, JD, 1955. Bar: U.S. Dist. Ct. (D.C. dist.) 1955, N.Y. 1958, U.S. Ct. Appeals (D.C. cir.) 1956, U.S. Dist. Ct. (so. and ea. dist.) N.Y. 1959. Assoc. Winthrop, Stimson, Putnam & Roberts, N.Y.C., 1957-61; v.p. Arcady Corp., 1963-68; gen. ptnr. Gaymark Assocs., 1964-93; counsel Skadden, Arps, Slate, Meagher & Flom, N.Y.C., 1968—; pres., chief exec. officer Sterling Capital Corp., 1980-93; gen. ptnr. Hopewell Ptnrs., 1985-93. Pres., chief exec. officer Marathon Securities Corp., N.Y.C., 1968-78, Highland Capital Corp., N.Y.C., 1972-84. Editor Columbia Law Rev., 1954-55. Mem. bd. visitors Columbia Law Sch., 1984—; bd. dirs. Hopewell Found., Inc., N.Y.C., 1958-93, Four Oaks Found., Inc., N.Y.C., 1984-93, Blue Ridge Found., Inc., N.Y.C., 1985-93; trustee Columbia U., 1988—, Columbia U. Press, Inc., 1990-93. Mem. ABA, Assn. of Bar of City of N.Y., Phi Beta Kappa. Jewish. Home: 876 Park Ave New York NY 10021-1832 Office: 919 3rd Ave New York NY 10022-3902

ROBBINS, ELIZABETH, stained glass artist, designer; b. N.Y.C., Dec. 17, 1941; d. Victor Ganales and Sylvia Sherrie (Woolf) R.; m. Jarvis Myers; children: Lorraine, Benjamin. BS in Art Edn., So. Conn. State Coll.; attended, Yale U., Cooper Union, N.Y.C., Silvermine (Conn.) Guild, Betzalel Art Sch., Jerusalem, Israel, Victoria & Albert Mus., London, Northeastern U., Boston, Wolverhampton (Eng.) Coll. Staff graphic layout and design Jarrett Press, N.Y.C., 1960-63; owner, operator Unique Boutique, Jerusalem, Israel, 1964-66; mem. staff, trainer Isratypeset, 1967-72; costume designer MGM, Israel, 1967-72; graphic designer Time-Life Book Divsn., Amsterdam, Holland, 1973; originator, operator The Darkroom, Cambridge, Mass., 1976-82; owner, operator Elizabeth Robbins Studios, 1982-96. Gallery showings include Hartford (Conn.) Courant Art Competition, 1956-59 (Best in Show award (sculpture) 1957, 2d Place award (painting) 1958, (sculpture) 1959, 3d Place award (sculpture) 1956), So. Conn. State Coll., New Haven, 1965, Yale, New Haven Group Show, 1965, Betzalel, Israel Group Show, 1970, Amalgamated Gallery, N.Y.C., 1984, Art on the Green, Newton, Mass., 1982-86, Abrams Gallery, Cambridge, Mass., 1987, Corning (N.Y.) Show, 1988, Metro Show, Washington D.C., 1988 (Hon. Mention), Goldmine Gallery, Manchester, Vt., 1988, Catamount Gallery, St. Johnsbury, Vt., 1989, New England Art Glass Show, Derby Line, Vt., 1990-93, Pitts., The Orchid As Art, 1992, 94, Ventura, Calif. Group Show, 1992, 94, San Francisco Harvest Show, Calif. 1993, 95; represented in various pub. collections, including Amchad/Assn. for Holocaust Survivors, Ramat Gan, Israel, Cobleigh Libr., Lyndonville, Vt., No. Vt. Regional Hosp., St. Johnsbury, Vt.; represented in numerous pvt. collections. Mem. Stained Glass Assn. Am., Vt. Coun. on the Arts, Vt. Handcrafters. Office: Elizabeth Robbins Studio Vail Circle Lyndonville VT 05851 Home: 4603 Jericho St White River Junction VT 05001-9317

ROBBINS, EMMETT TODD, systems analyst; b. Dallas, Nov. 26, 1962; s. Emmett and Willie Mae (Goodman) R. BA in Computer Sci., Morehouse Coll., 1984. Customer svc. coord. IBM, Atlanta, 1984; sr. data processing analyst AT&T Comm., 1985-87; sr. programs analyst Delta Air Lines, Inc., 1987-94; pres., CEO In Full View Window Svcs., Inc., 1989-94; computer support specialist GE Capital, Alpharetta, Ga., 1996-97; applications developer, 1997—; pres., CEO Proverb Investments, Inc., 1996—. MVS capacity planner Delta Air Lines, 1989-94; MICS System Adminstr., 1992-94; bd. dirs. Advanced Computer Techs. 2000 Inc. Mem., chmn. fin. com. Boy Scouts Am., Atlanta, 1990; asst. bus. mgr. New Birth Missionary Bapt. Ch., 1997—; bd. dirs. Jesse Draper Boys and Girls Club, 1993-95; mem. United Negro Coll. Fund employees com. Delta Air Lines, 1994. Recipient Ga. Key award 4-H Club of Am., 1980, Cert., Hoosier United Meth. Episc. Ch. Choir, 1990. Mem. Atlanta U. Computer Sci. Club, Kappa Alpha Psi (life, com. chmn. 1990-91, Polemarchs award 1991). Democrat. Avocations: tennis, basketball, reading, fishing. Home: 5175 Hermitage Dr Baton Rouge LA 70806-1826

ROBBINS, EUGENE WELDON, genealogist; b. Wichita Falls, Tex., Nov. 18, 1925; s. Clarence R. and Myrtle Otheny (Maguffee) R.; m. Betty Alice Day, Sept. 6, 1947; children: Marian Gail, Brian Andrew. BS, Tex. A&M, 1950. Info. dir. Houston (Tex.) C. of C., 1950-60; asst. to exec. v.p. Am. Road/Transp. Builders Assn., Washington, 1960-71; pres. Tex. Good Roads/Transp. Assn., Austin, Tex., 1971-85, Robbins Geneal. Collection, Spicewood, 1985—. Mem. adv. com. Tex. Transp. Inst., College Station; trustee Tex. A&M Rsch. Found., College Station. Author: Boggy Rangers, 1995. Sec.-treas. Edgewater Beach Neighborhood Assn., Spicewood. Lt.

USNR, 1943-46, PTO. Recipient Cert. of Appreciation, U.S. Dept. Commerce, Washington, 1970, Disting. Svc. award Better Roads and Transp. Coun., Washington, 1975, Scoop award Am. Assn. State Hwy. and Transp. Ofcls., Washington, 1977, Founders award Better Roads and Transp. Coun., Washington, 1988. Mem. Am. Assn. Ret. Persons, Am. Automobile Assn., Res. Officers Assn. (life), Ret. Officers Assn. (pres. Highland Lakes chpt.), Retreads (sec.-treas.), Slippery Rock Boosters Club Houston (founding mem.), Navy Mus. Found. (founding mem.). Home: 19517 Scenic Dr Spicewood TX 78669-1700

ROBBINS, FREDERICK CHAPMAN, retired physician, medical school dean emeritus; b. Auburn, Ala., Aug. 25, 1916; s. William J. and Christine (Chapman) Robbins; m. Alice Havemeyer Northrop, June 19, 1948; children: Alice, Louise. AB, U. Mo., 1936, BS, 1938; MD, Harvard U., 1940; DSc (hon.) , John Carroll U., 1955, U. Mo., 1958, U. N.C., 1979, Tufts U., 1983, Med. Coll. Ohio, 1983; LLD (hon.) , U. N.Mex., 1968. Diplomate Am. Bd. Pediatrics. Intern Children's Hosp., Boston, 1941—42, resident, 1940—41, resident in pediat., 1946—48; sr. fellow virus disease Nat. Rsch. Coun., 1948—50; staff rsch. divsn. infectious diseases Children's Hosp., Boston, 1948—50, assoc. physician, assoc. dir. isolation svc., assoc. rsch. divsn. infectious diseases, 1950—52; instr., assoc. in pediat. Harvard Med. Sch., 1950—52; dir. dept. pediatrics and contagious diseases Cleve. Met. Gen. Hosp., 1952—66; prof. pediatrics Case Western Res. U., 1950—80; dean Case Western Res. U. Sch. Medicine, 1966—80, dean emeritus, 1980—; prof. emeritus Case Western Res. U., 1987—, dir. Ctr. Adolescent Health Sch. Medicine; pres. Inst. Medicine, NAS, 1980—85. Vis. scientist Donner Lab. U. Calif., 1963—64. Pres. Soc. Pediatric Rsch. , 1961—62. Maj. U.S. Army, 1942—46. Decorated Bronze Star; co-recipient Nobel prize in physiology and medicine, 1954; recipient 1st Mead Johnson prize application tissue culture methods to study of viral infections, 1953, Med. Mut. Honor award, 1969, Ohio Gov.'s award, 1971, NASA Public Service Award, 1989, Frank and Dorothy Humel Hovorka Prize, Case Western Res. U., 1992, Benjamin Franklin Medal, Amer. Philosophical Soc., 1999. Mem.: Am. Philos. Soc., Am. Pediatric Soc, Am. Acad. Pediatrics, Am. Acad. Arts and Scis., Nat. Acad. Scis., Assn. Am. Med. Colls. (Abraham Flexner award 1987), Phi Gamma Delta, Sigma Xi, Phi Beta Kappa. Office: Case Western Res U Sch Med 10900 Euclid Ave Cleveland OH 44106-1712*

ROBBINS, GLORIA J. social worker; b. Rochester, N.Y., Nov. 11, 1938; d. Marvin and Rachel (Callner) Edelman; m. Ronald Robbins, Jan. 12, 1961; children: Joel, Michele. BS in Social Work, Adelphi U., Garden City, N.Y., 1979. Cert. social worker, Wash. Fellow N.Y. State Soc. Clin. Social Work; mem. NASW. Avocations: theater, hiking, travel. Home: 151 Academy St Poughkeepsie NY 12601-4514

ROBBINS, HENRY ZANE, public relations and marketing executive; b. Winston-Salem, N.C., Jan. 17, 1930; s. Romulus Mayfield and Vera Ethel (Daniel) R.; m. Barbara Anne Brown, Jan. 19, 1955; children: Zane Scott, Jill Stewart, Gail Ruth. AB, U. N.C., 1952; student, Emory U., 1952. Reporter Atlanta Constn., 1952; exhibit specialist Gen. Electric Co., Schenectady, 1952, employee relations specialist Cin., 1955, editor Schenectady, 1955, account supr. Winston-Salem, 1956-58, group supr. Schenectady, 1958-60; v.p., gen. mgr. Burson-Marsteller, Pitts. and Chgo., 1960-70, sr. v.p., 1970; pres., chief exec. officer SL&H-Robbins Inc., Chgo., 1970-72; also dir.; pres., chief exec. officer Beveridge Kraus Robbins & Manning, 1973-75; also dir.; pres., dir., chief exec. officer Beveridge and Robbins Inc., 1975-77; pres., chief exec. officer Financial Advt. of Ill., Inc.; mng. dir. Sports Mgmt. Group, 1975-77; dir. communications Arthur Andersen & Co., Chgo. and Geneva, Switzerland, 1977-81, dir. mktg. support services, 1981-89, dir. mktg. and comms., 1989-91; mem. Worldwide Alpha Group, 1991-96, exec. dir. global 1000 program, 1995—2000; prin. Arthur Andersen & Co., 1980—2000. Mem. journalism adv. com. Harper Coll., Palatine, Ill.; dir. Evanston Environ. Assn.; mem. Ladd Arboretum Commn., Evanston, Ill.; pub. rels. com. Chgo. Met. Crusade Mercy; mem. Nat. Task Force on Environment; cons. sec. Dept. Health, Edn. and Welfare, 1970; chmn. pub. rels. com. Honor Am. Day Com., 1970. Author: Vision of Grandeur, 1988, Globalizing the Enterprise, 2000; contbr. articles to profl. jours. Counselor Council of Mojave, 1972-74; gen. chmn. Chgo. Children's Classic Golf Tournament, 1974-77; chmn. Chgo. fin. com. Am.'s Freedom Train, 1976; chmn. fund devel. com. Presbytery of Chgo., 1977-83, maj. mission fund, 1977-79; dist. commr. Boy Scouts Am., 1976-79, chmn. Wildcat dist., 1980-83; mem. exec. bd. N.E. Ill. council, 1980-85; mem. Republican Citizens Com. Ill., 1960-61, Allegheny County (Pa.) Rep. Com., 1962-65; Trustee Roycemore Sch., Evanston, 1971-74; trustee, v.p. devel. Child and Family Services Chgo.; bd. dirs. Fellowship of Christian Athletes, U. N.C. Alumni Ill., Stockbrokers Assn. Chgo.; chmn. devel. com. Potawotamie Dist., 2000, chmn. fin. com., 2001. Served to 1st lt. AUS, 1952-54. Elected to N.C. Pub. Rels. Hall of Fame, 1994. Mem. Pub. Relations Soc. Am., Nat. Investor Relations Inst., Midwest Travel Writers Assn., Chgo. Ednl. TV Assn., Pub. Relations Counselors Roundtable, Am. Mgmt. Assn., Environ. Writers Assn. Am., Optimist Internat., Chgo. Assn. Commerce and Industry, Art Inst. Chgo., Univ. Club, Sunset Ridge Country Club, Optimist ClubChi Psi. Republican. Presbyterian. Home: 2759 Broadway Ave Evanston IL 60201-1556 Office: 33 W Monroe St Chicago IL 60603-5300

ROBBINS, HULDA DORNBLATT, artist, printmaker; b. Atlanta, Oct. 19, 1910; d. Adolph Benno and Lina (Rosenthal) Dornblatt. Student, Phila. Mus's. Sch. Indsl. Art, 1928-29, Prussian Acad., Berlin, 1929-31, Barnes Found., Merion, Pa., 1939. Poster designer and maker ITE Circuit Breaker Co. Inc., Phila., 1944; instr. serigraphy Nat. Serigraph Soc. Sch., N.Y.C., 1953-60; instr. creative painting Atlantic County Jewish Community Centers, Margate and Atlantic City, N.J., 1960-67. Represented by WIlliam P. Carl, Fine Prints, Boston, The Picture Store, Boston. One-man shows, Lehigh U. Art Galleries, 1933, ACA Galleries, Phila., 1939, 8th St. Gallery, N.Y.C., 1941, Serigraph Gallery, N.Y.C., 1947, Atlantic City Art Center, 1961, 71, numerous group shows, 2d Nat. Print ann. Bklyn. Mus., Carnegie Inst., Library of Congress, LaNapoule Art Found., Am. Graphic Contemporary Art; represented in permanent collections, including, Met. Mus. Art, N.Y.C., Mus. Modern Art, N.Y.C., Bibliotheque Nationale, Smithsonian Instn., Art Mus. Ont., Can., Victoria and Albert Mus., London, U.S. embassies abroad, Lehigh U., Princeton (N.J.) Print Club. Recipient Purchase prize Prints for Children, Mus. Modern Art, N.Y.C., 1941; prize 2d Portrait of Am. Competition, 1945; 2d prize Paintings by Printmakers, 1948 Mem. Am. Color Print Soc., Print Club, Graphics Soc., Serigraph Soc. (mem. founding group, charter sec., Ninth Ann. prize 1948, 49) Home and Office: 16 S Buffalo Ave Ventnor City NJ 08406-2635 *To cherish and express living through devotion to art.*

ROBBINS, JACK, artist; b. Baltimore, Md. s. John Adrian and Martha Rutledge Robbins; m. Brigid Smith Robbins; children: Margaret Frances, Benjamin Carter. BA, Ohio Wesleyan, Deleware, OH, 1977. Artist, Baltimore, Md., 1980—. Mem.: Balt. Watercolor Soc.

ROBBINS, JACK WINTON, lawyer; b. Flemington, Mo., Nov. 1, 1919; s. Winnie and Opal (Pitts) R.; m. Hilda Haynes, Feb. 2, 1946; children: Randel Bliss Brodrique, Mark Haynes Robbins. BS, U. North Tex., 1941; JD, Columbia U., 1943. Bar: N.Y. 1944, Pa. 1956, U.S. Supreme Ct. 1953. Law clk. N.Y. Ct. of Appeals, Albany, 1943-44; assoc. atty. Cravath, Swaine & Moore, N.Y.C., 1944-53; prosecutor Nuremberg (Germany) War Crimes Trials, 1946-48; counsel Pitcairn Trust Co., Jenkintown, Pa., 1953—. Bd. dirs. Upper Dublin Twp. Sch. Bd., Ft. Washington, Pa., 1960-73, Ursinus Coll., Collegeville, Pa., 1984—. Mem. ABA, Pa. Bar Assn., Phila. Bar Assn. Republican. Methodist. Home: 1206 Spring Ave Fort Washington PA 19034-1522 Office: Pitcairn Trust Co 165 Township Line Rd Jenkintown PA 19046-3531

ROBBINS, JACKIE WAYNE DARMON, agricultural and irrigation engineer; b. Spartanburg, S.C., Feb. 6, 1940; s. Jack Dennis and Laura Christina (Champion) R.; m. Betty Jo Wright, June 17, 1963 (dec. Jan. 1995); children: Jackie II, Robin C.D. m. Glenda Hudson, Apr. 11, 1996. BS, Clemson U., 1961, MS, 1965; PhD, N.C. State U., Raleigh, 1970. Registered profl. engr., La., Tex.; cert. irrigation designer. Asst. prof. engring. La. State U., Baton Rouge, 1963-65; engring. rsch. assoc. N.C. State U., 1965-70; assoc. prof. engring. U. Mo., Columbia, 1970-71; prof. engring. La. Tech. U., Ruston, 1971-88; pres., engr. Irrigation Mart, Inc., 1978—. Cons. irrigation systems design and engring.; cons. agtl. waste mgmt. processes and facilities; cons. crop prodn. techniques. Contbr. articles to Agrl. Engring., Jour. Water Pollution Control Fedn., others. E.C. McArthur fellow, 1962-63; NSF Hydrology Inst. fellow, 1965; NSF trainee, 1968; NSF grantee, 1977-78, others. Mem. NSPE, Am. Soc. Agrl. Engrs. (chair rural water supplies, vice chair land use group, vice chair S.W. Region, chair La. sect., numerous others), Irrigation Assn. (bd. govs. 1988-92, chair 1990-92, bd. dirs. 1994-96), La. Engring. Soc. (chair Monroe chpt.), Am. Soc. Engring. Edn., La. Agrl. Waste Mgmt. Com., Sigma Xi, Tau Beta Pi, Alpha Epsilon. Achievements include patent for drip irrigation hose. Home: 114 Deer Creek Rd Ruston LA 71270-1653 Office: Irrigation Mart Inc 3303 Mcdonald Ave Ruston LA 71270-7412 E-mail: jwdr@irrigation-mart.com.

ROBBINS, JACOB, biomedical researcher, endocrinologist; b. Yonkers, N.Y., Sept. 1, 1922; s. Samuel and Tillie (Sanoff) R.; m. Jean Adams, Sept. 4, 1949; children: Alice Elizabeth, Susan Lynn, Mark Samuel. AB, Cornell U., Ithaca, N.Y., 1944; MD, Cornell U., N.Y.C., 1947. Intern in medicine N.Y. Hosp., N.Y.C., 1947-48; resident Meml. Hosp., 1948-50, rsch. fellow, 1949-53, asst. attending physician, 1953-54; commd. sr. asst. surgeon USPHS, 1954, advanced through grades to med. dir., 1963, ret., 1989; rsch. scientist NIH, Bethesda, Md., 1954—; chief clin. endocrinology br. Nat. Inst. Diabetes, Digestive and Kidney Diseaes, NIH, 1963-92, chief endocrinology sect. genetics and biochemistry br., 1992-94; scientist emeritus NIH, 1995—. Asst. Sloan Kettering Inst., N.Y.C., 1953-54; instr. Cornell U. Med. Coll., 1950-54, George Washington U. Sch. Medicine, Washington, 1955-61; vis. scientist Carlsberg Lab., Copenhagen, 1959-60; vis. prof. Stellenbosch U., Capetown, South Africa, 1967, Gumma U., Maebashi, Japan, 1970. Editor-in-chief Endocrinology, 1968-72; editor rsch. monographs; also numerous articles on thyroid rsch., chpts. on thyroidology. Recipient Meritorious Svc. medal USPHS, 1971. Mem. Am. Thyroid Assn. (pres. 1974-75, Parke Davis award 1980, Disting. Svc. award 1983), Endocrine Soc. (Ingbar Disting. Svc. award 1995), Am. Soc. for Clin. Investigation, Assn. Am. Physicians, Am. Physiol. Soc., European Thyroid Assn. (hon.), Japan Endocrine Soc. (hon.), Italian Endocrine Soc. (hon.). Avocation: farming. Home: 7203 Bradley Blvd Bethesda MD 20817-2127 Office: NIH Bldg Bldg 10 Rm 6C201 Bethesda MD 20892

ROBBINS, JAMES EDWARD, electrical engineer; b. Renovo, Pa., May 11, 1931; s. James Edward and Marguerite Neva (Cleary) R.; m. Elizabeth Anne Caton, 1959 (div. July 1971); children: James, Katherine, Ellen; m. Dorothy Raye Bell, July 23, 1971; stepchildren: Mark, Lori. BEE, Pa. State U., 1958; MS in Math., San Diego State U., 1961. Registered profl. engr., Calif., Ariz. Rsch. engr. Astronautics divsn. Gen. Dynamics Co., San Diego, 1961-62; sr. engr. Kearfott divsn. Gen. Precision Co., San Marcos, Calif., 1962-65; sys. engring. specialist Teledyne Ryan Aerospace Co., San Diego, 1965-76; mgr. tech. ops. Electronics divsn. Gen. Dynamics Co., Yuma, Ariz., 1965-76; v.p. Cibola Info. Sys., 1982-84; cons. engr. Robbins Engring. Co., 1984-85; sr. engring. specialist Gen. Dynamics Svcs. Co., Ariz., 1985-90; sys. engr. Trimble Navigation, Sunnyvale, Calif., 1990—. Contbr. articles to profl. jours. With USN, 1951-55, Korea. Mem. Inst. Navigation, Nat. Soc. Profl. Engrs., Ariz. Soc. Profl. Engrs. (pres. we. divsn. 1986), Am. Legion, VFW (post comdr. 1963-65), Tau Beta Pi. Home: PO Box 1728 430 Ave Portola El Granada CA 94018-1728 Office: Trimble Navigation 645 N Mary Ave Sunnyvale CA 94085-2933 E-mail: jim_robbins@trimble.com., jim_robbins@earthlink.com.

ROBBINS, JANE BORSCH, library science educator, information science educator; b. Chgo., Sept. 13, 1939; d. Reuben August and Pearl Irene (Houk) Borsch; married; 1 child, Molly Warren. BA, Wells Coll., 1961; MLS, Western Mich. U., 1966; PhD, U. Md., 1972. Asst. prof. library and info. sci. U. Pitts., 1972-73; assoc. prof. Emory U., Atlanta, 1973-74; cons. to bd. Wyo. State Libr., 1974-77; assoc. prof. La. State U., Baton Rouge, 1977-79; dean La. State U. Sch. Library and Info. Sci., 1979-81; prof., dir. Sch. Library and Info. Studies U. Wis., Madison, 1981-94; dean, prof. Fla. State U. Sch. Info. Studies, Tallahassee, 1994—. Author: Public Library Policy and Citizen Participation, 1975, Public Librarianship: A Reader, 1982, Are We There Yet?, 1988, Libraries: Partners in Adult Literacy, 1990, Keeping the Books: Public Library Financial Practices, 1992, Balancing the Books: Financing American Public Library Services, 1993, Evaluating Library Programs and Services: A Manual and Sourcebook, 1994, Tell It! The Complete Manual of Library Evaluation, 1996; editor Libr. and Info. Sci. Rsch., 1982-92; contbr. articles to profl. jours. Bd. dirs. Freedom to Read Found., 1997-99. Mem.: ALA (councilor 1976—80, 1991—95), Fla. Libr. Assn. (bd. dirs. 1997—99), Wis. Libr. Assn. (pres. 1986), Assn. for Libr. and Info. Sci. Edn. (dir. 1979—81, pres. 1984), Am. Soc. Info. Sci., Beta Phi Mu (exec. dir. 2000—). Democrat. Episcopalian. Office: Fla State U Sch Info Studies Louis Shores Bldg Tallahassee FL 32306-2100 E-mail: robbins@lis.fsu.edu.

ROBBINS, JEANETTE LEE, sales and manufacturing executive; b. Portland, Oreg., July 21, 1956; d. Robert Lee and Norma Yvonne (Smith) Rassi; m. Michael Keith Robbins, May 22, 1981. A in Gen. Sci., Portland C.C., 1982. Cert. engring. aide, Oreg. With prodn. thrift Salvation Army, Portland, 1979, Goodwill Industries, Denver, 1983-87, St. Vincent De Paul, Portland, 1987-88; owner Job Devel. Rsch. Ctr., 1985—, Eye-Dea Devel. Sales & Mfg., Portland, 1988—. Detective scientist, 1980—; reviewer publs. and forms IRS, 1997—, U.S. Govt., Washington, 1997—, local bus map rev., 1998. Author: (textbook) Prime Factor Pattern, 1991, Prime Pattern of (Square) Root Ends, 1994; contbr. articles and book revs. to profl. publs. and books; artist, author: (visual aid) Artrithmetic, 1982, Patricia Mae, U.S. White House, 1996, Artrithmetic-Reference, 1997, Combination, 1998, Large Combination Deluxe, 1999. Corr., adviser, World Gov., Nat. Gov., State Gov., Local Gov., Private Citizen, Bus. Owners, 1978—, Dem. Nat. Com., Washington D.C., 1993—. With USAF, 1977. Mem. Pub. Libr. Sys. (rschr. 1978—), Nat. Geographic Soc. (corr. 1993—). Avocations: alpinist, photography, languages. Office: Eye Dea Devel Sales & Mfg PO Box 66221 Portland OR 97290-6221

ROBBINS, JEFFREY HOWARD, media consultant, research writer, educator; b. N.Y.C., Mar. 29, 1941; s. Stanley Samuel and Miriam (Cooper) R.; m. Marsha Sue Rimler, Nov. 3, 1984 (div. Dec. 1996); 1 child, Nina Camille. BSME, Carnegie Mellon U., 1962; MS in Physics, U. N.Mex., 1966, ABD in Physics, 1967; postgrad., U. Calif., Berkeley and L.A., 1963-64. Summer rsch. assoc. Linde Co., Tonawanda, N.Y., 1961; rsch. engr. N.Am. Aviation (Rockwell), Downey, Calif., 1962-64; summer rsch. assoc. Los Alamos (N.Mex.) Nat. Lab., 1965; sr. engr. Radio Engring. Labs., L.I., N.Y., 1968-70; engring. cons. PRD Electronics, Syosset, 1972-73; sr. cons. Bendix Corp., Teterboro, N.J., 1974-76; sr. engr. Giordano Assocs., Franklin Lakes, 1977-81; sr. applications engr. Racal-Redak, Mahwah, 1981-83; tech. media cons. Allied Signal Corp., Teterboro, 1983-92, U.S. Army, Picatinny Arsenal, N.J., 1992; tech. cons. Ford Motor Co., Lansdale, Pa., 1992-98, Visteon Automotive Electronics, Markham, Ont., Can., 1998—. Cons. Tyco Internat., Clark, N.J., 1998—; tech. cons., rsch. writer media literacy programs Packer Collegiate Inst., Bklyn., N.Y.C., 1992-93, On TV, Inc., N.Y.C., 1992; initiator, moderator Media Literacy Forum, 1995; evening sch. instr. New Sch. for Social Rsch., N.Y.C., 1979-85; presenter in field. Author: On Balance and Higher Education, 1970; contbr. articles to profl. jours. Organizer, co-moderator Future Impact of Artificial Intelligence, Robotics Forum, 1984. Recipient 1st prize for essay The World and I Mag., 1990; nominee Grawemeyer award in Edn., 1988; NDEA fellow, 1966-67, others; feature essay premier issue Plain mag., 1994. Mem. IEEE (presenter Internat. Symposium in Tech. and Soc. 1993, 96, 98, Internat. Soc. Sys. Scis. Conf. 1993, 95, 97, 99, 2000, initiator, moderator, media literacy forum Packer Collegiate Inst. 1995, presenter World Order Conf., Toronto 1999, 2001), N.Y. Acad. Scis., Sigma Xi, Phi Kappa Phi, Pi Tau Sigma. Home and Office: PO Box 335 Long Beach NY 11561-0335 E-mail: jrobbins@tycomltd.com., jhrobbins@erols.com.

ROBBINS, JENNIFER KAY, journalist; b. Cin., Nov. 10, 1962; d. Douglas Jay and Paula Jane (Wyatt) R.; m. Steven M. Hanger, Apr. 5, 1996; children: Cheyenne, Winston. A in Acctg., MacArthur State U., 1983; BS in Mass Comm., Auburn U., 1998. Acct. Small Bus. Svc., Montgomery, Ala., 1983-85, Computer Bus. Svcs., New Orleans, 1985-88, Ala. Assn. Realtors, Montgomery, 1990-93; owner, acct. Affordable Acctg., 1993-95; editor-in-chief AUMnibus, 1995-98; mng. editor Butler County News, Greenville, Ala., 1998-99; editor The Luverne (Ala.) Jour., 1999—. Founder, chairperson People Against Vetoing Edn., Montgomery, 1997; mem. PTA, Tallassee, Ala., 1995—; mem. leadership coun. Auburn U., 1997—. Recipient Emerging 30 award Montgomery Area C. of C., 1995, 3rd pl. news photography spot Coll. Press Assn., 1998. Mem. Soc. Profl. Journalists, Omicron Delta Kappa. Avocations: writing short stories, reading.

ROBBINS, JERRY HAL, educational administration educator; b. DeQueen, Ark., Feb. 28, 1939; s. James Hal and Barbara I. (Rogers) R. BA in Math, Hendrix Coll., 1960; M.Ed., U. Ark., 1963, Ed.D., 1966. Tchr. math. and music Clinton (Ark.) pub. schs., 1960-61; prin. Adrian (Mo.) High Sch., 1961-63; exec. sec. Ark. Sch. Study Council, Fayetteville, 1963-65; mem. faculty U. Miss., University, 1965-74, prof. ednl. adminstrn., 1970-74, chmn. dept. ednl. adminstrn., 1970-74; dean Coll. Edn., U. Ark., Little Rock, 1974-79; asso. v.p. for acad. affairs Ga. State U., Atlanta, 1979-84, dean Coll. Edn., 1984-90, prof. ednl. adminstrn., 1990-91; dean. Coll. Edn. Ea. Mich. U., Ypsilanti, 1991—. Co-author: (with S. B. Williams Jr.) Student Activities in the Innovative School, 1969, School Custodian's Handbook, 1970, Administrator's Manual of School Plant Administration, 1970. Mem. NEA, Am. Assn. Sch. Adminstrs., Am. Assn. Colls. Tchr. Edn. (dir. 1979-82, 2000—), Nat. Assn. Secondary Sch. Prins., So. Regional Council Ednl. Adminstrn. (pres. 1970-71), Tchr. Edn. Coun. State Colls. and Univs. (pres. 1998-99), Phi Delta Kappa, Kappa Delta Pi (v.p. chpt. devel. 1978-80, pres. elect 1980-82, pres. 1982-84, past pres. 1984-86) Mem. United Meth. Ch. Home and Office: 3384 Bent Trail Dr Ann Arbor MI 48108-9316 Office: Ea Mich U 310 Porter Bldg Ypsilanti MI 48197 E-mail: jerry.robbins@emich.edu.

ROBBINS, JOHN CLAPP, management consultant; b. Cleveland, Jan. 22, 1921; s. John Clapp and Esther Turner (Holland) R.; m. Louise Severance Nash, Jan. 10, 1951 (div. Oct. 1974); children: Anne Millikin, Julia Severance, John Nash; m. Beatrice Blair, Aug. 2, 1975 (dec. July 1994); m. Sylvia Hordosch, Dec. 20, 2000. AB, Harvard U., 1942. Copy boy, reporter, writer, promotion editor Cleve. Press, 1946-57; exec. internat. div. Mobil Oil Corp., N.Y.C., Istanbul, 1957-70; chief exec. officer Planned Parenthood/World Population, N.Y.C., 1970-75; prin. mgmt. cons. Stanford Research Inst., 1976-83; v.p. GPA Inc., N.Y.C., 1983—; pres. John Robbins Assocs. Spl. fin. cons. Internat. Helsinki Fedn., Vienna, Parkinson Disease Found., N.Y.C., Alan Guttmacher Inst., N.Y.C. Author: Too Many Asians, 1959. Bd. dirs., pres. Am. Hosp.. Istanbul; treas. Harvard Libr. in N.Y.C. Capt. AUS, 1942-45. Decorated Bronze Star, Purple Heart; Reid fellow, 1953 Mem. Internat. Planned Parenthood Fedn. London, N.Y. State Rep. Pro-Choice Alliance. Unitarian Universalist. Home and Office: 115 E 87th St New York NY 10128-1136 E-mail: Johnrobbins@rcn.com.

ROBBINS, KAREN DIANE, editor; b. Bloomington, Ill., Nov. 25, 1959; d. Harley Edward and Geraldine Elayne (Abell) H; m. Craig Douglas Robbins, May 25, 1992. Cert. Office Adminstrn./Info. Processing, Cert. Graphics Tech., Riverside (Calif.) C.C., 1993. Editor Rat and Mouse Tales, Am. Fancy Rat and Mouse Assn. Directory, Bylaws and Show Regulations/Standards book, Chapters book, Mouse Genetics book. Mem. Am. Fancy Rat and Mouse Assn. (founder). Home: PO Box 2589 Winnetka CA 91396-2589 Office: Am Fancy Rat Mouse Assn 9230 64th St Riverside CA 92509-5924 Fax: 818-592-6590.

ROBBINS, KENNETH CARL, biochemist; b. Chgo., Sept. 1, 1917; s. Samuel and Mary (Silberbrandt) R.; m. Pearl Podorowsky, Mar. 31, 1946; children: Paula Lange, Shelley R. BS, U. Ill., 1939, MS, 1940, PhD, 1944. Asst. prof. pathology Western Res. U. Sch. Medicine, Cleve., 1947-51; head protein sec. biochemistry rsch. The Armour Labs., Chgo., 1951-58; dir. biochemistry rsch., scientific dir. Michael Reese Rsch. Found., 1958-84; prof. medicine and pathology Pritzker Sch. Med./Univ. Chgo., 1970-87, prof. emeritus, 1987—; dir. exptl. pathology Michael Reese Hosp. and Med. Ctr., Chgo., 1984-86; rsch. scientist, prof. hematology and oncology medicine Northwestern Univ. Sch. Medicine, 1989-95, ret., 1995, emeritus, 1997—. Mem. hematol. study sect. NIH, Bethesda, Md., 1971-75, 76-80, blood diseases & resources adv. com. Nat. Heart, Lung, and Blood Inst., NIH, 1976-80; chmn. Gordon Conf. Hemostasis, N.H., 1975; mem. Internat. Com. on Thrombosis and Haemostasis, 1980-86, chmn. subcom. on Fibrinolysis, 1980-82; lectr. in field. Mem. editorial bd. Jour. Biol. Chemistry, 1975-80; contbr. articles to profl. jours. Recipient fouth Elwood A. Sharp award Wayne State U. Sch. Medicine, Detroit, 1971, Prix Servier Medal and Prize, Fifth Internal Congress Fibrinolysis, Malmo, Sweden, 1980; grantee NIH, Bethesda, 1960-95. Mem. Am. Assn. Immunologists, Am. Soc. Biochemistry and Molecular Biology, Am. Soc. Hematology, Soc. Exptl. Biology and Medicine. Achievements include 10 patents in field; discovery of fibrin stabilizing factor, pancreatic elastase zymogen-proelastase, mammalian enzymatic omega oxidation of fatty acids system; development of oral thrombolytic therapy, hybrid pasminogen activators. Home: Unit 36C 6101 N Sheridan Rd E Chicago IL 60660-6824 E-mail: kcrobb@northwestern.edu.

ROBBINS, LANNY ARNOLD, chemical engineer; b. Wahoo, Nebr., Apr. 3, 1940; s. Earl Willard and Mildred Irene (Hanson) R.; m. Connie Lou Polich, Feb. 24, 1962; children: James Alan, Debra Renea. BS, Iowa State U., 1961, MS, 1963, PhD, 1966. Rsch. engr., project leader Dow Chem. Co., Midland, Mich., 1966-73, rsch. specialist, 1973-76, assoc. scientist, 1976-83, rsch. scientist, 1983-88, sr. rsch. scientist, 1988-97, rsch. fellow, 1997—. Adj. prof. Va. Poly. Inst., Blacksburg, 1973-76, Mich. State U., Lansing, 1983; mem. indsl. adv. bd. Iowa State U., Ames, 1994—. Author (chpt.) Schweitzer's Handbook of Separation Techniques, 1997, Perry's Chemical Engineer's Handbook, 1997. Recipient H.H. Dow medal, 1993. Mem. AIChE. Republican. American Baptist. Achievements include patents for AquaDetox Aqueous Purification stripping devices and process, Sorbathene pressure swing adsorption vent emission control processes, liquid distributors for packed distillation, distillation process control. Home: 4101 Old Pine Trl Midland MI 48642-8892 Office: Dow Chem Co 1319 Bldg Midland MI 48667-0001

ROBBINS, LAWRENCE HARRY, anthropologist, educator; b. Washington, Nov. 22, 1938; s. Maurice and Edith R.; m. Martha Ann Edwards, Dec. 16, 1967; children: Daniel, Brian, Michael, Mark. AB, U. Mich., 1961, A.M., 1962; PhD, U. Calif., Berkeley, 1968. Asst. prof. U. Utah, 1967; mem. faculty Mich. State U., East Lansing, 1968—, prof. anthropology and African studies, 1977—, chairperson ANP dept., 1992-95. Vis. research asso. U. Nairobi, Kenya, 1969-70, Nat. Mus. Kenya, 1975-76; Fulbright vis. prof. U. Botswana, 1982-83; vis. archaeologist Nat. Mus. and Art Gallery, Botswana, 1982-83 Author: Stones, Bones and Ancient Cities, 1990; contbr. articles to profl. jours. Grantee NSF, 1965-66, 69-70, 75-77, 91-2000, Nat. Geographic Soc., 1987, 89. Mem. Am. Anthropol. Assn., Registry Profl. Archaeologists, Soc. Africanist Archeologists in Am., So. African Archeol. Soc., Botswana Soc. Office: Dept Anthropology Mich State U East Lansing MI 48824

ROBBINS, MARION LERON, agricultural research executive; b. Inman, S.C., Aug. 18, 1941; s. Jack Dennis and Christina (Champion) R.; m. Margaret Elanor Wilson, Sept. 25, 1965 (wid. Feb. 1995); children: Jack, Rona, Jeff, Kyle; m. Jeanette Rogers Robbins, May 10, 1996. BS, Clemson U., 1964; MS, La. State U., 1966; PhD, U. Md., 1968. Asst. prof. Iowa State U., Ames, 1968-72; rsch. scientist Clemson U., Charleston, S.C., 1972-83; resident dir. Sweet Potato Rsch. Sta., Chase, La., 1984-88, Calhoun (La.) Rsch. Sta., 1988—2001; coord. Calhoun Extension Sta., 2002—. Pres. La. Acad. Scis., 2001—, Sci. editor Hort Sci., 2001—, mem. awards com. La. Farm Bur., 1988—, Agribus. Coun., Monroe, 1988—. Editor Jour. Vegetable Crop Prodn., 1992—; assoc. editor Crop Prodn. jour., 1972-90; contbr. more than 200 articles, abstracts, rsch. papers and revs. to profl. and trade jours.; sci. editor HortScience, 2001—. Delegation leader People to People Internat., Spokane, Wash., 1985—. Mem. Am. Soc. for Hort. Sci. (dir., pres. so. region 1982-83), La. Acad. Scis. (sec. 1997—, pres.-elect 1999—, pres. 2001—), Rsch. Ctr. Adminstrs. Soc. (dir. 1985), Calhoun Civic Club (pres. 1994-95) Rotary Club (pres. 1987-88), Exch. Club (pres. 1976-77). Presbyterian. Achievements include development of 22 varieties and genetic lines of crop plants, including 2 All-American winners and an All-Am. designate. Office: Calhoun Rsch Extension Sta 321 Highway 80 E PO Box 488 Calhoun LA 71225-0539

ROBBINS, MARJORIE JEAN GILMARTIN, elementary education educator; b. Newton, Mass., Sept. 19, 1940; d. John and Helen (Arbuckle) Gilmartin; m. Maurice Edward Robbins, Aug. 1, 1962; children: John Scott, Gregory Dale, Kris Eric. BS in Edn., Gordon Coll., 1962; postgrad., U. Maine, Augusta, 1976, U. Maine, Orono, 1986, U. Maine, Portland, 1987. Cert. tchr. Tchr. Ctr. St. Sch., Hampton, N.H., 1962-64, Claflin Sch., Newton, 1965-66, Israel Loring Sch., Sudbury, Mass., 1966-67, Cheney Sch., Orange, 1967-69,

Palermo (Maine) Consolidated Sch., 1975—, head tchr., 1997—. Founder, tchr. Primary Edn. Program, Palmero, 1990—; dir., author Child Sexual Abuse Program, Palmero, 1988—; mem. Title I Com., 1995—, Health Curriculum Com., 1995—, health grant coord., 1997—. Mem. bd. Christian edn., mem. wellness team, facilitator for Skillful Tchr. course Winter St. Bapt. Ch., Gardiner, Maine, 1993—, mem. bd. missions, 1993-94; bd. dirs. Hillside Christian Nursery Sch., 1994—; coord. student assistance team Maine Sch. Union #51, 1993—, bd. dirs. United Team, 1993—, mem. publicity com., 1991-92; coord. Nursing Home Ministry, Gardiner. Mem. NEA, Maine Tchrs. Assn., Palermo Tchrs. Assn. (pres. 1984-86, 96-98), Maine Educators of the Gifted and Talented, Maine Sch. Union 51 (sec. certification steering com. 1988—, rep. gifted-talented com. 1976—), Palermo Tchrs. Assn. (treas. 1998—), Palermo Sch. Club (exec. bd. 19 85-88. Avocations: travel, swimming, camping, basketball. Home: 99 S Dondero Rd Robbins Ln Augusta ME 04330 Office: Palermo Consolidated Sch RR 3 Palermo ME 04354

ROBBINS, MARY, concert pianist; b. Shelby, N.C., Feb. 14, 1950; d. Clyde Hugh and Hazel Marguerite (Lovett) Robbins; m. Carl Brockman, Jan. 16, 1983. Student, Converse Coll., Spartanburg, S.C., 1968-71; BMusic, U. Tex., 1973, MMusic, 1975, D Musical Arts, 1992. Concert coord. Austin (Tex.) Virtuosi, 1980-82; piano clinician Alfred Music Pub., Van Nuys, Cailf., 1991-94; pianist various chamber orgns., Austin, 1976-91; pvt. piano instr. for adults and children, 1971—; tchg. asst., instr. piano U. Tex., 1971-75; founder, prin. pianist A. Mozart Fest, 1991—, artistic dir., 1991—. Accompanist U. Tex., Austin, 1971-84; invited lectr. Mozart Internat. Bicentennial Congress, Salzburg, Austria, 1991. Composer music and cadenzas following Mozart's style for his piano concertos, 1989—; composer, performer CD, A. Mozart Fest, 1998. Vol. music class tchr. First English Luth. Ch., Austin, 1992; founder combined groups Classical Music Consortium, Austin, 1997. Grantee Tex. Commn. on Arts, 1991, 93, City of Austin, 1992—. Mem. Austin Dist. Music Tchrs. Assn. (v.p. 1997-98, chair adult programs 1997—, chair festivals 1997-98, Pre-Coll. Tchr. of Yr. 1998), Mu Phi Epsilon. Lutheran. Avocations: cooking, entertaining, dancing, outdoor sports, visual arts. Home: 2600 La Ronde St Austin TX 78731-5924

ROBBINS, MARY ANN, secondary school educator; b. Vincennes, Ind., Oct. 2, 1944; d. Cecil D. and Mary E. (Kaufman) R. AS, Vincennes U., 1964; BS, Ind. State U., Terre Haute, 1966, MS, 1972. Cert. tchr. secondary math., Ind. Tchr. math. Northside Mid.Sch., Bartholomew Consol. Sch. Corp., Columbus, Ind., 1966—. Tchr. math. TV program Mathworks, Columbus, 1985, 89-92. Mem. NEA (life), Nat. Coun. Tchrs. Math., Ind. Coun. Tchrs. Math, Ind. State Tchrs. Assn., Columbus Educators Assn., Nat. Mid. Sch. Assn., Delta Kappa Gamma (treas. 1973-92). Democrat. Roman Catholic. Avocations: reading, travel. Home: 611 Willow Ln Columbus IN 47203-1533 Office: Northside Mid Sch 1400 27th St Columbus IN 47201-3107 E-mail: robbinsm@bosc.k12.in.us.

ROBBINS, NANCY LOUISE See MANN, NANCY LOUISE

ROBBINS, NANCY SLINKER, volunteer; b. New Kensington, Pa., Jan. 28, 1923; d. Charles Morris and Nancy Grace (Moore) Slinker; m. James Bingham Murray, Aug. 1, 1946 (div. 1959); m. Daniel Harvey Robbins, Nov. 21, 1964; children: Nancy Caroline, Christina Chapman. BA, Westminster Coll., 1945; grad., U. Pitts., 1946. Cert. tchr. Pa. Tchr. Lower Burrell Sch., New Kensington, 1945-48; asst. buyer Gimbel's, Pitts., 1951-53, buyer, 1953-57, La Salle's, Toledo, 1957-61, Sibley's, Rochester, N.Y., 1961-66. Editor: Fan Fare, 1980-81. Pres. bd. Woman's Edn. and Indsl. Union, Rochester, 1973-76, Women's Coalition for Downtown, Rochester, 1982-84; pres. bd. Ronald McDonald House, Rochester, 1986-90, adminstr. grants program, 1996—; chmn. Pub. TV Auction, Rochester, 1980. Recipient Jefferson award Am. Inst. Pub. Svc., 1988, Forman Flair award for outstanding volunteerism, 1990, DeWitt Clinton awrd for pub. svc. Masons, 1989. Avocations: antique collecting, travel, cooking. Home: 35 Schoolhouse Ln Rochester NY 14618-3231 E-mail: nandan0035@aol.com.

ROBBINS, NORMAN NELSON, lawyer; b. Detroit, Sept. 27, 1919; s. Charles and Eva (Gold) R.; m. Pamela Anne Eldred, April 22, 1946; children: Susan, Aimee. LLB, JD, Wayne State U., 1943. Bar: Mich. 1943. Pvt. practice, Birmingham, Mich., 1943—. Chmn. Mich. Bd. for Marriage Counselors, 1971-75; lectr. Inst. Continuing Legal Edn. Editor Mich. Family Law Jour., 1974—; mem. editorial bd. Am. Jour. Family Law; co-editor: Michigan Family Law, 2 vols., 1988; contbr. 600 articles to legal publs. Chmn. Wayne County unit Am. Cancer Soc., Detroit, 1971-76, Mich. Dept. Vets. Trust Fund, 1977-8. Capt. USMCR, 1943-46, PTO. Recipient Gov.'s award State of Mich., Cert. of Appreciation, Gov. of Mich., Cert. of Recognition, Detroit Common Coun. award Mich. Assn. Marriage Counselors, Lifetime Achievement award Mich. Family Law Sect. Mem. ABA (mem. family law coun. 1993-95, sr. editor ABA Family Adv. 1991—), Mich. Bar Assn. (chmn. family law sect. 1974-75), Oakland County Bar Assn., Am. Acad. Matrimonial Lawyers (pres. Mich. chpt. 1982), Am. Legion (judge adv. Mich. dept. 1968-69, comdr. Detroit chpt. 1970-71). Office: 5543 Tadworth Pl West Bloomfield MI 48322-4016

ROBBINS, OREM OLFORD, insurance company executive; b. Mpls., Feb. 5, 1915; s. Douglas Ford and Grace (Rorem) R.; m. Annette Strand Scherer, May 17, 1992; children: Ford M., Ross S., Gail R. Tomei, Cynthia R. Rothbard. BBA with distinction, U. Minn., 1936; BS in Law, William Mitchell Coll. Law, 1946, JD, 1948. Comml. rep. NW Bell Telephone Co., Mpls., 1936-48; dep. dir. U.S. Treas. Dept., 1948-49; sales rep. Conn. Gen. Life Ins. Co., 1949-56; founder, chmn. Security Life Ins. Co. Am., 1956—. Bd. dirs., past pres. Family and Children's Svcs., Mpls., 1968—; bd. govs., past chmn. Meth. Hosp., Mpls., 1960-90; past treas., bd. dirs. Goodwill/Easter Seals, St. Paul, 1958-68, 75-88; life trustee Hamline U., St. Paul, 1979—, chmn. bd. trustees, 1990-91. Col. U.S. Army, 1941-46. Decorated Legion of Merit; recipient Outstanding Achievement award U. Minn., 2001. Fellow Life Mgmt. Assn.; mem. Am. Soc. CLU (pres. Mpls. chpt. 1959), Health Underwriters Assn., Chartered Fin. Cons., Am. Legion, Skylight Club (Mpls.), Hole in the Wall Golf Club, Naples Yacht Club, Mpls. Club, Officer's Club, Masons. Republican. Methodist. Office: Security Life Ins Co Am 10901 Red Circle Dr Minnetonka MN 55343-9304 E-mail: oorobbins@securitylife.com.

ROBBINS, RAY C. manufacturing company executive; b. Syracuse, N.Y., Sept. 15, 1920; s. Frederick and Mary Elizabeth (Field) R.; children: Sandra Robbins Jannetta, Ray Charles Jr., Eric L. With Lennox Internat. Inc. (formerly Lennox Furnace Co.), 1940-48; asst sales mgr. Lennox Industries Inc. (formerly Lennox Furnace Co.), Syracuse, 1948-52; gen. mgr. new factory and sales office, Lennox Industries, Inc. (formerly Lennox Furnace Co.), Toronto, Ont., Can., 1952-67; dir. Lennox Can. and Timeplan Fin. Co. Ltd., 1953-65; pres. Lennox Can., 1965-69; exec. v.p. Lennox-Worldwide, 1969-70, pres., CEO, 1970-77; chmn. bd. Lennox Can., 1976-92; chmn. bd., chief exec. officer Lennox Industries Inc., 1977-80, chmn. bd., 1980-91, chmn. emeritus, 1991—. Bd. dirs. Lennox Internat., First Interstate of Iowa, Inc., Hawkeye Security Ins. Co., Des Moines, Fin. Security Group, Inc., Des Moines, Q-Dot, Garland, Tex.; pres., founder, bd. dirs. Exec. Inst., Inc., Dallas, 1983—; bd. advisor Internat. Exec. Svc. Corp., 1993—. Bd. dirs. Metro Toronto Big Bros., 1964-69, Queensway Gen. Hosp., 1957-69, Texx Found., 1979-81, Bus. Industry Polit. Action Com.; bd. govs., mem. exec. com. Iowa Coll. Found., 1975-78; v.p., mem. exec. bd. Mid-Iowa County Boy Scouts Am., 1972-78; mem. Pres.' Phys. Fitness Council, from 1979; exec. bd. Circle 10 council Boy Scouts Am., from 1979; mem. Dallas Citizens Council; bd. of govs. Nat. Women's Econ. Alliance Found.; bd. dirs. North Tex. Commn. Served with AUS, 1942-45, PTO. Mem. ASHRAE (life), Am. Refrigeration Inst. (bd. dirs. 1973-74, 78, life from 1979, v.p. 1975-76, chmn. 1977), NAM (bd. dirs. 1974-75, dir. at large 1976, dir. State of Iowa 1977-78, dir. State of Tex. 1979-92), Nat. Mgmt. Assn. (exec. adv. com. 1979-92), Gas Appliance Mfrs. Assn. (past bd. dirs.), Can. Gas Assn. (pres.), Can. Mfg. Assn. (chmn. Toronto dist.), U.S. C. of C. (Can.-U.S. sect.), Bus.-Industry Polit. Action Com. (bd. dirs. 1991). Clubs: Park Cen., Landmark Athletic, Aerobics Activity Ctr. (Dallas); Canyon Creek Country (Richardson, Tex.).

ROBBINS, REBECCA IRWIN, foundation executive; b. Franklin, Pa., Jan. 3, 1953; d. Forest B. and Alfreda Locke Irwin; m. Dale Charles Robbins, June 24, 1978; children: Anne, Theodore, Alison. BA, Grove City (Pa.) Coll., 1975. Reviewer Buffalo Courier Express, 1975-79; news editor, announcer WKSN-WHUG, Jamestown, N.Y., 1976-78; cmty. rels. asst. Jamestown (N.Y.) C.C., 1978-79; rsch. assoc. Chautauqua (N.Y.) Instn., 1979-83, grants coord., rsch. assoc., 1980-83; acting sec. Chautauqua Found., 1982—89; devel. officer Chautauqua (N.Y.) Instn., 1982-93; exec. dir. WCA Found., 1999—. Continuity dir. WFRA-WVEN Radios, Franklin, 1975—76; dir. Gebbie Found., Jamestown, 2000—, Carnahan-Jackson Found., Jamestown, 1983—93. Trustee Women's Christian Assn. Hosp., Jamestown, 1993—97; former bd. dirs. Jamestown Concert Assn., Busti Hist.Soc., So. Chautauqua County United Way, former pub. rels. chair of bd.; mem. Southwestern Mid. Sch. Compact team , 1996—2000; mem. cmty. coun. Roger Tory Peterson Inst., 1995—.

ROBBINS, ROBERT BERNARD, lawyer; b. Canton, Ohio, Aug. 31, 1951; s. Nathan H. and Evelyn (Cohen) R.; m. Melinda Abbot Street, Oct. 18, 1981; children: Julia Bates, Katherine Melinda, Caroline Rachel, Eli Street. AB, Cornell U., 1972; JD, Harvard U., 1975. Bar: D.C. 1975. Ptnr. Shaw Pittman LLP, Washington, 1976—, also chmn. corp. securities group. Chmn. D.C. Bar Commn. on Broker-Dealer Regulation, 1985-90; co-chmn. Ann. Course Study on Pvt. Placements and Regulation D, Am. Law Inst.-ABA, 1992—. Mem. D.C. Bar (steering com., sect. corp., fin. and securities law 1991-94, chmn. 1993-94). Office: Shaw Pittman LLP 2300 N St NW Washington DC 20037-1172 E-mail: robert.robbins@shawpittman.com.

ROBBINS, ROBERT MARVIN, accountant; b. Warren, Ohio, Aug. 2, 1924; s. Edward and May (Rubenson) R.; m. Phyllis Ann Dillon, Sept. 29, 1951; children: Michael C., Pat D., Robert J., Susan Jo Burkey. BSBA, Ohio State U., 1948; postgrad., NYU, 1972, 76, 79. CPA, Ohio. Sr. acct. Albert F. Turrell & Assocs. CPAs, Warren, Ohio, 1948-52; comptroller Harts Jewelry Stores, 1952-54; pvt. practice Warren, 1954-59; mng. ptnr. Griffith & Robbins, CPAs, 1959-65; owner R.M. Robbins & Assocs., CPAs, 1966-82; pres., mgr. R.M. Robbins & Assocs., Inc., 1982-98; retired. Sec. and acctg. cons. Ohio-Ont. Clean Fuels, Inc., Warren, 1986-90; area owner, franchisee Red Barn Restaurants, Omaha, 1968-72. Treas. Planned Parenthood, Youngstown, Ohio, 1970s; acct. Sisters of Humility of Mary, Villa Maria, Pa., 1978-83. Sgt. U.S. Army armored div., 1943-45, ETO. Mem. Am. Inst. CPAs, (mem. tax div. subcoms.), ACUTE, Ohio Soc. CPAs, Rotary, Exchange Club (treas. Warren chpt. 1968-73), Squaw Creek Country Club (past bd. dirs.), Elks, Buckeye Club (Warren), Ohio State U. Pres. Club. Avocations: flying, golf, history of American Revolution and Civil War. Home: 376 Wainwood Dr SE Warren OH 44484-4650

ROBBINS, STANLEY LEONARD, pathologist, educator; b. Portland, Maine, Feb. 27, 1915; BS, MIT, 1936; MD, Tufts U., 1940. Diplomate Am. Bd. Pathology. Intern Mallory Inst. Pathology, Boston, 1940-41, resident, 1941-44, asst. pathologist, 1945-53, assoc. dir., 1953-66, dir., 1966-72; asst. prof. Sch. Medicine, Boston U., 1947-50, assoc. prof., 1950-57, prof. pathology, 1957-80, chmn. dept. pathology, 1964-80; asst. prof. Med. Sch., Tufts U., Boston, 1947-50, prof. emeritus, 1990; vis. prof. Med. Sch., Harvard U., 1980—; pathologist Brigham and Women's Hosp., 1980—2002; ret., 2002. Vis. prof. U. Glasgow, Scotland, 1959-60, Hebrew U., Jerusalem, 1976-77; cons. VA Hosp., Boston, 1965-80, Univ. Hosp., Boston, 1970-80. Author: Robbins Pathologic Basis of Disease, 6th edit., 1991, Basic Pathology, 7th edit., 2002, Companion Handbook to Robbins Pathologic Basis of Disease, 4th edit., 2002 Trustee Boston Med. Libr., Combined Jewish Philanthropies; bd. dirs. Jewish Family Children's Svc.; past chmn. rsch. allocation com. Mass. Heart Assn. Fellow Am. Soc. Clin. Pathologists (hon.); mem. AAAS, U.S. and Can. Acad. Pathology (designated Disting. Pathologist 1990), Mass. Med. Soc. (Disting. Leader in Am. Medicine 1980), New Eng. Soc. Pathologists (pres. 1955), Am. Assn. Pathologists (Gold-Headed Cane award 1992), Am. Assn. Med. Mus., Am. Soc. Clin. Investigation, Alpha Omega Alpha. Home: 1010 Memorial Dr Cambridge MA 02138-4859

ROBBINS, STEPHEN J. M. lawyer; b. Seattle, Apr. 13, 1942; s. Robert Mads and Aneita Elberta (West) R.; m. Nina Winifred Tanner, Aug. 11, 1967; children: Sarah E.T., Alicia S.T. AB, UCLA, 1964; JD, Yale U., 1971. Bar: D.C. 1973, U.S. Dist. Ct. D.C. 1973, U.S. Ct. Appeals (D.C. cir.) 1973, U.S. Ct. Appeals (3d cir.) 1973, U.S. Dist. Ct. (ea. and no. dists.) Calif. 1982, U.S. Dist. Ct. (cen. dist.) Calif. 1983, Supreme Ct. of Republic of Palau, 1994. Pres. U.S. Nat. Student Assn., Washington, 1964-65; dir. scheduling McGovern for Pres., 1971-72; assoc. Steptoe & Johnson, 1972-75; chief counsel spl. inquiry on food prices, com. on nutrition and human needs U.S. Senate, 1975; v.p., gen. counsel Straight Arrow Pubs., San Francisco, 1975-77; dep. dist. atty. City and County of San Francisco, 1977-78; regional counsel U.S. SBA, San Francisco, 1978-80; spl. counsel Warner-Amex Cable Communications, Sacramento, 1981-82; ptnr. McDonough, Holland and Allen, 1982-84; v.p. Straight Arrow Pubs., N.Y.C., 1984-86; gen. legal counsel Govt. State of Koror, Rep. of Palau, Western Caroline Islands, 1994-95; pvt. practice law, 1986—. Adj. prof. govt. Calif. State U., Sacramento, 1999—. Staff sgt. U.S. Army, 1966-68. Mem. ABA (sect. urban, state and local govt. sect. real property, probate and trust law, sect. natural resources energy, environ. law, forum com. on affordable housing and cmty. devel.), D.C. Bar, State Bar of Calif., Urban Land Inst., Am. Hist. Assn., Supreme Ct. Hist. Soc., Acad. Polit. Sci., Chamber Music Soc. of Sacramento, Oreg. Shakespeare Festival, Shaw Island Hist. Soc. Democrat. Unitarian Universalist. Avocations: theatre, art, hiking. Office: 2150 3rd Ave Sacramento CA 95818-3102

ROBBINS, SUSAN PAULA, social work educator; b. Bklyn., Aug. 15, 1948; d. Harold Jess and Rose (Bernstein) R. AA, Manhattan C.C., 1972; BA summa cum laude, Hamline U., 1974; MSW, U. Minn., 1976; PhD, Tulane U., 1979. Adj. instr. dept. sociology and social work Augsburg Coll., Mpls., 1975-76; part-time instr. women's studies program U. Minn., 1976; rsch. and grant cons. Seminole Tribe of Fla., Hollywood, 1978-79, child and adolescent caseworker, program planning cons., 1979-80; coord. criminal justice/corrections program St. Mary's Dominican Coll., New Orleans, 1979-80; asst. prof. social work New Orleans Consortium, 1978-80, U. Houston, 1980-86, assoc. prof., 1986—, assoc. dean acad. affairs, 1998-2000. Cons. ABA Multi Door Program, Houston, Cmty. Svc. Option Program, Houston; mediator Dispute Resolution Ctrs., Houston, 1982—; trainer Tex. Dept. Protective Svcs. Tng. Inst., 1995—. Author (with others): Encyclopedia of Social Work, Social Workers' Desk Reference; contbr. articles and book chpts. to profl. jours. Women's Club of Mpls. fellow, 1975, Nat. Inst. of Mental Health fellow, 1976-78; recipient Nat. Faculty Excellence award Univ. Continuing Edn. Assn., 1998. Mem. NASW, Coun. on Social Work Edn., Social Welfare Action Alliance, Assn. for Cmty. Orgn. and Social Adminstrn., So. Sociol. Soc., Phi Kappa Phi (sec. Houston chpt. 1984—). Democrat. Jewish. Office: Univ Houston 4800 Calhoun Rd Houston TX 77204-4013 E-mail: srobbins@uh.edu.

ROBBINS, THOMAS EUGENE, writer; b. Blowing Rock, N.C., 1936; m. Terrie Hemingway (div.); m. Alexa d'Avalon, 1995; 1 child, Fleetwood Starr. Student, Washington and Lee U., 1954-56, U. Wash., 1963; degree in social sci., Va. Commonwealth U., 1959. Former copy editor Richmond (Va.) Times-Dispatch, Seattle Post-Intelligencer; art critic Seattle Times. Author: Guy Anderson, 1965, Another Roadside Attraction, 1971, Even Cowgirls Get the Blues, 1976 (Best Am. Short Story 1977), Still Life with Woodpecker, 1980, Jitterbug Perfume, 1984, Skinny Legs and All, 1990, Half Asleep in Frog Pajamas, 1994, Fierce Invalids Home from Hot Climates, 2000. With USAF. Named one of 100 Best Writers of 20th Century, Writer's Digets. Office: PO Box 338 La Conner WA 98257-0338

ROBBINS, THOMAS LANDAU, humanities researcher; b. N.Y.C., Oct. 13, 1943; s. Manuel Lee and Elly (Landau) R. AB, Harvard U., 1965; MA, U. N.C., 1968, PhD in Sociology, 1973. Instr., asst. prof. Queens Coll., 1971-78; instr. Cen. Mich. U., 1982-83; NIMH postdoctoral trainee in sociology Yale U., New Haven, 1979-81; sr. rsch. assoc. Santa Barbara (Calif.) Ctr. for Humanistic Studies, 1990—. Author: Cults, Converts and Charisma, 1988; co-editor: In Gods We Trust, 1981, 2d edit., 1990, Cults, Culture and the Law, 1985, Church-State Relations, 1987, Millennium, Messiahs and Mayhem, 1997, Misunderstanding Cults; assoc. editor Sociol. Analysis, 1984-90; edtl. cons. Nova Religio, 1997—; contbr. articles to various publs.; edtl. cons. Nova Religio. Mem. Soc. for the Sci. Study of Religion (exec. coun. 1988-91), Assn. for the Sociology Religion, (exec. coun. 1985-87), Am. Sociol. Assn., Soc. for the Study of Social Problems. Meher Baba. Home and Office: 427 4th St SW Apt 8A Rochester MN 55902-3226 *I am becoming concerned these days about threats to freedom of religion in the United States and Europe.*

ROBBINS, WILLIAM CURTIS, JR. television and motion picture producer, director, writer, news reporter, cameraman; b. Chgo., Dec. 24, 1948; s. William Curtis Sr. and Jean Vallee (Guyot) R. Grad. high sch., Santa Barbara, Clif., 1968; grad., Airline Sch. Pacific, Santa Monica, Calif., 1969, Danny Rouzer Sch. Motion Picture Photography, Hollywood, Calif., 1971. Producer Marine Movies, Santa Barbara, 1966-68, Looking Glass Films, Santa Barbara, 1972; producer, dir., writer, news reporter/cameraman Cinema Tech Films, Hollywood, 1972-76; producer, dir., writer, news reporter, cameraman Jimmy Oz Prodns., Temple City, Calif., 1976—. Founder, exec. dir. Corp. for Children's TV, 1987; cons. various cable and TV stas., 1973—. Producer TV film Flying Kids, 1988; producer, dir., writer: (short subjects) The Geni, 1988, The Watchdog, 1988, The Circus, 1988; author: Sunshine the Sea Otter, 1976, Her Father's Daughter, 1981, How To Land and Take Off Safely at Santa Catalina's Airport-in-the-Sky, 1989, Skyhawks: Air Rescue, 1995, Sunshine's New Adventure, 1997, (children's TV show) Beverly's Farm, 1991, Three Kids to the Moon, 1996; assoc. prodr. One Night on Earth, 2000. Accident prevention counselor FAA, 1982—. Mem. Soc. Motion Picture and TV Engrs., Order Iron Test Pattern (officer 1986—). Avocations: flying, underwater diving and photography. Email: (bus.) (home). Office: Jimmy Oz Prodns PO Box 128 Temple City CA 91780-0128 E-mail: jimmy_oz@hotmail.com., sky_king@hotmail.com.

ROBBINS, WILLIAM DAVID, retired police officer; b. Martins Ferry, Ohio, Dec. 22, 1930; s. Harold David and Hazel Clareice (Burnett) R.; m. Marion M. Ruckh, May, 1953; children: Christine Diana Gary, David Rock; m. Evelyn Clair Farley, Nov. 19, 1977; 1 child, Michael Allen. Student, U. Louisville, 1978, U. Ga., 1980. Officer Wheeling (W.Va.) Police Dept., 1957-76, detective, 1976-91, lt., 1991-94. With U.S. Army, 1952-53, Korea. Decorated Bronze Star; recipient numerous citations and commendations for police work. Mem. Fraternal Order of Police, Masons. Democrat. Roman Catholic. Avocations: shooting, golf, photography. Home: 58 Mount Wood Rd Wheeling WV 26003-2631

ROBBINS-WILF, MARCIA, educational consultant; b. Newark, Mar. 22, 1949; d. Saul and Ruth (Fern) Robbins; 1 child, Orin. Student, Emerson Coll., 1967-69, Seton Hall U., 1969, Fairleigh Dickinson U., 1970; BA, George Washington U., 1971; MA, NYU, 1975; postgrad., St. Peter's Coll., Jersey City, 1979, Fordham U., 1980; MS, Yeshiva U., 1981, EdD, 1986; postgrad., Monmouth Coll., 1986. Cert. elem. tchr., N.Y., N.J., reading specialist, N.J., prin., supr., N.J., adminstr., supr., N.Y. Tchr. Sleepy Hollow Elem. Sch., Falls Church, Va., 1971-72, Yeshiva Konvitz, N.Y.C., 1972-73; intern Wee Folk Nursery Sch., Short Hills, N.J., 1978-81, dir. day camp, 1980-81, tchr., dir., owner, 1980-81; adj. prof. reading Seton Hall U., South Orange, 1987, Middlesex County Coll., Edison, 1987-88; asst. adj. prof. L.I. U., Bklyn., 1988, Pace U., N.Y.C., 1988—. Ednl. cons. Cranford High Sch., 1988; presenter numerous workshops; founding bd. dirs. Stern Coll. Women Yeshiva U., N.Y.C., 1987; adj. vis. lectr. Rutgers U., New Brunswick, N.J., 1988. Chairperson Jewish Book Festival, YM-YWHA, West Orange, N.J., 1986-87, mem. early childhood com., 1986—, bd. dirs., 1986—; vice chairperson dinner com. Nat. Leadership Conf. Christians and Jews, 1986; mem. Hadassah, Valerie Children's Fund, Women's League Conservative Judaism, City of Hope; assoc. bd. bus. and women's profl. divsn. United Jewish Appeal, 1979; vol. reader Goddard Riverside Day Care Ctr., N.Y.C., 1973; friend N.Y.C. Pub. Libr., 1980—; life friend Millburn (N.J.) Pub. Libr.; pres. Seton-Essex Reading Coun., 1991-94. Co-recipient Am. Heritage award, Essex County, 1985; recipient Award Appreciation City of Hope, 1984, Profl. Improvement awards Seton-Essex Reading Council, 1984-86, Cert. Attendance award Seton-Essex Reading Counci, 1987. Mem. N.Y. Acad. Scis. (life), N.J. Council Tchrs. English, Nat. Council Tchrs. English, Am. Ednl. Research Assn., Coll. Reading Assn. (life), Assn. Supervision and Curriculun Devel., N.Y. State Reading Assn. (council Manhattan), N.J. Reading Assn. (council Seton-Essex), Internat. Reading Assn., Nat. Assn. for Edn. of Young Children (life N.J. chpt., Kenyon group), Nat. Council Jewish Women (vice chairperson membership com. evening br. N.Y. sect. 1974-75), George Washington U. Alumni Club, Emerson Coll. Alumni Club, NYU Alumni Club, Phi Delta Kappa (life), Kappa Gamma Chi (historian). Clubs: Greenbrook Country (Caldwell, N.J.); George Washington Univ. Avocations: reading, theatre. Home: 242 Hartshorn Dr Short Hills NJ 07078-1914 E-mail: dr.mrw349@aol.com.

ROBBOY, HOWARD ALAN, sociologist, educator; b. Phila., June 16, 1945; s. Benjamin and Irma Helen (Lee) R.; m. Candace Clark, July 7, 1977 (div. Dec. 1989). BA, Temple U., 1967; AM, Rutgers U., 1972, PhD, 1976. Asst. prof. Beaver Coll., Glenside, Pa., 1972-73, Trenton (N.J.) State Coll., 1976-82, assoc. prof., 1983—, chmn., 1988-94. Vis. asst. prof. U. Miss., 1977-81, 2001-02. Co-editor: Social Interaction, 1974, 83, 88, 4th edit., 1992. Mem. Am. Sociol. Assn., Soc. for Study of Social Problems, Soc. for Study of Symbolic Interaction, So. Sociol. Soc., Mid-South Sociol. Soc., Eastern Sociol. Soc. Democrat. Avocation: Oriental rugs. Home: 1600 Riverside Dr Trenton NJ 08618-5837 Office: Coll NJ Library Ct PO Box 7718 Ewing NJ 08628-0718

ROBBOY, STANLEY J. pathologist, educator; b. Cleve., Jan. 5, 1941; s. John and Sarah (Shapiro) R.; m. Anita Wyzanski, July 21, 1968 (div. 1981); children:: Elizabeth, Caroline; m. Marion Meyer, June 14, 1990. Student, U. Mich., 1958-61, MD, 1965. Diplomate Am. Bd. Pathology. Intern Mt. Sinai Hosp, Cleve., 1965-66; resident to chief in pathology Mass. Gen. Hosp., 1966-70, asst. in pathology, 1972-73, asst. pathologist, 1973-76, assoc. pathologist, 1976-84; resident in pathology Boston Hosp. for Women, 1970; instr. Tufts Med. Sch., 1968-69; asst. prof. pathology Harvard Med. Sch., Boston, 1972-76, assoc. prof., 1976-84; prof. pathology U. Medicine and Dentistry N.J.-N.J. Med. Sch., Newark, 1984—92, chmn. dept., 1984-89, prof. ob-gyn, 1990—92, pathologist-in-chief, 1984-89, dir. faculty practice service, 1985-89; prof. pathology, prof. ob-gyn Duke U., 1992—. Cons. pathologist St. Joseph Hosp., Paterson, N.J., 1985—, St. Barnabas Hosp., Livingston, N.J., 1985—, Beth Israel Hosp., Newark, 1985—, VA Med. Ctr., Durham, 1992-; pathologist (DES) Clear-Cell Adenocarcinoma Registry, 1972-83; pathologist, prin. investigator Nat. Collaborative Diethylstilbestrol project, 1974-82; vis. scientist New Eng. Primate Ctr., 1973-84; vis. prof. U. Shiraz Med. Sch., Iran, 1976; commr. N.J. Commn. on Cancer Research, 1987-92; sr. advisor East Asia Cons. Group, Boston, Los Angeles and Tokyo, 1984-85; reference panel for diagnostic and therapeutic tech. AMA, 1982—; mem. nat. med. com. Planned Parenthood Fedn. Am., 1990-93, vice chmn. com. on oncology, 1993; bd. dirs. Pamet Sys. Inc. Mem. editorial bd. Human Pathology, 1980-90, Cervix and the Low Female Genital Tract, 1983-94, Internat. Jour. Gynecologic Pathology, 1985-; book rev. editor, Informatics in Pathology, 1985-88, Pathology Rsch. and Practice, 1990--, Gynecologic Oncology, 1997--, InsScight, 1998--; contbr. articles to profl. jours. Trustee Am. Pathology Found., 1984-86. Served to maj. U.S. Army, 1970-72. Recipient Jr. Faculty award Am. Cancer Soc., 1972-75, Found. prize Am. Coll. Ob-Gyn, 1975; Pardee fellow U. Mich., 1961, Lederle Lab. fellow, 1962, Eliza Howell fellow, 1964, Ford Found. fellow, 1964-65; clin. fellow Am. Cancer Soc., 1967-68. Fellow Am. Soc. Clin. Pathologists (chmn. pathology telecommunications network com. 1983, task force on computers 1980-83, council on med. informatics 1983-84, planning and scope com. 1983-84, co-chmn. pathology communication network 1983-87), Coll. Am. Pathologists (alt. Mass. del. to house dels. 1981-84, co-chmn. pathology communication network 1983-85, alt. N.J. del. to house dels. 1985-92, exec. com. and advisor nomenclature and classification of disease 1975-80, editorial bd. Systematized Nomenclature Medicine 1976-80, gov. 1999--, vice chmn. coun. on pub. affairs 1999--), Soc. Gynecologic Oncologists Assocs.; mem. Arthur Purdy Stout Soc. Surg. Pathology (membership com. 1981-83), Internat. Acad. Pathology (edn. com. 1979-83, treas. 1993-2001, pres.-elect 2001--), Internat. Soc. Gynecologic Pathologists (chmn. membership com. 1982-84), Mass. Soc. Pathology (3d party relations 1978-84, chmn. computer com. 1981-84), N.J. Med. Soc., N.J. Soc. Pathology (edn. and profl. relations Coms. 1984-92, exec. com. 1985-92). Jewish. Office: Duke U Med Ctr PO Box 3712 Durham NC 27710-0001

ROBE, THURLOW RICHARD, engineering educator, university dean; b. Petersburg, Ohio, Jan. 25, 1934; s. Thurlow Scott and Mary Alice (McKibben) R.; m. Eleanora C. Komyati, Aug. 27, 1955; children: Julia, Kevin, Stephen, Edward. BSC.E., Ohio U., 1955, MS in Mech. Engring., 1962; PhD in Applied Mechanics, Stanford U., 1966. Engr. Gen. Electric Co., Niles, Ohio, Cleve., Erie, Pa., Evendale,Ohio, 1954-60; instr. Ohio U., Athens, 1960-63; asst. prof to prof., assoc. dean U. Ky., Lexington, 1965-80; dean Ohio U., Athens, 1980-96, Cruse W. Moss prof. Engring. Edn., 1992-96, dir. Innovation Ctr. Authority, 1983-96; dean emeritus, Moss prof. emeritus Russ Coll. Engring. and Tech., Ohio U., Athens, 1996—; pres., chmn. bd. Q.E.D. Assocs., Inc., Lexington, 1975-83. Trustee Engring. Found. Ohio, 1988-94; bd. govs. Edison Materials Tech. Ctr., 1987-96; dir. T. Richard and Eleanora K. Robe Leadership Inst., Ohio U., 1997—. Contbr. articles to profl. jours.; patentee trailer hitch. Bd. dirs. Athens County Cmty. Redevel. Corp., 1980-86; treas. South Lexington Little League, 1976-80; vice chmn. Thoroughbred dist., Boy Scouts Am., 1975-77; pres. Tates Creek H.S. PTA, Lexington, 1975-76; bd. dirs. U. Ky. Athletics Ass.n, 1975-80; trustee Ohio U. Found. Bd. Trustees, 1998—. Maj. USAF Res., 1955-85. Recipient Alumni medal of merit Ohio U., 1993; named Am. Coun. on Edn. Adminstrn. fellow, 1970-71, Ohio U. Alumnus of Yr., 1996, inductee Acad. Disting. Grads., Russ Coll. Engring. & Tech., 2001. Mem. ASME, NSPE (Profl. Engring. in Edn. exec. bd., ctrl. region vice-chmn. 1987-89), Am. Soc. Engring. Edn. (Outstanding Contbn. in Rsch. award 1966), Athens Reading Club, Athens Symposiarchs, Rotary, Sigma Xi, Tau Beta Pi, Omicron Delta Kappa, Alpha Lambda Delta. Office: Russ Coll Engring & Tech Ohio U Athens OH 45701 E-mail: robe@ohio.edu.

ROBECK, MILDRED COEN, educator, writer; b. Walum, N.D., July 29, 1915; d. Archie Blain and Mary Henrietta (Hoffman) Coen; m. Martin Julius Robeck, Jr., June 2, 1936; children: Martin Jay Robeck, Donna Jayne Robeck Thompson, Bruce Wayne Robeck. BS, U. Wash., 1950, MEd, 1954, PhD, 1958. Ordnance foreman Sherman Williams, U.S. Navy, Bremerton, Wash., 1942-45; demonstration tchr. Seattle Pub. Schs., 1946-57; reading clinic dir. U. Calif., Santa Barbara, 1957-64; rsch. cons. State Dept. Edn., Sacramento, 1964-67; prof., head early childhood edn. U. Oreg., Eugene, Oreg., 1967-86; vis. scholar West Australia Inst. Tech., Perth, 1985; v.p. acad. affairs U. Santa Barbara, Calif., 1987-95. Vis. prof. Victoria Coll., B.C. Can., summer 1958, Dalhousie U., Halifax, summer 1964; trainer evaluator U.S. Office of Edn. Head Start, Follow Thru, 1967-72; cons., evaluator Native Am. Edn. Programs, Sioux, Navajo, 1967-81; cons. on gifted Oreg. Task Force on Talented and Gifted, Salem, 1974-76; evaluator Early Childhood Edn., Bi-Ling. program, Petroleum and Minerology, Dhahran, Saudi Arabia, 1985. Author: Materials KELP: Kgn. Evaluation Learning Pot, 1967, Infants and Children, 1978, Psychology of Reading, 1990, Oscar: His Story, 1997, 2nd edit., 2000; contbr. articles to profl. jours. Evaluation cons. Rosenburg Found. Project, Santa Barbara, 1966-67; faculty advisor Pi Lambda Theta, Eugene, Oreg, 1969-74; guest columnist Oreg. Assn. Gifted and Talented, Salem, Oreg., 1979-81; editorial review bd. ERQ, U.S. Calif., L.A., 1981-91. Recipient Nat. Dairy award 4-H Clubs, Wis., 1934, scholarships NYA and U. Wis., Madison, 1934-35, faculty rsch. grants U. Calif., Santa barbara, 1958-64, NDEA Fellowship Retraining U.S. Office Edn., U. Oreg., 1967-70. Mem. APA, Am. Ednl. Rsch. Assn., Internat. Reading Assn., Phi Beta Kappa, Pi Lambda Theta. Democrat. Avocations: dyslexia research, historical research, duplicate bridge, writing. Home: 95999 Highway 101 S Yachats OR 97498-9714 E-mail: mrobeck@casco.net.

ROBEK, MARY FRANCES, business education educator; b. Superior, Wis., Jan. 30, 1927; d. Stephen and Mary (Hervert) R. BE, U. Wis., 1948; MA, Northwestern U., 1951; MBA, U. Mich., 1962, PhD, 1967. Tchr. Bergland (Mich.) High Sch., 1948, Tony (Wis.) High Sch., 1948-50, Sch. Vocat. and Adult Edn., Superior, 1950-58; prof. bus. edn. and office tech. Ea. Mich. U., Ypsilanti, 1958-93; instr. Jazyckova Gymnasium, Banská, Štiavnicá, Slovakia, 1994. Author: Information and Records Management, 1995. Assn. of Records Mgrs. and Adminstrs. fellow, 1992. Mem. Assn. Records Mgrs. and Adminstrs. (life), Inst. Cert. Mgrs. (pres. 1980-81, Emmett Leahy award 2000), Cath. Daus. Am., Delta Pi Epsilon, Delta Kappa Gamma, Pi Lambda Theta. Republican. Roman Catholic. Home: 515 Clough Ave Superior WI 54880 E-mail: RobekMary@aol.com. *Opportunity to do creative and innovative things without infringing on the rights of others is limited only by priorities set considering people and technology.*

ROBELOT, JANE, anchor; b. Greenville, S.C., Oct. 9, 1960; BA in Econs., Clemson U. News and sports dir., reporter WCCP-AM Radio, Clemson, S.C.; anchor, reporter WSPA-TV, CBS affiliate, Spartanburg, 1983-90; gen. assignment reporter WCAU-TV, Phila., 1990-92, co-anchor 6:00 PM news, 1991-92, co-anchor 11:00 PM news, 1992-95; co-anchor CBS Morning News, N.Y.C., 1995; news reader This Morning CBS News, 1995-96, co-anchor This Morning, 1996-99, co-anchor CBS Atlanta News, 1999—. Office: Sta WGNX-TV Meredith Corp 1810 Briarcliff Rd NE Atlanta GA 30329-4008

ROBENALT, JOHN ALTON, lawyer; b. Ottawa, Ohio, May 2, 1922; s. Alton Ray and Kathryn (Straman) R.; m. Margaret Morgan Durbin, Aug. 25, 1951 (dec. July 1990); children: John F., William A., James D., Robert M., Mary K., Margaret E., Thomas D.; m. Nancy Leech Kidder, Sept. 21, 1991. BA, Miami U., 1943; LL.B., JD, Ohio State U., 1948. Bar: Ohio 1948. Asst. atty. gen., Ohio, 1949-51; practice in Lima, 1951-59; acting municipal judge Lima Municipal Ct., 1955-59; partner Robenalt, Daley, Balyeat & Balyeat, 1959-82; ptnr. Robenalt, Kendall & Robenalt, 1983-85, Robenalt, Kendall, Rodabaugh & Staley, 1985-92, Robenalt & Robenalt, 1993—. Chmn. Lima March of Dimes, 1957-58; Bd. dirs. Lima Civic Center, pres., 1971-72; bd. dirs. Lima Rotating Fund; trustee Allen County Regional Transit Authority, Lima, pres., 1975— . Served with AUS, 1943-45. Mem. ABA, Ohio Bar Assn., Allen County Bar Assn. (pres. 1969-70), Am. Legion, Lima Automobile Club (bd. dirs., pres. 1975-82), Shawnee Country Club (pres. 1968-70), Ohio Automobile Club (trustee 1982-2002, chmn. 1995-97), Elks (bd. trustees 1991-97), Rotary, Delta Tau Delta, Phi Delta Phi. Home: 1755 Shawnee Rd Apt 700 Lima OH 45805-3857

ROBERGE, LAWRENCE FRANCIS, neuroscientist, biotechnology consultant, writer, bioethicist, educator; b. Springfield, Mass., Mar. 16, 1959; s. Donald Richard and Cornelia Marie (Daly) R. BS in Zoology and Psychology cum laude, U. Mass., 1985; MS in Biomed. Sci., U. Mass., Worcester, 1989; Biotech. Studies Cert., Becker Coll., 1994. Cert. radiation safety and protection. Sr. tech. Mass. Gen. Hosp., Boston, 1988; nuclear chemist Interstate Nuclear Svc., Springfield, 1989; tech. specialist NERAC, Tolland, Conn., 1989-93. Instr. Assumption Coll., Worcester, 1988—91, Quinsigamond C.C., Worcester, 1989, Orange County C.C., 2000—02, Yorktown U., 2001—; tchr. Prince Lifeskill Inst., Leicester, Mass., 1988—89; adj. faculty instr. Anna Marie Coll., Paxton, Mass., 1995—, Bay Path Coll., Longmeadow, Mass., 1996—, Lesley Coll., Cambridge, Mass., 1997—, Holyoke (Mass.) C.C., 1999—2000, Elms Coll., Chicopee, Mass., 1997—2000; biotech. tchr. Springfield (Mass.) H.S. of Sci. and Tech. Author: The Cost of Abortion, 1995; contbr. Precinct mem. Ludlow, Mass., 1978-81; bd. dirs. Great Awakening Ministries, Inc., 1994-95. Named Outstanding Young Man of Am., 1998; nominated Mass. Tchr. of Yr., 2000; recipient Disting. Svc. award U. Mass./Summa-United Asian Learning Ctr., 1998, Springfield Tchg. Excellence award, 2000. Mem. AAAS, Internat. Fedn. Advancement of Genetic Engring. and Biotech., N.Y. Acad. Sci., Cath. Assn. Scientists and Engrs., Biotech West (founder), Ctr. for Bioethics and Human Dignity, Soc. Cath. Social Scientists, World Future Soc., Univ. Faculty for Life. Achievements include research on reversible vasopressin control of hamster aggression, the role of steroids to control vasopressin expression in hamsters, biomedical and bioethical reviews on birth control vaccines and social, economic, demographic and medical effects of abortion on U.S. society, adverse effects of RU-486, fetal tissue research, condom technology, global population growth, natural family planning technologies, genetics, eugenics, genetic discrimination, cloning technology, social and economic aspects of the year 2000, biological weapons and bioremediation and introduced species. Home: 25 Lafayette Ave Middletown NY 10940-4101 E-mail: lroberge@map.com.

ROBERSON, BRUCE HEERDT, lawyer; b. Wilmington, Del., Mar. 7, 1941; s. A. L. and Virginia Amelia (Heerdt) R.; m. Mary E. Abrams; children: Cheryl Anne, David B., Douglas M. BS cum laude, Washington and Lee U., 1963; JD, U. Va., 1966. Bar: Va. 1966, Del. 1966, Fla. 1969. Assoc. Morris, Nichols, Arsht & Tunnell, Wilmington, 1966-67; assoc. Holland & Knight, Tampa, Fla., 1969-74; ptnr. Holland & Knight LLP, 1975—. Contbg. editor Pratt's Banking and Lending Institution Forms, 1992—. Capt. U.S. Army, 1967-69 Decorated Bronze Star. Fellow Am. Bar Found. (life), Fla. Bar Found.(life); mem. ABA (bus. law sect. com. on consumer fin. svcs. 1976—, banking law com. 1980—, savs. instns. com. 1989-96), Am. Judicature Soc., Fla. Bar Assn. (corp. banking and bus. law sect. exec. coun. 1978-86, chmn. banking law com. 1982-84), Del. Bar Assn., Va. Bar Assn., Hillsborough County Bar Assn., Univ. Club, Tampa Yacht and Country Club, Lambda Chi Alpha. Republican. Methodist. Office: Holland & Knight LLP PO Box 1288 Tampa FL 33601-1288 E-mail: broberso@hklaw.com.

ROBERSON, DEBORAH KAY, secondary school educator; b. Crane, Tex., Jan. 15, 1955; d. David B. and Virginia L. (King) Cole; m. Larry M. Roberson; children: Justin, Jenai, Julie. BS in Secondary Edn., Coll. S.W., 1981; MA in Sch. Adminstrn., Sul Ross State U., 1991. Cert. biology and history tchr., mid-mgmt. cert., supt. cert., Tex., biology and history tchr., secondary prin., supt., Okla. Sci. and social studies tchr. Andrews (Tex.) Ind. Sch. Dist., 1987-95; forum tchr. gifted social studies program, social studies dept. chair Ctrl. Mid. Sch., Broken Arrow, Okla., 1995—99; asst. prin. Ctrl. Middle Sch., 1999—2001; sci. tchr. 6th grade Jamison Mid. Sch., Pearland, Tex., 2001—. 7th grade history curriculum com. Andrews Ind. Sch. Dist., 1988, outdoor classroom com., 1989-90, chair sci. curriculum com., 1989-90, chair health curriculum com., 1990-91, Tex. pub. schs. open house com., 1989-90, 92-93, dist. textbook com., 1990-91; secondary edn. rep. Ptnrs. in Parliament, Berlin, 1993; site-based com. Broken Arrow Pub. Schs., 1995—, B.A.S.I.S. com., 1995—, nat. history day coord. Ctrl. Middle Sch., 1995, geography bee coord., 1995—, tech. com., 1996—, discipline com., 1996, remediation com., 1996—, Tools for Tomorrow Conf. com., 1996—, others; state geography com. Okla. State Dept. Edn., 1997. Prodr., dir.: Real History Radio, Broken Arrow Hist. Soc., 1997. Livestock leader Andrews County 4-H Program, 1985-89; vol. Am. Heart Assn., Andrews, 1988; vol., team mother Little League, Andrews, 1990; vol., treas. Mustang Booster Club, Andrews, 1993-95. Recipient Appreciation awards Mustang Booster Club, 1993, 94, VFW Ladies Aux. Post 10887 award, Broken Arrow, 1996—, Tchr. of Today award Masons, Broken Arrow, 1997, Nat. History Day Outstanding Tchr. award Tulsa C.C., 1997, Best Mannered Tchr. award Nat. Jr. Cotillion, 1999; Tchr. Program scholar Fulbright Meml. Fund, Japan, 1998. Mem. AAUW, Nat. Assn. Secondary Sch. Prins., Nat. Staff Devel. Coun., Assn. Tex. Profl. Educators (pres. local unit 1992-93, mem. resolutions com. 1994-95, Appreciation award 1993, sec. region 1993-94, v.p. region 1994-95), ASCD, Tex. Assn. Supervision and Curriculum Devel., Tex. Network for Continuous Quality Improvement, Nat. Coun. Social Studies, Okla. Assn. Supervision and Curriculum Devel., Okla. Alliance Geographic Edn., Okla. Assn. Secondary Sch. Prins., Coop. Orgn. Okla. Secondary Adminstrs., Redskins Booster Club (sec. 1996-97). Avocations: meeting people, travel, golf, rafting, hiking. Office: Jamison Mid Sch 2506 Woody Rd Pearland TX 77581 Home: 9402 Sunperch Ct Pearland TX 77584-2886

ROBERSON, DORIS JEAN HEROLD, retired social worker; b. N.Y.C., Oct. 15, 1924; d. Albert and Rosalind (Lowenstein) Herold; m. Lloyd Willis Roberson, Aug. 31, 1949; children: Lynn, Patricia, Katherine, Irene. BA cum laude, Mount Holyoke Coll., 1945; MSW, Fordham U., 1947. Cert. social worker, N.Y. Social worker Children's Aid Soc., N.Y.C., 1947-52, Yonkers (N.Y.) Pub. Schs., 1966-89; ret., 1989. Mem. NASW, Acad. Cert. Social Workers, N.Y. State Sch. Social Workers Assn., Phi Beta Kappa. Home: 145 Hoover Rd Yonkers NY 10710-3408

ROBERSON, JAMES O. foundation executive; m. JoAnn Roberson; children: Melanie Merrill, Sharyl Ritucci, James Jr., Trisha Sermersheim, Joel. AB in Journalism, Baylor U., 1956; student Indsl. Devel. Inst., U. Okla.; student Inst. Orgnl. Mgmt., U. Houston. Cert. econ. developer. Dir. info. West Tex. C. of C., Abilene, 1956-59; area devel. mgr. Mo.-Kans.-Tex. R.R., 1959-63; exec. dir. Albuquerque Indsl. Devel. Svc., 1963-65; dir. N.Mex. Dept. Devel., Santa Fe, 1965-69; mgr. Forward Metro Denver, 1969-72; dir. R.I. Dept. Econ. Devel., Providence, 1972-77; v.p., dir. new bus. devel. Howard Rsch. and Devel. Corp. subs. Rouse Co., Columbia, Md., 1977-79; sec. Md. Dept. Econ. and Community Devel., Annapolis, 1979-83; pres. Louisville C. of C., 1983-88; pres., CEO Rsch. Triangle Found. N.C., 1988—. Chmn. bd. dirs. Charlotte br. Fed. Res. Bank Richmond; cons., speaker in field. Editor West Tex. Today mag., 1956-59. Bd. dirs. N.C. Citizens for Bus. and Industry, N.C. Biotech. Ctr. Fellow Am. Econ. Devel. Coun. (past chmn.); mem. Indsl. Devel. Rsch. Coun., Nat. Assn. State Devel. Agys. (past pres.), Assn. Univ. Related Rsch. Parks (pres.).

ROBERSON, JESSIE HILL, federal agency administrator; Grad., U. Tenn. With DuPont, Ga. Power Co.; mgr. Rocky Flats Field Office Dept. Energy, Colo., 1996—99, asst. sec. environ. mgmt., 2001—. Mem. Def. Nuc. Facilities Safety Bd. Named Nat. Black Engr. of Yr. for profl. achievement in govt. Office: Dept Energy Environ Mgmt 1000 Independence Ave SW Washington DC 20585-0001*

ROBERSON, KELLEY CLEVE, health facility administrator; b. McAlester, Okla., July 11, 1950; s. Cleo Connie and Helen Frances (Sewell) R.; m. Georgia Lee Brown, Jan. 15, 1970; children: Kevin Christopher, Matthew Guy. BBA, Tex. Christian U., 1973; postgrad., U. Md., 1983-88, U. So. Calif., 1991-93. Cert. govt. fin. mgr. Commd. 2d lt. U.S. Army, 1973, advanced through grades to lt. col., 1992; exec. officer Med. Co., Ft. Carson, Colo., 1974; aviation sect. leader 377th Med. Co., Republic of Korea, 1975-76; ops. officer Aeromed. Evacuation Unit, Ft. Stewart, Ga., 1976-79, exec. officer Grafenwoehr, Germany, 1980-81; comdr. Med. Co. 2nd Armored Div., Garlstedt, Germany, 1981-83; compt. Walter Reed Army Inst. Rsch., Washington, 1983-88; comdr. Aeromed. Evacuation Unit, Hickam AFB, Hawaii, 1988-90; chief manpower Tripler Army Med. Ctr., Honolulu, 1990-92; chief resource mgmt., dep. comdr. adminstrn. Letterman U.S. Army Hosp. and Health Clinic, San Francisco, 1992-94; chief resource mgmt. Tripler Army Med. Ctr., Honolulu, 1994-97; chief program and budget U.S. Army Med. Dept., 1997-98; ret. U.S. Army, 1998; v.p., CFO Hawaii Health Sys. Corp., Honolulu, 1998-2000. COO/CFO Hawaii Health Sys. Corp., Honolulu, 2000—. Pres. Parents Club Damien Meml. High Sch., Honolulu, 1990-91; dir. Hawaii Health Sys. Found., 1999—, Hawaii Health Info. Corp., 1999—; bd. dirs. Alii Cmty. Care. Mem. Assn. Govt. Accts. (cert. govt. fin. mgr.), Am. Acad. of Med. Admintrs., Order Mil. Med. Merit, Am. Soc. Mil. Comptrs. (pres. Golden Gate chpt. 1992-93), Assn. U.S. Army, Ret. Officers Assn. United Methodist. Avocations: writing, golf, reading. Home: 2196 Halekoa Dr Honolulu HI 96821-1055 Office: Hawaii Health Sys Corp 3675 Kilauea Ave Honolulu HI 96816-2333 E-mail: kroberson@hhsc.org., kelleyroberson@hawaii.rr.com.

ROBERSON, KIP MICHAEL, library director, librarian; b. Indpls., Mar. 28, 1964; s. Walter Ulysses and Virginia Rose (Carrico) R.; life ptnr. Fred Kuhr. AS, Vincennes U., 1984; BS, U. So. Ind., 1987; MLS, Ind. U., 1989. Cert. libr. Mass. Reference libr. Lake County Pub. Libr., Merrillville, Ind., 1989-90, Morton Grove (Ill.) Pub. Libr., 1990-92, reference svcs. coord., 1992-93; dir. Ilsley Pub. Libr., Middlebury, Vt., 1993-95, Sharon (Mass.) Pub. Libr., 1995—. Mem. continuing edn. com. North Suburban Libr. Sys., Wheeling, Ill., 1991-93. Editor (newsletter) Reference Librs. Assn. Quarterly, 1991-93; asst. editor: Out in the Mountains, Burlington, Vt., 1994-95. Mem. Theatre Factory, Burlington, 1993-95; v.p. exec. bd. Old Colony Libr. Network, 1997-2000; v.p., exec. bd. 2000—. Acad. scholar Ind. U., Bloomington, 1988. Mem. ALA (com. mem. outstanding reference sources 1995-98), New Eng. Libr. Assn., Vt. Libr. Assn. (treas. 1994-95), Human Rights Campaign, World Wildlife Fund, Nat. Stonewall Dem. Found. Avocations: traveling, music, politics, trivia, current affairs. Home: Unit 4 119 Benefit St Providence RI 02903-1201 Office: Sharon Pub Libr 11 N Main St Sharon MA 02067-1299 E-mail: kipr@ocln.org.

ROBERSON, LINDA, lawyer; b. Omaha, July 15, 1947; d. Harlan Oliver and Elizabeth Aileen (Good) R.; m. Gary M. Young, Aug. 20, 1970; children: Elizabeth, Katherine, Christopher. BA, Oberlin Coll., 1969; MS, U. Wis., 1970, JD, 1974. Bar: Wis. 1974, U.S. Dist. Ct. (we. dist.) Wis. 1974. Legis. atty. Wis. Legis. Reference Bur., Madison, 1974-76, sr. legis. atty., 1976-78; assoc. Rikkers, Koritzinsky & Rikkers, 1978-79; ptnr. Koritzinsky, Neider, Langer & Roberson, 1979-85, Stolper, Koritzinsky, Brewster & Neider, Madison, 1985-93, Balisle & Roberson, Madison, 1993—. Adj. faculty U. Wis. Law Sch., Madison, 1978—. Co-author: Real Women, Real Lives, 1981, Wisconsin's Marital Property Reform Act, 1984, Understanding Wisconsin's Marital Property Law, 1985, A Guide to Property Classification Under Wisconsin's Marital Property Act, 1986, Workbook for Wisconsin Estate Planners, 2d edit., 1993, 3rd edit., 1997, 4th edit., 1999, Look Before You Leap, 1996, Family Estate Planning in Wis., 1992, rev. edit. 1996, The Marital Property Classification Handbook, 1999. Fellow Am. Acad. Matrimonial Lawyers (pres. Wis. chpt. 2001), Am. Bar Found. (del. family law coun. of cmty. property states 1996--, chair-elect 2002--); mem. ABA, Wis. Bar Assn., Dane County Bar Assn., Legal Assn. Women, Nat. Assn. Elder Law Attys., Internat. Soc. Family Law (del. family law coun. of cmty. property states 1996--). Office: Balisle and Roberson PO Box 870 Madison WI 53701-0870 E-mail: lr@mail.b-rlaw.com.

ROBERSON, MARK ALLEN, physicist, educator; b. Lufkin, Tex., Nov. 12, 1961; s. Roy and Thelma (Weist) R. AAS, Angelina County Jr. Coll., 1982; BSEE, Tex. A&M U., 1984; MS, Stephen F. Austin State U., 1989; PhD, Tex. Tech. U., 1994. From rsch. asst. to instr. Tex. Tech. U., Lubbock, 1990-95; instr. Vernon (Tex.) Regional Jr. Coll., 1995—. Robert A. Welch Found. fellow, 1991-94. Mem. AAAS, Am. Phys. Soc., Sigma Pi Sigma. Avocation: books. Office: Vernon Regl Jr Coll Vernon TX 76384-4092

ROBERSON, NATHAN RUSSELL, physicist, educator; b. Robersonville, N.C., Dec. 13, 1930; s. Nathan Russell and Myrtle (Taylor) R.; m. Ruth Haislip, June 19, 1954; children: David Wintner, Michael Taylor, Mary Russell. BS, U. N.C., 1954, MS, 1955; PhD, Johns Hopkins U., 1960. Jr. instr. Johns Hopkins U., Balt., 1955-60; research assoc. Princeton (N.J.) U., 1960-63; asst. prof. physics Duke U., Durham, N.C., 1963-68, assoc. prof., 1968-74, prof., 1974-98, prof. emeritus, 1998—. Instrumentation subcom. Nuclear Sci. Adv. Com., 1982-85; mem. energy sci. network steering com. Dept. Energy, 1987-90, nuclear physics panel on computer networks, 1988-90, dep. dir. Triangle U. Nuclear Lab., 1990-92; dir. Triangle Univs. Nuclear Lab., 1992-96, assoc. dir., 1996-98. Contbr. articles to profl. jours. Treas. N.C. Council Chs., 1974-79. Fellow AAAS, Am. Phys. Soc.; mem. IEEE, Phi Beta Kappa. Presbyterian. Home: 38 Stoneridge Pl Durham NC 27705 Office: Duke U Dept Physics Durham NC 27708

ROBERSON, PATT FOSTER, mass communications educator; b. Middletown, N.Y., Dec. 3, 1934; d. Gilbert Charles and Mildred Elizabeth (O'Neal) Foster; m. Murray Ralph Roberson Jr., May 10, 1963 (dec. 1968). AA, Canal Zone Jr. Coll., 1954; BA in Journalism, La. State U., 1957, MA in Journalism, 1973; MA in Media, So. U., Baton Rouge, 1981; PhD in Mass Communication, U. So. Miss., 1985. Exec. sec. Lionel H. Abshire and Assocs., AIA, Architects, Baton Rouge, 1958-60, Murrell and Callari, AIA, Architects, Baton Rouge, 1960-63; bus. mgr. So. Rev. La. State U., 1963-69; free-lance researcher, ind. contractor, 1969-74; rep. dept. info. State of La., 1974-75; asst. prof. mass. comm. So. U., 1976-86, assoc. prof. mass comm., 1986-93, prof. mass comm., 1993-96, prof. emeritus, 1996—. Reviewer Random House Pubs., N.Y.C., 1981; profl. devel. intern Baton Rouge Morning Advocate, 1991, Baker Observer, 1991-92; cons. advt. Baton Rouge Little Theater, 1971-96, 2002—, Baton Rouge Ballet Theatre, 1986—; reporter-photographer Canal Record, Seminole, Fla., 1967—; biographer of Edward Livermore Burlingame, John H. Johnson, Daniel Kimball Whitaker, (book) American mag. journalists series, Dictionary Literary Biography, Detroit, 1986-87; tutor Operation Upgrade, 1978-82; vol. reporter, photographer, proofreader The Platinum Record, Baton Rouge, 1996-99. Co-editor: La. State U. cookbook Tiger Bait, 1976; biographer Frank E. Gannett in Biographical Dictionary of American Journalism, 1987; freelance writer/editl. cons.; editl. bd. Am. Journalism, 1986-87; reviewer Longman Publs. 1991-92; contbr. articles to profl. jours. Mem. poll commn. East Baton Rouge Parish Govt., 1978-95; pres. Our Lady Lake Regional Med. Ctr., 1971-72; bd. dirs. Dist. Atty.'s Rape Crisis Commn., 1976-79, Plan Govt. Study Commn., 1973-76, Selective Svc. System Bd. 8, Baton Rouge, 1986-98, 2002—; docent Greater Baton Rouge Zoo, 1974-77; vol. ARC, 1989-99, Capital Area Ct.-Apptd. Spl. Adv., 1997-99; mem. East Baton Rouge Parish Commn. on Govtl. Ethics, 1992-93; mayoral appointee Baker Mobile Home Rev. Bd., 1990—; v.p. Baker Hist. and Cultural Found., 1990-93; mem. Baker Interclub Coun., 1990-91; organizer human-animal therapy svc. Baker Manor Nursing Home, 1994; mem. 1st class Citizens Basic Police Tng. Acad., Baton Rouge Police Dept., 1994; chairpub. rels., bd. dirs. Panama Canal Mus., 1998-2001. Mem. AAUP (sec.-treas. La. conf. 1988-89, sec. 1992-93, chmn. pub. rels. 1994-95), Assn. Edn. Journalism and Mass Comm., Am. Newspapers Pubs. Assn. (nat. coop. com. on edn. in journalism 1989-92), Women in Comm. (pres. Baton Rouge chpt. 1982, nat. judge Clarion awards 1987), Pub. Rels. Assn. La., La. State U. Journalism Alumni Assn. (pres. 1977), Soc. Profl. Journalists (pres. S.E. La. chpt. 1982), Am. Journalism Historians Assn., Oral History Assn., La. State U. Alumni Assn. (pres. East Baton Rouge Parish chpt. 1978-80), Popular Culture Assn., Investigative Reporters and Editors Assn., Baker C. of C., Toasmasters (adminstrv. v.p. Baton Rouge 1977), Pilot Club of Baker. Home: 2801 Allen Ct Baker LA 70714-2253

ROBERSON, ROBERT S. investment company executive; b. Mt. Kisco, N.Y., 1942; m. Barbara Drane, 1967; children: Elizabeth de V., Merritt B., Barbara D. BS, NYU, 1964; MBA, Coll. William and Mary, 1973. Various positions in fin. and bldg. industries, 1964-67; mem. N.Y. Produce Exchange, 1965-66; with Weaver Bros., Inc., Newport News, Va., 1967—, now pres., dir. Bd. dirs. First Peninsula Bank & Trust Co., Hampton, Va., 1977-78. Past dir. Peninsula Unit Am. Cancer Soc., Newport News; past dir. Heritage Coun. Girl Scouts U.S.A., Hampton; former trustee Newport News Pub. Libr., Va. Living Mus., Am. Assn. Mus., Newport News; former trustee Hampton Roads Acad., Newport News; former mem. bd. visitors to George Washington's Mt. Vernon Nat. Shrine; hon. dep. chief N.Y.C. Fire Dept.; pres., chief curator Golf Mus., Newport News; mem. bd. visitors, mem. exec. com., chmn. com. on devel. and alumni affairs Coll. William and Mary, Williamsburg, Va.; mem. bd. visitors and exec. com. Richard Bland Coll., Petersburg, Va. Decorated officer Order of St. John (England). Mem. Newcomen Soc. of the U.S., Hon. Fire Officers Assn., U.S. Golf Assn. (com. mem.), Gen. Soc. Colonial Wars, St. Nicholas Soc. of the City N.Y., Colonial Order Acorn, Sovereign Mil. Order of the Temple of Jerusalem (comdr.), Squadron A Assn., Pilgrims of the U.S./U.K., Union Club, The Brook, Church Club (N.Y.C.), Southampton Club (N.Y.), James River Country Club, Hampton Roads German Club (pres.), The Hundred Club (Newport News, Va.), N.Y. Yacht Club, Fishers Island Yacht Club (N.Y.), Rotary Internat. (Paul Harris fellow), Blue Key, Delta Sigma Pi. Republican. Episcopalian. Home: PO Box 3 Williamsburg VA 23187-0003

ROBERSON, SHIRLEY LOIS, nonprofit management executive; b. Worcester, Mass., Apr. 26, 1935; d. Paul T. Salmonsen and Ruth Mildred (Hofstra) Shimkus; m. William Virgil Roberson, June 20, 1961 (div. Nov. 1979); children: Kimberly, Marika. BA magna cum laude, Wheaton Coll., 1957; MEd, Worcester State U., 1960; postgrad. U. San Francisco. Tchr. Oxford Schs., Oxford, Mass., 1957-60, Army Dependent Schs., France, 1960-62, Laney Jr. Coll., Oakland, Calif., 1968-72; ptnr., cons. Roberson/Smit Assoc., Oakland, 1975-79; exec. dir. A Central Place, Oakland, 1977—. Pres., LWV, Oakland, 1973-75, conv. chmn., 1977; v.p. Community Devel. Commn., Oakland, 1976-78; program mem. Nonprofit Mgmt., San Francisco, 1980—; bd. dirs. YMCA, Oakland, 1981-84; v.p. bd. The Support Ctr., San Francisco, 1985; elder Montclair Presbyn. Ch., Oakland, 1985—. U. San Francisco scholar, 1984. Mem. Devel. Execs. Roundtable, Nonprofit Mgmt. Group, Wheaton Alumnae (council 1980—). Club: Last Monday (council 1976—) (Oakland). Avocations: skiing, backpacking, traveling, house construction, drama, painting. Home: 44 Cortez Ct Piedmont CA 94611-2323

ROBERT, CAVETT MCNEILL, JR. neurosurgeon; b. Douglas, Ariz., Jan. 16, 1940; s. Cavett Henry Robert Sr. and Gertrude Robin Buist; m. Sande Marie Skuce, Apr. 24, 1982; children: Wesley Anne, Ashley Cavett. BA, U. Pa., 1962, MD, 1966. Diplomate Am. Bd. Neurol. Surgery. Intern straight surg. UCLA, 1966-67, resident 1 rotating surg., 1967-68, resident in neurosurgery, 1968-73; house officer in neurology Nat. Hosp., Queen Sq., London, 1970-71; neurosurgeon Mt. Diablo Med. Ctr., Concord, Calif., 1973—, chmn. div. neurosurgery, 1983, 88, 89, vice chmn. dept. surgery, 1989-90, chmn. dept. surgery, 1990-91; neurosurgeon John Muir Med. Ctr., Walnut Creek, 1973—, chmn. neurosurgery sect., 1987-88, 97-98. Mem. clin. faculty U. Calif., San Francisco; lectr. in field. Contbr. articles to profl. jours. Lt. comdr. USNR, 1966-84. Fellow ACS; mem. AMA, Am. Assn. Neurol. Surgeons (mem. editl. bd. 1995-99), Congress Neurol. Surgeons, Calif. Assn. Neurol. Surgeons (No. dir. 1992-94, editor newsletter 1993-95, sec. 1994-96, 1st v.p. 1996-97, pres.-elect 1997-98, pres. 1998-99), We. Neurosurg. Soc., San Francisco Neurol. Soc., Calif. Med. Assn., Alameda-Contra Costa County Med. Assn. Avocations: Iron Man Triathlon, ultramarathons, multimedia computer developer, film editing, photography. E-mail: cavett@attbi.com.

ROBERT, PHYLLIS ANN, English educator; b. New Orleans, Sept. 30, 1942; d. Robert Jefferson and Ruth Mary (Aycock) De Blanc; m. William Paul Robert Jr., Aug. 6, 1966; children: Michele Annette, Jefferson De Blanc. BA, St. Mary's Dominican Coll., 1964; MA, U. New Orleans, 1995. English and French tchr. Ursuline Acad., New Orleans, 1965-68, tchr., 1990, 95—; tchr., student activities dir. Immaculata H.S., Marrero, La., 1976-80; tchr., chair English dept. St. Andrew the Apostle Sch., New Orleans, 1980-90; English tchr. Our Lady of Holy Cross Coll., 1995—; acad. dean Ursuline Acad., 1996-2000, asst. prin., 2000—. Chair Blue Ribbon Schs. Com., New Orleans, 1997—. Contbr. weekly column to Times-Picayune Newspaper, 1990-94. Sec. Tall Timbers Assn., New Orleans, 1984-87; pianist Holy Spirit Ch., New Orleans, 1985—. Mem. New Orleans Met. Piano Tchrs., Greater New Orleans Coun. Tchrs. English (exec. bd. 1995—), So. Assn. Colls. and Schs. Com. (chair 1996-97), La. Coun. Tchrs. English (bd. mem. 1998—). Office: Ursuline Acad 2635 State St New Orleans LA 70118-6399

ROBERT, VETTER SMITH, music educator; b. Houston, Apr. 19, 1956; s. David Lionel and Melba Ruth Vetter; m. Jaye Leeann Barnes, Feb. 17, 1966; children: Allison Vetter, Ashton Vetter, Austin Vetter. B Music Edn., U. North Tex., M Music Edn, 1982. Cert. tchr. Tex. Band dir. White Deer (Tex.) Ind. Sch. Dist., 1979—83, Reagan County Ind. Sch. Dist., Big Lake, 1983—. Dir. honor band; dir. UIL State Marching Band, 2001. Recipient Music Edn. grant, Dollar Gen., 2000. Mem.: Assn. of Tex. Small Sch. Bands (area & region coord. 2001—02, outstanding performance series 1999, top ten finalist 1999), Tex. Bandmasters Assn., Tex. Music Educators Assn. Republican. Avocations: camping, walking, bicycling, swimming. Home: 1007 Virginia Circle Big Lake TX 76932 Office: Reagan County High School 1111 12th St Big Lake TX 76932 Home Fax: 915-884-3021; Office Fax: 915-884-3021. Personal E-mail: bvetter@esc18.net. E-mail: bvetter@esc18.net.

ROBERTIELLO, GINA MARIE, criminal justice educator; b. Belleville, N.J., Feb. 26, 1969; d. Russell Gerard and Angela Mary (Castagnino) Pisano; m. Peter Michael Robertiello, Aug. 14, 1994; children: Brianna Christina, Gabriella Gina. BS in Adminstrn. of Justice, Rutgers U., New Brunswick, N.J., 1991; MA in Criminal Justice, Rutgers U., Newark, N.J., 1993, PhD in Criminal Justice, 2000. Adj. prof. Montclair (N.J.) State U., 1993-94, Rutgers U., Newark, 1994-96, Caldwell (N.J.) Coll., 1996; asst. prof. Monmouth U., Long Branch, N.J., 1994-96, Seton Hall U., South Orange, 1996—. Rsch. asst. Edna Mahan Correctional Facility, Clinton, NJ, 1991; internship coord. Rutgers U., New Brunswick, 1991, rschr., Newark, 1994—2000; citizen mem. staff Jersey City Police Dept., 1993; co-investigator COPS Project Seton Hall U., Rutgers U.; prin. investigator Perceptions of Police Behavior Rutgers U. Sch. Criminal Justice, Civilian-Police Acad., West Orange, NJ; prin. investigator Civilian Police Acad., Morris County, NJ. Contbr. chapters to books. Apptd. hon. dep. sheriff Bergen County, NJ, 1999; mem. acad. rev. com. Bergen County Sheriff's Dept., 1999; facilitator Pre Cana program St. Pius Ch., Montville, 1994—97, pvt. facilitator, 1997—. Mem.: Am. Criminal Justice Assn. (advisor 1996—), N.J. Assn. Criminal Justice Educators, Am. Soc. Criminology, Phi Delta Pi (advisor 1997—). Republican. Roman Catholic. Avocations: weight lifting, ballroom dancing, martial arts, crafts, reading. Home: 19 Crimson Ln Mine Hill NJ 07803-2444 E-mail: robertgi@shu.edu.

ROBERTO, JAMES BLAIR, physicist; b. Portland, Maine, Sept. 4, 1946; s. Michael Roberto and Marion Louise (Morris) R.; m. Jane Catherine Dowling, May 23, 1970; children: Andrew James, Timothy Aaron. SB, MIT, 1968; MS, Cornell U., 1970, PhD, 1974. Rsch. staff Oak Ridge (Tenn.) Nat. Lab., 1974—, divsn. dir., 1990-99, assoc. lab. dir., 1999—. Guest scientist KFA Juelich, Germany, 1977, MPI Garching, Germany, 1982; solid state scis. com. Nat. Rsch. Coun., 1993-2000, vice chair, com. on condensed matter and materials physics, 1996-99; bd. visitors physics dept. U. Tenn., 1999—. Co-author: Condensed Matter and Materials Physics, Basic Research for Tomorrow's Technology, 1999; chair adv. rev. bd. Jour. of Materials Rsch., 1992—. With USMC, 1970-72. Fellow AAAS; mem. Materials Rsch. Soc. (pres. 1991), Am. Phys. Soc. (chair divsn. of materials physics 1997-98), Am. Inst. of Physics (adv. com. Physics Today 2000—). Avocations: running, reading. Office: Oak Ridge Nat Lab PO Box 2008 Oak Ridge TN 37831

ROBERTON, DONALD K. telecommunications executive; b. Las Vegas, Nev., Oct. 29, 1941; s. Donald Nesbit and Mary Helen (Paterson) R.; m. Lupe W. Roberton, Nov. 9, 1985; children— Shannon Eillen, Dawn Christy, James, Monica, Angela. Cert., Colgate Darden, U. Va., 1981; cert. Mich. State U., 1977; Gen. plant supr. Centel Corp., Chgo., 1973-75; plant mgr. Central Telephone of N.C., Hickory, N.C., 1975-77, engring. mgr., 1977-78, gen. mgr., 1978-80; gen. mgr. Central Telephone of Va., Charlottesville, 1980-84; v.p. Fisk div. Centel Bus. Systems, Houston, 1984-85, v.p. customer service, 1985—. Bd. dirs. Jr. Achievement, Charlottesville, 1982-83; group chmn. United Fund, Hickory, N.C., 1978; bd. dirs. Adminstrv. Mgmt. Soc. Hickory, 1979-80. Served with U.S. Army, 1959-62. Recipient award for most improved operating performance Centel Corp., 1981. Republican. Lutheran. Club: Rotary. Home: 7918 Northbridge Dr Spring TX 77379-8732 Office: Centel Bus Systems-Group Staff 3838 N Belt East Suite 590 Houston TX 77032

ROBERTS, ALAN SILVERMAN, orthopedic surgeon; b. Apr. 20, 1939; s. Joseph William and Fannie (Margolies) S.; children: Michael Eric, Daniel Ian. BA, Conn. Wesleyan U., 1960; MD, Jefferson Med. Coll., 1966. Rotating intern Lankenau Hosp., Phila., 1966-67; resident in orthoaedics Tulane U. Med. Coll., 1967-71; pvt. practice specializing in orthopaedics and hand surgery L.A., 1971—. Mem. clin. faculty UCLA Med. Coll., 1971-76. Contbr. articles to profl. jours. With AUS, 1961. Riordan Hand fellow, 1969, Boyes Hand fellow, 1971. Mem. AMA, ACS, Am. Acad. Orthopaedic Surgeons, Calif. Med. Assn., L.A. County Med. Assn., Western Orthopaedic Assn., Riordan Hand Soc. Republican. Jewish.

ROBERTS, ALBERT DEE, internist; b. Ft. Worth, Mar. 7, 1930; s. Albert D. and Irene Burnett (Lewis) R.; m. Diane Truett, Dec. 22, 1952; children: Truett, Hillary. BS, So. Meth. U., 1951; MD, U. Tex. Southwestern, Dallas, 1954. Diplomate Am. Bd. Internal Medicine, Am. Bd. Nephrology. Pvt. practice, Dallas, 1960-75, 88-91; assoc. dean, prof. medicine U. Tex. Southwestern, 1975-88, prof. medicine, 1991—, Hartman prof. medicine, 1995—. Mem. ACP (master, gov. 1977-81, regent 1981-87, vice chair 1986-87), AMA, Am. Soc. Nephrology, Internat. Soc. Nephrology, Tex. Med Assn., Dallas County Med. Assn. Avocations: reading, music, tennis, travel. E-mail: albertroberts@swmed.edu.

ROBERTS, ALBERT ROY, social work educator; b. Bronx, N.Y., May 22, 1944; s. Harry and Evelyn (Schwartz) R.; m. Beverly Jean Schenkman, July 5, 1971; 1 child, Herbert. BA in Sociology, L.I. U., 1966, MA in Sociology, 1967; D Social Welfare, U. Md., Balt., 1978. Lectr. Rider Coll., Lawrenceville, N.J., 1970-71; asst. prof., chmn. Coppin State Coll., Balt., 1971-74; project dir. Am. Correctional Assn., College Park, Md., 1975-76; asst. prof. N.Y. Inst. Tech., Old Westbury, N.Y., 1976-78, Bklyn. Coll., CUNY, 1978-79; assoc. prof. U. New Haven, West Haven, Conn., 1979-81, Seton Hall U., South Orange, N.J., 1981-83; assoc. prof., chmn. Ind. U. Sch. Social Work, Indpls., 1984-89; prof. social work, program dir. Rutgers U., New Brunswick, N.J., 1989—. Manuscript reviewer Dorsey Press, Chgo., 1984-88, Hosp. and Cmty. Psychiatry, Washington, 1986-95, Longman Pubs., White Plains, N.Y., 1987-92; founding social work series editor Springer Pub. Co., N.Y.C., 1980—. Author: Sourcebook on Prison Education, 1971, Sheltering Battered Women, 1981, Battered Women and Their Families, 1984, Runaways and Non Runaways in an American Suburb, 1987, Helping Crime Victims, 1990; editor: Juvenile Justice: Policies, Programs and Services, 1989 (main selection Behavioral Sci. Book Club 1990), Crisis Intervention Handbook, 1990, Critical Issues in Crime and Justice, 1994, Crisis Intervention and Time-Limited Cognitive Therapy, 1995, Helping Battered Women, 1996, Visions for Change, 1996, Crisis Management and Brief Treatment, 1996; founding editor-in-chief Crisis Intervention and Time-Limited Treatment Jour., 1992—. Bd. dirs. Ind. chpt. Nat. Com. for Prevention Child Abuse, Indpls., 1986-89; mem. state adv. bd. for probation N.J. Supreme Ct., Trenton, 1991—; mem. N.J. Gov.'s Juvenile Justice and Delinquency Prevention Commn., 1991-95. Recipient award for outstanding article Correctional Edn. Assn., 1975. Fellow Am. Orthopsychiat. Assn.; mem. NASW, Acad. Criminal Justice Scis. (life), Am. Soc. Criminology, Nat. Coun. Juvenile and Family Ct. Judges (assoc.), Alpha Delta Mu. Avocations: hiking, bicycling, reading. Office: Rutgers U Adminstrn Justice Dept Lucy Stone Hall B 261 Piscataway NJ 08854 *The primary objective of a scholar and educator is to build the knowledge base in a selected area of expertise and to transmit it to one's students. My life has been devoted to setting important goals, overcoming adversity and persevering in order to achieve major accomplishments in both my personal and academic life.*

ROBERTS, ALIDA JAYNE, elementary school educator; b. Bristol, Conn., Aug. 11, 1967; d. James and Barbara Mae (Carlson) R. BA in Elem. Edn., Anna Maria Coll., Paxton, Mass., 1990; MS in Reading and Lang. Arts, Calif. State U., Fullerton, 1992; adminstrn. and supervision cert., U. Hartford, 1997, postgrad., 1999—. Cert. tchr., Conn., Mass. Elem. tchr. Rowland Unified Sch. Dist., Rowland Heights, Calif., 1990-94, Edgewood Elem. Sch., Bristol, Conn., 1994-95, Clara T. O'Connell Elem. Sch., Bristol, 1995-96, Edgewood Elem. Sch., Bristol, 1995-98, Chippers Hill Mid. Sch., Bristol, 1998—, softball coach, 1999—, asst. to prin., 2000—01. Tchr. Gifted and Talented Edn. After Sch. Program, West Covina, Calif., 1993-94, Chpt. 1 After Sch. Program, West Covina, 1993-94; intramural coach After Sch. Program Edgewood Elem. Sch., Bristol, Conn., 1994-95. Tchr. advisor PTA, La Puente, 1992-92, Clara T. O'Connell PTA, 1995-96. Bristol Fedn. Tchrs. scholar, 1986; Anna Maria Coll. grantee, 1986-90. Mem. NEA, ASCD, Internat. Reading Assn., Bristol Fedn. Tchrs., Nat. Coun. Tchrs. English, Conn. Coun. Tchrs. English, New Eng. League Middle Schs., Kappa Delta Pi. Avocations: reading, physical fitness. Home: 291 Morris Ave Bristol CT 06010-4418

ROBERTS, ANNE MCNATT, social services agency executive, educator; b. Oklahoma City, Aug. 31, 1954; d. Hoyt and Dollie (Shiplet) McN. MusB, U. Okla., 1977; postgrad., Am. Inst. Mus. Studies, Graz, Austria, 1982. Geol. technician Okla. Oil Industry, Oklahoma City, 1977-86; resource devel. coord. World Neighbors, 1986-87; cmty. dir. Okla. Alliance Against Drugs, 1987-89; exec. dir. Okla. Inst. for Child Advocacy, 1989—. Mem. adj. faculty St. Gregory's U., Shawnee, Okla., 2000—; vice chmn. Nat. Adv. Coun. on Maternal and Child Nutrition, Washington, 1994—; vice chmn. med. adv. com. Okla. Health Care Authority, Oklahoma City, 1995—; mem. Leadership Okla., Oklahoma City, 1998—. Mem. Joint Legis. Task Force on Child elfare Sys. Rev., Oklahoma City, 1999-2000, Okla. Gov.'s Task Force on Youth and Tobacco, Oklahoma City, 1998-2001. Named Preventionist of Yr., Okla. Assn. Prevention Profls. and Advs., 1995, Pub. Health Adv. of Yr., U. Okla. Coll. Pub. Health, 1997; recipient Dir.'s Cmty. Leadership award FBI, 1997, child abuse prevention award for outstanding individual svc. Okla. Interagy. Task Force on Child Abuse Prevention, 2000. Mem. Nat. Assn. Child Advs. (bd. dirs. 1997—, Child Adv. of Yr. award 2000), LWV, Okla. Acad. for State Goals, Okla. C. of C. Democrat. Baptist. Avocation: singing. Office: Okla Inst for Child Advocacy 420 NW 13th St Ste 101 Oklahoma City OK 73103 Fax: 405-236-5439. E-mail: aroberts@oica.org.

ROBERTS, ARCHIBALD EDWARD, retired career officer, writer; b. Cheboygan, Mich., Mar. 21, 1915; s. Archibald Lancaster and Madeline Ruth (Smith) R.; m. Florence Snure, Sept. 25, 1940 (div. Feb. 1950); children: Michael James, John Douglas; m. 2d, Doris Elfriede White, June 23, 1951; children: Guy Archer, Charles Lancaster, Christopher Corwin. Grad., Command and Gen. Staff Coll., 1952; student, U.S. Armed Forces Inst., 1953, U. Md., 1958. Enlisted U.S. Army, 1939, advanced through grades to lt. col., 1960; served in Far East Command, 1942, 53-55, ETO, 1943-45, 57-60; tech. info. officer Office Surgeon Gen., Dept. Army, Washington, 1950, Ft. Campbell, Ky., 1952-53, info. officer Camp Chicamauga, Japan, Ft. Bragg, N.C., Ft. Campbell, 1953-56, 1956-57, Ft. Benning, Ga., Wurzburg, Germany, 1957-58; spl. projects officer U.S. Army, Augsburg, Germany, 1959-60, U.S. Army Info. Office, N.Y.C., 1960-61; writer program precipitating Senate Armed Svcs. Hearings, 1962; ret., 1965. Mgr., salesman Nu-Enamel Stores, Asheville, N.C., 1937-38; co-owner, dir. Roberts & Roberts Advt. Agy., Denver, 1946-49. Author: Rakkasan, 1955, Screaming Eagles, 1956, The Marne Division, 1957, Victory Denied, 1966, The Anatomy of a Revolution, 1968, Peace: By the Wonderful People Who Brought You Korea and Viet Nam, 1972, The Republic: Decline and Future Promise, 1975, The Crisis of Federal Regionalism: A Solution, 1976, Emerging Struggle for State Sovereignty, 1979, How To Organize for Survival, 1982, The Most Secret Science, 1984; also numerous pamphlets and articles. Pres. Found. for Edn., Scholarship, Patriotism and Americanism, Inc.; founder, nat. bd. dirs. Com. To Restore Constn., Inc., 1965—. Recipient Merit award Am. Acad. Pub. Affairs, 1967, Good Citizenship medal SARa, 1968, Liberty award Congress of Freedom, 1969, Man of Yr. awards Women for Constl. Govt., 1970, Wis. Legis. and Rsch. Com., 1971; medal of merit Am. Legion, 1972, Spkr. of Yr. award We, The People, 1973, spl. tribute State of Mich., 1979; Arch Roberts Week named in his honor City of Danville, Ill., 1974. Mem.: SAR, Sons Am. Colonists, Airborne Assn., Res. Officers Assn. Home: 2218 W Prospect PO Box 986 Fort Collins CO 80522-0986 E-mail: comminc@webaccess.net.

ROBERTS, BETTY JO, retired librarian, speech therapist; b. Ft. Worth, Nov. 11, 1927; d. Harry Pullum and Mamie Josephine (Parker) Easton; m. Robert Lester Roberts, Jr.; children: Jo Lu, Lee Ann. Student, Tex. State Coll. Women, Denton, 1945-47, Tex. Wesleyan Coll.; BS, SW Tex. State U., 1952. Tchr. Milton H. Barry Sch. for Physical Rehab., Houston, United Cerebral Palsy Ctr., Ft. Worth, San Marcos Pub. Schs., 1952-53; supr. practice tchrs. S.W. Tex. State, 1952-53; tchr. Waco (Tex.) Ind. Schs., 1953-54; speech therapist Providence Crippled Children's Hosp., Waco; tchr. phonics, creative art Latin Am. Ctr., 1961-69; ch. librarian Trinity United Methodist Ch., 1979-88; ch. lib. Cen. United Methodist Ch., Tex., 1988-91. Compilor, Editor: Swedishes and More 1984. Democrat. Methodist. Address: 3248 Village Park Dr Waco TX 76708-1582

ROBERTS, BILL GLEN, retired fire chief, investor, consultant; b. Deport, Tex., June 2, 1938; s. Samuel Westbrook and Ann Lee (Rhodes) R.; m. Ramona Ryall, June 1, 1963 (dec. Nov. 1988); 1 child, Renee Ann; m. Johana R. Caines, Oct. 14, 2000. Student, So. Meth. U., 1968, North Tex. State U., 1974; grad. paramedic course, U. Tex. Southwestern Med. Sch., 1974; grad. Exec. Program for Fire Service, Tex. A&M U., 1978; AAS, El Centro Jr. Coll., Dallas, 1980; grad. exec. fire officer program, Nat. Fire Acad., 1989. With Dallas Fire Dept., 1958-82, lt., 1964-67, capt., 1967-71, div. fire chief, 1971-79, asst. fire chief, 1979-83; fire chief Austin (Tex.) Fire Dept., 1983-94. Tech. bd. dirs. Found. Fire Safety, Washington, 1982-85; adj. faculty Nat. Fire Acad., 1981-86; aft. State Life of Indpls., Dallas, 1962; owner Personnel Testing Lab., Dallas, 1963; real estate salesman Dale Copus Realtor, Dallas, 1963-66; salesman intercommunications equipment Chandler Sound, Dallas, 1966-67; field engr. IBM Corp., Dallas, 1968; cons. U. Tenn., 1974, Ga. Inst. Tech., 1974, Tex. Dept. Health Resources, 1973-78, Rand Corp., Washington, Mission Rsch., Santa Barbara, Calif., Macro Author: EMS Dallas, 1978; (with others) Anesthesia for Surgery Trauma, 1976, EMS Measures to Improve Care, 1980; contbr. articles to periodicals. Com. chmn. Dallas Jaycees, 1962-65; mem. task force Am. Heart Assn., Austin, 1973-83; bd. dirs. Brackenridge Hosp., 1989, Rehab. Hosp. Austin, 1992-94, Austin Police Pensions Bd., 1989, Capitol Area coun. Boy Scouts Am., 1989-92. Recipient John Stemmons Service award Dallas Fire Dept., 1979; Internat. Assn. Fire Chiefs scholar, 1967. Mem. Internat. Assn. Fire Chiefs, Am. Heart Assn., North Tex. Coun. of Govts. (regional emergency svc. adv. coun. 1973-79), Found. Fire Safety (tech. bd. dirs. 1982-85), Tex. Assn. Realtors, Rotary. Methodist. Home: 192 Hunter's Ridge Rd Canton NC 28716 E-mail: bglenrob@aol.com.

ROBERTS, BRADLEY EDWARD, finance company executive; b. Birmingham, Ala., Mar. 10, 1976; s. Ronald Graham and Pamela (O'Connor) Roberts; m. Elizabeth Reed Howell, May 5, 2001. BA in Econs., Hampden-Sydney Coll., Va., 1998; diploma, U. Econs., Prague, Czech Republic, 1997. Analyst Goldman, Sachs & Co., N.Y.C., 1998—2001; assoc. Wachovia Securities, Atlanta, 2001—. Mem.: Kappa Sigma. Home: 2397 Hurst Dr Atlanta GA 30305 Office: First Union Securities 3414 Peachtree Rd Ste 500 Atlanta GA 30326 Business E-Mail: broberts@wachoviasec.com.

ROBERTS, BRIAN L. communications executive; b. Phila., June 28, 1959; s. Ralph J. and Suzanne F. Roberts; m. Aileen Kennedy, Dec. 28, 1985; children: Sarah, Tucker, Amanda. Bachelor, U. Pa., 1981. V.p. ops. Comcast Cable Communications, Inc., Phila., 1985-86; exec. v.p. Comcast Corp., 1986-92, also bd. dirs., pres., dir., 1992—. Bd. dirs. The Bank of N.Y.; bd. trustees Simon Wiesenthal Ctr.; founding co-chair Phila. 2000; dir., exec. com. CableLabs. Vice chmn. The Walter Katz Found. Mem. Nat. Cable and Telecom. Assn. (chmn. 1995-96, treas., bd. dirs., exec. com.). Avocation: squash (All-American, silver medal with U.S. team 1981, 85 and 97). Office: Comcast Corp Fl 35 East Twr 1500 Market St Fl 33 Philadelphia PA 19102-2100*

ROBERTS, BRIAN MICHAEL, lawyer; b. Cin., May 28, 1957; s. Shearl Joseph and Mary Ruth (Christian) R.; m. Carol Denise Zimmerman, July 28, 1979; children: Nicholas Brian, Mary Katelin, Kevin Matthew. BS in Bus., Miami U., Oxford, Ohio, 1979; JD, U. Dayton, 1982. Bar: Ohio 1982, U.S. Dist. Ct. (so. dist.) Ohio 1983, U.S. Ct. Appeals (6th cir.) 1984, U.S. Supreme Ct. 1988. Ptnr. Jablinski, Folino, Roberts & Martin Co. LPA, Dayton, 1982—. Organizer, scheduler legal presentations to engaged couples Family Life Office, Archdiocese of Cin., Dayton, 1982-92. Mem. Ohio State Bar Assn., Ohio Acad. Trial Lawyers, Dayton Bar Assn., Miami Valley Trial Lawyers Assn., Assn. Trial Lawyers Am. Republican. Roman Catholic. Home: 3830 Gardenview Pl Dayton OH 45429-4517 Office: Jablinski Folino Roberts & Martin Co LPA PO Box 1266 Dayton OH 45402-9766 E-mail: brianr@jfrmlaw.com.

ROBERTS, BRIAN WAYNE, middle school educator, minister; b. Owensboro, Ky., Dec. 2, 1974; s. Clyde Wayne and Donna Lynn Roberts; m. Jenny Rebecca Westerfield. ThM, Luther Rice Sem., Lithonia, Ga., 2001. Ordained minister Green Brier Baptist, Utica, Ky., 1997; cert. tchr. Pastor New Life Bapt. Ch., Hawesville, Ky., 1997—2002, Sorgho (Ky.) Bapt. Ch., 2002—. Faculty sponsor Christian Student Fellowship, Owensboro, 1998—. Author: (study guide) God's Apocalypse: According to John, 1996. Student counselor Daviess/McLean Bapt. Assn., 1993—98, Ky. Wesleyan Meth. Workers, 1993—98. Recipient Elizabeth Munday Cmty. Svc. award, Ky. Wesleyan Coll., 1997. Mem.: Christian Educators Assn. Internat. R-Consevative. Avocation: University of Kentucky basketball. Home: 7030 Jack Hinton Rd Philpot KY 42366 Office: Daviess County Mid Sch 1415 E Fourth St Owensboro KY 42303

ROBERTS, BRUCE DAN, application developer, department chairman; b. Lorain, Ohio, Nov. 22, 1939; s. Dan Norman and Genevieve Ruth (Hancock) Roberts; m. Betsy Bancroft Barratt, Apr. 1965 (div. July 1972); stepchildren: Randall James Costanza, Richard Carl Costanza; m. Sandra Lee Walker Costanza, Sept. 30, 1972; children: Kenneth Lee, Kathryn Ann Roberts Packer. BA in Math., Physics, Econs., St. Lawrence U., Canton, N.Y., 1961; MSc in Systems Engring., U. Fla. Gainesville, Daytona Beach, 1966. From engr. to functional mgr. GE Aerospace, various locations , 1961—86; dir. Paoli Rsch. Ctr. Unisys, Paoli, Pa., 1986—89; v.p. engring. Unisys Electronic Systems, Fagan, Minn., 1989—92; v.p. devel. and prodn. Unisys Defense Systems Group, Tysons Corners, Va., 1992—96; sr. v.p. and group mgr. SAIT SAIC, San Diego, 1996—97; pres., ceo Cubic Defense Systems, 1997—. Mem. CASE adv. bd. Syracuse (N.Y.) U., 1984—86; mem. engring. dept. adv. bd, U. Minn., Mpls., 1990—92. Mem.: Sigma Pi Sigma, Pi Mu Epsilon, Phi Beta Kappa. Republican. Avocations: walking, hiking, coaching, sports. E-mail: bruce.roberts@cubic.com.

ROBERTS, BURK AUSTIN, lawyer; b. Albuquerque, Apr. 8, 1968; s. Thomas Franklin Jr. and Judy Jane Roberts; m. Cindy Rene Breaux, June 6, 1998. BA, U. Tex., 1989; JD, Baylor U., 1991. Bar: Tex. 1992. Ptnr. Roberts & Roberts LLP, Killeen, Tex., 1992—; city atty. City of Harker Heights, 1994—. Co-chair region 5 devel. Tex. Ctr. Legal Ethics & Professionalism, Austin, 1998-99. Mem. adv. bd. Killeen Salvation Army, 1993—, chair, 1996. Named Outstanding Young Man of Am., 1998. Fellow Tex. Bar Found., mem. Coll. State Bar Tex. Office: Roberts & Roberts LLP 324 E Avenue C Killeen TX 76541-5233

ROBERTS, BURTON BENNETT, lawyer, retired judge; b. N.Y.C., July 25, 1922; s. Alfred S. and Cecelia (Schanfein) R.; m. Gerhild Ukryn. BA, NYU, 1943, LL.M., 1953; LL.B., Cornell U., 1949. Bar: N.Y. 1949. Asst. dist. atty., New York County, 1949-66; chief asst. dist. atty. Bronx County, Bronx, N.Y., 1966-68, acting dist. atty., 1968-69, dist. atty., 1969-72; justice Supreme Ct. State N.Y., 1973-98, adminstrv. judge criminal br. Bronx County 12th Jud. Dist., 1984-98, adminstrv. judge civil br. Bronx County 12th Dist., 1988-98; ret., 1998; counsel Fischbein, Badillo, Wagner & Hording, 1999—. Pres. Bronx div. Hebrew Home for Aged, 1967-72. With U.S. Army, 1943-45. Decorated Purple Heart, Bronze Star with oak leaf cluster. Mem. Assn. Bar City N.Y., Am. Bar Assn., N.Y. Bar Assn., Bronx County Bar Assn., N.Y. State Dist. Attys. Assn. (pres. 1971-72) Jewish (exec. bd. temple). Home: 215 E 68th St Apt 19A New York NY 10021-5727 Office: Fischbein Badillo et al 909 3rd Ave New York NY 10022-4731 E-mail: broberts@fbwhlaw.com.

ROBERTS, CARL GEOFFREY, lawyer; b. Boston, June 17, 1948; s. Simon Matthew and Ruth (Gorfinkle) R.; m. Sharon Ash, Mar. 24, 1979. BA, Harvard U., 1970; JD, U. Pa., 1974. Bar: Pa. 1974, U.S. Dist. Ct. (ea. dist.) Pa. 1974, U.S. Ct. Appeals (3d cir.) 1978, U.S. Supreme Ct. 1980, U.S. Ct. Claims 1980, U.S. Dist. Ct. (mid. dist.) Pa. 1986. Law clk. U.S. Dist. Ct. (ea. dist.) Pa., Phila., 1974-76; assoc. Dilworth, Paxson, Kalish & Kauffman, 1978-82, ptnr., 1982-92, Ballard, Spahr, Andrews & Ingersoll, Phila., 1992—. Bd. dirs. Phila. Chamber Ensemble, sec., 1977-92, pres., 1992-95; mem. Hillel com. U. Pa., 1999—, chair 2001—; bd. dirs. Hillel of Greater Phila., 2000—. Mem. ABA (law practice mgmt. sect., editl. bd. sect. mag.). Office: Ballard Spahr Andrews & Ingersoll 1735 Market St Fl 51 Philadelphia PA 19103-7599

ROBERTS, CARYL, artist; b. N.Y.C., June 2, 1933; d. Robert Bernard and Miriam Francis Roberts; m. Martin Herbert Kahn, Oct. 31, 1954; children: David, Randy, Steven. Student, Pratt Inst., 1951, Sorbonne, 1952; BFA, Columbia U., 1956. Instr. East Ramapo Sch. Dist. # 1, Spring Valley, N.Y., 1969-90; freelance artist N.Y.C. and White Plains, 1970—. One-woman shows include Family Ct. New City, N.Y., 1977, Arts Coun. of Rockland, 1995, Armory Arts Ctr., West Palm Beach, Fla.; exhibited in group shows Ward-Nasse, N.Y.C., 1995—, Renaissance, Blauvelt, N.Y., PaintingsDirect.com.; slides of paintings archived with Nat. Mus. of Women in the Arts. Mem. Commn. on Gun Control, N.Y.C., 1960's, Correctional Assn., N.Y.C., 1960's; chair tree cert. Temple Beth Scholom, New City, 1970—. Mem. Rockland Ctr. for the Arts, Hopper Ho., Armory Arts Ctr., Arts Fedn. N.Y. Avocations: gardening, travel. Office: 89 Robinhood Ln New City NY 10956-6636

ROBERTS, CELIA ANN, librarian; b. Bangor, Maine, Feb. 6, 1935; d. William Lewis and Ruey Pearl (Logan) Roberts. AA, U. Hartford, 1957, BA, 1961; postgrad., So. Conn. State Coll., 1963—. With catalog, acquisition and circulation depts. U. Hartford Libr., 1956-65; libr. Simsbury Free Libr., Simsbury, Conn., 1965-69; reference libr. Simsbury Pub. Libr., 1969—. Tchr. ballet, 1965—66; tchr. genealogy, 1977—; ballet mistress Ballet Soc. Conn., Inc., 1968—70; with corps de ballet Conn. Opera Assn., 1963—64; active in prodns. Simsbury Light Opera Assn., 1964—69. Contbr. Vol. Family History Ctr., 1970—. Mem.: DAR (Abigail Phelps chpt.), AAUW (past pres. Greater Hartford chpt.), ALA, Simsbury Hist. Soc., Conn. Libr. Assn., Denison Soc., Inc., Conn. Hist. Soc., Soc. Mayflower Descs. Conn., Pro Dance, Ont. Geneal. Soc., New Eng. Historic and Geneal. Soc., Conn. Soc. Genealogists, Dance Masters Am. (Conn. Dance Tchrs. Club chpt.), New Brunswick Geneal. Soc., Daus. of Scotia, Simsbury Geneal. and Hist. Rsch. Libr., Chateauguay Valley Hist. Soc., Ellen Douglas Lodge #8. Unitarian Universalist. Office: Simsbury Public Libr 725 Hopmeadow St Simsbury CT 06070-2243 E-mail: croberts@simsbury.lib.ct.us.

ROBERTS, CHARLES PATRICK (PAT ROBERTS), senator; b. Topeka, Apr. 20, 1936; m. Franki Fann, 1969; children: David, Ashleigh, Anne-Wesley. BS, Kans. State U., 1958. Pub. Litchfield Park, Ariz., 1962-67; adminstrv. asst. to U.S. Senator Frank Carlson, U.S. Senate, Washington, 1967-68; adminstrv. asst. to U.S. Congressman Keith Sebelius U.S. Ho. of Reps., 1968-80; mem. 97th to 104th Congresses from 1st Kans. Dist., 1980-96, U.S. Senate from Kans., Washington, 1997—; mem. agr., nutrition and forestry com.; mem. armed svcs. com.; vice-chmn. ethics com.; mem. intelligence com. Served with USMC, 1958-62. Office: US Senate 302 Hart Senate Off Bldg Washington DC 20510-0001

ROBERTS, CHARLES S. application developer; b. Newark, Sept. 25, 1937; s. Ben and Sara (Fasten) R.; m. Wendy Shadlen, June 8, 1959; children: Lauren Roberts Gold, Tamara G. Roberts. BS in Chemistry, Carnegie-Mellon U., 1959; PhD in Physics, MIT, 1963. MTS, radiation physics rsch. AT&T Bell

Labs., Murray Hill, NJ, 1963-68, head info. processing rsch., 1968-73, head interactive computer systems rsch., 1973-82, head, advanced sys. dept. Denver, 1982-87, head software architecture planning dept. Holmdel, 1987-88; R&D mgr., system architecture lab. Hewlett-Packard Co., Cupertino, Calif., 1988-90, R&D mgr. univ. rsch. grants, 1990-92; prin. lab. scientist Hewlett-Packard Labs., Palo Alto, 1992-98; ret., 1998. Contbr. articles to profl. jours. Westinghouse scholar Carnegie Mellon U., 1955-59; NSF fellow MIT, 1959-63. Mem. IEEE, Assn. for Computing Machinery, Am. Phys. Soc., Sigma Xi, Tau Beta Pi, Phi Kappa Phi. Achievements include 2 patents on associative information retrieval and dithered display system; development of early UNIX operating system for 32-bit computers; research on Windows NT operating sys., on theory to explain electron loss in Van Allen Belts, on superimposed code techniques for associative information retrieval. Home: 108 Twelve Oaks Ln Ponte Vedra Beach FL 32082-3943 E-mail: csrob@acm.org.

ROBERTS, CHRIS, strategy and finance educator, researcher; b. New Castle, Pa., July 16, 1954; s. Samuel Bruce and Jan Roberts, Della V. Roberts (Stepmother), Sheldon S. Smith (Stepfather). BS in Mgmt., U. Utah, 1975, BS in Fin., 1981; MBA, U. Phoenix, Salt Lake City, 1986; PhD in Mgmt., U. Mass., 1995. Supr. Holiday Inns Reservation Ctr., Memphis, 1972—78; product mgr. Mountain Bell/Qwest Comms., Salt Lake City, 1978—89; assoc. prof. dept. HRTA U. Mass., Amherst, 1993—, assoc. dept. head dept. HRTA, 2001—. Contbr. ; editor: Jour. Hospitality and Tourism Edn. Mem.: Acad. Mgmt., Strategic Mgmt. Soc., Coun. Hotel, Restaurant & Instnl. Edn. (chair symposium com. 1998—2002, Outstanding Peer Reviewer 1999), Beta Gamma Sigma. Avocations: contract bridge, international travel. Home: PO Box 521895 Salt Lake City UT 84152-1895 Office: U Mass Flint 206A 90 Campus Center Way Amherst MA 01003-9247 Office Fax: 413-545-1235. Personal E-mail: q44q@yahoo.com. Business E-Mail: Q@hrta.umass.edu.

ROBERTS, CHRISTOPHER CHALMERS, lawyer; b. Washington, Oct. 12, 1950; s. Chalmers McGeagh and Lois (Hall) R.; m. Mary Hammond Higgins, Apr. 23, 1983; children: Kevin, Morgan, Rachel, Sarah. BA, Amherst Coll., 1972; JD, Georgetown U., 1975, MLT, 1981. Bar: Md. 1975, D.C. 1976, U.S. Dist. Ct. Md. 1978, U.S. Ct. Appeals (4th cir.) 1979, U.S. Dist. Ct. D.C. 1980, U.S. Ct. Appeals (D.C. cir.) 1980. Law clk. to presiding justice Ct. Appeals of Md., Annapolis, 1974-76; assoc. Shulman, Rogers, Gandal, Pordy & Ecker, P.A., Rockville, Md., 1978-83, ptnr., 1984—. Counsel Montgomery County Students Automotive Trades Found., Md., 1984-99. Editor: Jour. Georgetown Law, 1973—75; contbr. articles to legal jours. Mem. Amherst Alumni Assn. Washington (past officer, pres.). Office: Shulman Rogers Gandal Pordy & Ecker 11921 Rockville Pike Ste 300 Rockville MD 20852-2743 E-mail: croberts@srgpe.com.

ROBERTS, COKIE See ROBERTS, CORINNE BOGGS

ROBERTS, CORINNE BOGGS (COKIE ROBERTS), correspondent, news analyst; b. New Orleans, Dec. 27, 1943; d. Thomas Hale and Corinne Morrison (Claiborne) Boggs; m. Steven V. Roberts, Sept. 10, 1966; children: Lee Harriss, Rebecca Boggs. BA in Polit. Sci., Wellesley Coll., 1964; hon. degrees, Amherst Coll., Columbia Coll., Loyola U. of the South, Manhattanville Coll., Gonzaga U., Boston Coll., Hood Coll., Chestnut Hill Coll., Miss. Women's U., Notre Dame U. Md., Xavier U., St. Louis U., Duke U. Assoc. prodr., host Altman Prodns., Washington, 1964-66, prodr. L.A., 1969-72; reporter, editor Cowles Communications, N.Y.C., 1967; prodr. Sta. WNEW-TV, 1968, Sta. KNBC-TV, L.A., 1972-74; reporter CBS News, Athens, Greece, 1974-77; corr. Nat. Pub. Radio, Washington, 1977—, MacNeil/Lehrer Newshour, Washington, 1984-88; spl. Washington corr. ABC News, 1988-92; interviewer, commentator This Week With David Brinkley, 1992-96; co-anchor This Week, 1996—2002; chief congrl. analyst ABC News. Lectr. in field. Co-host weekly pub. TV program on Congress, The Lawmakers, 1981-84; producer, host pub. affairs program Sta. WRC-TV, Washington; producer Sta. KNBC-TV Serendipity, L.A. (award for excellence in local programming, Emmy nomination for children's programming); Author: We Are Our Mother's Daughters, 1998; contbr. articles to newspapers, mags. Bd. dirs. Dirksen Ctr., Pekin, Ill., 1988-95; bd. dirs. Fgn. Students Svc. Ctr., Washington, 1990—, Manhattanville Coll., Purchase, N.Y., 1991-99, Children's Inn at NIH, Bethesda, Md., 1992—. Recipient Broadcast award Nat. Orgn. Working Women, 1984, Everett McKinley Dirksen disting. reporting of Congress, 1987, Weintal award Georgetown U., 1988, Corp. Pub. Broadcasting award, 1988, Edward R. Murrow award Corp. Pub. Broadcasting, 1990, Broadcast award Nat. Women's Polit. Caucus, 1990, David Brinkley Comm. award, 1992, Mother of Yr. award Nat. Mothers' Day Com., 1992, Emmy award news and documentary, 1992. Mem. Radio-TV Corrs. Assn. (pres. 1981-82, bd. dirs. 1980-94), U.S. Capitol Hist. Soc. Roman Catholic.*

ROBERTS, DAVID DUNCAN, biochemist; b. Indiana, Pa., July 1, 1954; s. David and Sarah Edith (Nicely) R.; divorced; children: Benjamin Roberts, James Roberts; m. Nancy Smyth Templeton, Mar. 6, 1993; children: Lizette Templeton, Renee Templeton. BS Chemistry, MIT, 1976; PhD Biol. Chemistry, U. Mich., 1983. Sr. rsch. assoc. Clin. Assays/Div. Travenol Lab., Cambridge, Mass., 1976-79; staff fellow NIDDK, NIH, Bethesda, Md., 1984-86, sr. staff fellow, 1987, rsch. chemist, 1987-88; chief, biochem. pathology sect., lab. of pathology Nat. Cancer Inst., NIH, 1988—. Mem. NIDDK Cystic Fibrosis SCOR rev. com., NIH, 1994; ad hoc mem. pathobiochemistry study sect., NIH, 1989-95. Mem. editl. bd. Jour. Biol. Chemistry, 1995-2000; editor: Cell Surface Glycoconjugates: Structure and Function, 1993; contbr. articles to profl. jours.; patentee in field. Recipient Lee Murphy Meml. prize U. Mich., 1985, Walter J. Johnson Ann. prize for rsch. in life scis., Harcourt, Brace, Jovanovich, Phila., 1987. Mem. Am. Soc. Biochemistry and Molecular Biology, The Soc. for Glycobiology, AAAS. Office: NIH 10 Center Dr Msc 1500 Bethesda MD 20892-1500

ROBERTS, DAVID GLEN, prospector, investor; b. Plainview, Tex., Feb. 8, 1952; s. Doris Glen and Anna Grace (Mathis) R. Student, Tex. A&M U., 1970-71, Dallas Bapt. Coll., 1971-75; BA in Comm., U. Tex. Permian Basin, 1987. Lic. minister Bapt. Ch.; cert. profl. landman. Profl. stuntman, actor, 1972-76; mgr. Channel 100, Midland, Tex., 1976-78; owner D.G. Roberts Land Mgmt., 1978—, Diamond Developers Fire and Enviro-Safety Co.; regional mktg. dir. Nochar Inc.-Region 11, Midland, Tex., 1990-96; pub., owner Basin Voice newspaper. Cons. EPA, Indpls., 1991—. Appeared in film Giovanni & Ben, 1974, Drive In, 1976; theatre appearance at Globe Theatre, Odessa, Tex., 1975, Shakespeare in the Park, Dallas, 1976. Past chair Midland County Libertarian Party; past mem. exec. com. Dist. 31 Tex. Libertarian Party; organizer Sons of Liberty, Midland, 1990—. Mem. Am. Assn. Petroleum-Landmen, Five Aces, NRA, Tex. State Rifle Assn., Permian Basin Landman's Assn., N.O.R.M.L. Libertarian. Avocations: golf, motorcycling, hiking, shooting, photography. Office: Diamond Developers 3105 Barkley Ave Midland TX 79701-6215 E-mail: davy.roberts@bodywise.net.

ROBERTS, DAVID LOWELL, journalism educator, journalist; b. Lusk, Wyo., Jan. 12, 1954; s. Leslie James and LaVerne Elizabeth (Johns) R. BA, U. Ariz., 1979; MA, U. Nebr., 1997. Founder, editor, publisher Medicine Bow (Wyo.) Post, 1977-88; journalism instr. U. Wyo., Laramie, 1987-92; adviser U. Wyo. Student Publs., 1987-92; gen. mgr. Student Media Corp U No. Colo., Greeley, 1995-98; founder, publisher Hanna Herald, Wyo., 1979-80; asst. prof. mass comm. Missouri Valley Coll., Marshall, Mo., 2001—. Exch. reporter The Washington Post, 1982; freelance reporter Casper (Wyo.) Star-Tribune, 1978-83, various publs.; freelancer, 1977—. Co-author: (book) The Wyoming Almanac, 1988, 90, 94, 96, 2001; author: (book) Sage Street, 1991; columnist Sage Street, 1989-92. Chmn. Medicine Bow Film Commn., 1984; treas. Friends of the Medicine Bow Mus., 1984-88; pres. Medicine Bow Area C. of C., 1984; dir. Habitat for Humanity of Albany County, Laramie, 1991-92. Recipient Nat. Newspaper Assn. awards, over 40 Wyo. Press. Assn. awards, Five Editorial awards U. Wyo., Citizen of Yr. award People of Medicine Bow, 1986, Student Publs. awards U. Wyo., 1990, 92. Mem. Friends of Medicine Bow Mus. Mem. Green Party. Methodist. Avocations: writing, golf, visiting museums, photography. Home: 221 E Rosehill Marshall MO 65340

ROBERTS, DAVID POZZI, security management consultant; b. Holyhead, Anglesey, Wales, July 15, 1952; came to U.S., 1991; s. Alfred Pozzi Roberts and Nancy Brearey; m. Marianna Pacella, Mar. 31, 1994. , Chester Coll. Further Edn., U.K., 1969. Constable North Wales Police, 1972-77; constable, sgt. Met. Police/New Scotland Yard, London, 1977-84; chmn., mng. dir. Churchill Consultancy Group, Plc, 1984-90; dir. security Nippy Inc., Fort Lee, N.J., 1988-95; internat. cons. G.S.S. Security Svcs. Inc., N.Y.C., 1995—. Internat. mgmt. cons., 1984—. With Royal Air Force, 1969-72. Fellow Inst. Profl. Investigators, Inst. Dirs., Internat. Security Assn.; mem. World Assn. Detectives, I.N.T.E.L.N.E.T., Izaak Walton Lodge (founder). Anglican. Avocations: reading, writing, travel, shooting, fitness. Home: PO Box 625 Essex Fells NJ 07021-0625 Office: GSS Security Svcs Inc 750 8th Ave Ste 302 New York NY 10036-7005

ROBERTS, DELMAR LEE, editor; b. Raleigh, N.C., Apr. 9, 1933; s. James Delmer and Nellie Brockelbank (Tyson) R. BS in Textile Mgmt., N.C. State U., 1956; MA in Journalism, U. S.C., 1974. Product devel. engr. U.S. Rubber Co. (Uniroyal), Winnsboro, S.C., 1959-64; process improvement engr. Allied Chem. Co., Irmo, 1965-67; assoc. editor S.C. History Illustrated Mag., Columbia, 1970; editor-in-chief, editl. v.p. Sandlapper-The Mag. of S.C., 1968-74; mng. editor, art dir. Legal Econs. mag. of the ABA, Chgo., 1975-89, Law Practice Mgmt. mag. of the ABA, Chgo., 1990-2000, editor emeritus, 2000—. Editor: The Best of Legal Economics, 1979; freelance editor and/or designer of over 35 books. Active World Affairs Coun. Columbia, 1997—; 1st v.p. English-Speaking Union, 1996-97, pres. 1997—. With U.S. Army, 1956-58. Hon. fellow Coll. of Law Practice Mgmt., Golden, Colo., 1995—. Mem. Soc. Profl. Journalists, Capital City Club (Columbia), Phi Kappa Tau, Kappa Tau Alpha. Avocations: European travel, Turkish carpet/Kilim collecting, antique collecting.

ROBERTS, DENNIS WILLIAM, association executive; b. Chgo., Jan. 7, 1943; s. William Owen and Florence Harriet (Denman) R. BA in Journalism, U. N.Mex., 1968; MA in Legal Studies, Antioch U., 1982; MA, St. John's Coll., 1984. Cert. assn. exec. Gen. assignment reporter Albuquerque Pub. Co., 1964, sports writer, 1960-64, advt. and display salesman, 1967-68; dir. info. N.Mex. bldg. br. Asso. Gen. Contractors Am., Albuquerque, 1968-79, asst. exec. dir., 1979-82, dir., 1982—. Active United Way, Albuquerque, 1969-78; chmn. Albuquerque Crime Prevention Coun., 1982; bd. dirs. Rio Grande chpt. ARC, 1992-95, Albuquerque Lit. Coun., 1998—. Recipient Pub. Rels. Achievement award Assoc. Gen. Contractors Am., 1975, 78. Mem. N.Mex. Pub. Rels. Conf. (chmn. 1975, 82-83), Pub. Rels. Soc. Am. (accredited, pres. N.Mex. chpt. 1981, chmn. S.W. dist. 1984, chmn. sect. 1988), Am. Soc. Assn. Execs. (cert.), Contrn. Specifications Inst. (Outstanding Industry Mem. 1974, Outstanding Com. Chmn. 1978), Toastmasters Club (dist. gov. 1977-78, Disting. Dist. award 1978, Toastmaster of Yr. 1979-80), Masons, Shriners, Elks, Sigma Delta Chi (pres. N.Mex. chpt. 1969). Republican. Lutheran. Home: Apt 21 1410 Girard NE Albuquerque NM 87106 Office: Assn Gen Contractors 1615 University Blvd NE Albuquerque NM 87102-1717 E-mail: drobe80868@aol.com. *Personal philosophy: Set your priorities in life, then your goals. In pursuing your goals, visualize their accomplishment. Be persistent, and you will accomplish what you set out to accomplish. Learn to be fair to others and empathetic.*

ROBERTS, DON E. accountant; b. Bluefield, W.Va., Feb. 16, 1934; s. Frank P. and Lila T. (Thornburg) R.; m. Jacquelyn Joan Ballard, Dec. 30, 1956 (div. 1978); children: Donna, Bruce, Susan; m. Pamala Sue Allen, Nov. 25, 1978; children: Daryl, Dwight. Student, The Citadel, 1952; BSBA, Concord Coll., 1956; postgrad., U. of South Fla., 1977. Sr. acct. Lee W. McLain, CPA, Sarasota, Fla., 1956-62; prin. Don E. Roberts Co., 1962—. Leader 17 piece dance band "The Sophisticates". Treas. Sarasota (Fla.) 4H Found., 1966-76, treas. Sarasota Fair Assn., 1967-79. Named Hon. Mem. Sarasota 4H Found., 1978. Mem. Fla. Soc. Enrolled Agts. (pres. Sarasota chpt. 1986-88, Fla. pres. 1990-91), Fla. Accts. Assn. (pres. Sarasota chpt. 1966-69, mem. Fla. exec. bd. 1966-69, state pres. 2001-2002), Nat. Assn. Enrolled Agts., Nat. Assn. Pub. Accts., Fla. Accts. Soc. (1st v.p. 1999-00, pres.-elect 2000-01, pres. 2001—), Kiwanis Internat. (treas. Sarasota 1957-64, sec. 1966-68, 25 yr. Legion of Honor award 1984, 30 yr., 1989, 35 yr., 1994, life mem. 1988). Republican. Episcopalian. Avocation: Jazz. Home: 4873 Old Ranch Rd Sarasota FL 34241-9581 Office: Don E Roberts Co 3212 Southgate Cir Sarasota FL 34239-5514 E-mail: derea@aol.com.

ROBERTS, DONALD ALBERT, advertising, public relations, marketing and media consultant; b. Boston, Dec. 17, 1935; s. Albert Arthur and Linette Violette (Ouelette) R.; m. Gabrielle Dorothy St. Laurent, Apr. 20, 1957; children: Lynne Dianne, Tammy Denise. Student, U. Maine, 1987-88, 97-99. Program mgr., dir. sports Sta. WIMA-TV, Lima, Ohio, 1965-68; v.p., gen. mgr. Sta. WABK/WKME, Gardiner, Maine, 1968-74; pres., owner Sta. WRDO, Augusta, 1974-77; cons. group gen. mgr. Valley Communications, Bangor, 1977-78; pres., owner Roberts Advt. Agy., Augusta, 1977-78; v.p., gen. mgr. Sta. WLOB AM/FM, Portland, Maine, 1978-80, Sta. WKCG/WFAU, Augusta, 1980-83; pres., owner Roberts & Co., 1983—; exec. v.p. mktg., programming and advt. sales State Cable TV Corp., 1983-92; cons. gen. mgr. Capital Weekly Newspaper, 1993—. Cons. New Eng. Ziebart Dealers Assn., 1982—; cons. gen. mgr. Capital Weekly Newspaper, Augusta, Maine, 1994—. Contbr. articles to profl. jours. Pres. Auburn (Maine) City Coun., 1957-60; chmn. Jefferson-Jackson Dinner, Rockland, Maine, 1959, Preserve Augusta Neighborhood Assn., 1989—; del. Dem. State Conv., Bangor, 1980; city councilor-at-large of Augusta, 1990-94; mem. Augusta City Charter Commn., 1997-98; del. Maine Rep. Conv., 1996, 98, 2000. Named Maine Sportscaster of Yr. Nat. Sportscasters Assn., 1962, 63; recipient Tiger award Maine Broadcasting System, 1965. Mem. So. Kennebec Valley Realtors Assn., Cable Advt. Bur., Cable TV Adminstrs. and Marketers, Ohio Sportscasters Assn. (co-founder 1965), Maine Assn. Broadcasters (bd. dirs.), Kennebec Valley C. of C. (bd. dirs.). Avocations: politics, reading, golf. Home and Office: 44 Longwood Ave Augusta ME 04330-4131

ROBERTS, DONALD FRANK, JR. communications educator, educator; b. Seattle, Mar. 30, 1939; s. Donald Frank Sr. and Ruth Amalia (Geiger) R.; m. Karlene Hahn, 1963 (div. 1981): 1 child, Donald Brett; m. Wendy G. Roberts, Aug. 26, 1983; stepchildren: Richard L., David L., Katherine M. AB, Columbia U., 1961; MA, U. Calif., Berkeley, 1963; PhD, Stanford U., 1968. Instr., dept. English U. Hawaii, Honolulu, 1963-64; asst. dir. ednl. svc. bur. The Wall Street Jour., Princeton, N.J., 1964-65; asst. prof., rsch. assoc. dept. Comm., Inst. Comm. Rsch. Stanford (Calif.) U., 1970-76, assoc. prof., 1976-84, prof. Comm., 1984—, dir. Inst. Comm. Rsch., 1985-90, chmn. dept. Comm., 1990-96, Thomas More Storke Prof., 1991—. Cons. NIMH, 1970-71, Rand Corp., 1972-74, Sta. KQED-TV, 1975-77, Far West Lab. Ednl. Rsch. and Devel., 1978-79, FTC, 1978-80, Westinghouse Broadcasting, 1983-86, Soc. Nutrition Edn., 1984-86, The Disney Channel, 1986-87, WHO, 1988-89, SRI Internat., 1988-89, Carnegie Coun. Adolescence, 1989-90, NBC, 1992, Ctr. Disease Control, 1992, Children Now, 1992—, Software Pubs. Assn., 1994, Nickelodeon, 1994, JP Kids, 1995-97, MGM Animation, 1996—, DIC Entertainment, 1997—, Planet Lingo, 1997-2001, Sunbow Entertainment, 1999—, ABC/Disney TV Animation, 2000—, Disney Online, 2000—, Nelvana, Ltd., 2000—; bd. advisors Media Scope, 1992-94; bd. dirs. Recreational Software Adv. Coun., 1994-98; proposal reviewer NIMH, NSF, U.S. Agy. Internat. Devel., Can. Coun., John and Mary R. Markle Found., W.T. Grant Found.; spkr. numerous seminars, confs., symposia. Co-author: Process and Effects of Mass Communication, 1971, Television and Human Behavior, 1978, It's Not ONLY Rock and Roll, 1998, Kids & Media @ the New Millennium, 1999; mem. editl. bd. Jour. Broadcasting, 1980-88, Pub. Opinion Quarterly, 1981-86, Communicare, 1986—; editl. reviewer Commn. Rsch., Comm. Monograph, Comm. Yearbook, Human Comm. Rsch., Jour. Comm., Jour. Quarterly, Child Devel., Jour. Applied Psychology, Jour. Ednl. Psychology, Psychology Bull., Jour. Adolescent Health; contbr. articles to profl. jours, also monographs and book chpts. Fellow Human Scis. Rsch. Coun., Pretoria. South Africa, 1985, 1987, Fullbright Teaching fellow Inst. for Unterrichtstechnologie Und Medienpadagogic, Austria, 1987. Mem. APA, Internat. Comm. Assn., Assn. Edn. in Journalism and Mass Comm., Soc. Rsch. Child Devel., Soc. Personality and Soc. Psychology. Office: Stanford U Dept Comm McClatchy Hall Stanford CA 94305-2050 E-mail: droberts@stanford.edu.

ROBERTS, DONALD JOHN, economics and business educator, consultant; b. Winnipeg, Man., Can., Feb. 11, 1945; came to U.S., 1967; s. Donald Victor and Margaret Mabel (Riddell) R.; m. Kathleen Eleanor Taylor, Aug. 26, 1967. BA with honors, U. Man., 1967; PhD, U. Minn., 1972. Instr. dept. managerial econs. and decision scis. J.L. Kellogg Grad. Sch. Mgmt., Northwestern U., Evanston, Ill., 1971—72, asst. prof., 1972—74; assoc. prof. J. L. Kellogg Grad. Sch. Mgmt., Northwestern U., 1974—77; prof. J.L. Kellogg Grad. Sch. Mgmt., Northwestern U., 1977—80, Grad. Sch. Bus., Stanford (Calif.) U., 1980, Jonathan B. Lovelace prof., 1980—2001, assoc. dean, dir. rsch., 1987—90, dir. exec. program in strategy and orgn., 1992—, dir. global mgmt. program, 1994—, sr. assoc. dean, 2000—, John H. and Irene S. Scully prof., 2001—. Prof. (by courtesy) dept. econs. Stanford U., 1986—; vis. rsch. faculty U. Catholique de Louvain, Belgium, 1974-75; inaugural Clarendon lectr. mgmt. studies Oxford U., 1997; cons. bus., econs. and antitrust, 1976—; vis. fellow All Souls Coll., Oxford U., 1995, Nuffield Coll., Oxford U., 1999-00; vis. acad. fellow in leadership and orgn. McKinsey & Co., London, 1999-00. Co-author: Economics, Organization and Management, 1992;; assoc. editor Jour. Econ. Theory, 1977-92, Econometrica, 1985-87, Games and Economics Behavior, 1988—; mem. editl. bd. Am. Econ. Rev., 1991-95, Jour. Econs. and Mgmt. Strategy, 1991-98, Orgns. and Markets Abstracts, 1996—; contbr. articles to profl. jours. NSF grantee, 1973-93; rsch. fellow Ctr. Ops. Rsch. and Econometrics, Heverlee, Belgium, 1974, fellow Ctr. for Advanced Study in the Behavioral Scis., 1991-92. Fellow Econometric Soc. (coun. 1994-96); mem. Am. Econ. Assn., Beta Gamma Sigma. Home: 835 Santa Fe Ave Stanford CA 94305-1022 Office: Stanford U Grad Sch Bus Stanford CA 94305-5015 E-mail: roberts_john@gsb.stanford.edu.

ROBERTS, DONALD MUNIER, retired banker, trust company executive; b. Paterson, N.J., Aug. 3, 1935; s. Edward and Dorothy (Munier) R.; m. Sally D. Ingram, Sept. 6, 1958 (dec. Feb. 1978); 1 dau., Sarah M.; m. Mary Ayer Gordon, June 23, 1978; children: Edward (dec.), John, Martha. BS, Yale U., 1957; MBA, NYU, 1961. Exec. v.p., 1979-90; vice chmn., treas. U.S. Trust Co. N.Y., N.Y.C., 1990-95; retired, 1995. Bd. dirs. York (Pa.) Internat. Corp., Burlington Resources, Inc. Trustee, pres. St. Bernards Sch. Mem. N.Y. Road Runners Club Inc. (bd. dirs., past chmn.), Tau Beta Pi. Clubs: Links (N.Y.C.). Republican. Home: 10 Gracie Sq New York NY 10028-8031 Office: 18th Fl 645 Fifth Ave New York NY 10022-5910

ROBERTS, DONALD WILSON, pathologist, consultant; b. Phoenix, Jan. 20, 1933; s. Alpha Wilson and Rubye Clotilde (Finklea) R.; m. Mae Astrid Strand, June 17, 1959; children: Marc Donald, Sara Judith Roberts Roundy. BS, Brigham Young U., 1957; MS, Iowa State U., 1959; PhD, U. Calif., Berkeley, 1964. Postdoctoral Swiss Fed. Inst. Tech., Zurich, 1964-65; insect pathologist Boyce Thompson Inst. for Plant Rsch., Ithaca, N.Y., 1965-96; insect pathologist, res. prof. dept. biology Utah State U., Logan, 1997—. Cons. WHO, Kaduna, Nigeria, 1974, 76, Empresa Brasileira de Pesquisa Agropecuraria, Brasilia, Brazil, 1978, 79, 80, 94, 96; mem. sci. adv. bd. EcoSci. Corp., Worcester, Mass., 1990-95; project reviewer UN Devel. Program, Africa and South Am., 1993-96, USAID Africa, 1991-96; adj. prof. dept. entomology Cornell U., Ithaca, N.Y., 1993—, adj. prof. dept. plant pathology, 1994-99. Editor: (3 books) Diseases of Medically Important Arthropods, 1977, 80, 83, Invasion Processes of Fungi, 1983, Biotechnology in Pest Control, 1989; contbr. over 200 articles to profl. jours. Recipient Fulbright Sr. Rsch. scholarship Fulbright Found., Australia, 1985; named Family of Yr., Utah State U. Internat. Students, 1999. Mem. Soc. for Invertebrate Pathology (hon. 1998, founding mem., pres. 1988-90, Founder's Lectr. 1996), Entomol. Soc. Am. (Ea. br., Ciba-Geigy Recognition award 1985, 86, L.O. Howard Disting. Achievement award 1989), Am. Soc. Microbiology, Mycol. Soc. Am., Brazilian Entomol. Soc. (hon., recognition award 1996). Avocations: ballroom and swing dance. Office: Utah State U Dept Biology Logan UT 84322-5305 Fax: 435-797-1575. E-mail: dwroberts@biology.usu.edu.

ROBERTS, DORIS, actress; b. St. Louis, Nov. 4, 1930; d. Larry and Ann (Meltzer) R.; m. Michael E. Cannata, June 21, 1950; 1 child, Michael R.; m. William Goyen, Nov. 10, 1963 (dec.) Student, NYU, 1950-51; studies with, Sanford Meisner, Neighborhood Playhouse, N.Y.C., 1952-53, Lee Strasberg, Actors' Studio, 1956. Ind. stage, screen and TV actress, 1953—. Profl. stage debut, Ann Arbor, Mich., 1953; appeared in summer stock Chatham, Mass., 1955; Broadway debut in The Time of Your Life, 1955; other Broadway and off-Broadway appearances include The Desk Set, 1955, The American Dream, 1961, The Death of Bessie Smith, 1961, The Office, 1965, The Color of Darkness, 1963, Marathon 33, 1963, Secret Affair of Mildred Wilde, 1972, Last of the Red Hot Lovers, 1969-71, Bad Habits, 1973 (Outer Circle Critics award 1974), Cheaters, 1976, Fairie Tale Theatre, 1985, The Fig Tree, 1987, It's Only a Play, 1992; movie debut Something Wild, 1961, movies include Barefoot in the Park, 1968, No Way to Treat a Lady, 1973, A Lovely Way to Die, 1969, Honeymoon Killers, 1969, A New Leaf, 1970, Such Good Friends, 1971, Little Murders, 1971, Heartbreak Kid, 1972, Hester Street, 1975, The Taking of Pelham, One, Two, Three, 1974, The Rose, 1979, Good Luck, Miss Wyckoff, 1979, Rabbit Test, 1979, Ordinary Hero, 1986, #1 with a Bullet, 1987, For Better or for Worse-Street Law, 1988, National Lampoon's Xmas Vacation, 1989, Used People, 1992, The Night We Never Met, Momma Mia, 1994, Walking to Waldheim, 1995, The Grass Harp, 1995, A Fish in the Bathtub, 1997, My Giant, 1998, All Over the Guy, 2001, Dickie Roberts-Child Star, 2002; TV debut on Studio One, 1958, Mary Hartman, Mary Hartman, 1975, Mary Tyler Moore Hour, 1976, Soap, 1978-79, Angie, 1979-80, Remington Steele, 1984-88, Lily Tomlin Comedy Hour, Barney Miller, Alice, Full House, Perfect Strangers, Sunday Dinner, A Family Man, The Fig Tree (PBS), 1987, (TV films) The Story Teller, 1979, Ruby and Oswald, 1978, It Happened One Christmas, 1978, Jennifer: A Woman's Story, 1979, The Diary of Anne Frank, 1982, A Letter to Three Wives, Blind Faith, 1989, The Sunset Gang, 1990, Crossroads, 1993, Dream On, 1993, The Boys, 1993, A Time To Heal, 1994, A Mom For Christmas, Murder She Wrote, Step By Step, Burk's Law Walker, Texas Ranger, 1994, Amazing Grace, 1995, High Society, 1996, Everybody Loves Raymond, 1996—, A Thousand Men and a Baby, 1997, One True Love, 2000, Sons of Miseltoe, 2001. Recipient Emmy award, NATAS, 1984—85, 2001, Emmy nominations, 1986, 1988, 1991, 1998—99, 2001, 2002, winner Viewers for Quality TV, 1998—99, Am. Comedy Awards, 1999, TV Guide award, 2001—02. Mem. SAG, AFTRA, Actors Equity Assn., Dirs. Guild Am.

ROBERTS, DORIS EMMA, epidemiologist, consultant, medical/surgical nurse; b. Toledo, Dec. 28, 1915; d. Frederic Constable and Emma Selina (Reader) Roberts. Diploma, Peter Bent Brigham Sch. Nursing, Boston, 1938; BS, Geneva Coll., Beaver Falls, Pa., 1944; MPH, U. Minn., 1958; PhD, U. N.C., 1967. RN Mass. Staff nurse Vis. Nurse Assn., New Haven, 1938—40; sr. nurse Neighborhood House, Millburn, NJ, 1942—45; supr. Tb Baltimore County Dept. Health, Towson, Md., 1945—46; Tb cons. Md. State Dept. Health, Balt., 1946—50; cons., chief nurse Tb program USPHS, Washington, 1950—57, cons. divsn. nursing, 1958—63; chief nursing practice br. Health Resources Adminstrn., HEW, Bethesda, Md., 1966—75; adj. prof. U. N.C. Sch. Pub. Health, 1975—92. Cons. WHO, 1961—82. Contbr. articles to profl. jours. With USPHS, 1945—75. Recipient Disting. Alumna award, Geneva Coll., 1971, Disting. Svc. award, USPHS, 1971, Outstanding Achievement award, U. Minn., 1983. Fellow: APHA (v.p. 1978—79, Disting. Svc. award Pub. Health Nursing sect. 1975, Sedgwick Meml. medal 1979), Am. Acad. Nursing (hon.); mem.: Am. Nursing Assn., Inst. Medicine of NAS, Sigma Theta Tau, Delta Omega. Democrat. Episcopalian. Avocations: needlepoint, gardening, reading. Home: 9707 Old Georgetown Rd Apt 1112 Bethesda MD 20814-1746

ROBERTS, E. F. lawyer, educator; b. 1930; m. Alice A. Dunn, July 4, 1955; children: Martha, Ernest III, Michael, Marianne. BA, Northeastern U., Boston, 1952; LL.B., Boston Coll., 1954. Bar: Mass. 1954. Asst. prof. law Villanova U., Pa., 1957-59, assoc. prof. law, 1959-60, prof. law, 1960-64, Cornell U., Ithaca, N.Y., 1964-96, Edwin H. Woodruff prof. law, emeritus prof., 1996. Vis. prof. Nottingham U., Eng., 1962-63, Harvard U., 1983; mem. edn. panel Environ. Law Reporter, 1971-80; cons. in field. Author: Public Regulation on Title Insurance, 1960, Land Use Planning, 2d edit., 1975, Law and the Preservation of Agricultural Land, 1982, (with Strong et al) McCormick on Evidence, 5th edit., 1999. Mem. Am. Law Inst. (life). Office: Cornell U Sch Law Ithaca NY 14853 E-mail: roberts@postoffice.law.cornell.edu.

ROBERTS, EDWARD BAER, technology management educator; b. Chelsea, Mass., Nov. 18, 1935; s. Nathan and Edna (Podradchik) Roberts; m. Nancy Helen Rosenthal, July 14, 1959; children: Valerie Jo Friedman, Mitchell Jonathan, Andrea Lynne. BSEE, MSEE, MIT, 1958, MS in Mgmt., 1960, PhD in Econs., 1962. Founding mem. system dynamics program MIT, 1958-84, instr., 1959-61, asst. prof., 1961-65, assoc. prof., 1965-70, prof., 1970—, David Sarnoff prof. mgmt. of tech., 1974—, assoc. dir. research program on mgmt. of sci. and tech., 1963-73, chmn. tech. and health mgmt. group, 1973-88, chmn. mgmt. of tech. and innovation, 1988-99, chmn. ctr. for entrepreneurship, 1992-94, 97—, co-dir. internat. ctr. rsch. mgmt. tech., 1993-2000, dir. mgmt. of tech. program, 1980-89, co-chmn., 1989-99, chmn. mgmt. tech. innovation and entrepreneurship, 1999—. Co-founder, dir. Med. Info. Tech., Inc., Westwood, Mass., 1969—; co-founder, gen. ptnr. Zero Stage Capital Group, 1981—99; bd. dirs. Advanced Magnetics, Inc., Cambridge, Pegasystems, Inc., Cambridge, SOHU.com, Inc., Beijing, PR Restaurants, LLC, Andover, Mass. Author: (book) The Dynamics of Research and Development, 1964, Systems Simulation for Regional Analysis, 1969, The Persistent Poppy, 1975, The Dynamics of Human Service Delivery, 1976, Entrepreneurs in High Technology, 1991; prin. author, editor: book Managerial Applications of System Dynamics, 1978; editor (with others): Biomedical Innovation, 1981; editor: Generating Technological Innovation, 1987, Innovation, 2002; mem. editl. bd.: IEEE Trans. on Engring. Mgmt., mem. editl. bd.: Jour. Tech. Mgmt., mem. editl. bd.: Indsl. Mktg. Mgmt., mem. editl. bd.: Jour. Engring. and Tech. Mgmt., mem. editl. bd.: Jour. Product Innovation Mgmt., mem. editl. bd.: Sloan Mgmt. Rev., mem. editl. bd.: Tech. Forecasting and Social Change. Mem.: IEEE, Tau Kappa Alpha, Eta Kappa Nu, Tau Beta Pi, Sigma Xi. Home: 300 Boylston St Apt 1102 Boston MA 02116-3940 Office: MIT 50 Memorial Dr Cambridge MA 02142-1347

ROBERTS, EDWARD GRAHAM, librarian; s. Samuel Noble and Frances Johnson (Boykin) R.; m. Anna Jean Walker, Nov. 12, 1949; children: Galer Walker, Edward Graham, John Boykin. BA, U. South, 1943; BA in Library Sci., Emory U., 1948; PhD, U. Va., 1950. Curator manuscripts Duke U., Durham, N.C., 1948-52; dir. libraries (Drake U.), Des Moines, 1952-56; dir. Southeastern Interlibrary Research Facility, Atlanta, 1956-59; asst. prof. info. sci. Ga. Inst. Tech., 1963-66, assoc. prof., 1966-69, prof., 1969-73, assoc. dir. libraries, 1966-71, dir. libraries, 1971-84, dir. emeritus, 1984—. Chmn. info bank com. Ga. Tech. Service Program, Atlanta, 1965-67; mem. exec. bd. Southeastern Library Network, Atlanta, 1973-74; library cons. So. Regional Edn. Bd., Atlanta, 1958-59 Compiler, editor: Southeastern Supplement to the Union List of Serials, 1959; author: Literature of Science and Engineering, 1966, 2d edit.,1969. Served with U.S. Army, 1942-43. Mem. ALA, Southeastern Library Assn., Ga. Library Assn. Democrat. Episcopalian. Home: 1639 Adelia Pl NE Atlanta GA 30329-3807

ROBERTS, EDWIN ALBERT, JR. newspaper editor, journalist; b. Weehawken, N.J., Nov. 14, 1932; s. Edwin Albert and Agnes Rita (Seuferling) R.; m. Barbara Anne Collins, June 14, 1958; children: Elizabeth Adams, Leslie Carol, Amy Barbara, Jacqueline Harding. Student, Coll. William and Mary, 1952-53, NYU, evenings 1955-58; AA in Coll. & Cmty. Svc., St. Petersburg Jr. Coll., 1994. Reporter N.J. Courier, Toms River, 1953-54, Asbury Park (N.J.) Press, 1954-57; reporter Wall Street Jour., N.Y.C., 1957, editorial writer, 1957-63; news editor Nat. Observer, Silver Spring, Md., 1963-68, columnist, 1968-77; editorial writer, columnist Detroit News, 1977-78, editorial page editor, 1978-83; editor editorial page Tampa Tribune, 1983—. Author: Elections, 1964, 1964, Latin America, 1965, The Smut Rakers, 1966, Russia Today, 1967; Editor anthology: America Outdoors, 1965. Recipient Disting. Reporting Bus. award U. Mo., 1969; Pulitzer prize for distinguished commentary, 1974 Mem. Am. Soc. Newspaper Editors, Nat. Conf. Editorial Writers Office: 202 S Parker St Tampa FL 33606-2308

ROBERTS, ERNST EDWARD, marketing consultant; b. Wheeling, W.Va., Dec. 19, 1926; s. Charles Emmitt and Virginia Mae (Stephenson) R.; m. Donna Clare Davis, Dec. 27, 1949; children: Ernst Edward II, Carol Lee Roberts Gaydac. BS, U.S. Mil. Acad., 1949; MBA, Xavier U., Cin., 1954; MS in Mech. Engring., U. So. Calif., 1957; grad. with distinction, Air War Coll., 1970. Commd. 2nd lt. U.S. Army, 1949, advanced through grades to brig. gen., 1971, served as officer in combat Korea, 1950-52; prof. mil. sci. Xavier U., Cin., 1952-54; mgmt. asst. to asst. comdt. U.S. Army Air Def. Sch., Fort Bliss, Tex., 1957-60; admissions officer U.S. Mil. Acad., West Point, N.Y., 1961-62, asst. to supt. (pres.), 1962-64, dir. admissions, 1964-65; comdg. officer 3d Missile Battalion, 71st Arty., Fed. Republic of Germany, 1965-67; staff officer Gen. Staff U.S. Army, Washington, 1968-70; comdg. officer NATO Air Defense Arty. Group, Germany, 1970-71; comdg. gen. 38th Air Def. Arty. Brigade, Korea, 1971-72; asst. comdt. U.S. Army Air Def. Sch. and Ctr., Fort Bliss, Tex., 1972-74; retired U.S. Army, 1974; v.p. bldg. and property mgr. El Paso (Tex.) Nat. Bank and Corp., 1974-79, sr. v.p., dir. personnel and tng., 1979-83, exec. v.p., dir. mktg., 1983-92; mktg. cons., 1992—. Mem. exec. mgmt. com. Tex. Commerce Bank, El Paso, 1983-92; vis. lectr. mktg. Webster U. Mem. bd. advisors SBA; mem. mayor's Citizens Com. on Police Dept. Matters, El Paso; mem. Task Force to Evaluate Mgmt. of Sheriff's Dept.; head bond-issue campaign, El Paso.; adv. dir. Armed Services YMCA, past pres.; adv. dir. nat. bd. dirs. Armed Svcs. YMCA, El Paso Community Found.; past pres. U. Tex.-El Paso Eldorados; mem. bd., trustee Found. Lighthouse for Blind; chmn. adv. bd. dirs. El paso Bus. Com. for Arts; chmn. capital fund drive com. Rio Grande Girl Scouts Am., Plaza Theatre-Plaza Park Restoration bd.; past mem. campaign cabinet United Way El Paso County; chmn. Capital Fund Drive, Air Def. Artillery Mus., Ft. Bliss, Tex.,; bd. dirs. City of El Paso, mem. steering com. Safe 2000; bd. dirs. Crimestoppers of El Paso. Decorated D.S.M., Legion of Merit, Silver Star, Meritorious Svc. medal; recipient Pro Eclesio Et Pontifice, Vatican, 1971; Conquistador award City of El Paso, Liberty Bell award Legal Community El Paso, 1988. Mem. Am. Inst. Banking, Assn. U.S. Army (Gen. Army Omar N. Bradley chpt.), El Paso C. of C. (mem. armed forces com., chmn. spl. task force to evaluate chamber mgmt.), Mil. Order World Wars (chpt. chmn. citizen of yr. award 1996-2001), U.S. Army Air Def. Arty. Assn. (past pres.), El Past Club (past pres., bd. dirs.), Rotary (past pres.). Republican. Roman Catholic. Home: 8212 Antero Pl El Paso TX 79904-2401

ROBERTS, ESTHER LOIS, patent attorney, piano educator, composer, writer; b. Rockwood, Tenn. d. Reva Gretchen (Crowder) H. BA in Biology, BA in Botany, BM in Piano Lit./Pedagogy, MM in Piano Lit./Pedagogy, U. Tenn., Knoxville; JD, U. Tenn, Knoxville, 2001. Pvt. piano instr., Knoxville; law clk. Baker, McReynolds, Byrne, O'Kane & Shea; patent atty. Dept. of Energy, Oak Ridge, Tenn., 2001—. Composer (youth choir cantata) Children of Love, (soprano solo) Corn Husk Moon; author: (children's book series) Sam the Horse, Sam Gets Ready for School, others, 1996; contbr. to Tenn. Law Review. Mem. ABA (student mem.), Okla. Bar Assn., Tenn. Bar Assn., Am. Musicians Coll., Am. Indian Horse Registry, Great Smoky Mountain Indian Horse Club (pres.), Crossroads Dressage Soc., Nat. Soc. DAR, Scottish Clan Donnachaidh. Christian Scientist. Home and Office: Starlight Farm PO Box 32663 Knoxville TN 37930-2663 E-mail: starlight.farm@worldnet.alt.net.

ROBERTS, EVAN ELIJAH, JR. structural engineer, architect; b. Goree, Tex., Feb. 28, 1922; s. Evan Elijah and Mable Sue (Wilfong) R.; m. Colleen Verne Moore, Sept. 29, 1944; children: Charles Evan, Margaret Ann. BS in Archtl. Engring., Tex. Tech U., 1948; MS in Meteorology, Calif. Inst. Tech., 1952. Draftsman Haynes & Kirby, Lubbock, Tex., 1948-54; ptnr. Stiles, Roberts and Messersmith, 1954-77, Roberts-Johnson, Lubbock, 1977-80; v.p. Fanning, Fanning & Agnew, Inc., 1980-84; pres. Roberts and Thoma, Inc., 1980-96; chmn. bd. RTR Engrs., Inc., 1996—. Chmn. bd. dirs. Lubbock YMCA, 1968-70; chmn. bd. dirs. Lubbock Regional Mental Health Mental Retarded Ctr., Lubbock, 1986-88; mem. Lubbock City Bldg. Bd. Appeals, 1967-74. Capt. USAF, 1942-55. Named Disting. Engr., Tex. Tech U. Coll. Engring., 1976. Mem. NSPE, AIA (pres. Lubbock chpt. 1964), Am. Arbitration Assn. (arbitrator), Tex. Soc. Profl. Engrs. (pres. South Plains chpt. 1962, Engr. of Yr. 1991), Khiva Temple. Presbyterian. Avocations: travel, golf, photography, bridge. Home: 9408 Vicksburg Ave Lubbock TX 79424-4842 Office: RTR Engrs Inc 2574 74th St Ste 202 Lubbock TX 79423-1440

ROBERTS, FRANCIS STONE, advertising executive; b. Scranton, Pa., Aug. 15, 1944; s. Gordon Link and Eleanor Swartz (Stone) R.; children: Francis Stone, Link McGregor. BA, Grove City (Pa.) Coll., 1966; A.M.P., U. Chgo., 1984. With media dept., then account exec. Compton Advt. Inc., N.Y.C., 1966-69; account exec. Tatham-Laird & Kudner Advt., 1969-70; account supr., v.p. SSC&B Advt. Inc., 1970-78, sr. v.p., mgmt. supr., 1994; group exec. v.p. SSC&B: Lintas Advt. Worldwide, 1987-89; COO, pres. Lintas, N.Y., 1990-94; mem. policy and ops. coms., chmn. strategy rev. bd. Lintas N.Y.; also dir. Lintas N.Y. and U.S.A.; CEO, chmn. The CEO-Gotham Grp., N.Y.C., 1994-95; chmn., CEO Gotham Inc., 1995—; mng. dir. Gotham Ltd., London, 1996—. Mem. bd. dirs. Am. Assn. Advertising Agencies, Am. Advertising Fedn., The Ad Coun.; bd. trustees Pro Ad PAC. Emergency rm. com. Lenox Hill Hosp., Grove City Coll. alumni coun., 1999—. Mem. William Penn Charter Alumni Assn. (pres. N.Y. chpt. 1984-88), Ad Club N.Y., The Union League N.Y. Clubs: New Canaan Field, New Canaan Winter, New Canaan Country. Republican. Presbyterian. Home: 28 Landing Dr Dobbs Ferry NY 10522 Office: Gotham Inc Fl 17 100 5th Ave New York NY 10011-6996 also: Gotham: Paris 33 Rue Vernet 75008 Paris France E-mail: fsrgotham@aol.com.

ROBERTS, GEORGE BERNARD, JR. management and government relations consultant, former state legislator; b. Andover, Mass., June 13, 1939; s. George Bernard and Helene F. (Eversen) R.; m. Margaret Fay Edmunds, Aug. 26, 1967; children: Abigail Emerson, Jessica Swift. BS, U. N.H., 1964, M.P.A., 1967. Ptnr. Roberts Real Estate Assocs., Gilmanton, N.H., 1966—; mem. N.H. Ho. of Reps., 1967-80, majority leader, 1971-74, speaker, 1975-76, 77-78, 79-80; pres. Policy Mgmt. Assocs., Concord, N.H., 1980—. Pres. and treas. Concord, Concord Coach Soc. Del. Nat. Rep. Conv., 1972-76; mem. N.H. Constl. Conv., 1974, 84; N.H. Rep. Party Fin. Com.; pres. Nat. Conf. State Legislatures, 1979-80; chmn. exec. com. 1st Congl. Soc. Gilmanton. Mem. Nat. Rep. Legislators Assn. (founding, past pres.), Masons, Shriners, Scottish Rite, Historic Dist. Commn. Rilmanton, Sigma Alpha Epsilon. Republican. Office: Gilmanton Policy Mgmt Assocs 4 Park St Ste 100 Concord NH 03301-6313

ROBERTS, GEORGE J. information technology executive; Regional mgr. north ctrl. region Oracle Corp., Redwood City, Calif., 1990, group v.p. ctrl. sales divsn., 1990—97, sr. v.p. Bus. Online Application hosting initiative, 1997—98, sr. v.p. N.Am. sales, 1998—99, exec. v.p. N.Am. sales, 1999—. Office: Oracle Corp 500 Oracle Pkwy Redwood City CA 94085*

ROBERTS, GLORIA JEAN, writer; b. Bklyn., Aug. 4, 1959; d. Albert Brown and Alma Julia Ruth Brooks; m. Floyd D. Roberts, Apr. 23, 1982; stepson: Charles Richard Roberts. Student, Ohio Art Inst, 1977-81. Author: The Stienhardt Memoirs, 1998, vol. 2, 2000, Maxx Mann Series, 1998;one-woman shows include C.W. Post Coll., Brookville, N.Y., 1997, exhibited in group shows at Harborsfield Gallery, Greenlawn, N.Y., 1999—2000, Ward-Nasse Gallery, N.Y.C., 2001—; composer: Love 'Em and Leave Em Behind, 2000, Thoughts of a X-Mas Long Ago, 2001. Fundraiser Ackerman for Senate, N.Y.C., 1994. Mem. John Lennon Supper Club (pres., founder). Democrat. Avocations: collecting teddy bears, photography, poetry, yoga, tennis. Home: 205 Duncan Elder Dr Greenlawn NY 11740-2429 E-mail: gjroberts@aol.com.

ROBERTS, HAROLD ROSS, medical educator, hematologist; b. Four Oaks, N.C., Jan. 4, 1930; s. Walter Lee and Matilda Alicia (Daughtry) R.; m. Marilyn Claassen; children— Eric Michael, John Claassen BS, U. N.C., 1952, MD, 1955. Research assoc. U. N.C., Chapel Hill, 1961-62, instr. medicine, 1962-64, asst. prof., 1964-67, assoc. prof., 1967-70, prof., 1970—, chief hematology, 1968-77, dir. Hemophilia Treatment Ctr., 1977-80, dir. Ctr. for Thrombosis and Hemostasis, 1978—, co-chief hematology and oncology, 1979-81, chief hematology, 1981—. Vis. prof. U. Aarhus, Denmark, 1973-74; dir. clin. coagulation lab. N.C. Meml. Hosp., Chapel Hill, 1977— Assoc. editor Thrombosis & Hemostasis, 1975-81; editor Hemostasis, 1975-83; mem. editorial bd. Blood, 1976-82, assoc. editor, 1983— ; contbr. articles to profl. jours. Chmn. Orange County Bd. Adjustment, N.C. Recipient Disting. Career award Temple U. Health Sci. Ctr., Stockholm, 1983 Fellow ACP; mem. Assn. Am. Physicians, Am. Soc. for Clin. Investigation, AMA, Internat. Soc. on Thrombosis and Hemostasis Anglican. Avocations: arborist; ornithology; philosophy. Home: 2502 Jones Ferry Rd Chapel Hill NC 27516-9369 Office: U NC Chapel Hill Sch Medicine Ctr Thrombosis & Hemostasis Campus Box 7015 Chapel Hill NC 27514

ROBERTS, HARRY MORRIS, JR. lawyer; b. Dallas, June 10, 1938; s. Harry Morris and La Frances (Reilly) R.; m. Nancy Beth Johnson, Mar. 7, 1964; children: Richard Whitfield, Elizabeth Lee. BBA, So. Meth. U., 1960; LLB, Harvard U., 1963. Bar: Tex. 1963, U.S. Dist. Ct. (no. dist.) Tex. 1964, U.S. Ct. Appeals (5th cir.) 1972, U.S. Supreme Ct. 1971. Assoc. Thompson & Knight, Dallas, 1963-69, ptnr., 1970-75, sr. ptnr., 1975—. Lawyer; b. Dallas, June 10, 1938; s. Harry Morris and La Frances (Reilly) R.; m. Nancy Beth Johnson, Mar. 7, 1964; children: Richard Whitfield, Elizabeth Lee. BBA, So. Meth. U., 1960; LLB, Harvard U., 1963. Bar: Tex. 1963, U.S. Dist. Ct. (no. dist.) Tex. 1964, U.S. Ct. Appeals (5th cir.), 1972, U.S. Supreme Ct. 1971. Assoc. Thompson & Knight, Dallas, 1963-69, ptnr., 1970-75, sr. ptnr., 1975—; chmn. real estate, probate and trust law sect. State Bar Tex., 1984-85; vis. scholar U. Tex. Law Sch., 1986. Contbr. articles to legal jours. Trustee Shelter Ministries of Dallas, 1982— (chmn. bd. trustees 1992-95). Mem. ABA, Dallas Bar Assn. (chmn. real estate sect. 1981), Am. Bar Found., Tex. Bar Found., Dallas Bar Found., Am. Coll. Real Estate Lawyers, Tex. Coll. Real Estate Attys. (vice chair, bd. dirs. 1990-93). Episcopalian. Clubs: Salesmanship (Dallas), Dallas Country. Contbr. articles to profl. jours. Trustee Shelter Ministries of Dallas, 1982—, chmn. bd. trustees, 1992-95. Mem. ABA, Dallas Bar Assn. (chmn. real estate sect. 1981), Am. Bar Found., Tex. Bar Found., Dallas Bar Found., Am. Coll. Real Estate Lawyers, Tex. Coll. Real Estate Attys. (vice-chmn., bd. dirs. 1990-93), Salesmanship Club (Dallas), Dallas Country Club. Episcopalian. Office: Thompson & Knight 1700 Pacific Ave Ste 3300 Dallas TX 75201-4693 E-mail: robertsh@tklaw.com.

ROBERTS, JAMES ALLEN, urologist; b. Beach, N.D., May 31, 1934; s. Earl Fernando and Maria Ellen Roberts; m. Hilda Peachy Roberts, Nov. 29, 1986; children from previous marriage: Jennifer Lou Roberts Walsh, Mary Ellen Roberts Wargo, Thomas Jay. MD, U. Chgo., 1959. Diplomate: Am. Bd. Urology. Intern U. Chgo. Sch. Medicine, 1959-60, resident in urology, 1961-65; mem. faculty Tulane U. Med. Sch., New Orleans, 1971-99, prof. emeritus urology, 1975—, assoc. chmn., 1986—; sr. research scientist, head dept. urology Tulane Regional Primate Research Center, Covington, 1972-99; prof. emeritus, 1999—; fellow Fogarty Sr. Internat. NIH, 1984. Mem. editorial bd. Am. Jour. Kidney Diseases and Urol. Rsch.; contbr. articles to profl. jours. Bd. dirs. Highland Park Hosp., 1985-87. Recipient grants NIH, Original Rsch. award Southern Med. Assn., 1990, Cert. Achievement Am. Urological Assn., 1997; Fulbright Sr. scholar, 1999-2000. Fellow ACS; mem. St. Tammany Parish Med. Soc. (pres. 1979), Soc. Rsch. on Calculous Kinetics, La. Urol. Soc., Am. Urol. Assn., Soc. Univ. Urologists, Nat. Kidney Found., Soc. Exptl. Biology and Medicine, Nat. Inst. Health (SAT study sect. 1995-99), Sigma Xi. Office: 285 Roberts Dr Hendersonville NC 28739-9457 E-mail: jrhr285@home.com.

ROBERTS, JAMES CARL, communications executive, engineer; b. Orlando, Fla., May 6, 1953; s. James Ira and Avis Jean (Marg) R.; m. Lynne K. Lovvorn, Sept. 29, 1980; children: William D, Christine N., Jameson S., Michael B. BSEE, U. Miss., 1974; MBA, Newport (Calif.) U., 1988, DBA, 1992. Registered profl. engr., Kans. Pres. Accent Communications, Lakeland, Fla., 1977-80; engring. mgr. Motorola Corp., Foster City, Claif., 1980-83; regional mgr. MCI, Washington, 1983-84; dir. McCaw Communications, Denver, 1984-86; pres., chief exec. officer Communications Group Internat., 1986-97; chief exec. officer Metro Page of Fla., Boca Raton, 1988-97, Metrotek Ariz., Phoenix, 1988-97; founder, pres. VDC Corp., Greenwich, Conn., 1997-98; CEO, bd. chmn. Telecom. Wireless Corp., 1998—. Chief operating br. Tri-Pro, Denver, 1988-97, CGI, Inc., Denver, 1986-97, Metro, Inc., Ft. Meyers, Fla., 1988-97, CGI, Denver, 1992-97, Albania, 1992-97; bd. dirs. Malta Cellular, Valeta; chmn., gen. dir. CGI-MT of Serbia, Yugoslavia, 1990-92; gen. dirs., chmn. Serbia Cellular, 1989-92. Author: Cellular for Malta, 1987. Staff sgt. USAF, 1969-77. Mem. Cellular Telephone Industry Assn., Telocator, Colo. Arabian Assn., Intercircle, Internat. Arabian Assn., Met. Club, St. James Club. Republican. Baptist. Office: VDC 75 Holly Hill Ln Greenwich CT 06830-6098

ROBERTS, JAMES HAROLD, III, lawyer; b. Omaha, Aug. 11, 1949; s. James Harold Jr. and Evelyn Doris (Young) R.; m. Marilyn Novak, June 29, 1974; children: Jessica Noël, Meredith Caitlin. BA, U. Notre Dame, 1971; JD, St. Louis U., 1974. Bar: Iowa 1974, U.S. Ct. Mil. Appeals 1974, U.S. Supreme Ct. 1979, D.C. 1981. Govt. contract atty. U.S. Gen. Acctg. Office, Washington, 1978-83, U.S. Dept. Treasury, Washington, 1983-88; pvt. practice Van Scoyoc Kelly PLLC, 1988—. Editor St. Louis U. law rev., 1973-74. Served to capt. JAGC, U.S. Army, 1974-78, lt. col. USAR/NG, 1978-99. Mem. ABA (pub. contract law sect.), D.C. Bar Assn., Fed. Bar Assn. Roman Catholic. Home: 308 N Monroe St Arlington VA 22201-1736 Office: Van Scoyoc Kelly PLLC 101 Constitution Ave NW Ste 675E Washington DC 20001-1737 E-mail: jroberts@vsklaw.com.

ROBERTS, JAMES LEWIS, medical sciences educator; b. Lima, Peru, Oct. 23, 1951; U.S. citizen; s. David and Mary (Fuller) R.; m. Mariann Blum, Mar. 7, 1986. BS, Colo. State U., 1973; PhD, U. Oreg., 1977. Fellow U. Calif., San Francisco, 1977-79; asst. prof. Columbia U., N.Y.C., 1979-86, assoc. prof., 1986; dir., prof. Mt. Sinai Sch. Medicine, 1986-90, prof., 1990-2001, U. Tex., San Antonio, 2001—. Cons. Calif. Biotech., Mountain View, Calif., 1986-88, NIH, Bethesda, Md., 1979—. NIH Rsch. grantee, 1979—, NSF Rsch. grantee, 1981-84, 95-99, Mellon Found. Rsch. grantee, 1980-84. Mem. AAAS, Soc. for Neurosci., Endocrine Soc., Internat. Endocrine Soc., N.Y. Acad. Scis., Am. Soc. Biochemists and Molecular Biologists. Achievements include research in biosynthesis and regulation of the ACTH endorphin and gonadotropin releasing hormone precursor, glucocorticoid and estrogen regulation of gene expression, gene structure. Office: U Tex Health Sci Ctr Dept Pharmacology, MC6205 7703 Floyd Curl Dr San Antonio TX 78229-3900 E-mail: robertsjl0@uthscsa.edu.

ROBERTS, JAMES MCGREGOR, retired professional association executive; b. Moncton, N.B., Can., Nov. 24, 1923; came to U.S., 1949, naturalized, 1956; s. Roland M. and Edith M. (Shields) R.; m. Thelma E. Williams, May 6, 1944; 1 dau., Jana M. B.Commerce, U. Toronto, Ont., Can., 1949. Auditor Citizens Bank, Los Angeles, 1949-54; auditor Acad. Motion Picture Arts and Scis., Hollywood, Calif., 1954—, controller, 1956-71, exec. dir., 1971-89, exec. sec. acad. found., 1971-89, exec. cons. Calif., 1989-92, 1990-93; ret., 1994. Served as pilot Royal Can. Air Force, World War II. Home: 4968 Lerkas Way Oceanside CA 92056-7428 E-mail: thejim@worldnet.att.net.

ROBERTS, JAMES OWEN, financial planning executive, consultant; b. Madison, Wis., Aug. 19, 1930; s. John William and Sada (Buckmaster) R.; m. Georgianna Timmons, Jan. 30, 1954; children: Stephen, Susan, Ellen, Timmons. BS, Ohio State U., 1952; MBA, Case Western Res. U., 1970. With Owens-Ill., Inc., Toledo, 1952-71, food divsn. mgr. N.Y.C., 1963-66, br. mgr. Cleve., 1966-71; mgr. corp. fin. Stone & Webster Securities Corp., 1971-74; from regional dir. to pres. Mgmt. Planning, Inc., 1976-96, chmn., 1996—. Bd. dirs. Zaxis Internat., Inc.; lectr. valuation and bus. ownership succession. Contbr. articles to profl. jours. Trustee Applewood Ctrs. Found., 1996—, Soc. for the Blind, Cleve., 1983—86, Ohio Motorists Assn., 1985—94, chmn., 1990—92; pres. Childrens Svcs., Inc., 1986—88; trustee Great Lakes Theatre, co-chmn., 1998—2001; elder Fairmount Prresbyn. Ch. 1st lt. USAF, 1952—54. Mem. Cleve. Skating Club, Nassau Club, Huron Yacht Club, Chgo. Athletic Assn. Republican. Avocations: sailing, skiing, hiking, photography. Home: 2323 Stillman Rd Cleveland OH 44118-3520 Office: Mgmt Planning Inc 545 Hanna Bldg Cleveland OH 44115 also: 101 Poor Farm Rd Princeton NJ 08540-1941 E-mail: jroberts@mpival.com.

ROBERTS, JEANNE ADDISON, retired literature educator; b. Washington; d. John West and Sue Fisher (Nichols) Addison; m. Markley Roberts, Feb. 19, 1966; children: Addison Cary Steed Masengill, Ellen Carraway Masengill Coster. AB, Agnes Scott Coll., 1946; MA, U. Pa., 1947; PhD, U. Va., 1964. Instr. Mary Washington Coll., 1947-48; instr., chmn. English Fairfax Hall Jr. Coll., 1950-51; tchr. Am. U. Assn. Lang. Center, Bangkok, Thailand, 1952-56; instr. Beirut (Lebanon) Coll. for Women, 1956-57, asst. prof., 1957-60, chmn. English dept., 1957-60; instr. lit. Am. U., Washington, 1960-62, asst. prof., 1962-65, asso. prof., 1965-68, prof., 1968-93. Dean faculties Am. U., 1974; lectr. Howard U., 1971-72; seminar prof. Folger Shakespeare Libr. Inst. for Renaissance and 18th Century Studies, 1974; dir. NEH Summer Inst. for High Sch. Tchrs. on Teaching Shakespeare, Folger Shakespeare Libr., 1984, 85, 86; dir. NEH summer inst. Va. Commonwealth U. 1995, 96 Writings By and About Women in The English Renaissance. Author: Shakespeare's English Comedy: The Merry Wives of Windsor in Context, 1979, The Shakespearean Wild: Geography, Genus and Gender, 1991; editor: (with James G. McManaway) A Selective Bibliography of Shakespeare: Editions, Textual Studies, Commentary, 1975; (with Peggy O'Brien) Shakespeare Set Free, vol. 1, 1993, vol. 2, 1994, vol. 3, 1995, (with Georgianna Ziegler) Shakespeare's Unruly Women, 1997; contbr. articles to scholarly jours. Danforth Tchr. grantee, 1962-63; Folger Sr. fellow, 1969-70, 88. Mem. MLA (chmn. Shakespeare div. 1981-82), Renaissance Soc. Am., Milton Soc., Shakespeare Assn. Am. (trustee 1978-81, 87-89, pres. 1986-87), AAUP (pres. Am. U. chpt. 1966-67), Southeastern Renaissance Conf. (pres. 1981-82), Phi Beta Kappa, Mortar Board, Phi Kappa Phi. Episcopalian. Home: 4931 Albemarle St NW Washington DC 20016-4359

ROBERTS, JERRY, newspaper editor; Polit. editor city desk San Francisco Chronicle, editl. pg. editor, 1995-98, mng. editor, 1998—2002; exec. editor Santa Barbara News-Press, 2002—. Office: Santa Barbara News-Press 715 Anacapa St Santa Barbara CA 93101 Mailing: PO Box 1359 Santa Barbara CA 93102 E-mail: jroberts@newspress.com.*

ROBERTS, JO ANN WOODEN, school system administrator; b. Chgo., June 24, 1948; d. Tilmon and Annie Mae (Wardlaw) Wooden; m. Edward Allen Roberts Sr. (div.); children: Edward Allen Jr., Hillary Ann. BS, Wayne State U., 1970, MS, 1971; PhD, Northwestern U., 1977. Speech, lang. pathologist Chgo. Bd. Edn., 1971-78, adminstr., 1978-88; dir. spl. svcs. Rock Island (Ill.) Pub. Schs., 1988-90; supt. Muskegon Hts. (Mich.) Pub. Schs., 1990-93; deputy supr. Chgo. Pub. Schs., 1993-96; supt. of schs. Hazel Crest (Ill.) Sch. Dist. #152 1/2, 1996-98; cons. Chgo. Pub. Schs., 1998-2000, dep. accountability svcs., 1999—, IntrVention officer, 2000—. Instr. Chgo City C.C., 1976-77; project dir. Edml. Testing Svc., Evanston, Ill., 1976-77; exec. dir. Nat. Speech, Lang. and Hearing Assn., Chgo., 1984-86; hon. guest lectr. Govs. State U., University Park, Ill., 1983-86; cons. in field. Author: Learning to Talk, 1974. Trustee Muskegon County Libr. Bd., 1990, Mercy Hosp. Bd., Muskegon, 1990, St. Mark's Sch. Bd. Dirs., Southborough, Mass., 1989, United Way Bd., Muskegon, 1990; mem. Mich. State Bd. Edn. Systematic Initiative in Math and Sci., 1991, Gov. John Engler Mich. 2000 Task Force, 1991, Chpt. II Adv. Commn., 1991. Recipient Leadership award Boy Scouts Am., 1990; named finalist Outstanding Young Working Women, Glamour Mag., 1984, Outstanding Educator, Blacks in Govt., 1990. Mem. Am. Assn. Sch. Adminstrs., Nat. Alliance Black Sch. Educators, Mich. Assn. Sch. Adminstrs., Assn. Supervision & Curriculum Devel., Phi Delta Kappa. Avocations: creative writing, peotry, modern dance, theater, drawing. Address: Chgo Pub Schs 125 S Clark St Chicago IL 60603-5200

ROBERTS, JOHN CHARLES, law educator; b. Aberdeen, S.D., Feb. 29, 1940; s. Jacob John Schmitt and Leona (Blethen) Blake; m. Kathleen Kelly (div. 1985); children: Katherine, John Charles Jr.; m. Lynn Dale Friedman, Dec. 22, 1985; 1 child, Emily Sara. BS, Northwestern U., 1961; LL.B., Yale U., 1968. Bar: U.S. Dist. Ct. D.C. 1969, Mich. 1981. Assoc. Covington & Burling, Washington, 1968-71; assoc. dean, lectr. Yale U. Law Sch., New Haven, 1971-77; gen. counsel U.S. Senate Com. on Armed Services, 1977-80; adj. prof. law Washington Coll. Law, Am. U., 1978-80; dean, prof. law Wayne State U. Law Sch., Detroit, 1980-86; prof., dean Law Sch. DePaul U., Chgo., 1986-96, v.p. for univ. advancement, 1996-97, prof. law, 1997—. Mem. exec. com. Inst. for Continuing Legal Edn., Chgo., 1988-91. Mem. adv. com. Mich. Psychiat. Soc., 1980-86; bd. dirs. Constl. Rights Found., 1992-96. Lt. USN, 1961-65. Mem. ABA, Assn. Am. Law Schs. (mem. exec. com., chmn. sect. instn. advancement 1987-88, chmn., sec. adminstrn. law schs. 1993-94), Order of Coif. Democrat. Avocations: collecting modern first editions. Office: DePaul U Coll Law 25 E Jackson Blvd Chicago IL 60604-2289

ROBERTS, JOHN D. chemist, educator; b. L.A., June 8, 1918; s. Allen Andrew and Flora (Dombrowski) Roberts; m. Edith Mary Johnson, July 11, 1942; children: Anne Christine, Donald William, John Paul, Allen Walter. AB, UCLA, 1941, PhD, 1944; D in Natural Scis. (hon.) , U. Munich, 1962; DSc (hon.) , Temple U., 1964, Notre Dame U., 1993, U. Wales, 1993, Scripps Rsch. Inst., 1996. Instr. chemistry UCLA, 1944—45; NRC fellow chemistry Harvard U., 1945—46, instr. chemistry, 1946, MIT, 1946, asst. prof., 1947—50, assoc. prof., 1950—52; vis. prof. Ohio State U., 1952, Stanford U., 1973—74; prof. organic chemistry Calif. Inst. Tech., 1953—72, inst. prof. chemistry, 1972—88, inst. prof. chemistry emeritus, lectr., 1988—, dean of faculty, v.p., provost, 1980—83, lectr., 1988—, chmn. divsn. chemistry and chem. engring., 1963—68, acting chmn., 1972—73. Bd. dirs. Huntington Med. Rsch. Insts., 1984—99, Organic Syntheses Inc.; Robert Noyce vis. prof. sci. Grinnell Coll.,

2001. Author: Basic Organic Chemistry Part I, 1955, Nuclear Magnetic Resonance, 1958, Spin-Spin Splitting in High-Resolution Nuclear Magnetic Resonance Spectra, 1961, Molecular Orbital Calculations, 1961; author: (with M.C. Caserio) Basic Principles of Organic Chemistry, 1964, 2d edit., 1977, Modern Organic Chemistry, 1967; author: (with R. Stewart and M.C. Caserio) Organic Chemistry-Methane To Macromolecules, 1971; author: At The Right Place at the Right Time, 1990, ABCs of FT-NMR, 2000; contbg. editor: McGraw-Hill Series in Advanced Chemistry, 1957—60; editor: Organic Syntheses, Vol. 41, 1961; : Spectroscopy, mem. editl. bd.: Organic Magnetic Resonance in Chemistry, mem. editl. bd.: Asymmetry, mem. editl. bd.: Tetrahedron Computer Methodology. Trustee L.S.B. Leakey Found., 1983—92; bd. dirs. Coleman Chamber Music Assn.; adv. com. Calif. Competitive Tech., 1989—. Co-recipient Robert A. Welch award, 1990; named Hon. Alumnus, Calif. Inst. Tech., 1990, SURF dedicatee, 1992; named one of Most Influential Chemists of Last 75 yrs., Chem. and Engring. News, 1998; recipient Alumni Profl. Achievement award, UCLA, 1967, Nichols medal, 1972, Tolman medal, 1975, Michelson-Morley award, 1976, Norris award, 1978, Pauling award, 1980, Theodore Wm. Richards medal, 1982, Willard Gibbs Gold medal, 1983, Golden Plate award, Am. Acad. Achievement, 1983, Priestley medal, 1987, Madison Marshall award, 1989, Nat. Medal Sci., NSF, 1990, Glenn T. Seaborg medal, 1991, Award in nuclear magnetic resource, 1991, Svc. to Chemistry award, 1991, History Maker award, Pasadena Hist. Soc., 1994; fellow, Guggenheim, 1952—53, 1955—56. Mem.: AAAS (councillor 1992—95), NAS (councillor 1980—83, com. on sci. and engring. pub. policy 1983—87, Chem. Scis. award 1999), Am. Acad. Arts and Scis., Am. Philos. Soc. (coun. mem. 1983—86), Am. Chem. Soc. (chmn. organic chemistry divsn. 1956—57, award pure chemistry 1954, Harrison Howe award 1957, Roger Adams award in organic chemistry 1967, Arthur C. Cope award 1994, Chem. Pioneer award 1994, Nakanishi prize 2001), Phi Lambda Upsilon, Phi Lambda Upsilon, Sigma Xi. Office: Calif Inst Tech Crellin Lab Pasadena CA 91125-0001

ROBERTS, JOHN DERHAM, lawyer; b. Orlando, Fla., Nov. 1, 1942; s. Junius P. and Mary E. Roberts; m. Malinda K. Swineford, June 11, 1965; 1 child, Kimberlyn Amanda. Cert., Richmond (Va.) Bus. Coll., 1960; BS, Hampden-Sydney (Va.) Coll., 1964; LLB, Washington & Lee U., 1968. Bar: Va. 1968, Fla. 1969, U.S. Supreme Ct. 1969, U.S. Ct. Customs and Patent Appeals 1970, U.S. Tax Ct. 1970, U.S. Ct. Appeals (5th cir.) 1970, U.S. Ct. Appeals (9th cir.) 1974, U.S. Supreme Ct. 1969. Law clk. U.S. Dist. Ct., Jacksonville, Fla., 1968-69; assoc. Phillips, Kendrick, Gearhart & Aylor, Arlington, Va., 1969-70; asst. U.S. Atty. mid. dist. Fla. U.S. Dept. Justice, Jacksonville, 1970-74, Dist. of Alaska, Anchorage, 1974-77, U.S. magistrate judge, 1977—. Bd. dirs. Teen Challenge Alaska, Anchorage, 1984-93; chmn. Eagle Scout Rev. Bd., 1993—; bd. dirs. Alaska Youth for Christ, 1993-96; govs.'s Prayer Breakfast Com., 1994—, vice-chair, 1998—. Recipient Citizenship award DAR, Anchorage, 1984, plaque, U.S. Navy, Citizen Day, Adak, Alaska, 1980. Mem. ABA, Nat. Conf. Spl. Ct. Judges (exec. bd. 1985-92), 9th Cir. Conf. Magistrates (exec. bd. 1982-85, chmn. 1984-85), Alaska Bar Assn., Anchorage Bar Assn., Chi Phi, Psi Chi, Phi Alpha Delta. Republican. Office: US Magistrate Judge 222 W 7th Ave Unit 46 Anchorage AK 99513-7504

ROBERTS, JOHN J. accounting firm executive; b. 1945; With Coopers & Lybrand, 1967—, ptnr., 1974—, dep. chmn., 1991—, chief oper. officer, 1994-98; global mng. ptnr. PricewaterhouseCoopers, 1998—. Office: PricewaterhouseCoopers 1301 Avenue Of The Americas New York NY 10019-6022

ROBERTS, JOHN PETER LEE, cultural advisor, administrator, educator, writer; b. Sydney, Australia, Oct. 21, 1930; s. Noel Lee and Myrtle Winifred (Reid) R.; m. Christina Van Oordt, July 28, 1962; children— Noel, Christina, Olga. Student, State Conservatorium Music, New South Wales; MA, Carleton U., 1988; DFA (hon.), U. Victoria, 1992; LLD (hon.), U. Man., 1997. With CBC Radio, Toronto, Can., 1955—, producer, 1955—, head music and variety, 1971—, spl. adv. music and arts, 1975; sr. advisor cultural devel., head office Ottawa, 1983-87; mem. exec. bd. Internat. Music Centre, Vienna, 1968-80, first chmn. radio and comml. rec. group, 1969-70, hon. mem., 1980; mem. exec. bd. Internat. Inst. Music Dance and Theatre, 1969-75; bd. govs. Can. Conf. Arts, 1970-76; exec. bd. Internat. Music Coun., Paris, 1973-79; v.p. Internat. Music Council, 1975, pres., 1978-79, Can. Music Centre, Toronto, 1971-77, dir. gen., 1977-81; pres. Can. Music Council, 1968-71, 75-77; dir. Festival Singers of Can., 1965-78, Elmer Iseler Singers, 1979-81, Toronto Mendelssohn Choir, 1969-81, Nat. Youth Orch. Can., 1973-80; chmn. 1st World Music Week, 1975, Internat. Music Day, 1975-82; v.p. Internat. Inst. Audio-Visual Communication and Cultural Devel. (Mediacult), Vienna, 1976-87, pres., 1987-93, Internat. Rsch. Inst. for Media, Communication, Cultural Devel., Vienna, 1993-95. V.p. Musicians Internat. Mus. Aid Fund, Geneva, 1978—79; pres. Les Jeunesses Musicales du Can., 1979—83; jury chmn. Internat. Vocal Competition, Rio de Janeiro, 1979, Esther Honen's Calgary Internat. Piano Competition, 1996; spl. advisor to chmn. Can. Radio-TV and Telecomm. Commn., 1981—83; sr. advisor cultural devel. CBC, 1983—87; dean Faculty of Fine Arts, U. Calgary, 1987—95, adj. prof., 1995—; vis. fellow McGill Inst. Study of Can., McGill U., Montreal, 1995—96; bd. dirs. Esther Honen's Internat. Piano Competition, 1994, chmn., 96, 2000. Mem. editorial bd. Can. Music Book, 1970-77 Mem. exec. bd. dirs. Can. Nat. Commn. for UNESCO, 1976-80; founding pres. Glenn Gould Found., Toronto, 1983—. Decorated Order of Can. (mem., 1983, officer, 1996); Cross of Honour for Sci. and the Arts (Austria). Mem. Can. assn. Fine Arts Deans (chmn. 1989-93), Internat. Coun. Fine Arts Deans (bd. dirs. 1992-94). Office: U Calgary Faculty Fine Arts 2500 University Dr NW Calgary AB Canada T2N 1N4

ROBERTS, JONATHAN S. interventional cardiologist; b. West Palm Beach, Fla., July 26, 1956; s. Hyman J. and Carol A. Roberts; m. Amy B. Roberts, Mar. 6, 1988; children: Arille L., Emily M., Jillian B., Joshua E. BS, U. Fla., 1978; MD, U. Miami, 1982. Diplomate in internal medicine, cardiovascular diseases and interventional cardiology Am. Bd. Internal Medicine. Intern Emory U., Atlanta, 1982-83, resident, 1983-85, fellow, 1986-90; acting chief cardiology VA Hosp., 1990-91; interventional cardiologist Miami Cardiology Group, 1992—. Named one of Best Drs. in South Fla., Miami Metro mag., 1998, 2000, 2001. Fellow Am. Coll. Cardiology. Office: Miami Cardiology Group 8950 N Kendall Dr Ste 601 Miami FL 33176-2139

ROBERTS, JUDITH MARIE, librarian, educator; b. Bluefield, W.Va., Aug. 5, 1939; d. Charles Bowen Lowder and Frances Marie (Bourne) Lowder Alberts; m. Craig Currence Jackson, July 1, 1957 (div. 1962); 1 child, Craig, Jr.; m. Milton Rinehart Roberts, Aug. 13, 1966 (div. 1987). BS, Concord State Tchrs. Coll., 1965. Libr., Cape Henlopen Sch. Dist., Lewes, Del., 1965-91; with Lily's Gift Shop, St. Petersburg, Fla., 1991—. Pres. Friends of Lewes Pub. Libr., 1986-90; chmn. exhibits Govs. Conf. Librs. and Info. Svcs., Dover, Del., 1978; mem. Gov.'s State Library Adv. Coun., 1987-91. Mem. ALA, NEA, Del. State Edn. Assn., Sussex Help Orgn. for Resources Exchange (pres. 1984-85), Del. Library Assn. (pres. 1982-83), Del. Learning Resources Assn. (pres. 1976-77). Methodist. Business E-Mail: skyoff1@juno.com. E-mail: robertsjud@aol.com.

ROBERTS, JULIA FIONA, actress; b. Smyrna, Ga., Oct. 28, 1967; d. Betty and Walter Roberts; m. Lyle Lovett, Jun. 27, 1993 (div. 1995); m. Daniel Moder, July 4, 2002. Film appearances include Blood Red, 1986, Satisfaction, 1987, Mystic Pizza, 1988, Steel Magnolias, 1989 (Acad. Award nominee, Golden Globe award), Pretty Woman, 1990 (Acad. Award nominee, Golden Globe award), Flatliners, 1990, Sleeping With the Enemy, 1991, Hook, 1991, Dying Young, 1991, The Player, 1992, The Pelican Brief, 1993, I Love Trouble, 1994, Ready to Wear (Prêt-à-Porter), 1994, Something To Talk About, 1995, Mary Reilly, 1996, Everybody Says I Love You, 1996, Michael Collins, 1996, My Best Friend's Wedding, 1997, Conspiracy Theory, 1997, Stepmom, 1998, Notting Hill, 1999, Runaway Bride, 1999, Erin Brokovich, 2000 (Acad. award for Best Actress), The Mexican, 2001, America's Sweethearts, 2001, Ocean's Eleven, 2001, Full FRontal, 2002; TV appearances include: AFI's 100 Years...100 Movies, 1998, In the Wild, 1998; TV movies include Baja Oklahoma, 1988 Named Female Star of the Yr., Nat. Assn. Theatre Owners, 1991; recipient People's Choice awards Favorite Motion Picture Actress, 1991, 98, Favorite Comedy/Dramatic Motion Picture Actress, 1992, Favorite Dramatic Motion Picture Actres, 1994; recipient Woman of Yr. award Hasty Pudding Theatricals, 1997, Spl. award Internat. Star of Yr., ShoWest Conv., 1998. Office: ICM 8942 Wilshire Blvd Beverly Hills CA 90211-1934*

ROBERTS, KATHARINE ADAIR, retired bookkeeper; b. Columbus, Ga., June 4, 1930; d. William Lynn and Ella Miller (Adair) R. BA, U. Redlands, 1955; postgrad., San Bernardino Valley Coll., 1971-74, Calif. State U., San Bernardino, 1975-78. Bookkeeper Rettig Machine Shop, Inc., Redlands, Calif., 1970-97, ret., 1997. Pres. Dem. Study Club, San Bernardino, 1967-68, Redlands Dem. Club, 1976, Wilsonian Club, San Bernardino, 1986, World Federalist Assn., Redlands/San Bernardino chpt., 1987—; mem. San Bernardino County Dem. Ctrl. Com., treas. 1977-80; San Bernardino leader World Federalist Assn. Program-Ptnrs. for Global Change. Mem. Dem. Luncheon Club (George E. Brown Amb. of Peace award 2000), Humane Soc. of San Bernardino Valley, Redlands Humane Soc., Redlands Dem. Club (treas.), LWV, Inland Empire Debating Soc. (treas.). Democrat. Home: 798 W 18th St San Bernardino CA 92405-4235

ROBERTS, KATHLEEN JOY DOTY, secondary education educator; b. Jamaica, N.Y., Apr. 19, 1951; d. Alfred Arthur and Helen Caroline (Sohl) Doty; m. Robert Louis Roberts, Nov. 24, 1974; children: Robert Louis, Michael Sean, Kathleen Meagan. BA in Edn., CUNY, 1972, MS in Spl. Edn., 1974; cert. advanced study in ednl. adminstrn., Hofstra U., 1982; postgrad., Nova Southeastern U. Cert. sch. adminstrn., tchr. math., N.Y.; cert. N.Y. Dept. Mental Hygiene; lic. spl. edn. supr., ednl. dminstr., N.Y. Tchr. health conservation Woodside (N.Y.) Jr. H.S., 1973-77; coord. spl. edn. dept. Ridgewood (N.Y.) Jr. H.S., 1977-81; adminstrv. asst., health, compliance and mainstream coord. Grover Cleveland H.S., Ridgewood, 1981—, also coord. transition linkage, resource tchr. mentor, 1981—. Grant writer. Author: Closed Circuit Television and Other Devices for the Partially Sighted, 1971, National Society Colonial Daughters of the Seventeenth Century Lineage Book (Centennial Remembrance edit.), 1999, Universal Design in Online Learning Environments (Society for Information Technology and Teacher Education), 2002, (conf. procs. of SITE of AACE) Universal Design in Online Learning Environments, 2002. Legis. chmn. Fairfield Jr. and Sr. H.S. PTA and Massapequa coun., 1987-92. Mem.: ACM, DAR, NEA, Internat. Soc. Tech. in Edn., N.Y. State Tchrs. Assn., Colonial Dames of the XVII Century, Pilgrim Edward Doty Soc., Colonial Daus. 17th Century (pres. 1985—91, 2000—, registrar, historian Founders chpt. 1991—94, nat. chmn. hist. activities com. 1988—91, nat. councillor, publicity chmn. 1991—94, centennial com. 1994—96, registrar gen. nat. soc. 1997—2000). Republican. Home: 52 Hicksville Rd Massapequa NY 11758-5843 Office: Grover Cleveland HS 2127 Himrod St Flushing NY 11385-1299

ROBERTS, KENNETH LEWIS, investor, lawyer, foundation administrator; b. Dungannon, Va., Dec. 12, 1932; s. Clarence Eugene and Katherine (Osborne) R.; m. Anne Foster Cook, Sept. 10, 1955 (dec. Dec. 5, 1999); children— Kenneth L., Patrick Hagan Foster. BA, Vanderbilt U., 1954, LLB, 1959. Bar: Tenn. Assoc. prof. law Vanderbilt U., 1959-60; assoc. Waller, Lansden & Dortch, Nashville, 1960-66; exec. v.p. Commerce Union Bank, 1966-71; pres., CEO, dir. Cen. Nat. Bank, Richmond, Va., 1971-76; pres., CEO First Am. Nat. Bank, Nashville, 1976-90; dir. First Am. Corp., 1976-90, vice-chmn., 1976-77, pres., CEO, 1977-79, chmn., CEO, 1979-90; pres., exec. dir. FRIST Found., 1991—. Past pres. Cen. Nat. Corp. Trustee Vanderbilt U.; bd. dirs. Leadership Nashville, Montgomery Bell Acad., Country Music Found. Lt. Chem. Corps, AUS, 1955-57. Mem. ABA, Tenn. Bar Assn., Nashville Bar Assn., Nashville C. of C., Belle Meade Country Club, Univ. Club, Ponte Vedra (Fla.) Inn & Club. Office: FRIST Found 3319 W End Ave Ste 900 Nashville TN 37203-6827

ROBERTS, KRISTIE, researcher; b. Atlanta, Dec. 1, 1970; d. Joe Charles and Brucie May Roberts. BA, Fort Valley State Coll., 1993; MPA, Albany State Coll., 1995; postgrad., Jackson State U., 1998—. Field dir. Flint River Girl Scout Coun., Albany, Ga., 1995-96, dir. membership svcs., 1996-97, fund devel. mgr., 1997-98; dir. 2000 Friends Mentoring Program Albany/Dougherty Cmty. Partnership for Edn., 1998; rschr. Jackson (Miss.) State U., 1998—. Contbr. articles to profl. jours. Regent's Opportunity scholar Albany State Coll., 1995, Departmental Tuition scholar Dept. Pub. Policy, Jackson State U., 1998-2001, African-Am. Leadership Program scholar U. Md., 1999—. Mem. Am. Soc. Pub. Adminstrs., Conf. Minority Pub. Adminstrs., PPAD Student Assn. (v.p. 1998-99), PPAD Toastmasters Internat. (pres. 1998—, Leadership award 2001), Public Policy Adminstrn. Avocations: reading, traveling, bowling, singing. Home: PO Box 2104 Jackson MS 39225-2104 Office: Jackson State Univ Box 18 3825 Ridgewood Rd Jackson MS 39211 Fax: 601-432-6322. E-mail: kroberts1201@yahoo.com.

ROBERTS, LARRY SPURGEON, biological sciences educator, zoologist; b. Texon, Tex., June 30, 1935; s. E. Fowler and Frances Wray (Huggins) R.; m. Maria Elek, Feb. 7, 1962; children: Gregory Lorinc, Bruce Tibor, Teresa Margit, Eric Miklos. BS, So. Meth. U., 1956; MS (NSF fellow), U. Ill., 1958; DSc, Johns Hopkins U., 1961. Cert. scuba instr. Nat. Assn. Underwater Instrs. From asst. prof. to prof. zoology U. Mass., Amherst, 1963-79; prof. biol. scis. Tex. Tech U., Lubbock, 1979-90, chmn. dept., 1979-84. Adj. prof. biol. scis. U. Miami, 1990-99, Fla. Internat. U., 1990-93, 99—. Author: (with others) Foundations of Parasitology, 1977, 6th edit., 2000, Integrated Principles of Zoology, 1979, 11th edit., 2000, Biology of Animals, 1982, 7th edit., 1998, The Underwater World of Sport Diving, 1991, Animal Diversity, 3d edit., 2003. Mem. Amherst Dem. Town Com., 1968-79, vice chmn., 1972-76; mem. Amherst Town Meeting, 1966-76; mem. Amherst Zoning Bd. Appeals, 1972-75, vice chmn., 1972-75; recorder West Tex. Dems., 1985-86; mem. Dade County Dem. Exec. Com., 1991—. NIH postdoctoral trainee, 1961-63; NIH fellow, 1969-70; recipient Disting. Service cert. Mass. Tchrs. Assn., 1979 Mem. AAAS, ACLU (vice chmn. Hampshire County chpt. 1966-68, bd. dirs. Lubbock chpt. 1985-89, vice chmn. 1988-89, bd. dirs. Miami, Fla. chpt. 1991—, 1st v.p. 1998-2000, treas. 2000—, Fla. State bd. dirs.), Am. Soc. Parasitologists (Henry Baldwin Ward medal 1971, council mem. at large 1980-83, v.p. 1984-85, 96-97, pres. 1998-99), Am. Micros. Soc. (v.p. 1974-75, exec. com. 1978-81), Mass. Soc. Profs. (pres. 1977-78), Soc. Protozoologists, N.Y. Acad. Scis., Am. Soc. Tropical Medicine and Hygiene, Wildlife Disease Assn., Southwestern Assn. Parasitologists (v.p. 1982, pres. 1983), Southeastern Soc. Parasitologists (pres. elect 1993, pres. 1994), Internat. Soc. Reef Studies, Crustacean Soc., Am. Acad. Underwater Scis., Sigma Xi. Home: 27700 SW 164th Ave Homestead FL 33031-2846 E-mail: RobertsLS@cs.com.

ROBERTS, LAWRENCE GILMAN, telecommunications company executive; b. Dec. 21, 1937; s. Elliott John and Elizabeth (Gilman) R.; m. June Ellen Stuller, 1959 (div. 1973); children: Paul, Kenny. BS, MIT, 1959, MS, 1960, PhD, 1963. Dir. info. proc. Advanced Rsch. Projects Agy. U.S. Dept. Def., Arlington, Va., 1969-73; pres., CEO, GTE Telenet Corp., Vienna, 1973-82; pres. DHL, Redwood City, Calif., 1982-83; chmn., CEO, NetExpress, Inc., Foster City, 1983-93; pres. ATM Systems, Santa Clara, 1993-98; chmn. chief tech. officer Caspian Networks, Palo Alto, 1998—. Recipient L.M. Ericsson award for comms. Mem.: IEEE (Internet award 2000), NAE (Draper award 2001), Assn. Computing Machinery (SIGCOM award), Am. Fedn. Info. Processing (Harry Goode award, W. Wallace McDowell award), IEEE Computer Soc., Sigma Xi. Office: Caspian Networks 170 Baytech Dr San Jose CA 95134 E-mail: lroberts@caspiannetworks.com.

ROBERTS, LEIGH MILTON, psychiatrist; b. Jacksonville, Ill., June 9, 1925; s. Victor Harold and Ruby Harriet (Kelsey) R.; m. Marilyn Edith Kadow, 1946; children: David, Carol Troxell, Paul, Nancy Mills. BS, U. Ill., 1945, MD, 1947. Diplomate: Am. Bd. Psychiatry and Neurology. Intern St. Francis Hosp., Peoria, Ill., 1947-48; gen. practice medicine Macomb, 1948-50; resident in psychiatry U. Wis. Hosps., Madison, 1953-56; staff psychiatrist Mendota (Wis.) State Hosp., 1956-58; mem. faculty U. Wis. Med. Sch., Madison, 1959-89, prof. psychiatry, 1971-89, acting chmn. dept., 1972-75. Cons. in psychiatry, 1989-; mem. spl. rev. bd. Wis. Parole Bd. Sex Crimes Law, 1962-88, forensic cons., 1988—; mem. Dane County Disabilities Bd., 1962-66, Wis. Planning Com. Mental Health, 1963-65, Wis. Planning Com. Health, 1969-71, Wis. Planning Com. Vocat. Rehab., 1966-68, Wis. Planning Com. Health Centers, 1967-71, Wis. Mental Health Adv. Com., 1973-78; bd. dirs. Methodist Hosp., Madison, Dane County Rehab. House, Dane County Assn. Mental Health; cons. in field. Editor: Community Psychiatry, 1966, Comprehensive Mental Health, 1968; contbr. articles profl. jours. Pres. Wis. Council Chs., 1976-78; bd. dirs. Madison Campus Ministry, St. Benedict Center; trustee N.Central Coll., Naperville, Ill. Served with USNR, 1943-45, 50-53. Decorated Bronze Stars, Purple Heart. Fellow Am. Psychiat. Assn. (bd. trustees 1981-84), Wis. Psychiat. Assn. (pres. 1967) Methodist. Home and Office: 722 Sauk Ridge Trl Apt A Madison WI 53705-1157 *Life is a precious gift whose journey is molded and shaped by cumulative experiences and relationships. Religious belief and practice which provides future-oriented hope, disciplined accountability and living service are balanced by professional psychiatric vistas on the uniqueness and worth of each human person.*

ROBERTS, LEONARD H. retail executive; b. Chgo., Feb. 19, 1949; s. Jack and Goldie (Solomon) R.; m. Laurie Susan Osser, Aug. 20, 1967; children: Dawn, Adina, Melissa. BS in Chemistry and Mktg., U. Ill., 1971; JD, DePaul U., 1974. Food scientist Armour Foods, Chgo., 1968-71, Cen. Soya, Chgo., 1971-74; govt. lobbyist Ralston Purina Co., St. Louis, 1974-76, dir. mktg., 1976-78, mng. dir. Raltech Madison, Wis., 1978-81, v.p. food service ops. St. Louis, 1981-85; pres., chief exec. officer Arby's Inc., Atlanta, 1985-89; chmn. bd., chief exec. officer Shoney's Inc., 1989-93; pres. Radio Shack, Fort Worth, Tex., 1993—, Tandy Corp., Fort Worth, 1996—; chmn. pres. & CEO Radioshack Corp., Tex. Bd. dirs. Ghirardelli Chocolate Co., Tandy Corp. Holder numerous patents on Soya protein research. Active United Way Met. Tarrant County, 1994, Nat. Crime Prevention Coun., 1994, Clark U. Students in Free Enterprise, Girl Scouts U.S., Harris Meth. Bd.; mem. exec. com. Fort Worth Symphony. Recipient Pvt. Sector Initiative award Office Pres. of U.S., Washington, 1987, Disting. Achievement award B'nai B'rith, Restaurant Bus. Leadership award, 1991, Golden Plate award Nations Restaurant News, 1991, Wall St. Bronze Critics award, 1992. Mem. ABA, Ill. Bar Assn. Home: 3516 Briarhaven Rd Fort Worth TX 76109-3128 Office: RadioShack 100 Throckmorton St Ste 1800 Fort Worth TX 76102-2800

ROBERTS, LEONARD ROBERT, English language educator, poet; b. Cohoes, N.Y., Mar. 13, 1947; s. Raymond Richard and Margery Elizabeth (Trudeau) R.; m. Denise Geiger, Nov. 12, 1972 (div. June 1978); m. Nancy Jean Crane, Dec. 31, 1981; 1 child, Joshua Roberts; stepchildren: Tamara Day, Bradford Day. BA in English, Siena Coll., Loudonville, N.Y., 1970; MA in English, U. Dayton, 1972; PhD in English, Lehigh U., 1975. Prof. English Northampton C.C., Bethlehem, Pa., 1974—. Vis. prof. poetry Lafayette Coll., Easton, Pa., 1983-85; Fulbright lectr. Janus Pannonious U., Pécs, Hungary, 1988-89, U. Turku, Finland, 1994; judge numerous poetry competitions; condr. workshops and readings in poetry. Author: Cohoes Theater, 1980, From the Dark, 1984, Sweet Ones (Great Lakes & Prairies award 1988), Black Wings, 1989, Learning About the Heart (Silverfish Rev. Ann. chapbook competition winner 1992), Dangerous Angels, 1993, The Million Branches: Selected Poems and Interview, 1993, Counting the Black Angels, 1994, The Trouble-Making Finch, 1998, The Silent Singer: New and Selected Poems, 2001; contbr. poetry to jours. including Am. Poetry Rev., Antaeus, Antioch Rev., Boston Rev., Calif. Quar., Ga. Rev., Ind. Rev., Mass. Rev., Mich. Quar. Rev., Poetry Australia, Paris Rev.; translator: (books) The Selected Poems of Sándor Csoóri, 1992, Call to Me in My Mother Tongue, 1990, Selected Poems of Sándor Csoóri, 1989; translator articles in jours. With USCGR, 1968-74. Recipient Nat. Poetry Series award, 1988, Pa. Coun. on the Arts Writing awards in poetry, 1981, 86-87, 89, 91, 00, Soros Found. Transl. awards for Hungarian transl., 1989-90, 92, 97, Nat. Endowment for Arts Writing awards in poetry, 1984, 89, John Simon Guggenheim Meml. award, 1990-91, Pushcart Prize XVI Best of the Small Presses award for Gift Shop in Pecs, 1991, Witter-Bynner Transl. award, 1991-92, others, Nat. Faculty award in fine arts Am. Assn. Cmty. and Jr. Colls., 1987, Internat. Award for tchg. excellence Coll. Leadership program of Internat. Conf. on Excellence, Austin, Tex., 1989, Prof. Joseph A. Buff award for Alumni of the Yr., Career Achievement, Siena Coll., 1991, Disting. Alumni of Yr. award Lehigh U., 1993, Translation award NEH, 1999, Nat. Endowment fellowship for Coll. Tchrs. and Scholars, 1999. Mem. MLA, Poetry Soc. Am., Poets and Writers, Pa. Coun. on the Arts (adv. bd. 1990—). Democrat. Roman Catholic. Avocations: basketball, swimming, house re-building. Home: 2443 Wassergass Rd Hellertown PA 18055-2111 Office: Northampton CC Dept English Bethlehem PA 18020

ROBERTS, LORIN WATSON, botanist, educator; b. Clarksdale, Mo., June 28, 1923; s. Lorin Cornelius and Irene (Watson) R.; m. Florence Ruth Greathouse, July 10, 1967; children: Michael Hamlin, Daniel Hamlin, Margaret Susan. BA, U. Mo., 1948, MA, 1950; PhD in Botany, U. Mo.-Columbia, 1952. Asst. prof., then assoc. prof. botany Agnes Scott Coll., Decaur, Ga., 1952-57; vis. asst. prof. Emory U., 1952-55; mem. faculty U. Idaho, 1957—, prof. botany, 1967-91, prof. botany emeritus, 1991—; Fulbright research prof. Kyoto (Japan) U., 1967-68; research fellow U. Bari, Italy, 1968; Cabot fellow Harvard, 1974; Fulbright teaching fellow North-Eastern Hill U., Shillong, Meghalaya, India, 1977; Fulbright sr. scholar and fellow Australian Nat. U., Canberra, 1980; sr. researcher U. London, 1984; pres. botany sect. 1st Internat. Congress Histochemistry and Cytochemistry, Paris, 1960; Alexander von Humboldt vis. fellow Australian Nat. U., 1992. Author: Cytodifferentiation in Plants, 1976 (with J.H. Dodds) Experiments in Plant Tissue Culture, 1982, 2d edit., 3d edit. 1995, 1985 (with P.B. Gahan and R. Aloni) Vascular Differentiation and Plant Growth Regulators, 1988; contbr. articles to profl. jours. Served with USAAF, 1943-46. Decorated chevalier de l'Ordre du Merit Agricole France, 1961; Alexander von Humboldt fellow, 1992. Fellow AAAS; mem. N.W. Sci. Assn. (pres. 1970-71), Bot. Soc. Am., Am. Soc. Plant Physiologists, Internat. Assn. Plant Tissue Culture, Am. Inst. Biol. Scis., Idaho Acad. Scis., Sigma Xi, Phi Kappa Phi, Phi Sigma. Home: 920 Mabelle St Moscow ID 83843-3834

ROBERTS, LOUISE NISBET, philosopher, educator; b. Lexington, Ky., Apr. 21, 1919; d. Benjamin and Helen L. Nisbet; m. Warren Roberts, June 14, 1952 (dec.); children: Helen Ward Roberts Hill, Valeria Lamar Roberts Emmett. AB, U. Ky., 1942, MA, 1944; PhD, Columbia U., 1952. Instr. philosophy Fairfax Hall, Waynesboro, Va., 1943-44, Fairmount Casements, Ormond Beach, Fla., 1944-45; mem. faculty Newcomb Coll., Tulane U., 1948—, prof. philosophy, 1969-85, dept. head, prof. emeritus, 1985—. Contbr. articles to profl. jours. Univ. scholar, 1945-46. Mem. AAUW (fellow 1947-48, pres. New Orleans chpt. 1986-88), DAR (vice regent New Orleans chpt. 1987-90, 2002--), So. Soc. Philosophy and Psychology, Phi Beta Kappa (chpt. pres. 1956-57), Delta Delta Delta (fellow 1946-47). Democrat. Episcopalian. Office: Tulane U Dept Philosophy New Orleans LA 70118

ROBERTS, LYNN NOVAK, government employee; b. Dayton, Ohio, Sept. 17, 1941; d. George Vincent and Marjorie Alice Novak; children: Janet Lynn Geier-Moriarty, Rosalie Catherine Geier. BA in English cum laude, U. Ala., 1978. Level III cert. U.S. Army Acquisition Corps. Sec. pvt. sector, 1965-72; contract specialist Dept. of Def., Redstone Arsenal, Ala., 1972—. Author of poetry, articles and short stories. Bd. dirs. Humane Soc., Huntsville, Ala., 1993-94; active animal rescue. Mem. Dog Writers' Assn. Am. (judge 1994). Democrat. Avocations: hiking, camping, reading, boating, research on current novels. Home: 87 Stoney Brook Dr Union Grove AL 35175 E-mail: lynn.roberts@redstone.army.mil.

ROBERTS, LYNNE JEANINE, physician; b. St. Louis, Apr. 19, 1952; d. H. Clarke and Dorothy June (Cockrum) R.; m. Richard Allen Beadle Jr., July 18, 1981; children: Richard Andrew, Erica Roberts. BA with distinction, Ind. U., 1974, MD, 1978. Diplomate Am. Bd. Dermatology, Am. Bd. Pediatrics, Am. Bd. Laser Surgery. Intern in pediats. Children's Med. Ctr., Dallas, 1978-79, resident in pediats., 1979-80; resident in dermatology U. Tex. Southwestern Med. Ctr., 1980-83, chief resident in dermatology, 1982-83, asst. instr. dermatology and pediatrics, 1983-84, asst. prof., 1984-90, assoc. prof., 1990-99; prof., 1999—; physician Cons. Dermatol. Specialists, Dallas, 1990-93; pres. Lynne J. Roberts, MD, PA, 1993—. Dir. dermatology Children's Med. Ctr., Dallas, 1986-2000; dermatology sect. chief Med. City Dallas Hosp., 1994-95, 95-97. Contbr. articles to profl. jours., chpts. to books. Recipient Scholastic Achievement Citation Am. Med. Women's Assn., 1978. Fellow Am. Acad. Dermatology, Am. Soc. Laser Medicine and Surgery (bd. dirs. 1994-97); mem. Soc. Pediatric Dermatology, Am. Soc. Dermatologic Surgery, Tex. Med. Assn., Dallas Zool. Soc., Dallas Arboretum, Kappa Alpha Theta, Alpha Omega Alpha. Avocations: horseback riding, reading, fishing, swimming, camping. Office: Ste 330 7502 Greenville Ave Dallas TX 75231

ROBERTS, MARGARET HAROLD, editor, publisher; b. Aug. 18, 1928; AB, U. Chattanooga, 1950. Editor, pub. series Award Winning Art, 1960-70, New Woman mag., Palm Beach, Fla., 1971-84; editor, pub. BONKERS mag., 1992—2001. Author: juvenile book series Daddy is a Doctor, 1965. Office: PO Box 189 Palm Beach FL 33480-0189

ROBERTS, MARGOT MARKELS, business executive; b. Springfield, Mass., Jan. 20, 1945; d. Reuben and Marion (Markels) R.; children: Lauren B. Phillips, Debrah C. Herman. BA, Boston U. Interior designer Louis Legum Furniture Co., Norfolk, Va., 1965-70; buyer, mgr. Danker Furniture, Rockville, Md., 1970-72; buyer W & J Sloane, Washington, 1972-74; pres. Bus. & Fin. Cons., Palm Beach, Fla., 1976-80, Margot M. Roberts & Assocs., Inc., Palm Beach, 1976—. Dealer 20th century Am. art and wholesale antiques Margot M. Roberts, Inc., Palm Beach, 1989—; v.p., dir. So. Textile Svcs. Inc., Palm Beach. Pres. Brittany Condominium Assn., Palm. Beach, 1983-87; v.p. South Palm Beach Civic Assn., 1983-88; South Palm Beach Pres.'s Assn., 1984-88; vice chmn. South Palm Beach Planning Bd., 1983-88, 90-91; chair Palm Beach County Beach and Shores Coun., 1998—; elected town commr. Town South Palm Beach, Fla., 1991-92, elected vice mayor, 1992-93, elected mayor, 1993—, elected chair Palm Beach Countywide Beaches and Shores Bd., 1998—; apptd. Commn. on Status of Women of Palm Beach County, 1992-95; voting mem. Palm Beach Country Mcp. League, 1991—; apptd. Palm Beach County Intergovtl. Planning and Rev. exec. com., 1999; vice chair Commn. Status of Women of Palm Beach County, 1994-95; bd. dirs. Palm Beach County Juvenile Justice Bd., 1998-99. Mem. Nat. Assn. Women in Bus., Palm Beach C. of C. Republican. Office: Town Hall South Palm Beach 3577 S Ocean Blvd Palm Beach FL 33480-6450

ROBERTS, MARIE DYER, retired computer systems specialist; b. Statesboro, Ga., Feb. 19, 1943; d. Byron and Martha (Evans) Dyer; m. Hugh V. Roberts, Jr., Oct. 6, 1973 (dec. 2001). BS, U. Ga., 1966; student, Am. U., 1972. Cert. sys. profl.; cert. in data processing. Mathematician, computer specialist U.S. Naval Oceanographic Office, Washington, 1966-73; sys. analyst, programmer Sperry Microwave Electronics, Clearwater, Fla., 1973-75; data processing mgr., asst. bus. mgr. Trenam, Simmons, Kemker et al, Tampa, 1975-77; mathematician, computer specialist U.S. Army C.E., Savannah, Ga., 1977-81, 83-85, Frankfurt, West Germany, 1981-83; ops. rsch. analyst U.S. Army Constrn. Rsch. Lab., Champaign, Ill., 1985-87; data base adminstr., computer sys. programmer South Pacific divsn. U.S. Army C.E., San Francisco, 1987-93; computer specialist, IDEF repository coord. Functional Process Improvement Expertise/Def. Info. Sys. Agy, Arlington, Va., 1993-95; computer specialist Ctrl. Integration Def. Info. Sys. Agy., MacDill AFB, Fla., 1995—, ret., 2001. Instr. computer scis. City Coll. of Chgo. in Frankfurt, 1982-83. Author: Harris Computer Users Manual, 1983. Recipient Sustained Superior Performance award Dept. Army, 1983, 2 Nat. Peformance Rev. Hammer awards V.P. Al Gore, 1996, DISA Dirs.'s award for Project of Yr., 1999. Mem. Assn. Info. Tech. Profls., U. Ga. Alumni Assn., Sigma Kappa. E-mail: hurob@juno.com.

ROBERTS, MARK (ROBERT ELLIS SCOTT), actor, writer; b. Denver, June 9, 1921; s. Ward Ellis and Daisy (Hobson) Scott; m. Audrey von Clemm (dec.); children: Ward Ellis II, Margot, Jeffrey Frazier. Student, U. Kans., 1940-41; BA, U. Ariz., 1943. Cert. tchr. life, Calif. Ind. TV, stage, film actor, 1944—. Co-founder Kairos Theater, Los Angeles, 1964; dir. Theater Arts Program of Los Angeles, 1975-79. Novelist: The Only Man in Hollywood, 1980; playwright Summer's Welcome, 1954; film actor: (as Robert Scott) Girl in the Case, The Black Arrow (serial), One Mysterious Night, 1944, Ten Cents A Dance, 1945, Prison Ship, 1945, Gilda, 1946, The Unknown, 1946, Shadowed, 1946, Dead Reckoning, 1946, (as Mark Roberts) Taxi, 1950, Onionhead, 1955, The Money Jungle, 1957, Once is Not Enough, 1975, Posse, 1976, For the Boys, 1991, Intersection, 1993; actor: (TV series lead roles) The Front Page, 1950, Miss Susan, 1951, Three Steps to Heaven, 1953, Date With Life, 1955, The Brothers Brannigan, 1959-60, (TV episodes) Kraft Theatre, Philco Playhouse, Studio One, Suspense, Playhouse 90, FBI, Dan August, Perry Mason, Cannon, Highway to Heaven, Who's the Boss, Murder She Wrote, L.A. Law, Murphy Brown, (Broadway prodns.) Stalag 17, 1951, The Sacred Flame, 1952, (Chgo. prodn.) Dial 'M' For Murder, 1953 (Los Angeles prodn.), Garden Distict, 1958-59, Mornings at Seven, 1986, Summer and Smoke, 1991. Mem. Acad. Motion Picture Arts and Scis., Actors Equity Assn., Screen Actors Guild, AFTRA, Writers Guild Am. West, ASCAP, Phi Delta Theta (pres. U. Ariz. chpt. 1942). Democrat. Presbyterian. Avocation: collecting American and early California art, songwriting. E-mail: scout9@earthlink.net.

ROBERTS, MARK SCOTT, lawyer; b. Fullerton, Calif. s. Emil Seidel and Theda (Wymer) R. BA in Theater, Pepperdine U., 1975; JD, Western State U., 1978; cert. civil trial advocacy program, U. Calif., San Francisco, 1985; cert. program of instrn. for lawyers, Harvard U., 1990. Bar: Calif. 1980, U.S. Dist. Ct. (cen. dist.) Calif. 1980, U.S. Supreme Ct. 1989, U.S. Ct. Mil. Appeals 1989, U.S. Tax Ct. 1990. Prin. Mark Roberts & Assocs., Fullerton, Calif., 1980—. Instr. bus. law Biola U., La Mirada, Calif., 1980-84; judge pro tem Orange County Superior Ct., Santa Ana, 1989—; adj. prof. wills and trusts Trinity Law Sch., Santa Ana, 2000—. Co-author: Legacy-Plan, Protect and Preserve Your Estate, 1996, Generations Planning Your Legacy, 1999. Mem. Calif. State Bar Assn., Orange County Bar Assn. (charter), Nat. Network Estate Planning Attys. Office: Mark Roberts & Assocs 1440 N Harbor Blvd Ste 900 Fullerton CA 92835-4122

ROBERTS, MARKLEY, economist, educator; b. Shanghai, China, Sept. 3, 1930; s. Donald and Frances Charlotte (Markley) R.; m. Jeanne Addison, Feb. 19, 1966; children: Addison, Ellen. AB, Princeton U., 1951; MA, Am. U., 1960, PhD, 1970. Reporter Washington Star newspaper, 1952-57; legis. asst. Office of Senator Hubert Humphrey of Minn., Washington, 1957-62; legis. asst., economist AFL-CIO, 1962-96, asst. dir. econ. rsch. dept., 1989-96. Bd. dir., vice chmn. Econ. Edn. Found. for Clergy, 1972-80; chmn. labor research adv. council Bur. Labor Stats.-Dept. Labor, 1972-96; adj. prof. econs. U. Md., 1966—, George Washington U., 1972-96; treas. Inst. Learning in Retirement, 2002—. Contbr. numerous articles on labor and econ. affairs, tech., productivity to various publs.; author monographs in field. Mem. D.C. Democratic Central Com., 1964-68; ward III coordinator Washington Mayor Walter Washington, 1974-78; bd. dirs. Laymen's Nat. Bible Com. Inc., N.Y.C., 1972-82. Mem. UN Assn. (bd. dirs., v.p. nat. capitol area chpt. 1995—), Am. Econ. Assn., Indsl. Rels. Rsch. Assn. (exec. bd. 1975-77), Am. Polit. Sci. Assn., Nat. Acad. Social Ins., Assn. Evolutionary Econs., Am. Statis. Assn., Nat. Consumers League (bd. dirs. 1991-99), Newspaper Guild, Ams. for Dem. Action (exec. bd. 1992—), Social Democrats USA. Democrat. Episcopalian. Home: 4931 Albemarle St NW Washington DC 20016-4359

ROBERTS, MARY BELLE, clinical social worker; b. Sept. 27, 1923; d. Joseph Gill and Inez Wilson (Garvey) Roberts. BS, U. Mich., 1948, MSW, 1950. Cert. social worker Md., lic. clin. social worker Fla. Instr. dept. psychiatry U. Ala. Med. Coll., 1950—53; psychiat. social worker divsn. mental hygiene Ala. Dept. Pub. Health, 1950—52, acting dir., dir., 1952—53; sr. psychiat. social worker bur. mental health divsn. cmty. svc. Pa. Dept. Welfare, 1954—55; cons. psychiat. social work cmty. svc. br. NIMH, USPHS, HEW, 1955—64; pvt. practice psychiat. social work, 1964—68; caseworker Family Svc., Miami, Fla., 1968—70, Family and Childrens Svc., Miami, 1971—75; casework cons. United Family and Children Svcs., 1975—85; clin. social worker Family Counseling Svcs., 1985—90; pvt. practice clin. social work, 1990—; lic. clin. social worker Apogee, Inc., 1994—96. Home: 8126 SW 105th Pl Ocala FL 34481-9132

ROBERTS, MARY VESLEY, interior designer/decorator; b. Omaha, June 24, 1939; m. Peter Roberts, Sept. 19, 1981; children from previous marriage: Charles Jr., Scott, Sally. Student, U. Fla., 1957-60. Model Jantzen Inc., Portland, Oreg., 1958-60; stewardess Northwest Airlines, Washington, 1961-62; interior decorator 800 House Furniture & Design, Portland, 1973-74; prin. Mary Roberts Interiors, Oswego, Oreg., 1975—. Decorator Christiensen Motor Yacht Corp. Fund raiser Oreg. Mus. Sci. and Industry, March of Dimes; chmn. Fabric of Life Benefit for AIDS, Portland, 1991, 93; mem. Jr. League of Portland, 1973—; mem. adv. bd. Salvation Army, 1995—, Dougy Ctr., 1996—. Republican. Roman Catholic. Avocations: gardening, tennis, swimming, reading.

ROBERTS, MAURA M. retired secondary school educator; b. Washington, Mar. 2, 1944; d. John E. and Mary M. (McCann) Martin; m. Charles D. Roberts, Aug. 15, 1987; 1 child, Caragh M. McLaughlin. AB, U. Mass. at Lowell, 1965; MAT, Salem State Coll., 1973. Cert. tchr. English, Mass. Tchr. English Hilton Head (S.C.) Prep Sch.; with Concord (Mass.)-Carlisle Sch. Dist.; tchr. English, instr. understanding learning course Concord-Carlisle Sch. Dist.; ret., 2000. Adj. instr. Fitchburg State Coll. Mem. edn. adv. bd. Orchard House Mus., Concord, 1994-98. Mem. ASCD, Nat. Coun. Tchrs. English, Concord Carlisle Tchrs. Assn., Mass. Tchrs. Assn.

ROBERTS, MEL (MELVIN RICHARD KELLS), retired film editor; b. Toledo, Aug. 26, 1923; s. Paul Mickle and Letha Ellen (Mize) Kells. BA, U. So. Calif., 1950, postgrad., 1951. Film editor Graphic Films, Hollywood, Calif., 1951-52; music editor Salt of the Earth, Ind. Film Co., 1952-53; film editor Ford Found., Columbia Pictures, 1953-62; cinematographer and film editor Wexler Films, 1956-62; still photographer L.A., 1962-81; video prodr., dir., 1993-97. Photographer, pub. (books) Mel Roberts Male, Rex, California Boys-Photographs from the 1960s-1970s, 2000, Mel Roberts California Boys-Photographs from the 1960s and 1970s, 2001, Mel Roberts California Boys-The Wild Ones, and others, photographer Uniforms, 1998, Male Bonding 2, 1998; editor: (films) Paul Coates Confidential File, Tim McCoy Show, Rudy Vallee Prodns., (documentaries) City That Disappears, Graphic Films, prodr., dir.: (films) Classic Males Videos, 1993; editor: (documentary) Segregation and the South, 1957;Exhibited in group shows at David Aden Gallery, Venice, Calif., 1998, 2000—01, one-man shows include, 2000, Jerry Miller Gallery, Palm Springs, Calif., 2002. Sgt. USAF, 1943-45, PTO. Avocations: collecting classic films and film publications, music. Office: 1335 N La Brea Ave Apt 2102 Hollywood CA 90028-7526 also: care Lilo Korenjak Fremersbergstrasse 16 A 76530 Baden Baden Germany

ROBERTS, MELVILLE PARKER, neuroanatomist, neurosurgeon, educator; b. Phila., Oct. 15, 1931; s. Melville Parker and Marguerite Louise (Reimann) R.; m. Sigrid Marianne Magnusson, Mar. 27, 1954; children: Melville Parker III, Julia Pell, Erik Emerson. BS, Washington and Lee U., 1953; MD, Yale U., 1957. Diplomate: Am. Bd. Neurol. Surgery. Intern Yale Med. Ctr., 1957, neurosurg. resident, 1958-60, 62-64, Am. Cancer Soc. fellow in neurosurgery, 1962-64, instr., 1964; asst. prof. surgery Sch. Medicine U. Va., Charlottesville, 1965-69; practice medicine specializing in neurol. surgery Hartford, Conn., 1970-1998; mem. staff Hartford Hosp.; asst. prof. surgery Sch. Medicine U. Conn., Farmington, 1970-71, assoc. prof., 1972-75, assoc. prof. neurology, 1974-77, chmn. divsn. neurosurgery, 1971-84, prof. surgery, 1975—, acting chmn. dept. neurology, 1973-77, acting chmn. dept. surgery, 1974-77, William Beecher Scoville prof. neurosurgery, 1976-98, prof. emeritus, 1998—. James Hudson Brown rsch. fellow Yale U., 1957. Author: Atlas of the Human Brain in Section, 1970, 2d edition, 1987, The Brain Atlas, 1998; mem. editl. bd.: Conn. Medicine, 1973-98; contbr. articles to profl. jours. Capt. M.C., U.S. Army, 1960-61. Fellow Royal Soc. Medicine (London); mem. Am. Assn. Neurol. Surgeons, Soc. Neurol. Surgeons, Congress Neurol. Surgeons (bd. dirs. joint spinal sect. with Am. Assn. Neurol. Surgeons, chmn. ann. meeting 1987, sci. program chmn. ann. meeting 1988), Assn. for Rsch. in Nervous and Mental Diseases, New Eng. Neurosurg. Soc. (bd. dirs. 1976-79, pres. 1989-91), Soc. Brit. Neurol. Surgeons, Rsch. Soc. Neurol. Surgeons, Soc. Rsch. into Hydrocephalus and Spina Bifida, Conn. Acad. Arts and Sci., Vereingung Schweizer Neurochirugen, Mory's Assn., Graduate Club, Beaumont Med. Club (pres. 1988)(New Haven, Conn.) , Sloane Club, Naval Club (London). Episcopalian. Home: 15 The Courtyard 70B Hampton Rd Teddington England TW11 OJF Address: 48 Hickory Dr South Glastonbury CT 06073-3212

ROBERTS, MICHAEL DEAN, psychologist; b. Kalamazoo, July 26, 1947; s. Harold Dean and Norreen Margaret (Cloney) R.; m. Nancy Ann Zuidema, Aug. 16, 1969; 1 child, Ashley Ann. BA, Western Mich. U., 1969, MA, 1972; PhD, Ga. State U., 1974. Lic. clin. psychologist. Psychologist Palm Beach Mental Health Ctr., West Palm Beach, Fla., 1974-76; clin. dir. Region VII Mental Health Ctr., Columbus, Miss., 1976-81; exec. dir. Communicare, Oxford, 1981—. Adj. prof. U. Miss., Oxford, 1982—. Fellow APA, Miss. Psychol. Assn. (pres. 1988, Disting. Svc. award 1985), Miss. Assn. of Community Mental Health Progs. (pres. 1984), Miss. Bd. Psychol. Examiners (exec. sec. 1987), Rotary (bd. dirs. 1986, 90), Oxford C. of C. Republican. Avocations: tennis, sports cars. Bus. Home: 951 Frontage Rd #53 Oxford MS 38655-5130 Office: Communicare 152 Highway 7 S Oxford MS 38655-5392 E-mail: mdr@dixie-net.com., mandn@dixie-net.com.

ROBERTS, MICHAEL JOSEPH, journalist; b. Canton, Ohio, Nov. 22, 1954; s. Francis Joseph and Flora Louise (Taylor) R.; m. Lynn Ellen Lantry Streetman, 1973 (div. 1984); children: Amy Kathleen, Jennifer Anne. BS in Speech and Telecomms., Kent State U., 1979. Cert. master wildlife conservationist, Fla. News dir. WNYN Radio, Canton, 1979-80, WTAL Radio, Tallahassee, 1980-82; broadcast journalist WCTV TV, 1982-90; mng. editor WCTV News (CBS), 1990-95; journalist, cons. Spl. Projects Group, 1995—; assignment editor WTXL/WBXT News, 1999—. Spl. projects cons. Freestyle Prodns., Fla., 1989-90; mem. tng. cadre manhunt exercise U.S. Army Spl. Forces/Blue Ridge Tech. Coll., Hendersonville, N.C., 1989-94. Author screenplay: Diamondback, 1989; prodr. TV documentaries: Common Ground: A Citizen Summit, 1989, Vietnam: Beyond the Battles, 1991; editor, pub. newsletter Threat Level; co-creator spl. ops. Basic Sniper course. Bd. dirs. Big Bend chpt. ARC, Tallahassee, 1990; mem. Tallahassee-Krasnodar Sister City Program; master wildlife conservationist U. Fla.-IFAS, Gainesville. Recipient Nat. Broadcast award UPI, 1989, Outstanding Documentary award UPI, 1989, Best Documentary award AP, 1991, Best Overall Coverage award AP, 1991, 93, 94, Best Newscast award AP, 1991, 92, 94, FBI Dir.'s Exceptional Svc. citation, 2000. Mem. Am. Soc. Law Enforcement Trainers, Vietnam Vets. Am. (POW/MIA award 1993), Fla. Swat Assn., Sigma Delta Chi. Avocations: collecting firearms, shooting sports, cooking. Office: Spl Projects Group PO Box 37205 Tallahassee FL 32315-7205

ROBERTS, NANCY MIZE, retired librarian, composer, pianist; b. Corsicana, Tex., Apr. 19, 1931; d. Edward Harvey and Llora Inez (Huffman) Mize; m. Sam Butler Roberts, July 26, 1952 (dec.); children: Sam Butler Roberts Jr., John Daniel Roberts (dec.). Attended, Corsicana H.S. Cert. county librarian. Inventory clk. Oil City Iron Works, Corsicana, 1949-51; programmer KAND Radio, 1959-60; libr. Corsicana Pub. Libr., 1966-69, 70-73; owner dress shop Hang-Up, Corsicana, 1969-70; women's editor Corsicana Daily Sun, 1973-75; libr. Corsicana Pub. Libr., 1975-96; staff libr. Corsicana H.S., 1999—; libr. aide Corsicana Ind. Sch. Dist., 2000—. Composer: (church anthems) Clap Your Hands, Two Commandments, God Moves in A Mysterious Way, I Must Tell Jesus. Bd. dirs. Warehouse Living Arts, Women's Clubhouse Assn., 1996-99, Consicana Pub. Libr. Bd., 1997—. Recipient Lifetime Achievement award Northeast Tex. Library Assn., 1996. Mem. Women's Clubhouse Orgn. Democrat. Methodist. Avocations: playing piano, arranging music, writing reviews, directing plays, singing. Home: 1443 W 3rd Ave Corsicana TX 75110-4409

ROBERTS, NICKOLENA GRECO (NICKY ROBERTS), small business owner; b. Syracuse, N.Y., Aug. 14, 1951; d. William James and Eileen (Knox) Greco; m. Robert B. Hegley, Dec. 27, 1974 (dec. 1983); m. Galen E. Roberts, Jan 2, 1987; children: Vera, David, Nicholas. Diploma, Gen. Motors Sch. Mdsing. and Mgmt., 1981, 82. Lead dancer Maori Polynesian Restaurant, W. Palm Beach, Fla., 1970-72; sales/mgmt. WJNO Radio, W. Palm Beach, 1970-76, WIRK & WNGS Radio, W. Palm Beach, 1976-80; truck/fleet mgr. Bob Hegley Inc., Clewiston, Fla., 1980-82; owner, pres. Nicky Hegley Chevrolet, Clewiston, Fla., 1983-87; v.p., co-owner, Roberts Auto Collection, Inc., Lake Wales, Fla., 1987—; account exec. Highlands Media Co., Inc., Sebring, Fla., 1990-92; advt. cons. Morris Comms. Corp. (dba Newschief Pub. Group), 1994—. Sec., Airport Authority, Clewiston, 1983-86; bd. dirs. Actor's Community Theater, 1983-86; mem. Bus. Improvement Council, 1984-85. Mem. Nat. Assn. Female Execs., Sales Mktg. Execs., C. of C. Jehovah's Witness. Avocations: polynesian dancing, flying, reading, crafts, snow skiing.

ROBERTS, ORAL (GRANVILLE ORAL ROBERTS), clergyman; b. nr. Ada, Okla., Jan. 24, 1918; s. Ellis Melvin and Claudius Priscilla (Irwin) R.; m. Evelyn Lutman, Dec. 25, 1938; children: Rebecca Ann (dec.), Ronald David (dec.), Richard Lee, Roberta Jean. Student, Okla. Bapt. U., 1942-44, Phillips U., 1945-47; LLD (hon.) , Centenary Coll., 1975; MDiv, Oral Roberts U., 1981; DD, Internat. Ch. Foursquare, 1988. Ordained to ministry Pentecostal Holiness Ch., 1936, United Meth. Ch., 1968. Evangelist, 1936-41; pastor Fuquay Springs, N.C., 1941, Shawnee, Okla., 1942-45, Toccoa, Ga., 1946, Enid, Okla., 1947; began worldwide evangelistic ministry thru crusades, radio, TV, printed page, 1947; founder Oral Roberts Evangelistic Assn., Inc., Tulsa, 1948, Univ. Village Retirement Center, 1970, City of Faith Med./Research Ctr., 1981, Healing Outreach Ctr., 1986; founder, pub. Miracles Now mag., Daily Blessing mag.; founder, pres. Oral Roberts U., Tulsa, 1963-93, chancellor, 1993—. Founding chmn. Internat. Charismatic Bible Ministries, 1986. Author over 122 books including: If You Need Healing, Do These Things, 1947, God is a Good God, 1960, If I Were You, 1967, Miracle of Seed-Faith, 1970, The Miracle Book, 1972, A Daily Guide to Miracles, 1975, 3 Most Important Steps to Your Better Health and Miracle Living, 1976, How to Get Through Your Struggles, 1977, Don't Give Up, 1980, Your Road to Recovery, 1986, Attack Your Lack, 1985, How to Resist the Devil and His Demons, 1989, Fear Not!, 1989, A Prayer Cover Over Your Life, 1990, Is God Your Source?, 1992, Unleashing the Power of Praying in the Spirit, 1993, (autobiography) Expect a Miracle, My Life and Ministry, 1995, A Thousand Times More!, 1997, Don't Park Here!, 1997, Keys to Success, 1998, Seed-Faith 2000, 1999, Still Doing the Impossible, 2002; also numerous tracts, brochures, Bible commentaries. Recipient Outstanding Am. Indian of Yr. award Am. Indian Expn., 1963; inducted into Okla. Hall of Fame, 1972; named Oklahoman of Yr., Am. Broadcasters Assn., 197, One of 50 Most Influential Oklahomans, Okla. Today mag., 2000. Mem.: Rotary. Office: Oral Roberts U 7777 S Lewis Ave Tulsa OK 74171-0001

ROBERTS, PATRICIA LEE, education educator; b. Coffeyville, Kans. d. Philip Lee Brighton and Lois Ethel Wortham; m. James E. Roberts, Oct. 5, 1953; children: James Michael, Jill Frances. BA, Calif. State U., Fresno, 1953, MA, 1964; EdD, U. Pacific, 1975. Lifetime tchg. diploma; sch. adminstrn. cert. Prof. edn. Calif. State U., Sacramento, 1969—. Cons. in field. Author (textbooks): Alphabet: A Handbook of ABC Books and Book Extensions for the Elementary Classroom, 2d edit., 1994, A Resource Guide for Elementary School Teaching, 5th edit., 2000, Literature-Based History Activities for Children, Grades 4-8, 1997, Literature-Based History Activities for Children, Grades 1-3 , 1998, Integrating Language Arts and Social Studies for Kindergarten and Primary Children, 1996, A Guide for Developing an Interdisciplinary Thematic Unit, 3d edit., 2002, Taking Humor Seriously in Children's Literature, 1997, Multicultural Friendship Stories and Activities for Children Ages 5-14, 1997, Family Values Through Children's Literature, Grades K-3, 1999. Named Disting. Alumnae of Yr., U. Pacific, 1975-76. Mem. Internat. Reading Assn., Nat. Coun. Rsch. on English.

ROBERTS, PATRICK FRANCIS, air transportation executive, consultant; b. Dayton, Ohio, Dec. 4, 1947; s. Frederick Charles Roberts, Virgina Mae Roberts; m. Rosalie Bonacci; children: Alexis Bonacci-Roberts, Adrianna Bonacci-Ronerts. Prototype model maker numerous engrng. firms, Dayton, Ohio, 1970—77; bioenging. rschr. Biomed. Rsch. Lab., Wright-Patterson AFB, 1980—88; spl. ops. flight test mgr. Spl. Ops. Forces SPO, 1988—96, Electronic Combat SPO, Wright-Patterson AFB, 1996—2000; dir. aircraft moderization flight test Aircraft Moderization SPO, 2000—01; test mgr. for F-16 program Develop. Sys. Office, USAF, 2001—. Cons. electronic combat on supersonic aircraft PEOAVN, Redstone Arsenal, 1998—. Author: (book) Project Basketball, 1997. V.p. Kettering Basketball Club, Kettering, 1999—2001; founder, pres. SheDemons Basketball Club, Southwestern Ohio, 1999—Pres. Recipient Pride Achievement award, Military Airlift Command, 1967, Lockheed Golden Screwdriver award, Lockheed Corp., 1970, Notable Achievement award for devel. meals ready to eat aerial delivery sys. for PROVIDE PROMISE, Bosnia-Herzegovina, HQ Aero. Sys. Ctr., 1993, Notable Achievement award for mng. and coord. quick response modification and test for Life Line Flare installation, 1993, Mgr. of Yr., HQ Aero. Sys. Ctr., 1993. Avocation: coaching youth sports.

ROBERTS, PATRICK KENT, lawyer; b. Waynesville, Mo., Feb. 9, 1948; s. J. Kent and Winona (Clark) R.; m. Jeanne Billings, April 17, 1976; children: Christopher, Kimberly, Courtney. Student, U. Ill., Urbana, 1970; AB, U. Mo., 1970, JD, 1973. Bar: Mo. 1974, U.S. Dist. Ct. (we. dist.) Mo. 1974, U.S. Ct. Appeals (8th cir.) 1979. Lawyer U.S. Senator Stuart Symington, Columbia, Mo., 1973-76; ptnr. Daniel, Clampett, Powell & Cunningham, Springfield, 1976—2001; of counsel Cunningham, Harpool & Cordonnier, 2002—. Adj. faculty Webster U., 2000—. Mem. ctrl. com. Greene County Dems., Springfield, 1982-84, 88-90. Mem. ABA, Mo. Orgn. Def. Lawyers, Mo. Bar Assn., Springfield Met. Bar Assn. Lodges: Rotary. Democrat. Methodist. Office: Cunningham Harpool & Cordonnier PO Box 10306 3171 E Sunshine St Springfield MO 65804-2056

ROBERTS, PAUL, chef; Master sommelier Cafe Annie, Houston. Recipient Krug Cup. Achievements include being the only Master Sommelier in the State of Tex. and 1 of only 50 in country; becoming the first person in six years to pass the very intense Master Sommelier's test. Office: 1728 Post Oak Blvd Houston TX 77001*

ROBERTS, PAUL CRAIG, III, economics educator, author, columnist; b. Atlanta, Apr. 3, 1939; s. Paul Craig and Ellen Lamar (Dryman) R.; m. Becky B. Bickerstaff, 1959 (div. 1968); m. Linda Jane Fisher, July 3, 1969 (div. 1994); children: Becky Ellen, Stephanie Bradford, Pendaran Struan Sherman. BS, Ga. Inst. Tech., 1961; postgrad., U. Calif., Berkeley, 1962-63, Merton Coll., Oxford (Eng.) U., 1964-65; PhD (Earhart fellow), U. Va., 1967. Asst. prof. econs. Va. Poly. Inst., 1965-69; assoc. prof. U. N.Mex., 1969-71; rsch. fellow Hoover Instn., Stanford U., 1971-77, sr. rsch. fellow, 1978—; mem. U.S. Congl. Staff, 1975-78; asst. sec. of treasury for econ. policy Dept. Treasury, Washington, 1981-82; William E. Simon prof. polit. economy Georgetown U. Ctr. for Strategic and Internat. Studies, 1982-93; chmn. Inst. for Polit. Economy, 1985—, John M. Olin fellow, 1994—. Disting. adj. scholar Ctr. Strategic and Internat. Studies, Washington, 1993-96; adj. scholar Cato Inst., 1987-93, disting. fellow, 1993-96; assoc. editor, columnist Wall St. Jour., N.Y.C., 1978-80; columnist Bus. Week, 1983-98, Fin. Post, Can., 1988-89, Liberation, Paris, 1988-89, Erfolg, Fed. Rep. of Germany, 1988, Washington Times, 1988—, San Diego Union, 1988-92, Le Figaro, Paris, 1992-96, Investors Bus. Daily, 1998—; nationally syndicated columnist Scripps Howard News Svc., 1989-97, Creators Syndicate, 1997—; contbr. editor: Nat. Rev., 1993—, Reason Mag., 1993-95, World Trade mag., 1997—; mem. Pres.-elect Reagan's Task Force on Tax Policy, 1980; dir. Value Line Investment Funds, N.Y.C., A. Schulman, Akron, Ohio; cons. Morgan Guaranty Trust Co., Lazard Freres Asset Mgmt., 1983-97; pres. Econ. & Communication Svcs. Inc.; cons. Dept. Commerce, 1983, Dept. Def., 1983-84; mem. adv. bd. Marvin and Palmer, 1986-96, Am. studies program Harding U.; mem. ad. com. Ctr. for the Am. Founding; mem. Wright Investors' Svc. Internat. Bd. Econ. and Invesmtent Advisors; bd. dirs. Com. on Present Danger; trustee Intercollegiate Studies Inst., Com. on Developing Am. Capitalism; mem. selection com. Frank E. Seidman disting. award in Polit. Economy; pres. Inlet Beach Water Co., 2000—. Author: Alienation and the Soviet Economy, 1971, new edit., 1990, Marx's Theory of Exchange, 1973, new edit., 1983, The Supply-Side Revolution: An Insider's Account of Policymaking in Washington, 1984, The Cost of Corporate Capital in the U.S. and Japan, 1985, Meltdown: Inside the Soviet Economy, 1990, The New Color Line: How Quotas and Privilege Destroy Democracy, 1995; The Capitalist Revolution in Latin America, Oxford U. Press, 1997, The Tyranny of Good Intentions, 2000, Chile: Dos Visiones-la Era Allende-Pinochet, 2000; mem. editl. bd. Modern Age, Intercollegiate Rev.; contbg. editor Harper's Mag. Drafted original Kemp-Roth Bill, 1976. Recipient Meritorious Svc. award Dept. Treasury, 1982, Pub. Svc. award GSA, 1991, Warren Brookes award for Excellence in Journalism, 1992; Am. Philos. Soc. grantee, 1968; named to Chevalier de la Légion d'Honneur, 1987, Gridiron Secret Soc., U. Ga.; Nat. Chamber Found. fellow, 1984-85. Mem. Mont Pelerin Soc., Beethoven Soc., Am. Soc. French Legion of Honor, U.S. C. of C. (taxation com.), Polanyi Soc. Home and Office: 169 Pompano St Panama City FL 32413-7245 E-mail: pcr@digitalexp.com.

ROBERTS, PAUL DALE, state agency administrator, writer; b. Fresno, Calif., Jan. 17, 1955; s. Paul Marceau and Rosemarie Roberts; m. Patricia Mary Mitchell, Mar. 24, 1964; 1 child, Jason Randall Porter. AA, Sacramento City Coll., 1977; diploma in pvt. investigations, Ctrl. Investigation & Security, 1984. Office asst. I, Dept. Benefit Payments, Sacramento, 1976-77; firefighter Calif. Divsn. Forestry, Colfax, 1977; key data operator Dept. Justice, Sacramento, 1977-78; intelligence analyst, spl. forces instr. U.S. Army Mil. Intelligence, Seoul, Korea, 1979-84; office asst. 1 Calif. State Lottery Commn., 1987-89; law libr. Employment Devel. Dept., Sacramento, 1989-92; office asst. II, Calif. Dept. Health Svcs., 1992-98, chief cert. support, 1992-93; supervising program technician II Dept. Cmty. Svcs. and Devel., State Calif., 1998-2000; divsn. supr. polit. reform Sec. of State, 2000—. Office asst I, Calif. Lottery Commn., 1987-89; disaster courier dept. social svcs. Gov.'s Office of Emergency Svcs., L.A., 1994. Author: Organization of D.E.A.T.H. (Destroy Evildoers and Teach Harmony), 1984, The Cosmic Bleeder, 1991, Madam Zara, Vampiress, 1993, People's Comic Book Newsletter, 1996, The Legendary Dark Silhouette, 1997, Vacationing in Dublin, Ireland and Newry, Northern Ireland, 1997, (comic book) The Legendary Dark Silhouette, 1997, Jazma Universe Online!, 1998, Jazma League of Justice, 1999, Jazma Man/Jazma Girl, 2000, My Adventures in Brazil, 2001. Sgt. U.S. Army Mil. Police, 1973-76. Democrat. Roman Catholic. Avocations: private pilot, tennis, photography, hot air balloon/glider riding, sky diving. Home: 5606 Moonlight Way Elk Grove CA 95758-6837 Office: 1500 11th St Rm 495 Sacramento CA 95814 Fax: 916-653-5045. E-mail: proberts@ss.ca.gov.

ROBERTS, PAUL FRANKLIN, II, financial executive; b. Laredo, Tex., Apr. 16, 1949; s. Paul Franklin and Bernice Clevenger (Alworth) R.; m. Martha Diane Dow, Dec. 19, 1970; children: Averi Alison, Briana Alane, Paul Franklin III. BS in Math. cum laude, S.W. Tex. State U., 1970; M of Pub. Fin. Mgmt., The Am. U., 1983; postgrad., George Mason U., 1989-95. Team leader U.S. Army Communications Command, Fort Huachuca, Ariz., 1975-77; dep. comptroller U.S. Army Combined Arms Ctr., Fort Leavenworth, Kans., 1977-79; tech. dir. Comptroller of Army, Pentagon, Washington, 1981-82, dir. mgmt.engring., 1982-84; supr. program analyst U.S. Army Material Command, Alexandria, 1984-85, chief productivity mgmt. div., 1985-89; dir. resource mgmt. U.S. Army Devel. & Employment Agy., Fort Lewis, Wash., 1984-85; chief productivity improvement div. Asst. Sec. of Def., Pentagon, Washington, 1989-90; dir. investment Asst. Sec. of Army, Pentagon, 1990-95, dir. bus. resources, 1995-98; CFO, chief adminstrv. officer NOAA, Dept. Commerce, 1998—2000, Nat. Tech. Info. Svc., Dept. Commerce, Washington, 2000—. Mem. sr. exec. svc. Fed. Civil Svc., 1990—. Author: (study) Functional Army Manpower Evaluation, 1981. Dist. scout commr. Cochise dist. Boy Scouts Am., 1975—77, asst. scoutmaster George Washington dist., 1998—2000, asst. dist. commr. Tomahawk dist., cubmaster George Washington Dist., 1995—98; bd. dirs. Marriage Encounter/United Meth. Ch., 1986—88, jurisdictional exec. couple, 1986—88, state exec. couple, 1981—84. Recipient Eagle Scout award, 1962. Mem.: Ctr. for Study of Presidency, Am. Assn. Program and Budget Analysts, Am. Soc. for Pub. Adminstrn., Sr. Exec. Assn., Delta Tau Delta. Methodist. Avocations: golf, basketball, baseball card collecting. Home: 8011 Lake Pleasant Dr Springfield VA 22153-3005 Office: 5285 Port Royal Rd Springfield VA 22161-0001 E-mail: proberts@ntis.gov.

ROBERTS, PHILIP JOHN, history educator, editor; b. Lusk, Wyo., July 8, 1948; s. Leslie J. and LaVerne Elizabeth (Johns) R. BA, U. Wyo., 1973, JD, 1977; PhD, U. Wash., 1990. Bar: Wyo. 1977. Editor Lake Powell Chronicle, Page, Ariz., 1972-73; co-founder Medicine Bow (Wyo.) Post, 1977; pvt. practice in law Carbon and Laramie County, Wyo., 1977-84; historian Wyo. State Hist. Dept., Cheyenne, 1979-84; editor Annals of Wyo., 1980-84, 95—; owner, pub. Capitol Times, 1982-84; co-editor Wyo. History Jour., 1995-96; editor, 1996-97; owner, pub. Skyline West Press, Seattle, 1985-90; prof. history U. Wyo., Laramie, 1990—. Indexer Osborne-McGraw-Hill, Berkeley, 1988-95; guest lectr. media law, Dubai, United Arab Emirates, 1996, Cairo, 2001; mem. editl. bd. Annals of Wyo., 1990-95. Author: Wyoming Almanac, 1989 (pub. annually), Buffalo Bones: Stories from Wyoming's Past, 1979, 82, 84, Readings in Wyoming History, 1994, 96, 2000, Penny for the Governor, A Dollar for Uncle Sam: The Politics of Taxation in Washington, 2002; contbr. articles to profl. jours. Cand. for gov. of Wyo., 1998; chmn. Albany County Dem. Party, 1999-2001; pres. Albany County Hist. Soc., 2000-02; mem. Albany County Hist. Preservation Commn., 2000—; bd. mem. Laramie Plains Mus., 2000—. With USMC, 1970-72. Mem. Wyo. State Hist. Soc. (life), Wyo. State Bar, Pacific N.W. Historians' Guild, 9th Judicial Cir. Hist. Soc., Western History Assn., Am. Hist. Assn., Orgn. of Am. Historians, Albany County Hist. Soc. (pres. 2000-02). Office: U Wyo Univ Sta PO Box 4286 Laramie WY 82071-4286 E-mail: philr@uwyo.edu.

ROBERTS, PRISCILLA WARREN, artist; b. Montclair, N.J., June 13, 1916; d. Charles Asaph and Florence (Berry) R. Student, Art Students League, 1937-39, Nat. Acad., 1939-43. Represented in permanent collections Met. Mus., Cin. Art Mus., Canton (Ohio) Art Inst., Westmoreland County Mus. Art, Pa., IBM, Dallas Mus., Walker Art Ctr., Mpls., Butler Inst., Youngstown, Ohio, Nat. Mus. Am. Art, Washington, Nat. Mus. Women in the Arts, Washington. Recipient Proctor prize, 1947, popular prize Corcoran Biennial, 1947, prize Westmoreland County Mus., 3d prize Carnegie Internat., Pitts., 1950, Nat. Mus. Women in Arts, Washington, Snite Mus., U. Notre Dame, Ind. Mem. Nat. Acad. Design (Hallgarten prize 1945), Allied Artists Am. (Zabriskie prize 1944, 46), Catherine Lorillard Wolfe Assn. (hon.). Address: PO Box 716 Georgetown CT 06829-0716

ROBERTS, RALPH JOEL, telecommunications, cable broadcast executive; b. N.Y.C., Mar. 13, 1920; s. Robert and Sara (Wahl) Roberts; m. Suzanne Fleisher, Aug. 23, 1942; children: Catherine, Lisa, Ralph Jr., Brian, Douglas. BS in Econs., U. Pa., 1941; LHD (hon.), Holy Family Coll., 1994. Account exec. Aitken Kynett Advt., Phila., 1946-48; v.p. Muzak Corp., N.Y.C., 1948-50; pres., chief exec. officer Pioneer Industries, Inc., Darby, Pa., 1950-61; pres. Internat. Equity Corp., Bala Cynwyd, 1961-83; chmn. bd., Comcast Corp., Phila., 1969—; chmn., chief exec. officer Sural Corp. (merger with Internat. Equity Corp. 1983); chmn. Comcast Corp., Phila. Trustee, chmn. conflict interest com. Albert Einstein Med. Ctr.; bd. dirs. Phila. Electric Co., Phila. Nat. Bank, Corestates. Bd. dirs. regional NCCJ; trustee Brandywine Mus. and Conservancy, charter mem. World Bus. Coun.; past mem. mentor program and Benjamin Franklin assocs. U. Pa.; bd. dirs. Phila. Orch., 1993; past v.p. Family Svc. Phila.; past bd. dirs., mem. budget and fees com. State Coll. and Univ. Dirs.; mem. re-regulation and legis. affairs coms. Nat. Cable TV Assn.; past mem. Gov.'s Rev. of Govt. Mgmt., Inc. Lt. USNR, 1942-45. Reipient Americanism award Anti-Defamation League of B'nai B'rith, Brotherhood award NCCJ, 1989, award for outstanding svc. to cable TV industry Walter Kaitz Found., 1990, Acres of Diamonds Entrepreneurioal Excellence award Entrepreneurial Inst. Temple U., 1991, Disting. Vanguard award for leadership Nat. Cable TV Assn., 1993, Golden Plate award Am. Acad. Achievement, 1994, PAL award Police Athletic League Phila., 1995, Edward Powell award for cmty. svc. City of Phila., 1995, Joseph P. Wharton award U. Pa., 1995, Whitney M. Young Jr. Leadership award Urban League Phila., 1997, Disting. Cmty. Leadership award Operation Understanding, 1997, Cable TV Hall of Fame award, 2000, Mensa Achievement award, 2000, Heroes of Liberty award Liberty Mus., 2000, William Penn award Greater Phila. C. of C., 2002; named to Broadcasting and Cable Hall of Fame, 1993. Avocations: tennis, travel. Home: Sural Farm 505 Fairview Rd East Fallowfield Township PA 19320-4451 Office: Comcast Corp 1500 Market St Fl 33E Philadelphia PA 19102-4782

ROBERTS, RANDOLPH WILSON, health and science educator; b. Scranton, Pa., Oct. 8, 1946; s. S. Tracy and Alecia Francis (Sullivan) R.; m. Martha Jeanne Burnite, July 12, 1969 (div. Dec. 1985); children: Gwendolyn Suzanne, Ryan Weylin; m. Ava Elaine Brown, June 17, 1989. AB in Biology, Franklin & Marshall Coll., 1968, MA in Geoscis., 1974; MS in Sci. Teaching, Am. U., 1977; MS in Counseling, Western Md. Coll., 1990; CHES, Towson State U., 1993; postgrad., U. Md., Johns Hopkins U., Loyola Coll., Md. Cert. tchr., counselor, health educator, health edn. specialist (CHES), tax cons. Tchr. Woodlawn Jr. High Sch., Balt., 1968-73, Deer Park Jr. High/Mid. Sch., Randallstown, Md., 1973-87, Franklin Mid. Sch., Reisterstown, 1987-89; counselor and chmn. health/sci. dept. Balt. County Home & Hosp. Ctr., 1989—. Math and sci. tchr. Loyola H.S., Towson, Md., 1981-86, Talmudical Acad., Pikesville, Md., 1983-86; health educator Loyola Coll., Md., 1994; ednl. cons. Scott Fetzer co., Chgo., 1981-86; founder, pres. Tax Assistance, Ltd., Owings Mills, Md., 1981—; curriculum cons. Balt. County Bd. Edn., Towson, 1977, 78, 93, 95, 96; founder Building Children, 1982—; photographer Am. Sch. Pictures, 1993-98. Author: Earth Sciences Workbook, 1979. Mem. Glyndon (Md.) Meth. Ch., 1993—, scholarship com. chmn., handbell choir mem., Christian edn. com., liturgist, mem. adminstrv. coun.; treas. Boy Scouts Am. Pack 315, Reis, Md., 1986-90, Webelos Den leader, 1987-90, advancement chmn., com. mem. Troop 315, 1990-93; fin. ptnr./treas. Bare Hills Investment Group, 1994-98; founder, pres. Manor Enterprises, 2001. Mem.: AAHPERD, ACA, NEA, Am. Assn. Health Edn., Chesapeake Bay Found., Nature Conservancy, Balt. Rd. Runners, Eta Sigma Gamma, Mu Upsilon Sigma, Phi Delta Kappa. Avocations: travel, gardening, running, investing. Home: 9 Indian Pony Ct Owings Mills MD 21117-1210 Office: Home and Hosp Ctr 6229 Falls Rd Baltimore MD 21209-2120

ROBERTS, RAY CROUSE, JR. retired economics educator; b. Burlington, N.C., Jan. 8, 1929; s. Ray Crouse and Bessie (Cloniger) R.; m. Alice Suzanne Molnar, June 24, 1952; children: David, Rebecca, Eric, Mark. AB, Duke U., 1950; MS, U. N.C., 1957, PhD, 1961. Indsl. engr. Glen Raven Cotton Mills, N.C., 1952-54; asst. prof., assoc. prof., prof. econs. Old Dominion Coll., Norfolk, Va., 1956-67, chmn. dept. econs., 1962-67; vis. assoc. prof. econs. Duke U., 1964-65; dean Sch. Bus. Adminstrn., Winthrop Coll., Rock Hill, S.C., 1967-69; Frederick W. Symmes prof. econs. Furman U., Greenville, 1969-95, chmn. dept. econs., 1969-73, 85-88, 1993-94, acting v.p. for acad. affairs, dean, 1994-95; ret., 1995—. Served to 1st lt. USMCR, 1950-52; col. Res. ret. Mem. Am. Arbitration Assn. (nat. labor panel). Democrat. Methodist.

ROBERTS, RICHARD, mechanical engineering educator; b. Atlantic City, Feb. 16, 1938; s. Harold and Marion (Hofman) R.; m. Rochelle S. Perelman, Oct. 2, 1960; children: Lori, Lisa, Scott. BSME, Drexel U., 1961; MSME, Lehigh U., 1962, PhD in Mech. Engring., 1964. Asst. prof. mech. engring. Lehigh U., Bethlehem, Pa., 1964-68, assoc. prof., 1968-75, prof., 1975—. Editor: Proceedings of the Thirteenth Nat. Symposium on Fracture Mechanics, 1980, ASME PVP Division's Design Handbook, Materials and Fabrication, Vol. III. Recipient W. Sparagen award Am. Welding Soc., 1972, Adams Meml. award, 1981. Home: 317 Bierys Bridge Rd Bethlehem PA 18017-1142 Office: Lehigh Univ MSE/200 W Packer Bethlehem PA 18015

ROBERTS, RICHARD JOHN, molecular biologist, consultant, research director; b. Derby, Eng., Sept. 6, 1943; came to U.S., 1969; s. John Walter and Edna Wilhelmina (Allsop) R.; m. Elizabeth Dyson, Aug. 21, 1965 (dec.); children: Alison, Andrew; m. Jean E. Tagliabue, Feb. 14, 1986; children: Christopher, Amanda. BS, Sheffield (Eng.) U., 1965, PhD, 1968. Rsch. fellow Harvard U., Cambridge, Mass., 1969-70, rsch. assoc., 1971-72; sr. staff investigator Cold Spring Harbor Lab., N.Y., 1972-87, asst. dir., 1987-92; rsch. dir. New England Biolabs, 1992—, cons. New Eng. Biolabs, Beverly, Mass., 1974-92; sci. adv. bd. Genex, Rockville, Md., 1977-85, Molecular Tool, Balt., 1994—. Contbr. articles to profl. jours. Recipient Nobel prize in Physiology and Medicine, Nobel Foundation, 1993. John Simon Guggenheim Found. fellow, 1979. Fellow Royal Soc.; mem. Am. Soc. Microbiology, Am. Soc. Biol. Chemists. Office: New Eng Biolabs 32 Tozer Rd Beverly MA 01915-5599*

ROBERTS, ROBERT, III, retired lawyer; b. Shreveport, La., July 22, 1930; s. Robert and Mary Hodges (Marshall) R.; m. Susan F. Forrester, Mar. 16, 1974; children: Robert (dec.), Marshall, Francis T. Kalmbach Jr., Ellen K. Tizian, Lewis K.F. Kalmbach, Samuel A. Kalmbach. BA, La. State U., 1951, JD, 1953. Bar: La. 1953, U.S. Dist. Ct. (we. dist.) La. 1958, U.S. Ct. Appeals (5th cir.) 1966, U.S. Supreme Ct. 1975. Assoc., then ptnr. and shareholder Blanchard, Walker, O'Quin & Roberts and predecessor, Shreveport, 1955-99, of counsel, 1999—; ret. Former pres. Family Coun. and Children's Svcs.; former mem. Peabody study com. Caddo Parish Schs.; former chmn. legal div. United Way. 1st lt JAGC, U.S. Army, 1953-55. Mem. ABA, La. State Bar Assn. (former chmn. mineral law sect., former mem. ho. dels., former mem. bd. govs.), La. State Law Inst. (sr. officer, law reform agy. coun. 1962—, mineral code adv. com., civil code lease adv. com.), Soc. Bartolus, Shreveport Bar Assn. (pres. 1981), Shreveport Club. Office: Blanchard Walker O'Quin & Roberts PO Box 1126 Shreveport LA 71163-1126

ROBERTS, ROBERT, engineering organization executive, think-tank executive; Pres. Syracuse Rsch. Corp., Syracuse, N.Y. Office: Syracuse Rsch Corp 6225 Running Ridge Rd North Syracuse NY 13212-2510

ROBERTS, ROBERT WINSTON, social work educator, dean; b. Balt., July 23, 1932; s. Kelmer Swan Roberts and Lettie Mae (Collins) Johnston; m. Helen Elizabeth Perpich, Mar. 4, 1964 (div. Aug. 1997). BA with high honors, San Francisco State U., 1957; MSW, U. Calif., Berkeley, 1959; D in Social Welfare, Columbia U., 1970. Caseworker Edgewood Protestant Orphanage, San Francisco, 1959-62, Jewish Family Service, San Francisco, 1962-63; research assoc. U. Calif., Berkeley, 1963-65; research analyst Family Service Assn. Am., N.Y.C., 1965-69; asst. prof. U. Chgo., 1967-70; prof. U. So. Calif., Los Angeles, 1970-90, dean sch. social work, 1980-88, dean emeritus, prof. emeritus, 1990—. Vis. prof. Western Australia Inst. Tech. (now Curtin U.), Perth, 1976-77, Chinese U. Hong Kong and U. Hong Kong, 1980; cons. Crittenton Services, Los Angeles, 1970-72, James Weldon Johnson Community Ctr., N.Y., 1966-67; bd. dirs. El Centro, Los Angeles. Editor: The Unwed Mother, 1966; co-editor: Theories of Social Casework, 1970, Child Caring: Social Policy and the Institution, 1973, Theories of Social Work with Groups, 1976, Theory and Practice of Community Social Work, 1980; editorial bd. Social Work Jour.; contbr. articles to profl. jours. Staff sgt. USAF, 1950-54; sgt. 1st class USAR, 1956-59. Fellow NIMH, 1957-58, 65-67, Crown Zellerbach Found., 1958-59; recipient Outstanding Educator award Los Amigos de la Humanidad, 1979; named Disting. Assoc., Nat. Acad. Practice in Social Work, 1985. Mem. ACLU, NASW (chmn. social action com. 1960-61), Council on Social Work Edn. (bd. dirs. 1970-73, del. to assembly 1971-72, commn. minority groups 1972-73). Avocations: cooking, reading, travel, photography. Office: U So Calif Montgomery Ross Fisher Rm 21 Los Angeles CA 90089-0001

ROBERTS, RODNEY GLEN, electrical engineering educator; b. Hot Springs, Ark., Aug. 15, 1965; s. Victor Allen and Maylene Roberts; m. Qing Wan R. BSEE, BS in Math., Rose-Hulman Inst. Tech., 1987; MSEE, Purdue U., 1988, PhD, 1992. NRC fellow, rsch. scientist Wright-Patterson AFB, Dayton, Ohio, 1992-94; asst. prof. elec. engring. Fla. State U., Tallahassee, 1994-99, assoc. prof. elec. engring., 1999—. Assoc. editor (rsch. jours.) Intelligent Automation and Soft Computing, 1997—, Internat. Jour. Robotics and Automation, 1998—. NASA/ASEE Summer Faculty fellow, Kennedy Space Ctr., 1996, 97; David G. Ross fellow, Purdue U., 1989-90. Mem. IEEE (sect. chmn. 1996-97, 2000—, sect. sec. 1997-99), Tau Beta Pi, Eta Kappa Nu, Pi Mu Epsilon. Avocation: piano. Office: FAMU-FSU Coll Engring 2525 Pottsdamer St Tallahassee FL 32310-6046 E-mail: rroberts@eng.fsu.edu.

ROBERTS, SAMUEL SMITH, television news executive; b. Port Chester, N.Y., Feb. 8, 1936; s. Robert M. and Lillian (Smith) R.; m. Harriet Rubin, July 27, 1975; children: Rachel, David; children by previous marriage: Nancy, Pamela. BS, Northwestern U., 1957. With UPI, N.Y.C., 1961, Capital Cities Broadcasting, Providence, 1962, CBS News, 1962-95; sr. prodr. CBS Evening News, N.Y.C., 1978-81, nat. editor, 1982-84, fgn. editor, 1984-87; exec. prodr. CBS News Prodns., 1992-95, 20th Century, 1994-95; pres. Roberts Media Internat., N.Y.C., 1995-96; v.p., gen. mgr. TV programming Electronic Media Co., N.Y. Times, 1996-99; Frances L. Wolfson chair U. Miami, Coral Gables, Fla., 1999—. Served to lt. USN, 1957-61. Office: U Miami Sch Comm PO Box 248127 Coral Gables FL 33124-8127

ROBERTS, SANDRA BROWN, realty company executive; b. Boston, May 26, 1939; d. Frederick Thomas and Christine (Peyton) Brown; m. Joseph Peter Roberts Aug. 26, 1962 (div. May 1984); children: Christine, Joseph, Paul. BA, Boston Coll., 1981. Lic. real estate broker, Mass. Owner, mgr. real estate, Wellesley, Mass., 1963—; pres. Riverview Realty, 1970—; comml. realtor Boston, 1974—. Cons. Berkshire Hathaway, New Bedford, Mass., 1983-87; asst. to pres. BHR, Inc., New Bedford, 1988-2000. Founder, pres., bd. dirs. Friends of Ft. Washington, Inc.; active Friends of Boston Ballet, 1983—. Mem. DAR (Boston Tea Party chpt. regent 1983-84, 84-85), Navy League U.S., New Eng. Hist. Geneal. Soc., Boston Coll. Club (bd. dirs.), Order of Crown of Charlemagne (life), Order of Lafayette). Republican. Roman Catholic. Home and Office: 52 Kenilworth Rd Wellesley MA 02482-7428 Office: Friends Ft Washington Inc 1 Post Office Sq Ste 310 Boston MA 02109-2106

ROBERTS, SIDNEY, biological chemist; b. Boston, Mar. 11, 1918; s. Samuel Richard and Elizabeth (Gilbert) R.; m. Clara Marian Szego, Sept. 14, 1943. BS, MIT, 1939; postgrad., Harvard U., 1939-41; MS, U. Minn., 1942, PhD, 1943. Instr. physiology U. Minn. Med. Sch., 1943-44, George Washington U. Med. Sch., 1944-45; rsch. assoc. Worcester Found. Exptl. Biology, Shrewsbury, Mass., 1945-47; asst. prof. physiol. chemistry Yale U. Med. Sch., 1947-48; mem. faculty U. Calif. Med. Sch., Los Angeles, 1948—, prof. biol. chemistry, 1957—; chmn. acad. senate UCLA, 1989-90; mem. adv. panel regulatory biology NSF, 1955-57, adv. panel metabolic biology, 1957-59; mem. metabolism study sect. NIH, 1960-63; basic sci. study sect. Los Angeles County Heart Assn., 1958-63. Cons. VA Hosp., Long Beach, Calif., 1951-55, Los Angeles, 1958-62, Pew Fin. Biomed. Scholar Program, 1992-; air conservation tech. adv. com. Los Angeles County Lung Assn., 1972-76 Author articles, revs.; editor med. jours. Served to 2d lt. AUS, 1944-48. MIT Nat. Entrance scholar, 1935; Guggenheim fellow, 1957-58. Fellow AAAS; mem. Am. Physiol. Soc., Endocrine Soc. (v.p. 1968-69, Ciba award 1953), Brit. Biochem. Soc., Soc. Neurosci., Am. Chem. Soc. (exec. com. div. biol. chemistry 1956-59), Am. Soc. Biol. Chemists, Am. Soc. Neurochemistry, Internat. Soc. Neurochemistry, Phi Beta Kappa, Sigma Xi (pres. UCLA chpt. 1959-60). Home: 1371 Marinette Rd Pacific Palisades CA 90272-2627 Office: UCLA Sch Med Dept Biol Chemistry Los Angeles CA 90095-1737 E-mail: sr@ucla.edu.

ROBERTS, SIDNEY I. lawyer; b. Bklyn., Nov. 29, 1913; s. David I. and Ray (Bleicher) Robinovitz; m. Arlene Lee Aron, June 4, 1961; 1 son, Russell Lewis. BBA, CCNY, 1935; LL.B. magna cum laude, Harvard U., 1938. Bar: N.Y. 1938; C.P.A., N.Y. With Michael Schimmel & Co. (C.P.A.s), N.Y.C., 1938-39, S.D. Leidesdorf & Co. (C.P.A.s), N.Y.C., 1939-49; with firm Roosevelt, Freidin & Littauer, 1950-56, Anderson & Roberts, N.Y.C., 1956-57, Roberts & Holland, N.Y.C., 1957-94. Adj. prof. law Columbia U., 1971-78; mem. adv. council Internat. Bur. Fiscal Documentation. Author (with William C. Warren): U.S. Income Taxation of Foreign Corporations and Nonresident Aliens, 1966; author: (with others) Annotated Tax Forms: Practice and Procedure, 1970; editor: Legislative History of United States Tax Conventions, 18 vols., 1986—2001; contbr. articles to profl. jours. Mem. Internat. Bar Assn., ABA (sect. on taxation, council dir. 1970-73, chmn. com. on cooperation with state and local bar assns. 1968-70, chmn. com. on taxation of fgn. income 1963-64), N.Y. State Bar Assn. (tax sect. exec. com. 1967-87, chmn. com. on tax sect. planning 1968-70, chmn. com. on tax policy 1970-72), Assn. of Bar of City of N.Y., N.Y. State Soc. CPA's, Internat. Fiscal Assn. (mem. exec. com. 1972-77, pres. U.S.A. br. 1972-73). Jewish. Office: 145 Central Park W New York NY 10023-2004 E-mail: arsir@erols.com.

ROBERTS, STANLEY DWAYNE, physician, medical educator; b. Edmonton, Alta., Can., Sept. 17, 1959; came to U.S., 1994; s. Stan and Margaret Rosslyn (Rye) R.; m. Debra Elizabeth Bell, Aug. 20, 1981; children: Matthew, Brent, Michelle, Jared, Bradley. BSc with honors, U. Alta., Edmonton, 1980, BSc in Psychology with distinction, 1981, MD, 1985; grad., IHC Inst., 1999. Diplomate in family practice and sports medicine Am. Bd. Family Practice; cert. Family Medicine and Emergency Medicine, Coll. Family Physicians of Can. Resident in family medicine U. Alta., 1985-87; resident in physical rehab. and sports medicine McMaster U., Hamilton, Ont., Can., 1987-88, resident in emergency medicine Can., 1988-89, asst. prof. family and emergency medicine Can., 1989-94; med. dir., internat. med. cons. Med. Emergency, Inc., Toronto, Can., 1990-94; chief emergency svcs. Queensway Gen. Hosp., Can., 1992-94; employee health physician, family physician Norman (Okla.) Regional Hosp., 1994-95; family physician Bigstone Creek Indian Reserve, Alberta, 1995, 96; pvt. family practice Provo, Utah, 1996-97; faculty physician Utah Valley Family Practice Residency, 1997—; emergency physician Utah Valley Regional Med. Ctr., 1997—; assoc. team physician Brigham Young U., 1999—. Med. dir. Redcliff Ascent Wilderness Behavioral Reclamation Program Youth, 2000—; moderator, planner Telemedicine Can./USA Broadcasts, 1990—98; team doctor World Cup Speed Skating, 1999; dir. Utah Valley Sports Medicine Fellowship, 1999—; site physician 2002 Winter Olympics and Paralympics/Ice Hockey, Sledge Hockey; cons. Global Emergency Medicine Support; developer internat. tng. program for physicians, Nepal, 2000, Western Samoa, 01, Fiji, 01. Contbr. articles to profl. jours.; guest radio talk shows; developer internat. tng. program in emergency medicine: Art in EM = Advanced Resuscitation Training in Emergency Medicine. Chmn. coms. life support Heart and Stroke Found. (Can.) Ont., 1991-93; scoutmaster Boy Scouts Am., Kaysville, Utah, 1995, Orem, Utah, 1998-99. Recipient Achievement award for internat. distinction in music Govt. Alberta, 1976, Disting. Lectr. award Thailand and Asia Coll. Surgeons, 1993. Mem. AMA, Am. Acad. Family Physicians, Utah Med. Assn., Coll. Family Physicians (Can.), Am. Med. Soc. for Sports Medicine, Am. Coll. Sports Medicine. Mem. Lds Ch. Avocations: mountain biking, photography, family enrichment. Office: Utah Valley Sports Medicine Fellowship 1134 N 500 W Ste 102 Provo UT 84604-3380 E-mail: uvdrober@ihc.com.

ROBERTS, SUSAN STURGEON, art educator, writer; b. Aurora, Colo., Aug. 15, 1953; d. Thomas James Sturgeon, Lela Selby Nagle; m. Eugene Arden Roberts. BS, Calif. State Polytechnic U., 1978—78. Tchr. Redlands Unified Sch. Dist., Redlands, Calif., 1978—80; needle arts tchr. Grants Pass, Oreg., 1974—. Double knits designer Western Textile MIll., Ontario, Calif., 1978. Author: (book) The Complete Needlepoint Guide 400+ Needlepoint Stitches, 2000; sculpture. Mem.: Embroiderer's Guild Am. Inc. (program dir. 2001—02, asst. editor 1973—76), Am. Needlepoint Guild Inc. Office: 450 Genverna Glen Grants Pass OR 97527-9570 Home Fax: 541-471-0917; Office Fax: 541-471-0917. Personal E-mail: susanroberts15@hotmail.com. Business E-Mail: susanroberts15@hotmail.com.

ROBERTS, SUZANNE CATHERINE, artist; b. San Antonio, Oct. 27, 1953; d. Thomas Simons and Marceline Margaret (Conrady) Garrett; m. Ted Blake Roberts, May 22, 1976; 1 child, Elizabeth. BS in Radio-TV-Film, U. Tex., 1975, B of Journalism, 1977; MA in Interdisciplinary Studies, Corpus Christi (Tex.) State U., 1982, MS in Gen. Counseling, 1989; MA in Polit. Sci., S.W. Tex. State U., 1995. News announcer Sta. KIXL Radio, Austin, Tex., 1976, Sta. KSIX Radio, Corpus Christi, 1977-78; news anchor Sta. KZTV-TV, 1979, news reporter, 1977-80; news announcer, reporter Sta. KRYS-AM-FM, 1983-87; freelance reporter United Press Internat., Austin, 1989-94, Tex. State Network, Austin, 1995-97, Des Moines, 1997-2000; artist, 1998—.

ROBERTS, TERI ALANE, accountant, educator, civic activist; b. Mission Hills, Calif., Oct. 25, 1963; d. Alan Lewis and Barbara Ann (Taylor) R. BA in Speech Comm., Calif. State U., Northridge, 1990, BA in Polit. Sci. with honors, 1993, MA in Polit. Sci., 1997, MA in History Progress. Peer educator on rape Discovering Alternatives to Today's Encounters, Northridge, 1996-97; dir. Save the Animals Fund, Pasadena, Calif., 1997. Vol. Ga. Mercer for City Coun., Encino, Calif., 1997; mem. planning com., presenter at workshop Ending Violence Against Women Conf., Northridge, 1997; mem. planning com. Rainbow Sisters Project, L.A., 1999. Recipient Commendation for Rainbow Sisters Project, L.A. County, 1999. Mem. Polit. Sci. Club Calif. State U. (dir. fundraising 1992-93, dir. graduation com. 1992-93), Student Speech Comm. Assn. Calif. State U. (dir. social activities 1987-88), Delta Sigma (life). Democrat. Avocations: reading, dancing, church activities. Home: 8545 Balboa Blvd Apt 250 Northridge CA 91325-3531 E-mail: teriroberts@socal.rr.com.

ROBERTS, THEODORE HARRIS, banker; b. Gillett, Ark., May 14, 1929; s. D. Edward and Gertrude (Harris) R.; m. Elisabeth Law, July 17, 1953; children: Susan, William (dec.), Julia, John. BA in Govt., Northwestern State U., 1949; MA in Polit. Sci., Okla. State U., 1950; postgrad., U. Chgo. Grad. Sch. Bus., 1956. With Harris Trust and Savs. Bank, Chgo., 1953-82; exec. v.p., sec., treas. Harris Bank and Harris Bankcorp Inc., 1971-82, dir., exec. com., 1975-82; pres. Fed. Res. Bank St. Louis, 1983-85; chmn. bd., chief exec. officer Talman Home Fed. Savs. & Loan, Chgo., 1985-92; pres. LaSalle Nat. Corp., 1992-95, retired. Sr. cons. ABN AMRO, 1995—. Mem. Chgo. Club, Comml. Club Chgo., Econ. Club Chgo., Exmoor Country Club (Highland Park, Ill.). Office: 135 S La Salle St Ste 1162 Chicago IL 60603-4500

ROBERTS, THOMAS ANDREW, II, development executive; b. Jersey City, Sept. 5, 1949; s. Thomas Andrew and Muriel Cecelia (Burt) R.; m. Myrtle Beatrice Mumford, Sept. 15, 1971 (div. May 1991); children: Chantey P., Thomas Andrew III; m. Yvonne Coleta Belefanti, Apr. 3, 1994; children:

Andrew Belefanti, Oliver Basilio. BA, Rutgers U., 1973; JD, Seton Hall U., 1977. Bar: N.J. 1984. Cmty. specialist City of Newark, 1970-73; area coord. project Jersey City Redevel. Agy., 1973-75; dir. housing Urban League Essex County, Newark, 1976; dist. supr. Nat. Neighborhood Reinvestment Corp., Washington, 1977-85; lawyer East Orange, N.J., 1985-88; exec. dir. Camden (N.J.) Redevel. Agy., 1988-2000, NOAH Devel. Corp., Belle Glade, Fla., 2000—. Bd. dirs. A Better Camden Corp. Pres. Camden Coun. on Alcohol Abuse, 1990-2000; trustee, vice chmn. CamCare Health Corp., Camden, 1990-2000; trustee South Jersey Mus. Art, Lawnside, 1996-99, Camden Empowerment Zone Corp., 1996-2000; advisor Explorer Post 2044, Camden, 1995-97; fellow Leadership N.J., 1999. Mem. Fencing Acad. South Jersey (instr. 1997-2000). Presbyterian. Avocation: fencing. Home: 168 Park Rd N Royal Palm Beach FL 33411 Office: 601 Covenant Dr Belle Glade FL 33430-5728 E-mail: noahdev@ix.netcom.com.

ROBERTS, THOMAS GEORGE, retired physicist; b. Ft. Smith, Ark., Apr. 27, 1929; s. Thomas Lawrence and Emma Lee (Stanley) R.; m. Alice Anne Harbin, Nov. 14, 1958 (dec. 1994); children: Lawrence Dewey, Regina Anne; foster child, Marcia Roberts Dale; m. Betty Howard McElyea, July 28, 1995. AA, Armstrong Coll., 1953; BS, U. Ga., 1956, MS, 1957; PhD, N.C. State U., 1967. Rsch. physicist U.S. Army Missile Command, Huntsville, Ala., 1958-85; cons. industry and govt. agys., 1970—, SAIC, Huntsville, Ala., 1997-2001; owner Technoco, 1985-96. Contbr. articles to profl. jours.; patentee in field. Sgt. USAF, 1948-52. Fellow Am. Optical Soc.; mem. Am. Phys. Soc., IEEE, Huntsville Optical Soc. Am. (pres. 1980, 92), Toastmaster Internat. (pres. 1963). Episcopalian. Achivements include research in laser physics, optics, particle beams and instrumentation; diagnostic devices and techniques development.

ROBERTS, THOMAS HEYM, city and regional planner, consultant; b. Cleve., Jan. 28, 1928; s. Burke Brockway and Charlotte (Heym) R.; m. Jacquelyn Kline, June 4, 1950; children: Judith, Mark, Holly, Tod. BSCE, Case Inst. Tech., 1950; M of Regional Planning, U. N.C., 1952. Planning asst. City Planning Commn., Cleve., 1950, sr. planner Youngstown, Ohio, 1952-54, County Planning Bd., Charleston County, S.C., 1954-56; various positions to planning dir. Atlanta Region Metro. Planning Commn., Atlanta, 1956-66; dir. of planning Metro. Washington Coun. Govts., 1966-69; exec. dir. Am. Inst. Cert. Planners, Washington, 1969-72; dir. of planning Atlanta Regional Commn., 1972-78; pres. Thomas H. Roberts and Assocs., Atlanta, 1978—. Contbg. author: Lincoln Institute of Land Policy, 1985, 86, Land Development Control Law, 1986, The Practice of State and Regional Planning, 1986, Urban Planning, 1988. Fellow Am. Inst. Cert. Planners; mem. Am. Planning Assn. (bd. dirs. 1974-77, v.p. 1977-78, pres. 1978). Unitarian-Universalist. Avocations: quartet singing, vocal arranging, guitar. Home and Office: 4241 Smithsonia Ct Tucker GA 30084-2627

ROBERTS, THOMASENE BLOUNT, entrepreneur; b. Americus, Ga., Sept. 5, 1943; d. Thomas Watson and Mary Elizabeth (Smith) Blount; m. Henry Lee Roberts, Apr. 24, 1970 (div. 1991); 1 child, Asha Maia. Student, Fisk U., 1960-63; BA, Morris Brown Coll., 1965; MA, Atlanta U., 1970, postgrad., 1979-82, Clark Atlanta U. Social worker Gate City Day Nursery Assn., Atlanta, 1965-66; ticket agt. Delta Air Lines, Inc., 1966-68; clk. accounts payable Kraft Foods, Inc., Decatur, 1968; cons. family svcs. Atlanta Housing Authority, 1970-72, supr. family svcs., 1972-73, mgr. family relocation, 1974-79; grad. rsch. asst. Sch. Edn. Atlanta U., 1979-82; city coun. asst. City of Atlanta, 1984-88, rsch. asst. Dept. Pub. Safety, 1988; dir. govtl. rels. Morris Brown Coll., Atlanta, 1988-93; owner TBR Ent., 1993—2002; adminstrv. analyst human svcs. City of Atlanta, 1995-97, adminstrv. analyst, prin. dept. adminstrv. svcs., 1997; owner Dream Catcher Events, Inc., 1997—; psychol. svcs. specialist City of Atlanta, 1998—2002. Researcher/intern Project Focus Teen Mother Program, Atlanta, 1981-82; moderator Nat. Black Women's Health Project, Atlanta, 1985; workshop leader Assn. Human Resources Mgrs., Atlanta, 1989; pres.'s rep. U. Ctr. Devel. Corp., Inc., 1989-93; cons. entrepreneur devel. workshop Morris Brown Coll. Chairperson Ida Prather YWCA Cmty. Bd., Atlanta, 1985-90; bd. dirs. YWCA Met. Atlanta, 1986-90, Met. Atlanta Coalition 100 Black Women, 1988-90, 92-2001, sec., mem. bd. dirs., 1994-96, 1st v.p., 1997-2000; trustee Hammonds House Mus., 1995-2001; active fund dr. com. Jomandi Prodn., 1988-89; v.p. maj. gifts com. Camp Best Friends, City of Atlanta, 1989; mem. Multi-Cultural Leadership Group, Gov.'s Coun. on Developmental Disabilities, 1990; bd. dirs. Atlanta Black/Jewish Coalition, 1997-2000; apptd. mem. Atlanta Sister Cities Commn.; presenter, cons. Youth Motivation Task Force, 1998-2001. Mem. Atlanta-Trinidad/Tobago Exch. (sec., treas. 1983-89, Pt. of Spain cert. 1986), Nat. Polit. Congress Black Women (corr. sec. 1989-90), Nat. Assn. for Equal Opportunity Higher Edn. (coll. liaison 1988-93), Coun. for Advancement-Support of Edn., Info. Forum, Atlanta Urban League, Inc., Nat. Assn. for Equal Opportunity in Higher Edn. (Disting. Alumni award 1991), Nat. Soc. Fund-Raising Execs. (cert. 1992), Nat. Soc. Fund-Raising Execs. Leadership Inst., Friends of Morehouse Sch. Medicine, Assn. Bridal Cons., Internat. Spl. Events Soc. (v.p. programs 2001-02), Atlanta Bus. League, Delta Sigma Theta (pub. rels. asst. 1986-89). Avocations: dancing, theatre, music, film, art. Home and Office: 1817 King Charles Rd SW Atlanta GA 30331-4909 Fax: (404) 344-0378.

ROBERTS, TONY (DAVID ANTHONY ROBERTS), actor; b. N.Y.C., Oct. 22, 1939; s. Kenneth and Norma R.; 1 child, Nicole. BS, Northwestern U., 1961. Movie debut in The Million Dollar Duck, 1971; other film appearances include Star Spangled Girl, 1971, Play It Again, Sam, 1972, Serpico, 1974, The Taking of Pelham, One Two Three, 1974, Annie Hall, 1977, Lovers Like Us, 1977, Just Tell Me What You Want, Stardust Memories, 1980, A Midsummer Nights Sex Comedy, 1982, Question of Honor, 1982, Packin' It In, 1983, Amityville IIID, 1983, Hannah and her Sisters, 1986, 18 Again!, 1988, Popcorn, 1990, Switch, 1991; TV movies The Lindbergh Kidnapping Case, 1976, Girls in the Office, 1979, If Things Were Different, 1980, A Question of Honor, 1982, Our Sons, 1992, Not in My Family, 1993, The American Clock, 1993, Perry Mason: The Case of the Jealous Jokester, 1995; regular on TV series The Edge of Night, 1963-65, Rosetti and Ryan, 1977, The Four Seasons, 1986, The Lucy Arnaz Show, 1987, The Thorns, 1989; other TV appearances include The Way They Were, 1980; Broadway debut in Something about a Soldier, 1962; toured with nat. co. of Come Blow Your Horn, 1962; other Broadway stage appearances Take Her, She's Mine, 1964, Never Too Late, Barefoot in the Park, The Last Analysis, 1964, Don't Drink the Water, 1966, How Now, Dow Jones, 1967 (nominated for Tony award), Play It Again, Sam, 1969 (nominated for Tony award), Promises, Promises, 1971, Sugar, 1972, Absurd Person Singular, 1974, Murder at the Howard Johnson's, 1979, They're Playing Our Song, 1981, Doubles, 1985, Arsenic and Old Lace, 1986, Jerome Robbins Broadway, 1990, The Seagull, 1992, Tale of the Allergist's Wife, 2002; London debut in Promises, Promises, 1969 (London Critics Poll award as Best Actor in Musical), 1974; appeared in: Darkroom, Yale Repertory Theatre, New Haven, Hamlet, Otterbein Coll. (Ohio) Winter Drama Festival, 1975, Taming of the Shrew, Atlanta, 1978, Let 'Em Eat Cake, Berkshire Theatre Festival, Serenading Louis, Acad. Festival Theatre; The Seagull, Saratoga Performance Arts Festival, 1985, Who's Afraid of Virginia Woolf, 1986, (voice) audio books The Short Forever, 2002, Leadership, 2002. Served in U.S. Army. Mem. SAG (bd. dirs. 1990—, v.p. of NY div.,2001-), Actors Equity Assn. (governing coun. 1968-74) Office: Innovative Artists 1505 10th Ave Santa Monica CA 90401*

ROBERTS, VERNA DEAN, music educator; b. Sherman, Tex., Apr. 11, 1925; d. Vern Holbrook and Sarah Aileen Wells (Shoffner) Smith; m. James Bruce Roberts, Jan. 22, 1947; children: Gregory Bruce, Debra Deane, Pamela Anne. B in Music Edn., Phillips U., 1947; MS in Elem. Edn., Okla. State U., 1950; postgrad., U. Ill., 1960—, William R. Rainey Coll., 1960—. Pvt. tchr. piano, 1940—; pvt. tchr. voice, 1945—; music instr. pub. schs. Durant, Stillwater, Southard, Okla., 1947-51, Sacred Heart of Mary High Sch., Rolling Meadows, Ill., Elk Grove Village (Ill.) High Sch.; dir. children's choirs, adult choirs Okla., Ill.; singer with choruses & show choirs; music adjudicator Okla., Ill. Faculty mem. Am. Coll. Musicians Piano Guild Hall of Fame. Charter mem., elder, deacon, Sunday Sch. tchr., dir. adult & children's choirs, dir. stewardship drive, treas. Christian Women's Fellowship & Circle, Christian Ch. (Disiples of Christ), Arlington Heights, Ill. Mem. Nat. Music Tchrs. Assn., Ill. State Music Tchrs. Assn. (state membership chmn.), Northwest Suburban Music Tchrs. Assn. (1st v.p., 2nd v.p., chmn. numerous coms.), Assn. Disciples Musicians, Ill. Music Assn., Arts Coun. Co-op. Republican. Avocations: music performance, reading, poetry, swimming, cooking. Office: Roberts Sch Music 623 Sycamore Dr Elk Grove Village IL 60007-4624

ROBERTS, VICTORIA LYNN P. antique expert; b. N.Y.C., Sept. 15, 1953; d. Edgar Alan Parmer and Nina Joyce (Ash) Gross; m. George E. Roberts, Dec. 1, 1978 (div. 1985); 1 child, Joshua Henry. BA in Polit. Sci., Am. govt., const. law, Yale U., 1998; MBA, Fairfield U., 1999. Pres. High Gear Creative Svcs., Savannah, Ga., 1979-81; v.p. Rossignol Modeling Agy., N.Y.C., 1981-82; mgr., dir. Parc Monceau Antiques, Westport, Conn., 1982-85; pres., owner, CEO Victoria & Cie LLC, Custom Furniture Mfg., Norwalk, 1985—; pres., owner L.L.C. Custon Furniture Mfg. Antiques tchr. Sacred Heart U., Fairfield, Conn., 1988, 89, Norwalk Community Coll., 1989; antique lectr. various hist. socs., Conn., 1989-90; speaker in antiques field; antique expert seminars to interior designers, Norwalk, 1989; creator, sole contbr. spls. on antiques CNBC TV, 1989, 90. Antiques editor Brooks Community Newspaper, Westport, 1989-91; contbr. Antiques Mag., 1991—. Mem. Appraisers Assn. Am. (sr.), Coll. Arts Assn., Yale Club (N.Y.C. admissions com. mem.), Alpha Sigma Lambda. Avocations: scenic photography, bicycling, history, rose gardening. Office: Stamford Industrial Park Canal Street Stamford CT 06902 E-mail: victoria@victoriacie.com.

ROBERTS, WALTER HERBERT BEATTY, anatomist, educator; b. Field, B.C., Can., Jan. 24, 1915; came to U.S., 1956, naturalized, 1965; s. Walter McWilliam and Sarah Caroline (Orr) R.; m. Olive Louise O'Neal, Sept. 1, 1937; children: Gayle, Sharon, David. MD, Coll. Med. Evangelists (later Loma Linda U.), 1939. Intern St. Paul's Hosp., Vancouver, B.C., 1938-40; med. dir. Rest Haven Hosp. Sanitarium and Hosp., Sidney, Vancouver Island, 1940-53; post doctoral trg. White Meml. Hosp., Los Angeles, 1946-47, hosp., Edinburgh, Scotland, 1953-55; instr. in anatomy Loma Linda U., 1955-58, asst. prof. anatomy, 1959-62, asso. prof., 1962-70, prof., 1971—, chmn. dept. anatomy, 1974-81; prof. emeritus. Mem. Sigma Xi, Alpha Omega Alpha. Adventist. Home: 11366 Campus St Loma Linda CA 92354-3302 Office: Loma Linda Univ Dept Path & Human Anatomy Divsn Human Anatomy Loma Linda CA 92350-0001

ROBERTS, WALTER RONALD, political science educator, former government official; b. Waltendorf, Austria, Aug. 26, 1916; came to U.S., 1939, naturalized, 1944; s. Ignatius and Elizabeth (Diamant) R.; m. Gisela K. Schmarak, Aug. 22, 1939; children: William M., Charles E., Lawrence H. MLitt, Cambridge (Eng.) U., 1940, PhD, 1980. Research asst. Harvard U. Law Sch., 1940-42; writer, editor Voice of Am., 1942-49; press officer U.S. del. to Austrian Treaty talks, 1949, 55; fgn. affairs officer Dept. State, 1950-53; dep. asst. dir. USIA, 1954-60; counselor of embassy for pub. affairs Am. Embassy, Belgrade, Yugoslavia, 1960-66; diplomat-in-residence Brown U., Providence, 1966-67; counselor U.S. Mission to Internat. Orgns., Geneva, 1967-69; dep. assoc. dir. USIA, Washington, 1969-71, assoc. dir., 1971-74; dir. diplomatic studies Ctr. Strategic and Internat. Studies Georgetown U., 1974-75; exec. dir. Bd. Internat. Broadcasting, 1975-85; diplomat-in-residence George Washington U., 1986-96; sr. advisor U.S. Adv. Commn. on Pub. Diplomacy, 1998—. Author: Tito, Mihailovic and the Allies, 1941-45, 73, paperback, 1987, (with Terry L. Deibel) Culture and Information: Two Foreign Policy Functions, 1976; contbr. articles to profl. pubs. Apptd. mem. U.S. Adv. Commn. on Pub. Diplomacy, 1991-97, sr. advisor, 1998—; bd. dirs. Salzburg Seminar, 1993-97, Coun. Sr. Fellows, 1998—, Pub. Diplomacy Found., 1996—; bd. dirs. Pub. Diplomacy Inst., George Washington U., 2001—. Recipient Disting. Honor award USIA, 1974 Mem. Washington Inst. Fgn. Affairs, Coun. Fgn. Rels., Oxford-Cambridge Com., USIA Alumni Assn. (bd. dirs. 1995-98), Met. Club. Home: 4449 Sedgwick St NW Washington DC 20016-2713

ROBERTS, WILBUR EUGENE, dental educator, research scientist, wine importer; b. Lubbock, Tex., Nov. 16, 1942; s. Wilbur Eugene Roberts and Elva Etna (Chance) Turnwall; m. Cheryl Ann Jones, June 6, 1967; children: Jeffery Alan, Carrie Jean. DDS, Creighton U., 1967; PhD in Anatomy, U. Utah, 1969; cert. in orthodontics, U. Conn., 1974; DHC in Medicine (hon.), Lille (France) U., 1996. Diplomate Am. Bd. Orthodontics. Rsch. fellow U. Utah, Salt Lake City, 1967—69; postdoctoral fellow U. Conn., Farmington, 1971—74; from asst. prof. to prof. dentistry U. Pacific, San Francisco, 1974—88; prof. chmn. dept. orthodontics Ind. U., Indpls., 1988—93, chmn. dept. oral and facial devel., 1993—97, prof. physiology and biophysics Sch. Medicine, 1988—2000, dir. grad. orthodontics program Sch. Dentistry, 1988—; head orthodontics sect., 1997—; mem. steering com. Biomechs. and Biomaterials Rsch. Ctr. Ind. U.-Purdue U., Indpls., 1990—96; NRC sr. rsch. assoc. NASA Ames Rsch. Ctr., Moffett Field, Calif., 1982—83; Jarabak prof. orthodontics Ind. U., Indpls., 2001—; CEO, sec.-treas. VinElite Imports, Inc., 1999—. Dir. Bone Rsch. Lab. U. Pacific, 1980—88, dir. Oral Devel. Clinic, 1980—86, Dr. Fred West Meml. lectr., 1989, 97; rsch. cons. Neodontics Corp., Laguna Nigel, Calif., 1982—85, Denar Corp., Anaheim, Calif., 1985—87, Nobelpharma AG, Goteborg, Sweden, 1988, Dental Implant Clin. Rsch. Group, Ann Arbor, Mich., 1991—, Align Tech., Mountain View, Calif., Oral Medicine and Biology Study sect. NIH, 1992—96, Rsch. Coun. ADA, 1992; accreditation cons. in orthodontics ADA Coun. on Dental Accreditation, 1996—; task force on faculty recruitment Am. Assn. of Orthodontics, 1998—; adj. prof. mech. engring. Purdue U., Indpls., 1990—; assoc. prof. implantology, maxillofacial surgery U. Lille, France, 1987—; guest prof. U. Western Ont., Canada, 1987; Dr. George Grieve Meml. lectr. Can. Dental Assn., 1993; mem. internat. affairs com. Ind. U.-Purdue U., Indpls., 1995—; sci. cons. Align Tech. Corp.; U.S. importer Mud House Wine Co. Ltd., Marlbourgh, New Zealand, Oakridge Vineyards, Ltd., Australia; ptnr. Vinters of Zuperb Zinfandel, Paso Robles, Calif. Contbr. sci. articles to profl. jours. Rep. campaign worker, Contra Costa County, Calif., 1980-82; ch. sch. supt. San Ramon Valley Meth. Ch., Alamo, Calif., 1979-81; adult ministries council San Ramon Valley Meth. Ch., Danville, Calif., 1984-86; sci. cons. St. Isadore Sch. and San Ramon Valley High Sch., Danville, 1978-86; chmn. bldg. com. Sunrise at Geist United Meth. Ch., Indpls.; mem. planning bd. Vols. in Medicine, Indpls., 2000-2001. Lt. comdr. USN, 1969-71, Vietnam. Decorated Navy Commendation medal; named Eminent scholar, Okla. U., 1995; recipient Cosmos Achievement award, NASA, 1981, 1988, 1992, medal, City of Paris, 1989, City of Rouen, France, 1991, Rsch. award, Ind. U. Sch. Dentistry, 1993, Gold Medallion award, U. of Pacific Sch. Dentistry, 2001. Fellow: Am. Coll. Dentists, Internat. Coll. Dentists; mem.: Pacific Dental Rsch. Found. (pres. 1976—80), Am. Assn. Dental Rsch., Med. Dental Guild Calif. (pres. 1982—83, Gold Key award 1985), Conf. of the Co. of Wine Tasters of Normandy (pres. Ind. med. chpt. 1992—97, Master of the Cave 1997—2001, Baron of Honor 1999, Master of Embassies 2001—), Omicron Kappa Upsilon. Avocations: fishing, skiing, enology. Home: 8260 Skipjack Dr Indianapolis IN 46236-8429 Office: Ind U Sch Dentistry Sch Dentistry Sect Orthodontics 1121 W Michigan St Indianapolis IN 46202-5211 E-mail: werobert@iupui.edu.

ROBERTS, WILLIAM B. lawyer, business executive; b. Detroit, Aug. 23, 1939; s. Edwin Stuart and Marjorie Jean (Wardle) R.; m. Cathleen Anne Thompson, Sept. 1, 1962; children: Bradford William, Brent William, Katrina Marjorie. BA, Mich. State U., 1961; JD with distinction, U. Mich., 1963; China law diploma, U. East Asia, Macau, 1989. Bar: Mo. 1964, Fla. 1983, U.S. Dist. Ct. (ea. dist.) Mo. 1964, U.S. Dist. Ct. (mid. dist.) Fla. 1993. Mem. firm Thompson & Mitchell, St. Louis, 1963-67; atty. Monsanto Co., 1967-70; sr. exec. v.p. adminstrn., sec., gen. counsel Chromalloy Am. Corp. (successor Segua Corp. N.Y.), St. Louis, 1970-78, exec. v.p.-adminstrn., gen. counsel, sec. Clayton, Mo., 1978-82; pvt. practice law, 1983-87; mng. ptnr. Roberts and Nordahl, St. Louis and Naples, Fla., 1988-89, Law Offices of William B. Roberts, St. Louis and Naples, 1989-90, Darrow & Roberts, P.A., Naples, 1992-93; pres., mng. dir. Law Offices of William B. Roberts, 1994—, Kansas City, Mo., 1999—. Pres., mng. dir. The Fairborne Group, Ltd., St. Louis and Naples, 1988-91, William B. Roberts & Assocs. Co., Merger and Acquisitions Specialists, 1982—; mem. exam. com. of policyowners Northwestern Mut. Life Ins. Co., Milw., 1978; del. to U.S.-China Joint Session on Trade Investment and Econ. Law, Beijing, 1987; sports rep. Steve Carlton, St. Louis Cardinals, Phila. Phillies baseball clubs, 1987-89; pres., CEO Tropical Tracks, Inc., Naples, 1994—. Mem. ABA, Fed. Bar Assn. (Mid. Dist. Fla.), Mo. Bar Assn., St. Louis Bar Assn. (chmn. antitrust sect. 1973), Fla. Bar Assn., Collier County Bar Assn., Delta Theta Phi. Methodist. Home: 133 Crestview Terr Lake Placid FL 33852 Also: 321 NE Landings Dr Lees Summit MO 64064-1586

ROBERTS, WILLIAM D. broadcasting executive; b. Drummondville, Que., Can. BA, Trent U., Peterborough, Ont., 1973; MBA, St. Mary's U., Halifax, N.S., 1976; MA, Sorbonne, Paris, 1977; Diploma in Broadcast Mgmt., U. Notre Dame, Ind. Sr. policy analyst CRTC, Ottawa, Ont., 1980-84; sr. v.p. Can. Assn. of Broadcasters, 1984-89; sr. dir. gen. TV Ontario, Toronto, 1989-96; sec. gen. N.Am. Nat. Broadcasters Assn., 1996—. V.p. Couchiching Inst. for Pub. Affairs, Toronto, 1993—; fellow Calumet Coll., York U., Toronto, 1996—, Massey Coll., U. Toronto, 1997—. Avocations: karate, scuba diving. Office: North American National Broadcasters Assn NABA PO Box 500 Sta A Toronto ON Canada M5W 1E6

ROBERTS, WILLIAM EVERETT, lawyer; b. Pierre, S.D., May 12, 1926; s. Everett David and Bonnie (Martin) R.; m. Cynthia Cline, July 18, 1953; children: Catherine C. Roberts-Martin, Laura M., Nancy F., David H. BS, U. Minn., 1947; LLB, Yale U., 1950. Bar: Ind. 1950, U.S. Supreme Ct. 1964. Employee, ptnr. Duck and Neighbours, Indpls., 1950-58; ptnr. Cadick, Burns, Duck & Neighbours, 1958-60, Roberts, Ryder, Rogers & Scism, Indpls., 1960-85, Barnes & Thornburg, Indpls., 1986-93, of counsel, 1994—. Pres., bd. dirs. Park-Tudor Sch., Indpls., 1982-83; elder Second Presbyn. Ch., Indpls., 1962—; trustee Indpls. Mus. Art, 1978—; pres. New Hope of Ind., Indpls., 1986-87. Fellow Am. Bar Found.; mem. ABA, Ind. Bar Assn., Indpls. Bar Assn., Rotary, Meridian Hills Country Club (pres. 1983-84). Republican. Home: 10466 Spring Highland Dr Indianapolis IN 46290-1101 Office: Barnes & Thornburg 11 S Meridian St Ste 1313 Indianapolis IN 46204-3535

ROBERTS, WILLIAM JOHN JAMES, electrical engineer; b. Adelaide, Australia, May 30, 1967; s. Peter and Patricia Florence Roberts. BE with honors, U. Adelaide, 1992; PhD in Info. Tech., George Mason U., 1996. Sr. rsch. scientist Def. Sci. and Tech. Orgn., Salisbury, Australia, 1990-2000; sr. engr. Atlantic Coast Techs., Inc., Silver Spring, Md., 2000—. Office: Atlantic Coast Techs Inc 11499 Columbia Pike Silver Spring MD 20904-2535 E-mail: wjjroberts@hotmail.com.

ROBERTS, WILLIAM LEWIS, clinical pathologist; b. Columbus, Ohio, July 23, 1960; s. William Warren and Kathryn (Butler) R.; m. Wendy Lee Higginson, Aug. 5, 1989. BS in Chemistry, Ohio State U., 1982; PhD in Pharmacology, Case Western Res. U., Cleve., 1988, MD, 1990. Resident Yale-New Haven Hosp., 1990-92; postdoctoral fellow Yale U., New Haven, 1992-95; asst. prof. U. Miss. Med. Ctr., Jackson, 1995-98; assoc. prof. pathology U. Utah, Salt Lake City, 1998—. Contbr. articles to profl. jours. Fellow Coll. Am. Pathologists; mem. Am. Soc. Clin. Pathology, Am. Assn. Clin. Chemistry, Acad. Clin. Lab. Physicians and Scientists, Phi Beta Kappa, Phi Kappa Phi, Alpha Omega Alpha. Republican. Pentecostal Ch. Achievements include development of high temperature polymeric liquid crystals; characterization of the glycolipid membrane anchor of erythrocyte acetylcholinesterase; characterization of membrane-binding domain of brain acetylcholinesterase; research on the mechanism of action of antileishmanial antimony compounds. Home: 8574 Snowville Dr Sandy UT 84093-1009 Office: ARUP Labs 500 Chipeta Way Salt Lake City UT 84108-1221 E-mail: william.roberts@aruplab.com.

ROBERTS-DEGENNARO, MARIA, social work educator; b. Austin, Minn., Oct. 10, 1947; d. Clinton M. and Laura E. (DeMets) Becker; m. Paul DeGennaro, July 7, 1984; 1 child, Matthew. B of Social Work, U. Minn., 1970, MSW, 1976; PhD, U. Tex., 1981. Family counselor Hennepin County Welfare Dept., Mpls., 1970-73; coord. YMCA, 1973-74; dist. project coord. Child Abuse and Neglect Project, Phoenix, 1976-77; prof. San Diego State U., 1980—; dir. Interdisciplinary Ctr., San Diego State U., 1987-90; dir. Interdisciplinary Program on Early Intervention San Diego State U., 1989-94. Contbr. articles to profl. jours. Mem. Assn. on Community Orgn. and Social Adminstrn., Nat. Assn. Social Workers, Coun. on Social Work Edn. Office: San Diego State U Sch Social Work San Diego CA 92182

ROBERTS-HARVEY, BONITA, elementary education educator; b. Detroit, June 24, 1947; d. Walter James and Mattie Louise Hall; father, Dolphus Hall Sr.; 1 child, Paula Renee. BA, Grand Valley State U., 1974; cert. in continuing edn., Western Mich. U., 1987; MA in Edn. Leadership, Mich. State U., 1998. Art specialist Jenison (Mich.) Pub. Schs., 1974—, JEA pub. rels. rep., 1994—. Visual/performing artist Summer at Arts Place-Grand Rapids C.C., 1980-92; cons. art edn. Detroit Inst. Art, 1988; adj. instr. Grand Rapids C.C., 2000-. Bd. dirs., performing artist Robeson Players, Grand Rapids, Mich., 1973-94, Cmty. Cir. Theatre, Grand Rapids, 1981-84, 97—, Coun. Performing Arts for Children, Grand Rapids, 1981-88, Grand Rapids Art Mus., 1997; active First Cmty. African Meth. Episc. Ch., NAACP. Mem. ASCD, NEA (del., regional rep.), Nat. Fine Arts Caucus, Nat. Art Edn. Assn., Mich. Art Edn. Assn., Mich. Edn. Assn. (tri-county pub. rels. 1994-95, regional del.), Mich. Alliance Arts Edn., Nat. Mus. Women in Arts, Jenison Edn. Assn. (pub. rels. 1993—), Delta Sigma Theta, Delta Kappa Gamma. Avocation: performing/visual arts advocate. Office: Jenison Pub Schs 8375 20th Ave Jenison MI 49428-9230

ROBERTSON, A. HAEWORTH, actuary, benefit consultant, foundation executive; b. Oklahoma City, May 10, 1930; s. Albert Haeworth and Bonnie Tennessee (Duckett) R.; m. Mary Adeline Kissee, Feb. 3, 1952 (div. July 1979); children— Valerie Lynn, Alan Haeworth, Mary Kathryn. *Robertson is a descendant of Reverend George Robertson: born in Struan, Scotland, 1662, granted a Master of Arts degree from St. Andrews University (1681-83). Reverend Robertson served as a schoolmaster in Perthshire, Scotland, was licensed by the Bishop of London in 1692 for the Anglican Church, and served as chaplain on board a man-of-war, 1692. He immigrated to Virginia in 1692 and served as rector of Bristol Parish, Virginia, from 1693 until his death in 1739. He was the first minister of the Old Blandford Church in Petersburg, Virginia (constructed in 1735 and restored in 1901 as a Confederate shrine).* BA in Math., U. Okla., 1951; MA in Actuarial Sci., U. Mich., 1953. Actuary Wyatt Co., Washington and Dallas, 1955-58; actuary Bowles, Andrews & Towne, Dallas, 1958-60; v.p., actuary W. Alfred Hayes & Co., St. Louis, 1960-63; pres. First Am. Security Life Ins. Co. Mo., 1964-68; pvt. practice internat. cons. actuary Barbados and Ghana, 1969-72; sr. actuary ILO, Geneva, Switzerland, 1973-75; chief actuary U.S. Social Security Adminstrn., Balt., 1975-78; mng. dir. William M. Mercer, Inc., Washington, 1978-88; pvt. practice, internat. cons., actuary Kuwait, Turkey, Guyana, Zimbabwe, China, The Philippines, 1988—. Chmn. Retirement Bd. Actuaries, Dept. Def., 1984-95; mem. Edn. Benefits Bd. Actuaries, 1985-95; pres., founder Retirement Policy Inst. Inc., 1986—. *While serving as chief actuary, Robertson concluded that serious financial and design problems lay ahead for social security and Medicare that would require significant changes in the systems. He resigned in 1978 to have the time and freedom to bring this message to the public via three books, more than 100 articles, and hundreds of public appearances. This mission has been the principal focus of his professional life since 1975. Currently he believes that the nation has waited so long to acknowledge the problems and take remedial action that a smooth transition to more viable systems is impossible.* Author: The Coming Revolution in Social Security, 1981, Social Security: What Every Taxpayer Should Know, 1992, The Big Lie: What Every Baby Boomer Should Know About Social Security and Medicare, 1997. Served to 2d lt. USAF, 1953-55 Recipient Commrs. citation, Social Security Adminstrn., Washington, 1976, Arthur J. Altmeyer award, HEW, Washington, 1978, Disting. Alumni award, Ctrl. H.S., Oklahoma City, 1997. Fellow Soc. Actuaries (bd. govs. 1979-81, v.p. 1985-87), Conf. Cons. Actuaries; mem. Am. Acad. Actuaries, Internat. Actuarial Assn., Internat. Assn. Cons. Actuaries, U.K. Inst. Actuaries (assoc.), Cosmos Club, Phi Beta Kappa, Phi Eta Sigma, Phi Kappa Sigma. Republican. Methodist.

ROBERTSON, ABEL L., JR. pathologist; b. St. Andrews, Argentina, July 21, 1926; came to U.S., 1952, naturalized, 1957; s. Abel Alfred Lazzarini and Margaret Theresa G. (Anderson) R.; m. Irene Kirmayr Mauch, Dec. 26, 1958; children: Margaret Anne, Abel Martin, Andrew Duncan, Malcolm Alexander. BS, Coll. D.F. Sarmiento, Buenos Aires, Argentina, 1946; MD suma cum laude, U. Buenos Aires, 1951; PhD, Cornell U., 1959. Fellow tissue culture div. Inst. Histology and Embryology, Sch. Medicine Inst. Histology and Embryology, 1947-49; surg. intern Hosp. Ramos Mejia, Buenos Aires, 1948-50; fellow in tissue culture research Ministry of Health, 1950-51; resident Hosp. Nacional de Clinicas, 1950-51; head blood vessel bank and organ transplants Research Ctr. Ministry of Health, 1951-53; fellow dept. surgery and pathology Sch. Medicine Cornell U., N.Y.C., 1953-55; asst. vis.

surgery U. Hosp. N.Y., 1955-60; asst. prof. research surgery Postgrad. Med. Sch. NYU, 1955-56; asst. vis. surgeon Bellevue Hosp., 1955-60; assoc. prof. research surgery NYU, 1956-60, assoc. prof. pathology Sch. Medicine and Postgrad Med. Sch., 1960-63; staff mem. div. research Cleve. Clinic Found., 1963-73, prof. research, 1972-73; assoc. clin. prof. pathology Case Western Res. U. Sch. Medicine, Cleve., 1966-72, prof. pathology, 1973-82, dir. interdisciplinary cardiovascular research, 1975-82; exec. head dept. pathology Coll. Medicine, U. Ill., Chgo., 1982-88; prof. pathology Coll. Medicine U. Ill., 1982-93, prof. emeritus, 1993—; vis. prof. emeritus cardiovascular med. Core Analysis Lab., Stanford U. Coll. Medicine, 1995—, cardiac pathologist, 2000—. Rsch. fellow N.Y. Soc. Cardiovasc. Surgery, 1957-58; mem. rsch. study subcom. of heart com. N.E. Ohio Regional Med. Program, 1969—. Mem. internat. editorial bd.: Atherosclerosis, Jour. Exptl. and Molecular Pathology, 1964—, Lab. Investigation, 1989—, Acta Pathologica Japonica, 1991—; contbr. articles to profl. jours. Recipient Research Devel. award NIH, 1961-63 Fellow AAAS, Am. Coll. Cardiology, Am. Coll. Clin. Pharmacology, Am. Heart Assn. (established investigator 1956-61, nominating com. coun. on arteriosclerosis 1972), Royal Microscopical Soc., Royal Soc. Promotion Health (Gt. Britain), Am. Geriat. Soc., N.Y. Acad. Scis., Cleve. Med. Library Assn.; mem. AMA, AAUP, Am. Soc. for Investigative Pathology, Am. Inst. Biol. Scis., Am. Judicature Soc., Am. Soc. Cell Biology, Am. Soc. Pathologists, Am. Soc. Nephrology, Assn. Am. Physicians and Surgeons, Assn. Computing Machinery, Electron Microscopy Soc. Am., Assn. Pathology Chmn., Internat. Acad. Pathology, Soc. Cardiovasc. Pathology, Internat. Cardiovasc. Soc., Internat. Soc. Cardiology (sci. council on arteriosclerosis and ischemic heart disease), Internat. Fed. on Genetic Engring. and Biotechnology, Internat. Soc. for Heart Rsch., Internat. Soc. Nephrology, Internat. Soc. Stereology, Pan Am. Med. Assn. (life, councillor in angiology 1966), Ill. Registry Anatomical Pathology (treas. 1985-87), Chgo. Pathology Soc., Reticuloendothelial Soc. Leucocyte Biology, Soc. Cryobiology, Tissue Culture Assn., Ohio Soc. Pathologists, Electron Microscopy Soc. Northeastern Ohio (pres., trustee 11966-68), Heart Assn. Northeastern Ohio, N.Y. Soc. Cardiovasc. Surgery, N.Y. Soc. Electron Microscopists, Cuyahoga County Med. Soc., Cleve. Soc. Pathologists, The Oxygen Soc., Sigma Xi. Home: PO Box 3125 340 5th Ave Half Moon Bay CA 94019-3125 Fax: 650-712-0357. E-mail: alrrob@pol.net.

ROBERTSON, AMY L. systems analyst; b. Gadsden, Ala., Oct. 16, 1970; d. James David and Shirley (Pierce) Robertson. BS, Jacksonville (Ala.) State U., 1993. Sys. analyst Blue Cross Blue Shield of Ala., Birmingham, 1993-98; programmer analyst II, Federated Sys. Group, Norcross, Ga., 1998-99; sys. analyst Met. Life, Alpharetta, 1999—. Post leader Explorer Scouts, Birmingham, 1997—98; supporter Adopt-a-platoon, 1999; dir. Miss Colonial Mall Gadsden Pageant, 2002—; judge Miss Ala. Prelim.; bd. dirs. Miss Atlanta Scholastic Pageant, 2001—02. Mem. Leadership Devel. Assn., Jacksonville State U. Alumni Assn. Baptist. Office: Met LIfe 2400 Lakeview Pkwy Ste 200 Alpharetta GA 30004-7902

ROBERTSON, ANDREW, dancer; b. Carleton Place, Ontario, Can. Student, Nat. Ballet Sch., Toronto, Royal Winnipeg Ballet Sch. With Royal Winnipeg Ballet; mem. corps de ballet N.Y.C. Ballet, 1992—98, 2000—; with Am. Ballet Theatre, 1998—2000. Dancer (ballets) Chaconne, A Midsummer Nights Dream, The Nutcracker, Prodigal Son, Tschaikovsky Ste No. 3, Symphonic Dances, Concerti Armonici, West Side Story Ste., Variations Sérieuses. Office: NYC Ballet NY State Theatre 20 Lincoln Ctr Plz New York NY 10023-6913*

ROBERTSON, ARMAND JAMES, II, judge; b. San Diego, Sept. 23, 1937; s. Armand James and Muriel H. R.; m. Marion Sperry, Aug. 11, 1962; children: Armand James, Laura Marie. A.M. in Econs, Stanford U., 1960; LL.B., Harvard U., 1965. Bar: Calif. 1966. Law clk. to Charles M. Merrill, U.S. Ct. Appeals (9th cir.), 1965-66; assoc. firm Howard, Prim, Rice, Nemerovski, Canady & Pollak, San Francisco, 1966-71, ptnr., 1971-77; dir. Howard, Rice, Nemerovski, Canady, Robertson & Falk (P.C.), San Francisco, 1977-95; judge of the Superior Ct. City and County of San Francisco, 1995—. Bd. dirs. St. Francis Found., 1996—, chmn., 1999—. Lt. (j.g.) USN, 1960-62. Mem. Am. Law Inst., ABA (antitrust sect.), CPR Inst. for Dispute Resolution, Phi Beta Kappa. Home: Edgewood Ave San Francisco CA 94117-3713 Office: San Francisco Superior Ct 400 Mcallister St Rm 210 San Francisco CA 94102-4512

ROBERTSON, BEVERLY CARRUTH, retired steel company executive; b. Texarkana, Ark., May 16, 1922; s. Glenn C. Robertson (dec.); m. Ruth Mulcare, Oct. 31, 1945 (dec. Oct. 1993); children: Glenn J., Beverly R. Dodds, Rebecca A. Robertson Deans; m. Charlotte Doty Lawler, June 2, 1995. In sales Nat. Supply Co., Laurel, Miss., 1941-51; purchasing agt. Kirby Petroleum co., Houston, 1951-54; exec. v.p. mktg. Lone Star Steel Co., Dallas, 1954-85, exec. v.p., 1985-86; pres., dir., chief exec. officer LSSCO Trading Corp., 1985-86; owner BSEER Enterprises, Dallas, 1986—; ptnr. Clayton Equipment Co., 1992-97, retired, 1997—. Chmn. Sir Alec Inc., 1985-94; cons. Pipeco, Inc., Houston, 1986-88; exec. v.p. mktg. and procurement Nat. Pipe and Tube Co., Houston, 1988-89; pres., CEO Tex. Am. Pipe & Supply Co., Inc., Dallas, 1989—; cons. Ipsco Steel, Inc., Camanche, Iowa, 1991-92. Served to capt. USAF, 1943-46, ETO. Named Supplier of Yr. Petroleum Industry Buyers group Nat. Assn. Purchasing Mgmt., 1982 Mem. Dallas Country Club, Dallas Petroleum Club. Republican. Episcopalian. Home: PO Box 12688 Dallas TX 75225-0688

ROBERTSON, CAREY JANE, musician, educator; b. Culver City, Calif., Apr. 18, 1955; d. Robert Bruce and Marjorie Ellen (Greenleaf) Coker;l m. Brian Collins Robertson, June 28, 1975 (div. July 1985); 1 child, Sean Kalen. BMus, Calif. State U., Northridge, 1977; MMus, U. So. Calif., L.A., 1979, PhD of Mus. Arts, 1987. Organist/choir dir. Village Meth. Ch., North Hollywood, Calif., 1972-75, St. Bede's Episcopal Ch., Mar Vista, 1975-79; organist interim St. Alban's Episcopal Ch., Westwood, 1985; organist Covenant Presbyn. Ch., Westchester, 1985-90; organist/choir dir. St. David's United Ch., West Vancouver, B.C., Can., 1990-91; prin. organist Claremont (Calif.) United Ch. of Christ, 1991—; music educator Fontana Unified Sch. Dist. Prof. organ Claremont Grad. U., 1991—, New Calif. Conservatory, Buena Park, Calif., 2002—; concert organist Am. Guild of Organists, throughout U.S. and Can., 1974—; cons. Sch. Theology, U. B.C., 1990. Bd. dirs. Ruth and Clarence Mader Found., Pasadena, Calif., 1993—. Recipient Music Tchrs. Nat. Assn. Wurlitzer Collegiate Artist award, 1980; Irene Robertson scholar, 1977, 78. Mem. Am. Guild Organists (historian, sec. 1985-92, exec. com. 1983-85, sub-dean Pasadena chpt., 1998-99), Pi Kappa Lambda (Scholastic award 1987). Avocations: scuba diving instructor, water skiing. Home: 633 Maple Way Upland CA 91786-4511

ROBERTSON, CHARLES JAMES, museum director emeritus; b. Houston, Sept. 12, 1934; s. Charles James and Felide Corinne (O'Brien) R. BA, U. Va., Charlottesville, 1956; MA, Harvard U., 1958; student, U. London Courtauld Inst., 1960; JD, George Washington U., 1964. Atty. Dow, Lohnes & Albertson, Washington, 1964-69; adminstr. Richard H. Chamberlain, M.D. & Assoc., Phila., 1969-75; assoc. dir. N.C. Mus. Art, Raleigh, 1975-77; deputy dir. Smithsonian Am. Art Mus., Washington, 1977—2001. Treas., exec. com. Am. Assn. Mus., Washington, 1982-84; mem. adv. com. Octagon House Mus., Washington, 1989-97, chmn. 1993-96; bd. dirs. Victorian Soc. in Am., Phila., 1990—, v.p., 1994-2000; mem. Hist. Preservation Rev. Bd. of the Dist. of Columbia, 1992—; bd. regents Am. Archtl. Found., Washington, 1993-96; trustee Cosmos Club Preservation Found., Washington, 1993—, treas., 1999—. Contbr. articles to profl. jours. Pres. Dupont Circle Conservancy, Washington, 1978-92; v.p., bd. mem., Dupont Circle Citizens Assn. Washington, 1980-83, 86. Recipient Rumrill fellowship Harvard U., Cambridge, Mass., 1956-57. Mem. Cosmos Club, Phi Beta Kappa, Delta Theta Phi.

ROBERTSON, DALE WAYNE, minister; b. Anderson, S.C., Apr. 6, 1954; s. William Eural and Avis Louise (O'Barr) R.; m. Beth Brown, Nov. 21, 1978; children: Miranda Renee, Christi Alisha. BTh, Brainerd Theol. Seminary, Spartanburg, S.C., 1985; MTh, Immanuel Bapt. Theol. Seminary, Peachtree City, Ga., 1988, MDiv, 1989, DD, 1990. Lic. and ordained to ministry So. Bapt. Conv., 1981. Assoc. evangelist Greater Life Evangelism Assn., Owasso, Okla., 1978-81; minister First Bapt. Ch., Colcord, 1981-83, Bowman (Ga.) Bapt. Ch., 1983-85, Morningside Bapt. Ch., Valdosta, Ga., 1985—. Chmn. evangelism com. Hebron Assn., Elberton, Ga., 1984, Valdosta (Ga.) Assn., 1989; mem. com. on order of bus. Ga. Bapt. Conv., Atlanta, 1989, v.p., 1990, moderator, 1990, vice moderator, 1991, mem. pers. com., 1991, mem. resolutions com., 1991, nominating com., 1995-96, structure study com., 1995-96, time place preaching com., 1995-96, vice chmn. Ga. Baptist Convention Exec. Com., 1996-97, exec. com. mem. Ga. Baptist Convention, 1996-2001, mem. adminstrn. com., 1996-2001; mem. com. on coms., 1991; pres. Ga. Bapt. Preaching conf., 1993-94. Com. mem. Coms. of Southern Baptist Convention. Mem. Valdosta Bapt. Assn. (moderator 1992-94), Ga. Alumni Luther Rice Sem. (treas. 1993-94, pres. 1994-95, mem. relocation com. 1999-2000, mem. State Mo. budget com. 2000-2001, mem. cooperative program budget com. 2000-2001, mem. com. on coms. exec. com. 2000-2001, mem. new ch. membership com. 2000-2001, pres. Ga. Bapt. conv. 2001-). Home: 1125 N Lakeshore Dr Valdosta GA 31605-5917 Office: Morningside Bapt Ch PO Box 2405 Valdosta GA 31604-2445 *In a day of questioned morality and extreme permissiveness, the greatest challenge we face is to remain faithful in sharing the never-changing truths of Scripture to an ever changing world.*

ROBERTSON, DAVID ALLAN, JR. English educator; b. Chgo., July 30, 1915; s. David Allan Robertson and Anne Victoria Knobel; m. Beridge Ruth Leigh Mallory, June 18, 1940 (dec. Sept. 1953); children: Anne (Mrs. Robert Acheson Spencer), Susan, Allan; m. Victoria Adams Bryer, Oct. 10, 1964 (div. June 1988); children: Struan, Isabel, Samuel; m. Harriet Cooper Frothingham, Dec. 21, 1991. AB, Princeton U., 1936, MA, 1939, PhD, 1940. Instr. English, Barnard Coll. Columbia U., N.Y.C., 1940-42, 45-47, asst. prof., 1947-50, assoc. prof., 1950-56, prof., 1956-68, McIntosh prof., 1968-86, prof. emeritus, 1986—, chmn. dept., 1956-59, 64-67, 1975-77. Mem. commn. on English Coll. Entrance Exam Bd., 1959-64; mem. adv. bd. Victorian Studies, 1959-66, 75-87; mem. adv. coun. dept. English, Princeton U., 1970-92, chmn., 1977-82, libr., 1973-76, mem. dept. art and archaeology, 1974-85, chmn., 1977-82. Author: George Mallory, 1969, reprinted, 1999, Sir Charles Eastlake and the Victorian Art World, 1978, North of India, 1999; contbr. articles and revs. to profl. jours. Mem. coun. Friends of Princeton U. Libr., 1976—, chmn., 1991-95. Lt. comdr. USNR, 1942—, ret. Henry fellow Trinity Coll., Cambridge U., 1937-38, Howard Found. fellow, 1953-54. Mem. MLA, English Inst. (asst. sec. 1946, sec. 1947-48, editor English Inst. Essays 1946-48), Century Assn., Am. Alpine Club (co-editor jour. 1947-52), Nassau Club. Home: 75 Arreton Rd Princeton NJ 08540

ROBERTSON, DAVID WAYNE, pharmaceutical executive; b. Dumas, Tex., July 30, 1955; s. R.L. and N.C. R. BS, Stephen F. Austin State U., 1977; MS, U. Ill., 1978, PhD, 1981. Sr. medicinal chemist Eli Lilly and Co., Indpls., 1981-84, rsch. scientist, 1985-87, sr. rsch. scientist, 1988-89, rsch. group leader, 1988-89, dir. cen. nervous system rsch., 1990-91; v.p. medicinal chemistry Ligand Pharms., Inc., San Diego, 1991-92, v.p. rsch., 1992-93, v.p. discovery rsch., 1993-96; exec. dir. R & D DuPont Pharm. Co., Wilmington, 1996-99; v.p. rsch. Pharmacia & Upjohn, Kalamazoo, 1999—2001; exec. dir. global rsch. and devel. Pfizer, Ann Arbor, 2002—. Contbr. articles to profl. jours. Mem. Soc. for Neurosci., Am. Soc. Pharmacology and Exptl. Therapeutics, Am. Chem. Soc. Office: Pfizer Global Rsch & Devel 2800 Plymouth Rd Ann Arbor MI 48105

ROBERTSON, DON B. composer, author; b. Denver, Apr. 4, 1942; s. Donald B. and Lois (Schlenzig) R.; (div.); children: Rhonda, Heather, Marianne. Composer, performer (record albums) Dawn, 1969, Celestial Ascent, 1980, Resurrection, 1981, Starmusic, 1982, Spring, 1984, Anthem, 1986, Castles in the Sun, 1988; composer: Kopavi, Ballet for Orchestra and Chorus, 1993, Southern Wind (String Quartet), 1998; author: Tabla: A Rhythmic Introduction to Indian Music, 1968, Salve Festa Dies: Ancient Music for Modern Times, 1993, Accessing Transport Networks, 1996. With USN, 1960-64. Mem. Audio Engring. Soc., NARAS. Avocation: railroad buff.

ROBERTSON, DONALD MARSHALL, orthopaedic physician; b. Brockville, Ont., Can., Jan. 28, 1929; came to U.S., 1966; s. Duncan Marshall and Olive Gertrude (Mizener) R.; m. Beverly June Rice, May 1949 (div. Sept. 1967); m. Mary Evelyn Styles McInnis, Sept. 8, 1967; 1 stepchild, Stephen C. McInnis; children: Don Scott, James Neal. MD, U. Ottawa, Can., 1953. Diplomate Am. Bd. Disability Analysts. Gen. practice and surg. preceptorship, Can., 1953-60; pvt. practice surgery and gen. practice, Morrisburg, Ont., 1960-66; pvt. practice gen. medicine, Machias, Maine, 1966-97; pvt. practice surgery, 1966-93; pvt. practice orthopaedic medicine, 1978—. Mem. resident staff Ottawa Gen. Hosp., 1952-53; mem. active staff Winchester (Ont.) and Dist. Meml. Hosp., 1953-66, Cornwall (Ont.) Gen. Hosp., 1958-66, Hotel Dieu Hosp., Cornwall, 1966-68, Maine Coast Meml. Hosp., Ellsworth, 1966-69; hon. staff Down East Cmty. Hosp., Machias, 1968—, med. dir., 1993-97; affiliate staff Ea. Maine Med. Ctr., Bangor, 1972—; med. examiner State of Maine; preceptor in family medicine Boston U. Faculty Medicine; participant 1st Internat. Conf. on Low Back Pain and Its Relation to Sacroiliac Joint, U. Calif., San Diego, 1992, 2d Internat. Conf. on Low Back Pain, Lumbar Spine and Pelvis, 1995. Fellow Royal Soc. Health; mem. AMA, Am. Soc. Abdominal Surgeons, Am. Back Soc., Am. Assn. Orthopaedic Medicine, Am. Acad. Family Physicians (recognition as tchr. 1976, 84, 86), Maine Med. Assn. (ho. of dels. 1968—, pes. 1986-87, exec. com.), Washington County Med. Soc. Episcopalian. Avocations: boating, art, literature. Home: Rte 1A PO Box 211 Harrington ME 04643 Office: 6 West St Machias ME 04654-1024

ROBERTSON, DONNA VIRGINIA, architect, educator, dean; b. Richmond, Va., Feb. 26, 1952; d. Charles Henry and Florence (Givens) R.; m. Robert M. McAnulty, May 24, 1986; 1 child, Robertson. Cert. theater arts studies, Webster Coll., St. Louis, 1972; BA, Stanford U., 1974; MArch, U. Va., 1978. Registered arch., N.Y. Asst. prof. Harvard U., Cambridge, Mass., 1983-84; asst. prof. Barnard Coll. Columbia U., N.Y.C., 1984-92; dean Sch. Arch. Tulane U., New Orleans, 1992-96; dean Coll. Arch. Ill. Inst. Tech., Chgo., 1996—; ptnr. Robertson McAnulty Archs., 1986—; owner Donna V. Robertson Archs., N.Y.C., 1982-86; sr. designer Kohn Pedersen Fox Archs., 1980-82, Mitchell Giurgola Archs., N.Y.C., 1979-80. Adj. asst. prof. Barnard Coll., Columbia U., N.Y., 1982-83, dir. arch. program, fall 1985-92; vis. critic in design Harvard U., Cambridge, fall 1990, U. Va., Charlottesville, fall 1991; organizer, panelist Arch. and Lit. Symposium, N.Y.C., 1985; jury chair Am. Collegiate Schs. Arch., Boston, 1996; mem. bd. dirs. Nat. Archtl. Accrediting Bd., 2000—. Prin. arch. Fishback residence, New Orleans, Sunkel residence, New Orleans, Pisar residence, N.Y.C., Dachs residence, N.Y.C. Mem. AIA (juror annual design hons. awards 1996, educators and practitioners network), Chgo. Network-Internat. Women's Forum, Raven Soc., Arts Club (Chgo.), Phi Beta Kappa. Office: Ill Inst Tech 3360 S State St Chicago IL 60616 E-mail: robertson@iit.edu.

ROBERTSON, EDWARD NEIL, dentist; b. Rumford, Maine, Mar. 3, 1950; s. Edward Norris and Edith Louise (Kirk) R.; children (from first marriage): Christie Portia, Juliet Melissa (dec.), Jenni Celia, Edward Noah, Jessica Edith; m. Gordana Robertson, Mar. 18, 1998; children: Olivia, Gordon. BS in Biology, Antioch Coll., Yellow Springs, Ohio, 1973; MS in Epidemiology, Ohio State U., 1977; DDS, Case Western Res. U., 1983. Faculty adv. to med. students Ohio State U., Columbus, 1975-77; rsch. cons. Ohio Dept. Health, 1976-77; rsch. assoc. UCLA, 1977; epidemiologic/statis. cons. L.A., 1977; medic J & L Steel Corp., Cleve., 1979-84; pvt. practice Cleveland Heights, Ohio, 1983-94, Lyndhurst, 1995-2000. Mem. adj. faculty Cuyahoga C.C., Cleve., 1986-88; assoc. prof. Sch. Dentistry Case Western Res. U., 1991-96; asst. prof. Case Western Res. U. Sch. Dentistry, Cleve., 1997—; pvt. contractor Indian Health Svc. Dental Clinic, Pine Ridge, S.D., 1999-2000; clin. instr. U. Md. Dental Sch., 1999-00. Pres. Robertson Family Assn. of N.Am., 1986-88. Recipient numerous rsch. grants. Mem. Acad. Gen. Dentistry, U.S. Dental Inst., Acad. Laser Surgery. Avocations: soccer, cross-country skiing, camping, canoeing, sailing. Office: Beachwood Med Bldg 24755 Chagrin Blvd Ste 145 Beachwood OH 44122-5692 E-mail: dentalned@aol.com.

ROBERTSON, EDWIN DAVID, lawyer; b. Roanoke, Va., July 5, 1946; s. Edwin Traylor and Norma Burns (Bowles) R.; m. Anne Littelle Ferratt, Sept. 7, 1968, 1 child, Thomas Therit. BA with honors, U. Va., 1968, LLB, 1971. Bar: N.Y. 1972, U.S. Ct. Appeals (2d cir.) 1972, U.S. Dist. Ct. (ea. and so. dists.) N.Y. 1973, U.S. Supreme Ct. 1975, U.S. Dist. Ct. (ea. dist.) Mich. 1986. Assoc. Cadwalader, Wickersham & Taft, N.Y.C., 1972-80, ptnr., 1980—. Bd. dirs. Early Music Found. N.Y.C., 1983-99, chmn., 1993-99; bd. dirs. Oratorio Soc. of N.Y.C., 1988—, sec., 1991—. 1st lt. USAF, 1971-72. Echols scholar. Mem. ABA, Fed. Bar Coun., N.Y. County Lawyers Assn. (chmn. bankruptcy com. 1983-87, chmn. fin. com., bd. dirs. 1985-88, 95-99, 2000—, investment com. 1992—, exec. com. 1996—, treas. 2001—), N.Y. State Bar Assn. (ho. of dels. 2001—), Assn. Bar City N.Y., Soc. Colonial Wars, Down Town Assn., Jefferson Soc., Echols Scholar, Order of Coif, Phi Beta Kappa, Phi Kappa Psi. Republican. Episcopalian. Home: 315 E 72nd St New York NY 10021-4625 Office: Cadwalader Wickersham & Taft 100 Maiden Ln New York NY 10038-4818 E-mail: darob@cwt.com.

ROBERTSON, EDWIN OSCAR, banker; b. Speedwell, Tenn., May 28, 1923; s. John M. and Etta (Mayes) R.; m. Althea Maxine Moyers, June 3, 1948 (dec. Nov. 1970); children: Edwin Glenn, Craig Eric; m. Sarah Alice Parkman, Nov. 16, 1974. BS in Agr., U. Tenn., 1950; LLD (hon.), Lincoln Meml. U., 1984. Supr. vets. farm tng. County of Claiborne, Tazewell, Tenn., 1950-52; agr. rep. Citizens Bank, New Tazewell, 1952; v.p., agr. rep. Nat. Bank, Middlesboro, Ky., 1953-57; chmn. bd., chief exec. officer Comml. Bancgroup, Inc., Harrogate, Tenn., 1976—; pres., chief exec. officer Comml. Bank, Middlesboro, 1958—, chmn., CEO Harrogate, 1988—. Chmn. bd. Comml. Bank, Harrogate, 1976—, chmn., CEO, 1988—; mem. Govt. Task Force on Banking, Ky., 1983; trustee Lincoln Meml. U., Harrogate, 1974—; bd. dirs. Cumberland Devel. Corp., Middlesboro. Gov. Ruritan Nat. Tenn. Dist., 1954-55; bd. dirs. Middlesboro Indsl. Commn., 1962—, Ky. C. of C., 1983-84. With USAF, 1943-45. Mem. Rotary. Republican. Baptist. Avocations: farming, horseback riding. Home: PO Box 100 Harrogate TN 37752-0100

ROBERTSON, FLORENCE WINKLER, advertising and public relations agency executive; b. Hampton, Va., Sept. 11, 1945; d. Fred Felty Jr. and Florence Bernice Schnopp; m. John Park Winkler, Jr., June 24, 1967 (div. 1977); m. James Milton Robertson, Oct. 21, 1982. AA, Palm Beach Jr. Coll., 1965; BA, U. South Fla., 1967. Reporter Lexington (Ky.) Leader, 1967-70; freelance writer, 1971-76; TV and radio news reporter Sta. KCRG, Cedar Rapids, Iowa, 1972-73; asst. dir. pub. rels. Coe Coll., 1973-78; info. specialist Cedar Rapids Pub. Schs., 1979-83; advt. mgr. Smulekoff's Fine Home Furnishings, Cedar Rapids, 1984-93; owner, mgr. Fox Ridge Advt., 1993-2000; pub. rels. SAFE Coalition of Cedar Rapids, 2000—. Program dir. Ctrl. City Main St., 2002—. Pres. Home Fire Safety Task Force Ea. Iowa, 1983-86; chmn. Cedar Rapids Promotion Com., 1986-87; bd. dirs. Grant Wood Area chpt. ARC, Linn County Far Bur., 1994-99; organizer, bd. dirs. Cedar Rapids Christmas Parad, 1985-95. Recipient regional award Coun. for Advancement and Support Edn., 1975, 77, 78, nat. award, 1977; Gov.'s award for volunteerism, 1986, pub. svc. award Nat. Policy Officers Assn., City of hively, Ky., Am. Legion, 1970, nat. awad Nat. Sch. Pub. Rels. Assn., 1981, 83. Mem. Nat. Mgmt. Assn. (v.p. 1993-95, Local Mgr. of Yr. award 1995). Home: 3794 Toddville Rd Toddville IA 52341-9773

ROBERTSON, GREGORY HOWARD, civil engineer; b. Ellensburg, Wash., Nov. 2, 1962; s. John Paul and Bernadine Francis Robertson; m. Martha Jane Fleck, Aug. 2, 1986; children: Alice Nicole, Noah James. BSCE, Marquette U., 1985. Registered profl. engr., Mont., Wyo. Asst. civil engr. Ebasco Svcs., Inc., Bellevue, Wash., 1986; sr. constrn. engr. Bechtel Civil, Inc., San Francisco, 1986-89; sr. engr. Collier County Govt., Naples, Fla., 1989-91; coord. zoning and land use Sweetwater County Govt., Green River, Wyo., 1991-95; asst. county engr. Douglas County Govt., East Wenatchee, Wash., 1995-2000; dir. of pub. works Missoula County Govt., 2000—. Mem. ASCE (mem. pub. works com. 1992—, mem. land use tech. com. 1992—), Am. Inst. Cert. Planners (mem. ethics com. 1993—, cert.), Am. Planning Assn., Nat. Assn. County Engrs., Wyo. Planning Assn. (chair legis. com. 1991-95). Roman Catholic. Avocations: amateur radio, bicycling, hiking, fly fishing, Green Bay Packers. Home: 1941 36th St Missoula MT 59801-8918 Office: Missoula County Govt 6089 Training Dr Missoula MT 59808 E-mail: groberts@co.missoula.mt.us.

ROBERTSON, HORACE BASCOMB, JR. retired law educator; b. Charlotte, N.C., Nov. 13, 1923; s. Horace Bascomb and Ruth (Montgomery) R.; m. Patricia Lavell, Aug. 11, 1947; children— Mark L., James D. BS, U.S. Naval Acad., 1945; JD, Georgetown U., 1953; MS, George Washington U., 1968. Commd. ensign U.S. Navy, 1945, advanced through grades to rear adm., 1972; line officer, 1945-55; law specialist, 1955-68; spl. counsel to sec. Navy, Washington, 1964-67, judge adv., 1968-76; spl. counsel to chief naval ops. Washington, 1970-72; dep. judge adv. gen. Navy Dept., 1972-75, judge adv. gen., 1975-76; prof. law Duke U., 1976-89, sr. assoc. dean, 1986-89, ret., 1990; Chas H. Stockton chair of internat. law Naval War Coll., Newport, R.I., 1991-92. Decorated D.S.M. Mem. ABA, Am. Soc. Internat. Law. Methodist. Home: 9 Silver Maple Ct Durham NC 27705-5642 Office: Duke U Sch Law Durham NC 27708 E-mail: hbr@law.duke.edu.

ROBERTSON, HUGH DUFF, lawyer; b. Grosse Pointe, Mich., Mar. 14, 1957; s. Hugh Robertson and Louise (Grey) Bollinger; m. Mercedes Dano, May 3, 1997. BBA in Fin., U. Wis., Whitewater, 1978; JD, Whittier Coll., 1982. Bar: Calif. 1983, U.S. Tax Ct. 1984. Pres., CEO, A. Morgan Maree Jr. & Assocs., Inc., L.A., 1979—. Mem. ABA (forum com. on entertainment 1982—), State Calif., L.A. County Bar Assn., Beverly Hills Bar Assn., Acad. TV Arts and Scis., Am. Film Inst., Phi Alpha Delta. Republican. Episcopalian. Avocations: sports, swimming. Office: A Morgan Maree Jr & Assocs 1125 Gayley Ave Los Angeles CA 90024-3403

ROBERTSON, HUGH DUNBAR, biomedical researcher, consultant; b. Boston, June 12, 1943; s. Randal McGavock and Florence French (Dunbar) R.; m. Janet Abernathy, July 6, 1968; children: Andrew Dunbar, Michael Henry. BA in Life Scis., Harvard U., 1964; PhD in Genetics, Rockefeller U., 1969. Whitney postdoctoral fellow MRC Lab. of Molecular Biology, Cambridge, Eng., 1969-72; asst. prof. genetics Rockefeller U., N.Y.C., 1972-78, assoc. prof. genetics, 1978-88; assoc. prof. biochemistry Med. Coll. Cornell U., 1989-97, prof. biochemisty Med. Coll., 1997—. Chair sci. adv. bd. Enzo BioChem, Inc., N.Y.C., 1981-87; co-founder, chair sci. adv. bd. Innovir Labs., Inc., N.Y.C., 1989-98; organizer Cold Spring Harbor (N.Y.) RNA meeting, 1983, 84, 86, 93; cons. in field. Mem. editl. bd. Virology, 1982-88, RNA Jour., 1995-99; contbr. more than 115 articles to profl. jours. on RNA rsch. Patentee ribozyme compositions and methods. Bd. dirs. Christodora Charitable Found., N.Y.C., 1984—, v.p., 1995-96; mem. Canterbury Choral Soc., N.Y.C., 1973—, bd. chair, 1989-95, pres., 1988-89. Recipient Rsch. Excellence award McKnight Found., 1983; grantee NIH, 1979—, NSF, 1973-91, USDA, 1978-84, N.Y. State, 1993—, Am. Cancer Soc., 1978-82—. Mem. Am. Soc. Virology (founding mem., 1982—, admission com. 1982-88), RNA Soc. (founding mem. 1993—), Appalachian Mountain Club, Mass. Audubon Soc. Democrat. Episcopalian. Achievements include discovery of discovery of first two RNA processing enzymes; discovery of replication mode for viroid-like pathogens, including that causing human hepatitis delta; design of discovery of hepatitis C translation start signals. Avocations: choral singing, hiking near country home in Berkshire County, Mass., research on RNA evolution. Home: 430 E 63rd St New York NY 10021-7918 Office: Cornell U Weill Med Coll Dept Biochemistry 1300 York Ave New York NY 10021-4805 E-mail: hdrober@mail.med.cornell.edu.

ROBERTSON, JACK CLARK, accounting educator; b. Marlin, Tex., Apr. 27, 1943; s. Rupert Cook and Lois Lucille (Rose) R.; m. Caroline Susan Hughes, Oct. 23, 1965; children: Sara Ellen, Elizabeth Hughes. Student, Rice U., 1961-63; BBA with honors, U. Tex., Austin, 1965, M in Profl. Acctg., 1967; PhD, U. N.C., 1970. CPA, Tex. Tax acct. Humble Oil and Refining Co., Houston, 1964-65; auditor Peat, Marwick, Mitchell & Co., 1965-66; acct. Wade, Barton, Marsh CPAs, Austin, Tex., 1966-67; asst. prof. U. Tex., 1970-74, assoc. prof., 1974-79, Price Waterhouse auditing prof., 1979-84, C.T. Zlatkovich Centennial prof. acctg., 1984—. Acad. assoc. Coopers & Lybrand, N.Y.C., 1975-76; acad. fellow U.S. Securities and Exchange Commn. Office of the Chief Acct., Washington, 1982-83; Erskine fellow U. Canterbury, Christchurch, New Zealand, 1988; tng. the trainers instr. Vilnius, Lithuania, 1993; lectr. in field. Contbr. articles to profl. jours. Lay reader St. Matthews Episcopal Ch., Austin, 1972-75, mem. vestry, 1973-75, 77-79, 84-86, treas., 1974-75, 77-96, chmn. bldg. fund, 1976-87, chmn. everymen. canvass, 1980, sr. warden, 1986; del. Diocese of Tex. Coun., 1993-95; Trompetista El Grupo Valor Latino, Miembro comite del obispo Iglesia San Francisco de Asis, 2000—, treas., 2002–. Mem. AICPA, Am. Acctg. Assn. (sec.-treas. auditing sect. 1976-77, v.p. auditing sect. 1977-78, pres. auditing sect. 1978-79, chmn. auditing stds. com. 1980-81, chmn. SEC liaison com. 1983-84, historian auditing sect. 1999-2001), Tex. Soc. CPAs (vice-chmn., profl. ethics com. 1986-94, 95-97, Presdl. citation 1994), Assn. Cert. Fraud Examiners (regent emeritus, cert.), Phi Kappa Phi, Beta Gamma Sigma, Beta Alpha Psi. Office: U Tex Dept Acctg CBA 4M 202 Austin TX 78712 E-mail: jack.robertson@bus.utexas.edu.

ROBERTSON, JAMES, judge; b. Cleve., May 18, 1938; s. Frederick Irving and Doris Mary (Byars) R.; m. Berit Selma Persson, Sept. 19, 1959; children: Stephen Irving, Catherine Anne, Peter Arvid. AB, Princeton U., 1959; LLB, George Washington U., 1965. Bar: D.C. 1966, U.S. Supreme Ct. 1969. Assoc. Wilmer, Cutler & Pickering, Washington, 1965-69, ptnr., 1973-94; U.S. dist. judge D.C., 1994—; chief counsel Lawyers Com. for Civil Rights Under Law, Jackson, Miss., 1969-70, dir. Washington, 1970-72, co-chmn., 1985-87. Co-chmn. D.C. Lawyers Com. for Civil Rights Under Law, Washington, 1982-84; mem. com. on grievances U.S. Dist. Ct., 1988-92, vice chmn., 1989-92; bd. dirs. South Africa Legal Svcs. and Edn. Project, Inc., 1987-01, pres., 1989-94; bd. dirs. D.C. Prisoners Legal Svcs., Inc., 1992-94. Editor in chief George Washington Law Rev., 1964-65. Lt. USN, 1959-64. Fellow Am. Coll. Trial Lawyers, Am. Bar Found.; mem. ABA, D.C. Bar (bd. govs. 1986-93, pres.-elect 1990-92, pres. 1991-92), Am. Law Inst. Home: 3318 N St NW Washington DC 20007-2807 Office: US Courthouse Rm 6315 333 Constitution Ave NW Washington DC 20001-2854

ROBERTSON, JAMES COLE, consultant; b. Washington, June 8, 1929; s. Gordon and Florence Virginia (Cole) R.; m. Pauline Taylor, May 27, 1957; children: Lindsay Gordon, Preston Taylor. AS, Okla. State U., 1950; BS, U. So. Calif., 1954. Inspector Factory Ins. Assn., Charlotte, N.C., 1954-56; sr. instr. U. Md., College Park, 1956-62; asst. state fire marshal State Md., Balt., 1962-64, state fire marshal, 1964-82; cons. Nat. Fire Protection Assn., Quincy, Mass., 1982-85; dir. Dept. Emergency Svcs., Gainesville, Fla., 1985-86; asst. chief Gainesville Fire-Rescue Dept., 1986-88; regional rep. so. and ctrl. states Nat. Fire Protection Assn., Quincy, 1988-93; cons. Mizelle, Hodges & Assocs., Inc., Gainesville, 1993—. Fire protection cons. to cities and counties. Author: Introduction to Fire Prevention, 5th edit., 2000. Comdr. USCGR, ret. Mem. Fire Marshals Assn. N.Am. (hon. life, pres. 1969-70), Nat. Fire Protection Assn. (life, com. chmn. 1972-82), Sons Confederate Vets. Camp, Gainesville Sunrise Rotary. Republican. Episcopalian. Home: 3235 NW 31st St Gainesville FL 32605-2164 Office: Mizelle Hodges & Assocs Inc PO Box 716 Gainesville FL 32602-0716 E-mail: Robbie4771@aol.com.

ROBERTSON, JAMES MUELLER, civil engineer, educator; b. Champaign, Ill., Apr. 18, 1916; s. William Spence and Gertrude (Mueller) R.; m. Margaret Dillinger, Oct. 23, 1943; children: Bruce D., Alan S. BSCE, U. Ill., 1938; MS, U. Iowa, 1940, PhD, 1941. Asst. physicist U.S. Navy Dept., Taylor Model Basin, 1941-42; mem. engring. faculty, dir. Water Tunnel Pa. State U., 1942-54; rsch. engr. Douglas Aircraft, Santa Monica, Calif., 1944-45; prof. theoretical and applied mechanics U. Ill., Urbana, 1954-82, acting head dept., 1982, prof. emeritus, 1982—. Cons. U.S. Army, various indsl. orgns., 1957-73; vis. lectr. hydraulic engring. Kans. State U., 1967; course instr. TAPPI, 1969; lectr. U. Tenn. Space Inst., 1973; vis. prof. civil engring. Colo. State U., 1974; adj. prof. mech. engring. Naval Postgrad. Sch., 1984; bd. dirs. Internat. Mgmt. and Engring. Ltd., Colo., Terabyte, Inc., Boulder, Colo. Author: Hydrodynamics in Theory and Application, 1965; contbr. numerous articles to profl. publs. Sec., v.p., pres. Summit County Sr. Citizens, Frisco, Colo., 1983-97; sec. Skylin Six Area Agy. on Aging Coun., Frisco, 1986-95, chair, 1995-96; bd. dirs. Breckenridge (Colo.) Music Inst., 1984-95, sec., 1989-93, mem. adv. coun., 1995-2002. Recipient Alumni Honor award, Coll. Engring., 1989. Fellow ASCE (life, Hilgard prize 1955), ASME (life); mem. Sigma Xi, Phi Eta Sigma, Chi Epsilon, Tau Beta Pi, Phi Kappa Phi. Achievements include co-design of hydrodynamics research water tunnel at Pennsylvania State University. Home: 14091 E Marina Dr Apt 202 Aurora CO 80014-3712

ROBERTSON, JAMES WOOLSEY, lawyer; b. Ft. Sam Houston, Tex., Aug. 6, 1942; s. Robert Charles Lee and Marjorie Evelyn (Woolsey) R.; 1 child, William Angus; m. Laura Ann Koons, Apr. 24, 1993. BBA, U. Tex., 1966, JD, 1967. Bar: Tex.; cert. real estate law specialist. Ptnr. Locke Liddell & Sapp L.L.P., Houston, 1971—, chmn. fin. com., 1985-90, chmn. banking and real estate sect., 1992-98. Chancellor Episcopal Ch. Holy Spirit, Houston, 1984-92, trustee, 1984-87; bd. dirs., sec. Lighthouse for the Blind, Houston, 1998—. Lt. comdr. USCGR, 1968-71. Mem. State Bar Tex., Houston Bar Assn., Houston Real Estate Lawyers Coun. Republican. Avocations: golf, fly fishing, skiing, hunting. Office: 600 Travis St Ste 3200 Houston TX 77002-3095

ROBERTSON, JANE RYDING, marketing executive; b. Dallas, Apr. 11, 1953; d. Ronald and Olive Stacey (Hodgkinson) Pearce; m. James Randall Robertson, May 25, 1974; children: James Andrew, Jessica Ryding. Assoc. degree, Tyler Jr. Coll., 1972; BS, Tex. Tech U., 1974. Store mgr. trainee Montgomery Ward, Dallas, Lubbock, Tex., 1974-75; dist: sales rep. Max Factor & Co., Dallas, 1975-78; sr. asst. buyer cosmetics Sanger Harris, 1978-88, also cosmetic mktg.-divisional mktg. account exec., 1978-88; v.p. mktg. Dallas Market Ctr., 1988-90; dir. mktg.-pub. rels. Galleria/Hines Dallas, 1990—. Dir. pub. rels. Easter Seals, 1996—2000; mem. corp. adv. bd. So. Meth. U., 2000—; mem. nat. bd. dirs. Susan G. Komen Found. for Breast Cancer, Dallas, 1990—95; bd. dirs. Ctr. for Profl. Selling, Baylor U., Waco, 1989—95. Mem. Internat. Coun. Shopping Ctrs. (sr. cert. mktg. dir.), Fashion Group Internat., Univ. Club (bd. dirs. profl. women's com. 1990-92). Methodist. Avocations: reading, youth activities, interior decorating. Office: Galleria/Hines Dallas 13355 Noel Rd Ste 250 Dallas TX 75240-6820 E-mail: jane_robertson@hines.com.

ROBERTSON, JEAN ELLIS, art critic, art history educator; b. Mt. Kisco, N.Y., Oct. 15, 1950; d. Douglas Hosmer and Ruth Geissinger Robertson; m. Craig Milton McDaniel, June 12, 1976. BA, U. Pa., 1971, MA, 1973, PhD, 1983. Co-dir. So. Ohio Mus., Portsmouth, 1978-83; assoc. curator Columbus (Ohio) Mus. Art, 1984-88; instr. art history Ind. State U., Terre Haute, 1989-94; asst. prof. art history Herron Sch. Art, Ind. U.-Purdue U., Indpls., 1995-2001, assoc. prof. art history, 2001—. Coun. mem. Ohio Humanities Coun., Columbus, 1979-86; state curator Ind. Com., Nat. Mus. Women in the Arts, Washington, 1997-2000; vis. prof. art history Rose-Hulman Inst. Tech., Terre Haute, 1992-94. Co-author: Painting as a Language: Material, Technique, Form, Content, 2000; curator, author (exhbn. catalogue) Exploring Maps, 1992; curator, editor (exhbn. catalogue) Matter Mind Spirit: 12 Contemporary Indiana Women Artists, 1999; mem. editl. bd. Dialogue, 1985-89; Ind. corr. New Art Examiner, Chgo., 1995-99; contbg. editor Arts Indiana, 2001—. Named writer's resident, Millay Colony for the Arts, Austerlitz, N.Y., 1994, Mary Anderson Ctr. for the Arts, Mt. St. Francis, Ind., 1996, Vt. Studio Ctr., 2001; recipient Pres. Arts and Humanities Initiative award, Ind. U., 2001; fellow Dissertation fellow, U. Pa., Phila., 1976—77, Creative Renewal Arts fellow, Arts Coun. Indpls., 1999—2000; grantee Faculty Devel. grantee, Ind. U.-Purdue U., Indpls., 1997, 1998, 1999, internat. enhancement grantee, Ind. U., 2000. Mem. Internat. Assn. Art Critics (Am. sect.), Am. Assn. Mus., Coll. Art Assn., Women's Caucus for Art, Midwest Art History Soc. Home: 402 Buckingham Dr Indianapolis IN 46208-3612 E-mail: jerobert@iupui.edu.

ROBERTSON, JEANNE BENNETT, interior designer and artist; b. San Francisco, May 21, 1916; d. Willard Winslow and Mary Louise (Weymann) Bennett; m. Charles Bennett Robertson, July 5, 1941; children: David Bennett, Philip Bennett, Anne Louise Robertson Thomas. AB, U. Calif., 1938. Playground dir. San Francisco Recreation Dept., 1939-41, Washington D.C. Recreation Dept., 1941-42; pilot WASP, Sweetwater, Tex., 1943-44, Long Beach, Calif., 1943-44; pvt. practice interior design San Francisco & Honolulu, 1967—. Artist Art a la Carte Gallery, Honolulu, 1987—, The Gallery at Ward Ctr. Mem. AAUW (pres. 1983-85), Hawaii Watercolor Soc. (leader workshops 1975—, pres. 1979), Assn. Hawaiian Artists, Gen. Fedn. Women (pres. 1988), Nat. League Am. Pen Women (pres. 1992-94). Republican. Avocations: swimming, golf, fundraising.

ROBERTSON, JERALD LEE, physicist; b. Webbs Cross Roads, Ky., Oct. 4, 1935; s. Marvin Lee and Eva Lee (Wheat) R.; m. Carol Ann Sanderson, Aug. 29, 1963 (div. Jan. 1970). BS in Physics and Chemistry, Wilmington (Ohio) Coll., 1960; postgrad., Amherst (Mass.) Coll., 1961, U. Dayton, 1964-65. Cert. hazardous materials mgr., master gardener. Trainee, indsl. mgr. Ralston Purina, Sharonville, Ohio, 1961-63; rsch. physicist Monsanto Rsch., Dayton, 1963-68; graphic arts engr. Formica Corp., Evendale, Ohio, 1968-70; tech. svcs. mgr. Color Pac Inc., Franklin, 1970-73; tech. svcs. rep. GE, Coshocton, 1972-77; tech. svcs. mgr. Cin. Milacron, 1978-82; mgr. R&D Kornylak Corp., Hamilton, Ohio, 1983—. Sec. Elmwood Pl. Cmty. Urban Restoration Project, 1983; mem. citizen adv. bd. Henkel Corp., Cin., 1994-99; chmn. M.C. Watershed Coun., 1996-97; mem. Consensus Forum Hamilton County Environ. Priorities Project, 1996-98; bd. dirs. Hamilton Safety Coun., Rivers Unltd.-MCRP, Cin. Author: (with others) Pulp and Paper, 1980; columnist (weekly article) Suburban Press, 1983-85; contbr. articles to profl. jours.; photo exhibit Urban Appalachian Mus. Councilman Village of Elmwood Place, Ohio, 1992-96, candidate for mayor, 1983, 87, 93, 99; chmn. Mill Creek Watershed Steering Com., Cin., 1994-96; chmn. Citizens for Sensible Waste Mgmt., Cin., 1990-93; chmn. cmty. panel Bicentennial Commn., Cin., 1987; mem. sr. olympics basketball, 1992-2000; mem. adv. bd. Port Authority; bd. appraisers Millcreek Valley Conservancy Dist.; mem. pub. adv. com. Hamilton County Solid Waste Dist., 1998; mem. Hamilton County Recycling Subcom., 2000, Hamilton County Storm Water Com.; mem. Hamilton County Environ. Action Commn., 2001-. Recipient Cmtys. United for Action Environ. award, 1997, Alumni Vol. award Wilmington Coll., 1999. Mem. Ayn Rand Inst., CATO Inst., Objectivist Ctr. Avocation: wine tasting, hosta gardening. Home: 111 Township Ave Cincinnati OH 45216-2425

ROBERTSON, JERI ELIZABETH, special education educator, writer; b. Wilmington, Del., Apr. 19, 1954; d. William Christopher and Mabel May McCurdy; m. Merrill Robertson, June 16, 1954; children: Merrill, Jerry Christopher, Walter. Student, St. Augustineis Coll., Raleigh, NC, 1973—76; BS in Spl. Edn. cum laude, Va. Union U., 1978; MEd in Adminstrn. and Supervision cum laude, Va. Commonwealth U., 1993. Cert. spl. edn. tchr. Tchr. Richmond (Va.) Pub. Schs., Chesterfield County Schs., Richmond, Hanover Learning Ctr., Richmond, Charles City (Va.) County Schs., Richmond, Powhatan County Schs., Richmond. Mem.: NEA, Am. Assn. Curriculum Devel., Va. Commonwealth U. Alumni Assn., Carnegie Found. for Advancement of Tchg., Richmond Parents Monthly. Avocations: horseback riding, swimming, tennis, writing. Home: 8806 Playground Dr Richmond VA 23237

ROBERTSON, JERRY EARL, retired manufacturing company executive; b. Detroit, Oct. 25, 1932; s. Earl Howard and Nellie (Wright) R.; m. Joanne Alice Wesner, Sept. 3, 1955; children: Scott Clark, Lisa Kay, Stuart Todd. BS, Miami U., Oxford, Ohio, 1954; MS, U. Mich., 1956, PhD, 1959. With Minn. Mining & Mfg. Co., St. Paul, 1963-94, tech. dir. med. products div., 1973-74, dept. mgr. surg. products dept., 1974-75, gen. mgr. surg. products div., 1975-79, div. v.p. surg. products div., 1979-80, group v.p. health care products and services, 1980-84, exec. v.p. life scis. sector, 1984-86, exec. v.p. life scis. sector and corp. svcs., 1986-94; ret., 1994. Bd. dirs. Coherent, Inc., Choice Hotels Internat., Steris Corp. Bd. reference MAP Internat., Brunswick, Ga., 1986-94; bd. dirs. Project HOPE, 1988-98, Manor Care Inc., 1989-98, Cardinal Health Distbn., Inc., 1991-99. Mem. Pharm. Mfrs. Assn. (bd. dirs. 1984-89), Health Industry Mfrs. Assn. (bd. dirs. 1982-91, chmn. 1990-91). Unitarian Universalist. Office: Minn World Trade Ctr 30 7th St E Ste 3050 Saint Paul MN 55101-4921

ROBERTSON, JOEL THOMAS, railroad executive; b. Milo, Maine, Aug. 30, 1947; s. Paul Russell Robertson and Denice Luella Stevens; m. Patricia Rae Willinski, Mar. 13, 1970 (div. May 1990); children: Jason Thomas, April Dawn Robertson Bishop; m. Marie Paulette Melvin, Dec. 31, 1994; 1 child Stuart Spencer Stratton. BS, W.Va. State U., 1982; MA, Marshall U., 1986. Cert. safety mgr. World Safety Orgn., 85. Agt. Bangor (Maine) & Aroosook R.R., 1966—70, Can. Pacific Rwy., St. John, 1970—80; hazardous materials inspector Fed. RR Adminstrn., Washington, 1980—2001, hazardous materials specialist, 2001—. Transp. cons. Union Carbide Corp., Danbury, Conn., 1989—90; expert witness/accident investigator Collins, Collins & Dinardo, Buffalo, 1989—; bus. devel. cons. Brothers Coal Cons., Charleston, W.Va., 1989—90, TransMar Inc., Spokane, Wash., 1994, Coal Tech. Corp., Bristol, Va., 1989—97; appearance on nat. news program ABC Wide World News Tonight, 1985; interviewed by Tass Soviet News Agy., 89. Contbr. articles to profl. publs. Organizer, master of ceremonies First Joint Chem. Industry/Rwy. Safety Symposium, W.Va., 1985, Celebration of Engring. Career Day, Huntington, 1989; sci. advisor Bush White House Space Coun., Washington, 1989. Recipient Commendation, Gov. of W.Va., 1985. Mem.: Am. Soc. Profl. Engrs. (exec. affiliate 1983—89), Engrs. Club of Huntington (pres. 1987—88), Kiwanis (pres. West Huntington chpt. 1989—90). Republican. Mem. Lds Ch. Avocations: fund-raising activities, event organizing, photography, travel, writing. Home: 1606 NE Hughes Rd Washougal WA 98671 Office: Fed RR Adminstrn 703 Broadway Ste 650 Vancouver WA 98660 E-mail: joel313@aol.com.

ROBERTSON, JOHN ARCHIBALD LAW, nuclear scientist; b. Dundee, Scotland, July 4, 1925; s. John Carr and Ellen (Law) R.; m. Betty-Jean Moffatt, June 26, 1954; children: Ean Stuart, Clare Deborah, Fiona Heather. BA, Cambridge (Eng.) U., 1950, MA, 1953. Sci. officer U.K. Atomic Energy Authority, Harwell, Eng., 1950-57; research officer Atomic Energy Can. Ltd., Chalk River, Ont., 1957-63, head reactor materials br., 1963-70, dir. fuels and materials div., 1970-75, asst. to v.p., 1975-82; dir. program planning Atomic Energy Can. Ltd. (Research Co. Head Office), 1982-85; cons., 1985—. Mem. Atomic Energy Control Bd.'s Adv. Com. on Nuclear Safety, 1988-97. Author: Irradiation Effects in Nuclear Fuels, 1969, Decide the Nuclear Issues for Yourself: Nuclear Need Not Be Unclear, 2000; editor: Jour. Nuclear Materials, 1967-71. Served to capt., Royal Engrs. Brit. and Indian armies, 1943-47. Recipient W.B. Lewis medal Can. Nuclear Assn., 1987, W.J. Kroll Zirconium medal W.J. Kroll Inst. for Extractive Metallurgy, 1993. Fellow Royal Soc. Can. E-mail: jalrober@magma.ca.

ROBERTSON, JOSEPH E., JR. ophthalmologist, educator; b. Jackson County, Ind., July 24, 1952; s. Joseph E. and Virginia Faye (Baxter) R.; children: Kathryn Faye, Charles Joseph. BS cum laude, Yale U., 1974; MD, Ind. U., 1978; MBA, U. Oreg., 1997. Diplomate Am. Bd. Ophthalmology. Intern Bapt. Med. Ctr., Birmingham, Ala., 1978-79; resident Oreg. Health Sci. U., Portland, 1979-82; pvt. practice Vancouver, Wash., 1982-83; fellow Oreg. Health Sci. U./Devers Hosp./Good Samaritan Hosp., Portland, 1983-84; vitreous surgery fellow Steve Charles, M.D., Memphis, 1984-85; asst. prof. Oreg. Health Sci. U., Portland, 1985-92, assoc. prof., 1992-97, prof., chmn. dept. opthalmology, 1997—. Interim dean Oreg. Health Sci. U. Sch. Medicine, Portland, 2001—02. Contbr. articles to profl. jours., chpts. to books; editor videotapes. Apptd. mem. Oreg. Commn. for the Blind, 1988-94. Mem. Am. Acad. Ophthalmology (Oreg. rep. to coun. 1992-95, COVE com. 1988-93, skills transfer adv. com. 1994-98, nat. chair and state coord. Diabetes 2000), Oreg. Acad. Ophthalmology (pres. 1990-91), U. Medical Group (exec. com. 1997—; v.p. 1998—), Oreg. Med. Assn. Democrat. Presbyterian. Avocations: snow skiing, windsurfing, snowboarding, hiking, jogging. Office: Casey Eye Inst OHSU 3375 SW Terwilliger Blvd Portland OR 97201-4197

ROBERTSON, JOSEPH EDMOND, grain processing company executive; b. Brownstown, Ind., Feb. 16, 1918; s. Roscoe Melvin and Edith Penina (Shields) R.; m. Virginia Faye Baxter, Nov. 23, 1941; 1 son, Joseph Edmond, Jr. *Wife Virginia Baxter, BS Kansas State University, Kentucky Colonel, and she is a member of Traveler's Century and Circumnavigator's Clubs. She provided many of the notes Joe Robertson used in writing On Kilroy's Trail, published and released October, 1998. Son Joe Jr, BS Yale 1970, MD Indiana University 1978, MBA University of Oregon, 1997. He is director of Casey Eye Institute and chairman of Department of Ophthalmology at Oregon Health Science University, Portland Oregon. Grandchildren, Katie, 18,attends St. Paul's School, and Charles Joseph, 16, attends also attends St.Paul School.* BS, postgrad., Kans. State U., 1940. Cereal chemist Ewing Mill Co., 1940-43, flour milling engr., 1946-50, feed nutritionist, 1951-59; v.p., sec. Robertson Corp., Brownstown, Ind., 1960-80, pres., 1980-97, chmn., 1997—. Forest products tech. writer Forest Products Jour., 1973-78. Author: On Kilroy's Trail, 1998. Mem. Kans. State U. Varsity Basketball Team, 1937-40; pres. Jackson County (Ind.) Welfare Bd., 1948-52; mem. Ind. Port Commn., 1986-91; mem. Ind. Gov.'s Coun. of Sagamores of the Wabash. Served with USAAF, 1943-45. Named to Hon. Order Ky. Cols.; recipient Brownstown (Ind.) First Lifetime Achievement award, 1999. Mem. Hardwood Plywood Mfrs. Assn. (v.p. affiliate div. 1971-73, 87-88, internat. lectr. forest products industry 1973-97), Am. Assn. Cereal Chemists, Assn. Operative Millers, Am. Legion, Brownstown C. of C. (dir. All Am. city program 1955), Kans. State U. Alumni Assn. (life), Blue Key, Phi Delta Theta, Phi Kappa Phi, Alpha Mu. Clubs: Internat. Travelers Century (L.A.), Circumnavigators Club (N.Y.C.), Elks. Presbyterian. Home: Lake and Forest Club 1268 E Lake Shore Dr PO Box A Brownstown IN 47220 Office: 200 N Front St Brownstown IN 47220-1040

ROBERTSON, KENNETH CARL, music educator; b. Bethany, Mo., Oct. 14, 1963; s. Hal Dean and Iretha Elaine Robertson. MusB Edn., MusB Performance, Drake U., 1986; MusM, Conservatory of Music, Kansas City, Mo., 1988. Cert. Orff- Schulwerk Music Specialist 1999. Organist 1st Christian Ch., Pattonsburg, Mo., 1976—82, Glen Echo Christian Ch., Des Moines, 1982—86, Congl. United Ch. Of Christ, Prairie Village, Kans., 1986—89; organist/choirmaster St. Charles Ch., Gladstone, Mo., 1989—91; organist Pk. Christian Ch., Kansas City, 1991—99; music tchr. North Kans. City Schs., 1993—. Soloist Drake U. Choir, Des Moines, 1982—86; dance accompanist Alvin Ailey Dance Co., Kansas City, Mo., 1987—87. Singer: (recording) Handel's Messiah, 1983, (radio live performance) Three French Songs - Bernstein, 1984. Recipient Ctrl. Iowa 1st Pl. Music, Yamah Corp. Competition, 1979, 5 #1 music ratings, State of Mo., 1978—82. Mem.: Music Educators Nat. Conf., Am. Orff-Schulwerk Assn. Office: Gracemor Elem Sch 5125 N Sycamore Kansas City MO 64119 Office Fax: 816-413-6425. Personal E-mail: kcrmusic@aol.com. E-mail: krobert1@nkcsd.

ROBERTSON, LAWRENCE MARSHALL, JR. neurosurgeon; b. Denver, Feb. 4, 1932; s. Lawrence M. and Mildred Eleanor (Blackwood) R.; m. Joan T. White, May 13, 1958 (div. Oct. 1973); children: Colette M., Michele E., Laurienne J., Lawrence M. III; m. Lee Ann Crawford, Sept. 24, 1982; one child, William M. BA, U. Colo., 1954; MD, U. Colo., Denver, 1957; postgrad., U. Denver, 1981-85. Diplomate Am. Bd. Med.-Legal Analysis in Medicine and Surgery, Am. Bd. Clin. Neurol. Surgery, Am. Bd. Forensic Medicine. Intern Kings County Hosp., Bklyn., 1957-58; resident in gen. surgery St. Joseph Hosp., Denver, 1958-59; resident in neurology U. Colo., 1959-60; resident in neurosurgery Boston City Hosp., 1960-64; fellow in neurosurgery Lahey Clinic, Boston, 1963; practice medicine specializing in neurosurgery Denver, 1964—. Contbr. articles on malpractice to legal jours. Capt. USNR, 1979-83, 85. Recipient Continuing Edn. Cert., Am. Assn. Neurol. Surgeons and Cong. Neurol. Surgeons, 1976, 1980-83, Physicians Recognition award AMA 1976-79, 80-83, 84-87. Fellow Internat. Coll. Surgeons, Royal Coll. Surgeons; mem. AAAS, ACS, AMA, Colo. Neurosurg. Soc., N.Y. Acad. Scis., Naval Res. Assn., U.S. Naval Inst., Interurban Neurosurg. Soc., Rocky Mountain Traumatologic Soc., Phi Alpha Delta. Office: Colo Neurosurgery PC 1635 Gilpin St Denver CO 80218-1632

ROBERTSON, LEON H. management consultant, educator; b. Atlanta; s. Grady Jospeh and Pearline (Chandler) R. BS in Indsl. Mgmt., Ga. Inst. Tech., 1957, MS, 1959; postgrad., U. Okla.-Norman, 1958, U. Mich., 1961; PhD in Bus. Adminstrn., Ga. State U., 1968. Mgr. mgmt. cons. divsn. Arthur Andersen & Co., Atlanta, 1960-65; prof. bus. adminstrn. Ga. State U., 1965-75; corp. v.p. Tex. Gas Corp., Owensboro, Ky., 1975-78, sr. v.p., 1982-83; chmn., CEO Am. Carriers, Inc., Overland Park, Kans., 1978-88; chmn. bd. dirs. Midwest Coast Transport, 1988-89; prof. mgmt., dir. divsn. bus. adminstrn. U. Mo., Kansas City, 1990-96, prof. Internat. Acad. Programs, 1996-98, dir. Ctr. for Internat. Bus., 1999—. Office: Univ of Mo-Kansas City Henry W Bloch Sch Bus & Pub Admn 5110 Cherry St Kansas City MO 64110-2426

ROBERTSON, MARIAN ELLA (MARIAN ELLA HALL), small business owner, handwriting analyst; b. Edmonton, Alta., Can., Mar. 3, 1920; d. Orville Arthur and Lucy Hon (Osborn) Hall; m. Howard Chester Robertson, Feb. 7, 1942; children: Elaine, Richard. Student, Willamette U., 1937-39; BS, Western Oreg. State U., 1955. Cert. elem., jr. high. tchr., supt. (life) Oreg.; cert. graphoanalyst. Tchr. pub. schs., Mill City, Albany, Scio and Hillsboro, Oreg., 1940-72; cons. Zaner-Bloser Inc., Columbus, Ohio, 1972-85, assoc. cons., 1985-89; pres. Write-Keys, Scio, 1980-90; owner Lifelines, Jefferson, Oreg., 1991-94. Tchr. Internat. Graphoanalysis Soc., Chgo., 1979; instr. Linn-Benton Community Coll., 1985-89. Master gardener vol. Marion County, Oreg. State U. Extension Svc., 1992; floriculture judge Marion County Fair, 1992; master gardener clinic Oreg. State Fair, 1992; sr. intern 5th Congl. Dist. Oreg. , Washington1984, mem. sr. adv. coun.; mem. precinct com. Rep. Ctrl. Com., Linn County, 1986, alt. vice chair, 1986, parliamentarian, 1988—; candidate Oreg. State Legislature, Salem, 1986; del. N.W. Friends Yearly Meeting, Newberg, Oreg., 1990—92; clk. Marion Friends Monthly Meeting, 1992—93. Mem.: Internat. Platform Assn., Altrusa Internat., Port Orford Heritage Soc. (hon.), Knife and Fork Club. Republican. Mem. Soc. Of Friends. Avocations: piano, organ, violin, gardening, writing. Home: 2757 Pheasant Ave SE Salem OR 97302-3170

ROBERTSON, MARK ALLEN, lawyer; b. San Antonio, May 6, 1963; s. David Hearne and Margie Louise (McCleskey) R. BA, So. Meth. U., 1985; JD, Columbia U., 1989. Ptnr. Fulbright & Jaworski, L.L.P., Houston, 1989-2001, N.Y.C., 2001—. Editor (contbg.): 2002 ABA Antitrust Discovery Handbook; prodr.: (plays) Glass Bottom Cadillac, 1995. Bd. dirs. Houston Black Tie Dinner, Inc., 1997-2001; class fundraising chair So. Meth. U., Dallas, 1995—; mem. adminstrv. bd. St. Paul's United Meth. Ch., Houston, 1991-97. Mem. ABA, NY Bar Assn., D.C. Bar Assn., Tex. Bar Assn., Houston Bar Assn. (chair antitrust and trade regulation sect. 1998-99), Pi Kappa Alpha (regional pres. 1997—, Advisor of Yr. Internat. Chpt. 1995, So. Meth. U. N.Y.C. Alumni exec. com. 2002-), N.Y.C. Bar Chorus. Avocations: travel, singing, golf. Office: Fulbright & Jaworski LLP 666 Fifth Ave New York NY 10103-3198

ROBERTSON, MARK WAYNE, investment specialist; b. St. Louis, June 28, 1929; s. Harold LaGrand and Mabel Margaret (Mangels) R.; 1 child, A. Rafael Nuncio. Student, U. Houston, 1949-51. Cost acct. Mo. Pacific Railroad, Houston, 1951-55; contract adminstr. Air Cruisers Co., Belmar, N.J., 1955-57; right of way cons. Tex. Hwy. Dept., Houston, 1957; land mgr. Houston Natural Gas Co., 1957-71; adminstrv. asst. Houston Pile Line Co., 1971-84; real estate broker, investor, 1975—; pvt. practice as investor Kerrville, Tex., 1984—. Co-owner several small businesses and distributorships. Profl. artist. Fundraiser John Tower for Senator, Houston, Am. Heart Assn., Houston, 1971-81; officer Mended Hearts Assn., Houston, 1971-81; 2d v.p. Hill County Art Foun., Kerrville, 1989-92, treas., 1990-91, adv. bd. 1996—; sr. mem. Soc. Ambs. St. Joseph Hosp., 1989—; adv. Butt Holdworth Libr., 1991, 96; cultural adviser to mayor, 1991-97; mem. adv. bd. Kerr Arts and Cultural Ctr., 2001. Cpl. U.S. Army, 1951-53. Mem. Internat. Right of Way Assn. (officer 1958-83), Kerrville Art Club (pres. 1990), Art League of Houston, Nat. Soc. Painters in Casein and Acrylic, Allied Artists in Am., River Art Group. Roman Catholic. Avocation: owner of a small ranch resort. E-mail: marcos@ktc.com.

ROBERTSON, MELVINA, construction company executive; b. Guilford, Mo., June 3, 1934; d. Charlie Gale and Christina Gertrude (Nelson) Turner; m. Ponnie Leonard Robertson, June 3, 1955; children: Raymond Edward, Richard Leonard. Student, Cen. Mo. State Coll., 1966. Mgr. Knowles Restaurant, Kansas City, Mo., 1954-55; v.p. P.L. Robertson Concrete Found. Co., Inc., Ozark, 1972-90, pres., 1990—. Mem. Rose Soc. of Ozark, Nat. Audubon Soc. Mem. Reorganized Lds Ch. Avocation: reading.

ROBERTSON, MICHAEL SWING, minister; b. Boston, July 20, 1935; s. Charles Stuart and Elizabeth (Swing) R.; m. Margaret Filoon, Sept. 17, 1960 (dec. Oct. 1996); children: Michael Swing, Ashlee Whipple, Christopher Filoon, Andrew Stuart; m. Emily Erickson, Feb. 22, 1998. AB, Harvard U., 1957, grad. Advanced Mgmt. Program, 1979. With Robertson Factories, Inc., 1957-80, exec. v.p., 1968-73, pres., 1973-79, chmn. bd., 1979-80; dir. Robertson-Swing Co., 1980—; pres. The Berkley Co. Inc., 1981-90, Reactions Inc., 1985-90; treas. Falmouth Marine Inc., 1981-88; pres., treas. Orchard Computer Inc., 1984-91, chmn., treas., 1991-93; exec. sec. Nat. Assn. Congl. Christian Chs., Oak Creek, Wis., 1991-97; minister Pilgrim Congregational Ch., Taunton, Mass., 2000—; ch. coord. Cmty. Faith Alliance, Milw., 1997-2000; pres. Congl. Leadership Inst. Piedmont Coll., Ga., 1997—; exec. dir. Cmty. Village, Ltd., 1998-2000; pastor Pilgrim Congrl. Ch., Taunton, 2001—. V.p. adv. coun. Coll. of Bus. and Industry, Southeastern Mass. U., North Dartmouth, Mass., 1979-91; selectman, Town of Berkley, Mass., 1974-80, chmn. 1979-80; mem. Pres.'s Adv. Com. for Trade Negotiations, 1983-86; bd. dirs. Mass. Easter Seal Soc., 1977-91, pres. 1982-83; bd. dirs. Nat. Easter Seal Soc., 1985-91, Wis. Easter Seal Soc., 1994-95; chmn. Berkley Rep. Town com., 1977-91; mem. Pilgrim Congl. Ch., Taunton, Cmty. Bapt. Ch., Milw.; Rep. nominee U.S. Senate from Mass., 1976, nominee for Mass. state auditor, 1982; co-chmn. Mass Reagan for Pres. Com., 1980; Bristol

County coord. Reagan/Bush campaign; co-chmn. Mass. Dole for Pres. Commn., 1987; chmn. Southeastern Mass. campaign Harvard Coll., 1981; chmn. Friends of Harvard Track, 1986-91; trustee Barnstable County Hosp., 1985-90, chmn., 1988. Mem. Harvard Varsity Club, Falmouth Yacht Club, Harvard Club of Boston. Home: 7 Swing Lane Falmouth MA 02540 Office: Pilgrim Congrl Ch 45 Broadway Taunton MA 02780-3120 Fax: 508-828-9147. E-mail: miker@cape.com. *Accept responsibility with enthusiasm and gratitude. Our individual freedom is unmatched in history, compelling us to remain true to our heritage and our God.*

ROBERTSON, PATRICIA AILEEN, adult and geriatric nurse; b. Washington, Dec. 15, 1950; d. John Thomas and Virginia Aileen (Parker) Dickmeyer; m. Lee Eiden; children: Jason Earle, Alyssa Michelle. BS, U. Mass., 1973; BSN with honors, George Mason U., 1982, MSN, 1999. RN, Va.; cert. adult and geriatric nurse practitioner; ARNP Va., Wash. Staff nurse, perdiem intravenous therapist Inova Fairfax Hosp., St. Joseph's Hosp., Tacoma Gen. Hosp., Tacoma; pediatric nurse, health educator Western Clinic; nurse cons., intravenous therapy educator Pharmacy Corp. Am., Seattle; developer, dir. Careline health adv. and case mgmt. program Weyerhaeuser, Tacoma; cons. Home IV Therapy Agys.; cons. UR Case Mgmt. Olympic Counseling Svcs., Tacoma; program developer Coord. Adolescent Assessment Ctr.; adult and geriatric nurse practitioner Arlington (Va.) Free Clinic, Fairfax County Pub. Safety Occupl. Health Clinic; staff nurse vascular access team INOVA Fairfax (Va.) Hosp. Developer, AIDS edn. program for high sch. students and corp. employee, 1990; cons. alzheimer's dementia unit Weatherly Inn, 1992; speaker in field. Vol. NP Arlington Free Clin. Named Pierce County Nurse of Yr. nominee, 1986. Mem. ANA, Am. Coll. Nurse Practitioners (task force on End of Life/palliative care), Am. Coll. Nurse Practitioners in Women's Health, Am. Acad. Pain Mgmt., Nat. League Nursing, Nat. Assn. Vascular Access Networks, Wash. State Nurses Assn., Intravenous Nurses Soc., South Sound AIDS Network, Healthcare Providers Coun. Wash., Va. Coun. Nurse Practitioners, Sigma Theta Tau. Achievements include design and development of peripheral and central venous access device charts for teaching to patients and staff. Home and Office: 8621 Cherry Dr Fairfax VA 22031-2136 E-mail: proberts@cco.net.

ROBERTSON, PAUL JOSEPH, lawyer, educator; b. Chgo., Dec. 31, 1963; s. Mary Ellen (Statom) R. BSBA in Mktg., Georgetown U., Washington, 1985; BA in Sociology, St. Leo (Fla.) Coll., 1988; MBA, JD, U. Ill., 1992. Bar: Ill. 1992, D.C. 2002, U.S. Dist. Ct. (no. dist.) Ill. 1992, U.S. Ct. Appeals (7th cir.) 1992. Counsel Region V U.S. Dept. Health and Human Svcs., Chgo., 1992-93, staff atty. Social Security Adminstrn., 1993-94, sr. atty. Office Gen. Counsel Bethesda, Md., 1994—. Lectr. NIH, Found. for Advanced Edn. in Scis., Bethesda, 1995—; mem. black employees fed. adv. com. NIH, 1994-97. Campaign aide, FEC compliance, com. to elect Carol Moseley-Braun for U.S. Senate, Chgo., 1992. 1st lt. USAF, 1985-88. Decorated Air Force Meritorious Achievement Medal; recipient Joseph W. Rickert Award for Cmty. Svc., Faculty of Law, U. Ill., 1992. Mem. ABA, Nat. Bar Assn., Chgo. Bar Assn., Am. Legion, Masons. AME Ch. Avocations: Lacrosse, basketball, travel, reading, wine tasting. Office: NIH Bldg 31 -50 Rm 2B Bethesda MD 20892-0001

ROBERTSON, RAYMOND ELIOT, research chemist; b. St. Louis, Aug. 17, 1940; married BS, Cen. Mo. State U., 1962; MS, Colo. State U., 1971; PhD, U. Wyo., 1976. Research chemist Tretolite Co., Webster Groves, Mo., 1963-69; instr. E. Wyo. Coll., Torrington, 1975-76; research chemist Laramie (Wyo.) Energy Tech. Ctr., 1976-83; sr. research chemist, mgr. div. Western Research Inst., Laramie, 1983—. Mem. Am. Chem. Soc. Office: Western Research Inst 365 N 9th St Laramie WY 82072-3380

ROBERTSON, RICHARD EARL, physical chemist, educator; b. Long Beach, Calif., Nov. 12, 1933; s. Earl Austin and A. Isobel (Roberts) R.; m. Joyce W. Conger, Sept. 4, 1955 (div. 1972); children: Christopher, Jill; m. Patricia L. Richmond, Apr. 20, 1974. BA, Occidental Coll., L.A., 1955; student, UCLA, 1955-56; PhD, Calif. Inst. Tech., 1960. Phys. chemist rsch. lab. GE, Schenectady, N.Y., 1960-70; staff scientist Ford Motor Co., Dearborn, Mich., 1970-86; prof. materials sci. and engring. U. Mich., Ann Arbor, 1986—, dir. Macromolecular Sci. and Engring. Ctr., 1995-2000. Contbr. articles to profl. jours. Postdoctoral fellow Washington U., St. Louis, 1959-60. Fellow Am. Phys. Soc.; mem. Am. Chem. Soc., Sigma Xi. Office: U Mich Dept Materials Sci Eng Ann Arbor MI 48109-2136 E-mail: rer@umich.edu.

ROBERTSON, RICHARD ROBERT, grain milling executive; b. Seymour, Ind., Aug. 20, 1934; s. Richard Shields Robertson and Cora DeAlba; m. Ruth Ann Horstman, June 25, 1957; children: Richard Andrew, Susan Lynn. BS in Grain Milling, Kans. State U., Manhattan, 1956. Flour miller The Robertson Corp., Brownstown, Ind., 1979-89, v.p., 1989-97, pres., 1997-98, also bd. dirs. Bd. dirs. Engineerd Wood Rsch. Found., Tacoma, 1990-98. Author: A History of the American Roller Mills. Bd. dirs. Meml. Hosp. Found., Seymour, 1982—2002. Col. USAF, 1956—79. Mem. Assn. Operative Millers, Am. Assn. Cereal Chemists, Forest Products Soc., Elks. Presbyterian. Avocations: birding, antique phonographs, historic grist mills. Office: The Robertson Corp PO Box A Brownstown IN 47220-0301

ROBERTSON, RUTH ANN, systems analyst, engineer; b. Oak Ridge, Tenn., Nov. 20, 1959; d. Arnold Powell and Beatrice (Lazaroff) Litman. BME, Ga. Inst. Tech., 1982; postgrad., U. Redlands, Calif., 1991. Engring. intern IBM, Gaithersburg, Md., 1980-81; packaging engr. Hughes Aircraft Co., El Segundo, Calif., 1982-85; field engr. Spectrum Control, Inc., Valencia, 1985-86; pres. Precision Jaunt, El Segundo, 1986-87; sr. systems analyst Marquardt Co., Van Nuys, Calif., 1987-91, Axcom Computer Cons., Springfield, Mo., 1991-92; open systems product mgr. DataTrade, Inc., 1992-96; mgr.product realization Dayco Products, Inc., 1996-99; MIS mgr. S.W. Mo. State U., 1999-2000; UNIX adminstr. Cox Med. Ctr., 2000—. Mem. Whitehead Leadership Soc., Tau Beta Pi, Phi Tau Sigma. Office: Cox Med Ctr Computer Svcs 1423 N Jefferson Ave Springfield MO 65802 E-mail: ruth.robertson@coxhealth.com.

ROBERTSON, SAMUEL HARRY, III, transportation safety research engineer, educator; b. Phoenix, Oct. 2, 1934; s. Samuel Harry and Doris Bryle (Duffield) R.; m. Nancy Jean Bradford, 1954 (div. 1989); children: David Lyle, Pamela Louise; m. Linda Faye O'Neill, 1999. BS, Ariz. State U., 1956; D in Aviation Tech. (hon.), Embry-Riddle Aero. U., 1972. Registered profl. engr.; cert. comml. pilot--fixed wing, rotary wing, glider and balloon. Chief hazards divsn. Aviation Safety Engring. and Rsch., Phoenix, 1960-70; pres. Robertson Rsch. Engrs., 1960-70; rsch. prof., dir. Safety Ctr. Coll. Engring. and Applied Scis., Ariz State U., Tempe, 1970-79; pres. Robertson Research Inc., 1970-86, Robertson Aviation Inc., 1977-86, Internat. Ctr. for Safety Edn., 1982-96; pres., CEO Robertson Research Group, Inc., Tempe, 1986—, Robertson Aviation, LLC, Tempe, 1995—. Airplane design and accident investigator, 1961—; instr. aircrash investigation Internat. Ctr. Safety Edn., 1960—, inst. aerospace safety U. So. Calif., 1962-70, Armed Forces Inst. Pathology, 1970-90, Dept. Transp. Safety Inst., 1970-89; pres. Pine Springs Ranch, Inc, 1976—; adv. bd. Rio Salado Bank, Tempe, 1985-94; mem. adv. coun. Ctr. Aerospace Safety Edn., Embry-Riddle Aero. U., Daytona Beach, Fla., 1986—, trustee, 1992—; pres. Devil Dog Rsch., Inc., 1990—, Robertson Land & Cattle Inc., 1990—; comml. pilot, 1957—. Contbr. over 85 articles to profl. jours.; patentee applying plastic to paper, fuel system safety check valves, crash resitant fuel system, safety aircraft seats; holder FAA STC's various fuel systems, fuel system components; designer, developer, mfr. crash resistant fuel systems for airplanes, helicopters, championship racing cars. Pilot USAF, 1956-60, Ariz. Army NG 1960-61, 70-74, Ariz. Air NG, 1961-69. Recipient Contbns. Automotive Racing Safety award CNA, 1976, Adm. Luis De Florez Internat. Flying Safety award, 1969, Cert. Commendation Nat. Safety Coun., 1969, Gen. W. Spruance award for safety edn., SAFE Soc., 1982; holder Nat. Speed Record for one class of drag racing car, 1955-62, 5 nat. records for flying model aircraft, 1950-56; named to Ariz. Aviation Hall of Fame, 1996, OX5 Aviation Pioneers Hall of Fame, 1996, U.S. Army Aviation Hall of Fame, 2001, Army Aviation Assn. Am. Hall of Fame, 2001. Mem. AIAA, Internat. Soc. Air Safety Investigators (Jerome Lederer Aircraft Accident Investigation award, 1981), Aerospace Med. Assn., Exptl. Aircraft Assn., Soc. Automotive Engrs., Soc. Exptl. Test Pilots, Am. Helicopter Soc., Nat. Fire Protection Assn., Aircraft Owners and Pilots Assn., U.S. Automobile Club (tech. com.). Home: PO Box 58 Pine Springs Ranch Williams AZ 86046 Office: 1024 E Vista Del Cerro Dr Tempe AZ 85281-5709

ROBERTSON, SAMUEL LUTHER, JR. special education educator, therapist, researcher; b. Houston, Apr. 28, 1940; s. Sam L. and Portia Louise (Burns) R.; children: Samuel Luther IV, Sean Lee (dec.), Ryan William, Susan Elizabeth (dec.), Henry Philmore. BS, McMurry U., 1969; MA, Hardin-Simmons U., 1973; PhD, U. Tex., 1993. Cert. tchr., adminstr., counselor, prevention specialist, Tex.; lic. chem. dependency counselor, lic. clin. mental health counselor, advanced addiction counselor., Tex. Instr., coach, athletic dir. Tex. and La. schs., 1969-94; social worker, supr. Children's Protective Svcs., Abilene, Tex., 1978-79; instr., adminstr. Harlandale Sch. Dist., San Antonio, 1980-84, 87-90; adminstr. night sch. Harlandale Ind. Sch. Dist., 1988-89; instr. Edgewood Ind. Sch. Dist., 1985-87; developer, instr., integrated unit program, 1990—; CEO The Educative Inst., 1992—. CEO Educative Therapeutic Processes, 1972—; co-founder, dir. Inst. Organizational Personal Devel.; adj. prof. San Antonio Coll.; lectr. U. Tex. at San Antonio. Author: (play) The Challenged, 1965, Dream Poems, 1998; (poem) Trains in the Night, 1969; (screenplay) Tom & Jane, 2000; dir. (film) Tom & Jane, 2001. State co-chmn. Youth for Kennedy-Johnson, Tex., 1960; mem. W. Tex. Dem. Steering Com., Abilene, 1962-63; founding dir. Way Off Broadway Cmty. Theater, Eagle Pass, Tex., 1971-72; founding bd. dirs. Battered Women's Shelter, Abilene, 1978-79; v.p. bd. dirs. Mental Health Assn., San Antonio, 1980-83, bd. dirs Palmer Drug Abuse Program, San Antonio, 1985-87; pres., bd. dir. Alcoholic Rehab. Ctr., 1985-86, 1987-92; vice-chmn. Civilian and Mil. Addictive Programs, San Antonio, 1991-92; author, implementer Cmty. Vitalization Program, 1994—; mem. vestry St. George Episcopal Ch., mem. sch. bd., 1999—; mem. standards chair Tex. Certification Bd. of Addiction Profls.; chmn. 1999—. Named Tchr. of Yr. Southside Ind. Sch. Dist., San Antonio, 1970-71, Harlandale Alternative Ctr., San Antonio, 1987-88; Vol. of Yr., Mental Health Assn., San Antonio, 1982, Alcoholic Rehab. Ctr., San Antonio, 1992-93. Mem. ACA, NEA, Am. Mental Health Counseling Assn., Tex. State Tchrs. Assn., Am. Ednl. Rsch. Assn., Am. Assn. Sch. Adminstrs., Tex. Assn. Addiction Professionals, Nat. Alcoholism and Drug Abuse Counselors, N.Mex. Mental Health Counselors Assn., N.Mex. Profl. Counselors Assn., Phi Kappa Phi, Kappa Delta Pi. Episcopalian. Avocations: reading, writing, travel, theater, sports. Office: Educative Therapeutic Processes 339 E Hildebrand Ave San Antonio TX 78212-2412 *I have participated in my life, my family's life, and my community's life in a responsible fashion through the Grace of God.*

ROBERTSON, SANDRA DEE (GRAEN), tax director; b. Denver, Nov. 7, 1953; d. Fredrick Philip Arthur Graen and Dorothea Stone (Bell) Kohler; m. Charles E. Robertson Jr., Aug. 4, 1973 (Jan. 1985); 1 child, Daniel Philip. BS in Bus. cum laude, U. Colo., 1980. CPA, Colo., Ga. Staff acct. Brock, Cordle & Assocs., CPA's, Boulder, Colo., 1980-82; corp. tax acct. Storage Tech. Corp., Louisville, 1983-87; state tax supr. RJR Nabisco, Inc., Atlanta, 1987-89; mgr. Ernst & Young CPA's, 1989-91; dir. state and local taxes Equifax Inc., 1991-94; dir. state and local tax Ga.-Pacific Corp., 1994—. Bd. dirs. Com. on State Taxation. Served with U.S. Army, 1972-75. Mem. AICPA, Toastmasters, Beta Gamma Sigma. Democrat. Avocations: Russian language and history, Cajun and Zydeco music and dance, reading. Home: 450 Rock Springs Rd NE Atlanta GA 30324-5102

ROBERTSON, SARA STEWART, private investor, entrepreneur; b. N.Y.C., Feb. 4, 1940; d. John Elliott and Mary Terry (Schlamp) Stewart; m. James Young Robertson, Nov. 29, 1975 (dec. Mar. 1988). BA, Conn. Coll., 1961; MBA, Am. U., 1969. From trainee to officer First Nat. Bank/First Chgo. Corp., 1969-75, v.p., 1975-92; prin. Royall Enterprises, Chgo., 1992—; prin., dir. Zeppelin Press, Inc., Miami, Fla., 1995—. Chair individuals fundraising, exec. com. Youth Guidance, Chgo., 1993-95. Bd. dirs. Harbor House Condominium Assn. Chgo., 1990-92; trustee Sherwood Conservatory Music, 1993—, chair bd. devel., 1993-95, 97-99; mem. allocations com. and family priority grants com. United Way-Chgo., 1992-95; co-founder, v.p., sec.-treas. Animal Support Kindness and Kinship, Inc., 1999-2001, v.p., sec., 2001—. Mem.: Club 13 Palm Beach (pres. 1996—98). Home and Office: 339 Westminster Pl West Palm Beach FL 33405-1652 E-mail: saisairob@aol.com.

ROBERTSON, SHIRLEY PIERCE, human services administrator; b. Clanton, Ala., Oct. 26, 1948; d. Herbert O. Pierce and Myrtice Dean Duke; m. David Robertson, July 11, 1969; children: Amy, Pam, Matthew. BS in Sociology, Jacksonville (Ala.) State U., 1985, BS in Social Work, 1988. LCSW. Social worker foster care Etowah Co. Dept. Human Resources, Gadsden, Ala., 1987—. Vol. Girl Scouts Am., Glencoe, Ala., 1982-86, Big Brothers/Big Sisters Am., Gadsden, 1996; vol., coord. Estis Comm. Clearing Ho., Gadsden, 1986; bd. dirs. Rose Haven, Gadsden, 2001; tchr. youth dept. College Heights Bapt. Ch. Recipient Cmty. Svc. Vol. award Ala. State Dept. Human Resources, Montgomery, 1986. Mem. Ala. State Employee's Assn. Avocations: church activities, computers, reading, swimming, antiques. Home: 301 W Air Depot Rd Glencoe AL 35903 Office: Etowah Co Dept Human Resources 741 Forrest Ave Gadsden AL 35901 E-mail: JaxStMom@aol.com.

ROBERTSON, STERLING CLIFTON, music educator; b. Tientsin, Tiangjin, China, Jan. 22, 1928; arrived in U.S., 1932; s. Sterling Clifton and Mary Letitia (Grimes) Robertson. Student, Tex. Christian U., 1945—47, U. Tex., 1948—50, Julliard Sch. Music, N.Y.C., 1952—53, Columbia U., 1952—53; grad., Ft. Worth Conservatory Music, 1945. Tchr. piano, N.Y.C., 1950—70, San Antonio, 1970—. Staff pianist Four Seasons Hotels, San Antonio, Hyatt Regency, San Antonio, Wyndham-St. Anthony, San Antonio; concert pianist Carnegie Hall, 1961, 63, Royal Danish Ballet, various locations. Grantee grantee for piano study with George Copeland, Fairfield Found. and William Hale Harkness/Rebekah Harkness, 1952—53. Democrat. Avocations: theatre, film, art. Mailing: 314 Bryn Mawr Dr San Antonio TX 78209

ROBERTSON, TED ZANDERSON, judge; b. San Antonio, Sept. 28, 1921; s. Irion Randolf and Aurelia (Zanderson) R.; m. Margie Gardner. Student, Tex. A&I, 1940-42; LL.B., St. Mary's U., San Antonio, 1949. Bar: Tex. 1949. Chief civil dept. Dist. Atty.'s Office, Dallas County, Tex., 1960-65; judge Probate Ct. 2, 1965-69, Juvenile Ct. 2, Dallas County, 1969-75, 95th Dist. Ct., Dallas County, 1975-76, Ct. Civil Appeals, 5th Supreme Jud. Dist., Dallas, 1976-82, Supreme Ct. Tex., Austin, 1982; of counsel Frank Branson P.C., Dallas, 1989—. Guest lectr. So. Meth. U., Dallas, Dallas County Juvenile Bd., Tex. Coll. of the Judiciary, 1970-82 Active Dallas Assn. for Retarded Children; active Dallas County Commn. on Alcoholism, Dallas County Mental Health Assn. Served as yeoman USCG, 1942-46. Recipient Golden Gavel St. Mary's U., San Antonio, 1979; named Outstanding Alumnus St. Mary's U., 1981 Mem. Am. Judicature Soc., Tex. Bar Assn., Dallas Bar Assn., Dallas County Juvenile Bd. Lodges: Masons; Lions. Democrat. Methodist. Home: 6233 Highgate Ln Dallas TX 75214-2157 Office: Frank Branson 4514 Cole Ave Ste 1800 Dallas TX 75205-4185

ROBERTSON, TIMOTHY JOEL, statistician, educator; b. Denver, Oct. 4, 1937; s. Flavel P. and Helen C. (Oliver) Girdner; m. Joan K. Slater, Aug. 18, 1959; children— Kelly, Jana, Doug, Mike BA in Math., U. Mo., 1959, MS in Math., 1961, PhD in Stats., 1966. Asst. prof. Cornell Coll., Mt. Vernon, Iowa, 1961-63; prof. stats. U. Iowa, Iowa City, 1965—. Vis. prof. U. N.C., Chapel Hill, 1974-75, U. Calif.-Davis, 1983-84; Eugene Lukacs Disting. vis. prof. Bowling Green State U., 1991-92; vis. lectr. Com. Pres. Statis. Soc., 1971-74. Author: (with F.T. Wright and R.L. Dykstra) Order Restricted Statistical Inference; assoc. editor Am. Math. Monthly, 1977-81; mem. editl. bd. Comms. in Stats., 1981-92; assoc. editor Jour. Am. Statis. Assn., 1990-96; contbr. numerous articles to profl. jours. Recipient Collegiate Teaching award U. Iowa, 1990. Fellow Am. Statis. Assn. (council 1974-75), Inst. Math. Stats., Internat. Statis. Inst.; mem. Math. Assn. Am., Sigma Xi, Sierra Club Democrat. Avocations: canoeing, camping, bicycling, walking. Home: 673 Garfield Rd West Branch IA 52358-8574 Office: University of Iowa Dept Stats/Actuarial Sci Iowa City IA 52242

ROBERTSON, WILLIAM, IV, foundation administrator; b. Glen Ridge, N.J., Sept. 12, 1943; s. William R. III and Shirley (Anderson) Volpe; m. Harriette Alicia Sorenson, May 30, 1970; children: Paige, William V. BS, Parsons Coll., Fairfield, Iowa, 1966; MA, Sam Houston State U., 1969. Staff officer Nat. Acad. Scis., Washington, 1971-79; program officer Andrew W. Mellon Found., N.Y.C., 1979—. Trustee Rumson (N.J.) Country Day Sch., 1984-91, Ctr. for Plant Conservation, St. Louis, 1985-96. Office: Andrew W Mellon Found 140 E 62nd St New York NY 10021-8124 E-mail: wr@mellon.org.

ROBERTSON, WILLIAM ABBOTT, arbitrator, mediator, lawyer; b. San Francisco, Apr. 7, 1947; s. William Abbott Jr. and Roxana D. Robertson; children: Sara W., Claire S. BA, U. Calif., Davis, 1969; JD, U. Pacific, 1980. Bar: Calif. 1980, U.S. Dist. Ct. (no. and ea. dists.) 1981, U.S. Ct. Appeals (9th cir.) 1981. Atty. Rodeno & Robertson, Napa, Calif., 1984-94, Robertson Law Office, Napa, 1994-95; pvt. practice mediation and arbitration, Cotati, Calif., 1995—. Judge pro tem Napa Consol. Cts., 1982-96; assigned arbitrator Napa and Solano County Superior Cts., 1984-96. Avocations: ranching, quarter horses. Office: Robertson Mediation Office PO Box 550 Cotati CA 94931-0550

ROBERTSON, WILLIAM WITHERS, lawyer; b. Morristown, N.J., Nov. 3, 1941; s. Thomas Withers and Jessie (Swain) R.; m. Elizabeth Jeanne Robertson; children: Barbara Ellen, William Withers, Jessie Swain Wilt. BA, Rutgers U., 1964, LL.B., 1967. Bar: N.J. 1968. Law sec. to judge Superior Ct. N.J., 1967-68; asst. U.S. atty., 1972-76; 1st asst. U.S. atty., 1978-80; U.S. atty. Dist. N.J., 1980-81; chief Newark Organized Crime Strike Force, 1976-78; ptnr. Hannoch Weisman, Roseland, N.J., 1981-99, Robertson, Freilich, Bruno & Cohen, LLC, Newark, 1999—. Mng. editor Rutgers Law Rev., 1966-67. Trustee Rutgers U., 1984-88. Served to capt. JAGC USAR, 1968-72. Mem. Nat. Assn. Former U.S. Attys. (bd. dirs. 1990-93, pres. 2002-2003), Rutgers U. Law Sch. Alumni Assn. (pres. 1990-91), Rutgers U. Alumni Fedn. (pres. 1981-83). Office: Robertson Freilich Et Al 4th Fl 1 Riverfront Plz Newark NJ 07102-5401 E-mail: wrobertson@rtbclaw.com.

ROBERTSON, WYNDHAM GAY, university official, journalist; b. Salisbury, N.C., Sept. 25, 1937; d. Julian Hart and Blanche Williamson (Spencer) R. AB in Econs., Hollins Coll., Roanoke, Va., 1958. Rsch. asst. Standard Oil Co., N.Y.C., 1958-61; rschr. Fortune Mag., 1961-67, assoc. editor, 1968-74, bd. of editors, 1974-81, asst. mng. editor, 1981-86; bus. editor Time Mag., 1982-83; v.p. comm. U. N.C., Chapel Hill, 1986-96. Bd. dirs. Media Gen. Inc. Contbr. numerous articles to Fortune Mag. Trustee Thomas S. Kenan Inst. for the Arts, Nat. Humanities Ctr., Hollins U. Recipient Gerald M. Loeb Achievement award, U. of Conn., 1972. Mem. Phi Beta Kappa. Episcopalian.

ROBICHAUX, JOHN W. art educator, writer; b. Thibodaux, La., Dec. 11, 1948; s. Abe J. Robichaux, Muriel R. Robichaux; m. Sandra Ann Champagne. BA, Nicholls State U., Thibodaux, LA, 1973, MEd, 1976. Founder Chama Sch. of Landscape Painting, Chama, N.Mex., 2000—, dir., 2000—. Artist Studio Robichaux, Thibodaux, 1999—2001. Author: Hensche on Painting, 1998; editor: The Art of Seeing and Painting, 1988. Office: Chama School of Landscape Painting PO Box 1275 Thibodaux LA 70301 Personal E-mail: johnrobichaux@yahoo.com. Business E-Mail: chamaschool@yahoo.com.

ROBILLARD, ALAIN RICHARD, civil engineer; b. Juvisy, Essonne, France, Oct. 9, 1945; s. Henri Desire Robillard and Suzanne Albertine Gourdon; m. Fabienne Pia Idrac; two children. Engr., ETP, Paris, 1968. Registered civil engr. Co-instr. divsn. DDE74, Annecy, France, 1970-72; tech. mgr. Cogedim, Paris, 1972-73; mng. dir. Seralp-Beteralp, Lyon, France, 1979-84; project dir. Salahaldeen Univ., Baghdad, 1984-86; design mgr. Eurotunnel, London, 1986-87; v.p. Autoroutes Du Sud de France, Paris, 1987—2001, sr. exec. officer, 2002—. Chevalier Ordre du Merite, France, 1996. Avocation: nat. prof. skiing. Office: Autoroutes Du Sud de France 100 Ave de Suffren 75015 Paris France

ROBILLARD, EDMOND, priest; b. LeGardeur, Que., Can., Dec. 20, 1917; s. William and Marie (Lachapelle) R. B Arts and Scis., Coll. de l'Assomption, 1936; postgrad., Couvent Dominicain d'Ottawa, 1938-41; Licentiate in Theology, Cath. U. Am., 1943; ThD, U. Montreal, Can., 1944-45. Joined Dominican Order, Roman Cath. Ch., ordained priest, 1941. Prof. theology Coll. Dominicain, Ottawa, Ont., Can., 1943-50; prof. U. Montreal, 1955-83, prof. titulaire, 1970—83. Pres. Soc. des Ecrivains canadiens, 1973-77; sec. Soc. Letters of Que., 1977-83. Author: De l'analogie et du concept d'etre, 1963, John Henry Newman: L'idee d'universite, 1968, John Henry Newman: Conferences sur la Doctrine de la justification, 1980, Reincarnation: Illusion or Reality, 1982, Quebec Blues on Suicide, 1983, Nos Racines chrétiennes, 1985, La messe catholique de tous les dimanches de l'année sur des chorals de J. S. Bach, 1986, Tout ce qu'il vous dira, Faites-le, 1987, S. Justin: Itinéraire philosophique, 1989, Qui aime connaît Dieu, 1989, La sagesse et les Sentences, 1991, Jeux d'hiver et d'enfer, 1995, Le Discours poétique, 1996, Blaise Pascal: Le pari sur l'incertain, 1996, L'Expérience De La Trinité dans les Âmes Saintes d'après Saint Thomas D'Aquin, 1997; La Rédemption: une amoureuse Folie de Dieu, 1998, Les Saintes et Saints de la Liturgie Canadienne, 1999, Journal de Josephine, 2000, Memoires d'Une Enfance, 2001, Dieu Est Mort, 2002, Du Temps que le Goglu chantait, 2001; mem. editl. bd. jour. Carrefour Chretien, 1984—; contbr. to profl. jours. Mem. Soc. Can. Theologie, Assn. Can. Francaise L'avancement Scis., Quebec Writers Assn. (gen. pres., regional pres.), Académie des Lettres du Québec. Address: Les Péres Domínicains Montreal QC Canada H3T 1B6 Office: 2715 Chemin Ste Catherine Montreal QC H3T 1B6 Canada Fax: 514-731-0676.

ROBILLARD, JAMES L. educator; b. Milw., Feb. 5, 1926; s. Lionel Ovila Robillard and Diana Helen (Jenny) Rousseau. PhB, Marquette U., 1950; cert., Laval U., Quebec, Can., 1948; MA, U. Wis., 1951; ABD, U. Wis., Milw., 1999. Asst. d'Anglais Ministere de l'Edn. Lycee Chaptal, Paris, 1951-52; prof. de l'Anglais Ecole Superieure de Guerre Champs de Mars, 1951-52; lectr., tour mgr. Am. Express, Chgo., 1953-60; spl. asst. to pres. U. Chgo., 1960-62; exec. dir. Jesuit Rsch. Coun. Am., Washington, 1962-67; cons. edn. nat. urban coalition Call for Action, John W. Gardner, 1967; cons. edn. Stanwick Corp., Arlington, Va., 1968-69; lectr., tour mgr. Cartan Tours, Inc., Rolling Meadows, Ill., 1977-82; mgr. Tauck Tours, Inc., Westport, Conn., 1982-87; lectr., tour dir. Princess Tours cruises, Seattle, 1989, Globus Gateway Tours, N.Y.C., 1990, Mayflower Tours, Inc., Downers Grove, Il., 1992, Travel Am., Inc., West Allis, Wis., 1993; writer, rschr. Lamers Tours, Inc., Milw., 1995—, U. Wis., Milw., 1975—. Video/lectr. Channel 10/36 PBS Milw., 1999. Author: The Jesuit Order and Higher Education in the U.S., 1789-1966; co-author: Jesuit Colleges and Universities of the United States, 1967; contbr. articles to profl. publs. State rep. for Wis. Alliance Franco-Americans in Midwest, 1982—; orgn., rep. French Bastille Days, Milw., 1982-97; bd. dirs. Am. Geog. Soc. Collection Golda Meir Libr., U. Wis., Milw., 2000—. With USN, 1944-46. Recipient Chevalier des Palmes Acad., Min. Edn. Nat., Paris, 1987, L'Ordre des Francophones d'Amerique, Langue Francaise, Que., 1993. Mem. Shorewood Hist. Soc. (rschr. centennial com. 1999—, v.p. 1993-96), Alliance Francaise de Milw. (liaison rep. 1990-98), Colonial Dames of Wis., 17th Century (cons. 1999—), French-Colonial History of Wis. (rschr., cons. 1976—). Roman Catholic. Avocations: piano, French folk music, cooking. Home: 1809 E Marion St Marion Manor # 201 Milwaukee WI 53211-2037 Office: Alliance Franco-Am Midwest 1155 E 56th St Chicago IL 60637-1530

ROBILLARD, JEAN JULES, engineering educator, researcher; b. Enguinegatte, France, Mar. 28, 1924; s. Jules Auguste and Augustine Marie (Delaroziere) R. MS, U. de Lille, France, 1945; DSc, Sorbonne U., Paris, 1947. Rsch. engr. L.M. Ericsson, Stockholm; cons. Gen. Dynamics, Rochester, N.Y.; staff scientist Motorola, Scottsdale, Ariz.; lab. rsch. scientist CBS, N.Y.C.; prof. rsch. scientist U. N.Mex., Las Cruces; prof., dir. materials sci. lab. U. Tex., El Paso. Dir. Cue Inc. (D. Nokia) Newton Upper Falls, Mass.; cons. Ricoh Co., Tokyo, Tektronix, Beaverton, Oreg., Fuji Photo Film, Tokyo. Author, editor: Industrial Applications of Holography, 1988, Nonlinear Optical Materials, 1991, Optical Data Processing and Holography, 1992, Non-Silver Photographic Processes, 1973. Recipient awards CRCM, 1993, IMIQ, 1997. Mem. SPSE (Charles Ives award 1964), SPIE, SID. Roman Catholic.

ROBILLARD, LUCIENNE, Canadian government official; b. Montreal, Canada; BA, Coll. Basile-Moreau, 1965; MA in Social Work, U. Montreal, 1967; Diploma in Adminstrn., École des hautes études commerciales, Montreal, 1983, MBA, 1986. Social worker, clin. practitioner Maisonneuve-Rosemont Hosp.; appt. min. of labour and fed. campaigns Que., 1995-96; sr. adminstr. Centre de svcs. sociaux Richelieu; youth leader in a kibbutz Israel, 1969-72; apptd. pub. curator City of Quebec, Canada, 1986-89; elected mem. Quebec Nat. Assembly for Chambly, 1989; apptd. min. cultural affairs,

1989-90; apptd. min. higher edn. and science, 1990-92; apptd. min. of edn., 1992-93; min. edn. and science, 1993-94; min. health and social svcs., 1994-95; minister of labor, minister responsible for fed. campaign, 1995; elected mem. parliament Saint-Henri-Westmount, 1995—; min. citizenship and immigration, 1996-99; re-elected to parliament Westmount-Ville-Marie, 1997—; pres. Treas. Bd., 1999—; min. infrastructure., 1999—. Pres. Treasury Bd., Min. responsible for intrastructure; mem. Corp. professionelle des travailleurs sociaux de Québec, 1967—; mem. editl. com. (book) Le travail social et la santé au Québec, 1984-86, departmental study com. psychiatric svcs., Montreal region, 1984-85; pres. Commn. adminstrv. des svcs. de santé mentale of the Conseil régional de la Montérégie, 1983-86, Association des praticiens de service social en milieu de santé du Québec, 1984-86; cons. mental health dossier Rochon Commn., 1986. Mem. editl. com. Le Travail Social et la Santé du Québec, 1985. Mem. Corp Professionelle des Travailleurs Sociaux du Que. Office: 140 O'Connor St East Tower 9th Fl Ottawa ON Canada K1A OR5*

ROBIN, CLARA NELL (CLAIRE ROBIN), English language educator; b. Harrisonburg, Va., Feb. 19, 1945; d. Robert Franklin and Marguerite Ausherman (Long) Wampler; m. Phil Camden Branner, June 10, 1967 (div. May 1984); m. John Charles Robin, Nov. 22, 1984 (div. Dec. 1990). BA in English, Mary Washington Coll., 1967; MA in English, James Madison U., 1974; postgrad., Jesus Coll., Cambridge, Eng., 1982, Princeton U., 1985-86, Auburn U., 1988, U. No. Tex., 1990-91. Cert. tchr. English, French, master cert., Tex. Tchr. 7th grade John C. Myers Intermediate Sch., Broadway, Va., 1967-68; tchr. 10th grade Waynesville (Mo.) H.S., 1968-70; tchr. 6th, 7th, 8th grades Mary Mount Jr. Sch., Santa Barbara, Calif., 1970-72; tchr. 9th grade Forest Meadow Jr. H.S. Richardson (Tex.) Ind. Sch. Dist., 1972-78, tchr. 10th grade Lake Highlands H.S., 1972-84; tchr. 11th, 12th grades Burleson (Tex.) H.S. Burleson Ind. Sch. Dist., 1986—. Instr. composition Hill Coll., 1992-94. Contbg. author: (book revs.) English Journal, 1989-94, (lit. criticism) Eric, 1993. Vol. Dallas Theater Ctr., 1990—96; active Kimbell Art Mus., Ft. Worth, 1990—, Modern Art Mus., Ft. Worth, 1992—, KERA Pub. TV, Dallas, 1990—, Amon Carter Mus., Ft. Worth, 2001—; mem. MOMA, N.Y.C., 1995—, Whitney Art Mus., 2002—, Amon Carter Museum ,Ft. Worth, 2002—. Fellow NEH, 1988, 89, 92, 95, Fulbright-Hays Summer Seminar, 1991; ind. study grantee Coun. Basic Edn., 1990; recipient Chpt. Achievement award Epsilon Nu Delta Kappa Gamma, 1993, Honorable Mention Tex. Outstanding Tchg. of the Humanities award, 1995, Burlesson Independent Sch. Dist., Campus Ednl. Improvement Com., 1997-2000, Dist. Ednl. Improvement Com., 1998-2001. Mem.: United Educators Assn., Nat. Coun. Tchrs. English (spring conf. presenter 2000, 2002), Acad. Am. Poets, Epsilon Nu of Delta Kappa Gamma (1st v.p. 1988—94, v.p. 1992—94, profl. affairs com. 1996—98, comms. chair 1998—). Avocations: bicycling, travel, reading, writing, theater. Home: 4009 W 6th St Fort Worth TX 76107-1619 Office: Burleson High Sch 100 NW John Jones Dr Burleson TX 76028-5648 E-mail: crbkrd@aol.com.

ROBINER, DONALD MAXWELL, lawyer, former federal official; b. Detroit, Feb. 4, 1935; s. Max and Lucia (Chassman) Robiner; m. Phyllis F Goodman; children: Brian Roberts, Marc Roberts, Steven Ralph, Lawrence Alan. BA, U. Mich., 1957; postgrad., Wayne State U., 1957-58; JD, Case Western Res. U., 1961. Bar: Ohio 1961, US Supreme Ct 1964, US Ct Appeals (6th cir) 1965. Assoc. Metzenbaum, Gaines, Schwartz, Krupansky, Finley & Stern, Cleve., 1961-67; ptnr. Metzenbaum, Gaines, Krupansky, Finley & Stern, 1967-72; v.p. Metzenbaum, Gaines, Finley & Stern Co., L.P.A., 1972-77, Gaines, Stern, Schwarzwald & Robiner Co., Cleve., 1977-81; exec. v.p., sec. Schwarzwald, Robiner & Rock Co. LPA, 1981-90; prin. Buckingham, Doolittle & Burroughs Co. LPA, 1991-94; U.S. Trustee Ohio and Mich. region 9 U.S. Dept. of Justice, 1994—2001; of counsel Selkin, Billick & Harrold Co., LPA, Beachwood, Ohio, 2002—. V.p., sec. Richard L. Bowen & Assocs. Inc., Cleve., 1969—94; acting judge Shaker Heights Mcpl. Ct., 1973; mem. bd. bar examiners State of Ohio, Columbus, 1974—79; life mem. 6th Cir. Jud. Conf.; mediator alt ernate dispute resolution panel U.S. Dist. Ct. (no. dist.) Ohio, 1993—94. Sec. Friends of Beachwood Libr. Inc, Ohio, 1981—88; sec. Friends of Beachwood Libr. Inc., 1981—96, trustee, 1981—96. Recipient Cert Appreciation, Ohio Supreme Ct, 1974—79, Appreciation Award, Am Soc Appraisers, 1975. Mem.: Cleve. Bar Assn., Ohio Coun. Sch. Bd. Attys. (mem. exec. com. 1990—94), Am. Arbitration Assn. (Serv Award 1975), Comml. Law League Am., Am. Bankruptcy Inst., Jud. Conf. 8th Appellate Dist. Ohio (life), KP. Home: 3094 Richmond Rd Beachwood OH 44122-3247 Office: Commerce Park Four 23240 Chagrin Blvd Ste 450 Beachwood OH 44122 Fax: 216-831-1326. E-mail: DonRobiner@msn.com.

ROBINETT, BETTY WALLACE, linguist, educator; b. Detroit, June 23, 1919; d. Henry Guy and Beulah (Reid) Wallace; m. Ralph F. Robinett, Apr. 10, 1952 (dec. div. 1960); 1 child, Richard Wallace. BA, Wayne State U., 1940; MA, U. Mich., 1941, PhD, 1951. Instr., adminstrv. asst. English Lang. Inst., U. Mich., Ann Arbor, 1945-50; cons. Dept. Edn., San Juan, P.R., 1950-51, 52-57; lectr. English, U. Mich., 1951-52, 55-56; asso. prof. English InterAm. U., San German, P.R., 1957-59; asst. prof. English and linguistics Ball State U., Muncie, Ind., 1959-63, assoc. prof. English and linguistics, 1963-67, prof., 1967-68; prof. dept. linguistics U. Minn., Mpls., 1968-88, dir. program in English as a second lang., 1968-80, acting asst. v.p. acad. affairs, 1979-80, asst. v.p. acad. affairs, 1980-84, assoc. v.p. acad. affairs, 1984-88, prof. emerita, 1988, Morse alumni disting. tchg. prof. emerita, 1996; chmn. Univ. Senate Consultative Com., 1977-78. Vis. prof. Pa. State U., 1994-95; chmn. adv. panel on English tchg. USIA, 1988-93. Author: with (C.H. Prator) Manual of American English Pronunciation, 1972, 4th edit., 1985, Teaching English to Speakers of Other Languages, Substance and Technique, 1978, (with J. Schachter) Second Language Learning: Contrastive Analysis, Error Analysis and Related Aspects, 1983, (with Virginia F. Allen) Easy Latin Crossword Puzzles: Quid Pro Quo, 1999, Easy French Crossword Puzzles: Le mot Juste, 2002; editor Tesol Quar., 1967-72. Internat. Programs travel grantee, 1972, 77; recipient Morse-Amoco award for Excellence in Teaching, 1977 Mem. Tchrs. English to Speakers of Other Langs. (pres. 1974, James Alatis Svc. award 1990), Assn. Tchrs. ESL (chmn. 1976-77), Am. Assn. Applied Linguistics (v.p., pres. 1980-82), Linguistic Soc. Am. (life). Home: 1936 Park Forest Ave State College PA 16803-1329 E-mail: brobin4049@aol.com.

ROBINETT, TIMOTHY DOUGLAS, lawyer; b. Long Beach, Calif., Mar. 27, 1967; s. Clyde A. and Jeanne K. Robinett; m. Erica Sandra Behrens, June 7, 1997. BA, U. Calif., Berkeley, 1989; JD, Loyola U., 1993. Bar: Calif. 1993, U.S. Dist. Ct. (cen., so., no. and ea. dists.) Calif. 1993. Ptnr. Manning, Leaver, Bruder & Berberich, L.A., 1993—. Mem. L.A. County Bar Assn. Office: Manning Leaver Bruder & Berberich 5750 Wilshire Blvd Ste 655 Los Angeles CA 90036-3637

ROBINETTE, BETTY LOU, occupational health and infection control nurse; b. Richlands, Va., Nov. 24, 1941; d. John H. and Eva M. (Crawford) Brown; m. Daniel G. Robinette, Dec. 1, 1961; children: Daniel G. Jr., Brian L., Lisa D. Diploma, Va. Bapt. Hosp., Lynchburg, 1961; tng. infection control, U. Va., 1977. RN, Va. Nurse Highsmith Meml. Hosp., Fayetteville, N.C., 1962; supr., head nurse Clinch Valley Clinic and Hosp., Richlands, Va., 1962-63; nurse Bristol (Tenn.) Meml. Hosp, 1963-65; sch. nurse Wythe County Sch. Bd., Wytheville, Va., 1966-67; staff nurse, supr. Wythe County Cmty. Hosp., 1972—, employee health nurse coord. infection control practitioner, 1976—, team leader continuous quality improvement, 1994, safety officer, 1997—. Mem. Assn. Practitioners Infection Control, SW Va. AIDS Coalition.

ROBINETTE, CHRISTOPHER JOHN, lawyer; b. Raleigh, N.C., June 22, 1971; s. Kim V. and Billie Kaye Robinette; m. Amanda Irene Lenz, Oct. 13, 1996. BA, Coll. William and Mary, 1993; JD, U. Va., 1996. Bar: Va. 1996, U.S. Dist. Ct. (we. dist.) Va. 1997, U.S. Ct. Appeals (4th cir.) 1997, U.S. Dist. Ct. (ea. dist.) Va. 1998. Assoc. Tremblay & Smith LLP, Charlottesville, Va., 1996—. Contbr. to profl. jours. Adv. bd. mem. Salvation Army, Charlottesville, Va., 1997—; mem. Recreational Facilities Authority, Albemarle County, Va., 1998—. Mem. Va. State Bar (young lawyers divsn., litigation sect.), Va. Trial Lawyers' Assn., Charlottesville-Albermarle Bar Assn. Avocations: reading, jogging, weight lifting, traveling. Office: Tremblay & Smith LLP 105-109 E High St Charlottesville VA 22902 E-mail: chris.robinette@tremblaysmith.com.

ROBINETTE, JOSEPH ALLEN, theater educator, playwright; b. Rockwood, Tenn., Feb. 8, 1939; s. Paul Henry and Willie Merle (Ghormley) R.; m. Helen Marie Seitz; children: John, Anne, Michael, Christopher, Andrew. BA, Carson-Newman Coll., 1960; MA, So. Ill. U., 1966, PhD, 1972. Tchr. Bearden H.S., Knoxville, Tenn., 1962-63; instr. Arkansas City (Kans.) Jr. Coll., 1963-64, U. Hawaii, Hilo, 1968-69, So. Ill. U., Carbondale, 1965-68, 69-71; prof. theatre arts Rowan U., Glassboro, N.J., 1971—. Author 39 pub. plays and musicals, 1972—; authorized dramatizer Charlotte's Web, Stuart Little, The Lion, The Witch and the Wardrobe, The Paper Chase, A Rose for Emily, others. Founding mem. Opera for Youth, 1978—. Recipient various ASCAP awards, 1975—; recipient Charlotte Chorpanning cup for outstanding writing of children's plays, Children's Theatre Assn. Am., 1976. Mem. Am. Alliance for Theatre in Edn. Home: PO Box 11 Richwood NJ 08074-0011 Office: Rowan U 201 Mullica Hill Rd Glassboro NJ 08028-1702

ROBINOWITZ, CAROLYN BAUER, psychiatrist, educator; b. Bklyn., July 15, 1938; d. Milton Leonard and Marcia (Wexler) Bauer; m. Max Robinowitz, June 10, 1962; children: Mark, David AB, Wellesley Coll., 1959; MD, Washington U., 1964. Diplomate Am. Bd. Psychiatry and Neurology. Chief physician tng. NIMH, Bethesda, Md., 1968-70; dir. pediatric liaison U. Miami Sch. Medicine, Fla, 1970-72, dir. child psychiatry tng., 1971-72; dir. edn. George Washington U. Sch. Medicine, Washington, 1972-74; project dir. Psychiatrist as Tchr., 1973-75; dep. med. dir. Am. Psychiat. Assn., 1976-86, dir. Office Edn., 1976-87, sr. dep. med. dir., 1986-94, COO, 1986-94. Assoc. dean Georgetown U. Sch. Medicine, 1995—98, dean, 1998—2000, lectr., 1976—82, professorial lectr., 1982—94, prof., 1995—2000, clin. prof., 2000—; dir. Am. Bd. Psychiatry and Neurology, Evanston, Ill., 1979—86, sec., Ill., 1984, v.p., Ill., 85, pres., Ill., 86; clin. prof. psychiatry and behavioral scis., child health and devel. George Washington U., 1984—98, 2001—; professorial lectr. Uniformed Svcs. U. of Health Scis., 1986—. Editor: Women in Context, 1976; contbr. articles to jours., chpts. to books Admissions com. Wellesley Coll. Club, Washington, 1983-84; active Boy Scouts Am. Served with USPHS, 1966-69 Recipient NIMH Mental Health Career Devel. award, 1966-70, NIMH grantee, 1974-94. Fellow Am. Psychiat. Assn. (Disting. Svc. award 1991, Vestermark award 1995, Adminstrv. Psychiatry award 1999), Am. Coll. Psychiatrists (bd. dirs. 1993-96, 1st v.p. 1996-97, pres. 1999-2000, past pres. 2000—, Bowis award 1994, Disting. Svc. award 2001—); mem. AMA (coun. on sci. affairs 2001--), Assn. for Acad. Psychiatry (pres. 1994-95, dir. 1992-96), Group for Advancement of Psychiatry (dir. 1982-84, pres. 1989-91), Coun. Med. Splty. Socs. (dir. 1977-82, pres. 1981-82). Office: #514 5225 Connecticut Ave NW Washington DC 20015 E-mail: carolynrobinowitz@usa.net.

ROBINOWITZ, CHARLES, lawyer; b. White Plains, N.Y., Sept. 29, 1942; s. Seymour and Shirley (Horowitz) R.; m. Selene Bea Greenberg, June 17, 1973; children: Scott, Mark. BA, Cornell U., 1964; LLB, U. Va., 1968. Bar: Oreg. 1969, N.Y. 1969, U.S. Dist. Ct. (all dists.) Oreg. 1969, U.S. Ct. Appeals (9th cir.) 1973, U.S. Supreme Ct. 1974. Law clk. U.S. Dist. Ct., N.Y.C., 1968-69; assoc. Dusenbery, Martin et al, Portland, Oreg., 1969-71; pvt. practice, 1971—. Bd. dirs. Jewish Fedn. Portland, 1991-97; pres. Cornell Club Oreg., 1991-95, Temple Beth Israel, Portland, 1988-94; bd. dirs. Friends of Chamber Music, Portland, 1975-79. Mem. ABA, ATLA, Oreg. Trial Lawyers Assn., Oreg. State Bar Assn., Multnomah County Bar Assn. Avocations: running, classical music. Office: 1211 SW 5th Ave Ste 1150 Portland OR 97204-3729 E-mail: cr@teleport.com.

ROBINOWITZ, MAX, pathologist, consultant; b. Washington, Aug. 11, 1936; s. William and Stella (Chaikin) R.; m. Carolyn Landeck Bauer, June 10, 1962; children: Mark, David L. BS, Georgetown U., 1957, MD, 1961. Med. intern Barnes Hosp., St. Louis, 1961-62, asst. resident, Internal Medicine, 1962-63; resident in pathology Mt. Sinai Hosp., N.Y.C., 1963-67; asst. chief clin. pathology Walter Reed Army Med. Ctr., Washington D.C., 1968-69; asst. pathologist Armed Forces Inst. of Pathology, 1969-70; pathologist Mt. Sinai Med. Ctr., Miami Beach, Fla., 1970-72; asst. prof. pathology U. Miami, 1970-72; asst. prof. pathology, Sch. of Medicine Georgetown U., Washington D.C., 1972-75; pathologist Armed Forces Inst. of Pathology, 1976-90. Sr. med. officer Divsn. Clin. Lab. Devices, Office Device Evaluation, CDRH, FDA, Rockville, Md., 1990—; prof. pathology USPHS, Bethesda, Md., 1980—; clin. assoc. pathology Georgetown U. Med. Sch., Washington, 1976—. Maj. U.S. Army, 1967-69. Mem. AACC, AOA, USCAP, CAP, ASCP. Office: FDA HFZ-440 2098 Gaither Rd Rockville MD 20850-4017

ROBINS, BETTY DASHEW, antiques and arts dealer; b. N.Y.C., Feb. 14, 1923; d. Leon and Esther (Turits) Dashew; m. Arthur Joseph Robins, Sept. 26, 1948; children: Lisa Dale, Michael Lee. BA, NYU, 1952. Field staff Pearl Buck Open Door, N.Y.C., 1944-45; dir. MacArthur House, San Francisco, 1945-47, Georgetown House, Washington, 1948-50; asst. curator S. Asian Collection Mus. of Art and Archaeology, U. Mo., Columbia, 1967-68; owner BDR Assocs. Arts and Antiques, 1976—. Founding mem., 1st pres. Columbia Art League, 1959-61; gen. chmn. 1st Tenn. Artist Craftsman Fair, Nashville, 1971-72; bd. mem. Mus. Assocs., Mus. Art and Archaeology, U. Mo., 1975-85, Boone County Hist. Soc., 2001—; mem. S. Asian studies com., 1976-85; coord. Festival of India, 1985-86, Festival of China, 1986-87, Peace Through the Arts, 1987-88, yr.-long programs commemorating 50th anniversary India independence, Columbia, 1997; mem. profl. visual arts adv. com. Mo. Arts Coun., 1980-82; cons. Denver Art Mus., 1991-92; advisor India Arts exhibit U. Mo. Mus. Art and Archaeology, 1997; organizer gallery exhibits, such as carved coconut Scrapers of Malaysia, India, Indonesia, Nat. Inst. of Pub. Adminstrn., Kuala Lumpur, 1989, Traditional Arts of India and U.S.A., U. Mo., 1989, Healing Imagery of Malaysia and U.S.A., U. Mo., 1991, Decorative Arts India, Stephens Coll., 1998, Storytelling through the Everyday Art of Mo. and India, Boone County Hist. Mus., 1998. Co-author: Everyday Art of India, 1968; contbr. articles to profl. jours. Bd. dirs. PAST (hist. preservation of Mo.), 1978-79. Named Woman of the Yr., Women in Comms., 1977-78, Vol. of Yr., Vol. Action Coun., 1983; recipient Quiet Hero award Columbia Pub. Schs., 1998. Home: 2316 Woodridge Rd Columbia MO 65203-1550

ROBINS, JAMES DOW, counselor; b. Athens, Ga., Oct. 17, 1952; s. Gerald Burns and Fay Ann Robins; m. Sharon Eileen Parker, Apr. 12, 1974 (div. 1976). BA in Psychology, SUNY, Albany, 1981; BA in Comm. cum laude, Tex. A&M U., 1981, MA in Secondary Edn., 1982; ABA, cert. legal asst., Southwestern Paralegal Inst., 1984; MS in Guidance and Counseling, Tex. A&M U., 1993. Bar: Tex., 1985; cert. counselor, psychologist, English and speech tchr., legal asst., Tex. Program dir. University City, Inc., Athens, 1971-73; sta. mgr. Bethany Broadcasting, Houston, 1973-76; program coord. for radio and TV, Tex. A&I U., Kingsville, 1977-82; dir. pub. rels. Kleberg Meml. Hosp., 1983-84; legal asst., cons. Kleberg, Dyer, Redford & Weil, Corpus Christi, Tex., 1984-86; tchr. English lit. Brownsville (Tex.) Ind. Sch. Dist., 1986-90; dir. testing and assessment, dir. suicide intervention Kingsville Ind. Sch. Dist., Kingsville, 1993—, counselor, 1993—. Cons. Conner Mus., Kingsville, 1981-82. Author: The School Counselor: A Profession in Transition, 1993; contbr. articles to various publs. Recipient Disting. Svc. award for Excellence in Broadcasting, Tex. A&M, 1980-81. Mem. ACA (profl.), Tex. Counseling Assn., Mensa, The Blues Found. (internat. voting mem.), State Bar of Tex. (legal asst. div. 1985), Am. Counseling Assn., Tex. Counselors Assn., Tex. Sch. Counselors Assn., Tex. Assn. for Humanistic Edn. and Devel., Tex. Assn. for Multi-Cultural Counseling and Devel., Am. Assn. Assessment in Counseling, World Wildlife Fedn., Gulf Coast Counseling Assn., Gulf Coast Assn. for Counseling and Devel., The Blues Found., Phi Delta Kappa , Alpha Chi. Methodist. Avocations: writing, guitar, computers. Home: 515 University Blvd Kingsville TX 78363-4242 E-mail: jrobins@intcomm.net.

ROBINS, JUDY ROSELYN, interior designer; b. Cleve., Sept. 2, 1948; d. Stanley and Esther (Resnick) Waxman; m. Kenneth Michael Robins, Sept. 26, 1971. AAS, Fashion Inst. Tech.; BS, N.Y.U., 1970, MA, 1972. Fabric coordinator Celanese Corp., N.Y.C., 1970-71; merchandiser Bayly Corp., Denver, 1973-74; instr. Metro State Coll., Denver, 1977-81; self-employed interior designer, Denver, 1975—; mem. bd. Waxman Industries. Mem. steering com. Alliance Contemporary Art; women's bd. Nat. Jewish Hosp., 1978-80, bd. dirs., 1984-88; trustee Denver Art Mus., 1986-96, collections com., devel. com.; bd. dirs., v.p. leadership Allied Jewish Fedn., assoc. campaign chmn., 1985, gen. chmn. 1987-88; bd. govs. Nat. Jewish Ctr. for Immunology and Respiratory Medicine; bd. dirs. congregation Jewish Family and Children's Svc. Colo., 1975-83, Anti-Defamation League, 1987-90; v.p. Mizel Mus. Judaica; founding mem. Young Women's Leadership Cabinet United Jewish Appeal, 1977-82, Nat. Jewish Ctr. Bd., 1984-87, Nat. Women's Bd., 1984—; mem. steering com. Denver Art Mus., trustee, 1986—; bd. mem. Nat. Found. for Jewish Culture. Recipient Young Leadership award Allied Jewish Fedn., 1977. Recipient Afkey award Denver Art Mus., 1995. Mem. United Jewish Appeal (nat. women's div. exec. com. 1985—, nat. vice chair 1990—). Address: 2165 E Alameda Ave Denver CO 80209-2710

ROBINS, LEE NELKEN, medical educator; b. New Orleans, Aug. 29, 1922; d. Abe and Leona (Reiman) Nelken; m. Eli Robins, Feb. 22, 1946 (dec. Dec. 1994); children: Paul, James, Thomas, Nicholas; m. Hugh Chaplin, Aug. 5, 1998. Student, Newcomb Coll., 1938-40; BA, Radcliffe Coll., 1942, MA, 1943; PhD, Harvard U., 1951. Mem. faculty Washington U., St. Louis, 1954—, prof. sociology in psychiatry, 1968-91, prof. sociology, 1969-91, prof. social sci., prof. social sci. in psychiatry, 1991-2000, prof. emeritus, 2001—. Past mem. Nat. Adv. Coun. on Drug Abuse; past mem. task panels Pres.'s Commn. on Mental Health; mem. expert adv. panel on mental health WHO; Salmon lectr. N.Y. Acad. Medicine, 1983; Cutter lectr. Harvard U., 1997. Author: Deviant Children Grown Up, 1966; editor 11 books; mem. editl. bd. Psychol. Medicine, Jour. Studies on Alcohol, Social Psychiatry and Psychiatric Epidemiology, Epidemiol. e Psichiat. Sociale; contbr. articles to profl. jours. Recipient Rsch. Scientist award USPHS, 1970-90, Pacesetter Rsch. award Nat. Inst. Drug Abuse, 1978, Radcliffe Coll. Grad. Soc. medal, 1979, Sutherland award Am. Soc. Criminology, 1991, Nathan B. Eddy award Com. on Problems of Drug Dependence, 1993, Spl. Presdl. Commendation Am. Psychiat. Assn., 1999, Am. Acad. Arts and Scis., 1999, Commendation and Appreciation award Harvard Inst. Psychiat. Epidemiology and Genetics, 2000; rsch. grantee NIMH, Nat. Inst. on Drug Abuse, Nat. Inst. on Alcohol Abuse and Alcoholism. Fellow Am. Coll. Epidemiology, Royal Coll. Psychiatrists (hon.), Am. Soc. Psychiatrists (hon.), Soc. Study of Addiction (hon.); mem. APHA (Rema Lapouse award 1979, Lifetime Achievement award sect. on alcohol and drug abuse 1994), Internat. Fedn. Psychiat. Epidemiology (com.1992-2002), World Psychiat. Assn. (sect. com. on epidemiology and cmty. psychiatry, 1985-2002, co-chmn. sect. on rsch. instruments in psychiatry), Soc. Life History Rsch. in Psychopathology, Am. Coll. Neuropsychopharmacology, Inst. Medicine, Am. Psychopath. Assn. (pres. 1987-88, Paul Hoch award 1978). Office: Washington U Med Sch Dept Psychiatry Saint Louis MO 63110 E-mail: lro6@aol.com.

ROBINS, MARJORIE MCCARTHY (MRS. GEORGE KENNETH ROBINS), civic worker; b. Oct. 4, 1914; d. Eugene Ross and Louise (Roblee) McCarthy; m. George Kenneth Robins, Nov. 9, 1940; children: Carol Robins Von Arx, G. Stephen, Barbara A. Robins Foorman. Mem. Mo. Libr. Commn., 1937-38; mem. bd. St. Louis Jr. League, 1945, 46; mem. bd. Occupational Therapy Workshop of St. Louis, 1941-46, pres., 1945, 46; mem. bd. Ladue Chapel Nursery Sch., 1957-60, 61-64, pres. bd., 1963, 64; past regional chmn. United Fund; past mem. St. Louis Met. Youth Commn., St. Louis Health and Welfare Coun.; bd. dirs. Internat. Inst. of St. Louis, 1966-72, 76-82, 83-92, sec., 1968, v.p., 1981; bd. dirs. Mental Health Assn. St. Louis, 1963-70, Washington U. Child Guidance and Evaluation Clinic, 1968-78; bd. dirs. Cen. Inst. for Deaf, 1970—, v.p., 1975-76, pres., 1976-78; bd. dirs. Met. St. Louis YWCA, 1954-63, 64-74, pres. bd., 1960-63, trustee, 1977—; mem. nat. bd. YWCA, 1967-79, nat. v.p., 1973-76; vol. tchr. remedial reading clinic St. Louis City Schs., 1968-71; trustee John Burroughs Sch., 1960-63, John Burroughs Found., 1965-80, Roblee Found., 1972—, Nat. YWCA Retirement Fund, 1979-88; bd. dirs. Gambrill Gardens United Meth. Retirement Home, 1979-85, Thompson Retreat and Conf. Center, 1981-87; bd. dirs. Springboard to Learning Inc., 1980-98, v.p., 1980-90; tutor I Have A Dream Found., 1995-98. Mem. Archaeol. Inst. Am. (bd. dirs. 1993-95, 97-00, treas. St. Louis chpt. 1985-87, 93-95), Vassar Club (sec. and pres. 1939-40), Wednesday Club (dir. 1968-70, 77-79, 80-81, 93-95), St. Louis. Home: 45 Loren Woods Saint Louis MO 63124-1903

ROBINS, MITCHELL JAMES, management consultant; b. Detroit, May 23, 1956; s. Melvin M. Robins and Judith (Bell) Martin; m. Amy Elizabeth Green, July 2, 1978; children: Alexander Philip, Sean Lewis, Emily Dinah. BBA, U. Mich., 1977; postgrad., U. Detroit, Oakland U. CPA, Mich., Fla., Ind., Nev., Calif. Exec. mgr. GM; founder, mng. ptnr., CEO Robins-Assocs., CPAs and Cons., Southfield, Mich., 1981—, founder, mng. ptnr. La Jolla, Calif., 1980—; founder, mgr., ptnr. Lumedics, Ltd., Paris. Bd. dirs. Campus Distbn., Inc., Ann Arbor, Mich., Internat. Med.-Dental Hypnotherapy Assn., LumeDics Ltd., San Diego; mem. Restaurant Bus. Research Adv. Panel, N.Y.C. Mem. steering com. Rep. 300 Com. of Mich., Oakland County, zoning bd. appeals City of Farmington Hills, Rep. Senatorial Inner Circle; mem. Carmel Valley Planning Bd., 1997. Named Nat. Rep. Congl. Com. Businessman of the Yr., 1999. Mem. AICPA, ABA, Mich. Assn. CPA's, Mich. Soc. Planning Ofcls., Assn. MBA Execs., U. Mich. Alumni Assn., Internat. Platform Assn. Clubs: Economic (Detroit), Detroit Athletic, Heritage Hills Country, Skyline. Republican. Avocations: golf, tennis, history, politics, travel. Home: 12885 Ralston Cir San Diego CA 92130-2447 Fax: 858-551-1215. E-mail: mrobinsooo@usa.net.

ROBINS, NATALIE, poet, writer; b. Bound Brook, N.J., June 20, 1938; d. Louis Robins and Mildred (Levy) Robins-Vogel; m. Christopher C.H. Lehmann-Haupt, Oct. 3, 1965; children: Rachel Louise, Noah Christopher. BA, Mary Washington Coll., Fredericksburg, Va., 1960. Author: (poetry) Wild Lace, 1960, (poetry) My Father Spoke of His Riches, 1966, (poetry) The Peas Belong on the Eye Level, 1971, (poetry) Eclipse, 1981, (non-fiction) Savage Grace, 1985 (Edgar award Mystery Writers of Am., 1985), (non-fiction) Alien Ink, 1992 (Hefner Found. 1st Amendment award, 1992), (non-fiction) The Girl Who Died Twice, 1995, Living in the Lightning: A Cancer Jour., 1999; contbr. Self mag., 1996-97. E-mail: nrobins@speakeasy.net.

ROBINS, NORMAN ALAN, strategic planning consultant, former steel company executive; b. Chgo., Nov. 19, 1934; s. Irving and Sylvia (Robbin) Robins; m. Sandra Ross, June 10, 1956; children: Lawrence Richard, Sherry Lynn. BSChemE, MIT, 1955, MSChemE, 1956; PhD in Math., Ill. Inst. Tech., 1972. Asst. mgr. process sys. and controls Inland Steel Co., East Chicago, Ind., 1962—67, assoc. mgr. process sys. and controls, 1967—72, dir. process rsch., 1972—77, v.p. rsch., 1977—84, v.p. technol. assessment, 1984—86, v.p. strategic planning, 1986—91; ret., 1991; ind. cons. in strategic planning, 1991—. Mem. bd. edn. Homewood-Flossmoor HS, Ill., 1974—77. Mem.: AIChE, AIME (Nat. Open Hearth Conf. award 1972).

ROBINS, REED W. music recording executive; b. Richmond, Va., June 4, 1957; BA in Music Composition, Va. Commonwealth, 1981; cert., Rec. Inst. Am., 1984. Owner Synergy Prodns., Richmond, 1984, N.Y.C., 1984-95, Macintyre Music Rec., N.Y.C., 1995—; pres. Changing Tones Records, 1995—; owner Tactus Music Pub., 1995—. Composer (film score): The Painter, 1993; prodr. music recs. including Songs of Jimi Hendrix for Solo Jazz Piano, 1995, My Happiness, 1995. Mem. ASCAP, Am. Music Ctr. Office: Macintyre Music 874 Broadway New York NY 10003-1222 E-mail: reed@changingtones.com.

ROBINS, ROBERT SIDWAR, political science educator, administrator; b. Spangler, Pa., Apr. 20, 1938; s. Sydney and Katherine (Sidwar) R.; m. Marjorie McGann, Nov. 25, 1959; children: Anthony P., Nicholas A. BA, U. Pitts., 1959; MA, Duke U., 1961, PhD, 1963. Prof. polit. sci. Tulane U., New Orleans, 1965—, chmn. dept. polit. sci., 1979-90, dep. provost, 1991-98. Acad. visitor Inst. Commonwealth Studies, U. London, 1969-70, 78-79, mem. 1987-88; sr. assoc. mem. St. Antony's Coll., Oxford, Eng., 1972-73; vis. scholar Hastings Ctr., 1982; vis. scientist Tavistock Clinic, London, 1987-88. Author: Political Institutionalization and the Integration of Elites, 1976 (Carnegie Commn. report) Legislative Attitudes Toward Higher Education in Louisiana, 1968, Psychopathology and Political Leadership, 1977, Disease and Political Leadership, 1990; co-author: When Illness Strikes the Leader, Political Paranoia; contbr. articles to profl. publs. Vice chmn. Elections Integrity Commn., State of La., 1981-82 Recipient Excellence in Teaching award Tulane U., 1978; Fulbright scholar, 1961-62 Mem. Am. Polit. Sci. Assn., Internat. Soc. Polit. Psychology, New Orleans Fgn. Relations Assn. (bd. dirs.) Avocations: carpentry; gardening. Home: Dept Polit Sci New Orleans LA 70118-5118 Office: Tulane U Dept Polit Sci New Orleans LA 70118

ROBINS, RONALD ALBERT, JR. lawyer; b. Columbus, Ohio, Nov. 19, 1963; s. Ronald Albert and Barbara (Feibel) R.; m. Mary Wales Leslie, Nov. 29, 1967. BA, Duke U., 1985; JD, Harvard U., 1989. Jud. clk. Hon. Milton Pollack, N.Y.C., 1989-90; assoc. Davis Polk & Wardwell, 1990-93, Vorys Sater Seymour and Pease LLP, Columbus, 1993-96, ptnr., 1997—. Chmn. alumni bd. Columbus Acad., 1997-99; chmn. adv. bd. for Columbus, Duke U., 1998—. Mem. Columbus Bar Assn. Office: Vorys Sater Seymour and Pease LLP 52 E Gay St Columbus OH 43215-3161 E-mail: rarobins@vssp.com.

ROBINSON, ADELBERT CARL, lawyer, judge; b. Shawnee, Okla., Dec. 13, 1926; s. William H. and Mayme (Forston) R.; m. Paula Kay Settles, Apr. 16, 1988; children from previous marriage: William, James, Schuyler, Donald, David, Nancy, Lauri. Student, Okla. Bapt. U., 1944-47; JD, Okla. U., 1950. Bar: Okla. 1950. Pvt. practice, Muskogee, Okla., 1956-97; with legal dept. Phillips Petroleum Co., 1950-51; adjuster U.S. Fidelity & Guaranty Co., 1951-54, atty., adjuster-in-charge, 1954-56; ptnr. Fite & Robinson, 1956-62, Fite, Robinson & Summers, 1963-70, Robinson & Summers, 1970-72, Robinson, Summers & Locke, 1972-76, Robinson, Locke & Gage, 1976-80, Robinson, Locke, Gage & Fite, 1980-83, Robinson, Locke, Gage, Fite & Williams, Muskogee, 1983-95, Robinson, Gage, Fite & Williams, Muskogee, 1995-97. Police judge City of Muskogee, 1963—64, mcpl. judge, 1964—70; prin. justice 84Temp. Divsn. 36 Okla. Ct. Appeals, 1981—84, spl. dist. judge, 1997—; pres., dir. Wall St. Bldg. Corp., 1969—78, Three Forks Devel. Corp., 1968—77, Rolo Leasing Inc., 1971—97, Suroya II Inc.1, 1977—99; mng. ptnr. RLG Ritz, 1980—97; ptnr. First City Real Estate Partnership, 1985—94; del. to U.S./China Jt. Session on Trade, Investment and Econ. Law, Beijing, 1987. Chmn. Muskogee County (Okla.) Law Day, 1963, Muskogee Area Redevel. Authority, 1963, Muskogee County chpt. Am. Cancer Soc., 1956; pres., bd. dirs. United Way of Muskogee Inc., 1980-88, v.p., 1982, pres., 1983; bd. dirs. Muskogee Cmty. Concert Assn., Muskogee Tourist Info. Bur., 1964-68; bd. dirs., gen. counsel United Cerebral Palsy Eastern Okla., 1964-68; trustee Connors Devel. Found., Connors Coll., 1981-99, chmn., 1987-89; active Muskogee Housing Authority, 1992-95. With inf. AUS, 1945-46. Mem. ABA, Okla. Bar Assn. (chmn. uniform laws com. 1970-72, chmn. profl. coop. com. 1965-69, past regional chmn. grievance com.), Muskogee County Bar Assn. (pres. 1971, mem. exec. coun. 1971-74), Okla. Assn. Def. Counsel (dir.), Okla. Assn. Mcpl. Judges (dir.), Muskogee c. of C., Delta Theta Phi., Rotary (pres. 1971-72). Methodist. Home: 3702 Club Estates Dr Muskogee OK 74403 Office: Muskogee County Courthouse PO Box 1350 Muskogee OK 74402-1350

ROBINSON, AGNES CLAFLIN, educational administrator; b. N.Y.C., Oct. 2, 1918; d. Crittenden Hull and Agnes Sanger (Claflin) Adams; m. Albert Lewis Robinson (div.); children: Nicholas Adams, John Claflin, Hugh Wesley, James Allen, Lewis Stewart. AB, Barnard Coll., 1941; MS, NYU, 1949. Tech. asst. BEll Telephone Labs., Whippany, N.J., 1943-44; v.p. Family Service Assn., Morristown, 1946-48; bd. dirs. Adult and Child Guidance Clinic, San Jose, Calif., 1955-58; v.p. Palo Alto (Calif.) Mental Health Soc., 1959-63; pres. PTA, Palo Alto, 1961-63; trustee Palo Alto Unified Sch. Dist., 1963-73, pres., 1965-67. Chmn. Drug Abuse Bd., Palo Alto, 1971-74; mem. adv. bd. Nairobi Day Schs., East Palo Alto, 1969-72; mem. adv. bd. Child Care Now, 1972-73; mem. Calif. Post-Secondary Edn. Commn., 1974-80, chmn., 1978-80; advisor to pub. affairs com. YWCA, 1974-2002; mem. Mid-Peninsula Com. for Integrated Edn., 1974-80; bd. dirs. Addiction Research Found., 1974-78, pres., 1974-77; bd. dirs. Mid-Peninsula Learning Ctr. 1980-83; pres. New Ways to Work, 1976-79; mem. spl. legis. com. Calif. Student Fin. Aid Study Group, 1979; mem. Palo Alto Human Rels. Commn., 1981-82; bd. govs. Calif. Cmty. Colls., 1982— , pres., 1986-87; mem. accreditation coms. Western Assn. Schs. and Colls., 1989-97; co-chair Palo Alto com. Study Circles for Racial Understanding, 1998-2000. Author: (with Ruth McAneny Loud) New York, New York! A Knickerbocker Holiday for You and Your Children, 1946. Mem. NAACP (life), PTA (life), Sierra Club (life), Radcliffe Club of Mid-Peninsula. Democrat. Home: 1765 Fulton St Palo Alto CA 94303-2943 E-mail: acr1765@aol.com.

ROBINSON, ALEXANDER JACOB, clinical psychologist; b. St. John, Kans., Nov. 7, 1920; s. Oscar Frank and Lydia May (Beitler) R.; m. Elsie Louise Riggs, July 29, 1942; children: Madelyn K., Alicia A., David J., Charles A., Paul S., Marietta J., Stephen N. BA in Psychology, MS in Clin. Psychology, Ft. Hays (Kans.) State U., 1942; postgrad., U. Ill., 1942-44. Cert. psychologist, sch. psychologist. Chief psychologist Larned (Kans.) State Hosp., 1948-53, with employee selection, outpatient services, 1953-55; sch. psychologist County Schs., Modesto, Calif., 1955-61, Pratt (Kans.) Jr. Coll., 1961-66; fed. grantee, writer assoc. dir. Exemplary Federally Funded Program for Spl. Edn., Pratt, 1966-70; dir. spl. edn., researcher Stafford County Schs., St. John, 1970-81, ret., 1981. Supr. testing and data Incidence of Exceptional Children in Kansas, Kans. State U., Ft. Hays, 1946; writer, asst. dir. Best Exemplary Federally Funded Program on Spl. Edn., Pratt, 1966-70; fed. grantee, researcher, writer, study dir. Edn. for the High-Performance Child, St. John, 1970—, Psychogenesis of the Sociopathic Personality, a longitudinal study. Minister, The Ch. of Jesus Christ. Served to 2d lt. U.S. Army, 1944-46, PTO. Mem. N.Y. Acad. Scis., Libr. of Congress. Lodges: Lions (program chmn. St. John 1974-76). Achievements include research on normal children with a learning disability and their specific developmental requirement. Avocations: history, ethnology, cultural anthropology, music, literature. Home and Office: 202 Grandview St Saint John KS 67576-2100

ROBINSON, ALICE HELENE, English language educator, administrative assistant; b. Cleve., Oct. 16, 1946; d. Alford B. and Willie Helena (Knuckles) R. BA, Cleve. State U., 1968, MA, 1992; postgrad., John Carroll U. Cert. tchr., Ohio. English language educator Cleve. Bd. Edn., Ohio. Presenter 1st Celtic Conf. Cleve. State U., 1993. Cleve. Edn. Fund scholar, 1991. Mem.: Cleve. Mus. Art. Episcopalian. Avocations: collecting stamps, plates, and artifacts, word puzzles, logic problems. Home: 3344 E 142nd St Cleveland OH 44120-4009 Office: Cleve Bd Edn 1380 E 6th St Cleveland OH 44114-1606

ROBINSON, ALICE JEAN MCDONNELL, retired drama and speech educator; b. St. Joseph, Mo., Nov. 17, 1922; d. John Francis and Della M. (Mavity) McDonnell; m. James Eugene Robinson, Apr. 21, 1956 (dec. 1983). BA, U. Kans., 1944, MA, 1947; PhD, Stanford U., 1965. Tchr. Garden City (Kans.) High Sch., 1944-46; asst. prof. Emporia (Kans.) State U., 1947-52; dir. live programs Sta. KTVH-TV, Hutchinson-Wichita, Kans., 1953-55; assoc. prof. drama and speech U. Md. Baltimore County, Balt., 1966-99, rsch. theatre history. Author: The American Theatre: A History in Slides, 1992, Betty Comden and Adolph Green: A Bio-Bibliography, 1993; co-editor: Notable Women in the American Theatre, 1989; appeared in plays, including Landscape, 1983, Tartuffe, 1985, Rockaby, 1990. Mem. Am. Soc. Theatre Rsch., Assn. Theatre Higher Edn., Phi Beta Kappa. Republican. Avocations: travel, reading, acting, directing. Home: 111 N Main St Caldwell KS 67022-1535

ROBINSON, ANGELA TOMEI, clinical laboratory technologist; b. Bklyn., June 5, 1957; d. Leo James and Nina Angela T.; m. John C. Robinson, Sept. 27, 1987. BS, St. John's U., 1979, MS, 1985. Cert. lab. technologist. Exec. sec. Stead-fast Temporaries, Inc., N.Y.C., 1975—79; chief med. technologist Winthrop-U. Hosp., Mineola, 1979—98, adminstrv. lab. coord., edn. coord., lab. info. mgr., 1998—; coord., founder Nat. Med. Lab. Week, 1981—; tech. supr., lab. mgr., cons. Hilton Med. Group, Hempstead, 1993—96; lab. technologist Cardiovasc. Group, Garden City, 1996—2000, asst. lab. mgr., 2000—. Lab. cons. Gastroenterology Group, Mineola, NY, 1998—2000; staff contbr. newsletter Winthrop-U. Hosp., Mineola, 1981—, in pub. rels., 1981—, com. mem., clin. instr. for retng. personnel in lab., chmn. com. to petition salary increases, 1987—90, mem. Vision 2000 redesign team, 1997—98; adj. prof. seminar C.W. Post Coll., Westbury, NY, 1992—, edn. coord., NY, 1998—; adj. prof. SUNY-Farmingdale, 1999—, advisor, 1999; guest lectr. SUNY-Stony Brook, 1995—; rep. Nassau Suffolk Health Manpower Plan, 1991; team mem. vision 2000 NIH, 1997—98; com. rep. SJU Ann. Clin. Lab Sem., 1998—. Author: (poetry) Our World's Best Loved Poems, 1984 (2d place merit cert. 1983) contbr. articles to profl. jours.; lectr. ednl. seminars and confs. Singer Blessed Sacrament Ch. Choir, Bklyn., 1971-73, coord., singer ch. folk group, 1971-79; mem. Mothers Against Drunk Driving, 1985-87, Nat. Rep. Congl. Com., 1984-86, Am. Health Found., 1986-87, DAV, 1984-87; fundraiser Statue of Liberty/Ellis Island Found., 1985-86, 95-96, Hands Across Am., 1986, U.S. Olympic Team Spirit, 1992—, U.S. English First, Nat. Mus. Am. Indians. Recipient cert. of merit N.Y. State Senate, 1985, citation Gov. N.Y. State Pres. Soc., 1975; award St. John's U. Med. Tech. Alumni, 1992 Mem. Am. Soc. Clin. Lab. Sci., Profl. Stds. Coalition Clin. Lab. Pers., Am. Soc. Clin. Pathologists (registered), Made in the U.S. Found., N.Y. State Soc. Clin. Lab. Sci. (chmn. govt. liason com., state bd. dirs. 1988—, Outstanding Med. Tech. Student award 1979, Member of Yr. award 1995, founding officer Nassau-Suffolk chpt. 1985-86, bd. dirs., seminar moderator 1985-87, pres.-elect 1986-87, 90-91, pres. 1991—, membership com. 1991, state chairperson 1993—), Profl. STDS Coalition (pub. rels. chair 1993—, co-chair 1997—), Theta Phi Alpha (alumni chmn. 1976-77, alumni-collegiate rep. 1986-87). Avocations: piano, guitar, gardening, singing, tennis.

ROBINSON, ANNETTMARIE, entrepreneur; b. Fayetteville, Ark., Jan. 31, 1940; d. Christopher Jacy and Lorena (Johnson) Simmons; m. Roy Robinson, June 17, 1966; children: Steven, Sammy, Doug, Pamela, Olen. BA, Edison Tech. U., 1958; BA in Bus., Seattle Community Coll., 1959. Dir. -perss. Country Kitchen Restaurants, Inc., Anchorage, 1966-71; investor, 1971—. Cons. Pioneer Investments, Anchorage, 1983—, M'RAL, Inc. Retail Dry Goods, Anchorage, 1985; owner Cons. Co., Reno, 1998—. Mem. Rep. Presdl. Task Force, Washington, 1984—, Reps. of Alaska, Anchorage, 1987; mem. chmn. round table YMCA, Anchorage, 1986—; active Sta. KWN2, KQLO, Reno, Nev.; active in child abuse issues and prosecution; dir., sec. Hunter Lake Townhouse Assn., Reno, Sta. KSRU and KHOG-Radio, KIHM Cath. Radio, Reno, 1996—, KOZZ Radio, 2000—; ; mem. Cmty. Assn. Inst. Condo/Coop./Townhouse Law, 1999—. Named Woman of Yr. Lions, Anchorage, 1989, marksman first class Nat. Rifle Assn., 1953. Mem. Porsche Club of Am. (racing team 1998—). Avocations: Egyptology, theology, archeology, shooting, fishing.

ROBINSON, ANTHONY CHRISTOPHER, novelist, educator; b. Biskupitz, Germany, Mar. 10, 1931; came to U.S., 1931; s. Henry Morton and Gertrude (Ludwig) R.; m. Mary Chika, Nov. 16, 1957 (dec. Mar. 1976); children: Jennifer Eve, Henry David; m. Tatiana Padwa, Feb. 14, 1998. BA, Columbia Coll., N.Y.C., 1953; MA cum laude, Columbia U., 1960; grad., Phillips Acad., Andover, Mass. Prof. English, dir. creative writing SUNY, New Paltz, 1964-2000, prof. English emeritus, 2000—. Vis. prof. U. Paris, 1971-72. Author: A Departure From the Rules, 1960 (Bread Loaf fellow 1960), The Easy Way, 1963, Home Again, Home Again, 1969, The Whole Truth, 1990, The Member-Guest, 1991. Lt. USNR, 1953-56. Democrat. Roman Catholic. Avocations: golf, fly fishing, golf club making, hiking. Home: 153 Huguenot St New Paltz NY 12561 E-mail: robinsoa@newpaltz.edu.

ROBINSON, ARTHUR HOWARD, geography educator; b. Montreal, Que., Can., Jan. 5, 1915; s. James Howard and Elizabeth (Peavey) R.; m. Mary Elizabeth Coffin, Dec. 23, 1938 (dec. Jan. 1992); children: Stephen Michael, Patricia Anne; m. Martha Elizabeth Rodabaugh Phillips, Feb. 6, 1993. BA, Miami U., Oxford, Ohio, 1936, LittD, 1966; MA, U. Wis., 1938; PhD in Geography, Ohio State U., 1947, DSc (hon.), 1984. Sec. to mem. Ohio Bd. Liquor Control, 1936; asst. geography U. Wis., 1936-38, Ohio State U., 1938-41; chief map div. OSS, 1941-46; mem. faculty U. Wis., 1945—, prof. geography, 1951-80, prof. emeritus, 1980—, chmn. dept., 1954-58, 66-68, Lawrence Martin prof. cartography, 1967—; dir. Univ. Cartographic Lab., 1966-73; hon. cons. cartography Library of Congress, 1974-80. Chief map officer U.S. Delegation Quebec and Cairo confs., World War II; pres. Internat. Cartographic Assn., 1972-76 Author: Look of Maps, 1952, Early Thematic Mapping in the History of Cartography, 1982; co-author: Elements of Geography, 4th edit., 1957, Elements of Cartography, 6th edit., 1995, Fundamentals of Physical Geography, 3rd edit., 1977, The Nature of Maps, 1976; co-editor: Cartographical Innovations, 1987; editor Am. Cartographer, 1974-76; also articles; designer Robinson map projection, 1963. Served to maj. AUS, 1944-45. Decorated Legion of Merit; recipient Carl Mannerfelt medal Internat. Cartographic Assn., 1981, Helen Culver Gold Medal Geog. Soc. Chgo., 1983, John Oliver LaGorce medal Nat. Geog. Soc., 1988, Silver medal Brit. Cartographic Soc., 1991; Guggenheim rsch. fellow, 1964, 78. Fellow Brit. Cartog. Assn.; mem. Can. Cartog. Assn., Assn. Am. Geographers (coun. 1960-65, pres. 1963), Am. Congress Surveying and Mapping (hon.; chmn. cartography divsn. 1971), Am. Geog. Soc. (life, O.M. Miller medal). Home: 7707 N Brookline Dr Apt 302 Madison WI 53719-3526 E-mail: ahrobins@facstaff.wisc.edu.

ROBINSON, ARTHUR RICHARD, civil engineer, educator; b. Bklyn., Oct. 28, 1929; s. Harry and Ruth Anna (Bodner) R. BCE, Cooper Union, N.Y.C., 1951; MS, U. Ill., 1953, PhD, 1956. From rsch. assoc. to asst. prof. U. Minn., Mpls., 1955-60; assoc. prof. U. Ill., Urbana, 1960-63, prof., 1963-93; prof. emeritus, 1993—. Contbr. articles to profl. jours. Mem. ASCE (Moisseiff award 1970, Walter L. Huber rsch. prize 1969), ASME. Achievements include research on wave propagation problems in solids with applications to dynamic contact and crack mechanics, and on numerical methods applied to a number of static and dynamic problems of importance in structural mechanics. Office: U Ill Dept Civil Engring 3146 Newmark CE Lab 205 N Mathews Ave Urbana IL 61801-2350

ROBINSON, BARBARA PAUL, lawyer; b. Oct. 19, 1941; d. Leo and Pauline G. Paul; m. Charles Raskob Robinson, June 11, 1965; children: Charles Paul, Torrance Webster. AB magna cum laude, Bryn Mawr Coll., 1962; LLB, Yale U., 1965. Bar: N.Y. 1966, U.S. Dist. Ct. (so. and ea. dists.) N.Y. 1975, U.S. Tax Ct. 1972, U.S. Ct. Appeals (2d cir.) 1974. Assoc. Debevoise & Plimpton (formerly Debevoise, Plimpton, Lyons & Gates), N.Y.C., 1966-75, ptnr., 1976—. Mem. adv. bd. Practicing Law Inst.; bd. dirs. Am. Arbitration Assn., 1987—, Sch. Choice Scholarships Found. Mem. bd. editors: Chase Jour., 1997—2001; contbr. articles. Mem. adv. coun., bd. visitors CUNY Law Sch., Queens, 1984—90; mem. Coun. on Fgn. Rels.; trustee Trinity Sch., 1982—86, pres., 1986—88; bd. dirs. Found. for Child Devel., 1989—, chmn., 1991—2000; bd. dirs. Catalyst, 1993—, Fund Modern Cts., 1990—, Wave Hill, 1994—, Garden Conservancy, 1996—, Lawyers Com. for Civil Rights Under Law, 1997—, The William Nelson Cromwell Found., 1993—, Irish Legal Rsch. Found. Inc., 1996—, Citizens Union Found. Inc., 1996—; trustee Bryn Mawr Coll., 2000—. Recipient Laura Parsons Pratt award, 1996. Fellow Am. Coll. Trust and Estate Counsel, Am. Bar Found., N.Y. Bar Found.; mem. ABA (mem. commn. on women in profession 1999—), N.Y. State Bar Assn. (vice chmn. com. on trust adminstrn., trusts and estates law sect. 1977-81, ho. of dels. 1984-87, 90-92, mem. com. ann. award 1993-94), Assn. of Bar of City of N.Y. (chmn. com. on trusts, estates and surrogates cts. 1981-84, judiciary com. 1981-84, coun. on jud. adminstrn. 1982-84, chair nominating com. 1984-85, 99—, mem. exec. com. 1986-91, chair 1989-90, v.p. 1990-91, pres. 1994-96, chair com. on honors 1993-94, mem. com. on long-range planning 1991-94, co-chair coun. on childen 1997-99), Assn. of Bar of City of N.Y. Fund Inc. (bd. dirs., pres.), Women's Forum, Yale Coun., Yale Law Sch. Assn. N.Y. (mem. devel. bd., exec. com. 1981-85, pres. 1988-93), Order of the Coif, Yale Club, Washington Club. Office: Debevoise & Plimpton 919 Third Ave New York NY 10022 E-mail: bprobinson@debevoise.com.

ROBINSON, BARRY R. lawyer; b. Dover, Ohio, Dec. 8, 1946; AB, Princeton U., 1969; JD cum laude, Ohio State U., 1972. Bar: Ohio 1972. Ptnr. Baker & Hostetler, Columbus, Ohio. Fellow Am. Coll. Trust and Estate Counsel; mem. ABA, Ohio State Bar Assn., Columbus Bar Assn. Office: Baker & Hostetler Capital Sq 65 E State St Ste 2100 Columbus OH 43215-4260

ROBINSON, BERNARD LEO, retired lawyer; b. Kalamazoo, Feb. 13, 1924; s. Louis Harvey and Sue Mary (Starr) R.; m. Betsy Nadell, May 30, 1947; children: Robert Bruce, Patricia Anne, Jean Carol. BS, U. Ill., 1947, MS, 1958; JD, U. N.Mex., 1973. Bar: N.Mex. 1973, U.S. Supreme Ct. 1976. Rsch. engr. Assn. Am. Railroads, 1947-49; instr. arch. Rensselaer Poly. Inst., 1949-51; commd. 2d lt. U.S. Army, 1945, advanced through grades to lt. col., 1965, ret., 1968; engr. Nuclear Def. Rsch. Corp., Albuquerque, 1968-71; lawyer, 1973-85, Silver City, N.Mex., 1985-89, Green Valley, Ariz., 1989-90, Sierra Vista, 1990-91; pres. Robinson Fin. Svcs., Tucson, 1993-95. Dist. commr. Boy Scouts Am., 1960-62. Decorated Air medal. Mem. ASCE, ABA, Ret. Officers Assn., DAV, Assn. U.S. Army, VFW. Home: 11821 N Pyramid Point Dr Tucson AZ 85737-3726

ROBINSON, BETTY HEFNER, artist; b. Greer, S.C., Apr. 1, 1928; d. Roy Culvin and Leona (Lee) Hefner; m. Richard Edmond Robinson, Aug. 14, 1953; children: Mark Richard, John Anderson. BA, Meredith Coll., 1949; postgrad., Feree Sch. Art, 1949-50, Vt. Studio Sch., 1985, 87. Instr. art Va. Intermont Coll., Bristol, 1950-51; tchr. art George Wythe High Sch., Wytheville, Va., 1951-53; artist pvt. practice, Signal Mountain, Tenn., 1960-91, Georgetown, S.C., 1991—. One-woman shows include The Hunter Mus. Am. Art, Chattanooga, Tenn., 1978, Cumberland Gallery, Nashville, 1989, Sumter (S.C.) Gallery Art, 1994, The Wells Gallery, Charleston, S.C., 1995, Gallery C, Raleigh, N.C., 2001, Franklin G Burroughs-Siemeon B Chapin Mus., Myrtle Beach, S.C., 2002. Recipient Top award S.C. Watercolor Soc. Exhibit, 1998; Va. Ctr. Creative Arts fellow, Sweetbriar, 1992. Mem. Nat. Watercolor Soc. (assoc.), S.C. Watercolor Soc., Tenn. Watercolor Soc. (life, dir. 1980-89, pres. 1982), Georgetown Watercolor Soc. dir. 1992-99, pres. 1994-96). Presbyterian. Avocation: reading. Home: 321 Freeman Dr Georgetown SC 29440-5916

ROBINSON, BEULAH LOBDELL, retired educator; b. Chico, Calif., Dec. 19, 1928; d. James Britton and Beulah May (Shirley) L.; m. Gordon Sidney Taylor, Aug. 9, 1953; (div. Jan., 1964); 1 child, Allis Rosemary; m. Charles Dwayne Robinson, July 15, 1967 (dec.). BA, U. Calif., Berkeley, 1950. Cert. tchr., adminstr., Calif. Supt., prin. Manzanita Sch. Dist., Gridley, Calif., 1974-81; elem., middle sch. prin. Williams (Calif.) Unified Sch. Dist., 1981-84; dir., elem. sch. prin. Chico (Calif.) Unified Sch. Dist., cons., 1984-98; ret. Named Adminstr. of Yr. Butte County Adminstrs. Assn., 1995. Mem. ASCD, LWV, AAUW, Assn. of Calif. Sch. Adminstrs. (pres. region 2, 1981-82, 2000-01, del. state assembly, 1981-86, pres.-elect region 2 ret. charter 1999-2000, Adminst. of Yr. 1980), Bidwell Mansion Assn., Chico Mus. Assn. (pres., bd. dirs.). Avocations: reading, travel, theater, opera. Home: 938 W 12th Ave Chico CA 95926-2142

ROBINSON, BRENDA KAY, editor, public relations professional; b. Flint, Mich., May 15, 1946; d. Albert Coleburn and Kathryn Mary (Salay) Moore; m. Richard F. Robinson, Feb. 6, 1970; 1 child, Kelly Dawn. AS in Fashion, Garland Jr. Coll., 1967. Actress Actor's Workshop and Repertory Co., West Palm Beach, Fla., 1980-82; asst. store mgr. Pavo Real Sculpture Gallery, Boca Raton, 1987-88; freelance artist, illustrator, coloring book designer Troy, Mich., 1972—; freelance editor, writer Delray Beach, Fla., 1995—; v.p., editor Dick Robinson Co., 1979—; pub. rels. dir. Unity of Delray Beach Ch., 1996-99; sales office profl. Mens Dept. and Designer Salon, Saks Fifth Ave., Troy, Mich., 1968-72. Cons. Mary Kay Cosmetics, 1983-84. Author, illustrator (coloring book with text) Boca Raton Animal Shelter Coloring Book, 1993. Puppeteer Kids on the Block shows Assn. for Retarded Citizens, West Palm Beach, Fla., 1981-85; bd. treas. Windemere House Condominium Assn., Delray Beach, 1993, bd. sec., 1994. Republican. Avocations: Web surfing, walking, Bichon Frise dogs, Native American drumming. Home and Office: 250 S Ocean Blvd Apt 252 Delray Beach FL 33483-6752 E-mail: brenda515@aol.com.

ROBINSON, BRUCE EUGENE, physician, educator, researcher; b. East St. Louis, Ill., Sept. 13, 1951; s. Eugene Leslie and Melba Irene (Johnson) R.; m. Sandra Patricia Eick, Dec. 28, 1974; children: Scott, Lynn, Carlin, Sarah. BS, U. Ctrl. Fla., 1972; MD, U. South Fla., 1975, MPH, 1993; postgrad., Harvard U., 1987-88. Diplomate Am. Bd. Internal Medicine and Geriatrics. Resident in internal medicine U. South Fla., Tampa, 1979—81; registrar in geriatric medicine Amersheim (Eng.) Gen. Hosp., 1981; prof. divsn. geriatric medicine U. South Fla., 1985—; chief sect. geriatric medicine James A. Haley VA Hosp., Tampa, 1985—98; med. dir. Hospice of Hillsborough, 1985—95; chief geriat. Sarasota Meml. Hosp., 1998—; med. dir. Lakeside Terr., 2000—, Plymouth Harbor, Pines of Sarasota, 2002—. Med. dir. Skilled Nursing Facility, Tampa Gen. Hosp., 1989-98. Assoc. editor: Geriatric Review Syllobus, 1989; contbr. Lt. comdr. USN, 1976-79. USPHS grantee VA Hosp., 1984-86, USPHS grantee, 1988; Hartford Found. scholar, Fellow ACP, Am. Geriatrics Soc. (edn. com. 1986-91), Gerontol. Soc. Am. Avocations: music, fishing. Office: Sarasota Meml Hosp 1700 S Tamiami Trl Sarasota FL 34239-3555

ROBINSON, CHARLENE G. mental health nurse, educator; b. Mt. Union, Pa., Jan. 10, 1932; d. Lester and Clarabelle (Parsons) Garman; m. John W. Robinson, Dec. 21, 1951 (dec.); children: John W. Jr., Susan, Cheryl, Lester, Nancy. Diploma, Temple U., 1954; BSN, U. Louisville, 1983, MSN, 1986; MEd, Western Ky. U., 1984. Asst. prof. nursing Elizabethtown (Ky.) Community Coll.; staff nurse Ireland Army Hosp., Ft. Knox, Ky.; asst. mgr. psychiatry J.C. Blair Meml. Hosp., Huntingdon, Pa.; nursing instr. Kauai Community Coll., Lihue, Hawaii; asst. mgr. psychiatry J.C. Blair Meml. Hosp., Huntingdon; retired. Home: 7337 E Applewood Dr Inverness FL 34450-2520

ROBINSON, CHARLES DAVID, financial services executive; b. Warren, Ohio, Sept. 26, 1944; s. Lee Elmo and Dora Mae (Wheeler) R.; m. Sharon Ann Dillon, June 20, 1980; 1 child from previous marriage, Heather Lynn. Student, Ventura (Calif.) Jr. Coll., 1962, Harvard U., 1964; BA, Am. U., 1966; MA, Ohio State U., 1979. CFP. Mershon fellow Ohio State U., Columbus, 1966-72; dir. tng. NATPAC-SOUTH Inc., Washington, 1973-74; field underwriter N.Y. Life, Bailey's Cross-Roads, Va., 1974-75; dir. debate W.T. Woodson High Sch., Fairfax, 1975-80; exec. account rep. VALIC, 1980-89, unit mgr., 1981-86, dist. mgr. Phoenix, 1990-91, regional mgr., 1991-95; regional v.p. VAMCO, 1991-95; v.p. nat. markets VALIC, Houston, 1995—. Editor, author: (booklet) Mutual Fund Sales Kit, 1992, (brochures) New Mexico Alternative Retirement Plan, 1991, Arizona Optional Retirement Plan, 1991; co-developer: Portfolio Optimizer Asset Allocation Software, 1994. Asst. to chmn. conv. coms. Bush Campaign Republican Nat. Conv., New Orleans, 1988; chmn. Fairfax County Tchrs. for Vivian Watts, Va., 1979. Mem. Inst. Cert. Fin. Planners, Phi Alpha Theta, Alpha Tau Omega. Avocations: golf, tennis, skiing. Office: VALIC 2929 Allen Pkwy Ste 800 Houston TX 77019-7104

ROBINSON, CHARLES EMANUEL, systems engineer, consultant; b. Hayes, Clarendon, Jamaica, Jan. 14, 1946; came to U.S., 1986; s. Charles E. and Ethlyn C. (Singh) R.; m. Joy B. Cassanova, July 31, 1971; children: Sonya, Monique, Nicole, Kimberley. Student, Nat. Tech. Schs., L.A., 1966. Radio technician Chin's Radio & TV, Kingston, Jamaica, 1964-66; solid state technician Wonards Radio Engring., 1966-68; instrument technician Ewarton Plant, Aluminum Co. Can., Jamaica, 1968-69; sr. field tech. engr. Ruel Samuels Ltd., Kingston, 1969-77; mng. dir. MSS Ltd., 1977-80, Robinson Assocs., Mandeville, Jamaica, 1980-86; design engr. Seaboard Electronics, New Rochelle, N.Y., 1986-95, mgr. tech. svc., 1988-95; sys. engr. Mobile-Comm, Ridgeland, Miss., 1995-2000; RF engr. Metawave Comms., 2000—. Mem. IEEE, Am. Mgmt. Assn. Avocations: photography, reading, electronic circuit design and simulation, writing computer programs in C++. Home: 612 Parkway Blvd Coppell TX 75019-6000 E-mail: charles-r@att.net.

ROBINSON, CHARLOTTE HILL, artist; b. San Antonio, Nov. 28, 1924; d. Lucius Davis and Charlotte (Moore) Hill; m. Floyd I. Robinson, Mar. 1943; children: Floyd I. Jr., Lawrence H., Elizabeth H. Student, Incarnate Word Coll., 1943-45, NYU, 1947-48, Corcoran Sch. Art, 1951-52. Painting instr. Art League No. Va., Alexandria, 1967-75. Condr. Art World Seminar Washington Women's Art Ctr., 1975-80, drawing workshop Smithsonian Instn. Resident Assocs. Program, Washington, 1977; program dir. Nat. Women's Caucus for Art, 1979; project coord., exhbn. curator The Artist and the Quilt, nat. mus. traveling exhbn., 1983-86; vis. artist S.W. Craft Ctr., San Antonio, 1983-85; lectr. WFUV 90 FM, Fordham U., N.Y.C., 1990, San Antonio Art Inst., 1991, Nat. Mus. for Women in Arts, Washington, 1991, Iowa State U., Ames, 1991; panelist Nat. Mus. Women in Arts, 1997, Woman and the Arts, Douglass Coll./Rutgers U., 1998, Washington Women's Caucus for Art at the Millenium Art Ctr., 2001. Editor: The Artist & The Quilt, 1983; one-person shows include Thames Sic. Ctr., New London, Conn., 1991, Brunner Gallery & Mus., Iowa State U., 1991, 92, San Antonio Art. Inst., 1991, Fordham U., 1991, de Andino Fine Arts, Washington, 1992, Masur Mus. Art, Monroe, La., 1993, 96, 2001, Lee Hansley Art Gallery, Raleigh, N.C., 1993, 97, 2001, Sol Del Rio, San Antonio, 1995, 97-98, 1812 Artic Gallery, Virginia Beach, Va., 1995, Savannah Coll. Art and Design, 1997, Duke U. Sch. Law, 1998, No. Va. C.C., 1999, McLean Project for the Arts, 2002; exhibited in group shows at Franklin Square and Watkins Gallery, Washington, 1992, Rutgers U., New Brunswick, N.J., 1992, 96, 98, Brody's Gallery, Washington, 1992, Lee Hansley Art Gallery, Raleigh, 1993, 96, 98-2001, Emerson Gallery, McLean, 1993, 95, 99, No. Va. C.C., 1994, 99, Harvard U., 1996, Ceres Gallery, N.Y.C., 1999-2000, Millennium Art Ctr., Washington, 2001. Trustee Bronx (N.Y.) Mus., 1977; bd.

dirs. Washington Women's Art Ctr., 1977, New Art Examiner, 1985-86; nat. bd. dirs. Women's Caucus for Art, 1983-84. Recipient Concourse award Corcoran Sch. Art, 1952; Telfair Acad. Art scholar, Savannah, Ga., 1959; Nat. Endowment for Arts grantee, 1977-81; fellow Va. Ctr. for Creative Arts, Sweet Briar, Va., 1985. Address: Lee Hansley Gallery 225 Glenwood Ave Raleigh NC 27603

ROBINSON, CHRISTINE MARIE, mathematics educator; b. Savannah, Ga. d. Aaron Sr. and Lucille (Jones) Williams; m. Amos Robinson, Aug. 2, 1953; children: Michael Anthony, Pamela Michele. BS in Math. magna cum laude, Savannah State U., 1951; MA, U. Mich., 1965. Instr. in math. Chatham County Bd. of Instruction, Savannah, 1951-64, Duval County Bd. of Instruction, Jacksonville, Fla., 1964-71, master and resource tchr., 1971-76; prof. math. Fla. C.C., 1976-99, ret., 1999. Mem. faculty task force Fla. Dept. Edn./Fla. Assn. C.C., Tallahassee, 1979-81; on-site coord. Fla. Devel. Edn. Assn. Conv., Jacksonville, 1986; chmn. Fla. C.C. EA/EO Com., Jacksonville, 1988, 89. Mem. YWCA, Jacksonville, 1989—; vol. driver Wheels for Cancer-AKA Sorority, Jacksonville, 1986; chmn. United Way, Jacksonville, 1987. Recipient Outstanding Faculty Mem. award Fla. Community Coll., 1987, Teaching Excellence award U. Tex., 1988; scholar U. Mich., U. Ill.; grantee NSF. Mem. Am. Math. Assn. Two-Yr. Colls., Fla. Devel. Edn. Assn. (bd. dirs. Jacksonville chpt. 1983-86), Fla. Assn. C.C., Math. Assn. Am., So. Assn. Colls. and Schs. (Fla. com.), LWV, Alpha Kappa Alpha. Democrat. Roman Catholic. Avocations: reading, piano, dancing, bicycling. Home: 7426 Simms Dr Jacksonville FL 32209-1023

ROBINSON, CLAYTON DAVID, minister, educator; b. Pasadena, Calif., Oct. 30, 1955; s. Gary Garth and Gay Elizabeth Clara (Guilmette) R.; m. Kimberly Ann Cole, June 18, 1977; children: Christina Mary, Kathleen Joy, Jonathan David. BA, So. Calif. Coll., 1975; MA, Azusa (Calif.) Pacific U., 1976; MDiv, Fuller Theol. Sem., 1978, PhD in Ministry, 1986. Ordained to ministry Internat. Ch. of the Foursquare Gospel, 1982. Co-pastor Foursquare Gospel Ch., Huntington Beach, Calif., 1975-82, pastor, founder Mission Viejo, 1982-88, pastor Arcadia, 1988-91, pastor, founder Laguna Niguel, 1991—. Mem. faculty Life Bible Coll., L.A., 1985-92; mem. adj. faculty So. Calif. Coll., Costa Mesa, 1985; mem. faculty, Berean Bible coll., 2002-; youth dir. Orange County (Calif.) Foursquare Chs., 1974-86; founder, dir. The Net Coffee House, Huntington Beach, 1981-82; Saddleback divsn. supt. Foursquare Chs., 1994-2002. Orange county regional Supt. Foursquare Ch. Divsn. Supt. at large, Orange County Dist. Foursquare Ch. 2002- Author: The Revelation, 1976, 2d edit. 1991, The Antichrist, 1980, A Strategy for Church Growth and Renewal, 1986; editor, author: Church Planting, 1991; editl. advisor Ministry Advantage Mag., 1994—2000; contbr. numerous articles to profl. jours. Founder, pres. New Life Tng. Ctr., 1998—.

ROBINSON, CLEO PARKER, artistic director; Degree in Dance Edn. Psychology, Denver U., DFA (hon.), 1991. Founder, exec. artistic dir., choreographer Cleo Parker Robinson Dance, Denver. Mem. dance, expansion arts and inter-arts panels NEA; bd. dirs. Denver Ctr. Performing Arts; tchr. in workshops. Co-creator (documentary) African-Americans at Festae, Run Sister Run, (film) Black Women in the Arts, (music video) Borderline. Apptd. Nat. Coun. on Arts, 1999. Recipient Thelma Hill Ctr. for the Performing Arts award, 1986; Choreography fellow NEA; named one of Colo. 100, 1992; named to Blacks in Colo. Hall of Fame, 1994. Mem. Internat. Assn. Blacks in Dance (2nd v.p.). Office: Cleo Parker Robinson Dance 119 Parker Ave W Denver CO 80205

ROBINSON, DANIEL BARUCH, retired banker; b. Hamilton, Ont., Can., Dec. 4, 1937; s. David A. and Zelda (Frank) R.; m. Marta A. Calero, May 7, 1960; children— Allegra, Robert B.Commerce, McMaster U., Hamilton, Ont., 1960; postgrad., U. Mich., 1969, Harvard U., 1971, Pontif Universidade Católica do Rio de Janeiro, 1979, Georgetown U., 1994, 96. Chartered acct. Vice pres. fin. Comsur, La Paz, Bolivia, 1971-72; fin. dir. Light Servicos, Rio De Janeiro, Brazil, 1972-78; sr. fin. analyst The World Bank, Washington, 1978-79; v.p. fin. Jari Florestal, Rio De Janeiro, 1979-80, Manalta Coal, Calgary, Alta, Can, 1981-82; exec.v.p. Atomic Energy Can. Ltd., Mississauga, Ont., 1983-85; rep. Interam. Devel. Bank, Barbados, 1985-89, Washington, 1989-99. Pres. Canadian Club, Rio de Janeiro, 1974-75 Recipient Highest Standing prize Chartered Accts. Assn., 1961; Price, Waterhouse and Co. scholar, 1959 Mem. Inst. Chartered Accts. Ont., Canadian Inst. Chartered Accts., Fin. Execs. Inst. Clubs: Rio de Janeiro Yacht, Jockey Club do Rio de Janeiro, Itanhangá Golf (Rio de Janeiro), Sandy Ln. Property Owners Assn. (Barbados). Avocations: reading; translating from Spanish and Portuguese to English. Home: 352 Bay St S Hamilton ON Canada L8P 3J9 Fax: 905-527-4744. E-mail: drobinson11@cogeco.ca.

ROBINSON, DANIEL N. psychology and philosophy educator; b. N.Y., Mar. 9, 1937; s. Henry S. and Margaret R.; children: Tracey, Kimberly; m. Francine Malasko, 1967. BA, Colgate U., 1958; MA, Hofstra U., 1960; PhD, CUNY, 1965. Rsch. psychologist, electronics rsch. labs. Columbia U., 1960-65, asst. dir. sci. honors program electronics rsch. labs., 1964-68, sr. rsch. psychologist, electronics rsch. labs., 1965-68, asst. dir. of life scis. electronics rsch. labs., 1967-68; asst. prof. dept. psychology Amherst Coll., 1968-70, assoc. prof., 1970-71; dir. grad. program dept. psychology Georgetown Univ., 1981-83, chmn. dept. psychology, 1973-76, 85-91, assoc. prof., 1971-74, prof., 1974—, adj. prof. philosophy, 1996—, disting. rsch. prof. and prof. psychology, 1998—2001, disting. prof. emeritus, 2002—. Vis. lectr. psychology Princeton U., 1965-68; vis. prof. Folger Shakespeare Inst., 1977; vis. sr. mem. Linacre Coll., vis. lectr. philosophy Oxford (Eng.) U., 1991—, faculty fellow, 1999—, philos. faculty, 2002—; vis. prof. Princeton U., 2001; adj. prof. Columbia U., 2002—; cons. NIH, 1967-70, NSF, 1965-75, PBS, 1978-84, 1985-88, MacArthur Found., 1985, Atty. Gen's. Task Force on Crime, 1980, HHS, NIH, 1988. Author: Psychology: A Study of Its Origins and Principles, 1972, The Enlightened Machine: An Analytical Introduction to Neuropsychology, 1973, 80, Psychology: Traditions and Perspectives, 1976, An Intellectual History of Psychology, 1976, The Mind Unfolded: Essay's on Psychology's Historic Texts, 1978, Systems of Modern Psychology: A Critical Sketch, 1979, Psychology and Law: Can Justice Survive the Social Sciences?, 1980, An Intellectual History of Psychology-Revised Edition, 1981, 3rd edit., 1995, Toward A Science of Human Nature: Essays on the Psychologies of Hegel, Mill, Wundt, and James, 1982, Philosophy of Psychology, 1985, Aristotle's Psychology, 1989, (with William R. Uttal) Foundations of Psychobiology, 1983, (with Sir John Eccles) The Wonder of Being Human: Our Mind and Our Brain, 1984; editor Heredity and Achievement, 1970, Readings in the Origins and Principles of Psychology, 1972, Significant Contributions to the History of Psychology, 1977-78, Annals of Theoretical Psychology, 1990, Social Discourse and Moral Judgment, 1992, Wild Beasts and Idle Humours: Legal Insanity from Antiquity to the Present, 1996; editor Jour. Theoretical and Philosophical Psychology, 1997-2002; contbr. chpts. to books, reference books, articles to profl. jours. Recipient Inst. for Advanced Study in the Humanities fellow, U. Edinburgh, 1986-87; Pres's. medal Colgate U., 1986, Pub. Svc. award Gen. Svcs. Adminstrn., 1986. Fellow APA (past pres. divsns. 24 and 26, Lifetime Achievement award Divsn. History of Psychology 2001, Disting. Contbn. award Divsn. Theoretical and Philos. Psychology 2001), Brit. Psychol. Soc.; mem. Sigma Xi, Psi Chi. Home: 300 E Main St Middletown MD 21769 Office: Columbia U. Dept Psychology New York NY 10027

ROBINSON, DAVID ALTON, climatologist, geography educator; b. Hackensack, N.J., May 13, 1955; s. Thomas George and Lois Joan (Coombs) R.; m. Virginia Keating Johnson, May 1, 1983; children: Douglas, Andrew. BS in Geology with honors, Dickinson Coll., 1977; MS in Geology, MPhil in Geology, Columbia U., 1981, PhD in Geology, 1984. Rsch. asst. Lamont-Doherty Earth Obs. Columbia U., Palisades, N.Y., 1977-78, grad. rsch. asst., 1978-84, assoc. rsch. scientist, 1984-88; asst. prof. dept. geography Rutgers U., New Brunswick, N.J., 1988-91, assoc. prof., 1991-95, prof., 1995—, state climatologist, 1991—, assoc. dir. Walton Ctr. for Remote Sensing and Spatial Analysis, 1995—, chmn. dept. geography, 1996—. Adj. prof. Coll. New Rochelle (N.Y.). 1984-87, Bergen C.C., Paramus, N.J., 1986-88; vis. scientist U.S. Nat. Climatic Data Ctr., Asheville, N.C., 1988; adj. assoc. rsch. scientist Lamont-Doherty Earth Obs., 1988—; mem. several panesl NRC; spkr. and cons. in field. Contbr. chpts. to books and articles to profl. jours. Rsch. grantee NSF, 1983—, NASA, 1986—, others. Mem. Assn. Am. Geographers (pres. climate splty. group 1996-97). Am. Assn. State Climatologists (pres. elect 2002—), Am. Meteorol. Soc., Am. Geophys. Union, North Jersey Weather Observers (pres. 1986-87), Sigma Xi. Avocations: weather watching, singing, running, sports. Office: 54 Joyce Kilmer Ave Piscataway NJ 08854-8045 E-mail: drobins@rci.rutgers.edu.

ROBINSON, DAVID BRADFORD, scientific writer, poet; b. Richmond, Va., Apr. 14, 1937; s. Albert Lewis and Martha Ellen (Lovern) R. BS, U. Miami, 1959, MS, 1961; D of Jurisprudence, Calif. Ctrl. U., 1961, MA, 1994; AA, Miami-Dade C.C., 1970; DSc, Northwestern Coll., 1978, PhD, 1979, MA, 1994. Author: Characteristics of Cesium, 1978, Collected Poems, 1987. Founder Ronald Reagan Rep. Ctr., Washington; exhibitor Statue of Liberty, Port of N.Y., 1986; mem. Heritage Found., 1989; sustaining sponsor Ronald Reagan Presdl. Found., 1987; charter mem. Ronald Reagan Trust; charter mem. Honor Roll Rep. Presdl. Task Force, 1990, life mem., 1989, Commemorative Honor Roll, 1991; mem. Nat. Rep. Senatorial Com. with Presdl. Commn., 1992; founding sponsor, founding mem. Space Life Sta., 1989; spkrs. citizen task force Inaugural Mem. Cert. of Honor; life mem. Rep. Nat. Com. Recipient 2d pl. Amateur Trophy, Capablanca Chess Club, 1964, Presdl. Sports award bicycling, 1976, Presdl. Achievement award Rep. Nat. Com., 1982, Cert. Good Standing Rep. Presdl. Task Force, 1982-85, Presdl. Merit medal, 1982, Appreciation cert. Sen. Paula Hawkins, 1986, Golden Poet Trophy award World of Poetry, 1987, Silver Anniversary Album, Nat. Geog. Soc., 1990, Pres. Ronald Reagan Appreciation cert., 1988, Pres. Bush Congl. Victory Squadron Recognition cert., 1989, Affidavit of Life Membership, Cert. from Rep. Nat. Com., Bush Inaugural/Freedom medal, 1989, World Time-Capsule cert., 1990, Am. in Space medal, 1990, Cert. of Appreciation, Nat. Rep. Congl. Com., 1990, Pegasus Time Capsule plaque, 1991, Congl. Merit cert. Nat. Rep. Congl. Com., 1992, Battle of Normandy Found. Appreciation award, 1993, Presdl. Legion of Merit medal, 1993, Congl. Order of Liberty award, 1993, Appreciation cert. Sen. Kay Bailey Hutchinson, 1993, Rep. Presdl. award, 1994, Albert Einstein medal Brit. Bur. Degree Promotion, 1994, Cert. of Appreciation, The Golden Heart Club, Mil. Order of Purple Heart Svc. Found., Congl. Order of Freedom, 1995, Cert. of Meritorious Svc. Rep. Party Planning Com., 1996, Cert. Appreciation World War II Meml., 1997, Chmn.'s Honor Roll cert., Rep. Nat. Com., 1997, Eisenhower Commn., 1997, Caesar medal Trinity Broadcasting Network, 1998, Cert. Recognition Rep. Nat. Com., 1999, Jubilee Yr. Blessing Cert. His Holiness John Paul II/Missionary Assn. Mary Immaculate, 1999, Cert. of Appreciation Concerns of Police Survivors, 2000, Cert. of Appreciation Rep. Nat. Com., 2000, Cert. Appreciation, Planetary Soc., 2001. Mem. Am. Air Mus. (Brit., founder 1991), Battle of Normandy Meml. Mus. (charter 1988), Sigma Xi, Russian Club, Phi Theta Kappa. Avocation: chess. E-mail: super@earthling.net.

ROBINSON, DAVID BROOKS, retired naval officer; b. Alexandria, La., Oct. 26, 1939; s. Donald and Marion (Holloman) R.; m. Gene Kirkpatrick, Aug. 1, 1964; children: Kirk, David. Student, Tex. A&M U., 1958-59; BS, U.S. Naval Acad., 1963; MS in Physics, Naval Postgrad. Sch., Monterey, Calif., 1969. Commd. ensign USN, 1963, advanced through grades to vice admiral, 1993; comdg. officer USS Canon and USS Ready, Guam, 1969-71; adminstrv. aide to Chmn. Joint Chiefs Staff, Washington, 1971-74; comdg. officer USS Luce, Mayport, Fla., 1976-78; surface comdr. assignment officer. and dir. fiscal mgt. and procedural control divsn. Naval Mil. Pers. Cmd., 1979-81; mem. Fgn. Service Inst. Exec. Seminar, Washington, 1982; comdg. officer USS Richmond K. Turner, Charleston, S.C., 1983-84; chief of staff, comdr. Naval Surface Force, Atlantic Fleet, Norfolk, Va., 1984; exec. asst. and sr. aide to vice chief Naval Ops., Washington, 1985, dir. Manpower and Tng. div., 1986, dir. Surface Warfare div., 1987-88; cmdr. cruiser destroyer group 8, 1988-89; vice dir. and subsequently dir. operational plans and inter-operability directorate Joint Staff, Washington, 1989-91; dep., chief of staff to comdr. U.S. Pacific Fleet, 1991-93, comdr. naval surface force, 1993-96; ret. USN, 1996. Decorated Navy Cross, Def. D.S.M., D.S.M., Legion of Merit with 4 gold stars, Bronze Star, Purple Heart. Mem. Optimists (pres. Oakton, Va. 1986-87). Methodist. Avocations: golf, cycling, stamp collecting, reading.

ROBINSON, DAVID CLINTON, reporter; b. Goffstown, N.H., Nov. 5, 1963; s. Clinton and Barbara Lee (Ploss) R.; m. Karen Ruth Eckhardt, July 3, 1992; children: Laura Lee, Lindsay Lee, Clinton Nelson. AB, Syracuse U., 1985. Reporter The Buffalo News, 1985—. Bd. dirs. ToyTown USA Found., 1998—. Mem. Buffalo Newspaper Guild (exec. com. 1989-98, vice chmn. 1991-92). Office: The Buffalo News 1 News Plz Buffalo NY 14203-2994

ROBINSON, DAVID E. telecommunications industry executive; BS in Econs., Bates Coll.; MBA, Dartmouth Coll. Various positions Gen. Instrument Corp., 1983, founding dir. fiber optics transmission bus., 1988; mgmt. positions AT&T Network Sys., 1993—95; sr. v.p., gen. mgr. digital network sys. broadband comms. sector (formerly Gen. Instrument Corp.) Motorola, Inc., 1995—2000, exec. v.p. Ill., pres. broadband comms. sector. Office: Motorola Inc 1303 E Algonquin Rd Schaumburg IL 60196*

ROBINSON, DAVID HOWARD, lawyer; b. Hampton, Va., Nov. 24, 1948; s. Bernard Harris and Phyllis (Canter) R.; m. Nina Jane Briscoe, Aug. 20, 1979. BA, Calif. State U., Northridge, 1970; JD, Cabrillo Pacific U., 1975. Bar: Calif. 1977, U.S. Dist. Ct. (so. dist.) Calif. 1977, U.S. Ct. Claims, 1979, U.S. Supreme Ct. 1980. Adminstr. Cabrillo Pacific U. Coll. Law, 1977; assoc. Gerald D. Egan, San Bernardino, Calif., 1977-78, Duke & Gerstel, San Diego, 1978-80, Rand, Day & Ziman, San Diego, 1980-81; pvt. practice, 1981-88; ptnr. Robinson and Rubin, 1988-95; dep. atty. gen. State of Calif., 1995—. Mem. Foothills Bar Assn. (bd. dirs., past treas.). Office: 110 West A St San Diego CA 92101-3711

ROBINSON, DAVID MASON, cell physiologist; b. July 7, 1932; came to U.S., 1969, naturalized, 1979. s. Thomas Leon Mason and Mabel (Orr) R.; m. Jean Marcia Smith, Sept. 10, 1965; children: Jane Leonie Mason, Simon Henry Mason; m. Christine Parfitt, July 1998. BSc with 1st class honors, U. Durham, 1955, PhD, 1958; BM, BChir, Oxford (Eng.) U., 1964. Mem. sci. staff Namulonge Rsch. Sta., Kampala, Uganda, 1959-61; rsch. officer, tutor Hope Dept. Zoology Oxford (Eng.) U., 1961-63; mem. sci. staff, biophysics group Med. Rsch. Coun., Radiobiol. Rsch. Unit, Harwell, Eng., 1963-66; prin. sci. officer, head cell biology Microbiol. Rsch. Establishment, Porton, Eng., 1966-69; asst. rsch. dir., head cell biology ARC Blood Rsch. Lab., Bethesda, Md., 1969-73; prof. biology, assoc. mem. Vincent Lombardi Cancer Rsch. Ctr., Georgetown U., Washington, 1974-80; prin. sci. officer, head cell biology Microbiol. Rsch. Establishment, Porton, Eng., 1966-69; asst. rsch. dir., head cell biology ARC Blood Rsch. Lab., Bethesda, Md., 1969-73; prof. biology, assoc. mem. Vincent Lombardi Cancer Rsch. Ctr., Georgetown U., Washington, 1974-80, adj. prof. anatomy and cell biology Sch. Medicine, 1982-90; adj. prof. liberal studies Georgetown U., 1980—. Assoc. dir. sci. programs, divsn. heart and vascular disease Nat. Heart, Lung and Blood Inst., NIH, Bethesda, Md., 1980-94, acting dir., 1993, dir. vascular rsch. program, 1994-2001, dep. dir. divsn. heart and vascular diseases, 2000—; mem. faculty biology and genetics NIH Grad. Sch., 1981-86; mem. faculty Brookings Inst., 1994-99, Nat. Def. U., 1995—. Author: (with G. A. Jamieson) Mammalian Cell Membranes, 5 vols., 1973-76; contbr. articles to profl. jours. Capt. 1st Royal Green Jackets, 43d and 52d, Brit. Ter. Army, 1062-65. Recipient Vicennial medal Georgetown U., 1992; named Disting. Vis. Prof. of Yr., Baylor Coll. Medicine, 1997, Presdl. Lectr., Am. Venous Forum, 1998; Philip Buckle Meml. scholar U. Durham, 1958, Empire Cotton Growing Corp. postgrad. scholar, 1957. Mem.: Am. Soc. Cell Biology, Soc. Cryobiology (sec. 1975), Soc. Complex Carbohydrates, Biophys. Soc., Royal Green Jackets Assn., Sigma Xi (pres. Georgetown chpt. 1978), Alpha Sigma Nu (hon.). Democrat. Episcopalian. Home: Stoneleigh Cottage PO Box 2164 Shepherdstown WV 25443-2164 Office: NIH Rm 9158 MSC 7940 Two Rockledge Ctr Bethesda MD 20892-7956 E-mail: dr14j@nih.gov.

ROBINSON, DAVID ZAV, non-profit agency consultant; b. Montreal, Que., Can., Sept. 29, 1927; s. Benjamin and Antonia (Seiden) R.; m. Nan Senior, Sept. 6, 1954; children: Marc, Eric. AB, Harvard U., 1946, AM, 1947, PhD, 1950. Asst. dir. rsch. Baird-Atomic Inc., Cambridge, Mass., 1949-59, 60-61; sci. liaison officer Office Naval Rsch., London, 1959-60; sci. advisor staff Office of Pres., Washington, 1961-67; v.p. acad. affairs NYU, 1967-70; v.p. Carnegie Corp. N.Y., N.Y.C., 1970-80, exec. v.p., 1981-85, exec. v.p., treas., 1986-88; exec. dir. Carnegie Commn. on Sci Tech. and Govt., 1988-97; cons., 1997—. Dir. Urban Research Corp., Chgo., 1968-75; cons. Congressional Office of Tech. Assessment, 1975-78; mem. com. women in sci. NRC, 1975-82, chair com. on tchr. testing, 1999-2000; mem. vis. com. dept. chemistry Harvard U., 1977-83; physics dept. Princeton U., 1970-76 Mem. N.Y. Energy Rsch. and Devel. Authority, 1971-77; trustee CUNY, 1976-81, Amideast, 1983-88, Citizen Union Found., 1985—, Inst. Schs. of the Future, 1986—, N.C. Sch. Sci. and Math., 1989-97, Santa Fe Inst., 1987—, Prep for Prep, 1989-98. Mem. AAAS, Optical Soc. Am., Coun. on Fgn. Rels., Am. Contract Bridge League, Fedn. of Am. Scientists Coun., Bar Assn. of City of N.Y. (commn. on future of CUNY 1999—), Harvard Club (N.Y.C.). Office: 437 Madison Ave New York NY 10022-7001

ROBINSON, DAVIS ROWLAND, lawyer; b. N.Y.C., July 11, 1940; s. Thomas Porter and Cynthia (Davis) R.; m. Suzanne Walker, June 11, 1966; children: Christopher Champlin II, Gracyn Walker. BA magna cum laude, Yale U., 1961; LLB cum laude, Harvard U., 1967. Bar: N.Y. 1968, D.C. 1971, U.S. Supreme Ct. 1972. Fgn. svc. officer U.S. Dept. State, Washington, 1961-69; assoc. Sullivan & Cromwell, N.Y.C., 1969-71; assoc., then ptnr. Leva, Hawes, Symington, Martin and Oppenheimer, Washington, 1971-81; the legal adviser U.S. Dept. State, 1981-85; ptnr. Pillsbury, Madison & Sutro, 1985-88, Le Boeuf, Lamb, Greene & MacRae LLP, Washington, 1988—2002, of counsel, 2002—. Dir. Mid. East Policy Coun., Washington, 1999—. Pres. Harvard Legal Aid Bur., 1966-67. Mem. Assn. of Bar of City of N.Y., Am. Law Inst. (adviser fgn. rels. law of U.S.), Am. Soc. Internat. Law, Coun. on Fgn. Rels., Phi Beta Kappa. Office: Le Boeuf Lamb Greene & MacRae LLP 1875 Connecticut Ave NW Washington DC 20009-5728 Business E-Mail: drrobins@llgm.com.

ROBINSON, DEBORAH J. counselor, educator, educational consultant; b. Buffalo; d. Daniel L. and Barbara A. Robinson. BA, Canisius Coll., Buffalo, 1974; MS in Student Pers. Adminstrn., Buffalo State Coll., 1981. Notary pub., N.Y. Counselor U. Buffalo-Buffalo Ednl. Talent Search, 1982; residential mgr. Women's Residential Resource Ctr., Buffalo, 1986-88; GED coord. aide and tutor JUSENDO, 1988-89; counselor, coord. Trott ACCESS Ctr. Niagara County C.C., Sanborn, N.Y., 1989-91, coord. women in tech. program, 1992, CEOSC counselor, 1992-93, placement counselor, 1993-95, counselor, 1995—. Cons. Cmty. Action Orgn., Edn. Task Force, Buffalo; mem. Ellicott Dist. Concerned Taxpayers, Buffalo; evaluator commn. on higher edn. Middle States Assn. Colls., 1998—. Recipinet Niagara County Black Achievers, Inc. award, 1998. Mem. AAUW, Career Devel. Orgn., Di GAmma. Avocations: collecting elephants, reading, stock market. Office: Niagara County CC 3111 Saunders Settlement Rd Sanborn NY 14132-9487

ROBINSON, DEREK SCOTT, mathematician, educator; b. Montrose, Scotland, Sept. 25, 1938; s. Stanley Scott and Helen Annan Robinson; m. Judith Ann Pounds; children: Ewan, Gavin. PhD, Cambridge U., England, 1963. Prof. U. of Ill., Urbana, Ill., 1968—. Contbr. articles to profl. jours.; editor: Jour. Group Theory, 1999—; contbr. chapters to books. Mem.: Am. Math. Soc. Office: Dept of Mathematics Univ of Ill 1409 W Green Urbana IL 61801

ROBINSON, DIXIE FAYE, educator; b. Lexington, Ky., Feb. 7, 1944; d. John David and Betty Lou (Taylor) Moore; m. Jim Darrell Robinson, June 25, 1978. BA, Georgetown (Ky.) Coll., 1966; MA in Edn., Ball State U., 1972; postgrad., Miami U., Oxford, Ohio, 1989—, Ind. U., 1990-92. Cert. tchr., Ind. Tchr. Richmond (Ind.) Community Schs., 1966-91, adminstr., 1991-97, alt. sch. tchr., 1997—. Team leader Richmond Community schs., 1983-90, mentor tchr., 1989-91, coop. learning staff devel. mem., 1989-91, coord. ptnrship in edn., 1990-91, site-base convenor, 1990-91; v.p. Richmond Area Reading Coun., 1984. Pres. Historic Richmond, Inc., 1982; tour guide Richmond-Wayne County Tourism Bur., 1986-87; vice-chmn. Richmond Area Rose Festival, 1988-89; adv. bd. Palladium Item, Richmond, 1990. Recipient Hoosier Meritorious award Ind. Sec. of State, 1986, Nat. Energy Edn. Devel. award, Washington, 1991, Exemplary Program award for alternative schs. State of Ind., 2001; grantee Newspapers in Edn., 1986. Mem. NEA, NAFE, ASCD, Nat. Mid. Sch. Assn., Assn. Tchr. Educators, Nat. Assn. Secondary Sch. Prins., Nat. Coun. Tchrs. English (Ctr. of Excellence award 1988-91), Ind. Coun. Tchrs. of English (Hoosier Tchr. English 1991), Ind. Middle Level Inst., Richmond Area Reading Coun., Kappa Delta Gamma, Phi Delta Kappa. Avocations: historic preservation, antiques, community affairs, reading, travel. Home: 100 NW 8th St Richmond IN 47374-4055

ROBINSON, DONALD LEONARD, social scientist, educator; b. Buffalo, Dec. 28, 1936; s. Sidney Smith and Marion Esther (Hershiser) R.; m. Molly McCaslin Jahnige, Jan. 1, 1983; children: John Samuel, David Wynn; stepchildren: Katherine Jahnige, Paul Jahnige. BA, Yale U., 1958; MDiv, Union Theol. Sem., 1962; PhD, Cornell U., 1966. Instr. govt. Cornell U., Ithaca, N.Y., 1965-66; asst. prof. Smith Coll., Northampton, Mass., 1966-71, assoc. prof., 1971-78, prof., 1978—, Sylvia Dlugasch Bauman chair Am. studies, 1990-93, dir. Am. studies, 1979-85, chmn. dept. govt., 1997-2000, Charles N. Clark prof., 1998—. Cons. Ford Found., 1986-88, 91-92, Media and Society, 1986-87, Comm. on Operation of U.S. Senate, 1976; dir. Project '87, 1977-78; vis. prof. Doshisha U., Kyoto, Japan, 1989; vis. fellow polit. sci. Yale U., 1999, St. Antony's Coll., Oxford, 1999. Author: Slavery in the Structure of American Politics, 1765-1820, 1971, To the Best of My Ability: The Presidency and the Constitution, 1987, Government for the Third American Century, 1989; mem. editorial bd. Presdl. Studies Quar., 1987—; editor: Reforming American Government: The Bicentennial Papers of the Committee on the Constitutional System, 1985; co-editor: The Constitution of Japan: A Documentary History of Its Framing and Adoption, 1998; co-author: Partners for Democracy: Creating the New Japanese State Under MacArthur, 2002. Adminstr. New Eng. Regional Commn., 1973; chmn. Dem. City Com., 1978-80, Northampton Planning Bd., 1980-82; warden St. John's Episcopal Ch., 1981-85; trustee Diocese of Western Mass., 1988—; mem. select bd., Ashfield, Mass., 1992-2001. Rockefeller Bros. fellow, 1958-59; Kent fellow, 1962-66; Project '87 fellow, 1980; fellow Ctr. for Study Democratic Insts., 1971; Phi Beta Kappa vis. scholar, 1988-89; recipient Anisfield-Wolf award, 1971 Mem. Am. Polit. Sci. Assn., Cosmos Club, Phi Beta Kappa. Home: Norton Hill Rd Ashfield MA 01330 Office: Smith Coll Dept Govt Northampton MA 01063-0001 E-mail: drobinso@smith.edu.

ROBINSON, DONALD PETER, musician, retired electrical engineer; b. Phila., Jan. 27, 1928; s. Warren Frederick and Marcella Theresa (Derry) R.; m. Beatrice Graves, Sept. 22, 1951 (dec.); children: Donald, Stephen, Sharon Robinson-Byrd, Michael; m. Mary Katherine Robertson, June 9, 1990. A.A., Temple U. Sch. Tech., 1956. Sr. engr./technician Gen. Electric Co., Utica, N.Y., 1956-89, ret., 1989; organist emeritus St. Joseph-St. Patrick's Ch., Utica, 1983— ; minister music/organist St. Paul's Baptist Ch., Utica, 1961-88; organist Utica Council K.C., 1969— ; organist/choir dir. 4th degree assembly Central N.Y. dist. K.C., 1985— ; producer, host Organ Loft radio program WLFH, Little Falls, N.Y., 1962-90; pipe organ cons. Served with AUS, 1948-54. Mem. Am. Guild Organists (past dean central N.Y. chpt.), Am. Theatre Organ Soc., Nat. Assn. R.R. Passengers (bd. dirs.), K.C. (past faithful navigator 4th degree assembly). Roman Catholic. Home: 715 Garfield Ave Rockford IL 61103-6023

ROBINSON, DONALD WARREN, educator, artist; b. New Bedford, Mass., Sept. 18, 1932; s. Warren Fowler and Mary Irene (Johnson) R.; m. Dolores Carol Lee, July 9, 1955; 1 child, Richard Allen. BFA, U. Ga., 1953; MFA, Columbia U., 1954; EdD, Rutgers U., 1983. Instr. art Wagner Coll., summer 1953, Gettysburg (Pa.) Coll., 1954-55; tchr., head dept. art elem. and secondary schs. Edison Twp., N.J., 1957-67; vice prin. John Adams Jr. H.S., Edison, 1967-73; prin. M.L. King Sch., 1973-86, H. Hoover Mid. Sch., Edison, 1986-90; pvt. cons. in field. Workshop leader N.Y.C. Tchrs., S.I. Mus., N.Y., 1961-63. Works exhibited in Va., N.J., Md., Pa., N.Y. and Ga. Elder, Presbyn. Ch. Served with USN, 1955-57. Mem. John Dewey Soc., Art Students League N.Y. (life), Guild of Creative Art (exhibiting mem.), Art Alliance, Am. Artist Profl. League, N.J. Prins. and Suprs. Assn., Printmaking Coun. N.J., Phi Kappa Phi, Kappa Delta Pi, Phi Delta Kappa. Home: 55 Frost Ave W Edison NJ 08820-3157 E-mail: dwrobbie29@aol.com.

ROBINSON, DOROTHY K. lawyer; b. New Haven, Feb. 18, 1951; children: Julia Robinson Bouwsma, Alexandra Toby Bouwsma. BA in Econs. with honors, Swarthmore Coll., 1972; JD, U. Calif., Berkeley, 1975; MA (hon.), Yale U., 1987. Bar: Calif. 1975, N.Y. 1976, Conn. 1981, U.S. Ct. Appeals (2d cir.) 1975, U.S. Dist. Ct. (so. dist.) N.Y. 1981. Assoc. Hughes Hubbard & Reed, N.Y.C., 1975-78; asst. gen. counsel Yale U., New Haven, 1978-79, assoc. gen. counsel, 1979-84, dep. gen. counsel, 1984-86, gen. counesl, 1986-95, dir. fed. rels., 1986-88, acting sec., 1993, v.p., gen. counsel, 1995—. Mem. Calif. Law Rev., 1973-75. Trustee Hopkins Grammar Day Prospect Hill Sch., New Haven, 1983-88, sec., 1986-88; trustee Wenner-Gren Found. Anthrop. Rsch., 1991—; bd. dirs. Cold Spring Sch., New Haven, 1990-95; mem. adv. bd. Conn. Mental Health Ctr., New Haven, 1979-89; bd. dirs. Nat. Assn. Ind. Coll. and Univs., 1995-98; mem. alumni coun. Swarthmore Coll., 1999-2002. Fellow Ezra Stiles Coll. Yale U., Am. Bar Found.; mem. ABA, Nat. Assn. Coll. and Univ. Attys. (bd. dirs. 1987-90), Conn. Bar Assn., Calif. Bar Assn., Assn. Bar City N.Y., Phi Beta Kappa. Office: Yale U Office of Gen Counsel PO Box 208255 New Haven CT 06520-8255

ROBINSON, DOROTHY MARIE, poet, educator; b. San Francisco, Mar. 24, 1947; d. Andrew and Phebe Ophelia Robinson. BA, Univ. Calif., Berkeley, CA, 1965; MA, St. Mary's Coll., Moraga, CA, 1979. California Administrative Credential State of Calif., California Lifetime Teaching Credential State of Calif. Educator Berkeley Unified Schools, Berkeley, Calif., 1971—73, Pitts. Unified Schools, Pittsburg, 1974—84, Oakland Unified Schools, Oakland, 1984—88, Vallejo Unified Schools, Vallejo, 1998—99, San Francisco Unified Schools, San Francisco, 1999—2000, Hayward Unified Schools, Hayward, 1998—. Author: (books of poetry) I Believe I'll Tell, Ain't No Secrets. Mem.: Calif. Teacher's Assn., Nat. Edn. Assn. Home: 5303 Fallon Ave Richmond CA 94804-4710

ROBINSON, EARL, JR. marketing and economic research executive, transportation executive, business educator, retired air force officer; b. St. George, Bermuda, Nov. 5, 1954; s. Willie Earl and Jeanette (Wilson) Robinson; m. Indera Rodgers, Dec. 11, 1999; children: Aiyana Spring, Jasmine Summer, Earl III. BA in Radio, TV, U. Detroit, 1976; MS in Mgmt., Troy State U., 1986; postgrad., Old Dominion U., 1986—; MS in Conputer Info. Sys., U. Detroit, 1998; PhD in Legal Letters, Sunbelt Paralegal Inst., 1999. Commd. lt. USAF, 1976, advanced through grades to lt. col., 1992, gen. officer aide, adminstrv. staff officer Germany, 1982-85, with tactical air command Hampton, Va., 1986-88, mem. faculty Air Command and Staff Coll. Montgomery, Ala., 1989-92, comdr. recruiting squadron Clinton Twp., Mich., 1992-94, ret., 1994; pres. Power-Base USA, 1994—; chief advisor solar energy co., 1994—; exec. dir. Detroit Tranist Authority, 1994-95, 1995—. Maj. prof. Spring Arbor (Mich.) Coll., 1992—; adj. prof. Faulkner U., Montgomery, 1991—; pres., CEO ERJ Corp. Ltd., Hampton, Va., 1986-88; pres. Paddle King Corp., Zaragoza, Spain, 1980-82; cons. Inst. Def. Analysis. Inventor info. resource mgmt. system. Mem. Nat. Tech. Assn. (publicity chmn. 1984-85), Urban Youth Action (case worker 1984-85), Housing Opportunity, Inc., Hampton Host Lions Club, Tuskegee Airmen (past chpt. pres.). Avocations: computers, reading, table-trennis, team sports, fishing, golf. Home: 1035 Roslyn St Mount Clemens MI 48043-2934

ROBINSON, EARL JAMES, academic administrator, information systems and statistics educator, consultant; b. Wilmington, Del., Apr. 15, 1949; s. Harry and Minerva Ruth (James) R.; m. Karen Frances Smith, July 5, 1980; children: Ruth Frances, Sarah Rebecca. AB, Davidson Coll., 1971; MS, Bucknell U., 1973; PhD, U. Ga., 1977. Asst. prof. U. Ga., Athens, 1977-78, St. Mary's U., Halifax, N.S., Can., 1978-81, assoc. prof. Can., 1981-84, chmn. dept. Can., 1981-84; assoc. prof., chmn. St. Joseph's U., Phila., 1984-91; dean, prof. Coll. Bus. Minot (N.D.) State U., 1991-94; exec. v.p. acad. affairs, dean faculty, prof. Briar Cliff Coll., Sioux City, Iowa, 1994-98; pres., prof. Lees-McRae Coll., Banner Elk, N.C., 1998—. Cons. Mgmt. Rsch. Assocs., Halifax, 1978-84; pres., cons. Robinson & Assocs., Phila., 1984-91, Minot, N.D., 1991-94, Sioux City, Iowa, 1991-98, Banner Elk, 1998—. Contbr. numerous articles to profl. jours. Recipient Golden M award St. Mary's U., 1981; grantee St. Joseph's U., 1985, St. Mary's U., 1982, Ashland Oil Corp., 1973, FAA, 1977, NSF, 1978. Mem.: AAUP, Am. Assn. Higher Edn., Sigma Phi Epsilon (social chmn. 1969—70, chpt. counselor 1988—91, nat. coms. 1996), Sigma Xi. Episcopalian. Avocations: choral music, flying. Home: PO Box 1856 Banner Elk NC 28604-1856 Office: Lees-McRae Coll PO Box 128 Banner Elk NC 28604-0128 E-mail: robinson@lmc.edu.

ROBINSON, EDGAR ALLEN, retired oil company executive; b. Boston, Dec. 12, 1933; s. Herbert and Ruth (Solomon) R.; m. Ruth Enid Schwartz, July 24, 1956; children: Jeffrey Michael, Laurie Karen. AB, Brown U., 1955; MBA, Harvard U., 1960. Fin. analyst Exxon Corp., N.Y.C., 1960-66, asst. treas., 1966-70; corp. planning mgr. Esso Europe Inc., London, 1970-72; pres. Esso Africa Inc., 1972-75; dep. contr. Exxon Corp., N.Y.C., 1975-79; sr. v.p. Exxon Co. U.S.A., Houston, 1979-83; v.p., treas. Exxon Corp., Irving, Tex., 1983-99; ret., 1999. Bd. dirs. bus. Arts Fund, Houston, 1980-83, chmn., 1983; trustee Houston Ballet Found., 1980-83, Brown U., Providence, 1982-88; mem. Dean's adv. com. U. Chgo. Bus. Sch., 1984—, chmn., 1990-94; bd. dirs. Dallas Zoo, 1992-2000; pres. Dallas Zool. Soc., 1998-99; bd. govs. Dallas Symphony, 1993—; bd, dirs. Dallas Jewish Coalition for the Homeless, 1995—, pres., 1998-2000, trustee Am. Trust for the British Libr., 2000—; bd. dirs. Dallas Theatre Ctr., 2000—, Greenwall Found., 2000—. Home: 5001 Drexel Dr Dallas TX 75205-3112 E-mail: eartexas@aol.com.

ROBINSON, EDNA EARLE, real estate company executive; b. Mt. Vernon, Tex., Dec. 21, 1938; d. Thomas Colquitt and Myrtle Lee (McGill) Lindsey; m. Raymond Roy Robinson, Jr., June 3, 1960; 1 child, Randall Ray. BA, Baylor U., 1960. Cert. profl. sec. Office mgr., sec. Blanchard, Walker, O'Quin & Roberts, Shreveport, La., 1963-76; v.p. Shreveport Pub. LLC, 1976-2000, Snap One, Inc., Shreveport, 1983—, Snap Two, Inc., Shreveport, 1985—, Beaird Properties, LLC, Shreveport, 2000—. Sec.-treas. Charles T. Beaird Found., Shreveport, 1976—; pres. Shreveport Single Rm. Occupancy, Inc., 1995-99; bd. dirs. Shreveport-Bossier Svc. Connection, 2001—. Mem. Shreveport C. of C. (leadership coun. 1987—), River Cities Network (treas. 1996-99, v.p. 2000—, pres. 2001), Profl. Secs. Internat. (treas., sec., v.p., pres. Pelican chpt. 1971-90), Cert. Profl. Sec. Acad., Cert. Profl. Secs. of La. (charter). Baptist. Avocations: reading, boating, travel. Home: 533 Hunters Run Bossier City LA 71111-8171 Office: Beaird Properties LLC 330 Marshall St Ste 1112 Shreveport LA 71101-3015 E-mail: ednalrobinson@aol.com.

ROBINSON, EDWARD LEE, retired physics educator, consultant; b. Clanton, Ala., Nov. 6, 1933; s. Alonzo Lee and Ollie Sarah (Mims) R.; m. Shirley Anne Burnett (div. Sept. 1972); children: Edward Lee Jr., James Allan, Paul David; m. Linda G. Moon, 1990. AB with honors, Samford U., 1954; MS, Purdue U., 1958, PhD, 1962. Dir. Cyclotron Lab. Samford U., Birmingham, Ala., 1961-67, asst. prof. physics, chmn. dept., 1961-62, assoc. prof., chmn. dept., 1962-66, prof., chmn. dept., 1966-67; assoc. prof. U. Ala., 1967-77, co-radiation safety officer, 1967-85, dir. Van de Graaff Accelerator Lab., 1970-91, acting chmn. dept., 1973-74, prof. physics, 1977-91, adj. prof. forensic sci., 1983-91, cons. in applied physics and accident reconstrn., 1991—. Cons. Hayes Internat. Corp., Birmingham, 1963-68, So. Rsch. Inst., Birmingham, 1968-69; rschr. Oak Ridge (Tenn.) Nat. Lab., 1968, 74-75, 82, U. Md., College Park, 1966, 67; bd. overseers Samford U., 1999—. Active Birmingham YMCA; mem. at large nat. coun., chmn. sci. adv. com. for explorer scouting Boy Scouts Am., 1999—. Mem. Am. Phys. Soc., Soc. Automotive Engrs., AAAS, Ala. Acad. Sci. (life, v.p. 1964-65), Tex. Assn. Accident Reconstrn. Specialists (bd. dirs.), numerous other nat. and internat. profl. assns. Baptist. Achievements include discovery, co-discovery of six radioisotopes. Avocations: handball, scuba diving. Home: 233 Oakmont Rd Birmingham AL 35244-3264 E-mail: elrobinson@charter.net.

ROBINSON, EDWARD NORWOOD, lawyer; b. Roseboro, N.C., June 18, 1925; s. Edward Croswell and Lolita (Underwood) R.; m.Pauline L. Gray, Mar. 20, 1952; children: Edward Norwood Jr., James Gray, Michael Lindsay, Mark Alvin. BS in Engring., U.S. Mil. Acad., 1945; JD, Duke U., 1952. Atty. Robinson & Lawing, L.L.P., Winston-Salem, N.C. N.C. civilian aide to Sec. of Army, 1994-2001; apptd. to 5th Dist. Acad. Selection Bd.; mem. ethics com. Bowman Gray Sch. Medicine; bd. visitors Duke U. Sch. Law, Wake Forest U. Sch. Law, Duke Divinity Sch.; lectr. in field. Co-editor Duke Law Jour. Past pres. Winston-Salem Rotary Club; past campaign chmn. United Way; past pres. C. of C.; past pres. local chpt. ARC; past dir. Winston-Salem Housing Found.; mem. Centenary United Meth. Ch., Winston-Salem, tchr. Chapel class, chmn. bd. stewards; past chmn. Winston-Salem Dist. United Meth. Ch., Ch. Ext.; past dir., campaign chmn. Triad United Meth. Home. 1st Lt. U.S. Army, 1942-49. Recipient Charles L. Rhyne award Duke U. Law Alumni, 1997. Fellow Am. Coll. Trial Lawyers; mem. ABA (antitrust and litigation sects.), U.S. 4th Cir. Jud. Conf. (life), N.C. Bar Assn. (past dir.), Forsyth County Bar Assn. (past pres.), Pvt. Adjudication Ctr. Duke U. (past chmn. bd.), U.S. Mil. Acad. Assn. Grads. (bd. trustees emeritus), Order of the Coif, Joseph Branch Inns of Ct., Am. Inns of Ct. Avocations: golf, travel. Office: Robinson and Lawing LLP 370 Knollwood St Ste 600 Winston Salem NC 27103-1830 E-mail: nrobinson@robinson-lawing.com.

ROBINSON, EDWARD T., III, lawyer; b. Glen Cove, N.Y., May 23, 1932; s. Edward Jr. and Helen (Rahilly) R.; m. Lynn Simmons; children: Edward IV, Wendy, Christopher, Jeffrey, Lesley, Michael. AB, Holy Cross Coll., 1954; JD, Georgetown U., 1960. Bar: N.Y. 1961, U.S. Ct. Appeals (2d cir.) 1966. Counsel Royal-Globe Ins. Co., Mineola, N.Y., 1960-64; pvt. practice, Oyster Bay, 1964-70, 91-2000; ptnr. Robinson & Cincotta, 1970-85, Robinson & Lynch, Oyster Bay, 1985-91; counsel Cammarata & Cronin LLP, 2000—. Mem. adv. bd. Chgo. Title Ins. Co., N.Y.C., 1982-2000, Fleet Bank, 1989-95, United Cerebral Palsy, 1980—; mem. Nassau County Commn. on Govt. Revision, 1993—; mem. County Exec. Blue Ribbon Panel on Criminal Justice; mem. exec. coun. N.Y. State Conf. Bar Leaders, 1986-90; counsel Oyster Bay-East Norwich Ctrl. Sch. Dist., 1966-2000; mem. N.Y. State grievance com. 10th Jud. Dist., 1995—. Mem. Nassau County Traffic and Parking Violations Bur.; pres. Holy Cross Coll. Club, L.I., 1989-90; trustee Nassau County coun. Boy Scouts Am.; chmn. Forget-Me-Not Ball, United Cerebral Palsy. Recipient Community Svc. award Nassau County coun. Boy Scouts Am.; named Man of Yr. United Cerebral Palsy, Nassau County, 1979. Mem. N.Y. State Bar Assn. (del., v.p. 1992-95, mem. ho. of dels. 1995—), Nassau County Bar Assn. (pres. 1986-87), Oyster Bay C. of C. (pres. 1976-79), Meadowbrook Golf Club, Country Club La Romana (Dominican Republic). Republican. Roman Catholic. Avocations: golf, tennis, jazz music. Home: 60 Calvin Ave Syosset NY 11791-2106 Office: 34 Audrey Ave Unit 3 Oyster Bay NY 11771-1595

ROBINSON, ELAINE, consultant; b. Rochester, N.Y., June 14, 1944; d. Frederick William and Dorothy Christine (Bauman) Robinson; m. John Peter Loiello, Aug. 7, 1971. AAS, Broome C.C., Binghamton, N.Y., 1964; BA, SUNY, Cortland, 1966. Caseworker Monroe County Dept. Social Svcs., Rochester, 1966-73; social worker Westminster Social Svcs., London, 1974-79; vol. coord./scheduler Carter/Mondale Presdl. Com., Washington, 1979-80; dep. to the dir. Nat. Abortion Rights Action League, 1982-87; sr. cons. Loiello Assocs. Internat., 1988-89; adminstr. Comms. Consortium, 1989-90; v.p. Gowran Internat., 1990-93, pres., 1994—2000; assoc. Washington Adv. Group, 2002. Home: 1661 Crescent Pl NW Apt 608 Washington DC 20009-4050 E-mail: gowran@erols.com.

ROBINSON, ELLA GARRETT, editor, writer; b. Decatur, Ala., Apr. 12, 1954; d. Calvis Clemon and Jewell Helms Garrett; m. Daniel Robinson, May 7, 1976. BA, Samford U., Birmingham, AL, 1972—76. Editl. asst. Woman's Missionary Union, Birmingham, Ala., 1976—94; copy editor/writer freelance, Pleasant Grove, 1994—. Author: (book) A Guide to Literary Sites of the South, 1998. Mem.: Ala. Media Profls. Home: 735 Seventh Pl Pleasant Grove AL 35127 Personal E-mail: ERobnson@aol.com.

ROBINSON, ELLA SCALES, language educator; b. Wedowee, Ala., Apr. 16, 1943; d. Leslie S. and Mary Ella (Mcpherson) Scales; m. John W. Robinson (dec. Feb. 1986); 1 child, John W. BS, Ala. State U., 1965; MA, U. Nebr., 1970, PhD, 1976. Tchr. English Selma (Ala.) Pub. Schs., 1965-69; rsch. asst. English dept. U. Nebr., Lincoln, 1969-70, tchr. asst. English dept., 1971-75, asst. prof. English, 1981-91; asst. prof. English, dir. freshman English U. Ill., 1975-78; asst. prof. English Atlanta U., 1978-80; assoc. prof. English Tuskegee (Ala.) U., 1994-2001; head humanities and fine arts dept. Concordia Coll., Selma, Ala., 2001—, head English dept., 2000—. Author: (poetry) Selected Poems, 1995, To Know Heaven, 1996, Love, The Seasons and Death, 1996, Poems: Angels in the Sun, 1996, Heritage: Tuskegee Poems a Celebration, 1997. Mem. NCTE, NAACP (life), MLA, African Lit. Assn., Lincoln Nebr. Chaparral Poets. Democrat. Methodist. Avocations: poetry, gardening, cooking, painting. Home: 6607 Luxembourg Cir Montgomery AL 36117-3447

ROBINSON, EMILY SUE, music educator; b. Henryetta, Okla., Mar. 1, 1952; d. William Gilbert and Frances (Meyer) Campbell; m. Robert Thomas Robinson, Apr. 16, 1972; children: Juliette Renae Kidd, Tamara Kaye Clemence, Samuel Thomas. MusB, Oklahoma City U., 1974; MusM, U. Okla., 1990. Piano instr., Midwest City, Okla., 1976—; accompanist Rose State Coll., 1986—, adj. prof., 1988—2000, prof., 2000—; accompanist Midwest Choral Soc., 1992—2000. Organist Midwest Blvd. Christian Ch., Midwest City, 1971-74; accompanist Chouteau Acad. Ballet, Oklahoma City, 1972-75, music dir. Eastminster United Presbyn. Ch., Del City, 1975—. Mem. Okla. Music Tchrs. Assn. (adjudicator 1994—), Ctrl. Oklahoma Music Tchrs. Assn. (historian 1996-98). Home: 332 W Campbell Dr Midwest City OK 73110-3318 Office: Rose State Coll 6420 SE 15th St Midwest City OK 73110-2704 Fax: 405-733-7427.

ROBINSON, EMMA HAIRSTON, artist, educator; b. Lexington, N.C., Sept. 13, 1942; d. Cardell and Martha Ann (McCarter) Hairston; m. Daniel Louis Robinson, Dec. 26, 1963; 1 child, Gardell Lewis. BFA, Howard U., 1990, MFA, 1992. Sec. Dept. Navy, Washington, 1968-70, NSF, Washington, 1970-81; artist, tchr., lectr. Arts for Aging, Bethesda, Md., 1990—. CEO Impace, 1997; office mgr., cons. Nat. Assn. Minority Contractors, Washington, 1993-94. Lucy E. Moten fellow, 1989; Spl. Talent scholar, 1988-92. Mem. Nat. Conf. Artists, New D.C. Collage Soc., Nat. Coun. Negro Women, Washington Area Lawyers for Arts, Golden Key Nat. Honor Soc., Order of Ea. Star, Zeta Phi Beta. Democrat. Avocations: music, linguistics, travel, gardening. Home: 1523 Church St NW Washington DC 20005-1905

ROBINSON, ENDERS ANTHONY, geophysicist, educator, writer; b. Boston, Mar. 18, 1930; s. Edward Arthur and Doris Gertrude (Goodale) Robinson; m. Eva Arborelius, Sept. 9, 1962 (div. 1973); children: Anna, Erik Arthur, Karin; m. Joyce McPeake, Aug. 8, 1992. *Enders Robinson is the ninth-generation descendent of the carpenter Samuel Wardwell(1643-1692) who was executed in Salem for witchcraft on September 22,1692. The magistrate who tracked him down was John Hathorne, the great-great grandfather of author Nathaniel Hawthorne. In his book, The House of the Seven Gables, the fictional Colonel Pyncheon is based upon John Hathorne, and the fictional wizard Matthew Maule upon Wardwell. The land disputes between Pyncheon and Maule in the book are like those between John Hathorne and Wardwell in real life.* BS in Math., MIT, 1950, MS in Econs., 1952, PhD in Geophysics, 1954. Dir. geophys. analysis group MIT, Cambridge, Mass., 1952-54, instr. math., 1955-56; geophysicist Gulf Oil Corp., Pitts., 1954-55; petroleum economist Standard Oil Co. N.J., N.Y.C., 1956-57; asst. prof. stats. Mich. State U., East Lansing, 1958; asst. prof. math. U. Wis., Madison, 1958-61, assoc. prof. math. (with tenure), 1961-62; dep. prof. stats. Uppsala (Swedeñ) U., 1960-64; v.p., dir. Digicon Inc., Houston, 1965-70; pres. Robinson Rsch. Inc., 1970-82; vis. prof. theoretical and applied mechanics Cornell U., Ithaca, NY, 1981-82; McMan prof. geophysics U. Tulsa, 1983-93; Maurice Ewing and J.L. Worzel prof. geophysics Columbia U., N.Y.C., 1993—2000, prof. emeritus, 2000—. *Citation for the Ewing Gold Medal, 2001: For a lifetime of remarkable achievements that began while he was in MIT graduate school, when he in essence invented the field of digital seismic data processing, and has continued to at least today when he is receiving the Best Paper in Geophysics award in addition to the Maurice Ewing medal. These outstanding achievements are, however, merely bookends to an astonishing career. The progress in our science over the last fifty years in large part has evolved from the work of Enders Robinson whose extraordinary scientific legacy we recognize today with the highest honor of the Society of Exploration Geophysicists.* Author: (book) Seismic Inversion and Deconvolution, Dual Sensor Technology, 1999, 31 other books on sci., tech. and history; editor: Internat. Jour. Imaging Sys. & Tech., 1988—; mem. editl. bd.: Multidimensional Sys. and Signal Processing, An Internat. Jour., 1990—. 2d lt. U.S. Army, 1950—51. Recipient Donald G. Fink Prize award, IEEE, 1984, Achivement award, Thayer Acad. Alumni, 1997, Alexander von Humboldt Rsch. award for sr. U.S. scientists, 1999. Mem.: Nat. Rsch. Coun. (com. undiscovered oil and gas resources), Nat. Acad. Engring. (petroleum and mining sect.), European Assn. Geoscientists and Engrs. (Conrad Schlumberger award 1969), Soc. Exploration Geophysicists (hon. Classic Paper award 1953, 1957, Best Paper award 1964, Reginald Fessenden medal 1969, father of deconvolution 1983, Best Paper award 2001, Maurice Ewing Gold medal 2001), Renaissance Inst. Washington, N.Y. Athletic Club, MIT Club N.Y. Office: Trump Place 160 Riverside Blvd #6U New York NY 10069-0705 Business E-Mail: ear11@columbia.edu.

ROBINSON, EVELYN EDNA, educator; b. St. John, Maine, Feb. 23, 1911; d. Registe Jalbert and Olive Michaud; m. Carl Robinson, July 19, 1939; children: Robert, James. BA in Math., U. Maine, 1934; MS, U. N.H., 1963; MEd, Hillyer Coll. U., 1960. Tchr. English and math. Ft. Kent (Maine) H.S., 1934; tchr. English and math., coach girls basketball Madewaska (Maine) H.S., 1935-55; tchr. math. Stamford (Conn.) H.S., 1955-56; tchr. math and English, Bristol (Conn.) H.S., 1956-63; prof. math. Worcester (Mass.) State Coll., 1963-77, chmn. dept., 1970-77. Coord. cmty. bus. Worcester State Coll., 1970-77, class advisor, 1968-72, salary equity bd., 1971-73. Vol. libr. Madawaska Pub. Libr., 1936-55; lector Christ the King, Worcester, 1974-2000. Mem. Delta Kappa Gamma. Republican. Roman Catholic. Avocations: decorating, flower arrangements, ceramics, tailoring. Home: 12 Brookside Ave Worcester MA 01602

ROBINSON, FLORINE SAMANTHA, marketing executive; b. Massies Mill, Va., Feb. 4, 1935; d. John Daniel and Fannie Belle (Smith) Jackson; m. Frederick Robinson (div. 1973); children: Katherine, Theresa, Freda. BS, Morgan State U., 1976; postgrad., U. Balt., 1977-81, Liberty U., 1987. Writer, reporter Phila. Independent News, 1961-63; freelance writer, editor Balt., 1963-71; asst. mng. editor Williams & Wilkins Pubs. Inc., Balt, 1971-76; mktg. rep., then mktg. mgr. NCR Corp., Balt., 1977-93; assoc. minister, trustee Christian Unity Temple, 1976—; pres. ABCOM, Inc., 1993—. Bd. dirs. Armstrong & Bratcher, Inc., Balt. Editor: Stedman's Medical Dictionary, 1972; contbr. articles to profl. jours. Active PTA, Balt., 1963-65; bd. dirs. Howard Pk. Civic Assn., Balt., 1967—, pres. 1991—; leader, cons. Girl Scouts USA, 1970-73. Recipient Excellence in Rsch. award Psi Chi, 1976, Citizen citation Mayor of Balt. Mem. NAFE, Mid-Atlantic Food Dealers Assn., Am. Soc. Notaries, Internat. Platform Assn., Edelweiss Club, Order of Eastern Star. Democrat. Avocation: piano. Home: 3126 Howard Park Ave Baltimore MD 21207-6715

ROBINSON, FRANKLIN WESTCOTT, museum director, art historian; b. Providence, May 21, 1939; s. Charles Alexander Robinson Jr. and Celia (Sachs) Stillwell; m. Margaret Dredge, Aug. 14, 1967; 1 child, John Alexander. BA, Harvard U., 1961, MA, 1964, PhD, 1970. Instr. Wellesley Coll., 1968-69; asst. prof. Dartmouth Coll., 1969-75; assoc. prof. Williams Coll., 1975-79; dir. Williams Coll. Mus., 1976-79, Mus. of Art, R.I. Sch. Design, Providence, 1979-92, Herbert F. Johnson Mus. Art, Cornell U., Ithaca, N.Y., 1992—. Author: Gabriel Metsu, 1975, Seventeenth Century Dutch Drawings from American Collections, 1977, Dutch and Flemish Paintings from the Ringling Mus, 1980. Fulbright fellow, 1961-62; recipient Claiborne Pell award R.I. State Coun. Arts, 1992. Mem. Assn. Art Mus. Dirs., Coll. Art Assn. Clubs: Century, Hope. Office: Herbert F Johnson Mus Art Cornell University Ithaca NY 14853-4001

ROBINSON, FRED COLSON, English language educator; b. Birmingham, Ala., Sept. 23, 1930; s. Emmett Colson and Morwenna Hope (Bennett) R.; m. Helen Caroline Wild, June 21, 1959; children: Lisa Karen, Eric Wild. BA, Birmingham So. Coll., 1953; MA, U. N.C., 1954, PhD, 1961; DLitt (hon.), Williams Coll., 1985; MA (hon.), Yale U., 1989. Instr. Stanford (Calif.) U., 1960-61, asst. prof., 1961-65, assoc. prof., 1967-71, prof. English philology, 1971-72; asst. prof. Cornell U., Ithaca, N.Y., 1965-66, assoc. prof., 1966-67; prof. Yale U., New Haven, 1972-83, Douglas Tracy Smith prof., 1983—, chmn. medieval studies, 1975-78, 80. Vis. prof. Harvard U., Cambridge, Mass., 1983; mem. pub. com. Medieval Acad. Monographs, Cambridge, 1987-90. Author: Old English Literature: Select Bibliography, 1970, Beowulf and the Appositive Style, 1985, The Tomb of Beowulf, 1993, The Editing of Old English, 1994; co-author: A Bibliography...on Old English Literature, 1980, Old English Verse Texts from Many Sources: A Comprehensive Collection, 1991, A Guide to Old English, 6th edit., 2001, Beowulf: An Edition with Relevant Shorter Texts, 1998; editor Old English Newsletter, 1966-73, Early English MSS in Facsimile, 1971—, Anglo-Saxon England, 1972—, Anglistica, 1981—; contbr. more than 85 articles to scholarly jours. Trustee Yale Univ. Library Assocs., New Haven, 1986-89, 91-95, 97—. With U.S. Army, 1954-56. Recipient Disting. Vis. Scholar award U. Ala., 1999; fellow Guggenheim Found., 1974-75, Am. Coun. Learned Socs., 1968-69, Inst. Social and Econs. Rsch., Rhodes U., 1978, Japan Soc. for Promotion Sci., 1989; grantee NEH, 1976, 79, 81, 85, Am. Philos. Soc., 1973, 85; named Professore solo per ricerca Univ. di Roma "La Sapienza", 2000. Fellow AAAS, Medieval Acad. Am. (pres. 1983-84, Haskins medal 1984), Brit. Acad. (corr., Sir Israel Gollancz prize 1997), Meddeleeue-verenigung van Suidelike Afrika (corr.); mem. Finnish Acad. of Sci. and Letters (fgn. mem.), New Eng. Medieval Conf. (pres. 1982-83), Conn. Acad. Arts and Scis. (pres. 1980-85), Internat. Soc. Anglo-Saxonists (elected hon.), Elizabethan Club (bd. govs. 1986-88, v.p. 1989-90, pres. 1990-92), Manuscript Club (v.p. New Haven chpt. 1990-92), Phi Beta Kappa. Episcopalian. Office: Yale Univ Dept English New Haven CT 06520

ROBINSON, GAIL PATRICIA, retired mental health counselor; b. Medford, Oreg., Dec. 31, 1936; d. Ivan T. and Evelyn H. (Hamilton) Skyrman; m. Douglas L. Smith; children: Shauna J., James D. BS in Edn., Oreg. State U., 1958, PhD in Counseling, 1978; MS in Counseling, Western Oreg. State Coll., 1974. Lic. profl. counselor, Oreg. Tchr. Monterey (Calif.) Pub. Schs., 1958-59, Corvallis (Oreg.) Pub. Schs., 1959-62, 69-75, counselor, 1977-81; pvt. practice Corvallis, 1977-95. Vol. therapist Children's Svcs. divsn., Linn and Benton Counties, 1982-83; asst. prof. Western Oreg. State coll., 1977, counselor, 1982-83; mem. grad. faculty Oreg. State U., Corvallis, 1978-95; presenter workshops, lectr. in field. Contbr. articles to profl. jours. Mem. Benton County Mental Helath Citizens Adv. Bd., 1979-85, chair, 1982-83; trustee WCTU Children's Farm Home, 1978-84, chair child welfare com., 1982-83, pres., 1984; mem. Old Mill Sch. Adv. Bd., 1979-85, chair, 1979-81; bd. dirs. Cmty. Outreach, 1979-83; mem. Benton Com. for Prevention of Child Abuse, 1979-85, v.p., 1982; mem. Oreg. Bd. Lic. Profl. Counselors and Therapists, 1989-95, chair, 1989-90. Mem. ACA (govt. rels. com. 1988-91, professionalization com. 1988-92, pres. 1996-97), Am. Mental Health Counselors Assn. (chair consumer and pub. rels. com. 1988-91, bd. dirs. Western region 1989-91, chair strategic planning com. 1994-95, pres. 1992-93), Oreg. Counseling Assn. (chair licensure liaison com. 1985-91, exec. bd. 1985-88, steering com. 1986-87, register editorial com. 1985-86, Disting. Svc. award 1985, 87, Leona Tyler award 1989), Oreg. Mental Health Counselors Assn.

ROBINSON, GARRY LEWIN, television news executive; b. Kansas City, Mo., Oct. 26, 1951; s. Calvin Luin and Reba Kathleen (Owen) R.; m. Linda Sue Payton, Oct. 21, 1973 (div. 1982); children: Penny Lynn, Larry Calvin II, Jeff Noel. BS, Ark. State U., 1981. Cert. tech. Dynatech Newstar and AP Newscenter Computer Sys. Various positions Sta. KAWW-AM-FM, Heber Springs, Ark., 1969-76, dir. news, ops., 1978; asst. news dir. Sta. KARV-AM, Russellville, 1976-78; ops. mgr., news dir. Sta. KCON-AM, Conway, 1978-79; asst. news dir. Sta. KTVE-TV, El Dorado, 1979-81; mging. producer Sta. KAIT-TV, Jonesboro, 1981-84; newscast producer Sta. KOLD-TV, Tucson, 1984-85; newscast producer, now news ops. mgr. Sta. KSLA-TV, Shreveport, La., 1984—, exec. prodr., 10 PM prodr., newsroom computer sys. mgr., 1985—, exec. producer, computer system mgr., 1985—, new opers. mgr. Bd. dirs. North Ark. Fire Dist., Russellville, 1977; bd. advisors City Cable TV Commn., Conway, 1978; chmn. drama div. Conway Regional Arts Commn., 1977-78; advisor Explorer Scouts, Shreveport, 1987. Recipient numerous reporter awards Ark. AP, Little Rock, 1969-84, Radio Documentary award Am. Assn. Women in Radio and TV, Little Rock, 1978, various TV news awards La., Tex., Ark., AP Broadcasters Assn., 1985-90. Mem. Radio TV News Dirs. Assn. (Edward R. Murrow award 1987), Sigma Delta Chi (North La. chpt.) (bd. dirs. 1987). Clubs: Phi Eta Sigma (pres. 1970-71). Democrat. Baptist. Avocations: reading, writing, guitar, computers, outdoor sports. Home: 5063 Town North Dr Shreveport LA 71107-2843 Office: Sta KSLA-TV 1812 Fairfield Ave Shreveport LA 71101-4431 E-mail: garry@garryrobinson.com., garry@shreve.net.

ROBINSON, GLENDA CAROLE, pharmacist; b. Johnson City, Tenn. d. Harry and Jackie Evelyn Bowers; m. Richard Haynes Robinson, 1967 (div. 1985); children: Rachel Corianne, Fredrick David. BS in Pharmacy, U. Tenn.,

1967. Pharmacist supr. Sommers Drug Stores, San Antonio, 1968-69; staff pharmacist Crawford Long Hosp., Atlanta, 1971-72, Rich's Pharmacy, Atlanta, 1973-74; relief staff pharmacist Atchley Drug Ctr., Greeneville, Tenn., 1977-86; staff pharmacist Takoma Hosp. Pharmacy, 1983-86, Greene Valley Developmental Ctr., Greeneville, 1987-91, dir. pharmacy, 1991—. Mem. First Dist. Pharmacy Assn. East Tenn., Greeneville Jr. Women's Club (sec., internat. affairs chair), Greeneville Morning Rotary Club (pres., Polio Plus chair, Outstanding Rotarian 1996-97, Found. Dist. Svc. award 1998-99), Soc. Cicero.

ROBINSON, HARLO LYLE, lawyer; b. Shelley, Idaho, Mar. 10, 1925; s. Clarence and Vilate (Hainey) R.; m. Janet Allen Alderson, Dec. 28, 1969; children— Thomas Allen, Harlo Todd. B.S., U. Utah, 1949; J.D., U. Calif.-Berkeley, 1952. Bar: Calif. 1953, Hawaii 1970. Gen. counsel Dillingham Corp., Honolulu, 1968-76; assoc. Ikazaki, Lo, Youth & Nakano, 1976-77; of legal counsel Bob Pomery Cons., Tehran, Iran, 1977-79, Saudi Arabia Parsons, Yanbu, Saudi Arabia, 1979— . Assoc. editor Calif. Law Rev., 1951-52. Adv. bd. Southwestern Legal Found., Dallas, 1971-82. Republican. Mem. Christian Ch. Home: 696 Kalanipuu St Honolulu HI 96825-2421

ROBINSON, HAROLD OSCAR, clergyman, educator; b. Trenton, N.J., Apr. 21, 1943; s. Oscar Alexander and Emma (Gale) R.; m. Alice Louise Steele, Sept. 21, 1991; children: Kheesa L., Harold Oscar. BA, Rutgers U., 1973, MEd, 1974; MDiv, Hood Theol. Sem., Salisbury, N.C., 1998. Ordained deacon A.M.E. Zion Ch., 1989, elder, 1991. Pastor Jonesboro (Tenn.) A.M.E. Zion Ch., 1989-90, Brown Hill A.M.E. Zion Ch., Locust, N.C., 1990-94; 1st resident missionary, presiding elder African Meth. Episcopal Zion Ch., South Africa, 1994-96; assoc. min. Little Rock A.M.E. Zion Ch., Charlotte, N.C., 1996-2000; prof. humanities Shaw U., Kannapolis, 1997-2001; tchr. social studfies A.L. Brown H.S., 1999-2001. Chmn. diversity task force Cabarrus County Schs., Concord, N.C., 1997-99; asst. prof. Essex County Coll., Newark, 1975-79; mgr. safety, security and law enforcement N.J. Job Corps Ctr., Edison, 1978-83. Editor: A History of African Americans in Cabarrus County, N.C., 1992 (book awrd 1993); book editor A.M.E. Zion Quar. Rev., 1998-99. Nat. Boy Scout dir. A.M.E. Zion Ch., Charlotte, 1994-2000; grad. Challenge Greensboro Clas I, 1989, Leadership Cabarrus, 1994; del. Dem. Nat. Conv., N.Y.C., 1980. Recipient Heritage award Livingstone Coll., Salisbury, N.C., 1997; named to Hon. Order Ky. Cols., 1994; named lt. col., aide-de-camp State of Tenn., 1994. Mem. NAACP (pres. 1991-93), Phi Beta Sigma. Avocations: camping, reading, collecting African American art. Home: 3735 Rock Hill Church Rd Concord NC 28027-6688

ROBINSON, HELEN MARGARET, emergency physician, internist; b. Atlanta, 1950; d. Richard Martin and Frances (Gibbs) Robinson; m. John Michael O'Farrell, July 24, 1974 (div. Dec. 1991); children: John R., Kevin D., William R. BA, Emory U., 1972; MD, Med. Coll. Ga., 1976. Diplomate Am. Bd. Emergency Medicine, Am. Bd. Internal Medicine. Intern Ga. Bapt. Hosp., Atlanta, 1976-77, resident in internal medicine, 1977-79; emergency physician Huntsville (Ala.) Hosp., 1985—, vice chmn. dept. emergency medicine, 1994—2000, chmn. dept. emergency medicine, 2001—. Fellow Am. Coll. Emergency Physicians; mem. AMA, Med. Assn. State of Ala., Madison County Med. Soc. Office: Huntsville Hospital 101 Sivley Rd SW Huntsville AL 35801-4470

ROBINSON, HENRY, III, office manager, legal consultant; b. Balt., Jan. 16, 1960; s. Henry II and Minnie Louise (Anderson) R.; m. Margaret Taylor, Apr. 11, 1979 (dec. June 1981); 1 child, Henry IV. ASB, Internat. Corr. Schs., 1991; JD, La Salle U., Mandeville, La., 1997; paralegal diploma with honors, paralegal diploma with honors, Sch. Paralegal Studies, 1998. Cert. paralegal. Correctional officer Md. Penitentiary, Balt., 1979-81; electrician Md. Correctional Inst., Hagerstown, 1983-88; office mgr. State Use Industries, 1988-97; with refrigeration shop Md. House of Correction, Jessup, 1998-2000, wood assembly, 2000—01, refrigeration apprentice, 2001—; with SUI Wood Assembly Plant, Jessup, 2000—01. Facilitator Alternative to Violence, 1993—, chmn. follow-up com., 1998; chairperson follow-up com. Alternative To Violence Project, Inc., 1998. Recipient cert. of appreciation Cmty. Correctional Svcs. Com., 1995, 96. Mem. Lifestyles (chmn. 1993-94, 2d v.p. 1994-95, cert. 1994, 95), Ravens Roost (sec.-treas. 1998-99), Jessup Gavel Club (v.p. 1998-99). Jehovah'S Witness. Avocations: powerlifting, volleyball, scramble, most sports, corresponding.

ROBINSON, HENRY WARD, meteorologist; b. Schoharie, N.Y., June 30, 1940; s. Frank Locklyn and Esther (Lawyer) R.; m. Muriel Scott, Aug. 15, 1964; children: Katherine, Heather, David. BS, SUNY, Oneonta, 1964; MS, Pa. State U., 1970. Tchg. asst. Pa. State U., State College, 1968-72; instr. Upsala Coll., East Orange, N.J., 1973-75; analyst Computer Sci. Corp., Silver Spring, Md., 1975-78; meteorologist Nat. Westher Svc. NOAA, 1978—. Adj. prof. Montgomery Coll., Germantown, Md., 1983—; mentor NASA Goddard Space Flight Ctr. Ea. Region Remote Sensing Applications Ctr.; vis. instr. NSF program Notre Dame U., South Bend, Ind.; data stream instr., adv. Am. Meteorol. Data Stream Project. Contbr. numerous articles to profl. jours.; writer, coord., dir., editor tng. videos tornado Climatology, 1981, NOAA Weather Radio—Operation and Maintenance, 1981, AFOS Crash—Degraded Mode Operation, 1982; prodr. video Station Workshop on the Recent Developments in Model Output Statistics and Perfect Prognosis Techniques, 1987; exec. prodr. NEXRAD Precursor Module—NEXRAD Hydrometeorological Processing, 1990. Mem. Am. Meteorol. Soc. (bd. sch. and popular meteorol. and oceanographic edn., contbg. editor operational terms Glossary of Meteorology), Am. Geophys. Union. Home: 19622 Enterprise Way Montgomery Village MD 20886

ROBINSON, HERBERT HENRY, III, educator, psychotherapist; b. Leavenworth, Wash., Mar. 31, 1933; s. Herbert Henry II and Alberta (Sperber) R.; m. Georgia Murial Jones, Nov. 24, 1954 (div. 1974); children: Cheri Dean Asbury, David Keith, Peri Elizabeth Layton, Tanda Rene Graff, Gaila Daire. Grad. of Theology, Bapt. Bible Coll., 1959; BA in Philosophy/Greek, Whitworth Coll., 1968; MA in Coll. Teaching, Ea. Wash. U., 1976; postgrad., Gonzaga U., 1980—. Cert. psychotherapist, perpetrator treatment program supervision; nat. bd. cert. counselor. Choir dir. Twin City Bapt. Temple, Mishawaka, Ind., 1959-61; min. Inland Empire Bapt. Ch., Spokane, 1961-73; tchr. philosophy Spokane (Wash.) C.C., 1969-72; dir. Alternatives to Violence, Women in Crisis, Fairbanks, Alaska, 1985-87; tchr. pub. rels. U. Alaska, 1986-87; dir. Alternatives to Violence Men Inc., Juneau, 1988-89; tchr. leadership mgmt. U. Alaska S.E., 1988-89; min. Sci. of Mind Ctr., Sandpoint, Idaho, 1989-92; dir., therapist Tapio Counseling Ctr., Spokane, 1991—; cert. psychotherapist, supr. perpetrator treatment program Wash. Cons. Lilac Blind/Alpha Inc./Marshall Coll., Spokane, 1975-85, Alaska Placer Mining Co., Fairbanks, 1987; tchr. Spokane Falls C.C., Spokane, 1979-85; seminar, presenter Human Resource Devel., Spokane and Seattle, Wash., Pa., 1980; guest trainer United Way/Kellogg Found. Inst. for Volunteerism, Spokane, 1983. 1st trombone San Diego Marine Band, 1953-56, Spokane Symphony, 1961; bd. dirs. Tanani Learning Ctr., Fairbanks, 1987; mem. consensus bldg. team Sci. of Mind Ctr., Sandpoint, 1989-92. Cpl. USMC, 1953-56. Mem. ACA, Assn. for Humanistic Edn. and Devel., Assn. for Religious Values in Counseling, Internat. Assn. Addictions and Offender Counselors, Internat. Assn. Marriage and Family Counselors, Am. Assn. Profl. Hypnotherapists, Masterson Inst. Office: Tapio Counseling 5325 E Sprague Ave Spokane WA 99212-0820

ROBINSON, HOBART KRUM, management consulting company executive; b. Quincy, Mass., Oct. 8, 1937; s. Hobart Krum and Charlotte Elizabeth (Hall) R.; m. Gerd Ingela Janhede, Oct. 17, 1964; children: Steven Whitney, Karina Jill, Peter Danforth. BA, Williams Coll., 1959; MBA, Columbia U., 1964. Market analyst Mobil Chem. Co., Richmond, Va., 1964-67; mgr. program analysis and control Polaroid Corp., Cambridge, Mass., 1967-69; exec. v.p., dir. Simplex Wire and Cable, Inc., North Berwick, Maine, 1969-73; sr. engagement mgr. McKinsey and Co., Inc., N.Y.C., 1973-76, prin. Copenhagen, 1977-81, N.Y.C., 1985-89, Stockholm, 1989-95, dir. adminstrn. Eastern Europe, 1993-95, dir. adminstrn. N.Y.C., 1995-98; pres., CEO Brink's Inc., Darien, Conn., 1981-84; ret., 1998. Dir. Burlington No. Air Freight, Inc., Newport Beach, Calif., 1982-84. Pres. Am. Club in Copenhagen, 1980-81; dir. Fulbright Commn., Copenhagen, 1980-81; vice chair Williams Coll. Alumni Fund, 1999—. Lt. USNR, 1959-62. Mem. Innis Arden Golf Club (Old Greenwich, Conn.) (gov. 1982-87, prse. 1986-87), Tournament Players Club (Ponte Vedra, Fla.), Taconic Golf Club (Williamstown, Mass.), Sky Club (N.Y.C.), Marsh Landing Country Club (Ponte Vedra, Fla.), Sawgrass Country Club (Ponte Vedra). Republican. Episcopalian. Home: 94 Ide Rd Williamstown MA 01267-2815 Home Fax: 413-458-1787. E-mail: bartrobin@aol.com.

ROBINSON, HOWARD NEIL, plastic surgeon; b. St. Louis, June 5, 1946; s. William S. and Adaline S. Robinson; m. Jeantte Shatkin, Dec. 18, 1976; children: Dallas, Amanda, Dustin. AB, St. Louis U., 1968, MD, 1972. Diplomate Am. Bd. Plastic Surgery. Resident gen. surgery U. Fla., 1972-74, St. John's Mercy Med. Ctr., St. Louis, 1974-76, burn fellow, 1976-77; resident plastic surgery U. Ill., 1977-79; pres. Howard N. Robinson, M.D., P.A., Pembroke Pines, Fla., 1980—. Author: (with others) Looseleaf Textbook of Surgery, 1976; contbr. articles to profl. jours. Mem. Am. Soc. Plastic Surgeons, Am. Soc. Aesthetic Plastic Surgeons, Lipoplasty Soc. N.Am., Fla. Soc. Plastic Surgeons, Grtr. Miami Soc. Plastic Surgeons (pres. 1994-95), Broward County Soc. Plastic Surgeons (pres. 1990-91). Republican. Office: 601 N Flamingo Rd Ste 317 Pembroke Pines FL 33028-1011 E-mail: HRobin1014@aol.com.

ROBINSON, HUGH GRANVILLE, consulting management company executive; b. Washington, Aug. 4, 1932; s. James Hill and Wilhelmina (Thomas) R.; 1 stepchild, Mia; children by previous marriage: Hugh Granville, Susan K. Student, Williams Coll., 1949-50; BS, U.S. Mil. Acad., 1954; MS, MIT, 1959; LLD, Williams Coll., 1983. Commd. 2d lt. U.S. Army, 1954, advanced through grades to maj. gen., 1983; platoon leader, co. comdr. Co. B, 185th Engrs. Bn., Korea, 1955; platoon leader, ops. officer 74th Engr. Co., Korea, 1955-56; br. chief Engr. Supply Control Office, St. Louis, 1956-58; chief Catalog and Authorization div. Engr. Supply Control Agy., Orleans, France, 1960-62; co. comdr. 553d Engr. Bn., Orleans, 1962-63; chief combat br. War Plans divsn. Engr. Strategic Studies Group, Washington, 1963-65; Army asst. to armed forces aide to Pres., 1965-69; comdr. 39th Engr. Bn., Vietnam, 1969-70; br. chief war plans divsn. Office Dep. Chief Staff for Ops., Washington, 1970-71; assigned Nat. War Coll., 1972; comdr. 3rd regt. U.S. Corps Cadets, West Point, N.Y., 1973-74, U.S. Army Engr. Sch. Brigade, Fort Belvoir, Va., 1974-76; dist. engr. U.S. Army Engr. Dist., L.A., 1976-78; dep. dir. civil works office Chief of Engrs., Washington, 1978-80; comdr. Southwestern Divsn., U.S. Army C.E., 1980-83; ret., 1983; v.p. Southland Corp., Dallas, 1983-88; pres. Cityplace Devel. Corp.; sr. v.p. Grigsby Brandford Powell, Inc., 1988-94; now chmn., CEO The Tetra Group, Inc., Dallas, 1989—. Mem. Mississippi River Commn., 1980-83, bd. engrs. for rivers and harbors, 1980-83, Coastal Engring. Rsch. Bd., 1980-83; bd. dirs. Circuit City Stores, Inc., Guaranty Bank, IMCO Recycling; chmn. Dallas Fed. Res. Bd., 1991; adv. bd. TXU; with Tex. Pub. Broadcasting, LBJ Found., 1989—. Mem. nat. bd. dirs. Keep Am. Beautiful, 1981-85; bd. dirs. Dallas Symphony, 1981-85, Dallas United Way, 1984-92, Baylor U. Med. Ctr. Found., 1983-91, Dallas Opera, 1983-90, Dallas Citizens Coun., 1987-91, Greater Dallas C. of C., 1986-91, Vietnam Vets Meml. Fund Tex.; chmn. African Am. Mus., Dallas Youth Svcs. Corp.; trustee Dallas Mus. Fine Arts, 1988-93; mem. adv. coun. U. Tex. Engring. Fedn., 1991—. Mem. Am. Soc. Mil. Engrs. (past sec. Orleans chpt., regional v.p. Tex., pres. Dallas chpt.), Assn. U.S. Army, Dallas Black C. of C., ASCE Methodist. Office: The Tetra Group Inc 2501 Oak Lawn Ave Ste 201 Dallas TX 75219

ROBINSON, HUGH R. retired marketing executive; b. Syracuse, N.Y., Sept. 18, 1922; s. Frank J. and Gladys (Hunt) R.; m. Evelyn De Mattia, Nov. 24, 1949; children: Susan, Hugh R., Patrice. BS, Syracuse U., 1949. Dist. mgr. Syracuse China, 1949-59; with Royal Worcester Porcelain Co., N.Y.C., 1959-77, v.p. sales, 1971-75, pres., 1975-76, Royal Worcester Spode, Inc., 1977, Lance Internat., N.Y.C., 1977-84; v.p., dir. Caithness Glass Inc., 1980-84; v.p. sales amnd mktg. Weil Ceramics & Glass Inc., 1985-86, CEO, exec. v.p., 1986-88; CEO LLadro U.S.A. Inc., 1988-91; v.p. Lladro Realty, Inc., 1988-94, Lladro Galleries, Inc., 1988-94; retired, 1994. Advisor Lladro Group, Valencia, Spain, 1991-97; cons. in giftware industry. Served with USAAF, 1942-46. Mem. Alumni Assn. Syracuse U. Home: 4723 61st Avenue Dr W Bradenton FL 34210-4029

ROBINSON, HURLEY, surgeon; b. L.A., Feb. 25, 1925; s. Edgar Ray and Nina Madge (Hurley) R.; m. Mary Anne Rusche, Mar. 14, 1953; children: Kathleen Ann Robinson Petschke, Mary Elizabeth, Lynda Jean Robinson Lamb, William Hurley, Patricia Kay Robinson Hardy, Paul Edgar. Student, U. Calif., Berkeley, 1943, U. Calif., Santa Barbara, 1946-48; BS, Northwestern U., 1950, MD, 1952. Diplomate Am. Bd. Surgery. Intern Wesley Meml. Hosp., Chgo., 1952-53; resident in gen. surgery Milw. County Hosp., 1953-57; surgeon Abbott Med. Group, Ontario, Calif., 1957-59; pvt. practice Upland, 1959-64; ptnr. Robinson & Schechter Surg. Med. Group, 1964-92. Instr. dept. surgery San Bernardino County Med. Ctr., San Bernardino, Calif., 1959-79; sr. surg. staff San Antonio Cmty. Hosp., Upland, 1958—, trustee, 1979-81, pres. med. staff, 1980; mem. staff Pomona (Calif.) Valley Med. Ctr.; exec. com. San Bernardino (Calif.) County Med. Ctr., 1974, adv. bd., 1974; clin. asst. vascular surgery The London Hosp., 1973; cons. in field. Contbr. articles to Wis. Med. Jour. Chmn. troop com., camp dr. Boy Scouts Am., Upland, 1970-72. With U.S. Army, 1943-46. Fellow ACS, Am. Coll. Chest Physicians, Am. Coll. Angiology; mem. AMA, Am. Med. Soc. Vienna, Calif. Med. Assn., San Bernardino County Med. Soc., Tri-County Surg. Soc. So. Calif. (pres.), Pan-Pacific Surgical Assn., Soc. Clin. Vascular Surgery, L.A. Surg. Soc. Republican. Presbyterian. Office: 124 Garnet Ave Newport Beach CA 92662-1009

ROBINSON, IRWIN JAY, lawyer; b. Bay City, Mich., Oct. 8, 1928; s. Robert R. and Anne (Kaplan) R.; m. Janet Binder, July 7, 1957; children: Elizabeth Binder Schubiner, Jonathan Meyer, Eve Kimberly Wiener. AB, U. Mich., 1950; JD, Columbia U., 1953. Bar: N.Y. 1956. Assoc. Breed Abbott & Morgan, N.Y.C., 1955-58; asst. to ptnrs. Dreyfus & Co., 1958-59; assoc. Greenbaum Wolff & Ernst, 1959-65, ptnr., 1966-76; sr. ptnr. Rosenman & Colin, N.Y.C., 1976-90; of counsel Pryor, Cashman, Sherman & Flynn, 1990-92; sr. ptnr. Phillips, Nizer, Benjamin, Krim & Ballon, N.Y.C., 1992-99; pvt. practice, 1999—. Treas. Saarsteel, Inc., Whitestone, N.Y., 1970—. Bd. dirs. Henry St. Settlement, N.Y.C., 1960-85, Jewish Cmty. Ctr. Assn. N.Am., N.Y.C., 1967-94, mem. adv. bd., 1998—; bd. dirs. Heart Rsch. Found., 1989-94, pres., 1991-93. Mem. ABA, N.Y. State Bar Assn., Assn. Bar City of N.Y., Internat. Bar Assn., Thai-Am. C. of C. (founder, bd. dirs. 1992-95, pres. 1992-95), Vietnam-Am. C. of C. (founder, bd. dirs. 1992-95, pres. 1992-95), Philippine-Am. C. of C. (bd. dirs. 1960-98), Sunningdale Country Club, The Desert Mountain Club. Jewish. Home: 4622 Grosvenor Ave Bronx NY 10471-3305 Office: care Kramer Levin Naftalis & Frankel 919 3d Ave 40th Fl New York NY 10022-3902 E-mail: ijrjbr@aol.com.

ROBINSON, JACK ALBERT, retail drug stores executive; b. Detroit, Feb. 26, 1930; s. Julius and Fannie (Aizkowitz) R.; m. Aviva Freedman, Dec. 21, 1952; children: Shelby, Beth, Abigail. B in Pharmacy, Wayne State U., 1952. Founder, chief exec. officer, chmn. bd. Perry Drug Stores, Inc., Pontiac, Mich., 1957-95; founder, chmn., pres. JAR Group LLC, Bloomfield, 1996. Former bd. dirs. Riser Foods, Inc.; former corp. dir. R & B Inc. Chmn. Wayne State U. Fund, Detroit, 1986, Concerned Citizens for the Arts in Mich., 1990, 91—; chmn. ann. fund Detroit Symphony Orch.; bd. dirs. United Way of Pontiac, Mich., 1986, United Found. of Detroit, 1986, Pontiac Area Urban League, Cmty. Found., S.E. Mich., Detroit Svc. Group, Save Orch. Hall, Inc., Cranbrook Inst. Sci., Jewish Fedn. Apts., Wetzman Inst. Sci., Holocaust Meml. Ctr., Harper-Grace Hosp., Detroit; past dir. Pontiac Symphony Boys Club, Detroit Osteo. Hosp.; pres. United Jewish Found. Met. Detroit, 1992, Greater Detroit Interfaith Round Table NCCJ, 1994-95, co-chmn., 1992; pres. Jewish Fedn. Met. Detroit, 1992-94. Recipient Disting. Alumni award Wayne State U. Coll. Pharmacy, 1975, Eleanor Roosevelt Humanities award from State of Israel, 1978, B'nai B'rith Youth Svcs. Am. Tradition award, 1982, Wayne State U. Disting. Alumni award, 1985, Tree of Life award Jewish Nat. Fund, 1985, Disting. Citizen award Pontiac Boy Scouts Am., 1985, Corp. Leadership award Wayne State U., 1985, Booker T. Washington Bus. Assn. Brotherhood award, 1986, Humanitarian award March of Dimes, 1987, award Weizmann Rsch. Inst., 1987, Humanitarian award Variety Club, 1988, Fred M. Butzel award Jewish Fedn. Met. Detroit, 1991, B'nai B'rith Great Am. Traditions award, 1991, Cmty. Svc. award Am. Arabic and Jewish Friends, 1995, Outstanding Philanthropic award Nat. Soc. Fundraising Execs., 1999, Mich. Hall of Fame award in Real Estate and Retailing, Internat. Coun. Shopping Ctrs., 2001; named Entrepreneur of Yr. Harvard U. Bus. Sch., Detroit, 1982. Mem.: Econ. Club (bd. dirs. Detroit chpt.), Am. Found. for Pharm. Edn. (bd. dirs.), Am. Pharm. Assn., Nat. Assn. Chain Drug Stores (chmn. 1987, Lifetime Achievement award 1995, Robert B. Begley award 1995). Avocations: skiing, jogging, photography, classical music, glass collecting. Office: JAR Group LLC Ste 330 38500 N Woodward Ave Bloomfield Hills MI 48304-2961

ROBINSON, JACK FAY, clergyman; b. Wilmington, Mass., Mar. 7, 1914; s. Thomas P. and Ethel Lincoln (Fay) R.; m. Eleanor Jean Smith, Sept. 1, 1937 (dec. 1966); 1 child, Alice Virginia Dungey; m. Lois Henze, July 16, 1968; stepchildren: Susan Bently, Cynthia Berkeley, Charles Henze. AB, Mont. State U., 1936; BD, Crozer Theol. Sem., 1939; AM, U. Chgo., 1949, postgrad., 1950-52. Ordained to ministry Bapt. Ch., 1939. Min. Bethany Ch., American Falls, Idaho, 1939-41, 1st Ch., Council Grove, Kans., 1944-49; ordained (transfer) to ministry Congl. Ch., 1945; min. United Ch., Chebanse, Ill., 1949-52, 1st Ch., Argo, 1954-58, Congl. Ch., St. Charles, 1958-64; assoc. min. Plymouth Congl. Ch., Lansing, Mich., 1964-66; tchr. Chgo. Pub. Schs., 1966-68; min. Waveland Ave. Congl. Ch., Chgo., 1967-79; interim pastor Chgo. Met. Assn. Interim pastor United Ch. of Christ, First Congl. Ch., Des Plaines, Ill., 1979, Bethany United Ch., Chgo., 1980, Eden United Ch. of Christ, Chgo., 1983-84, St. Nicolai Ch., Chgo., 1984, Grace United Ch. of Christ, Chgo., 1985-86, Christ Ch. of Chgo., 1987, First Congl., Evanston, Ill., 1987-88, First Congl. Ch., Brookfield, Ill., 1988-89, Steger, Ill., 1990-91, Berwyn, Ill., 1992, Immanual United Ch. of Christ, Streamwood, Ill., 1993, Immanuel United Ch. of Christ, Bartlett, 1994; assoc. pastor, calling min. of visitation People's Ch., Chgo., 1990-93; hist. cons. Bell & Howell Co., Chgo., 1981-82; coord. Inst. Cont. Learning Roosevelt U., 1998—. Author: The Growth of the Bible, 1969, From A Mission to a Church, 1976, Bell & Howell Company: A 75 Year History, 1982; co-author: Harza: 65 Years, 1986, History of the Illinois Conference, United Church of Christ, 1990. Assoc. Hyde Park dept. Chgo. YMCA, 1942-44, U. Chgo. Libr., 1952-54; chmn. com. evangelism Kans. Congl. Christian Conf., 1947-48; city chmn. Layman's Missionary Movement, 1946-49; trustee Congl. and Christian Conf. Ill., v.p., 1963-64; mem. exec. coun. Chgo. Met. Assn. United Ch. of Christ, 1968-70, sec. ch. and ministry com., 1982-88; mem. gen. bd. Ch. Fedn. Greater Chgo., 1969-71; mem. Libr. Bd. Coun. Grove, 1945-49; dean Northside Mission Coun. United Ch. of Christ, 1975-77, sec. pers. com. Ill. Conf. United Ch. of Christ, 1986-88; bd. dirs. Tri-Village United Way, 1996—; coord. Inst. Continued Learning Roosevelt U., Schaumburg, Ill., 1998—. Mem. Chgo. Coun. Fgn. Rels. Recipient Pres.' award Congl. Christian Hist. Soc. Home: 321 E Morse Ave Bartlett IL 60103-4168

ROBINSON, JAMES D., III, corporate executive, investor; b. Atlanta, Nov. 19, 1935; m. Bettye Bradley (div.); 4 children; m. Linda Gosden, 1984. BS, Ga. Inst. Tech., 1957; MBA, Harvard U., 1961. Officer various depts. Morgan Guaranty Trust Co. of N.Y., N.Y.C., 1961-66, asst. v.p., staff asst. to chmn. bd. and pres., 1967-68; gen. ptnr. White, Weld & Co., 1968-70; exec. v.p. Am. Express Co., N.Y.C., 1970-75, pres., dir., 1975-77, chmn. bd. dirs., CEO, 1977-93. Pres., CEO Am. Express Internat. Banking Corp., 1970-73; chair Am. Express Credit Corp., 1973-75; co-founder, gen. ptnr. RRE Ventures, 1994—; chmn., CEO RRE Investors LLC; bd. dirs. Coca Cola Co., Bristol-Myers Squibb Co., Novell, Inc., First Data Corp., Screaming Media Inc.; chair Violy Byorum & Ptnrs. Holdings; former co-chair Bus. Roundtable. Author: Inflation Overkill, 1994, Full Steam Ahead, 2000. Active Bus. Coun., Coun. on Fgn. Rels., U.S. Japan Bus. Coun., Dean's Adv. Coun. Roberto C. Goizueta Sch. Bus. Emory U., Exec. Adv. Bd., Ivan Allen Coll.; hon. co-chair bd. Meml. Sloan-Kettering Cancer Ctr., former chair bds. of overseers and mgrs. Meml. Sloan-Kettering Cancer Ctr.; hon. mem. The Brookings Instn.; mem. bd. dirs. Nat. Acad. Found.; mem. Pres.' Cir. The Asia Soc.; bd. dirs., chair emeritus N.Y.C. Partnership and C. of C., Inc.; chair emeritus World Travel & Tourism Coun.; former chair Internat. Trade and Investment Task Force of the Bus. Roundtable, former chair svcs. policy adv. com.; former chmn. adv. com. on trade and policy negotiations United Way of Am.; former mem. Coun. on Competitiveness; former trustee Alfred P. Sloan Found. mem. Dewitt Wallace Found. Lt. USNR, 1957-59. Mem. Japan Soc. (bd. dirs.), Econ. Club (N.Y.C.). Office: RRE Ventures 126 E 56th St Fl 22 New York NY 10022-3613

ROBINSON, JAMES ALFRED, retired educator; b. Phila., May 13, 1939; s. James Alfred Sr. and Evelyn (Perry) R.; children: James, John, Marge Robinson Balais; m. Gladys Acaba, Mar. 9, 1996. BS, Cheyney (Pa.) U., 1961; postgrad., Temple U., 1966-68, Goddard Coll., 1989-90, C.C. Phila., 1989. Middle sch. tchr. Phila. Pub. Sch. System, 1962-95. Chmn. J.A. Robinson Assocs. Video Prodn. Cons., Phila., 1988—; video prodn. cons. In Search of History:The Underground Railroad, History channel, 1999; video documentarian. Media arts fellow Mid-Atlantic region Pitts. Filmmakers NEA, Pa. Coun. for Arts, 1993. Mem. HTML Writers Guild. Baptist. Avocations: photography, music, tennis.

ROBINSON, JAMES ARTHUR, policy scientist; b. Blackwell, Okla., June 9, 1932; s. William L. and Ethel Bell (Hicks) R.; children: Adelaide, Luke. AB, George Washington U., 1954, DPS (hon.), 1977; MA, U. Okla., 1955; PhD, Northwestern U., 1957. Congl. fellow Am. Polit. Sci. Assn., 1957-58; Instr. polit. sci. Northwestern U., 1958-59, asst. prof., 1959-62, assoc. prof., 1962-64; prof. polit. sci. Ohio State U., Columbus, 1964-71; dir. Mershon Center, 1967-70, v.p. acad. affairs, provost, 1969-71; pres., prof. polit. sci. Macalester Coll., St. Paul, 1971-74; pres. U. West Fla., Pensacola, 1974-88, pres. emeritus, 1988—, Regents prof., 1988—. Author: (with R. C. Snyder) National and International Decision Making, 1961, Congress and Foreign Policy Making, rev. edit, 1967, House Rules Committee, 1963, (with J. Baum) Party Primaries in Taiwan, 1999, (with D. Brown and E. Moon) Appraising Steps in Democratization: Elections in Taiwan, 1986-2000, 2000. Congl. fellow Am. Polit. Sci. Assn., 1957-58. Mem.: Cosmos (Washington).

ROBINSON, JAMES LEROY, architect, educator, developer; b. July 12, 1940; s. Willie LeRoy and Ruby Nell Robinson; m. Martha Robinson; children: James LeRoy II, Kerstin Gunilla, Maria Theresa Narvaez, Jasmin Marisol, Ruby Nell, Kenneth Arne. BArch, So. U., 1964; MCP, Pratt Inst., 1972. Arch. Pt. of N.Y. Authority, 1964; arch., store planner W.T. Grant, 1964; with Herbst & Rusciano, AIA, 1965; arch. Carson, Lundin & Shaw, N.Y.C., 1966, Kennerly, Slomanson & Smith, N.Y.C., 1967-69, arch.-on-bus., 1969; pres. Robinson Archs., P.C., 1969—. V.p. J&K Constrn. Cons., Inc.; vis. prof. CUNY; adj. prof. Pratt Inst. Prin. works include Stuyvesant Heights Christian Ch., David Chavis House, Fulton Ct. Houses, Sinclair Houses, Hamilton Heights Terr., Eliot Graham Houses, Sojourner Truth Houses, Nehemiah Plan, Casas Theresa, N.Y.C. Postal Data Ctr., Mt. Carmel Bapt. Ch., Consol. Edison Collection Ctr., Jasmin Houses, CityHomes CD&E, The Promenade, Gore Residence & Tse Residence. Bd. dirs. Boys Club Am. With U.S. Army, 1966. Decorated knight Order of St. John, Knight of Malta; recipient AIA Design award, 1976; Martin Luther King fellow Pratt Inst., 1972. Mem. Am. Arbitrators Assn. (arbitrator), N.Y. Coun. Black Archs. Democrat. Address: 55C DeLancey St New York NY 10002-2804 E-mail: jackrabbit85@hotmail.com.

ROBINSON, JAMES R. medicare auditor; b. Columbia, SC, Dec. 10, 1973; BS in acctg., U. SC, 1995—98, BS in fin., 2000. Asst. sr. auditor Palmetto Goverment Benefits Adminstr., Columbia, SC, 1998—2002. Named Eagle Scout, Boy Scouts of Am., 1989. Home: PO Box 5098 Columbia SC 20250 Personal E-mail: originalacctant@yahoo.com.

ROBINSON, JAMES WILLIAM, retired management consultant; b. Bklyn., Feb. 22, 1919; s. Charles Edward and Adelaide (Reimer) R.; m. Dorothy L. Luckow, July 5, 1946; 1 child, Joan Barbara. AB, Cornell U., 1940, LLB, 1942. Bar: N.Y. 1942. Assoc. atty. Whitman, Ransom & Coulson, 1946-57; with Westvaco Corp., N.Y.C., 1957-69, sec., 1966-69; prin., mng. dir. Georgeson & Co. Inc., 1969-82; mng. dir. Morrow & Co., 1982-90; pres. J.W. Robinson Assocs., Inc., Gig Harbor, Wash., 1990—. Mem. adv. com. shareholder comms. SEC; com. on shareowner comms. N.Y. Stock Exch., 1986-92. Editor: Tender Offers Handbook, Proxy Rules Handbook. Capt. AUS, 1942-46. Decorated Bronze (V) Star medal. Mem. ABA, N.Y. State Bar Assn., Assn. Bar City N.Y., Am. Soc. Corp. Secs., Canterwood Country Club, Phi Delta Phi, Lambda Chi Alpha. Home and Office: 4820 Old Stump Dr NW Gig Harbor WA 98332-8899

ROBINSON, JAY (JAY THURSTON ROBINSON), artist; b. Detroit, Aug. 1, 1915; s. Carter Boston and Marie Rose (Steger) R.; m. Dorothy June Whipple, Sept. 15, 1937 (dec. 1968); children: Theodore Carter, Thomas

Whipple, James Jay; m. Anne Frances Helen Posch, Nov. 5, 1970 (dec. 1999). BA, Yale U., 1937; MFA, Cranbrook Acad. Art, 1943. One-man shows include, Guggenheim Mus. Non-Objective Painting, N.Y.C., 1947, Milch Galleries, N.Y.C., 1948, 51, 53, 54, 55, 56, J.B. Speed Art Mus., Louisville, 1953, Dayton Art Inst., 1953, Phila. Art Alliance, 1957, Monede Gallery, N.Y.C., 1961, 62, Raymond Burr Galleries, Beverly Hills, Calif., 1963, xxth Century West Gallery, N.Y.C., 1968, E. Kuhlik Gallery, N.Y.C., 1971, New Canaan Soc. for Arts, 1983, Broome St. Gallery, N.Y.C., 1994, group shows include, Guggenheim Mus., 1947, 49, Carnegie Inst., Pitts., 1949, Des Moines Art Center, 1950, Butler Inst., Youngstown, Ohio, 1953, also Audubon Artists, N.Y.C., Corcoran Gallery, Washington, Mich. Artists, Detroit, NAD, N.Y.C., Pa. Acad., Phila., Provincetown (Mass.) Annual, Va. Biennial, Richmond; represented in permanent collections, including, Detroit Inst. Art, Houston Mus. Fine Art, Witte Meml. Mus., San Antonio, Philbrook Art Center, Tulsa; Berea Coll., Goucher Coll., Fisk U.; represented also in corp. collections, including, IBM; Republic Steel Co., Bristol-Myers Squibb, portrait painter, designer china and textiles; illustrator: Seventeenth Summer (Maureen Daly), 1948, The New York Guide Book, 1964; contbr. illustrations to other books. Served with OSS, 1943; Served with USN, 1943-46. Louis Comfort Tiffany Found. award, 1950; various purchase awards Am. Acad. Arts and Letters, 1951-64; Outstanding Alumnus award Detroit Country Day Sch., 1966 Home: 305 E Landing Williamsburg VA 23185-8254 *I have always been drawn to the theme of Man in His Environment. By extension to our own, I love jazz music, many of whose players I have painted; classic cars; Japanese gardens; good company and active social life. Travel enables me to see what others have done and are doing.*

ROBINSON, JEANNE LOUISE, lecturer, writer; b. Portland, Oreg., Sept. 12, 1946; d. Louis Darell and Mary Louise (Lane) Gentry; m. Gini Mario Martini, June 13, 1965 (div. 1968); children: Deborah Corinna Martini, Darell James Martini; m. Joseph Ira Robinson, Dec. 5, 1998. Student, Northwestern Coll. Bus., Portland, 1968, Mt. Hood Community Coll., Gresham, Oreg., 1986. Receptionist, sec. to pres. Met. Printing Co., Portland, 1969-73; adminstrv. asst. Lifespring, Inc., 1974-77; cons. Jeanne Mort Co., Boring, Oreg., 1978-80; office mgr. Beef Palace Provisioners, Gresham, 1980-82; bus. cons. Boring, 1983-90; owner Good As New Doll Hosp., 1990-92; adminstrv. projects mgr. Profl. Svc. Industries, Portland, 1992-98; treatment sec. River-Bend Youth Ctr., 1999—2002. Co-compiler: Lebanon Pioneer Cemetery, 1991, rev. edit. 1995, Visitors' Guide to Oregon Historic Cemeteries, 1999. Apptd. to Oreg. Pioneer Cemetery Commn., 1995 (chair, 1995-99). Mem. Geneal. Coun. Orgn. (sec. 1991-94), Fellowship of Brethren Genealogists, Geneal. Forum of Oreg., Ind. Geneal. Soc. (charter), Oreg. Hist. Cemeteries Assn. (pres. 1992-96, exec. dir. 1997-2002), Lebanon Geneal. Soc. Avocation: genealogy. Home: 16385 SE 232nd Dr Boring OR 97009-8179 E-mail: ohca@integrity.com.

ROBINSON, JENNIFER LYNN, nursing educator; b. Washington, Dec. 28, 1958; d. John and Jennie (Mucha) Robinson. Diploma, Washington Hosp. Sch. Nursing, 1979; BSN, Wheeling Jesuit Coll., 1990; MSN with clin. specialty in cardiopulmonary nursing, U. Pitts., 1995. RN, Pa.; CCRN. Med.-surg. staff nurse Washington Hosp., 1979-83, nurse trainer med. info. sys., 1983, staff nurse CCU, 1984-86, asst. nurse mgr. CCU, 1986-91, instr. critical care class, 1990—, nurse educator, 1991—. ACLS instr. Washington Hosp. Mem.: AACN, Washington Hosp. Sch. Nursing Assn., Alpha Sigma Nu, Alpha Sigma Lambda, Sigma Theta Tau, Nat. Honor Soc. Nurses. Office: Washington Hosp Sch Nursing 155 Wilson Ave Washington PA 15301-3336 E-mail: sonlib@pulsenet.com.

ROBINSON, JOE SAM, neurosurgeon; b. Atlanta, July 21, 1945; s. Joe Sam and Nell (Mixon) R.; m. Elizabeth Ann Moate, Apr. 3, 1982; children: Joe Sam III, Edward Richard, Thomas McRae. AB cum laude, Harvard Coll., 1967; MD, U. Va., 1971; MS, Northwestern U., 1975. Surg. intern Emory U., 1971-72, resident in surgery, 1972-73; resident in neurosurgery Northwestern U., 1973-78; instr. U. Ill., 1978-79, Yale U., 1979-81; pres. Ga. Neurosurg. Inst. P.A., Macon, 1981—. Prof., chief neurosurgery Mercer U. Sch. Medicine, Macon, 1986; chief surgery Med. Ctr. Ctrl. Ga., Macon, 1989—, vice chmn. surgery, 1991-97, chmn. dept. surgery, 1996—; vis. neurosurgeon China, 1992, Konaus Acad. Neurosurgery Inst., Lithuania, 1992; clin. prof. Med. Coll. Ga., 2002. Lt. col. USANG, 1972-95. Fellow Internat. Coll. Surgeons (vice regent 1983-93); mem. Am. Assn. Neurol. Surgeons, Congress Neurol. Surgeons, AAAS, Ga. Neurosurg. Soc., Alpha Omega Alpha. Republican. Methodist. Office: Ga Neurosurg Inst PA 840 Pine St Ste 880 Macon GA 31201-7525

ROBINSON, JOHN WILLIAM, IV, lawyer; b. Atlanta, Apr. 29, 1950; s. J. William III and Elizabeth (Smith) R.; m. Ellen Showalter, Dec. 28, 1976; children: William, Anna. BA with honors, Washington & Lee U., 1972; JD, U. Ga., 1975. Bar: Fla., Ga., U.S. Dist. Ct. (no., so. and mid. dists.) Fla., U.S. Ct. Mil. Appeals, U.S. Ct. Appeals (5th and 11th cirs.), U.S. Supreme Ct.; cert. labor & employment law, civil trial and bus. litigation lawyer, Fla., Nat. Bd. Trial Advocacy. Trial atty. Nat. Labor Rels. Bd., New Orleans, 1975-76; trial def. counsel 8th infantry U.S. Army, Mainz, Germany, 1977-78, trial counsel 8th infantry Germany, 1979; law clerk, commr. Ct. Mil. Review, Washington, 1980; atty. Fowler, White, Boggs & Banker, PA, Tampa, Fla., 1980—, head labor and employment law dept., 1993—, dir., 1998—, sec./treas, ops. com., 2001—. Mem. faculty U. Md., 1977-79; arbitrator U.S. Dist. Ct. (mid. dist.) Fla. Editor-in-chief: Employment & Labor Relations Law, 1991-95; editor: Developing Labor Law, 1982—, Model Jury Instructions for Employment Litigation, 1994—; editor: Employment Litigation Handbook, 1998. Chmn. Tampa Bay Internat. Trade Coun., 1990-91, Rough Riders Dist. Boy Scouts Am., 1990; legal counsel Drug Free Workplace Task Force, 1999-00, Greater Tampa C. of C., 1996, gen. counsel, bd. dirs., 1999—. Capt. U.S. Army, 1976-80. Named one of Best Lawyers in Am. for labor and employment law. Mem. ABA (divsn. dir. 1996-2000, chmn. employment and labor rels. com. 1993-96, litigation sect., mem. coun., chmn. com. on multijurisdictional practice 2000—), Fla. Bar Assn. (chmn. labor and employment law sect. 1992-93), Wash. & Lee U. Bd. (pres. nat. alumni bd. 1990-91, trustee 1995—), Rotary (pres. Tampa Bay chpt.), Am. Inn of Ct. (pres., dir. and barrister). Avocations: tennis, history. Office: Fowler White Boggs Banker PA 501 E Kennedy Blvd Tampa FL 33602-5237

ROBINSON, JOHN ALAN, logic and computer science educator; b. Halifax, Eng., Mar. 9, 1930; came to U.S., 1952; naturalized citizen, 1990. s. Harry and Clara (Pilkington) R.; m. Gwen Groves, Dec. 18, 1954; children: Alan Groves, Hugh Parke Custis, Gwen Owen. BA in Classics with honours, Corpus Christi Coll., Cambridge (Eng.) U., 1952; MA, 1955; MA in Philosophy, U. Ore., 1953; MA, Princeton, 1963, PhD, 1956; D in Applied Sci. honoris causa, Leuven, 1988; D in Philosophy honoris causa, Uppsala, 1994. Operations research analyst E.I. du Pont de Nemours & Co., Inc., 1956-60; post-doctoral research fellow U. Pitts., 1960-61; mem. faculty Rice U., 1961-67, prof. philosophy, 1964-65, prof. computer sci. and philosophy, 1965-66, prof. computer sci., 1966-67; disting. prof. logic and computer sci. Syracuse U., 1967-84, Univ. prof., 1984-92, univ. prof. emeritus, 1993—. Cons. in applied math. divsn. Argonne Nat. Lab., 1961-67, Stanford Linear Acceleration Ctr., 1966-68; vis. rsch. fellow Australian Nat. U., 1989; Fujitsu vis. prof. U. Tokyo, 1991-92. Author: Logic: Form and Function, 1979; founder, editor-in-chief Jour. Logic Programming, 1984-86; contbr. articles to profl. jours. Served with RAF, 1948-49. Recipient Sr. U.S. Scientists prize Humboldt Found., 1995, Herbrand award, 1996; Guggenheim Found. fellow, 1967-68; hon. rsch. fellow U. Edinburgh, 1967—. Fellow Am. Assn. for Artificial Intelligence; mem. Kokusai Bunka Kaikan (Tokyo). Home and Office: 96 Highland Ave Greenfield MA 01301-3606

ROBINSON, JOHN BECKWITH, development management consultant; b. Portland, Oreg., May 23, 1922; s. Jewell King and Arvilla Agnes (Beckwith) R.; m. Dilys Walters, Sept. 8, 1945; children— John Gwilym, David Gwyn. BA, U. Oreg., 1944; postgrad., U. Shrivenham, Eng., 1945, U. Oxford, 1946, Am. U., 1947. Staff Bur. Budget, 1948, 51-52; sr. program and budget officer UNESCO, 1948-51; chief personnel policy Mut. Security Agy., Washington, 1952-54, program officer Guatemala, 1954-59, planning officer, later acting asst. dep. dir. for program and planning, 1959-61; dep. U.S. rep. devel. assistance com. OECD, 1961-64; asst. dir. devel. policy Pakistan, 1964-68; dep. dir. North Coast Affairs, AID, State Dept., Washington, 1969-71; dep. mission dir. U.S. Econ. Aid Program, Colombia, 1971-73, mission dir. Dominican Republic, 1973-76, Honduras, 1976-79; privatization adviser Gov. of Costa Rica, 1986-88; prin. assoc. J.B. Robinson & Assocs. (devel. mgmt. cons.), 1979—. Mem. faculty, fellow Harvard U., 1968-69; cons. NATO, 1951, UN, 1959 Served to 1st lt., inf. AUS, 1943-46, ETO. Mem. Oriental Club (London), DACOR BACON House (Washington), Minchinhampton Probus Club (pres. 1983-84). Episcopalian. Address: Anglezarke The Hithe Rodborough Common Stroud GL5 5BN Gloucestershire England also: 7130 SW Gable Pky Portland OR 97225-2620 *Summary: always do more than what is asked for the task at hand. The extra effort always leads to unexpected opportunities for career advancement. Helping others to realize their potential has its own rewards and their success helps to realize your own hopes and aspirations, and improve your own quality of life and satisfaction in a life well-spent. Never underestimate the contribution of your wife and family.*

ROBINSON, JOHN BOWERS, JR. bank holding company executive; b. Laconia, N.H., Oct. 9, 1946; s. John Bowers and Lee (Osborn) R.; m. Jane Frances Moore, Aug. 31, 1968; children: John Paul, Claire Frances, David Moore, Leanne Elizabeth, Gregory Joseph, Peter August. BA, Fairfield U., 1968; MBA, Adelphi U., 1977. V.p., asst. to pres. Hempstead Bank, N.Y., 1977-79, exec. v.p., 1979-81, pres., 1981-82; v.p. planning Norstar Bancorp, Inc., Albany, 1982-84, exec. v.p., 1984-87, pres., 1987-88; mng. dir. govt. banking FleetBoston Fin. (formerly Fleet Fin. Group), 1988—. Mem. Albany Med. Ctr., 1989—. Pres. bd. trustees Doane Stuart Sch., Albany, N.Y., 1996—. Mem. Ft. Orange Club, Schuyler Meadows Club. E-mail: john b. Home: 81 Old Niskayuna Rd Loudonville NY 12211-1349 Office: FleetBoston Fin Mail Code NYEH 34303C Peter D Kiernan Plz Albany NY 12207 E-mail: john_b_robinson@fleet.com.

ROBINSON, JOHN GWILYM, conservationist; b. Paris, Nov. 22, 1949; s. John Beckwith and Dilys (Walters) R.; m. Linda Cox, June 8, 1974; children: David Andrew Cox, Amanda Siân Cox. BA in Zoology with honors, Swarthmore Coll., 1971; PhD in Zoology, U. N.C., 1977. Postdoctoral fellow dept. zool. rsch. Nat. Zool. Park, Smithsonian Instn., Washington, 1977-80, zoologist, 1980-83; affiliate assoc. curator Fla. Mus. Natural History, Gainesville, 1983-98; affiliate assoc. prof. dept. wildlife and range scis. U. Fla., 1983-85, assoc. prof., 1985-90, courtesy prof., 1990-98, dir. program for studies in tropical conservation, 1980-90; dir. wildlife conservation internat. Wildlife Conservation Soc. (former N.Y. Zool. Soc.), Bronx, N.Y., 1990-93, v.p. internat. conservation, 1993-99, sr. v.p., 1999—. Program dir. integrated approaches to tng. in conservation and sustainable devel. Pew Charitable Trusts, Phila., 1988-93; chmn. adv. group Sustainable Use Initiative, World Conservation Union, 1995-99, mem. steering com. Species Survival Commn., 1991-99, regional mem. N.Am. and Caribbean, 1991—, primate specialist Species Survival Commn., 1985—, vice chmn. sustainable use specialist group, 1992-99. Mem. editl. bd. Primates, 1991-98; bd. editors Conservation Biology, 1993—; sci. com. Conservation and Mgmt., 1993—; editor: (with L.D. Navarro) Diversidad Biologica en La Reserva de la Biosphera de Sian Ka'an, 1990, (with K. H. Redford) Neotropical Wildlife Use and Conservation, 1991, (with E.L. Bennett) Hunting for Sustainability in Tropical Forests, 2000; contbr. articles to profl. jours., chpts. to books. Mem. tech. adv. bd. Fundaçao Biodiversitas, Brazil, 1989—; mem. coun. advisors Branger Found., Venezuela; bd. dirs. Wild Things Inc., 1992-97, Global Coral Reef Alliance, 1992-97, Greentree Group, Inc., 1993-97, Sociedade Civil Mamirauá, Brazil, Sócio Efetivo, 1993—; bd. dirs. World Parks Endowment, Inc., 1994—. Mem. AAAS, Am. Soc. Primatologists (conservation com. 1984-88), Internat. Primatological Soc. (election com. 1990—, Martha T. Galante endowment overview com. 1989—, conservation com. 1986-92), Assn. Tropical Biology, Fauna and Flora Preservation Soc., Soc. for Conservation Biology (bd. govs. 1999-2002). Office: Wildlife Conservation Soc 185th St and Southern Blvd Bronx NY 10460 E-mail: jrobinson@wcs.org.

ROBINSON, JOHN LEWIS, geography educator; b. Leamington, Ont., Can., July 9, 1918; s. William John and Emily Laverne (Dunphy) R.; m. Josephine Rowan, Oct. 14, 1944; children: David, Jo-Anne, Patricia. BA, Western Ont. U., 1940; MA, Syracuse U., 1942; PhD, Clark U., 1946; LLD (hon.), Western Ont. U., 1984; DSc (hon.), U. B.C., 1994. Geographer N.W.T. Adminstrn., Ottawa, Ont., 1943-46; prof., head dept. geography U. B.C., Vancouver, 1946-68, prof. geography, 1968-85, prof. emeritus, 1985—. Author 14 books on aspects of regional geography of Can., including British Columbia: 100 Years of Geographical Change, 1973, Themes in the Regional Geography of Canada, 1983, 2d edit., 1989; contbr. articles to profl. jours. Recipient citation of merit Assn. Am. Geographers, 1966; Massey medal Canadian Geog. Soc., 1971 Mem. Canadian Assn. Geographers (pres. 1956, citation for service to profession 1976) Office: U BC Dept Geography Vancouver BC Canada V6T 1Z2

ROBINSON, JOHN MINOR, lawyer, retired business executive; b. Uniontown, Pa., Mar. 18, 1910; s. John M. and Martha (Downs) R. AB, Harvard U., 1932, LL.B, 1935. Bar: Calif. 1936. Assoc. firm Macdonald & Pettit, 1935-41; partner firm Musick, Peeler & Garrett, 1947-77; v.p., sec. Consol. Western Steel div. U.S. Steel Corp. (and predecessors), 1941-57. Mem. Calif. Club (past pres. L.A.), Pacific Union Club (San Francisco), Cypress Point Club (Pebble Beach, Calif.), Royal and Ancient Golf Club of St. Andrews (Fife, Scotland). Office: 9500 Center St Carmel CA 93923-8552

ROBINSON, JOHN RITCHEY, surgeon; b. West Palm Beach, Fla., Jan. 13, 1961; s. John Ritchey and Elizabeth Jean Robinson; m. Donna Kisiel Robinson, Aug. 31, 2000. BA, Northwestern U., Evanston, Illinois, 1978—82; BS, U. Fla., Gainesville, 1982—84; MD, U. So. Fla., Tampa, 1984—88. Diplomate Am. Bd. of Neurol. Surgery. Surg. internship Cleve. Clinic Found., Cleveland, Ohio, 1988—89, neurosurgical residency, 1989—94; fellow neurosurgery Allegheny Cereval Hosp., Pittsburgh, Pa., 1993—94, Barrow Neurologic Inst., Phoenix, 1994—96; physician Martin Meml. Hosp., Stuart, Fla., 1996—, co dir. ctr. spinal surgery, 1996—, dir. surg. icu, 1997—98, 2001—. Lectr. in field. Mem.: AMA, congress of neurol. surgeons spine sect., Am. heart assn. stroke coun., Am. assn. of neurol. surgeons, Am. bd. of neurol. surgery. R-Consevative. Roman Catholic. Avocations: golf, computers, computers. Office: Center Cranial Spinal Surgery 509 Riverside Drive Suite 203 Stuart FL 34994

ROBINSON, JOHN VICTOR, lawyer; b. Harare, Zimbabwe, July 9, 1958; s. Denis Antony Beck and Elizabeth Jill R. BA, Rhodes U., Grahamstown, South Africa, 1983; MA, Oxford (Eng.) U., 1985; JD, U. Richmond (Va.), 1986. Bar: Va. Assoc. atty. Hunton & Williams, Richmond, Va., 1986-89, McSweeney, Burtch & Crump, Richmond, 1989-93, Cantor, Arkema & Edmonds, P.C., Richmond, 1993-97; pvt. practice, 1997—. Past mem. regional com. Nat. Trial Competition, Richmond; apptd. adminstrv. hearing officer Va. Supreme Ct.; adj. asst. prof. Law U. Richmond Sch. Law. Rhodes scholar Oxford U., 1983-85. Mem. ABA, Va. Bar Assn., Bar Assn. City of Richmond. Office: 7102 Three Cropt Road Richmond VA 23226-3615

ROBINSON, JOSEPH EDWARD, geology educator, consulting petroleum geologist; b. Regina, Sask., Can., June 25, 1925; came to U.S., 1976; s. Webb Gabriel Wilton and Blanche Marion (Schiefner) R.; m. Mary Corrine Maclaughlin, Nov. 1, 1952 (div. 1977); children: Joseph Christopher, John Edward, Timothy Webb. B.Eng., McGill U., 1950, M.Sc., 1951; PhD, U. Alta., 1968. Registered profl. engr., Que., Can. Geophysicist Imperial Oil Ltd., Can., 1951-68; sr. geologist Union Oil Co. Can., Calgary, Alta., Can., 1968-76; cons. geologist J.E. Robinson & Assocs., Syracuse, N.Y., 1976—; prof. geology Syracuse U., 1976-91, prof. emeritus, 1991—. Author: Computer Applications in Petroleum Geology, 1982. Served with Can. Navy, 1943-46, ETO. Mem. Am. Assn. Petroleum Geologists, Soc. Exploration Geologists, Soc. Ind. Profl. Earth Scientists, Can. Assn. Petroleum Geologists, Internat. Assn. Math. Geology (assoc. editor 1976-78) Home: 837 Ackerman Ave Syracuse NY 13210-2906 Office: Syracuse U Dept Geology Syracuse NY 13244-0001

ROBINSON, JOYCE MCPEAKE, administrator; b. Newark, July 28, 1941; d. Salvatore and Wilhelmina (Cervetto) Guinta; m. John David McPeake, June 15, 1963 (div. Aug. 1974); children: John Paul, David Samuel; m. Enders Anthony Robinson, Aug. 8, 1992. BA in English, Tufts U., 1962; MA in English, Boston U., 1965, EdD, 1979. Asst. to dean women & dept. adminstrn. Boston U., 1962-63, 65-67; reading specialist Hingham (Mass.) Pub. Schs., 1963-64; reading and learning specialist Manter Hall Sch., Cambridge, Mass., 1964-67; reporter Patriot Ledger, Quincy, 1967-69; dir. Christ Luth. Sch., Scituate, 1971-74; prin. and reading specialist Scituate Pub. Schs., 1974-80; chair English, dir. reading programs St. Andrew's Sch., Boca Raton, Fla., 1980-88; chair English, learning specialist Broadwater Acad., Exmore, Va., 1988-89; dir. learning resources, English Fountain Valley Sch., Colorado Springs, Colo., 1989-91; asst. prin. Islamic Saudi Acad., Alexandria, Va., 1991-93; chair English Masters Sch., Dobbs Ferry, N.Y., 1993-94; head QUEST program Dwight Sch., N.Y.C., 1994—96, head of sch., 1996—. Adj. prof. Nova U., Ft. Lauderdale, Fla., 1984-88, St. Thomas U., Miami, Fla., 1987-88; sch. evaluator Fla. Coun. Ind. Schs., 1985-88; cons. in field. Author: Teaching Study Skills, 1987, Wordworks, 1990; contbr. (poetry) Rhyme and Reason, 1987; editor: How to Double Your Child's Grades in School, 1997; contbr.: Fostering Creativity in Children, K-8, 2000. Coord. Am. Inst. Fgn. Study, Boston, 1987; parent agt. Hamilton Coll. Parents Fund, Clinton, N.Y., 1986—; mem. town adv. com. Scituate Town Com., 1975-80. Mem. Nat. Coun. Tchrs. English, Am. Acad. Poets, Nat. Assn. Ind. Schs., Fla. Coun. Librs., Ea. Ednl. Rsch. Assn. (membership chair 1993-95), Internat. Reading Assn., Coun. Exceptional Children, Modern Lang. Assn., Hemingway Soc., Am. Assn. Ednl. Rsch. (bd. mem. 1996—), Nat. Acad. Ednl. Rsch. Home: 160 Riverside Blvd Apt #6U New York NY 10069 Office: Dwight Sch 291 Central Park W New York NY 10024-3002 E-mail: jrobinson@dwight.edu.

ROBINSON, JUDY ANN, nurse; b. Whiteville, N.C., May 19, 1947; d. Harry Elwood and Sarah (Nobles) Robinson; children: Michele, Rachel, Shannon. RN, High-Smith Rainey Hosp., Fayetteville, N.C., 1968. RN, N.C. Staff nurse Century Care Nursing Home, Whiteville, N.C., 1968, Columbus County Hosp., Whiteville, 1965-68; head nurse Onslow County Hosp., Jacksonville, 1965-70; staff nurse, head nurse Columbus County Hosp., Whiteville, 1971-89; pediat. coord. Bladen County Health, Elizabethtown, N.C., 1989-91; contract nurse Columbus County Home Health, Whiteville, 1991-96, patient care coord., 1996—. Tchr., instr. South Eastern C.C., Whiteville, 1999; staff nurse Premier Living Nursing Home, 1998-99. Home: PO Box 54 Whiteville NC 28472-0054 Office: 706 N Thompson St Whiteville NC 28472-3428

ROBINSON, JUNE KERSWELL, dermatologist, educator; b. Phila., Jan. 26, 1950; d. George and Helen S. (Kerswell) R.; m. William T. Barker, Jan. 31, 1981. BA cum laude, U. Pa., 1970; MD, U. Md., 1974. Diplomate Am. Bd. Dermatology, Nat. Bd. Med. Examiners, Am. Bd. Mohs Micrographic Surgery and Cutaneous Oncology. Intern Greater Balt. Med. Ctr., Hanover, N.H., 1974, resident in medicine, 1974-75; resident in dermatology Dartmouth-Hitchcock Med. Ctr., Hanover, N.H., 1975-78, chief resident, clin. instr., 1977-78, instr. in dermatology, 1978; fellow Mohs; chemosurgery and dermatologic surgery NYU Skin and Cancer Clinic, N.Y.C., 1978-79; instr. in dermatology NYU, 1979; asst. prof. dermatology Northwestern U. Med. Sch., Chgo., 1979, asst. prof. surgery, 1980-85, assoc. prof. dermatology and surgery, 1985-91, prof. dermatology and surgery, 1991-98; prof. medicine and pathology, dir. divsn. dermatology Cardinal Bernardin Cancer Ctr., Loyola U. Med. Ctr., 1998—, program leader skin cancer clin. program, 1998—. Mem. consensus devel. conf. NIH, 1992; mem. panel on use of sunscreens Internat. Agy. for Rsch. on Cancer, WHO, 2000; lectr. in field. Author: Fundamentals of Skin Biopsy, 1985, also audiovisual materials; editor: (textbooks) Atlas of Cutaneous Surgery, 1996, Cutaneous Medicine and Surgery: An Integrated Program in Dermatology, 1996; mem. editl. bd. Archives of Dermatology, 1988-97; sect. editor The Cutting Edge: Challenges in Med. and Surg. Therapeutics, 1989-97; contbg. editor Jour. Dermatol. Surgery and Oncology, 1985-88; mem. editl. com. 18th World Congress of Dermatology, 1982; contbr. numerous articles, abstracts to profl. publs., chpts. to books. Bd. dirs. Northwestern Med. Faculty Found., 1982-84, chmn. com. on benefits and leaves, 1984, nominating com. 1988. Grantee Nat. Cancer Inst., 1985-91, Am. Cancer Soc., 1986-89, Skin Cancer Found., 1984-85, Dermatology Found., 1981-83, Northwestern U. Biomed. Rsch., 1981, Syntex, 1984. Fellow: Am. Coll. Chemosurgery (chmn. sci. program ann. meeting 1983, chmn. publs. com. 1986—87, chmn. task force on ednl. needs 1989—90, co-editor bull. 1984—87); mem.: Chgo. Dermatol. Soc., Women's Dermatol. Soc. (pres. 1990—92, Wilma Bergeld, MD Visionary and Leadership award 2002), Soc. Investigative Dermatology, Am. Soc. Dermatol. Surgery (pres. 1994—95), Dermatology Found. (trustee 1995—98), Am. Acad. Dermatology (asst. sec.-treas. 1995—98, sec.-treas. 1998—2001, bd. dirs. 1993—95, Stephen Rothman Lectr. award 1992, Presdl. citation 1992, 2000), Am. Dermatol. Assn., Am. Cancer Soc. (pres. Ill. divsn. 1996—98). Home: 132 E Delaware Pl Apt 5806 Chicago IL 60611-4951

ROBINSON, KAREN VAJDA, clinical dietitian; BS in Home Econs., Montclair State Coll., 1980; MS in Health Scis./Dietetics, James Madison U., 1992. Cert. food svc. sanitation mgr., N.J. 1984. Dietitian Roosevelt Hosp., Edison, N.J., 1980-85; asst. mgr. UVA (U. Va.) Dining Svcs., Charlottesville, 1985-86; temp. sales sec., mem. banquet prep. staff Boar's Head Inn, 1986-88; head diet counselor Diet Ctr., 1986-90; dietetic intern VA Med. Ctr., Hampton, Va., 1991; pub. health nutritionist Cen. Shenandoah Health Dist., Waynesboro (Va.) Health Dept., 1993-97; clin. dietitian Yonkers Gen. Hosp., 1999—2001; outpatient dietitian St. John Riverside Hosp./Parkcare Pavilion, Yonkers, 2001—; clin. dietitian St. John Riverside Hosp., 2002—. Grad. dietetic intern mentor, 1993—97; cons. dietitian Hebrew Hosp. Home, Bronx, NY, 1998; food svc. mgr. Sodexho Marriott Svcs., Morningside House Nursing Home, Bronx, 1998—99; clin. dietitian Yonkers Gen. Hosp., 1999—2001; cmty. svcs. instr. Westchester C.C., Valhalla, NY, 2001—; in/out patient dietitian Park Care Pavilion (formerly Yonkers Gen. Hosp.), 2001—; clin. dietitian St. John's Riverside Hosp., Yonkers, 2002—. Contbr. articles to local newspapers. Mem. Charlottesville Health Promotion Coalition, 1993-97. Mem.: Westchester Rockland Dietetic Assn. (health fairs chair 1998—2001, scholarship com. 2000, pub. rels. co-chair 2000—01, sec. 2001—, grantee 2000), Va. Dietetic Assn. (exec. bd. 1996—97), Blue Ridge Dietetics Assn. (mem. exec. bd. 1993—97, editor newsletter 1993—96, nat. nutrition month coord. 1993—95, pres.-elect 1995—96, scholarship com. 1996, pres. 1996—97), Va. Pub. Health Assn. (sec. 1995, awards chair 1996—97), Dietitians in Nutrition Support, Gerontol. Nutritionists Practice Group, Consultant Dietitians in Health Care Facilities, Am. Assn. Family and Consumer Scis. (cert.), Am. Dietetic Assn. (registered). Home: PO Box 488 Tarrytown NY 10591-0488

ROBINSON, KATHY M. music educator; b. Phila., June 30, 1959; d. Jason and Betty Jane (Miller) R. BS in Music Edn., Lebanon Valley Coll., 1981; MM in Music Edn./voice performance, Northwestern U., 1986; PhD in Music Edn., U. Mich., 1996. Elem. vocal music tchr. Lampeter (Pa.) Strasburg Sch., 1983-84, Sch. Dist. # 65, Evanston, Ill., 1988-90; asst. prof. music edn. Temple U., Phila., 1995-99, Eastman Sch. Music, Rochester, NY, 1999—. Vis. instr. music Gustavus Adolphus Coll., St. Peter, Minn., 1988; lectr. music edn. U. Mich., Ann Arbor, 1994, Ann Arbor, 95; vocal music tchr., dir. Umculo: The Kimberley Project, Kimberley, South Africa, 1997—; profl. singer in regional choirs operas in east and midwest, 1984—. Church organist, choir dir. St. Paul United Ch. of Christ, Chelsea, Mich., 1990-95. Mem.: ASCD, Internat. Soc. for Music Edn., Soc. for Ethnomusicology, N.Y. State Sch. Music Assn., Am. Guild Organists, Am. Orff-Schulwerk Assn., Music Educators Nat. Conf. Democrat. Lutheran. Avocations: singing, cooking, travel. Home: 330 Orchard Park Blvd Rochester NY 14609 Office: Eastman Sch Music 26 Gibbs St Rochester NY 14604-2599 E-mail: krobinson@esm.rochester.edu.

ROBINSON, KAYNE, political organization officer; Donna Robinson. B, Drake U. With Des Moines Police Dept.; dep. Iowa chmn. Dole Presdl. campaign, 1988; Iowa chmn. Gramm Presdl. campaign, 1996; chmn. Iowa Reps., 1999—2001. With USMC. Named Police Officer of the Yr. Iowa Assn. Women Police. Mem. NRA (1st v.p.). Office: 521 E Locust St Des Moines IA 50309-1939*

ROBINSON, KENNETH CHARLES, finance educator; b. Macon, Ga. s. Charles William Robinson and Joyce R. Sorrow. BBA, U. Ga., 1984, MBA, 1991, PhD, 1995. Gen. mgr., CFO Shoe Shack, Inc., Macon, 1984-90, controller, buyer, 1990-91, mgmt. advisor, 1991-94; grad. tchg. asst. U. Ga., Athens, 1991-95; lectr. U. Wollongong, NSW, Australia, 1995-96; assoc. prof. strategy & entrepreneurship Kennesaw (Ga.) State U., 1996—. Mem. rels. com. Greater Macon C. of C., 1988—90, vice chmn. small bus. coun., 1989—90. Recipient Heizer Best Doctoral Dissertation award, Entrepreneurship Divsn., Acad. Mgmt., 1996, Mescon/Coles Best Empirical Paper award, Acad. Mgmt., 1999, Best Paper award, Entrepreneurship/Ethics Track, So. Mgmt. Assn., 2001; fellow Kauffman Ctr. Entrepreneurial Leadership, 1994, Comer fellow, U. Ga., 1994. Mem.: Strategic Mgmt. Soc., U.S. Assn. Small Bus. and Entrepreneurship (Runner-Up award 1999), Acad. Mgmt. (mem. exec. com. entrepreneurship divsn. 1996—, chair awards com. 1998—).

Presbyterian. Avocations: travel, skiing, scuba diving, hiking. Home: 2953 Lookout Pl NE Atlanta GA 30305 Office: Kennesaw State U Coles Coll Bus 1000 Chastain Rd NW Kennesaw GA 30144-5591 Fax: 770-423-6606.

ROBINSON, KENNETH JOHN, emergency medicine physician; b. Hanover, N.H., Mar. 17, 1964; s. Kenneth J. and Lilla F. (Finizio) R. BS in Biochemistry cum laude, U. Vt., 1986; MD, U. Pitts., 1991. Bd. cert. in emergency medicine, 1995. Intern, resident Geisinger Med. Ctr., Danville, Pa., 1991-94; staff Hartford (Conn.) Hosp., 1994—, John Dempsey Hosp., Farmington, Conn., 1994—; asst. prof. dept. traumatology and emergency medicine U. Conn. Sch. Medicine. Med. dir., co-program dir., LIFE STAR Helicopter program Hartford Hosp.; presenter and spkr. in field. Mem. AMA, Am. Coll. Emergency Physicians, Air Med. Physician's Assn. (chair membership com. 1996—, trustee 1998—), Nat. Assn. Emergency Medical Svcs. Physicians, Wilderness Med. Soc. Office: Hartford Hosp 80 Seymour St Hartford CT 06102-8000

ROBINSON, KENNETH LARRY, insurance company executive; b. Carrollton, Ga., Sept. 20, 1944; s. Tommy Esper and Annie Eunie (Bowie) R.; m. Peggy Marie Tally, Jan. 20, 1967 (div. Feb. 1974); 1 child, Toni Marie; m. Malinda Gayle York, Jan. 11, 1975; 1 child, Tommy Eric. Student, U.S. Armed Forces Inst., Quantico, Va., 1964; cert., Life Ins. Mktg./Rsch. Assn., Atlanta, 1982, Life Underwriters Tng. Coun., Montgomery, Ala., 1987. Dist. mgr. United Family Life Ins. Co., Atlanta, 1967-77, Mut. Savs. Life Ins. Co., Decatur, Ala., 1978-88; agy. mgr. Robinson Ins. Agy., Montgomery, 1989; regional mgr. Nat. Security Ins. Co., Elba, 1989-97, agy. devel., 1997—. Master mgr., United Family Life Ins. Co., Atlanta, 1975-77; president's advisory coun., Mut. Savs. Life Ins. Co., Decatur, 1985-87, pres.' club, 1987. Recipient Cert. Achievement Cotton States Ins. Co., 1989. Mem. Nat. Assn. Life Underwriters, Lions. Republican. Baptist. Avocations: golf, fishing. Home: 3364 W Mildred St Mobile AL 36605-4124

ROBINSON, KENNETH PATRICK, lawyer, electronics company executive; b. Hackensack, N.J., Dec. 12, 1933; s. William Casper and Margaret Agnes (McGuire) r.; m. Catherine Esther Lund, Aug. 26, 1961; children: James, Susan. BS in Elec. Engring., Rutgers U., 1955; JD, NYU, 1962. Bar: N.Y. 1962, U.S. Ct. Appeals (fed. cir.) 1990. With Hazeltine Corp., Greenlawn, N.Y., 1955-88, patent counsel, 1966-69, gen. counsel, 1969-88, sec., 1971-88; v.p. Hazeltine Rsch. Inc., Chgo., 1966-88; of counsel Brumbaugh, Graves, Donohue & Raymond, N.Y.C., 1989-92; prin. Kenneth P. Robinson, Huntington, N.Y., 1992—. Dir. Hazeltine Ltd., London, 1973-80; dir. Imlac Corp., Needham, Mass., 1978-83. Served to 1st lt. USAF, 1955-57. Mem. ABA, IEEE, Am. Intellectual Law Assn., Licensing Execs. Soc. Roman Catholic. Home: 137 Darrow Ln Greenlawn NY 11740-2923 Office: 474 New York Ave Huntington NY 11743-3542

ROBINSON, LAURIE OVERBY, former assistant attorney general; b. Washington, July 7, 1946; d. Kermit and Ethel Esther (Schlasinger) Overby; m. Craig Baab, Oct. 22, 1977 (div. 1991); 1 child Teddy Baab ; m. Sheldon Krantz, Dec. 8, 1991. BA in Polit. Sci. magna cum laude, Brown U., 1968. Desk editor Cmty. News Svc., N.Y.C., 1968-71; asst. staff dir. sect. criminal justice ABA, Washington, 1972-74, dir. sect. criminal justice, 1979-93; assoc. dep. atty. gen. U.S. Dept. Justice, 1993-94, asst. atty. gen. Office Justice Programs, 1994-2000; mem. Nat. Com. to Prevent Wrongful Executions, 2000—; sr. fellow program on crime policy U. Pa. Jerry Lee Ctr. Criminology. Mem. ex-officio, bd. regents Nat. Coll. Dist. Attys., Houston, 1979—93; adv. bd. Fed. Sentencing Reporter, N.Y.C., 1990—; chair Nat. Forum Criminal Justice, Washington, 1991—93; bd. dirs. Nat. Ctr. Victims of Crime. Mem. RAND Criminal Justice Adv. Bd.; mem. Clinton transition com. Dept. Justice, 1992; trustee Vera Inst. Justice, 2001—; bd. dirs. Police Found. Mem.: ABA, Phi Beta Kappa. Democrat. Business E-Mail: robinsol@sas.upenn.edu. E-mail: laurieorob@aol.com.

ROBINSON, LAWRENCE BRANDON, investment company executive; b. Omaha, Aug. 31, 1932; s. Lawrence and Gladys (Brandon) R.; m. Eva Anderson, Feb. 28, 1972; children: Tish, Lindsey, Amanda. BA, Grinnell Coll., 1954; JD, U. Colo., 1959. Bar: Colo. 1959. ptnr. Robinson, Sullivan and Bullard, Boulder, Colo., 1959-71; pres. The Chesapeake Bay Co., Boulder, 1965—, La Jolla(Calif) Investment Co., 1979—; gen. ptnr. La Jolla Shores Plaza Partnership, 1975—; pres. Barclays Ltd., La Jolla, 1968—; mcpl. judge, Boulder, 1967-70; city atty., Vail, Colo., 1969-74. Served with USAF, 1955-57. Mem. La Jolla Beach and Tennis Club, Fairbanks Ranch Country Club. Home: PO Box 2736 Rancho Santa Fe CA 92067

ROBINSON, LEE E. composer, personal financial analyst; b. Clairton, Pa., Aug. 20, 1950; s. Lee E. and Madeline H. Robinson. BS in Indsl. Mgmt., W.Va. Inst. Tech., Montgomery, 1972. Leader Lee Robinson and ISKA Jazz Quartet, Pitts., 1979—; music prodr., writer Motif, 1987; composer I Dream a World, 1992, 93; v.p., co-founder Pitts. Film Workers, 1993-96; founder, dir. Edge of Art-Works, Pitts., 1994—; co-founder I/O Jazz Duet, N.Y.C., 1996—. Accompianist Dance Alloy, Pitts., 1999—, Melanie Miller Dance, 1999. Composer: Public Broadcasting Svc., Jobs: A Way out?, 1996, I/O jazz duet Japan Tour, 2000, (film) With Abandon, 2000; music for films and theatre. Mem. Am. Soc. Composers, Authors and Pubs., Wilkinsburg Art Alliance (v.p.). Achievements: hiking, mountain biking, travel, kite flying, exotic sports cars. Home: 2750 Locust Dr Pittsburgh PA 15241

ROBINSON, LEONARD HARRISON, JR. international government consultant, business executive; b. Winston-Salem, N.C., Apr. 21, 1943; s. Leonard Harrison and Winnie Cornelia (Thomas) R.; children: Kimberly Michelle, Rani Craft. NSF cert., Bennett Coll., Greensboro, N.C., 1959; BA, Ohio State U., 1964; postgrad., SUNY, Binghamton, 1966-67, Am. U., 1982-89, Harvard U., 1991; LLD (hon.), Shaw U., Raleigh, N.C., 1983; LHD (hon.), Huston-Tillotson Coll., 1991. Vol. Peace Corps, Bihar, India, 1964-66; assoc. dir. for India Peace Corps, Madras, 1967-70; dir. recruitment Peace Corps., Washington, 1970-71; dir. inner-city programs EPA, 1971-72; dir. mgmt. Family Planning Internat. Assistance, N.Y.C., 1972-74, Africa dir. Accra, Ghana and Nairobi, Kenya, 1974-77; task force dir. U.S. Ho. Reps., Washington, 1977-78; dir. population Africa AID, 1978-79; dir. Internat. Devel. Ctr. Battelle Inst., 1979-83; dep. asst. sec., sr. exec. svc. Dept. State, 1983-85; pres. African Devel. Found., 1985-90; dep. asst. sec. state, sr. exec. svc. Dept. State, 1990-93; vice chmn., COO Washington Strategic Consulting Group, Inc., 1993-97; founder, pres. LHR Internat. Group, Inc., 1997—; exec. v.p., then pres. and CEO Nat. Summit on Africa Secretariat, 1997—. Cons. area studies U. Mo. Peace Corps, summer 1966; mgmt. analyst ATAC, Washington, 1971; mem. U.S. presdl. del. to Dakar, Senegal, 1987, to Malawi, Mozambique, and Uganda, Sept. 1988, to Mali, Uganda, and Kenya, Dec. 1988, v.p.'s visit to Africa, 1991; hon. consul Govt. Sao Tome and Principe, 1996—. Author: monographs Assessment and Analysis of Population Attitudes in Tanzania, 1981, Analyze African Official Attitudes Concerning U.S. Population Assistance in Lesotho, Tanzania, Senegal and Togo, 1981. Adviser Population Resource Ctr., N.Y.C., 1978-82; adviser internat. program for health and tng., U. N.C., Chapel Hill, 1980-84; vice-chmn. New Directions Task Force Rep. Party, Montgomery County (Md.), 1982-83; adv. coun. Nat. Coun. Returned Peace Corps Vols., 1987—; bd. dirs. Washington Ballet, 1982-85, 86-91, v.p. bd. dirs. 1988-90; bd. dirs. Friends of Smithsonian Mus. African Art, Washington, 1982-84, Coalition for Equitable Representation in Govt., Montgomery County, Montgomery County Bd. Soc. Svcs., 1986-89, Joint Agrl. Consultative Corp., 1985-86, Alan Gutmacher Inst., 1992-96, Friends of the U. of Natal, South Africa, 1995—. Decorated commandeur de l'Ordre National du Niger, 1989; recipient Africare Disting. Svc. award, 1990, Key to the City of Greensboro, N.C., 1991, Christian D. Maxwell Disting. Svc. award Liberian Com. for Relief, Resettlement and Reconstruction, 1993; hon. counsel for the Govt. of Sao Tome and Principe, Ctrl. Africa; sr. fellow U. Mass. John W. McCormack Inst. Mem. Soc. Internat. Devel. (dir. 1982), Am. Pub. Health Assn. (sec. population sect. 1979-81), Coun. on Fgn. Rels., C. of C. of D.C. (dir. 1979-82), Metro Club Washington, Kappa Alpha Psi, Sigma Pi Phi. Office: Nat Summit on Africa Secretariat Enos Cosby Internat House 1218 16th St NW Washington DC 20036-3202 *Human life is precious and extraordinary. I have strived to live to the fullest, by being productive, impact-oriented, and successful in contributng to the improvement of people's lives. This quest has brought me happiness and fulfillment.*

ROBINSON, LESTER W. airport executive; B in Bus. Adminstrn., Mich. State U., 1973. CPA. With Coopers & Lybrand; CFO 1st Independence Corp., Detroit, 1980-83, pres., CEO, 1989-91; auditor gen. Wayne County, 1988-89, dept. dir. airports fin. & adminstrn. dept. airports, 1991-93, CFO dept. budget, 1993-95, dir. dept. airports, 2000—; corp. fin. rep. 1st Mich. Corp., 1995-2000. Office: Dept Aviation Detroit Met Airport Williams Rogell Dr Detroit MI 48242*

ROBINSON, LOIS HART, retired public relations executive; b. Freeport, Ill., Aug. 9, 1927; d. Seril N. and Cora (Stabenow) Hart; m. Noel M. Henze, Nov. 15, 1947 (div. 1964); children: Susan Henze Bentley, Cynthia Henze Berkeley, Charles Henze; m. Jack Fay Robinson, July 16, 1968. Student, Oakton C.C., 1976-77, Northwestern U., 1977-81. Med. sec. Freeport Meml. Hosp., 1945-47; sec. No. Ill. Corp., 1947-49; adminstrv. asst. to supt. schs. Cmty. Sch. Dist. 303, St. Charles, Ill., 1962-68; exec. sec. Bell & Howell Co., Chgo., 1969-73, supr. corp. rels., 1973-79, mgr. corp. comm., 1979-85, mgr. corp. comm. svcss., 1985-88; pres., dir. Bell & Howell Found., 1983-88; freelance writer Evanston, Ill., 1989-91. Bd. dirs. Evanston Ecumenical Action Coun., 1991-93, Tri-Village United Way, 1996-97, Friends of Judson Coll., 1998—, Friends Bartlett Libr., 1997—. Recipient Effie award Am. Mktg. Assn., 1983. Mem. United Ch. of Christ. Home: 321 E Morse Ave Bartlett IL 60103-4168

ROBINSON, LYNDA HICKOX, artist; b. Bakersfield, Calif., June 26, 1932; d. George Philip and Naida (Hathaway) Hickox; m. Arthur C. Robinson; children: Jill, Scott. BA, U. Calif., Berkeley, 1953; MA, Mills Coll., 1957. 1st v.p. San Francisco Women Artists, 1985-86, pres., 1986-87; chair exhbns. com. East Bay Women Artists, Montclair, Calif., 1994—. Invited artist Glasgow Scotland City of Culture Exhbn., 1990. Dancer, tchr. dance, 1957-82; photographer, 1982-89, painter, 1990—; exhbns. include San Francisco Women Artists Gallery, 1992-94, Kaiser Cmty. Gallery, 1992-02, Alta Bates Cmty. Gallery, 1994-02, Valley Art Ctr. Gallery, 1992-02, Royal Ground Gallery, 1994-02; represented in permanent collections Fuji Vending, Dr. Louise Annand MacFarquar, Prof. and Mrs. Fred Casmir; contbr. artworks to jours. and mags. Recipient Tchg. fellowship Mills Coll., 1954, Francis Coen cash award, 1993. Mem. Phi Beta Kappa.

ROBINSON, MALCOLM KENNETH, surgeon; b. Phila., Nov. 22, 1961; s. James Herbert and Soiesette Elaine (Furlonge) R. AB, Harvard U., 1983, MD, 1987. Diplomate: Am. Bd. Surgery; cert. nutrition support physician. Surgery intern, resident Brigham and Women's Hosp., 1987-95, attending surgeon, asst. dir. metabolic support svc., 1994-2000; instr. surgery Harvard Med. Sch., 1994-2000; dir. metabolic support svc. Brigham and Women's Hosp., 2000—; asst. prof. surgery Harvard Med. Sch., Boston, 2000—. Med. dir. Nutritional Rsch. Ctrs., Hopkinton, Mass., 1996-98. Mem. editl. bd. Jour. Parentoral and Enteral Nutrition, 1996. Recipient Nat. Rsch. Svc. award NIH, 1990-92, supplemental grant NIH, 1995-98. Fellow ACS; mem. AMA, Soc. Surgery Alimentary Tract, Assn. Acad. Surgery, Am. Soc. Parentoral and Enteral Nutrition (Maurice Shils award 1996-97). Office: Brigham & Womens Hosp Dept Surgery 75 Francis St Boston MA 02115-6106

ROBINSON, MARGUERITE STERN, anthropologist, educator, consultant; b. N.Y.C., Oct. 11, 1935; d. Philip Van Doren and Lillian (Diamond) Stern; m. Allan Richard Robinson, June 12, 1955; children: Sarah Penelope, Perrine, Laura Ondine. BA, Radcliffe Coll., 1956; PhD, Harvard U., 1965. Assoc. scholar Inst. for Ind. Study (now Bunting Inst.) Radcliffe U., Cambridge, Mass., 1964-65; asst. prof. anthology Brandeis U., 1965-72, assoc. prof., 1972-78, prof., 1978-85, dean Coll. Arts and Scis., 1973-75; assoc. fellow Inst. Internat. Devel. Harvard U., Cambridge, 1978-80, fellow Inst. Internat. Devel., 1980-85, inst. fellow Inst. Internat. Devel., 1985-2000, inst. fellow emeritus Inst. Internat. Devel., 2000—; dir. Cultural Survival Inc., 1981-99, Am. Inst. Indian Studies, Chgo., 1977—, chmn., 1983-84. Cons. Ministry of Fin., Govt. of Indonesia, Jakarta, 1979-92, USAID, 1992-98, Banco Solidario, Bolivia, 1993-95, Bank Rakyat Indonesia, 1994-98, World Bank, 1994-95, Bank Danamon Indonesia, 1995-96, Office of the Comptroller of the Currency, 1996-99, UNESCO, 1997, World Bank, 1997-2002, Bank of Tanzania, 1997, Microfin. Tng. Program Econs. Inst., Boulder, Co., 1995-2002, Dept. for Internat. Devel., U.K., 2000, Women's World Banking, 2000-2002. Author: Political Structure in a Changing Sinhalese Village, 1975, Local Politics: The Law of the Fishes, 1988, Pembiayaan Pertanian Pedesaan, 1993, The Microfinance Revolution, Vol. 1: Sustainable Finance for the Poor, 2001; contbg. author: Cambridge Papers in Social Anthropology 3, 1962, Cambridge Papers in Social Anthropology 5, 1968, Enterprises for the Recycling and Composting of Municipal Solid Waste, 1993, The New World of Microenterprise Finance, 1994, New Perspectives on Financing Small Business in Developing Countries, 1995, Assisting Development in a Changing World, 1997, Agricultural Development in the Third World, 1998, Strategic Issues in Microfinance, 1998, Microfinance: Conversations with the Experts, 1999; contbr. articles to profl. jours. Mem. internat. coun. advisors Calmeadow Found., 1996—; pres. The Greatest Gift Corp. Fellow NIH, 1964-65; grantee NSF, 1966-70, Ford Found., 1972-74, 79, Calmeadow Found., 1994; fellow Indo-Am. Fellowship Program-Indo-U.S. Subcommn. on Edn. and Culture, 1976-77, Am. Inst. Indian Studies, 1976-77; grantee Calmeadow Found., 1994. Fellow Am. Anthrop. Assn., Soc. Bunting Inst. Fellows; mem. Assn. Asian Studies, India Internat. Centre. Home and Office: 505 Chestnut Hill Ave Brookline MA 02445-4149

ROBINSON, MARIETTA S. lawyer; BA, U. Mich., 1973; JD, UCLA, 1978. Bar: Calif. 1978, Mich. 1979, U.S. Dist. Ct. (ea. dist.) Mich. 1979, U.S. Ct. Appeals (6th cir.) 1983, U.S. Supreme Ct. 1989. Data processing mktg. rep. IBM Corp., Flint, Mich., 1973-75; assoc. The Bank of Bermuda Legal Dept., Hamilton, 1978-79; from assoc. to ptnr. Dickinson, Wright, Moon, VanDusen & Freeman, Detroit, 1979-94; ptnr. Sommers, Schwartz, Silver & Schwartz, P.C., Southfield, Mich., 1985-89; owner Law Offices of Marietta S. Robinson, Detroit, 1989—. Dem. nominee for Mich. Supreme Ct., 2000; adj. prof. U. Detroit Sch. of Law, 1982-83, Wayne State U., Detroit, 1983-84; lectr. in field. Contbr. articles to profl. jours. Trustee Dalkon Shield Claimants Trust, 1989-97; appointee Gov. James Blanchard, State of Mich. Bldg. Authority, 1985-89, State Bar Mich./Mich. State Med. Soc. Coalition, 1993—. Named one of ten Mich. Lawyers of Yr., Lawyers Weekly, 2000. Fellow ABA, Internat. Soc. Barristers (bd. govs.), Am. Bar Found., Mich. State Bar Found.; mem. State Bar Mich., State Bar Calif., ATLA, Mich. Trial Lawyers Assn., Women Lawyers Mich., Detroit Bar Assn., Oakland Bar Assn., U.S. Ct. Appeals (6th cir.) Jud. Conf. (life). Office: 180 Oakland Ave Ste 260 Birmingham MI 48009- E-mail: mrobin6510@aol.com.

ROBINSON, MARK LEIGHTON, oil company executive, petroleum geologist, horse farm owner; b. San Bernardino, Calif., Aug. 4, 1927; s. Ernest Guy and Florence Iola)Lemmon) R.; m. Jean Marie Ries, Feb. 8, 1954; children; Francis Willis, Mark Ries, Paul Leighton. AB cum laude in Geology, Princeton U., 1950; postgrad., Stanford U., 1950-51. Geologist Shell Oil Co., Billings, Mont., Rapid City, S.D., Denver, Midland, Tex., dist. geologist Roswell, N.Mex., 1957-60, divsn. mgr., 1961-63, Jackson, Miss., 1964-65, Bakersfield, Calif., 1967-68, mgr. exploration econs. N.Y.C., 1969; ctrl. office staff BIPM (Royal Dutch Shell Oil Co.), The Hague, The Netherlands, 1966; pres., chmn. bd. dirs. Robinson Resource Devel. Co., Inc., Roswell, 1970—. Chmn., pres. Como Petroleum Corp., Roswell, 1994—. Campaign chmn. Chaves County Rep. Com., Roswell, 1962; mem. alumni schs. com. Princeton U., 1980—; vestry St. Andrew's Episcopal Ch., Roswell, N.Mex., 1999-2002. With USNR, 1945-46. Mem. Assn. Petroleum Geologists, Stanford U. Earth Scientists Assn., Yellowstone Bighorn Rsch. Assn., Am. Horse Show Assn., SAR, Sigma Xi. Episcopalian. Achievements include discovery of Lake Como oil field, Miss., 1971, McNeal oil field, Miss., 1973, North Deer Creek gas field, Mont., 1983, Bloomfield East oil field, Mont., 1986, West Cat Claw Draw gas field, N.Mex., 1997, Southeast Cemetary Gas Field, N.Mex., 2000. Home: 2003 Southridge Rd Roswell NM 88203-9346 Office: Robinson Resource Devel Co Inc PO Box 1227 Roswell NM 88202-1227

ROBINSON, MARSHALL ALAN, economics educator, foundation executive; b. Berkeley, Calif., Feb. 16, 1922; s. Webster Richard and Evelyn (Casey) R.; m. Ynid Douglas Rankin, June 5, 1944 (div. 1973); children: Joan Douglas, Margaret Elaine, Richard Webster; m. Flavia Derossi, Oct. 1974. AB, U. Calif.-Berkeley, 1943; MA, Ohio State U., 1948, PhD, 1950. Instr. econs. Ohio State U., 1948-50; asst. prof. econs. Tulane U., 1951-53; research asso. Nat. Bur. Econ. Research, 1951-52; asst. prof. econs. Dartmouth Coll., 1953-55; sr. staff mem., asst. to pres. Brookings Instn., 1955-60; prof. econs., dean Grad. Sch. Bus., U. Pitts., 1960-63; dir. econ. devel. and adminstrn. program Ford Found., 1964-67, program officer in charge higher edn. and research, 1967-71, dep. v.p. edn. and research, 1971-73, v.p. resources and environ., 1973-79; pres. Russell Sage Found., N.Y.C., 1979-86; vis. prof. Grad. Sch. CUNY, 1986-89; fellow Inst. Social and Policy Studies Yale U., 1989-91; v.p. Daniele Agostino Found., 1992—. Author: An Introduction to Economic Reasoning, 1956, 5th edit., 1981, The National Debt Ceiling, 1959. Bd. dirs. Belgium-Am. Ednl. Found., 1981-96; trustee Antioch U., 1987-90. Served to 1st lt. USMCR, 1943-45, PTO. Decorated Royal Order of Leopold, Belgium. Mem. Am. Econs. Assn., N.Y. Sci. Policy Assn., Coun. on Fgn. Rels., Century Assn., Alpha Delta Phi.

ROBINSON, MARTIN (MARTY ROBINSON), television and radio broadcaster, media consultant; b. Chgo., Sept. 7, 1932; s. Edward Emmanuel Robinson and Florence Ruth (Cohen) Mayer; m. Mary Alice Wellingham, May 31, 1959; children: Paul Edward, Jill Marie. Broadcaster, host Stas. WAAF, WGN and WNIB, Chgo., 1956-58, Sta. WFMT, Chgo., 1958-93, Sta. WTTW-TV, Chgo., 1971-99. Speaker, concert narrator; lectr. Lyric Opera Chgo.; media cons. J. Walter Thompson, Hill & Knowlton, Burson Marsteller, Newell & Matthews, 1973—. Host, narrator programs (Peabody award, 15 Emmy awards, 8 Ohio State awards, Chgo. and San Francisco Film Festival Gold medals); prodr., host nationally syndicated opera program The First Fifty Years, 1967-93. Served with USN, 1950-53. Recipient Emmy awards, 1977, 78. Avocations: biking, weight training, the Internet. Office: 5 Lynnbrook Dr Prospect Heights IL 60070-1022 E-mail: martyrob@home.com.

ROBINSON, MARY CATHERINE, artist; b. Oshkosh, Wis., Aug. 18, 1934; d. Edward Charles Leupold and Nora Alice O'Laughlin; m. Charles Benjamin Robinson, Sept. 10, 1960; children: Charles Edward, Jeanne Marie, David James. Student, U. Wis., Milw., 1953—54, Ringling Art Sch., Sarasota, Fla., 1954—56, Layton Art Sch., Milw., 1957—58. Owner Tree Top Studio, Nokomis, Fla. Represented by. Recipient First prize painting, Fla. State Fair, 1959; scholar, Ringling Art Sch., Sarasota, 1954—56, Layton Art Sch., Milw., 1957—58. Mem.: N.Y. Soc. Portrait Artists, Am. Soc. Portrait Artists, U.S. Tennis Assn. Avocations: painting, sculpting, tennis, photography, fishing. Home: 1609 Hammock Dr Nokomis FL 34275

ROBINSON, MARY ELIZABETH GOFF, retired historian, researcher; b. East Providence, R.I., Jan. 3, 1925; d. Newell Darius and Eva Agnes (Crane) Goff; m. Charles Albert Robinson, July 30, 1954; 1 child, Thomas Goff (dec.). BA, Wheaton Coll., Norton, Mass., 1947. Cataloger, fine arts Chester County Hist. Soc., Pa., 1973-80, trustee, 1974-80. Cataloger artifacts Chadds Ford (Pa.) Hist. Soc., 1992-95. Co-author: (monograph) Ada Clendenin Williamson, 1983, (history) The Ingalls and the Hoyts, The Crane Sawmill, The Ingalls-Crane House, 1995; author: (monograph) The Life of a Young Entrepreneur at the Turn of the Twentieth Century, 1992; editor: A Quiet Man from West Chester, 1974. Mem. Jr. League, Providence, 1957-62, Providence Athenaeum, 1955-63, Providence Preservation Soc., 1959-63, Brandywine Conservancy, Del. Symphony Orch., Winterthur Mus.; donor Newell D. Goff Fund Chester County Cmty. Found.; founder Chester County Artists Register Chester County Art Assn., acting libr., 1994—. Donor T. Morris Longstreth Libr. endowment West Chester U., Greater Lewes (DE) Found., Friends of Lewes Pub. Libr.. Mem. AAUW, R.I. Hist. Soc. (trustee 1994-99, founder Newell D. Goff Inst. for I & E Studies), Danville (Vt.) Hist. Soc., Hershey's Mill Country Club, Hope Club (Providence). Avocations: writing, reading, hiking, travel.

ROBINSON, MARY FRANCES, retired French language educator; b. Dec. 16, 1918; BA, Wilson Coll., 1940; MA, Syracuse U., 1947, PhD, 1954. Instr., asst. prof., assoc. prof. French, Wake Forest U., Winston-Salem, N.C., 1952-68, prof., 1968-89, prof. emerita, 1989—, chmn. Romance lang. dept., 1967-74, 78-82.

ROBINSON, MARY JEAN, retired elementary school educator; b. Commerce, Tex., Oct. 16, 1929; d. Younger Edward and Maggie Belle (Sanders) Flynt; m. Ray Leon Robinson; children: Douglas, Cathy, John, Vicki. BS, West Tex. State U., 1960; MS in Edn., Tex. Tech U., 1980. Tchr. elem. sch. Amarillo (Tex.) Ind. Sch. Dist., 1960-61, Perryton (Tex.) Ind. Sch. Dist., 1961, elem. tchr. music, 1977-80; tchr. elem. sch. Booker (Tex.) Ind. Sch. Dist., 1961-75; elem. tchr. music Waka (Tex.) Ind. Sch. Dist., 1975-77; tchr. music Acton Elem. Sch., Duncanville, Tex., 1980-92, ret., 1992, appraiser music/elem., 1984-86. Part-time music tchr. Eustace Ind. Sch. Dist., 1993-95; part-time min. of music, 1st United Meth. Ch., Mabank, 1993—; min. music 1st United Meth. Ch., Mabank, 1993-2001; clinician music workshops Lipscomb County/Leander, Tex., 1961-80, Ennis, Tex., others; pres. High Sch. Ex-Students Commerce Assn., 1988-91. Bd. dirs. mus.'s Perryton Country Club, 1973-80, Avanti Community Theater, Avanti Com. Chorus, Mabank Garden Club; dir. music 1st Bapt. Ch., Booker, 1976-77, pianist, 1965-73; accompanist Booker Bank Notes; elected mem. hosp. bd. Lipscomb County, Tex., 1977-81; pres. Henderson County Arts Coun., 1999-2002; sec. Booker Community Fund, 1978-800; exec. bd. dirs., v.p. Duncanville Women's League, 1985-86, chmn., 1987-89; life mem. Acton PTA, program chair, 1981-82, 86-88, Tex. chpt. PTA, 1984; pianist Duncanville Rotary. Named Best Citizen City of Booker, 1969, Woman of Month Perryton Bus. and Profl. Women, 1978, Wyatt's Tchr. of Month 1986; recipient Life Mem. award Nat. chpt. PTA, 1992, Achievement award Kappa Upsilon 1992, Alpha State Delta Kappa Gamma Achievement award, 1995. Mem. Tex. Music Educators, Duncanville Regional Arts Assn. (chair edn. and publicity 1983-87, exec. bd. dirs. 1985-87), Tex. Ret. Tchrs. Assn. (scholarship chmn.), Avanti Community Theater, Delta Kappa Gamma (state music chmn. 1989-91, state membership com. 1991-93, state membership chmn. 1993-95, area IX coord. 1995-97, achievement awards com. 2002—). Republican. Methodist. Avocations: aerobics, travel, reading.

ROBINSON, MARY JO, pathologist; b. Spokane, Wash., May 26, 1954; d. Jerry Lee and Ann (Brodie) R. BS in Biology, Gonzaga U., 1976; DO, Coll. Osteo. Medicine and Surgery, U. Med. Health Scis., 1987. Diplomate Nat. Bd. Osteo. Med. Examiners, Am. Osteo. Bd. Pathology; cert. anatomic pathology, lab. medicine and dermatopathology. Med. technologist Whitman Comty. Hosp., Colfax, Wash., 1977-81, Madigan Army Med. Ctr., Ft. Lewis, 1981-83; intern Des Moines Gen. Hosp., 1987-88; resident in pathology Kennedy Meml. Hosp., Stratford, N.J., 1988-92; asst. prof. pathology Sch. Medicine U. Medicine and Dentistry of N.J., 1995—; staff pathologist Kennedy Meml. Hosp., Cherry Hill, N.J., 1995—; fellow in dermatopathology Jefferson Med. Coll., Phila., 1994. Fellow Coll. Am. Pathologists; mem. AMA, Am. Osteo. Coll. Pathologists (1st prize resident paper 1992), Am. Osteo. Assn., Am. Soc. Clin. Pathologists, N.J. Assn. Osteo. Physicians and Surgeons. Avocations: astronomy, antiques, science fiction. Office: Kennedy Health Systems UMDNJ Sch Med Mgmt Svc Ctr 500 Marlboro Rd Cherry Hill NJ 08034- E-mail: m.robinson@kennedyhealth.org.

ROBINSON, MARY LOU, federal judge; b. Dodge City, Kans., Aug. 25, 1926; d. Gerald J. and Frances Strueber; m. A.J. Robinson, Aug. 28, 1949; 3 children. BA, U. Tex., 1948, LL.B., 1950. Bar: Tex. 1949. Ptnr. Robinson & Robinson, Amarillo, 1950-55; judge County Ct. at Law, Potter County, Tex., 1955-59, (108th Dist. Ct.), Amarillo, 1961-73; assoc. justice Ct. of Civil Appeals for 7th Supreme Jud. Dist. of Tex., 1973-77, chief justice, 1977-79; U.S. dist. judge No. Dist. Tex., Amarillo, 1979—. Named Woman of Year Tex. Fedn. Bus. and Profl. Women, 1973. Mem. Nat. Assn. Women Lawyers, ABA, Tex. Bar Assn. (Outstanding 50-Yr. Lawyer award 2002), Amarillo Bar Assn., Delta Kappa Gamma. Presbyterian. Office: US Dist Ct Rm 226 205 E 5th Ave # F13248 Amarillo TX 79101-1559

ROBINSON, MARY LU, retired accountant, artist; b. Bloomington, Ind., Nov. 11, 1919; d. Louis Cleveland and Ruby Olive (King) Welch; m. Robert Newlin Robinson, Sept. 27, 1948; children: Richard Louis, Rebecca Jane. Student, Ind. U., Bloomington, 1937-40, Ind. U., South Bend, 1954-55, Tex. Christian U., Ft. Worth, 1989, 90, 99. Ptnr. Robert N. Robinson, CPA, South Bend, 1950-82. Exhibited in group shows at Composers, Authors, Artists Am., N.Y.C., 1990, Soc. Watercolor Artists, Ft. Worth, 1989—, Internat. Soc. Exptl. Artists, 1992, Womans Club, Ft. Worth, 1989—. Den mother Boy Scouts Am., South Bend, 1956-59. Mem. DAR, Nat. Assn. Pen Women, Inc. (chpt. pres. 1999—), Colonial Dames XVIIC (chpt. pres. 1995-97), Daus. Colonial Wars (state pres. 1992-95), Magna Charta Soc., Colonial Order of the Crown, Daus. Am. Colonists, Daus. of 1812, Washington Family Descs., Nat. Trust Historic Preservation, Order Eastern star (assoc. matron 1969-70), Johnson County Master Gardner Assn. Avocations: geneology, travel, history, bridge, gardening. Home: 3915 W 57th Ter Shawnee Mission KS 66205-3148 E-mail: marylrobinson@sbcglobal.com.

ROBINSON, MAURA, artist; b. Norwalk, Conn., Nov. 27, 1956; d. Victor Anthony and Amy (Abraham) R.; m. William Lindsley Ward. BFA, SUNY, Purchase, 1978. One-woman shows include: Art Space, L.A., 1989, Genovese Gallery, Boston, 1992, Woodward Gallery, N.Y.C., 1998; group shows include: Genovese Gallery, 1988, 89, 90, Art Space, L.A., 1991, Gallery V, Kansas City, Mo., 1994, Woodward Gallery, N.Y.C., 1998, 99, 1995, 96, 2000, 01, Bauer Mus., Ind., 2001. E-mail: studiomr@aol.com.

ROBINSON, MAUREEN LORETTA, retired secondary school educator; b. N.Y.C., May 17, 1945; d. Arthur Vincent and Paula (Dillon) R.; m. Derish Michael Wolff, Feb. 13, 1992. BA in English, Wagner Coll., 1967; MS, CUNY, 1970. Cert. tchr. secondary sch. English, K-12 reading, N.Y. Tchr. English Curtis H.S., S.I., N.Y., 1968-95, coord. student activities, 1985-94. Vis. lectr. Coll. of S.I., 1982; guest lectr. NYU, 1991, Pace U., N.Y.C., 1993; dir. Soc. de Management de Projets Internat., Paris, 1996—. Elected mem. Somerset Hills Bd. Edn., Bernardsville, NJ, 1997—; v.p. Somerset County Ednl. Svcs. Commn., Raritan, 2000—02; bd. dirs. Bernardsville Garden Club, pres., 1997—99, pub chair, 1995—97, 2001—, sec., 1999—2001; bd. dirs. Friends of the Bernardsville Libr., pub. chair, 1996—2002; trustee Somerset Hills Edn. Found., 1996—97; class agt. Wagner Coll., 1995—, trustee, 1998—, vice-chair, 2001; pres. Somerset County Ednl. Svcs. Commn., Raritan, 2002—; bd. dirs. Clarence Dillon Pub. Libr. Staff sgt. USAR, 1979—85. Recipient Human Rels. award Greater N.Y. Region of NCCJ, 1994, Army Achievement medal Dept. of the Army, 1983. Mem. AAUW, Wagner Coll. Nat. Alumni Assn. (1st v.p. 1999-2001, mem. at large 2000—). Avocations: reading, gardening, skiing, cooking, travel. Home: 160 Jockey Hollow Rd Bernardsville NJ 07924-1312 E-mail: mrobidwolf@aol.com.

ROBINSON, MICHAEL FRANCIS, private art dealer and appraiser; b. London, Oct. 6, 1954; came to U.S., 1978; s. Canon Joseph and Anne (Antrobus) R. Student, The King's Sch., Canterbury, Eng., 1968-72; LLB, King's Coll., London U., London, 1976; postgrad., The Coll. Law, London, 1976-77, Centre Study European Law, London & Luxembourg. Head rare books Brentano's, Inc., N.Y.C., 1978-81, Phillips Auctioneers, N.Y.C., 1981-85, auctioneer fine arts, 1982-85; pres. M.F. Robinson & Assocs., 1985—. Cons. to mus. and pvt. collectors, IRS, 1989-2000; Prforzheimer lectr. N.Y. Pub. Libr., N.Y.C., 1989; chmn. writers panel San Francisco Internat. Antique Fair, 1989, 90. Author articles Archtl. Digest, Connosieur, Art and Auction, Manuscripts and other mags.; contbg. editor The Am. Book Collector, 1985-89, Art and Auction, 1989-96; assoc. editor Jour. Guild of Bookworkers; editor Treasures of Eton College, The Pierpont Morgan Library, 1990; joinr editor, co-author: In August Co. The Collections of the Pierpont Morgan Library, 1991-92, Mark Twain: An American Voice to the World, 1996. Chmn. The Bach Ensemble, N.Y., 1984-99; cons. to dept. of history, Presbyn. Ch. U.S.A., 1999-2000. Mem. The Hon. Soc. Inner Temple (Duke of Edinburgh Scholar 1974), The Manuscript Soc., The Hardwick Soc. Clubs: The Worshipful Co. of Wax Chandlers (London), Westside (Georgetown). Lodges: Masons (curator 1984—). Episcopalian. Avocation: music before 1800. Office: PO Box 1947 Middleburg VA 20118-1947

ROBINSON, MICHAEL HILL, retired zoological park director, biologist; b. Preston, Eng., Jan. 7, 1929; came to U.S. 1984; s. Samuel and Ethel (Hill) R.; m. Barbara Cragg Robinson, May 19, 1955 (divorced). BS, U. Wales, U.K., 1963; DPhil, U. Oxford, Eng., 1966; DSc (hon.), U. Westminster, Eng., 2000. Tchr. sci. U.K. Secondary Schs., 1953-60; sr. sci. master Camborne Grammar Sch., 1958-60; biologist Smith. Tropical Research Inst., Panama, 1966-71; vis. lectr. U. Pa., Phila., 1969; reader in biology New U. Ulster, No. Ireland, 1971; biologist Smithsonian Tropical Research Inst., Panama, 1971-84, asst. dir., 1980, acting dir., 1980-81, dep. dir., 1981-84; dir. Nat. Zool. Park, Washington, 1994-2000; sr. scientist Smithsonian Tropical Rsch. Inst., 1999—. Contbr. articles to profl. jours. Mem. Soc. for Study of Animal Behavior, Soc. for Strays. Address: 8291 SW Bent Oak Ct Stuart FL 34997

ROBINSON, MICHAEL WARING, public relations executive, writer; b. N.Y.C., Nov. 8, 1963; s. Thomas Porter Jr. and Vanessa (Gillespie) Robinson. BA, Syracuse U., 1985. Writer, reporter N.Y. Times, N.Y.C., 1985-89; news summary writer The White House, Washington, 1989; spokesman U.S. Dept. Justice, 1989-91; sr. account exec. Hager Sharp Inc., 1991-93; media dir. The Jefferson Group, 1993-95; media rels. assoc. dir. NASDAQ Stock Market/Nat. Assn. Securities Dealers, 1995-98; sr. media rels. adviser Mobil Corp., 1998-99; v.p. corp. comms. Friedman, Billings, Ramsey Group, Inc., 1999—2001; dir. office pub. affairs, policy eval. and rsch. U.S. Securities and Exchange Commn., 2001—. Author Op-Ed page The Christian Sci. Monitor, 1994. Pub. rels. com. Smithsonian-Young Benefactors, Washington; judge PR News Patinum awards, 1999. Recipient Silver Inkwell award Internat. Assn. Bus. Communicators, 1994. Republican. Avocations: tennis, sailing. Home: 5217 Marlyn Dr Bethesda MD 20816-1972

ROBINSON, NANCY NOWAKOWSKI, academic administrator; b. Pitts., Nov. 2, 1945; d. Theodore Joseph Nowakowski and Martha Radick; 1 child David A. BA cum laude, U. Pitts., 1983, MA, 2000. Pres. City of God Found., Pitts., 2000—02, bd. dirs.; assoc. Sisters of the Holy Family of Nazareth, Pitts., 1998—; bd. dirs., treas. Extrasolar Planetary Found., Pitts., 1980—97. Recipient Sister Noel Kernan award, Seton Hill Coll., 1999; grantee Dorot Found. grantee for study in Israel, 1999, Pax Christi grantee, Pax Christi, 1999. Mem.: Soc. Bibl. Lit., Am. Acad. Religion. Roman Catholic. Avocations: travel, outdoors, Jewish/Catholic relations, history. Business E-Mail: nancy1@pitt.edu.

ROBINSON, NAOMI JEAN, educational training systems educator; b. Storm Lake, Iowa, Oct. 10, 1951; d. Wendell and Norma (Wright) Robinson. BA, Buena Vista Coll., 1973; MAEd., George Washington U., 1978. Tchr. elem. schs., Storm Lake, Iowa, 1973—75; edn. specialist intern U.S. Army, Ft. Monroe, Va., 1976—78, edn. and test specialist Ft. Eustis, 1978—79, tng. systems analyst White Sands Missile Range, N.Mex., 1979—82, tng. effectiveness analysis study coord., 1983—85, analyst ops. rsch. and tng. systems, 1985—87, edn. specialist, dir. tng. tech. field Advanced Concepts Team Ft. Huachuca, Ariz., 1987—88, edn. specialist, dir. tng. lab. Tng. Devel. and Analysis Directorate, N.J. N.G. High Tech. Tng. Ctr. Ft. Dix, NJ, 1988—90, program mgr., COR Tng. Devel. and Analysis Directorate for TRADOC tng. mission support contract, 1990—94, chief spl. projects team, 1994—96, acting divsn. chief tng. rsch and studies divsn., 1990—91; chief TRADOC tng. Mission Support Contract Br., 1991—94; chmn. Tng. Devel. Revitalization Joint Task Force Pentagon, Washington, 1994—96; dir. ops. support divsn. and exec. officer tng. devel. analysis activity Ft. Monroe, Va., 1996—97; asst. dep. chief of staff Tng. Hdqs. 5th Army, Ft. Sam Houston, Tex., 1997—. Author: Guidelines for Development of Skill Qualification Tests, 1977, Standard Operating Procedure for TRADOC Training Mission Support Contract, 1991, 1992. V.p. Young Reps., 1972—73. Mem.: NAFE, Iowa Edn. Assn., Human Factors Soc., Federally Employed Women (1st v.p. chpt. 1982—83, 1984—85), Bus. and Profl. Women Club. Republican. Presbyterian. Home: 13999 Old Blanco Rd Apt 3311 San Antonio TX 78216-7790 Office: Hdqs 5th US Army Ste 146 Bldg 16 Rm 110 1400 E Grayson St Fort Sam Houston TX 78234-7000 Business E-Mail: robinsonn@samhou.5tharmy.army.mil.

ROBINSON, NEAL, government agency administrator; Dir. Air Force Cryptologic Office, Ft. Meade, Md.; commd. USAF, advanced through grades to brig. gen., intelligence officer, flight comdr., chief ops mgmt., chief intelligence directorate of ops., Middle East analyst, assoc. dir. ops. for command, control, intelligence, surveillance and reconnaissance, dir. of intelligence U.S. European Command Germany; vice comdr. Air Intelligence Agy., Lackland AFB, Tex. Office: Dir Cryptologic Office 9800 Savage Rd, Ste 6202 Fort George G Meade MD 20755*

ROBINSON, NEIL CIBLEY, JR. lawyer; b. Columbia, S.C., Oct. 25, 1942; s. Neil C. and Ernestine (Carns) R.; m. Judith Ann Hunter, Sept. 4, 1971 (div. Nov. 1979); 1 child, Hunter Leigh; m. Vicki Elizabeth Kornahrens, Mar. 2, 1985; children: Neil C. III, Taylor Elizabeth. BS in Indsl. Mgmt., Clemson U., 1966; JD, U. S.C., 1973. Bar: S.C. 1974, U.S. Ct. Appeals (4th cir.) 1974, U.S. Dist. Ct. S.C. 1976. Asst. to dean U. S.C. Law Sch., Columbia, 1973-74; law clk. to Hon. Charles E. Jr. Simons Jr. U.S. Dist. Ct. S.C., Aiken, 1974-76; assoc. Grimball & Cabaniss, Charleston, S.C., 1976-78; ptnr. Grimball, Cabaniss, Vaughan & Robinson, 1978-84; ptnr., pres. Robinson, Wall & Hastie, P.A., 1984-91; ptnr., exec. com. Nexsen, Pruet, Jacobs, Pollard & Robinson, 1991—. Permanent mem. 4th Cir. Jud. Conf., 1982—; pres. Coastal Properties Inst., Charleston, 1981—. Bd. dirs. Southeastern Wildlife Exposition, Charleston, 1987—, pres. 1994-99, Charleston Maritime Festival, 1993-99, pres. 1994-98, Parklands Found. of Charleston County; pres. S.C. Tourism Coun., Columbia, 1991-99; co-founder, chmn. Charleston Planning Project Pub. Edn., 1996—; bd. dirs. Charleston Edn. Found., Clemson U. Humanities Found., Charleston Edn. Network, chmn. bd. dirs., 2000—; edn. adv. bd. Coll. of Charleston; adv. bd. for design, Clemson U. Cpl. USMCR, 1960-66. Recipient Order of Palmetto, Gov. David Beasley, S.C., 1996. Mem. ABA, Urban Land Inst. (recreational devel. coun.), S.C. Bar Assn., Fed. Bar Assn., S.C. Def. Trial Lawyers Assn., Hibernian Soc. (mgmt. com. 1984—, sec. 1998-2000, chmn. 2000—), Kiawah Club, Haig Point Club, Country Club of Charleston, Phi Delta Phi. Presbyterian. Avocations: golf, hunting. Home: PO Box 121 Charleston SC 29402-0121 Office: Nexsen Pruet Jacobs Pollard & Robinson 200 Meeting St Ste 301 Charleston SC 29401-3156 E-mail: nrobinson@npjp.com.

ROBINSON, PAUL ARNOLD, historian, educator, writer; b. San Diego, Oct. 1, 1940; s. Joseph Cook and Beryl Marie (Lippincott) R.; m. Ute Brosche, Aug. 3, 1964 (div. Aug. 1967); 1 child, Susan Marie. BA, Yale U., 1962; postgrad., Free U. Berlin, 1962-63; PhD, Harvard U., 1968. Asst. prof. history Stanford U. (Calif.), 1967-73, assoc. prof., 1973-80, prof. history, 1980—, Richard W. Lyman prof. in the humanities, 1994—. Author: The Freudian Left, 1969, The Modernization of Sex, 1976, Opera and Ideas: From Mozart to Strauss, 1985, Freud and His Critics, 1993, Ludwig van Beethoven: Fidelio, 1996, Gay Lives: Homosexual Autobiography from John Addington Symonds to Paul Monette, 1999, Opera, Sex, and Other Vital Matters, 2002; editor: Social Thought in America and Europe, 1970; contbg. editor The New Republic, 1979-85. Guggenheim fellow, 1970-71, Stanford Humanities Ctr. fellow, 1984-85, 96-97, Inst. for Advanced Study fellow, 1990-91. Mem. Am. Acad. Arts and Scis., Am. Hist. Assn. Home: 671 Santa Ynez St Palo Alto CA 94305-8542 Office: Stanford Univ Dept History Stanford CA 94305 E-mail: paul.robinson@forsythe.stanford.edu.

ROBINSON, PETER, retired paleontology educator, consultant; b. N.Y.C., N.Y., July 19, 1932; s. Edward and Carol Nye (Rhoades) R.; m. Patricia Ellen Fisher, Sept. 11, 1954 (div. Mar. 1980); children: Diane Elizabeth, Nathan; m. Paola D'Amelio Villa, Dec. 8, 1984 BS, Yale U., 1954, MS, 1958, PhD, 1960. Instr. Harpur Coll. SUNY, Binghamton, 1955-57; rsch. assoc. Yale Peabody Mus., New Haven, 1960-61; curator geology U. Colo. Mus., Boulder, 1961—, asst. prof. natural history, 1961-67, assoc. prof., 1967-71, prof., 1971—2002, dir. mus., 1971-82, prof. geol. sci., 1971—2002; ret., 2002. Geologist Colo. Nubian Expdn., Sudan, 1962-66; chief Colo. Paleontol. Expdn., Tunisia, 1967-81 ; mem. geol. adv. group Colo. Bur. Land Mgmt., Denver, 1983-91. Mem. AAAS, Soc. Vertebrate Paleontology (pres. 1977-78), Australian Mammal Soc., Soc. Española Paleontologia, Sigma Xi Democrat. Home: 912 Hover Ridge Cir Longmont CO 80501-4141 Office: Mus U Colo Campus Box 265 Boulder CO 80309 E-mail: peter.robinson@colorado.edu.

ROBINSON, PETER BULLENE, musician, composer, songwriter; b. Kansas City, Mo., July 2, 1949; s. David Weaver and Margaret Evelyn (Sherwood) R.; m. Mary Healy Fasenmyer, Dec. 29, 1984; children: Nathan, Evie. BA in English, Princeton (N.J.) U., 1972. Staff asst. U.S. Senator Robert Dole, Washington, 1973-74; pianist, band leader Muehlebach Hotel, Kansas City, 1975-79; legis. asst. U.S. Rep. Larry Winn Jr., Washington, 1979-82; freelance pianist and composer, 1982—; resident pianist Hotél Sófitel, 1997-98. Performances include Jefferson Hotel, 1983-84, Ritz-Carlton Hotel, 1984-88, 92-97, Georgetown Inn, 1988-89, Old Ebbitt Grill, 1989-90, Hotel Sofitel, 1997-98; performer, composer (rec.) Peter Robinson Live in Washington, 1984, (compact discs) Originally, 1989, Peter Robinson Presents Songs of the Season, 1993, Dancin', 1994, The Kansas Song, 1996. Founder Bullene Music "Music is Our Middle Name". Mem. ASCAP, D.C. Fedn. Musicians (exec. bd. dirs. 1994-96). Home: 4302 Locust Ln Bethesda MD 20816-2522

ROBINSON, PREZELL RUSSELL, academic administrator; b. Batesburg, S.C., Aug. 25, 1922; s. Clarence and Annie (Folks) R.; m. Lulu Harris, Apr. 9, 1950; 1 dau. AB in Econs. and Social Sci., St. Augustine's Coll., 1946, hon. degree; MA in Sociology and Econs., Cornell U., 1951, Ed.D. in Sociology-Ednl. Adminstrn., 1956; D.C.L. (hon.), U. of the South, 1970; L.H.D., hon. degree, Cuttington U. Coll., Monrovia, Liberia; L.H.D., Voorhees Coll., 1981, hon. degree; L.H.D., Episcopal Theol. Sem., 1982; LL.D. (hon.), Bishop Coll., 1979; D.C.L., Columbia U., 1980, hon. degree; DHL (hon.), Kenyon Coll., 1988; hon. degree, Va. Theology Sem., Alexandria, Barton Coll., Campbell U., N.C. State U., Shaw U. Tchr. social sci., French Bettis Jr. Coll., Trenton, S.C., 1946-48; sucessively registrar, tchr., acting prin. high sch., acting dean jr. coll., instr., dir. adult edn. Voorhees Jr. Coll., Denmark, 1948-56; prof. sociology, dean coll. St. Augustine's Coll., Raleigh, N.C., 1956-64, exec. dean, 1964-66, acting pres., 1966-67, pres., 1967-95, pres. emeritus, 1995—. Pres. United Negro Coll. Fund, Inc., 1978-81, Nat. Assn. Equal Opportunity Higher Edn., 1981-84, N.C. Assn. Coll. & U., Cooperating Raleigh Colls., 1981, 86—; bd. dirs. Learning Inst. N.C.; scholar-in-residence Nairobi (Kenya) U., 1973; vis. lectr. Dept. State del. to African nations, 1971, 73, 78; dir. Wachovia Bank & Trust Co.; vice chmn. N.C. State Bd. Edn., mem., 1973-99, vice-chmn., 1994-99. Contbr. articles to profl. publs. Mem. exec. com. N.C. Edn. Com. on Tchr. Edn.; mem. N.C. Bd. Edn.; chmn. bd. Assn. Episcopal Colls.; mem. Mayor's Community Relations Com.; vice chmn. Wake County div. Occoneechee coun. Boy Scouts Am., 1959-67; chmn. Wake Occoneechee coun., 1963-66, mem. exec. com., from 1965; vice chmn. Wake County chpt. ARC; chmn. edn. div. United Fund of Raleigh, mem. budget com., 1965— ; mem. exec. com. Wake County Libraries.; trustee Voorhees Coll. Fulbright fellow to India, summer 1965; former U.S. Pres. George Bush appointee U.S. Alt. Rep. or Public Member Amb. Gen. Assembly of U.N., N.Y., 1992, 96. Served with AUS, 1942. Recipient Distinguished Alumni award Voorhees Coll., 1967, Silver Anniversary award N.C. Community System, 1989; decorated Star of Africia Liberia; recipient numerous service awards and citations; named one of the most effective coll. pres.s in U.S. Coun. for Advancement and Support of Edn., Washington, 1986; Univ. fellow Cornell U., 1954, rsch. fellow, 1955, 56; Fulbright fellow, 1965. Mem. AAAS, Nat. Assn. Collegiate Deans and Registrars, Am. Acad. Polit. and Social Sci., Am. Sociol. Soc., N.C. Sociol. Soc. (exec. com.), Ctrl. Intercollegiate Athletic Assn. (exec. com.), N.C. Assn. Ind. Colls. and Univs. (dir.), Raleigh C. of C. (A.E. Finley Disting. Svc. award 1989), So. Sociol. Assn., Am. Acad. Polit. Sci., N.C. Lit. and Hist. Soc., N.C. Hist. Soc., Delta Mu Delta, Phi Delta Kappa, Phi Kappa Phi, Alpha Kappa Mu, Phi Beta Lambda. Protestant Episcopalian (lay reader). Home: 821 Glascock St Raleigh NC 27604-2317 Office: St Augustine's Coll 1315 Oakwood Ave Raleigh NC 27610-2247

ROBINSON, PRISCILLA JANE, artist; b. Washington, May 13, 1948; d. Charles C. and Pauline Bates; m. Edward Robinson, June 7, 1970; 1 child, Alexander. BFA, U. Ariz., 1970. Sculptures exhibited Eagle Air Freight lobby, Houston, 1998, Tokyo Electron Am., Austin, Tex., 1996, Shell Oil and Chevron Oil, Houston, 1997. Studio: 2811 Hancock Dr Austin TX 78731-5012 E-mail: pjr@priscillarobinson.com.

ROBINSON, RANDAL D. lawyer; b. Newark, Apr. 2, 1949; s. Paul Alden and Bonnie J. C. R.; m. C. Brittney Copeland, Oct. 1, 1993; children: Brandon M., Frances M. BA, Denison U., 1971; JD, Capital U., 1975. Bar: Ohio 1975, U.S. Dist. Ct. (so. dist.) Ohio 1983, U.S. Ct. Appeals (6th cir.). Assoc. Harris, Lias & Strip, Columbus, Ohio, 1975-79; ptnr. Burman & Robinson, 1979—. Instr. bus. law Columbus (Ohio) Tech. Inst., 1983-84; instr., lectr. Franklin County Trial Lawyers Assn., 1998. Mem. ABA, Am. Arbitration Assn., Nat. Panel Arbitrators, Ohio State Bar Assn., Columbus Bar Assn. (lectr. family law legal assts. program 1980-82), Comml. Law League Am., Austin Healey Club N. Am., Inc. (bd. dirs., gen. counsel 1976—). Office: Burman & Robinson 601 S High St Fl 2 Columbus OH 43215-5680

ROBINSON, RAYMOND EDWIN, musician, music educator, writer; b. San Jose, Calif., Dec. 26, 1932; s. Elam Edwin and Zula Mai (Hatley) R.; m. Ruth Aleen Chamberlain, Mar. 12, 1954; children: Cynthia Rae, Greg Edwin, David L., Brent Steven, Jeffrey Vernon. BA, San Jose State U., 1956; MMus, Ind. U., 1958, D in Mus. Edn., 1969; LHD, Westminster Choir Coll., 1987; postdoctoral study, Cambridge U., England, 1987-89, Jagiellonian U., Poland, 1995. Instr. music Ind. U., Bloomington, 1958-59; music critic Portland Reporter, 1962-63, Balt. Evening Sun, 1964-68; founder, tchr. seminar for music adminstrs., 1972—; chmn. divsn. fine arts Cascade Coll., Portland, Oreg., 1959-63; dean Peabody Inst., Balt., 1963-69; pres. Westminster Choir Coll., Princeton, N.J., 1969-87; vis. fellow Wolfson Coll. U. Cambridge, England, 1987—89, England, 2002—; disting. prof. choral studies, choral condr. Palm Beach Atlantic U., West Palm Beach, Fla., l989—; pres. Prestige Publs. Inc., 1978—, 1992-95; music critic Palm Beach (Fla.) Post, 1991—; prof. Sch. Ch. Music Knox Theol. Sem., Ft. Lauderdale, Fla., 1989—; vis. prof. U. Miami, 2001—. Choral condr. Palm Beach C.C., Lake Worth, Fla., 1992-93; condr.-in-residence, dir. music First Presbyn. Ch., West Palm Beach, 1989-97; dir. music Coral Ridge Presbyn. Ch., Ft. Lauderdale, Fla., 1997—; spl. guest choral condr. Palm Beach Opera, 1990—; interim condr. Choral Soc. Palm Beaches, 1992; condr. Ray Robinson Chorale, 1994—, Cambridge, Eng., 1987-89, Kiev, Ukraine, 1997, Budapest, 1997, Cracow, 2002, Coral Ridge Presbyn. Ch., 1997—; vis. prof. U. Miami, Fla., 2001-2002. Author: The Choral Experience, 1976, Choral Music, 1978; Krzysztof Penderecki, A Guide to His Works, 1983, A Study of the Penderecki St. Luke Passion, 1983, John Finley Williamson: A Centennial Appreciation, 1987; co-author: German Diction for the Choral Singer, 1992, A Bach Tribute: Bach Essays in Honor of William H. Scheide, 1993; co-author, editor: Studies in Penderecki, 1998; editor: Labyrinth of Time: Five Addresses fo the End of the Millenium; editor The Choral Tradition Series, Hinshaw Music Inc., 1978—. Bd. dirs. Balt. Symphony Orch., 1967-69, Am. Boy Choir Sch., 1970-73, N.Y. Choral Soc., 1972—, Palm Beach Atlantic U. choral series Hinshaw Music Inc., 1990—; bd. dirs. Palm Beach County Coun. Arts, chmn. profl. artists com., mem. task force for master plan, 1990-92; mem. cultural plan com. Palm Beach County Cultural Coun., 1992—; mem. task force for edn. Fla. Philharm. Orch., 1994—. Recipient Disting. Alumni Merit award Ind. U., 1975, Disting. Alumni award Sch. Music Ind. U., 1973, Disting. Alumni award San Jose State U., 1990. Mem. Coll. Music Soc. (life), Am. Choral Dirs. Assn. (life, chmn. rsch. and publs. com. 1986—), Internat. Heinrich Schütz Soc. (chmn. Am. sect. 1984-87), Univ. Club N.Y., Nassau Club Princeton, Govs. Club West Palm Beach. Presbyterian. Home: 2413 Medina Way West Palm Beach FL 33401-8019 E-mail: robinsre@pbac.edu.

ROBINSON, RICHARD M. technical communication specialist; b. Bklyn., Nov. 28, 1934; s. Allen and Syd (Bell) R.; m. Rochelle Wolf, Dec. 25, 1967; children: Michelle P., Steven E. BS in Physics, Rensselaer Poly. Inst., Troy, N.Y., 1956, MS in Tech. Comm., 1959. Assoc. engr. Convair-Astronautics, San Diego, 1956-57; tech. writer Raytheon, Andover, Mass., 1957-58; pubs. engr. Hazeltine Electronics, Little Neck, N.Y., 1959-61; sr. pubs. engr. Sperry Gyroscope, Great Neck, 1961-68; mgr. editl. svcs. Grumman Corp., Bethpage, 1968-94; tech. comm. specialist/cons. Setauket, 1995—. Adj. faculty Suffolk County C.C. Contbr. articles to profl. jours.; referee papers IEEE Trans. on Profl. Comm. Mem. IEEE (life sr., conf. chmn. 1989, tech. activities bd. 1992-93, Profl. Com. Soc. adminstrv. com. 1977-97, Profl. Com. Soc. pres. 1992-93, Alfred N. Goldsmith award 1983, 3d Millennium medal 2000), Soc. Tech. Comms. (sr. mem.), Miramar Ski Club (pres. 1966-67), Amateur Ski Instrs. Assn. (cert. instr.). Home and Office: 10 Penelope Dr Setauket NY 11733-2010 E-mail: r.robinson@ieee.org.

ROBINSON, RICHARD ALLEN, JR. human resources development trainer, consultant; b. Ellensburg, Wash., Aug. 21, 1936; s. Richard Allen and Rosa Adele (Oswald) R.; m. R. Elaine Whitham, Sept. 8, 1956; children: Sharon E. Robinson Losey, Richard Allen, René L. Rivera. BA, U. Wash., 1958; postgrad., U.S. Army Command and Gen. Staff Coll., 1969-70; MA, U. Mo., 1971. Commd. 2d lt. U.S. Army, 1958, advanced through grades to lt. col., 1972, various infantry assignments including command, 1958-72, R&D assignments including dep. dir. test of behavioral sci., 1975-77, ret., 1979; chief office orgn. and employee devel. Wash. Dept. Social and Health Svcs., Olympia, 1979—; pvt. practice orgn. and mgmt. devel. cons./trainer, 1979—. Contbg. author: Games Trainers Play, vol. II, 1983. Decorated Legion of Merit with oak leaf cluster, Bronze Star. Mem. ASTD. Office: DSHS Mail 8425 27th St W Tacoma WA 98466-2722 E-mail: robbyr@msn.com.

ROBINSON, RICHARD FRANCIS, writer, author, genealogist; b. Passaic, N.J., June 13, 1941; s. Francis Ward and Evelyn (Burnett) R.; m. Brenda Kay Moore, Feb. 6, 1970; 1 child, Kelly. Student, Coll. of William & Mary, 1959-60; BA in Journalism, Mich. State U., 1964; student, Nat. Geneaol. Soc. course, 2000. Reporter, columnist North Jersey Herald News, Passaic, 1964-67; med. writer, reporter The Oakland Press, Pontiac, Mich., 1967-75; staff reporter Nat. Enquirer, Lantana, Fla., 1975-79; staff writer Hank Meyer Assocs., Miami, 1987-88; pres. Dick Robinson Co., Delray Beach, 1979—. Co-author: GeneWeaver Users Manual for Version 1.0, Clooz Version 1.2 Users Manual, 2000; editor: Foot and Leg Function, 1988—90; contbr. numerous articles to publs. including Geneal. Computing: Quar. Jour. Delegate Mich. State Rep. Conv., Detroit, 1970; mem. exec. bd. Mich. Fedn. Young Reps., 1970; mem. website com. Bd. for Certification of Genealogists. Recipient First Pl. award AP, 1973. Mem. Am. Med. Writers Assn. (bd. dirs. 1984-85, chmn. trade book awards com. 1986, founding pres. Fla. chpt. 1983-84, pres. 1986-88), Nat. Assn. Sci. Writers, Assn. Profl. Genealogists, Nat. Geneal. Soc., N.Y. Geneal. and Biog. Soc., Geneal. Soc. N.J., Passaic County (N.J.) Hist. Soc., Delray Beach Tennis Ctr. Avocations: tennis, computers, genealogy. Home and Office: 250 S Ocean Blvd Apt 252 Delray Beach FL 33483-6752 E-mail: rfr252@aol.com. *To succeed at anything in life, honestly believe you can do it well-and you will.*

ROBINSON, RICHARD GARY, management consultant, accountant; b. Oakland, Calif., Aug. 17, 1931; s. William Albert and Inez Wilhelmina (Zetterblad) R.; m. Rosemary Elsen, June 18, 1955 (dec. Dec. 1963); m. Lorraine Mary Deshaies, Nov. 13, 1965 (dec. Feb. 1984); children: Elisabeth Claudine (dec.), Christopher Paul. BBA, U. Minn., 1955; grad., Indsl. Coll. Armed Forces, 1972; M in Internat. Mgmt., Am. Grad. Sch. Internat. Mgmt., 1980; ABD in Internat. Econs., U. Denver. CPA, Colo., N.Mex.; cert. mgmt. cons. Commd. 2d lt. USAF, 1955, advanced through grades to maj., dir. radar ops. tactical air warfare, comdr. strategic missile operation and maintenance functions, project mgr., dir. mgmt. info. sys. Dept. Def. activities S.E. Asia; ret., 1976; pvt. practice Colorado Springs, Colo., 1976—; mng. ptnr. A-Action Acctg. & Tax Profls., 1994-96, Santa Fe Bus. Solutions, LLC, 1999—; pres. Bus. Devel. Specialists, Santa Fe, 1980—. Cons. People to People Project Assist to Baltic States Govts. on Trade and Econ. Legis.; dir., CFO Unique Equipment Co.; bd. dirs. United Air Freight Ltd.; CFO, bd. dirs. U.S. Gaming Fin. Corp.; adv. bd. Pegasus Learning Co., Inc.; adj. faculty Embry Riddle Aero. U., Luke AFB, Ariz.; faculty U. Phoenix; adj. prof. econs. and internat. bus. Regis U., Colorado Springs; U. So. Colo. Bus. adv. coun. Colo. Internat. Trade Office; bd. dirs. Santa Fe Family YMCA. Decorated Meritorious Svc. medal with oak leaf cluster, AF Commendtion medal with 2 oak leaf clusters. Mem. Colorado Springs Estate Planning Coun., Estate Planning Coun. Santa Fe, Internat. Bus. Assn. of the Rockies (past pres.), Colo. Springs World Affairs Coun. (bd. dirs.), Am. Mktg. Assn., Armed Forces Comm. and Electronics Assn., Am. Mgmt. Assn., Nat. Assn. Accts., Inst. Mgmt. Cons., Assn. Polit. Risk Analysts, N.Am. Soc. Corp. Planning. Lutheran. Home: HC 75 Box 315 13 Camino Potrillo Lamy NM 87540-9623 Office: 1 Caliente Rd Ste F Santa Fe NM 87508-8162 E-mail: rgrcpa@attglobal.net.

ROBINSON, ROBERT ARMSTRONG, pension fund executive; b. Waterbury, Conn., Sept. 11, 1925; s. Robert and Ethel (Armstrong) R.; m. D. Ann Harding, June 7, 1947; 1 child, Gayllis Robinson Ward. AB magna cum laude, Brown U., 1950, MA, 1952; postgrad., U. Ill., 1954-55; Litt. D., Episcopal Theol. Sem. Ky., 1971; D.C.L., U. South, 1972; LL.D., Nashotah House, Oconomowoc, Wis. Instr. English Brown U., 1950-53; instr. English, asst. prof. rhetoric U. Ill., 1953-56; trust officer Colonial Bank & Trust Co., Waterbury, 1956-63, v.p., trust officer, 1963-65, sr. trust officer, 1965-66; v.p., sec. Ch. Pension Fund and Affiliates, Ch. Life Ins. Corp., Ch. Ins. Co., Ch. Agy. Corp., Ch. Hymnal Corp., 1966-67, exec. v.p., 1967-68, pres., dir., 1968-91; pres. emeritus Ch. Pension Fund and Affiliates, Ch. Life Ins. Corp., et al., 1991—. Mgr. East Side House Settlement; bd. dirs. Seabury Press, Inc.,

Mariners Instl. Funds, Inc., Mariner Tax Free Instl. Fund, UST Master Funds, Morehouse Pub. Co., Inc., Mariner Funds Trust, Mariner Equity Trust, Pigmy Corp., U.S.T. Master Tax Free Funds, U.S.T. Master Variable Series, Inc., Rosiclare Lead and Fluorspar Mining Co., Infinity Funds, Inc., others; cons. to exec. dir. Pension Benefit Guaranty Corp.; dir. Infinity Mutual Funds, Excelsior Mut. Funds. Trustee Hillspeak, Eureka Springs, Ark., Canterbury Cathedral Trust in Am., Hoosac Sch. Washington Nat. Cathedral, Nashotah Theol. Sem., Wis., H.B. and F.K. Bugher Found., Living Ch. Found.; mem. exec. com. N.Y. couns. Boy Scouts Am., Ch. Pensions Conf.; mem. econ. adv. bd. Columbia U. Grad. Sch. Bus. Adminstrn, mem. John Carter Brown Libr. Assoc. With inf. AUS, 1943-46. Decorated Bronze Star, Purple Heart with oak leaf cluster, Mil. Order of the Purple Heart, Knights of Malta, Order St. John. Mem. Am. Numis. Soc. (councillor), Conn. Bankers Assn. (v.p., head trust divsn.), Am. Numis. Assn., Newsomen Soc., St. Andrew's Soc. (N.Y.C.), Brown Club (N.Y.C.), Union League Club (N.Y.C.), Church Club (N.Y.C.) (pres. 1991—), Country Club of New Canaan, Athenaeum Club (London), Pilgrims, Union, Met. Clubs (Washington), Yeaman's Hall Club (Charleston, S.C.), Phi Beta Kappa. Republican. Episcopalian (vestryman). Clubs: St. Andrew's Soc. (N.Y.C.), Brown (N.Y.C.), Union League (N.Y.C.), Church (N.Y.C.), Country of New Canaan, Athenaeum (London), Pilgrims, Union, Met. (Washington), Yeaman's Hall (Charleston, S.C.). Home: 2 Hathaway Common New Canaan CT 06840-5737 Office: 800 2nd Ave New York NY 10017-4709

ROBINSON, ROBERT BLACQUE, foundation administrator; b. Long Beach, Calif., Apr. 24, 1927; s. Joseph LeRoi and Frances Hansel R.; m. Susan Amelia Thomas, Jan. 21, 1960; children: Victoria, Shelly, Blake, Sarah. Student, Oreg. State Coll., 1946; BA, UCLA, 1950; student, U. Hawaii. Partner, Pritchard Assocs. (Mgmt. Cons.), Honolulu, 1956-58; asst. dir. Econ. Planning and Coordination Authority, Hawaii, 1959; dep. dir. dept. econ. devel. State of Hawaii, 1960-63; asst. mgr. Pacific Concrete and Rock Co., Ltd., Honolulu, 1963-66, exec. v.p. and gen. mgr., 1966-68, pres. and gen. mgr., 1968-75, chmn., 1976-77; pres. C. of C. of Hawaii, Honolulu, 1977—. Bd. govs. Hawaii Employers Coun., 1969-74, mem. exec. com., 1969-74, vice chmn., 1973-74; bd. dirs. Pacific Aerospace Mus., 1982-86; mem. Hawaii Tourism Conf., 1977, chmn., 1981-82; bd. dirs. Aloha United Fund, 1970-76, sec., 1972, v.p., 1973-76; bd. dirs. Oahu Devel. Conf., 1970-75; treas., bd. dirs. Crime Stoppers Hawaii, 1981—; mem. Hawaii Joint Coun. on Econ. Edn., 1985—; bd. dirs. Jr. Achievement Hawaii, 1967-73, pres., 1969; bd. dirs. Hawaii Ednl. Coun., 1974-75, Health and Community Services Coun. Hawaii, 1982-84; mem. exec. com. Hawaii Conv. Ctr. Coun., 1984—, Interagency Energy Conservation Coun., State of Hawaii, 1978—; trustee Cen. Union Ch., 1983-86; bd. dirs. Waikiki Improvement Assn. Inc., 1986—; mem. Ctr. for Tropical and Subtropical Aquaculture industry Adv. Coun., 1987—; chmn. Mayor's Adv. Com. on Pacific Nations Ctr., 1988-89. Lt. comdr. USNR, 1945-46, ret. Mem. Japan-Am. Conf. of Mayors and C. of C. Pres. (mem. Am. exec. com. 1974—), Am. Soc. Assn. Execs. (past dir. Hawaii chpt.), Hawaii Execs. Coun. (found. , Young Pres. Assn. (past mem.), Aloha Soc. Assn. Execs., C. of C. Hawaii (dir. 1972-75, chmn. 1975), Coun. of Profit Sharing Industries (past dir. Hawaii sect.), Cement and Concrete Products Industry of Hawaii (pres. 1968), Hawaii Mfrs. Assn. (past dir.), Navy League of U.S. (Hawaii council), Engring. Assn. Hawaii, Pacific Club, Rotary, Sigma Chi. Home: 1437 Kalaepohaku St Honolulu HI 96816-1804 Office: C of C Hawaii 735 Bishop St Ste 220 Honolulu HI 96813-4816

ROBINSON, ROBERT CRIBBEN, librarian, information company executive; b. Madison, Wis., June 16, 1950; s. Robert Cribben and Elizabeth (Mahoney) R.; m. Julie Baxter, June 10, 1978; children: Megan, Kerry. BA, Allegheny Coll., 1972; MLS, U. Md., 1973. Asst. program libr. Nat. Pub. Radio, Washington, 1974-75, news libr., 1975-94, sr. libr., 1994—. Pres. Robinson Info. Co., Arlington, 1985—. Mem. Spl. Libr. Assn., Nat. Geneal. Soc., Photog. Soc. Am., Investigative Reporters and Editors, Soc. Am. Archivists, Potomac Soc. Stereo Photographers (pres. 1985-87), Internat. Assn. Sound Archivists.. Home: 6231 21st St N Arlington VA 22205-2036 Office: Nat Pub Radio 635 Massachusetts Ave NW Washington DC 20001-3753

ROBINSON, ROBERT EARL, chemical company executive; b. Covington, Ky., Aug. 3, 1927; s. Adolph Earl and Frances Elizabeth (Rouse) R.; m. Myrtle Caroline Tonne, June 10, 1951; children: Linda Ann, Carol Eileen Robinson Cranford, Timothy John. AB, Berea Coll., 1949; MS, Purdue U., 1951, PhD, 1953; postgrad., U. Cin., 1962-64. Project leader U.S. Indsl. Chems., Cin., 1953-64; group leader Stauffer Chem. Co., Weston, Mich., 1964-65; rsch. dir. Cardinal Chem. Co., Columbia, S.C., 1965-66; exec. v.p. Lindau Chems. Inc., 1966-86, pres., 1986—. Dir. Richland Land Devel. Co., Columbia. Contbr. articles to profl. jours. and encys.; 25 patents in field. Fundraiser Am. Cancer Soc., Columbia, 1991; mem. bd. dirs. S.C. Philharmonic Orch., 1993-99, 2000—. With U.S. Army, 1946-47. Fellow Am. Inst. Chemists; mem. AAAS, Am. Chem. Soc. (chair divsn. small chem. bus. 1993, 98), N.Y. Acad. Scis., Baker St. Irregulars, Sherlock Holmes Soc. London, Mensa. Avocations: Sherlock Holmes, computer science, serious music. Home: 6117 Lakeshore Dr Columbia SC 29206-4331 Office: Lindau Chems Inc 731 Rosewood Dr Columbia SC 29201-4633

ROBINSON, ROBERT L. former financial service company executive, lawyer; b. Ridgeway, Va., Feb. 22, 1936; s. Gerald L. and Annie (McBride) R.; m. Audrey M. Allen, July 30, 1960; children: Robert, Diane, Kelly. BA, Va. State Coll., 1957; LL.B., Harvard U., 1960; MBA, U. Conn., 1976. Bar: N.Y. 1961, Pa. 1978. Atty. N.Y. Central Ry. Co., N.Y.C., 1960-63; asst. gen. counsel Crane Co., 1963-71; counsel Xerox Corp., Stamford, Conn., 1971-77; v.p., asst. gen. counsel and sec. INA Corp., Phila., 1977-82; sr. v.p., gen. counsel investment group CIGNA Corp., Bloomfield, Conn., 1982-84, sr. v.p., asst. gen. counsel, corp. sec., 1984-87, sr. v.p., gen. counsel property & casualty group Phila., 1987-88, sr. v.p., chief counsel litigation and ins., 1988-2000; ret., 2000. Dir. Phila. Reinsurance Corp., Am. Arbitration Assn., CPR Inst. for Dispute Resolution. Served to lt. U.S. Army, 1957. Mem. ABA, Pa. Bar Assn., Westchester-Fairfield Corp. Counsel Assn. (founder, bd. dirs. pres. 1976-77), Great Oak Yacht Cub, Harvard Club (N.Y.C.), Merion Cricket Club, Phila. Club., Phila. Cricket Club. Republican. Office: 451 Moreno Rd Wynnewood PA 19096 E-mail: rakr@erols.com.

ROBINSON, ROBERT WHITEHILL, financial advisor; b. Nashville, Jan. 23, 1967; s. Robert Wallace and Judith Logan (Whitehill) R. BA in Polit. Sci., Vanderbilt U., 1990. V.p. sales and ops. TBI Steel, Jackson, Tenn., 1987-91; pres. Student Asset Mgmt., Nashville, 1989-91; with Hamilton Securities Group, Washington, 1991-96, bd. dirs., 1992-96; fin. advisor Am. Express Fin. Advisors, Inc., Alexandria, Va., 1997—. Republican. Episcopalian. Office: Am Express Fin Advisors 4900 Seminary Rd Ste 100 Alexandria VA 22311-1811

ROBINSON, RONALD ALAN, manufacturing executive; b. Louisville, Mar. 23, 1952; s. J. Kenneth and Juanita M. (Crosier) R.; m. Joan Parker, 1986; children: Rex, Jay. BS, GA Inst. Tech., 1974; MBA, Harvard U., 1978. Staff engr., asst. to exec. v.p. ops. Dual Drilling Co., Wichita Falls, Tex., 1978-80; v.p. Dreco, Inc., Houston, 1980-84, pres., dir. subs. Triflo Industries Internat., Inc.; pres., COO Ramteck Sys., Inc., 1984-87; chmn., CEO Denver Techs. Inc., 1988-95; pres. Svedala Industries, Inc., 1996-99; pres., CEO Alamo Group Inc., Seguin, Tex., 1999—. Manufacturing executive; b. Louisville, Mar. 23, 1952; s. J. Kenneth and Juanita M. (Crosier) R.; m. Joan Parker, 1986; children: Rex., Jay. BS, Ga. Inst. Tech., 1974; MBA, Harvard U., 1978. Staff engr., asst. to exec. v.p. ops. Dual Drilling Co., Wichita Falls, Tex., 1978-80; v.p. Dreco, Inc., Houston, 1980-84, pres., dir. subs. Triflo Industries Internat. Inc.; pres., COO Ramteck Systems, Inc., 1984-87; chmn. and CEO Denver Techs. Inc., 1988-95; pres. Svedala Industries, Inc., 1996-99; Pres. and CEO, Alamo Group Inc, 1999—. Recipient Optimist Internat. Citizenship award, 1970; Gardiner Symonds fellow, 1977. Mem. Harvard Alumni Assn. Recipient Optimist Internat. Citizenship award, 1970; Gardiner Symonds fellow, 1977. Mem. Harvard Alumni Assn. Home: 4815 Newstead Pl Colorado Springs CO 80906-5935 Office: Alamo Group Inc 1502 E Walnut St Seguin TX 78155-5202

ROBINSON, RONALD GENE, military contract negotiator, educator; b. Detroit, June 13, 1952; s. John Henry and Linnie (Mattingly) R.; m. Cheryl Lee Robinson, Aug. 27, 1982 (div. July 2000); children: Ronald Jr., Lindee Marie, Ryan John; m. Dee Robinson, May 6, 2001. AA, Schoolcraft Coll., 1972; B in Gen. Studies, U. Mich., 1974; MA, Western Mich. U., 1977. Cert. govt. contracting level III. Prof. polit. sci. Schoolcraft Coll., Livonia, Mich., 1976—; contract negotiator U.S. Army, Warren, 1981—. Pres. R&B Advt. Agy., Warren, 1996-98. Author: Judicial Character, 1977; columnist The County Line, Warren, 1990-97, The Warren Examiner, 1996-97. Candidate Warren City Coun., 1991, nominee, 1995; chmn. Hartsig Pk. Homeowners Assn., Warren, 1990-97; precinct del. Livonia Rep. Party, 1974-81; mem. Oakland County Young Reps., 2000—; bd. dirs. Warren-Centerline Right to Life, 1991—. Mem. So. Polit. Sci. Assn. Avocations: swimming, travel, dancing, playing Stratego, playing pool. Personal E-mail: rgr11897@aol.com.

ROBINSON, RONALD MICHAEL, financial executive, financial consultant; b. N.Y.C., May 1, 1942; s. Arthur John and Matilda (Siegel) R.; m. Mary Jane Reemelin, Feb. 25, 1972; children: Scott Edward, Elizabeth Drew. BS, Ohio State U., 1964; MBA, U. Pa., 1966. CPA, Pa. Fin. mgr. Am. Airlines, Inc., N.Y.C., 1969-72; mgmt. cons. Coopers & Lybrand, Phila., 1973-75; pres. Robinson Assocs., Inc., Paoli, Pa., 1975-81; dir. fin. and adminstrn., chief fin. officer Presbyn. Homes, Inc., Camp Hill, 1982-99. Bd. dirs. Healthamerica, Mems. First Fed. Credit Union; Continuing Care Rx, Advosave.com, Presbyterian Apts., Cumberlund Crossings. Mem. Carlisle (Pa.) Borough Coun., 1988-92. Home: 1214 Georgetown Circle Carlisle PA 17013-3548 Office: Presbyn Homes Inc PO Box 908 Carlisle PA 11701 Fax: (717) 258-8727. E-mail: robinsonr@mindspring.com.

ROBINSON, ROSCOE ROSS, nephrologist, educator; b. Oklahoma City, Aug. 21, 1929; s. Roscoe and Tennie (Ross) R.; m. Ann Allen, Aug. 24, 1952; children: Susan, Brooke. BS, U. Ctrl. Okla., 1949; MD, U. Okla., 1954, LHD, 1994. Diplomate: Nat. Bd. Med. Examiners, Am. Bd. Internal Medicine (asso. mem. bd. govs. 1975-78, mem. 1979-82, chmn. test com. on nephrology 1979-82). Intern in medicine Duke U. Med. Ctr., Durham, N.C., 1954-55, jr. asst. resident in medicine, 1955-56, chief resident, instr. medicine, 1957-58, assoc. in medicine, 1960-62, asst. prof. medicine, dir. div. nephrology, 1962-65, assoc. prof. medicine, dir. div. nephrology, 1965-69, prof. medicine, dir. div. nephrology, 1969-78, Florence McAlister prof. medicine, dir. div. nephrology, 1978-81, assoc. v.p. health affairs NC, 1976-81; chief exec. officer Duke U. Hosp., 1976-81; prof. medicine Vanderbilt U. Med. Ctr., Nashville, 1981—, vice chancellor health affairs, 1981-97, vice chancellor emeritus, 1997—; vice chair Duke U. Health Sys., 1998—2001. Am. Heart Assn. rsch. fellow, vis. fellow dept. medicine Columbia-Presbyn. Med. Ctr., N.Y.C., 1956-57; clin. investigator Durham VA Hosp., 1960-62, attending physician, 1962-81; cons. nephrology Fayetteville and Asheville, N.C., Research Triangle (N.C.) Inst., 1964-81; nat. cons. to surgeon gen. USAF, 1970-89; chmn. N.C. Kidney Coun. Region 21, Dept. HEW, 1977-81; sr. investigator N.C. Heart Assn., 1962-74. Mem. editl. bd. Archives Internal Medicine, 1970-80, Seminars in Nephrology, 1972-93, Mineral and Electrolyte Metabolism, 1977-92; mem. editl. com. Fogerty internat. com. Monograph on Prevention of Kidney and Urinary Tract Disease; cons. editor renal diseases: Cecil Textbook of Medicine, 15th edit., 16th edit.; contbr. articles to profl. jours. Trustee Montgomery Bell Acad., Nashville, 1982—, Duke U., 1992—2000, vice chmn. health sys., 1998—2001; bd. dirs. AMA Found., 1999—2001, mem. exec. com., 1993—99. Fellow: ACP; mem.: Nat. Inst. Diabetes, Digestive and Kidney Diseases (nat. adv. coun. 1987—90), Soc. Med. Adminstrs. (pres.-elect 1989—91, pres. 1991—93), Assn. Acad. Health Ctrs. (bd. dirs. 1985—91, chmn. 1989—90, 1989—90), Kidney Found. N.C., Nat. Kidney Found. (sci. adv. bd. 1970—75, bd. dirs. 2000—01), Am. Soc. Nephrology (councillor 1977—80, pres.-elect 1980—81, pres. 1981—82, John Peters award 1992), Internat. Soc. Nephrology (editor Kidney Internat. Jour. 1971—84, exec. com. 1972—95, v.p. 1984—87, pres.-elect 1987—90, pres. 1990—93, Hamburger award 2001), Am. Soc. Artificial Internal Organs (councillor 1968—71), Am. Physiol. Soc., So. Soc. Clin. Investigation (councillor 1977—80), Am. Soc. Clin. Investigation, N.C. Heart Assn. (sr. investigator 1962—74, bd. dirs. 1971—72, exec. com.), Am. Heart Assn., European Dialysis and Transplant Assn., Assn. Am. Physicians, Am. Fedn. Clin. Rsch. (councillor So. sect. 1968—71), Am.Clin. And Climatol. Assn., Alpha Omega Alpha. Home: 501 Jackson Blvd Nashville TN 37205-3427 Office: Vanderbilt U Med Ctr Ste 2000 Village at Vanderbilt Nashville TN 37232

ROBINSON, ROXANA BARRY, writer, art historian; b. Pine Mountain, Ky., Nov. 30, 1946; Student, Bennington Coll., 1964-66; BA, U. Mich., 1969. Art cataloguer Sotheby's, N.Y.C., 1970-74; exhbn. dir. Terry Dintenfass Gallery, 1974-76; freelance writer, 1976—. Author: (novel) Summer Light, 1988 (Washington Irving award Westchester Libr. Assn.), This Is My Daughter, 1998 (Notable Book Yr. award N.Y. Times 1998, Washington Irving award Westchester Libr. Assn.), (biography) Georgia O'Keeffe: A Life, 1989 (Notable Book Yr. award N.Y. Times 1989, Washington Irving award Westchester Libr. Assn.), (short stories) A Glimpse of Scarlet, 1991 (Notable Book Yr. award N.Y. Times 1991), Asking For Love, 1995 (Washington Irving award Westchester Libr. Assn., Notable Book of Yr Nat. Libr. Assn.). Bd. trustees Katonah Mus. Art, 1980—, Eugene Lang Coll., N.Y., Nat. Humanities Ctr., N.C., 1995—. PEN Am. Ctr., N.Y., 1998—. Recipient Lit. Lion award N.Y. Pub. Libr., 1991; fellow Nat. Endowment Arts, 1987, MacDowell Colony, 1999, John S. Guggenheim Found. fellow, 2000. Office: c/o Lynn Nesbit Janklow-Nesbit 445 Park Ave New York NY 10022

ROBINSON, RUTH CARLESON, secondary education educator; b. Salem, Oreg., Aug. 27, 1937; d. Richard Victor and Opal Charlotte Carleson; m. Kenneth Oliver Robinson, Aug. 2, 1959; children: Grant Kenneth, Victoria Ruth. BS, Oreg. State U., 1959. H.s. tchr. Hillsboro (Oreg.) Sch. Dist., 1959-60, Gresham-Barlow Sch. Dist., Gresham, Oreg., 1976—. Site coun. Sam Barlow H.S., Gresham, 1994—2002, chair site coun., 1998—2002. Contbr. Portland Opera Assn., 1982—, Portland Classical Chinese Garden, Portland Art Mus. Mem. AAUW, NEA, Oreg. Edn. Assn., Gresham-Barlow Edn. Assn. (v.p. 1994-95, pres. 1995-96), Multnomah County UniServ (sec. 1989-92, pres. 1993-95). Avocations: opera, travel, collecting. Home: 2934 NE 38th Ave Portland OR 97212-2854 Office: Sam Barlow HS 5105 SE 302d Ave Gresham OR 97080

ROBINSON, RUTH HUBBARD, retired elementary school educator; b. Orangeburg, SC, Sept. 18, 1926; d. Charles Harrison and Sarah Hook Hubbard; m. John Samuel Robinson (dec. Aug. 22, 1996); children: Tyrone, Lynn Miller, Elton; children: Tyrone, Lynn Miller, Elton. BA in English, Claflin U., Orangeburg SC, 1948; MS in Edn., S.C. State U., 1957. Cert. English S.C. Dept. Edn., elem. edn. S.C. Dept. Edn., reading S.C. Dept. Edn. English tchr. Orangeburg County Tng. Sch., Elloree, SC, 1948—49, Norway (S.C.) H.S., 1951—53; elem. sch. tchr. Allendale (S.C.) Tng. Sch., 1957—59, Bethlehem Elem. Sch., St. Matthews, 1961—63; elem. reading tchr. Orangeburg Sch. Dist. 5, 1963—86; ret. Author: (book of poetry) Images, 1996, poetry. Co-founder, chair Robinson Scholarship Fund of St. Luke Presbyn. Ch. (USA), Orangeburg, 1994. Recipient Meritorious Svc. award, St. Luke Presbyn. Ch. Bd. Deacons, 1983, Golden Poet award, World of Poetry, 1988, Grand Prize in Quilting, Orangeburg (SC) County Fair, 2000, 2001. Mem.: VFW Aux. (charter), NAACP (life), Claflin U. Nat. Alumni (life). Democrat. Presbyterian. Avocations: quilting, travel, reading, volunteering. Home: 279 Oakridge Dr NE Orangeburg SC 29115

ROBINSON, SALLY WINSTON, artist; b. Detroit, Nov. 2, 1924; d. Harry Lewis and Lydia (Kahn) Winston; m. Eliot F. Robinson, June 28, 1949; children: Peter Eliot, Lydia Winston, Sarah Mitchell, Suzanne Finley. BA, Bennington Coll., 1947; postgrad., Cranbrook Acad. Art, 1949; grad., Sch. Social Work, Wayne U., 1948, MA, 1972; MFA, Wayne State U., 1973. Psychol. tester Detroit Bd. Edn., 1944; psychol. counselor and tester YMCA, N.Y.C., 1946; social caseworker Family Svc., Pontiac, Mich., 1947; instr. printmaking Wayne State U., Detroit, 1973—. Tchr. children's art Detroit Inst. Art, 1949-50, now artistic advisor, bd. dirs. drawing and pring orgn. One-woman shows include , U. Mich., 1973, Wayne State U., 1974, Klein-Vogel Gallery, 1974, Rina Gallery, 1976, Park McCullough House, Vt., 1976, Williams Coll., 1976, Arnold Klein Gallery, 1977, exhibited in group shows, Bennington Coll., Cranbrook Mus., Detroit Inst. Art, Detroit Artists Market, Soc. Women Painters, Soc. Arts and Crafts, Bloomfield Art Assn., Flint Left Bank Gallery, Balough Gallery, Detroit Soc. Woman Painters, U. Mich., U. Ind., U. Wis., U. Pitts., Toledo Mus., Krannert Mus., Represented in permanent collections , Detroit, N.Y.C., Birmingham, Bloomfield Hills. Bd. dirs. Planned Parenthood, 1951—, mem. exec. bd., 1963—; bd. dirs. PTA, 1956-60, Roeper City and Country Sch., U. Mich. Mus. Art, 1978; trustee Putnam Hosp. Med. Rsch. Inst., 1978; mem. Gov.'s Commn. Art in State Bldgs., 1978-79; mem. art and devel. coms. So. Vt. Art Ctr., 1987-88; mem. vol. com. Marie Selby Gardens; patron Graphic Art Studio, U. So. Fla., Tampa; patron, benefactor Clark Mus., Williamstown, Mass. Fellow: Williams Coll. Mus. Art (mem. visiting com.); mem.: Bloomfield Art Assn. (program co-chmn. 1956), Birmingham Soc. Women Painters (pres. 1974—76), Detroit Soc. Women Painters, Detroit Artists Market (dir. 1956—, hon. bd. mem.), Founders Soc. Detroit Inst. Art, Bennington Coll. Alumnae Assn. (regional co-chmn. 1954), Cosmopolitan Club (N.Y.C.), Am. Club (Sarasota, Fla., bd. dirs.), Burlington Vt. Garden Club, Oaks Club (Fla.), Women's City Club (coord. art shows Detroit 1950), Village Women's Club (Birmingham, Mich.). Unitarian Universalist. Home: 209 Hills Point Rd Charlotte VT 05445-9698 also: 840 N Casey Key Rd Osprey FL 34229-9779

ROBINSON, SAMUEL WILLIS, JR. information sciences specialist; b. Charlotte, N.C., Aug. 6, 1927; s. Samuel Willis and Gladys Pamelia (DeArmon) R.; m. Ramona Del Hatfield, Jan. 27, 1951; children: Sharon, Michael, Susan, Lorraine. BS in Physics, Davidson Coll., 1949; MS in Physics, Clemson U., 1951. Aerospace rsch. scientist Nat. Com. for Aeronautics, Langley AFB, Va., 1951-53; aerospace engr., mgr. Lockheed Ga. Co., Marietta, 1953-70; info. specialist Lockheed Calif. Co., Burbank, 1970-90, computer cost analyst Info. Svcs. div., 1982-90; ret., 1990. Regional dir. Simulation Couns., Atlanta, 1960-70; cons. Computer Usage Billing, Burbank, 1987-90. Patentee in field. With USNR, 1945-46. Mem. Phi Beta Kappa, Sigma Pi Sigma. Presbyterian. Avocations: personal computer applications, golf duffer. Home: 2752 E Ponderosa Dr Apt 185 Camarillo CA 93010-4816

ROBINSON, SARA CURTIS, arts administrator; b. Amarillo, Tex., Jan. 6, 1967; d. Don Teel Curtis and Suzanne (Stokes) Brent; m. Benjamin Rowland Robinson, Oct. 5, 1991; children: Rowland Wyatt, Tristan Rodman. BA, Pine Manor Coll., 1989. Asst. dir. Sorota Fine Arts, Boston, 1989; asst. to curator Asiatic art Mus. Fine Arts, 1990-91; from devel. officer to dir. devel. Bank of Boston Celebrity Series, 1992—. Mem. Women in Devel., Boston, 1993-96, Boston Arts Mktg. Group, 1992-94. Mem. Jr. League Boston, 1990-95, com. chair, 1993; mem. Mass. Advocates for the Arts, Boston, 1993-96, Cultural Diversity Com. for the Arts, Boston, 1993-96; com. Newbury St. League Auction, Boston, 1989. Mem. Internat. Soc. Performing Arts Adminstrs., Nat. Soc. Fundraising Execs. Episcopalian. Office: Bank of Boston Celeb Series 20 Park Plz Ste 1032 Boston MA 02116-4309

ROBINSON, SCHARN, lawyer, author, researcher; b. Albany, N.Y., Jan. 5, 1968; d. David McKinley and N. Ruth Penn R. BA, Union Coll., 1990; Phd, U. Mich., 1995; JD, U. Calif., Berkeley, 1998. Assoc. O'Melveny & Myers LLP, Washington, 1998—2001, Paul, Hastings Janofsky & Walker LLP, 2001—. Polit. sci. vis. prof. Union Coll., Schenectady, N.Y., 1995, SUNY, Albany, 1995, U. of the West Indies, Barbados, 1996; sociology vis. prof. St. Mary's of Calif., Moraga, Calif., 1998, U. Calif. Berkeley Ext., 1998. Vol. Berkeley Cmty. Law Ctr., 1996, San Francisco Coalition on Homelessness, San Francisco, 1996. Scholar Harry S. Truman Found., Stanley Becker scholar; fellow NSF; named to Acad. Hall of Fame City of Schenectady, 2000; recipient Bailey prize. Mem. ABA, Am. Polit. Sci. Assn. (fellow), Nat. Bar Assn., Phi Sigma Alpha. Avocations: tennis, jazz, kickboxing. Home: 4708 Queens Grove St White Plains MD 20695

ROBINSON, SHARON BETH, health science association administrator; b. Balt., Sept. 28, 1959; BS, Towson State U., 1981; MS, Johns Hopkins U., 1986. Exec. asst. Congress of Neurol. Surgeons, Balt., 1983-86; office adminstr. Md. Inst. Emergency Med. Svcs., 1986-87; coord. spl. projects U. Md. Med. Systems, 1986-88; adminstr. Am. Bd. Med. Genetics, Bethesda, Md., 1988—, Am. Coll. Med. Genetics, Bethesda, 1992-98, Am. Bd. Genetic Counseling, Bethesda, 1993—. Mem. Catonsville Community Coll. Alumni Assn. (bd. dirs. 1984-89, sec. 1986, v.p. 1987, pres. 1988). Office: ABMG/ABGC 9650 Rockville Pike Bethesda MD 20814-3998 E-mail: srobinson@genetics.faseb.org.

ROBINSON, SHAWNA, race car driver; b. Des Moines, Nov. 30, 1964; 2 children. Big-rig tractor driver Great Am. Truck Racing Tour, 1980; racecar driver Huffman Racing, 1991. Named winner, Dash Race, 1988, Most Popular Driver, 1988, Rookie of the Yr., 1988, winner, Talladega Pole award, 2000; recipient 3d pl., Goody's Dash Series, 1988, 4th pl., Bondo/Mar-Hyde Series Race, 1999, 2d pl., First Plus Fin. 200, 1999. Office: c/o BAM Racing 11881 Vance Davis Dr Charlotte NC 28269*

ROBINSON, STACEY MUKAI, lawyer, associate; b. Honolulu, Apr. 8, 1969; d. Stanley Yukiyoshi and Elaine Tsuruko Mukai; m. John Henry Robinson, Mar. 9, 1996. BA cum laude, Williams Coll., 1991; JD, U. Va., 1995. Bar: Hawaii 1996, U.S. Dist. Ct. Hawaii 1996, U.S. Ct. Appeals (9th cir.) 1996. Assoc. McCorriston, Miho, Miller, Mukai, Honolulu, 1996—. Mem. ABA, Hawaii State Bar Assn. Office: McCorriston Miller Mukai MacKinnon LLP 500 Ala Moana Blvd Ste 5-400 Honolulu HI 96813-4989 E-mail: robinson@m4law.com.

ROBINSON, STEPHEN K. astronaut; b. Sacramento, Oct. 25, 1955; s. William and Joyce Robinson. BS in Mech. Engring., U. Calif., Davis, 1978; MS in Mech. Engring., Stanford U., Calif., 1983; PhD in Mech. Engring., Aeronautics, Astronautics, Stanford U. Rsch. scientist NASA Ames, Mountain View, Calif., 1979—90; chief exptl. flow physics br. NASA Langley Rsch. Ctr., Hampton, Va., 1990—93; fellow MIT Man Vehicle Lab., Cambridge, Mass., 1993—94; leader aerodynamics and acoustics element NASA Langley Gen. Aviation Tech., Hampton, 1994; astronaut Johnson Space Ctr., Houston, 1995—. Recipient Ames Honor award, NASA, 1989, G.M. Low Meml. Engring. fellowship, NASA/Space Club, 1993. Mem.: AIAA (Tech. Paper award (co-author) 1992), Exptl. Aircraft Assn., Aerospace Med. Assn. Achievements include conducted experiments in space spending over 497 hours in that environment. Avocations: art, canoeing, hiking, music, antique aircraft. Office: Astronaut Office NASA Johnson Space Ctr Houston TX 77058

ROBINSON, STEPHEN MICHAEL, applied mathematician, educator; b. Columbus, Ohio, Apr. 12, 1942; s. Arthur Howard and Mary Elizabeth (Coffin) R.; m. Chong-Suk Han, May 10, 1968; children: Diana Marie, James Andrew. BA, U. Wis., 1962, PhD, 1971; MS, NYU, 1963; Doctor honoris causa, Univ. Zürich, 1996. Adminstr. U. Wis., Madison, 1969-72, asst. prof., 1972-75, assoc. prof., 1975-79, prof. indsl. engring. and computer scis., 1979—, chmn. dept. indsl. engring., 1981-84. Cons. to various agys. Dept. Def., 1971—. Editor: Math. of Ops. Rsch., 1981-86, assoc. editor, 1975-80, Jour. Ops. Rsch., 1974-86, Math. Programming, 1986-91; mem. bd. editors Annals Ops. Rsch., 1984-99, Set-Valued Analysis, 1992-99, Jour. Convex Analysis, 1994—; adv. editor Math. of Ops. Rsch., 1987—, Ops. Rsch. Letters, 2002-; mem. editl. bd. Springer Series in Ops. Rsch., 1996—; contbr. numerous articles to profl. jours. Trustee Village of Shorewood Hills, Wis., 1974-76, mem. fin. com. , 1973-87; bd. overseers Simon's Rock Coll., Great Barrington, Mass., 1991-2002. Capt. U.S. Army, 1963—69, Korea, Vietnam. Decorated Legion of Merit, Bronze star, Air medal, Army Commendation medal with 2 oak leaf clusters; recipient John K. Walker Jr. award, Mil. Ops. Rsch. Soc., 2001. Mem. Inst. for Ops. Rsch. and Mgmt. Scis. (mem. Ops. Rsch. Soc. Am. coun. 1991-94, sec. 2000—), Inst. Indsl. Engrs., Soc. Indsl. and Applied Math., Math. Programming Soc. (mem.-at-large of coun. 1991-94, George B. Dantzig prize 1997), Madison Club. Home: 1014 University Bay Dr Madison WI 53705-2251 Office: U Wis Dept Indsl Engring 1513 University Ave Madison WI 53706-1572 E-mail: smrobins@wisc.edu.

ROBINSON, STEWART MARSHALL, mathematician, educator; b. Schenectady, N.Y., Jan. 7, 1934; s. Samuel and Ruth (Englebardt) R.; m. Valerie Countway, July 7, 1960; children: Zachary, Benjamin, Elliott. BS, Union Coll., 1955; PhD, Duke U., 1959. Rsch. asst. Duke U., Durham, N.C., 1959; asst. prof. U. R.I., Kingston, 1959-61, Smith Coll., Northampton, Mass., 1961-64; assoc. prof. math. Union Coll., Schenectady, 1964-68, Cleve. State U., 1968-94; adj. prof. math. Case Western Res. U., Cleve., 1994—. Treas. Greater Cleve. Coalition for Cleve. Environment, 1993—; dir. Stop Targeting Ohio Poor, Cleve., 1996—. Mem. Am. Math. Soc., Math. Assn. Am. Home: 3334 Berkeley Rd Cleveland Hts OH 44118-2075 Office: Case Western Res U Yost Hall 218 Cleveland OH 44106

ROBINSON, SUSAN MITTLEMAN, data processing executive; b. Bklyn., Nov. 18, 1941; d. Samuel and Ida (Priest) Mittleman; m. Sheldon N. Robinson, June 5, 1962; children: Edward Bruce, Nancy Michelle, Jonathan Scott, Karen Barbara, Judith Lynn. AAS in Computer Sci., BCC, Lincroft, N.J., 1981; BBA, CUNY, 1962; MS in Computer Sci., Fairleigh Dickinson U., 1983; postgrad., Seton Hall U., 1983-85. Engr. asst. United Technologies, East Hartford, Conn., 1962-64; programmer, sys. analyst Litton Industries (Sweda), Pine Brook, N.J., 1981-83; asst. prof. data processing Mercer Coll., West Windsor, 1983-85; adj. instr. data processing Brookdale C.C., Lincroft, 1983—; coord. MIS N.J. Dept. Health and Sr. Svcs., Trenton, 1985—, NT LAN adminstr. N.J., 1994—, world wide web webmaster; med. data set liaison N.J. Dept. Health and Sr. Svcs. and HCFA, 1996—. Outsource cons. Medicare/Medicaid, Trenton, 1989—; cons. Health Care Fin. Authority, Balt., 1995—. Author (reference material) Info-Henco, 1987, Automated Survey Processing Environment Users Training Manual, 1993; developer computerized sys. to help patients and their family select a nursing home. Exec. bd. Temple Beth Am, Parsippany, N.J., 1972-80. Mem. SAS Users Group, N.J. DOH Prime Users Group. Avocations: knitting, puzzle-solving, travel. Office: NJ Dept Health and Sr Svcs PO Box 367 Trenton NJ 08625-0367

ROBINSON, THEODORE CURTIS, JR. lawyer; b. Chgo., Jan. 22, 1916; s. Theodore Curtis and Edna Alice (Willard) R.; m. Marynel Werner, Dec. 28, 1940; children: Theodore Curtis III, Peter S. BA, Western Res. U., 1938, LLB, 1940. Bar: Ohio 1940, U.S. Dist. Ct. (no. dist.) Ohio 1946, U.S. Ct. Appeals (8th cir.) 1948, U.S. Dist. Ct. (we. dist.) Wis. 1950, U.S. Dist. Ct. (we. dist.) N.Y. 1950, U.S. Ct. Appeals (6th cir.) 1950, Ill. 1957, U.S. Dist. Ct. (no. dist.) Ill. 1957, U.S. Ct. Appeals (7th cir.) 1964, U.S. Supreme Ct. 1972. Assoc. Davis & Young, Cleve., 1940; law clk. no. dist. ea. divsn. U.S. Dist. Ct., 1940-42; assoc. Leckie, McCreary, et al, 1945-52; ptnr. McCreary, Hinslea & Ray, 1953-57, McCreary, Hinslea, Ray & Robinson, Chgo., 1957-90; counsel Ray, Robinson, Hannin & Carle, 1990-91, Ray, Robinson, Carle, Davies & Snyder, Chgo., 1991-98, ret., 1998. Mem. exec. com. Maritime Law Assn. of U.S., N.Y.C., 1981-83; pres. Propellor Club of U.S., Chgo., 1966-67; sec., treas. Internat. Shipmasters Assn., Chgo., 1958-91. Contbr. articles to profl. law reviews. Lt. USCG, 1943-45. Fellow Am. Coll. Trial Lawyers; mem. ABA, Chgo. Bar Assn. (com. chmn. 1973), Internat. Assn. Def. Counsel, Order of Coif, Traffic Club Chgo. (dir. 1986, 87), Whitehall Club (N.Y.), Nat. Eagle Scout Assn. Republican. Avocations: gardening, golf, reading. E-mail: mwrtcr@aol.com.

ROBINSON, VERNA COTTEN, retired librarian, property management owner; b. Enfield, N.C., Oct. 6, 1927; d. Ernest and Ida (Faulcon) Cotten; m. Elbert Crutcher Robinson, Aug. 14, 1953 (dec. Feb. 1992); children: Angela, Elbert Cotten. BS, N.C. Cen. U., 1948; MS in Libr. Sci., Carnegie Mellon U., 1950. Br. libr. Blyden br. Norfolk (Va.) Pub. Libr., 1950-51; serials libr. Howard U., Washington, 1951-52; sch. libr. Spingarn H.S., 1952-53, Cardozo H.S., Washington, 1955-60, Roosevelt H.S., Washington, 1960-67, 70-85; ret. D.C. Pub. Schs., 1985. Pres. Robinson Property Mgmt., Inc., Washington, 1993—; bd. dirs. New Birth Corp., Miami, Fla. V.p. D.C. Assn. Sch. Librs., Washington, 1972-74; vice-chair Diaconate Lincoln Congrl. Temple/United Ch. of Christ, 1999—, chair, 2000—. Recipient Elder Wise Woman award, Ctrl. Atlantic Conf. of United Ch. of Christ, 2002, Pioneer's Achiever's award United Ch. Christ, 1995; Daisy Scarborough scholar N.C. Cen. U., 1946-48, Carnegie Libr. Alumni scholar Carnegie Libr. Sch. Alumni Assn., 1948-50. Mem. African Am. Women's Assn. (internat. com. 1992-95), Delta Sigma Theta (tuition scholar Grand chpt. 1948-50). Avocations: reading, walking.

ROBINSON, VIANEI LOPEZ, lawyer; b. Houston, Mar. 6, 1969; d. David Tiburcio and Romelia Gloria (Guerra) Lopez; m. Noel Keith Robinson, Jr., Apr. 16, 1994. AB in Psychology cum laude, Princeton U., 1988; JD, U. Tex., 1991. Bar: Tex. 1991; mediator's cert. Assoc. Bracewell & Patterson LLP, Houston, 1991-94, Wagstaff Law Firm, Abilene, Tex., 1994-97; owner Robinson Law Firm, 1997—. Contbr. articles to profl. jours., chpts. to School Law in Texas, A Practical Guide, 1996, Texas Employment Law, 1998; weekly wine columnist (with Keith Robinson), Abilene Reporter News. Bd. dirs. Ctr. for Contemporary Arts, pres., 2000, sec., 2001; mem. adv. bd., Day Nursery of Abeline. Presdl. scholar, Nat. Merit scholar, Nat. Hispanic scholar, 1985, Vinson & Elkins scholar U. Tex. Sch. Law, Austin, 1988-91. Fellow Tex. Bar Found.; mem. ABA, State Bar Tex. (minority dir. 2000-05, various coms.), Coll. of the State Bar of Tex. (bd. dirs. 2000-01), Tex. Young Lawyers Assn. (bd. dirs. 1994-97), Abilene Bar Assn., Abilene Young Lawyers Assn., Big Country Soc. for Human Resource Mgmt. (pres. 1999). Avocations: theater and dance, fine art, food and wine. Home: 2410 Wyndham Ct Abilene TX 79606-4370 Office: Robinson Law Firm First Nat Bank Tower 400 Pine St Ste 1070 Abilene TX 79601-5173 Fax: 915-677-6044. E-mail: vlr@robinsonlawfirm.com.

ROBINSON, W. LEE, lawyer; b. Rome, Sept. 24, 1943; m. Irene Scales, 1966; children: Christine, Jacquelyn. BS, Ga. Inst. Tech.; MBA, JD, Mercer U., 1985. With Robinson Hardware Store, Macon, Ga., 1954-86; mem. Ga. Senate, Atlanta, 1975-83; mayor City of Macon, Macon, 1988-92; pvt. practice, 1985—. 2d lt. U.S. Army; col. USAR. Decorated Bronze Star with two oak leaf clusters, Legion of Merit with oak leaf cluster. Named to U.S. Army Officer Candidate Sch. Hall of Fame. Mem. Ga. Assn. Criminal Def. Lawyers, Macon C. of C. (former bd. dirs.), Macon Bar Assn. Address: 3824 Overlook Ave Macon GA 31204-1325 Office: 201 2nd St Ste 580 Macon GA 31201-8282 also: PO Box 4852 Macon GA 31208-4852 E-mail: wlrmcnlaw@aol.com.

ROBINSON, WALTER GEORGE, arts management and funding consultant; b. London, June 18, 1911; s. Walter and Annie (Ledger) R.; m. Ruth V. Holden, Sept. 14, 1941 (dec. Mar. 1987); stepchildren: Malcolm D. Whitman III, Gail W. Hughes; m. Vesta H. Bogle, May 31, 1990. Student, NYU, 1943; D.F.A. (hon.), Mpls. Coll. Art and Design, 1975. Engaged in investment bus., N.Y.C., 1928-33; with Bass River Savs. Bank, South Yarmouth, Mass., 1934-60, pres., 1952-60; dir. Cape & Vineyard Electric Co., 1958-60, Hyannis Trust Co., until 1960; pres. Mpls. Soc. Fine Arts, governing and supporting orgn. for Mpls. Inst. Arts, Mpls. Coll. Art and Design, Children's Theatre Co., 1960-72, vice chmn., treas., sec., 1972-75; acting dir. Mpls. Sch. Art, 1962-63; acting pres. Mpls. Coll. Art and Design, 1974-75; dir. resource devel. Mus. Fine Arts, Boston, 1975-77; arts mgmt. and funding cons., 1977—; pres. Am. Art Advocates, Inc., 1984-87. Trustee Farmers & Mechanics Savs. Bank. Vice pres. Cape Cod Hosp., 1955-60; chmn. Mpls. Com. for Urban Environment, 1968-70, 72-74; mem. Minn. State Arts Council, 1967-73, Minn. Heritage Preservation Commn., 1972-75; chmn. Mpls. Bicentennial Commn., 1974-75; mem. Minn. Com. on Esthetic Environment, 1973-75; founding dir. E.B. Kelley Found., Hyannis, Mass., 1954-87, v.p., 1985-87; bd. dirs. Tyrone Guthrie Theatre Found., Mpls., 1960-70; trustee Northwestern Hosp., 1967-74, Am. Assn. Museums, 1973-75. Mem.: Skylight, Minneapolis, Minnesota (Mpls.). Home: Damariscotta, Maine. Died 2002.

ROBINSON, WARREN A. (RIP ROBINSON), lawyer; b. Denver, Mar. 23, 1957; s. William A. and Mary Jane Robinson; m. Janice M. Koerwer, Aug. 18, 1979; children: John William, Robert Joseph, Matthew Laurence, Sarah Elizabeth. BA, Seton Hall U., 1979; JD, U. Denver, 1982. Bar: Colo. 1982, U.S. Dist. Ct. Colo. 1982, U.S. Ct. Appeals (10th cir.) 1984. Assoc. Greengard, Blackman & Senter, Denver, 1982-83; assoc., ptnr. Silver & Hayes, P.C., 1983-89; ptnr. Silver, Robinson & Barrick, P.C., 1989-91; shareholder Robinson & Schuyler, P.C., 1991-2000; pvt. practice Littleton, Colo., 2000—. Mem. Colo. Bar Assn., Arapahoe County Bar Assn. Democrat. Christian. Avocations: sports, stained glass, coaching children. Office: 7931 S Broadway # 308 Littleton CO 80122 E-mail: warjd@aol.com.

ROBINSON, WILKES COLEMAN, retired federal judge; b. Anniston, Ala., Sept. 30, 1925; s. Walter Wade and Catherine Elizabeth (Coleman) R.; m. Julia Von Poellnitz Rowan, June 24, 1955; children: Randolph C., Peyton H., Thomas Wilkes Coleman. AB, U. Ala., 1948; JD, U. Va., 1951. Bar: Ala. 1951, Va. 1962, Mo. 1966, Kans. 1983. Assoc. Bibb & Hemphill, Anniston, Ala., 1951-54; city recorder City of Anniston, 1953-55; judge Juvenile and Domestic Relations Ct. of Calhoun County, Ala., 1954-56; atty. legal dept. GM&O R.R., Mobile, 1956-58; commerce counsel, asst. gen. atty. Seaboard Air Line R.R., Richmond, Va., 1958-66; chief commerce counsel Monsanto Co., St. Louis, 1966-70; gen. counsel, v.p. Marion Labs., Inc., Kansas City, Mo., 1970-79; pres. Gulf and Gt. Plains Legal Found., 1980-85, also bd. dirs.; atty. Howard, Needles, Tammen & Bergendoff, 1985-86, also bd. dirs.; v.p. S.R. Fin. Group, Inc., Overland Park, Kans., 1986-87; judge U.S. Ct. Fed. Claims, Washington, 1987-97, sr. judge, 1997—. Bd. govs. Kansas City Philharmonic Orch., 1975-77. Served with USNR, 1943-44. Mem. Indian Bayou Golf Club, Scottish Rite, Phi Beta Kappa (past treas. Kansas City, Mo. chpt.), Phi Eta Sigma, Phi Alpha Theta, Kappa Alpha. Episcopalian. Home: 12 Weekewachee Cir Destin FL 32541-4426 Office: US Ct Fed Claims US Cts Bldg 717 Madison Pl NW Washington DC 20439-0002

ROBINSON, WILLIAM ADAMS, lawyer; b. Flushing, N.Y., Sept. 7, 1936; s. William E. and Marjorie Robinson. BA in Internat. Econs., Stanford U., 1958, postgrad. Law Sch., 1960—62; JD, Golden Gate U., 1964. Bar: (Calif.) 1965, (U.S. Supreme Ct.) 1984. Assoc. Barfield, Barfield & Dryden, San Francisco, 1970—71; ptnr. Goldeen, Goldeen & Robinson, Lafayette, 1966—70; assoc. Miller, Van Dorn & Bowen, San Francisco, 1970—71; sr. trial counsel Calif. State Automobile Assn., 1971—96; mediator, arbitrator, pvt. adminstrv. law judge Law Offices William A. Robinson, 1996—. Dep. sheriff Santa Clara County, Calif., 1962; claims authorizer Social Security Adminstrn., San Francisco, 1963—64; lectr. C.E.B. Golden Gate U. Law Sch., 1978—; referee State Bar Ct. state and fed. jud. arbitrator; prof. Monterrey Coll. Law. Author: Practicing California Judicial Arbitration, CEB, 1983—89. Pres. Easter Seal Soc., Marin County, Calif., 1978—79. Capt. politico-mil. affairs USNR, 1955—88. Mem.: Bar Assn. San Francisco (chmn. arbitration com.), Am. Arbitration Assn. (arbitrator), U.S. Naval Order, Tiburon Yacht Club (commodore 1983), Naval Air Sta. Aero Club. Office: 3033 Strawberry Hill Rd Pebble Beach CA 93953-2922

ROBINSON, WILLIAM ANDREW, health service executive, physician; b. Phila., Jan. 31, 1943; s. Colonial Washington and Lillian Dorothy (Ivey) R.; m. Jacqueline Ellen Garcia, Mar. 28, 1980; 1 child, David Alan; 1 child by previous marriage, William Andrew Jr. BA, Hampton U., 1964; MD, Meharry Med. Coll., 1971; MPH, Johns Hopkins U., 1973. Diplomate Nat. Bd. Med. Examiners; lic. physician, Md. Rotating intern George W. Hubbard Hosp., Nashville, 1971-72, emergency rm. physician, 1972; med. officer gastrointestinal drug sect., bur. drugs FDA USPHS, HEW, Rockville, Md., 1973-75; dep. dir. office health resources opportunity USPHS, HHS, 1975-80, dep. dir. bur. health professions health resources adminstn., 1980-87, chief med. officer health resources and svcs. adminstn., 1987-89, dep. asst. sec. minority health, dir. office minority health Washington, 1989-91, acting adminstr. health resources and svcs. adminstn. Rockville, 1993-94, chief med. officer health resources and svcs. adminstrn., 1991—, dir. Office Pub. Health Affairs, 1996-97, dir. Ctr. for Quality, 1997—. Chmn. sr. execs. performance rev. bd. Office of Asst. Sec. for Health, 1990-91; pub. health svc. rep. 2d Internat. Conf. on Health Promotion, Adelaide, South Australia; health cons. com. on interior and insular affairs U.S. Ho. of Reps., Washington, 1982-83; appointed field faculty dept. family and comty. health Meharry Med. Coll., 1979; U.S. rep. to WHO Primary Health Care Conf., Alma Ata, Kazahkstan. Mem. nat. editl. bd. Jour. Health Care for the Poor and Underserved, 1991; contbr. articles to profl. jours. Capt. U.S. Army, 1964-67. Recipient Nat. Urban Coalition Comty. Health Svc. award, 1972, Letter of Appreciation, Chmn. Congl. Black Caucus Health Braintrust, U.S. Ho. of Reps., 1988. Mem. AMA, APHA, Am. Acad. Family Physicians, Blacks in Govt., Fed. Physicians Assn., Nat. Med. Assn., Sr. Execs. Assn., Delta Omega (Alpha chpt.). E-mail: brobinson@hrsa.gov.

ROBINSON, WILLIAM I. sociologist, journalist; b. N.Y.C., Mar. 28, 1959; s. Howard Sydney and Jo-Ann Phyllis Robinson; m. Gloconda Lucia Robinson, May 10, 1985 (div. Oct. 9, 2000); children: Amaru Alejandro, Tamara Yoconda. BA, Friends World Coll., N.Y.C., 1982; M, U. N.Mex., 1992, PhD, 1994. Editor, reporter Agencia Nueva Nicaragua, Managua, 1982-87; Washington bur. chief Agencia Nueva Nicaragua Internat. News Agy., Washington, 1987-90; news analyst, cons. Latin Am. Data Base, Albuquerque, 1990-94; prof. sociology U. N.Mex., 1994-96, U. Tenn., Knoxville, 1996-98, N.Mex. State U., Las Cruces, 1998-2001, U. Calif., Santa Barbara, 2001—. Author: David & Goliath, 1987, A Faustian Bargain, 1992, Promoting Polyarchy, 1996. Mem.: Internat. Studies Assn., Latin Am. Studies Assn., Am. Sociol. Assn., Global Studies Assn., Phi Kappa Phi. Avocation: Latin dance. Office: U Calif Santa Barbara Dept Sociology Santa Barbara CA 93106

ROBINSON, WILLIAM P. academic administrator, consultant, speaker; b. Elmhurst, Ill., Sept. 30, 1949; s. Paul Frederick and Lillian (Horton) R.; m. Bonnie Van Laan, Aug. 10, 1974; children: Brenna Kay, Benjamin Paul, Bailley Kay. Student, Moody Bible Inst., Chgo., 1967-70; AB, U. No. Iowa, 1972; postgrad., Princeton (N.J.) Theol. Sem., 1972-73; MA, Wheaton Coll., 1975; PhD, U. Pitts., 1979. Assoc. minister First Presbyn. Ch., Pitts., 1975-77; instr. U. Pitts., 1977-79; asst. prof. sch. continuing studies Nat. Coll. Edn., Evanston, Ill., 1979-80, dean sch. continuing studies, 1980-84, sr. v.p., 1984-86; pres. Manchester Coll., North Manchester, Ind., 1986-93, Whitworth Coll., Spokane, Wash., 1993—. Bd. dirs. Coun. Indep. Colls., Ind. Colls. Wash., Whitworth Coll.; cons., speaker for U.S. corps. and svc. orgns. Bd. dirs. Wash. Friends of Higher Edn., Spokane Symphony; vol. various orgns., especially prion work and hunger projects. Recipient various acad. awards. Mem. Nat. Assn. Ind. Colls. and Univs., Coun. Ind. Colls., Spokane Country Club, Spokane Club. Presyterian. Avocation: sports. Office: Whitworth Coll Office of Pres 300 W Hawthorne Rd Spokane WA 99218-2515*

ROBINSON, WILLIAM PHILIP, III, lawyer; b. Providence, Jan. 30, 1940; s. William Philip and Dorothy Frances (Hayes) R.; m. Marlene H. Zieky, Sept. 1, 1974; children: Jeffrey, Kevin, Courtney. BA, U. de Louvain, Belgium, 1962; MA, U. R.I., 1966; PhD, U. Conn., 1971; JD, Boston Coll., 1975. Bar: R.I. 1975, Mass. 1985, U.S. Ct. Appeals (1st cir.) 1977, U.S. Supreme Ct. 1989. Instr. U. Conn., Storrs, 1967-71; law clk. U.S. Ct. Appeals, Boston, 1975-77; assoc. Edwards & Angell, Providence, 1977-81, ptnr., 1981—. Bd. trustees Providence Country Day Sch., East Providence, 1991-97. Mem. East Greenwich Sch. Com., 1988-96, vice chmn., 1990-94; mem. exec. com. R.I. Assn. of Sch. Coms.; mem. East Greenwich Dem. Town Com., 1988—; mem. Fed. Bd. Bar Examiners, R.I., 1994—; mem. R.I. Jud. Performance Evaulation Com., 1993—, R.I. Bd. Govs. for Higher Edn., 2000—. Mem. Boston Coll. Law Sch. Alumni Assn. (v.p. R.I. chpt. 1990-93, pres. 1993-97, nat. del. 1997—), Order of Coif, Phi Beta Kappa. Democrat. Roman Catholic. Avocations: reading, skiing, golf, literary translation. Office: Edwards & Angell 2800 Financial Plz Providence RI 02903 E-mail: wrobinson@ealaw.com.

ROBINSON, ZELIG, lawyer; b. Balt., July 7, 1934; s. Morton Matthew and Mary (Ackerman) R.; m. Karen Ann Bergstrom (div. Oct. 1987); children: John, Christopher, Kristin; m. Linda Portner Strangmann, Dec. 23, 1987. BA, Johns Hopkins U., 1954; LLB, Harvard U., 1957. Bar: Md. 1958. Legis. analyst Md. House of Dels., Annapolis, 1958; tech. asst. IRS, Washington, 1958-60; pvt. practice Balt., 1960-62; assoc. gen. counsel commerce com. U.S. Ho. of Reps., Washington, 1962-64; assoc. Weinberg & Green, Balt., 1964-66; special legal cons. commerce com. U.S. Ho. of Reps., Washington, 1966-68; pvt. practice Balt., 1966-72; mem. Gordon, Feinblatt, Rothman, Hoffberger & Hollander, LLC, 1972—. Bd. dirs. Durapak Mfg. Co., Balt., Vac Pac, Inc., Balt., Universal Die Casting Co., Inc., Saline, Mich.; chmn. Balt. City Minimum Wage Commn., 1974-82, Md. Pub. Broadcasting, 1991-95; mem. Gov.'s. Commn. to revise Md. Code, Annapolis, 1968-89. Contbr. articles to profl. jours. Bd. dirs., v.p./sec. Gov.'s Mansion Found., Annapolis, Md.; v.p. bd. dirs. Md. Cmtys. and Citizens Fund, Chestertown, Md.; sec. bd. dirs. William Donald Schaefer Civic Fund; bd. dirs. Md. Arts Pl., Balt., Balt. Coalition of Homeowners, 1989—, Everyman Theatre, 2002–; mem. Found. for Md. Pub. Broadcasting; bd. dirs., pres. Celebration 2000, Inc., 1998—; founder, bd. dirs. Baltimore Efficiency and Econ. Found., 1999—. With U.S. Army, 1958. Mem. ABA, Md. State Bar Assn. (laws com., internat. law com.). Democrat. Office: Gordon Feinblatt Rothman Hoffberger & Hollander LLC 233 E Redwood St Baltimore MD 21202-3332 E-mail: zrobinson@gfrlaw.com.

ROBINSON-PANT, ANNA PATRICIA, education educator; b. Buenos Aires, Sept. 28, 1960; arrived in Eng., 1963; d. Roger John and Jean Josephine Robinson; m. Mahesh Prasad Pant; children: Benjamin Prasad, Anita Cathleen. BA in English Lit. with Honors, MA, Cambridge (Eng.) U., 1983; MSc in Social Policy and Planning, London Sch. Econ./Polit. Sci., 1989; PhD in Edn., U. Sussex, Eng., 1997. Primary sch. tchr. St. Dominics Sch., London, 1984-85; tchr. trainer Vol. Svcs. Overseas, Nepal, 1985-87, field officer Nepal, 1990-93; literacy/devel. vol. Indian Tribal Women's Trust, 1988; desk officer for Nepal and Bangladesh Action Aid U.K., 1989-90; rsch. asst. Inst. Devel. Studies, U.K., 1994; freelance rschr. various agys. in Nepal and U.K., 1998-2000; lectr. U. East Anglia, U.K., 2000—. Author: The Jumping Boy, 1985, The Magic Ink, 1986, The Marble Tree, 1987, Why Eat Green Cucumber at the Time of Dying?, 2001 (UNESCO award for internat. lit. rsch.); contbr. bhpt. to book: Ethnographic Perspectives, 2000. Recipient UNESCO Internat. award for lit. rsch., 1998. Mem. Edn. for Devel. Avocations: music, flute, piano, freelance journalism. Office: U East Anglia Ctr Applied Rsch in Edn. Norwich NR4 7TJ England E-mail: a.robinson-pant@uea.ac.uk.

ROBISON, CAROLYN LOVE, retired librarian; b. Orlinda, Tenn., Aug. 9, 1940; d. Fount Love and Martha Desha (Jones) R. BA, Denison U., 1962; MLS, Emory U., 1965; PhD, Ga. State U., 1982. Tchr. Dag Hammarshjold Jr. H.S., Wallingford, Conn., 1962-64; asst. libr., lectr. Architecture Libr., Ga. Inst. Tech., Atlanta, 1965-67; head circulation Ga. State U., 1967-71, asst. prof., then assoc. prof., asst. libr., 1971-75, prof., assoc. libr., 1975-98, ret., 1998. Active Friends of Atlanta-Fulton County Pub. Libr., 1981—98. Recipient Woman of Achievement award YWCA, 1989. Mem. ALA, AAUP, Ga. Libr. Assn., Delta Kappa Gamma, Phi Kappa Phi, Kappa Delta Pi. Republican. Presbyterian. Home: 1057 Capital Club Cir NE Atlanta GA 30319-2662 E-mail: clrobison@mindspring.com.

ROBISON, CHARLES BENNETT, legal consultant; b. Lewistown, Ill., Jan. 6, 1913; s. Marvin Thomas and Minnie Dell (White) Robison; m. Katherine Louise Parkins, Sept. 23, 1939 (dec. Dec. 1996); children: Kenneth P, Peter C, Dianne R Marcell, Alice R Berntson. AB cum laude, Knox Coll., 1934; JD, Northwestern U., 1937. Bar: Ill 1937. Assoc. Meyers & Matthias and predecessors, Chgo., 1938-73; v.p., gen. counsel Protection Mut. Ins. Co., Park Ridge, Ill., 1973-78; cons., counsel Meyers & Matthias, Matthias & Matthias, Chgo., 1978-83; legal cons. Luth. Brotherhood, Mpls., 1983-2000, Nat. Fraternal Congress Am., Naperville, Ill., 1983-2000; ret., 2000. Mem adv bd NW suburban coun Boy Scouts Am, 1959—84. Maj AUS, 1941—45. Recipient Silver Beaver, Boy Scouts Am, 1959. Mem.: ABA, Ill State Bar Asn, Asn Fraternal Benefit Counsel, Fedn Ins and Corp Counsel Found (pres 1975—93), Fedn Ins and Corp Counsel (past pres), Lions (pres Des Plains 1983—84, Melvin Jones Fellow Award 1998). Republican. Congregationalist. Home: 1639 Campbell Ave Des Plaines IL 60016-6636

ROBISON, CLARENCE, JR. surgeon; b. Tecumseh, Okla., Dec. 9, 1924; s. Clarence Sr. and Margaret Irene (Buzzard) Robison; m. Patricia Antoinette Hagee, May 27, 1951; children: Timothy D., Paul D., John D., Rebecca A. AS, Stanford U., 1943; MD, U. Okla., 1948. Intern Good Samaritan Hosp., Portland, Oreg., 1948-49; fellow pathology and oncology U. Okla., 1949-51; pathologist USAF Hosp., Cheyenne, Wyo., 1951-53; resident in surgery Okla. U. Health Scis.-VA Svc., Oklahoma City, 1953-56; mem. faculty surgery dept. Okla. U. Health Scis., 1956-57, clin. prof. surgery, 1957—. Mem. bd. advisors Mercy Health Ctr., Oklahoma City, 1974—81, sec. staff, 1974—84, chief surgery, 1992—95. Presdl. elector Dems., 1960; mem. Commn. Mission Indian Nations Presbytery, 1980—91; elder Presbyn. Ch.; bd. dirs. Okla. Found. Quality Assurance, Oklahoma City, Found. Sr. Citizens, 1964—. Capt. USAF, 1951—53. Fellow: ACS, Am. Cancer Soc. (past pres. Okla. divsn., exec. com., bd. dirs., nat. bd. dirs.), Southwestern Surg. Soc.; mem.: SAR, AMA (del. organized med. staff sect. Oklahoma City 1989—, alt. del. AMA Okla. 1991—93, 1996—98), Oklahoma City Surg. Soc. (pres. 1967—69), Okla. Surg. Assn. (sec., treas. 1966—68), Okla. State Med. Assn. (alt. trustee Okla. 1989—92, trustee 1993—96), Oklahoma County Med. Soc. (bd. dirs. 1989—93), Men's Dinner Club, Petroleum Club, Sportsman Club, Knights Templar, Shriners (Royal Order Jesters), Masons (32 degree). Office: 4200 W Memorial Rd Ste 508 Oklahoma City OK 73120-9331 E-mail: nmijr@yahoo.com.

ROBISON, FREDERICK MASON, financial executive; b. Danville, Ill., May 30, 1934; s. Frederick A. and Katherine L. (Mason) R.; m. Nancy Jane Potter, Aug. 18, 1956; children: Frederick B., Christopher M. BS, U. Ill., 1956, JD, 1959. Tax mgr. Arthur Andersen & Co., Chgo., 1959-65; treas. Warnaco, Inc., Bridgeport, Conn., 1965-76; v.p. Emery Air Freight, Wilton, 1976-86, treas., 1976-79, sec., 1979-82, controller, 1979-86; v.p., controller Burlington Air Express, Irvine, Calif., 1986-88; sr. v.p. fin., chief fin. officer Sebastain Internat., Inc., Woodland Hills, 1988-96. Vice chmn. Town Council, Monroe, Conn., 1971-73, mem., 1969-73, bd. edn., Monroe, 1973-79, chmn., 1975-79. Mem. Fin. Execs. Inst. (dir. So. Conn. chpt. 1973-75, pres. 1977-78) Republican. Presbyterian. Home: 508 W Bay St Dunn NC 28334-5602

ROBISON, JULIE THOMPSON, gerontologist, educator; b. Mt. Kisco, N.Y., Aug. 6, 1968; d. Edward Thorwald and Nancy (Cale) Thompson;; m. Neal Evans Robison Jr, Aug. 8, 1992; children: Lucy Hobart, Evan Winslow. BA, Georgetown U., 1990; MA, Cornell U., 1993, PhD, 1995. Psychologist Nat. Inst. on Aging, Washington, 1990-91; rsch. asst. Cornell U., Ithaca, N.Y., 1991-95; post-doctoral fellow Yale U., New Haven, 1995-97, rsch. assoc., 1995-98; sr. scientist Braceland Ctr. for Mental Health and Aging Hartford Hosp., 1997—; asst. prof. medicine U. Conn., Farmington, 1999—. Co-contbr.: 25 articles to profl. jours.; co-contbr. chpts. to 5 books. Alumni interviewer Georgetown U., 1993—; vol. First Steps program Harford Hosp., 2000—; trustee Alzheimers Resource Ctr. Conn., 2000—. Rsch. grantee Donaghue Found., 1997-99, Hartford Hosp., 1999-01, ManorCare Found., 2000-01, Alzheimers Assn., 2002—. Mem. Gerontol. Soc. Am. Avocations: motherhood, sailing, reading, skiing. Office: Braceland Ctr Mental Health & Aging Inst Living Hartford Hosp 200 Retreat Ave Hartford CT 06106 E-mail: jrobiso@harthosp.org.

ROBISON, MARSHA GAIL, career planning administration; b. Charleroi, Pa., Nov. 24, 1953; d. Lou H. and Marian Alice (Robinson) Skokut; children: Justin, Maya. BS in Mech. Engring., Calif. Poly. U., Pomona, 1976. Cert. tchr., Calif. CAD packaging designer Gen. Dynamics, Pomona, 1972-80, Singer Librascope, Glendale, Calif., 1980-81; ind. cons. Hughes, ITT, Rockwell, L.A., 1981-83; pres. CAD Counsel, Simi Valley, Calif., 1982—, MicroAcad., North Hollywood, 1987—. Mem. Nat. Computer Graphics Assn. Office: 4195 Valley Fair St Ste 205A Simi Valley CA 93063-2900 E-mail: cad_mgr@pacbell.net.

ROBISON, OLIN CLYDE, political science educator, former college president; b. Anacoco, La., May 12, 1936; s. Audrey Clyde and Ruby (Cantrell) R.; div.; children: Gordon Reece, Blake Elliott, Mark Edward. BA, Baylor U., 1958, LLD, 1979; D.Phil., Oxford (Eng.) U., 1963; LHD (hon.), Ehrenburger-Johannes Gutenberb U., Mainz, Fed. Republic Germany, 1977, Monterey Inst. Internat. Studies, 1982, Hofstra U, 1988; LLD (hon.), U. Vt., 1989, Middlebury Coll., 2000. Dean students San Marcos (Tex.) Acad., 1963-64; regional officer Peace Corps, Washington, 1964-65, dir. univ. affairs, 1965-66; spl. asst. dep. under-sec. for polit. affairs Dept. State, Washington, 1966-68; asso. provost for social scis. Wesleyan U., Middletown, Conn., 1968-70; provost, dean faculty, sr. lectr. govt. and legal studies Bowdoin Coll., Brunswick, Maine, 1970-75; prof. polit. sci. Middlebury (Vt.) Coll., 1975-95, pres., 1975-90, pres. emeritus, 1990—, prof. emeritus, 1995—; pres. Salzburg Seminar, 1991—. Chmn. Am. Collegiate Consortium, 1987-94; cons. State Dept., 1968-72, 77-88; bd. dirs. Investment Co. Am., Am. Mut. Fund, Bank of Vt., 1989-92, The Noel Group, N.Y.C, 1989-91, AMCAP, ACMAP Mut. Fund; cons. Paine Webber Mitchell Hutchins Inc., Am. Coun. Life Ins., 1968-81, Washington Forum, Met. Life Ins. Co. Bd. dirs. Atlantic Info. Center for Tchrs., London, 1970-77, Am. Com. on U.S.-Soviet Rels., Washington; chmn. Vt. com. Rhodes Scholarship Trust, 1976-77; bd. dirs. Am. Coun. Young Polit. Leaders, 1968-78, 81-90, Inst. East-West Security Studies, N.Y.C., Nat. Spinal Cord Injury Assn., Washington, Atlantic Coun. U.S., 1973-78, 81-91, U.S. Commn. for United World Coll. Schs.; mem. U.S. Adv. Commn. on Public Diplomacy, 1978-83, chmn., 1978-81, visiting comm. Harvard Div. Sch., Cambridge, Mass., 1980-86, adv. commn. Harvard U., Ctr for Middle Ea. Studies, Cambridge, 1992-96; U.S. del. Conf. on Security and Coop. in Europe, Belgrade, 1977-78; U.S. del. Conf. on Security and Coop. in Madrid, 1980, in Vienna, 1986-87; bd. dirs. Nat. Endowment for Democracy, 1984-92; bd. dirs., chmn. Chatham House Found., 1985-93. Named Ehrenburger Johannes Gutenberg Universität, Mainz, Fed. Republic Germany, 1977;

Rockefeller Found./Aspen Inst. fellow, 1978-79; Presdl. fellow Aspen Inst. Humanistic Studies, 1979-80, Harry Luce fellow Aspen Inst., 1982-83. Mem. Internat. Inst. Strategic Studies (London), Soc. Values in Higher Edn., Council Fgn. Rels., Royal Inst. Internat. Affairs (bd. dirs. 2000—). Clubs: Federal City (Washington); Century (N.Y.C.); United Oxford and Cambridge (London). Baptist. Office: Salzburg Seminar The Marble Works PO Box 886 Middlebury VT 05753-0886

ROBISON, PAULA JUDITH, flutist; b. Nashville, June 8, 1941; d. David Victor and Naomi Florence R.; m. Scott Nickrenz; Dec. 29, 1971; 1 child, Elizabeth Hadley Amadea Nickrenz. Student, U. So. Calif., 1958-60; BS, Juilliard Sch. Music, 1963. Founding artist, player Chamber Music Soc., N.Y.C., 1970-90, NY ChoroBand, 1994; co-dir. chamber music Spoleto Festival, Charleston, S.C., 1978-88; Filene artist-in-residence Skidmore Coll., Saratoga Springs, N.Y., 1988-89; mem. faculty New Eng. Conservatory Music, 1991—2001; co-dir. Gardner Chamber Orch., Boston, 1995—. Faculty Juilliard Sch., N.Y.C., 1978-82; annual concert series, Met. Mus. Art, N.Y., 1990—, With Art series, N.Y., 2000, Mass MOCA, 2001. Soloist with various major orchs., including N.Y. Philharm., London Symphony Orch.; player, presenter Concerti di Mezzogiorno, Spoleto (Italy) Festival, 1970—; commd. flute concertos by Leon Kirchner, Toru Takemitsu, Oliver Knussen, Robert Beaser, Kenneth Frazelle; premiered works by Pierre Boulez, Elliott Carter, William Schuman, Thea Musgrave, Carla Bley; premiered Rio Days Rio Nights, Music Theatre Group prodn. in N.Y.C., 1998; participant Marlboro Music Festival, 1999—; author: The Paula Robison Flute Warmups Book, 1989, The Andersen Collection, 1994, Paula Robison Masterclass: Paul Hindemith, 1995, The Sidney Lanier Collection, 1997, Frank Martin: Ballade, 2002; recs. on CBS Masterworks, Music Masters, Vanguard Classics, New World Records, Omega, Arabesque, Sony Classical, King Recs., Mode Recs. Recipient First prize Geneva Internat. Competition, 1966, Adelaide Ristori prize, 1987; named Musician of Month, Musical Am., 1979, House Musician for Isamu Noguchi Garden Mus., N.Y.C., 1988; Martha Baird Rockefeller grantee, 1966; Nat. Endowment for Arts grantee, 1978, 86; Fromm Found. grantee, 1980; Housewright Eminent scholar Fla. State U., 1990-91. Recipient Disting. Svc. award, Music Tchrs. Nat. Assn., 1989, Laurence Lesser Presdl. award, 1999, Lifetime Achievement award, USDAN Ctr. Arts, 2000, Hon. Citizen for Life award, City of Charleston, 2002. Mem. Sigma Alpha Iota (hon.). Office: care Matthew Sprizzo 477 Durant Ave Staten Island NY 10308-3006

ROBISON, RICHARD EUGENE, architect; b. Wichita, Kans., Oct. 30, 1951; s. Robert Dale and Corene (Tiffany) R.; m. Manola Cristina Gomez Pantoja, Dec. 20, 1975; children: Amy Elizabeth, Harriet Paige. Student, Baker U., 1969-71; B Environ. Design, U. Kans., 1974. Lic. profl. architect, Kans.; cert. constrn. specifier. Architect U.S. Peace Corps, Khouribga, Morrocco, 1974-75, OFESUR, Valencia, Venezuela, 1975-78; instr. U. Carabobo, 1979-80; architect, ptnr. R.G. Asesores SRL, 1978-83; architect Van Doren-Hazard-Stallings, Inc., Topeka, 1983-87, Heery Internat., Inc., Atlanta, 1987-92, Lord, Aeck, and Sargent, Inc., Atlanta, 1992-94, prin., 1994—. Instr. So. Coll. Tech., 1992. Co-author automated specifications writing system Sweet Spec, 1989, Spec System, 1990. Mem. AIA, Constrn. Specifications Inst., So. Bldg. Code Congress Internat., Assn. Preservation Tech. Internat., Am. Inst. Conservation. Avocations: music, theater. Home: 7484 Waters Edge Dr Stone Mountain GA 30087-6132 Office: Lord Aeck and Sargent Inc 1201 Peachtree St NE 400 Colony Sq NE Ste 300 Atlanta GA 30361-3500

ROBISON, VICTOR JAMES, JR. retired military officer; b. Youngstown, Ohio, Apr. 29, 1920; s. Victor James Robison and Babe Albert. BS, Case Western Res. U., 1942, MA, 1948; Qualified Comms. Officer, US Naval Acad. Grad. Sch., 1943; student, Sorbonne U., Paris, 1949-50, Columbia U., 1950-51. Commd. ensign USN, 1943, advanced through grades to comdr., comms. officer USS Taylor, 1943-45, tng. officer US Naval Res. Tng. Ctr. Balt., 1952-55, asst. ops. officer USS Worcester Mediterranean and Pacific, 1955-56; US Naval attaché US Embassy, Warsaw, 1957-58; officer in charge Jt. Comm. Ctr. Navy Liaison Group, USN, Ft. Ritchie, Md., 1958-61; US Naval attaché U.S. Embassy, Brussels, 1962-66; asst. curator for Navy Dept., Office Chief of Naval Ops. USN, Washington, 1966-69, ret., 1969; English tchr. Corcoran Coll. Art, Washington, 1969—70; pvt. practice appraiser Navy artifacts and memorabilia Washington and Annapolis, Md., 1970-84. Decorated Order of Leopold II, 1966, Navy Unit commendation, others. Mem. VFW, Am. Legion, Fleet Res. Assn., Smithsonian Instn., Beta Theta Pi. Avocations: philately, jogging, poetry, learning. Home: 423 7th St SE Washington DC 20003-2756

ROBISON, WILBUR GERALD, JR. research biologist; b. Cheyenne, Wyo., Dec. 27, 1933; s. Wilbur Gerald and Irene (Decker) R.; m. Lucia Maria Panuncio, Sept. 20, 1957; children: Sylvia Lee, Stanley Jay, Nancy Kay, Lydia Joy. BA, Brigham Young U., 1958, MA, 1960; PhD, U. Calif., Berkeley, 1965; postgrad., Harvard U., 1966. Postdoctoral rsch. fellow Harvard Med. Sch., Boston, 1965-66; asst. prof. biology U. Va., Charlottesville, Va., 1966-72; sr. staff fellow Nat. Eye Inst., NIH, Bethesda, Md., 1972-76, geneticist, cell biologist, 1976-83, head exptl. anatomy, 1983-85, head pathophysiology, 1985—, acting head pathology, 1988—. Contbr. articles to profl. publs., chpts. to books. Mem. AAAS, Am. Diabetes Assn., Assn. for Rsch. in Vision and Ophthamology. Mem. Lds Ch. Achievements include development of rat model for diabetic retinopathy and demonstration of prevention with aldose reductase inhibitors. Home: 1306 Gresham Rd Silver Spring MD 20904-1436 Office: Nat Eye Inst NIH Bldg 6 Rm 316 Bethesda MD 20892-2735 E-mail: robisong@nei.nih.gov.

ROBISON, WILLIAM CHRISTOPHER, management accountant; b. York, Pa., July 31, 1961; s. Gerald Austin and Gale Louise (Woods) R.; m. Joanne Gazvoda, June 21, 1986; children: Kelly Ann, Rachel Noel. BS magna cum laude, Waynesburg Coll., 1984. Cert. mgmt. acct. Fin. analyst First Nat. Bank Washington, Pa., 1984-89; sr. fin. analyst Mellon Bank, Pitts., 1989-2000; mgmt. acct. RHI Mgmt. Resources, 2001—. Mem. Inst. Mgmt. Accts., Toastmasters Internat. (Competent Toastmaster and Competent Leader). Democrat. Roman Catholic. Avocation: Se Jong Tae Kwan Do. E-mail: wcrobison@juno.com.

ROBISON, WILLIAM ROBERT, lawyer; b. Memphis, May 5, 1947; s. Andrew Cliffe and Elfrieda (Barnes) R. AB, Boston U., 1970; JD, Northeastern U., 1974. Bar: Mass. 1974, D.C. 1975, U.S. Dist. Ct. Mass. 1975, U.S. Ct. Appeals (1st cir.) 1975, U.S. Dist. Ct. Conn. 1977, U.S. Supreme Ct. 1977, Calif. 1978, U.S. Dist. Ct. (cen. dist.) Calif. 1979, U.S. Ct. Appeals (9th cir.) 1979. Assoc. Meyers, Goldstein, et al, Boston, 1975-76, Cooley, Shrair, et al, Springfield, Mass., 1976-78, Hertzberg, et al, Los Angeles, 1978-79, Marcus & Lewi, Santa Monica, Calif., 1980-81; pvt. practice, 1981—. Lectr. Northeastern U., Boston, 1975-76; judge pro-tem., Mcpl. Ct., Los Angeles, 1984—, Los Angeles Superior Ct., 1987—. Co-author: Commercial Transactions, 1976. Bd. dirs. Boston Legal Asst. Project, 1972-75, Action for Boston Community Devel., Inc., 1971-75. Mem. ABA, Los Angeles County Bar Assn., Santa Monica Bar Assn. (Cert. of Appreciation 1987). Democrat. Unitarian Universalist. Home and Office: 2546 Amherst Ave Los Angeles CA 90064-2712 E-mail: billrobison@prodigy.net.

ROBITAILLE, LUC, professional hockey player; b. Montreal, P.Q., Can., Feb. 17, 1966; With Hull Olympiques Major Jr. Hockey League, Que., 1983-84, L.A. Kings, 1984-94, Pitts. Penguins, 1994-95, N.Y. Rangers, 1995-97, L.A. Kings, 1997—2001, Detroit Red Wings, 2001—. Scored winning goal for nat. team of Can. at 1994 World Hockey Championship. Recipient Guy LaFleur trophy, 1985-86, Can. Hockey Player of Yr. award, 1985-86, Calder Meml. trophy, NHL Rookie of Yr., 1986-87; named to NHL All-Star team, 1987, 88, 90-91, 92-93; mem Stanley Cup Championship team 2002 Office: Detroit Red Wings Joe Louis Arena 600 Civic Center Detroit MI 48226*

ROBLE, CAROLE MARCIA, accountant; b. Bklyn., Aug. 22, 1938; d. Carl and Edith (Brown) Dusowitz; m. Richard F. Roble, Nov. 30, 1969. MBA with distinction, N.Y. Inst. Tech., 1984. CPA, Calif., N.Y. Compt. various orgns. various orgns., 1956-66; staff acct. ZTBG CPA'S, L.A., 1966-67; sr. acct. J.H. Cohn & Co., Newark, 1967-71; prin. Carole M. Roble, CPA, South Hempstead, N.Y., 1971-90; ptnr. Roble & Libman, CPAs, Baldwin, 1990-93; prin. Carole M. Roble, CPA, 1993—. Speaker, moderator Found. for Acctg. Edn., N.Y., 1971—; lectr. acctg. various schs. including New Sch., Queens Coll., Empire State Coll., Touro Coll., N.Y. Inst. Tech., N.Y.C., Parsons Sch., 1971—. Guest various N.Y. radio and TV stas., 2 noted various newspapers. Treas. Builders Devel. Corp. of L.I., Westbury, N.Y., 1985; dir. Women Econ. Devels. of L.I., 1985-87. Recipient Sisterhood citation Nat. Orgn. Women, 1984, 85, cert. of Appreciation Women Life Underwriters, 1988, Women in Sales, 1982, 84; named top Tax Practitioner Money Mag., 1987, one of Top 100 Most Influential People, Acctg. Today, 1999. Mem. AICPA (mem. small firm advocacy com. 1996—), Am. Acct. Assn. (auditing sect.), Am. Soc. Women Accts. (pres. N.Y. chpt. 1980-81), Am. Woman's Soc. CPAs, Nat. Conf. CPA Practitioners (trustee L.I. chpt. 1981-82, sec. 1982-83, treas. 1983-84, v.p. 1984-85, 1st v.p. 1985-86, pres. 1986-87, nat. nominating com. 1983-84, 88-89, nat. continuing profl. edn. chmn. 1988-90, nat. treas. 1991-94, nat. v.p. 1994-96, exec. v.p. 1996-98, first woman nat. pres. 1998-99), Calif. Soc. CPAs, N.Y. State Soc. CPAs (bd. dirs. Nassau chpt. 1981-86, 91-93, bd. dirs. profl. devel., 1982-86, sec., mem. fin. acctg. standards com. 1990-95), Kiwanis (program chmn. County Seat chpt. 1989-90, sec. 1990-91, pres. 1991-92), Baldwin C. of C. (treas. 1990-93). Avocations: golf, gourmet cuisine, water skiing, music. Home: 626 Willis St Hempstead NY 11550-8000

ROBLES, ELIODORO GONZALES, consulting company executive, educator; b. Paniqui, Tarlac, The Philippines, July 3, 1923; s. Mariano Abraham and Lucia (Gonzales) R.; m. Rosario Palaganas Lavitoria, Oct. 30, 1964; children: Michael, Elmer, Eliodoro Jr., Marilou, Jonathan, Jay. BS in Polit. Sci., Far Eastern U., 1953; MA in Internat. Rels., Cornell U., 1954; MA in Polit. Economy, Harvard U., 1955, PhD in Polit. Economy, 1959. Cert. tchr., Calif.; cert. C.C. instr., Calif. C.C.; cert. C.C. supr., Calif. C.C. Instr. Far Eastern U., Manila, 1952-53; tech. cons., staff asst. Embassy of the Rep. of Indonesia in the Philippines, 1950-53; spl. asst. on fgn. econ. policies Program Implementation Office of the Pres. of the Philippines, 1962-64; prof. econs. and polit. sci., dean Grad. Sch. Far Eastern U., Manila, 1959-64; econ. officer, dep. dir. for econ., cultural, social affairs S.E. Asia Treaty Orgn. (SEATO), Bangkok, 1964-74; project dir. San Francisco Unified Sch. Dist., 1975-79; sr. assoc. Devel. Assocs., Inc., Walnut Creek, Calif., 1979—; evaluation specialist including polit. economist USAID, various locations, 1984-85, edni. adminstrn. specialist Manila and Islamabad, Phillipines and Pakistan, 1987, tng. specialist, Asia Narcotics Edn. Program, 1988-89, polit. economist, 1992—. Presenter, attendee numerous confs., seminars and workshops including Nat. Conf. on Sch. Sys. and Bilingual Edn., San Jose, Calif., 1975, Conf. on Bilingual Edn.: Asian Am. Bilingual Materials Devel. Ctr., Berkeley, Calif., 1975, Ctr. for Ednl. Devel., San Francisco, Calif., 1975, among others. Author: Economic Analysis, 1966, The Philippine in the Nineteenth Century, 1969. Lt. col. Philippine Army, 1941-46; 1st lt. inf. U.S. Army, 1946-49. Recipient scholarship Fulbright Assn., 1954; Telluride fellow Cornell U., 1954, Fletcher fellow Harvard U., 1954-55, Newberry fellow Newberry Libr., 1957-58. Mem. Fulbright Assn., Filipino Am. Tchrs. Assn., Far Eastern U. Alumni Assn. (bd. dirs., adviser 1991—), Harvard Club San Francisco. Democrat. Methodist. Avocations: general gardening, orchid growing, stamp and coin collecting. Home: 1335 Greenway Dr Richmond CA 94803-1204 Office: Devel Assocs Inc 1475 N Broadway Walnut Creek CA 94596-4649 E-mail: erobles@devassoc.com.

ROBLES-GALIANO, ESTELA, artist, educator; b. Mayaguez, P.R., Mar. 28, 1943; d. Jose Javier Robles-Santiago and Ana Teresa Galiano-Vincenty; m. Jose Arturo Hernandez-Calero, Dec. 26, 1964; children: Arturo Hernandez, Javier Hernandez, Eduardo Hernandez. BA, U. P.R., Mayaguez, 1963. Prof. Cath. U. P.R., Aguadilla, 1965—72, Interamerican U. P.R., Aguadilla, 1967—68; instr. art U. P.R. Telephone directories and tourist guide. Founder-pres. Nat. Exhbn. Day of Puerto Rican Artist Painter, Corp., Aguadilla, 1998—2000. Named one of Women Who Make History, Senate of P.R., Capitol, San Juan, 1998; recipient Homage, Women Cívic Club Aguadilla, Mayaguez, 1988, Unión Mujeres Americanas, Mayagüez, Aguadill, 1992—93, Exch. Club Aguadilla, 1992. Mem.: Am. Soc. Portrait Artists, Assn. Watercolorists P.R. (signature mem. and chair publicity 1998—2000), Nat. Mus. Women in the Arts. Home: PO Box 462 Aguadilla PR 00605 Personal E-mail: estelarg@coqui.net.

ROBOCK, ALAN, meteorology educator; b. Boston, Sept. 7, 1949; s. Stefan Hyman Robock and Shirley Ruth (Bernstein) Fox; m. Sherri Lynne Carpini West, May 12, 1990; children: Brian, Daniel. BA, U. Wis., 1970; SM, MIT, 1974, PhD, 1977. Vol. Peace Corps, The Philippines, 1970-72; rsch. scientist Lawrence Livermore (Calif.) Lab., 1973; asst. prof. dept. meteorology U. Md., College Park, 1977-82, assoc. prof., 1982-96, prof., 1996-97; prof. dept. environ. scis. Rutgers U., New Brunswick, NJ, 1998—. Dir. Ctr. Environ. Prediction Rutgers U., 2001-; snow forecaster Montgomery County (Md.) Pub. Schs., 1980-81; state climatologist State of Md., 1991-97; vis. rsch. scientist Princeton U., NOAA/Geophys. Fluid Dynamics Lab., 1994-95. Editor Jour. Climate and Applied Meteorology, 1985-87, Jour. Geophys. Research-Atmospheres, 2000—; assoc. editor Revs. Geophysics, 1994-2000, Jour. Geophys. Rsch.-Atmospheres, 1998-2000; contbr. articles to profl. publs., chpts. to books. Fellow Am. Meteorol. Soc.; mem. AAAS (Congressional sci. fellow 1986-87), Am. Geophys. Union. Avocations: tennis, Bob Dylan music, travel, politics. Office: Rutgers U Dept Environ Scis 14 College Farm Rd New Brunswick NJ 08901-8551 E-mail: robock@envsci.rutgers.edu.

ROBOL, RICHARD THOMAS, lawyer; b. Norfolk, Va., Feb. 8, 1952; s. Harry James and Lucy Henley (Johnson) R. BA, U. Va., 1974; JD, Harvard U., 1978. Bar: Va. 1979, Ohio 1996, U.S. Dist. Ct. (ea. dist.) Va. 1979, U.S. Ct. Appeals (4th cir.) 1979, U.S. Dist. Ct. (we. dist.) Va. 1981, U.S. Supreme Ct. 1982, D.C. 1991, U.S. Ct. Appeals (4th, 6th and 9th cirs.) 1995. Law clk. to presiding justice U.S. Dist. Ct. (ea. dist.) Va., 1978-79; ptnr. Seawell, Dalton, Hughes & Timms, Norfolk, 1979-87, Hunton and Williams, Norfolk, 1987-92; exec. v.p., gen. counsel Columbus Am. Discovery Group, Inc., 1992—. Adj. prof. U. Dayton Law Sch.; asst. prof. mil. sci. Capital U.; pro bono counsel Nat. Commn. for Prevention Child Abuse, Norfolk, 1983, Tidewater Profl. Assn. on Child Abuse, 1983, Parents United Va., 1981-82, Sexual Abuse Help Line, 1983-86; mem. Boyd-Graves Conf. on Civil Procedure in Va., 1981-87. Contbr. articles to law revs.; contbg. editor: International Law for General Practitioners, 1981. Bd. dirs. Va. Opera Assn. Guild, Norfolk, 1983-87, Tidewater br. NCCJ, 1991-92; deacon Ctrl. Bapt. Ch., Norfolk, 1980-83. Capt. USAR, 1992—. Fulbright scholar, 1974. Mem. Va. State Bar Assn. (bd. dirs. internat. law sect. 1984-87, chmn. 1982-83), Va. Young Lawyers Assn. (cir. rep. 1984-88), Va. Assn. Def. Attys., Maritime Law Assn., Norfolk-Portsmouth Bar assn. (chmn. speakers bur. 1987-88), Assn. Def. Trial Attys. (chmn. Va. 1987), Def. Rsch. Inst., 1982-88. Avocations: camping, rowing, scuba diving. Home: 60 Kenyon Brook Dr Worthington OH 43085-3629 Office: Columbus Am Discovery Group 433 W 6th Ave Columbus OH 43201-3136 E-mail: robol@ee.net.

ROBOLD, ALICE ILENE, retired mathematician, educator; b. Delaware County, Ind., Feb. 7, 1928; d. Earl G. and Margaret Rebecca (Summers) Hensley; m. Virgil G. Robold, Aug. 21, 1955; 1 son, Edward Lynn. BS, Ball State U., 1955, MA, 1960, EdD, 1965. Substitute elem. tchr. Am. Elem. Sch., Augsburg, Germany, 1955-56; instr. Ball State U., Muncie, Ind., 1960-61, tchg. fellow, 1961-64, asst. prof. math. scis., 1964-69, assoc. prof., 1969-76, prof., 1976-98; ret., 1998. Mem. Nat. Coun. Tchrs. Math., Ind. Coun. Tchrs. Math. Mem. Ch. of God.

ROBRENO, EDUARDO C. federal judge; b. 1945; BA, Westfield State Coll., 1967; MA, U. Mass., 1969; JD, Rutgers U., 1978. With antitrust divsn. U.S. Dept Justice, Phila., 1978-81; ptnr. Meltzer & Schiffrin, 1981-86, Fox, Rothschild, O'Brien & Frankel, Phila., 1987-92; judge U.S. Dist. Ct. for Ea. Dist. Pa., 1992—. Mem. Jud. Conf. Com. on Bankruptcy Rules. Fellow Am. Law Inst. Office: US Courthouse Rm 3810 Philadelphia PA 19106

ROBSON, DONALD, physics educator; b. Leeds, Eng., Mar. 19, 1937; came to U.S., 1963; s. Albert and Rose Hannah (Parbutt) R.; m. Joy Olivia Burkitt Findlay, Aug. 1960 (div. May 1971); children: Donald Peter, David Ian, Karen Joy; m. Martha Breitenlohner, Aug. 26, 1971 (div. Sept. 1999); m. Kimberly G. Kitchen, Dec. 18, 1999; 1 child, Nadirah Berge. BSc, U. Melbourne, Australia, 1959, MSc, 1961, PhD, 1963. Rsch. assoc. Fla. State U., Tallahassee, 1963-64, asst. prof. physics, 1964-65, assoc. prof., 1965-67, prof., 1967—, chmn. dept. physics, 1985-91, Disting. prof., 1990—. Editor: (with J.D. Fox) Isobaric Spin in Nuclear Physics, 1966, Nuclear Analogue States, 1976; assoc. editor Nuclear Physics A., 1972-96; contbr. more than 100 articles to profl. jours. Chmn. bd. trustees Southeastern Univ. Rsch. Assn., 1996-98. Fulbright scholar, 1963-64; A.P. Sloan fellow, 1966-67; Alexander Von Humboldt sr. scientist, 1976-77. Fellow Am. Phys. Soc. (co-recipient Tom W. Bonner prize 1972). Avocations: chess, golf, running. Office: Fla State U Dept Physics Tallahassee FL 32306

ROBSON, MARTIN CECIL, surgery educator, plastic surgeon; b. Lancaster, Ohio, Mar. 8, 1939; children: Karen Iredell, Douglas Spears, Martin Cecil Robson III. Student, Northwestern U., 1957—59; BA, Johns Hopkins U., 1961, MD, 1964. Diplomate Am. Bd. Surgery, Am. Bd. Plastic Surgery . Intern U. Chgo. Hosps. and Clinics, 1964—65; resident in surgery Balt. City Hosp., 1965—67, Brooke Gen. Hosp., Ft. Sam Houston, Tex., 1967—69; resident in plastic surgery Yale-New Haven Hosp., 1971—73; instr. dept. surgery Yale U. Sch. Medicine, New Haven, 1973—74, asst. prof. plastic surgery, 1973—74, assoc. prof., 1974; assoc. prof., chief plastic surgery U. Chgo., 1974—77, prof. and chief plastic surgery, 1977—83; dir. U. Chgo. Burn Center, 1976—83; prof., chmn. divsn. plastic and reconstructive surgery Wayne State U., Detroit, 1983—88; dir. Detroit Med. Ctr. Burn Ctr., 1983—88; Truman Blocker Disting. prof., chief divsn. plastic surgery U. Tex. Med. Br., 1988—93; dir. surg. svcs. Shriners' Burn Inst., Galveston, Tex., 1988—93; prof. surgery U. South Fla., Tampa, 1993—2001, prof. surgery emeritus, 2001—, chair divsn. surgery rsch., 1993—97; chmn. surg. svc. Bay Pines (Fla.) VA Med. Ctr., 1993—97. Chmn., pres. Am. Bd. Plastic Surgery , 1996—97. Mem. editl. bd.: Jour. Trauma. Maj. M.C. U.S. Army, 1967—71, col. M.C. USAR, 1991—97. Fellow: ACS, Royal Australasian Coll. Surgeons (hon.); mem.: Am. Bd. Med. Specialties, Am. Assn. Plastic Surgery, Wound Healing Soc. (pres. 1995—96, Lifetime Sci. Achievement award 1998), Am. Surg. Assn., Am. Burn Assn. (pres. 1985—86, Disting. Svc. award), Plastic Surgery Rsch. Coun. (chmn. 1983—84), Royal Coll. Surgeons of England (hon.), Alpha Omega Alpha, Phi Delta Theta, Nu Sigma Nu. E-mail: mcrobson@earthlink.net.

ROBSON, SYBIL ANN, film producer; b. Tulsa, Dec. 8, 1956; d. John Nicholas and Alma Robson. BFA, So. Meth. U., 1979. Anchor, reporter Sta. WRR-AM Radio, Dallas, 1976-78; researcher Sta. WFAA-TV, 1977-78; polit. researcher ABC News, Paris, 1978-79; anchor, reporter Sta. KOLR-TV, Springfield, Mo., 1979-80, Sta. WFMY-TV, Greensboro, N.C., 1980-83, Paramount Pictures, L.A., 1983-86; investor Robson Investments, 1982—; film producer Bernhard/Robson Entertainment, 1987-91; pres., film producer Robson Entertainment, Beverly Hills, Calif., 1992—. Mem. Earth Communications Office; mem. Hollywood Women's Political Com. Mem. Am. Film Inst., Ind. Feature Project, Women in Film, Environ. Media Assn., Sigma Delta Chi. Avocations: snow skiing, tennis, piano.

ROBY, ANNIE BETH BRIAN, librarian; b. Lorenzo, Tex., Nov. 20, 1935; d. William Preston and Zona Inez (Cherry) Brian; m. Alexander Eugene Roby, Dec. 23, 1955; children: Rodney, Renee Setser, Rebecca Jordan. BS, Sul Ross State U., Alpine, Tex., 1968; BLS, U. North Tex., Denton, 1986. Cert. tchr., Tex., librarian Am. Libr. Assn., Tex. Tchr. Ector County Ind. Sch. Dist., Odessa, Tex., 1968-73, Bangs (Tex.) Ind. Sch. Dist., 1973-74, libr., 1990-92; tchr. Brownwood (Tex.) Ind. Sch. Dist., 1974-82, libr. coord., 1992—; libr. Howard Payne U., Brownwood, 1987-89. Cons. Bangs Ind. Sch. Dist., 1990-92, Brownwood Ind. Sch. Dist., 1992—. Mem. Tech. Com., Brownwood, 1995-96; sec. Jr. Twentieth Century Book Club, Brownwood, 1997—. Grantee J.R. Beadel Found., 1995-97. Mem. ALA, AAUW, Tex. Libr. Assn., Rotary, Phi Delta Kappa. Baptist. Avocations: piano, swimming, water skiing, creative writing, sewing. Home: 2505 Southside Dr Brownwood TX 76801-5611 Office: Brownwood Ind Sch Dist 2100 Slayden St Brownwood TX 76801-5456

ROBY, B. ANDREW, music educator; b. Harlan, Ky., July 23, 1959; s. Billy E. and Bobbie Z. (Gatewood) R.; m. Mary D. Martin, June 23, 1982; children: Rachel Karis, David Andrew. MusB, Union U., 1981; M in Ch. Music, So. Bapt. Theol. Sem., 1985, D in Musical Arts., 1991. Mem. faculty Asbury Coll., Wilmore, Ky., 1987-90, Shorter Coll., Rome, 1990-93, Union U., Jackson, Tenn., 1993—, chair dept. music, 1994—. Conductor chorus, vocal soloist recitals. Interim min. music 1st Baptist Ch., Savannah, Tenn., 1993-94, Paris, Tenn., 1994-96, Ripley, Tenn., 1998-99, Jackson, 1999—, Meridian Bapt. Ch., Jackson, 1996-98, 1st Bapt. Ch., Jackson, 1999—; v.p. Andrew Jackson Sch. PTO, Jackson, 1996-97. Mem. Nat. Assn. Tchrs. Singing (state chair auditions 1989-90, state gov. 1997—) Am. Choral Dirs. Assn. (editor newsletter 1993-98), Rotary. Democrat. Avocations: racquetball, bicycling, traveling. Home: 201 Laurie Cir Jackson TN 38305-3046 Office: Union U 1050 Union U Dr Jackson TN 38305

ROBY, CHRISTINA YEN, data processing and information systems specialist; b. Shanghai; came to U.S., 1980; d. Hai Zhou and Yun Qui (Zhang) Yen; m: Ronald L. Roby; 1 child, Colin H. BS, Jiao-Tung U., Shanghai, 1957; MS, U. Balt., 1986. Lic. engr., Peoples Republic of China. Chief mech. engr. Shenyang Valve Rsch. Inst., China, 1958-1980; computer system operator U. Balt., 1984, rsch. asst., 1984-86; sales assoc. V. F. Assocs., Inc., Balt., 1986-88; system analyst Computer Data Systems, Inc., Rockville, Md., 1988-89; sys. analyst State Md., Balt., 1989-98; lead advanced sys. analyst State of Md., 1998—. Instr. Community Coll. of Balt., 1986, 88; cons. Nat. Ins. Agency, Balt., 1988. Author: Guide to Using MS-DOS, 1988; contbr. author Japanese-Chinese Electrical Mechanical Industry Dictionary, 1980; transl., editor Analysis of Gas, Impurities and Carbide in Steel, 1961; contbr. articles to profl. jours. Vol. tutor U. Balt., 1983; vol. tchr. Chinese Lang. Sch., Balt., 1985-86, 90—, v.p., 1998—; lectr. Internat. Festival Exhbn., 1986, vice prin., Chinese Lang. Sch. of Baltimore, 1998—. Recipient cert. of appreciation Chinese Lang. Sch., 1986. Mem. NAFE, Sci. and Tech. Assn., Beta Gamma Sigma, Delta Mu Delta. Avocations: calligraphy, meditation, Tai-Chi, foreign languages. E-mail: croby2@yahoo.com.

ROBY, JASPER, bishop; Sr. bishop, exec. head Apostolic Overcoming Holy Ch. of God, Inc., Birmingham, Ala. Office: Apostolic Overcoming Holy Church God Inc 1120 24th St N Birmingham AL 35234-3131

ROBY, PAMELA ANN, sociology educator; b. Milw., Nov. 17, 1942; d. Clark Dearborn and Marianna (Gilman) R.; m. James Peter Mulherin, July 15, 1977 (div. 1987). BA, U. Denver, 1963; MA, Syracuse U., 1966; PhD, NYU, 1971. Instrn. ednl. sociology NYU, 1966; asst. prof. George Washington U., Washington, 1970-71; asst. prof. sociology and social welfare Brandeis U., Waltham, Mass., 1971-73; chair cmty. studies bd. U. Calif., Santa Cruz, 1974-76, 79, assoc. prof., 1973-77, prof. sociology and women's studies, 1977—, dir. sociology doctoral program, 1988-91, chair sociology dept., 1998-2001. Vis. scholar U. Wash., Seattle, 1991-92; mem. anthropology, linguistics and sociology panel NSF, Washington, 1993; mem. sociology program rev. com. Northeastern U., Boston, 1990; assessor Social Scis. and Humanities Rsch. Coun. Can., Toronto, 1993; cons. James Irvine Found., San Francisco, 1986; vice chair Nat. Commn. on Working Women, Washington, 1977-80; mem. social sci. rsch. rev. com. NIMH, Washington, 1976-78; Re-evaluation Counseling (coll. and U. faculty reference person), 1980—. Author: Women in the Workplace, 1981; editor: The Poverty Establishment, 1974, Child Care: Who Cares? Foreign and Domestic Infant and Early Childhood Development Policies, 1973-75; co-author: The Future of Inequality, 1970; adv. editor: Sociol. Quar., 1990-93, Gender and Society, 1986-89. Andrew W. Mellon sr. scholar Wellesley Coll., 1978-79; vis. fellow Indian Coun. Social Sci. Rsch., 1979. Mem. Soc. for Study Social Problems (pres. 1996-97), Sociologists for Women in Soc. (pres. 1978-80), Am. Sociol. Assn. (chair sect. on sex and gender 1974-78, exec. coun. mem.-at-large 1975-78), Internat. Sociol. Assn. (rsch. coun. mem.-at-large 1978-82), Pacific Sociol. Assn. (v.p. 1996-97), Ea. Sociol. Assn. (exec. coun. mem.-at-large 1973-74), Re-evaluation Counseling (internat. ref. person for coll. and univ. faculty), Phi Beta Kappa, Alpha Kappa Delta. Avocations: camping, hiking, painting, swimming, pen and ink drawing. Office: U Calif Dept Sociology C8 Santa Cruz CA 95064

ROCCA, CHRISTINA B. federal agency administrator; married; 2 children. BA in History, King's Coll., London, 1980. Intelligence officer CIA, 1982—97; fgn. affairs advisor Senate Sam Brownback; asst. sec. of state South Asian affairs U.S. Dept. of State, Washington, 2001—. Office: US Dept of State South Asian Affairs 2201 C St NW Washington DC 20520-6243 Office Fax: 202-735-4333.*

ROCCO, RON, artist; b. Ft. Hood, Tex., Nov. 21, 1953; s. Raymond and Dorothy Ann (D'Angelo) R. Student, Fordham U., 1972; BFA, SUNY, Purchase, 1976; MS in Visual Studies, MIT Ctr. for Advanced Visual Studies, 1983. Artist-in-residence Exptl. TV Ctr., Owego, N.Y., 1982—; guest lectr., artist-in-residence The Banff (Alta., Can.) Ctr., 1987; artist-in-residence Kunstlerhaus Bethanian, Berlin, 1991; artist-in-residence inter. studio program Kunst and Complex, Rotterdam, Netherlands, 1993. Guest lectr. various univs., 1977-90; mem. UN Internat. Conf. on Communication Tech. and Traditional Cultures, N.Y.C., 1983; bd. dirs. Art & Sci. Collaborations, Inc. Performance at The Solomon R. Guggenheim Mus., N.Y.C., 1983; works exhibited: Arnot Art Mus., Elmira, N.Y., 1976, The Showing Room, N.Y.C., 1979, IV Biennale Internazionale Danteesca, Ravenna, Italy, 1979, The Ithaca Festival, N.Y., 1979, Gallery Danielli, Toronto, Can., 1981, Pratt Inst., Brooklyn, 1981, The Fifth Floior Studio, N.Y.C., 1981, Herbert F. Johnson Mus., Ithaca, 1981, The Asia Soc., N.Y.C., 1985, Video Image Invitational, Found. Georgio Ronchi, Capri, Italy; Bronx Mus. Art, N.Y., 1985; Internat. Exhibit of Computer Art Forms, Kortijk, Belgium, 1986, P.S.1 Mus./MOMA Inc., N.Y.C., 1987, Found. Artgarden, Amsterdam, The Netherlands, 1989, The Katonah (N.Y.) Mus. Art, 1990, The Bklyn. Mus., 1990, Fundacao Rocha, Fortalesca, Brazil, 1991, Kunstlerhaus Bethanien, Berlin, 1991, Amerika Haus, Berlin, 1992, Rotunda Gallery, N.Y.C., 1996, Neuberger Mus. Art, Purchase, N.Y., 1996, Warehouse Galerie, Amsterdam, 1993, ISEA95/Internat. Exhbn. Electronic Art, Montreal, 19995, Sylvia White Gallery, N.Y.C., 1996, The Brooklyn Mus., 1997, List Ctr. MIT, Cambridge, 1997, Snug Harbor Cultural Ctr., N.Y.C., 1998, U. Mass., Lowell, 1999, Campo and Campo, Antwerp, Belgium, 1999, Galerie Volcker and Freunde, Berlin, Germany, 2000, Islip Art Mus., N.Y., 2000, Collaborative Concepts, Beacon, N.Y., 2001, ABC NO RIO and The Hudson Guild, N.Y.C., 2001; artistic dir. Laser Sculpture/Dance, 1981; producer, dir. Zaroff's Tale, 1983 (N.Y. State Coun. on Arts grantee); co-dir., collaborator Buddah Meets Einstein at the Great Wall, 1985 (Nat. Endowment Arts award); collaborator, sculptor Light and Sound Sphere Study, 1986 (N.Y. State Coun. on Arts grantee); collaborator Communicating Vessels, 1998 (sponsors: CBK/Centrum Bildende Kunst, Rotterdam and Netherlands Consul to N. Am.). Founder, dir. Ithaca Artists Coop., 1977-80; pub. commns. N.J. Light Rail Project, West Ave. Station, 1997. Creative and Performing Arts Coun. grantee Cornell U., Ithaca, N.Y., 1977, expansion arts program grantee Nat. Endowment Arts, 1977-79; recipient Netherland-Am. Found. award, 1989, Art Matters award, 1989, N.Y. Found. for the Arts award, 1989, The Found. for Contemporary Performance Arts award, 1989, Sculpture award, Ithaca Art Assn., 1976. Mem. ACLU, Film/Video Arts, Am. Assn. Mus. Buddhist. Studio: 59 Harrison Ave Brooklyn NY 11211-8115 E-mail: rr192@columbia.edu.

ROCEK, JAN, chemist, educator; b. Prague, Czech Republic, Mar. 24, 1924; came to U.S., 1960, naturalized, 1966; s. Hugo and Frida (Loebl) Robitschek; m. Eva Trojan, June 26, 1947; children: Martin, Thomas. MS, Tech. U., Prague, 1949, PhD, 1953. Scientist Czechoslovak Acad. Sci., Prague, 1953-57, sr. scientist, 1957-60; vis. scientist U. Coll., London, 1958; research fellow Harvard U., 1960-62; asso. prof., then prof. Cath. U. Am., 1962-66; prof. chemistry U. Ill., Chgo., 1966-95, acting head dept., 1980-81, head dept., 1981-93, vice chancellor rsch., dean grad. coll., 1993-95, acting dean Grad. Coll., 1969-70, dean Grad. Coll., 1970-79, asso. mem. Ctr. for Advanced Studies, 1968-69; ret., 1995. Vis. scholar Stanford U., 1979-80, Cambridge U., 1980 Contbr. articles to profl. jours. Mem. Am. Chem. Soc., AAAS, Czechoslovak Soc. Arts and Scis. in Am., AAUP, Sigma Xi (pres. chpt. 1976-77, 85-86), Phi Kappa Phi. Home: 2636 Laurel Ln Wilmette IL 60091-2202 E-mail: rocek@uic.edu.

ROCH, LEWIS MARSHALL, II, ophthalmic surgeon, medical entrepreneur; b. Mineola, Tex., Aug. 13, 1934; s. Lewis Marshall and Gladys Irene (Hoover) R.; m. Lois Afton Price; children: Lewis Marshall Roch III, Katrina Ann Seitz. BA, U. Tex., Austin, 1955; MD, U. Tex. Southwestern, 1959. Diplomate Am. Bd. Ophthalmology. Intern USPHS Hosp., Boston, 1959-60, resident in ophthalmology New Orleans, 1960-63, dep. chief ophthalmology, 1963-64, chief opthalmology Seattle, 1964-67; attending ophthalmic surgeon Ball Meml. Hosp., Muncie, Ind., 1967—, chmn. dept. surgery, chmn. clin. staff, 1975, chmn. exec. com., 1980-93; founder, CEO, med. dir. The Eye Ctr. Group, 1985—, 1985—, The Surgi Ctr. Group, Muncie, 1985—. Ho. of dels. Ind. State Med. Assn., 1975-87; exec. com. Ind. Acad. Ophthalmology, 1978-82; bd. dirs. Cardinal Health Ptnrs.; clin. asst. prof. Ind. U. Sch. Medicine, 1978—. Chmn. Muncie-Delaware Devel., 2000—; mem. Ball State U. Bus. Forecasting Roundtable, 2000—; exec. v.p. Muncie-Delaware Econ. Devel.; trustee Minnetrista Cultural Ctr., 2002—. Fellow ACS, Am. Acad. Ophthalmology; mem. AMA, Ind. State Med. Assn., Muncie Acad. Medicine (pres. 1981-82), Am. Soc. Cataract and Refractive Surgeons, Am. Coll. Physicians Execs., Muncie-Delaware C. of C. (bd. dirs. 1999—). Republican. Achievements include first to work in outpatient ambulatory surgery; innovation in intraocular lens implantation in cataract surgery; integration of physician's practices with hospital health care delivery systems. Avocations: treaking, gardening, woodworking. Home: 2006 E Robinwood Dr Muncie IN 47304-2857 Office: The Eye Ctr Group LLC 200 N Tillotson Ave Muncie IN 47304-3988 E-mail: lmroch@comcast.net.

ROCH, THIERRY GEORGE, hotel association executive; b. N.Y.C., Feb. 19, 1962; s. George Jacques and Sabine Yvette R. BS in Civil Enging., U. Va., 1984. Transportation planner RBF & Assocs., Newport Beach, Calif., 1984-87; comml. leasing assoc. Berens Asset Mgmt., 1987-92; from dir. member rels. to v.p. corp. industry affairs Am. Hotel & Motel Assn., Washington, 1992-99; exec. dir. Hist. Hotels of Am., 1999—. Office: Nat Trust for Hist Preservation 1795 Massachusetts Ave NW Washington DC 20036 E-mail: thierry-roch@nthp.org.

ROCHA, GUY LOUIS, archivist, historian; b. Long Beach, Calif., Sept. 23, 1951; s. Ernest Louis and Charlotte (Sobus) R. BA in Social Studies and Edn., Syracuse U., 1973; MA in Am. Studies, San Diego State U., 1975; postgrad., U. Nev., 1975—. Cert. archivist Am. Acad. Cert. Archivists. Tchr. Washoe County Sch. Dist., Reno, 1975-76; history instr. Western Nev. C.C., Carson City, 1976; curator manuscripts Nev. Hist. Soc., Reno, 1976-81, interim asst. dir., 1980, interim dir., 1980-81; state adminstr. archives and records Nev. State Libr. and Archives, Carson City, 1981—. Hist. cons. Janus Assocs., Tempe, Ariz., 1980, Rainshadow Assocs., Carson City, 1983—. Co-author: The Ignoble Conspiracy: Radicalism on Trial in Nevada, 1986, The Earp's Last Frontier: Wyatt and Virgil Earp in Nevada 1902-1905, 1988; contbr. to books and govt. study; host weekly radio talk show Sta. KPTL, Carson City, 1988-2000, KUNR/NPR, Reno, 2001-; hist. cons. to documentary Las Vegas, A&E Network, 1996, documentary Hoover Dam, PBS Network, 1999. Mem. Washoe Heritage Coun., Reno, 1983-85; editl. bd. Nev. Hist. Soc., Reno, 1983—; mem. Washoe County Dem. Ctrl. Com., Reno, 1984-87; ex-officio mem. Nev. Commn. Bicentennial U.S. Constn., 1986-91. Mem. Conf. Intermountain Archivists (coun. mem. 1979-87, v.p. 1984-85, pres. 1985-86), No. Nev. Pub. Adminstrs. Group (pres. 1986-87), S.W. Labor Studies Assn., State Hist. Records Adv. Bd. (dep. coord. 1984-86, coord. 1986—), Westerners Internat. Nev. Corral (dep. sheriff 1980-81, sheriff 1984-85, mem. state coords. steering com. 1985-87, vice chmn. 1986-87), Soc. Am. Archivists, Western History Assn., Nat. Assn. Govt. Archives and Records Adminstrs., Orgn. Am. Historians. Home: 1824 Pyrenees St Carson City NV 89703-2331 Office: Nev State Libr & Archives 100 N Stewart St Carson City NV 89701-4285

ROCHA, LUIZ ALBERTO OLIVEIRA, engineering educator; b. Alegrete, Brazil, Dec. 26, 1958; s. Antonio Portilho and Maria de Lourdes Oliveira Rocha; m. Maria Ema da Silva, Jan. 9, 1982; children: Antonio da Silva, Ana Paula da Silva. Bacharel Mech. Engring. Automobile, Mil. Inst. Engring., Rio de Janeiro , 1991; Master, Pontificie U. Cath.- PUC, Rio de Janeiro, 1995; PhD, Duke U., 2002. Lic. Mech. Engr., 1991. Engr. Ford of Brazil, Sao Paulo, Brazil, 1992; engr. projects Inst. R&D, Rio de Janeiro, 1992—96; prof. Found. U. Fed. of Rio Grande, Rio Grande, Brazil, 1996—. Roman Catholic. Office: Duke U Dept Mech Engring & Mat Sci Durham NC 27708-300 Business E-Mail: lar2@duke.edu.

ROCHA, MARILYN EVA, retired clinical psychologist; b. San Bernardino, Calif., Oct. 23, 1928; d. Howard Ray Gonding and Laura Anne (Johanson) Walker; m. Hilario Ursala Rocha, Mar. 25, 1948 (dec. Feb. 1971); children: Michael, Sherry, Teri, Denise. AA, Solano Jr. Coll., 1970; BA, Sacramento State U., 1973, MA, 1974; PhD, U.S. Internat. U., 1981. Psychologist Naval Drug Rehab. Ctr., U.S. Navy, San Diego, 1975-85, chief psychologist, 1983-84; staff clin. psychologist Calif. Youth Authority No. Reception Ctr. Clinic, 1985-92, El Paso de Robles Sch., Paso Robles, Calif., 1992-2000; ret., 2000. Dir. Self-Help Agys., San Diego. Author short story. Vol. counselor Hamonium, San Diego, 1976-77, SMRC Planning Group Scripps/Miramar Ranch, 1982-85; leader Vacaville coun. Cub Scouts/Boy Scouts Am., Calif., 1957-62, 4-H, also Brownie's. Recipient Outstanding Svc. award CYA, 1993, Woman of the Yr. award, 1995. Mem. APA, PTA (hon., life), Calif. Scholastic Fedn., Am. Assn. Suicidology, Friends of the Libr. (sec.), Friends of the Adobes, Multi-floral Garden Club (membership chmn.), Delta Zeta. Democrat. Unitarian Universalist. Home: Morning Glory Ranch 4625 Ross Dr Paso Robles CA 93446-9379 E-mail: mgranch@webtv.net.

ROCHA, OSBELIA MARIA JUAREZ, librarian, assistant principal; b. Odessa, Tex., Aug. 3, 1950; d. Tomas R. and Maria Socorro (Garcia) Juarez; m. Ricardo Rocha, July 8, 1972; children: Nidia Selina, René Ricardo. AA, Odessa Coll., 1970; BA, Sul Ross State U., 1972; MA, Tex. A&I U., 1977; MLS, Tex. Woman's U., 1991; Mid-Mgmt. Cert., U. Tex. of the Permian Basin, 1999. Cert. life provisional reading specialist, learning res. tchr., secondary english, math., Tex.; cert. mid-mgmt. adminstr. Math. tchr. Del Rio (Tex.) Jr. High Sch., 1972-78; reading tchr. Del Rio High Sch., 1978-79; math. tchr. Ector High Sch., Odessa, 1979-81, Permian High Sch., Odessa, 1981-88; libr. Blackshear Elem. Magnet Sch., 1988-93, Bowie Jr. H.S., Odessa, 1993-95, Ector Jr. H.S., Odessa, 1995-96, Permian H.S., Odessa, 1996-2000; asst. prin. Big Spring H.S., Tex., 2000—02; prin./curriculum dir. Weimar HS I.S.D., 2002—. Reviewer of children's and adolescents' books for MultiCultural Rev.; author articles. Mem. ASCD, Tex. Assn. Secondary Sch. Prins., Tex. Assn. Bilingual Edn., Tex. Reading Assn., Tex. Libr. Assn., Tex. Elem. Prins. and Suprs. Assn., Tex. Coun. Women Sch. Execs., Beta Phi Mu, Delta Kappa Gamma. Roman Catholic. Avocations: reading, needlework, camping, baking. Home: PO Box 279 Weimar TX 78962-0279 Office: Weimar HS 506 S Main St Weimar TX 78962 E-mail: osbeliar@yahoo.com., orocha@esc3.net.

ROCHBERG, GEORGE, composer, educator; b. Paterson, N.J., July 5, 1918; s. Morris and Anna (Hoffman) R.; m. Gene Rosenfeld, Aug. 18, 1941; children: Paul Bernard (dec.), Frances Ruth. BA, Montclair State Tchrs. Coll., 1939, LHD, 1962; BMus, Curtis Inst. Music, 1948; MA, U. Pa., 1949, MusD (hon.), 1988, Phila. Mus. Acad., 1964, Curtis Inst. Music, 1988. Faculty Curtis Inst. Music, 1948-54; Fulbright fellow Am. Acad., Rome, 1950-51; editor, dir. publs. Theo. Presser Co., Bryn Mawr, Pa., 1951-60; chmn. Music dept. U. Pa., 1960-68; ret., 1983; Annenberg prof. humanities U. Pa., 1979. Commd. to compose ballet music for Anna Sokolov, Lincoln Center Fund, 1965; recordings include numerous others; (recipient Gershwin Meml. award 1952, Soc. for Publ. Am. Music award 1956, Koussevitzky commn. 1957, Naumberg Rec. award 1961); Composer: Symphony No. 1, 1948-49, Night Music, 1949, String Quartet No. 1, 1952, Serenata d Estate, 1955, Symphony No. 2, 1956, La Bocca della Verita, 1958, String Quartet No. 2, 1959-61, Blake Songs, 1961, Time-Span (II), 1962, Trio for Violin, Cello and Piano, 1963, Zodiac, 1964, Black Sounds, 1965, Contra Mortem et Tempus, 1965, Music for the Magic Theater, 1965, Symphony No. 3, 1969, Tableaux for chamber ensemble, 1968, String Quartet No. 3, 1972, Violin Concerto premiered by Isaac Stern, 1975, Piano Quintet (Nat. Endowment for Arts commn.), 1975, Symphony No. 4, 1976, Sonata Seria, 1998, 3 Elegiac Pieces, 1998; monodrama Phaedra, 1976, String Quartet No. 4, 1979 (1st place Kennedy Center Friedheim award), The Confidence Man, an Opera, 1981, Piano Trio No. 2 (for Beaux Arts Trio), 1983, Symphony No. 5, Chgo. Symphony, 1986, Symphony No. 6, Pitts. Symphony, 1987, Muse of Fire for flute and guitar, 1989, Piano Trio No. 3 (for Beaux Arts Trio), 1991, Sonata for Violin and Piano, 1988, Sonata-aria for Cello and Piano, 1992, Concerto for Clarinet and Orchestra, 1994-95, Chromaticism: Symmetry in Atonal and Tonal Music, 1996, Circles of Fire for 2 Pianos, 1997; (chamber concerto for guitar and ensemble) Eden: Out of Time and Out of Space, 1997, Sonata Seria for piano, 1998, Three Elegiac Pieces for Piano, 1999. Served to 2d lt., inf. AUS, 1942-45, ETO. Decorated Purple Heart with cluster; gold medal in music Brandeis Creative Arts award, 1985; Nat. Inst. Arts and Letters grant, 1962; Fromm Found. commn., 1965; Guggenheim fellow, 1957, 1966-67; Nat. Endowment for Arts grant, 1972-73 Mem. Am. Acad. Arts and Scis., Am. Musicological Soc., ASCAP (Life-Achievement award 1999). *I have always clung fast to these fundamentals: that music was given man so he could express the best he was capable of; that the best he was capable of had to do with his deepest feelings; that his deepest feelings are rooted in what I believe to be a moral order in the universe which underlies all real existence.*

ROCHDI, MYRIAM, pharmacist, researcher; b. Eaubonne, Paris, France, Apr. 2, 1964; d. Ahmed and Francoise (Loiseleux) R. PharmD, Sch. of Pharmacy, Paris, 1987. Rsch. fellow Nat. Inst. Health and Med. Rsch., Paris, 1989-94; dir. biopharmaceutics SkyePharma AG, San Diego, 1995—. Mem. Am. Assn. Pharm. Sci. E-mail: myrochdi@yahoo.com.

ROCHE, GERARD RAYMOND, management consultant; b. Scranton, Pa., July 27, 1931; s. Joseph Arthur and Amelia Jane (Garcia) R.; m. Marie Terotta, Apr. 27, 1957; children: Mary Margaret, Anne Elizabeth, Paul Joseph. BS in Acctg., U. Scranton, 1953; MBA, NYU, 1958. Mgmt. trainee AT&T, Phila., 1955-56; account exec. ABC-TV, N.Y.C., 1956-58; sales and mktg. positions Kordite Corp. subs. Mobil Oil Co., Macedon, N.Y., 1959-63; assoc. Heidrick & Struggles, Inc., N.Y.C., 1964-68, ptnr., 1968—, mgr. N.Y., 1968-73, mgr. East, 1973-77, pres., chief exec. officer 1978-81, chmn., 1981-2000, sr. chmn., 2000—. Bd. dirs. Value Am. Corp. Former trustee Cath. U. Am., U. Scranton; bd. dirs. Covenant House, N.Y.C. Served to lt. USN, 1953-55. Mem. Univ. Club, Sky Club, Yale Club, Sleepy Hollow Country Club (bd. govs.), Blind Brook Club, The Golf Club of Purchase, Loblolly Pines C. C., Knights of Malta, Alpha Sigma Nu (past treas.), Community Anti-Drug Coalitions of America (bd. dirs.). Roman Catholic. Office: Heidrick & Struggles Inc 245 Park Ave Fl 43 New York NY 10167-0152 E-mail: grr@h-s.com.

ROCHE, JAMES G. federal agency administrator; Capt. U.S. Navy, 1960-83; Office Sect. Defense, 1975-79; sr. profl. staff mem. Senate Select Com. Intelligence, 1979-81; princ. dep. dir. policy planning staff U.S. Dept. State, 1981-83; staff dir. U.S. Senate Com. on Armed Svcs.; v.p., dir. analysis ctr. Northrop Grumman, 1984-89, v.p., special asst. to chmn., pres., CEO, 1989-91, v.p., adv. devel. planning, 1991-; corp. v.p., pres. Northrop Grumman's Elec. Sensors, Systems Sector, 1998—2001; secy. airforce U.S. Dept. Def., Washington, 2001—. Office: US Dept Def Secy Air Force 1670 Air Force Pentagon Washington DC 20330-1670 Office Fax: 703-695-8809.*

ROCHE, JOHN JEFFERSON, lawyer; b. N.Y.C., Apr. 12, 1934; s. William and Florence E. (Garvey) R.; m. Judith J. Stackpole, Sept. 4, 1980; 1 child from previous marriage, Forrest B. AB, Brown U., 1957; LL.B., Boston U., 1964. Bar: Mass. 1964, U.S. Tax Ct. 1976. Asst. atty. gen. Dept. Atty. Gen., Boston, 1964-67; ptnr. Hale and Dorr, 1967-90; pvt. practice Cambridge, Mass., 1991-2001; ptnr. Taylor, Ganson & Perrin LLP, Boston, 2001—. Trustee The Hotchkiss Sch., 1986-91, Archaeol. Inst. Am.; bd. dirs. Indian Soc., Bostonian Soc. Served with U.S. Army, 1959-62. Fellow Am. Coll. Trusts and Estates, Internat. Acad. Estate and Trust Law; mem. ABA, Mass. Bar Assn., Boston Bar Assn., Masons, Wig and Penn Club (London), Winchester Country Club. Republican. Congregationalist. Office: John J Roche & Assocs Ste 405 160 Federal St Boston MA 02110-1700

ROCHE, JOHN EDWARD, educator, human resources consultant; b. St. Albans, N.Y., Nov. 11, 1946; s. John F. and Carolyn C. (Miller) R.; m. Valerie Vastola; children: Christopher B., Danielle, Ryan J., Jennifer M. BA, Marist Coll., 1968, MBA, 1975; MS in Edn., SUNY, New Paltz, 1974; EdD, Nova Southeastern U., 1998. Tchr. Kingston (N.Y.) City Schs., 1968-76; employment supr. ACLI Internat. Inc., N.Y.C., 1976-78; dir. pers. Balfour MacLaine Internat., 1978-80; mgr. employee rels. Harcourt Brace Jovanovich, 1980-82; nat. dir. pers. Hayt, Hayt & Landau, Great Neck, N.Y., 1982-86; pres. Pers. Mgmt. Svcs., 1983-86, Martin-Roche Assocs., Inc., Levittown, 1986-94; prof. instrnl. tech. N.Y. Inst. Tech., Old Westbury, 1989-2000, chair Sch. Edn. Manhattan Campus, 1997-2000, acting dir. Ctr. Labor & Indls. Rels., 2000; assoc. dean Sch. Continuing Studies L.I. U., Bklyn., 2000—; pres. Human Resources Dept. Inc., Syosset, N.Y., 1994—, L.I. Bus. Network, Inc., 1994-2000. Pres. Martin-Roche Internat. Ltd., Plainview, N.Y., 1992-94. Exec. dir. Jr. Achievement, Kingston, 1972-76, coach Syosset Baseball Assn., CYO Basketball Assn.; human resource com. mem. Adults and Children with Learning and Devel. Disabilities, 1990—. Mem. ASTD, WorldatWork (cert. compensation profl.), Soc. for Human Resource Mgmt. (cert. sr. profl. in human resources), KC (grand knight 1967-68). Republican. Roman Catholic. Avocations: astronomy, photography. Home: 17 Meadow Ln Sysoset NY 11791-4126 Office: L I Univ Sch Continuing Studies Brooklyn NY 11201 E-mail: roche@liu.edu., jeroche@juno.com.

ROCHE, JOHN JAMES, investment banker; b. Chgo., June 28, 1961; s. Thomas Michael and Joyce Ann (Kappel) R. BS, Marquette U., Milw., 1983, postgrad., 1987, 89. Money market trader Sanwa Bank Ltd., Chgo., 1984-86; asst. v.p. Chem. Bank, N.Y.C., 1986-88; v.p. First Chgo. Capital Markets, 1988—. Mem. Delta Sigma Pi. Republican. Roman Catholic. Home: 1408 W Norwood St Chicago IL 60660-2404 Office: First Chgo Capital Markets 1 S First National Plz Ste 33 Chicago IL 60603-2000

ROCHE, JUDITH, poet, secondary school educator; b. Detroit, Sept. 9, 1941; d. Lawrence George Nault and Aline Bernice Tabor; m. Thomas McCutcheon Roche, Dec. 17, 1960 (div. June 1972); children: Tari, Robin. BA, Ea. Mich. U., 1967; MA, New Coll. of Calif., San Francisco, 1986. Tchr. various schs., Mich., Wash.; lit. arts dir. One Reel, Seattle, 1985—; artist in residence Wash. State Arts Commn., 1985—, Seattle Arts & Letters, 1995—2000, Mus. of Glass, Tacoma, 2000—01. Author: (poetry collections) Ghosts, Myrrh/My Life as a Screamer, 1985—94; editor: (anthologies) First Fish First People, 1998 (Am. Book award), Ergo, 1987—94. Recipient award, Artists Trust, Seattle, 1997; fellow, Seattle Arts Commn., 1998. Mem.: PEN. Unitarian Universalist. Office: One Reel 1725 Westlake N Seattle WA 98109

ROCHE, KAREN RUTH, plastic surgeon; b. Pitts., Dec. 11, 1948; d. Joseph Stephen and Gertrude Marie (Otto) R.; m. Kenneth John Sapos, 1966 (div. 1971); 1 child, John D. Sapos; m. Roger Kent Galey, Sept. 23, 1977; children: Erin, Heather, Roger Kent Jr. BS magna cum laude, U. Pitts., 1971, MD, 1975. Diplomate Am. Bd. Plastic Surgery, Nat. Bd. Med. Examiners. Resident in gen. surgery Hosps. of U. Health Ctr. of Pitts., 1975-77, Western Pa. Hosp., Pitts., 1978-79, burn care fellow, 1979-80, plastic surgery resident, 1980-82; pvt. practice, 1982-92, Plastic Surgery of Pitts., 1992—. Tchg. fellow in gen. surgery, U. Pitts., 1976-77, clin. asst. prof. plastic surgery, 1986—; chief of surgery U. Pitts. Med. Ctr. Passavant, 1990-91, chief of head and neck surgery, UPMC, Passavant, 1999-00. Fellow ACS; mem. Am. Soc. Plastic Surgeons, Am. Soc. Aesthetic Plastic Surgery, Inc., Pa. Med. Soc., Allegheny County Med. Soc. (dir. 1995-2000), Ohio Valley Soc. Plastic and Reconstructive Surgery, Greater Pitts. Plastic Surgery Soc. (sec.-treas. 1990-91, pres. 1992-93), Robert H. Ivy Soc. (bd. dirs. 1995). Republican. Presbyterian. Avocations: skiing, hiking. Home: 108 Hawthorne Rd Pittsburgh PA 15238-2322 Office: Plastic Surgery of Pitts 9370 Mcknight Rd Ste 404 Pittsburgh PA 15237-5953 E-mail: galey108@aol.com.

ROCHE, KEVIN EAMONN (EAMONN ROCHE), architect; b. Dublin, Ireland, June 14, 1922; came to U.S., 1948, naturalized, 1964; s. Eamon and Alice (Harding) R.; m. Jane Tuohy, June 10, 1963; children: Eamon, Paud, Denis, Anne, Alice. B.Arch., Nat. U. Ireland, 1945; D.Sc. (hon.), Nat. U. Ireland, 1977; postgrad., Ill. Inst. Tech., 1948; D.F.A. (hon.), Wesleyan U., 1981, Yale U., 1995. With Eero Saarinen and Assocs., Bloomfield Hills, Mich., 1950—61; ptnr. Kevin Roche John Dinkeloo and Assocs., Hamden, 1966—. Prin. works include Ford Found. Hdqs., 1967, Oakland (Calif.) Mus, 1968, Met. Mus. Art, N.Y.C., Creative Arts Ctr., Wesleyan U., Middletown, Conn., 1971, Fine Arts Ctr., U. Mass., 1971, Union Carbide Corp. World Hdqs., Conn., Gen. Foods Corp. Hdqs., Rye, N.Y., 1977, 1978, Conoco Inc. Hdqs., Houston, 1979, Central Pk. Zoo, N.Y.C., 1980, DeWitt Wallace Mus. Fine Arts, Williamsburg, Va., 1980, Bouygues World Hdqs., Paris, 1983, J.P. Morgan and Co. Hdqs., N.Y.C., 1983, UNICEF Hdqs., N.Y.C., 1984, Leo Burnett Co. Hdqs., Chgo., 1985, Corning (N.Y.) Inc. Hdqs., 1986, Merck & Co. Hdqs., N.J., 1987, Dai Ichi Hdqs./Norinchukin Bank Hdqrs., Tokyo, 1989, Nations Bank Hdqs., Atlanta, 1989, Pontiac Marina Pvt. Ltd., Singapore, 1990, Metropolitano, Madrid, 1990, Borland Internat. Headquarters, Scotts Valley, Calif., 1990, Tanjong & Binariang/Ampang Tower, Kuala Lumpur, Malaysia, 1993, Mus. Jewish Heritage Holocaust Meml., N.Y.C., 1993, Tata Cummins Pvt. Ltd., Jamshedpur, India, 1994, Vis. Ctr., Columbus, Ind., 1994, Cummins Engine Co. APEX Mfg. Facility, 1994, Lucent Techs. Hdqs., Murray Hill, N.J., 1996, Wuxi Newage Cummins, Wuxi, China, 1996, Total Sys. Svcs. Corp. Headquarters, Columbus, Ga., 1997, student housing and student union NYU, N.Y.C., 1997—, ctrl. athletic facility MIT, Cambridge, 2000, Lucent Tech. R & D Facilities, various locations including The Netherlands and Germany, 1995—, Shiodome Block B Devel., Tokyo, 1997—, Santander Ctrl. Hispano, Madrid, 2001--, Station Place, Washington, 2001--. Mem. Fine Arts Commn., Washington; trustee Am. Acad. in Rome, 1968-71, Woodrow Wilson Center for Scholars in Smithsonian Instn. Recipient Creative Arts award Brandeis U., 1967; A.S. Bard award City Club N.Y., 1968, 77, 79; award Gov. of Calif., 1968; N.Y. State award Citizens Union N.Y., 1968; total design award Am. Soc. Interior Design; Pritzker Archtl. prize, 1982; Albert S. Bard award, 1990. Fellow AIA (medal of honor N.Y. chpt. 1968, Gold Medal award 1993, 25-yr. award 1995), AAAS; mem. NAD (academician), AAAL (pres. 1994-97), Am. Acad. Arts and Letters (Brunner award 1965, Gold medal 1990), Académie d'Architecture (Grand Gold medal 1977), Mcpl. Art Soc. N.Y. (Brendan Gill prize 1989), Acad. di San Luca. Office: Kevin Roche John Dinkeloo & Assocs PO Box 6127 20 Davis St Hamden CT 06517-3501

ROCHE DE COPPENS, PETER GEORGE, sociologist, educator; b. Vevey, Switzerland, May 24, 1938; s. George Sebastian and Alice Emmanuela (De Coppens) Roche de C.; m. Marian Karpacz, May 27, 1977 (dec. 1991); m. Marie Teresa Crivelli, Sept. 16, 2002. BS, Columbia U., 1965; MA, Fordham U., 1966, PhD, 1973; MSW, U. Montreal, 1978. Prof. sociology, anthropology East Stroudsburg (Pa.) U., 1970—. Instr. sociology Fordham U., N.Y.C., 1968-69, tchg. fellow, 1965-68; cons. UN, N.Y.C., 1997; v.p. Internat. Inst. Integral Human Studies, Montreal, 1977-97; cons. UN; ady. prof. faculty edn. McGill U., Montreal, 1998—. Author: The Development of the New Man, 1989, 98, The Art of Joyful Living, 1991, The Sociological Adventure, 1991, 96, Divine Light and Fire, 1992, Divine Light and Love, 1994, The Initiatory Path for the Year 2000, 1994, The Levels of Human Counciousness, 1996, , Love Vitamins, 1998; contbr. articles to mags.; host tv program Soul Sculpture. E-mail: proche@esu.edu.

ROCHELLE, DUDLEY CECILE, lawyer; b. Franklinton, La., Sept. 10, 1950; s. James Cecil and Mildred Grace (Stennis) R. BA in Polit. Sci., La. State U., 1972; JD, Yale U., 1975. Bar: Ga. 1976, U.S. Dist. Ct. (no. dist.) Ga. 1976, U.S. Ct. Appeals (5th cir.) 1976, U.S. Tax Ct., U.S. Ct. Appeals (11th cir.) 1997; cert. arbitrator and mediator. Vista atty. Atlanta Legal Aid Soc., 1975-76; law clk. to Hon. Joel J. Fryer Fulton County Superior Ct., Atlanta, 1976-77; trial atty. U.S. Dept. Labor, 1977-82; assoc. Hendrick Spanos & Phillips PC, 1982-88, shareholder (ptnr.), 1988-94, Spanos & Rochelle, P.C., Atlanta, 1994-97; shareholder Littler Mendelson, P.C., 1997—. Bd. dirs. Ga. Pub. Policy Found., 1996—, Midtown Alliance, Atlanta, 1982-92; mem. adv. bd. Coverdell Leadership Inst., Atlanta, 1996—. Mem. State Bar Ga. (mem. labor sect.), Atlanta Bar Assn. (mem. labor/employment sect., chairperson alt. dispute resolution com. 1986-92, mem. bench and bar com. 1982-87), Christian Legal Soc., Federalist Soc., Yale Club Ga. (bd. dirs. 1982-86), So. Inst. Bus. and Profl. Ethics (bd. dirs.). Republican. Avocations: outdoor activity, scuba diving, music. Home: 2745 Brook Grove Ct Atlanta GA 30339-5329 Office: Littler Mendelson PC 3348 Peachtree Rd NE Ste 1100 Atlanta GA 30326-1447 E-mail: DRochelle@littler.com.

ROCHELLE, LUGENIA, academic administrator; b. Maple Hill, N.C., July 14, 1943; d. John Edward and Ruby Lee (Holmes) R. BA, St. Augustine's Coll., 1965; MS, N.C. A & T State U., 1969; D of Pedagogy, Barbar-Scotia Coll., 1993. Cert. tchr., N.C. Tchr. French, English Butler High Sch., Barnwell, S.C., 1965-67; instr. English N.C. A & T State U., Greensboro, 1970-77, St. Augustine's Coll., Raleigh, N.C., 1977-86, dir. freshman studies program, 1986-91, dean lower coll., 1991-95, asst. to v.p. acad. affairs, 1991-92; dir. gen. studies, asst. prof. English Voorhees Coll., Denmark, S.C., 1996-98, spl. asst. to pres. external affairs SC, 1999—2002, dir. Hons. Coll. S.C., 1999—, dean, Coll. of General Studies, 2002—. Dir. Mellon program St. Augustine's Coll., Raleigh, 1980-83; adv. bd. cooperating Raleigh Colls., 1986—, Off to Coll., Montgomery, Ala., 1993—; mem. profl. practices commn. N.C. Dept. Pub. Instrn., 1994-96; coord. Title III, coord. Bd. Trustees Rels.; dir. Ctr.

Excellence in Humanities, Vorhees Coll., April 2000—; Hostess for Radio Talk Show, Views and News from Voorhees Coll., Sept. 2001—. Author: English Manual of Writing, 1980, (with others) Off to College, 1997, 98, reprinted, 1999, 2000, 01; editor: Can't Nobody Do You Like Jesus, 1998. Judge oratorical contests, Optimist Club, Raleigh, 1985-93; chair pro tem Raleigh Bicentennial Hist. Com., Raleigh, 1991-92; initiated, effected chartering of Phi Eta Sigma St. Augustine's Coll., 1995; bd. dirs. Garner Rd. YMCA, Raleigh, 1994-1996; coord. Honda Campus All-Star Challenge, 1996—; lay min., sec. vestry St. Philip's Episcopal Ch., 1997—; instnl. rep. S.C. Women in Higher Edn., Voorhees Coll., 1998—. Nat. teaching fellow N.C. A & T State U., Greensboro, 1968-70. NCTE Fellow Nat. Coun. Tchrs. English; mem. ASCD (assoc.), Cardinal Club. Avocations: reading, collecting antique birds, travel. E-mail: rochelle@voorhees.edu.

ROCHELLE, VICTOR CLEANTHUS, lawyer, consultant; b. El Reno, Okla., Nov. 4, 1918; s. Floyd Emerson and Goldie Opal (Dunbar) R.; m. Marjorie Armitage, Dec. 20, 1946 (div. 1956); children— Vickie Adrianne, Margo Renee; m. Patricia Ann Leary, Mar. 20, 1964; children— Elizabeth Ann, Linda Raquel. B.A., U. Tex., 1940; LL.B., Columbia U., 1947. Bar: Tex. 1948, U.S. Dist. Ct. Ill. 1953. Assoc. Tom Hartley, Atty., Pharr, Tex., 1947-49; assoc. Kelly, Looney, McLean & Littleton, Edinburg, Tex., 1949-52; personal injury supr. Country Mut. Ins. Co., Chgo., 1952-57, claims mgr., 1957-61, Bloomington, Ill., 1961-69; cons., dir. litigation Country Mut., Country Casualty, Mid-Am., 1969-84; ins. law cons., 1984— ; lectr. in field; arbitrator Mut. Casualty, 1965-70. Served to lt. comdr., USN, 1941-45. Mem. ABA, Tex. Bar Assn., Ill. Bar Assn., McLean County Bar Assn., Internat. Assn. Ins. Counsel, Property Loss Bur., Def. Research Inst., Am. Judicature Soc. Republican. Address: 27 Lateer Dr Normal IL 61761-3925

ROCHESTER, MICHAEL GRANT, geophysics educator; b. Toronto, Ont., Can., Nov. 22, 1932; s. Reginald Baillie Rochester and Ruth Ellen (Bonwick) Rochester Konrad; m. Elizabeth Manser, May 9, 1958; children— Susan, Fiona, John. BA with honors, U. Toronto, 1954, MA, 1956; PhD, U. Utah, 1959. Aerodynamicist A. V. Roe Can. Ltd., Malton, Ont., 1954-55; lectr. geophysics U. Toronto, 1959-60, asst. prof., 1960-61, U. Waterloo, Ont., 1961-65, assoc. prof., 1965-67, Meml. U. Nfld., St. John's, Can., 1967-70, prof., 1970-98, univ. research prof., 1986—, prof. emeritus, 1998—. Mem., officer Nat. Spiritual Assembly of Baha'is of Can., 1963-92. Grantee NRC, Natural Scis. and Engring. Research Council Can. Fellow Royal Soc. Can.; mem. Internat. Union Geodesy and Geophysics (Can. nat. com. 1971-75, 84-88), AAAS, Am. Geophys. Union, Can. Assn. Physicists, Can. Geophys. Union (Tuzo Wilson medal, 1986), Internat. Astron. Union (commn. rotation of the Earth 1973—), Royal Astron. Soc. London, Sigma Xi Avocations: hiking, swimming, history. Office: Meml Univ Nfld Dept Earth Scis Saint John's NF Canada A1B 3X5 E-mail: mrochest@mun.ca.

ROCHETTE, ANN ROBINSON, clinical manager; b. Pawtucket, R.I., Sept. 7, 1951; d. Vincent J. and Mary E. (Flynn) Robinson; m. Richard Rochette, June 27, 1982; children: Michael, Stephen. Diploma, St. Joseph Hops. Sch. Nursing, Providence, 1973; BS in Nursing, Salve Regina Coll., 1977; MS in Nursing, Boston U., 1981. Cert. pediatric advanced life support. Clin. nurse specialist pediatric critical care R.I. Hosp., Providence, 1981-83, clin. instr. pediatrics nursing, 1983-88, asst. dir. pediatric nursing, 1988-92; asst. prof. R.I. Coll., 1992-98; clin. mgr. Hasbro Children's Hosp., 1998—. Mem. ANA, Sigma Theta Tau.

ROCHETTE, EDWARD CHARLES, association executive; b. Worcester, Mass., Feb. 17, 1927; s. Edward Charles and Lilia (Viau) R.; m. Mary Ann Ruland, July 29, 1978; children by previous marriage— Edward Charles, Paul, Philip. Student, Washington U., St. Louis, Clark U. Exec. editor Krause Publs., Iola, Wis., 1960-66; acting exec. dir. Am. Numismatic Assn., Colorado Springs, Colo., 1967-68, exec. v.p., 1972-87, ret., 1987; editor jour. The Numismatist, 1968-72; exec. dir. Am. Numismatic Assn., 1998—. Bd. overseers Inst. Philatelic and Numismatic Studies, Adelphi U., Garden City, N.Y., 1979-81; chmn. medals com. Colo. Centennial Bicentennial Commn., 1976; mem. adv. panel Carson City Silver Dollar program Gen. Services Adminstrn., 1979-80; numismatic cons. U.S. Olympic Com. USOC, 1995—; mem. U.S. Assay Commn., 1965. Served with USN, 1944-46. Recipient Gold medal for syndicated column Numismatic Lit. Guild, 1980, 86-88; inducted to Numismatic Hall of Fame, 2000. Mem. Am. Numis. Assn. (life, medal of merit 1972, Numismatic Hall of Fame 2000), Am. Soc. Assn. Execs., Colo. Soc. Assn. Execs. (pres. 1988-89). Lodges: Pikes Peak Kiwanis (pres. 1987-88). Democrat. Roman Catholic. Office: Am Numis Assn 818 N Cascade Ave Colorado Springs CO 80903-3208 E-mail: rochette@money.org.

ROCHETTE, LAURA CHRISTINE, literature educator; b. Montgomery, Ala. , Sept. 6, 1963; d. Kenneth Ferdinand Rochette and Patricia Mary Francoeur. MA, Middlebury Coll., Vt., 1996; BA, U. Calif. L.A., 1985. English tchr. Marlborough Sch., L.A., 1988—. Mem.: UCLA Alumni Assn., Modern Lang. Assn. Avocations: singing, writing, reading, cooking, travel. Office: Marlborough Sch 250 S Rossmore Ave Los Angeles CA 90004 E-mail: laura.rochette@marlboroughschool.org.

ROCHETTE, LOUIS, retired shipowner and shipbuilder; b. Quebec City, Que., Can., Feb. 19, 1923; s. Evariste and Blanche (Gaudry) R.; m. Nicole Barbeau, Oct. 12, 1968; children: Louise (dec.), Anne, Guy. M. Commerce, Laval U., Que., 1948. Chartered acct., Que. Chief auditor Sales Tax Govt. Que., Quebec City, 1955—65; treas. Davie Ltd., Lauzon, 1965—76; chmn., CEO Davie Ltd., 1976—81; exec. v.p. Marine Industries, Ltd., Montreal, 1965—76; pres., CEO Soconav Inc., Quebec, 1976—86; pres. Gesconav Inc., 1986—. Past chmn. Lloyd's Com. for Can. Author: Le Reve Separatiste, 1969. Bd. dirs. Gov. Coun. for Can. Unity; gov. Laval U. Found, Quebec Opera Found. Pilot RCAF, 1943-45, ETO. Fellow Inst. Chartered Accts. Can., Can. Inst. Mgmt. Accts. Home and Office: 17 Ocelots Road Saint Anne Des Lacs QC Canada J0R 1B0 *Whatever success I have met with throughout my career was mainly achieved through perseverance in the face of what often looked like insurmountable obstacles.*

ROCHLIS, JAMES JOSEPH, manufacturing company executive; b. Phila., Apr. 12, 1916; s. Aaron and Gussie (Pearlene) R.; m. Riva Singer, Mar. 21, 1943; children: Jeffrey A., Susan J. Ed. pub. schs. Salesman Mid-City Tire Co., Phila., 1945-46, gen. mgr., 1946-49; pres. Ram Rubber Co., 1948-49; rep. Blair & Co., 1949-61, bus. analyst, 1955-61; pres., chief exec. officer Baldwin-Montrose Chem. Co., Inc., N.Y.C., 1961-68; v.p. Chris-Craft Industries, Inc., 1968-69; pres. Chris-Craft Corp., Pompano Beach, Fla., 1969-71; exec. v.p. Chris-Craft Industries, Inc., N.Y.C., 1969-87, also bd. dirs.; pres. Baldwin-NAFI Industries div. Chris-Craft Industries, 1968—, Chris-Craft Internat., 1977-87, Chris-Craft Indsl. Products, Inc., Pompano Beach, 1981-86, chmn., bd. dirs., cons., 1986—. Bd. dirs. Montrose Chem. Co. Calif., Torrance and Mex., So. Mass. Cablevision Corp., N.Y.C., Piper Aircraft Corp., Lock Haven, Pa., Chris-Craft Pacific, Inc., Calif. Mem. AIAA, Fin. Analysts Soc. Phila., Soc. Naval Architects and Marine Engrs., Antique and Classic Boat Soc. Clubs: Lotus (N.Y.C.). Home: 150 E 69th St New York NY 10021-5704 also: 10601 Wilshire Blvd Los Angeles CA 90024-4518 Office: Chris-Craft Industries Inc 767 5th Ave New York NY 10153-0023 E-mail: jrochlis@aol.com.

ROCHOWICZ, JOHN ANTHONY, JR. mathematician, mathematics and physics educator; b. Reading, Pa., Mar. 20, 1950; s. John Anthony and Sara Jane (Binckley) R. BS in Math., Albright Coll., 1972; MS in Math., Lehigh U., 1974; secondary edn. cert. math., Albright Coll., 1975; EdD in Ednl. Tech., Lehigh U., 1993. Cert. secondary teaching, Pa. Math. tchr. Bethlehem (Pa.) Cath. High Sch., 1980-81; instr. math. Pa. State U.-Berks, Reading, 1982-84, Kutztown (Pa.) U., 1983-84, Lehigh County C.C., Schnecksville, Pa., 1984, Alvernia Coll., Reading, 1984, Reading (Pa.) Area C.C., 1984-86; prof. math. Alvernia Coll., 1985—. Recipient Alumni Educator award Albright Coll., Reading, 1987. Mem. AAUP, Math. Assn. Am., Assn. for the Advancement Computing in Edn., Assn. for Ednl. Communications and Tech., Nat. Coun. Tchrs. Math.; contbr. articles to scientific jours. Democrat. Roman Catholic. Avocations: collecting music, computers, calculators, billiards, swimming. Home: 41 Columbia Ave SCM Reading PA 19606-1316 Office: Alvernia College 400 Saint Bernardine St Reading PA 19607-1799

ROCK, ALLAN MICHAEL, Canadian government official; b. Ottawa, Ont., Can., Aug. 30, 1947; s. James Thomas and Anne (Torley) R.; m. Deborah Kathleen, June 24, 1983; children: Jason, Lauren, Andrew, Stephen. BA, U. Ottawa, 1968, LLB, 1971. Certified specialist in civil litigation. Sr. ptnr. Fasken Campbell & Godfrey, Toronto; min. of justice, atty. gen. Govt. of Can., 1993-97, min. of health, 1997—2002, min. of industry, 2002—. Treas. Law Soc. Upper Can., 1992-93; bencher Law Soc., 1983, 87, 91; former chmn. discipline and legal edn. coms.; past chmn. litigation dept. Fasken Campbell Godfrey. Fellow Am. Coll. Trial Lawyers. Office: 11th Fl East Tower 235 Queen St Ottawa ON Canada K1A 0H5

ROCK, ARTHUR, venture capitalist; b. Rochester, N.Y., Aug. 19, 1926; s. Hyman A. and Reva (Cohen) Rock; m. Toni Rembe, July 19, 1975. BS, Syracuse U., 1948; MBA, Harvard U., 1951. Gen. ptnr. Davis & Rock, San Francisco, 1961-68, Arthur Rock & Assocs., San Francisco, 1969-80. Mem. exec. com. Teledyne, Inc., L.A., 1961-94; dir. emeritus, founder, past chmn., chmn. exec. com., lead dir. Intel Corp., Santa Clara, Calif.; bd. dirs. Echelon Corp., San Jose, Calif.; bd. govs. Nasdaq Stock Market, Inc. Trustee Calif. Inst. Tech.; pres. Basic Fund; bd. dirs. San Francisco Opera Assn., 1970-92, San Francisco Mus. Modern Art; mem. vis. com. Harvard U. Bus. Sch., 1982-88. Recipient Medal of Achievement Am. Electronics Assn., 1987, Am. Acad. Achievement, 1989, Lifetime Achievement in Entrepreneurship and Innovation award U. Calif., 1999; named to Jr. Achievement Hall of Fame, 1990, Calif. Bus. Hall of Fame, 1990, Bay Area Bus. Coun. Hall of Fame, 1995, Arents Pioneer medal Syracuse U., 1997, Outstanding Dir., Corp. Am., 1999, SDForum Visionary award, 2001. Office: 1 Maritime Plz Ste 1220 San Francisco CA 94111-3502

ROCK, BARRY DAVID, social work educator; b. Bklyn., Nov. 26, 1942; s. Paul and Molly (Moldowsky) R.; m. Marjorie Ann Greenberg, Dec. 6, 1964; children: Nanette, Joanna. BA, CUNY, Flushing, 1965; MSW, Adelphi U., 1969; DSW, CUNY, N.Y.C., 1983. Cert. social worker, N.Y. Caseworker Bur. Child Welfare, N.Y.C., 1965-67; social worker, supr. Hillside Hosp. L.I. Jewish Med. Ctr., Glen Oaks, N.Y., 1969-81, dir. dept. social work New Hyde Park, 1984-96; dir. program rev. and evaluation N.Y.C. Dept. Mental Health, Mental Retardation & Alcoholism, N.Y.C., 1981-84; dir. dept. social work L.I. Jewish Med. Ctr., New Hyde Park, N.Y., 1984-96; adj. faculty, rschr. Fordham U., Grad. Sch. Social Svc., N.Y.C., 1996-97, assoc. prof., 1997—. Officer adv. bd. Columbia U. Sch. Social Work, N.Y.C., 1985-97; cons. U. Haifa (Israel) Sch. Social Work, 1987-88, McQuade Children's Svcs., New Windsor, N.Y., 1997; chair adv. bd. Adelphi U. Sch. Social Work, Garden City, N.Y., 1990-97. Author, reviewer, guest editor Social Work in Health Care, 1992-97; reviewer Am. Jour. Managed Care, 1996-97; co-editor: Social Work in the Era of Devolution: Toward a Just Practice, 2001. Recipient Social Work Rsch. award Herman Goldman Found., L.I. Jewish Med. Ctr., 1985-96, Rsch. on Elderly award Selma B. Harris Fund, L.I. Jewish Med. Ctr., 1989-96, Bartlett award N.Y. Cmty. Trust, Fordham U., 1997—; tng. grantee NIMH, Hunter Coll., CUNY, 1986-89. Mem. NASW, APHA, Acad. Cert. Social Workers, Am. Hosp. Assn., Gerontol. Soc. Am., N.Y. Acad. Scis., Hastings Ctr. E-mail: rock@fordham.edu.

ROCK, GAIL ANN, obstetrical and gynecological nurse; b. Maquokela, Iowa, Mar. 24, 1960; d. Robert William and Mary Anne (Franzen) Scheckel; m. William Beale Rock III, June 6, 1981; 1 child, William Beale IV. Chiropractic Asst., Palmer Coll. Chiropractic, Davenport, Iowa, 1979; AAS in Nursing, North County Community Coll., Saranac Lake, N.Y., 1987; BSN, SUNY, Plattsburg, 1992-95; MSN, Shenandoah U., 1999. Cert. resolve thru sharing counselor, inpatient obstet. nurse; cert. childbirth educator; cert. lactation cons.; cert. nurse midwife. Staff nurse ob-gyn. Adirondack Med. Ctr., Saranac Lake, N.Y., 1987-90, nurse mgr. ob-gyn., 1990-95; nurse mgr. birth ctr. Preston Meml. Hosp., Kingwood, W.Va., 1995-98; staff nurse-high risk perinatal Inova, Fairfax, Va., 1998—; nurse midwife Birth Ctr. Blue Ridge, Charlottesville, 1999-2000, No. W.Va. Nurse Midwives/Cindy Brown & Assocs., LLC, Kingwood, W.Va., 2000—02, Women's Care Ptnrs., Altoona, Pa., 2001—. Women's care partners, Altoona, Pa., 2001-; group educator sibling and new parent classes, Saranac Lake, 1991-95; mem. Garrett County Pub. Health Childbirth Edn., 1995-2000. Mem. NAFE, Internat. Lactation Cons. Assn., Assn. Women's Health Obstet. and Neonatal Nurses, Am. Coll. Nurse Midwifery, Sigma Theta Tau. Home: 880 Trap Run Rd Friendsville MD 21531-1509 Office: Women's Care Ptnrs 2613 8th Ave Ste 1B Altoona PA 16602-2039 E-mail: grock@iceweb.net.

ROCK, JOHN AUBREY, gynecologist and obstetrician, educator; b. Corpus Christi, Tex., Oct. 21, 1946; s. William A. and Burta (Wheeler) R.; children: John Aubrey Jr., Deborah Ellen, Daniel Authur; m. Martha Miller. BS in Zoology, La. State U., Baton Rouge, 1968; MD, La. State U., New Orleans, 1972. Asst. prof. Johns Hopkins U. Sch. Medicine, Balt., 1978-80, assoc. prof., 1980-87, prof. ob-gyn, 1987-92, prof. pediatrics, 1988-92, dir. reproductive endocrinology, 1979-91, dep. dir. med. sch., 1985-88; chmn. Union Meml. Hosp., 1991-92; James Robert McCord prof., chmn. dept. ob-gyn. Emory U. Sch. Medicine, Atlanta, 1992—. Cons. Dept. Army, Washington, 1982-93, NASA, Houston, 1988—; chmn. ad hoc com. on in vitro fertilization State of Md., 1985. Author: Reparative and Constructive Surgery of the Female Generative Tract, 1983, Endometriosis, 1988, TeLinde's Operative Gynecology, 1991, 8th edit., 1995, Reproductive Endocrinology, Surgery and Technology, 1995; mem. editl. bd. Fertility and Sterility jour., 1986-94, Gynecology Surgery, 1989—. Fellow ACOG; mem. Am. Gynecol. and Obstet. Soc., Soc. Gynecol. Surgeons (pres. 1998-99), Am. Soc. for Reproductive Medicine (pres. 1996-97), Soc. Gynecologic Investigation, Soc. Reproductive Surgeons (pres. 1986), World Endometriosis Soc. (pres. 2000-02), Rotary, Phi Kappa Phi. Methodist. Office: Emory U WMB Dept OB-GYN 1639 Pierce Dr Rm 4208 Atlanta GA 30322-0001

ROCK, MARY ANN, fine artist, educator, consultant; b. St. Louis, Mar. 2, 1931; d. Clobert Bernard and Mary Henrietta (Jones) Broussard; m. William Ralph Rock, Mar. 18, 1960 (div. Sept. 1967); 1 child, John Henry C. BS, Bennett Coll., 1952; postgrad., Chgo. Art Inst., 1953-54, So. Ill. U., Carbondale, 1955. Instr. arts and crafts Presidio Hill Sch., San Francisco, 1966-71; dir. gallery Cannery House Gallery, Friday Harbor, Wash., 1974-76; co-founder Island Artisans, 1980-85; gallery asst. Waterworks Gallery, 1986-95; with European study tour, 1996; patron sponsored painting sabbatical, 2001—03. Guest instr. Spring St. Sch., Friday Harbor, 2001, 02. Author, illustrator: DreamKeeper, 1995; illustrator brochures; one-woman and group shows include 13th Salon Internat. del Alpha, Lyon, France, 7th Whatcomb County Museum Bellingham, 1988, Portland C.C., 1990, Chetwynn Stapleton Gallery, Portland, 1989-98, Waterworks Gallery, Friday Harbor, 1986—. Presenter art workshops Friday Harbor Elem. Sch., 1976, 87, Portland C.C., 1989, 90, guest instr. Spring St. Sch., 2001; curator African art exhibit NAACP, San Francisco, 1961. Vt. Studio Ctr. fellow, Johnson, Vt., 1999. Democrat. Avocations: collecting ethnic artifacts, skiing, rock climbing, travel, reading.

ROCK, PAUL ELLIOT, sociologist, educator; b. London, Aug. 4, 1943; s. Ashley Rock and Charlotte Carnegie Dickson; m. Barbara Ravid, Sept. 25, 1965 (dec. 1998); children: Matthew, Oliver. BSc in Sociology, London Sch. Econs., 1964; DPhil, U. Oxford, Eng., 1970. Asst. lectr. London Sch. Econs. and Polit. Sci., 1967-70, lectr., 1970-76, sr. lectr., 1976-83, reader, 1983-85, prof. sociology, 1985-95, prof. social instns., 1995—. Vis. prof. Princeton U., 1974-75; vis. scholar Ministry of Solicitor Gen., Ottawa, Can., 1981-83; cons. BBC. Author: A View from the Shadows, 1986, Helping Victims of Crime, 1990, The Social World of an English Crown Court, 1993, Reconstructing A Women's Prison, 1996, After Homicide, 1998. Fellow Ctr. for Advanced Study of The Behavioral Scis., Stanford, Calif., 1996; social sci. fellow Nuffield Found., 1985, 96. Fellow Royal Soc. Arts, Brit. Acad. Office: London Sch Econs Polit Sci Houghton St London WC2A 2AE England E-mail: p.rock@lse.ac.uk.

ROCK, ROSALIND, international business consultant, educator; b. N.Y.C., Dec. 14, 1937; d. Samuel and Beatrice (Schildhaus) R.; m. Michael C. Young, Feb. 1, 1967; children: Tracy Beth, Todd Alden. BA, CUNY, 1959, MS in Edn., 1963; MBA, NYU, 1985. Tchr. elem. schs., N.Y.C., 1961-67; creator, implementor pilot project Boggle in the Classroom, Parker Bros., 1968; coord. group sales Pepsico's Summerfare Arts Festival, 1980; ednl. cons. Northside Devel. Ctr., 1981; mktg. dir. real estate investments Saxon Capital, N.Y.C., 1986-88; pres. Rock Internat. Investments, bus. cons. represents companies, govt. agencies, and devel. zones in China, India and Eastern Europe, seeking strategic partners, 1989—. Author: (children's rec.) Let's Create, 1972, (syndicated children's page for TV data) Channel Marker, 1974-79. Mem. Fin. Women's Assn., Women's Econ. Round Table. Office: Rock Internat Investments 1065 Park Ave New York NY 10128-1001 E-mail: rockintl@aol.com.

ROCK, WILLIAM BOOTH, producer, announcer; b. Bridgeport, Conn., July 15, 1947; s. Ben Bernard Rock and Elsie (Booth) Doyle; m. Jamie Lorain DeSenti, June 16, 1950; children: James Dillon, Sean Dillon, Joel Rock. BA in Communication Arts, Seton Hall U., 1969. Announcer various radio stas., 1965-70, Sta. WYNY-FM, N.Y.C., 1981-96, United Stas. Radio Network, N.Y.C., 1986-91; sta. mgr. Sta. WSOU-FM, South Orange, N.J., 1968-69; program dir. Sta. WTRY-AM/FM, 1970-71, Sta. WMEX-AM, 1972-73; asst. program dir. Sta. WNBC-AM, N.Y.C., 1974-77; v.p. programming Insilco Broadcast Group, Conn., Fla., Okla., La., 1977-81; pres. Bill Rock Prodns., Stratford, Conn., 1981—; co-host Country Takes Manhattan, 1993. Instr. Sta. WIXY-AM Sch. Broadcasting, Cleve., 1970-71, Conn. Sch. Broadcasting, Stratford, 1985-86. Prodr.: (TV series) Airshow, 1987, Kennedy Ctr.--A Unique Perspective, 1989; voice (comedy series) SJS Entertainment (bought by SFX radio network), 1989—90, 1992—, (nat. radio network spls.) UNISTAR Radio Network, including Motor City Beat, U.S. Hall of Fame, Diana Ross and the Supremes Story, 4 Tops, Temptations 25th Anniversary, 1987—, Class of '66 Radio Reunion, 1991, daily voice (nationally syndicated radio comedy series novels) SFX Radio Network WINSTAR Radio Svcs. (now Excelsior Radio Networks), 1993—, voice of news 12 N.J., 1996—, NBC Nightly News Promos, 1996—2000, Weekend Nightly News, 1996—2000, Meet the Press, 1996—2001, Dateline NBC Europe, 1996—, NBC Asia, 1996—, prime time billboards, 1996—, Saturday Night Live, 1996—, others, announcer MSNBC shows Weekend Mag., Judge and Jury, McLaughlin Report, CNBC, spl. edit. Headliners & Legends, others, 1996—, voice NBC/Radioshack Network, 1998—2000, host (nat. syndicated series) A Day in the Country, —. Pub. rels. officer USCG Aux., vice comdr. flotilla 24-2, divsn. PA officer divsn. 24, asst. PA officer dist. 1, comdr. flotilla 24-2, 2001, commd.. officer 24-2, 2001—02, boat crew qualified, patrol and comms. specialist; v.p. bd. dirs. Conn. Air and Space Ctr.; commr. Stratford Harbor and Waterfront, 2001, vice chmn., 2002; pres. The 71 Corp.; Bd. dirs. New Haven County Advt. Club, Sikorsky Archives, 1990—96; bd. dirs., chmn. bus. plan Guenster Rehab. Ctr. Recipient MacEchern award, 1984, silver medal N.Y. Internat. TV Film Festival, 1985, bronze statue Telly awards, 1990-96, 99, 2000, Mercury award, 1990, Pinnacle awards, 1990, 2000, Excellence award Conn. Bds. Edn., 1995, Communicator award, 1996, 99, Key to Paterson, N.J.; inductee WSOU (Seton Hall U.) Hall of Fame, 1998; commendation for Meritorious Service, U.S. Coast Guard, 2000, Superior Profl. Leadership Achievement award, 2001. Mem. AFTRA, Fairfield County Advt. Club, N.J. County Music Assn. (life), Sikorsky Archives. Avocations: aviation, musician, seamanship and navigation. Home and Office: 850 Housatonic Avenue Ext Stratford CT 06615-6029 E-mail: brock@snet.net.

ROCKALL, ARTHUR ALLISON, automotive designer; b. Detroit, Jan. 25, 1929; s. Arthur Thomas and Leaon Cleo (Barnett) R.; m. Betty Melton Ploussard Coff (div. 1979); 1 child, Yvonne Leigh Hausch; m. Diane Margaret Dunn, Aug. 4, 1984. BFA, Wayne State U., 1993; MA in Fine Arts, Ea. Mich. U., 1995; hon. degree, Schoolcraft Coll., 1998. With Ford Motor Co., Dearborn, Mich., 1952-87, master modeler, 1968-76, design supr., 1976-87. Cons. Ford Motor Co., 1987-89; sculptor, 1964-67. One man shows at Ford Gallery, 1995, Lansing Art Gallery, 2002; exhibited in group shows at 1st Presbyn. Ch., Northville, 1993-2000, Toledo Sculpture Guild, 1995-96, Flatlanders Gallery, Ella Sharp Mus., Jackson, 1999-2000, 02, Greater Lansing Artists, Kresge, 2000, Potter Ctr., Jackson, 2000-01, Lansing Gallery Art, 2000, Christian Art Show, Lansing, 2001. Pres. Met. Detroit Ski Coun., 1977-79, Northville (Mich.) Hist. Soc., 1988-91; v.p. Northville Arts Commn., 1995-97; v.p. Stockbridge Area Arts Coun., 2000-01, pres., 2002. Master sgt. USAAF, 1950-52. Named Disting. Alumni, Schoolcraft Coll., Livonia, Mich., 1995, one of Key People, Northville Hist. Soc., 1997; recipient Merit award Northville 1st Presbyn. Ch., 1998, 99. Mem. AAUW, Stockbridge Artist Assn., Ea. Mich. Art Alumni, Toledo Sculpture Guild, Jackson Civic Art Assn. Avocations: travel, walking. E-mail: rockyrockall@hotmail.com.

ROCKALL, DIANE MARGARET, librarian, consultant, archivist; b. Detroit, Dec. 16, 1945; d. John Joseph Dunn and Shirley Lena (Book) Dunn Cunningham; m. Arthur Allison Rockall, Aug. 4, 1984. BA in Journalism, Wayne State U., 1970, MLS, 1977, MA, 1995; AAS (hon.), Schoolcraft Coll., 1998. Cataloguer reference dept. Detroit News, 1964-71, photo classifier, 1971-77, asst. supr. reference dept., 1977-80, head reference dept., 1980-87; library cons. Rockall Ltd., Northville, Mich., 1987-90; rschr., archivist Rockall Unltd., 1990—. Archivist Northville Hist. Soc., 1990-97. Co-author: Step By Step Through Northville, 1989; author: A Powerful Voice for 75 Years: A History of the League of Women Voters of Michigan, 1995, Art at the Millennium, 1999; dir. audio tapes Northville Oral History Project; contbr. articles to profl. jours. Newsletter editor, bd. dirs. Jackson Civic Art Assn.; mem. Stockbridge Area Artists. Recipient Spirit of Detroit award Detroit br. NOW, 1979, Community Enrichment award AAUW (Northville), 1991, Key People award Northville Hist. Soc., 1991; LWV grantee, 1989. Mem. AAUW (pres., program v.p., chair pub. policy, mem. nominations com.), Wayne Libr. Sci. Alumni (pres., v.p., editor), Spl. Librs. Assn. (Mich. chpt., pres., bd. dirs.), Northville Hist. Soc., LWV (pres. Northville 1990-92), Women of Wayne (pres. 1995-96, western regional v.p., rec. sec., newsletter editor). Mem. United Ch. of Christ. Avocations: walking, travel, drawing.

ROCKART, JOHN FRALICK, information systems researcher; b. N.Y.C., June 20, 1931; s. John Rachac and Janet (Ross) R.; m. Elise Jean Feldmann, Sept. 16, 1961; children: Elise B. Liesl, Scott F. AB, Princeton U., 1953; MBA, Harvard U., 1958; PhD, MIT, 1968. Sales rep. IBM, 1958-61, dist. med. rep., 1961-62, fellow in Africa, 1962-64; instr. MIT, Cambridge, Mass., 1966-67; asst. prof. IBM, 1967-70, assoc. prof., 1970-74, sr. lectr., 1974—; dir. MIT, 1976—. Bd. dirs. Keane, Inc., Boston, Comshare, Inc., Ann Arbor, Mich. Co-author: Computers & Learning Process, 1974, Rise of Managerial Computing, 1986, Executive Support Systems, 1988 (Computer Press Assn. 1989); contbr. articles to profl. jours. Trustee New Eng. Med. Ctr., Boston. Lt. USN, 1953-56. Mem. Assn. for Computing Machinery, Inst. for Mgmt. Sci., Ops. Rsch. Soc. Am., Soc. for Info. Mgmt. (bd. dirs. mem. at large 1989-94), Weston (Mass.) Golf Club, Lake Sunapee Country Club (New London, N.H.). Republican. Unitarian Universalist. Home: 150 Cherry Brook Rd Weston MA 02493-1308 Office: CISR MIT Sloan Sch Mgmt 3 Cambridge Ctr NE20-336 Cambridge MA 02142

ROCKBURNE, DOROTHEA GRACE, artist; b. Montreal, Que., Can; Student, Black Mountain Coll.; PhD (hon.) , Coll. of Creative Studies, Detroit, 2002. Milton and Sally Avery Disting. prof. Bard Coll., 1986. Trustee Ind. Curators Inc., N.Y., Art in Gen.; artist in residence Am. Acad. in Rome, 1991; vis. artist Skowhegan Sch. Printing and Sculpture, 1984; Rockefeller Found. resident Bellagio (Italy) Conf. and Study Ctr., 1997. One-person shows include Sonnabend Gallery, Paris, 1971, New Gallery, Cleve., 1972, Bykert Gallery, N.Y.C., 1970, 72, 73, Galleria Toselli, Milan, Italy, 1972, 73, 74, Galleria D'Arte, Bari, Italy, 1972, Lisson Gallery, London, 1973, Daniel Weinberg Gallery, San Francisco, 1973, Galerie Charles Kriwin, Brussels, 1975, Galleria Schema, Florence, Italy, 1973, 75, 92, John Weber Gallery, N.Y.C., 1976, 78, Galleria la Polena, Geona, Italy, 1977, Tex. Gallery, Houston, 1979, 80, 81, Xavier Fourcade Gallery, N.Y.C., 1981, 82, 83, 85, 86, David Bellman, Toronto, 1980, 81, Margo Leavin, Calif., 1982, Arts Club of Chgo., 1987, André Emmerich Gallery, N.Y.C., 1988, 89, 91, 92, 94, 95, 10 yr. retrospective Rose Art Mus., 1989, P. Fong & Spratt Galleries, San Jose, Calif., 1991, Sony Music Hdqs., N.Y.C., 1993, Frederick Spratt Gallery, San Jose, 1994, Guild Hall Mus., Easthampton, N.Y., 1995, Portland Mus. of Art, Maine, 1996, Ingrid Raab Gall., Berlin, 1997, Art in Gen., N.Y., 2000, Lawrence Rubin, Greenberg, Van Doren, N.Y., 2000; group shows include Whitney Mus. Am. Art, 1970, 73, 77, 79, 82, Mus. Modern Art, N.Y.C., 71, 73, 84, 86, 93, 94, Buenos Aires, 1971, Kolner Kunst Market, Cologne, Germany, 1971, Stedelijk Mus., Holland, 1971, Spoleto (Italy) Festival, 1972, Palazzo Taverna, Rome, 1973, Nat. Gallery Victoria, Melbourne, Australia, 1973, Art Gallery NSW, Sydney, 1973, Auckland (New Zealand) City Art Gallery, 1973, Inst. Contemporary Art, London, 1974, Mus. d'Arte de la Ville, Paris, 1975, Galerie Aronowitsch, Stockholm, 1975, Stadtiches Mus., Manchengladbach,

Germany, 1975, Galleria D'Arte Moderna, Bologna, Italy, 1975, Art Gallery Ont., Toronto, Can., 1975, Mus. Fine Art, Houston, 1975, Contemporary Arts Ctr., Cin., 1973, 75, 81, Mus. Contemporary Art, Chgo., 1971, 77, 86, Corcoran Gallery of Art, Washington, 1975, 87, Städtisches Mus., Leverkusen, Germany, 1975, Cannaviella Studio d'Arte Rome, 1976, Phila. Coll. Art, 1976, 83, Balt. Mus. Art, 1976, New Mus., N.Y.C., 1977, 80, 84, 83, Renaissance Soc. of U. Chgo., 1976, Lowe Art Mus., U. Miami, Fla., 1976, Inst. Contemporary Art, Boston, 1976, Seibu Mus. Art, Tokyo, 1976, N.Y. State Mus., Albany, 1977, Drawing Ctr., 1977, Kansas City (Mo.) Art Inst., 1977, Smithsonian Inst., Washington, 1977, Kassel, Fed. Republic Germany, 1972, 77, Ackland Art Ctr., Chapel Hill, N.C., 1979, 84, Milw. Art Ctr., 1978, 81, Biblioteca Nacional, Madrid, 1980, Gulbenkian Mus., Lisbon, Portugal, 1980, Bklyn. Mus., 1981, 89, Guggenheim Mus., 1982, 88, 89, Albright Knox Art Gallery, Buffalo, 1979, 80, 88, 89, Kuustforeningen Mus., Copenhagen, 1980, Venice Biennale, 1980, Cranbrook (Mich.) Acad. Art, 1981, Mus. Fine Arts, Boston, 1983, Contemporary Arts Mus., Houston, 1983, Norman Mackenzie Art Gallery, U. Regina, Sask., Can., 1983, Galleriet, Sweden, 1983-84, Seattle Art Mus., 1979-84, Nat. Mus. Art., Osaka, Japan, 1984, Fogg Art Mus., Cambridge, Mass., 1984, Am. Acad. and Inst. Arts and Letters, N.Y.C., 1984, 87, L.A. County Mus. Art, 1984, 86, Wadsworth Atheneum, Hartford, Conn., 1981, 84, Evehart Mus., Pa., 1984, Grey Art Gallery, NYU, 1977, 84, 87, Avery Ctr. Arts, Bard Coll., N.Y., 1985, 87-88, Stamford (Conn.) Mus., 1985, Aldrich Mus., Conn., 1979, 82, Bronx Mus. Arts, N.Y.C., 1985, High Mus., Atlanta, 1975, 81, Phila. Mus. Art, 1986, Nat. Gallery Art, Washington, 1984, Mus. Art, Ft. Lauderdale, Fla., 1986, Nat. Mus. Women in Art, Washington, 1987, Xavier Fourcade Gallery, 1983, 86, 87, L.A. County Mus. Modern Art, 1986-87, The Hague, The Netherlands, 1986, Carnegie-Mellon Art Gallery, Pitts., 1979, 87, Balt. Mus. Art, 1975, 76, 88, Ctr. for Fine Arts, Miami, 1989, Milw. Art Mus., 1989, Cin. Art Mus., 1989, New Orleans Mus., 1989, Denver Art Mus., 1989, Parrish Art Mus., South Hampton, N.Y., 1990, 91, Margo Leavin Gallery, L.A., 1991, Mus. of Modern Art, N.Y.C., 1991, Guild Hall Mus., East Hampton, N.Y., 1991, Am. Acad., Rome, 1991, Mus. Contemporary Art, L.A., 1991, Hunter Coll., N.Y., 1991, Centro Cultural/Arte Contemporanea, Mexico City, 1991, Hilton, San Jose, Calif., 1992, Hillwood Art Mus., L.I., N.Y., 1992, Am. Acad. and Inst. Arts and Letters, 1992, Neuberger Mus., 1992, Statue of Liberty Group, 1993, Foster Harmans Galliers of Am. Art, Sarasota, Fla., 1993, Kohn-Abrams Gallerie, L.A., 1993, The Gallery at Bristol Myers Squibb, N.J., 1993, Friends of Art and Preservation in Embassies, N.Y.C., 1993, Just Art, N.Y.C., 1993, Mus. Modern Art, N.Y.C., 1994, TZ Art and Co., N.Y.C., 1996, Andre Emmerich Gallery, N.Y.C., 1993, Nat. Gallery of Art, Washington, 1994, 97, Fred Spratt Gallery, San Jose, Calif., 1994, RAAB Galarie, Berlin, 1994, Gallary at Bristol Myer Squibb, N.J., 1994, Moma, N.Y.C., 1994, N.Y. Studio Sch., N.Y.C., 1995, Aldrich Mus., Conn., 1995, Rose Art Mus., Brandeis U., 1996, White Columns, N.Y., 1996, 65 Thompson Street Gallery, N.Y.C., 1996, Fifth Ave. Lobby Gallery, 1997, Addison Gallery Am. Art Philips Acad., Andover, Mass., 1997, Fine Arts Mus. San Francisco, 1997, Wexner Ctr. Aarts., Columbus, 1997, Art Resources Tranfer, Inc. Dorfman Projects, 1998, Art Asset, L.L.C., N.Y.C., 1998, Dieu Donne Papermill, Inc., N.Y.C., 1998, LaSalle Ptnrs. NationsBank Plaza, Charlotte, N.C., 1998, P.S.1-primarily Structural, 1999, Gemini Gall. Prints, 1998, Amer. Acad. of Arts & Letters, 1999—, Parson's Sch. Design, N.Y., 1999, David A. Damson Gallery, Washington, 1999, Parrish Art Mus., Southampton, N.Y., 1999, Adamson Gallery, Wash. D.C., 1999, Parsons Sch. of Design, N.Y., 1999, L.A. Museum of Contemporary Art, 1999, Nevberger Museum of Art, Purchase, N.Y., 2000, David Dorsky Gallery, N.Y., 2000, Laurence Rubin, Greenberg, Van Doren Fine Art, N.Y.C., 2000, Armory Ctr. Arts, Pasadena, Calif., 2001, The Ralls Collection, D.C., 2001, The Rena Sophia Mus., Spain, 2002, Carrie Secrist Gallery, Chgo., 2002 Am. Acad. Ceremonial Exhbn., 2001, The Geffen Contemporary, Calif., 2002, The Krannert Art Mus., Ill., 2002, Artemis Greenberg Van Doren Fine Art, N.Y.C., 2002, The Shelby Gallery, Fla., 2002, The Nat. Acad. of Design, N.Y.C., 2002, The Armory Show, N.Y.C., 2002, The Nat. Gallery of Art, D.C., 2001, Armory Ctr. for the Arts, Pasadena, 2001, others; print exhbns. include Kate Ganz, Ltd., Six Women Artists, N.Y.C., 2001; represented in permanent collections Milw. Art Ctr., Mus. Modern Art N.Y.C., Fogg Mus., Cambridge, Mass., Phila. Mus. Art, High Mus. Art, Atlanta, Houston Mus. Fine Arts, Corcoran Gallery, Washington, Mpls. Art Inst., Mpls. Art Mus., Met. Mus. Art, N.Y.C., Guggenheim Mus., N.Y.C., Ludwig Mus., Aachen, Fed. Republic Germany, Holladay, Washington, Saatchi, London, Bard, Albright-Knox Art Gallery, Buffalo, Whitney Mus. Am. Art, N.Y.C., U. Mich., Ann Arbor, Ohio State U., Columbus, Gilman Paper Co., N.Y., Auckland (New Zealand) City Art Mus., Portland (Oreg.) Art Mus., Aaken Art Mus., Oberlin, Ohio, Highhold Internat., S. Africa, U. Ohio Art Gallery, Columbus, HHK Charitable Found., Milw., Art Gallery Ont., Toronto, Can., Nat. Mus. Women in Art, Washington, Chase Manhattan Bank, N.Y.C.; installations: Hilton Hotel, San Jose, Calif., Sony Music Hdqs., Aldridge Mus., Conn., Edward T. Gignoux Courthouse, Portland, Maine, Ann Arbor, Mich. Recipient Witowsky prize, 72d Am. Exhbn., Art Inst., Chgo., 1976, Creative Arts award, Brandeis U., 1985, Bard Coll., 1986, Jimmy Ernst Lifetime Achievement award in art, Am. Acad. Arts and Letters, 1999, The Pike award, Nat. Acad. of Art and Design, 177th Ann. Exhbn., 2002, Adolph and Clara Obrig prize, Nat. Acad. Design, 177th Ann. Exhbn., 2002; fellow, Guggenheim fellow, 1972; grantee, Nat. Endowment Arts, 1974, Am. Acad. Rome, 1991. Mem. Am. Acad. Arts and Letters.

ROCKEFELLER, ALLISON HALL W. conservationist; b. Manhattan, N.Y., Nov. 20, 1958; d. George Carroll and JoeAnn (Feeley) Whipple; m. Peter Clark Rockefeller, Dec. 19, 1987; 2 children. BA, Hamilton Coll., Clinton, N.Y., 1980. Asst. dir. pub. rels. Sotheby's Internat. Realty, N.Y.C., 1980-83; dir. pub. rels. and corp. comms. Douglas L. Elliman & Co., 1983-88; founder residential sales divsn. Elliman East; residential sales assoc. Brown Harris Stevens, N.Y.C., 1988-90; founder Henry Hudson Soc. of Historic Hudson Valley, Inc., 1988—; trustee, devel. com. mem. Mus. of City of N.Y., 1993—; trustee, chmn. devel. com. Student Conservation Assn., Charlestown, N.H., 1987-95, chmn. bd., 1995—. Mem. Pres.'s coun. Mission Soc., N.Y.C., 1994—. Mem. Nat. Soc. Fund Raising Execs., Delta Psi. Presbyterian. Avocations: horticulture, historic houses, American history, writing, landscape architecture. Office: 30 Rockefeller Plz Rm 5600 New York NY 10112-0002

ROCKEFELLER, DAVID, banker; b. N.Y.C., June 12, 1915; s. John Davison Jr. and Abby Greene (Aldrich) R.; m. Margaret McGrath, Sept. 7, 1940 (dec. Mar. 1996); children: David, Abby A., Neva, Margaret D., Richard G., Eileen M. BS, Harvard Coll., 1936; student, London Sch. Econs.; PhD, U. Chgo., 1940; LLD (hon.), Columbia U., 1954, Bowdoin Coll., 1958, Jewish Theol. Sem., 1958, Williams Coll., 1966, Wagner Coll., 1967, Harvard U., 1969, Pace Coll., 1970, St. John's U., 1971, Middlebury, 1974, U. Liberia, 1979, Rockefeller U., 1980, Am. U., 1987, U. Miami, 1988; DEng (hon.), Colo. Sch. Mines, 1974, U. Notre Dame, 1987. Sec. to Mayor Fiorello H. La Guardia, 1940-41; asst. regional dir. Office Def., Health and Welfare Services, 1941-42; asst. mgr. for. dept. Chase Nat. Bank, N.Y.C., 1946-47, asst. cashier, 1947-48, 2d v.p., 1948-49, v.p., 1949-51, sr. v.p., 1951-55; exec. v.p. Chase Manhattan Bank (Chase Nat. Bank merged with Bank of Manhattan), 1955-57; vice chmn. bd. Chase Manhattan Bank, 1957-61, pres., chmn. exec. com., 1961-69, chmn., 1969-81, CEO, 1969-80. Chmn. Chase Internat. Adv. Com., 1981-99, Rockefeller Group, Inc., 1981-95, N.Y. Clearing House, 1971-78, Ctr. for Intern-Am. Rels., 1966-70, Overseas Devel. Coun., U.S.-USSR Trade and Econ. Coun. Inc.; chmn. Internat. Exec. Svc. Corps., 1964-68; chmn. Rockfeller Ctr. Properties Trust, Inc., 1996—. Author: Unused Resources and Economic Waste, 1940, Creative Management in Banking, 1964. Active Urban Devel. Corp., N.Y. State Bus. Adv. Coun., 1968-72, U.S. Adv. Com. on Reform on Internat. Monetary System, 1973-77, U.S. exec. com. Dartmouth Conf. Bd. Inst. Internat. Econs., Am. Friends of LSE, U.S. Hon. Fellows LSE, Bus. Com. for Arts; founding mem. Commn. on White House Fellows, hon. mem., 1964-65; exec. com., chmn. Downtown Lower Manhattan Assn., 1958-75; trustee Rockefeller U., 1940-95, Carnegie Endowment Internat. Peace, Hist. Hudson Valley, 1981—; chmn. Rockefeller Bros. Fund, 1981-87, vice-chmn., 1968-80; hon. trustee Rockefeller Family Fund; life trustee U. Chgo.; trustee, chmn. bd., exec. com. Mus. Modern Art, 1962-72, 87-93; bd. overseers Harvard Coll., 1954-60, 62-68; co-founder Trilateral Commn., 1973-91, N.Am. chmn. 1981-92, hon. chmn., 1992; hon. chmn. Internat. House, 1940—, dir., 1940-63; pres. Morningside Heights, Inc., 1947-57, chmn., 1957-65; chmn. Am. Soc., 1981-92, hon. chmn., 1992—, N.Y.C. Partnership, 1979-88. Capt. AUS, 1942-45, NATOUSA, ETO. Decorated Legion of Honor France, Order of Arts and Letters; Order of the Liberator San Martin, Argentina, Order of Valor, Rep. of Cameroun, Order of Boyaca, Colombia, Order of Christopher Columbus, Domincan Republica, Nat. Order of Merit, Ecuador, Knight Comdr.'s Cross of the Order of Merit, Germany, Order of the Republic, Guinea, Gwengha Medal of the Rep. of Korea,, Order of the Aztec Eagle, Mexico, Order of the Throne, Morocco, Hilal-i'Quaid-e-Azam, Pakistan, Order of Vasco Nunez de Balboa, Panama, Order of Manuel Amador Guerrero, Panama, Nat. Order of Merit/Grand Cross, Paraguay, Order of Merit, Italy, Order of Southern Cross, Brazil, Order of the White Elephant and Order of Crown, Thailand, Order of the Cedars, Lebanon, Order of the Sun, Peru, Nicholas Copernicus award, Porland, Order of Prince Henry the Navigator, Portugal, Nat. Order of the Lion, Rep. of Senegal, Order of Francisco de Miranda, Venezuela, Order of the Humane African Redemption, Liberia, Order of the Crown, Belgium, Nat. Order of Ivory Coast, Grand Cordon Order of Sacred Treasure, Japan, Order Bernardo O'Higgins, Chile, others; recipient Merit award N.Y. chpt. AIA, 1965, Gold medal Nat. Inst. Social Scis., 1967, AIA medal of Honor for City Planning N.Y.C., 1968, Charles Evans Hughes award NCCJ, 1974, World Brotherhood award Jewish Theol. Sem, 1953, C. Walter Nichols award NYU, 1970, Regional Planning Assn. award, 1971; Hadrian award, World Monuments Fund, 1994, U.S. Presdl. Medal of Freedom, 1998. Mem. Council Fgn. Relations (dir. 1949-51, v.p. 1951-70, chmn. 1970-85), Japan Soc. (hon. chmn.), Internat. House (hon. chmn.), Bilderberg Conf., Harvard Club, Univ. Club, Century Club, The Links, The Knickerbocker. Avocation: sailing. Address: 30 Rockefeller Plz Rm 5600 New York NY 10112-0002

ROCKEFELLER, EDWIN SHAFFER, lawyer; b. Harrisburg, Pa., Sept. 10, 1927; s. Edwin S. and Nancy Rhea (McCullough) R.; m. Marilie Gould Wallace, Dec. 22, 1952; children: Ben Wallace, Edwin Palmer. AB, Yale U., 1948, LLB, 1951, M in Internat. Pub. Policy, Johns Hopkins U., 1989. Bar: Conn. 1951, D.C. 1956, U.S. Supreme Ct. 1957. Atty., FTC, 1956-61, asst. to gen. counsel, 1958-59, exec. asst. to chmn., 1960-61; pvt. practice, Washington, 1961—; ptnr. Schiff Hardin & Waite, Washington, 1981-93, of counsel, 1994-2001; mem. USIA Inspection Team, Pakistan, 1971; adj. prof. Georgetown U. Law Ctr., Washington, 1985-87. 1st lt. JAGC, U.S. Army, 1953-56. Mem. ABA (chmn. sect. antitrust law 1976-77, ho. of dels. 1979-82), Chevy Chase Club, Met. Club (Washington), Yale Club (N.Y.C.). Author: Antitrust Questions & Answers, 1974; Desk Book of FTC Practice & Procedure, 3d edit., 1979; Antitrust Counseling for the 1980s, 1983. Office: Apt 1114 2801 New Mexico Ave NW Washington DC 20007-3940

ROCKEFELLER, HARRY ANDREW, software engineer; b. New Haven, Jan. 27, 1950; s. Harry Andrew and Margaret Pearl (Grundy)_R.; m. Johnnie Marie Gwartney, June 4, 1977; children: Jeremy, Toby, Timothy. BS, Oral Roberts U., 1971; MS, SUNY, Stony Brook, 1975. Chemistry instr. Oral Roberts U., Tulsa, 1975-80; chemist Dowell, 1980-81, rsch. chemist, 1981-85, sr. rsch. chemist, 1985-86; sr. engr. Flight Safety Internat., Broken Arrow, Okla., 1987-92, prin. engr., 1992—. Contbr. articles to profl. jours. Asst. soccer coach Broken Arrow Soccer Club, 1990-93, head coach, 1993—; deacon Arrow Heights Bapt. Ch., 1988—, R.A. dir., 1992—, Sunday sch. tchr., 1989—. Republican. Home: 4936 S Narcissus Ave Broken Arrow OK 74011-4217 Office: Flight Safety Internat 2700 N Hemlock Cir Broken Arrow OK 74012-1123

ROCKEFELLER, JOHN DAVISON , IV (JAY ROCKEFELLER), senator, former governor; b. N.Y.C., NY, June 18, 1937; s. John Davison III and Blanchette Ferry (Hooker) R.; m. Sharon Percy, Apr. 1, 1967; children: John, Valerie, Charles, Justin. BA, Harvard U., 1961; student, Japanese lang. Internat. Christian U., Tokyo, 1957-60; postgrad. in Chinese, Yale U. Inst. Far Eastern Langs., 1961-62. Apptd. mem. nat. adv. council Peace Corps, 1961, spl. asst. to dir. corps, 1962, ops. officer in charge work in Philippines, until 1963; desk officer for Indonesian affairs Bur. Far Eastern Affairs, U.S. State Dept., 1963; later asst. to asst. sec. state for Far Eastern affairs; cons. Pres.'s Commn. on Juvenile Delinquency and Youth Crime, 1964; field worker Action for Appalachian Youth program, from 1964; mem. W.Va. Ho. of Dels., 1966-68; sec. of state W.Va., 1968-72; pres. W.Va. Wesleyan Coll., Buckhannon, 1973-75; gov. State of W.Va., 1976-84; U.S. senator from W.Va., 1985—; mem. vets. affairs com., fin. com., commerce, sci. and transp. com.; chmn. Sen. steel caucus, Bipartisan Com. on Comprehensive Health Care. Chmn. Nat. Commn. on Children, natural resources and environ. com. Nat. Govs. Assn., 1981-84, Dem. Tech. and Comms. Com., Sen. Steel Caucus, Bipartisan Com. on Comprehensive Health Care; mem. Vets. Affairs Com., Fin. Com., Commerce, Sci. and Transp. Com. Contbr. articles to mags. including N.Y. Times Sunday mag. Trustee U. Chgo., 1967—; chmn. White House Conf. Balanced Nat. Growth and Econ. Devel., 1978, Pres.'s Commn. on Coal, 1978-80, White House Adv. Com. on Coal., 1980; active Commerce, Sci., and Transp. Com., Fin. Com.; ranking mem. Vet. Affairs Com. Office: US Senate 531 Hart Senate Bldg Washington DC 20510-0001*

ROCKEFELLER, LAURANCE S. philanthropist; b. N.Y.C., May 26, 1910; s. John Davison, Jr. and Abby Greene (Aldrich) R.; m. Mary French, Aug. 15, 1934; children: Laura Rockefeller Chasin, Marion French Rockefeller Weber, Lucy Rockefeller Waletzky, Laurance. BA, Princeton U., 1932; LLD (hon.), SUNY Sch. Forestry at Syracuse U., 1961, U. Vt., 1968; D.Pub. Svc. (hon.), George Washington U., 1964; LHD (hon.), Tex. Tech. Coll., 1966, Duke U., 1981, Marymount Coll., 1983; HHD (hon.), Princeton U., 1987. Chmn. Rockefeller Center, Inc., 1953-56, 58-66, dir., 1936-78; founding trustee, pres., chmn. Rockefeller Bros. Fund, 1958-80, vice chmn., 1980-82, adv. trustee, 1982-85. Dir. Ea. Airlines, 1938-60, 77-81, adv. dir., 1981-87; chmn. Woodstock Resort Corp.; bd. dirs. Readers Digest Assn., 1973-93. Mem. Nat. Cancer Adv. Bd., 1972-79; hon. chmn. N.Y. Zool. Soc., 1975; life trustee Wildlife Conservation Soc.; Meml. Sloan-Kettering Cancer Ctr., 1947-60, chmn. 1960-82, hon. chmn. 1982—; chmn. Citizens Adv. Coun. on Environ. Quality, 1969-73, Jackson Hole Preserve, Inc., pres., 1940-87, chmn. and trustee, 1987-96, chmn. emeritus and trustee, 1997—; commr. Palisades Interstate Pk. Commn., 1939-78, pres., 1970-77, commr. emeritus, 1978—; chmn. Outdoor Recreation Resources Rev. Commn., 1958-65, N.Y. State Coun. of Pks., 1963-73, White House Conf. on Natural Beauty, 1965; life mem. corp. MIT; trustee emeritus Princeton U.; hon. trustee Nat. Geog. Soc.; trustee Alfred P. Sloan Found., 1950-82, Greenacre Found., Nat. Pk. Found., 1968-76, Sleepy Hollow Restorations, 1975-87, chmn., 1981-85; trustee Hist. Hudson Valley, 1987—, chmn. emeritus, 1997—; chmn. Woodstock Found., 1968-97, chmn. emeritus, 1997—; hon. dir. Nat. Wildflower Ctr., 1988—. Decorated commandeur de Ordre Royal du Lion, Belgium, 1950; comdr. most excellent Order Brit. Empire, 1971; recipient Conservation Service award U.S. Dept. Interior, 1956, 62, Horace Marden Albright Scenic Preservation medal, 1957, Disting. Service medal Theodore Roosevelt Assn., 1963, Audubon medal, 1964, Nat. Inst. Social Scis. award, 1959, 67, Alfred P. Sloan, Jr. Meml. award Am. Cancer Soc., 1969, Medal of Freedom, 1969, Cert. of Award, Am. Assn. for Cancer Research, 1980, James Ewing Layman's award Soc. Surg. Oncology, 1980, Congl. gold medal, 1990, McAneny Hist. Pres. medal, 1993, Chmn.'s award Nat. Geograph. Soc., 1995, Theodore Roosevelt Nat. Park medal of honor, 1995, Lady Bird Johnson Conservation award Lifetime Achievement, 1997, Gov.'s Parks & Preservation award, N.Y., 1997. Mem. Am. Conservation Assn. (pres. 1958-80, chmn. 1980-85, hon. chmn. 1985—), Princeton Club, University Club, Brook Club, Capitol Hill Club, Cosmos Club, Boone and Crockett Club, Knickerbocker Club, Lotos Club (N.Y.C.), Sleepy Hollow Club (Tarrytown). Office: 30 Rockefeller Plz Rm 5600 New York NY 10112-0002

ROCKEFELLER, WINTHROP P. lieutenant governor; b. Sept. 17, 1948; s. Winthrop Rockefeller Sr.; m. Lisenne Rockefeller; children: Andrea, Katherine, Winthrop Jr., William, Colin, John, Louis. Student, Oxford U.; grad. Ranch Mgmt. Program, Texas Christian U., 1974. Lt. gov. State of Ark., 1996—. Chmn. Pres. Coun. on Rural Am., 1991-93, Juvenile Justice Adv. Group; bd. dirs. Ark. Crime Commn., Tex. Christian U.; mem. Ark. State Police Commn., 1981-95; pres. Ark. Cattlemen's Assn., 1976-78. Vice-chmn. Winthrop Rockefeller Found., Ark. Cancer Rsch. Ctr., Ark. Arts Found.; founder, chmn. Internat. Billfish Conservation, U.S. Marshal's Assn.; trustee Winthrop Rockefeller Charitable Trust. Mem. Ducks Unlimited (trustee emeritus).*

ROCKEL, VIANA EILEEN, university fundraiser, consultant; b. Pueblo, Colo., Feb. 10, 1953; d. Duane Albert and Mary Vinta (Ames) Rockel; m. Douglas Ray Heeren, July 22, 1972 (dec.); children: Douglas Ray, Valissitie Christina; m. Eric Damian Kelly, May 31, 1980 (div. 1996); stepchildren: Damian Charles, Eliza Jane. BS, U. So. Colo., 1985; MS, Iowa State U., 1992. V.p. bd. dirs. Color Radio, Ltd., Leadville, Colo., 1980-83; mktg. cons. U. Park Mchts. Assn., Pueblo, 1985; mktg. and pub. rels. specialist Pueblo C.C., 1980-85; rsch. asst. Leadership Inst. for a New Century Iowa State U., Ames, 1990-93; rsch. asst. Iowa State U./Ames Rsch. Inst. for Studies in Edn., 1992-93; asst. to sr. v.p. for external affairs Drake U., Des Moines, 1993-99; asst. dir. corp. and found. rels. U. Iowa Found., Iowa City, 1999—. Advt. cons. Seal Pharmacy, Pueblo, 1984-85; freelance grant and tech. writer for human svc. agys. and ednl. instns., 1991—; community coll. student assessment and accountability cons. in field. Bd. dirs. Pueblo Girls Club, 1986-89; active Jr. League of Pueblo, 1982-85; vol. tng. Channel 8 Auction, Pueblo, 1980-88, Leadership Pueblo, 1986; dir. So. Colo. Sci. Olympiad, 1989-90. Mem. AAUW (bd. dirs. 1987), State Bd. Community Colls. (rep., mem. mktg. com. 1985-90), Am. Assn. Women in Community and Jr. Colls., Coll. Student Pers. Assn., Kiwanis, Colo. Press Club, So. Press Club, Alpha Chi, Phi Kappa Phi. Avocations: art, hydroponics, geoponics, reading, hiking. Home: 223 S Westminster St Iowa City IA 52245-4942 Office: U Iowa Found PO Box 4550 Iowa City IA 52244-4550

ROCKEMANN, DAVID DOUGLAS, health services administrator; b. Jefferson City, Mo., Mar. 9, 1954; s. Raymond William and Irene Pauline (Strobel) R.; m. Margaret Ann Perkinson, June 20, 1986. BA in Sociology, U. Mo., 1976, MS in Community Devel., 1978. State health planner State Health Planning Devel. Agy., Jefferson City, 1978; health cons., research assoc. Syncaredian Health Assn., Walnut Creek, Calif., 1978-79; asst. dir. day care Jewish Home for the Aged, San Francisco, 1979; adminstr. St. Regis Retirement Ctr., Hayward, Calif., 1979-82; dir. aging services Community and Econ. Devel. Assn., Chgo., 1982-86; exec. dir., chief exec. officer Community Nutrition Network, 1986-87; dir. of bus. devel. Health Services div. John Knox Village, Lee's Summit, Mo., 1987-89; adminstr. Ctr. on Rural Elderly, U. Mo., Kansas City, 1989-90; dir. program devel. geriatric svcs. Chestnut Hill Hosp. Healthcare, Phila., 1991-92; adminstr. Twining Village Continuing Care Retirement Ctr., South Hampton, 1992-95, Riddle Village Continuing Care Retirement Cmty., Media, 1995-96; v.p. Plexus Group, Quakertown, 1996-98; reg. dir. Cathedral Rock, St. Louis, 1998—. Cons. Wade West Inc., San Francisco, 1979; rschr. Calif. Dept. Health Svcs., San Francisco, 1978-79; rsch. asst. Ctr. for Rsch. in Social Behavior, Columbia, Mo., 1977-79; gerontology rsch. cons. Ctr. for Aging, U. Mo., Kansas City, 1987-90; cons. Diversified Health Svcs., Plymouth Meeting, Pa., 1990-91. Author: Outreach to the Elderly, 1983, Older Women Living in a Continuing Care Retirement Community: Marital Status and Friendship Formation, 1996; (with others) Health Care Trends, 1978, Consumer's Guide to Nursing Homes, 1978. Mem. adv. coun. Suburban Cook County Area Agy. on Aging, Chgo., 1983—84; bd. mem. Elder Abuse Coun., Kansas City, Mo.; legis. adv. State of Ill. Spl. Com. on Aging, Chgo., 1918; coord., moderator Mid-Am. Congress on Aging, Kansas City, Mo., 1985, mem. planning com. Chgo., 1986; presenter XIV meeting Internat. Assn. Gerontology, Acapulco, Mexico, 1989, presenter XV meeting Budapest, Hungary, 1993, presenter XVI meeting Adelaide, Australia, 1997, presenter XVII meeting Vancouver, Canada, 2001. Adminstrn. on Aging scholar U. Mo., 1977-78; Older Americans Act grantee, 1982-87. Mem. Gerontol. Soc. Am. (presenter ann. sci. meeting 1992, 93, 94, 95, 97, 98, 99, 2000), Am. Soc. on Aging (presenter ann. meeting 1989, 90, 94, 98), Am. Coll. Health Care Adminstrs. Lutheran. Office: Cathedral Rock 415 Ft Worth Club Bldg 306 W 7th St Fort Worth TX 76102

ROCKENSIES, JOHN WILLIAM, mechanical engineer; b. N.Y.C., May 30, 1932; s. John William and Wilma (Mercz) R.; m. Marion Pauline Peachman, Sept. 16, 1956; children: Kenneth John, Karen Martha Rockensies Steinbeck. B of Mech. Engring., CCNY, 1954, M of Mech. Engring., 1960; postgrad., Bklyn. Polytechnic Inst., 1955, Columbia U., 1956. Registered prof. engr., N.Y. Jet engine performance and compressor devel. Curtiss Wright Corp., Woodridge, N.J., 1954-56; product devel. engr. Sperry Gyroscope Corp., Lake Success, N.Y., 1956-60; sr. exptl. test engr. Pratt & Whitney Corp., East Hartford, Conn., 1960-62; project engr. Stratos Corp., Bayshore, N.Y., 1962; prin. propulsion engr. Republic Aviation Corp., Farmingdale, 1963-64; power plant design engr., group and project leader, project engr., engr. specialist and mgr. Grumman Aerospace Corp., Bethpage, 1964-95; retired, 1995; contract staff engr. Northrop-Grumman Corp., Bethpage, N.Y., 1996-98. Mem. SAE E-32 Engine Condition Monitoring com., 1983; instr. navigation Smithtown Bay Power Squadron. Author tech. papers in field. Deacon, trustee, elder First Presbyn Ch. of Smithtown. Recipient Apollo Achievement award NASA, Washington, 1970. Assoc. fellow AIAA (mem. air breathing propulsion tech. com. 1996—); mem. NSPE, ASME, U.S. Power Squadrons (sr. navigator). Avocations: sailing, boating, jogging, camping, travel, model aircraft. Home: 65 Parnell Dr Smithtown NY 11787-2428 E-mail: jrock8@optonline.net.

ROCKENSIES, KENNETH JULES, physicist, educator; b. N.Y.C., June 10, 1938; s. John William and Wilma (Mercz) R.; m. Eileen Regina Dros, June 6, 1970; children: Kevin John, Patricia Ann, Regina Marie. BS in Physics, Polytech. U. Bklyn., 1960, MS in Physics, 1962; postgrad., NYU, 1965-67; Adelphi U., 1969-75, Nova U., 1992—. Physicist We. Union Telegraph, N.Y.C., 1962-63; prof. CUNY, Bklyn., 1963-93, Coll. Misericordia, Dallas, 1993—. Author: The Rotational Interferometer, 1962, The Effect of Class Size on Achievement in College Physics, 1995. Mem. NSTA, Am. Assn. Physics Tchrs., Soc. Coll. Sci. Tchrs., Optical Soc. Am. Achievements include rsch. in interferometry, relativistic optics, electrostatic data storage, electrosensitive recording papers and statis. studies in edn. Office: College Misericordia 301 Lake St Dallas PA 18612-1090

ROCKETT, D. JOE, lawyer, director; b. Cushing, Okla., May 3, 1942; s. Gordon Richard and Hazel Peggy (Rigsby) R.; m. Mary Montgomery, Aug. 31, 1963; children: David Montgomery, Ann Morley. BA, U. Okla., 1964, JD, 1967. Bar: Okla. 1967, U.S. Dist. Ct. (we. dist.) Okla. 1968. Assoc. Kerr, Davis, Irvine & Burbage, Oklahoma City, 1967-69, Andrews Davis Legg Bixler Milsten & Price, Oklahoma City, 1969-73, mem., 1973—, also bd. dirs., pres., 1986-90, 96-00. Securities law advisor Oil Investment Inst., Washington, 1984-87. Bd. dirs. Myriad Gardens Conservatory, Oklahoma City, 1987—, chmn., 1991-92. Mem. ABA (fed. regulation of securities and partnership coms. of bus. law sect. 1984), Okla. Bar Assn. (securities liaison com. 1983, chmn. bus. assocs. sect. 1985, securities adminstr.'s select com. 1986—). Avocations: sailing, fishing, skiing. Office: Andrews Davis Legg Bixler Milsten & Price 500 W Main St Ste 500 Oklahoma City OK 73102-2275 E-mail: djrockett@andrewsdavis.com.

ROCKETT, KAY, civic worker; b. Jackson, Miss., Nov. 2, 1941; d. Louis Newbern and Rita (Hall) R.; 1 child, Barbara. B.A., U. Miss., 1963; M.A., Miss. Coll., 1975. Past treas. Rockett Enterprises; social columnist Northside Sun, Jackson. Chmn.'s advisor U.S. Congrl. Adv. Bd.; bd. dirs. Hinds County Heart Assn. (Outstanding Service award 1975), Miss. Opera Assn. (chmn. statewide opera gala 1980), Miss. Ballet Theatre, Juvenile Diabetes Found of Jackson, Miss. Mus. Art; membership chmn. Jackson Music Assn., 1979; active mem. Jackson Symphony Encore Club, Hinds County Heart Assn. Century Club, Miss. Opera Curtain Raisers. Mem. D.A.R., United Daus. Confederacy, First Families of Va., Colonial Dames XVII Century, Chi Omega. Republican. Baptist. Clubs: Country of Jackson, Capitol City Petroleum of Jackson, Cotillion of Jackson (advisor), University, Miss. Debutantes Mothers of Miss. (2d v.p.). Home: 6069 Old Canton Rd # 343 Jackson MS 39211-3335

ROCKLAND, LAWRENCE HOWARD, psychiatrist, educator; b. N.Y.C., Apr. 13, 1932; s. Milton and Bess Sherry Rockland; m. Charlotte Francis Roberts, June 29, 1957; children: Nancy, Thomas, Peter. BS, Union Coll., 1952; MD, Albany Med. Ctr., 1956. Diplomate Am. Bd. Psychiatry and Neurology. Rsch. psychiatrist NIMH, Bethesda, Md., 1959—61; pvt. practice Scarsdale, Larchmont, NY, 1961—; instr. psychiatry Georgetown Med. Coll., Washington, 1961—63; asst. prof. psychiatry Albert Einstein Coll. Medicine, N.Y.C., 1967—76; assoc. prof. clin. psychiatry Cornell U. Med. Coll., 1982—99; prof. psychiatry emeritus Weill/Cornell Med. Coll., 1999—; assoc. prof. clin. psychiatry U. Mass. Med. Coll., Worcester, 1999—. Cons. Montgomery County Child Clinic, Rockville, Md., 1962—66, US Peace Corps, Washington, 1963—66, Carson Adult Family Clinic, Westfield, Mass., 1999—. Contbr. articles to profl. jours., chapters to books; author: Supportive

Therapy, 1989, Supportive Therapy for Borderlines, 1992, (Italian edit.) La Terapia di Sostegno, 1994. Surgeon USPHS, 1959—2001. Fellow: Am. Psychoanalytic Assn. (exec. coun. 1976—79, 1985—2001), Am. Psychiat. Assn. (life); mem.: Group for Advancement Psychiatry, Sigma Xi, Phi Beta Kappa, Alpha Omega Alpha. Avocations: music, hiking, physical exercise, reading. Home and Office: 216 Lincoln Ave Amherst MA 01002

ROCKLEN, KATHY HELLENBRAND, lawyer; b. N.Y.C., June 30, 1951; BA, Barnard Coll., 1973; JD magna cum laude, New England Sch. Law, 1977. Bar: N.Y. 1978, U.S. Dist. Ct. (so. and ea. dists.) N.Y. 1982, U.S. Dist. Ct. (no. dist.) Calif. 1985. Interpretive counsel N.Y. Stock Exchange, N.Y.C.; 1st v.p. E.F. Hutton & Co. Inc.; v.p., gen. counsel and sec. S.G Warburg (U.S.A.) Inc.; mem. Proskauer Rose LLP, N.Y.C. Mem. exec. com. lawyers divsn. Am. Friends Hebrew U.; mem. lawyers' divsn. exec. com. ADL. Mem. N.Y. State Bar Assn., N.Y. Women's Bar Assn., Assn. Bar City N.Y. (v.p., chmn. exec. com., chmn. drugs and law com., chmn. fed. legis. com., securities law com., sec. 2d century com., sex and law com., young lawyers'com., corp. law com.). Office: Proskauer Rose LLP 1585 Broadway New York NY 10036 E-mail: krocklen@proskauer.com.

ROCKOFF, MARK ALAN, pediatric anesthesiologist; b. Jersey City, Apr. 13, 1948; s. Aaron and Rose Rockoff; m. Elizabeth Sceery, Aug. 6, 1978; children: Benjamin, Jillian, Michael. BS, MIT, 1969; MD, Johns Hopkins U., 1973. Diplomate Am. Bd. Pediatrics, Am. Bd. Critical Care Pediatrics, Am. Bd. Anesthesiology. Pediatric intern and resident Mass. Gen. Hosp., Boston, 1973-75, anesthesia resident, 1975-77, assoc. dir. pediatric ICU, 1979-81; neuroanesthesia fellow U. Calif., San Diego, 1978-79; assoc. dir. ICU Children's Hosp., Boston, 1981-89, assoc. anesthesiologist-in-chief, 1988—; med. dir. operating rm., 1992-99; prof. anaesthesia Harvard Med. Sch., Boston, 1999—. Editor jours. Survey of Anesthesiology, 1984-94, Jour. Neurosurg. Anesthesiology, 1994-98. Fellow: Soc. Critical Care Medicine, Am. Acad. Pediats., Am. Soc. Anesthesiologists; mem.: Soc. Pediat. Anesthesia (pres. 1996—98), Am. Bd. Anesthesiology (dir. 2000—). Office: Children's Hosp 300 Longwood Ave Boston MA 02115-5737

ROCKOFF, S. DAVID, radiologist, physician, educator; b. Utica, N.Y., July 21, 1931; s. Samuel and Sarah (Rattinger) R.; m. Jacqueline Garsh; children—Lisa E., Todd E., Kevin D. AB, Syracuse U., 1951; MD, Albany Med. Coll., 1955; M.Sc. in Medicine, U. Pa., 1961. Diplomate: Am. Bd. Radiology. Intern U.S. Naval Hosp., Bethesda, Md., 1955-56; resident and fellow in radiology, USPHS trainee dept. radiology p. of U. Pa., Phila., 1958-61; staff radiologist NIH, Bethesda, Md., 1961-65; asst. prof. radiology Yale U. Sch. Medicine, New Haven, 1965-68, assoc. prof., 1968; asst. attending radiologist Yale-New Haven Med. Center, 1965-68; assoc. prof. radiology Washington U. Sch. Medicine, St. Louis, 1968-71; asst. radiologist Barnes and Allied Hosps., 1969-71; cons. radiologist VA Hosp., 1969-71, Homer G. Phillips Hosp., St. Louis, 1968-71; prof. radiology George Washington U. Sch. Medicine, Washington, 1971—, chmn. dept. radiology, 1971-77, head pulmonary radiology, 1978—, interim chmn. dept. radiology, 1989-90, prof. emeritus radiology, 1993—. Cons. NIH, 1972—; vis. prof. Hadassah U., Beersheba U., Rambam Hosp., Israel, 1977; cons. in radiology VA Hosp., Washington, 1972-77, U.S. Naval Med. Center, Bethesda, 1973-77; mem. diagnostic radiology adv. com. NIH, 1973-76; mem. Cancer Research Manpower Rev. Com., NIH, 1978 Editor-in-chief: Investigative Radiology, 1965-76; editor-in-chief emeritus, 1976—; editor Jour. Thoracic Imaging, 1985; reviewer Jour. Computed Tomography, 1997—; contbr. numerous articles to med. jours. Served with USN, 1955-58; Served with USPHS, 1961-63. Recipient numerous USPHS grants. Fellow Am. Coll. Radiology (pres.-elect D.C. chpt. 1976), Am. Coll. Chest Physicians; mem. Am. Fedn. Clin. Research, D.C. Med. Soc. (mem. med.-legal com. 1975-78), AMA, Radiol. Soc. N.Am. (mem. roster of disting. sci. advisors Rsch. and Edn. Found. 1999), Assn. Univ. Radiologists, Soc. Thoracic Radiology (pres. 1983-84, exec. dir. 1984-87). Home: PO Box 675650 Rancho Santa Fe CA 92067-5650

ROCKOWITZ, NOAH EZRA, lawyer; b. N.Y.C., Apr. 11, 1949; s. Murray and Anna Rae (Cohen) R.; m. Julie Rachel Levitan, Dec. 24, 1978; children: Shira Aviva, Leora Civia, Dahlia Yaffa. BA, Queens Coll., 1969; JD, Fordham U., 1973. Bar: N.Y. 1974, U.S. Dist. Ct. (so and ea. dists.) N.Y. 1974, U.S. Ct. Appeals (2d cir.) 1974. Tchr., chmn. social studies dept. Intermediate Sch. 74, Queens, N.Y., 1969-73; atty. Cahill Gordon & Reindel, N.Y.C., 1973-78; corp. sec., asst. gen. counsel Belco Petroleum Corp., 1978—85; v.p., gen. counsel Hudson Gen. Corp., Great Neck, N.Y., 1985-98, sr. v.p. NY, 1988—2001; sr. v.p., gen. counsel GlobeGround N.Am. LLC, 2001—. Trustee, exec. com., chmn. bd. edn. The Solomon Schechter Sch. Westchester; trustee Beth El Synagogue of New Rochelle; Westchester adv. com. Bd. Jewish Edn. Greater N.Y. Mem. ABA, Am. Soc. Corp. Secs., N.Y. State Bar Assn., Assn. of Bar of City of N.Y., Am. Corp. Counsel Assn., Phi Beta Kappa. Office: GlobeGround NAm LLC 111 Great Neck Rd PO Box 355 Great Neck NY 11022-0355

ROCKSTEIN, MORRIS, science writer, editor, consultant; b. Toronto, Ont., Can., Jan. 8, 1916; came to U.S., 1923; s. David and Mina (Segal) R.; children: Susan M. Bumgarner, Madelaine Jo Sottile. AB magna cum laude, Bklyn. Coll., 1938; MA, Columbia U., 1941; PhD, U. Minn., 1948; cert., Oak Ridge (Tenn.) Inst. Nuclear Studies, 1950. Research asst. entomology U. Minn., St. Paul, 1941-42; asst. prof., assoc. prof. zoophysiology Wash. State U., Pullman, 1948-53; asst. prof., then assoc. prof. physiology NYU Sch. Medicine, N.Y.C., 1953-61; prof. physiology U. Miami Sch. Medicine, 1961-81, chmn. dept., 1967-71; pres. Cortisol Med. Research, Inc., 1983-85. Chmn. sci. adv. bd. Anorexia Nervosa Inst., Melbourne, Fla., 1983-85, Fla. Med. Ctr., Lauderdale Lakes, 1971-78; cons. entomology APHA, 1961-78; del. White House Conf. on Aging, Washington, 1961, 71; cons. insect physiology Sect. Tropical Medicine and Parasitology NIH, Washington, 1962-66, NASA, 1980-92, BIOS, 1983-85; mem. corp. Marine Biol. Lab., 1961—, trustee, 1961-63, life mem., trustee emeritus, 1993—; vis. lectr. Minority Insts. FASEB MARCPROG, 1983-88. Sr. author: Biology of Human Aging, 1978; editor: (with G.T. Baker) Molecular Genetic Mechanisms in Development and Aging, 1972, Development and Aging in the Nervous System, 1973, Physiology of Insecta, 6 vols., 1973-74, Theoretical Aspects of Aging, 1977; (with R.T. Goldman) Physiology and Pathology of Human Aging, 1978, Biochemistry of Insects, 1978; editor Miscellaneous Publs. and Thos Say Found. Monographs, 1983-92; contbr. articles to profl. jours. Mem. resource and mgmt. com. Area Agy. on Aging, 1988-90. Served with USAAF, 1942-46, lt. comdr., USPHS res., 1951-81. NRC fellow in natural scis. U. Minn., 1946-48; recipient Disting. Alumnus award Bklyn. Coll., 1959, Outstanding Alumnus Achievement award U. Minn., 1977, Post 50th Alumni Lifetime Achievement award Bklyn. Coll. Alumni Assn., 1998, A.C. Hodson Meml. award lectr. U. Minn., 1999; named knight comdr. of merit Knights of Malta, 1982. Fellow AAAS (life, mem. coun. 1962-64), Gerontol. Soc. (pres. 1965-66), Entomol. Soc. Am. (life mem.); mem. Internat. Assn. Gerontology (mem. exec. coun. 1963-66), Internat. Assn. Prolongation of Human Life Span (v.p. 1974-92), Am. Physiol. Soc., Am. Soc. Zoologists, Soc. Gen. Physiologists, Sunflower Soc. Miami (v.p. 1986-88), Army-Navy Club, Coral Gables Country Club (bd. dirs. Fleet 1994-96, 97-98), Phi Beta Kappa, Sigma Xi. E-mail: rocky-1@webtv.net.

ROCKSTROH, DENNIS JOHN, journalist, screenwriter; b. Hermosa Beach, Calif., Feb. 1, 1942; s. Philip Herman and Alicia (Rubio) R.; m. Le Thi Que Huong, May 2, 1970; children: Bryan Benjamin, Paula Kim-Mai. Student, San Luis Rey Coll., 1960-61, El Camino Coll., 1961-62, San Fernando Valley State Coll., 1965-67. Reporter Thousand Oaks (Calif.) News Chronicle, 1966-67; tchr. Girls' High Sch., Qui Nhon, Vietnam, 1967-70; instr. Dalat U./Vietnamese Mil. Acad., 1970-71, Ohlone Coll., Fremont, Calif., 1984—; freelance war corr. Dispatch News Svc., Vietnam, 1967-71; city editor Santa Paula (Calif.) Daily Chronicle, 1972-73; reporter San Jose (Calif.) Mercury News, 1973-90, columnist, 1990—. Guest lectr. U. Calif., Berkeley, 1987-91. Vol. Internat. Vol. Svcs., Vietnam, 1967-71; bd. dirs. San Jose unit ARC, 1978, Hope Rehab., San Jose, 1976-77. With U.S. Army, 1962-65, Vietnam. Co-recipient Pulitzer prize for Loma Prieta earthquake coverage, 1989; decorated Army Commendation Medal for Valor, 1965. Mem. Soc. Profl. Journalists, St. Anthony's Sem. Alumni Assn., Nat. Soc. Newspaper Columnists. Roman Catholic. Home: 3573 Tankerland Ct San Jose CA 95121-1244 Office: San Jose Mercury News 3890 Mowry Ave Ste 202 Fremont CA 94538-1447 E-mail: drockstroh@sjmercury.com., drockstroh@yahoo.com.

ROCKSWOLD, GAYLAN LEE, neurosurgeon; b. Valley City, N.D., Dec. 11, 1940; s. E. Palmer and Myrna Christine R.; m. Mary Helen Garnass, June 27, 1964; children: Sarah Beth, Payl Gaylan, Nathan Kristopher. BA, St. Olaf Coll., 1962; MD, U. Minn., 1966, PhD, 1976. Diplomate Am. Bd. Neurol. Surgery. Intern Hennepin County Gen. Hosp., Mpls., 1966-67; gen. surgery resident USPHS Hosp., Balt., 1967-68; med. assoc. sect. neurosurgery Nat. Cancer Inst., 1969; med. fellow dept. surgery U. Minn., Mpls., 1969; med. assoc. Nat. Cancer Inst., Balt., 1969; from instr. to prof. U. Minn., Mpls., 1974-92, prof., 1992—; chief neurosurgery divsn. Hennepin County Med. Ctr., 1977—. Pres. Neurosurgical Assocs., Ltd., Mpls., 1997—; adv. bd. Mpls. Neurosci. Inst.,1992—, v.p. 1998—; presenter in field. Author: (with others) 11 chpts. in books; contbr. over 45 articles in profl. jours. Adv. THINK First Head and Spinal Cord Injury Prevention Program, Mpls., 1990-91; mentor Mentor Connection Program for High Sch. Students, Mpls., 1995-96. Recipient Recognition award Minn. Head Injury Assn., Mpls., 1993; Smith-Kline-French Foreign fellow Malawi, East Africa, 1965. Mem. ACS (Minn. chpt. com. on trauma), AMA. (Minn. state chpt.), Am. Assn. Surgery of Trauma, Neurosurg. Soc. Am., Am. Assn. Neurological Surgeons, Congress Neurological Surgeons, Minn. Neurosurg. Soc. (sec., treas., v.p., pres. 1989-95), Hennepin County Med. Soc., Hitchcock Surg. Soc., The Wilderness Soc., Phi Beta Kappa, Alpha Omega Phi. Lutheran. Avocations: sailing, backpacking, reading history and biographies, canoeing, fishing. Office: Hennepin County Medical Ctr 701 Park Ave Minneapolis MN 55415-1623 E-mail: rocks001@maroon.tc.umn.edu.

ROCKWELL, BRUCE MCKEE, retired banker and foundation executive; b. Denver, Dec. 18, 1922; s. Robert B. and Florence (McKee) R.; m. Virginia Packard, Apr. 22, 1950; children— David, Jane, Sarah. BA, Yale U., 1945. Exec. sec. to mayor City of Denver, 1947-51; pub. rels. and advt. account exec. William Kostka & Assocs., 1952-53; with Colo. Nat. Bank, Denver, 1953-85, pres., 1970-75, chmn., CEO, 1975-85, also dir.; pres. Colo. Trust, Denver, 1985-91; sr. cons. BBC, Inc., 1991. Chmn., bd. dirs. The Denver Partnership, Inc., Kaiser Permanente, 1980-92; bd. dirs. Am. Pub. Welfare Assn., 1989-91; chmn. Denver Urban Renewal Authority, 1958-68; nat. coun. Salk Inst., 1978-84; trustee C.C. Denver, Com. Econ. Devel., 1979-85, Denver Symphony Orch., 1974-77, Denver Art Mus., 1965-72, 82-86, Denver Health Authority, 1995—; trustee Colo. Hist. Soc., 1980—, chmn., 1986-87; mem. Colo. Moffat Tunnel Comm., 1997-98. Ensign USNR, 1945-46. Named Colo. Bus. Man of Yr., Colo. Bus. mag., 1976, Rotary Club, 1984. Mem. Assn. Res. City Bankers (dir. 1975-85), Denver C. of C., Univ. Club, Tennis Club. Home: 2800 S University Blvd #18 Denver CO 80210

ROCKWELL, DON ARTHUR, retired psychiatrist; b. Wheatland, Wyo., Apr. 24, 1938; s. Orson Arthur and Kathleen Emily Rockwell; m. Frances Pepitone-Arreola, Dec. 23, 1965; children: Grant, Chad. BA, Wash. U., 1959; MD, U. Okla., 1963; MA in Sociology, U. Calif., Berkeley, 1967. Diplomate Am. Bd. Psychiatry and Neurology. Intern in surgery San Francisco Gen. Hosp., 1963-64; resident in psychiatry Langley-Porter Neuropsychiatric Inst. U. Calif. Med. Ctr., San Francisco, 1964-67; instr. dept. psychiatry U. Calif. Sch. Medicine, Davis, 1969-70, asst. prof., 1970-74, assoc. prof., 1974-80, acting. assoc., dean curricular affiars, 1979-80, acting assoc. dean student affairs, 1980, assoc. dean student affairs, 1980-82, prof., 1980-84; career tchr. NIMH, 1970-72; assoc. psychiatrist Sacramento Med. Ctr.; med. dir. U. Calif. Med. Ctr., Davis, 1982-84; prof., vice chmn. dept. psychiatry and biobehavioral scis. UCLA, 1984-96; dir. UCLA Neuropsychiat. Hosp., 1984-95; chief profl. staff Neuropsychiat. Inst., UCLA, 1984-85, also dir. outpatient svcs. Chmn. U. Calif. Hosp. Dirs. Council, 1988-89; cons. Nat. Commn. on Marijuana, Washington, 1971-73. Co-author: Psychiatric Disorders, 1982; contbr. chpts. to books; articles to profl. jours. Mem. bd. visitors U. Okla. Sch. Medicine; chmn. hosp. dirs. coun. U. Calif. Hosp.; mem. governing coun. AHA Psychiat. Hosp.; mem. County of Santa Barbara Civil Grand Jury, 2001—02; bd. dirs. Bereavement Outreach, Sacramento, 1974—84, Suicide Prevention, Yolo County, 1969—84. Fellow Am. Psychiat. Assn., Am. Coll. Psychiatrists, Am. Coll. Mental Health Adminstrs.; mem. AMA (gov. coun. psych. hosp.), Am. Sociologic Assn., Calif. Med. Assn. (med. staff survey com.), Cen. Calif. Psychiat. Assn. (sec.-pres. 1977-78), U. Okla. Alumni Assn. (trustee 1981-86), Alpha Omega Alpha. Home: 1816 E Las Tunas Rd Santa Barbara CA 93103-1744 E-mail: rockwell@west.net.

ROCKWELL, ELIZABETH GOODE, dance company director, consultant, educator; b. Portland, Oreg., Sept. 10, 1920; d. Henry Walton and Elizabeth (Harmon) Goode; m. William Hearne Rockwell, Feb. 3, 1948; children: Enid, Karen, William. BA, Mills Coll., 1941; MA, NYU, 1946. Instr. dance Monticello Jr. Coll., Alton, Ill., 1941-42; dir. masters program in dance Smith Coll., Northampton, Mass., 1946-48; 1st dir. dance dept. High Sch. of Performing Arts, N.Y.C., 1948-51, 53-54; dir. Elizabeth Rockwell Sch. Dance, Bedford, N.Y., 1956-86, Rondo Dance Theater Internat. Dance Touring Co., Bedford, 1971-93; tchr. continuing dance classes CCAE, 1994—; with Martha Graham, 1944-46; with Hanya Holm, 1946-48; with José Limon, 1949-52. Mem. adv. ednl. com. Calif. Ctr. for Arts, Escondido, Calif., 1993-95, dir. dance classes, 1994—; tchr. master class, choreographer Waitukubuli Dance Theater, Dominica, 1999; dir. prime dance performance Artists Coming of Age, U. San Diego, 1999. Choreographer (suite of dances) Jazz Suite, 1966, (50-minute dances) Catch the Wind, 1969, Genesis, 1972, (narrative modern ballet) The Executioner, 1974, Decathalon, 1982; dir. (subscription series) Dance-Art-Poetry-Jazz, 1978-79, (dance/music 1600-1900) Stages in Ages, 1981, (Am. dance revivals) Masterpieces of American Dance, 1982-84, Dances of the Decades, 1985-90, (revival & new choreography) Dances of Our Times, 1991; dir. dance workshops for Calif. Ctr. Arts, 1994, 95, 96; creator, founder performing group of older dancers Golden Connections Dance Ensemble of Women, CCAE, (touring San Diego area), 1996—. Bd. dirs. Coun. for Arts in Westchester, White Plains, N.Y., 1978-79, affiliate, 1978— Recipient Medal for Performance, Israeli Army, 1966, Award for Excellence in Arts Edn. Alumnae of High Sch. of Performing Arts, 1990, Tommy Dance award of distinction San Diego Area Dance Alliance, 1999; various grants N.Y. State Coun. on Arts, 1971-93, Coun. Arts in Westchester, 1973-92, dance touring program grant Nat. Endowment for Arts, 1975-79. Mem. Am. Dance Guild, Westchester Dance Coun. (program dir. 1965-69), Assn. Am. Dance Cos., San Diego Area Dance Alliance (bd. dirs. 1995—). Avocations: writing, swimming, touring, reading. Home: 205 Tampico Gln Escondido CA 92025-7359

ROCKWELL, KAY ANNE, elementary education educator; b. Brighton, Mich., Feb. 12, 1952; d. Philip Oscar and Patricia Irene (Bennett) Newton; m. Lawrence Edward Rockwell, Aug. 23, 1975. BA in Social Sci. & Elem. Edn. cum laude, Spring Arbor Coll., 1974; MA in Early Childhood Edn., Ea. Mich. U., 1981. Dir. child care St. Luke's Luth. Day Care Ctr., Ann Arbor, Mich., 1980-82; tchr. 3d grade Colo. Christian Sch., Denver, 1982-94; tchr. 1st grade Front Range Christian Sch., Littleton, Colo., 1994—. Chmn. Nat. Children's Book Week Colo. Christian Sch., 1993-94, chmn. ACSI spelling bee, 1991-94, 95-98, chmn. ACSI speech meet, 1985-86; mem. Bible curriculum com., chmn. reading curriculum com. Front Range Christian Sch., 1999-2000, mem. edn. com., 1999-2001. Spring Arbor Coll. scholar, 1972-74. Office: Front Range Christian Sch 4001 S Wadsworth Blvd Littleton CO 80123-1358

ROCKWELL, RICHARD COOK, association executive; b. Tyler, Tex., June 1, 1942; s. Richard Stauffer and Louis (Cook) R.; m. Phyllis Rolston, Mar. 19, 1969 (div. 1986); children: Jeffrey David, Stephen Dane. BA, U. Tex., 1964, MA, 1966, PhD, 1970. Dir. Social Sci. DAta Libr., U. N.C., Chapel Hill, 1969-76; fellow Boys Town Ctr., Omaha, 1976-79; staff assoc. Social Sci. Rsch. Coun., N.Y.C., 1979-91; exec. dir. Inter-univ. Consortium for Polit. and Social Rsch., Ann Arbor, Mich., 1991—. Mem. standing com. on START, Internat. Geosphere/Biosphere Programs, Stockholm, 1990—; exec. com. Global Change Program, U. Mich., 1992—. Coantbr. articles to profl. jours.; editor: AIDS in Africa, 1988. Mem. AAAS, Am. Statis. Assn. (Bur. of Census adv. com. 1991—), Phi Beta Kappa. Democrat. Unitarian Universalist. Office: ICPSR/ISR U Mich 426 Thompson St Ann Arbor MI 48104-2321

ROCKWELL, R(ONALD) JAMES, JR. laser and electro-optics consultant; b. Cin., May 7, 1937; s. Ronald James and Mary Cornelius (Thornton) R.; m. Diane Lundin, Feb. 3, 1968; children: James Gregory, Christopher Derrick. BS, U. Cin., 1960, MS, 1964. Directing physicist, assoc. prof. laser scis., laser research labs. Med. Center, U. Cin., 1963-76; dir. continuing edn. services Electro-Optical Systems Design Jour., Cin., 1976-77; v.p. laser/electro-optics Control Dynamics, Inc., 1977-79; pres. Rockwell Assocs., Inc. (cons. lasers, optics and electro-optics), 1979-89; pres., chief exec. officer Rockwell Laser Industries (cons. lasers, optics and electro-optics), 1989—. Exec. com. safe use lasers com. Am. Nat. Standards Inst., 1971-2000, chmn. control measures tech. com., 1971—; exec. sec. Laser Inst. Am., 1976-77, dir., 1972-92, pres., 1974; mem. adv. com. Laser History Project, 1983-89; dir. Laserworks, Inc., Rockwell Devel. Co.; cons. WHO, Internat. Electrotechnical Commn., founder Consortium of Laser and Tech. Cons., 1988; mem. tech. com. Laser Fire Protection of the Nat. Fire Protection Assn., 1991—. Co-author: Lasers in Medicine, 1971; author: Laser Safety Training Manual, 1982, Laser Safety in Surgery and Medicine, 1985, Laser Safety: Concepts, Analysis and Controls, 1992, Laser Safety: Modularized Training Package, 1994, Users Guide for Laser Safety, 1997, Multi-Lingual Laser Safety Training Program, 1998, Laser Accidents, a 30 Year Review, 2000, Medical User's Guide for Laser Safety, 2000; created software program: Laser Hazard Analysis, 1987, LAZAN for Windows, 1995, SKYZAN for Windows, 1996; co-developer: LASERNET page on the World-Wide Web (Internet), 1996; contbr. chpts. to books and articles to profl. jours.; editor jours. in field; mem. editl. bd. Jour. Laser Applications, 1994-99. Co-chmn. Internat. Laser Safety Conf., 1990, 92, mem. planning com., keynote spkr., 1997. Recipient Pres.' award Laser Inst. Am., 1985, Safety and Health award Am. Welding Soc., 2001. Fellow: Laser Inst. Am.; mem.: IEEE, Internat. Laser Display Assn., Midwest Bio-Laser Inst., Am. Soc. Laser Medicine and Surgery, N.Y. Acad. Scis., Newcomen Soc., Delta Tau Delta (dir. acad. affairs, nat. bd. dirs. 1975—83, D.S.C. award 1985), Sigma Xi (nat. lectr. 1971—75). Methodist. Achievements include designer, builder portable laser entertainment system in laser light artistic shows; patentee in field; co-developer laser safety awareness training program for world-wide web. Home: 6282 Coachlite Way Cincinnati OH 45243-2920 Office: PO Box 43010 7754 Camargo Rd Cincinnati OH 45243-2661 E-mail: BigJimR@aol.com.

ROCKWELL, THEODORE, nuclear engineer; b. Chgo., June 26, 1922; s. Theodore G. and Paisley (Shane) R.; m. Mary Juanita Compton, Jan. 25, 1947; children: Robert C. (dec.), W. Teed, Lawrence E., Juanita C. BS in Engring, Princeton U., 1943, Chem.E. (MS), 1945; grad. courses, Oak Ridge, 1944-49; D.Sc. (hon.), Tri-State U., 1960. Registered profl. engr., D.C. Process improvement engr. Manhattan Project, Oak Ridge, 1944-45; head shield engring. group Oak Ridge Nat. Lab., 1945-49; nuclear engr., naval reactors br. AEC, also nuclear propulsion divs. Navy Bur. Ships, 1949-55, tech. dir., 1955-64; founding officer, dir. MPR Assos., Inc., Washington, 1964—; research asso. Johns Hopkins U. Center Fgn. Policy Research, 1965-66. Chmn. Atomic Indsl. Forum Reactor Safety Task Force, 1966-72; mem. adv. group artificial heart program NIH, 1966; cons. to Joint Congl. Com. on Atomic Energy, 1967; founding officer, dir. Radiation, Sci. & Health, Inc., 1996—. Author: The Rickover Effect: How One Man Made a Difference, 1992; co-author: Shippingport Pressurized Water Reactor, 1958, Arms Control Agreements/Designs Verification, 1968; co-founder Princeton Engr.; editor: Reactor Shield Design Manual, 1956; contbg. editor New Realities, 1988-92; contbr. sci. articles to profl. publs., non-tech. articles nat. mags.; holder patents, patent applications for neutron-absorbing cermets and plastics, also others. Mem. adv. council dept. chem. engring. Princeton U., 1966-72. Recipient Disting. Civilian Svc. medal USN, 1960, Disting. Svc. medal AEC, 1960, Lifetime Contbn. award Am. Nuclear Soc. (1st, now known as Rockwell award), 1986. Fellow Am. Nuclear Soc., Am. Soc. Psychical Rsch. (life); mem. AAAS (rep. of Parapsychol. Assn. to AAAS 1975-87), N.Y. Acad. Scis., Soc. for Sci. Exploration, U.S. Psychotronic Assn. (dir. 1988-91), Nat. Inst. for Discovery Sci. (sci. adv. bd. 1995—), Nat. Acad. Engring., Authors Guild, Writers Ctr., Washington Ind. Writers, Cosmos Club (Washington), Nat. Press Club. Presbyterian (elder). Address: 3403 Woolsey Dr Chevy Chase MD 20815-3924 E-mail: tedrock@cpcug.org.

ROCKWELL, WINTHROP ADAMS, lawyer; b. Pittsfield, Mass., May 7, 1948; s. Landon Gale Rockwell and Ruth (Adams) Lonsdale; m. Barbara Washburn Wood, June 20, 1970; children: Samuel Adams, Madeleine McCord. AB, Dartmouth Coll., 1970; JD, NYU, 1975. Bar: Minn. 1975, U.S. Dist. Ct. Minn. 1975. Asst. newsman fgn. desk N.Y. Times, N.Y.C., 1970-71; asst. to pres. Dartmouth Coll., Hanover, N.H., 1971-72; assoc. Faegre & Benson, Mpls., 1975-79; assoc. chief counsel Pres.'s Commn. on Accident at Three Mile Island, Washington, 1979; assoc. Faegre & Benson, Mpls., 1979-82, ptnr., 1983—, chmn. diversity com., 1990-95, head gen. litigation group, 1995—. Bd. dirs., v.p. Children's Theatre, Mpls., 1982-83; bd. dirs. Actors Theatre St. Paul, 1975-79, Trinity Films, Mpls., 1978-82, Minn. Ctr. for Book Arts, 1996—; mem. adv. bd. Univ. Minn. Joint Degree Program in Law, Health and the Life Scis. Brit.-Am. Project fellow, 1987. Mem. ABA, Minn. Bar Assn., Hennepin County Bar Assn., Am. Agrl. Law Assn., Adirondack 46ers, Adirondack Mountain Club. Avocations: writing, tennis, mountaineering, gardening. Home: 1901 Knox Ave S Minneapolis MN 55403-2840 Office: Faegre & Benson 2200 Wells Fargo Ctr 90 S 7th St Ste 2200 Minneapolis MN 55402-3901 E-mail: wrockwell@faegre.com.

ROCKWOOD, IRVING E., JR. publisher; b. Norwood, Mass., Dec. 13, 1944; s. Irving E. and Cassie A. (Richardson) R.; m. Nancy E. Wilcox, June 14, 1969; children: Catherine Anne, Margaret Elaine. BA in Polit. Sci., No. Ill. U., 1967, MA in Polit. Sci., 1969. Sales rep. Coll. Divsn. Houghton Mifflin Co., Geneva, 1970-72, maths. editor Coll. Divsn. Boston, 1972-74; editor, math. and econs. Coll. Divsn. D.C. Heath, Lexington, Mass., 1974-76; gen. editor U. Wis. Press, Madison, 1976-79; exec. editor Longman, Inc., N.Y.C., 1979-85; pres. Irving Rockwood & Assocs., Inc., Chappaqua, N.Y., 1985-89; pub. Dushkin Pub. Group, Guilford, Conn., 1989-95; editor and pub. Choice, Middletown, 1995—. Mem. rsch. libr. delegation Citizen Amb. Program People to People, S. Africa, 1997; chair grants subcom. Horace Greeley Edn. Fund, Chappaqua, N.Y., 1989-95. Mem. Am. Polit. Sci. Assn., Soc. for Scholarly Pub., Am. Soc. Assn. Execs., ALA, Assn. Coll. and Rsch. Librs. Mem. Ch. of Christ. Avocations: reading, hiking, do-it-yourself projects, choral singing. Office: Choice 100 Riverview Ctr Middletown CT 06457-3401 E-mail: irockwood@ala-choice.org.

ROCKWOOD, LINDA LEE, lawyer; b. Cedar Rapids, Iowa, July 25, 1950; d. Robert Walter and Dorothy Jean (Rehberg) Sorensen; children: Holly Lynn, Christian Douglas. BA, U. Denver, 1972; JD, U. Tex., 1984. Bar: Colo. 1984, U.S. Dist. Ct. Colo., U.S. Ct. Appeals (10th cir.). Econ. and consumer research analyst May Dept. Stores, St. Louis, 1973-75; asst. dir. Ctr. for Study Am. Bus., Washington U., 1975-77; mgr. Mid-Columbia Symphony, Richland, Wash., 1978-79; assoc. Holland & Hart, Denver, 1984-88; shareholder, dir. Parcel, Mauro & Spaanstra, 1988-98, pres., 1996-98; ptnr. Faegre & Benson, 1998—, adminstrv. ptnr., 2001—. Author: New Mines From Old Environmental Considerations in Remining and Reprocessing of Waste Materials, 1991, The Alcan Decisions: Causation Through the Back Door, 1993, RCRA Demystified: The Professional's Guide to Hazardous Waste Law, 1996, Citizen Suits: Public Interest or Private Advocacy, 2000, Institutional Controls: Brownfields Superweapon or Ultimate Trojan Horse?, 2000. Bd. dirs. Colo. Hazardous Waste Mgmt. Soc., 1986, 89-91, pres., 1987-88; mem. Mayor's Convention Ctr. Task Force, 1997-99, Ctrl. Platte Valley Devel. Coun., 1999—. Mem. Colo. Bar Assn. (exec. coun. environ. law sect. 1987-90), Environ. Law Inst., Rocky Mountain Mineral Law Found., Order of Coif, Phi Beta Kappa. Office: Faegre & Benson LLP 2500 Republic Plaza 370 17th St Denver CO 80202-5665 E-mail: lrockwood@faegre.com.

ROCQUE, VINCENT JOSEPH, lawyer; b. Franklin, N.H., Nov. 27, 1945; s. Francis Albert and Mary Helen (O'Grady) R.; m. Emily Adams Arnold, May 31, 1969; children: Amanda Adams, Peter O'Connor, Caroline Quin. BA magna cum laude, Georgetown U., 1967; JD, Columbia U., N.Y.C., 1970. Bar: D.C. 1971, U.S. Supreme Ct., 1973. Assoc. Hogan & Hartson, Washington, 1970-73; counsel, spl. asst. to commr. Barbara Franklin U.S. Consumer Product Safety Commn., 1973-77; asst. dir. bur. trade regulation U.S. Dept. Commerce, 1977-80; ptnr. Sullivan & Worcester, 1980-90; pvt. practice law, 1990—. V.p., co-pres. Janney Pub. Elem. Sch. PTA, Washington, 1982-84; vol. coord. homeless shelters Cath. Charities, Washington and Silver Spring, Md., 1984-90. Staff sgt. USAR, 1969-75. Mem. ABA (adminstrv. law and regulatory practice sect., internat. law and practice sect., bus. law sect.), Fed. Bar Assn. (adminstrv. law and internat. law sects.), Mid-Atlantic Literary Edification Soc., Nat. Capital YMCA, Phi Beta Kappa. Roman Catholic. Avocations: reading, travel, American Civil War history, basketball. Office: 1155 Connecticut Ave NW Ste 110 Ste 400 Washington DC 20036-4306

RODA, JOSEPH FRANCIS, lawyer; b. Lancaster, Pa., June 22, 1949; s. Frank Edward and Mary Virginia (Reeder) R.; m. Dianne M. Nast, Aug. 23, 1980; children: Michael, Daniel, Joseph, Joshua, Anastasia. AB, Harvard Coll., 1971; JD, U. Pa., 1974. Bar: Pa. 1974, U.S. Dist. Ct. (ea. dist.) Pa. 1975, U.S. Dist. Ct. (mid. dist.) Pa. 1981, U.S. Ct. Appeals (3d cir.) 1981, U.S. Supreme Ct. 1982. Law clk. to judge U.S. Dist. Ct. (ea. dist.) Pa., Phila., 1974-75; assoc. Kohn, Savette, Marion & Graf, P.C., 1975-80; pvt. practice Lancaster, 1980—. Mem. ABA, ATLA, Am. Coll. Trial Lawyers, Pa. Trial Lawyers Assn. (ho. dels.), Pa. Bar Assn. (ho. of dels), Internat. Acad. Trial Lawyers, Lancaster Country Club, Hamilton Club (Lancaster). Avocations: sports, piano. Home: 1059 Sylvan Rd Lancaster PA 17601-1923 Office: 801 Estelle Dr Lancaster PA 17601-2130 E-mail: rodanast@aol.com.

RODBELL, CLYDE ARMAND, distribution executive; b. Atlanta, Aug. 16, 1927; s. Joseph Hirsch and Fannie (Turetzky) R.; m. Cecile Rosenson, Mar. 27, 1949 (div.); children: Marsha, Jeffrey, Keith, Kim; m. Robin Graham McKenzie Rodbell, Dec. 15, 1974; 1 child, Lindsey. BBA, Emory U., 1949. Chmn. Apex Supply Co. Inc., Atlanta, 1949—. Co-chmn. George Bush Presdl. Fund Raising, Ga., 1988-89; mem. State of Ga. Electoral Coll., 1989, exec. commr. Am. Bicentenial Pres. Inaugural Bus. Adv., 1989, Pres' Commn. on White House Fellowships, 1989-92. With U.S. Army, 1945. Mem. Wholesale Assn. Ga., Southern Wholesalers Assn., Am. Supply Assn., Standard Club, Rotary Club. Republican. Jewish. Avocations: reading, gardening, antiquing, politics, fund raising.

RODDEN, JOHN GALLAGHER, communications educator, writer; b. Phila., Oct. 18, 1956; s. John and Rose Gallagher Rodden. BA, LaSalle U., Pa., 1978; MA, U. Va., 1982, PhD, 1987. Asst. prof. U. Va., 1983-89, U. Tex., 1989-93. Author: the Politics of Literary Reputation, 1989, Performing the Literary Interview, 2001, Repainting the Little Red Schoolhouse: A History of East Germany, Textbook Reds, 2002, The Worlds of Irving howe, 2002, Orwell: The Politics of Reputation, 2001; editor: Lionel Trilling, 1999, Conversations With Isabel Allende, 1999, Understanding George Orwell's Animal Farm, 2000. Recipient dissertation award Nat. Comm. Assn., 1988, 1st place book award Nat. Communication Assn., 1990, Nat. Champion in persuasive speaking, Nat. forensic Assn., 1978. Roman Catholic. Avocation: running. Home: 2502 Nueces St Apt 212 Austin TX 78705-4835

RODDICK, DAVID BRUCE, construction company executive; b. Oakland, Calif., Oct. 31, 1948; s. Bruce Ergo and Hortensia Cabo (Castedo) R.; m. Sharon Ann Belan, May 25, 1975; children: Heather Marie, Christina DeeAnn. BSCE, U. Calif., Davis, 1971. Engr. Bechtel Corp., San Francisco, 1971-77, contract specialist, 1977-78; subcontract adminstr. Boecon Corp., Richland, Wash., 1978-79; constrn. mgr. BE&C Engrs., Inc., Vancouver, 1979-81; contracts mgr. Boecon Corp., Tukwila, 1981-83; sr. constrn. mgr. BE&C Engrs., Inc., Wichita, Kans., 1983-84; project mgr., v.p. ops. Carl Holvick Co., Sunnyvale, Calif., 1984-88, also corp. sec. bd. dirs.; v.p., gen. mgr. Brookman Co. div. B.T. Mancini Co., Inc., Milpitas, 1988-92; v.p., sec., CFO B.T. Mancini Co., Inc., 1992-98, sr. v.p. ops., CFO, corp. sec., 1998-2000, exec. v.p., CFO, corp. sec., 2000—. Mem. devel. com. San Jose (Calif.) Mus. Assn., 1993—95; mem., dir. Constrn. Fin. Mgmt. Assn., 1995—, pres. Silicon Valley chpt., 1990—; pres. Reed Sch. PTA, San Jose, 1985—88, San Jose Coun. PTAs, 1988—89; trustee Heart of Valley Bapt. Ch.; bd. dirs. Vinehill Homeowners Assn., 1975—77. Lt. col. C.E. USAR, 1969—99. Decorated Army Achievement medal, 1988, Commendation medal, 1991, 96, 98, meritorious svc. medal, 1998, 99; recipient Calif. State PTA Hon. Svc. award, 1988, Bronze de Fluery medal Army Engr. Assn., 1998. Mem. Am. Soc. Civil Engrs., Res. Officers Assn. (life), Am. Arbitration Assn. (mem. panel arbitrators), Am. Subcontractors Assn., Engr. Regimental Assn. (life), Calif. Aggie Alumni Assn., Ill. State Geneal. Soc., Floor Covering Installation Contractors Assn., Oreg. Calif. Trails Assn., Santa Maria Valley Geneal. Archtl. Engring. Inst. (founding mem.), Soc., Army Engr. Assn. (de Fleury medal 1998), U. Calif.-Davis Century Club, Sigma Nu. Republican. Office: B T Mancini Co Inc 876 S Milpitas Blvd Milpitas CA 95035-6311

RODE, LEIF, retired real estate personal computer consultant; b. Copenhagen, Aug. 24, 1926; arrived in US, 1948, naturalized, 1960; s. Stig and Kirsten (Bay) Rode; children: Christian, Lise. BS magna cum laude, Columbia U., 1959. Cert. auditor; ChFC, CLU. Mgr. East Asiatic Co., N.Y.C., 1952-54; various auditing positions N.Y. Life Ins. Co., 1954-70, asst. gen. auditor, 1970-71, gen. auditor, 1971-82, sr. v.p., gen. auditor, 1982-87, cons., 1987-89; real estate agt. Weichert Realtors, Holmdel, N.J., 1989-90, Fraybern Realtors, Holmdel, 1990-92, Colts Neck (N.J.) Realty, 1992-98; ret, 1998. Mem. Bd. Edn., Colts Neck, 1975—76, v.p., 1976—78; bd. dirs. Sports Found., Inc., 1973—75, pres., 1975—77; trustee Bayshore Cmty. Hosp., Holmdel, 1986—87. With Royal Danish Navy, 1946—47. Recipient Award of Honor, NY State Soc CPAs, 1960; scholar Merle M Hoover, 1960. Mem.: NJ Asn Realtors (munic liaison to Colts Neck Twp 1989—94, state legis comt 1990—93, new products and technology comt 1990—92, vice chair 1992, chmn 1993, bd dirs 1993, real estate personal computer consult 1995—98), Monmouth County Bd Realtors (mem constn and by-laws comt 1989—92, co-chair 1991—92, strategic planning comt 1992—93), Am Soc CLU and Chartered Fin Consults, Inst Internal Auditors. Lutheran. Home and Office: 18 Sandhurst Rd Lakewood NJ 08701 E-mail: llrode@aol.com.

RODEFER, JEFFREY ROBERT, lawyer, prosecutor; b. Santa Fe, Mar. 29, 1963; s. Robert Jacob and Joanne D. (Thomas) R. BS, U. Nev., 1985; JD, cert. dispute resolution, Willamette U., 1988. Bar: Calif. 1990, Nev. 1990, U.S. Dist. Ct. Nev. 1990, U.S. Dist. Ct. (ea. dist.) Calif. 1990, U.S. Ct. Appeals (9th cir.) 1990, Colo. 1991, Oreg. 1997, U.S. Supreme Ct. 1997; cert. arbitrator, Nev. Legal intern Willamette U. Legal Aid Clinic, Salem, Oreg., 1987-88; legal rschr. transp. divsn. Nev. Atty. Gen. Office, Carson City, 1989-90, dep. atty. gen. taxation divsn., 1990-93, dep. atty. gen. gaming divsn., 1993-99, sr. dep. atty. gen. gaming divsn., 1999-2001, asst. chief dep. atty. gen. gaming divsn., 2001—02; corp. compliance officer, assoc. gen. counsel Boyd Gaming Corp., Las Vegas, 2002—. Author: Nevada Property Tax Manual, 1993, Nevada Gaming Law Index, 1999; contbr. articles to Nev. Lawyer. Contbg. mem. U. Nev. Coll. Bus. Adminstrn. and Athletic Dept., Reno, 1992, Willamette U. Coll. Law, Ann. Law Fund, Salem, 1992; active Nat. Parks and Recreation Assn., Washington, 1991; mem. First Christian Ch. Mem. Internat. Assn. Gaming Attys., U. Nev. Coll. Bus. Alumni Assn., Am. Inns of Ct. (Bruce R. Thompson chpt.), State Bar Nev. (functional equivalency com. 1993—, chmn. gaming law sect. 2000—), Phi Delta Phi. Republican. Office: Boyd Gaming Corp 2950 Industrial Rd Las Vegas NV 89109-1150 Office Fax: 702-696-1111. E-mail: jeffreyrodefer@boydgaming.com.

RODELL, PAUL ARTHUR, history educator; b. Chgo., Sept. 19, 1945; s. Gustave George and Helen Christine (Nelson) R.; m. Tan Lee Gek, Nov. 18, 1973 (dec. June 1986). BA, No. Ill. U., 1968; MA, SUNY, Buffalo, 1982, PhD, 1992. Adj. faculty Inst. Industry Studies N.Y. State Sch. Indsl. and Labor Rels., Cornell U., 1989-92; asst. prof. dept. history Ga. So. U., Statesboro, 1992—. Mem. Asia coun. U. Sys. Ga., 1995—; Asian studies com. Ga. So. U., Statesboro, 1994—. Author: Culture and Customs of the Philippines, 2002; editor Jour. Commonwealth and Post-Colonial Studies, 2000; contbr. chpts. to books, articles to profl. jours. Program tech. rep.'s asst. agr. U.S. Peace Corps, Manila, 1970-71, vol., Botolan, Zambales, The Philippines, 1968-70. Recipient Rsch. grant Fulbright-Hays Com., The Philippines, 1980-81, Scholar-in-Residence, Luce Found., 1991-92, grant Nat. Endowment for Humanities, Honolulu, 1993, Spl. Initiatives award Ga. So. U., 1995-96, Libr. Support grant Japan Found., 1996. Mem. Assn. Third World Studies (life, exec. dir. 1992—, Presdl. award 2000), Assn. Asian Studies (exec. coun. Philippine studies group 1995-98), Savannah Coun. on World Affairs, World History Assn. Avocations: music, travel, wines, reading. Office: Ga So Univ Dept History Statesboro GA 30460-8054 E-mail: rodell@gasou.edu.

RODEMAN, FREDERICK ERNEST, accountant; b. Chgo., Jan. 29, 1938; s. Ernest August and Elizabeth Mae (Penrod) R.; m. Marilyn Kay Paul, June 17, 1967. BBA, Ind. U., 1959; cert. bank controllership, U. Wis., 1975; MBA, De Paul U., 1976. CPA, Ind., Wis. Auditor Arthur Andersen & Co., Chgo., 1959-67; acct. mgr. A.B. Dick & Co., 1967-72; controller Beloit (Wis.) State Bank, 1972-77; pvt. practice acctg. Beloit, 1977—. Mem. Am. Inst. CPA's. Republican. Baptist. Home and Office: 2372 Tara Ct Beloit WI 53511-1938

RODEMEYER, MICHAEL LEONARD, JR. lawyer; b. Balt., May 25, 1950; s. Michael Leonard and Claire Isabel (Gunther) R.; m. Dorrit Carolyn Green, June 7, 1975; children: Justin, Christoffer. AB, Princeton U., 1972; JD, Harvard U., 1975. Bar: Md. 1977, D.C. 1980, U.S. Ct. Appeals (10th cir.) 1980. Atty. Fed. Trade Commn., Washington, 1976-81, atty. advisor, 1981-84; counsel Subcom. on Natural Resources, Agr. Rsch. & Environ., 1984-88; staff dir., counsel U.S. Ho. of Reps., 1988-90, house com. on sci., chief dem. counsel, 1990-98; asst. dir. for environment White House Office of Sci. and Tech. Policy, 1998-99, dem. legis. dir., 1999-2000; exec. dir. Pew Initiative on Food and Biotech., 2000—. Democrat. Avocations: computing, bicycling. Home: 6000 Harvard Ave Glen Echo MD 20812-1114 Office: Pew Initiative on Food and Biotech 1331 H St NW Ste 900 Washington DC 20005 E-mail: mrodemeyer@pewagbiotech.org.

RODEN, DAN MARK, clinical pharmacologist ,cardiologist, medical educator; b. Montreal, Can., Apr. 15, 1950; came to U.S., 1978; s. Rudolph George and Eva (Vonchovsky) R.; m. Rosemary Wetherill, Dec. 29, 1972; children: Mark McKenzie, Paul Joseph, Rosemary Claire. BSc, McGill U., 1970, MD, 1974. Diplomate Am. Bd. Internal Medicine, Am. Bd. Cardiovascular Disease, Am. Bd. Clinical Cardiac Electrophysiology, Am. Bd. Clinical Pharmacology; Lic. physician, Quebec, Canada and Tenn.; Cert. Med. Coun. of Canada, Nat. Bd. Med. Examiners. Intern Royal Victoria Hosp., Montreal, Can., 1974-75, resident Can., 1975-76, 77-78; pvt. practice Can., 1976-77; rsch. fellow clin. pharmacology Vanderbilt U., Nashville, 1978-81, fellow cardiol., 1980-81, asst. prof., 1981-85, assoc. prof., 1985-89, prof. Med. and Pharmacology, 1989—, also dir. divsn. clin. pharmacology, 1992—. Del. 4th U.S.-USSR Symposium on Sudden Death, Birmingham, Ala., 1985; mem. Nat. VA Merit Review Cardiovasc. Disease com., 1986-88, chmn. 1988-89; ad hoc reviewer, Pharmacology Study and Cardiovasc. and Pulmonary Study sects., NIH, mem. Cardiovasc. and Pulmonary Study sect., 1991-94, chmn. 1994-96; adv. panel cardiovasc. and renal drugs, U.S. Phamacopeial Conv., 1990-95; mem. external adv. com., Pharmacological Scis. Tng. Grant, Columbia U., 1992—; mem. Clin. Cardiac Electrophysiology Test Writing com., Am. Bd. Internal Medicine, 1992—; mem. adv. com., Vanderbilt Clin Rsch. Ctr., 1989-91, chmn. 91-92, faculty appointments and promotions, Vanderbilt U. Dept. Med., 1992-95; mem. instl. review bd., Vanderbilt U. Dept. Health Scis., 1991-93, chmn. 1993-94. Author 27 book chpts., over 150 abstracts and 130 articles to profl. jours.; mem. editl. bd. Jour. Cardiovasc. Electrophys., 1990—; mem. adv. bd. The Med. Letter (newsletter), 1991—. Fellow Am. Coll. Physicians, Am. Coll. Cardiology (annual scientific session program com. 1992-93), Royal Coll. Physicians of Can.; mem. Am. Fedn. Clin. Rsch., Am. Soc. Clin. Pharmacology Therapeutics (bd. dirs. 1994—, chmn. cardiovasc. and pulmonary sect., 1995—), North Am. Soc. Pacing and Electrophysiol., Cardiac Electrophysiol. Soc., Biophysical Soc., Am. Soc. Pharmacol. and Experimental Therapeutics, So. Soc. Clin. Investigation, Am. Soc. Clin. Investigation, Am. Heart Assn. (clinician-sci.t award, 1981-86, long-range planning com. 1995—, basic sci. coun. exec. com. 1995—) Office: Vanderbilt U 532B Medical Rsch Bldg 1 Nashville TN 37232-0001

RODEN, JON-PAUL, retired educator and labor union organizer, educational consultant; b. Vernon, Conn., July 15, 1943; s. Paul James and Evelyn Mary Roden. BS, SUNY, Oswego, 1965; MS, Ctrl. Conn. State U., 1970. Cert. pioneer in professionalism Nat. Bd. Profl. Tchg. Stds. Tchr. elem. sch. Vernon Pub. Schs., 1965-68, tchr. anatomy and physiology, 1969-79, tchr. computer sci., 1980-82, dist. chmn. computer sci., 1982-2000, staff devel. presentor, 1986—; union organizer Conn. Edn. Assn., Hartford, 2000—, state treas.; ret. Tech. advisor Capitol Region Edn. Coun., 1981-85; presenter Inst. for Tchrs. and Learning, Conn. Dept. Edn., 1990-91, N.E. Holmes Group, Boston, 1994; mem. adv. com. Affiliate Newsletter Svc., 1992—; provider mgr. Conn. Dept. Edn., 1994-98; mem. Legis. Task Force on ednl. tech., 1995-97; mem. Legis. Task Force on tchrs. retirement health ins. sys., 2000-2001; mem. Conn. stakeholders com. Nat. Bd. Profl. Tchg. Stds, 1995—, cons. 1995; mem. educator preparation program rev. com. Conn. State Bd. Edn., 1996-99; mem. nat. parent-tchr. adv. coun. Am. Online; presenter Nat. Sch. Bd. Assn. Tech. Conf., 1995, 96, 97, 98; keynote spkr. Minn. High Success Consortium, 1997; mem. bd. examiners Nat. Coun. Accreditation Tchr. Edn.; mem. tech. adv. commn. Nat. Coun. State Edn. Affiliates, 1999-2001; presenter NEA, Chgo., 2000; mem. task force on Conn. low performing schs. Assoc. editor: Logo Activities, 1985; writer, editor numerous teaching guides. Pres. U. Conn. Friends of Soccer, 1987-89; corporator Newington (Conn.) Children's Hosp., 1978-98; mem. Vernon Rep. Town Com., 1978-98; celebrant Celebration of Excellence Conn. State Dept. Edn., 1991, 95, 99; bd. govs. Conn. Children's Hosp., 1995—; mem. adv. bd. Vernon Law Enforcement Block Grant, 1997-2000; mem. Vernon Recreation Commn., 1978-84, chmn., 1982-84; mem. Vernon Traffic Authority, 1988-94, 96—, vice chair, 1996—; spl. dep. sheriff Tolland County, Conn., 1977-82; notary pub., Conn., 1972—, registered lobbyist Conn. gen. assembly. Recipient Ofcl. Citation of Recognition Conn. Gen. Assembly, 1991, 95, 96, Celebration of Excellence Emeritus award Conn. State Dept. Edn., 1999; nominated Disney Tchr. awards, 2000. Mem.: NEA (design com. 1995, conv. del. 1995, 1996, presenter 1995, 2000, tchr./cons. Washington 1995—, panelist N.E. regional leaders conf. Phila. 1997, panelist N.E. regional leaders conf. Rochester 1999), ASCD, Conn. Computer Educators, Conn. Edn. Assn. (editl. bd. 1991—, presenter Mid-winter confs. 1995, presetner Summer Leadership confs. 1993—2001), Nat. Coun. State Edn. Affiliates (tech. com. 1999), Shriners, Elks, Masons, Delta Kappa Epsilon, Phi Delta Kappa (chpt. pres. 1994—96, exec. bd. 1991—, internat. doctoral dissertation com., selection com. 1995). Roman Catholic. Avocations: racquetball, cycling, skiing. Home: 105 Maple Ave Vernon Rockville CT 06066-5400 Office: Connecticut Edn Assn Capitol Pl 21 Oak St #500 Hartford CT 06106

RODEN, MARTIN S. engineering educator, writer; b. N.Y.C., Aug. 14, 1942; s. Leonard and Rose Roden. BSEE, Poly. U., N.Y.C., 1963; MSEE, Poly. U., 1965; PhD, Kensington U., 1982. Staff engr. Bell Tel. Labs., Whippany, NJ, 1963—68; prof. Calif. State U., L.A., 1968—. Cons. Hughes Aircraft, Fullerton, Calif., 1972—94. Author: (textbooks) Electronic Design, 2001. Bd. chair United Way, San Gabriel Valley, Calif., 1994. Named Disting. Engring. Educator of Yr., Engrs. Coun., L.A., 1997; recipient Excellence in Tchg. award, AT&T, 1990. Fellow: Inst. for Advancement of Engring.; mem.: IEEE (sr.; chair L.A. chpt. 1999—, Millennium medal 2000), Am. Soc. Engring. Edn. Office: Calif State U LA 5151 State University Dr Los Angeles CA 90032 Fax: 323-343-4547. E-mail: mroden@calstatela.edu.

RODENBAUGH, MARCIA LOUISE, retired elementary school educator; b. Pitts., Nov. 11, 1942; d. F. Thomas and Lucy Indiana (Fry) Wimer; m. John Anthony Lee, Mar. 21, 1964 (div. Nov. 1971); m. Richard Allan Rodenbaugh, Aug. 3, 1975 (div. Dec. 1989); stepchildren: Ken, Tiffany, Tricia. BA in Edn., Westminster Coll., New Wilmington, Pa., 1964, MEd in Remedial Reading, 1966. Tchr. North Hills Sch. Dist., Pitts., 1964-69, Ctrl. Bucks Schs., Doylestown, 1969-92, sabatical, 1993—2001. Fellow Pa. Writing Project, West Chester U., 1990; presenter in field. Author children's books: Marci Books (set of 6), 1983-99. Pres. Maple Leaf Day Care Ctr. Bd., Warminster, Pa., 1971; pres. Wesley Coll. Parents Assn., Dover, Del., 1985-86; vol. Meals on Wheels, Phila. inner-city schs.; local judge History Day, Ursinus Coll.; home tutor. Mem. NEA, AAUW, Pa. Edn. Assn., Ctrl. Bucks Edn. Assn. Republican. Presbyterian. Avocations: skiing, sailing, writing, piano, church choir. Home: 7-16 Aspen Way Doylestown PA 18901-2756 Office: Ctrl Bucks Sch Dist 315 Weldon Dr Doylestown PA 18901-3525

RODENBECK, SVEN ERICH, environmental engineer; b. Ft. Eustis, Va., Oct. 2, 1955; s. Eric Otto and Herma (Grawi) R.; m. Pamela Jo Foster, July 27, 1991; children: Erika Hahn, Johanna Sophia. AA in Gen. Studies, St. Petersburg Jr. Coll., 1975; BS in Gen. Studies, BS in Environ. Engring., U. Ctrl. Fla., 1978; MS in Environ. Engring., U. Md., 1983; ScD in Environ. Health, Pub. Health, Tulane U., 1997. Registered profl. engr., Md., Fla.; diplomate AAEE. Capt. USPHS, 1999, field engr. Indian Health Svc. Mont., 1979, field engr. Rocky Boy (Mont.) Indian Reservation, 1979-81; environ. engr. pollution control sect., environ. protection br. Divsn. Safety, NIH, Bethesda, Md., 1981-86, environ. compliance officer environ. protection br., 1986-87; environ. engr. office health assessment Agy. for Toxic Substances and Disease Registry, Atlanta, 1987-89, environ. engr. med. waste group, office of assoc. adminstr., 1989-90, environ. engr. cons. divsn. health assessment and cons., 1990-91; environ. engr. cons. Tulane U. Sch. Pub. Health and Tropical Medicine, New Orleans, 1991-93; environ. engr. cons., divsn. health assessment and cons. Agy. for Toxic Substances and Disease Registry, Atlanta, 1993-95, acting sect. chief health assessment and cons. divsn., 1995-96, environ. engr. cons. divsn. health assessment and cons., 1996-98, sect. chief health assessment and cons. divsn., 1998—; chief of staff, chief engr. USPHS, 1999—. Water quality officer Nat. Scout Jamboree, Ft. A.P. Hill, Va., 1989, chief of staff PHS chief engineer, 1999—. Contbr. articles to profl. publs.; author report to congress: The Public Health Implications of Medical Waste, 1990. Named PHS Engr. of Yr., NSPE, 1997; recipient numerous USPHS awards , including Commendation medal, 1987, 1990, 2001, Achievement medal, 1984, 1989, citation, 1981, Surgeon Gen.'s Exemplary Svc. medal, 1996, Field Med. Readiness Badge, 1996. Mem. ASCE, Am. Acad. Environ. Engrs. (diplomate, trustee), Water Environ. Fedn., Nat. Wildlife Fedn., Assn. of Mil. Surgeons of U.S. (life), Nat. Audubon Soc., Ret. Officers Assn., Commd. Officers Assn. of USPHS, Consumers Union (life), UCF Alumni Assn., Soc. Am. Mil. Engrs. (Hollis medal 2001), Delta Tau Delta. Lutheran. Home: 1229 Hadaway Ct Lawrenceville GA 30043-4668 Office: Mailstop E-32 1600 Clifton Rd NE Atlanta GA 30329-4018 E-mail: srodenbeck@cdc.gov.

RODENBERGER, CHARLES ALVARD, aerospace engineer, consultant; b. Muskogee, Okla., Sept. 11, 1926; s. Darcy Owen and Kathryn Martha (Percival) R.; m. Molcie Lou Halsell, Sept. 3, 1949; children: Kathryn Sue Wilcox, Charles Mark. Student, U. Ark., 1944-45; BS in Gen. Engring., Okla. State U., 1948; MSM.E., So. Meth. U., 1959; PhD in Aero. Engring., U. Tex.-Austin, 1968. Registered profl. engr., Tex. Petroleum engr. Amoco Oil Co., Levelland, Tex., 1948-51; chief engr. McGregor Bros., Odessa, 1953; petroleum engr. Gen. Crude Oil Co., Hamlin, 1954; sr. design engr. Gen. Dynamics, Ft. Worth, 1954-60; aerospace engr. NASA, Houston, summer 1962; prof. aerospace engring. Tex. A&M U., College Station, 1960-82, prof. emeritus, 1982—; chmn. bd. Meiller Research, Inc., 1967-82; pres. JETS, Inc., N.Y.C., 1977-79; cons. Southwest Research Inst., Gen. Motors Corp., Gen. Dynamics. Patentee hypervelocity gun and orthotic device. Served with USAAF, 1945; served with USAF, 1951-53. NSF fellow, 1964-65; recipient Disting. Teaching award Tex. A&M U., 1962 Fellow AIAA (assoc.); mem. Nat. Soc. Profl. Engrs. (v.p. 1980-81), Tex. Soc. Profl. Engrs., ASME, Am. Soc. for Engring. Edn., Sigma Xi. Methodist. Home: 8377 FM 2228 Baird TX 79504-4813 E-mail: crodenberg@aol.com.

RODENBURG, CLIFTON GLENN, lawyer; b. Jamestown, N.D., Apr. 5, 1949; s. Clarence and Dorothy Irene (Peterman) R.; m. Donna Michele Stockman, Mar. 1, 1980. BS, N.D. State U., 1971; JD, U. N.D., 1974; M.L.I.R., Mich. State U., 1976. Bar: N.D. 1974, U.S. Dist. Ct. N.D. 1974, U.S. Ct. Appeals (8th cir.) 1974, Minn. 1980, U.S. Supreme Ct. 1980, S.D. 1983, Nebr. 1984, U.S. Dist. Ct. Minn. 1984, U.S. Dist. Ct. Nebr. 1984, Wis. 1985, U.S. Dist. Ct. Wis. 1985, Mont. 1986, U.S. Dist. Ct. Mont. 1986, bd. cert. Creditors' Rights Law, Am. Bd. Cert. Ptnr. Johnson, Rodenburg & Lauinger, Fargo, N.D., 1976—; pres., gen. counsel Rodenburg Group, Inc., 1980—. Contbg. editor: The Developing Labor Law, 1976-80; drafter N.D. garnishment statutes, 1982. Mem. Acad. Comml. and Bankruptcy Law Specialists.

RODENHAUSEN, JOHN E. sales executive; BS in Bus. Adminstrn., Mktg., Ursinus Coll, Collegeville Pa.; student elec. engring., Pa. State U., U.S. Marine Corps. Asst. engr. . asst. tech. contract mgr. Burroughs Corp., 1965—68; regional sales mgr., OEM mktg. mgr., Mohawk Data Scis. Corp., 1968—75; sales exec. Digital Equipment Corp., 1975—79; sales exec. to dist. mgr. Harris Corp. Info. Terminal Groups, 1979—83; dir. ctrl. area Motorola Computer Systems, 1984—86; strategic acct. mgr. Digital Equip. Corp., 1986—93; corp. accts. mgr. Exide Electronics Corp., 1993—96; dir. data ctr. group APC, 1997—2000; mktg. cons. Caterpillar Corp., 2000; v.p. sales Catalyst Power/ABB Corp., 2001—. Home: 3006 Wintergreen Dr Carlsbad CA 92008

RODER, HANS MARTIN, retired physicist, consultant; b. Schenectady, N.Y., June 30, 1930; s. Johann Nikolaus and Elsa Margarethe (von Kujawa) R.; m. Mary Margaret Ball, Aug. 4, 1951; children: Jenny Brooks, Nicholas, Renate Pearson. BA in Chemistry, U. Colo., 1955, postgrad. in chemistry and physics, 1955-60. Physicist divsn. cryogenics Nat. Inst. Stds. and Tech. (formerly Nat. Bur. Stds.), Boulder, Colo., 1955-66, leader data compilation group, 1966-73, physicist divsn. thermophysics, 1973-87. V.p., sec. Doggie Biscuits, Inc., Breckenridge, Colo., 1989—. Contbr. to books: Technology and Uses of Liquid Hydrogen, 1964, Transport Properties of Fluids, 1990; editor: The Nat. Ski Patrol Ski Mountaineering Man., 1980; contbr. over 75 articles to profl. jours. Patrol leader Nat. Ski Patrol, Loveland Basin, Colo., 1962-87, ski mountaineering advisor, Denver, 1978-85. 1st lt. AUS, 1952-54. Recipient Gold Medal award U.S. Dept. Commerce, 1966, Tech. and Utilization award NASA, 1967, 68, 70, 71; R.B. Scott Meml. award Cryogenic Engring. Conf., 1969. Avocations: skiing, hiking, mountain climbing. Home: PO Box 684 340 W Buffalo Dillon CO 80435

RODGERS, BILLY RUSSELL, chemical engineer, research scientist; b. Fitzgerald, Ga., Sept. 5, 1936; s. Jimmie R. and Ruby Doris (Morris) R.; divorced; children: Cheryl, Donna, Angie, Rusty. AA, U. Fla., 1956, BSChemE with high honors, 1966, MS in Engring., 1967; PhD, U. Tenn., 1980. Project leader Shell Devel. Co., 1968-72; group leader Keene Corp. Fluid Handling, Cookeville, Tenn., 1972-74, Oak Ridge (Tenn.) Nat. Lab., 1974-92; sr. engr. Walk Haydel & Assocs., New Orleans, 1992-94; pres. Rodgers USA Enterprises, Orange Park, Fla., 1992—, Intelligent Cons., Orange Park, 1993—; qualifying agt./mgr. Rodgers Constrn. Co., 1996—. Author 3 books in field; contbr. articles to profl. publs. Fellow AIChE (bd. dirs. 1993-97, chmn. fuels and petrochem. divsn. 1992-95, chmn. program com. fuels and petrochem. divsn. 1990-92). Republican. Achievements include 1 patent in field. Avocation: computers. Office: Rodgers USA Enterprises 794 Foxridge Center Dr Orange Park FL 32065-8716

RODGERS, CAROLYN MARIE, literature educator, writer; b. Chgo. d. Clarence and Bazella Helen Rodgers. BA, Roosevelt U., Chgo., 1981; MA, U. Chgo., 1984. Literary anthology adviser Harold Washington Jr. Coll., Chgo.; English lectr., creative writing instr. Columbia Coll. Contbr. poems to jours., articles to profl. jours.; author: (novels) Speak as Liberators, Natural Process, Brothers and Sisters, Spectrum in Black, The Black Poets, To Gwen, With Love, Jump Bad, Black Spirits, Purpose in Literature, Geography of Poets, To Hoyt W. Fuller/Homage, Understanding the New Black Poetry, No More Masks, Giant Talk, You Better Believe It, Exploring Life Through Literature, Counterpoint, I had been Hungry All the Years, Contemporary Black Poetry, Black Sister Anthology, Renewal, Sturdy Black Bridges, Confirmation, No Crystal Stairs, Nommo, The Souls of My Black Sisters, No More Masks, In Search of Color Everywhere, Daughters of Africa, Language Issues, Black Women Writers 1950-1980. Recipient Author's Poet Laureate award, Soc. Midland, award, Nat. Endowment of the Arts, 1970; fellow Gwendolyn Brooks fellowship; grantee Pen grants. Roman Catholic. Address: PO Box 804271 Chicago IL 60680-4104 Office: Eden Press PO 8084 Chicago IL 60680 also: PO Box 804271 Chicago IL 60680

RODGERS, CINDY WHITFIELD, artist; b. Dallas, Jan. 19, 1955; d. Harold D. and Phena D. Whitfield; m. Robert E. Rodgers, May 1, 1981. Student, Kans. U., 1973—75. Travel agt. Donacyn Travel, Kansas City, Kans., 1975—79, Preston Travel, Dallas, 1980—82; mgr. Shade Tree Enginetrics, Nevada, 1982—2001; self employed painter, 1990—. Chmn. bd. dirs. Automobili Italiane Car Show, Dallas, 1993—97; bd. dirs. Corinthian Vintage Auto Racing, Dallas, 1998—; paintings on exhibit Montecello Gallery, Dallas. Recipient Best of Show, Automobili Italiane Concours, 1990, 2d place, Corinthian Vintage Auto Racing, 2001. Mem.: Oil Painters Assn., Outdoor Painters Soc., Assoc. Creative Artists (2d pl. mini-show 2001). Office: Shad Tree Enginetrics 1101 W Cook Nevada TX 75173

RODGERS, CLIFTON EUGENE, trade association administrator; b. Harrisburg, Pa., Sept. 15, 1954; s. Clifton Eugene and Jean Rodgers; m. Shelley Church Rodgers; children: Henry A. children: John S. BA in History and Lit., Hampshire Coll., 1978. Corp. sales rep. Mellon Bank, NA, Pitts., 1979—81; spl. asst. to exec. v.p.s Fannie Mae, Washington, 1981—83; mgr. secondary mktg. The First Boston Corp., N.Y.C., 1983—85; v.p. F. S. Phillips Co., Inc., Bethesda, Md., 1985—91; dir. Office of Bus. Liaison U.S. Dept. Treasury, Washington, 1991—93; asset mgr. J.E. Robert Co., Alexandria, Va., 1993—94; v.p. Legg Mason, Bethesda, 1994—96; sr. v.p. The Real Estate Roundtable, Washington, 1996—. Dir. Starlight Children's Found., L.A.,

1998—, founding pres. Washington, 1998—2001; vestry mem. Christ Ch.; pres. The Decade Soc., 1989—90. Mem.: Urban Land Inst. (program com. 2000—02). Episcopalian. Office: The Real Estate Roundtable 1420 New York Ave NW Washington DC 20005 Office Fax: 202-639-8442. Business E-Mail: crodgers@rer.org.

RODGERS, DANIEL TRACY, history educator; b. Darby, Pa., Sept. 29, 1942; s. Oliver Eliot and Dorothy (Welch) R.; m. Irene Wylie, 1971; children: Peter Samuel, Dwight Oliver. AB, BS in Engring., Brown U., 1965; PhD in History, Yale U., 1973. Instr. history U. Wis., Madison, 1971-73, asst. prof., 1973-78, assoc. prof., 1978-80; assoc. prof. history Princeton (N.J.) U., 1980-86, prof., 1986-98, Henry Charles Lea prof. history, 1998—, chair, 1988-95, 97-98. Fulbright lectr., Frankfurt, Fed. Republic Germany, 1983-84. Author: The Work Ethic in Industrial America, 1860-1920 (Frederick Jackson Turner award 1978), 1978, Contested Truths: Keywords in American Politics since Independence, 1987, Atlantic Crossings: Social Politics in a Progressive Age, 1998 (Ellis W. Hawley award 1979, George Louis Beer prize 1979). Recipient Chancellor's award U. Wis., Madison, 1978, Ellis W. Hawley award Am. Hist. Assn., 1999; Am. Coun. Learned Socs. fellow, 1976, NEH fellow, 1987-88, Ctr. for Advanced Study in Behavioral Scis. fellow, 1991-92; Woodrow Wilson Ctr. fellow, 1999-2000. Office: Princeton U Dept History Princeton NJ 08544-0001 E-mail: drodgers@princeton.edu.

RODGERS, FRANK, librarian; b. Darlington, Eng., July 28, 1927; came to U.S., 1956; s. Charles Bede and Frances (Page) R.; m. Sarah Louise Edelson, Dec. 18, 1971; children: Hilda Marie, Norah Frances. BA with honors, King's Coll., U. Durham, 1947; diploma librarianship, London U., 1952. Libr. Poplar Tech. Coll., London, 1951-53, St. Martin's Sch. Art, 1953-56; sr. libr. adult svcs. divsn. Akron (Ohio) Pub. Libr., 1956-59; asst. reference libr. U. Ill., 1959-64; chief reference libr., then asst. dir. pub. svcs. Pa. State U. Librs., 1965-69; dir. Portland (Oreg.) State U. Libr., 1969-79; dir. librs. U. Miami, Fla., 1979-97. Mem. Oreg. adv. coun. librs., 1973-74; bd. dirs. Pacific N.W. Bibliog. Ctr., 1973-77; tech. adv. com. librs. Columbia Regional Assn. Govts., 1976-79; vis. fellow U. Southampton Eng., 1975-76; pres. Oreg. Libr. Assn., 1974-75; mem. nominating com. Southeastern Libr. Network, 1984-85; bd. dirs. S.E. Fla. Libr. Info. Network, 1984-97, pres. 1991-92; mem. exec. coun. Assn. Caribbean U. Rsch. and Instl. Librs., 1985-88; chmn. local organizing com. for 1981 and 1987 confs. in Miami; mem. Fla. Libr. Network Coun., 1985-91; NEH challenge grant rev. panel, 1987, Howard U. ann. inspection team, 1989, Reaffirmation com., Tex. Christian U., 1993. Author, editor various libr. publs., guides. Sr. fellow Grad. Sch. Libr. and Info. Sci. UCLA, 1983; grantee Coun. Libr. Resources, 1975-76. Fellow Libr. Assn. U.K.; mem. ALA, Assn. Rsch. Librs. (office mgmt. studies adv. com. 1981-83, stats. and measurements com. 1993-96), Assn. Specialized and Coop. Libr. Agys. (membership promotion com. 1994-96, chair 1990 program com.), Assn. Southeastern Rsch. Librs. (chmn. membership com. 1982-97). Address: 7a Avenida Norte #25 Antigua Guatemala E-mail: frodgers@conexion.com.gt.

RODGERS, FREDERIC BARKER, judge; b. Albany, N.Y., Sept. 29, 1940; s. Prentice Johnson and Jane (Weed) R.; m. Valerie McNaughton, Oct. 8, 1988; 1 child: Gabriel Moore. AB, Amherst Coll., 1963; JD, Union U., 1966. Bar: N.Y. 1966, U.S. Ct. Mil. Appeals 1968, Colo. 1972, U.S. Supreme Ct. 1974, U.S. Ct. Appeals (10th cir.) 1981, U.S. Ct. Appeals (fed. cir.) 2001. Chief dep. dist. atty., Denver, 1972-73; commr. Denver Juvenile Ct., 1973-79; mem. Mulligan Reeves Teasley & Joyce, P.C., Denver, 1979-80; pres. Frederic B. Rodgers, P.C., Breckenridge, Colo., 1980-89; ptnr. McNaughton & Rodgers, Central City, 1989-91; county ct. judge Gilpin County Combined Cts., 1987—. Presiding mcpl. judge cities of Breckenridge, Blue River, Black Hawk, Central City, Edgewater, Empire, Idaho Springs, Silver Plume and Westminster, Colo., 1978-96; chmn. com. on mcpl. ct. rules of procedure Colo. Supreme Ct., 1984-96; mem. gen faculty Nat. Jud. Coll. U. Nev., Reno, 1990—, elected to faculty coun., 1993-99 (chair 1999). Author: (with Dilweg, Fretz, Murphy and Wicker) Modern Judicial Ethics, 1992; contbr. articles to profl. jours. Mem. Colo. Commn. on Children, 1982-85, Colo. Youth Devel. Coun., 1989-98, Colo. Family Peace Task Force, 1994-96. Served with JAGC, U.S. Army, 1967-72; to maj. USAR, 1972-88. Decorated Bronze Star with oak leaf cluster, Air medal. Recipient Outstanding County Judge award Colo. 17th Judicial Dist. Victim Adv. Coalition, 1991; Spl. Community Svc. award Colo. Am. Legion, 1979. Fellow Am. Bar Found., Colo. Bar. Found. (life); mem. ABA (jud. div. exec. coun. 1989-2000, vice-chair 1996-97, chair-elect 1997, chair 1998-99, mem. Ho. of Dels. 1993—, jud. divsn. del. to ABA nominating com. 2000-01, bd. govs. Dist. 11 2001—), Colo. Bar Assn. (bd. govs. 1986-88, 90-92, 93-99), Continental Divide Bar Assn., Denver Bar Assn. (bd. trustees 1979-82), First Jud. dist. Bar Assn. (trustee 2000—), Nat. Conf. Spl. Ct. Judges (chmn. 1989-90), Colo. County Judges Assn. (pres. 1995-96), Colo. Mcpl. Judges Assn. (pres. 1986-87), Colo. Trial Judges Coun. (v.p. 1994-95, sec. 1996-97), Denver Law Club (pres. 1981-82), Colo. Women's Bar Assn., Am. Judicature Soc., Nat. Coun. Juvenile and Family Ct. Judges, Federalist Soc. for Law and Pub. Policy Studies, Judge Advs. Assn., Univ. Club (Denver), Arlberg Club (Winter Park), Marines Meml. Club (San Francisco), Rotary (charter pres. Peak to Peak 2000—, Paul Harris fellow 1996). Episcopalian. Office: Gilpin County Justice Ctr Central City CO 80427-0398 E-mail: frederic.rodgers@judicial.state.co.us.

RODGERS, GERALDINE ELLEN, retired elementary educator, researcher; b. Newark, Dec. 20, 1925; d. Charles Joseph and Katharine Geraldine (Murtha) R. BS in Elem. Edn. magna cum laude, Fairleigh Dickinson U., 1963; MA in Nat. History, William Paterson Coll., 1967. Elem. tchr. Wayne (N.J.) Twp. Schs., 1963-85. Sabbatical leave to observe the teaching of beginning reading in U.S., Holland, Sweden, Germany, Austria and France, 1977-78; rschr. in field, 1978—; spkr. in field. Author: Why Jacques, Johann and Jan Can Read, 1979, The Case for the Prosecution in the Trial of Silent Reading Comprehension Tests, 1981, The Wary Reader's Guide to Psychol-inguistics: Subjective VS. Objective Readers, 1982, The Flat Earth of American Reading Instruction, 1983, A Counter-Report on the Report of the Commission on Reading, 1985, The History of Beginning Reading: From Teaching by "Sound" to Teaching by "Meaning", 1995, 2d edit., 2001, The Hidden Story, 1998; contbr. articles to profl. jours. Vol. Lyndhurst Twp. Schs., 1998—2002. Republican. Roman Catholic. Avocations: gardening, traveling, classical music, natural history.

RODGERS, GILBERT M. energy executive; s. Dana B. and Emma Katherine M. Rodgers; m. Janet C. Lowers, Sept. 11, 1966; children: Anna, Andrew. B in Elec. Engring., Union Coll., 1962; MS, Ohio State U., 1963; PhD, Stanford U., 1972; grad. cert. in bus. mgmt., Harvard U., 2002. V.p. corp. devel. Data Resources Inc., Lexington, Mass., 1978—85; v.p. Dun & Bradstreet, Cambridge, 1986—89; vis. prof. Inst. de Estudios Superiores de la Empresa, Barcelona, 1988—89; co-founder, exec. v.p. Faneuil Group, Boston, 1989—96; pres. Faneuil Internat., 1996—97; dir. Cambridge (Mass.) Energy Rsch. Assocs., 1997—. Mem. adv. bd. FTTX Systems, Clinton, Wash., 2000—. Musician: Classical Chorals, 2002 (FEA Cert. of Outstanding Achievement, 1975). Mem. zoning com. Capitol Hill Restoration Soc., Washington, 1973—77. Fellow Sci. and Tech. fellow - Brookings Instn., Ford Found., 1968—69; grantee, U.S. Army Corps of Engrs., 1963. Mem.: Internat. Assn. Energy Economists, Assn. Energy Engineers, U.S. Equestrian Assn., Norfolk Hunt Club. Avocations: competetive horseback riding, sailing, swimming. Home: 283 North St Medfield MA 02052 Office: Cambridge Energy Rsch Assocs 20 University Rd Cambridge MA 02138 Office Fax: 617-497-0423. Personal E-mail: gilrodgers@aol.com. E-mail: grodgers@cera.com.

RODGERS, GRACE ANNE, university official; b. South Bend, Ind., Apr. 19, 1936; d. Morris and Barbara Mae (Hamm) Morrow; m. Eugene M. Rodgers, July 7, 1956; children: Craig Eugene, Kimberly Sue. BS, Ind. State U., 1981; pub. mgmt. cert., Ind. U., South Bend, 1991, MPA, 1993. Dir. spl. programs Ivy Tech. State Coll., South Bend, 1990-94, mktg. cons., 1994; mem. assoc. faculty dept. pub. affairs--non-profit marketing and environ. Ind. U., 1994—, dir. internships-student svcs. Sch. Pub.-Environ. Affairs, 1994—, dir. cmty. links, 1997—. Author: (manuals) Resume and Beyond, 1990, Strategic Marketing Plan, 1994. Mem. Youth Svcs. Bur., South Bend Recipient Indiana U. South Bend Student Gov. Lifetime Achievement award. Mem. Ind. U. Sch. Pub. end Environ. Affairs Alumni Assn. (adv. coun. 1993—), Ind. U.-South Bend Alumni Assn., Ind. State U. Alumni Assn., Phi Theta Kappa (hon., award for outstanding svc. 1993), Pi Alpha Alpha (sec. 1996—). Republican. Methodist. Avocations: travel, reading, classical music. Home: 17120 Killarney Ct Granger IN 46530-9771 Office: Ind U 1800 Mishawaka Ave South Bend IN 46615-1621 E-mail: profgrac@aol.com.

RODGERS, JAMES BEALL, surgeon; b. Martinsburg, W.Va., 1923; s. Decatur Hedges and Anne Leitch (Lancaster) R.; m. Anne English Colcord, Jan. 2, 1950; children: David, Alan, Alice. BA, U. Va., 1945, MD, 1948. Diplomate Am. Bd. Surgery. Intern Colum-Presbyn. Med. Ctr., N.Y.C., 1948-50, resident in surgery, 1952-57; assoc. clin. prof. surgery Columbia P&S, 1956-92; sr. attending surgeon emeritus St. Lukes, Roosevelt Hosp. Ctr., N.Y.C., 1957-92, ret., 1992. Fellow ACS; mem. Century Assn.

RODGERS, JAMES FOSTER, association executive, economist; b. Columbus, Ga., Jan. 15, 1951; s. Laban Jackson and Martha (Jackson) R.; m. Cynthia Lynne Bathurst, Aug. 20, 1975. BA, U. Ala., Tuscaloosa, 1973; PhD, U. Iowa, 1980. Fed. intern Office Rsch. and Stats., Social Security Adminstrn., Washington, 1976-77; rsch. assoc. Ctr. Health Policy Rsch., AMA, Chgo., 1979-80, rsch. dir., 1980-82, asst. to dep. exec. v.p. AMA, 1982-85; dir. AMA Ctr. Health Policy Rsch., 1985-96, v.p. health policy, 1996—. Contbr. articles on health econs. to profl. jours. Pharm. Mfrs. Assn. grantee, 1978; NSF grantee, 1978; Hohenberg fellow, 1969-70 Mem. Am. Econ. Assn., Am. Soc. Assn. Exec., Am. Statis. Assn. Home: 2233 N Orchard St Chicago IL 60614-3713 Office: AMA Ctr for Health Policy Rsch 515 N State St Chicago IL 60610-4325

RODGERS, JANET AHALT, nursing educator, dean; b. Hershey, Pa. d. Harold A. and Margaret L. (Bittle) Ahalt; m. Terry C. Rodgers. BSN, Wagner Coll., 1957; MA in Psychiat.-Mental Health Nursing, NYU, 1964, PhD Nursing, 1971; cert., N.Y. Med. Coll., 1973. RN, N.Y. Staff N.Y. State Psychiat. Inst., N.Y.C., 1957-59, head nurse, 1959-61; asst. DON Psychiat. Treatment Ctr., 1961-62; group therapist Creedmoor State Hosp., Queens, N.Y., 1963; instr. Wagner Coll., S.I., 1964-66, asst. prof., 1966-68, lectr. psychiat. nursing, 1969-70; asst. prof. psychiat. nursing Lehman Coll. CUNY, 1971-74, coord. psychiat. nursing Lehman Coll., 1971-76, assoc. prof., dep. chmn., 1974-77; prof., chairperson dept. nursing Old Dominion U., Norfolk, Va., 1977-79; cons., 1979-81; prof., chair dept. nursing Lycoming Coll., Williamsport, Pa., 1981-87; dean., prof. Philip Y. Hahn Sch. Nursing U. San Diego, 1987—. Vis. assoc. prof. Sch. Nursing U. Pa., 1981; presenter in field. Contbr. articles to profl. jours. Mem. adv. bd. Lee Hawkins Endowment Fund, Norfolk, Va., 1978-83, N.Y.C. Com. for Children, 1973-77, Bronx Health Manpower Consortium Bd., 1975-76, Ea. Va. Health Edn. Consortium, 1977-79; mem. health adv. bd. Divine Providence Hosp.-Cmty. Mental Health Ctr., 1985-87; bd. dirs. Regional Home Health Svcs., Williamsport, Pa., 1982-87, Divine Providence Hosp., Williamsport, 1986-87, San Diego Hospice, 1989-92, Am. Lung Assn. San Diego and Imperial Counties, 1994-96, Am. Heart Assn., 1996-2000, Assn. Calif. Nurse Leaders, 1996-98; bd. trustees Scripps Health, San Diego, 1998—, The Whittier Inst. for Diabetes, 2001; exec. ptnr. Cmty. Health Improvement Ptnrs., San Diego County, 1999—. Recipient Diane F. Cooper Lifetime Achievement Award, 2002. Fellow Am. Orthopsychiat. Assn., Am. Acad. Nursing; mem. ANA, Am. Assn. Colls. Nursing (bd. dirs. 1987-94, pres.-elect 1990-92, pres. 1992-94, Wagner Coll. Alumni Assn. Achievement award 1977), Wagner Coll. Nat. Alumni Assn. (bd. dirs. 1999—), NYU Alumni Assn. (v.p. 1970-72, Mary Barr Alumni award Sch. Nursing 1993), Pi Lambda Theta, Kappa Delta Pi, Phi Kappa Phi, Sigma Theta Tau (Beta Upsilon and Zeta Mu chpts.). Office: U San Diego Hahn Sch Nurs & Health Svcs 5998 Alcala Park San Diego CA 92110-2492 E-mail: rodgers@acosd.edu.*

RODGERS, JOHN JOSEPH, III, educational administration consultant, educator; b. Jamaica, N.Y., Oct. 13, 1941; s. John Joseph Rodgers, Edith (McInerney) Rodgers; m. Iris Rodgers; children: Janet, John Joseph IV, Yvette. BS, Fordham U., 1962; Profl. diploma, St. Johns U., 1970, EdD, 1979; postgrad., CUNY, Flushing. Asst. prin. N.Y.C. Bd. Edn., 1972-82; prin. Howard T. Herber Sch., Malverne, N.Y., 1982-85, Norman Thomas H.S., N.Y.C., 1988-96, Matawan Regional H.S., Aberdeen, N.J., 1996-97; cons. on ednl. adminstrn. Valley Stream, NY, 1999—; prof. math. Farleigh Dickinson U., Madison, N.J., 1999-2001; prof. ednl. adminstrn. Coll. New Rochelle, N.Y., 2000-01; dean acad. affairs Five Towns Coll., Dix Hills, NY, 2001—02; acad. dean Bus. Informatics Ctr., The Coll. for Bus., Valley Stream, 2002—. Mem. ASCD, Am. Assn. Sch. Adminstrs., Math. Assn. Am., Nat. Assn. Secondary Sch. Prins. Home: 350-34 N Corona Ave Valley Stream NY 11580-3403 E-mail: jrodgers@thecollegeforbusiness.com., pelicula419@hotmail.com.

RODGERS, LAWRENCE RODNEY, physician, educator; b. Clovis, N.Mex., Mar. 9, 1920; s. Samuel Frank and Lillian (O'Connor) R.; m. Ivy Lorna Piper, Aug. 6, 1943; children: Lawrence Rodney (dec.), Ivy Elizabeth, George Piper. BS, West Tex. State U., 1940; MD, U. Tex., 1943. Diplomate Am. Bd. Internal Medicine. Intern Phila. Gen. Hosp., 1943-44, resident in medicine, 1946-49; assoc. internist Tumor Inst., U. Tex. M.D. Anderson Hosp., Houston, 1949—; chmn. dept. medicine Hermann Hosp., 1966-71; assoc. prof. clin. medicine Baylor U., 1949—; prof. clin. medicine U. Tex., 1972—. Editor: Harris County Physician, 1976-80. Bd. dirs. Tex. Med. Found.; trustee Houston Mus. Med. Sci., 1981. Served to maj. M.C. AUS, 1944-46. Decorated Bronze Star with two oak leaf clusters; recipient Ashbel Smith Disting. Alumnus award U. Tex. Med. Br.-Galveston, 1993, Mastership award Am. Coll. Physicians, 1996. Fellow ACP (gov. for Tex. 1979-83, Laureate Internist Tex. award 1994); mem. AMA (del. 1975-94), Tex. Med. Assn. (elected emeritus), Harris County Med. Soc. (exec. bd. 1978-82, v.p. 1984), Am. Heart Assn., Houston Soc. Internal Medicine (pres. 1974), Houston Acad. Medicine (pres. 1981), Houston Philos. Soc. (pres. 1993-94), Doctor's Club Houston (bd. govs. 1984-88, pres. 1986).

RODGERS, LOUIS DEAN, retired surgeon; b. Centerville, Iowa, Nov. 24, 1930; s. John James and Anna Alice (Spraguer) R.; m. Gretchen Lynn Hendershot, Feb. 19, 1954; children: Cynthia Ann, Elizabeth Dee. MD, U. Iowa, 1960. Diplomate Am. Bd. Surgery. Intern Broadlawns Hosp., Des Moines, 1960-61; resident Meth. Hosp., 1961-65; pvt. practice, 1965-95. Chmn. dept. surgery Iowa Meth. Ctr., Des Moines, 1980-84, chief gen. surgery, 1982-95; clin. assoc. prof. surgery U. Iowa, Iowa City, 1983-95, ret., 1995 . Mem. steering com. gov.'s campaign Iowa Rep. Com., 1982; bd. dirs. Iowa Meth. Med. Found., Des Moines, 1983, Des Moines Synthony, 1984-90, Des Moines Children's Home, 1987-93. Staff sgt. U.S. Army, 1951-54. Recipient Disting. Alumni award Centerville Schs. Found., 1993; named Surg. Tchr. of Yr., Iowa Meth. Med. Ctr., 1978, 84. Fellow ACS (liaison to cancer com. 1973); mem. Western Surg. Assn. (Iowa trauma com. 1983), Iowa Acad. Surgery (pres. 1982-83), Throckmorton Surg. Soc. (pres. 1986), Des Moines Golf and Country. Republican. Home: 13138 Cedar Crest Ln Des Moines IA 50325

RODGERS, LYNNE SAUNDERS, women's health nurse; b. Winchester, Va., May 11, 1956; d. Ronald Otho and Anne Coleman Saunders; m. Joseph Rodgers, Dec. 21, 1985; children: Joseph Anthony, John Robert, Stephanie Lynne. BSN, George Mason U., 1978. Cert. inpatient obstetric nursing, childbirth educator, counselor, Resolve Through Sharing, perinatal grief counselor. Clin. nurse specialist in labor and delivery Bethesda (Md.) Naval Hosp., 1978-87; labor and delivery staff nurse clinician INOVA Fairfax Hosp., Falls Church, Va., 1987—; clinician, staff nurse in obstetrics Fauquier Hosp., Warrenton, 1990—. Recipient finalist, NSAI Song Contests. Mem. Assn. Women's Health Obstetric and Neonatal Nurses. Office: Fauquier Hosp 500 Hospital Dr Warrenton VA 20186-3099 E-mail: rodgersl@fauquierhospital.org.

RODGERS, MARY COLUMBRO, English educator, academic administrator, writer; b. Aurora, Ohio, Apr. 17, 1925; d. Nicola and Nancy (DeNicola) Columbro; m. Daniel Richard Rodgers, July 24, 1965; children: Robert, Patricia, Kristine. AB, Notre Dame Coll., 1957; MA, Western Res. U., 1962; PhD, Ohio State U., 1964; postgrad., U. Rome, 1964-65; EdD, Calif. Nat. Open U., 1975, DLitt, 1978. Tchr. English Cleve. elem. schs., 1945-52, Cleve. secondary schs., 1952-62; supr. English student tchrs. Ohio State U., 1962-64; asst. prof. English U. Md., 1965-66; assoc. prof. Trinity Coll., 1967-68; prof. English D.C. Tchrs. Coll., 1968—; pres. Md. Nat. U., 1972—; chancellor Am. Open U., 1965—; dean Am. Open U. Acad.; ret., 2000; ind. rschr., 2002—. Author numerous books and monographs, latest works include: A Short Course in English Composition, 1976, Chapbook of Children's Literature, 1977, Comprehensive Catalogue: The Open University of America System, 1978-80, Open University of America System Source Book, V, VII, VII, 1978, Essays and Poems on Life and Literature, 1979, Modes and Models: Four Lessons for Young Writers, 1981, Open University Structures and Adult Learning, 1982, Papers in Applied English Linguistics, 1982, Twelve Lectures on the American Open University, 1982, English Pedagogy in the American Open University, 1983, Design for Personalized English Graduate Degrees in the Urban University, 1984, Open University English Teaching, 1945-85: Conceptual History and Rationale, 1985, Claims and Counterclaims Regarding Instruction Given in Personalized Degree Residency Programs Completed by Graduates of California National Open University, 1986, The American Open University, 1965 to 1985: History and Sourcebook, 1986, New Design II: English Pedagogy in the American Open University, 1987, The American Open University, 1965 to 1985: A Research Report, 1987, The American Open University and Other Open Universities: A Comparative Study Report, 1988, Poet and Pedagogue in Moscow and Leningrad: A Travel Report, 1989, Foundations of English Scholarship in the American Open University, 1989, Twelve Lectures in Literary Analysis, 1990, Ten Lectures in Literary Production, 1990, Analyzing Fact and Fiction, 1991, Analyzing Poetry and Drama, 1991, Some Successful Literary Research Papers: An Inventory of Titles and Theses, 1991; author 19 publs., 1991-2001. Fulbright scholar U. Rome, 1964-65. Fellow Cath. Scholars; mem. U.S. Distance Learning Assn., Poetry Soc. Am., Nat. Coun. Tchrs. English, Am. Ednl. Rsch. Assn., Am. Acad. Poets, Ohioana Libr. Assn., Pi Lambda Theta. Home and Office: Coll Heights Estates 3916 Commander Dr Hyattsville MD 20782-1027 E-mail: openuniv@aol.com.

RODGERS, ROBERT AUBREY, physicist; b. Huntsville, Ala., May 10, 1967; s. Aubrey and Peggy Joyce Rodgers; m. Rocio Palacios, Oct. 25, 1997. BS, U. Ala., Huntsville, 1990, MS, 1992; MS in Health Physics, Ga. Inst. Tech., 1993; postgrad., U. Tex. Health Sci. Ctr., Houston, 2001—. Diplomate Am. Bd. Radiology Med. Nuclear Physics, Am. Bd. Sci. Nuclear Medicine, Am. Bd. Nuclear Medicine Physics and Instrn., Am. Bd. Radiology Diagnostic Radiologic Physics, Am. Bd. Sci. Nuclear Physics Radiation. Grad. student physics rschr. Polarization and Lens Design Lab., U. Ala., Huntsville, 1991-92; grad. student med. physics rschr. Emory U.-Ga. Inst. Tech., Atlanta, 1992-94; staff med. health physicist, officer USAF, Lackland AFB, Tex., 1996-97, diagnostic med. physics fellow, 1997-98, chief diagnostic med. physics element, 1998-2000; company grade officer of quarter 759 MDTS, 1999; company grade officer of quarter 81 MDSS MDG, 2001; assoc. chief med. physics Keesler AFB, 2000—01; grad. rsch. asst. electron rsch. group dept. radiation physics M.D. Anderson Cancer Ctr., Houston, 2001—. With civilian instrn. program Air Force Inst. Tech. Decorated Air Force Commendation medal with two oack leaf clusters; scholar Honor Scholar, U. Ala., Huntsville, 1988—89, scholar, 1986—87. Mem. Am. Assn. Physicists in Medicine, Health Physics Soc., Air Force Assn., Soc. Photo-Optical Instrumentation Engrs., Soc. Nuclear Medicine. Baptist. Achievements include research on development of scattering polarimeter and measurement/analysis of diffraction grating polarization and efficiency properties, validation of compton scatter and attenuation correction methods for cardiac SPECT imaging.

RODGERS, STEPHEN JOHN, lawyer, physician, consultant; b. Phila., July 10, 1943; s. Harry Edward Rodgers and Antoinette Julia (Battaglini) Muckenfuss; m. Roberta Elaine Rhine, Sept. 21, 1974; children: Abigail Elizabeth, Rebecca Elizabeth. MD, Hahnemann U., 1969; JD, Widener U., 1989. Bar: Pa. 1990, N.J. 1990; med. lic., Pa., Del., N.J. Pvt. practice in family practice and emergency medicine Del. Pain Clinic, Wilmington, 1975-89, asst. dir., 1989-92; pvt. practice as medicolegal cons., 1992—. Mem. Med. Assistance and Health Svcs. Adv. Bd., N.J., 1996-98; chair Task Force on Ind. Med. Exam., Dept. Labor and Industry, Commonwealth of Pa., 1996-98. Comdr. USN, 1968-75; capt. USNR, 1975—; surgeon gen. N.J. Naval Militia Joint Command. Fellow Am. Acad. Family Physicians, Am. Acad. Disability Evaluating Physicians, Am. Acad. Emergency Medicine, Am. Coll. Legal Medicine; mem. Aerospace Med. Assn., Pa. Bar Assn. (health care com. 1991—), Del. Acad. Medicine, N.J. Acad. Family Physicians (ho. of dels. 1989, 90, 91), Vietnam Vets. of Am. Republican. Roman Catholic. Avocations: equestrian, pro bono veterans and disability advocate. Home: PO Box 54 Alloway NJ 08001-0054 Office: Ste 30 1701 Augustine Wilmington DE 19803 E-mail: D.elOccMed@dol.net.

RODGERS, STEVEN EDWARD, tax practitioner, educator; b. Pierre, S.D., Feb. 8, 1947; s. Thomas Edward and Dorothy Zoe (Barker) R.; m. Donna Lynn Joyner, June 10, 1984; 1 child, Michelle Ann. Student, State U. S.D., 1964-65, U. Calif., Berkeley, 1968-72; cert., Coll. for Fin. Planning, 1986-87; fellow, Nat. Tax Practice Inst., 1988-89. CFP, Enrolled Agent. Collection mgr. Cenval Leasing-Ctrl. Bank, Long Beach, Calif., 1972-77; tax preparer Rodgers Tax Svc., Las Vegas, 1977-78; CEO Rainbow Tax Svc. Inc., 1978—. Pres. Rainbow Tax Svc., Inc., Las Vegas, 1978-90. Author: Marketing To Build Your Tax Practice, 1994. Active Amnesty Internat., Mensa; chmn. Best in the West Edn. Found., Las Vegas, 1994—, Nat. Assn. Enrolled Agents Edn. Found., 1995-96. With U.S. Army, 1965-68, Vietnam. Mem. Nat. Assn. Enrolled Agts. (nat. sec. 1989-90, nat. treas. 1991-92, nat. edn. chair 1994-95, named Tax Educator of the Yr., 1995), Nat. Assn. Enrolled Agents Edn. Found. (chair 1995-96), Nev. Soc. Enrolled Agts. (charter pres. 1985-86, fellow edn. found.), So. Nev. Assn. Tax Cons. (pres. 1981-82), Nat. Soc. Pub. Accts., Vietnam Vets. Am. Home: 1101 Cahill Ave Las Vegas NV 89128-3335 Office: Rainbow Tax Svc Inc 6129 Clarice Ave Las Vegas NV 89107-1401

RODGERS, SUZANNE HOOKER, ergonomics consultant, physiologist; b. Rochester, N.Y., Dec. 26, 1939; d. John Ashmead and Priscilla May (Bodman) Rodgers. AB, Vassar Coll., 1961; PhD, U. Rochester Med. Ctr., 1967. Postdoctoral fellow USPHS Middlesex Hosp., London, 1966-68; ergonomist Eastman Kodak Co., Rochester, N.Y., 1968-82; cons., 1982—. Author: Working With Backache, 1985; tech. editor, prin. author Ergonomic Design for People at Work, 1983, 86. Bd. dirs., chmn. com., v.p. Rochester Philharm. Orch. Inc., Rochester, 1969-75; bd. dirs. Opera Theatre Rochester, 1969-75; bd. dirs., chmn. com., pres. Monroe County Bd. Health, Rochester, 1979-88. Mem. Soc. Mfg. Engrs., Human Factors and Ergonomics Soc., (pres. Western N.Y. chpt. 1971-72), Am. Coll. Sports Medicine. Avocations: photography, sailing, gardening, reading, enjoying silent films. Home and Office: 169 Huntington Hls Rochester NY 14622-1121 E-mail: shrodgers@aol.com.

RODGMAN, ALAN, chemist, consultant; b. Aberdare, Wales, Feb. 7, 1924; came to U.S., 1954, naturalized, 1961; s. Arch and Margaret (Llewellyn) R.; m. Doris Curley, June 7, 1947; children: Eric, Paul, Mark. BA in Chemistry, U. Toronto, 1949, MA in Organic Chemistry, 1951, PhD in Organic Chemistry, 1953. Rsch. asst. med. rsch. dept. U. Toronto, 1947-51, rsch. assoc., 1951-54; tchr., courses in organic chemistry, phys. chemistry, math. Chem. Inst. Can., 1951-54; sr. rsch. chemist R.J. Reynolds Tobacco Co., Winston-Salem, N.C., 1954-65, head smoke rsch. sect., 1965-75, mgr. analytical rsch., 1975-76, dir. rsch., 1976-80, dir. fundamental rsch. and devel., 1980-87; cons. in field, 1987—. Adj. prof. Wolfe's U., Maple, Ont., Canada, 1993—. Mem. editorial bd. Tobacco Sci., 1963-67 (Vol. 31 Tobacco Sci. dedicated in his name 1987), Beiträge zur Tabakforschung Internat., 1978-87. Mem. Tobacco Working Group, Nat. Cancer Inst., 1976-77, Tech. Study Group on Cigarette and Little Cigar Fire Safety, 1984-87, Sci. Commn. Cooperation Ctr. for Sci. Rsch. Relative to Tobacco, 1982-84. With Royal Can. Navy, 1942-45. Mem. Coun. for Tobacco Rsch. (industry tech. com. 1956-62), Chem. Inst. Can., Can. Chem. Soc., Am. Chem. Soc., N.Y. Acad. Scis., Sigma Xi Episcopalian. Home: 2828 Birchwood Dr Winston Salem NC 27103-3410

RODIBAUGH, ROBERT KURTZ, retired judge; b. Elkhart County, Ind., July 2, 1916; s. Ralph Leedy and Rose (Kurtz) R.; m. Doris Ann Siekemeyer, Jan. 1, 1942 (dec.); children: David L., Bob K.; m. Eunice Margaret Cline, Nov. 25, 1972. BSc, U. Notre Dame, 1940, JD, 1941. Bar: Ind. 1941, U.S. Dist. Ct. (no. dist.) Ind. 1946, U.S. Ct. Appeals (7th cir.) 1972, U.S. Supreme Ct. 1965. Dep. pros. atty. Ind. 60th Jud. Cir., St. Joseph County, 1948-50, 53-57; judge U.S. Bankruptcy Ct., No. Dist. Ind., South Bend, 1960-99, ret., 1999. Lectr. in law U. Notre Dame, 1973; atty. St. Joseph County Bd. Zoning Appeals, 1958-60. V.p. No. Ind. coun. Boy Scouts Am., 1967-77; bd. dirs. St. Joseph County chpt. ARC, 1970-77. Capt. U.S. Army, 1941-46, PTO. Recipient Silver Beaver award Boy Scouts Am., 1969. Mem. ABA, Seventh Fed. Cir. Bar Assn., Ind. Bar Assn., St. Joseph County Bar Assn. (gov.

1953-56), Comml. Law League, Nat. Conf. Bankruptcy Judges (dir. 1977-79), Exch. Club, Masons, DeMolay Club (Legion of Honor), Shriners, Rotary (South Bend, Ind. chpt.). Office: US Bankruptcy Ct PO Box 7003 401 S Michigan St South Bend IN 46601-2365

RODIGER, WILLIAM KING, telecommunications and media industry consultant; b. Norwalk, Conn., Oct. 6, 1961; s. Walter Gregory and Elizabeth (King) Rodiger; m. Heather L. McKinney, Oct. 20, 1990; 1 child, Jonathan Amory. BS in Physics, Dickinson Coll., 1984; MS in Computer Engring., Syracuse U., 1986. Grad. rsch. asst. N.Y. State Ctr. for Computer Applications/Software Engring., Syracuse, 1985-86; staff engr. IBM Data Systems Divsn., Kingston, N.Y., 1986-89; systems engr. IBM Nat. Sci. Mktg., White Plains, 1989-91; mktg. cons. IBM North Am., Waltham, Mass., 1991—. Patentee NxM round robin switching matrix; coherence control; look-ahead priority arbitration. Trustee Sudbury (Mass.) United Meth. Ch., 1994-97. Mem. IEEE Computer Soc., Assn. Computing Machinery, Boston Computer Soc. Home: 193 Morse Rd Sudbury MA 01776-1716 Office: IBM 404 Wyman St Ste 1 Waltham MA 02451-1280

RODIN, HOWARD ALAN, periodontist; b. Bronx, N.Y., Oct. 21, 1942; s. David and Edna (Fialkow) R.; m. Gail Sandra Stein, July 8, 1967; children: Dennis, Stephanie. BS, Fairleigh Dickinson U., 1964, MS in Physiology, 1966; DDS, Howard U., 1970; cert. in periodontics, Columbia U., 1973. Intern Sydenham Hosp., N.Y.C., 1970-71; staff dept. virology Mt. Sinai Hosp., 1964-66; fellow Fairleigh Dickinson U., 1971; pvt. practice Babylon, N.Y., 1973-82, Smithtown, 1978—; staff dept. spl. surgery St. John's Hosp., 1979-81, 85-91. Cons. NYU Med. Ctr./Goldwater Meml. Hosp., 1995-97; planning com. Greater L.I. Dental Meeting, 1973-97, gen. chmn., 1985; asst. clin. prof. periodontics Columbia U., 1986-88; pres. L.I. Acad. Periodontists, 1986-90; mass disaster forensic identification team TWA Flight 800; mem. forensic identification team World Trade Ctr., 2001. Contbr. articles to profl. jours. Fellow Am. Coll. Dentists (chmn. N.Y. sect. 2002), Internat. Coll. Dentists, Pierre Fauchand Acad., Acad. Dentistry Internat., N.Y. Acad. Dentistry, Suffolk Acad. Medicine (pres. 1992-93, bd. trustees 1990-95), Am. Acad. Osseointegration; mem. ADA (del., alt. del. 1989-2001), Am. Acad. Forensic Scis., Am. Soc. Forensic Odontology, Internat. Assn. Dental Rsch. (periodontal rsch. com. 1984—, implantology rsch. com. 1995—, Hatton award 1968), Am. Assn. Oral Biologists, Internat. Acad. Periodontists, Am. Acad. Periodontology, Suffolk County Dental Soc. (bd. dels. 1981—, pres. 1991), N.Y. State Soc. Periodontists (bd. dirs.), Northeastern Soc. Periodontists, N.Y. Acad. Scis., Suffolk Soc. Forensic Dentistry (exec. com. 1995—), Columbia U. Periodontal Alumni Assn. (trustee 1996—), Sigma Xi, Alpha Omega (pres. 1985-87).

RODIN, JUDITH SEITZ, academic administrator, psychology educator; b. Phila., Sept. 9, 1944; d. Morris and Sally R. (Winson) Seitz. AB, U. Pa., 1966; PhD, U. Columbia, 1970. Asst. prof. psychology NYU, 1970—72; assoc. prof. Yale U., 1975—79, prof., dir. grad. studies, 1982—89, Philip R. Allen prof. psychology, medicine and psychiatry, 1984—94, chmn. dept. psychology, 1989—91, dean Grad. Sch., 1991—92, provost, 1992—94; pres. U. Pa., Phila., 1994—, prof. psychology, medicine and psychiatry, 1994—. Chmn. John D. and Catherine T. MacArthur Found. Rsch. Network on Determinants and Consequences of Health-Promoting and Health-Damaging Behavior, 1983-93; vice chair coun. press. U. Rsch. Assn., 1994-95, chair, 1995-96; mem. Ind. Panel to Review Safety Procedures at The White House, 1994-95; chair adv. com. Robert Wood Johnson Found., 1994—; mem. Pres. Clinton's Com. Advisors Sci. and Tech., 1994—; mem. Coun. Competitiveness, 1997—; mem. nominating com. N.Y. Stock Exch., 1998—; bd. dirs. Aetna, Electronic Data Sys., AMR. Author: (with S. Schachter) Obese Humans and Rats, 1978, Exploding the Weight Myths, 1982, Body Traps, 1992; chief editor Appetite Jour., 1979-92; contbr. articles to profl. jours. Mem. Pa. Task Force on Higher Edn. Funding, 1994; bd. dirs. Catalyst, N.Y.C., 1994—; trustee Brookings Inst., 1995—; pres. steering com. Am. Reads, 1997—. Fellow Woodrow Wilson Found., 1966-67, John Simon Guggenheim Found., 1986-87; grantee NSF, 1973-82, NIH, 1981—. Fellow AAAS, APA (bd. sci. affairs 1979-82, pres. divsn. 38 health psychology 1982-83, Outstanding Contbn. award 1980, Disting. Sci. award 1977), Am. Acad. Arts and Scis., Soc. Behavioral Medicicine; mem. AAUW (mem. exec. com. 1996—), Am. Philosophical Soc., Inst. Medicine of NAS, Acad. Behavioral Medicine Rsch., Ea. Psychol. Assn. (exec. bd. 1980-82), Phi Beta Kappa, Sigma Xi (pres. Yale chpt. 1986-87). Office: U Pa Office of the Pres 100 College Hall Philadelphia PA 19104-6380 also: University of Pennsylvania 3451 Walnut Philadelphia PA 19104*

RODINO, VINCENT LOUIS, insurance company executive; b. N.Y.C., June 25, 1929; s. Vincenzo and Sofia (De Toro) R.; m. Marie Green; children: Peter Vincent, Vincent Douglas. BA, NYU, 1957. CLU. With The Equitable Fin. Cos., N.Y.C., 1946—, chief mktg. services sector, 1983-84, chief traditional products sector, 1984-86, chmn., chief exec. officer Traebco subs., 1984-86, chief sales support sector, 1986-89; dep. pres. northeastern region Equitable Ins. Cos., 1989-92; bd. dirs. Traebco subs. The Equitable. Trustee Life Underwriter Tng. Council, Washington, 1987. Served as sgt. U.S. Army, 1951-53. Mem. Assn. Advanced Life Underwriting, Nat. Assn. Life Underwriters, N.Y.C. Chpt. CLUs. E-mail: vrodino@prodigy.net.

RODITE, ROBERT R.R. engineering scientist; b. Easton, Pa., Oct. 17, 1942; s. Victor James and Alice Cecilia (Zatovich) R.; m. Patricia Ann Sule, Apr. 8, 1967; children: Colleen P., Robert J. BSEE, Lafayette Coll., 1964; MSEE, Caif. Inst. Tech., 1965. Rsch. engr., mgr. mfg. rsch. lab. IBM, Endicott, N.Y., 1965-70, mfg. engring. mgr. electronic packaging mfg., 1970-72, devel. engring. mgr. electronic packaging engring., 1972-77, program dir. corp. engring., programming & tech. staff Armonk, 1977-79, product engring. mgr., sr. engr. multichip module devel. East Fishkill, 1979-81, system mgr., sr. tech. staff mem. fin. industry devel. Charlotte, N.C., 1981-92, sr. tech. staff mem. corp. tech. strategy devel. staff Armonk, 1992-93; pres. Rodite Assocs., Inc., Charlotte, N.C., 1993—; lectr. math. Belmont Abbey Coll., 2001. Workgroup mem. Am. Nat. Standards Inst. Com. X9B Stds. Com., 1991-97; chmn. IBM Image Processing and Visualization Interdivisional Tech. Liaison Com., 1992-93; lectr. math. Belmont Abbey Coll., 2001. Contbr. articles to profl. jours.; patentee in field. Asst. scoutmaster Boy Scouts Am., Charlotte, 1991, 92; mid. sch. basketball asst. coach, Charlotte, 1991-92, 93-94; com. mem. Town County Consolidation Com., Endicott, 1970s; Cath. sch. bd. mem. Diocese of Charlotte, 1988-90. Tau Beta Pi fellow Calif. Inst. Tech., 1964. Mem. IEEE (sr.), Assn. for Info. and Image Mgmt. Internat. (designated Master Info. Tech. 1997, cert. document Image Architech, Laureate of Info. Technologies 1998), Phi Beta Kappa, Tau Beta Pi, Eta Kappa Nu. Avocations: personal computers, camping. Home: 9664 Chaumont Ln Charlotte NC 28277-2140 E-mail: rodite@email.com.

RODLEY, LAURA, writer; b. Wilmington, Del., Dec. 15, 1955; d. James Corbett and Sheila Craig Steen; married, Apr. 10, 1982; children: Lily Tyla, Emilene Sumner Claire, Joseph Ambrose. BA, Norwich U., 1997. Cert. nursing asst., 1991. Owner, mgr. Violet the Wonder Pony Party Co., Shelburne Falls, Mass., 1992-97; painter's assoc. Thurston Munson, Greenfield, 1997-98; salesperson Shelburne Falls, 2000—. Contbr. poems to lit. jours.; watercolor exhbns. include Greenfield Pub. Libr., 1992, Salmon Falls Marketplace, Shelburne Falls, Twice Upon a Time, Brattleboro, Vt., 1997, others; permanent collections Greylock Animal Hosp., North Adams, Mass., Franklin Nursing and Rehab. Ctr., Greenfield, Greenfield Town Hall; quilts exhibited Heritage State Park, 1986, Berkshire Quilt Festival, Berkshire C.C., Williams Coll. Student Union Bldg., 1989, elsewhere. Recipient cert. appreciation, Selectmen of Greenfield, 1999. Mem. Wild Women's Writers Group, Ashfield Serve, Deerfield Valley Art ASsn., Old Deerfield Painting Group. Home: P O Box 63 Shelburne Falls MA 01370

RODMAN, ALPINE C. arts and crafts company executive; b. Roswell, N.Mex., June 23, 1952; s. Robert Elsworth and Verna Mae (Means) R.; m. Sue Arlene Lawson, Dec. 13, 1970; 1 child, Connie Lynn. Student, Colo. State U., 1970-71, U. No. Colo. Ptnr. Pinel Silver Shop, Loveland, Colo., 1965-68, salesman, 1968-71; real estate salesman, 1971-73; mgr. Traveling Traders, Phoenix, 1974-75; co-owner Deer Track Traders, Loveland, 1975-85; pres. Deer Track Traders, Ltd., 1985—. Author: The Vanishing Indian: Fact or Fiction?, 1985. Mem. Civil Air Patrol, 1965-72, 87-92, dep. comdr. for cadets, 1988-90; cadet comdr. Ft. Collins, Colo., 1968, 70, Colo. rep. to youth tng. program, 1969, U.S. youth rep. to Japan, 1970. Mem. Bur. Wholesale Sales Reps., Western and English Salesmen's Assn. (bd. dirs. 1990), Internat. Platform Assn., Indian Arts and Crafts Assn. (bd. dirs. 1988-94, exec. com. 1989-92, v.p. 1990, pres. 1991, market chmn. 1992), Crazy Horse Grass Roots Club. Republican. Office: Deer Track Traders Ltd PO Box 448 Loveland CO 80539-0448 *Personal philosophy: I believe that most good and bad in the world comes out of respect or lack of respect for one's self, fellow man, environment and creator.*

RODMAN, ELISE, physician; b. Boston, Apr. 22, 1953; d. Leonard and Doris (Brudnick) R. BS, Tufts U., Medford, Mass., 1975; MD, Tufts U., Boston, 1979. Diplomate Am. Bd. Internal Medicine, Am. Bd. Endocrinology and Metabolism. Resident in medicine Tufts New Eng. Med. Ctr., Boston, 1979-82, fellow in endocrinology, 1982-85; physician Peabody (Mass.) Med. Assocs., 1985—. Instr. Tufts U., 1984—; exec. com. mem. Salem Hosp., 1994-96. Author: (with others) Prolactinomas: Practical Diagnosis and Management, 1986; contbr. articles to profl. jours. Bd. dirs. Spotlighters of Lynnfield, Mass., 1992-94. Fellow Am. Coll. Endocrinology; mem. AMA, Mass. Med. Soc., Endocrine Soc., Am. Diabetes Assn., Am. Assn. Clin. Endocrinology, Alpha Omega Alpha (pres. Tufts Med. Sch. chpt. 1978-79). Avocations: musical theatre, singing, piano. Office: Peabody Med Assocs 2 Essex Ctr Dr Peabody MA 01960-1600

RODMAN, FRANCIS ROBERT, psychoanalyst, writer; b. Boston, Feb. 3, 1934; s. Wilfred and Sarah Frieda (Kraus) R.; m. Inger Marianne Andersson, Aug. 17, 1961 (dec. Sept. 1974); children: Ingrid, Simone; m. Katharine Newton; children: Sarah, Nicholas. AB cum laude, Harvard U., 1955; MD, Boston U., 1959. Diplomate Am. Bd. Psychiatry and Neurology. Intern San Francisco Hosp., 1959-60; resident in psychiatry UCLA, 1960-63; staff psychiatrist children's divsn. Camarillo (Calif.) State Hosp., 1963-64; pvt. practice psychiatry, Encino, Calif., 1964-66; tng. in psychoanalysis L.A. Psychoanalytic Soc. and Inst., 1965-71; pvt. practice psychoanalysis, Beverly Hills, Calif., 1968—. Mem. Ctr. for Advanced Psychoanalytic Studies, Princeton, N.J., 1978—; bd. advisors Lucy Daniels Found., Cary, N.C., 1998—. Author: Not Dying: A Memoir, 1977, Keeping Hope Alive, 1986; editor: The Spontaneous Gesture-Selected Letters of D.W. Winnicott, 1987. Capt. M.C., U.S. Army, 1966-68. Mem. Am. Psychiat. Assn., Am. Psychoanalytic Assn., So. Calif. Psychiat. Soc., L.A. Psychoanalytic Soc. and Inst., Am. PEN, PEN West. Office: 450 N Bedford Dr Ste 211 Beverly Hills CA 90210-4306 Fax: (310) 275-6764.

RODMAN, LEIBA, mathematician; b. Riga, Latvia, June 9, 1949; came to U.S., 1985; s. Zalman and Haya Rodman; m. Ella Levitan, Feb. 2, 1983; children: Daniel, Ruth, Benjamin, Naomi. Diploma in maths., Latvian State U., 1971; MA in Statis., Tel Aviv (Israel) U., 1976, PhD in Maths., 1978. Instr. Tel Aviv U., 1976-78, sr. lectr., 1981-83, assoc. prof., 1983-85; postdoctoral fellow U. Calgary, Can., 1978-80; from assoc. to full prof. Ariz. State U., Tempe, 1985-87; prof. math. Coll. William and Mary, Williamsburg, Va., 1987—. Author: Introduction to Operator Polynomials, 1989, (with others) Matrix Polynomials, 1982, Matrices and Indefinite Scalar Products, 1983, Invariant Subspaces of Matrices with Applications, 1986, Interpolation of Rational Matrix Functions, 1990, Algebraic Riccati Equations, 1995; co-editor: Contributions to Operator Theory and Its Applications, 1988. Mem. IEEE, Am. Math. Soc., Math. Assn. Am., Internat. Linear-Algebra Soc., Soc. Indsl. and Applied Maths. Office: Coll of William & Mary Dept Math PO Box 8795 Williamsburg VA 23187-8795 E-mail: lxrodm@math.wm.edu.

RODMAN, LEROY ELI, lawyer; b. N.Y.C., Feb. 22, 1914; s. Morris and Sadie (Specter) R.; m. Toby Chertcoff, Mar. 14, 1943; children: John Stephen, Lawrence Bernard. AB, CCNY, 1933; JD (James Kent scholar), Columbia, 1936. Bar: N.Y. 1937. Practiced in, N.Y.C., 1937-43, 46—; law sec. to U.S. dist. judge Bklyn., 1936; law asst. Am. Law Inst., N.Y.C., 1937; chief food enforcement unit N.Y. Regional Office, OPA, 1942-43; mem. firm Lawrence R. Condon, N.Y.C., 1937-42; ptnr. Joseph & Rodman, 1946-53; sr. ptnr. Rodman, Maurer & Dansker, 1964-73, Carro, Spanbock, Londin, Rodman & Fass, N.Y.C., 1973-78, Rodman & Rodman, N.Y.C., 1978-89, Teitelbaum, Hiller, Rodman, Paden & Hibsher, P.C., N.Y.C., 1990-96; of counsel Morrison, Cohen, Singer & Weinstein LLP, 1996—. Sec. Ameribrom, Inc., Clearon Corp. Editorial bd.: Columbia Law Rev, 1934-36; Contbr. articles to legal jours. V.p. Ctrl. Synagogue, pres. brotherhood, 1958—60, hon. trustee; bd. dirs. Manhattan coun. Boy Scouts Am., v.p., 1961—68, pres., 1972—75, exec. bd. Greater N.Y. coun. Capt. JAGD U.S. Army, 1943—46. Recipient Certs. Svc., Silver Beaver award Boy Scouts Am., 1962, Eagle Scout. Fellow: Am. Coll. Trust and Estate Counsel; mem.: ABA, Judge Adv. Assn., Assn. of Bar of City of N.Y., N.Y. County Lawyers Assn., Metropolis Country Club (White Plains, N.Y.) (sec. 1976—77, 1980—82, v.p. 1977—78, bd. govs. 1976—82), Univ Club (N.Y.C.), Phi Beta Kappa. Jewish. Home: 535 E 86th St New York NY 10028-7533 Office: 750 Lexington Ave New York NY 10022-1200

RODMAN, PETER WARREN, government official; b. Boston, Nov. 24, 1943; s. Sumner and Helen Rhoda (Morris) R.; m. F. Veronique Boulad, Apr. 13, 1980; children: Theodora, Nicholas. BA summa cum laude, Harvard U., 1964, JD, 1969; BA, MA, Oxford (Eng.) U., 1966. Staff mem. NSC, Washington, 1969-77; fellow in diplomatic studies Ctr. for Strategic and Internat. Studies, 1977-83; dir. rsch. Kissinger Assocs., 1982-83; mem. policy planning council Dept. of State, 1983-84, dir. policy planning staff, 1984-86; dep. asst. to pres. for nat. security affairs (fgn. policy) NSC, 1986-87, NSC counselor, spl. asst. to pres. for nat. security affairs, 1987-90; fellow Johns Hopkins Fgn. Policy Inst., 1990-93; dir. Middle East and Eurasian studies Ctr. for Strategic and Internat. Studies, 1994-95; dir. nat. security programs Nixon Ctr., 1995-2001; asst. sec. def. for internat. security affairs Dept. of Def., 2001—. Author: More Precious Than Peace: The Cold War and the Struggle for the Third World, 1994; sr. editor Nat. Rev., 1991-99; contbr. articles to profl. jours. V.p. World Affairs Coun., Washington, 1996-2001; trustee Freedom House, 1997-2001. Mem. Coun. on Fgn. Rels., Internat. Inst. for Strategic Studies, Atlantic Coun. U.S., Cosmos Club. Office: 2400 Defense Pentagon Rm 4E838 Washington DC 20301-2400 E-mail: prodman@nixoncenter.org.*

RODMAN, RAYMOND G. insurance company executive; b. Topeka, Aug. 2, 1946; s. John T. and Wilma D. (Cox-Betts) R.; m. Sherri L. Shughart, Aug. 31, 1968; children: Eric, Erin, Tara, Charisse. BS in Math., Emporia State U., 1970; MBA, Ill. State U., 1980. CLU, ChFC, CPCU, cert. data processing profl. Programmer State Farm Ins., Bloomington, Ill., 1970-72, analyst, 1973-75, team leader, 1975-77, project leader, 1977-80, supt., 1980-86, mgr., 1986-90, IS mgr., 1990—. Chmn. economy subcom., steering com. 2020 Planning Com., Normal, Ill., 1995-96; mem. McLean County Bd., 1990—. Mem. CPCU Soc., CLU Soc. Republican. Baptist. Home: 719 N School St Normal IL 61761-1620 Office: State Farm Insurance 3 State Farm Plz # K2 Bloomington IL 61791-0002

RODMAN, SUE A. wholesale company executive, artist, writer; b. Ft. Collins, Colo., Oct. 1, 1951; d. Marvin F. Lawson and Barbara I. (Miller) Lawson Shue; m. Alpine C. Rodman, Dec. 13, 1970; 1 child, Connie, Lynn. Student, Colo. State U., 1970-73. Silversmith Pinel Silver Shop, Loveland, Colo., 1970-71; asst. mgr. Traveling Traders, Phoenix, 1974-75; co-owner, co-mgr. Deer Track Traders, Loveland, 1975-85; v.p. Deer Track Traders, Ltd., 1985—. Author: The Book of Contemporary Indian Arts and Crafts, 1985, also numerous children's articles and short stories. Mem. U.S. Senatorial Club, 1982-87, Rep. Presdl. Task Force, 1984-90; mem. CAP, 1969-73, 87-90, pers. officer, 1988-90. Mem. Internat. Platform Assn., Indian Arts and Crafts Assn., Western and English Sales Assn., Crazy Horse Grass Roots Club. Mem. Am. Baptist Ch. Avocations: museums, piano, recreation research, fashion design. Office: Deer Track Traders Ltd PO Box 448 Loveland CO 80539-0448

RODMAN, SUMNER, insurance company executive; b. Malden, Mass., Aug. 5, 1915; s. Nathan Markel and Sara Ruth (Slater) Rodman; m. Helen Rhoda Morris, July 2, 1942; children: Peter Warren, John Slater. AB cum laude, Harvard U., 1935. CLU. Ins. broker, employee benefits specialist Aetna Life Ins. and Annuity Co., Boston, 1935-98; with Rodman Ins. Agy., Inc., Needham; life ins. adviser, 1953—. Pres. Boston Life Ins. and Trust Coun., 1958—59. Bd. dirs. Boston Estate Planning Coun., 1960—85, pres., 1958; mem. Anti-Defamation League B'nai Brith, World Affairs Coun. Boston; bd. dirs. Jewish Family and Children's Svc., 1953—85; mem. Am. Jewish Com.; hon. trustee Temple Israel, Boston; bd. dirs. Youth Tennis Found. New Eng., 1963—85, Simons-Gutman Found., 1965—, Alzheimers Assn. Ea. Mass., 1990—97; hon. trustee Combined Jewish Philanthropies of Greater Boston, 1967—. Served to capt. AUS, ETO. Fellow CLU Inst., 1952, 1961. Mem.: New Eng. Tennis Assn. (bd. dirs. 1966—68, Hall of Fame 1992), Am. Soc. CLUs (pres. 1972—73), Boston Life Underwriters Assn. (pres. 1965—66), Am. Coll. (trustee 1971—74), Million Dollar Round Table (life), Wightman Tennis Ctr. Club (Weton, Mass.), Harvard Varsity Club (Boston), Harvard Club (Boston), Newton Club (Mass.), Squash and Tennis Club, Masons, Golden Key Soc. Jewish. Home: 94 Vine St Chestnut Hill MA 02467-3050 Office: Rodman Ins Agy Inc 145 Rosemary St Needham MA 02494-3238 E-mail: srodman@rodmanins.com.

RODNE, KJELL JOHN, healthcare administrator; b. July 6, 1948; came to U.S., 1959; s. Johannes and Margit (Gautun) R.; m. Kathleen Anne Gordon, Sept. 21, 1966; children: Jay Robert, Lee Eric. BS, U. Minn., Duluth, 1971; MSW, 1985; cert., Univ. Assn. Human Resources, 1995; PMA sci. of success diploma, personal computer tng. program diploma, , 1996. Asst. youth dir. YMCA, Duluth, 1967-68; counselor Northwood, 1968-71; team leader, 1971-76; social worker, 1976-77; program dir., 1977-85; pers. dir. City of Duluth, 1985-86, adminstrv. asst., 1986-92; mgmt. cons., 1992-93; adminstr. Northwood West, 1993-95; dir. quality assurance, 1995-96; CEO Duluth Bethel Soc., 1996-97; dir. program ops. Youth Continum, New Haven, 1997-2000; dir. St. Croix Boys Camp, 2000—. Bd. dirs. Minn. Coun. Residential Teatment Ctrs., St. Paul, 1977-85, 93-96. Mem. Duluth City Coun., 1978-85, pres., 1981; bd. dirs. United Devel. Achievement Ctr., Duluth, 1981-85, United Way of Duluth, 1981-89, Duluth Econ. Devel. Authority, 1989-92, Arrowhead Growth Alliance, 1990-92, Northspan, 1991-92. Mem. Lake Superior Assn. Labor Mgmt. (bd. dirs. 1989-92), Internat. City Mgrs. Assn. (pub. policy com. 1991-95), Nat. Assn. Homes for Children. Democrat. Home: 1511 N 64th St Superior WI 54880-5958 E-mail: ingolf@aol.com.

RODNEY, JOEL MORRIS, dean, campus executive officer; b. Bklyn., Nov. 9, 1937; s. Samuel Seymour and Jane (Loorya) R.; m. Judith DeStefano, July 22, 1994; children from previous marriage: Jonathan, Adam, Benjamin. BA cum laude, Brandeis U., 1959; PhD, Cornell U., 1965; attended, Inst. Ednl. Mgmt. Harvard U., 1976. From instr. to assoc. prof. Wash. State U., Pullman, 1963-70; chmn. div. social scis., assoc. prof. history Elmira (N.Y.) Coll., 1970-72, coordinator flood relief and community planning, 1973; dean arts and sci., prof. history Widener Coll., Chester, Pa., 1973-76, acting chief acad. officer, dean, 1976-77, chief acad. officer, dean, 1977-81, dir. univ. grad. programs, 1979-81; v.p. acad. affairs Salisbury (Md.) State Coll., 1981-86; provost Rockford (Ill.) Coll., 1986-90; CEO, dean U. Wis. -Washington County, West Bend, 1990—. Editor Albion, 1967-78; contbr. articles to profl. jours. Vice chmn. Md. Gov.'s Com. on Employment of Handicapped, 1985-86, chmn. and mem. Lower Shore divsn., 1983-86; chmn. adv. bd., mem. Crozer-Chester Med. Health Ctr., Chester, 1974-77; project evaluator NEH, 1986, RSA, 1993; mem., sec. Delaware County Mental Health/Mental Retardation Bd., 1975-81; adv. bd. Rehab. Inst. of Chgo., 1988-94; mem. coun. Ct. of Gov.'s Regents Coll., London, 1986-90, Rock Valley Coll. Indsl. Coun., Rockford, 1989-90; bd. dirs. Moraine Symphony Orch., 1990-93, Welcome Home, Inc., 1990—, pres., 1992—; citizens adv. bd. West Bend Bank One, 1991, Washington County Vol. Ctr., 1991-92; bd. dirs. The Threshold, 1992—, vice chair, 1990-2000, chair, 2000; apptd. to State Wis. Coun. Phys. Disabilities, 1994, vice chmn., 1995, chmn., 1996-2000; exec. com. Moraine area Tech. Prep. Coun., 1994—; mem. Wis. Gov.'s Com. on Persons with Disabilities, 1994-97, vice chmn., 1996; mem. adv. bd. S.E. Wis. Area Health Edn. Coun., 1995-96, West Bend Art Mus., 1996-2001, chair, 1999-2001; mem. West Bend C. of C. Ambs., 1995—; mem. Washington County Growth Mgmt. Task Force, 1996—, chair, 1999—; del. Washington County Reps., 1997—; bd. dirs. Kettle Moraine YMCA, 1999—. Recipient Disting. Service award Widener Meml. Sch., 1978, Award of merit Md. Gov.'s Com. on Employment of Handicapped, 1984; named to Legion of Honor, Chapel of Four Chaplains, 1978; honoree West Phila. Vets. and Handicapped Employment Com., 1977. Mem. Am. Assn. Acad. Deans, Conf. on Brit. Studies, Am. Assn. Univ. Adminstrs., Nat. Spinal Cord Injury Assn. (bd. dirs. Ill. chpt. 1988-90), Rotary, Phi Alpha Theta. Republican. Home: 229 Bittersweet Dr West Bend WI 53095-4907 Office: U Wis Washington County 400 S University Dr West Bend WI 53095-3619

RODNING, CHARLES BERNARD, surgeon; b. Pipestone, Minn., Aug. 4, 1943; s. Selmer Bernard and Ida Amanda (Selness) R.; m. Mary Elizabeth Lipke, June 15, 1968; children: Christopher Bernard, Soren Piers, Kai Johannes. BS, Gustavus Adolphus Coll., St. Peter, Minn., 1965; MD, U. Rochester, 1970; PhD, U. Minn., 1979. Diplomate Am. Bd. Med. Examiners, Am. Bd. Surgery. Intern, asst. resident dept. surgery U. Rochester Sch. Medicine and Dentistry, 1970-72; assoc. resident to chief resident, med. fellow dept. surgery U. Minn. Health Scis. Ctr., Mpls., 1972-79; prof. dept cell biology and neurosci. U. South Ala., Mobile, 1981—, prof. dept. surgery, 1981—, vice chmn. dept. surgery, 1981—, dir. gen. surgery, 1996—. Field liaison physician Commn. on Cancer-ACS, Chgo., 1984—; mem. med. adv. bd. Ala. Organ & Tissue Ctr., Birmingham, 1988—. Author: Elan Vital, 1988, Wode and Ston, 1988, Sorrowful Wheel, 1989, Ponderings, 1990, The Sea Rises in the West, 1991, Stepping Stones, 1991, Snowbound Below the Firn Line, 1991, Love Knot, 1994, Papering Dreams, 1994, Carry Onward, 1996, Swaying Grass, 1998, Tradition of Excellence: Pictorial History of Surgical Education at the Mobile General Hospital and University of South Alabama College of Medicine and Medical Center, 1999; reviewer: Jour. Histochem. Cytochem., 1988—; contbr. (articles) Clin. Anatomy, —, Surg. Endoscopy, Pharos, Jours. Thoracic Cardiovasc. Surgery, So. Med. Jour., others. Bd. dirs. Mobile Mental Health Ctr., Mental Health Found. of S. Ala., Mobile Med. Mu. Comdr. USN, 1974-81. Recipient Physicians Recognition award AMA, 1980, 85, 88, 91, 95, 99, 02, Bacaner Rsch. award Minn. Med. Found., 1979, Humanism in Medicine award Arnold P. Gold Found., Healthcare Found. N.J., 2002, Howard L. Holley award Med. Assn. State Ala., 2002. Fellow ACS, Internat. Coll. Surgeons (vice regent Ala. chpt. 1989—); mem. Iota Delta Gamma, Alpha Omega Alpha, Phi Kappa Phi. Office: U South Ala Dept Surgery Med Ctr USA 2451 Fillingim St Mobile AL 36617-2238 E-mail: crodning@usamail.usouthal.edu.

RODNUNSKY, SIDNEY, lawyer, educator; b. Edmonton, Alta., Can., Feb. 3, 1946; s. B. and I. Rodnunsky; m. Teresita Asuncion; children: Naomi, Shawna, Rachel, Tevie, Claire, Donna, Sidney Jr. BEd, U. Alberta, 1966, LLB, 1973; MEd, U. Calgary, 1969, grad. diploma, 1990; BS, U. of State of N.Y., 1988; MBA, Greenwich U., 1990. Served as regional counsel to Her Majesty the Queen in Right of the Dominion of Can.; former gov. Grande Prairie Regional Coll.; now prin. legal counsel Can. Nat. exec., Alta. coord. for gifted children, ombudsman, SIG coord. Mensa Can.; past pres. Grande Prairie and Dist. Bar Assn., Alta Tchrs. Assn., Aspenview. Author: Breathalyzer Casebook; editor: The Children Speak. Decorated knight Grand Cross Sovereign and Royal Order of Piast, knight Grand Cross Order of St. John the Baptist; knight Hospitaller Order St. John of Jerusalem; Prince of Kiev, Prince of Trabzon, Prince and Duke of Rodari, Duke of Chernigov, Count of Riga, Count of St. John of Alexandria; named to Honorable Order of Ky. Colonels; named adm. State of Tex.; recipient Presdl. Legion of Merit. Mem. Law Soc. Alta., Law Soc. Sask., Can. Bar Assn., Inst. Can. Mgmt., Phi Delta Kappa. Address: PO Box 92 Whale Cove NU Canada X0C 0J0 E-mail: wonderfulschool@hotmail.com.

RODOLFA, EMIL RAYMOND, psychologist; b. San Jose, Nov. 23, 1952; s. Joseph and Louise R.; m. Mary Jo Pyne, Jan. 6, 1979; children: Kit, Joie. BA, San Jose State U., 1976; MS in Counseling, Calif. State U., Hayward, 1977, MS in Edn. (Rsch.), 1978; PhD, Tex. A&M U., 1981. Lic. psychologist Calif., Nev. Psychologist, dir. tng. Humboldt State U., Arcata, Calif., 1981-88; psychologist, assoc. dir. U. Calif., Davis, 1988—, dir., 2002. Pres. Assn. Counseling Ctr. Tng. Agys., 1996-98. Fellow APA; mem. Assn. Psychology Post-doctoral and Internship Ctrs. (vice-chmn. 1998—), Assn. Counseling Ctr. Tng. Agencies (pres. 1996-98, chmn. Coun. Chairs Tng. Couns., 1996-98), State Calif. Bd. Psychology (v.p. 2001). Office: Counseling Ctr U Calif Davis CA 95616 E-mail: errodolfa@ucdavis.edu.

RODOLFF, DALE WARD, engineer, sales executive, consultant; b. Casa Grande, Ariz., Aug. 5, 1938; s. Norval Ward and Mary Louise (Grasty) Rodolff; m. Kathleen Pennington, Sept. 3, 1960 (div. July 1983); children: David Ward (dec.), Julia Ann. BS in Mining Engring., U. Ariz.; PMD, U. Cape

Town; postgrad., Denver Sem. Registered profl. engr., Republic of South Africa. Supt. smelting and fabricating Inspiration Consol. Copper Co., Claypool, Ariz., 1960-72; smelter and refinery supt. Palabora Mining Co, Phalaborwa, Republic of South Africa, 1972-74; asst. mgr. Empress Nickel Mining Co., Gatooma, Zimbabwe, 1974-77; smelter supt. Magma Copper Co., San Manuel, Ariz., 1977-81; v.p., gen. mgr. Sentinel Mgmt. Corp., Tucson, 1981-82; dir., mgr. metallurgy Outokumpu Engring. Inc., Denver, 1982-86, mgr. N.Am., 1986-96, also bd. dirs.; supt. flash smelting and flash converting Kennecott Utah Copper, 1996-97. Cons., pres. D.W. Rodolff Cons. Corp., 1986—; pres. Bus. Performance Svcs., Inc., 1986-90; dir. Grace Ministries, 1995-99; chmn. Mountain Area Crisis Pregnancy Ctr., 2001—. Contbr. articles to tech. jours.; inventor scrap rod feed system, 1970. Pres. Y Men's Club, Miami, Ariz., 1969. Kennecott scholar U. Ariz., 1959. Mem. AIME (metall. soc., soc. mining engrs., chmn. smelter div. 1970, 71, pyro metall. com. 1973-77), Mining and Metall. Soc. Am. Avocations: flying, skiing, Christian endeavors. Home and Office: 6527 S Jungfrau Way Evergreen CO 80439-5308

RODOVICH, ANDREW PAUL, magistrate; b. Hammond, Ind., Feb. 24, 1948; s. Andrew H. and Julia (Makar) R.; m. Gail Linda Patrick, May 27, 1972; children: Caroline Anja, Mary Katherine, James Patrick. BA, Valparaiso (Ind.) U., 1970, JD, 1973. Bar: Ind. Ptnr. Hand, Muenich & Rodovich, Hammond, 1973-78; chief dep. prosecutor Lake County Prosecutor's Office, Crown Point, Ind., 1979-82; U.S. magistrate U.S. Dist. Ct., Hammond, 1982—. Referee Hammond City Ct., 1978; adj. prof. Valparaiso Law Sch., 1985—. Fellow Ind. Bar Found.; mem. Nat. Coun. U.S. Magistrates, Delta Theta Phi. Republican. Avocations: sports. Home: 7207 Baring Pky Hammond IN 46324-2218 Office: US Dist Ct 136 Federal Bldg Hammond IN 46320-1529

RODOVICH, ARLENE GUYOTTE, administrator, small business owner; b. Springfield, Mass., Mar. 21, 1935; d. Walter L. Guyotte and Dorothy (Hawley) Bigelow; m. Robert F. Rodovich, Sept. 30, 1955; 1 child, Heidi E. Pepyne. AA, Greenfield (Mass.) Community Coll., 1977. Cert. profl. property mgr. Sec., bookkeeper Gordon E. Ainsworth Assocs., South Deerfield, Mass., 1954-60; from jr. clk. to dir. U. Mass. Property and Inventory Control, Amherst, 1966—. Owner Conway (Mass.) Bus. Service, 1958—. Author: (manual) Property Management, 1972. Chmn. fin. com., zoning bd. appeals, Conway, 1975—, selectman, 1991—; vice chair Franklin/Hampshire Employment and Tng. Mem. Nat. Property Mgmt. Assn. (v.p. profl. devel. 1987—, v.p. fin. 1988, pres. 1989-90, Property Person of the Yr. 1984, Property Person of the Yr. Eastern region 1986), Mass. Fedn. Bus. and Profl. Women (2d v.p. 1986—, 1st v.p. 1987-88, pres. elect 1988—, pres. 1989-90). Avocations: needlepoint, travel. Home: Ashfield Rd Conway MA 01341 Office: U Mass Goodell Bldg Amherst MA 01341

RODOWSKY, LAWRENCE FRANCIS, retired state judge; b. Balt., Nov. 10, 1930; s. Lawrence Anthony and Frances (Gardner) R.; m. Colby Fossett, Aug. 7, 1954; children: Laura Rodowsky Ramos, Alice Rodowsky-Seegers, Emily Rodowsky Savopoulos, Sarah Jones Rodowsky, Gregory, Katherine Rodowsky O'Connor. AB, Loyola Coll., Balt., 1952; LLB, U. Md., 1956. Bar: Md. 1956. Ct. crier, law clk. U.S. Dist. Ct. Md., 1954-56; asst. atty. gen. State of Md., 1960-61; assoc., ptnr. firm Frank, Bernstein, Conaway & Goldman, Balt., 1956-79; judge Ct. Appeals Md., Annapolis, 1980-2000, rules com., 1969-80. Lectr., asst. instr. U. Md. Law Sch., 1958-68, 87-91; reporter jud. dept. Md. Constl. Conv. Commn., 1966-67. Chmn. Gov. Md. Commn. Racing Reform, 1979. Fellow Am. Coll. Trial Lawyers; mem. Md. Bar Assn., Balt. Bar Assn. Roman Catholic. Home: 4306 Norwood Rd Baltimore MD 21218-1118 Office: 620 CM Mitchell Jr Courthse 100 N Calvert St Baltimore MD 21202 E-mail: Lawrence.Rodowsky@courts.state.md.us.

RODRIGUE, GEORGE P. newspaper editor; Exec. editor, v.p. news The Press Enterprise, Riverside, Calif., 1998—. Office: The Press Enterprise 3512 14th St Riverside CA 92501-3878

RODRIGUES, WILLIAM PATRICK, JR. city planner; b. Fullerton, Calif., June 17, 1971; s. William Patrick Rodrigues, Sr. and Hazel Katherine Groves. BS in Urban and Regional Planning, Calif. State Polytech. U., Pomona, 1994. Planning intern City of Perris, Calif., 1994-95; planning aide City of Glendora, 1995-98, asst. planner, 1998-2001; assoc. planner City of Santa Monica, 2001—. Mem. Am. Inst. Cert. Planners (cert.), Am. Planning Assn. (Calif. chpt., Orange County chpt.), Glendora Mcpl. Employees Assn. (v.p. 2000, pres. 2001). Republican. Roman Catholic. Avocations: golf, baseball, basketball, racquetball. Office: City of Santa Monica City Planning Divsn Rm 212 PO Box 2200 Santa Monica CA 90407-2200

RODRIGUES LIMA, KRISTINE ROOP, clinical social worker; b. Norwood, Mass., Dec. 8, 1948; d. John Wesley and Emily (Lawrence) Roop; m. Otavio A. Rodrigues Lima, July 21, 1979; 1 child, Kathryn. Student, U. Manchester, Eng., 1968-69; BA in English, Allegheny Coll., 1970; MSW, Smith Coll., 1973. Lic. ind. clin. social worker; bd. cert. diplomate. Assessor and counselor adoptive applicants Family and Children's Svcs., Pitts., 1970-71; group therapist St. Jude Halfway House, Jamaica Plain, Mass., 1971-73; clin. social worker Children's Friend and Family Svc., Salem, 1973-77, Head Start, Action, Inc., Gloucester, 1977, Marlborough (Mass.)-Westborough Community Mental Health Clinic, 1977-79; pvt. practice Cambridge, Mass., 1977—; psychotherapist and counselor Health Integration Svcs., Inc., Peabody, 1979-82; dir. South End Christian Counseling Ctr., Boston, 1982-84; ptnr. Advent Counseling Assn., Cambridge, 1983—; dir. Milestone Counseling Assocs., 1990—. Deacon, film/discussion moderator Newton (Mass.) Presbyn. Ch.; tchr. How Families Work program Southborough (Mass.) Pub. Libr., Creative Parenting program Marlborough Pub. Libr.; co-chmn. Project Home Again and World Vision, Newton, 1990. Mem. Acad. Cert. Social Workers. Avocations: piano, hiking, tailoring. Office: 144A Mt Auburn St Cambridge MA 02138-5776

RODRIGUEZ, AGUSTIN ANTONIO, surgeon; b. Hato Rey, P.R., Aug. 20, 1961; s. Agustin and Esther Rodriguez (Gonzalez) R.; m. Liana Esther Lopez, 1993; children: Agustin Andrés, Claudia Sofía, Alvaro Agustin. AB in Biology, Harvard Coll., 1982; MD, U. P.R., San Juan, 1986. Diplomate Nat. Bd. Med. Examiners, Am. Bd. Surgery, Am. Bd. Gen. and Vascular Surgery. Intern Boston U. Med. Ctr., 1986-87, resident in surgery, 1988-93, acad. trainee surgery; vascular fellow Tufts U., New England Med. Ctr., 1993-95; asst. prof. surgery Tufts U. Sch. Medicine, Boston, 1995—. Assoc. prof. surgery Sch. Medicine U. P.R., San Juan, 1996—. Contbr. articles to profl. jours. Fellow ACS; mem. AMA, Am. Numismatic Soc., Am. Numismatic Assn., Mass. Med. Soc., N.Y. Acad. Scis., European Soc. Vascular Surgery (assoc.), Am. Venous Forum, Interam. Coll. Physicians and Surgeons, Am. Soc. Clin. Vascular Surgery, Assn. Acad. Surgery, Soc. Am. Gastrointestinal and Endoscopic Surgeons, Coll. Med. Surgeons Puerto Rico, Cirujanos Vasculares de Habla Hispana, Alpha Omega Alpha. Republican. Home: 1924 Calle Sauco Rio Piedras PR 00927-6718 Office: U PR Sch Medicine Dept Surgery San Juan PR 00936-5067 E-mail: Agustinr@asem.net.

RODRIGUEZ, ANNABELLE, state attorney general; BA, JD, U. P.R. From asst. solicitor gen. to solicitor gen. P.R. Dept. Justice; ptnr. Martino, Odell & Calabria, Hato Rey, PR, 1993—96; judge U.S. Dist Ct. (P.R. dist.), 1996; atty. gen. Commonwealth of P.R., 2001—. Office: Atty Gen PO Box 9020192 San Juan PR 00902*

RODRIGUEZ, ANTONIO JOSE, lawyer; b. New Orleans, Dec. 7, 1944; s. Anthony Joseph and Josephine Olga (Cox) R.; m. Virginia Anne Soignet, Aug. 23, 1969; children: Henry Jacob, Stephen Anthony. BS, U.S. Naval Acad., 1966; JD cum laude, Loyola U. of the South, New Orleans, 1973. Bar: La. 1973, U.S. Dist. Ct. (ea. dist.) La. 1973, U.S. Ct. Appeals (5th cir.) 1973, U.S. Dist. Ct. (mid. dist.) La. 1975, U.S. Dist. Ct. (we. dist.) La. 1977, U.S. Ct. Appeals (11th cir.) 1981, U.S. Supreme Ct. 1987, U.S. Dist. Ct. (so. dist.) Miss. 1991, U.S. Ct. Appeals (4th cir.) 1991, U.S. Ct. Appeals (1st cir.) 1997, U.S. Ct. Internat. Trade, 1991. Assoc. Phelps, Dunbar, Marks, Claverie & Sims, New Orleans, 1973-77; ptnr. Phelps Dunbar, 1977-92, Fowler Rodriguez Kingsmill Flint, Gray & Chalos, LLP, New Orleans, 1992—. Prof. law Tulane U., New Orleans, 1981—; mem. nat. rules of the road adv. coun. U.S. Dept. Transp., Washington, 1987-90, chmn. nat. navigation safety adv. coun., 1990-94, mem., 2000—; spkr. on admiralty and environ. Co-author: Admiralty-Limitation of Liability, 1981—, Admiralty-Law of Collision, 1990—; author: (chpt.) Benedict on Admiralty, 1995—; assoc. editor Loyola Law Rev., 1971-73; contbr. articles to profl. maritime and environ. jours. Bd. dirs. Greater New Orleans Coun. Navy League, 1988—, Propeller Club of New Orleans, 1997—. Lt. USN, 1966-70; capt. USNR, 1970-95. Decorated Navy Commendation medal; recipient Disting. Pub. Svc. award U.S. Dept. Transp., 1993. Fellow La. Bar Found.; mem. ABA, La. State Bar Assn., La. State Law Inst., Maritime Law Assn. U.S. (proctor 1975—), New Orleans Bar Assn., Southeastern Admiralty Law Inst., Assn. Average Adjusters U.S., Assn. Average Adjusters U.K., Naval Res. Assn. (chpt. pres. 1982-84), U.S. Naval Acad. Alumni Assn. (chpt. pres. 1981-83), Bienville Club, Phi Alpha Delta, Alpha Sigma Nu. Republican. Roman Catholic. Home: 4029 Mouton St Metairie LA 70002-1303 Office: Fowler Rodriguez Kingsmill Flint Gray & Chalos LLP 201 Saint Charles Ave Fl 36 New Orleans LA 70170-1000

RODRIGUEZ, CARLOS AUGUSTO, lawyer; b. Havana, Cuba, Sept. 1, 1954; came to U.S., 1960; s. Urbano and Estela (Cardenas) R.; m. Valerie Carr, May 27, 1989. BA magna cum laude, Furman U., 1977; JD, U. Fla., 1980. Bar: Fla. 1980, U.S. Ct. Appeals (5th cir.) 1981, U.S. Dist. Ct. (so. dist. and trial bar) Fla. 1984, U.S. Ct. Appeals (11th cir.) 1995; bd. cert. civil trial atty. Asst. pub. defender Broward County Pub. Defender's Office, Ft. Lauderdale, Fla., 1980-83, chief asst. pub. defender, 1983-85; assoc. Fazio, Dawson & DiSalvo, 1985-87; sole practice, 1987—. Assoc. prof. U. Miami Sch. Law, Miami, 1983-85; lectr. criminal procedure Nova Law Cen., Ft. Lauderdale, 1983-85, lectr. on law Broward Community Coll., Ft. Lauderdale, 1983-87; mem. Nuisance Abatement Bd., 1989—, chmn., 1996—; vice chmn. Marine ADv. Bd., 1990. Mem. Marine Adv. Bd., Broward, Fla., 1986-96; rep. Primary Rep. Port Everglades Commn., Broward, 1984. Mem. ABA, ATLA, Am. Bd. Trial Advocacy, Acad. Fla. Trial Lawyers, Broward County Bar Assn., Phi Beta Kappa. Republican. Roman Catholic. Avocations: scuba diving, fishing, water and snow skiing. Home: 2448 SE 12th St Pompano Beach FL 33062-7040 Office: 633 S Andrews Ave Ste 402 Fort Lauderdale FL 33301-2857 Fax: 954-463-9492.

RODRIGUEZ, DAVID GONZALEZ, JR. priest, art and religion educator; b. San Antonio, June 9, 1947; s. David Campos and Maria Beatrice (Gonzalez) R. BFA, Coll. St Francis, 1979; M in pastoral studies, Loyola U., 1984; M in divinity, Cath. Theo. Union, 1988; M in arts inter-discipline, Columbia Coll., 1993; MFA, Md. Inst. Coll. Art, 1995. Cert. elem. tchr., art tchr., Ill. Clk. USAF, 1968-72; tchr. St. Ann's Cath. Sch., Great Falls, Mont., 1969-72; sales & design Gen. Men's Wear, San Antonio, 1972-73; tchr. art and religon St. Jude's Cath. Sch., New Lenox, Ill., 1974-79; tchr. cont. edn. Joliet Jr. Coll., 1976-77; tchr., chair fine arts Providence H.S., 1979-84; tchr., chair arts & religion Hales Francisan H.S., Chgo., 1984—; priest Chgo. and Joliet Dioc., 1989—; chaplain Cruise Lines, Fla., 1989—. Art teach core mem. Chgo. Cath. H.S., 1989—; art dept. evaluator Ill. North Cen., Chgo., 1990—; curriculum staff and evaluator Hales Franciscan H.S., 1990—; adj. faculty art edn. dept. The Sch. of Art Inst. Chgo., 1994—, apprentice tchr. supr., 1995—. One-man show Courtyard Gallery, Chgo., 1997; exhbns. include Fox Gallery, Balt., 1999, Alex Gallery, Washington, 1999, South Shore Cultural Ctr., Chgo., 2000; represented in permanent collections at Mus. Sci. & Industry, Chgo., Sco. of Art Inst. Chgo., Columbia Coll., Chgo. Juror fine arts Art Reach, Chgo., 1990—; mem. Arts Basics, Art. Inst. Chgo., 1990—; mem. Gt. Falls Symphony Chorus. With USAF, 1968-72. Coca-Cola fellow Md. Inst. Coll. Art, 1991-95. Mem. Nat. Cath. Edn. Assn., Nat. Art Edn. Assn., Cath. Edn. Archdiocese of Chgo., Facets Cinema, Art Inst. Chgo., Mex. Fine Arts Mus. Roman Catholic. Avocations: dance, remodeling design, floral design, cooking, choreography, painting. Home: 5225 S Greenwood St Chicago IL 60615-2623 Office: Hales Franciscan HS Province 4930 S Cottage Grove Ave Chicago IL 60615-2623

RODRIGUEZ, DONNA JEANNE ANGLIN, dietitian, writer; b. Albuquerque, July 21, 1953; d. Randolph Sterling and Audrey Miriam (Kubach) Anglin; m. Ralph A. Rodriguez, Feb. 19, 1977. BS, N.Mex. State U., 1975; MS, U. N.Mex., 1996. Cert. nutrition support dietitian; registered dietitian. Clin. dietitian U. N.Mex. Hosp., Albuquerque, 1977-91, nutrition support coord., 1991-95, rsch. coord., 1995-96, vis. prof./lectr., 1996-97; profl. healthcare writer Lovelace Healthcare Innovations, Albuquerque, 1997-98; clin. dietitian West Albuquerque Dialysis Ctr., 1999—. Assoc. editor: (jour.) Support Line, 1996—; contbr. articles to profl. jours., chpts. to books. Mem. Am. Soc. Parenteral and Enteral Nutrition, N.Mex. Soc. Parenteral and Enteral Nutrition, Am. Dietetic Assn., N.Mex. Dietetic Assn., Am. Burn Assn. (chmn. nutrition spl. interest group 1994-96). Avocations: camping, needlework.

RODRIGUEZ, EDWARD JOHN, educational software developer; b. San Antonio, Mar. 27, 1959; s. Robert Benedict and Maria Alicia Rodriguez. BA in Journalism, U. N.Mex., 1981; MBA, Pepperdine U., 1997. Sports reporter, photographer KOAT-TV, Albuquerque, 1978; news announcer KUNM Radio, 1978-79; news reporter, photographer KOB-TV, 1979-83; pres. Kismet Prodn. Corp., 1983-87; asst. coord. Columbia Pictures TV, L.A., 1988-93; adminstr. UCLA Med. Ctr., 1994-95; pres. Evening Star Prodns., L.A., 1996—. Recipient 1st pl. N.Mex. State Wrestling Championship, 1976, 1st pl. award S.W. Creative Writing Assn., 1977, 1st pl. TV comml. award ADDY, Albuquerque, 1985. Avocation: judo (black belt). Home and Office: 3741 S Bentley Ave Apt 2 Los Angeles CA 90034-6927

RODRIGUEZ, ELENA GARCIA, retired pension fund administrator; b. Havana, Cuba, Mar. 21, 1944; came to U.S., 1959; d. Eliseo and Elena (Suarez) Garcia; divorced; children: Victor, Yvonne, Daniel. B in Profl. Studies, Barry U., 1983; MS in Mgmt., St. Thomas U., 1985; postgrad., U. Phila., 1989, UCLA, 1990. With City of Miami, Fla., 1969-95, pension adminstr., 1978-95, ret., 1995. Author: General and Sanitation Pension Benefit Booklet, 1982, Fire and Police Pension Benefit Booklet, 1982, Retirement Planning Booklet, 1985; author numerous programs dealing with pension and acctg. for pension assets. Mem. Leadership Miami, 1985—; mediator Cir. Ct., family, County Ct. Mem. Nat. Assn. Security Dealers (arbitrator and mediator), Fed. Emergency Mgmt. Agency, Internat. Found. Employee Benefit Plans, Internat. Pers. Mgmt. Assn., Inst. Fiduciary Edn., Assn. Conflict Resolution, Fla. Assn. City Clks., N.Y. Stock Exch. (arbitrator and mediator), Better Bus. Bur. (arbitrator, mediator). Republican. Roman Catholic. Avocations: growing orchids, stained glass, tile mosaics, painting.

RODRIGUEZ, ENSOR, physician, scientist; b. San Juan, P.R., Jan. 11, 1937; s. Ensor A. Rodriguez and Josefina Lopez; m. Aida Lucia Herrera, Sept. 3, 1957; children: Jose E., Marisela, Marisol, David E. MPH, Harvard U., 1958; MD, U. Salamanca, Spain, 1961; PhD, The Johns Hopkins U., 1976. Diplomate Am. Bd. Preventive Medicine. Commd. med. officer USAF, 1964, advanced through grades to col., 1976; deputy dir. Aerospace Med. Rsch. Lab., Dayton, Ohio, 1978-80; med. dir. USAF Hosp., Patrick AFB, Fla., 1980-82; staff surgeon USAF Sys. Command, Washington, 1982-84; corp. med. dir. Atlantic Richfield Co., L.A., 1984-92; intern Dist. Hosp., Arecibo, P.R.; residency Sch. Pub. Health Harvard U.; resident Sch. Aerospace Medicine USAF; cons. PACT, L.A., 1993—. Fellow Ctr. Performance Humana. Office: PACT 121 S Hope St Apt 2 Los Angeles CA 90012-5002 E-mail: rodensor@aol.com.

RODRIGUEZ, FERDINAND, chemical engineer, educator; b. Cleve., July 8, 1928; s. José and Concha (Luís) R.; m. Ethel V. Koster, July 28, 1951; children: Holly Edith, Lida Concha. BS, Case Western Res. U., 1950, MS, 1954; PhD, Cornell U., 1958. Devel. engr. Ferro Corp., Bedford, Ohio, 1950-54; asst. prof. chem. engring. Cornell U., 1958-61, assoc. prof., 1961-71, prof., 1971—. On sabbatic leave at Union Carbide Corp., 1964-65, Imperial Chem. Industries, Ltd., 1971, Eastman Kodak Co., 1978-79; cons. to industry. Author: Principles of Polymer Systems, 4th edit., 1996; contbr. numerous articles to profl. jours.; songwriter. Served with U.S. Army, 1954-56. Recipient Excellence in Teaching award Cornell Soc. Engrs., 1966, Edn. Achievement award Hispanic Engr. Mag., 1991. Fellow Am. Inst. Chem. Engrs.; mem. Am. Chem. Soc., Soc. Hispanic Profl. Engrs., Soc. Plastics Engrs. Lutheran. Home: 107 Randolph Rd Ithaca NY 14850-1720 Office: 230 Olin Hall Cornell U Ithaca NY 14853 E-mail: FR13@cornell.edu.

RODRIGUEZ, FRED HENRY, JR. pathologist, educator; b. New Orleans, Oct. 5, 1950; s. Fred Henry and Lorraine Esther (Fitzpatrick) R.; m. Susan Marilyn Miller, Dec. 22, 1973; children: Alison Patricia, Fred Henry, Kathryn Lorraine, David Miller. BS in Biology, U. New Orleans, 1972; MD, La. State U., 1975. Diplomate in anat. and clin. pathology, immunopathology Am. Bd. Pathology, mem. immunology test com., 1988-94. Pathology intern Charity Hosp., New Orleans, 1975-76, resident in pathology, 1976-79, co-chief resident, 1978, vis. pathologist, 1979—; instr. dept. pathology La. State U. Med. Ctr., 1978-80, asst. prof., 1980-83, assoc. prof., 1983-93, prof., 1993—, asst. prof. dept. med. tech., 1980-83, assoc. prof., 1983-93, prof., 1993—, assoc. dir. diagnostic electron microscopy lab., 1978—; staff. pathologist VA Med. Ctr., 1979—, chief lab. svc., 1984—, v.p. med. staff, 1990. Author, co-author sci. articles; author course manual for slide series, course manual for clin. pathology. Bd. dirs. Ronald McDonald House, New Orleans, 1982-89. Recipient biol. scis. faculty award U. New Orleans, 1972; Am. Cancer Soc. grantee, 1974. Fellow Coll. Am. Pathologists (VA adminstrv. del. Ho. of Dels. 1988—); mem. AMA (Physicians Recognition awards), So. Med. Assn., Am. Soc. Clin. Pathologists (immunology exam. com. bd. registry 1986-92, cons. R&D com. 1988-94, bd. govs. 1991—, adv. coun. 1991—, sec. 1995-99), Am. Soc. Clin. Pathologists (bd. dirs. 1999—), Internat. Acad. Pathology, U. New Orleans Alumni Assn. (awards and scholarship com. 1986—), Alpha Omega Alpha, Phi Eta Sigma, Beta Beta Beta, Phi Kappa Phi. Office: 1601 Perdido St # 113 New Orleans LA 70112-1262

RODRIGUEZ, GENO (EUGENE RODRIGUEZ), artist, arts administrator; b. N.Y.C., June 2, 1940; s. Eugenio and Juana (Lopez) R.; m. Janice Rooney, Oct., 1966; 1 dau., Samantha Marisol. Student, Internat. Peoples Coll., Elsinor, Denmark, 1961-62; nat. diploma in art, Hammersmith Coll. Art, London, 1966. Founder, pres., exec. dir. Alternative Center for Internat. Arts Alternative Museum, N.Y.C., 1975—; instr. photography Sch. Visual Arts, 1978-82, Rutgers U., 1977-79; founder, dir. Alternative Mus., 1982. Mem. Artists Cert. Appeals Bd., N.Y.C., 1979, spl. artist task force N.Y. State Council on Arts, 1981; panelist, cons. NEA, Dept. Cultural Affairs N.Y.C.; curator Internet exhbns.; lectr. in field. Exhibited in one-man shows Il Diaframa Gallery, Milan, Italy, 1979, Mus. Contemporary Arts, Caracas, Venezuela, 1979, Real Art Ways Gallery, Hartford, Conn., 1980, Cayman Gallery, N.Y.C., 1980, CEPA Gallery, Buffalo, 1987, Sheldon Meml. Art Gallery U. Nebr., Lincoln, 1989; group shows include Autoren Gallery, Munich, 1980, Miss. Mus. Art, Jackson, 1981, Palacio de Minerias, Mexico City, 1981, J.A.M. Gallery, N.Y.C., 1981, Chrysler Mus., Norfolk, Va., 1981, Am. Indian Gallery, 1982, Roger Litz Gallery, N.Y., 1982, Tweed Gallery, N.J., 1983, Baumgartner Gallery, Washington, 1983, Municipality of Genoa, Italy, 1984, Phila. Arts Alliance, 1985, Jayne H. Baum Gallery, N.Y.C., 1985-86, Gerald Melberg Gallery, Charlotte, N.C., 1985, Eupherat Gallery, Calif., 1986, N.Y. State Mus., Albany, 1986, Hillwood Art Gallery, N.Y., 1986, Stux Gallery, Boston, 1986, San Diego Mus. Art, 1987, Alternative Mus., N.Y.C., 1987, Graham Modern, N.Y.C., 1987, Internat. Ctr. Photography, N.Y.C., 1987, Haggerty Mus. Art Marquette U., Milw., 1988, Herter Art Gallery U. Mass., 1989, Nat. Mus. Am. Art Smithsonian Instn., 1989; represented in permanent collections Internat. Ctr. Photography, N.Y.C., Mus. City of N.Y., Met. Mus. Art, N.Y.C., Everson Mus. Art, Syracuse, N.Y., Am. Mus. Natural History, N.Y.C., Mus. Contemporary Art, Caracas, Venezula; author: The Islands: Worlds of the Puerto Ricans, 1974, Mira, Mira, Mira Puerto Rican New Yorkers, 1975. Active Clinton/Gore Presdl. Transition Team for Arts and Humanites, 1992. Served with USN, 1959-63. Recipient Phelps-Stokes Fund award, 1977; Ludwig Vogelstien Found. award, 1981; Nat. Endowment for Arts fellow, 1979 Mem. Am. Assn. Mus. (exec. mem. curators com. 1985). Office: Apt 9A 32 W 82nd St New York NY 10024-5622

RODRIGUEZ, GEORGE P. poet, editor; b. N.Y.C., Oct. 22, 1949; s. Francis Joseph Rodriguez and Josephine Rosemary Malfa; 1 child Gregory. AA, St. John's U., 1973. Democrat. Roman Catholic. Avocation: collecting. Home: 495 N Washington Ave Titusville FL 32796

RODRIGUEZ, GRISELL, librarian, educator; b. Chgo., Apr. 3, 1967; d. Luciano and Margarita (Valazquez) Rodriguez. BA in Philosophy, U. Puerto Rico, Mayaguez, 1993; MLS, U. Wis., 1996. From cataloger to patents libr. U. Puerto Rico, Mayaguez, 1996—2000, automation dept. head, 2000—. Grantee Hispanic Serving Instns. grant, U.S. Dept. Edn. Mem.: ALA, Assn. Coll. & Rsch. Libr. Avocations: reading, music, exercise, travel. Home: Casa G-1 Urb Vista del Rio Anasco PR 00610 Office: Univ Puerto Rico Libr PO Box 9022 Mayaguez PR 00681-9022 Office Fax: 787-265-5456. E-mail: g.rodriguez@rumlib.uprm.edu.

RODRIGUEZ, IRENE TOBIAS, artist, art educator; b. Cleve., Dec. 1, 1942; d. Howard A. and Matilda M. (Cook) Tobias; m. Randy Vanek (div.) children: Keith A., Heather G. Johnson; m. Ricardo S. Rodriguez, June 1, 1991; step children: Richard, Tracy Hugus. BS in Art Edn., Bowling Green State U., 1964; postgrad. studies, Hiram (Ohio) Coll., 1973, U. Calif., Berkeley, 1980-87. Cert. tchr., Ohio. Art instr. Mentor (Ohio) Schs., 1964-66, Cardinal Schs., Middlefield, Ohio, 1966-68, Jefferson (Ohio) Area Local Schs., 1974-91, N. Canton (Ohio) Pub. Libr., 1991-93; instr. art adult edn. Canton (Ohio) Local Schs., 1995; art instr. Canon Mus. of Art, 1993-2000, pvt. practice, N. Canton, Ohio, 1991—. Designer Trinity United Ch. of Christ, 1991; designer Stark County Power Squadron, Canton, 1992—, Dock of the Bay Yacht Club, Sandusky, Ohio, 1997. Inventor: Board Game; artist; paintings shown in numerous exhbns in Ohio; painting, photograph reproduced in "The Ensign", 1995, 97, 99; represented in pvt. collections Dept. Commerce, State of Ohio, Grape Jamboree Collection, Geneva, Ohio. Recipient numerous awards including Artist Mag., 1987. Mem. Canton Artists League, Canton Mus. of Art, U.S. Power Squadrons, Stark County Squadron (officer 1995—). Avocation: boating. Home and Office: 1447 Jonathan Ave SW North Canton OH 44720-4117

RODRIGUEZ, JESUS ALONZO, chiropractor; b. Juarez, Chih, Mex., Jan. 10, 1950; arrived in U.S., 1959; s. Salvador Alonzo Rodriguez, Consuelo Martinez; m. Maria Cecilia Guevara, Apr. 5, 1974; children: Alejandro, Adrian, Vanessa, Omar. AA, El Paso C.C., 1976; BS, U. Tex. El Paso, 1982; D of Chiropractic, Tex. Chiropractic Coll., 1986. Dr. chiropractic, El Paso, 1987—. Asst. instr. chiropractic Tex. Chiropractic Coll., Pasadena, 1985—86, head intern radiology, 1985—86. E-4 USAF, 1969—73, Vietnam. Recipient award, League United Latin-Am. Citizens, 1989. Mem.: El Pa;so Chiropractic Assn., Tex. Chiropractic Assn., Chiropractic Rehab. Assn., Am. Chiropractic Assn. Democrat. Avocations: writing, reading. Office: 1420 Geronimo Bldg 8 Ste 1 El Paso TX 79925

RODRIGUEZ, JOSÉ L. biochemist; b. Bayamo, Oriente, Cuba, Sept. 7, 1953; arrived in U.S., 1992; s. Angel Lorenzo Rodriguez, Juana Garcia; m. Maria de los Angeles Sierra, July 29, 1976; children: Luis Enrique, Maria Denisse. BS in Biochemistry, U. Havana, 1974; BSChE, HPI Jose A. Echau, Cuba, 1988. Cert. med. technologist Fla. Chief biochemistry dept. A.A. Aballi Children's Hosp., Havana, Cuba, 1980—92; prof. St. Louis Career Acad., Mo., 1992—. Prof. biol. sci. Carlos J. Finby Inst. Health, Havana, 1985—90; cons. A.A. Aballi Hosp., Havana, 1985—92. Contbr. Mem.: NSTA. Avocation: Avocations: sports, music, stamp collecting, reading. Home: 4050 Tholossin Ave Saint Louis MO 63116-3635 Office: Saint Louis Career Acad 3125 S Kingshighway Blvd Saint Louis MO 63139-1107

RODRIGUEZ, JUAN ALFONSO, technology corporation executive; b. Santiago, Cuba, Feb. 10, 1941; came to U.S., 1953; s. Alfonso and Marie Madeleine (Hourcadette) R. BEE, CCNY, 1962; MEE, NYU, 1963. Engr. IBM, Poughkeepsie, N.Y. and Boulder, Colo., 1963-68, engring. mgr., 1968-69; dir. tech. Storage Tech. Corp., Louisville, 1969-74, v.p. engring., 1974-77, v.p., gen. mgr. disk, 1977-79, v.p., gen. mgr. optical disk Longmont, 1979-85; pres., CEO Exabyte Corp., Boulder, 1985-87, CEO, 1987-90; chmn., 1987-92; pres. Sweetwater Corp., 1992-93, chmn., 1992-95, also bd. dirs.; prof. elec. and computer engring. and engring. mgmt. U. Colo., 1992—, co-exec. dir. Ctr. for Entrepreneurship, 1994-2000; chmn. Datasonix, 1992-96, Vixel, 1995-99; chmn., CEO Ecrix Corp., 1996—2001; chief technologist, bd. dirs. Exabyte Corp., 2001—. Mem. devel. coun. Coll. Engring. U. Colo., 1990-92; Decisionism Corp.; mem. engring. adv. bd. CCNY, bd. dirs. Colo. Advanced Tech. Enterprise, 1994-98; Robert J. Appel Disting. lectr. law and tech. Law Sch. U. Denver, 1990. Patentee in field. Bd. dirs. Boulder YMCA, 1982-87, U. Colo. Artist Series, 1988-92; mem. bd. govs. Boulder County United Way, 1989-93, chairperson campaign, 1992; commr. Colo. Advance Tech. Inst., 1988-92. Recipient Ind. Quality award Rocky Mountain sect. Am. Soc. Quality Control, 1990, Gen. Palmer award for Outstanding Engr. in Industry The Am. Cons. Engrs. Coun. of Colo., 1995; named Boulder Spirit Entrepreneur of Yr., 1989, Entrepreneur of the Decade Boulder C. of C., 1994, Hispanic Engr. of Yr., Entrepreneur Hispanic Engr. Nat. Achievement Awards

Coun., 1995; finalist Entrepreneur of Yr., Arthur Young & Inc Mag., 1989. Fellow IEEE; mem. Computer Soc. of IEEE (mem. steering com. on mass storage 1981-93), Soc. Photo-Optical Instrumentation Engrs., Boulder C. of C. (chmn. entrepreneurs support program 1989), Greater Denver C. of C. (bd. dirs. 1990-91). Office: Univ Colo PO Box 425 Boulder CO 80309-0425

RODRIGUEZ, JULIO, information technology executive; b. N.Y.C., Feb. 6, 1935; s. Julio Rodriguez and Dora Torres; m. Olga Zatsepina, Jan. 8, 1996; children: Richard, Ronald, Anne Marie, Matthew. BS in Edn., SUNY, Cortland, 1957; MA in English, Queens Coll., 1963; cert. in adminstrn., Hofstra U., 1966; MA in Psychology, NYU, 1971. English and comm. arts tchr. Brentwood and East Islip Schs., Suffolk County, N.Y., 1957-65; instr. edn. and psychology Adelphi Suffolk Coll., Oakdale, 1965-67; rsch. asst. N.Y. City U. Ctr. for Urban Edn., N.Y.C., 1965-67; dep. dean tchr. edn. Adelphi Suffolk Coll., Oakdale, 1967-69; spl. cons. to pres. N.Y.C. Bd. Edn., N.Y.C., 1969-71; exec. v.p. Monserrat Assoc., 1971-73; sr. mgr. quality control RCA Corp., Cherry Hill, N.J., 1973-76; exec. dir. Iprus Inst., N.Y.C., 1982-88; pres. Culturelink Corp., 1988-98; v.p. tng. Global Privacy Solutions, Washington, 1998—. Dir. Mercy Coll. Culture Link Ctr., Dobbs Ferry, N.Y., 1993-95.; U.S. rep. non-govt. orgn. UN Consulate, N.Y.C., 1977-80; spkr., panelist in field; adj. prof. Lehman Coll. CUNY, 1997—. Editor, pub. art/history book: Portraits of the Puerto Rican Experience, 1984; tech. cons. film: The Sun and the Moon, 1988; editor jour. Hispanics and HIV, 1986. Pres. Citizens for Lyndon Johnson, Suffolk County, 1964; mem. com. N.Y.C. Mayoral Transition, 1986. Recipient Civic award Inst. Puerto Rican Culture, 1985. Mem. APA, Am. Anthropol. Assn. Avocations: singing, fishing, travel. Home: 34 Hillside Ave Apt 4C New York NY 10040-4805 E-mail: culturelink@worhdnet.att.net.

RODRIGUEZ, LENOIR, secondary school educator; b. San Antonio, Feb. 9, 1943; d. Leonardo and Maria Luisa Lara; m. Louis Rodriguez, Dec. 30, 1967; children: Anna Laura, Angela. BA, Our Lady of the Lake U., San Antonio, 1965; MEd, Our Lady of the Lake U., 1967. Tchr. English Lanier H.S., San Antonio, 1965—69, Whittier Mid. sch., San Antonio, 1969—84, Brackenridge H.S., San Antonio, 1984—99, curriculum coord., 1999—. Home: 12810 Varrientos San Antonio TX 78233 Office: Brackenridge High Sch 400 Eagleland San Antonio TX 18210

RODRIGUEZ, LEONARD, foundation administrator; b. Phoenix, Jan. 27, 1944; s. Jesus H. and Manuela (Razo) R.; m. Jo Ann Gama, Jan. 16, 1965 ; 1 child, Lena Teresa. BS in Mktg., Ariz. State U., 1981, MPA, 1995. Cert. tchr., Ariz. Adminstrv. svcs. officer Title XX Adminstrn., Phoenix, 1979-81, Block Grants Adminstrn., Phoenix, 1981-84; property mgmt. mgr. State of Ariz., 1984-86; pres. LTR Mgmt. Svcs., 1986-93; dir. PALS computer literacy program N.W. Resources and Learning Ctr., 1989-91; program cons. City of El Mirage, 1989-91; master tchr. Rio Salado C.C., 1989-91; project dir., exec. dir. Westside Coalition for Substance Abuse Prevention, 1990-91; mem. cpht. svcs. Make-A-Wish Found. of Am., 1993-97; found. adminstn., 1997—. Adj. clin. instr., faculty assoc. Ariz. State U., 1979-89; cons. Applied Econs. Curriculum, Jr. Achievement of Cen. Ariz., Inc., 1987; nat. tng. cons. Ctr. Substance Abuse Prevention, Housing & Urban Devel., Macro Internat., Washington, 1992-93. Chmn. community rels. minority recruitment program Ariz. State U., Tempe, 1985-86; bd. dirs. Concilio Latino de Salud, Inc., pres. 1993-94, Friendly House, Inc., Phoenix, 1985-87, pres., 1987; mem. community problem solving coordinating com. Valley of the Sun United Way, 1988; alliance chmn. Gov.'s Office of Drug Policy, mem. statewide exec. com., 1991; program cons. Cada Uno, Inc., 1990-91; adult literacy coord. Chandler Pub. Libr., 1992-93; tng. cons. Phoenix Fight Back Program, 1992-93; outreach coord. Hemophilia Assn., Ariz., 1992-93. Mem. Am. Soc. Public Adminstrn., Ariz. Adminstrs. Assn., Counterparts (founder 1986), Hispanic C. of C., Vesta Club (chmn. scholarship com. 1983), Rotary (pres. 1987-88, voting del. internat. conv. 1987). Avocations: painting, sculpture, late 19th century art. Home: 6225 N 30th Way Phoenix AZ 85016-2212

RODRIGUEZ, LOUIS JOSEPH, university president, educator; b. Newark, Mar. 13, 1933; m. Ramona Dougherty, May 31, 1969; children: Susan, Michael, Scott. BA, Rutgers U., 1955; MA, La. State U., 1957, PhD, 1963. Dean, Coll. Bus. Adminstrn., Alcee Fortier Disting. prof. Nichols State U., Thibodaux, La., 1958-71; dean Coll. Bus. U. Tex.-San Antonio, 1971-72, v.p. acad. affairs, dean faculty, 1972-73; dean Sch. Profl. Studies U. Houston-Clear Lake City, 1973-75, vice-chancellor, provost, 1975-80; pres. Midwestern State U., Wichita Falls, Tex., 1981—2000; ret., 2000; Hardin Found. prof. Midwestern State U., Wichita Falls, Tex., 1994—. Vice chmn. Coun. Tex. Pub. Univ. Pres. and Chancellors, 1992-93; mem. formula and health professions edn. adv. coms. Tex. Higher Edn. Coordinating Bd. Author 4 books; contbr. over 50 articles to profl. jours. Chmn. bd. Tex. Council on Econ. Edn., Houston, 1981-83; bd. dirs. Joint Council on Econ. Edn., N.Y.C., 1981-83, Goodwill Industries Am., Washington, 1976-82, Robert Priddy Found., 1993-96, Wichita Falls Met. Y.M.C.A., 1999-2000, 4A Economic Devel. Bd., 2000—, Wichita Falls Area Cmty. Found., 1999-2001; pres. Wichita Falls Bd. Commerce and Industry, 1988-89, Clear Lake City Devel. Found., Houston, 1976-77, Goals for Wichita Falls, Inc., 1983; mem. internat. adv. com. Tex. Higher Edn. Coordinating Bd.; pres. United Way Greater Wichita Falls, 1998-99. Recipient Tchr. Edn. Supportive Pres. award Am. Assn. Colls. Tchr. Edn., 1991, Disting. Citizen award N.W. coun. Boy Scouts Am., 1998; named Wichitan of the Yr., 1987; Ford Found. grantee, 1964; Fulbright fellow, 1976 Mem. Am. Assn. State Colls. and Univs. (bd. dirs.), So. Assn. Colls. and Schs. (Commn. on Colls.), Assn. Tex. Colls. and Univs. (pres. 1988-89), Rotary (pres. Downtown Wichita Falls club 1990-91). Mem. Ch. of Christ. Home: 2403 N Elmwood Cir Wichita Falls TX 76308-3813

RODRIGUEZ, MANUEL ALVAREZ, pathologist; b. Guantanamo, Cuba, Nov. 12, 1946; came to U.S., 1961, naturalized, 1970; s. Manuel and Maria Teresa (Alvarez) R.; children: Austin B., Matthew J. BSc in Biology, U. Nev., 1966; MT, St. Alexius Hosp., Bismarck, N.D., 1969; BSc in Medicine, U. N.D., 1971; MD, U. Tex., Galveston, 1973; flight surgeon training, Brooks AFB, San Antonio, 1992. Diplomate Am. Bd. Pathology. Rotating intern Meml. Med. Ctr., Corpus Christi, Tex., 1973-74; commd. USPHS, 1974, advanced through grades to comdr., 1993; gen. surgery resident USPHS Hosp., New Orleans, 1974-75, anatomic/clin. pathology resident, 1975-76, U. N.D. Sch. Medicine, Grand Forks, 1976-77, Touro Infirmary Hosp., New Orleans, 1977-79; pvt. practice Houston, 1979-89; sr. med. officer USPHS-USCG Med. Clinic, New Orleans, 1990-92; flight surgeon, sr. med. officer USPHS-Brooks AFB, San Antonio, 1992, USPHS-USCG Air Sta. Med. Clinic, Sitka, Alaska, 1992-96; clin. dir. USPHS, El Centro, Calif., 1997-98; sr. med. officer PHS Indian Health Ctr., White Earth, Minn., 1998—. Instr. pathology La. State U. Med. Sch., Baton Rouge, 1979-80; tchg. fellow pathology U. N.D. Med. Sch., Grand Forks, 1976-77. Contbr. articles to profl. jours. Dir. charitable donations mil. ann. drive USPHS-USCG, New Orleans, Sitka, 1990-96, Miami Lakes, Fla., 1996. Fellow Am. Acad. Family Practice, Coll. Am. Pathologists. Avocation: writing professional articles. Home: PO Box 354 Dakota City NE 68731

RODRIGUEZ, MIQUEL, prosecutor; b. San Jose, Calif. BA in Econs., BA in Polit. Sci., Cornell U., 1983; JD, Harvard U., 1986. Bar: Pa. 1988, D.C. 1990, Calif. 1990, U.S. Dist. Ct. Wis., U.S. Dist. Ct. Pa. 1988, U.S. Dist. Ct. D.C. 1989, U.S. Dist. Ct. Ky. 1988, U.S. Dist. Ct. Mont. 1989, U.S. Dist. Ct. Hawaii 1989, U.S. Dist. Ct. (so., no., ea., ctrl. dists.) Calif. 1990, U.S. Ct. Appeals (9th cir.) 1990. Law clk. to Hon. Diarmuid F. O'Scannlain U.S. Ct. Appeals 9th cir., 1986-87; trial atty. civil rights divsn. U.S. Dept. Justice, Washington, 1987-90; assoc. ind. counsel Office of Ind. Counsel Kenneth Starr, 1994-95; asst. U.S. atty. criminal and appellate divsns. Office of U.S. Atty., Sacramento, 1990-94, asst. U.S. atty. criminal divsn. ea. dist., 1995—. Contbr. articles to profl. jours. Office: Office of US Atty Federal Courthouse Sacramento CA 95814

RODRIGUEZ, NESTOR JOAQUIN, insurance broker; b. Tulua-Valle, Colombia, Jan. 23, 1959; came to U.S., 1982; s. Pedro Pablo and Edna Lucia R.; m. Ligia Carolina Urroz, Apr. 16, 1988; children: Veronica Alexandra, Mauricio Javier. Degree in Computer Engring., U. INCCA of Colombia, Bogota, 1981; B of Profl. Studies, Barry U., 1989. CLU, ChFC, CFP. V.p. Uniflor, Ltda., Bogota, Colombia, 1979-81; pres. Universal Growers, Inc., Miami, Fla., 1982-84; gen. mgr. The Life Ins. Co. of VA, 1985-92, Interamerican Ins. Brokers, Miami, 1992-96; pres. VMR Ins. Group, Weston, 1996—. Ins. cons. Best-Dorsey Ins., Inc., Coral Gables, Fla., 1996—; spkr. in field; exec. dir. rsch. book Economic Impact Colombia Community, 1992. Author: (insurance guide) Manual del Inversionista, 1990. Founder The Kiwanis Club of Colombia, 1989; dir. Colombian-Am. C. of C., Miami, 1990-92. Recipient Nat. Quality/Sales/Health awards, Fort Lauderdale, 1987-91, Pres.'s awards The Life Ins. Co. of Va., 1990-92; named to Million Dollar Round Table, 1987. Mem. CLU Soc., ChFC Soc., Nat. Assn. Life Underwriters. Republican. Roman Catholic. Avocations: youth coach soccer, golf, little league coach, biking. Office: VMR Ins Group 2222 Ponce De Leon Blvd Ste 400 Coral Gables FL 33134-5039 Home: 1892 Hidden Trail Ln Weston FL 33327-1456

RODRIGUEZ, RAMON, activist, educator; b. Lompoc, Calif., Aug. 16, 1949; s. Ramon Rodriguez and Augustina Pina; m. Grasiela Romero, Aug. 7, 1982. BA, U. Calif., Santa Cruz, 1973; JD, Hastings Coll. Law, 1976. Lifetime cert. c.c. tchr. Instr. Moorpark (Calif.) Coll., 1976-78; housing coord. Commn. on Human Concerns, Ventura, Calif., 1980-85; contracts specialist Pvt. Industry Coun., 1987-88; instr. Ventura Coll., 1989—. Contbr. articles to L.A. Opinion, L.A. Times, Ventura Star, others, 1996—. Organizer S.W. Voter Registration Project, L.A., 2000; vol. elections offices County of Ventura, 1992—; mem. Ventura County Dem. Cen. Com., 1996-2000; co-founder Ventura County Urban League, 1984; founder, chmn. N.Am. Civil Rights Orgn., 1996; vol. St. Vincent de Paul, 2002—; bd. commrs. Ventura Housing Authority, 1984-91. Mem. ABA (cons. 1998), ACLU (bd. dirs.), Am. Polit. Sci. Assn., Hispanic Nat. Bar Assn., Mex.-Am. Polit. Assn., 1999—; Acad. Polit. Sci. (v.p., exec. sec. 1992-96), Hastings Alumni Assn., Santa Clara Valley Dem. Club (founder, pres. 1996). Democrat. Roman Catholic. Avocations: reading, writing, book collecting, classical music. Email: rjrdz@aol.com;nacro'97.

RODRIGUEZ, RICK, newspaper executive editor; b. Salinas, Calif., Apr. 5, 1954; Grad., Stanford U., 1976, Guadalajara, Mex. Newspaper intern Salinas Californian; reporter Fresno (Calif.) Bee, Sacramento (Calif.) Bee, asst. mng. editor, mng. editor, 1993—98, exec. editor & sr. v.p., 1998—. Mem. Pulitzer Prize juries 1994, 95. Mem. Calif. Chicano News Media Assn. (co-founder Sacramento chpt., past bd. dirs.). Office: Sacramento Bee 2100 Q St Sacramento CA 95816-6899*

RODRIGUEZ, ROMAN, physician, child psychiatrist, educator; b. N.Y.C., Jan. 21, 1951; s. Roman Rodriguez and Margarita (Castillo) Torres. BS in Biology, St. Mary's Coll. Calif., 1972; MD, U. Calif., San Francisco, 1976. Diplomate Nat. Bd. Med. Examiners, Am. Bd. Psychiatry and Neurology-Adult Psychiatry, Child and Adolescent Psychiatry. Resident in gen. psychiatry Menninger Found., Topeka, 1976-79, fellow in child psychiatry, 1978-80; resident physician Topeka VA Med. Ctr., 1976-79; dir. psychiat. svcs. Youth Ctr., Topeka, 1979-80; assoc. med. dir. Mission/SE Adolescent Day Treatment Ctr., San Francisco, 1980-81; staff psychiatrist, med. advisor Youth Guidance Ctr., 1980-82; clin. dir. Growing Mind Corp., San Rafael, Calif., 1980-85; pvt. practice child psychiatry San Francisco, San Rafael, 1980-85; child team leader dept. psychiatry Kaiser Permanente Med. Ctr., South San Francisco, 1985-93, physician well being com., 1990-94, chief dept. psychiatry, 1994—. Med. staff Children's Hosp., San Francisco, 1980-85, St. Luke's Hosp., San Francisco, 1981-85, Marin Gen. Hosp., Greenbrae, Calif., 1983-87; asst. clin. prof. U. Calif., San Francisco, 1981—, mem. admissions com. Sch. Medicine, 1980-85; examiner Am. Bd. Psychiatry and Neurology, Inc., 1992—. Bd. dirs. Canal Cmty. Alliance, San Rafael, 1985-86, Cmty. Health Ctr. Marin, Fairfax, Calif., 1985-86, Bahia de Rafael Fourplex, San Rafael, 1986, Village in the Park Homeowners Assn., Daly City, 1991-95; trustee Sacred Heart Cathedral H.S., 1994—. Mem. Am. Psychiat. Assn., Am. Acad. Child and Adolescent Psychiatry, No. Calif. Regional Assn. Child and Adolescent Psychiatry (editor newsletter 1993—), No. Calif. Psychiat. Soc., Calif. Med. Assn., San Mateo County Med. Soc. Republican. Roman Catholic. Office: Kaiser Permanente Med Ctr Dept Psychiatry 1200 El Camino Real Dept South San Francisco CA 94080-3299 E-mail: drroman@msn.com.

RODRIGUEZ, SONIA, dancer; b. Toronto, Ont., Can. Student, Princess Grace Acad., Monaco. Mem. Nat. Ballet Can., Toronto, Canada, 1990—2000, prin. dancer Canada, 2000—. Dancer (ballets) Giselle, The Sleeping Beauty, Coppélia, The Nutcracker, The Merry Widow, Onegin, The Taming of the Shrew, Jewels, Lead pas de deux Désir, Apollo, dancer Cruel World, Terra Firma, The Four Seasons. Office: Walter Carsen Ctr Nat Ballet Can 470 Queens Quay West Toronto ON Canada M5V 3K4*

RODRIGUEZ, TERESA IDA, elementary education educator, educational consultant; b. Levittown, N.Y., Oct. 10, 1951; d. George Arthur and Frieda (Diaz) R. BA in Secondary Edn., Hofstra U., 1973, MA in Bilingual Edn., 1978; profl. diploma in multicultural leadership, L.I. U., 1990. Cert. permanent nursery, kindergarten, elem. Spanish 7-12, bilingual K-6, ESL tchr., sch. dist. adminstr., sch. adminstr., supr., N.Y. Bilingual elem. tchr. Long Beach (N.Y.) Pub. Schs., 1973-76, Hempstead (N.Y.) Pub. Schs., 1976-79; account exec. Adelante Advt., N.Y.C., 1979-81; adminstrv. asst. Assocs. and Nadel, 1981-84; freelance outside prop and set decorator for TV commls., 1984-88; tchr. ESL Central Islip (N.Y.) Pub. Schs., 1988-92; ednl. cons. Houghton Mifflin Co., Princeton, N.J., 1992-95; tchr. 5th grade Central Islip (N.Y.) Pub. Schs., 1995—. Cons. on tchr. tng. Staff Devel. Ctr. Islips, Central Islip, 1989—; cons. on staff devel. Nassau Bd. Coop. Ednl. Svcs., Westbury, N.Y., 1990—, edn. instrn. specialist IBM, 1991; presenter confs., workshops, seminars; cons. and grant writer, N.Y.C. and suburbs. Exhibited in group shows for photography, also one-woman show, 1999. Grantee N.Y. State Div. Bilingual Edn., 1988-90, Staff Devel. Ctr. Islips, 1988, Suffolk Bd. Coop. Ednl. Svcs., 1989; WLIW Pub. TV mini grantee; Pres.'s fellow L.I.U., 1989-90. Mem. ASCD, Internat. Reading Assn. (presenter nat. conf. 1992, 93), N.Y. State ASCD, Suffolk Reading Coun., Smithtown Township Arts Coun. Avocations: tennis, photography, bicycling, swimming. Home: 30 Wheelwright Ln Levittown NY 11756-5233 Office: 545 Clayton St Central Islip NY 11722-3021

RODRIGUEZ, TIMOTHY ALLEN, language educator; b. Fond Du Lac, Wis., July 11, 1958; s. Donald William and Margaret Ann Rodriguez; m. Kathryn Marie Hébert, July 9, 1988; children: William Joseph, Kathryn Ann, Bryan Allen. BS, Western Ill. U., 1982, MS, 1984; PhD, U. Iowa, 1995. Tchr. bilingual edn. Danville (Ill.) Sch. Dist. 118, 1982-83, Houston Ind. Sch. Dist., 1984-86; ESL tchr. Palm Beach (Fla.) County Sch. Dist., 1986-88, 95-97, Martin County Sch. Dist., Stuart, Fla., 1988-91, 98-99; asst. prof. Western Ill. U., Macomb, 1993-95; adj. prof. Nova Southeastern U., Ft. Lauderdale, Fla., 1996-2000; asst. prof. U. Findlay, Ohio, 2001—. Vis. prof. Fla. Atlantic U., 2000-01, Port St. Lucie; validator Nat. Bd. for Profl. Tchg. Stds. Contbr. articles to profl. jours.; presenter Internat. TESOL Conf., 1996. Mem. Internat. TESOL, Internat. Reading Assn., Nat. Assn. Bilingual Edn., Sunshine State TESOL (bd. dirs. 1998-2001).

RODRIGUEZ, VINCENT ANGEL, lawyer, director; b. Cayey, P.R., 1921; s. Vicente and Maria (Antongiorgi) R. BS, Harvard U., 1941; LLB, Yale U., 1944. Bar: N.Y. 1947. Assoc. Sullivan & Cromwell, N.Y.C., 1944-56, ptnr., 1956—. Mem. Council Fgn. Relations, ABA, Assn. Bar City N.Y., Am. Soc. Internat. Law Clubs: River (N.Y.C.). Home: 4521 Fisher Island Dr Miami FL 33109-0156 Office: Sullivan & Cromwell 125 Broad St Fl 28 New York NY 10004-2489

RODRIGUEZ, VIVIAN N. lawyer, accountant; b. Riverdale, N.Y., Dec. 16, 1969; d. Felix and Maria Rodriguez. AA in Bus., Miami Dade C.C., Miami, Fla., 1989; B of Acctg., Fla. Internat. U., Miami, 1991, M of Acctg., 1992; JD, U. Miami, 1995, LLM in Taxation, 2001. Bar: Fla.; CPA, Fla. Acct. Norman A. Eliot & Co., Miami, 1991-96; atty., acct. Managed Recovery Svcs. Corp., 1996-97; sole practitioner, 1997—2001; atty. Office Chief Counsel/IRS/Dept. Treasury, 2001—. Mem. ABA, AICPA, ATLA, Am. Assn. Atty.-CPAs, Fla. Assn. Atty.-CPAs, Fla. Inst. CPAs, Dade County Bar Assn., Fla. Bar. Republican. Roman Catholic. Avocation: science fiction.

RODRIGUEZ, WILLIAM JULIO, physician; b. Ponce, P.R., June 18, 1941; BS, MD, Georgetown U., Washington, 1967; PhD, Georgetown U., 1975. Intern U. Hosp., San Juan, PR, 1967—68; intern and resident Univ. Hosp., P.R., 1967-72; resident in pediatrics U. Hosp., 1970—72; fellow Children's Hosp., Washington, 1972-75; attending in infectious disease Children's Hosp. Nat. Med. Ctr., 1975—; pediat. sci. dir. Pediatric Team, CDER.FDA, 2000—; med. officer USN, 1968—70. Assoc. chief infectious disease and microbiology rsch. Children's Hosp. Med. Ctr., 1979—80, chief infectious disease and microbiology, 1980—83, chmn. infectious disease dept., 1983—2000; cons. staff Hosp. for Sick Children, Washington, 1985—2000, Shady Grove Adventist Hosp., Rockville, Md., 1988—2001, Holy Cross Hosp., Silver Spring, Md., 1988—2001, Columbia Hosp. for Women, 1990—2000; prof. emeritus pediat. George Washington Med. Sch., 2000—. Contbr. articles to profl. jours. MARC fellow, XIII, 1973-76. Fellow Infectious Disease Soc.; mem. AAAS, APS, AAP, SPR, Am. Fedn. Clin. Rsch., Am. Soc. Microbiology, Assn. of Puerto Ricans in Sci. & Engring. Office: FDA 5600 Fisherslune HFD 950 Rm 5A-33 Rockville MD 20857 E-mail: rodriguezw@cder.fda.gov.

RODRIGUEZ, XAVIER, state official, educator; BA, Harvard U., 1983; MPA, JD, U. Tex., 1987. Cert.: Tex. Bd. Legal Specialization (labor and employment law). Ptnr. Fulbright & Jaworksi; justice Supreme Ct. State of Tex., 2001—. Served Judge Advs. Gen's. Corps.; lectr. continuing legal edn. courses. Contbr. chapters to books. Past pres. Respite Care San Antonio; San Antonio C. of C.; vice chmn. State Bd. Educator Certification; mem. bd. dirs. San Antonio Area Found.; mem. adv. bd. to dean St. Mary's U. Sch. Law, U. Tex. at San Antonio Coll. Social and Behavioral Scis. Officer USAR, 1983. Named 40 under 40 Rising Stars, San Antonio Bus. Jour. Fellow: Tex. Bar Found.; mem.: ABA (seven-mem. standing com. on legal assts.), State Bar of Tex. (immediate past. chmn. labor and employment law sect. , standing com. on legal assts.). Office: Supreme Ct PO Box 12248 Austin TX 78711*

RODRIGUEZ ARROYO, JESUS, gynecologic oncologist; b. Arecibo, P.R., Jan. 11, 1948; s. Jesus Rodriguez and Blanca Arroyo; m. Annie Arsuaga, June 3, 1972; children: Ivan, Patricia. BS, U. P.R., San Juan, 1968, MD, 1972, postgrad., 1976. Diplomate Am. Bd. Ob-Gyn. Assoc. dir. gynecologic oncology Oncology Hosp., Rio Piedras, P.R., 1978-83; assoc. prof. ob-gyn, dir. gynecologic oncology U. Hosp. Sch. Medicine, 1978-85; gynecologic oncologist Met. Hosp., 1979-88, Auxilio Mutuo Hosp., P.R., 1981-98; obstetrician, gynecologist San Pablo Hosp., Bayamon, 1981-98, Ashford Meml. Community Hosp., 1983-98. Cons. gynecologic oncology Tchrs. Hosp., Hato Rey, P.R., 1979-86, Hermanos Melendez Hosp., Bayamon, 1979-98; instr. ob-gyn. U. P.R. Sch. Medicine, 1976-78, asst. prof., 1978-83, assoc. prof., 1984, dir. gynecologic oncology sect., 1978-84. Contbr. articles to med. jours. Mem. Citizen Ambassador Cancer Mgmt. Del. to USSR, 1990. Mem. AAAS, Am. Coll. Surgeons, P.R. Med. Assn. (jud. ethical coun. 1990-91), Internat. Gynecologic Cancer Soc., Soc. Gynecologic Oncologists, Dorado Beach Hotel, Caparra Country Club. Home: 1910 Pasionaria St Urban Santa Maria San Juan PR 00927 Office: Caribbean Oncology & Gyn Assn PO Box 194557 San Juan PR 00919-4557 E-mail: caribbeanoncology@hotmail.com.

RODRIGUEZ-CAMILLONI, HUMBERTO LEONARDO, architect, historian, educator; b. Lima, Peru, May 30, 1945; came to U.S., 1963; s. Alfonso and Elda (Camilloni) R.; m. Mary Ann Alexanderson, July 1, 1972; children: Elizabeth Marie, William Howard. BA magna cum laude, Yale U., 1967, MArch, 1971, MPhil, 1973, PhD, 1981. Rsch. asst. Sch. Architecture Yale U., 1964-70, teaching fellow dept. history art, 1971-72, 74-75; chmn. research dept. Centro de Investigacion y Restauracion de Bienes Monumentales Instituto Nacional de Cultura, Lima, 1973; restoration architect OAS, Washington, 1976—; prof. Sch. Architecture Tulane U., New Orleans, 1975-82; prof., dir. Henry H. Wiss Ctr. Theory and History of Art and Architecture, Coll. Architecture and Urban Studies Va. Poly. Inst. and State U., Blacksburg, 1983—, dir. Ctr. for Preservation and Rehab. Tech., Coll. Architecture, 1986—. Vis. prof. U. Ill., Chgo., 1982-83; reviewer, cons. Choice, 1975—; mem. interim bd. dirs. Ctr. Planning Handbook Latin-Am. Art, 1978-87; cons., adviser Internat. Exhbn. and Symposium Latin-Am. Baroque Art and Architecture, 1980; mem. adv. bd. Mountain Lake Symposium on Art and Architecture Criticism, 1985—. Internat. Symposium Luis Barragan, 1990; coord., advisor exhbn. Tradition and Innovation: Painting, Architecture and Music in Brazil, Mex. and Venezuela between 1950-80, 1991, Internat. Art History Colloquium, 1993, 48th Internat. Congress of Americanists, 1994, Congress Internat. Union Architects, 1996, 49th Internat. Congress Americanists, 1997, 2nd European Assn. for Archtl. Edn./Archtl. Rsch. Ctrs. Consortium Conf., 2000; coord., adv. exhbn. Frank Lloyd Wright: An Architect in America, 1995, The Jesuits, Conference II: Cultures, Scis. and the Arts, 1540-1773, 2002. Author: (with Walter D. Harris) The Growth of Latin American Cities, 1971; (with Charles Seymour, Jr.) Italian Primitives, The Case History of a Collection and its Conservation, 1972, Religious Architecture in Lima of the Seventeenth and Eighteenth Centuries: The Monastic Complex of San Francisco el Grande, 1984; contbg. editor Handbook of Latin American Studies, 1987—, The Retablo Facade as Transparency: A Study of the Frontispiece of San Francisco, Lima, 1991, Tradición e Innovación en la Arquitectura del Virreinato del Perú, Constantino de Vasconcelos y la Invención de la Arquitectura de Quincha en Lima Durante el Siglo XVII, 1994, (with Graziano Gasparini) Arquitectura Iberoamericana, 1997, Manuel de Amat y Junyent y la Navona de Lima: un ejemplo de diseño urbano barroco del siglo XVIII en el virreinato del Perú, 1999, (with Mehdi Setareh) Monticello's Dome: Development of an Integrated Resource for the Study of Thomas Jefferson's Architecture, 2000; contbg. editor: The Dictionary of Art, 1991-96, Encyclopedia of Twentieth Century Architecture, 1999. Named Ellen Battell Eldridge fellow, 1970-72, Robert C. Bates Jr. fellow Jonathan Edwards Coll., Yale U., 1970-71, Social Sci. Rsch. Coun. fellow, 1972-74, Yale Concilium Internat. Studies fellow, 1972-73, Giles Whiting fellow, 1974-75, NEH fellow Columbia U., 1983, Hobart and William Smith Colls. fellow, 1987, U. Ill. fellow, 1990, Edilia De Montequin fellow, 1991, NEH fellow U. N.Mex., 1992. Mem. Internat. Archive of Women in Architecture (treas. 1999—), Soc. Archtl. Historians (bd. dir. 1977-80, past. pres., past sec. South Gulf chpt.) SE sect. Soc. Archtl. Historians, Coll. Art Assn. Am., SE Coll. Art Conf., Latin Am. Studies Assn., Assn. Latin Am. Art, Assn. Preservation Va. Antiquities, New River Valley Preservation League (bd. dir. 1987—), Nat. Trust Historic Preservation, Save our Cemeteries (past dir.), Preservation Resource Ctr. (past bd. dir.), Assn. for Preservation Tech., Blacksburg Regional Art Assn. (bd. dir), Inter-Am. Inst. Advanced Studies in Cultural History (bd. dirs. 1996—), KC, Tau Sigma Delta, Phi Beta Delta. Roman Catholic. Office: Va Poly Inst and State U Coll Architecture & Urban Studies Blacksburg VA 24061-0205 E-mail: hcami@vt.edu. *As an educator across the years, I have come to realize that the true art of teaching consists of reaching both the human mind and the human heart.*

RODRIGUEZ-DIAZ, JUAN E. lawyer; b. Ponce, P.R., Dec. 27, 1941; s. Juan and Auristela (Diaz-Alvarado) Rodriguez de Jesus; m. Sonia de Hostos-Anca, Aug. 10, 1966; children: Juan Eugenio, Jorge Eduardo, Ingrid Marie Rodriguez. BA, Yale U., 1963; LLB, Harvard U., 1966; LLM in Taxation, NYU, 1969. Bar: N.Y. 1968, P.R. 1970. Assoc. Baker & McKenzie, N.Y.C., 1966-68, McConnell, Valdes, San Juan, P.R.; undersec. Dept. Treasury P.R., 1971-73; mem. Sweeting, Pons, Gonzalez & Rodriguez, 1973-81; pvt. practice San Juan, 1981-94, Totti & Rodriguez-Diaz, 1994—. Bd. dirs. Ochoa Indsl. Sales Corp., Ensco Caribe, Inc., Industrias Vassallo, Inc. Bd. govs. Aqueduct and Sewer Authority P.R., 1979-84; mem. adv. com. collective bargaining negotiation of P.R. elec. Power Authority to Gov. P.R., 1977-78; bd. govs. P.R. coun. Boy Scouts Am., mem. transition com., 1984-85; mem. adminstrv. coun. Ballajá. Mem. N.Y. State Bar Assn., P.R. Bar Assn., AFDA Club, Berwind Country Club, Palmas de Mar Country Club. Office: Suite 1200 416 Ave Ponce De Leon Hato Rey San Juan PR 00918-3418 E-mail: JERD@TRDLAW.com.

RODRIGUEZ-FIGUEROA, R. VILMARIE, pharmaceutical executive; b. Aibonito, P.R., Nov. 27, 1961; d. Hector Jose Rodríguez and Aurea Esther Figueroa; m. Efrain Flores-Colon, Aug. 12, 1983; children: Veronica A., Andre S. BS in Life Scis. magna cum laude, U. P.R., Cayey, 1983; MS in Chemistry magna cum laude, San Diego State U., 1990. Rsch. assoc., grad. teaching asst. San Diego State U., 1984-89; safety and health specialist Rohr, Inc., Chula Vista, Calif., 1989-92; environ. health & safety specialist Bechman Instruments, Carlsbad, 1992-94; sr. indsl. hygienist San Diego Gas & Elec., 1994-96; assoc. dir. environ. health and safety Ligand Pharms., San Diego, 1996—. Instr. Southwestern Coll., Chula Vista, 1989—; mem. hearing bd. Air Pollution Control Dist., San Diego, 2000—; cons. Internat. Health & Safety, Chula Vista, 1996—. Cubmaster Boys Scouts Am., Chula Vista, 1999—; tchr. Bonita (Calif.) Valley Christian Ctr., 1992-98; dist. mem., rep. New Progressive Party, Cayey, 1981-83. Mem. Am. Indsl. Hygiene Assn. (spl. interest 1999—), Am. Indsl. Hygiene Assn. (pres. San Diego local sect. 1995-96), Biosafety Network San Diego (dir. 1999—), Indsl. environ. Assn., Binat. Air Quality Alliance. Avocations: mountain biking, baking, choral singing. Office: Ligand Pharms 10275 Sci Ctr Dr San Diego CA 91910-1117

RODRIGUEZ-FRANSON, JULIE ISABEL, counselor; b. Jacksonville, Fla., Jan. 22, 1969; d. William Julio and Julie Anne Rodríguez; m. Tad Aaron Franson, Jan. 4, 1997; children: William Christopher, Matthew Aaron. BA, Georgetown U., 1991; MA, George Washington U., 1994. Nat. cert. counselor Nat. Bd. Cert. Counselors. Elem. sch. counselor Family Support Ctr., Bethesda, Md., 1994-96; youth and family counselor Mental Health Assn. Linkages to Learning, Rockville, 1995-99; lower sch. counselor Holton-Arms Sch., Inc., Bethesda, 1995—. Mem. ACA, APA, Nat. Bd. Cert. Counselors. Roman Catholic. Avocations: hiking, arts and crafts. Office: Holton-Arms Sch Inc 7303 River Rd Bethesda MD 20817 Business E-Mail: jrodriguezfrans@holton-arms.edu.

RODRIGUEZ-LAGUNA, ASELA, Spanish language and literature educator; b. San Germán, P.R., Dec. 6, 1946; came to U.S., 1968; d. Ramon Rodriguez and Eugenia Seda; m. Elpidio Laguna, June 21, 1975; children: Asela M., Maria E., Alexandra. BA, U. P.R., Mayaguez, 1968; MA, U. Ill., 1971, PhD, 1973. Asst. prof. Spanish Rutgers U., Newark, 1973-79, assoc. prof. Spanish, 1979—. Dir. study abroad program in Spain, Rutgers U., 1992, 94, 96, 99, acting dir. Dept. Puerto Rican and Hispanic Caribbean Studies. Author: G.B. Shaw en el Mundo Hispánico, 1981; editor: Images and Identities: The Puerto Rican in Two World Contexts, 1987, The Global Impact of Portuguese Language and Culture, 2001. Mem. exec. com. N.J. Coun. for Humanities, New Brunswick, 1987-92. Recipient Paul Robeson Faculty award, 2001; named Prof. of Yr., 2001; grantee NEH, N.J. Coun. Humanities, Dodge Found., 1983, Delmas Found., Luso-Am. Found., 1998. Mem. MLA, Am. Assn. Tchrs. of Spanish and Portuguese, Latin Am. Studies Assn., Lions. Home: 283 Newman St Metuchen NJ 08840-2643 E-mail: arlaguna_andromeda@rutgers.edu.

RODRIGUEZ-LOPEZ, JULIO ARNALDO, surgeon, researcher; b. Caguas, P.R., May 17, 1956; s. Julio Rodriguez and Marcelina Lopez; m. Rebeca Garcia, Mar. 5, 1983; children: Rebeca, Erica, Alexandra. MD, Ctrl. East U., San Pedro Macoris, Dominican Republic, 1982. Diplomate Am. Bd. Surgery. Intern then resident Ponce (Puerto Rico) Regional Hosp., 1985-92; fellow in vascular surgery Ariz. Heart Inst., Phoenix, 1992-93; mem. staff Healthwest Regional Med. Ctr.-Columbia, 1993—; pvt. practice, 1993-97; staff mem. Ariz. Heart Hosp. Adj. asst. prof. affiliate faculty divsn. clin. edn. Midwestern U. Mem. AAAS, ACS, Internat. Soc. Endovascular Surgery, Ariz. Coll. Surgeons, Maricopa County Med. Soc., Cirujanos Vasculares de Habla Hispana. Office: Ariz Heart Inst 2632 N 20th St Phoenix AZ 85006-1339

RODRIGUEZ-SAINS, RENE S. physician, surgeon, educator; b. Santiago, Cuba, July 25, 1952; came to U.S., 1960, naturalized, 1968; s. Emilio Rene Rodriguez and Caridad Sains; m. Juanita Laszlo, Aug. 31, 1974; children: Daniel Rene, Diana. BA cum laude, CUNY, 1973; MD, NYU, 1977. Diplomate Nat. Bd. Med. Examiners, Am. Bd. Ophthalmology. Dermatology rsch. fellow NYU Med. Ctr., N.Y.C., 1973-77, intern dept. medicine, 1977-78; resident in ophthalmology Manhattan Eye, Ear and Throat Hosp., 1978-81, chief resident in ophthalmology, 1980-81, asst. attending surgeon, 1981-85, assoc. attending surgeon Ophthalmic Plastic & Reconstructive Surgery, Ocular Tumor & Orbital Clinic, 1985-89, surgeon dir. Ophthalmic Plastic & Reconstructive Surgery Clinic, 1989-93, surgeon dir., chief Ocular Tumor & Orbital Clinic, 1989-93; attending surgeon, chief Manhattan Eye, Ear And Throat Hosp., N.Y.C., 1993—, attending surgeon ophthalmic plastic and reconstructive surgery clinic, 1993—, dir. internat. fellowship program, 1991—. Heed Ophthalmic Found. fellow Manhattan Eye, Ear and Throat Hosp.-N.Y. Hosp., Cornell U. Med. Ctr., 1981-82, resident instr. dept. ophthalmology, 1983-85; adj. asst. prof. dermatology NYU, 1981-88; clin. asst. prof. ophthalmology, Mt. Sinai Med. Ctr.; attending surgeon Dept. Ophthalmology, Plastic and Reconstructive Surgery divsn., Bronx VA Hosp., 1985-88; clin. asst. prof. Dept. Ophthalmology, NYU Med. Ctr., 1988—. Mem. med. adv. bd. Skin Cancer Found., 1980—; mem. NYU Malignant Melanoma Clin. Coop. Group, 1981—; bd. dirs. Orbital Disease Found., 1994—; mem. Barraquer Inst. Barcelona, Spain, N.Y. Soc for Clin. Ophthalmology. Contbg. editor Jour. Dermatologic Surgery ad Oncology, 1980-90; co-author: Malignant Melanoma, 1979; contbr. articles to med. jours. Fellow Am. Coll. Surgeons, Am. Acad. Facial Plastic and Reconstructive Surgery, Am. Soc. Ophthalmic Plastic and Reconstructive Surgery, N.Y. Acad. Medicine; mem. AMA, N.Y. State Ophthalmol. Soc., Am. Assn. Ophthalmology, Assn. Rsch. in Vision and Ophthalmology, Manhattan Ophthalmologic Soc., N.Y. County Med. Soc., Med. Soc. State N.Y., Am. Acad. Ophthalmology. Office: 178 E 71st St New York NY 10021-5119

RODTS, GERALD EDWARD, JR. neurosurgeon, spine specialist, educator; b. July 18, 1961; BA in Biology, Princeton U., 1983; MD, Columbia U., 1987. Diplomate Am. Bd. Neurol. Surgery. Resident in neurosurgery UCLA, 1987-94; fellow in spine surgery/neurosurgery Emory U., Atlanta, 1994-95, asst. prof. neurosurgery, 1995-99, assoc. prof. neurosurgery, 1999—. Author textbooks on spinal surgery; contbr. articles to med. jours. Achievements include research in computer-assisted image-guidance in spinal surgery and minimally-invasive spinal surgery. Office: Emory Clinic Neurosurgery 550 Peachtree St NE Ste 806 Atlanta GA 30308-2247

ROE, BENSON BERTHEAU, surgeon, educator; b. L.A., July 7, 1918; s. Hall and Helene Louise (Bertheau) R.; m. Jane Faulkner St. John, Jan. 20, 1945; children: David B., Virginia St. John. AB, U. Calif., Berkeley, 1939; MD cum laude, Harvard U., 1943. Diplomate Am. Bd. Surgery, Am. Bd. Thoracic Surgery (dir. 1971-83, chmn. bd. 1981-83, chmn. exam. com. 1978, chmn. long-range planning com. 1980, chmn. program com. 1977). Intern Mass. Gen. Hosp., Boston, 1943-44, resident, 1946-50; nat. rsch. fellow dept. physiology Med. Sch., Harvard U., 1947, instr. surgery, 1950; Moseley Traveling fellow Harvard. U. at U. Edinburgh, Scotland, 1951; asst. clin. prof. surgery U. Calif., San Francisco, 1951-58, chief cardiothoracic surgery, 1958-76, prof. surgery, 1966-89, emeritus prof., 1989—; pvt. practice medicine specializing in cardiothoracic surgery, 1952-85. Sr. scientist Cardiovascular Rsch. Inst., 1956-89; cons. thoracic surgery VA Hosp., San Francisco Gen. Hosp., Letterman Army Hosp., St. Lukes Hosp., Blue Shield of Calif., Baxter Labs., Ethicon, Inc.; bd. dirs. Control Laser Corp.; vis. prof. U. Utah, U. Ky., U. Gdansk, Poland, Nat. Heart Hosp., London, U. Ibadan, Nigeria, Sanger Clinic, Charlotte, Rush-Presbyn. Hosp., Chgo., Penrose Hosp., Colorado Springs. Mem. editl. bd. Annals of Thoracic Surgery, 1969-82, Pharos, E-medicine; editor 2 med. texts; author 21 textbook chpts.; contbr. 174 articles to profl. jours. Bd. dirs. United Bay Area Crusade, 1958-70, mem. exec. com., 1964-65; bd. dirs. chmn. exec. com. San Francisco chpt. Am. Cancer Soc., 1955-57; bd. dirs. San Francisco Heart Assn., 1964-72, pres., 1964-65, chmn. rsch. com., 1966-71; mem. various coms. Am. Heart Assn., 1967-70; pres. Miranda Lux Found., 1982-94; trustee Avery-Fuller-Welch Found.; bd. dirs. Internat. Bioethics Inst., Point Reyes Bird Observatory. Served with Med. Svc. Corps, USNR, 1944-46. Inductee Rowing Hall of Fame, 1979, U. Calif. Athletic Hall of Fame, 1995. Fellow Am. Coll. Cardiology, ACS (chmn. adv. coun. thoracic surgery, program chmn. thoracic surgery, cardiovascular com.), Polish Surg. Assn. (hon.); mem. Am. Assn. Thoracic Surgery (chmn. membership com. 1974-75), AMA (residency rev. com. for thoracic surgery), Am. Surg. Assn., Pacific Coast Surg. Assn., Calif. Acad. Medicine (pres. 1974), Calif. Med. Assn., Soc. Univ. Surgeons, Soc. Thoracic Surgeons (pres. 1972, chmn. standards and ethics com.), Soc. Vascular Surgery (v.p.). Clubs: Cruising of Am, Pacific Union, St. Francis Yacht, Calif. Tennis. Office: U Calif Div Cardiothoracic Surgery U Calif M593 San Francisco CA 94143-0118 E-mail: ghotieg@earthlink.net.

ROE, BRUCE A. chemistry educator, researcher; b. N.Y.C., Jan. 1, 1942; s. Sanford Joseph and Ann M. (La Marca) R.; m. Judy Ann Pessek, June 7, 1963; children: Nathaneal Peter, Caroline Mary. BA in Chemistry, Math., and Physics, Hope Coll., 1963; MA in Chemistry and Biochemistry, Western Mich. U., 1967, PhD in Chemistry and Biochemistry, 1970. H.s. chemistry and biochemistry tchr. Marshall (Mich.) Pub. Schs., 1963-68; grad. tchg. fellow Western Mich. U., Kalamazoo, 1968-70; NIH postdoctoral rsch. fellow SUNY, Stony Brook, 1970-73; asst. prof. chemistry Kent (Ohio) State U., 1973-77, assoc. prof. chemistry and rsch., 1977-81; assoc. prof. pathology and biology Northeastern Ohio U. Coll. Medicine, Rootstown, 1977-81; prof. biochemistry U. Okla., Norman, 1981—, adj. prof. biochemistry and molecular biology, 1981—, George Lynn Cross Rsch. prof., 1997—, mem. radiation safety bd., chairperson DNA recombinant com., 1989—. Author: DNA Isolation and Sequencing: Essential Techniques Serise, 1999; editor Biotechniques, 1990—; mem. editl. bd. Genome Rsch.; contbr. more than 160 articles to profl. jours. including Geonomics, Sci., Human Molecular Genetics, Nucleic Acids Rsch., Biochemistry, among others. Elder First Presbyn. Ch., Norman. Recipient numerous grants. Mem. AAAS, Am. Soc. for Biochemistry and Molecular Biology. Home: 2822 Walnut Rd Norman OK 73072 Office: U Okla Dept Chemistry 620 Parrington Oval Rm 311 Norman OK 73019 E-mail: broe@ou.edu.

ROE, BYRON PAUL, physics educator; b. St. Louis, Apr. 4, 1934; s. Sam S. and Gertrude Harriet (Claris) R.; m. Alice Susan Krauss, Aug. 27, 1961; children: Kenneth David, Diana Carol. BA, Washington U., St. Louis, 1954; PhD, Cornell U., 1959. Instr. physics U. Mich., Ann Arbor, 1959-61, asst. prof., 1961-64, assoc. prof., 1964-69, prof., 1969—. Guest physicist SSC Lab., 1991. Author: Probability and Statistics in Experimental Physics, 1992, 2d edit., 2001, Particle Physics at the New Millennium, 1996 (Libr. Sci. Book Club selection). CERN vis. scientist Geneva, 1967, 89; Brit. Sci. Rsch. Coun. fellow, Oxford, 1979; recipient inventor's prize CDC Worldtech, Edina, Minn., 1982, 83. Fellow Am. Phys. Soc. Home: 3610 Charter Pl Ann Arbor MI 48105-2825 Office: U Mich Physics Dept 500 E University Ave Ann Arbor MI 48109-1120 E-mail: byronroe@umich.edu.

ROE, CHARLES BARNETT, lawyer; b. Tacoma, June 25, 1932; s. Charles Brown and Gladys Luvena (Harding) R.; m. Marilyn Marie Quam, July 31, 1954; children: Sharon Lynn De Groot, Jeannine Carole Roe Dellwo. AB, U. Puget Sound, 1953; postgrad. U. Calif., Berkeley, 1957-58; JD, U. Wash., 1960. Bar: Wash. 1960, U.S. Dist. Ct. (ea. and we. dists.) 1960, U.S. Ct. Appeals (9th cir.) 1963, U.S. Supreme Ct. 1963, U.S. Ct. Appeals (D.C. cir.) 1964. Asst. atty. gen. depts. natural resources, conservation, water resources and pollution control commn., State of Wash., Olympia, 1960-70, asst. dir. dept. water resources, 1967-69, sr. asst. atty. gen., 1970-90; of counsel Perkins Coie, Olympia, 1991—; chief counsel dept. ecology and nuclear waste, 1970-85, Nuclear Waste Bd., 1983-90; counsel natural resources com. Wash. Ho. of Reps., Olympia, 1970; adj. prof. Gonzaga U. Sch. Law, Spokane, 1973-76, U. Puget Sound Law Sch., 1985-90; contractor Nat. Water Commn., Washington, 1970-71. Rep., Western States Water Coun., Salt Lake City, 1970-90; sec. Olympia Audubon Soc., 1962-63; chmn. bd. mgrs. United Chs., Olympia, 1967-68. Served to 1st lt. USAF, 1954-57. Mem. ABA (chmn. water resources com. natural resources sect. 1981-83), Wash. State Bar (chmn. environ. law sect. 1971-72), Washington Cts. Hist. Soc. (bd. dirs. 1998—), Mason, Rotary, Kappa Sigma, Phi Delta Phi. Mem. United Ch. of Christ. Home: 2400 Wedgewood Dr SE Olympia WA 98501-3841 Office: 111 Market St NE Olympia WA 98501-6965

ROE, GERALD BRUCE, director, writer; b. Cushing, Wis., June 16, 1940; s. Fred Walter and Maybell Meranda (Swenson) R.; m. Laurel A. Nagel, Sept. 12, 1964 (dec. Feb. 1990); children: Stephen, David. BA, U. Minn., 1964, postgrad., 1969-71; MA, Coll. St. Thomas, 1967. Tchr. St. Anthony Padua H.S., Mpls., 1965-68, Ctrl. H.S., St. Paul, 1968-69; asst. to dir. bur. recommendations U. Minn., Mpls., 1973; assoc. dir. ednl. placement U. Iowa, Iowa City, 1974—. Co-author: (with Rebecca Anthony) Over 40 and Looking for Work, 1991, The Curriculum Vitae Handbook, 1994, 2d edit., 1998, 101 Grade A Resumés for Teachers, 1994, 2d edit., 1998; contbr. articles to profl. jours. Bd. dirs. Iowa City Cmty. Theatre, 1994-98. Mem. Phi Delta Kappa (chpt. 0005, v.p. 1990-94, pres. 1994-97). Avocation: theatre. Office: Univ Iowa Ednl Placement 302 Lindquist Ctr N Iowa City IA 52242-1529 E-mail: gerald-roe@uiowa.edu.

ROE, MARK J. law educator; b. N.Y.C., Aug. 8, 1951; m. Helen Hsu, Aug. 12, 1974; children: Andrea Hsu, Jessica Hsu. BA, Columbia U., 1972; JD, Harvard U., 1975. Bar: N.Y. 1976. Atty. Fed. Res. Bank, N.Y.C., 1975-77; assoc. Cahill Gordon & Reindel, 1977-80; prof. Rutgers U. Law Sch., Newark, 1980-86, U. Pa. Law Sch., 1986-88, Columbia U. Law Sch., N.Y.C., 1988-2001, Harvard Law Sch., Cambridge, Mass., 2001—. Author: Strong Managers, Weak Owners: The Political Roots of American Corporate Finance, 1994, Corporate Reorganization and Bankruptcy, 2000, Political Determinants of Corporate Governance, 2002. Office: Harvard Law Sch 435 W 116th St Cambridge MA 02138 E-mail: mroe@law.harvard.edu.

ROE, MARY ANN, postmaster; b. Greenwich, Conn., Jan. 10, 1945; d. Frederick Johnston and Doris Irene Capp; m. Robert Andrew Roe, June 17, 1966; children: Jeffrey Brian, Jennifer Yvonne. Student, S.W. Mo. State U., 1969, N.E. Mo. State U., 1970. Clk. U.S. Postal Svc., Brookfield, Mo., 1977-82, supt. postal ops., 1983-93, postmaster, 1993—. Author: Roe's Reference, 1987; contbr. articles to mags. Sec.-treas. Busy Women's Club, Brookfield, 1990—; asst. leader Girl Scouts U.S.A., Brookfield, 1990-99. Recipient Best Column award Show Me Postmaster, 1997. Mem. Nat. Assn. Postmasters U.S. (instr. conv. 1996, 97, 2001, Mo. Career Devel. com. 1996-98, state editor 1999—). Methodist. Avocations: reading, sewing, travel. Office: US Postal Svc 104 N Grant St Wheeling MO 64688-9998

ROE, RICHARD C. industry consultant, former home furnishings manufacturing executive; b. Des Moines, Jan. 4, 1930; s. Lloyd E. and Mary E. (Nuzum) R.; m. Sally McGlothlen, Dec. 27, 1952; children: Stephen James, Julie Ann. BS in Gen. Engring, Iowa State U., 1952. Registered profl. engr., Iowa, Ind., Ill. Indsl. engr. Maytag Co., Newton, Iowa, 1952-56; gen. mgr. mfg. Schnadig Corp., Chgo., 1956-66; v.p. mfg. Sealy Inc., 1966-76, group v.p., 1976-86, pres., 1987-89; cons. to industry, 1989—. Bd. dirs. Schnadig Corp., Chgo. Patentee in field. Former chmn. adv. com. dept. mgmt., mem. adv. coun. Coll. Bus., Iowa State U. Recipient profl. achievement citation in engring. Iowa State U., 1989. Mem. NSPE, Inst. Indsl. Engrs., Internat. Sleep Products Assn. (former chmn., pres., Exceptional Svc. award 1989), Elks. Home: 8355 E Via De La Luna Scottsdale AZ 85258-3572 Office: 1429 River Rd Lakeview AR 72642

ROE, ROGER ROLLAND, JR. lawyer; b. Mpls., Dec. 31, 1947; s. Roger Rolland Roe Jr.; m. Paula Speltz, 1974; children: Elena, Madeline. BA, Grinnell Coll., 1970; JD, U. Minn., 1973. Bar: Minn. 1973, U.S. Dist. Ct. Minn. 1974, U.S. Ct. Appeals (8th cir.) 1977, U.S. Supreme Ct. 1978, Wis. 1988, U.S. Dist. Ct. Nebr. 1995, U.S. Dist. Ct. (ea. and we. dists.) Wis. Law clk. to Hon. Judge Amdahl Hennepin County Dist. Ct., Mpls., 1973-74; from assoc. to ptnr. Rider, Bennett, Egan & Arundel, 1974-91; mng. ptnr. Yaeger, Jungbauer, Barczak, Roe & Vucinovich, PLC, 1992-2000; ptnr. Best & Flanagan LLP, 2000—. Mem. nat. panel arbitrators Am. Arbitration Assn.; judge trial practice class and moot ct. competitions law sch. U. Minn.; guest lectr. Minn. Continuing Legal Edn. courses. Fellow Internat. Soc. Barristers; mem. ATLA (guest lectr.), Am. Bd. Trial Advs. (diplomat, Minn. chpt. pres. 1996-97), Minn. Trial Lawyers Assn., Million Dollar Round Table, Mich. Trial Lawyers Assn. Avocations: golfing, downhill skiing. Office: Best & Flanagan LLP 225 S 6th St # 4000 Minneapolis MN 55402

ROE, THOMAS COOMBE, former utility company executive; b. Dover, Del., Sept. 22, 1914; s. John Moore and Elizabeth Lindale (Cooper) R.; m. Emma Lillian Scotton, Oct. 16, 1937 (dec.); children: Thomas C., Margaret Ruth (dec.); m. Carolyn Scotton, May 4, 2002. BS in Elec. Engring, U. Del., 1935; DHL (hon.), Wesley Coll., 1987. With Eastern Shore Public Service, 1936-43; with Delmarva Power & Light Co., 1943—; pres. subs. Delmarva Power & Light Co., 1971-76, chmn. bd., 1976-79, dir., 1971-80, ret., 1980. Hon. trustee Peninsula Regional Med. Ctr., Salisbury, Md.; hon. trustee, former chmn. Wesley Coll., Dover, Del.; former trustee Wesley Theol. Sem., Washington. Served with AUS, 1941-45. Mem.: Rotary (past pres.). Republican. Methodist.

ROE, THOMAS LEROY WILLIS, pediatrician; b. Bend, Oreg., Sept. 1, 1936; MD, U. Oregon Health Scis. U., Portland, 1961. Diplomate Am. Bd. Pediatrics. Intern U. Calif., San Francisco, 1961-62, resident, 1962-64; physician Sacred Heart Med. Ctr., Eugene, Oreg.; pvt. practice Peace Health Med. Group, 1969—; clin prof. pediatrics U. Oreg., Portland, 1985—. Fellow Am. Acad. Pediatricians; mem. AMA, North Pacific Pediatrics Soc. E-mial. Office: Peace Health Med Clinic 1162 Willamette St Eugene OR 97401-3568 E-mail: troe@peacehealth.org.

ROE, W. BARTON, engineering executive; b. N.Y.C., Aug. 29, 1955; s. Kenneth Andrew R.; m. Lynne Roe, 1983; 4 children. BS in Mech. Engring., U. Pa., 1978; MSEE, Stevens Inst. Tech., 1987. Engr. analyst Sargent & Lundy Engrs., Chgo., 1978-80; engr. Stone & Webster Engring. Co., N.Y.C., 1980-85; supr. mech. thermal group Am. Rocket Co., Camarillo, Calif., 1987; project engr. Burns & Roe Group Inc., Oradell, N.J., 1988-92, v.p. bus. devel., 1992-96, v.p. infrastructure, 1996—, also bd. dirs. Bd. dirs. Polar Molecular Corp., 1991-92. Mem. ASME (sect. dir. 1998-2001), IEEE, NSPE, Greenwich Country Club, Psi Upsilon (trustee 2000-2001). Avocations: golfing, skiing. Office: Burns and Roe Group Inc 800 Kinderkamack Rd Oradell NJ 07649 E-mail: broe@roe.com.

ROE, WANDA JERALDEAN, artist, retired educator, lecturer; b. Batesville, Ark., Nov. 9, 1920; d. William Melvin and Luna Eva (Cockrum) Finley; m. Roy A. Roe, Dec. 25, 1940; children: Ramona Jeraldean, Roy A. II. BS in Edn., U. Cen. Ark., Conway, 1954; MS in Edn., Ark. State U., 1965; diploma Exec. Devel. Ctr., U. Ill., 1984; postgrad., U. Ark., 1981. Cert. educator, Ark.; lic. profl. counselor, Ark. Counselor Fountain Lake H.S., Hot Springs, Ark., 1965-68; instr. art and home econs. Foreman (Ark.) H.S., 1968-72; profl. counselor Pea Ridge (Ark.) H.S., 1972-83; instr. art No. Ark. C.C., Rogers, 1980-90; profl. artist Rogers (Ark.) Art Guild Gallery, 1983-94, Big Spring Gallery, Neosho, Mo., 1989-98, Ark. Artists Registry, Little Rock, 1983—; instr. art Wishing Springs Gallery, Bella Vista, Ark. Dir. workshops State Dept. Edn., Little Rock, 1965-83; supr. for practice tchrs. and counselor interns. Ark. Colls. and Univs., 1968-83; art instr. War Eagle Seminar, 1996; presenter in field. Exhibited in one-person show at Walton Art Ctr., 1996; contbr. poetry to mags.; mem. editorial adv. bd. Cmty. Pubs. Inc., 1994-97; art work pub. Internat. Bu.. Delta Kappa Gamma Soc., 2001. Mem. State Adv. Coun. for Gifted/Talented Edn., Little Rock, 1989-96; mem. Ark. Leadership Acad., 1996, G/T Coalition, 1996-97; juror for art contests; guide for County Constn. Day, Benton County, 1987; pres. United Meth. Women, Pea Ridge, 1973-75; cmty. vol.; sec. Benton County Dem. Ctrl. Com., 1996-2002; White House vol., 1996; mem. rsch. bd. advisors Internat. Directory of Disting. Leadership, 1992—. Travel Study grantee Delta Kappa Gamma, 1987; named Art Educator of Yr., N.W. Art Educators Assn., 1983; recipient numerous art awards. Mem.: AAUW (state pres. 1985—87, state exec. bd.), Rogers Art Guild (pres. 1991—92), Ozark Pastel Soc. (pres. 1990—93, Signature mem.), Internat. Assn. Pastel Socs. (Outstanding Vol. award 1997), Spiva Art Ctr., Ark. Art Educators Assn. (Svc. award for contbn. to art profession 1997), Nat. Art Educators Assn., Dem. Women's Club (v.p. 1996—98), Village Art Club (pres. 1998—2001, bd. dirs. 2002—), Delta Kappa Gamma (stete pres. 1983—85, internat. nominations com. 1998—2002, state exec. bd.). Democrat. Methodist. Avocations: music, lecturing, directing workshops.

ROE, WILLIAM THOMAS, behavioral engineer, educator, researcher; b. N.Y.C., July 7, 1944; s. William T. and Harriet E. (Higgins) Roe; m. Susan C. Kane, Aug. 30, 1972. BA in Engring./Indsl. Psychology, Calif. State U.-Northridge, 1971, MA in Human Factors/Applied Exptl. Psych, 1978; postgrad., Walden U. Rsch. asst. XYZYX Info. Corp., Canoga Park, Calif., 1973-74; mem. psychol. staff Manned Systems Scis. Inc., Northridge, 1974-75; rsch. psychologist Inst. Safety and Systems Mgmt., U. So. Calif., L.A., 1975-76; mgr., account exec. systems and data processing Mgmt. Recruiters So. Calif., Encino, 1976-79; resource evaluation analyst Samaritan Health Svc., Phoenix, 1979; sr. methods analyst Valley Nat. Bank, 1979-81; indsl. engr. City of Scottsdale, Ariz., 1981-84; prof. psychology Phoenix Coll., 1984—. Author: Ergonomic Models of Human Performance: Source Materials for the Analyst, 1975, Behavioral Engineering: Paradigm for Human Transformation, 1988, Mind-Body Psychology: Source Materials for Medical Education, 1995; contbr. With USN, 1961—67, Vietnam. Recipient Recognition certs., San Fernando Valley chpt. Data Processing Mgmt. Assn., 1978, Phoenix chpt Data Processing Mgmt. Assn., 1983, Tchg. Excellence award, NISOD, 1996. Mem.: APA (divsns. 2, 15, 21, 27, 46), We. Psychol. Assn., Human Factors Soc., Am. Psychol. Soc., Am. Counseling Assn. Office: Phoenix Coll 1202 W Thomas Rd Phoenix AZ 85013-4208

ROEBUCK, JAMES RANDOLPH, JR. state legislator; b. Phila., Feb. 12, 1945; m. Cheryl Arrington. BA cum laude, Va. Union U., 1966; MA, U. Va., 1969, PhD, 1977. Lectr. Drexel U., 1970-77, asst. prof., 1977-84; legis. asst. Office of Mayor, Phila., 1984-85; mem. Pa. Ho. of Reps., Harrisburg, 1985—. Chmn. Pa. Legis. Black Caucus, 1998-2000; mem. Pa. History and Mus. Commn., 1990-95; bd. dirs. Pa. Higher Ednl. Assistance Agy., 1995—. Author: The Shaping of William Howard Tafts View of East Asia 1900-1908; co-editor: Biographical Dictionary of Internationalists, 1983. Recipient Young Leadership award Hamilton Watch Co., 1966, Outstanding Svc. award Va. Union U. Alumni Assn., 1973, Legion of Honor award Chapel Four Chaplains, 1980. Mem. Nat. Black Caucus State Legislators, Alpha Phi Alpha. Address: 4800 Baltimore Ave Philadelphia PA 19143-3419 E-mail: jroebuck@panhouse.net.

ROEBUCK, JOSEPH CHESTER, leasing company executive; b. Detroit, Feb. 6, 1946; s. Joseph Leonard and Stella (Grochocki) R.; m. Susan A. Hatala, Mar. 26, 1977; children: Christopher, Jennifer. AA, Northwood Inst., 1966; BS in Bus., Ctrl. Mich. U., 1968. Sales IBM Corp., Southfield, Mich., 1968-70; prin. Roebuck, Schaden & Assocs., Detroit, 1970-73; salesman U.S. Leasing, Birmingham, Mich., 1973-76; sales mgr. Federated Fin., Southfield, 1977-82; v.p. Corp. Funding, Inc., Birmingham, 1982-97; pres. Corp. Resources, Inc., 1984-2000; v.p. asset mgmt. svcs. Inacom Corp., Omaha, 1997—. Mem. Oakland Hills Country Club. Republican. Roman Catholic. Avocations: golf, flying, travel, racquetball, automobile collecting.

ROECK, THOMAS J., JR. airline financial executive; b. Berwyn, Ill., June 21, 1944; s. Thomas Joseph and Ruth R. (Lovings) R.; m. Carol A. Hansen, Sept. 29, 1973 BS in Acctg., U. So. Calif., 1971. With Global Marine Inc., L.A., 1966-84, asst. treas., 1973-78, treas., 1978-80, v.p., treas., 1980-84; sr. v.p., chief fin. officer Western Air Lines, Inc., 1984-87; v.p. fin. adminstrn. Delta Air Lines Inc., Atlanta, 1987-88, sr. v.p. fin., chief fin. officer, 1988-97; chair exec. com. Chamberlin Edmonds & Assocs. Served as sgt. U.S. Army, 1968-70, Korea

ROEDDER, EDWIN WOODS, geologist; b. Monsey, N.Y., July 30, 1919; s. Hans and Edna (Woods) R.; children: Spencer, Lucy; m. Margaret Reinhart, Nov. 3, 1994. BA, Lehigh U., 1941; MA, Columbia U., 1947, PhD, 1950; DSc (hon.), Lehigh U., 1976. Rsch. engr. Bethlehem Steel Corp., Bethlehem, Pa., 1941-46; predoctoral fellow Geophys. Lab., Carnegie Inst., Washington, 1946-47; asst. in geology Columbia U., N.Y.C., 1946-49; asst. prof., assoc. prof. U. Utah, Salt Lake City, 1950-55; chief solid state group U.S. Geol. Survey, Washington, 1955-60, staff geologist, 1960-62, geologist, 1962-73, rsch. geologist, 1974-87; assoc. Harvard U., 1987—; scientist emeritus U.S. Geol. Survey, Washington, 1987—. Mem. or cons. various adv. bds, vis. coms., panels for U.S. govt. and several universities. Author: Composition of Fluid Inclusions, 1972, Fluid Inclusions, 1984; editor: Research on Mineral Forming Solutions, 1965, Fluid Inclusion Research (ann. book), 1968—; patentee in field. Recipient Exceptional Sci. Achievement medal NASA, 1973, Disting. Svc. medal U.S. Dept. Interior, 1978, Abraham Gottlob-Werner medaille Deutschen Min. Gesellschaft, 1985, Cyril Purkyne medal Czech Geol. Survey, 1991, first H.C. Sorby medal, 1993, First N.P. Ermakov prize for disting. svc. to thermobarogeochemical rsch., 1999; grantee NSF, others. Fellow AAAS, Am. Geophys. Union (pres. V.G. and P. sect. 1978-80), Mineral Soc. Am. (v.p. 1981-82, pres. 1982-83, Washington A. Roebling medal 1986); mem. NAS, Geochem. Soc. (sec. 1967-70, v.p. 1975-76, pres. 1976-77), Soc. Econ. Geologists (R.A.F. Penrose medal 1988). Avocations: music, travel, stamp collecting. Office: Harvard U Dept Earth & Planetary Scis Cambridge MA 02138 E-mail: roedder@shore.net.

ROEDDER, WILLIAM CHAPMAN, JR. lawyer; b. St. Louis, June 21, 1946; s. William Chapman and Dorothy (Reifeiss) R.; m. Gwendolyn Arnold, Sept. 13, 1968; children: William Chapman, Barcley Shane. BS, U. Ala., 1968; JD cum laude, Cumberland U., 1972. Bar: Ala. Law clk. to chief justice Ala. Supreme Ct., Montgomery, 1972; ptnr. McDowell Knight Roedder & Sledge, L.L.C., Mobile, Ala., 1997—. Comments editor Cumberland-Samford Law Rev.; contbr. articles to legal publs. Mem.: ABA (vice chair com. trial tactics, torts and ins. practice 1995—96), Def. Rsch. Inst., Ala. Def. Lawyers Assn., Fedn. Def. and Corp. Counsel (chmn. products liability sect. 1990—93, bd. dirs. 1993—2000, regional v.p. 1994—96, exec. com. 1997—, sec.-treas. 1999—2000, pres.-elect 2000—01, pres. 2001—02, chmn. bd. dirs. 2002—), Mobile County Bar Assn. (past sec., past chmn. ethics com. 1988—90, grievance com. 1994—96), Ala. State Bar Assn., Order of Barristers, Curia

Honoris, Phi Alpha Delta (pres. 1971—72). Home: 211 Levert Ave Mobile AL 36607-3219 Office: McDowell Knight Roedder & Sledge LLC PO Box 350 Mobile AL 36601-0350 E-mail: broedder@mcdowellknight.com.

ROEDER, REBECCA EMILY, software engineer; b. Findlay, Ohio, Nov. 2, 1959; d. Brian Eldon and Barbara Lee (Melton) R.; m. Stephen William Bigley, May 28, 1983. BS in Edn. and Computer Sci., Bowling Green State U., 1983, MS in Computer Sci., 1993. Sys. analyst NCR Corp., Dayton, Ohio, 1983-84; sr. sys. analyst Unisys (Burroughs) Corp., Detroit, 1984-88; asst. dir. St. Vincent Med. Ctr., Toledo, 1988-95; sr. cons. Advanced Programming Resources, Inc., Columbus, 1996; sr. software engr. Qwest Comm., Dublin, 1996—2002; sys. analyst Ohio Bur. of Worker's Compensation, Columbus, 2002—. Active Sta. WGTE/WGLE Pub. Radio, Toledo, 1984—96, Sta. WOSU Pub. Radio, Columbus, 1996—, Sta. WCBE Radio, Columbus, 1996—98, 2001, Toledo Mus. Art, 1988—96, Toledo Zoo, 1993—96, Dawes Arboretum, 1996—, Stratford Festival Friend, 1997—, Columbus Zoo, 1997—, Columbus Symphony Orch. Concerto Club, 1998—; presenter Women in Sci. Career Day, Lourdes Coll., 1992. Marathon scholar Marathon Oil Co., Findlay, 1978, Hancock scholar Findlay Area C. of C., 1978. Mem. Assn. for Computing Machinery. Unitarian Universalist. Avocations: instrumental and choral music, drum and bugle corps, reading. Home: 4964 Vicksburg Ln Hilliard OH 43026-5740 Office: BWC 30 W Spring St Columbus OH 43215-2256

ROEDER, RICHARD KENNETH, business owner, lawyer; b. Phila., Oct. 11, 1948; s. Walter August and Gloria (Miller) R.; 1 child, William Frederick. AB, Amherst Coll., 1970; JD, U. Calif., Berkeley, 1973, Cambridge U., 1973-74. Assoc. Paul, Hastings, Janofky & Walker, L.A., 1974-81, ptnr., 1981-90; founding ptnr. Aurora Capital Group, 1990—. Office: Aurora Capital Group Ste 2100 10877 Wilshire Blvd Los Angeles CA 90024-4341

ROEDER, ROBERT GAYLE, biochemist, educator; b. Boonville, Ind., June 3, 1942; s. Frederick John and Helene (Bredenkamp) R.; m. Suzanne Himsel, July 11, 1964 (div. 1981); children: Kimberly, Maxine, Michael; m. Cun Jing Hong, June 2, 1990. BA summa cum laude (Gilbert scholar), Wabash Coll., 1964, DSc (hon.), 1990; MS, U. Ill., 1965; PhD (USPHS fellow), U. Wash., 1969. Am. Cancer Soc. fellow dept. embryology Carnegie Instn. Washington, Balt., 1969-71; asst. prof. biol. chemistry Washington U., St. Louis, 1971-75, assoc. prof., 1975-76, prof., 1976-82, prof. genetics, 1978-82, James S. McDonnell prof. biochem. genetics, 1979-82; prof. lab. biochemistry and molecular biology Rockefeller U., N.Y.C., 1982—, Arnold O. and Mabel S. Beckmann prof. molecular biology and biochemistry, 1985—. Cons. USPHS, 1975-79, Am. Cancer Soc., 1983-86. Recipient Dreyfus Tchr.-Scholar award Dreyfus Found., 1976, molecular biology award NAS-U.S. Steel Found., 1986, outstanding investigator award Nat. Cancer Inst., 1986—, Louisa Gross Horowitz award Columbia U., 1999, Gairdner Found. Internat. award, 2000, Dickson prize, 2001, ASBMB-Merck award, 2002; co-recipient Lewis S. Rosenstiel award for disting. work in basic med. scis. Brandeis U., 1995, Passano award Passano Found., Inc., 1995, Alfred P. Sloan prize GM Cancer Rsch. Found., 1999; grantee NIH, 1972—, NSF, 1975-79, Am. Cancer Soc., 1979-85. Fellow AAAS, Am. Acad. Arts & Scis., Am. Acad. Microbiology, N.Y. Acad. Scis.; mem. NAS, Am. Chem. Soc. (Eli Lilly award 1977), Am. Soc. Biol. Chemists, Am. Soc. Microbiologists, Harvey Soc. (pres. 1994), Phi Beta Kappa. Home: 504 E 63rd St Apt 36P New York NY 10021-7933 Office: Rockefeller U 1230 York Ave New York NY 10021-6399 E-mail: roeder@mail.rockefeller.edu.

ROEDERER, JUAN GUALTERIO, physics educator; b. Trieste, Italy, Sept. 2, 1929; came to U.S., 1967, naturalized, 1972; s. Ludwig Alexander and Anna Rafaela (Lohr) R.; m. Beatriz Susana Cougnet, Dec. 20, 1952; children: Ernesto, Irene, Silvia, Mario. PhD, U. Buenos Aires, 1952. Research scientist Max Planck Inst., Gottingen, W.Ger., 1952-55; group leader Argentine Atomic Energy Commn., Buenos Aires, 1953-59; prof. physics U. Buenos Aires, 1959-66, U. Denver, 1967-77, U. Alaska, Fairbanks, 1977-93, prof. emeritus, 1993—, dir. Geophys. Inst., 1977-86, dean Coll. Environ. Scis., 1978-82. Vis. staff Los Alamos Nat. Lab., 1969-81; chmn. U.S. Arctic Research Com., 1987-91; sr. adviser Internat. Ctr. Theoretical Physics, Trieste, Italy, 1998—. Author: Dynamics of Geomagnetically Trapped Radiation, 1970, Physics and Psychophysics of Music, 1973, 3d edit., 1995; contbr. articles to profl. jours. Nat. Acad. Sci. NASA sr. research fellow, 1964-66 Fellow AAAS, Am. Geophys. Union (Edward A. Flinn III award, 2000); mem. Assn. Argentina de Geodestas y Geofisicos (hon.), Nat. Acad. Sci. Argentina (corr.), Nat. Acad. Sci. Austria (corr.), Third World Acad. Scis. (assoc.), Internat. Assn. Geomagnetism and Aeronomy (hon.). Lutheran. Achievements include research on plasma and energetic particles in earth's and Jupiter's magnetosphere, policy issues for Arctic, perception of music. Home: 105 Concordia Dr Fairbanks AK 99709-3029 Office: U Alaska Geophys Inst Fairbanks AK 99775-7320 E-mail: jgr@gi.alaska.edu.

ROEDIGER, JANICE ANNE, artist, educator; b. Trenton, N.J. d. John and Anne Balint; m. Paul Margerum Roediger; children: Pamela Anne, Matthew Paul, Joan Margaret. Student, Beaver Coll., 1975-78; grad. cert., Pa. Acad. Fine Arts, 1988. Instr. multi-media Jane Law Long Beach Island Gallery, Surf City, N.J., 1992-95; instr. drawing Long Beach Island Found., Loveladies, NJ, 1994—2002. Docent Mus. Am. Art, Pa. Acad. Fine Arts, Phila., 1992—. Exhibited in group shows at Rittenhouse Galleries, Phila., 1988-94, Phila. Mus. Art, ASR Gallery, 1992—, Schaff Gallery, Cin., 1995-96, Lambertville (N.J.) Gallery of Fine Arts, 1997—. Mem. vestry, rector's warden St. Anne's Episcopal Ch., Abington, Pa., 1970-73; chair med. staff aux. Abington Meml. Hosp., 1973-7, chair scholarship com., 1974; coord. student com. Pa. Acad. Fine Arts, Phila., 1986-88; active Phila. Mus. Art, 1972—. Recipient Rohm & Haas Outstanding Achievement award Pa. Acad. Fine Arts, 1987, Pearl Van Sciver award Woodmere Mus., 1991, Blumenthal award Cheltenham Ctr. for Arts, 1991, Pres. award, 2001, Lance Lauffler award for visionary painting Pa. Acad. Fine Arts, 1988, Award of Merit Long Beach Island Found., 1994, 96, Woodmere Mus. Memorial Endowment Awd., 1999. Mem. Nat. Mus. Women in Arts, Phila. Art Alliance, Artists Cultural Exch. (bd. dirs. 1989—). Episcopalian. Avocations: writing, collecting, golf, walking, travel. Home: 1244 Rydal Rd Rydal PA 19046-1415 Studio: 1913 Evernsey Ave Abington PA E-mail: imjanroe@aol.com.

ROEDIGER, PAUL MARGERUM, hospital administrator; b. Princeton, N.J., June 30, 1932; s. Paul Otto and Helen Mae (Margerum) R.; m. Janice Ann Balint, Aug. 18, 1956; children: Pamela, Matthew, Joan. AB, Princeton U., 1954; MD, Jefferson Med. Coll., 1958. Dir. med. edn. Abington (Pa.) Meml. Hosp., 1965—, chief divsn. gen. internal medicine, 1972-2000. Vestry mem. St. Ann's Episcopal Ch., Abington, 1965—. Fellow ACP, Coll. Physicians of Phila. Home: 1244 Rydal Rd Rydal PA 19046 Office: 1200 York Rd Dixon Bldg Abington PA 19001-3800 E-mail: amhgme@amh.org.

ROEG, NICOLAS JACK, film director; b. London, Aug. 15, 1928; s. Jack Nicolas and Mabel Getrude (Silk) R.; m. Susan Rennie Stephen, May 12, 1957; children: Joscelin Nicolas, Nicolas Jack, Lucien John, Sholto Jules; m. Theresa Russell, 1985; children: Maximilian Nicolas Sextus, Statten Jack. Student Brit. schs.; LittD honoris causa, Hull (Eng.) U., 1995. Cinematographer films The Caretaker, 1963, Masque of Red Death, 1964, Fahrenheit 451, 1966, A Funny Thing Happened on the Way to the Forum, 1966, Far from the Madding Crowd, 1967, Petulia, 1968; co-dir. film Performance, 1970; dir. films Walkabout, 1970, Don't Look Now, 1973, Glastonbury Fayre, 1973, The Man Who Fell to Earth, 1976, Bad Timing, 1980, Eureka, 1982, Insignificance, 1985, Castaway, 1986, 89, Track 29, 1987, Aria, 1987, The Witches, 1988-89, Cold Heaven, 1990, Heart of Darkness, 1994, Two Deaths, 1994, Hotel Paradise, 1995, Full Body Massage, 1995, Samson & Delilah, 1996; dir. TV films: Sweet Bird of Youth, 1989, Heart of Darkness, 1994; exec. producer Without You I'm Nothing, 1989, Young Indy, 1991, The Sound of Claudia Schiffer, 1999—; writer (screenplays) Night Train, 2000, Ivanhoe, 2000. Decorated comdr. Brit. Empire. Fellow Brit. Film Inst.; mem. Dirs. Guild Am., Dir. Guild Gt. Britain, Acad. Motion Picture Arts and Scis., Assn. Cinematograph, TV and Allied Technicians.

ROEHL, ANTHONY C. lawyer; b. Mpls., Apr. 10, 1975; s. Darrell I. Roehl, Carla J. Roehl; m. Eileen M. Murfee. BSBA, U. Fla., 1997; JD, U. Mich., 2002. Editl. writer Ind. Fla. Alligator, Gainesvilee, 1994—96; sr. cons. Peterson Worldwide, Tampa, 1997—99. Puzzle; author: 2001: A Tax Return Odyssey, 2002; composer: (Model) P-51D's Nuts!, 2002. Vol. Bush 2000, Ann Arbor, 2000—02. Mem.: Federalist Soc. Lutheran. Avocations: reading, writing, sports. Home: 2208 Gables Dr Atlanta GA 30319

ROEHL, JERRALD J. lawyer; b. Austin, Tex., Dec. 6, 1945; s. Joseph E. and Jeanne Foster (Scott) R.; m. Nancy J. Meyers, Jan. 15, 1977; children: Daniel J., Katherine C., J. Ryan, J. Taylor. BA, U. N.Mex., 1968; JD, Washington and Lee U., 1971. Bar: N.Mex. 1972, U.S. Ct. Appeals (10th cir.) 1972, U.S. Supreme Ct. 1977. Practice of law, Albuquerque, 1972—; pres. Roehl Law Firm P.C. and predecessors, 1976—. Lectr. to profl. groups; real estate developer, Albuquerque. Bd. advs. ABA Jour. 1981-83; bd. editors Washington and Lee Law Rev., 1970-71. Bd. dirs. Rehab. Ctr. of Albuquerque, 1974-78; mem. assocs. Presbyn. Hosp. Ctr., Albuquerque, 1974-82; incorporator, then treas. exec. com. Ctr. City Coun., 1991-98, law coun. Washington & Lee U. Law Sch., 2002—. Recipient award of recognition State Bar N.Mex., 1975-77. Mem. ABA (award of achievement Young Lawyers div. 1975, council econs. of law practice sect. 1978-80, exec. council Young Lawyers div. 1979-81, fellow div. 1984—, council tort and ins. practice sect. 1981-83), N.Mex. Bar Assn. (pres. young lawyers sect. 1975-76), Albuquerque Bar Assn. (bd. dirs. 1976-79), N.Mex. Def. Lawyers Assn. (pres. 1983-84), Sigma Alpha Epsilon, Sigma Delta Chi, Phi Delta Phi. Clubs: Albuquerque County, Albuquerque Petroleum. Roman Catholic. Home: 4411 Constitution Ave NE Albuquerque NM 87110-5721 Office: Roehl Law Firm PC 300 Central Ave SW Albuquerque NM 87102-3298 E-mail: jjr@roehl.com.

ROEHL, NANCY LEARY, marketing professional, educator; b. Natick, Mass., Mar. 25, 1952; d. Norman Leslie and Dorothy (Holmquist) Pidgeon; m. Patrick J. Leary, Sept. 17, 1977 (div. May 1984); m. Patrick F. Roehl, July 2, 1995. AA, Mass Bay Coll., Wellesley, Mass., 1979; BS, Lesley Coll., Cambridge, Mass., 1988; MA in Edn./Arts and Scis., U. South Fla., 1992. Cert. tchr., Fla. Sec. GTE Corp., Needham, Mass., 1973-78; coord. edn. Cullinet Software Inc., Westwood, 1983-84, adminstrv. asst., 1984-85, mgr. adminstrn., 1985-86; specialist product mktg. Cullinet Co., 1986-88; v.p. mktg. and adminstrn. Jonathan's Landscaping, Bradenton Beach, Fla., 1988-89; tech. support staff A Plus Tax Product Group, Arthur Andersen, Inc., Sarasota, 1989-90; cons. Palmetto, 1990—; tchr. Manatee County, 1992—, corp. shopper, 2000—. Contbr. articles to profl. jours. Mem. AAUW, Nat. Coun. for Social Studies, Fla. Cmty. Assn. Mgrs., Nat. Trust for Hist. Preservation, Phi Kappa Phi. Office: 1 Hurricane Ln Bradenton FL 34205

ROEHM, MACDONELL, JR. executive; b. Semerang, Indonesia, July 6, 1939; s. MacDonell and Mary Bennett (Cobb) R.; m. Nedra Ann Zeth, May 11, 1974. BA, Colgate U., 1961; MBA, Harvard U., 1966. Fin. analyst Exxon Corp., 1966-68; asso. Lazard Freres, N.Y.C., 1968-71; gen. partner J. Bush & Co., 1971-73; v.p. planning and devel. Cerro Corp., 1973-75; v.p., treas. N L Industries, Inc., 1976-79; sr. v.p. ops., devel. and planning N L Petroleum Services/N L Industries, Inc., Houston, 1979-80; pres. N.L. Shaffer/NL Industries, Inc., 1980-82; exec. v.p. NL Industries, Inc., 1982-85; ptnr. AEA Investors, Inc., 1985-94; chmn., pres., CEO Bill's Dollar Stores, Inc., 1994-98; chmn., CEO Crooked Creek Capital LLC, 1998—. Served with USN 1961-64. Decorated Silver Star, Bronze star, Purple Heart.

ROEHMHOLDT, JOHN MICHAEL, urologist, educator; b. Buffalo, Jan. 3, 1960; s. Robert Louis and Mary Elizabeth Roehmholdt; m. Sheliah Joan Jung, Aug. 25, 1990; children: Peter, Max, Julie. BA in Biology summa cum laude, Canisius Coll., Buffalo, 1981; MD cum laude, Albany Med. Coll., 1985. Diplomate Am. Bd. Urology; lic. capt. USCG. Pvt. practice; resident surgery U. Wis. Hosp. and Clinics, Madison, 1985-87, resident in urology, 1987-90; pvt. practice, Amherst, N.Y., 1990—. Clin. instr. urology SUNY, Buffalo, 1996—; mem. staff DeGraff Meml. Hosp., North Tonawanda, N.Y., pres. med. staff, 1995, dir., 1996-97; mem. trustee coun. Kaleida Health Sys., Buffalo, 1998—. Bd. dirs. West Seneca Devel. Ctr. chpt. N.Y. State ARC, 1994—; chmn. stewardship and devel. com. parish coun. Sts. Peter and Paul Ch., Williamsville, N.Y., 1999—, pres. parish coun., 2001-02. Recipient physician's recognition award AMA, 2000. Fellow ACS; mem. AMA (Physicians Recognition award 2000), Am. Urol. Assn., Buffalo Urol. Soc. (pres.-elect 2001-02, pres. 2002-2003), Olcott Yacht Club (N.Y.) (sr. mem., fleet surgeon 1998—), Alpha Omega Alpha. Office: Northtown Urology Assocs PC 3800 Sheridan Dr Amherst NY 14226

ROEHRIG, C(HARLES) BURNS, internist, health policy consultant; b. Brookline, Mass., Jan. 21, 1923; s. Gilbert Haven and Helen (Burns) R.; m. Patricia Joan Orme, July 22, 1952; children— Joan Russell Roehrig Vater, Jennifer Orme Roehrig Munn, Charles Burns, Jr. Student, Amherst Coll., 1941-43, Vanderbilt U., 1943-44; MD, U. Md., 1949; cert. in internal medicine, U. Pa., Phila., 1953. Diplomate Am. Bd. Internal Medicine. Intern Boston City Hosp., 1949-50; resident in internal medicine and diabetes Joslin Clinic, New Eng. Deaconess Hosp., Boston, 1952-54; practice medicine specializing in internal medicine and diabetes, 1954-91; chief of staff, pres. med. adminstrv. bd. New Eng. Deaconess Hosp., 1972-75; dir., mem. exec. com. Blue Shield of Mass., Inc., 1977-88; exec. com. Met. Boston Hosp. Coun., 1982-86; physician adv. coun. Mass. Hosp. Assn., Burlington, 1982-86. Editor: Today's Internist, Washington, 1987-99; contbr. articles to profl. jours. Bd. dirs. Camping Svcs. Bd., Greater Boston YMCA, 1966—; mem. physician adv. group Health Care Financing Adminstrn., Washington, 1983-88; mem. adv. panel on physician payment and med. tech. Office of Tech. Assessment, U.S. Congress, Washington, 1984-85; chmn. Federated Coun. for Internal Medicine, Washington, 1985-86; trustee New Eng. Deaconess Hosp. Capt. (flight surgeon) USAF, 1949-52. Fellow ACP; mem. AMA (chmn. coun. on long range planning and devel., Chgo.), New Eng. Diabetes Assn. (pres. 1963-64), Mass. Soc. Internal Medicine (pres. 1971-72), Am. Soc. Internal Medicine (pres. 1984-85), Country Club of Hilton Head, Wellesley (Mass.) Country Club. Republican. Episcopalian. E-mail: eddesk@aol.com.

ROELANDTS, WILLEM P. data processing executive; BEE, Rijks Hogere Technische Sch., Belgium. Various position including sr. v.p. Hewlett-Packard, 1966—96; CEO, pres. Xilinx, San Jose, 1996—. Spkr. in field. Mem.: Fabless Semiconductor Assn. (pres.), Tech. Network (bd. dirs.), Semiconductor Industry Assn. (bd. dirs.). Office: Xilinx Inc 2100 Logic Dr San Jose CA 95124-3400 Office Fax: 408-559-7114.

ROELLER, HERBERT ALFRED, biology and medical scientist, educator; b. Magdeburg, Germany, Aug. 2, 1927; came to U.S., 1962; s. Alfred H. and Elfriede (Wartner) R.; m. Manuela R. Buresch, Dec. 20, 1957. Abiturium, Christian Thomasius Schule, Halle/Saale, 1946; PhD, Georg August U., Goettingen, 1962; MD, U. Muenster, 1955. Project assoc. zoology U. Wis., Madison, 1962-65, asst. prof. pharmacology, 1965-66, rsch. assoc. zoology, 1966-67, assoc. prof. zoology, 1967-68; prof. biology Tex. A&M U., 1968-83, prof. biochemistry and biophysics, 1974-83, dir. Inst. Devel. Biology, 1973-83, Disting. prof., 1977—, Alumni prof., 1980-85. V.p. rsch. Zoecon Corp., Palo Alto, Calif., 1968-72, sci. adv., 1972-85, chief scientist, Zoecon Rsch. Inst., Palo Alto, 1985-88; sci. advisor Syntex Rsch., Palo Alto, 1966-68, European Cmty., 1988—, Affymax Rsch. Inst., Palo Alto, 1989-96; corp. advisor Symyx Techs., Sunnyvale, Calif., 1996—; mem. adv. panel regulatory biology, divsn. biol. and med. scis. NSF, 1969-72; mem. Internat. Centre Insect Physiology and Ecology, Nairobi, Kenya, 1970—, dir. rsch., 1970-75. Mem. editl. bd. Jour. Chem. Ecology, 1974—; Contbr. articles to profl. jours. Recipient Disting. Achievement award for research Tex. A&M U., 1976. Fellow Tex. Acad. Sci.; mem. German Acad. Naturforscher Leopoldina, AAAS, Am. Soc. Zoologists, Entomol. Soc. Am., Am. Soc. Devel. Biology, Sigma Xi.

ROELLIG, LEONARD OSCAR, physics educator; b. Detroit, May 17, 1927; s. Oscar Otto and Laura K. (Rutz) R.; m. B. Pauline Cowdin, June 20, 1952; children: Thomas Leonard, Mark Douglas, Paul David. AB, U. Mich., 1950, MS, 1956, PhD, 1959. From asst. prof. to prof. physics Wayne State U., Detroit, 1958-78, dean, 1971-72, asso. provost, 1972-76; pres. Central Solar Energy Research Corp., Detroit, 1977; prof. physics CCNY, 1978-96, prof. emeritus, 1996—; vice chancellor acad. affairs CUNY, 1978-83. Vis. prof. Univ. Coll., London, 1968-69, Tata Inst. Fundamental Rsch., Bombay, India, 1973, Paul Scherrer Inst., Villigen, Switzerland, 1991-92; chmn. bd. advisers Midwest Regional Solar Energy Planning Venture, 1977. Co-author: Positron Annihilation, 1967; contbr. articles to profl. jours. Bd. dirs. Luth. Publicity Bur., 1981-91, v.p., 1984-85, pres., 1985-89; v.p. Grosse Pointe (Mich.) Human Rels. Coun., 1969-70. With USN, 1945-46, U.S. Army, 1950-52. Recipient Wayne State U. Fund Research Recognition award, 1963, Probus Club award for acad. achievement, 1968, Probus Club award for acad. leadership, 1977 Mem. Am. Phys. Soc. Home: 4520 Sioux Dr Boulder CO 80303-3733 Office: U Colo Dept Physics Boulder CO 80302 E-mail: loroellig@aol.com.

ROELLIG, PAUL DAVID, publishing executive; b. Ann Arbor, Mich., May 20, 1958; s. Leonard Oscar and Bonita Pauline (Cowdin) R.; m. Kim Elizabeth Urshalitz, June 15, 1985; children: David, Brittany, Corrie. Spl. asst. to sec. U.S. Dept. Edn., Washington, 1985-88; dept. assoc. dir. policy devel. White House, 1988-90; chmn., CEO Bulletin News Network, Inc., McLean, Va., 1990—. CEO Profl. Football Coaches, Inc., Vienna, Va., 2001—. Pub. White House Bulletin, 1990—, Bulletin's Morning Digest, 1993—, Bulletin's Frontrunner, 1996—, NFLcoaches.com, 2001—. Home: 10514 Birnham Rd Great Falls VA 22066-3202 Office: BNN Ste 501 8150 Leesburg Pike Vienna VA 22182-2714

ROELS, OSWALD ALBERT, oceanographer, educator, business executive; b. Temse, Belgium, Sept. 16, 1921; came to U.S., 1958, naturalized, 1965; s. Ghisleen and Elvire (Heirwegh) R.; m. Dorothy Mary Broadhurst, Sept. 16, 1950; 1 dau., Margaret Ann Roels Talarico. BS, U. Louvain, Belgium, 1940, MS, 1942; PhD, 1944. Prof. Columbia U., N.Y.C., 1960-75, CCNY, 1969-76; prof., dir. dept. marine sci. U. Tex., Austin, 1976-80; chmn. Maritek Corp., Corpus Christi, Tex., 1980-92; pres. Bradley Barges Inc. Adj. prof. Rockefeller U., N.Y.C., 1969-80; vis. research prof. Laval U., Que., Can., 1972-80; dir. mariculture research Port Aransas (Tex.) Marine Lab., U. Tex. Marine Sci. Inst., 1976-80 Author numerous articles in field.; assoc. editor: Nutrition Revs., 1961-68. Served with Belgian Army, 1940. Recipient Postdoctoral award U. Brussels, 1945, Postdoctoral award U. Liverpool, Eng., 1946, Postdoctoral award Sorbonne, 1957; Research Career Devel. award NIH, 1962-65; WHO fellow, 1957; Hoffman-LaRoche vis. lectr., 1974 Mem. AAAS, Am. Chem. Soc., Am. Inst. Nutrition, Am. Soc. Biol. Chemists, Am. Soc. Limnology and Oceanography, Chemici Lovanienses, Inst. Environ. Scis., Inst. Food Tech., Internat. Conf. Biochem. Lipids, Marine Tech. Soc., N.Y. Acad. Scis., N.Y. Lipid Club, Photoelectric Spectrometry Group Gt. Britain, World Mariculture Soc. Home: 4345 Rosecliff Dr Charlotte NC 28277-8657

ROEMBACH, JEANINE LOUISE, adult, child and adolescent psychiatrist; b. Wichita, Kans., June 24, 1952; d. Theodore Leon Jr. and Donna Esther (Whitwam) Roembach; m. Gregory Darwin Clark, Dec. 4, 1976; children: Haley Rebecca, Emily Katherine, Benjamin Michael, Claire Isabelle. MD, U. Kans., Wichita and Kansas City, 1975. Pediatric intern U. Kans., Wichita, 1975-76; rotating intern Menninger Sch. Psychiatry, Topeka, 1976-77, psychiatry resident, 1977-80, child psychiatry fellowship, 1979-82; clin. psychiatrist, supr., instr. Menninger Inst. and Karl Menninger Sch. Psychiatry, 1976-94; staff psychiatrist Columbus (Ind.) Regional Med. Ctr., 1994-97, MeritCare, Fargo, N.D., 1997—. Tarlton Morrow prof. Karl Menninger Sch. Psychiatry, Topeka; examiner Am. Bd. Psychiatry and Neurology; asst. dir. Presch. Day Treatment Ctr., 1976-93, dir. 1993-94. Fellow Am. Acad. Child and Adolescent Psychiatry. Avocations: cooking, gardening, needlework, piano, reading. Office: MeritCare 700 1st Ave S Fargo ND 58103-1802

ROEMER, ELIZABETH, astronomer, educator; b. Calif., Sept. 4, 1929; d. Richard Quirin and Elsie Roemer. BA with honors, U. Calif., Berkeley, 1950, PhD (Lick Obs. fellow), 1955. Tchr. adult class Oakland pub. schs., 1950-52; lab technician U. Calif. at Mt. Hamilton, 1954-55; grad. research astronomer U. Calif. at Berkeley, 1955-56; research asso. Yerkes Obs. U. Chgo., 1956; astronomer U.S. Naval Obs., Flagstaff, Ariz., 1957-66; asso. prof. dept. astronomy, also in lunar and planetary lab. U. Ariz., Tucson, 1966-69, prof., 1969-97; prof. emerita, 1997—; astronomer Steward Obs., 1980-97, astronomer emerita, 1997—. Chmn. working group on orbits and ephemerides of comets commn. 20 Internat. Astron. Union, 1964-79, 85-88, v.p. comm. 20, 1979-82, pres., 1982-85, v.p. commn. 6, 1973-76, 85-88, pres., 1976-79, 88-91; mem. adv. panels Office Naval Research, Nat. Acad. Scis.-NRC, NASA; researcher and author numerous publs. on astrometry and astrophysics of comets and minor planets including 79 recoveries of returning periodic comets, visual and spectroscopic binary stars, computation of orbits of comets and minor planets. Recipient Dorothea Klumpke Roberts prize U. Calif. at Berkeley, 1950, Mademoiselle Merit award, 1959; asteroid (1657) named Roemera, 1965; Benjamin Apthorp Gould prize Nat. Acad. Scis., 1971; NASA Spl. award, 1986. Fellow AAAS (council 1966-69, 72-73), Royal Astron. Soc. (London); mem. Am. Astron. Soc. (program vis. profs. astronomy 1960-75, council 1967-70, chmn. div. dynamical astronomy 1974), Astron. Soc. Pacific (publs. com. 1962-73, Comet medal com. 1968-74, Donohoe lectr. 1962), Internat. Astron. Union, Am. Geophys. Union, Brit. Astron. Assn., Phi Beta Kappa, Sigma Xi. Office: U Ariz PO Box 210092 Lunar & Planetary Lab Tucson AZ 85721-0092

ROEMER, JOHN ALAN, financial executive; b. Milw., June 9, 1949; s. John Edward and Jeanette Luella (Fleischmann) R.; m. Janet Frances Maloney, Aug. 8, 1970; children: John Robert, Joseph Michael. BSBA in Acctg., Suffolk U., 1977; MBA, Rensselaer Poly. Inst., 1983. Supr. reimbursement Univ. Hosp., Boston, 1977-79; dir. fin. planning Champlain Valley Physician Med. Ctr., Plattsburgh, N.Y., 1979-84; contr. Arnot Ogden Meml. Hosp., Elmira, 1984-85; dir. fiscal svcs. Bershire Med. Ctr., Pittsfield, Mass., 1985-87; v.p. fin. Franklin Med. Ctr., Greenfield, 1987-91; sr. fiscal cons. Regional Office Brim Healthcare, Inc., Madison, Wis., 1991-94; CFO Eagle Publishing Group, Pittsfield, Mass., 1994-95; prin. Roemer Bus. Svcs., 1995—; CFO, East Galbraith Healthcare Cmty., Cin., 1998-99; sr. v.p., CFO Cmty. HealthCare Partnership, Inc., Mason, 1999—2000; assoc. Resources Connection, Cin., 2000—. Fellow Healthcare Fin. Mgmt. Assn.; mem. DAV, Ea. English Springer Spaniel (treas. 1991, v.p. 1987-88), KC (Appreciation award 1983). Roman Catholic. Home: 4321 Wilderness Way Mason OH 45040-7243 E-mail: roemerja@att.net.

ROEMER, TIMOTHY J. congressman; b. South Bend, Ind., Oct. 30, 1956; m. Sarah Lee Johnston, 1989. BA in pol. sci, U. Calif., San Diego, 1979; MA, PhD in internat. rels., U. Notre Dame, 1986. Staff asst. to congressman John Brademas U.S. Congress, def., trade and fgn. policy advisor to senator Dennis DeConcini; mem. U.S. Congress from 3rd Ind. dist., 1991—, mem. economic and ednl. opportunity com., mem. sci. com., mem. edn. and the workforce com., mem. permanent select committee on intelligence. Adj. prof. Am. U. Office: US Ho of Reps 2352 Rayburn Hob Washington DC 20515-0001 also: 217 N Main St South Bend IN 46601-1216*

ROEMING, ROBERT FREDERICK, foreign language educator; b. Milw., Dec. 12, 1911; s. Ferdinand August and Wanda E. (Radtke) R.; m. Alice Mae Voss, Aug. 30, 1941; 1 child, Pamela Alice. BA in Econs./Acctg., U. Wis., 1934, MA in Italian, 1936, PhD in French, 1941. Mem. faculty U. Wis.-Milw., 1937—, prof. French and Italian, 1956—, assoc. dean Coll. Letters and Sci., asst. to provost for devel. of spl. programs, 1957-62, sole dir. dept. lang. labs., 1964-70, dir. English as 2d lang., 1967-70, founder and dir. Ctr. Twentieth Century Studies, 1970-74, prof. emeritus, 1980—; founder, chief investigator Camus Bibliography Research Collection, Golda Meir Library, 1985—. Rep. D.C. Heath Co., 1943-46; cons., 1946-50; cons. computer systems Harnischfeger Corp., Milw., 1953-57; chmn. tech. sect. Internat. Congress on Fgn. Lang. Tchg., Pädagogisches Zentrum, Berlin, summer 1964; guest InterAm. Congress of Linguists, Montevideo, Uruguay, 1966; ofcl. guest Romanian govt. 10th Internat. Congress Linguists, summer 1967; dir. Insts. in Adult Basic Edn., 1969, U.S. Office Edn.; pres., treas. Electronic Rsch. Instruments Co., Inc., Nashotah, Wis., 1969-93. Author: In the Land of the Immortals, 1934, (with C.E. Young) Introduction to French, 1951, Camus, A Bibliography, 1969, rev. and augmented computer-microfiche, 15th edit., 2000, Little Magazine Catalog, 1976, 77 (NEH grantee); editor: Modern Lang. Jour, 1963-70; contbr. numerous monographs and articles to profl. jours., 72 taped radio programs on French Black lit. Chmn. bldg. commn. Village of Chenequa, Wis., 1972-88; trustee, chmn. Midwest chpt. Jose Greco Found. for Hispanic Dance, Inc., 1970-76; mem. Wis. Bd. Nursing, 1977-79, chmn., 1979; mem. numerous nat. conservation orgns. and local civic groups. Decorated chevalier, officier, commandeur Ordre Palmes Académiques (France); recipient Travel award Italian Govt., summer, 1934. Mem. MLA (life, index com. 1970-79), Nat. Fedn. Modern Lang. Tchrs. Assn. (exec. com.

1963-70), Verband Deutscher Schriftsteller, Wis. News Photographers Assn. (hon. life, Pres.'s award 1972), Soc. des Etudes Camusiennes, Am. Assn. of French Acad. Palms, Wis. Assn. for the Blind and Physically Handicapped, Chenequa Country Club, Lake Country Racquet and Athletic Club, Phi Eta Sigma, Phi Kappa Phi, Tau Kappa Epsilon. Achievements include research in application of the computer to humanities, applied linguistics and contemporary French and Italian Literature. Home: 6078 N Oakland Hills Rd Nashotah WI 53058 Office: U Wis-Milw Golda Meir Libr W240 2311 E Hartford Ave Milwaukee WI 53211-3175 Fax: 414-229-6791.

ROEN, DUANE HARLEY, English educator; b. River Falls, Wis., Feb. 19, 1949; s. Harley Eldon and Doris June (Bennett) R.; m. Maureen Ann Earley, Apr. 3, 1978; children, Nicholas James, Hanna Elizabeth. Cert. secondary English tchr., Wis. Tchr. English, New Richmond (Wis.) H.S., 1972-77; instr. U. Minn., 1977-81; asst. prof. U. Nebr., Lincoln, 1981-82, U. Ariz., Tucson, 1982-88, assoc. prof., 1988-93, coord. grad. studies, 1990-92, dir. grad. program in rhetoric composition and tchg. English, 1995-99; prof. English Ariz. State U., Tempe, 1995—, dir. Ctr. Learning and Tchg., 1999—; prof. Syracuse U., 1993-95, dir. of writing program, 1993-95. Cons. in field. Author (with others) Becoming Expert: Writing and Learning in the Disciplines; editor: (with others) Richness in Writing: Empowering ESL Students, 1989, A Sense of Audience in Written Communication, 1990; contbr. articles to profl. jours. Kelly Research grantee U. Nebr, 1982. Mem. Nat. Coun. Tchrs. English, Nat. Conf. Rsch. English, Ariz. English Tchrs. Assn. (exec. bd., treas. 1983-85). Avocations: genealogy, softball, refinishing furniture. Home: 2021 E Carmen St Tempe AZ 85283-3302 Office: Ariz State Univ PO Box 870101 Tempe AZ 85287-0101 E-mail: duane.roen@asu.edu.

ROEN, SHELDON R. publisher, psychologist; b. N.Y.C. s. Morris Rosenthal and Gussie (Weininger) R.; m. Selma Lois Pollets, Feb. 21, 1954; children—Randa M., Marjorie A., Harris L. BS, City U. N.Y., 1950, MA, 1951; PhD, Columbia U., 1955; postgrad., New Sch. Social Research, 1951-53, Harvard Sch. Pub. Health, 1961-62. Diplomate: Am. Bd. Examiners in Profl. Psychology. Tchr. pub. schs., N.Y.C., 1950-53; chief Clin. Psychology Svc., Ft. Sill, Okla., 1955-58; instr. Cameron Coll., Okla. A. and M. U., 1956-58; asst. prof. U. N.H., 1958-60; asst. chief psychol. services Mass. Mental Health Center, Boston, 1960-63; instr. Harvard, 1961-63; rsch. assoc. Med. Sch., 1960-63; dir. rsch. S. Shore Mental Health Center, Quincy, Mass., 1962-66; assoc. prof. dept. psychology Tchrs. Coll., Columbia, N.Y.C., 1966-72; dir. Psychol. Consultation Center, 1966-72; chmn. bd., pres., psychologist Human Scis. Press, N.Y.C., 1972—. Lectr. L.I. U., summer 1958, Tufts U., 1961-62; mem. N.H. Gov.'s Com. on Spl. Edn., also Study Com. on Mental Health Reorgn., 1961-62; cons. VISTA program OEO, 1966-67; mem. juvenile problems research rev. com. NIMH, 1968-69; mem. research rev. com. Title III Elementary and Secondary Edn. Act project application Ohio Dept. Edn., 1969-72; mem. mental health coordinating com. local sch. dist. 5, N.Y.C., 1969-72; mem., research dir. work incentive program for welfare recipients Wharton Sch. Pa., U.S. Dept. Labor, 1969-72; mem. mental health and community control com. N.Y. Psychologists for Social Action, 1969-72 Authors, editor books.; Editor: Mass. Psychol. Assn. Newsletter, 1963-65, Community Mental Health Jour; contbr. articles to profl. jours. and chpts. to books. Chmn. bd. trustees Bristol Acres Sch., Taunton, Mass., 1965-67. Fellow Am. Psychol. Assn. (mem. com. pre-coll. behavioral scis. 1968-71, founder div. 27 community psychology div. 1969, chmn. subcom. pre-high sch. behavioral sci. 1969-72), Am. Pub. Health Assn.; Am. Orthopsychiat. Assn. (com. on research edn. 1965-67), Am. Sociol. Assn.; mem. New Eng. Psychol. Assn. (steering com. 1965-68), N.H. Psychol. Assn. (legis. chmn. 1961-62) Office: 3205 Beacon St Pompano Beach FL 33062-1207

ROENICK, JEREMY, professional hockey player; b. Boston, Jan. 17, 1970; Center Chgo. Blackhawks, 1988-96, Phoenix Coyotes, 1996—2001, Phila. Flyers, 2001—. Named The Sporting News NHL Rookie of the Yr., 1989-90. Played in NHL All-Star Games, 1991-94. Office: Philadelphia Flyers First Union Center Complex 3601 S. Broad Street Philadelphia PA 19148*

ROER, ROBERT DAVID, physiologist, educator; b. N.Y.C., Oct. 15, 1952; s. Edwin Marvin and Dorothy Barbara (Blaymore) R.; m. Marjorie Elizabeth Smith, May 29, 1976; 1 child, Sara Elizabeth. BS, Brown U., 1974; PhD, Duke U., 1979. Asst. prof. U. N.C., Wilmington, 1979-85, assoc. prof., 1985-90, prof., 1990—, dean Grad. Sch., 2002—. Contbr. articles to various jours. and publs. Grantee NSF, NASA, N.C. Biotech. Ctr., N.C. Sea Grant. Mem. AAUP, Am. Physiol. Soc., Soc. Integrative & Comparative Biology, Crustacean Soc., Sigma Xi, Phi Kappa Phi. Office: Univ North Carolina 601 S College Rd Wilmington NC 28403-5955 E-mail: roer@uncw.edu.

ROES, NICHOLAS A. communications executive; b. Jersey City, Dec. 26, 1952; s. Nicholas R. and Mimi (Maresca) R.; m. Nancy Bennett. BS in Edn., U. Bridgeport, 1974, MA in Bus. and Pub. Mgmt., 1983; PhD in Addictions Treatment, Westbrook U., 1997. Registered investment advisor SEC, credentialed substance abuse counselor NY, credentialed alcohol and substance abuse counselor, credentialed justice counselor, registered addiction specialist. Chmn. bd. Tchr. Update, Inc., Saddle River, N.J., 1976—; pres., cons., author Nicholas A. Roes & Assocs., 1979—; mng. ptnr. Barryville (N.Y.) Investors, 1985—; exec. dir. New Hope Manor, residential substance abuse treatment ctr. for women, Barryville, N.Y., 1992—. Dir. NAR Prodns., 1987, Idea Group, Inc., 1986—; instr. Marist Coll., Poughkeepsie, N.Y., 1989—. Author: Helping Children Watch TV, 1978, rev., 1992, America's Lowest Cost College, 1977, 10th edit., 1997, Gambling for Fun, 1988, Pick Your Own, 1989, Solutions for The Treatment Resistant Addicted Client, 2001; editor (newsletter) Tchr. U pdate, 1977; columnist The Investment Column, 1980—. Exec. dir. New Hope Manor, Barryville, 1992—. Mem. Internat. Assn. Fin. Planners, Direct Mail Club of N.Y., EDPRESS, C. of C., Mensa, Internat. Platform Assn. Avocation: music. Office: Nicholas A Roes & Assocs PO Box 205 Saddle River NJ 07458-0205 E-mail: nickaroes@aol.com.

ROESCH, BRENDA LYNNETTE, landscape architect, community planner; b. Anaheim, Calif., July 29, 1973; d. Roy Thomas and Teresa Ann Langheld; m. James Ronald Roesch, Aug. 21, 1999. BS in Landscape Arch., Calif. Poly. State U., 1995; MBA, U. Tex., San Antonio, 2002. Registered landscape arch.; cert. planner Am. Inst. Cert. Planners; cert. arborist Internat. Soc. Arborists. Landscape arch. Travis AFB, Fairfield, CAlif., 1995-96, Hdqs. Air Force Ctr. for Environ. Excellence, San Antonio, 1996—. Com. mem. Neighborhood Greenway Orgn., San Antonio, 2001—. Mem. Am. Planners Assn. Avocations: swimming, skiing, fitness, gardening, travel. Home: 13282 Hunters Breeze San Antonio TX 78230 Office: Hdqs USAF Ctr for Environ Excellence 8107 Aeromedical Rd San Antonio TX 78235 Office Fax: 210-536-9004. Personal E-mail: jroesch@satx.rr.com. Business E-Mail: brenda.roesch@brooks.af.mil.

ROESCH, CLARENCE HENRY, banker; b. Egg Harbor City, N.J., Aug. 22, 1925; s. Joseph Aloysius and Bertha (Heumann) R.; m. Helen Regina Owens, Sept. 25, 1954; children: Kathleen Marie, Helena Patricia, Maryanne Cornelia. BBA, Rutgers U., 1949, postgrad., 1961; certificate, Am. Inst. Banking, 1961; grad., Trust Sch., Bucknell U., 1971. Cert. internal auditor, data processing auditor. Bookkeeper, teller, head teller, asst. sec., trust officer, auditor Egg Harbor Bank & Trust Co., 1949-61; bank examiner Phila. Fed. Res. Bank, 1962-65; chief auditor Am. Bank & Trust Co. of Pa. (name changed to Meridian Bancorp Inc. 1985), Reading, 1966-88, v.p. audit dept., 1968-88, ret. officer, 1988; parish sec. St. Benedict Ch., Plowville, 1989-99; sr. staff auditor Nat. Penn Bank, Boyertown, 1990-97. Census enumerator, 2000; mem. faculty Berks County chpt. Am. Inst. Banking, 1966-68; instr. bank auditing Bank Adminstrn. Inst., U. Richmond, 1968; pres., past mems. chpt. Am. Banking Inst., Atlantic County, N.J., 1958-59. Budget com. Berks County chpt. United Way, 1967-73; bd. dirs. Berks Reading Coun. Camp Fire, 1966-93, chmn. fin. com., 1973, 75, treas., 1974-84; instr. 55 Alive Program AARP, 1989-93. Recipient John Johnston award as outstanding banker N.J., 1955; award U.S. Savs. Bond Com., 1961; Luther Halsey Gulick award for vol. services Camp Fire, 1975; John C. Collier award for outstanding bus. and fin. services, 1981, Blue Ribbon award for vol. services Camp Fire, 1984, award for corp. vol. of yr. Meridian Bancorp Inc., 1984, 85, Outstanding Svc. in Fin. Mgmt. award Camp Fire, 1988. Mem. Inst. Internal Auditors (dir. ctrl. Pa. chpt.), Berks County Bankers Assn., Travelers Protective Assn., Berks Reading C. of C., Bank Administration Inst. (past pres., dir. Penn-Jersey chpt.), Spring Lawn Optimist Club (bd. dirs. 1992, Key Mem. award 1992, chmn. fin. and budget com. 1992-94). Home: 6-E Doral Dr Reading PA 19607-3379

ROESCH, JOSEPH GERARD, priest, theology studies educator; b. Queens, NY., Oct. 30, 1960; s. William Bernard and Kathleen Joan Roesch. BA in English, St. Joseph U., Phila.; ThM, Catholic U. Am., Washington. Ordained priest Roman Cath. Ch. Cath. Priest Congregation of Marians of the Immaculate Conception, Washington, 1992—. Avocations: jogging, reading, attending plays.

ROESCH, ROBERT EUGENE, dentist; b. July 10, 1951; s. Wilber H. and Vivian (Reese) R.; m. Susan M. Tuttle, Aug. 25, 1973. BA, Midland Luth. Coll., 1973; DDS, U. Nebr., 1976. Pvt. practice, Fremont, Nebr., 1979—; mem. bd. Three Rivers Pub. Health Dept., 2002—. Dental cons. Dodge County Am. Cancer Soc., Fremont, 1984—98. Campaign chmn. Fremont United Way, 1987, v.p., 1988; mem. orgn. com. Main St. Fremont, 1995—, chmn. orgn. com., 1998—, 2nd v.p., 1998, 1st v.p., 1999; pres. Sinai Luth. Ch. Coun., Fremont, 1983—84, bd. dirs., 1987—90; mem. endowment com. Sinai Luth. Ch., 1990—94; bd. dirs. Main St. Fremont, 1997—. Master: Acad. Gen. Dentistry (v.p. region 10 1990—91, dir. 1991—93, trustee 1993—94, budget and fin. com. 1994—99, 1997, 1998, 1999, spkr. to house 1999—); fellow: Internat. Coll.Dentistry, Internat. Acad. Dentistry; mem.: ADA (alt. del. 2000, 2001), Acad. Gen. Dentistry, Fremont Indsl. Found., Fremont C. of C. (diplomate 1985—94, vice-chmn. memberships and membership svcs. 1989—90, bd. dirs. 1991—94, vice-chmn. pub. affairs 1992—94), Fremont Wellness Coun. (bd. dirs. 1996—98), Omaha Dist. Dental Soc. (bd. dirs.), Am. Equilibration Soc., Am. Assn. Functional Orthodontists, Am. Orthodontic Soc., Nebr. Dental Assn. (v.p. 2000—02, pres.-elect 2001, pres. 2002), Nebr. Acad. Gen. Dentistry (pub. info. officer 1983—85, sec., treas. 1985—88, pres.-elect 1988—89, pres. 1990—92, exec. dir. 1992—94, cont. edn. chmn. 1994—, legis. chmn. 1997—), Acad. Operative Dentistry, Midland Coll. Alumni (bd. dirs. 1981—87, pres. 1983—84), Salmon Soc., Fremont Cmty. Players, Fremont Tennis Assn., Dodge County Hist. Soc., R.V. Tucker Nebr. Study Club, Tri Valley Dental Study Club (sec.-treas. 1983, v.p. 1984, pres. 1985, v.p. 1989), Midland Luth. Coll. Boosters Club (bd. dirs. 1988—94), Main St. Ambs. (co-chmn. 1997—98, chmn. 1998—2000, pres. 2000), Optimists (bd. dirs. 1981—83, 1984—88, pres. 1987, bd. dirs. Fremont club 1991—93), Am. Legion. Avocations: tennis, traveling. Home: 2137 Nye Dr Fremont NE 68025-2210 Office: 553 N Broad St Fremont NE 68025-4930 E-mail: pnurse6256@aol.com.

ROESELER, WOLFGANG GUENTHER JOACHIM, city planner; b. Berlin, Mar. 30, 1925; s. Karl Ludwig and Therese (Guenther) R.; m. Eva Maria Jante, Mar. 12, 1947; children: Marion, Joanie, Karl. PhD, Philipps State U. of Hesse, Marburg, Germany, 1949; LLB, Blackstone Sch. Law, Chgo., 1958. Assoc. planner Kansas City (Mo.) Planning Commn., 1950-52; city planning dir. City of Palm Springs, Calif., 1952-54; sr. city planner Kansas City, 1954-56; prin. assoc. Ladislas Segoe & Assocs., Cin., 1956-64; dir. urban and regional planning Howard, Needles, Tammen & Bergendoff, cons., Kansas City and N.Y.C., 1964-68; owner W.G. Roeseler, Cons. City Planner and Transp. Specialist, Bryan, Tex., 1969—. Head dept. urban and regional planning Tex. A&M U., 1975-81, 85-88, prof., 1975-90, dir. Tex A&M Ctr. Urban Affairs, 1984-88, exec. officer for edn. Coll. of Architecture, 1987-88, prof. emeritus, 1990—. Author: Successful American Urban Plans, 1982; author tech. reports; contbr. articles to profl. jours. Fellow Am. Inst. Cert. Planners; mem. Am. Planning Assn., Transport Planners Coun., Urban Land Inst. Home: 2508 Broadmoor Dr Bryan TX 77802-2803

ROESER, RONALD O. lawyer, consultant; b. Berwyn, Ill., May 6, 1950; s. John O. and Mary Jean (Marsden) R.; m. Susan Marie Gill, July 22, 1972; children: Michelle Marie, Michael Franklin. BA, So. Ill. U., 1972; JD, DePaul U., 1975. Bar: Ill. 1975, U.S. Dist. Ct. (no. dist.) Ill. 1975, U.S.Tax. Ct. 1975, U.S. Ct. Appeals (7th cir.) 1975. Assoc. Imming & Faber, Elgin, Ill., 1975-77; ptnr. Imming, Faber & Roeser, 1977-81, Imming & Roeser, Elgin, 1981-83, Roeser & Vucha, Elgin, 1983-84, Roeser, Vucha & Carbary, Elgin, 1984—. Mem. Fed. Trial Bar, Ill. Bar Assn., Kane County Bar Assn., Chgo. Bar Assn., Ill. Trial Lawyers Assn., Dundee Jaycees (treas., bd. dirs. 1975—, Outstanding Merit awards 1976, 78, 81), Lions. Republican. Roman Catholic. Avocations: history, reading, contact sports. Home: 34w921 Duchesne Dr Dundee IL 60118-3101 Office: Roeser & Vucha 920 Davis Rd Elgin IL 60123-1390

ROESER, THOMAS FRANCIS, columnist, commentator; b. Evanston, Ill., July 23, 1928; s. Harold Nicholas Roeser and Frances Catherine Cleary; m. Lillian Kathleen Prescott, Oct. 10, 1959; children: Thomas F. Jr., Mary Catherine, Michael J., Jeanne Marie. BA in English, St. John's U., 1950. Asst. to rep. Albert Quie and rep. Walter Judd U.S. Capitol, Washington, 1958-60; asst. to gov. of Minn. St. Paul, 1960-63; v.p. The Quaker Oats Co., Chgo., 1964-91; asst. sec. of commerce U.S. Commerce Dept., Washington, 1969—; dir. congl. rels. U.S. Peace Corps, 1970; pres. Thomas F. Roeser & Assocs., Chgo., 1991—. Op-ed columnist Chicago Tribune, 1995-97, Chicago Sun Times, 1997-; dist. prof. pub. policy Roosevelt U., Chgo., 1997; radio talk show host WLS-AM. Chmn. Cath. Citizens Ill., Chgo., 1996—, City Club Chgo., 1996—. Kennedy fellow Harvard U., Cambridge, 1977, Woodrow Wilson Internat. fellow, Princeton, N.J., 1979-80, Sr. fellow Heartland Inst., Chgo. Mem. Better Govt. Assn. (bd. dirs. 1980—), Chgo. Athletic Assn., Skyline Club. Republican. Roman Catholic. Office: Thomas F Roeser & Assocs 333 N Michigan Ave Ste 932 Chicago IL 60601-3907

ROESLER, JOHN BRUCE, lawyer; b. Portland, Oreg., Oct. 9, 1943; s. Bruce Emil and Charlotte Amanda (Naess) R.; m. Kathryne Elise Nilsen, Aug. 14, 1965; children: Paul, Mark, Nico. BA, U. Kans., 1966, JD, 1971. Bar: Mo. 1971, N.Mex. 1979, Colo. 1998, U.S. Dist. Ct. (we. dist.) Mo. 1971, U.S. Dist. Ct. N.Mex. 1979, U.S. Dist. Ct. Colo. 1998. U.S. Ct. Appeals (10th cir.) 1979, U.S. Ct. Appeals (5th cir.) 1988, U.S. Ct. Appeals (4th cir.) 1992, U.S. Supreme Ct. 1987. Assoc. The Gage Firm, Kansas City, Mo., 1971-74; civil rights advocate State of N.Mex. Human Rights, Santa Fe, 1977-78; law clk. Hon. Edwin L. Felter N.Mex. Supreme Ct., 1978-79; asst. dist. atty. Taos (N.Mex.) Dist. Atty.'s Office, 1979-80; asst. spl. pros. Santa Fe Dist. Atty.'s Office, 1980-82; pvt. practice Santa Fe, 1982-97; of counsel Roth, Van Amberg, Gross, Rogers & Ortiz, 1991-94; spl. asst. atty. gen. Colo. Atty. Gen's Office, 1997-99; assoc. Jones & Keller, Denver, 1999-2000; pvt. prac., 2000—. Instr. John Marshall Law Sch., Chgo., summer, 1974; spkr. edn. law and civil rights issues U. Miami Law Sch., 2000, Nat. Com. for Prevention of Child Abuse, Chgo., 1989, Little Rock, 90. Author: (books) How To Find the Best Lawyers, In Harm's Way: Is Your Child Safe in School; mem. law rev. U. Kans. Sch. Law, 1970-71; contbr. articles to profl. jours. and treatise. Mem. Colo. Bar Assn., Denver Bar Assn., Colo. Trial Lawyers Assn. Democrat. Roman Catholic. Avocations: skiing, hiking, gardening. Home: 2571 S Sherman St Denver CO 80210-5725 Office: 303 E 17th Ave Ste 700 Denver CO 80203

ROESLER, ROBERT HARRY, media consultant; b. Hammond, La., Oct. 5, 1927; s. Albert N. and Hilda (Schwartz) R.; m. Cloe Alferez, May 7, 1955; children: Kim, Bob, Toby. Student, Tulane U. Mem. sports staff Times Picayune, New Orleans, 1949-94, sports editor, 1964-80; exec. sports editor Times Picayune and States-Item, 1980-94; sports coord. New Orleans Met. Conv. and Visitors Bur., 1994—; CEO Roesler Media Cons. Chmn. faculty coun., Student Publs. Bd., U. New Orleans, 1998-2001. Author: Fair Grounds: Big Shots and Long Shots, 1998. Vice-chmn. Navy Recruiting Dist.; mem. assistance coun., New Orleans, 1992-96. With USN, WWII, Korean conflict. Mem. Profl. Football Writers Assn. Am. (pres. 1976-77), Nat. Turf Writers Assn., Football Writers Am., Am. Legion, Navy League U.S., New Orleans Press Club (pres. 1959-60, sports writing awards). Home: 6958 Colbert St New Orleans LA 70124-2334 Office: 1520 Sugar Bowl Dr New Orleans LA 70112-1255 E-mail: roesler@cox.net.

ROESLER, ROSE PIEPER, retired geriatrics nurse; b. Chgo., May 27, 1923; d. Albert G. L. and Rose C. (Kenitz) Pieper; m. Gerald O. Roesler, Dec. 22, 1951; children: Jon E. Roesler, Julia R. Roesler Utroske. Diploma in nursing, Walther Meml. Hosp., Chgo., 1944; postgrad., Cook County Hosp., Chgo., 1945. RN, Ind. Cert. to train nursing aides, Ind. U. Acting oper. rm. supr. Children's Meml. Hosp., Chgo., 1946-47; surg. nurse Hines VA Hosp., Maywood, Ill., 1947-49; staff nurse Luth. Home for the Aged, Arlington Heights, 1955-56; staff nurse labor and delivery, post partum Sherman Hosp., Elgin, 1956-58, 61-62; staff nurse post-partum, labor and delivery N.W. Community Hosp., Arlington Heights, 1962-66; float nurse Luth. Gen. Hosp., Park Ridge, 1966-70; med./surg. nurse N.W. Community Hosp., Arlington Heights, 1975; surg. nurse Sears, Roebuck and Co., Schaumburg, 1971-73; staff nurse the in-svc. dir. Willows Rehab. Ctr., Valparaiso, Ind., 1977-80, 82-84, program dir. nurse's aide tng., 1987-88; surg. asst. Valparaiso Eye Clinic, 1980. Instr. nursing aide classes Willows Rehab. Ctr., Valparaiso, 1989. Capt. ANC., 1945-46, 49-52.

ROESNER, LARRY AUGUST, civil engineer; b. Denver, Mar. 14, 1941; s. Walter George and Sarah Jane (Merrick) R.; m. Kathleen Ann Fahrenbruch, Dec. 13, 1964; children: David John, Kevin Walter, Nathan August, Melissa Jane. BS, Valparaiso (Ind.) U., 1963; MS, Colo. State U., 1965; PhD, U. Wash., Seattle, 1969. Registered profl. engr., Calif., Colo. From assoc. engr. to prin. engr. Water Resources Engrs., Inc., Walnut Creek, Calif., 1968-77; from assoc. to v.p. Camp Dresser & McKee Inc., Annandale, Va., 1977-85, sr. v.p., dir. water resources Maitland, Fla., 1985-92, chief tech. officer, 1992-98; dean Camp Dressert & McKee Corp. U., 1998-99; Harold H. Short prof. urban water infrastructure systems Colo. State U., Ft. Collins, 1999—, interim head dept. civil engring., 2000. Guest lectr., cons. urban hydrology and surface water quality; NRC exec. com. Wastewater Mgmt. in Urban Coastal Areas, 1992; chair Engring. Found. Conf. Stormwater Mgmt.-Sustainable Urban Water Resources in the 21st Century, 1997, NRC study panel Oil in the Sea, 2001; urban wet weather adv. Water Environ. Rsch. Found.; U.S. del. to joint IHR/IWA com. on urban drainage. Contbr. articles to profl. jours. Recipient Water Resource Planning and Mgmt. Divsn. Svc. to the Profession award 1999. Fellow ASCE (chmn. 1995 water resources planning and mgmt. div. splty. conf., nat. Walter L. Huber civil engring. rsch. prize 1975); mem. NAE, Am. Acad. Environ. Engrs. (diplomate), Am. Water Resources Assn., Water Environ. Fedn. (chmn. urban quality runoff task force), Tau Beta Pi (eminent engr.). Republican. Lutheran. Achievements include development of mathematical models for U.S. government agencies including QUAL-II stream quality model for the EPA; an urban stormwater management model, the dynamic hydraulics model SWMMEXTRAN for storm drainage and sewer systems. Home: 5926 Huntington Hills Dr Fort Collins CO 80525-7118 Office: Colo State U Dept Civil Engring Fort Collins CO 80523-1372 E-mail: roesner@engr.colostate.edu. *An environmental engineer is a caretaker in God's garden, the earth. The challenge for the environmental engineer is to maintain a balance between the needs of people and those of nature so that we may both use and enjoy the garden. It is the responsibility of the environmental engineer to leave the garden a little nicer than he found it.*

ROESNER, PETER LOWELL, manufacturing company executive; b. Winchester, Ind., July 3, 1937; s. Lowell LeClair and Martha Christine (Overmyer) R.; children: Peter Lowell II, David Brandon, John Franklin. Student, Durham (Eng.) U., 1957-58; BA, DePauw U., 1959; JD, U. Mich., 1962; MBA, Harvard U., 1964. Bar: Ind. 1962, N.J. 1992. Asst. to pres. Overmyer Corp., Muncie, Ind., 1964-65, corp. sec., 1965-69, pres., 1969-84, also dir.; pres. Clinitemp Inc., Indpls., 1985-88; pres., owner Middletown (N.J.) Interiors Inc., 1993—. Dir. Mchts. Nat. Bank, 1974-84 Trustee Purdue U., 1978. Mem. Ind. Mfrs. Assn. (dir. 1970-82, pres. 1975, chmn. Phoenix Award com. 1974), Glass Packaging Inst. (trustee 1981-84), ABA Episcopalian.

ROESSER, JEAN WOLBERG, state legislator; b. Washington, May 8, 1930; d. Solomon Harry Wolberg and Mary Frances Brown; m. Eugene Francis Roesser, Aug. 3, 1957; children: Eugene Francis, Jr., Mary Roesser Calderon, Anne. BA, Trinity Coll., Washington, 1951; postgrad. in econs., Cath. U. of Am., 1951-53. Congl. relations asst. U.S. Info. Agy., Washington, 1954-58; news reporter for Montgomery County Coun., Suburban Record, 1983-86; mem. Md. Ho. of Dels., Annapolis, 1986-94, Md. Senate, Annapolis, 1994—; mem. fin. com., ethics com. State Senate, Md. Gen. Assembly, 1994—, joint com. welfare reform, 1996—, joint com. healthcare delivery & financing, 1996—, joint budget & audit com., 1997—, chair joint com. on welfare reform, 2002. Former mem. Md. Gov.'s Task Force on Energy; former pres. Montgomery County Fedn. Rep. Women, Potomac Women's Rep. Club; former 3d v.p. Md. Fedn. Rep. Women; founding mem. Montgomery County Arts Coun.; alt. del. Rep. Nat. Conv., 1992, del., 1996. Named one of Md.'s Top 100 Women, Daily Record, 2002; recipient Cmty. Achievement award, Washington Psychiat. Soc., 1994, 1998, Trinity Coll. Leadership award, 1994, Common Cause Md. award, 1993, Md. Underage Drinking Preventio Coalition award, 1994, Legislator of the Yr. award, Montgomery County Med. Soc., 1996, 2000, Best in Class award, Md. C. of C., 1997, Cmty. Svc. award, Washington Psychiatric Soc., 1998, Legislator of Yr. award, Md. State's Atty.'s Assn., 2000. Mem. Women Legislators Md., also area citizens assns. and chambers commerce. Republican. Roman Catholic. Home: 10830 Fox Hunt Ln Potomac MD 20854-1553 Office: James Senate Office Bldg 437 Miller 11 Bladen St Annapolis MD 21401-8012

ROESSLER, CAROL ANN, state legislator; b. Madison, Wis., Jan. 16, 1948; d. John J. and Lucile E. (Kraner) Murphy; m. Paul Roessler. BS, U. Wis., Oshkosh, 1972. Dir. nutrition program for older adults County of Winnebago, Wis., 1973-82; mem. Wis. Assembly, Madison, 1983-87, Wis. Senate from 18th dist., Madison, 1987—. Instr. pre-retirement planning Fox Valley Tech. Inst., 1978-81. Home: 1506 Jackson St Oshkosh WI 54901-2942 Office: PO Box 7882 Madison WI 53707-7882 E-mail: Sen.Roessler@legis.state.wi.us.

ROESSLER, P. DEE, lawyer, former judge, educator; b. McKinney, Tex., Nov. 4, 1941; d. W.D. and Eunice Marie (Medcalf) Powell; m. George L. Roessler, Jr., Nov. 16, 1963 (div. Dec. 1977); children: Laura Diane, Trey. Student, Austin Coll., 1960-61, 62-64, Wayland Bapt. Coll., 1961-62; BA, U. West Fla., 1968; postgrad., East Tex. State U., 1975, U. Tex.-Dallas, 1977; JD, So. Meth. U., 1982. Bar: Tex. 1982, U.S. Dist. Ct. (ea. dist.) Tex. 1983, U.S. Dist. Ct. (no. dist.) Tex. 1983, U.S. Supreme Ct. 2000. Tchr. Van Alstyne Ind. Sch. Dist., Tex., 1968-69; social worker Dept. Social Svcs., Fayetteville, N.C., 1971-73, Dept. Human Svcs., Sherman and McKinney, 1973-79, 81; assoc. atty. Abernathy & Roeder, McKinney, 1982-85, Ronald W. Uselton, Sherman, 1985-86; prof., program coord. for real estate Collin County C.C., McKinney, 1986-87, prof. criminal justice, 1986-91, legal asst., 1986-99; asst. county atty. Grayson County, Tex., 1999-2000; solo practice, 2000—. Mcpl. judge City of Mckinney Mcpl. Ct., 1986-89; mem. Tex. State Bar Com. on Legal Assts., 1990-94, Tex. State Bar Com. on Child Abuse and Neglect, 1996-2001. Mem. Collin County Shelter for Battered Women, 1984-86, chmn., 1984-85; v.p. Collin County Child Welfare Bd., 1986, pres., 1987-88, 96-97, treas., 1989, mem., 1985-89, 94-98; Rep. jud. candidate Collin County, 1986; chmn. bd. Tri County Consortium Mental Health Mental Retardation, 1984-85; mem. Tex. Area 5 Health System Agy., 1979, Collin County Mental Health Adv. Bd., 1978-79; trustee Willow Park Hosp., HCA, 1987-88; chair Collin County Criminal Justice Sub-com., 1987-88; mem. Collin County Pub. Responsibility Com., 1991-96, chair, 1994-95; bd. dirs. Ct. Apptd. Spl. Advocates, 1991-95. Mem. Collin County Bar Assn., Plano Bar Assn. Baptist. Avocations: gardening, reading, writing, traveling. Home: 5 Shadybrook Cir Melissa TX 75454-8912 Office: 1600 1st Ave Mc Kinney TX 75069

ROETENBERG, AARON DAVID, retail consultant; b. Harrisburg, Pa., July 3, 1958; s. Barnet and Etta Rae (Miller) R. AA, Harrisburg Area C.C., 1978; BS, Bloomsburg State U., 1980. Buyer Bon-Ton Stores, York, Pa., 1980-97; retail implementation specialist Tru Serv Corp., Chgo., 1997-2000; retail cons., 2000—. Sec., bd. dirs. York Coun. Jewish Chs., 1996-98; bd. dirs. Ohev Sholom Congregation, York, 1996-2000. Mem. Zeta Psi Alumni Assn., Nat. Eagle Scout Assn. Avocations: martial arts, kayaking, genealogy, golf. Home: 711 N Franklin St York PA 17403-1005 E-mail: aaronr@gte.net.

ROETHEL, DAVID ALBERT HILL, consultant; b. Milw., Feb. 17, 1926; s. Albert John and Elsie Margaret (Hill) R.; children: Elizabeth Jane, Susan Margaret. BS, Marquette U., 1950, MS, 1952; cert., Oak Ridge Sch. Reactor Tech., 1953. Chem. engr. naval reactors br. AEC, Washington, 1952-57; mgr. profl. relations, asst. to exec. sec. Am. Chem. Soc., 1957-72; exec. dir. Nat. Registry in Clin. Chemistry, 1967-72, Am. Assn. Clin. Chemists, Washington, 1968-70, Am. Orthotic and Prosthetic Assn., 1973-76, Am. Acad. Orthotists and Prosthetists, Am. Bd. Cert. in Orthotics and Prosthetics, 1973-76; exec. dir., fellow Am. Inst. Chemists, Washington, 1977-90, bd. dirs., exec. com., 1981-90, exec. dir. Nat. Certification Commn. in Chemistry and Chem. Engring., 1977-90, exec. dir., trustee Am. Inst. Chemists Found., 1982-90, sec., 1990; pres. Peachtree Promotions, 1991—; dir. Chemical Heritage Found., 1992-98; v.p., treas. Cons. Consortium, 1994-98, pres., 1998-2000, bd. dirs., 1992—. Sec., vice chmn., then chmn. Intersoc. Com. on Health Lab.

Svcs., 1966-72; v.p. Pensions for Profls., Inc., Washington, 1970-72; vice chmn., then chmn. Engrs. and Scientists Joint Commn. on Pensions, 1978-80, vice chmn., 1985-87, chmn., 1988-90, 94-95, sec., 1996-97; mem. Commn. Profls. in Sci. and Tech., 1978-96, sec.-treas., 1979-82, bd. dirs., 1989-96, v.p., 1990-91, exec. com., 1990-93, 95; sec. gen. 7th Internat. Congress in Orthotics and Prosthetics, 1975-76, 2d World Congress in Prosthetics and Orthotics, 1975-77; chmn. U.S. arrangements Can.-Am. Chem. Congress, 1982-84; bd. dirs. China-U.S. Sci. Exchanges, 1985-89. Editor: Almanac, 1973-76, Chemist, 1977-90. Mem. Md. Gov.'s Com. on Sci. Devel., 1969; bd. dirs. Episcopal Ctr. for Children, 1991-97, sec., 1992-93, pres., 1993-95; mem. Episcopal Sr. Ministries Coun., 2002—. Served with U.S. Army Air Corps, 1944-46, CBI. Recipient Outstanding Svc. award Intersoc. Com. on Health Lab. Svcs., 1972, Appreciation awards Nat. Reg. in Clin. Chemistry, 1972, Engrs. and Sci. Com. on Pensions, 1996, Stewart R. Macdonald award., Consultans Consortium, 2001. Mem.: Washington Acad. Scis. (DCIC rep. 2000—), Chem. Soc. Washington (bd. dirs. 2000—02), D.C. Inst. Chemists (sec. 1992—94, bd. dirs. 1992—, pres.-elect 1995—97, pres. 1998—99, Honor Scroll award 1999), Am. Inst. Chemists, Coun. Engring. and Sci. Soc. Execs. (bd. dirs. 1983—86), Am. Chem. Soc. (dir. fed. credit union 1967—70, pres. 1968—70), Sports Car Club Am. (local officer 1960—74, bd. dirs. 1964—67, vice chmn., sec. 1967, 1975—76, bd. dirs. 1975—77, historian 1989—), Pi Mu Epsilon, Sigma Gamma Chi, Alpha Chi Sigma (nat. dist. counselor 1964—68, nat. profl. rep. Washington chpt. 1986—, bd. dirs. 1986—, pres. 1989—90, grand prof. alchemist 1992—94, pres. 1995—98, sec. 1998—, newsletter editor 1998—, pres. 1963—64, Profl. Achievement award 1986). E-mail: Droethel@juno.com.

ROETHENMUND, OTTO EMIL, financial and banking executive; b. Thun, Switzerland, Sept. 1, 1928; came to U.S., 1951, naturalized, 1957; s. Franz and Berta (Dallenbach) R.; m. Ermina Grassi, May 7, 1955; children— Robert, Denise. MA, U. Neuchatel, 1948. Mgmt. trainee Kantonalbank, Bern, 1948-51; exec. trainee J. Henry Schroeder Banking and Trust Corp., N.Y.C., 1951-56; with Deak-Perera Group, 1956—, vice chmn., group partner, 1962—; v.p., then sr. v.p. Deak & Co. (holding co.), 1962-74, exec. v.p., 1974-80, pres., chief exec. officer, 1980-86; pres., dir. Inter-Nation Capital Mgmt. Corp., 1986—. Lectr. internat. monetary and investment seminars. Served to lt. Swiss Army, 1948-51. Decorated knight Mil. Order Sts. Salvador and Brigitta (Sweden). Mem. Explorers Club, Met. Club (N.Y.C.), Westchester Country Club. Home: 2 Shore Rd Rye NY 10580-1031 Office: Inter-Nation Capital Mgmt Corp 230 Park Ave Rm 2600 New York NY 10169-0699 E-mail: oeratincm@aol.com.

ROETMAN, ORVIL M. retired airplane company executive; b. Slayton, Minn., Aug. 28, 1925; s. Ernest Gilbert and Olava (Christianson) R.; m. Lavera Jones, Mar. 14, 1948 (dec.); 1 child, Debra Roetman Caldwell; m. Arlis M. Olson, Sept. 17, 1999. BA, U. Minn., 1950; BS in Aerospace Engring., U.S. Naval Post. Grad. Sch., 1955; JD, George Washington U., 1965; postgrad., Naval War Coll., 1961. Bar: D.C. 1966. Commd. ensign U.S. Navy, 1945, advanced through grades to comdr., 1962, ret., 1965; sole practice law Washington, 1965-66; in legal svcs. Boeing Co., Seattle, 1966-67, dir. contract adminstrn., 1968, dir. internat. sales, 1971-79, v.p. internat. sales, 1979-83, v.p. contracts, 1983-87, corp. v.p. govt. and internat. affairs, 1988-90, ret., 1990. Bd. dirs. higher edn. Concordia U. Sys. E-mail: oroetman@aol.com.

ROETT, RIORDAN, political science educator, consultant; b. N.Y.C., Sept. 10, 1938; s. Riordan Jr. and Marion (Underwood) R. BA, Columbia U., 1959, MIA, 1962, PhD, 1968. Postdoctoral fellow Ctr. for Internat. Studies, MIT, Cambridge, Mass., 1966-67; asst. prof., assoc. prof. polit. sci. Vanderbilt U., Nashville, 1967-73; prof. polit. sci. Sch. Advanced Internat. Studies, Johns Hopkins U., Washington, 1973—. Sr. polit. analyst internat. capital markets Chase Manhattan Bank, N.Y.C., 1983-95; sr. advisor World Econ. Forum, Geneva; bd. dirs. Global Ptnrs. Income Fund, Emerging Markets Income Fund I & II, Salomon Bros. Worldwide Income Fund, Emerging Markets Floating Rate Fund, Salomon Bros. 2008 Worldwide Dollar Govt. Term Trut. Editor, co-author: Latin America, Western Europe, and the U.S.: Reevaluating the Atlantic Triangle, 1985, Mexico and the U.S.: Managing the Relationship, 1988, Paraguay: The Legacy of Personalist Politics, 1990, Mexico's External Relations in the 1990's, 1991, Political and Economic Liberalization in Mexico, 1993, The Challenge of Institutional Reform in Mexico, 1995, The Mexican Peso Crisis: International Perspectives, 1996, Brazil Under Cardoso, 1997, Mexico's Private Sector: Recent History, Future Challenges, 1998, Mercosur: Regional Integration, World Markets, 1999, Brazil: Politics in a Patrimonial Society, 5th edit. 1999. Fulbright fellow, 1962. Mem. Latin Am. Studies Assn. (v.p. 1977, pres. 1978), Coun. on Fgn. Rels., Cosmos Club. Democrat. Roman Catholic. Home: 2301 Connecticut Ave NW Apt 1B Washington DC 20008-1730 Office: Johns Hopkins U SAIS 1740 Massachusetts Ave NW Washington DC 20036-1903 E-mail: rroett@jhu.edu.

ROFF, ALAN LEE, lawyer, consultant; b. Winfield, Kans., July 2, 1936; s. Roy Darlis and Mildred Marie (Goodaile) R.; m. Sonyia Ruth Anderson, Feb. 8, 1954; 1 child, Cynthia Lee Roff Edwards; m. Molly Gek Neo Tan, July 21, 1980. BA with honors and distinction, U. Kans., 1964, JD with distinction, 1966. Bar: Okla. 1967. Staff atty. Phillips Petroleum Co., Bartlesville, Okla., 1966-75, sr. atty., 1976-85, sr. counsel, 1986-94; cons. in Asia, 1995—. Mem. editl. bd. Kans. Law Rev., 1965-66. Precinct com. man Rep. Party, Lawrence, Kans., 1963-64; assoc. justice Kans. U. Chancery Club; mem. Kans. U. Young Reps. Elizabeth Reeder scholar U. Kans., 1965-66, Eldon Wallingford award, 1964-66. Mem. ABA, Okla. Bar Assn., Washington County Bar Assn., Phoenix Club (Bartlesville) (bd. dirs. 1985-86, gen. counsel 1986-91), Order of the Coif, Masons, Hon. Order Ky. Cols., Phi Alpha Delta, Pi Sigma Alpha. Mem. First Christian Ch. Avocation: travel. Home and Office: 2247 Mountain Dr Bartlesville OK 74003-6954

ROFF, J(OHN) HUGH, JR. energy company executive; b. Wewoka, Okla., Oct. 27, 1931; s. Hugh and Louise Roff; m. Ann Green, Dec. 23, 1956; children— John, Charles, Andrew, Elizabeth, Jennifer AB, U. Okla., 1954, LL.B., 1955. Bar: Okla., Mo., N.Y. Law clk. to presiding justice U.S. Ct. Appeals (10th cir.), 1958; atty. Southwestern Bell Telephone Co., St. Louis, 1959-63, AT&T, N.Y.C., 1964-68; v.p., gen. atty. Long Lines, 1969-73, gen. atty., 1973-74; chmn., pres., chief exec. officer United Energy Resources, Houston, 1974-86; chmn. PetroUnited Terminals Inc., 1986-98, Roff Resources LLC, Houston, 1998—. Past chmn. Cen. Houston Inc.; mem. adv. bd. Ctr. for Strategic and Internat. Studies, Washington; mem. coun. overseers Jones Sch. Bus. Adminstrn., Rice U.; trustee Baylor Coll. Medicine; past chmn. adv. bd. The Salvation Army, Houston. 1st lt. U.S. Army, 1955-58. Mem. Order of Coif, Phi Beta Kappa, Beta Theta Pi. Clubs: Houston Country, Coronado, Houstonian. Office: 333 Clay St Ste 4300 Houston TX 77002-4103 E-mail: hughroff@roffresources.com.

ROFF, WILLIAM ROBERT, history educator, writer; b. Glasgow, Scotland, May 2, 1929; came to U.S., 1969; s. Robert Henry William and Isabella (Anderson) R.; m. Susanne Rabbitt, Aug. 2, 1978; children: Sarah, Emily. BA, U. New Zealand, 1957, MA, 1959; PhD, Australian Nat. U., 1965. Lectr. history Monash U., Australia, 1963-66; lectr., sr. lectr. U. Malaya, Malaysia, 1966-69; assoc. prof. Columbia U., N.Y.C., 1969-73, prof., 1973-90, prof. emeritus, 1990—. Vis. prof. Yale U., 1971, L'Ecole des Hautes Etudes en Sciences Sociales, Paris, 1985; vis. fellow Australian Nat. U., 1974; hon. fellow Edinburgh U., Scotland, 1992—. Author: The Origins of Malay Nationalism, 1967, (with others) In Search of Southeast Asia, 1971, Bibliography of Malay and Arabic Periodicals, 1972; author, editor: Kelantan: Religion, Society and Politics, 1973; editor: Islam and the Political Economy of Meaning, 1987. Guggenheim Found. fellow 1973; Rockefeller Found. fellow, 1982 Mem. Royal Asiatic Soc. (life), Assn. for Asian Studies, Asian Studies Assn. Australia, Brit. Soc. for Middle East Studies, Middle East Studies Assn. Avocation: parenting. Home: 29 Shore St Cellardyke Fife Scotland E-mail: williamroff@compuserve.com.

ROFFÉ, SARINA, cultural organization administrator; b. Bklyn., Feb. 16, 1955; d. Abe J. and Reneé (Salem) Missry; m. David Roffé, June 4, 1974; children: Simon, Honey, Abraham. BA in Journalism, U. Md., 1992. Reporter Gazette Newspaper, Gaithersburg, Md., 1991—93; news editor Richner Publs., Lawrence, NY, 1993—94; mng. editor Queens Tribune, 1994; interpreter of deaf Montgomery County Pub. Schs., Rockville, Md.; writer, editor freelance Bklyn.; dir. pub. affairs NYC Dept. Juvenile Justice, 1996—2002; founder, exec. dir. NY Speech Ctr., Inc., 1995—; nat. dir. comms. Jewish Nat. Fund, 2002—. Contbg. author: Choices in Deafness-A Parent's Guide, 1987, contbg. author: Cued Speech Resource Guide for Parents, 1993, contbg. author: Jewish Cooking in America, 1994; contbr. articles to profl. jours. Pres. Montgomery County Assn. Hearing Impaired Children, Silver Spring, 1981—83; fundraising v.p., treas. B'nai B'rith Women, Gaithersburg, 1975—93; dir. Magen David Sephradic Congregation Bd., Rockville, 1989—93. Named Best in the Bus., Am. Correctional Assn., 1999; recipient 1st Pl. award, Am. Sephradic Fedn., 1991. Mem.: Soc. for Profl. Journalists, Nat. Cued Speech Assn. (pres.), Sephardic Voters League (v.p. 1999—), Hadassah, Nat. Registry of Interpreters for Deaf, Jewish Women Internat., Acad. Women Achievers of the YWCA, Deadline Club. Democrat. Jewish. Avocation: Mid East cooking. E-mail: sarinaroffe@aol.com.

ROFFMAN, BLAINE YALE, pathologist; b. Omaha, Jan. 30, 1935; s. Sam and Ruth (Wintroub) R.; m. Judith Ileane Ferdinand, June 29, 1958; children: Shari, Carin, Linda. BA, State U. of Iowa, 1956; MD, U. Nebr., Omaha, 1961. Diplomate Am. Bd. Pathology, Am. Bd. Forensic Medicine. Intern Marion County Gen. Hosp., Indpls., 1961-62; resident in internal medicine U. Nebr. Med. Ctr., Omaha, 1964-65, resident in pathology, 1965-68; pathologist Physicians Lab., 1968—; assoc. prof. pathologist U. Nebr. Med. Ctr., 1968—; pres. Physicians Lab., Omaha, 1975—. Lab. dir. Midlands Community Hosp., Papillion, Nebr., 1968-2000. Pres. Temple Israel, Omaha, 1982; bd. dirs., Jewish Fedn. Found., Omaha, 1987—, chair, 2000-02. Capt. USAF, 1962-64. Fellow Coll. Am. Pathologists (com. mem.), Am. Soc. Clin. Pathology, Am. Acad. Forensic Sci.; mem. AMA, Metro. Omaha Med. Soc. (pres. 1992-93), Nebr. Assn. Pathologists (pres. 1974), Nat. Assn. Med. Examiners. Home: 616 N 162 St Omaha NE 68118-2500 Office: Physicians Lab 4840 F St Omaha NE 68117-1428 E-mail: quincy201@pol.net., byroffman@physlab.com.

ROFFMAN, HOWARD, motion picture company executive; b. Phila. Student, U. Pa.; JD, U. Fla. Assoc. Morgan, Lewis & Bockius, Washington; from legal counsel to gen. counsel Lucasfilm, Ltd., San Rafael, Calif., 1980-84, acting COO, 1984-85, v.p. licensing, 1986-99; pres. Lucas Licensing, 1999—. Author: Presumed Guilty, 1974, Understanding the Cold War, 1976, The Edge of Desire, 1995, Three, 1996, Tales, 1997, Pictures of Fred, 1998, Jagged Youth, 2000, Johan Paulik, 2001, Pictures of Kris, 2002. Mem. Calif. Bar Assn., Washington Bar Assn., Licensing Industry Merchandising Assn. Office: Lucas Licensing Ltd PO Box 10148 San Rafael CA 94912-0148

ROGAL, GARY JEFFREY, cardiologist; b. Newark, Nov. 20, 1952; s. David and Bert Shane Rogal; m. Camille Elizabeth Rogal, Oct. 18, 1981; children: David, Jennifer, Sarah. BA, George Washington U., 1974, MD, 1978. Diplomate Am. Bd. Internal Medicine, Am. Bd. Cardiovasc. Disease. Resident in internal medicine L.I. Jewish-Hillside Med. Ctr., 1978-81; resident in cardiology U. Rochester-Strong Meml. Hosp., 1981-84; asst. prof. medicine Albany (N.Y.) Med. Coll., 1984-86; chief cardiology St. Barnabas Health Care Sys., Livingston, N.J., 1998—; pvt. practice gen. and interventional cardiology, 1986—. Fellow Am. Coll. Cardiology; mem. Phi Beta Kappa. Avocations: photography, skiing, resistance/aerobic training. Office: Diagnostic and Clin Cardiology PA 769 Northfield Ave West Orange NJ 07052-1198

ROGALSKI, CAROL JEAN, clinical psychologist, educator; b. Chgo., Sept. 25, 1937; d. Casimir Joseph and Lillian Valentine Rogalski. BS, Loyola U., Chgo., 1961; PhD, NYU, 1968; cert. in psychoanalysis, Postgrad. Ctr. Mental Health, 1973. Lic. clin. psychologist, N.Y., Ill. Rsch. assoc. William Alanson White Inst., N.Y.C., 1961-66; rsch. asst., intern Hillside Hosp., Glen Oaks, N.Y., 1966-68; cons. Mt. Sinai Hosp., N.Y.C., 1968-73; staff psychologist Westside VA Hosp., Chgo., 1974—; clin. asst. prof. psychiatry Med. Sch. U. Ill., 1996—. Mem. editorial bd. Internat. Jour. Addictions, 1994-98; contbr. articles to profl. publs. Mem.: Chgo. Soc. for Psychotherapy Rsch. (chair 1988—91), Communal Studies Assn. Avocation: watercolors. Office: Westside VA Hosp 820 S Damen Ave Chicago IL 60612-3728 E-mail: carol.rogalski@med.va.gov.

ROGALSKI, LOIS ANN, speech and language pathologist; b. Bklyn. d. Louis J. and Filomena Evelyn (Maro) Giordano; m. Stephen James Rogalski, Jun e 27, 1970; children: Keri Anne, Stefan Louis, Christopher James, Rebecca Blair, Gregory Alexander. BA, Bklyn. Coll., 1968; MA, U. Mass., 1969; PhD., NYU, 1975. Lic. speech and lang. pathologist, N.Y. Speech, lang. and voice pathologist Rehab. Ctr. of So. Fairfield County, Stamford, Conn., 1969, Sch. Health Program-P.A. 481, Stamford, 1969-72, pvt. practice speech, lang. and voice pathology Scarsdale, N.Y., 1972—. Cons. Bd. Coop. Ednl. Svcs., 1976-79, Handicapped Program for Preschoolers for Alcott Montessori Sch., Ardsley, N.Y., 1978—; rsch. methodologist Burke Rehab. Ctr., 1977. Mem. profl. adv. bd. Found. for Children with Learning Disabilities, 1978—; bd. dirs. United Way of Scarsdale-Edgemont, 1988-89; instr. religious instr. CCD Immaculate Heart of Mary Ch., Scarsdale, 1991—; bd. dirs. Scarsdale Teen Ctr., Inc., 1998—. Fellow Rehab. Svcs. Adminstrn., 1968-69; N.Y. Med. Coll., 1972-75. Mem. N.Y. Speech & Hearing Assn., Westchester Speech & Hearing Assn., Am. Speech, Hearing & Lang. Assn. (cert. clin. competence), Coun. for Exceptional Children, Assn. on Mental Deficiency, Am. Acad. Pvt. Practice in Speech Pathology & Audiology (bd. dirs., treas. 1983-87, pres. 1987-89), Internat. Assn. Logopedics & Phoniatrics, Sigma Alpha Eta. Office: PO Box 331H Scarsdale NY 10583-8831 Fax: 914-725-7341.

ROGAN, JAMES E. federal agency administrator, former congressman; m. Christine Apffel. BA in Polit. Sci., U. Calif., Berkeley, 1979; JD, UCLA, 1983. Past atty. Lillick McHose and Charles (now Pillsbury, Madison and Sutro), L.A.; past dep. dist. atty. L.A. County; judge Glendale (Calif.) Mcpl. Ct., 1990—93, presiding judge, 1993—94; past mem. Calif. Assembly, 1994—96, assembly majority leader, 1996; mem. U.S. Congress from 27th Calif. dist., 1996—2001; mem. house jud. com., mem. commerce com., asst. minority whip; ptnr. Venable, Baetjer, Howard & Civiletti, Washington, 2001; under secy. of commerce for intellectual property, 2001—; dir. US Patent & Trademark Office, 2001—. Adj. prof. trial advocacy Sch. Law Southwestern U.; adj. prof. criminal law Coll. Law Glendale U.; past adj. prof. criminal law Glendale C.C.; mem. Selective Svc. Sys. U.S. Govt., 1981—. Office: US Patent & Trademark Office Crystal Plaza 3 Rm 2C02 Washington DC 20231 Fax: 202-225-5828.*

ROGAN, ROBERT WILLIAM, management educator, consultant, osteopath, psychiatrist; b. Buffalo; BA, MBA, SUNY, Buffalo; cert. in data processing, Cornell U.; DO, W.Va. Sch. Osteo. Medicine, 1983; postgrad., Virginia Beach, 1986-88; JD, Regent U., 1990. Bar: Pa. 1992; diplomate Nat. Bd Examiners for Osteo. Medicine and Surgery, cert. in psychiatry NC Psychiat. Assn.; data processor, data educator. Assoc. prof. bus. West Liberty (W.Va.) State Coll., 1976-79; chief intern Metro Health Ctr., Erie, Pa., 1983-84; asst. prof. computer sci. Gannon U., 1984-85; asst. prof. mgmt. Slippery Rock (Pa.) U., 1985-86; practice medicine specializing in osteopathy Harborcreek Family Practice, Erie, Pa., 1985; resident physician Univ. Med. Ctr.-East Carolina U., Greenville, N.C., 1992-96. Temp. physician Oceana (W.Va.) Med. Ctr., 1992-95; rschr., tchr. law Inst. Fine Mechanics and Optics, St. Petersburg, Russia, 1993, Poland, 1994; part-time radio announcer Sta. WGHB, Farmville, N.C., 1993-96; psychiat. and mgmt. cons., critical incident stress debriefer, 1996—; asst. prof. W.Va. U. Sch. Medicine, 1999—; chmn. ethics com. William R. Sharpe Hosp., 2000—. Counselor Contact Crisis Care, Lewisburg, W.Va., 1980—81; med. vol. Jamaica, 1988, Haiti, 1989, Calcutta, India, 1992, Marshall U. Sch. Medicine, 1990—91; constrn. vol. Japan, 1991, Senegal, West Africa, 2000, Ecuador, 2001; mem. Hist. Preservation Commn., City of Greenville, 1995—96, disaster vol., 2001—. Scholar U. Buffalo, N.Y. State Bd. Regents; grantee NSF, Cornell U.; Group for Advancement of Psychiatry fellow, 1995-96. Mem. Am. Osteo. Assn., N.C. Psychiat. Assn. (psychiatry and law rep. 1994-96, mem. econ. affairs com. 1995-96, mem. exec. coun. 1994-96). Avocations: travel, sports, volunteering. E-mail: nagor36@earthlink.net.

ROGAN, STEPHEN JOSEPH, software implementation consultant; b. N.Y.C., Dec. 7, 1955; s. Robert F. and Agnes (O'Connor) R.; m. Laurie E. Leblanc, May 27, 1984; children: Daniel, Julianne. BS, Fairfield (Conn.) U., 1977; MBA, Pace U., 1982. CPA, Conn.; cert. prodn. and inventory mgmt.; JAVA cert. Acctg. coord. Greenwich (Conn.) Assocs., 1978-83; br. contr. Nat. Guardian, Norwalk, Conn., 1984-85; contr. L'Amy Inc., Shelton, 1986-88, v.p. fin. and adminstrn., 1989-93; v.p. ops. Silhouette Optical, Northvale, N.J., 1994-95; cons. Price Waterhouse Coopers (formerly Coopers-Lybrand), Westport, Conn., 1996—. Coach Jr. Boys Basketball, Norwalk; asst. coach Jr. Boys Soccer and Baseball, Norwalk; usher, greeter St. Philip's Ch., Norwalk. Mem. Ednl. Soc. Resource Mgmt., Conn. Soc. CPAs (mem. tech. com.), Mensa, Intertel. Republican. Roman Catholic. Avocations: power boating, downhill skiing, travel, personal computers. Home: 27 Algonquin Rd Norwalk CT 06851-1809 Office: Price Waterhouse Coopers 300 Atlantic St Stamford CT 06901-3522

ROGASH, JOSEPH ALAN, meteorologist, educator; b. Boston, Aug. 6, 1953; s. Alfred and Marylyn Lorraine Rogash; m. Charlotte Mae Johnson; children: Lindsay, Lisa. BS in History, U. Mass., Boston, 1975; BS in Physics, U. Mass., Dartmouth, 1980; MS in Atmospheric Sci., Colo. State U., 1982. Cert. secondary sch. tchr. Mass. Meteorologist U.S. Dept. of Def., White Sands Missile Range, N.Mex., 1983—86; adj. prof. meteorology U. Memphis, 1992; meteorologist/lead forecaster Storm Prediction Ctr., Norman, Okla., 1994—2000; meteorologist Nat. Weather Svc., Santa Teresa, N.Mex., 2000—. Leader heavy rain forecasting program Storm Prediction Ctr., Norman, 1996—2000. Contbr. articles to profl. jours. Participant meteorol. outreach to pub. schools Nat. Weather Svc., El Paso, Tex., 2000—. Mem.: Mo. Acad. of Sciences, Nat. Weather Assn. Avocations: weightlifting, hiking, photography, history. Office: Nat Weather Svc 7950 Airport Rd Santa Teresa NM 88008 Business E-Mail: Joseph.Rogash@noaa.gov.

ROGATZ, PETER, physician; b. N.Y.C., Aug. 5, 1926; s. Julian and Sally (Levy) Rogatz; m. Marjorie Plaut, June 10, 1949; children: Peggy Joy, William Peter. BA, Columbia Coll., 1945; MD, Cornell U., 1949; M.P.H., Columbia U., 1956. Intern Lenox Hill Hosp., N.Y.C., 1949-50, resident, 1950-51, VA Hosp., Bronx, N.Y., 1951-52, N.Y. Hosp., N.Y.C., 1952-53; dep. dir. Montefiore Hosp., 1960-63; dir. L.I. Jewish Med. Center, 1964-68, Univ. Hosp., SUNY, Stony Brook, 1968-71; sr. v.p. Blue Cross/Blue Shield of Greater N.Y., 1971-76; prin., founding ptnr. RMR Health and Hosp. Mgmt. Cons., Inc., Roslyn Heights, N.Y., 1976-84; v.p. med. affairs Vis. Nurse Service, 1984-91; med. dir. Staff Builders, Inc., 1992-98. Prof. cmty. medicine SUNY, Stony Brook, 1968—94; mem. N.Y.C. Mayor's Commn. on Delivery of Health Svcs., 1967; v.p. Health and Welfare Coun. of Nassau County, 1968—72; bd. dirs. Cmty. Coun. Greater N.Y., 1974—77; mem. Task Force on N.Y.C. Crisis, 1976—81; chmn. bd. dirs. Cmty. Health Program affiliated with L.I. Jewish Med. Ctr., 1989—94; chmn. bd. dirs. Managed Health Inc., 1990—94. Author: Organized Home Medical Care in New York City, 1956; co-author (with Eli Ginzberg): Planning for Better Hospital Care, 1961; contbr. articles to profl. jours. Bd. dirs. Choice in Dying, 1994—2000, Compassion in Dying of N.Y., 1998—. Recipient Dean Conley award, Am. Coll. Hosp. Adminstrs., 1975; fellow, Commonwealth Fund, 1955. Fellow: ACP, Am. Coll. Preventive Medicine, N.Y. Acad. Medicine, APHA; mem.: N.Y. County Med. Soc., N.Y. State Med. Soc., N.Y. Pub. Health Assn., Am. Hosp. Assn., AMA. Home and Office: 76 Oakdale Ln Roslyn Heights NY 11577-1535

ROGAWSKI, MICHAEL ANDREW, neurologist, neuroscientist; b. L.A., Apr. 8, 1952; s. Alexander Simon and Elise (Berwin) R.; m. Julie Beth Schweitzer; children: David S., Elizabeth T., Alexander J. BA, Amherst (Mass.) Coll., 1974; MD, PhD in Pharmacology, Yale U., 1980. Diplomate Am. Bd. Med. Examiners. Resident, fellow, neurology Johns Hopkins Hosp., Balt., 1982-85; mem. active staff Warren Grant Magnusson Clin. Ctr., NIH, Bethesda, 1987—; sr. investigator, chief Epilepsy Rsch. sect. Nat. Inst. Neurol. Disorders & Stroke, NIH, 1990—. Former mem. neuropharmacology and neurochemistry study sect. NIMH. Mem. editl. bd.: Molecular Pharmacology, mem. editl. bd.: Epilepsy Rsch., mem. editl. bd.: Synapse, mem. editl. bd.: Cellular and Molecular Neurobiology CNS Drug Reviews, mem. editl. bd.: Pharmacology and Therapeutics, exec. editor: Neuropharmacology; editor: Neurotransmitter Actions in the Vertebrate Nervous System, 1985, Current Protocols in Neuroscience, 1997—. Mem. Am. Acad. Neurology, Am. Epilepsy Soc. (bd. dirs.), Am. Soc. Pharmacology and Exptl. Therapeutics (Epilepsy Rsch. award), Soc. Neurosci., Am. Soc. for Exptl. Neurotherapeutics, Phi Beta Kappa. Achievements include research on neurophysiology and neuropharmacology and patents for anticonvulsant drugs. Home: 9637 Cold Star Ct Columbia MD 21046-2072 Office: Nat Inst Neurol Disorders & Stroke Bethesda MD 20892 E-mail: michael.rogawski@nih.gov.

ROGE, BRET ALAN, lawyer; b. Milw., Jan. 31, 1959; s. Albert Harland and Gloria May Roge; m. Jill Marie Munson, Aug. 23, 1997; children: Seth Alan, Evan William. BBA in Acctg. sum cum laude, U. Wis., Milw., 1981; JD cum laude, Marquette U., 1984. Bar: Wis. 1984; CPA. Tax mgr. Arthur Young & Co., Milw., 1984-89; ptnr. Michael Best & Friedrich LLP, 1989—. Contbr. chpts. to books. Bd. dirs. Waukesha County Econ. Devel. Corp., Waukesha, Wis., 1998. Mem. ABA, AICPA (Elijah Watt Sells award 1984), Wis. Inst. CPA, Mil. Bar Assn., Beta Gamma Sigma. Avocations: biking, skiing, golfing. Office: Michael Best & Friedrich LLP 100 E Wisconsin Ave Milwaukee WI 53202-4107

ROGÉ, RONALD WILLIAM, financial planner, investment management executive; b. Bklyn., Mar. 7, 1947; s. Frederick William and Nancy (Rinaldo) R.; m. Patricia Mack, March 29, 1970; 1 child, Steven. AAS, N.Y.C. Community Coll., 1968; BS, L.I. U., 1970; MS, Poly. U., Bklyn., 1975. SEC registered investment advisor; cert. fin. planner. Planning engr. N.Y. Tel. Co., N.Y.C., 1970-78, product mgr., 1978-83; mgr. fin. planning NYNEX Enterprises, 1983-85, staff dir. employee benefits, 1986-90; pres. R.W. Rogé & Co., Inc., Bohemia, N.Y., 1986—. Apptd. adv. bd. TIAA/CREF Inst., 1999—. With USN, 1966-72. Named One of Am.'s Best Fin. Advisors, Worth mag., 1994-2002, One of Am.'s Best Fin. Advisors for Drs., Med. Econs. mag., 1998, 99, 2000, 01. Mem. Nat. Assn. Personal Fin. Advisors (bd. mem., dir. and v.p. consumer awareness, chmn. pub. rels. com. 1993-95, 96, dir. N.E./Mid Atlantic region, nat. bd. dirs. 1994-96, dir. and sec. 1995-96). Republican. Roman Catholic. Avocations: tennis, golf. Home: 86 Woodview Ln Centereach NY 11720-4060 Office: RW Rogé and Co Inc 630 Johnson Ave Ste 103 Bohemia NY 11716-2618 E-mail: ron@rwroge.com.

ROGEL, STEVEN R. forest products company executive; BS in Chem. Engring., U. Wash., 1965. With St. Regis Paper Co., 1965-70; asst. mgr. St. Anne-Nackawic Pulp and Paper, Nackawic, N.B., Can., 1970-72; tech. dir. Willamette Industries, Inc., Albany, Oreg., 1972-95, pres., CEO, 1995-97, Weyerhaeuser Co., Tacoma, 1997—, chmn., 1999—. Bd. dirs. Kroger Co. Trustee Pacific U.; bd. dirs. Pacific Harbors coun. Boy Scouts Am. Mem. Am. Forest and Paper Assn. (bd. dirs.). Office: 33663 Weyerhaeuser Way S Federal Way WA 98003-9620*

ROGENESS, MARY SPEER, state legislator; b. Kansas City, Kans., May 18, 1941; d. Frederic A. and Jeannette (Hybskmann) Speer; m. Dean Rogeness, Aug. 31, 1964; children: Emily, James, Paul. BA, Carleton Coll., 1963. Computer analyst Dept. Def., Ft. Meade, Md., 1963-66; freelance writer, editor Longmeadow, Mass., 1982-91; mem. Mass. Ho. of Reps., Boston, 1991—. Editor: Reflections of Longmeadow, 1983. Mem. Longmeadow Rep. Town Com., 1983—; bd. dirs. Goodwill Industries Hartford-Springfield, 1996—; mem. Longmeadow Sch. Com., 1982-88. Mem. Am. Legis. Exch. Coun., World Affairs Coun. of Western Mass. Office: Mass House of Reps State House Boston MA 02133

ROGER, JERRY LEE, school system administrator; b. Chase, Kans., Mar. 11, 1945; s. LeRoy J. and Lottie E. (Maphet) R.; m. Tucky Saint Smith, 1995. BS, U. Tulsa, 1966, MA, 1969, EdD, 1975. Cert. tchr., supt., Okla. Math. tchr. Kansas City (Mo.) Pub. Schs., 1966-67, Shawnee Mission (Kans.) Pub. Schs., 1967-71; rsch. asst. Tulsa Pub. Schs., 1972-73, rsch. coord., 1973-81, adminstrv. asst., 1981-90, rsch. dir., 1990-95, dir. planning and assessment, 1995-2000; chmn. U. Phoenix Sch. Gen. Studies, Tulsa, 2000; dir. acad. affairs U. Phoenix, 2001—. Adj. instr. Tulsa Jr. Coll., 1975-88; adj. asst. prof. U. Tulsa, 1980-85; sr. faculty U. Phoenix, Tulsa campus, 1998-2000. Contbr. book revs. to Tulsa Sunday World, 1990-92. Paul Harris fellow; Rotary benefactor. Mem. NEA, Am. Ednl. Res. Assn., Nat. Book Critics Cir., Nature Conservancy, Nat. Conf. for Cmty. and Justice, Phi Delta Kappa. Home: 3538 S Winston Ave Tulsa OK 74135-2045 Office: U Phoenix 10810 E 45th St Tulsa OK 74146-3818 E-mail: Jerry.Roger@apollogrp.edu.

ROGERS, AILENE KANE, retired secondary school educator; b. Jamaica, N.Y., Jan. 17, 1938; d. Daniel H. and Helen (Shirkey) Kane; m. Edward Lee Rogers, Nov. 18, 1961 (dec. Mar. 1998); children: Ruth, John, Helen, Daniel (dec.). BA, Middlebury Coll., 1959; MS, Am. U., 1963; MS in Environ. Sci.,

George Mason U., 1998. Asst. dir. program Student Conservation Assn., Charlestown, N.H., 1959-60, dir., 1960; teaching asst. Am. U., Washington, 1961-62; naturalist Nat. Park Svc., 1966-68; tchr. sci. Hauppauge (N.Y.) Middle Sch., 1972-73, Oak Grove Coburn Sch., Vassalboro, Maine, 1974-75, head sci. dept., 1976-79; tchr. sci. lower sch. Nat. Cathedral Sch., Washington, 1979-82, tchr. sci. upper sch., 1982-2000, head sci. dept., 1989-93, 94-95; ret., 2000; cons. Cornell Coop. Ext., Suffolk County Vanderbilt Mus., 2002—. Counselor Sci. Camp, The Potomac Sch., McLean, Va., summers 1982-88, 90, dir. sci. camp, 1986-88, co-dir., 1991; cons. Nat. Geographic Soc. Edn. Programs, 1982-89, Nat. Geographic Soc., 1980-92, Greenhouse Crisis Found., 1991, Nat. Assn. Biology Teachers, 1993; lectr. Young Assoc. Program Smithsonian Inst., Jan., Feb., 1988, 89; facilitator Com. for Math. and Sci., Washington, 1993-95; cons. marine biology program Cornell Extension Svcs./Vanderbilt Mus., Centerport, N.Y., 2002--. Founder Setauket Environ. Ctr., 1970, bd. govs., 1970-72; bd. dirs. Student Conservation Program, 1970-79; cons. Sch. Wide Environ. Edn. Program, N.Y.C., 1978, Population Reference Bur., 1995; cons. edn. programs Nat. Geog. Soc., 1980—; founder, chmn. Pittston (Maine) Conservation Commn., 1975-78; co-pres. McLean High Sch. Student-Parent-Tchr. Assn., 1982-84; mem. State Team D.C., Mid-Atlantic Consortium Math. and Sci. Edn.-Dwight D. Eisenhower Nat. Program Math. and Sci. Edn., 1989-94; marine sci. tchr. oceans program Phillips Acad., Andover, Mass., 1996. Chopinsky fellow for Ukrainian Ednl. Exch., 1994; NSF grantee, 1962. Mem. Nat. Parks and Conservation Assn., Student Conservation Assn., Nature Conservancy (dir. Maine chpt. 1976-78). Home: 91 Little Neck Rd Centerport NY 11721-1615

ROGERS, ALAN VICTOR, former career officer; b. Hannibal, Mo., Nov. 13, 1942; s. Julian Alan and Gladys Cuneo R.; m. Linda Rae Peterson, May 8, 1966; children: Kimberly Rae, Krista Anne, Peter Alan. BS in Mil. Sci., USAF Acad., 1964; MBA with distinction, Harvard Bus. Sch., 1972; grad. with distinction, Air War Coll., 1980. Commd. 2d lt. USAF, 1964, advanced through grades to maj. gen., 1989, ret., 1993; combat fighter pilot 355th Tactical Fighter Wing, Takhli, Thailand, 1966-67; jet pilot instr. Flying Tng. Wing, Williams AFB, Ariz., 1967-69; student Harvard Bus. Sch., Cambridge, Mass., 1970-72; pers. officer Cols. Group USAF Pentagon, Washington, 1972-75; student Air War Coll., Maxwell AFB, Ariz., 1980; wing comdr. 5th Bomb Wing, Minot AFB, N.D., 1982-84, 96th Bomb Wing (1st B-1 Wing), Dyess AFB, Tex., 1984-86; dir. ops. SAC, Offutt AFB, Nebr., 1986-89; asst. chief of staff ops. Supreme HQ Allied Powers Europe NATO, Mons, Belgium, 1989-91; dir. J-7 Joint Staff, Pentagon, Washington, 1991-93; assoc. Burdeshaw Assocs., Ltd., Bethesda, Md., 1993-94; prin. Gemini Consulting, Morristown, N.J., 1994-97; sr. v.p., gen. mgr. Fed. Defense Group, Am. Mgmt. Sys., Inc. , Fairfax, Va., 1997—2002. Mem., mil. adviser C. of C., Minot, N.D., 1982-84, Abilene, Tex. 1984-86. Decorated Defense Disting. Svc. Medal, Legion of Merit, D.F.C. with two oak leaf clusters, Purple Heart, Def. Superior Svc. medal, Disting. Svc. medal, Def. Disting. Svc. medal; recipient Am. U. Leadership award, 2000. Mem.: Nat. Def. Industry Assn. (bd. dirs.), Daedalians (chpt. pres. 1986), Nat. Eagle Scout Assn., Red River Valley Fighter Pilots Assn., Sabre Soc., USAF Acad. Assn. Grads. (bd. dirs. 1999—), Air Force Assn. Republican. Roman Cathlic. Avocations: skiing, travel, antiques. Home: 4600 32nd Rd N Arlington VA 22207-4406 E-mail: alanvrogers@aol.com.

ROGERS, ALICE LOUISE, retired bank executive, writer, researcher; b. McLoud, Okla., Feb. 18, 1929; d. John Edmond and Katy McNora (Williams) Stanka; m. Jesse Ray Rogers, Apr. 18, 1948; children: Jimmy Allen Rogers, Bonnie Kay Calhoun. Student, Am. Inst. Banking, 1967-69. Clk. typist loan dept. Security Pacific Nat. Bank, L.A., 1960-64; office mgr., adminstrv. asst. to v.p. loan adminstn. divsn. City Nat. Bank, Beverly Hills, 1964-75, credit mgr. Pershing Square branch, 1975-77. Author, editor: Dance Bands and Big Bands Reference Book and Price Guide, 1986, Dance Bands, Big Bands and Swing Reference Book and Price Guide, 1993; contbr. articles to DISCoveries mag., Internat. Assn. of Jazz Record Collectors Jour., Joslin's Jazz Jour., Dancing USA mag., Am.'s Registry of Outstanding Profls. Mem.: Big Band Acad. Am., Internat. Assn. Jazz Record Collectors. Republican. Avocations: phonograph record collection, researching jazz and dance information, postcard collection. Home: 700 Clark St Apt 108 Deming NM 88030-4589

ROGERS, ANN, small business owner; b. Malakoff, Tex., Jan. 7, 1933; d. Alvin and Lillian (Looney) Workman; m. Clemon Wayne Rogers, Mar. 2, 1951 (dec. Aug. 24, 1978); children: Larry Wayne, David Keith. AS, Cedar Valley Coll., 1995. Farmer, Malakoff, 1939-47; labeling maching operator Figaro Co., Dallas, 1948; advt. mgr. Sears, Roebuck & Co., 1949-87; mgr. Hutchins, Tex., 1979-95; pres. Plastic Grinders, Inc., 1992-94. City Coun. Woman, City Hutchins, 1980-82, mem. zoning bd., 1983-85. Mem. Phi Theta Kappa, Alpha Zeta Omicron. Democrat. Baptist. Avocations: photography, painting, printmaking, sewing, flower gardening. Home: PO Box 92 Hutchins TX 75141-0092

ROGERS, ARTHUR HAMILTON, III, lawyer; b. Florence, S.C., Apr. 19, 1945; s. Arthur Hamilton Jr. and Suzanne (Wilson) R.; m. Karen Lyn Hess, June 22, 1968; children: Sarah Elizabeth, Thomas Hess. BA, Rice U., 1967; JD, Harvard U., 1970. Bar: Tex. 1970. Assoc. Fulbright & Jaworski LLP, Houston, 1970-74; participating assoc. Fulbright & Jaworski L.L.P., 1974-77; ptnr. Fulbright & Jaworski, L.L.P., 1977—; gen. counsel Lifemark Corp., 1981-82. Sec. Mosher, Inc., Houston, 1984-97. Bd. dirs. Alley Theatre, Houston, 1990—, v.p. fin., 2001—, mem. exec. com., 2001—; bd. dirs. Autry House, 1994-97; mem. exec. com. Rice U. Fund Coun., Houston, 1993-99, vice chmn., 1996-97, chmn., 1997-98. Mem. ABA, State Bar Tex., Assn. of Rice Alumni (treas. 1995-97), Petroleum Club of Houston, The Forest Club. Episcopalian. Home: 5309 Bordley Dr Houston TX 77056-2323 Office: Fulbright & Jaworski LLP 1301 Mckinney St Fl 51 Houston TX 77010-3031 E-mail: arogers@fulbright.com.

ROGERS, BARBARA J. musician; b. Teaneck, N.J., June 7, 1951; m. Richard D. Weis. MusB with highest distinction, Eastman Sch. Music, 1973; MusM in Piano Accompanying, U. So. Calif., 1974; D Mus. Arts in Piano Performance, U. Cin., 1992. Choir dir. Westminster United Presbyn. Ch., Ontario, Calif., 1980-84; instr., staff accompanist U. La Verne, 1981-85; grad. tchg. asst. U. Cin. Conservatory Music, 1985-88; pvt. piano tchr. and vocal coach, Ontario, Calif., 1977-85, N.Y., N.J., 1988-99; dir. music The Presbyn. Ch., New Brunswick, N.J., 1994-99, founding dir. summer music day camp, 1996-99. Freelance performer, N.Y. and N.J. met. area, 1988-99, Twin Cities Minn. area, 1999—; dir. music Cmty. Presbyn. Ch. Sand Hills, Kendall Park, N.J., 1988-93; accompanist Cantabile Chamber Chorale, Bound Brook, N.J., 1992-99; piano faculty Northwestern Coll., St. Paul, 2000—; cons. and presenter in field. Co-composer: children;s bibl. music It's Good!, 1993, composer choral anthems, songs, works for organ, chamber music. Mem. Music Tchrs. Nat. Assn., Internat. Alliance for Women in Music, Choristers Guild, Soc. for Am. Music, Am. Guild Organists, Soc. Composers, Inc., Am. Composers Forum, Minn. Music Tchrs. Assn.

ROGERS, BARBARA JEAN (B.J. ROGERS), writer, editor; b. Chgo., Apr. 23, 1949; d. Louis Herman and Bernice (Millunchick) Block; m. Malcolm Leland Rogers Jr., Feb. 17, 1979; children: Anna Elizabeth, Sara Randall. BA cum laude, U. Ill., 1971; MLAS, Vanderbilt U., 1999. Freelance proofreader, copy editor, author Thomas Nelson Pubs., Nashville, 1979-94; v.p. Rogers Graphics, 1980-82; proofreader, editor Typecraft Co., 1982-88; editor creative svcs. Vanderbilt U., 1993—. Assoc. critic STAGES, 1991—; gen. mgr. Am. Negro Playwright Theatre, Nashville, 1992-94; artistic staff asst. Tenn. Repertory Theatre, Nashville, 1990-93; cast mem., bus. mgr. So. Stage Prodns. and Tenn. Repertory Theatre, 1982, prodn. mgr., 1983, gen. mgr., 1985-86; studio booker, Soundshop, Inc., Nashville, 1977; nat. traffic mgr. Sammy & Co., 1975; post-prodn. coord. Studio Seven, Inc., Chgo., 1973-75; mem. libr. staff Chgo. Hist. Soc., 1968-71. Producer, dir. Nashville Arts Hark Awards, Greater Nashville Arts Found., 1991, Hungry Ear Prodns., 1989, Dark Horse Theatre; dir. Welcome to 1998. Founding mem. Tenn. Repertory Theatre Artistic Co., 1987; co-founder, artistic dir. Nashville Early Music Ensemble; founding pres. Nashville Opera Chorus, 1989, soprano, 1989-97; house mgr., costume designer Dark Horse Theatre/Nashville Shakespeare Festival, 1990-92; costume designer Belmont U. Opera Workshop, Nashville, 1991-97, Actors' Playhouse, Nashville, 1993; box office mgr. Kingston Mines Theatre, Gill Community Arts Ctr., Unity Theatre, Chgo., 1969-75; sec. Bellevue (Tenn.) Civic Coun., 1980-81; edn. ctr. dir. Heartlands Acad. Trust, 1986-90. Mem. AFTRA (bd. dirs. Nashville chpt. 1984-92), Actors' Equity Assn. Office: Vanderbilt U Creative Svcs 850 Baker Bldg 110 21st Ave S Nashville TN 37203-2416

ROGERS, BENJAMIN TALBOT, former consulting engineer, solar energy consultant; b. Cleve., Oct. 4, 1920; s. Benjamin Talbot and Marie Aline (Miller) R.; m. Dale Hays, Sept. 11, 1961 (dec. Nov. 1975); children: Leslie, Phyllis. BS in Mech. Engring., U. Wis., 1944. Registered profl. engr., N.Mex., Colo., Ariz., Tex. Mech. engr. Black & Veatch, Kansas City, Mo., 1946-49; staff mem. U. Calif., Los Alamos, N.Mex., 1949-76; cons. engring., 1949-76, Embudo, N.Mex, 1976-80, 81-2000; ret., 2000. Vis. prof. Ariz. State U., 1980-81, 84; v.p. Barkmann & Rogers Cons. Engrs., Santa Fe, N.Mex., 1964-70. One-man shows include Millicent Rogers Mus., Taos, N.Mex., 1994, Roller Mill Mus., Cleveland, N.Mex., 1995, Ariz. State U. Coll. Architecture, Tempe, 1996, First State Bank Taos, 1997 (Artist of Month 1997), Johnson Gallery, Madrid, N.Mex., 1998-99; contbr. articles to tech. and profl. jours.; 6 patents in field of optics, high speed photography and explosive tech. Commr. Rinconada Cmty. Acequia, Embudo, 1961-70; v.p. adv. bd. Embudo Presbyn. Hosp., 1972; pres. Embudo Valley Health Found., 1974. 1st lt. C.E., 1942-46. Recipient Solar Design award HUD, Dept. of Energy, Solar Energy Rsch. Inst., 1978, Peter van Dresser award N.Mex. Solar Energy Assn., 1983, Maharishi award Maharishi Found., 1984; grantee Graham Found. for Advanced Studies in Fine Arts, 1992, 95. Fellow ASHRAE; mem. ASME (life), NSPE (life), Am. Soc. Materials (life). Republican. Home: PO Box 2 Embudo NM 87531-0002

ROGERS, BERNARD WILLIAM, military officer; b. Fairview, Kans., July 16, 1921; s. William Henry and Lora (Haynes) R.; m. Ann Ellen Jones, Dec. 28, 1944; children: Michael W., Diane E., Susan A. Student, Kans. State Coll., 1939-40; BS, U.S. Mil. Acad., 1943; BA (Rhodes scholar), Oxford (Eng.) U., 1950, MA, 1954, DCL (hon.), 1983; grad., Command and Gen. Staff Coll., 1954-55, Army War Coll., 1959-60; LLD, Akron U., 1978, Boston U., 1981. Commd. lt. U.S. Army, 1943, advanced through grades to gen., 1974; aide to supt. U.S. Mil. Acad., 1945-46, comdt. cadets, 1967-69; aide to high commr. Austria Gen. Mark W. Clark, 1946-47; bn. comdr. Korea, 1952; exec. to comdr.-in-chief Far East Command, 1953-54; mil. asst. to Chief Staff U.S. Army, 1956-59; exec. to chmn. (Joint Chiefs of Staff), 1962-66; asst. div. comdr. (1st Inf. Div.), Vietnam, 1966-67; comdg. gen. (5th Inf. Div.), Ft. Carson, Colo., 1969-70; chief legis. liaison Dept. Army, 1971-72, dep. chief of staff for personnel, 1972-74; comdg. gen. U.S. Army Forces Command, 1974-76; chief of staff U.S. Army, 1976-79; supreme allied comdr. Europe; comdr. in chief (U.S. European Command), 1979-87; ret. U.S. Army, 1987. Former bd. dirs. Atlantic Coun. U.S., George C. Marshall Found., Gen. Dynamics Co., Kemper Nat. Ins. Co., Thomas Industries; former sr. cons. The Coca-Cola Co.; chmn. USO World Bd. of Govs., 1988-94. Decorated DSC, Def. DSM with oak leaf cluster, DSM of Army, Navy and Air Force, Silver Star, Legion of Merit with 3 oak leaf clusters, D.F.C. with 2 oak leaf clusters, Bronze Star medal with V device; hon. fellow Univ. Coll., Oxford U.; recipient Disting. Svc. Citation U. Kans., 1984, Disting. Grad. award U.S. Mil. Acad., 1995, Assn. U.S. Army George C. Marshall medal, 1999. Mem.: VFW, Mil. Order of World Wars, Ret. Officers Assn., Assn. Am. Rhodes Scholars, Assn. U.S. Army (bd. dirs.), Soc. 1st Inf. Divsn., Am. Soc. French Legion of Honor, Alibi, Alfalfa, Army and Navy Club, The Pilgrims, Army-Navy Country Club, Phi Delta Theta.

ROGERS, BRENDA ANN, community health clinical specialist; b. Boston, Feb. 28, 1952; d. John C. and Catherine (O'Connor) Rogers; m. Joseph Parisi, Aug. 28, 1976; children: Jonathan, Jeremy. AS, Northeastern U., 1974; BS, Boston Coll., 1982, MS summa cum laude, 1989; grad. clin. specialist in mental health, Mass. Gen. Hosp., 2000. RN, Mass.; cert. hypnotherapist. Pres. Profl. Nurse, Boston, 1982—; pvt. practice Brighton, 1982—; co-owner Cmty. CARE Solutions Inc., Boston. Mem. ANA (cert. family nurse practitioner), Mass. Nurses Assn. Home: 8 Newcastle Rd Brighton MA 02135-1817 Office: Cmty CARE Solutions Inc 20 McKenna West Roxbury MA 02132 also: Profl Nurse Health Care Svc 300 Market St Brighton MA 02135-2131 E-mail: PNURSE6256@aol.com., CommunicaCareSolutions@msn.com.

ROGERS, BRENDA GAYLE, educational administrator, educator, consultant; b. Atlanta, July 27, 1949; d. Claude Thomas and Louise (Williams) Todd; m. Emanuel Julius Jones Jr., Dec. 17, 1978; children: Lavelle, Brandon, Albre Jede, Briana Adanne. BA, Spelman Coll., 1970; MA, Atlanta U., 1971, EdS, 1972; PhD, Ohio State U., 1975; postgrad., Howard U., 1980, Emory U., 1986. Program devel. specialist HEW, Atlanta, 1972; rsch. assoc. Ohio State U., Columbus, 1973-75; asst. prof. spl. edn. Atlanta U., 1975-78, program adminstr., 1978—, CIT project dir., 1977-91, exec. dir. Impact project, 1992—. Tech. cons. Dept. Edn., Washington, 1978-93, 96, 97-98, cons. Head Start, 1990-91; cons. Princeton Testing Svcs., 1996—; due process regional hearing officer Ga. State Dept. Edn., Atlanta, 1978-84, adv. bd., 1980-84; regional cons. Access project, 1995—; mem. parent adv. coun. APS, 1988—; cons. program devel. Ga. Respite Care, Inc., 1988-89; mem. exec. bd., pres. PTA Stone Mountain elem. Sch., 1989-92; mem. test verification panel Edn. Testing Svcs., Princeton, N.J., 1995-96; cons. So. Assn. Colls. & Univs., 1998. Mem. Ga. Assessment Project com. Atlanta Pub. Schs. Adv. Coun., 1986—; bd. dirs. Mountain Pines Civic Assn., 1988—; mem. Grady Meml. Hosp. Cmty. Action Network, Atlanta, 1982-83; exec. bd. PTA Shadow Rock Elem. Sch., 1992-94. Recipient disting. svc. award Atlanta Bur. Pub. Safety, 1982, Mountain Sch. PTA, 1995, award Atlanta Pub. Sch. Sys., 1980, 82, 83, 89-90, Disting. Svc. award CAU, 1998; fellow Ohio State U., 1972-74, Howard U., 1980. Mem. NAFE, Assn. for Retarded Citizens, Coun. for Exceptional Children, So. Assn. Colls. and Univs. (cons. com. 1998—), Nat. Assn. Learning Disabilites, Phi Delta Kappa, Phi Lambda Theta. Democrat. Roman Catholic. Avocation: gourmet cooking. Office: Clark Atlanta U James P Brawley Atlanta GA 30314-3913 E-mail: dr.brenda.rogers@mediaone.net.

ROGERS, BRIAN DEANE, retired librarian; b. New London, Conn., June 26, 1937; s. Albert Nash and Janette (Loofboro) R.; m. Carol Mallett, May 18, 1962; children: Alison, Paul, Amy. BA, Alfred U., 1959; MLS, Rutgers U., 1967. Asst. registrar Salem (W. Va.) Coll., 1964-66; libr. staff Wesleyan U., Middletown, Conn., 1967-75; librarian Conn. Coll., New London, 1975-93, spl. collections libr., 1993-99. Mem. State Adv. Council on Libraries, Hartford, 1976, chair 1977; mem. library bd. Mystic Seaport Maritime Mus., Mystic, Conn., 1987—. Contbr. The Battery Park City Broadsheet (N.Y.C.), 1998—. Mem. accreditation teams New England Assn. Sch. & Colls., 1985-90. Served with U.S. Army, 1961-64. Mem. Eugene O'Neill Soc. (bd. dirs. 2001—). Clubs: Columbiad (Meriden, Conn.); Acorn (Hartford, Conn.). Home: 114 Library St Mystic CT 06355-2420

ROGERS, BRYAN LEIGH, artist, art educator; b. Amarillo, Tex., Jan. 7, 1941; s. Bryan Austin and Virginia Leigh (Bull) R.; m. Cynthia Louise Rice; 1 child, Kyle Austin Rogers. BE, Yale U., 1963; MS, U. Calif., Berkeley, 1966, MA, 1969, PhD, 1971. Design engr. Monsanto Co., Texas City, Tex., 1962; research engr. Rocketdyne, Canoga Park, Calif., 1963-64; research scientist Lawrence Livermore (Calif.) Lab., 1966; lectr. U. Calif., Berkeley, 1972-73; fellow Akademie der Bildenden Künste, Munich, 1974-75; prof. art San Francisco State U., 1975-88; head prof. sch. art Carnegie Mellon U., Pitts., 1988-99, dir. Studio for Creative Inquiry, 1989-99; dean, prof. Sch. of Art and Design U. Mich., Ann Arbor, 2000—. Fellow Ctr. Advanced Visual Studies MIT, Cambridge, Mass, 1981. Editor Leonardo Jour., San Francisco, 1982-85. One-man shows include: Laguna Beach (Calif.) Mus. Art, 1974, DeSaisset Art Gallery U. Santa Clara, Calif., 1974, San Francisco Mus. Modern Art, 1974, Baxter Art Gallery Calif. Inst. Tech., Pasadena, 1979, Contemporary Crafts gallery, Portland, Oreg., 1987; group exhbns. include: Berkeley (Calif.) Art Ctr., 1969, Hansen-Fuller Gallery, San Francisco, 1970, San Francisco Arts Commn. Gallery, 1984, Clocktower Gallery, N.Y.C., 1984, Otis-Parsons Gallery, L.A., 1985, P.P.O.W. Gallery, N.Y.C., 1985, 18th Internat. Bienal, São Paulo, Brazil, 1985, MIT, Cambridge, 1990, Objects Gallery, Chgo., 1992, ARTEC 93 Internat Biennale, Nagoya, Japan, 1993, Chgo. Cultural Ctr., 1993, Am. Iron and Steel Expo., Pitts., 1993, Pitts. Ctr. for Arts, 1994, Allegheny Coll. Gallery, Meadville, Pa., 1997, Aichi Art Ctr., Nagoya, Japan, 1997. Fellow NEA, Washington, 1981, 82, Deutscher Akademischer Austauschdienst, Fed. Republic of Germany, 1974, NSF, Washington, 1965-69; recipient SECA award San Francisco Mus. Modern Art, 1974. Office: Sch Art & Design Univ Michigan Ann Arbor MI 48109 E-mail: blrogers@umich.edu.

ROGERS, C. B. lawyer; b. Birmingham, Ala., July 10, 1930; s. Claude B. Rogers and Doris (Hinkley) Rogers Lockerman; m. Patricia Maxwell DeVoe, Dec. 22, 1962; children: Bruce Lockerman, Evelyn Best, Brian DeVoe. AB, Emory U., 1951, LL.B., 1953. Bar: Ga. 1953. Adj. prof. litigation Emory U., 1968-70; assoc., then partner firm Powell, Goldstein, Frazer & Murphy, 1954-76; partner firm Rogers & Hardin, Atlanta, 1976—. Fellow Am. Coll. Trial Lawyers; mem. Am. Law Inst., Capital City Club (Atlanta). Democrat. Episcopalian. Home: 1829 W Wesley Rd NW Atlanta GA 30327-2019 Office: Rogers & Hardin International Tower 229 Peachtree St NE Ste 2700 Atlanta GA 30303-1638 E-mail: cbr@rh-law.com.

ROGERS, CANDACE MARIE, nursing educator; b. Mt. Pleasant, N.Y., June 24, 1948; d. Arthur Trice and Catherine Marie (Bartow) Marrow; widowed; m. Samantha Lynn, Joseph Micheal, Amiee Louise. AAS, Thomas Nelson C.C., 1973; BSN, Hampton Inst., 1983; MSN, Hampton U., 1986; postgrad., U. Ala., Birmingham, 1993—. LPN, RN, Va. Med. nurse Riverside Regional Med. Ctr., Newport News, Va., 1969-70, critical care nurse, 1970-71, charge nurse, 1971-73, primary nurse, 1973-77, acting head nurse, 1977, head nurse, 1977-79, staff nurse, 1979-80, IV nurse, 1980-86; nurse mgr. Riverside Rehab. Inst., 1986-89; asst. prof. Norfolk (Va.) State U., 1989—, curriculum coord., 1993-94, AD program coord., 1994-95, acting dept. head, 1995-98, interim dept. head, 1998-99. Contbr. articles to profl. publs. Leader Colonial Coast coun. Girl Scouts U.S., Newport News, 1989-93, products coord. svc. team, 1990-93; CPR instr. Peninsula chpt. ARC, 1989-91. Capt. USAR, 1990—. Mem. ANA, VACADNE, Nat. League Nurses, Va. League Nurses (chair membership com. 1999—), Va. Nurses Assn. (chair conv. planning com. 1990-92), Dist. 10 Nurses Assn., Sigma Theta Tau (treas. 1991-93, sec. 1993-95), Chi Eta Phi. Democrat. Baptist. Avocations: crocheting, reading. Office: Norfolk State U 700 Park Ave Unit 3109 Norfolk VA 23504-3993 Home: 5 Widgeon Court Smithfield VA 23430

ROGERS, CARLETON CARSON, JR. trade show and convention executive; b. Chgo., Nov. 5, 1935; s. Carleton Carson and Eleanor (Lowell) R.; m. Loretta Zirkel; children: Kirsten Anne, Mark, Brett. BS in Bus. Adminstrn., Am. U., 1957; postgrad., Northwestern U., 1957, Chgo.-Kent Coll. Law, 1957-58. Mgmt. trainee Ill. Bell Telephone Co., Chgo., 1959-61; sales mgr. Programs Internat., 1961-64, pres., 1964-71, Internat. Spkrs. Networks, Elgin, 1971-75; show mgr. Indsl. & Sci. Conf. Mgmt., Chgo., 1975-78; pres. Expo Mgmt., Inc., 1978-82, Trade Expositions and Assoc. Mgmt. Ltd., Chgo., 1982-92, expn. Mmgt., Inc., Elgin, 1992-99, National Show Mgmt., Inc., Elgin, 1999—. Adj. prof. Roosevelt U., Chgo. Pres. Kane County (Ill.) Young Republican Club, 1962-64; trustee Gail Borden Pub. Libr., Elgin; bd. dirs. Area C Coun. on Aging for Ill., Upper Kane County chpt. Am. Heart Assn., Chgo. Conv. and Tourism Bur.; mem. adminstrv. bd., pres. bd. trustees First United Meth. Ch., Elgin.; sec.-treas.. found. pres. Ctr. for Exhbn. Industry Rsch. Mem. Internat. Assn. Exhibit Mgmt. (chmn. bd., recipient Disting. Svc. award), Masons, Shriners, Omicron Delta Kappa, Alpha Tau Omega. Home: 11n937 Almora Ter Elgin IL 60123-4805 Office: Nat Show Mgmt Inct PO Box 7084 Elgin IL 60121-7084 E-mail: expomgmt@juno.com.

ROGERS, CAROLYN KAY, nurse; b. Binghamton, N.Y., Nov. 29, 1933; d. Annetta Evelyn (Coffman); m. Donald Alvin Rogers, Aug. 29, 1952; children: Jeffrey, Lee, Constance, Eric, Kyle. RN, Binghamton City Hosp.; BSN, Syracuse U., 1967, MSN, 1975. RN, N.Y. Nursing dir. Midtown Hosp., Syracuse, N.Y., 1956-62; nursing instr. Crouse Irving Hosp., 1965-67; community health supr. Oswego County (N.Y.) Dept. Health, 1967-75; community health nurse cons. N.Y. State Dept. Health, Syracuse, 1975-78, program dir. home care/ambulatory care office health systems, 1978-90, program dir. ambulatory care, 1990-92, program dir. home care, 1992-95. Adj. prof. Syracuse U. Coll. Nursing, 1990-91, visitors com., 1975—. Mem. sch. bd. Cen. Square (N.Y.) Community Sch., 1976-78; pres. Caughdenoy (N.Y.) United Meth. Women, 1991-94, pres. Oubanio dist., 2000—. Mem. N.Y. League for Nursing, Sigma Theta Tau. Avocations: travel, Bible study, cooking. Home: 299 Schilly Rd Central Square NY 13036-3453 also: 9820 Booth Bay Dr Fort Pierce FL 34945-2432

ROGERS, CHARLES EDWIN, physical chemistry educator; b. Rochester, N.Y., Dec. 29, 1929; s. Charles Harold and Maybelle (Johnson) R.; m. Barbara June Depuy, June 12, 1954; children: Gregory Newton, Linda Frances, Diana Suzanne. BS in Chemistry, Syracuse U., 1954; PhD in Phys. Chemistry, SUNY at Syracuse U., 1957. Rsch. assoc. dept. chemistry Princeton U., 1957-59, Goodyear fellow, 1957-59; mem. tech. staff Bell Telephone Labs., Murray Hill, N.J., 1959-65; assoc. prof. macromolecular sci. Case Western Res. U., Cleve., 1965-74, prof., 1974-98, prof. emeritus, 1998—. Sr. vis. fellow Imperial Coll., U. London, 1971; assoc. dir. Ctr. for Adhesives Sealants Coatings, Case Western Res. U., 1984-88, dir., 1988-91; co-dir. Edison Polymer Innovation Corp., Ctr. for Adhesives, Sealants and Coatings, 1991-97; cons. to polymer and chem. industries; devel. overseas ednl. instns. Editor: Permselective Membranes, 1971, Structure and Properties of Block Copolymers, 1977; contbr. numerous articles to profl. jours.; patentee in field. Served with U.S. Army, 1946-49. Mem. Am. Chem. Soc., Am. Phys. Soc., N.Am. Membrane Soc., Cleve. Coatings Soc., The Adhesion Soc. Home: 8400 Rockspring Dr Chagrin Falls OH 44023-4645 Office: Case Western Reserve U Dept Macromolecular Sc Cleveland OH 44106-7202 E-mail: cer@po.cwru.edu.

ROGERS, CHARLES RAY, minister, religious organization administrator; b. Grapevine, Tex., Nov. 26, 1935; s. Arlin Avery and Bessie Lorene (Deaton) R.; m. Oma Fay Hines, Aug. 21, 1954; children: Sheree Gay Rogers Saberjissa, Charles Denne Ray, Robin Celeste Rogers Eddins. MS in Christian Edn., Faith Bible Coll., 1980, DD in Humanities (hon.), 1981; B of Theology, M of Theology, Ctrl. Am. Theol. Sem., Escuintla, Guatemala, 2000; D of Ministry in Humanities (hon.), Sem. of Theol. Missions, Escuintla, Guatemala, 1992. Pastor various Bapt. chs., Athens, Dallas, Ft. Worth, 1960-64, various interdenominational chs., Houston, Longview, 1965-69; pres. Evangelism in Action, Ft. Worth, 1969—. Bd. dirs. World Ministry Fellowship, Plano, Tex., dir. world missions, 1970—; leader over 100 Mission, humanitarian trips Evangelism in Action, Ft. Worth, 1976—. Author: Joy, 1979, Handbook for Victorious Living, 1980, How to Develop Christian Love, 1981; vocalist (rec.) Charlie, 1981. Republican. Avocations: golf, tennis, swimming, running, computers. Home: 6417 Rogers Dr Fort Worth TX 76180-4817 Office: Evangelism in Action PO Box 820724 Fort Worth TX 76182-0724

ROGERS, CHERYL LYNN, music and dance educator; b. Tyler, Tex., Sept. 14, 1949; d. Lewis Barton and Edna Elaine (Hunt) Whisenant; m. Carl Michael Rogers, May 23, 1971; children: Jennifer Leigh, Christopher Lewis. AA, Tyler Jr. Coll., 1969; B. Music Edn., North Tex. State U., 1971; MA, Stephen F. Austin State U., 1972; EdD, Texas A&M Commerce, Commerce, 1997. Math. instr. Kilgore (Tex.) Ind. Sch. Dist., 1972-73, jr. high choral dir., 1973-75; instr. music Tyler Jr. Coll., 1975-88, dir. music and dance, 1988—. Dir. Concert Chorus, Chamber Singers, Harmony and Understanding, Tyler, 1980—; adjudicator All-Region, All-Area Vocal Auditions, Tyler, 1975—. Mem. Tyler Friends of the Gifted, 1990—; social com. mem. Hollytree Country Club, Tyler, 1989-90; v.p. edn. Women's Symphony League, Tyler, 2001—; mem. adminstrv. bd. Marvin United Meth. Ch., Tyler, 1984—; yearbook commn. chmn. Kilgore Music Club, 1974-75. Grad. Teaching fellow Stephen F. Austin State U., 1971-72. Mem. Am. Choral Dirs. Assn., Tex. Music Educators Conf., Tex. Assn. Music Schs. (pres.), Tex. Jr. Coll. Tchr. Assn., Nat. Assn. Tchrs. Singing, Tex. Choral Dirs. Assn., Mortar Bd., Alpha Chi, Pi Kappa Lambda, Phi Theta Kappa, Kappa Delta Pi Edn. Honor Soc. Republican. Avocations: needlepoint, reading. Office: Tyler Jr Coll PO Box 9020 Tyler TX 75711-9020 E-mail: crog@tjc.tyler.cc.tx.us.

ROGERS, DANFORTH WILLIAM, lawyer; b. Buffalo, May 13, 1937; s. William Silliman and Grace W. (Danforth) R.; m. Carol Robinson, Sept. 9, 1961; children: Danforth W.S., Ninon M. BA, Yale U., 1959; JD, Cornell U., 1962. Assoc. LeBeouf, Lamb & Leiby, N.Y.C., 1963-65, Palmer & Serles, N.Y.C., 1965-69, ptnr., 1970-78, Gifford Woody Palmer & Serles, N.Y.C., 1978-85, Townley & Updike, N.Y.C., NY, 1985—95; atty. pvt. practice, 1996—. Mem. ABA, N.Y. State Bar Assn., Assn. Bar City of NY, Am. Contact Bridge League, North River Power Squad., Sons Revolution N.Y. Home and Office: 13 E 9th St New York NY 10003-5910

ROGERS, DAVID, playwright, novelist, actor; b. N.Y.C. s. George and Deborah (Samuels) Rosenberg; m. June Lois Walker, Oct. 14, 1962; children— Dulcy Dru, Amanda Brooke. Student, Am. Theatre Wing Sch., 1948, 49. N.Y.C. prodns. include Ziegfeld Follies, 1957, Vintage '60, 1960, New Faces of 1962, Fun City, 1967, Charlie and Algernon, 1980 (Tony award nomination); London prodns. include Jubilee Girl, 1956, Young at Heart, 1961, Flowers for Algernon, 1979, Killing Jessica, 1986; pub. plays include Tom Jones, 1964, Flowers for Algernon, 1969, Brave New World, 1970, F.L.I.P.P.E.D, 1971, Here and Now, 1973, Soft Soap, 1982, Rehearsal for Murder, 1983; pub. musicals include Best of Broadway, 1961, Cheaper by the Dozen, 1969, The Hobbit, 1972, The Truth About Cinderella, 1974, The Dream on Royal Street, 1981; TV The Hero; opera, 1966 (winner Prix d'Italia Concorso Internat. Per Opere Radiofoniche e Televisive), Carol Burnett show, 1970; novels Oh Eden, 1974, The Bedroom Set, 1976, Somewhere There's Music, 1977, The Great American Alimony Escape, 1979, The In-Laws, 1979; actor Broadway prodns. Doubles, 1985, George Abbott's Broadway, 1987, A Funny Thing Happened on the Way to the Forum, 1997, (off Broadway) Down the Garden Paths, 2000, internat. tour Grand Hotel, 1991; regional theatre appearances include Players Theatre, Columbus, 1992, Birmingham (Mich.) Theatre, Jupiter (Fla.) Theatre, 1993, Great Lakes Theatre Festival, Cleve., 1994, Phoenix Theatre, Purchase, N.Y., 1995, Denver Ctr. Theatre Co., 1996, Repertory Theatre of St. Louis, 1998, Cin. Playhouse in the Park, 1998, Westport (Ct.) Playhouse, 1998, San Jose Repertory Theatre, 1999 (Dean Goodman Choice award), Va. Stage Co., Norfolk, 2000, Fla. Studio Theatre, Sarasota, 2002; TV guest appearances on Law and Order, 2000, Law and Order: Criminal Intent, 2001. Served with U.S. Army, 1951-52, Korea. Mem. SAG, Dramatists Guild, Writers Guild Am. East, AFTRA, Broadcast Music Inc., Actors Equity. Clubs: Theatre Artists Workshop (Westport, Conn.) (bd. dirs. 1985).

ROGERS, DAVID ANTHONY, electrical engineer, educator, researcher; b. San Francisco, Dec. 21, 1939; s. Justin Anthony and Alice Jane (Vessey) R.; m. Darlene Olive Hicks, Feb. 20, 1965; 1 child, Stephen Arthur. BSEE cum laude, U. Wash., 1961, PhD in Elec. Engring., 1971; MSEE, Ill. Inst. Tech., 1964; MDiv cum laude, Trinity Evang. Div. Sch., Deerfield, Ill., 1966. Registered profl. engr., Wash. Assoc. engr. Ford Aero., Newport Beach, Calif., 1961; tech. asst. IIT Rsch. Inst., Chgo., 1963, grad. fellow, 1963-64; predoctoral lectr. U. Wash., Seattle, 1964-65, 66-71, acting asst. prof., 1971-72; asst. prof. State U. of Campinas, Brazil, 1972-77, assoc. prof., 1977-80; assoc. prof. elec. engring. N.D. State U., Fargo, 1980-86, prof., 1986—. External MS thesis examiner Poly. Sch. U. Sao Paulo, Brazil, 1974; external PhD thesis examiner Inst. Tech., Banaras Hindu U., India, 1989, 91, 95; rschr. microwaves, fiber optics, electromagnetics, profl. and rsch. ethics, tech. and soc., engring. edn.; faculty seminar (interdisciplinary, multi-cultural and internat. studies 1991-94); presenter N.D. State U.-Bush Found. Industry-Ethics Inst., 1995-96. Co-author: Fiber Optics, 1984; mem. editl. rev. bd. IEEE Transactions Microwave Theory and Techniques, 1987-97; contbr. articles to profl. publs. including IEEE Transactions on Antennas and Propagation, Transactions on Edn., Transactions on Microwave Theory and Techniques, Jour. Quantum Electronics, Electronics Letters, Radio Sci., Engring. Edn., Computers in Edn. Jour. Mem. rev. panel NSF, Quantum Electronics Waves and Beams program, 1989; mem. tech. paper rev. com. Internat. Symposium on Recent Advances in Microwave Tech., China, 1989, 97, Reno, 1991, India, 1993, Ukraine, 1995, Spain, 1999; reviewer procs. ASEE/IEEE Frontiers in Edn. Conf., Phoenix, 1998, San Juan, P.R., 1999, Kansas City, 2000, others; judge N.D. Sci. Olympiad, 1987-95, S.E. N.D. Regional Sci. and Engring. Fair, 1993, 95-96; reviewer SBMO/IEEE MTT-S Internat. Microwave and Optoelectronics Conf., Natal, Brazil, 1997, Belem, Brazil, 2001; vol. examiner FCC Amateur Radio Exams thru Am. Radio Relay League. 2d lt. Signal Corps, U.S. Army, 1961-62. NSF Summer fellow, 1965; grantee Ford Found., 1969-70, TELEBRAS (Brazil), 1973-80, NSF, 2001–. Mem. IEEE, IEEE Antennas and Propagation Soc., Am. Soc. Engring. Edn. (internat. and other divsn., grantee summer 1984), N.D. Acad. Sci., Am. Geophys. Union, Applied Computational Electromagnetics Soc., Am. Sci. Affiliation, Am. Radio Relay League (life), Order of Engr., IEEE Edn. Soc., Microwave Theory and Techniques Soc., Sigma Xi, Tau Beta Pi, Eta Kappa Nu. Evangelical. Office: ND State U Elec Computer Engring Dept Fargo ND 58105

ROGERS, DAVID FREEMAN, aerospace engineering educator; b. Theresa, N.Y., Sept. 3, 1937; s. Lewis Freeman and Gladys Marion Zoller; m. Nancy Ann Nuttall, Sept. 5, 1959; children: Stephen David, Karen Nanci, Ransom Robert. B in Aero. Engring., Rensselaer Poly. Inst., 1959, MS in Aero. Engring., 1960, PhD, 1967. Asst. prof. U.S. Naval Acad., Annapolis, Md., 1964-67, assoc. prof., 1967-74, prof., 1974—, dir. aeronautics, 1999—. Fujitsu rsch. prof. Royal Melbourne Inst. Tech.; hon. rsch. scholar U. Coll. London, 1977-78. Author: Mathematical Elements for Computer Graphics, 1976, 2d edit. 1990; Procedural Elements for Computer Graphics, 1985, 2d edit., 1997, Laminar Flow Analysis, 1992, Flying Adventures, Vols. 1-2, 1999, An Introduction to NURBS: with Historical Perspective, 2001; editor Meml. edit. for P. Bezier, CAD Jour., 2001; mem. editl. bd. Visual Computer, CAD, the Computer Aided Design Jour.; contbr. articles to profl. jours. David F. Rogers Chair in Aerospace Engineering named in his honor, 2000. Avocations: flying, photography, sailing. Office: US Naval Acad Aerospace Engring Dept Annapolis MD 21402 Fax: 410-293-2591.

ROGERS, DAVID HUGHES, finance executive; b. Chgo., May 21, 1947; s. Joseph Gordon and Viola Winifred (Hughes) R.; Bonnie Hope Sinai, 1997; children: Kirsten Morgan, Loren Avery, Daniel Jay. BA, U. Mich., 1968; PhD, Columbia U., 1975. Economist Fed. Res. Bank of Cleve., 1974-75; asst. treas. B.F. Goodrich Co., Akron, Ohio, 1975-82; exec. v.p., chief fin. officer First Tex. Savs. Assn., Dallas, 1982-83; sr. exec. v.p., chief operating officer PriMerit Bank, Las Vegas, 1984-87, pres., dir., 1987-91, vice chmn., 1991-92; COO, The Baird Cos., 1992-99; v.p., chief fin. officer Norall Labs., 1999—2001; v.p., relationship mgr. Wells Fargo Bank, Nev., 2001—. Adj. prof. econs. C.C. of So. Nev., 1998—. Author: Consumer Banking in New York, 1975; also articles. Bd. dirs. Boulder Dam Area coun. Boy Scouts Am., 1986—; bd. dirs. Nev. Sch. Arts, 1988-98; chmn. Las Vegas Bus. Bank, 1995-99. Office: Wells Fargo Bus Banking 770 E Warm Springs Las Vegas NV 89119 E-mail: DHRogers@lvcm.com.

ROGERS, DAVID JOHN, lawyer; b. Lawrence, Mass., Aug. 13, 1960; s. James Martin and Eleanor Elizabeth (Jones) R. BA, Coll. William and Mary, 1982; JD, U. Pitts., 1988. Bar: N.H. 1988, Mass. 1989. Contract adminstr. Sanders Assocs., Inc., Nashua, N.H., 1983-85; assoc. Devine, Millimet, Stahl & Branch, Manchester, 1988-89; ptnr. Carpenito & Rogers, PA, Salem, 1989-90; asst. corp. counsel City of Nashua, 1991; pvt. practice Londonderry, N.H., 1991-98; atty. Landmark Title, Inc., Manchester, 1998-2000. Mem. Worker's Compensation Appeals Bd., State of N.H., 1993—. Active Salem Youth Com., 1989-95; fin. com. West Congl. Ch., Haverhill, Mass., 1990-95. U. scholar U. Pitts., 1988. Mem. Mass. Bar Assn., N.H. Bar Assn., Young Lawyers Com. Republican. Avocations: golf, running, reading, community theater. Home: 20 Cindy Dr Hooksett NH 03106-2003 Office: 1244 Hooksett Rd Ste 7 Hooksett NH 03106

ROGERS, DEBORAH DEE, English language educator; b. Boston, Apr. 20, 1949; BA with honors, Rutgers U., 1971; MA, U. Calif., Berkeley, 1974; MPhil with distinction, Columbia U., 1979, PhD, 1983. Rsch. asst. Yale Edition of Johnson, 1979-81; instr. CUNY, Columbia Coll., 1980-82; asst. prof. U. Maine, Orono, 1982-89, assoc. prof., 1990-96, prof., 1996—. Sec. seminar on 18th-century European culture Columbia U., 1979-81; manuscript cons. U. Press New Eng., Broadview Press, Prentice Hall, Praeger, Addison Wesley Longman, Univ. Presses of Fla., Macmillan. Author: Bookseller as Rogue: John Almon and the Politics of Eighteenth-Century Publishing, 1986, The Critical Response to Ann Radcliffe, 1994, Ann Radcliffe: A Bio-Bibliography, 1995, Two Gothic Classics by Women, 1995; contbr. articles to scholarly jours.; referee Publs. of the MLA, Tulsa Studies in Women's Lit., Utopian Studies, Studies in Eighteenth-Century Culture, Eighteenth Century Fiction, Nineteenth Century Contexts. Faculty rsch. grantee, 1984, 87, 2000, Women in Curriculum rsch. grantee, 1989, 93, NEH travel grantee, 1992-93; Pres.'s fellow Columbia U., 1978-79. Mem. MLA (chair, organizer Samuel Johnson bicentennial celebration 1984), Nat. Coun. Tchrs. English, Am. Studies Assn. (presenter), Am. Soc. for 18th-Century Studies (presenter). Office: U Maine Dept English 304 Neville Hl Orono ME 04469-0001

ROGERS, DEBORAH S. biologist, writer; b. Japan, Oct. 11, 1954; d. Dilwyn J. and Priscilla H. Rogers; children: Even Pay, Maria Miller. BA, Augustana Coll., Sioux Falls, S.D., 1975; MS, U. Wis., 1979. Rschr. Ctr. for Alternative Mining Devel. Policy, Madison, Wis., 1979—80; ecologist The Nature Conservancy, Pierre, SD and Mandan, ND, 1981—82; dir. Tech. Info. Project, Rapid City and Pierre, 1982—94; rschr./writer Rapid City, 1995—; human biology/ecology instr. Oglala Lakota Coll., Kyle, 2001—. Mem. Advocates for Music Edn., Rapid City, SD, 2000—02; bd. advisors No. Prairies Land Trust, Sioux Falls, 2001—02; apptd. Governor's Mining Task Force, Pierre, 1987; bd. dirs. Dakota Choral Union, Rapid City, 1999. Named West River Notable, Rapid City Jour., 1991, featured South Dakotan, S.D. Pub. TV, 1990; recipient Keller Conservation award, Spearfish Canyon Preservation Trust, 1995. Mem.: Am. Anthropol. Assn. Office: Oglala Lakota Coll 127 Knollwood Rapid City SD 57701 Personal E-mail: dsrogers1231@aol.com. E-mail: drogers@olc.edu.

ROGERS, DIANA FLORENCE, research scientist; b. Kenmore, N.Y., Nov. 2, 1967; d. Richard Max Dolmatin and Susan Deborah (Ness) Byington; m. James Scott Rogers, Feb. 2, 1991; children: James Richard, Amanda Jane. BS in Chemistry magna cum laude, U. Hartford, 1997—; postgrad., Rensselaer Polytechnic Inst., 1997—. Tutor, lab. instr. dept. chemistry, lab. U. Hartford, Conn., 1994-96, rschr. dept. chemistry, 1995; rschr. dept. polymer sci. U. Conn., Storrs, 1996. Vol. Ctr. Sch., Willington, Conn., 1997—; class agt. U. Hartford, rep., 1996—. Summer fellow NASA Space Found., 1995, fellow, 1996; alumni scholar U. Hartford, 1994-95; recipient Soc. for Applied Spectroscopy award NY sect., 2001-02. Mem. Am. Chem. Soc., U. Hartford Chemistry Club (v.p. 1994-95, pres. 1995-96), N.Y. Sect. Soc. Applied Spectroscopy (award 2001-2002), Sigma Xi. Home: 10 Depot Rd Unit 1023 Willington CT 06279-1641

ROGERS, DONALD ROBERT, retired pathologist, consultant; b. Tacoma, Apr. 7, 1932; s. John Robert and Thelma Ethel (Neely) R.; m. Georgia Lee Miller, June 9, 1956; children: Steven, Julie BS, U. Puget Sound, 1954; MD, U. Wash., 1958. Diplomate Am. Bd. Pathology. Intern Mpls. Gen. Hosp., 1958-59; resident U. Wash., Seattle, 1963-66; pathologist Humana Hosp., Anchorage, 1967-94, ret., 1994. Med. examiner State of Alaska, 1967-94; cons. forensic pathology. Contbr. articles to profl. jours. Bd. dirs. Am. Cancer Soc., Alaska, 1967—, nat. del. dir., 1983-84. Lt. comdr. USN, 1959-62. Fellow Coll. Am. Pathologists; mem. ACS (mem. Anchorage unit 1967-94), Ala. State Med. Assn. (pres. 1989-91), Anchorage Med. Soc. (pres. 1972), Nat. Assn. Med. Examiners, Rotary. Republican. Home and Office: 921 Old Klatt Rd Anchorage AK 99515-3254

ROGERS, DOUGLAS GEORGE, pediatrician, endocrinologist; b. Ann Arbor, Mich., Apr. 24, 1954; s. Paul LeRoy and Marion (Johnson) R.; m. Kathryn Mierle, Feb. 26, 1977; children: Dana, Theresa, Sharon, Kimberly. Student, U. Mich., 1972-75; MD, Chgo. Med. Sch., 1978. Diplomate Am. Bd. Pediat., Am. Bd. Pediat. Endocrinology. Intern and resident in pediat. Cardinal Glennon Childrens Hosp., St. Louis, 1978-81; fellow in pediat. endocrinology St. Louis Childrens Hosp., 1983-85; asst. prof. Baylor Coll. Medicine, Houston, 1985-88; chmn. pediat. Hamot Med. Ctr., Erie, Pa., 1988-91; head sect. pediat. endocrinology Cleve. Clinic, 1991—. Med. dir. Camp Ho Mita Koda for Diabetic Children, Newberry, Ohio, 1996—. Author: (chpt.) Pediatric Cardiology, 1990; contbr. articles to profl. jours. Bd. dirs. Juvenile Diabetes Found., Cleve., 1994—2001. Named Disting. Alumnus, Chgo. Med. Sch., 1996. Fellow Am. Acad. Pediat.; mem. The Endocrine Soc., Lawson Wilkins Pediat. Endocrine Soc. Avocations: biking, swimming. Office: Cleveland Clinic 9500 Euclid Ave # A-120 Cleveland OH 44195-0002

ROGERS, EARL LESLIE, artist, educator; b. Oakland, Calif., July 8, 1918; s. Robert Ray and Addie Myrtle (Dice) R.; m. Eileen Estelle MacKenzie, Apr. 9, 1945; children: Leslie Eileen, Brian Donald (dec.). Student, L.A. Valley Coll., 1949-52, Northridge State U., 1958-59, UCLA Extension, 1967, Sergei Bongart Sch. Art, 1967-68; AA, Pierce Coll., 1958; MA equivalency, Merced Coll., 1996. Cert. tchr., Calif. Various positions City of L.A., Van Nuys, Calif., 1948-55, Reseda, 1955-68; pvt. practice Canoga Park, 1948-68; art tchr. Mariposa (Calif.) County High Sch., 1969-70; art instr. Merced (Calif.) County Coll., 1970—. Instr. Earl Rogers Studio Workshop, Mariposa, Calif., 1969—; art dir. Yosemite Nat. Park, Calif., 1973; instr. art Asilomar Conf. Grounds, Pacific Grove, Calif., 1980; juror various art orgns., 1971-95; demonstrator Clovis (Calif.) Art Guild, 1971, 89, Sierra Artists, Mariposa, 1972, 81, 82, 84, 91, 2000, Merced Art League, 1976, Yosemite Western Artists, Oakhurst, Calif., 1973, Madera (Calif.) Art Assn., 1978, Chowchilla (Calif.) Art Guild, 1983, 86, 87, 89, 91, Soc. Western Artists, 1981, 89, 93, 97. One-man shows include L.A. City Hall, 1968, Merced Coll., 1969, 1995, Mariposa Title Co. Bldg., 1969, Coffee's Gallery, 1970, Bear Valley Hist. Bon-Ton, Calif., 1999, others, exhibited in group shows at West Valley Artists Assn., 1966—68, L.A. City Hall, 1967, Tosemite Nat. Park, 1973, Soc. Western Artists, 1977—78, Cannon Bldg. Rotunda, Washington, 1982, Mother Lode Gallery, Columbia, Calif., 1977—78, Arbor Gallery, Merced, 1988, 1998, 2001, Gold Country Gallery, 1990—91, Merced Coll., 1969—92, 1996, Mariposa County Arts Coun., 1999, at others, Represented in permanent collections John C. Freemont Hosp., Mariposa, Mariposa County Arts Coun., Mariposa Mus. and History Ctr. Asst. scout master Boy Scouts of Am., Canoga Park, Calif., 1956-58; art instr. L.A. Recreation Corps, L.A. Parks and Recreation Dept., 1967. Mem. Soc. Western Artists (Neva Rall Meml. award 1978), Mariposa Mus. and Hist. Ctr. (life), Pastel Soc. West Coast. Avocations: piano and books. Home and Office: 5323 State Hwy 49 N Mariposa CA 95338-9503

ROGERS, EDWARD SAMUEL, communications company executive; b. Toronto, May 27, 1933; s. Edward Samuel and Velma Melissa (Taylor) R.; m. Loretta Anne Robinson, Sept. 25, 1963; children: Lisa Anne, Edward Samuel, Melinda Mary, Martha Loretta. BA, Trinity Coll., U. Toronto, 1956; LLB, Osgoode Hall Law Sch., 1961; DSc (hon.), Clarkson U., 1989; LLD (hon.), U. Victoria, 1990; LLD, York U., 1994. Bar: Ont., 1962. Founder, prin. Rogers Telecomm. Ltd., Toronto, 1960—; pres., CEO Rogers Comm. Inc., 1978—; vice chmn. Rogers Cablesystems Ltd., Rogers Media Inc., Toronto, also bd. dirs. Bd. dirs. The Hull Group, The Toronto Dominion Bank, Can. Pub. Corp., Rogers Cable TV Ltd., Rogers Cablesystems Ltd.,Toronto Blue Jays Baseball Club. Bd. dirs. Jr. Achievement Can. Mem. Royal Can. Yacht Club, Albany Club, Granite Club, York Club, Muskoka Golf & Country Club, Rideau Club Ottawa, Lyford Cay Club (gov.), Balboa Bay Club, Sigma Chi (Beta Omega chpt.). Progressive Conservative. Mem. Anglican Ch. Office: Rogers Comm Inc 333 Bloor St E Toronto ON Canada M4W 1G9

ROGERS, ELYSE MACFADYEN, communications and foundation executive; b. Kearny, N.J., Sept. 28, 1932; d. Frank H. and Silvia (Simms) MacFadyen; m. Edward W. Rogers, July 18, 1952; children: Pamela, Cynthia, Jenifer. RN, Mountainside, 1953; BS, Ind. U., 1957; MA, Purdue U., 1973. Pres. Sci. Syntax Services, Midland, Mich., 1976-81; exec. v.p. OAK Assoc. KK, Tokyo, 1981-84; pres. MAC Internat. Ltd., 1984-87, MAC Internat. Ltd.-USA, Midland, 1987—; asst. v.p. Herbert H. and Grace A. Dow Found., 1990—. Vice chmn. Asian Pacific Council Am. C. of C., Japan, 1985-87; bd. govs. Am. C. of C., Japan, 1985-87. Author: Staying Healthy in Japan, 1983, Cross Cultural Dialogues, 1985, Home Nursing Care, 1978; columnist: Japan Times, Yomiuri Shimbun, and Tokyo Weekender, 1980—; contbr. articles to profl. jours. Bd. dirs. Midland Symphony Orch., 1995-2002, chair, 1998-2000; bd. dirs. MidMich. Health, 1995—, MidMich. Med. Ctr., 1998—; bd. dirs. MicMich. Vis. Nurse Assn., 1990-96, chair, 1995-96; bd. fellows Saginaw Valley State U., 1997—; bd. govs. Northwood U., 2000-. Recipient Disting. Woman award Mitten Bay coun. Girl Scouts U.S., 1997, Athena award Athena Found., 1998. Mem. Am. Med. Writers Assn. (fellow), Fgn. Exec. Women (founder, pres. 1981-84), Am. Soc. Journalists and Authors, Detroit Women Writers, Mich. Non Profit Assn. (bd. dirs. 1999—), Fgn. Corrs. Club of Japan, Midland Country Club, Rotary, Zonta. Republican. Episcopalian.

ROGERS, ERNEST MABRY, lawyer; b. Demopolis, Ala., Sept. 22, 1947; s. James B. and Ernestine B. (Brewer) R.; m. Jeanne Edwards, Dec. 15, 1979; children: Gilbert B., Katherine B., Mary C. BA, Yale U., 1969; JD, Harvard U., 1974. Bar: Ala. 1974, U.S. Dist. Ct. (no. dist.) Ala. 1975, U.S. Ct. Appeals (5th cir.) 1976, U.S. Ct. Appeals (11th cir.) 1981, U.S. Supreme Ct. 1981, U.S. Ct. Claims 1983, U.S. Ct. Appeals (6th cir.) 1987. Law clk. to judge U.S. Dist. Ct. (no. dist.) Ala., 1974-75; ptnr. Bradley, Arant, Rose & White, Birmingham, Ala., 1981—. Contbr. articles to profl. jours. Fellow Am. Coll. Constrn. Lawyers; mem. Am. Arbirtation Assn., Kiwanis. Episcopalian. Office: Bradley Arant Rose & White 1400 Park Place Tower 2001 Park Pl Ste 1400 Birmingham AL 35203-2736 Business E-Mail: mrogers@barw.com.

ROGERS, EUGENE CHARLES, retired investment firm executive; b. Bklyn., Sept. 29, 1932; s. Eugene Aloysius and Agnes Hilda (Scharbach) R.; m. Anita Therese Tobin, May 13, 1961; 1 son, Eugene Charles. BBA, St. John's U., Bklyn., 1954; MBA, N.Y. U., 1960. C.P.A., N.Y. Staff accountant Haskins & Sells (C.P.A.s), N.Y.C., 1954-60, Bache & Co., N.Y.C., 1960-62; controller, then chief fin. officer Reynolds Securities Inc., 1962-72, v.p., treas., 1972—; 1st v.p., treas. Dean Witter Reynolds Inc., 1978-81, sr. v.p., treas., 1981—. Guest lectr., panelist in field. Bd. advisors Coll. Bus. Adminstrn., St. John's U. Served with U.S. Army, 1954-56. Mem. N.Y. State Soc. C.P.A.'s, Fin. Execs. Inst., Fin. Club of N.Y. U. Grad. Sch. Bus., Securities Industry Assn. (past pres. fin. mgmt. div.), Sun and Surf Beach Club, World Trade Ctr. Club, Hempstead Golf and Country Club. Roman Catholic. Home: 15 Whitby Ct Rockville Centre NY 11570-1641

ROGERS, EUGENE JACK, medical educator; b. Vienna, Austria, June 13, 1921; came to U.S., 1937; s. Louis and Malvina (Haller) R.; m. Joyce M. Lighter, Feb. 9, 1952; children: Jay A., Robert J. BS, CCNY; M.B., Chgo. Med. Sch., 1946, MD, 1947. Diplomate Am. Bd. Phys. Medicine and Rehab. Intern Our Lady of Mercy Med. Ctr. and Cabrini Meml. Hosps., N.Y.C., 1946-48; resident Madigan Hosp., Tacoma, 1951, Mayo Clinic, Rochester, Minn., 1951, N.Y. Med. Coll. Met. Med. Ctr., 1953-55; USPHS fellow, 1955-56; ship's surgeon U.S. Lines, Grace Lines, N.Y.C., 1948-49; indsl. physician Abraham & Strauss Stores, Bklyn., 1949-51; practice medicine specializing in phys. medicine and rehab., 1956-73; dir. rehab. service, attending physician N.Y. City Hosp. Dept., 1955-73; prof. and chmn. dept. rehab. medicine Chgo. Med. Sch., North Chicago, Ill., 1973—. Cons. N.Y.C. Mayor's Adv. Com. for Aged, 1957; asst. prof. SUNY Downstate Med. Sch., Bklyn., 1958-73; med. dir. Schwab Rehab. Hosp., Chgo., 1973-75; acting chief rehab. service VA Center, North Chicgo, 1975-77; chmn. Ill. Phys. Therapy Exam. Com., 1977-78; examiner Am. Bd. Phys. Medicine and Rehab., 1983; sec., dir. Microtherapeutics, Inc., 1972 Editor: Total Cancer Care, 1975; contbr. articles to med. jours.; contbg. editor Ill. Med. Jour., 1983-89 Served to capt. U.S. Army, 1951-53. Recipient Bronze medal Am. Congress Rehab. Medicine, 1974 Fellow ACP, Am. Acad. Phys. Medicine and Rehab. (Cert. of Appreciation 1993); mem. Ill. Med. Soc. (chmn. workmen's compensation com. 1980-83), Ill. Soc. Phys. Medicine and Rehab. (pres. 1983-84), Chgo. Med. Sch. Faculty Assembly (spkr. 1978-80), Chgo. Med. Sch. Alumni Assn. (exec. com., asst. treas. 1983-93, treas. 1993—, sec. 1995-97, 1st v.p. 1999—, pres. 2001, Presdl. plaque Greater N.Y. chpt., Disting. Alumnus award 1980), Odd Fellows (pres. 1961-62), Alpha Omega Alpha, Phi Lambda Kappa (trustee 1980). Home: 1110 N Lake Shore Dr Chicago IL 60611-1054 Office: Finch U Health Scis Chgo Med Sch 3333 Green Bay Rd North Chicago IL 60064-3037 E-mail: eugenerogers@worldnet.att.net. *To render good medical care: Prevent disease, evaluate the patient, treat the condition, educate patient and family, restore function, support group referral, on-line medical knowledge maintenance, never neglect or lie to or for patients.*

ROGERS, FRANCES EVELYN, author, retired educator and librarian; b. Mobile, Ala., Aug. 30, 1935; d. James Richard Graves and Jessie Reynolds (Butler) Lay; m. Jay Dee Rogers, Mar. 22, 1957; children: Laura, Larry. BA, North Tex. State U., 1957; MSLS, Our Lady of the Lake U., San Antonio, 1975. Cert. tchr., libr., Tex. Tchr. Ector County Ind. Sch. Dist., Odessa, Tex., 1958-59; social dir. svc. club Lackland AFB, San Antonio, 1960-61; tchr. San Antonio Ind. Sch. Dist., 1965-70; tchr., libr. Northside Ind. Sch. Dist., San Antonio, 1970-90, ret., 1990. Author: (hist. novels) Midnight Sins, 1989, Texas Sins, 1989, Wanton Slave, 1990, Surrender to the Night, 1991, A Love So Wild, 1991, Sweet Texas Magic, 1992, Desert Fire, 1992, Desert Heat , 1993, Flame, 1994, Raven, 1995, Angel, 1995, Wicked, 1996, The Forever Bride, 1997, Betrayal, 1997, Hot Temper, 1997, Crown of Glory, 1998, Lone Star , 1999, Longhorn, 2000, Devil in the Dark, 2001, The Loner , 2001, The Grotto, 2002, The Ghost of Carnal Cove, 2002, (contemporary novels) Golden Man, 1999, Second Opinion, 1999, (hist. novels under name Keller Graves) Brazen Embrace, 1987, Rapture's Gamble , 1987, Desire's Fury , 1988, Velvet Vixen, 1988, Lawman's Lady, 1988. Sec., vol. Opera Guild San Antonio, 1980—; pres. San Antonio Romance Authors, 1997. Recipient Spirit of Romance award Rom Con, 1996, Prism Award Romance Writers Am., 1997, Tex. Gold award East Tex. Romance Writers Am., 1998. Mem. Nat. Soc. Arts and Letters. Home: 2722 Belvoir Dr San Antonio TX 78230-4507 E-mail: Erogers722@aol.com.

ROGERS, FRANCES NICHOLS, assistant principal; b. Fontana Dam, N.C., July 25, 1944; d. Fred Edward and Violet Bernice (Slagle) Nichols; m. Terry William Rogers, July 3, 1970. BA in English, Berea Coll., 1966; MA in Elem. Edn., U. Ky., 1968; postgrad., U. N.C., 1992. Tchr. intern Breathitt County Schs., Jackson, Ky., 1966-68; tchr. elem. sch. Haywood County Schs., Waynesville, N.C., 1968-72, resource program developer, 1972-75, 77-83, asst. prin., 1983-89, 92-98, prin., 1989-92. Pres. Haywood County Chpt. N.C. Edn. Assn., 1969-70. Author: Mount Zion United Methodist Church: A History 1850-1982, 1982; author of poems; contbr. articles to profl. jours. Mem. Youth for Christ, Waynesville, 1980—. Named Outstanding Young Educator Waynesville Jaycees, 1968-69, Leader of Am. Elem. Edn., 1971. Mem. N.C. Ret. Sch. Pers., NEA, N.C. Edn. Assn. Methodist. Avocations: travel, reading, gardening. Home: 138 Mayapple Trail Clyde NC 28721-9718

ROGERS, FRANK ANDREW, restaurant, hotel executive; b. Indpls., May 9, 1931; s. Andrew Jackson and Jane (Safford) R.; m. Beulah Frances White, Sept. 28, 1971; children: Jane, Debra, Anne, Gina, Andrea. BA in Bus., Ind. U., 1967. Chmn., pres., CEO Brown County Fed. Savs. and Loan, NAshville, Ind., 1963-80, Bloomington (Ind.) Nat. Bank, 1980-88; chmn., CEO Lake Shore Bank, Michigan City, Ind., 1984-88; pres. Nashville Hillside Corp., 1966—, Ordinary Corp., Nashville, 1974—, Brown County Inn, Inc., Nashville, 1992—; mgr. AbeMartin Lodge, 1962-66, 89—; pres. Nashville House, Inc., 1959—. Bd. dirs., chmn. First Bank Greenwood, Ind., Ind. Emergency Mgmt. Found. Mem., pres. Nashville Town Bd., 1959-62, Brown County Sch. Bd., Nashville, 1972-75, Monroe County Conv. and Visitors Bur., Bloomington, Ind.; bd. dirs. Bloomington Hosp., Citizens Bank of Cen. Ind., 1988-90, Brown Cmty. YMCA, 1999-; bd. dirs., pres. Brown County Conv. and Visitors Commn. Served with USN, 1950-54. Mem. VFW, Lions, Am. Legion, Ind. U. Alumni Assn. Home and Office: Nashville House PO Box 187 Nashville IN 47448-0187 E-mail: hhouse8007@aol.com.

ROGERS, FRANKLIN ROBERT, former language and literature educator, writer, literary critic; b. N.Y.C., July 25, 1921; s. Verner Brownell and Anna Elizabeth (Willard) R.; m. Mary Ann Cate, May 26, 1946; 1 child, Bruce David. BA, Fresno State Coll., 1950, MA, 1952; PhD, U. Calif., Berkeley, 1958. Instr. U. Wis.-Milw., 1958-60, asst. prof., 1960-63, U. Calif., Davis, 1963-64; assoc. prof. San Jose State Coll., 1964-68, prof., 1968-86; assoc. prof. U. Lyon, France, 1969-71, U. Paris Sorbonne, 1975-76; seminar lectr. Inst. des Hautes Etudes Sci., Burres-sur-Yvette, France, 1976, Kyoto Am. Studies summer seminar, Kyoto, Japan, 1986; ret., 1986. Fulbright prof. Lyon, 1966-67 Editor: Simon Wheeler, Detective by Mark Twain, 1963, Mark Twain's Satires and Burlesques, 1967, Roughing it by Mark Twain, 1972; author: Mark Twain's Burlesque Patterns, 1960, The Pattern for Mark Twain's Roughing It, 1961; co-author (with Mary Ann Rogers): Painting and Poetry, 1985, Occidental Ideographs, 1991; author: (novels) Two Roads to Poona, 2002; contbr. articles. Staff Sgt. U.S. Army signal corps radio intelligence, 1942-46. Mem. MLA. Avocations: painting, woodworking. Home: 206 Woodland Rdg Los Gatos CA 95033-7810 E-mail: frrogers@email.sjsu.edu.

ROGERS, FRED BAKER, medical educator; b. Trenton, N.J., Aug. 25, 1926; s. Lawrence H. and Eliza C. (Thropp) R. AA, Princeton U., 1947; MD, Temple U., 1948; MS in Medicine, U. Pa., 1954; MPH, Columbia U., 1957; spl. student, Johns Hopkins U., 1962. Diplomate: Am. Bd. Preventive Medicine. Intern Temple U. Hosp., Phila., 1948-49, chief resident physician, 1953-54; USPHS fellow Temple U. Sch. Medicine, 1954-55, asst. prof. preventive medicine, 1956-58, assoc. prof., 1958-60, prof., 1960-90, prof. emeritus, 1991—, chmn. dept., 1970-77. Lectr. epidemiology Columbia U. Sch. Pub. Health, 1957-68, Sch. Nursing, U. Pa., 1964-67; cons. USN Hosp.,

Phila., 1964-73 Author: A Syllabus of Medical History, 1958, Help-Bringers: Versatile Physicians of N.J, 1960, Epidemiology and Communicable Disease Control, 1963, Studies in Epidemiology, 1965, (with A.R. Sayre) The Healing Art, 1966, (with M.E. Cashel) Your Body is Wonderfully Made, 1974; mem. editorial bd. Am. Jour. Pub. Health, 1967-73; contbr. articles to profl. jours. With M.C. USNR, 1950-53, Korea, capt. (ret.) USNR. Recipient Chapel of Four Chaplains award, 1982. Fellow ACP; mem. AMA (past chmn. sect. preventive medicine), Am. Pub. Health Assn., Royal Soc. Medicine of London (hon.), Sigma Xi, Alpha Omega Alpha, Phi Rho Sigma. Clubs: Campus (Princeton); Franklin Inn (Phila.); Charaka (N.Y.C.); Osler (London). Home: 333 W State St Apt 6K Trenton NJ 08618-5722 Office: Temple U Sch Med Philadelphia PA 19140

ROGERS, FRED MCFEELY, television producer and host; b. Latrobe, Pa., Mar. 20, 1928; s. James Hillis and Nancy (McFeely) Flagg; m. Sara Joanne Byrd, July 9, 1952; children: James Byrd, John Frederick. MusB, Rollins Coll., 1951; MDiv, Pitts. Theol. Sem., 1962; DHL (hon.), Thiel Coll., 1969; HHD (hon.), Eastern Mich. U., 1973; LittD (hon.), St. Vincent Coll., 1973; DD (hon.), Christian Theol. Sem., 1973, Washington and Jefferson Coll., 1984, Westminster Coll., 1987; LHD (hon.), Yale U., 1974, Lafayette Coll., 1977, Washington and Jefferson Coll., 1984, Linfield Coll., 1982, Duquesne U., 1982, Slippery Rock Coll., 1982, U. S.C., 1985, MacMurray Coll., 1986, Drury Coll., 1986, Bowling Green State U., 1987; DFA (hon.), Carnegie-Mellon U., 1976; MusD (hon.), Waynesburg Coll., 1978, U. Ind., 1988; LLD (hon.), Hobart and William Smith Colls., 1985, U. Conn., 1991, Ind. U., Pa., 1992, Boston U., 1992, Moravian Coll., 1992; hon. degree, Goucher Coll., 1993, U. Pitts., 1993, N.C. State, 1996; DHL (hon.), U. W.Va., 1995; D Pub. Svc. (hon.), Edinboro (Pa.) U., 1998; hon. degree, Westminster Choir Coll., 1999, Marist Coll., 1999, Old Dominion U., 2000; LHD, Marguette U., 2001, Middlebury Coll., 2001. Adj. prof. U. Pitts., 1976; C.E.O., Family Comm., Inc., Pitts.; asst. producer NBC, N.Y.C., 1951-53; exec. producer Sta. WQED, Pitts., 1953-62; producer, host CBC, Toronto, Ont., 1962-64; exec. producer, host Mister Rogers' Neighborhood (PBS), Pitts., 1965—; prodr., host Old Friends, New Friends PBS interview series, 1979-81; host Fred Rogers' Heros PBS, 1994. Author: Mister Rogers Talks with Parents, 1983, Mister Rogers' First Experiences Books, 1985, Mister Rogers' Playbook, 1986, Mr. Rogers Talks About Divorce, 1987, Mister Rogers-How Families Grow, 1988, You are Special, 1994, Let's Talk About It: Divorce, 1995, Let's Talk About It: Adoption, 1996, Dear Mister Rogers, 1996, Let's Talk About Stepfamilies, 1999, Let's Talk About It: Extraordinary Friends, 2000, The Giving Box, 2000; producer five audio cassettes of original songs-Many Ways to Say I Love You, audio cassettes and CD Bedtime, 1992, Growing, 1992, You Are Special, 1995, Coming and Going, 1997; composer: Mr. Rogers' Songbook, Mister Rogers EZ Play Today Songbook, 1998, It's a Beautiful Day with Mister Rogers Songbook, 1998; host, writer, producer five one hour video-cassettes home videos CBS, 1987-88, eight 30 minute home videos, 1995-96. Chmn. child devel. and mass media forum White House Conf. on Children; mem. Esther Island Preserve Assn.; bd. dirs. McFeely Rogers Found.; hon. chmn. Nat. PTA, 1992-94. Recipient Children's Trust award Children's Med. Ctr., Chgo., 1997, Pittsburgher of Yr. award Pitts. mag., 1997, Lifetime Achievement TV Critics Assn., 1997, Lifetime Achievement Nat. Acad. TV Arts and Scis., 1997, Lifetime Achievement award Gold Angel Internat. Angel Awards, 1998, Emmy award for performer, children's series, 1999, Spirit of Am. award Nat. Coun. for the Social Studies, 1999, Pa. Founder's award Pa. Hist. and Mus. Commn., 1999, Parents' Choice Classic award, 1999; star on Hollywood Walk of Fame, Hollywood C. of C., 1998; inducted to TV Hall of Fame Nat. Acad. TV Arts and Scis., 1999, Library of Congress LIveing Legend Award, 2000, Lifetime Acievement Award, 2000, National Exceptional Service Award, Salvation Army, 2000, Strong Kids award YMCA, 2001, Mental Health award Psychology Today, 2001, Christophers award, 2001, James Bryant Conant award Edn. Commn. of States, 2001. Mem. Luxor Ministerial Assn., Nat. Assn. TV Program Execs. Presbyterian. Office: 4802 5th Ave Pittsburgh PA 15213-2957 *Every person in this life is so much more than meets the eye or ear. I'm continually surprised at the complexity of all those whom I'm fortunate enough really to get to know.*

ROGERS, GAIL ELIZABETH, library director; b. Charlotte, N.C., May 6, 1947; d. James Yates and Marian Elizabeth (Church) Rogers. BA, Salem Coll., 1969; MLS, U. N.C., 1971. Cert. libr., Ga. Br. libr. Atlanta Pub. Libr., 1970-77; br. coord. Dekalb Libr. System, Decatur, Ga., 1977-82; asst. dir. West Ga. Regional Libr., Carrollton, 1982-83, Cobb County Pub. Libr., Marietta, Ga., 1983-90, dir., 1991—. Mem. Leadership Cobb, Cobb County, 1985-86. Mem. ALA, Ga. Libr. Assn. (2d v.p. 1987-89), Southeastern Libr. Assn. (v.p.-pres. elect. 1990-92, pres. 1992-94), Urban Librs. Coun., Kiwanis Club Marietta (bd. dirs. 1991-92, sec. 1992-93, sec.-treas. 1993-94, pres. 1995-96). Office: Cobb County Public Lib 266 Roswell St SE Marietta GA 30060-2005

ROGERS, GARDNER SPENCER, railroad company executive; b. Bryn Mawr, Pa., Sept. 16, 1926; s. Gardner Spencer and Frances (Lloyd) R.; m. Margaret Elizabeth Windsor, July 18, 1954; children: Ann Rogers Wilbanks, Barbara Rogers Coombs. Student, Episc. Acad., 1940-44, MIT, 1944-45; BS, U. Colo., 1951. Registered profl. engr., Calif. With We. Pacific R.R. Co., San Francisco, 1947-70, engr. costs, valuation and stats., 1964-69, asst. to gen. mgr. planning and control, 1969, asst. gen. mgr., 1970; gen. mgr. Civil & Mech. Maintenance Pty. Ltd., Perth, Australia, 1970-77; mgr. We. Australian ops. Fluor Australia Pty. Ltd., 1971-73, gen. mgr. ry. divsn., 1973-77; gen. mgr. Pilbara Industries, 1971-73; dir. budgets and control Consol. Rail Corp., 1978-79, sr. dir. budgets, planning and control, 1980, dir. corp. planning, 1981-87; cons., 1987—2001. Adv. com. on R.R. property ICC, 1966-70; mem. spl. adv. team R.R. Ofcls. to U.S. Govt., 1962. Mng. trustee Daniel B. Gardner Trust, Chgo.; alt. trustee Cathedral Sq. Found., Perth; vestryman Ch. of Eng., 1971-77, mem. synod and provincial synod, 1973-77, memn. diocesan coun., 1974-77, bd. dirs. sch.'s trust, 1975-77; vestryman, chmn. fin. com., sr. warden St. Mary's-by-the-Sea Episc. Ch., Pacific Grove, Calif., 1989-91; vestryman, chmn. stewardship com., jr. warden St. Mark's Epis. Ch., Medford, Oreg., 1996-98. Mem. Instn. Engrs. Australia, Am. C. of C. in Australia (bd. dirs., v.p., chmn. We. Australian exec. com. 1976-77), Swanleigh (chmn. exec. com. 1974-77, coun.), Am. Mgmt. Assn., Am. Ry. Engr. Assn. (sec. com. 11 1983-87), Epis. Diocese of El Camino Real (bd. dirs. 1991-93, lay Eucharistic Min. 1991-94), Diocese of Oreg. (lay Eucaristic Min. 1995—, lic. lay reader 1996—), Ry. and Locomotive Hist. Soc., Soc. of Cin., Mil. Order Loyal Legion (vice comdr.), Colo. Alumni Assn. No. Calif. (pres. 1951-52), Rogue Valley Manor (pres. residents coun. 1999-2000), Berkeley Tennis Club, Pacific Ry. Club, Commonwealth Club, Australian-Am. Club, Alpha Tau Omega (high coun. 1964-68, 82-90). Home: 2410 Rogue Valley Manor Dr Medford OR 97504-4512 Personal E-mail: grogersRVM@charter.net.

ROGERS, GARRY LEE, minister, medical technician; b. Asheville, N.C., May 29, 1950; s. Kenneth Ledbetter and Annie Faye (Freeman) R.; m. Judy Gaynelle Plemmons, Octo. 6, 1973; children: Angela Dawn, Andrea Gaynelle, Steffan Garry, Shaana Lynette. EMT-IV Tech., Asheville Buncombe Tech. Coll., 1984; B of Ministry, Internat. Bible Sem., Plymouth, Fla., 1985; student N.T. Study Series, Moody Bible Inst., 1985; M in Bible Theology, DD (hon.), Internat. Bible Sem., Plymouth, Fla., 1986; cert., Fruitland Bapt. Bible Inst., 1994; grad., Foley Belsow Locksmith Inst., 2001. Lic. to ministry So. Bapt. Conv., 1969, ordained, 1973. Music dir. New Liberty Bapt. Ch., Asheville, 1967-73, assoc. pastor, 1975-76; pastor Mt. Pleasant Bapt. Ch., Hot Springs, N.C., 1973-74, Jones Valley Bapt. Ch., Leicester, 1976-90, Emmanuel Bapt. Ch., Clyde, NC, 1990—2002. Med. technician Tempoe Inc., Asheville, 1983-93; sec. New Found. Bapt. Sunday Sch. Conv., Asheville, 1983-85, moderator, 1984-90; mem. gen. bd. Bapt. State Conv., Cary, N.C., 1984-87; trustee Christian Action League, Raleigh, N.C., 1987—, nominating com., 1994; chaplain West Buncombe Fire Dept., 1985-92, 99—, Erwin H.S. Bus. Dirvers Assn., 1986, Buncombe County Sheriffs Dept., 2000—. Author: Prayer and Praying, 1986. Vol. fireman and EMT-D West Buncombe Fire Dept., Asheville, 1983—; pres. Olivette Cmty. Watch, Asheville, 1990—; mem. com. on coms. Haywood Bapt. Assn., 1994—, mem. ordination com., 1996-98, 1999-2002. Recipient Bold Mission 100% Increase in Giving award, Bold Mission 100% Increase in Baptisms award N.C. Bapt. Conv., 1977-82, 20 Yr. award West Buncombe Fire Dept., 1998. Mem. N.C. Firemans Assn., Buncombe County Sch. Bus Drivers Assn., N.C. Athletic Officials Assn. Democrat. Home: 520 Olivette Rd Asheville NC 28804-9672 E-mail: GLROG@MSN.COM. *One of the greatest joys a person can experience in this life is the receiving of others and the giving of oneself. Everyone should experience this joy in life.*

ROGERS, GARTH WINFIELD, lawyer; b. Fort Collins, Colo., Nov. 4, 1938; s. Harlan Winfield and Helen Marie (Orr) R.; m. Joanne Kathleen Rapp, June 16, 1962; children: Todd Winfield, Christopher Jay, Gregory Lynn, Clay Charles. BS, U. Colo., 1958, LLB, 1962. Bar: Colo. 1962; U.S. Dist. Ct. Colo. 1962. Law clk. to presiding justice U.S. Dist. Ct., Denver, 1962-63; assoc. Allen, Stover & Mitchell, Ft. Collins, 1963-68; ptnr. Allen, Rogers & Vahrenwald, 1968-97; ret., 1997. Articles editor Rocky Mountain Law Rev., 1961-62. Past bd. dirs. Salvation Army, Ft. Collins, Ft. Collins C. of C., United Way of Ft. Collins, Trinity Luth. Ch., Ft. Collins, others; bd. dirs. Poudre Sch. Dist. Bd. Edn. Mem. ABA, Colo. Bar Assn., Larimer County Bar Assn. Avocations: Nicaragua projects, participative sports, amateur writing, reading. Office: 215 W Oak St Ste 202 Fort Collins CO 80521-2734

ROGERS, GARY STEVEN, consultant; b. Houston, Aug. 3, 1951; s. Boyd A. and Eleanor V. (Bouldin) R.; m. Esperanza G. Calderon, Aug. 17, 1976 (div. 1992); children: Jonathan, Christopher. BA, U. North Tex., Denton, 1973, MA, 1976, PhD, 1983. Lic. psychologist, Tex. Program dir. Western State Hosp., Staunton, Va., 1983-85; pvt. practice in psychology Psychol. Devel. Assocs., Abilene, Tex., 1985-88; owner Courtech Sys., Inc., 1991—, On-Site Computer Support, Inc., 1997—. Avocations: personal computing, chess. Home: 3933 Ridgway Rd Abilene TX 79606

ROGERS, H. DENNIS, lawyer; b. Miami, Mar. 20, 1948; s. Charles Edward and Dorothy Belle (Bannister) R.; m. Mary Kathleen Kelly, Aug. 26, 1978; children: Kristen Marie, Matthew David. BA (with honors), Fla. State U., 1970; JD, U. Fla., 1979. Bar: Fla. 1984, U.S. Ct. Appeals (11th cir.) 1984, U.S. Dist. Ct. (mid. dist.) Fla. 1982. Atty. Blake & Assocs., P.A., Tampa, Fla., 1981-84, Jacobs, Robbins, Gaynor, Burton et al, Tampa, 1984-86, Foley & Lardner, Tampa, 1986-93, Carey & Florin, P.A., Clearwater, Fla., 1993-96; ptnr. Mitchell & Rogers, P.A., Tampa, 1996, Florin, Roebig, Walker, Huddlestein & Rogers, P.A., 1997-2000; pvt. practice Clearwater, Fla., 2000—. Barrister Justice William Glenn Terrell Inn of Ct., 1992-94. Bd. dirs. Hampton Lakes Homeowners Assn., Tampa, 1990, vp. Recipient Pro Bono award Bay Area Vol. Lawyers Program, 1985, 90, 91. Mem. ATLA, Fla. Bar Assn. (litigation sect.), Clearwater Bar Assn., Acad. Fla. Trial Lawyers, Greater Tampa Sertoma Club. Avocations: golf, music, swimming, fishing, computers. Office: H Dennis Rogers PA Ste 200 28163 US Hwy 19 Clearwater FL 33761-2696 E-mail: hdrogers@tampabay.rr.com.

ROGERS, HAROLD DALLAS (HAL ROGERS), congressman; b. Barrier, KY, Dec. 31, 1937; BA, U. Ky., 1962, LLB, 1964. Bar: Ky. 1964. Pvt. practice, Somerset, Ky., 1967-69; Commonwealth atty. Pulaski and Rockcastle counties, 1969-80; mem. 97th-107th Congresses from 5th Dist. Ky., 1981—, mem. appropriations com., subcom. transp., commerce, justice state, energy and water. With KY and NC Nat. Guard, 1957—64. Republican. Office: US Ho of Reps 2406 Rayburn Hob Washington DC 20515-1705*

ROGERS, HON PAULLETTO, researcher, writer; b. Washington, Aug. 22, 1961; s. Paulleto Rogers I and Dorothy L.R. Rogers; children: Alexis R. Roycia July, Ambre L. Majasticaa, Ericka J. Student, Wayne County C.C.; cert. computer ops., Mother Waddles Sch. Cert. paralegal; notary pub. Pres. C.C.OA, L.A., 1983; gen. operator CBOU, 1983—; regent agent Security MGN, 1984; collector Nat. Credit Corp., L.A., 1985; craftman Vinyl Indsl. Products, Chgo., 1986; field insp. Mortgage Svcs. Assoc., Inc., 1995; sales cons. Swepo, 1996; legal tech. Probone Legal Svcs., 1997; directorate Prousa Internat. Projects 2001, 1998. Substaining member Rep. Platform Commn., 1986; substaining sponsor Ronald Reagan Presdl. Found., Libr., and Ctr. Pub. Affairs, Ventura County, Calif., 1988; sponsor Statue of Liberty Ellis Island Centennial Commn., 1985, Ronald Reagan Congressional-Vicotry Fund, 1987; advisorate Senate Adv. Coun., 1997; co-founder Justice Inst.; vol. Mother Waddles-Petr. Mission Support; del. at large Del. Adv. Coun.; legal adv. Alexis, Ambre, Dorthy-Lewis, Paul, Paulleto, Rogers, Sutton, Profl. Corp., 2001. Creator, founder The Collectionals Survey. At-large-del. Rep. Presdl. Task Force, 1992—, lobbyist, 1994—; activist U.S. Def. Com., 1985; lobbyist Prousa Legal Corpsusa, 1999; del. Wayne County Clk. Office; Mich. state advisor Rep. Senatorial Com.; mem. Jaycees, 1981, GOPAC, congl. VIP, 1984; GOP Victory Fund sponsor NRCC, 1984; supporter KIDSFIRST YESMI, 2000; assoc. mem. Ch. Tae Adv., 2000—. Decorated Rogers Coat of Arms, Medieval Knight, Chevron, 2000; recipient Cert. Recognition, NRCC, 1990, Cert. Appreciation, Presdl. Commn. A.A., 1990, Presdl. award Rep. Presdl. Legion of Merit. Mem. Oahspe (assoc.), World Peace Tonite/Freedom Inst. (assoc.), 2nd Ch. of Tae. Avocations: copyrights, activism, lobbying, community investing. Home: PO Box 27473 Detroit MI 48227-0473 Office: 13426 Strathmoor Sta/Sta Hy PO Box 27473 Detroit MI 48227-0473

ROGERS, HOWARD H. chemist; b. N.Y.C., Dec. 26, 1926; s. Julian Herbert and Minnie (Jaffa) R.; m. Barbara Kniaz, Mar. 27, 1954 (div. 1978); children: Lynne, Mark David, Susan; m. Maureen Dohn, Dec. 28, 1978. BS in Chemistry, U. Ill., 1949; PhD in Inorganic Chemistry, MIT, 1953. Research group leader Allis-Chalmers Mfg. Co., West Allis, Wis., 1952-61; sr. tech. specialist Rocketdyne div., Rockwell, Canoga Park, Calif., 1961-70; chief research scientist Martek Instruments, Newport Beach, 1970-73; scientist Boeing Satellite Systems, Torrance, 1973—. Developer nickel-hydrogen battery; patentee; contbr. sci. papers to profl. publs. in field. With USN, 1944—46. Recipient Lawrence A. Hyland Patent award Hughes Aircraft Co., 1987. Mem. Electrochem. Soc. (chmn. So. Calif./Nev. sect. 1976-78), Am. Chem. Soc., Sigma Xi. Home: 18361 Van Ness Ave Torrance CA 90504-5309 Office: Boeing Satellite Systems B231/2019 PO Box 2999 Torrance CA 90509-2999 E-mail: howard.rogers@alum.mit.edu. *In my 75 plus years of living experience I have found that these two items are vital: focus on what you intend to do, not what you have already done; complete honesty to yourself and to others in interpreting and reporting results is mandatory.*

ROGERS, ISABEL WOOD, retired religious studies educator; b. Tallahassee, Aug. 26, 1924; d. William Hudson and Mary Thornton (Wood) R. BA, Fla. State U., 1945; MA, U. Va., 1947; MRE, Presbyn. Sch. Christian Edn., 1949; PhD, Duke U., 1961; DD (hon.), Austin Coll., 1986; LLD (hon.), Westminster Coll., 1988; LHD, Centre Coll., 1989. Campus min. 1st Presbyn. Ch., Milledgeville, Ga., 1949-52; campus chaplain Ga. Coll., Milledgville, 1952-61; prof. applied Christianity Presbyn. Sch. Christian Edn., Richmond, Va., 1961-98; ret., 1998. Elder Ginter Pk. Presbyn. Ch., Richmond, 1976-79, 89—; moderator of Gen. Assembly, Presbyn. Ch. U.S.A., 1987-88; lectr. Presbyn. chs. Author: The Christian and World Affairs, 1965, In Response to God, 1969, Our Shared Earth, 1980, Sing A New Song, 1981, Toward a Liberating Faith: A Primer on Feminist Theology, 1999. Vol. Richmond Community Action Program, 1968-75, YWCA, Women's Advocacy Program, 1982—; bd. dirs. Massanetta Conf. Ctr., Richmond, 1987—. Du Pont fellow U. Va., 1946. 47, Kearns fellow Duke U. Mem. Soc. Christian Ethics, Phi Kappa Phi, Phi Beta Kappa. Democrat. Avocations: hiking, jogging, tennis, gardening, stamp collecting. Home: 1214 Palmyra Ave Richmond VA 23227-4435

ROGERS, JACK DAVID, plant pathologist, educator; b. Point Pleasant, W.Va., Sept. 3, 1937; s. Jack and Thelma Grace R.; m. Belle C. Spencer, June 7, 1958. BS in Biology, Davis and Elkins Coll., 1960; MF, Duke U., 1960; PhD, U. Wis., 1963. From asst. prof. to prof. Wash. State U., Pullman, 1963-72, chmn. dept. plant pathology, 1986-99. Contbr. articles to profl. jours. Recipient William H. Weston Teaching Excellence award Mycological Soc. Am., 1992. Mem. Mycological Soc. of Am. (pres., 1977-78), Am. Phytopathol. Soc., Botanical Soc. Am., British Mycological Soc.

ROGERS, JAMES ALLAN, music director, hymnologist, author, editor; b. Canton, Ohio, June 27, 1944; s. Herbert Miller and Edna Mae (Schmeltzer) R.; m. Janet Elizabeth Wiant, May 7, 1947; children: Joel Andrew, Jeffry Aaron. BMus, Baldwin Wallace Coll., Berea, Ohio, 1966; M.Sacred Music, Northwestern U., 1968, Garret Sem., 1968. Diaconal minister, cert. dir. music Meth. Ch. Dir. music Calvary Presbyn. Ch., Canton, Ohio, 1968-69, Maple Grove United Meth. Ch., Columbus, 1969-75, First United Meth. Ch., Springfield, Ill., 1975—. Asst. carillonneur Thomas Rees Carillon, Springfield, 1980—. Contbr. articles to profl. jours. Bd. dirs. Springfield Choral Soc., Cmty. Concert Assn., Springfield, Opera Theater of Springfield. James A. Rogers Hymnol. Libr. at Boston U. named in his honor. Mem. Hymn Soc. U.S. and Can. (life, chmn. promotion com. 1975-80), Am. Guild Organists, Choristers Guild, Fellowship of United Meth. in Music, Worship and the Arts, Guild of Carillonneurs of N.Am., Phi Mu Alpha. Home: 26 Mishawaka Dr Rochester IL 62563-9473 Office: First United Meth Ch 501 E Capitol Ave Springfield IL 62701-1813

ROGERS, JAMES BEELAND, JR. investment company executive; b. Balt., Oct. 19, 1942; s. james Beeland and Ernestine Barbara (Brewer) R. BA cum laude, Yale U., 1964; BA with honors, MA in Politics, Philosophy/Econ. Balliol Coll., Oxford U., Eng., 1966. Investment analyst Bache & Co., N.Y.C., 1968-69, R. Gilder & Co., N.Y.C., 1969-70; asst. to chmn. Neuberger & Berman, 1970-71; with Arnhold and S. Belichroeder, Inc., 1971-73; exec. v.p. Soros Fund Mgmt., N.Y.C., 1973-80; chmn. bd. Rogers Holdings, 1980—. Adj. prof. Columbia U. Sch. Bus., 1983-85, prof. fin., 1986-90; host The Profit Motive with Jim Rogers, TV show, 1989-90; co-host, commentator various TV shows, 1992—; vis. prof., Columbia U., 1994-96; columnist, 1995—. Author: Investment Biker: On the Road with Jim Rogers, 1994, Driving Around the World on Millennium Adventure, 1999—2001. Home: 352 Riverside Dr New York NY 10025-2731 E-mail: Jim@jimrogers.com.

ROGERS, JAMES CURTIS, movie producer, publisher, screenwriter; b. Sandston, Va., May 21, 1930; s. James Allen and Julia Pollard (Curtis) R. BA, U. Calif., Berkeley, 1961; BS, William and Mary Coll.; MA, PhD, Columbia Pacific. Sec., treas., CEO Rojet Theatre Co., Atlanta, 1954; prof. Capitol Radio and Electronics Inst., Washington, 1955; tech. writer Guided Missile Rocket dept. RCA Svc. Co., Alexandria, Va., Cherry Hill, N.J.; sec., treas., CEO Hawkeye Records, Iowa City, 1961-63; tchr. Calvert County H.S., Prince Frederick, Md., 1964; child protective officer Social Svc. Bur., Richmond, Va., 1964-68; head master Lyceum Ednl. Com., Gloucester, 1968-70; pub. Lyceum Publs., Richmond, 1968-92; producer, agt. YoungStar Prodns., 1989-91; pub., editor FutureWend Publs., 1991—. Ethics cons. The Matrism Orgn., Richmond, 1988—; publs. officer U.S. Coast GuardAux., Richmond, 1986-87. Author: Foreign Language With a Smile, 1965—, The Kidnapping, 1995; editor It's Your Choice Mag., 1993; author plays. Adminstr. Julie and Jim Rogers scholarship fund, Richmond, 1988—; scoutmaster Robert E. Lee Coun., Boy Scouts Am., Richmond, 1948-52, sea scout skipper, 1948-52; dir. Children's Theatre Project, Berkeley, 1959. Mem. Thalian Soc., Am. Inst. Hypnosis, Coll. Med. Hypnotists, Scriptwriter Network, Acad. for Polit. and Social Sci. Avocations: piano/organ public performance, foreign languages. Office: Apt 104 1511 Wilcox Ave Los Angeles CA 90028-7337

ROGERS, JAMES DEVITT, judge; b. Mpls., May 5, 1929; s. Harold Neil and Dorothy (Devitt) R.; m. Leanna Morrison, Oct. 19, 1968. AB, Dartmouth Coll., 1951; JD, U. Minn., 1954. Bar: Minn. 1954, U.S. Supreme Ct. 1983. Assoc. Johnson & Sands, Mpls., 1956-60; sole practice, 1960-62; judge Mpls. Municipal and Dist. Ct., 1959-91. Mem. faculty Nat. Judicial Coll. Bd. dirs. Mpls. chpt. Am. Red Cross, chmn. service to mil. families and vets. com.; bd. dirs. Minn. Safety Council, St. Paul, 1988-91. Served to sgt. U.S. Army, 1954-56. Mem. ABA (chmn. nat. conf. spl. ct. judge, spl. com. housing and urban devel. law, traffic ct. program com., chmn. criminal justice sect., jud. adminstrn. div.), Nat. Jud. Coll. (bd. dirs.), Nat. Christmas Tree Grower's Assn. (pres. 1976-78), Mpls. Athletic Club. Congregationalist. Office: 14110 Prince Pl Minnetonka MN 55345-3027

ROGERS, JAMES EDWIN, geology and hydrology consultant; b. Waco, Tex., Feb. 24, 1929; s. Charles Watson and Jimmie (Harp) R.; m. Margaret Anna Louise Bruchmann, Oct. 10, 1957; 1 child, James Frederick. Student, Rice U., 1947-49, Baylor U., 1953; BS, U. Tex., 1955, MA, 1961. Geologist U.S. Geol. Survey, St. Paul, 1956-59, Alexandria, La., 1959-63, supervisory hydrologist, 1963-85; ind. cons., 1985—. Cons. geol. survey for map State of La., Baton Rouge, 1982-85, mapping com., 1997—, mem. adv. bd. La. geol. survey, 1998—. Author: Water Resources of Kisatchie Well-Field Area Near Alexandria, Louisiana, 1981, Preconstruction and Simulated Postconstruction Ground-Water Levels at Urban Centers in the Red River Navigation Project Area, Louisiana, 1983, Red River Waterway Project - Summary of Ground-Water Studies by the U.S. Geological Survey, 1962-85, 1988; co-author: Water Resources of Vernon Parish, Louisiana, 1965, Water Resources of Ouachita Parish, Louisana, 1972, Water Resources of the Little River Basin, Louisana, 1973. Scoutmaster Boy Scouts Am., Alexandria, 1971, 72. Sgt. U.S. Army, 1950-52, Japan. Fellow Geol. Soc. Am.; mem. Gem Mineral and Lapidary Soc. Ctrl. La. (pres. 1972, 86-87, 94-96), Baton Rouge Geol. Soc., Phi Beta Kappa. Presbyterian. Avocations: numismatics, minerals, genealogy, travel, history. Home and Office: 4008 Innis Dr Alexandria LA 71303-4738

ROGERS, JAMES EUGENE, electric and gas utility executive; b. Birmingham, Ala., Sept. 20, 1947; s. James E. and Margaret (Whatley) R.; m. Robyn McGill (div.); children: Chrissi, Kara, Ben; m. Mary Anne Boldrick, Oct. 28, 1977. BBA, U. Ky., 1970, JD, 1974. Asst. atty. gen. Commonwealth Ky., Louisville; asst. chief trial atty. Fed. Energy Regulation Commn., Washington, dep. gen. counsel litigation and enforcement; law clk. to presiding justice Supreme Ct Ky., Louisville; ptnr. Akin, Gump, Strauss, Hauer & Feld, Dallas, Akin Gump Strauss Hauer & Feld, Houston, 1985-86; formerly pres. Transwestern Pipeline; pres., CEO, chmn. Cinergy Corp. (formerly PSI Resources, Inc.), Cin., 1994—. Bd. dirs. CINergy Corp., Fifth Third Bank, Edison Electric Inst., Duke Realty Investments, Inc. Trustee Nat. Symphony Orch.; bd. dirs. Cin. Mus. Assn., The Nature Conservancy-Ind. chpt., U. Ky. Bus. Partnership Found. Mem. Ky. Bar Assn., D.C. Bar Assn., Meridian Hills Country Club, Crooked Stick Golf Club, Queen City Club, Met. Club. Baptist. Avocations: tennis, biking, skiing, golf. Office: Cinergy Corp 139 E Fourth St Cincinnati OH 45202-0960*

ROGERS, JAMES FREDERICK, banker, management consultant; b. Centerville, Iowa, June 27, 1935; s. John W. and Mildred Holly (Morris) R.; m. Janet L. Marsden, June 27, 1957; children: Jennifer Burke, John William. AB, U. Mo., 1957; postgrad., Rutgers U. Grad. Sch. Banking, 1970-72. With Am. Security and Trust Co., Washington, 1959-85, exec. v.p., 1980-83. Bd. dirs., pres. Am. Security Corp., 1983-85; cons. B.E.I.-Golembe Assocs., 1985-93; chmn. Nat. Bank of No. Va., 1988-89. Commr. Arlington County Planning Commn., 1979-80; asst. treas. Kennedy Ctr. Performing Arts; pres., trustee Leonard Wood Found.; trustee Friends of Nat. Zoo, Greater Washington Rsch. Ctr., Washington Dulles Task Force, Arena Stage, Sch. Commerce U. Va. Officer AUS, 1958-59. Mem. D.C. Bankers Assn. (pres. 1984-85), Davenport Soc., U. Mo., Met. Club (Washington), Chevy Chase Club. Presbyterian. Home: 4201 38th Rd N Arlington VA 22207-4554

ROGERS, JAMES GARDINER, accountant, educator; b. St. Louis, May 6, 1952; s. Gardiner and Virginia Joy (Goodbar) R.; m. Barbara May Baird, Feb. 14, 1976; children Andrew Baird, Benjamin Baird, Samuel Baird. BA, Washington and Lee U., 1973; MBA, Am. U., 1975. CPA, Pa. Credit officer loan workout div. Phila. Nat. Bank, Phila., 1975-78; mgr. cash and banking Gen. Waterworks Corp., 1978-81, asst. treas., 1981-85; v.p. fin., treas. Phila. Presbyn. Homes, Inc., 1985-88; exec. dir. devel. Eastern U., St. Davids, 1988—. Ptnr., bd. dirs. PC Mgmt. Enterprises, Inc., Bryn Mawr, Pa.. Treas. Lower Merion Bapt. Ch., Bryn Mawr, 1978-85; v.p. Lupus Foundn. of Am., Inc., Washington, 1985-87, asst. v.p., 1982-85, bd. dirs., 1977—; pres., bd. dirs. Pa. Lupus Foundn., Wayne, 1973—, bd. dirs.; elder Proclamation Presbyn. Ch., 1996—. Mem. Mensa. Clubs: Merion Cricket (Haverford, Pa.). Republican. Avocations: reading, microcomputers, tennis, skiing. Home: 308 Chamounix Rd Wayne PA 19087-3612 Office: Eastern Coll Saint Davids PA 19087 E-mail: jrogers@eastern.edu., JGRogers.CPA@verizon.net.

ROGERS, JAMES THOMAS, lawyer; b. Denver, Oct. 3, 1941; s. John Thomas and Elizabeth (Milligan) R. JD, U. Wis., 1966. Bar: Wis. 1966, U.S. Tax Ct. 1976, U.S. Ct. Claims, 1975, U.S. Ct. Customs and Patent Appeals, 1975, U.S. Supreme Ct. 1973. Chmn., Madison (Wis.) Legal Aid Soc., 1965-66; dist. atty. Lincoln County (Wis.), 1967, 69-73; spl. dist. atty. pro tem Oneida County (Wis.), 1972, Price County (Wis.), 1972-76, Lincoln County (Wis.), 1976-84; spl. city atty. City of Wausau (Wis.), 1973, 74, 77; ptnr. Rogers & Bremer, Merrill, Wis., 1973-89; prin. Rogers Criminal Law Offices, Merrill, 1989—. bd. dirs. Merrill Fed. Savings & Loan Assn., 1990—, Home Supply Co-Op., Wausau, 1995—. Chmn. Judiciary Com., N.E. Crime Control Commn., 1971-72. Chmn., Lincoln County Republican Com., 1971-73; pub. defender bd. State of Wis., 1988—, 2d vice chmn., 1989-93, 1st vice chmn.,

1993—. Bd. dirs. Wis. Judicare, 1990-92. Mem. State Bar Wis. (spl. com. on prosecutorial improvements 1983-89, spl. com. to rev. criminal sanctions 1987-88, conv. and entertainment com. 1989-93), Lincoln County Bar Assn. (pres. 1969-70), Wis. Dist. Attys. Assn. (life), ABA (liaison drunk driving com. of criminal justice sect., vice chmn. asset and investment mgmt. com. sec. econs. of law practice, marriage and cohabitation com. family law sect., def. svcs. commn. criminal law sect., liaison criminal justice sect.), Nat. Assn. Criminal Def. Lawyers (state and local def. bar liaison com., ad hoc subcom. on property of DNA evidence), Assn. Trial Lawyers Am. (constl. challenge com. 1988-92), Wis. Acad. Trial Lawyers (chmn. constl. challenge com. 1988-91), bd. dirs. 1985-91), Tex. Trial Lawyers Assn., N.Y. State Trial Lawyers Assn., Wis. Assn. Criminal Def. Lawyers (sec. 1986-87, pres.-elect 1987-88, pres. 1988-89, bd. dirs. 1986—, liaison to ABA criminal justice sect.), Wausau Club. Home: PO Box 438 1408 E 8th St Merrill WI 54452-1537

ROGERS, JAMES THOMAS, trade association executive; b. Columbus, Ohio, Mar. 30, 1947; s. Charles Bernard and Joanne R.; m. Janet Carol Baker, Jan. 3, 1951; children: Mark, Kimberly, Matthew, Scott. BS, Ohio State U., 1970; MA, 1972. Dir. pub. affairs Ohio Coun. Retail Merchants, Columbus, 1973-78; mgr., state govt. rels. PPG Industries, Pitts., 1978-79; dir. state rels., lobbyist Food Mktg. Inst., Washington, 1979-81, Nat. Restaurant Assn., Washington, 1981-84, sr. dir. govt. rels., 1984-87; pres., CEO Food Industry Alliance N.Y. State, Albany, 1987—. Mem. N.Y. State Adv. Coun. of Vocat. and Ednl. Svcs. for Individuals with Disabilities SUNY/State Edn. Dept., Albany, 1990-97. Bd. dirs. Capital Dist. Youth for Christ, Albany, 1997-2002. Mem. Food Industry Assn. Execs., Am. Soc. Assn. Execs., Kappa Tau Alpha. Home: 50 Edison Dr Niskayuna NY 12309 Office: Food Industry Alliance NY State 130 Washington Ave Albany NY 12210 Fax: (518) 434-9962. E-mail: rogers2434@aol.com., jim@fiany.com.

ROGERS, JAMES VIRGIL, JR. retired radiologist and educator; b. Johnson City, Tenn., Oct. 7, 1922; s. James Virgil and Mary Ruth (Collins) R.; m. Mildred Vandivere, June 9, 1945 (div. 1985); children: Rebecca Jean, James V. III, Janet Marie, Susan Margaret; m. Mary Lujean Craven, Mar. 18, 1989. BS, Emory U., 1943, MD, 1945. Intern Kings County Hosp., N.Y.C., 1945-46; resident in radiology Grady Meml. Hosp., Altanta, 1947-48, Emory U. Hosp., Altanta, 1948-50; instr. Emory U. Sch. Medicine, Atlanta, 1950-51, assoc., 1950-53, asst. prof., 1954-60, assoc. prof., 1960-64, prof., 1965-93; ret. Chief radiology svc. Emory U. Hosp., Atlanta, 1971-80, vice chmn. dept. radiology 1973-78, acting chmn., 1978-80; dep. sect. head Emory Clinic, Atlanta, 1971-78, sect. head, 1978-80, chief radiology svc., 1982-91; cons. radiology 3d Army Hdqrs., Atlanta; examiner Am. Bd. Radiology, 1970-79, site inspector for residency programs, 1972-83. Contbr. articles to profl. jours. Pres. Palestine Human Rights campaign of Ga., Atlanta, 1990, 1996-97. 1st lt. M.C., U.S. Army, 1946-47. Fellow Am. Coll. Radiology (councilor); mem. Radiol. Soc. North Am., Am. Roentgen Ray Soc., So. Radiologic Conf. (past pres.), Ga. Radiologic Soc. (past pres.), Atlanta Radiologic Soc. (past. pres.), AMA, So. Med. Assn. (past pres. radiology sect.), Druid Hills Golf Club, Am. Legion. Republican. Methodist. Avocations: golf, fishing. Home: 3845 Shore Blvd Oldsmar FL 34677-5615

ROGERS, JEAN GREGORY, retired lawyer; b. Panama City, Fla., Dec. 15, 1934; d. William Green and Jean (Balkom) Gregory. BA in English, Agnes Scott Coll., Decatur, Ga., 1956; LLB, U. Md., Balt., 1962. Bar: Md. Ct. Appeals, 1963, U.S. Supreme Ct., 1968, U.S. Dist. Ct., Md., 1968, U.S. Ct. Appeals (4th cir.), 1969, U.S. Ct. Appeals (5th cir.), 1985, U.S. Ct. Appeals (10th cir.), 1988. Asst. county solicitor Office of County Solicitor Balt. County, Towson, Md., 1963-68; sole practitioner pvt. practice, 1963-68; asst. U.S. atty. Office of U.S. Atty. Dept. Justice, Balt., 1968-73; asst. regional counsel Fed. Hwy. Adminstrn., 1973-75, regional counsel Fort Worth, Tex., 1975-96, ret., 1996. Project com. SP20-6, Nat. Coop. Hwy. Rsch. Program Nat. Rsch. Coun., Transp. Rsch. Bd., Washington, 1986-96; Group Coun. on Legal Resources, Transp. Rsch. Bd., Washington, 1979-82. Recipient Superior Achievement award, Fed. Hwy. Adminstr., 1980. Mem.: ABA. Presbyterian. Home: 3608 Bechler Ln Winston Salem NC 27106

ROGERS, JEANNE VALERIE, art educator, artist; b. Islip, N.Y., Dec. 1, 1935; d. Joseph Oliver and Louise Valerie (Bayer) Fields; m. James Aubrey Rogers, Jan. 1, 1956; children: Bradley, Tyler, Lisa, Todd. BFA in Ceramics Design, Alfred U., 1957; MS in Art Edn., SUNY, New Paltz, 1962; postgrad., L.I. U., 1986-90, Parsons Sch. Design, 1988-90. Cert. art edn. tchr. K-12, elem. tchr., N.Y. Elem. art tchr. Sayville (N.Y.) Sch. Dist., 1957-61, high sch. art tchr., 1987-90; art tchr. Bayport (N.Y.)/Bluepoint Sch. Dist., 1980; art dir., art tchr. The Hewlett Sch., East Islip, N.Y., 1984-87; field supr. of student tchrs. Dowling Coll., Oakdale, 1990—; high sch. art tchr. Torah Acad., Commack, 1991—; instr. watercolor painting Staff Devel. Ctr. of The Islips, East Islip 45, N.Y.C., 1996—. Instr. oil painting adult edn. East Islip High Sch., 1961-62; dir. children's art Summer Outdoor Art Workshops, East Islip, 1967-78; adj. prof. Dowling Coll., 1991-92, art cons., 1990—; instr. watercolor painting for tchrs. Staff Devel. Ctr. of the Islips, East Islip H.S., N.Y., 1996—. Co-author/illustrator: Suffolk Scribes Calligraphic Poetry, 1980 (Libr. award East Islip, 1980); exhibited juried show at Babylon (N.Y.) Citizens Coun. Arts, 1994 (Best in Show award), Invitational Exhibit of Women Artists, Patchogue, N.Y., 1995; reader children's poetry Women in the Arts cable TV show, 1974; contbr. painting as cover design Suffolk Woman Watch Newspaper (premier issues), 1994. Instr. life saving and water safety ARC, Islip, 1955-61; tchr. Sunday sch. Presbyn. Ch., Islip, 1957-63; instr., dir. lifesaving and water safety Shoreham Beach Club, Sayville, 1965-70; instr. preschool, youth and adult swimming Bayshore YMCA, Lasalle Acad., Oakdale, 1971-88, instr., swim dir., 1983-88; art judge C. of C. Summerfest, Sayville, 1990. Recipient award of merit in painting, Nat. League Am. PEN Women, Vanderbilt Mus., Centerport, N.Y., 1993, 94, Chem. Bank award for painting Arts Coun., 1992, East Islip Pub. Libr., 1992, hon. mention Huntington Township Art League, Northport Spoke Gallery, N.Y., 1991, HTAL winners show Hutchins Gallery, CW Post Campus/L.I. U., 1991, Honorable Mention Huntington Twp. Art League, Northport Spoke Gallery, N.Y., 1991, others. Mem. AAUW (implementation chair soc.'s reflection in arts study 1972-74, legis. chair Islip area br. 1972-74, cultural interests chair 1973-75), summer socials chmn. General and Ednl. grants Fundraising, 1995—, historian 1996—), Suffolk Scribes (charter mem., corr. sec. 1988-89), Nat. League Am. PEN Women (corr. sec. 1996-97), South Shore Watercolor Soc., South Bay Art Assn., N.Y. State Tchrs. Assn., L.I. Art Tchrs. Assn. Republican. Presbyterian. Avocations: tennis, swimming, ballroom dancing, reading, travel. Home: 274 Marilynn Ct East Islip NY 11730-3315

ROGERS, JOAN LISSO, social worker, psychotherapist; b. New Orleans, Sept. 11, 1946; d. James Miginn and Elissa (Lavorgna) Lisso; m. Curtis C. Rogers Jr., July 13, 1968 (div. 1974); 1 child, Curtis Charles III. BA, Newcomb Coll., New Orleans, 1968; MSW, Tulane U., 1974. Clin. social worker III New Orleans Mental Health Ctr.; dir. student mental health svc. U. New Orleans, 1977-81; employee counselor Hotel Dieu Hosp., 1981; child care coord. East Jefferson Mental Health, Metairie, La., 1981-83; coord. adult and adolescent children of alcoholics program Harahan, 1988-89; dir. schizophrenia rehab. project Harahan, Haraha, 1988-89. Pvt. practice, New Orleans, 1977—; family/group therapist River Oaks Psychiat. Hosp., New Orleans, 1977-90; cons. Parents Anonymous, New Orleans, 1990, Impaired Profl. Com., New Orleans, 1990. Active Women's Breakfast, New Orleans, 1990—, Century Club Contemporary Arts Ctr., New Orleans, 1989—; Friends of Zoo, New Orleans, 1985—, Friends of Aquarium, New Orleans, 1990—. Mem. NASW, La. Group Psychotherapy Soc., Am. Group Psychotherapy Assn. (assoc.), Am. Assn. Marriage and Family Therapy (clin.). Avocations: dancing, art collecting, renovation. Office: 744 Dante St New Orleans LA 70118-1014 Fax: 504-866-1982.

ROGERS, JOE, lieutenant governor; m. Juanita Kay; children: Trent, Jordan, Haley. Degree in bus., Colo. State U.; JD, Ariz. State U. Past law clk. to Hon. Robert Broomfield U.S. Dist. Ct.; assoc. Davis, Graham & Stubbs, Colo., 1989-93; staff counsel to Sen. Hank Brown U.S. Congress, Washington, 1993-95; lt. gov. State of Colo., 1998—. Past atty. Lend-A-Lawyer Program, Colo. Mem. Denver Bar Assn. (bd. dirs. credit union 1990-93), Colo. Bar Assn., Sam Carey Bar Assn. Office: Lt Govs Office 130 State Capitol Denver CO 80203-1792*

ROGERS, JOHN ALVIN, retired technical educator, writer, publisher; b. Dennison, Ohio, Dec. 19, 1946; s. William Arlington and Friedarika Albestina (Schulte) R. B of Gen. Studies, N.Mex. Inst. Mining and Tech., 1974; MS in Resource Geography, Oreg. State U., 1976; postgrad., U. Ariz., 1982. Reporter The Evening Chronicle, 1974; cons. writer Forest Service Research Lab, USDA, Corvallis, Oreg., 1976; rsch. assoc. divsn. econ. and bus. rsch. U. Ariz., Tucson, 1977, rsch. assoc. engring. experiment sta., 1977-78, rsch. assoc. Water Research Ctr., 1979, rsch. assoc. Sch. Renewable Natural Resources, 1980-81, rsch. assoc. libr. dept. acquisitions, 1981-82; intern Pima County Assn. Govts., 1979; engring. asst. divsn. environ. health Pima County Health Dept., 1980; tutor writing Pima Community Coll., 1982-83, assoc. faculty dept. writing, teaching asst. dept. reading, 1983-84; tech. writer Hamilton Test Systems, Tucson, 1984; sr. tech. writer E-Systems, Inc., Greenville, Tex., 1985-91; adj. prof. geography Tyler (Tex.) Jr. Coll., 1991; ind. cons. documentation and rsch. svcs. Tyler, 1992-93; edn. materials specialist Avalon Software, Tucson, 1993-94; pres. Sci. Probes Tech. Writing, Publ., and Tng. Svcs., 1994—. Vol. facilitator pub. participation program Pima County Planning Dept., 1978; mem. So. Ariz. Environ. Coun., 1982-85, editor bull., 1982-84, rep. basin study com. 1983-84, pres., 1982-83, chair program and edn. 1983-84; vol. hydrologist Ariz. Land Dept., Tucson, 1983; reader grants Tandy Corp., Tucson, 1983; cons. environmentalist Tex Com. on Natural Resources, 1989-93. Editor Wordsmith's Forge Quar., 1991-93; contbr. articles and papers to profl. publs. Vol. leader wildlife and ecology project Hunt and Rockwall Counties (Tex.) 4-H, 1985-90. With USN, 1967-71, Vietnam, with Res. Mem. VFW, Noncommd. Officers Assn. (life), Vietnam Vets Am. (life), Audubon Soc. (coord. field trips Tucson chpt. 1994), Nature Conservancy, Mus. Natural History. Home: 4716 W Knollside St Tucson AZ 85741-4630

ROGERS, JOHN HEADLEY, educator; b. Richmond, Ky., Mar. 8, 1947; s. Glenn Clive and Agnes Amerine R. BA, Ctr. Coll., 1969; MA, Ind. U., 1973, PhD, 1977. Tchr. Pendelton County H.S., Falmouth, Ky., 1969-71; lectr. Ind.-Purdue U., Indpls., 1977-80, Morehead (Ky.) State U., 1980-81; prof. English Vincennes (Ind.) U., 1982—. Contbg. author: British Romantic Poets, 1990, British Romantic Writers, 1991; 18th Century Literary Biographers, Encyclopedia of the Essay, 1997; editor: British Short Fiction, 1918-1945, 1996. Pres. Old Town Players Cmty. Theatre, Vincennes, 1993-96, v.p., 1991-93. Mem. AAUP, Nat. Coun. Tchrs. English, Modern Lang. Assn., Popular Culture Assn., Phi Delta Kappa (found. rep., pres. 2000—). Democrat. Methodist. Avocations: theatre, travel, reading, music. Home: 1507 E Saint Clair St Vincennes IN 47591-4817 Office: Vincennes U 1002 N 1st St Vincennes IN 47591-1500

ROGERS, JOHN JAMES WILLIAM, geology educator; b. Chgo., June 27, 1930; s. Edward James and Josephine (Dickey) R.; m. Barbara Bongard, Nov. 30, 1956; children: Peter, Timothy. BS, Calif. Inst. Tech., 1952, PhD, 1955; MS, U. Minn., 1952. Lic. geologist, N.C. From instr. to prof. Rice U., Houston, 1954-75, master Brown Coll., 1966-71, chmn. geol. dept., 1971-74; W.R. Kenan Jr. prof. geology U. N.C., Chapel Hill, 1975-97, W.R. Kenan Jr. prof. geology emeritus, 1997—. Author: A History of the Earth, 1993, History and Environment of North Carolina's Piedmont, 1999; co-author: Fundamentals of Geology, 1966, Precambrian Geology of India, 1987; co-editor: Holocene Geology of Galveston Bay, 1969, Precambrian of South India, 1983, Basalts, 1984, African Rifting, 1989, People and the Earth, 1998; regional editor Jour. African Earth Scis., 1982-93; contbr. articles to profl. jours. Fellow Geol. Soc. Am., Geol. Soc. India, Geol. Soc. Africa (hon.); Am. Assn. Petroleum Geologists. Home: 1816 Rolling Rd Chapel Hill NC 27514-7502 Office: U of NC Dept Geology CB 3315 Chapel Hill NC 27599-0001

ROGERS, JOHN RUSSELL, manufacturing company executive, engineer; b. St. Louis, May 12, 1929; s. John Flint and Faye (Russell) R.; m. Lorraine Esther Klockenbrink, Sept. 15, 1951; children: John Oliver, Gail Joanne. AB in Econs., Washington U., St. Louis, 1951. Registered profl. engr., Mo., Ill. Mfg. engr. Day Brite Lighting Inc., St. Louis, 1957-59, plant supt. Tuptlo, Miss., 1959-64; plant mgr. White Rodgers Ltd., Markham, Ont., Can., 1964-66; ops. mgr. Metal Goods Corp., St. Louis, 1966-71; v.p., prin. Ross & Baruzzini, Inc., Cons. Engrs., 1971-84; pres. John R. Rogers Assocs., Inc., Cons. Engrs., 1984—. Bd. dirs. Grace Hill Settlement House, St. Louis, Grace Hill Child Devel. Bd.; pres. Thompson Ctr., St. Louis, 1984. Capt. U.S. Army, 1951-54. Mem. NSPE, Inst. Indsl. Engrs. (sr.), Am. Cons. Engrs. Coun., Assn. Profl. Materials Handling Cons. (pres. 1986-88, bd. dirs.), Materials Handling & Mgmt. Soc. (v.p. 1983—, bd. dirs.), Soc. Mfg. Engrs. (sr.), Rotary. Avocations: tennis, amateur radio, wood carving. Home and Office: John Rogers Assocs Inc 10332 Richview Dr Saint Louis MO 63127-1433

ROGERS, JOHN S. retired union official; b. Scranton, Pa., Nov. 19, 1930; Student, U. Wis., 1959-61, U. Mich., 1963; student spl. studies, Am. U., 1965-66, Harvard U. Bus. Sch., 1967. Internat. rep. United Brotherhood of Carpenters and Joiners of Am., Washington, 1958-65, asst. to gen. pres., 1966-74, dir. edn., 1971-82, mem. gen. exec. bd., 1974-78, gen. sec., 1978-91, ret., 1992. Sec.-treas. Suffolk County (N.Y.) Dist. Coun. Carpenters, 1957-58; v.p. N.Y. State Bldg. and Constrn. Trades Council, 1974-78, N.Y. State Fedn. Labor, 1974-78; pres. N.Y. State Coun. Carpenters, 1974-78; vice chmn. N.Y. State Commn. Jobs and Energy; mem. Suffolk County Pub. Employment Rels.s Bd.; vis. lectr. George Meany Ctr. Labor Studies. Author numerous trade union leadership mans. and instructional materials, 1966-79. Bd. dirs. L.I. action com. Assn. Help for Retarded Children, 1956-60; labor co-chmn United Cerebral Palsy, N.Y.C., 1977-78; v.p. Leukemia Soc. Mem. Harvard Trade Union Alumnae Assn. Home: 2713 Cranbrook Dr Boynton Beach FL 33436-5717

ROGERS, JON MARTIN, financial consultant, financial company executive; b. Piedmont, S.C., June 4, 1942; s. James Robert and Eunice (Ashley) R.; m. E. Jeanette Owen, June 16, 1962; children: E. Elaine, Jonette Marie, Melissa Anne. BS, Clemson U., 1964, MS, 1966; PhD in Fin. Mgmt., LaSalle U., 1994. CLU, Chartered Fin. Cons. Sales rep. Met. Life, Greenville, S.C., 1969-71, dist. sales mgr. Atlanta, 1972-74, regional sales mgr. Milw., 1975-81, Liberty Corp., Greenville, 1982-88; chmn. bd., chief exec. officer Rogers Fin. Group, 1989-2000; CEO Rogers Fin. Group LLC, 2000—. Ptnr. J&J Enterprises, Piedmont, S.C., 1975—; registered securities rep. Royal Alliance Assocs., Inc., N.Y.C., 1986—; adj. prof. Webster U. Mem. C. of C., Greenville, 1985-86; pres. Rep. Party precinct, Piedmont, 1988; bd. dirs. Optomist Club, Greenville, 1985; deacon, chmn. Washington Ch., Pelzer, S.C., 1985-87, 93-94. Capt. U.S. Army, 1967-69, Vietnam. Decorated Bronze Star. Mem. Nat. Assn. Life Underwriters (v.p. 1972-73, recipient awards), Internat. Assn. Fin. Planners, Nat. Assn. Securities Dealers, Million Dollar Round Table, Gideons Internat. Club (S.C. pres. 1985-87), Child Evangelism Fellowship (bd. dirs. 1988-89), Rotary Internat. (bd. dirs., pres. 1996-97). Baptist. Avocations: photography, golf, walking. Home: 21 Fairway Dr Piedmont SC 29673-9167 Office: Rogers Fin Group Inc 1 Whitsett St Greenville SC 29601-3136 E-mail: jrogers6@msn.com.

ROGERS, JUDITH W. federal judge; b. 1939; AB cum laude, Radcliffe Coll., 1961; LLB, Harvard U., 1964; LLM, U. Va., 1988; LLD (hon.), D.C. Sch. Law, 1992. Bar: D.C. 1965. Law clk. Juvenile Ct. D.C., 1964-65; asst. U.S. atty. D.C., 1965-68; trial atty. San Francisco Neighborhood Legal Assistance Found., 1968-69; atty. assoc. atty. gen.'s office U.S. Dept. Justice, 1969-71, atty. criminal divsn., 1969-71; gen. counsel Congl. Commn. on Organization of D.C. Govt., 1971-72; coordinator legis. program Office of Dep. Mayor D.C., 1972-74, spl. asst. to mayor for legis., 1974-79, corp. counsel, 1979-83; assoc. judge D.C. Ct. Appeals, 1983-88, chief judge, 1988-94; cir. judge U.S. Ct. Appeals-D.C. Cir., 1994—. Mem. D.C. Law Revision Commn., 1979-83; mem. grievance com. U.S. Dist. Ct. D.C., 1982-83; mem. exec. com. Conf. Chief Justices, 1993-94. Bd. dirs. Wider Opportunities for Women, 1972-74; mem. vis. com. Harvard U. Sch. Law, 1984-90; trustee Radcliffe Coll., 1982-88. Recipient citation for work on D.C. Self-Govt. Act, 1973, Disting. Pub. Svc. award D.C. Govt., 1983, award Nat. Bar Assn., 1989; named Woman Lawyer of Yr., Women's Bar Assn. D.C., 1990. Fellow ABA; mem. D.C. Bar, Nat. Assn. Women Judges, Conf. Chief Justices (bd. dirs. 1988-94), Am. Law Inst., Phi Beta Kappa. Office: US Ct Appeals 333 Constitution Ave NWRm 5800 Washington DC 20001-2866*

ROGERS, JUSTIN TOWNER, JR. retired utility company executive; b. Sandusky, Ohio, Aug. 4, 1929; s. Justin Towner and Barbara Eloise (Larkin) R. AB cum laude, Princeton U., 1951; JD, U. Mich., 1954. Bar: Ohio 1954. Assoc. Wright, Harlor, Purpus, Morris & Arnold, Columbus, 1956-58; with Ohio Edison Co., Akron, 1958-93, v.p., then exec. v.p., 1970-79, pres., 1980-91, chmn. bd., 1991-93; ret., 1993. Past mem. coal adv. bd. Internat. Energy Agy. Past pres., trustee Akron Cmty. Trusts, Akron Child Guidance Ctr.; past chmn. Akron Assoc. Health Agys., U. Akron Assocs., Ohio Electric Utility Inst.; past chmn., trustee, mem. exec. com. trustees Akron Gen. Health Sys.; trustee Sisler McFawn Found., Cmty. Health Ventures, Inc., VNS-Hospice Found.; former trustee Stan Hywet Hall & Gardens; past dir. Edison Elec. Inst., Elec. Power Rsch. Inst., Assn. of Edison Illuminating Co.'s. Mem. Portage Country Club, Mayflower Club, Rockwell Springs Trout Club (Castalia, Ohio), Princeton Club (N.Y.C.), Phi Delta Phi, Beta Gamma Sigma.

ROGERS, KAREN BECKSTEAD, gifted studies educator, researcher, consultant; b. L.A., Nov. 28, 1943; d. Maurice Webster and Helen Dorothy (Nalty) Beckstead; m. William Geoffrey Rogers, Sept. 11, 1965; children: Jeanne Elizabeth Rogers Armstrong, Jennifer Lynn Rogers Hasbrouck, William Carey. BA in Humanities, U. Calif., Berkeley, 1965; MA in Spl. Edn., San Diego State U., 1969; MA in Ednl. Psychology, U. Minn., 1983, PhD in Curriculum and Instrn. Sys., 1991. Cert. elem. tchr., Calif. Pace project coord. West Jr. Paul Schs., 1975-77; Omnibus project dir. Jr. League of Mpls., 1978-83; instr. U. Minn., Mpls., 1985—95; gifted studies instr. U. St. Thomas, St. Paul, 1984-87, asst. prof. gifted studies, 1987-93, assoc. prof. gifted studies, 1993-98, prof., 1999—. Cons., Burnsville, Minn., 1978—. Author: Ability Grouping and Gifted Learners, 1991 (Early Scholar award, 1991); contbg. editor Roeper Rev., 1994—, contbg. reviewer Jour. Secondary Gifted Edn., 1994—, Jour. for the Edn. of the Gifted, 1994—, Gifted Edn. Internat., 1998—, Gifted Child Quarterly, 1997—; contbr. 90 articles to profl. jours.; contbr. (chpts.) Re-forming of Gifted Education; Talent Development in Context. Docent Mpls. Inst. Arts, 1975—. Recipient Lifetime Achievement award Minn. Coun. for Gifted and Talented, 1989. Mem. Coun. for Exceptional Children (pres. The Assn. for the Gifted 1994-96), Nat. Assn. for Gifted Children, Am. Ednl. Rsch. Assn. Democrat. Avocations: art collecting, art history, music appreciation, writing, reading. Home: 14004 Whiterock Rd Burnsville MN 55337-4717 Office: U St Thomas MOH 217 1000 Lasalle Ave Minneapolis MN 55403-2025 E-mail: kbrogers@stthomas.edu.

ROGERS, KATE ELLEN, interior design educator; b. Nashville, Dec. 13, 1920; d. Raymond Lewis and Louise (Gruver) R.; diploma Ward-Belmont Jr. Coll., 1940; BA in Fine Arts, George Peabody Coll., 1946, MA in Fine Arts, 1947; EdD in Fine Arts and Fine Arts Edn., Columbia U., 1956. Instr., Tex. Tech. Coll., Lubbock, 1947-53; co-owner, v.p. Design Today, Inc., Lubbock, 1951-54; student asst. Am. House, N.Y.C., 1953-54; asst. prof. housing and interior design U. Mo., Columbia, 1954-56, assoc. prof., 1956-66, prof., 1966-85, emeritus, 1985—, chmn. dept. housing and interior design, 1973-85; mem. accreditation com. Found. for Interior Design Edn. Rsch., 1975-76, chmn. stds. com., 1976-82, chmn. rsch., 1982-85. Mem. 1st Bapt. Ch., Columbia, Mo.; bd. dirs. Meals on Wheels, 1989-91. Nat. Endowment for Arts rsch. grantee, 1981-82. Fellow Interior Design Educators Coun. (pres. 1971-73, chmn. bd. 1974-76, chmn. rsch. com. 1977-78); mem. Am. Soc. Interior Designers, (hon., medal of honor 1975), Am. Home Econs. Assn., Columbia Art League (adv. bd. 1988-93), Pi Lambda Theta, Kappa Delta Pi, Phi Kappa Phi (hon.), Gamma Sigma Delta, Delta Delta Delta (Phi Eta chpt.), Phi Upsilon Omicron, Omicron Nu (hon.). Democrat. Author: The Modern House, USA, 1962; editor Jour. Interior Design Edn. and Research, 1975-78.

ROGERS, KATHIE ANNE, accountant; b. Patchogue, N.Y., Aug. 20, 1951; d. William Arthur and Rosemary Anne (Falvey) Rogers; m James M. Castiglione, Sept. 27, 1969 (div.); children: James W., John S.; m. Timothy L. Buckley, July 21, 2002. AAS, Suffolk C.C., Riverhead, N.Y., 1982; BBA, Dowling Coll., 1984; MST, L.I. U., 1990; DBA, Nova Southeastern U., 2000. CPA, N.Y. Acct. Center Moriches (N.Y.) Libr., 1983—; adj. asst. prof. Suffolk C.C., Riverhead, 1987-94; instr., lectr. L.I.U.-C.W. Post Campus, Brookville, N.Y., 1992-94; asst. prof., chair dept. St. Francis Coll., Brooklyn Heights, 1994-2000; asst. prof. Suffolk C.C., Riverhead, 2000—. Mem. AICPA, Am. Acctg. Assn., Avocation: fitness enthusiast.

ROGERS, KEITH JOHNATHAN, artist; b. Ketchikan, Alaska, Aug. 25, 1940; s. Ralph Dawson and Charlotte Edna (Mercer) R.; m. Nilda Lou Yanke, Oct. 24, 1975 (div. Dec. 1987); children: David Keith, Faline Marie, Nathaniel Aaron. BA, Washington State U., 1976. Represented by Art Concepts Gallery, Tacoma. One man show East Pike Gallery, Seattle, 1993; exhibited in group shows at Tacoma Mall, Wash. (1st. place, hon. mention), 1968, Carnegie Art Mus., Walla Walla, 1977, Pendleton Art Show (hon. mention) Oreg., 1982, 47th Annual Lake Worth Art League Nat. Art Show, Lake Worth Fla. (1st. place in oils), 1988, Art Concepts Gallery, Tacoma, 1990, Shadowflight Gallery, Seattle, 1991, Annikin Gallery, Friday Harbor, 1994; contbr ink drawings to mags. such as The Artist's and American Artist. Donated paintings to March of Dimes Auction, 1959, others. Puffin Found. grantee, 1991. Avocations: canoeing, sailing, boating, restoring antique automobiles.

ROGERS, LEE FRANK, radiologist; b. Colchester, Vt., Sept. 24, 1934; s. Watson Frank and Marguerite Mortimer (Cole) R.; m. Donna Mae Brinker, June 20, 1956; children: Michelle, Cynthia, Christopher, Matthew. BS, Northwestern U., 1956, MD, 1959. Commd. 2d lt. U.S. Army, 1959, advanced through grades to maj., 1967; rotating intern Walter Reed Gen. Hosp., 1959-60; resident radiology Fitzsimons Gen. Hosp., 1960-63; ret., 1967; radiologist Baptist Meml. Hosp., San Antonio, 1967-68, U. Tex. Med. Sch., San Antonio, 1968-71, dir. residency tng., radiologist Houston, 1972-74; prof., chmn. dept. radiology Northwestern U. Med. Sch., Chgo., 1974-95; editor-in-chief Am. Jour. Roentgenology, Winston-Salem, N.C., 1995—; prof. radiology Bowman Gray Sch. Medicine Wake Forest Univ. Fellow Am. Coll. Radiology (past pres.), Am. Roentgen Ray Soc. (past pres.); mem. Assn. U. Radiologists (past pres.), Radiol. Soc. N.Am., Am. Bd. Radiology (past pres.), Alpha Omega Alpha. Episcopalian. Office: Am Jour Roentgenology 101 S Stratford Rd Ste 303 Winston Salem NC 27104-4224 *The source of most problems is previous solutions.*

ROGERS, LINDA GIBBONS, artist; b. L.A., Sept. 10, 1935; d. Louis Alberto and Louise Marie Gibbons; m. John W. Rogers, Dec. 27, 1955; children: Steve, Matthew, Glenn. BA, ucla, 1957; MA, Calif. State U., Long Beach, 1978, MFA, 1988. Cert. secondary sch. tchr. Calif. Art instr. L.A. City Schs., 1957—62, Tustin (Calif.) Adult Edn., 1973—83, Saddleback Cmty. Coll., Tuston, 1984—85; exhibitor Laguna (Calif.) North Gallery, 1998—. Exhibited in group shows at Laguna Art Fair, 1979—, Watercolor West, Riverside, Calif., 1979—. Mem.: Watercolor West (publicity chmn. 1979—, award 1980). Republican. Presbyterian. Home: 14721 Iverness Way Tustin CA 92780

ROGERS, LINDA LEE, artist; b. Bisbee, Ariz., Aug. 6, 1954; d. Raymond Boyd and Mary Lois (Dees) Mortenson; m. Richard Alan Rogers, Apr. 23, 1977. BA in Art, W. N.Mex. U., 1997. PADI diver basic/rescue. Keypunch operator WNMU, Silver City, N.Mex., 1973-76, UV Industries, Fierro, 1976-78; data analyst Gray & Gray, Inc., Silver City, 1978-82, 82-90; EMT-I Gila Regional Med. Ctr., 1988-92; artist Desert Reef Ind., Pinos Altos. Photographer: Studies in Black and White, 1997, White-tail Deer (Best of Show Grant County Art Guild 1997), Perspectives V, 1997; artist: (painting) Aquaology (Best of Show Grant County Art Guild 1996). Recipient 1st pl. photography award Grant County Art Guild, Pinos Altos, N.Mex., 1995, 96, Bookstore award W. N.Mex. U./McGay Gallery, Silver City, 1995, 1st pl. S.W. N.Mex. Ceramics Assn. divsn., 1998, Grant County Art Guild, 1998, Jubilation Gallery, 1998-99, Peterson's Photographic Mag., 1998, 75th Ann. Gila Wilderness Show, 1999, Stellei Gallery, Las Cruces, 1999, Potter's Guild Las Cruces, 2000. Mem. We. N.Mex. U. Art Club (treas. 1997), Grant County Art Guild (treas. 1995-96), Women's Caucus for Art. Avocations: scuba diving, photography, pottery, environmental issues, animal rights/rescue. Office: Desert Reef Industries PO Box 53078 Pinos Altos NM 88053-3078 E-mail: linda@desertreef.com.

ROGERS, LORENE LANE, university president emeritus; b. Prosper, Tex., Apr. 3, 1914; d. Mort M. and Jessie L. (Luster) Lane; m. Burl Gordon Rogers, Aug. 23, 1935 (dec. June 14, 1941). BA, N. Tex. State Coll., 1934; MA (Parke, Davis fellow), U. Tex., 1946, PhD, 1948; DSc (hon.), Oakland U., 1972; LLD,

Austin Coll., 1977. Prof. chemistry Sam Houston State Coll., Huntsville, Tex., 1947-49; research scientist Clayton Found. Biochem. Inst. U. Tex., Austin, 1950-64, asst. dir., 1957-64, prof. nutrition, 1962-80, assoc. dean Grad. Sch., 1964-71, v.p. univ., 1971-74, pres., 1974-79, mem. exec. com. African grad. fellowship program, 1966-71; research cons. Clayton Found. for Research, Houston, 1979-81. Vis. scientist, lectr., cons. NSF, 1959-62; cons. S.W. Research Inst., San Antonio, 1959-62; mem. Grad. Record Exams Bd., 1972-76, chmn., 1974-75; adv. com. ITT Internat. Fellowship, 1973-83; dir. Texaco, Inc., Gulf States Utilities, Republic Bank, Austin. Bd. dirs. Tex. Opera Theatre, Austin Lyric Opera; chmn. bd. trustees Texaco Philanthropic Found.; chmn. council of presidents Nat. Assn. State Univs. and Land-Grant Colls., 1976-77, mem. exec. com., 1976-79; mem. com. on identification of profl. women Am. Council on Edn., 1975-79, mem. com. on govt. relations, 1978-79; mem. target 2000 project com. Tex. A&M U. System; mem. ednl. adv. bd. John E. Gray Inst., Lamar U., Beaumont, Tex. Eli Lilly fellow, 1949-50; Recipient U. Tex. Students Assn. Teaching Excellence award, 1963; Disting. Alumnus award N. Tex. State U., 1972; Outstanding Woman of Austin award, 1950, 60, 71, 80; Disting. Alumnus award U. Tex., 1976; Honor Scroll award Tex. Inst. Chemists, 1980 Fellow Am. Inst. Chemists; mem. AAAS, Am. Chem. Soc. (sec. 1954-56), Am. Inst. Nutrition, Am. Soc. Human Genetics, Nat. Soc. Arts and Letters, Assn. Grad. Schs. (internat. edn. com. 1967-71), Sigma Xi, Phi Kappa Phi, Iota Sigma Pi, Omicron Delta Kappa. Achievements include research in hydantoin synthesis, intermediary metabolism, biochem. nutritional aspects of alcoholism, mental retardation, congenital malformations. Home: 4 Nob Hill Cir Austin TX 78746-3650

ROGERS, LOUIS JEROME, writer, educator; b. N.Y.C., Jan. 9, 1943; s. George and Hilda Aronowitz; children: Jennifer, Andrew, Peter. BA, CCNY, 1968; MA, NYU, 1970. Lectr. Hunter Coll., Bronx, NY, 1971—74; pub., editor-in-chief Innter Paths Mag., N.Y.C., 1976—84; writer, prodr. (TV series) Turning Inward , 1980—87; consulting editor Prentice Hall Press, 1988—89; pub., editor-in-chief PIR Publs., 1988—2001; affiliate prof. Sacred Heart U., Fairfield, Conn., 2000—. Author: Ladder to the Sky, Coming Alive, Mirror of the Unseen, Layla & Majnun, The Fire of Love, Islands of the Blessed. Served with USAR. Avocations: sailing, hiking, walking, bicycling. Home: 26 Reichert Cir Westport CT 06880 Office: Sacred Heart U 3131 Park Ave Fairfield CT 06432

ROGERS, MAL DAVID, JR. chemical engineer; b. July 26, 1922; BSChemE, U. Okla., 1948, M of Chem. Engring., 1949; cert. in nuc. engring., Pa. State U. and Argonne Nat. Lab., 1957. Chem. engr. Pure Oil, Wyo., 1949-51, Shell Chem., Deer Park, Tex., 1951-56; sr. chem., nuclear engr. Gen. Dynamics, Ft. Worth, 1956-59; sr. chem. engr., tech. staff Tex. Instruments, Dallas, 1959-90. Lt. USAF, 1942-45. Decorated DFC, Purple Heart; recipient Air medals with 2 oak leaf clusters USAF. Mem. N.Y. Acad. Scis. Home: 1240 Derby Dr Richardson TX 75080-5834

ROGERS, MALCOLM AUSTIN, museum director, art historian; b. Scarborough, Yorkshire, Eng., Oct. 3, 1948; s. James Eric and Frances Anne (Elsey) R. MA, Magdalen Coll., U. Oxford, Eng., 1976; DPhil, Christ Ch., U. Oxford, 1976. Asst. keeper Nat. Portrait Gallery, London, 1974-83, dep. dir., 1983-94; Ann and Graham Gund dir. Mus. Fine Arts, Boston, 1994—. Author: Blue Guide: Museums and Galleries of London, 1983; contbr. articles to profl. publs. Mem. Harvard overseers' com. Visit the Art Mus.; trustee Found. for the Arts, Nagoya, Japan, Wednesday Evening Club of 1777, Club of Odd Volumes. Fellow Soc. Antiquaries. Avocations: wine and food, travel, opera. Home: 540 Chestnut Hill Ave Brookline MA 02445-4155 Office: Mus Fine Arts 465 Huntington Ave Boston MA 02115-5597 E-mail: mrogers@mfa.org.

ROGERS, MARGARET ELLEN JONSSON, civic worker; b. Dallas, Aug. 7, 1938; d. John Eric and Margaret Elizabeth (Fonde) Jonsson; m. Robert D. Rogers; children: Emily, Erik, Laura. Student, Skidmore Coll., 1956-57, So. Meth. U., 1957-60. Civic worker, Dallas. Dir. Sta. KRLD radio, Dallas, 1970-74; dir. 1st Nat. Bank, Dallas, 1976-85, vice-chmn. dirs. trust com.; trustee Meth. Hosps., 1972-82, mem. exec. com., 1977-82, corp. bd. mem., 1990-94, mem. fin. com., 1990-93. Bd. dirs. Lamplighter Sch., 1967—; past mem. vis. com. dept. psychology MIT; mem. vis. com. Stanford U. Librs., 1984-90; bd. dirs. Callier Ctr. Communication Disorders, 1967-90, Winston Sch., 1973-85; bd. dirs., mem. exec. com. Episc. Sch., 1976-83; chmn. Crystal Charity Ball; co-chmn. nat. major gifts com. Stanford Centennial Campaign; bd. dirs. Children's Med. Center, Hope Cottage Childrens' Bur., Baylor Dental Sch., Dallas Health and Sci. Mus., Dallas YWCA, Day Nursery Assn.; mem. devel. bd. U. Tex., Dallas, 1988-90; bd. govs. The Dallas Found., 1988-95, chmn. investment com. 1991-92; trustee So. Meth. U., mem. investment com., 1988—, chmn. investment com., 1992-99; mem. vis. com. Dedman Coll., 1989-90; life trustee Dallas Mus. Art, mem. investment com.; mem. collectors com. Nat. Gallery Art; bd. dirs. Dallas Arboretum, 1991-92; trustee, mem. fin. com. Monterey Bay Aquarium, 1995—, chair devel. com., 1995-2000, mem. fin. com., 2000—. Mem. internat. coun. Mus. Modern Art; pres. MJR Fund, Jonsson Found. Margaret Jonsson Charlton Hosp. of Dallas named in her honor, 1973.

ROGERS, MARK CHARLES, physician, educator; b. N.Y.C., Oct. 25, 1942; s. Gerald and Inez (Kaufman) R.; m. Elizabeth Ann London, Dec. 30, 1972; children: Bradley, Meredith. BA, Columbia U., 1964; MD, SUNY, Syracuse, 1969; MBA, U. Pa., 1991; PhD (hon.), U. Ljubljana Slovenia, 1995. Diplomate Am. Bd. Anesthesiology (examiner 1982-96), Am. Bd. Pediatrics. Intern Mass. Gen. Hosp., Boston, 1969-70, resident, 1973-75, Boston Children's Hosp., 1970-71; fellow Duke U. Med. Ctr., Durham, N.C., 1971-73; asst. prof. dept. anesthesiology and critical care medicine Johns Hopkins U., Balt., 1977-79, assoc. prof., 1979-80, prof., chmn. dept., 1980-93, assoc. dean Sch. Medicine, 1990-93, dir. pediatric ICU, 1977-93; CEO Duke Hosp. and Health Network, 1993-96; sr. v.p. Perkin Elmer, Wilton, Conn., 1996-98; pres. Paramount Capital, N.Y.C., 1998—. Pres. Critical Care Found., Balt., 1981-96; cons. WHO, Bangkok, 1982-83. Editor in chief: Yearbook of Critical Care, 1983-96, Textbook of Pediatric Intensive Care, 1987, 91, 96, Principles and Practices of Anesthesiology, 1990; editor: Perioperative Management, 1989, dep. editor in chief Critical Care Medicine Jour., 1990-96. Maj. U.S. Army, 1975-77. Recipient Club of Mainz award, Mainz, Fed. Republic of Germany, 1981, award Assn. Univ. Anesthetists, 1980; Fulbright scholar, Ljubljana, Yugoslavia, 1990. Mem. Inst. Medicine. Home: 85 Lukes Wood Rd New Canaan CT 06840-2202 Office: Paramount Capital 787 7th Ave New York NY 10019-6018 E-mail: rogersmc@paramountcapital.com.

ROGERS, MEGAN ELIZABETH, mental health therapist; b. Bradford, Pa. d. James Russell and Martha Ann (Spencer) R.; m. Thomas J. Sarac, Oct. 17, 1992; 1 child, Isaac W. Sarac. BA in Psychology with deptl. honors., Coll. of Wooster, 1985; MA in Psychology, U. Chgo., 1991; Pys. D. in Clin. Psychology, Minn. Sch. Profl. Psychology, 2001. Social worker Selfhelp Cmty. Svcs., N.Y.C., 1985-87; tchg. asst. U. Chgo., 1988-89; rsch. asst. U. Chgo. Hosp., 1988-90; mental health therapist Counseling and Personal Devel., Phillips, Wis., 1991-94; intern in clin. psychology Battle Creek VA Med. Ctr., 1998-99; prof. psychology Inver Hills C.C., Minn., 2001—. Contbr. articles to profl. jours. Coord. soup and bread program, Wooster, 1982-85. U. Chgo. fellow, 1989. Mem. APA, Phi Beta Kappa. Democrat. Presbyterian. Home: 3401 Glen Oaks Ave White Bear Lake MN 55110

ROGERS, MICHAEL ALAN, writer; b. Santa Monica, Calif., Nov. 29, 1950; s. Don Easterday and Mary Othilda (Gilbertson) R.; m. Donna Rini, Oct. 9, 2000. BA in Creative Writing, Stanford U., 1972. Assoc. editor Rolling Stone Mag., San Francisco, 1972-76; editor-at-large Outside mag., 1976-78; vis. lectr. fiction U. Calif., Davis, 1980; sr. writer Newsweek mag., San Francisco, 1983—; mng. editor Newsweek InterActive, 1993-97; exec. prodr. broadband divsn. The Wash. Post Co., 1995-96; v.p. Washingtonpost.Newsweek Interactive, 1996—. Editor, gen. mgr. Newsweek.MSNBC.com, N.Y.C., 1998—. Author: Mindfogger, 1973, Biohazard, 1977, Do Not Worry About The Bear, 1979, Silicon Valley, 1982, Forbidden Sequence, 1988; contbr. articles to mags., newspapers. Recipient Disting. Sci. Writing award AAAS, 1976, Best Feature Articles award Computer Press Assn., 1987. Mem. Author Guild, Sierra Club. Achievements include patents for for multimedia storytelling technology. Avocations: travel, hiking. Office: Newsweek 251 W 57th St New York NY 10019-1802

ROGERS, MICHAEL BRUCE, orthodontist; b. Augusta, Ga., Aug. 25, 1945; s. Bruce Latimer and Dorothy (Baird) R.; m. Elizabeth Bennett, Dec. 21, 1968; children: Bruce, Kay, Alison, Lisa. Student, Emory U., 1963-65, DDS, 1969; cert. in orthodontics, Med. Coll. Ga., 1973. Diplomate Am. Bd. Orthodontists. Pvt. practice orthodontia, Augusta, 1973—. Part-time asst. clin. prof. Sch. Dentistry, Med. Coll. Ga., Augusta, 1973—. Capt. Dental Corps U.S. Army, 1971-73. Army Commendation Medal. Fellow: Ga. Acad. Dental Practice, The Internat. Acad. Dentists, Pierre Fauchard Acad., Ga. Dental Assn. (hon.; spkr.. of ho. 1999—), Internat. Acad. Dental Studies, Am. Coll. Dentists; mem.: Ea. Dist. Dental Soc. (pres. 1982—83), Med. Coll. Ga. Orthodontic Alumni Assn. (pres. 1981—83), Ga. Assn. Orthodontists (v.p. 1983—84, pres. 1984—85, exemplary svc. award), So. Assn. Orthodontists (spokesperson, sec.-treas. 1993—95, dir. 1995, pres. 2000), Am. Assn. Orthodontists (Ga. del., chmn. mem., ethics and jud. conderns, spkr. of house 1995—97, trustee 2001), ADA (del.), Omicron Kappa Upsilon, Psi Omega (pres. 1967—68). Roman Catholic. Home: 3214 Candace Dr Augusta GA 30909-3259 Office: 3545 Wheeler Rd Augusta GA 30909-6517

ROGERS, MIKE, congressman; b. June 2, 1963; BA, Adrian Coll. Spl. agt. FBI; small bus. owner; mem. Mich. Senate from 26th dist., 1995-2000; vice chmn. judiciary com. Mich. Senate, mem. fin. svc., human resources, labor and vet affairs coms., mem. reappropriations com., mem. tech. and energy commn., mem. banking and fin. com.; mem. U.S. Congress from Mich. 8th dist., Washington, 2001—; mem. fin. svcs. and transp. coms. Office: District Office 1327 E. Michigan Ave. Lansing MI 48912*

ROGERS, MILLARD FOSTER, JR. art museum director emeritus; b. Texarkana, Tex., Aug. 27, 1932; s. Millard Foster and Jessie Bell (Hubbell) Rogers; m. Nina Olds, Aug. 3, 1963; 1 child Seth Olds. BA with honors, Mich. State U., 1954; MA, U. Mich., 1958; studied with, John Pope-Hennessy; LHD, Xavier U., 1987. Gosline fellow Victoria and Albert Mus., London, Eng., 1959; curator Am. art Toledo Mus. Art, 1959-67; coord. Ford Found. intern program; dir. Elvehjem Art Ctr., prof. art history U. Wis., Madison, 1967-74; dir. Cin. Art Mus., 1974-94, dir. emeritus, 1994—. Vis. scholar Principia Coll., Elsah, Ill., 1982, Elsah, 84; pres. Mariemont Preservation Found., Ohio, 1982—91, Ohio, 1995—2001; adj. prof. U. cin., 1987—91. Author: Randolph Rogers, American Sculptor in Rome, 1971, Spanish Paintings in the Cincinnati Art Museum, 1978, Favorite Paintings from the Cincinnati Art Museum, 1980, Sketches and Bozzetti by American Sculptors, 1800-1950, 1988, Rich in Good Works: Mary M. Emery of Cincinnati, 2000, John Nolen and Mariemont: Building a New Town in Ohio, 2001. With AUS, 1954—56. Named Outstanding Citizen of Mariemont, 1991. Mem.: Am. Assn. Mus., Assn. Art Mus. Dirs. (hon.), Phi Beta Kappa. Office: 3610 Pleasant St Cincinnati OH 45227

ROGERS, NATHANIEL SIMS, banker; b. New Albany, Miss., Nov. 17, 1919; s. Arthur L. and Elizabeth (Bouton) R.; m. Helen Elizabeth Ricks, July 3, 1942; children— Alice, John, Lewis. AB, Millsaps Coll., 1941; MBA, Harvard U., 1947. With Deposit Guaranty Bank and Trust Co., Jackson, Miss., 1947-69, 1st v.p., 1957-58, pres., dir., 1958-69, 1st City Nat. Bank Houston, 1969-81, chmn., 1982-84; pres. 1st City Bancorp. of Tex., Houston, 1970-83, chmn., 1983-85, also bd. dirs. Chmn. Jackson United Givers Fund, 1957, pres., 1959, bd. dirs., 1958-61; pres. Andrew Jackson area coun. Boy Scouts Am., 1962; trustee Miss. Found. Ind. Colls., 1959-69; past pres., trustee Millsaps Coll.; trustee Methodist Hosp., Houston; chmn. ofcl. bd. Meth. ch. Lt. (s.g.) USNR, 1942-46. Named Outstanding Young Man of Year Jackson Jr. C. of C., 1955. Mem. Am. Bankers Assn. (pres. 1969-70), Miss. Bankers Assn. (pres. jr. banker sect. 1952-53, pres. 1964-65), Robert Morris Assocs. (pres. S.E. chpt. 1954-55, nat. dir. 1959-62), Assn. Res. City Bankers (bd. dirs. 1980-83), Jackson C. of C. (pres. 1962), Houston C. of C. (chmn. 1979-80), Young Pres.'s Orgn., Millsaps Coll. Alumni Assn. (pres. 1955-56), Newcomen Soc., Phi Beta Kappa, Omicron Delta Kappa, Kappa Alpha. Methodist.

ROGERS, OSCAR ALLAN, JR. college president; b. Natchez, Miss., Sept. 10, 1928; s. Oscar Allan and Maria Pinkie (Jackson) R.; m. Ethel Lee Lewis, Dec. 20, 1950; children— Christopher, Christian, Christoff. A.B., Tougaloo Coll., 1950; S.T.B., Harvard U., 1953, M.A.T., 1954; Ed.D., U. Ark., 1960; postgrad. U. Wash., 1968-69; LHD (hon.), Oklahoma City U., 1992,. Ordained to ministry Congl. Ch., 1953, Baptist Ch., 1955, Methodist Ch., 1962. Asst. pastor St. Mark Congl. Ch., Roxbury, Mass., 1951-54; dean-registrar Natchez Jr. Coll., Miss., 1954-56; pres. Ark. Bapt. Coll., Little Rock, 1956-59; dean students prof. social sci. and edn. Jackson State U., Miss., 1960-68, dean Grad. Sch., 1969-84; pres. Claflin Coll., 1984-94, pres. emeritus, 1994—; postdoctoral fellow U. Wash., Seattle, 1968-69; pastor Asbury-Kingsley Charge, Bolton and Edwards (Miss.) United Meth. Ch., 1962-84, Merton (Miss) Cir. United Meth. Chs., 1994-96. Served with USN, 1946-47. Recipient Order of the Palmetto Gov. Campbell (S.C.), 1994. Mem. Conf. Deans of Black Grad. Schs. (pres. 1975-76, treas. 1979-84), AAUP, NAACP, Phi Delta Kappa, Kappa Delta Pi, Alpha Phi Alpha. Democrat. Author: My Mother Cooked My Way Through Harvard with These Creole Recipes, 1973; Mississippi: The View from Tougaloo, 1979. Home and Office: 5932 Holbrook Dr Jackson MS 39206-2062

ROGERS, PATRICIA JUNE, clinical social worker; b. Cordele, Ga., June 15, 1930; d. Culma and Sara Van (Tison) Harris; m. William Judson Rogers, Apr. 30, 1961. BA, Tift Coll., 1951; MSW, Tulane U., 1963. Diplomate Am. Bd. Examiners in Clin. Social Work; lic. clin. social worker, Fla. Pub. welfare worker State of Ga., Tifton, 1951-56, sr. child welfare worker Savannah, 1957-60; dist. child welfare supr. State of Fla., Jacksonville, 1963-65; caseworker Family Counseling Svc., 1965-68; sr. clin. social worker Guidance Ctr., Inc., Daytona Beach, Fla., 1968-73, Human Resources Ctr., Daytona Beach, 1973-79, outpatient team leader, 1974-81, component dir., 1981; program dir. Act Corp., 1981-97; clin. cons. Our Chldrn. First, 1997—. Child and family therapist Counselling Assocs., Ormond Beach, Fla., 1985-95. Dep. registrar County of Volusia, Fla., 1990—. Mem. AAUW (mem.-at-large), NASW (cert., Social Worker of Yr. 1981), Am. Assn. Marriage and Family Therapists (clin. mem.). Democrat. Home: 918 Pineapple Rd Daytona Beach FL 32119-2543 Office: Our Children First 51 S Ridgewood Ave Daytona Beach FL 32114-4929

ROGERS, PATTIANN, poet, writer, poet, educator; b. Joplin, Mont., Mar. 23, 1940; d. William Tall, Irene Tall; m. John Robert Rogers; children: John, Arthur. BA, U.of Mo., 1961; MA, U.Houston, 1981. Vis. asst. prof. So. Meth. U., Dallas, 1985, U. of Houston, Houston, 1986; field faculty Vt. Coll. Norwich U., Montpelier, Vt., 1986—89; vis. writer U. of Tex., Austin, Tex., 1987; Richard Hugo disting. poet-in-residence U. of Mont., Missoula, Mont., 1988; vis. asst. prof. U. of Tex., 1988—89, U. of Mont., 1993; assoc. prof. U. of Ark., Fayetteville, Ark., 1993—97; vis. prof. Wash. U., St. Louis, 1995. Lectr. in field. Author: The Expectations of Light, 1981 (Best book of Poetry, 1982), The Tattooed Lady in the Garden, 1986, Legendary Performance, 1987, Splitting and Binding, Soerette Diehl Fraser/Natalie Ornish Poetry Award from the Texas Institute of Letters, 1989, Geocentric, 1993, Firekeeper, New and Selected Poems, 1994 (Natalie Ornish award for Poetry , 1995), Eating Bread and Honey, 1997, the Dream of the Marsh Wren, Writing as Reciprocal Creation, 1999, Song of the World Becoming, New and Collected Poems, 1981 - 2001, 2001, numerous poems. Recipient Theodore Roetheke prize, Poetry N.W. U. of Washington, 1981; fellow, Guggenheim Found., 1984—85, Lannan Found., 1991; grantee, Nat. Endowment for the Arts, 1982, 1988, Residency in Bellagio, Italy, Rockefeller Found., 2000. Home: 7412 Berkeley Cir Castle Rock CO 80108

ROGERS, PAUL A'COURT, management consulting executive; b. Detroit, Oct. 12, 1939; s. Noel and Jessie (Adams) Rogers; 1 child Ashley. BSBA, U. Md., 1982. Field engr. Gen. Dynamics, Pomona, Calif., 1962—65, project mgr., 1968—72; field engr. Hughes Aircraft Co., L.A., 1965—68; sys. engr. Sci. Mgmt. Assocs., Riverdale, Md., 1972—73, program mgr., 1975—82, corp. planner, 1982—; pres. R & M Assocs., 1989—; pres., CEO Parinc Corp. Project mgr. Sys. Cons., Washington, 1973—75; bd. dirs. Applied Sys. Planning, Mut. Human Concerns. Served with USNR, 1959—62. Mem.: Am. Soc. Naval Engrs., Project Mgmt. Inst., Am. Mktg. Assn., Am. Mgmt. Assn., Naval Inst. Democrat. Presbyterian. Home: 7524 Republic Ct Alexandria VA 22306 E-mail: paul_acourt@msn.com.

ROGERS, PAUL GRANT, lawyer, former congressman; b. Ocilla, Ga., June 4, 1921; s. Dwight L. and Florence (Roberts) R.; m. Rebecca Bell, Dec. 15, 1962; 1 child, Rebecca Laing. BA, U. Fla., 1942, JD, 1948, LLD; LLD (hon.), Fla. Atlantic U., U. Md., Duke U., L.I. U.; DSc (hon.), George Washington U., U. Miami, Albany Med. Coll. of Union U.; D.Sc. (hon.), Commonwealth U. Va.; HHD (hon.), Nova U.; LHD (hon.), N.Y. Med. Coll., N.Y. Coll. Podiatric Medicine, Hahnemann Med. Coll.; DMedSci (hon.), Med. U. S.C. Bar: Fla. 1948. Partner Burns, Middleton, Rogers, Farrell & Faust, 1952-69; mem. 84th-95th congresses from 11th Dist. Fla., 1955-79; chmn. house subcom. on health and environ. Hogan & Hartson, Washington, 1979—, ptnr., 1979—. Trustee Cleve. Clinic Found.; bd. dirs. Am. Cancer Soc., Scripps Rsch. Inst.; co-chmn. Nat. Coalition on Health Care; chmn. Nat. Osteoporosis Found., Friends of Nat. Libr. Medicine, Rsch! Am.; mem. nat. coun. Washington U. Sch. Medicine; mem. dean's coun. Harvard Sch. Pub. Health. Recipient Pub. Welfare medal Nat. Acad. Scis., 1982, Sea Grant award, 1985, Yr. 2000 award Nat. Cancer Inst., 1987, Albert and Mary Lasker Found. award for pub. svc., 1993, Hugo Schaefer award APHA, 1994, NOF Leadership award, 1995, Maxwell Finland award, 1996, Disting. Svc. award Am. Cancer Soc., 1997, Disting. Am. award Nat. Cmty. Pharmacists Assn., 1998, Environment Golden Eagle award Nat. Assn. Physicians, 1999, Paul G. Rogers award Assn. Acad. Health Ctrs., 1999, Golden Eagle award Physicians for the Environment, 1999. Mem. ABA, Fla. Bar Assn. (gov. jr. sect. 1952-53), Palm Beach County Bar Assn., D.C. Bar Assn., Inst. Medicine of NAS, Phi Delta Phi, Phi Delta Theta. Methodist (steward). Office: Hogan & Hartson 555 13th St NW Ste 1200 Washington DC 20004-1109

ROGERS, PETER PHILLIPS, environmental engineering educator, city planner; b. Liverpool., England, Apr. 30, 1937; came to U.S., 1960, naturalized, 1977; s. Edward Joseph and Ellen (Duggan) R.; m. Suzanne Ogden, Oct. 24, 1998; children: Christopher, Justin. B in Engring., Liverpool U., 1958; MS, Northwestern U., 1961; PhD, Harvard U., 1966. Asst. engr. Sir Alfred McAlpine & Sons Ltd., Cheshire, Eng., 1958-60; mem. faculty Harvard U., 1966—, Gordon McKay prof. environ. engring., 1974—, prof. city planning, 1974—. Mem. Center Population Studies, Harvard U. Sch. Pub. Health, 1974—; cons. World Bank, UN, U.S. Agy. for Internat. Devel., Govt. India, Govt. Pakistan, Govt. Bangladesh, Govt. Nepal, Govt. Italy, Govt. Costa Rica, Commonwealth P.R. Co-author: Urbanization and Change, 1970, Land Use and The Pipe: Planning for Sewerage, 1975, Resource Inventory and Baseline Study Methods for Developing Countries, 1983, Systems Analysis for River Basin Management, 1985, Evaluacion de Projectos de Desarrollo, 1990, America's Waters, 1993, Water in the Arab World, 1994, Measuring Environmental Quality in Asia, 1997, Science with a Human Face, 1997. Mem. World Commn. for Water in 21st Century. Gordon McKay tchg. fellow 1961; Radley rsch. student, 1962-64; doctoral dissertation fellow Resources for Future 1964-65; recipient Clemens Herschel prize Harvard U., 1964; Guggenheim fellow, 1973, 20th Century Found. fellowship, 1989. Mem. Third World Acad. Scis. (corr.), Indian Inst. Agrl. Engring. (life), Cosmos Club (Washington), Sigma Xi. Home: 20 Berkeley St Cambridge MA 02138 Office: Harvard U 116 Pierce Hall Cambridge MA 02138

ROGERS, PIER CAMILLE, management educator; b. Chgo., July 24, 1953; d. Walter Eugene and Alpha (Spikner) R.; m. David Nathaniel Heywood, July 23, 1983; 1 child, Gabriel Alexander Heywood. BA, Wellesley Coll., 1975; MA, MS, Boston U., 1977; PhD, N.Y.U., 1991. Coll. advisor Pine Manor Coll., Chestnut Hill, Mass., 1976-78; legis. liaison Mass. Dept. Pub. Welfare, Boston, 1977-79; agy. rels. mgr. United Way Mass. Bay, Inc., 1979-83; rsch. assoc. N.Y.C. Bd. Edn., 1984-85; lectr. N.Y.U., 1991-92; asst. project dir. La Guardia C.C., Long Island City, N.Y., 1990-92; asst. prof. non-profit mgmt. The New Sch. for Social Rsch., N.Y.C., 1992-99; chief oper. officer Assoc. Black Charities, 2001—; cons., Wagner Sch. at NYU, 2000; rsch. scholar Yale U., 1999-2000; lectr. Yale Div. Sch., 1999-2000. Evaluation cons. La Guardia C.C., 1992-93, 95, 97-98, United Way of N.Y.C., 1990, 94; mem. faculty South African Nonprofit Mgmt. Inst., New Sch. for Social Rsch., summer 1994, 95; Kellogg vis. fellow at PONPO, Yale U., vis. lectr. Yale Divinity Sch., 1998-99; advisor Privitization of Culture project NYU/New Sch. Mem. family life com. Unity Bapt. Tabernacle, Mt. Vernon, N.Y., 1988—; edl. adv. com. Bridges & Boundaries, N.Y.C., 1991; annual fund vol. Riverdale Country Sch., Bronx, N.Y., 1993—; mem. exec. com. Jack & Jill Am., Westchester chpt., 1992—, hist. 1999—. Mem. Am. Soc. Pub. Adminstrn., Assn. Rsch. Nonprofit Orgns. and Voluntary Action (bd. dirs. 1997—), Conf. Minority Pub. Adminstrns., Partnership African Am. Endowment Devel. (mem. nat. adv. coun.), Ctr. for Preventive Psychiatry (bd. dirs. 1999—). Avocations: collecting African American art, reading mysteries. Office: Associated Black Charities 105 E 22nd St New York NY 10010

ROGERS, RANDALL LLOYD, mechanical engineer; b. Madison, Ind., Apr. 11, 1923; s. Ernest Ellsworth and Lena Eugenia (Green) R.; m. Jane Coleman, Aug. 16, 1952; children: Susan, Betsy, Gerrit, Carol, Mary. BA in Physics and Math., Hanover Coll., 1951; MEd, Am. Internat. Coll., Springfield, Mass., 1957; cert. in computer tech., Worcester Poly. Inst., 1963; cert. in US explosive saftey laser tech., U. Mich., 1964; cert. in metallurgy, U. Ky. Registered profl. engr.; gen. tel. lic. Radio, tel. & chronograph technician Jefferson Proving Ground, Madison, Ind., 1943-45, test dir. 20mm cannon sect., 1945-52; mech. engr. rsch. & engring. Springfield (Mass.) Armory, 1952-67; mech. engr. Benet Weapons Lab. Watervliet (N.Y.) Arsenal, 1967-94. Math. tchr. evening radio, TV, Springfield, Mass., 1957-67. Co-author The History of Milton (Ind.) Baptist Church, 1992, (six vols. written for Benet Weapons Lab.) 20mm Gatling Type Guns, 1970; author numerous reports on ammunition acceptance and exptl. tests; editor radar drawings and tests. Mem. ins. commn., Monson, Mass., 1966, Watervliet Arsenal Mus. Soc., N.Y., 1992; pres. Silver St. Chapel, Monson. With USN, 3 mos. Commn. Ky. Col., State of Ky., 1947. Mem. Am. Soc. Metals, Masons, Shriners (Legion of Honor, pres. Hampshire). Baptist. Achievements include utilization of aircraft, police and fixed stations for ammunition testing; graphical method for determining rate of fire of automatic cannons; 120mm plans for rapid fire gun loader. Avocations: Leicester Cable TV-Channel 13, genealogy, mil. history. Home: 2 Tanglewood Rd Leicester MA 01524-1618

ROGERS, RAYMOND JESSE, retired federal railroad associate administrator; b. Eugene, Oreg., Mar. 1, 1941; s. Raymond Everett and Virginia Elaine (Simpkins) R.; m. Joan Katherine Peterson, June 6, 1964 (div. Aug. 1974); 1 child, Virginia Arlene; m. Kim Lien Nguyen, Dec. 26, 1974; children: Kim Lan, Vincent Minh. Student, Santa Rosa (Calif.) Jr. Coll., 1960-61, U.S. Army Non-commd. Officer Acad., Anchorage, Alaska, 1963, U. Md., 1967-74, Fed. Exec. Inst., Charlottsville, Va., 1981. Lic. real estate agt., Va. Sr. asst. mgr. Household Fin. Corp., Md., 1964-67; contract specialist Dept. Navy, Washington, 1967-71; contract svcs. officer AID, Saigon, Vietnam, 1971-76; contracting officer Dept. Transp., Fed. R.R. Adminstrn., Washington, 1976-80, dir. fin. svcs., 1980-84, assoc. adminstr. for adminstrn., 1984—2002, CFO, CIO, 1994—2002. Leader local group Boy Scouts Am., Vienna, Va., 1987-92, Izaac Walton League of Am., Am. Legion, Am. Assn. of Retired Persons. Sgt. U.S. Army, 1961-64. Decorated Vietnam Civilian Svc. medal. Mem. U.S. Sr. Exec. Svc., Fed. Exec. Inst. Alumni Assn. Avocations: fishing, hiking, camping, waterskiing. Home: 102 Yeonas Dr SW Vienna VA 22180-6557

ROGERS, RHONWYN VONCELLE, therapist, psychology educator; b. Atlanta, Mar. 11, 1949; d. Billy Rudolph Smith and Nonye S. Shepherd; m. Robert Lewis Rogers, Sr., Dec. 12, 1970; children: Robiaun Leurise Charles, Robert Lewis, Jr. BA, Bennett Coll., Greensboro, N.C., 1970; MEd, Georgia State U., Atlanta, 1978; EdD, U. Sarasota, Fla., 2001. Cert. N. Am. Assn. Masters in Psychology. Planner, evaluator Econ. Opportunity Atlanta, 1970-73; sch. psychometrist N.W. Ga. Cesa, Rome, 1979-85; exec. dir. Archdiocese of Atlanta, 1986-92; practicum New Vision Counseling Ctr., State Mountain, Ga., 1997-98; advanced practicum Hub Counseling and Psychoeducational Ctr., Tucker, 1999-2000; adj. prof. Gordon Coll., Barnsville, 2001—. Bd. dirs. Interfaith Coalition of Met. Atlanta; adv. bd. Glenmary Rsch. Ctr., Atlanta; adv. com. Atlanta Olympic Games; cons. Pres. Jimmy Carter's Symposium for Interfaith Leaders. Cons. King Day, The Martin Luther King Svc., Atlanta, 1988-91, Pres. Nelson Mandela's Tour, Atlanta; vol. Beginners Paradise Preschool, Atlanta, 1996-97. Grantee Funding Oral History Program, Private Found., 1992. Mem. Nat. Assn. Sch. Psychologist, ACA, APA, Assn. Transpersonal Psychology, Ga. Assn. Sch. Psychologist. Avocations: Karate, dancing, singing, quilting, travel. Home: 3059 Pomona Way East Point GA 30344 E-mail: ms.roneewiz@att.net.

ROGERS, RICHARD DEAN, federal judge; b. Oberlin, Kans., Dec. 29, 1921; s. William Clark and Evelyn May (Christian) R.; m. Helen Elizabeth Stewart, June 6, 1947; children— Letitia Ann, Cappi Christian, Richard Kurt. BS, Kans. State U., 1943; JD, Kans. U., 1947. Bar: Kans. 1947. Ptnr. firm Springer and Rogers (Attys.), Manhattan, Kans., 1947-58; instr. bus. law Kans. State U., 1948-52; partner firm Rogers, Stites & Hill, Manhattan, 1959-75; gen. counsel Kans. Farm Bur. & Service Cos., 1960-75; judge U.S. Dist. Ct., Topeka, 1975—. City commr., Manhattan, 1950-52, 60-64, mayor, 1952, 64, county atty., Riley County, Kans., 1954-58, state rep., 1964-68, state senator, 1968-75; pres. Kans. Senate, 1975. Served with USAAF, 1943-45. Decorated Air medal, Dfc. Mem. Kans., Am. bar assns., Beta Theta Pi. Clubs: Masons. Republican. Presbyterian. Office: US Dist Ct 444 SE Quincy St Topeka KS 66683

ROGERS, RICHARD F. construction company executive, architect, engineer; b. Chgo., July 25, 1942; s. Frank S. and Emily H. (Novak) R.; m. Christina L. Rogers, June 30, 1963; children: Mitchell, Cynthia. B in Architectural Engineering, U. Ill., Chgo., 1964. Registered architect, Ill., Wis., Mich., profl. engr., Ill. Architect Einstein Assocs. Inc., Skokie, Ill., 1963-69; v.p. Land Am. Corp., Chgo., 1969-70; project architect M.A. Lombard Constrn. Co., Alsip, Ill., 1970-73; sr. project mgr. W.E. O'Neil Constrn. Co., Chgo., 1973-78; pres. A.C.M. Assocs. Inc., Mt. Prospect, Ill., 1978—. Mem.: AIA. Office: 1306 S Wolf Rd Wheeling IL 60090-6444

ROGERS, RICHARD HUNTER, lawyer, business executive; b. Flushing, N.Y., Sept. 11, 1939; s. Royden Harrison and Frances Wilma (Hunter) R.; children: Gregory P., Lynne A., Reade H. BS in Bus. Adminstrn, Miami U., 1961; JD, Duke, 1964. Bar: Ill. 1964, Ohio 1973. Atty. Continental Ill. Nat. Bank, Chgo., 1964-65; sr. atty. Brunswick Corp., 1965-70; corporate counsel The A. Epstein Cos., Inc. (real estate developers), 1970-73; v.p., gen. counsel, sec. Price Bros. Co., Dayton, Ohio, 1973-82; v.p., divsn. mgr. Water Systems Tech. div. Price Bros. Co., 1982-85; pres. Internat. divsn. Price Bros. Co., 1986—88; pvt. practice law, 1988—; pres. Richard H. Rogers & Assocs. LPA. Pres. adv. coun. Miami U. Bus. Sch.; bd. dirs. Red and White Club, Miami U.; mem. Washington Twp. Task Force on Future Govt.; trustee Woodhaven, Inc.; mem. Washington Twp. Zoning Commn., 1990—, chmn., 1999—. Mem. ABA (forum com. on constrn.), Ill. Bar Assn., Ohio Bar Assn., Dayton Bar Assn. (chmn. corp. law dept. com. 1983-84, exec. com. 1986-87, editor Bar Briefs 1990-91), Miami U. Alumni Assn. (pres.), Miami U. Pres.'s Club. Office: 7333 Paragon Rd Ste 200 Dayton OH 45459-4157 Address: PO Box 751144 Dayton OH 45475-1144 E-mail: rhrlawoffice@aol.com.

ROGERS, RICHARD LEE, educator; b. N.Y.C., Sept. 17, 1949; s. Leonard J. and Beverly (Simon) R.; m. Susan Jane Thornton, Aug. 14, 1976; children: Caroline, Meredith. BA, Yale U., 1971, MA in Religion, 1973; postgrad., U. Chgo., 1977-80; MS in Edn., Bank St. Coll. Edn., N.Y.C., 1989. Tchr. Foote Sch., New Haven, 1974-77; devel. assoc. U. Chgo., 1980-81, spl. asst. to v.p. planning, 1981-82; spl. asst. to pres. New Sch. Social Rsch., N.Y.C., 1982-83, sec. of corp., then v.p., sec., 1983-94; pres. Coll. for Creative Studies, Detroit, 1994—. Office: Coll for Creative Studies 201 E Kirby St Detroit MI 48202-4048 E-mail: rrogers@ccscad.edu.

ROGERS, RICHARD MEAD, food service executive; b. Montclair, N.J., Oct. 7, 1942; s. George and Doris Hayward Rogers; m. Joan Ruperti Gerdau, Oct. 26, 1968; children: Gregory Theophilus, Alec Nicoll Mead. BA in Econ., Hobart Coll., 1963; postgrad., U. Pa., 1964. CFA. Securities analyst Union Svc. Corp., N.Y.C., 1964, 65-67; v.p. White, Weld & Co., Inc., 1967-74; portfolio mgr. GE Pension Trust, Stamford, Conn., 1974-76; pres. The Otto Gerdau Co., N.Y.C., 1976-89, Rogers Internat. Ltd., Portland, Maine, 1990—. Fundraiser Portland Symphony Orch., 1996—; vestry St. John's Episcopal Ch., Stamford, 1972-76; grand argentier Commanderie De Bordeaux, N.Y.C., 1989—, grand chambellan, 2000—. With USAR, 1964-65. Mem. Choral Art Soc., Camphill Found. (treas. 1996—2001), Prouts Neck Country Club, Prouts Neck Yacht Club, The Cumberland Club. Republican. Avocations: sailing, singing, golfing, tennis, chess. Home: Chiara 21 Atlantic Dr Scarborough ME 04074 Office: Rogers Internat Ltd 58 Fore St Portland ME 04101

ROGERS, RICHARD MICHAEL, judge; b. Lorain, Ohio, Dec. 8, 1944; s. Paul M. and Lillie (Morris) R.; m. Sophia Lydia Wagner, Dec. 23, 1967; children: L. Danielle, David K., Marisa D., Matthew D. BA, Ohio No. U., 1966, JD, 1972. Bar: Ohio 1972, U.S. Dist. Ct. (no. dist.) Ohio 1973. Assoc. Martin, Hall & Rogers, Marion, Ohio, 1972-76; ptnr. Rogers & Rogers, 1976-81; asst. law dir., police prosecutor City of Marion, 1973-74; pub. defender, 1975; asst. county prosecutor Marion County, 1976-81; village solicitor La Rue, Ohio, 1976-81; judge Marion Mcpl. Ct., 1982-88, Common Pleas Ct., 1989—; mem. traffic rules rev. commn. Ohio Supreme Ct., 1989—. Judge dist. competition Nat. Bicentennial Competition on Constitution and Bill of Rights, 1988, judge state competition, 1988—, judge nat. competition, 1989, 93, 95; instr. faculty Ohio Jud. Coll. Mem. Marion Active 20/40 Svc. Club, 1973-84, treas., 1976-80, bd. dirs., 1976-84, pres., 1980-81; chmn. bd. dirs., pres., co-founder Marion Area Driver Re-edn. Project, 1974-81; pres. Big Bros./Big Sisters Marion County, 1986-87, bd. dirs., 1984-88; mem. sch. bd. St. Mary's Elem. Sch., 1985-88, v.p., 1986, bd. dirs. Marion Cath. High Sch. Endowment Fund, 1986—, v.p., 1991—; mem. Marion Cath. Jr./Sr. High Sch. Bd., 1988-94, pres., 1990-91; mem. fellow in criminal justice steering com. Marion campus Ohio State U., 1996—; mem. paralegal adv. com. Marion Tech. Coll., 1994-96; trustee Ohio State Bar Found., 1997-99. With U.S. Army, 1968-69. Mem. Ohio State Bar Assn. (modern cts. com. 1982-85, jud. adminstrn. and legal reform com. 1982-93, legis. subcom. of jud. adminstrn. and legal reform com. 1989-93, coun. dels. 1991-93, bd. govs. 1996-99, chmn. govt. affairs com. 1998-99, vice-chair criminal justice com. 2001—), Marion County Bar Assn. (pres. 1985-86), Ohio Jud. Conf. (gen. adminstrn. 1984-85, vice chair family matters video com. 1991—, chmn. subcom. legal matters video, civil law and procedure com. 1991-95, editl. bd. Ohio Jury Instrn. 1995—), Ohio Bar Coll., Marion County Law Libr. Assn. (trustee 1982—, pres. 1991-93), Ohio Common Pleas Judges Assn., Delta Theta Phi, Sigma Pi. Republican. Methodist. Avocations: golf, scuba diving. Home: 310 Edgefield Blvd Marion OH 43302-5802 Office: Common Pleas Ct Marion County Courthouse 100 N Main St Marion OH 43302-3089 *Notable cases include: Hines vs. Thermal-Gard of Ohio, Inc., 1988, applicability of home solicitation sales acts, Augenstein vs. Augenstein, deeds sufficient to convey, reserve life estate, Scioto Conservancy Dist., Establishment of Conservancy Dist.*

ROGERS, RITA, artist, conservator; b. Miami, Fla., Feb. 28, 1936; d. James Louis Rogers and Selma Lazeroff; m. David Randal McCarthy, Dec. 26, 1958 (div. Dec. 1988); children: Daniel, Teresa, Sara, Judith, Elizabeth, Andrew. Student, Arts Students League, 1952-54, Worcester Mus. Sch., Yale U., 1956; BA, Bard Coll., 1957; postgrad., Columbia U., 1957-58. Mgr. Ark Press, Portsmouth, R.I., 1970-81; reviews editor Anyart Jour., Providence, 1975-79; writer Art New England, Boston, 1982-83; conservator Redwood Libr., Newport, R.I., Preservation Soc. Newport. Instr. painting Stonehill Coll., Brockton Mus., Elderhostel; instr. painting and printmaking Portsmouth Abbey Sch.; instr. printmaking Newport Art Mus.; instr. mural painting workshop Arts Reach, Festival for Disabled; lectr. in field. One-woman shows include Newport Art Assn., 1977, Stonehill Coll., North Easton, Mass., 1979, Wheeler Gallery, Providence, 1979, Hartford (Conn.) Coll. Women, 1982, Ilgenfritz Gallery, Newport, 1983, Sarah Doyle Gallery, Providence, 1984, Hilson Gallery, Deerfield, Mass., 1984, Portsmouth (R.I.) Abbey Sch., 1985, Bridgewater (Mass.) State Coll., 1986, Providence Coll., 1988, Hydrangea House Gallery, Newport, 1990, Arnold Art Gallery, Newport, 1990, DeBlois Gallery, Newport, 1992, Gallery One, Providence, 1992, Salve Regina U., Newport, 1996, Boarshead Gallery, Newport, 1999, Deblois Gallery, Newport, 2000, premier Etage, Newport, 2001; exhibited in group shows at Hera Gallery, Wakefield, R.I., 1987, Salve Regina Coll., Newport, 1987, Joan Hodgell Gallery, Sarasota, Fla., 1990, Warwick (R.I.) Art Mus., 1991, 92, 93, Swinburne Sch., Newport, 1992, numerous others; represented in permanent collections. Recipient Martha Rockwell Millet prize Bristol (R.I.) Mus., 1983, 2d prize R.I. State Coun. Arts, 1989, Best in Show award Warwick Mus., 1991, 92, 1st Pl. award Warwick Mus., 1993; named Artist-in-residence R.I. State Coun. Arts, 1981, Artists-in-the-schs. R.I. State Coun. Arts, 1989; grant-in-aid R.I. State Coun. Arts, 1976; Painting fellow Ossabaw Found., 1981, Yaddo, 1981, 85, Va. Ctr. Creative Arts, 1982, 84, 86; grantee Adolph and Esther Gottlieb Found., 1982; Artist Project grantee R.I. State Coun. Arts, 1991. Office: 23 3rd St Newport RI 02840-2422

ROGERS, RITA DORIS LUCK, family nurse practitioner; b. Lincoln County, Kans., Feb. 6, 1948; d. Ernest F. and Rea N. (Nelson) Luck; m. Eugene W. Rogers, Mar. 15, 1969; children: R. Michelle, Sara J (dec.), Brandon G. Diploma, Wesley Sch. Nursing, 1969; BSN cum laude, Ft. Hays State U., 1992, MSN, 1996. RN, ARNP, Kans., Mo., Nebr.; cert. family nurse practitioner ANCC, AANP. Float, relief charge nurse Wesley Med. Ctr., Wichita, 1969-71; charge nurse Mitchell County Hosp., Beloit, Kans., 1971-72; dir. PHN III Jewell County Health Dept., Mankato, 1973-74; office nurse Dr. A.T. Llana, Superior, Nebr., 1975-76; head nurse, evening supr. Jewell County Hosp., 1977-97; family nurse practitioner Dr. Judith Butler, Superior, 1997-99; interim dir. nursing Sterling (Kans.) Presbyn. Manor, 1998-99, Kansas City Presbyn. Manor, 1999; nurse cons. Presbyn. Manors Mid-Am., Wichita, Kans., 1999—; interim nurse practitioner Statcare Minor Emergency Ctr., Salina, 2000. Allied health adj. faculty Cloud C.C., Concordia, Kans., 1988—' Perkins grant coord. North Ctrl. Kans. Area Vo-Tech., Beloit, 1988; county chair Am. Cancer Soc., Mankato, 1972-74; sec. Jewell County Mental Health Assn., 1973-75; parliamentarian Dist. XII Kans. State Nurses Assn., Topeka, 1975-79; infection control com. Brodstone Meml. Hosp., Superior, Nebr., med. staff mem., 1997-98; mem. nursing standards com. Presyn. Manors of Mid-Am., 1998—. Columnist Rap with Rita, 1973-74. County and club leader 4-H, Jewell County, 1977-91, 2000—; tchr. Sunday sch. Luth. Ch., Mankato, 1979-82. Scholar Kans. Health Found., 1993, Midwest Organ Bank, 1994, Ft. Hays State U., 1994, Dane G. Hansen Found., 1994, Kans. Nurses' Found. Wesley Alumni, 1995. Mem. Am. Acad. Nurse Practitioners, Great Plains Nurse Practitioner Soc., Nebr. Nurse Practitioners, Ft. Hays Grad. Nurses Assn., Ft. Hays Alumni Assn., Sigma Theta Tau. Avocations: gardening, crocheting, computing, family. Home: Rte 2 Box 252 309 N Columbus St Jewell KS 66949-9582 Office: PO Box 20440 6525 E Mainsgate Wichita KS 67208-1440 Fax: 785-428-7929. E-mail: rrogers2@pmma.org.

ROGERS, ROBERT BURNETT, naval officer; b. Plainfield, N.J., May 25, 1931; s. Jack Willoughby and Margaret (Snyder) R.; m. Jeanne Weaver, Mr. 15, 1956 (dec. Sept. 1978); children: Robert Burnett (dec.), Steven Michael, John Weaver, Kathryn Patricia; m. Marolyn Maybelline Templeton, May 25, 1981. BS, U.S. Naval Acad., 1954; MS, George Washington U., 1968. Commd. ensign U.S. Navy, 1954, advanced through grades to rear adm., 1981; comdg. officer U.S.S. Austin, Norfolk, Va., 1977-78; asst. chief of staff Naval Surface Force Atlantic, Atlantic Fleet, Norfolk, 1978-80, dep. comdr. Norfolk, 1982-83; comdr. Destroyer Squadron Eight, Mayport, Fla., 1980-81; dep. chief of staff Supreme Allied Command Atlantic, Norfolk, 1981-82; comdr. Amphibious Group Two, 1983-86; dir. logistics Atlantic Fleet, 1986, ret., 1986. City Commr. Fernandina Beach, 1994, mayor, 1996-97, city commr., 1999-2002. Decorated Legion of Merit with 4 gold stars; recipient William S. Sims award Navy League U.S. Mem. U.S. Naval Inst., Marine Corps. Assn. Roman Catholic. Home: 2056 Oak Marsh Dr Fernandina Beach FL 32034-2407

ROGERS, ROBERT REED, manufacturing company executive; b. Oak Park, Ill., Feb. 22, 1929; s. Glen Charles and Lucile (Reed) R.; m. Barbara June Fain, Feb. 22, 1951 (div.); children: Robin, Janeen, Kevin; m. Celeste Sim, Sept. 29, 1993. BS in Chemistry, Berea Coll., 1951; MBA, Ill. Inst. Tech., 1958, postgrad., 1959-62. Asst. mgr. metallurgy rsch. dept. Armour Rsch. Found., Ill. Inst. Tech., Chgo., 1955-56, faculty econs. dept., 1956—62; cons. McKinsey & Co., Inc., 1962-64; mgr. devel. planning, profl. group Litton Industries, Inc., 1964-67; pres. N.Am. subs. Muirhead & Co., Ltd., 1967-68; group v.p. Am. Electric Inc. subs., City Investing Co., 1968-70; pres. Cleartight Corp., 1971-73, Newport Internat. Metals Corp., 1973-76, Kensington Assocs., Inc., Newport Beach, Calif., 1976-83; pres., chmn. bd. Proteus Group, Inc., 1981-83; pres., chmn. bd. dirs. Comparator Sys. Corp., 1983-96; chmn. bd. UltraCard, Inc., 1997-98, Vantage Assocs. Inc., Newport Beach, 1998—. Officer USN, 1951-55. Decorated Knight of Grace Sovereign Order St. John; Machinery and Allied Products Inst. fellow, 1956-62; Berea Coll. grantee. Mem. Navy League, Mensa, Intertel. Democrat. Mem. Ch. Of Religious Science. Home: 311 Bay Hill Dr Newport Beach CA 92660-5235 Office: MagnaCarda Inc 5001 Birch St Newport Beach CA 92660-2116 Business E-Mail: rrr@magnacardainc.com. E-mail: rogersrr@compuserve.com.

ROGERS, ROBERT ERNEST, medical educator; b. West Palm Beach, Fla., Nov. 16, 1928; s. Jessie H. and Willie L. (Bahr) Rogers; m. Barbara Ann Hill, May 16, 1950; children: Robert E. Jr., Stephanie Ann Thompson, Cheri Lee Heck. BS, John B. Stetson U., 1949; MD, U. Miami, 1957. Diplomate Am. Bd. Ob-gyn. Commd. 1st lt. M.C., U.S. Army, 1952, advanced through grades to col., 1971; intern Brooke Gen. Hosp., San Antonio, 1957-58, chief resident ob-gyn, 1960-61; resident in ob-gyn Jackson Meml. Hosp., Miami, Fla., 1958-60; fellow gynecology M.D. Anderson Hosp., Houston, 1965-66; asst. chief ob-gyn Tripler Army Med. Ctr., Honolulu, 1966-69; chmn. ob-gyn Walter Reed Med. Ctr., Washington, 1969-70, Madigan Army Med. Ctr., Tacoma, 1970-74; ret. U.S. Army, 1974; prof. Ind. U. Sch. Medicine, Indpls., 1974—, also chief gynecol. div., 1974—; chief ob-gyn svd. Wishard Meml. Hosp., 1983-87. Contbr. articles to profl. jours. Mem.: ACOG (chmn. gynecol. practice com., commr. practice), AMA, Internat. Soc. Advancement Humanistic Studies Medicine (pres. 1997—98), Soc. Gynecol. Oncologists, Soc. Gynecol. Surgeons (pres. 1983—84). Office: Ind U Sch Medicine 550 University Blvd Indianapolis IN 46202-5149 E-mail: Bobberogers@insightbb.com., reroger@iupui.edu.

ROGERS, ROBERT HAMER, small business executive; b. Great Falls, S.C., Mar. 18, 1928; s. Robert Hamer and Clara Elizabeth (Ellenberg) R.; m. Marjorie Amplis Hoyle, Oct. 4, 1952 (dec.). Student, Howard Bus. Coll., 1955. Owner Bobby's Music Shop, Shelby, N.C., 1948—. Treas., chair Dem. Party, Cleveland County, 1960-70, 10th dist. chair, 1985-90; chair Goodwin House Found., 1990-95; chair Isothermal Planning and Devel. Commn., 1997-2000. Sgt. U.S. Army, 1950-52. Mem. Optimist Club (pres., treas., internat. gov., lt. gov., v.p.). Democrat. Methodist. Office: Bobby's Music Shop 215 E Marion St Shelby NC 28150-4609

ROGERS, ROBERT MARK, physician; b. Upper Darby, Pa., June 9, 1933; s. John Francis and Clara (Baumann) R.; m. Sandra Betz, Feb. 14, 1968; children: Janet Marie, Robert Mark, Linda, William Bradford, David Philip. BA cum laude, LaSalle Coll., Phila., 1956; MD, U. Pa., 1960. Intern Hosp. of U. Pa., 1960-61, chief emergency svcs., 1968-69, founder, dir. respiratory ICU, 1968-72, dir. pulmonary disease sect. tng. program, 1970-72; resident Case Western Res. U. Hosps., Cleve., 1961-63; fellow in pulmonary disease VA Hosp., 1963-64, U. Pa., 1964-65, postdoctoral trainee in physiology, 1966-68, asst. prof. medicine and assoc. in physiology, 1968-72; prof.medicine, assoc. prof. physiology Okla. Health Scis. Ctr. Coll. Medicine, 1972-80, also chief pulmonary disease sect., dept. medicine, dir. clin. pulmonary physiology lab. hosp. and clinics; dir. Comprehensive Lung Ctr. U. Pitts. Med. Sch., 1990-97, chief pulmonary, allergy and critical care medicine, 1980-96, prof. medicine, 1980—. Editor: Respiratory Intensive Care, 1977; mem. editl. bd. Current Opinion in Pulmonary Medicine and Critical Care; contbr. rsch. articles to profl. publs. Mem. ACP (U.S. rep. to Chinese Med. Assn. 1979, founding editor-in-chief audio cassettes program 1978-80), Am. Thoracic Soc. (founding dir. Learning Resources Ctr. 1971-77, Presdl. commendation 1977, Outstanding Achievement award 2002), Am. Fedn. Clin. Rsch., Am. Coll. Chest Physicians (Presdl. citation 1998), Am. Physiol. Soc., Soc. Critical Care Medicine, Am. Heart Assn., Ctrl. Soc. Clin. Rsch., So. Soc. Clin. Rsch., Pa. Thoracic Soc. (pres. 1985-88), Coll. Physicians Phila. Home: 4116 Bigelow Blvd Pittsburgh PA 15213-1408 Office: U Pitts Sch Medicine 628 NW Montefiore Hosp 3459 Fifth Ave Pittsburgh PA 15213 E-mail: rogersrm@msx.upmc.edu.

ROGERS, RONALD, public relations executive; Pres., CEO Rodgers & Assocs., L.A. Office: 1875 Century Park E Ste 300 Los Angeles CA 90067-2504*

ROGERS, RUBY ELIZABETH, artist; b. New Kensington, Pa., June 24, 1952; d. Claude Ray and Dora Jean (Remaley) Downing; m. Kenneth Michael Rogers, June 26, 1970; children: Aaron Nathan, Jason Edward. Student, Fed. Tax and Bus. Sch., Chgo., 1990, NRI Sch. Computer Programming, Washington, 1990-93, ICS Sch. Med. Tng., Scranton, Pa., 1996—. Owner Kenneth M. Rogers Gen. Contractor, Claysville, Pa., 1975-90, Art by R. Rogers, Claysville, 1991—; mem. staff Home and Cmty. Based Svcs., Inc. United Cerebal Palsy of Southwestern Pa., 1998—. Exhibited in group show at Calif. State Coll., 1969 (cert. of merit Washington County Fedn. Women's Clubs). Occupl. therapy vol. Washington (Pa.) Hosp., 1994-96, United Cerebral Palsy of Southwestern, Inc., Washington, 1994—; ptnr. Spl. Olympics, 1996098; mem. The Shepherd's Guide, Christian Advertisers Orgn., 1995-99; mem. WQED Pitts. Pub. Broadcasting, 1990—. Mem. AAUW, Nat. Mus. Women in Arts. Republican. Lutheran. Avocations: reading, walking, gardening. Home and Office: 1285 Templeton Run Rd Claysville PA 15323-1147

ROGERS, RUTHERFORD DAVID, librarian; b. Jesup, Iowa, June 22, 1915; s. David Earl and Carrie Zoe (Beckel) R.; m. E. Margaret Stoddard, June 4, 1937; 1 child, Jane Shelley; m. Bernette W. Barton, Feb. 28, 2002. BA, U. No. Iowa, 1936, Litt.D., 1977; MA, Columbia, 1937, BS (Lydia Roberts fellow), 1938; D.Library Adminstrn. (hon.), U. Dayton, 1971. Asst. N.Y. Pub. Library, 1937-38; reference librarian Columbia Coll. Library, Columbia U., 1938- 41, acting librarian, 1941-42, librarian, 1942-45; research analyst Smith, Barney & Co., N.Y.C., 1946-48; dir. Grosvenor Library, Buffalo, 1948-52, Rochester Pub. Library, 1952-54; chief personnel office N.Y. Library, 1954-55; chief reference dept., 1955-57; chief asst. librarian of Congress, Washington, 1957-62, dep. librarian of, 1962-64; dir. univ. libraries Stanford U., 1964-69; univ. librarian Yale U., 1969-85, univ. librarian emeritus, 1985—. Founder, chmn. bd. dirs. Rsch. Librs. Group, Inc.; mem. Exam. Com. for Pub. Librarians' Certs., N.Y. State, 1951-54; mem. U.S. Adv. Coun. Coll. Libr. Resources; bd. govs. Yale U. Press; bd. dirs., v.p. H.W. Wilson Found., 1969-98; chmn. program mgmt. com. Internat. Fedn. Libr. Assns. Author: Columbia Coll. Library Handbook, 1941, (with David C. Weber) University Library Administration, 1971; also articles in profl. jours. Served from pvt. to 1st sgt. Air Transp. Command USAAF, 1942-43; from 2d lt. to capt., planning officer, chief, spl. Planning Div., Office Asst. Chief Staff, Plans, Air Transport Command 1943-46. Decorated officier de L'Ordre de la Couronne Belge; recipient U. No. Iowa Alumni Achievement award, 1958, Disting. Alumni award Columbia U. Sch. Libr. Svc., 1992, medal Internat. Fedn. of Libr. Assns., 1977. Fellow Am. Acad. Arts and Scis.; mem. A.L.A. (chmn. com. Intellectual Freedom 1950-51), (1950-60), (2d v.p. 1965-66), (mem. exec. bd. 1961-66), (trustee endowment fund), Assn. Research Libraries (dir., pres. 1967-68), N.Y. Library Assn., AAUP, Bibliog. Soc. Am., Assn. Coll. and Reference Libraries, Blue Key, Kappa Delta Pi, Sigma Tau Delta, Theta Alpha Phi. Clubs: Grolier; N.Y. Library (N.Y.C.), Columbia U. (N.Y.C.), Yale (N.Y.C.); Cosmos (Washington), Kenwood Country (Washington); Roxburghe (San Francisco); Book of Calif. Home: 1081 Lakemont Ct Winter Park FL 32792-5025

ROGERS, SHARON J. education consultant; b. Grantsburg, Wis., Sept. 24, 1941; d. Clifford M and Dorothy L (Beckman) Dickau; m. Evan D Rogers, June 15, 1962 (div. Dec. 1980). BA summa cum laude, Bethel Coll., St. Paul, 1963; MA in Libr. Sci., U. Minn., 1967; PhD in Sociology, Wash. State U., Pullman, 1976. Lectr., instr. Alfred (N.Y.) U., 1972-76; assoc. prof. U. Toledo, 1977-80; assoc. dean Bowling Green (Ohio) State U. Librs., 1980-84; univ. libr. George Washington U., Washington, 1984-92, asst. v.p. acad. affairs, 1989-92, assoc. v.p. acad. affairs, 1992-97, co-dir. Univ. Teaching Ctr., 1990-97; cons. in higher edn. and librs., 1997—. Mem Online Computer Library Ctr Users Coun, 1985—92; pres. Online Computer Library Ctr Users Coun., 1989—90, rsch. advt. com., 1990—92; trustee Online Computer Library Ctr. Users Coun., 1992—2002; chair Online Computer Library Ctr Users Coun, 1996—99; exec dir Assn Libr. and Info. Sci. Edn., 1997—2000. Contbr. articles to profl jours. Bd dirs CapAccess, 1993—97, treas, 1993—95; bd dirs ACLU, Toledo, 1978—84. Fellow Jackson, Univ Minn, 1964—65; grantee NSF, Wash State Univ, 1969—72. Mem.: ALA (exec coun 1987—91, pub comt 1989—93, chair 1990—93), Universal Serials and Book Exchange (bd dirs, treas 1987), Washington Research Library Consortium (bd dirs 1987—90), Am Sociological Asn, Asn Col and Research Libraries (pres 1984—85). Home: 2922 24th St N Arlington VA 22207 E-mail: sroger7@attglobal.net.

ROGERS, SHEILA WOOD, elementary and secondary school educator; b. Louisville, May 10, 1949; d. John Cornelius and Gladys Virginia (Moody) Wood; m. Franklin Don Rogers, Mar. 23, 1969; children: Pamela, Rachel. BA in Math., Christopher Newport Coll., 1974; MEd in Computer Edn., Hampton U., 1986. Tchr. Hampton (Va.) City Schs., 1974-86; instructional specialist York County Pub. Schs., Yorktown, Va., 1986-91; tchr. York County (Va.) Schs., 1991—. Math. cons. Nat Diffusion Network, Washington, 1988-90; York County rep. Consortium for Interactive Instrn., Norfolk, Va., 1986-91; facilitator Star Schs. Tech. Edn. Rsch. Ctrs., U. Va., Boston, Charlottesville, 1989-91; coord. computer contest U. Wis., Peninsula Coun. of Math. of Va., Hampton, Newport News, 1980-86. Pres. PTA, R. E. Lee Elem. Sch., Hampton, 1987-89, C. A. Lindsay Middle Sch., Hampton, 1989-91; pres. on coun. Hampton Coun. of PTAs, 1990-91, 1st v.p., 1991-93; dir. preschool choirs West Hampton Bapt. Ch., Hampton, 1988—. Mem. NEA, Va. Edn. Assn., York County Edn. Assn. (sec. 1996-2002, v.p. 2002—), Va. Coun. Tchrs. Math., Peninsula Coun. Tchrs. Math., Greater Peninsula Swimming Assn. (rep. 1989-96), Delta Kappa Gamma (mem. Gamma Phi chpt.). Baptist. Avocations: music, reading, handcrafts. Home: 109 Prince James Dr Hampton VA 23669-3609 Office: Grafton Mid Sch Grafton Dr Yorktown VA 23693

ROGERS, SHERRY ANNE, physician; b. Syracuse, N.Y., Apr. 15, 1943; d. Rodney Wellington and Jayne Hammond; m. Robert Hamilton Rogers, June 30, 1970. BA, Syracuse U., 1969; MD, SUNY, 1969-70. Intern Health Scis. Ctr. Syracuse, 1969-70; pvt. practice pediat., Auburn, N.Y., 1970-71; emergency physician Cmty. Gen. Hosp., Syracuse, 1971-72; pvt. practice family medicine, 1972-85; pvt. practice environ. medicine, 1978—. Lectr. in field. Author: (book) Tired or Toxic?, 1990, Wellness Against All Odds, 1994, Chemical Sensitivity, 1995, You Are What You Ate, The E.I. Syndrome, 1997, Depression Cured At Last, 1997, No More Heartburn, 2000, The Cure is in the Kitchen, The Scientific Basis of Environmental Medicine Techniques, 2000, Total Wellness, 2000, 2001, Pain Free in 6 Weeks, 2001; editor (ed environm med sect): Internal Medical World Report, 1992—93; contbr. articles to profl jours, book. Office: NE Ctr Environ Med 2800 W Genesee St Syracuse NY 13219-1451

ROGERS, SHERYL ANN, small business owner, educator; b. Hillsdale, Mich., Nov. 29, 1949; d. Floyd Orlando and Pauline Doris Foulk; m. Richard Hobart Rogers, Apr. 20, 1968 (div. May 1976); children: Jeffrey L., Paul Michael; m. Richard Reyes Ramirez, Feb. 15, 1993. BA magna cum laude, Hillsdale Coll., 1988. Cert. secondary edn. Mich., Ohio, Tex. Computer specialist Hillsdale Cmty. Health Ctr., Hillsdale, Mich., 1979—86; tchr. North Ctrl. HS, Pioneer, Ohio, 1988—89; tchr. pvt. sch. Seville, Spain, 1990—91; tchr. Brownsville (Tex.) Ind. Sch. Dist., 1991—97; owner Daybreak Moving and Storage, San Benito, Tex., 1992—. Agent Paul Arpin Van Lines, Greenwich, RI, 2000—. Recipient Grace Nichols prize for Spanish, 1987, 1988; scholar Margaret E. Wadley scholarship, 1985, 1986, Velma Knight scholarship, 1985, 1986. Mem.: Houston Womens Bus. Coun., Harlingen Hispanic C. of C., Brownsville C. of C., Southwest Movers Assn. Avocations: movies, music, travel, home interior, dogs. Home and Office: RR 6 Box 117-G San Benito TX 78586 Fax: 956-350-6177. E-mail: texasmover@aol.com.

ROGERS, STEPHEN HITCHCOCK, former ambassador; b. Flushing, N.Y., June 21, 1930; s. Francis Walker and Julia (Wheeler) R.; m. Kent Brain, June 23, 1956; children: Kryston R. Fischer, F. Halsey, Julia L., John H. BA, Princeton U., 1952; MA, Columbia U., 1956; MPA, Harvard U., 1962. Fgn. svc. officer Dept. of State, 1956-93; econ. counselor Am. Embassy, London, 1970-72; counselor U.S. Mission to OECD, Paris, 1972-75; office dir. Bur. Inter.-Am. Affairs Dept. of State, Washington, 1975-78; econ. counselor Am. Embassy, Mexico City, 1978-82; prof. Nat. Def. U., Washington, 1982-85; econ. counselor Am. Embassy, Pretoria, South Africa, 1986-90, amb. Mbabane, Swaziland, 1990-93. Bd. dirs. Cen. Atlantic Conf., United Ch. of Christ, 2000—. Lt. (jg) USN, 1952-55. Recipient Outstanding Civilian Svc. award Dept. of Army, 1985. Mem. Am. Fgn. Svc. Assn., Nassau Club (Princeton, N.J.). Mem. United Ch. of Christ. Home: 3803 Ivydale Dr Annandale VA 22003-2006

ROGERS, STEVEN CHARLES, electronics technician; b. Perryton, Tex., July 21, 1953; s. Billy Dale Rogers and Patricia Ann (Higgins) Garward; m. Bunjong Chettha, Jan. 25, 1974; children: Mongkon, Nopadon, Johnny, Thomas. Sales rep. Hawkins Subway, Cocoa Beach, Fla., 1991; laborer Norrell Temp. Svcs., Dayton, Ohio, 1991, CBS Temp. Svcs., Dayton, 1991-92; sales rep. Jolly Pirate Doughnuts, 1992; security pers. Am. Security, Ft. Walton Beach, Fla., 1992, Pinkerton Security, Ft. Walton Beach, 1992-95; electronics assemblyman Manpower Temporary Svcs., 1995; constrn. worker Greg Cartwright, 1995; electronics assembler Mfg. Tech. Inc., 1995-98. Contbr. poetry to The Garden of Life, 1995, Poetic Voices of America, 1995, Back Road Travels, 1995, Spirit of the Age, 1995, also others. With USAF, 1971-91. Baptist. Avocations: reading, chess, fishing. Home: 2004 Las Vegas Trail Navarre FL 32566 Office: Metric Systems Corp 645 Anchors St NW Fort Walton Beach FL 32548-3888

ROGERS, STEVEN RAY, physicist; b. Tachikawa, Honshu, Japan, Dec. 6, 1952; came to U.S., 1953; s. Culis Doyle Martin and Mary Lu (Bowles) Rogers; m. Robina Rae Behel, Dec. 27, 1975; children: Miranda Rae, Kellina Gail. BA in Math./Physics magna cum laude, U. No. Colo., 1975; MS in Physics, Kans. State U., 1977. Rschr., instr. Kans. State U., Manhattan, 1975-79; tech. staff ElectroMagnetic Applications, Lakewood, Colo., 1979-82; lead engr. MITRE Corp., Colorado Springs, 1982—. Cons., advisor on system survivability and hardening North Am. Aerospace Def. Command * U.S. Space Command, Colorado Springs, 1982—; adj. prof. Webster U., Colorado Springs, 1994. Contbr. articles to Jour. Physics: Atomic & Molecular, IEEE Transactions on Nuclear Sci. and other profl. jours. Mentor for gifted students Colorado Springs Schs. #20, 1992-93; host family for cadet USAF Acad., Colorado Springs, 1994-98. Recipient Program Recognition award MITRE Corp., 1988, 1996. Mem. IEEE (sr., chmn. Pikes Peak sect. 1993-94), Sigma Pi Sigma, Lambda Sigma Tau. Achievements include co-invention of global situation awareness information distribution system (patent); co-founder of programs that sustain the survivability of NORAD and U.S. Space Command systems; evaluation and integration of NORAD systems. Home: 5510 Broadmoor Bluffs Dr Colorado Springs CO 80906-7971 Office: MITRE Corp 1150 Academy Park Loop Ste 212 Colorado Springs CO 80910-3716

ROGERS, SUSAN (SUE ROGERS), data processing consultant; b. Jonesboro, Ark., Aug. 22, 1949; d. Eric J. Jr. and Suzanne (Payne) Rogers; m. Joseph Edward Aldrich, July 3, 1974 (div. Mar. 1985); m. Walter J. Wakefield, Oct. 1, 1994; stepchildren: Alisha M. Wakefield, Jeremy W. Wakefield. BS in Math, U. Ark., 1975. Cert. computer programmer. Chief programmer State Ark. Dept. Fin. and Adminstrn., Little Rock, 1973-76; programmer, analyst Dillards Dept. Stores, 1976-77; mem. profl. staff Cutler-Williams Inc., Dallas, 1977-79; sr. tech. cons. Sterling Software (formerly Informatics Gen.), 1979-86; pvt. practice cons., 1986-87; programmer, analyst Fed. Res. Bank, 1988-89; pvt. practice, 1989—; tchr. disabled students Dallas County Community Coll., 1990-92. Tchr. jewelry making Dallas Community Coll., 1988-91. Exhibitions at State Fair of Tex., 1985-87, Plano Art Assn., 1985, Arlington Art Assn., 1986, North Lake Coll., 1987. Vol. arts and crafts program Dallas County Juvenile Detention Ctr., 1985-89. Mem. Craft Guild of Dallas, Soc. Creative Anachronism, North Tex. Herb Club, Mensa. Home and Office: 2925 Seymour Dr Dallas TX 75229-4932

ROGERS, THEODORE COURTNEY, investment company executive; b. Lorain, Ohio, Aug. 25, 1934; s. William Theodore and Leona Ruth (Gerhart) Rogers; m. Elizabeth B. Barlow, June 28, 1984; children from previous marriage: Pamela Ann Rogers Harmon, Thomas Courtney Jr. BS in Social Sci., Miami U., Oxford, Ohio, 1956, LHD (hon.), 2001; postgrad., Johns Hopkins U., 1957; MBA summa cum laude, Marquette U., 1968. With Armco Inc., 1958-80; pres. Olympic Fastening Systems, 1970-74; with Bathey Mfg. Co. subs., 1970, group v.p. indsl. products, 1971-74; exec. v.p. Nat. Supply Co. subs., Houston, 1974-76, pres., 1976-80, v.p. parent co., 1976-79, group v.p. parent co., 1979-80; pres., COO NL Industries, Inc., N.Y.C., 1980-82, pres., CEO, 1982-83, chmn., pres., CEO, 1983-87; ptnr. Am. Indsl. Ptnrs., N.Y., 1987—. CEO & chmn. Bucyrus Internat.; chmn. Stanadyne Automotive Corp., Consoltex Inc.; bd. dirs. Gt. Lakes Carbon Corp., chmn. Nat. coun. Theatre Comm. Group; trustee St. John's Coll.; bd. dirs. United Cerebral Palsy Rsch. and Ednl. Found., Inc., Lincoln Ctr. Peforming Arts, City Ctr. Music and Drama, Nat. Ocean Industries Assn.; chmn. bd. dirs. Theatre for New Audience; former chmn. Ctr. Cmty. Interests; emeritus chmn. N.Y.C. Ballet; bd. dirs., trustee Ballet Rev. Qur. Lt. USN, 1956—58. Mem.: Poets and Writers (bd. dirs.), Bus. Roundtable, World Press Orgn., N.Y. Soc. Libr. (trustee), Petroleum Equipment Suppliers Assn. (bd. dirs.), Grolier Club, Sky Club, Houston Country Club, Achilles Track Club (founder, bd. dirs.), Century Assn. (N.Y.), Ramada Club, Links Club, Econs. Club (N.Y.), Univ. Club (Milw.), Union Club (Cleve.), Met. Club (Washington), Beta Gamma Sigma (bd. dirs.). Office: Am Indsl Ptnr 551 5th Ave Ste 3800 New York NY 10176-0001

ROGERS, THEODORE OTTO, JR. lawyer; b. West Chester, Pa., Nov. 17, 1953; s. Theodore Otto and Gladys (Bond) R.; m. Hope Tyler Scott, Nov. 7, 1981; children: Helen Elliot, Theodore Scott, Robert Montgomery Bond. AB magna cum laude, Harvard U., 1976, JD cum laude, 1979. Bar: N.Y. 1980, U.S Ct. Appeals (2nd cir.) 1984, U.S. Dist. Ct. (so. and ea. dists.) N.Y. 1980, D.C. 1981, U.S. Ct. Claims, 1982, U.S. Supreme Ct. 1983, U.S. Ct. Appeals (6th and 10th cirs.) 1983, U.S. Ct. Appeals (1st cir.) 1984, U.S. Ct. Appeals (fed. cir.) 1986. From assoc. to ptnr. Sullivan & Cromwell, N.Y.C., 1979—. Co-author: (books) Employment Litigation in New York, 1996, Employment Law DeskBook for Human Resources Professionals, 2001. Mem. U.S. Presdl. Transition Team, 1980. Fellow Coll. Labor and Employment Lawyers; mem. N.Y. State Bar Assn. (co-chair individual rights and responsibilities com. labor and employment law sect.), Assn. of Bar of City of N.Y. (labor and employment law). Republican. Home: 535 E 86th St New York NY 10028-7533 Office: Sullivan & Cromwell 125 Broad St Fl 28 New York NY 10004-2489 E-mail: rogerst@sullcrom.com.

ROGERS, THOMAS FRANCIS, foundation administrator; b. Providence, Aug. 11, 1923; s. Thomas Francis and H. Ann (Flaharty) R.; m. Estelle E. Hunt, July 6, 1946; children: Clare, Judith Reynolds, Hope Grove. BS cum laude, Providence Coll., 1945; MA, Boston U., 1949. Rsch. assoc. Radio Rsch. Lab. Harvard U., Cambridge, Mass., 1944-45; TV engr. Bell and Howell Co., Chgo., 1945-46; electronics scientist AF Cambridge Rsch. Ctr., Cambridge, Mass., 1946-54; assoc. group leader MIT Lincoln Lab., 1951-53; lab. head AF Cambridge Rsch. Ctr., Bedford, Mass., 1954-59; div. head and steering com. mem. MIT Lincoln Lab., 1959-64; asst. dir. def. rsch. and engring. Office of Sec. Def., Washington, 1964-65, dep. dir. def. rsch. and engring., 1965-67; dir. rsch. and tech. Office of Sec. HUD, 1967-69; v.p. The Mitre Corp., Washington, Bedford, 1969-72; chmn. The Sophron Found., McLean, Va., 1980—; dir. U.S. Congress Office of Tech. Assessment Study on Civilian Space Stas. and U.S. Future in Space, Washington, 1982-84; from pres. to chief scientist The Space Transp. Assn., Arlington, Va., 1992—. Founding chmn. bd. dirs. External Tanks Corp., Boulder, Colo.; bd. dirs. Internat. Radio Satellite Corp., Washington, Space Destinations Svcs., Inc., 1994—; chmn. bd. dirs. Luna Corp., Great Falls, Va., 1991—; dir. Share Space Found., 2000; chmn. POLARIS Command-Comm. Co., USN, 1960-64; mem. Satellite Comm. Panel, Pres.'s Sci. Adv. Com., 1961-63; mem. Dept. Def. NASA Satellite Comm. Com., 1961-64; U.S.A. del. UN Conf. on Applications of Sci. and Tech. by Lesser Developed Nations, Geneva, 1963; mem. Fed. Aeronautics and Astronautics Coordinating Bd., 1965-67, Fed. Coun. on Sci. and Tech., 1967-69; mem. Space Program Adv. Coun., NASA, 1971-73, chmn. applications com., 1972-73; mem. NAS com. on regional emergency med. comm. systems, 1976-78, space applications bd. com. on NASA space comms. 1986-87, com. on antenna, satellite broadcasting and emergency preparedness for Voice of Am., 1986-88, adv. com. study space transp. U.S. Congrl. Office Tech. Assessment, 1994-95. Contbr. articles to jours., chpts. to books. Trustee X-Prize Found., 1995—. Recipient Outstanding Performance award CSC, 1957, cert. commendation Sec. Navy, 1961, Meritorious Civilian Svc. award and medal, Sec. Def., Constrn.'s Man of Yr. award Engring. News Record, 1969, Space Pioneer award Nat. Space Soc., 1988, Best Vision of the Future awrd Space Frontier Found., 1997, NASA Disting. Pub. Svc. award, 1999. Fellow IEEE (mem. aerospace policy com., chmn. 1991-95, Profl. Achievement award 1995); mem. Internat. Acad. Astronautics, Cosmos Club (Washington). Home and Office: 10655 Gramercy Pl Columbia MD 21044-7437

ROGERS, THOMAS SYDNEY, communications executive; b. New Rochelle, N.Y., Aug. 19, 1954; s. Sydney Michael Rogers Jr. and Alice Steinhardt; m. Sylvia Texon, Oct. 9, 1983; children: Robert, Jessica, Jason. BA, Wesleyan U., 1975; JD, Columbia U., 1979. Bar: N.Y. 1980, U.S. Dist. Ct. (so. and ea. dists.) N.Y. 1980, U.S. Ct. Appeals (D.C. cir.) 1981. Legis. aide to Congressman Richard Ottinger U.S. Ho. Reps., Washington, 1975-76, sr. counsel subcom. telecommunications, 1981-86; assoc. Lord, Day & Lord, N.Y.C., 1979-81; v.p. policy planning and bus. devel. Nat. Broadcasting Co., Inc., 1987-88; pres. NBC Cable, 1988-89, NBC Cable & Bus. Devel., 1989-99; exec. v.p. NBC, N.Y.C., 1992-99; vice chmn. NBC Internet, 1999; chmn., CEO Primedia, Inc., 1999—. Pres., CEO internat. coun. Nat. Acad. TV Arts and Scis., 1994-97, chmn., 1998-99; lectr. in field. Named one of Outstanding Young Men in Am., 1985. Mem. N.Y. State Bar Assn., Internat. Radio and TV Soc. Office: Primedia Inc 745 5th Ave Fl 23D New York NY 10151-0099

ROGERS, THOMASINA, federal commissioner; Student, Northwestern U.; JD, Columbia U. Chmn. Adminstrv. Conf. U.S., Washington, 1994-95; presdl. pers. staff The White House; dep. legal counsel, then legal counsel EEOC; mem. Occupl. Safety and Health Rev. Commn., 1998—. Bd. dirs. Children's Nat. Med. Ctr. Mem. Am. Arbitration Assn. (bd. dirs.) Office: Occupl Safety and Health Rev Commn 1120 20th St NW Washington DC 20036-3406*

ROGERS, TINA KAREN PROFITT, administrative assistant, writer; b. Irvine, Ky., May 10, 1963; d. Tracy Gene Profitt and Marylan Katherine (Hunley) Taylor; m. David Ray Rogers, Aug. 27, 1983 (div. Aug. 1997); children: Katherine Shanee, Autumn Gene. With First Security Nat. Bank, Lexington, Ky., 1980—83, Merryl Lynch, Lexington, 1983—86, Dr. Granacher, Lexington, 1993—95, Mecedes Benz Co., Lexington, 1995—97, The Bristol Group, Lexington, 1997—99, Lexing Granite Co.-Rock of Ages, Lexington, 1999—; indep. cons. Avon, 1995—. Pres. 4-H Club, Clay City, Ky., 1973—75; advocate Domestic Violence, Lexington, 1997; budget com. mem. Tates Creek Elem. Sch., 1990—95; tchr. Ch. at Tatesbrook, 1989—99. Democrat. Avocations: painting, woodworking, hiking, swimming, crafts. Home: 2816 Winter Garden Lexington KY 40517

ROGERS, WARD JUNIOR, retired industrial designer; b. Savanna, Ill., May 8, 1924; s. Charles Clarence Rogers and Lucille Mae Woods; m. Marilyn Ruth Edwards, May 30, 1945; children: Douglas, Renee, Toni, Ward J. Grad., Mpls. Sch. Fine Arts, 1947. Chef Old Elm Club, Highland Park, Ill., 1947—49; engr. Clinton Engine, Manquota, Iowa, 1950—51; engr., indsl. designer GE, Morrison, Ill., 1951—71; art dir. Color Arts Inc., Racine, Wis., 1971—74; owner Dairy Bar, Mt. Carroll, 1976—86; custodian US Post Office, 1973—91. Freelance designer Savanna Fabricators, Sterling (Ill.) Ambulance. Author: (column) Remember When, 1980. Pres. Art Guild, Morrison, Ill.; chmn. Mt. Carroll Hist. Soc., 1998—; precinct com. Dem. Party, Morrison. S/sgt. USMC, 1941—45, PTO, 2d lt. reserves U.S. Army, 1949. Mem.: VFW (life), Indsl. Design Inst., Am. Legion. Avocations: antiques, records, collecting cars, painting. Home: 207 E Rapp St Mount Carroll IL 61053

ROGERS, WARREN JOSEPH, JR. journalist; b. New Orleans, May 6, 1922; s. Warren Joseph and Rose Agatha (Tennyson) R.; m. Hilda Kenny, Dec. 23, 1943 (dec.); children: Patricia Ann, Sean; m. Alla Bilajiw, Dec. 26, 1973; 1 son, Michael (dec.). Student, Tulane U., 1940-41, La. State U., 1951. Copy boy, cub reporter New Orleans Tribune, 1939-41; copyreader, columnist New Orleans Item, 1945-47; reporter A.P., Baton Rouge, 1947-51, Washington, 1951-53, diplomatic corr., 1953-59; mil., fgn. affairs corr. assignments abroad Wash. Bur. N.Y. Herald Tribune, 1959-63; chief Washington corr. Hearst Newspapers, assignments abroad, 1963-66; Washington editor LOOK mag., 1966-69, chief, 1969-70; mil., fgn. affairs corr. Washington bur. Los Angeles Times, 1970-71; Washington columnist Chgo. Tribune-N.Y. News syndicate, 1971-73; v.p. pub. affairs Nat. Forest Products Assn., Washington, 1973-76; editorial dir. Plus Publs., 1977-78, v.p., editor-in-chief, 1978-79; free-lance, 1979—. Washington bur. chief The Trib of N.Y., 1977-78; editor White House Weekly, 1981-89; exec. editor Associated Features, Inc., Washington editor, 1992—; editor This Week in the White House, 1989-90, Georgetown Courier, 1991-92; bd. dirs. Nat. Press Found., Internet Guide, Inc.; founder Robert F. Kennedy Journalism awards; lectr. presdl. politics, mil. and fgn. affairs. Author: The Floating Revolution, 1962, Outpost of Freedom, 1965, (with others) An Honorable Profession: A Tribute to Robert F. Kennedy, 1968, (with Paul Watson) Sea Shepherd, 1982, When I think of Bobby: A Personal Memoir of the Kennedy Years, 1993. Served with USMCR, 1941-45. Recipient citation Overseas Press Club N.Y., 1963, Disting. Svc. award Nat. Press Found., 1991. Mem.: Nat. Press (pres. 1972), Federal City Club, Gridiron Club, Washington Ind. Writers. Home: 1622 30th St NW Washington DC 20007-2903 *In more than 50 years of reporting, I have learned that people yearn for the truth, as long as it is about somebody else. But they go to almost any length to conceal it or put a spin on it when it is about themselves. Yet, telling the truth is what a reporter must do. No wonder we rank behind Congress in the popularity polls.*

ROGERS, WAYNE L. political organization administrator; m. Valerie; children: Courtney, Kellyn. MBA, U.S. Naval Acad.; postgrad., Georgetown U. Pres. Synergics, Inc., Annapolis, Md.; chair Md. Dem. Party. Mem. nat. fin. bd., Leadership 2000 com. Dem. Nat. Com. Office: 188 Main St Ste 1 Annapolis MD 21401*

ROGERS, WILLIAM, psychologist, behavior specialist, writer, lecturer, journalist; BA in Broadcast Journalism, L.A. Inst. Arts, 1970; BA in Psychology, We. Ill. U., Macomb, 1979; MS in Counseling Psychology, Our Lady of the Lake U., San Antonio, 1989; PhD in Psychology, Columbia Pacific U., San Rafael, Calif., 1993; postgrad., Rollo May Ctr. Social Rsch. Saybrook Inst., San Francisco, 1994. Fgn. and domestic correspondent ABC News, NBC News, UPI Internat., KTRH Radio News, WOAI Radio News, 1970-85. Exec. dir. Behavior Rsch. Inst. San Antonio. Author: The Technology of Behavior, 1993, The Behavior Management Handbook, 1994, Creating Positive Behavior, 1995, Recovered Memory and Other Assaults Upon the Mysteries of Consciousness, 1995, Behavior and Consequences, 1997, Kids in Chaos, 1997, Humpty Dumpty was Pushed, 1999; feature stories include Cmty. Responsibility, Behavior and Consequences, 1974, Missing Children, 1984; contbr. articles to profl. jours., TV and radio shows. Recipient George Foster Peabody Nomination Tex. Med. Assn., Wendall mays Pub. Svc. award Tex. Bar Assn., Gov.'s award AP, Tex. Assn. Broadcasters, Radio-T.V. News Dirs. Assn., Tex. Legislature Commendation, League of United Lat. Am. Citizens award Tex. State Network News, Coastal Bend Planning Commn. Spl. Svc. award, Headliner's News award, AP honors (5), UPI awards (13); citation ABA, U.S. Senate, Spl. Citation City of Corpus Christi, Tex., Spl. Resoultion of Commendation Tex.Ho. Reps., Exceptional Recognition Entered Into Perpetuity State of Tex. Archives; recognized as founder of Behavior Mgmt. Philosophy and Methodology (Existential-Realism). Office: Behavior Rsch Inst 3614 Hunters Circle San Antonio TX 78230

ROGERS, WILLIAM CECIL, political science educator, consultant; b. Manhattan, Kans., 1919; s. Charles Elkins and Sadie (Burns) R.; m. Mary Jane Anderson, Aug. 31, 1941; children: Shelley, Faith, Mary Sarah. BA, U. Chgo., 1940, MA, 1941, PhD, 1943. Asst. to dir. Pub. Adminstrn. Clearing House, Chgo., 1943-47; lectr. internat. relations U. Chgo., 1945-47; asst. prof. U. Va., 1947-48; asso. prof. polit. sci. Western Res. U., 1948-49; dir. World Affairs Center, U. Minn., Mpls., 1949-84; cons. Minn. Internat. Ctr., 1984—. Dir. Program Info. on World Affairs, Mpls. Star and Tribune, 1951-73. Author: Community Education in World Affairs, 1956, A Guide to Understanding World Affairs, 1966, Global Dimensions in U.S. Education: The Community, 1972; co-author: The Winter City Book, 1980. Pres. Minn. Jazz Sponsors, 1966-67; chmn. Mpls. Com. on Urban Environ., 1976-80. Mem. Nat. Univ. Extension Assn. (past sec.-treas.), Winter Cities Assn. (co-founder 1982). Home: 3510 Mckinley St NE Minneapolis MN 55418-1511 Office: 711 E River Rd Minneapolis MN 55455-0369

ROGERS, WILLIAM CORDELL, financial executive; b. Louisville, Apr. 16, 1943; s. Delbert Clifton and Nelle Frances (Grimsley) R.; m. Elaine Elizabeth Nicolay, Apr. 10, 1966; children: William C. II, Erin D., Nicole M., Shannon D. AA, Lincoln Coll., 1969; BS, Ill. State U., 1971; MBA, U. Phoenix. Corp. fin. cons. DEN, Inc. CPAs, Tempe, Ariz., 1977-83; v.p., treas. Dahlberg Industries, Scottsdale, 1983-91; CFO Act II Printed Cirs. Inc., Tempe, 1991—2000; controller TeleDirect Internat., Inc., Scottsdale, 2001—; self-employed fin. analyst. Cons., Scottsdale, 1977—; instr. econ. Lincoln Coll., 1972-77. With U.S. Army, 1964-67, Vietnam. Decorated Army Commendation medal; recipient Dow Jones award Dow Jones-Wall St. Jour., 1969. Mem. Rotary (bd. dirs. Scottsdale club 1986—, pres., Paul Harris fellow 1985—). Republican. Avocations: golf, reading, music. Home: 8549 E Turney Ave Scottsdale AZ 85251-2831 Office: TeleDirect Internat Inc 17255 N 82d St Scottsdale AZ 85255

ROGERS, WILLIAM DILL, lawyer; b. Wilmington, Del., May 12, 1927; m. Suzanne Rochford, Sept. 7, 1926; children: William Rogers, Daniel. BA, Princeton U., 1948; LL.B., Yale U., 1951. Bar: D.C. 1952, U.S. Supreme Ct. 1954. Ptnr. Arnold & Porter, Washington, intermittently 1953—; dep. U.S. coordinator Alliance for Progress, AID, 1962-65; pres. N.Y. Ctr. Inter.-Am. Relations, 1965-72; asst. sec. of state inter-Am. relations Dept. State, 1974-76, undersec. of state for econ. affairs, 1976-77; mem. law faculty Cambridge U., Eng., 1982-83. Sr. counselor Bipartisan Commn. on Central Am., 1983-84; vice chmn. Kissinger Assocs. Inc. Author: The Twilight Struggle: The Alliance for Progress and U.S.-Latin-American Relations, 1967. Co-chmn. U.S.-Mexico Binat. Commn.; bd. dirs. Coun. Fgn. Rels., 1981-90. Mem. Am. Soc. Internat. Law (pres. 1971-73), ABA. Office: Arnold & Porter 555 12th St NW Washington DC 20004-1206

ROGERS, WILLIAM FENNA, JR. supermarket executive, management consultant; b. Higgsinville, Mo., Dec. 25, 1912; s. William Fenna and Emily S. (Moose) R.; m. Thelma Ann Hooper, June 15, 1940 (dec. Mar. 1982); m. Ethel Allene Burgess, Aug. 6, 1983; stepchildren: Dorothy H. Nance, Linda H. Connors. BA, Ark. Coll., 1933; postgrad. U. Ark., 1933, Tulane U., 1935, U. Fla., 1938-39. Vocat. adv. Nat. Youth Adminstrn., Little Rock, 1936-38; chief field ops. U.S. Employment Svc., Little Rock, 1938-43, chief supr. tng., Washington, 1946-47; asst. dir. Civilian Pers. Divsn., U.S. Dept. Navy, Washington, 1947-55; mem. productivity team Nat. Mgmt. Coun., Paris, 1952; lectr. U.S. Internat. Fair, Amsterdam, 1963; v.p. indsl. rels. Giant Food, Inc., Washington, 1955-75; mgmt. cons., Falls Church, Va., 1975—; trustee Teamster Warehouse Fund, 1956—, Carpet Layers Funds, 1968—; lectr. Am. U., 1949-69; pres. Chateau Devel. Corp., Fairfax, Va., 1978-83. Mem. selection bd. U.S. Postal Svc., 1969-77; elder New York Ave. Presbyn. Ch., Washington, 1948-72, cons. Lincoln commn., 1984—, chmn., 1989—; elder Falls Church Presbyn. Ch., 1980-83, sunday sch. supt., 1984-88; mem. Falls Church Village Preservation and Improvement Soc., 1967—; chmn. bur. edn. and employment Greater Washington Bd. Trade, 1974-76. Served to lt. comdr. USNR, 1943-64. Mem. ASTD (life), Am. Legion Res. Officers Assn., Naval Res. Assn., Alpha Psi Omega, Kappa Gamma, Pi Kappa Delta, Iota Lambda Sigma. Club: Internat. Town and Country (dir. 1959-61) (Fairfax, Va.). Avocations: golf, fishing. Home: 9229 Arlington Blvd Apt 258 Fairfax VA 22031-2508

ROGERS, WILLIAM RAYMOND, college president emeritus, psychology educator; b. Oswego, N.Y., June 20, 1932; s. William Raymond and A. Elizabeth (Hollis) R.; m. Beverley Claire Partington, Aug. 14, 1954; children: John Partington, Susan Elizabeth Apple, Nancy Claire Glassman. BA magna cum laude, Kalamazoo Coll., 1954; BD, U. Chgo. and Chgo. Theol. Sem., 1958; PhD, U. Chgo., 1965; MA (hon.), Harvard U., 1970. Cons., staff counselor Counseling and Psychotherapy Rsch. Ctr., U. Chgo., 1960-62; tchg. fellow, counselor to students Chgo. Theol. Sem., 1961-62; asst. prof. psychology and religion, dir. student counseling Earlham Coll., Richmond, Ind., 1962-68, assoc. prof. psychology and religion, assoc. dean of Coll., 1968-70; vis. lectr. pastoral counseling Harvard U. Div. Sch., Cambridge, Mass., 1969-70, prof. religion and psychology Div. and Edn. Schs., 1970-80, faculty chmn. clin. psychology and pub. practice, 1970-72, chmn. counseling and cons. psychology, 1979-80; prof. psychology and religious studies Guilford Coll., Greensboro, N.C., 1980—, pres., 1980-96, pres. emeritus, 1996—. Bd. dirs. BB&T, Kendal Corp. Author: The Alienated Student, 1969, Project Listening, 1974, Nourishing the Humanistic in Medicine, 1979; Contbr. articles to profl. jours. Bd. dirs. Greensboro Symphony Soc.; mem. Cemala Found.; mem. Moses Cone-Wesley Long Cmty. Health Found. Danforth Found. fellow, Blatchford Traveling fellow U. Chgo. and Chgo. Theol. Sem. Mem.: Islesboro Hist. Soc. (pres. 1999—2002), So. Assn. Colls. and Schs., Nat. Assn. Ind. Colls. and Univs., Friends Com. on Nat. Legislation, Friends Assn. Higher Edn., Soc. Values in Higher Edn., Tarratine Club of Dark Harbor (bd. govs.), Rotary (past pres.). Mem. Soc. Of Friends. Home: 661 Main Rd Islesboro ME 04848-4201

ROGGE, JAMES ALAN, education educator; b. Akron, Ohio, Mar. 18, 1952; s. Arthur Denver and Violet Rogge; m. Ruth Moss, Dec. 22, 1974. BA, U. South Fla., 1974; MEd, U. Miami, 1976; EdS, Nova U., 1994. Cert. tchr., Fla. Asst. city planner City of Ormond Beach, Fla., 1977-78; tchr. 5th grade Beacon Hill Pvt. Sch., Hollywood, 1978-79; tchr. social studies/gifted Broward County Schs., Ft. Lauderdale, 1979-82, 91-92, Dade County Schs., Miami, 1982-91; instr. reading Broward C.C., Ft. Lauderdale, 1992—, Miami C.C., 1994-97, Nova U., Ft. Lauderdale, 1997—. Mem. scholarship com. U. South Fla., Ft. Lauderdale, 1989-91, mem. com. collegewide equal opportunity, 1994-95, multicultural, 2000-01, student success, 2001—. Grantee Broward C.C., 1993, 94, 01. Mem. Internat. Reading Assn., Broward County ESOL Coun., Chronicle of Higher Edn. Avocations: travel, speedwalking, skiing, writing, chess. Office: Broward CC North Campus 1000 Coconut Creek Blvd Coconut Creek FL 33066 E-mail: roggej@yahoo.com.

ROGGE, KATHLEEN RUTH, domestic engineer, art educator, nurse; b. Loma Linda, Calif., Nov. 11, 1946; d. Robert Edward Donaldson and Virginia Ruth (Hassig) Rosenlind; m. David George Rogge, May 16, 1970 (div. 2002); children: Aaron David, Rebekah Ruth, Sarah Hadassah. LPN. Domestic engr., Camino, Calif., 1970-76, Rogge Farm, Vita, Man., Can., 1976-97; adult edn. instr. Shevchenko Sch., 1986, 90-96. Pres. Figure Skating Club, Vita, Manitoba, Can., 1983; activity dir., cons., C. of C., Vita, 1981-85. Avocations: teaching, fitness, children, reading. Home: 5840 Margo Dr Lincoln NE 68510-5028

ROGILLIO, KATHY JUNE, musician, piano rebuilder, educator; b. Baton Rouge, Nov. 4, 1950; d. David Hunter and Thelma Ruth (Tucker) R. MusB, La. State U., 1972, MusM, 1974. Organist Plains Presbyn. Ch., Zachary, La., 1963-73; teacher's aid Gifted/Talented East Baton Rouge Parish, Baton Rouge, 1974-75; staff accompanist La. State U., 1975-76; music enrichment tchr. Episcopal H.S., 1976-77; organist, choirmaster Grace Episcopal Ch., St. Francisville, La., 1977-82; piano-technician So. U., Baton Rouge, 1977-84; apprentice in piano rebuilding and concert tuning, 1978-81; music tchr., organist, choirmaster St. Patrick's Episcopal Day Sch. and Ch., Zachary, La., 1985-86; vis. organist, dir. Numerous Chs., La. and Miss., 1982—; piano rebuilder pvt. practice, Zachary, La., 1986—. Ind. contract work Santi Falcone, Falcone Piano Co., Haverhill, Mass., 1987-88, part time organist/choirmaster St. Patrick's Episcopal Ch., Zachary, La., 1999-2000; pvt. piano tchr. La. Sch. for Visually Impaired, 2000—; recitalist, vis. organist. Arranger: Piano-Trio Arrangement Brahms Intermezzo Opus 118, #2, 1986 (2d pl. Composer's Guild Farmington, Utah, 1986). Treas. Beulah Plains Cemetery Assn., Zachary, La., 1987; mem. Landowners for Equitable Flood Control, Zachary, La., 1994—; Dem. candidate for U.S. Ho. of Reps. from 6th Dist. La., 2000. Mem. Am. Guild Organists, Baton Rouge Musicians' Assn. (exec bd. 1990-92, v.p. 1992-94. pres. 1994-96), La. Endowment for the Humanities, La. Pub. Broadcasting, Pi Kappa Lambda (profl. mus. hons. frat.). Democrat. Episcopalian. Avocations: needlework, cooking, animals. kathyjrogillio.com. Home and Office: Artist Pianos 18153 Barnett Rd Zachary LA 70791-8114 E-mail: k.rogillio@worldnet.att.net.

ROGIN, GILBERT LESLIE, editor, author; b. N.Y.C., Nov. 14, 1929; s. Robert I. and Lillian Carol (Ruderman) R. Student, State U. Iowa, 1947-49; AB, Columbia, 1951. Editor-at-large Miller Pub., L.A., 1955—. Author: The Fencing Master, 1965, What Happens Next?, 1971, Preparations for the Ascent, 1980. Served with AUS, 1952-54. Recipient award for creative work in lit. Am. Acad. Inst. Arts and Letters 1972 Home: 21 W 10th St New York NY 10011

ROGLIERI, JOHN LOUIS, health facility administrator; b. Plainfield, N.J., June 24, 1939; s. Vito and Grace Mary (DeCristofaro) R.; m. Geraldine Ann Piller, June 15, 1963; children: Maria Roglieri Friedman, Anna Roglieri Healy, John. BSChemE, AB in Applied Scis., Lehigh U., 1960; MD, Harvard U., 1966; MS in Bus., Columbia U., 1978. Diplomate Nat. Bd. Med. Examiners. Intern Bellevue Hosp., Columbia Svc., 1966-67; resident Presbyn. Hosp.,

N.Y.C., 1969-71, dir. divsn. ambulatory medicine, 1973-75, v.p. ambulatory svcs., 1975-82, dir. employee health svc., 1988-92; fellow Harvard Med. Sch., Boston, 1971-73; asst. dir. lab. computer sci. Mass. Gen. Hosp., 1972-73, dir. ambulatory screening clinic, 1972-73; med. dir. N.Y. Health Plan, Inc., N.Y.C., 1988-92; corp. med. dir. Sanus Corp. Health Sys., Ft. Lee, N.J., 1992-95, NYL Care Health Plans Inc., N.Y.C., 1996-99; physician Web Link, Inc., Englewood, N.J., 2000-2001; med. dir. N.Y. Life Ins. Co., 2001—. Cons. Nat. Ctr. Health Svc. Rsch. and Devel., 1973-75; dir. clin. scholar program Columbia U., 1975-77, asst. prof. clin. medicine Coll. Physicians and Surgeons, 1973—; health edn. cons. Basic Internat. Investments, 1975-76; v.p., bd. dirs. AMA-RCO Internat., N.Y.C., 1975-85; mem. adv. bd. Western and Upper Manhattan Regional Perinatal Network, Coll. Physicians and Surgeons, N.Y.C., 1975-80; appeared in various TV and radio programs. Author: Odds on Your Life, 1980; mem. editl. bd. Managed Care, 1992—, Jour. Applied Rsch. in Health Adminstrn., 1979-81, Hosp. Physician, 1997—; book rev. cons. Acad. Press, Inc., N.Y.C.; contbr. articles to profl. publs. Capt. USPHS, 1967-69. Mem. APHA, Am. Fedn. Clin. Rsch., Am. Soc. Internal Medicine, N.Y. State Soc. Internal Medicine, Soc. for Rsch. and Edn. in Primary Care Internal Medicine, Nat. Assn. Managed Care Physicians. Roman Catholic. Avocations: surfcasting, woodworking. Office: Columbia Presbyn Med Ctr 161 Fort Washington Ave New York NY 10032-3713

ROGO, KATHLEEN, safety engineer, researcher; b. Carrollton, Ohio, Sept. 28, 1952; d. Silvio and Mary (Siragusano) R. Grad. high sch., Carrollton; PhD in Med. Sci. (hon.), Ohio Valley Pathologists, Inc., 1992. Cert. histotechnologist, emergency med. technologist, safety engr. Rsch. pathology trainee Aultman Hosp., Canton, Ohio, 1970-75, supr. anatomic pathology, 1974-75; lab. mgr. W. Morgan Lab., 1973-74; supr. anatomic pathology Dr.'s Hosp., Massillon, Ohio, 1975-78; emergency med. technician Canton Fire Dept., 1976-81; safety engr. Ashland Oil Co., Canton, 1980-82; rsch. pathologist assoc., med. cons, v.p. Ohio Valley Pathologists, Inc., Wheeling, W.Va., 1990—. Mem. Am. Soc. Clin. Pathology (cert. histotechnician), Am. Soc. Safety Engrs. (cert.), Am. Soc. Emergency Med. Technicians (cert.), Ohio State Med. Soc., Internat. Platform Assn. Democrat. Roman Catholic. Avocations: professional model, dancer and musician.

ROGOFF, ALICE ELIZABETH, writer, editor; b. New Rochelle, N.Y., Aug. 10, 1949; d. Julian Rogoff and Gladys Charlotte (Pollak) Rogoff Sternberg; m. David Henry Williams, Mar. 2, 1989. BA in Anthropology, Grinnell Coll., 1971; MA in English/Creative Writing, San Francisco State U., 1980, MA in Drama, 1990. Tchr. Rural Inst., Ukiah, Calif., 1993-95; co-editor Haight Ashbury Lit. Jour., San Francisco, 1984—; dir. Sr. Reading Theatre, 1997—. Bd. dirs. Bay Area Ctr. for Art and Tech., San Francisco, 1994-96, Rural Inst., Ukiah, 1992. Co-editor: (anthologies) Noe Valley: An Anthology of Poetry, 1974, This Far Together, 1996. Mem. newsletter com. San Franciscans for Tax Justice, 1995-96; mem. working com.. War Resisters League, West San Francisco, 1979. Zellerbach Family Fund grantee for editl. work. Mem. Coun. Lit. Mags. and Presses, Nat. Writers Union (steering com. Local 3, head fiction and poetry caucus 1999-2001). Avocations: music, natural science, hiking, dogs and cats. Home: 558 Joost Ave San Francisco CA 94127-2408 E-mail: alicerogoff@yahoo.com.

ROGOFF, JEFFREY SCOTT, lawyer; b. Manhasset, N.Y., May 11, 1968; s. Arnold Steven and Paula Rogoff. BA, Binghamton U., 1990; JD, NYU, 1993. Bar: N.J. 1993, U.S. Dist. Ct. N.J. 1993, U.S. Dist. Ct. (so. and ea. dists.) N.Y. 1994, U.S. Dist. Ct. (no. and we. dists.) N.Y. 2000, U.S. Ct. Appeals (3d cir.) 1998. Law clk. Magistrate Judge Michael Dolinger U.S. Dist. Ct. (so. dist.) N.Y., N.Y.C., 1993-94; assoc. Kronish, Lieb, Weiner & Hellman, 1994-95, Schindel, Farman & Lipsius LLP, N.Y.C., 1995-2000; solicitor U.S. Dept. Labor, 2000—. Mem. Phi Beta Kappa. Jewish. Home: 11 Furman Dr Wayne NJ 07470-5304 Office: US Dept Labor Office of Solicitor 201 Varick St Room 983 New York NY 10014 E-mail: rogoff-jeffrey@dol.gov.

ROGOFF, JEROME HOWARD, psychiatrist, psychoanalyst, forensic expert; b. Detroit, Dec. 21, 1938; s. Abraham Solomon and Sarah Riva (Epstein) R.; (div. 1983); m. Erika Kathleen Keller, Sept. 25, 1983. BA cum laude, Harvard Coll., 1960; MD, Case Western Reserve U., 1965. Diplomate Am. Bd. Psychiatry and Neurology. Physician Peace Corps USPHS, Kathmandu, Nepal, 1966-68; clin. fellow psychiatry Harvard Med. Sch., Boston, 1975-79; staff psychiatrist Westwood (Mass.) Lodge Hosp., 1972-74; assoc. clin. prof. psychiatry Tufts Med. Sch., Boston, 1977-86; assoc. chief, psychiatry and dir., inpatient Psychiatry, day hosp. Faulkner Hosp., 1975-94; pvt. practice psychiatry, psychoanalysis and forensic psychiatry, 1994—. Cons. psychiatrist Mass. Parole Bd. Probate Ct. Plymouth County, Mass., LEAA, Washington, 1971-78; med. psychiat. dir. ct. diversion program Boston TASC-A, 1974-75; treas., bd. dirs. Guild for Continuing Edn., Boston, 1981-95; founding dir. Law and Psychiatry Resource Ctr., Boston, 1983—; adj. prof. Simmons Sch. Social Work, Boston, 1981-85; lectr. in psychiatry Harvard Med. Sch., Boston, 1986-94, 2001-. Chmn. psychiatry team Combined Jewish Philanthropies, Boston, 1978-83, assoc. chmn. med. team, 1984-87, mem. social planning and allocations com., 1991-98, mem. cmty. svcs. com., 1998—, chmn. chronic mental illness com., 1999-2000, mem. disabilities com., 2000—; bd. dirs. Jewish Vocat. Svc., Boston, 1987-91. Fellow Am. Psychiat. Assn. (pub. affairs rep. 1988-92, 93-94, mem. budget com. 1996-2002, assembly rep. 2000—, disting. fellow 2002-); mem. Mass. Psychiat. Soc. (councillor 1988-94, chair pub. affairs com. 1988-92, 93-94, chair nominating com. 1990, 2000, pres.-elect 1998-99, pres. 1999-00), Am. Psychoanalytic Assn., Boston Psychoanalytic Soc., Am. Acad. Psychiatry and Law. Democrat. Avocations: cabinetry, carpentry, cooking, classical music, languages. Home and Office: 659 Chestnut St Waban MA 02468-2035 *Two guiding principles, both from my father: "When in doubt, do the right thing." Sounds trite and naive, but turns out in the event to be profound; one almost always knows deep down what the right thing is. "When you are born, you cry, and everyone around you laughs. So live your life that when you come to leave it, you laugh, and everyone around you cries." On my profession of psychiatry and psychoanalysis: psychotherapy adds insight to injury.*

ROGOFF, KENNETH SAUL, economics educator; b. Rochester, N.Y., Mar. 22, 1953; s. Stanley Miron and June Beatrice (Goldman) R.; m. Evelyn Jane Brody, Aug. 18, 1979 (div. 1989); m. Natasha Lange, June 25, 1995; children: Gabriel, Juliana. BA/MA in Econs., Yale U., 1975; PhD in Econs., MIT, 1980. Economist Internat. Monetary Fund, Washington, 1983; economist, sect. chief Internat. Fin. div., Bd. Govs. of the Fed. Res. Sys., 1979-84; assoc. prof. econs. U. Wis., Madison, 1985-89; prof. econs. U. Calif., Berkeley, 1989-92; prof. econs. and internat. affairs Princeton (N.J.) U., 1992—; Charles and Marie Robertson prof. of internat. affairs Princeton U., 1995-98; prof. econs. Harvard U., 1999—; econ. counselor, dir. rsch. IMF, 2001—. Vis. scholar San Francisco Fed. Res., 1990-92, World Bank, Washington, 1989, IMF, Washington, 1988-94. Author books and contbr. articles to profl. jours. Alfred P. Sloan Rsch. fellow, 1986-87, Hoover Instn. Nat. fellow, 1986-87, NSF fellow, 1985—, John Simon Guggenheim fellow, 1998. Fellow Econometric Soc., Am. Acad. Arts and Scis.; mem. Am. Econ. Assn., Internat. Grandmaster Chess. Office: Harvard U Econs Dept Littauer Ctr Cambridge MA 02138-3001 E-mail: krogoff@harvard.edu.

ROGOFF, PAULA DRIMMER, English and foreign language educator; b. N.Y.C. d. George and Florence (Levine) Drimmer; m. Arnold Stevan Rogoff; children: Jeffrey Scott, Eric Todd, Brian Craig. BA cum laude, Hunter Coll., 1961; MEd summa cum laude, William Paterson Coll., 1979. Cert. elem. tchr., ESL tchr., supr., N.J. Tchr. handicapped Herricks Bd. Edn., Williston Park, N.J.; tchr. reading compensatory edn. Oakland (N.J.) Bd. Edn.; tchr., coord. gifted-talented program N. Haldeon (N.J.) Bd. Edn.; ESL adult tchr., h. s. students Passaic County Tech. Inst., Wayne, N.J. Presenter Children's Libr. programs. Named Tchr. of Yr., Passaic County Tech. Inst., 1999-2000. Mem. ASCD, NEA, TESOL, Internat. Platform Assn., N.J. Edn. Assn., Phi Beta Kappa, Phi Lambda Theta, Kappa Delta Pi. Home: 11 Furman Dr Wayne NJ 07470-5304 Office: Passaic County Tech Inst 45 Reinhardt Rd Wayne NJ 07470

ROGOLS, SAUL, food scientist; b. Cambridge, Mass., July 27, 1933; s. Barney Barkan and Dora (Cohen) R.; m. Donna Janelle, May 25, 1985. BSc in Biology and Chemistry, Antioch Coll., 1955; MSc in Bacteriology and Biochemistry, Ohio State U., 1958, PhD, 1960, postgrad., 1961-62; MBA, Ohio U., Lancaster, 1982. Cert. med. technician; cert. instr. ARC. Tech. dir. quality control/quality assurance A. E. Staley Mfg. Co., 1961-79; med. technologist Children's Hosp., Columbus, Ohio, 1961-75; materials control mgr. Essex Group div. United Technologies, 1979-80; dir. quality assurance Hexcel Corp., 1980-82; sr. scientist Amstar Corp., 1982-84; sr. food scientist Grain Processing Corp., 1986-91; dir. tech. svcs., sr. scientist Penford Corp., Englewood, Colo., 1991-98; ret., cons. agrl. products Penwest Foods Co., 1998—. Mem. adv. bd. Chem. Week Mag.; contbr. articles to profl. jours.; patentee in field. Fellow Am. Inst. Chemists; mem. TAPPI, Am. Assn. Cereal Chemists (charter mem. carbohydrate div.), Am. Chem. Soc. (biol. chemistry div.), Inst. Food Technologists (carbohydrate exec. com.), Am. Assn. Candy Technologists, N.Y. Acad. Sci., Sigma Xi. Avocation: model ship building. Home: 23573 Pondview Pl Golden CO 80401-5761 E-mail: sjrogols@aol.com.

ROGOSKI, PATRICIA DIANA, financial executive; b. Chgo., Dec. 29, 1939; d. Raymond Michael and Bernice Rose (Konkol) R. BS in Acctg. and Econs., Marquette U., 1961, postgrad., 1965-66, NYU, 1966-68, St. John's U., N.Y.C., 1975-76; cert. mgmt. acct., 1979. Sr. fin. analyst Blackhawk Mfg. Co., Milw., 1961-66; mgr., sr. analyst Shell Oil Co., N.Y.C., 1966-71; mgr. data processing Bradford Nat./Penn Bradford, Pitts., 1971-75; asst. mgr. fin. controls ITT, N.Y.C., 1975-79; v.p., comptr. ITT Consumer Fin. Corp., Mpls., 1979-80; sr. v.p. fin. ITT Fin. Corp., St. Louis, 1980-84; v.p., exec. asst., group exec. ITT Coins, Secaucus, N.J., 1984-85; pres. Patron S., Ltd., Wilmington, Del., 1986—; CFO, sr. v.p. Guardsmark, Inc., Memphis, 1989-94; sr. v.p. Peoplemark, Inc., 1989-94. Bd. dirs. St. Louis Repertory Theater, 1983-84. Named to Acad. Women Achievers, YWCA, N.Y.C., 1980. Mem. Fin. Execs. Inst., Inst. Mgmt. Acctg., Econ. Club, Memphis Symphony Chorus. Avocation: duplicate bridge. Office: Patron S Ltd 2711 Centerville Rd Ste 400 Wilmington DE 19808-

ROGOVIN, JOHN A(NDREW), lawyer; b. Washington, July 10, 1961; s. Mitchell and Sheila Ann (Ender) R. AB, Columbia U., 1983; JD, U. Va., 1987. Bar: N.Y. 1989, D.C. 1990. Law clk. hon. Laurence Silberman U.S. Ct. Appeals (D.C. Cir.), Washington, 1987-88; assoc. Kramer, Levin et al, N.Y.C., 1988-89, O'Melveny & Myers, Washington, 1990-92, spl. counsel, 1996-97, ptnr., 1997-2001; dep. transition counsel Presdl. Transition, Little Rock, 1992-93; asst. to atty. gen. U.S. Dept. Justice, Washington, 1993, dep. asst. atty. gen. Civil Divsn., 1993-96; dep. gen. counsel FCC. Mem. ABA, D.C. Bar Assn. Office: Fed Comm Commn Dep Gen Counsel Washington DC 20554 E-mail: Jrogovin@omm.com.

ROGOVIN, MILTON, documentary photographer, retired optometrist; b. N.Y.C., Dec. 30, 1909; s. Jacob and Dora (Shainhouse) R.; m. Anne Setters, Apr. 7, 1942; children: Ellen, Mark, Paula. BS in Optics and Optometry, Columbia U., 1931; MA in Am. Studies, SUNY, Buffalo, 1972; DFA (hon.), U. Buffalo, 1994, Buffalo State Coll., 1994, D'Youville Coll., 1994. Optometrist, Buffalo, 1931-75; freelance documentary photographer, 1958—. Author: Milton Rogovin: The Forgotten Ones, 1985, Portraits in Steel, 1993, Windows That Open Inward, 1999, The Bonds Between Us, 2001, (triptychs) Buffalo's Lower West Side Revisited. Served with U.S. Army, 1942-45. Recipient W. Eugene Smith Meml. Fund award, 1983, Gov.'s award N.Y. State Coun. on Arts, 2000; Libr. of Congress acting as repository for Milton Rogovin's negatives and photographs, 1999—. Home: 90 Chatham Ave Buffalo NY 14216-3109

ROGOW, LOUIS MICHAEL, oncologist, educator; b. Jersey City, June 20, 1944; s. Irving and Helen (Grollman) R.; m. Enid Zazeela, Jan. 24, 1982; children from previous marriage: Ilisa, Jay. BS, Trinity Coll., 1965; MD, Hahnemann U., 1969. Diplomate Nat. Bd. of Med. Examiners; cert. radiology, radiation oncology. Instr. radiology Radiation Oncology N.Y. Med. Coll., N.Y.C., 1973-75, asst. prof., 1975-77; CEO Ideal Window Mfg., Bayonne, N.J., 1980—; dir. radiation oncology, hyperthermia John F. Kennedy Med. Ctr., Edison, 1977-95; ret., 1995. Clin. asst. prof. radiology, U. Medicine and Dentistry, Rutgers Med. Sch., New Brunswick, N.J., 1983-95; instr. Sch. Nuc. Medicine Tech., John F. Kennedy Med. Ctr., Edison, N.J., 1984-95; bd. dirs. JFK Med. Ctr. Found.; CEO VT, LLC, Camden, N.J., 1997—. Contbr. articles to profl. jours. Bd. trustees Am. Cancer Soc. (N.J. divsn.); bd. dirs. Resource Ctr. for Women and Their Families, Somerset County, N.J., 1993-2000; bd. dirs. Cancer Care, N.J. divsn., 1996-2000; adv. bd. Cancer Care N.J., 2000—; pres. Helen and Irving Rogow Found., 2000—. Clin. fellow Am. Cancer Soc., 1971, 73, faculty fellow Am. Cancer So., 1975, 76; recipient Ptnrs. in Caring award N.J. Sen., 1999. Fellow Am. Coll. Radiology; mem. Am. Soc. Therapeutic Radiology and Oncology, Am. Endocurie Therapy Soc., Am. Radium Soc., N.Y. Cancer Soc., Oncology Soc. N.J.,), Somerset Hills Handicapped Riders Club. Office: Ideal Window Mfg Box 48 100 W 7th St Bayonne NJ 07002-1133 E-mail: dr@idealwindowmfg.com.

ROGOWSKY, ROBERT ARTHUR, trade commission operations director, professor; b. Vancouver, B.C., Can., Mar. 12, 1951; s. Michael Randall and Ruth Ann (Wellman) R.; m. Linda Sue George, June 17, 1972; children: Vanessa, Heather, Tara, Nichole, Alexis. BA in Econs., Boston U., 1973; MA in Econs., U. Va., 1975, PhD in Econs., 1982. Asst. prof. dept. econs. George Mason U., Fairfax, Va., 1977-78; rsch. economist Bur. Econs. FTC, Washington, 1979-83; econ. advisor to commrs. Consumer Product Safety Commn., 1983-84, acting exec. dir., asst. to dir., 1984; pres. Econ. Edn. for Clergy, Inc., Bethesda, Md., 1985-86; exec. asst. to chmn. Internat. Trade Commn., Washington, 1986-87; dep. dir. Bur. Consumer Protection FTC, 1987-89; dir. office of industries U.S. Internat. Trade Commn., 1989-92, dir. ops., 1992—; adj. prof. George Mason U. Instr. U. Va., 1976-77; econ. rschr. Am. Enterprise Inst., 1976; econ. rsch. analyst Econ. Policy Office, U.S. Dept. Justice, 1974-75; presenter in field. Contbr. articles to profl. jours. Mem. Am. Mgmt. Assn., Am. Econs. Assn., Assn. Christian Economists. Lutheran. Home: 709 Miller Ave Great Falls VA 22066-2917 Office: US International Trade Comm Operations 500 E St NW Washington DC 20436-0003

ROGUL, JUNE AUDREY, fundraising executive, government relations specialist; b. N.Y.C., Dec. 30, 1942; d. Caroll Mitchell and Gail (Arkin) Silver; m. Marvin Rogul, Mar. 17, 1974; children: Jonathan, Daniel. BA, Tufts U., 1964; MS, Columbia U., 1966. Cmty. orgn. specialist D.C. Redevel. Land Agy., Washington, 1966-70; asst. to the dir. Prime Minister's Commn. on Disadvantaged Children & Youth, Jerusalem, Israel, 1971-72; rep. Nat. Conf. Soviet Jewry, Washington, 1973-75; lobbyist Am. Israel Pub. Affairs Com., 1975-77; dir. JWB, 1980-82, GNK Assocs., Washington, 1982-83; dir. Washington region Am. Com. for Weizmann Inst. Sci., 1983-98, dir. govt. rels., 1992-98; dir. nat. outreach New Israel Fund, 1998—. Assoc. The Kahn Pub. Policy Report, Washington, 1982-83; cons., rep. Na'Amat U.S.A., Washington, 1982-89; cons. in field. Del. Allied Civic Group, Silver Spring, Md., 1978-79; chmn. Linden Civic Assn., Silver Spring, 1978-79; appointee Montgomery County Housing Policy Implementation Com., Rockville, Md., 1979; mem. Joint Action Com. for Polit. Affairs, 1982—, co-chmn. Washington chpt., 1992. Mem. Assn. Fundraising Profls., Nat. Jewish Dem. Coun. Democrat. Avocations: travel, foreign languages, jogging, skiing. Home: 6132 Roseland Dr North Bethesda MD 20852 E-mail: june@nif.org.

ROGULA, JAMES LEROY, consumer products company executive; b. Rock Island, Ill., Nov. 8, 1933; s. Andrew and Nellie Pearl (Cook) R.; m. Adelaide F. Dittbrenner, May 29, 1960; children: James Lyle, Adelaide Ann, John Andrew. BA, Knox Coll., 1955; MBA, NYU, 1964. Group product mgr. Am. Chicle Co., Long Island City, N.Y., 1958-66; v.p. new product devel. Carter Wallace, Inc., N.Y.C., 1966-72; v.p. new products J.B. Williams Co., 1972-74; sr. v.p. E.J. Brach & Sons, Chgo., 1974-77; v.p., gen. mgr. A.E. Staley Mfg. Co., Oak Brook, 1977-80; exec. v.p. Booth Fisheries Corp., Chgo., 1980-82; v.p., gen. mgr. Arm & Hammer div. Church & Dwight, Inc., Princeton, NJ, 1982-90; pres. Am. Candy Co., Richmond, Va., 1990-94; group exec. v.p. N.Am. bus. groups Scotts Co., Marysville, Ohio, 1994—2001; pres., personal care domestic Church & Dwight Co. Inc., Princeton, 2001—. With U.S. Army, 1956-58. Mem. Sunset Ridge Country Club, Wedgewood Country Club. Home: 4 Grange Rd Pennington NJ 08534 Office: 469 N Harrison St Princeton NJ 08540-3510

ROHACK, JOHN JAMES, cardiologist; b. Rochester, N.Y., Aug. 22, 1954; s. John Joseph and Margaret Elizabeth (McLaughlin) R.; m. Charlotte McCown, Dec. 7, 1980; 1 child, Elisha Monique Feigle. BS, U. Tex., El Paso, 1976; MD, U. Tex., Galveston, 1980. Diplomate Am. Bd. Internal Medicine. Intern internal medicine U. Tex. Med. Br. Hosps., Galveston, 1980-81, resident internal medicine, 1981-83, chief resident internal medicine, 1983-84, fellow cardiology, 1984-86; instr. medicine U. Tex. Med. Br., 1983-86; asst. prof. medicine Tex. A&M Coll. Medicine, College Station, 1986-95, assoc. prof., 1995—, sect. chief cardiology, 1989-97. Assoc. med. dir. Scott and White Health Plan Bryan Coll. Sta., 1995-97; assoc. med. dir. for med. ops. Scott and White Health Plan and Clinic, 1997-2000, med. dir. Health Plan, 2000—; bd. dirs. Health for All Clinic, v.p., 1994-96; mem. Accreditation Coun. on Continuing Med. Edn., 1995-99, Liaison Com. on Med. Edn., 1999-2001; med. dir. Fitlife Ctr. Tex. A&M U., College Station, 1990-97; mem. bd. commrs. Joint Commn. on Accreditation of Healthcare Orgns., 2002-. Bd. dirs. Am. Heart Assn., Brazos Valley College Station, 1987-97, Tex. affiliate Austin, 1991-98, 1st v.p., 1994-95, pres.-elect, 1995-96, pres., 1996-97. Fellow ACP, Am. Coll. Cardiology (bd. dirs. Tex. chpt. 1992-97); mem. AMA (alt del. ho. of dels. 1984-93, del. 1993-2001, coun. on med. edn. 1995-2001, chair elect 1996-97, chair 1997-98, trustee 2001—), Tex. Med. Assn. (exec. coun. med. student sect. 1981-82, ho. of dels. 1982—, trustee 1994-2002, pres.-elect 1999-2000, pres. 2000-2001). Avocations: golf, gardening, reading, ranching. Office: Scott and White Clinic 2401 S 31st St Temple TX 76508-0001

ROHAN, VIRGINIA BARTHOLOME, college development director; b. Helena, Mont., Apr. 19, 1939; d. William Franklin and Virginia Marie (Gibson) Bartholome; m. William Patrick Rohan, Dec. 29, 1962; children: Virginia Marion, William Patrick Jr., Christopher James. AB summa cum laude, St. Teresa's Coll., 1960; MA in Am. Lit., Cath. U. Am., 1961; postgrad., Kans. U., 1961-62; PhD in English, U. Mass., 1974. Instr. western civilization program Kans. U., Lawrence, 1961-62; instr. English St. Joseph Coll., Emmitsburg, Md., 1962-63; lectr. English U. Mass., Amherst, 1975-76; research assoc. Smith Coll. Devel. Office, Northampton, Mass., 1976-77, asst. dir. for founds., 1977-80, dir. devel. svcs., 1980-89; asst. v.p. devel. U. Vt., Burlington, 1989-90, interim v.p. for devel. and alumni rels., 1990-92; dir. devel. Hampshire Coll., Amherst, 1992—. Lectr. English Holyoke (Mass.) C.C., 1976-77, Mt. Holyoke Coll., South Hadley, Mass., 1977-78; mem. faculty, mgmt. Inst. for Women in Higher Edn., Wellesley, Mass., 1983, 93; pres. Investments Unltd. Inc., Northampton, 1983-84. Author: (play) The Happy Prince, 1959; contbr. articles to profl. jours. Treas., bd. dirs. Friends WFCR (pub. radio), Amherst, 1983-85. Fellow Woodrow Wilson Found., 1960-61. Mem. Women in Devel. Western Mass. (co-founder, chairperson 1983-85), Coun. for Advancement and Support of Edn. (mem. faculty, panelist, chairperson roundtable, discussant 1979-94), Kappa Gamma Pi, Pi Beta Phi. Office: Hampshire Coll Amherst MA 01002

ROHATYN, FELIX GEORGE, ambassador; b. Vienna, Austria, May 29, 1928; came to U.S., 1942, naturalized, 1950; s. Alexander and Edith (Knoll) R.; m. Jeannette Streit, June 9, 1956; children: Pierre, Nicolas, Michael; m. Elizabeth Fly, May 31, 1979. BS, Middlebury (Vt.) Coll., 1948; LLD (hon.), Adelphi U., Bard Coll., Hofstra U., 1981, L.I. U., 1981, Middlebury Coll., 1982, Fordham U., 1983; LLB (hon.), NYU, 1979, Brandeis U., 1987. With Lazard Freres & Co., LLC, N.Y.C., 1948—, mng. dir., 1960—97; amb. to France Paris, 1997—2001; with Rohatyn Assocs., N.Y.C., 2002—. Bd. dirs. Comcast Corp., LVMH, Inc., Fiat, Inc., Suez, Inc., Publicis; mem. bd. govs. N.Y. Stock Exch., 1968—72. Served with AUS, 1951-53, Korea. Office: Rohatyn Assocs LLC 30 Rockefeller Plz 50th Fl New York NY 10020

ROHDE, BRUCE C. food company executive, lawyer; b. Sidney, Nebr., Dec. 17, 1948; BS, Creighton U., 1971, JD cum laude, 1973. Bar: Nebr. 1974, U.S. Dist. Ct. Nebr. 1974, U.S. Tax Ct. 1975, U.S. Ct. Appeals (8th cir.) 1976, U.S. Ct. Appeals (5th cir.) 1979, U.S. Supreme Ct. 1980, U.S. Claims Ct. 1981, U.S. Ct. Appeals (D.C. cir.) 1982. Lawyer McGrath, North, Mullin & Kratz, Omaha, to 1996; vice chmn., pres. ConAgra Inc., 1996—97, CEO, 1997—, chmn., 1998—. Bd. dirs. Valmont Industries Inc. Vice chmn. bd. dirs. Creighton U.; chmn. bd. dirs. Strategic Air and Space Mus. Mem. ABA (corp., banking and bus law sect., taxation sect., antitrust law sect., litigation sect.), Assn. Trial Lawyers Am., Nebr. Assn. Trial Lawyers, Nebr. State Bar Assn., Nebr. Soc. CPAs, Omaha Bar Assn., Beta Gamma Sigma, Beta Alpha Psi. Address: ConAgra Inc 1 ConAgra Dr Ste 302 Omaha NE 68102*

ROHDE, JAMES VINCENT, software systems company executive; b. O'Neill, Nebr., Jan. 25, 1939; s. Ambrose Vincent and Loretta Cecilia R.; children: Maria, Sonja, Daniele, Olga. B of Comml. Sci., Seattle U., 1962. Chmn. bd. dirs., pres. Applied Telephone Tech., Oakland, Calif., 1974; v.p. sales and mktg. Automation Electronics Corp., 1975-82; founder, pres., CEO, chmn. Am. Telecorp, Inc., Redwood City, Calif., 1982-99; founder, vice-chmn., bd. dirs. Ceon Corp., 1999—. Chmn. exec. com., chmn. emeritus Pres.'s Coun. Heritage Coll., Toppenish, Wash., 1985—; chmn. bd. dirs. Calif. chpt. Coun. of Growing Cos., 1990-93. Bd. dirs. Ind. Colls. No. Calif., 1991-93. Named U.S. Dept. Commerce Export Exec. Yr. No. Calif., 1993. Mem. Am. Electronics Assn. (bd. dirs. 1992-94, vice-chmn. No. Calif. coun. 1992-93, chmn. 1993-94). Republican. Roman Catholic. Office: Ceon Corp 720 Bay Rd Redwood City CA 94063-2469 E-mail: jrohde@ceon.com.

ROHDE, TAMERA ANNETTE, oncological nurse; b. Norfolk, Nebr., Sept. 1, 1957; m. Mark Rohde, Oct. 22, 1983. Diploma, Bishop Clarkson Meml. Hosp. Sch. Nursing, Omaha, 1981; BSN, Bishop Clarkson Meml. Hosp. Coll. Nursing, Omaha, 1984. RN, Iowa, Nebr.; cert. oncology nurse. Staff nurse, bone marrow transplant unit Bishop Clarkson Hosp., 1981-84; staff nurse Baylor Med. Ctr., Dallas, 1984-85; asst. nursing dir. Siouxland Regional Cancer Ctr., Sioux City, Iowa, 1987—.

ROHE, WILLIAM MICHAEL, urban planning educator; b. N.Y.C., Apr. 23, 1950; s. Victor Joseph and Grace (White) R.; m. Jamie Stone, June 10, 1989. AAS, SUNY, Farmingdale, 1970; BS, SUNY, Buffalo, 1972; M Regional Planning, Pa. State U., 1975, PhD in Man Environ. Rels., 1978. Asst. prof. Pa. State U., University Park, 1977-78; asst. prof. city, regional planning U. N.C., Chapel Hill, 1978-85, assoc. prof., 1985-92; prof., 1992—; Dean E. Smith prof., 1994-97; dir. Ctr. for Urban and Regional Studies U. N.C., Chapel Hill, 1994—. Cons. Rsch. Triangle Inst., Rsch. Triangle Park, N.C., 1979-96, Urban Systems Rsch. and Engring., Cambridge, Mass., 1985-87, Abt assoc., Cambridge, Mass.; HUD vis. scholar, Washington, 1984-85; gov. bd. Urban Affairs Assn., 2000—. Author: Planning with Neighborhoods, 1985, Sustainable Nonprofit Housing Devel., 1998; mem. editl. bd. Jour. Am. Planning Assn., Jour. Planning Lit., Jour. Planning Edn. and Rsch., Jour. Urban Affairs; assoc. editor: Housing Policy Debate; contbr. articles to profl. jours. Mem. Chapel Hill Planning Commn., 1980-86; Chapel Hill Small Area Planning Com., 1990-94. Grantee Nat. Inst. Justice, 1982, HUD, 1987, 95, 97, 98, rsch. grantee Ford Found., 1988, 91, 2001, Fannie Mae Found., 1994, 1997, 99, Neighborhood Reinvestment Corp., 1997, 98. Mem. AAUP (pres.-elect U. N.C. chpt. 1990-91, pres. 1991-93), Am. Planning Assn. (Best Paper award 1992, 95), Assn. Collegiate Schs. of Planning (exec. com. 1993-95, Best Paper award 1996). Avocation: tennis, sailing. E-mail: brohe@unc.edu.

ROHLF, F. JAMES, biometrician, educator; b. Blythe, Calif., Oct. 24, 1936; BS, San Diego State Coll., 1958; PhD in Entomology, U. Kans., 1962. Asst. prof. biology U. Calif., Santa Barbara, 1962-65; assoc. prof. statis. biology U. Kans., 1965-69; assoc. prof. biology SUNY, Stony Brook, 1969-72, prof., 1972—, chmn. dept. ecology and evolution, 1975-80, 90-91. Statis. cons. N.Y. Pub. Svc. Commn., 1975-78, IBM, 1977-81, U.S. EPA, 1978-80; vis. scientist IBM, Yorktown Heights, N.Y., 1976-77, 80-81; vis. prof. U. Rome, 1997, 99. Fellow: Am. Acad. Arts and Scis.; mem.: Internat. Fedn. Classification Socs. (pres. 1975—78), Classification Soc. (pres. 1975—78, bd. dirs. 1994—, editl. bd. 1984—), Soc. Systematic Biologists, Biometric Soc. Achievements include research and development of statistical methods and software for geometric morphometrics and applications of multivariate analysis to systematics and population biology. Office: SUNY at Stony Brook Dept Ecology And Evolution Stony Brook NY 11794-5245 E-mail: rohlf@life.bio.sunysb.edu.

ROHLFING, FREDERICK WILLIAM, lawyer, political consultant, retired judge; b. Honolulu, Nov. 2, 1928; s. Romayne Raymond and Kathryn (Coe) R.; m. Joan Halford, July 15, 1952 (div. Sept. 1982); children: Frederick W., Karl A., Brad (dec.); m. Patricia Ann Santos, Aug. 23, 1983. BA, Yale U., 1950; JD, George Washington U., 1955. Bar: Hawaii 1955, Am. Samoa 1978. Assoc. Moore, Torkildson & Rice, Honolulu, 1955-60; ptnr. Rohlfing, Nakamura & Low, 1963-68, Hughes, Steiner & Rohlfing, Honolulu, 1968-71, Rohlfing, Smith & Coates, Honolulu, 1981-84; sole practice, 1960-63, 71-81, Maui County, 1988—; dep. corp. counsel County of Maui, Wailuku, Hawaii,

1984-87, corp. counsel, 1987-88; land and legal counsel Maui Open Space Trust, 1992-97, also bd. dirs. Polit. cons., 1996, 98; magistrate judge U.S. Dist. Ct. Hawaii, 1991-96. Active Hawaii Ho. Reps., 1959-65, 80-84, Hawaii State Senate, 1966-75; U.S. alt. rep. So. Pacific Commn., Noumea, New Caledonia, 1975-77, 1982-84; Maui adv. coun. State Reapportionment Commn., 2001; hon. chmn. Maui coms. George W. Bush for Pres. Capt. USNR, 1951-87. Mem. Hawaii Bar Assn., Maui Country Club, Naval Intelligence Profls. Avocations: ocean swimming, golf. Home and Office: 2807 Kekaulike Ave Kula HI 96790

ROHLOFF, CLAIRE MARIE, interior designer, educator; b. Dover, N.J., Mar. 17, 1945; d. Harold Alfred and Margaret Clara (Grether) Rohloff. Diploma, Bryn Mawr Hosp., 1966; BFA magna cum laude, Kean Coll. N.J., 1980; MS in Interior Design, Pratt Inst., 1984; grad., Meridian Shiatsu Inst., 1997. RN N.J., cert. internat. cert. bodywork and massage profl., practitioner Asian bodywork; master gardener. Asst. head nurse neuropsychiat. inst. Morristown (N.J.) Meml. Hosp., 1966-70; clinic nurse Morris County Aftercare Clinic Drug Abusers, Morristown, 1970-72; charge nurse psychiat. unit Overlook Hosp., Summit, N.J., 1975-81, interior design tech. and facilities devel., 1981-83; propr. Innovative Interiors; asst. prof. Kean Coll., 1979-80, prof., 1980-90, Trenton State Coll., 1990-92; co-owner Light lines Holistic Health Ctr., Clinton, N.J., 1992-97; owner, tchg. classes in Shiatsu and Yoga East West Inst. Inc., 1997—. Cons. Sweets electronic divsn., McGraw Hill. Mem.: Alpha Sigma Lambda. Presbyterian. Home: 383 Bloomsbury Rd Bloomsbury NJ 08804-3208

ROHLOFF, LORI LUANNE, artist, former special education educator; b. Calgary, Alberta, Can., June 23, 1961; came to U.S., 1977; d. Robert John and Catherine Anne (Sled) R.; m. Leon A. Peek, 1993. BS in Psychology, U. N. Tex., 1984; BA in Edn., Tex. Women's U., 1991. Cert. tchr. spl. edn., Tex.; cert. art edn. 1-12, Tex. Spl. edn. art educator Jane Marshall Elem., Middle Sch., Denton, Tex., 199-91; spl. edn. educator high sch. Sanger (Tex.) Ind. Sch. Dist., 1991—; tchr. secondary art Sanger High Sch., 1994—. One-woman shows include Connectivity, 1992, E. Gallery, 1998; exhibited in group shows at North Tex. Area Arts League, 1993 (Best of Show), 95, Martha Robbins Ann. Exhb., 1997, Dallas Visual Art Ctr., 1997, Tex. Womans U. Gallery, 1997., Mem. Mortarboard. Democrat. Episccopalian. Avocations: photography, jogging, gardening.

ROHM, ROBERT HERMANN, sculptor, educator; b. Cin., Feb. 6, 1934; s. Hermann George and Anna Katherine (Sager) R.; m. Patricia Jean Cutlip, Dec. 6, 1959 (div. 1978); children: Hans Tobin, Kyle Curtis. B in Indsl. Design, Pratt Inst., 1956; MFA in Sculpture, Cranbrook Acad. Art, 1960. Instr. Columbus (Ohio) Coll. Art and Design, 1956-59, Pratt Inst., Bklyn., 1960-65; prof. art U. R.I., Kingston, 1965-95, pres. emeritus N.Y., 1996—. One-man shows: O.K. Harris Gallery, N.Y.C., 1970, 72, 73, 75, 77, 80, 83, 84, 86, 89, 92, 94, 97, 99, 2002, Parker St. 470 Gallery, Boston, 1970, 72, Univ. Rochester, N.Y., 1971, N.S. Coll. Art, Halifax, 1970, Worcester Art Mus. (Mass.), 1978, Univ. R.I., 1981, 88, 94, Nielsen Gallery, Boston, 1985, 86, 92, 93, 2001, La Jolla Mus. Contemporary Art, Calif., 1985, Lenore Gray Gallery, Providence, 1990, 93, 95, Wheeler Gallery, Providence, 1996, R.I. Coll., Providence, 1998; group shows include Boston Mus., 1974, Whitney Mus., N.Y.C., 1962, 64, 69, 70, 73, 83, Va. Mus., Richmond, 1970, Fogg Mus., Cambridge, Mass., 1971, Seattle Art Mus., 1969, Vancouver Art Mus., B.C., Can., 1970, N.J. State Mus., Trenton, 1969, R.I. State Coun. on Arts, 1973, 82, Vassar Coll., 1971, Inst. Contemporary Art, Boston, 1975, Miss. Mus. Art, Jackson, 1979-80, Grey Art Gallery, NYU, 1980, Montclair (N.J.) Art Mus., 1978, Aldrich Mus. Contemporary Art, Ridgefield, Conn.,1981, 82, SUNY-Plattsburgh, 1981, Zone Gallery, Springfield, Mass., 1982, Cumberland Gallery, Nashville, 1986, 93, Allan Frumkin Gallery, N.Y.C., 1985, Beitzel Fine Arts Inc., N.Y.C., Addison Gallery Am. Art, Andover, Mass., 1989, Nielsen Gallery, Boston, 1990-91, 99, Soma Gallery, San Diego, 1993, Palo Alto (Calif.) Cultural Ctr., Centre Coll., Danville, Ky.; represented in permanent collections Columbus Gallery Fine Art, Finch Coll., N.Y.C., Pa. State U., Kunsthalle, Zurich, Va. Mus. Fine Arts, Mus. Modern Art, N.Y.C., U. N.Mex., Albuquerque, Albright-Knox Gallery, Buffalo, Whitney Mus. Am. Art, N.Y.C., Met. Mus. Art, N.Y.C., Rose Art Mus., Brandeis U., Waltham Mass., Mus. Fine Art, Boston, Mus. of Contemporary Art, Chgo., Newport (R.I.) Art Mus., Tucson Mus. of Art, Ariz., Flint Inst. Arts, Mich., Butler Inst. Am. Art, Youngstown, Ohio, Munson-Williams Proctor Arts Inst. Mus. Art, Utica, N.Y. Grantee Guggenheim Found., 1964, R.I. State Council on Arts, 1973, 82, 93, NEA, 1974, 86; recipient Cassandra Found. award, 1967, award Boston 200 Bicentennial Commn., 1975. Achievements include subject of numerous articles in jours. and catalogues. E-mail: bob_rohm@hotmail.com.

ROHN, DAVID RIIS, reporter, columnist, educator; b. Columbus, Ohio, May 3, 1946; s. Robert Jones and Ann Janet Rohn; m. Madelaine Berger Rohn, Dec. 4, 1980; children: Robert Morris, Jacob Samuel. BA, Marietta (Ohio) Coll., 1968. Reporter, columnist The Indpls. News, 1968-82, chief editl. writer, columnist, 1982-99; environ. writer The Indpls. Star, 1999—2002; instr., mem. adj. faculty Ind. U., Indpls., 1980—. Bd. dirs. Eagle Creek Pk. Found., Indpls., 1998-2000; mem. Juries 2000 Com., Indpls., 1998-2000. Recipient Chris Savage award Ind. U., 1974, 1st Amendment award Ind. Bar Assn., Indpls., 1979, Sagamore of the Wabash, Gov. Frank O'Bannon, Indpls., 1999. Mem. Soc. Profl. Journalists (Bronze medallion 1983), Indpls. Lit. Club, Indpls. Press Club (bd. dirs. 1972-74), Amos Butler Audubon Soc., Friends of Corkscrew Swamp. Avocations: birding, archery. E-mail: davidrohn@aol.com.

ROHN, REUBEN DAVID, pediatric educator and administrator; b. Israel, Apr. 12, 1945; came to U.S., 1954; s. Aryeh and Rachel (Brenner) R.; m. Judith Semel, Sept. 6, 1971; 1 child, Karen. BA cum laude, Bklyn. Coll., 1967; MD, N.Y. Med. Coll., 1971. Diplomate Am. Bd. Pediat., Am. Bd. Pediatric Endocrinology, Am. Bd. Pediatrics-Adolescent Medicine. Intern in pediat. Montefiore Hosp., Bronx, N.Y., 1971-72, resident in pediat., 1972-74; fellow in adolescent medicine U. Md. Hosp., Balt., 1974-76; preceptor in pediat. Johns Hopkins U. Sch. Health Svcs., 1975-76; asst. prof. dept. pediat. Ea. Va. Med. Sch., Norfolk, 1976-82; coord. pediat. clerkship Ea. Va. Med. Sch., Children's Hosp. of King's Daus., 1977-90; prof. dept. pediat. Ea. Va. Med. Sch., 1989—; adj. prof. chemistry Old Dominion U., 1984—; dir. adolescent medicine/endocrinology Children's Hosp. of King's Daus., 1976—. Mem. curriculum com. Ea. Va. Med. Sch., 1977-79, clerkship coords. com. 1977-90, genetics com., 1978-80, evaluation com. 1979-91, chmn. selectives com., 1981-82, ad hoc com. on consultation, 1982-83, student progress com., 1983-85, student health com., 1985-87, LCME com. on curriculum, 1990-92; mem. child abuse com. Children's Hosp. of King's Daus., 1976-80, chmn. adolescent adv. com., 1976-80, patient care com. 1980-94, nutrition com. 1980-94, utilization rev. com., 1980-82, med. records com., 1987-89, gen. med./surg. task force com., 1987-88, chmn. dept. promotions com., 1990—; bd. dirs. Pediat. Faculty Assocs., 1994-98, mgmt. com. Children's Specialty Group, 1998-2000; spkr. in field. Reviewer Jour. Adolescent Health Care, 1986—, mem. editl. bd., 1989-92; contbr. articles to profl. jours. Mem. Norfolk Sch. Health Coun., 1977—, mem. ad hoc com. infant screening program for hypothroidism Commonwealth of Va., 1977-79, cons., 1979—; mem. cmty. adv. bd. Norfolk Adolescent Pregnancy Prevention Svc. Project, 1981-83; bd. dirs. Elizabeth River chpt. Am. Diabetes Assn., 1982-85, South Hampton Roads chpt. 1985-93; mem. adv. com. Norfolk-Virginia Beach Jr. League, 1987-88; judge ann. Health Edn. Fair, Norfolk Pub. schs., 1980-94; pres. VA/Carolines chpt. Soc. Adolescent Medicine, 1998-2000. Recipient grant Bressler Rsch. Fund, 1975-76, Biomed. Rsch. Devel. grant Ea. Va. Med. Sch., 1978, 78-79, 79-80. 81-82, 83-84, Children's Health Found. grant, 1988-89. Fellow: Am. Acad. Pediat. (youth and adolescence com. Va. chpt. 1978—2000); mem.: Lawson Wilkins Pediat. Endocrine Soc., Soc. Adolescent Medicine (abstract reviewer 1984—91), Sigma Xi. Avocations: photography, folk dancing. Home: 4653 Larkwood Dr Virginia Beach VA 23464-5815 Office: Childrens Hosp Kings Daus 601 Childrens Ln Norfolk VA 23507-1910 E-mail: rrohn@chkd.com.

ROHNER, BONNIE-JEAN, small business owner, computer consultant; b. Waltham, Mass., Aug. 2, 1946; d. Gerrit John and Marjorie Lorraine (Hollis) R.; children: David Harrison Sackett, Amanda Marjorie Sackett. BFA in Fashion, Pratt Inst., Bklyn., 1967; BA in Biology, Adelphi U., Garden City, N.Y., 1983; MS, CIS, U. New Haven, Conn., 1993. Freelance fashion designer, Garden City, 1971-76; owner, mgr. The Printing Workshop, Massapequa, N.Y., 1976-78; personnel mgr. Doron Ltd., Norwich, Conn., 1978-79; computer related trainer Gen. Dynamics, Groton, 1979-89; acad. computing coord. Three Rivers Com./Tech. Coll., Norwich, 1989-94; owner, mgr. bytestream, Norwichtown, Conn., 1993—. Computer cons. U. New Haven, Groton, 1990-92; tech. advisor Countywide Network Com., 1989-90; sec. Connbug, Rocky Hill, Conn., 1992-93; tech. cons. on Internet Am. Online, 1996—. Mem. NAFE, AAUW, AAUP, ACM, Women's Network of S.E. Conn. Avocations: creative writing, internet.

ROHNER, RALPH JOHN, lawyer, educator, university dean; b. East Orange, N.J., Aug. 10, 1938; AB, Cath. U. Am., 1960, JD, 1963. Bar: Md. 1964. Teaching fellow Stanford (Calif.) U., 1963-64; atty. pub. health div. HEW, 1964-65; prof. law Cath. U. Am. Sch. Law, Washington, 1965—, acting dean, 1968-69, assoc. dean, 1969-71, dean, 1987-95; staff counsel consumer affairs subcom. U.S. Senate Banking Com., 1975-76; cons. Fed. Res. Bd., 1976-83, chmn. consumer adv. council, 1981; cons. FDIC, 1978-80; spl. counsel Consumer Bankers Assn., 1984—. Cons. U.S. Regulatory Coun., 1979-80. Co-author: Consumer Law: Cases and Materials, 1979, 2d edit., 1991; co-author, editor The Law of Truth in Lending, 1984, republished, 2000. Bd. dirs. Migrant Legal Action Program, Inc., Washington, Automobile Owners Action Coun., Washington, Credit Rsch. Ctr., Georgetown U., Am. Fin. Svcs. Assn. Edn. Found. Conf. on Consumer Fin. Law. Mem. ABA, Am. Law Inst., Coll. of Consumer Fin. Svcs. Lawyers. Home: 10909 Forestgate Pl Glenn Dale MD 20769-2047 Office: Cath U Sch Law 620 Michigan Ave NE Washington DC 20064-0001 E-mail: rohner@law.edu. *We learn from those we teach, we are inspired to write by those who read, and we should serve as examples to those who aspire.*

ROHNER, THOMAS JOHN, JR. urologist; b. Trenton, N.J., Jan. 1, 1936; s. Thomas J. and Julia (Kanyo) R.; m. Jessie Rohner; children: Christopher, James. BA, Yale U., 1957; MD, U. Pa., 1961. Diplomate Am. Bd. Urology. Intern Hosp. U. Pa., Phila., 1961-62, resident in gen. surgery, 1962-64, resident in urology, 1964-67; asst. prof. surgery M.S. Hersey Med. Ctr., Pa. State U., Hershey, 1970-71, assoc. prof., 1971-75, prof., 1975—, chief urol. divsn., 1970-2000; assoc. dean for clin. affairs M.S. Hershey Med. Ctr., Pa. State U., 1996-99, interim chair dept. surgery, 1998-99, chief of med. staff, 1999-2000. Bd. dirs. Highmark, Inc.; corp. mem. Pa. Blue Shield, 1991—. Contbr. articles to profl. jours. Served to maj. M.C., U.S. Army, 1967-69. USPHS fellow, 1969-70; grantee HEW, 1971-76, USPHS, 1971-76 Fellow ACS (pres. ctrl. Pa. chpt. 1983-84, bd. govs. 1991-97); mem. AMA, Am. Urol. Assn. (pres. mid-Atlantic sect. 1986-87), Urol. Assn. Pa., Phila. Urol. Soc. (pres. 1980-81), Assn. Acad. Surgeons, Am. Bd. Urology (trustee 1995-2001), Pa. Med. Soc., Dauphin County Med. Soc., Soc. Pediat. Urology, Soc. Univ. Urologists (pres. 1990-91), Nat. Urol. Forum, Societe Internationale d'Urologie, Transamerican Urol. Rschrs., Internat. Continence Soc., Coll. Physicians of Phila. Home: 2907 Mt Gretna Rd Elizabethtown PA 17022-9689 Office: Milton S Hershey Med Ctr Pa State Univ PO Box 850 Hershey PA 17033-0850 E-mail: trohner@psu.edu.

ROHR, DAVIS CHARLES, aerospace consultant, business executive, retired air force officer; b. Burlington, Wis., Oct. 29, 1929; s. Charles Davis Rohr and Dorothy Elizabeth (Hahn) Rohr Larson; m. Gayle Lynn White, Aug. 22, 1959; children— Ellen Louise, Jean Elizabeth Student, Northwestern U., 1947-48; B.Sc., U.S. Mil. Acad., 1952; MA, U. Wash., 1960. Commd. 2d lt. USAF, 1952, advanced through grades to maj. gen, 1980, fighter pilot Ohio, Korea, Japan, 1954-58; asst. prof. history USAF Acad., Colo., 1960-64; fighter pilot, squadron ops. officer Idaho and, Fed. Republic Germany, 1965-69; fighter squadron comdr. Vietnam, 1969-70; country dir. S.Am. Office of Sec. of Def., Washington, 1970-73; exec. officer, dep. dir. maintenance Hdqrs. Tactical Air Command, 1973-75; tactical fighter wing comdr. Tex., Utah, 1976-79; chief Office of Mil. Coop., Cairo, 1979-81; dir. plans and policy U.S. European Command, Stuttgart, Fed. Republic Germany, 1981-84; dep. comdr. in chief U.S. Cen. Command, MacDill AFB, Fla., 1984-87, ret.; aerospace cons., 1988—. Adj. prof. history Paradise Valley C.C., 1991-94; real estate broker, 1991—. Decorated Def. D.S.M., 2 Def. Superior Service medals, Legion of Merit with cluster, D.F.C., Meritorious Service medal, Air medal with 14 clusters, Air Force Commendation medal, Purple Heart

ROHR, DONALD GERARD, history educator; b. Toledo, Oct. 10, 1920; s. Lewis Walter and Marie (Pilliod) R.; m. Joan Willis Michener, Sept. 14, 1948; children: Karen, Kristin. BA, U. Toronto, Ont., Can., 1943, MA, 1949; PhD, Harvard U., 1958. Instr., then asst. prof. Williams Coll., 1953-59; mem. faculty Brown U., 1959—, prof. history, 1963-86, emeritus, 1986—, chmn. dept., 1960-65, 66-69, 72-74, sec. faculty, 1969-72, assoc. dean faculty and acad. affairs, 1976-81; adminstv. dir. Howard Fedn., 1989-92. Author: The Origins of Social Liberalism in Germany, 1963, (with Robert Ergang) Europe Since Waterloo, 1967; editor: Travel Diaries of John Carter Brown, 1822-1824. Served with AUS, 1943-46, ETO. Mem. Am. Hist. Assn., Conf. Group Ctrl. European History, Providence Com. Fgn. Rels. (sec. 1968-81, chmn. 1981-92), Thomas Becket Fedn. (v.p. 1983-84, pres. 1984-86), English Speaking Union (pres. Providence br. 1986-88), U. Club, Faculty Club (Providence, pres. 1981-83). Roman Catholic. Home: 71 Grotto Ave Providence RI 02906-5609

ROHR, DWIGHT MASON, news director, radio marketing consultant; b. Covington, Va., July 18, 1952; s. Edward Mason and Betty (Eppling) R.; m. Betty Erwin, Aug. 1, 1977; children: Christopher Mason, Joseph Michael. AAS in Bus. Mgmt., Dabney S. Lancaster C.C., Clifton Forge, Va., 1997. Cert. radio operator; cert. radio mktg. cons. Audio engr. WJBR, Wilmington, Del., 1971-72; announcer WASA/WHDG, Havre de Grace, Md., 1972-73; news dir. mktg. WKEY Inc., Covington, 1974—. Active Stonewall Jackson Area coun. Boy Scouts Am., 1990-99; dir. cmty. rels. ARC, Covington, 1975-98; mem. adv. bd. Salvation Army, Covington, 1995-2001—, Alleghany County chpt. March of Dimes, 2001—; city coucilman, Covington, 1997-98; mountaineer Amateur Radio Emergency Svc. Recipient Scouter of Yr. awrd VFW Post 1033, 1994, Dist. award of merit Boy Scouts Am., 1995, Silver Beaver, 1998; named to Outstanding Young Men of Am., 1980. Mem. Soc. Profl. Journalists, Radio TV News Dirs. Assn., Masons, Scottish Rite, Va. Mountain Amateur Radio Club, Covington Ruritan Club. Avocations: amateur radio, broadcasting, coin collecting. Home: 347 E Gray St Covington VA 24426-2109 E-mail: wkeywiqo@aol.com., wiqo@aol.com.

ROHR, JAMES EDWARD, banker; b. Cleve., Oct. 18, 1948; s. Charles E. and Loretta (Kramer) R.; m. Sharon Lynn Chambers, Dec. 29, 1970; children— Julie, James, Kristen. BA, Notre Dame U., 1970; MBA, Ohio State U., 1972. From comml. banking officer to pres. Pitts. Nat. Bank, 1974-89, chmn., CEO, 1989-93, pres., CEO, 1993—; vice-chmn. PNC Bank Corp., 1989-92, pres., 1992—, COO, 1998—; CEO, pres. PNC Fin. Svcs. Group, Inc., Pitts., 2000—, chmn., 2001—. Bd. dirs. Allegheny Techs. Corp. Mem. adv. bd. Salvation Army, Pitts., 1983—; chair Civic Light Opera; bd. dirs. Greater Pitts. coun. Boy Scouts Am., Cultural Trust, Carnegie-Mellon U. Mem. Am. Bankers Assn., Fin. Svcs. Roundtable, Allegheny Conf., Orgn., Pa. Bus. Roundtable (vice chmn.), Duquesne Club (dir.). Roman Catholic. Office: PNC Financial Services Group Inc 249 5th Ave Pittsburgh PA 15222-2709

ROHR, RICHARD DAVID, lawyer; b. Toledo, Aug. 31, 1926; s. Lewis Walter and Marie Janet (Pilliod) R.; m. Ann Casey, Aug. 25, 1951; children: Martha, Elizabeth, Matthew, Sarah, Margaret, Thomas. BA magna cum laude, Harvard U., 1950; JD, U. Mich., 1953. Bar: Mich. 1954, U.S. Dist. Ct. (so. dist.) Mich. 1954, U.S. Ct. Appeals (6th cir.) 1960, U.S. Supreme Ct. 1961. Assoc. Bodman, Longley & Dahling, L.L.P., Detroit, 1954-58, ptnr., 1958-75, mng. ptnr., 1975-2000. Adj. prof. U. Mich., Ann Arbor, 1976-82. With U.S. Army, 1945-46. Mem. ABA, Detroit Bar Assn., Mich. Bar Assn., Renaissance Club, Detroit Athletic Club, Order of Coif, Phi Beta Kappa. Roman Catholic. Home: 441 Rivard Blvd Grosse Pointe MI 48230-1627 Office: Bodman Longley Dahling LLP 100 Renaissance Ctr Ste 34 Detroit MI 48243-1001

ROHRABACHER, DANA, congressman; b. Coronado, Calif., June 21, 1947; s. Donald and Doris Rohrabacher; m. Rhonda Carmont, Aug. 1997. Student, L.A. Harbor Coll., 1965-67; BA in History, Long Beach State Coll., 1969; MA in Am. Studies, U. So. Calif., 1976. Reporter City News Svc./Radio West, L.A.; editorial writer Orange County Register, 1979-80; asst. press. sec. Reagan for Pres. Campaign, 1976, 80; speechwriter, spl. asst. to Pres. Reagan White House, Washington, 1981-88; mem. 101st-102nd Congresses from Calif. dist., 1989-93, 103d-106th Congress from 45th dist. Calif., 1993—. U.S. del. Young Polit. Leaders Conf., USSR; disting. lectr. Internat. Terrorism Conf., Paris, 1985; mem. Internat. Rels. com.; chmn. sci. subcom. on space and aeroautics. Recipient Disting. Alumnus award L.A. Harbor Coll., 1987. Avocations: surfing, white water rafting. Office: US Ho Reps 2338 Rayburn HOB Washington DC 20515*

ROHRABACHER, JANET HAMMOND, geneologist, archivist; b. Williamston, Mich., Apr. 24, 1913; d. Herbert Moore and Anna Eugenia (Lane) Hammond; m. Albert Hazen Rohrabacher (dec.); children: Ardenne Anna Brigham, Jeffrey. Tchg. cert., We. Mich. U., Kalamazoo, 1936; degree in Practical Nursing, McPherson Nursing Sch., Howell, Mich., 1965; student, Mich. State U., East Lansing, 1940. Cert. Geneologist, LPN. Nurse Mich. State Sanatorium, Howell, 1939-41, Ingham County Chest Hosp., Lansing, 1940, Ea. Mich. Sanatorium, Ypsilanty, 1941, McPherson Hosp., Howell, 1942-66; archivist Howell Carnegie Libr., 1977-2001. Writer Bicentennial History of Howell. Chmn. Livingston County Civil War Obs. Com., 1963; active Bicentennial Com. Howell, 1973-77, Mich. State Sesquicentennial Com., 1985-89; sec. Howell Archives Bd., 1977—. Recipient award Mich. Geneol. Coun., 1991. Mem. DAR (award 1976), Livingston County Historical Soc. (charter, founder), Ancient and Honorable Artillery Soc. Mass, Descendents of Early Quakers, Palatines Am., Detroit Soc. Geneol. Rsch. Methodist. Avocations: antique collecting, square dancing, genealogical lecturing. Home: 407 W Highland Rd Apt A1 Howell MI 48843

ROHRBACH, HEIDI A. lawyer; b. Buffalo, Jan. 25, 1953; d. William R. and A.T. R.; m. Leonard Lance, Aug. 9, 1996; 1 child, Peter R. Frank. BA, Northwestern U., Evanston, Ill., 1974; JD, Vanderbilt U., Nashville, 1977. Bar: N.Y., 1978. V.p., asst. gen. counsel J.P. Morgan Chase & Co., N.Y.C., 1985—. Office: JP Morgan Chase & Co 270 Park Ave Fl 40 New York NY 10017-2014

ROHRBACH, PETER THOMAS, writer; b. N.Y.C., Feb. 27, 1926; s. James P. and Kathryn Ann (Foley) R.; m. Sheila Sheehan, Sept. 21, 1970; 1 child, Sarah. MA, Cath. U., Washington, 1952. Editl. cons. Harvard U., Urban Inst., Nat. Urban Coalition, HEW, Dept. Transp. Author 16 books including: The Largest Event, 1994, Conversation with Christ, 1994, Journey to Carith, 1966, American Issue, 1984, Stagecoach East, 1983; (booklets) Find, 1985, Many Missions, 1986; Editor: The Wright Brothers, The Jet Age, Prelude to the Space Age, Messerschmitt (winner Prix Aéronautique in France 1981); editor jour. Spiritual Life, Air and Space mag.; writer TV and motion picture scripts for comml. and pub. prodns. including Wally's Workshop and PBS's series on aging; contbr. articles to profl. jours. Mem. Authors Guild, PEN.

ROHRBAUGH, LISA ANNE, librarian; b. Girard, Ohio, Sept. 17, 1956; d. John Michael and Josephine Antoinette (Oliva) Sultan; m. Paul Hugh Rohrbaugh Jr., July 28, 1979. BA, Youngstown State U., 1978; MLS, Kent State U., 1979. Libr.. readers assistance dept. Youngstown (Ohio) Pub. Libr., 1979-86; libr., researcher Ajax Magnethermic Corp., Warren, Ohio, 1986-90; asst. reference libr. Youngstown State U., 1990-93; dir. East Palestine (Ohio) Meml. Pub. Libr., 1993—. Translator articles dealing with electronics and induction heating/melting tech. from Spanish, German and French into English; mem. Ohio Regional Libr. Sys. Reviewer for Libr. Jour. Recipient Quest '91 Creative Scholarship award Youngstown State U., 1991. Mem. Ohio Libr. Coun., Rotary (pres. E. Palestine (Ohio) 1999-2000). Avocations: reading, cooking, baseball. Office: East Palestine Meml Pub Libr 309 N Market St East Palestine OH 44413-2153

ROHRBAUGH, NOVA R, retired music educator; b. Brodbecks, Pa., Jan. 28, 1915; d. Adam Kaltreider and Florence Viola Grote; m. Norman S Rohrbaugh, Oct. 13, 1934; children: Machree M Baumgardner, Marlet R, Laura J Summers. BM, U. Ext. Conservatory, Chicago, IL, 1961. Music tchr. Conewago Twp., Hanover, Pa., 1956—59; elem. tchr. Southwester Sch. Dist., 1959—69; music tchr. Conewago Valley Sch. Dist., 1970—74, Spring Grove Sch. Dist., Spring Grove, 1970—78. Pvt. music tchr., Pa., 1941—2000. Composer: (choral anthem) I Want to Live for the Master , The Lord is My Light , author several books of poetry, (childrens book) Chester the Nosy Pig , Daisy the Little Gosling , Benny the Little Goat. Vol. Hanover Hall Nursing Home, Homewood Retirement Ctr, Hanover, Pa., 1982—2001. Recipient Editors Choice Award, Nat. Libr. of Poetry, 1994, 1995. Mem.: Am. Assoc Ret. Persons (sec. 1986—2000, outstanding svc. to cmty. 1992). Democrat-Npl. United Church Of Christ. Avocations: sewing, quilting, writing poetry and childrens stories. Home: 120 Amy Ln New Oxford PA 17350

ROHRBAUGH, WAYNE JOSEPH, chemical company executive; b. York, Pa., Aug. 13, 1948; s. Clair Joseph and Mary Elizabeth Rohrbaugh; m. Phyllis Theresa Leonard, June 19, 1971; children: Stephanie Elaine, Michael Wayne, Daniel Philip, Christine Marie. BS in Chemistry with honors, Drexel U., 1971; PhD in Phys. Chemistry, Iowa State U., 1977. Rsch. asst. Ames Lab./U.S. Dept. Energy, Ames, Iowa, 1971-76; assoc. prof. chemistry Wesley Coll., Dover, Del., 1976-78; group leader material structure rsch. Mobil R&D Corp., Paulsboro, N.J., 1978-90; mgr. analytical sect. ICI Americas, Inc., Wilmington, Del., 1990-94; rsch. mgr. corp. R&D dept. Ashland Chem. Co., Columbus, Ohio, 1994-96, dir. corp. R&D dept., 1996—. Adj. prof. chemistry Rowan Coll., Glassboro, N.J., 1980-88; guest scientist Brookhaven (N.Y.) Nat. Lab., 1985-88. Contbr. articles to profl. jours. Mem. council Ames Cmty. Coun. on Drugs, 1973, All-Univ. Cmty. Coun., Ames, 1975, Wesley Coll. Coun., Dover, 1977, 78. Recipient Outstanding Young Men of Am. citation U.S. Jaycees, 1978. Mem. Am. Chem. Soc. (undergrad. award in analytical chemistry 1970, South Jersey sect. chmn. 1987-88, sec. Carothers Award com. 1991-92), Indsl. Rsch. Inst., Dirs. Indsl. Rsch., Analytical Lab. Mgrs. Assn. (pres.), Coun. for Chem. Rsch., Sigma Xi, Phi Lambda Upsilon, Pi Lambda Phi. Republican. Roman Catholic. Achievements include zeolite structure research; led group that solved the framework molecular structures of ten zeolite compositions, one of which, ZSM-18, represents the only known aluminosilicate structure containing rings of three (Si,Al)-O species. Office: Ashland Chemical Co PO Box 2219 Columbus OH 43216-2219 E-mail: wrohrbaugh@ashland.com.

ROHRBOUGH, ELSA CLAIRE HARTMAN, artist; b. Shreveport, La., Sept. 26, 1915; d. Adolph Emil and Camille Claire (Francis) Hartman; m. Leonard M. Rohrbough, June 19, 1937 (dec. Jan. 1977); children: Stephen, Frank, Leonard. Juried exhbns. (painting) Massur Mus. Art, Monroe, La., Mobile (Ala.) Art Gallery, Gulf Coast Juried Exhibit, Mobile, Juried Arts Nat., Tyler, Tex., Greater New Orleans Nat., La. Watercolor Soc. Internat., Ky. Watermedia Nat., So. Watercolor Ann., La. Women Artist, many others. One-woman shows include Le Petit Theatre du Vieux Carre, New Orleans World Trade Ctr.'s Internat. House, Singing River Art Assn., Pascagoula, Miss., La. Font Inn, Pascagoula, Mandeville (La.) City Hall, St. Tammany Art Assn., Covington, La., others; exhibited in groups shows at 1st Guaranty Bank, Hammond, La., St. Tammany Art Assn., Ft. Isabel Gallery, Covington, S.E. La. State U. Mem.: St. Tammany Art Assn. (bd. dirs. 1985—86, 1987, instr. 1977—78, classes chmn. 1986—88), La. State Assn. (pres. 1998—2000), Nat. League Am. Pen Women (v.p. S.E. La. br. 1986—87, 2002—, pres. 1987—92, 1994—98). Republican. Roman Catholic. Avocations: sewing, flower arranging, gardening, ethnic cooking, American antiques. Home: 100 Christwood Blvd Apt 106 Covington LA 70433-4601

ROHREN, BRENDA MARIE ANDERSON, therapist, educator; b. Kansas City, Mo., Apr. 18, 1959; d. Wilbur Dean and Katheryn Elizabeth (Albright) Anderson; m. Lathan Edward Rohren, May 10, 1985; 1 child, Amanda Jessica. BS in Psychology, Colo. State U., 1983; MA in Psychology, Cath. U. Am., 1986. Lic. mental health practitioner. Mental health therapist, sr. case mgr. Rappahannock Area Community Svcs. Bd., Fredericksburg, Va., 1986-88, mental health therapist, case mgmt. supr., 1988; rsch. assoc. Inst. Medicine, NAS, Washington, 1988-89; supr. adult psychiat. program Lincoln (Nebr.) Gen. Hosp., 1989, program supr. mental health svcs., 1989-91; adj. instr. S.E. Community Coll., Lincoln, 1990—; assessment & referral specialist Rivendell Psychiat. Ctr., Seward, Nebr., 1993-95; therapist Lincoln Day Treatment Ctr., Lincoln, 1993-95. Adj. instr. Coll. of St. Mary, 1994—2001; therapist Rape/Spouse Abuse Crisis Ctr., Lincoln, 1996—2002; substance abuse counselor Independence Ctr., Lincoln; computer cons. Syscon Corp., Washington, 1983—84. Author: (report) Bottom Line Benefits: Building Economic Success Through Stronger Families; editor: (newsletter) Alliance for Mentally Ill, Lincoln, 1993-2002. Active Nat. Alliance for the Mentally Ill-Lincoln, Nebr. Domestic Violence/Sexual Assault Coalition. Mem. APA (assoc.), ACA, Nebr.

Psychol. Assn. (assoc.), Nebr. Counseling Assn Democrat. Roman Catholic. Avocations: interior decorating, reading, landscaping, camping. Home: 3821 S 33rd St Lincoln NE 68506-3806 Office: SE Community Coll 8800 O St Lincoln NE 68520-1299

ROHRER, GEORGE JOHN, retired lawyer; b. Elmira, N.Y., Oct. 24, 1931; s. George J. and Lois (Hess) R.; m. Martha M. Jacobs, Jan. 6, 1952; children: Jacquelyn D. Berbusse, Michael A., John S. JD with distinction, Pacific Coast U., 1967. Bar: Calif. 1969, U.S. Dist. Ct. (ctrl. dist.) 1969. Incentive dir. Blue Chip Stamp Co., L.A., 1963-69; gen. ptnr. Songer Leavell Rohrer & Jorgensen, Bellflower, Calif., 1969-80; sr. ptnr. Rohrer & Holtz, Anaheim, 1980-94; ret., 1994. Panel atty. Calif. Assn. of Realtors/State, Hotline, Calif. 1977-94; Founder/Dir. Midcities Nat. Bank, Bellflower, 1981-90; trustee S.E. area Bar Assn., Norwalk, Calif., 1974-75. Pres. Bellflower Kiwanis Club, 1972-73; dir. Los Cerritos Y.M.C.A., Bellflower, 1977-78; vol. counsel Am. Radio Relay League, 1987-92. Mem. Orange County Bar Assn., Los Angeles County Bar Assn., Orange County Amicus (pro bono), Bellflower C. of C. (pres. 1975-76), Masons, Shriners. Republican. Avocations: amature radio, fishing, travel. E-mail: kb6fo@artelco.com.

ROHRER, HEINRICH, physicist; b. Buchs, Switzerland, June 6, 1933; Diploma in physics, Swiss Inst. Tech., Zurich, 1955, PhD in Physics, 1960; D. Sci. (hon.), Rutgers U., 1987, Marseille (France) U., 1988, Madrid U., 1988, Tsukuba (Japan) U., 1994, Frankfurt (Germany) U., 1996, Tohoku (Japan) U., 2000. Rsch. asst. Swiss Inst. Tech., Zurich, 1960-61; postdoctoral Rutgers U., New Brunswick, N.J., 1961-63; with IBM Rsch. Lab., Zurich, 1963-97; rschr. CSIC, Madrid, 1997-2000, RIKEN, Waco, Japan, 1998, Tohoku U., Sendai, Japan, 1998—. Vis. scholar U. Calif., Santa Barbara, 1974-75. Co-recipient King Faisal Internat. prize for sci., 1984, Hewlett Packard Europhysics prize, 1984, Nobel prize for Physics, 1986, Cresson medal Franklin Inst., Phila., 1987; IBM fellow, 1986; named to Nat. Inventors Hall of Fame, 1994. Fellow Royal Microscopical Soc. (hon.); mem. NAS (fgn. assoc.), Swiss Acad. Tech. Scis., Swiss Phys. Soc. (hon.), Swiss Assn. Engring. and Architecture (hon.), Zurich Phys. Soc. (hon.). Office: Rebbergstr 9d CH 8832 Wollerau Switzerland E-mail: h.rohrer@gmx.net.

ROHRER, JANE CAROLYN, gifted education specialist, academic administrator, poet, consultant; b. Faribault, Minn., July 17, 1940; d. Christian A. and Lydia G. (Hilleboe) R.; children: Paula Eisenrich, Lisa Eisenrich, Peter Eisenrich. BS in English, U. Minn., 1962, MA in English, 1964; MA in Edn., Boise (Idaho) State U., 1976; PhD in Spl. Edn./Gifted, Kent State U., 1992. Tchr. English Lompoc (Calif.) High Sch., 1962-63; gifted and talented facilitator Boise Sch. Dist., 1976-84, spl. edn. cons. tchr., 1984-89, spl. edn. adminstrv. intern, 1989-90; faculty Kent (Ohio) State U., 1991-92; dir. Tchr. Edn. Program Sierra Nev. Coll., Incline Village, Nev., 1993-1996, dean acad. programs, 1995-1996, dean faculty, 1997-99, v.p. acad. affairs, 1999—, acting pres., 2001. Mem. Nev. Statewide Task Force on Tchr. Edn., Nev. State English Framework Commn.; numerous publs. and conf. presentations. Choir dir., La., Japan, Idaho, Ohio, Nev., 1966-98. Whittenberger fellow Boise State U., 1975-76. Mem. Ch. Women United, Coun. Exceptional Children (state bd. dirs. 1987-88), Nat. Assn. Gifted Children, S.W. Regional Spl. Edn. Adv. Bd., Idaho Talented and Gifted Assn. (state pres. 1988-89), Nev. Assn. Colls. of Tchr. Edn. (sec.-treas.), Mortar Bd., Phi Beta Kappa, Eta Sigma Upsilon, Pi Lambda Theta, Phi Delta Kappa. Avocations: reading, music, swimming, hiking, writing. E-mail: jrohrer@sierranevada.edu.

ROHRER, REED BEAVER, lawyer; b. Langley AFB, Va., June 15, 1954; s. Richard L. and Elaine (Beaver) R.; children: Christopher S., Jennifer R. BBA, U. Hawaii, 1977; JD, Pepperdine U., 1980; LLM in Taxation, U. San Diego, 1981. Bar: Hawaii 1981, U.S. Dist. Ct. Hawaii 1981, U.S. Tax Ct. 1981. Tax specialist Grant Thorton (Alexander Grant), Honolulu, 1981-83; assoc. Oliver, Cuskaden & Lee, 1983-85; corp. counsel Bishop Trust Co. Ltd., 1985-89; v.p., corp. counsel Wall St. Fin. Corp., Irvine, Calif., 1989-92; prin. Law Firm of Reed B. Rohrer, Honolulu, 1992-94; ptnr. Rottenger & Rohrer, 1994—96; prin. Reed B. Rohrer, 1996—. Pres. TRAC Systems, Inc.; bd. dirs. Rohrer Investment Corp., Cozy U.S.A., Inc.; co-trustee Hawaii Cemetery Trusts, 2001--; spkr. in field. Author: (with others) Wills and Trusts Formbook, 1987; contbr. articles to profl. jours. Mem. ABA, Hawaii Bar Assn. (chmn. tax sect. 1988, estate and gift tax com.). Republican. Avocations: flying, surfing, diving, sailing. Home: 7852 Makaaoa Pl Honolulu HI 96825- Office: 735 Bishop St Ste 325 Honolulu HI 96813-3916

ROHRER, SUSAN EARLEY, film producer, writer, director; b. Richmond, Va., Mar. 24; d. Charles Marion Jr. and Gloria Jean (Ripley) Earley; m. Mark Brooks Rohrer. BA in Art cum laude, James Madison U. Prodr., dir., co-story writer (tv shows) Never Say Goodbye, 1988 (Emmy award, Humanitas Prize finalist), Terrible Things My Mother Told Me, 1988 (Emmy nomination, Gold award Nat. Ednl. Film Festival); producer, dir. (tv movies) For Jenny With Love (TV Movie award), Mother's Day, 1989 (3 Image award nominations), producer, dir., writer (tv show) The Emancipation of Lizzie Stern, 1991 (Angel award, Bronze award Nat. Ednl. Film Festival, Emmy nomination, Monitor award finalist, TV Movie award), If I Die Before I Wake, 1993 (Emmy nomination, Humanitas Prize finalist, Cine Golden Eagle, TV Movie award); dir. (TV show) Sweet Valley High, 1996; dir. TV pilot Dojo Kids, 1996; prodr., dir., co-writer About Sarah, TV movie, 1998 (award of excellence Film Adv. Bd., Best of Festival award Breckenridge Film Festival, The Christopher award, Angel award, N.Y. Festivals finalist). Recipient Resolution of Recognition Virginia Beach City Coun., 1988. Mem. ATAS, SAG, Writers Guild Am., Dirs. Guild Am. also: Irv Schechter Co care Irv Schechter 9460 Wilshire Blvd Ste 300 Beverly Hills CA 90212

ROHRER, SUSAN JANE, mayor; b. Springfield, Ill., Apr. 30, 1945; d. Russell Shriver and Margaret (Shumaker) Rohrer. AB, MacMurray Coll., 1967; MS, U. Ill., 1971, PhD, 1973. Cert. tchr. spl. K-14, H.S., Gen. Adminstr. K-12, Ill. Instr., Virden Jr. H.S., Ill., 1967-69; asst. to dean U. Ill. Coll. Medicine-Urbana, 1974-75, adminstrv. assoc., 1975-80; asst. prin. Virden Jr. and Sr. H.S., 1983-84, prin., 1984-87; sports writer News Gazette Newspaper, Champaign, Ill., 1973-74; owner Home Care Svcs., Inc., 1990—; co-owner Capitol Foods, Inc., Springfield, Ill., 1992-96. Dir. Dana Thomas Found., Springfield, Ill., 1989, Virden Unit 4 Sch. Bd.; sec. Virden Sch. Bd., 1992-93, v.p., 1993-94; mayor Virden. Ill., 1993—. Methodist. Home: 121 W Hill St Virden IL 62690-1232

ROHRICH, RODNEY JAMES, plastic surgeon, educator; b. Eureka, S.D., Aug. 5, 1953; s. Claude and Katie (Schumacher) R.; m. Diane Louise Gibby, July 3, 1990; children: Taylor Rodney, Rachel Nicole. BA summa cum laude, N.D. State U., 1975; MD with honors, Baylor Coll., 1979. Diplomate Am. Bd. Plastic Surgery, Nat. Bd. Med. Examiners. Instr. surgery Harvard Med. Sch. Mass. Gen. Hosp., Boston, 1985-86; asst. prof. U. Tex. Southwestern Med. Ctr., Dallas, 1986-89, assoc. prof., 1989-91; chief plastic surgery Parkland/Zale Univ. Med. Ctr., 1989-99; prof., chmn. dept. plastic surgery U. Tex. Southwestern Med. Ctr., 1991—, Betty and Warren Woodward chair in plastic surgery, 1999. Pres., faculty senate U. Tex., crystal charity ball disting. chair in plastic surgery. Mem. editl. bd. Selected Readings in Plastic Surgery, The Cleft Palate and Craniofacial Jour.; co-editor Plastic and Reconstructive Surgery Jour., 1998—; contbr. articles to med. jours. Bd. dirs. Save-the-Children Found., Dallas, March of Dimes, Dallas, Dallas for Children; class mem. Leadership Dallas, 1989-90; mem. Adopt-A-Sch., Dallas Summer Mus. Guild, Dallas Mus. Art, Dallas Symphony Assn., Tex. Health Found., Youth Leadership Dallas. Grantee Urban Rsch. Fund, 1982, United Kingdom Ltd. Ednl. Rsch. Fund, 1983, Oxford Cleft Palate Found., 1983, Am. Assn. Plastic Surgeons, 1985, Plastic Surgery Ednl. Found., 1985, 89, 90, U. Tex. Health Sci. Ctr. Dept. Surgery, 1986, Howmedica, 1989, ConvaTec-Squibb, 1989, 91, ConvaTec, 1991; recipient Disting Svc. award Plastic Surg. Ednl. Found., 1997, Alumni Achievement award, N.D. State U., 1997. Mem. AAAS, ACS, AMA (Thomas Cronin award 1988, 90, Clifford C. Snyder award 1990), Am. Assn. Hand Surgery, Am. Burn Assn., Am. Cleft Palate Assn., Am. Soc. Law and Medicine, Am. Soc. Maxillofacial Surgeons, Am. Soc. for Surgery the Hand, Am. Soc. Plastic and Reconstructive Surgeons, Am. Trauma Soc., British Med. Assn., Nat. Vascular Malformations Found. Inc. (med. and sci. adv. bd.) Tex. Med. Assn., Tex. Soc. Plastic Surgeons, Mass. Gen. Hosp. Hand Club, Dallas County Med. Soc., Assn. Acad. Chmn. Plastic Surgery, Dallas Soc. Plastic Surgeons, Harvard Med. Sch. Alumni Assn., Inst. for Study of Profl. Risk, Plastic Surgery Rsch. Coun., Reed O. Dingman Soc. Plastic Surgeons, So. Med. Assn. Republican. Roman Catholic. Office: U Tex Southwestern Med Ctr Dept of Plastic Surgery 5323 Harry Hines Blvd Dallas TX 75390-9132 E-mail: Rod.Rohrich@UTSouthwestern.edu.

ROHRMAN, DOUGLASS FREDERICK, lawyer; b. Chgo., Aug. 10, 1941; s. Frederick Alvin and Velma Elizabeth (Birdwell) R.; m. Susan Vitullo; children: Kathryn Anne, Elizabeth Clelia, Alessandra Claire. AB, Duke U., 1963; JD, Northwestern U., 1966. Bar: Ill. 1966. Legal coord. Nat. Communicable Disease Ctr., Atlanta, 1966-68; assoc. Keck, Mahin & Cate, Chgo., 1968-73, ptnr., 1973-97, Lord, Bissell and Brook, Chgo., 1997—. Exec. v.p., dir. Kerogen Oil Co., 1967—; chmn. bd. visitors Nicholas Sch. of Environment Duke U., 1993-2001. Co-author: Commercial Liability Risk Management and Insurance, 2 vols., 1978, 86, Lenders Guide to Environmental Law: Risk and Liability, 1993; contbr. articles on law to profl. jours. Vice chmn., commr. Ill. Food and Drug Commn., 1970-72. Lt. USPHS, 1966-68. Fellow: Am. Numismatic Soc. (life; chmn. adv. com.); mem.: ABA, William Preston Few Assn. (mem. pres. coun.), Duke U. Alumni Assn., James B. Duke Soc., Selden Soc., Am. Soc. Law and Medicine, Environ. Law Inst., 7th Cir. Bar Assn., Chgo. Bar Assn. (chmn. com. food & drug law 1972—73), Am. Numismatic Assn. (life), Wigmore Club, Mich. Shores Club, Legal Club. Democrat. Epsicopalian. Home: 520 Brier St Kenilworth IL 60043-1064 Office: Lord Bissell & Brook 115 S La Salle St Ste 3200 Chicago IL 60603-3902

ROHSE, ELAINE DAHL, newswriter; b. Portland, Oreg., Apr. 12, 1920; d. Henry Dahl and Irene Lillian Hartman; m. Homer F. Rohse, 1942. BA, U. Oreg., 1942. Columnist News-Register, McMinnville, Oreg., 1969—. Freelance writer to numerous profl. jours. Served McMinnville City Coun., 1971—75. Recipient distinguished svc. award, Dayton FFA Chaoter, 2000, svc. plaque, Mid-Valley Rehab., Oregon, 1995. Mem.: Yamhill County Rep. Ctrl. Commn. (v.p.), Yamhill County Hist. Soc. (life; pres.). Avocations: travel, golf, hiking, bridge, reading. E-mail: rohse@onlinemac.com.

ROHSENOW, WARREN MAX, retired mechanical engineer, educator; b. Chgo., Feb. 12, 1921; s. Fred and Selma (Gorss) R.; m. Katharine Towneley Smith, Sept. 20, 1946; children— John, Brian, Damaris, Sandra, Anne. BS, Northwestern U., 1941; M.Eng., Yale, 1943, D.Eng., 1944. Teaching asst., instr. mech. engring. Yale, 1941-44; mem. faculty Mass. Inst. Tech., 1946-85, prof. mech. engring., 1955-85, dir. heat transfer lab., 1954-85, prof. emeritus, 1985. Bd. dirs. Dynatech Corp., Thermal Process System. Author: (with Choi) Heat Mass and Momentum Transfer, 1961; Editor; Developments in Heat Transfer, 1964, (with Hartnett) Handbook of Heat Transfer, 1973, 3d edit., 1998. Served as lt. (j.g.) USNR, 1944-46; mech. engr. gas turbine div. Engring. Expt. Sta. Annapolis, Md. Recipient Pi Tau Sigma gold medal Am. Soc. M.E., 1951; award for advancement sci. Yale Engring. Assn., 1952; merit award Northwestern Alumni, 1955 Fellow Am. Acad. Arts and Scis., Nat. Acad. Engring., ASME (hon. mem., Heat Transfer Meml. award 1967, Max Jakob Meml. award 1970, ASME medal 2001); mem. Sigma Xi, Tau Beta Pi, Pi Tau Sigma. Home: 32 Carroll St Falmouth ME 04105-1908

ROIF, HENRY IRVING, aeronautical engineer, electronic engineer; b. Lima, Peru, Dec. 15, 1955; came to U.S., 1991; s. Israel Meyer and Raquel (Rotstain) R. BSEE, Nat. U. Engring., Lima, 1984; MS in Aero. Engring., Israel Inst. Tech., Haifa, 1989; comml. pilot, Escuela de Aviacion Civil Peru, Lima, 1981. Flight test engr. Quiet Tech. Venture, Miami, Fla., 1996—. Mem. IEEE, AIAA, Aerospace and Electronics Systems Soc., IEEE Comm. Soc., Inventors Soc. South Fla. Jewish. Avocations: hang gliding, scuba diving, outdoors, music; achievements include 17 patents including aircraft landing taxing system, special project for the recovery of the ozone layer; patent pending on automobile automatic steering and cruise guidance control, airport surface movement detection system; electromagnetic fields for protection of airplanes from lightning; automatic parking for airplanes. Office: 1551 NE 167th St Apt 711 North Miami Beach FL 33162-2964 Fax: (305) 947-6082. E-mail: hroif@ieee.org.

ROIG, MIGUEL, psychology educator; b. Havana, Cuba, Sept. 28, 1956; came to U.S., 1970; s. Miguel Roig Tur and Peregrina (Bermudez) Mayans; m. Maryellen Reardon, Aug. 6, 1988; children: Michael John, Elena Graham. BA, Jersey City State Coll., 1979; MA, St. John's U., 1981; PhD, Rutgers U., 1989. Adj. instr. Essex County Coll., Newark, 1982-84, Kean Coll., Union, 1983-86, Montclair (N.J.) State Coll., 1983-87; tests & measurement specialist N.Y.C. Dept. Pers., N.Y.C., 1984-87; instr. Wagner Coll., Staten Island, N.Y., 1987-89; assoc. prof. St. John's U., 1989—. Contbr. articles to profl. jours; inventor shampoo dispenser, 1991. Recipient Faculty Merit award St. John's U., 1991-92, 93-94, 95-96, 98-99. Mem. APA, AAAS, Am. Psychol. Soc., Am. Soc. Psychical Rsch., Parapsychol. Assn. (assoc.). Avocations: surf fishing, bird-watching, metal detecting, gardening, fossil collecting. Home: 31 Lincoln Ave Rumson NJ 07760-2050 Office: St John's U. 300 Howard Ave Staten Island NY 10301-4496 E-mail: roigm@stjohns.edu.

ROISMAN, HANNA MASLOVSKI, classics educator; b. Wroclaw, Poland; d. Leon and Eugenia (Shlager-Katz) Maslovski; m. Joseph Roisman, Aug. 5, 1971; children: Elad L., Shalev G. BA in Classics, MA in Classics, Tel Aviv U., Ramat Aviv, Israel, 1977; PhD in Classics, U. Wash., 1981. Lectr. classics Tel Aviv U., 1981-87, sr. lectr. classics, 1987-90; assoc. prof. classics Colby Coll., Waterville, Maine, 1990-94, prof., 1994—. Jr. fellow Ctr. Hellenic Studies, Washington, 1985—86; vis. scholar U. Wash., Seattle, 1983, Cornell U., Ithaca, NY, 1989, Ithaca, 1995—96, Ithaca, 2001—02, vis. assoc. prof., 1986—94, vis. prof. (summers), 1995—97, 2000—02; sec. Israel Soc. for Promotion of Classical Studies, 1987—89. Author: Loyalty in Early Greek Epic and Tragedy, 1984, Nothing is as it Seems: The Tragedy of Implicit in Euripides' Hippolytus, 1999; co-author: The Odyssey Re-Formed, 1996; co-editor: Essays on Homeric Epic, 1993, Studies in Roman Epic, 1994, Essays on the Drama of Euripides, 1997, Essays on Homeric Epic, 2 vols., 2002; editor: Text and Presentation, Jour. Comparative Drama Conf., 1999—2000; contbr. articles to profl. jours. AAUW fellow, 1980-81. Office: Colby Coll Mayflower Hill Waterville ME 04901 E-mail: hroisman@colby.edu.

ROITSCH, PAUL ALBERT, pilot; b. Hermosa Beach, Calif., Oct. 15, 1926; s. George Arthur and Margaret (Pattillo) R.; m. Phyllis T.A. McCoy, Aug. 26, 1955; children— Sharon Elise, Alison Carol, Paul Eric. BA, U. So. Calif., 1952; postgrad. U.S. Navy Test Pilot Sch., 1965. Copilot, navigator Pan Am. Airways, San Francisco, 1952-53, pilot, 1955-64, asst. chief pilot tech., Jamaica, N.Y., 1965-69, chief pilot tech., 1969-73, line pilot, 1973-86, pres. Paul Roitsch Assocs., Internat. Aviation Cons., Greenwich, Conn., 1986—, pilot Civil Air Transport, 1954-55; bd. dirs. Pan Am Hist. Found., 1993—, v.p., 1994—, exec. v.p., 1995—. With USN, 1944-49, 53-54. Mem. AIAA, Soc. Automotive Engrs. (airplane handling qualities and flight deck design com., recipient cert. of appreciation 1981), Internat. Soc. Air Safety Investigators. Home: 39 John St Greenwich CT 06831-2608 Office: PO Box 786 Greenwich CT 06836-0786

ROIZMAN, BERNARD, virologist, educator; b. Chisinau, Rumania, Apr. 17, 1929; arrived in U.S., 1947, naturalized, 1954; s. Abram and Liudmilla (Seinberg) Roizman; m. Betty Cohen, Aug. 26, 1950; children: Arthur, Niels. BA, Temple U., 1952, MS, 1954; ScD in Microbiology, Johns Hopkins, 1956; DHL (hon.), Gov.'s State U., 1984; MD (hon.), U. Ferrara (Italy), 1991; DSc (hon.), U. Paris, 1997, U. Valladolid, Spain, 2001. From instr. microbiology to asst. prof. Johns Hopkins Med. Sch., 1956—65; mem. faculty div. biol. scis. U. Chgo., 1965—, prof. microbiology, 1969-84, prof. biophysics, 1970—, chmn. com. virology, 1969-85, 88-01, Joseph Regenstein prof., 1981-83, Joseph Regenstein Disting. Svc. prof., 1984—, chmn. dept. molecular genetics and cell biology, 1985-88. Bd. dirs., co-founder Aviron, Inc., 1992—; convener herpes virus workshop, Cold Spring Harbor, NY, 1972; lectr. Am. Found. for Microbiology, 1974—75; mem. spl. virus cancer program devel. rsch. working group Nat. Cancer Inst., 1967—71, cons. inst., 1967—73; mem. steering com. human cell biology program NSF, 1971—74, cons. found., 1972—74; mem. adv. com. cell biology and virology Am. Cancer Soc., 1970—74; chmn. herpes virus study group Internat. Commn. Taxonomy of Viruses, 1971—73; mem. Internat. Microbiol. Genetics Commn. Internat. Assn. Microbiol. Scis., 1974—81; mem. sci. adv. coun. N.Y. Cancer Inst., 1971—88; mem. adv. bd. Leukemia Rsch. Found., 1972—77; mem. herpes-virus working team WHO/FDA, 1978—81; mem. bd. sci. cons. Sloan Kettering Inst., N.Y.C., 1975—81; mem. study sect. exptl. virology NIH, 1976—80; mem. task force on virology Nat. Inst. Allergy and Infectious Disease, 1976—77; mem. external adv. com. Emory U. Cancer Ctr., 1973—81, Northwestern U. Cancer Ctr., 1979—89; cons. Inst. Merieux, Lyon, France, 1979—91; mem. com. to establish vaccine priorities Nat. Inst. Medicine, 1983—85; chmn. sci. adv. bd. Tampa Bay Rsch. Inst., 1983—, chmn. bd. trustees, 1991—. Editor: (book) Herpes Viruses, Vol. 1, 1982, Herpes Viruses, Vol. 2, 1983, Herpes Viruses, Vols. 3 and 4, 1985, The Human Herpesviruses, 1993, Infectious Diseases in an Age of Change, 1995; adv. editor: Progress in Surface Membrane Science, 1972, editor-in-chief: Jour. Infectious Agts. and Disease, 1992—96, mem. editl. bd.: Jour. Hygiene, 1985—91, mem. editl. bd.: Infectious Diseases, 1965—69, mem. editl. bd.: Jour. Virology, 1970—, mem. editl. bd.: Jour. Intervirology, 1972—85, mem. editl. bd.: Archives of Virology, 1975—81, mem. editl. bd.: Virology, 1976—78, mem. editl. bd.: , 1983—, mem. editl. bd.: Microbiologica, 1978—, mem. editl. bd.: Cell, 1979—80, mem. editl. bd.: Gene Therapy, 1994; contbr. scientific papers, chapters to books. Trustee Goodwin Inst. Cancer Rsch., 1977—. Named hon. prof., Shandong Acad. Med. Scis., China, 1985; recipient Lederle Med. Faculty award, 1960—61, Career Devel. award, USPHS, 1963—65, Pasteur award, Ill. Soc. Microbiology, 1972, Esther Langer award for Achievement in Cancer Rsch., 1974, Outstanding Alumnus in Pub. Health award, Johns Hopkins U., 1984, ICN Internat. prize in Virology, 1988, J. Allyn Taylor Internat. prize in Medicine, 1997, Bristol-Myers Squibb award for Disting. Infectious Disease Rsch., 1998; fellow Travelling, Internat. Agy. Rsch. Against Cancer, Karolinska Inst., Stockholm, 1970; grantee Facutly Rsch. Assoc., Am. Cancer Soc., 1966—71, USPHS/NIH, 1958—, Am. Cancer Soc., 1962—90, NSF, 1962—79; scholar Am. Cancer Soc., Pasteur Inst. Paris, 1961—62. Fellow: Japanese Soc. for Promotion of Sci., Am. Acad. Arts and Scis.; mem.: NAS, Johns Hopkins U. Soc. Scholars, Chinese Acad. Engring. (fgn.), Hungarian Acad. Scis. (fgn.), Brit. Soc. Gen. Microbiology, Am. Soc. Molecular Biology and Biochemistry, Am. Soc. Virology, Am. Soc. Microbiology, Am. Assn. Immunologists, Am. Acad. Microbiology, Inst. Medicine, Quadrangle Club (Chgo.). Home: 5555 S Everett Ave Chicago IL 60637-1968 Office: U Chgo MB Kovler Viral Oncology Labs 910 E 58th St Chicago IL 60637-1432

ROJANY, LISA ADRIENNE, publishing company executive, writer; b. L.A., Feb. 14, 1964; d. Aviezer Rojany and Mary Marks; m. Kristian Buccieri, Apr. 9, 2000. B of Comms. magna cum laude, UCLA, 1986; cert. in translation, Sorbonne U., Paris, 1987; M English and Am. Lit., Brown U., 1990. Newspaper journalist UCLA Daily Bruin, Together Newsmag., L.A., 1985-86; English tutor Paris, 1986-87; writer, reviewer TV Guide, L.A., 1987-88; freelance editor, writer Creative Ideaz and Editl. Svcs. of L.A., 1985—; sr. editor Intervisual Books, Santa Monica, 1991-93; editl. dir. Price Stern Sloan divsn. Penguin Putnam Pub., L.A., 1993-97, Gateway Learning Corp., 1997; west coast publ. dir. Golden Books Family Entertainment, L.A., 1998-2000; editl. dir. bus. devel. MyPotential.com, 2000-01; editor/writer, pres. Editl. Svcs. of L.A., 2001—. Proofreader MIT U. Press, Cambridge, Mass., 1990, Fidelity, Inc., Boston, 1990, Heinle & Heinle Pubs., Inc., Boston, 1990; correlator, proofreader Houghton Mifflin Co., Boston, 1990; spkr. in field. Author: (childrens books) The Hands-on Book of Big Machines, 1992, Exploring the Human Body, 1992 (10 Best New Parenting Books, Child Mag., 1993), King Arthur's Camelot, 1993 (Book of the Month Club selection, 1993), The Story of Hanukkah, 1993, Where's That Pig?, 1993, Santa's New Suit, 1993, Jake and Jenny on the Town, 1993, 1996, Andrews & McMeel Mini Pop-Up Quote Books, 1993, Alice in Wonderland, 1994, Token of Love and Spring Gardens, 1994, Mickey Mouse: Where's the Picnic, 1994, Winnie the Pooh: The Suprise Party, 1994, Make Your Own Valentines, 1994, Make Your Own Valentines, 3d edit., 1996 (Pub.'s Weekly Bestseller list , 1994, Pub.'s Weekly Bestseller list , 1995), Melvin Martian, Dumbo's Circus Train, 1995, Cinderella's Coach, 1995, The Magic Feather, 1995 (Parents Choice Silver Honor award, 1995), Pandora's Box (CD ROM), 1995, Over in the Meadow (CD ROM), 1995, Tell Me About When I Was a Baby, 1996, Gold Diggers: The Novelization, 1996, Hanukkah Candles, 1995, Dragonheart: The Jr. Novelization, 1996, Giant Animal Fold-Outs: Big Trucks & Bigger Diggers, 1996, Giant Giants & Magic Mermaids, 1996, Hippo & Pals, 1996 (Am. Booksellers Pick of the List, 1995), Kangaroo & Company, 1996 (Am. Booksellers Pick of the List, 1995), Dena Dinosaur, Morty Monster, Wanda Witch, 1996, Code Blue: In the Emergency Room, 1996, Code Blue: Making the Grade, 1996, Leave It to Beaver: The Novelization, 1997, Love You Because...Love, Barbie, 1999, Make Your Own Valentine Cards, 2000; co-author: (books) Fund Your Future, 2001 (NY Times Bus. Hardcover Bestseller list #10 , 2002, NY Times hardover bus. bestseller, 2001); ghostwriter: childrens books Dinotopia Pop-Up Book, 1993, ghostwriter: childrens books Sliding Surprise Books, 1993—97, ghostwriter: childrens books The Facts of Life, 1994, ghostwriter: childrens books All Mixed Up, 1994, ghostwriter: childrens books Little Merlin's Book of Magic Pets, 1994, ghostwriter: childrens books Claverie Fairytale Theater, 1994. Vol. kids activity days Dutton's Books, Brentwood, Calif., 1996; spkr. UCLA Extension, 1993-98; mem. comms. bd., fin. com. UCLA, 2002-. Recipient one of 10 Best New Parenting Books award Child Mag., 1993. Mem. PEN Ctr. U.S.A. West (editor-in-chief 1992-95), Soc. Children's Book Writers and Illustrators (manuscript reviewer 1995—), Internat. Women's Writing Guild, Author's Guild, Brown Alumni Assn. (interviewer 1995-98), UCLA Alumni Assn. (bd. dirs., comms., fin. com. 2002—), Phi Beta Kappa. Avocations: parenting twins, reading, hosting discussion salon, rollerblading, walking. Office: 142 Voyage Mall Marina Del Rey CA 90292 E-mail: creativeideaz@attbi.com.

ROJAS, CARLOS, Spanish literature educator; b. Barcelona, Spain, Aug. 12, 1928; s. Carlos and Luisa (Vila) R.; m. Eunice Anne Mitcham, Mar. 19, 1966; children: Carlos, Eunice Anne. MA, U. Barcelona, 1951; PhD, U. Cen., Madrid, 1955; PhD (hon.), U. Simón Bólivar, Barranquilla, Colombia, 1985. Teaching asst. U. Barcelona, 1951-52; fgn. asst. U. Glasgow, Scotland, 1952-54; asst. prof. Rollins Coll., Winter Park, Fla., 1957-60, Emory U., Atlanta, 1960-63, assoc. prof., 1963-68, prof., 1968-80, Charles Howard Candler prof. Spanish lit., 1980-96, Charles Howard Candler prof. emeritus, 1996. Author: Auto de fe, 1968 (Premio Nacional de Literatura 1968), Azana, 1973 (Planeta award 1973), El Igenioso Hidalgo y Poeta F.G. asciende a los infiernos, 1980 (Nadal award 1980), El Sueno de Sarajevo, 1982, El Jardin de las Hespèrides, 1988, El Jardin de Atocha, 1990, Yo, Goya, 1990, Proceso A Godoy, 1992, Salvador Dali, or the Art of Spitting on Your Mother's Portrait, 1993, Alfonso de Borbón Habla Con El Demonio, 1995, !Muera La Inteligencia! !Viva La Muerte! Salamanca, 1995, The Garden of Janus, 1996, Crónica de la Guerra Civil Española, 1996; co-author, contbg. editor Spanish Civil War documents, Momentos estelares de la guerra de España, 1996, La Vida y la Época de Carlos IV, 1997, Los Borbones Destronados, 1997, El bastardo del Rey, 1999, The Garden of the Hesperides, 1999, Puneta La Espaneta, 2000. Recipient Premio Espejo de España award, Madrid, 1984, Encomienda al Mérito Civil, King of Spain, 1986, Univ. Scholar/Tchr. award Emory U., 1987, Arts and Scis. award of Distinction, Emory U., 2001; honoree of yr. Philol. Assn. of Carolinas, 1987. Mem. MLA, Am. Assn. Tchrs. Spanish and Portuguese, Assn. Doctores y Licenciados Españoles en los Estados Unidos (bd. dirs.), South Atlantic MLA (hon.). Avocation: painting. Home: 1378 Harvard Rd NE Atlanta GA 30306-2413 Office: Emory U Dept Spanish Atlanta GA 30322-0001 E-mail: crojas@emory.edu.

ROJAS, EDDY M. engineering educator; b. San Jose, Costa Rica, Feb. 26, 1969; came to U.S., 1993; s. Jorge L. Rojas and Hannia Molina; m. Denise Murillo, Aug. 10, 1991. MSCE, U. Colo., 1995, MA in Econs., PhD in Civil Engring., U. Colo., 1997. Registered civil engr., Costa Rica. Rschr. Earthquake Engring. Lab. U. Costa Rica, San Jose, 1991, instr., 1991-93; asst. prof. U. Buffalo, 1997—2001, U. Wash., 2001—. Contbr. papers to profl. jours. Recipient Making Virtual Teams Work award, Constrn. Industry Inst., 2000, Tech. Transfer for Mex. Electrical Contracting Firms award, Electrical Contracting Found., 2000, Automating N.Y. State Dept. Transp. Data Collection, 1998, Millennium Generation award, Electrical Contracting Found., 2001. Mem. ASCE (mem. constrn. rsch. coun. 1997—, computing in constrn. com. 1997—). Roman Catholic. Office: U Washington 116 Architecture Box 351610 Seattle WA 98195-1610 E-mail: er@u.washington.edu.

ROJAS, VICTOR HUGO MACEDO, retired vocational education educator; b. Mollendo, Peru, Jan. 11, 1923; came to U.S., 1944; s. Mariano A. and Maria Santos (Macedo) R.; m. Mary Emily Bush, Apr. 28, 1945 (dec. 1984). AA, Miami-Dade C.C., 1982; BS in Vocat. Edn., Fla. Internat. U., 1986. Cert. tchr.,

Fla. Automotive mechanic various Ford dealerships, Miami, Fla., 1945-60; automotive technician East Tenn. Motors, Knoxville, 1960-63, Tally-Embry Ford, Inc., Miami, 1964-66, shop foreman, then mgr., 1966-75, master technician, automotive instr., 1973-75; instr. automotive tech. Dade County Pub. Schs., 1975-91; ret., 1991. Adviser, sponsor Vocat.-Indsl. Clubs Am., Miami, 1988-91. Contbr. articles to newspapers. With Armada Peruana, 1940-44, USN, 1945. Recipient Cert. of Achievement Motor Age mag., 1961, 62, St. Mary's Cathedral, Miami, 1988, Automotive Svc. Excellence award Nat. Inst. Automotive Svc., 1975. Mem. Am. Legion (historian 1989), Elks. Democrat. Roman Catholic. Avocations: music, ballroom dancing, reading, writing, photography. Home: 2365 Ainsworth Ave Spring Hill FL 34609-4402

ROJAS WAHL, ROY UWE, research scientist; b. Braunschweig, Germany, Dec. 12, 1965; s. Jaime Rojas, Gertraud Rojas Wahl; m. Mireille Noromalala Legoutte; children: Cyril, Amelie. Dr. rer. nat., Technische Universitaet, Braunschweig, 1995. Rsch. asst. Tex. A&M U., College Station, 1993—96; prin. rsch. chemist Unilever Rsch. U.S., Edgewater, NJ, 1996—99, product scientist, 1999—2002; sr. chemist Exxon Mobile R&E Co., Annandale, 2002—. Author: (Invention) Peroxynitrite as a novel fabric bleaching reagent, 1999, (Publication) Hydroperoxide Formation in Model Collagens and Collagen Type I, 2002, Peroxynitrite as a novel stain bleaching reagent, 2001, Analytical studies on the oxidative degradation of reactive textile dye Uniblue A, 2000, Role of hydroxypropylcellulose in free radical induced reactions of the anthraquinone based textile dye,Uniblue A, 2000, Mechanistic studies on 3-N-morpholinesydnonimine (SIN-1) as a new precursor molecule for the fabric bleach, 2000, Mechanistic studies on the decomposition of water soluble azo-radical initiators, 1998, The selective functionalization of saturated hydrocarbons. Part 32. Distinction between the FeII-FeIV and FeIII-FeV manifolds in Gif chemistry. The importance of carboxylic acids for alkane activation. Evidence for a dimeric iron , 1996, Determination of ligand environment in solution in Gif type systems using quantitative 13C-NMR-spectroscopy, 1996, The importance of carboxylate ligands in the differentiation of catalase reactivity from Gif ketonization systems, 1996, Further evidence for the FeII-FeIV and FeIII-FeV manifolds in the substitution of saturated hydrocarbons, 1995, The FeII-FeIV and FeIII-FeV manifolds in an expanded world of Gif chemistry, 1994, Diastereoselective alkylations at η2-manganese complexes, 1994. Assoc. writer - Urgent Actions Amnesty Internat., Germany, 1989—91. Air surveillance operator, 1985—86, Goslar. Mem.: Am. Chem. Soc. Achievements include patents for peroxynitrite as a novel fabric bleaching reagent. Avocations: 16th Century history, contempoary and modern classical music. Home: 516 North St Teaneck NJ 07666 Office: Exxon Mobile Research and Engring 1545 Rt 22 E Annandale NJ 08801 Business E-Mail: roy.rojas-wahl@unilever.com.

ROJO, RUTH M. nutritionist, consultant; b. San Antonio, Oct. 23, 1938; d. Fernando Sosa and Margie Macias Rojo; children: Amina Ruth. Dr. Naturopathy, Clayton Coll. Natural Health, Birmingham, AL, 1996, United State Sch. Naturopathy, Atlanta, GA, 1999; PhD Nutrition, Am. Holistic Coll. Nutrition, Birmingham, AL, 1996; Dr. Naturopathic Medicine, Colo. U. Naturopathic Medicine, Denver, CO, 1999. Board Certified Naturopath Am. Naturopathic Med. Certification and Accreditation Bd. Pres. / founder Tex. State Naturopathic Med. Assn., San Antonio, 1998—; tex. rep. Am. Naturopathic Med. Assn., Las Vegas, Nev., 1998—, bd. mem., 2000—. Lectr. Sun Harvest / Whole Foods, San Antonio, 1998—2002, U. Tex., San Antonio, 1998—2002. Author: (book) Priority 1 - A Guide to Natural Health. Legislative chair NE Bexar County Rep. Women's Club, San Antonio, 2001—02. Recipient Hall of Fame Award, Tex. State Naturopathic Assn., 2000. Avocations: painting, walking, reading, sports. Office: Ruth M Rojo ND PhD 8026 Vantage Dr Suite 101 San Antonio TX 78230 Office Fax: 210-340-1303.

ROKACH, ABRAHAM JACOB, structural engineering and computer software consultant; b. N.Y.C., Nov. 14, 1948; s. David and Sara (Biro) R.; m. Pninah Abigail Kacev, June 19, 1977; children: David, Aaron Zvi, Moshe Mordecai, Aryeh Raphael Pesach, Chaya Esther, Malka Rachel, Isaac Elazar. B of Engring., CCNY, 1969; MSCE, MIT, 1970. Registered structural engr., Ill., profl. engr., N.Y. Pres. Rokach Engring. P.C., Chgo., 1984—, Hypermedia Systems Inc., Chgo., 1989—. Adj. prof. structural engring. U. Ill., Chgo., 1984-87; consulting editor McGraw-Hill, 1990-93. Author: Guide to Load and Resistance Factor Design of Structural Steel Buildings, 1986, Schaum's Outline of Structural Steel Design, 1991, The Bibilical Tabernacle, 1998, Ezekiel's Temple, 1999; editor: Manual of Steel Construction, 1994. Fellow, grantee NSF; recipient Cert. Honor, Structural Engrs. Assn. Ill., 1985. Fellow ASCE. Home and Office: 3314 W Rance Ter Lincolnwood IL 60712-3831

ROKHVARGER, ANATOLY EFIM, materials science and ceramic technology scientist; b. Moscow, July 24, 1937; came to U.S., 1991; s. Efin Laser and Avgustina Naum (Leschiner) R.; m. Zina Gregory Mikhelson, Feb. 17, 1965; 1 child, Avgustina. MS, Mendeleev Chem.-Tech. U., Moscow, 1959, PhD, 1967; cert., Moscow U., 1965; DS, Tech. U., Leningrad, USSR, 1986. Engr. Electronic Industry Design Inst., Moscow, 1959-63; rschr. Bldg. Materials Inst., 1964-68; project leader, head dept. Ceramic Industry Analytical Ctr., 1969-91; rsch. prof. Poly. U., Bklyn., 1992—; v.p. R&D Nucon Sys., Inc., N.Y.C., N.Y., 1996-2000. Vis. scientist Rutgers U. Ctr. Ceramic Rsch., Piscataway, N.J., 1998-99. Author 3 books, 1 textbook in field; contbr. over 175 articles to profl. jours. Named One of the Greatest Innovators of 20th Century Am. Ceramic Soc. Achievements include development of nine advanced technological systems and six ceramic products; research in application of system analysis, quality assurance methods in ceramic engineering; invention of cost-effective technology of gas impenetrable and thick-walled ceramics used for ultimate safe and durable ceramic containers for nuclear and hazardous waste; including techniques for their mass production and seamless covering using microwave; industrial processing of high temperature superconductor continuous wire and other shaped products for all electrical and electronic needs, using such Y-Ba-Cu-O powder, silicone compound and silver. Office: Polytechnic U 6 Metrotech Ctr Brooklyn NY 11201-3840 E-mail: aerokhv@aol.com.

ROKKE, DOUGLAS LIND, physicist, educator; b. Apr. 22, 1949; BS, Western Ill. U., Macomb, 1975; MS, U. Ill., Urbana, 1986, PhD, 1992. Staff physicist U. Ill., Urbana, 1977-96; asst. prof. Jacksonville (Ala.) State U., 1998-2000; health physicist U.S. Army Res., various locations, 1986—; cons. govtl. and non-govtl. agencies, 2000—. E-mail: envirodoc22@hotmail.com.

ROKKE, ERVIN JEROME, college president; b. Warren, Minn., Dec. 12, 1939; s. Edwin K. and Joan (Ivery) R.; m. Pamela Mae Patterson, June 6, 1962; children: Lisa Mae, Eric Scott. Student, St. Olaf Coll., 1957-58; BS, USAF Acad., 1962; MPA, Harvard U., 1964, PhD in Polit. Sci., 1970. Commd. 2d lt. USAF, 1962, advanced through grades to lt. gen., 1994; intelligence officer Pacific Air Forces, Hawaii, Japan, 1965-68; assoc. prof. dept. polit. sci. USAF Acad., Colorado Springs, Colo., 1968-73, permanent prof., 1976-80, dean of faculty, 1982-86; plans officer NATO Hdqrs., Brussels, 1973-76; air attache Am. Embassy, London, 1980-82, def. attache Moscow, 1987-89; sr. staff Nat. Security Agy., Ft. Meade, Md., 1989-91; dir. intelligence Hdqrs. European Command, Stuttgart, Fed. Republic Germany, 1991-93; assigned to Hdqs. USAF, Washington, 1993-94; pres. Nat. Def. U., Ft. Lesley J. McNair, DC, 1994-97, Moravian Coll. and Moravian Theol. Sem., 1997—. Cons. Dept. State, 1969. Editor: American Defense Policy, 1973. Decorated Def. Disting. Svc. medal, Disting. Svc. medal, Def. Superior Svc. medal, Legion of Merit. Mem. Coun. on Fgn. Rels., Falcon Found. Lutheran. Avocations: reading, skiing, squash. Home: 79 W Church St Bethlehem PA 18018-5821 Office: Moravian Coll 1200 Main St Bethlehem PA 18018-6614 E-mail: chass01@aol.com.

ROKOSZ, GREGORY JOSEPH, emergency medicine physician, lawyer, educator; b. Passaic, N.J., Mar. 27, 1955; s. Ferdinand and Stella D. (Wirkowski) R.; m. Christine M. Muller, Oct. 1, 1983; 1 child, Stefanie Lee. BA in Biol. Scis. with honors, Rutgers U., 1977; DO, Des Moines U., 1980; JD magna cum laude, Seton Hall U., 1999. Diplomate Am. Bd. Emergency Medicine, Am. Bd. Osteo. Emergency Medicine, Am. Osteo. Bd. Family Physicians. Intern Met. Hosp., Phila., 1980-81; resident in family practice Union (N.J.) Hosp., 1981-82, emergency dept. physician, 1982-94, 98, dir. med. edn., 1993-2001, v.p. med. affairs, 1994-2000, sr. v.p. med. and acad. affairs, 2001—; dir. transitional yr. residency program, 2000—02; v.p. med. edn., 2000—; med. dir. N.J. Paramedic Registry Exam., 1990-94; mobile ICU insp. N.J. Dept. Health, Office EMS, Newark, 1990-94. Mem. N.J. Bd. Med. Examiners, Trenton, 1994—, v.p., 1997—99, pres., 1999—2001; clin. instr. dept. emergency medicine U. Medicine and Dentistry Sch. Osteo. Medicine, Stratford, 1992—93, asst. clin. prof., 1993—; asst. prof. emergency medicine N.Y. Coll. Osteo. Medicine/N.Y. Inst. Tech., Old Westbury, 1994—96, assoc. prof., 1996—, clin. asst. dean, 1997—; assoc. prof. dept. medicine St. George's U. Sch. Medicine, 2001—; assoc. mem. PRO of N.J., 1991—; dir. emergency medicine residency program Newark (N.J.) Beth Israel Med. Ctr., 1998—99; expert witness in emergency medicine; vice-chmn. N.Y. Coll. Osteo. Medicine Ednl. Consortium, 1999—; mem. accreditation rev. com. Accreditation Coun. for Continuing Med. Edn., 2000—. Contbg. author: Continuous Quality Improvement for Emergency Departments, 1994; mem. Seton Hall Law Rev., 1997-99. Fellow Am. Coll. Emergency Physicians, Am. Coll. Osteo. Emergency Physicians; mem. ABA, Am. Osteo. Assn., Am. Coll. Osteo. Family Physicians, Assn. Osteo. Dirs. and Med. Educators, Am. Coll. Physician Execs., Assn. for Hosp. Med. Edn., Grad. Med. Edn. Coun. N.J. (mem. adv. bd. 1997—). Republican. Roman Catholic. Avocations: skiing, sports, cultural events, music, family activities. Home: 8 Wildlife Run Boonton NJ 07005-9043 Office: St Barnabas Med Ctr 95 Old Short Hills Rd Livingston NJ 07039

ROKOSZ, MICHAEL JOHN, research scientist; b. Coburg, Germany, Nov. 29, 1946; s. Michal and Janina (Falkowska) R.; m. Susan Marie Winkler, June 28, 1986; 1 child, Aleksandra Janina. BS in Physics, U. Detroit, 1970. Rsch. engr. Chrysler Corp., Highland Park, Mich., 1972-75, rsch. scientist, 1975-79, Ford Motor Co., Dearborn, 1979—. Tutorial instr. Denver X-Ray Conf., Denver, 1985, 87; instr. Sunya X-Ray Clinic, Albany, 1980-89. Contbg. author: Advances in X-Ray Analysis, 1982, 85, 86, 89. Comm. leader's coun. United Way Comm. Svcs., Detroit, 1995-97; trustee Mich. chpt. NMSS, Southfield, 1985—. Recipient Hope award Mich. Chpt. Nat. Multiple Sclerosis Soc., 1994, Heart of Gold award United Way Cmty. Svcs., 2001. Mem. Engring. Soc. Detroit (mem. strategic planning com., by-laws com., advanced composites conf. planning com., chair of Info. Tech. Spl. Interest Group, coll. fellows 2001), Sigma Xi (pres. Ford chpt. 1993-94). Achievements include devel. of software drivers, data collection software and data analysis software for the first VAX-730 controlled X-ray spectrometer installation in the world; solid state nuclear magnetic resonance applications research. Avocations: computers, hunting, fishing. Office: Ford Motor Co 20000 Rotunda Dr Dearborn MI 48124-3958

ROLAND, ALEX FREDERICK, history educator; b. Providence, Apr. 7, 1944; s. George Hayes and Alice Ruth (Thurber) R.; m. Elizabeth Ann Sullivan, June 31, 1979; children: Quentin H. Hopkins, Michael K., Christopher S., Daniel H. BS, U.S. Naval Acad., Annapolis, Md., 1966; MA, U. Hawaii, 1970; PhD, Duke U., 1974. Historian NASA, Washington, 1973-81; assoc. prof. Duke U., Durham, N.C., 1981-87, prof. history dept., 1987—, chair dept. history, 1996-99. Johnson prof. mil. history U.S. Mil. History Inst., Carlisle, Pa., 1988—89; Dr. Leo Shifrin prof. mil.-naval history U.S. Naval Acad., 2001—; resident fellow Dibner Inst., Cambridge, Mass., 1994—95. Author: Underwater Warfare in the Age of Sail, 1978, Model Research, 1985, The Military-Industrial Complex, 2001; co-author: Men in Arms, 5th edit., 1991, Strategic Computing, 2002; editor: A Spacefaring People, 1985; co-editor: Atmospheric Flight, 2000. Capt. USMC, 1966-70. Mem. Soc. History Tech. (pres. 1995-96), Soc. Mil. History (v.p. 2001-). Office: Duke U Dept History Durham NC 27708 E-mail: alex.roland@duke.edu.

ROLAND, ANNE, registrar Supreme Court of Canada; b. Neuilly-sur-Seine, France, 1947; d. Pierre Philippe Roland and Geneviève Lehman; m. Alphonse Morisette, Dec. 3, 1975; 1 child, Julien. BA Philosophy, Caen, France, 1965; diploma, Inst. Supérieur d'interprétation et de traduction, 1969; lic. in law, Paris, 1969; LLB, U. Ottawa, 1979. Bar: Quebec 1980. Legal trans., revisor, Can., 1971-75; chief trans. svcs. customs and excise Sec. of State, Can., 1975-76; spl. asst. to chief justice Can., 1976-81; chief law editor Supreme Ct. Can., 1981-88, dep. registrar, 1988-90, registrar, 1990. Mem. Can. Bar Assn., Assn. Can. Ct. Adminstrs., Assn. Francophone Jurists, Can. Inst. Adminstrn. Justice, Assn. Reporters Jud. Decisions. Office: Supreme Ct Can Office Reg 301 Wellington St Ottawa ON Canada K1A 0J1

ROLAND, BILLY RAY, electronics company executive; b. Grandview, Tex., June 12, 1926; s. Marvin Wesley and Minnie Mae (Martin) R.; m. Ruth Ranell Sheets, Mar. 9, 1950 (div. 1982); children: Carl Ray and Darla Kay (twins); m. Linda Sue Leslie, Feb. 21, 1986 (div. Nov. 1991); m. Martha Kay Redford, May 17, 1993. BS, Tex. Christian U., 1954. CPA, Tex. Ticket and baggage agt. Southwestern Greyhound Co., Ft. Worth, 1943-44, 46-51; supr. acctg. dept. Tandy Leather Co., 1954-60; controller, asst. sec., treas. Tandy Corp., 1960-75; v.p., 1978-85; ret.; controller, asst. sec., treas. Tandy Crafts, Inc., 1975-78. V.p., treas. David L. Tandy Found., 1966—; mng. trustee James L. and Eunice West Charitable Trust, 1980-91; treas. Benjamin F. Johnston Found., 1984—. Served with U.S. Army, 1944-46. Mem. AICPA, Tex. Soc. CPAs, Colonial Country Club, Petroleum Club, Eagle Mountain Country Club. Republican. Methodist. Home: 8937 Random Rd Fort Worth TX 76179-2739

ROLAND, CATHERINE DIXON, entrepreneur; b. Andalusia, Ala., Mar. 9, 1939; d. Charles and Thelma (Chapman) Dixon; m. Henry F. Roland, Dec. 16, 1966 (div. Nov., 1976); 1 child, Charles H.; stepchild, Vickie Roland Little. Student, Huntingdon Coll., 1954-56; BS, Auburn U., 1956-59; MA in History, U. Ala., Tuscaloosa, 1965-66. Sec. Dixon Lumber Co., Inc., Andalusia, 1969-74, v.p., 1974-78; land and timber owner, mgr. Catherine D. Roland & Co., 1978—. Owner Sta. WCTA, andalusia, 1947-75, bd. dirs., 1972-75; owner, bd. dirs. D & G Property Ltd., Perth, Australia, 1967—, Covington County Bank, 1979—, So. Nat. Corp., 1985—. Chmn. Thelma Dixon Found., Andalusia, 1981—; mem. Rep. Senatorial Inner Cir., Washington, 1980—, 2d Congl. Com., Montgomery, Ala., 1980—, Andalusia Pub. Libr. Friends, Inc., 1981—; mem. adv. coun. Mises Inst. Auburn (Ala.) U., Auburn and Washington, 1983-85, Coll. Bus. Auburn U., 1987—; mem. Com. of 100, Huntington Coll., 1978, trustee, 1978—, vice chmn. bd. trustees 1985-93; bd. dirs. Women Health, Birmingham, Ala., 1978-82, Health Svcs. Found., 1982—, Andalusia Hosp., 1980-82. Named countess Huntingdon Coll., Montgomery, 1978, named to Hall of Honor, 1980; recipient commendation for Outstanding Svc. and Leadership, 1980, Loyalty award, 1988. Mem. DAR, Nat. Soc. Colonial Dames XVII Century, Ams. of Royal Descent, Dames of Magna Charter, Forest Landowners Assn., Ala. Landowners Assns., Ala. Wildlife Fedn., Andalusia Area C. of C., Auburn Alumni Assn., Huntingdon Coll. Alumni Assn. (chmn. Andalusia area chpt. 1983—), Am. Legion, Study Club. Methodist. Avocations: numismatics, reading, horses, tennis.

ROLAND, CHARLES GORDON, physician, medical historian, educator; b. Winnipeg, Man., Can., Jan. 25, 1933; s. John Sanford and Leona (McLaughlin) R.; m. Marjorie Ethel Kyles, 1953 (div. 1973); children: John Kenneth, Christopher Franklin, David Charles, Kathleen Siobhan; m. Connie Rankin, 1979. Student, U. Toronto, Ont., Can., 1952-54; MD, BSc, U. Man., 1958, DSc (hon.), 1997. Intern St. Boniface Hosp., Man., 1958-59; pvt. practice medicine specializing in family medicine Tillsonburg, Ont., 1959-60, Grimsby, 1960-64; sr. editor Jour. Am. Med. Assn., Chgo., 1964-69; head sect. publs. Mayo Clinic, 1969-70, chmn. dept. biomed. communications, 1970-77; prof. history medicine, prof. biomed. communications, coordinator family practice track, chmn. adminstrv. com. dept. family medicine Mayo Med. Sch., 1971-77; mem. admissions, edn. and curriculum coordinators coms., hon. mem. med. staff West Lincoln Meml. Hosp., Grimsby; mem. grants com. Hannah Inst. History of Medicine, Toronto, 1974-77, 87-91, mem. publs. com., 1991-95; Jason A. Hannah prof. history of medicine McMaster U., Hamilton, Ont., Can., 1977-99, Hannah prof. emeritus Can., 1999—, assoc. mem. dept. history. Can., 1978-96, chmn. archives com. Faculty of Health Scis. Can., 1983-98; chmn. spl. grants com. Hannah Inst. for History of Medicine, 1981-85; Sid W. Richardson vis. prof. Inst. Med. Humanities U. Tex. Med. Br., Galveston, 1984; prof. emeritus McMaster U., 1999—. Mem. devel. adv. com. Assoc. Med. Svcs., 1999—; inaugural Osler-McGovern lectr. Green Coll., Oxford U., Eng., 2001. Author: (with L.S. King) Scientific Writing, 1968, (with J.P. McGovern) William Osler, The Continuing Education, 1969, Good Scientific Writing, 1971, William Osler's The Master Word in Medicine: A Study in Rhetoric, 1972, (with L.S. Baker) You and Leukemia: A Day at a Time, 1976, (with P. Potter) An Annotated Bibliography of Canadian Medical Periodicals, 1826-1975, 1979, Clarence Meredith Hincks 1885-1964: Mental Health Crusader, 1990, Courage Under Seige:: Starvation, Disease and Death in the Warsaw Ghetto, 1992, Harold Nathan Segall: Pioneer Canadian Cardiologist, 1995, Long Night's Journey Into Day: Prisoners of War in the Far East, 1941-45, 2001; editor: (E.P. Scarlett) In Sickness and In Health, 1972; co-editor: An Annotated Checklist of Osleriana, 1976, vol. 2, 2000, Sir William Osler 1849-1919: A Selection for Medical Students, 1982, Health Disease and Medicine: Essays in Canadian History, 1984, Bibliography of Secondary Sources in Canadian Medical History, 1985, 2nd edition, 2000, (with J.P. McGovern) The Collected Essays of Sir William Osler (3 vols.), 1985; editor, author introduction: Medical Topography of Upper Canada, 1985; (with Richard Golden) Sir William Osler: An Annotated Bibiography with Illustrations, 1987; co-editor: The Persisting Osler, 1984, The Persisting Osler II, 1994, The Persisting Osler III, 2001; editor in chief Can. Bulletin of Med. History, 1987-90; mem. editorial adv. bd. Canadian Family Physician, 1964-72, Chest, 1966-95, Med. Communications, 1971-75, Postgrad. Med. Jour., London, 1967-72, Mayo Clinic Procs., 1969-77, Bioscis. Communications, 1975-80, Ont. Med. Rev., 1979-84, HSTC Jour., 1980-87, Can. Bull. Med. History, 1983-90, Med. History (London), 1982-87, Jour. History of Medicine and Allied Scis., 1991-94, 96—. Mem. bd. curators Osler Library, McGill U., Montreal, 1981—. Recipient Jason A. Hannah medal Royal Soc. Can., 1994. Fellow AAAS (council 1969-74), Am. Med. Writers Assn. (pres. 1969-70); mem. Can. Med. Assn., Am. Assn. History Medicine (sec.-treas. 1976-80, publs. com. 1979-85), Acad. Medicine Toronto (Grogan lecture com. 1978-83), Am. Mil. Inst., Internat. Inst. Prisoners of War, Soc. Internat. d'Histoire de la Medicine (internat. del. for Can. 1983-86), Can. Soc. for History of Medicine (v.p. 1982-87, pres. 1993-95), Soc. Med. History Chgo. (sec.-treas. 1966-69), Can. Ctr. for Studies in Hist. Horticulture (exec. com. 1982-89), Council Biology Editors, Med. Hist. Club Toronto (pres. 1977-78), Ont. Hist. Soc., Can. Hist. Assn., Bibliog. Soc. Can., Am. Osler Soc. (sec.-treas. 1975-85, v.p. 1985-86, pres. 1986-87), Japan Osler Soc. (hon.), Royal Soc. Medicine (London), Royal Can. Mil. Inst., Champlain Soc. (Toronto), History of Second World War (Can. com.), Soc. Army Hist. Research, Sigma Xi. Clubs: Univ. (Rochester); Osler (London); Alpine of Can.; Literary (Chgo.). Office: McMaster U 3N10-HSC Med Ctr 1200 Main St W Hamilton ON Canada L8N 3Z5 E-mail: rolandc@mcmaster.ca.

ROLAND, DAVID LEONARD, broadcast production educator; b. Port Jefferson, N.Y., Oct. 2, 1948; s. Leonard Ernest and Dorothy (Stewart) R.; m. Susan Mary Becht, July 10, 1971 (dec. Nov. 1979); m. Theresa Regina Ryan, Dec. 27, 1980. BS, Empire State Coll., 1976; MA, L.I. U., 1981. Tchr. photography Bd. Coop. Ednl. Svcs., Patchoque, N.Y., 1975-85, tchr. TV prodns., graphic arts module leader, 1985—. Video arts prof. Five Towns Coll., Dix Hills, N.Y. Dir. CBS TV Worth Teaching Video (cert. merit), Camp Pa-gua-tuck Video (Outstanding Svc. award); audio engr. Children of the Cradle. Named Disting. Occupational Tchr. of Yr. State of N.Y., 1988. 020. Vocat. Indsl. Clubs Am. (advisor 1976—, chair), Internat. TV Assn., L.I. Media Arts Com., Assn. of BTC Educators. Home: 523 Washington Ave Riverhead NY 11901-2742 Office: Eastern Suffolk BOCES 350 Martha Ave Bellport NY 11713-1525

ROLAND, DONALD EDWARD, advertising executive; b. Dalhart, Tex., Nov. 14, 1942; s. Vernon O. Roland and Doris M. (Cox) Roland Hutson; m. Kathleen Marie Bennett, Feb. 1, 1964; children; Aileen, Donald E., Jenny. BS, Calif. State U., L.A., 1964; MA, U. Calif., Riverside, 1967; cert. exec. mgmt., UCLA. Dir. computer graphics Times Mirror Press, L.A., 1966-78, plant mgr., 1978-81, v.p. prodn., 1981-83; group v.p. ops. Treasure Chest Advt., Glendora, Calif., 1983-84, sr. v.p. ops., 1984-93, exec. v.p., 1993-94, pres., CEO, 1995-2000; pres., CEO, chmn. Vertis Inc., Balt., 2000—. Republican. Home: 4 Norwood Rd Annapolis MD 21401-1227 Office: Vertis Inc PO Box 17102 Baltimore MD 21297-1102 E-mail: droland@vertisinc.com.

ROLAND, GERARD, economics educator; b. Jemappes, Belgium, Oct. 3, 1954; s. Yves and Marie Thérèse (Leclercq) R.; m. Heddy Riss, Nov. 18, 1980; children: Elsa, Florence, Juliette. PhD in Econs., U. Libre Brussels, 1988. Asst. U. Libre Brussels, 1983-88, maitre de conf., 1988-91, prof., 1991-2001, U. Calif., Berkeley, 2001—. Program dir. on transition econs. Ctr. for Econ. Policy Rsch., London, 1995—; vis. prof. U. Cath. Louvain, 1989, Ecole des Hautes Etudes en Scis. Sociales, Paris, 1990, U. Calif., Davis, 1991, London Sch. Econs., 1993, Collegium Budapest, 1993, Stanford U., 1994, 95, Inst. for Internat. Econ. Studies, Stockholm, 1995; William Davidson Inst. vis. chair Mich. Bus. Sch., 1997. Contbr. articles to profl. jours. Soldier Belgian Air Force, 1974. Fellow Ctr. Advanced Studies Behavioral Scis., Stanford U., 1998-99, Ctr. for Econ. Rsch. and Grad. Edn.-Econ. Inst., Prague, 1999-2001. Office: U Calif-Berkeley Dept Econ 605 Evans Hall # 3880 Berkeley CA 96720-3880 E-mail: groland@clb.ac.be.

ROLAND, JOHN, newscaster; b. Pitts., Nov. 25, 1941; s. John Roland and Marion (Costlow) Gingher. BA in English., U. Calif., Long Beach, 1963. Rschr. NBC News, L.A., 1966-69; reporter KTTV, 1969; anchorman Fox News, N.Y.C., 1970—. Recipient Emmy award, 1978, 83, Pub. Svc. award Am. Fed. Govt. Employees Assn., 1974, Cert. of Appreciation, Goldwater Hosp., N.Y., 1975, N.Y. City Patrolman's Benevolent Assn. Journalism award, 1982, Good Samaritan award Bronx C. of C., 1983, Excelsior award N.Y.C. Coun., 1983, Man of the Yr. award N.Y.'s Finest Found., 1989; named Crimefighter of the Week, N.Y. Daily News, 1983. Mem. N.Y.C. Police Dept. Detective Endowment Assn. (hon.), Sigma Alpha Epsilon. Avocations: boating, tennis, golf. Office: WNYW TV Fox Broadcasting Co 205 E 67th St New York NY 10021-6050

ROLAND, MELISSA MONTGOMERY, accountant; b. Houston, Mar. 6, 1961; d. John Edgar and Mariann (Guggino) Montgomery; m. Larry Dean Roland, Sept. 20, 1984. BBA, Tex. A&M U., 1983. CPA, Tex., cert. fraud examiner, Tex. Audit sr. Arthur Andersen & Co., Houston, 1983-87; cons. mgr.-performance improvement group Ernst & Young, San Antonio, 1988-91; COO Roy Smith Shoes, Inc. d/b/a Accenté, Houston, 1991-96; v.p., COO 3d Coast Mgmt., Inc., Jacksonville, Fla., 1996—. Bd. dirs., treas. Grandparents Outreach, San Antonio, 1989—. Mem. AICPA, Tex. Accts. and Lawyers for the Arts (adv. bd.), Tex. Soc. CPAs, Young Reps., Jr. League Jacksonville, S.W. Found. Forum. Presbyterian. Avocations: running, scuba diving, weight lifting, bicycling. Office: 515 Rutile Dr Ponte Vedra Beach FL 32082-2319

ROLAND, PETER SARGENT, otolaryngologist; b. Washington, Apr. 3, 1947; s. Joseph Morgan and Mary Hellen (Banker) R.; m. Melinda Clair Gill, Feb. 22, 1989; children: Evelyn, Jason, Britney, Kenzey. BA, Rockford Coll., 1969; MD, U. Tex., 1976. Resident in otolaryngology Pa. State U.-M.S. Hershey Med. Ctr., Hershey, 1976-80; asst. prof. otolaryngology Uniformed Svcs. U. Health Scis., Washington, 1980-84; fellow in otology, neurotology and skull base surgery EAR Found., Nashville, 1984-85; prof., vice chmn. otolaryngology, head and neck surgery U. Tex. Southwestern Med. Ctr., Dallas, 1985-2001, prof., chmn. otolaryngology, head and neck surgery, 2001—. Chief otolaryngology Parkland Meml. Hosp., Dallas, 1990—. Served to lt. comdr. USNR, 1980-84. Fellow Am. Otol. Soc., Am. Neurotol. Soc., Am. Acad. Otolaryngology; mem. Alpha Omega Alpha. Avocations: running, reading, hiking. Home: 2117 Clearspring Dr S Irving TX 75063-3393 Office: U Tex Southwestern Med Ctr 5323 Harry Hines Blvd Dallas TX 75390-7208 E-mail: peter.roland@utsouthwestern.edu.

ROLAND, RAYMOND WILLIAM, lawyer, mediator, arbitrator; b. Ocala, Fla., Jan. 3, 1947; s. Raymond W. and Hazel (Dunn) R.; m. Jane Allen, Dec. 28, 1968; children: John Allen, Jason William. BA, Fla. State U., 1969, JD, 1972. Bar: Fla. 1972, U.S. Dist. Ct. (no. dist.) Fla. 1973, U.S. Dist. Ct. (mid. dist.) Fla. 1985, U.S. Ct. Appeals (5th cir.) 1974, U.S. Ct. Appeals (11th cir.) 1983, U.S. Supreme Ct. 1985; cert. cir. ct. mediator. Assoc. Keen, O'Kelley & Spitz, Tallahassee, 1972-74, ptnr., 1974-77; ptnr., v.p. McConnaughhay, Roland, Maida & Cherr, P.A., 1978-97; cir. mediator U.S. Ct. Appeals 11th Cir., 1997—2002. Diplomate mem. Fla. Acad. of Profl. Mediators, Inc.; adj. prof. Bapt. Coll. Fla. Bd. dirs. So. Scholarship Found., Tallahassee, 1985-89, 98-99, v.p. 1989; bd. visitors Bapt. Coll. Fla. Mem. Internat. Assn. Def. Coun., Def. Rsch. Inst., Fla. Bar, Tallahassee Bar Assn. (treas. 1979), Kiwanis (life, lt. gov. 1984- 85), Capital City Kiwanis Club (Kiwanian of Yr. 1978, pres. 1979), Fla. Kiwanis Found. (life fellow). Republican. Baptist. Avocations: reading, hiking, camping, golf. Home: 328 Jefferson Dr Atlanta GA 30350

ROLAND, REGINA E. elementary school educator; b. Evanston, Ill., Aug. 1, 1949; d. Melvin J. and Rosemary G. (Malone) Ahrens; m. James I. Roland, Feb. 14, 1970. BA, No. Ill. U., 1971; MEd, Nat. Louis U., 1985. Educator St. John the Bapt. Sch., Winfield, Ill., 1972—74; Spanlsh/ESL/bilingual tchr. Des Plaines (Ill.) Cmty. Consol. Sch. Dist., 1974—. Presenter workshops in field. Co-author: A Hat for All Seasons, Hats on the Go; contbr. articles to mags. Scholar, Ill. State67. Mem.: NEA, Assisi Animal Found. Roman Catholic. Avocations: reading, walking, jewelry-making, writing, volunteer work. Home: 61 Dundee Ln Barrington IL 60010 E-mail: Regina@avenew.com.

ROLATER, FREDERICK STRICKLAND, history educator, consultant; b. McKinney, Tex., July 22, 1938; s. Frederick Gladstone and Vern (Strickland) R.; m. Jeannette Baker, Aug. 5, 1960. BA, Wake Forest U., 1960; MA, U. So. Calif., 1963, PhD, 1970. Assoc. prof. history Blue Mountain (Miss.) Coll., 1963-64; chmn. dept. social studies Grand Canyon Coll., Phoenix, 1964-67; Fulbright prof. history U. Kyushu and Seinan Gakuin U., Fukuoka, Japan, 1987-88; prof. history, dir. grad. studies dept. history Middle Tenn. State U., Murfreesboro, 1967-2000; prof. ch. history Korea Bapt. Theol. U./Sem., Taejon, Republic of Korea, 2000—. Author: Japanese Americans, 1991; contbr. articles to profl. jours. Mem. exec. bd. So. Bapt. Hist. Commn., Nashville, 1984-92; chmn. history com. Tenn. Bapt. Conv., Brentwood, Tenn., 1984-85, 98-2000; mem. hist. com. Bapt. World Alliance, Seoul, Korea, 1990; mem. Rutherford County Hist. Com., Murfreesboro, 1980-83. Recipient Meritorious Svc. award Tenn. Bapt. Conv., 1991; Nat. Merit scholar, 1956-60. Mem. Tenn. Bapt. Hist. Soc. (pres.), Gideons Internat., Concord Bapt. Assn. (moderator 1998-2000), Phi Beta Kappa. Office: Korea Baptist Theological Seminary Gu Daejeon 305-358 Republic of Korea E-mail: frolater@mtsu.edu., frolater@hotmail.com.

ROLEN, SCOTT BRUCE, baseball player; b. Jasper, Ind., Apr. 4, 1975; m. Niki Warner, Feb. 2, 2002. 3d base Phila. Phillies, 1993—2002, St. Louis Cardinals, 2002. Named Nat. League Rookie Player of the Yr., The Sporting News, 1997, Baseball Writers Assn. of Am., 1997. Office: c/o St Louis Cardinals 250 Stadium Plaza Saint Louis MO 63102*

ROLES, FORREST HANSBURY, lawyer; b. Balt., Aug. 19, 1942; s. Forrest and Agnes (Campbell) R.; m. Emily Lynn McPhail, Feb. 25, 1967; children: Margaret Jean, Elizabeth Jane. BA, Davidson Coll., 1964; LLB, W.Va. U., 1967. Bar: U.S. Dist. Ct. (so. dist.) W.Va. 1967, U.S. Ct. Appelas (4th cir.) 1971, U.S. Supreme Ct. 1978. Assoc. Jackson & Kelley, Charleston, W.Va., 1967-72, ptnr., 1972-82, Smith, Heenan & Althen, Charleston, 1983-97, Hennan, Althen & Roles, Charleston, 1997—. Bd. dirs. Concord Coll. Found., 1996—, chmn. 1999—; bd. dirs. Kanawha County Pub. Defender, Charleston, 1986—. Named among Best Lawyers in Am. Woodward/White, Inc., 1995—. Republican. Home: 904 Bird Rd Charleston WV 25314-1401 Office: Box 2549 1380 BB&T Sq Charleston WV 25329 E-mail: froles@harlaw.com.

ROLES, SHERRY LYNN, family nurse practitioner; b. Warren, Ohio, Mar. 9, 1961; d. Willie Edward and Donis May (Cutright) Ailstock; m. Gene Worth Roles, Dec. 10, 1988; children: Tawnie Danielle, Marshall Adam. BSN summa cum laude, U. Ctrl. Okla., 1992; MSN, Fla. State U., 1995. RN, Fla.; cert. advanced nurse practitioner; cert. BLS, ACLS. Staff nurse Bay Med. Ctr., Panama City, Fla., 1993, Riverdell Hosp., Panama City, 1993-94; family nurse practitioner North Fla. Med. Ctr., Bristol, Fla., 1995—. Lt. USN, 1988-93. Mem. AACN, Am. Assn. Nurse Practitioners, Fla. Rural Health Assn., Sigma Theta Tau.

ROLETT, ELLIS LAWRENCE, medical educator, cardiologist; b. N.Y.C., July 10, 1930; s. Daniel Meyer and Mary Elaine (Warshaw) R.; m. Virginia Ann Vladimir, Mar. 25, 1956; children: Roderic Lawrence, Barry Vladimir, Daniel Alfred. BS, Yale U., 1952; MD cum laude, Harvard U., 1955. Diplomate: Am. Bd. Internal Medicine, Am. Bd. Cardiovas. Disease. Intern, resident in medicine Mass. Gen. Hosp., Boston, 1955-56, 59-61; asst. resident N.Y. Hosp.-Cornell U. Med. Ctr., N.Y.C., 1956-57; Am. Heart Assn. research fellow Peter Bent Brigham Hosp., Boston, 1961-63; mem. faculty U. N.C., Chapel Hill, 1963-74, then prof., 1971-74; prof. UCLA, 1974-77; chief cardiology VA Wadsworth Hosp., L.A., 1974-77, Dartmouth-Hitchcock Med. Ctr., Hanover, N.H., 1977-87; prof. Dartmouth Med. Sch., 1977-97; prof. medicine active emeritus U. Dartmouth, 1997—. Vis. scientist August Krogh Inst., Copenhagen, 1984; mem. merit rev. bd. Cardiovasc. studies VA, 1976-79, chmn., 1978-79; mem. regional rsch. rev. com. New Eng. Am. Heart Assn., 1978-83; mem. sci. bd. Stanley J. Sarnoff Endowment for Cardiovasc. Sci., 1992-97, chmn., 1994-95, bd. dirs., 1997-2000; mem. lit. sect. rev. com. Nat. Libr. Medicine, 1995-99, chmn., 1998-99; dir. Vt.-Karelia (Russia) Med. Project, 1992—. Bd. dirs. N.H. affiliate Am. Heart Assn., 1978-85; pres. N.H. affiliate Am. Heart Assn., 1983-85. Served to capt. M.C. USAF, 1957-59. Recipient Lederle Med. Faculty award, 1965-68, USPHS Career Devel. award, 1967-72; grantee USPHS/NIH, 1964-76, VA Merit Rev. Rsch. Program, 1975-77, Mathers Found., 1984-86, 93-96, Am. Heart Assn., 1989-91. Mem. AAAS, Am. Coll. Cardiology, Am. Fedn. Clin. Research, Am. Heart Assn., Am. Physiol. Soc., Internat. Soc. Heart Research, Phi Beta Kappa, Alpha Omega Alpha Home: 4 Balch Hill Ln Hanover NH 03755-1622 Office: Dartmouth Med Sch Hanover NH 03755 E-mail: ellis.rolett@dartmouth.edu.

ROLEWICZ, ROBERT JOHN, estimating engineer; b. Chgo., Sept. 16, 1954; s. Frank Joseph and Margaret Mary (Ahlbach) R.; m. Vicki Lynn Heggeland, Sept. 1, 1985; children: Heather Margaret, Jeremy Robert. Diploma, Washburne Trade Sch., 1977. Level II inspector Kropp Forge Co., Chgo., 1974-77, chief cost estimator, 1978-88, mgr. estimating, chief estimating engr., 1989—. Pres. Kropp Employees Fed. Credit Union, 1986-88; founding mem. Metalworking Industry Adv. Coun., 1990. Committeeman Citizens to Reelect Jack Kubik, Cicero, Ill., 1984-96, Citizens to Reelect Judy Baar Topinka, Cicero, 1984-96; vol. instr. Boys Club, Cicero, 1975-84; bd. dirs. Cicero Family Svc. and Mental Health Ctr., 1979-87; supporter Cicero Police Benevolent Assn., 1990—, Misericordia Home for Developmentally Disabled, 1974—, Seguin Sch. for Retarded Citizens Assn., Inc., 1985—, Berwyn Libr. Bldg. Fund, Nat. Parks and Conservation Assn., 1990—; local area children's soccer coach; vol. cmty. based holiday baskets for needy families, 1979—, cmty. based drug awareness forum, 1985—; mem. Nat. Arbor Day Found., 2000— Recipient Hold My Hand award Children's Ctr. Cicero, 1982. Mem. VFW (life), Metalworking Industry Adv. Coun. (founding mem.), Vets. of Vietnam War Inc, Vietnam Vets. Am. Inc., Czechoslovak Soc. Am, Vietnow, Sacred Heart League, Cicero Hist. Soc., Brookfield Zoo, St. Jude League, Nat. Audubon Soc., St. Patrick H.S. Alumni Club, Kropp Key Club (pres. 1984—, Golden Anvil award 1989), Elks (mag. editor 1976—, exalted ruler 1981-82, 94-95, 2000-2001, v.p. N.E. dist., P.E.R. plaque 1982, Elk of Yr. award Cicero-Berwyn 1989, 93, Govt. Rels. award 1989, Grand Lodge Order of Elks Disting. Citizenship award 1999, Grand Exalted Rulers Commendation award 1998-99, Grand Lodge Trail Blazer award 2000--01), Moose, Handyman Club Am., Nat. Home Gardening Club (charter mem. 2001—). Republican. Roman Catholic. Avocations: jogging, swimming, camping, canoeing, hiking. E-mail: rolewicz@webtv.net.

ROLEY, JEFF W. foundation representative; b. Normal, Ill., Dec. 6, 1960; s. Wayne F. and Betty R. Roley; m. Shelley G. Roley, July 15, 1994; children: Alexandria Elizabeth, Baley Renae. BS in Econs., Ill. State U., Normal, 1985. Sr. cons. Banc One Securities Corp., Columbus, Ohio, 1993-95; gift planner U. Ill. Found., Urbana, 1995—. Bd. mem., treas. Christian Campus Found., U. Ill., Urbana; chmn., deacon first Christian Ch.-Cmty. Impact Ministry, Champaign, Ill. Named Layperson of Yr., Kiwanis Internat., 1999. Mem. Nat. Com. on Planned Giving, Nat. Soc. Fund Raising Execs., East Ctrl. Ill. Estate Planning Coun. Office: U Ill Found 1305 W Green St # Mc-386 Urbana IL 61801-2945 E-mail: roley@uif.uillinois.edu.

ROLF, HOWARD LEROY, mathematician, educator; b. Laverne, Okla., Nov. 25, 1928; s. James Walter and Edith (Yoho) R.; m. Anita Jane Ward, June 24, 1961; children: James Scott, Jennifer Jane, Stephanie Kaye, Rhonda Mary. BS, Okla. Baptist U., 1951; MA, Vanderbilt U., 1953, PhD, 1956. Instr. math. Vanderbilt U., 1954-56, asst. prof., dir. computer ctr., 1959-64; asst. prof. Baylor U., 1956-57, prof., 1964-98, dir. acad. computing, 1968-70, chmn. dept. math., 1971-97. Assoc. prof. Georgetown (Ky.) Coll., 1957-59; cons. in field. Author: (with William C. Brown) Mathematics, 1982, Finite Mathematics, 1988, 91, 94, 99, 2002, Mathematics for Management, Social and Life Sciences, 1991. Mem. Math. Assn. Am. (chmn. Tex. sect. 1977), Sigma Xi, Pi Mu Epsilon, Golden Key. Baptist. Home: 4096 Speegleville Rd Waco TX 76712-4033

ROLFE, PAULA GRACE, educational administrator; b. Perth Amboy, N.J., Mar. 12, 1942; d. Fredrick Carl and Mae (Sapun) Lamp; m. George William Rolfe, Jr., July 4, 1965; 1 child, George William III. BA, Montclair (N.J.) State Coll., 1964; MS, Ill. State U., 1969; EdD, Auburn U., 1982. Tchr. Edison (N.J.) Twp. Pub. Schs., 1964-67, Pekin (Ill.) Pub. Schs., 1967-68, 1969-70, Guardian Angel Orphanage, Peoria, 1967-71; substitute tchr. Montgomery (Ala.) Pub. Schs., 1974-77; grad. teaching asst. Auburn (Ala.) U., 1979-80; owner, dir. Sylvan Learning Ctr., Shreveport, La., 1983—. Mem. Mayor's Commn. for Women of Bossier City (La.) Inc., 1987-2000, 1st v.p., 1990—, pres., 1991-92. Mem. Am. Bus. Women's Assn. (Woman of the Yr. 1988, Srebo chpt. sec. 1990—, pres. 1991-92), Am. Home Econs. Assn., Am. Assn. for Adult and Continuing Edn., Quota Club (rec. sec. 1997-98, 1st v.p. 1998-99, pres. 1999-2000), Montclair State Coll. Alumni Assn., Ill. State U. Alumni Assn., Auburn U. Alumni Assn. Methodist. Avocations: swimming, boating, cross-stitching, gardening.

ROLFE, ROBERT MARTIN, lawyer; b. Richmond, Va., May 16, 1951; s. Norman and Bertha (Cohen) R.; m. Catherine Dennis Stone, July 14, 1973; children: P. Alexander, Asher B., Joel A., Zachary A. BA, U. Va., 1973, JD, 1976. Bar: Va. 1976, N.Y. 1985, U.S. Dist. Ct. (ea. and we. dists.) Va. 1976, U.S. Ct. Appeals (4th cir.) 1976, U.S. Ct. Appeals (2d cir.) 1979, U.S. Dist. Ct. (ea. dist.) Mich. 1985, U.S. Ct. Appeals (D.C. cir.) 1985, U.S. Dist. Ct. (so. and ea. dists.) N.Y. 1985, U.S. Ct. Appeals (7th cir.) 1995, U.S. Ct. Fed. Claims, 1997, U.S. Supreme Ct. 1979. Assoc. Hunton & Williams, Richmond, 1976-83, ptnr., 1983—, co-head litigation, intellectual property and antitrust team, mem. exec. com., 1998—. Contbr. articles to profl. jours. Trustee Jewish Family Supporting Found.; bd. dirs. Jewish Family Svcs., Richmond, pres., 1993-95; bd. mgrs., 2d v.p. Congregation Beth Ahabah, 1995-97, 1st v.p., 1997-99. Fellow Am. Bar Found.; mem. ABA (litig. sect.), Va. Bar Assn., Va. State Bar, Richmond Bar Assn., Am. Arbitration Assn. (comml. arbitrators panel), Order of Coif (Alumni award for acad. excellence U. Va. 1976). Home: 18 Greenway Ln Richmond VA 23226-1630 Office: Hunton & Williams Riverfront Plz East Tower PO Box 1535 Richmond VA 23218-1535 also: 200 Park Ave New York NY 10166-0005

ROLFE, RONALD STUART, lawyer; b. N.Y.C., Sept. 5, 1945; s. Nat and Florence I. (Roth) R.; m. Sara Darehshori, June 1, 2002; 1 child, Andrew. AB, Harvard U., 1966; JD, Columbia U., 1969. Bar: N.Y. 1969, U.S. Ct. Appeals (2d cir.) 1970, U.S. Dist. Ct. (so. and ea. dists.) N.Y. 1971, U.S. Supreme Ct. 1973, U.S. Dist. Ct. (no. dist.) Calif. 1982, U.S. Ct. Appeals (6th and 5th cirs.) 1982, U.S. Ct. Appeals (9th cir.) 1983, U.S. Dist. Ct. (ea. dist.) Ky. 1984, U.S. Ct. Appeals (7th and 10th cirs.) 1989, U.S. Ct. Appeals (fed. cir.) 1991, U.S. Ct. Appeals (3d cir.) 1992, U.S. Ct. Appeals (4th cir.) 1991. Law clk. to judge U.S. Dist. Ct. (so. dist.) N.Y., 1969-70; assoc. Cravath, Swaine & Moore, 1970-77, ptnr., 1977—. Sec. bd. trustees Allen-Stevenson Sch., 1981—91, pres., 1992—; trustee Lawrenceville Sch., 1987—, v.p., 2001—. Fellow: Am. Bar Found.; mem.: ABA, Am. Law Inst., Fed. Bar Coun. (trustee 1989—94), Assn. Bar City NY, NY State Bar Assn., Turf and Field Club (N.Y.C.), Stanwich Club (Greenwich, Conn.), Univ. Club, Union Club. Office: Cravath Swaine & Moore Worldwide Plz 825 8th Ave 40th Fl New York NY 10019-7475 E-mail: rrolfe@cravath.com.

ROLFE, STANLEY THEODORE, civil engineer, educator; b. Chgo., July 7, 1934; s. Stanley T. and Eunice (Fike) R.; m. Phyllis Williams, Aug. 11, 1956; children: David Stanley, Pamela Kay, Kathleen Ann. BS, U. Ill., 1956, MS, 1958, PhD, 1962. Registered profl. engr., Pa., Kans. Supr. structural-evaluation sect. ordnance products divsn. U.S. Steel Corp., 1962-69, divsn. chief mech. behavior of metals divsn., 1969; A.P. Learned prof. civil engring. U. Kans., 1969—, chmn. civil engring. dept., 1975-98, Charles E. Spahr prof., 1999. Chmn. metall. studies panel ship rsch. com. Nat. Acad. Scis., 1967-70 Co-author: Fracture and Fatigue Control in Structures— Applications of Fracture Mechanics; co-author: textbook Strength of Materials; contbr. numerous articles to profl. jours. T.R. Higgins lectr., 1980; Recipient Sam Tour award Am. Soc. Testing Materials, 1971, H.E. Gould Distinguished Teaching award U. Kans., 1972, 75, AWS Adams Meml. Educator award, 1974; U. Ill. Civil Engring. Disting. Service award, 1985, U. Ill. Coll. Engring. Alumni Honor award Disting. Service in Engring., 1987; U. Kans. Irvin E. Youngberg research award, 1985. Mem. ASME, ASTM, ASCE (hon.; chmn. task force on fracture, State of Art award 1983, Ernest E. Howard award 2001), Nat. Acad. Engring., Soc. Exptl. Stress Analysis, Am. Soc. Engring. Edn., Chi Psi. Presbyterian. Home: 821 Sunset Dr Lawrence KS 66044-2433

ROLFES, LEONARD JOSEPH, pediatrician; b. New Orleans, Apr. 23, 1923; s. Frederick John and Catherine (Cunningham) R.; m. Elizabeth Browder, June 19, 1954; children: Frederick, James, Katherine, Elizabeth, Leonard, Jr., Anne. BS, Tulane U., 1949, MD, 1951. Diplomate Am. Bd. Pediatrics. Resident in pediatrics Charity Hosp., New Orleans, 1954-55, U. Chgo., 1955-57; pediatrician Hamilton Med. Group, Lafayette, La., 1957-92; cons. pediatrician Charter-Cypress Hosp., 1992-2000. Clin. faculty Tulane Med. Sch., New Orleans, 1959-92. Lt. comdr. USN, 1943-65. Fellow Am. Acad. Pediatrics. Roman Catholic. Avocations: computers, golf. Home: 408 Beverly Dr Lafayette LA 70503-3112 E-mail: lrolfes@worldnet.att.net.

ROLFES, RICHARD JAMES, radiologist; b. Cin., Apr. 12, 1960; s. Robert Joseph and Dolores Ann R.; m. Mary Beth, June 14, 1986; children: Matthew, Lauren, Bradley. BA, U. Cin., 1982; MD, Ohio State U., 1986. Diplomate Am. Bd. Radiology, Nat. Bd. Med. Examiners, cert. Bd. Nuclear Cardiology. Resident in radiology U. Fla., Gainesville, 1986-90; fellow in MRI and nuclear medicine The Christ Hosp., Cin., 1990-91; staff radiologist Anderson Mercy Hosp., 1991-94, The Christ Hosp., Cin., 1994-99; assoc. med. dir., fellowship dir. Proscan Imaging, 1999—. Mem. Rep. Nat. Com., 1991—. Mem. Am. Coll. Radiology, Radiol. Soc. N.Am., Clin. Magnetic Resonance Soc., Soc. Nuclear Medicine, Inst. Clin. PET, Ohio State Radiol. Soc. Roman Catholic. Avocations: travel, family. Office: Proscan Imaging 5400 Kennedy Ave Cincinnati OH 45213-2624

ROLISON, DEBRA ROSE, research chemist; b. Sioux City, Iowa, May 26, 1954; d. James Patrick Rose and Romaine Barbara Schurman. BS, Fla. Atlantic U., 1975; PhD, U. N.C., 1980. Rsch. chemist Naval Rsch. Lab., Washington, 1980—99, head advanced electrochem. materials sect., 1999—. Mem. editl. adv. bd. Jour. electroanalytical chemistry Elsevier, Lausanne, Switzerland, 1995—; mem. editl. adv. bd. Ency. of Nanoscience and Nanotechnology Marcel Dekker, N.Y.C., 2001—; chair 2001Gordon Rsch. Conf. Electrochemistry Gordon Rsch. Confs., West Kingston, RI, 2001. Author (with M. Fleischmann, S. Pons, P. Schmidt): (book) Ultramicroelectrodes, 1987; author: (book chpt.) Doing chemistry with nanostructures-What's the little deal?, 1996, A "Title IX" challenge to academic chemistry[0085] or[0085] Isn't a millennium of affirmative action for white men sufficient?, 2000. Recipient Alan Berman Rsch. Publ. award, Naval Rsch. Lab., 2001. Mem.: Materials Rsch. Soc., Am. Chem. Soc. (editl. adv. bd. Analytical Chemistry 1990—92, editl. adv. bd. Langmuir 2000), Soc. for Electroanalytical Chemistry (life; dir., seac bd. of directors 1997—2001, editor SEAC Comms. 1997—2002). Home: 1821 N Tuckahoe St Arlington VA 22205 Office: Naval Rsch Lab 4555 Overlook Ave SW Washington DC 20375 Business E-Mail: rolison@nrl.navy.mil.

ROLL, DAVID LEE, lawyer; b. Pontiac, Mich., May 1, 1940; s. Everett Edgar and Garnette (Houts) R.; m. Nancy E. Spindle, Aug. 17, 1963; children: Richard, Molly. BA cum laude, Amherst Coll., 1962; JD, U. Mich., 1964. Bar: Mich. 1965, U.S. Dist. Ct. (ea. dist.) Mich. 1965, U.S. Ct. Appeals (6th cir.) 1969, D.C. 1974, U.S. Dist. Ct. D.C. 1975, U.S. Supreme Ct. 1975, U.S. Ct. Appeals (4th cir.) 1976, U.S. Ct. Appeals (D.C. cir.) 1983, U.S. Ct. Appeals (3rd and 11th cirs.) 1985, U.S. Ct. Appeals (9th cir.) 1992, U.S. Ct. Appeals (fed. cir.) 1993. Assoc. Hill, Lewis, Detroit, 1965-70, ptnr., 1970-72; asst. dir. gen. litigation Bur. of Competition Fed. Trade Commn., Washington, 1972-75; ptnr. Steptoe & Johnson, 1975-93, chmn., 1993-98. V.p. bus. devel., bd. dirs. eLawForum, 2000—. Mem. ABA (chair Robinson Patman Act com., antitrust sect. 1984-86, Clayton Act com., antitrust sect. 1986-88, Energy Litigation com., litigation sect. 1992-93, mem. task force on indsl. competitiveness 1987, coun., antitrust sect. 1988-91, author, editor antitrust sect.), Lex Mundi (bd. dirs., chair competition com.). Office: 1330 Connecticut Ave NW Washington DC 20036-1704 E-mail: droll@steptoe.com.

ROLL, IRWIN CLIFFORD (WIN ROLL), advertising, marketing and publishing executive; b. N.Y.C., Aug. 21, 1925; s. Arnold and Bertha (Vogel) R.; m. Marilyn Witlin, Apr. 10, 1949; children: Richard J., Douglas W. BBA magna cum laude, CCNY, 1948; postgrad., Columbia U., 1952. Asst. advt. mgr. Standard Motor Products, Inc., Long Island City, N.Y., 1948-50; advt. and sales promotion exec. RCA, Harrison, N.J., 1950-54; account exec. Fuller & Smith & Ross, Inc., N.Y.C., 1954-59, group v.p., 1959-66; pres., dir. Henderson & Roll, Inc., advt. and pub. relations agy., 1966-77; pres., dir., chief exec. officer Henderson, Roll & Friedlich, Inc., 1977-79; chmn. bd., treas., chief exec. officer, dir. Listfax Corp., nat. computerized info. services co., 1966-79; pres., CEO Win Roll and Co., Inc., N.Y.C., 1979-89, 99—; chmn. bd. Roll-Bender Research, 1980-82, Devonshire Communications, Ltd., 1980-83; sr. v.p. Tradewell Industries, Inc., 1983-87. Exec. v.p. Internat. Mktg. Sys. Inc., 1988-90; pres. Concord Cons. Group, 1990—; corp. devel. dir. Ind. Media Svcs., Inc., 1990-92; pres. Maco Pub. Co., 1992- 94; pres., treas., bd. dirs. Megaworld, Inc., 1994-99. Mem. mktg. com. Nat. Multiple Sclerosis Soc., 1958-98; bd. dirs. Westchester County chpt. Multiple Sclerosis Soc., 1983-89; pres. Rosedale Residential Assn., 1983-85, bd. dirs., 1980-2000. With U.S. Army, 1943-46, ETO. Mem. Ad-Net Nat. Advt. Orgn. (bd. dirs. 1983-90, pres. 1986-88), Beta Gamma Sigma (bd. dirs., v.p. N.Y. Alumni chpt. 1986-89, pres. 1989-91, adv. bd. 1991—). Home: 2558 Downeyville Ave Henderson NV 89052 Fax: 702-614-5117. E-mail: winroll@webtv.net.

ROLL, JOHN MCCARTHY, judge; b. Pitts., Feb. 8, 1947; s. Paul Herbert and Esther Marie (McCarthy) R.; m. Maureen O'Connor, Jan. 24, 1970; children: Robert McCarthy, Patrick Michael, Christopher John. BA, U. Ariz., 1969, JD, 1972; LLM, U. Va., 1990. Bar: Ariz. 1972, U.S. Dist. Ct. Ariz. 1974, U.S. Ct. Appeals (9th cir.) 1980, U.S. Supreme Ct. 1977. Asst. pros. atty. City of Tucson, 1972-73; dep. county atty. Pima County (Ariz.), 1973-80; asst. U.S. Atty. U.S. Attys. Office, Tucson, 1980-87; judge Ariz. Ct. Appeals, 1987-91, U.S. Dist. Ct. Ariz., 1991—. Mem. criminal justice mental health standards project ABA, 1980—83, mem. com. model jury instrns. 9th circ., 1994—2001, chair com. model jury instrns. 9th circ., 1998—2001; mem. panel workshop criminal law CEELI Program, Moscow, 1997; mem. U.S. Jud. Conf. Adv. Com. Criminal Rules, 1997—. Contbr. Merit Selection: the Arizona Experience, Ariz. State Law Jour., 1991, The Rules Have Changed: Amendments ot the Rules of Civil procedure, Defense Law Jour., 1994, Ninth Cir. Judges' Benchbook on Pretrial Proceedings, 1998, 2000, 2002. Coach Frontier Baseball Little League, Tucson, 1979-84; mem. parish coun. Sts. Peter and Paul Roman Cath. Ch., Tucson, 1983-91, chmn., 1986-91; mem. Roman Cath. Dioceses Tucson Sch. Bd., 1986-90. Recipient Disting. Faculty award Nat. Coll. Dist. Attys., U. Houston, 1979, Outstanding Alumnus award U. Ariz. Coll. Law, 1992. Mem. Fed. Judges Assn., KC (adv. coun. 1991). Republican. Office: US Dist Ct 405 W Congress Tucson AZ 85701

ROLL, MARILYN RITA BROWNLIE, social worker; b. Bay City, Mich., Dec. 7, 1946; d. John P. and Rita (Himpele) Brownlie; m. Charles S. Roll Jr., Dec. 28, 1968; 1 child, Brian. BS, Cornell U., 1969; MSW, Rutgers U., 1986. Lic. clin. social worker, N.J.; cert. practitioner in psychodrama, cert. in EMDR, cert. in Imago relationship therapy for couples and singles, cert. in clin. hypnosis, cert. family life educator, cert. secondary sch. tchr., cert. sch. social worker, N.J., cert. parent effectiveness instr., cert. stepfamily counselor, ACSW; diplomate clin. social work. High sch. home econs. tchr. Scotch Plains Fanwood High Sch., NJ, 1970, 1973—78; dir., co-founder, program developer Family Life Resources, Fanwood, N.J., 1982—; sch. social worker Somerset Elem. Sch., North Plainfield, 1984-85; psychotherapist, intervention counselor Resolve Community Counseling Ctr., Scotch Plains, 1985-87; pvt. practice psychotherapist Westfield, N.J., 1987—. Evaluative cons. Bank St. Coll. for Internat. Work and Family Life Study, N.Y.C., 1986; program developer, parent educator The Mothers Ctr., Scotch Plains, 1977-83. Researcher: (book-Time, Inc.) The Preschool Years, 1983-85. Mem. Sch. Dist. Substance Abuse com., Scotch Plains, 1987-88. Mem. Nat. Assn. Social Workers, Nat. Coun. on Family Rels., The Am. Orthopsychiat. Assn., Am. Soc. Group Psychotherapy and Psychodrama, Am. Soc. Clin. Hypnosis, The Stepfamily Found., Family Resource Coalition, Alumni Assn. of Sch. of Social Work Rutgers U., Alumni Assn. Cornell Univ. Sch. Human Ecology, Phi Lambda Theta. Home: 184 Burns Way Fanwood NJ 07023-1604 Office: 128 S Euclid Ave Westfield NJ 07090-5103

ROLLAND, ALAIN P. pharmaceutical executive; b. Landivisiau, France, Oct. 26, 1959; s. Alexandre and Gabrielle (Bizien) R.; m. Corine Lhuissier, July 11, 1981; children: Gabriel, Alix, Benjamin. BA in Math, Physics, Landerneau, France, 1976; Pharm D., Rennes U., France, 1981, DEA in Pharmacokinetics, 1983, PhD, 1987. Scientist Ciba-Geigy Pharms., Horsham, U.K., 1987-88; head formulation rsch. group CIRD Galderma, Sophia Antipolis, France, 1989-93; dir. gene delivery GeneMedicine, Inc., The Woodlands, Tex., 1993-96, v.p. gene delivery scis., 1996-97, v.p. rsch., 1997-98; v.p. R & D, The Woodlands Ctr. Head, Valentis Inc., 1999—. Reviewer for several scientific jours.; mem. editl. bd. Advanced Drug Delivery Revs., Jour. of Controlled Release, Jour. of Pharmacy and Pharmacology; editor books in field; patentee in field; contbr. articles to profl. jours. Recipient prize Found. of French Pharm. Industry for Rsch., 1987, Claude Bernard Assn., 1987, French Acad. of Pharmacy, 1987. Mem. Am. Controlled Release Soc., Internat. Soc. for Gene Therapy, Am. Chem. Soc., European Working Group on Human Gene Transfer and Therapy, Am. Assn. Pharm. Scientists, n.Y. Acad. Sci., Am. Soc. Gene Therapy. Achievements include devel. of delivery system to target anti-cancer drugs to the liver for treatment of hepatoma and creation of gene medicine for the prevention and treatment of human diseases. Avocations: horseback riding, squash, watercolor printing, flute, reading. Office: Valentis Inc 8301 New Trails Dr The Woodlands TX 77381-4248

ROLLAND, LUCIEN GILBERT, paper company executive, director; b. St. Jerome, Que., Can., Dec. 21, 1916; s. Olivier and Aline (Dorion) R.; m. Marie de Lorimier, May 30, 1942; children: Nicolas, Natalie, Stanislas, Dominique, Christine, Etienne, David. Student, Coll. Jean de Brebeuf, Montreal, U. Montreal, BA, BASc., C.E., also D.C.Sc. (hon.), 1960. Registered profl. engr. With Rolland Paper Co. Ltd. (name changed to Rolland inc. 1979), 1942—, v.p., gen. mgr., 1952, pres., gen. mgr., 1952-78, pres., CEO, 1978—, chmn., pres., CEO, 1984, chmn., CEO, 1985, chmn., 1991. Cons. in field, 1995; chmn. bd. Tarascon, Inc. Bd. govs. Notre-Dame Hosp., Montreal Children's Hosp., Montreal Gen. Hosp., Hôpital Marie Enfant. Decorated Knight Comdr. Order St. Gregory, officer Order of Can. Mem. Can. Pulp and Paper Assn. (hon.), Corp. Profl. Engrs., Montreal Bd. Trade, Province of Que., C of C, Montreal C. of C., Engring. Inst. Can. Home: Apt B-60 1321 Sherbrooke St W Montreal QC Canada H3G 1J4 Office: Tarascon Inc 1200 McGill College #1100 Montreal QC Canada H3B 4G7

ROLLE, ANDREW, historian, writer; b. Providence, Apr. 12, 1922; m. Frances Squires, Dec. 1945 (div.); children: John Warren, Alexander Frederick, Julia Elisabeth.; m. Myra Moss, Nov. 1983. BA, Occidental Coll., 1943; MA, UCLA, 1949, PhD, 1953; grad., So. Calif. Psychoanalytic Inst., 1976. Am. vice consul, Genoa, Italy, 1945-48; editorial asso. Pacific Hist. Rev., 1952-53; from asst. prof. to Cleland prof. history Occidental Coll., 1953-88; rsch. scholar Huntington Libr., San Marino, Calif., 1988—. Author: Riviera Path, 1946, An American in California, 1956, reprinted, 1982, The Road to Virginia City, 1960, reprinted, 1989, Lincoln: A Contemporary Portrait, 1961, (with Allan Nevins, Irving Stone) California: A History, 1963, rev. edits., 1963, 69, 78, 87, 98, 2002, Occidental College: The First Seventy-Five Years, 1963, The Lost Cause: Confederate Exiles in Mexico, 1965, 1992, The Golden State, 1967, rev. edit., 1978, 1989, 2000, California, A Student Guide, 1965, Los Angeles, A Student Guide, 1965; Editor: A Century of Dishonor (Helen Hunt Jackson), 1964, Life in California (Alfred Robinson), 1971, Voyage to California (Jour. of Lucy Herrick), 1998; The Immigrant Upraised, 1968, The American Italians: Their History and Culture, 1972, Gli Emigrati Vittoriosi, 1973; (with George Knoles others) Essays and Assays, 1973, (with others) Studies in Italian American Social History, 1975, (with others) Los Angeles: The Biography of a City, 1976, 2d edit., 1991, (with Allan Weinstein and others) Crisis in America, 1977, The Italian Americans: Troubled Roots, 1980, 2d edit. 1985, Los Angeles: From Pueblo to Tomorrow's City, 1981, 2nd edit.,

1995, Occidental College: A Centennial History, 1986, John Charles Frémont: Character as Destiny, 1991, Henry Mayo Newhall and His Times, 1992, Westward the Immigrants, 1999. Served to 1st lt. M.I. AUS, 1943-45, 51-52. Decorated Cavaliere Ordine Merito Italy; recipient silver medal Italian Ministry Fgn. Affairs; Commonwealth award for non-fiction; Huntington Library-Rockefeller Found. fellow; resident scholar Rockefeller Found. Center, Bellagio, Italy Fellow Calif. Hist. Soc.; mem. Phi Beta Kappa. Office: Huntington Libr Rsch Div San Marino CA 91108

ROLLE, MARTHA COLLINS (MARTHA TRAUDT COLLINS), lawyer; b. Colorado Springs, Colo., July 23, 1952; d. Verne O.M. and Helen Louise Traudt; m. Alexander F. Rolle; children: Joseph T. Collins, Alexander S. Rolle. BS in Math., U. Nebr., 1974; JD, U. Colo., 1977. Bar: Colo. 1977, N.Y. 1997. Assoc. Holme Roberts & Owen LLC, Denver, 1977-82, ptnr., 1983—. Contbg. author: Rocky Mountain Mineral Law Foundation's Law of Federal Oil and Gas Leases, 1988; author: Hedging Transactions for Oil and Gas Producers: Rocky Mountain Mineral Law Foundation Special Institute, 1995; contbr. articles to profl. jours. Mem. ABA, Colo. Bar Assn., Denver Bar Assn., N.Y. Bar Assn., Order of Coif, Phi Beta Kappa. Office: Heathcoat House 20 Savile Row London W1S 3PR England E-mail: rollem@hro.com.

ROLLE, MYRA MOSS See MOSS, MYRA

ROLLENCE, MICHELE LYNETTE, molecular biologist; b. Takoma Park, Md., Nov. 23, 1955; d. John Francis and Martha Jo (Jackson) R.; m. David H. Specht, June 3, 1978 (div. Sept. 1982). AA, Montgomery Coll., 1976; BS, U. Md., 1978; MS, Johns Hopkins U., 1995. Lab. technician Dairy and Food Labs., San Francisco, 1979-81; rsch. asst. Genex Corp., Gaithersburg, Md., 1981-82, rsch. assoc., 1982-86, sr. rsch. assoc., 1986-88, rsch. scientist, 1989-93; rsch. assoc. Genetic Therapy, Inc., 1993—. Contbr. articles to profl. publs.; patentee in field. Pres. Explorer Post div. Boy Scouts Am., Gaithersburg, 1973; youth advisor Neelsville Presbyn. Ch., Germantown, Md., 1990. Recipient Nat. Exploration award TRW/Explorers Club, 1973. Mem. AAAS, Am. Soc. Genetic Therapy, Am. Soc. Microbiology, DAR, Pleasant Plains of Damascus. Democrat. Presbyterian. Avocations: bell choir, guitar, dance, hiking. Office: Genetic Therapy Inc 9 W Watkins Mill Rd Gaithersburg MD 20878-4021 E-mail: michele.rollence@pharma.novartis.com.

ROLLER, DAVID ISAAC, financial services company executive; b. Bklyn., Jan. 13, 1949; s. Morton and Helen (Deligtisch) R.; m. Susan Firtle, June 3, 1973; children: Aviva Natanya, Yael Elisheva. BA, L.I. U., 1971; MA, NYU, 1980, PhD, 1983, Cleo Soc., Oakland, Mich., 1991; DD, N.W. Ecumenical Inst., Petaluma, Calif., 1992. Ordained rabbi, 1980; cert. religious counselor. Rabbi North Rockland Jewish Cmty. Ctr., Pomona, N.Y., 1980-81; educator, asst. rabbi Old Westbury (N.Y.) Hebrew Congregation, 1982-83; rabbi Beth Emek Congregation, Livermore, Calif., 1983-85; pres., founder Roller Fin. Assocs., 1985—. Guest rabbi High Holidays, East Bay Chavuarah, Danville, Calif., 1990-93; chaplain Masonic Home for Adults, Union City, Pa., 1992—; mem. Sys Op AOL-Jew Comm Bd., 1995—. Mem. Internat. Assn. Fin. Planners, Am. Coun. Life Underwriters, Am. Assn. Rabbis, East Bay Bd. Rabbis, Masons (chaplain 1985-86), Mensa, Rotary. Republican. Jewish. Avocations: photography, reading.

ROLLER, DUANE WILLIAMSON, archaeologist, educator; b. Lafayette, Ind., Oct. 7, 1946; s. Duane Henry Dubose and Marjorie Fair (Williamson) R.; m. Letitia Jean Kaminski, Feb. 18, 1984. BA, U. Okla., 1966; MA, 1968; PhD, Harvard U., 1971. Asst. prof. Franklin and Marshall Coll., Lancaster, Pa., 1971-74, Wilfrid Laurier U., Waterloo, Ont., 1974-84, assoc. prof. classics, 1982-86; asst. prof. Ohio State U., 1986-89, assoc. prof., 1989-93, prof., 1993-98, prof. Greek and Latin, 1998—. Exec. mem. Can. Archaeol. Inst., Athens, 1982-87; dir. Tanagra Survey Project, Greece, 1985—, Southern Messapia Survey, Italy, 1989—. Author: Tanagran Studies: the Building Program of Herod the Great; contbr. editor Internat. Rwy. Traveller; contbr. articles on classical archaeology and classical studies to profl. jours. Charles Eliot Norton fellow Harvard U., 1970; Fulbright scholar, 1995, 2000; recipient rsch. awards Social Scis. and Humanities Rsch. Coun. Can., 1980, 84, Nat. Geographic Soc., 1990, NEH, 1993, 2000.. Mem. Archaeol. Inst. Am. Democrat. Avocations: railway passenger travel. Office: Ohio State U Lima OH 45804

ROLLER, MARION, sculptor; Student, Vesper George Sch. Art, Boston, Art Students League, N.Y.C.; BA in Art, Queens Coll., 1980. Sculptor in residence, 1999-2000. Instr. Fashion Inst. Tech., N.Y.C., Sculpture Ctr.; head design dept. Traphagen Sch. of Fashion. Exhbns. include The Newark Mus., 1995-96, Nat. Acad. Design, N.Y., 1994, Nat. Sculpture Soc., N.Y., 1996-97, Scottsdale, Ariz., Serravezza, Italy, 1994, Transco Mus., Phila., U.S. Mint, San Francisco, Denver, Albany (N.Y.) Inst. History and Art, Pittsfield (Mass.) Mus., Fedn. Internat. de la Medaille, Helsinki, Finland, Budapest, Hungary, 1993, Price Waterhouse Galleries, N.Y.C., 1997, Janus Gallery, Santa Fe, Chesterwood, Stockbridge, Mass., 1997, Hillsdale (Mich.) Coll., 1997, Nat. Sculpture Soc., 2000, 2001, UN, N.Y.C., 1995, Cannon House Rotunda, Washington, Butler Inst. of Am. Art, 2001, Nat. Acad. Annual, 2001, others; commns. include Nassau Ctr. for Emotionally Disturbed Children, St. Mary's Children and Families Found., Traphagen Sch. Fashion, Rosemary Harris Meml., Brookgreen Gardens, medal Nat. Acad. Design, Butler Mus., others; contbr. articles, book reviews to Sculpture Review. Recipient Helen Gapen Oehler Meml. award Allied Artists, 1991, Samuel Cashwan Meml. award Audubon Artists, 1992, Audubon Artists award, 1994, Pen & Brush award for Watercolor, 1997, Nat. Sulpture Soc. Annual Exhibit award, 1998, Lou Magnani award Salmagundi Club, 1998, Gold medal of Honor 56th Annual Audubon Artists Exhibit, 1998, medal Internat. Exhibit of Medallic Art Museum Beelden ann Vee, 1998, award for Medallic Sculpture Pen & Brush, 1999, medal of Ethel Traphagen Medallic Art Co., 2001. Fellow Nat. Sculpture Soc. (sec., Kalos Kagathos Found. prize, C. Percival Dietsch Sculpture prize, Tallix Foundry prize, Edith H. & Richman Proskauer prize, Joel Meisner Foundry award); mem. Nat. Acad. Design (academician), Audubon Artists (treas., past pres., Gold medal of honor, Art Students League award, 1999), The Pen & Brush (chmn. sculpture sect., Pen and Brush award for watercolor, 1997, Bronze medal for sculpture, Chaim Gross Found. award, 1996, Samuel Cashwan meml. award, 1992, Margaret Sussman award 2000, Charlotte Dunwiddie award for medallic art 2000), Allied Artists Am. (past pres., Silver medal honor, Sybil and Bob Porton award, Helen Gapen Oehler Meml. award, 1991), Am. Medallic Sculpture Assn., Fine Arts Fedn. (bd. mem.). Address: 30 W 60th St New York NY 10023-7902

ROLLER HALL, GAYLE ALINE, gifted and talented education educator; b. L.A., Dec. 3, 1959; d. Willard E. and Ruby A. (Meek) Roller; m. Samuel Hall, May 20, 1995. BA in Elem. Edn., Hendrix Coll., 1982; M in Elem. Edn., Ark. Tech. U., 1985, MS in Edn. Gifted and Talented, 1992. Cert. elem. edn., gifted K-12. Substitute tchr. Ft. Smith (Ark.) Pub. Schs., 1982-84; grad. asst. Ark. Tech. U., Russelville, 1984-85; gifted and talented tchr. Russellville (Ark.) Schs., 1985-86; gifted and talented adminstr., coord., tchr. Hartford (Ark.) Sch., 1986—. Vis. lectr. Ark. Tech. U., Russellville, 1987-89; conf. presentor, 2000. Mem. Circle K. Svc. Orgn., Conway, Ark., 1978-82, Big Sister Youth Svcs., Conway, 1978-81; asst. leader 4-H Hartford, 1988-93, main leader, 1993-94. Mem. Ark. Edn. Assn. (pub. rels. com. 1990-93), Hartford Edn. Assn. (pres. 1992-94). Baptist. Avocations: needle crafts, reading, working with children and plants. Office: Hartford Sch PO Box 489 Hartford AR 72938-0489 Home: RR 2 Box 1275 Howe OK 74940-9207

ROLLERI, DENISE MARIE, radiation therapist, business owner; b. Phila., Mar. 16, 1950; d. Albert J. and Marie (Fenerty) R. diploma, diploma, Bryn Mawr Sch. Radiol. Tech., Pa., 1976. Chief technologist dept. radiation therapy Bryn Mawr Hosp., 1970-75; sr. staff therapist Thomas Jefferson U. Hosp., Phila., 1976-85; supr. radiation oncology dept. St. Peter's Med. Ctr., New Brunswick, N.J., 1985-87; pres., CEO, R.T. Temps Inc., Wayne, Pa., 1987—, R.T. Career Edn., Wayne, 1995—. Pres. Radnor (Pa.) Young Reps., 1976-77, Mem. Am. Hosp. Assn., Soc. Radiation Oncology Adminstrs., Am. Soc. Radiol. Tech. Avocations: boating, walking, pet therapy. Office: RT Temps Inc PO Box 404 Wayne PA 19087-0404

ROLLETTE, HAROLD HENRY, insurance company executive; b. Cazenovia, Wis., May 6, 1939; s. Henry Harold and Eva Gertrude (Jessop) R.; m. Joanne Krueger, Oct. 24, 1959 (div. 1964); m. Mary Jean Hirschinger, Aug. 31, 1968 (dec. July 1995); children: Christopher, Renee; m. Nancy Jo Larsen, June 5, 1997. BA, Madison Bus. Coll., Wis., 1962. Underwriter Gen. Casualty Cos., Madison, 1962-66, mktg. rep., 1966-73, sales mgr. Ill. Freeport, 1973-75, br. mgr. Springfield, Ill., 1975-79, asst. mktg. mgr. Madison, 1979-81, br. mgr., resident sr. v.p. Sun Prairie, Wis., 1981—. Bd. dirs. Sun Prairie Indsl. Devel. Corp., 1989—. Mem. Sun Prairie C. of C. (bd. dirs. 1984-86), Leions. Republican. Lutheran. Avocations: woodworking, golf, hunting, fishing. Office: Gen Casualty Cos One General Dr Sun Prairie WI 53596

ROLLIN, BERNARD ELLIOT, philosophy educator, consultant on animal ethics; b. N.Y.C., Feb. 18, 1943; s. Phillip and Yetta Ethel (Bookchin) R.; m. Linda Mae Schieber, Aug. 30, 1964; 1 child, Michael David Hume. BA, CCNY, 1964; PhD, Columbia U., 1972. Preceptor Columbia U., N.Y.C., 1968-69; asst. prof. philosophy Colo. State U., Ft. Collins, 1969-73, assoc. prof., 1973-78, prof., 1978—, prof. physiology and biophysics, 1980—, dir. bioethical planning, 1981—, prof. animal scis., univ. disting. prof., 2000—. Cons. Can., Australian, South African, The Netherlands, and U.S. govts., various univs. and agys. including U. Calif., Berkeley, Wash. State U., U. Fla., USDA, NIH, 1980—, United Airlines, Denver, 1985—, Nat. Livestock Ethics Coun., 1997—, Pfizer, 1998, McDonalds, 1998; lectr. on animal ethics, 1978—. Author: Natural and Conventional Meaning, 1976, Animal Rights and Human Morality, 1981, 2d edit., 1992 (Outstanding Acad. Book award Choice Mag. Am. Assn. U. Librs., 1982, Gustavus Meyers Ctr. award for study of human rights 1993), The Unheeded Cry, 1989, 2nd edit., 1998, The Experimental Animal in Biomedical Research, 1990, vol. 2, 1995, The Frankenstein Syndrome: Ethical and Social Issues in the Genetic Engineering of Animals, 1995, Farm Animal Welfare, 1995, Veterinary Ethics, 1998; mem. editl. bd. Jour. AVMA, Between the Species, Agrl. Ethics, Acta Semiotica et Linguistica, Studies in Animal Welfare Sci., numerous others; contbr. articles to profl. jours. Recipient Harris T. Guard award Colo. State U., 1981, honors prof., 1983; Waco F. Childers award Am. Humane Assn., 1982, svc. award Colo. Vet. Med. Assn., 1983, Disting. Faculty award Colo. State U. Coll. Vet. Med., 1993, Gustavus Myers Human Rights award 1994, Brownlee award Animal Welfare Found. Can., 1994; named Eddy prof., 2001. Jewish. Avocations: weightlifting, horseback riding, motorcycles. Office: Colo State U Dept Philosophy Fort Collins CO 80523-0001

ROLLIN, BETTY, writer, television journalist; b. N.Y.C., Jan. 3, 1936; d. Leon and Ida R.; m. Harold M. Edwards, Jan. 21, 1979. BA, Sarah Lawrence Coll., 1957. Assoc. features editor Vogue mag., 1964; sr. editor Look mag., 1965-71; network corr. NBC News, N.Y.C., 1971-80, contbg. corr., 1985—2002; network corr. ABC News Nightline, 1982-84. Contbr. corr. Religion and Ethics Newsweekly PBS; lectr. in field. (profl. actress): on state and TV, 1958—64; author: I Thee Wed, 1962, Mothers Are Funnier Than Children, 1964, The Non-Drinkers' Drink Book, 1966, First, You Cry, 1976, reissue, 2000, Am I Getting Paid for This?, 1982, Last Wish, 1985, reissue, 1998; columnist: Hers, N.Y. Times; contbr. articles. V.p. Death With Dignity Nat. Ctr., 1997—. Office: care NS Bienstock Inc 1740 Broadway New York NY 10019-4315

ROLLINS, ALDEN MILTON, documents librarian; b. Billerica, Mass., July 31, 1946; s. Alden Milton and Agnes Morgan (Simpson) R. BA, Am. U., 1968; MLS, U. R.I., 1973. Cert. geneal. record specialist, Bd. for Certification of Genealogists., Vt., N.H. Documents libr. U. Alaska Libr., Anchorage, 1973—. Author: The Fall of Rome: A Reference Guide, 1983, Rome in the Fourth Century A.D., 1991, Vermont Warnings Out, 1995. With U.S. Army, 1969-71. Mem. Nat. Geneal. Soc., Geneal. Soc. Vt., N.H. Geneal. Soc., New Eng. Hist. Geneal. Soc., N.H. Hist. Soc., Vt. Hist. Soc. (life), Piscataqua Pioneers (life). Avocation: genealogy. Home: 221 E 7th Ave Apt 114 Anchorage AK 99501-3639 Office: U Alaska Libr Govt Documents 3211 Providence Dr Anchorage AK 99508-4614

ROLLINS, ALFRED BROOKS, JR. historian, educator; b. Presque Isle, Maine, May 28, 1921; s. Alfred Brooks and Clarissa (Jack) R.; m. Ernestine Emma McMullin, Nov. 6, 1942 (dec. Aug. 28, 1972); children: John Douglas, Nancy Jane, James Scott; m. Faith Kenyon, June 16, 1973 (dec. Mar. 8, 1979); m. Helen Anrod Jones, Feb. 28, 1981. BA, Wesleyan U., Middletown, Conn., 1942, MA, 1946; PhD, Harvard U., 1953. From instr. to prof. history State U., N.Y. at New Paltz, 1948-63; prof., chmn. dept. history State U. N.Y. at Binghamton, 1964-67; dean U. Vt., Burlington, 1967-70, v.p. acad. affairs, 1970-76; pres. Old Dominion U., Norfolk, Va., 1976-85, prof. history, 1976-91, pres. emeritus, prof. emeritus, 1991—. Cons. oral history project John F. Kennedy Library, 1965 Author: Roosevelt and Howe, 1962; Editor narrative: Franklin D. Roosevelt and the Age of Action, 1960, Woodrow Wilson and the New America, 1965; Contbr. articles to profl. jours. Served to 1st lt. USAAF, 1943-46. Decorated D.F.C., Air medal with four clusters. Mem. Am. Hist. Assn., Orgn. Am. Historians, Phi Beta Kappa, Chi Psi.

ROLLINS, ARLEN JEFFERY, osteopathic physician; b. Cleve., June 30, 1946; s. Lee Roy and Celia (Madorsky) R.; m. Deborah Joyce Gross, Dec. 18, 1971 (div.); children: Aaron Jason, Howard Philip, Lee Craig. AB, Miami U. of Ohio, 1968; DO, Chgo. Coll. Osteo. Medicine, 1973; MS in Occupl. Medicine Environ. Health, U. Cin., 1984. Diplomate Am. Bd. Preventive Medicine. Intern Phoenix Genl. Hosp., 1973-74; resident in environ. health/occupl. medicine Cin. Gen. Hosp.-U. Cin., 1974-77; plant physician Ford Motor Co., Cin., 1974-77, Walton Hills, Stamping Plant Divsn., Cleve., 1987—. Assoc. med. dir. East Side Occupl. Health Ctr., Cleve., 1977-79; med. dir. Ferro Corp., Cleve., 1979—, S.K. Wellman Corp., Cleve., 1979-87, Morgan Matroc, 1979—; pres. Occupl. Health Mgmt. Cons.; cons. occupl. health Ohio Bell Telephone Co., Cleve., 1981-87; cons. Occupl. Health Ctr., Univ. Hosps. of Cleve.; dir. occupl. health program Bedford Med. Ctr. Univ. Hosps. Cleve., 1990-99; corp. med. cons. Cleve.-Cliffs Inc., 1998—. Fellow Am. Acad. Occupl. Medicine, Am. Occupl. Med. Assn., Am. Coll. Preventive Medicine; mem. Ohio State Med. Assn., Cleve. Acad. Medicine (pub. health and immunization com., med.-legal com.), Western Res. Med. Dirs. Assn., Am. Osteo. Assn., Am. Osteo. Acad. Pub. Health and Preventive Medicine (past bd. dirs.). E-mail: arlenrollins@worldnet.att.net.

ROLLINS, EDWARD TYLER, JR. newspaper executive; b. Durham, N.C., May 23, 1922; s. Edward Tyler and Bessie (Steed) R.; m. Frances Louise Page, Oct. 5, 1963; children: Edward Tyler III, William Lawson. AB, U. N.C., 1947. V.p., asst. sec. Durham (N.C.) Herald Co., 1949-69, v.p., sec.-treas., 1969-81, pres., pub., 1982-88, chmn., bd. dirs., 1985—. Pres. Durham Radio Corp. Stas. WDNC-AM, WDCG-FM, 1982-88. Bd. dirs. Chowan Coll. Graphic Arts Found., 1986-95; bd. dirs. Sch. of Journalism Found. of N.C., 1982-88; mem. Friends of Duke Art Mus., mem. adv. bd. N.C. Nat. Bank, 1979-89; mem. Gov.'s Bus. Coun. on Arts and Humanities, 1989-90; mem. Duke Pres.'s Art Mus. com., 1994—; trustee Meredith Coll., Raleigh, N.C., 1966-69, Durham Pub. Libr., 1961-81; former bd. dirs. Durham Salvation Army; pres. Durham YMCA, 1952; former bd. dirs. Family Svc. Assn.; supporter N.C. Symphony. With U.S. Army, 1943-46. Mem. Newspaper Assn. Am., N.C. Press Assn., So. Newspaper Publs. Assn., The English Speaking Union, Durham C. of C. (bd. dirs. 1969), Kiwanis, Hope Valley Country Club, Univ. Club, Carolina Club. Presbyterian. Office: Durham Herald Co Inc 2828 Pickett Rd Durham NC 27705-5613

ROLLINS, JAMES CALVIN, baseball player; b. Oakland, Calif., Nov. 27, 1978; Grad., Encinal HS, 1996. Profl. baseball player Phila. Phillies, 2000—. Co-recipient NL Cool Papa Bell award, Negro League Hall of Fame; named 5th Best Rookie in Major Leagues, Baseball Am., 3d Best in Nat. League; named to Topps Major League Rookie All-Star team, MLB mgrs. . Avocation: recreational activities. Office: Philadelphia Phillies Veterans Stadium 3501 South Broad Street Philadelphia PA 19148*

ROLLINS, JUDITH ANN, sociologist, educator, researcher, writer; b. Boston; d. Edward Bryant and Edith Frances (Wade) R. BA, Howard U., 1970, MA, 1972; PhD, Brandeis U., 1983. Instr. Sociology Fed. City Coll., Washington, 1972-77; asst. prof. Sociology N.E. U., Boston, 1983-84, Simmons Coll., Boston, 1984-89, assoc. prof. Sociology, 1989-92; assoc. prof. Africana studies, sociology Wellesley (Mass.) Coll., 1992-95, prof. Africana studies and sociology, 1995—. Author: Between Women, 1985 (Am. Sociol. Assn. award 1987), All Is Never Said, 1995. Office: Wellesley Coll Dept Africana Studies Wellesley MA 02481 E-mail: jrollins@wellesley.edu.

ROLLINS, JUNE ELIZABETH, elementary education educator; b. Turin, N.Y., June 24, 1929; d. Jay Elihue and Mildred (Evans) Hoskins; m. Clair Austin Rollins, June 28, 1952; children: Timothy, Teri June, Scott, Tracy. BS in Music, Fredonia (N.Y.) State U., 1950. Cert. tchr. nursery, kindergarten, elem. edn., music, N.Y. Tchr. instrumental and vocal music Greenwood (N.Y.) Ctrl. H.S., 1968-71, Greenwood Ctrl. Sch., 1950-58, 59-68, Whitesville Ctrl., 1958-59; tchr. kindergarten Greenwood Ctrl. Sch., 1965-68, tchr. 3rd grade, 1971-97, tchr. pre-K, 1997—2001, tchr. music, 2001—. Tchr. piano. Organist, choir dir., tchr. Bible sch. and Sunday sch. Greenwood Meth. Ch., 1972—; organist Andover Meth. Ch., 1995—; dir. Greenwood Cmty. Band, 1999—2000. Recipient Spl. Mission Recognition award Meth. Ch. for Music, 1981, Spl. Recognition award Music Dean Dist. United Meth. Houghton Coll., 1992, Gen. Douglas MacArthur Youth award Grand Lodge of State of N.Y., 1994, Outstanding Educator award Twin Tiers of N.Y. and Pa., 1995; named Outstanding Citizen West Greenwood Grange, 1992; featured in Evening Tribune, Hornell, N.Y., 1990. Mem. Delta Kappa Gamma (publicity chair 1989—, sec. 1994-97). Methodist. Avocations: flower gardening, crafts, needlework, quilling. Home: 2671 Main St Greenwood NY 14839 Office: Greenwood Ctrl Sch PO Box 936 Greenwood NY 14839-0936

ROLLINS, LISA L. journalist; b. Jan. 16, 1965; BS in Journalism, U. North Tex., 1996; MS in Mass Comm., Middle Tenn. State U., 1998, EdS in Higher Edn., 2000. Instr. journalism Middle Tenn. State U., Murfreesboro, 1997—, asst. dir. news and pub. affairs Tenn., 2000—; corr. Jour. Comms., Franklin, 1999—. Host/exec. producer on FM radio, Nashville. Mem. Soc. Profl. Journalists (nat. bd. 1998—). E-mail: lrollins@mtsu.edu.

ROLLINS, SONNY (THEODORE ROLLINS), composer, musician; b. N.Y.C., Sept. 7, 1930; s. Walter and Valborg (Solomon) R.; m. Dawn Finney, 1956 (div.); m. Lucille Pearson, Sept. 7, 1959. Ed. high sch., N.Y.C.; ArtsD, Bard Coll., 1992, Long Island U., 1998, Wesleyan U., 1998, Duke U., 1999; D of Music, New Eng. Conservatory of Music, 2002. Concert tours in Europe, Far East, 1973— ; composed, scored and played music for motion picture Alfie; more than 100 original compositions recorded for Milestone, Fantasy-Prestige compositions include Way Out West, also others. Recipient numerous awards Guggenheim fellow, 1972 Home: RR 9 # G Germantown NY 12526

ROLLMAN, STEVEN ALLAN, communication educator; b. N.Y.C., Aug. 3, 1947; s. Leo and Margot (Seelenberger) R.; m. Nancy Sue Toberen, June 15, 1973; 1 child, Benjamin Allan. BA, C.W. Post Coll., 1970; MA, Ohio U., 1972; PhD, Pa. State U., 1977. Instr. Pa. State U., University Park, 1976; asst. prof. James Madison U., Harrisonburg, Va., 1977-83, assoc. prof., 1983-95, coord. interpersonal communication, 1986-90, prof., 1995—. Cons. various sch. dists., Va., 1978—, Swissair, Zurich, 1971-72; book reviewer Choice, 1982—. Contbr. articles to profl. jours.; editor: Virginia Journal of Communication, 1980-81. Mem. Nat. Comm. Assn., So. States Comm. Assn., Va. Speech Comm. Assn., Internat. Listening Assn. Avocations: computers, music, film, automobiles, tennis. Home: 608 Wyndham Woods Cir Harrisonburg VA 22801-1668 Office: James Madison U Sch Speech Cmn Harrisonburg VA 22807-2106

ROLL-PREISSLER, AUDREY, artist; b. N.Y.C., Oct. 31, 1932; m. Detlev Preissler, Mar. 26, 1955 (div. 1983); children: Karen, Erik(dec.) , Kurt, Susanne; m. Norman Shapiro, June 30, 1993. Student, F.I.T., N.Y.C., Art Students' League. Tchr. U. Wyo., Truman U., Colo. State U., Ctrl. Wyo. Coll., Jackson. Juror for art shows, scholarships, 1983—; presenter workshops and seminars in field. One woman shows at Curfman Gallery, Ft. Collins, Colo., Dooly Gallery, Park City, Utah, Inkfish Gallery, Denver, Inter-Am. Bank, Washington, UN Bldg., N.Y.C. (award 1970); exhibited in group shows at U.S. Embassies, Ireland, Alaska Visual Arts Ctr., Anchorage, Art Zone, Denver, Bklyn. Mus., Capricorn Gallery, Washington, Cork Gallery, Kennedy Ctr., N.Y.C., Colorado Springs (Colo.) Fine Art Ctr., Minn. Mus. Art, St. Paul, Nicolaysen Mus., Casper, Wyo., Palm Springs (Calif.) Desert Mus., Pirates' Contemporary Art Oasis, Denver, Rehoboth (Del.) Art League, Smithsonian Inst., Washington, Ucross Found., U. So. Calif., Long Beach, Wyo. State Capitol Bldg., Cheyenne, Yellowstone Art Ctr., Billings, Mont.; represented in numerous pub. and pvt. corp. collections, including Amtrak, Apache Oil Co., Houston, AT&T, Washington, Ford Motor Co., Dearborn, Mich., Immokallee Found., Inc., Naples, Fla., Wyo. State Mus., Snow King Resort Hotel, Jackson, Wyo., Truman Libr., Independence, Mo., U.S. State Dept., Washington, W.E. Weiss Found., Jackson, Whitney Gallery of Art, Cody, Wyo., others; illustrator children's books. Recipient award Wyo. Arts Coun., 1985. Home: PO Box 7532 Jackson WY 83002-7532

ROLLS, BARBARA JEAN, nutrition educator, laboratory director; b. Washington, Jan. 5, 1945; d. Howard Julian and Patricia Jane (Pratt) Simons; m. Edmund Thomson Rolls, Sept. 6, 1969 (div. Jan. 1983); children: Melissa May, Juliet Helen. BA, U. Pa., 1966; PhD, Cambridge (Eng.) U., 1970; MA (hon.), Oxford (Eng.) U., 1970. Mary Somerville rsch. fellow Oxford U., 1969-72, IBM rsch. fellow, 1972-74; jr. rsch. fellow Wolfson Coll. Oxford U., 1974-75; E.P. Abraham rsch. fellow Green Coll. Oxford U., 1979-82, fellow in nutrition, 1983-84; assoc. prof. psychiatry Johns Hopkins U. Sch. Medicine, Balt., 1984-91, prof. psychiatry, 1991-92, dir. Lab. for Study Human Ingestive Behavior, 1984—; Jean Phillips Shibley prof. biobehavioral health Pa. State U., State College, 1992-94, prof., Helen A. Guthrie chair nutrition, 1994—. Mem. Nat. Diabetes and Digestive and Kidney Diseases Adv. Coun., 1994-98; cons. in field. Author: Thirst, 1982, Carbohydrates and Weight Management, 1998, Volumetrics: Feel Full on Fewer Calories, 2000; mem. editl. adv. bd. Jour. Appetite, 1981—; mem. editl. bd. Am. Jour. Physiology, 1985-99, Trends in Food Sci. and Tech., 1991-93, Am. Jour. Clin. Nutrition, 1992-98, Obesity Rsch., 1992—, Nutrition Rev., 1993-97; contbr. articles to profl. jours. Recipient Rolleston Meml. prize Oxford U., 1974, Merit award NIH, 1997—, Internat. award for Modern Nutrition, 2001; Thouron scholar Cambridge U., 1966-69; Med. Rsch. Coun. (U.K.) grantee, 1969-84, NIH grantee, 1987—. Mem. Am. Physiol. Soc., Soc. for Study Ingestive Behavior (bd. dirs. 1986-90, pres.-elect 1990-91, pres. 1991-92), N.Am. Assn. for Study Obesity (coun. 1991-93, v.p. 1994-95, pres.-elect 1995-96, pres. 1996-97), Am. Soc. Nutritional Scis. (award in human nutrition 1995), Am. Soc. Clin. Nutrition. Office: Pa State U 226 Henderson Bldg University Park PA 16802-6501

ROLLS, STEVEN GEORGE, chief financial officer; Joined BF Goodrich Co., Richfield, Ohio, 1981; asst. treas.; CFO Canadian and aerospace bus.; v.p., controller; CFO Convergys Corp. (subs. Cin. Bell Inc.), 1998—. Office: Convergys Corp PO Box 1638 Cincinnati OH 45201-1638

ROLNIK, ZACHARY JACOB, publishing company executive; b. Bayonne, N.J., Oct. 2, 1961; s. Joseph and Katie (Simon) R. BA, U. Rochester, 1982; M. in Pub. Policy, Harvard U., 1984. Ops. analyst, presdl. mgmt. intern U.S. Dept. Treasury, Washington, 1984-85; sr. editor, pub. Kluwer Acad. Pubs., Norwell, Mass., 1985-95, v.p., dir., 1996—. Home: 146 Pleasant St Hanover MA 02339-1844 Office: Kluwer Acad Pubs 101 Philip Dr Norwell MA 02061-1677

ROLOF, MARCIA CHRISTINE, sales executive; b. Green Bay, Wis., Sept. 1, 1950; adopted d. William August Rolof and Marcella S. (Rantanen) R.; m. Gerald W. Mattson, July 5, 1969 (div. 1974); 1 child, Shannon M. Mattson; m. Louis Glenn Mitchell, Nov. 12, 1994. Mgr., sales rep. Cameo Photography, 1980-82; tchr., physically challenged resource coord. U. Wis., 1982-85; dist. mgr. Women's Specialty Retail Group, U.S. Shoe, 1985—91; corp. adminstr. FLC, Inc., Houston, 1992—94; dist. mgr. The Avence, 1994—96; gallery dir. Phillips Art, Inc., Anderson Fine Art, 1996—. Tutor, reading and lang. Pasadena Ind. Sch. Dist., Houston Author: Tie the Moon to Your Car (My Cancer, My Way), 1994; author short stories; spokesperson childrens pub. radio series. Network vol. U. Tex. M.D. Anderson Cancer Ctr., Houston, 1993—; vol. counselor R to R Cancer Soc., Houston, 1994. Mem. Houston C. of C., Pasadena C. of C.

ROLOFF, MARVIN L. publishing executive; m. Shirley Sekas, June 27, 1959; children: Reed, Ross, Robyn. BA, Wartburg Coll., 1955; postgrad., U. Iowa, 1956; BD, Wartburg Theol. Sem., 1960, DD (hon.), 1997; ThM, Princeton Theol. Sem., 1961. Ordained to ministry Luth. Ch., 1961. Pastor youth and edn. Grace Luth. Ch., Green Bay, Wis., 1961-65; editor Augsburg Pub. Ho., Mpls., 1965-70, sr. editor children's curriculum divsn. parish edn., 1970-71, curriculum editl. dir. divsn. parish edn., 1971-74, dir. media resources divsn. life and mission in congregation, 1974-76, dir. edn. resources bd. of publ., 1976-87; dir. ednl. resources pub. Pub. Ho. of Evangelical Luth. Ch. Am., 1988-91; v.p. mktg. Augsburg Fortress, Pubs., 1991-93, v.p. customer resources and relationships, 1993-95, acting pres., CEO, 1995-96, pres., CEO, 1996—. Vis. prof. Christian edn. Luther Northwestern Theol. Sem., 1981, 83, 89, instr. Christian Edn. Inst., summers 1976-90; cons., chairperson youth/adult and children's coms. Curriculum Selection Conf. of Armed Forces, 1971-91; mem. resource planning groups Evangelical Luth. Ch. Am.; mem. publ. com. Augsburg Fortress, Pubs. Mem. Assn. Profs. and Rschrs. in Religious Edn., Protestant Ch.-Owned Pubs. Assn. (mem. edn. com., chair armed forces com. 1993—, mem. exec. com., bd. dirs. 1993—), Nat. Coun. Chs. (Augsburg Fortress, Pubs. rep. to ministries in Christian edn. com., mem. unit com. 1988—, mem. budget and fin. com. 1992—, mem. Bible translation and utilization com. 1994—). Protestant Ch.-Owned Pubs. Assn. (pres. 1998—). Office: Augsburg Fortress Pubs 100 S 5th St Ste 700 Minneapolis MN 55402-1219 Fax: 612-330-3583.

ROLSHOVEN, ROSS WILLIAM, legal investigator, artist; b. Mandan, N.D., Oct. 20, 1954; s. Raymond Paul and Bernice June (Mastel) R.; divorced; children: Ashley Anna, Carsen Ross. BA in Bus. Adminstrn., U. N.D., 1976. Lic. pvt. investigator, N.D., Minn. Claims adjuster, investigator Border Area Adjustments, Grand Forks, N.D., 1976-84; owner, mgr. Great Plains Claims, Inc., 1984—. Chmn. N.D. Claims Seminar, Grand Forks, 1988; guest lectr. U. N.D. Law Sch., 1993-96. Photographic exhibits include Artifacts, 1992 (1st pl. award 1992), Spirit of the Buffalo, 1992 (1st pl. award 1992), Grey Morn' on the Red, 1991 (Merit award 1991); featured artist Custer County Art Show, Miles City, Mont., 1995, Western Lines Art Exhibit at Empire Art Ctr., 2000; American Artists/ American Horses Exhibit, Ruidoso, N. Mex., 2000; sculpture How the West Was Won, 1992 (2d pl. award 1992); solo show N.D. Mus. Art Inventions & Imagination, 2002. Mem. N.D. Mus. Art; patron Grand Forks Fire Hall Theater, 1988-92; mem. Fargo/Moorhead Art Assn., 1992; mem. bldg. restoration com. North Valley Arts Coun.; trustee, chmn. N.D. Cowboy Hall of Fame, 1998—; chmn. Ctrl. Bus. Dist. Authority, Grand Forks, 1998-2000. Recipient Svc. Recognition award United Way, 1984, Hist. Preservation award N.D. Hist. Soc., 1990, Buckskinner award Roughrider Internat. Art Show Com., 1994, 2d Pl. award Fargo Regional Art Show, 1994-95. Mem. Nat. Assn. Legal Investigators, Minn. Assn. Detectives, Red River Valley Claims Assn. (pres. 1986-87), Upper Red River Valley Claims Assn. (pres. 1988-89), Dakota Masters Club Swim Club. Avocations: photography, painting, horseback riding, swimming, archaeology. Office: Great Plains Claims Inc 220 S 3d St Grand Forks ND 58201-6345

ROLSTON, HOLMES, III, theologian, educator, philosopher; b. Staunton, Va., Nov. 19, 1932; s. Holmes and Mary Winifred (Long) R.; m. Jane Irving Wilson, June 1, 1956; children: Shonny Hunter, Giles Campbell. BS, Davidson Coll., 1953; BD, Union Theol. Sem., Richmond, Va., 1956; MA in Philosophy of Sci., U. Pitts., 1968; PhD in Theology, U. Edinburgh, Scotland, 1958. Ordained to ministry Presbyn. Ch. (USA), 1956. Asst. prof. philosophy Colo. State U., Ft. Collins, 1968-71, assoc. prof., 1971-76, prof., 1976—. Vis. scholar Ctr. Study of World Religions, Harvard U., 1974-75; official observer UNCED, Rio de Janiero, 1992. Author: Religious Inquiry: Participation and Detachment, 1985, Philosophy Gone Wild, 1986, Science and Religion: A Critical Survey, 1987, Environmental Ethics, 1988, Conserving Natural Value, 1994, Genes, Genesis and God, 1999; assoc. editor Environ. Ethics, 1979—; mem. editorial bd. Oxford Series in Environ. Philosophy and Pub. Policy, Zygon: Jour. of Religion and Sci.; contbr. chpts. to books, articles to profl. jours. Recipient Oliver P. Penock Disting. Svc. award Colo. State U., 1983, Coll. award for Excellence, 1991, Univ. Disting. Prof., 1992; Disting. Russell fellow Grad. Theol. Union, 1991, Disting. Lectr., Chinese Acad. of Social Scis., 1991, Disting. Lectr., Nobel Conf. XXVII, Gifford Lectr., U. Edinburgh, 1997; featured in Fifty Key Thinkers on the Environment, 2001. Mem. AAAS, Am. Acad. Religion, Soc. Bibl. Lit. (pres. Rocky Mountain-Gt. Plains region), Am. Philos. Assn., Internat. Soc. for Environ. Ethics (pres. 1989-94), Phi Beta Kappa. Avocation: bryology. Home: 1712 Concord Dr Fort Collins CO 80526-1602 Office: Colo State U Dept Philosophy Fort Collins CO 80523-0001

ROLSTON, STEPHEN LOYAL, application developer, consultant; b. Phoenix, Dec. 30, 1955; s. Loyal Grant and Barbara Louise Rolston; life ptnr. Jerrie Dailey; children: Amanda Henderson, Jillian Lee. BA, U. Nev., Las Vegas, 1985. Program mgr. Honeywell Systems Inc, Campbell, Calif., 1998—2000; software cons. Camstar Sys. Inc, 2000—. Contbr. poetry and stories to anthologies. Sgt. USAF, 1975—80. Avocations: history, war gaming, fencing. Home: #352 39 W Julian St San Jose CA 95110 Personal E-mail: stephenr@camstar.com. Business E-Mail: stephenr@camstar.com.

ROLWING, RICHARD JOSEPH, writer; b. Indpls., Mar. 18, 1929; s. Edward Merlin and Rose Blanch (Marbaugh) R.; m. Patricia Ann Gardner, Aug. 24, 1964; children: Jonathan, Julia, Richard, Mary, Patrick. BA, Cath. U. Am., 1955; BD, Kenrick Sem., 1962; MA, U. Notre Dame, 1964; postgrad., U. Iowa, 1965-68. Asst. prof. theology U. Dayton and Xavier U., Cin., 1968-75; asst. mgr. Atlantic and Pacific Grocery, Columbus, 1975-77; v.p. Capital Concepts, 1980-86; ins., securites salesman, 1986-90. Author: Israel's Original Sin, 1994, My Daily Constitution, 2000. Mem. Am. Philos. Assn., Am. Cath. Philos. Assn., Soc. Christian Ethics, Soc. Philosophy Religion, Soc. Christian Philosophers, Am. Maritain Assn., Am. Acad. Religion, Cath. Bibl. Assn., Federalist Soc., Internfaith Orgn. Ctrl. Okla., Cath. Coun. Intercultural Afffairs, Fellowship Cath. Scholars, Cardinal Newman Soc., Am. Family Assn., Columbus Real Estate Assn. Roman Catholic.

ROM, MARTIN (MELVIN ROM), investor; b. Detroit, Mar. 2, 1946; s. Jack and Thelma (Meyer) R.; m. Barbara Miller, July 12, 1970. BA magna cum laude, U. Mich., 1967. Founder MultiVest, Inc., Southfield, Mich., 1969, pres., 1969-73, chmn. bd., chief exec. officer, 1973-75; pres. Real Estate Securities and Syndication Inst., Nat. Assn. Realtors, Washington, 1975-76, dir., bd. govs., 1972-77; pres. Martin Rom Co., Inc., 1976—. Vice chmn. Sports Illus. Ct. Clubs, Inc., 1977-79; bd. dirs. Mocatta Corp., 1979-80; founder, dir. Real Age, Inc., 1994—; mem. joint com. Nat. Assn. Securities Dealers-Nat. Assn. Realtors, 1975-76; mem. adv. com. on market instruments Commodity Futures Trading Commn., 1975-76; mem. Com. on Gold Regulations, 1974-75. Author: Nothing Can Replace the U.S. Dollar . . . and It Almost Has, 1975; Adv. bd.: Housing and Devel. Reporter, Washington. Trustee U. Chgo. Found. Mem. Phi Beta Kappa. Home and Office: 60 Quarton Ln Bloomfield Hills MI 48304-3456 E-mail: mrom@compuserve.com.

ROMA, AIDA CLARA, artist; b. Phila., July 17, 1924; d. Carlo and Giustina S. R.; widowed; 7 children. Student, Camden County Coll., 1990-99. Dental Dr. Martin Apother, Runnemede, N.J., 1956-66; owner Rogers Auto Sales, 1966-90; tchr. St. Joseph's Sch., Camden, 1955-56. Author: Jealousy, 1999, My 2 Best Friends, 2001; actor: (of poems). Art tutor, Haddenfield, N.J.; v.p. Girl Scouts Am., Runnemede, 1964; sec. Boy Scouts Am., 1960; mem. St. Teresa's Choir, 1993—, Atlantic City Choirs. Recipient numerous awards. Mem. Sons of Italy. Republican. Avocation: singing. Home: PO Box 2076 Laurel Springs NJ 08021

ROMA, JOHN RICHARD, civil engineer, executive; b. Somerville, Mass., Oct. 15, 1944; s. John A. and Anna J. (Keane) R.; m. Jean M. Reardon, Aug. 10, 1974; children: Joy M., John J., Jennifer G. A in CE, Wentworth Inst., Boston, 1965; BSCE, Northeastern U., Boston, 1969, MBA, 1985; MSCE, MIT, 1976. Prof. engr., Mass. Supr. Raymond Internat., N.Y.C., 1969-70; engr. Golder Gass Assocs., Cambridge, Mass., 1972-74; project mgr. Arthur Schofield, Inc., Wayland, 1976-78, Peabody N.E. Inc., N. Easton, 1979; mgr. ground anchors, mktg. mgr. Franki Found. Co., Boston, 1980-85; v.p., gen. mgr. New Eng. Found. Co. Inc., Quincy, 1985—. Mem. indsl. prof. adv. com. Wentworth Inst., Boston, 1984—. Mem. Town Bd. Examiners, Arlington, Mass., 1983-98; mem. troop 368 com. Boy Scouts Am., Arlington, 1990-97; mem. parish coun. St. Camillus Ch., Arlington, 1993—. Lt. U.S. Army Corp Engrs., 1970-72, Vietnam. Mem. ASCE, The Moles. Home: 3 Sagamore Rd Arlington MA 02476-7034 Office: New Eng Found Co Inc 77 Federal Ave Quincy MA 02169-7752

ROMA-DEELEY, LOIS, poet, English educator; b. Amityville, N.Y., Mar. 5, 1950; d. Louis Frank Sr. and Josephine R.; m. Peter Michael Deeley; children: Peter Deeley Jr., Melissa Deeley Rothslisberger. BA, Ariz. State U., 1984; MFA, 1988; PhD, Union Inst., 2000. Instr. writing and poetry Writer's Voice, Paradise Valley, Ariz., 1993; lectr. Ariz. State U., Tempe, 1993-94; prof. English, Paradise Valley C.C., 1994—. Author: poems; editor, peer editor: (textbook) Women's Rights, 1994; editor, co-poetry editor: National Forum; contbr. chpts. to books. Mem. Assoc. Writing Programs, Phi Kappa Phi (pres. Ariz. State U. chpt. 1994-95). Recipient 1st hon. mention XIX Tucson Internat. Poetry Festival, Emily Dickinson award, 2001, 2002. Office: Paradise Valley CC 18401 N 32d St Phoenix AZ 85032 Fax: (602) 787-7285. E-mail: lois.roma-deeley@pvmail.maricopa.edu.

ROMAGUERA, MARIANO ANTONIO, consulting engineer; b. Mayaguez, P.R., May 4, 1928; s. Jose Mariano and Aminta (Martinez) R.; BS, MIT, 1950; MS, U. P.R., 1975; m. Virginia Casablanca, July 3, 1952; children: Jose Mariano, Jorge Enrique, Alberto, Ana Maria. Asst. engr. Arturo Romaguera, Cons. Engr., Colombia, 1950-51; asst. engr. Ingenio Providencia, Palmira, Colombia, 1951; shift engr. Central Igualdad and Western Sugar Refinery, Mayaguez, 1954; erection engr., asst. project mgr., Pradera Valle, Colombia, 1954-55, plant supt., chief engr., 1955-57; project engr. Ingenior Providencia, Palmira, Colombia, 1957, chief engr. ops. and maintenance, 1958-64; exec. v.p. Romaguera & Vendrell Devel. Corp., Mayaguez, P.R., 1964-68; pres. RomaVel, Inc., Mayaguez, 1965-68, Yagueka Equipment, Inc., 1968-78, Mariano A. Romaguera and Assocs., Engrs., Appraisers and Cons., Mayaguez, 1974—; sr. ptnr. Camino, Romaguera & Assocs., 1976—; sr. ptnr. M/E Appraisers, 1976—; cons. engr. Sugar Corp. P.R., Commonwealth of P.R., Biomass Steam Generation Rsch.; bd. Pres., Yagueka dist. P.R. coun. Boy Scouts Am., 1965-69, mem. exec. bd. P.R. coun.; chmn. ARC, 1966; bd. dirs. Mayaguez YMCA; mem. MIT Ednl. Coun.; mem. bd. regents Catholic U. of P.R. With Army, 1952-54, Korea. Recipient Silver Beaver award P.R. coun.l Boy Scouts Am., 1969. Mem. NSPE, ASME (pres. S.W. P.R. group), Am. Soc. Appraisers, P.R. Bd. Appraisers and Examiners, Instituto de Evaluadores de P.R., Colegio Ingenieros y Agrimensores de P.R. (past pres. Mayaguez dist.), Instituto de Ingenieros Mecanicos de P.R., P.R. Soc. Profl. Engrs., Assn. Engring. Socs., Am. Right of Way Assn., Internat. Soc. Sugar Cane Technologists, P.R. Assn. Real Estate Bds., brd. examiners, P.R., appraises, 1997—, Regent Catholic U. P.R., Mayaguez Campus, Mayaguez Bd. Realtors, M.I.T. Alumni Assn., Nu Sigma Beta, Alpha Phi Omega. Roman Catholic. Lodge: Rotary. Home: 16 Calle Peral N Mayaguez PR 00680-4855 Office: PO Box 1340 Mayaguez PR 00681-1340

ROMAINE, HENRY SIMMONS, investment consultant; b. N.Y.C., May 30, 1933; s. Theodore Cole and Cornelia (Simmons) R.; m. Susan Donaldson; children: Henry, Hilary, Kathryn. BA, Harvard U., 1954. Asst. security analyst Mutual Life Ins. Co., N.Y.C., 1958-60, investment analyst, 1960-61, investment specialist, 1961-64, asst. dir. investments, 1964, dir. investments, 1964-66, asst. v.p. for securities investment, 1966-68, 2d v.p. for securities investment, 1969-71, v.p. for securities investment, 1971-72, sr. v.p., 1972-78, sr. v.p., chief investment officer, 1976-78, exec. v.p., 1978-81, pres., 1981-86; vice chmn., chief investment officer Am. Gen. Corp., Houston, 1986-93. Dir. MONY Life Ins. Co. of Can.; chmn. bd. MONY Real Estate Investors, 1978-86; mem. adv. bd. Chem. Bank, 1974-93. Served with USN, 1954-57. Mem. Links Club, Harvard Club. Home: 7 Conquest Ave Sullivans Island SC 29482-9779

ROMAN, ANDREW MICHAEL, lawyer, educator; b. Pitts., Aug. 19, 1951; s. James Andrew and Lois Roman; m. Heather Lynne Harms; children: Rebecca Lynne, Carolyn Elizabeth. BA, Bucknell U., 1973; JD, Duquesne U., 1976. Bar: Pa. 1976. Law clk. U.S. Dist. Ct. (we. dist.) Pa., Pitts., 1976-77; assoc. Eckert Seamans Cherin & Mellott, 1977-84, ptnr., 1985-91; dir. Cohen & Grigsby, P.C., 1991—, v.p. tech., 1998—. Adj. prof. law Duquesne U. Sch. Law, Pitts., 1993—; arbitrator Fed. Ct. Arbitration Panel, Pitts., 1991—; faculty mem. seminar on bad faith litigation in Pa. Nat. Bus. Inst., 1995, 99, 2000, 01. Editor-in-chief Duquesne Law Rev., 1976, A New Look at the Broad Form Nuclear Exclusion, Risk Management, 1995. Bd. dirs. Codes Rev. Bd., Mt. Lebanon, Pa., 1991—, The Extended Court House, Inc., 1997—; mem. vestry St. Paul's Episcopal Ch., Mt. Lebanon, 1995-98. Recipient Am. Jurisprudence awards Lawyers Coop. Pub. Co., 1974; T. Robert Brennan scholar Duquesne U. Sch. Law, 1974, Duquesne U. Sch. Law scholar, 1975. Mem. ABA, Am. Arbitration Assn. (mem. panel 1991—), Pa. Bar Assn., Allegheny County Bar Assn., Duquesne U. Law Alumni Assn. (treas. 1985-86, bd. dirs. 1988-90, pres. 1992-93). Office: Cohen & Grigsby PC 11 Stanwix St Ste 15 Pittsburgh PA 15222-1312

ROMAN, ANTONIO REGINO, cardiologist, internist; b. Phila., Jan. 24, 1959; s. Rafael and Cecilia Roman; m. Lori Ann Roman, June 27, 1992; children: Antonio Regino Jr., Thomas Franklin, Matthew Adam. BA, Fordham U., Bronx, 1980, MA, 1981; MPH, Universidad Del Valle, Cali, Colombia, 1982; MD, U. Rochester, N.Y., 1986. Diplomate Am. Bd. Internal Medicine with subspecialty in cardiology; testamur in electrocardiography, echocardiography and perioperative transesophageal echocardiography; Am. Bd. Nuclear Cardiology. Intern in medicine Yale Affiliated Hosp., Danbury, Conn., 1986-87, resident in medicine, 1987-89; fellow in cardiology SUNY-Buffalo, 1989-92; attending in emergency medicine Twin Cities Physician Group, Buffalo, 1992-93; pvt. practice Jamestown Area (N.Y.) Medical Assocs., 1994—. Fulbright scholar, 1981-82. Fellow ACP, Am. Coll. Cardiologists, Am. Coll. Chest Physicians, Interam. Coll. Physicians. Democrat. Roman Catholic. Avocation: marathon running. Office: Jamestown Area Med Assocs 31 Sherman St Jamestown NY 14701-7079 Home: 46 Grandview Ave Lakewood NY 14750-1644 E-mail: regino@aol.com.

ROMAN, ERNAN, marketing executive; b. Quito, Ecuador, Oct. 5, 1950; came to U.S., 1958; s. Murray Roman and Eva Cseko; m. Sheri Joan Struhl, May 13, 1979; children: Elias Vale, Helaina Mali. BA, Antioch Coll., 1972; MBA, Fairleigh Dickinson U., 1983. Account exec. CCI Telemarketing, N.Y.C., 1971-73, dir. sales, 1973-77, v.p. mktg., 1977-82, sr. v.p. mktg., 1982-83; pres. Ernan Roman Direct Mktg., Douglas Manor, N.Y., 1983—. Pioneered methodology of integrated direct mktg. and consensual database opt-in. Author: Integrated Direct Marketing: Techniques and Strategies for Success, 1988, Integrated Direct Marketing: The Cutting Edge Strategy for Synchronizing Advertising, Direct Mail, Telemarketing and Field Sales, 1995; contbr. to mktg. books, numerous profl. jours. Mem. Direct Mktg. Assn. (Mktg. Leader award 1981, Echo award 1985). Avocations: photography, collecting art, boating, scuba diving, skiing.

ROMAN, GREGG WILLIAM, geneticist, researcher; b. Passaic, N.J., May 25, 1964; s. William Edward and Anna Elizabeth R.; m. Beth Carole, Oct. 18, 1987; children: Jacob, Maxwell. BS, U. N.H., Durham, 1986, MS, 1989; PhD, U. Pa., Phila., 1995. Postdoc. fellow Baylor Coll. Medicine, Houston, 1995-2000, instr., 2000-01, asst. rsch. prof., 2001—. Inventor Plant genes for sensitivity to ethylene and pathogens, 1996; contbr. articles to profl. jours.; patentee in field. Phillip O'Bryan Montgomery fellow Damon Runyun-Walter Winchell Cancer Rsch. Fund, 1995-98; NIH grantee, 2002—. Mem. AAAS. Office: Dept Cell Biology Baylor College of Medicine Houston TX 77030 E-mail: roman@bcm.tmc.edu.

ROMAN, STANFORD AUGUSTUS, JR. medical educator, dean; b. N.Y.C. s. Stanford Augustas and Ivy L. (White) D.; m. Norma Dabney Roman; children: Mawiyah Lythcott, Jane E. Roman-Brown. AB, Dartmouth Coll., 1964, MA (hon.), 1992; MD, Columbia U., 1968; MPH, U. Mich., 1975. Diplomate Nat. Bd. of Med. Examiners. Intern in medicine Columbia U.-Harlem Hosp. Ctr., N.Y.C., 1966—69, resident in medicine, 1969—71, chief resident in medicine, 1971—73; 1972assoc. dir. ambulatory care Columbia U. Harlem Hosp., 1972—73; instr. medicine Columbia U., 1972—73; asst. physician Presbyn. Hosp., 1972—73; clin. dir. Healthco, Inc., Soul City, NC, 1973—74; dir. ambulatory care, asst. prof. medicine/sociomed. scis. Boston City Hosp., Boston, 1974—78; asst. prof. medicine U. N.C., Chapel Hill, 1973—74; asst. dean Boston U. Sch. Medicine, 1974—78; med. dir. D.C. Gen. Hosp., Washington, 1978—81; from assoc. dean acad. affairs to dep. dean Dartmouth Med. Sch., Hanover, NH, 1981—87, assoc. prof., 1981—87, dep. dean, 1986—87; dean, v.p., prof. medicine Morehouse Sch. Med., Atlanta, 1987—89; sr. v.p., med. and profl. affairs Health and Hosps. Corp., N.Y.C., 1989—90; dean med. sch., prof. cmty. health and social medicine CUNY, 1990—; interim pres. CCNY, 1999—2001. Dir. Boston Comprehensive Sickle Cell Ctr., 1975—78; bd. dirs. Winifred Masterson Burke Rehab. Hosp., White Plains, NY, 1993—94; mem. Dartmouth Hitchcock Med. Ctr. Bd. of Medicine, NY, 1993—98; trustee Dartmouth Coll., Hanover, NH. Contbr. to book chpts. and profl. jours. and editls. Fellow N.Y. Acad. Medicine; mem. AMA, APHA, Nat. Med. Assn., N.Y. State Coun. Grad. Med. Edn., N.Y. State Dept. Edn. Bd. Medicine. Democrat. Episcopalian. Avocations: photography, travel, music.

ROMANA, KATHLEEN, writer, artist; b. Boston, Oct. 30, 1957; Student, Mus. Sch. Art, Boston, 1973-75; diploma, Butera Sch. Art, Boston, 1979; AA, Back Bay C.C., Boston, 1981. Freelance illustrator various advt. agys., Boston, 1981-92, freelance copywriter, 1990-92; poet/writer Austin, Tex., 1993—; owner Odyssey Vintage Clothing Store, 2000—. Author, poet, illustrator: Dreamscapes and Other Wanderings, 1998; author, editor, illustrator: Thy Kingdom Come, 1998; author of poetry included in anthologies: Outstanding Poets of 1998, The Isle of View, 1998, Daydreams, 2000, Tides of Memory, 2000, Treasured Poems of America, 2000, Internat. Libr. Poetry, 2000, Ovations, 2001, Best Poems and Poets of 2001 (anthologies) Homecomings, The Silence Within, Acclamations. Recipient Editors Choice award and Poet of Merit award Internat. Libr. Poets, Pres.'s award for Lit. Excellence, Iliad Press, 2001, The Pres. award Literary Excellence, 2002; others. Mem. Internat. Soc. Poets (disting.), Nat. Libr. Poetry. Avocations: Samurai saber, Tai Chi. Office: Odyssey Vintage Clothing 1108 Koening Ln Austin TX 78756

ROMANCE, MARY C. library director; b. Rabat, Morocco, June 20, 1957; d. Francis Joseph and Ann (Pickert) Romance. BA in Orgnl. Comms. and Mgmt., U. Mich., Ann Arbor, 1979; MLS, Rutgers U., New Brunswick, N.J., 1992. Libr. coord. Bernardsville (N.J.) Pub. Libr., 1991-93; libr. dir. Rockaway (N.J.) Borough Pub. Libr., 1993-94, Lincoln Park (N.J.) Pub. Libr., 1994-97, Roxbury Twp. Pub. Libr., Succasunna, N.J., 1997—. V.p., 1998, pres., 1999, M.A.I.N. Inc. Planning Coun.. Mem. Roxbury Area C. of C. (bd. dirs.). Office: Roxbury Public Library 103 Main St Succasunna NJ 07876-1417

ROMANI, JOHN HENRY, health administration educator; b. Milan, Italy, Mar. 6, 1925; s. Henry Arthur and Hazel (Pettengill) R.; m. Barbara A. Anderson; children: David John, Paul Nichols, Theresa A. Anderson. BA, MA, U. N.H., 1949; PhD, U. Mich., 1955. Instr. U. N.H., 1950-51; instr. U. Mich., Ann Arbor, 1954-55, assoc. prof., asst. to assoc. dean Sch. Pub. Health, 1961-69, assoc. v.p., 1971-75, chmn. health planning and adminstrn., 1975-80, prof., 1971-93, prof. emeritus pub. health adminstrn., 1993—; interim chair Pub. Health Policy and Adminstrn., 1991-92. Asst. prof. We. Mich. U., 1956-57; assoc. dir. Cleve. Met. Svcs. Commn., 1957-59; assoc. prof. U. Pitts., 1959-61; vice chancellor, prof. U. Wis.-Milw., 1969-71; rsch. fellow Brookings Instn., 1955-56; mem. task force Nat. Commn. on Orgn. Cmty. Health Svcs., 1963-66; dir. staff Sec.'s Com. on Orgn. Health Activities, HEW, 1965-66; dir. Govtl. Affairs Inst., 1969-75, chmn., 1970-72; trustee Pub. Adminstrn. Svc., 1969-75, chmn., 1973-75; mem. Delta Dental Plan Mich., 1972-78, bd. dirs. 1972-78, chmn. consumers' adv. coun., 1975-77; bd. dirs. Ctr. for Population Activities, 1975-81, chmn., 1975-81; lifetime vis. prof. Capital U. Economics and Bus., Beijing, 1996—; rsch. assoc. Human Scis. Rsch. Coun., Pretoria, South Africa, 1999—. Author: The Philippine Presidency, 1956; editor: Changing Dimensions in Public Administration, 1962; contbr. articles to profl. jours. Mem. Citizens League, Cleve., 1957-59; mem. Ann Arbor Citizens Coun., 1965-69; bd. dirs. Southeastern Mich. Family Planning Project, 1975-77; trustee Congregational Summer Assembly, 1982-85; commr. Accrediting Commn. on Edn. for Health Svcs. Adminstrn., 1989-95. Served with AUS, 1943-46, ETO. Fellow Am. Pub. Health Assn. (chmn. program devel. bd. 1975-77, exec. bd. 1975-80, governing coun. 1975—, pres. 1979, chmn. publs. bd. 1984-88), Royal Soc. Health (hon.), Am. Polit. Sci. Assn. (life); mem. ASPA (past mem. coun.), Population Assn. Am., Phi Kappa Phi, Pi Sigma Alpha, Pi Gamma Mu, Delta Omega. Home: 2670 Bedford Rd Ann Arbor MI 48104-4010 Office: 2670 Bedford Rd Ann Arbor MI 48104-4010

ROMANI, PAUL NICHOLAS, government official; b. L.I., N.Y., May 14, 1943; m. Patricia Elsie Riley, July 26, 1968; children: Michele P., Christopher P. BBA, George Washington U., 1967, MBA, 1968, DPA with distinction, 1975. Lic. real estate broker, Va.; cert. EEO counselor; CFP, CNA; cert. net. engr. Assoc. professorial lectr. George Washington U., 1970-72; sci. adminstr. NSF, Washington, 1972-82; sci. and tech. fellow The White House, 1982-83, dir. fin. and adminstrn. automated systems div., 1983-85, dir. adminstrv. ops., 1985-91; dir. Fed. Fin. Instns. Exams. Coun., 1991-98; CEO R3 Cons. Svcs. Inc., 1999—; cons. The White House, Washington, 2001—. Dir. adminstrn., comptr. Pres.' Edn. Summit with Govs., Charlottesville, Va., 1989; cons. to Pres. Nixon's Adv. Coun. on Mgmt. Improvement, 1970. Author: Principal Investigator Guide to Research Proposal Development, 1998; mem. editl. adv. panel Bur. Bus. Practice, 1997—; contbr. articles to profl. jours. Bd. dirs. scholarship fund City of Alexandria, Va., 1992—. Humble Oil fellow, 1968, McGraw-Edison fellow George Washington U., 1971-73; recipient Disting. Svc. award Exec. Office of the Pres., 1989, Disting. Svc. award Fed. Fin. Instns. Exam. Coun., 1992, Spl. Achievement award, 1995. Mem. Am. Soc. Pub. Adminstrn., Soc. Gen. Systems Rsch., Soc. Am. Value Engrs., Tex. State Soc., Alpha Kappa Psi. Roman Catholic. Office: R3 Cons Svcs Inc Mills Bldg 1700 Pennsylvania Ave NW Washington DC 20006-4704 E-mail: r-cubed@erols.com.

ROMANO, ANGELA, pediatric cardiologist; b. Bklyn., Jan. 30, 1954; d. Joseph and Mary R.; m. Andrew Adesman. BA, Barnard Coll., 1976; MD, Columbia U. Coll. Phys. Surg., 1980. Diplomate Am. Bd. Pediatrics, Am. Bd. Cardiology. Resident, chief resident Babies Hosp., N.Y.C., 1980-84; fellow in cardiology Children's Hosp. Phila., 1984-87; attending pediat. cardiologist Schneider Children's Hosp., New Hyde Park, N.Y., 1987—. Fellow Am. Coll. Cardiology, Am. Acad. Pediatrics; mem. Pediat. Cardiology Soc. Greater N.Y. Office: Schneider Children's Hosp Pediatric Cardiology New Hyde Park NY 11042 E-mail: romano@lij.edu.

ROMANO, JOSEPH ANTHONY, healthcare education and marketing consultant; b. Bklyn., Sept. 5, 1946; s. Anthony Wilbur and Anne (Fusco) R.; m. Linda Rose Giacalone, Sept. 23, 1972; children: Nicholas Joseph, Christine Dianne. Student, Villanova U., 1964-66; BS Pharm. Sci., Columbia U., 1970, D Pharmacy, 1972. Clin. resident Lenox Hill Hosp., N.Y.C., 1970-72; asst. dean, asst. prof. Columbia U., 1972-76, SUNY, Buffalo, 1976-78; assoc. dean, assoc. prof. U. Wash., Seattle, 1978-83; assoc. dir. medicine Pfizer Labs., N.Y.C., 1983-85, product mgr., 1985, asst. to pres., 1985-87; sr. v.p., group dir. Hill & Knowlton, Inc., 1987-88; exec. dir. external affairs Novartis, 1988-89; pres., COO Visual Med. Mktg., 1989-92; vice chair Nelson Communications, Inc. Worldwide (divsn. Publicis), 1992-2001; chmn., CEO SCIENS Worldwide Healthcare Comms., 1996-2001; co-chmn. Nelson Profl. Sales, 1998-2000. Mem. U.S. Nat. Adv. Com. Health Profls., Washington, 1980-86. Co-author: Clinical Pharmacology, 1980, Pharmacy State Board Reviews, 1976, 78, 85, The Vitamin Book, 1985, 99; cons. editor Med. Intercom, N.Y.C., 1986-89; contbr. articles to profl. jours. Fellow Royal Soc. Health London; mem. Am. Pharm. Assn., Am. Soc. Healthcare Pharmacists, Am. Assoc. Study Headaches, Nat. Headache Found., U.S. Golf Assn., Rho Chi. Avocations: photography, philately, golf, music, cooking. E-mail: josephromano@earthlink.net.

ROMANO, LOUIS, JR. industrial gas company executive; b. Bridgeport, Conn., July 3, 1945; s. Louis and Santa (Cutuli) R.; m. J. Johnson (div. June 1986), children: Marjorie S., Angela J.; m. Ann Elizabeth Fox Berk, Aug. 27, 1988. BS in Engring., U.S. Naval Acad., 1967; postgrad., Manhattan Coll., 1975, George Washington U., 1991. Sales engr. Union Carbide Corp., Chgo., 1974-77, asst. sales mgr. Houston, 1977-81; divsn. sales mgr. Union Carbide Indsl. Svcs. Co., 1981-83; product mgr. Linde div. Union Carbide, Danbury, Conn., 1983-87; worldwide market mgr. Union Carbide Indsl. Gases Inc., 1987-92, Praxair Inc., Danbury, 1992, dir. merchant products ctrl. region, 1992—; dir. Global Procurement, 1998—. Contbr. articles to profl. jours. Vol. Spl. Olympics, Conn., 1988—; bd. dirs. Kleinwood Mcpl. Utility Dist., Spring, Tex., 1981-83; mentor Whisonier Middle Sch., Brookfield, Conn.; chmn. Diabetes Assn. Greater Cleve., 1995—. With USN, 1967-74, lt. comdr. USNR, 1974-88. Mem. AICE, Am. Chem. Soc., Cleve. Chem. Assn. (bd. dirs. 1995—), Sales & Mktg. Eecs. (v.p., bd. dirs.), Navy League, U.S. Naval Acad. Alumni Assn. Republican. Avocations: tennis, bridge, scuba diving, golf. Home: 2507 Hollyberry Ln Palm City FL 34990

ROMANO, RAY, actor, comedian; b. Forest Hills, N.Y., Dec. 21, 1957; Stand-up comedian; sit-com actor. Actor: (T.V. series) Everybody Loves Raymond, 1996— (Best Actor, Quality Comedy from Viewers for Quality TV

, 1998, TV Critics Assn. award for outstanding ind. achievement in comedy, 1999, nominated for Emmy award as outstanding lead actor in comedy series, 1999, nominated for Golden Globe award as best performance by actor in comedy , People's Choice award for favorite male TV performer, 2002, nominated for Screen Actors Guild award as outstanding performance by a male actor in comedy series, 2002, TV Guide Favorite Actor in a Comedy award, Funniest Male Lead in a TV Series at 14th Ann. Am. Comedy award), (T.V. guest appearances in) Dr. Katz Professional Therapist, 1995, The King of Queens, 1998, Hollywood Squares, 1998—, Becker, 1998, Who Wants to Be a Millionaire, 1999; author: Everything and a Kite.*

ROMANO, REBECCA KAY, counselor; b. Zanesville, Ohio, Mar. 26, 1958; Charles Ronald Fulkerson and Margaret Jane (Kiser) Williams; m. Richard Ralph Romano, May 24, 1986; children: Nicholas Robert, Kaitlin Kristine. BA, Walsh U., 1980; MEd, Bowling Green State U., 1981, 82. Lic. profl. counselor; nat. cert. counselor; sex offender treatment provider, Colo. Day program instr. Devel. Opportunities, Cañon City, Colo., 1983-85; clin. behavior specialist Pueblo Regional Ctr. Colo. Divsn. Devel. Disabilities, 1985-86; career devel. tchr. Colo. Dept. Corrections, Cañon City, 1986-87, facility mental health therapist, 1987—2002, devel. disabilities coord., 1991—2002, facility mental health coord., 1995—2002. Therapist sex offender treatment team Colo. Dept. Corrections, 1986—, clin. team leader, 2002--, co-chair state com. to devel. lifetime supervision stds. for devel. disabled sex offenders; presenter in field. Mem. ACA, AAUW, Am. Assn. Mental Retardation (past state bd. dirs. 1987-91), Am. Correctional Assn., Nat. Assn. for Dually Diagnosed, Colo. Assn. Mental Health Counselors, Women of the Evang. Luth. Ch. Am. (exec. bd. mem., newsletter editor 1997, confirmation youth mentor, Sunday Sch. tchr. 1998—). Lutheran. Avocations: reading, gardening, bicycling, volleyball, walking. Office: Colo Dept Corrections ACC Clin Svcs Box 3-- Canon City CO 81215

ROMANOFF, MARJORIE REINWALD, retired education educator; b. Chgo., Sept. 29, 1923; d. David Edward and Gertrude (Rosenfield) Reinwald; m. Milford M. Romanoff, Nov. 6, 1945; children: Bennett Sanford, Lawrence Michael, Janet Beth (dec.). Student, Northwestern U., 1941-42, 43-45, Chgo. Coll. Jewish Studies, 1942-43; BEd, U. Toledo, 1947, MEd, 1968, EdD, 1976. Tchr. Old Orchard Elem. Sch., Toledo, 1946-47, McKinley Sch., Toledo, 1964-65; substitute tchr., 1964-68; instr. Mary Manse Coll., 1974; instr. children's lit. Sylvania (Ohio) Bd. Edn., 1977; supr. student tchrs. U. Toledo, 1968-73, 85—, instr. advanced comms., 1977, rschr., 1973-74; instr. Am. Lang. Inst., 1978—2002. Part-time asst. prof. elem. edn. Bowling Green (Ohio) State U., 1978—88; chair rsch. com. Am. Lang. Inst., U. Toledo, 1985—94, asst. prof. elem. edn. in lang. arts, 1985—87, part time asst. prof. elem. edn., ESL specialist, 1978—2002; presenter numerous workshops and demonstrations in children's lit. and analysis of tchr. behavior, 1976—99. Author: Language and Study Skills: For Learners of English, Prentice Hall Regents, 1991. Trustee Children's Svcs. Bd., 1974-76; pres. bd. Cummings Treatment Ctr. for Adolescents, 1978-80; mem. Crosby Gardens Adv. Bd., 1976-82, Cmty. Planning Coun., 1980-84, Citizens Rev. Bd. of Juv. Ct., 1979—; mem. allocations com. Mental Health and Retardation Bd., 1980-81; mem. Bd. Jewish Edn., 1976—, pres., 1982-84; mem. Jewish Family Svc., 1978-85, v.p., 1980-85; mem. allocations com. Jewish Welfare Fedn., 1980, 89-91; bd. dirs. Family Life Edn. Coun., 1984-90, sec., 1988-90; mem. budget and allocations com. Jewish Fedn., 1989-93; bd. dirs. Friends Toledo-Lucas County Librs., 1991—, bd. pres., 1991-93; program chair U. Toledo Women's Commn., 1991-93; bd. dirs. Ohio Friends of Pub. Librs., 1992-94; presenter ann. conf. N.W. Ohio Libr. Assn., 1993, Bowling Green State U., 1997; condr. workshop Internat. Conf./Teaching Langs., U. Cin., 1996. Named One of Ten Women of Yr., St. Vincent's Hosp., Guild, 1984, Outstanding Instructional Staff Woman, U. Toledo, 1990. Mem. Tchrs. English to Speakers Other Langs. (presenter 1986, presenter Internat. TESOL Atlanta 1993), Nat. Soc. for Study Edn., Toledo Libr. Legacy Found., Orgn. Rehab. and Tng. (named Outstanding Woman in Cmty. Svc. 1987), Hadassah (chpt. pres. regional bd. 1961-64), Northwestern U. Alumni Assn., Phi Kappa Phi, Phi Delta Kappa, Kappa Delta Pi (pres./faculty adv. 1971-75, Point of Excellence award 1992), Pi Lambda Theta (chpt. pres. 1978-80, nat. com. 1979-84). Democrat. Home: 2514 Bexford Pl Toledo OH 43606-2414 E-mail: MRR1923@aol.com.

ROMANOFF, MILFORD MARTIN, building contractor; b. Cleve., Aug. 21, 1921; s. Barney Sanford and Edythe Stolpher (Bort) R.; m. Marjorie Reinwald, Nov. 6, 1945; children: Bennett S., Lawrence M., Janet Beth (dec.). Student, U. Mich. Coll. Arch., 1939-42; BBA, U. Toledo, 1943. Pres. Glass City Constrn. Co., Toledo, 1951-55, Milford Romanoff, Inc., Toledo, 1956—. Co-founder Neighborhood Improvement Found. Toledo, 1960; active Lucas County Econ. Devel. Com., 1979—, Childrens Svcs. Bd. Lucas County, 1981—97, Arthritis Bd. Dirs., Crosby Gardens Bd. Advisors, 1983—96, Toledo Met. Area Govt. Exec. Com., 1996—; citizens adv. bd. Recreation Commn. Toledo, 1973—86; campus adv. com. Med. Coll. Ohio, 1980—; trustee Cummings Treatment Ctr. for Adolescents, 1981—; pres. Toledo Lodge, 1958—59, Cherry Hill Nursing Home, 1964—85; bd. dirs. Anti-Defamation League, 1955—60, Ohio Hillel Orgns., Lucas County Dept. Human Svcs., Arthritis Assn., 1995—, Comprehensive Addiction Svc. Sys., 1998, Kidney Found. Northwestern Ohio, 1986—, sec., 1989; vice chmn. Comprehensive Addiction Svc. Sys., 1999; chmn. Toledo Amateur Baseball and Softball Com., 1979—81; cons. U.S. Care Corp., 1985—; bd. govs. Toledo Housing for Elderly, 1982—84, sec., 1989, pres. bd. govs., 1990—, pres., 1991—; bd. adv. Ret. Sr. Vol. Program, 1987—89, chmn., 1988—90, 1993—, sec. adv. bd., 1990—; vice chmn. adv. bd. Salvation Army, 1986—87, chmn. adv. bd., 1988—90, ct. apptd. spl. advocate adv., bd. treas., 1988—; chmn. Mental Health Adv. Bd., 1983—84, sec., 1989; bd. dirs. Toledo Urban Forestry Commn., 1991—, pres., 1993, 1995, Lucas County Dept. Human Svcs. Bd.; adv. coun. Renaissance Sr. Apts., 1997, chmn. adv. coun., 1999; adv. bd. Lucas Co. Correctional Facility, 1999—; vice chmn. Compass Bd., 2000—; bd. dirs. Area Office on Aging of Northwest Ohio, 2001, Lucas County Mental Health, 2001; chair Compass Corp. for Recovery Svcs., 2002—; active Dem. Precinct Com., 1975—78; trustee Temple Brotherhood, 1956—58, bd. dirs., 1981—; pres. Ohio B'nai Brith, 1959—60. Mem.: Mental Health Bd. of Lucas County, Toledo Zool. Soc., Juvenile Justice (adv. bd.), U. Mich. Alumni Assn., Econ. Opportunity Planning Assn. Greater Toledo (adv. bd.), Nat. Coun. on Alcoholism & Drug Dependence, Toledo Mus. Art (assoc.), U. Toledo Alumni Assn., Hadassah (assoc. Toledo chpt., juvenile correctoin bd. 2000—), Masons (Outstanding Cmty. Svc. award of Lucas County 2001), Zeta Beta Tau. Home and Office: Milford Romanoff Inc 2514 Bexford Pl Toledo OH 43606-2414

ROMANOFF, STANLEY M., JR. human resource specialist; b. Toledo, Feb. 3, 1948; s. Stanley M. and Helen (Feinberg) R.; children: Erika Lee, Jennifer Lyn, Tara Marie, Erin Michele. BBA, U. Cin., 1970. Pers. supr. assembly div. GM, Norwood, Ohio, 1969-72; pers. mgr. Diamond Internat. Corp., 1972-73; property mgr., investment counselor Romanoff Enterprises, Toledo, 1973-77; pers. adminstr. wage and salary United Telephone Co. Ohio, Mansfield, 1977-79; compensation and benefits mgr. United Inter-Mountain Telephone Co., Bristol, 1979-84, employee rels. mgr., 1984-86; human resources cons. Romanoff Enterprises, Tenn., 1986-87; bus. mgr. Magna Internat., Livonia & Southfield, Mich., 1987-94, dir. human resources and bus. systems, 1994-97; mgr. human resources Brother Industries, Memphis, 1998—. Mem. Am. Compensation Assn., Am. Mgmt. Assn., Soc. for Human Resource Mgmt., Am. Soc. of Employers, Soc. Human Resources, Memphis, Leadership Bartlett. Office: 2025 Ambergate Ln Cordova TN 38016-4455

ROMANO-MAGNER, PATRICIA R. English studies educator, researcher; b. N.Y.C., Mar. 22, 1928; d. Al and Nicole (Siriani) Romano; m. Ralpha M. Magner, Dec. 24, 1954. AA, BA, L.A. City Coll.; MA, Calif. State U., L.A.; D (hon.), Stanford U., Cambridge (Eng.) U., Queens Coll. Master tchr. Burbank (Calif.) Unified Sch. Dist., L.A. City Schs., Stanford (Calif.) U. Sch. for the Gifted; prof. Calif. State U., L.A. Mem. AAUP (award 2000), Am. Legion Auxillary, Sierra Club, Natural Resources Defense Coun., The Friends of the William J. Clinton Presidential Libr. (founding mem.). Republican. Avocation: horseback riding. Home: 5975 N Odell Ave Chicago IL 60631-2358

ROMANOSKI, BARBARA ANN, neonatology nurse; b. Tokyo, Mar. 22, 1954; d. John Thomas and Vitolda Helen (Pupa) R. LPN, diploma, Laramie County Community Coll., 1984; AS in Nursing, SUNY, 1987, BSN, 1989. RN; cert. neonatal intensive care nurse. Evening charge RN hemodialysis Biomed. Applications, Pine Brook, N.J., 1985-91; staff LPN/GN-med.-surg./ob.-gyn. Clara Maass Med. Ctr., Belleville, 1987-88; staff nurse/evening charge RN renal transplant and hemodialysis St. Barnabas Med. Ctr., Livingston, 1988; staff nurse emergency rm. Union Hosp., Union; staff nurse ICU/critical care unit Meadowlands Med. Ctr., Secaucus, 1990-91; staff nurse telemetry St. Barnabas Med. Ctr., Livingston, 1991—, staff nurse neonatal ICU, 1992—, diabetes nurse educator, pediatrics, 2001—. Mem. AACN, Assn. Women in Health, Obstetric, and Neonatal Nurses, Nat. Assn. Neonatal Nurses. Home: 41 Yantacaw Pl Nutley NJ 07110-1250 E-mail: tinytotrn@aol.com.

ROMANOV, VOLODYMYR ALEXEEVICH, computer science educator, researcher; b. Kamynino, Kursk, Russia, Jan. 23, 1960; s. Alexey Filippovich and Olga Sergeevna Romanov; m. Svitlana Egorivna Chystova, Oct. 16, 1981; children: Olga Volodymyrivna, Volodymyr Volodymyrovych. MD, Nat. U., Kharkov, Ukraine, 1983, PhD, 1987. Cert. computer scis. and nuc. physics. Rschr. Nuc. Phys. Lab., Kharkiv, Ukraine, 1983-88; prof. State Tech. Univ. Agr., 1988-96; head Info. Tech. Ctr., 1996-2000. Vice-head Com. Young Rschrs., Kharkiv, 1984-91; editor Regional TV, Kharkiv, 1985-87; prof. State Tech Univ. Agr., Kharkiv, 1996-2000, prof. Newton Coll., Montreal, 2000—. Author: (with S. Troubnikov) Nuclear Forces, 1992, (with I. Furman) Programmed Microcontrollers, 2000; contbr. articles to profl. jours. Mem. Can. Info. Processing Soc. Russian Orthodox. Avocations: Russian literature, history, music. Home: Apt 81 4645 Bourret Montreal QC Canada H3W 1K9 Office: 2900 Decarie # 3575 Cote-St Luc Montreal QC Canada H3X 2T8 E-mail: volodymyr_romanov@yahoo.com.

ROMANOWITZ, BYRON FOSTER, architect, engineer; b. Covington, Ky., Nov. 14, 1929; s. Harry Alex and Mildred (Foster) R.; m. Mildred Elaine Gize, June 15, 1957; children: Laura Ann, Mark Walter, Cynthia Ellen. BS in Civil Engring, U. Ky., 1951; M.F.A. in Architecture, Princeton, 1953. Instr. sch. architecture Princeton U., 1954; architect Brock & Johnson, Lexington, 1958-59, Johnson & Romanowitz, Architects, Lexington and Louisville, 1960-2000; ret., 2000. Pres. Ky. Bd. examiners and Registration of Archs., 1975-91; instr. U. Ky. Sch. Architecture, 1996, 2000. Prin. works include U. Ky. campus bldgs., 1959-96, Ea. Ky. U. campus bldgs., 1959-77, Centre Coll., Danville, Ky., campus bldgs., 1967-89, Georgetown (Ky.) Coll. campus bldgs., 1964-84, Asbury Coll., Wilmore, Ky., 1972-78, Asbury Theol. Sem., 1978-93, Berea Coll. bldgs., 1978-91, Transylvania U. bldgs., 1974-98, U. Louisville, 1990-98, 11 downtown Lexington office bldgs.; leader Men of Note Orch., 1986—, Jazzberry Jam Combo, 1993—. Mem. Lexington Urban Renewal Commn., 1963-69; chmn. adv. bd. Salvation Army, 1971-72; trustee Midway (Ky.) Coll., 1986-95. With USNR, 1955-58; lt. comdr. Res. Recipient award of merit nat. archtl. competition AIA/Ednl. Facilities Lab., 1966 Fellow AIA (1st honor awards Ky. archtl. competition 1959, 61, 68, 70, 73, 78, 80, 81, pres. East Ky. chpt. 1965); mem. Ky. Soc. Architects (pres. 1966), Masons, Rotary, Lexington Club, Navy League, Tau Beta Pi, Phi Mu Alpha, Phi Sigma Kappa. Home: 2057 Lakeside Dr Lexington KY 40502-3016

ROMANOWSKI, THOMAS ANDREW, physics educator; b. Warsaw, Poland, Apr. 17, 1925; came to U.S., 1946, naturalized, 1949; s. Bohdan and Alina (Sumowski) R.; m. Carmen des Rochers, Nov. 15, 1952; children: Alina, Dominique. BS, Mass. Inst. Tech., 1952; MS, Case Inst. Tech., 1956, PhD, 1957. Rsch. assoc. physics Carnegie Inst. Tech., 1956-60; asst. physicist high energy physics Argonne Nat. Lab., Ill., 1960-63, assoc. physicist, 1963-72, physicist, 1972-78; prof. physics Ohio State U., Columbus, 1964-92, prof. emeritus, 1992-98; sr. scientist Argonne Nat. Lab., 1992; physicist U.S. Dept. Energy, Washington, 1992-98; cons. in pvt. practice, 1998—. Contbr. articles to profl. jours. and. and papers to sci. meetings, seminars and workshops. With high energy program U.S. Dept. Energy, 1993-98. Served with C.E. AUS, 1946-47. Fellow Am. Phys. Soc., AAAS; mem. Lambda Chi Alpha. Achievements include research in nuclear and high energy physics. Home: 319 Tano Rd Santa Fe NM 87506-8823 E-mail: romanowski@santafe-newmexico.com.

ROMANS, DONALD BISHOP, corporate executive; b. Louisville, Apr. 22, 1931; s. Albert D. and Moneta (Bishop) R.; m. Marilyn Yvonne Neff, June 13, 1953 (dec. Aug. 2000); children: Rebecca Ann, Jennifer. BS, U. Louisville, 1953; MBA, Harvard U., 1958. Mgr. internal auditing and data processing, mem. contr. staff Container Corp. Am., Chgo., 1958-62; successively asst. to pres., asst. treas., treas., v.p. fin., sr. v.p. fin., exec. v.p. Trans Union Corp., 1962-81; exec. v.p., chief fin. officer Sunbeam Corp., 1981-82, Bally Mfg. Corp., Chgo., 1982-87; fin. cons., 1987; pres. Romans and Co., 1987-93. Bd. dirs. Burnham Fund Inc., N.Y.C.; trustee Zweig Series Trust, N.Y.C.; life trustee St. Mary of Nazareth Hosp. Capt. USMCR, 1953-56. Mem. Econ. Club. Republican. Avocations: tennis, boating. Home: 39 S Sheridan Rd Lake Forest IL 60045-3269 E-mail: dbromans@telocity.com.

ROMANS, JOHN NIEBRUGGE, lawyer; b. Bklyn., May 23, 1942; s. John McDowell and Helen Pond (Niebrugge) R.; m. Caroline Ward; children: John A., Andrew C. BA, Williams Coll., 1964; LLB, Columbia U., 1967. Bar: N.Y. 1967, U.S. Dist. Ct. (so. and ea. dist.) N.Y. 1971, U.S. Ct. Appeals (2d cir.) 1971, U.S. Ct. Appeals (3rd cir.) 1976, U.S. Ct. Appeals (4th and 7th cirs.) 1987, U.S. Ct. Appeals (9th cir.) 1992, U.S. Ct. Appeals (11th cir.) 1996, U.S. Supreme Ct. 1971. Ptnr. Curtis, Mallet-Prevost, Colt & Mosle, N.Y.C., Katten Muchin & Zavis, N.Y.C., Rosen Weinhaus, LLP, N.Y.C. Lectr. on air law topics at various seminars. Contbr. articles to profl. jours. Trustee Summit (N.J.) Unitarian-Universalist Ch., 1978, Mamaroneck Pub. Libr. Dist., 1990-99; mem. budget com. Village of Mamaroneck, 2001—, chmn, 2002; dir. The Univ. Glee Club NYC, 1993—. Lt. USNR, 1968-71. Mem. Assn. Bar City N.Y. (aero. com. 1983-85, chmn. 1986-89, 92-94, 2000-02, products liability com. 1989-91), Larchmont (N.Y.) Yacht Club. Avocation: sailing. Office: Rosen Weinhaus LLP 40 Wall St 32d Fl New York NY 10005-1304

ROMANS, JOHN THOMAS, economics educator; b. Yonkers, N.Y., Dec. 26, 1933; s. William M.A. and Alice Jane (Thomas) R.; m. Joanne Fielding Jacobson, Mar. 28, 1959; children: Kelly, Duncan. BS, Cornell U., 1955; MS, U. Tenn., 1957; PhD, Brown U., 1963. Lectr. econs. SUNY, Buffalo, 1960, asst. prof., assoc. prof., 1967—, dir. grad. studies in econs., 1985—. Cons. Bur. Econ. Analysis, U.S. Dept. Commerce, Washington, 1968-80; expert witness on econ. losses, N.Y. State, 1980—. Author: Capital Exports and Growth among U.S. Regions, 1965; contbr. articles to profl. jours. Pres. Temagami (Ont., Can.) Lakes Assn., 1987-89. Mem. Am. Econ. Assn., Nat. Assn. Forensic Economists, Conf. on Income and Wealth. Democrat. Avocations: fishing, hiking, canoeing. Home: PO Box 761 Anna Maria FL 34216-0761

ROMANSKY, MONROE JAMES, physician, educator; b. Hartford, Conn., Mar. 16, 1911; s. Benjamin and Henrietta (Levine) R.; m. Evelyn Muriel Lackman, Jan. 10, 1943; children: Stephen, Gerald, Michael, Richard. AB, U. Maine, 1933; MD, U. Rochester, 1937. Diplomate: Am. Bd. Internal Medicine. Intern Strong Meml. Hosp.-U. Rochester, N.Y., 1937-38, asst. resident, 1938-39, James Gleason Research fellow studies on relationship of kidneys to hypertension, 1939-40, chief resident, 1940-41, instr. in medicine, 1941-42; investigator Office Sci. Research and Devel., Surgeon Gen. U.S., 1941-42; chief biochemistry and antibiotic research Walter Reed Army Hosp., 1942-46; asso. prof. Sch. Medicine, George Washington U., Washington, 1946—, prof. medicine, 1957—; dir. George Washington U. med. div. D.C. Gen. Hosp., 1950-69; dir. infectious diseases research lab. and infectious diseases div. D.C. Gen. Hosp., 1950-69. Cons. internal medicine antibiotics Walter Reed Army Hosp., Washington, 1946— ; Cons. internal medicine antibiotics VA Hosp., Washington, 1952— , NIH, Bethesda, Md., 1953— , Surgeon Gen. USAF, 1966— ; mem. Asian influenza adv. com. D.C., 1956-61; mem. ad hoc adv. com. Bur. Medicine FDA, 1966-67; examiner Am. Bd. Internal Medicine, 1965, 67, 69 Editorial bd.: Antimicrobial Agts. and Chemotherapy, 1961-72; Contbr. to profl. jours. Trustees council U. Rochester, 1965— . Served with M.C., AUS, 1942-46. Decorated Legion of Merit; recipient Founders award Tau Epsilon Phi, Disting. Career award U. Maine. Fellow ACP (adv. bd. to gov. D.C. 1969—); mem. Am. Soc. Internal Medicine, Am. Fedn. Clin. Research, Soc. Exptl. Biology and Medicine, Am. Soc. Microbiology, Infectious Diseases Soc. (founding council 1963-66), Soc. Med. Cons. to Armed Forces, Sigma Xi, Alpha Omega Alpha. Clubs: Woodmont Country. Achievements include pioneer work in prolonging action of penicillin, requiring only single daily injection, Romansky Formula, 1944; nutritional studies in obesity as related to weight reduction. Home: 5600 Wisconsin Ave Chevy Chase MD 20815-4405

ROMANSTEIN, STANLEY E. music educator, researcher; b. Columbia, Sc, Jan. 24, 1956; s. S.E. and Syble Byrd Romanstein; children: Jonathan Michael. PhD, College-Conservatory of Music , U. of Cin., Cincinnati, OH, 1990; MM, College-Conservatory of Music, U. of Cin., Cincinnati, OH, 1980. Chair, dept. of music St. Lawrence U., Canton, NY, 1987—96; exec. dir. Balt. Sch. for the Arts, Baltimore, Md., 1996—2000; devel. dir. Weisman Art Mus., Minneapolis, Minn., 2000—01; pres. & ceo MN Humanities Commn., Saint Paul, 2001—. Bd. of directors MN Chorale, Minneapolis, Minn., 2000—, Dale Warland Singers, Saint Paul, Minn., 2002—. Jewish. Office: MN Humanities Commission 987 East Ivy Avenue Saint Paul MN 55106

ROMAS, NICHOLAS ACHILLES, urologist, educator; b. Endicott, N.Y., Jan. 17, 1936; s. Peter Angelo and Stavroula Romas; m. Serene Karikas, June 19, 1968; children: Stavra Nicole, Eva Maria, Pamela Stephanie. AB, Colgate U., 1958; MD, Columbia U., 1962. Bd. cert. urologist, 1974. Asst. prof. clin. urology Columbia U. Coll. Physicians and Surgeons, N.Y.C., 1970-78, assoc. prof. clin. urology, 1978-89, prof. clin. urology, 1989—; dir. urology St. Luke's-Roosevelt Hosp. Ctr., 1984—. Editor: Prostate Acid Phosphatase Measurement, 1982; contbr. articles to profl. jours. Maj. USAF, 1968-70. Mem. Am. Urol. Assn. (rsch. com. 1990—, fin. com. 1991—, pub. com. 1998—, pres-elect NY sect. 2002), N.Y. Acad. Medicine (adv. com. 1986—, sec. urology sect. 1987-88, chmn. 1988-89). Greek Orthodox. Achievements include research in the role of prostate acid phosphates in different stages of prostate cancer. Office: St Lukes-Roosevelt Hosp Ctr 1000 10th Ave New York NY 10019-1147

ROMA-SCOTT, MARY LOU, music educator; b. Jersey City, Nov. 25, 1949; d. Mario Gerard Roma and Mary Louise (De Rosa) Roma Crimaldi; m. Richard Dean Scott, Sept. 13, 1970; children: Kimberly, David. BA in Music Edn. and Piano Performance, N.J. City U., 1971, MA in Music Edn., 1975. Instr. music Clarendon Elem. Sch., Secaucus, N.J., 1971-73; instr. piano Metuchen, 1973—; instr. presch. music, 1975-77; instr. music Marlboro (N.J.) Mid. Sch., 1977-78, Jersey City State Coll., 1978-87, Middlesex County Coll., Edison, N.J., 1984—; instr. piano dept. performing arts Red Bank Regional H.S., Little Silver, 1991-98; instr. music Moss Sch., Metuchen, 1997—; choral dir. Metuchen H.S., 1997—. Cons. Piano Consortium, N.Y.C., 1980—. Mem. bd. recreation com., Metuchen, 1980-85; Dem. com. woman, Metuchen, 1978-81. Named one of Outstanding Young Women of Am., 1981. Mem. NEA, Music Educators Assn., Piano Tchrs. of Am. (Genia Robiner Tchg. award 1990-91), N.J. Music Educators Assn. Avocations: gardening, swimming, cooking. Home: 35 Stoneham Pl Metuchen NJ 08840-1661 Office: Metuchen Bd of Edn Main St Metuchen NJ 08840

ROMATOWSKI, JANE A. education educator, associate dean; b. Detroit, Mar. 21, 1932; d. John and Mary (Reiter) Pecherski; m. Stanley P. Romatowski, July 4, 1960; children: Marie E. Romatowski Thomas, Nancy J. Romatowski Valentini. BA, Marygrove Coll., 1953; postgrad., Harvard U., 1954; MEd, U. Detroit, 1957; EDD, Wayne State U., 1972. Cert. elem. tchr., Mich. Tchr. Detroit Pub. Schs., 1953-62; critic tchr. Wayne State U., Detroit, 1954-60; substitute tchr. various pub. schs., Wyandotte, Trenton, Detroit, 1965-67; lectr. U. Mich. Sch. Edn., Dearborn, 1972-73; asst. prof. edn. U. Mich., 1973-77, assc. prof., 1977-83, prof., 1983—, asst. dean, 1988-89, interim dean, 1989-90, assoc. dean, 1990—. Presenter in field; cons. CATS Project Oak Park (Mich.) Schs., 1974-76. Co-author: Calliope, 1981, Ethnic Pride, 1983; contbr. articles to profl. jours. Commr. Trenton Pub. Libr., 1970-74. Recipient Susan B. Anthony award, 1992, Soroptomist Women Helping Women award, 1993, Marygrove Coll. Alumna of the Yr. award, 1994, Mich. Assn. of Governing Bds. Disting. Faculty award, 1995, Woman of Achievement award Western Wayne County YWCA, 1999; Young Author's Conf. grantee Mich. Coun. for Arts, 1978-79, Disting. Student Orgn. Advisor award U. Mich., 1998, Disting. Faculty Svc. award, 1997. Mem. Internat. Reading Assn., Mich. Reading Assn., Nat. Coun. Tchrs. English, Assn. for Edn. Young Children (nat., Mich., Detroit chpts.), Am. Assn. Colls. Tchr. Edn., Mich. Assn. Tchr. Educators, Soroptomist Soc. (Midwest region, judge 1987-90), Pi Lambda Theta, Delta Kappa Gamma. Roman Catholic. Avocations: reading, theater, films, recreational sports. Office: U Mich Dearborn 4901 Evergreen Rd Dearborn MI 48128-2406

ROMBACH, LOUIS HERMAN, lawyer, chemist; b. Cin., Apr. 4, 1926; s. Charles and Mathilda Elizabeth (Lauck) R.; m. Ann Marie O'Brien, June 9, 1951; children: Louis J., Linda M., Stephen E., Charles M., Thomas A. BS in Chemistry, Xavier U., 1948, MS in Chemistry, 1949; PhD in Chemistry, U. Cin., 1953; JD, Temple U., 1964. Bar: U.S. Patent and Trademark Office 1963, Del. 1965, U.S. Dist. Ct. D.C. 1965, U.S. Ct. Appeals (D.C. cir.) 1965, U.S. Claims Ct. 1966, U.S. Ct. Appeals (fed. cir.) 1982. Rsch. chemist Du Pont Co., Wilmington, Del., 1953-64; sr. counsel Dupont Co., 1965-91; ret., 1991. Patentee in polymer chemistry; contbr. articles to profl. jours. Pres. Pembrey Civic Assn., 1993-95. Ensign USN, 1944-46. Cancer rsch. fellow NIH, 1951-53. Mem. Am. Chem. Soc., Am. Inst. Chemists, Royal Soc. Chemistry, Del. Bar Assn., D.C. Bar Assn., Sci. Rsch. Soc. Am., Xavier U. Nat. Alumni Assn. (founder, first pres. Del. Valley chpt. 1993-95), Phi Alpha Delta, Phi Lambda Upsilon. Avocations: running, tennis, computers, travel. E-mail: LHROM@JUNO.COM.

ROMBERGER, JOHN ALBERT, scientist, historian; b. near Klingerstown, Pa., Dec. 25, 1925; s. Ralph T. and Carrie (Bahner) R.; student Hershey Jr. Coll., 1947-49; BA, Swarthmore Coll., 1951; MS, Pa. State U., 1954; PhD, U. Mich., 1957; postdoctoral, Calif. Inst. Tech., 1957-60; m. Margery Janet Davis, June 17, 1951; children: Ann I., Daniel D. Plant physiologist, Forest Physiology Lab., U.S. Forest Service, U.S. Dept. Agr., Beltsville, Md., 1961-82; vis. scientist Swedish U. Agrl. Scis., Alnarp, 1983, Inst. Agrl. Scis., Zamosc, Poland, 1985, Agrl. U., Warsaw, 1988. Served with AUS, 1945-46. Fellow Poland-U.S. Interacad. Exchange Program, U. Silesia, Katowice, 1981, 83. Fellow AAAS; mem. Am. Soc. Plant Physiologists, Bot. Soc. Am., Soc. for History Tech., Pa. German Soc., Sigma Xi. Author: Meristems, Growth, and Development in Woody Plants, 1963, (with Z. Hejnowicz and J.F. Hill) Plant Structure: Function and Development, 1993; editor: Internat. Rev. Forestry Research, 1963-70, Beltsville Symposia in Agrl. Research, 1976-78. Contbr. articles on devel. and theoretical biology to profl. jours. Home: 320 Tennessee Ave Elizabethville PA 17023-9640

ROMEO, ANTHONY ALBERT, orthopedic surgeon; b. Walnut Creek, Calif., Nov. 8, 1961; s. Sam J.W. and Patricia Ann (DeFilippo) R.; m. Laura Lee Sawicki, June 30, 1984; children: Brianna, Alyssa, Danielle, Christin, Sabrina. MD, St. Louis U., 1987. Cert. orthopedic surgery. Intern Cleve. Clin. Found., 1987-88, resident, 1988-92; advanced clin. experience shoulder/elbow orthopedic surgery U. Wash., Seattle, 1992-93; active staff Rush Presbyn. St. Luke's Med. Ctr., Chgo., 1993—, Oak Park (Ill.) Hosp., 1994—. Asst. prof. orthopedics Rush Med. Coll., Chgo., 1993—. Mem. AMA, Am. Acad. Orthopaedic Surgeons, Am. Shoulder and Elbow Surgeons Soc., Notre Dame Orthopedic Soc., Alpha Omega Alpha. Office: Midwest Orthopaedics 1725 W Harrison St Ste 1063 Chicago IL 60612-3836 also: Midwest Orthopaedics 610 S Maple Ste 1400 Oak Park IL 60304-1022

ROMEO, PETER JOHN, lawyer; b. Darby, Pa., Aug. 1, 1942; s. Joseph Paul and Rose Marie (Beckett) R.; m. Nancy Virginia Schmidt, July 15, 1972; children: Christopher, Jeffrey, Michael. BSBA, Georgetown U., 1964; JD, George Washington U., 1967, LLM, 1969. Bar; Va. 1968, U.S. Dist. Ct. D.C. 1969, U.S. Supreme Ct. 1972; CPA, D.C. Acct. Schumaker & Yates, Washington, 1964-69; atty. U.S. Securities and Exchange Com., 1969-72, spl. counsel, 1972-79, chief counsel div. corp. finance, 1980-84; ptnr. Hogan & Hartson LLP, 1984—. Author: The Registration Process, 1985 (updated biannually); co-author: Comprehensive Section 16 Outline, 1984 (updated annually), Section 16 Reporting Guide, 1989, Section 16 Forms and Filing Handbook, 1991 (updated 1993, 96, 2000), Section 16 Treatise and Reporting Guide, 1994; contbr. articles to profl. jours. Mem. ABA (mem. fed. regulation securities com.), D.C. Bar Assn., Va. State Bar. Roman Catholic. Office: Hogan & Hartson LLP 555 13th St NW Washington DC 20004-1161 E-mail: pjromeo@hhlaw.com.

ROMEO, ROSS VICTOR, army officer; b. Detroit, Nov. 4, 1958; s. Salvatore Victor and Carol Ann (Kunart) R.; children: Christian, Ross II, Andie. BA, U. Mich., 1981; MA, Boston U., 1987; MBA, U. Md., 1994; PhD, Hamilton U., 1999. Commd. 2d lt. U.S. Army, 1983, advanced through ranks to lt. col., 1987, co. commdr. Fed. Republic Germany, 1986-89; mgr. worldwide intercomputer network Def. Communications Agy., Washington, 1989-92; v.p. 21st Century Investments; dir. Army network and Systems Ops. Ctr., 1997—. Selected DCA Co. Grade Officer of Yr., 1990. Mem. Armed Forces Communications-Electronics Assn., Am. Assn. Individual Investors, Nat. Assn. Investors Corp., U. Mich. Alumni Assn. Avocations: pvt. investing, cons. for investment firms. Home: PO Box 1030 Sierra Vista AZ 85636-1030 Office: Def Communications Agy The Pentagon Washington DC 20303-0001 E-mail: decillion@earthlink.net.

ROMER, CHRISTINA DUCKWORTH, economist, educator; b. Alton, Ill., Dec. 25, 1958; d. Clifford Lee and Carol (Greer) Duckworth; m. David Hibbard Romer, Aug. 20, 1983; children: Katherine, Paul, Matthew. BA, Coll. William & Mary, Williamsburg, Va., 1981; PhD, MIT, Cambridge, Mass., 1985. Asst. prof. Princeton (N.J) U., 1985—88; acting assoc. prof. U. Calif., Berkeley, 1988—90, assoc. prof., 1990—93, prof., 1993—97, Class of 1957 prof., 1997—. Rsch. assoc. Nat. Bur. Econ. Rscsh., Cambridge, Mass., 1990—; mem. rsch. adv. bd. Com. for Econ. Devel., Washington, 1994—98; mem. editl. bd. Jour. Econ. History, 1994—97. Editor: (book) Reducing Inflation, 1997; contbr. articles to profl. jours. Recipient Presdl. Young Investigator award, NSF, 1989—94; fellow, John Simon Guggenheim Meml. Found., 1998—99. Mem.: Econ. History Assn. (nominating com. 2001—02), Am. Econs. Assn. (exec. com. 2000—03). Democrat. United Church Of Christ. Achievements include research in statistics that provided new evidence on the effects of monetary policy. Showed that historical macroeconomic indicators overstate the size of business cycles before World War II. Office: Univ Calif Dept Econs Berkeley CA 94720-3880

ROMER, DANIEL, university official, psychologist, educator; b. Caracas, Venezuela, Apr. 19, 1947; came to U.S., 1948; s. Adolf and Eleanor (Rittermann) R.; m. Lauren B. Alloy, Jan. 4, 1985; 1 child, Adrienne. AB, Dartmouth Coll., 1969; PhD, U. Ill., Chgo., 1974. Rsch. fellow Dept Mental Health, Chgo., 1976-79; vis. asst. prof. Northwestern U., Evanston, 1979-81; adj. assoc. prof. U. Ill., 1981-89; assoc. rsch. dir. Leo Burnett Co., Chgo., 1982-89; sr. rschr. Annenberg Sch. for Comm., U. Pa., Phila., 1990—2000, sr. fellow Ctr. for Cmty. Partnerships, 1996—, rsch. dir. Annenberg Pub. Policy Ctr., 2001—, rsch. dir. Inst. for Adolescent Risk Comm., 2001—. Mem. nat. expert panel on adolescent STD prevention Ctr. for Disease Control and Prevention, Atlanta, 2000-01; mem. rev. panels NIH, Washington, 1994-97, 98—. Mem. editl. bd. Jour. Exptl. Social Psychology, 1988-91, Youth and Society, 2001—; contbr. over 60 articles to psychol. and pub. health jours., chpts. to books. Grantee NIMH, 1992—, Ford Found., 1994. Mem. APA, APHA. Office: Annenberg Pub Policy Ctr 3620 Walnut St Philadelphia PA 19104 E-mail: dromer@asc.upenn.edu.

ROMER, ROBERT HORTON, physicist, educator; b. Chgo., Apr. 15, 1931; s. Alfred Sherwood and Ruth (Hibbard) R.; m. Diana Haynes, June 12, 1953 (dec. Feb. 1992); children: Evan James, David Hibbard, Theodore Haynes; m. Betty Steele, June 25, 1994. BA, Amherst Coll., 1952; PhD in Physics, Princeton U., 1955. Faculty Amherst (Mass.) Coll., 1955—, prof. physics, 1966—, chmn. dept., 1966—. Research asso. Duke, 1958-59; guest physicist Brookhaven Nat. Lab., 1963—; vis. prof. physics Voorhees Coll., 1969-70 Author: Energy—An Introduction to Physics, 1976, Energy Facts and Figures, 1984. NSF fellow Princeton, 1952-55, U. Grenoble, France, 1964-65 Fellow AAAS, Am. Phys. Soc.; mem. Am. Assn. Physics Tchrs. (asso. editor jour. 1968, book rev. editor 1982-88, editor 1988—), Phi Beta Kappa, Sigma Xi. Achievements include research in low temperature physics, solar energy, electromagnetic theory. Home: 104 Spring St Amherst MA 01002-2332 E-mail: rhromer@amherst.edu.

ROMERO, FREDDIE JOSEPH, lawyer; b. Roswell, N.Mex., July 23, 1956; s. Fred Fresquez and Beatriz Rose (Kimbrell) R.; m. Lorena Helen Hickman, Apr. 25, 1987. BA in Govt., N.Mex. State U., 1978; JD, U. N.Mex., 1981. Bar: N.Mex. 1981, U.S. Dist. Ct. N.Mex. 1982, U.S. Ct. Appeals (10th cir.) 1982. Asst. city atty. City of Albuquerque, Albuquerque, 1981-82; assoc. atty. Atwood, Malone, Mann and Turner, Roswell, 1982-87, ptnr., 1987-95, Cusack, Jaramillo, Romero and Assoc., Roswell, 1995—. Bd. dirs. Counseling Assocs. Inc., Roswell, 1984-89, pres., 1989-90; bd. dirs. Chaves County Hist. Soc., Roswell, Roswell Hispano C. of C., 1993—. Mem. ABA, N.Mex. Trial Lawyers Assn., Chaves County Bar Assn., N.Mex. Hispanic Bar Assn., Am. Inns of Ct. (barrister, southeastern N.Mex. chpt.), Young Lawyers N.Mex. Assn. (dir. 1987-88), State Bar of N.Mex. (libr. com. 1988-89, chmn. trial practice sect. 1992-93, bd. dirs. supreme ct. disciplinary bd. 1993—. Democrat. Roman Catholic. Avocations: N.Mex. colonial and territorial hist. rsch., legal philosophy, Basketball. Office: Cusack Jaramillo Romero and Assocs 123 W 4th St Roswell NM 88201-4709

ROMERO, JORGE ANTONIO, neurologist, educator; b. Bayamon, P.R., Apr. 15, 1948; s. Calixto Antonio Romero-Barcelo and Antonia (de Juan) R.; m. Helen Mella, June 20, 1970 (div. 1983); children: Sofia, Jorge, Alfredo, Isabel; m. Cheryl Raps, Aug. 1994; 1 child, Jessica. SB, MIT, 1968; MD, Harvard U., 1972. Diplomate Am. Bd. Psychiatry and Neurology. Intern U. Chgo. Hosp. and Clinics, 1972-73; resident Mass. Gen. Hosp., Boston, 1975-78; rsch. fellow in pharmacology NIMH, Bethesda, Md., 1973-75; asst. prof. neurology Harvard Med. Sch., Boston, 1979-92; mem. staff VA Med. Ctr., Brockton, Mass., 1979-92; assoc. physician Brigham and Women's Hosp., Boston, 1980-92; chmn. dept. neurology Ochsner Clin. Baton Rouge, 1993-97; assoc. clin. prof. neurology La. State U. Sch. Medicine, 1996-97; assoc. attending physician Baylor U. Med. Ctr., Dallas, 1998—. Cons. Mass. Mental Health Ctr., Boston, 1987-92. With USPHS, 1973-75. Recipient Career Devel. award VA, 1979. Mem. Am. Acad. Neurology. Office: 3600 Gaston Ave Dallas TX 75246 E-mail: romero.jorge@worldnet.att.net.

ROMERO, JOSEFINO TABERNILLA, nurse anesthetist; b. Tayabas, Quezon, The Philippines; came to U.S., 1963; s. Melanio Merca and Teodorica (Tabernilla) R. Diploma, Quezon Meml. Hosp., 1961; cert. nurse anesthetist, Mt. Carmel Hosp., Detroit, 1968; D in Art, U. Found., Malta, 1986. RN, Mich. Psychiat. nurse Nat. Mental Hosp., Manila, 1961-63; operating room nurse St. Vincent Hosp., Worcester, Mass., 1963-64, Michael Reese Hosp., Chgo., 1964-65, Sarnia (Canada) Gen. Hosp., 1965-66; operating room nurse, nurse anesthetist Quezon Meml. Hosp., 1971-72; nurse anesthetist Mt. Carmel Hosp., 1973-74, Brent Hosp., Detroit, 1974-86, Straith Hosp., Southfield, Mich., 1986—. Exhibited paintings in numerous one-man shows including Beijing Internat. Conv. Ctr., 1991, Pontiac Art Ctr., 1989, Troy Libr. and Gallery, 1989, Scarab Club Detroit, 1989, Lawrence St. Gallery, Pontiac, Mich., 1989, Acad. Art Gallery, Paris, 1988, Gallert in the Grove, Canada, 1987, Southfield Civic Ctr., 1986, Electric Fantasy Gallery, 1986, Philippine Orgn. and Filipino Artists, Chgo., 1978, others; exhibited in several group shows including Detroit Press Club, 1989, Mich. Design Ctr., 1988, Philippine Cultural Ctr., Ayala Mus., Casa de Communidad de Tayabas, 1997, Seattle Asian Art Mus., 1997, Gov.'s Mansion-The Philippine, 1998, Galleria Romero, The Philippines, 1998. Named one of Outstanding Men. Mich., City of Detroit, 1976, Outstanding Alumnus quezon Meml. Hosp. Sch. Nursing, 1994; recipient Albert Einstein award Internat. Acad. Found., 1991, Merit award Mich. Ann. Art Festival, 1975, Cert. of Appreciation Gov. of Mich., 1986, Quezon medal honor (The Philippines), 1997. Mem. Am. Assn. Nurse Anesthetists, Mich. Assn. Nurse Anesthetists, Filipino Nurse Assn., Beijing Watercolor Soc., Scarab Club Detroit (bd. dirs. 1988—), Knights of Rizal, Internat. Assn. Educators for World Peace. Roman Catholic. Avocations: photography, travel, tennis. Home: 2230 S Shore Ct Rochester Hills MI 48307

ROMERO, PATRICIA WATKINS, historian, educator, researcher; b. Delaware, Ohio, July 28, 1934; d. Warren Arthur Watkins and Jean Virginia (Beatty) Alexander; divorced; children: Stephen, Arthur, Jeffrey. BA, Cen. State U., 1964; MA, Miami (Ohio) U., 1965; PhD, Ohio State U., 1971. Assoc. for rsch. Assn. Study of African-Am. Life History, Washington, 1965-72; assoc. prof. U. South Fla., Tampa, 1972-74; vis. fellow Johns Hopkins U., Balt., 1975-89; asst. prof. history Towson (Md.) U., 1989-93, assoc. prof., 1993-98, prof., 1998—. Vis. assoc. prof. So. Meth. U., Dallas, 1984; cons. Raintree Steck-Vaughn Pubs., Newark, 1994—. Author: (books) E. Sylvia Pankhurst: Portrait of a Radical, 1987, Lamu: History, Society, Family in an East African Port City, 1997, Profiles in Diversity: Women in the New South Africa, 1998; editor: Jour. Colonialism and Colonial History, 1999—. Mem. adv. bd. House of Ruth, 1990—, Child Reach Internat., 1991—. Episcopalian. Office: Towson U Towson MD 21204 E-mail: promero@towson.edu.

ROMERO-BARCELÓ, CARLOS ANTONIO, former congressman, former governor of Puerto Rico, former mayor of San Juan; b. Sept. 4, 1932; s. Antonio S. Romero and Josefina Barceló; m. Kathleen Donnelly, Jan. 2, 1966; children: Juan Carlos, Melinda Kathleen; children by previous marriage: Carlos, Andrés. BA, Yale U., 1953; LLB, U. P.R., 1956; LLD (hon.), U. Bridgeport, 1977. Bar: P.R. 1956. Mem. Herrero-Frank & Romero-Barceló, 1956-58; ptnr. Rivera-Zayas, Rivera-Cestero & Rúa, San Juan, 1958-63, Segurola, Romero & Toledo, San Juan, 1963-68; pres. Citizens for State 51, 1965-67; mayor PR, 1969-77; gov. P.R., 1977-85; pres. New Progressive Party, 1974-85, 89-91; P.R.'s at-large rep. U.S. Ho. Reps., Washington, 1992-2000; mem. edn. and workforce and resources com. 106th Congress, also ranking mem. pub. lands and nat. parks subcom. Office: Centro de Seguros Bldg 701 Ponce de Leon Ave # 412 San Juan PR 00907 E-mail: rbarcelo@prtc.net.

ROMERO-GONZÁLEZ, GUIDO MAURICIO, psychiatrist, educator, consultant; b. Santafe de Bogota, Colombia, Nov. 15, 1960; s. Carlos Guillermo Romero and Dora Cecilia Gonzalez. MD, Colegio Mayor del Rosario, Bogota, 1989, cert. in ednl. resources, 1995. Med. intern Hosp. Univ. del Valle, Cali, 1983-84, Med. Social Svc./Primary Attention Unit, Planadas, 1985; emergency rm. med. coord. Hosp. San Blas, Bogota, 1986-87; med. resident in psychiatry Hosp. San Jose, 1986-89; med. cons. in psychiatry Hosp. San Blas, 1989-93; chief human rights dept. Mil. U., 1995-97. Neurophysiology instr. K. Lorenz U., Bogota, 1988—89; mental health prof. Colegio Mayor del Rosario, Bogota, 1990—; mental health cons. Ministry of Health, Bogota, 1990—91, Ombudsman Office, Bogota, 1992—97, chief divsn. mental health, 1997—2000; dir. of course: Human Rights Colegio Mayor del Rosario, dir. of course: HIV/AIDS, 1997—2000; invited asst. prof. psychiatry Yale U., New Haven, 2000—; participant World Health Conf. UCLA, 1998; founder, pres. CT Latino P.FLAG Inc., 2002—. Author: Psychotherapy, 1994, Special Mental Health Assistant in Special Case of Masacre de Trujillo-Valle, 1995, Nat. Policy of Mental Health of Colombia, 1997, Risk Reduction in Addiction Behavior, 1997; contbr. articles to profl. jours. including Rev. Colegio Mayor del Rosario. Tech. dir. Fundacion Conaccion, Bogota, 1987-88, exec. dir., 1988-94; sci. dir. Fundacion por La Salud, Bogota, 1994-2000. Recipient Rafael Pombo scholarship Colegio Mayor del Rosario, 1970-72, hon. scholarship, 1973-77. Mem. Soc. Colombiana de Psiquiatria, Asociacion Medica Rosarista (hon.). Mem. Conservative Party. Jewish. Avocations: music, beach volleyball, art. Home: 1169 Forest Rd New Haven CT 06515 Office: 950 Campbell Ave Bldg 36 Allingtown CT 06516 E-mail: gromero@claustro.urosario.edu.co., alexandrohefestion@msn.com., mauricio.romero-gonzalez@yale.edu.

ROMESBURG, KERRY D. university president, former state education administrator; b. Akron, Ohio, Mar. 12, 1945; s. Bert Lewis and Edna (Bartlett) R.; m. Judy Kaye Land, July 2, 1965; children: Rod A., Donald A. BA, Ariz. State U., 1967, MA, 1968, PhD, 1972. Tchr. math. East H.S., Phoenix, 1969-70; asst. dir. instl. rsch. Ariz. State U., Tempe, 1972-73; planning analyst Ariz. Bd. Regents, Phoenix, 1973-74; exec. dir. Ariz. Commn. Post Secondary Edn., 1974-75, Alaska Commn. Postsecondary Edn., Juneau, 1975; pres. Utah Valley St. Coll., Orem, Utah, 1996—. Mem. Western Interstate Commn. on Higher Edn., Boulder, Colo., 1977—, chmn., 1981-82; mem. Western Tech. Manpower Coun., 1982—; mem. Nat. Adv. Coun. for United Student Aid Funds, N.Y.C., 1978—. Recipient Outstanding Alumnus award Ariz. State U., 1982; NDEA fellow, 1972. Mem. State Higher Edn. Exec. Officers, Nat. Adv. Coun. State Postsecondary Planning Commns., Am. Assn. Higher Edn., NEA. Office: Utah Valley State College 800 W University Pkwy Orem UT 84058-0001*

ROMEU, JORGE LUIS, mathematics educator, writer; b. Havana, Cuba, Dec. 10, 1945; came to U.S., 1980; s. Maunuel E. and Raquel (Fernandez) R.; m. Zoila Barreiro, July 25, 1970; children: Jorge Luis, Ricardo, Rafael. Lic. in Math., U. Havana, 1973; MS in Ops. Research, Syracuse U., 1981, M in Philosophy, 1987, PhD, 1990. Applied mathematician Cuban Inst. Petroleum, Havana, 1972-73, Ministry Pub. Works, Havana, 1974-76, Ministry Agr., Havana, 1977-79; research engr. IIT Research Inst., Rome, 1982-85; sr. engr. IIT Rsch. Inst., 1998—; assoc. prof. math. SUNY, Cortland, 1985-98, assoc. prof. emeritus, 1998—. Adj. prof. Syracuse U., 1988—; practicing faculty IME, 1999—; dir. Juarez-Lincoln-Marti Internat. Edn. Project, 1995—; ednl. cons. Fundayacucho, Venezuela, 1998, Acad. Specialist, U.S. Dept. of State, Mex., 2000. Author: Los Unos Los Otros Etc., 1971, La Otra Cara de la Moneda, 1983, A Practical Guide to Statistical Analysis of Material Property Data, 1999; frequent contbr. Syracuse Post-Standard, Hispanic Link News Svc.; contbr. articles to Syracuse Herald, Miami Herald; prodr., dir., condr. (weekly radio program) Sobremesa, 1994-98; frequent panelist Mesa Redonda program, Radio Marti/VOA. Recipient Disting. Collaborator award Cuban Assn. Journalists, Dr. Nuala M. Drescher Minority Faculty award SUNY, 1989, Saaty award Am. Jour. Math. and Mgmt. Scis., 1997, Profl. Devel. award Mohawk Valley Exec. Engring. Coun., 2002; scholar French Govt., 1964, Spanish Govt., 1978, Fulbright scholar to Mexico, 1994; named to Fulbright Spkr. Specialist Roster Program, 2001. Fellow Inst. Stats., Royal Stats. Soc. (chartered statis. fellow); mem. Am. Statis. Assn. (human rights nat. com. 1985-87), Mgmt. and Ops. Rsch. Soc. Cen. N.Y. (past pres.), Assn. for Study of Cuban Economy (bd. dirs.), Las Palmas Club (founder, pres. 1984-88). Roman Catholic. Avocations: music, history, writing. Home: 201 Rugby Rd Syracuse NY 13203-1440 Office: IIT Rsch Inst 201 Mill St Rome NY 13440-6916 also: PO Box 6134 Syracuse NY 13217 E-mail: jromeu@cat.syr.edu.

ROMEY, WILLIAM DOWDEN, geologist, educator; b. Richmond, Ind., Oct. 26, 1930; s. William Minter and Grace Warring (Dowden) R.; m. Lucretia Alice Leonard, July 16, 1955; children: Catherine Louise Keener, Gretchen Elizabeth Tanzer, William Leonard. AB with highest honors, Ind. U., 1952; student, U. Paris, 1950-51, 52-53; PhD, U. Calif. at Berkeley, 1962. Asst. prof. geology and sci. edn. Syracuse U., 1962-66, assoc. prof., 1966-69; exec. dir. earth sci. ednl. program Am. Geol. Inst., 1969-72; prof., chmn. dept. geology St. Lawrence U., Canton, N.Y., 1971-76, prof., 1976—, prof., chmn. dept. geography, 1983-93; prof. emeritus, 1993—. Ednl. cons., 1962—; NAS visitor USSR Acad. Sci., 1967; vis. geoscientist Am. Geol. Inst., 1964-66, 71; earth sci. cons. Compton's Ency., 1970-71; adj. prof. Union Grad. Sch., 1974—; mem. bd. rsch. advisers and readers Walden U., 1981—; prof. Grad. Sch. Am., 1993—; travel writer and cruise ship lectr., 1990—. Author: (with others) Investigating the Earth, 1967, (with J. Kramer, E. Muller, J. Lewis) Investigations in Geology, 1967, Inquiry Techniques for Teaching Science, 1968, Risk-Trust-Love, 1972, Consciousness and Creativity, 1975, Confluent Education in Science, 1976, Plus Ça Change..., 1996; co-editor: Geochemical Prospecting for Petroleum, 1959; assoc. editor: Jour. Coll. Sci. Tchg., 1972-74, Geol. Soc. Am. Bull., 1979-84, Jour. Geol. Edn., 1980—; editor-in-chief: Ash Lad Press, 1975—; contbr. articles on geology, geography and edn. to profl. pubs. Bd. dirs. Onondaga Nature Ctrs., Inc., 1966—69. Served to lt. j.g. USNR, 1953—57, lt . comdr. res. Woodrow Wilson Found. fellow, 1959-60, 61-62; NSF sci. faculty fellow U. Oslo, 1967-68 Fellow AAAS, Geol. Soc. Am., Explorers Club; mem. Nat. Assn. Geology Tchrs. (v.p. 1971-72), N.Y. Acad. Scis., Nat. Assn. Geology Tchrs. (pres. 1972-73), Assn. Am. Geographers, Am. Geophys. Union, Geol. Soc. Norway, Can. Assn. Geographers, Assn. for Can. Studies in U.S., Phi Beta Kappa, Sigma Xi, Phi Delta Kappa. Home and Office: PO Box 294 East Orleans MA 02643-0294

ROMIG, EDGAR DUTCHER, clergyman; b. N.Y.C., July 6, 1921; s. Edgar Franklin and Ella Woodruff (Dutcher) R. BA, Princeton U., 1942; MDiv, Episcopal Theol. Sch., Mass., 1951; DD (hon.), Va. Theol. Sem., 1969. Ordained deacon Episcopal Ch., 1951, priest, 1952. Asst. minister Trinity Ch., Boston, 1951-53; rector Grace Ch., North Attleboro, Mass., 1953-58, St. Stephen's Ch., Lynn, 1958-64, Ch. of Epiphany, Washington, 1964-92. Dep. Episcopal Gen. Conv., 1973, 76, 79, 82, 85, 88, 91. Author: Trinity Church in the City of Boston, 1953; contbr. articles to various jours. Ambulance driver Am. Field Svc., 1942-43, NATOUSA; with AUS, 1943-45, ETO. Decorated Bronze Star, Purple Heart. Mem. Century Club (N.Y.C.), Princeton Club (N.Y.C.), Met. Club. Democrat. Home: 4000 Cathedral Ave NW Apt 217B Washington DC 20016-5265

ROMIG, THOMAS J. military officer; b. Manhattan, Kans., Dec. 27, 1948; Grad., Nat. War Coll., Armed Forces Staff Coll.; BS, Kans. State U., 1970; JD with honors, Santa Clara U., 1980. Commd. U.S. Army, 1971, advanced through grades to maj. gen., mil. intelligence officer NC, Ft. Huachuca, Ariz.; trial counsel, sr. trial counsel, chief of legal assistance and chief criminal law 2d Armored Divsn., Ft. Hood, Tex., 1980—83; instr. internat. and operational law Judge Advocate Gen.'s Sch., Charlottesville, Va., 1984—87, plans officer, pers., plans and tng. office, 1988—90; staff judge advocate 32d Army Air Def. Command, Darmstadt, Germany, 1990—93, chief pers./asst. chief pers., plans and tng. office, 1993—95; staff judge advocate V Corps, Heidelberg, Germany and Taszar, Hungary, 1996—98; asst. judge advocate gen. for mil. law and ops. Office of the Judge Advocate Gen., Rosslyn, Va., 1998, judge advocate gen. Washington. Decorated Legion of Merit, Meritorious Svc. medal with 4 oak leaf clusters, Army Commendation medal, Army Achievement medal, Nat. Def. Svc. medal with 1 bronze service star, Armed Forces Svc. medal, NATO medal. Office: Office of the Judge Advocate General US Army Pentagon Washington DC 20310-1500*

ROMINE, JOAN MARIE WINTERS, financial officer, treasurer; b. Teaneck, N.J., July 13, 1951; d. Robert Grant and Joan Clare (Mooney) Winters; m. Mario Alejandro Romine, Oct. 31, 1972 (div. Dec. 1985); children: Jeremy Patrick, Kelly Marie, Christopher Grant. BS in Acctg., Kean U., 1988; postgrad. in Fine Arts, Coll. of New Rochelle, 1969-72. CFO, sec.-treas. Hanita Cutting Tools, Inc., Montainside, N.J., 1988-95; controller Magic Cinemas, L.L.C., Livingston, 1995-96; CFO, treas. Clearview Cinema Group, Inc., Chatham, 1996—. Republican. Avocations: travel, photography, painting, Bible history. Home: 2330 Morse Ave Scotch Plains NJ 07076-2138 Office: Clearview Cinema Group Inc 97 Main St Chatham NJ 07928-2407

ROMINGER, M. KYLE, lawyer; b. Indpls., Mar. 5, 1968; s. Roger Kyle and Phyllis Rae Rominger; m. Jennifer Lynn Gist, July 16, 1994. BS in Ecology, Ethology and Evolution, U. Ill., 1990; JD, U. Louisville, 1997. Bar: Ill. 1997, U.S. Dist. Ct. (ctrl. dist.) Ill. 1997. Intern Office of Gov., Office of Dept. of Transp., State of Ill., Springfield, 1989; rsch. asst. U. Ill., Champaign, 1989; project mgr. Ill. EPA, Springfield, 1991-94; assoc. Giffin, Winning, Cohen & Bodewes, 1997-99; asst. counsel Ill. EPA, 1999—. Mem. ABA, Ill. Bar Assn., Sangamon County Bar Assn. Office: 1021 N Grand Ave E Springfield IL 62702-4059 E-mail: kyle.rominger@epa.state.il.us.

ROMJUE, JOHN LAWSON, historian, writer; b. Washington, Oct. 4, 1936; s. Lawson Rodney Romjue, Joanne Romjue; m. Ingeborg Gertrud Schaefer, Mar. 25, 1961; children: Martin John, Kristin Elisabeth. BA in History and Polit. Sci., U. Mo., 1962, MA in Modern English History and German Lit., 1963. Staff historian USN Facilities Engring. Command, Port Hueneme, Calif., 1966—69; command historian US Army Combat Devel. Experimentation, Fort Ord, 1969—74; staff historian, dep. staff historian field programs Mil. Hist. Office US Army Tng. and Doctrine Command, Fort Montrose, Va., 1974—85, chief hist. studies and publs. Mil. Hist. Office, 1985—98. Author: American Army Doctrine for the Post-Cold War, 1996, The Army of Excellence, 1993, Out of the Riven Century, 2001. Specialist 5 U.S. Army, 1957—61. Grantee Fulbright Commn., 1963—64. Mem.: Va. Writers Club (1st v.p. 1995—96, bd. govs. 1997—2001). Republican. Lutheran. Home: 105 Lochmere Ct Yorktown VA 23693

ROMMER, JAMES ANDREW, physician; b. Newark, Aug. 22, 1952; s. Thomas Colman and Hortense (Marsh) R.; m. Linda Joan Anderson, Oct. 7, 1979; children: Elizabeth Anne, Nicole Marie. BS, Haverford Coll., 1974; MD, Cornell U., 1978. Diplomate Am. Bd. Internal Medicine. Intern N.Y. Hosp., Cornell Med. Ctr., N.Y.C., 1978-79, resident in internal medicine, 1978-81; fellow in internal medicine Johns Hopkins Med. Sch., Balt., 1981-82; pvt. practice Livingston, N.J., 1982—. Attending physician St. Barnabas Med. Ctr., Livingston, 1984—, exec. com., 1990, 94, 96, v.p. med. staff, 2001; co-chief divsn. of internal medicine, 1996-99, clin. chief dept. medicine, 1996-98; asst. clin. prof. Mt. Sinai Sch. Medicine, N.Y.C., 1998. Fellow Am. Coll. Physicians; mem. AMA, Am. Soc. Internal Medicine, Alpha Omega Alpha. Avocations: tennis, reading, jogging. Office: 349 E Northfield Rd Livingston NJ 07039-4802 E-mail: JRommer176@aol.com.

ROMNEY, CARL F. seismologist; b. Salt Lake City, June 5, 1924; m. Barbara Doughty; children: Carolyn Ann, Kim. BS in Meteorology, Calif. Inst. Tech., 1945; PhD, U. Calif., Berkeley, 1956. Seismologist U.S. Dept. Air Force, 1955-58; asst. tech. dir. Air Force Tech. Applications Center, 1958-73; dep. dir. Nuclear Monitoring Research Office, Def. Advanced Research Projects Agy., 1973-75, dir., 1975-79; dep. dir. Def. Advanced Research Projects Agy., 1979-83; dir. Ctr. Seismic Studies, 1983-91; v.p. Sci. Applications Internat. Corp., 1987—2001. Tech. adviser U.S. reps. in negotiations Test Ban Treaty; mem. U.S. del. Geneva Conf. Experts, 1958, Conf. on Discontinuance Nuclear Weapons Tests, 1959, 60; negotiations on threshold Test Ban Treaty, Moscow, 1974; mem. U.S. del. Peaceful Nuclear Explosions Treaty, Moscow, 1974-75 Contbr. articles to tech. jours. Recipient Exceptional Civilian Service award Air Force, 1959, Exceptional Civilian Service awards Dept. Def., 1964, 79; Pres.'s award for Distinguished Fed. Civilian Service, for outstanding contbns. to devel. of control system for underground nuclear tests, 1967; Presdl. Rank of Meritorious Exec., 1980; inducted in Hall of Honor, Air Intelligence Agy., 1996. Achievements include research on earthquake mechanism, seismic noise; generation, propagation, detection seismic waves from underground explosions. Home: 4105 Sulgrave Dr Alexandria VA 22309-2629 E-mail: cromney@earthlink.net.

ROMNEY, CHRISTOPHER MARTIN, vocational school educator; b. Niagara Falls, N.Y., Dec. 26, 1952; s. Edwin Clarence and Charlotte Jean (Dalton) R. BS in Edn., SUNY, Buffalo, 1985, MS in Edn., 1990; MEd in Adminstrn. and Supervision, Niagara U., 1997. Cert. coop. work study coord. Tech. tchr. Cattaraugus (N.Y.) Cen. Sch., 1985-86; vocat. edn., gen. ednl. devel. tchr. Orleans-Niagara Bd. Coop. Ednl. Svcs., Medina, N.Y., 1986-87; vocat., spl. edn. tchr. Orleans-Niagara Bd. Coop. Ednl. Svcs. East, Sanborn, 1987-89; vocat. educator Orleans-Niagara Bd. Coop. Ednl. Svcs. West, 1989-90, math., sci. tchr., 1990—. Troop leader Medina coun. Boy Scouts Am., 1987-89. Mem. Nat. Assn. Secondary Sch. Prins., Nat. Sci. Tchrs. Assn., Vocat. Indsl. Clubs Am. (co-chief, advisor ON-BOCES), Bd. Coop. Ednl. Svcs. Tchrs. Assn. (chmn. 1990-93), SUNY Buffalo Alumni Assn., Epsilon Pi Tau, Phi Delta Kappa. Avocations: fishing, boating. Office: Orleans-Niagara BOCES 3181 Saunders Settlement Rd Sanborn NY 14132-9487

ROMNEY, RICHARD BRUCE, lawyer; b. Kingston, Jamaica, Dec. 29, 1942; came to U.S., 1945, naturalized, 1956; s. Frank Oswald and Mary Ellen (Burton) R.; m. Beverly Cochran, Sept. 11, 1965 (dec. 1984); children: Richard Bruce, Jr., Stephanie Cochran; m. Lynthia H. Walker, Aug. 14, 1988; children: Alisa Dawn, Kristen Elizabeth. BA, U. Pa., 1964; JD, U. Va., 1972. Bar: N.Y. 1973, U.S. Ct. Appeals (2d cir.) 1975; registered foreign lawyer, Law Soc. Eng. and Wales. Assoc. Dewey, Ballantine, Bushby, Palmer & Wood, N.Y.C., 1972-80, ptnr., 1981—. Mem. editl. bd. U. Va. Law Rev., 1970-72. Served to lt. USN, 1964—68. Mem. ABA, N.Y. State Bar Assn., Assn. Bar City N.Y., Order of Coif. Home: 35 Deerfield Rd Chappaqua NY 10514-1604 Office: Dewey Ballantine LLP 1301 Avenue Of The Americas New York NY 10019-6022 E-mail: rromney@dbllp.com.

ROMNEY, SEYMOUR LEONARD, physician, educator; b. N.Y.C., June 8, 1917; s. Benjamin and Anne (Senter) Romney; m. Shirley Gordon, Nov. 4, 1945; children: Benjamin, Mary, Tim, Anne. AB, Johns Hopkins, 1938; MD, N.Y. U., 1942. Intern Beth Israel Hosp., Boston, 1942-43; resident Boston Lying-in Hosp., Free Hosp. for Women, Boston, 1946-51; fellow, instr. Harvard Med. Sch., 1947-51, asst. prof. obstetrics and gynecology, 1951-57; prof., chmn. dept. gynecology and obstetrics Albert Einstein Coll. Medicine, N.Y.C., 1957-72, prof., 1972-89, prof. emeritus, 1989—, dir. research gynecol. oncology, 1972—. Dir. obstetrics and gynecology Bronx Mcpl. Hosp. Ctr., N.Y.C., 1957-72; cons. WHO. Chair Soc. of Physicians for Reproductive Choice and Health; bd. dirs. NARAL, N.Y., Mass., Planned Parenthood, N.Y.C.; mem. Nat. Abortion & Reproductive Rights Action League. Served to lt. M.C. USNR, 1943-45. Mem. ACOG, AAAS, Nat. Abortion and Reproductive Rights Action League, Am. Assn. Med. Colls. (life), Am. Gynecol. and Obstet. Soc., Soc. Gynecologic Investigation, Am. Assn. Cancer Rsch., Population Assn. Am., N.Y. Obstet. Soc., N.Y. Acad. Medicine, N.Y. Acad. Sci. Home: Glenbrooke Dr White Plains NY 10605-5008 Office: Einstein Coll Morris Park Ave Bronx NY 10460-2534

ROMO, JOSÉ LEÓN, library consultant; b. Roswell, N.Mex., July 16, 1930; s. Jose L. and Barbara (Romero) R. BA in Theology and Spanish, Coll. of Santa Fe, 1974; postgrad., Colegio Sant' Anselmo, Rome, 1975-76; MA in LS, U. Denver, 1980. Monk Order of St. Benedict, Pecos, N.Mex., 1970-75, 76-78, Rome, 1975-76; reference, libr. instrn. libr. Coll. St. Benedict, St. Joseph, Minn., 1980-84, St. John's U., Collegeville, 1980-84; reference libr., instr. Laredo (Tex.) Jr. Coll.-Laredo State U., 1984-87; libr. dir. St. Vincent de Paul Sem., Boynton Beach, Fla., 1988-96; libr. cons. Benedictine Order, Portales, N.Mex., 1996—. Latin Am. Affairs scholar, U. N.Mex., 1948-50; U. Denver. Libr. Sci. fellow, 1979-80. Mem. ALA, Am. Coll. and Rsch. Librarians, Am. Theol. Libr. Assn. Office: Benedictine Order Oblate 1716 S Ave B Portales NM 88130-7327

ROMOFF, JEFFREY ALAN, health care executive; b. N.Y.C., Nov. 30, 1945; s. Richard Warren and Evelyn (Alter) Romoff; m. Vivian Irene Goodman, Aug. 25, 1966 (dec. June 1983); children: Jennifer Ann, Rebecca Lynn; m. Maxine Ketterer, July 28, 1984 (div. July 1966); m. Michele M. McKenney, Apr. 1977 (div. Dec. 2001). BS magna cum laude in Social Scis., CCNY, 1967; M.Phil. in Polit. Scis., Yale U., 1971. Teaching fellow Yale U., 1969-70, teaching assoc., 1970-71; exec. dir. Central Naugatuck Valley Mental Health Council, Waterbury, Conn., 1971-73; regional programing dir. Western Psychiat. Inst. and Clinic (U. Pitts.), 1973-74, assoc. dir. div. edn. and research, 1974-75; assoc. dir. Western Psychiat. Inst. and Clinic, 1975—; adj. asst. prof. pub. health U. Pitts., 1981—, instr. psychiatry, 1982—, assoc. v.p. health scis., 1984-86, vice chancellor health scis., 1986-92; exec. v.p. U. Pitts. Med. Ctr., 1986-92; sr. vice chancellor for Health Adminstrn. U. Pitts., 1992—; pres. UPMC Health Sys., 1992—. N.Y.C. Regents scholar CCNY, 1963-67 Mem. Am. Hosp. Assn. (governing coun. sect. for mental health and psychiat. scvs. 1986-89), Am. Psychiat. Assn. (chmn. joint com. with Am. Hosp. Assn. 1983-84), Hosp. Assn. Pa., Coun. Psychiat. Svc. Providers (exec. com. 1981-84) Jewish. Home: 3208 Fox Run Rd Allison Park PA 15101-1506 Office: UPMC Health Sys Forbes Tower 200 Lothrop St Ste 11045 Pittsburgh PA 15213-2546

ROMOSER, GEORGE KENNETH, political and social science educator; b. Kingston, N.Y., Sept. 14, 1929; s. Carl August and Alva (Becker) R.; m. Mechthild von Tresckow, Apr. 30, 1967; children: Alexandra Ada, Valerie Anna. AB, Rutgers U., 1951; A.M., U. Chgo., 1954, PhD, 1958. Research asst. Nat. Opinion Research Center, 1953; fellow Social Sci. Rsch. Coun., 1953-54; lectr. Indiana Univ., 1954—55; asst. Freiburg (Germany) U., 1955-56; instr. Ohio State U., 1957-61; from asst. prof. to assoc. prof. Conn. Coll., 1963-67; assoc. prof., prof. polit. sci. U. N.H., Durham, 1961-62, 67-96, chmn. dept., 1968-71, prof. Internat. Affairs, 1986-93, course dir. Internat. Perspective Ctr., 1986-88, dir. program on tech., society and values, 1996-2000. Fulbright prof. Faculty of Law, Mainz U., Fed. Republic Germany, 1962-63; dir. Emigre Meml. German Internship Programs, 1965—; vis. prof. Free U., Berlin, 1964, Mannheim U., 1968, 82-83, Johns Hopkins, Bologna, Italy, 1969, Munich U., 1973-74, U. Pa., 1986, Kobe U., Japan, 1988-89, Bowdoin Coll., 1990, Freiburg U., Germany, 1993-94, Fulbright Sr. Prof.; adj. prof. Mannheim U., Fed. Republic Germany, 1983—; Fulbright sr. rsch. fellow Munich U., 1974; Rockefeller fellow Aspen Inst. for Humanistic Studies, 1978-79; rsch. fellow Inst. on Far Ea. Studies, Kyungnam U., Republic of Korea, 1997; cons. Com. on Internat. Exchange of Persons, 1965-66; NEH fellow Yale U., 1993; co-founder Conf. Group on German Politics, 1968—, chmn., 1968-84, regional dir., 1984-87; founder, dir. New Eng. Workshops on German Affairs, 1980—; co-founder Pacific Coast Workshops on German Affairs, 1983-93; commuting fellow Ctr. European Studies Harvard U., 1983—; founder The Japanese Circle, 1989—. Co-author: West German Politics in the Mid-Eighties, 1985, Germany's New Politics, 1995; contbr. articles to profl. jours., books. Chmn. com. on govtl. reorgn. Democratic party N.H., 1962. Decorated Civilian Knight's Cross Fed. Republic of Germany, 1972. Mem. Am. Coun. on Germany, Internat. Polit. Sci. Assn., Am. Polit. Sci. Assn., New England Circle, Nat. Assn. Scholars, Phi Delta Theta, Pi Sigma Alpha, Delta Phi Alpha, Phi Alpha Theta. Home: 22 Worster Rd Eliot ME 03903-1113 Office: PO Box 345 Durham NH 03824 E-mail: gkr@hopper.unh.edu.

ROMULUS, RENEE MICHELLE, corporate executive; b. Newport News, Va., Feb. 14, 1963; d. Rennie Dick and Eleanor Nowitcky; m. Mark Romulus, Feb. 19, 1981 (div. Aug. 1997); children: Ashley, Laura, Shannon. BSBA in MIS, Old Dominion U., 1987; MS in Bus. Mgmt., Johns Hopkins U., 1994; Masters Cert. in Project Mgmt., George Washington U., 1998. cert. instr. and cons. in mng. orgnl. change. Cofounder, owner, operator Creative Post Techs., Inc., Virginia Beach, Va., 1986-91; sys. engr. retail NCR, Richmond, 1988-89, sect. mgr. sys. svcs. divsn. Washington, 1990-91, tech. cons. Ams. Profl. Svcs., 1991-92, change mgmt. cons. Ams. Profl. Svcs., 1992-94, dir. profl. svcs. learning Ams. Profl. Svcs. Dayton, Ohio, 1994-97, mng. ptnr. customer edn. svcs., 1997-99, dir. human rels. global integration, 1999—. Tchr. Ch. of Jesus Christ of Latter-Day Saints, Beavercreek, Ohio, 1994-97. Mem. ASTD, Soc. for Human Resources Mgmt. (sr. profl. in human resources). Mem. Lds Ch. Avocations: continuing improvement, professional self-development. Office: 1700 S Patterson Blvd Dayton OH 45479-0001 Home: 13222 Shady Ridge Ln Fairfax VA 22033-1509

ROMZEK, BARBARA S(UE), public administration educator; b. Mt. Clemens, Mich., Aug. 3, 1948; d. Lawrence John and Theresa Agnes (Kociba) R.; m. David Alan Greenamyre, May 19, 1984; children: Wallis Greenamyre Romzek, Spencer Romzek Greenamyre. BA, Oakland U., 1970; MA, Western Mich. U., 1972; PhD, U. Tex., Austin, 1979. Asst. instr. U. Tex., Austin, 1977-79; asst. prof. polit. sci. U. Kans., Lawrence, 1979-85, rsch. assoc. Ctr. for Pub. Affairs, 1981-84, assoc. prof. pub. adminstrn., 1985-95, chairperson Dept. Pub. Adminstrn., 1988-93, prof. pub. adminstrn., 1995—. Cons. pub. affairs various local, state, nat. and internat. orgns., 1980—; interim dir. human resources Bd. Pub. Utilities, Kansas City, Kans., 1986; guest scholar Brookings Instn., 1995. Co-author: American Public Administration: Politics and the Management of Expectations, 1991, New Governance for Rural America: Creating Intergovernmental Partnerships, 1996; co-editor: New Paradigms for Government: Issues for the Changing Public Service, 1994; mem. editorial bd. Pub. Adminstrn. Rev., 1987-90, Adminstrn. and Soc., 1990—, Jour. Pub. Adminstrn. Rsch. and Theory, 1990-93, Am. Jour. Polit. Sci., 1994—, Jour. Pub. Adminstrn. Edn., 1994—; contbr. articles to profl. jours. Recipient Mosher award ASPA, 1988; dissertation fellow AAUW, Washington, 1978-79. Mem. Am. Polit. Sci. Assn. (pub. adminstrn. sect. chairperson 1988-89, mem. pub. adminstrn. sect. exec. coun. 1986-91, mem. Gaus award com. 1989, nat. coun. 1992-94, chair com. organized sects. 1993—), Am. Soc. Pub. Adminstrn. (governing bd. Kans. chpt. 1983-84, Brownlow award com. 1987, Moshers award com. 1989, chair Levine award com. 1993-95, vice chair task force confs. 1994-95, Webb award com. 1996-97), Acad. Mgmt. (Levine award com. 1989, exec. com. pub. sector div. 1989-95), Nat. Assn. Schs. of Pub. Affairs and Adminstrn. (exec. coun. 1990-93, dissertation award com. 1988-89, com. chair 1989, commn. on peer rev. and accreditation 1989-92, rsch. com. 1987-90, joint task force on local govt. edn. with Internat. City Mgmt. Assn. 1987-90, task force on edn. for state and local pub. svc. 1991-93, Staats award com. 1994-95, com. chair 1994-95, nominating com. 1996, constn. com. 1996-97), Internat. City Mgmt. Assn. (task force on continuing edn. and profl. devel. 1991-93, bd. regents ICMA U. 1996—), League Kans. Mcpls. (spl. com. on future 1989), Pi Alpha Alpha (nat. coun. 1989-93). Avocations: reading, golf, travel. Office: U Kans Dept Pub Adminstrn 318 Blake Hall Lawrence KS 66045-7508

RONA, PETER ARNOLD, oceanographer, researcher, educator; b. Trenton, N.J., Aug. 17, 1934; s. Gustav G. and Elizabeth Rona; m. Donna Cook, Aug. 16, 1974; 1 child, Jessica. AB, Brown U., 1956; MS, Yale U., 1957, PhD, 1967. Exploration geologist Standard Oil Co., N.J., 1957-59; rsch. assocs. Hudson Labs, Columbia U., Dobbs Ferry, N.Y., 1960-69; sr. rsch. geophysicist NOAA, Miami, Fla., 1969-94; prof. marine geology and geophysics Inst. Marine and Coastal Scis., Rutgers U., New Brunswick, N.J., 1994—. Cons. on seafloor resources UN, N.Y.C., 1970—; trustee, advisor Internat. Oceanographic Found., Miami, 1981-95; cruise lectr. Royal Caribbean Line, 1991; organizer Atlantic Deep Sea Rsch. Ctr., 1994—, Ocean Sys. Engring. Ctr.; Geraldine R. Dodge lectr. Liberty Sci. Ctr., 1999. Author: The Central North Atlantic, 1980; editor: Seafloor Spreading Centers, 1981, Hydrothermal Processes at Seafloor Spreading Centers, 1983; contbr. over 250 articles to profl. jours. Trustee Mus. Sci., Miami, 1974—, also past chmn.; officer Dade County Cultural Affairs Coun., Miami, 1979-84. Recipient Shepard medal Soc. Econ. Paleontologists and Mineralogists, 1986, gold medal U.S. Dept. Commerce, 1987, outstanding sci. paper award NOAA, 1989, Hans Pettersson Bronze medal of the Royal Swedish Acad. of Scis., 1999. Fellow Geol. Soc. Am. (assoc. editor 1975-82), AAAS, Explorers Club; mem. Am. Geophys. Union (assoc. editor 1988-92), Am. Assn. Petroleum Geologists, Soc. Econ. Geologists, Brown U. Club, Sigma Xi. Office: Rutgers U Inst Marine & Coastal Scis 71 Dudley Rd New Brunswick NJ 08901-8521 E-mail: rona@imcs.rutgers.edu.

RONALD, PAULINE CAROL, retired art educator; b. York, Yorkshire, Eng., Feb. 28, 1945; came to U.S., 1966; d. Peter Vincent Leonard and Doris Annie Hume-Shotton; m. James Douglas Ronald, July 16, 1966 (div. 1986); 1 child, Alexia Denise; m. James Donald Wadsworth, Feb. 15, 1991 (div. July 1994). Diploma, Harrogate Sch. Art, Yorkshire, 1965, U. New Castle, Upon Tyne, 1966; MA, Ball State U., 1977. Cert. art tchr., Ind. Art tchr. Knightstown (Ind.) Schs., 1966-67, Dunkirk (Ind.) Schs., 1967-68, Richmond (Ind.) High Sch., 1968-98; ret., 1998. Part time tchr. Ind. U., Earlham Coll., Richmond 1974-84; set painter Richmond Civic Theatre. Exhibited in numerous group shows; illustrator History of Wayne County, History of Centerville, 1996. Coach State Acad. Fine Arts State Team Champions, 1988, 96, 2d Pl. for the state, 1989, 95, 97; bd. dirs., mem. permanent collection com. Richmond Art Mus. Recipient Best Set Painting awards, also numerous awards for drawing and painting, Indpls. Art Mus. Mem. NEA, Ind. State Tchrs. Assn., Art Assn. Richmond, Indpls. Mus. Art. Avocations: painting, gardening, cooking, reading, sailing. Home: PO Box 142 Hell West Bay Grand Cayman Island England

RONALD, PETER, utility executive; b. Duluth, Minn., Aug. 26, 1926; s. George W. and Florence (Jones) R.; m. Mary Locke Boyd, Nov. 25, 1950; children: Peter Webb, Pauline Morton, Samuel Herschel. BA, U. Va., 1950. With Louisville Gas & Electric Co., 1950-88, treas., 1962—, v.p., 1969-82, sr. v.p., 1982-88, dir., 1979-89. Bd. dirs., mem. exec. com. Bus. Devel. Corp. Ky., 1967-75, pres., 1971-72; bd. dirs. Louisville Community Chest, 1967-72, v.p., 1969-72; bd. dirs., v.p. Louisville Rehab. Ctr., 1964-82, pres., 1970-71; bd. overseers Louisville Country Day Sch., 1967-70; trustee Children's Hosp. Found., 1978-81, sec.-treas., 1978-81; bd. govs. Captiva (Fla.) Civic Assn., 1990-94, v.p., 1992; commr. Captiva, Fla. Erosion Prevention Dist., 1996-98. With USNR, 1945-46. Mem. Louisville Country Club, Captiva Yacht Club, Zeta Psi. Home: 4710 Indian Hills Green Louisville KY 40207-1366 also: PO Box 877 Captiva FL 33924

RONALTER, CHELSEA MARIA, artist, graphics designer; b. Manchester, N.H., Jan. 30, 1974; d. Lynn Elise Ronalter, Donald E. and Lynn Elise R.. AA in Commercial Design and Illustration, Manchester (N.H.) Cmty. Tech. Coll., 1997; AA in Interior Design, Hesser College, Manchester, NH, 2001; postgrad., Notre Dame College, Manchester, NH , 2001—. Graphic designer Notre Dame Coll., Manchester, NH, 1998—. Event planner Notre Dame Coll., Manchester, NH, 1999—2000. Mem.: Phi Theta Kappa Honor Soc. Roman Catholic. Avocations: art, literature, history. Office: Notre Dame Coll 2321 Elm Street Manchester NH 03104

RONAN, WILLIAM JOHN, management consultant; b. Buffalo, Nov. 8, 1912; s. William and Charlotte (Ramp) R.; m. Elena Vinadé, May 29, 1939; children: Monica, Diana Quasha. AB, Syracuse U., 1934; PhD, NYU, 1940, LLD, 1969; certificate, Geneva Sch. Internat. Studies, 1933. Mus. asst. Buffalo Mus. Sci., 1928-30; with Niagara-Hudson Power Co., 1931; transfer dept. N.Y.C.R.R., 1932; Penfield fellow internat. law, diplomacy and belles lettres, 1935; Univ. fellow, 1936; editor Fed. Bank Service, Prentice-Hall, Inc., 1937; instr. govt. N.Y. U., 1938, exec. sec. grad. div. for tng. in pub. services, 1938, asst. dir., 1940, asst. prof. govt., dir. grad. div. for tng. pub. service, 1940, assoc. prof. govt., 1946-47, prof., 1947, dean, grad. sch. pub. adminstrn. and social service, 1953-58; Cons. N.Y.C. Civil Service Commn., 1938; prin. rev. officer, negotiations officer U.S. Civil Service Commn., 1942; prin. div. asst. U.S. Dept. State, 1943; cons. Dept. State, 1948, Dept. Def., 1954; dir. studies N.Y. State Coordination Commn., 1951-58; project mgr. N.Y. U.-U. Ankara project, 1954-59; cons. ICA, 1955, N.Y. State Welfare Conf.; adminstrv. co-dir. Albany Grad. Program in Pub. Adminstrn.; 1st dep. city adminstr. N.Y.C., 1956-57; exec. dir. N.Y. State Temporary Commn. Constl. Conv., 1956-58; sec. to Gov. N.Y., 1959-66; chmn. interdept. com. traffic safety, commr. Port Authority N.Y. and N.J., 1967-90, vice chmn., 1972-74, chmn., 1974-77; with UTDC Corp., West Palm Beach, Fla. Trustee Crosslands Savs. Bank; chmn. bd. L.I. R.R., 1966-74; chmn. Tri-State Transp. Com., N.Y., N.J., Conn., 1961-67; chmn. interstate com. New Haven R.R., 1960-63; chmn. N.Y. Com. on L.I. R.R., 1964-65; mem. N.Y. State Commn. Interstate Coop., 1961, N.Y. State Com. Fgn. Ofcl. Visitors, 1961, N.Y. State Coordination Commn., 1960; mem. N.Y. Civil Svc. Commn., Temporary State Commn. on Constl. Conv., 1966-67; chmn. N.Y. State Met. Commuter Transp. Authority, 1965-68, Met. Transp. Authority, 1968-74, Tri-Borough Bridge and Tunnel Authority, 1968-74, N.Y.C. Transit Authority, 1968-74, Manhattan and Bronx Surface Transit Operating Authority, 1968-74; chmn. bd., pres. 3d Century Corp., 1974-94; mem. Commn. Critical Choices for Am., 1973—, acting chmn., 1975—; mem. urban transp. adv. com. U.S. Dept. Transp.; sr. adviser Rockefeller family, 1974-80; pres. Nelson Rockefeller Collection, Inc., 1977-80; trustee Power Authority of State of N.Y., 1974-77; cons. to trustees Penn Ctrl. Transp. Co.; vice chmn. bd. CCX, Inc.; sec.-treas. Sarabam Corp. N.V.; chmn., dir. UTDC (U.S.A.) Inc., 1987-88; chmn. UTDC Corp., 1989-94, Transit Svcs. Corp., 1989-94; cons. Herzog Transit Svcs., 1995-99, Dime Savs. Bank, Metal Powder Products Inc., Flomet Inc., 1997—, Internat. Mining and Metals Inc., Quadrant Mgmt. Inc., 1990—, Ohio Highspeed Rail Authority, 1991-93; chmn. N.Y. and N.J. Inland Rail Rate Com.; dir. Nat. Mgmt. Coun., 1951. Author: Money Power of States in International Law, 1940, The Board of Regents and the Commissioner, 1948, Our War Economy, 1943, (with others), articles in profl. jours.; adviser: Jour. Inst. Socio-Econ. Studies. Mem. U.S. FOA, Am. Public Health Assn.; staff relations officer N.Y.C. Bd. Edn.; Mem. Nat. Conf. Social Work, Nat. Conf. on Met. Areas, Citizens Com. on Corrections, Council on Social Work Edn.; bd. dirs. World Trade Club; adv. bd. World Trade Inst.; mem. 42d St. Redevel. Corp., chmn., 1980-94; mem. Assn. for a Better N.Y.; bd. advisers Inst. for Socioecon. Studies, 1977—; dir. Nat. Health Council, 1980-86; dep. dir. policy Nelson Rockefeller campaign for Republican presdl. nomination, 1964; mem. N.Y. State Gov.'s Com. on Shoreham Nuclear Plant, 1983-85, Nassau County Indsl. Devel. Authority, 1982-90, U.S. Dept. Transp. Com. on Washington and Capital Dist. Airports, 1985-86; bd. dirs. Ctr. Study Presidency, 1986-90, Alcoholism Council of N.Y., 1986—; trustee N.Y. Coll. Osteopathic Medicine, 1986-91; v.p. Am. Cancer Soc., Palm Beach. Served as lt. USNR, 1943-46. Mem. ASPA, NEA, Am. Polit. Sci. Assn., Am. Acad. Pub. Adminstrn., Civil Svc. Assembly of U.S. and Can., Internat. Assn. Met. Rsch. and Devel., Nat. Mcpl. League, Mcpl. Pers. Soc., Citizens Union of N.Y., Nat. Civil Svc. League, Am. Acad. Polit. and Social Sci., L.I. Assn. Commerce and Industry (dir.), Internat. Inst. Adminstrv. Scis., Am. Fgn. Law Assn., Internat. Union Pub. Transport (mgmt. com., v.p.), Am. Pub. Transit Assn. (chmn. 1974-76), Nat. Def. Transp. Assn. (v.p. for Mass transit), English Speaking Union (bd. dirs. Palm Beach), Met. Opera Club, Maidstone Club, Devon Yacht Club, Knickerbocker Club, Hemisphere Club, Harvard Club, Creek Club, Wings Club, Traffic Club, Univ. Club, Am. Club Riviera, Beach Club (Palm Beach), Everglades Club. Home: 525 S Flagler Dr West Palm Beach FL 33401-5922 also: Villa La Pointe Du Cap Ave de La Corniche 06230 Saint Jean Cap Ferrat France E-mail: wjram@aol.com.

RONAYNE, JOAN BERNICE, business strategy consultant; b. Needham, Mass., Sept. 23, 1966; d. Joseph Stephen and Joan Bernice (Mack) Ronayne. AB magna cum laude, Harvard U., 1988, MBA, 1993. Rsch. assoc. Ctr. for Strategic and Internat. Studies, Washington, 1985; analyst Union Francais de Banques-Locabail, Paris, 1986; cons. Alternative Investment Corp., Boston, 1987; cons., mgr. rsch. assocs. Monitor Co., Cambridge, Mass., 1988-91; investment banking assoc. Goldman Sachs, N.Y.C., 1992; real estate investment banking assoc. Merrill Lynch & Co., 1993-96; investment banking assoc. in tech. sect. Cowen & Co., Boston, 1996—. Cons. in field; joint participant Washington Internat. Studies Ctr. Program and Harvard Summer in Washington Program, 1985. Bus. editor Harvard Crimson, Cambridge, Mass., 1984-88. Mem. Needham Town Meeting, 1989-94; religious edn. tchr. St. Joseph's Parish, Needham, 1989-90; mem. vis. fellows com. John F. Kennedy Sch. Govt., Cambridge, 1985-87; mem. exec. bd. Harvard Crimson Key Soc., 1985-88. John Harvard scholar, 1986, 87, Kosciuszko Found. scholar, 1991; recipient Cert. of Appreciation, Archdiocese of Boston, 1990, Elizabeth Cary Agassiz award Radcliffe Coll., 1986, 87, 88. Mem. NAFE, Radcliffe Club, Harvard Club, Rotary (Goodwill Ambassador to Soviet Union 1990), Phi Beta Kappa. Avocations: travel, sports. Home: 15 Douglas Rd Needham MA 02492-4503 Office: Cowen & Co 2 International Pl Boston MA 02110-4104

RONAYNE, MICHAEL RICHARD, JR. academic dean; b. Boston, Apr. 29, 1937; s. Michael Richard and Margaret (Fahey) R.; m. Joanne Maria, Aug. 7, 1971; 1 child, Michelle Eileen. BS, Boston Coll., 1958; PhD, U. Notre Dame, 1962. Instr. chemistry Providence Coll., 1962-63, asst. prof. chemistry, 1963-64; rsch. chemist Panametrics, Inc., Waltham, Mass., 1964-66; asst. prof. chemistry Suffolk U., Boston, 1966-67, assoc. prof., 1967-70, prof., chmn. dept. chemistry, 1970-72, dean Coll. Arts and Sci., 1972—. Reaccreditation vis. team mem. New Eng. Assn. Schs. and Colls., Winchester, Mass., 1974-80, Mass. Dept. Edn., Boston, 1975; mem. acad. adv. com. Mass. Bd. Higher Edn., Boston, 1977. Contbr. articles to sci. jours., profl. publs. Mem. Winchester Sch. Com., 1983-92, chmn., 1984-85, 86-87; mem. Winchester Town Meeting, 1983-98, mem. town capital planning com., 1983-84, town coun. on youth, 1987-88, 89-90; mem. exec. com., bd. dirs. Mass. Bay Marine Studies Consortium, 1985-87; project dir. U.S. Dept. of Edn. Title III Grants. Shell Oil Corp. fellow, 1958-59, AEC fellow 1959-62; recipient Contbns. in Sci. and Edn. citation New Eng. Sch. Art and Design, Boston, 1991; named to Matignon High Sch. Alumni Achievement Hall of Fame, 1997. Mem. AAAS, Am. Chem. Soc., Am. Conf. Acad. Deans, Coun. for Liberal Learning, Am. Assn. for Higher Edn., Sigma Xi, Phi Alpha Theta, Phi Gamma Mu, Sigma Tau Delta, Omicron Delta Epsilon, Sigma Zeta, Pi Sigma Alpha. Office: Suffolk U Beacon Hill Boston MA 02114 E-mail: mronayne@suffolk.edu.

RONCAL, ROGELIO, psychiatrist; b. Bataan, Philippines, 1939; MD magna cum laude, Manila Ctrl. U., 1962. Diplomate Am. Bd. Psychiatry and Neurology, Am. Bd. Forensic Medicine. Intern French Hosp., N.Y.C., 1963; resident in psychiatry Middletown PC-N.Y. Psychiat. Inst., 1965-67; physician Horton Meml. Hosp., Middletown, N.Y.; founding dir. Middletown Alcohol Treatment Ctr. (now R. Ward Addictions, Treatment Ctr.), 1974—; pvt. practice., 1974-89; clin. dir. Middletown Psychiat. Ctr., N.Y.; attending psychiatrist Mid Hudson Psychiat. Ctr., New Hampton, 1984-95; med. dir. chemical dependency program Pius XII Youth and Family Svcs., 1995—. Instr. clin. psychiat. Columbia U.; psychiatrist N.Am. Province Order Carmelites, 1975-95; med. cons. N.Y. State Divsn. Alcoholism and Alcohol Abuse, 1981-84; pychiat. cons. McQuade Found. for Children, 1974-81; attending psychiatrist N.Y. State Dept. Corrections, 1992-95. Maj. M.C., USAR, 1983. Recipient Life Achievement award Alcoholism and Drug Abuse Coun. Orange County, N.Y., 2001, medal of honor MCU Coll. Medicine, 2000; donor M. Roncal achievement award for acad. excellence given to delinquent youth in group homes served by Pius XII Youth and Family Svcs., 1990-95. Fellow: APA, Am. Acad. Integrative Medicine, Am. Psychiat. Assn. (life); mem.: Acad. Internat. Med. Study, Manila Ctrl U. Med. Alumni Assn. (pres. N.E. chpt. 1998, pres. found. in Am. 1999), West Hudson Psychiat. Soc. (sec. 1979, pres. 1981), N.Y. State Med. Soc. (task force on smoking cessation 1997—), Am. Soc. Addiction Medicine, Am. Acad. Psyciat. Adminstrn., Am. Coll. Forensic Examiners, Orange County Med. Soc., Am. Coll. Physician Execs., Am. Med. Dirs. Assn., Med. Staff Orgn. Middletown Psychiat. Ctr., Med. Staff Orgn. Mid-Hudson Forensic Psychiat. Ctr. (pres. 1995). Office: Youth and Family Svcs 224 Main St Goshen NY 10924-2157 Fax: 914-294-1402. E-mail: Rogerfely@aol.com.

RONCO, WILMA LILLEY, chief operating officer; b. Pottstown, Pa., Oct. 9, 1948; d. William Arthur and Anna May (Lines) Lilley; m. Arthur C. Smith, Aug. 15, 1992; children: William Matthew, Daniel Christopher. BS, Boston U., 1975; MBA, Northeastern U., 1987. Cert. spl. edn. tchr. Spl. needs tchr. Ipswich (Mass.) Pub. Schs., 1975-77; 2nd grade tchr. Acton (Mass.) Pub. Schs., 1977-78; nursery sch. tchr. Community Nursery Sch., Lexington, Mass., 1979-80; dir. early intervention program Marlboro Early Intervention, 1988-2000; chief program officer Thom Child and Family Svcs., 2000—. Pres. Community Nursery Sch., Lexington, 1987-88. Chair fin. com. Follen Cmty. Ch., Lexington, 1990-95, pres. bd., 2000-01; mem. appropriations com. Town of Lexington, 1988-90. Mem. Pi Lambda Theta, Beta Gamma Sigma. Democrat. Unitarian Universalist. Avocations: skiing, world travel, scuba diving.

RONDE, JOHN HERMAN, author, translator; b. Lonneker, Overyssel, The Netherlands, July 12, 1929; s. Johannes Maria Ronde and Lamberdina Hulsschreuder. BA in Econs., Columbia U., 1973, MA in Social Studies, 1974, MPhil in Geography, 1983. Substitute tchr. N.Y.C. H.S., 1985-86, 92-93; asst. geographer U.S. Census Bur., N.Y.C., 1988-91. Author: Migration, Social Infrastructure and Urban Development in Selected German Cities, and Housing Policy and Supply in the Federal German Republic (1970-85), 1996, Urban Development and Migration in Kiel with Reference to City Center and Fringe Area Development Initiatives, 1971-84, Philosophical Interpretations of Modern Science, The Developing New World View of Man and His Activities for The Fulfillment of His Needs, An Introduction To and A Discussion of A Model of The Location of Man and His Activities, or: Geography as a Theory of Man. Mem.: AAAS, Am. Chem. Soc. (nat. affil.), N.Y. Acad. Scis. Democrat. Avocations: collecting and playing music, collecting books on history and philosophy of science. Home: 75 E 3d St New York NY 10003-9015

RONDEAU, ANN E. career officer; b. San Antonio; Diploma in History, Eisenhower Coll., 1973; Grad., Officer Candidate Sch., 1974. Commd. 2d lt. USN, 1974, advanced through grades to rear adm.; various assignments to exec. officer Fast Sealift Squad. One, New Orleans, 1987-89; asst. for polit.-mil. analysis Chief of Naval Operation (CNO), 1989-90; various to mil. asst. to Prin. Deputy Under Sec. of Def. for Policy, 1995-96; assigned to Navy's Quadrenniel Def. Rev. Support Office, 1997—; dep. chief of staff Shore Base Mgmt. N46/U.S. Pacific Fleet. Decorated Def. Superior Svc. medal, Legion of Merit, Def. meritorious Svc. medal (2 times), Navy Meritorious Svc. medal (2 times), Navy Commendation medal (3 times); recipient Groben award for Leadership Eisenhower Coll.

RONDEAU, CLEMENT ROBERT, petroleum geologist; b. Ironwood, Mich., July 6, 1928; BS, Tulane U., 1955. Geol. supr. Texaco, Inc., New Orleans, 1955-63; area mgr. Pubco Petroleum Corp., 1963-69; cons. petroleum geologist Harahan, La., 1969—; owner Natural Gas Exploration Co., 1977—. Mem. AAAS, Am. Assn. Petroleum Geologists, Soc. Exploration Geophysicists, New Orleans Geol. Soc., N.Y. Acad. Sci., The Explorers Club, Internat. Platform Assn., Phi Beta Kappa, Sigma Gamma Epsilon. Democrat. Roman Catholic. Home: 612 S Beach Blvd Bay Saint Louis MS 39520-4203 Office: Natural Gas Exploration Co 632 Strafford Dr Harahan LA 70123-5036 E-mail: gasfinder@aol.com.

RONDEAU, DORIS JEAN, entrepreneur, consultant; b. Winston-Salem, N.C., Nov. 25, 1941; d. John Delbert and Eldora Virginia (Klutz) Robinson; m. Robert Breen Corrente, Sept. 4, 1965 (div. 1970); m. Wilfrid Dolor Rondeau, June 3, 1972. Student Syracuse U., 1959-62, Fullerton Jr. Coll., 1974-75; BA in Philosophy, Calif. State U.-Fullerton, 1976, postgrad., 1976-80. Ordained to ministry The Spirit of Divine Love, 1974. Trust real estate clk. Security First Nat. Bank, Riverside, Calif., 1965-68; entertainer Talent, Inc., Hollywood, Calif., 1969-72; co-founder, dir. Spirit of Divine Love, Huntington Beach, Calif., 1974—; pub., co-founder Passing Through, Inc., Huntington Beach, 1983—; instr. Learning Activity, Anaheim, Calif., 1984—; chmn. bd., prin. D.J. Rondeau, Entrepreneur, Inc., Huntington Beach, 1984—; co-founder, dir. Spiritual Positive Attitude, Inc., Moon In Pisces, Inc., Vibrations By Rondeau, Inc., Divine Consciousness, Expressed, Inc., Huntington Beach, Doris Wilfrid Rondeau, Inc., Huntington Beach, Calif. Author, editor: A Short Introduction To The Spirit of Divine Love, 1984; writer, producer, dir. performer spiritual vignettes for NBS Radio Network, KWVE-FM, 1982-84; author: Spiritual Meditations to Uplift the Soul, 1988. Served with USAF, 1963-65. Recipient Pop Vocalist First Place award USAF Talent Show, 1964, Sigma chpt. Epsilon

Delta Chi, 1985, others. Mem. Hamel Bus. Grads., Smithsonian Assocs., Am. Mgmt. Assn., Nat. Assn. Female Execs. Fax: (714) 841-3286. Avocations: long-distance running, body fitness, arts and crafts, snorkeling, musical composition.

RONDEAU-BASSETT, CHERYL MARYANN, small business owner; b. Ortonville, Minn., Oct. 21, 1952; d. Walter T. and Martha Evelyn (King) Quade; m. Mark J. Rondeau, Oct. 21, 1971 (div. 1985); children: Christopher, Samuel, Daniel, Sally, Joseph, Patrick; m. Scott D. Bassett, Feb. 26, 1994. BA, Mount Marty Coll., Yankton, S.D., 1988; postgrad., S.D. State U., 1992. Proprietor Wilmot (S.D.) Cafe, 1972-73; from salesperson to dist. mgr. Beeline Fashions Inc., Wilmot, 1973-79; salesperson Century 21 - Accent Realty, Lebanon, Oreg., 1978-79; sales and mktg. dir. Hercules Metal, Corona, S.D., 1983-86; sales cons. Mary Kay Cosmetics, Wilmot, 1986-87; pub., editor Wilmot Enterprise, 1988-99; owner Gigglotti's Sidewalk Cafe, Wilmot, 1999—. Internat. Soc. Weekly Newspaper Editors grad. asst., dept. journalism S.D. State U., 1992-94; presenter in field; computer trainer Connecting Point Computer Ctr., Sioux Falls, 1998-99; mass. comms. dir., bus. instr. Sisseton-Wahpeton C.C., S.D., 1996-98; adj. instr. Mt. Mary Coll., Watertown, S.D., 1996—. Dir., producer: Welcome Home Jennifer, 1990; dir., creator: After the Storm, 1991; dir. Just A Little Bit Country, 1995. Organizer Citizens for Edn., Wilmot, 1986-89; organizer, 1st pres. student body orgn. Harmony Hill Ctr., Watertown, S.D., 1986-88; chmn. Wilmot Summer Recreation, 1989-91; vice chmn. Roberts County Dems., Sisseton, 1989-93; cons., advisor Roberts County Econ. Devel. Com., 1991-93; dir. Ground Hog Day in Branson, 1994; people to people citizen amb. to U.S./China Joint Conf. on Women's Issues, 1995. Recipient Community Svc. award Mount Marty Coll., 1988, scholar. Mem. NAFE, AAUW, Soc. Profl. Journalists, Nat. Fedn. Press Women, Nat. Newspaper Assn., S.D. Newspaper Assn., S.D. Press Women's Assn., Mo. Valley Adult Edn. Assn. Nat. Fedn. Ind. Bus., Am. Legion Aux., Wilmot Alumni Assn. (pres., com. chair), Wilmot Community Club, Kappa Delta Pi. Lutheran. Avocations: music, gardening, cooking, reading, horseback riding. Home: PO Box 296 Wilmot SD 57279-0296 Office: Gigglotti's PO Box 37 Wilmot SD 57279-0037 E-mail: crondeau@tnics.com.

RONDEPIERRE, EDMOND FRANCOIS, insurance executive; b. N.Y.C., Jan. 15, 1930; s. Jules Gilbert and Margaret Murray (Moore) R.; m. M. Anne Lerch, July 5, 1952; children: Aimee S., Stephen C., Peter E., Anne W. BS, U.S. Mcht. Marine Acad., 1952; JD, Temple U., 1959. Bar: D.C. 1959, Conn. 1988, U.S. Supreme Ct. 1992. Third mate Nat. Bulk Carriers, 1952-53; field rep. Ins. Co. N.Am., Phila., 1955-59, br. mgr., 1959-61, asst. sec. underwriting, 1965-67, asst. gen. counsel, 1967-70, sr. v.p., gen. counsel, 1970-76; v.p., dep. chief legal affairs INA Corp., 1976-77; v.p., gen. counsel Gen. Reins. Corp., Stamford, Conn., 1977-79, sr. v.p., corp. sec., gen. counsel, 1979-94, sr. v.p., 1994-95; pres., dir. ARIAS-US, 1994-99, dir. emeritus, 1999—. Bd. dirs. Arias-US. Lt. USN, 1953-55. Mem. ABA, Conn. Bar Assn., D.C. Bar Assn., Inter-Am. Bar Assn., Soc. CPCU, Internat. Assn. Def. Counsel (past bd. dirs.), AIDA Reins. and Ins. Arbitration Soc. (dir., pres.), Stamford Yacht Club, Wee Burn Country Club. Roman Catholic.

RONDESTVEDT, KAREN ANNE, librarian, educator; b. Ann Arbor, Mich., Mar. 30, 1948; d. Christian S. Jr. and Estelle S. Rondestvedt; m. Matias G. Aranda, Nov. 26, 1988. BA, Oberlin Coll., 1972; MA, PhD, U. Chgo., 1986. Slavic libr. asst. U. Chgo., 1972-85; Slavic bibliographer librs. U. Pitts., 1985-2000; curator for Slavic and East European collections Stanford (Calif.) U., 2001—. Editor (jour.) Slavic East European Information Resources, 2000—, (book series) Slavic & East European Librarianship, 2000—. Mem. Am. Assn. for Advancement of Slavic Studies (chair bibliography and documentation com. 1996-98), Polish Inst. Arts & Scis. of Am. Democrat. Unitarian Universalist. Avocations: cooking, travel. Office: Green Libr ASRG 3rd Flr Stanford Univ Stanford CA 94305-6004

RONDINELLI, DENNIS A(UGUST), business administration educator, researcher; b. Trenton, N.J., Mar. 30, 1943; s. August P. and Vincentia Rondinelli; m. Soonyoung Chang, Dec. 19, 1976; children: Linda, Lisa. BA, Rutgers U., 1965; PhD, Cornell U., 1969. Asst. prof. urban affairs U. Wis., Milw., 1971-73; assoc. prof. grad. sch. of mgmt. Vanderbilt U., Nashville, 1973-76; assoc. prof. planning Maxwell Sch. of Citizenship and Pub. Affairs Syracuse U., N.Y., 1976-79, prof. social scis., 1979-86; prin. scientist and sr. policy analyst Office for Internat. Programs, Research Triangle Inst., Research Triangle Park, N.C., 1986-90; Glaxo Disting. Internat. Prof. Mgmt. Kenan-Flagler Bus. Sch. Cons. World Bank, U.S. Dept. State, UN Devel. Program, Govts. of Colombia, South Korea, Can., Indonesia, Philippines, China, India, mem. com. of experts on pub. adminstrn., United Nations Econ. and Social Coun., 2002—. Author: Decentralization and Development: Policy Implementation in Developing Countries, 1983, Applied Methods of Regional Analysis: The Spatial Dimensions of Development Policy, 1985, Development Administration and U.S. Foreign Aid Policy, 1987, Urban Services in Developing Countries: Public and Private Roles in Urban Development, 1988, Planning Education Reforms in Developing Countries, 1990, Development Projects as Policy Experiments, 1993, Privatization and Economic Reform in Central Europe, 1994, Expanding Sino-American Business and Trade: China's Economic Transition, 1994, Great Policies: Strategic Innovations in Asia and the Pacific, 1995, Policies and Institutions for Managing Privatization, 1996, Market Reform in Vietnam, 1999; mem. editl. adv. bd. Policy Sciences: Politics, Adminstrn., and Change, contbr. articles to jours. Captain U.S. Army, 1965-72. Decorated Julio Lieras Order of Merit (Colombia), 1988; recipient Rural Devel. medal Republic of Vietnam, 1971, Ethnic Minorities Devel. medal, 1971, W. Bloomberg award for excellence in futures studies, 1997, Weatherspoon Disting. Rsch. award, 1997; East-West Ctr. sr. fellow, 1975-76, Pacific Basin Rsch. Ctr./Soka U. of Am./Harvard U. rsch. fellow, 1991-92. Avocations: gardening, writing nonfiction. Office: Kenan-Flagler Bus Sch U NC CB #3490 Chapel Hill NC 27599-3490 E-mail: dennis_rondinelli@unc.edu.

RONDON, EDANIA CECILIA, lawyer; b. Santiago, Cuba, Oct. 22, 1960; came to U.S., 1965; d. Edalio Marcelino and Ylia Nayda (Jacas) R.; m. Antonio Omar Maldonado, Sept. 5, 1987. BA, Syracuse U., 1982; JD, Boston U., 1985. Bar: N.J. 1985, U.S. Ct. Appeals (3d cir.) 1985. Assoc. Thomas A. Declemente, P.C., Union City, N.J., 1985-88; pub. defender City of Union City, 1985—; assoc. ins. def. James D. Butler, P.A., Jersey City, 1988-93; assoc. Edania C. Rondon, P.A., Union City, 1993—. Mem. ABA, Hudson County Bar Assn. Democrat. Roman Catholic. Home: 630 Slocum Ave Ridgefield NJ 07657-1837 Office: Edania C Rondon PA 3700 Bergenline Ave Ste 201 Union City NJ 07087-4847

RONEY, JOHN HARVEY, lawyer, consultant; b. L.A., June 12, 1932; s. Harvey and Mildred Puckett (Cargill) R.; m. Joan Ruth Allen, Dec. 27, 1954; children: Pam Roney Peterson, J. Harvey, Karen Louise Hanke, Cynthia Allen Harmon. Student, Pomona Coll., 1950-51; BA, Occidental Coll., 1954; LLB, UCLA, 1959. Bar: Calif. 1960, D.C. 1976. Assoc. O'Melveny & Myers, L.A., 1959-67, ptnr., 1967-94, of counsel, 1994—; gen. counsel Pa. Co., 1970-78, Baldwin United Corp., 1983-84; dir. Coldwell Banker & Co., 1969-81, Brentwood Savs. & Loan Assn., 1968-80. Spl. advisor Rehab. of Mut. Benefit Life Ins. Co., 1991-94; cons., advisor to Rehab. of Confederation Life Ins. Co., 1994-95; mem. policy adv. bd. Calif. Ins. Commn., 1991-95. Served to 1st lt. USMCR, 1954-56. Mem. ABA, Calif. Bar Assn. (ins. law com. 1991-95, chmn. 1993-94), L.A. County Bar Assn., D.C. Bar Assn., N.Y. Coun. Fgn. Rels., Pacific Coun. on Internat. Policy, Conf. Ins. Counsel, Calif. Club, Sky Club (N.Y.), Gainey Ranch Golf Club (Scottsdale), L.A. Country Club. Republican. Home: The Strand Hermosa Beach CA 90254 Office: 400 S Hope St Ste 1665 Los Angeles CA 90071-2801 E-mail: jroney@omm.com.

RONEY, PAUL H(ITCH), federal judge; b. Olney, Ill., Sept. 5, 1921; m. Sarah E. Eustis; children: Susan M., Paul Hitch Jr., Timothy Eustis. Student, St. Petersburg Jr. Coll., 1938—40; BS in Econs., U. Pa., 1942; LLB, Harvard U., 1948; LLD, Stetson U., 1977; LLM, U. Va., 1984. Bar: N.Y. 1949, Fla. 1950. Assoc. Root, Ballantine, Harlan, Bushby & Palmer, N.Y.C., 1948—50; ptnr. Mann, Harrison, Roney, Mann & Masterson (and predecessors), St. Petersburg, Fla., 1950—57; pvt. practice, 1957—63; ptnr. Roney & Beach, St. Petersburg, 1963—69, Roney, Ulmer, Woodworth & Jacobs, St. Petersburg, 1969—70; judge U.S. Ct. Appeals (5th cir.), 1970—81, U.S. Ct. Appeals (11th cir.), St. Petersburg, 1981—86, chief judge, 1986—89, sr. cir. judge, 1989—. Adv. com. on adminstrv. law judges U.S. CSC, 1976—77; pres. judge U.S. Fgn. Intelligence Surveillance Ct. of Rev., 1994—2001; lectr. Stetson U. Coll. of Law. With U.S. Army, 1942—46. Fellow: Am. Bar Found.; mem.: ABA (chmn. legal adv. com. Fair Trial-Free Press 1973—76, task force on cts. and public 1973—76, jud. adminstrn. divsn., chmn. appellate judges conf. 1978—79, Gavel Awards com. 1980—83), Jud. Conf. U.S. (subcom. on jud. improvements 1978—84, exec. com. 1986—89, com. to review circuit coun. conduct and disability orders 1991—93), Nat. Jud. Coll. (faculty 1974—75), St. Petersburg Bar Assn. (pres. 1964—65), Fla. Bar Assn., Am. Law Inst., Am. Judicature Soc. (bd. dirs. 1972—76). Office: US Ct Appeals Barnett Tower One Progress Plz 200 Central Ave Saint Petersburg FL 33701-3326 Fax: 727-893-3851.*

RONEY, RAYMOND G. educator, publisher; b. Phila., July 26, 1941; s. Wallace and Rosezell (Harris) R.; m. Ruth Agnes Westgaph, May 2, 1970; 1 child, Andre. BA in Polit. Sci., Cen. State U., Wilberforce, Ohio, 1963; MLS, Pratt Inst., Bklyn., 1965. Head reference dept. Howard U., Washington, 1965-66; dir. libr. and info. svcs. Nat. League of Cities/U.S. Conf. Mayors, 1967-70; dir. libr. svcs. Washington Tech. Inst., 1970-78; deputy dir. learning resources U. D.C., 1978-84; dean instrnl. svcs. El Camino Coll., Torrance, Calif., 1984—; pub. Libr. Mosaics Mag., Culver City, 1989—. Pres. Yenor, Inc., Culver City, Calif., 1989—. Author: (books) Introduction to AV for Technical Assistants, 1981, AV Tech. Primer, 1988. Pres. Shepard Park Citizens Assn., Washington, 1973-83; chmn. Friends of Libr., L.A. Southwest Coll., 1993—. Recipient Adminstrv. Excellence award INTELECOM, Pasadena, Calif., 1993, Outstanding Adminstr. of Yr. award Calif. Assn. Postsecondary Adminstrs., 1997. Mem. ALA, Coun. on Libr. Media Technology (officer, bd. dirs., Outstanding Leadership award 1994), Calif. Acad. and Rsch. Librs. (program chmn.), Learning Resources Assn. of Calif. C.C. (bd. dirs.). Avocations: music, reading, travel. Office: El Camino Coll 16007 Crenshaw Blvd Torrance CA 90506-0001

RONEY, ROBERT KENNETH, retired aerospace company executive; b. Newton, Iowa, Aug. 5, 1922; s. Louie Earl and Hazel Iona (Cure) R.; m. Alice Lorraine Mann, Oct. 6, 1951; children: Stephen P., Karen Margaret Dahl. BSEE, U. Mo., 1944; MSEE, Calif. Inst. Tech., 1947, PhD, 1950. Engr. rsch. Jet Propulsion Lab. Calif. Inst. Tech., Pasadena, 1948-50, Hughes Aircraft Co., Culver City, Calif., 1950-54, mgr. sys. analysis, 1955-59, dir. tech. R&D, 1960, assoc. mgr. space sys. divsn., 1961-68, mgr. space sys. divsn., 1968-70, v.p. asst. group exec., 1970-85, sr. v.p. corp. tech., 1986-88, ret., 1988. Mem. adv. bd. Dept. Transp. Comml. Space Transp., 1984-87, Engring. Sch. U. Kans., 1988-91. Lt. (j.g.) USNR, 1944-46, PTO. Recipient Honor award for Disting. Svc. in Engring. U. Mo.-Columbia, 1979. Fellow IEEE; mem. NAE, Caltech Assocs. Home: 1105 Georgina Ave Santa Monica CA 90402-2027

RONG, SHU, materials scientist, researcher; b. QingDao, ShanDong, China, Oct. 15, 1972; s. Yuexin Shu and Yong Li; m. Hua G Shu. Ph.D(hon.) , China Acad.Sci U. Sci.Tech.China, Hefei, 1993—98; M in Materials Sci., U. Houston - Clearlake, 2002. Rsch. engr. U. Science and Tech. China, Hefei, China, 1994—98; cons RHIC, Houston, 2001; rsch. software engr. Rock Solid Images, 2001—. Author: (Journal) several papers; contbr. articles to profl. jours. Mem.: AAAS, Am. Phys. Soc. Home: 10815 Montverde Houston TX 77099 Office: Rock Solid Images 2600 S. Gessner Ste 650 Houston TX 77099

RONG, XIUJIANG JOHN, medical physicist, researcher; m. Xiaobo Du, Mar. 26, 1988; children: Jimmy, William. MS, U. Mo., 1990, PhD, 1996. Health physicist China Inst. of Atomic Energy, Beijing, 1984—87; radiol. physicist Lab. of Indsl. Hygiene, China Ministry of Health, 1987—90; postdoctoral rsch. fellow U. of Mich. Med. Ctr., Ann Arbor, 1997—99; rsch. assoc. M.D. Anderson Cancer Ctr., Houston, 1999—2001, resident, 2001—. Reviewer: Med. Physics Jour., reviewer: Chinese Jour. Radiological Medicine and Protection. Recipient Outstanding Student award, Peking U., 1983, Advanced Sci. and Tech. award, China Ministry of Health, 1993, Cert. of Merit for Sci. Exhibit, Radiol. Soc. of N.Am., 1997, Hon. Mention Poster Award, Med. Imaging Symposium of the Internat. Soc. for Optical Engring., 1998, 2001. Mem.: Am. Assn. Physicists in Medicine. Office: M D Anderson Cancer Ctr 1515 Holcombe Blvd Box 56 Houston TX 77030 Office Fax: 713-745-0581. Business E-Mail: jrong@di.mdacc.tmc.edu.

RONG, YIMING, manufacturing engineering educator; b. Harbin, China, Sept. 3, 1958; arrived in U.S., 1985; s. Yanmo Rong and Kunyi Shen; m. Jiaoshi Dong, June 12, 1984; 1 child Zhixin (Blake). BS in Mech. Engring., Harbin U. Sci. & Tech., 1981; MS in Mfg. Engring., Tsinghua U., Beijing, 1984; MS in Indsl. Engring., U. Wis., 1987; PhD in Mech. Engring., U. Ky., 1989. Instr. Tsinghua U., 1984-85; postdoctoral rsch. assoc. U. Ky., Lexington, 1990; asst. prof. mfg. systems So. Ill. U., Carbondale, 1990-96, assoc. prof. mfg. sys., 1996-98; assoc. prof. mfg. engr. Worcester (Mass.) Poly. Inst., 1998—. Faculty rsch. assoc. Wright-Patterson AFB, Dayton, Ohio, 1995; vis. assoc. prof. U. Ill., Urbana, 1996; adj. prof. Dalian U. Tech., China, 2000—, Harbin U. Sci. & Tech., 1996—, Huazhong U. Sci. & Tech., Wuhan, China, 1998—; adj. assoc. prof. Tsinghua U., Beijing, 1994—96. Author: (book) Computer-Aided Fixture Design, 1999; editor, organizer Procs. Symposium Mfg. Engring./Computer-Aided Tooling, 1995, Procs. Symposium Mfg. Engring./Concurrent Design of Product & Mfg. Processes, 1998, Symposium Mfg. Engring./Decision Making in Design and Mfg., 1999. Pres. Chinese Friendship Assn., Lexington, 1988—89; faculty advisor Chinese Students and Scholars Assn., 2002—. Chinese Students Assn., 2002—. Recipient Rsch. Initiation award, NSF, 1993—96; grantee Rsch., USAF Office Sci. Rsch., 1995—96, NSF, 1997—, 2001, 2001—, Dept. Energy, 2001—, Pratt & Whitney Rsch. Ctr., 1996—97, Caterpillar, 1998—, Ford, 1999—, Delphi Automotive Sys., 1999—. Mem.: ASME, Chinese Mech. Engring. Soc., Am. Soc. Engring. Edn., Soc. Mfg. Engrs. Achievements include development of of first comprehensive computer-automated modular and dedicated fixture design techniques and systems; of tolerance analysis method for manufacturing processes with multiple setups; of an automated setup and fixture planning technique and system; of fixture design analysis and verification technique; exploration of flexible fixturing with phase-change materials; modeling of machingin chip formation/breaking and heat treatment processes. Office: Worcester Poly Inst Mech Engring Dept 100 Institute Rd Worcester MA 01609-2280 Fax: 508-831-5178. E-mail: rong@wpi.edu.

RONIS, MARTIN JORN JANIS, pediatrics researcher and educator; b. Huddersfield, Yorkshire, Eng., Apr. 8, 1961; came to U.S., 1985; s. Fritz and Helga (Nicks) R.; m. Lisa Ricketson, May 16, 1992. BA in Natural Scis., Cambridge U., Eng., 1982; PhD in Biochemistry and Physiology, Reading (Eng.) U., 1985. Teaching asst., instr. biochemistry Reading U., 1982-85; postdoctoral rsch. assoc. toxicology program N.C. State U., Raleigh, 1985-87; vis. rsch. assoc. dept. physiol. chemistry Karolinska Inst., Stockholm, 1987-89; instr. dept. pediatrics U. Ark. Med. Scis., Little Rock, 1989-90, asst. prof., 1990-96, tenured assoc. prof. Ark. Children's Hosp. Rsch. Inst., 1996—2002, prof., 2002—. Ad hoc reviewer sea grant instl. program Hancock Inst. Marine Studies, U. So. Calif., 1990, La. Bd. Regents, LEQSF Grant Program, 1992. Ad hoc reviewer Alcohol: Clin. and Exptl. Rsch., Gastroenterology, others; contbr. articles to profl. jours. Grantee Nat. Inst. Alcohol Abuse and Alcoholism, 1990—, Nat. Inst. Drug Abuse, 1992-95, Nat. Inst. Environ. Health Sci., 1994-99, EPA, 1995-96, USDA, 1995—. Mem. Internat. Soc. Study of Xenobiotics, Soc. Toxicology, Soc. for Study of Reproduction, Acad. Sci., Sigma Xi. Democrat. Avocations: bicycling, reading, brewing. Home: 7214 Apache Rd Little Rock AR 72205-5002 Office: U Ark Med Scis Dept Pediatrics Slot 512-20B Little Rock AR 72205

RONN, AVIGDOR MEIR, chemical physics educator, consultant, researcher; b. Tel Aviv, Nov. 17, 1938; came to U.S., 1959; m. Linda Ann Tenney, Aug. 25, 1963; children: David A., Karin J. BS in Chemistry, U. Calif., Berkeley, 1963; AM in Phys. Chemistry, Harvard U., 1964, PhD in Phys. Chemistry, 1966. Rsch. asst. Nat. Bur. Standards, 1966-68; from asst. prof. to assoc. prof. chemistry Poly. Inst. Bklyn., 1968-73; prof. chemistry Bklyn. Coll. CUNY, 1973-2000, Broeklundian prof. Bklyn. Coll., 1987-90, dir. Laser Inst., 1987—; sr. rsch. fellow Long Island Jewish Med. ctr, 1992—, Albert Enstein Med. Coll., 1992—; pres. PhoDyne Technologies, Inc., Great Neck, N.Y., 1995—. Exec. officer PhD program in chemistry CUNY, Manhattan, 1984-90, exec. dir. Applied Sci. Inst., Bklyn., 1987-90; vis. prof. U. Tel Aviv, 1971-72; Fulbright Sr. scholar U. Sao Paulo, Brazil, 1983-84; v.p., gen. mgr. Lic Industries, Inc., Suffern, N.Y., 1979-80. Author: (with others) Advances in Chemical Physics, 1980, Techniques of Chemistry, 1981. Pres. Towne House 27, Inc., Great Neck, 1984—. 1st sgt. Israeli Army, 1956-58. Alfred P. Sloan Found. fellow, 1971-73, OAS fellow, U. Sao Paulo, Brazil, 1973. Mem. Israel Chem. Soc., Am. Phys. Soc., Am. Chem. Soc., SPIE, Am. Assn. Laser Medical & Surgery, Phi Beta Kapp. Achievements include 6 patents for Laser Initiated Chain Reactions for Producing a Sintered Product, Method for Forming Patterns on Substrate or Support, Production of Chain Reaction by Laser Chemistry, Preparation of Metal Containing Polymeric Materials via Laser Chemistry, Method of Molecular Species Alteration by Nonresonant Laser Induced Dielectric Breakdown, Plasma Assay Spectrometer; 2 patents on method for assaying photosentizing drug in whole blood; 1 patent on assaying photosentizing drug in plasma; 1 patent on optical cable assembly; 1 patent on assaying photosensitizing drug in tissue. Address: LI Jewish Med Ctr New Hyde Park NY 10040 E-mail: aronn@lij.edu.

RONNING, CHARLOTTE JEAN, foreign language educator; b. Billings, Mont., Dec. 19, 1953; d. Charles and Ruth Alice (Johnson) R. BA, Mont. State U., Billings, 1978, BS, 1980; MA, U. Colo., 1995. Nat. cert. counselor. Sales/office mgr. Clint Faubions, Denver, 1980-81; office mgr. Virginia Horn Travel, 1981-82; sales, instr. R.B. Bonar & Assocs., 1982-86; fgn. lang. educator Cherry Creek Schs., 1987—. Student Fgn. Study League, Europe, 1970; Dale Carnegie course instr., N.Y.C., 1982-87; sponsor Cherry Creek in Costa Rica, 1988. Mem. Fgn. Lang. Proficiency Com., Denver, 1993—; v.p. Bromley Commons, Denver, 1994—, U. Madrid, 1997. Mem. ACA, Colo. Counseling Assn., Chi Sigma Iota, Alpha Lambda Delta, Alpha Mu Gamma, Kappa Alpha Theta. Republican. Presbyterian. Avocations: piano, golf, skiing. Home: 350 Detroit St Apt 207 Denver CO 80206-4361

RONNING, DEBRA DIANE, music educator; b. DuBois, Pa., Sept. 6, 1950; d. Orville Melford and Isabelle E. Ronning; m. Frederick F. Ritsch, Dec. 21, 1991; 1 child, Anne Ronning Ritsch. BS, Indiana U. of Pa., 1972, MA, 1975. Nat. cert. tchr. of music. Adj. faculty mem., dir. preparatory divsn. Elizabethtown (Pa.) Coll., 1985-88, lectr. in music, dir. preparatory divsn., 1988—. Artist in residence Elizabethtown Coll., 1983-85. Bd. dirs. Elizabethtown Child Care Ctr., 1996-99. Mem. Nat. Guild Piano Tchrs. (judge), Fedn. Musicians, Pa. Music Tchrs. Assn. (chair for jr. high competitions 1993-95, v.p. 1995-97, pres. 1997—), Music Tchrs. Nat. Assn. (pres.-elect Eastern divsn. 2000—). Office: Elizabethtown Coll FAPA Elizabethtown PA 17022

RONNINGSTAM, ELSA FRIDEBORG, psychologist, educator; b. Boden, Sweden, Oct. 17, 1950; came to U.S., 1985; d. Yngve Fritjof and Frideborg (Rönnberg) Karlsson. BA, U. Umeå, Sweden, 1971; MSc, U. Stockholm, 1976, PhD, 1988. Clin. psychologist dept. psychiatry Huddinge Hosp., Stockholm, 1980-85, 87-88; rsch. fellow in clin. psychology, psychosocial rsch. program McLean Hosp., Harvard Med. Sch., Belmont, Mass., 1985-87, rsch. and clin. fellow, 1989-90; instr. in psychology Harvard Med. Sch., 1990-95, asst. prof. psychology, 1996—; asst. psychologist McLean Hosp., 1990-95, assoc. psychologist, 1996—. Author: (in Swedish) Bereavement in Childhood, 1978; editor: Disorders of Narcissism-Diagnostic Clinical and Empirical Implication, 1997. Swedish Am. Found. scholar, 1989-91. Office: McLean Hosp Psychol Rsch Pr 115 Mill St Belmont MA 02478-1041 E-mail: ronningstam@email.com.

RONSHAGEN, JUDITH P. pharmacist; b. Manchester, N.H. d. Romeo M. and Eleanor M. (Dionne) Patrick; m. Eugene O. Ronshagen, May 10, 1986. BS in Pharmacy, Mass. Coll. Pharmacy, 1970. Staff pharmacist Notre Dame Hosp., Manchester, N.H., 1970-71, Gosselin Pharmacy, Manchester, 1971-72, Sacred Heart Hosp., Manchester, 1972-77, Elliot Hosp., Manchester, 1977-82, asst. dir. pharmacy, 1982-95, pharmacy sys. coord., 1995—. Staff pharmacist Howes Pharmacy, Goffstown, N.H., 1976—; mem. N. H. Bd. Pharmacy, Concord, 1983-93, sec., 1989-92, v.p., 1992-93; mem. Drug Utilization Bd., 1993-96; trustee Mass. Coll. Pharmacy and Allied Health Scis., Boston, 1992—; adv. bd. mem. Marion Merrell Dow, Cin., 1988, APHA's Voice of Pharmacy, Washington, 1993-95, Roche Pharmaceutical, Nutley, N.J., 1994-96. Recipient Alumni Achievement award Mass. Coll. Pharmacy and Allied Health Scis., Boston, 1983; named Pharmacist of the Yr., N.H. Pharmacists Assn., Concord, 1985. Mem. Am. Soc. Healthcare Pharmacists (bd. dirs. 1983-86), Bd. Pharmaceutical Specialties (bd. mem. 1995-2000), New Eng. Coun. Hosp. Pharmacists (bd. mem., pres. 1978, 2000, Program Chair of Yr. 1981, 83, 89, 93), N.H. Soc. Hosp. Pharmacists (sec.-treas. 1974-76, pres. 1976-78, Pharmacist of the Yr. 1981). Avocations: traveling, reading, golf. Home: 15 Autumn Ln Londonderry NH 03053-2958 Office: Elliot Hosp 1 Elliot Way Manchester NH 03103-3599

RONSON, BONNIE WHALEY, literature educator; b. Tampa, Fla. d. Terrell Allen and Audie Lou Whaley; 1 child, Tyler Beeby. BA, Mercer U., 1975; MEd, U. Tampa, 1980; DPA, Nova U., 1989. Prof. English, Hillsborough C.C., Tampa, 1988—. Author: (books) Lessons All Around You, 1998, More Lessons All Around You, 1999. Home: 3143 Lakestone Dr Tampa FL 33618 Office: Hillsborough C C Ybor City Campus Tampa FL 33610 Home Fax: 813-908-5791. E-mail: drronson@gte.net.

RONSON, RAOUL R. publishing executive; b. Fiume, Italy, Mar. 22, 1931; came to U.S., 1951; s. Mirko and Margaret (Fischer) Ruzicka; m. Susan Kohn, July 22, 1962; 1 child, Paul. DBA, U. Rome, 1950; MA, New Sch Social Research, 1957; postgrad., Inst. for Advanced Internat. Studies, U. Miami, 1967-68, NYU, 1974. Fgn. corr., freelance writer, 1953-59; treas. Daron Enterprises, Inc., 1959-63; pres. Seesaw Music Corp., N.Y.C., 1963—, Okra Music Corp., N.Y.C., 1963-77, Ulsyra Prodn. Corp., N.Y.C., 1963—. Pres. The Composers Press, 1972-76; acad. lectr. Am., Australian, New Zealand univs. and conservatories; vis. lectr. Youngstown (Ohio) State U., 1985—, Finch Coll., N.Y.C., Eastman Sch. Music, Rochester, N.Y., Wake Forest U., Winston-Salem, N.C. Producer documentary films, 1959—, classical music recs., 1963—, The Dana Recording Project (nominated 2 Grammy awards). Mem. Emergency Control Bd. Office of Mayor, N.Y.C., 1973-82, Fed. Emergency Mgmt. Agy., Washington, 1982-84; rsch. analyst Office of the Sec. Def., Res. Affairs, The Pentagon, Washington, 1984-91; liaison officer U.S. Mil. Acad., West Point, N.Y., 1988-97. With M.I., AUS, 1952-54, USAR, 1955-91, ret. 1991. Decorated Legion of Merit, Def. Superior Svc. medal, Def. Meritorious Svc. medal, Army Meritorious Svc. medal, Army Commendation medal, Def. Identification badge Office Sec., Korean Svc. medal, UN Svc. medal, medal from Korean pres.; recipient numerous other awards and decorations; Grammy award nominee for Classical Prodr. of the Yr., 1993. Mem. Am. Polit. Sci. Assn., Am. Acad. Polit. and Social Sci., Internat. Platform Assn., Civil Affairs Assn., Sibelius Soc. (bd. dirs. 1978-85), Nat. Acad. Rec. Arts and Scis., Masons. Home: 825 W End Ave New York NY 10025-5349 Office: 2067 Broadway New York NY 10023-2806

RONSON, SUSAN, administrative assistant; b. N.Y.C., June 30, 1940; d. Solomon Blondheim and Harriet (Lustbader) Kohn; m. Raoul Ronson, July 22, 1962; 1 child, Paul. Student, Miami U., Oxford, Ohio, 1958-60; cert., Katharine Gibbs, N.Y.C., 1960-61, Emergency Mgmt. Inst., Emmitsburg, Md., 1983, Nat. Def. U., Washington, 1988. Sec. Doubleday & Co., N.Y.C., 1961-65; freelance editor, 1965-73; exec. sec. Howard Needles Tammen & Bergendoff, 1974-87; exec. asst., facilities adminstr. The Capital Group Cos., Inc., 1987—; exec. asst., dir. Seesaw Music Corp., 1988—. Adminstrv. officer, Fed. Emergency Mgmt. Agy., N.Y.C. Mem. Nat. Def. Exec. Res., Assn. of Nat. Def. Exec. Reserve (exec. v.p. and dir. N.Y. met. chpt. 1988-97). Republican. Avocations: ballet, reading, music, cooking. Home: 825 W End Ave New York NY 10025-5349 Office: The Capital Group Cos Inc 630 5th Ave Fl 36 New York NY 10111-0100

RONY, PETER R. chemical engineering educator; b. Paris, June 29, 1939; came to U.S., 1940; s. George Jury and Rosette R.; m. Myriam Eliette Paiz, Dec. 23, 1961; children— Karen, Karl, Paul, Glenn, Marianne. B.S., Calif. Inst. Tech., 1960; Ph.D., U. Calif.-Berkeley, 1965. Assoc. prof. chem. engring. Va. Poly. Inst., Blacksburg, 1971-75, prof., 1975— ; trustee CACHE, Inc., Austin, Tex. Author: 8080A Microcomputer Programming and Interfacing, 1975, also 8 other books. recipient Faculty Service award Nat. Univ. Extension Assn., 1978; Delos/Tektronix award for Excellence in Lab. Instrn., Am. Soc. Engring. Educators, 1984; Dreyfus Found. tchr.-scholar, 1973. Mem. IEEE (sr.; editor-in-chief IEEE Micro 1983-85), Am. Chem. Soc., Am. Inst. Chem. Engrs. Avocations: swimming; microcomputers. Home: 1501 Highland Cir Blacksburg VA 24060-5668

RONZETTI, THOMAS A. TUCKER, lawyer, law educator; b. Ft. Meade, Md., Oct. 15, 1964; s. Thomas Anthony and Anna Susan (Arcieri) R.; m. Nancy Ellen Dennebaum, June 23, 1990; children: Michael Hogan, Cara Grace, Emma Faith. BA in Econs., Duke U., 1987; JD, U. Miami, 1992. Bar: Fla. 1992, U.S. Dist. Ct. (so. dist.) Fla. 1993, U.S. Ct. Appeals (11th cir.) 1996, U.S. Supreme Ct. 1998. Law clk. Judge Edward B. Davis, Miami, Fla., 1992-93; assoc. Valdez-Fauli, Cobb, et al, 1993-94; asst. county atty. Dade County Atty., 1994—2001; of counsel Kozyak, Tropin & Throckmorton, P.A., 2001—. Instr. U. Miami Sch. Law, 1992—. Editor-in-chief: U. Miami Law Rev., 1991—92. Mem. Order of the Coif. Avocations: guitar, boating, fishing. Office: Kozyak Tropin & Throckmorton PA 200 S Biscayne Blvd Ste 2800 Miami FL 33131-

RONZHIN, ANATOLY IVANOVICH, physicist, engineer; b. Moscow, July 1, 1945; s. Ivan Pavlovich Ronzhin and Lidia Konstantinovna Ronzhina; m. Nina Dmitrievna Tikhomirova, May 16, 1969; children: Dmitriy, Michael. MS in Physics, MEPHI, Moscow, 1968; PhD, JINR, Dubna, Russia, 1978, IHEP, Protvino, Russia, 1990. Rschr. JINR, Dubna, 1968—70, sr. scientist, 1970—74; leading scientist IHEP, Protvino, 1974—93; engring. physicist Fermilab, Batavia, Ill., 1993—. Contbr. articles to profl. jours.; inventor in field. Avocations: swimming, skiing, travel. Home: 2529 Wydown Ln Aurora IL 60504 Office: Fermilab Batavia IL 60510

ROOBOL, NORMAN RICHARD, chemist, educator; b. Grand Rapids, Mich., Aug. 19, 1934; s. Pleune and Henrietta (Sietsema) Roobol; m. Joan Lois Ezinga, Aug. 15, 1957; children: Kerri Linda, Michael Eric, Victoria May, Sara Elizabeth Angelique. BS, Calvin Coll., 1958; PhD in Organic Chemistry, Mich. State U., 1962. Rsch. chemist Shell Oil Co., Emeryville, Calif., 1962-65; asst. prof. chemistry GMI Engring. Inst., Flint, Mich., 1965-68, assoc. prof., asst. head dept. math., sci., 1968-72, prof., 1972-89; pres. NR Painting Cons. Co., Peachtree City, Ga., 1989—. Rhodes prof., Russelsheim, Germany, 1980—81; tchr. short courses paint; cons. coatings application processes; spkr. indsl. painting methods; painting advisor, instr. Outboard Marine Corp., 1986—2001, Bombardier Can., 1988—, Compaq-Asia, Singapore, 1991—, Harley-Davidson, 1992—, Metagal Comercie e Industri, San Paulo, Brazil, 1996—, Decometal S.A., Panama City, Panama, 1997—, J. R. McDermott Corp., Jebel Ali, 2000—; adj. prof. Kent (Ohio) State U., 1986—, Okla. State U., 1994—, U. Wis., 1998. Author: (book) Painting Problems Solved, 1987, Industrial Paint and Powder Principles and Practices, 1991, Industrial Paint and Powder Principles and Practices, 3d edit., 2002; monthly columnist, tech. editor: Indsl. Paint and Powder Jour.; contbr. articles to profl. jours. Sr. advisor Flint Sci. Fair. With Signal Corps U.S. Army, 1954—56. Fellow Johnson, 1957—58, NSF, 1960—62, Dow, 1961—62. Fellow: Am. Inst. Chemists; mem.: AAUP, Assn. Finishings Proc. (v.p. profl. devel. coun.), Soc. Mfg. Engrs. (bd. dirs.), Am. Sci. Affiliation, Pi Tau Sigma (chpt. sr. adviser 1979—86), Alpha Tau Omega, Sigma Xi. Achievements include patents in field. Home and Office: Powder Coating & Painting 507 Haddington Ln Peachtree City GA 30269-3340 E-mail: norm@roobol.net.

ROOD, DAVID S. linguistics educator; b. Albany, N.Y., Sept. 14, 1940; s. J. Henry and Pearl B. (Stanley) R.; m. Juliette A. Victor; 1 child, Jennifer. AB, Cornell U., 1963; MA, U. Calif., Berkeley, 1965; PhD, U. Calif., 1969. Instr. U. Colo., Boulder, 1967-69, asst. prof., 1969-77, assoc. prof., 1977-82, prof., 1982—; vis. prof. U. Köln, Germany, 1998-99. Author: Wichita Grammar, 1975, Siouan Languages Archive, 1982; (with others) Beginning Lakhota, 1976; editor Internat. Jour. of Am. Linguistics, 1981-2002; contbr. numerous articles to profl. jours. NSF grantee, 1972-96, NEH grantee, 1972-96, Volkswagen Stiftung grantee, 2000—. Mem. Linguistic Soc. Am., Soc. for Study Indigenous Langs. Am., Soc. for Linguistic Anthropology, Tchrs. of English to Speakers Other Langs. Office: U Colo Dept Linguistics 295 UCB Boulder CO 80309-0295 E-mail: rood@colorado.edu.

ROOF, BETTY SAMS, internist; b. Columbia, S.C., Apr. 13, 1926; d. Grover Melton Saunders and Lucinda Wood (Sams) R.; m. Herman Hugh Fudenberg (div.); children: Drew Douglas, Brooks Roberts, David Melton, Hugh Haskell. BS, U. S.C., Columbia, 1944; MD, Duke U., 1949. Diplomate am. Bd. Internal Medicine, Am. Bd. Endocrinology and Metabolism. Vol. vis. investigator Rockefeller Inst., N.Y.C., 1949-50; intern Presbyn. Hosp., 1950-51, asst. resident, 1951-53, asst. physician, 1953-55; attending physiican Francis Delafield Hosp., 1954-55; clin. and rsch. fellow dept. medicine Mass. Gen. Hosp., Boston, 1955-56; rsch. fellow Harvard U., 1955-56; rsch. fellow dept. pathology Mass. Gen. Hosp., 1957-58; rsch. assoc. dept. microbiology and pathology Rockefeller Inst., 1956-57, 58-59; asst. rsch. physician Cancer Rsch. Inst., U. Calif., San Francisco, 1962-63, assoc. rsch. physician, 1967-71, lectr. medicine, 1971-74, clin. prof., 1974; assoc. prof. medicine Med. U. S.C., Charleston, 1974-80, prof., 1980-2000, prof. emeritus, 2000. Asst. dean, Med. U. S.C., Charleston, 1989-2000. Contbr. articles to profl. jours. Mem. Library Bd., Mill Valley, Calif., 1965-68; mem. Tamaplais Nursery Sch. Bd., Mill Valley, 1968. Am. Cancer Soc. trainee, 1953-55; grantee Am. Cancer Soc., USPHS, Koebig Trust Fund; USPHS fellow, 1949-50. Mem. Am. Assn. Cancer Rsch., Am. Diabetes Assn. (Woman of Valor award 1995, 99), Western Soc. Clin. Rsch., Endocrine Soc., Internat. Endocrine Soc., Am. Soc. for Bone and Mineral Rsch., Charlestown Med. Soc., ACP, Am. Fedn. Clin. Rsch., So. Soc. Clin. Investigation, Waring Libr. Soc., Soc. for Destitute Widows and Children of Dec. Physicians, Pilot Club of Charleston (S.C. (v.p. 1988-89, pres. 1990-91), Phi Beta Kappa, Alpha Omega Alpha. Home: 675 Ft Sumter Dr Charleston SC 29412-4333 Office: Med U SC 96 Jonathan Lucas St Ste 323 Charleston SC 29425-8900

ROOF, HOLLY LOUGHLIN, artist, educator; b. Grand Rapids, Mich., Nov. 28, 1960; d. Richard Ellis and Sandra (Braudy) Loughlin; m. James Roger Roof Jr., Aug. 26, 1986; children: Ben, Bethany. BA, Albion Coll., 1982; MBA, U. Denver, 1990. Ski instr. Vail Resorts, Colo., 1983-92; owner Alpine Gardener, Avon, 1987-93; adj. instr. Colo. Mountain Coll., Eagle, 1993—; artist freelance, 1983—. Computer cons. Eagle, Colo., 1992—, bus. cons., 1990—. Artist: (paintings) Mother Earth, 1997, The Hockey Player, 1993 (hon. mention 1995), (woodcut prints) Well Suited, 1990 (1st prize 1991), Hip Deep, 1997 (res. champion 1997). Recipient Grand Champion award Eagle County Fair, 1996, hon. mention awards Glenwood Springs Art Guild, Colo., 1993, 94, Purchase prize, 1994, 96, 98. Avocations: skiing, golf, gardening.

ROOF, MICHAEL KITCHING, demographer, researcher; b. Lexington County, S.C., Dec. 18, 1921; s. Michael Lowman and Eunice Ernestine (Kitching) R.; m. July 24, 1949 (div. Sept. 1970); children: Michael Kitching Jr., Melanie June Roof Brown, Brian Eugene; m. Kristina Marietta Medrano, Dec. 18, 1976. Student, Am. U., 1954-57; BA, George Washington U., 1956; postgrad., U.S. Dept. Agr. Grad. Sch., 1979-83. Manpower splst. Office of Prodn. Mgmt. and War Prodn. Bd., Washington, 1941-46; labor editor Bur. Nat. Affairs, Inc., 1947-48; demographer rsch. divsn. ref. svc. The Libr. of Congress, 1949-64; sr. demographer fgn. manpower rsch. office U.S. Bur. Census, Suitland, Md., 1958-59, expert demographic cons. fgn. manpower rsch. office, 1960-61, demographer, statistician Ctr. Internat. Studies Washington, 1977-89; ret., 1989; cons. to the demography as UN adviser various orgns., So. Calif., 1965-70, 72-76. Cons.; UN employee Govt. Iran, Iranian Ministry Health, UN specialist demography and evaluation Iranian family planning program; developed projects in field; tchr. in field. Author: (monograph) Angelenos on the Move: 1960-74, 1975, (mongraph) Detailed Statistics on the Population of Israel, 1950-84, with Projections to 2010, 1984, (monograph) Jordan Population and Manpower Estimates and Projections: 1979 to 2010, 1987; co-author: (monograph) Detailed Statistics on the Population of Turkey, 1950-82, with Projections to 2000, 1982, (monograph) Palestinian Population: 1950-84, 1985, The Roof (Rueff, Ruff) Family and Kinfolk of Central South Carolina: 1748-1999, 1999; contbr. numerous articles to profl. jours., chpts. to books. Mem. Population Assn. Am., Internat. Union Scientific Study of Population. Democrat. Lutheran. Avocations: geneaolgy, aerobic activities, swimming, softball. Home: 306 E Custis Ave Alexandria VA 22301-1202

ROOK, JUDITH RAWIE, television producer, writer; b. Long Beach, Calif., Jan. 25, 1942; d. Wilmer Ernest and Margaret Jane (Towle) Rawie; children: Daryn Simons, Dawn Reinard; m. Tim Rook. BBA, Loyola-Marymount Univ., 1964; BA in Visual Arts.Comms., U. Calif., San Diego, 1978. Statis. analyst Smith, Kline Internat., 1964-66; syndicated columnist Environ. Forum, 1971-74; prodr./writer PBS series Focus, 1980, Achieving, 1982; dir. IABC, San Francisco, 1982; dir. programming Westinghouse Cable, 1983-85; dir. devel. Embassy/Nelson Home Entertainment, 1985-87; ptnr. Real Magic, 1987-89; prodr., writer, ptnr. BrantHol Prodns., 1990-93; prodr., writer Close Encounters, 1990-93, Christmas Comes to Silverton, 1990-93, R2 Group One Creative Moment, 1994-95, Close-Up: The 60s, A Film and Art Festival, 1996-97; assoc. prodr. Fox Latin Am. Billboard Music Awards, 1998-2000. Mem. adv. bd. U. Calif. Irvine Screenwriting/Film Prodn., 1996—; mem. adv. bd. Univ. Art Mus., 1996-97, co-pres. contemporary coun., 1996-97; mem. exec. bd. Long Beach Mus. Art, 1995-96; bd. dirs. Counseling 4 Kids, 1998—, bd. sec., 2001—. Nominee Emmy award; recipient You Make the Difference award; grantee, Theatre 40 Playwright's Forum. Mem. Am. Film Inst., Women in Film (dir. seminars on women in film festivals), IFP West. Democrat. Episcopalian. E-mail: tirook@earthlink.net.

ROOK, VICKI LYNN, safety specialist; b. Denton, Tex., Oct. 14, 1954; d. Lonzo Lester and Myrtle Jodelle (Williams) Roberts; m. Rickey Hugh Rook, Jan. 27, 1979; children: Brandon Nicholas, Katy Lynn. Student, Richland Jr. Coll., Dallas, 1974-75. Safety supr. United Parcel Svc., Dallas, 1975-81; pers., safety adminstr. Boeing Airport Equipment, Carrollton, Tex., 1981-83; safety rep. Loral Vought Sys. Corp., Grand Prairie, 1983-95; sr. safety specialist Fed. Express Corp., Dallas, 1995—. Mem. workers comp claims mgmt. various cos., Dallas, 1975—; mgr. union contract negotiation Boeing Airport Equipment, Dallas, 1983; com. mem. mgmt. safety program tng. Fed. Express, Memphis, 1997—. Tchr. Sunday sch. Walnut Ridge Bapt. Ch., Mansfield, Tex., 1997—, 1st Bapt. Ch., Grand Prairie, 1980-82, counselor ch. camp, 1980-82; vol. ednl. TV Loral Vought Sys., Dallas, 1993. Named Safety Specialist of Yr. Fed. Express, 1997. Mem. Am. Soc. Safety Engineers, Nat. Safety Coun. Republican. Office: Fed Express Corp 1220 River Bend Dr Dallas TX 75247-4918

ROOKE, ALLEN DRISCOLL , JR. civil engineer, consultant; b. San Antonio, Oct. 5, 1924; s. Allen Driscoll and Jean Edna (Lackner) R.; m. Betty Ruth Whitson, Oct. 17, 1949; children: Victoria Lynn Lewis, Cornelia Ruth. BSCE, Tex. A&M U., 1957; MSCE, Miss. State U., 1980. Registered profl. engr., Miss. Enlisted U.S. Army, 1942, advanced through grades to brig. gen., ret., 1984; rsch. civil engr. U.S. Army Corps Engrs., Vicksburg, Miss., 1958-83; ptnr. F.B. Rooke & Sons, Woodsboro, Tex., 1964—; sr. engr. Sci & Tech. Corp., Vicksburg, Miss., 1984-95. Bd. dirs. First Nat. Bank, Woodsboro, 1985—. Author/co-author numerous tech. publs. Mem. Res. Officers Assn. U.S. (dept. pres. 1980-82, svc. award 1980, 84), Assn. of U.S. Army, Ret. Officer's Assn. (chpt. v.p. 1985-86), Soc. Am. Mil. Engrs. (post v.p. 1979). Clubs: Army and Navy Vicksburg (pres. 1980, 82). Episcopalian. Avocation: chess. Home: PO Box 732 Woodsboro TX 78393-0732 E-mail: adrooke@mycidco.com.

ROOKE, DAVID LEE, retired chemical company executive; b. San Antonio, May 2, 1923; s. Henry Levi, Jr. and Annie (Davidson) R.; m. Esthermae Litherland, June 2, 1945; children— Eugene, Mark, Paul, Bruce. BS in Chem. Engring, Rice Inst., Houston, 1944; postgrad., U. Houston. With Dow Chem., Midland, Mich., 1946-88, v.p. ops., 1977-78; pres. Dow U.S.A., 1978-82; v.p. Dow Chem. Corp., 1978-82, exec. v.p., 1982-83, sr. v.p., 1983-86, sr. cons., 1986-88, ret., 1988, also bd. dirs. Bd. dirs. Dow Corning Corp., James Avery Craftsman, Inc. Nat. exec. bd. Boy Scouts Am., 1979-86; bd. dirs. Meth. Mission Home, San Antonio. Served with USNR, 1944-46. Mem. AICE, United Meth. Reporter Found. (Dallas). Methodist.

ROOKS, CHARLES S. foundation administrator; b. Whiteville, N.C., June 29, 1937; BA in English, Wake Forest Coll., 1959; Rockefeller Brothers fellow, Harvard U., 1959-60; MA in Polit. Sci., Duke U., 1964, PhD in Polit. Sci., 1968. Rsch. assoc. Voter Edn. Project, Atlanta, 1969-70, dir. tech. assistance programs, 1970-71, dep. dir., 1971-72; exec. dir. Southeastern Coun. of Founds., 1972-78; dir. mem. svcs. Coun. on Founds., Washington, 1979-80, v.p., 1981-82, acting CEO, 1981-82; exec. dir. Meyer Meml. Trust, Portland, Oreg., 1982—. Instr. polit. sci. Duke U., Durham, N.C., 1963, 65-67; asst. prof. of govt. Lake Forest Coll., Ill., 1967-69; asst. prof. polit. sci. Clark Coll., Atlanta, 1969-71; bd. dirs. Pacific Northwest Grantmakers Forum, Forum of Regional Assns. of Grantmakers; mem. adv. bd. Neighborhood Partnership Fund (Oreg. Cmty. Found.); mem., adv. bd. Giving in Oreg. Coun.; co-chair Northwest Giving Project. Contbr. articles to profl. jours. Home: 2706 SW English Ct Portland OR 97201-1622 Office: Meyer Memorial Trust 1515 SW 5th Ave Ste 500 Portland OR 97201-5450

ROOKS, JUDITH PENCE, midwifery, public health consultant; b. Spokane, Wash., Aug. 18, 1941; d. Lawrence Cyrus and Christine Atrice (Snow) Pence; m. Peter Geoffrey Bourne, Mar. 1972 (div.); m. Charles Stanley Rooks, Sept. 21, 1975; 1 child, Christopher Robert. BS, U. Wash., 1963; MS, Cath. U. Am., 1967; MPH, Johns Hopkins U., 1974. Cert. edpidemiology, nursing, nurse-midwifery, mediation. Staff nurse The Clin. Ctr., NIH, Bethesda, Md., 1965; asst. prof. nursing dept. San Jose (Calif.) State Coll., 1967-69; epidemiologist Ctrs. for Disease Control, Atlanta, 1970-78; asst. prof. dept. ob-gyn. Oreg. Health Sci. U., Portland, 1978-79; expert Office of the Surgeon Gen., Dept. HHS, Washington, 1979-80; project officer U.S. AID, 1980-82; prin. investigator Sch. Pub. Health Columbia U., N.Y.C., 1988-89, assoc. Pacific Inst. for Women's Health, 1993-2001; cons. Portland, 1982—. Mem. tech. adv. com. Family Health Internat., Research Triangle Park, N.C., 1986-97; mem. midwifery adv. com. Frontier Nursing Svc., Hyden, Ky., 1997—; mem. com. Inst. of Medicine NAS, Washington, 1983-85; academic faculty cmty.-base nurse-midwifery edn. program Frontier Sch. Midwifery and Family Nursing, Hyden, Ky., 1993-95; dir. N.Y. Acad. Medicine/Maternity Ctr. Assn. evidence-based symposium on The Nature and Management of Labor Pain, 1999-01. Author: Midwifery and Childbirth in America, 1997; co-author: Nurse-Midwifery in America, 1986, Reproductive Risk in Maternity Care and Family Planning Services, 1992; mem. editl. bd. Birth, 1996—; editl. cons. Jour. Nurse Midwifery, 1992-2000, Jour. Midwifery and Women's Health, 2002--; contbr. articles to profl. jours. Mem bd. advisors World Affairs Coun. Oreg., Portland, 1987-90; bd. dirs. Planned Parenthood of the Columbia/Willamette, Portland, 1987-90; chm. Ga. Citizens for Hosp. Abortion, Atlanta, 1969-70; assoc. Pacific Coun. on Internat. Policy, 1995-97. Recipient nat. award Nat. Perintal Assn., 1999. Mem. APHA (chair com. on women's rights 1982-83, mem. governing coun. 1976-77, 79-82, Martha May Eliot award for svc. to mothers and children 1993, Hattie Hemschemeyer award for cont. outstanding contbns. to nurse-midwifery and maternal and child health care 1998), Am. Coll. Nurse-Midwives (life, pres. 1983-85). Avocations: gardening, walking, reading, traveling, cooking. Home and Office: 2706 SW English Ct Portland OR 97201-1622 E-mail: jprooks1@home.com.

ROOMANN, HUGO, architect; b. Tallinn, Estonia, Mar. 25, 1923; came to U.S., 1951, naturalized, 1957; s. Eduard August and Annette (Kask) R.; m. Raja R. Suursoho, Sept. 15, 1945; children— Katrin-Kaja, Linda-Anu. *"Raja R. Roomann's book "Urban Growth and the Development of an Urban Sewer System, City of Cincinnati 1800-1915" was published in 2001."This was shown to be inserted right after "Linda Anu"* BS, Inst. Tech. Carolo Wilhelmina, Braunschweig, W. Ger., 1950; M.F.A. in Arch. (scholar 1956-57), Princeton U., 1957. Archtl. engr. Austin Co., Roselle, N.J., 1951-54; archtl. designer Epple & Seaman, Newark, 1954-55, 57-61; propr. Hugo Roomann, Cranford and Elizabeth, N.J., 1961-66; partner A.M. Kinney Assocs. (Architects and Engrs.), Cin., N.Y.C. and Chgo., 1966-89. Dir. architecture, v.p. corp. ops. A.M. Kinney, Inc., Cin., 1967, 77, 89; dir. Walter Kidde Constructors, Inc., 1973, A.M. Kinney, Inc., A.M. Kinney Assocs. Inc., Chgo.; pres. Design Art Corp., 1986. Prin. works include Grad. Rsch. Ctr. for Biol. Scis., Ohio State U., 1970, Lloyd Libr., Cin., 1968, offices, labs. and mfg. facilities, Miles Labs., West Haven, Conn., 1969, Am. Mus. Atomic Energy, Oak Ridge, 1975, Renton K. Brodie Sci. Ctr., U. Cin., 1970, EPA Nat. Labs., Cin., 1975, NALCO Tech. Ctr., Naperville, Ill., 1979, Brown & Williamson Corp. Hdqrs., Louisville, 1983, U. Cin. Kettering Lab., 1989. Pres. Citizens League, Elizabeth, N.J., 1966, Estonian Heritage Assn. Cin., 1991-94; bd. dirs., pres. Inter-Ethnic Coun. of Greater Cin., 1992-95. Recipient Top Ten Plant award Factory mag., 1967, Top Ten Plant award Modern Mfg. mag., 1970 Mem. AIA (Ohio chpt. award for Renton K. Brodie Sci. Ctr. 1971, for NALCO Ctr. 1980), Cin. Preservation Assn., Princeton Club. Lutheran. Office: 2856 Observatory Ave Cincinnati OH 45208-2340

ROONEY, ANDREW AITKEN, writer, columnist; b. Albany, N.Y., Jan. 14, 1919; s. Walter S. and Ellinor (Reynolds) R.; m. Marguerite Howard, Mar. 21, 1942; children: Ellen, Martha, Emily, Brian. Student, Colgate U., 1942. Writer-producer CBS-TV News, 1959—; newspaper columnist Tribune Co. Syndicate, 1979—. Author: (with O.C. Hutton) Air Gunner, 1944, The Story of Stars and Stripes, 1946, Conquerors' Peace, 1947, The Fortunes of War, 1962, A Few Minutes with Andy Rooney, 1981, And More By Andy Rooney, 1982, Pieces of My Mind, 1984, Word for Word, 1986, Not That You Asked, 1989, Sweet and Sour, 1992, My War, 1995, Sincerely, Andy Rooney, 1999, Common Nonsense, 2002; TV programs include An Essay on War, Mr. Rooney Goes to Washington, Mr. Rooney Goes to Dinner; regular commentator-essayist: 60 Minutes, 1978—. Served with AUS, 1941-45. Decorated Air Medal, Bronze Star.; recipient awards for best written TV documentary Writers Guild Am., 1966, 68, 71, 75, 76, Emmy awards, 1968, 78, 81, 82 Office: CBS News 524 W 57th St New York NY 10019-2924

ROONEY, CAROL BRUNS, dietitian; b. Milw., Dec. 20, 1940; d. Edward G. and Elizabeth C. (Lemke) Bruns; m. George Eugene Rooney Jr., July 1, 1967; children: Steven, Sean. BS, U. Wis., 1962; MS, U. Iowa, 1965. Registered dietitian; cert. nutrition specialist; disting. health care food svc. adminstr.; cert. dietitian, Wis. Intern VA Med. Ctr., Hines, Ill., 1962-63, resident in nutrition and food svc. Iowa City, 1963-65, dietitian nutrition clinic Hines, 1965-67, 69-70, chief clin. dietetics, 1970-71, chief adminstrv. dietetics, 1971-73, clin. dietitian Memphis, 1967-68; asst. chief nutrition and food svc. Zablocki VA Med. Ctr., Milw., 1974-85, chief nutrition and food svc., 1985-96, divsn. mgr. cons. care, 1996-98, cons. nutrition and food svc. mgmt., 1995—, bus. enterprise mgr., 1998-2000. Adj. lectr. Loyola U. Coll. Dentistry, Maywood, Ill., 1969-72; investigator nutrition VA/Med. Coll. Wis., Milw., 1975-2000, co-dir. ann. clin. nutrition symposium, Milw., 1979-94; chmn. task force on ration allowance VA, Washington, 1977-84, mem. nutrition and food svc. spl. interest users group Washington, 1983-85, chmn. tech. adv. group region IV, 1986; mem. Dept. Vets. Affairs Mktg. Ctr. Subsistence Task Force, 1991-95, dietetic internship adv. bd. St. Luke's Hosp., Milw., 1983-87; mem. Dept. Vets. Affairs Nat. Cost Containment Ctr. Nutrition & Food Svc. Benchmarking Tech. Adv., 1995-96; lectr. in field, 1965—; mem. Dept. Vets. Affairs, Nutrition and Food Svc. Policy Manual Rev. Task Force, 1992-96, Dept. Vets. Chiefs, Food and Nutrition Svc. Mentor Group, 1992-96. Author: (videocassette) VA Ration Allowance as a Management Tool 1976; editor: Nutrition Principles and Dietary Guidelines for Patients Receiving Chemotherapy and Radiation Therapy, 1980; contbr. articles to profl. jours., 1978—. Mem. profl. edn. com. Milw. South unit Am. Cancer Soc., 1976-86, bd. dirs. Milw. South unit, 1984-86, Milw. div., 1986-87, Wis. div., 1987-91, media spokesperson, 1983-91, del. to Milw. div., 1984-85, mem. organizational and expansion com. Milw. div., 1986-87, profl. edn. com. Milw. div., 1986-87, Wis. div., 1987-91, mem. taking control Wis. div., 1987-91, chmn. nutrition Wis. div., 1989-91; mem. med. adv. com. YMCA Met. Milw., 1985—; mem. Marquette U. High Sch. Mothers Guild, 1990-94. Named Dept. Vets. Affairs Dietitian of Yr., 1994; recipient Disting. Svc. award, Am. Cancer Soc. Milw. South unit, 1980, Women of Achievement award, Girl Scouts USA Milw. area, 1987, Leadership award, VA, 1989, Dept. Vets. Affairs Fed. Women's Program cert. merit for outstanding profl. leadership, 1994, commendation, Dept. Vet. Affairs, 2000, rsch. grantee, Paralyzed Vets. Am., 1981—83. Fellow Am. Dietetic Assn. (registered, practice groups in mgmt. responsibilities in health care delivery, gerontology nutrition 1980-2000, dietetics in phys. medicine and rehab. 1983-97, clin. nutrition mgmt. 1987—, amb. nat. media spokesperson 1983-89, Resource Amb. 1991—, Outstanding Svc. award 1983-89), FADA; mem. AAUW, Am. Soc. Health Care Food Svc. Adminstrs. (dir.-at-large Wis. chpt. 1993-95, pres.-elect Wis. chpt. 1995-96, pres. 1996-97, immediate past pres. 1997-98, Disting. Health Care Food Svc. Adminstr. 1995—), Wis. Dietetic Assn. (co-chmn. divsn. mgmt. practice 1976-77, chmn. 1977-78, bd. dirs. 1981-83, coord. cabinet 1984-91, pres. 1988-89, chmn. nominating com. 1989-90, chmn. long-range planning com. 1989-90, legis. com. 1988—, Wis. Medallion award 1986), Milw. Dietetic Assn. (cmty. nutrition and clin. dietetics and rsch. coms. 1975-76, chair ad hoc com. for nutrition and oncology patients 1976-79, clin. dietetics and rsch. study group 1981-90, chair 1983-85, pres. 1982-83, by-laws com. 1983-84, chair policies and procedures com. 1983-87, pub. rels. com. 1983-87, chair nominating com. 1984-85), Fed. Execs. Assn., Leadership Vets. Affairs Alumni Assn. (charter, life), Phi Upsilon Omicron, Kappa Delta, Kappa Delta Alumnae Assn., Milw. Kappa Delta Alumnae Assn. (rep. Milw. Panhellenic coun. 1998-99, treas. 1999—). Avocations: tennis, golf. Home: 18230 Le Chateau Dr Brookfield WI 53045-4922

ROONEY, DANIEL M. professional football team executive; b. 1932; s. Arthur Joseph and Kathleen (McNulty) R. Former salesman advt., editor Pitts. Steelers Program; now pres. Pitts. Steelers; mem. exec. coms. NFL. Office: Three Rivers Stadium 3400 S Water St Pittsburgh PA 15203-2349*

ROONEY, JOHN PHILIP, law educator; b. Evanston, Ill., May 1, 1932; s. John McCaffery and Bernadette Marie (O'Brien) R.; m. Jean Marie Kliss, Feb. 16, 1974 (div. Oct. 1988); 1 child, Caitlin Mairin. BA, U. Ill, 1953; JD, Harvard U., 1958. Bar: Ill. 1958, Calif. 1961, Mich. 1975, U.S. Tax Ct. 1973. Assoc. lawyer Chapman & Cutler, Chgo., 1958-60, Wilson, Morton, San Mateo, Calif., 1961-63; pvt. practice San Francisco, 1963-74; prof. law Cooley Law Sch., Lansing, Mich., 1975—. Author: Selected Cases (Property), 1985; contbr. articles to profl. jours. Pres. San Francisco coun. Dem. Clubs, 1970. 1st lt. U.S. Army, 1953-55. Recipient Beattie Teaching award Cooley Law Sch. Grads., 1979, 90, 92. Fellow Mich. Bar Found.; mem. ABA (real estate fed. tax problems com., title ins. com.), Ingham County Bar Assn., Univ. Club. Democrat. Unitarian Universalist. Office: Cooley Law Sch 300 S Capitol Ave Lansing MI 48933-1586 E-mail: rooneyj@cooley.edu.

ROONEY, KEVIN DAVITT, lawyer; b. Springfield, Mass., June 23, 1944; s. Davitt Michael and Elizabeth Isabel (Wlodyka) R.; m. Annette Eloise Benevento, Nov. 11, 1972; children: Kathryn Denise, Mary Elizabeth. BA, St. Marys Coll., 1966; JD, George Washington U., 1975. Bar: Va. 1975, D.C. 1977. Computer systems analyst VA, Washington, 1967-68, 70-73; chief legal programs and budget Dept. Justice, 1973-77, exec. asst. to assoc. atty. gen., 1977, asst. atty. gen. for adminstrn., 1977-84; prin. Rooney & Assocs, 1984-87, 90-94, Rooney & Barry, Washington, 1987-89; assoc. dir. Exec. Office for Immigration Rev. Dept. Justice, Falls Church, Va., 1995-97, asst. dir. Fed. Bur. Prisons Washington, 1997-99, dir. Exec. Office for Immigration Rev. Falls Church, Va., 1999-2001, acting commr. Immigration and Naturalization Svc., 2001—. Bd. dirs., v.p. Joint Action in Cmty. Svcs., Inc., Washington, 1988-94. With U.S. Army, 1968-70. Mem. ASPA, Fed. Bar Assn., Va. Bar Assn., D.C. Bar Assn. Office: Dept Justice Immigration Naturlization 425 Eye St NW Washington DC 20536

ROONEY, MARIA DEWING, photographer; b. N.Y.C., July 25; d. Madeleine L'Engle Franklin; m. John Bryan Rooney, Jan. 21, 1984; children: Bryson, Alexander. BFA, Phila. Coll. Art. Tchr. photography Bishop Bright Grammar Sch., Leamington Spa, Eng., Mid-Warwickshire Sch. of Further Edn., Leamington Spa, 1976-80; photographer, owner The Studios, Shipston-on-Stour, Eng., 1977-80; photographer Gary Studios & Comini Studios, Dallas, 1980-83; pvt. practice Mystic, Conn., 1990—. Exhibitions include Warwick (Eng.) Gallery, Derby (Eng.) Coll. Art Gallery, Bath (Eng.) Pl. Cmty. Ctr., Midland Group Galley, Nottingham, Eng., Wimbledon Sch. Art, London, Warwich U. Arts Ctr., Birmingham, Eng., Essex Art Assn., 1998, R. J. Julia, Madison, Conn., 1998, State Capitol Hartford, Conn., 1999; contbr. photographs Anytime Prayers, 1994, Mothers and Daughters, 1997, Mothers and Sons, 1999, photographs published in Co-Optic Publs., London, 1976—80; prodr.: series greeting cards with personal photography. Mem. Child and Family Svcs. Mem.: AAUW, Mystic Art Assn., Essex Art Assn. (photography award 1997, 2002). Avocations: sailing, writing. Home and Office: 77 High St Mystic CT 06355 E-mail: vlad0121@aol.com.

ROONEY, MATTHEW A. lawyer; b. Jersey City, May 19, 1949; s. Charles John and Eileen (Dunphy) R.; m. Jean M. Alletag, June 20, 1973 (div. Dec. 1979); 1 child, Jessica Margaret; m. Diane S. Kaplan, July 6, 1981; children: Kathryn Olivia, S. Benjamin. AB magna cum laude, Georgetown U., 1971; JD with honors, U. Chgo., 1974. Bar: Ill. 1975, U.S. Dist. Ct. (no. dist.) Ill. 1975, U.S. Ct. Appeals (7th cir.) 1990. Law clk. to cir. judge U.S. Ct. Appeals (7th cir.), Chgo., 1974-75; assoc. Mayer, Brown, Rowe & Maw, 1975-80, ptnr., 1981—. Assoc. editor U. Chgo. Law Rev., 1973. Fellow Am. Coll. Trial

Lawyers; mem. ABA, 7th Cir. Bar Assn., Order of Coif, Phi Beta Kappa. Democrat. Roman Catholic. Avocations: jogging, golfing. Home: 2718 Sheridan Rd Evanston IL 60201-1754 Office: Mayer Brown Rowe & Maw 190 S La Salle St Ste 3100 Chicago IL 60603-3441 E-mail: mrooney@mayerbrownrowe.com.

ROONEY, PAUL C., JR. lawyer, retired; b. Winnetka, Ill., Oct. 23, 1943; s. Paul C. and Mary K. (Brennan) R.; m. Maria Elena Del Canto, Sept. 6, 1980. BA, Harvard U., 1963, LLB, 1966. Bar: Mass. 1968, N.Y. 1972, Fla. 1980, U.S. Dist. Ct. (ea. and so. dists.) N.Y., U.S. Ct. Appeals (2d cir.). Ptnr. White & Case, N.Y.C., 1983-98, ret., 1998. Served to lt. USNR, 1966-69. Mem. N.Y. State Bar Assn., Univ. Club (N.Y.C.), Mashomack Preserve (N.Y.), Sharon Country Club (Conn.). Home: 417 Park Ave New York NY 10022-4401 also: 11 Lilac Ln Sharon CT 06069-0271 Office: White & Case 1155 Avenue Of The Americas New York NY 10036-2787

ROONEY, PAUL GEORGE, mathematics educator; b. N.Y.C., July 14, 1925; s. Geoffrey Daniel and Doris Elizabeth (Babcock) R.; m. Mary Elizabeth Carlisle, June 20, 1950; children: Francis Timothy, Elizabeth Anne, Kathleen Doris, John Edward, James Carlisle. B.Sc., U. Alta., 1949; PhD, Calif. Inst. Tech., 1952. Asst. prof. math. U. Alta., 1952-55; asst. prof. U. Toronto, 1955-60, assoc. prof., 1960-62, prof., 1962-91, prof. emeritus, 1991—. Dir. Commonwealth Petroleum Co., Calgary, 1946-59 Editor in chief Can. Jour. Math. 1971-75; contbr. articles to profl. jours. Bd. dirs. Francis F. Reeve Found., 1954-85. Served with Can. Army, 1943-45. Fellow Royal Soc. Can.; Mem. Can. Math. Soc. (councillor 1960-64, 66-70, 76-78, v.p. 1979-81, pres. 1981-83), Am. Math. Soc., Math. Assn. Am. Office: U Toronto Dept Math Toronto ON Canada M5S 1A1 E-mail: rooney@math.toronto.edu.

ROONEY, PHILLIP B. service company executive; BA magna cum laude, St. Bernard Coll. Various positions, including pres. Waste Mgmt., 1969-97; various positions including pres. mgmt. svcs. Service Master Co., Downers Grove, Ill., 1997—. Trustee Notre Dame U.; mem. fin. coun. Archdiocese of Chgo.; chmn. sister Cities Internat.; mem. Civic Leadership Coun. of El Valor; dir. Ill. Tool Works. Recipient Semper Fidelis award Marine Corps Scholarship Found., Outstanding Svc. to Mil. award USO, El Valor's Corp. Visionary award, Man of Yr. award Ill. Viet Nam Vets. Mem. Econ. Club of Chgo. Office: ServiceMaster Co One Service Master Way Downers Grove IL 60515 E-mail: prooney@svm.com.

ROONEY, WILLIAM RICHARD, magazine editor; b. New Brunswick, N.J., Mar. 12, 1938; s. William Richard and Bernadette (Huether) R.; m. Rita Ann Scherer, July 20, 1963; children: Karen, Kevin, Brian, Kristin. BS in English, St. Peter's Coll., Jersey City, 1959. Asst., then assoc. editor Marine Engring./Log mag., N.Y.C., 1960-64; assoc. editor Outdoor Life mag., 1964-72, mng. editor, 1972-76, sr. editor, 1976-77; editor articles Sports Afield ann. outdoor mags., 1983-90; editor Am. Forests mag., Washington, 1977-95, v.p. for publs., 1991-95; book editor Safari Press, 1996—; mng. editor Am. Guardian mag., Fairfax, Va., 1997—, Am. Hunter mag., Fairfax, 1997-99, Wildlife Soc., Bethesda, Md., 1999—. Contbr. to: Complete Outdoors Ency, 1972; others. With AUS, 1959-60. Mem. Outdoor Writers Assn. Am. Roman Catholic. Home: 7916 Carrie Ln Manassas VA 20111-2548 Office: 5410 Grosvenor Ln Bethesda MD 20814-2144

ROOP, JAMES JOHN, public relations executive; b. Parkersburg, W.Va., Oct. 29, 1949; s. J. Vaun and Mary Louise (McGinnis) R.; m. Margaret Mary Kuneck (div. 1982); m. Susan Lynn Hoell (div. 1989); m. Daisy P. Billue, 1990 (div. 1999). BS in Journalism, W. Va. U., 1971. Various account mgmt. postions Ketchum Pub. Rels., Pitts., 1972-77, v.p., 1977-79, Burson-Marsteller, Chgo., 1979-81; sr. v.p. Hesselbart & Mitten/Watt, Cleve., 1981-84, exec. v.p., 1984-86, pres., 1986-87, Watt, Roop & Co. (formerly Hesselbart & Mitten/Watt), Cleve., 1987-96; chmn., pres., CEO James J. Roop Co., 1996—. Contbr. articles to profl. jours. Mem. Leadership Clevel.; bd. dirs. Ctr. for Families and Children, Boys Hope, Kidney Found., Police Athletic League, Econs. Am. Fellow Pub. Rels. Soc. Am. (chmn. investor rels. sect. 1984-85, chmn. honors and awards com. 1995); mem. Nat. Investor Rels. Inst. (chpt. pres. Cleve./Akron chpt., sr. investor rels. roundtable), Cleve. Skating Club, Mayfield Country Club. Republican. Home: 2697 Scarborough Rd Cleveland Heights OH 44106-3241 Office: James J Roop Co 650 Huntington Bldg 925 Euclid Ave Cleveland OH 44115-1408

ROOP, JOSEPH MCLEOD, economist; b. Montgomery, Ala., Sept. 29, 1941; s. Joseph Ezra and Mae Elizabeth (McLeod) R.; m. Betty Jane Reed, Sept. 4, 1965; 1 dau., Elizabeth Rachael. BS, Ctrl. Mo. State U., Warrensburg, 1963; PhD, Wash. State U., Pullman, 1973. Economist Econ. Rsch. Svc., U.S. Dept. Agr., Washington, 1975-79; sr. economist Evans Econs., Inc., 1979-81; staff scientist Battelle Pacific N.W. Nat. Lab., Richland, Wash., 1981—. Adj. prof. dept. econs. Wash. State U., 1999—; with Internat. Energy Agy., Paris, 1990-91. Contbr. tech. articles to profl. jours. Served with U.S. Army, 1966-68. Dept. Agr. Coop. State Rsch. Svc. rsch. grantee, 1971-73. Mem. Am. Econ. Assn., Econometric Soc., Internat. Assn. Energy Econs., Am. Statis. Assn. Home: 715 S Taft St Kennewick WA 99336-9587 Office: PO Box 999 MSIN K6-05 Richland WA 99352-0999 E-mail: joe.roop@pnl.gov., jroop715@worldnet.att.net.

ROOP, RALPH GOODWIN, retired oil marketing company executive; b. Snowville, Va., June 23, 1915; s. Guy C. and Ora (Goodwin) R.; married; children: Nancie Roop Kennedy, Paterson Roop Webster. BS, Va. Poly. Inst., 1936; MS, Cornell U., 1937. Various positions So. States Coop., Richmond, Va., 1937-66; pres. and/or chmn. bd. Petroleum Marketers, Inc., 1954-88, dir., mem. exec. com., 1988—. Trustee Va. Wesleyan Coll., Norfolk, 1982—; bd. dirs. Suhor Found., 1988—, Trinity Found., Richmond. Named Oil Man of Yr., Va. Petroleum Jobbers Assn., 1983. Mem. Va. Petroleum Council (chmn. 1964-67), Va. Oil Men's Assn. (pres. 1975-76), Am. Petroleum Inst., Richmond C. of C. (past bd. dirs.). Methodist. Avocations: travel, photography, fishing. Home: 2300 Cedarfield Pkwy Apt 363 Richmond VA 23233-1945

ROORDA, JOHN FRANCIS, JR. business consultant; b. Evanston, Ill., Jan. 16, 1923; s. John Francis and Sadie M. (Daley) R.; m. Elizabeth Mulcahy, July 2, 1949; children: Elizabeth Roorda Barker, John F., Ann Roorda Hollis. BSChemE, Purdue U., 1943, PhD, 1949. With Shell Oil Co., 1949-83; gen. mgr. combined oil products/chem. econs. dept., 1973-74; v.p. planning and econs., 1974-77; v.p. Shell Devel. Co., Houston, 1977-78; v.p. corp. planning Shell Oil Co., 1978-83; pres. John Roorda, 1983—. Coordinator Exec. Service Corps, Houston, 1985— Served to lt. (j.g.) USNR, 1943-46. Recipient Disting. Engring. Alumnus award Purdue U., 1976, Outstanding Chem. Engr. award Purdue U., 1993. Mem. Sigma Xi. Roman Catholic. E-mail: graycell@houston.rr.com.

ROOS, BARBARA DIANE, educational director; b. Boston, Jan. 10, 1956; d. Robert Anthony and Helene (Gallipeau) R. BFA, U. Bridgeport, 1978. Cert. mgmt., U. Neb., 1991. Staff asst. Assn. Am. Med. Coll., Washington, 1982-86; ednl. dir. Nat. Rural Electric Coop. Assn., Arlington, Va., 1986—. Vol. Jr. League of Washington, 1994—, violence intervention program, Arlington, 1990—. Office: Child Welfare League of America 440 First St NW 3rd Flr Washington DC 20001-2085

ROOS, CASPER, actor; b. N.Y.C., Mar. 21, 1925; s. Jacob and Sabina (Uhlenbusch) R.; m. Shirley Anne Nicholson, June 27, 1953; 1 child, Pieter Nicholson. Student, N.Y. Coll. Music. Treas. Actors Equity Found., N.Y.C., 1982-88; co-chmn. research subcom. Nat. Theater Com., N.Y.C., 1983—. Prin. actor Shenandoah, N.Y.C., 1975-78, Brigadoon, N.Y.C., 1979-80, My One and Only, N.Y.C., 1982-85, Into the Light, 1986, Man of La Mancha, Zurich, 1988, (Broadway prodn.) Shenandoah Revival, 1989; numerous regional theater prodns. Served with U.S. Mcht. Marines, 1943-46. Mem. Actors Equity (treas. 1982-88, councilor 1964-79, 88-93). Home: PO Box 11 Gilbertsville NY 13776-0011 *Don Quixote wanted to 'add a little grace to the world.' I, too, would like to add a 'little' to this world, whether it be grace or laughter or tears to an audience or service to my colleagues. If, like Don Quixote, I look a little foolish, so be it. I prefer a life of striving for the ultimate to the easier smug acceptance of the status quo.*

ROOS, CHARLES EDWIN, physicist; b. Chgo., Apr. 23, 1927; s. Charles Frederick and Mary Barkuloo Roos; m. Anne Friedrich, Aug. 30, 1952; children: Margit Josephine, Alice Marie, Carlton Friedrich, Charles David. BA in Zoology, U. Tex., Austin, 1948; PhD in Physics, Johns Hopkins U., 1953. Faculty assoc. in physics Johns Hopkins U., Balt., 1953-54; asst. prof. physics U. Calif., Riverside, 1954-59; rsch. fellow Calif. Inst. Tech., Pasadena, 1955-67; assoc. prof. physics Vanderbilt U., Nashville, 1959-65, prof. physics, 1965-89, prof. emeritus, 1989—; chmn. Nat. Recovery Tech., 1982—. Regular visitor, Be.. Labs., Holmdale, N.J., 1973-76, scientific assoc. CERN, Geneva, Switzerland, 1969-80, founder, dir. Am. Magnetics, Oak Ridge, Tenn., 1966-85, mng. ptnr. Seofon Assocs., Baytown, Tex., 1960—; prin. investigator, NSF, 1955-89, U.S. Dept. Energy, 1970—. Contbr. over 140 articles to profl. jours.; U.S. and fgn. patentee in field. Mem. Condominium bd, 817 5th Ave. Condominium, N.Y.C., 1975—, pres. bd., 1999—. With USN, 1945-46. Recipient Tibbets award, SBA, 1996, Nat. Conservation medal, DAR, 1992; guest Nobel awards, Royal Acad. Physics, Stockholm, 1989; sr. NATO fellow, NSF, Max Planck Inst., 1968. Fellow Am. Physics Soc.; mem. Cosmos Club, Cumberland Club. Avocations: cross-country skiing, scuba diving. Office: 566 Mainstream Dr Ste 300 Nashville TN 37228-1234 E-mail: ceroos@comcast.net.

ROOS, DANIEL, engineering educator; b. Bklyn., Apr. 12, 1939; s. Sigmund and Anita (Sperling) R.; m. Eva Bonis, June 1, 1969; children— Richard Joseph, Linda Suzanne. BS in Civil Engring, M.I.T., 1961, MS, 1963, PhD, 1966. Mem. faculty MIT, Cambridge, 1963—, assoc. prof. civil engring., 1970-76, prof., 1976—, head transp. systems div., 1977-78, dir. Ctr. for Transp. Studies, 1978-85, dir. Ctr. Tech., Policy and Indsl. Devel., 1985-97, Japan Steel Industry prof., 1985—, mem. Commn. on Indsl. Productivity, 1987-89, assoc. dean engring. systems, 1997—, spl. asst. provost and chancellor, 1996—, co-dir. Ford Indsl. Ptnrships, dir. engring. sys. divsn., 1998—. Founder, dir. Multisystems Inc., Cambridge, 1965—85; chmn. com. to assess advanced vehicle and hwy techs. NRC, 1990—91, mem. com. on fuel economy, 1991—92; dir. Internat. Motor Vehicle Program, 1980—99; co-dir. Lean Aircraft Initiative, 1992—97; mem. coun. indsl. relationships MIT, 1996—97. Author: ICES System Design, 1964; The Future of the Automobile, 1984, Auto Futures, 1990; co-author: Made in America, 1989, The Machine That Changed the World, 1990; contbr. articles to profl. jours. Mem. U.S. Task Force on Transp., 1969. Recipient Shingo Prize for Excellence in Mfg. Rsch., 1994. Mem. ASCE (Frank M. Masters Transp. Engring. award 1989), Assn. Computing Machinery, Ops. Research Soc. (treas. transp. sci. sect. 1970-71), Transp. Research Bd. (chmn. para-transit com. 1974-80, group coun. 1980-84), Coun. Univ. Transp. Ctrs. (pres. 1983). Achievements include developing Dial-A-Ride transp. concept, 1965; dir. Internat. Motor Vehicle. Home: 28 Baskin Rd Lexington MA 02421-6929 Office: MIT Engring Sys Divsn 77 Massachusetts Ave Cambridge MA 02139-4307 E-mail: roos@mit.edu.

ROOS, JANE MAYO, art history educator; b. N.Y.C., Feb. 14, 1943; d. Maurice Arthur and Katherine Haverkamp Mayo; m. Michael Roos, Apr. 17, 1971 (div. Dec. 1993); 1 child, Katherine; m. William Howard Griesar, June 12, 1999. BA, Coll. New Rochelle, 1964; MA, Hunter Coll., 1974; PhD, Columbia U., 1981. Editor Holt, Rinehart and Winston, N.Y.C., 1966-71; prof. art history Hunter Coll. and Grad. Ctr. CUNY, 1985—. Vis. lectr. Christie's Grad. Program Connoisseurship, N.Y.C., 1999—. Author: Early Impressionism and the French State 1866-1874, 1996; co-author: Rodin's Monument to Victor Hugo, 1998, The Landscapes of France, 1995; contbr. articles to profl. jours. Curator A Painter's Poet: Stéphane Mallarmé, 1999. Columbia U. grantee, 1975, 76, 81, Samuel H. Kress Found. grantee, 1977, 78, 79, Rsch. and Travel grantee Am. Coun. Learned Socs., 1987, , CUNY Rsch. and Travel grantee, 1991, 94, 98, 99, 2000, Florence Gould Found. grantee, 1999; Postdoctoral fellow J. Paul Getty Truste, 1987-88. Mem. Coll. Art Assn. Am., Assn. Historians Nineteenth-Century Art. Avocations: travel, gardening, yoga. Home: 40 Clinton Ave Dobbs Ferry NY 10522 Office: Hunter Coll and Grad Ctr 695 Park Ave New York NY 10021

ROOS, KATHLEEN MARIE, special education educator; b. Kansas City, Mo., Feb. 1, 1962; d. Edward Joseph Jr. and Teresa Angela (Houlihan) R. BS in Edn., Avila Coll., 1984, MS in Edn. Exceptionalities, 1987. Tchr. behavior disorder and learning disabled Ctr. Sch. Dist. 58, Kansas City, 1985—. Mem. Richards-Gebaur Cmty. Coun., Kansas City, 1985—, mem. scholarship com., 1989—, chmn. 1998, 99, mem. airshow com., 1988-92, corr. sec., 1991-92, v.p., 1993-94, pres., 1994-95, 2000, chmn. 31st ann. awards banquet, co-chair 5 Las Vegas Nights; mem. Whiteman AFB Cmty. Coun., 1994—. Mo. State Dept. grantee, 1988. Mem. Mo. Nat. Edn. Assn., Coun. Exceptional Children (bldg. rep. 1986-89), Ctr. Edn. Assn. (bldg. rep. 1986-89), Ctr. Elem. PTA (treas. 1990-91), Richards-Gebaur Mil. Club (adv. bd. 1994-98). Roman Catholic. Avocations: needlework, sewing, quilting, water skiing, skiing. Home: 401 Sandra Ln Belton MO 64012-4205 Office: Ctr Elem Sch 8401 Euclid Ave Kansas City MO 64132-2207

ROOS, NESTOR ROBERT, consultant; b. St. Louis, Aug. 19, 1925; s. Maurice and Fannie (Friedman) R.; m. Fay Weil, July 8, 1951; children: Marilyn Roos Hall, Eileen Roos Ruddell, Robert F. BBA, Washington U., St. Louis, 1948; MSBA, Washington U., 1949; DBA, Ind. U., 1959. Instr. bus. La. State U., Baton Rouge, 1949-51; teaching fellow Ind. U., Bloomington, 1951-53; asst. prof. Ga. State U., Atlanta, 1953-55; prof. U. Ariz., Tucson, 1955-86, prof. emeritus, 1986; chmn. Risk Mgmt. Pub. Co., 1976—, cons. editor, 1990—. Cons., expert witness in field; bd. dirs. Blue Cross-Blue Shield Ariz., sec., 1993-95, chair, 1998-2001; mem. Ins. Dirs. Adv. Com., Phoenix, 1987—, Reverse Mortgage Adv. Com., Tucson, 1988-90. Author: (with others) Multiple Line Insurers, 1970, Governmental Risk Management Manual, 1976, Industrial Accident Prevention, 1980. Bd. dirs. Handmaker Geriatric Ctr., Tucson, 1987-92; pres. Temple Emanu-El, Tucson, 1981-83. With U.S. Army, 1943-45, ETO. Grantee Nat. Inst. Occupational Safety and Health, 1975. Mem. Risk and Ins. Mgmt. Soc., Western Risk and Ins. Assn. (pres. 1972-73), Public Risk and Ins. Mgmt. Assn. (dir. edn. and tng. 1982-89). Democrat. Jewish. Avocations: gardening, golf. Home: 7311 E Camino De Cima Tucson AZ 85750-2212 Office: Risk Mgmt Pub Co 2030 E Broadway Blvd Ste 106 Tucson AZ 85719-5908 E-mail: NES999@aol.com.

ROOS, SONYA INGRID, interior designer, educator, business owner; b. London, Oct. 24, 1940; came to U.S., 1945; d. Henry S. and Emily (Reich) Rosenfeld; m. Leo Roos, Jan. 29, 1961; children: Joel, Lori, Robin. AS in Interior Design, West Valley Coll., 1980; BA, Newark State Tchrs. Coll., 1971; student, CUNY, 1958-61. Cert. tchr., N.J.; lifetime credential Calif. coll. instr. in interior design. Interior designer Creative Interiors, San Jose, Calif., 1980-81; part-time instr. in interior design West Valley Coll., Saratoga, 1980-85, Saddleback Community Coll., Mission Viejo, 1986—; dir. interior design dept. Forma Decor, Newport Beach, 1985-86; interior designer Rolf Broms & Assocs., Laguna Niguel, 1986—, designer, owner, 1990—. Part-time instr. Orange Coast Community Coll., Costa Mesa, Calif., 1986-89, Rancho Santiago Coll., Santa Ana, 1988-90; guest lectr. pvt. orgns. Mem. Am. Soc. Interior Designers (allied), Internat. Interior Designers Assn. (allied), C. of C., Hadassah. Avocations: reading, social dancing, skiing, water skiing. Home: 3711 Blue Canyon Dr Studio City CA 91604-3802

ROOS, SYBIL FRIEDENTHAL, retired elementary school educator; b. L.A., Jan. 29, 1924; d. Charles G. and Besse (Weixel) Friedenthal; m. Henry Kahn Roos, May 8, 1949 (dec. Dec. 1989); children: Catherine Alane Cook, Elizabeth Anne Garlinger, Virginia Ann Bertrand. BA in Music, Centenary Coll., 1948; MEd, Northwestern State U., 1973. Cert. elem. edn. tchr., spl. edn. tchr. Tchr. Caddo Parish Schs., Shreveport, 1968-75, Spring Branch Ind. Schs., Houston, 1975-85; vol. Houston Grand Opera/Guild, 1979—, Houston Mus. of Fine Arts/Guild, 1990—, Houston Symphony Soc./Guild, 1997—. Author tchrs. guides. Pres. Nat. Coun. Jewish Women, Shreveport, 1958, Houston Grand Opera Guild, 1989-91; bd. dirs. Mus. Fine Arts; area coord. Spl. Olympics, Shreveport, 1974-75; mem. Houston Symphony League, Houston Ballet Guild; bd. dirs. U. Houston Moore Sch. Music. With USN, 1944-46. Mem. AAUW (pres. Spring Valley Houston chpt. 1985-87), Houston Grand Opera Guild, Houston Symphony League, Houston Ballet Guild, Mus. of Fine Arts Guild (bd. dirs.), U. Houston Sch. of Music (bd. dirs.) Am. Needlepoint Guild, Delta Kappa Gamma (bd. dirs., treas. 1987-89), Phi Mu. Republican. Avocations: music, tennis, needlepoint, volunteering. Home: 10220 Memorial Dr Apt 78 Houston TX 77024-3227 E-mail: s.roos@worldnet.att.net.

ROOSA, JAN BERTOROTTA, clinical psychologist; b. Champaign, Ill., Apr. 19, 1927; s. Walter Laidlaw and Giannina (Bertorotta) R.; m. Joan Herr. BS, U. Ill., 1950; MA, U. Denver, 1951, PhD, 1957. Coord., clin. psychologist Child Rsch. Coun., Kansas City, Mo., 1954-57, dir. neighborhood rsch. project, 1957; supr., psychologist State Hosp., Fulton, 1957-59; chief of psychotherapy VA Hosp., Kansas City, 1959-63; clin. psychologist in pvt. practice, Kansas City area, 1963—. Dir., co-founder Learning Resource Ctr., Kansas City, 1969-79; dir. Gestalt, Social Competence Inst., Kansas City, 1969-89; active Conflict Resolution of Met. Kansas City; dir. Competence and Cooperation Group, 1992—. Author: Situation-Options-Consequences-Simulation: A Technique for Teaching Social Skills, 1973, Psychological and Social Competence Model and Skills, 1975, 88, 92; creator SOCCSS and SOCCSS: A Decision Making Process, 1973, 96, The Competence and Cooperation Based Program, 1995. Served with USN, 1945-47, 51-52. Mem. APA, Greater Kansas City Psychol. Assn., Mo. Psychol. Assn., Kans. Assn. Profl. Psychologists, Mental Health Profls., Nat. Register Health Providers in Psychology. Office: 9229 Ward Pkwy Ste 370 Kansas City MO 64114-3334 E-mail: jbroosa@sky.net.

ROOSE-CHURCH, LISA ANN, reporter, secondary school educator; b. Barstow, Calif., Apr. 23, 1964; d. Beverly Jean Robinson; m. Raymond Lee Church, Aug. 16, 1986. BS, Ctrl. Mich. U., 1986. Cert. secondary sch. tchr. Freelance writer, Haslett, Mich., 1977-95; corr. Morning Sun, Mt. Pleasant, 1985; editor, pub. Poetry Magic Pubs., Haslett, 1987-95; news editor, reporter The Daily Herald, Columbia, Tenn., 1995-2000; state corr. The Tennessean, Nashville, 2000-01; substt. tchr. Marshall County Schs., Lewisburg, 2000—; copy-editor, reporter Daily News Jour., Murfreesboro, 2001—. Membership processor Mich. Edn. Data Network Assn., East Lansing, 1991-95. Pub., editor poetry books; contbr. numerous articles to newspapers. Coach 8th grade volleyball, Potterville, Mich., 1987. Recipient 3rd place non-deadline reporting Tennessee Assoc. Press. Mng. Editor's Contest, 1999, 3rd place deadline category, 2000. Office: Daily News Jour 224 N Walnut St PO Box 68 Murfreesboro TN 37130 Fax: (810) 885-1831. E-mail: lisarchurch@aol.com.

ROOSEVELT, RUTH BARRONS, international trading consultant, artist; b. Oak Park, Ill., Aug. 15, 1934; d. James Roy and Elizabeth Bellinger (Howell) Barrons; m. Robert Armstrong Anthony, Feb. 1959 (div. 1967); 1 child, Graham Barrons Anthony; m. William Donner Roosevelt, June 1969 (div. Oct. 1979). BA, Wheaton Coll, 1956; JD, U. Mich., 1959. Bar: Calif. 1959, N.Y. 1980; cert. master hypnotist Nat. Guild Hypnotists, Internat. Assn. Counselors and Therapists master hypnotist. Fin. advisor Drexel Bernham Lambert, N.Y.C., 1979-81; head internat. moneyline trading desk Rudolf Wolff, 1981-86; v.p. Thomson McKinnon, 1986-89, Prudential Securities, N.Y.C., 1989-92; dir. Wall St. Hypnosis. Ctr., 1992—. Author: (book) Complete Guide to Trader Trouble Shooting, 1995, (audio) Power Trading for Power Profits, 1995, Exceptional Trading: The Mind Game, 1999, Twelve Habitudes of Highly Successful Traders, 2001; co-author: (book) Living in Step, 1976; artist (paintings), 1959—. Mem. Nat. Guild Hypnotists, Internat. Assn. Counselors & Therapists, N.Y. Artists Equity, N.Y. Bar Assn., Calif. Bar Assn. Home: 165 William St New York NY 10038-2605 Office: Wall St Hypnosis Ctr 165 William St New York NY 10038-2605 E-mail: traderruth@aol.com.

ROOSEVELT, THEODORE, IV, investment banker; b. Jacksonville, Fla., Nov. 27, 1942; s. Theodore III and Anne Mason (Babcock) R.; m. Constance Lane Rogers, Aug. 1, 1970; 1 child, Theodore Roosevelt V. AB, Harvard U., 1965, MBA, 1972. Assoc. Lehman Bros., N.Y.C., 1972-76; corp. v.p. Lehman Bros. Kuhn Loeb, 1976-82; sr. v.p. Lehman Comml. Paper Inc., 1982-85; mng. dir. Lehman Brothers (formerly Shearson Lehman Bros., Inc.)., 1985—. Chmn., bd. dirs. Lehman Bros. Fin. Products, Inc.; dir. Inst. for Environment and Natural Resources, U. Wyo. Mem. League of Conservation Voters; trustee Pew Ctr. for Global Change; mem. N.Y. State Park Recreation and Hist. Preservation Commn. for City of N.Y.; trustee Am. Mus. Natural History; commr. Hudson River Park Conservancy. Mem.: Fgn. Policy Assn., Coun. Fgn. Rels., The Econ. Club N.Y., Harvard Club (N.Y.C.), Explorers Club, The Heights Casino Club (Bklyn.), Edgartown Yacht Club, The Links (N.Y.C.). Republican. Home: 1 Pierrepont St Brooklyn NY 11201-3302 Office: Lehman Bros 745 7th Ave 20th Fl New York NY 10019

ROOT, ALAN CHARLES, diversified manufacturing company executive; b. Essex, Eng., Apr. 11, 1925; came to U.S., 1951, naturalized, 1959; s. Charles Stanley and Lillian (Collins) R. BA, Oxford U., 1943; MA, Cambridge U., 1951; MBA, Stanford U., 1953. Rsch. analyst Dow Chem. Co., Midland, Mich., 1954—55; mgr. mktg. rsch. GE Co., 1955—61; v.p. bus. planning Mosler Safe Co., Hamilton, Ohio, 1961—70; v.p. corp. planning Am. Standard Inc., N.Y.C., 1970—76, sr. v.p. ops. svcs., 1976—86, sr. v.p., 1986—88, sr. advisor, 1989. Trustee 1995 Trust Fund; sr. advisor Unit Ice, 1995—; bd. dirs. Am.-Standard Energy Inc., Amstan Trucking Inc., 1976-86. Trustee, treas. N.J. Chamber Music Soc., 1988—95; mem. Sheriff's Jury, N.Y. Cty., 1971—79; bd. dirs., chmn. Brit. Schs. and Univs. Found., 1970—2002, hon. dir., 2002—. Capt. Brit. Army, 1944—48, capt. Brit. Army, 1944—48. Admission to Order of St. John of Jerusalem sanctioned by Her Majesty Queen Elizabeth II, 1986, comdr., 1994. Mem. AIChE (assoc. producer TV series Midland sect. 1955), Pilgrims U.S., Newcomen Soc. N.Am., Univ. Club (N.Y.C.). Home: 4934 Mount Pleasant Ln Las Vegas NV 89113-0114 Fax: 702-227-8885. *Good luck meant that my industrial career drew on the education I enjoyed as a young man. Professional advancement came by building on prior experience at each step and through long-term, managerial continuity.*

ROOT, ALLEN WILLIAM, pediatrician, educator; b. Phila., Sept. 24, 1933; s. Morris Jacob and Priscilla R.; m. Janet Greenberg, June 15, 1958; children: Jonathan, Jennifer, Michael. AB, Dartmouth Coll., 1955, postgrad. Med. Sch., 1954-56; MD, Harvard U., 1958. Diplomate Am. Bd. Pediatrics (mem. bd. 1985—), Am. Bd. Pediatric Endocrinology (mem. bd. 1985-90, chmn. 1990). Intern Strong Meml. Hosp., Rochester, N.Y., 1958-60; resident in pediatrics Hosp. U. Pa., Phila., 1960-62; fellow in pediatric endocrinology Children's Hosp. of Phila., 1962-65; assoc. physician in pediatrics U. Pa. Sch. Medicine, 1964-66, asst. prof. pediatrics, 1966-69; assoc. prof. pediatrics Temple U. Sch. Medicine, Phila., 1969-73, prof., 1973; asst. physician in endocrinology Children's Hosp. Phila., 1965-69; chmn. divsn. pediatrics Albert Einstein Med. Center., Phila., 1969-73; prof. pediatrics U. South Fla. Coll. Medicine, Tampa, 1973—, prof. biochemistry, 1987—, assoc. chmn. dept. pediatrics, 1974-99, dir. sect. pediatric endocrinology, 1973-96. Dir. univ. tchg. svcs. All Children's Hosp., St. Petersburg, 1973-89; mem. Fla. Infant Screening Adv. Coun., 1979—, chmn., 1994—; mem. Hillsborough County Thyroid Adv. Com., 1980; mem. med. adv. com. Nat. Pituitary Agy., 1974-78, mem. growth hormone subcom., 1972-79, 81-85. Author: Human Pituitary Growth Hormone, 1972; editor: (with C. La Cauza) Problems in Pediatric Endocrinology, 1980; mem. editl. bd. Jour. Pediats., 1973-81, Jour. Adolescent Health Care, 1979-95, Jour. Pediat. Endocrinology and Metabolism, 1985—, Jour. Clin. Endocrinology and Metabolism, 1993-96, 2001—, Growth, Genetics and Hormones, 1993—, Pediats. in Rev., 1995-2001; assoc. editor Adolescent and Pediat. Gynecology, 1992—. USPHS grantee; Birth Defects Found. grantee. Mem. AAAS, Am. Pediatric Soc., Soc. Pediatric Rsch., Lawson Wilkins Pediatric Endocrine Soc. (treas. 1979-88, pres. 1988-89), Endocrine Soc., Am. Acad. Pediatrics, Am. Fedn. Clin. Rsch., Soc. Exptl. Biology and Medicine, Soc. Nuclear Medicine, N.Y. Acad. Sci., Phila. Coll. Physicians, Phila. Endocrine Soc. (bd. dirs. 1971-72, treas. 1973), Dartmouth Coll. Alumni Coun., Dartmouth Club. Office: 801 6th St S Saint Petersburg FL 33701-4816 E-mail: roota@allkids.org.

ROOT, CHARLES JOSEPH, JR. finance executive, consultant; b. Pierre, S.D., July 26, 1940; s. Charles Joseph and Hazel Ann (Messenger) R.; 1 child from previous marriage, Roseann Marie; m. Sharon Lee, June 24, 1995; stepchildren: Nichole Marie Marcillac, Monique Marie Marcillac. Student, San Francisco Jr. Coll., 1963-65, La Salle Extension U., 1970-71, Coll. of Marin, 1971-72, Am. Coll. Life Underwriters, 1978-82. Registered investment advisor; charter fin. cons.; cert. fin. planner. Estate planner Bankers Life Co., San Francisco, 1966-78; fin. planner Planned Estates Assocs., Corte Madera, Calif., 1978-81; mng. dir. Double Eagle Fin. Corp., Santa Rosa, 1981—, investment advisor, 1983—; personal bus. mgr., 1987—. V.p. Big Bros. of Am., San Rafael, Calif., 1976-80; treas. com. to elect William Filante, San Rafael, 1978, Cmty. Health Ctrs. of Marin, Fairfax, Calif., 1982-83, Wellspring Found., Philo, Calif., 1981-85; treas., bd. dirs. Ctr. for Attitudinal Healing, Tiburon, Calif., 1989-92; bd. dirs. Pickle Family Circus, San Francisco, 1988, United Way Sonoma Lake, Mendocino Counties, 1993—; bd. dirs. Redwood Empire Estate Planning Coun., Santa Rosa, Calif., 1992—, v.p. programs, 1993, pres. 1995-96). Mem. Internat. Assn. Fin. Planners, Coll. Fin.

Planning (cert. fin. planner 1988), Registry of fin. Planning, Nat. Assn. Life Underwriters, Marin County Assn. Life Underwriters (v.p. 1971-76, editor newsletter 1976-80), Rotary (Paul Harris Fellow 1980). Republican. Avocations: pilot, downhill skiing, scuba diving, golf. Office: Double Eagle Fin Corp PO Box 2790 Santa Rosa CA 95405-0790

ROOT, DAVID LEIGH, advertising company executive; b. Toledo, Aug. 14, 1950; s. Robert William and Mary Josephine (Gardner) R.; BA, Hillsdale Coll., 1972; m. Kay Fuhrman, July 15, 1972; children— Whitney, Jay. Real estate regional mgr. Root Outdoor Advt., Inc., Toledo, 1972-74, v.p. real estate, 1974-76, exec. v.p., 1976-81, CEO, pres., 1981-98; chmn., CEO The Root Co., 1998—; v.p. Root & Devel. Inc., 1974-85; v.p. Root Parking Systems, 1974-85, pres., CEO, 1985—; mem. adv. bd. Mid-Am. Bank & Trust, 1980—; dir. Traffic Audit Bur., Inc. Mem. fin. com. ARC, 1982; trustee Wellness Cmty., Black Swamp Conservancy. Mem. Nat. Fedn. Ind. Bus., Inst. Outdoor Advt., Outdoor Advt. Assn. Am. (bd. dirs. 1987—), Outdoor Advt. Assn. Ohio, Toledo C. of C., Better Bus. Bur., Delta Tau Delta. Clubs: Belmont Country (Perrysburg, Ohio); Toledo, Carranor Hunt and Polo, Birchwood Farms Country Club, Hillsboro Club, St. Ann's Hunt, Ringneck Ridge Hunt. Office: Root Comm Inc 21 S Erie St Toledo OH 43602-1233

ROOT, EDWARD LAKIN, education educator, university administrator; b. Cumberland, Md., Dec. 5, 1940; s. Lakin and Edna Grace (Adams) R. BS, Frostburg (Md.) State Coll., 1962, MEd, 1966; EdD, U. Md., 1970. Cert. tchr., Md. Tchr. Allegany County Bd. of Edn., Cumberland, 1962-66; grad. fellow U. Md., College Park, 1966-67, fellow, 1967-69; with Frostburg State U., 1969-99, prof., head edn. dept., 1980-87, dean, 1987-95, prof., head MEd. adminstrn., 1995-99. Mem. gubernatorial appointee to Md. State Bd. Edn., 1999—, Profl. Stds. Bd. Md., Balt., 1980-87, 95-99, Cert. Rev. Bd. Md., Balt., 1987-90, Md. Task Force Adminstrn., Balt., 1985-88, Md. Task Force: Essentials in Tchr. Edn., 1995, Md. Task Force: Prisoners of Time and Response; task force tchr. assessment, 1995-97, Md. Task Force on Tchr. Quality, 2001—, Md. Task Force on Disadvantaged but Capable Students, 2000—. Mem. Allegany County (Md.) Planning and Zoning Bd. Appeals, 1995-96. Mem. ASCD, Nat. Assn. Secondary Sch. Prins., Nat. Soc. for the Study of Edn., Mensa, Elks, Shriners, Masons, Phi Delta Kappa. Democrat. Methodist. Avocation: photography. Home: 100 Pennsylvania Ave Cumberland MD 21502-4236 Office: Frostburg State U College Ave Frostburg MD 21532-1724

ROOT, GERALD EDWARD, legal administrator; b. Gridley, Calif., May 5, 1948; s. Loris Leo Root and Mary Helen (Wheeler) Murrell; m. Tricia Ann Caywood, Feb. 13, 1982 (widowed); children: Jason Alexander, Melinda Ann. AA in Bus., Yuba C.C., Marysville, Calif., 1968; BA in Psychology, Calif. State U., Sonoma, 1974; MA in Social Sci., Calif. State U., Chico, 1977; EdD, U. San Francisco, 2002. Gen. mgr. Do-It Leisure Therapeutic Recreation, Chico, 1977-79; CETA projects coord. City of Chico, 1980-81; exec. dir. Voluntary Action Ctr., Inc., South Lake Tahoe, Calif., 1981-83; devel. dir. Work Tng. Ctr., Inc., Chico, 1983-92; exec. dir. North Valley Rehab. Found., 1986-92; dir. comms. and cmty. outreach Superior Ct. of Calif., County of Sacramento, 1992—2000, project mgr. self-represented litigants action plan initiative, 2000—02, project mgr. virtual courthouse tour--distance learning, 2001—02, project mgr. collaborative pub. edn. youth leadership program, 2002—. Project mgr. Juvenile Detention Alternatives Initiative, 1992-98, Feather River Industries Vocat. Tng., 1991, Creative Learning Ctr. Constrn., 1988-89, Correctional Options-Drug Ct., 1994, Violence Prevention Resource Ctr., 1995-96, Communities That Care-Juvenile Delinquency Prevention Initiative, 1995, Securing the Health and Safety of Urban Children Initiative, 1995-97, Joint Cabinets Youth Work Group/Child Welfare League Am., 1996-97, Task Force on Fairness-The Juvenile Justice Initiative, 1994-97, SacraMentor, Inc., CA Wellness Found., 1994-95, Violent Injury Prevention Coalition/Calif. Dept. Health and Human Svcs., 1995—, Domestic Violence Coord. Coun., Sacramento County, 1995-98, Family Violence Summit, 1997, Ptnrs. in Protection Conf. 1997 Child Abuse Prevention Coun., The Drug Store, Calif. Nat. Guard drug demand reduction program, 1996-97, disporportionate minority confinement rsch. com. Criminal Justice Cabinet, 1997-99, Court Cmty.-Focused Strategic Plan, 1998-2002, Sunrise Recreation and Park Dist. 10 Yr. Master Plan, 1999-2000; steering com. Multicultural Family Violence Prevention Conf., 1996-2001; presenter in field. Bd. dirs. Cmty. Action Agy., Butte County, Calif., 1990-92, ARC, Butte County, 1989-90, Sunrise Recreation and Park Dist., 1996-2001; adv. bd. Butte C.C. Dist., 1987-92, Cmty. Svcs. Planning Coun., 1994-96; blue ribbon task force for strategic plan Calif. Found. for Parks and Recreation, 2000. Grantee AAdminstrv. Office of the Cts./Calif. Jud. Coun., Annie E. Casey Found., USDA, U.S. Dept. Justice, Robert Wood Johnson Found., Calif. Office Criminal Justice Planning, U.S. Dept. Labor, Office Juvenile Justice and Delinquency Prevention, Sacramento Criminal Justice Cabinet, Calif. Wellness Found., Calif. Endowment; recipient Ralph N. Kleps award Calif. Judicial Coun., 2000. Office: Superior Ct Calif County of Sacramento 720 9th St Sacramento CA 95814-1302 E-mail: gerald.root@saccourt.com.

ROOT, JAMES BENJAMIN, landscape architect; b. Detroit, Jan. 26, 1934; s. William Jehial and Helen Elizabeth (English) R. BBA, Memphis State U., 1960; B Landscape Architecture, U. Ga., 1966. Registered landscape architect; lic. real estate agt., Va. Asst. prof. W.Va. U., Morgantown, 1973-75, 93; pvt. practice Charlottesville, Va., 1976-85, 91—; site planner LBA, PH&R, Charles P. Johnson & Assocs., Fairfax, 1986-90. Pvt. practice as golf course architect, Charlottesville, 1976—; instr. Parkersburg C.C., 1975, Piedmont Va. C.C., 1981. Author: Fundamentals of Landscaping and Site Planning, 1985; contbr. articles to profl. jours., also poetry. Mem. Planning Commn., Marietta, Ohio, 1972. Mem. Nat. Golf Found., Elks, Va. Writers Club. Avocation: playing piano. Office: PO Box 7017 Charlottesville VA 22906-7017

ROOT, JANET GREENBERG, private school educator; b. Atlantic City, May 16, 1936; d. Louis and Edith (Shapiro) Greenberg; m. Allen W. Root, June 15, 1958; children: Jonathan, Jennifer, Michael. BS, U. Md., 1958. Tchr. Bd. Edn., Brighton, N.Y., 1958-60; dir. music/art parent program, chmn. dept. arts-humanities Shorecrest Prep. Sch., St. Petersburg, Fla., 1989—. Trustee Shorecrest Prep. Sch., 1980—86, 1990—96, 1998—, dir. cultural enrichment program, 1978—; mem. ednl. bd. Bayfront Ctr., 1993—2000; mem. art com. Tampa Bay Holocaust Mus.; trustee Salvador Dali Mus., 1998—, chmn. edn. com.; mem. long range bldg. com.; trustee Order of Salvador, 1999—. E-mail: jroot@shorecrest.org.

ROOT, JOAN SCHIMPF, civic worker, museum trustee; b. Phila., Jan. 25, 1926; d. Henry Leonard and Josephine Abbott (Sibson) Schimpf; m. Stanley W. Root, Jr., Sept. 3, 1949; children: Henry W., Louise A., Walter W. (dec.). BA, Skidmore Coll., 1947. Chmn. mus. guide program Phila. Mus. Art, 1971—74, mem. exec. com. Friends of Mus., 1975—77, pres. women's com., 1977—80, ex-officio trustee, 1977—80, trustee, 1980—96, hon. trustee, mem. exec. com., 8085, mem. nominating com.; bd. dirs. Phila. Hospitality, Inc., 1992—2001, mem. chmn.'s coun., 2001—; port warden, mem. exec. com. Phila. Maritime Mus. (name now Independence Seaport Mus.), 1975—78, mem. capital projects com., 1980, mem. intern selection com., 1981—83; bd. dirs. Friends Ind. Nat. Hist. Park, 1975—78, mem. capital projects com., 1980, mem. intern selection com., 1981—83; mem. trustee com. Mus. Coun. Phila., 1981; mem. exec. com. U.S. Assn. Mus. Vols., 1980—82; bd. dirs. Goldei Paley Design Ctr., Phila. Coll. Textiles and Sci., 1982—85; mem. Morris Arboretum Meml. Coun., U. Pa., 1985—92; trustee Fairmount Park Coun. Hist. Sites, 1985—91; mem. long range planning com. Friends of Art, Philharm. Galleries, Naples, Fla., 2001. Mem. Internat. Coun. Mus., Am. Assn. Mus., Vol. Com. Art Mus., Ea. Nat. Parks and Monuments Assn., Am. Craft Coun., Nat. Trust Hist. Preservation, Acorn Club. Republican. Episcopalian. Address: 16 Hounds Run Ln Blue Bell PA 19422-2456

ROOT, JONATHAN DAVID, company executive; b. Dec. 18, 1959; AB, Dartmouth Coll., 1982; MD, U. Fla., 1986; MBA, Columbia U., 1995. Dir. neurology-neurosurgery spl. care unit N.Y. Hosp., N.Y.C., 1986-95; asst. prof. neurology Cornell Med. Ctr., 1986-95; gen. ptnr. U.S. Venture Ptnrs., Menlo Park, Calif., 1995—. Office: 2180 Sand Hill Rd Ste 300 Menlo Park CA 94025-6953 E-mail: jroot@usvp.com.

ROOT, LAURA LEE, personal care industry executive; b. Oxnard, Calif., Mar. 8, 1953; d. Robert James Dodge and Barbara Louis (Forest) Mickle; m. Thomas Mayfield Root, Aug. 8, 1987; children: Virginia Anne, Robert William, Sara Michelle. Grad., Internat. Esthetic/Cosmetology, Vancouver, 1997. Diplomate Internat. Com. Aesthetics. Paralegal Hughes Hubbard & Reed, L.A., 1987-89; owner, esthetician Face to Face, McMinnville, Oreg., 1994-96, Body & Soul Esthetic Retreat, McMinnville, 1997-98; owner Esthetic Edn. Resource, Phoenix, 1999—, Enlightenment Skincare, 2000—. Author: The Complete Guide to Microdermabrasion: Treatment, Technique & Technology, 1999, Techniques and Protocols for the Medical Skin Care Clinic, 2001, (booklet) Professional Salon Services, 1995, Ultrasound and E-Stim: Applicaton and Techniques in Medical Aesthetics, 2002, (leaflet) Hip & Cellulite Reduction, 1997; contbr. articles to profl. jours. Republican. Avocations: Russian Classic ballet, private pilot, motorcycles. Office: Esthetic Edn Resource 5025 E Bluefield Ave Scottsdale AZ 85254

ROOT, M. BELINDA, chemist; b. Port Arthur, Tex., May 2, 1957; d. Robert A. and Charlene (Whitehead) Lee; m. Miles J. Root, Nov. 8, 1980; children: Jason Matthew, Ashley Erin. BS in Biology, Lamar U., 1979; MBA, U. Houston, 1994. Asst. chemist Merichem Co., Houston, 1979-81, project chemist, 1982-84, instrument chemist, 1984-85, quality assurance coord., 1986-89, product lab. supr., 1989-91; quality control supr. mfg. Welchem Inc. subs. Amoco, 1991—; mgr. Quality Control Petrolite Corp., 1993; mgr. quality control/quality assurance Akzo-Nobel Chems., Pasadena, Tex., 1994—, mgr. quality and environ. svcs., 1999—. Mgr. Quality and Environ. Svcs. (Lazko Nobel Chems), 1999—. Editor (newsletter) Merichemer, 1989-91. Mem. MADD, 1989—, PTA, 1988—. Recipient Gulf Shore Regional award Cat Fanciers Assn., 1981, Disting. Merit award, 1990. Mem. Am. Soc. Quality Control (cert. quality auditor, quality engr.), Am. Chem. Soc., United Silver Fancier (sec. 1980-82), Lamar U. Alumni Assn., Houston Area Lab Mgrs. Group (chair 2000-01), Beta Beta Beta (sec. 1978-79), Beta Gamma Sigma. Avocations: camping, gardening. Office: Akzo-Nobel Chem Inc 13000 Baypark Rd Pasadena TX 77507-1104

ROOT, NILE, photographer, educator; b. Dec. 11, 1926; s. Victor Nile and Ella May (Holaway) R.; m. Abigail Barton Brown, Feb. 5, 1960; 1 child, James Michael. Student, U. Denver, 1968; MS in Instrnl. Tech., Rochester Inst. Tech., 1978. Microphotographer U.S. Dept. Commerce, Field Info. Agt. Tech., Federal Republic Germany, 1946-48; free-lance photographer, 1949-51; pres. Photography Workshop, Inc., Denver, 1952-60; dir. dept. biophotography and med. illustration Rose Meml. Med. Ctr., 1960-70; dir. med. illustration dept. Children's Hosp., 1970-71; dir. Photography for Sci., 1971-72; prof. biomed. photog. comms. Rochester (N.Y.) Inst. Tech., 1972-86; chmn. dept., 1974-86; prof. emeritus Coll. Imaging Arts and Scis., 1986—. Travel writer, photographer, Japan, China, S.E. Asia, 1986-89; writer, photographer, Tucson, 1989—; dir. HEW project for devel. of field, 1974-77. Contbr. illustrations to med. textbooks; represented in numerous mus. photog. exhibits and numerous pvt. collections. Served with USN, 1945—46. Recipient numerous awards for sci. photographs; Eisenhart Outstanding Tchr. award Rochester Inst. Tech., 1986; named 1st Ann. Faculty fellow Sch. Photog. Arts and Scis., Rochester Inst. Tech., 1979. Fellow Biol. Photog. Assn. (registered, emeritus, bd. govs. 1977-79, Louis Schmidt award 1986); mem. Ctr. Creative Photography. Democrat. Home and Office: 7812 E Elida St Tucson AZ 85715-5009 E-mail: niler314@aol.com.

ROOT, NINA J. librarian, author; b. 1934; d. Jacob J. and Fannie (Slivinsky) R. BA, Hunter Coll.; MSLS, Pratt Inst.; postgrad., USDA Grad. Sch., 1964-65, CUNY, 1970-75. Reference and serials libr. Albert Einstein Coll. Medicine Libr., Bronx, N.Y., 1958-59; asst. chief libr. Am. Cancer Soc., N.Y.C., 1959-62; chief libr. Am. Inst. Aeros. and Astronautics, 1962-64; head ref. and libr. svcs. sci. and tech. divsn. Libr. Congress, Washington, 1964-66; mgmt. cons. Nelson Assocs., Inc., N.Y.C., 1966-70; dir. libr. svcs. Am. Mus. Natural History, 1970-97; freelance mgmt. cons. and libr. planning, 1970-99. Trustee Barnard Found., 1984-91; mem. libr. adv. coun. N.Y. State Bd. Regents, 1984-89, trustee Metro, 1987-92; bd. dirs. Hampden/Booth Libr. Players, 1990-97, Sutton Area Cmty., 1997-2001; trustee Mercantile Libr. N.Y., 1993-95; dir. emerita Libr. AMNH, 1998—. Recipient Meritorious Svc. award Libr. of Congress, 1965, Founders medal SHNH, 1997. Mem. ALA (preservation com. 1977-79, chmn. libr./binders com. 1978-80, chmn. preservation sect. 1980-81, mem. coun. 1983-86), Spl. Librs. Assn. (sec. documentation group N.Y. chpt. 1972-73, 2d v.p. N.Y. 1975-76, treas. sci. and tech. group N.Y. 1975-76, mus. arts and humanities divsn. program planning chairperson-conf. 1977), Archons of Colophon (convener 1978-79), Soc. for Hist. of Natural History (N.Am. rep. 1977-85), N.Y. Acad. Scis. (mem. publs. com. 1975-80, 89-91, archives com. 1976-78, search. com. 1976), Explorers Club. Home: 400 E 59th St New York NY 10022-2342

ROOT, PHYLLIS IDALENE, writer; b. Ft. Wayne, Ind., Feb. 14, 1949; d. John Howard and Margaret Esther (Trout) R.; children: Amelia, Ellen. BA, Valparaiso U., 1971. Tchr. complete scholar program U Minn., 1997—; tchr. MPA writing for children Vt. Coll., 1998—. Author: Moon Tiger, 1985, Soup for Supper, 1986, The Listening Silence, 1992, The Old Red Rocking Chair, 1992, Coyote and the Magic Words, 1993, Sam Who Was Swallowed By a Shark, 1994, Rosie's Fiddle, 1997, One Windy Wednesday, 1996, Contrary Bear, 1996, Mrs. Potter's Pig, 1996, Aunt Nancy and Old Man Trouble, 1996, The Hungry Monster, 1996, What Baby Wants, 1998, One Duck Stuck, 1998, Aunt Nancy and Cousin Lazybones, 1998, Turnover Tuesday, 1998, Grandmother Winter, 1999, Here Comes Tabby Cat, 2000, Hey Tabby Cat, 2000, Meow Monday, 2000, Foggy Friday, 2000, Kiss the Cow, 2000, All for the Newborn Baby, 2000, Rattletrap Car, 2001, Soggy Saturday, 2001, Mouse Goes Out, 2002, Mouse All Year Round, 2002, Oliver Finds His Way, 2002, Big Momma Makes the World, 2002, What's That Noise? (with M. Edwards), 2002. Mem. Authors Guild, Soc. Children's Book Writers and Illustrators. Avocations: gardening, sailing, canoeing.

ROOT, STANLEY WILLIAM, JR. lawyer, retired; b. Honolulu, Mar. 2, 1923; s. Stanley William and Henrietta E. (Brown) R.; m. Joan Louise Schimpf, Sept. 3, 1949; children: Henry, Louise. AB, Princeton U., 1947; LLB, U. Pa., 1950. Bar: Pa. 1950, U.S. Ct. Mil. Appeals 1951, U.S. Supreme Ct. 1971. Ptnr. Foley, Schimpf & Steeley, Phila., 1952-69, Ballard, Spahr, Andrews & Ingersoll, Phila., 1970-91, of counsel, 1992-97; ret., 1998. Lectr. Pa. Bar Assn., 1970-80; bd. dirs. Boardman-Hamilton Co., sec. 1980-98. Exec. v.p. Chestnut Hill Cmty. Assn., Phila., 1978; with Whitpain Farm Assn., Blue Bell, Pa., 1987, 90, pres., 1992-94; with St. Paul's Ch. Vestry, Phila., 1969-75; bd. dirs. Lansdale (Pa.) Med. Group, 1972-95, E.B. Spaeth Found. Wills Hosp., Phila., 1975-88, Chevalier Jackson Clinic, Phila., 1965-88; trustee Civil War Libr. and Mus., 1985-93, v.p., 1989, sec., 1992-93, mem. adv. bd., 1993-95; trustee Soc. Protestant Episc. Ch., Pa. Diocese, 1955-95. Lt. col. U.S. Army, 1942-45, ETO, 1950-52, Korea. Decorated Bronze Star; recipient Pa. Commendation medal State of Pa., 1962; named Comdr. Phila. chpt. Mil. Order Fgn. Wars, 1972. Mem. Union League (pres. 1983-85), Sunnybrook Golf Club, Royal Poinciana Golf Club, Brit. Officers Club, Mil. Order Loyal Legion. Republican. Episcopalian. Avocations: golf, tennis, fishing. Home: 16 Hounds Run Ln Blue Bell PA 19422-2456 Office: Ballard Spahr Andrews & Ingersoll 51st Fl 1735 Market St Fl 51 Philadelphia PA 19103-7599 E-mail: stanislaw16@aol.com.

ROOT, WILLIAM LUCAS, electrical engineering educator; b. Des Moines, Oct. 6, 1919; s. Frank Stephenson and Helen (Lucas) R.; m. Harriett Jean Johnson, Dec. 10, 1918; children: William Lucas Jr., Wendy Elizabeth Root Cate. BEE, Iowa State U., 1940; MEE, MIT, 1943, PhD in Math., 1952. Staff mem. MIT Lincoln Lab., Lexington, Mass., 1952-61, group leader, 1959-61; lectr. Harvard U., Cambridge, 1958-59; visitor U. Wis., Madison, 1963-64; vis. prof. Mich. State U., East Lansing, 1966, 68, U. Calif., Berkeley, 1966-67; prof. aerospace engring. U. Mich., Ann Arbor, 1961-87, prof. emeritus, 1988—. Vis. fellow U. Cambridge (Eng.), 1970; mem. U.S. Army Sci. Bd., 1979-82. Co-author: Random Signals and Noise, 1958 (Russian and Japanese transls.); assoc. editor: (IEEE) Information Theory Transactions, 1977-79; Soc. Indsl. and Applied Math. Jour. Applied Mathematics, 1962-72; contbr. 65 articles to profl. jours., book chpts. and conf. procs. Served to lt. USMCR, 1943-45. NSF Sr. postdoctoral fellow, 1970, vis. fellow Cambridge Clare Hall, 1970; recipient Claude E. Shannon award IEEE Info. Theory Soc., 1986, Career Achievement award ComCon Conf. Bd., 1987. Life fellow IEEE (vice chmn. adminstrv. com. info. theory group 1965-66); mem. Am. Math. Soc. Home: PO Box 3785 Ann Arbor MI 48106-3785 Office: U Mich Dept Aerospace Engring Ann Arbor MI 48109

ROOT, WILLIAM PITT, poet, educator; b. Austin, Minn., Dec. 28, 1941; s. William Pitt and Bonita Joy (Hilbert) R.; m. Judith Carol Bechtold, 1965 (div. 1970); 1 dau., Jennifer Lorca; m. Pamela Uschuk, 1987. BA, U. Wash., 1964; MFA, U. N.C. at Greensboro, 1967; postgrad., Stanford, 1968-69. Asst. prof. Mich. State U., 1967-68; tchr. writing Mid-peninsula Free U., 1969; writer-in-residence Amherst Coll., U. Southwestern La., 1976, U. Mont., 1978, 80, 83-84; with poet-in-schs. program state art councils Oreg., Miss., Idaho, Ariz., Vt., Mont., Wyo., Wash., Tex., 1971—; Distinguished writer-in-residence Wichita State U., 1976; vis. writer in residence U. Mont., 1978, 80, 83-86, Hunter Coll., N.Y.C., 1986—; vis. writer NYU, 1986. Vis. writer Westside Young Men's Hebrew Assn., N.Y.C., 1988, Pacific Lutheran U., 1990. Author: The Storm and Other Poems, 1969, Striking the Dark Air for Music, 1973, The Port of Galveston, 1974, Coot and Other Characters, 1977, 7 Mendocino Songs, 1977, A Journey South, 1977, Fireclock, 1981, Reasons for Going It on Foot, 1981, In the World's Common Grasses, 1981, The Unbroken Diamond: Nightletter to the Mujahideen, 1983, Invisible Guests, 1984, Faultdancing, 1986, Trace Elements from a Recurring Kingdom, 1994; collaborated (with filmmaker Ray Rice) on poetry films Song of the Woman and the Butterflyman (Orpheus award 1st Internat. Poetry Film Festival 1975), 7 For a Magician, 1976, Faces, 1981. Rockefeller Found. grantee, 1969-70; Guggenheim Found. grantee, 1970-71; Nat. Endowment for Arts grantee, 1973-74; U.S./U.K. Bicentennial Exchange Artist, 1978-79, Wallace Stegner creative writing fellow Stanford U., 1968-69; recipient 1st prize univ. poetry contest Acad. Am. Poets, 1966, Atlantic Young Poet award, 1967, Stanley Kunitz Poetry award, 1981, Guy Owen Poetry Prize, 1982, Pushcart Prize (Poetry), 1977, 1980, 1985; named Poet Laureate of Tucson, 1997—. Address: CUNY Hunter Coll Dept Eng 695 Park Ave New York NY 10021-5024 E-mail: wpropoet@attglobal.net. *With Rilke I believe the measure of one's life consists in a growing capacity to engage ever more fully in that dance between what we call will and what we call fate until the result is a contagion of vitality powerful enough to dissipate the spell of habits and to recreate in oneself that first spirit which is intuitive, sympathetic, and clear. Poems simply record the complex effort.*

ROOT-BERNSTEIN, ROBERT SCOTT, biologist, educator; b. Washington, Aug. 7, 1953; s. Morton Ira and Maurine (Berkstresser) Bernstein; m. Michèle Marie Root-Bernstein, Sept. 2, 1978; children: Meredith Marie, Brian Robert. AB, Princeton U., 1975, PhD, 1980. Postdoctoral fellow Salk Inst. for Biol. Studies, La Jolla, Calif., 1981-82, rsch. assoc., 1983-84; from asst. to assoc. prof. Mich. State U., East Lansing, 1987-96, prof., 1996—. Cons. Parke-Davis Pharm. Rsch. Divsn., Ann Arbor, 1990-96, Chiron Corp., 1992-96; mem. adv. bd. Soc. for Advancement Gifted Edn., Chgo., 1987-92; Sigma Xi nat. lectr., 1994-96. Author: Discovering, 1989, Rethinking AIDS, 1993, Honey, Mud, Maggots and Other Medical Marvels, 1997, Sparks of Genius, 1999; columnist The Scis. mag., 1989-92; contbr. numerous articles to profl. jours. MacArthur Found. fellow, 1981-86; recipient D.J. Ingle Meml. Writing prize, 1988. Mem. Phi Beta Kappa (hon.), Sigma Xi. Avocations: drawing, painting, photography, cello. Office: Mich State U Dept Physiology Biomed & Phys Scis Bldg East Lansing MI 48824 E-mail: rootbern@msu.edu.

ROOTE, DAVID JAMES, state agency administrator; b. Pitts, May 25, 1960; s. Jay Campbell and Blanche Marie R.; m. Diane, Sept. 24, 1994; children: Steven, Andrew. BCE, Pa. State U., 1983. Registered profl. engr., Pa. Constrn. inspector Pa. Dept. Transp., Uniontown and Pitts., 1984-86; water qualtiy specialist Pa. Dept. Environ. Protection, Greensburg, 1987—. Mem. AIChE, Western Pa. Water Pollution Control Fedn., Lions (environ. chmn. 1996—, pres. Jeannette club 1993-94). Avocations: shotokan karate, fishing, hunting, reading, computer activities. Office: Pa Dept Environ Protection Rd #2 Box 603-C Greensburg PA 15601 E-mail: Droote@state.pa.us.

ROOTENBERG, SHARYN MICHELE, lawyer; b. Bklyn., Mar. 15, 1969; d. Jacob and Ruth Rootenberg. BA, SUNY, Albany, 1990; JD, Yeshiva U., 1995. Bar: N.Y. 1995, N.J. 1995, U.S. Ct. Appeals (2d cir.) 1997. Legis. aide N.Y. State Assembly, Albany and Bklyn., 1988-90; assoc. Herzfeld & Rubin, N.Y.C., summer 1993, Edmonds & Beier, N.Y.C., summer 1994; asst. corp. counsel N.Y.C. Corp. Counsel, Family Ct. Divsn., Bklyn., 1995-97, N.Y.C. Corp. Counsel, Appeals Divsn., N.Y.C., 1997—. Mediator pilot pro bono project, ABA, 1994-96. Committeeperson Kings county Dem. Com., Bklyn., 1992-96. Mem. ABA, N.Y. State Bar Assn., Assn. of Bar of City of N.Y. (com. mcpl. affairs, Outstanding Asst. Corp. Counsel award 1999), N.Y. County Lawyers Assn. Office: NYC Corp Counsel Appeals Divsn 100 Church St Fl 6 New York NY 10007-2601

ROOTS, KEITH DYLAND, academic administrator; b. Richmond, Va., Oct. 2, 1965; s. Samuel and Willie Tina (Perkins) R.; m. Kenna Lea Ose, July 11, 1998. BA in Govt., U. Va., 1986; MEd, U. Tex., 1991. Dist. exec. Stonewall Jackson Area Coun. Boy Scouts Am., Wanesboro, Va., 1986-89; asst. to pres. Longwood Coll., Farmville, 1991-95; asst. to provost U. Va., Charlottesville, 1998—2001, asst. dir. corp. and found. rels., 2001—02, assoc. dir. found. rels., 2002—. Recipient Eagle Scout award Boy Scouts Am., 1980; Am. Assn. State Colls. & Univs. fellow, 1993. Mem. Am. Assn. Higher Edn., Rotary, Alpha Phi Omega (nat. bd. dirs.). Avocations: sports, coin collecting, Scouting memorabilia. Office: U Va PO Box 400807 Charlottesville VA 22904-4807

ROOZEN, MARY LOUISE, public relations executive; b. Mar. 31, 1921; d. Edward E. and Margaret (May) Silverman; m. Edwin Cramer Roozen, Sept. 18, 1943; children: Mary Katrina Roozen Hass, Joanna Roozen Satorius, Margaret Roozen Monahan. BA in Speech, U. Wis., 1942. With Met. Milw. Assn. Commerce, 1942-43; adminstrv. asst. Curative Workshop of Milw., 1968-69; adminstrv. asst. mktg. Marine Corp., Milw., 1969-70, mktg. officer, 1970-73, asst. v.p., 1973-76, v.p. pub. rels., 1976-84; devel. dir. VNA Milw., 1989-90. Dir. Germantown Marine Bank, 1977-83; v.p. Marine Bank, N.A., Milw., 1977-87, cons. corp. pub. relations, 1987-93; curator Marine Collection of Wis. Art, 1969-87, v.p. Marine Found., 1980-87; bd. dirs. Plaza Bldg. Mgmt., 1980-87. Bd. dirs. Neighborhood House, Milw., 1963-78, co-chair capital fund dr., 1984; pres. Temp, 1980-81; chair 440th Tactical Air Wing Comty. Coun., USAFR, 1988, dir. 1985-90; bd. dirs. Curative Workshop, Milw., 1970-78, Wis. Humane Soc., 1976-85, Friends of Art, Milw., 1980-84, Ozaukee Humane Soc., 1983-86, Vol. Ctr. Greater Milw., Friends of PBS Channel 10/36, bd. dirs. Red Bus. Corp., 1993-2002; docent Milw. Art Mus., Am. Heritage Soc., Fine Arts Soc., 1991—. Recipient Recognition award Nat. Ctr. for Voluntary Action, 1977. Mem. Pub. Rels. Soc. Am. (chair fin. instns. sect. 1983-85, exec. com. 1980-84), Wis. Sr. Pub. Rels. Forum, Nat. Assn. Bank Women (chmn. Milw. group 1976-77), Women's Club of Wis. (mem. fin. com. 1983-85, mem. art com. 1993-94, mem. house com. 1994-95), River Tennis Club. Episcopalian. Home and Office: 7716 N Boyd Way Milwaukee WI 53217-3209

ROOZENDAAL, LEONARDUS MARTINUS, not-for profit administrator; b. Goes, The Netherlands, Apr. 7, 1956; s. Dina van Zweden; m. Sarah Ruth Simon; children: Leah Adriana, Ana Catarina. Degree in Clin. Chemistry, Laboratorium Sch., Goes, 1975; degree in Biochemistry, Dr. Struycken Inst., Breda, The Netherlands, 1979; MPH, Johns Hopkins U., Balt., 1986. Mgr. lab. Netherlands Devel. Orgn., Tahoua, Niger, 1981-84, coord. primary health care Cameroon, 1987-90; mgr. health project CARE, Zinder, Niger, 1991-93, mgr. health sector Quito, Equador, 1993-96, dep. dir. Kisumu, Kenya, 1996-99, dir. Nairobi, Kenya, 1999—2002. Chmn. bd. dirs. Wedco Enterprise Devel. Ltd., Nairobi, 1999-2000, Rural Enterprise Agri-Bus. Project, 2000-01; mem. exec. com. Non Govtl. Orgns. Coun., 2000-01; trustee CARE pension fund, Nairobi, 1999-2001, dir., Khartoum, Sudan, 2002—. Avocations: reading, art collecting, travelling, family outings, cinema. Office: CARE 151 Ellis St NE Atlanta GA 30303-2420 E-mail: leo@care.or.ke.

ROPER, BERYL CAIN, writer, publisher, retired library director; b. Long Beach, Calif., Mar. 1, 1931; d. Albert Verne and Ollie Fern (Collins) Cain; m. Max H. Young, Aug. 22, 1947 (div. 1958); children: Howard, Wade, Debra, Kevin, John R., Christopher; m. George Albert Roper, Mar. 24, 1962 (dec. July 1978); children: Ellen, Georgianne; m. Jack T. Hughes, Sept. 21, 1993 (dec. May 2001). BA, West Tex. State U., 1986; MA, Tex. Womans U., 1989. Libr. clk. Cornette Libr., West Tex. State U., Canyon, 1981-87; dir. Clarendon (Tex.) Coll. Libr., 1988-96. Lectr. in history and archaeology; owner Aquamarine Publs. Editor, pub.: In the Light of Past Experience, 1989, Transactions of the Southwest Federation of Archaeological Societies, 1993, Greenbelt Site, 1996, Presbyterian Mission Work in New Mexico: Memoirs of Alice Blake, 1997;

author, pub.: Trementina, 1990, Trementina Revisited, 1994, Seekers After Truth, 1998; author articles on women and history. Mem. Clarendon Archaeol. Soc. (charter, v.p. 1990-91), Tex. Libr. Assn., Tex. Intertribal Indian Orgn., Pi Gamma Mu, Beta Phi Mu, Alpha Chi, Phi Alpha Theta. Republican. Mem. Lds Ch. Avocations: music, gardening, decorating, remodeling old houses, genealogy. Office: Aquamarine Publs 8001 Cattle Dr Canyon TX 79015 E-mail: beryl0I@sprynet.com.

ROPER, BIRDIE ALEXANDER, social sciences educator; b. New Orleans; d. Earl and Ethel (Charmer) Alexander; m. Morris F. Roper; 1 child, Andree Marie Driskell. BS, U. Dayton, 1949; MA, Azusa Pacific U., 1971, Claremont Grad. Sch., 1978, PhD, 1980. DON Flint Goodridge Hosp., New Orleans, 1954, 55; sch. nurse, health educator, classroom tchr. L.A. Unified Sch. Dist., 1963-91; extended day prof. social scis. dept. Pasadena City Coll., 1972—; clin. instr. dept. nursing Calif. State U., San Bernardino, 1993—. Researcher, author, cons. in gerontology. Editor: (newsletter Calif. Nurses Assn.) Vital Signs. Mem. ANA, Am. Soc. Univ. Profs., Am. Soc. on Aging, Inst. for Rsch. on Aging, Nat. Coun. on Aging, Nat. Gerontol. Nursing Assn., Nat. Assn. Profl. Geriatric Care Mgrs., Phi Delta Kappa (bd. mem. San Antonio chpt. 1981-92), Alpha Kappa Alpha. Home and Office: 1700 Heritage Park Rd Charleston SC 29407-5839

ROPER, HARRY JOSEPH, lawyer; b. Bridgeport, Conn., Apr. 15, 1940; BEE, Rensselaer Poly. Inst., 1962; LLB, NYU, 1966. Assoc. Neuman, Williams, Anderson & Olson, Chgo., 1966-70, ptnr., 1970-90, Roper & Quigg, Chgo., 1990—. Home: 611 W Fullerton Pky Chicago IL 60614-2613 Office: Roper & Quigg 200 S Michigan Ave Chicago IL 60604-2402

ROPER, JEFFREY SEAN, state agency administrator; b. Antioch, Calif. s. Larry G. and Marta M. R. B, Boise State U., 1994. Ops. mgr. Eddie Bauer, Inc., Seattle, 1996-98; exec. dir. PDCA, Washington State Coun., 1998—. Bd. dirs. Treasure Valley Red Cross, Boise, 1991-97, Sojourner Pl., Seattle, 2000—. Avocations: traveling, reading, cooking, gardening. Office: PDCA Washington State Coun 870 SW 136th St Seattle WA 98166 Fax: (206)246-5616. E-mail: jroperpdca@hotmail.com.

ROPER, JOHN MARLIN, SR. federal magistrate judge; b. Greenville, Ala., Dec. 11, 1942; s. Marlin Ross and Ruby Lois (Martin) R.; m. Virginia Gene Kerth, Apr. 2, 1966; 1 son, John Marlin. BS, Auburn U., 1964; JD, Tulane U., 1968. Bar: Ala. 1968, Miss. 1974. Counselor, program dir. Juvenille Delinquency Instn., New Orleans, 1966-69; sr., law clk. to judge U.S. Dist. Ct. (so. dist.) Miss., 1969-75, magistrate judge, 1975—. Mem. Fed. Magistrate Judges Assn. (dir. 5th cir. 1976-82, nat. officer 1982-86, nat. pres. 1986-87, security com. jud. conf. 1987-89, budget com. jud. conf. 1989-97). Methodist. Office: US District Court Ste 150 725 Martin Luther King Blvd Biloxi MS 39530-2267

ROPER, SALLY ANN, health facility coordinator; b. Hazelton, Pa., Aug. 24, 1950; d. Robert H. and Margaret F. (Baskin) Walk; children: Julia Kane, Laurie Kane. Diploma in nursing, Kings County Hosp., 1972; cert. health adminstrn., Kings Coll., 1995, MS in Healthcare Adminstrn., 1996; student, Bklyn. Coll., Luzerne County C.C.; BA in Mgmt. Health svcs., Ottawa U., 1992. RN, Pa.; cert. ACLS instr., BLS instr. Nurse Kings Highway Hosp., Bklyn.; staff nurse ICU, CCU Kings County Hosp.; staff nurse progressive care Nesbitt Meml. Hosp., Kingston, Pa., quality improvement coord.; performance improvement coord. Wyoming Valley Health Care Sys.; dir. quality mgmt. N.E. Health and Hospice Care, Inc. Mem. Nat. Assn. for Healthcare Quality, Am. Coll. Healthcare Execs., Pa. Assn. for Healthcare Quality. E-mail: nehhquality@dfnow.com .

ROPER, WILLIAM LEE, dean, physician; b. Birmingham, Ala., July 6, 1948; s. Richard Barnard and Jean (Fyfe) R.; m. Maryann Roper, Jan. 14, 1978 AA, Fla. Coll., 1968; BS, U. Ala, 1970, MD, 1974, M.P.H., 1981. Diplomate Am. Bd. Pediatrics, Am. Bd. Preventive Medicine. Intern, resident in pediatrics U. Colo. Med. Ctr., Denver, 1974-77; health officer Jefferson County Dept. Health, Birmingham, 1977-82, 83; White House fellow Washington, 1982-83; spl. asst. to Pres. for health policy, 1983-86; adminstr., Health Care Finance Adminstrn. HHS, 1986-89; dep. asst. to pres. for domestic policy The White House, 1989-90; adminstr. Agy. for Toxic Substances and Disease Registry and dir. Ctrs. for Disease Control and Prevention, Atlanta, 1990-93; sr. v.p. Prudential Health Care, Roseland, NJ, 1994-97; pres. Prudential Ctr. for Health Care Rsch., Atlanta, 1993-95; dean sch. pub. health U. N.C., Chapel Hill, 1997—. Mem. Inst. Medicine of NAS, Phi Beta Kappa, Alpha Omega Alpha Republican. Home: 10424 Stone Chapel Hill NC 27517-8549 Office: U NC 170 Rosenau Hall Campus Box 7400 Chapel Hill NC 27599-7400

ROPES, DAVID GARDNER, marketing executive; b. Coral Gables, Fla., Feb. 19, 1947; s. Lawrence Gardner and Jean (Newell) R.; m. M. Cassandra McGinnis, Aug. 21, 1968; children: Alexandra, Micheal. BS in Journalism, U. Fla., 1968. Pub. relations asst. Philip Morris U.S.A., N.Y.C., 1968-69, asst. to pres., 1972-74, mktg. mgr., 1974-77; account supr. William Esty Co., 1977-80; advt. mgr. Pepsi-Cola U.S.A., Purchase, N.Y., 1980-82; v.p. advt. and media Pizza Hut, Inc., Wichita, Kans., 1982-87; v.p. advt. Pepsi-Cola Co., Somers, N.Y., 1987-90; sr. v.p. global mktg. Reebok Internat., Boston, 1990-97; dir. corp. advt. and integrated mktg. Ford Motor Co., Detroit, 1997-2000; exec. v.p. mktg., bus. devel. Zuniversity.com., Stamford, Conn., 2000—01; co-founder, CMO MarketEcho, New Canaan; mktg. cons., 2002—. Capt. U.S. Army, 1969-72, Vietnam. Named one of Top 100 Advt. Execs. Advt. Age mag., 1986. Mem. Assn. Nat. Advt. (bd. dirs. 1997—), U. Fla. Alumni Assn. (bd. dirs. 1995-98, Disting. Alumni 1994), Ad Coun. (bd. dirs. 1997—), Detroit Aircraft Club (bd. dirs. 1998). Republican. Roman Catholic. Avocations: golf, tennis. E-mail: dropes100@yahoo.com.

ROPP, STEPHEN CHAPMAN, political scientist; b. Durham, N.C., Apr. 25, 1941; s. Theodore and Elizabeth Chapman Ropp; m. Jo-Carol Hall, June 9, 1966; children: Samantha May Howell, Elizabeth Eleanor. BA, Allegheny Coll., 1963; MA, U. Wash., 1965; PhD, U. Calif., Riverside, 1971. Asst. prof. polit. sci. N.Mex. State U., Las Cruces, 1972—77, assoc. prof. polit. sci., 1977—83, prof. polit. sci., 1983—84; Milward Simpson Disting. prof. polit. sci. U. Wyo., Laramie, 1983—84, prof. polit. sci., 1985—2002. Vis. prof. polit. sci. N.Mex. State U., Las Cruces, 1983—84; cons. Kissinger Commn. on Cen. Am., Washington, 1983—84; expert witness U.S. Senate Fgn. Rels. Com., Washington, 1986; mem. nat. screening com. Fulbright Program, Washington, 2000—02. Author: (book) Panamanian Politics, 1981; co-editor: Central America: Crisis and Adaptation, 1984, The Power of Human Rights, 1999. Sgt. U.S. Army, 1965—68. Named Clarence Seibold prof., U. Wyo., 2001; named one of Top 65 Fgn. Policy Experts in U.S., Nat. Jour., 1990; recipient Sr. Fulbright award, Fulbright Program, 1999. Mem.: Am. Polit. Sci. Assn. (Outstanding Tchg. award 2000), Internat. Studies Assn., Latin Am. Studies Assn. Methodist. Avocations: hiking, swimming, basketball, skating. Home: 1484 N 22d St Laramie WY 82072 Office: U Wyo Dept Polit Sci PO Box 3197 Laramie WY 82071 E-mail: sropp@uwyo.edu.

ROPPOLO, JUSTIN KYLE, investment company executive; b. Austin, Tex., Feb. 20, 1978; s. James Ignatius and Patricia Gail Roppolo; m. Brandi Ballard, May 20, 2000. BA in Agrl. Econs., Tex. A&M U., 2000. Real estate agt. Lakeview Realty, Richland Chambers, Tex.; credit analyst First Nat. Bank, Fairfield, 2002; investment rep. Edward Jones, Leander, 2002—. Avocations: hunting, fishing, playing sports. Home: 301 Fairfield Loop Leander TX 78641 E-mail: justinroppolo@hotmail.com.

ROPSKI, GARY MELCHIOR, lawyer; b. Erie, Pa., Apr. 19, 1952; s. Joseph Albert and Irene Stefania (Mszanowski) R.; m. Barbara Mary Schleck, May 15, 1982. BS in Physics, Carnegie-Mellon U., 1972; JD cum laude, Northwestern U. Sch. Law, 1976. Bar: Ill. 1976, U.S. Patent and Trademark Office 1976, U.S. Dist. Ct. (no. dist.) Ill. 1976, U.S. Ct. Appeals (7th cir.) 1977, U.S. Dist. Ct. (ea. dist.) Wis. 1977, U.S. Ct. Appeals (3d cir.) 1981, Pa. 1982, U.S. Ct. Claims 1982, U.S. Ct. Appeals (fed. cir.) 1982, U.S. Supreme Ct. 1982, U.S. Dist. Ct. (ea. dist.) Mich. 1984, U.S. Dist. Ct. (no. dist.) Calif. 1986. Assoc. Brinks Hofer Gilson & Lione, Chgo., 1976-81, shareholder, 1981—. Adj. prof. patents and copyrights Northwestern U. Sch. Law, Chgo., 1982-97. Contbr. numerous articles to profl. jours. Mem. ABA, Internat. Bar Assn., Internat. Trademark Assn., Am. Intellectual Property Law Assn., Ill. Bar Assn., Intellectual Property Law Assn. Chgo., Chgo. Bar Assn., Univ. Club, Chgo. Yacht Club. Roman Catholic. Office: Brinks Hofer Gilson & Lione Ste 3600 455 N Cityfront Plaza Dr Chicago IL 60611-5599 E-mail: gropski@brinkshofer.com.

ROQUE, FRANCIS XAVIER, auxiliary bishop; b. Providence, Oct. 9, 1928; s. Warren Edward Roque and Mary Loretta Gallagher BA, Saint John's Sem., 1950. ordained priest Roman Catholic, 1953. Parish priest Diocese of Providence, 1953-61; army chaplain U.S. Army, 1961-83; bishop Archdiocese for Mil. Svcs. USA, Washington, 1983—. Served to col. U.S. Army, 1961-83, Vietnam Decorated Bronze Star Office: Archdiocese for Mil Svcs USA PO Box 4469 Washington DC 20017-0469 E-mail: froque@milarch.org.

RORAT, EDWARDA, pathologist, educator; b. Warsaw, Poland; came to U.S., 1959; d. Jan Rorat and Stephanie Buczkowska; m. Orest Filipowicz (div. 1965). MD, Pomeranian Med. Acad., Poland, 1959. Resident L.I. Jewish Queens Hosp. Ctr., L.I., N.Y., 1961-65; Asst. attending pathologist Queens Hosp. Ctr., 1965-66, L.I. Jewish-Hillside Med. Ctr. SUNY, Stony Brook, 1965-66, assoc. attending pathologist anatomic pathology & cytology, 1966-77; cons. in gynecol. pathology Columbia-Presbyn. Med. Ctr., N.Y.C., 1972-77; assoc. attending pathologist in anat. pathology Beth Israel Med. Ctr., 1977-83, pathologist in charge cytology lab., 1977—, attending pathologist, 1983—. Clin. asst. prof. pathology SUNY, Stony Brook, 1971-77; adj. asst. prof. pathology Coll. Physicians and Surgeons, Columbia U., 1974-77; asst. prof. pathology Mt. Sinai Sch. Medicine, 1977-87, assoc. prof. pathology, 1988—. Contbr. articles to med. jours. Fellow Coll. Am. Pathologists, Am. Coll. Obstetricians and Gynecologists (assoc.); mem. Am. Soc. Clin. Pathologists, Internat. Acad. Pathology, Am. Soc. Cytology, Internat. Soc. Gynecol. Pathologists, N.Y. State Pathologists Soc., Pathologists Club N.Y. Home: 345 E 56th St Apt 18B New York NY 10022-3739 Office: Beth Israel Med Ctr 16th St New York NY 10003

ROREM, NED, composer, author; b. Richmond, Ind., Oct. 23, 1923; s. Clarence Rufus and Gladys (Miller) R. Student, Northwestern U., 1940-42, Curtis Inst., Phila., 1943; BA, Juilliard Sch. Music, 1946, MA, 1948; D.F.A. (hon.), Northwestern U., 1977, Curtis Inst., 1982. Slee prof., composer-in-residence Buffalo U., 1959-61; prof. composition U. Utah, 1965-67, Curtis Inst., 1980—, Yale U., New Haven, 1998—, Manhattan Sch. of Music, 1995—. Guest composer New Music New Haven Series Sch. Music Yale U., 1998, vis. prof., 1998-99; composer-in-residence Lakes Chamber Music Festival, 1999. Composer: symphonies No. 1, premiere Vienna, Austria, 1951, No. 2, premiere La Jolla, Calif., 1956, No. 3, premiere with Leonard Bernstein and N.Y. Philharmonic, 1959, Three Piano Sonatas, 1949, 50, 54, Lento for Strings, 1950, Design for Orch., 1954, Pilgrims for Strings, 1958, Eagles for Orch., 1958, Lions, 1964, Ideas for Easy Orch, 1961, Piano Concerto No. 2, 1951, 3d Piano Concerto, 1970, Eleven Studies, 1959, Water Music, 1966, Sun; for voice and orch., commd. by N.Y. Philharmonic, 1966, Air Music for Orch. 1974 (Pulitzer prize 1976), Assembly and Fall, 1975, Sunday Morning for Orch., 1977, Remembering Tommy, 1981; numerous chorus works, latest being Letters from Paris, 1965; for chorus and orch., commd. by Koussevitzky Found. in Library of Congress, Little Prayers, 1972, Whitman Cantata, 1982, An American Oratorio, 1983, Homer, 1986, Seven Motets, 1986, Te Deum, 1986, What is Pink?, 1987, The Death of Moses, 1987, Goodbye My Fancy, 1988; operas A Childhood Miracle, 1952, Three Sisters Who Are Not Sisters, 1969, Fables, 1970, Bertha, 1968, Miss Julie, 1964 (Ford Found. grantee), Hearing, 1976, Cycles: War Scenes, 1969, Six Songs for High Voice and Orchestra, 1954, Six Irish Poems, 1951, Poems of Love and the Rain, 1964, Ariel for Voice, clarinet and piano, 1971, Last Poems of Wallace Stevens for voice, cello and piano, 1971, Serenade for voice, violin, viola and piano, Women's Voices, 1975, The Nantucket Songs, 1979, Three Calamus Poems, 1982, The Schuyler Songs, 1987, Day Music and Night Music for Violin, 1972-73, Etudes for Piano, 1975, Book of Hours for flute and harp, A Quaker Reader for Organ, 1976, The Santa Fe Songs, 1980, Remembering Tommy, 1980, Views From the Oldest House for organ, 1981, Winter Pages, 1981, Picnic on the Marne, 1982, Dances for Cello, 1983, Violin Concerto, 1984, Organ Concerto, 1985, String Symphony, 1985, Septet: Scenes from Childhood, 1985, Trio: End of Summer, 1985, Quintet: Bright Music, 1988, Diversions for Brass Quintet, 1989, Trio (Spring Music), 1990, Three Organbooks; The Auden Poems, Trio for Violin, Cello, Piano, 1990, Swords and Plowshares (for 4 solo voices and orch.), 1991, Third Quartet, 1991, Fourth Concerto for Piano (left hand) and Orch., 1991, Present Laughter for mixed chorus, piano and brass, 1993, Fourth Quartet, 1994, Songs of Sadness for quartet of baritone, guitar, clarinet and cello, 1994, More Than a Day for countertenor and orch., 1995, Six Variations for Two Pianos, 1995. Evidence of Things Not Seen, 1997; Autumn Music for Violin and Piano, 1997, Six Organ Pieces, 1998, Double Concerto for Violin, Cello and Orchestra, 1998, An Oboe Book, 1999, Aftermath, 2002, Trio (oboe, violin, piano), 2002; commns. for U.S. Bicentennial include compositions for, Cin. Symphony, N.C. Symphony, Nat. Endowment of the Arts, Am. Harp Soc.; Author: The Paris Diary of Ned Rorem, 1966, Music from Inside Out, 1967, The New York Diary, 1967, Music and People, 1968, Critical Affairs, 1970, Pure Contraption, 1973, The Later Diaries, 1974, An Absolute Gift, 1978, Setting the Tone, 1983, Paul's Blues, 1985, The Nantucket Diary, 1987, Settling the Score, 1988, Knowing When To Stop, 1994, Other Entertainment, 1996, Dear Paul, Dear Ned, 1997 (letters between Paul Bowles and Ned Rorem), Lies: A Diary (1986-1999), 2000 A Ned Rorem Reader, 2002; also articles newspapers, mags., Recs. for, Columbia, Decca, Odyssey, Desto, Phillips, Premier, C.R.I., Westminster, Orion, New World Records. Recipient Music Libraries Assn. award for song Lordly Hudson 1948, Gershwin Meml. award 1949, Lili Boulanger award 1950, Nat. Inst. Arts and Letters award 1968, Pulitzer prize in music 1976, Grammy award for Best Orchestral Rec., 1989; Fulbright fellow Paris, 1951-52; Guggenheim fellow, 1957-58, 77-78 Mem.: AAAL (pres. 2000—), ASCAP, PEN, Am. Acad. Arts & Letters (pres. 2000—), Soc. Friends. Mem. Soc. Of Friends. Address: PO Box 764 Nantucket MA 02554-0764

RORER, JOHN WHITELEY, publisher, consultant; b. Phila., Aug. 4, 1930; s. Ronald Erle and Hazel (Whiteley) R.; m. Beverly Case, June 6, 1953. BS, U. Pa., 1952; MBA, Drexel U., 1956. Credit analyst Phila. Nat. Bank, 1954-56; with Curtis Pub. Co., Phila., 1956-68; dir. purchasing Chilton Pub. Co., Phila., 1968-70; founding pres. Focus Bus. Weekly, Bus. News, Inc., Phila., 1968—, pres., pub., 1974—; owner Pubs. Systems Assocs., Upper Darby, Pa., 1979—. Mem. Phila. World Affairs Council, 1979—. Served to capt. U.S. Army, 1952-54. Mem. Nat. Assn. Bus. Publs. (co-founder, bd. dirs. 1978-81), Nat. Assn. Indsl. Advt., Mktg. and Communications Execs. Assn., Union League Club, Engrs. Club (Phila.), Downtown Club. Republican. Episcopalian. Avocation: economics research. Home: 7520 Rogers Ave Upper Darby PA 19082-1907 Office: 1015 Chestnut St Philadelphia PA 19107-4316

RORER, LEONARD GEORGE, psychologist, writer; b. Dixon, Ill., Dec. 24, 1932; s. Leonard Gleason and Marion Emma (Geyer) R.; m. Gail Evans, Apr. 30, 1958 (div. May 11, 1964); children: Liat, Eric Evans; m. Nancy McKimens, Jan, 9, 1969 (div. Jan. 19, 1976); 1 child, Mya Noelani. BA, Swarthmore Coll., 1954; PhD, U. Minn., 1963 . Rsch. assoc., then assoc. dir. Oreg. Rsch. Inst., Eugene, 1963-75; prof. psychology Miami U., Oxford, Ohio, 1975-93, dir. clin. psychology tng. program, 1976-86; pres. Oreg. Psychol. Assn., 1973-75. NIMH spl. rsch. fellow U. Calif., Berkeley, 1967-68; fellow Netherlands Inst. Advanced Study, 1971-72; postdoctoral fellow Inst. for Rational-Emotive Therapy, 1982-83. Fellow APA (coun. reps. 1968-72), Am. Psychol. Soc. (charter), We. Psychol. Assn.; mem. Midwestern Psychol. Assn., Assn. Advancement Behavior Therapy, Soc. Multivariate Exptl. Psychology. Author articles in field, mem. editorial bds. profl. jours. Home: 407 High St Santa Cruz CA 95060-2613

RORICK, MARVIN HORTON, III, physician, neurologist; b. Toledo, Apr. 22, 1952; s. Marvin Horton Jr. and Mary (Foster) R.; m. Lindsay Barksdale, Dec. 3, 1983; children: Paige, Kathleen. BS, Tufts U., 1974; MS, MIT, 1978; MD, U. Cin., 1984. Diplomate in neurology Am. Bd. Psychiatry and Neurology. Ptnr. physician Riverhills Healthcare, Cin., 1987—; active tchg. staff Christ Hosp., 1992—, Jewish Hosp., Cin., 1992—, Bethesda Hosp., Cin., 1992—. Bd. dirs. Coun. for Epilepsy, Life Ctr.; mem. adv. bd. Hospice Cin.; active Indian Hill Ch. Mem. Acad. Medicine of Cin. (sec. 1996-97, treas. 1997-98, pres. 1998-99), Cin. Country Club, Moraine Country Club (Dayton, Ohio). Republican. Episcopalian. Avocations: golf, squash, platform tennis. Office: Riverhills Healthcare 111 Wellington Pl Cincinnati OH 45219-1758

RORICK, WILLIAM CALVIN, librarian, educator, portrait artist; b. Elyria, Ohio, June 23, 1941; s. Harold R. and Edythe E. (Harris) R.; m. Anne L. Sherbondy, Aug. 21, 1971. BA in Econs. and Bus. Adminstrn., Ohio Wesleyan U., 1963; MusB in Music History and Lit., U. Utah, 1968; MusM in Music History and Lit., Northwestern U., 1970; MLS, Pratt Inst., 1974; MA in Musicology, NYU, 1982; trainee in portraiture, various art schs., workshops, 1990—. Curator orchl.-choral libr., reference asst., office mgr. Manhattan Sch. Music Libr., N.Y.C., 1970-74; music reference libr. CUNY Queens Coll. Music Libr., Flushing, 1974-96, instr., 1974-79, asst. prof., 1979-96, asst. prof. emeritus, 1996—, mem. senate nominating com., del.-at-large arts divsn., 1984-86. Contbr. articles and revs. to profl. jours. Bd. deacons South Britain (Conn.) Congl. Ch., 1998—. Grantee Rsch. Found. CUNY, 1981-84; recipient regional and nat. art awards including Best in Show Conn. Classic Arts Assn. Mem. Am. Musicological Soc., Am. Printing History Assn., Assn. for Recorded Sound Collections, Internat. Assn. Music Librs., Libr. Assn. CUNY (chmn. grants com. 1978-80, mem. publs. com. 1979-81, editor Directory 1980-81, del. 1983-85), Music Libr. Assn. (program chmn. Greater N.Y. chpt. 1977-79, sec.-treas. 1979-81, chpt. chmn. 1983-85, mem. nat. subcom. on basic music collection 1977-79, chmn. nat. membership com. 1979-82, mem. Music Pubs. Assn. joint com. 1986-88), Am. Soc. Portrait Artists, Sonneck Soc., Conn. Classic Arts, Inc. (publicity chmn. 1996—), Portrait Soc. of Am., Inc., Portrait Soc. Atlanta, Beta Phi Mu. Home: 63 Beacon Hill Dr Southbury CT 06488-1914

RORIE, CONRAD JONATHAN, scientist, naval officer; b. Henning, Tenn., Oct. 28, 1930; s. Elvy and Lena (Jenkins) R.; m. Patricia Paris Cunliffe, Feb. 7, 1952; children: Michael Stephen, Catherine Jean, Patrick Jonathan. BS, Union U., Jackson, Tenn., 1952; MSEE, U.S. Naval Postgrad. Sch., 1961; PhD in Elect. Engring., Vanderbilt U., 1970. Enlisted USN, 1952, advanced through grades to adm., 1971; comdg. officer various ships, 1957-72; comdr. U.S. Naval Surface Weapons Ctr., Dahlgren, Va., 1974-77; dep. comdr. for surface combatants and weapons systems engr. Naval Sea Systems Command, Washington, 1977-81; comdr. Naval Surface Forces Middle Pacific & Naval Base Pearl Harbr, Hawaii, 1981-84. Planning dir. Johns Hopkins U., Applied Physics Lab., 1984—; mem. numerous naval bd. for officer career devel., chmn. Weapons Systems Mgr./Ordnance Adv. Bd. to Naval Postgrad. Sch. President Hawaii Navy Relief Soc. and Red Cross, 1980; chmn. Combined Fed. Campaign Charity Dr., 1981; bd. dirs. Govs. for Navy Charity Retail Store, 1981; commissioning chmn. USS Antietam, 1987, USS Arleigh Burke, 1991; mem. panel Navy/Civilian U. Lab., 1988; mem. curricula rev. com. Naval Postgrad. Sch., 1977-81; bd. dirs. Historic USS Constellation, 1996; mem. warfare sys. adv. panel for 21st century aircraft carriers. Decorated Legion of Merit (4), Meritorious Svc. medal with gold star; recipient Ann. Disting. Alumnus award Union U., 1975, Am. Spirit of Honor medal, APL Disting. Svc. award Johns Hopkins U., 1998; named Tenn. Number One State Future Farmer, 1948; C.J. Rorie annual award for Excellence established in his honor, 1987, Navy Surface Warfare Ctr. established in his honor. Mem. Naval Inst., Am. Soc. Naval Engrs., Nat. Security Indsl. Assn., AIAA, Am. Astronaut. Soc., U.S. Navy League, Armed Forces Communications and Electronics Assn., Mil. Order of Carabao, Masons, Bapt. Club, Sigma Xi, Eta Kappa Nu, Alpha Tau Omega. Home: 12412 Hooper Ct Fulton MD 20759-9645 Office: Johns Hopkins U Applied Physics Lab Johns Hopkins Rd Laurel MD 20707 E-mail: conradrorie@aol.com.

RORIE, NANCY CATHERINE, retired elementary and secondary school educator; b. Union County, N.C., May 31, 1940; d. Carl Evander and Mary Mildred (Pressley) R. BA, Woman's Coll. U. N.C., 1962; MEd, U. N.C., 1967; EdD, Duke U., 1977. Cert. curriculum and instrnl. specialist, social studies tchr. for middle and secondary levels, English tchr., N.C. Social studies and English tchr. Guilford County Schs., Greensboro, NC, 1962—67; social studies instr. Lees-McRae Coll., Banner Elk, 1967—76; social studies tchr. Monroe (NC) City Schs., Monroe, 1977—93; social studies and lang. arts tchr. Union County Schs., 1993—2002; ret., 2002. Mem. Prof. Educators N.C., Phi Alpha Theta, Kappa Delta Pi. Democrat. Baptist. Home: 2401 Old Pageland Monroe Rd Monroe NC 28112-8163

RORIG, KURT JOACHIM, chemist, research director; b. Bremerhaven, Germany, Dec. 1, 1920; came to U.S., 1924, naturalized, 1929; s. Robert Herman and Martha (Grundke) R.; m. Helen Yonan, Mar. 20, 1949; children: James, Elizabeth, Miriam. BS, U. Chgo., 1942; MA, Carleton Coll., 1944; PhD, U. Wis., 1947. Lectr. Loyola U., Chgo., 1950-62; chemist to dir. Chem. Research G.D. Searle & Co., 1947-87; pres. Chemo-Delphic Cons. Ltd., 1987—. Adj. prof. chemistry U. Ill., Chgo., 1989—. Patentee in field. Mem. Sch. Bd., Wilmette, Ill., 1969-71. Mem. Am. Chem. Soc. (dir. Chgo. sect.), Am. Soc. Pharm. and Exptl. Therapeutics, N.Y. Acad. Scis., AAAS, Chgo. Chemists Club (past pres.) Presbyterian. Home and Office: 337 Hager Ln Glenview IL 60025-3329

RORISON, MARGARET LIPPITT, reading consultant; b. Wilmington, N.C., Feb. 6, 1925; d. Harmon Chadbourn and Margaret Devereux (Lippitt) R. AB, Hollins Coll., 1946; MA, Columbia U., 1956; Diplôme de langue, L'Alliance Française, Paris, 1966; postgrad., U. S.C., 1967-70, 81—. Market and editorial researcher Time, Inc., N.Y.C., 1949-55; classroom and corrective reading tchr. N.Y.C. public schs., 1956-65; TV instr. ETV-WNDT, Channel 13, N.Y.C., 1962-63; grad. asst., TV instr. U. S.C., Columbia, 1967-70; instrnl. specialist in reading S.C. Office Instrnl. TV and Radio, S.C. Dept. Edn., 1971-81; reading cons. S.C. Office Instrnl. Tech., 1982—. Author instrnl. TV series: Getting the Word (So. Ednl. Communications Assn. award 1972, Ohio State award 1973, S.C. Scholastic Broadcasters award 1973), Getting the Message, 1981. Episcopalian. Home: 460 S 23rd St Wilmington NC 28403-0200

RORKE, LUCY BALIAN, neuropathologist; b. St. Paul, June 22, 1929; d. Aram Haji and Karzouhy (Ousdigian) Balian; m. Robert Radcliffe Rorke, June 4, 1960. AB, U. Minn., 1951, MA, 1952, BS, 1955, MD, 1957. Diplomate Am. Bd. Pathology. Intern Phila. Gen. Hosp., 1957-58, resident anat. pathology and neuropathology, 1958-62, asst. neuropathologist, 1963-67, chief pediat. pathologist, 1967-68, chief neuropathologist, 1968-69, chmn. dept. anat. pathology and chief neuropathologist, 1969-73, chmn. dept. pathology, 1973-77, pres. med. staff, 1973-75; practice medicine specializing in neuropathology Phila., 1962—; neuropathologist Children's Hosp., 1965—, pres. med. staff, 1986-88, acting pathologist-in-chief, 1995-2000. Cons. neuropathologist Wyeth Rsch. Labs., Radnor, Pa., 1961-87, Wistar Inst. Anatomy and Biology, Phila., 1967-93; assoc. prof. pathology U. Pa. Sch. Medicine, Phila., 1970-73, prof., 1973—, clin. prof. neurology, 1979—, clin. prof. pediats., 1997—; forensic neuropathologist Office of Med. Examiner, Phila., 1977—. Author: Myelinization of the Brain in the Newborn, 1969, Pathology of Perinatal Brain Injury, 1982; mem. editl. bd. Jours. Neuropathology Exptl. Neurology, 1980-85, 93—, Pediat. Neurosurgery, 1984-2002, Child's Nervous System, 1984-88, Brain pathology, 1990-95; contbr. articles to profl. jours. NIH fellow in neuropathology, 1961-62; NIH grantee for study of neonatal brain, 1963-68; recipient Meritorious Svc. award to neuropathology Am. Assn. Neuropathologists, 1999. Fellow Coll. Am. Pathologists; mem. Phila. Gen. Hosp. Med. Staff (pres. 1973-75), Phila. Neurol. Soc. (v.p. 1971-72, editor Transactions 1973, pres. 1975-76), Am. Assn. Neuropathologists (exec. council 1976-85, v.p. 1979-80, pres. 1981-82), Am. Neurol. Assn., AMA, Burlington County Med. Soc., Phila. Coll. Physicians (trustee 2002), Am. Soc. Neuroradiology (hon.). Home: 120 Chestnut St Moorestown NJ 08057-2937 Office: Childrens Hosp of Phila 324 S 34th St Philadelphia PA 19104-4304 E-mail: Rorke@email.chop.edu.

RORSCHACH, RICHARD GORDON, lawyer; b. Tulsa, Aug. 9, 1928; s. Harold Emil and Margaret (Hermes) R.; m. Martha Kay King, Dec. 23, 1979; children by previous marriage: Richard Helm, Reagan Cartwright, Andrew Maxwell. BS, MIT, 1950; MS, U. Okla., 1952; JD, U. Houston, 1961. Bar: Tex. 1961; lic. prof. engr., Tex. Cons. civil engr. Freese & Nichols, Ft. Worth, 1955; cons. engr. Freese, Nichols & Turner, Houston, 1955-56; petroleum engr. Marathon Oil Co., Bay City, Tex., 1956-57, Houston, 1957-61, atty., 1961-64; ptnr. Broady, Kells & Rorschsch, Houston, 1964-68, Ragan, Russell & Rorschach, Houston, 1968-80, Kilgore, Tex., 1980—. Mem. exec. com.

Colonial Royalties Co., Tulsa, 1970-77; officer Little River Oil & Gas Co., 1980-88; mng. ptnr. Pentagon Oil Co., 1988—; pres. Nat. Assn. Royalty Owners-Tex., 1993-96; chmn. Nat. Assn. Royalty Owners, Inc., 1996-99, bd. dirs., 1999-2000; mem. exec. com. Nat. Assn. Royalty Owners, Inc.; owner, breeder, exhibitor Arabian Horses Shadowbrook Farm, Kilgore, Tex., 1980—. Author: How to Protect Your Royalty Interests: Texas Perspectives, Vols. 1 & 2, 2002. Served to 1st lt. C.E., AUS, 1952-54, Korea. Mem. ASME, ASCE, Tex. Bar Assn., Rotary Club (pres. Kilgore chpt. 1984-85), Sigma Xi, Sigma Alpha Epsilon. Republican. Presbyterian. Home: RR 4 Box 210 Kilgore TX 75662-9023 Office: 1100 Stone Rd PO Box 1934 Kilgore TX 75663-1934 E-mail: rgr@kilgore.net.

RORTY, RICHARD MCKAY, philosophy educator; b. N.Y.C., Oct. 4, 1931; s. James Hancock and Winifred (Raushenbush) R.; m. Amelie Sarah Oksenberg, June 15, 1954 (div. 1972); 1 son, Jay; m. Mary R. Varney, Nov. 4, 1972; children: Patricia, Kevin. BA, U. Chgo., 1949, MA, 1952; PhD, Yale U., 1956; DHL, Northwestern U., 1992, Fla. Internat. Univ., 1994. Instr. philosophy Yale U., 1955-57; instr. Wellesley Coll., 1958-60, asst. prof., 1960-61; mem. faculty Princeton U., 1961-82, prof. philosophy, 1970-81, Stuart prof. philosophy, 1981-82; Univ. prof. humanities U. Va., 1982—. Author: Philosophy and the Mirror of Nature, 1979, Consequences of Pragmatism, 1982, Contingency, Irony and Solidarity, 1989, Objectivity, Relativism and Truth, 1991, Essays on Heidegger and Others, 1991. Served with AUS, 1957-58. Guggenheim fellow, 1973-74; MacArthur fellow, 1981-86. Mem. Am. Philos. Assn. (pres. Eastern div. 1979), Am. Acad. Arts and Scis. Home: 402 Peacock Dr Charlottesville VA 22903-9725 Office: 412 Cabell Hall Charlottesville VA 22903

ROSA, DOMENICO, mathematics educator; b. L'Aquila, Abruzzi, Italy, Apr. 19, 1947; came to U.S., 1957; s. Emidio Pio and Assunta (Rosa) R.; m. Julia Margaret Pelletier, July 24, 1976; children: Robert Francis, Katherine Elizabeth. BA, Tufts U., 1970; MS, McMaster U., 1971, PhD, 1974. Actuarial asst. The Hartford (Conn.) Ins. Group, 1975-79, sr. actuarial, 1979-83; asst. prof. to prof. Teikyo Post U., Waterbury, Conn., 1983-95, prof., 1995—. Contbr. papers to profl. jours. Mem. Am. Math. Soc., Math. Assn. Am. Democrat. Roman Catholic. Avocations: history, politics. Office: Teikyo Post Univ 800 Country Club Rd Waterbury CT 06708-3240

ROSA, FREDRIC DAVID, construction company executive; b. Monroe, Wis., Oct. 31, 1946; s. Fredric Carl Rosa and Irene (Sommers) Rosa Figi; m. Melanie A. Downs, May 31, 1986; children: Mark, Katherine. BBA in Mktg., U. Wis., 1968. Dir. mktg. Swiss Colony Stores, Inc., Monroe, 1968-80; pres. Videotape Indsl. Prodns., Inc., Madison, Wis., 1980-82; agt. VR Bus. Brokers, Colorado Springs, Colo., 1982-83; sales rep. NCR Corp., Denver, 1983-85; prin. F. D. Rosa & Assocs., Denver, Aspen and Eagle, Colo., 1985-89; pres. Peak Benefit Cons., Colorado Springs, 1989-95; registered prin. Nexus Fin. Programs, Inc., Colo., 1990-92, Nutmeg Securities Ltd., Colorado Springs, 1992-94; sales staff Am. Airlines, Colo., 1993-95. Cons. Kolb-Lena Cheese Co., Lena, Ill., 1983-85; instr. The Am. Coll., Bryn Mawr, Pa., 1990-91, A.D. Banker & Co., Overland Park, Kans., 1995-97; owner Fred Rosa Constrn., Colorado Springs, 1990-94, Lakewood, Colo., 1995—. Contbr. articles to trade publs. and newspapers. Mem. Am. Soc. CLU and Chartered Fin. Cons., Mensa, Internat. Legion of Intelligence, Delta Sigma Pi (life). Methodist. Avocations: big game hunting, skiing, camping, travel. Home and Office: Fred Rosa Constrn 1270 Cody St Lakewood CO 80215-4897 E-mail: roosa1660@iwon.com.

ROSA, HELEN, dean; Dean U. Central del Caribe Sch. Medicine, Bayamon, PR, 2002—. Office: Univ Central del Caribe Sch Medicine Office of Admissions Call Box 60-327 Bayamon PR 00960-6032*

ROSA, IDAVONNE TAYLOR, retired community health nurse; b. Ft. Worth, Aug. 10, 1921; d. William Oscar and Minnie Belle (White) Taylor; m. John Moore Rosa (dec.); children: Walter E. Rose, Jimie Lee Rose. Diploma in nursing, U. Cen. Ark., 1974; postgrad., Ark. State U. RN, Ark.; lic. social worker, Ark.; cert. disaster nurse ARC. Vol. Peace Corps, Afghanistan, 1968-72; dir. nursing Pioneer Nursing Home, Melbourne, Ark., 1974-79; dir. ind. living svcs. East Ark. Agy. on Aging, Jonesboro, 1980-97; Izard county supt. White River Area Agy. on Aging, 1997-98; health care cons., educator, 1999—; owner guest house Patzcuaro, Mexico. Chmn. nursing adv. coun. Delta Tech. Inst., 1994-97; home care nursing cons., 2000. Mem. steering com., Ark. rep. Nat. Silver Haired Congress, 1994-95; del. White House Conf. on Aging, Washington, 1995; tng. coord. disaster com. Craighead County chpt. ARC, 1995—; pres. Mid-Am. Congress on Aging, 1988-89, chmn. presdl. adv. bd., 1990-95; mem. Melbourne Planning and Zoning Commn., 1997—. Mem. S.W. Soc. on Aging, Ark. Nursing Home Nurses Assn., Ark. Gerontol Soc. (bd. dirs. 1993-95). Home: PO Box 214 Melbourne AR 72556-0214

ROSA, MARGARITA, agency chief executive, lawyer; b. Bklyn., Jan. 5, 1953; d. Jose and Julia (Mojica) R.; 1 child, Marisol Kimberly Rosa-Shapiro. BA in History cum laude, Princeton U., 1974; JD, Harvard U., 1977. Bar: N.Y. Assoc. Rosenman & Colin, N.Y.C., 1977-79, Rabinowitz & Boudin, N.Y.C., 1981-84; staff atty. Puerto Rican Legal Def. Edn. Fund, 1979-81; teaching fellow Urban Legal Studies program CUNY, 1984-85; gen. counsel N.Y. State Div. Human Rights, N.Y.C., 1985-88, exec. dep. commr., 1988-90, commr., 1990-95; exec. dir. Grand St. Settlement, 1995—. Vice chmn. N.Y. State Task force on ADA Implementation, 1991-95; mem. N.Y. Gov.'s Task Force on Sexual Harassment, 1992; mem. Mayor's Commn. on the Judiciary, 2002--; bd. dirs. Pub. Interest Law Found., NYU Law Sch., 1982-84; adj. prof. law Fordham Law Sch., 1995; adj. prof. pub. policy Wagner Grad. Sch. NYU, 1995—, Baruch Coll. Exec. MPA program, 1998; bd. dirs. Martin Luther King Jr. Commn. N.Y. State, 1990-95, Feminist Press CUNY, 1990-95; mem. adv. bd. N.Y.C. Ind. Budget Office, 1996-2001, vice chair, 2000-01; mem. adv. bd. Women in Mgmt. Inst., Wagner Grad. Sch., NYU, 1995—. Bd. dirs. N.Y. Civil Liberties Union, 1981-86, Lower East Side Family Union, N.Y.C., 1982-84, United Neighborhood Houses, 1995-97, Legal Svcs. for Children, 1999—, Non-Profit Coordinating Com., 2001—. Recipient Hispanic Women Achievers award N.Y. State Gov.'s Office Hispanic Affairs, 1990, Woman of Excellence award CUNY, 1992, Oscar García Rivera award P.R. Bar Assn., 1996, N.Y. State Atty. Gen.'s award for disting. pub. svc. in the legal profession, 2002; Lombard Assn. fellow Office of U.S. Atty., So. Dist. N.Y., 1975; Revson Teaching fellow Charles Revson Found., 1984-85. Mem. N.Y. State Bar Assn. (com. on minorities in the profession 1997—), Assn. Bar City N.Y. (commn. future of CUNY 1999—). Office: Grand St Settlement 80 Pitt St New York NY 10002-3516

ROSA, PETER MANUEL, university administrator, researcher; b. N.Y.C., Nov. 22, 1946; s. Pedro and Raquel (Ramirez) R.; m. Pamela Ann Greene, Aug. 10, 1968; children: Kimberly Ann, Peter Martin. BA, Cen. Conn. State U., 1968, MS, 1974; PhD, U. Conn., 1981. Tchr. Bristol (Conn.) Cen. High Sch., 1968-72; admission officer Cen. Conn. State U., New Britain, 1972-83; researcher, lobbyist Conn. Dept. Higher Edn., Hartford, 1983-87; higher edn. lobbyist Conn. State Univ. System, 1987-96, acad. adminstr. New Britain, 1996-98; v.p. student affairs Ctrl. Conn. State U., 1998—. Dean, faculty Nat. Assn. Coll. Admission Counselors, Hampton (Va.) Inst., 1988-92. Alderman, asst., majority leader New Britain Common Coun., 1989-91, 93; mem. Latino and Puerto Rican Affairs Commn., 1995-97; bd. dirs. Conn. Assn. Bds. Edn., 1995-99. Nat. Hispanic Leadership fellow N.J. Dept Higher Edn., 1985. Mem. Conn. Assn. Latin Ams. in Higher Edn. (pres. 1983), Nat. Assn. Coll. Admission Counselors, New Britain Bd. Edn. (vice chair 1997-98, pres. 1998-99). Democrat. Roman Catholic. Avocations: politics, baseball, reading, music. Home: 521 Shuttle Meadow Ave New Britain CT 06052-1826 Office: Ctrl Conn State U New Britain CT 06050 E-mail: rosa@ccsu.edu.

ROSA, RAYMOND ULRIC, retired banker; b. New Britain, Conn., Jan. 30, 1927; s. Kenneth E. and Regina (Chenette) R.; m. Irene M. Asselin, Feb. 5, 1949; children: R. James, David M., Cathryn P., Michael F., Nancy A., Kenneth E. AS, Hillyer Coll., 1949. CPA, Conn. Pvt. practice pub. accounting, Manchester, Conn., 1949-52; auditor Auditors of Pub. Accounts, State of Conn., Hartford, 1952-65; dir. Fed.-State Relations Dept. Finance and Control, Conn., 1965-69; dep. commr. Finance and Control, 1969-71; sr. v.p., auditor Soc. Savings, Hartford, 1971-90, ret., 1990. Mem. Windsor Locks (Conn.) Bd. Fin., 1973—81; pres. Savs. Bank Forum, 1981—82; trustee, sec.-treas. Mease Manor, Inc., Dunedin, Fla., 1995—2001, vice chmn., Fla., 2001—. Treas. Mental Health Assn. Conn., 1974-77, v.p., 1977-80, pres., 1980-83; bd. dirs. Nat. Assn. Mental Health, 1977-85, v.p. region 1, 1982-83; bd. dirs. Combined Health Appeal of Greater Hartford, 1982-90. Served with USNR, 1944-46. Mem. AICPA, Conn. Soc. CPAs, Conn. Soc. Govtl. Accts., KC, Dunedin Country Club (bd. dirs. 1997-2000, v.p. 1998-99, pres. 1999-00), Suffield Country Club (bd. govs. 1984-91). Home: 2060 Golf View Dr Dunedin FL 34698-2330

ROSADO, RODOLFO JOSE, psychologist, educator; b. N.Y.C., Jan. 9, 1959; s. Rodolfo Jose and Maria (Gonzalez) R.; m. Ruth Laura Morrison, June 11, 1982; children: Emily Hope, Adam Philip. BS in Psychology, Fordham U., Bronx, N.Y., 1979, MA in Clin. Psychology, 1986, PhD in Clin. Psychology, 1992. Diplomate in clin. psychology and child psychology Am. Bd. Psychol. Specialties; lic. psychologist, N.Y., Conn. Psychology tng. fellow N.Y. Med. Coll., Valhalla, 1979-81; clin. psychology intern Hall-Brooke Hosp., Westport, Conn., 1982-83; therapist Child Guidance Ctr., Bridgeport, 1983-85, office coord., 1985-90, program dir., 1990-93; asst. prof. Fairfield (Conn.) U., 1993-97, program dir. coll. access, 1995-96; pvt. practice specializing in psychol. evaluations Norwalk, Conn., 1993—. Initial Rev. Group profl. reviewer USPHS, Rockville, Md., 1990-95; regional adv. com. Dept. Children & Families, Bridgeport, 1995—; oversight collaborative Bridgeport Futures, 1994-95; faculty co-sponsor SALSA Hispanic Students Assn., Fairfield U., 1995-97; bd. dirs., clin. cons. R.E.A.C.H. Program, Riverside, Conn.; bd. dirs. Side by Side Charter Sch., Norwalk, Conn., 2002--. Author, moderator TV show Conversation in Edn., 1994; co-author proposal Empowerment Zone Grant, 1994; author proposal Comprehensive Child & Adolescent Svc., 1993. Mem. Youth Svc. Bur., City of Bridgeport, 1991-93; family preservation initiative Conn. Dept. Children & Families, Bridgeport, 1995-2000; coach Little League Baseball, 2000-02; asst. coach Biddy Basketball Youth Program, Norwalk, 2001-02; sec. bd. dirs. Side by Side Charter Sch., Norwalk, Conn., 2002—. Recipient N.Y. Regents scholarship, 1975-79, scholarship Fordham U., Bronx, 1975-79, Appreciation award for collaborative support State of Conn. Dept. Children & Families, 1995, Outstanding Contbns. to Latino Cmty. Recognition award Puerto Rican/Latino employees of Human Resources Adminstrn. and Affiliated Agys., Dept. Homeless Svcs. and Adminstrn. for Children's Svcs., 1999. Mem. APA, Am. Coll. Forensic Examiners, Hispanic Assn. Mental Health and Allied Professions (exec. com., treas. 1988-92), Conn. Coalition for Children of Alcoholics (steering com. 1986-87), Sigma Xi. Avocation: racquetball, hiking. Office: 71 East Ave Ste U Norwalk CT 06851

ROSALDO, RENATO IGNACIO, JR. cultural anthropology educator; b. Champaign, Ill., Apr. 15, 1941; s. Renato Ignacio and Mary Elizabeth (Potter) R.; m. Michelle Sharon Zimbalist, June 12, 1966 (dec. Oct. 1981); children: Samuel Mario, Manuel Zimbalist; m. Mary Louise Pratt, Nov. 26, 1983; 1 child, Olivia Emilia Rosaldo-Pratt. AB, Harvard U., 1963, PhD, 1971. Asst. prof. cultural anthropology Stanford (Calif.) U., 1970-76, assoc. prof., 1976-85, prof., 1985—, Mellon prof. interdisciplinary studies, 1987-90, dir. Ctr. for Chicano Rsch., 1985-90, chair anthropology, 1994-96, Lucie Stern prof. social scis., 1993—. Author: Ilongot Headhunting 1883-1974, 1980, Culture and Truth, 1989. Recipient Harry Benda prize Assn. for Asian Studies, 1983; Guggenheim fellow, 1993. Fellow Am. Acad. Arts and Scis. Avocations: poetry, swimming, drawing, dancing. Home: 2520 Cowper St Palo Alto CA 94301-4218 Office: Stanford U Dept Anthropology Palo Alto CA 94305-2145

ROSALES, SANDRA JOHNSON, school system administrator; b. Riverside, Calif., June 21, 1944; d. William Emory Johnson and Mildred Alice (Alford) Wimer; m. Wynn Neal Huffman, Feb., 1962 (div. May 1967); 1 child, Kristen Lee; m. Steven Jack Herrera, June, 1985 (div. Dec. 1997); m. Mario Rosales, Sept. 22, 2000. AA in Purchasing Mgmt., Fullerton Coll., 1983; BSBA, U. Redlands, 1985, MA in Mgmt., 1988. Sr. purchasing clk Fullerton (Calif.) Union High Sch. Dist., 1969-77, buyer, 1977-79, coord. budgets and fiscal affairs, 1979-83; asst. dir. fin. svcs. Downey (Calif.) Unified Sch. Dist., 1983-85; dir. acctg. Whittier (Calif.) Union High Sch. Dist., 1985-89; asst. supt. bus. Whittier City Sch. Dist., 1989-91, Oxnard Elem. Sch. Dist., 1991—. Cons. Heritage Dental Lab., El Toro, Calif, 1981-97. Spl. dep. sheriff Santa Barbara (Calif.) County Sheriff's Mounted Posse, 1986-90; spl. dep. marshal U.S. Marshals Posse, Los Angeles, 1987-95. Mem. Calif. Assn. Sch. Bus. Ofcls. (treas. S.E. sect. 1985, mem. acct. R & D com. 1983-89, mem. chief bus. ofcls. com. 1989-92), So. Calif. Paraders Assn. (exec. sec. 1976-97), Calif. State Horsemens Assn. (regional v.p. 1986-87, sec. 1988), Alpha Gamma Sigma. Avocations: horseback riding, golf, reading, micro-computers, model trains. Office: Oxnard Elem Sch Dist 1051 S A St Oxnard CA 93030-7442 Home: 1900 Muirfield Dr Oxnard CA 93030

ROSALES, SUZANNE MARIE, hospital coordinator; b. Merced, Calif., July 23, 1946; d. Walter Marshall and Ellen Marie (Earl) Potter; children: Anita Carol, Michelle Suzanne. AA, City Coll., San Francisco, 1966. Diplomate Am. Coll. Utilization Review Physicians. Utilization review coord. San Francisco Gen. Hosp., 1967-74; mgr. utilization review/discharge planning UCLA Hosp. and Clinics, 1974-79; nurse III Hawaii State Hosp., Kaneohe, 1979-80; review coord. Pacific Profl. Std. Review Orgn., Honolulu, 1980-81; coord. admission and utilization reviewq The Rehab. Hosp. of the Pacific, 1981-85; coord. Pacific Med. Referral Project, 1985-87; dir. profl. svcs. The Queen's Healthcare Plan, 1987-88; utilization mgmt. coord. Vista Psychiat. Physician Assocs., San Diego, 1989; admission coord. utilization review San Francisco Gen. Hosp., 1989-91, quality improvement coordinator, 1991—. Cons. Am. Med. Records Assn. Contbr. articles to profl. jours. Mem. Nat. Assn. Utilization Review Profls. Home: 138 Alta Vista Way Daly City CA 94014-1402 Office: San Francisco Gen Hosp 1001 Potrero Ave San Francisco CA 94110-3594

ROSALSKY, BARBARA ELLEN, artist, home health aide; b. N.Y.C., Nov. 16, 1948; d. Ellis M. Rosalsky and Claire (Schwartz) Rosalsky Shapiro; m. Dennis Robinson. BA, SUNY, Plattsburgh, 1970. Sales girl Cambridge (Mass.) Artist mag., 1970-71; artist Pillar of Fire mag., Zarephath, N.J., 1977; home health aide CMR, Bound Brook, 1978—; designer New Brunswick (N.J.) Tomorrow, 1980-87; art therapist Middlesex Hosp., New Brunswick, 1981-83. Solo exhibitions include The Bird and Me, 1980; group exhibitions include Other Artists Other Art, 1983. Mem. Cultural Arts Commn., Piscataway, N.J., 1993—. SUNY Plattsburgh scholar, 1970. Mem. Women's Caucus Art, Marriott Swim Club. Democrat. Avocations: piano, swimming, dancing, hiking, print making. Home: 114 Woodland Rd Piscataway NJ 08854-4222

ROSAN, ROBERT CARL, retired physician; b. Dec. 1, 1927; BA magna cum laude, Colo. U., 1952; MD, Albany Med. Coll., 1957. Resident and fellow in pathology Harvard U./Boston U., 1957—63; asst. prof. pathology Stanford U., Palo Alto, Calif., 1963—70; asst. prof. pathology and pediatrics St. Louis Med. Sch., 1970—76; asst. prof. pathology U. Tex., Houston, 1976—78; resident in pediat. U. Tex. Med. Br., Galveston, 1978—79; resident in psychiatry Tex. Rsch. Inst., 1979—82; asst. prof. psychiatry U. Tex., Houston, 1982—88, U. Buffalo, 1988—97; ret. Contbr. more than 40 articles to sci. publs; co-inventor of laser microprobe; co-discoverer of bronchopulmonary dysplasia. Active Unitarian Ch., Boulder, Boston, Palo Alto, St. Louis, Houston, 1950-88. Home: 36 Whitney Pl Buffalo NY 14201-2315

ROSAND, DAVID, art history educator; b. Bklyn., Sept. 6, 1938; s. Johan Herbert and Frieda (Grotenstein) R.; m. Ellen Fineman, June 18, 1961; children: Jonathan, Eric. AB, Columbia Coll., 1959; MA, Columbia U., 1962, PhD, 1965. Instr. art history Columbia U., N.Y.C., 1964-67, asst. prof., 1967-69, assoc. prof., 1969-73, prof., 1973-95, chmn. Soc. of Fellows in the Humanities, 1979-83, Meyer Schapiro prof. art history, 1995—. Author (with Michelangelo Muraro): Titian and the Venetian Woodcut, 1976, Titian, 1978; author: Painting in Cinquecento Venice: Titian, Veronese, Tintoretto, 1988, rev. edit., 1997, The Meaning of the Mark: Leonardo and Titian, 1988; author: (with others) Places of Delight: The Pastoral Landscape, 1988; author: Robert Motherwell on Paper, 1997, Myths of Venice: The Figuration of a State, 2001, Drawing Acts: Studies in Graphic Expression and Representation, 2002; editor: Titian: His World and His Legacy, 1982; editor: (with Robert W. Haning) Castiglione: The Ideal and the Real in Renaissance Culture, 1983; editor: Interpretazioni Veneziane, 1984. Mem. bd. advisors CASVA Nat. Gallery Art., 1990-94. Fulbright Commn. fellow, 1962-63; NEH fellow, 1971-72, 85-86, 91-92; John S. Guggenheim Meml. Found. fellow, 1974-75. Mem. Coll. Art Assn. Am., Renaissance Soc. Am. (mem. exec. bd. 1981—), Save Venice, Inc. (bd. dirs.), Ateneo Veneto (fgn.), Am. Acad. Arts and Scis. Home: 560 Riverside Dr New York NY 10027-3202 Office: Columbia U Dept Art History & Archaeology 826 Schermerhorn Hall New York NY 10027 E-mail: dr17@columbia.edu.

ROSARIO-GUARDIOLA, REINALDO, dermatologist; b. Santurce, P.R., Sept. 17, 1948; s. Tomas and Avarena (Guardiola) Rosario; m. Fe Milagros Rivera, Aug. 19, 1972; children: Amarillis, Reinaldo, Gadiel. BS, U. P.R., 1968, MD, 1972. Rsch. fellow photobiology Harvard Med. Sch., Boston, 1976-77; asst. prof. U. P.R. Sch. of Medicine, Rio Piedras, 1979—; chief, dermatology sect. San Juan VA Hosp., 1979—. Bd. dirs. Wesleyan Acad. Guaynabo, P.R., 1990-99. Grantee Dermatology Found., 1978. Fellow Am. Acad. Dermatology; mem. P.R. Dermatol. Soc. (pres. scientific com. 1978-79, pres.-elect 1999-2000, pres. 2000-01), Harvard-MGH House Officers Club, Alpha Omega Alpha. Office: 652 Munoz Rivera Ave Ste 3170 San Juan PR 00918-4261

ROSARIO-OLMEDO, CARMEN GLORIA, principal; b. Mayaguez, P.R., Jan. 4, 1940; d. Rafael and Emilia (Derieux) Rosario; m. William Galindo, Apr. 19, 1968 (div. 1974); m. Ruben Eduardo Olmedo, Dec. 25, 1976. BA, CCNY, 1963; MA, NYU, 1982; profl. diploma, L.I. U., 1987. Cert. elem. prin., asst. prin., sch. dist. adminstr., sch. adminstr. and supr., permanent tchg. cert., N.Y.C. Tchr. N.Y.C. Bd. Edn., 1963-89, asst. prin., 1989-95, prin. I.A., 1995-97, prin., 1997—. Curriculum designer Cmty. Sch. Dist. 17, Bklyn., 1965-66, tchr. trainer, 1967-70; exch. tchr. trainer, San Juan, P.R., 1970-71; founder, artistic dir. Children in the Arts, Bklyn., 1979-86; coord. sch. vol. program Pub. Sch. 316, Bklyn., 1988-95. Contbr.: The Mexican Family, 1979, The Chilean Family Structure, 1982. Mem. Puerto Rican Educator's Assn., N.Y.C., 1979—, Atlas, N.Y.C., 1972-93. Recipient Women's Hist. Month award Borough Pres. Office, 1986; Fulbright scholar, 1972, 82, NDEA grantee U.S. Office Edn. Inst. for Tchg. Disadvantaged Children, 1965-66, exch. program grantee N.Y.C. Bd. Edn., 1970-71. Mem. ASCD, Counsel of Supervisors and Adminstrs., Nat. Assn. P.R. Women, Hispanic Orgn. Latino Actors, Fulbright Assn. (life). Avocations: acting, anthropology, artist, traveling, writer, archaeology. Home: 176 Prospect Park W Brooklyn NY 11215-5285 Office: Pub Sch 316 750 Classon Ave Brooklyn NY 11238-4685 E-mail: colmedo@nycboe.nycenet.edu.

ROSATI, SHARON WETMORE, social worker; b. Montpelier, Vt., Feb. 19, 1963; d. Duane Paul and Ann Jeannette (Hoadley) Wetmore; m. Paul David Rosati, Sept. 19, 1986; children: Patrick Jung, Jayna Elizabeth. AS with honors, Suny, Delhi, 1983; BS cum laude, Suny, Brockport, 1985; MSW, U. Buffalo, 1993. CSW, ACSW. Sociotherapist, asst. supr., social worker Hillside Children's Ctr., Rochester, N.Y., 1985-97; social worker Wayne Finger Lakes BOCES, Shortsville, NY, 1997—. Mem. NASW, Assn. Child Care Workers. Avocation: photography. Home: 24 Portage St Rochester NY 14621-4212 Office: Red Jacket Edn Ctr 1506 Rt 21 Shortsville NY 14548 E-mail: srosati@wflboces.org.

ROSATO, ANTHONY DOMINICK, mechanical engineer, educator; b. Bklyn., Aug. 28, 1953; s. Michael Joseph and Betty (Rispoli) R. BME, Pratt Inst., 1975; MS in Theoretical and Applied Mechanics, Northwestern U., 1979; MS in Applied Maths., Carnegie Mellon U., 1981, PhD in Mech. Engring., 1985. Devel. engr. Green Fan Co., Beacon, NY, 1975—77; rsch. asst. dept. civil engring. Northwestern U., Evanston, Ill., 1977—79; tchg. asst. mech. engring. and maths. Carnegie Mellon U., Pitts., 1979—82, rsch. asst., 1981—84, rsch. assoc. dept. mech. engring., 1985—86; adj. faculty dept. exact scis. Carlow Coll., 1986; asst. prof. mech. engring. N.J. Inst. Tech., Newark, 1987—93, assoc. prof. mech. engring., 1993—2002, prof. mech. engring., 2002—, dir. Particle Tech. Ctr., 1995—99, dir. Granular Sci. Lab., 2000—, coord. undergrad. rsch. in mech. engring., 2000—. Faculty Gov.'s Sch. in Scis., Drew U., Madison, N.J., 1988; vis. faculty fellow, physicist dept. earth scis. Lawrence Livermore (Calif.) Nat. Lab., 1989, 90; Joliot professorship Ecole Superieure de Physique et de Chimie Industrielles, Laboratoire H.M.P., Paris, 1994; mem. nat. materials adv. bd. NRC, 1995; vis. scientist The Lovelace Insts., Albuquerque, 1995-96; vis. assoc. prof. mech. engring. Worcester Poly. Inst., 1995; assoc. chmn. mech. engring. grad. studies, N.J. Inst. Tech., 2001—. Assoc. editor Mechanics Rsch. Comms.; reviewer Jour. Computational Physics, Applied Mechanics Reviews, EuroPhysics Letters, Internat. Jour. Multi Flow, Powder Tech., Jour. Fluid Mechanics, Physics of Fluids, Mechanics Rsch. Comm., Internat. Jour. Multiphase Flow, NSF, Phys. Rev. Letters, Phys. Rev. E; contbr. articles to profl. jours. Chair sci. com. IUTAM Symposium, Cape May, N.J., 1999. Fellow ASME; mem. AIChE (particle tech. forum), Am. Soc. Engring. Edn. (program chair elect grad. studes divsn. 1995), Am. Acad. Mechanics, N.J. Inst. Tech. Ctr. for Applied Maths., Sigma Xi, Tau Beta Pi, Pi Tau Sigma. Roman Catholic. Office: NJ Inst Tech Mech Engring Dept University Heights Newark NJ 07102 E-mail: rosato@adm.njit.edu.

ROSBERG, DAVID WILLIAM, plant sciences educator; b. Superior, Wis., Jan. 3, 1919; s. Albert and Hulda (Sundin) R.; m. Helen Dana McDonald, Nov. 8, 1941; children— David William, Dana Karin. BA, St. Olaf Coll., 1940; postgrad., Tex. A&M Coll., 1940-41; MS, Ohio State U., 1947, PhD, 1949. Grad. asst. biology dept. Tex. A&M U., College Station, 1940-42, lab asst. Tex. Agrl. Exptl. Sta., 1942, asst. prof. plant physiology and pathology dept., 1949-54, asso. prof., 1954-58, prof., 1958-60, prof., head dept. plant scis., from 1960, prof. emeritus, 1981—. Insp. R.R. Perishable Inspection Agy., N.Y.C., 1941; grad. asst. dept. botany Ohio State U., 1946-48, research asst.; Research Found., 1948-49; lab. asst. Battelle Meml. Inst., Columbus, O., 1948 Named Disting. Alumnus Ohio State U., 1972 Mem. AAAS, Am. Phytopath. Soc., Tex. Acad. Sci., Sigma Xi, Phi Kappa Phi, Gamma Sigma Delta Home: 11630 Sh # 30 College Station TX 77845 Office: Tex A&M U Dept Plant Scis College Station TX 77843-0001

ROSBERG, MERILEE ANN, education educator; b. Oak Park, Ill., June 1, 1942; d. Andrew Clark and Martha (Kester) Adamson; m. William H. Rosberg, Aug. 17, 1963; children: Peter E., Trent W. AB, Augustana Coll., 1963; MA, U. Iowa, 1971, PhD, 1985. Tchr. Cedar Rapids (Iowa) Pub. Schs., 1963-65, Internat. Sch. Kuwait, 1965-67, N. Winnisheik Cmty. Schs., Decorah, Iowa, 1967-69, St. Mark's Luth. Ch. Presch., Cedar Rapids, 1969-71; staff tng. specialist Linn County Day Care Svcs., 1971-76; dir. early childhood program Jane Boyd Comty. House, 1976-86; prof., divsn. chair Mt. Mercy Coll., 1986—. Vis. prof. U. Sts Cyril & Methodius, Veliko Turnovo, Bulgaria, 1992, Czech Tech. U., Prague, Czech Rep., 1990. Fulbright scholar U. Brunei Darusalam, 1994-95. Mem. Nat. Assn. Early Childhood Edn., Nat. Coun. Tchrs. English, Internat. Readign Assn., Orgn. Mondiale Pour L'Education Prescolaire (U.S. nat. com.). Avocations: reading, travel. Home: 1900 Bever Ave SE Cedar Rapids IA 52403-2715 Office: Mt Mercy Coll 1330 Elmhurst Dr NE Cedar Rapids IA 52402-4763 E-mail: merilee@mmc.mtmercy.edu.

ROSBERGER, DANIEL FREDRIC, vitreoretinal surgeon; b. N.Y.C., Nov. 8, 1959; s. Henry and Anne (Waldman) R.; m. Sonam Tshering, Dec. 8, 1996. AB, Cornell U., 1981; PHD, Med. U. S.C., 1988; MD, Cornell U., 1990. Diplomate Am. Bd. Ophthalmology. Intern N.Y. Hosp., 1990-91, resident, 1991-94; fellow Johns Hopkins Hosp., Balt., 1994-96; asst. prof. Cornell U. Med. Coll., N.Y.C., 1996—.

ROSCH, ELLIOTT CARL, internist; b. N.Y.C., July 29, 1952; s. Maurice Charles and Bea (Horowitz) R. BA, Brown U., 1974; MD, U. Pa., 1978. Diplomate Am. Bd. Internal Medicine. Pvt. practice, Yonkers, N.Y., 1981—; med. dir. Riverside Med. Group. V.p., chmn. homeless svcs. Jewish Coun. Yonkers, 1992—. Office: Riverside Med Group 1010 N Broadway Yonkers NY 10701-1303

ROSCH, JOHN THOMAS, lawyer; b. Council Bluffs, Iowa, Oct. 4, 1939; s. H.P. and Phebe Florence (Jamison) R.; m. Carolyn Lee, Aug. 18, 1961; children: Thomas Lee, Laura Lee. BA, Harvard U., 1961, LLB, 1965. Bar: Calif. 1966, U.S. Dist. Ct. (no. dist.) Calif. 1966, U.S. Dist. Ct. (ea. dist.) Calif. 1967, U.S. Ct. Appeals (9th cir.) 1966. Assoc. McCutchen, Doyle, Brown & Enersen, San Francisco, 1965-72, ptnr., 1972-73, 75-93; office mng. ptnr. Latham & Watkins, 1994—. Dir. Bur. Consumer Protection, FTC, Washington, 1973-75 Contbr. articles profl. jours. Fellow Am. Bar Found., Am. Coll. Trial Lawyers; mem. ABA (past chmn. antitrust sect.), State Bar Calif., San

Francisco Bar Assn., Calif. State and Antitrust and Trade Regulation Sect. (past sect. chair). Republican. Episcopalian. Office: Latham & Watkins 505 Montgomery St Fl 19th San Francisco CA 94111-2552

ROSCOE, STANLEY NELSON, psychologist, aeronautical engineer; b. Eureka, Calif., Nov. 4, 1920; s. Stanley Boughton and Martha Emma (Beer) R.; m. Margaret Hazel Brookins, Dec. 21, 1948 (dec.); children: Lee Marin Roscoe Bragg, Jack; m. Elizabeth Frances Lage, Mar. 12, 1977 (dec.); 1 child, Catherine Marie; m. Gayle Buchanan Karshner, Mar. 15, 1990. AB in Speech and English, Humboldt State U., 1943; postgrad., U. Calif., Berkeley, 1942, 46; MA in Psychology, U. Ill., 1947, PhD in Psychology, 1950. Cert. psychologist, Calif. Research asst. U. Ill., Urbana-Champaign, 1946-50, research assoc., 1950-51, asst. prof., 1951-52; assoc. dir. Inst. Aviation, head aviation rsch. lab., Savoy, 1969—75, prof. aviation, psychology, aero. and astronautical engring., 1969—79, prof. emeritus, 1979—; prof. psychology N.Mex. State U., Las Cruces, 1979-86, prof. emeritus, 1986—; with Hughes Aircraft Co., Culver City, Calif., 1952-69, 75-77, dept. mgr., 1962-69, sr. scientist, 1975-77; tech. adviser, cons. in field. Pres. Illiana Aviation Scis. Ltd., Las Cruces, N.Mex., 1976—; v.p. Aero Innovation, Inc., Montreal. Author: Aviation Psychology, 1980, Flightdeck Performance: The Human Factor, 1990,, Heydays in Mattole, 1996, Predicting Human Performance, 1997, Keeping the Picture: The Measurement of Flow Control, 1999; editor: Aviation Research Monographs, 1971-72, Heydays in Humboldt, 1991, From Humboldt to Kodiak, 1992; assoc. cons. editor: Human Factors Jour., 1982—, Internat. Jour. Aviation Psychology, 1991—; contbr. more than 200 articles to profl. jours.; patentee, inventor in field. 1st lt. AC, U.S. Army, 1943-46. Fellow APA (divsn. of applied and engring. psychology, Franklin V. Taylor award 1976), Human Factors and Ergonomics Soc. (pres. 1960-61, Jerome H. Ely award 1968, 73, 89, 91, Alexander C. Williams award 1973, Paul M. Fitts award 1974, Pres.'s award 1990), Royal Aero Soc. (Eng.); mem. IEEE, AIAA, Inst. Navigation, Assn. Aviation Psychologists (ann. career award 1978), Aerospace Human Factors Assn. (Paul T. Hansen award 1994), Sigma Xi, Phi Kappa Phi, Phi Sigma, Chi Sigma Epsilon. Home: 2750 Sunnygrove Ave Mckinleyville CA 95519-7912 Office: PO Box 4498 Las Cruces NM 88003-4498 E-mail: roscoe@aero.ca.

ROSCOPF, CHARLES BUFORD, lawyer; b. Marvell, Ark., Apr. 21, 1928; s. Emmett Lee and Sally Virginia (King) R.; m. Mary Anne Maddox, Aug. 22, 1954; children— Charles David; Ann Karen. Student, Hendrix Coll., 1948-50; JD, U. Ark., 1954. Bar: Ark. bar 1954, U.S. Dist. Cts 1955, 64, U.S. Supreme Ct. bar 1965. Pvt. practice, Helena, Ark., 1954—; assoc. firm Burke, Moore & Burke, 1954-58; ptnr. firm Burke & Roscopf, 1958-64; sr. ptnr. Roscopf and Roscopf, P.A., 1964—. Mem. Ark. Ho. of Reps., 1953-58; del. Ark. Constl. Conv., 1968; mem. Ark. Probate Drafting Com.; mem. Ark. State Bd. Law Examiners, 1973-79; spl. justice Ark. Supreme Ct. Served with USN, 1946-48; served with USAFR, 1962-68. Fellow Am. Bar Found., Ark. Bar Found. (pres. 1995-96); mem. ABA, Ark. Bar Assn. (pres. 1990-91), Am. Law Inst., Rotary (Paul Harris fellow), Masons, Shriners, Kappa Sigma. Methodist. Home: 117 Avalon Pl Helena AR 72342-1715 Office: Helena Nat Bank Bldg PO Box 610 Helena AR 72342-0610

ROSE, ANITA, journalist, minister; b. Marquette, Mich., Apr. 25, 1957; d. Thomas Kyle and Juanita Evelyn Hubbard; m. Robert G. Rose, Oct. 6, 2000; children: Angela, Zachary Hubbard, Thomas, John. AAS, Kaskaskia Coll., 1977; BA, East Tenn. State U., 2000. Sales dir. Mary Kay Cosmetics, Inc., Dallas, 1977—80; broadcast sec. Wets - TV, Johnson City, Tenn., 1995—98; CEO Broken Hearts Ministries, Jonesborough, 1996—. Author: (book) How to Get Mr. Right. Not!, 1994, Comforts in a Time of Storm, 1997. Team mem. Presdl. Prayer Team, Orange, Calif., 2001—02; gop team leader Rep. Nat. Com., Washington, 2000—02. Named Famous Poet, Hollywood Famous Poets Soc., 2001. Mem.: Pi Gamma Mu (life Honors 2000), Psi Chi (life Honors 2000). Avocation: travel. Home: 490 Sand Valley Rd Jonesborough TN 37659 Office: Broken Hearts Ministries 490 Sand Valley Rd Jonesborough TN 37659 Personal E-mail: therosebuds@cs.com. Business E-Mail: brokenheartsinc@cs.com.

ROSE, ANITA CARROLL, retired educator; b. New Bedford, Mass., Oct. 14, 1922; d. Louis Arthur and Aline (Chicoine) Carroll; m. Anthony E. Rose, Sept. 24, 1955 (dec.); children: Anthony David, Stephen Arthur. BA, U. Mass., Dartmouth, 1971; MAT, R.I. Coll., 1975. Exec. sec. Berkshire-Hathaway, Inc., New Bedford, 1941-55, New Bedford Cancer Soc., 1956-59; tchr. French and English New Bedford Pub. Schs., 1971-88; ret., 1988. Clk. Friends of Coastline Elderly Svcs., Inc., 1991-93; bd. dirs. Our Lady's Haven, 1995—. Pres. New Bedford Jr. Women's Club, 1950-51, Fairhaven Mothers' Club, 1967-69, book chmn., 1989-91, sunshine chmn., 1991-93, nominating com. chmn., 1993—; v.p. Cath. Women's Club, 1957-59, del. Coun. of Women's Orgns., 1989-91; active Fairhaven Town Mtg., Mass., 1965—; trustee Millicent Libr., Fairhaven, 1980—; rec. sec. Fairhaven Improvement Assn., 1982-99; sec. Fairhaven Rep. Town Com., 1980—; bd. dirs. St. Anne Credit Union, New Bedford, 1988—, asst. treas., investment com. 1991-93, pres., chmn. bd., 1993—; adv. coun. Coastline Elderly Svc. Inc., 1988-92; del. Mass. Rep. Conv., 1974, 82, 86, 90, 94, 98; mem. YWCA, Old Dartmouth Hist. Assn., Friends of the Zeiterion Theatre, Friends New Bedford Festival Theatre. Testimonial dinner in her honor for years of cmty. svc. Fairhaven Improvement Assn., 1997. Mem. AAUW (pres. Coll. Club New Bedford 1983-85, 1st v.p. 1989-91, del. nat. conv. 1981, 83, 85, 93, chmn. nominating com. Mass. divsn. 1988-90, chmn. art study group 1992—, honored Mass. chpt. 1986), Tri-County Music Assn. (pres. 1992-95, bd. dirs. 1988—), R.I. Coll. Alumni Assn., U. Mass.-Dartmouth Alumni Assn., Southeastern Mass. Assn. Social Studies, Libr. Assocs. U. Mass.-Dartmouth, Mil. Order World Wars, Ret. Officers Assn., Am. Ex-Prisoners of War, St. Joseph's Couples Club (pres. 1987-88, 2001-02), Fairhaven Colonial Club (2d v.p. 1988-89), MONETA Assocs. Investment Club (chmn. 1998-99), Republican Club Southeastern Mass., Greater New Bedford Garden Club, Friends of Buttonwood Park Zoo. Avocations: travel, music, theater. Home: 49 Laurel St Fairhaven MA 02719-2817 E-mail: fairhavenacr@msn.com.

ROSE, ARDEN ELAINE, artist, painter; b. Boston, Nov. 30, 1944; BA in Philosophy, U. Calif., Berkeley, 1966, MSW, 1968; student in oil, watercolors and pastels, De Young Mus. Art Sch., San Francisco, 1968-71; pvt. instrn. with Hilda Kidder, Acad. Fine Arts, Vienna, Austria; pvt. instrn., Royal Coll. Portrait Painters, Edinborough, Scotland. Editor: Arden Rose, The Vision of A Painter, 1992; author: Interacting Through Creative Arts Activities, 1976; one-woman shows include Louise M. Davies Symphony Hall, San Francisco, 1982, Arden Rose Art Studios, Santa Barbara, Calif. and French West Indies, 1985—; exhibited in group shows Galerie Marumo, L.A., 1982, Salon d'Autumne, Paris, 1987, Musée Guimet, Paris, 1988, Festivale Internat., Osaka, 1988, Companile Galleries, Inc., Chgo., 1985, others. Mem. Los Angeles County Art Museum, L.A. Recipient Cert. of Excellence, N.Y. Soho Internat. Art Competition, 1992; named Am. Artist guest of honor Fêtes des Impressionistes, French Govt., 1993, 94. Mem. L.A. County Art Mus. Home: PO Box 90625 Santa Barbara CA 93190-0625

ROSE, ARTHUR ROYAL, financial planner, tax consultant; b. Red Bank, N.J., July 22, 1955; s. Melvin S. and Margaret L. R. BS in Bus. summa cum laude, BA in Psychology summa cum laude, Monmouth U., 1986, MBA, 1990. CFP; Accredited tax preparer; registered investment advisor, N.J.; enrolled agt. IRS. CFO, Interphase Industries Inc., Red Bank, 1986-91; pres. World-View Inc., 1991—. Advisor Smilco LLC, Red Bank. Mem. Inst. Cert. Fin. Planners. Office: World-View Inc 114B Monmouth St Red Bank NJ 07701-1109

ROSE, BRITA MAY, web site designer; b. Cuffley, Hertfordshire, Great Britain and Northern Ireland, Aug. 9, 1964; d. John Harold and Irene Evelyn Burden; m. Wesley Anthony Rose, Jan. 19, 1961. BA in History/Philosophy with honors, CUNY, Bklyn., 1997. Dir. Athenaclassicdesigns, Bklyn., 2000—. Web site designer Bklyn Coll., 1999—. Vol. animal rescuer, Bklyn., 1995—2002; bd. of deacons The Village Ch., Greenwich Village, 1997—2002; bd. dirs. So. Exposure Relief Org., N.Y.C., 1999—2000. Scholar Ford Colloquium scholar, Bklyn Coll., 1994—96, Judith Rothenberg scholar, 1996—97. Mem.: ASPCA, Nat. Campaign for Tolerance (cert. of tolerance), Mid. East Web, Defenders of Wildlife, Golden Key. Liberal. Avocations: travel, writing, horseback riding, dancing, music. Home: 4611 6th Ave Brooklyn NY 11220 Personal E-mail: britamayrose@hotmail.com.

ROSE, CAROL ANN, retired air transportation executive; b. Toledo; d. Donald Lucien and Dorothy Josephine (Maus) Edmunds; m. Saul Rose, Feb. 3, 1971 (div. 1976). BA, Kent State U., 1963. Entertainer, restaurant supr. S.S. Aquarama Cruiseship, Cleve., 1961-63; airline reservation agt. United Airlines, 1963-68, internat. passenger svc. rep. Miami, Fla., 1969-70, V.I.P. customer svc. receptionist-expediter Phila., 1971-79, account exec., 1980-84, spl. events mgr. Chgo., 1984-87, red carpet club coord., 1987-88, corp. meeting planner, 1988-90, comml. aircraft weight and balance planner Seattle, 1991-96, comms. coord., 1996-98, mktg. and promotion coord., 1998-99, coord. workers compensation-comm./return to work Chgo., 1999—2001; ret., 2001. Speaker Am. Mktg. Assn., Chgo., 1989. Author: Red Carpet Club Procedure Manual-O'Hare, 1987, Corporate Meeting Planners Manual, 1989, United Airlines Foundation Community Connection Report; Editor: Sky Lines Seattle Station Newsletter, 1992, United Airlines Workers' Compensation Newsletter, 1999. Recipient Oustanding Svc. award Airline Passengers Assn., Phila., 1981, Outstanding Contbn. award Muscular Dystrophy Assn.-Jerry Lewis Telethon, Las Vegas, 1985, 86, 89, Leadership award United Way Campaign, Chgo., 1988. Mem. Meeting Planners Assn., Mgmt. Club (v.p. 1983, pres. 1984), Women United (exec. bd. 1982-83), Delta Zeta. Avocations: reading, aerobic walking, writing prose for spl. events, social dancing. E-mail: carol.rose@ual.com.

ROSE, CAROLYN BRUCE, interior designer, educator; b. Gunnison, Miss., Oct. 10, 1930; d. John Douglas and Emmye Elizabeth (Bowe) Simmons; m. James Frederick Rose, Sept. 7, 1953; children: James Frederic, Phillip Douglas, Elizabeth Bowe. BS, Miss. Women's U., 1952; MS, Delta State U., 1952. Tchr. Inverness (Miss.) H.S., 1952; elem. sch. tchr. John D. Overstreet Elem. Sch., Starkeville, Miss., 1952-53, Misawa (Japan) AFB Dependent Sch., 1954-55; nursery sch. tchr. L.I., N.Y., 1954-55; owner Rose Designs, Dallas, 1968-88; exec. v.p. Handel's Specialty Shops, 1988. Sec. women's com. Dallas Theatre Ctr., 1965-74; bd. dirs. women's com. Dallas Civic Opera, 1978-83; mem. Opera Action, 1965-70; rsch. com. head Noted Cookery Cookbook, Dallas Symphony Orch., 1968; chmn. charity events Investment Bankers Wives' Com., 1978; local chmn., judge Dallas County 4-H; bd. dirs. Chorus of Santa Fe, 1985-86, Family Restoration Network, Dallas, 1985, Scarborough Prodns., Dallas Comm. Ctr., 1986; nat. adv. bd. Santa Fe Opera, 1986-89. Home chosen for Dallas Designer's Homes Tour, 1981. Mem. Miss. Edn. Assn., Miss. Opera Assn. Inc. (bd. dirs. 1991—), Guild of Miss. Opera. Republican.

ROSE, CHARLES, television journalist; B in History, JD, Duke U.; postgrad., NYU. Interviewer Sta. WPIX-TV, N.Y.C., 1972; mng. editor Bill Moyers Internat. Report, 1974—; exec. producer Bill Moyers Jour., 1975—; corr. U.S.A.: People in Politics, PBS, 1976; polit. corr. NBC News, 1976-77; co-host A.M. Chgo., 1978; host The Charlie Rose Show Sta. KXAS-TV, Dallas, Ft. Worth, 1979-81, Sta. WRC-TV, Washington, 1981-83; former host, interviewer CBS News Nightwatch, 1984—; exec. prodr., exec. editor and host The Charles Rose Show, 1991—; corr. Sixty Minutes II, 1999—. Producer: (TV program) A Conversation with Jimmy Carter (Peabody award). Recipient News and Documentary Emmy award for Conversation with Roger Payne, 1992, Cable ACE award, 1992. Office: 499 Park Ave New York NY 10022-1240

ROSE, CHARLES ALEXANDER, lawyer; b. Louisville, June 14, 1932; s. Hector Edward and Mary (Shepard) R.; m. Moncie Watson; children: Marc, Craig, Lorna, Gordon, Alex, Sara. BA, U. Louisville, 1954, JD, 1960. Bar: Ky. 1960, U.S. Ct. Appeals (6th cir.) 1970, Ind. 1978, U.S. Supreme Ct. 1978. Pvt. practice, Louisville, 1960-63; assoc. Jones, Ewen & McKenzie, 1963-65; ptnr. Curtis & Rose, 1965-81, Weber & Rose, Louisville, 1981—. Organist Scottish Rite Temple, Louisville. Lt. USAF, 1954-56. Mem. ABA, Ky. Bar Assn., Ind. Bar Assn., Louisville Bar Assn., Am. Soc. Hosp. Attys., Am. Bd. Trial Advocates, Brandeis Soc., Fedn. Ins. Counsel, River Road Country Club, Pendennis Club (Louisville), Jefferson Club. Republican. Episcopalian. Office: 400 W Market St Ste 2700 Louisville KY 40202-3358

ROSE, CHARLES DAVID, consulting company executive; b. Corpus Christi, Dec. 28, 1939; s. Robert Chester and Gladys (Blackmon) R.; m. Mary Ann McKinney, Apr. 23, 1965; children: David, Elizabeth, Katherine. BS in Physics magna cum laude, La. Tech. U., 1964; postgrad., Iowa State U. From engr. to dist. level supr. staff ops. South Ctrl. Bell Telephone Co., 1964-70; mgr. sales and engring. Hycaloader Co., 1970-74; owner Charles Rose Cons., Monroe, La., 1974—. Contbr. numerous articles to profl. jours. Mem. ASTM (various coms.), Am. Statis. Assn., Am. Soc. for Quality Control. Achievements include devel. of fractal variogram model for use in geostatistics; designated U.S. expert for ISO on coal sampling. Home: 4404 Landlewood Ct Dallas TX 75287-5142 Office: Charles Rose Cons PO Box 797425 Dallas TX 75379-7425

ROSE, DANIEL, real estate company executive, consultant; b. N.Y.C., Oct. 31, 1929; s. Samuel B. and Belle (Bernstein) R.; m. Joanna Semel, Sept. 16, 1956; children: David Semel, Joseph Benedict, Emily, Gideon Gregory. Student, Yale U., 1947-50; cert. of proficiency in Russian lang., U.S. Air Force Program, 1951; BA, Syracuse U., 1952; postgrad., U. Paris. With Dwelling Mgrs., Inc., N.Y.C., 1954—, pres., 1960—, vice-chmn., sec.-treas. Baltic-Am. Enterprise Fund, 1994—; dir. Dreyfus Tax Exempt Bond Fund Inc., 1976-82, Dreyfus Money Market Fund, Inc., 1980-82; pres., CEO Rose Assocs., Inc., N.Y.C., 1980-99, chmn., 1999—, 22 Dreyfus Funds, 1992—. Assoc. fellow Pierson Coll. Yale U., 1974—; bd. govs., hon. life mem. Technion-Israel Inst. Tech.; bd. dirs., grants com. Realty Found. N.Y.; vice-chmn. Lionel Trilling seminars Columbia U., 1977—; bd. dirs. Ventures in Edn.; trustee, mem. exec. and compensation and benefits coms. U.S. Trust Co. of N.Y., 1982-92; trustee, vice-chmn. mixed use devel. coun. Urban Land Inst., 1986-93; exec. com. Urban Land Found., 1989—, gov., 1993—; designated Cert. Property Mgr. Inst. for Real Estate Mgmt. Expert adv. to sec. HUD, 1972; expert/cons. to commr. edn. HEW, 1974; cons. HUD panel on urban devel., 1984-86; dir. N.Y. Coun. Humanities, 1980-86, N.Y. Conv. Ctr. Devel. Corp., 1980-90, Get Ahead Found., 1989-98, Fifth Ave. Assn., 1989-98; mem. Governor's Task Force on Housing, 1975, Task Force on Taxation, Mcpl. Assistance Corp., 1976-77, Planning Commn. Theatre Adv. Group, coun. of fellows, vis. com. to grad. faculty, bd. overseers Ctr. for Study of N.Y.C. affairs New Sch. for Social Rsch.; overseers com. to visit Ctr. Internat. Affairs Harvard U., 1992-98; Mcpl. Broadcasting System, 1977-78, MIT Ctr. for Real Estate Devel.; donor Daniel Rose chair urban econs., trustee NYU N.Y. Inst. for Humanistic Studies, Mus. of City of N.Y., 1984-90; chmn. bd. trustees, Horace Mann-Barnard Sch., 1971-74, trustee, 1962-89, hon. trustee, 1989— ; v.p., assoc. treas., bd. dirs. Police Athletic League of N.Y., vice chmn. Cen. Harlem Facility; founder and pres. Harlem Ednl. Activities Fund Inc., YM & YWHA of the Bronx, 1963-67; v.p. N.Y. Landmarks Conservancy, bd. dirs. 1977-90; bd. dirs. Jewish Cmty. Ctrs. Assn., 1970—, pres. 1974-78, hon. pres. 1978—; v.p. World Confedn. of Jewish Cmty. Ctrs., 1977-83; former trustee and exec. com. mem. Fedn. of Jewish Philanthropies of N.Y., chmn. standing functional com. on cmty. ctrs., 1969-73; ptnr. N.Y.C. Partnership, 1990—; treas., bd. dirs. Citizens Housing and Planning Coun. of N.Y., 1972—; chmn. Dem. platform adv. com., 1984 Nat. Conv.; bd. advisors Dem. Leadership Coun., 1992—, Progressive Policy Inst.; trustee Dem. Nat. Com., 1988; chmn. Del. Svcs. Host Com., N.Y.C.; bd. trustees MBA of N.Y. Scholarship Found., Inc., 1996—. Served with USAF, 1951-54. Mem. Internat. Inst. Strategic Studies (dir. Am. com. for IISS 1987—), Coun. on Fgn. Rels., Fgn. Policy Assn. (bd. dirs. 1971—, chmn. fgn. policy assocs. 1972-75), East-West Inst. (bd. dirs. 1982—, treas. 1988—, co-chmn. fin. com. 1990—, chmn. exec. com. 2000—), Am. Soc. Real Estate Counselors (mem. publs.-rsch. com.), Real Estate Bd. of N.Y. Inc. (chmn. housing com. 1975—, mem. bd. govs. 1977-80, 90—, mem. REBNY Found.), Assn. of Yale Alumni (del.-at-large 1978-81, class of 1951 del. 1986-89), Century Assn. (N.Y.C.), Coffee House, Yale, Union League Club, Cosmos (Washington), Quaker Ridge Country Club, Noyac Country Club, Econ. Club N.Y. Office: Rose Associates Inc 200 Madison Ave Fl 5 New York NY 10016-3912 E-mail: drose@rosenyc.com.

ROSE, DANIEL ASA, writer, editor; b. N.Y.C., Nov. 20, 1949; s. Gilbert Jacob and Anne Kaufman Rose; m. Laura Love Rose, Nov. 30, 1974 (div. 1981); children: Alexander Edward, Marshall; m. Shelles Elaine Roth, Sept. 5, 1993; children: Spencer Conrad Roth-Rose, Jeremy Adam Roth-Rose. AB, Brown U., 1971. Book editor Success, N.Y.C., 1980—83; travel columnist Esquire, 1984—90; food editor R.I. Montals, Providence, 1995—2001; travel editor Madison, N.Y.C., 1997—2000; arts and culture editor The Forward, 2000—. Author: Flipping for It, 1987, short stories; contbr. articles to publs. Recipient O'Henry prize, N.Y.C., 1980, New Eng. Booksellers award, Boston, 2001. Mem.: PEN (Fiction award 1996, 1997), Authors Guild, Phi Beta Kappa. Home: 13 & Bay State Rd Rehoboth MA 02769 Office: The Forward 45 E 33rd St New York NY 10016

ROSE, DAVID ALLAN, investment manager; b. N.Y.C., Feb. 15, 1937; s. Edward William and Marion (Nadelstein) R.; m. Frances Helaine Dushman, Aug. 16, 1959; children: Evan Denali, Mitchell Franklin. BS in Acctg., Queens Coll., 1958; MBA, Syracuse U., 1968; LLD (hon.), U. Alaska, 1999. Fin. mgr. U.S. Army, Fort Richardson, Alaska, 1961-75, comptroller, 1975; exec. dir. Alaska Mcpl. Bond Bank Authority, Anchorage, 1975-82, Alaska Indsl. Devel. Authority, Anchorage, 1980; co-owner Downtown Investment Co., 1980—, Downtown Delicatessen, Inc., Anchorage, 1976—; CEO, Alaska Permanent Fund Corp., Juneau, 1982-92; chmn., CEO, Alaska Permanent Capital Mgmt. Co., Inc., Anchorage, 1992—. Fin. advisor Fin. Green Lake Dam, Sitka, Alaska, 1977, Fin. Dutch Harbor Port, Unalaska, Alaska, 1979-80, Fin. Kenai-Anchorage Pipeline, Anchorage, 1979-80, Fin. Pulp Mill Pollution Control, Ketchikan, Alaska, 1979-80. Mem. City Coun., Anchorage, 1971-75, Borough Assembly, Anchorage, 1971-75, Mcpl. Assembly, Anchorage, 1975-80; pres. Alaska Mcpl. League, 1975, Mcpl. Assembly, Anchorage, 1975-77; vice chmn. endowment fund Alaska Pacific U., 1994—; chair Anchorage Concert Assn. Endowment, 2000—; chair organizing com. Unity Park Found., 2002—. Recipient Golden Man award Boys Club Alaska, Anchorage, 1974, Decoration for Meritorious Civilian Service, U.S. Army, 1975, Pub. Service award City and Borough, Juneau, 1986, Lions Internat. awards, awards for fundraising Am. Diabetes Assn., Disting. Svc. medal State of Alaska, 1999; named Pub. Adminstr. Yr. ASPA, Alaska chpt., 1986, Alaskan of Yr. Denali award, 1997. Mem. Rotary (awards). Republican. Jewish. Avocations: boating, gardening. Office: Alaska Permanent Capital 900 W 5th Ave Ste 601 Anchorage AK 99501-2044 E-mail: apcm@alaska.net.

ROSE, DAVID L., lawyer; b. Ft. Monmouth, N.J., Feb. 18, 1955; s. Llewellyn Paterson and Bebe (Faulk) R.; m. Laura Marie Jarvis, Sept. 3, 1989; children: Allison Michelle, Jessica Morgan, Ashley Elizabeth. BA in Comm., U. Colo., 1980; JD, Ariz. State U., 1991. Bar: Ariz. 1991, U.S. Dist. Ct. Ariz. 1991, U.S. Ct. Appeals (9th cir.) 1993, U.S. Supreme Ct. 1997. Law clk. Bonn & Anderson, Phoenix, 1988-91, Maricopa County Superior Ct., Phoenix, 1990-91; lawyer Anderson, Brody, Levinson, Weiser & Horwitz, 1991-92, Brandes, Lane & Joffe, Phoenix, 1992-93; pvt. practice, 1993—; lawyer Rose & Hildebrand, P.C., 1997—. Editor: Missive, 1992. Bd. dirs. Maricopa County Family Support Adv. Com., Phoenix; adv. coun. Washington Sch. Dist., Phoenix; mem. Ariz. State Legis., Domestic Rels. Reform Com., Phoenix. Mem. Maricopa County Bar Assn. (adv. family law com.), ABA (adv. family law sect.), Nat. Congress for Men (pres.), Father's for Equal Rights of Colo. (pres.). Avocations: aviation, computer systems. Office: 1440 E Washington St Phoenix AZ 85034-1109

ROSE, DEBORAH, epidemiologist; b. N.Y.C., Mar. 14, 1950; d. Frederick Phineas and Sandra (Priest) R.; m. Jan A.J. Stolwijk, Sept. 16, 1990; 1 child, Sarah Leia. BA, Yale U., 1972; SM, Harvard U., 1975; MPH, Yale U., 1977, PhD, 1989. Epidemiologist Nat. Inst. Occupl. Safety and Health, Rockville, Md., 1978-79; assoc. in rsch. II dept. epidemiology and pub. health Yale U., New Haven, 1986-88, lectr. Sch. Nursing, 1986-88; epidemiologist Nat. Ctr. Health Stats., Hyattsville, Md., 1989—. Cons. to the Min. of Health, Hungary, 1999—. Mem. adv. bd. Dwight Hall at Yale, New Haven, 1982—, v.p., 2002-; trustee Carnegie Instn. Washington, 2001—. Recipient Elm-Ivy award Yale U., 1987, Alumni award Assn. Yale Alumni, 1997, Mary E. Ives award New Haven Free Pub. Libr., 1999. Mem.: APHA, Soc. Epidemiol. Rsch., Sigma Xi. Avocations: computer consulting, bonsai. Home: 4414 Harbour Town Dr Beltsville MD 20705-1081 Office: Nat Ctr Health Stats 6525 Belcrest Rd Rm 870 Hyattsville MD 20782-2003 E-mail: debrose@erols.com.

ROSE, DONALD L., physician, educator; b. St. Charles, Mo., July 20, 1911; s. William Albert and Estelle Mattie (Sherry) R.; m. Martha Jane Koontz, Mar. 6, 1937; children: Nancy Kathryn Rose Harling, William Donald. BA, U. Colo., 1933, MA, MD, 1936. Diplomate Am. Bd. Phys. Medicine and Rehab. Intern Miami Valley Hosp., Dayton, Ohio, 1936-37, resident, 1937-38; rsch. assoc. Kettering Inst. Med. Rsch., 1938-41; asst. prof. sch. medicine Univ. Kans., Kansas City, 1947-49, assoc. prof., 1949-51, prof., 1951-74, prof. emeritus, 1974—. Cons. Phys. Med. Surgeon Gen.'s Office, Washington, 1957-65, nat. cons. USAF, 1959-61; bd. govs. Am. Bd. Phys. Medicine and Rehab., Rochester, Minn., 1957-67. Contbr. chpt. An Atlas of Amputations, 1947, Postgraduate Medicine and Surgery, 1951, Therapeutic Heat, 1958. Med. advisor NFIP Wyandotte County, Kansas City, 1947-60, Johnson County chpt., 1950-60, MDA Kansas City, 1965-74. Fellow Baruch Found., Boston, 1946-47. Mem. AMA, Am. Acad. Phys. Medicine and Rehab. (pres. 1953-54, Disting. Clin. award 1983), Am. Congress Rehab. Medicine (pres. 1957-58), Kans. Med. Soc., Wyandotte County Med. Soc. Republican. Methodist. Avocations: golf, boating. Home: 226 Concordia Dr Bella Vista AR 72714-2430

ROSE, DONALD JAMES, computer science educator; b. Santa Ana, Calif., May 25, 1944; 1 child, Tamar Rose. BA, U. Calif., Berkeley, 1966; AM, Harvard U., 1967, PhD, 1970. Instr. applied math. Harvard U., Cambridge, Mass., 1970; asst. prof. math. U. Denver, 1970-72; asst. prof. applied math. Harvard U., 1972-74, assoc. prof., 1974-77; prof., chmn. dept. computer sci. Vanderbilt U., Nashville, 1977-78; researcher Bell Labs., Murray Hill, N.J., 1978-84; prof., chmn. dept. computer Sci. Duke U., Durham, N.C., 1984-91, prof., 1991—. Cons. MCNC, Research Triangle Park, 1984-89, Bell Labs, Murray Hill, 1984-98, Tanner Rsch. Pasadena, Calif., 1993-94. Co-editor: Sparse Matrices and Their Applications, 1972, Sparse Matrix Computations, 1976; contbr. more than 50 articles to profl. jours. Mem. IEEE, Am. Math. Soc., Math. Assn. Am., Assn. Computing Machinery, Soc. Indsl. Applied Math. Office: Duke U Dept Computer Sci PO Box 90129 Durham NC 27708-0129 E-mail: djr@cs.duke.edu.

ROSE, DONALD MCGREGOR, retired lawyer; b. Cin., Feb. 6, 1933; s. John Kreimer and Helen (Morris) R.; m. Constance Ruth Lanner, Nov. 29, 1958; children: Barbara Rose Mead, Ann Rose Weston. AB in Econs., U. Cin., 1955; JD, Harvard U., 1958. Bar: Ohio 1958, U.S. Supreme Ct. 1962. Asst. legal officer USNR, Subic Bay, The Philippines, 1959-62, with Office of JAG The Pentagon, Va., 1962-63; assoc. Frost & Jacobs, LLP, Cin., 1963-70, ptnr., 1970-93, sr. ptnr., 1993-97, ret. ptnr., 1997. Co-chmn. 6th Cir. Appellate Practice Inst., Cin., 1983, 90, mem. 6th Cir. adv. com., 1990-98, chmn. subcom. on rules, 1990-94, chmn., 1994-96. Trustee Friends of Cin. Pks., Inc., 1980-89, 93-98, pres. 1980-86; trustee Am. Music Scholarship Assn., Cin., 1985-88; pres. Social Health Assn. Greater Cin. Area Inc., 1969-72; co-chmn. Harvard Law Sch. Fund for So. Ohio, Cin., 1985-87; pres. Meth. Union, Cin., 1983-85; chmn. trustees Hyde Pk. Cmty. United Meth. Ch., Cin., 1974-76, chmn. coun. on ministries, 1979-81, chmn. adminstrv. bd., 1982-84, chmn. mem. canvass, 1985, chmn. staff parish rels. com., 1988-90, chmn. commn. missions, 1993-95; trustee Meth. Theol. Sch. Ohio, vice chmn. devel. com., 1990-94, sec. 1992-94, chmn. devel. com., 1994-98, vice chmn., 1998, chmn., 1999—; loaned exec. United Way, Cin., 1999. Lt. USNR, 1959-63. Mem. Cin. Bar Assn., Cin. Citizens Police Assn., On Air Reader, Cin. Assn. for Blind, Univ. Club (Cin.), Cin. Country Club, Boothbay Harbor Yacht Club. Republican. Avocations: sailing, golf. Home: 8 Walsh Ln Cincinnati OH 45208-3435 also: 11 Blackstone Rd Boothbay Harbor ME 04538-1943 E-mail: dmrose@fbtlaw.com.

ROSE, DWIGHT DEAN, music educator; b. Omaha, Apr. 6, 1970; s. Marvin Alan Rose (Deceased) and Betty Jane Rose. BA, Midland Luth. Coll., Fremont, NE, 1993; MA Music Ed., Univ. Nebr., Omaha, NE, 2002. Music educator Laurel-Concord Schools, Laurel, Nebr., 1993—97, Lyons-Decatur Schools, Lyons, 1997—2002. Recipient Snider Young Band Dir., Nebr. State Bandmasters Assn., 1998. Mem.: Music Educators Nat. Conf., Nebr. Music Educators Assn., Nebr. State Bandmasters Assn. Office: Lyons-Decator Public Schools PO Box 526 Lyons NE 68038

ROSE, ELIHU, real estate executive; b. N.Y.C., Mar. 30, 1933; s. Samuel B. and Belle (Bernstein) R.; m. Susan Wechsler, Feb. 6, 1965; children: Amy, Isabel, Abigail. BS, Yale U., 1954; MA, NYU, 1969, PhD, 1978. Vice chmn. Rose Assocs., N.Y.C., 1956—. Trustee Tchrs. Coll., Columbia U. Contbr.

articles to profl. mil. jours. Trustee Jewish Mus. N.Y., 1992—; former chmn. bd. dirs. Internat. Ctr. Photography; bd. dirs. Sta. WNET (PBS), Lincoln Ctr. theater, 1992—, Nat. Mus. Am. History, Smithsonian Instn. Fellow Am. Acad. Arts and Scis.; mem. Internat. Inst. Strategic Studies, Coun. Fgn. Rels., Century Assn., Union League Club, Yale Club of N.Y., Army and Navy Club (Washington). Office: Rose Assocs 200 Madison Ave New York NY 10016-3903

ROSE, ELIHU ISAAC, lawyer; b. Bklyn., Nov. 27, 1941; s. Aaron Henry and Frances (Klinger) R.; m. Gail Roberta Cohen, Aug. 22, 1964; children: Melissa Kaye, Heidi Jill. AB, Columbia U., 1963, MBA, 1965; JD, St. John's U., Bklyn., 1968. Bar: N.Y.; CPA, N.Y. Sr. tax acct. Price Waterhouse & Co., N.Y.C., 1967-71; dir. taxes Exec. Monetary Mgmt., Inc., 1971-79; pres. Elihu I. Rose, P.C., Lake Success, N.Y., 1979—. Mem. ABA, AICPA, N.Y. State Bar Assn., N.Y. State Soc. CPAs, Bar Assn. Nassau County, Estate Planning Coun. L.I. Office: 1983 Marcus Ave Ste 129 New Hyde Park NY 11042-1016 E-mail: roselaw@sprintmail.com.

ROSE, ERNST, dentist; b. Oldenburg, Germany, July 22, 1932; came to U.S., 1940, naturalized, 1946; s. William and Elsie (Lowenbach) R.; m. Shirley Mae Glassman, Dec. 24, 1960 (div. Dec. 1997); children: Ruth Ellen, Michele Ann, Daniel Scot, Seth Joseph; m. Sally Rayen Dunn, Mar. 14, 1998; 1 stepchild, Toby Meritt. BS, Georgetown U., 1955; DDS, Western Res. U., 1963. Intern Waterbury (Conn.) Hosp., 1964; pvt. practice dentistry Hubbard, Ohio, 1964-96. Pres., treas. Dr. Ernst Rose, Inc.; lab. instr. Ohio State U., Columbus, 1956-57; dental adviser Assoc. Neighborhood Ctr. Mem. Liberty Twp. Zoning Commn., 1967-74, 88-92, vice chmn., chmn., 1970-74, 90; chmn. Hubbard (Ohio) Urban Renewal Com., 1968-74; mem. Brotherhood Bd., 1967—, treas., 1971-73, 88-90, pres. 1975-77, 90-92, 97-99, temple bd. dirs., 1975-84, 89-95, 97—; bd. dirs. The Playhouse, 2000-2001, Victorian Players, 2000-. With AUS U.S. Army, 1957—59, Enimitok nuclear testing. Mem. ADA, Ohio Dental Assn., Corydon Palmer Dental Soc. (mem. coun. 1983-87), Warren Dental Soc., Hubbard C. of C. (bd. dirs. 1967-97, v.p. 1995-97), Jewish Chataugua Soc. (life), Alpha Omega (coun. mem. 1968—, sec. 1970-71, v.p. 1971-72, pres. 1972-73, pres. 1989-90, 99-2000), B'nai B'rith (pres. 1970-71, trustee 1971—), Rotary (sec. 1999-2001, Paul Harris fellow, vice chmn. Kashrut com. 1983-85, chmn. Kashrut com. 1985-94, vice chmn. Mikvah com. 1983-93). Home: 3509B Somerset Dr Youngstown OH 44505-1779

ROSE, FRANKLIN ARTHUR, plastic surgeon; b. Denver, Oct. 21, 1951; s. Albert and Selma R.; m. Cindi Harwood; children: Erica, Benjamin. BS cum laude, U. Wis., 1973; MD, U. Colo., 1977. Diplomate Am. Bd. Plastic Surgery, Nat. Bd. Med. Examiners. Subintern in plastic surgery Stanford U. Sch. Medicine, Palo Alto, Calif., 1976; intern gen. surgery U. Calif., Davis, 1977-78; resident gen. surgery Yale U., New Haven, 1978-79, Albert Einstein Coll. of Medicine Hosps., N.Y.C., 1979-80; resident plastic surgery Baylor Coll. Medicine, Houston, 1981-83, fellow in plastic surgery and microsurgery, 1980-81; fellow in aesthetic plastic surgery NYU Inst. Plastic and Reconstructive Surgery, 1983; plastic surgeon, ptnr. Tex. Inst. Plastic Surgery, Houston, 1984—. Contbr. articles to profl. jours.; presented rsch. and papers to sci. confs., symposiums. Med. student senator U. Colo. Senate, 1977. Grantee: Gore & Assocs., Xomed Inc., Heyer Schulte Co., Am. Soc. for Aesthetic Plastic Surgery, Inc. Mem. AMA, Tex. Med. Assn., Harris County Med. Assn., Am. Soc. Plastic and Reconstructive Surgeons Inc., Lypolisis Soc. N. Am., Am. Acad. Cosmetic Surgery, S. Baron Hardy Soc., John Converse Soc. Avocations: tennis, golf, skiing. Office: Tex Inst Plastic Surgery 6624 Fannin St Ste 2200 Houston TX 77030-2334

ROSE, GAIL ELAINE, wholesale trade company manager; b. Chgo., Sept. 14, 1949; d. Edward Vincent and Ollove Lorraine (Ruska) Ruzicka. AAS, Morton Coll., 1969; BA, Nat.-Louis U., Evanston, Ill., 1984. Dental asst. Merrill Shepro, DDS, LaGrange Park, Ill., 1968-71; dental asst. instr. Morton Coll., Cicero, 1969-71; dental asst. Bernard C. Marker DDS, Niles, 1971-73; adminstrv. asst. KYB Corp. Am., Oak Brook, 1973-78, adminstrv. mgr. Lombard, 1978-87, dir. adminstrv. dept., 1987-90, v.p. adminstrn., 1990-99, KYB Am. LLC, Lombard, 1999—. Mem., assoc. Ill. Sheriffs' Assn., 1982—; mem. Rep. Nat. Com., Washington, 1980—. Mem. Women of Moose. Roman Catholic. Avocations: physical fitness, bicycling, reading. Office: KYB America LLC 140 N Mitchell Ct Addison IL 60101-1490

ROSE, GEORGE ANDREW, software developer, information systems specialist; b. Mt. Clemens, Mich., Dec. 17, 1950; s. George Hubert and Geraldine Marie (Benoit) R. BA, BSW in Psychology and Biology, Ea. Mich. U., 1975; MBA in Internat. Fin., George Washington U., 1987. Inpatient substance abuse therapist St. Joseph's Hosp., Mt. Clemens, Mich., 1974-77; dep. twp. clk. Twp. of Clinton (Mich.), 1977-79; social worker Bur. Rehab, Washington, 1979-84; sr. social worker Comprehensive Alcohol and Drug Abuse Ctr., 1984-88; contract mgmt. UMWA Health and Retirement Funds, 1988-91; dir. software devel., info. svcs. United Seniors Health Coop., 1993-98; pres., CEO The Portsmouth Group, Inc., 1997—. Home: 2929 Connecticut Ave NW Ste 306 Washington DC 20008-1435 Office: The Portsmouth Group Inc Ste 605 1522 K St Washington DC 20005 E-mail: georgerose@portsmouthgroup.net.

ROSE, GILBERT JACOB, psychiatrist, writer, psychoanalyst; b. Malden, Mass., May 9, 1923; s. M. Edward and Sara (Freedman) R.; m. Anne Kaufman, Mar. 10, 1946; children: Renee Rose Shield, Daniel Asa, Cecily Rose Itkoff, Aron Dana. AB, Harvard U., 1944; MD, Boston U., 1947. Diplomate Am. Bd. Psychiatry and Neurology. Asst. clin. prof. psychiatry Med. Sch. Yale U., New Haven, 1961-67; assoc. clin. prof. psychiatry Yale U. Med. Sch., 1967-83, lectr. in psychiatry Med. Sch., 1983-87; instr. Western New Eng. Psychoanalytic Inst., 1970-76; pvt. practice Rowayton, Conn., 1955—. Author: Power of Form: A Psychoanalytic Approach to Aesthetic Form, 1980, expanded edit., 1992, Trauma & Mastery in Life & Art, 1987, expanded edit., 1996, Necessary Illusion: Art as Witness, 1996. Capt. USAF, 1953-55. Recipient Founders' Disting. Tchg. prize, The Western New Eng. Psychoanalytic Soc., 2000—02. Fellow Am. Psychiat. Assn. (life), Am. Coll. Psychoanalysts; mem. Am. Psychoanalytic Assn. (life), Yale U. Muriel Gardiner Program for Psychoanalysis and the Humanities. Avocations: traveling, sailing, art, music. Home and Office: PO Box 215 Norwalk CT 06853-0215

ROSE, HUGH, management consultant; b. Evanston, Ill., Sept. 10, 1926; s. Howard Gray and Catherine (Wilcox) R.; m. Mary Moore Austin, Oct. 25, 1952; children: Susan, Nancy, Gregory, Matthew, Mary. BS in Physics, U. Mich., 1951, MS in Geology, 1952; MBA with highest distinction, Pepperdine U., 1982. Mgr. Caterpillar, Inc., Peoria, Ill., 1952-66; v.p., mktg. mgr. Cummins Engine Co., Columbus, Ind., 1966-69; pres., CEO Cummins Northeastern, Inc., Boston, 1969-77; pres. Power Systems Assocs., L.A., 1980-83, C.D. High Tech., Inc., Austin, Tex., 1984-87; mgmt. cons. Rose and Assocs., Tucson, 1984, 87—. Polit. cartoonist. Contbr. articles to profl. jours. Bd. dirs. Raymond Alf Mus., Claremont, Calif., 1975—, Comstock Found., Tucson, 1988, Environ. Edn. Exch., 1991, Heart Ctr. U. Ariz., Tucson, 1992. With USAAF, WWII. Fellow AAAS; mem. Acacia, Soc. Vertebrate Paleontology, Beacon Soc. Boston (pres. 1979-80), Algonquin Club Boston (v.p., bd. dirs. 1974-80), Duxbury Yacht Club, Longwood Cricket Club, Skyline Country Club, Phi Beta Kappa (pres. Greater Tucson Assn.), Delta Mu Delta, Sigma Gamma Epsilon, Sigma Pi Sigma, Beta Beta Beta, Sigma Xi. Republican. Presbyterian. Office: Rose & Assocs 5320 N Camino Sumo Tucson AZ 85718-5132

ROSE, HUGH, retired economics educator; b. London, July 20, 1920; came to U.S., 1960, naturalized, 1977; s. William and Ann (Ogus) R. Student, Oxford (England) U., England, 1939-40, 45-47, Nuffield Coll., 1950-52. Lectr. in econs. Rhodes U., South Africa, 1947-50, lectr. South Africa, 1952-53; lectr. in econs. Exeter U., England, 1954-60; assoc. prof. econs. U. Rochester, N.Y., 1961-63, prof., 1965-70; assoc. prof. econs. U. Toronto, Can., 1963-65; hon. rsch. assoc. Harvard U., Cambridge, Mass., 1969-70; prof. econs. Johns Hopkins U., Balt., 1970-91. Author: Macroeconomic Dynamics, 1991; contbr. articles. With British Army, 1940-45. Home: 112 Cross Keys Rd Apt D Baltimore MD 21210-1536 Office: Johns Hopkins U Dept Econs 3400 N Charles St Dept Econs Baltimore MD 21218-2680 E-mail: hrose@charm.net.

ROSE, ISRAEL HAROLD, mathematics educator; b. New Britain, Conn., May 17, 1917; s. Abraham and Dora (Dubrow) R.; m. Pearl Nitzberg, Jan. 24, 1942 (div. Feb. 1956); 1 son, Steven Philip; m. Susan Ann Lazarus, Mar. 26, 1961; children: Dora, Eric. Student, CCNY, 1934-36; AB, Bklyn. Coll., 1938, A.M., 1941; PhD, Harvard, 1951. Tutor, instr. Bklyn. Coll., 1938-41; instr. Pa. State Coll., 1942-46; asst. prof. U. Mass., 1948-54, assoc. prof., 1954-60; faculty Hunter Coll., 1960-68, prof. math., 1965-68, chmn. dept., 1966-68; prof. math. Lehman Coll., CUNY, 1968-82, prof. emeritus, 1983—, chmn. dept., 1968-72, 80-82, resident prof., 1983—. Vis. asst. prof. Mt. Holyoke Coll., 1951-52, vis. assoc. prof., 1954-55, 58-59; sci. cons. AID, India, summer 1965 Author: A Modern Introduction to College Mathematics, 1959, Algebra: An Introduction to Finite Mathematics, 1963, Vectors and Analytic Geometry, 1968, Elementary Functions: A Precalculus Primer, 1973, (with Esther R. Phillips) Elementary Functions, 1978. NRC predoctoral fellow Harvard, 1946-48; fellow Fund Advancement Edn., 1952-53 Mem. Am. Math. Soc., Math. Assn. Am. (chmn. Met. N.Y. sect. 1973-75), Nat. Council Tchrs. Math., Assn. Tchrs. Math. New Eng. (pres. Conn. Valley sect. 1956-57), Sigma Xi (pres. Hunter Coll. chpt. 1966-67) Home: 18 Floral Dr Hastings On Hudson NY 10706-1202 Office: Lehman Coll Bedford Park Blvd W Bronx NY 10468

ROSE, JACOBUS, producer; s. Alfred and Fanchon Rose. BSBA, U. Redlands, 1984. V.p. bus. affairs Sound FX Inc., Burbank, Calif., 1979-82; v.p. mktg. and ops. Glen Genn Sound, Hollywood, 1982-85; sound dir. Walt Disney, Touchstone Pictures, Burbank, 1985-88, dir. visual effects, sound and post prodn. svcs., 1988-89, prodn. exec., 1990-93, The Completion Bond Co., Century City, Calif., 1991-94; prodn. supr. "Streetfighter" Universal Pictures, 1994. Co-prodr.: Arabian Knights, 1995, Ace Ventura--When Nature Calls, 1996, Bad Moon, 1996, Steal This Movie, 1999; exec. prodr.: Splitsville, 1998; (co-exec. prodr.): Orgazmo, 1997; prodr.: Kill You Twice, 1997, Facade, 1997, Election, 1998, Flutie: An American Hero, 1999, Deadlocked, 1999, The Linda McCartney Story, 2000, Blonde, 2000, Superfire, 2001, Extream Team, 2001, Hearts of Men. Avocations: tennis, skiing, scuba, skydiving, travel. E-mail: jakerose@skylarkfilms.com.

ROSE, JALEN, professional basketball player; b. Detroit, Jan. 30, 1973; s. Jeanne R. Student, U. Mich. Guard Denver Nuggets, 1994-96, Ind. Pacers, 1996—2002, Chicago Bulls, 2002—. Named Honorable Mention All-Am., AP, 1991; set Michigan freshman scoring record, 1991; selected as All-Am., Parade Magazine, Third-Team All-Am., USA Today; set Nuggets' rookie record for assists, 1994-95 season; named to All-Rookie Second Team, NBA, 1995 Office: Chicago Bulls United Center 1901 W. Madison St. Chicago IL 60612*

ROSE, JAMES TURNER, aerospace consultant; b. Louisburg, N.C., Sept. 21, 1935; s. Frank Rogers and Mary Burt (Turner) R.; m. Daniele Raymond, Sept. 15, 1984. BS with high honors, N.C. State U., 1957. Aero. rsch. engr. NASA, Langley Field, Va., 1957-59; project engr. NASA (Mercury and Gemini), Langley Field, Va. and Houston, 1959-64; program sys. mgr. McDonnell Douglas Astronautics Co (MDAC), St. Louis, 1964-69; mgr. shuttle ops. and implementation (MDAC) McDonnell Douglas Astronautics Co., 1969-72, mgr. shuttle support (MDAC), 1972-74, mgr. space processing programs, 1976-83; dir. electrophoresis ops. in space McDonnell Douglas Astronautics Co (MDAC), 1983-86; dir. space shuttle engring. NASA, Washington, 1974-76, asst. adminstr. comml. programs, 1987-91; aerospace cons., 1992—. Chmn. Fla. Space Bus. Roundtable, 1995-98. Recipient Lindberg award for mgmt. leadership AIAA, 1983, Presdl. Meritorious Rank award, 1989, NASA Exceptional Svc. medal, 1990, Laurels award Aviation Week, 1990, Aerospace Contribution to Soc. award AIAA, 1993. Mem. Phi Kappa Phi. Epsicopalian.

ROSE, JED EUGENE, research scientist; b. Dayton, Ohio, June 8, 1952; s. Sigmund Paul and Sarah (Rock) R.; m. Frederique Behm, May 16, 1987; children: Justin Paul, Andrew Marc. BA in Physics, U. Calif., Berkeley, 1973; PhD in Neurosci., U. Calif., San Diego, 1978. Rsch. psychologist VA Med. Ctr., L.A., 1981-88, rsch. health scis. specialist, 1988-89, Durham, N.C., 1989—. Asst. rsch. psychologist UCLA, 1980-86, assoc. rschr., 1986-89; assoc. med. rsch. prof. Duke U., Durham, 1989—. Contbr. articles to Pharmacology, Biochemistry and Behavior Jour. Drug and Alcohol Dependence, Clin. Pharmacology and Therapeutics, Chest. Nat. Inst. on Drug Abuse grantee, 1981—. Fellow APA (co-chair membership dr. 1994—); mem. Soc. Neurosci. Achievements include patents for Method and Apparatus for Reduction in the Incidence of Tobacco Smoking, Aerosol for Use in the Reduction of Tobacco Smoke, Agonist-Antagonist Combination to Reduce the Use of Nicotine and Other Drugs. Office: VA Med Ctr Nicotine Rsch Lab 2200 W Main St Ste B150 Durham NC 27705-1106

ROSE, JEFFREY RAYMOND, economist, educator, negotiator; s. Albert and Thelma R.; m. Sandra Black; 1 child, Adam. BA with honors, U. Toronto, 1968, M.Indsl. Relations, 1983; postgrad., London Sch. Econs., 1968-69. Planner planning dept. City of Toronto, 1976-80; pres. local 79 Can. Union Pub. Employees, Toronto, 1980-83, nat. pres. Ottawa, Ont., 1983-91; dep. min. intergovtl. affairs Govt. of Ont., Toronto, 1991-95; sr. fellow Harrowston program in conflict mgmt.-negotiation U. Toronto, 1995—. Gen. v.p. Can. Labour Congress, 1983—91. Exec. mem. Ont. New Dem. Party, 1982-91; bd. dirs. Inst. for Rsch. on Pub. Policy, 1988-91; mem. fed. coun. New Dem. Party, 1988-91; co-chmn. Ont.-Que. Commn. for Cooperation, 1991-95. Home: 55 Sunnydene Crescent Toronto ON Canada M4N 3J5

ROSE, JOAN L. computer security specialist; b. N.Y.C., June 27, 1946; d. Vincent A. LaVertu and Joan Ellis; children: Robert, Lauren. BA, CUNY, Bklyn., 1967. Cert. info. sys. security profl. Internat. Info. Sys. Security Cert. Consortium. Programmer Met. Life Ins., N.Y.C., 1967-68; sys. analyst Western Electric, Oklahoma City, 1968-74, Pacific Intermountain Express, Oakland, Calif., 1974-78, Chevron, San Francisco, 1978-99; security adminstrn. mgr. Safeway, Inc., Walnut Creek, 1999—; dep. project mgr. SHARE (IBM Users Group), Chgo., 1998—. Project mgr. GUIDE (IBM Users Group), Chgo., 1983—98. Participant Habitat for Humanity, 1995—. Mem.: Info. Sys. Security Assn. (Bay Area chpt. treas. 1983—). Democrat. Home: 3299 Pine Valley Rd San Ramon CA 94583-3633 Office: Safeway Inc 2800 Ygnacio Valley Rd Walnut Creek CA 94598-3592 E-mail: joan.rose2@safeway.com.

ROSE, JOAN MARIE, medical/surgical nurse; b. Fresno, Calif., Aug. 12, 1952; d. Hobert Lee and Ila Marie (Jacobson) Hamilton; m. Steven Arthur Westenrider, May 1, 1976 (div. Dec., 1984); m. Richard Lee Rose, Aug. 6, 1994; children: John Rose, Dan Rose, Denise Haight. AS in Nursing, Fresno City Coll., 1987; extended edn. tchg. credential, Calif. State U., 2002. RN. Nurse Valley Med Ctr., Fresno, Calif., 1988-95; RN Nancy Hinds Hospice, 1996—. Instr. Dinuba Adult Sch. for Vocat. Nursing Students, 2002—. Author: (book) Dreams Come True, 1996; also poetry. Avocations: writing, reading, walking, bike riding, gardening.

ROSE, JOANNA SEMEL, cultural activist; b. Orange, N.J., Nov. 22, 1930; d. Philip Ephraim and Lillian (Mindlin) Semel; m. Daniel Rose, Sept. 16, 1956; children: David S., Joseph B., Emily, Gideon G. Cert., Shakespeare Inst., U.K., 1951; BA summa cum laude, Bryn Mawr Coll., 1952; postgrad., St. Hilda's Coll., Oxford U., 1953. Chmn. adv. bd. Partisan Rev., N.Y.C.; mem. exec. com. Am. Friends of St. Hilda's Coll., former chmn.; former pres. bd. dirs., current bd. dirs. Paper Bag Players, N.Y.C.; former bd. dirs., current mem. adv. coun. Poets and Writers, Inc., Nat. Dance Inst., N.Y.C. Bd. dirs. Bay Street Theatre, Sag Harbor, Eldridge St. Project, N.Y.C., Am. Friends Jewish Mus. Greece; assoc. fellow Berkeley Coll. Yale U.; mem. N.Y. Inst. for the Humanities. Mem. Cosmopolitan Club, Bryn Mawr Club of N.Y., LVIS East Hampton. Home: 895 Park Ave New York NY 10021-0327 also: 1 Lily Pond Ln East Hampton NY 11937

ROSE, JODI, opera company founder and artistic director; b. Phila., Nov. 27, 1952; d. Hubert Michael and Rita Gervase (Schubert) Rosenberger; m. Edward A. Caycedo; children: Gervase-Teresa, Thomas Schubert, Tanya-Katrina, Edward-Michael. Student, Vienna (Austria) Hochshule, 1973; BS in Edn. and Music, Chestnut Hill Coll., Phila., 1974; postgrad. in performing arts, NYU, 1976-77. Leading roles in 35 musicals or operas throughout country, U.S. and Europe, 1974-87; founder, artistic dir. Opera on the Go, Ltd., Jamaica Estates, N.Y., 1988—. Produced, staged and choreographed many children's and adult operas, including Goldilocks, Little Red Riding Hood, The Tortoise and the Hare, The Pirate Captains, Telephone, Sweet Betsy from Pike, The Medium, and La Pizza Con Funghi. Founder, dir. musical theater workshops for youth, Queens Theater, N.Y., 1993— Recipient numerous cmty. and corp. grants, as well as grants from N.Y. State Coun. on Arts; selected as guest performers at Lincoln Ctr., N.Y.C.; recipient 8-yr. grant N.Y.C. Dept. Youth Svcs. Republican. Roman Catholic. Avocations: ballroom dancing, scuba diving, water skiing, swimming, horseback riding. Home and Office: 1212 Huntcliff Trace Aiken SC 29803

ROSE, JOEL ALAN, legal consultant; b. Bklyn., Dec. 26, 1936; s. Edward Isadore and Adele R. Rose; m. Isadora Fenig, Apr. 12, 1964; children: Susan, Terri Angstriech. BS in Econs., NYU, 1958; MBA, Wharton Grad. Sch., U. Pa., 1960. Asst. purchasing agt. Maidenform Inc., N.Y.C., 1960-62; personnel dir. E.J. Korvette Inc., 1962-66; mgmt. cons. Daniel J. Cantor & Co. Inc., Phila., 1966—, sr. v.p., 1987—; mgmt. cons. to legal profession. Coord. Ann. Conf. on Law Firm Mgmt. and Econs. Author: Managing the Law Office; mem. adv. bd. Law Office Economics and Management, 1987; contbg. columnist N.Y. Law Jour., 1984—, Nat. Law Jour. Extra, 1996—, Phila. Legal Intelligencer, 1995—, L.A. Daily Times, 1999—, Legal Times of Washington, 1998—, N.J. Law Jour., 2000-, The Barrister, 1995-; also articles to profl. jours.; bd. editors Acctg. for Law Firms; editl. adv. bd. Corp. Counsel's Guide to Law Dept. Mgmt. With U.S. Army, 1960, Res., 1960-66. Fellow Coll. of Law Practice Mgmt.; mem. ABA (chmn. acquisition and mergers com., practice mgmt. sect., large law firm interest group), Inst. Mgmt. Cons., Am. Arbitration Assn. (nat. panel), Adminstrv. Mgmt. Soc. (past chpt. pres.), Am. Mgmt. Assn., Assn. Legal Adminstrs. Office: Joel A Rose & Assoc Inc PO Box 162 Cherry Hill NJ 08003-0162

ROSE, JOHN CHARLES, physician, educator; b. N.Y.C., Dec. 13, 1924; s. Hugh Stanley and Marie-Louise (Delury) R.; m. Dorothy Anne Donnelly, June 26, 1948; children— Nancy, Ellen, John Charles, Richard, Christopher. BS, Fordham U., 1946; MD magna cum laude, Georgetown U., 1950, D.Sc. (hon.), 1973; LL.D. (hon.), Mt. St. Mary's Coll., 1973. Diplomate: Am. Bd. Internal Medicine, Am. Bd. Family Practice. Intern Walter Reed Army Hosp., 1950-51; resident, research fellow Georgetown U., VA hosps., Washington, 1950-54; established investigator Am. Heart Assn., 1954-57; instr., asst. prof. medicine Georgetown U., 1954-57, coord. med. edn., 1957-58, assoc. prof. physiology and biophysics, 1958-60, prof., 1960-91, chmn. dept. physiology and biophysics, 1958-63, dean Sch. Medicine, 1963-73, 78-79, prof. medicine, 1973-91, prof. emeritus, 1991—, vice chancellor Med. Ctr., 1984-87. Assoc. editor Am. Family Physician, 1955-62, chief med. editor, 1962-88; assoc. editor Acad. Medicine, 1992-95; contbr. articles to sci. publs. Trustee Charles E. Culpeper Found., 1986-96. Served to 2d lt. USAAF, 1943-45. Decorated Air medal. Master ACP; mem. Am. Physiol. Soc., Soc. Exptl. Biology and Medicine (nat. councillor 1962-63), Am. Heart Assn. (fellow sect. circulation). Clubs: Cosmos (Washington). Home: 5710 Surrey St Chevy Chase MD 20815-5520 E-mail: jrosemd@earthlink.net.

ROSE, JOHN DAVID, cardiologist; b. Denver, 1946; BA magna cum laude, Wesleyan U., 1968; MD, U. Pa., 1972. Diplomate Am. Bd. Internal Medicine, Am. Bd. Cardiovascular Disease. Intern Hosp. U. Penn, Phila., 1972-73, resident in medicine, 1973-75; fellow in cardiology N.C. Meml. Hosp., Chapel Hill, 1975-77; prof. medicine East Carolina U., Greenville, N.C. Mem. staff Pitt County Meml. Hosp., Greenville. Mem. Alpha Omega Alpha. Address: 1800 W 5th St Greenville NC 27834-2888

ROSE, JOHN THOMAS, finance educator, department chairman; b. Ft. Worth, Aug. 20, 1943; s. Paul Pittman and Francis Nan (White) R.; m. Sandra Kaye Rolen, Sept. 5, 1969; children: Melanie Ann, Leah Nan, Lynnelle Renee. BA with honors, Tex. A&M U., 1965; MA, Washington U., St. Louis, 1968, PhD, 1976. Economist Bd. Govs. of FRS, Washington, 1972-82, sr. economist, 1982-84; prof. fin., Harriette L. & Walter G. Lacy, Jr. chair banking Baylor U., Waco, Tex., 1984—, acting chmn. dept. fin. ins. and real estate, 1996-97, chmn. dept., 1997—. Contbr. articles to profl. jours. Bd. visitors Abilene (Tex.) Christian U., 1989-92. Capt. U.S. Army, 1969-71. Decorated Bronze Star U.S. Army; recipient Disting. Bus. Prof. award, 1988, Hankamer Sch. Bus. Baylor U., 1988; Econ. Devel. Adminstrn. U.S. Dept. of Commerce fellow, 1966-69; Ernst & Young Found. Rsch. grantee, 1991. Mem. Am. Fin. Assn., So. Fin. Assn., Southwestern Fin. Assn., Fin. Mgmt. Assn., Omicron Delta Epsilon, Beta Gamma Sigma. Mem. Ch. of Christ. Office: Baylor U Hankamer Sch of Bus Dept Fin Ins and Real Estate PO Box 98004 Waco TX 76798-8004 E-mail: jt_rose@baylor.edu.

ROSE, JONATHAN CHAPMAN, lawyer; b. Cleve., June 8, 1941; s. Horace Chapman and Katherine Virginia (Cast) R.; m. Susan Anne Porter, Jan. 26, 1980; 1 son, Benjamin Chapman. AB, Yale U., 1963; LL.B. cum laude, Harvard U., 1967. Bar: Mass. 1968, D.C. 1972, U.S. Supreme Ct. 1976, Circuit Ct. Appeals 1977, Ohio 1978. Law clk. Justice R. Ammi Cutter, Mass. Supreme Jud. Ct., 1967-68; spl. asst. to U.S. pres., 1971-73; gen. counsel Coun. on Internat. Econ. Policy, 1973-74; assoc. dept. atty. gen. U.S. Dept. Justice, 1974-75; dept. asst. atty. gen. U.S. Dept. Justice (Antitrust Div.), 1975-77, asst. atty. gen. Office of Legal Policy, 1981-84; ptnr. firm Jones, Day, Reavis & Pogue, Washington, 1977-81, 84—. Prin. Ctr. for Excellence in Govt.; pres. Yale Daily News Found.; bd. govs. Yale Alumni Assn., 1996-99. 1st lt. U.S. Army, 1969-71. Mem. ABA, D.C. Bar Assn., Mass. Bar Assn., Ohio Bar Assn., Fed. Bar Assn., Am. Law Inst. Clubs: Met, Chevy Chase, Union, Yale, Harvard. Republican. Episcopalian. Office: Jones Day Reavis & Pogue 51 Louisiana Ave NW Washington DC 20001-2113 E-mail: jcrose@jonesday.com.

ROSE, JOSEPH HUGH, clergyman; b. Jewett, Ohio, Nov. 21, 1934; s. Joseph Harper and Lottie Louella (VanAllen) R.; m. Nila Jayne Habig, Feb. 14, 1958; children: J. Hugh II, Stephanie Jayne, David William, Dawnella Jayne. ThB, Apostolic Bible Inst., St. Paul, 1955, DD, 1990. Ordained United Pentecostal Ch. Assoc. min. Calvary Tabernacle, Indpls., 1956-73; Ind. youth sec. United Pentecostal Ch., 1958-60, Ind. youth pres., 1960-72, bd. edn. Mo., 1974—, presbyter Ohio dist., 1975-97, hon. life presbyter Ohio, 1997; pastor Harrison Hills Ch., Jewett, Ohio, 1973—. Editor, Ind. Dist. News, 1959-70; narrator radio svc. Harvestime, 1961—. Republican. Avocations: travel. Office: United Pentecostal Ch 8855 Dunn Rd Hazelwood MO 63042-2212 E-mail: jhrhhupc@eohio.net., jhrose@upci.org.

ROSE, JUDY HARDIN, nursing administrator; b. Shelbyville, Ky., Sept. 14, 1956; d. T.J. and Martha Bell (Ricketts) Hardin; m. Jake E. Rose Jr., Feb. 14, 1980; 1 child, Natalie Adele. Student, Western Ky. U., Bowling Green, 1974-75; AS, Ky. State U., Frankfort, 1979; BSN, U. Louisville, 1995. Cert. CPR instr., HIV counselor, jr. instr., ARC. Tchr. expectant mother classes Family Med. Ctar., Campbellsburg, Ky., 1978; acting shift supr. Kings Daus. Hosp., Shelbyville, 1979-80; charge nurse Cen. State Hosp., Louisville, 1982-87; registered nurse Rice-Audubon Vocat. Edn., 1987-94; charge nurse Johnson-Breckinridge Treatment Ctr., 1994-98; nurse adminstr. Dept. Juvenile Justice, Louisville, 1998—2002. Advisor Youth of Newburg, 1991-92; youth sponsor, youth dir. cross tng. Henry Christian Ch., 1992-97, youth counselor, 1997, AbandonedBaby Proj., Inc., 1998-99. Home: 4009 Evergreen Rd Crestwood KY 40014-9230 Office: Dept of Juvenile Justice 10510 Lagrange Rd Louisville KY 40223-1277

ROSE, KATHERINE CAST, volunteer; b. Akron, Ohio; d. John Frederick and Amy (Motz) Cast; m. Horace Chapman Rose, Oct. 1, 1938; 1 child, Jonathan Chapman. AB, Wellesley Coll., 1929. Actress Cleve. Play House, Chautauqua Repertory Co., 1929-36; trustee Goodrich Social Settlement, 1936-43, Jr. League Cleve., Nat. Cathedral Assn., Washington, 1948-56, 59-65, Children's Theatre of Washington, 1947-49, Cleve. Internat. Youth Leaders, Cleve. Playhouse. Chmn. box com. Nat. Symphony Orch., 1947-48; mem. adv. coun. Nat. Inst. Mental Health, 1956-59; co-chmn. Ohio Citizens for Eisenhower, 1952, 56; vice chmn. women's divsn. Nat. Citizens for Eisenhower's Congrl. Com., 1954; mem. adv. coun. Nat. Accident Prevention Bur., 1959-63; chmn. Blueprint for Life, Cleve., 1963. Mem. Intown (Cleve.) Club, Sulgrave (Washington) Club. Republican. Episcopalian. Home: 5955 Ranleigh Manor Dr Mc Lean VA 22101-2428

ROSE, KATHLEEN NOLAN, health facility administrator; b. Milford, Mass., Jan. 23, 1945; d. Bernard J. Nolan and Grace D. Mueller; m. Stephen W. Rose, Jan. 24, 1970; children: Sheila, Adam. Diploma, St. Vincent Hosp. Sch. Nursing, Worcester, Mass., 1966; BS, St. Joseph's Coll., Windham, Maine, 1987; postgrad., St. Joseph's Coll., North Windam, Maine. Staff nurse

ICU St. Vincent Hosp., 1966-69; community health nurse MVCS-Vis. Nurse Svc., Oak Bluffs, Mass., 1969-77; nursing supr. MVCS-Vis. Nurse/Homemaker Svcs., 1977-80; dir. quality assurance Martha's Vineyard Hosp., 1980-81, DON, 1981-92; nursing coord. Cape Cod Hosp., Hyannis, 1992-95; exec. dir. AIDS Alliance of Martha's Vineyard, Vineyard Haven, 1995-2001; pres., CEO Vineyard Nursing Assn., Oak Bluffs, 2001—. Office: Vineyard Nursing Assn PO Box 2093 PO Box 2568 Oak Bluffs MA 02557

ROSE, L. STEVEN See JASHEL, LARRY

ROSE, LEATRICE, artist, educator; b. N.Y.C., June 22, 1924; d. Louis Rose and Edna Ades; m. Sol Greenberg (div.); children: Damon, Ethan; m. Joseph Stefanelli, Oct. 10, 1975. Student, Cooper Union, 1941-45, Arts Students League, 1946, Hans Hoffman Sch., 1947. Solo exhbns. include Hansa Gallery, N.Y.C., 1954, Zabriskie Gallery, N.Y.C., 1965, Landmark Gallery, N.Y.C., 1974, Tibor de Nagy Gallery, N.Y.C., 1975, 78, 81, 82, Elaine Benson Gallery, Bridgehampton, N.Y., 1980, Armstrong Gallery, N.Y.C., 1985, Benton Gallery, Southampton, N.Y., 1987, Cyrus Gallery, N.Y.C., 1989; group exhbns. include Sam Kootz Gallery, N.Y.C., 1950, Peridot Gallery, N.Y.C., 1952, Poindexter Gallery, N.Y.C., 1959, Tanager Gallery, N.Y.C., 1960, 62, Riverside Mus., N.Y.C., 1964, Frumkin Gallery, N.Y.C., 1964, Pa. Acad. Fine Arts, Phila., 1966, N.Y. Cultural Ctr., 1973, The Queens (N.Y.) Mus., 1974, 83, Nat. Acad. Design, N.Y.C., 1974, 75, 76, 92, 93, Weatherspoon Art Gallery, Greensboro, N.C., 78, 81, Whitney Mus. Am. Art, N.Y.C., 1978, Albright-Knox Gallery, Buffalo, 1978, 81, Met. Mus. Art, 1979, Vanderwoude Tananbaum Gallery, N.Y.C., 1982, Benton Gallery, 1986, 87.; public collections include Albrect Gallery, St. Joseph, Mo., Guild Hall Mus., East Hampton, N.Y., Tibor de Nagy, Met. Mus. Art. Grantee N.Y. State Coun. Arts, 1974, The Ingram Merrill Found., 1974, AAUW, 1975, NEA, 1977, Esther and Aldolph Gottlieb Found., 1980, 88; recipient Altman prize NAD, 1974, Phillips prize NAD, 1992, award AAAL, 1992, Am. Inst. Art award. Mem. NAD. Avocations: reading, walking. Office: 463 West St Apt A924 New York NY 10014-2038

ROSE, LOIS LYNN HALL, psychiatric social worker; b. Detroit, Apr. 5, 1951; d. Walter Leroy and Dorothy (Lausten) Hall; m. James Michael Rose, June 16, 1973; children: Steven Charles, Sarah Christine, Matthew James. BA with high honors, Mich. State U., 1973; MSW, U. Mich., 1975. Cert. social worker, Mich. Social worker trainee Wayne State U. Mental Health Clinic, Detroit, 1974; psychiat. social worker trainee Neuro Psychiat. Hosp., U. Mich. Hosp., Ann Arbor, 1974-75; med. social worker Wyandotte (Mich.) Gen. Hosp., 1975-76; psychiat. social worker W. Shore Mental Health Clinic, Muskegon, Mich., 1976-81, Rose & Rose Attys., Montague, 1981—. Bd. dirs. White Lake Community Fund, Whitehall, Mich., 1985-90, pres., 1986-90; troop leader Girl Scouts U.S.A., Montague, 1985-91; mem. White Lake Arts Coun. Avocations: downhill skiing, travel. Office: Rose & Rose Attys 8787 Ferry St Montague MI 49437-1232

ROSE, MARGARETE ERIKA, pathologist; b. Esslingen, Germany, Feb. 12, 1945; came to U.S., 1967; d. Wilhelm Ernst and Lina (Schurr) Pfisterer; m. Arthur Caughey Rose, Feb. 3, 1967; children: Victoria Anne, Alexandra Julia, Frederica Isabella. MD, U. So. Calif., L.A., 1972. Diplomate Am. Bd. Anatomic and Clin. Pathology. Pathologist St. Joseph Med. Ctr., Burbank, Calif., 1977-78, Glenview Pathology Med. Group, Culver City, 1979—. Dir. anatomic pathology Glenview Meml. Pathology, Culver City, 1988—; dir. Life Chem. Lab., Woodland Hills, Calif.; co-dir., lab. Holy Cross Med. Ctr., Mission Hills, Calif., 1994-95, chmn. dept. pathology, Brotman Med. Ctr., Culver City, Calif., 2002—; med. dir. Lab., City of Angels Med. Ctr., L.A., 2002—; bd. dirs. Women in Recovery, Inc. Mem. Because I Love You, L.A., 1994. Fellow Am. Soc. Pathology, Coll. Am. Pathology. Avocations: cross-stitching, gardening, traveling. Office: Brotman Med Ctr Dept Pathology 3828 Hughes Ave Culver City CA 90232-2716

ROSE, MARIAN HENRIETTA, physics researcher; b. Brussels, Belgium; (parents Am. citizens); m. Simon Rose, Oct. 20, 1948 (dec. Jan. 1981); children: Ann, James, David, Simon. BA, Barnard Coll., 1942; MA, Columbia U., 1944; PhD, Harvard U., 1947. Teaching fellow Harvard U., Cambridge, Mass., 1945-46; adj. asst. prof. Courant Inst., N.Y.C., 1947-48, rsch. assoc., 1951-65, sr. rsch. scientist, 1965-75; vis. fellow Yale U., New Haven, 1981-93. Bd. dirs. Minna-James-Heineman Stiftung, Essen, Fed. Republic of Germany. Contbr. articles to profl. jours. Bd. dirs. Jay Heritage Ctr., Rye, N.Y.; mem. Wetlands Control Commn., Bedford, N.Y., 1992-99, Conservation Bd., Bedford, 1989-93; pres. Croton Watershed Clean Water Coalition, 1997—. Mem.: Sierra Club (conservation chair Atlantic chpt. 1992—95, del. at large to Westchester County Environ. Mgmt. Coun. 1994—, chair N.E. regional conservation com. 1995—98, conservation chair Atlantic chpt. 1998—2000, steering com. Atlantic chpt. 2000—02, del. at large N.E. regional conservation com., del. at large Atlantic chpt., exec. com. Atlantic chpt.), Sigma Xi, Phi Beta Kappa. Avocations: skiing, hiking. E-mail: marianr451@aol.com.

ROSE, MARK ALLEN, humanities educator, educator; b. N.Y.C., Aug. 4, 1939; s. Sydney Aaron and Rose (Shapiro) R.; m. Ann Bermingham; 1 son, Edward Gordon. AB summa cum laude, Princeton, 1961; LittB, Merton Coll., Oxford (Eng.) U., 1963; PhD, Harvard, 1967. From instr. to assoc. prof. English Yale U., 1967-74; prof. English U. Ill., Urbana, 1974-77; prof. U. Calif., Santa Barbara, 1977—, chmn. dept. English, 1987-89; dir. U. Calif. Humanities Rsch. Inst., 1989-94, chmn. dept. English, 1997—2001. Author: Heroic Love, 1968, (fiction) Golding's Tale, 1972, Shakespearean Design, 1972, Spenser's Art, 1975, Alien Encounters, 1981, Authors and Owners, 1993; editor: Twentieth Century Views of Science Fiction, 1976, Twentieth Century Interpretations of Antony and Cleopatra, 1977, (with Slusser and Guffey) Bridges to Science Fiction, 1980, Shakespeare's Early Tragedies, 1994, (CD-ROM) Norton Shakespeare Workshops. Woodrow Wilson fellow, 1961, Henry fellow, 1961-62, Dexter fellow, 1966, Morse fellow, 1970-71, NEH fellow, 1979-80, 90-91. Mem. MLA, Renaissance Soc. Am., Shakespeare Soc. Am., Phi Beta Kappa. Home: 1135 Oriole Rd Montecito CA 93108-2438 Office: English Dept U Calif Santa Barbara CA 93106

ROSE, MATTHEW K. rail transporation executive; Sr. v.p. mdse. bus. unit Burlington No./Santa Fe Corp., 1996-97, sr. v.p., COO, 1997-99, pres., COO, 1999—. Office: Burlington No Santa Fe Corp 2650 Lou Menk Dr 2nd Fl Fort Worth TX 76131-2830*

ROSE, MICHAEL DEAN, lawyer, educator; b. Johnstown, Pa., Oct. 22, 1937; BA, Ohio Wesleyan U., 1959; JD, Case Western Res. U., 1963; LLM, Columbia U., 1967. Bar: Ohio 1963. Assoc. firm Porter, Stanley, Treffinger & Platt, Columbus, Ohio, 1963-66; asst. prof. law Ohio State U., 1967-69, assoc. prof., 1969-72, prof., 1972-99, Lawrence D. Stanley prof. law, 1987-99, prof. emeritus, 1999—. Staff asst. to chief counsel IRS, Washington, 1970-71. Author: (with Leo J. Raskind) Advanced Federal Income Taxation: Corporate Transactions, 1978, (with Joseph S. Platt) A Federal Taxation Primer, 1973, Hornbook on Federal Income Taxation, 3d edit., 1988; editor Selected Federal Taxation Statutes and Regulations, 1973-99, Ohio Will Manual, 1986—. Fellow Am. Coll. Trust and Estate Counsel; mem. Am. Law Inst. Home: 1327 Friar Ln Columbus OH 43221-1527 Office: Ohio State U 55 W 12th Ave Columbus OH 43210-1338 E-mail: rose.4@osu.edu.

ROSE, MICHAEL LEONARD, film, television and video producer; b. St. Paul, Aug. 9, 1952; s. Robert L. and Beverly Bain (McKee) R.; m. Carol L. King, 1991. BA, UCLA, 1978, MFA, 1990. Media dir. Com. to Bridge the Gap, L.A., 1980-82; producer KPFK Pacifica, 1982-83, GM, Detroit, 1983-92, Network USA, Inc., Rockville, Md., 1993-96; producer 30-part documentary series Automobiles, 1995—; prodr., writer, dir. Michael Rose Prodns., Santa Monica, Calif., 1996—. Producer (film) Character, 1984 (Cine award 1984, 96), (videotape) A New Me, 1985 (U.S. Industry award 1985), Safety Belts for Dummies and People, 1986 (ITVA award, U.S. Industry award, Nat. Com. Films for Safety award); producer, writer (videotape) I Need the Earth and the Earth Needs Me, 1990 (Cine Golden Eagle award, Nat. Edn. Film and Video award 1991), (film) A Tale of Two Cities, 1990 (Expo of Short Film and Video Award, Outstanding Student Documentaty Bklyn. Arts Coun. 1991); dir. pub. svc. announcement Eye Exam, 1988 (ITVA award 1988); producer The Game of Your Life, 1989 (Am. Film and Video award, ITVA award), Precious Cargo, (TV series) Wheels of Survival, Dream Machines, Ultimate Autos. Active, producer Mahaffey for Coun. campaign, Detroit, 1989; producer radio comml. Friends of the Nuclear Freeze, L.A., 1982. Recipient E.P. Ingersoll award Soc. Automotive Historians, 1998, Nat. Ednl. Media Network award, 1998; scriptwriting grantee Calif. Coun. for Humanities, 1999. Mem.: Dirs. Guild Am., Internat. Documentary Assn. (bd. dirs.). Office: 1526 14th St Ste 105 Santa Monica CA 90404-3320 E-mail: michaelrose@mrpi.tv.

ROSE, MICHAEL ROBERTSON, evolutionary biology educator, consultant; b. Iserlohn, Germany; s. James Barry and Charlotte Julia Rose; children: Darius, Caitlin, Liam, Muireann. BS, Queen's U., Kingston, Ont., Can., 1975, MS, 1976; PhD, U. Sussex, Eng., 1979. NATO sci. fellow U. Wis., Madison, 1979-81; asst. prof. Dalhousie U., Halifax, N.S., Can., 1981-85, assoc. prof. Can., 1985-87; assoc. prof. evolutionary biology U. Calif., Irvine, 1987-90, prof., 1990—. Author: Evolutionary Biology of Aging, 1991, Adaptation, 1996, Darwin's Spectre, 1998. Recipient President's prize Am. Soc. Naturalists, 1992, Busse award World Congress Gerontology, Adelaide, Australia, 1997. Mem. Soc. for Study Evolution. Avocation: music. E-mail: mrrose@uci.edu.

ROSE, NOEL RICHARD, immunologist, microbiologist, educator; b. Stamford, Conn., Dec. 3, 1927; s. Samuel Allison and Helen (Richard) R.; m. Deborah S. Harber, June 14, 1951; children: Alison, David, Bethany, Jonathan. BS, Yale U., 1948; MA, U. Pa., 1949, PhD, 1951; MD, SUNY, Buffalo, 1964; MD (hon.), U. Cagliari, Italy, 1990; ScD (hon.), U. Sassari, Italy, 1992; Order of the First Class (hon.), Ctrl. U. Venezuela, 1997. From instr. to prof. microbiology SUNY Sch. Medicine, Buffalo, 1951-73, dir. Center for Immunology, 1970-73, dir. Erie County Labs., 1964-70; dir. WHO Collaborating Center for Autoimmune Disorders, 1968—; prof. immunology and microbiology, chmn. dept. immunology and microbiology Wayne State U. Sch. Medicine, 1973— 82; prof., chmn. dept. immunology and infectious diseases Johns Hopkins U. Sch. Hygiene and Pub. Health, Balt., 1982-93, prof. medicine and environ. health scis., 1982—, prof. molecular microbiology and immunology, 1993—; prof. pathology Johns Hopkins U. Sch. Medicine, 1994—; dir. Johns Hopkins Autoimmune Disease Rsch. Ctr., 1998. Cons. in field. Editor: (with others) International Convocation on Immunology, 1969, Methods in Immunodiagnosis, 1973, 3d rev. edit., 1986, The Autoimmune Diseases, 1986, 2d edit., 1992, 3d edit., 1998, Microbiology, Basic Principles and Clinical Applications, 1983 Principles of Immunology, 1973, 2d rev. edit., 1979, Specific Receptors of Antibodies, Antigens and Cells, 1973, Manual of Clinical Laboratory Immunology, 1976, 6th edit., 2002, Genetic Control of Autoimmune Disease, 1978, Recent Advances in Clinical Immunology, 1983, Clinical Immunotoxicology, 1992, Manual of Human Immunology, 1997; editor in chief Clin. Immunology and Immunopathology, 1988-98; contbr. articles to profl. jours. Recipient award Sigma Xi, 1952, award Alpha Omega Alpha, 1976, Lamp award, 1975, Faculty Recognition award Wayne State U. Bd. Govs., 1979, Pres.'s award for excellence in teaching, 1979, Disting. Service award Wayne State U. Sch. Medicine, 1982, U. Pisa medal, 1986, U. Venezuela medal, 1998; named to Acad. Scholars Wayne State U., 1981; Josiah Macy fellow, 1979 Fellow AAAS, APHA, Am. Acad. Allergy and Immunology, Am. Acad. Microbiology, Assn. Med. Lab Immunologists; mem. Acad. Clin. Lab. Physicians and Scientists, Am. Assn. Immunologists, Am. Soc. Investigative Pathology, Am. Soc. Clin. Pathologists, Am. Soc. Microbiology (hon.; Abbott Lab. Clin. and Diagnostic Immunology award 1993), Brit. Soc. Immunology, Coll. Am. Pathologists, Sociètè Française d'Immunologie, Can. Soc. Immunology, Soc. Exptl. Biology and Medicine Coun., Clin. Immunology Soc. (sec., treas., pres. 1993), Austrian Immunology Soc. (hon. mem.), Sigma Xi (pres. Johns Hopkins U. chpt. 1988), Alpha Omega Alpha, Delta Omega. Office: Johns Hopkins U 615 N Wolfe St Baltimore MD 21205-2103

ROSE, NORMAN, retired lawyer, retired accountant; b. N.Y.C., July 7, 1923; s. Edward J. and Frances (Ludwig) R.; div.; children: Ellen, Michael; m. Judith Rose; stepchildren: Dwight, Audrey, Jason. BBA, CCNY, 1947; JD, N.Y. Law Sch., 1953. Bar: N.Y. 1954, U.S. Dist. Ct. (ea. dist.) N.Y. 1956, U.S. Tax Ct. 1956, U.S. Dist. Ct. (so. dist.) N.Y. 1960, U.S. Supreme Ct. 1961, U.S. Ct. Appeals (2d cir.) 1967, Fla. 1979. Pvt. practice, N.Y.C., 1954-69, Ft. Lauderdale, Fla., 1979-91; ptnr. Dean, Falanga & Rose, Carle Pl., N.Y., 1979-81. Referee Small Claims Ct., N.Y.C., 1959-69; arbitrator Accident Claims Tribunal, Am. Arbitration Assn., 1960-65; C.P.A., N.Y.C., 1951-57; lectr. in field. Author law note Liability of Golfer to Person Struck by Ball, 1959 (Hon. Mention 1960). Pres. Nassau South Shore Little League, Lawrence, N.Y., 1966-68; treas. 5 Towns Dem. Club, Woodmere, N.Y., 1966-67; chmn. United Fund, Village of Lawrence, 1967. Capt. USAF, 1943-45, ETO. Decorated DFC, Air medal with 5 oak leaf clusters, Silver Star, Purple Heart. Mem. ATLA (sustaining), Acad. Fla. Trial Lawyers (sustaining), N.Y. State Assn. Plaintiffs Trial Lawyers, N.Y. State Bar Assn., Fla. Bar, Nassau County Bar Assn. (chmn. med-legal com. 1975-77), Lawyer/Pilots Bar Assn., Pompano Beach Power Squadron (safety officer), Masons, Shriners. Home: #2111 3200 Port Royale Dr N Apt 2111 Fort Lauderdale FL 33308-7808 E-mail: normierose@aol.com.

ROSE, PATRICIA, artist, educator; 1 child Nicholas Flores. BA, U. Calif., Berkeley, 1968; MA, Roosevelt U., 2002. Cert. elem., secondary tchr. Ill. Tchr. Chgo. Pub. Schs., 1991—95; dir. Ravenswood Gallery and Studios, 1995—96; founder, dir. Art Odyssey, Wilmette, 1997—; tchr. Muslim Cmty. Ctr. Full Time Sch., Morton Grove, 1999—2000; instr. gifted edn. and arts Sch. of Art Inst., Chgo., 2001. Exhibited in group shows at Union League Club, Chgo., 1999, Montserrat Gallery, N.Y.C., 2000, Ann. Chgo. Art Open, 2000, Art Odyssey, Willmette, 2002. Mem.: Ill. Assn. Gifted Children, Nat. Assn. Gifted Children. Avocations: theater , social science.

ROSE, PAUL LAWRENCE, history educator; b. Glasgow, Scotland, Feb. 26, 1944; m. Susan Ellen Kaplow, June 3, 1969; children: Alexander, Olivia, Zoe, Ariel. BA, MA, Oxford U., Eng., 1968; D in History, U. Paris, 1973. Vis. lectr. UCLA, 1968-69; research assoc. Toronto U., 1969-70; instr. St. John's U., N.Y., 1970-71; APS research fellow Cambridge (Eng.) U., 1974-75; from lectr. to sr. lectr. to reader/research prof. James Cook U., Australia, 1974-84; prof. history Newcastle U., Australia, 1984-85, Haifa (Israel) U., 1985-92, Reuben Hecht prof. Zionist history, 1987-92; Roberts prof. York U., Can., 1990-92; Mitrani prof. Jewish studies/European history Pa. State U., 1992—. Author: The Italian Renaissance of Mathematics, 1975, Bodin and the Great God of Nature, 1980, German Question/Jewish Question, 1990, Wagner-Race and Revolution, 1992, Heisenberg and the Nazi Atomic Bomb Project, 1998. Recipient various research awards; Am. Philos. Soc. grantee, Am. Coun. Learned Socs. grantee, Australian Rsch. Commn. grantee. Fellow Royal Hist. Soc.; mem. Am. Hist. Assn., Inst. for Advanced Study. Avocations: music, chess, billiards. Office: Pa State U Dept History Weaver Bldg 106 University Park PA 16802 E-mail: plr2@psu.edu.

ROSE, PETER ISAAC, sociologist, writer; b. Rochester, N.Y., Sept. 5, 1933; s. Aaron E. and Lillian (Feld) R.; m. Hedwig Hella Cohen, Mar. 25, 1956; children: Elisabeth Anne, Daniel Eric. AB, Syracuse U., 1954; MA, Cornell U., 1957, PhD, 1959. Instr. Goucher Coll., 1958-60; mem. faculty Smith Coll., Northampton, Mass., 1960—; prof., 1967-73; chmn. dept. sociology and anthropology Smith Coll., 1967-74, 79-80, Sophia Smith prof., 1973—; dir. Am. Studies Diploma program, 1973—; mem. grad. faculty U. Mass., 1961—; sr. fellow Kahn Inst., 2000—. Fulbright prof. U. Leicester, Eng., 1964-65, Kyoto (Japan) Am. Studies Inst., Flinders U., Australia, 1970; vis. prof. Wesleyan U., Middletown, Conn., 1966-67, U. Colo., 1968, Yale U., 1970, Clark U., 1970-71, Doshisha U., Kyoto, Japan, fall 1999; vis. scholar Harvard U., 1983, 84-85, vis. prof., spring 1984; vis. scholar Chinese Acad. Social Sci., Beijing, 1986; resident scholar Rockefeller Study Ctr., Bellagio, Italy, summer 1987; vis. fellow St. Catherine's Coll., Oxford, spring, 1995,Stanford U., 1996, Liguria Study Ctr., Bogliasco, Italy, spring 1998, fall 2001. Author: They and We, 1964, 5th edit., 1997, The Subject is Race, 1968, Strangers in Their Midst, 1977, Mainstream and Margins, 1983, Tempest-Tost, 1997, Guest Appearances and Other Travels in Time and Space, 2002; co-author: Sociology, 1977, 2d edit., 1982, Understanding Society, 1978, 3d edit., 1968; editor: The Study of Society, 1967, 4th edit., 1977, The Ghetto and Beyond, 1969, Americans From Africa, 1970, rev. edit., 2001, Nation of Nations, 1972, reissued, 1981, Seeing Ourselves, 1972, rev. edit., 1975, Socialization and the Life Cycle, 1979, Working With Refugees, 1986, Interminority Relations in the U.S., 1993, Professorial Passions, 1998; co-editor: Through Different Eyes, 1973. Mem. Am. Sociol. Assn. (mem. coun. 1974-77), Mass. Sociol. Assn. (pres. 1967-68), Soc. Study of Social Problems (v.p. 1968-69), Ea. Sociol. Soc. (v.p. 1970-71, pres. 1991-92). Home: 66 Paradise Rd Northampton MA 01060-2907 E-mail: prose@smith.edu.

ROSE, PETER EDWARD, former professional baseball player and manager; b. Cin., Apr. 14, 1941; s. Harry Rose; m. Karolyn Ann Englehardt (div.); children: Fawn, Peter; m. Carol Woliung, Apr. 1984; children: Cara, Tyler. Player Cin. Reds, 1963-78, player mgr., 1984-87, mgr., 1987-89; player Phila. Phillies, 1979-83, Montreal Expos, 1984; host weekly radio show Pete Rose on Baseball Sta. WCKY, Cin., 1992; now host syndicated show Talk Sports with Pete Rose Sta. WGTO-AM, Orlando, Fla. Author: (with Bob Hertzel) Charlie Hustle, 1975, Winning Baseball, 1976, (with Peter Golenback) Pete Rose on Hitting, 1985, (with Roger Kahn) Pete Rose: My Story, 1989; TV appearances include Babe Ruth, 1991, Arli$$, 1996, Savage Skies, 1996, Veronica's Closet, 1997, Wrestlemania XIV, 1998, Wrestlemania XV, 1999, Wrestlemania XVI, 2000. Named Nat. League Rookie of Yr., 1963, Most Valuable Player, 1973, Most Valuable Player World Series, 1975, Nat. League Player of Yr. The Sporting News, 1968, Ball Player of Decade, 1979; named to Nat. League All-Star Team, 1965, 67-71, 73-79, 80-81. Achievements include being second player in baseball history to exceed 4000 hits, all time leader in hits. Office: PO Box 33906 Indialantic FL 32903

ROSE, PETER GRAHAM, gynecologic oncologist; b. Beverly, Mass., Mar. 11, 1955; MD, Boston U., 1955. Cert. in ob-gyn., specialty in gynecol. oncology. Resident in surgery Vanderbilt U., Nashville, 1981-83; resident in ob-gyn. Ohio State U., Columbus, 1983-86; fellow in gynecologic oncology Roswell Park, Buffalo, 1986-88; with MetroHealth Med. Ctr., Cleve. Prof. Case Western Res. U. Mem. ACOG, Am. Soc. Clin. Oncology. Office: MetroHealth Med Ctr Cancer Care Pavillion #2017 2500 MetroHealth Dr Cleveland OH 44109

ROSE, RICHARD LOOMIS, lawyer; b. Long Branch, N.J., Oct. 21, 1936; s. Charles Frederick Perrott and Jane Mary (Crotta) R.; m. Marian Frances Irons, Apr. 1, 1960; children: Linda, Cynthia, Bonnie. BA, Cornell U., 1958; JD, Washington and Lee U., 1963. Bar: N.Y. 1963, Conn. 1965, U.S. Dist. Ct. (so. dist.) N.Y. 1964, U.S. Dist. Ct. Conn. 1965, U.S. Ct. Appeals (2d cir.) 1965, U.S. Supreme Ct. 1970. Assoc. Cummings & Lockwood, Stamford, Conn., 1965-71, ptnr., 1971-91, Kleban & Samor, P.C., Southport, 1991-93; of counsel Whitman Breed Abbott & Morgan, Greenwich, Conn., 1993-95; prin. Roberts, Rose & Bates, P.C., Stamford, 1995—. Bd. dirs. and sec. Index Corp.; mem. adv. com. Conn. Banking Commr. on Conn. Securities Laws, 1982—; dir. Conn. World Trade Assn. Editor: Washington and Lee Law Rev. Chmn. Fgn. Trade Zone Com. to Mayor of City of Bridgeport, Conn., 1988-90; mem. fgn. trade awareness com. S.W. Area Industry and Commerce Assn., Task Force, 1987-88; bd. dirs. German Sch. of Conn., Inc., 1992—. 1st lt. U.S. Army, 1958-60, Korea. Mem. ABA, Conn. Bar Assn. (exec. com. corp. sect.), Internat. Bar Assn., New Canaan Country Club, Phi Delta Phi, Omicron Delta Kappa, Phi Delta Theta. Republican. Office: Roberts Rose & Bates PC PO Box 15630 1055 Washington Blvd Stamford CT 06901-2216

ROSE, ROBERT NEAL, brokerage house executive; b. Chgo., Feb. 27, 1951; s. James Allan Rose and Hazel (Gordon) Kaufman; m. Anna Yvette Trujillo, Aug. 23, 1981; children: David James, Michelle Elizabeth, Daniel Jonathan. BS, Georgetown U., 1973; MPA, Harvard U., 1995. Trader Salomon Bros., N.Y.C., 1974-75; project coord. Latin Am. Merrill Lynch Govt. Securities, 1975-76; dir. fed. govt. affairs Pub. Service of N.Mex., Albuquerque, 1977-78; exec. dir. Gov. Jerry Apodaca, Washington, 1979-80; expert cons. U.S. Dept. Commerce, 1980-81; asst. treas. Am. Express Internat. Bank, N.Y.C., 1981-82; sr. v.p. Refco, Inc., 1982-84; v.p., mgr. Thomson McKinnon Securities, 1984-88; sr. v.p. Lehman Bros., 1988-92; mng. dir. Credit Agricole Futures Inc., 1992-95; sr. mng. dir. Bear Stearns, 1995—. Cons. BDM Corp., McLean, Va., 1981-88; Presdl. appointee J. William Fulbright Fgn. Scholarship Bd., 1993-97; bd. dirs. Shenandoah U. Sch. Bus. Mem. Dem. conv. site selection com., 1989-90; arrangements com. Dem. Conv., San Francisco, 1984, rules com., L.A., 2000; fin. chmn. Conn. Dem. State Ctrl. Com., 1993; chmn. nat. fin. coun. Dem. Nat. Com., 1998-99; trustee Conservative Synagogue of Westport, 2000-02; exec. com. Conn. Yankee Coun. Boy Scouts Am., 2000—. Wexner Heritage Found. fellow, 1992-94. Jewish. Avocations: skiing, tennis. Home: 326 Bayberry Ln Westport CT 06880-1315 Office: 383 Madison AVe New York NY 10179 E-mail: robrose@att.net.

ROSE, ROBERT DIDIER, neurophysiologist; b. Washington, Oct. 10, 1954; s. Richard Contee and Mary Estill (Martin) R. AB, Transylvania U., 1976; MS, Emory U., 1981; PhD, SUNY, Stony Brook, 1986. Tchg. asst. Emory U., 1977-81, SUNY, Stony Brook, 1981-82, NIMH predoctoral rsch. fellow, 1982-84, rsch. asst., 1984-86; rsch. assoc. prof. dept. pharmacology U. Pitts. Med. Sch., 1987-88; clin. neurophysiologist dept. neurosurgery U. Pitts. Med. Ctr., 1992; clin. fellow Ctr. Clin. Neurophysiology U. Pitts. Sch. Medicine, 1992-97; asst. prof. dept. biol. scis. Duquesne U., Pitts., 1988-90; asst. prof. dept. biology Slippery Rock (Pa.) U., 1991-92; vis. prof. dept. anatomy and histology U. Pitts. Dental Sch., 1998—; COO Neurex, Inc., 1999—. Pres., CEO Neuro-Resource, 1998—; cons. Computational Diagnostics, Inc., Pitts., 1992—; cons. dept. otolaryngoloty Children's Hosp. of Pitts., 1994—, NuVasive, Inc., 2000—; adj. faculty mem. C.C. of Allegheny County, Pitts., 1988—; trainee activities com. Ctr. for Neurosci., U. Pitts., 1988—; naturalist-cons. Queens Coll. Ctr. for Environ. Edn., 1982-84; grant reviewer U.S.-Israel Bination Sci. Found., Tel Aviv, 1990—; mem. panel NSF, Washington, 1990, 92; lectr., reviewer in field. Contbr. articles, chpts., abstracts to profl. publs. Fellow Marine Biol. Lab., Woods Hole, Mass., 1978, Luft-Brückendank fellow Inst. Tierphysiologie und Angewandte Zoologie, Arbeitsgruppe Neurobiologie, Freie U. Berlin, 1979, Deutscher Akademischer Austauschdienst fellow, 1979, NIMH/NRSA fellow SUNY-Stony Brook, 1982-84; grantee Emory U., 1978-81, Freie U., 1979, Hunkele Devel. Fund, 1988, State of Pa., 1989, NSF, 1989-91, Copeland Found., 1992-94, Children's Hosp. of Pitts., 1994, 94-95. Mem. AAAS, Am. Soc. Neurophysiol. Monitoring, Soc. Neurosci. Avocations: white water kayaking, fishing, skiing, rugby. Office: 440 Broadway Pitcairn PA 15140-1447

ROSE, ROBERT E(DGAR), state supreme court justice; b. Orange, N.J., Oct. 7, 1939; BA, Juniata Coll., Huntingdon, Pa., 1961; LL.B., NYU, 1964. Bar: Nev. 1965. Dist. atty. Washoe County, 1971-75; lt. gov. State of Nev., 1975-79; judge Nev. Dist. Ct., 8th Jud. Dist., Las Vegas, 1986-88; justice Nev. Supreme Ct., Carson City, 1989—, chief justice, 1993-94, 1999-2000. Office: Nev Supreme Ct Capitol Complex 201 S Carson St Carson City NV 89701-4702

ROSE, ROBERT ERNEST, gas & oil drilling industry executive; MBA, So. Meth. U. Drillship ops. mgr., area mgr., drilling divsn. v.p. Global Marine, Inc., Houston, 1964-76; sr. exec. positions Atwood Oceanics, Inc., Diamond M Co., Kaneb Svcs., Inc.; pres., CEO Diamond M. Co. & Diamond Offshore Drilling, Inc., until 1998; CEO, pres. Global Marine, Inc., Houston, 1998—2001, chmn. bd. dirs., 1999—, Global Santa Fe, 2001—. Bd. dirs. Am. Bur. Shipping, Offshore Energy Ctr., Am. Petroleum Inst., Grey Wolf, Inc. Bd. dirs. Sam Houston Area Coun., Boy Scouts Am., Am. Petroleum Inst., Nat. Ocean Industries Assn. Office: Global Santa Fe Corp 777 N Eldridge Pkwy Ste 800 Houston TX 77079-4493

ROSE, ROBERT GORDON, lawyer; b. Newark, June 25, 1943; s. Harry and Ann Shirley (Gordon) R.; m. Ellen Nadley Berkowitz, July 2, 1966; children: Lisa Pauline, Michael Allan. BA, SUNY, Buffalo, 1965; MA, Columbia U., 1969; JD, Seton Hall U., 1974. Bar: N.J. 1974, U.S. Dist. Ct. N.J. 1974, U.S. Ct. Appeals (3rd cir.) 1974, U.S. Ct. Appeals (2nd cir.) 1975. Law clk. to Hon. John J. Gibbons U.S. Ct. Appeals (3rd cir.), Newark, 1974-75; assoc. Pitney, Hardin, Kipp & Szuch, Morristown, N.J., 1975-80, ptnr., 1980—. Mem. com. on unauthorized practice of law Supreme Ct. N.J., 1989—, apptd. com. chair, 2000. Contbr. articles to profl. jours. Recipient Disting. Grad. award Seton Hall U. Law Sch., 2000. Mem. ABA, N.J. Bar Assn., Morris County Bar Assn. (trustee 1989-90). Avocations: travel, philately. Office: Pitney Hardin Kipp & Szuch Park Ave at Morris County PO Box 1945 Morristown NJ 07962-1945 E-mail: rrose@phks.com.

ROSE, ROBERT MICHAEL, materials science and engineering educator; b. N.Y.C., Apr. 15, 1937; s. Lawrence Lapidus and Lillian (Rosen) R.; m. Martha Gibbs, Oct. 15, 1961; children: Cynthia J., James L., Joshua S. S.B., MIT, 1958, Sc.D., 1961. Registered profl. engr., Mass. Asst. prof. materials sci. and engring MIT, Cambridge, 1961-66, assoc. prof., 1966-72, prof., 1972—; dir. MIT Concourse program, 1988—; prof. health scis. and tech. Harvard Med. Sch.- MIT, 1978-90; dir. Cryoelectro Assocs., Wenham, Mass., 1978-90. Author: Structure and Properties of Materials, 1964, Practical Biomechanics for the Orthopedic Surgeon, 1979, 92, The Chicken From Minsk, 1995. Recipient Kappa Delta prize Am. Acad. Orthopedic Surgeons, 1973 Mem. Am. Soc. Metals (vice chmn. 1971-72, Bradley Stoughton prize, chmn. 1972-73), Metal Soc. AIME, Dolphin Yacht Club (Marblehead, Mass.), Boston Yacht Club. Jewish. Home: 18 Morgan St Wenham MA 01984-1114 Office: Room 4-132 MIT 77 Massachusetts Ave Cambridge MA 02139-4301 *I would share my thoughts with you if I were satisfied with what I am. But I submit to you that anyone who is truly satisfied with his personal success doesn't understand the nature of his own achievement.*

ROSE, ROBERT WILLIAM (ROBIN), JR. forest regeneration scientist, educator; b. Bryn Mawr, Pa., July 9, 1945; s. Robert William Rose and Anne (Foulke) Corson; m. Marion Bray, Sept. 4, 1977; children: Robert Wistar, Andrew Blair; m. Li-Wen Lee, Apr. 1, 1995. BA in History, U. Conn., 1968; MS in Forestry, U. Vt., 1975; PhD in Forestry, N.C. State U., 1980. Forest regeneration scientist Westvaco Corp., Summerville, S.C., 1979-86; prof., dir. Nursery Tech. Coop. Oreg. State U., Corvallis, 1986—, dir. Vegetation Mgmt. Rsch. Coop., 1993—, pres.-elect faculty senate, 1999. Co-author: Propagation of Pacific Northwest Native Plants, 1998. Served with USAF, 1968-72, Vietnam. Decorated Bronze Star. Mem. Internat. Soc. Tropical Foresters (country v.p. 1999—). Episcopalian. Avocation: nature photography. Home: 2500 NW Princess St Ste 204 Corvallis OR 97330 Office: Oreg State U Forest Sci Dept Jefferson St Corvallis OR 97331

ROSE, ROSLYN, artist; b. Irvington, N.J., May 28, 1929; d. Mark and Anne Sarah (Green) R.; m. Franklin Blou, Nov. 26, 1950; 1 child, Mark Gordon Blue (dec.). Student, Rutgers U., 1949-51, Pratt Ctr. for Contemporary, Printmaking, N.Y.C., 1969; BS, Skidmore Coll., 1976. Artist. One-woman shows include Midday Gallery, Caldwell, N.J., 1972, Caldwell Coll., 1972, Kean Coll., Union, N.J., 1973, Art Corner Gallery, Millburn, N.J., 1974, Brandeis U., Mass., 1974, Newark Mus., 1974, George Frederick Gallery, Rochester, N.Y., 1981, Robbins Gallery, Washington, 1981, Arnot Art Mus., Elmira, N.Y., 1982, Douglas Coll. Rutgers U., New Brunswick, 1987, Nathans Gallery, West Paterson, N.J., 1984, 86, 89, 97, 99, The Pen and Brush, N.Y.C., 1998; exhibited in group shows at Seattle Art Mus., Portland (Oreg.) Mus., NYU U., Montclair Art Mus., N.J., Women in the Arts, Florence and Naples, Italy, Art Ctr. Athens, Greece, Middlesex County Mus., Piscataway, N.J., New Century Artists, N.Y.C., Noyes Mus., Oceanville, N.J., Grounds for Sculpture, Hamilton, N.J., others; represented in permanent collections including N.J. State Mus., Trenton, Citibank of N.Y., Russia, N.J. State Libr., Trenton, Roddenbery Meml. Libr., Cairo, Ga., Rosenberg Libr., Galveston, Tex., Period Gallery, Omaha, Cambridge Art Assn., Cambridge, Mass., Newark Mus., Newark Pub. Libr., AT&T, BASF Wyandotte Corp., First Fed. Bank, Rochester, Gulf & Western Industries, Irving Trust Co., N.Y., McAllen Internat. Mus., Tex., Nabisco Brands Corp., East Hanover, N.J., Verizon, Readers Digest Collection, Voorhees-Zimmerli Mus., Rutgers U., New Brunswick, N.J., The Noyes Mus. (study collection), Oceanville, N.J., others; featured artist New Century Artists Gallery, N.Y.C., 1998-2001, Internat. Soc. Exptl. Artists, 1999-2000; creator UNCIF cards, 1979-80. Recipient graphic award Westchester (N.Y.) Art Soc., 1973, Best-in-Show award Livingston (N.J.) Art Assn., 1971, Best-in-Show award N.J. Ctr. for Visual Arts, Summit, 1969, Mixed Media Merit award Salmagundi Club, N.Y.C., 1995, Exptl. Art award Western Colo. Art Ctr., 2000; numerous others. Mem.: Nat. Collage Soc. Inc., Collage/Assemblage Soc. NY, Internat. Soc. Exptl. Artists, N.Y. Artists Equity, Nat. Assn. Women Artists (v.p. 1997—2001, exec. bd. 2001—, Innovative Painting award 1990), Period Gallery (Alternative Photography award 2000, 2001), Pen and Brush Club N.Y.C. (Mixed Media award 1996, 1997, 1998, Photography award 2000, 2001). Office: Roslyn Rose Studios 321 Newark St Hoboken NJ 07030-2434 E-mail: bluerosestudios@yahoo.com.

ROSE, RUTH ORMSBY, retired English educator; b. Chgo. d. John Alexander and Nellie Arnold Rose. BA, Smith Coll., 1926; MA, Harvard U., 1927, PhD, 1929. Instr. English Coker Coll., Hartsville, S.C., So. Ill. Tchrs. Coll., Wheaton Coll., Norton, Mass., Milwaukee Downer, Western Coll., Oxford, Ohio; prof., head dept. English MacMurray Coll., Jacksonville, Ill.; ret., 1973. Home: Newtonville, Mass. Died July 29, 2002.

ROSE, SARAH ELIZABETH, genealogist, counselor; d. Harry Silber Agsanian and Bernice Marchita Phillips; 7 children. Graduate with hon., Officer's Acad. U.S. Army, 1976; BA in Social Sci., San Jose State U., 1980. Cert. Profl. Genealogist 2002. Dir. of religious sch. Umpqua Valley Havurah, Roseburg, Oreg., 1990—91. Author: (book) Many Branches, One Tree , 1997, World Wide Roots, 2001; contbr. poetry to various pub. With U.S. Army, 1974—77. Decorated Nat. Def. Svc. Medal US Army; recipient Cold War Recognition Cert., US Dept. of Def., 1974—77. Mem.: Pioneers of Kans., Pioneer Families Nebr., Ill. Priarie Pioneers, Am. First Families, Nat. Soc. DAR, The Winthrop Soc. (assoc.), Nat. Soc. Daughters of the Am. Colonists, Nat. Soc. Colonial Dames XVII Century, The Am. Legion. Avocations: native american crafts, collecting masks. Personal E-mail: genealogical2002@yahoo.com.

ROSE, SELWYN H. chemical company executive; b. N.Y.C., May 1, 1933; s. Rubin and Ruth Rosenthal; m. Helen Diana De Mov, July 25, 1957; children: Michelle, Wendy, Suzanne. BS, CCNY, 1954; MS, Ohio State U., 1958, PhD, 1961; MBA with honors, U. Chgo., 1979; CFP, Coll. Fin. Planning, 1994. Sr. rsch. chemist Pennwalk Corp., King of Prussia, Pa., 1961-65; dept. mgr. Horizons Inc., Beachwood, Ohio, 1965-72, dir. rsch., 1972-74; mgr. long range rsch. De Soto Inc., Des Plaines, Ill., 1974-79; dir. rsch., cen. rsch. lab. Borg-Warner Chems., 1979-85; v.p. tech. Parker Chem. Co., Madison Heights, Mich., 1985-88; gen. mgr. rsch. and devel. Himont Inc., Wilmington, Del., 1988-91, v.p. product devel., 1991-93; pres. SHR Fin. Advisors, 1993—. Contbr. articles to profl. jours.; patentee in field. 1st lt. U.S. Army, 1954-56. Recipient IR 100 award Indsl. Rsch. mag., 1971, award Roon Found., 1979. Mem. Am. Chem. soc., Nat. Assn. Personal Fin. Advisors, Fin. Planners Assn. Achievements include development of polyphosphazene polymers. Home: 1503 Evergreen Ln Wilmington DE 19810-4431

ROSE, SUSAN A. SCHULTZ, retired theological librarian; b. Mountain Lake, Minn., Dec. 22, 1911; d. David. D. and Anna (Eitzen) Schultz; m. Delbert R. Rose, Dec. 27, 1986. BA, John Fletcher Coll., 1940; BSLS, U. Ill., 1946, MLS, 1949; LittD (hon.), Houghton Coll., 1974. Dean women John Fletcher-Kletzing Coll., University Park, Iowa, 1940-45; asst. libr. Bethany (Okla.) Coll., 1946-47; dir. libr. svcs. Asbury Theol. Sem., Wilmore, Ky., 1949-78, ret., 1978; cons. grad. schs. theology librs. The Philippines, 1978-80, 85-86, Nairobi, Kenya, 1983-84, Zagreb, Yugoslavia, 1984, Taiwan, Korea, Japan, 1987, Allahabad, India, 1989, Kericho, Kenya, 1989, Manila, 1990, Wesly Bible Seminary, Jackson, Miss., 1987-93, Kaohsiung, Taiwan, 1992, Owerri, Nigeria, 1993. Mem. exec. com. 1st Alliance Ch., Lexington, Ky., 1958-61, 66-73; del. to nat. coun. Christian and Missionary Alliance, Columbus, Ohio, 1964, to Nat. Congress on Edn., St. Paul, 1970 Contbr. articles to profl. jours. Sunday sch. tchr. 1st Alliance Ch., Lexington, 1951-70; mem. libr. bd. Withers-Jessamine County Libr., Nicholasville, Ky., 1966-77. Recipient Outstanding Spl. Libr. of Yr. award Ky. Trustees Assn., 1967, Disting. Svc. award Asbury Theol. Sem., 1974, Emily Russell award Assn. Christian Librs. , 1974, Disting. Alumnus award Vennard Coll. (successor to John Fletcher-Kletzing Coll.), 1982. Mem. Am. Theol. Libr. Assn. (ret., exec. sec. 1967-71, dir. 1974-77), Wesley Theol. Soc. (ret.; Lifetime Achievement award 2000), Christian Holiness Assn., Ky. Libr. Assn. (bd. dirs. 1960—, sect. chair 1966-67). Mem. Christian and Missionary Alliance. Home: Shell Point Village 3905 Lucina Fort Myers FL 33908-1671 *To me life is two-dimensional. Total commitment to God is basic, then, neither knowingly exploit another nor permit another to exploit me. By helping others set worthy goals and achieve them I have found fulfillment. What a joy, years later to hear: "You changed my life course for the better. Thank You!".*

ROSE, SUSAN CAROL, restaurant executive, chef, consultant; b. Rochester, N.Y., Jan. 29, 1942; d. Frederick Raymond Smith and Grace Eunice (Read) Smith Drum; m. Larry Anthony Rose, Jan. 5, 1963 (div. Jan. 1976); children: John David, Karen Michelle Haines, Patricia Anne. Student, Monroe Community Coll., Rochester, 1959-60; cert. exec. steward, Innisbrook Resort, 1976; student, St. Petersburg Jr. Coll., Tarpon Springs, Fla., 1978-80, Pinellas Voc. Tech., 1987—. With Blue Cross-Blue Shield, Rochester, 1959-67; from coffee service mgr to exec. steward Innisbrook Resort, Tarpon Springs, 1974-84; catering team supr. Bon Appetit Restaurant, Dunedin, Fla., 1984, Bounty Caterers, Dunedin, 1984; asst. mgr. trainee Wendy's Internat., Largo, Fla., 1984; store mgr. Long John Silver's, 1984-85; exec. steward, banquet chef, room service mgr., cons. Sandestin Beach Hilton, Destin, Fla., 1985; day mgr. Shells Restaurant, Clearwater, 1986-87; sous chef, kitchen mgr. Saltwaters Seafood Grille, Palm Harbor, 1987; exec. steward Adam's Mark Caribbean Gulf Resort, Clearwater Beach, 1987—; chef/kitchen mgr. Seafood Broiler, 1990-91; chef Hwy. Ribbery Restaurant, 1991, Boomerangs Cafe, 1992; galley supr., cook Empress Cruise Lines, 1992-94; chef Wards Seafood, 1994—; chef/kitchen mgr. Wilson Sports Lounge, Dunedin, Fla., 1997-98; chef Belleair Country Club, Largo, 1997-98. Garde manger 94th Aero Squadron Restaurant, Las Fontanas Restaurant; mgr. Beef O'Brady's, 1997; cons. restaurant mgmt. Mem. Nat. Assn. Female Execs., Hospitality Industry Assn., Smithsonian Inst. Assocs., Holiday Inn Priority Club, Internat. Travel Club, Encore Travel Club, Clearwater Jaycees. Democrat. Roman Catholic. Avocations: school, music, reading, bowling. Home: 1162 Jackson Rd Clearwater FL 33755-4605

ROSE, SUSAN PORTER, consultant; b. Cin., Sept. 20, 1941; d. Elmer Johnson and Dorothy (Wurst) Porter; m. Jonathan Chapman Rose, Jan. 26, 1980; 1 child Benjamin Chapman. BA, Earlham Coll., 1963; MS, Ind. State U., Terre Haute, 1970; HDL (hon.) , Rose-Hulman Inst. Tech., 2002. Staff asst. Congressman Richard L. Roudebush, Washington, 1963-64; asst. dean George Sch., Bucks County, Pa., 1964-66; asst. dir. admissions Mt. Holyoke Coll., South Hadley, Mass., 1966-71; asst. dir. correspondence First Lady (Mrs. Nixon) The White House, 1971-72, dir. of scheduling to First Lady (Pat Nixon), 1972-74, to First Lady (Betty Ford), 1974-77; spl. asst. to asst. atty. gen. Office Improvements in Adminstrn. Justice, Washington, 1977-79; spl. asst. to dep. asst. atty. gen. Justice Mgmt. divsn. U.S. Dept. Justice, 1978-81; chief of staff to Mrs. Bush, asst. to v.p. Office of V.P. of U.S., 1981-89; dep. asst. to Pres. of U.S., chief of staff to First Lady (Barbara Bush) The White House, 1989-93; commr. U.S. Commn. Fine Arts, 1993-98; cons. McLean, Va., 1993—. Bd. dirs. Barbara Bush Found. for Family Lit.; bd. trustees Bush Presdl. Libr. and Ctr. Recipient Disting. Alumni award, Earlham Coll., 1992, Ind. State U., 1991. Mem.: Ind. Acad. Home: 5955 Ranleigh Manor Dr Mc Lean VA 22101-2428

ROSE, TERRI KAYE, obstetrical gynecological nurse practitioner, forensic exam nurse; b. Joplin, Mo. children: Meghan, Kaisley. Lic. vocat. nurse cert., Rancho Santiago Coll., 1979, ADN, 1982; nurse practitioner cert., Harbor-UCLA Med. Ctr., 1984; BSN, Calif. State U., Dominguez Hills, 1992; postgrad., U Ala, Birmingham, 1992-95, Calif. State U., San Jose, 1996; postgrad. nurse midwife classes. Cert. nurse practitioner, Calif., Ariz., advanced practice nurse, Mo., pub. health nurse, Calif. Staff nurse Coastal Communities Hosp., Santa Ana, Calif., 1979-82, charge nurse obs., 1982-85; ob.-gyn. nurse practitioner Huntington Beach (Calif.) Community Clinic, 1984-87; charge nurse labor and delivery Western Med. Ctr., Santa Ana, 1985; ob.-gyn. nurse practitioner with pvt. practice physician Huntington Beach, 1987-89; patient educator Healthdyne Perinatal Svcs., Smyrna, Ga., 1989-95; staff nurse labor and delivery Citizen's Hosp., Talladega, Ala., 1991; family planning nurse practitioner OACAC, Springfield, Mo., 1992-93; prenatal nurse practitioner, clin. coord. S.W. Regional Prenatal Clinic, 1993-94; women's health care nurse practitioner, clin. coord. Family Health Care Clinic, 1994-96; clin. instr. U. Mo., St. Louis, 1995—; ob-gyn. nurse practitioner Fresno, Calif., 1996-97; charge nurse ob-gyn. practitioner perinatology El Centro, 1997-98; staff nurse labor and delivery Crown Nursing Agy., Springfield, Mo., 1999-2000. Mem. ANA (cert. high risk perinatal nurse 1984-89, elected to Nat. Registry Cert. Nurses in Advanced Practice 1988), Assn. Women's Health, Obstetrics, and Neonatal Nursing (cert. obstetrics and gynecolog. nurse practitioner, co-chair planning com. Dist. VII Mo. sect. conf.). Home: 1713 A Redbird Dr Webb City MO 64870

ROSE, THOMAS ALBERT, artist, art educator; b. Washington, Oct. 15, 1942; s. Francis John and Ann Elizabeth (Voelkel) R.; m. Mary Melinda Moyer, Aug. 21, 1965; children: Sarah, Jessica. Student, U. Wis., 1960-62; BFA, U. Ill., 1965; MA, U. Calif., Berkeley, 1967; postgrad., Lund (Sweden) U., 1967-68. Instr. U. Calif., Berkeley, 1968-69, N.Mex. State U., Las Cruces, 1969-72; faculty mem. U. Minn., Mpls., 1972—, prof. art, 1983—, Fesler-Lampert chair in humanities, 2001—. Author: Winter Book, 1995; one-man shows include Clock Tower, N.Y.C., 1977, Truman Gallery, N.Y.C., 1977-78, Rosa Esman Gallery, N.Y.C., 1979, 81, 82, Marianne Deson Gallery, Chgo., 1984-86, Robert Thomson Gallery, Mpls., 1986, 91, 92, 95, Deson Saunders Gallery, Chgo., 1989, Mpls. Inst. Art, 1992, Weisman Art Mus., Mpls., 1994, Tweed Mus., Duluth, Minn., 1995, Steinbaum/Krauss Gallery, N.Y.C., 1996, 99, Brevard Mus. Art, Melbourne, Fla., 1997, Gensler Arch., Washington, 1999, Flanders Gallery, Mpls., 2000, Bernice Steinbaum Gallery, Miami, Fla., 2001; exhibited in group shows at Walker Art Ctr., Mpls., 1974, 76, 77, Whitney Mus. Downtown, N.Y.C., P.S. #1, N.Y.C., 1978, Wave Hill, Bronx, N.Y., 1981, Hirshhorne Mus., Washington, 1981, Am. Ctr. in Paris, 1982, Harvard U. Sch. Architecture, 1983, Cultural Ctr., Chgo., 1983, Hal Bromm Gallery, N.Y.C., Sheldon Mus., Lincoln, Nebr., 1989, Tampa (Fla.) Mus., 1988, MCAD, Mpls., 1996, Minn. Mus. Art, 1996, Socrates Sculpture Park, N.Y.C., Fla. Internat. U., Miami, 1997; represented in permanent collections Walker Art Ctr., Joslyn Mus., Omaha, Park St. Lofts, Springfield, Mass., U. Minn., Mpls., Am. Lung Assn. Target Ctr., Mpls., St. Lukes Episcopal Ch., Mpls.; set designer: Fool for Love, Cricket Theater, Mpls., 1985, Circus, Theater de Jeune Lune, 1986; project dir. Works of Art in Pub. Places for Humphrey Inst. Pub. Affairs, Mpls., 1988; prin. works include Minn. Zoo, Marine Edn. Ctr., Sacred Heart U., Fairfield, Conn., Berniece Steinbaum Gallery, Miami, 1999. Named Rockefeller resident, Bellagio, Italy, 1993; recipient McKnight Artist fellow, 1995, travel fellow, Dayton-Hudson/Jerome, 1990, 1995, Jerome Found. Arts, 1993—94, Mellon Found., 1993, Fesler-Lampert Chair in Humanities, 2002; fellow, Nat. Endowment for Arts, 1977, 1981, Bush Found., 1979, Minn. State Arts Bd., 1979, 1984, McKnight Found., 1981, McKnight Found. Rsch., 1993—96, McKnight Photography, 2002; grantee, Arts Bd. Opportunities, 1993. Home: 91 Nicollet St Minneapolis MN 55401-1513 Office: Univ Minn 208 Studio Arts 23D S Avenue Minneapolis MN 55425 E-mail: rosex00l@umn.edu.

ROSE, TODD ALAN, lawyer; b. Merced, Calif., Oct. 26, 1962; s. William Arthur and Mary (Brooks) R.; m. Teresa Gail Suiter, June 1, 1991; children: Miranda Brooke, Savannah Leigh, Emily Jane, Thomas Pierce. BS, Murray State U., 1988; JD, Vanderbilt U. Law Sch., 1991. Bar: Tenn. 1991, U.S. Dist. Ct. (we. dist.) Tenn. 1992. Asst. dist. atty. State of Tenn., Paris, 1994-97; mem. Burch, Porter & Johnson, P.L.L.C., 1991-94, 97—. Office: Burch Porter & Johnson PLLC 107 W Blythe St Paris TN 38242-4150

ROSE, WIL, foundation executive; b. Townsend, Ohio, Sept. 13, 1931; s. William Marion and Dorothy Louise (Arnold) R.; m. Anna Marie Thielmann, Mar. 4, 1952 (div. 1976); children: Sharon, Dan; m. Princess Pale Moon, Oct. 7, 1977; children: Michael, Robert, John Mark. AA in Comml. Photography, Santa Monica City Coll., 1956; LitD, Ashland U., 1982. With motion picture prodn. dept. Moody Inst. Sci., Santa Monica, Calif., 1955-57; assoc. dir. Internat. Libr. Project, Europe and Asia, 1957-58; pres., founder DATA Internat., Palo Alto, Calif., 1958-66; pres. Gen,. Eisenhower's People to People, Inc., Kansas City, 1966-68; dir. Involvement, Inc., Palo Alto, Calif., 1968-69; pres. TransService corp., 1969-73; CEO Am. Indian Heritage Found., Falls Church, 1973—; pres., founder PlanAm. Consulting, Va., 1981—. Co-founder and Charitable devel. officer Nat. Heritage Found. Inc., Falls Church, Va., 1968—; pres. Nat. Leadership Inst. 1977-78; pres., founder Nat. Found. for Philanthropy, Mpls., 1978-80; bd. devel. officer Congrl. Awards for Youth, Fairfax, Va., 1978—; mem. presdl. task force Reagan Adminstrn., Washington, 1984. Staff sgt. USMC, 1950-54, Korea. Decorated Purple Heart; recipient Nat. Achievement award SERTOMA Internat., 1964; named One of Five Outstanding Young Men, Calif. Jaycees, 1962, One of Ten Outstanding Young Men in U.S., U.S. Jaycees, 1966. Mem. Rotary Club (various com. chmn.), 1962—. Avocations: writing, speaking.

ROSE, WILLIAM, retired business executive; b. Waukegan, Ill., Nov. 7, 1919; s. Louis and Bertha Rose; m. Vivian May Gulledge, July 15, 1951; children: Whyland, Calvin, Marcia. LittD (hon.), Shimer Coll. Pres. Jobs Temporaries, Waukegan, 1951-86, ret., 1986. Fin. chmn. Boy Scouts Am., 1959-60, bd. dirs., 1966-71; mem. Lake County (Ill.) Mental Healt Adv. Com., 1971-80, bd. auditors Shields Twp., Ill., 1957-61; justice of peace Lake County, 1956-61, police magistrate, 1959-61; bd. dirs. Shimer Coll., Lake County Mental Health Clinic, 1957-68, United Community Services, 1964-71, Lake County Crime Commn., 1969-75; treas. Lake County Econ. Devel. Corp., 1982-83; bd. dirs., v.p. Lake County Welfare Council, 1963; bd. dirs. Pvt. Industry Council, 1977-83. Served with Signal Corps, AUS, 1944-46. Mem. Ind. Office Svcs. Inst. (pres. 1971-73), Nat. Assn. Temporary Svcs. (dir. 1975-78), Lake County Mental Health Soc. (pres. 1951), Waukegan-North Chgo. C. of C. (bd. dirs. 1968-74, pres. 1976), Am. Legion (comdr. 1951), VFW. Jewish (treas. congregation 1968-74, pres. 1976). Lodge: B'nai B'rith. Clubs: Waukegan Exchange (pres. 1963-64), North Shore Craftsman (pres. 1965). Home: 1075 E Victory Dr Ste 118 Lindenhurst IL 60046-7917

ROSE, WILLIAM KENNETH, astronomy educator; b. Ossining, N.Y., Aug. 10, 1935; s. Kenneth W. and Shirley Hazel (Near) R.; m. Sheila Luba Tuchman, Apr. 3, 1961; children: Kenneth W., Edward W., Cindy E. AB, Columbia U., 1957, PhD in Physics, 1963. Mem. rsch. staff Princeton (N.J.) U., 1963-67; asst. prof., assoc. prof. MIT, Cambridge, 1967-71; assoc. prof. astronomy U. Md., College Park, 1971-76, prof., 1976—. Author: Astrophysics, 1973, Stars, Galaxies and Cosmology, 1989, Advanced Stellar Astrophysics, 1998; also numerous articles. E-mail: wrose@astro.umd.edu.

ROSE, WILLIAM SHEPARD, JR. lawyer; b. Columbia, S.C., Mar. 9, 1948; s. William Shepard and Meta Cantey (Boykin) R.; m. Frances John Hobbs, Aug. 11, 1973; children: Katherine Cummings, William Shepard, III, Whitaker Boykin. BA in English, U. South, 1970; JD, U. S.C., 1973; LLM in Taxation, Georgetown U., 1976. Bar: S.C. 1973, Ohio 1977, D.C. 1974, U.S. Dist. Ct. D.C. 1976, U.S. Tax Ct. 1976, U.S. Supreme Ct. 1976, U.S. Ct. Claims Ct. 1978, U.S. Ct. Appeals (10th cir., 5th cir., 4th cir.) 1987, U.S. Ct. Appeals (3d, 6th, 7th, 8th, 9th and 11th cirs.) 1988. Trial atty. Office of Chief Counsel IRS, Washington, 1973-77; assoc. Frost & Jacobs, Cin., 1977-80, McNair Law Firm PA, Hilton Head Island, S.C., Washington, 1980-83, ptnr., 1983-87, 89—. Asst. atty. gen., tax divsn. U.S. Dept. Justice, Washington, 1987-89; chmn., dir. Sea Pines Montessori Sch., 1983-86, Hilton Head Broadcasting, 1983-87, MBR Corp., Adwell Corp., Links Group, Inc., Hilton Head Prep. Sch., 1986-87, 89-93, dir. Boys & Girls Club of Hilton Head Island, 1992—, Hilton Head Humane Soc., 1985, Nickel Plate Properties, Inc., Lima Lake Inc., Lakeside Corp., The Nickel Plate Line, Inc. Contbr. articles to profl. jours. Asst to chmn. bus. fundraising Beaufort County United Way, Hilton Head Island, 1984; vice chmn. Beaufort County Rep. Party, 1991-92, 93, chmn., 1992-93, vice chmn., 1993-95; mem. Beaufort County Transp. Com., 1994-95; commr. Sea Pines Pub. Svc. Dist., South Island Pub. Svc. Dist. Mem. ABA (past co-chmn. subcom. tax sect.), Am. Coll. Tax Counsel, Ohio Bar Assn., D.C. Bar Assn., S.C. Bar Assn., Beaufort County Bar Assn., Hilton Head Bar Assn., S.C. Yacht Club (bd. govs. 1989-94, exec. com. 1993-94, rear commodore 1993-94), Caroliniana Ball. Republican. Episcopalian. Home: 11 Jessamine Pl Hilton Head Island SC 29928-4255 Office: PO Drawer 7787 52 New Orleans Rd Ste 204 Hilton Head Island SC 29928-4780 E-mail: rrose@mcnair.net.

ROSE-ACKERMAN, SUSAN, law and political economy educator; b. Mineola, N.Y., Apr. 23, 1942; d. R. William and Rosalie Rose; m. Bruce A. Ackerman, May 29, 1967; children: Sybil, John BA, Wellesley Coll., 1964; PhD, Yale U., 1970. Asst. prof. U. Pa., Phila, 1970-74; lectr. Yale U., New Haven, 1974-75, asst. prof., 1975-78, assoc. prof., 1978-82; prof. law and polit. economy Columbia U., N.Y.C., 1982-87; Ely prof. of law and polit. econ. Yale U., New Haven, 1987-92, co-dir. Ctr. Law, Econ. and Pub. Policy, 1988—, Luce prof. jurisprudence law and polit. sci., 1992—. Panelist Am. studies program Am. Coun. Learned Socs., 1987-90; review panelist, faculty Fulbright Commn., 1993-96; vis. rsch. fellow World Bank, 1995-96; fellow Ctr. for Advanced Study in the Behavioral Scis. Author: (with Ackerman, Sawyer and Henderson) Uncertain Search for Environmental Quality, 1974 (Henderson prize 1982); Corruption: A Study in Political Economy, 1978; (with E. James) The Nonprofit Enterprise in Market Economies, 1986; editor: The Economics of Nonprofit Institutions, 1986; (with J. Coffee and L. Lowenstein) Knights, Raiders, and Targets: The Impact of the Hostile Takeover, 1988, Rethinking the Progressive Agenda: The Reform of the American Regulatory State, 1992, Controlling Environmental Policy: The Limits of Public Law in Germany and the United States, 1995, Corruption and Government: Causes, Consequences and Reform, 1999; contbr. articles to profl. jours.; bd. editors: Jour. Law, Econs. and Orgn., 1984—, Internat. Rev. Law and Econs., 1986—, Jour. Policy Analysis and Mgmt., 1989—, Polit. Sci. Quar., 1988—. Guggenheim fellow 1991-92, Fulbright fellow, Free U. Berlin, 1991-92; fellow Ctr. for Advanced Study in the Behavioral Scis., Stanford, Calif., 2002, Collegium Budapest, 2002. Mem. Am. Law and Econs. Assn. (bd. dirs. 1993-96, 2002-), Am. Econ. Assn. (mem. exec. com. 1990-93), Am. Polit. Sci. Assn., Assn. Am. Law Schs., Assn. Pub. Policy and Mgmt. (policy coun. 1984-88, treas. 1998-2000). Democrat. Office: Yale U Law Sch PO Box 208215 New Haven CT 06520-8215

ROSEBERG, CARL ANDERSSON, sculptor, educator; b. Vinton, Iowa, Sept. 26, 1916; s. Swan Bernard and Selma (Olson) R.; m. Virginia M. Gorman, Aug. 23, 1942. B.F.A., U. Iowa, 1939, postgrad., 1939-41, M.F.A., 1947; postgrad., Cranbrook Acad. Art, summers 1947-48, U. Hawaii, 1950-51, U. Va., summer 1964, Mysore (India) U., summer 1965, Tyler Sch. Art, Temple U., summer 1967. Faculty Coll. William and Mary, Williamsburg, Va., 1947—, prof. fine arts, 1966-82, prof. emeritus, 1982—, William and Mary Heritage fellow, 1968-82. Founding bd. mem. 20th Century Gallery, Williamsburg.; active judge various art groups Exhibited one man shows at Radford Coll., 1962, Roanoke Fine Art Gallery, 1962-63, Norfolk Mus., 1963, Asheville (N.C.) Gallery Art, 1963, Longwood Coll., 1966, Phi Beta Kappa Hall, William and Mary Coll., 1970; 35 yr. retrospective William and Mary Coll., 1982; retrospective Twentieth Century Gallery, 1983; exhibited in numerous group shows; represented in permanent collections at U. Iowa, Springfield (Mo.) Mus., Va. Mus. Fine Arts, Colonial Williamsburg, Chrysler Mus. Norfolk, Rockingham County Citizens Com., Longwood Coll., Farmville, Va., Thalhimer Bros., Inc., Swem Libr., Coll. William and Mary, Patriot's Colony '98, others; designer, creator bronze meml. plaque honoring Donald W. Davis for, Millington Hall, Coll. William and Mary, 1970, bronze plaque honoring William G. Guy, Rogers Hall, 1975; I.L. Jones, Jr., Bruton Parish Ch., 1985. designer: James City County Bicentennial Medallion, 1976; designer, creator Carter O. Lowance Bronze Medallion Marshall-Wythe Sch. Law Coll. William and Mary, 1989, Bronze Medallion honoring 300th Ann. Coll. William and Mary, 1991, Bronze Medallion honoring L. I'Anson Marshall-Wythe Sch. Law, 1991. Served to comdr. USNR, 1941-45, 50-52; ret. Res. Recipient Thomas Jefferson award, 1971, numerous art awards, Cheek award William & Mary, 1993. Fellow Internat. Inst. Arts and Letters; mem. Am. Audubon Artists, Fulbright Assn., Res. Officers Assn. Am., Va. Watercolor Soc., Navy League U.S., Williamsburg German Club, Mid. Plantation Club, Masons, Lambda Chi Alpha. Presbyterian. Home: PO Box 1468 Williamsburg VA 23187-1468

ROSEBERRY, EDWIN SOUTHALL, retired state agency administrator; b. Roanoke, Va., July 4, 1925; s. Edwin Alexander and Gladys Edmonia (Southall) R.; m. Mary Louise Sprengel, Sept. 2, 1949 (dec. 1978); children: Edwin Jr., David, Kevin; m. Alice Proffit Boger, Dec. 27, 1980; 1 stepdaughter, Elizabeth Leigh Boger. BS in Commerce, U. Va., 1949. Registered sanitarian, Hawaii, Va. Store mgr. Allied Arts, Charlottesville, Va., 1949-51; retail credit sales mgr. B.F. Goodrich Co., 1951-53; environ. health specialist Dept. of Health, 1953-84, Dept. of Labor, Honolulu, 1987-2000; ret., 1999. Self-employed photographer, Charlottesville, 1949-85, Honolulu, 1985—. Contbr. photographs: The Inward Eye, 1986. Election ofcl. State of Hawaii, Honolulu, 1988—. With USN, 1944-46. Recipient numerous nat. awards Eastman Kodak Co., nat. newspapers, and photography mags., 1951-69. Mem. VFW (life), Am. Indsl. Hygiene Assn., Austrian Hawaiian Club (v.p., bd. dirs. 1985), Antique Auto Assn. (pres. Piedmont region 1964), Hawaii Photo Soc. (v.p. 1989), Elks (tiler and inner guard 1985), Am. Legion (dept. historian, VFW jr. vice commdr.), Mason (32 degree), Shriners (sojourners, heroes of '76, eastern star), Pi Delta Epsilon. Episcopalian. Avocations: photography, stamp collecting, antique automobiles, figure skating. Home: Carriage Hill Apts #302 820 Beverly Dr Charlottesville VA 22911

ROSEBERRY, ELIZABETH ANN, neonatologist; b. Athens, Ohio, Jan. 26, 1947; d. Horace Hewell and Margaret Elizabeth (Ross) Roseberry; m. Massimo Costa, June 15, 1974 (div. Sept. 9, 1982); m. Matthew Martin Hine, June 14, 1986 (div. Oct. 15, 1989). BS in Biology cum laude, Wake Forest U.,

1968; MS in Zoology, Oreg. State U., 1970; postgrad., U. Ariz., 1974-76; MD, U. Tex., Houston, 1985. Diplomate in pediatrics and in neonatal-perinatal medicine Am. Bd. Pediatrics; lic. physician Tex., Va., W.Va. Lab. technician III Litton-Bionetics, Inc., Bethesda, Md., 1971-74; lab. technician II depts. pharmacology and anesthesiology U. Ariz. Med. Ctr., Tucson, 1974-75, rsch. asst. dept. anesthesiology, 1975-76; rsch. asst. II, dept. lab. medicine, Biol. Scis. Group U. Conn., Farmington and Storrs, 1977-78; technician I Forest Sci. Lab. Tex. A&M U., College Station, 1979-80; rsch. assoc. dept. survery Divsn. Immunology and Organ Transplantation, U. Tex., Houston, 1980-81; resident in pediatrics U. Tex. Med. Br., Galveston, 1985-88, fellow in neonatology, 1988-90; affiliate neonatologist Fairfax Neonatal Assocs., P.C., Falls Church, Va., 1990-92; assoc. neonatologist Pediatrix Med. Group, Charleston, W.Va., 1992-98; prin. NeoHealth, Port Arthur, Tex., 1998-2001; assoc. neonatologist Ctrl. Ohio Newborn Medicine, Inc., Columbus, 2001—. Staff neonatologist Fairfax Hosp., Falls Church, 1990—92, Potomac Hosp., Woodbridge, Va., 1990—92, Women and Children's Hosp., Charleston Area Med. Ctrs., 1992—98, Mary Washington Hosp., Fredericksburg, 1993—98, Alexandria (Va.) Hosp., 1993—98, Virginia Beach (Va.) Gen. Hosp., 1994—98, St. Joseph Hosp., Houston, 1997—98, Park Plz. Hosp., Houston, 1997—98; clin. asst. prof. pediat. W.Va. U. Sch. Medicine, 1993—94; dir. NICU Park Pl. Med. Ctr., Port Arthur, 1998—2001, Med-Jefferson Hosp., Nederland, Tex., 1998—2001, St. Mary Hosp., 1998—2001, Orange (Tex.) Bapt. Hosp., 1998—2001, Marion (Ohio) Gen. Hosp., 2001—. Contbr. articles to profl. jours. Recipient Minnie L. Maffett award, 1989-90. Fellow Am. Acad. Pediatrics; mem. AMA (Physician Recognition award 1988-91, 92—), Tex. Med. Assn., Med. Soc. Va., Jefferson County Med. Soc. Avocations: gardening, theater. Home: 1446 Eagle Pass Dr Marion OH 43302 Office: Ctrl Ohio Newborn Medicine 300 E Town St 4th Fl Columbus OH 43215-5535 E-mail: erosebe@attglobal.net.

ROSEBERY, RICHARD JAY, manufacturing company executive; b. Gary, Ind., May 5, 1935; s. William J. and Vivian Ethel (Schnell) R.; m. Charleen Annette Bennett, July 30, 1966; children: Susan Dare, Richard J., Jr. BS in Elec. Engring., Purdue U., 1957. Program mgr. Emerson Electric, St. Louis, 1957-62; v.p. elec. engring. and contracting group Dynalectron Corp., McClean, Va., 1962-72; v.p. corp. affairs Arthur Corp., Phoenix, 1972-74; v.p., treas., CFO Elcor Corp., Dallas, 1975-93, exec. v.p., chief fin. and adminstrv. officer, 1993-96, vice-chmn., chief fin. and adminstrv. officer, 1997—2001; also bd. dirs. Exec. v.p. Elcor Svc. Corp.; chmn. bd. dirs., CEO Chromium Corp.; v.p., bd. dirs. Elk Corp. Am.; chmn. bd. dirs. Ortloff Corp.; v.p. bd. dirs. Ortloff Internat. Corp., Ortloff Engrs., Ltd., Elk Corp. of Ala., Elk Corp. of Ark., Elk Corp. of Tex., Elk Corp. of Dallas; chmn. bd. dirs., pres. G.A. Industries Corp., M. Machinery Co., M. Svc. Co. Mem. fin. United Way, Midland, Tex., 1985-87, pres. Dallas chpt., 1997-98. Mem. Fin. Execs. Internat. (area dir. 1999—), Conf. Bd., Am. Mgmt. Assn., Nat. Assn. of Mfrs., U.S. C. of C., Tex. C. of C., Dallas C. of C. Home: 5703 Club Oaks Dr Dallas TX 75248-1119 Office: Elcor Corp Wellington Ctr Ste 1000 14643 Dallas Pkwy Dallas TX 75254-8890 E-mail: richardroseberry@aol.com.

ROSEBORO, BRIAN CARLTON, federal agency administrator; m. Valeri Roseboro; 2 children. BS in Econs., U. Rochester; MBA, Columbia U. Chief dealer fng.-exch. desk N.Y. Fed. Res. Bank; v.p. fng.-exch. options 1st Nat. Bank Chgo.; risk mgmt. advisor fgn.-exch. trading Swiss Bank Co., N.Y.C.; dep. dir. mkt. risk mgmt. Am. Internat. Group; asst. sec. fin. mkts. U.S. Dept. Treasury, Washington, 2001—. Office: US Dept Treasury Fin Mkts 1500 Pennsylvania Ave Washington DC 20220*

ROSEBROUGH, CAROL BELVILLE, cable television company executive; b. Ironton, Ohio, June 5, 1940; d. Lindsey and Bessie (Reed) Belville; m. John R. Rosebrough, Mar. 4, 1960 (dec. Nov. 1974); children: G. Suzanne, John R., Rebecca J. Student, Columbia (Mo.) Coll., 1958-59; BSBA, Franklin U., 1985. Cons. CBR and Assocs., Columbus, 1978-82; dir. adminstrn. United Cerebral Palsy Columbus and Franklin County, 1972-82; bus. mgr. Times Mirror, Newark, 1982-83, ops. mgr., 1983-85, gen. mgr. Logan/Waverly/Greenfield, Ohio, 1985-86, Times Mirror doing bus. as Dimension Cable Svcs., Marion, 1986-88; v.p., gen. mgr. Cable TV div. Susquehanna Comms. (formerly Times Mirror and Cox Comms.), Williamsport, Pa., 1988—. Fllow Betsy Magness Leadership Inst., 1999—. Bd. dirs United Way, Marion County, 1987-88, Lycoming County, 1989-2000, Williamsport/Lycoming C. of C., 1995-2000. Named one of Pa.'s Best 50 Women in Bus., 1997, One of Top 100 Bus. Persons in the State of Pa., 1997-99; fellow Betsy Magness Leadership Inst., 1999-2000. Mem. Ohio Cable TV Assn. (bd. dirs. 1986-88), Pa. Cable TV Assn. (bd. dirs. 1990-96), Pa. Edn. Comms. Systems (bd. dirs. 1990—), Pa. Rural Devel. Coun. (exec. com. telecomms. task force 1992-95), Mid-Ohio Regional Planning Commn. (transp. com. 1980-82), Internat. Women's Writers Guild, Internat. Assn. Counselors and Therapists. Avocations: writing, reading, music, arts/therapies. Office: Susquehanna Comms 330 Basin St Williamsport PA 17701-5216 E-mail: crosebro@suscom.com.

ROSEBUSH, JAMES SCOTT, international management and public affairs consultant, former government official; b. Flint, Mich., June 1, 1949; s. Kenneth F. and Jacqueline (Porter) R.; m. Nancy Paull, May 18, 1974; children: Claire Haisley, Lauren Culver. BA, The Principia, Elsah, Ill., 1971; MA, Boston U., 1973. Cons., Boston, 1972-76; v.p. Nat. Chamber Found., Washington, 1976-79; assoc. dir. corp. contbn. Standard Oil Co., Cleve., 1979-81; dir. Office Bus. Liaison, U.S. Dept. Commerce, Washington, 1981, spl. asst. to pres. for pvt. sector initiatives, Washington, 1981-82; dept. asst. to pres., chief staff for First Lady The White House, 1982-86; pres. James Rosebush & Co., 1986—. Lectr. Georgetown U., Washington, 1977-79, George Washington U., Washington, 1977-79; presdl. appointee Nat. Mus. Svcs. Bd. Author: First Lady, Public Wife, 1987; contbr. articles to profl. jours. Mem. rev. com. United Way, Cleve., 1979; mem. community relations com. Cleve. Orch., 1979; bd. dirs. Phillips Collection Mus. Recipient Internat. award Rotary Internat., 1970 Republican. Avocations: tennis, skiing, reading, travelling. Office: 1250 24th St NW Ste 350 Washington DC 20037-1124 E-mail: jsrosebush@aol.com.

ROSEFIELDE, STEVEN SHELLEY, economics educator; b. Bklyn., Aug. 18, 1942; s. Louis Rosefielde and Roslyn (Seitzman) Leiber; m. Susan Joyce Geller, June 20, 1965; children: Justine, David. AM in Soviet Regional Studies, Harvard U., 1966, MA, 1967, PhD, 1972. Adj. prof. nat. security U.S. Naval Postgrad. Sch., Monterey, Calif., 1978-85; asst. prof. econs. U. N.C., Chapel Hill, 1972-76, assoc. prof., 1977-85, prof., 1985—. Author: Soviet International Trade, 1973, World Communism, 1980, False Science, 1987; author, editor: Economic Welfare and Socialism, 1983. Mem. Atlantic Econ. Soc. (exec. com.). Home: 1409 Arboretum Dr Chapel Hill NC 27517-9117 Office: U NC Dept Econs Gardner Hall Clb # 3305 Chapel Hill NC 27514

ROSEFSKY, JONATHAN BENENSOHN, pediatrician; b. Johnson City, N.Y., June 28, 1939; s. I.J. and Elsie S. Rosefsky; m. Sue Perel, 1964; children: Katherine, Douglas, Matthew. AB, Cornell U., 1960; B in Med. Sci., Dartmouth U., 1962; MD, Harvard U., 1964. Diplomate Am. Bd. of Pediatrics; lic. Pa., Va. Intern in surgery Vanderbilt Univ. Hosp., Nashville, 1964-65; resident in pediatrics Children's Hosp. Med. Ctr., Boston, 1965-67; pediatrician USAF Med. Corps, Langley AFB, Va., 1967-69; dir. neonatal ICU United Health Svcs. Hosp., Johnson City, N.Y., 1969-74; pvt. practice Binghamton, 1969-86; pres. Notation Systems, Inc., 1981-89; asst. dir. clin. devel. McNeil Consumer Products Co., Ft. Washington, Pa., 1986-89; dir. med. svcs., sr. dir. med. affairs Wyeth-Ayerst Labs., St. David's, Pa., 1989—99; pres. Fluidmotive, Inc., Haverford, 2000—. Cons. in pediatrics, N.Y. State Dept. Social Svcs., Albany, 1976-86, FDA adv. com. on Gen. Hosp. and Personal Use Devices, Rockville, Md., 1986; industry rep. FDA adv. com. on immunology devices, Rockville, 1987-93; asst. prof. pediatrics, Jefferson Med. Sch., Phila., 1987—. Contbr. Chmn. Citizen's Adv. Com. to Mayor of Binghamton, N.Y., 1971; active chmn.'s coun. Phila. Mus. of Art. Capt. (M.C.) USAF, 1967-69. Recipient Physician's Recognition award, AMA, 2000, 2001—. Fellow Am. Acad. Pediat., Am. Coll. Nutrition, Am. Coll. Physician Execs.; mem. Harvard Club (N.Y.C.), Green Valley Country Club. Avocations: skiing, swimming, photography, foreign languages, travel. Home: 251 Montgomery Ave Haverford PA 19041-1862 E-mail: fluidmotive.inc@att.net.

ROSEGARTEN, RORY, talent manager, television and theater producer; b. N.Y.C., Feb. 12, 1962; s. Robert Joel and Rita Honey (Mandel) R.; m. Wendy Jill Korn, May 4, 1991; children: Danielle Sydney, Ryan Harris. Student, Ariz. State U., 1980-81. Pres. The Conversation Co., Ltd., Great Neck, N.Y., 1983—. Prodr.: (broadway musical) Late Nite Comic, 1987; exec. prodr.: (CD) Robert Klein: Let's Not Make Love, 1990, Ray Romano: Live at Carnegie Hall, 2002; (TV series) Everybody Loves Raymond, 1996—, New Joke City, 2000-01; (TV spl. HBO) Robert Klein: It All Started Here, 1996, Sketch Pad, 2001; (CD) Brian Regan: Live, 1997; (TV spl. Showtime) Something's Wrong with the Regan Boy, 1992, A Pair of Jokers: Brian Regan and Dennis Regan, 1991; (TV spl., DVD) Clint Holmes: A Night to Remember, 2001, (CD) Ray Romano: Live at Carnegie Hall, 2002. Bd. govs. Comic Relief, 1999—; assoc. bd. dirs. Parker Jewish Geriat. Inst., New Hyde Park, N.Y., 1995-98. Mem. NATAS, Friars Club. Avocations: autograph and memorabilia collecting, ice hockey, water skiing. Office: The Conversation Company Ltd 1044 Northern Boulevard Suite 304 Roslyn NY 11576

ROSEGGER, GERHARD, economist, educator; b. Bruck/Mur, Austria, July 28, 1930; came to U.S., 1954, naturalized, 1961; s. Walter and Irmgard Elsa (Stark) R.; m. Clara Louise Tretter, July 17, 1954; children: Karin Andrea, Michael Lorenz, Nora Lynn, Thomas Martin. Dr.iur., U Graz, Austria, 1953; MBA, U. Pa., 1954. From instr. to asst. prof. Rutgers U. Coll. of S. Jersey, Camden, N.J., 1956-61; asst. prof. Case Inst. Tech., Cleve., 1962-65; assoc. prof. Case Western Res. U., 1965-75, prof. econs., 1975—, Frank Tracy Carlton prof. econs., 1978—, emeritus, 1997—; Fulbright vis. prof. U. Innsbruck, Austria, 1983-84, 91. Vis. prof. U. Cin., 1988, U. Kassel, Germany, Helsinki (Finland) Sch. Econs., 1991, Vienna Tech. U., 1995-98, vis. rsch. scholar U. Waikato, Hamilton, N.Z., vis. prof. Donau-U. Krems, 1995-98. Author: The Economics of Production and Innovation, 1980, 2d edit., 1986, 3d edit., 1995, (with others) Evaluating Technological Innovations, 1980, Technological Progress and Industrial Leadership, 1984; contbr. chtps. to books, numerous articles to profl. jours. Fulbright scholar, 1950-51; recipient research and travel grants. Mem. Am. Econ. Assn., Inst. Mgmt. Scis., Sigma Xi. Mem. Christian Ch. (Disciples Of Christ). Home: 15719 Chadbourne Rd Cleveland OH 44120-3333 Office: Case Western Reserve Univ Economics Dept Cleveland OH 44106

ROSE-HEIM, WILLIAM BENTLEY, minister, mediator, author; b. Syracuse, N.Y., Aug. 29, 1955; s. William Bentley and Marilynn Ann Rose; m. Irma Diana Ruiz, Jan. 4, 1975 (div. Oct. 1985); children: Daniel Joseph, Christina Marie, Elizabeth Ann; m. Donna Rae Heim, May 16, 1986; children, Zachariah Shalom, Nathaniel Mir. AA, Riverside (Calif.) City Coll., 1979; BA, Rockhurst Coll., 1980; MDiv, St. Paul Sch. Theology, Kansas City, Mo., 1986; grad., Ark. Leadership Acad., 1997. Ordained to ministry Christian Ch., 1987. Pastoral assoc. Curé of Ars Cath. Ch., Leawood, 1979-83, St. Francis Xavier Cath. Ch., Kansas City, 1983-85; pastoral asst. St. Luke Presbyn. Ch., 1985-87; co-pastor 1st Christian Ch., Odessa, Mo., 1987-93; sr. pastor, 1993-96; mental health therapist West Cen. Mo. Mental Health Ctr., Warrensburg, 1990-95; assoc. regional minister Christian Ch., Ark., 1996-2000; co-pastor N.W. Area Christian Ch. Mid-Am., 2000—; mem. adj. faculty St. Paul. Sch. Theology, 2000—. Instr. in theology Rockhurst High Sch., Kansas City, 1980-84; vol. chaplain intern VA Med. Ctr., 1986-89, asst. chief chaplain, 1988; moderator Christian Ch. Mid Am., 1994-96; founder, mediator Helping Hand Dispute Resolution Svcs., 1991-96. Contbr. Co-founder Odessa Alanon Family Group, 1987-90, Odessa R/7 Friends for Youth, 1987—; sec. bd. dirs. Odessa Habitat for Humanity, 1989-90; co-founder Odessa Outreach-West Cen. Mo. Mental Health Ctr., 1990; co-founder, acting exec. dir. Odessa Cmty. Svc. Ctr., 1991; coach Ark. Leadership Acad., 1999—; 2d v.p. Ark. Interfaith Conf.; v.p. Ark. Friends for Better Schs., 1999; mem., bd. dirs. Our House Homeless Shelter, 1997-99; mem. Disciples of Christ Hist. Soc.; pastor, counselor Gen. Conf. Disciples Men, 1998-99; co-founder, sec. Interfaith Disaster Recovery Team, 1998-2000; mem. Renewing Rural Mo., 2000-2002; chaplain Cameron Fire Dept., 2001. Recipient Ark. Traveler award Ark. Leadership Acad., 2000. Avocations: rock-climbing, music composition, writing, woodcraft, guitarist. Home: 705 E 3rd St Cameron MO 64429-1951 Office: Christian Ch MidAm PO Box 353 811 S Walnut Cameron MO 64429 E-mail: brh@nwareacc.org. *Lead us to places You call home by Your good Spirit O my God.*

ROSEIG, ESTHER MARIAN See FOGEL, ESTHER MARIAN

ROSEL, CAROL ANN, artist; b. Dodge City, Kans., June 12, 1944; d. John Elbert and Mary Claire (Wetmore) Frazier; m. Herbert Carey Zortman, Aug. 21, 1960 (div. Jan. 1989); children: Elaine Marie, Anita Louise, Stanley Dale; m. George D. Rosel, Sept. 22, 1990 (dec. June 1995). Student, Ctrl. Coll., McPherson, Kans., 1961; BFA cum laude, Ft. Hays State U., 1994. Cert. machine embroidery instr. Dress designer Ms. Cosmo Ltd., Wichita, Kans., 1975-76; designer artistic embroidery garments, 1977-80, 99; owner Carol Ann's Gallery, Liberal, Kans.; part time music tchr. W. Mid. Sch., 1999—. Part-time art tchr. C.C.s, Baker Art Ctr., Seward County C.C., U.S. D 480, Liberal, part-time music tchr.; singer A Touch of Class; developer The Tour (the Life of Christ). One-woman show Ft. Hays Libr., 1993. Mem. Baker Art Ctr., Liberal, 1989—, Hays (Kans.) Arts Coun., 1993, Carnegie Ctr. of Arts, Dodge City; solo pianist ch. weddings and comty. functions; mem. Glory Rd. Singers, 1999; mem. cast Wild West Show, 2001, Touch of Class Ladies Group; vol. Make A Wish Found.; tchr. Sunday sch. Recipient All Am. Scholar Collegiate award, 1994, Grand Champion award State Fair, 1989, 90, 95, 97, 98, Purple Champion award, 1990, others; named Woman of World, 1995-96, Internat. Women of World, 1996-97, Internat. Woman of Yr., 1995-96. Mem.: Liberal C. of C., So. Gospel Music Assn., Mid. Am. Arts and Crafts Assn., Baker Art Ctr., Lions Club, Christian Life Drama Club, Art Club, Pinnacle Honor Soc. Republican. Avocations: piano, singing, dramatics, oil painting. Home and Office: 2901 Westview Dodge City KS 67801

ROSELL, SHARON LYNN, physics and chemistry educator, researcher; b. Wichita, Kans., Jan. 6, 1948; d. John E. and Mildred C. (Binder) R. BA, Loretto Heights Coll., 1970; postgrad., Marshall U., 1973; MS in Edn., Ind. U., 1977; MS, U. Wash., 1988. Cert. profl. educator, Wash. Assoc. instr. Ind. U., Bloomington, 1973-74; instr. Pierce Coll. (name formerly Ft. Steilacoom (Wash.) Community Coll.), 1976-79, 82, Olympic Coll., Bremerton, Wash., 1977-78; instr. physics, math. and chemistry Tacoma (Wash.) Community Coll., 1979-89; instr. physics and chemistry Green River Community Coll., Auburn, Wash., 1983-86; researcher Nuclear Physics Lab., U. Wash., Seattle, 1986-88; asst. prof. physics Cen. Wash. U., Ellensburg, 1989—. Mem. faculty senate Ctrl. Washington U., 1992-98. Lector and dir. Rite of Christian Initiation of Adults, St. Andrew's Ch., Ellensburg, Wash., 1993—, mem. parish coun., 1995-2000. Mem. Am. Phys. Soc., Am. Assn. Physics Tchrs. (rep. com. on physics for 2-yr. colls. Wash. chpt. 1986-87, v.p. 1987-88, 94-95, pres. 1988-89, 95-96, past pres. 1996-97), Am. Chem. Soc., Internat. Union Pure and Applied Chemistry (affiliate), Pacific Northwest Assn. Coll. Physics (bd. dirs. 1997-99, 2001—, treas. 2002-), Soc. Physics Students (councilor zone 17 1998—). Democrat. Roman Catholic. Avocations: leading scripture discussion groups, reading, writing poetry, needlework. Home: 1100 N B St Apt 2 Ellensburg WA 98926-2570 Office: Cen Wash U Physics Dept Ellensburg WA 98926 E-mail: rosells@cwu.edu. *Personal philosophy: Every human being is born with a unique set of talents and gifts with which to serve the Lord and other people; the greater the gift, the greater the obligation to serve.*

ROSELLA, JOHN DANIEL, clinical psychologist, educator; b. Phila., Sept. 12, 1938; s. Orazio and Angela Theresa (Cardone) Rosella; m. Rose Mary Theresa Malloy, Nov. 14, 1964; children: Anne-Marie, John Daniel Jr. BS in Psychology, Villanova U., 1961; MEd Temple U., 1966, postgrad. Temple U., 1969—72, PhD Walden U., 1981. Diplomate Am. Bd. Forensic Examiners, Am. Bd. Psychol. Spltys., Profl. Acad. Custody Evaluators, cert. hypnotherapist, lic. psychologist, Pa.; cert. in edn. St. Joseph's U., 1963. Tchr., counselor Father Judge H.S., Phila., 1962—67; counselor Bristol Twp. Sch. Dist., Bucks County, 1967—69; prof., dept. social & behavioral scis. Bucks County C.C., 1994, subject area coord., 1995, Newtown, Pa., 1968—, founder coll. reading and study skills program, 1968—70, founding chmn. dept. basic studies, 1970—76; dir. psychol. svcs. Fairless Hills (Pa.) Med. Ctr., 1978—89, dir. clin. svcs., 1989—96; asst. clin. prof. Widener U., 1990—. Cons. Office of Vocat. Rehab., 1977—; psychol. cons. Eugenia Hosp.19890, 1980—, Bur. Disability Determination, 1982—, Human Growth Ctr., Inc., 1982—, Crestview North Nursing Home and Rehab. Ctr., 1990—; cons. staff psychologist Attleboro Nursing Home and Rehab. Ctr., 1993—2001, Pickering Manor Nursing Home, 1997—2001; clin. assoc. prof., Dept. Mental Health Scis. Hahnemann U., 1982—94; cons. Bucks County (Pa.) Family Ct., 1985—; grad. clin. supr. Coll. of N.J., 1985—86; grad. counseling intern supr. Rider Coll., 1988—95; participant 1st Internat. Colloquium on Family Health, Sri Lanka, 1983, Australia, 88; ednl. profl. travel Italy and Switzerland, 1991; lectr. in field. Author: Reading and Study Skills: A Counseling Approach, 1970, Effects of the Basic Studies Program on the Academic Achievement of High Risk Students, 1973—74, The Professor and the Law, 1975, Research in Hypnosis for Students, 1976, Marriage and Family Therapy: Its Evolution from Revolution, 1980, others; author: (audiotapes) Developing Successful Study Skills, Guided Imagery Exercises; author: articles. Active Right to Read Task Force, 1972—73; project dir. Fairless Hills Psychiat. Hosp. bldg. program, 1982—83; pres. bd. trustees Friends of the Libr. Found., Bucks County C.C., 1984—; co-founder Newtown Twp. Dem. Party, 1978, 1st vice chmn., 1979—80, Dem. committeeman, 1989—92; mem. 8th Congressional Dist. Adv. Coun. on Health Care, 1981—83; bd. dirs. Valley Day Sch., 1978—81; Bucks County Cmty. Ctrs., 1980—85. Recipient Man of Yr. award, Assn. to Advance Ethical Hypnosis, 1976, Disting. Tchg. recognition, Phi Theta Kappa, 1981, 1983, Faculty Svc. award, 1989, Profl. AChievement award, Bucks County C.C. Alumni Assn., 1991. Fellow: Pa. Psychol. Assn., Internat. Coun. for Sex Edn. and Parenthood of Am. U.; mem.: APA, Profl. Acad. Custody Evaluators, Pa. Assn. Marriage and Family Therapy, Am. Assn. Marriage and Family Therapy, Am. Coll. Forensic Examiners, Sons of Italy, KC, Am. Legion. Office: Offices at Oxford Crossing Ste 202 333 S Oxford Valley Rd Fairless Hills PA 19030-2626

ROSELLE, DAVID PAUL, university president, mathematics educator; b. Vandergrift, Pa., May 30, 1939; s. William John and Esther Suzanne (Clever) R.; m. Louise Helen Dowling, June 19, 1967; children— Arthur Charles, Cynthia Dowling BS, West Chester State Coll., 1961; PhD, Duke U., 1965; LLD, West Chester U., 1994; hon. degree, Westchester U., Soha U., Japan. Asst. prof. math. U. Md., College Park, 1965-68; assoc. prof. math. La. State U., Baton Rouge, 1968-73, prof., 1973-74, Va. Poly. Inst. and State U., Blacksburg, 1974-87, dean grad. sch., 1979-81, dean research and grad. studies, 1981-83, provost, 1983-87, chmn. Commn. on Rsch., 1981-83, chmn. Commn. on Grad. Studies, 1983-87; prof. U. Ky., 1987-90, pres., 1987-90; prof. math., pres. U. Del., 1990—. Pres. COMAP, Inc., Lexington, Mass., 1986-95; bd. dirs. William Trust Corp., VTLS, Inc. Editor: Proc. of the First Louisiana Conf. on Combinatorics, Graph Theory and Computing, 1970, Proc. of the Second Louisiana Conf. on Combinatorics, Graph Theory and Computing, 1971; mem. editorial bd. The Bicentennial Tribute to American Mathematics, 1977; contbr. numerous research articles to profl. jours. Mem. Del. Roundtable, 1990—, Bus.and Pub. Edn. Coun., 1990—; trustee Winterthur Mus., 1991—; bd. dirs. Del. Acad. Medicine, 1991—, Med. Ctr. Del., 1991—; mem. USAID adv. com. vol. fgn. aid, 2000—. Named Outstanding Alumnus West Chester State Coll., 1979; Westinghouse Coop. scholar, 1957; NSF grantee, 1965-75; Teaching Excellence Cert., 1978; Digital Equipment grant, 1984; Nat. Coun. Tchrs. Math. Cert. of Appreciation, 1984; founding fellow of Inst. for Combinatorics and Its Applications, 1990; numerous invited addresses at univs. and profl. soc. meetings. Mem. Am. Math. Soc., Math. Assn. Am. (sec., fin. com., exec. com., com. on publs. 1975-84; com. on spl. funds 1985—; chmn. com. on accreditation 1985; numerous other coms.). Home: 47 Kent Way Newark DE 19711-5201 Office: U Del Rm. 104 Hullihen Hall Newark DE 19716-0099 E-mail: roselle@udel.edu.*

ROSELLE, PAUL LUCAS, material scientist; b. Balt., Mar. 9, 1960; s. William Charles and Marsha (Lucas) R.; m. Dori Lynn Knoff, June 1, 1985; children: Anna Kristen, Lucas Vernon. BS in Chemistry, U. Wis., Milw., 1982, MS in Material Sci., 1985. Cert. haz-mat first responder, Eastman Kodak Co.; cert. haz-mat technician, AlFalight Inc. Rsch. scientist Kodak Rsch. Labs. (Microelectronics Tech. Divsn.), Rochester, N.Y., 1985-94; R&D project mgr. Planar Sys., Lake Mills, Wis., 1994-99, active matrix liquid crystal display (AMLCD) process mgr., 1999-2000; dir. high power laser diode processing AlFaLight, Inc., Madison, 2000-01, v.p. of Madison ops., 2001—. Mfg. process evaluation team Semiconductor Rsch. Corp., 1991-94; monodispersed advanced colorant system RFP team mem. U.S. Display Consortium, patterned glass inspection RFP team mem. Contbr. articles to profl. jours. AFS student, Austria, 1977. Recipient patent award Eastman Kodak, 1994. Mem. NRA (cert. firearms instr. 1993—), Soc. for Info. Display (sec. exec. program com. 1997-98). Achievements include patents for micro liquid crystal displays having circular cover glass and viewing area free of spacers, low temperature insitu image reversal process for microelectronic fabrication, method of making a two phase charge coupled device, plasma etching indium tin oxide using a deposited silicon nitride mask, plasma etching indium tin oxide, forming planar ITO gate electrode array structures, etching indium tin oxide, gaseous cleaning method for silicon devices, process to eliminate the reentrant profile in double polysilicon gate structures. Office: AlFalight Inc 1832 Wright St Madison WI 53704 E-mail: proselle@alfalight.com.

ROSELLE, WILLIAM CHARLES, librarian; b. Vandergrift, Pa., June 30, 1936; s. William John and Suzanne Esther (Clever) R.; m. Marsha Louise Lucas, Aug. 2, 1959; 1 child, Paul Lucas. BA, Thiel Coll., 1958; MLS, U. Pitts., 1963. Lic. profl. guide State of Mont., 1978. Mem. faculty Milton Hershey (Pa.) Sch., 1960-62; trainee Pa. State Library, 1962-63; asst. catalog librarian Pa. State U., 1963-65; engring., math. librarian U. Iowa, 1965-66, library adminstrv. asst., 1966-69, asst. dir. libraries, 1969-71; prof., dir. library U. Wis.-Milw., 1971-89; dir. univ. library system U. Pitts., 1989-90; pvt. cons. Thiensville, Wis., 1991—. Chmn. Morris Fromkin Meml. Lectr. Com., 1972-89; chmn. planning task force on computing U. Wis. System, 1973-74, mem. library planning study com., 1978-79, co-chmn. library automation task force, 1983-85; chmn. computing mgmt. rev. team U. Wis.-Stout, 1976; chmn. Council for U. Wis. Libraries, 1981-82; library cons. Grambling (La.) State U., Viterbo Coll., LaCrosse, Wis., N.C. A&T U., Greensboro, Mt. Mary Coll., Milw., U. Ill. at Chgo., Milw. Sch. Engring., Bklyn. Coll., U. South Ala., Concordia Coll., Milw., Metrics Rsch. Corp., Cardinal Stritch Coll., Milw., N.Y. Inst. Tech., Indiana U. of Pa., Med. Coll. Wis., Wis. Luth. Coll., Milw.; participant Library Adminstrs. Devel. Program, U. Md., 1973, micrographics seminar Nat. Microfilm Assn., 1973, Mgmt. Skills Inst., Assn. Rsch. Libraries, Kansas City, Mo., 1977, Meadowbrook Symposium Midwest Library Network, 1976; mem. sect. geography and map libraries Internat. Fedn. Library Assns. and Instns., 1978-83; mem. bldg. com. Ctr. for Rsch. Libraries, 1980-82. Editorial cons. The Quest for Social Justice, 1983, Current Geographical Publications, 1978-89; contbr. articles to profl. jours. Pres. Thiensville (Wis.) Village Bd., 1987; bd. dirs. Charles Allis Art Mus., 1979-84. Served with AUS, 1958-60. Named Disting. Alumnus, Thiel Coll., 1985 Hon. fellow Am. Geog. Soc.; mem. Spl. Libraries Assn. (spl. citation 1979), ALA (life), Iowa Library Assn. (chmn. audit com. 1968-70, chmn. intellectual freedom com. 1969-70), Wis. Library Assn., Midwest Acad. Librarians Conf. (chmn. 1969-71), AAUP (treas. U. Iowa chpt. 1969-70), Coun. Wis. Libraries (chmn. 1973-74), Soc. Tympanuchus Cupido Pinnatus, Internat. CBX Owners Assn., Milw. Civil War Round Table, Ozaukee Corvette Club, Beta Beta Beta, Beta Phi Mu, Phi Alpha Theta, Phi Kappa Phi, Phi Delta Kappa. Lutheran. Home: 324 Sunny Ln Thiensville WI 53092-1334

ROSELLI, JOHN ANTIMO, finance company executive; b. Jan. 17, 1954; BS, MIT, 1978. Tech. mgr. MKI Securities, Inc., N.Y.C., 1985-87; tech. dir. Kidder Reports, Inc., 1987-91; treas. Lamborn Securities, Inc., 1992—2000; founder risk mgmt. practice Parson Group LLC, 1999—2001. Cons. in field. Home: 4-74 48th Ave Apt 3T Long Island City NY 11109

ROSELLI, RICHARD JOSEPH, lawyer; b. Chgo., Mar. 2, 1954; s. H. Joseph and Dolores Roselli; m. Lisa McNelis; children: Nicholas Joseph, Christiana Elise, Alexandra Grace, Michaela Luciana, Anthony Santino. BA, Tulane U., 1976, JD, 1980. Bar: Fla. 1981, U.S. Dist. Ct. (so. dist.) Fla. 1981, U.S. Ct. Appeals (5th and 11th cirs.); bd. cert. civil trial lawyer. Assoc. Krupnick & Campbell, Ft. Lauderdale, Fla., 1981-84; ptnr. Krupnick, Campbell, Malone, Roselli, 1984-91, Krupnick Campbell Malone Roselli Buser Slama & Hancock P.A., Ft. Lauderdale, 1999—2002; mng. ptnr. Krupnick Campbell Malone Roselli Buser Slama Hancock McNelis Liberman & McKee P.A., 1999—2001, Roselli & Roselli PA, Ft. Lauderdale, 2002—. Trustee Fla. Dem. Party, 1992-95. Mem. ATLA (pres.' coun. 1996-97), Am. Bd. Trial Advocates, Am. Soc. Law and Medicine, So. Trial Lawyers Assn. (founder),

Acad. Fla. Trial Lawyers (bd. dirs. 1987—, exec. com. 1990-97, sec. 1993, treas. 1994, pres. elect. 1995, pres. 1996, chmn. Fla. lawyers action group-PAC 1996, Golden Eagle award, 1989, 1996, 98, Silver Eagle award, 1990, Crystal Eagle award 1995), Broward County Trial Lawyers (bd. dirs.), Trial Lawyers for Pub. Justice, Lawyer Pilots Bar Assn., St. Jude Catholic Ch. Office: Ste 600 3471 N Federal Hwy Fort Lauderdale FL 33306

ROSEMAN, ARNOLD DAVID, lawyer; b. N.Y.C., Apr. 10, 1917; s. Samuel Victor and Pauline (Kaplan) R.; m. Rose L. Mirkin, June 20, 1948 (dec. 1991); children: Paula Saler, Robert L. BS, CCNY, 1938; JD, Harvard U., 1941. Bar: N.Y. 1941, J.S. Dist. Ct. (so. and ea. dists.) N.Y. 1946, U.S. Ct. Appeals (2d cir.) 1948, U.S. Supreme Ct. 1960. Sole practice, N.Y.C. and Westchester, 1941—. N.Y. State commr. of investigation, 1974-75; acting city judge New Rochelle (N.Y.), 1972; spl. dist. atty. Westchester County, N.Y., 1977-78; lectr. N.Y. State Bar, 1979-82. Author: (with others) Basic Criminal Practice, 1979-8[9]6. Whip and minority leader Westchester Bd. Suprs., 1957-67; chmn. Cmty. Chest, 1956-57. Served to capt. USAAF, 1941-46, PTO. Mem. ABA, N.Y. State Bar Assn., Westchester County, Eastchester, and New Rochelle Bar Assn., Lions (pres. 1974), VFW, Am. Legion, Elks. Address: 670 White Plains Rd Ste 115 Scarsdale NY 10583-5027 Fax: 914 472-5074.

ROSEMAN, CHARLES SANFORD, lawyer; b. Jersey City, Feb. 26, 1945; s. Leon and Edith (Neidorf) R.; children: Rochelle Lynn, Loren Scott. BA, Calif. State U., 1968; JD, U. San Diego, 1971. Bar: Calif. 1972, U.S. Dist. Ct. (so. dist.) Calif. 1972, U.S. Dist. Ct. (cen. dist.) Calif. 1975, U.S. Supreme Ct. 1980, U.S. Claim Ct. 1990. Assoc. Greer, Popko, Nickoloff & Miller, San Diego, 1972-73; ptnr. Roseman & Roseman, 1973-78, Roseman & Small, San Diego, 1978-82, Frank, Roseman, Freedus & Mann, San Diego, 1982-86, Roseman and Mann, 1986-92; pvt. practice San Diego, 1992—; judge pro tem San Diego County Superior Ct., 1975—; also arbitrator, mediator, 1977—. Bd. dirs. Glenn Aire Cmty. Devel. Assn., San Diego, 1972-73, Big Bros. San Diego County, 1973-81,; bd. dirs. San Diego County Anti-Defamation League, 1985—; chmn. exec. com. 1984-85, assoc. nat. commr., 1995—; bd. dirs. San Diego County Legal Aid Soc., 1988-89, Tifereth Israel Synagogue, pres. 1982-84, Homeys Youth Found., 2002--. Mem. ABA, ATLA, Consumer Attys. of Calif. (Recognition of Experience award 1985), Calif. Bar Assn., Am. Arbitration Assn. (arbitrator, panel 1985—), San Diego Bar Assn., Consumer Attys. of San Diego (bd. dirs. 1982-84), U. San Diego Sch. Law Alumni Assn. (bd. dirs. 1972-73), B'nai B'rith (pres. 1978). Democrat. Office: Law Offices Charles S Roseman & Assocs 170 Laurel St San Diego CA 92101-1419 E-mail: csr1@flash.net.

ROSEMAN, JACK, computer services company executive; b. Lynn, Mass., June 13, 1931; s. Abraham and Bessie (Guz) R.; m. Judith Ann Rosenthal, Feb. 21, 1960; children: Laura, Alan, Shari. BA, Boston U., 1954; MS, U. Mass., 1955. Instr. U. Mass., 1958-60; dir. info. processing CEIR, Inc., Washington, 1960-66; v.p. KMS Tech. Ctr., 1966-70; pres., bd. dirs. On-Line Systems, Inc., Pitts., 1970-79; pres., chmn. United Computing Internat. subs. of SPRINT, 1979-80; pres., bd. dirs., later chmn. Actronics, 1981-85; pvt. investor, ptnr. J.R. Assocs., Pitts., 1988-92; chmn. of bd. dirs. Omega Systems, 1994-96. Disting. adj. prof. Donald H. Jones Ctr. Entrepreneurship, 1992—2000, assoc. dir., 1992—2001; John Thorne prof. entrepreneurship Carnegie Mellon U., 2000—01; dir. emeritus Pitts. High Tech. Coun.; rsch. staff whirlwind project computation ctr. MIT, 1997—2000; chmn. Cerebellum, Inc., 1997—2000; dir. Roseman Inst., 2002—; bd. dirs. Acustica, Inc.; advisor Vivismo, Inc.; bd. dirs. Safe Drive Tech. Trustee Kobold Found. Recipient Judges' award, Ernst & Young, and Merrill Lynch Inc. mags.

ROSEMAN, JANET LYNN, writer, dance educator; b. Meriden, Conn., Nov. 29, 1954; d. Sidney and Theodora (Tobea) R. BS in Counseling, Syracuse U., 1976; MS in Dance Therapy, Lesley Coll., 1978; PhD in Dance Theory and Criticism, The Union Inst., 12001. Prof. journalism San Jose (Calif.) State U., 1987-90, City Coll. San Francisco, 1987-93; prof. English Golden Gate U., San Francisco, 1990, San Francisco Art Inst., 1989; prof. journalism Coll. Marin, San Rafael, Calif., 1988-90; prof. dance San Francisco State U., 2000; dance critic Oakland (Calif.) Tribune, 1990—. Dance critic Oakland Tribune, Dance Spirit, Dance USA, Marin Ind. Jour., San Francisco Bay Times, Dance Israel, San Mateo Times, Metro, UPI, The Sun Sentinel, among others; guest lectr. U. R.I., 1997, Internat. Assn. for Psychology and the Performing Arts, Miami, 1998, CORD: Congress on Rsch. on Dance, 1999, Toronto Can. and the Hague, The Netherlands, 1999, U. Capetown, South Africa, 1999, San Francisco State U., 2000, Grad. Theol. Union Ctr. for Woman, Holy Names Coll., Jewish Cmty. Ctr., Book Passage, GAIA Books Gualala Arts Ctr., Sir Francis Drake Lit. Festival, Falkirk Cultural Ctr., Film Arts Found., Alumnae Resources, Cody's Books, Two Sisters Bookstore, Barnes and Noble, Borders Books. Author: Gumps Since 1861: A San Francisco Legend, 1995, rev. edit., 2000, The Way of the Woman Writer, 1995, Beach Blanket Babylon, 1997, Dance Masters: Interviews with Legends of the Dance, 2001; contbr. articles to numerous profl. jours. Grantee Harvard U., The Kittredge Fund., 1998, Swann Found. for Caricature and Cartoon, 1989, Ludwig Vogelstein Writers, 1990, San Jose State U., The Author's Guild, others. Mem. Dance Critics Assn., Congress on Rsch. on Dance, Soc. Dance History Studies. Avocations: ballet, pointe, pool playing, attending museums. E-mail: dancejan@aol.com.

ROSEMAN, MARTIN RICHARD, publisher, consultant, lecturer; b. East Orange, N.J., Aug. 4, 1958; s. Jack Melvin and Esther Shirley (Beshunsky) Roseman; m. Carolina Villacorta, Dec. 8, 2001; children from previous marriage: Fabricio, Shirley. BA, Hampshire Coll., 1980; MS, Rutgers U., 1987. Rschr., editor Consumer Fedn. Am., Washington, 1977; pres. Matrix Audio Video, West Hatfield, Mass., 1980-86; founder, pres. MAC Consulting, Miami Beach, Fla., 1980—; dir. mktg. Profl. Audio Cons., Millburn, N.J., 1986-96; v.p. Les Enfants, South Orange, 1990-97. Chief cons. Sony Latin Am., 2001; lectr. CEDIA Expo, 1999. Profl. musician, 1974—. Lobbyist Pub. Citizen, Washington, 1977; sponsor Save the Children, Westport, Conn., 1991-97; ptnr. NJPIRG, Trenton, N.J.; Frontline sponsor Greenpeace, Washington. Mem. Profl. Audio Video Retailers Assn., Custom Electronics Design and Installation Assn., Home Theater Specialists Assn., Nat. Trust for Hist. Preservation. Democrat. Jewish. Avocations: musical performance and composition, computer science, antiquities. E-mail: info@macmrkt.com.

ROSEMAN, SAUL, biochemist, educator; b. Bklyn., Mar. 9, 1921; s. Emil and Rose (Markowitz) R.; m. Martha Ozrowitz, Sept. 9, 1941; children: Mark Alan, Dorinda Ann, Cynthia Bernice. BS, CCNY, 1941; MS, U. Wis., 1944, PhD, 1947; MD (hon.), U. Lund, Sweden, 1984. From instr. to asst. prof. U. Chgo., 1948-53; from asst. prof. to prof. biol. chemistry, also Rackham Arthritis Research Unit, U. Mich., 1953-65; Ralph S. O'Connor prof. biology Johns Hopkins U., Balt., 1965—, chmn. dept., 1969-73; dir. McCollum-Pratt Inst., 1969-73, chmn. dept. biology , dir., 1988-90. Cons. NIH, NSF, Am. Cancer Soc., Hosp. for Sick Children, Toronto; sci. counselor Nat. Cancer Inst.; Lynch lectr. U. Notre Dame, 1989; Van Niel lectr. Stanford U., 1992. Author articles on metabolism of complex molecules containing carbohydrates and on solute transport.; former mem. editorial bd.: Biochemistry, Jour. Biol. Chemistry. Served with AUS, 1944-46. Recipient Sesquicentennial award U. Mich., 1967, T. Duckett Jones Meml. award Helen Hay Whitney Found., 1973, Rosenstiehl award Brandeis U., 1974, Internat. award Gairdner Found. award, 1981, Townsend Harris award CUNY, 1987, Spl. award 11th Internat. Symposium on Glycoconjugates, 1991, Karl Meyer award Soc. Glycobiology, 1993. Fellow Am. Acad. Microbiology; mem. Am. Soc. Biol. Chemists, Am. Soc. Cell Biology, Am. Acad. Arts and Scis., Nat. Acad. Scis., Am. Chem. Soc., Am. Soc. Microbiologists, Biochem. Soc. Japan (hon.). Office: Johns Hopkins U 34th Charles St Baltimore MD 21218

ROSEMAN, SUSAN CAROL, artist; b. Phila., June 20, 1950; d. Myer and Jeanette (Lewin) R.; m. James Robert Feehan, Feb. 21, 1985. Student, Art Inst. Pitts., 1967; 5-yr. cert., Pa. Acad. Fine Arts, 1973. Painter, printmaker, Pipersville, Pa., 1973—; sign painter Rose Moon Signs and Design, 1984—; curator Cafe Gallery, Rosemont, N.J., 1986—; pres. Riverbank Arts Inc., Stockton, 1994—. Lectr. painting William Allen High Sch., Allentown, Pa., 1976; bd. dirs. Open Space Gallery, Allentown, 1980-81; mem. publicity and exhbn. com. Abington Art Ctr., Jenkintown, Pa., 1978-81; curator Gallery at Vineyards, New Hope, Pa., 1990; juror student show Pa. Acad. Fine Arts, Phila., 1990, Shad Festival, Lambertville, N.J., 1990, Plastic Club, Phila., 1994. One-woman shows include Moravian Coll., Bethlehem, Pa., 1980, Gallery 500, Elkins Park, Pa., 1981, 20th Century Gallery, Phila., 1983; exhibited in group shows at Women in the Arts, William Penn Mus., Harrisburg, Pa., 1981-82, Japan Internat. Artists Soc., Prefectural Mus. of Nara and Chiba, Japan, 1981-82, Trenton (n.J.) State Coll., 1986, Fellowship of Pa. Acad. Fine Arts, James A. Michener Art Mus., Doylestown, Pa., 1992, Woodmere Art Mus., 1994, Mus. Am. Art of Pa. Acad. Fine Arts, 1996, others; represented in permanent collections. Recipient 2nd pl. award Allentown Art Mus., 1979, Purchase prize 10th Biennial Nat. Printshow, Critics Choice award Lehigh Art Alliance, 1983; scholar Pa. Acad. Fine Arts, 1972; fellow Baum Sch. Art, 1980-81; LHP Found. grantee, 1994—. Mem. Woodmere Art Mus., Pa. Acad. Fine Arts Alumni Assn. (co-chmn. exhbns. 1990-92, bd. dirs. 1991-92). Avocations: collecting art, antiques. Home and Office: 6588 Groveland Rd Pipersville PA 18947-1402

ROSEMANN, PHILIPP WOLFRAM, philosopher, educator; b. Frankfurt/Main, Hesse, Germany, Feb. 24, 1964; s. Herwart Heinrich and Helga Gertrud (Steinbuechel) R. Candidate Philosophy, U. Hamburg, Germany, 1986; MA in Medieval Philosophy, Queen's U., Belfast, No. Ireland, 1989; Lic. Philosophy, Cath. U. Louvain, Belgium, 1991, D Philosophy, 1995. Warburg scholar Warburg Inst. U. London, 1987-88; tchg. fellow Queen's U., Belfast, 1988-90; rschr. Cath. U. Louvain, 1990-93, lectr., 1995-96, Uganda Martyrs U., Nkozi, 1996-97; prof. U. Dallas, 1997—. Co-author (with Werner Welte): (books) Alltagssprachliche Metakommunikation im Englischen und Deutschen, 1990; author: Omne ens est aliquid: Introduction à la lecture du "système" philosophique de saint Thomas d'Aquin, 1996, Omne agens agit sibi simile: A "Repetition" of Scholastic Metaphysics, 1996, Understanding Scholastic Thought with Foucault, 1999; editor: Robert Grosseteste, Tabula, 1995, Dallas Medieval Texts and Translations; co-editor (with M. Lejeune): Business Ethics in the African Context Today, 1996; co-editor, editor, traduire, interpreter with S.G. Lofts: books Editor, translator, interpreter: Essais de méthodologie philosophique, 1997; editor (assoc. editor): Am. Cath. Philos. Quar.; contbr. articles to newspapers. Mem. Soc. Internat. pour l'Étude de la Philosopie Médiévale, Martin-Heidegger-Gesellschaft, AAUP, Am. Philos. Assn., Am. Cath. Philos. Assn., Soc. Promotion Eriugenian Studies, Uganda Soc., Tex. Medieval Assn. Roman Catholic. Avocations: running, weight lifting. Home: 2517 Wynnewood Dr Dallas TX 75224-2667 Office: U Dallas Dept Philosophy 1845 E Northgate Dr Irving TX 75062-4736 E-mail: rosemann@udallas.edu.

ROSEMARIN, CAREY STEPHEN, lawyer; b. Englewood, N.J., Aug. 19, 1950; s. Jack L. and Muriel Ruth (Gordon) R.; m. Joan Maxine Lafer, June 17, 1973; children: Benjamin Joseph, Meryl Ruth. BS, U. Mich., 1972; MS, Pa. State U., 1974; JD, U. Tenn., 1978. Bar: Tenn. 1978, Ill. 1982, U.S. Dist. Ct. (ea. dist.) Tenn. 1978, U.S. Dist. Ct. (no. dist.) Ill. 1982. Rsch. assoc. Union Carbide Corp., Oak Ridge Nat. Lab., 1974-80; asst. regional counsel U.S. EPA, Chgo., 1980-86; ptnr. Katten, Muchin, & Zavis, 1986-90, Jenner & Block, Chgo., 1990-99; prin. Law Offices of Carey S. Rosemarin, P.C., Northbrook, Ill., 1999—. Bd. dirs. Congregation Beth Judea, Long Grove, Ill. Mem. ABA, Tenn. Bar Assn., Chgo. Bar Assn. (chmn. environ. law com. 1985-86), Environ. Law Inst. (assoc.). Jewish. Avocations: licensed glider pilot, bicycling. Office: Law Offices of Carey S Rosemarin PC 500 Skokie Blvd Ste 510 Northbrook IL 60062-2893 Fax: 312-896-5786. E-mail: csr@rosemarinlaw.com.

ROSEMBERG, EUGENIA, physician, educator, medical research administrator; b. Buenos Aires, Argentina, Apr. 25, 1918; came to U.S., 1948, naturalized, 1956; d. Pedro and Fanny (Hestrin) R. BS, Liceo Nacional de Senoritas, Buenos Aires, 1936; MD, U. Buenos Aires, 1944. Intern Hosp. Pirovano, Buenos Aires, 1940-41; resident Hosp. Nacional de Clinicas, U. Hosp., U. Buenos Aires, 1941-44, assoc. in pediatrics, 1943-48; instr. in anatomy Hosp. Nacional de Clinicas, U. Hosp., U. Buenos Aires (Med. Sch.), 1940-46, instr. pediatrics, 1946-48; practice medicine specializing in pediatrics, 1946-48; research in endocrinology Balt., 1948-51, Worcester, Mass., 1955—; Mead Johnson fellow dept. endocrinology Johns Hopkins Med. Sch., Balt., 1948-49; vis. scientist Med. Sch., U. Montevideo, Uruguay, 1950; research fellow NIH, Bethesda, Md., 1951-53, Nat. Inst. Arthritis and Metabolic Diseases, 1951-53, Med. Research Inst. and Hosp., Oklahoma City, 1953; mem. staff Worcester Found. Exptl. Biology, Shrewsbury, Mass., 1953-62; research dir. Med. Research Inst. of Worcester, Inc., 1962—; cons. Center for Population Research, Nat. Inst. Child Health and Human Devel., NIH, 1969-70, chief contraceptive devel. br., 1970-71; prof. pediatrics U. Md. Hosp., Balt., 1970-73; prof. medicine U. Mass. Med. Sch., Worcester, 1972—; mem. staff Worcester City Hosp., 1955-85, sec. human experimentation com., 1965-83, chmn., 1984-85, dir. clin. research, 1972-85. Sec. subcom. on gonadotropins Nat. Hormone and Pituitary Program, Nat. Inst. Arthritis, Diabetes, Digestive and Kidney Diseases, 1965-69, chmn., 1969-85, mem. med. adv. bd., 1969-72, 73-85, sec. subcom. on standards endocrinology study sect., 1968 Author: Gonadotropins, 1968, (with C.A. Paulsen) The Human Testis, 1970, Gonadotropin Therapy in Female Infertility, 1973, (with C. Gual) Hypothalamic Hypophysiotropic Hormones—Physiological and Clinical Studies, 1973; Mem. editorial bd.: Giner, 1970—, Procs. 1st Ann. Meeting Am. Soc. Andrology, supplement, Vol. 8, 1976, Andrologia, 1978—, Jour. Andrology, 1979-82, Internat. Jour. Andrology, 1978—; assoc. editor: Reproduccion, 1970—, Andrologia jour, 1974-77; Contbr. articles and book chpts. on research in endocrinology to med. texts and jours.; Translator: from Spanish Diagnosis and Treatment of Endocrine Disorders in Childhood and Adolescence (L. Wilkins). Patentee in field, U.S., Can., Europe. Fellow AAAS; mem. Am. Med. Women's Assn., Endocrine Soc. U.S. (mem. com. pub. affairs 1971, v.p. 1975-76), Soc. for Research in Biology of Reproduction, Soc. for Study of Reproduction, Am. Fertility Soc., Peru Fertility Soc. (fgn. corr.), N.Y. Acad. Scis., New Eng. Cardiovascular Soc., Am., Mass. heart assns., Argentine Endocrine Soc., Argentine Pediatric Soc., Sociedad Argentine Para El Estudio de la Esterilidad., Pan Am. Med. Women's Alliance, Am. Soc. Andrology (program chmn. 1975-76, exec. council 1976-78, chmn. publ. com. 1975-80, Disting. Andrologist award 1982), Internat. Com. for Study Andrology (exec. council 1976-79)

ROSEN, ANA BEATRIZ, electronics executive; b. Guayaquil, Ecuador, May 16, 1950; came to U.S., 1962; d. Luis A. and Luz Aurora (Rodriguez) Moreira; m. Manuel Jose Farina, Dec. 15, 1979 (dec. Apr. 1990); children: Kevin Farina, Mark Farina; m. Michael G. Rosen, June 6, 1992 (dec. Oct. 2001). AA, Latin-Am. Inst., 1971. Adminstr. asst. M&T Chem. Inc., N.Y.C., 1971-75; mgr. sales Singer Products Co., 1975-78; v.p. Argil Internat. Ltd., 1978-83; pres. KMA Enterprises Inc., Bklyn., 1983-94, KMA Industries Inc., Palm Beach Gardens, Fla., 1994—. Mem. U.S Trade Adv. Bd.; v.p. Miro Sales, Inc. Bd. dirs. Palm Beach County chpt. ARC. Mem. ARC, World Trade Coun. (Palm Beach County), Gold Coast Bus. and Profl. Women of the Palm Beaches, County Bus. & Profl. Coun. Roman Catholic.

ROSEN, ARTHUR DAVID, neurobiology educator; b. Bklyn., Sept. 19, 1935; s. Elihu and Gertrude (Simonson) R.; m. Patricia Dailey, Dec. 24, 1997. BA, Columbia U., 1956; MD, SUNY, Bklyn., 1960. Diplomate Am. Bd. Psychiatry and Neurology. Intern Bklyn. Jewish Hosp., 1960-61; fellow in neurophysiology SUNY, Bklyn., 1961-62; resident in neurology Kings County Hosp., 1962-64; asst. prof. medicine SUNY, 1966-73, assoc. prof. neurology Stony Brook, 1973-80, prof. neurology, 1980-98, prof. neurology emeritus, 1998—; prof. biol. scis. Purdue U., West Lafayette, Ind., 1998—; clin. prof. neurology Ind. U. Sch. of Medicine, 1998—. NIH/NRSA fellow in neurobiology, 1993-94. Contbr. articles to Jour. Neurophys., Exptl. Neurology, Jour. Neurol. Sci., Am. Jour. Physiology, 1960-2001. Lt. comdr. USNR, 1964-66. Grantee NINDB, 1971, NIH, 1973, VA, 1974, 77, Haemoneties Inst., 1985, KROC Found., 1985. Fellow Am. Acad. Neurology; mem. Am. Neurol. Assn., Soc. for Neuroscience, Biophys. Soc., Sigma Xi. Achievements include research on demonstration of antidromic activity in the CNS and demonstration of effect of magnetic fields on several biological systems. Address: Purdue U Dept Biol Scis Lilly Hall Lafayette IN 47907 E-mail: arosen@bilbo.bio.purdue.edu.

ROSEN, ARTHUR MARVIN, advertising executive; b. N.Y.C., Dec. 28, 1930; s. Joseph and Cornelia (Grob) R.; m. Maureen Elizabeth Reilly; children: Ellen Jessica, Deborah Lynn, Daniel Joshua. BA, CUNY, 1952; MA, Yale U., 1953; postgrad., Columbia U., 1955-57, Dartmouth Coll. Analyst research Dancer-Fitzgerald-Sample, N.Y.C., 1955-56; supr. research Benton and Bowles, 1956-61; account exec. Young and Rubicam, 1961-66; v.p. account supr. Grey Advt., 1966-69; pres. Met. Diagnostic, 1969-73; v.p. group mgmt. Grey Advt., 1973-81; exec. v.p. Sudler and Hennessey, 1981-94; mktg. cons. Himmel Nutrition, Inc., 1994-95, Martin Himmel, Inc., 1994-95. Spkr. in field. Contbr. articles to profl. jours. Pres. Temple Beth Or, Washington Twp., N.J., 1973-74; chmn. Soc. Families, Colgate U., 1983-84; study leader ILEAD, Dartmouth Coll.; study leader Adventures in Learning, Colby-Sawyer Coll. Cpl. U.S. Army, 1953-55. Republican. Jewish. E-mail: ponderosen@tds.net.

ROSEN, ARYE, microwave, optoelectronics and medicine researcher; b. June 26, 1937; BSEE cum laude, Howard U., 1963; MScE, Johns Hopkins U., 1965; MSc in Physiology, Thomas Jefferson U., 1975; PhD in Elec. Engring., Drexel U., 1993. Registered profl. engr., B.C., Can. Disting. mem. tech. staff Sarnoff Corp. subs. SRI, Princeton, N.J., 1967—; assoc. in medicine Jefferson Med. Coll., Phila., 1977—; rsch. prof. Biomed. Engring. and Sci. Inst., Drexel U., adj. prof. elec. and computer engring., 1981—. Co-editor: High-Power Optically Activated Solid-State Switches, 1993, New Frontiers in Medical Device Technology, 1995; contbr. more than 150 articles to profl. jours. Recipient Microwave prize 16th European Microwave Conf., 1986, Disting. Alumni award Drexel U. Coll. Engring., Elec. and Computer Engring. Dept., 1997, IEEE MTT-S Microwave Application award, 2000, IEEE Third Millenium medal, 2000, IEEE Reg. I award, 1989. Mem.: IEEE (mem. MMT-S tech. com. for light-wave tech. 1979—, mem. MTT-S tech. program com., chmn. MTT-S tech. com. on biol. effects and med. applications, mem. editl. bd., assoc. editor IEEE Jour. Light-Wave Tech., editl. bd. Transactions on Microwave Theory and Techniques, editl. bd. Microwave and Optical Tech. Letters, mem. tech. com. IEEE Internat. Conf. Microwaves in Medicine 1991, ednl. activities bd., mem.-at-large health care engring. policy com., Disting. Microwave lectr. 1997—2001), Nat. Acad. Engring., NY Acad. Scis. Achievements include 50 patents in the fields of engineering and medicine, including Percutaneous Transluminal Microwave Catheter Angioplasty, Method and Apparatus for High Frequency Catheter Ablation, Catheter with Distally Located Integrated Circuit Radiation Generator, Electrical Phase Shifter Controlled by Light, Direct DC to RF Conversion by Impulse Excitation, Light Controlled Antennas, High Power Optical Switch, Radiation Protection Circuit for Protection Against Gamma Ray and Neutron Radiation. Office: David Sarnoff Rsch Ctr CN 5300 Princeton NJ 08543-5300

ROSEN, BENSON, business administration educator; b. Detroit, Oct. 9, 1942; s. David and Laura R.; m. Brenda M. Leibroder, Dec. 17, 1966; children: Gregory Scott, David Loren. BS, Wayne State U., 1964, MA, 1968, PhD, 1969. Asst. prof. U. N.C., Chapel Hill, 1969-74, assoc. prof., 1974-80, prof. bus. adminstrn., 1980—, Hanes prof., 1992, sr. assoc. dean acad. affairs, 1995-98. Vis. prof. U. Minn., 1981; cons. to bus., industry, govt.; cons. EEOC. Author: Becoming Aware, 1976; Older Employees: New Roles for Valued Resources, 1985; mem. editorial rev. bd. Acad. Mgmt. Jour., 1978-84; contbr. articles to profl. jours. Bd. dirs. SHRM Found., 1994-2001. Recipient Young Scholars award Spencer Found., 1976, 78, Disting. Rsch. award, 1993, PhD Teaching award, 1994; NSF grantee, 1973-75; Adminstrn. on Aging grantee, 1978-80. Fellow APA; mem. Acad. Mgmt., Soc. Human Resource Mgmt. ben. Office: U NC CB 3490 Kenan Flagler Bus Sch Chapel Hill NC 27599-3490 E-mail: Ben_Rosen@unc.edu.

ROSEN, BERNARD, engineer, engineering company executive; b. Bklyn., Mar. 31, 1927; s. Hyman and F. Rosen; m. Janice Raskin; children: Steven. Stuart, Roberta Sue. BEE, City Coll. N.Y., 1950; MEE, Poly. Tech. U., 1957. Registered profl. engr., N.Y. From mgr. to v.p. Watkins Johnson, Palo Alto, Calif., 1964—94, ret., 1994. Bd. dirs. Jr. Achievement, Santa Clara, Calif.; math tutor Los Altos/Mountain View Adult Edn., Sunnyvale/Cupertino Adult Edn. Mem. Am. Mgmt. Assn., IEEE, AFCEA, Tau Beta Pi, Eta Kappa Nu, Sigma Xi.

ROSEN, BERNARD CARL, sociologist, social psychologist, educator; b. Phila., July 1, 1922; s. Morris and Sophie Slaviter Rosen; m. Shirley Rosenbluth, Sept. 10, 1950; 1 child, Michele Beth. BA, Temple U., 1948; MA, Columbia U., 1950; PhD, Cornell U., 1952. Instr. Yale U., New Haven, 1952-53; asst. prof. U. Conn., Storrs, 1953-61; prof. U. Nebr., Lincoln, 1961-66, Cornell U., Ithaca, N.Y., 1966-93, prof. emeritus, 1993—. Vis. prof. U. São Paulo, Brazil, 1960-61, Escola Sociologia-Politica, São Paulo, 1963-64, Harvard U., 1966, London Sch. Econs., 1973-74, U. Padua, Italy, 1983-84; cons. Upjohn Inst. for Employment Rsch., 1965, NSF, 1966-89, USAID, 1990, Hunter Coll. Edn. in Depressed Areas Project, 1963, U. Chgo. Study of Adolescence Project, 1963; organizer Conf. on Socialization of Competence, Social Sci. Rsch. Coun., Puerto Rico, 1965, Conf. on Ednl. Aspirations of Can. Youth, Carleton U., Ottawa, 1970, Symposium on Family Structure and Personality, Soc. Rsch. in Child Deve., 1963, Conf. of Personality Deve. Among H.S. Youth, Social Sci. Rsch. Coun., 1963, Nat. Com. for Vis. Scientists, 1978. Author: The Industrial Connection, 1982, Women, Work and Achievement, 1989, Winners and Losers of the Information Revolution, 1998, Masks and Mirrors: Generation X and the Chameleon Personaltiy, 2001, Adolescence and Religion, 1965; co-author: (with A.M. Rattazzi, A. C. Tajoliand D. Capozza) Aspettative Di Istruzione E Occupazione Nei Giovani, 1988; contbr. articles to profl. jours., chpts. to books; co-editor: Achievement in American Society, 1969;ssoc. editor Sociometry, 1966-79; mem. editl. bd. Luso-Brazilian Rev., 1966-71; reviewer jours. in field. With U.S. Army, 1943-46, WW II. Decorated 2 combat stars; ssch. grantee NSF, 1968-73, NIMH, 1956-57, 58-62, Harvard U. 1957, U. Calif., Berkeley, 1964. Avocations: art collecting, travel, visiting museums. Home: 895 Highland Rd Ithaca NY 14850-1475 Office: Dept Sociology Uris Hall Cornell U Ithaca NY 14853

ROSEN, BETH DEE, travel agency executive; b. N.Y.C., June 27, 1945; BA, Queens Coll., 1967, MA, 1970; cert. adminstrn. and supervision, CUNY, 1982. Tchr. N.Y.C. Bd. Edn., 1967-2001; lectr. City U. N.Y., 1971-73; pres. Uniglobe Rainbow Travel Inc., Middletown, N.J., 1982-94; dir. Uniglobe Rainbow Travel Sch., 1983-87; travel counselor Excel Travel, Middletown, NJ, 1994—2001, Carlson Wagonlit Travel, 2002—. Mem. reader adv. panel Conde Nast Traveler, 1991, mem. travel agt. adv. panel, 1996—; master cruise counselor, Aussie specialist, Princess cruise expert. Columnist "The Courier" newspaper, Middletown, N.J. Avocations: whale watching, bell collecting. Office: Carlson Wagonlit Travel 26802 Cherry Hills Blvd Sun City CA 92586

ROSEN, BRUCE IRA, psychiatrist, researcher, educator; b. Nov. 26, 1945; married; 2 children. BA, U. Vt., 1967; MD, Loyola U., 1971. Diplomate Am. Bd. Psychiatry and Neurology, Am. Bd. Geriatric Psychiatry. Resident in psychiatry L.I. Jewish-Hillside Med. Ctr., New Hyde Park, N.Y., 1971-74, psychotherapy fellowship, 1974-75; dir. dept. psychiatry St. Catherine Siena Med. Ctr., Smithtown, 1976—; assoc. prof. clin. psychiatry SUNY, Stony Brook, 1976—, supr. PGY II and III residents in psychiatry, 1986—. Mem. exec. com. St. John's Hosp., Smithtown, 1979—; consulting psychiatrist U. Hosp., Stony Brook, 1980—; rschr. U. Vt., 1966-67, Suffolk County Mental Health Project, 1991-96; prin. investigator various clin. drug trials; lectr. in field. Fellow Am. Psychiat. Assn. (Suffolk County dist. br. exec. com. 1980-90, sec. 1982-84, chmn. legis. com. 1981-85, alt. del. area II coun. 1982-86, 86-90, pres. 1985-86, bd. dirs. 1992—); mem. AMA, N.Y. State Med. Soc., Suffolk County Med. Soc. Home and Office: 222 Middle Country Rd Ste 210 Smithtown NY 11787-2814 E-mail: shrink296@aol.com.

ROSEN, CAROL MENDES, artist; b. N.Y.C., Jan. 15, 1933; d. Bram de Sola and Mildred (Bertuch) Mendes; m. Elliot A. Rosen, June 30, 1957. BA, Hunter Coll., 1954; MA, CUNY, 1962. Tchr. art West Orange (N.J.) Pub. Schs., 1959-85. Co-curator exhibit Printmaking Coun. N.J., Somerville, 1981; exhibit curator 14 Sculptors Gallery, N.Y.C., 1988; collection: Nat. Collection of Fine Arts, Smithsonian Instn., Newark Mus., N.J. State Mus., Bristol-Myers Squibb, AT&T, Noyes Mus., N.Y. Pub. Libr., Zimmerli Art Mus., Mus. of Modern Art, Whitney Mus., Yale U., Skimore, Libr. Collection Bklyn. Mus., Victoria & Albert Mus., Nat. Art Gallery, London, Mus. of Tolerance, L.A., Tel Aviv U. and The Jewish Nat. & Univ. Libr., Jerusalem, Houghton Libr., Harvard U., Clark Art Inst., Williams Coll. Mus. Art, Nat. Mus. Women in Arts. Contbr. articles to arts mags. Recipient Hudson River Mus. award, Yonkers, 1983; fellow, N.J. State Coun. Arts, 1980, 1983. Jewish. Avocations: gardening, reading. Home: 10 Beavers Rd Califon NJ 07830-3433

ROSEN, CHARLES, II, lawyer; b. New Orleans, Jan. 29, 1925; s. Louis Leucht and Nita (Silverstein) R.; m. Mary Alice Waldauer (div. 1976); children: Charles III, Virginia, Jane, James Louis; m. Sandra Reed (div. 1995); m. Emily Hart, 1995. BA, Tulane U., 1948, LLB, 1951. Bar: La. 1951. Assoc.

Rosen, Kammer, Wolff, Hopkins & Burke, New Orleans, 1951-55, Jones, Walker, Waechter, Poitevent, Carrere & Denegre, New Orleans, 1955-58, ptnr., 1958-90; spl. counsel Locke, Purnell, Rain, Harrell (now Locke Liddell & Sapp), 1990-97; of counsel Sullivan Stolier & Resor, 1997—. Past chmn. and mem. exec. com. Golf & Sports Attractions, Inc., ret. mem. Fore Kids Found. Past trustee Touro Synagogue; hon. trustee Touro Infirmary; chmn. lawyers div. Jewish Fedn. Greater New Orleans, 1969; past chmn. lawyers div. United Fund. 1st lt. U.S. Army, 1944-46, PTO. Mem. ABA, La. Bar Assn., New Orleans Bar Assn., Am. Coll. Real Estate Attys., Anglo Am. Real Property Inst., So. Golf Assn. (past bd. dirs.), New Orleans Golf Assn. (past pres., past bd. dirs.), Tulane Green Wave Club (past bd. dirs.), Lakewood Country Club (past pres., bd. dirs.). Republican. Avocation: golf. Home: 410 Northline Metairie LA 70005-4452 Office: Sullivan Stolier & Resor 909 Poydras St Ste 2600 New Orleans LA 70112-4022 E-mail: attorney@ssrlawfirm.com.

ROSEN, CHARLES ABRAHAM, electrical engineer, consultant; b. Toronto, Ont., Can., Dec. 7, 1917; came to U.S., 1950; s. Morris and Ida (Muscet) R.; m. Blanche Jacobson, May 15, 1941; children: Hal, Steven, Naomi, Sema. BEE, Cooper Union, 1940; M in Engring., McGill U., 1950; PhD, Syracuse U., 1957. Founder, CEO Electrolabs Registered, Montreal, Can., 1946-50; semiconductor designer GE, Syracuse, N.Y., 1950-52, mgr. dielectrics group, 1952-57; mgr. applied physics SRI Internat., Menlo Park, Calif., 1957-62, dir. artificial intelligence, 1962-78; founder, chmn. Machine Intelligence Corp., Sunnyvale, 1980-85; co-founder, dir. Ridge Vineyards, Cupertino, 1962-87; CEO Cultured Foods Corp., San Francisco, 1988-92, also bd. dirs.; pvt. practice cons. Atherton, Calif., 1988—. Cons. Ricoh Rsch., Menlo Park, 1989-2001, Food Machinery, Sunnyvale, 1989-2001; adv. com. Nat. Rsch. Coun., Washington, 1990-92; dir. Techniquip Corp., Livermore, Calif., 1995—, Electric Mobility Sys., Los Altos, Calif., 1996-2000. Co-author Principles of Transistor Circuits, 1953, Solid State Dielectric Design, 1959; contbr. articles to profl. jours.; patentee in field. P.O. Air Force, Can., 1944-45. Recipient Engelberger award Robot Inst. Am., 1982. Fellow IEEE (Taylor award 1975), Am. Assn. Artificial Intelligence; mem. AAAS, Am. Physical Soc. Avocations: winemaking, horticulture, hydroponics, inventions. Home: 139 Tuscaloosa Ave Atherton CA 94027-4016 E-mail: rosenca@attglobal.net.

ROSEN, CHARLES BURKE, surgeon; b. Bismarck, N.D., May 28, 1959; MD, Mayo Med. Sch., 1984. Diplomate Am. Bd. Surgery. Resident in gen. surgery Mayo Grad. Sch. Medicine, Rochester, Minn., 1984-89, fellow in transplant surgery, 1989-91; mem. staff, assoc. prof. surgery U. Fla. Coll. Medicine, Gainesville; surgical dir., liver transplantation Mayo Clinic, Rochester, MN. Mem. AMA, Assn. Acad. Surgery, Am. Soc. Transplant Surgeons, Southwestern Surg. Congress. Office: Mayo Clinic 200 1st St SW Rochester MN 55905-0002

ROSEN, CLIFFORD JAMES, internist; b. Utica, N.Y., Feb. 18, 1950; s. Harry N. and Harriett P. (Rubin) R.; m. Donna Peckham, June 17, 1973; (div. Dec. 1983); 1 child, Aaron; m. Rebecca Harless, Aug. 7, 1986; 1 child, Isaac. BS, U. Maine, 1971; MD, SUNY, Syracuse, 1975. Diplomate Nat. Bd. Med. Examiners, Am. Bd. Internal Medicine. Chief resident in medicine U. Mass./Berkshire Med. Ctr., Pittsfield, 1978-79, instr. medicine, 1978-79; fellow in endocrinology Dartmouth Hitchcock Med. Ctr., Hanover, N.H., 1982-84; cooperating prof. nutrition U. Maine, Orono, 1986-88, rsch. asst. prof., 1988-91, rsch. assoc. prof., 1991-94; clin. assoc. prof. Tufts U. Sch. Medicine, Boston, 1991-94, Boston U. Sch. Medicine, 1993—; rsch. prof. U. Maine, 1995—, prof. nutrition, 1999—. Adv. bd. Inst. Cellular Rsch., Bangor, 1991-93; exec. dir. Maine Ctr. for Osteoporosis Rsch.; chief medicine St. Joseph Hosp., Bangor, 1989-99. Editor-in-chief Jour. Clin. Densitometry, 1998—; editor Osteoporosis in Clin. Medicine, 1995—; contbr. chpts. to books, articles to profl. jours. Founder Physicians for Nat. Health Plan, Maine, 1991; com. person Am. Health Reform Com., Washington, 1993. Recipient Katherine Musgrave award Maine Nutrition Coun., Augusta, 1994, Excellence in Aging Rsch. award Glenn Found., 1996. Mem. Am. Fedn. Clin. Rsch., Soc. of Insulin Growth Factor Rschrs., Endocrine Soc., Am. Soc. Bone and Mineral Rsch. (bd. dirs. adult bone and mineral working group 1993—, pub. affairs com. 1994—, pres.-elect, pres.), Soc. Clin. Densitometry (founding mem.). Democrat. Jewish. Avocations: running, gardening. Home: 16 Mckinley St Bangor ME 04401-3830 Office: St Joseph Hosp Maine Ctr Osteoporosis Rsch Bangor ME 04402 E-mail: rofe@aol.com.

ROSEN, DAVID MICHAEL, public relations administrator, public affairs consultant; b. Cambridge, Mass., Mar. 26, 1945; s. Maynard S. and Irma (Leavitt) R.; m. Nina J. Glick, Apr. 8, 1967; children: Michelle, Elisabeth. BA, Boston U., 1967, MS, 1977. Reporter The Day, New London, Conn., 1968-69, Boston Herald, 1969-73; polit. writer UPI, Boston, 1973-76, State House bur. chief, 1976-77; polit. commentator WGBH-TV, 1975-77; pub. affairs cons., 1977-79; pub. info. dir. U.S. Commodity Futures Trading Commn., Washington, 1979-80; dir. pub. rels. Harvard U., Cambridge, Mass., 1980-84, assoc. v.p., 1984-85, U. Chgo., 1986-88; v.p. Nicolazzo Assocs., Boston, 1988; chief of staff Office of Lt. Gov., 1988-89; v.p. Brandeis U., Waltham, Mass., 1989-93; cons. David Rosen Assocs., Boston, 1993; dir. pub. rels. Yeshiva U., N.Y.C., 1993-99; assoc. v.p. pub. affairs Emerson Coll., Boston, 2000—. Cons. U.S. GAO, Washington, 1977-79, Mass. Ins. Divsn., Boston, 1977-78, Harvard U., 1977-80, Radcliffe Coll., 1993, New Eng. Bd. Higher Edn., 1993, Clark U., 1993, Pilgrim Health Care, 1993; substitute tchr. Boston Pub. Schs., 1967-68. Author: Protest Songs in America, 1977. Avocations: piano, running. Home: 157 Bishops Forest Dr Waltham MA 02452-8800 Office: Emerson Coll Pub Affairs 120 Boylston St Boston MA 02116-4624 E-mail: david_rosen@attbi.com., david_rosen@emerson.edu.

ROSEN, DIANE, artist; b. N.Y.C. m. Peter Voletsky, May 5, 1988; 1 child, Emily Blanche. BA cum laude, Goucher Coll., 1970; postgrad., Columbia U., 1975-76, Art Students League, N.Y.C., 1976-79, NAD, 1979-80. Co-owner, creative dir. Inkwell Graphics, N.Y.C., 1975-79; instr. studio art Birch Wathen Sch., 1976-80; freelance illustrator, 1980-84; instr. figure drawing Parsons Sch. Design, 1983-85; v.p., creative dir. Wilcox & Assocs., 1985-89; owner, mgr., prin. artist Diane Rosen Studio, 1990—. Guest lectr. creativity NYU, N.Y.C., 1985; art dir. film prodn. co. FIT, N.Y.C., 1992. Murals executed in London, 1991, N.Y.C., 1993, Washington, 1994, San Antonio, 1996; exhibited works in shows at Bard Coll., Annandale on Hudson, N.Y., 1979, Bond Gallery, N.Y.C., 1987, Two Visions Gallery, Washingtonville, N.Y., 1994, Walter Wickiser Gallery, N.Y.C., 1995, Mark Gruber Gallery, New Paltz, N.Y., 1996—; S.E. Feinman Gallery, N.Y.C., 1998-99, Wyckoff Gallery, 1999-2001, Butler Inst. Am. Art, Youngstown, Ohio, 2002; represented in permanent collection of Pastel Soc. Am. Designer promotional lit. N.Y.C. Mayor's Voluntary Action Coun., 1974; children's art vol. Mt. Sinai Hosp., N.Y.C., 1976; art and design vol. Jewish Assoc. Svcs. for Aged, N.Y.C., 1989-91; logo design vol. Negro Ensemble Co., N.Y.C., 1990; mem. adv. bd. Orange County Arts Coun. Recipient President's award Pastel Soc. West Coast, 1992, Pen and Brush award Pen and Brush Club, N.Y.C., 1993, A & A Giffuni Purchase award Pastel Soc. Am., 1995; French Govt. fellow Inst. Internat. Edn., 1981. Mem. Pastel Soc. Am. (bd. dirs.), Salamagundi Club, Allied Artists Am. (assoc.), Am. Artists Profl. League, Hudson Valley Pastel Soc. Avocations: photography, writing, hiking, biking.

ROSEN, EDEN RUTH, promoter, public advocate, merchandiser, consultant, writer; b. Chgo., Sept. 25, 1951; d. David and Mary Naomi (Katz) R. BA in Psychology with honors, Northeastern Ill. U., 1972. With customer advt. dept. Capitol Records, Los Angeles, 1980-82, 83-85; promoter The André Martel Show, Burbank, Calif., 1982-86; merchandiser P. J. Clark, 1985; coordinator A. J. Masters Fan Club, 1986-88; sec. TV and music adminstrn. L.A., 1986-87; co-founder ERPP Enterprises, Burbank, 1986-89. Libr. met. Youth Symphony Orch., Chgo., 1966—68; part-time pub. rels. asst. to Patti Maturkanic, 1989—90; promotions coord. Internat. Promotions, 1990—93; cmty. svcs. facilitator Vascular Dementia, 1997—2001; exec. dir. ERBS, 1993—98; mem. CAL-OSHA Workplace Security Adv. Com.; city chpt. head Lettermen Fan Club, San Fernando Valley, 1978—84; sprk. in field. Author: Do Managers Really Know How to Manage?/How to Lose or Keep a Good Hardworking Employee, 2000, A Daughter's Lament: The Trials & Tribulations of a Family Caregiver, 2001; founder Conversations with Psychologists; author Opportunity World Mag., L.A. Jobs Mag., Apt. Age Mag., 2000; contbr. to Directory of Psychology Employment, 1970-73. Freshman orientation leader, 1972. Recipient Leadership award, 1972, Svc. award, 1972, Go-Getter award Acad. Country Music Christmas Party Com., 1991. Mem. Modern Music Masters (life), Psi Chi (pres., v.p. 1970-73). E-mail: RosenEden@hotmail.com.

ROSEN, ELIZABETH, library executive; b. Mount Vernon, N.Y., May 25, 1937; d. Edward Patrick and Deborah (Borgenicht) Flynn; m. Robert C. Maynard, 1957 (div. 1963); 1 child, Dori J.; m. Bernard Rosen, July 17, 1963; 1 child, Sara-Ann. BA, St. Francis Coll., 1986; postgrad., L.I. U., 1988-90. Staff acct. The Ford Found., N.Y.C., 1986-87, supr./accounts payable, 1987-90; contr. The Morgan Libr., 1990-94, CFO, 1994-98, CFO, sys. officer, 1998-2000, cons., 2000—. Mem. N.Y. State Soc. of CPAs. E-mail: lizrosen@aol.com.

ROSEN, ELLEN FREDA, psychologist, educator; b. Chgo., Jan. 28, 1941; d. Samuel Aaron and Clara Laura (Pauker) R. BA, Carleton Coll., 1962; MA, U. Ill., 1965, PhD, 1968. Instr. psychology U. Ill., Urbana, 1966-67; prof. Coll. William and Mary, Williamsburg, Va., 1967-99; adean grad. studies and dir. Ctr. for Urban Mental Health Rsch. Chgo. State U., 1999—. Cons. Ctr. for Teaching Excellence Hampton (Va.) U., 1988-94; sr. rsch. scientist Behavioral Rsch. Ctr., Hampton U., 1997-99. Author: Ednl. Computer Software, (with E. Rae Harcum) The Gatekeepers of Psychology, 1993; contbr. articles to profl. jours. Mem. Soc. for Computers in Psychology, Psychonomic Soc., Ea. Psychol. Assn., Am. Psychol. Soc. Office: Office Grad Studies LIB 338 Chgo State Univ Chicago IL 60628 E-mail: EF-Rosen@csu.edu.

ROSEN, FRED, travel company executive; b. Windsor, Ont., Can., May 19, 1926; arrived in U.S., 1946; s. Harry and Dora Rosen; m. Gertrude Rush, May 13, 1952; 1 child Robert Martin. Cert. Elec. Tech., Washington U., St. Louis, 1964; AA in Tourism, Forest Park C.C., St. Louis, 1993; Cert. Microcomputers, Meramec C.C., St. Louis, 2000. X-ray maint. staff Keleket X-Ray, Covington, Ky., 1953—54; whse. mgr. Western Shoe Jobbers, St. Louis, 1954—64, prodn. supr., 1977—92; owner Vanity Shoes, Kirkwood, 1964—77, Accessible Travel, St. Louis, 1997—. Contbg. editor: the Independence, 1997—98; author: (guidebook) How to Travel - A Guidebook for Persons with a Disability, 1997, How to Travel in Canada - A Guidebook for a Visitor with a Disability, 2000. Commr. Kirkwood Disabled Commn., 1984—91, Kirkwood Housing Authority, 1977—83, Kirkwood Human Rights, 1974—77. Sgt. 1st class U.S. Army, 1946—53, ETO. Mem.: Masons (worshipful master 1990—91, Achievement award 1991). Jewish. Avocations: dancing, cruising. Home: 144 Oakside Ln Saint Louis MO 63122-1211

ROSEN, GEORGE, economist, educator; b. St. Petersburg, Russia, Feb. 7, 1920; s. Leon and Rebecca (Rosenoer) R.; m. Sylvia Vatuk; 1 son, Mark. BA, Bklyn. Coll., 1940; MA, Princeton U., 1942, PhD, 1949. Prof. econs. Bard Coll., Annandale-on-Hudson, N.Y., 1946-50; economist Dept. State, Washington, 1951-54, Council Econ. Indsl. Research, Washington, 1954-55, MIT, CENIS, Cambridge, 1955-59, UN, N.Y.C., 1959-60, Ford Found., N.Y.C., Nepal and India, 1960-62, Rand Corp., Santa Monica, Calif., 1962-67; chief economist Asian Devel. Bank, Manila, Philippines, 1967-71; prof. econs. U. Ill.-Chgo., 1972-85, prof. econs. emeritus, 1985—, head dept., 1972-77; fellow Woodrow Wilson Internat. Ctr., Washington, 1989-90. Adj. prof. Johns Hopkins U.-Nanjing U. Ctr. Chinese-Am. Studies, 1986-87; cons. USAID, Egypt, 1994; book rev. editor Econ. Devel. and Cultural Change, 1988-2001; treas. Am. Com. for Asian Econ. Studies, 1990-95; Golden Jubilee spkr. Dept. Commerce Osmania U., Hyderabad, India, 1999; disting. spkr. Ctr. for Advanced Study of Internat. Devel., Mich. State U., East Lansing, 1999. Author: Industrial Change in India, 1958, Some Aspects of Industrial Finance in India, 1962, Democracy and Economic Change in India, 1966, 67, Peasant Society in a Changing Economy, 1975, Decision-Making Chicago-Style, 1980, Western Economists and Eastern Societies, 1985, Industrial Change in India 1970-2000, 1988, Contrasting Styles of Industrial Reform: China and India in the 1980s, 1992, Economic Development in Asia, 1996; contbr. The India Handbook, 1997. Ford Found. fellow NYU, 1971-72; grantee U. Ill., 1977-78, Social Sci. Research Council and Am. Inst. Indian Studies, 1980-81, Am. Inst. Indian Studies, 1983-84, 87-88, Rockefeller Found. Bellagio Study Ctr., 1984. Office: U Ill Dept Econs M/C 144 601 S Morgan St Chicago IL 60607-7121

ROSEN, GERALD ELLIS, federal judge; b. Chandler, Ariz., Oct. 26, 1951; s. Stanley Rosen and Marjorie (Sherman) Cahn; m. Laurie DeMond; 1 child, Jacob DeMond. BA, Kalamazoo Coll., 1973; JD, George Washington U., 1979. Researchist Swedish Inst., Stockholm, 1973; legis. asst. U.S. Senator Robert P. Griffin, Washington, 1974-79; law clk. Seyfarth, Shaw, Fairweather & Gerardson, Wash., 1979; from assoc. to sr. ptnr. Miller, Canfield, Paddock and Stone, Detroit, 1979-90; judge U.S. Dist Ct. (ea. dist.) Mich., 1990—. Mem. Jud. Evaluation Com. (co-chmn. 1983-88), Detroit; adj. prof. law Wayne State U., 1992—, U. Detroit Law Sch., 1994—; mem. U.S. Jud. Conf. Com. on Criminal Law; lectr. CLE confs., others. Co-author: Federal Civil Trials and Evidence, 1999, Michigan Civil Trials and Evidence, 2001; contbr. articles to profl. jours. Rep. candidate for U.S. Congress, Mich., 1982; chmn. 17th Congl. Dist. Rep. Com., 1983-85; mem. Mich. Criminal Justice Commn., 1985-87; mem. Birmingham Athletic Club; bd. visitors George Washington U. Law Sch., 2000—; bd. dirs. Focus Hope, 2000—. Fellow Kalamazoo Coll. (sr. 1972); recipient Career Achievement award Rolex/Intercollegiate Tennis Assn. Mem. Fed. Judges Assn. (bd. dirs.). Jewish. Office: US Courthouse 231 W Lafayette Blvd Rm 802 Detroit MI 48226-2707

ROSEN, GERALD HARRIS, physicist, consultant, educator; b. Mount Vernon, N.Y., Aug. 10, 1933; s. David A. and Shirley (Schapiro) R.; m. Sarah Louise Sweet, June 8, 1963; children: Lawrence A., Karlyn Rosen Aires. BSE. (Guggenheim Jet Propulsion scholar, Whiton Engring.-Physics scholar), Princeton U., 1955, MA (NSF predoctoral fellow), 1956, PhD, 1958. NSF predoctoral fellow Inst. Theoretical Physics, Utrecht, Netherlands, 1957-58; research asso. dept. aero. engring. Princeton, 1958-59; NSF postdoctoral fellow Inst. Theoretical Physics, Stockholm, 1959-60; tech. cons. weapon systems evaluation div. The Pentagon, 1960; prin. scientist Martin-Marietta Aerospace div., Balt., 1960-63; cons. to a tech. v.p. Southwest Research Inst., 1963-66; prof. physics Drexel U., Phila., 1966-73, M.R. Wehr prof. physics, 1973-98, prof. emeritus, 1998—. Cons. fin., indsl. and govt. agys., 1966—. Author: Formulations of Classical and Quantum Dynamical Theory, 1969, A New Science of Stock Market Investing, 1990; assoc. editor Bull. Math. Biology, 1982—; contbr. revs., articles to Math. Revs., Am. Phys. Soc., other profl. jours.; patentee in field. Sponsor San Antonio Chamber Music Soc., 1963-66; mem. Franklin Inst., 1967— ; mem. publ. bd. Soc. Math. Biol., 1983— . Fellow Am. Phys. Soc., AAAS; mem. Am. Math. Soc. Home: 415 Charles Ln Wynnewood PA 19096-1604 Office: Drexel U Dept Physics Philadelphia PA 19104 *The meaning of life has transcended human understanding up to the present time, but there are reasons to believe that future discoveries in science will illuminate the significance of life in nature. We must break completely free of non-rational dogma and illusion, and attempt to solve this mystery with factual clues revealed by scientific progress.*

ROSEN, GERALD ROBERT, editor; b. N.Y.C., Nov. 17, 1930; s. Sol and Essie (Shapiro) R.; m. Lois Lehrman, May 9, 1958; 1 son, Evan Mark. BS, Ind. U., 1951, MA, 1953. Intelligence analyst Dept. Def., N.Y.C., 1955-58; assoc. editor Challenge: The Mag. of Econ. Affairs, 1959-61, mng. editor, 1961-64, 65-66; sr. editor Dun's Rev., N.Y.C., 1964-65, nat. affairs editor, 1967—; exec. editor Dun's Rev. (now Bus. Month), 1978-90; editor IMF survey Washington, 1990-93; mng. dir. Global Insights Svcs., 1993—. Fin. corr. Westinghouse Broadcasting Co. Served with CIC U.S. Army, 1953-55. Mem. Soc. Am. Bus. and Econ. Writers, N.Y. Fin. Writers Assn., White House Corrs. Assn. Clubs: Nat. Press. Home: 3210 Grace St NW Washington DC 20007-3628

ROSEN, JAMES MAHLON, artist, art historian, educator; b. Detroit, Dec. 3, 1933; s. Joseph and Lillian Rosen; children: Phyllis Dresser, Shira Del, Jeremy-Joseph. Student, Cooper Union, 1956; BS, Wayne State U., 1957; MFA, Cranbrook Acad. Art, 1958. Mem. faculty dept. art Wayne State U., 1961-63, U. Hawaii, 1965-67; mem. faculty Santa Rosa (Calif.) Jr. Coll., 1967-84, U. Calif., 1987-88; Wm. Morris Eminent scholar in art Augusta Coll., 1989-96; prof., dir. Meyer Schapiro Program, 1996-00. Artist-in-residence, guest lectr. Deep Springs Coll., R.I. Sch. Design, Montclair State Coll., San Bernardino State Coll., Pa. Acad. Fine Arts; artist-in-residence Ferrara, Italy, artist-critic Vermont Studio Sch., 1988, 1992, 2001. Author: Notes From a Painter's Journal, 1960, An American Homage to Piero della Francesca, In the Realm of Light, William Bartram Sketches: The Field and the Image, Qualities of Camouflaging, 1970, On the Sheer Nonsense of Liking Anything, 1979, Imagination as an Event of the Physical World; exhbns. include Betty Parsons Gallery, N.Y.C., Donald Morris Gallery, Detroit, Gallery Paule Anglim, San Francisco, Mus. Modern Art Penthouse Show, Eva Gelfman Gallery, Baux-Xi Gallery, Toronto, La Jolla Mus. Contemporary Art; dir., curator William Bartram Art Exhbn.; represented in permanent collections in Mus. Modern Art, N.Y.C., Whitney Mus. Am. Art, Ga. Mus. Art, Syracuse U., Ashmolean Mus., U. Calif. Berkeley Mus., San Francisco Mus. Modern Art, Met. Mus. of Art, Cranbrook Mus. Art, Victoria and Albert Mus., London Denver Art Mus.; bd. dirs. Arts Meridian-A Cultural Jour. Ams.; commissions include Ascott Residencies, London, Occidental Grand Hotel, Atlanta, Fairmont Hotel, Chgo. Dir., co-founder Cape Pine Found. for the Arts, 2000; commr. Procurement of Art in Nfld., Can., 2000; bd. dirs. Ian Olson Environ. Peace Garden, Trepassey, Nfld., Can. Served with M.C., U.S. Army, 1953-55. Grantee Huntington Hartford Found., Yaddo, MacDowell Found., NEH, Djerassi Found. Arts, Ga. Coun. on Arts, James and Angela Baird Found., Nfld., Can. Mem. Am. Soc. Art, Religion and Culture (bd. dirs.), Soc. So. Painters (pres.), Soc. of Art, Religion and Contemporary Culture (bd. dirs.), Phi Kappa Phi (SE region 1997, Painter of the Yr. 1997, Louis K. Bell rsch. award 1999). Home: 2533 Tupelo Dr Augusta GA 30909 E-mail: jrosen@nf.sympatico.ca.

ROSEN, JAYNE HALPERN, interior designer; b. N.Y.C., Nov. 10, 1944; d. Max J. and Rosalind Halpern; m. Paul I. Rosen, June 21, 1970. Dir. interior design mktg. Regenbogen Assocs., New Hope, Pa., 1988—. Mem.: Am. Soc. Interior Designers (allied mem.).

ROSEN, JON HOWARD, lawyer; b. Bklyn., May 20, 1943; s. Eli and Vera Horowitz Rosen; children: Jason Marc, Hope Terry. BA, Hobart Coll., 1965; JD, St. John's U., 1968; postgrad. in bus., CCNY, 1969—71. Bar: N.Y. 1969, Calif. 1975, Wash. 1977. Atty. FAA, N.Y.C., 1968-71; regional atty., contract adminstr. Air Line Pilots Assn., N.Y.C., Chgo., L.A., San Francisco, 1971-77; pvt. practice Seattle, 1977-80; ptnr. Frank and Rosen, 1981-98, Frank Rosen Freed Roberts LLP, Seattle, 1999—2002, The Rosen Law Firm, 2002—. Instr. labor studies Shoreline C.C., 1978-90. Trustee Temple DeHirsch Sinai, 1991-98, v.p., 1998-00, pres.-elect 2000-01, pres., 2001—; chair Ward Springs Pk. Steering Com. Fellow: Coll. Labor and Employment Lawyers; mem.: ABA (union co-chmn. com. on employee rights and responsibilities 1992—96, union co-chmn. regional programs subcom. 1998—2000, union co-chmn. nat. programs. subcom. 2000—, union co-chmn. ADR in labor and employment law com. 2002—, co-regional EEOC liaison), Wash. State Trial Lawyers Assn. (past chair employment law com.), Nat. Employment Lawyers Assn. (founding state chair, state steering com. 1990—95), King County Bar Assn. (past chmn. aviation and space law sect., past chmn. Pacific Coast Labor and Employment Law Conf., past chmn. labor law sect.). Office: Rosen Law Firm 705 2nd Ave Ste 1200 Seattle WA 98104-1729 E-mail: jhr@jonroselaw.com.

ROSEN, JOSHUA NATHAN, lawyer; b. Chicago Heights, Ill., Aug. 9, 1966; s. Stanley and Margit (Kir-Stimon) R.; m. Wen-Ying Rosen. BA, U. Ill., 1988; JD, So. Ill. U., 1993. Bar: Ill. 1993, U.S. Dist. Ct. (so. dist.) Ill. 1994. Assoc. Craig & Craig, Mt. Vernon, Ill., 1994—. Mem. ABA, Ill. State Bar Assn., So. Ill. Am. Inn of Ct. (barrister). Office: Law Offices of Larry Kloenhamer 2 Rincon Ctr 121 Spear St Ste 410 San Francisco CA 94105

ROSEN, JUDAH BEN, computer scientist; b. Phila., May 5, 1922; s. Benjamin and Susan (Hurwich) R.; children— Susan Beth, Lynn Ruth. BSEE, Johns Hopkins U., 1943; PhD in Applied Math., Columbia U., 1952. Rsch. assoc. Princeton (N.J.) U., 1952-54; head applied math. dept. Shell Devel. Co., 1954-62; vis. prof. computer sci. dept. Stanford (Calif.) U., 1962-64; prof. dept. computer sci. and math. rsch. ctr. U. Wis., Madison, 1964-71; prof., head dept. computer sci. U. Minn., Mpls., 1971-92, fellow Supercomputer Inst., 1985—; sr. fellow Supercomputer Ctr., San Diego, 1993—; adj. rsch. prof. dept. computer sci. and engrin. U. Calif. San Diego, La Jolla, 1992—, bioinformatics grad. program faculty, 2001—. Fulbright prof. Technion, Israel, 1968-69, Davis vis. prof. 1980; invited lectr. Chinese Acad. Sci., Peking, 1980, Guilin, 1996, Samos, Greece, 2000; lectr., cons. Argonne (Ill.) Nat. Lab.; mem. Nat. Computer Sci. Bd. Author: Topics in Parallel Computing, 1992; editor: Nonlinear Programming, 1970, Supercomputers and Large-Scale Optimization, 1988; assoc. editor Global Optimization, 1990—, Annals of Ops. Rsch., 1984—; contbr. articles to profl. jours. and procs. Grantee NSF, 1995—, ARPA/NIST, 1994-97. Mem. Assn. Computing Machinery, Soc. Indsl. and Applied Math., Math. Programming Soc., European Acad. Scis. Achievements include research in supercomputers and parallel algorithms for optimization, computation of molecular structure and drug design by energy minimization and homology models, algorithms for structured approximation in signal processing. Home: 4771 Caminito Impersado San Diego CA 92130-2470 Office: U Calif San Diego Dept Computer Sci Engring 9500 Gilman Dr La Jolla CA 92093-0114 E-mail: jbrosen@cs.ucsd.edu.

ROSEN, KAREN, interior designer; b. N.Y.C., Jan. 14, 1946; d. Leon D. and Beatrice (Willett) Miller; 1 child, Meredith Lauren. Student, Boston U., 1964-66; BS in Elem. Edn., NYU, 1968; cert., N.Y. Sch. Interior Design, 1971. Pres. KMR Design Group, Inc., N.Y.C., 1974—. Color cons. to various mfrs. in design field; interior design work ranges from residential to pub. and comml.; designer custom furnishings; guest lectr. various coll. and real estate seminars; numerous radio and TV appearances; work featured in several major design mags. and newspapers. Recipient S.M. Hexter award for best residential interior, 1981. Mem. Internat. Interior Design Assn. Office: KMR Design Group Inc 80 E End Ave Apt 6E New York NY 10028-8015 E-mail: krmdesigngroup@aol.com.

ROSEN, LAWRENCE, anthropology educator; b. Cin., Dec. 9, 1941; s. George and Hannah (Persky) R. BA, Brandeis U., 1963; MA, U. Chgo., 1965, PhD, 1968, JD, 1974. Bar: N.C. 1975, U.S. Supreme Ct. 1979. Asst. prof. anthropology U. Ill., Urbana, 1968-70; mem. Inst. for Advanced Study, Princeton, N.J., 1970-71; assoc. prof. anthropology Duke U., Durham, N.C., 1974-77; prof. anthropology Princeton U., N.J., 1977—; Wm. Nelson Cromwell Prof., 2002. Adj. prof. Columbia U. Law Sch., 1979—; vis. prof. Northwestern U. Law Sch., Chgo., 1985-87, U. Pa. Law Sch., Phila., 1985-86, Georgetown Law Ctr., 1994; Lewis H. Morgan lectr. U. Rochester, 1985; vis. fellow Wolfson Coll. Oxford U., 1986, 2002-04, Corpus Christi Coll. Cambridge U., 1998-99. Co-author: Meaning and Order in Moroccan Society, 1978; author: Bargaining for Reality, 1984, The Anthropology of Justice, 1989, The Justice of Islam, 2000; editor: The American Indian and the Law, 1974, Other Intentions, 1995, The Culture of Islam, 2002. Legal asst. Native Am. Rights Fund, Boulder, Colo., 1973 Woodrow Wilson fellow, 1964, Guggenheim fellow, 1981, John & Catherine MacArthur Found. award, 1981, Fulbright fellow, 1991; vis. scholar Phi Beta Kappa, 1997. Fellow Am. Anthrop. Assn. E-mail: lrosen@princeton.edu.

ROSEN, LOUIS, physicist; b. N.Y.C., June 10, 1918; s. Jacob and Rose (Lipionski) R.; m. Mary Terry, Sept. 4, 1941; 1 son, Terry Leon. BA, U. Ala., 1939, MS, 1941; PhD, Pa. State U., 1944; DSc (hon.), U. N.Mex., 1979, U. Colo., 1987. Instr. physics U. Ala., 1940-41, Pa. State U., 1943-44; mem. staff Los Alamos Sci. Lab., 1944-90, group leader nuclear plate lab., 1949-65, alt. div. leader exptl. physics div., 1962-65, dir. meson physics facility, 1965-85, div. leader medium energy physics div., 1965-86, sr. lab. fellow, 1985-90, sr. fellow emeritus, 1990—; Sesquicentennial hon. prof. U. Ala., 1981. Mem. panel on future of nuclear sci., chmn. subpanel on accelerators NRC of NAS, 1976, mem. panel on instnl. arrangements for orbiting space telescope, 1976; mem. U.S.A.-USSR Coordinating Com. on Fundamental Properties of Matter, 1971-90. Author papers in nuclear sci. and applications of particle accelerators.; bd. editors: Applications of Nuclear Physics; co-editor Climate Change and Energy Policy, 1992. Mem. Los Alamos Town Planning Bd., 1962-64; mem. Gov.'s Com. on Excellence in N.Mex.; mem. N.Mex. Cancer Control Bd., 1976-80, v.p., 1979-81; co-chmn. Los Alamos Vols. for Stevenson, 1956; Dem. candidate for county commr., 1962; bd. dirs. Los Alamos Med. Ctr., 1977-83, chmn., 1983; bd. govs. Tel Aviv U., 1986. Recipient E.O. Lawrence award AEC, 1963, Golden Plate award Am. Acad. Achievement, 1964, N.Mex. Disting. Pub. Svc. award, 1978; named Citizen of Yr., N.Mex. Realtors Assn., 1973; Guggenheim fellow, 1959-60; alumni fellow Pa. State U., 1978; Louis Rosen prize established in his honor by bd. dirs. Meson

Facility Users Group, 1984; Louis Rosen Auditorium dedicated, 1995. Fellow AAAS (coun. 1989), Am. Phys. Soc. (coun. 1975-78, chmn. panel on pub. affairs 1980, div. nuclear physics 1985, mem. subcom. on internat. sci. affairs 1988). Home: 1170 41st St Los Alamos NM 87544-1913 Office: Los Alamos Sci Lab PO Box 1663 Los Alamos NM 87544-0600 *I have come to believe that only after one has learned to manage and set worthy goals for himself should he attempt to do so for others.*

ROSEN, MARTIN JACK, lawyer; b. L.A., Sept. 9, 1931; s. Irving and Sylvia (Savad) R.; m. Joan D. Meyersieck, Oct. 22, 1954; children: Dirk Rosen, Marika. BA, UCLA, 1953; JD, U. Calif., Berkeley, 1956. Pvt. practice, Merced, Calif., 1960-62, San Francisco, 1962-82; mem. Silver, Rosen, Fischer & Stecher, P.C., 1964-79. Lectr. Haas Sch. Bus., U. Calif., Berkeley, 1998. Author: Oral Histor, 2000. Past pres. Trust for Pub. Land, 1979-97. With USAF, 1958-60. Fellow internat. legal studies U. Calif. Law Sch./Inst. Social Studies, The Hague, 1956-57; conservation fellow Yale Sch. Forestry, 1999. Fax: 415-4594816. E-mail: kentwilds1@cs.com.

ROSEN, MARVIN, psychiatrist, pediatrician, educator; b. N.Y.C., Mar. 25, 1942; s. Eli and dorothy (Baron) R.; m. J. Teresa Shelby (div. July 1988); m. Cheryn Lee Grant, Mar. 26, 1989; 1 child, Geoffrey Howard. BA in Psychology cum laude, Columbia U., 1963, MD, 1967. Diplomate Am. Bd. Pediat., Am. Bd. Psychiatry and Neurology, Am. Bd. Child and Adolescent Psychiatry. Intern in pediat. Bronx (N.Y.) Mcpl. Hosp. Ctr., 1967-68, resident in pediat., 1968-70; fellow in child devel. Oreg. Health Scis. U., Portland, 1972-73, resident in adult and child psychiatry, 1980-84, clin. asst. prof. psychiatry, 1984—; pvt. practice pediat., Kaiser Permanente, Portland and Vancouver, Wash., 1973-80; pvt. practice adult, adolescent and child psychiatry, Portland, 1984—; psychiatric cons. Multnomah County CAPcacre, 2000. Clin. asst. prof. family medicine and psychiatry Coll. Osteo. Medicine Pacific; acting med. dir. psychiat. svcs. S.W. Wash. Hosps., Vancouver, 1984-85, cons. Adolescent Drug and Alcohol Treatment Ctr., 1984-97; cons. Elahan Mental Health Ctr., Vancouver, 1985, 87-88, Rosemont Sch., Portland, 1984-98, Children's Home Soc., Vancouver, 1990-94, Project for Cmty. Recovery, Portland, 1991-98, Trillium Family Svcs., Portland, 1997-98, 2000-2001, Conquest Ctr., Portland, 1996-98; dir. adolescent svcs. CPC Cedar Hills Hosp., Portland, 1987-88; vocat. rehab. cons. State of Wash., 1984-93; med. dir., cons. Project STOP and Transition Projects, Portland, 1984-94; med. dir., cons. Mainstream Youth, 1984-95; cons. family practice residency tng. program Family Care Med. Clinic, Portland, 1995-97; med. dir., cons. Native Am. Rehab. Assn., Portland, 1989-97, Nanitch Sahallie Youth Residential Adolescent Treatment Program, Keizer, Oreg., 1994-98, Stay Clean, Portland, 1996-99; cons. presch. program Rock Creek Therapeutic Day Care Program, 1996-98; psychiat. cons. Skamania County Counseling Ctr., Stevenson, Wash., 1984-98; Oreg. med. reviewer Managed Health Network, 1997-99 ; med. dir. cmty. counseling program Cascadia Behavioral Healthcare, Inc. (formerly Network Behavioral Healthcare, Inc.), Portland, 1998-2000, 2001--med. dir. Intensive Outpatient Ease Mgmt. Svcs., 1998--; med. dir. adolescent and adult behavioral health svds. Woodland Park Hosp., Portland, 1998-99; presenter in field. Contbr. articles to med. jours., including Jour. Am. Acad. Child and Adolescent Psychiatry, Pediatrics, Ob.-Gyn. Cons. Cath. Cmty. Svcs., Vancouver, 1989-92, 97-98. Maj. M.C., U.S. Army, 1970-72. Mem. Am. Psychiat. Assn., Am. Acad. Child and Adolescent Psychiatry (Am. Indian child com. 1991-96, substance abuse com. 1996-98), Oreg. Psychiat. Assn. (child psychiat. com. 1990-92, chmn. child psychiatry com. 2000-01, program com. 1985-94, gang com. 1997-2000), Oreg. Coun. Child and Adolscent Psychiatry (exec. coun. 1990-92, program chmn. 1985-92, v.p. 1999-2000, pres. 2000-01, past pres. 2001—), Alpha Omega Alpha. Office: PMB 291 6663 SW Beaverton Hillsdale Hw Portland OR 97225-1403 E-mail: topmarv@aol.com.

ROSEN, MARVIN ABRAHAM, music educator; b. Englewood, N.J., May 9, 1953; s. Sidney J. and Clarice M. (Solomon) R.; m. Beata Regina Rzeszodko, Oct. 24, 1986. BA in Music Edn., Trenton State Coll., 1975; MusM in Musicology, Manhattan Sch. Music, 1977; EdM in Music Edn., Columbia U., 1983, EdD in Coll. Tchg., 1985. Piano instr. New Sch. for Music Study, Princeton, N.J., 1979-82; pvt. piano instr., 1983—. Pianist Radio Boston WGBH/WNYC/WBAI/NY/WFLN PH, 1993-95; pianist-recital Moniuszko Soc., Warsaw, Poland, 1997; piano soloist for recordings Fred the Cat, Vision of Starry Night; lecture-recital Karlowicz Music Sch., Katowice, Poland, 1997, The Phillips Collection, Washington, 1998; author composer information in booklets; lectr. in field. Host weekly radio program Classical Discoveries WPRB 103.3 FM, Princeton, 1997. Mem. Kappa Delta Pi (Columbia U. chpt.), Princeton Music Club (pres. 1997—). Avocations: classic CD collecting, expert on classical recordings, baseball fan, 50's and 60's pop music. Office: Princeton Univ Store 36 University Pl Princeton NJ 08540-5116

ROSEN, MATTHEW STEPHEN, botanist, consultant; b. N.Y.C., Oct. 7, 1943; s. Norman and Lucille (Cass) R.; m. Deborah Louise Mackay, June 16, 1974 (div. Feb. 1983); children: Gabriel Mackay, Rebecca Mackay; m. Kay Eloise Williams, July 11, 1987. MFSc, Yale U., 1972; BS, Cornell U., 1967. Instr. ornamental horticulture SUNY-Farmingdale, 1968-69; landscape designer Manhattan Gardener, N.Y.C., 1969-70; instr. ornamental horticulture McHenry County Coll., Crystal Lake, Ill., 1972-74; coord. agrl. studies, asst. prof. biology, chemistry Mercer County Community Coll., West Windsor, N.J., 1974-79; adminstr. Des Moines Botanical Ctr., 1979-96, horticulture divsn. mgr., 1996—. Consulting dir. West Mich. Horticultural Soc., 1993; judge Communities in Bloom, 2001, Am. in Bloom, 2002; cons. in field. Contbr. articles to profl. jours. Com. chmn. United Way Cen. Iowa, 1982, divsn. chmn. 1983-86, 88-89, 91, 2000, group chmn. 1987, chmn. arts adv. com. 1985-86, pres. 1986, bd. dirs. Arts and Recreation Council, 1985-86, com. chmn., 1992; mem. career vocat. com. Des Moines Indsl. Sch. Dist., 1986, co-chmn., 1987, mem. Ptnrs. for Progress com., 1988-90, mem. sci. monitoring program, 1991, 92; chmn. Two Rivers Festival, 1987-88; active Des Moines Sister City Program, Kofu, Japan, 1984, delegation, 1989, Naucalpan, Mexico, 1986, 87, Shijiazhuang, China, 1986, 90, 92, 95, 97; mem. edn. com. Am. Assn. Botanical Gardens & Arboretum, mem. membership com., mem. conservation com., bd. dirs., 1997—; judge Cmtys. in Bloom and Am. in Bloom, 2001. Mem. Am. Assn. Botanical Gardens and Arboreta (edn. com.), Greater Des Moines C. of C. (team leader 1984—, chmn. new mem. sales, chmn. 8 O'clock new, Pres. Cabinet award 1983, 84, 85, Achievement award C. of C. Fedn. 1986, mem. exec. com. 1995, 96, 97), East Des MoinesC. of C. (bd. dirs. 1992—, v.p., sec. 1993—, pres.-elect 1994, pres. 1995, 96, sister cities commn. 1994, china chair 1995, 96, 97—, treas. 1995, 96, 97—), Greater Des Moines Conv. and Visitors Bur. (chmn. new mem. sales com. 1988-89), Iowa Advt. Rev. Coun., Affiliate Pres.'s Coun. of Chambers (chair 1995, 97), bd. of dirs. DM Gen. Hosp., 1994-95, 96, 97, Bd. Coun. Internat. Trade, Latinos Unidos (bd. dirs. 1996, 97), Greater Des Moines C. of C. (bd. dirs. 1995—, mem. exec. com. 1995—), Rotary, Phi Kappa Phi, Pi Alpha Xi. Democrat. Jewish. Avocations: photography, reading, model trains, collecting old books, writing. Home: 1042 22nd St West Des Moines IA 50265-2219 Office: Des Moines Botanical Ctr 909 E River Dr Des Moines IA 50316-2854 E-mail: msrosen@ci.des-moines.ia.us.

ROSEN, MEYER ROBERT, chemical engineer; b. Bklyn., Mar. 9, 1943; s. Philip and Jeanne (Rosenzweig) R.; children: Carrie, David; m. Selma Schwartz Mirman. BS, Poly. Inst. Bklyn., 1964, MS, 1966. Diplomate, Am. Bd. Forensic Engring. and Tech., cert. forensic examiner, profl. chemist, profl. chem. engr.; fire explosion investigator Nat. Cert. Bd., Nat. Assn. Fire Investigators. Rsch. engr. Union Carbide Corp., Tonawanda, N.Y., 1966-73, project scientist, 1973-79, devel. scientist Tarrytown and Boundbrook, N.J., 1979-92; dir. chemistry and fire investigation Inter-City Testing and Cons. Corp., Mineola, NY, 1993—; pres. Interactive Cons. Inc., 1993—. Cons. Brookfield Engring. Labs., Stoughton, Mass., 1979-81; cons. to chem. industry; course dir. Ctr. for Profl. Advancement, East Brunswick, N.J., 1994; adj. prof. chemistry Westchester C.C., 1970-84; exec. advisor Am. Bd. Forensic Engring. and Tech.; spkr. in field. Co-author: Rheology Modifier Handbook: Practical Use & Application, 2000; contbr. articles to profl. jours. including Polymer Plast. Tech. Engr., Jour. Coatings Tech., Jour. Coll. Interface Sci., Am. Jour. Acupuncture, Union Carbide World Mag., DCI Mag.; journalist Chem. Market Reporter, Global Cosmetic Industry; author 2 books on Hyperacusis ear disorder. Fellow Am. Coll. Forensic Examiners, Royal Soc. Chemistry London (chartered chemist), Am. Inst. Chemists (dir., exec. bd. dirs.), Am. Coll. Forensic Examiners; mem. ASTM (mem. various subcoms.), Am. Inst. of Chem. Engrs., Am. Chem. Soc. (divsn. colloid and surface chemistry, mem. noise com.), Am. Indsl. Hygiene Assn. (cons. spl. interest group), Am. Soc. Safety Engrs. (v.p.), Assn. Cons. Chemists and Chem. Engrs., Am. Assn. Colorists and Textile Chemists, Am. Med. Writers Assn., Nat. Assn. Sci. Writers, Soc. de Chimie Industrielle (Am. sect.), Nat. Fire Protection Assn., Soc. Indsl. Chemistry (Am. sect.), Am. Assn. Acupuncture and Oriental Medicine, Acupuncture Soc. Pa., Nat. Dental Acupuncture Soc. (exec. bd.), Nat. Alliance of Acupuncture and Oriental Medicine (bd. cert. in pain mgmt.), Nat. Hearing Conservation Assn. Achievements include 21 patents for process for fire fighting foams, antifoams; flocculation of phosphatic slimes, high molecular weight water soluble polymers and flocculating method, process for producing polymer water-in-oil emulsion, process for agglomerating ore concentrate utilizing clay and dispersions of polymer binders or dry powder binders, removal of residual ethylene oxide from poly(ethylene oxide); development of treatment of previously incurable ear disorder, seminar leader in Reflex-Correspondence Training. Publications include Polyox R Water Soluble Resin Worldwide Technical Literature; Rheology of Non-Newtonian Fluids; Energy Medicine; Auriculotherapy; Korean Hand Therapy. Office: Interactive Cons Inc PO Box 66 East Norwich NY 11732-0066 Fax: 516-922-3830. E-mail: meyer-rosen@earthlink.

ROSEN, MICHAEL HOWARD, real estate executive; b. N.Y.C., May 22, 1943; s. Irving Edward and Lilyan Ruth (Ruttenberg) R.; children: Daniel Matthew, Lenise Gayle. AB, Tufts U., 1965. Lic. real estate broker, N.Y., Md. Exec. v.p., dir. Rosen Orgn., Inc., N.Y.C., 1971-75; v.p. apt. ops. Monumental Properties, Inc. & Monumental Properties Trust, Balt., 1975-79; exec. v.p. Town and Country Mgmt. Corp., 1979-93; exec. v.p., chief oper. officer Town & Country Trust, 1993—. Commr. Wellwood Little League Baseball and Pikesville Basketball, 1981-82, Blue Devil Umpire Assn., 1982—, Mason Dixon Umpire Assn., 1989-99, pres., 1998-99; commr. Chesapeake Basin Collegiate Umpire Assn., 1996—, pres., 2000—; commr. W.Va. Inercollegiate Athletic Conf., 1997—, Mason Dixon Colligiate Umpire Assn., 1990—, pres., 2000; divsn. chmn. maj. firms divsn. United Way of Ctrl. Md., 1983-86; chmn. ctrl. mid. team, 1987—; bd. dirs. Cystic Fibrosis Found., 1983-88, Essex C.C. Found., 1990-94, Waxter Ctr. Sr. Citizens Found., 1989-94, Nat. Multi Housing Coun., 1994—, Md. Multi Housing Assn., 1997—; chmn. Life Line Ministries, Md., 1988-92; bd. dirs. Bapt. Family & children's Svcs., 1999—. Mem. Nat. Apt. Assn., Greater Balt. Bd. Realtors. Office: Town & Country Trust 100 S Charles St Ste 1700 Baltimore MD 21201-2777

ROSEN, MOISHE, religious organization founder; b. Kansas City, Mo., Apr. 12, 1932; s. Ben and Rose (Baker) R.; m. Ceil Starr, Aug. 18, 1950; children: Lyn Rosen Bond, Ruth. Diploma, Northeastern Bible Coll., 1957; DD, Western Conservative Bapt. Sem., 1986. Ordained to ministry Bapt. Ch., 1957. Missionary Am. Bd. Missions to the Jews, N.Y.C., 1956, minister in charge Beth Sar Shalom Los Angeles, 1957-67, dir. recruiting and tng. N.Y.C., 1967-70; leader Jews for Jesus Movement, San Francisco, 1970-73, exec. dir., 1973-96, founder, 1973—. Speaker in field. Author: Saying of Chairman Moishe, 1972, Jews for Jesus, 1974, Share the New Life with a Jew, 1976, Christ in the Passover, 1977, Y'shua, The Jewish Way to Say Jesus, 1982, Overture to Armageddon, 1991, The Universe is Broken: Who on Earth Can Fix It?, 1991, Demystifying Personal Evangelism, 1992, Witnessing to Jews, 1998. Trustee Western Conservative Bapt. Sem., Portland, Oreg., 1979-85, 86-91, Bibl. Internat. Coun. on Bibl. Inerrancy, Oakland, Calif., 1979-89; bd. dirs. Christian Advs. Serving Evangelism, 1987-91. Named Hero of the Faith, Conservative Bapt. Assn. Am., 1997. Office: Jews for Jesus 90 Miraloma Dr San Francisco CA 94127-1641 E-mail: MityMo@aol.com.

ROSEN, MYOR, harpist, educator; b. N.Y.C., May 28, 1917; s. Caesar and Rose (Seidenberg) R.; m. Esther Rosen, May 25, 1941; children: Linda, David. Diploma, Juilliard Sch. Music, 1940. Faculty Juilliard Sch. Music, 1947-69. Prin. harpist, Mexico Symphony Orch., 1941-42, Indpls. Symphony Orch., 1941-42, Mpls. Symphony Orch., 1943-44, staff harpist, CBS, Columbia Records and free lanced, 1945-60, prin. harpist, N.Y. Philharm., 1960-87; Composer incidental music for; NBC series Arts and the Gods, 1946, CBS Camera Three, 1947, Solomon, The King, 1948. Served with U.S. Army, 1945. Mem. Am. Fedn. Musicians, Bohemians. E-mail: roymnesor@juno.com. *Having been the fortunate recipient of a 7-year scholarship through the New York Philharmonic Symphony Society and the Juilliard School of Music when I began my career as a harpist, I can think of no greater honor than my privilege in having been accepted as principal harpist with the same organization which trained me. I now bend my efforts to train future harpists to excel in like manner. In my opinion, the most important function of a teacher is to teach his students how to teach themselves; self-development.*

ROSEN, NATHANIEL KENT, cellist; b. Altadena, Calif., June 9, 1948; s. David Leon and Frances Jean (Kaufman) R.; m. Jennifer Langham, Aug. 27, 1976 (div. 1986); m. Margo Shohl, May 21, 1989; children: Samuel Gregory, Stella Rosalie. Student, Pasadena (Calif.) City Coll., 1965-67; Mus.B., U. So. Calif., 1971. Teaching asst. U. So. Calif., 1968-75, mem. faculty 7th ann. Gregor Piatigorsky Seminar Sch. Music, 1984; asst. prof. Calif. State U. at Northridge, 1970-76; mem. faculty Manhattan Sch. Music, N.Y.C., 1982-88, 94—; now mem. faculty U. Ill., Urbana, 1988-94. Prin. cellist, Los Angeles Chamber Orch., 1970-76, Pitts. Symphony, 1977-79, concert cellist worldwide; recordings include Orientale: Romantic Music for the Cello. Recipient 1st prize Naumburg Competition, 1977, 1st prize Moscow Tchaikovsky Competition, 1978; Ford Found. grantee, 1970-71; Rockefeller Found. grantee, 1973-74 Mem. Violoncello Soc. N.Y., Century Assn. N.Y. Office: John Gingrich Mgmt Inc PO Box 1515 New York NY 10023-9462 also: North Star Recordings 95 Hathaway St Providence RI 02907-3760

ROSEN, PAUL PETER, pathologist; b. Bklyn., Aug. 16, 1938; s. George and Beate (Caspari) R.; m. Mary Sue, Aug. 7, 1994; children: Susan Deborah, Jonathan Daniel. BS, Swarthmore Coll., 1960; MD, Columbia U., 1964. Asst. attending pathologist Meml. Hosp., N.Y.C., 1970-73; asst. prof. pathology Cornell U. Med. Sch., 1972-78; assoc. attending pathologist Meml. Hosp., 1973-78, attending pathologist, 1978-98; assoc. prof. pathology Cornell U. Med. Sch., 1978-84, prof. pathology, 1984—; assoc. mem. Sloan Kettering Inst., 1980-84, mem. tenure title, 1984-98, Meml. Sloan-Kettering Cancer Ctr., N.Y.C., 1984-98; sr. cons. pathologist Dickstein Cancer Treatment Ctr., White Plains, N.Y., 1998-99; attending pathologist, chief of breast pathology N.Y. Presbyn. Hosp., N.Y.C., 1999—. Adj. prof. pathology N.Y. Med. Coll., Valhalla, N.Y., 1996-99. Author: Rosen's Breast Pathology, 1996, 2d edit., 2001, Breast Pathology: Diagnosis by Needle Core Biopsy, 1999; co-author: Tumors of the Mammary Gland, 1993; co-editor Pathology Annual, 1977-95, Revs. Pathology, 1996-98; contbr. more than 280 articles on diseases of breast to profl. jours. Mem. Internat. Acad. Pathology, Am. Soc. Clin. Pathologists, Soc. Surg. Pathologists, N.Y. Acad. Medicine.

ROSEN, RAYMOND, health facility executive; b. Louisville, Feb. 5, 1950; s. Sam and Olga Rosen; m. Deborah Joy Rubinow, June 25, 1972; children: Lisa, Jessica. BS, Pa. State U., 1972; MA, George Washington U., 1974. Adminstrv. resident York (Pa.) Hosp., 1973-74, asst. to pres., 1974-75, asst. adminstr.-adminstrn., 1975-77, asst. adminstr.-med. affairs, 1977-79, adminstr.-med. affairs, 1979-87, v.p. opers., 1987—. Pres. Young Adminstrs. Group Ctrl. Pa., 1980-82, Rabbit Transit, Inc., 1992—, vice chmn., 1989-92, chmn., 1992—; bd. dirs. Fedn. South Ctrl. Pa. Emergency Health Svcs., 1978-92, mem. adv. com., 1992-93, York County Emergency Health Svcs. Coun., 1978-92, Jewish Cmty. Ctr., 1986-91; divsn. chmn. United Way York County, 1988, York County Transp. Auth., 1995—. Fellow Am. Coll. Healthcare Execs. (regent south ctrl. Pa. 1991-95), mem. Am. Hosp. Assn., Hosp. Assn. Pa. (planning com. 1992—). Office: York Hosp 1001 S George St York PA 17403-3676

ROSEN, RHODA, obstetrician, gynecologist; b. Trenton, N.J., Jan. 17, 1933; d. Max and Gussie (Thierman) R.; m. Seymour Kanter, Aug. 19, 1956; children: Cynthia, Gregg, Larry, Brad. BA, U. Pa., 1954, MD, 1958. Diplomate Am. Bd. Obstetrics and Gynecology. Intern Albert Einstein Phila. Med. Ctr., 1958-59, resident, 1959-62, assoc. staff gynecology exec. com.; clin. prof. ob-gyn. Temple U. Med. Sch.; attending physician Rolling Hill Hosp., Elkins Park; pvt. practice ob-gyn. Phila., 1962—. Chmn. gynpathology com. Albert Einstein Med. Ctr., Phila.; arbitrator N.Y. Stock Exch. Bd. dirs. Joseph J. Peters Inst.; docent Barnes Found., Merion, Pa. Fellow ACOG, ACS; mem. AMA, Nat. Assn. for Arbitrators for N.Y. Stock Exchange, Pa. Med. Soc., Phila. Colposcopy Soc. (past pres.), Ex-Residents Assn. (past pres. Albert Einstein Med. Ctr.), Philadelphia County Med. Soc. (com.), Phila. Bar Assn. (com.). Jewish. Avocations: tennis, biking, art, swimming, music. Home: 1420 Locust St Apt 35K Philadelphia PA 19102

ROSEN, RICHARD DAVID, lawyer; b. Pitts., June 24, 1940; s. Benjamin H. and Bertha B. (Broff) R.; m. Ellaine H. Heller, June 23, 1963; children: Deborah H. Fidel, Jaime M. Cohen. BA, Yale U., 1962; JD, Harvard U., 1965. Bar: Pa. 1966, Fla. 1979. Mgr. Bachrach, Sanderbeck & Co., Pitts., 1965-70; mng. ptnr. Grant Thornton, 1970-76; chmn. tax dept. Baskin & Sears, 1977-78; pres. Gas Transmission, Inc., 1979—2000; dir., shareholder Cohen & Grigsby, 1989—. Bd. dirs., sec. Comml. Data Svcs., Sim Computer Leasing Corp., Pitts., Direct Mail Svc., Inc. Contbr. articles to profl. jours. Trustee Jewish Healthcare Found., 1995—, chmn. investment com., 2001—. Fellow Am. Coll. Trust and Estate Counsel; mem. ABA, Pa. Bar Assn. (mem. estate planning com. 1996—, chmn. 1998-2000), United Jewish Fedn. Greater Pitts. (chmn. profl. adv. com. 1997—), Green Oaks Country Club (dir. 1997—). Avocations: golf, tennis. Home: 1198 Beechwood Ct Pittsburgh PA 15206-4522 Office: Cohen & Grigsby PC 11 Stanwix St 15 Fl Pittsburgh PA 15222-1312 E-mail: rrosen@cohenlaw.com.

ROSEN, RICHARD LEWIS, lawyer, real estate developer; b. N.Y.C., Mar. 6, 1943; s. Morris and Lorraine (Levy) R.; m. Doris Ellen Bloom, Aug. 28, 1983. BA, Cornell U., 1965; JD, N.Y. Law Sch., 1968; cert., NYU Real Estate Inst., 1980. Bar: N.Y. 1968, U.S. Dist. Ct. (so. and ea. dists.) N.Y. 1972; lic. real estate broker. Pvt. practice, N.Y.C., 1971-73; ptnr. Rosen, Wise, Felzen & Salomon, 1973-79, Rosen & Felzen, N.Y.C., 1979-84, Rosen, Rudd, Kera, Graubard & Hollender, N.Y.C., 1985-88, Bell, Kalnick, Klee and Green, N.Y.C., 1989-90; shareholder Rosen, Einbinder & Dunn, P.C., 1990—. Contbg. author: Francising 101, The Complete Guide to Evaluating, Buying and Growing Your Franchise Business. Named Ea. States Lightweight Weightlifting Champion, 1968; N.Y. State Regents scholar. Mem. ABA (mem. Forum Com. on Franchising), Am. Assn. Franchises and Dealers (former chmn. legal steering com., chmn. fair franchising stds. com., chmn. alternate dispute resolution com., bd. dirs.), Franchise Lawyers Assn., Am. Franchise Assn., N.Y. State Bar Assn. (founding mem. franchise law com., chmn. mission statement com. of franchise law com.), Nat. Franchise Mediation Program (mem. steering com.), Assn. Bar City N.Y. (panel mem. com. on franchising, panel mem. com. on corp. law), Red Key Hon. Soc., Cornell U., Sphinx Head Hon. Soc., Cornell U., Spiked Shoe Soc., Cornell U., Ea. Intercollegiate Athletic Assn. (named Lightweight Football All Ea. Selection 1963, 64). Avocations: tennis, skiing, physical fitness, guitar, reading. Home: 1 Old Jericho Tpke Jericho NY 11753-1205 also: Lamb Ave Quogue NY 11959 Office: Rosen Einbinder & Dunn PC 641 Lexington Ave New York NY 10022-4503 E-mail: RLR@redlawfirm.com.

ROSEN, ROBERT ARNOLD, management company executive, real estate investor; b. N.Y.C., June 19, 1936; s. Louis and Helen (Weiss) R.; m. Florence Cohen, Oct. 23, 1960; children: David S., Kenneth A., Mark A., Emily B. BBA, CUNY, 1957, MBA, 1960; postgrad. (Ford Found. scholar), NYU, 1961; grad., Indsl. Coll. Armed Forces, Air War Coll., 1960, U.S. Air Force U.; various courses, Naval Edn. and Tng. Command. Sales promotion mgr. Leipzig & Lippe, Inc., 1956-58; advt. and sales promotion mgr. Zenith Radio, 1957-62; chmn., pres., founder Am. Bus. Resources Corp., 1963-64; v.p., dir. Royal Bus. Funds Corp., 1964-68; chmn., CEO Rosen Assocs. Mgmt. Corp., Jericho, N.Y., 1983—. V.p. corp. finance div., dir. Brand Grumet & Siegel, Inc., 1969-70; pres. Brand Grumet & Siegel Equities, Inc., 1970; former pres., chief operating officer Bell TV, Inc., N.Y.C.; pres., former chmn. bd. Holmes Protection, Inc.; former chmn. bd., pres. Union Small Bus. Investment Co., 1968-77, Skyway-Laguardia Corp.; dir. past chmn. bd. Okuraya Davos Internat., Inc.; chmn. bd., pres., chief exec. officer, treas. Suburban Broadcasting Corp., 1970-80; chmn., pres. Affiliated Communications Corp.; vice chmn., pres. Communication Services Corp.; pres. Wescom Corp.; pres. Androse Corp., 1983—; cons. Asian Devel. Bank, Albert Einstein Coll. Medicine, Nat. Housing Bank of Brazil; mem. U.S. Senatorial Bus. Adv. Bd.; lectr. Baruch Coll. Grad. Sch. Bus., CUNY, 1960-63; adj. prof. Fairleigh Dickinson U. Grad. Sch. Bus., 1968-75; pres., dean Internat. Inst. Real Estate Studies Ltd.; dir. Center for Real Estate Studies, Adelphi U.; adj. prof. mgmt. NYU; mem. faculty New Sch. for Social Research; guest lectr., mem. bd. advs. Fordham U.; prin. owner, developer shopping centers, comml. real estate throughout, U.S.; chmn. UN Trade and Tech. Adv. Mission to Israel, 1972, Econ. Devel. Com./UJA Fedn.; active Nat. Builder Mktg. Bd. Chmn. Borough Pres.'s of Manhattan Com. on Narcotics Addiction Control, 1970-75; N.Y. mem. adv. coun. U.S. Air Force Acad.; mem. editl. policy com. Internat. Property Investment Jour. of Hostra U. Law Sch.; mem. Navy Recruiting Dist., N.Y. Assistance Coun.; bd. dirs. The Film Forum, 1979-86, N.Y.C. Housing Partnership, Housing Partnership Devel. Corp.; bd. dirs. Intrepid, Sea Air Space Mus., trustee; chmn. Navy Task Force to Study Navy Budgeting, Acquisition and Procurement; mem. Pres.'s Pvt. Sector Survey on Cost Control (Grace Commn.); mem. N.Y. State Gov.'s Bus. Adv. Coun.; trustee Zachary and Elizabeth M. Fisher Found., Fisher House Found., Inc.; bd. dirs. Fed. Law Enforcement Found.; chmn. econ. devel. com. United Jewish Appeal/Fedn., also bd. dirs.; bd. dirs. L.I. Jewish Med. Ctr.; mem. corp. adv. bd. Queens Coll.; adv. bd. Roundabout Theatre. With USAFR and USNR, 1959-90, ret. as capt. USNR, 1990; rear adm. upper half N.Y. Naval Militia, comdr. Divsn. Mil. and Naval Affairs; naval aide to the Gov. Mem. Nat. Assn. Corp. Real Estate Execs., Soc. Internat. Devel., Internat. Inst. Valuers (SCV designation), NRA, Nat. Def. Exec. Res., Chief Execs. Orgn., Nat. lPres.'s Orgn., Young Pres.'s Orgn. (past chmn. Met. chpt.), Real Estate Bd. N.Y., Assn. for Better N.Y., Internat. Coun. Shopping Ctrs., Property Cons. Soc., Nat. Assn. Rev. Appraisers (cert. rev. appraiser), Air Force Assn., Res. Officers Assn., Nat. Guard Assn. (life), Naval Res. Assn. (life), U.S. Naval Inst., Navy League U.S., Naval War Coll. Found. (assoc.), Am. Legion, Naval Militia Assn. (chmn.), Jewish War Vets. U.S., Militia Assn. N.Y., U.S. Navy Pub. Affairs Assn., Alpha delta Sigma, Phi Sigma Delta, Sigma Alpha. Home: PO Box 8 Rhinebeck NY 12572 Home: 85-29 Wicklow Pl Jamaica Est NY 11432-2415 Office: Rosen Associates Mgmt Corp 33 South Service Rd Jericho NY 11753-1006 E-mail: rar@rosenmgmt.com.

ROSEN, ROBERT CHARLES, English language educator; b. Bklyn., Dec. 29, 1947; s. Morris R. and Beatrice (Greenberg) R. BS in Math., MIT, 1970; MA in English, Rutgers U., 1975, PhD, 1978. From asst. prof. to prof. English William Paterson U., Wayne, N.J., 1978—. Author: John Dos Passos: Politics and the Writer, 1981, Politics of Education: Essays from Radical Teacher, 1990, Literature and Society: An Introduction to Fiction, Poetry, Drama, Nonfiction, 3d edit., 2000, Against the Current: Readings for Writers, 1998; contbr. articles to profl. jours. Nat. Defense Edn. Act fellow, 1970-73, NEH fellow, 1980. Office: William Paterson U English Dept 300 Pompton Rd Wayne NJ 07470-2103 E-mail: rosenr@wpunj.edu.

ROSEN, ROBERT STEPHEN, theatre arts, humanities and English educator; b. N.Y.C., Mar. 20, 1947; s. George Bernard and Elaine Lucille (Lavinsky) R.; m. Mary Patricia Bush; 1 child, David Michael. BA, U. Pitts., 1969, PhD in secondary edn., 1987; MA, California U. of Pa., 1980. Cert. secondary edn. tchr. in English and Speech, N.Y., secondary sch. prin., Pa. Studio dir. WQED-TV, Pitts., 1968-69; tchr. The Village Acad., Bethel Park, Pa., 1969-71; tchr. communication skills, English, humanities, theatre arts Mt. Lebanon (Pa.) Sch. Dist., 1976—. Instr. edn. U. Pitts., 1986-89; mem. steering com. for arts Commonwealth of Pa., Pa. State U., 1988. Contbr. articles to compendium on schs. and the arts. Presenter Pitts. Assn. for Edn. of Young Children at Carnegie-Mellon U., 1988-90, Kennedy Ctr. for Performing Arts, AATE Think Tank on the Future of Theatre and Education, 1990, U. Pitts. Literacy Conf. 1991. Recipient Gift of Time Tributes, Am. Family Inst., 1989, 90, 1st Pl. award for creativity and excellence for directing Romeo and Juliet, Nat. H.S. Theatre Contest, 1992, Mt. Lebanon PTSA Outstanding Svc. award, 1997, finalist for Tchr. Excellence Found. award, 2000. Mem. ASCD (conf. presenter 1993), NEA, AFTRA, Am. Alliance Theatre and Edn. (secondary sch. chairperson for U.S. 1989-91, rsch. award 1989), Am. Ednl. Rsch. Assn., Inst. Ednl. Rsch. (Spl. Merit award 1989), Pa. Ednl. Rsch. Assn., Pa. Assn. Supervision and Curriculum Devel (conf. presenter 1991), Phi Delta Kappa. Avocations: swimming, writing. Home: 552 Oxford Blvd Pittsburgh PA 15243-1562 Office: Mt Lebanon Sch Dist 155 Cochran Rd Pittsburgh PA 15228-1360

ROSEN, ROBERT THOMAS, analytical and food chemist; b. Concord, N.H., Nov. 5, 1941; s. Maurice J. and Miriam M. (Miller) R.; m. Sharon Lynne Beres, Apr. 23, 1972. BA (cum laude), Nasson Coll.; PhD, Rutgers U. Sr. rsch. scientist Chem. Rsch. and Devel. Ctr., FMC Corp., Princeton, N.J., 1966-84; program dir. analytical support facilities, 1984—; assoc. dir. Ctr. for Advanced Food Technology, Rutgers U., New Brunswick, N.J., 1993—; rsch. prof. food sci. Rutgers U., 2000—. Contbr. articles and book reviews to profl. jours. Fellow Am. Inst. Chemists; mem. Am. Chem. Soc. Inst. Food Technologists, Phi Lambda Upsilon (hon.). Achievements include research in gas and liquid chromatography, free and glycosidically bound organic compounds in fruits and vegetables, determination of non-volatile and thermally labile pesticides and phytochemicals in food, natural products and the environment by liquid chromatography and mass spectrometry. Home: 347 Harrier Dr Jamesburg NJ 08831-5566 Office: Rutgers U Cook Coll Ctr for Advanced Food Tech New Brunswick NJ 08901 E-mail: Rosen@aesop.rutgers.edu.

ROSEN, SAM, economics educator emeritus; b. Balt., Apr. 1, 1920; s. Louis and Belle (Kurtz) R.; m. Mary Berman, Mar. 5, 1943; children— Michael David, Laura Elizabeth, Jonathan Donald. AB, U. Wis., 1942; MA, Harvard U., 1948, PhD, 1952. Asst. prof. econs. U. Wyo., Laramie, 1949-51, U. Del., Newark, 1952-57; assoc. prof. U. N.H., Durham, 1957-63, prof., 1963-74, Nashua Corp. prof. econs., 1974-85, emeritus prof. econs., 1985—. Vis. prof. Inst. Social Studies, Holland, 1969, People's Republic China, 1987; vis. Fulbright prof., Malta, 1975 Author: National Income, 1963, National Income and Other Social Accounts, 1972; Contbr. articles to profl. jours. Served to lt. USNR, 1942-45. Mem. AAUP (pres. U. N.H. chpt. 1962-63, 72-73), Am. Econ. Assn., Internat. Assn. Rsch. in Income and Wealth, Am. Fin. Assn., Ret. Faculty Assn. (chmn., bd. dirs.), N.H. Assn. for the Elderly (bd. dirs.), Seacoast Jazz Soc. (bd. dirs.). Office: Whittemore Sch Bus-Econs Mcconnell Hall Durham NH 03824

ROSEN, SANFORD JAY, lawyer; b. N.Y.C., Dec. 19, 1937; s. Alexander Charles and Viola S. (Grad) R.; m. Catherine Picard, June 22, 1958; children: Caren E. Andrews, R. Durelle Schacter, Ian D., Melissa S. AB, Cornell U., 1959; LLB, Yale U., 1962. Bar: Conn. 1962, Calif. 1974, D.C. 1974, U.S. Supreme Ct. 1966. Law clk. to Hon. Simon E. Sobeloff U.S. Ct. Appeals, Balt., 1962-63; prof. sch. law U. Md., 1963-71; assoc. dir. Coun. on Legal Edn. Opportunity, Atlanta, 1969-70; vis. prof. law U. Tex., Austin, 1970-71; asst. legal dir. Nat. ACLU, N.Y.C., 1971-73; legal dir. Mex.-Am. Legal Def. Fund, San Francisco, 1973-75; ptnr. Rosen, Remcho & Henderson, 1976-80, Rosen & Remcho, San Francisco, 1980-82; prin. Law Offices of Sanford Jay Rosen, 1982-86; sr. ptnr. Rosen & Phillips, 1986-89; prin. Rosen & Assocs., 1990; sr. ptnr. Rosen, Bien & Asaro, 1991—. Mem. Balt. Cmty. Rels. Commn., 1966-69; mem. com. Patuxent Instn., Md., 1967-69; ad hoc adminstrv. law judge Calif. Agrl. Labor Rels. Bd., San Francisco, 1975-80; interim monitor U.S. Dist. Ct. for no. dist. Calif., San Francisco, 1989, early neutral evaluator, 1987—, mediator, 1993—; judge pro tem San Francisco Superior Ct., 1991—; perm. atty. del. Jud. Conf. U.S. Ct. Appeal for 4th Cir.; atty. del. Jud. Conf. U.S. Ct. Appeals 9th cir., 1996-98. Contbr. articles to profl. jours. Mem. Com. on Adminstrn. of Criminal Justice, Balt., 1968; mem. adv. com. HEW, Washington, 1974-75. Mem. ABA, Assn. Trial Lawyers Am. (chair civil rights sect. 1993-94), D.C. Bar Assn., Calif. Bar Assn., Bar Assn. San Francisco. Avocations: reading, travel, movies. Office: Rosen Bien & Asaro 155 Montgomery St Fl 8 San Francisco CA 94104-4113 E-mail: srosen@rbalaw.com.

ROSEN, SAUL WOOLF, research scientist, health facility administrator; b. Boston, July 29, 1928; s. David Tsvi and Ida (Hannah) Sadwin; m. Mary Jean Westfall, June 14, 1959 (div. 1986); children: Craig, Laura, David; m. Deborah Susan Kieffer, Nov. 3, 1989. BA cum laude, Harvard U., 1947, MD, 1956; PhD, Northwestern U., 1955. Intern U. Calif. Med. Ctr., San Francisco, 1956-57, resident, 1957-58, sr. res., 1960-61; clin. assoc. Nat. Inst. Arthritis and Metabolic Diseases, Bethesda, Md., 1958-60, sr. investigator NIH, 1961-84; dep. dir. Clin. Ctr. NIH, 1984-90, acting dir. clin. ctr., 1990-94. Vis. scientist Nat. Inst. Med. Rsch., London, 1975-76. Contbr. articles to profl. jours. U.S. Rubber Co. fellow, Northwestern U., 1950. Fellow ACP; mem. Assn. Am. Physicians, Endocrine Soc. Avocations: opera, lexicography, philately, weightlifting. Home: 11801 Rockville Pike Apt 1204 Rockville MD 20852-2728 E-mail: saulrosen@earthlink.net.

ROSEN, SIDNEY, psychologist; b. Bklyn., May 19, 1917; s. Ezekiel and Fannie (Kornfeld) R.; m. Catherine Elkin Rosen; children: Mark, Daniel, Steven C., Amy S. BA, Bklyn. Coll., 1938; MA, New Sch. for Social Rsch., N.Y.C., 1948; PhD, U. Mich., 1952. Rsch. assoc. Inst. Soc. Rsch., Ann Arbor, Mich., 1951-57; lectr. in psychology U. Mich., 1952-53; asst. prof., assoc. prof. Marquette U., Milw., 1957-64, prof. psychology, 1964-68, U. Ga., Athens, 1968-87; fellow Inst. for Behavioral Rsch., 1970-83; ret., 1987. Contbr. articles to profl. jours. Fellow APA; mem. Am. Psychol. Soc., Soc. for Exptl. Social Psychology. Home: 198 Sunnybrook Dr Athens GA 30605-3348

ROSEN, SIDNEY MARVIN, lawyer; b. Detroit, June 27, 1939; s. Fred A. and Gertrude (Cole) R.; children: Jordan, Aviva. BS, U. Ariz., 1961, JD, 1964. Bar: Ariz. 1964, U.S. Dist. Ct. Ariz. 1964, Calif. 1965, U.S. Dist. Ct. (so. dist.) Calif. 1965, U.S. Supreme Ct. 1971. Asst. atty. gen. State of Ariz., Phoenix, 1964-66, spl. asst. atty. gen., 1968-69; assoc. Kirkwood, Kaplan, Russin & Vechi, Bangkok and Saigon, Vietnam, 1967-68; ptnr. Rosen, Chemal, Ocampo and Fontes, Phoenix, 1970—. Co-founder, law instr. Ariz. Bar Rev. Course, 1965-73; prof. internat. law Am. Grad. Sch. of Internat. Mgmt., Phoenix, 1975-76; former gen. counsel Nat. Speakers Assn., 1973-85. Candidate Dem. nomination for atty. gen. State of Ariz., 1974, U.S. Congress, 1976; mem. Ariz.-Mex. Gov.'s Commn., 1974—, counsel commerce and industry sect., 1974—; chmn. campaign Bonds for Israel, Ariz., 1980-85; founding chmn., exec. bd. Internat. Found. for Anticancer Drug Discovery, 1996—. Baird scholar, University scholar; recipient Speaker Preview Auditions First Pl. award Internat. Platform Assn., 1969-70, Silver Bowl award, 1969-70. Mem. Ariz. Bar Assn. (internat. relations com.), Calif. Bar Assn., Maricopa County Bar Assn., World Assn. Lawyers, Nat. Speakers Assn. (founder, former gen. counsel 1973-85), World Affairs Council, Hospitality Internat. (host), FIABCI (law instr. Internat. Real Estate Fedn. 1985-90, gen. counsel Ariz. chpt. 1985—), Ariz. World Trade Assn. (former bd. dirs.), Jaycees (treas. Ariz. chpt. 1969-70, ambassador to Philippine Islands 1969-70), Pan Am. Club of Ariz. (past pres.), Traveler's Century Club, Valley Forward Assn. (bd. dirs.), Phi Alpha Delta (pres. 1963-64). Lodges: Kiwanis. Democrat. Jewish. Avocations: stamp collecting, photography, world traveling, camping, scuba diving. Home: 2233 N Alvarado Rd Phoenix AZ 85004-1415 Office: Rosen Chenal Ocampo & Fontes 4323 N 12th St Ste 104 Phoenix AZ 85014-4506 Fax: (602) 263-9297. E-mail: baliinaz@aol.com.

ROSEN, STANLEY HOWARD, humanities educator, educator; b. Warren, Ohio, July 29, 1929; s. Nathan A. and Celia (Narotsky) R.; m. Francoise Harlepp, Sept. 5, 1955; children: Nicholas David, Paul Mark, Valerie. BA, U. Chgo., 1949, PhD, 1955; postgrad., Am. Sch. Classical Studies, Athens, Greece, 1955-56; D honoris causa, New U. Lisbon, 1997. Mem. faculty Pa. State U., 1956-94, prof. philosophy, 1966-94; Fulbright research prof. U. Paris, 1960-61; research fellow Humanities Research Inst., U. Wis., 1963-64; Inst. Arts and Humanities research sr. fellow Pa. State U., 1972—, Evan Pugh prof. philosophy, 1985-94; Bowne prof. philosophy Boston U., 1994—, univ. prof., 2000—. Vis. prof. U. Calif., San Diego, 1978, U. Nice, 1981, Scuola Superiore Pisa, 1989; vis. lectr. U. Barcelona, Spain, 1992; Priestly lectr. U. Toronto, 1997; Cardinal Mercier lectr. Louvain U., 1998. Author: Plato's Symposium, 1968, Nihilism, 1969, G.W.F. Hegel, 1974, The Limits of Analysis, 1980, Plato's Sophist: The Drama of Original and Image, 1983, Hermeneutics as Politics, 1987, The Quarrel Between Philosophy and Poetry, 1988, The Ancients and the Moderns, 1989, The Question of Being, 1993, Plato's Statesman: The Web of Politics, 1995, The Mask of Enlightenment, 1995, Metaphysics in Ordinary Language, 1999; editor: The Examined Life: A Treasury of Western Philosophy, 2000, The Elusiveness of the Ordinary, 2002. Research grantee Am. Philos. Soc., 1961; Research grantee Earhart Found., 1971, 73, 81, 2000. Mem. Metaphys. Soc. Am (pres. 1990-91). Home: 117 Brook St Wellesley MA 02482-6632 Office: 745 Commonwealth Ave Boston MA 02215-1401 E-mail: srosen@bu.edu .

ROSEN, STEVEN TERRY, oncologist, hematologist; b. Bklyn., Feb. 18, 1952; married, 1976; 4 children. MB, Northwestern U., 1972, MD, 1976. Genevieve Teuton prof., med. sch. Northwestern U., 1989—, dir. cancer ctr., 1989—. Dir. clin. programs Northwestern Meml. Hosp., 1989—. Editor-in-chief Jour. Northwestern U. Cancer Center, 1989—, Contemporary Oncology, 1990-95, Cancer Treatment and Rsch., 1995—, In Touch, 198—. Mem. AAAS, ACP, AMA, Am. Soc. Hematology, Am. Soc. Clin. Oncology, Ctrl. Soc. Clin. Rsch. Achievements include research in hematologic malignancies, lung cancer, breast cancer, biologic and hormonal therapies. Office: Northwestern U Olson Pavilion Rm 8250 303 E Chicago Ave Chicago IL 60611-3093

ROSEN, SUSAN A. C. English language educator; b. Glen Cove, N.Y., Apr. 10, 1956; d. Eli Cohen and Rosalie Eva Levine; m. Perry Mark Rosen, Aug. 5, 1979; children: Sara, Jake. BA in History, SUNY, Albany, 1978; MA in English, U. Md., 1983, PhD, 1994. Adj. asst. prof. English U. Md., University College, 1990-93; assoc. prof. English Anne Arundel C.C., Arnold, Md., 1994—. Project dir. Am. Insts. for Rsch., Washington, 1986-90. Author: (book) Introduction to Writing, 1995; contbr. articles to profl. jours. Recipient Excellence in Tchg. award NISOD, 2000. Home: 1401 Foggy Glen Ct Silver Spring MD 20906 Office: Anne Arundel C C 101 College Pkwy Arnold MD 21012 E-mail: sarosen@mail.aacc.cc.md.us.

ROSEN, WENDY LEE, librarian; b. Glen Cove, N.Y., Aug. 9, 1961; d. William I. and Marilyn L. (Miller) R. BA, SUNY, Stony Brook, 1983; MSLS, L.I. U., 1986. Libr. Stenotype Inst., Hicksville, N.Y., 1986; reference libr. Plainedge (N.Y.) Pub. Libr., 1986, Plainview (N.Y.)-Old Bethpage Pub. Libr., 1986-95, New Bern (N.C.) Craven County Pub. Libr., 1996—. Democrat. Jewish. Avocations: computers, Spanish, music, history, photography. Home: 46B Mulberry Ln New Bern NC 28562 E-mail: wendyrose@latinmail.com.

ROSEN, WENDY WORKMAN, arts management and publishing executive; b. Miami, Sept. 17, 1954; d. Robert L. and Mildred E. (Duck) Workman; m. Steven David Rosen, June 22, 1972, children: Rebecca, Jeffrey. AS, Santa Fe Coll., 1974; BS, U. Fla., 1976. Cert. exhbn. mgr. Advt. exec. Balt. News Am., 1978-80, Balt. Mag, 1980-82; pres. The Rosen Group, Inc., Balt., 1982—. Cons. Times Pub. Group, Balt., 1982; gen. ptnr. Mill Ctr. Artists Studios, Balt.; pres. Am. Craft Showroom; founder The Buyers Markets of American Crafts, founder Craft Bus. Inst. Author: Crafting as a Business, Cash For Your Crafts; pub.: Niche mag., Am. Style mag., Market Insider. Bd. mem. Craft Emergency Relief Fund. Mem. Natl. Assn. Exposition Mgrs., Glass Art Soc. Democrat. Jewish. Avocation: gardening. Office: The Rosen Agy 3000 Chestnut Ave Ste 300 Baltimore MD 21211-2769

ROSEN, WILLIAM, English language educator; b. Boston, July 1, 1926; s. Louis H. and Alice (Goldstein) R.; m. Barbara Cooper, Aug. 13, 1960; children: Judith Anne, Susan Eleanor. AB, Harvard U., 1948, AM, 1949, PhD, 1958. Instr. U. Wis., Madison, 1956-60; asst. prof. U. Conn., Storrs, 1960-63, assoc. prof., 1963-65, prof. English, 1965-92; prof. emeritus, 1992—; coordinator English grad. studies U. Conn., Storrs, 1979-80, 81-84, head English dept., 1987-92. Old Dominion prof. humanities Hampton Inst., Va., 1969-70; vis. fellow Clare Hall, Cambridge U., Eng., 1980-81, 88-89. Author: Shakespeare and the Craft of Tragedy, 1960; co-editor: Julius Caesar, 1963; contbr. articles to profl. jours. Vol. long term care adv., ombudsman program State of Conn., 1994—; mem. Town of Mansfield Commn. on Aging, 1995-99; mem. Mansfield Town Coun., 1999—; facilitator Ctr. for Learning in Retirement, 1994—. Pvt. U.S. Army, 1953-55. Mem. AAUP (v.p. 1974-75, pres. 1975-76, chief negotiator U. Conn. chpt. 1976-77, pres. Conn. emeritus assembly 2000—), MLA. Democrat. Jewish. Avocations: reading, gardening. Home: 233 Hanks Hill Rd Storrs Mansfield CT 06268-2333 Office: U Conn Dept English Storrs Mansfield CT 06268

ROSEN, WILLIAM WARREN, lawyer; b. New Orleans, July 22, 1936; s. Warren Leucht and Erma (Stich) R.; m. Eddy Kahn, Nov. 26, 1965; children: Elizabeth K., Victoria A. BA, Tulane U., 1958, JD, 1964. Bar: La. 1964, U.S. Dist. Ct. (ea. dist.) La. 1965, U.S. Ct. Appeals (5th cir.) 1965, U.S. Supreme Ct. 1984, U.S. Dist. Ct. (mid. dist.) La. 1985, Colo. 1989. Assoc. Dodge & Friend, New Orleans, 1965-68, Law Office of J.R. Martzell, New Orleans, 1968-70; pvt. practice, 1970-79, 89-90; ptnr. Lucas & Rosen (and predecessor firms), 1979-87, Herman, Herman, Katz & Cotlar, New Orleans, 1987-88, Rosen and Samuel, New Orleans, 1990-95; of counsel Rittenberg & Samuel, 1996-99; founder & dir. Litigation Consultation Svcs., 1996-99; ptnr. Rosen & Lundeen, L.L.P., 1999—. Adj. prof. trial advocacy Law Sch. Tulane U., 1988—, mem. adv. com. paralegal studies program, 1977-86, instr. bus. orgns., 1978, instr. legal interviewing, 1980-81; mem. adv. com. Paralegal Inst. U. New Orleans, 1990—, instr. legal interviewing and investigations, 1986-87; lectr. legal and paralegal fields; lectr. real and demonstrative evidence Nat. Edn. Network, 1993; lectr. new judges seminar La. Jud. Coll., 2000, 01. Author: (with others) Trial Techniques publ. La. Trial Lawyers Assn., 1981; columnist Briefly Speaking publ. New Orleans Bar Assn., 1993-2000. Mem. budget and planning com. Jewish Welfare Fedn., 1970-73; mem. adv. coun. on drug edn. La. Dept. Edn., 1973; mem. profl. adv. com. Jewish Endowment Found., 1982—; mem. exec. com. U.S. Olympic Com., La., 1982-84; bd. dirs. Planned Parenthood La., 1994-2001; pres. Dad's Club, Isidore Newman Sch., 1984-85, Uptown Flood Assn., 1982-85; bd. dirs. Jewish Children's Home Svc., 1973-76, Met. Crime Commn. New Orleans, 1976-82; spl. agt. Office Spl. Investigations USAF, 1958-61. Fellow, Inst. of Politics. Loyola U. Mem. ABA, ATLA (keyperson com. 1986-89, vice chmn. paralegal com. 1986-89, mem. family law adv. com. 1989-90, sec. family law sect. 1990-91, lectr. legal edn. 1979, 81, 83, 86, 88); mem. La. Bar Assn. (vice chmn. pub. rels. com. 1970-73, 88-89, past chmn. state youth drug abuse edn. program, vol. lawyers for arts 1986-96, chmn. sr. counsel com. 1995-96), Am. Arbitration Assn., Nat. Fedn. Paralegal Assn. (adv. coun. 1989-1998), Assn. Atty. Mediators (pres. La. chpt. 1995), Nat. Choice in Dying (legal adv. com. 1992-96), Nat. Edn. Network (lectr. legal edn. 1993), New Orleans Bar Assn. (CLE com. 1990-91, chmn. 1991-92, mem. alternative dispute resolution com. 1996-2000, panel moderator 1997), Inn of Ct. (master 1992—), Rotary Club New Orleans (bd. dirs. 1996-98, chmn. legal com. 1996—). Avocation: photography (included in Louisiana Photographers publ. Contemporary Arts Ctr. 1988). Office: Rosen & Lundeen 210 Baronne St Ste 704 New Orleans LA 70112-4132 Fax: 504-523-3370. E-mail: lcsno@aol.com.

ROSEN, YERETH JOSETTE, journalist; b. Washington, May 25, 1959; d. Martin M. and Judith Jacobs R.; m. Michael A. Tumey, June 27, 1999; 1 child, Jania Josette. BA, U. Va., 1981; MBA, U. Colo., 1986. Reporter The Pueblo (Colo.) Chieftain, 1983-85; regional corr. The Longmont (Colo.) Times Call, 1985-87; reporter The Anchorage Times, 1987-89; assoc. editor Alaska Mag., Anchorage, 1989-90; reporter Reuters Am., 1990—; spl. Akaska corr. The Bur. of Nat. Affairs, 1995—; freelance writer, 1989—. Mem. Nordic Ski Club of Anchorage, Congregation Beth Sholom. Mem. Alaska Press Club, Soc. of Profl. Journalists, Alaska Press Women/Nat. Fedn. of Press Women. Jewish.

ROSENAU, JAMES NATHAN, political scientist, author; b. Phila., Nov. 25, 1924; s. Walter Nathan and Fanny Fox (Baum) R.; m. Norah McCarthy, Aug. 5, 1955 (dec. July 1974); 1 child, Heidi Margaret; m. Pauline Vaillancourt, June 14, 1987 (div. 1993); m. Hongying Wang, Dec. 11, 1993; 1 child: Fan Elizabeth. AB, Bard Coll., 1948; AM, Johns Hopkins U., 1949; PhD, Princeton U., 1957. From instr. to prof. Rutgers U., New Brunswick, N.J., 1949-70; prof. Ohio State U., Columbus, 1970-73; prof. polit. sci. U. So. Calif., L.A., 1973-92; prof. internat. affairs George Washington U., 1992—. Research asst. Inst. Advanced Study, Princeton, N.J., 1953-54; research assoc. Princeton U., N.J., 1960-70; dir. Sch. Internat. Relations U. So. Calif., L.A., 1976-79; dir. Inst. for Transnat. Studies, U. Southern Calif., L.A., 1973-92. Author: Public Opinion and Foreign Policy, 1961, National Leadership and Foreign Policy, 1963, The Dramas of Politics, 1973, Citizenship between Elections, 1974, The Scientific Study of Foreign Policy, 1980, Turbulence in World Politics, 1990, The United Nations in a Turbulent World, 1992, Along the Domestic-Foreign Frontier, 1997; (play) Kwangju: An Escalatory Spree, 1991; co-author: American Leadership in World Affairs, 1984, Global Voices, 1993, Thinking Theory Thoroughly, 1995, 2nd edit., 2000, International Political Economy, 1995, Understanding Globalization, 1998; co-editor: Journeys through World Politics, 1989, Global Changes and Theoretical Challenges, 1989, Governance without Government, 1992, Strange Power, 2000, Information Technologies and Global Politics, 2002. Trustee Bard Coll., Annandale-on-Hudson, 1968-70, Odyssey Theater Ensemble, L.A., 1987-88. With U.S. Army, 1942-46. Ford Found. fellow, 1958-59, Guggenheim fellow, 1987-88; Rsch. grantee NSF, 1970, 73, 78-79, 83, 88, 92, 96, NEH grantee, 1976. Fellow World Acad. Art and Sci.; mem. Internat. Studies Assn. (pres. 1984-85), Am. Polit. Sci. Assn. (exec. council 1975-77) Democrat. Office: 2130 H St NW Washington DC 20037-2521 E-mail: jnr@gwu.edu.

ROSENAU, PETE, public relations executive; Owner, powersports franchises, import/export parts and accessories retail and wholesale operation; owner 6 new car franchises Honda, Hyundai, Mazda, Volkswagon, Toyota, Subaru, Mich.; chmn. Franco Pub. Rels. Group, 2002—. Bd. trustees YWCA Western Wayne County. Recipient Quality Dealer award, Time Mag., All-Star Dealer award (twice nominated), Sports Illustrated. Mem.: Henry Ford Cmty. Coll. (mem. found. bd.), BBB (serves exec. com.), Detroit Auto Dealers Assn. (past pres., exec. com., bd. dirs., co-chmn. 1997 and 1998 N.Am. Internat. Auto Shows, mem. bd. dirs. adv. ethics stds.). Office: Franco Pub Rels Group 400 Renaissance Ctr Ste 1050 Detroit MI 48243 Office Fax: 313-567-4486.*

ROSENBACH, LEOPOLD, engineer, consultant; b. Walbrzych, Poland, Jan. 10, 1947; came to the U.S., 1969; s. Samuel and Halina (Kormicz) R.; m. Pola Knott, Dec. 23, 1969; 1 child, Coleene Rosenbach. MSEE, Polytechnic, Wroclaw, Poland, 1968. Cert. mfg. engr. Mfg. mgr. Leviton Mfg. Co., Bklyn., 1973-77; mfg. engr. Eagle Electric, Long Island City, N.Y., 1977-78; electric mfg. engr. Standard Motor Products, 1979-83, product devel. mgr., 1984-87, design mgr., 1988-90, engring. mgr., 1991-93, dir. materials, 1994-96, dir. ops., 1996—. Contbr. numerous articles to sci. jours. Mem. IEEE, Am. Soc. Metals, Am. Purchasing Soc., Internat. Soc. for Hybrid Microelectronics (met. chpt. treas. 1988-89, sec. 89-90, pres. 90-91), Soc. Mfg. Engrs. Avocations: music, astronomy. Home: 10262 Cove Lake Dr Orlando FL 32836-3756 Office: Standard Motor Electronics 170 Sunport Ln Orlando FL 32809-7892 E-mail: leor@smpe.net.

ROSENBAUM, ALLAN, public administration educator, academic administrator, international governance advisor; b. N.Y.C., Oct. 5, 1940; s. Frances Lawrence; m. Judith M. Rosenbaum, June 16, 1963; children: Michelle, Amy. BA, U. Miami, 1962; MS in Edn., So. Ill. U., Carbondale, 1964; MA, U. Calif., Berkeley, 1967; PhD, U. Chgo., 1976. Adminstrv. asst. to lt. gov. State of Ill., Chgo., Springfield, 1968-69; dir. Woodlawn manpower planning survey Ctr. Urban Studies, U. Chgo., 1970-71; asst. prof. polit. sci. U. Wis., Madison, 1971-74, U. Conn., Storrs, 1974-77; sr. assoc., study dir. Nat. Inst. Edn., HEW, Washington, 1977-80; chief cons. appropriations subcom. on edn.-human resources Md. Gen. Assembly, Annapolis, 1981, dir. jobs initiative task force, 1982-83; assoc. prof., dir. Md. Inst. Policy Analysis and Rsch. U. Md. Grad. Sch., Balt., 1981-89, dir. Thomas M. Bradley Ctr. Employment and Tng. Edn.-Rsch., 1985-88; prof. pub. adminstrn., dean Sch. Pub. Affairs and Svcs., Fla. Internat. U., Miami, 1988-94, dir. Inst. for Pub. Mgmt., 1995—, coord. PhD program, 2000—. Advisor, cons. UN Devel. Program, govts. Argentina, Costa Rica, Paraguay, Peru, Poland, Ukraine, others; organizer, speaker State Treas.'s Conf. on Capital Debt Affordability in Md., 1987; mem. policy coun. Fla. Inst. Govt., 1988-89; chmn. 1991 ann. conf. program Policy Studies Orgn., 1990-91; co-prin. Consortium for Legis. Devel. in Latin Am., 1990-95; numerous presentations in field. Co-author: Poliscide, 1976, repub., 1989; author: Local Governence, 1997, Responding to Citizens Needs, 2001; editor-in-chief Policy Studies Rev., 1993-97; contbr. articles to profl. jours., chpts. to books and proc. Pres. Reston (Va.) Community Assn., 1987-88; chmn. sci. adv. com. Greater Miami Coalition for Drug Free Community, 1989-96, bd. dirs., 1990-97; mem. govt. rels. com. United Way Dade County, Miami, 1989-94. Fellow Ford Found., 1966-67, Nat. Inst. Mental Health, Pub. Policy fellow U Chgo., , 1967-70, U. Conn., 1975, Inst. for Ednl. Leadership, 1976-77; numerous govt. and found. grants. Mem. Nat. Assn. Schs. Pub. Affairs and Adminstrn. (exec. coun.), Am. Soc. for Pub. Adminstrn., Assn. for Pub. Policy Analysis and Mgmt., Am. Polit. Sci. Assn., Greater Miami C. of C. (task force on homelessness in South Fla. 1989-92, pub. affairs and state affairs coms. 1989-96), Internat. Inst. Adminstrv. Scis. (founding mem. working group on environ. mgmt. 1990-93, exec. coun. 2001-), Internat. Assn. Schs. and Insts. Adminstrn. (task force on women in pub. mgmt. 1990-93, v.p., bd. mgmt., chair ann. conf. 1995, 2000, pres. 2001-), Cosmos Club. Democrat. Jewish. Home: 5000 Riviera Dr Miami FL 33146-1741 Office: Fla Internat U Sch Pub Policy and Mgmt Univ Park Campus Miami FL 33199

ROSENBAUM, BELLE SARA, appraiser, interior designer, museum director, educator; b. N.Y.C., Apr. 1, 1922; d. Harry and Hinda (Sits) Heimowitz; m. Jacob H. Rosenbaum, Mar. 12, 1939; children: Linda Zelinger, Simmi Brodie, Martin, Arlene Levene. Cert., N.Y. Sch. Interior Design, 1945; MA in Judaic Art, PhD, U. B.C., 1997. Sr. mem. Am. Soc. Appraisers, Washington, 1979—; tchr. Judaica Yeshiva U., 1984—; dir. Mus. Contemporary Judaica; pres. Jarvis Designs, Inc., Union City, N.J., 1955-75, Design Assocs., BLS, Monsey, N.Y., 1970-78; v.p. Lord & Lady Inc., Union City, 1955-70, Cardio-Bionic Scanning, Inc., Spring Valley, N.Y., 1975-78; v.p., treas. Rapitech Sys., inc., 1985; exec. bd. State of Israel Bonds Orgn., 1992—. Author short stories, 1947-48, Chronicle of Jewish Traditions, 1992, Upon Thy Doorposts, 1996; contbr. articles on interior design to profl. jours. Chmn. bd. artifacts Rockland Holocaust Ctr., 1991—; trustee Rockland Ctr. Holocaust Studies, 1994; pres. Ednl. Ctr. Jewish Values Jerusalem Gt. Synagogue, Israel, 1998—; co-chair Nat. Jewish Art Week, 2000; curator arts Holocaust Mus. Rockland County, 2000; Bd. dirs. Midgal Ohr Schs., 1971—, Shaare Zedek Hosp., Jerusalem, 1998—, Jewish Fedn. Rockland County, 1999—, Riverdale (N.Y.) Jewish Mus., 1999—, Am. Guild Judaic Art, 1999—, Judaica Mus. Riverdale, 2001—.

ROSENBAUM, DAVID HERBERT, neurologist; b. Poona, India, Sept. 27, 1944; came to U.S., 1949; s. Edmund and Senta (Jacks) R.; m. Catherine Helen Taylor, May 15, 1983; children: Nicholas, Raphael, Colin. AB cum laude, Brown U., 1965; postgrad., Duke U. Sch. Medicine, 1965-67; MD, NYU, 1969. Diplomate Am. Bd. Psychiatry and Neurology; lic. physician, N.Y. Intern and resident internal medicine NYU/Bellevue Hosp., 1969-71; resident neurology Neurol. Inst. N.Y., 1971-74; assoc. prof. neurology and geriatrics Mt. Sinai Sch. Medicine, N.Y.C., 1974—96, assoc. clinical prof. neurology, 1996—; asst. chief neurology VA Med. Ctr., Bronx, 1990-96; pvt. practice Englewood, N.J., 2000—. Consulting neurologist N.Y. Med. Group, Bronx, 1996-2000. Mem. profl. adv. bd. Epilepsy Soc. N.Y.C., 1995—, bd. dirs., 1996—. Mem. Am. Acad. Neurology, Assn. for Rsch. in Nervous and Mental Diseases, Am. Epilepsy Soc., Epilepsy Found. of Am. Home: 230 Riverside Dr Ph J New York NY 10025-8655 Office: 97 Engle St Englewood NJ 07631 E-mail: dhrmd@nyc.rr.com.

ROSENBAUM, DAVID MARK, engineering executive, consultant, educator; b. Boston, Feb. 11, 1935; s. Frederick and Elizabeth (Gelman) R.; m. Karen Jeanne Smith, Dec. 27, 1964; children: Benjamin Micah, Shoshana Elizabeth. BSc, Brown U., 1956; MS, Renessaler Polytech. Inst., 1958; PhD, Brandeis U., 1964. Asst. rsch. prof. Boston U., 1964-65; assoc. prof. Polytech. U., Bklyn., 1969-70; pres. Network Analysis Corp., Glen Cove, N.Y., 1970-72; asst. dir. Office of Nat. Narcotics Intelligence, Washington, 1973-74; cons. to compt. gen. GAO, 1975-78; dir. Office of Radiation Programs EPA, 1978-81; pres. Tech. Analysis Corp., McLean, Va., 1981—. Cons. Dir. of Licensing, AEC, Washington, 1972-73. Author: Super Hilbert Space and the Quantum Time Operator, 1969, Liquefield Energy Gases Safety, 1978, A Statistical Procedure for Testing Pacemakers, 1978, Health Effects of Low-Level Radiation, 1981, A Statistical Procedure for Cluster Recognition with Application to Atlanta Leukemia Data, 1983. Mem. IEEE (sr.), Am. Phys. Soc. Office: Tech Analysts Corp # 202 6723 Whittier Ave Mc Lean VA 22101-4533 E-mail: dmrose@radix.net.

ROSENBAUM, ERNEST HAROLD, internist, oncologist, educator; b. Cleve., Jan. 5, 1929; s. Lionel Clarence Rosenbaum and Dora Beatrice Heldman; m. Isadora Ray, May 5, 1949; children: Eileen, Alexandra, Diane, Steven. BA, U. N.Mex., 1951; MD, U. Colo., 1956. Diplomate Am. Bd. Internal Medicine, Am. Bd. Oncology. Intern Stanford San Francisco Gen. Hosp., 1956-57, resident, 1957-58, Mt. Zion Hosp., San Francisco, 1958-59, New England Ctr. Hosp., 1961-63, fellow in hematology, 1961-63; mem. staff U. Calif. San Francisco/Mt. Zion Hosp. Med. Ctr.; clin. prof. medicine U. Calif. San Francisco, 1983—2002, Stanford (Calif.) Hosp. and Clinics, 2000—. Med. dir. Better Health Found., San Francisco, 1987—2002; bd. dirs. Susan B. Komen Found., San Francisco, 1989—2002; program dir. Cancer

Supportive Care Program, Complementary Medicine Clinic Stanford U. Sch. Medicine, 1999—, dlin. prof. medicine, 1999—. Med. advisor San Francisco Opera, 1988-2002. With USAF, 1959-61. Fellow ACP; mem. Calif. Med. Assn., San Francisco Med. Soc., Am. Soc. Clin. Oncologists. Jewish. Office: U Calif/Mt Zion Comprehensive Cancer Ctr 1600 Divisidero San Francisco CA 94115-3006 E-mail: ernie@pop.lmi.net.

ROSENBAUM, FRANCES, entrepreneur; b. Mt. Vernon, N.Y., Oct. 27, 1953; d. Zoltan and Barbara Trattner R.; m. Robert L. Ginsberg, June 2, 1974; children: Jonathan Zachary, Kori Julia, Bailey Laurel. BA, Brandeis U., 1975; MBA, Adelphi U., 1988. Lic. broker. Mgr., salesperson Tupperware Orgn., Bklyn., 1974-77; pres. Phran Brokerage, Inc., 1975-78; adminstrv. asst. M. Dunn Advt., N.Y.C., 1975-76; brokerage mgr. Guardian Life Ins. Co., 1976-82; pres. Infantessimal Planning, Inc., Oceanside, N.Y., 1984-94, Phran-Tek, Ltd., Oceanside, 1994—; creator, designer, founder LockerShockers.com website, 2001. Patentee Land Shark Privacy Shield, 1995; author: (children's play) The Frog Principal, 1994; editor/author/pub.: (newspaper) The Sweet Hollow Gazette, 1992-96; co-author spl. edn. video, 1996. Active Dem. Party, Huntington, N.Y., 1992-96; trustee Cmty. Awareness of Sweet Hollow, Melville, N.Y., 1992-96, Sunquam for Ednl. Equality, Melville, 1991-92; pres. Sunquam PTA, Melville, 1990-91, Signal Hill PTA, Dix Hills, N.Y., 1993-94; com. liaison Half Hollow PTA, Dix Hills, 1990-96. Recipient Jenkins award N.Y. PTA, 1991, Cmty. Svc. award Town of Huntington, N.Y., 1994. Mem. Nat. PTA (life, pres. local chpt. 1990-91, 93-94), Hadassah (life), Signal Hill PTA (past pres. 1994-96). Jewish. Avocations: piano, computers, writing, local politics, tennis. Office: Phran-Tek Ltd 157 Atlantic Ave Oceanside NY 11572-2005

ROSENBAUM, GREG ALAN, merchant banker, consultant; b. Toledo, Aug. 7, 1952; s. Marvin and Ida Edith (Millman) R.; m. Martha Jane Radlo, Sept. 3, 1978; children: Eli Samuel, Eve Hannah, Elliott Jacob. AB, Harvard U., 1974, M in Pub. Policy, JD, Harvard U., 1978. Bar: Ohio 1978, Ill. 1980. Summer assoc. Jones, Day, Reavis & Pogue, Cleve., 1977; tchg. fellow in govt. and social scis. Harvard U., Cambridge, Mass., 1976-78; cons. Boston Consulting Group, Boston and Chgo., 1978-82; v.p. Dyson-Kissner-Moran Corp., N.Y.C., 1982-87; mng. dir. Carlyle Group, Washington, 1987-88; pres. Palisades Assocs., Inc., Bethesda, Md., 1988—. Debating coach Harvard U., 1976-79; dir. Varlen Corp., Naperville, Ill., 1985-99, Richey Electronics, Inc., Garden Grove, Calif., 1993-99, McLaren/Hart Inc., Rancho Cordova, Calif., 1995-2000, Expressions Furniture, Inc., Anaheim, Calif., 1992-97, AMCO Corp., Chgo., 1993-97, The Whaler on Kaanapali Beach, 1999—, PlayCore Holdings, Inc., 2000—. Co-author: The Crime of Poverty, 1973, Beyond Politics, 1974, World Without Plenty, 1975. Dir. Lifeline, A Mental Retardation Partnership, Washington, 1993-98; baseball coach Potomac (Md.) Boys' Club, 1992-96; co-chair Harvard Debate Centennial, 1991—; mem. Harvard Law Sch. 20th Reunion gift com., 1997-98, 25th Reunion gift com., 1998-99. Winner Ames Moot Ct. competition Harvard Law Sch., 1976. Mem. ABA, Am. Forensic Assn. (nat. intercollegiate debate champion 1974, coach nat. intercollegiate debate champion 1979), Am. Acad. Polit. and Social Scis., Ctr. for Study of Presidency, Toledo Bar Assn., Chgo. Bar Assn., Phi Beta Kappa. Democrat. Jewish. Avocations: major league baseball, golf, computers, sports memorabilia. Office: Palisades Assocs Inc 9140 Vendome Dr Bethesda MD 20817-4021

ROSENBAUM, HAROLD L. conductor, music educator; b. Danville, Pa., Jan. 24, 1950; s. Abraham Jacob and Gertrude Rosenbaum; m. Edith Raymon. BA, CUNY, Queens, 1972, MA, 1974. Prof. Adelphi U., Garden City, N.Y., 1986-87, Juilliard Sch., N.Y.C., 1995-96, Queens Coll., CUNY, N.Y.C., 1980-98, 2001—02, dir. choirs, 1998—; prof. SUNY, Buffalo, 1997—. Adj. lectr. Queens Coll., CUNY, N.Y.C., 1972-80. Condr. over 1200 concerts in Am. and throughout Europe, 1973—, including Madeira Bach Festival, Portugal, Tanglewood Festival Contemporary Music, Juilliard Sch. Focus Festival; collaborations with Am. Symphony, Bard Festival Orch., Orch. St. Luke's, Bklyn. Philharm., PDQ Bach broadcasts; recordings with CRI, SONY Classical, Bridge Records, Capstone Records, Koch Internat. Bd. advisors Am. Soc. Jewish Music, N.Y.C., 1991-92, The Village Singers, N.Y.C., 1997—. Recipient Chorus Am. award ASCAP, 1991, 93; Winston Churchill travel fellow English Spkg. Union N.Y., 1983. Recipient Chorus Am. award ASCAP, 1991, 93; Winston Churchill Traveling fellow English-Speaking Union N.Y., 1983. Home and Office: 2 Cove Rd South Salem NY 10590

ROSENBAUM, JACOB I. lawyer; b. Cleve., Oct. 4, 1927; s. Lionel C. and Dora (Heldman) R.; m. Marjorie Jean Arnold, Apr. 20, 1952; children: Laura Rosenbaum, Alexander, Judith Bartell JD, U. N.Mex., 1951. Bar: N.Mex. 1951, Ohio 1952. Pres. Ohio Savs. Assn., Cleve., 1955-60, sr. v.p., 1960-92, also dir.; ptnr. Burke, Haber & Berick, 1955-79, Arter & Hadden, Cleve., 1979-94, of counsel, 1994—. Pres. Kiwanis Found. of Cleve., 1994—; active Judson Retirement Cmty., Cleveland Heights, 1990—, trustee, 1994, pres., 1992; trustee Cleve. Zool. Soc., 1983—, Cleve. Nat. Air Show, 1981—, pres., 1987—90, 1994—, pres. Found., 1995—2000; trustee Golden Age Ctrs. of Cleve., 1996—; pres. Temple Emanu El, University Heights, 1965—67, 1995—; bd. dirs. U. N.Mex. Law Sch. Mem.: Cleve. Execs. Assn. (pres. 1989, chmn. 1990), Greater Cleve. Bar Assn., Ohio Bar Assn. (chmn. aviation law com. 1981—84), Lawyer-Pilots Bar Assn. (pres. 1981—82, editor jour. 1982—97), Kiwanis Club of Cleve. (pres. 1970—71). Democrat. Jewish. Home: 28050 N Woodland Rd Cleveland OH 44124-4521 Office: Arter & Hadden 1100 Huntington Bldg 925 Euclid Ave Cleveland OH 44115-1475

ROSENBAUM, JAMES MICHAEL, judge; b. Ft. Snelling, Minn., Oct. 12, 1944; s. Sam H. and Ilene D. (Bernstein) Rosenbaum; m. Marilyn Brown, July 30, 1972. BA, U. Minn., 1966. Bar: (Minn) 1969, (Ill.) 1970, (U.S. Supreme Ct.) 1979. VISTA staff atty. Leadership Coun. for Met. Open Cmtys., Chgo., 1969-72; assoc. Katz, Taube, Lange & Frommelt, Mpls., 1972-77; ptnr. Rosenbaum & Rosenbaum, 1977-79, Gainsley, Squier & Korsh, Mpls., 1979-81; U.S. dist. atty. U.S. Dept. Justice, 1981-85; judge U.S. Dist. Ct., Minn., 1985—, chief judge, 2001—. 8th cir. rep. Jud. Conf. U.S., 1997—, mem. exec. com. , 1999—2001. Author: (booklet) Guide to Practice Civil Rights Housing, 1972; co-author: U.S. Courts Design Guide, 1991—96; contbr. Campaign chmn. People for Boschwitz, Minn., 1978; bd. vis. U. Minn. Law Sch. (pres. 1996-97). Mem.: FBA (bd. dirs.). Republican. Jewish. Office: US Courthouse 300 S 4th St Minneapolis MN 55415-1320

ROSENBAUM, LOIS OMENN, lawyer; b. Newark, Apr. 10, 1950; d. Edward and Ruth (Peretz) Omenn; m. Richard B. Rosenbaum, Apr. 4, 1971; children: Steven, Laura. AB, Wellesley Coll., 1971; JD, Stanford U., 1974. Bar: Calif. 1974, Oreg. 1977, D.C. 1974, U.S. Supreme Ct. 1990, Wash. 2001. Assoc. Fried, Frank, Harris, Shriver & Kampelman, Washington, 1974-75, Orrick, Herrington, Rowley & Sutcliffe, San Francisco, 1975-77, Stoel Rives LLP (formerly Stoel, Rives, Boley, Jones & Grey), Portland, Oreg., 1977-81, ptnr., 1981—. Mem. U.S. Dist. Ct. Mediation Panel. Bd. dirs. Providence Med. Found., 1990-95, Robison Jewish Home, 1994-97, Jewish Family & Child Svc., 1997-2000, Am. Jewish Commn., 2000—; past mem. Nat. Legal Com. Am. Jewish Com. Wellesley Coll. scholar, 1971. Mem. ABA, Multnomah County Bar Assn. (arbitration panel), Am. Arbitration Assn. (panel mem.), Multnomah Athletic Clubs, Wellesley Club (pres. 1987-88). Office: Stoel Rives LLP 900 SW 5th Ave Ste 2600 Portland OR 97204-1268 E-mail: lorosenbaum@stoel.com.

ROSENBAUM, MICHAEL FRANCIS, securities dealer; b. N.Y.C., Feb. 9, 1959; s. Francis Fels Jr. and Joyce (Keefer) R.; m. Elika Sosnick, Mar. 8, 1986; children: Erin Sosnick, Sarah Greer, Kira Keefer. AB, Princeton U., 1981. Cert. Nat. Assn. Securities Dealers. Product mgr. Sutro & Co., Inc., San Francisco, 1981-84; v.p. sales Pacific Securities, 1984-89; v.p., br. mgr. Rauscher Pierce Refsnes, 1989-92; v.p. sales Smith Mitchell Investment Group, 1992-93; sr. v.p. sales Gruntal & Co., Inc., 1993-94; sr. v.p. taxable fixed income Coast Ptnrs. Securities, 1994-99; sr. compliance examiner NASD Regulation, 1999-2001. Bd. dirs. S.G. Rosenbaum Found., N.Y.C. Trustee Princeton U. Rowing Assn. Democrat. Jewish. Avocations: skiing, sailing, dog breeding. Home: PO Box 1104 Ross CA 94957-1104 Fax: 415-925-2336. E-mail: mfr81@bloomberg.net.

ROSENBERG, A. IRVING, lawyer; b. Newark, Aug. 4, 1921; s. Sam and Dora Rosenberg; m. Toby Kalb, Dec. 12, 1943; children: Jeffrey, Elliot. Stenographic ct. reporting cert., Ct. Reporting Sch., Newark, 1940; Law Degree, Rutgers U., Newark, 1948. Bar: N.J. 1948. Office staf U.S. Secret Svc. Treasury Dept., Newark and N.Y.C., 1940-42; pvt. practice law, 1948—. Pres., dir. Psychic Studies Inst., Union, N.J., 1978—; lectr. in field. Author: Autobiography of the Unconscious, 1978; law rev. staff Rutgers Law Rev. Jour., 1941; contbr. articles to profl. jours. Comdr. Jewish War Vets. Post, Union, 1971-72; dir. C. of C., Union, 1975-85; chancellor comdr. Knights of Pythias, Union, 1985-86. With USN, 1942-45. Mem. Internat. Soc. for the Study of Multiple Personality and Dissociation (also N.J. chpt.), Am. Soc. for Psychical Rsch. Avocations: tennis, boating, antique collecting, trance mediumship and hypnosis. Office: 1227 Morris Ave Union NJ 07083-3307 E-mail: airvingrose@prodigy.net.

ROSENBERG, ALAN DAVID, accountant; b. Mt. Vernon, N.Y., Apr. 11, 1946; s. Benjamin Bernard and Miriam (Nierenberg) R.; m. Wendy Patricia Cutler, May 25, 1975; children: Kerri L., Joshua Z., Brian S. BS in Acctg., NYU, 1967; MBA in Taxation, Baruch Coll., 1970. CPA, N.Y. Sr. acct. Ernst & Ernst, N.Y.C., 1967-70; dir. acctg., CFO various firms, 1970-75; pres. Alan D. Rosenberg, CPA, P.C., N.Y.C., New Rochelle, N.Y., 1975—. Mem. AICPA (mem. tax practice mgmt. com. 1992—), N.Y. State Soc. CPAs, Inst. Mgmt. Accts., Nat. Conf. CPA Practitioners, Alliance of Practicing CPAs, Estate Planning Coun. Westchester County, Tax Soc. NYU. Jewish. Avocations: sports, reading, family activities. Office: 2 W 45th St Ste 1208 New York NY 10036-4212

ROSENBERG, ALAN GENE, newspaper editor; b. Chgo., Sept. 14, 1957; s. Earl David and Lorraine Faith (Blum) R.; m. Avis Beth Gunther-Rosenberg, Apr. 8, 1984; children: Ethan Elijah, Rebecca Greer, Jacob Sigmund. BS in Journalism, Northwestern U., 1978. From state staff reporter to asst. features editor Providence Jour., 1978—. Mem. Am. Assn. Sunday and Feature Editors. Office: Providence Jour 75 Fountain St Providence RI 02902-0050 E-mail: alan_rosenberg@projo.com.

ROSENBERG, ALAN STEWART, lawyer; b. N.Y.C., Mar. 29, 1930; s. Louis and Sadye (Knobler) R.; m. Ilse Rosenberg/Klein, Aug. 15, 1963; children: Gary, Robert. BA, Stanford U., 1949; LLB, Columbia U., 1952; LLM, NYU, 1960. Bar: N.Y. 1955. Assoc. Wolf Haldenstein Adler & Freeman, N.Y.C., 1955-56; ptnr., chmn. tax dept. Proskauer Rose Goetz & Mendelsohn, 1957—92. Contbr. articles to profl. jours. Mem. exec. com., bd. visitors Stanford (Calif.) U. Law Sch., 1982-85, advisor Humanities Ctr., 1985—, Jewish studies program, 1986—; chmn. bd. N.Y. Alliance for the Pub. Sch., 1988-91; mem. adv. com. on pub. issues Advt. Coun., 1991-94; bd. dirs., sec. Univ.-Urban Schs. Nat. Task Force Inc., 1981-96; mem. bd. visitors Columbia U. Law Sch., 1991-96; bd. dirs. Ctr. Ednl. Innovation, 2000—; bd. dirs., treas. Justice Resource Ctr., 1994-97; bd. dirs. The Abraham Fund; chmn. bd. dirs. Richalan Found. Lt. (j.g.) USN, 1952-55. Avocations: amateur opera singer; tennis. Home: 115 Central Park W New York NY 10023-4153 E-mail: aandi98@aol.com.

ROSENBERG, ALEX, mathematician, educator; b. Berlin, Germany, Dec. 5, 1926; came to U.S., 1949, naturalized, 1959; s. Theodore and Rela (Banet) R.; m. Beatrice Gershenson, Aug. 24, 1952 (div. Apr. 1985); children: Theodore Joseph, David Michael (dec.), Daniel Alex; m. Brunhilde Angun, June 14, 1985 BA, U. Toronto, 1948, MA, 1949; PhD, U. Chgo., 1951. From instr. to assoc. prof. math. Northwestern U., 1952-61; prof. math. Cornell U., Ithaca, N.Y., 1961-88, prof. emeritus, 1988—, chmn. dept., 1966-69; prof. U. Calif., Santa Barbara, 1986-94, chmn. dept., 1986-87, prof. emeritus, 1994—; mem. com. undergrad. program math. Math Assn. Am., 1966-76. Mem. Inst. Advanced Study, 1955-57; vis. prof. U. Calif., Berkely, 1961, 1979, U. Calif., Los Angeles, 1969-70, 82, U. London, Queen Mary Coll., 1963-64, U. Munich, 1975-76, E.T.H Zurich, 1976, U. Dortmund, 1984-85; trustee Am. Math Soc., 1973-83. Editor: Proc. Am. Math. Soc., 1960-66, Am. Math. Monthly, 1974-77; Contbr. articles to profl. jours. Recipient Humboldt Stiftung Sr. U.S. Scientist award U. Munich, 1975-76, U. Dortmund, 1981 Home: Heidestr 87 58239 Schwerte Germany

ROSENBERG, ALEX JACOB, art dealer, curator, fine arts appraiser, educator; b. N.Y.C., May 25, 1919; s. Israel and Lena (Zar) R. Student, Albright Coll., 1935-37, Sch. Phila. Mus. Art, 1937-40; BS, Phila. U., 1948; DHL (hon.), Hofstra U., 1989. completed Personal Property courses, levels I, II, III and IV, Am. Soc. of Appraisers, Uniform Standards of Profl. Appraisal Practice, 1994, 2000. Pres. Anserphone, 1959-66; sec., dir. Gen. Cablevision Tex., 1968-72; v.p., dir. Communicable, Inc., Fla., 1967-71, Gen. Cablevision Palatka, 1967-71, Beacon Cable Corp., 1966-71; pres., dir. Modern Cable Corp., 1966-71, B.F.C.-C.A.T.V. Corp., 1966-71; v.p., dir. Starfax Corp. Real Estate, 1968-70; gen. ptnr. Lakewood Plaza Assocs., N.J., 1973-92, Rostin Assocs., Austin, Tex., 1970-83; pres. Transworld Art Inc., Alex Rosenberg Gallery and Alba Edits., N.Y.C., 1968-89, Rostin Mgmt. Corp., 1986-89, The Abbot Group, 1987-89, Ardmore Affiliates Ltd., Alex Rosenberg Fine Art, 1985—, Neikrug-Rosenberg Assocs., 1989-97. Lectr. Parsons Sch. Design, N.Y.C., 1979—88; instr. appraising modern art NYU, 1992—95, adj. prof. appraising, 1995—; vis. prof. fine art Advanced Inst. Arts, Havana, Cuba, 1993—; organizer Henry Moore exhbn. Mus. Budapest, Bratislava and Prague, Hungary, 1993; co-curator Leonoid Sokov, Albright Coll., Reading , Pa., 2002. Curator An American Portrait, 1976—78, Mus. Fine Art, Havana, 1992—93, co-curator Romare Bearden as Printmaker, 1992—97, Leonid Sokov-Freedman Gallery, Reading, Pa., 2002, Henry Moore Mother and Child Exhbn., 1987—88, assoc. editor exhbn. catalogue. Trustee Alice Baber Art Fund, 1991-93, Phila. Coll. Textiles and Sci., 1992-95, Tel Aviv Mus. Art (mem. internat. bd. dirs., 1999—, trustee, 2000—); bd. dirs. Artists' Rights Today, 1974-80; mus. adv. bd. Hofstra Mus., Hempstead, N.Y., 1987-92; mem. collection and exhbn. com. Parrish Art Mus., Southhampton, N.Y., 1989-95; mem. adv. com. Pollock-Krasner House and Study Ctr., 2000—; trustee Guttman Inst., 1979-92; mem. exec. bd. Nat. Emergency Civil Liberties Com., 1970-98, treas., 1981-98; trustee Nat. Emergency Civil Liberties Found., 1964-98, chmn., 1992-98; nat. bd. dirs. and bd. dirs. local coun. SANE, 1974-83, bd. dirs. Ctr. for Constitutional Rights, 1998—; trustee, treas. New Lincoln Sch., 1968-71; trustee Givat Haviva Ednl. Found., N.Y.C., 1969—, chmn. exec. com., 1992-99, v.p., 1998—; trustee Givat Haviva Inst., Hadera, Israel, 1993-96, Stephen Wise Free synagogue, 1967-70, 73-76, 99-2000, Mus. Borough Bklyn., 1986-89; del. 28th World Zionist Congress, Jerusalem, 1972; mem. Cmty. Planning Bd. # 7, 1965-67, 70-72; mem. Lower West Side Anti-Poverty Bd., 1965-66, Lincoln Ctr. Cmty. Coun., 1968-74, Com. for Ind. Civilian Police Rev. Bd., 1967; mem. steering com. Com. Pub. Edn. and Religious Liberty; chmn. Am. Israel Civil Liberties Coalition, 1988-89; Dem. dist. leader, 1964-74, state committeeman, 1970-73, mem. county exec. com., 1964-74; del. Dem. Nat. Conf., 1968, 72; bd. dirs. Raoul Wallenberg Commn. of U.S., 1986-90, chmn., 1990-92; mem. print and drawing coun. Israel Mus., 1980-85; assoc. dir. Snug Harbor Cultural Ctr., S.I., 1982-88; mem. AAA del. to Pres. Coun. of Appraisal Orgns., 1995-96; bd. mem. Ludwig Found. of Cuba, 1995—, Am. Friends Ludwig Found. Cuba, 2000—; mem. Assn. Governing Bds. of Univs. and Colls., 1994-96, Nat. Registry of Forensic Examiners, 1994-96. Recipient Spl. prize Grenschen Triennial, Switzerland, 1976, Cuban Order of Culture, 1995, Cert. of Commendation, Am. Soc. Appraisers, 1993, Cert. for Disting. Svc., Appraisers Assn. of Am., 1993, Graham J. Littlewood III award for profl. excellence Phila. Coll. of Textiles and Sci., 1996, Alex and Carole Rosenberg Collection, Savannah Coll. of Art and Design, 1999, Alex Rosenberg Gallery Hofstra U., 1996—. Mem. Am. Soc. Appraisers (sr., bd. examiners 1987—, personal property com. 1987-89), Appraisers Assn. Am. (cert. mem., bd. dirs. 1990-96, v.p. 1992-94, 1st v.p. 1994, pres. 1994-96), Fine Art Pubs. Assn. (v.p., bd. dirs. 1981-83, pres. 1983-86, treas. 1986-89), Nat. Arts Club. Home and Office: 3 E 69th St New York NY 10021-4943 Fax: 212-628-4769.

ROSENBERG, ALISON P. public policy official; b. Miami, Fla., Sept. 5, 1945; d. Mortimer I. and Gail (Sklar) Podell; m. Jeffrey Alan Rosenberg, May 4, 1969; 1 child, Robert Aaron. BS in Econs., Smith Coll., 1967. Mng. officer Citibank, N.Y.C., 1967-69; legis. aide Senator Charles Percy, Washington, 1969-80; profl. staff mem. Senate Fgn. Rels. Com., 1981-85; assoc. asst. adminstr. Agy. for Internat. Devel., 1985-87; dir. African affairs Nat. Security Coun., 1987-88; dep. asst. sec. for Africa State Dept., 1988-92; asst. adminstr. for Africa Agy. for Internat. Devel., 1992-93; lead partnerships specialist (Africa) The World Bank, 1993—. E-mail: arosenberg@worldbank.org.

ROSENBERG, ARTHUR HENRY, internist; b. Phila., Mar. 14, 1934; MD, Columbia U., 1959. Diplomate in internal medicine, hematology and oncology Am. Bd. Internal Medicine. Intern U. Ill. Rsch. Edn. Hosps., 1959-60, resident in medicine, 1962-63, Mt. Sinai Hosp., N.Y.C., 1963-64, fellow in hematology, 1964-65; attending physician Greenwich Hosp.; chmn. dept. hematology and oncology, med. dir. Bendheim Cancer Ctr.; asst. prof. dept. medicine Yale U. Fellow Am. Coll. Physicians; mem. AMA, Am. Soc. Breast Diseases, Am. Soc. Clin. Oncology, Am. Soc. Hematology. Office: 77 Lafayette Pl Greenwich CT 06830-5426 E-mail: ahronc2000@yahoo.com.

ROSENBERG, CAROLE, art dealer, real estate broker; b. Bklyn., Nov. 16, 1936; d. Hugo and Mildred (Wilinsky) Clemente; m. Melvyn S. Sponder; m. Jerome A. Halsband; children: Michael S. Halsband, Kenneth L. Halsband; m. Alex J. Rosenberg, May 15, 1977. Student, Hunter Coll., 1954-56; BA, Bklyn. Coll., 1958; postgrad., NYU, 1961-62, 64-65. Tchr. N.Y.C. Sch. System, 1958-59, 61-63, Fla. Sch. System, Miami Beach, 1959-61; gallery owner and dir. Original Graphics/Carole Halsband Gallery, N.Y.C., 1971-76; assoc. editor Transworld Art Inc., 1974-78; exec. dir., curator Alex Rosenberg Gallery/Transworld Art Inc., 1978-87; exec. dir., v.p. Ardmore Affiliates Ltd., 1987—; real estate salesperson, 1986-91; real estate broker Carole Rosenberg Properties Internat. Ltd., 1992—. Treas. 3/69 Owners Corp., N.Y.C.1984-87, pres., 1987-91, v.p., 1991-93; chmn. bd. dirs. Friends of the Hofstra U. Arboretum, Hempstead, N.Y., 1991-94. Editor: (art catalogs) Henry Moore, Howard Kanovitz, Mark Tobey, Lila Katzen, 1975; assoc. editor (portfolio) An American Portrait, 1976. Mem. adv. bd. Women Beyond Borders, 1995—, Ludwig Found. Cuba, 1995—; mem. cmty. bd. Water Mill Ctr., 1999—; internat. bd. mem. Tel Aviv Mus. Art, 1999—; bd. dirs. Am. Friends of the Tel Aviv Mus., 2000—; mem. coun. Friends of Upper East Side Hist. Dist., N.Y.C., 1983—96; pres. Am. Friends of the Ludwig Found. of Cuba, 2000—, Lotos Club Found., Lotos Found., 2000—. Recipient Lotos medal of merit, 1995, Mgmt. Achievement Award for Innovation, N.Y. Habitat Mag., N.Y.C., 1989. Mem. Real Estate Bd. N.Y.C., Parrish Art Mus. (patron garden com.), Met. Mus. Art, Mus. Modern Art, Guggenheim Mus., Nat. Arts Club, Hort. Soc. N.Y., Lotos Club (mem. art com. 1989—, chmn. art com. 1992-98, dir. 1993-99), City Gardens Club, Women's City Club Am. Hort. Soc., N.Y. Hort. Soc., (Longhouse Res. garden comm. 1995—), Hort. Alliance of the Hamptons, Guggenheim Mus., Art Table. Democrat. Jewish. Avocation: gardening. E-mail: arfineart@aol.com.

ROSENBERG, CHARLES ERNEST, historian, educator; b. N.Y.C., Nov. 11, 1936; s. Bernard and Marion (Roberts) R.; m. Carroll Ann Smith, June 22, 1961 (div. 1977); 1 child, Leah; m. Drew Gilpin Faust, June 7, 1980; 1 child, Jessica. BA, U. Wis., 1956; MA, Columbia U., 1957, PhD, 1961; DHL, U. Wis., 1997. Fellow Johns Hopkins U., Balt., 1960-61; asst. prof. U. Wis., 1961-63; assoc. prof. U. Pa., Phila., 1965-68, prof. history, 1968—, chmn. dept., 1974-75, 79-83; prof. history of sci. Harvard U., 2001—. Bd. dirs. Mental Health Assn. Southeastern Pa., 1973-76, Library Co. of Phila., 1980—, Ctr. Advanced Study Behavioral Scis., 1999—. Author: The Cholera Years: The United States in 1832, 1849 and 1866, 1962, The Trial of the Assassin Guiteau: Psychiatry and Law in the Gilded Age, 1968, No Other Gods: On Science and Social Thought in America, 1976, The Care of Strangers: The Rise of America's Hospital System, 1987, Explaining Epidemics and Other Studies in the History of Medicine, 1992; editor Isis, 1986-89. Nat. Inst. Health Research grantee, 1964-70; Guggenheim Found. fellow, 1965-66, 89-90; Nat. Endowment Humanities fellow, 1972-73; Rockefeller Found. humanities fellow, 1975-76; fellow Inst. Advanced Study, 1979-80, Ctr. Advanced Study in Behavioral Scis., 1982-83. Fellow Am. Acad. Arts and Scis., Am. Philos. Soc.; mem. Inst. Medicine of NAS, Am. Assn. History of Medicine (William H. Welch medal 1969, coun. 1974-76, pres. 1992-94), History of Sci. Soc. (George Sarton medal 1995, coun. 1972-75), Soc. Social History of Medicine (pres. 1981), Orgn. Am. Historians (exec. bd. 1985-88). Home: 76 Brattle Cambridge MA 02138 Office: Harvard U Dept History of Sci Cambridge MA 02138 E-mail: rosenb3@fas.harvard.edu.

ROSENBERG, CHARLES MICHAEL, art historian, educator; b. Chgo., Aug. 3, 1945; s. Sandor and Laura (Fried) R.; m. Carol Ann Weiss, June 25, 1967; children: Jessica Rachel, Jasper Matthew. BA, Swarthmore Coll., 1967; MA, U. Mich., 1969, PhD, 1974. Asst. prof. SUNY, Brockport, 1973-80; assoc. prof. U. Notre Dame, Ind., 1980-96, prof., 1996—. Author: 15th Century North Italian Painting and Drawing: Bibliography, 1986, Art and Politics in Late Medieval and Early Renaissance Italy, 1990, Este Monuments and Urban Development in Renaissance Ferrara, 1997; contbr. articles to Art Bull., Renaissance Quar., others. Kress Found. fellow Kunsthistorisches Inst., Florence, Italy, 1971-73, Am. Coun. Learned Socs. fellow, 1977-78, NEH fellow, Brown U., 1979-80, Villa i Tatti, Florence, 1985-86, Rome prize Am. Acad. Rome, 2000-01. Mem. Coll. Art Assn., Renaissance Soc. Am., Centro di Studi Europa Della Corti, Italian Art Soc. Office: Notre Dame U Dept Art Art History & Design Notre Dame IN 46556 E-mail: rosenberg.1@nd.edu.

ROSENBERG, CLAUDE NEWMAN, JR. investment adviser; b. San Francisco, Apr. 10, 1928; s. Claude Newman and Elza (Wolff) R.; m. Louise Jankelson, Dec. 19, 1968; children: Linda Kay, Douglas Claude. BA, Stanford U., 1950, MBA, 1952. Research analyst J. Barth & Co., San Francisco, 1955-62, partner charge research, 1962-70; investment adviser, pres. Rosenberg Capital Mgmt., San Francisco, 1970-96. Lectr. and mem. adv. council Grad. Sch. Bus., Stanford; adv. bd. mem. Entrepreneur's Found., Hauser Ctr., Kennedy Sch. Govt., Harvard U.; founding chmn. The Philanthropic Rsch. Inst., 1997; founder, chmn. The Newtithing Group, 1997. Author: Stock Market Primer, 1962, rev., 1970, 76, 81, 87, The Common Sense Way to Stock Market Profit, 1968, rev., 1978, Psycho-Cybernetics and the Stock Market, 1970, Investing with the Best, 1986, rev., 1993, Wealthy and Wise, 1994. Bd. dirs. Jewish Welfare Fedn., Presbyn. Children's Cancer Research Center, Internat. Hospitality Center, Jewish Community Center; trustee San Francisco Ballet Assn., Univ. High Sch., San Francisco.; chmn. adv. council Stanford U. Sch. Bus.; chmn., founder Newtithing Group, 1997. Served with USNR, 1951-53. Recipient Arbuckle award Stanford U. Grad. Sch. Bus., 1984, Daniel I. Forrestal Leadership award Assn. of Investment and Mgmt. Rsch. 1992, Lilywhite award Employee Benefit Rsch. Inst., 1994, Bus. Statesman award Harvard Bus. Sch. Assn. of No. Calif., 1995, Lifetime Achievement award San Francisco C. of C., 1997, Fishes and Loaves Philanthropist award Cath. Charities, 1998. Mem. Fin. Analysts San Francisco, Alumni Assn. Stanford U. Grad. Sch. Bus. (pres.) Republican. Jewish religion. Clubs: Family (San Francisco), Concordia-Argonaut (San Francisco), Calif. Tennis (San Francisco), Family (San Francisco). Home: 2465 Pacific Ave San Francisco CA 94115-1237 Office: Four Embarcadero Center Fl 37 San Francisco CA 94111

ROSENBERG, DAN YALE, retired plant pathologist; b. Stockton, Calif., Jan. 8, 1922; s. Meyer and Bertha (Naliboff) R.; m. Marilyn Kohn, Dec. 5, 1954; 1 son, Morton Karl. AA, Stockton Jr. Coll., 1942; AB, Coll. of the Pacific, 1949; MS, U. Calif., Davis, 1952. Jr. plant pathologist State of Calif. Dept. Agr., Riverside, 1952-55, asst. plant pathologist Sacramento, 1955-59, assoc. plant pathologist Riverside, 1959-60, pathologist IV, 1960-63, program supr., 1963-71, chief exclusion and detectin, divsn. plant industry, 1971-76, chief nursery and seed svcs. divsn. plant industry, 1976-82, spl. asst. divsn. plant industry, 1982-87; pres. Health Inc., 1972-73. Agrl. cons., 1988—; mem. Citrus Rsch. Adm. Com., U. Calif., Riverside, 1992—; mem. Gov.'s Interagy. Task Force on Biotech., 1986—; agrl. cons. Calif. Avocado Commn., 1994—. Contbr. articles to profl. jours. Served with AUS, 1942-46, ETO. Mem. Am. Phytopath. Soc. (fgn. and regulatory com. 1975—, grape diseases sect. 1977-79, grape pests sect. 1979—), Calif. State Employees Assn. (pres. 1967-69), Sacto. Met. C. of C. (internat. trade com. 1993-97), N.Am. Plant Protection Orgn. (industry adv. group), Plant Patents Fruit Trees and Ornamental Trees. Home and Office: 2328 Swarthmore Dr Sacramento CA 95825-6867

ROSENBERG, DAVID ALAN, military historian, educator; b. N.Y.C., Aug. 30, 1948; s. Sidney and Fay (Breitman) R.; m. Deborah Lee Haines, July 1, 1973; 1 child, Rebecca Haines. BA in History, Am. U., 1970; MA in History, U. Chgo., 1971, PhD in History, 1983. Asst. historian, cons. Lulejian & Assocs., Inc., Falls Church, VA., 1974-75; instr. history U. Wis., Milw., 1976-78; pvt. practice cons., rschr. Chgo., Washington, 1978-82; asst. prof. history U. Houston, University Park, 1982-83; sr. fellow Strategic Concepts Devel. Ctr., Nat. Def. U., Washington, 1983-85; prof. strategy and ops. U.S. Naval War Coll., Newport, R.I., 1985-90; assoc. prof. history Temple U.,

Phila., 1990-2000, professorial lectr., 2001—; Adm. Harry W. Hill prof. maritime strategy Nat. War Coll., Washington, 1996—; sr. strategic rschr. U.S. Naval War Coll., 1998—. Mem. U.S. exec. com. four Nation Nuclear History Program, project dir. Berlin Crisis, 1989-95; cons. Office of Sec. Def., 1991-93, Office of Chief of Naval Ops., 1991—, Office of Sec. of Navy, 1992—; mem., chair Sec. Navy's Adv. Subcom. of Naval History, 1995—. Co-editor: (15 vol. book set) U.S. Plans for War, 1945-1950, 1990; contbr. articles to Jour. Am. History (2 awards nat. hist. assns. 1980), 22 others, also 16 book chpts. With USNR, 1982—. Recipient Meritorious Pub. Svc. award Dept. of Navy, 1995, Superior Civilian Svc. medal, 2000; Advanced rsch. scholar U.S. Naval War Coll., 1974-79; Ford Found grantee, 1985-86, MacArthur rsch. grantee 1987-88; MacArthur fellow 1988-93. Mem. Orgn. Am. Historians (Binkley-Stephenson article prize), Soc. for Historians of Am. Fgn. Rels. (Bernath article prize), Soc. for Mil. History, U.S. Naval Inst., Internat. Inst. for Strategic Studies. Jewish. E-mail: rosenbergd@ndu.edu.

ROSENBERG, DAVID MORTON, pediatrician; b. Milw. s. Samuel and Janette Molly Rosenberg; children: Nicole, Andrew, Nathan. BS, U. Wis., 1970; DO, Coll. Osteopathic Medicine and Surgery, 1974. Diplomate Am. Bd. Pediatrics. Intern Milw. Children's Hosp., 1974-75, resident, 1975-77; pvt. practice, 1977-95, Covenant Med. Group, 1995—. Apptd. clin. instr. pediatrics Med. Coll. Wis., 1977, aptpd. asst. clin. prof. pediatrics, 1985; bd. dirs. Wis. Independent Physicians Group Bd., 1982-85, 92-97; med. dir. Family Hosp. Well Baby Clinic of Teen Pregnancy Svc., 1980-85; med. dir. newborn nurseries Sinai Samaritan Med. Ctr., Milw., 1991-93. Fellow Am. Acad. Pediatrics; mem. Internat. Assn. Healthcare Practitioners, State Med. Soc. Wis., Milw. Pediatric Soc., Milw. County Med. Soc., Phi Delta Epsilon. Office: Covenant Med Group 7950 N Pt Wash Rd Fox Point WI 53217-3133 E-mail: drosenberg@covhealth.org.

ROSENBERG, ELLEN Y. religious association administrator; married; 2 children. Student, Goucher Coll.; BS in Edn., Mills Coll.; postgrad., Columbia U. Assoc. dean for acad. affairs Marymount Manhattan Coll., N.Y.C.; exec. dir. Women of Reform Judaism/Fed. Temple Sisterhoods, 1992—. Bd. dirs. Mazon, World Union for Progressive Judaism, Jewish Braille Inst. Am., Union Am. Hebrew Congregations. Office: WRJ 633 3rd Ave New York NY 10017-6706

ROSENBERG, ERIC LEE, internal medicine physician, educator; b. Stoneham, Mass., Mar. 8, 1957; s. Richard Harvey and Janice S. Rosenberg; m. Jane Rogers, May 16, 1981; children: Daniel, Emily. BA cum laude, Yale U., 1979; MD, U. Pa., 1983. Diplomate Am. Bd. Internal Medicine, cert. added qualifications in geriatrics. John C. Leonard fellow Hartford (Conn.) Hosp., 1986-87; pvt. practice Hartford, 1986-97; internal medicine physician ProHealth Physicians, PC, 1997—. Clin. instr. U. Conn. Sch. Medicine, Farmington, 1992—; cofounder, treas. ProHealth Physicians MSO, Inc., Farmington, 1992-97, chmn. fin. com., 1995-98, chmn. ancillaries com., 1997—. Fundraiser Greater Hartford YMCA, Glastonbury, Conn., 1998—; bd. dirs. Retreat Condominium Corp., Hartford, 1990-2000. Named one of Nation's Top Primary Care Physicians, Castle-Connolly, Inc., 2000. Fellow ACP; mem. Hartford County Med. Assn., Conn. State Med. Soc. Avocations: sailing, hiking. Office: ProHealth Physicians PC 1000 Avery Heights Hartford CT 06106 E-mail: erosenberg@prohealthmd.com.

ROSENBERG, FLORENCE PESSAH, lawyer; b. N.Y.C., Jan. 8, 1922; d. Morris A. Pessah and Fanny Cantor; m. June 1, 1985; children: Richard C., sherry A. Waldorf, Barret Craig. Student, CCNY, 1939-41; BA, St. John's Coll., Bklyn., 1944; JD, St. John's Coll., 1946. Bar: N.Y. 1946, Calif. 1961. Atty. Fed. Cts., L.A., 1961-65; assoc. Hirschberg, Goodman & King, 1966-68; atty. Crenshaw Legal Clinic, 1971-80; pvt. practice Encino, Calif., 1981-94, Calabasas, 1994—. Atty. domestic violence, Van Nuys, Calif., 1986—. Mem. L.A. Bar Assn. (Vol. 1988), San Fernando Bar Assn. (Pro Bono for Domestic Violence 1997). Home and Office: Apt B213 5450 Vesper Ave Sherman Oaks CA 91411-4231

ROSENBERG, GABRIEL JOSEPH, legal consultant, physician; b. Indpls., July 14, 1932; s. Pincus S. and Esther Edithe (Slutzky) R.; m. Francine Zelma Levinson, Nov. 29, 1959; children: Natalie, Teresa, Andrew, Laura (dec.). BA, Ind. U., 1954, MD, 1957. Rotating intern Cook County Hosp., Chgo., 1957-58; resident in pediatrics Riley Hosp. for Children, 1958-59, 61-62; pediatrician pvt. practrice, Indpls., 1962-67, Meth. Hosp. Ind., Indpls., 1967-88, dir. pediatric. med. edn., 1967-83, co-dir. PNA program, 1971-88, dir. med./pediatric residency program, 1983-85, dir. pediatrics, 1983-86, med. dir., 1986-87; legal cons. pediat. malpractice, pvt. practice, 1988—. Adj. asst. prof. nursing Ind. U. Sch. Nursing, 1976-88, asst. prof. pediatrics, 1972-88. Contbr. articles to profl. jours. Capt. USAF, 1959-61. Fellow Am. Acad. Pediatrics; mem. Am. Coll. Legal Medicine (assoc.), Am. Coll. Physician Execs., Ambulatory Pediatric Assn. Independent. Avocations: tennis, art, fishing, bridge.

ROSENBERG, GARY ARON, real estate development executive, lawyer; b. Green Bay, Wis., June 18, 1940; s. Ben J. and Joyce Sarah (Nemzin) R.; m. Gloria Davis, Nov. 1967 (div. 1975); children: Myra, Meredith; m. Bridgit A. Maile, Apr. 9, 1983. BS, Northwestern U., 1962, MBA, 1963; JD, U. Wis., 1966. Bar: Wis. 1966, Ill. 1967. Chmn., dir. The Rosenberg Found., 1960—; atty. U.S. SEC, Washington, 1966-67; pvt. practice Chgo., 1967-74; founder, chmn. bd., CEO UDC Homes, Inc. (formerly UDC-Universal Devel., L.P.), 1968-1995; chmn., CEO, dir. Canterbury Devel. Corp., 1986—; dir. Olympic Cascade Fin. Corp., 1996-98, Nat. Securities, Chgo., 1996—; chair, pres., CEO, dir. OneStop Shop, Inc., 1998—; dir. hometouch Ctrs., Inc. Mem. adv. bd. Kellogg Grad. Sch. Mgmt. Northwestern U., Evanston, Ill., 1985—, founder, chmn. adv. bd. Kellogg Real Estate Rsch. Ctr., 1986—, adj. prof., 1982—; founder Shadow Hill Entertainment Corp., Beverly Hills, Calif., 1990. Recipient Arts Edn. Svc. award Ill. Alliance for Arts Edn., Chgo., 1988, Kellogg Schaffner Disting. Alumni award Kellogg Grad. Sch. Mgmt., 1993. Mem. Nat. Assn. Home Builders (coun. 1989-90), John Evans Club. Avocations: skiing, hiking, climbing, tennis, golf, reading. Office: hometouch Ctrs Inc Ste 3660 676 N Michigan Ave Chicago IL 60611-2866 E-mail: bamgar@interaccess.com.

ROSENBERG, GARY MARC, lawyer; b. N.Y.C., June 4, 1950; s. David and Edna (Goldberg) R.; m. I. Denise Estes, July 3, 1971; children: Dena Elyse, Janna Beth, Adam Ilan. BA, Queens Coll., 1971; JD, Bklyn. Law Sch., 1974. Bar: N.Y. 1975, U.S. Dist. Ct. (so. dist.) N.Y. 1976, U.S. Supreme Ct. 1985. Pres. Rosenberg & Estis, P.C., N.Y.C., 1976—. Office: Rosenberg & Estis PC 733 3rd Ave New York NY 10017-3204

ROSENBERG, HELEN, sociology educator; b. Bad Reichenhal, Germany, Oct. 23, 1946; d. Nathan and Hannah Gertz; m. Howard L. Rosenberg, June 6, 1971; children: Lauren, Darren. PhD, Northwestern U., 1989. Group worker Clayton Halfway House, Chgo., 1967-68; rsch. scientist I Inst. for Juvenile Rsch., 1968-82; prin. rsch. investigator Thresholds Rsch. Inst., 1989-91; assoc. prof. U. Wis.-Parkside, Kenosha, 1991—. Vis. prof. Obafemi Awolowo U., Nigeria, 1995; vis. scholar program for law and justice studies, Northwestern U., 1999-2000; project coord. Cmty. Alternative Policing Strategy, Criminal Justice Dept. Loyola U., chgo., 1993; project dir. Survey of Racine (Wis.) Cmty. Policint Initiative, 1997-99. Co-author: The State Mental Patient and Urban Life: Moving In and Out of the Institution, 1994, Worlds of the Mentally Ill: How Deinstitutionalization Works in the City, 1991; contbr. chpts. to books, articles to profl. jours. Grantee Nat. Inst. Justice, 1997-99, Racine Police Dept., 1996, State of Ill., Wis. Tchg. Fellowship, 1994; fellow Ctr. for Urban Affairs Rsch., Northwestern, 1984-88. Office: 900 Wood Rd Kenosha WI 53144-1133 E-mail: rosenbeh@uwp.edu.

ROSENBERG, HERB, sculptor, educator; b. N.Y.C., Feb. 4, 1942; s. David and Eve Rosenberg; m. Jean Gustavson, Nov. 14, 1976 (div. Nov. 1998); 1 child, Andrew. BA, SUNY, Binghamton, 1964; MFA, Pratt Inst., 1967. Registered art therapist. Dir. art therapy studies N.J. City U., Jersey City, 1971—. Exhibited in solo shows at World's Fair, Brisbane, Australia, 1988, UNESCO, Paris, 1992, Grand Palais, Paris, 1994, BRAS. Bd. dirs. Hurley Found., N.Y.C., 1994—, Ctr. Bros d'Or Cultural Ctr., N.S., Can., 1996—, C.A.S.E. Mus., Jersey City, 1995—. Grantee Jersey City State Coll., 1979, 81, 84, 88; recipient Juror's award Hong Kong Mus. Art, 1992; named Sculptor of Yr., Hudson County Cultural Ctr., 1984. Mem.: Kans. Sculpture Soc., Australian Sculpture Soc., Am. Art Therapy Assn., Internat. Sculpture Soc., Art Therapy Assn. (chair 1984—86), Internat. Expressive Arts Assn., Am. Expressive Arts Assn. E-mail: pneuonce@aol.com.

ROSENBERG, JACOB JOSEPH, orthodontist; b. N.Y.C., July 15, 1947; s. Louis and Pearl (Flaster) R.; m. Marylynn Borteck; children: Jonathan, Carolyn, Hilary. BA, U. Vt., 1968; MS, Colo. State U., 1970; DDS with honors, SUNY, Buffalo, 1975; cert. in Orthodontics, Columbia U., 1977. Diplomate Am. Bd. Orthodontics. Practice dentistry specializing in orthodontics, Bethesda, Md., 1977-97; clin. asst. prof. orthodontics U. Md., Balt., 1997—. Alumni admission rep. U. Vt. Mem. ADA, Md. State Soc. Orthodontists (pres. 1986-87), Am. Assn. Orthodontists, Am. Bd. Orthodontics (mem. Coll. Diplomates), Orthodontic Edn. of Research Found., Alpha Omega. Avocations: golf, skiing, reading, photography, travel. Address: 9621 Reach Rd Potomac MD 20854-2857

ROSENBERG, JEROME DAVID, physicist; b. N.Y.C., June 15, 1920; s. Hyman D. and Hilda (Cantor) R.; m. Shirley Sirota, 1947; children: Jonathan, Hindy. BS in Physics, CCNY, 1948; postgrad., Nat. Bur. Standards Grad. Sch., 1949-52, George Washington U., 1952, U. Md., 1951-53, Cath. U. Am., 1953-54. Engr. officer USCG Acad., 1942, APA-34, 1943-45; dir. microphonics Nat. Bur. Standards, 1949-54; project mgr., mgr. test nuclear reactor Harry Diamond Labs., Washington, 1952-62; ops. mgr. tech. utilization NASA, 1962-64; program and project mgr. space applications program NASA Nat. Geodetic Satellite Prog., Satellites Pageos GEOS 1&2, 1964-72; dep. dir. comm. divsn. NASA, 1972-74, dir. tech. applications divsn., 1974-77, dir. office energy programs divsn. bus. mgmt., 1977-78; spl. assignment to solar applications & conservation, barriers and incentive br. Dept. Energy, 1978-79; leader solar energy group Mitre Corp., McLean, Va., 1979-80; prin. cons. energy and environ. divsn. Booz, Allen & Hamilton, Washington, 1980-82; sr. staff officer Bd. Telecomm. and Computer Applications, NRC-NAS, 1982-85. Exec. dir. NASA Alumni League, Washington, 1986—; mem. Outlook for Space Study Group, NASA planning group to develop U.S. space programs, 1975. Lt. (j.g.) USCG, 1943—44. Recipient NASA Exceptional Svc. medal, 1973. Mem. Fed. Exec. Inst., Sigma Pi Sigma. Office: NASA Alumni League 750 1st St NE Washington DC 20002-4241 E-mail: jerry@ssrinc.com.

ROSENBERG, JEROME IRA, lawyer; b. Passaic, N.J., June 9, 1931; s. Emanuel and Sylvia S. (Schwartz) R.; m. Dorothy Elaine Teninbaum, Aug. 21, 1955; children: Peter, Michael BA, NYU, 1953; LLB, Harvard U., 1956. Bar: N.Y. 1966, D.C. 1957, U.S. Supreme Ct. 1961. Tax law specialist IRS, Washington, 1960-63; counsel Hughes Hubbard & Reed LLP, N.Y.C., 1968—. Lectr. NYU Tax Inst. Contbr. articles to Jour. of Taxation Served as lt. USAF, 1957-60 Mem. N.Y. State Bar Assn., Assn. of Bar of City of N.Y., D.C. Bar Assn., Phi Beta Kappa. Office: Hughes Hubbard & Reed One Battery Park Plz New York NY 10004-1466 E-mail: rosenber@hugheshubbard.com.

ROSENBERG, JEROME LAIB, chemist, educator; b. Harrisburg, Pa., June 20, 1921; s. Robert and Mary (Katzman) R.; m. Shoshana Gabriel, Sept. 15, 1946; children— Jonathan, Judith. AB, Dickinson Coll., 1941; MA, Columbia U., 1944, PhD, 1948. Rsch. chemist S.A.M. Labs., 1944-46; Instr. chemistry Columbia U., 1946-48; rsch. assoc. (asst. prof.) inst. Radiobiology and Biophysics, U. Chgo., 1950-53; mem. faculty U. Pitts., 1953-91, chmn. dept. biophysics and microbiology, 1969-71, prof. biol. scis., 1976-91, dean faculty arts and scis., 1970-86, vice provost, 1978-89, chmn. biol. scis., 1989-90, interim chmn. communication, 1991, assoc. dean faculty arts and scis., 1991-92, rsch. integrity officer, 1992—, prof. emeritus biol. scis., 1991—, dir. Jewish studies program, 1991-99. Author: Photosynthesis, 1965; editor, reviser: Outline Theory and Problems of College Chemistry (Schaum), 1949, 58, 66, 80, 90, 97; contbr. articles to profl. jours. NSF sr. fellow Technion Israel Inst. Tech., 1962-63, AEC fellow U. Chgo., 1948-50; recipient Pitts. award Am. Chem. Soc., 1987. Mem. AAUP (nat. coun. 1968-69, pres. Pa. div. 1968-69). Home: 1029 S Negley Ave Pittsburgh PA 15217-1045 E-mail: shoshjerry@msn.com.

ROSENBERG, JEROME ROY, lawyer, accountant; b. N.Y.C., Oct. 5, 1926; s. Louis and May (Schack) R.; m. Julia Daniels, Apr. 21, 1968; children: Louise I., Daniel M. BS, NYU, 1949, JD, 1953, LLM in Taxation, 1972; postgrad., Oxford U., 1949. Bar: N.Y. 1956, U.S. Dist. Ct. (so. dist.) N.Y. 1985, U.S. Dist. Ct. (ea. dist.) N.Y. 1985, U.S. Claims Ct. 1977, U.S. Tax Ct. 1965, U.S. Supreme Ct. 1968. Acct. Apfel & Englander, CPAs, N.Y.C., 1950-52; with Abraham J. Briloff, CPA, 1952-54, Samuel Aronowitz & Co., CPAs, N.Y.C., 1955-57, David Berdon & Co., CPAs, N.Y.C., 1957-63; sole practice, 1964—; spl. tax counsel Jackson & Nash, 1964-70, Seward & Kissel, N.Y.C., 1968—. Lectr. NYU, 1972; co-founder N.Y. Tax Study Group, Inc. Author: Managing Your Own Money, 1979; asst. tech. editor Jour. Taxation, 1964; mem. editl. bd. Practical Acct., 1968-85; sr. tech. editor Income Tax Workbook, 1970-75. Served with USAF, 1943-45. Mem. ABA, AICPA, Assn. Bar City N.Y. (sr. lawyers com. 2001—), N.Y. Soc. CPAs (mem. exec. tax com. 1983-92, Disting. Svc. award 1993). Home: 50 Park Ave New York NY 10016-3075

ROSENBERG, JILL, realtor, civic leader; b. Shreveport, La., Feb. 17, 1940; d. Morris H. and Sallye (Abramson) Schuster; m. Lewis Rosenberg, Dec. 23, 1962; children: Craig, Paige. BA in Philosophy, Tulane U., 1961, MSW, 1965; grad., Realtor Inst., 1994. Cert. residential specialist Residential Sales Coun.; grad. Realtor Inst. 1993. Social worker La. Dept. Pub. Welfare, 1961-62, 63-64; genetics counselor Sinai Hosp., Balt., 1967-69; ptnr. Parties Extraordinaire, cons., 1973-77; realtor assoc. Robert Weil Assocs., Long Beach, Calif., 1982—. Mem. dean's adv. bd. Coll. Bus. Adninstrn. Calif. State U., Long Beach, 2001—. Pres. we. region Pres. we. region, 1972—73; v.p. Jewish Cmty. Fedn. Long Beach and West Orange County, 1983—86, bd. dirs., 1982—86; pres. Long Beach Cancer League, 1987—88, exec. bd. dirs., 1984—96; pres. Long Beach Jewish Cmty. Sr. Housing Corp., 1989—91; v.p. fundraising S.E. unit Long Beach Harbor chpt. Am. Cancer Soc., 1989—90; trustee St. Mary Med. Ctr. Found., 1991—; pres. nat. conf. NCCJ, 1994—96, bd. dirs., 1989—, Leadership Long Beach, 1992—2000, pres., 1994—95; hon. bd. govs., 2000—; mem. dean's adv. bd. Sch. Bus. Adminstrn. Calif. State U., Long Beach, 2001—; bd. dirs. Long Beach Symphony Assn., 1984—85, Westerly Sch. Assoc., 1991—2000, Phoenix Long Beach Mus. Art, 1992—98, Am. Diabetes Assn., Long Beach., Calif., 1997—99, Stramski Children's Devel. Ctr., Long Beach Meml. Med. Ctr., 1998—, Pub. Corp. for Arts, 2002—, Long Beach Day Nursery, 2000—. Recipient Young Leadership award Jewish Cmty. Fedn. Long Beach and West Orange County, 1981, Jerusalem award State of Israel, 1989, Hannah G. Solomon award Nat. Coun. Jewish Women, 1992, Alumnus of Yr. award Leadership Long Beach, 1995, Humanitarian award The Nat. Conf., 1997, Disting. Leadership award Calif. Assn. Leadership Programs, 2000; named Rick Racker Woman of Yr., 1999; scholar La. Dept. Pub. Welfare, 1962, NIMH, 1964. Mem. Rotary Club of Long Beach (bd. dirs. 2000-01). Office: Robert Weil Assocs 5220 E Los Altos Plz Long Beach CA 90815-4251

ROSENBERG, JOEL BARRY, government economist; b. Bronx, N.Y., Aug. 14, 1942; s. Benjamin and Miriam Dorothy (Yellin) R.; B.A., Queens Coll., 1964, M.A., 1966; Ph.D., Brown U., 1972; m. Judith Lynne Jackler, Aug. 26, 1965; children: Jeffrey Alan, Marc David. Cons., Commonwealth Svcs., Washington, 1970-71; asst. prof. econs. SUNY, Geneseo, 1971-75, Case Western Res. U., Cleve., 1975-76; mgr., industry economist IRS, Washington, 1976—. NDEA fellow, Brown U., 1966-69. Mem. Am. Econ. Assn., Nat. Assn. Bus. Economists, Am. Statis. Assn. Contbr. articles to profl. jours. Home: 16 Flameleaf Ct Gaithersburg MD 20878-5216 Office: IRS 500 N Capitol St NW Washington DC 20221-0003

ROSENBERG, JOHN DAVID, English educator, literary critic; b. N.Y.C., Apr. 17, 1929; s. David and Dorothy Lilian (Shatz) R.; m. Barbara E. Hatch, 1952 (div. 1969); m. Maurine Ann Hellner, June 11, 1972; 1 child, Matthew John. BA, Columbia U., 1950, MA, 1951, PhD, 1960; BA, Clare Coll., Cambridge U., 1953, MA, 1958. Editor-in-chief Columbia Rev., 1949-50; lectr. English Columbia U., N.Y.C., 1953-54, asst. prof., 1962-65, assoc. prof., 1966-67, prof. English, 1967—, William Peterfield Trent prof., 1994—; instr. CCNY, 1954-62; chmn. Columbia Coll. humanities program, 1970-73, dir. grad. studies in English, 1986-89. Vis. prof. English Harvard U., 1968, U.B.C., 1970, Princeton U., 1978; vis. fellow Clare Hall Cambridge U., England, 1969; guest lectr. U.S. Mil. Acad., Cambridge U., Lancaster U. Author: The Darkening Glass: A Portrait of Ruskin's Genius, 1961, The Fall of Camelot: A Study of Tennyson's Idylls of the King, 1973, Carlyle and the Burden of History, 1985; editor: The Genius of John Ruskin, 1963, 2nd edit., 98, Mayhew, 1968, Swinburne: Selected Poetry and Prose, 1968, The Poems of Alfred, Lord Tennyson, 1975; contbr. essays and reviews on English lit. to N.Y. Times Book Rev., N.Y. Rev. Books, Harper's mag., Hudson Rev. and profl. jours. Recipient Clarke F. Ansley award Columbia U., 1960, Disting. Svc. award Columbian Coll. Core Curriculum, 1997; Coun. for Rsch. in Humanities grant-in-aid, 1965; Euretta J. Kellett fellow Cambridge U., 1951-53, Edward Coe fellow, 1956-57, Samuel S. Fels fellow, 1959-60, Am. Coun. Learned Soc. fellow, 1965-66, 70, Lawrence H. Chamberlain fellow, 1965-66, Guggenheim fellow, 1968-69, NEH fellow, 1982-83. Mem. MLA (chmn. exec. com. Victorian divsn. 1970, exec. com. 1979-83), Tennyson Soc., Ruskin Assn., Camp Rising Sun Alumni Assn., Columbia Coll. Alumni Assn. (dir. 1980-82, Alexander Hamilton medal 1994), Phi Beta Kappa. Office: Columbia U Dept English 1150 Amsterdam Ave New York NY 10027-7051

ROSENBERG, LEE EVAN, financial planner; b. Bklyn., Nov. 6, 1952; s. Daniel and Rita (Blanket) R.; m. Saralee Hymen, Aug. 27, 1977; children: Zachary Martin, Alexandra Lynn, Taryn Jessica. BA, Bklyn. Coll., 1974. Cert. fin. planner. Underwriter Fin. Life Ins. Co., N.Y.C., 1974-75, Mony, N.Y.C., 1975-80; pres. Lee Rosenberg Assoc., 1980-83; co-founder, sr. ptnr. ARS Fin. Svcs. Inc., Valley Stream, N.Y., 1983—. Co-host radio show Moneytalk WBAB, L.I., 1991; guest Nat. CNBC TV show Money Club, 1995, 96; cons. fin. sections New Choices Mag., 1995—; mem. adv. bd. Forum for Investor Advice, 2000-2002. Author: (with Saralee Rosenberg) Destination Florida: Guide to a Successful Relocation, 1989, 50 Fabulous Places to Retire in America, 1991, 50 Fabulous Places to Raise Your Family, 1993, Retirement Ready or Not! How to Get Financially Prepared in a Hurry, 1993; contbr. chpt to Building a Successful Financial Planning Practice, 1988; contbr. articles to profl. jours.; guest CNBC Power Lunch, 1997, 98, 99, 2000, 01, 02; contbr. CNBC.com, 2000—. Named one of Best 200 Fin. Advisors in USA, Worth Mag., 1996, 97, 98. Mem. Internat. Assn. Fin. Planners, Internat. Assn. Registered Fin. Planners, Internat. Soc. Preretirement Planners, L.I. Inst. Cert. Fin. Planners (bd. dirs., pres. 1988—), Nat. Speakers Assn. (bd. dirs. N.Y. chpt.). Home: 5 Cobblers Ln Dix Hills NY 11746-5001 Office: ARS Fin Svcs Inc 125 Franklin Ave Ste 6 Valley Stream NY 11580-2108 also: 500 N Broadway Jericho NY 11753-2127 Office: 31301 Powerline Rd Ste 309 Boca Raton FL 33433 E-mail: contact@arsfinancial.com.

ROSENBERG, LEON JOSEPH, marketing educator; b. Atlanta, Oct. 9, 1918; s. Harry Manville and Gertrude Dora (Hassenbusch) R.; m. Phylis Jane Israel, Feb. 6, 1943 (dec. Mar. 1976); children: Joanne Rosenberg Larson, Paul Harvey; m. Louise Nachman Mayer, Oct. 15, 1977. BS in Indsl. Mgmt, Ga. Inst. Tech., 1939; MS (Univ. scholar), Columbia U., 1940; PhD, N.Y. U., 1967. Mem. staff Nat. Retail Mchts. Assn., N.Y.C., 1947-49; sr. research analyst Federated Dept. Stores, Inc., Cin., 1949-52; research dir. Sanger Harris Dept. Store, Dallas, 1952-56, gen. supt., 1956-67; assoc. prof. Coll. Bus. Adminstrn., U. Ark., Fayetteville, 1967-74; prof., mktg. and transp. Sam M. Walton Coll. Bus. Adminstrn., U. Ark., 1975-89; dept. head Coll. Bus. Adminstrn., U. Ark., 1986-88; prof. emeritus U. Ark., 1989—; mktg. cons., sales assoc. Lindsey & Assocs. Inc., Fayetteville, 1990—. Sales assoc., 1968—; disting. vis. prof. Calif. State U., San Bernardino, 1990. Contbr. articles to profl. jours. Pres. Jewish Family Svc., Dallas, 1960-62, Temple Shalom, Fayetteville, 1992-96; mem. exec. com. Dallas Jewish Fedn., 1963-67; bd. dirs. New Orleans Jewish Children's Regional Svc., 1962-73, 75—, Jewish Fedn. Ark., 1992-96; pres. N.W. Ark. unit B'nai B'rith, 1992—; bd. dirs. Washington County (Ark.) chpt. Am. Cancer Soc., 1979-86, pres., 1982-83. Capt. USAAF, 1940-46. Mem. Acad. Mktg. Sci., Am. Mktg. Assn., So. Mktg. Assn., S.W. Mktg. Assn., S.W. Small Bus. Inst. Assn., Econs. and Bus. History Soc. (trustee 1986-89), Masons, Alpha Phi Omega (svc. award 1971), Beta Gamma Sigma, Delta Nu Alpha. Home: 1923 E Joyce Blvd # 168 Fayetteville AR 72703 Office: Lindsey & Assocs Inc 3900 Front St Fayetteville AR 72703

ROSENBERG, LESLIE KAREN, media buyer; b. Camden, N.J., Mar. 3, 1949; d. Lorimer and Doris Selma (Kohn) R. BS in Radio, TV, Film, U. Tex., 1971. Continuity dir. WEAT-TV/AM/FM, West Palm Beach, Fla., 1971-74; media buyer Wm. F. Haselmire Advt., 1974-75, media dir., 1982-85; program and pub. svc. dir. WTBS-TV, Atlanta, 1975-78; nat. traffic coord. WXIA-TV, 1978-80; sr. sales asst. CBS Radio Spot Sales, 1980-82; acct. exec. WRMF-FM, West Palm Beach, 1985; media dir., acct. exec. Merlin Masters & Nomes Advt., 1985-88; pres., media dir. Media Magic Plus, 1988—; advt. coord. Hearx, Ltd., 1996-98; media dir. Fantasma Prodns., Inc., 1998—2001; mktg. mgr. Broward Ctr. for Performing Arts, 2001—. Communications adv. bd. Palm Beach Jr. Coll., Lake Worth, 1972-74. Talent, author various radio commercials (Addy award 1973, 74), talent various TV commercials (Addy award 1974). Bd. dirs. Lake Worth (Fla.) Playhouse, 1989-92, program co-chmn., 1989-91; mem. Internat. Cultural Exch. Program, 1984, 94, 97; producer Lake Worth Playhouse Internat. Cultural Exch. for 1994 trip to Eng., mem. com. for 97 trip to Eng., 1994-97. Mem.: NATAS, NAFE, U.S. Racquetball Assn. (dir. tournament control 1976—80), Advt. Club of the Palm Beaches (bd. dirs. 1983—85). Avocations: singing, tap dancing, theatre, reading, shopping. Office: Media Magic Plus PO Box 19962 West Palm Beach FL 33416-4962 E-mail: LKRose761@aol.com.

ROSENBERG, MANUEL, retail company executive; b. Boston, Apr. 26, 1930; s. Israel and Lillian (Wirin) R.; m. Audray Merle Gold, Aug. 28, 1955; children: Peter Neal, Beth Susan. AB, Harvard U., 1951, MBA, 1953. V.P. Filene's, Boston, 1967-73; pres., chief exec. officer Gimbel's, Phila., 1973-75, chmn. bd., chief exec. officer, 1975-77; exec. v.p. Garfinckel, Brooks Bros., Miller & Rhoads, Inc., Washington, 1977-79, pres., 1979-82, also dir.; chmn. bd., chief exec. officer Morse Shoe, Inc., Canton, Mass., 1982-92. Overseer Beth Israel Hosp., Boston; trustee Mass. Eye and Ear Infirmary, Boston; bd. govs. Am. Jewish Com.; mem. corp. Judge Baker Children's Ctr. Lt. USN, 1953-56. Mem. Univ. Club, Harvard Club. Home: 370 Beacon St Boston MA 02116-1002

ROSENBERG, MARC STEVEN, lawyer; b. N.Y.C., June 15, 1958; s. Marvin and Bette Rosenberg; m. Tina Rosenberg; children: Brett, James, Katherine. AB, Princeton U., 1980; JD, Harvard U., 1983. Bar: N.Y. 1984. Assoc. Cravath Swaine & Moore, N.Y.C., 1985-90, ptnr., 1990—. Office: Cravath Swaine & Moore 825 8th Ave Fl 38 New York NY 10019-7475

ROSENBERG, MARILYN ROSENTHAL, artist, visual poet; b. Phila., Oct. 11, 1934; m. Robert Rosenberg, June 12, 1955; 2 children. B in Profl. Studies in Studio Arts, SUNY, Empire State Coll., 1978; MA in Liberal Studies, NYU, 1993. Author, pub., creator unique and edit. poetry/painting books, (one-woman shows) Irvine Gallery, State U. Calif., Irvine, 1981, The Sandor Tezsler Libr. Gallery, Spartanburg, S.C., 1983, U. Wis., River Falls, 1984, 361 Degrees Gallery, Greenfield, Mass., 1987, UCLA Art Libr. Dickson Art Ctr., L.A., 1989-90 , Marymount Coll., Tarrytown, N.Y., 1993, McHenry County Coll., Crystal Lake, Ill., 1997, John Jay Coll., N.Y.C., 1999, Westchester CC, Valhalla, NY, 2002 , (two person exhbns.) SUNY Purchase Libr., 1982, The Hudson River Mus., Yonkers, N.Y., 1984, Women's Studio Workshop Inskirts Gallery, Rosendale, N.Y., 1986, Brownson Art Gallery, Purchase, N.Y., 1988 , (with collaborator) Westchester County Gallery, White Plains, N.Y., 1989, ,(group exhbns.) Long Beach (Calif.) Mus. Art, 1977, Kathryn Markel Fine Arts Gallery, N.Y.C., 1978 , Pratt Graphic Ctr. Gallery, N.Y.C, 1978, Polytechnic State U. Gallery, San Luis Obispo, Calif., 1979, Phila. Art Alliance, Glassboro State Coll., Pa., 1979, Ridotte del Treatro Comunale, Italy, 1980 , SUNY Purchase Gallery, 1982, Galerie Caroline Corre, Paris, 1983, Thorpe Intermedia Gallery, Sparkhill, N.J., 1983, U. Rochester Gallery, Rochester, N.Y., 1984, 14 Sculptors Gallery, N.Y.C., 1984 , Georgetown U., Washington, 1984, Franklin Furnace, N.Y.C., 1986, Douglas & Cook Colls., New Brunswick, N.J., 1985, City Without Walls, Newark, 1986, Galleri T.V., Malmo, Sweden , Post Machina Group and Am. Consulate, Bologna, Italy, 1986, Tech. U. Nova Scotia, Halifax, 1986, Museu Municipal, Figuira Da Foz, Portugal, 1987, King Stephen Mus., Szekesfehrvar, Hungary, 1987, Allen Meml. Art Mus., Oberlin, Ohio, 1987, Cultural Centre San Paulo, Brazil, 1988, Centro Cultural de la Caja de Ahorros de Valencia, Spain, 1988, Cooper Union Art, N.Y.C., 1989, San Francisco Craft and Folk Art Mus., 1990 , Alternatives Gallery, San Luis Obispo, Calif., 1990-91, San Antonio Art Inst., 1991, Sazama Gallery, Chgo., 1992, SUNY Oneonta, 1992, Ralston Fine Arts, Johnson City, Tenn., 1993, Va. Ctr. Craft Arts, 1993, Libr. Can., 1993 , Muee de la Post, Paris, 1993, Pratt Inst., N.Y.C., 1993, Musee de la Poste, Paris,

1993-94, Papertrail, Ottawa, Can., 1993-94, Nexus Found. Arts, Phila., 1994, Va. Ctr. Craft Arts, Richmond, 1994 , Libr. Nat. Mus. Women, Washington, 1994-95, Spirit Sq. Ctr. Arts, Charlotte, N.C., 1995, Ellipse Arts Ctr. Arlington, Va., 1995, Monterserrat Coll. Art Gallery, Beverly, Mass., 1995 , Yale U. Art Gallery Sculpture Hall, New Haven Conn., 1995, Harper Collins, N.Y.C., 1995, Brookfield Craft Ctr., Conn., 1995, Muscatine Art Ctr., Iowa, 1995, Sangre de Cristo Art Ctr., Pueblo, Colo., 1995, Lake George (N.Y.) Art Project, 1995, Mus. Nebr. Arts, U. Nebr., Kearny, 1995, The Gallery, Hastings-on-Hudson, N.Y., 1996, Ctr. for Book Arts, N.Y.C., 1996, Franklin Furnace, N.Y.C., 1996, Rutgers U., New Brunswick, 1996 , Harper Collins, N.Y., 1996, The Stamp Art Gallery, San Francisco, 1997, U. Alberta, Edmonton, Can., 1997, Finegood Art Gallery, West Valley, Calif., 1997, 98, Klutznick Nat. Jewish Mus., Washington, 1998 , Neuberger Mus. Art, Purchase, N.Y., 1998-99, Collins Gallery, U. Strathclyde, Glasgow, Scotland, 1998, Iona Gallery, Kingussie, 1998, Inst. de Artes Graficas de Oaxaca, Mex., 1998, Inverness Mus. & Art Gallery, 1999 , Biblioteca Mex., Mexico City, 1999, Kutztown U., Sharadin Art Gallery, 1999, Fla. Atlantic U., Boca Raton, Fla., 2000, U. Ctrl. Ark., Conway, Ark., 2000, Ocean Grove Libr., Victoria, Australia, 2000 , City Gallery, Szekesfehervar, Hungary, 2000, The Temple, Judea, Elkins Park, Pa., 2001, The Ctr. Book Arts, N.Y., 2001;Exhibited in group shows at Art Acad. Cin., 2002, Ohio State U. Librs., Columbus, 2002, Cuesta Coll. Art Gallery, San Luis Obispo, Calif., 2002, Pensacola Mus. Art, Fla., 2002, U. Indpls. Gallery, 2002; (pub. collections and archives) Atlantic Coll. Art Libr., Ga., Art Gallery New South Wales, Sydney, Australia, Artpool Art Rsch. Ctr., Budapest, Hungary, Bibliotheque Nat., Paris, R.I., Canberra Sch. Art Libr., Australia, Canadian Postal Mus. Archive, Ottawa, Electrografia Museo Internacional, La Mancha, Cuenca, Spain, Fogg Art Mus., Cambridge, Mass., Mus. Modern Art Libr., N.Y.C., The Ruth and Marvin Sackner Archive, Miami Beach, Fla., Tate Gallery Libr., London , Yale U. Libr., New Haven, Ct., Canberra Sch. Art Gallery, Sutralia, Cleve. Inst. Art Libr., Harvard U. Fogg Mus. and Houghton Libr., Cambridge, Mass., Rochester (N.Y.) Inst. Tech., Sch. Art Inst. Chgo. Libr. , Amherst (Mass.) Coll. Libr., Atlanta Coll. Art Libr., Bklyn Mus. Art Libr., Brown U. Libr. , Cleve. Inst. Art Libr., Dartmouth Coll., Sherman Art Libr., Georgetown U. Libr., The N.Y. Pub. Libr., R.I. Sch. Design , Stanford U. Libr., Temple U. Libr., Phila., U. Calif. at Davis, Santa Barbara Librs., U. Chgo. Libr., U. Utah, Mariott Libr., U. Va. Libr., Va. Commonwealth U. Libr. , Wellesley Coll. Libr. , Libr. Mus. Fine Arts, Boston , Sch. Mus. Fine Art Libr., Boston, Nat. Art Libr., Victoria and Albert Mus., London, King St. Stephen Mus., Hungary, L.I. U. Bklyn. Ctr. Libr., N.Y., Orleti Etexea, La maison de la Poesie, Laractz, Spain , Staatliche Mus. zu Berlin Prensiscehr Kultturbesitz Kunstbibiothek, (in various publs., periodicals, web sites, exhbn. catalogues prin. works). Home: 67 Lakeview Ave W Cortlandt Manor NY 10567-6415

ROSENBERG, MARK L. health agency administrator; b. Newark, July 30, 1945; m. Jill Alison Dimond; children: Julie, Ben. BA in Biology magna cum laude, Harvard Coll., 1967, MD cum laude, M of Pub. Policy, Harvard Coll., 1972. Diplomate Am. Bd. Internal Medicine, Am. Bd. Psychiatry and Neurology. Intern Mass. Gen. Hosp., Boston, 1972—73, resident in medicine, 1973—74; resident in preventive medicine Ctrs. for Disease Control, Atlanta, 1975—76; resident in psychiatry Beth Israel Hosp., Boston, 1980—83; clin. prof. dept. cmty. medicine and family practice Morehouse Sch. Medicine, Atlanta, 1984—93; clin. prof. psychiatry Emory U. Sch. Medicine, 1994—99; exec. dir. Task Force for Child Survival and Devel., 1999—; dir. sci. devel., dir. programs Ctr. for Child Well-being, 1999—. Dir. Nat. Ctr. for Injury Prevention and Control, Atlanta, 1994—99, acting assoc. dir. for pub. health practice, 1992—93; dir. divsn. injury control Ctr. for Environ. Health and Injury Control, 1989—92; spl. asst. for behavioral sci., office of dep. dir. CDC, Atlanta, 1989, advisor to dep. dir., 88, asst. dir. for sci. divsn. injury epidemiology and control, 1986—88, liaison officer office program planning and evaluation, 1979—80; assoc. dir. office extramural health programs Harvard Sch. Pub. Health, Boston, 1979—80; clin. fellow in psychiatry Harvard Med. Sch., Boston, 1980—83; vis. prof. dept. cmty. health Emory U. Sch. Medicine, Atlanta, 1984—91, clin. asst. prof. psychiatry, 1985—87, clin. assoc. prof., 1988—93; adj. prof. Emory U. Sch. Pub. Health, Atlanta, 1991—; clin. prof. dept. cmty. health and preventive medicine Morehouse Sch. Medicine, Atlanta, 1993—; staff physician Women's Med. Clinic, Atlanta, 1974—76, Harvard St. Neighborhood Health Ctr., Boston, 1976—77, Winchester (Mass.) Hosp., 1978—83; emergency rm. physician Burbank Hosp., Fitchburg, Mass., 1976—77, Harrington Hosp., Southbridge, Mass., 1976—77; vis. physician dept. psychiatry Grady Meml. Hosp., Atlanta, 1985—; lectr. and cons. in field. Author: Patients: The Experience of Illness, 1980, Violence in America: A Public Health Approach, 1990; mem. editl. bd. Violence and Victims, 1985—88, Violence, Aggression and Terrorism, 1986—; contbr. articles. Active Calif. Wellness Found., 1993—; bd. dirs. southeastern divsn., sci. adv. coun. Am. Suicide Found., 1990—. Recipient Coulter Lecture award, Am. ongress Rehab. Medicine, 1991, William S. one award, Am. Trauma Soc., 1991, Outstanding Achievement award, 1994, World Health Day award, Am. Assn. for World Health, 1993, Disting. Svc. award, Ga. Assn. Family and Marital Therapists, 1994, Disting. Achievement award, Disability Wellness Assn., 1998, Outstanding Svc. medal, USPHS, 2000, Meritorious Svc. medal, 2000, Disting. Svc. medal, 2000; fellow, Mass. Gen. Hosp., 1977—78, Mead-Johnson, 1982; scholar, John Harvard, 1964. Mem.: Alpha Omega Alpha, Inst. of Medicine of NAS, Phi Beta Kappa. Avocation: photography. Home: 972 Oakdale Rd NE Atlanta GA 30307-1272 Office: 750 Commerce Dr Ste 400 Decatur GA 30030

ROSENBERG, MARK B. political science educator, university official; b. Athens, Ohio, Aug. 15, 1949; married; 2 children. BA, Miami U., Oxford, Ohio, 1971; PhD in Polit. Sci., U. Pitts., 1976. Prof. polit. sci. Fla. Internat. U., Miami, 1976—, chmn. Caribbean L.Am. studies coun., 1977-79, founding dir. L.Am. and Caribbean Ctr., 1979—, founding/acting dean Coll. Urban and Pub. Affairs, 1994-97, vice provost for internat. studies, 1996-98, provost, acting pres., 1998—, acting pres., 1999-2000, provost, exec. v.p. acad. affairs, 2000—. Mem. exec. com. OLAM; mem. articulation coordination com. Fla. Bd. Edn.; mem. Coun. of Fgn. Relations, Pacific Coun. on Internet. Realtions. Author, editor, co-editor 6 books; former bd. editors Fla. Trend, Latin Trade; contbr. articles to profl. jours. Presdl. appointee U.S. Customs Dist. Export Coun.; mem. exec. com. OLAM, the Jewish Leadership Inst./Jewish Fedn. Miami; mem. statewide articulation coordination com. Fla. Bd. Edn. Mem. Greater Miami C. of C. (vice chair exec. com. for internat. econ. devel. 1992-94), Coun. Fgn. Rels., Pacific Coun. in Internat. Rels. Office: Fla Internat U University Park Pc 526 Miami FL 33199-0001

ROSENBERG, MARK LOUIS, lawyer; b. Lexington, Ky., Sept. 21, 1947; s. Edward George and Shirley Lee (Berkin) R.; m. Betty Adler, May 16, 1982; stepchildren: Aaron, Sarah Claxton; children: Eli, Daniel. BA, U. Mich., 1969; JD, harvard U., 1973; LLM in Taxation, Georgetown U., 1985. Bar: D.C. 1973, Md. 1991, U.S. Dist. Ct. D.C. 1973, U.S. Ct. Appeals (D.C. cir.) 1973. Asst. to v.p. George Washington U., 1973-75; counsel U.S. Ho. of Reps., Washington, 1975-77; sr. atty. FTC, 1977-85; ptnr. Gordon, Feinblatt et al, 1989-91; prin. Law Offices of Mark L. Rosenberg, 1991—; of counsel The Jacobovitz Law Firm, 1994-97. Mem. Fed. Bar Assn. (dep. sect. coord., Disting. Svc. award 1982, 83, 87). Democrat. Jewish. Home: 6101 Shady Oak Ln Bethesda MD 20817-6027 Office: Law Offices of Mark L Rosenberg 6917 Arlington Rd Ste 301 Bethesda MD 20814-5211

ROSENBERG, MICHAEL, lawyer; b. N.Y.C., Oct. 13, 1937; s. Walter and Eva (Bernstein) Rosenberg; m. Jacqueline Raymonde Combe, Apr. 29, 1966; children: Andrew James, Suzanne Jennifer. AB in Econs. with honors, Ind. U., 1959; LLB, Columbia U., 1962. Bar: NY 1963, US Ct Appeals (2d cir) 1975, US Dist Ct (ea dist so div) Mich 1989. From. dep. asst. atty. gen. to asst. atty. gen. N.Y. State Dept. Law, N.Y.C., 1963-66; assoc. Hellerstein, Rosier & Rembar, 1966-73; assoc. gen. counsel Gen. Instrument Corp., 1973-78; from assoc. gen. counsel to dep. gen. counsel U.S. Filter Corp., 1978-82; v.p., gen. counsel, sec. Alfa-Laval Inc., Ft. Lee, N.J., 1982-88; counsel Becker Ross Stone De Stefano & Klein, N.Y.C., 1988-89; ptnr. Rosenberg & Rich, White Plains, N.Y., 1989-95, Quinn, Marantis & Rosenberg, LLP, White Plains, 1995-97, Marantis, Rosenberg & van Nes, LLP, White Plains, 1997-2001; atty. Law Offices of Michael Rosenberg, 2001—. Mem Zoning Bd Appeals Town of North Castle, NY, 1995—. Mem.: ABA, Westchester County Bar Assn., NY State Bar Assn. Office: Law Offices of Michael Rosenberg 120 Bloomingdale Rd White Plains NY 10605

ROSENBERG, MICHAEL JOSEPH, financial executive; b. Passaic, N.J., Apr. 19, 1928; s. Emanuel and Sylvia Sarah (Schwartz) R.; m. Judith Ann Melnick, Dec. 6, 1964 (div. 1983); children: Ann Kirsten, Emily Jeanne; m. Kathleen Ann Jennings, Mar. 3, 1990. BS, Upsala Coll., 1951; MBA, NYU, 1955, postgrad., 1955-59. Asst. v.p. Meinhard & Co., N.Y.C., 1953-58, A.J. Armstrong Co., N.Y.C., 1958-59, Sterling Nat. Bank, N.Y.C., 1959-61; exec. v.p. Rosenthal & Rosenthal, Inc., 1961-96; chmn. Taurus Global, LLC, 2000—. Bd. dirs. D.V.L., Inc., N.Y.C.; dir. Am. com. Shenkar U.; mem. deptl. disciplinary com. Supreme Ct. NY Appellate Divsn. Contbr. numerous articles on comml. fin. to newspapers and mags. Bd. dirs., treas. Town Hall Found., N.Y.C., 1982—; treas. Citizens for Clean Air, N.Y.C., 1984, N.Y. Rd. Runners Found., 2002—; trustee NYU, 1997—. Capt. U.S. Army, 1951-53, Korea; col. N.Y. Nat. Guard, 1997—. Decorated Silver Star, Bronze Star; recipient Meritorious Svc. award NYU, 1983; Albert Gallatin fellow, 1981. Mem. Albert Gallatin Assocs. (chmn. 1984-87), NYU Bus. Forum (pres. 1981-82), NYU Grad. Sch. Bus. Adminstrn. Alumni Assn. (pres. 1978-79), NYU Ptnrs. (co-chmn. 1987-89, chmn. 1990-93), NYU Club (pres. 1975-77, 82-85). Avocations: skiing, tennis, running, sailing. Office: 53 Columbus Ave Ste 2 New York NY 10023-6917

ROSENBERG, NORMAN, surgeon, educator; b. N.Y.C., Apr. 25, 1916; s. Leo and Rose (Kamerman) R.; m. Ruth Harriet Feller, Nov. 30, 1940; children: Lois A. Rosenberg Ebin, Ralph. BA, U. Pa., 1934; MD, NYU, 1938. Diplomate Am. Bd. Surgery, Am. Bd. Gen. Vascular Surgery. Intern Mt. Sinai Hosp., N.Y.C., 1939-41, resident, 1942-43; practice medicine, specializing in vascular surgery New Brunswick, N.J., 1946-80; sr. attending surgeon St. Peters Med. Center, from 1946, now emeritus sr. attending surgeon; chief staff Middlesex Gen. Hosp., 1959-66, chief vascular surgery, 1960-86, dir. dept. surgery, 1975-81. Cons. surgeon Roosevelt Hosp., Metuchen, N.J., 1956-87 , Raritan Valley Hosp., Greenbrook, N.J., 1970-81, Somerset Hosp., Somerville, N.J., 1952-88 , J.F. Kennedy Hosp., Edison, N.J., 1969-88 ; clin. prof. surgery Robert Wood Johnson Med. Sch., U. Medicine and Dentistry N.J., New Brunswick, 1972-81, chief vascular surgery sect., 1981-86, prof. surgery, 1981-91, prof. emeritus, 1991—; cons. Johnson & Johnson Research Center, New Brunswick, 1954-78 Author: Handbook of Carotid Artery Surgery Facts and Figures, 1989, 2d edit., 1994; contbr. articles to books and profl. jours.; co-inventor modified bovine arterial graft Trustee Robert Wood Johnson Found., 1958-96. Capt. M.C., AUS, 1943-46. Fellow A.C.S., Southeastern Surg. Congress; mem. Soc. Vascular Surgery (sr.), Internat. Soc. Cardiovascular Surgery, Soc. Surgeons N.J. Home: 48 North Dr East Brunswick NJ 08816-1122

ROSENBERG, NORMAN JACK, agricultural meteorologist, educator; b. Bklyn., Feb. 22, 1930; s. Jacob and Rae (Dombrowitz) R.; m. Sarah Zacher, Dec. 30, 1950; children: Daniel Jonathon, Alyssa Yael. BS, Mich. State U., 1951; MS, Okla. State U., 1958; PhD, Rutgers U., 1961. Soil scientist Israel Soil Conservation Service, Haifa, 1953-55, Israel Water Authority, Haifa, 1955-57; asst. prof. agrl. meteorology U. Nebr., Lincoln, 1961-64, assoc. prof., 1964-67, prof. agrl. meteorology, 1967—, prof. agrl. engring., 1975—, prof. agronomy, 1976—, George Holmes prof. agrl. meteorology, 1981-87, prof. emeritus, 1987—, leader sect. agrl. meteorology, 1975-79, acting asst. vice chancellor for research, 1983-85; sr. fellow, dir. climate resources program Resources for the Future, Washington, 1987-92; chief scientist integrated earth studies energy sci. divsn. Battelle Pacific N.W. Nat. Lab., 1992—; scientist Joint Global Change Rsch. Inst., Pacific N.W. Nat. Lab. and U. Md., 2001—. Cons. Dept. State AID, NOAA, Oak Ridge Assoc. Univs., 1986-87, Elec. Power Rsch. Inst. 1989-92, Sandia Nat. Labs., 1990; mem. numerous ad hoc coms. and mem. standing com. on atmospheric sci. Nat. Acad. Scis./NRC, 1975-78, mem. bd. on atmospheric sci. and climate, 1982-85, mem. U.S. com. Internat. Geosphere-Biosphere Program, 1984-86, mem. panel on policy implications of climate change, 1990-91; mem. bd. coun. Agrl. Sci. and Tech.; vis. prof. agrl. meteorology Israel Inst. Tech., Haifa, 1968; trustee Nat. Inst. Global Environ. Change, 1992, vice-chmn., 1992-95, chmn., 1996-2000. Author: Microclimate: The Biological Environment, 1974, 2d edit., 1983, Chinese transl., 1983, Malay transl., 1987; editor: North American Droughts, 1978, Drought in the Great Plains: Research on Impacts and Strategies, 1980, Greenhouse Warming: Abatement and Adaptation, 1989, Toward an Integrated Impact Assessment of Climate Change: The MINK Study, 1993, Carbon Sequestration in Soils: New Science, Monitoring and Beyond, 1999; editor: (with V.C. Cole and K. Paustian) Mitigation of Greenhouse Gas Emissions by the Agricultural Sector, Spl. issue of Climate Change, 1998; editor: (with R.C. Izaurralde) Storing Carbon in Agricultural Soils: A multipurpose environmental strategy, Spl. issue of Climatic Change, 2001; tech. editor: Agronomy Jour., 1974—79, cons. editor: Agrl. and Forest Meteorology, cons. editor: Climatic Change; contbr. articles to profl. jours. Mem. Intergovernmental Panel on Climate Change, 1993—. Recipient Centennial medal Nat. Weather Svc., 1970; sr. fellow in sci., NATO, 1968, rsch. fellow U. Nebr., 1968, Lady Davis fellow Hebrew U., Jerusalem, 1977, nat. resources fellow Resources for Future, 1986; grantee State of Nebr., 1970-73, NSF, 1971-87, 96, U.S. Dept. Commerce, 1972-74, 80-82, 83-85, 88-89, NASA, 1972-73, 85-86, U.S. Dept. Interior, 1974-75, 77-79, 88—, USDA, 1979-82, 88-89, U. Nebr. Found., 1982, Nat. Ctr. Atmospheric Rsch., 1984-85, U.S. Dept. Energy, 1989-92, G. Gunnar Vetleson Found., 1987-92, UN Environ. Program, 1989, EPA, 1988-89, 98, NASA, 1995-97, 98, NOAA, 1996. Fellow AAAS (com. climate 1984-89, com. global change 1992-96, adv. panel Earth Explorer ency. 1992-95), Am. Soc. Agronomy, Am. Meteorol. Soc. (Outstanding Achievement in Bioclimatology award 1978, councillor 1981-84); mem. Am. Assn. State Climatologists (Nebr. rep. 1979-81), Arid Zone Soc. India, Sigma Xi, Alpha Zeta, Gamma Sigma Rho. Clubs: Cosmos (Washington). Jewish. Office: Joint Global Change Rsch Inst 8400 Baltimore Ave College Park MD 20740-2496 E-mail: nj.rosenberg@pnl.gov.

ROSENBERG, PAUL I. lawyer; b. Newark, Feb. 26, 1937; BS in Econs., U. Pa. Wharton Sch., 1959; MBA, NYU, 1964, JD, 1970, LLM, 1975. Bar: N.J. 1970, U.S. Dist. Ct. N.J. 1970, N.Y. 1982, U.S. Dist. Ct. (3rd dist.) N.Y. 1982, U.S. Tax Ct. 1983. Ptnr. Fox and Fox LLP, Livingston, 1974—. Contbr. articles to legal publs. Mem. Essex Co. Probate Early Settlement panel. Fellow Am. Coll. Trust and Estate Counsel (mem. nat. employee benefits in estate-planning, estate and gift tax com.); mem. ABA, Essex County Bar Assn., N.J. State Bar Assn. Home: One Belgrade Terr West Orange NJ 07052 Office: Fox and Fox LLP 70 S Orange Ave Livingston NJ 07039-4994

ROSENBERG, PIERRE MAX, museum director; b. Paris, Apr. 13, 1936; s. Charles and Gertrude (Nassauer) R.; m. Béatrice de Rothschild, July 29, 1981. Baccalauréat, Lycée Charlemagne, Paris; Licence, Law Faculty, Paris; Diplome, Louvre Sch., Paris. Chief curator dept. paintings Musée du Louvre, Paris, 1982-94, pres., dir., 1994—2001. Author: Chardin, 1963, 99, Peyron, 1983, (catalogue) La peinture francaise du XVIIe siècle dans les coll. américaines, 1981, (catalogue) Watteau, 1984, 96, Fragonard, 1987, Frères Le Nain, 1993, Poussin, 1994, G. de la Tour, 1997, D. Vivant Denon, 1999. Mem. Soc. Histoire Art Francais (pres. 1982-84), Com. Francais Histoire Art (pres. 1984-96), Acad. Francaise. Home: 35 rue de Vaugirard 75006 Paris France E-mail: pierre.rosenberg@wanadoo.fr.

ROSENBERG, RALPH, former state senator, lawyer, consultant, educator, foundation administrator; b. Chgo., Oct. 7, 1949; s. Nathan Benjamin and Rhea (Matlow) R.; m. Teresa Marie Sturm, July 11, 1989; children: Jacob Louis, Joel Patrick. BS in Commerce and Bus. Adminstrn., U. Ill., 1972; JD, Drake Law Sch., 1974. Bar: Iowa 1974. Sole practice Rosenberg Law Firm, Ames, Iowa, 1974—; mem. Iowa Ho. of Reps., Des Moines, 1981-90, Iowa Senate, Des Moines, 1990-94. Adj. faculty Des. Moines Area C.C., 1980—, Drake Law Sch., 1992, Upper Iowa U., 1993, Iowa State U., 1994—; dir. Environ. Planning Rsch. Group, Ames, 1976-77; exec. dir. Story County Legal Aid Soc., Nevada, Iowa, 1977-78; asst. Story County atty. County Attys. Office, Nevada, 1979-81; exec. dir., mng. atty. Youth Law Ctr., Des Moines, 1989-92; chair adv. bd. Inst. Pub. Leadership, 1994—; exec. dir. Coalition for Family and Childrens Svcs., 1995—; co-chair Iowans United for a Healthy Future. Author, editor: Public Interest Law, 1992; author: Family Theory, Law, Policy and Practice, 1994; editor: Descriptive Analysis of Iowa Environmental Agencies, 1977. Past chair Midwest Leadership Inst. of Coun. of State Govt.; bd. dirs. Jewish Cmty. Rels. Commn., Iowa Protection and Advocacy, regional adv. bd. Legal Svcs. Corp. Iowa, Child and Family Policy Ctr.; past bd. dirs. Co-op. Child Care Svcs., Cmty. Action Rsch. Group, Rural Iowa. Recipient Outstanding Contbn. to Well-being of Children award Youth and Shelter Svcs., 1992, Excellence in Svc. award Legal Svcs. Group, 1993, Iowa LWV Cornerstone award, 1994, Iowa Farmers' Union Friend of the Farmer award, 1994, Iowa Consumer Action Network Citizen Svc. award, 1994; named LEgislator of Yr., Sierra Club, 1988, Isaak Walton League, 1993, Common Ground award Inst. of Public Leadership, 1997; named Legis. Conservationist of Yr., Wildlife Soc., 1988, Elected Ofcl. of Yr., Iowa Corrections Assn., 1984. Mem.: Nat. Conf. State Legislators (criminal justice com. 1986—94), Iowa State Bar Assn. Home: 811 Ridgewood Ave Ames IA 50010-5823 Office: 1111 9th St Ste 390 Des Moines IA 50314-2527 E-mail: hn3957@earthlink.net.

ROSENBERG, RAYMOND DAVID, secondary education educator, consultant; b. Jersey City, Apr. 25, 1951; s. Fabulous Sam and Arlene (White) R.; m. JoAnn Gabriella Simchera, June 10, 1984; 1 child, Anna Teresa. BA, Boston U., 1974; MEd, William Paterson Coll., 1978, MEd in Sch. Adminstrn., 1994. Cert. tchr., N.J. Child care worker Bergen Residential Ctr., Rockleigh, N.J., 1975; substitute tchr. aide South Cliff Elem. Sch., Ft. Lee, 1975-76; mgr. Betty Gercek Residence, N.Y.C., 1977-78; tchr. Lodi (N.J.) Boy's and Girl's Club Preschool, 1979-80; tchr. reading Passaic County Tech. Vocat. High Sch., Wayne, N.J., 1980-82; specialist learning disabilities North Jersey Devel. Ctr., Totowa, 1983-84, adaptive switch tchr., 1986-87; ednl. specialist Div. Devel. Disabilities, Springfield, N.J., 1984-85, tchr. profoundly retarded students, 1987-89, tchr. medically frail, 1990-91; tchr. mildly retarded, emotionally disturbed students North Jersey Devel. Ctr., Totowa, 1992-93; learning disabilities tchr. Office of Edn., N.J., 1993-96; cons. youth consultation svcs. George Washington Sch. Annex, Hackensack, 1993-96; learning cons. child study team North Bergen (N.J.) H.S., 1996-98; GED tchr. Bergen C.C. Computer Learning Ctr., Paramus, 1998—. Learning disabilities tchr., cons., 1995-2000, cons. Juvenile Justice Commn., 1995—; pres. Ednl. Assessment Svcs., Inc.; sales assoc. Radio Shack, 2000—. Editor: Common Sense Newsletter, 1972, Jour. Learning Cons., 1996. Asst. scoutmaster Boy Scouts Am., Teaneck, N.J., 1980-83; mem. St. James Episcopal Ch., Sexton. Recipient Eagle Scout award Boy Scouts Am., Ridgefield, N.J., 1968. Mem. Nat. Eagle Scout Assn., Pi Lambda Theta (Beta Chi chpt.). Episcopal. Lodge: Order of Arrow. Avocations: applied behavior analysis, behavior modification, behavior therapy.

ROSENBERG, RICHARD F. physician, radiologist; b. N.Y.C., June 13, 1942; s. Henry J. and Sylvia (Harris) R.; m. Judith Wolf, May 5, 1985; 1 child, Glen. BA, Colgate U., 1964; MD, N.Y. Med. Coll., 1968. Diplomate Am. Bd. Radiology. Intern Met. Hosp., N.Y.C., 1968-69; resident Montefiore Hosp. and Med. Ctr., Bronx, N.Y., 1969-70, 72-74, chief resident, 1974; radiologist Lipsay & Rosenberg, Great Neck, 1974-78; dir. gastrointestinal radiology North Shore U. Hosp., Manhasset, 1978-82; radiologist, owner Great Neck Radiologists, 1982—. Mem. adv. bd. Bank of Great Neck, 1990-94. Contbr. articles to profl. jours. Lt. comdr. USN, 1970-72. Fellow Am. Coll. Gastroenterology; mem. Am. Coll. Radiology, Alpha Omega Alpha. Republican. Office: Great Neck Radiologists 935 Northern Blvd Great Neck NY 11021-5309

ROSENBERG, RICHARD MORRIS, banker; b. Fall River, Mass., Apr. 21, 1930; s. Charles and Betty (Peck) R.; m. Barbara K. Cohen, Oct. 21, 1956; children: Michael, Peter. BS, Suffolk U., 1952; MBA, Golden Gate U., 1962; LLB, Golden Gate Coll., 1966. Publicity asst. Crocker-Anglo Bank, San Francisco, 1959-62; banking services officer Wells Fargo Bank, N.A., 1962-65, asst. v.p., 1965-68, v.p. mktg. dept., 1968, v.p., dir. mktg., 1969, sr. v.p. mktg. and advt. div., 1970-75, exec. v.p., from 1975, vice chmn., 1980-83, Crocker Nat. Corp., 1983-85; pres., chief operating officer Seafirst Corp., 1986-87, also dir.; pres., chief operating officer, also bd. dirs. Seattle First Nat. Bank, 1985-87; vice chmn. bd. BankAm. Corp., San Francisco, 1987-90, chmn., CEO, 1990-96. Bd. dirs. Airborne Express, Pacific Life, MiFund; past chmn. Mastercard Internat.; past. pres. Fed. Res. Adv. Coun. Bd. dirs. San Francisco Symphony, United Way; trustee Calif. Inst. Tech.; bd. dirs. Am. Ctr. for Wine, Food and the Arts. Jewish. Office: Bank of Am CA5-705-11-01 555 California St San Francisco CA 94104- E-mail: richard.rosenberg@bankofamerica.com.

ROSENBERG, ROBERT ALLEN, psychologist, educator, optometrist; b. Phila., July 31, 1935; s. Theodore Samuel and Dorothy (Bailes) R.; m. Geraldine Bella Tishler, Sept. 3, 1961; children: Lawrence David, Ronald Joseph. BA, Temple U., 1957, MA, 1964; BS, Pa. Coll. Optometry, 1960, OD, 1961. Lic. optometrist, psychologist, Pa. Instr. Pa. Coll. Optometry, Phila., 1962-65, asst. prof., 1965-67; asst. prof. psychology Community Coll. Phila., 1967-76, assoc. prof., 1976—. Pvt. practice optometry, Roslyn, Pa., 1965-95; assoc. in practice optometry, Huntingdon Valley, Pa., 1995-98. Contbr. articles to profl. jours. Named Humanitarian Chapel of Four Chaplains Bapt. Temple, 1980. Fellow Am. Acad. Optometry; mem. Am. Optometric Assn., Pa. Optometric Assn., Bucks-Montgomery Optometric Assn., Alumni Assn. Pa. Coll. Optometry (v.p. 1992-98, sec. 1991—). Avocations: singing, acting, photography, writing, public speaking. Home: 970 Corn Crib Dr Huntingdon Valley PA 19006-3304 Office: Community Coll Phila 1700 Spring Garden St Philadelphia PA 19130-3991

ROSENBERG, ROBERT BRINKMANN, technology organization executive; b. Chgo., Mar. 19, 1937; s. Sidney and Gertrude (Brinkmann) R.; m. Patricia Margaret Kane, Aug. 1, 1959 (dec. Feb. 1988); children: John Richard Debra Ann; m. Maryann Bartoli Manrot, June 25, 1989. BSChemE with distinction, Ill. Inst. Tech., 1958, MS in Gas Tech, 1961, PhD in Gas Tech, 1964. Registered profl. engr., Ill. Adj. asst. prof. Ill. Inst. Tech., 1965-69; mem. staff Inst. Gas Tech., Chgo., 1962-77, v.p. engring. rsch., 1973-77; v.p. rsch. and devel. Gas Research Inst., Chgo., 1977-78, exec. v.p., sr. v.p., 1978-84, v.p., 1984-96; pres. RBR @ Vision, Burr Ridge, Ill., 1996—; also bd. dirs. IEA Internat. Ctr. for Gas Tech. Info. Tech. program dir. World Energy Congress, 1996—98. Author. Mem. Hinsdale (Ill.) Home Rule Ad Hoc Com., 1975-77; bd. dirs. Hinsdale Arts Coun., 1977-85, dir. emeritus, 1985-95; pres. Triangle Frat. Edn. Found., 1974-96, bd. dirs., 1996-2001, dir. emeritus; mem. vis. com. dept. chemistry U. Tex.; mem. adv. coun. U. Tex. Coll. Natural Scis. Found., 1990-95; pres. Lake Ridge Club Homeowners Assn., 2001—. Recipient Gas Industry Research award, 1985, Energy Exec. of Yr. award, 1987, Profl. Achievement award Ill. Inst. Tech. Alumni Assn., 1991. Mem. AIChE, Am. Gas Assn. (operating sect. award of merit 1989), Inst. Gas Engrs., Combustion Inst. (past treas. bd. cen. states sect.), Atlantic Gas Rsch. Exch. (chmn. mng. bd. 1980-96), Internat. Gas Union (U.S. rep. subcom. F-2 1974-83), Gas Appliance Engrs. Soc. (past trustee), Air Pollution Control Assn. (past sect. com. residential pollution sources), Triangle (svc. key and Outstanding Alumnus award 1987). Achievements include patents for 13 patents in field. Home: 28 Lake Ridge Club Dr Burr Ridge IL 60527-7937 Office: RBR @ Vision 28 Lake Ridge Club Dr Burr Ridge IL 60527-7937 E-mail: RBR@attbi.com.

ROSENBERG, ROGER NEWMAN, neurologist, educator; b. Milw., Mar. 3, 1939; s. Sol J. and Cora D. (Newman) R.; m. Adrienne Turick, June 24, 1962; children— Jennifer, Lara Student, Tufts U., 1957-60; BS, Northwestern U., 1961, MD with distinction, 1964. Diplomate Am. Bd. Psychiatry and Neurology. Intern Harvard Med. Service, Beth Israel Hosp., Boston, 1964-65; resident in neurology Neurol. Inst., Columbia U., N.Y.C., 1965-67, instr. neurology, 1967-68; research assoc. Lab. of Biochem. Genetics, NIH, Bethesda, Md., 1968-70; clin. instr. Howard U. Med. Sch., Washington, 1969-70; asst. prof. neuroscis. Sch. Medicine, U. Calif.-San Diego, 1970-71; assoc. prof. neuroscis. and pediatrics, attending neurologist Univ. Hosp., U. Calif.-La Jolla, 1971-74; prof., chmn. dept. neurology U. Tex. Southwestern Med. Ctr., Dallas, 1973-91, prof. physiology, 1976—, Zale Disting. chair, prof. neurology, 1990—, dir. Alzheimer's Disease Rsch. Ctr., 1989—. Attending neurologist Parkland Meml. Hosp. and Children's Med. Ctr., Dallas, 1974—, Zale Lipshy Univ. Hosp., 1990—; mem. staff Presbyn. Hosp., Dallas, 1974—, St. Paul's Hosp., Dallas, 1974—; cons. staff VA Hosp., Dallas, 1974—; mem. nat. med. adv. bd. Nat. Ataxia Found., Mpls., 1971—, Myasthenia Gravis Found., 1973; chmn. med. adv. bd., dir. med. sci. research Internat. Joseph Diseases Found., Livermore, Calif., 1977—; lectr. Japanese Soc. Neurology, 1987, 94, Chinese Neurol. Soc., 1987, Spanish Neurol. Soc., 1992; chmn. bd. sci. councilors NIH, 1984-86; pres. (hon.), Intl. French Soc. of Neurology Charcot Centenary Symposium, 1993. Editor Jour. Neurogenetics; mem. editl. bd. Neurology, 1977-82, 91-97, Trends in Neurosci., 1980-86, Current Opinion in Neurology & Neurosurgery, 1990—, Jour. of AMA, 1997—; chief editor Archives of Neurology, 1997—; contbr. articles to med. jours. Bd. dirs.

Winston Sch., Dallas, 1974-80 1st Woody Guthrie scholar, 1971; USPHS grantee; recipient Disting. Alumnus award Neurol. Inst., N.Y., 1994. Fellow AAAS; mem. Am. Acad. Neurology (chmn. sci. program com. nat. meetings 1979-84, elected councillor exec. bd. 1984-89, pres. 1991-93), Am. Neurochem. Soc., Tissue Culture Soc., Soc. Neurosci., Am. Fedn. Clin. Rsch., Soc. Pediat. Rsch., Internat. Child Neurology Assn., Am. Neurol. Assn. (1st v.p. 1987), Ctrl. Soc. Neurol. Rsch., Can. Congress Neurol. Scis. (hon.), Spanish Neurol. Soc. (hon. 1994), Sigma Xi, Alpha Omega Alpha (Merit award Northwestern U. Alumni Assn. 1986). Home: 4425 Wildwood Rd Dallas TX 75209-2801 Office: U Tex Southwestern Med Ctr Dallas TX 75235 E-mail: rrosen@mednet.sw.med.edu.

ROSENBERG, RUDY, chemical company executive; b. Feb. 26, 1930; came to U.S., 1949, naturalized, 1954; s. Hilaire and Frieda Rosenberg; m. Rose H. Wauters, Nov. 7, 1953; 1 child, Rudy. Student in classical studies, Atheneum Leon Lepage, Brussels, 1946. Buyer Lever Bros., Brussels, 1946-49; head biochem. divsn. Mann Rsch. Labs., N.Y.C., 1954-61, Gallard-Schlesinger, Carle Place, N.Y., 1961-75; pres. Accurate Chem. & Sci. Corp., Westbury, 1975—. Prin., v.p., Leeches U.S.A. Ltd. Served with U.S. Army, 1951-53. Mem. Reticuloendothelial Soc. Internat. Clubs: Antique Automobile, Rolls Royce, Puppetry Guild Greater N.Y. Democrat.

ROSENBERG, RUTH HELEN BORSUK, lawyer; b. Plainfield, N.J., Feb. 23, 1935; d. Irwin and Pauline (Rudich) Borsuk; children— Joshua Cohen, Sarah, Rebecca, Daniel, Miriam, Tziporah, Isaac AB, Douglass Coll., 1956; JD, U. Pa., 1963. Bar: Pa. 1964, N.Y. 1967, D.C. 1986, Md. 1987, Va. 1994, Mass. 1995, U.S. Ct. Appeals (3d cir.) 1969, U.S. Supreme Ct. 1969, U.S. Ct. Appeals (4th cir.) 1994. Law clk. Ct. Common Pleas, Phila., 1963-64; assoc. Blank, Rudenko, Klaus & Rome, 1964-67; atty. Office Corp. Counsel, City of Rochester, 1967-68; assoc. Nixon, Hargrave, Devans & Doyle, Washington, 1968-74, ptnr., 1975-99, Nixon Peabody LLP, Washington, 1999—. Vice chairperson character and fitness com. Appellate divsn. 4th dept. 7th Jud. Dist. N.Y. Supreme Ct., 1976-80, mem. grievance com., 1981-84. Bd. dirs. Soc. Prevention Cruelty to Children, 1976-77, N.Y. Civil Liberties Union, 1972-85, v.p. 1976-85; bd. dirs. Jewish Home and Infirmary, 1978-83, pres., 1980-83; v.p. Jewish Fedn. Rochester, 1983, Yachad, Inc., Jewish Cmty. Housing Devel. Corp., 1990-94; bd. dirs. Jewish Cmty. Coun., Greater Washington, 1989-93, Leadership Washington, 1990-91, Libr. Theatre, 1994-97, Op. Understanding, D.C., 1994-95. Mem. ABA, D.C. Bar Assn., Md. Bar Assn., Va. Bar Assn., Phi Beta Kappa. Office: Nixon Peabody LLP 401 9th St NW Ste 900 Washington DC 20004-2128 E-mail: rrosenberg@nixonpeabody.com.

ROSENBERG, SAMUEL NATHAN, French and Italian language educator; b. N.Y.C., Jan. 19, 1936; s. Israel and Etta (Friedland) R. AB, Columbia U., 1957; PhD, Johns Hopkins U., 1965. Instr. Columbia U., N.Y.C., 1960-61; lectr. Ind. U., Bloomington, Ind., 1962-65, asst. prof., 1965-69, assoc. prof. Ind., 1969-81, prof. dept. French and Italian, 1981-99, prof. emeritus, 2000—, chmn. dept., 1977-84. Author: Modern French CE, 1970, (with others) Harper's Grammar of French, 1983, (with W. Apel) French Secular Compositions of the 14th Century, 3 vols., 1970-72, (with H. Tischler) Chanter m'estuet: Songs of the Trouveres, 1981; translator: (with S. Danon) Ami and Amile, 1981, revised edit., 1996, Lyrics and Melodies of Gace Brulé, 1985, (with H. Tischler) The Monophonic Songs in the Roman de Fauvel, 1991, Lancelor-Grail Cycle, vol. 2, 1993, Chansons des trouvères, 1995, Songs of the Troubadours and Trouvères, 1997, (with others) Early French Tristan Poems, 2 vols., 1998. Pres. Mid-Am. Festival of the Arts, Inc., Bloomington, Ind., 1984-85. Woodrow Wilson Found. fellow, 1959-60; Fulbright fellow, 1960-61; Lilly Faculty fellow, 1986-87. Mem MLA, Am. Assn. Tchrs. French; mem. Medieval Acad. Am., Internat. Courtly Lit. Soc., Am. Literary Translators Assn. (bd. dirs. 2002--), Phi Beta Kappa Home: PO Box 1164 Bloomington IN 47402-1164 E-mail: srosenbe@indiana.edu.

ROSENBERG, SARAH ZACHER, institute arts administration executive, humanities administration consultant; b. Kelem, Lithuania, Jan. 10, 1931; came to U.S., 1938; d. David Meir Zacher and Rachel Korbman; m. Norman J. Rosenberg, Dec. 30, 1950; children: Daniel, Alyssa. BA in History, U. Nebr., 1970, MA in Am. History, 1973. Rsch. historian U. Mid-Am., Lincoln, Nebr., 1974-78, program developer dept. humanities, 1978-79, asst. dir. div. acad. planning, 1980-81, dir. program devel., 1981-82; exec. dir. Nebr. Humanities Coun., 1982-87, Nebr. Found. for Humanities, Lincoln, 1984-87, Am. Inst. for Conservation Hist. and Artistic Works, Washington, 1987-97, exec. dir. found., 1991-97; program officer, spl. cons. mus. div. NEH, 1987, external reviewer, 1981, 89; cons. strategic planning for nonprofit cultural instns., 1997—. Lay participant long-range planning conf. Nebr. Bar Assn., Hastings, 1986. Co-editor: The Great Plains Experience: Readings in the History of a Region, 1978; contbr. articles to profl. jours. Action mem. Hadassah, Lincoln, 1961—87, Tifereth Israel Synagogue, Lincoln, 1961—87, Beth El Congregation, Besthesda, Md., 1988—2001, Kol Shalom Congregation, 2001—; bd. dirs. Sta. KUCV, affiliate Nat. Pub. Radio, Lincoln, 1986—87, Lincoln Cmty. Playhouse, Lincoln, 1986—87. NEH grantee, 1981, 86, merit awards, 1983, 87; Humanities Resource Ctr. grantee, Peter Kiewit Found., 1984. Mem. Am. Hist. Assn., Western Hist. Assn., Alpha Theta. Democrat. Home: 8102 Appalachian Ter Potomac MD 20854-4050

ROSENBERG, SAUL ALLEN, oncologist, educator; b. Cleve., Aug. 2, 1927; BS, Western Res. U., 1948, MD, 1953. Diplomate Am. Bd. Internal Medicine, Am. Bd. Oncology. Intern Univ. Hosp., Cleve., 1953—54; resident in internal medicine Peter Bent Brigham Hosp., Boston, 1954—61; research asst. toxicology AEC Med. Research Project, Western Res. U., 1948—53; asst. prof. medicine and radiology Stanford (Calif.) U., 1961—65, assoc. prof., 1965—79, chief divsn. oncology, 1965—93, prof., 1970—95; prof. emeritus, 1995—; Am. Cancer Soc. prof. Stanford (Calif.) U., 1983—89, assoc. dean, 1989—92. Chmn. bd. No. Calif. Cancer Program, 1974—80. Contbr. articles to profl. jours. Served to lt. M.C. USNR, 1954—56. Master: ACP; mem.: Western Assn. Physicians, Western Soc. Clin. Rsch., Radiation Rsch. Soc., Calif. Acad. Medicine, Assn. Am. Physicians, Am. Soc. Clin. Oncology (pres. 1982—83), Am. Fedn. Clin. Rsch., Inst. Medicine NAS, Am. Assn. Cancer Rsch. Office: Stanford U Sch Medicine Div Oncology 269 Campus Dr Stanford CA 94305

ROSENBERG, SEYMOUR, psychologist, educator; b. Newark, Sept. 7, 1926; s. Morris and Celia (Weiss) R.; children: Harold Stanley, Michael Seth. BS, The Citadel, 1948; MA, Ind. U., 1951, PhD, 1952. Research psychologist USAF, San Antonio, 1952-58, U. Kans., Lawrence, 1958-59, Bell Telephone Labs., Murray Hill, N.J., 1959-65; vis. prof. psychology Columbia, N.Y.C., 1965-66; prof. psychology Rutgers U., New Brunswick, NJ, 1966—2000, chmn. dept. psychology, 1981-83, 94-95, prof. emeritus psychology. Adj. prof. Rutgers U. Med. Sch., 1974—2000; vis. scholar U. Leuven, Belgium, 1983, Belgium, 92, Univ. de Provence, France, 1990; panel mem. NSF, 1970—72. Cons. editor Jours. Personality and Social Psychology, 1968-69; assoc. editor, 1970-73; contbr. articles to profl. jours. Served with USN, 1945-46. Fellow Social Sci. Rsch. Coun., 1973—74; grantee grantee, NSF, 1965—90, NIMH, 1966—68, Rsch. scientist grantee, 1968—73. Fellow Am. Psychol. Assn.; mem. Soc. Exptl. Social Psychology, Psychometric Soc., Classification Soc., N.Y. Acad. Sci., Eastern Psychol. Assn. Home: 689 Canal Rd Somerset NJ 08873-7327 Office: Rutgers U Dept Psychology ED Livingston Campus New Brunswick NJ 08903 E-mail: srpsych@rci.rutgers.edu.

ROSENBERG, SHELI Z. investment company executive; Degree, Tufts U., Northwestern U. Atty. Cotton, Watt, Jones & King, 1966—70; mng. ptnr. Schiff Hardin & Waite, 1976—80; from gen. coun. to vice-chmn. Equity Group Investments, LLC, Chgo., 1980—2000, vice-chmn., 2000—. Bd. dirs. CVS Corp., Capital Trust, Cendant Corp., Dynegy, Inc., Manufactured Home Communities, Inc., Equity Residential Properties Trust, Equity Office Properties Trust, Ventas, Inc.; adv. bd. J.L. Kellogg Grad. Sch. Bus. N.W. Univ. Trustee Rush Presbyn. St. Luke's Med. Ctr., exec. com.; co-founder, pres. Ctr. for Exec. Women, J.L. Kellogg Grad. Sch. Bus., 2001—. Office: Equity Group Investments LLC 737 North Michigan Ave Ste 1405 Chicago IL 60611 E-mail: szr312@aol.com.

ROSENBERG, SHIRLEY SIROTA, publications executive; b. Bklyn. d. Charles and Donia (Rudoy) Sirota; m. Jerome D. Rosenberg; children: Jonathan, Hindy. BA, Bklyn. Coll. Freelance writer, 1968—; contract writer-editor Dept. HEW, Washington, 1968-72; writer, editor Smithsonian Instn., 1972-77; instr. George Washington U., 1979—99; pres. SSR, Inc., Washington, 1977—. Washington corr. Parent's mag.; cons. NSF, Nat. Task Force on Minorities, Women and the Handicapped in Sci. and Enging., Joseph P. Kennedy Inst., bd. dirs. Office of Commn., U.S. Holocaust Meml. Coun., Humanities mag. NEH, George Washington U. Pubs. Specialist program, ARC Blood Svcs. Author: The First Oil Rush, 1967, How Children Grow, 1971, Code of Ethics and Professional Standards for Print Media Professionals, 1981, 92, A National Conversation on Ameircan Pluralism and Identity, 1995, Living is a Lifelong Process, 1995, Staying Connected: A Guide for Parents on Raising a Teenage Daughter, 2000; editor-author: First Special Report on Alcohol and Alcohol Abuse, Forging Partnerships for Africa's Future Facility Study, Bureau of Engraving and Printing, Staying Connected: A Guide to parents on Raising A Teenage Daughter; contbr. articles to trade and profl. jours.; editor, coord. top level nat. and internat. position papers. Recipient 1st place award Soc. Tech. Communicators, 1983, Achievement award, 1990, Merit award Art Dirs. Club, 1984, 1st place award Washington Edpress, 1984, 86, 95, 96, 97. Mem. Am. Soc. Journalists and Authors, Assn. of Edit. Bus., Washington Women in Pub. Rels., Nat. Assn. Govt. Communicators (1st Pl. award 1981, 95, 2d Pl. award 1990).

ROSENBERG, THEODORE ROY, financial executive; b. Nyack, N.Y., Aug. 6, 1933; s. Rebecca Sheer R.; m. Eleanor Schmalsteig, Feb. 19, 1956 (div); children: Bradley Scott, Martha Ann; m. Mary Frances McVay, Sept. 21, 1991. BS, U. Conn., 1955; MBA, U. Pa., 1964. Commd. 2nd lt. U.S. Army, 1955, advanced through grades to col., 1976, retired, 1982; portfolio mgr. The Burney Co., Falls Church, Va., 1979—, v.p. mktg., 1982-94, v.p., 1994-95, pres., 1995—2001. Bd. dirs. Army Transp. Mus., U. Conn. Found., 1995-2001. Decorated Legion of Merit, Bronze Star; recipient Vietnam Medal of Honor, Govt. of Vietnam, 1966; inducted into Alumni Hall of Fame, U. Conn. Sch. Bus. Adminstrn., 1994. Mem. U. Pa. Mid-Atlantic Regional Adv. Bd., Wharton Club of Washington (Man of Yr. 1995). Avocations: scuba diving, snorkeling, golf. Office: The Burney Co 121 Rowell Ct Falls Church VA 22046-3174 E-mail: burney_ted@prodigy.net.

ROSENBERG, VICTOR I. plastic surgeon, educator; b. N.Y.C., Nov. 15, 1936; s. Leonard C. and Sarah G. (Berger) R.; m. Deborah Iskoe, Jan. 2, 1966; children: Spencer, Ria. AB, NYU, 1957; MD, Chgo. Med. Sch., 1961. Diplomate Am. Bd. Plastic Surgery. Intern Beth Israel Hosp., N.Y.C., 1961-62, resident, 1962-63, 64-66, Beekman Downtown Hosp., 1963-64, Bronx Mcpl. Hosp., 1966-67, Mt. Sinai Hosp., N.Y.C., 1967-68; pvt. practice in plastic surgery, 1968—. Assoc. attending surgeon Beth Isreal Hosp., 1968—; assoc. attending surgeon Beekman Downtown Hosp., 1968—, chief plastic surgery, 1976-80; attending surgeon N.Y. Infirmary-Beekman Downtown Hosp., 1980-98, dir. cosmetic surgery, 1984-97; asst. attending surgeon Mt. Sinai Hosp., N.Y.C., 1968—; asst. clin. prof. Mt. Sinai Sch. Medicine CUNY. Comdr. USN, 1968-70. Fellow ACS, Internat. Coll. Surgeons; mem. Am., N.Y. Regional socs. plastic and reconstructive surgeons, Am. Soc. Aesthetic Plastic Surgery, AMA, Am. Cleft Palate Assn., N.Y. Acad. Medicine, N.Y. State, N.Y. County Med. Socs., Pan Am. Med. Assn. (diplomate sect. plastic surgery), Friars Club. Office: 4 Sutton Pl New York NY 10022-3056

ROSENBERG, VICTOR LAURENCE, management educator, entrepreneur; b. Monroe, La., June 26, 1944; s. Leonard Herman and Gertrude Edna (Mazer) R.; m. Margaret States Miller, Aug. 15, 1965 (div. 1985); children: Michael Jerome, Ambriel States, Shamain Ilya, Arilim Gordon; m. Nina Greever Edwards, Apr. 30, 1988; children: Jennifer Edwards. BS in Engring., MIT, 1966; MS in Engring., Boston U., 1987, DBA in Strategy, 1991. V.p. Chesapeake Life Ins. Co., Balt., 1967-72, pres., 1979-82; program mgr. Xerox Co., Stamford, Conn., 1972-78; chmn. bd. dirs. Datatel, Alexandria, Va., 1978-79, 1978-79; asst. to pres. Atex div. Eastman Kodak, Bedford, Mass., 1982-85; v.p. cons. Tech. Fin. Svcs., Boston, 1985-88; cons. health care Boston U., 1985—; asst. prof. mgmt. Keene State Coll., 1991-93, Worcester (Mass.) State Coll., 1993-94, Northeastern U., Boston, 1994—; chair dept. mgmt. Becker Coll., Worcester, 1996—. Founder, pres. Achiya Nursing Tech., Nashua, N.H., 1987-91; lectr. Sch. Mgmt. Tech., Boston U., 1987-90, U. Lowell, Worcester Poly.; mgmt. cons. New Eng. Med. Ctr., Boston, 1986-87; vol. mgmt. cons. Roger Williams Hosp., Boston City Hosp., Mass. Gen. Hosp., Hahnemann Hosp.; bd. dirs. McIntrye Cons., 1991—. Contbr. articles to profl. publs. Founding dir. MIT Enterprise Forum of Washington, 1981; curriculum advisor Community Coll. Balt., 1972; active MIT Edn. Council, 1978. Mem. Clowns of Am., Phi Kappa Sigma. Clubs: MIT of Balt. (pres. 1980-82). Republican. Jewish. Home: 4 Bayberry Ln Framingham MA 01701-3031

ROSENBERGER, BRYAN DAVID, lawyer; b. Johnstown, Pa., Oct. 8, 1950; s. Clarence Haines and Ida Rae (Neiderheiser) Rosenberger; m. Barbara Leah Byer, July 14, 1977; children: Laura Michelle, Lisa Renee. BS, Juniata Coll., 1971; JD, Coll. of William and Mary, 1974. Bar: Pa 1974. Assoc. Eckert Seamans Cherin & Mellott, Pitts., 1974-82, ptnr., 1983—, chmn. corp. and bus. dept., 1992-98, mem. exec. com., 1994-98, also bd. dirs., chmn. bus. div., 2001—. Active new leadership bd Pittsburgh Symphony Soc, 1990—98. Mem.: ABA, Allegheny County Bar Assn, Pa Bar Assn. Home: 1358 Oakledge Ct Upper Saint Clair PA 15241-3540 Office: Eckert Seamans Cherin & Mellott 600 Grant St Ste 4400 Pittsburgh PA 15219-2702 Business E-Mail: bdr@escm.com.

ROSENBERGER, CAROL, concert pianist; b. Detroit, Nov. 1, 1935; d. Maurice Seiberling and Whilamet (Gibson) R. B.F.A., Carnegie-Mellon U., 1955; postgrad., Acad. Performing Arts, Vienna, 1956-59. In charge of artists and repertoire Delos Internat. Mem. artist faculty U. So. Calif., Calif. State U., Northridge, Immaculate Heart Coll.; vis. artist numerous colls. and univs. Internat. concert career, 1964—; New York debut, 1970; appeared several times at Carnegie Hall; soloist Am. Symphony, Nat. Symphony, Royal Philharmonic, San Diego Symphony, Detroit Symphony, Houston Symphony, St. Louis Symphony, Indpls. Symphony, Los Angeles Chamber Orch.; performed world premiere of Buenaventura; piano concerts with Philippine Philharmonic, 1977, Am. Symphony, 1977; recital series in Am., European, Asian music capitals; recordings include Hindemith's Four Temperaments with London Royal Philharm., Water Music of the Impressionists (one of 25 Best Classical CDs of All Time, Stereo Rev., Recording of Yr., Gramophone mag., All-time Gt. Recording, Billboard mag.), works of Beethoven, Schubert, Szymanowski, Night Moods, 1989, Perchance To Dream, Lullabys for Children and Adults, 1989, Reveries: Music of Chopin, Such Stuff as Dreams, Singing on the Water, Mozart Adagios, (with N.Y. Chamber Symphony) Fantasy Variations on a Theme of Youth (Howard Hanson), 1991 (Grammy nomination), Haydn D Major Concerto, Nights in the Gardens of Spain, Beethoven Concerto No. 4, (with Seattle Symphony) Burleske, Piano Concerto of Howard Hanson, (with L.A. Chamber Orch.) Shostakovich 1st Piano Concerto, others; prodr., co-prodr. Music for Young People Series, others; author script for narration of The Firebird (Stravinsky) (Notable Recording award ALA);contbr. articles to music publs. Recipient Steinway Centennial medal, 1954, Critics Choice award Gramaphone mag., 1980, 10/10 award CD Rev. Mem. Nat. Acad. Rec. Arts and Scis. Achievements include being chosen to represent Am. women musicians by Nat. Commn. on Observance Internat. Womens Year, 1976. Office: Delos Internat Inc 1645 Vine St Ste 340 Los Angeles CA 90028-8842

ROSENBERGER, CAROLYN ANN, art educator; b. Beaver Dam, Wis., Nov. 27, 1945; d. Gust Albert and Ethel May (Linck) Pomering; m. Randy Byron Rosenberger, Aug. 3, 1968; 1 child, Shiloh Rae. BS, U. Wis., 1967, postgrad., 1969-94. Founder, advisor Ann. H.S. Art Show, Iola, Wis., 1967-2002, H.S. Art Club, 1972-2002; art tchr., supr. Summer Sch. Art Program, Amherst, Wis., 1969-71; art tchr. adult night sch. Fox Valley Tech., Iola, 1970-80; supr. to student who won Milw. Jour. Art Calendar Contest, 1971, 76, 82, 83, 85, Waupaca Fine Arts Festival, Waupaca, Wis., 1969-2002, Statewide H.S. Art Day, Oshkosh, Wis., 1979, 93, 94, 97, 99, Bi-State X-mas Card Design Contest, Waupaca, Wis., 1985, 90, 91, 91, 93; in charge of h.s. gifted/talented exhibits, 1990-2002; accepted exhibitor Ctrl. Wis. Art Tchrs. Exhibit, Stevens Point, 1984; judge Wis. Regional Art Assn. Exhibit, Wausau, 1992; tchr. Wis. Valley Art Assn., Wausau, 1993, 94, 95, 96, 97, 98, 99, 99, 2000, 2001, 2002; founder, chmn. Art on Track Profl. Art/Craft Fair, Iola, 1991, 92, 93, 94, 95, 96, 97, 98, 99, 2000, 2001, 2002. One-person shows include Cen. Wis. Cultural Ctr., Wisconsin Rapids, 2002; exhbns. include Wis. Edn. Assn., Madison, 1989 (purchase award and award of merit, 1990, purchase awards, 1992, 93, 94, 96, 98, 2000, 02), Shawano Arts and Crafts Fair, 1990 (2d place prize), Wisconsin Rapids Arts and Crafts Fair, 1990 (1st place award), New London Mid-Winter Art Exhibit, 1991 (prize), Winnebagoland Art and Crafts Fair, Oshkosh, 1991, 99 (prize), 10 State Art Fair, 1992 (Excellence award), Milw. War Meml. Mus., 1992 (merit award), Art Works Gallery, Green Bay, 1993, Wausau Ctr. for Visual Arts, 1992, 93, 94, 98, 99, 2001, 2002, Neville Mus., Green Bay, 1993, 94, 95, 97, 99, Bonifas Art Ctr., Escanaba, Mich., Nat. Exhibit Mequon, Wis., 1993, 94, Waupaca 31st Fine Arts Festival Exhibit, 1994 (prize and purchase award 1994, top purchase award prize 1998-2002), Marshfield's New Visions Gallery, 1994, 95, 97, 2001, 2002, Nicolet Coll., Rhinelander, 1994, Wausau Ctr. Visual Arts, 1993, 98, 2000, 2001, 2002 Wausau 8-State Mid-Winter Exhibit, 1995, 98, 2000, 2001, 2002, Waupaca Pub. Libr., 1996, 98, 99, Alexander House Gallery and Mus., Port Edwards, 1996, Hardy Gallery, 1996, Lawton Gallery, Green Bay, 1999, Art at the Arboretum, Appleton, Wis., 1999, 2000, 01, Seippel Ctr., Beaver Dam, Wis., 2000, Prairie Art Ctr., Oshkosh, 2002, Appleton Art Ctr.'s Inaugural Exhibit, 2002, Secura Ins. Co.'s Fine Art Exhbn., Appleton, 2002, Wis. Edn. Assn., Madison, 2002. Leader, camp councilor United Meth. Youth, Iola, 1967-68; founding mem. Iola Jaycettes, 1976, local dir.; organizer Art in the Park Iola Centennial, 1992. Named Jaycette of Yr. Iola Jaycettes, 1979, Tchr. of Yr. Iola-Scandinavia Tchrs. Assn., 1979; recipient Best of Show Trophy winner Scandinavian Fine Arts Show, 1977, 78, 79, 81, 82, 83, Award of Merit, Eagle River Artarama, 1991, 97, Best of Show award Wis. Rapids, 1995, Best of Painting award Marshfield Art Fair, 1996. Mem. Wis. Art Edn. Assn., Nat. Art Edn. Assn., Wis. Women in the Arts, Midwest Watercolor Soc., Wis. Painters and Sculptors Inc., Ctr. for the Visual Arts in Wausau, Hardy Gallery, Northeastern Wis. Arts Coun., Appleton Art Ctr. Methodist. Avocations: painting, camping, photography, pool. Home: PO Box 203 Iola WI 54945-0203 Office: Iola Scandinavia Sch 540 S Jackson St Iola WI 54945-9115 E-mail: carolynrosenberg@hotmail.com.

ROSENBERGER, JANICE WHITEHILL, speech and language pathologist; b. Newport, Vt., Sept. 27, 1943; d. Clarence Arthur and Doris Martha Jordan; children: Gregory, Karen, Andrew. AA, Orange Coast Coll., 1974; student, Portland (Oreg.) State U., 1974-75; BS, No. Ill. U., 1977; MS, Marquette U., 1978; postgrad., U. Vt., 1981-82, cert., 1990. Accounts receivable clk. Yankton (S.D.) Coll., 1963-66; libr. researcher Microwave Instruments Co., Corona del Mar, Calif., 1973; tchr. ESL Libertyville (Ill.) Sch. Dist., 1978-80; tchr. GED Mundelein (Ill.) High Sch., 1979-80; speech-lang. pathologist Barre (Vt.) City Schs., 1981-83, Orleans Essex Vis. Nurses Assn. and Hospice, Inc., Newport, Vt., 1983-2000. Workshop presenter Coll. Lake County, Grayslake, Ill., 1980; exec. sec. Paul Rosenberger Appraiser, North Troy, Vt., 1982-99; recorder, auditor, mem. profl. health adv. com., 1984-94, support group facilitator, 1992-93; facilitator, time keeper Newport Early Action Team, 1986-98; speech-lang. pathologist Orleans and Essex North Supervisory Union, Derby, Vt., 1987-90, mem. infectious control com., 1996-97. Editor books. Pres. ch. women's group, North Troy, 1987—89; mem. Hosp. Aux., 1986—97; sec. Friendly Class Union, 1986—88, v.p., 2000—; election judge state govt., Mundelein, 1978—79; supr., mem. United Ch. Christ, 1984—; mem. Vt. Conf. Christian Edn. Cluster, 1982—84. Recipient Jr. Women's Club award, 1974, Editing Internat. award, 1981, Activity Achievement award, 1985, Outstanding Contbn. award, 1990, Award Continuing Edn., 1993, Pres.'s award, 1980, Dedicated Svc. plaque for committent to provision of speech svcs. in N.E. kingdom, 1995. Mem.: After 5 Club (telephone chmn. 1984—85, bible coord. 1985—90, 1993—94, chmn. 1992—93, area rep. 1994—98, coord. 1999—2000, spkr. 1995—). Avocations: music, writing, exercise, reading. Home: Rte 101 PO Box 631 North Troy VT 05859-0631

ROSENBERGER, MARGARET ADALINE, retired elementary school educator; b. Micanopy, Fla., Oct. 1930; d. Eugene David and Lillian Adeline (Bauknight) Rosenberger. Student, Stetson U., 1946—48; BA in Edn., U. Fla., 1949, MEd, 1952. Drama sec. Nat. Youth Adminstrn., Gainesville, Fla., 1939—40; clk. U.S. Army, Camp Blanding, 1940—46; tchr. J.J. Finley, Gainesville, 1949—52; prin., tchr. Micanopy Jr. H.S., 1952—55; gen. supr. Alachua County Schs., Gainesville, 1955—57; tchr. U.S. dep. Sch., Heidelberg, Germany, 1957—58; elem. supr. Alachua County Schs., 1958—59; tchr. U.S. Army Dependents' Sch., Heidelberg, Germany, 1957—58; prin. Littlewood Elem. Sch., Gainesville, 1959—73, Prairie View Elem. Sch., Gainesville, 1973—82, ret., 1982. Mem. sch. adv. com. Prairie View Elem. Sch., 1975—82. Contbr. poems to mags. & papers; co-author: Reflections of Light, 1995; contbr. articles, . Pres. Children's Commn., Gainesville, 1956—57; dir. The Village Chorus, 1987—; mem. Gainesville Schs. PTA, 1959—82; mem. PTA Micanopy, 1952—55; Dem. candidate Fla. House Rep., 1974; pianist/organist The Village Vespers on Sunday Evenings, 1990—; bd. dir. Foster Grandparents, Gainesville, 1974—76; chmn. bd. dir. No. Fla. Retirement Village, Inc., 1982—86, bd. rep. to residents, 1986—, v.p. bd. dir., 1981—82. Mem.: Internat. Soc. Poets, Am. Soc. Composers, Authors & Pub., Altrusa Internat. Club Gainesville (chmn. internat. com., chmn. newsletter, spkr. for programs), Order of Eastern Star, Delta Kappa Gamma (internat. soc. 1959—). Democrat. Baptist. Avocations: stamp collecting, coin collecting, book collecting, post card collecting, creative writing. Home: 410 SW Wacahoota Rd Micanopy FL 32667 Mailing: 8015 NW 28th Place B 110 Gainesville FL 32606

ROSENBERGER, THAD ALLEN, research scientist; b. Mansfield, Ohio, Sept. 6, 1967; s. Arnold Joseph and Eula Faye Rosenberger; m. Theodora M. Kung. PhD, Ohio State U., 1999. Rsch. scientist NIH/Nat. Inst. Aging, Bethesda, Md., 1999—. Contbr. articles to profl. jours. Mem. Am. Soc. for Neurochemistry, Internat. Soc. for Neurochemistry. Home: 751 Sykesville Rd Sykesville MD 21784 Office: NIH/Nat Inst Aging 9000 Rockville Pike Bethesda MD 20892 E-mail: plsetn@mail.nih.gov.

ROSENBERGER, TIMOTHY JOSEPH, transportation planning consultant; b. Cleve., June 5, 1962; s. Warren Joseph and Shirley Ann Rosenberger; m. Elaine Welsh, July 29, 1989; children: Timothy Joseph Jr., Tessa Elaine, William Warren. AB, Youngstown State U., 1981; MS in Urban Studies, Cleve. State U., 1991. Planning analyst Greater Cleve. RTA, 1992-94; assoc. planner Parsons Brinckerhoff, Inc., Balt., 1994-97; sr. planner Parsons Brinckerhoff Europe Ltd., London, 1997-99, Parsons Brinckerhoff Ohio, Cleve., 1999—. Mem. AICP (cert.) Avocations: reading, gardening.

ROSENBERRY, WILLIAM KENNETH, lawyer, educator; b. St. Louis, Aug. 14, 1946; s. William Hugh and Shirley Anne (Love) Rosenberry; m. Linda Lou Lang, Aug. 24, 1968 (div. Jan. 1985); children: Ashlie Anne, Allison Renee; m. Donna L. Pruitt; stepchildren: Corey David Pruitt, Lindsey Lee Pruitt. BBA, U. Tex., Arlington, 1967; JD, Baylor U., 1970. Bar: Tex. 1970, Colo. 1991, U.S. Dist. Ct. (no. dist.) Tex. 1971, cert.: (specialist in comml. real estate law), Tex. (residential real estate law). Assoc. Hinds & Chambers, Arlington, 1970-71; ptnr. Duke, Rosenberry, Duke & Jelinek, 1971-76; pvt. practice, 1976—. Mem. faculty U. Tex., 1991—; bd. dirs. Equitable Bank, NA, Arlington, Equitable Bankshares, Dallas; gen. mgr. Triple R. Properties; escrow officer Am. Title Co., 1984—. Pres. Pantego Christian Acad. Boosters, Arlington, 1990—92; mem. Arlington City Zoning Bd., 1989—92; bd. dirs. Baylor Bear Found. of Baylor U., Childrens Charities Ft. Worth, v.p., 1999—; bd. dirs. Ft. Worth Charities, Inc. Named, Outstanding Young Men in Am., 1980; recipient Outstanding Part-Time Faculty Tchg. award, U. Tex. Dept. Real Estate and Fin., 1992. Mem.: Arlington Bar Assn. (bd. dirs. 1987), Arlington Rep. Club, Arlington Sportsmans Club. Mem. Pantego Bible Ch. Avocation: Avocations: fishing, hunting, jogging.. Office: 3010 W Park Row Dr Arlington TX 76013-2048

ROSENBLATT, ADYLIN ISABELLE, social worker; b. N.Y.C., Apr. 3, 1926; d. Morris James and Goldie Sylvia (Goldman) Lipson; m. Murray Rosenblatt; children: Karin Ann, Daniel Bernard. BA, Hunter Coll., 1947; MA, U. Chgo., 1953; MSW, San Diego State U., 1971. Diplomate in clin. social work. Recreation swim instr. 110th St. Community Ctr., N.Y.C., 1947-49; rsch. asst. Sociology Dept. Cornell U., Ithaca, N.Y., 1949-50, U. Chgo., 1951-53; psychiat. social worker Adult Protective Svcs., San Diego, 1973-76; prin. investigator U. Calif., San Diego State U., La Jolla, 1971, 73; dir. social svcs. Tri City Hosp., Oceanside, Calif., 1976-77, Green Hosp. of Scripps U., La Jolla, 1977-79; pvt. practice La Jolla, San Diego, 1979—. Bd. dirs. Ceder Community Ctr., 1973-77, NASW Health Coun. (sec. 1977); family advocacy rep. Marine Corps Recruit Depot, San Diego, 1985. Contbr. articles profl. jours. Mem. La Jolla Shores Assn. (bd. dirs. 1997-99).

Fellow World Fedn. Mental Health; mem. NASW (v.p. 1974-80, chmn. counseling and psychotherapy referall svc. 1983-84), ARC (disaster mental health svcs. divsn. 1996—), Soc. Clin. Social Work, Compeer (bd. dirs. 1985-90), Cognitive Soc. of San Diego, Am. Soc. on Aging, Am. Assn. Social Work with Groups (bd. mem. San Diego chpt. 1995—). Avocations: swimming, walking, reading, community work. Office: Adylin Rosenblatt PO Box 2066 La Jolla CA 92038-2066

ROSENBLATT, ALBERT MARTIN, state appeals court judge; b. N.Y.C., Jan. 17, 1936; s. Isaac and Fannie (Dachs) R.; m. Julia Carlson, Aug. 23, 1970; 1 child, Elizabeth. BA, U. Pa., 1957; LLB (JD), Harvard U., 1960. Bar: N.Y. 1961.. Dist. atty. Dutchess County, N.Y., 1969-75, county judge, 1976-81; justice N.Y. State Supreme Ct., 1982-89, justice, appellate divsn., 1989-98; justice N.Y. Ct. Appeals, 1999—. Instr. judge N.Y. State, 1987-89; vis. prof. Vaar Coll., 1993; moderator N.Y. State Fair Trial Free Press Conf., 2000, 2001; creator Dutchess County 1st consumer protection bur., 1973; instr. newly elected state supreme ct. judges and county judges; asst. dist. attys., 1974, 75; instr. law tng. N.Y. State Police Acad., 1997; lectr. Nat. Dist. Attys. Assn., 1968-74; mem. vis. faculty trial advocacy workshop Harvard Law Sch., 1998, 99. Mem. bd. editors N.Y. State Bar Jour., 1992—; contbr. articles on law to profl. jours. and popular mags. Bd. dirs. United Way Cmty. Chest, 1970; bd. dirs. Bardavon 1869 Opera House, Dutchess County Hist. Soc.; mem. adv. bd. Jewish Cmty. Ctr., 1987—; pres. Hist. Soc. Cts. of State of N.Y., 2002—. With USAR, 1960-66. Mem. N.Y. State Bar Assn. (named Outstanding Prosecutor 1974, Outstanding Jud. Svcs. award 1994), N.Y. State Dist. Attys. Assn. (pres. 1974, Frank S. Hogan award 1987, Jud. Svcs. award 1994), Profl. Ski Instrs. Am. (cert. 1984—), Baker St. Irregulars Club (former assoc. editor Baker St. Jour.). Republican. Jewish. Home: 300 Freedom Rd Pleasant Valley NY 12569-5431 Office: 10 Market St Poughkeepsie NY 12601-3228

ROSENBLATT, ARTHUR ISAAC, architect, former museum director; b. N.Y.C., Aug. 31, 1931; s. Harry and Helen (Satz) R.; m. Ruth Anne Turteltaub, Aug. 5, 1956; children: Paul Mark, Judith Alice. Diploma in architecture, Cooper Union, 1952; BArch, Carnegie-Mellon U., 1956. Registered architect, N.Y. Designer Katzman Assocs., N.Y.C., 1956-57, Isadore & Zachary Rosenfield, N.Y.C., 1957-60, Skidmore, Owings & Merrill-Harrison, Abramovitz, Pomerance and Breines, N.Y.C., 1960-61; chief designer Irwing S. Chanin, Architect, 1961-65; first dep. commr. N.Y.C. Dept. Parks, Recreation and Cultural Affairs, 1966-68; v.p., vice dir. Met. Mus. Art, N.Y.C., 1968-86; dir. capital projects N.Y. Pub. Libr., 1982-86; dir. U.S. Holocaust Meml. Mus., Washington, 1986-88; v.p. Grand Cen. Partnership, N.Y.C.; assoc. dir. Bryant Park Restoration Corp., 1989-95; v.p. 34th St. Partnership, 1991-95; prin. RKK&G Mus. & cultural Facilities Cons., Inc., 1995—. Faculty Sarah Lawrence Coll., Bronxville, N.Y., 1967-69; dir. capital projects N.Y. Pub. Libr., N.Y.C., 1982-86; cons. arch. Butler Mus. Am. Art, 1980, Whitney Mus. Am. Art, N.Y.C., 1981, Chrysler Mus. Art, Norfolk, Va., 1982, Internat. Ctr. Photography, N.Y.C., 1985-86, Mus. and Archive Acad. Hebrew Lang., Jerusalem, Newport Harbor Art Mus., 1990-91, J.B. Speed Art Mus., Louisville, 1992, Museo de Arte de Ponce, Ponce, P.R., 1995, P.R. Tourism Co., Commonwealth of P.R., 1995, Museo de Arte de P.R., 1996-2000, Songwriters Hall of Fame Mus., 1997, Am. Craft Mus., 1999, Ctr. Jewish History, 1999, Auschwitz Jewish Cultural Ctr., Poland, 1999, City Mus. of Washington, Hist. Soc. Washington, 2000, Saginaw Art Mus., 2001, Latvian Contemporary Art Ctr., Riga, Latvia, 2001. Author: Temple of Dendur, 1978, John Wiley & Sons Building Type Basics for Museums, 2000; co-author: Movie Song Catalog, 1993; contbr. articles to mags. and jours. Vice chmn. cmty. planning bd. # 8, N.Y.C., 1964-66; trustee The Cooper Union, 1983-86; commr. N.Y.C. Coun. Environment; pres. Met. Hist. Structures Assn.; presl. appointee Nat. Mus. Svc. Bd. of the Inst. of Mus. and Librs. Svcs., Washington, 1995. With U.S. Army, 1953-55. Nat. Endowment for the Arts grantee, 1981. Fellow AIA (pres. N.Y. chpt. 1982-83, spl. citation 1978, Thomas Jefferson award for pub. architecture 1998), Nat. Inst. for Archtl. Edn. (bd. dirs. 1978); mem. Mcpl. Art Soc., Archtl. League N.Y. (pres. 1970-72), Met. Historic Structures Assn. (pres.), Century Assn., Players Club, Salmagundi Club of N.Y. (chmn. bd. dirs.). Home: 1158 5th Ave New York NY 10029-6917 Office: 48 W 25th St New York NY 10010-2708 E-mail: rkkg@att.net.

ROSENBLATT, HOWARD MARSHALL, lawyer, financial professional; b. Jacksonville, Fla., May 4, 1947; s. Harry and Gertrude (Schulman) R.; m. Eve Darlene Ackerman, Feb. 22, 1976; children: Raphael Tzvi, Micah Jacob. BAE, U. Fla., 1969, JD, 1981. Bar: Fla. 1982; CLU, ChFC. Tchr. Duval County Bd. Pub. Instrn., Jacksonville, 1969-70; field underwriter Mut. Life Ins. Co. of N.Y. (The MONY Group), Gainesville, Fla., 1971—; registered rep. MONY Securities Corp., 1974—; pvt. practice law, 1983—. Chmn. Alachua County U.S. Constn. Bicentennial Commn., 1986-87; Dem. candidate for Fla. Ho. of Reps., 1988, 2000; bd. dirs. Alachua County divsn. Am. Cancer Soc., 1993-98; bd. dirs. Planned Parenthood North Ctrl. Fla., 1994-2000, treas., 1996-98; pres. Congregation B'nai Israel, 1993-95. Recipient Fred West Meml. award Fla. Jaycees, 1983. Fellow Life Underwriter Tng. Coun.; mem. ABA, The Fla. Bar (chmn. member benefits com. 1995-96), 8th Jud. Cir. Bar Assn., Am. Judicature Soc., Assn. for Women Lawyers (pres.-elect chpt. 2001-02), Fla. Assn. Ins. and Fin. Advisors (v.p. region IV 1987-91 chaplain, 1992-93), Gainesville Assn. Ins. and Fin. Advisors (pres. 1982-84, Agt. of Yr. 1974, 84, 87), Gainesville Estate Planning Coun. (pres. 1982-83), Million Dollar Round Table (life, membership communication com., found. knight), Am. Soc. Fin. Svc. Profls. (local pres. 1981, sponsor Gold Key Soc., pres. 2001--), Fla. Blue Key, B'nai B'rith (pres. Gainesville lodge 1974-75, 76-77, Gainesville unit 1994--). Democrat. Avocations: golf, teaching, reading, youth-related activities. Office: 2830 NW 41st St Ste J Gainesville FL 32606-6667 E-mail: howard_rosenblatt@mony.com., hrcampaign@hotmail.com.

ROSENBLATT, JASON PHILIP, English language educator; b. Balt., July 3, 1941; s. Morris D. and Esther (Friedlander) R.; m. Zipporah Marton, June 2, 1964; children: Noah David, Raphael Mark. BA, Yeshiva U., 1963; MA, Brown U., 1966, PhD, 1969. Asst. prof. English U. Pa., Phila., 1968-74, Georgetown U., Washington, 1974-76, assoc. prof., 1976-83, prof. English, 1983—. Vis. lectr. English lit. Swarthmore (Pa.) Coll., 1972-73; cen. exec. com. Folger Inst./Folger Shakespeare Libr., Washington, 1976-88. Author: Torah and Law in "Paradise Lost", 1994; co-editor: Not in Heaven: Coherence and Complexity in Biblical Narrative, 1991; mem. editl. bd. Milton Studies, 1992—; contbr. articles to scholarly pubs. Recipient Virginia Graham Healey award, 1998-99; Guggenheim Found. fellow, 1977-78, NEH fellow, 1990-91, Folger Shakespeare Libr./NEH fellow, 1999-2000. Mem. MLA (del. assembly 1989-91, exec. com. div. religion and lit. 1982-86), Milton Soc. Am. (exec. com. 1977-80, James Holly Hanford award 1989, v.p. 1998, pres. 1999), Milton Seminar, Phi Beta Kappa. Democrat. Jewish. Avocations: Talmud study, music, swimming. Office: Dept English Georgetown Univ PO Box 571131 Washington DC 20057-1131 E-mail: rosenblj@georgetown.edu.

ROSENBLATT, JOAN RAUP, mathematical statistician; b. N.Y.C., Apr. 15, 1926; d. Robert Bruce and Clara (Eliot) Raup; m. David Rosenblatt, June 10, 1950. AB, Barnard Coll., 1946; PhD, U. N.C., 1956. Intern Nat. Inst. Pub. Affairs, Washington, 1946-47; statis. analyst U.S. Bur. of Budget, 1947-48; rsch. asst. U. N.C., 1953-54; mathematician Nat. Inst. Standards and Tech. (formerly Nat. Bur. Standards), Washington, 1955—, asst. chief statis. engring., 1963-68, chief statis. engring. lab., 1969-78, dep. dir. Ctr. for Applied Math., 1978-88; dep. dir. Computing and Applied Math. Lab., Gaithersburg, 1988-93, dir., 1993-95, guest rschr. Statis. Engring. Divsn., 1996—. Mem. com. on indsl. rels. Dept. Stats. Ohio State U., 1981-90; mem. adv. com. in math. and stats. USDA Grad. Sch., 1971—; mem. Com. Applied and Theoretical Stats., Nat. Rsch. Coun., 1985-88. Mem. editorial bd. Communications in Stats., 1971-79, Jour. Soc. for Indsl. and Applied Math., 1965-75, Nat. Inst. Stds. and Tech. Jour. Rsch., 1991-93; contbr. articles to profl. jours. Chmn. Com. on Women in Sci., Joint Bd. on Sci. Edn., 1963-64. Rice fellow, 1946, Gen. Edn. Bd. fellow, 1948-50; recipient Fed. Woman's award, 1971, Gold medal Dept. Commerce, 1976, Presdl. Meritorious Exec. Rank award, 1982. Fellow AAAS (chmn. stats. sect. 1982, sec. 1987-91), Inst. Math. Stats. (coun. 1975-77), Am. Statis. Assn. (v.p. 1981-83, dir. 1979-80, Founders award 1991), Washington Acad. Scis. (achievement award math. 1965); mem. AAUW, Royal Statis. Soc. London, Philos. Soc. Washington, Internat. Statis. Inst., Bernouilli Soc. Probability and Math. Stats., Caucus Women Stats. (pres. 1976), Assn. Women Math., Exec. Women Govt., Phi Beta Kappa, Sigma Xi (treas. Nat. Bur. Standards chpt. 1982-84). Home: 2939 Van Ness St NW Apt 702 Washington DC 20008-4628 Office: Nat Inst Stds and Tech 100 Bureau Dr Stop 8980 Gaithersburg MD 20899-8980

ROSENBLATT, KARIN ANN, cancer epidemiologist; b. Chgo., Apr. 22, 1954; d. Murray and Adylin Rosenblatt. BA, U. Calif., Santa Cruz, 1975; MPH, U. Mich., 1977; PhD, Johns Hopkins U., 1988. Postdoctoral fellow U. Wash., Seattle, 1987-89; staff scientist Fred Hutchinson Cancer Rsch. Ctr., 1989-91; asst. prof. U. Ill., Champaign, 1991-97, assoc. prof., 1997—. Vis. scientist Fred Hutchinson Cancer Rsch. Ctr., 1999-2000; vis. scholar U. Wash., 1999-2000. Fellow Am. Coll. Epidemiology; mem. APHA (governing councilor epidemiology sect. 1988-2000), Internat. Epidemiologic Assn., Internat. Genetic Epidemiology Soc., Soc. for Epidemiologic Rsch. Office: Dept Cmty Health 120 Huff Hall MC 588 1206 S 4th St Champaign IL 61820-6920

ROSENBLATT, LESTER, naval architect; b. N.Y.C., Apr. 13, 1920; s. Mandell and Rosa (Wolff) R. BS, CCNY; BS in Naval Architecture and Marine Engring., U. Mich., 1942; DSc (hon.), Webb Inst. Naval Architecture, 1993. Registered profl. engr., N.Y., Mass. Naval architect John H. Wells, Inc., 1942-47; naval acrhitect USN Pearl Harbor Navy Yard, 1944-46; co-founder, chmn., chief exec. officer, naval architect M. Rosenblatt & Son Inc., Naval Architects and Marine Engrs., N.Y.C. and throughout U.S., 1947-2000. Designer maj. ships, U.S. and fgn. Contbr. numerous tech. papers. Trustee (hon.) Webb Inst. Naval Architecture; mem. United Jewish Appeal N.Y., Maritime Friends of Seamen's Ch. Inst. Recipient U. Mich. Sesquicentennial award in ship design, 1967, 1st Rosenblatt-Mich. award, U. Mich., 1992; Admiral's honoree SUNY Maritime Coll., 1992. Fellow Soc. Naval Architects and Engrs. (pres. 1978-80, nat. chmn. membership com. 1964-78, mem. coun. and exec. com., Land medalist, hon. mem., chmn. N.Y. sect. 1961-62); mem. Am. Bur. Shipping, Bur. Veritas, Am. Soc. Naval Engrs. (Harold Saunders award 1987), Marine Soc. N.Y. (hon.), Internat. Maritime Hall of Fame, Soc. Marine Cons., N.Y. Yacht Club, Tau Beta Pi. Office: Lester Rosenblatt Inc 8 E 83rd St New York NY 10028-0418 E-mail: lrosenblatt@mrosenblatt.amsec.com.

ROSENBLATT, LOUISE MICHEL, emerita educator; b. Atlantic City, Aug. 23, 1904; d. Samuel and Jennie (Berman) R.; m. Sidney Ratner, June 1932; 1 child, Jonathan. BA with honors, Barnard Coll., 1925; cert. d'etudes francaises, U. Grenoble, France, 1926; D in Comparative Lit., U. Paris, 1931; postgrad., Columbia U., 1932-34; LHD (hon.), U. Ariz., 1991. Instr. English Barnard Coll., 1927-38; asst. prof. English Bklyn. Coll., 1938-48; assoc. chief Western European sect., chief ctrl. reports sec Bur. Overseas Intelligence, Office War Info., 1943-45; prof. English edn. NYU, N.Y.C., 1948-72, prof. emerita, 1972—. Vis. prof. Rutgers U., 1972-75; mem. faculty insts. in English Northwestern U., Mich. State U., U. Pa., U. Ala., U. Alta. (Can.), Auburn U., U. Mass., 1978-96; vis. prof. U. Miami (Fla.), 1996-2001; participant Conf. Methods in Philosophy and the Scis., sec., 1941-42; cons. in field. Author: L'idée de l'Art pour l'Art, 1931, reprinted, 1976, Literature as Exploration, 1938, 5th rev. edit., 1995, Arabic transl., 1999 (cited as Book of Century by Mus. Edn. 1999); (with William S. Gray) Reading in an Age of Mass Communication, 1949, Research Development in the Teaching of English, 1963, The Reader, The Text, The Poem: The Transactional Theory of the Literary Work, 1978, rev. paperback edit., 1994; (with Robert Parker) Developing Literacy, 1983; (with Charles Cooper) Researching Response to Literature, 1984; (with Patricia Demers) The Creating Word, 1985, Writing and Reading: The Transactional Theory, 1988; (with Jana Mason) Reading and Writing Connections, 1989; contbr. chpts. to Transactions With Literature, 1990, Handbook of Research on the English Language Arts, 1990, Theoretical Models of the Reading Process, 4th edit., 1994; contbr. articles to profl. jours. Recipient NYU Great Tchr. award, 1972, Nat. Coun. Tchr. English Disting. Svc. award, 1973, Russell award for disting. rsch., 1980, Leland Jacobs award Lit., 1981, Disting. Alumna award Barnard Coll., 1990, Disting. Rsch. award Nat. Conf. Rsch. English, 1990, Lifetime Achievement award John Dewey Soc., 2001; named to N.J. Lit. Hall of Fame, 1988, Internat. Reading Assn. Hall of Fame, 1992, Outstanding Educator in Lang. Arts, 1999; Franco-Am. Exch. fellow, 1925-26, Guggenheim fellow, 1942-43. Mem. MLA, Am. Soc. Aesthetics, Nat. Coun. Tchrs. English (James C. Squire award 2002), Nat. Conf. Rsch. English, Am. Comparative Lit., Soc. Advancement of Am. Philosophy, Internat. Comparative Lit. Assn., Phi Beta Kappa. Home: 11 Cleveland Ln Princeton NJ 08540-3049

ROSENBLATT, MICHAEL, medical researcher, educator; b. Lund, Sweden, Nov. 27, 1947; s. Arthur Rosenblatt and Jean (Strosberg) Bialer; m. Patricia Ellen Regenbogen, Aug. 23, 1969; children: Anna Miriam, Adam Richard. AB summa cum laude, Columbia U., 1969; MD magna cum laude, Harvard U., 1973. Diplomate Am. Bd. Internal Medicine. Intern then resident Mass. Gen. Hosp., Boston, 1973-75, clin. rsch. fellow in endocrinology and metabolism, 1975-77, chief endocrine unit, 1981-84; instr. in medicine Harvard U., 1976-78, asst. prof. medicine, 1978-82, assoc. prof. medicine, 1982-85; v.p. for biol. rsch. Merck Sharp & Dohme Rsch. Labs., 1984-87, v.p. for biol. rsch. and molecular biology, 1987-89, sr. v.p. rsch. Pa., 1989-92; dir. divsn. health sci. and tech. Harvard-MIT, 1992-98; Ebert prof. molecular medicine Harvard Med. Sch., Boston, 1992-98; chief divsn. bone and mineral metabolism Beth Israel Hosp., 1992—2000. Faculty dean acad. programs Beth Israel Deaconess Med. Ctr., Harvard Med., 1996—2000, George R. Minot prof. med., 1996—; exec. dir. Carl J. Shapiro Inst. Edn. and Rsch. at Harvard Med. Sch. and Beth Israel Deaconess Med. Ctr., 1996—2000, pres., 1999—2001. Editor: Atrial Natriuretic Factor Endocrinology and Metabolism Clinics of N.Am., 1987; contbr. numerous sci. articles on parathyroid hormone and calcium metabolism to leading sci. jours. Recipient Vincent du Vigneaud award Gordon Confs., Kingston, R.I., 1986, Fuller Albright award Am. Soc. for Bone and Mineral Rsch., 1986, citation Japan Endocrine Soc., Tokyo, Taiwanese Osteoporosis Soc., Tainan. Fellow AAAS; mem. The Endocrine Soc., Am. Soc. for Biochemistry and Molecular Biology, Am. Soc. for Clin. Investigation, Am. Soc. Bone and Mineral Rsch. (pres. 1997-98), Assn. Am. Physicians, Inter-Urban Clin. Club (pres. 1997-98). Home: 130 Lake Ave Newton MA 02459-2108 Office: Beth Israel Deaconess Med Ctr 330 Brookline Ave # FD-230 Boston MA 02215-5400 E-mail: mrosenbl@caregroup.harvard.edu.

ROSENBLATT, MURRAY, mathematics educator; b. N.Y.C., Sept. 7, 1926; s. Hyman and Esther R.; m. Adylin Lipson, 1949; children: Karin, Daniel BS, CCNY, 1946; MS, Cornell U., 1947, PhD in Math., 1949. Asst. prof. statistics U. Chgo., 1950-55; assoc. prof. math. Ind. U., 1956-59; prof. probability and statistics Brown U., 1959-64; prof. math. U. Calif., San Diego, 1964—. Vis. fellow U. Stockholm, 1953; vis. asst. prof. Columbia U., 1955; guest scientist Brookhaven Nat. Lab., 1959; vis. fellow U. Coll., London, 1965-66, Imperial Coll. and Univ. Coll., London, 1972-73, Australian Nat. U., 1976, 79; overseas fellow Churchill Coll., Cambridge U., Eng., 1979; Wald lectr., 1970; vis. scholar Stanford U., 1982 Author: Statistical Analysis of Stationary Time Series, 1957, Random Processes, 1962, (2d edit), 1974, Markov Processes, Structure and Asymptotic Behavior, 1971, Studies in Probability Theory, 1978, Stationary Sequences and Random Fields, 1985, Stochastic Curve Estimation, 1991, Gaussian and Non-Gaussian Linear Time Series and Random Fields, 2000; mem. editl. bd. Jour. Theoretical Probability. Recipient Bronze medal U. Helsinki, 1978; Guggenheim fellow, 1965-66, 71-72 Fellow Inst. Math Statistics, AAAS; mem. Internat. Statis. Inst., Nat. Acad. Scis. Office: U Calif Dept Math La Jolla CA 92093 also: PO Box 2066 La Jolla CA 92038-2066 E-mail: mrosenblatt@ucsd.edu.

ROSENBLATT, PAUL CONRAD, family educator; b. Chgo., Sept. 25, 1938; s. Harry and Rose (Albaum) R.; m. Judith E. Spitzner, Jan. 29, 1958 (div. 1983); children: Seth, Ira; m. Sara E. Wright, June 9, 1984; 1 child, Emily. Student, U. Ill., Chgo., 1955-57; AB, U. Chgo., 1958; PhD, Northwestern U., 1962. From. asst. prof. to assoc. prof. U. Mo., Columbia, 1962-67; from. assoc. prof. to prof. U. Minn., St. Paul, 1969—. Vis. prof. Northwestern U., Evanston, Ill., 1978; vis. assoc. prof., lectr. U. Calif., Riverside, 1966-69. Author: The Family in Business, 1985, Farming Is in Our Blood, 1990, Metaphors of Family Systems Theory, 1994, Multiracial Couples, 1995, Parent Grief: Narratives of Loss and Relationship, 2001, Help Your Marriage Survive the Death of a Child, 2001; editl. bd. Rural Sociology, 1993-95, Family Bus. Rev., 1991-96, Jour. Rural Cmty. Psychology, 1988-95, 97—, Jour. Family and Econ. Issues, 1998—, Jour. Loss and Trauma, 1995—, Death Studies, 2001—, Mortality, 2001—. Mem. APA, Soc. Cross-Cultural Rsch. (past pres.), Nat. Coun. Family Rels., Am. Anthrop. Assn., Soc. Applied Anthroplogy, Rural Sociol. Soc., Internat. Work Group on Death, Dying and Bereavement, Assn. for Death Edn. and Counseling. Office: U Minn Dept Family Social Sci 290 McNeal Hall Saint Paul MN 55108 E-mail: prosenbl@tc.umn.edu.

ROSENBLATT, PAUL GERHARDT, judge; b. 1928; AB, U. Ariz., 1958, JD, 1963. Asst. atty. gen. State of Ariz., 1963-66; adminstrv. asst. to U.S. Rep., 1967-72; soel practice Prescott, Ariz., 1971-73; judge Yavapai County Superior Ct., 1973-84, U.S. Dist. Ct. Ariz., Phoenix, 1984—. Office: US Dist Ct 230 N 1st Ave Phoenix AZ 85025-0230 also: 401 W Washington St Phoenix AZ 85003-2117

ROSENBLATT, PETER RONALD, lawyer, former ambassador; b. N.Y.C., Sept. 4, 1933; s. William and Therese Amalia (Steinhardt) Rosenblatt; m. Naomi Henriette Harris; children: Therese Sarah Sonenshine, Daniel Harris, David Steinhardt. BA, Yale U., 1954, LL.B., 1957; postgrad. fellow, Tel-Aviv U., 1971. Bar: N.Y. 1959, D.C. 1969. Teaching asst. history Yale U., New Haven, 1954-55; asst. dist. atty. N.Y. County, 1959-62; asso. Stroock & Stroock & Lavan, N.Y.C., 1962-66; dep. asst. gen. counsel AID, Washington, 1966; mem. White House staff, 1966-68; jud. officer, chmn. bd. contract appeals U.S. Post Office Dept., 1968-69; v.p., dir. EDP Technology, Inc., 1969-71; chmn. bd. Internat. Devel. Services, 1969-71; spl. cons. to Senator Edmund S. Muskie, 1970-72; practice law Washington, 1972-77, 81-91; founding ptnr. Heller & Rosenblatt, 1991—. Personal rep. of Pres. with rank amb. to conduct negotiations on future polit. status of Trust Ter. of Pacific Islands, Washington, 1977-81; mem. Mid. East study group Dem. Adv. Coun. Elected Ofcls., 1974-76; bd. dirs. MediSense, Inc., 1983-96. Sec., chmn. exec. com. Coalition for a Dem. Majority, 1973-77, pres., 1983-93; bd. dirs. Com. on Present Danger, 1976-77, 82-93; mem. U.S. Nat. Com. Pacific Econ. Cooperation, 1986, sec., 1987—; bd. govs. Haifa (Israel) U., 1990-94, 98—; sec.-treas. Fund for Democracy and Devel., 1991-94, pres., 1994—; mem. adv. coun. Nixon Ctr., 1994—; mem. task force on fgn. policy Dem. Policy Commn., 1986; bd. govs. Am. Jewish Com., 1998—, UN Watch, 2000—, chmn., bd. govs. Koppelman Inst. on Am. Jewish-Israeli Rels., 1999-2002; bd. advisors Jewish Inst. for Nat. Security Affairs, 2000—; exec. com. The Alliance for Am. Leadership, 2001—. Mem. ABA, N.Y., D.C. Bar, Coun. Fgn. Rels. Jewish. Office: Heller & Rosenblatt 1101 15th St NW Ste 205 Washington DC 20005-5002 E-mail: ffdd@erols.com.

ROSENBLATT, ROGER, writer; b. N.Y.C., Sept. 13, 1940; m. Virginia Rosenblatt; children: Carl, Amy, John. PhD in English and Am. Lit., Harvard U.; hon. doctorate, U. Md., Claremont Grad. Sch., U. Utah, Pace U., Brigham Young U. Tchr. lit. and creative writing Harvard U., 1968-73; dir. edn. NEH, 1973-75; lit. editor The New Republic, 1975-78; columnist Washington Post, mem. editorial bd., 1976-79; essayist, sr. writer Time, 1980-88; essayist MacNeil/Lehrer News Hour, PBS, 1983—; columnist, editor-at-large Life mag., 1989-92; editor-at-large Time, Inc., 1999—2001. Univ. Prof. writing L.I. U. Author: Black Fiction, 1974, Children of War, 1983 (Robert F. Kennedy Book prize), Witness: The World Since Hiroshima, 1985, Life Itself: Abortion in the American Mind, 1992 (Melcher award), The Man in the Water, 1994, Coming Apart, 1997, Consuming Desires, 1999, Rules for Aging, 2000, Where We Stand, 2002, (plays) Free Speech in America, 1991, And, 1992, Bibliomania, 1993. Fulbright scholar, Dublin, Ireland, 1965; recipient numerous journalistic honors including two George Polk awards, George Foster Peabody award, Emmy award.

ROSENBLATT, STEPHEN PAUL, marketing and sales promotion company executive; b. N.Y.C., Feb. 13, 1935; s. Jack Aaron and Ruth (Kloth) R.; m. Dorothy Freedman, Apr. 7, 1962; children: Gregg, Amy, Robert. BEd, NYU, 1957. Tchr. art N.Y.C. Schs., 1957-58; art dir. Morse Internat., N.Y.C., 1958-65; v.p. L.C. Gumbinner Advt., 1966-71; group mktg. dir. Norcliff Thayer, Tarrytown, N.Y., 1971-75; pres. BMS Mktg. Services, Inc., N.Y.C., 1975-89, The Promotion Group Inc. subs. Doctus PLC, N.Y.C., 1989-91, SPQR Inc., Yorktown Heights, N.Y., 1991-93, ret., 1993. Home: 1451 White Hill Rd Yorktown Heights NY 10598-3543

ROSENBLATT, SUZANNE MARIS, performance artist, poet, visual artist; b. Hackensack, N.J., July 2, 1937; d. David and Rose (Richman) Freedman; m. Adolph Leon Rosenblatt, Mar. 26, 1961; children: Sarah, Eli, Joshua. BA, Oberlin Coll., 1959. Artist, tchr. Artreach, Milw., 1988-98. Author, illustrator: Everyone Is Going Somewhere, 1976, Memorandance, 1978, Changes in the Lake, 1982, Shorelines, 1991; illustrator: On the Waterbed They Sank to Their Own Levels (Sarah Rosenblatt), 2000; one-woman shows include at Magin Gallery Performing Arts Ctr., Milw., 1976-86, L.I. Univ. Gallery, Bklyn., 1980, Piano Gallery, Milw., 1988, 2000, Gallery of Wis. Art., Milw., 1993. Mem. and performer various environ., peace, civil rights orgns. Grantee Jr. League, 1989, 94, 96, Bader Found., 1993. Avocations: swimming, biking, dancing, Tai Chi, Gardening. Home: 4211 N Maryland Ave Milwaukee WI 53211-2062

ROSENBLEETH, RICHARD M. lawyer; b. Phila., Mar. 20, 1932; s. Morris B. and Henrietta (Friedman) R.; m. Judith A. Alesker, June 20, 1954; children— Dori, Lyn BS in Econs., U. Pa., 1954, JD, 1957. Bar: Pa. 1958, U.S. Supreme Ct. 1961. Asst. dist. atty. City of Phila., 1957-62; assoc. Richman, Price & Jamieson, 1962-65; ptnr. Blank, Rome, Comisky & McCauley, Phila., 1965-97; gen. coun. MBIA Muni Svcs. Co., 1998-2001, Arbitration and Mediation Svcs., Phila., 2001—. Mem. Civil Justice Reform Act Adv. Group, U.S. Dist. Ct. (ea. dist.) Pa., 1991—; co-chair Mayor Rendell's Transition Task Force on the Law Dept., 1991; judge pro tem Phila. Ct. Common Pleas, 1992—. Pres. Merion Park Civic Assn., Pa., 1967; mem. Citizens Crime Commn., Phila., 1979-87; commr. Youth Svcs. Coordinating Commn., Phila., 1979-85; Pa. state mem. chair U.S. Supreme Ct. Hist. Soc., 1994-95; pres., Corp. Alliance for Drug Edn., 1998-2000, chmn. Pa. Conv. Ctr. Authority, 1996-2000. Fellow Am. Coll. Trial Lawyers (chmn. Pa. state com. 1993-94), Internat. Acad. Trial Lawyers, Am. Bar Found.; mem. ABA, Pa. Bar Assn., Phila. Bar Assn., Phila. Bar Found. (pres. 1994). Avocations: golf; art collecting. Office: One Logan Sq 8th Fl Philadelphia PA 19103-6998 E-mail: rosenbleeth@hotmail.com.

ROSENBLOOM, ARLAN LEE, physician, educator; b. Milw., Apr. 15, 1934; s. Harris Phillip and Esther (Schneider) R.; m. Edith Kathleen Peterson, Sept. 14, 1958; children: Eric David, Maliah Jo, Disa Lynn, Harris Phillip. BA, U. Wis., 1955, MD, 1958. Diplomate Am. Bd. Pediatrics, Am. Bd. Pediatric Endocrinology, Am. Coll. Epidemiology. Intern Los Angeles County Gen. Hosp., 1958-59; resident in gen. practice Ventura County Hosp., Ventura, Calif., 1959-60; physician-in-chief Medico Hosp., Kratie, Cambodia, 1960-61; med. officer Pahang, Malaysia, 1961-62; resident in pediatrics U. Wis. Hosp., Madison, 1962-63, 64-65, fellow in pediatric endocrinology, 1963-64, 65-66; asst. prof. pediatrics U. Fla., Gainesville, 1968-71, asso. prof., 1971-74, prof., 1974-96, disting. svc. prof. emeritus, 1996—, founder, chief div. endocrinology, 1977-94; dir. Office for Internat. Health Programs, 1995-99; mem. Ctr. for African Studies U. Fla., mem. Ctr. for Latin Am. Studies. Assoc. dir. Clin. Research Center, 1969-74, dir., 1974-80; dir. Nat. Found. March of Dimes Birth Defects Center, 1969-73; med. dir. Gainesville Youth Clinic, 1972-74; mem. adv. com. Nat. Disease and Therapy Index; mem. Fla. Com. Children and Youth, 1972; data work group chmn. Nat. Diabetes Commn., 1975; mem. epidemiology and disease control study sect. NIH, 1978-82; vis. prof. McMaster U. Med. Centre, 1974-75; hon. prof. Ctrl. U. Quito, Ecuador, 2001; cons. epidemiologist Boston U. Health Policy Inst., West Africa, 1983-84; mem. affiliate faculty dept. clin. psychology U. Fla., 1984—; pres., dir. Fla. Camp for Children and Youth with Diabetes, 1970-90; dir. N. Fla. Regional Diabetes Program Children and Youth, 1974-88; dir. U. Fla. Diabetes Rsch. Edn. and Treatment Ctr., 1977-90; clin. and sci. adv. bd. Children's Diabetes Found., Denver, 1978-86; dir. N. Fla. Regional Diabetes and Endocrine Program for Children and Youth, 1988-96; asst. med. dir. Children's Med. Svcs., Dist. 3/13, 1986-2000, med. dir., 2001—; med. dir. Med. Foster Care Prgm., 1995-2000; mem. nat. diabetes adv. bd. NIH, 1990-94; internat. cons. Inst. for Endocrinology, Metabolism and Reproduction, Quito, Ecuador, 1990-99; mem. panel on devices FDA, 1999—. Editor Acta Paediactria Belgica, 1979-82, Today in Medicine (Diabetes), 1989—; mem. editl. bd. European Jour. Pediat., 1982—, Jour. Pediat. Endocrinology and Metabolism, 1983—, Clin. Pediat., 1989-2002, Diabetes Care, 1992-95, Jour. Clin. Endocrinology and Metabolism, 1995-2000, Clin. Diabetes, 1996-99, Pediatric

Diabetes, 1999—; contbr. numerous articles to profl. jours. Epidemiologist smallpox eradication program USPHS, Yaounde, Cameroon, 1966-68, comdr. inactive Res., 1968-69, capt. Ready Res., 1987—. Recipient Faculty Rsch. prize U. Fla. Coll. Medicine, 1994, U. Wis. Med. Alumni Citation, 1995, U. Fla. Blue Key Disting. Faculty award, 1995. Mem. Am. Acad. Pediatrics, Am. Diabetes Assn. (bd. dirs. 1986-90), Brit. Diabetic Assn., Fla. Diabetes Assn. (dir.), Alachua County Med. Soc., Internat. Soc. Pediatric Adolescent Diabetes, Endocrine Soc., Lawson Wilkins Pediatric Endocrine Soc., Am. Pediatric Soc., Soc. Pediatric Rsch. Home: 2902 SW 1st Ave Gainesville FL 32607-3002 Office: Children's Med Svcs Ctr 1701 SW 16th Ave Bldg B Gainesville FL 32608-1153 E-mail: rosenal@peds.ufl.edu.

ROSENBLOOM, BERT, marketing educator, consultant, writer; b. Phila., Feb. 2, 1944; s. Max and Dora (Cohen) R.; m. Pearl Friedman, Aug. 18, 1968; children: Jack Alan, Robyn. BS, Temple U., 1966, MBA, 1968, Ph.D, 1974. Instr. mktg. Rider Coll., Trenton, N.J., 1968-72, asst. prof., 1972-74; asst. prof. mktg. Baruch Coll. CUNY, 1974-76; assoc. prof. Drexel U., Phila., 1976-80, prof., 1980-85, G. Behrens Ulrich prof. mktg., 1985-98, assoc. dean grad. programs, 1994-97, Rauth chair electronic commerce mgmt., 1999—. Vis. scholar Higher Sch. Commerce Paris, 1993; cons. editor mktg. Random House, N.Y.C., 1977—; exec. dir. Safe Guard Scientific E-Commerce Mgmt. Ctr., 1999-2000, sr. rsch. fellow, 2000—; cons. in field; mem. bd. dirs. Reality Landscaping Corp., 1991—, McKee Real Estate Devel. Corp., 1991—; vis. disting. prof. Hannon U., Japan, 2000; vis. disting. scholar U. St. Gallen, 2000; Disting. vis. fellow Sogang U., Korea, 2001. Author: Marketing Channels, 1978, 3d edit., 1987, Market Functions and the Wholesaler Distribution, 1987, Marketing Channels: A Management View, 5th edit., 1997, 6th edit., 1999, Retail Marketing, 1981, Direct Selling Channels, 1993, Wholesale Mktg. Channels, 1994; editor Jour. Mktg. Channels, 1989—, Jour. Consumer Mktg., Jour. Global Mktg., Jour. Acad. Mktg. Sci.; contbr. articles to profl. jours. Mem. E-Commerce Commn., Mayor Phila., 1999—. Named Disting. Erskine fellow U. Canterbury, New Zealand, 1986; recipient Outstanding Educator award Chapel of Four Chaplains, 1984, Nomura Fund Collaborative rsch. award U. Rykus, Japan, 1998; rsch. award Distbn. Rsch. and Edn. Found., 1986, rsch. award Direct Selling Found., 1986, 91, 96, Literati Club award for excellence, 2002; Nat. Assn. Wholesaler Distbrs. grantee, 1991; honored as disting. prof. Retail Mktg. Inst. of Australia, 1985. Fellow Acad. Mktg. Sci. (bd. govs. 1978-89); mem. Internat. Mgmt. Devel. Assn. (pres. 1992-94), Am. Mktg. Assn. (v.p. Phila. chpt. 1978-79), Beta Gamma Sigma. Office: Drexel U Sch Bus 32d and Market Sts Philadelphia PA 19104

ROSENBLOOM, CARL F. pediatrician; b. Boston, Mar. 2, 1942; s. David and Rose (Laskey) R.; m. Lois Millen, Feb. 10, 1968; children: Deborah, Jonathan. BA, Boston U., 1963; MD, U. Vt., 1967. Diplomate in pediatrics and adolescent medicine Am. Bd. Pediatrics. Pediatric intern and resident Montefiore Hosp.-Albert Einstein Coll. Medicine, Bronx, N.Y., 1967-70; pediatrician Pentucket Med., Haverhill, Mass., 1973—; med. dir. Bradford (Mass.) Coll., 1968-95. Chmn. bd. health City of Haverhill, 1988—, sch. physician, 1988—; pres. med. staff Hale Hosp., Haverhill, 1991-93, trustee, 1980-85, 95—. Lt. comdr. USN, 1970-72. Fellow Am. Acad. Pediatrics, Soc. for Adolescent Medicine; mem. N.Am. Soc. for Pediatric and Adolescent Gynecology, Mass. Med. Soc. Office: Pentucket Med 1 Park Way Haverhill MA 01830-6278

ROSENBLOOM, DANIEL, investment banker, lawyer; b. N.Y.C., Feb. 11, 1930; s. Sol and Florence (Vogel) R. BA, U. Va., 1951, JD, 1954; LLM, NYU, 1960. Bar: Va. 1954, N.Y. 1956. Atty. Paskus, Gordon & Hyman, N.Y.C., 1956-61; v.p., sec., gen. counsel Phila. & Reading Corp., 1962-67; ptnr. First Manhattan Co., 1967—. Trustee Nat. Found. for Facial Reconstruction, NYU Med. Ctr., Univ. Va. Law Sch. Found. 1st lt. AUS, 1954—56. Mem. Sunningdale Country Club, Farmington Country Club, Harmonie Club, Atlantic Golf Club, Phi Alpha Delta, Phi Epsilon Pi. Office: First Manhattan Co 437 Madison Ave New York NY 10022-7001

ROSENBLOOM, DAVID HARRY, political science and law educator; b. N.Y.C., Aug. 27, 1943; s. Jerome and Rita R. BA, Marietta Coll., 1964, LLD (hon.), 1994; MA, U. Chgo., 1966, PhD in Polit. Sci., 1969. Asst. prof. U. Kans., Lawrence, 1969-71; fellow Am. Soc. Pub. Adminstrn. U.S. Civil Svc. Commn., Washington, 1970-71; vis. sr. lectr. Tel Aviv (Israel) U., 1971-73; asst. prof. U. Vt., Burlington, 1973-75, assoc. prof., 1975-78; vis. assoc. prof. Syracuse (N.Y.) U., 1978-79, prof., 1979-89, disting. prof., 1988-90, Am. U., Washington, 1990—. Author: (Books) Federal Service and Constitution, 1971, Public Administration, 1993, 4th edit., 1998, Public Administration and Law, 1997, Building a Legislative-Centered Public Administration, 2000. Mem. Clinton-Gore Transition Team, U.S. Office Pers. Mgmt., Washington, 1992. Recipient Charles Levine Meml. award for excellence and Disting. Rsch. award Am. Soc. for Pub. Adminstrn. and Nat. Assn. Schs. of Pub. Affairs and Administration, Washington, 1992, 93, Thomas Dye award for outstanding svc. Policy Studies Orgn., 1996, Dwight Waldo award for outstanding contbns. to lit. and leadership of Pub. Adminstrn., Am. Soc. Pub. Adminstrn., Washington, 1999, Louis Brownlow Book award Nat. Acad. Pub. Adminstrn., 2001. Fellow Nat. Acad. Pub. Adminstrn. Recipient John Gaus award for exemplary scholarship in joint tradition polit. sci. and pub. adminstrn. Am. Polit. Sci. Assn., 2001. Office: American U 4400 Massachusetts Ave NW Washington DC 20016-8001 E-mail: rbloom@american.edu.

ROSENBLOOM, DONALD THEODORE, orthodontist, sleep disorders specialist; b. N.Y.C., May 22, 1927; s. Joseph and Sarah (Daniels) R.; m. Belle Leah Rosenbloom; children: Ira Seth, Mindy Sharon. DDS, NYU, 1950, postgrad., 1956-60. Diplomate Am. Bd. Orthodontics. Orthodontist, sleep disorders specialist in pvt. practice, Paramus, N.J., 1961—. Author: (text book) Review of Current Knowledge in Orthodontics, 1974; editor: (text book) Dynamics of Dental Practice Administration, 1976. 1st lt. U.S. Army, 1952-54, Austria. Fellow Am. Coll. Dentists, Internat. Coll. Dentists; mem. N.J. Soc. Orthodontics, Sleep Disorders Dental Soc., Bergen County Dental Soc. (pres. 1972-73). Avocations: jewelry, sculpture, tennis, photography, computers. Home and Office: 185 Prospect Ave Hackensack NJ 07601-2210

ROSENBLOOM, H. DAVID, lawyer; b. N.Y.C., May 26, 1941; s. Milton M. and Rose Gold R.; m. Carla L. Peterson, June 23, 1968; children: Sarah Alix, Julia Micol. AB, Princeton U., 1962; postgrad. (Fulbright scholar), U. Florence, Italy, 1962-63; JD, Harvard U., 1966. Bar: N.Y. 1967, D.C. 1968. Spl. asst. to Arthur J. Goldberg U.S. amb. to UN, 1966-67; law clk. to Abe Fortas U.S. Supreme Ct., 1967-68; assoc. Caplin & Drysdale, Washington, 1968-72, ptnr., 1972-77, 81—. Spl. asst. to dep. asst. sec. for tax policy Dept. Treasury, Washington, 1977, internat. tax counsel, 1978—81; lectr. Harvard U. Law Sch., 1984—87, 1990—93, 1995—96, 1999, Pub. Fin. Tng. Inst., Taipei, Taiwan, 1985—86, Taipei, 1989, Stanford U. Law Sch., 1988, Inst. Tecnologico Autonomo d' Mex., 1993, 95, 97, Columbia U. Law Sch., 1997, U. Pa. Law Sch., 1998, NYU Law Sch., 2000—, U. Commerciale Luigi Bocconi, Milan, 2001—; mem. faculty of law U. Sydney, 2001. Mem. D.C. Bar Home: 2948 Garfield Ter NW Washington DC 20008-3507 Office: 1 Thomas Cir NW Washington DC 20005-5802

ROSENBLOOM, JOEL, molecular biologist, educator; b. Denver, July 18, 1935; s. Isadore and Ida (Berman) R.; m. Joan Caplan, June 8, 1958; children: Aaron, Eric. AB, Harvard U., 1957; MD, U. Pa., 1962, PhD, 1965. Asst. prof. med. sch. U. Pa., Phila., 1968-72, assoc. prof. dental sch., 1972-75, prof., 1978—. Contbr. articles to profl. jours. Recipient Flory award U. Adelaide, 1989. Mem. Am. Soc. Biology and Molecular Biology, Biophysical Soc. Home: 923 Nicholson Rd Wynnewood PA 19096-1639 Office: U Pa Rsch Ctr in Oral Biology 4010 Locust St Philadelphia PA 19104-3507 E-mail: jrosen@biochem.dental.upenn.edu.

ROSENBLOOM, LEWIS STANLEY, lawyer; b. Fort Riley, Kans., Feb. 28, 1953; s. Donald and Sally Ann (Warsawsky) R.; m. Rochelle Leavitt, Dec. 16, 1973; children: Micah, Shaina. BA, Lake Forest Coll., 1974; JD with high honors, DePaul U., 1977. Bar: Ill. 1977, U.S. Dist. Ct. (no. dist.) Ill, 1977, U.S. Ct. Appeals (7th cir.) 1979, U.S. Supreme Ct. 1983, U.S. Ct. Appeals (9th cir.) 1987, U.S. Ct. Appeals (3rd cir.) 1993. Sr. acct. Gale, Takahasi & Channon, Chgo., 1973-74; law clk. to Hon. Robert L. Eisen U.S. Dist. Ct. (no. dist.) Ill., 1976; assoc. Nachman, Munitz & Sweig, Ltd., 1976-82, prin., 1982-87; ptnr., co-chmn. involvency, bankruptcy & bus. reorgn. dept. Winston & Strawn, 1987-93; ptnr., sr. corp. reorgn. counsel McDermott, Will & Emery, 1994—; chmn. distressed transactions SBU. Mem. bd. advisors to bankruptcy, comml. law advisor Bus. Laws, Inc., 1988—; lectr. in field. Contbr. articles to profl. jours. Mem. adv. com. and fin. subcom. Ill. Bd. Higher Edn., Springfield; mem. state edn. and legal aid subcom. Ill. Coun. on Children and Youth Welfare, Chgo. Coll. scholar Lake Forest Coll., 1973-74. Fellow Am. Coll. Bankruptcy; mem. ABA (bus. bankruptcy com. 1982—, chmn. new and pending bankruptcy legis. com. 1982-85, chmn. transp. reorganizations com. 1985-88), Chgo. Bar Assn. (bankruptcy reorganization com., co-chmn. sub-com. on retention and fees 1987-88). Office: McDermott Will & Emery 227 W Monroe St Ste 3100 Chicago IL 60606-5096 E-mail: lrosenbloom@mwe.com.

ROSENBLOOM, MINDY SHARON, psychiatrist; d. Donald T. and Belle L. Rosenbloom; m. Stuart T. Schwartz. BA summa cum laude, Barnard Coll., 1981; MD, U. Medicine/Dentistry of N.J., 1985. Diplomate Am. Bd. Psychiatry and Neurology, Am. Bd. Geriatric Psychiatry. Intern Brown U., Providence, 1985-86, resident in psychiatry, 1986-89; med. dir. East Bay Mental Health Ctr., Barrington, R.I., 1989—; adjunct prof. URI Sch. Nursing. Clin. asst. prof. dept. psychiatry and human behavior Brown U., Providence; spkr. in field. Mem. APA, Cmty. Psychiatrists of R.I. (chair), Phi Beta Kappa. Office: East Bay Mental Health Ctr 2 Old County Rd Barrington RI 02806-1602

ROSENBLOOM, SANFORD M. lawyer; b. Phila., Sept. 24, 1928; s. Fred L. and Pauline B. (Basen) R.; m. Irene Nelson, 1961 (div. 1974); m. Willa Glazer, Nov. 21, 1976 BS, U. Pa., 1951; JD, Rutgers U., 1955. Bar: Pa. 1956, U.S. Dist. Ct. (ea. dist.) Pa. 1956, U.S. Ct. Appeals (3d cir.) 1957. Ptnr. Schnader, Harrison, Segal & Lewis, Phila., 1955-93, ret., 1993. Mem. Phila. Bar Assn. (former officer and chmn. com. real estate sect.), Pa. Bar Assn. (former ho. of dels., chmn. real property, probate and trust law sect. 1991-92), Bala Golf Club (Phila.), Palm Aire Golf Club (Pompano Beach, Fla.). Republican. Jewish. Avocations: tennis, golf. Home: 2401 Pennsylvania Ave Apt 20b32 Philadelphia PA 19130-7717 Office: Schnader Harrison Segal et al 1600 Market St Ste 3600 Philadelphia PA 19103-7287

ROSENBLUM, EDWARD G. lawyer; b. Union City, N.J., Aug. 2, 1944; s. Milton and Frances (Nardi) R.; m. Charis Ann Schlatter, Dec. 1, 1971; children: Deborah, Michelle. BA, Rutgers U., 1966, JD, 1969. Bar: N.J. 1969. Ptnr. Rosenblum & Rosenblum, P.A., Jersey City, 1971-79, Secaucus, N.J., 1979-93, Rosenblum Wolf & Lloyd, P.A., Secaucus, 1994—, Teaneck, 1998—. Lectr. in field. Author: N.J. Lawyer, 1980, N.J. Municipalities, 1987. Active Table to Table, Englewood, N.J. Mem. N.J. State Bar Assn. (vice chmn. tax ct. rules com. taxation sect. 1984—, chmn. real property tax com. 1984—, vice chmn. taxation sect. 1987—, chmn.-elect 1987, chmn. 1988-89, Supreme Ct. com. on tax ct. 1982-92). Office: 300 Frank Burr Blvd Teaneck NJ 07666

ROSENBLUM, ELIZABETH PARKER, retired statistical consultant, nurse; b. Ironton, Ohio, Nov. 17, 1929; d. Carlos and Frances Van Valkenburg Parker; m. Marvin Rosenblum, May 30, 1959; children: Dore, Mendel, Jessie, Rebecca, Sarah. BS in Nursing, U. Va., 1957, MS in Edn., 1982, PhD in Research in Edn., 1985. Instr. nursing U. Va., Charlottesville, 1957-59, Piedmont Va. Community Coll., Charlottesville, 1975-76; asst. prof. rsch. in edn. U. Va., 1985-91, statis. cons., 1991-2000; ret., 2000. Appointed mem. Albemarle County (Va.) Sch. Bd., 1976-78. Mem. Assn. Women in Math, LWV. Democrat. Jewish.

ROSENBLUM, HAROLD ARTHUR, grocery distribution executive; b. Sharon, Pa., Jan. 5, 1923; s. H. David and Carol (Thaler) R.; m. Irene F. Rosen, June 25, 1950; children— Julia M., Mark A., Lee S., Joel N., Ruth C. (dec.) Student, Western Res. U., 1939-40; AB cum laude, Harvard, 1943, JD, 1949. Bar: Pa. 1949. With Sharon div. Peter J. Schmitt Co. (formerly Golden Dawn Foods, Inc.), Sharon, 1950-85; pres. Golden Dawn Foods, Inc., 1961-80, chmn. bd., 1980-83, treas., 1961-73. Sec. H.M. Pollock Co., Kittanning, Pa., 1982-90. Mem. Mercer County Mental Health/Mental Retardation Bd., 1967-90, chmn., 1967-70, 80-81, sec., 1984-90; chmn. Community Council Com. Mental Health/Mental Retardation, 1965-67, Shenango Valley Jewish Fedn., 1964—; pres. Friends of Buhl Henderson Library, 1973-75; treas. Mercer County Mental Health Assn., 1964-66; bd. dirs. Mercer County Cmty. Mental Health & Counseling Ctr., 1959-82, sec., 1961-63, pres., 1963-65; v.p. Mercer County Drug and Alcohol Coun., Inc., 1973-74; mem. exec. bd. Shenango Valley Human Rels. Coun., 1960-68; mem. econ. devel. com. Multi-County Manpower Devel. Corp., 1972-73; mem. Sharon Human Relations Commn., 1969-88 , sec., 1984, chmn. 1985-86; sec. Mercer County Comprehensive Health Planning Bd., 1972-74, mem. adv. com., 1971-74; charter mem. Pa. Freedom of Choice in Family Planning; mem. Mercer County Commn. on Drug and Alcohol Abuse, 1973-78; mem. adv. bd. Shenango Valley Campus, Pa. State U., 1976; exec. com. Mercer County br. NAACP, 1964-71; pres. bd. dirs. Playhouse 600, 1973-76; bd. dirs. Sharon Regional Health System (formerly Sharon Gen. Hosp.), 1964—, sec., 1966-77, chmn., 1977-96, home health adv. com., 1973—; mem. Mayor's Com. for Arts, 1973-75; trustee-at-large Pa. council Union Am. Hebrew Congregations, 1966-76, 85-90; bd. dirs. Shenango Valley Urban League, 1971-73, Pa. Mental Health Assn., 1968-72; bd. dirs. Mercer County Edn. and Rehab. Ctr. (formerly Mercer County Crippled Children's and Adults Soc.), 1981-94, exec. com., 1983-94, sec., 1986-92; bd. dirs. Family and Children's Svc. of Youngstown Area Jewish Fedn., 1981—, sec., 1986-87, v.p., 1987-89, pres. 1990-92; bd. dirs. Temple Beth Israel, Sharon, 1951-63, 82-89, v.p., 1956-58, pres., 1958-63, 84-87 ; bd. dirs. Cmty. Food Warehouse, 1983-88 , pres., 1985-86; Youngstown State U. Human Services Devel. Adv. Bd., 1986-92; adv. bd. Behavioral Health Ctr., 1988—. Served with AUS, 1943-46. Buhl Day honoree, 1985. Mem. Nat. Am. Wholesale Grocers Assn. (bd. govs. 1964-66), Shenango Valley C. of C. (bd. dirs. 1969-71, treas. 1970, Person of Yr. 1985). Clubs: Rotary (Sharon) (pres. 1978-79), Sharon Country (Sharon), University (Sharon) (fin. sec., pres. 1978-79); F.H. Buhl (dir. 1977-79). Home: 1700 Hannah Ct Sharon PA 16146-3818 E-mail: harirene@infonline.net.

ROSENBLUM, JEFFREY IRA, consulting economist; b. N.Y.C., Mar. 12, 1956; s. Charles and Sylvia Lilian (Silverstein) R.; m. Monica Rosales, Sept. 15, 2000. BS, SUNY, Brockport, 1983; PhD, U. Tex., 1992. Analyst Pub. Utility Commn. of Tex., Austin, 1986-91, asst. mgr., 1991-94; mgr. KPMG Peat Marwick LLP, N.Y.C., 1994-96, sr. mgr. Dallas, 1996-99, KMPG LLP (formerly KPMG Peat Marwick), Short Hills, N.J., 1999-2001, Arthur Andersen LLP, Roseland, NJ, 2001—02; ind. cons., 2002—. Mem. Am. Econ. Assn., Law and Econs. Assn. Home: 108 Old Farm Rd Milford PA 18337-9497 Office: Arthur Andersen LLP 105 Eisenhower Pkwy Roseland NJ 07068-1099 E-mail: jeffr3@mercurylink.net.

ROSENBLUM, JOHN WILLIAM, finance educator; b. Houston, Jan. 1, 1944; s. H. William and Susan (Ullmann) R.; m. Carolyn Edith Jones, Sept. 12, 1964; children: J. Christopher, Kathryn, Nicholas. AB, Brown U., 1965; MBA, Harvard U., 1967, DBA, 1972. Instr. Harvard U. Bus. Sch., Boston, 1969-72, asst. prof., 1972-75, assoc. prof., 1975-79; prof. Darden Grad. Sch. Bus. Adminstrn., U. Va., Charlottesville, 1979-80, assoc. dean, 1980-82, dean, 1982-93, Tayloe Murphy prof., 1993—; dean Jepson Sch. Leadership Studies, U. Richmond, Va., 1996-2000. Bd. dirs. Chesapeake Corp., Cone Mills Corp., The Providence Jour. Co., Grantham, Mayo, Van Otterloo, Thomas Rutherfoord, Inc. Co-author: Strategy and Organization, 1973, (2d edit.), 1977, Cases in Political Economy-Japan, 1980. Bd. dirs. Landmark Vols. Mem. Phi Beta Kappa, Omicron Delta Kappa. Home: 854 Crozet Ave Crozet VA 22932-9803

ROSENBLUM, MARTIN JACK, historian; b. Appleton, Wis., Aug. 19, 1946; s. Sander and Esther Pearl (Ressman) R.; m. Maureen Rice, Sept. 6, 1970; children: Sarah Terez, Molly Dvora. BS in English, U. Wis., 1969; MA in English, U. Wis., Milw., 1971, PhD in English, 1980. Lectr. U. Wis., Milw., 1970-80, acad. staff, 1980-93; historian Harley-Davidson, 1993—. Author: The Holy Ranger, 1989, (CD) Free Hand, 1991, Down on the Spirit Farm, 1994, (CD) No Freedom, Honey, 2000, Places to Go, 2000, Spirit Fugitive, 2001; editor: Harley-Davidson: 1903-1993, 1994, Harley-Davidson Lore, 1999, Harley-Davidson Lore, vol. II, 2000; author: (CD boxed set) Pilgrimage Farm Trilogy, 2002, The Holy Ranger's Free Hand, 12th anniversary edit., 2002. Mem. Am. Motorcyclist Assn. (life), Am. Historic Racing Motorcycle Assn., Harley Owners Group (life), Ugly Motorcycle Club, Single Action Shooting Soc., Colt Collector's Assn. Home: 2521 E Stratford Ct Milwaukee WI 53211-2635 Office: Harley-Davidson Motor Co 3700 W Juneau Ave Milwaukee WI 53208-2865 E-mail: spiritfugitive@aol.com.

ROSENBLUM, MARTIN JEROME, ophthalmologist; b. N.Y.C., Apr. 7, 1948; s. Philip and Rita (Steppel) R.; m. Zina Zarin, May 31, 1975; children: Steven David, Richard James. BS, Bklyn. Coll., 1968; MD, U. Ariz., 1973; postgrad., Columbia U., 1977. Diplomate Am. Bd. Ophthalmology, Nat. Bd. Med. Examiners. Intern Cornell U., N.Y.C., 1973-74; resident N.Y. Med. Coll., 1975-78, instr., 1978-79; practice medicine specializing in eye surgery St. Petersburg, Fla., 1979—. Chief ophthalmology Edward White Hosp.; asst. clin. prof. ophthalmology, U. So. Fla.; attending surgeon St. Anthony's Bayfront Med. Ctr., Palms of Pasadena, St. Petersburg Gen. Hosp., Am. Soc. for Cataract and Refractive Surgery, Columbia Ctr. Spl. Surgery; surgeon dir. Suncoast Eye Clinic, Pa. Fellow ACS, Am. Acad. Ophthalmology; mem. AMA, Am. Soc. Ophthalmic Plastic and Reconstructive Surgery, Fla. Med. Assn., Fla. Soc. Ophthalmology, Pinellas County Med. Soc., Bayou Country Club. Republican. Jewish. Avocations: tennis, golf, travel, skiing. Home: 9035 Baywood Park Dr Largo FL 33777-4630 Office: 2200 16th St N Saint Petersburg FL 33704-3106 E-mail: mjreye@aol.com.

ROSENBLUM, MARVIN, mathematics educator; b. Bklyn., June 30, 1926; s. Isidore and Celia (Mendelsohn) Rosenblum; m. Frances E. Parker, May 30, 1959; children: Isidore, Mendel, Jessie, Rebecca, Sarah. BS, U. Calif.-Berkeley, 1949, MA, 1951, PhD, 1955. Instr. math. U. Calif.-Berkeley, 1954-55; asst. prof. U. Va., Charlottesville, 1955-59, assoc. prof., 1960-65, prof., 1965-2000, Commonwealth prof., prof. emeritus. Mem. Inst. Advanced Study, 1959-60 Served with USNR, 1944-46. Jewish. Office: U Va Dept Math Kerchof Hall Charlottesville VA 22903

ROSENBLUM, RICHARD MARK, utility executive; b. N.Y.C., Apr. 28, 1950; s. Victor Sigmund and Julia R.; m. Michele E. Cartier, Aug. 30, 1979; children: Gialisa, Jeremy Scott. BS, MS, Rensselaer Poly. Inst., 1973. Startup engr. Combustion Enginrg., Inc., Windsor, Conn., 1973-76; engr. So. Calif. Edison Co., Rosemead, 1976-82; project mgr. San Onofre Nuclear Generating Sta., 1982-83, tech. mgr., 1983-84, nuclear safety mgr., 1984-86, mgr. quality assurance, 1986-89, mgr. nuclear regulatory affairs, 1989-93, v.p. engring. and tech. svcs., 1993-95, v.p. distbn., 1996-98, sr. v.p. T&D, 1998—. N.Y. State Regents scholar, 1968-73. Office: 2244 Walnut Grove Ave Rosemead CA 91770-3714 E-mail: richard.rosenblum@sce.com.

ROSENBLUM, ROBERT, art historian, educator; b. N.Y.C., July 24, 1927; s. Abraham H. and Lily M. (Lipkin) R.; m. Jane Kaplowitz, June 23, 1977; children: Sophie Lila, Theodore Abraham. BA, Queens Coll., 1948; MA, Yale U., 1950; PhD, NYU, 1956; MA (hon.), Oxford U., 1972; ArtsD (hon.), Queens Coll., 1992. Mem. faculty U. Mich., Ann Arbor, 1955-56, Princeton (N.J.) U., 1956-66, Yale U., New Haven, 1966-67; mem. faculty NYU, N.Y.C., 1967—, prof. fine arts, 1967—. Part-time curator Guggenheim Mus., N.Y.C., 1996—. Author: Cubism and Twentieth Century Art, 1960, Transformations in Late Eighteenth Century Art, 1967, Ingres, 1967, Frank Stella, 1971, Modern Painting and the Northern Romantic Tradition, 1975, The International Style of 1800, 1976, Andy Warhol: Portraits of the 70s, 1979, 19th Century Art, 1984, The Dog in Art From Rococo to Post-Modernism, 1988, The Romantic Child From Runge to Sendak, 1989, Paintings in the Musee d'Orsay, 1989, The Jeff Koons Handbook, 1992, Andy Warhol Portraits, 1993, Mel Ramos: Pop Images, 1994, The Paintings of August Strindberg, The Structure of Chaos, 1995, On Modern American Art, 1999, 1900: Art at the Crossroads, 2000. Served with U.S. Army, 1945-46. Recipient Frank Jewett Mather award for art criticism, 1981 Fellow Am. Acad. Arts and Scis.; mem. Coll. Art Assn. Am., l'Ordre des Arts et des Lettres (commandeur). Office: NYU Dept Fine Arts Washington Sq N New York NY 10003-6688

ROSENBLUM, SCOTT S. lawyer; b. N.Y.C., Oct. 4, 1949; s. Harold Lewis and Greta Blossom (Lesher) R.; m. Barbara Anne Campbell, Oct. 29, 1977; children: Harold, Emma, Casey. AB summa cum laude, Dartmouth Coll., 1971; JD, U. Pa., 1974. Bar. U.S. Dist. Ct. (so. dist.) N.Y. 1975. From assoc. to ptnr. Stroock & Stroock & Lavan, N.Y.C., 1974-91; ptnr. Kramer, Levin, Naftalis & Frankel, 1991—, mng. ptnr., 1994-2000. Mem. N.Y. bd. govs., vice chmn. Mid. East Quarterly, Phila., 1994—; bd. dirs. Dovenmuehle Mortgage, Inc., Schaumburg, Ill, Greg Manning Auctions, Inc., West Caldwell, N.J., Temco Svc. Industries, Inc., N.Y.C., I.T. Internat. Theatres Ltd., Herzlia, Israel, Investec Ernst & Co., N.Y.C. Co-author: Public Limited Partnerships and Roll-Ups, Securities Law Techniques, The Practitioner's Guide to Transactions and Litigation, 1995. Trustee Village of Saltaire, N.Y., 1993—. Mem. ABA (high tech. com. 1983-84), Assn. Bar City N.Y. (corps. com. 1991-94), Phi Beta Kappa. Avocation: sailing. Home: 19 Wildwood Cir Larchmont NY 10538-3426 Office: Kramer Levin Naftalis & Frankel 919 3rd Ave New York NY 10022-3902 E-mail: srosenblum@kramerlevin.com.

ROSENBLUM, STEPHEN SAUL, chemist, researcher; b. Bklyn., Sept. 26, 1942; s. Leon Abraham and Gertrude Rosenblum; m. Ellen Patricia McLaughlin, Jan. 5, 1972; children: Andrew Edward, Leah Frances. AB in Chemistry, Columbia U., 1963; PhD in Chemistry, U. Calif., Berkeley, 1969. Research fellow in physics Calif. Inst. Tech., Pasadena, 1969-70; guest lectr. physics Freie U., Berlin, Federal Republic of Germany, 1970-72; vis. staff mem. Hahn-Meitner Institut, Federal Republic of Germany, 1972-74; postdoctoral Los Alamos (N.Mex.) Nat. Lab., 1974-77; staff scientist Lawrence Berkeley Lab., 1977-85; sr. engr. Varian Assocs., Palo Alto, Calif., 1985-91; sr. rsch. scientist Kobe Steel USA Applied Electronics Ctr., 1991-95; sr. scientist Advanced Energy Industries, Inc., Milpitas, 1995—. Contbr. articles on materials science to profl. jours.; patentee in field. Fellow Am. Inst. Chemists; mem. Fedn. Am. Scientists, ACLU, Am. Phys. Soc., Am. Chem. Soc., Am. Vacuum Soc., Sierra Club, Phi Beta Kappa. Avocations: gardening, sailing, fly fishing.

ROSENBLUM, STEWART IRWIN, recording industry executive; b. New York, NY; m. Andrea Bonnie Reiter, Feb. 5, 1978; children: Theodore, Scott, Jonathan. BA with honors, Hofstra U., 1969; JD, St. John's U., Queens, N.Y., 1972. Bar: N.Y. 1973, Pa. 1988, U.S. Dist. Ct. (ea. and so. dists.) N.Y. 1975, U.S. Dist. Ct. (mid. dist.) Pa. 1997. V.p. bus. affairs to pres. Reiter Records, Ltd., East Stroudsburg, Pa., 1989—; v.p. One Hot Note Music, Inc., Cold Spring Harbor, N.Y., 1989—; pvt. practice, 1973-99, East Stroudsburg, Pa., 1994—, Patchogue, 1999—. Mem. Pa. Bar Assn., Pi Gamma Mu. Republican. Avocations: reading, sports. Home and Office: 308 Penn Est East Stroudsburg PA 18301-9023 E-mail: stewrose@aol.com.

ROSENBLUM, VICTOR GREGORY, political science and law educator; b. N.Y.C., June 2, 1925; s. George and Vera (Minster) R.; m. Louise Rann, Feb. 21, 1946; children: Susan, Ellen, Laura, Keith, Jonathan, Peter, Warren, Joshua. AB, Columbia U., 1945, LL.B., 1948; PhD, U. Calif.-Berkeley, 1953; D.H.L., Hebrew Union Coll., 1970; D.L., Siena Heights Coll., 1982, Wabash Coll., 1998. Bar: Ill., N.Y., U.S. Supreme Ct. Lectr. polit. sci. U. Calif., Berkeley, 1949-52, asst. prof. polit. sci., 1953-57; assoc. prof. polit. sci. Northwestern U., 1958-63, prof. polit. sci. and law, 1963-68, 70-88, Nathaniel L. Nathanson prof., 1988—; pres. Reed Coll., Portland, Oreg., 1968-70. Sr. legal cons. project on bankruptcy govtl. studies div. Brookings Instn., 1964-69; vis. Fulbright lectr. Sch. Law U. Louvain, Belgium, 1966-67, vis. prof., 1978-79, 91-92; mem. Adminstrv. Conf. U.S., 1982-96. Editor in chief Adminstrv. Law Rev., 1958-62; author: Law As A Political Instrument, 1955, (with A.D. Castberg) Cases on Constitutional Law: Political Roles of the Supreme Court, 1973, (with Frances Zemans) The Making of a Public Profession, 1981; contbr. to law revs., also law and polit. sci. books. Staff assoc. Govtl. Affairs Inst., Washington, 1952-53; cons., assoc. counsel Subcom. on Exec. and Legis. Reorgn., Com. on Govt. Ops., U.S. Ho. of Reps., 1956-57; bd. dirs. Center for Adminstrv. Justice, 1972-78. Mem. ABA (council sect. adminstrv. law 1962-65, 72-75, chmn. 1977-78), Fed. Bar Assn., Am. Polit. Sci. Assn., Law and Soc. Assn. (pres. 1970-72), Am. Judicature Soc. (dir. 1982-90, chmn. bd. 1985-86), Assn. Am. Law Schs. (exec. com. 1984-88, pres. 1987), Consortium of Social Sci. Assns. (pres. 1987-88), Phi Beta Kappa, Pi Sigma Alpha. Democrat. Jewish. Home: 2025 Sherman Ave Evanston IL 60201-3268 Office: Northwestern U Sch Law 357 E Chicago Ave Chicago IL 60611-3059 E-mail: v-rosenblum@law.northwestern.edu.

ROSENBLUM, WILLIAM F., JR. lawyer; b. N.Y.C., May 11, 1935; AB cum laude, Princeton U., 1957; JD, Columbia U., 1960. Bar: N.Y. 1961, U.S. Dist. Ct. (so. dist.) N.Y. 1965. Gen. atty. Stanley Warner Corp., 1964-66; assoc. Leon, Weill & Mahony, 1967-70, Finley, Kumble, Wagner & Heine, 1970-74; pvt. practice, 1975; v.p. legal affairs Rep. Nat. Bank N.Y., 1976-82, Rep. N.Y. Corp., 1982-86, sr. v.p., dep. gen. counsel, corp. sec., 1987—2001;

mng. dir., gen. counsel NuVerse Advisors LLC, N.Y.C., 2001—. Mem.: ABA (mem. bus. law sect.), Assn. of Bar of City of N.Y. (mem. futures regulations com. 1987—90, fgn. and comparative law com. 2000—, futures and derivatives regulation com.), N.Y. State Bar Assn. (mem. sect. bus. law, commodities and derivatives regulation 1990—). Office: 645 Fifth Ave New York NY 10022

ROSENBLUM GREVÉY, ESTELLE, retired dean, nursing educator; b. Davenport, Iowa, Feb. 8, 1933; d. Dan and Cecil (Spiewak) Masters; m. Sidney Rosenblum, Aug. 30, 1953 (dec. 1988); children: Jay Douglas, Gail Rae, Paul Mitchell; m. Jack Grevey, Mar. 31, 1996; stepdaughter: Eileen Grevey Hillson. Student, U. Iowa, 1950-53; BSN, Wayne State U., Detroit, 1956; MSN, U. Tex., El Paso, 1981; PhD, U. N.Mex., 1979, MA in Audiology, 1971. Head nurse Northville (Mich.) State Hosp., 1956; head nurse, supr. Sister Kenny Polio/Rehab. Hosp., 1957-60; pub. health nurse Englewood County Health Dept., 1961-62; nursing supr. Bernalillo County Indian Hosp., Albuquerque, 1962-63, asst. dir. nursing, 1963-64; clin. tchr. U. N.Mex. Coll. Nursing, Albuquerque, 1964-65, inst. to prof., 1972-86, dean and prof. nursing, 1986-93, dean and prof. emerita, 1993—; sch. nurse West Mesa High Sch., Albuquerque, 1967-69. Internat. nursing cons.; dir. ANA Approved CE program, Profl. Seminar Cons., 1979-89; spkr. Hong Kong Nurse Educators Soc., 1985; founder convenio U. N.Mex. and U. Mex., 1990, first nurse midwifery grad. program, U. N.Mex., 1989, first nurse practitioner program at grad. level, 1987. Author: Fundamentals of Hearing for Health Professionals, 1981; contbr. articles to profl. jours., chpts. to book. Bd. dirs. U. N.Mex. Found., 1996—, bd. sec. 2000-04; docent City of Albuquerque, 1996—; chair recognition com. Jewish Cmty. Ctr., 1998—. USPHS grantee, 1989; recipient Centennial Disting. Alumni award, U. N.Mex., 1989, Helene Fuld award to Coll. Nursing, U. N.Mex., 1987, Sigma Delta Tau Nat. Disting. Alumni award, 1988, State N.Mex. Gov.'s Disting. Svc. award, 1993, Estelle H. Rosenblum Thesis award U. N.Mex. Coll. Nursing, 1995; Rosenblum-Weiss Ctr. for Nursing Excellence in women and children's health care established at U. N.Mex., 2000. Fellow Am. Acad. Nursing; mem. Am. Assn. Colls. of Nursing (emeritus, exec. devel. series 1988-92), Am. Colls. Nursing (bd. dirs. 1990-92), N.Mex. Nurses Assn. (pres. 1975), N.Mex. Health Resources (bd. dirs. 1986-88), The Rotary Club of Albuquerque (Harvest ball fundraiser 1994—), Sigma Theta Tau (founder, pres. Gamma Sigma chpt. 1974-76, Mentor award), Phi Kappa Phi.

ROSENBLUTH, MARION, educator, consultant, psychotherapist; b. Chgo., Apr. 4, 1928; d. Edwin William and Louise (Sulzberger) Eisendrath; m. Paul Richard Rosenbluth, June 16, 1950 (dec. Nov. 1972); children: Daniel, Jane Baldwin, Thomas, James, Catherine Rothschild. BA, Harvard U., 1949; MSW, Cath. U. of Am., 1951; PhD, U. Ill., 1986. Lic. clin. social worker, Ill. Clin. therapist Chgo. Dept. of Health, 1973-80; pvt. practice Chgo., 1980—; prof. Loyola U., 1986—; cons. Inst. for Clin. Social Work, 1988—. Cons. student health Loyola U., 1978-80; psychiat. cons. Circuit Ct. of Chgo. Domestic Rels. Divsn., 1995—; womens bd. dirs. U. Chgo. Bd. dirs. Chgo. Area Project, 1978—, Rec. for the Blind, Chgo., 1980—, Inst. Psychiatry Northwestern U. Mem. NASW, Coun. on Social Work Edn., Bd. Examiners Clin. Social Work (diplomate), Ill. Soc. Clin. Social Work, Arts Club of Chgo., Cliff Dwellers, Friday Club. Office: 676 N St Clair St Chicago IL 60611-2927 E-mail: mers03@aol.com.

ROSENBLUTH, MARSHALL NICHOLAS, physicist; b. Albany, N.Y., Feb. 5, 1927; s. Robert and Margaret (Sondhein) Rosenbluth; m. Sara Unger, Feb. 6, 1979; children from previous marriage: Alan Edward, Robin Ann, Mary Louise, Jean Pamela. BA, Harvard U., 1945; MS, U. Chgo., 1947, PhD, 1949. Instr. Stanford U., 1949—50; staff mem. Los Alamos Sci. Lab., 1950—56; sr. research adviser Gen. Atomic Corp., San Diego, 1956—67; prof. U. Calif., 1960—67, Inst. for Advanced Study, Princeton (N.J.) U., 1967—80; dir. Inst. for Fusion Studies, U. Tex., 1980-87; prof. U. Calif., San Diego, 1987—92; chief U.S. scientist Internat. Thermonuclear Engring. Reactor, 1992—. Lectr. with rank prof. in astrophys. scis. Princeton U., also vis. sr. research physicist , Plasma Physics Lab., 1967—80; Andrew D. White vis. prof. Cornell U., 1976; cons. AEC, NASA, Inst. Def. Analysis. Served with USNR, 1944—46. Recipient E.O. Lawrence award, 1964, Albert Einstein award, 1967, Maxwell prize, 1976, Enrico Fermi award, Dept. Energy, 1985, Nat. medal of Sci., Pres. U.S., 1998, Disting. Assoc. award, U.S. Dept. Energy, 2002, Hannes Alfuen prize, European Phys. Soc., 2002. Mem.: NAS, Am. Acad. Arts and Scis., Am. Phys. Soc. (Nicholson medal for humanitarian svc. 2000), Am. Philos. Soc. Home: 2311 Via Siena La Jolla CA 92037-3933 Office: U Calif San Diego Dept Physics 9500 Gilman Dr La Jolla CA 92093-0319

ROSENBLUTH, MORTON, periodontist, educator; b. N.Y.C., Sept. 28, 1924; s. Jacob and Eva (Bigeleissen) R.; m. Sylvia Fradin, July 2, 1946; children: Cheryl Bonnie, Hal Glen. BA, NYU, 1943, grad. program in periodontia, oral medicine, 1946, DDS, 1946. Diplomate Am. Bd. Periodontology. Intern Bellevue Hosp., N.Y.C., 1946-47, resident, 1947; individual practice dentistry, 1947-59; individual practice periodontia North Miami Beach, Fla., 1960—; individual practice periodontia, TMJ, implantology Bay Harbor Islands , 1995—. Periodontist Mt. Sinai Hosp., N.Y., Polyclinic Hosp. and Med. Sch. N.Y., Mt. Sinai Hosp., Miami Beach, Fla., Parkway Gen. Hosp.; chief dental dept. North Miami Gen. Hosp.; chmn. periodontia sect. Dade County Rsch. Ctr.; clin. assoc. prof. divsn. oral and maxillofacial surgery U. Miami Sch. Medicine; assoc. clin. prof. Southeastern U. Health Scis.; assoc. prof. Nova Southeastern U. Coll. Dental Medicine; lectr. throughout U.S.A., Israel, Mexico, Rome, Teheran, Bangkok, Hong Kong, Tokyo, Honolulu, Jamaica, Paris, London, Sicily, Budapest, Berlin, Luxembourg, South Africa and others; vis. lectr. U. Tenn. Dental Coll., NYU Dental Coll.; cons. VA Hosp., Miami. Contbr. articles to profl. jours. Mem. adv. bd. U. Fla. Coll. Dentistry; mem. profl. adv. bd. North Dade Children's Ctr., Hope Sch. Mentally Retarded Children; mem. sci. adv. com. United Health Found.; chmn. Dental divsn. United Fund of Dade County, Combined Jewish Appeal; nat. chmn. Hebrew U. Sch. Dental Medicine; bd. dirs. Health Planning Coun. South Fla.; pres. Condominium Assn.; bd. dirs. and bd. overseers Am. Friends of Hebrew U.; mem. med. adv. bd. Dade-Broward Lupus Found.; trustee Jewish Congregation, 1961-64. With AUS, 1943-44, as capt. USAF, 1951-52. Recipient Maimonides award State of Israel, 1979. Fellow Am. Coll. Dentists, Internat. Coll. Dentists; mem. ADA, Am. Acad. Periodontology, Am. Assn. Hosp. Dental Chiefs, Am. Acad. Dental Medicine, Am. Soc. Advancement Gen. Anesthesia in Dentistry, Am. Soc. Periodontists, Fla. Soc. Periodontists, Northeastern Soc. Periodontists, Fla. Dental Soc. (chmn. coun. on legislation), Miami Dental Soc., Miami Beach Dental Soc., East Coast Dental Soc. (sec.-treas. 1968, pres. 1971-72), North Dade Dental Soc. (pres. 1963-64), Fedn. Dentaire Internat., Fla. Acad. Dental Practice Adminstrn., Alpha Omega (pres. 1978-78, internat. regent 1973-75, internat. editor 1975-77, internat. pres.-elect 1977-78, internat. pres. 1979, chmn. bd. Alpha Omega Found. 1985-90), Am. Dental Interfrat. Coun. (pres. 1981-82), Nocoma Club (pres. 1958-60), NYU Century Club (local chmn.), Jockey Club (bd. govs.), KP, Masons, Kiwanis (bd. dirs. 1965), Chaine Des Rotisseurs (Miami Beach charge de missions). Home: 11111 Biscayne Blvd Apt 857 Miami FL 33181-3404 Office: 1166 Kane Concourse Bay Harbor Islands FL 33154-2000

ROSENBURGH, DWAYNE MAURICE, electronics engineer; b. Balt., Sept. 16, 1960; s. Samuel Boston and Lucille Anita (Hopkins) R.; m. Deborah Francine Muse, Mar. 23, 1985; 1 child, Lauren Stefanie. BS, Morgan State U., 1982; MS, George Washington U., 1997, postgrad., 1999—. Rsch. assoc., physics dept. Morgan State U., Balt., 1982-83; physicist Dept. of Def., Ft. Meade, Md., 1983-85, electronic engr., 1985—, sr. electronic engr. Bd. dirs. Technologies and More, Inc. Contbr. articles to profl. jours. Dep. comdr. for cadets, Civil Air Patrol, USAF Aux., Balt., 1984-86. Mem. IEEE (sr.), Internat. Freelance Photographers Orgn., Am. Radio Relay League, Am. Amateur Racquetball Assn., U.S. Chess Fedn., Mensa. Avocations: amateur radio, sports, chess. E-mail: d.rosenburgh@ieee.org.

ROSENBURGH, STEPHEN ARUTHUR, executive; b. Peterborough, Ont., Can., July 15, 1951; came to U.S., 1993; s. Donald Joseph and Evelyn Mabel (Poole) R.; children: Lara Aislynn, Meghan Lynne, Jana Michelle. BA in Polit. Sci., Laurentian U., 1973; grad diploma in pub. adminstrn., Carelton U., 1974, MA in Adminstrn. and Mktg., 1975; cert. mgmt., Harvard U., 1997. Exec. officer Govt. Ont., Mgmt. Bd. Cabinet, Toronto, Can., 1975-77; sr. v.p. York-Hannover, 1977-83; pres. Morewood Industries, Ltd., Ottawa, Ont., 1983-89; sr. v.p. Bramalea, Ltd., Toronto, 1990-91; pres. Carelton County Mgmt., Ottawa, 1989-96, Jordan Homes, Charlotte, N.C., 1993-95; chmn., CEO Enterprise Devel. Internat., Fairfax, Va., 1996—; dir. Consol. Stone Industries, 1998—; pres. U.S. Land Investments, Charlotte, N.C., 1998—. Baptist. Home: 6944 Garden Terrace Ct Charlotte NC 28210

ROSENBUSH, STUART WILLIAM, cardiologist; b. Chgo., Jan. 31, 1951; s. Walter and Rena R.; m. Miriam Strilky, Jan. 19, 1974; children: Eric, Lara, Aaron. BS, U. Ill., 1972, MD, 1976. Diplomate Am. Bd. Internal Medicine, Am. Bd. Cardiovascular Diseases; cert. in interventional cardiology. Intern in internal medicine Michael Reese Med. Ctr., Chgo., 1976-77, resident in internal medicine, 1977-79; fellow in cardiology Rush Presbyn. St. Luke's Med. Ctr., 1979-81, attending cardiologist, 1981—. Asst. prof. medicine Rush Med. Coll., Chgo., 1982—. Fellow Soc. for Cardiac Angiography and Interventions. Fellow ACP, Am. Coll. Cardiology, Am. Heart Assn. (clin. coun.). Office: Assocs in Cardiology 1725 W Harrison St Chicago IL 60612-3828 also: 9701 Knox Ave Skokie IL 60076-1256

ROSENDAL, HANS ERIK, meteorologist; b. Lyngby, Denmark, July 19, 1931; s. Kaj and Anna Katrine (Hansen) R.; m. Angela Karlos, Dec. 20, 1958; children: Erik P., Dana G., Paul A. BS, U. Wis., 1960; MS, U. Mich., 1965. Meteorologist U.S. Weather Bur., Washington, 1960-65; state climatologist Nat. Weather Svc., Madison, Wis., 1965-73, meteorologist Milw., 1973-74, Phoenix, 1974-76, Honolulu, 1976—. Editor Mariners Weather Log, 1962-64. Recipient Gold medal U.S. Dept. Commerce, Honolulu, 1992. Fellow Am. Meteorol. Soc. (spl. award 1992). Lutheran. Home: 1242 Mokapu Blvd Kailua HI 96734-1847 Office: Nat Weather Svc U Hawaii at Manoa Honolulu HI 96734 E-mail: hans.rosendal@noaa.gov., rosendalhe@aol.com.

ROSENDALE, GEORGE WILLIAM, aircraft company executive; b. Keenan, Okla., Nov. 4, 1933; s. John Webster and Laura Lee (Schawo) Rosendale; m. Penney Sue Tillotson, Dec. 27, 1964; children: James Christopher, Kathleen Marie, John Charles. Student ., Okla. Bapt. U., 1957—58; student, U. Wichita, 1958—63; BA in English, Wichita State U., 1969, MS in Adminstrn., 1971. Diplomate Pers. Accreditation Inst., 1977. Engring. draftsman Skyline Corp., Wichita, Kans., 1952, Boeing Aircraft Co., Wichita, 1953, O.A. Sutton Corp., Wichita, 1956, engring. checker, 1856—56; various positions Cessna Aircraft Co., 1958—98, pers. rep., 1967—69, tng. supr., 1969—73, mgr. employee tng. and devel., 1973—84, mgr. pers. projects, 1984—85, mgr. mgmt. resource devel., 1985—87, adminstr. internat. assembly programs, 1987—88, mgr. material fin. and adminstrn., 1988—98; mgr. material TAD Tech., 1999—2000. Vocat. instr. Wichita Pub. Schs., 1963; pers. adviser Wichita Police Res., 1969—73; treas. Haysville Police Res., 1975—91; chmn. bd. dirs. Corp. Employment Resources, Inc., 1987—88. Area comdr. United Fund, Wichita, 1971; sec. Haysville Jr. Football League, Haysville, Kans., 1973—75; study com. chmn. Wichita Cmty. Planning Coun., 1972—73; mem. Haysville Planning Commn., 1976—86, chmn., 1977—79, 1980—84; exec. com. Kans. State Employment and Tng. Coun., 1979—82. Served with U.S. Army, 1953—56. Recipient Campaign award, United Fund of Wichita, 1969—71, Outstanding Svc. Plaque award, Am. Cancer Soc., 1978—79, 1981—82, SER Individual Support award, 1979, others. Mem.: Optimist (chmn. cmty. svc. 1985—88, v.p. Haysville club 1986—87, pres. 1987—88, lt. gov. Kans. dist. 1988—89, dir. 1989—92), Psi Chi. Home: 424 W Hollywood St Wichita KS 67217-5934

ROSENDHAL, JEFFREY DAVID, federal science agency administrator, astronomer; b. Bklyn., June 21, 1941; s. Louis and Beulah (Goldsmith) R.; m. Sharon E. Katzman, Dec. 27, 1964 (div. Jan. 25, 1989); children: Martin Andrew, Rachel Lynn; m. Ellen R. Anderson, Feb. 14, 1992. BA, Williams Coll., 1962; MS, U. Ill., 1963; PhD, Yale U., 1968. Vis. asst. prof. astronomy U. Wash., Seattle, 1968-69; asst. prof. U. Wis., Madison, 1969-71, U. Ariz., Tucson, 1971-74; with NASA, Washington, 1974—, mgr. advanced programs and tech., astrophysics divsn., 1978-80, asst. assoc. adminstr. advanced planning Office Space Sci., 1980-81, asst. assoc. adminstr. sci. Office Space Sci., Applications, 1981-87, spl. asst. to assoc. adminstr. for space sci. and applications, 1987-89, 92-93, spl. asst. for policy Office Exploration, 1989-90, asst. dir. exploration (internat.) Office Aeronautics, Exploration and Tech., 1990-91, asst. dir. strategic planning Astrophysics Divsn. Office of Space Sci., 1993-96, asst. assoc. adminstr./edn. and outreach Office Space Sci., 1996-2001, edn. and pub. outreach dir. Office of Space Sci., 2001—. Vis. prof. internat. rels. George Washington U., 1988-89; mem. staff energy subcom. House Sci. Space and Tech. Com., 1992. Mem. editl. adv. bd. Jour. Brit. Interplanetary Soc., 1988—; contbr. articles to Astrophys. Jour., Astrophysics and Space Sci., Physics Today, Issues in Sci. and Tech., Acta Astronautica, other jours. and conf. procs. Recipient NASA Sr. Exec. Svc. Performance awards, 1980, 82-86, 96, 99, 2000, Outstanding Leadership medal, 1984, group achievement awards, 1986 (2), 95, 96, European Space Agy. Team Achievement award, 1983, 85, 86, Presdl. award of Meritorious Exec. in Sr. Exec. Svc., 1987; NSF grantee, 1971, 72-73; NASA fellow Yale U., 1966-68; hon. Woodrow Wilson fellow, 1962. Fellow: AIAA (assoc.); mem.: Sr. Execs. Assn., Internat. Astron. Union, Internat. Acad. Astronautics, Royal Astron. Soc., Am. Astron. Soc. (divsn. planetary scis.), Astron. Soc. Pacific, Cosmos Club, Phi Beta Kappa. Achievements include discovery of the variability of the microturbulence in early-type high luminosity stars; direction of the selection of flight experiments for every major NASA scientific mission 1980-1988; development of strategic and implementation plans for incorporating education and the public understanding of science into space science research programs and missions; establishment of a national support network for space science education; creation of one of the largest programs in astronomy and space science education ever undertaken. Home: 11446 Links Dr Reston VA 20190-4813 Office: NASA Hdqrs Office Space Sci Code S Washington DC 20546 E-mail: jeffrey.rosendhal@hq.nasa.gov., enjrosend@erols.com.

ROSENDHAL, RACHEL LYNN, information technology executive; b. Madison, Wis., Sept. 17, 1970; d. Jeffrey and Sharon Rosendhal. BA in Math. and Psychology, Coll. William and Mary, 1992; MS in Ops. Rsch., Stanford U., 1995. Team lead product support Hire.com, Austin, Tex., 1999—. Treas. bd. dirs. Bouldin Creek Condominiums Home Owners Assn., Austin, 1999—2002. Mem.: INFORMS (treas. Austin chpt. 1999—2000, v.p. Austin chpt. 2000—01). Home: 802 South First St # 225 Austin TX 78704 Office: Hirecom 200 Academy Dr Austin TX 78704 Personal E-mail: rrosendhal@hotmail.com. E-mail: rachel@hire.com.

ROSENDIN, RAYMOND JOSEPH, electrical contracting company executive; b. San Jose, Calif., Feb. 14, 1929; s. Moses Louis and Bertha C. (Pinedo) R.; m. Jeanette Marie Bucher, June 30, 1951 (dec. Feb. 1967); children: Mark R., Patricia A., Debra M., Cynthia C., David R.; m. Nancy Ann Burke, July 6, 1984; children: Raymond M., Callie R., Blake W. Student engring., San Jose State U., 1947-48; BSE.E., Heald's Engring. Coll., San Francisco, 1950. V.p., CEO Rosendin Electric, Inc., San Jose, Calif., 1953-59, exec. v.p., CEO, 1969-75, pres., CEO, 1975-94, chmn., CEO, 1995-2000, chmn., 2000—, former dir. Former dir. Community Bank, San Jose Bd. fellows U. Santa Clara, Calif., 1966-93, pres. bd., 1969-72, bd. regents, 1972-82; bd. dirs. United Way, Santa Clara, 1970-74; O'Connor's Hosp., San Jose, 1979-85, Community Hosp., Los Gatos, Calif., 1968-74. Recipient Man of Yr. award Santa Clara Valley Youth Village, 1963, Optimist of Yr. award Optimist Club, San Jose, 1970 Mem. C. of C. Greater San Jose (past dir.), Nat. Elec. Contractors Assn. (past pres., gov., dir.) Clubs: St. Claire (San Jose). Republican. Roman Catholic. Avocation: boating. Office: Rosendin Electric Inc 880 Mabury Rd San Jose CA 95133-1021

ROSENDORFF, CLIVE, cardiologist; b. Bloemfontein, South Africa, Mar. 28, 1938; m. Daphne Avigail Lynn, Dec. 30, 1962; children: Bryan Peter, Nicola, Adam. BSc with honors, U. Witwatersrand, Johannesburg, South Africa, 1958, MBBCh, 1962, MD, 1977, DSc Medicine, 1984; PhD U. London, 1969. Med. cert., N.Y. Lectr., cons. medicine St. Thomas Hosp., London, 1965-69; prof., chmn. physiology U. Witwatersrand Med. Sch., Johannesburg, 1970-91, dean, 1987-90; prof., assoc. chmn. medicine Mt. Sinai Sch. Medicine, N.Y.C., 1991—; chief medicine VA Med. Ctr., Bronx, N.Y., 1991—. Vis. prof. Yale U., 1969-70, U. Calif., San Francisco, 1977, Hosp. Lariboisiere, Paris, 1991; rsch. fellow Am. Heart Assn., Yale U., 1969-70. Author: Clinical Cardiovascular and Pulmonary Physiology, 1988, Essential Cardiology: Principles and Practice, 2001, over 170 rsch. papers. Fellow ACP, Royal Soc. South Africa, Royal Coll. Physicians, Am. Coll. Cardiology. Achievements include research in cardiovascular disease. Office: Mt Sinai Sch Medicine Box 9000 Dept Medicine 1 Gustave L Levy Pl New York NY 10029-6500 also: VAMC Med Ctr Med Svc 130 W Kingsbridge Rd Bronx NY 10468-3904 E-mail: clive.rosendorff@med.va.gov.

ROSENE, RALPH WALFRED, consulting company executive; b. Davenport, Iowa, Mar. 21, 1938; s. Raymond Walfred and Lavern (Marre) R.; m. Linda Roberts, Aug. 3, 1957; children: Leigh, Russell, Tim. Grad. high sch. Sales Mpls. Star/Tribune, 1958-66, sales mgr., 1966-68; advt. dir. Rapid City (S.D.) Jour., 1968-72, ops. mgr., 1972-74, gen. mgr., 1974-76; chief exec. officer First Am. Systems, Rapid City, 1976-82; sr. ptnr. Target Systems, Inc., Dallas, 1982-85, pres., 1985—, CEO, 1990-97; cons. mgr. EASI Sys., Inc., Ft. Worth, 1997-98, dir. corp. devel. U.S. personnel, 1998-99, COO, U.S. personnel, 1999-2000, exec. cons. U.S. personnel, 2000—; cons., 2000—. Spkr. and seminar leader in field. Contbr. to numerous nat. industry publs. Chmn. bd. Community Action Agy., Rapid City, 1970-71; developer Leadership Sch. Mem. Rapid City S.D. C. of C. (chmn. bd. 1980), Toastmasters (pres. Dallas chpt. 1986), CEO Network (mem. local bd.). Office: 222 Country Rd 2430 Mineola TX 75773 E-mail: ralphr@uspersonnel.com.

ROSENFELD, ALBERT HYMAN, science and medical writer; b. Phila., May 31, 1920; s. Samuel and Annie (Zeiffert) R.; m. Lillian Elizabeth Snow, Aug. 24, 1948; children: Robert, Shana. *Albert Rosenfeld's parents came over from Franz Josef's Austro-Hungarian Empire around the turn of the century and met in Philadelphia, where all nine of their children were born. Albert was the youngest. Wife Lillian Snow was born in Muskogee, OK, raised in Pampa, TX, and recently retired as chief research librarian for American Institute of CPAs in NYC. Son Robert was born in Santa Fe, NM and teaches philosophy at the University of Massachusetts and Suffolk University in Boston. Daughter Shana, born in NY, is a librarian at the Yonkers Public Library.* BA in History and Social Scis., N.Mex. State U., 1950, DLett (hon.), 1971. Freelance mag. writer, corr., Santa Fe, 1950-56; sci. editor Life mag., N.Y.C., 1956-69; mng. editor Family Health mag., 1969-71; writer, prodr. Time-Life Video, 1971-72; sci. editor, columnist Saturday Rev., 1973-79; cons. on future programs March of Dimes Birth Defects Found., White Plains, N.Y., 1973—; adj. asst. prof. U. Tex. Med. Br., Galveston, 1973-98. Bd. dirs. RegeneRx, Biopharms., Inc., Bethesda, Md., Totts Gap (Pa.) Med. Rsch. Labs.; mem. sci. bd. Alliance for Aging Rsch., Washington, 1995—. Author: The Quintessence of Irving Langmuir, 1962, The Second Genesis, 1969, Prolongevity II, 1985; co-author: Responsible Parenthood, 1980; contbr. articles to profl. publs. Sgt. U.S. Army, 1942-45, ETO. Recipient award for leadership in med. journalism Lasker Found., 1967, Nat. Mag. award Columbia U., 1975, James P. Grady medal Am. Chem. Soc., 1981. Mem. AAAS, World Future Soc., Nat. Assn. Sci. Writers, Authors Guild, N.Y. Acad. Scis., Coun. for Advancement of Sci. Writing (bd. dirs., past pres.), Smithsonian Assocs., Hastings Ctr. Democrat. Jewish. Avocations: music, sketching, tennis, baseball, hiking. E-mail: alrosenf@westnet.com.

ROSENFELD, ARNOLD SOLOMON, retired newspaper editor; b. N.Y.C., Apr. 18, 1933; s. William and Sarah (Cohen) R.; m. Ruth Doris Lilly, Sept. 30, 1956 (dec. Sept. 1996); children— William Bennett, Jonathan Andrew, Lauren; m. Rosalin Coletti, Dec. 5, 1999. Student, U. Houston, 1951; Profl. Journalism fellow, Stanford U., 1967. Mem. staff Houston Post, 1953-67; assoc. editor Detroit mag., Detroit Free Press, 1967; editor Detroit mag., 1968; mng. editor Dayton Daily News, Ohio, 1968-76, editor, 1976-80, Dayton Daily News and Jour. Herald, 1980-84, Austin Am.-Statesman, Tex., 1984-88, Atlanta Jour.-Constitution, 1988-89; editor-in-chief Cox Newspapers, Atlanta, 1989-2000; ret.; dir. The Temple, 1994-98. Editor: A Thomason Sketchbook, 1969. Pres. Temple Israel Dayton, 1984; bd. dirs. Antioch U., 1978-84, Huston-Tillotson Coll., 1987-89, Genesis Shelter, 1998—. With AUS, 1951-53. Recipient Editorial Writing award A.P. Mng. Editors Assn. Tex., 1966; Tex. Theta Sigma Phi award, 1969, 72; Media award Nat. Assn. Mental Health, 1976 Mem. Am. Soc. Newspaper Editors Found. (bd. dirs., treas. 1992—). Home: 5875 Riverwood Dr NW Atlanta GA 30328-3728

ROSENFELD, ARTHUR F. federal agency administrator; b. Allentown, Pa. m. Carla Toledo. BA, Muhlenberg Coll., 1970; MBA, Lehigh U., 1974; JD, Villanova U., 1979. Bar: D.C. 1979, U.S. Supreme Ct., U.S. Ct. Appeals (4th, 5th and D.C. cirs.). Labor atty. U.S. C. of C., Washington, 1979—84; atty. Hansell & Post, 1984—86; numerous positions including counsel for regulations divsn. employee benefits, spl. asst. to silicitor of labor, assoc. deputy sec. labor U.S. Dept. Labor, 1986—97; sr. labor advisor to chmn. James M. Jeffords Senate Com. Health, Edn., Labor and Pensions, 1997—2001; gen. counsel Nat. Labor Rels. Bd., 2001—. Office: NLRB 1099 14th St NW Washington DC 20570-0001*

ROSENFELD, ARTHUR H. lawyer, publisher; b. Bklyn., May 24, 1930; s. Abraham and Sadie (Albert) R.; m. Lois E. Glantz, Apr. 15, 1956; children: Felicia Ann, Carolyn Jane, Sara Ellen. Student, St. Andrew's U., 1950-51; AB, Union Coll., Schenectady, 1952; JD, Harvard U., 1955; postgrad., CCNY, 1962-63. Bar: N.Y. 1955. Pres. Warren, Gorham & Lamont, Inc., N.Y.C., 1970-81, Internat. Thomson Profl. Pub., N.Y.C., 1981-84; chmn. bd. Rosenfeld, Emanuel Inc., Larchmont, N.Y., 1984-88; pres. Prentice Hall Tax & Profl. Ref., N.Y.C., 1988-89, Maxwell Macmillan Profl. and Bus. Reference Div., Englewood Cliffs, N.J., 1989-92; chmn. Arthur H. Rosenfeld Assocs., 1991—; Civic Rsch. Inst., Inc., 1992—. Bd. dirs. Coun. Econ. Priorities, 1990—. Mem. ABA, N.Y. State Bar Assn., Am. Assn. Pubs. (exec. coun. 1991), Harvard Club. Democrat. Office: 2067 Broadway Ste 50 New York NY 10023 E-mail: ahrcri@aol.com.

ROSENFELD, AZRIEL, computer science educator, consultant; b. N.Y.C., Feb. 19, 1931; s. Abraham Hirsh and Ida B. (Chadaby) R.; m. Eve Hertzberg, Mar. 1, 1959; children— Elie, David, Tova BA, Yeshiva U., 1950, M.H.L., 1953, MS, 1954, D.H.L., 1955; MA, Columbia U., 1951, Ph.D, 1957; D.Tech. (hon.), Linkoping U., Sweden, 1980; D of Tech. (hon.), Oulu U., Finland, 1994; LHD (hon.), Yeshiva U., 2000. Ordained rabbi, 1952. Physicist Fairchild Controls Corp., N.Y.C., 1954-56; engr. Ford Instrument Co., Long Island City, N.Y., 1956-59; mgr. research electronics div. Budd Co., Long Island City and McLean, Va., 1959-64; prof., dir. Ctr. for Automation Rsch. U. Md., College Park, 1964-2001, Disting. univ. prof., 1995-2001, prof. emeritus, 2001—. Vis. asst. prof. Yeshiva U., N.Y.C., 1957-63; pres. ImTech, Inc., Silver Spring, Md., 1975-92 Author, editor numerous books; editor numerous jours. Recipient Info. Sci. award Assn. for Intelligent Machinery, 1998. Fellow IEEE (Emanuel R. Piore award 1985), IEEE Computer Soc. (Harry Goode Meml. award 1995), IEEE Sys., Man and Cybernetics Soc. (Norbert Wiener award 1995), Washington Acad. Scis. (Sci. Achievement award 1988), Am. Assn. for Artificial Intelligence (founding), Assn. Computing Machinery (founding); mem. Math. Assn. Am., Machine Vision Assn. (bd. dirs. 1984-88, Pres.'s award 1987), Internat. Assn. Pattern Recognition (pres. 1980-82, K.S. Fu award 1988, founding fellow 1994), Assn. Orthodox Jewish Scientists (pres. 1963-65), Nat. Acad. Engring. of Mex. (corr.). Home: 6701 Park Hgts Ave Apt 3G Baltimore MD 21215-2442 Office: U Md Ctr Automation Rsch Computer Vision Lab College Park MD 20742-3275 E-mail: ar@cfar.umd.edu.

ROSENFELD, DAVID LEONARD, radiologist; b. Englewood, N.J., Apr. 13, 1942; MD, U. Pitts., 1967. Diplomate in radiology and pediatric radiology Am. Bd. Radiology, cert. additional qualification in pediatric radiology. Intern Harrisburg Hosp., 1967-68; resident in radiology Montefiore Hosp., Bronx, 1968-71; with St. Peter's Med. Ctr., New Brunswick, N.J., Robert Wood Johnson Univ. Hosp.; clin. prof. radiology U. Medicine and Dentistry N.J., 1994—. Fellow: Am. Coll. Radiology; mem.: Soc. for Pediat. Radiology, Am. Inst. Ultrasound in Medicine, Radiol. Soc. N.Am. Office: Univ Radiology Group 579 Cranbury Rd East Brunswick NJ 08816-5405 E-mail: orchiddoc@rcn.com.

ROSENFELD, EDWARD, travel company executive; b. Phila. Cert. Travel Agt., Inst. Cert. Travel Agents, Wellesly, Mass., 1978. Cert. Inst. Cert. Travel Agts., 1978. V.p. Cefra Travel, Scottsdale, Ariz., 1973—; pres. Learco Travel Enterprises, Phoenix, 1985—. Cons. Am. Soc. Travel Agts., 1980-85, Indian Nation, Ariz., 1999-2001. Author: Outside Sales, A Travel Book, 1990. Mem. ICTA. Office: Learco Travel Enterprises PO Box 26750 Scottsdale AZ 85255-0129 E-mail: learco@earthlink.net.

ROSENFELD, HAROLD LEE, plastic surgeon; b. N.Y.C., May 19, 1940; s. Sam and Rose Rosenfeld; children: Ariel Margaret, Samuel Jordon. AB, Occidental Coll., 1961; MD, U. So. Calif., 1965. Diplomate Am. Bd. Plastic Surgery. Resident in gen. surgery Huntington Meml. Hosp., Pasadena, Calif., 1969-70, Queen of Angels Hosp., L.A., 1970-72; resident in plastic surgery La. State U., New Orleans, 1972-74; travelling fellow in plastic surgery No. Europe, 1974; clin. instr. plastic surgery La. State U., New Orleans, 1974-75, Loma Linda (Calif.) U., 1985-93; clin. asst. prof. plastic surgery U. So. Calif., L.A., 1987—. Mem. staff Huntington Meml. Hosp., Pasadena, 1975—, chmn. plastic surgery, 1996—; mem. staff St. Luke Med. Ctr., Pasadena, 1975—, chief plastic surgery, 1992-94, chief of surgery, 1994; cons. in plastic surgery Good Samaritan Hosp., L.A., 1975—; staff Arcadia (Calif.) Meth. Hosp., 1975—, Orthopaedic Hosp., L.A., 1999—. Cons. Citizens Dem. Cons., Washington, 1996. Lt. USN, 1966-68. Fellow ACS; mem. Am. Soc. Plastic and Reconstructive Surgery, Am. Soc. Aesthetic Surgeons, Am. Assn. Hand Surgery, Calif. Soc. Plastic Surgery, Calif. Med. Soc., Am. Soc. for Laser Medicine and Surgery, Pasadena Med. Assn. (pres. 1999-2002). Avocation: bonsai. Office: Harold Rosenfeld 39 Congress St # 300 Pasadena CA 91105-3024

ROSENFELD, HARRY LEONARD, rabbi; b. Cleve., June 25, 1955; s. Nathan and Frances (Skrall) R.; m. Michele Lynn Hope, May 29, 1988. BS in Psychology, John Carroll U., 1976; MA in Hebrew Letters, Hebrew Union Coll., 1980. Ordained rabbi, 1981. Asst. rabbi Temple Israel, Memphis, 1981-84; rabbi Congregation Beth Sholom, Anchorage, 1984-2000; sr. rabbi Temple Beth Zion, Buffalo, 2000—. Adj. prof. Alaska Pacific U., Anchorage, 1987-2000, SUNY, Buffalo; exec. com. Alaska, Am. Israel Polit. Affairs Com., Anchorage, 1986-92. Bd. dirs. Cath. Social Svcs., Anchorage, 1991-2000; pres. United Way Anchorage, 1985-90; mem. Mcpl. Health and Human Svcs. Commn., Anchorage, 1986-88, Anchorage Mcpl. Equal Rights Commn., 1986; mem. Rabbinic Cabinet, United Jewish Appeal, 1994—, mem. exec. bd., 1994—, mem. exec. bd. Network of Ind. Cmtys., 1995-99. Mem. Ctrl. Conf. Am. Rabbis (ch. state com. 1985-86), Assn. Reform Zionists. Office: Temple Beth Zion 700 Sweet Home Rd Amherst NY 14226-1497 E-mail: rabbiharryrosenfeld@attglobal.net.

ROSENFELD, HARRY MORRIS, editor; b. Berlin, 1929; s. Sam and Esther Laja Rosenfeld; m. Anne Hahn, Feb. 28, 1953; children: Susan, Amy, Stefanie. BA, Syracuse U., 1952; postgrad., NYU, 1954, Columbia U., 1955-59. With N.Y. Herald Tribune, 1954-66, fgn. editor, 1962-66; mng. editor Herald Tribune News Svc., 1959-62; with Washington Post, 1966-78, fgn. editor, 1969; asst. mng. editor Met. News, 1970-74, Nat. News, 1974-76, Outlook/Book World, 1976-78; editor Times Union and Knickerbocker News, Albany, N.Y., 1978-88, L.A. Herald Examiner, 1985, The Times Union and Sunday Times Union, 1978-96; editor-at-large, columnist The Times Union, Albany, N.Y., 1996—. Dir. daily Watergate coverage for Washington Post (newspaper award Pulitzer Gold medal for pub. svc.); vice-chmn. N.Y. Fair Trial Free Press Conf., 1985-98, vice chmn. emeritus, 1998—; co-chmn. N.Y. State Reporters Com. for Freedom of Press; mem. adv. com. Harvard Journalism Fellowship for Advanced Studies in Pub. Health; Pulitzer juror, 1987-88, 96, 97. Commr. N.Y. State Regents Commn. on Libr. Svcs. Recipient Black United Front award, 1973, First Amendment award Anti-Defamation League-B'nai B'rith, L.A., Outstanding Alumni award, Syracuse U. Coll. of Arts and Scis., 1993, Media Responsibility award N.Y. State Martin Luther King Jr. Inst. for Non-Violence, 1993. Mem. Am. Soc. Newspaper Editors, N.Y. State AP Assn. (pres. 1983, 3d pl. column award 1983, 85, 1st pl. column award 1987), N.Y. State Soc. Newspaper Editors, Internat. Press Inst., UPI Fgn. News Com. (rep. for N.E.), Soc. Profl. Journalists (adv. bd. Albany chpt.), and 3 commns. on Cameras in the Cts. (adv. comm.). Office: Times Union PO Box 15000 Albany NY 12212-5000 E-mail: hrosenfeld@timesunion.com.

ROSENFELD, JOEL CHARLES, surgeon; b. Phila., Nov. 5, 1948; MD, Jefferson Med. Coll., 1974. Diplomate Am. Bd. Surgery. Intern Pa. Hosp., Phila., 1974-75, resident, 1975-79, fellow in vascular surgery, 1981-82; surgeon St. Luke's Hosp., Bethlehem, Pa., 1987—, gen. surgery residency program dir., 1995—. Mem. AMA, ACS, Internat. Soc. Cardiovasc. Surgery, Soc. for Clin. Vascular Surgery, Assn. Program Dirs. Surgery, Assn. for Acad. Surgery. Office: Progressive Physicians 301 W Broad St Bethlehem PA 18015 E-mail: rosenfj@slhn.org.

ROSENFELD, LYLE MARTIN, computer engineer; b. Bklyn., Mar. 20, 1953; s. Morris and Leslie (Schectman) R.; m. Sharon Rhonda Seidner, May 24, 1981; children: Leslie Rachel, Robert. BS, U. So. Calif., 1979, MS in Computer Engring., 1980. Manufacturers certification from: Compaq, Packard Bell, Epson, Apple, AST, NCR, ATT, Panasonic, Okidata, DFI, TRIGEM, Pionex, Star Micronics, Canon, Zenith, NEC, Data Products, Nexar, Patriot, Toshiba. Design engr. Merganthaler Co., L.I., N.Y., 1980-85; v.p., prin. MPI Computer Distbn. Inc., N.Y.C., 1985—. Author life agy. mgmt. system, gen. agy. mgmt. system and comprehensive fin. planning analysis software. Bd. dirs. Adloptive Parents Com., L.I., N.Y. With USN, 1976-80. Mem. Assn. Field Svc. Mgrs. (cert. computer engr.), Odd Fellows. Republican. Jewish. Avocations: fishing, travel, family, the internet.

ROSENFELD, MARK KENNETH, real estate developer; b. Jackson, Mich., Mar. 17, 1946; s. Nathan and Marjorie N. (Leopold) R.; children: Edward Robert, Zachary, Alix Caitlin. BA, Amherst Coll., 1968; S.M., MIT, 1970. With Jacobson's, Jackson, 1972—, v.p., real estate group mgr., 1976-78, exec. v.p., 1978-82, pres, 1982-93, chmn., CEO, 1993-96; chmn. Wilherst Developers Inc., 1997—. Bd. dirs. Ramco-Gershenson Property Trust, Ecliptic Sys., Inc., Kurt Gaum Inc. With U.S. Army, 1969-70. Jewish. E-mail: mark.rosenfeld@wilherst.net.

ROSENFELD, MARTIN JEROME, management consultant to law firms, educator; b. Flint, Mich., Oct. 3, 1944; s. Israel Edward and Lillian Edith (Natchez) R.; m. Marcy Tucker Colman; 1 child, Joshua; stepchildren: Jessica Colman, Zachary Colman. BA, Mich. State U., 1968, MHA, 1978; MBA with high honors, Ind. No. U., 1979. Adminstr. Care Corp., Grand Rapids, Mich., 1969-70, Chandler Convalescent Ctr., Detroit, 1970-71, Grand Community Hosp., Detroit, 1971-73; exec. v.p., chief exec. officer Msgr. Clement Kern Hosp. Spl. Surgery, Warren, 1973-84; pres. M.J. Rosenfeld Assocs., 1984-85; COO Dickinson, Wright, Moon, Van Dusen & Freeman, 1985-88; acting COO New Ctr. Hosp., Detroit, 1995-96; prin. Rosenfeld LLC, Farmington Hills, 1988—; instr. U. Phoenix, 2001—. Instr. Marygrove Coll., 1975-80; assoc. prof. Mercy Coll., Detroit, 1978-80; mem. faculty Inst. on Continuing Legal Edn., Ann Arbor, Mich., Inst. Law Firm Mgmt., Ann Arbor; instr. Legal Tech '87, Chgo. Author papers in field. Mem. editl. bd. The Human-Size Hosp.; mem. panel of experts The Health Care News. V.p. Detroit chpt. Jewish Nat. Fund, 1978—; pres. Cranbrook Village Homeowners Assn., 1977; chmn. Community Hosps. of Southeastern Mich., 1981-84; mem. tech. work group Comprehensive Health Planning Coun. of Southeastern Mich., 1981-84; mem. fin. mgmt. com., mem. hosp. affairs bd. Greater Detroit Area Hosp. Coun., 1981-84; bd. dirs., com. chmn. Detroit Symphony Orch., 1984-90; bd. dirs., mem. fund raising com. Detroit Met. Orch., 1984-87. Mem. ABA, Assn. Legal Adminstrs., Am. Assn. Health Care Cons., Royal Soc. Health, Am. Podiatry Assn. (com. hosps. 1981-84), Warren C. of C. (com. chmn. 1975), Nat. Assn. Legal Search Cons., Nat. Assn. Pers. Svcs., Mich. Assn. Pers. Svcs., Sanford Rose Assocs. Dirs. Assn. (pres. 1993-95, treas. 1995-97). Office: Rosenfeld LLC 3278 Middlebelt Road Suite A Farmington Hills MI 48334-1770 E-mail: mjr@rosenfeldllc.com.

ROSENFELD, MICHAEL G. medical educator; Prof. dept. medicine U. Calif. Med. Sch., La Jolla, 1996—. Mem. NAS. Office: U Calif San Diego Sch Medicine Howard Hughes Med Inst 9500 Gilman Dr Room 345 La Jolla CA 92093-0648

ROSENFELD, RONALD A. federal agency administrator; Grad., Law Sch. Sec. of commerce State of Okla.; dep. asst. sec. for single family housing Dept. HUD, 1989, gen. dep. asst. sec. housing, FHA commr., pres. Govt. Nat. Mortgage Assn., 2001—. Office: Dept HUD Govt Nat Mortgage Assn 451 7th St SW Washington DC 20410-9000

ROSENFELD, SARENA MARGARET, artist; b. Elmira, N.Y., Oct. 17, 1940; d. Thomas Edward and Rosalie Ereny (Fedor) Rooney; m. Robert Steven Bach, June 1958 (div. 1963); children: Robert Steven, Daniel Thomas; m. Samson Rosenfeld III, June 5, 1976. Student, Otis/Parson Art Inst., L.A., 1994-98, Idyllwild Sch. Music and Arts, 1994-98. One-woman shows include Robert Dana Gallery, San Francisco, Gordon Gallery, Santa Monica, Calif., Hespe Gallery, San Francisco, Art Expressions, San Diego, L.A., La Jolla, Calif., Aspen, Colo., New Orleans, Honolulu, La Sierra U., Riverside, Calif., U. Enklinik, Bochum, Germany, Ruhr U., Germany, Universitatsklinikum Benjamin Franklin, Berlin, 2002, exhibited in group shows at Ergane Gallery, N.Y.C., Orlando Gallery, Sherman Oaks, Calif., Gallery 444, San Francisco, Bradford Gallery Blue Sq., Newport Beach, Calif., 2001, L.A., Soho, N.Y.C., Santa Barbara, Calif., Tanglewood, Mass., Johannesburg, South Africa. Mem. vol., animal handler Wildlife Waysta., Angeles Nat. Forest, Calif.; vol. animal keeper L.A. Zoo. Recipient Best of Show award Glendale Regional Arts Coun., 1984-85, 1st pl. awards Santa Monica Art Festival, 1982, 83, 84, 85, 86, Sweepstakes award and 1st pl., 1986, Purchase prize awards L.A. West C. of C., 1986-87, Tapestry in Talent Invitational San Jose Arts Coun., 1986, 1st pl. awards Studio City and Century City Arts Couns., 1976-84, 1st award Pacific Palisades Art Affair XII, 1997, Sherman Oaks Fall Arts Festival, 1997. Mem. Nat. Mus. of Women in the Arts. Republican. Home: 6570 Kelvin Ave Canoga Park CA 91306-4021

ROSENFELD, STEPHEN SAMUEL, newspaper editor; b. Pittsfield, Mass., July 26, 1932; s. Jay C. and Elizabeth R.; m. Barbara Bromson, Oct. 28, 1962; children: David, Rebecca, Emmet, James. BA, Harvard U., 1953;; MA, Columbia U., 1959. Reporter Berkshire Eagle, Pittsfield, 1955-57; successively reporter, fgn. corr., editorial writer, columnist, editor editorial page Washington Post, 1959-2000. Co-author: (with Barbara Rosenfeld) Return from Red Square, 1967; author: The Time of Their Dying, 1977. Served to 1st lt. USMC, 1953-55. Mem. Coun. on Fgn. Rels., Alexandria Lit. Soc. Home: 202 S Saint Asaph St Alexandria VA 22314-3744

ROSENFELD, STEVEN B. lawyer; b. N.Y.C., Apr. 12, 1943; s. Eugene David and Laura (Sipin) R.; m. Naomi Eve Winkler, Aug. 21, 1965; children: Kathryn Anne, Elizabeth Jane. BA, Columbia Coll., 1964; LLB, Columbia U., 1967. Bar: N.Y. 1967, D.C. 1984, U.S. Dist. Ct. (so. dist.) N.Y. 1969, U.S. Dist. Ct. (ea. dist.) N.Y. 1970, U.S. Ct. Appeals (2d cir.) 1971, U.S. Ct. Appeals (3d cir.) 1974, U.S. Ct. Appeals (Fed. cir.) 1978, D.C. 1979, U.S. Supreme Ct. 1979, U.S. Ct. Appeals (5th cir.) 1982, U.S. Ct. Appeals (6th and D.C. cirs.) 1984, U.S. Ct. Appeals (4th and 9th cirs.) 1987, U.S. Ct. Appeals (1st cir.) 1989, U.S. Ct. Appeals (10th cir.) 1991. Law clk. to Hon. Charles M. Metzner U.S. Dist. Ct. (so. dist.) N.Y., 1967-68; assoc. Rosenman & Colin, N.Y.C., 1968-71; dep. gen. counsel N.Y. State Commn. on Attica, N.Y.C., Batavia, N.Y., 1971-72; assoc. Paul, Weiss, Rifkind, Wharton & Garrison, N.Y.C., 1972-75, ptnr., 1976—. Lectr. Columbia U. Sch. Law, 1995—; chmn. N.Y.C. Conflict of Interest Bd., 2002—. Contbr. articles to profl. jours. Bd. dirs. N.Y. Assn. New Ams., N.Y.C., 1973-95; trustee Dalton Sch., N.Y.C., 1988-94; trustee Putney Sch. Putney, Vt., 1995-2001, N.Y. Theatre Workshop, 1996—. Mem. N.Y. State Bar Assn. (ho. of dels. 1996-98), Assn. Bar City N.Y. (exec. com. 1992-96, v.p. 1998-99, past mem. various coms.), Legal Aid Soc. (pres. 1989-91, bd. dirs., exec. com. 1978-95). Democrat. Jewish. Avocations: opera and chamber music, theatre, tennis. E-mail: srosenfeld.paulweiss.com. Office: Paul Weiss Rifkind Et Al 1285 Ave of Americas New York NY 10019-6028

ROSENFELD, STEVEN IRA, artistic director, music publisher; b. Bklyn., May 24, 1949; s. Harry Allen and Rosina (DeStefano) R. BA, Southampton Coll., 1971; postgrad., St. Francis Coll., Bklyn., 1975—. V.p. mktg. JVC, Inc., Maspath, N.Y., 1972-74; dir. Yamaha Internat. Corp., Buena Park, Calif., 1974-75; v.p., gen. mgr. Audio Mktg. Cons., Yorktown, N.Y., 1976-88; pres. World Wide Mgmt., 1970—; dir. Parsec Electronics, Wilmington, Del., 1986-88; mng. dir. Westchester Shakespeare Festival, N.Y.C., 1987-90; dir. The Roger Hendricks Simon Studio, 1987—90; v.p. Barnett Labs., Houston, 1992-93; CEO Apple Pie Products, 1996—; pres., CEO The F.C. Sturtevant Co., 1998—; dir. The Neworld Order Recording Co., 1998—, New Canaan Capitol, 1996—, Waterline Filter Corp., 2000—. Editor (newspaper) The Windmill, 1968-69. Mem. Internat. Platform Assn., Audio Engring. Soc. (cert.), Soc. Audio Cons. (cert.), Nat. Trust, Nat. Acad. Rec. Arts and Scis. Jewish.

ROSENFELD, STEVEN IRA, ophthalmologist; b. N.Y.C., Nov. 18, 1954; s. Frederick and Pearl (Stern) R.; m. Lisa Allyson Klar, June 24, 1978; children: Michael, Julie. BA, Johns Hopkins U., 1976; MD, Yale U., 1980. Diplomate Am. Bd. Ophthalmology, Nat. Bd. Med. Examiners. Intern Yale-New Haven Hosp., 1980-81; resident Barnes Hosp., St. Louis, 1981-84; fellow Bascom Palmer Eye Inst., Miami, Fla., 1984-85; ptnr. in pvt. practice Delray Eye Assocs., Delray Beach, 1985—. Clin. instr. Bascom Palmer Eye Inst., 1985-90, asst. clin. prof., 1990-96, assoc. clin. prof., 1996—; assoc. examiner Am. Bd. Ophthalmology, Phila., 1993—. Author: The Eye in Systemic Disease, 1990, Lens and Cataract, 1996; contbr. articles to profl. jours. Recipient Harry Rosenbaum Rsch. award Washington U. Sch. Medicine, 1984; named one of Best Doctors in Am., 1996; Heed Ophthalmic Found. fellow, 1984. Fellow ACS, Am. Acad. Ophthalmology, Soc. Heed Fellows; mem. Castroviejo Corneal Soc., Eye Bank Assn. Am., Fla. Med. Assn., Fla. Soc. Ophthalmology, Assn. for Rsch. in Vision and Ophthalmology, Ocular Microbiology and Immunology Group, Phi Beta Kappa, Alpha Omega Alpha. Avocations: tennis, golf, fly fishing, lacrosse. Office: Delray Eye Assocs 16201 South Military Trail Delray Beach FL 33484-6503

ROSENFELD, WALTER DAVID, JR. architect, writer; b. N.Y.C., May 30, 1930; s. Walter David and Florence (Romann) R.; m. Marilyn Smith, Oct. 15, 1954; children: John W., Sarah E., Susannah, Elizabeth A. AB, U. Pa., 1952; postgrad., Ind. U., 1953-54, Yale U., 1954-55, 57-60. Registered architect, Mass., N.H.; cert. Nat. Coun. Archtl. Registration Bds.; cert. constrn. specifier. Draftsman, specifier Perry Dean Stewart, Boston, 1960-67; architect, specifier, v.p., prin. The Architects Collaborative, Cambridge, Mass., 1967-86, also dir., 1980-84; cons. architect Walter Rosenfeld CSI, Newton, 1986—. Author: The Practical Specifier, 1985; contbg. editor Progressive Architecture mag., 1980-94; contbr. articles to profl. jours. Pres. Friends of Newton Free Libr., Mass., 1970-72; chmn. Newton Ward 1 Dem. Com., 1974-80; vice chmn. designer sel. com. City of Newton, 1976-86; bd. dirs. Mass. Audubon Soc., 1987-99, Mass. Audubon Coun., 01—. Mem. AIA, Constrn. Spcifications Inst. (bd. dirs. Boston chpt. 1980-86, pres. Boston chpt. 1987-88), Boston Soc. Architects. Office: Walter Rosenfeld CSI PO Box 568 Edgartown MA 02539-0568

ROSENFIELD, JAMES HAROLD, communications executive; b. Boston, July 18, 1929; s. Harold and Beatrice (Garber) R.; m. Nancy Lee Stenbuck, Oct. 19, 1952; 2 children. BA, Dartmouth Coll., 1952; D of Comml. Sci. (hon.), St. John's U., 1981. TV network sales exec. NBC, N.Y.C., 1954-57; advt. mgr. Polaroid Corp., Boston, 1956-59; v.p. mktg. Airequipt, Inc., New Rochelle, N.Y., 1959-65; TV account exec. CBS, Inc., N.Y.C., 1965-67, dir. daytime sales, 1967-70, v.p. Ea. sales, 1970-75, v.p. network sales adminstrn., 1975-77, v.p., nat. sales mgr., 1977, pres. TV Network Div., 1977-81; exec. v.p. CBS/Broadcast Group, 1981-83, sr. exec. v.p., 1983-85; chmn., CEO John Blair Communications, Inc., 1987-93; pres. JHR Assocs., Consulting, 1993; mng. dir. Veronis, Suhler & Assocs., 1994-98; pres. JHR & Assocs., 1998—. Bd. dirs. Salon Interactive, Inc., Knit Media, Hotelevision, Global Vision-New Media, Columbia U. Sch. Pub. Health; mem. adv. bd. Pathfire, Inc., AdEact, Inc., Patriot Networks, Inc., EyeWonder, Inc. Mem. nat. bd. dirs. Jr. Achievement, Inc.; past alumni trustee Roxbury (Mass.) Latin Sch.; bd. dirs., former chmn. Adv. Coun. With Signal Corps, AUS, 1950-53. Mem. NATAS (bd. internat. coun.), Internat. Radio TV Soc. (past pres.).

ROSENFIELD, KENNETH, cardiovascular surgeon; b. Boston, Oct. 5, 1955; m. Janet M. Rosenfield; children: Cory Joseph, Hannah Rose, Emma Louise. BA, Dartmouth Coll., 1978; MD, U. Mass., 1982. Diplomate Am. Bd. Internal Medicine with subspecialty in cardiovascular surgery. Cardiovascular interventionist St. Elizabeth's Med. Ctr., Brighton, Mass. Cons., mem. adv. bd. various multiple device and pharm. cos. Office: Mass Gen Hosp Cardiology Divsn 55 Fruit St Bulfinch 105 Boston MA 02114

ROSENFIELD, M(ANUEL) C(HARLES), retired history educator, retired coastguard officer; b. Boston, Aug. 23, 1931; s. James Charles and Lillian Francis (Obelsky); m. Dora Rose Empson, Dec. 2, 1961; 1 child, Sarah Elizabeth. BA, Boston U., 1951, MA, 1957; PhD, U. London, 1961. Prof. history S.E. Mass. U. (name changed to the U. Mass.), Dartmouth, 1965-96. Contbr. articles to profl. jours. Rsch. fellow Inst. Hist. Rsch., London, 1961, Mus. of London, 1960; tchg. fellow Boston U., 1957. Fellow Royal Hist. Soc. U.K. (assoc.); mem. Hist. Assn. U.K., Am. Hist. Assn., London and Middlesex Archl. Soc., Bostonian Soc., Boston Athaeneaum. Home: PO Box 395 8 Marion Rd Mattapoisett MA 02739-0395 E-mail: mcri.ma.ultranet@rcn.com.

ROSENFIELD, ROBERT LEE, pediatric endocrinologist, educator; b. Robinson, Ill., Dec. 16, 1934; s. Irving and Sadie (Ospide) R.; m. Sandra L. McVicker, Apr. 14, 1973. BS, Northwestern U., 1956; MD, 1960. Diplomate Am. Bd. Pediat. Endocrinology. Intern Phila. Gen. Hosp. and Children's Hosp., Phila., 1960-63, 65-68; practice specializing in pediat. endocrinology; prof. pediats., medicine U. Chgo., 1968—. Vis. prof. U. Dundee, 1986-87. Contbr. articles to profl. jours. Capt. USMC, 1963-65. Fogarty Sr. Internat. fellow, USPHS, Weizmann Inst., Israel, 1977-78. Mem. Am. Bd. Pediat. (sub.-bd. pediatric endocrinology 1983-86), Am. Pediat. Soc., Lawson Wilkins Pediatric Endocrinology Soc., Endocrine Soc., Soc. Gynecol. Investigation, Soc. Dermatol. Investigation, Chgo. Pediat. Soc. (pres. 1981). Democrat. Jewish. Avocation: photography. Home: 1700 E 56th St Apt 3502 Chicago IL 60637-5099 Office: U Chgo Med Ctr 5841 S Maryland Ave Chicago IL 60637-1463

ROSENGART, TODD KENNETH, cardiothoracic surgeon, researcher; b. Bklyn., Jan. 24, 1960; s. Martin Rosengart and Barbara Kodish; m. Debra Helen Rosengart, June 15, 1989; children: Michael, Eric. BS with distinction, Northwestern U., Evanston, Ill., 1981; MD with distinction, Northwestern U., Chgo., 1983. Diplomate Am. Bd. Surgery, Am. Bd. Thoracic Surgery. Intern in gen. surgery NYU Med. Ctr., N.Y.C., 1983-84, resident in gen. surgery, 1984-85, resident and chief resident in gen. surgery, 1987-89; med. staff fellow NIH, Bethesda, Md., 1985-87; asst. thoracic surgeon N.Y. Hosp., 1989-90, thoracic surgeon, 1990-91; instr. Cornell U. Med. Coll., N.Y.C., 1989-90, asst. prof. surgery, 1991-93, asst. prof. cardiothoracic surgery, 1993-97, assoc. prof. cardiothoracic surgeery, 1997—; assoc. prof. cardiothoracic surgery Weill Med. Coll. Cornell U., 1998—; assoc. attending cardiothoracic surgeon N.Y. Presbyn. Hosp., 1997-99; chief cardiothoracic surg. Evanston (Ill.) Hosp., 1999—; assoc. prof. surgery Northwestern U. Med. Sch., 1999—. Sr. registrar Hosp. for Sick Children, London, 1991; asst. Harley St. Clinic, London, 1991; tchg. asst. NYU Med. Ctr., 1988-89; asst. attending surgeon Jamaica Hosp., 1993-96; United Hosp. Med. Ctr., 1994—; attending physician N.Y. Hosp. Med. Ctr. of Queens, 1995—; mem. Ctr. for Vascular Biology, 1996—; assoc. attending cardiothoracic surgeon N.Y. Hosp., 1997, N.Y. Presbyn. Hosp., 1998—; vis. assoc. prof. surgery Columbia U., 1997—; vis. assoc. attending surgeon Presbyn. Hosp., 1997—; manuscript reviewer, presenter, cons. in field. Editl. bd. Cardiac and Vascular Regeneration: Angiogenesis and Myogenesis, Basic th Therapeutic, 1999—; contbr. numerous articles to profl. publs., chpts. to books; patentee gene transfer therapy delivery devide and method, perfusion and occlusion device and method. Nat. Merit scholar, 1977; recipient rsch. award A.G. Morrow Soc., 1987, 97; grantee miles Labs., 1992—, N.Y. Heart Assn., 1994-97, Datascope Corp., 1995—, AccuLase, Inc., 1995—, St. Jude Med., 1996—, Picower Found., 1996—, U.S. Surg. Corp., 1996—, Thoracic Surgery Found. Rsch. and Edn. 1997-99, OrthoBiotech, 1997—, Baxter Healthcare Corp., 1998—, NIH, 1998—. Fellow ACS, Am. Coll. Cardiology, Am. Coll. Chest Physicians; mem. AAAS, Am. Fedn. Clin. Rsch., Am. Heart Assn. (sci. coun. on cardiothoracic and vascular surgery), Nat. Assn. for Bloodless Medicine and Surgery (bd. dirs. 1997—), Andrew Morrow Soc. Cardiac Surgeons, N.Y. Soc. Thoracic Surgery (membership com. 1994-97, chmn. membership com. 1998—, program com. 1994—, chmn. program com. 1997—), Soc. Thoracic Surgeons, Soc. Univ. Surgeons, N.Y. Acad. Scis., 21st Century Cardiac Surg. Soc. (pres., membership chmn. 1995-96, v.p. 1996-98), Spencer Soc. Surgeons, Alpha Omega Alpha, Phi Rho Sigma. Office: Evanston Northwestern Healthcare 2650 Ridge Ave Burch 100 Evanston IL 60201

ROSENGREN, PAUL GREGORY, lawyer; b. Oakland, Calif., Apr. 3, 1952; s. Jack Whitehead and Patricia Jean (Dorking) R.; m. Nikki Christine Ballard, Aug. 21, 1976. AB, Princeton U., 1974; MBA, JD, U. Calif., Berkeley, 1977. Bar: Calif. 1978, D.C. 1978, U.S. Ct. Appeals (5th cir.) 1979. Assoc. Covington & Burling, Washington, 1978; law clk. to justice U.S. Ct. Appeals (5th cir.), New Orleans and Baton Rouge, La., 1978-79; assoc. Gibson, Dunn & Crutcher, Washington, 1979-85; assoc. gen. counsel Fannie Mae, 1985-88, v.p., dep. gen. counsel, 1988-2000; gen. counsel, corp. sec. ARMILLAIRE Techs., Inc., Bethesda, 2000—. Note and comment editor U. Calif. Law Rev., 1975-77. Mem. Huntington Met. Area Task Force, Fairfax County, Va., 1984-85; bd. dirs., pres. Heritage Hill Townhouses Assn., Alexandria, Va., 1980-82. Mem. ABA, D.C. Bar Assn., Calif. Bar Assn., Washington Met. Area Corp. Counsel Assn., Am. Corp. Counsel Assn. Avocations: theatre, travel, tennis, reading. Office: 10411 Motor City Dr 4th Fl Bethesda MD 20817

ROSENHEIM, DONALD EDWIN, electrical engineer; b. N.Y.C., Mar. 23, 1926; s. Seymour Lawrence and Leah Rebecca (Rosenberg) R.; m. Judith Comfort Hyman, June 22, 1958; children— Micah Robert, Jay Aaron. BSEE magna cum laude, Poly. Inst. Bklyn., 1949; MS, Columbia U., 1957. Devel. engr. Servo Corp. Am., 1949-51; mem. rsch. staff IBM ., 1951—, asst. dir. rsch. divsn., 1972-73. Dir. San Jose (Calif.) Rsch. Lab., 1973-83, dir. tech. coordination, 1983-84; asst. dir. Almaden Rsch. Ctr., San Jose, 1984-92 Fellow IEEE; mem. Sigma Xi, Tau Beta Pi, Eta Kappa Nu. Home: 128 Smith Creek Dr Los Gatos CA 95030-2139 E-mail: jdrosenheim@msn.com.

ROSENHEIM, EDWARD WEIL, English educator; b. Chgo., May 15, 1918; s. Edward Weil and Fannie (Kohn) R.; m. Margaret Morton Keeney, June 20, 1947; children: Daniel Edward, James Morton, Andrew Keeney. BA, U. Chgo., 1939, MA, 1946, PhD, 1953. Publicity writer Pub. Relations Service, Chgo., 1939-40; instr. Gary (Ind.) Coll., 1946; faculty U. Chgo., 1947—, prof. English, 1962—, David B. and Clara E. Stern prof., 1980-88, prof. emeritus, 1988—, assoc. chmn. dept. English, 1967-75, dir. broadcasting for univ., 1954-57; dir. Nat. Humanities Inst., 1977-80. Disting. vis. prof. Pa. State U., 1961; Disting. lectr. Nat. Coun. Tchrs. English, 1967; mem. Ill. Humanities Coun., 1982—, pres., 1985-87. Author: What Happens in Literature, 1960, Swift and the Satirist's Art, 1963; editor: Selected Prose and Poetry of Jonathan Swift, 1958, Jour. Gen. Edn., 1954-56; co-editor: Modern Philology, 1968-88. Served to capt. inf. AUS, 1941-46. Recipient Alumni Svc. medal U. Chgo., 1990; Willet Faculty fellow, 1962, Guggenheim Meml. fellow, 1967. Mem. Am. Soc. 18th Century Studies, Johnson Soc. (pres. Central region 1971) Clubs: Quadrangle, Wayfarers, Caxton. Home: 5805 S Dorchester Ave Chicago IL 60637-1730 Office: 1050 E 59th St Chicago IL 60637-1559

ROSENHEIM, MARGARET KEENEY, social welfare policy educator; b. Grand Rapids, Mich., Sept. 5, 1926; d. Morton and Nancy (Billings) Keeney; m. Edward W. Rosenheim, June 20, 1947; children: Daniel, James, Andrew. Student, Wellesley Coll., 1943-45; JD, U. Chgo., 1949. Bar: Ill. 1949. Mem. faculty Sch. Social Service Adminstrn., U. Chgo., 1950—, assoc. prof., 1961-66, prof., 1966—, Helen Ross prof. social welfare policy, 1975-96, dean, 1978-83; lectr. in law U. Chgo., 1980-97. Vis. prof. U. Wash., 1965, Duke U., 1984; Helen Ross prof. emerita U. Chgo., 1996—; acad. visitor London Sch. Econs., 1973; cons. Pres.'s Commn. Law Enforcement and Adminstrn. Justice, 1966-67, Nat. Adv. Commn. Criminal Justice Stds. and Goals, 1972; mem. Juvenile Justice Stds. Commn., 1973-78; trustee Carnegie Corp. N.Y., 1979-87; trustee Children's Home and Aid Soc. of Ill., 1981—, chair, 1996-98; chair CHASI Sys. Inc., 1998-2001; dir. Nat. Inst. Dispute Resolution, 1981-89, Nuveen Bond Funds, 1982-97; mem. Chgo. Network, 1983—. Editor: Justice for the Child, 1962; contbr. ; editor: Pursuing Justice for the Child, 1976; editor: (with F.E. Zimring, D.S. Tanenhaus, B. Dohrn) A Century of Juvenile Justice, 2002; editor: (with Mark Testa) Early Parenthood and Coming of Age in the 1990s, 1992; contbr. articles to profl. jours. Home: 5805 S Dorchester Ave Chicago IL 60637-1730 Office: 969 E 60th St Chicago IL 60637-2677 E-mail: mrosenhe@midway.uchicago.edu.

ROSENHOUSE, HOWARD, retired lawyer; b. Bklyn., Oct. 15, 1939; s. Barnet and Sonia Rosenhouse. BA, Bklyn. Coll., 1960, MA, 1969; JD, Bklyn. Law Sch., 1963, LLM, 1965; MS, Pace U., 1975. Bar: N.Y. 1963, N.J. 1985, U.S. Dist. Ct. (so. and ea. dists.) N.Y. 1985, U.S. Dist. Ct. N.J. 1985, U.S. Supreme Ct. 1980. Tchr. social studies, guidance counselor, acting asst. prin. N.Y.C. Bd. Edn., 1963-79, counsel to bd. examiners, 1979-90, atty. at bd. edn., 1991-94. Pres. The Shores Homeowners Assn., Boca Raton, Fla. Mem. N.Y. State Bar Assn., Bklyn. Law Sch. Alumni Assn. Jewish.

ROSENHOUSE, IRWIN J. artist, designer; b. Chgo. B.F.A., Cooper Union, N.Y.C., 1950. Designer Mus. Modern Art, 1954-57, Harcourt, Brace & Co., 1957, Dell Books, 1963; tchr. art Mus. Modern Art, 1967-69, Pratt Graphic Center, N.Y.C., 1972, 85, Bklyn. Coll., 1972-73, Bklyn. Mus. Art Sch., 1974, Nassau C.C., 1972-99, N.Y. Tech. Coll., 1983-86; owner Rosenhouse Gallery, N.Y.C., 1963-72. Lectr. art, book illustration, design; preparer graphics for Arab-Israeli peace confs.: The Road to Peace, Convocation for Peace, N.Y.C., 1989-90; dir. monthly ednl. lecture series N.Y. Artist Equity, 1989-91; adj. prof. Nassau C.C., 1972-78. One-man shows N.Y.C., Bklyn., Easthampton, N.Y., Dance Theater Workshop Art Gallery, N.Y.C., 1992, also various colls. and mus. in U.S.; exhibited in group shows numerous mus., painting socs. exhbns. throughout U.S.; represented in permanent collections Met. Mus., N.Y. Pub. Libr., Everhart Mus., Cooper Union Mus., Bklyn. Coll. Collection; illustrator: (juvenile) Have You Seen Trees?, The Rabbis Bible, What Kind of Feet Does a Bear Have?. Served with U.S. Mcht. Marine, 1944-51. Recipient Louis Comfort Tiffany Found. award, 2 Huntington Hartford Found. awards, Billboard Ann. award, Illustrators Club award, 1st prize Rome Collaborative; record cover designs included in Smithsonian ethnic music collection. Address: c/o Sarfaty 54 Everit Ave Hewlett NY 11557 *Humanist imagery has been my main concern and the pursuit of a simple, direct image of nature.*

ROSENHOUSE, MICHAEL ALLAN, lawyer, editorial consultant; b. Chgo., Nov. 8, 1946; s. Seymour Samuel and Jeanne Mozette (Rosenthal) R. BA, Yale U., 1968; JD, U. Chgo., 1974. Bar: Ill. 1974, N.Y. 1982. Atty. in pvt. practice, Rochester, N.Y. Mng. editor: Am. Jurisprudence, 2d edit., 1991—93, mng. editor: Am. Law Reports (Fed.), 1991—93; editor: (newsletter) Bank Employment Law Report , 1998—99; author: Employment Law (Syracuse Law Rev.), 1998; columnist: The Daily Record, 2001—. Mem.: N.Y. State Bar Assn., Monroe County Bar Assn. (co-chair Disability Labor and Employment Law Commn. 1998—99), U. Chgo. Club of Rochester (bd. dirs. 1999—2001), Yale Alumni Assn. (schs. com. 1997—), U. Chgo. Law Sch. Alumni Assn. (bd. dirs. 1977—80). Avocation: squash, tennis, golf. Office: 70 Linden Oaks Rochester NY 14625 E-mail: mike@rosenhouse.com.

ROSENKER, MARK VICTOR, trade association executive; b. Balt., Dec. 8, 1946; s. Stanley and Irene (Moss) R.; m. Heather Beldon. BA in Communications, U. Md., 1969, postgrad., 1970-71; grad., USAF Air Command and Staff Coll., 1986, USAF Air War Coll., 1990. Asst. to events producer, relief engr. ABC-TV News, Washington, 1968-69; dep. dir. radio and TV Com. Reelect Pres., 1972; staff asst. to sec. U.S. Dept. Interior, 1972-73; account exec. Daniel Edelman Pub. Relations, Inc., 1973-75; dir. communications Motorized Bicycle Assn., 1975; dep. press sec. Pres. Ford Com., 1976; v.p. Electronic Industries Alliance, 1977—; asst. exec. dir. for external affairs UN for Organ Sharing, 1999—. Bd. of vis. Cmty. Coll. USAF, Maxwell, Ala., 1981-86; apptd. commr. Am. Battle Monument Commn., 1990-94. Active Campaign to Elect Reagan/Bush, Washington, 1980, 84, Campaign to Elect Bush/Quayle, 1988, 92—; sr. advisor Dole/Kemp Campaign, 1995-96. 1st lt. USAF, 1969-72, brig. gen. USAFR, 1972—. Recipient Chuck Docekal Meml. award, 1987, Am. Battle Monuments Commn. Meritious Svc. award, 1994. Mem. Am. Soc. Assn. Execs., Greater Washington Soc. Assn. Execs., Res. Officers Assn. Club, Capitol Hill Club, Army Navy Club. Avocations: sailing, tennis, skiing, golf. Home: 1626 Great Falls St Mc Lean VA 22101-5079 Office: United Network for Organ Sharing 1800 K St NW Washington DC 20006-2202

ROSENKILDE, CARL EDWARD, physicist; b. Yakima, Wash., Mar. 16, 1937; s. Elmer Edward and Doris Edith R.; m. Bernadine Doris Blumenstine, June 22, 1963 (div. Apr. 1991); children: Karen Louise, Paul Eric; m. Wendy Maureen Ellison, May 24, 1992. BS in Physics, Wash. State Coll., 1959; MS in Physics, U. Chgo., 1960, PhD in Physics, 1966. Fellow Argonne (Ill.) Nat. Lab., 1966-68; asst. prof. math. NYU, 1968-70; asst. prof. physics Kans. State U., Manhattan, 1970-76, assoc. prof., 1976-79; physicist Lawrence Livermore (Calif.) Nat. Lab., 1979-93, lab. assoc., 1994-95, participating guest, 1995-97, cons., 1974-79; chief scientist C.R. Sci., 1993-98. Astronomy instr. Los Positas Coll., 1997; part-time instr. physics Bellarmine Coll. Prep., 1999-2000; full-time instr., 2000—. Contbr. articles to profl. jours. Woodrow Wilson fellow, 1959-60. Mem. Am. Phys. Soc., Am. Assn. Physics Tchrs., Calif. Math. Coun. C.C., Am. Astron. Soc., Soc. for Indsl. and Applied Math., Am. Geophys. Union, Accoustical Soc. Am., Math. Assn., Am., Tubists Universal Brotherhood Assn., Phi Beta Kappa, Phi Kappa Phi, Phi Eta Sigma, Sigma Xi. Republican. Presbyterian. Achievements include rsch. in nonlinear wave propagation in complex media, theoretical physics, fluid dynamics. E-mail: crosenkilde@bcp.org.

ROSENKOETTER, GERALD EDWIN, engineering and construction company executive; b. St. Louis, Mar. 16, 1927; s. Herbert Charles and Edna Mary (Englege) R.; m. Ruth June Beekman, Sept. 10, 1949; children: Claudia Ruth, Carole Lee. BSCE, Washington U., St. Louis, 1951; MSCE, Sever Inst. Tech., St. Louis, 1957. Registered profl. engr. Colo., Del., D.C., Fla., Ga., Idaho, Kans., Mass., Mich., Mo., N.C., N.J., Ohio, Pa., Tex., Utah, Wis., Ind. Sr. structural engr. Sverdrup & Parcel, Inc., St. Louis, 1951-56, project engr., 1956-60, engrng. mgr. Denver, 1960-62; project mgr. Sverdrup & Parcel & Assocs., St. Louis, 1962-69, chief engr., 1969-74, v.p., 1974-80; pres., CEO SPCM, Inc., 1980-85; exec. v.p. Sverdrup Corp., 1985-88, vice-chmn., 1988-93; pres., CEO Sverdrup Hydro, Inc., 1988-93; engr. and fin. cons. Sarasota, 1993—. Assoc. prof. Washington U., 1955-60; ptnr. 3 Sverdrup Partnerships, 1977-93; expert witness Sverdrup & Parcel & Assocs., 1970-75; cons. engrng. and constrn. projects, 1993—; bd. dirs. 17 corps. Councilman City of Berkeley, Mo., 1956-58, councilman-at-large, 1958-60, chmn. city planning and zoning com., 1963-65; dir. Conservatory and Sch. Arts, St. Louis, 1989-92. Sgt. U.S. Army, 1945-46. Engrs. Club of St. Louis scholar, 1950. Mem. ASCE (chmn. continuing edn. 1965-66, named Outstanding Sr. Engrng. Student 1951), Bent Tree Country Club (Sarasota, Fla.). Lutheran. Avocations: golfing, travel. Address: 4368 Brandywine Dr Sarasota FL 34241-6107

ROSENKRANTZ, DANIEL J. computer science educator; b. Bklyn., Mar. 5, 1943; s. Harry and Ruth (Sirota) R.; m. Carole Jaffee, Aug. 2, 1969; children: Holly, Sherry, Jody, Andrew. BS, Columbia U., 1963, MS, 1964, PhD, 1967. With Bell Telephone Labs., Murray Hill, N.J., 1966-67; info. scientist GE Co. R & D Ctr., Schenectady, N.Y., 1967-77; prof. dept. computer sci. U. Albany-SUNY, 1977—, dept. chair, 1993-99; prin. computer scientist Phoenix Data Systems, Albany, 1983-85. Author: (with P.M. Lewis II and R.E. Stearns) Compiler Design Theory, 1976. Fellow ACM (editor-in-chief jour. 1986-91, area editor for formal langs. and models of computation 1981-86, mem. numerous conf. coms., Sigmod Contbns. award 2001); mem. IEEE Computer Soc., ACM Spl. Interest Group on Automata and Computability Theory (sec. 1977-79). Home: 1261 Cranbrook Ct Niskayuna NY 12309-1203 Office: U at Albany SUNY Dept Computer Sci Albany NY 12222-0001 E-mail: djr@cs.albany.edu.

ROSENKRANTZ, LINDA, writer; b. N.Y.C., May 26, 1934; d. Samuel H. and Frances (Sillman) R.; m. Christopher Finch, Feb. 2, 1973; 1 child, Chloe. BA, U. Mich., 1955. Founding editor Auction Mag., N.Y.C., 1967-72; columnist Copley News Svc., San Diego, 1986--. Author: Talk, 1968; co-author: Gone Hollywood, 1979, SoHo, 1981, Beyond Jennifer and Jason, 1988, Beyond Charles and Diana, 1992, Beyond Shannon and Sean, 1992, Beyond Sarah and Sam, 1992, The Last Word on First Names, 1995, Sotheby's Guide to Collecting Animation Art, 1998, My Life as a List: 207 Things About My (Bronx) Childhood, 1999, Beyond Jennifer and Jason, Madison and Montana, 1999, Baby Names Now, 2001.

ROSENKRANTZ, STEVEN JAY, lawyer; b. N.Y.C., Feb. 4, 1965; s. Michael and Rhona Sue (Dasheff) R. BA, Rutgers Coll., 1987; JD, Rutgers U. Sch. Law, 1991. Bar: Pa. 1994, D.C., 1996. Rsch. assoc. Fedn. Am. Scientists, Washington, 1993-94; rsch. asst. U.S. Dept. Justice, 1994-95; fgn. affairs specialist U.S. Arms Control & Disarmament Agy., 1995-99; spl. asst. office of undersec. state arms control U.S. Dept. State, 1998-2001, fgn. affairs officer Bur. Arms Ctrl., 2001—. Mem. Mid. East Inst., Phi Beta Kappa. Avocations: history, classical music, fencing, reading. Home: 1401 Blair Mill Rd Apt 1811 Silver Spring MD 20910-4875 Office: US Dept State Bur Arms Control Office Strat & Theater Def Washington DC 20520 Office Fax: 202-736-4082. E-mail: rosenkrantzsj@t.state.gov.

ROSENKRANZ, LINDA, English educator; b. Bryan, Tex., Jan. 25, 1943; d. Fred Louis and Laura Imogene (Gandy) Rosenkranz; children: Richard Mark Geppert, Nathan Jay Geppert, Gary Patrick Geppert. BA in English, Sam Houston State U., Huntsville, Tex., 1964; MA, U. St. Thomas, Houston, 1991. Coach girls' tennis and basketball Dickinson (Tex.) Ind. Sch. Dist., 1964-66; athletic dir. girls' sports Dickinson H.S., 1964-66; tchr. asst. Sam Houston State U., Huntsville, 1962-63; camp asst. dir. UN/UNESCO, Paris; resident tchr. Brit. prep sch.; faculty English Houston C.C. Sys., 1988—; instr. English S.W. Coll., Houston C.C., 1988—. Contbr. articles and poetry to profl. jours. Dir. Galveston County Head Start, Dickinson, 1966; dir. civic affairs Pleasant Run Farm Civic Assn., Cin., 1973-76; mem. Ashford Hills Civic Assn., Houston, 1993—. Recipient Outstanding Tchr. of the Yr. award Dickinson Ind. Sch. Dist., 1965, Outstanding Young Educator award Texas City Ind. Sch. Dist., 1966, Faculty Assn. Outstanding Tchr. award Houston C.C. Sys., 1998, numerous writing awards; Jesse Jones scholar, 1961. Mem. MLA, Two Yr. C.C. Assn. Avocations: gardening, writing, socio-political issues, literature, current events. Office: SW College/Houston CC Sys 10141 Cash Rd Stafford TX 77477 E-mail: rosenkranz_l@hccs.cc.tx.us.

ROSENKRANZ, ROBERT BERNARD, military officer; b. Paterson, N.J., Sept. 26, 1939; s. Irving Morton and Lucille (Kane) R.; m. Barbara Jean Larson, May 17, 1970; children: Stephen Robert, Deborah Anne, Diana Rebecca, Susan Leslie. BS, U.S. Mil. Acad., 1961; MA, U. Pa., 1969. Comd. 2d. lt. U.S. Army, 1961, advanced through grades to maj. gen., 1992, officer Fed. Republic of Germany, 1962-65, battalion exec. officer Korea, 1973-74, battery comdr. Vietnam, 1966-67, battalion and brigade comdr. Germany, 1977-79, 83-85; assoc. prof. U.S. Mil. Acad., West Point, N.Y., 1969-72; dir. soviet studies U.S. Army War Coll., Carlisle, Pa., 1981-83; sr. mil. asst. under sec. of def. Pentagon, Washington, 1986-88; dep. dir. Army Ops., Readiness and Mobilization U.S. Army Pentagon, 1988-89, dir. force programs, 1989-92; comdr. U.S. Army Optec, 1992-95; sr. v.p. range and logistics svcs. Dyncorp, Reston, Va., 1995-2001; v.p. force mgmt. and logistics MPRI, Alexandria, 2001—. Decorated Bronze Star, Air medal; recipient Superior Svc. medal U.S. Dept. Def., 1988, D.S.M., 1992, 95. Mem.: Nat. Def. Indsl. Assn., Internat. Test and Evaluation Assn., Assn. of the U.S. Army, Internat. Inst. Strategic Studies. Republican. Jewish. Avocations: jogging, reading, woodworking, golf, racquetball. Home: 3222 Wynford Dr Fairfax VA 22031-2828 E-mail: rrosenkranz@MPRI.com., rrosen007@aol.com.

ROSENKRANZ, STANLEY WILLIAM, lawyer; b. N.Y.C., Aug. 20, 1933; s. Jacob and Adele R.; m. Judith Ossinsky, Aug. 14, 1960; children: Jack Michael, Andrew Lawrence. BS in Acctg. U. Fla., 1955, JD with honors, 1960; LLM (Kenneson fellow), NYU, 1961. Bar: Fla. 1960, Ga. 1970, cert.: (tax lawyer). Mem. firm Macfarlane, Ferguson, Allison & Kelly, Tampa, Fla., 1961-68, 71-79; with King & Spalding, Atlanta, 1969-71, Holland & Knight, Tampa, 1979-86, Shear, Newman, Rosenkranz, Burton & Lamb, Tampa, 1986-2000, Ruden McClosky Smith Schuster & Russell, Tampa, 2000—. Adj. prof. Grad. Sch. Law, U. Fla., 1975-79, Grad. Coll. Bus. Adminstrn., U. Tampa, 1989, 97-99, Stetson U. Coll. Law. Pres. Congregation Schaarai Zedek, Tampa, 1981-83; bd. dirs. Union Am. Hebrew Congregations, 1990—, v.p. S.E. region, 1988-90, pres., 1992-96. With U.S. Army, 1955-57. Named Young Man of Year Tampa Jaycees, Fla., 1967 Mem. ABA, Am. Coll. Tax Counsel, Am. Law Inst., Fla. Bar Assn., Ga. Bar Assn., Greater Tampa C. of C. (bd. govs., chmn. anti-drug task force). Home: 1125 Shipwatch Cir Tampa FL 33602-5785 Office: 401 E Jackson St Fl 27 Tampa FL 33602-5233 E-mail: swr@ruden.com.

ROSENMAN, KENNETH D. medical educator; b. N.Y.C., Feb. 25, 1951; AB, Cornell U., 1972; MD, NY Med. Coll., 1975. Bd. cert. internal medicine; bd. cert. occupational and preventive medicine. Asst. prof. U. Mass., Amherst, 1979-81; dir. occupational and environ. health N.J. Dept. Health, Trenton, 1981-86; pvt. practice Plainsboro, N.J., 1986-88; assoc. prof. Mich. State U., East Lansing, 1988-93, prof., 1993—. Office: Mich State U 117 W Fee Hall East Lansing MI 48824-1316

ROSENMAN, ROBERT EDWARD, ceonomist, educator, researcher; b. Bklyn., Dec. 21, 1953; s. Lawrence and Harriet Rosenman; m. Pamela Ann Spahn, May 24, 1981; children: Emily, Jeremy. BA in Econs. and Polit. Sci., U. Pa., 1975, MA in Econs., 1977; PhD in Econs., U. Minn., 1982. Asst. prof. econs. U. N.H., Durham, 1982-83; prof. econs. Wash. State U., Pullman, 1983—, grad. program dir. dept. econs., 1994—. Contbr. articles to profl. jours. Commr. Pullman Meml. Hosp., 1992-99; mem. Gov.'s Oversight Subcom. for HRSA NIV/AIDS Rural Planning Grant, Seattle, 1990-91. Recipient citation of excellence for rsch. implications ANBAR, 1998. Mem. Am. Econ. Assn. Office: Wash State U Dept Econs Pullman WA 99164-4741 Office Fax: (509) 335-4362. E-mail: yamaka@wsu.edu.

ROSENMAN, STEPHEN DAVID, obstetrician and gynecologist; b. Bklyn., Sept. 4, 1945; s. Bernard and Theresa (Marks) R. m. Arlette de Greef, Dec. 26m 1970; children: Burt, Joelle. BA in Biology, Hofstra U., 1967; MD magna cum laude, Cath. U. of Louvain (Belgium), 1972. Diplomate Am. Bd. Ob-Gyn., voluntarily re-cert. 1991; lic. N.Y., Conn. Rotating intern Dalhousie U., Canada, 1972-73; ob-gyn. resident Bridgeport (Conn.) Hosp., 1973-75, chief resident, 1976-77, sr. attending physician ob-gyn., 1977—; pvt. practice Fairfield, Stratford, Trumbull, Conn., 1977-2000; chief gynecology, dir. residency program Bridgeport Hosp., 2000—; instr. ob-gyn. Yale U. Sch. Medicine. Named Tchr. of Yr., Bridgeport (Conn.) Hosp. 1977, 78, 80; featured in Conn. Mag. Fellow Am. Bd. Obstetrics, Am. Coll. Ob.-Gyn. Avocations: computer, reading. Office: Bridgeport Hosp 267 Grant St Bridgeport CT 06110

ROSENMANN, DANIEL, physicist, educator; b. Lima, Peru, Sept. 6, 1959; came to U.S., 1991; s. Lothar and Eva (Roiter) R.; m. Patricia Edith Alvarado, Jan. 21, 1989. BS in Physics, U. Nac. Mayor de San Marcos, Lima, Peru, 1986; postgrad., No. Ill. U., 1991-93. Instr. U. Nacional Mayor de San Marcos, Lima, 1982-91; tchr. Coll. Leon Pinelo, 1986-91; teaching asst. No. Ill. U., DeKalb, 1991-93, grad. rsch. asst., 1993; lab. grad. participantship Argonne (Ill.) Nat. Lab., 1993-96; rsch. lab. mgr. physics dept. No. Ill. U., DeKalb, 1994-96; sci. assoc. Argonne Nat. Lab., 1996—. Author: Lab. guide book, 1988, 89. Scholar, fellow Argonne Nat. Lab. 1993-96. Mem. AAAS, Am. Phys. Soc., N.Y. Acad. Scis., Nat. Geographic Soc., Sigma Xi, Sigma Pi Sigma. Home: 2512 Bordeaux Dr Apt 204 Naperville IL 60540-1830

ROSENN, BARAK M. physician; b. Jerusalem, Israel, Aug. 18, 1951; came to U.S., 1989; s. Joseph A. and Miriam A. Rosenn; m. Shulamit Rosenn. MD, Hebrew U. Hadassah, Jerusalem, 1983. Diplomate Am. Bd. Ob-Gyn. Resident in ob-gyn. Hadassah Med. Ctr., Jerusalem, 1983-89; fellow in maternal-fetal medicine U. Cin., 1989-91, asst. prof. ob-gyn., 1991-96, assoc. prof. ob-gyn., 1996—; dir. obstetrics maternal-fetal medicine St. Luke's Roosevelt Hosp. Ctr., N.Y.C., 2000—; assoc. prof. ob-gyn. Columbia U. Coll. Physicians and Surgeons, 2001—. Dir. perinatal svcs. The Christ Hosp., Cin., 1997—; dir. women's health svcs. dept. ob-gyn. U. Cin., 1991-96; mem. founding and organizing com. Diabetes in Pregnancy Study Group of N.Am., Cin., 1998—. Author 3 book chpts.; contbr. more than 35 articles to profl. jours. Maj. Israel Def. Forces, 1969-75. Mem. Soc. Gyn. Investigation, Soc. Maternal-Fetal Medicine, Nat. Perinatal Assn. (grantee 1989-93, Best Presentation award 1996), Am. Diabetes Assn., Soc. Perinatal Rsch. Office: St Luke's Roosevelt Hosp Ctr Dept Ob-Gyn 1000 10th Ave Ste 10-C New York NY 10019

ROSENN, HAROLD, lawyer; b. Plains, Pa., Nov. 4, 1917; s. Joseph and Jennie (Wohl) R.; m. Sallyanne Frank, Sept. 19, 1948; 1 child, Frank Scott. BA, U. Mich., 1939, JD, 1941; LLD, Coll. Misericordia, 1991. Bar: Pa. 1942, U.S. Supreme Ct. 1957. Ptnr. Rosenn & Rosenn, Wilkes Barre, Pa., 1948-54, Rosenn, Jenkins & Greenwald, Wilkes Barre, 1954-87, of counsel, 1988—. Mem. Pa. State Bd. Law Examiners, 1983-93, Pa. Gov.'s Justice Commn., 1968-73, Pa. Crime Commn., 1968-73, Fed. Jud. Nominating Com., Pa., 1977-79, Appellate Ct. Nominating Com., Pa., 1979-81; asst. dist. atty. Luzerne County, Pa., 1952-54. Chmn. United Jewish Appeal Campaign of Wyoming Valley, 1956, 84, ARC, Wilkes-Barre, 1958-60, life mem. bd.; pres. Pa. Coun. on Crime and Delinquency, Harrisburg, 1969-71; bd. dirs. Coll. Misericordia, Dallas, Pa., 1976-86, emeritus, 1986—, Hoyt Libr., Kingston, Pa., 1971-78, Nat. Coun. on Crime and Delinquency, N.Y.C., 1969-71, Jewish Cmty. Ctr. Wilkes-Barre, Pa., 1964-66; chmn. United Way Campaign of Wyoming Valley, 1975, chmn. of bd., 78-80; pres. Temple Israel of Wilkes Barre, 1972-74, chmn. bd. 1974-84, life mem. bd.; comdr. post 395 Am. Legion, Kingston, 1948; bd. dirs. Keystone State Games, 1982—, Jewish Fedn. Bd. of Greater Wilks-Barre, 1994—, St. Vincent de Paul Soup Kitchen, 1987-2000; trustee Wyoming Valley Vet.'s Hosp. Fund, 2002—. Capt. USAAF, 1942-45, ETO. Decorated medal with 6 bronze stars, European combatant cross French Govt.; named Golden Key Vol. of Yr., United Way of Pa., 1989; recipient Erasmus medal, Dutch Govt., Disting. Svc. award in Trusteeship, Assn. Governing Bds., Univs. and Colls., 1990, Disting. Cmty. Svc. award, Greater Wilkes-Barre Soc. Fellows Anti-Defamation League, 1991, Clara Barton honor award, Wyoming Valley chpt. ARC, 1992, Lifetime Achievement award, United Way of Wyoming VAlley, 1992, Outstanding Vol. Fundraiser award, Greater Pocono chpt. Nat. Soc. of Fundraising Execs., 1995, honoree, Wyoming Valley Interfaith Coun., 1986, Ethics Inst. N.E. Pa., 2001, inductee, Jr. Achievement Hall of Fame for N.E. Pa., 1997. Mem. ABA, Pa. Bar Assn., Am. Judicature Soc., The Pa. Soc., B'nai B'rith (pres. Wilkes Barre 1952-53, Cmty. Svc. award 1976), U. Mich. Club N.E. Pa. (pres. 1946-76), Westmoreland Club (Wilkes-Barre), Huntsville Golf Club (Lehman, Pa.). Republican. Jewish. E-mail: hr@rjglaw.com.

ROSENN, MAX, federal judge; b. Plains, Pa., Feb. 4, 1910; s. Joseph and Jennie (Wohl) Rosenn; m. Tillie R. Hershkowitz, Mar. 18, 1934; children; Keith S., Daniel Wohl. BA, Cornell U., 1929; LLB, U. Pa., 1932. Bar: Pa. 1932, U.S. Supreme Ct. 1955, Cts. of Philippines 1946. Gen. practice, Wilkes-Barre, Pa., 1932—70; spl. counsel Pa. Dept. Justice, 1939; asst. dist. atty. Luzerne County, 1942—44; solicitor various mcpl. boroughs, ptnr. Rosenn, Jenkins & Greenwald, Wilkes-Barre, 1954—70; sec. pub. welfare Pa., 1966—67; judge U.S. Ct. Appeals (3rd cir.), 1970—81, sr. judge, 1981—. Criminal procedure rules com. Supreme Ct. Pa., 1958—85; mem. Pa. Commn. to Revise Pub. Employee Laws, 1968—69; Pa. chmn. com. children and youth White House Conf., 1968—70. Contbr. articles to profl. jours. Active Pa. Bd. Pub. Welfare, 1963—66; chmn. study commn. Pa. Gov.'s Coun. for Human Svcs., 1966—67; exec. bd. Commonwealth of Pa., 1966—67; chmn. Commn. Met. Govt., 1957—58, Pa. Human Rels. Commn., 1969—70, Legis.-exec. Task Force Structure for Human Svcs., 1970, Flood Recovery Task Force, 1972; pres. Property Owners Assn. Luzerne County, 1955—57; alt. del. Rep. Nat. Conv., 1964; pres. Wyoming Valley Jewish Com., 1941—42; life trustee Wilkes-Barre Jewish Cmty. Ctr. Named a U.S. Courthouse in his honor, 1996, libr., U.S. Courthouse at Scranton in his honor, 2002. Fellow: Internat. Acad. Trial Lawyers, Am. Coll. Trial Lawyers; mem.: ABA, Am. Judicature Soc., Am. Soc. Law and Medicine (past assoc. editor), Am. Law Inst., Luzerne County Bar Assn., Pa. Bar Assn., Westmoreland Club, Masons (33rd degree), B'nai B'rith (life; pres. dist. grand lodge 1947—48, bd. govs., chmn. bd. dirs. Anti-Defamation League Pa., W.Va. and Del. 1955—58, nat. commr. 1964—), Alpha Epsilon Pi. Jewish. Office: US Ct Appeals Max Rosenn US CthseRm 235 197 S Main St Wilkes Barre PA 18701-1500

ROSENNE, MEIR, lawyer, government agency administrator; b. Iasi, Romania, Feb. 19, 1931; arrived in Israel, 1944; s. Jacob and Mina Rosenhaupt; m. Vera Ayai, June 9, 1959; children: Mihal, Dafna. MA in Polit. Sci., Inst. Polit. Sci., Paris, 1953; LLB, Sorbonne, U. Paris, 1955, PhD in Internat. Law with honors, 1957; grad., Inst. Internat. Studies, Paris, 1953. In govt. service, Israel, 1953—; consul Israel Consulate, N.Y.C., 1967-69; sr. lectr. in polit. sci. U. Haifa, Israel, 1969-71; coordinator Atomic Energy Commn. Israel, 1969-71; chief legal adviser Fgn. Office Israel, Jerusalem, 1971-79; Israeli amb. to France, Paris, 1979-83; Israeli amb. to U.S. Washington, 1983-87; pres. State of Israel Bonds, N.Y., 1989-93; ptnr. Balter, Guth, Aloni & Co., Jerusalem, 1994—. Chmn. overseas com. Jerusalem Bank; bd. dirs. Israel Discount Bank Holding, Ltd. Contbr. Chmn. internat. bd. govs. Share-Zedek Hosp., Jerusalem, 1989—94. Sgt. Israeli Air Force, 1948—50. Named comdr., Nat. Order French Legion of Honor; recipient Harold Weil medal, NYU Sch. Law, Elie Wiesel award. Mem.: French Assn. Internat. Law, Am. Soc. Internat. Law, Israeli Bar Assn., Soc. Internat. Law, Internat. Law Soc. France, Internat. Club Washington. Avocations: volleyball, swimming. Office: Balter Guth & Aloni 23 Hillel St Jerusalem Israel E-mail: mrosenne@bgalen.co.il.

ROSENOF, THEODORE DIMON, historian, educator; b. Newark, Sept. 15, 1943; s. Irving and Josephine Stella (Schmitt) R.; m. Patricia Mary Reilly, Aug. 31, 1985; children: Charles Reilly, Liza. BA, Rutgers U., 1965; MA, PhD, U. Wis., 1970. Vis. instr., vis. asst. prof. history Tex. Tech. U., Lubbock, 1975-77; vis. asst. prof. history Pan Am. U., Edinburg, Tex., 1977-78; rsch. assoc. U. Wis., Madison, 1978-79; asst. prof., assoc. prof. history Mercy Coll., Dobbs Ferry N.Y., 1979-89, prof. history, 1989—. Author: Dogma, Depression, and the New Deal: The Debate of Political Leaders over Economic Recovery, 1975, Patterns of Political Economy in America: The Failure to Develop a Democratic Left Synthesis, 1933-1950, 1983, Economics in the Long Run: New Deal Theorists and Their Legacies, 1933-1993, 1997, Realignment: The Theory that Changed the Way We Think about American Politics, 2003. Mem. Am. Hist. Assn., Orgn. Am. Historians. Democrat. Home: 75 Academy Ave Cornwall On Hudson NY 12520 E-mail: trosenof@hvc.rr.com.

ROSENOW, DORIS JANE, critical care nurse, nursing consultant; b. Sharon, Pa., Sept. 13, 1935; d. John J. and Mary F. (Koss) Skertic; m. Galen J. Rosenow, Dec. 14, 1957; children: Mary K. Gage, Gail E. Logan. Diploma in Nursing, St. Anthony de Padua Hosp., Chgo., 1955; BSN and BA in Psychology, Incarnate Word Coll., San Antonio, 1980; MSN, U. Tex. Health Sci. Ctr., San Antonio, 1984; PhD, U. Tex., 1990. RN, Tex.; cert. critical care RN. Critical care nurse Good Shephard Hosp., Longview, Tex., 1977, Brooke Army Med. Ctr., San Antonio, 1978-85; instr. Health Scis. Ctr. Tex. Tech. U., Odessa, 1985-88; asst. prof. Incarnate Word Coll., San Antonio, 1990-91, U. Tex., Galveston, 1991-92; assoc. prof. Tex. A&M Internat. U., Corpus Christi, 1992—. Researcher in field. Contbr. articles to profl. jours. Served to 1st lt. USAF, 1957-60. Mem. ANA, Tex. Nurses Assn., Scientific Rsch. Soc., Sigma Theta Tau (Nat. Honor Soc. 1984), Phi Kappa Phi (Nat. Honor Soc. 1990), Sigma Xi. Home: 15615 Boulder Creek St San Antonio TX 78247-2936

ROSENOW, EDWARD CARL, III, medical educator; b. Columbus, Ohio, Nov. 2, 1934; s. Oscar Ferdinand and Mildred Irene (Eichelberger) R.; m. Constance Donna Grahame, Sept. 7, 1957; children: Sheryl Lynn, Scott Edward. BS, Ohio State U., 1955, MD, 1959; MS in Medicine, U. Minn., 1969. Diplomate Am. Bd. Internal Medicine, Am. Bd. Pulmonary Diseases. Intern Riverside Meth. Hosp., Columbus, Ohio, 1959-60; resident in internal medicine Mayo Grad. Sch. Medicine, Rochester, Minn., 1960-65, clin. fellow in thoracic diseases, 1965-66; cons. in internal medicine (pulmonary diseases) Mayo Clinic, 1966; instr. in medicine Mayo Grad. Sch. Medicine, 1969-73; asst. prof. medicine Mayo Med. Sch., 1973-77, assoc. prof. medicine, 1977-80, prof. medicine, 1980; chmn. divsn. pulmonary and critical care medicine, 1987-94; assoc. dir. internal medicine residency program Mayo Clinic, Rochester, 1977-79, program dir. internal medicine residency program, 1979-84, sec. Mayo staff, 1979; pres. Mayo staff, 1986; Arthur M. and Gladys D. Gray prof. medicine Mayo Clinic, Rochester, 1987-96, prof. emeritus, 1996—. Cons. NASA, Houston. Capt. M.C., U.S. Army, 1962-64. Recipient Alumni Achievement award Coll. Medicine Ohio State U., 1989, Disting. Mayo Clinician award, 1994, Henry S. Plummer Disting. Internist award, 1994, Karis award Mayo Clinic, 1996, Disting. Alumnus award Mayo Found., 1998; Edward W. and Betty Knight Scripps Professorship named in his honor Mayo Med. Sch., 1994, Edward C. Rosenow, III, Outstanding Subsplty. fellow award established in his honor. Fellow ACP (gov. Minn. chpt. 1987-91, Ralph S. Claypoole Sr. award for Lifetime Dedication to Patient Care 1995, Minn. chpt. Laureate award 1994, Disting. Lectr. award 1996), Am. Coll. Chest Physicians (master fellow, editl. bd. CHEST 1973-78, editor spl. case reports 1975-90, com. on postgrad. med. edn. 1978-84, sci. program com. 1982, com. on undergrad. med. edn. 1981-82, co-chmn. sci. program com. Internat. Coll. Chest Physicians meeting, Sydney, Australia, 1985, regent 1984-88, pres. elect 1988-89, pres. 1989-90, pres. Chest Found. 1998—, Dist. Lectr. award); mem. AMA, So. Minn. Med. Assn., Minn. Thoracic Soc., Am. Thoracic Soc., Sigma Xi. Office: Mayo Clinic Div Pulmonary Diseases 200 1st St SW Rochester MN 55905-0002

ROSENOW, JOHN EDWARD, foundation executive; b. Lincoln, Nebr., Sept. 15, 1949; s. Lester Edward and Lucille Louise (Koehler) R.; m. Nancy Kay Hadley; children: Matthew, Stacy. BS in Agrl. Engring., U. Nebr., 1971. Dir. of tourism Nebr. Dept. Econ. Devel., Lincoln, 1971-79, interim dept. dir., 1985; founder Nat. Arbor Day Found., 1972, exec. dir. million-mem., 1979-94, pres., 1994—. Co-author: (book) Tourism: the good, the bad, and the ugly, 1979. Democrat. Mem. United Ch. of Christ. E-mail: arborday.org. Office: Nat Arbor Day Found 211 N 12th St Lincoln NE 68508-1422

ROSENQUIST, EDWARD ESTHER, physician associate; b. Surabaja, Indonesia, Oct. 15, 1954; came to U.S., 1960; s. Harold Arnold Rosenquist and Betsy (Noya) Dewitt; m. Christie Kay Rosenquist, Dec. 28, 1985; children: Hannah, Matthew, Joshua, Sarah. Cert. physician assoc., Johns Hopkins U., 1977; AA, Essex C.C., Balt., 1977; BA, Covenant Coll., 1986. Physician assoc. neurol. surgery Balt. City Hosps., 1979-84, U. Minn. Hosps. and Clinics, Mpls., 1987-93, Neurosurg. and Spinal Surgery Assocs., Rapid City, S.D., 1993-95, Thomas V. Rankin, M.D., Eau Claire, Wis., 1995-99, Marshfield Clinic, Eau Claire, 1999—; physician assoc. orthop. Chippewa Valley Orthop. and Sports Medicine, 2000—. Physician assoc. Johns Hopkins Med. Instns. Neurosurgery, Balt., 1979-84; physician assoc. ambulatory care Md. Dept. Corrections, Balt., 1978-79. Youth dir., deacon Loch Raven Presbyn. Ch., Towson, Md., 1982-84; soccer coach AYSO, 1999; Awana youth leader Calvary Bapt. Ch.; coach Eau Claire Luth. Sch. Basketball, 2000-01, Eau Claire United Soccer. Fellow Am. Assn. Surgeon Assts., Wis. Acad. Physician Assts., Am. Assn. Neurosurg. Physician Assts., Am. Acad. Physician Assts., Physician Assocs. Orthopedic Surgery, Am. Assn. Neurol. Surgery; mem. N.Am. Spine Soc., Am. Assn. Neurol. Surgeons (grantee 1993-94). Republican. Avocations: poetry, soccer, audio-electronics, bicycling, classic films. Home: 4330 S Pointe Ct Eau Claire WI 54701-3009 Office: Chippewa Valley Orth and Sports Med 3213 Stein Blvd Eau Claire WI 54701

ROSENQVIST, MARK BRYN, aquatic biologist, aquatic conservation educator; b. Milw., June 7, 1960; s. Rolf Bryn and Mary Jane Audrey (Simons) R.; m. Pamela Frances McKay, Oct. 5, 1991. AA, Coll. Lifelong Learning, 1993, BS, 1998. Comm. technician Dept. Def., Ft. Meade, Md., 1977-81; aquarist various employers, Md., D.C., Va., 1981-85, Tropic Seas Aquarium, Denver, 1985-88; mgr. breeding facility Windhover, Inc., 1987-88; aquaculture technician Aquatic Rsch. Organisms, Hampton, N.H., 1988-96, tech. mgr., 1996—. Conservation breeder Cyprinodon and Related Genera Study and Maintenance Group, Hampton, 1992—; coord. conservation breeding program Aquatic Conservation Network, Ottawa, Ont., Can., 1993-96, v.p., 1993-95; edn. cons. U. N.H. Coop. Ext. Svc., Durham, 1995—; mem. Freshwater Fish Taxon Adv. Group, Terrestrial Invertebrate Taxon Adv. Group; mem. adv. com. Rockingham County Aquaculture Edn. Ctr., 1996-99. Co-author: Aquatic Conservation Network Captive Breeding Guidelines, 1994; contbr. articles to profl. publs.; asst. prodr. video The Perfect Aquarium, 1987. Pres., bd. dirs. Aquaculture Edn. and Rsch. Ctr., 1999—; bd. dirs. Citizens for a Seacoast Aquarium, 1999—; mem. adv. com. plant and animal sci. program Seacoast Sch. of Tech., 1998—. Mem. Am. Assn. Zoos and Aquariums (assoc.), N.Am. Native Fishes Assn., Am. Livebearer Assn. Avocations: numismatics, diecast and tin vehicles, European Medieval and Renaissance studies. Home: 9 Grape St Newmarket NH 03857-1108 E-mail: aerc2000@aol.com.

ROSENSAFT, JEAN BLOCH, university administrator; b. N.Y.C., Jan. 6, 1952; d. Sam E. and Lilly Bloch; m. Menachem Rosensaft, Jan. 13, 1974; 1 child, Joana Deborah. BA in Art History, Barnard Coll., 1973; postgrad., NYU, 1978. Gallery lectr. in spl. exhbns. Mus. of Modern Art, N.Y.C., 1977-80; NEA lectr. on collections Modern Art Edn. Dept., 1979-80, spl. asst. for ind. sch. program, 1980-83, spl. asst. for publs., 1983-84; coord. pub. programs The Jewish Mus., N.Y.C., 1984-86, asst. dir. of edn., 1986-89; sr. nat. dir. for pub. affairs and institutional planning Hebrew Union Coll. Jewish Inst. of Religion, 1989—, exhbns. dir., 1994—. Author: Chagall and the Bible, 1987. Mem. collections and acquisitions com. U.S. Holocaust Meml. Mus., Washington, 1980—; mem. steering com. Coun. of Am. Jewish Mus., N.Y.C., 1995—; chair task force on the arts UJA/Fedn. Women's Task Force, N.Y.C., 1995—; v.p. Internat. Network of Children of Jewish Holocaust Survivors, N.Y.C., 1987—; chair Park Ave Synagogue H.S. Parents Assn., N.Y.C., 1993-96, sch. bd., 1993—, adv. bd. 1996—. George Welwood Murray fellow Barnard Coll., 1973. Home: 179 E 70th St New York NY 10021-5109 Office: Hebrew Union Coll Jewish Inst Religion 1 W 4th St New York NY 10012-1105

ROSENSAFT, LESTER JAY, management consultant, lawyer, business executive; b. Leominster, Mass., Jan. 11, 1958; s. Melvin and Beatrice (Golombek) R.; m. Elisabeth Amanda Lahti, July 29, 1992, 1 child, Mia Elisabeth. BS in Econs., Wharton Sch., U. Pa., 1978; JD, MBA, Case Western Res. U., 1981; LLM in Corp. Law, NYU, 1983. Bar: Ohio 1981, U.S. Dist. Ct. (no. dist.) Ohio 1982, U.S. Dist. Ct. (all dists.) N.Y. 1982, Mass. 1992. Practice corp. and comml. law, Ohio, 1981—. Reorgn. law fed. cts. Ohio, N.Y., 1982—; mem. firm. Hall, Rosensafi & Yen, Cleve. and Singapore, 1961-90; with Cons. to Mgmt., Inc., Clve., N.Y.C., Boston, Hong Kong, 1977—, v.p., 1977-80, pres., CEO, 1980-83, chmn., 1983-85; pres., CEO Eljay Devel. Corp., 1985-86; chmn., CEO Logistix Ltd., 1987-90; ptnr. Sanctuary Assocs., Boston, 1988-89; exec. v.p., CFO The Union Meat Co., East Hartford, Conn., 1989-90, also bd. dirs.; pres. Golub Enterprises II, Inc., 1989-90; also bd. dirs.; COO The CCC Fin. Orgn., Cleve., 1992-95, also bd. dirs.; pres., CEO, bd. dirs. ASA Investment Commn., Inc., N.Y.C., 1995—; pres., CEO ASA Adminstrn., Inc., Chgo., Greensboro, N.C., 1999—, also mem. bd. dirs; bd. dirs. ASA Acquisition Corp., 1998—, fin. and strategic planning com.; mem. ASA Mgmt. and Exec. Com., 1995—, ASA Investment Com., 1996-98; chmn. Chatham Fin., Cleve., N.Y.C., 1995-96; vice chmn. bd. dirs. Paramount Sys. Design Group, Inc., N.Y.C., 1982-89, v.p. corp. devel.; bd. dirs. Ameritech Corp., N.Y.C., 1983-85; v.p., CFO, bd. dirs. Chipurnoi Inc., L.I. City, N.Y.; v.p., CFO Kannerton Industries, N.Y.C., London, 1983-85; vice chmn., gen. counsel, bd. dirs. GIOIA Couture, Inc., Akron, Ohio, 1984-86; dir. Honeybee Robotics Ltd., Taiwan and N.Y.C., Pelletier Brothers, Inc., 1986-88, Advanced Radiator Techs., Inc., Fitchburg, Mass., 1987-88. Co-author: Industrial Development Survey for City of Leominster, 1978; contbr. articles to profl. jours. Ednl. cons., adviser indsl. devel. and strategic urbanism; cons. federally funded biomed. rsch. projects; active Combined Jewish Philanthropies; participant 40th Anniversary II Pres.'s Mission, 1987; chmn. Region V Outreach Mission, 1988; vice chmn. Regional Campaign Leadership Nission, 1991; mem. Russian Resettlement Com., 1988-91, Major Gifts Gala Com., 1989; assoc. alumni trustee U. Pa., 1991-95; active U. Penn. Seondary Com. Ctrl. Mass., U. Penn. Bd. Govs., Cleve., 1992-95; exec. adv. coun. Keene State Coll., 1984-88. Recipient APEX Grand award 1999, ESMA best of show award, 1999, numerous ACE awards, silver and gold Quill awards, 1996-99. Mem. ABA, Assn. Corp. Growth Turnaround Mgmt. Assn., Greater Cleve. Bar Assn., Ohio State Bar Assn., Assn. Bar City N.Y., Bankruptcy Lawers Bar Assn., N.Y.C. Reorgn. Roundtable, Internat. Soc. Strategic Planning Cons., Soc. Profl. Mgmt. Cons., Inst. Mgmt. Cons. (cert.), Coun. Cons. Orgns., Coll. Firm Prins., North Ctrl. Mass. C. of C. (dinsl. devel. com. 1984-86), Phi Alpha Delta (vice justice), Boca Pointe Golf and Racquet Club. Address: 9 Whispering Ivy Way Mendham NJ 07945-1241 Office: 146 W 57th St New York NY 10019

ROSENSAFT, MENACHEM ZWI, lawyer, author, foundation executive, community activist; b. Bergen-Belsen, Germany, May 1, 1948; came to U.S., 1958, naturalized, 1962; s. Josef and Hadassah (Bimko) R.; m. Jean Bloch, Jan. 13, 1974; 1 child, Joana Deborah. BA, MA, Johns Hopkins U., 1971; MA, Columbia U., 1975, JD, 1979. Bar: N.Y. 1980. Adj. lectr. dept. Jewish studies CCNY, 1972-74, professorial fellow, 1974-75; rsch. fellow Am. Law Inst., 1977-78; law clk. to judge U.S. Dist. Ct. (so. dist.) N.Y., N.Y.C., 1979-81; assoc. Proskauer, Rose, Goetz & Mendelsohn, 1981-82, Kaye, Scholer, Fierman, Hays & Handler, N.Y.C., 1982-89; v.p., sr. assoc. counsel Chase Manhattan Bank, 1989-93; spl. counsel Hahn & Hessen, 1994-95; sr. internat. counsel Ronald S. Lauder Found., 1995-97; exec. v.p. Jewish Renaissance Found., Inc., 1996-2000; ptnr. Ross & Hardies, 2000—. Author: Moshe Sharett, Statesman of Israel, 1966, Fragments, Past and Future (poetry), 1968, Not Backward to Belligerency, 1969; editor: Bergen Belsen Youth mag., 1965, Life Reborn, Jewish Displaced Persons 1945-1951, 2001; book rev. editor Columbia Jour. Transnat. Law, 1978-79; co-editor (with Yehuda Bauer) Antisemitism: Threat to Western Civilization, 1988; contbg. editor: Reform Judaism, 1993—; contbr. to various publs. including N.Y. Times, Washington Post, Newsweek, N.Y. Post, L.A. Times, N.Y. Daily News, Phila. Inquirer, Miami Herald, Internat. Herald Tribune, Jerusalem Post, Liberation, Paris, Davar, Tel Aviv, El Diario, Santiago de Chile, (with Joana D. Rosensaft) Fordham Internat. Law Jour., Columbia Human Rights Law Rev., Jewish Social Studies, Leo Baeck Inst. Year Book XXI, Columbia Jour. Environ. Law, (with Michael I. Saltzman) Tax Planning Internat. Rev., Fellowship, Reform Judaism, United Synagogue Rev., Forward, Midstream, N.Y. Jewish Week; dir., editor-in-chief Holocaust Survivors' Memoirs Project of World Jewish Congress, 2000—. Chmn. Internat. Network Children Jewish Holocaust Survivors, 1981-84, founding chmn., 1984—; nat. pres. Labor Zionist Alliance, 1988-91; chmn. commn. human rights World Jewish Congress, 1986-91, chmn. exec. com. Am. sect., 1986-90; mem. Gen. Coun. World Zionist Orgn., 1987-92; mem. U.S. Holocaust Meml. Coun., 1994-2000, chmn. content com., 1994-2000, chmn. collections and acquisitions com., 1996-2000, chmn. task force on procedures for com. on conscience, 1996, mem. exec. com., 1996—, chmn. governance com., 2001-02; mem. N.Y.C. Holocaust Meml. Commn., 1982-96, chmn. collections com., 1987-89; bd. dirs., exec. com. Nat. Com. for Labor Israel, 1988-91, 95-2001; mem. Am. Zionist Tribunal, 1988-90, chmn., 1990; sec. Am. Zionist Fedn., 1990-93; bd. dirs. Am. Jewish Joint Distbn. Com., 1988-91, Mercaz, 1991-97; mem. nat. adv. bd. United Synagogue Conservative Judaism, 1995—, also chmn. United Synagogue delegation to Nat. Jewish Cmty. Rels. Adv. Coun., 1994-97; mem. exec. com. Nat. Jewish Cmty. Rels. Adv. Coun., 1994-97; mem. N.Y. County Dem. Com., 1981-85; organizer, leader demonstration in Germany against Pres. Reagan's visit to Bitburg Cemetery and Bergen-Belsen concentration camp, 1985; del. meeting on recognition of Israel between five Am. Jews and leaders of Palestine Liberation Orgn., Stockholm, 1988; sec. Park Ave. Synagogue, 1998—, trustee, 1994—, chmn. Sherr Inst. Adult Jewish Studies, 1993—. Recipient Abraham Joshua Heschel Peace award, 1989, Parker Sch. recognition of achievement with honors in internat. and fgn. law, 1979, 400th Anniversary medal City of Warsaw, 1999, commendation Jewish Heritage Week, Comptroller of N.Y.C., 1999; Harlan Fiske Stone scholar, 1977-79. Mem. ABA, Phi Beta Kappa. Home: 179 E 70th St New York NY 10021-5109 Office: Ross & Hardies 65 E 55th St New York NY 10022-3219 E-mail: menachem.rosensaft@rosshardies.com.

ROSENSHINE, ALLEN GILBERT, advertising agency executive; b. N.Y.C., Mar. 14, 1939; s. Aaron and Anna (Zuckerman) R.; m. Suzan Weston-Webb, Aug. 31, 1979; children: Andrew, Jonathan. AB, Columbia Coll., 1960. Copywriter J.B. Rundle (advt.), N.Y.C., 1962-65; copywriter Batten, Barton, Durstine & Osborn, 1965, copy supr., 1967, v.p., 1968, asso. creative dir., 1970, sr. v.p., creative dir., 1975-77, exec. v.p., 1977-80, pres., 1980-82, chief exec. officer, 1981-86, chmn., 1983-86, also dir., mem. exec. com.; pres., chief exec. officer BBDO Internat., 1984-86, also bd. dirs.; pres., chief exec. officer Omnicom Group, 1986-88; chmn., chief exec. officer BBDO Worldwide, 1989—. Lectr. gen. studies Bklyn. Coll., 1961-65 Office: BBDO Worldwide Inc 1285 Avenue Of The Americas New York NY 10019-6028*

ROSENSHINE, ANITA S. social worker; b. N.Y.C., May 9, 1941; d. Emanuel and Gertrude Marion (Golden) Weinerman; m. Allen G. Rosenshine, Apr. 12, 1964 (div. 1980); children: Andrew, Jonathan; m. Ira Kornbluth, Apr. 24, 1987. AB, Barnard Coll., 1962; MA in History, NYU, 1964; MSW, Columbia U., 1979. Cert. bd. cert. diplomate in social work. Clin. social worker Hall-Brooke Hosp., Westport, Conn., 1979-82, Four Winds Hosp., Katonah, N.Y., 1982-89, Family Svc. League Clinic, Southampton, 1989—. Mem. Nat. Assn. Social Workers, Acad. Cert. Social Workers, N.Y. State Soc. Clin. Social Work Psychotherapists. Office: Family Svc League 300 Hampton Rd Southampton NY 11968-5030

ROSENSON, IRWIN DALE, accountant; b. Chgo., Oct. 5, 1934; s. Morris and Evelyn (Goldstein) R.; m. Mary Joan Bingham, Dec. 27, 1958; children: Deborah, Sandra, Dale. BS in Acctg., Roosevelt U., 1956. CPA, lic. ins. prodr.; securities lic.; accredited bus. advisor Nat. Soc. Accounts. Pres. N.W. Acctg. Svc., Mt. Prospect, Ill., 1984-2001, Des Plaines, 1987-2001. Mem. Ind. Accts. Assn. of Ill. (chmn. polit. action com. 1993-2001, pres. N.W. Suburban chpt. 1993-96), Ill. Soc. of CPAs, Nat. Soc. Accts. (state dir. for Ill.2000-01), Forest View Tennis Club. Jewish. Avocation: tennis. Office: Ste 7 834 E Rand Rd Mount Prospect IL 60056-2569

ROSENSTEEL, GEORGE THOMAS, physics educator, nuclear physicist; b. Balt., Sept. 30, 1947; s. Walter St. George and Marie Emily (White) R.; m. Tsetsa Dankova. BSc, U. Toronto, Ont., Can., 1973, PhD, 1975. Can. fellow NRC, 1976-78; prof. physics Tulane U., New Orleans, 1978—, chmn. dept., 1985-91. Vis. fellow Brit. Sci. and Engring. Coun., U. Sussex, Eng., 1986; vis. prof. Nat. Inst. Nuclear Theory, U. Washington, 1992, Inst. Theoretical Physics U. Gent, Belgium, 1999. Contbr. numerous articles to profl. jours. Delivered grad. sch. commencement address Tulane U., 1987; recipient 7 grants NSF, 1979—. Mem. Am. Phys. Soc., Am. Math. Soc., Sigma Xi (young scientist award 1987). Office: Tulane U Dept of Physics New Orleans LA 70118 E-mail: george.rosensteel@tulane.edu.

ROSENSTEIN, IRA H. radio producer, poet; b. N.Y.C., June 28, 1947; s. Joseph and Mildred Rosenstein; m. Nudjarin Unsin, June 7, 2000. BA, Queens Coll., N.Y.C., 1968; MFA, Brandeis U., Waltham, Mass., 1972. Reporter WBAI-FM Radio, N.Y.C., 1996-98; mgr. The Music Store and Flute Ctr., 1997—; prodr. WOR-AM Radio, 1998—. Author: (books of poetry) Left on the Field to Die, 1984, Twenty-Two Sonnets, 1986; editor: Starlight Poets 1, 1990, Starlight Poets 2: Sonnets, 1992. Office: PO Box 3102 Long Island City NY 11103-0102 E-mail: irar@iopener.net.

ROSENSTEIN, JAMES ALFRED, lawyer, mediator, negotiation facilitator; b. Phila., Jan. 4, 1939; s. Louis Charles and Natalie Selma (Stern) R.; m. Linda Merle Lederman, Sept. 7, 1969; 1 child, Judith Esther AB, Harvard U., 1961, JD, 1968. Bar: Pa. 1968. Assoc. Wolf, Block, Schorr and Solis-Cohen, Phila., 1968-76, ptnr., 1976-97; prin. Rosenstein Assocs., 1997—. Mem. adv. com. task force on condominiums Joint State Govt Commn., Pa. Gen. Assembly, 1977-79; mem. condominium-coop. steering com. Phila. City Planning Commn., 1980-81 Contbr. articles to profl. jours. Trustee Jewish Fedn. of Greater Phila., 1977—, mem. exec. com., 1989-97, 98—, chmn. com. on local svcs., 1986-89, sec., 1987-88, v.p., 1988-94, chmn. com. on allocations and planning, 1989-92; v.p. jewish Cmty. Rels. Coun., 1982-85, 89-90, 96-2000, pres., 2000-2002; trustee United Way of Greater Phila., 1979-84, bd. dirs., 1982-85, 91-97; pres. Hillel Greater Phila., 1981-83; vice chmn. Synagogue-Fedn. Coun. Greater Phila., 1995-97, chmn., 1997-99. Lt. USN, 1961-64. Mem. ABA (chmn. devel. and financing of condominium projects 1993-97), Pa. Bar Assn. (chmn. common interest ownership com. 1980-93, chmn. real property divsn. 1993-95, chmn. real property, probate and trust law sect. 1995-96), Phila. Bar Assn. (co-chmn. legis. rels. com. 1996-97), Am. Coll. Real Estate Lawyers, Coll. Cmty. Assn. Lawyers, Soc. Profls. in Dispute Resolution (co-chmn. comml. sect. 1998-2000), Coun. Jewish Fedns. (bd. dirs. 1986-98, chmn. com. on svcs. to aging 1991-94, chair nat. funding coun. 1996-98, exec. com. 1997-98), United Jewish Cmtys. Fedn. N.Am. (chmn. N.E. region 1998-2001). Office: Rosenstein Assocs 1650 Arch St 22nd Fl Philadelphia PA 19103-2047 E-mail: jrosenstein@earthlink.net.

ROSENSTEIN, LEONARD, real estate company executive; b. Phila., Aug. 4, 1922; s. Benjamin and Esther (Zibulski) R.; m. Eleanor M. Peterson, Mar. 11, 1960; children: Elissa L., Risa B., Tedd B. BS in Pharmacy, Temple U., 1943; BS in Pharmacy (hon.), New Orleans. Lic. pharmacist, Pa., N.J. Pres. Lincoln Pharmacy, Atlantic City, 1947-69, Mercy Ambulance, Las Vegas, Nev., 1971-73, Nev. Devel. and Realty Co., Las Vegas, 1973—, am. Mgmt. Co., Las Vegas, 1973—; chmn. Players Express Travel, 1990—. Editor: Temple University Apothecary, 1943. Chmn. Downtown Improvement Authority, Atlantic City, N.J., 1982-84; pres. N.J. Pharm. Assn., 1960; chmn., pres. Nat. Assn. Retail Druggists, Washington, 1969; commr. So. Nev. Regional Housing Bd., Las Vegas, 1993-94.; mem. Beth Sholem Congregation, 1971—. Cpl. U.S. Army, 1943-46, ETO. Recipient award Am. Legion, 1940, E.R. Squibb, 1960, Bowl of Hygea, A.H. Robbins, 1965; named Ky. Col., 1965—. Mem. Greater Las Vegas Realtor Assn., Inst. Real Estate Mgmt., Jewish War Vets, Am. Legion, Elks, Alpha Zeta Omega. Avocations: photography, reading. Home: 909 Cashman Dr Las Vegas NV 89107-4429 Office: Nev Devel & Realty Co 2980 Meade Ave Las Vegas NV 89102-0729

ROSENSTEIN, MARY ELISABETH MALLORY, retired clinical social worker; b. Los Gatos, Calif., Feb. 25, 1916; d. Merton Shannon and Mabel Beatrice (Penny) Mallory; m. Albert Rosenstein, Sept. 20, 1947; children: Nathan Stewart, Thomas Mallory. AB, U. Calif., Berkeley, 1937; MA in Social Work, U. Chgo., 1950. Licn. clin. social worker, marriage, family and child counselor, Calif. Caseworker Calif. Relief Adminstrn., San Francisco, 1938-40, San Francisco Children's Agy., 1940-42; caseworker foster home placement Oakland (Calif.) Family Svc., 1942-44; psychiat. social worker ARC Hosp. Svc., Oakland and Long Beach, Calif., 1946-51, Calif. Dept. Mental Health, L.A., Long Beach, Santa Ana, 1950-51; dist. supr. Calif. Dept. Mental Health, L.A., 1951-53; caseworker, acting dir. Family Svc. Assn. Rio Hondo Area, Whittier, Calif., 1954-81; pvt. practice, 1981-91; ret., 1991. Chmn. mental health study LWV, Whittier, 1974-76; workshop leader Montebello (Calif.) Child Study Workshop; chmn. liaison com. San Gabriel Valley Regional County Mental Health, Pasadena, Calif., 1976-81; cons. dist. teen mothers Montebello Unified Sch. Dist. Mem. Whittier Area Coordinating Coun., 1960—; pres. Birney Elem. Sch. PTA, Pico Rivera, Calif., 1957; cellist Rio Hondo Symphony Assn. Orch., Whittier, 1970-97; v.p., membership chmn. UN Assn., Whittier, 1968-97. Recipient commendation Calif. Legislature, 1981, U.S. Ho. of Reps., 1981, County of L.A., 1981, spl. citation UN Assn. U.S.A., 1996. Fellow Soc. for Clin. Social Workers; mem. NASW (diplomate in clin. social work), Acad. Cert. Social Workers, AAUW (Las Distinguitas award 1979), LWV. Democrat. Unitarian Universalist. Avocations: music, gardening, swimming, river rafting, live theater.

ROSENSTEIN, MELVYN, surgeon; b. N.Y.C., Jan. 3, 1940; s. David and Rachael Rosenstein; m. Joanne Belden McClure, Nov. 6, 1999; children: Michael, Peter, Joshua, Tracy. BS magna cum laude, Tufts U., 1961; MD, NYU, 1965. Pvt. practice urology, L.A., 1971—96; chief of surgery Brotman Med. Ctr., 1982—89, chief of staff, 1988—89. 1st lt. USAR, 1965—75. Fellow: ACS; mem.: L.A. County Med. Assn. (v.p. 1984). Home: 4335 Marina City Dr # 846 Marina Del Rey CA 90292 Fax: 310-306-0370. E-mail: MelRosenstein@earthlink.net.

ROSENSTEIN, NEIL, surgeon, genealogical researcher; b. Cape Town, South Africa, Oct. 31, 1944; came to U.S., 1969; s. Emanuel Boruchovich and Annie (Marine) R.; m. Mavis Joyce Naumann, Jan. 14, 1968; children: Joel, Ari, Moshe Baruch, Rafael Samuel, Jonathan Simcha. MD, U. Cape Town Med. Sch., 1967. Intern Tel Hashomer Hosp., Tel Aviv, 1968-69; surg. resident Mt. Sinai Hosp., Cleve., 1970-75, N.Y.C., 1970-75; mem. surg. staff Trinitas, Elizabeth , NJ, 1975—, The Union Hosp. , 2001—. Author: These Are the Generations, 1969, The Unbroken Chain, 1976, 90, The Margolis Family, 1984, The Gaon of Vilna and his Cousinhood, 1997; co-author: From King David to Baron David—A Rothschild Saga, 1989, Avnei Zikaron, 1999; editor: Latter Day Leaders, Sages and Scholars, 1982, The Feast and the Fast, 1984. Founder, pres. Jewish Geneal. Soc., N.Y.C., 1977-79; bd. dirs. YMHA, Union, N.J., 1990-2001; mem. adv. bd. Auschwitz Jewish Center Found., N.Y.C., 1999—; founder, dir. Computer Ctr. for Jewish Genealogy; rep. to genealogy com. Ctr. for Jewish History bd. dirs. Yeshiva U., N.Y., 2001—. Mem. Med. Soc. N.J., Union County Med. Soc. N.J., AmeriGroup NJ, Inc. (med. adv. com.). Republican. Jewish. Home: 185 Shelley Ave Elizabeth NJ 07208-1061 E-mail: Neil@Tali.com.

ROSENSTEIN, PETER D. educational association administrator; b. N.Y.C., Jan. 23, 1947; s. Heinz and Dorrit Rosenstein. BA, CCNY, 1969; MPA, Baruch U., 1978. Coord. local govt. Mayor's Office, N.Y.C., 1974-77; exec. dir. implementation unit White House Conf. on Handicapped Individuals, Washington, 1978-80; exec. dir. Am. Acad. Physician Assts., Alexandria, Va., 1981-84, Accts. for Pub. Interest, Washington, 1985-89, Nat. Assn. for Gifted Children, Washington, 1989—. Trustee U. D.C., Washington, 2000—. Issues coord. Williams for Mayor, Washington, 1998. Mem. Profl. Conv. Mgmt. Assn. (bd. dirs. Capital chpt. 1995-2000), Arts in Action (pres. 1995—), Masons. Democrat. Jewish. Avocations: travel, theater. Office: Nat Assn for Gifted Children 1707 L St NW Ste 550 Washington DC 20036-4212

ROSENSTEIN, ROGER G. hand surgeon; b. N.Y.C., July 28, 1949; s. Solomon Nathan and Beverly B. (Gutterman) R.; m. Rima Gail Kopelman, May 25, 1975; children: Melissa G., Hilary A., Aliza B. BA, Columbia U., 1971, MD, 1975. Diplomate Am. Bd. Orthopedic Surgery with qualifications in surgery of hand. Intern, surg. resident The Roosevelt Hosp., N.Y.C., 1975-77; resident in orthopedic surgery Columbia Presbyn. Med. Ctr., 1977-80; fellow in hand surgery Thomas Jefferson U., Phila., 1980-81; hand surgeon in pvt. practice Paramus, N.J., 1981—. Asst. clin. prof. orthopedic surgery U. Medicine and Dentistry N.J., Newark, 1986—; chief hand surgery sect. Hackensack (N.J.) U. Med. Ctr., 1989—. Contbr. articles to profl. jours. Fellow Am. Acad. Orthopedic Surgery; mem. Am. Soc. Surgery of the Hand, N.Y. Soc. Surgery of the Hand. Office: 22 Madison Ave Paramus NJ 07652-2721

ROSENSTOCK, LOUIS ANTHONY, III, lawyer; b. Petersburg, Va., July 27, 1941; BA, Washington and Lee U., 1963; JD, LLB, U. Richmond, 1966. Bar: Va. 1966. Judge 11th Jud. Dist., Petersburg, 1973-75; sole practice, 1975-98; purchasing agt., risk mgr., code enforcement support mgr. City of Petersburg, 1999—. Special asst. city atty., Petersburg. Capt. JAGC, U.S. Army, 1966-71. Mem. ABA, Va. State Bar, Petersburg Bar Assn. (pres. 1984-85). Office: City of Petersburg City Hall Annex 103 W Tabb St Petersburg VA 23803-3211 E-mail: labuy@techcom.net.

ROSENSTOCK, SUSAN LYNN, orchestra administrator; b. Bklyn., Nov. 2, 1947; BS, SUNY, Cortland, 1969; MBA, So. Meth. U., 1977, MFA, 1978. Asst. mgr. Columbus (Ohio) Symphony Orch., 1978-82; grants program dir., info. officer Greater Columbus Arts Coun., 1982-83, asst. dir. grants and adminstrn., 1983-84; dir. annual giving and spl. events Columbus Symphony Orch., 1984-86, dir. devel., 1986-90, orch. mgr., 1990-98, gen. mgr., 1998—. Panelist Ohio Arts Coun. Music Panel, 1986, 87, Challenge Grants Panel, 1991, J.C. Penney Gold Rule Award Judges Panel, 1993, 94. Mem. Am. Symphony Orch. League (devel. dirs. steering com. nat. conf. 1987, 88), Nat. Soc. Fund Raising Execs. (program com. Ctrl. Ohio chpt. 1988-94, chmn. program com. 1993, 94, bd. dirs. 1993-95, treas. 1995). Office: Columbus Symphony Orch 55 E State St Columbus OH 43215-4203 E-mail: susanr@columbussymphony.com.

ROSENSWEIG, RONALD ELLIS, scientist consultant; b. Hamilton, Ohio, Nov. 8, 1932; s. Herman and Deana (Meisel) R.; m. Ruth Evelyn Cohen, Sept. 5, 1954; children— Scott Elliot, Beth Ellen, Perry Ethan Chem. Engr., U. Cin., 1955; S.M., MIT, 1956, Sc.D., 1959. Asst. prof. dept. chem. engring. MIT, Cambridge, 1959-62; prin. scientist Avco Corp., Wilmington, Mass., 1962-69; pres., tech. dir., co-founder Ferrofluidics Corp., Burlington, 1969-73, also dir., 1969-85; rsch. assoc. Exxon Corp., Annandale, N.J., 1973-78, sr. rsch. assoc., 1978-85, sci. advisor, 1985-95; internat. rsch. chair Blaise Pascal, Paris, 1996-98. Vis. prof. U. Minn., Mpls., 1980, U. Chgo., 1990, Weizmann Inst. Sci., Israel, 1997. Author: Ferrohydrodynamics, 1985; contbr. articles to profl. jours.; patentee in field Fellow NSF, MIT, 1955-56; recipient IR-100 awards Indsl. Rsch. Pubs., 1968, 69, 71; named Young Engr. of Yr., Avco Corp., 1966, Disting. Engring. Alumnus U. Cin., 1986. Mem. Nat. Acad. Engring., Am. Inst. Chem. Engrs. (Alpha Chi Sigma award for rsch. 1985), Am. Phys. Soc., Magnetic Fluids Conf., Internat. Steering Com. (chmn. 1977-92). Jewish. Home: 34 Gloucester Rd Summit NJ 07901-3023 E-mail: resosen@comcast.net.

ROSENTHAL, AARON, management consultant; b. N.Y.C., July 12, 1914; s. Zelig and Sarah (Shapinsky) R.; m. Edna Blanche Finkel, Sept. 3, 1940; children— Stephen Mark, Marjorie Ann. BA, Coll. City N.Y., 1934, MS in Edn, 1935; postgrad., Georgetown U. Law Sch., 1937-39, Am. U., 1950-53. Dir. Internal Audit Service, VA, Washington, 1953-58; controller VA, 1958-60; dir. financial mgmt. NASA, 1960-61; comptroller NSF, 1961-69, Nat. Acad. Scis., 1969-76; exec. cons. Coopers & Lybrand. Fin. cons. to Ctr. for Devel. and Population Activities; fin. and mgmt. cons. to Joint Oceanographic Instns. Inc.; U.S. rep. supr. Radiation Effects Rsch. Found., Hiroshima, Japan; mem. nat. adv. coun. nat. Ctr. for Higher Edn. Mgmt. Systems; bd. dirs. TCOA, Inc., Manchester Center, Vt. Trustee Sci. Service Inc. Served with AUS, 1943-45. Recipient Exceptional Service award VA, 1960; Merit citation Nat. Civil Service League, 1957; Distinguished Service award NSF, 1969 Fellow AAAS; mem. Am. Soc. Pub. Adminstrn., Assn. Govt. Accts. Home: 3001 Veazey Ter NW Washington DC 20008-5454 Office: 2101 Constitution Ave NW Washington DC 20418-0007 E-mail: aared@starpower.net.

ROSENTHAL, ALAN SAYRE, government official; b. N.Y.C., Sept. 30, 1926; s. Morris S. and Elizabeth (Ralph) R.; m. Helen Miller, Sept. 8, 1951; children: Edward S., Susan L., Richard M., James M. AB, U. Pa., 1948; LL.B., Yale U., 1951. Bar: N.Y. 1952. Asst. in instrn. Yale U. Law Sch., 1950-51; law clk. to U.S. Circuit Judge Henry W. Edgerton, Washington, 1951-52; atty. appellate sect., civil div. Justice Dept., 1952-72, asst. chief, 1958-72; adminstrv. judge atomic safety and licensing appeal panel AEC (now Nuclear Regulatory Commn.), Washington, 1972-91, chmn., 1972-88; adminstrv. judge pers. appeals bd. GAO, 1991-96, chmn., 1992-94; adminstrv. judge atomic safety and licensing bd. panel Nuclear Regulatory Commn., 1999—. Mem. ethics panel Montgomery County Bd. Edn., 1987-93; lectr. law U. Pa., 1981-83, Am. U., 1991-92. Pres. Kensington Elem. Sch. PTA, 1966-67; pres. North Chevy Chase Swimming Pool Assn., 1974-76; chmn. trustees Cedar Ln. Unitarian Universalist Ch., 1970-71; bd. dirs. Montgomery chpt. ACLU, 1967-69. Served with USAAF, 1944-46. Recipient John Marshall award Justice Dept., 1969, Disting. Svc. award Nuclear Regulatory Commn., 1988. Mem. Order of Coif, Phi Beta Kappa, Pi Gamma Mu, Delta Sigma Rho Home: 3203 Kent St Kensington MD 20895-3210 E-mail: rsnthl@aol.com.

ROSENTHAL, ALBERT JAY, advertising agency executive; b. Chgo., Sept. 30, 1928; s. Harry and Jennie (Comm) R.; m. Rhoda R. Rosenstein, June 18, 1950; children: Jayne, Michael, James, Nancy. BA, U. Ill., 1950. Reporter Transradio Press., Chgo., 1950-51; columnist Lerner Newspapers, 1951-53; creative dir. Elliot, Jaynes & Baruch, 1953-61; chmn. Albert Jay Rosenthal & Co., Chgo. and N.Y.C., 1961-85; chmn. Midwest div. HBM/Creamer-Albert Jay Rosenthal, Chgo., 1985-88, Della Femina, McNamee WCRS, Inc., Chgo., 1988-93; chmn. DFM/Tatham, 1993; founder, pres. Franchising & Licensing World Ctr., 1994-98; v.p. mktg., chief mktg. officer Terry Farms Inc., Wayzata, Minn., 1998—. Weekly columnist Franchising and You, Chgo. Sun-Times. Bd. dirs. Ill. Arts Alliance Found., Ill. Arts Alliance, Court Theatre U. Chgo.; mem. sustaining fund com. Ravinia Festival Assn.; mem. mktg. com. World Bus. Coun., Washington; vice chmn. Chgo. Internat. Film Festival; v.p. Gastro-Intestinal Rsch. Found. U. Chgo. Named one of Chgo. Ten Outstanding Young Men, Chgo. Jr. Assn. of Commerce, 1962, Advt. Man of Yr., Alpha Delta Sigma, 1978, Communicator of Yr., Jewish United Fund, 1988 Jewish. Home: 1110 N Lake Shore Dr Apt 32N Chicago IL 60611-1022

ROSENTHAL, ALBERT LESTER, dermatologist, educator; b. New Bedford, Mass., July 25, 1926; s. Myer and Ruth Naomi (Gourse) R.; m. Carol Ash, July 30, 1969; children: Robert, Jill, Bruce. BA magna cum laude, Tufts U., 1946, MD, 1951. Diplomate Am. Bd. Dermatology. Intern R.I. Hosp., Providence, 1951-52, asst. resident surgery, 1952-53; asst. resident dermatology Mass. Gen. Hosp., Boston, 1955-56; asst. in dermatology NYU, 1958-60; practice medicine specializing in dermatology Trenton, N.J., 1958—; attending dermatologist Mercer Hosp., 1958—, chief dermatologist, 1958-93; chief dermatology Helene Euld Hosp., 1973-85; assoc. in dermatology U. Pa., Phila., 1969-73; assoc. prof. dermatology Hahnemann Med. Coll., 1973-87, clin. prof. dermatology, 1987—; mem. staff Grad. Hosp. Pa., 1969-73, Hamilton Hosp., chief dermatologist, 1972-76. Contbr. numerous articles on dermatology to med. jours. Trustee Friend of the N.J. State Mus., 1972—, chmn. bd. trustees, 1980-82, v.p. fine arts, 1978-80; gov. appointee adv. coun. N.J. State Mus., 1994-2000; adv. bd. Princeton Sr. Resource Ctr., 1997—, Am. Art Newark Mus., 1998-2002; mem. Mercer County Cultural and Heritage Commn., 1982-2000, chmn., 1984-2000; mem. Mercer County Open Space Preservation Commn., 1992-2000; founding mem. Leader's Soc. Dermatology Found., 1988; gov. appointee Bd. Trustees N.J. State Mus., 2000—. Served to capt., M.C., USAF, 1953-55. Mem. Am. Acad. Dermatology, Pa. Acad. Dermatology, Noah Worcester Dermatology Soc., Phila. Dermatology Soc. (pres. 1984-85), N.J. Dermatology Soc., N.J. Med. Soc., Mercer Med. Soc., AMA. Jewish. Office: 74 Franklin Corner Rd Lawrenceville NJ 08648-2102 E-mail: carosentha@aol.com.

ROSENTHAL, AMNON, pediatric cardiologist; b. Gedera, Israel, July 14, 1934; came to U.S., 1949, naturalized, 1959; s. Joseph and Rivka Rosenthal; m. Prudence Lloyd, July 22, 1962; children: Jonathan, Eben, Nathaniel. MD, Albany Med. Coll., 1959. Intern Buffalo Children's Hosp., 1959-60; resident in pediatrics Children's Hosp. Med. Center, Boston, 1960-62, resident in pediatric cardiology, 1965-68; asso. prof. pediatrics Children's Hosp. Med. Center and Harvard U. Med. Sch., Boston, 1975-77; prof. pediatrics C.S. Mott Children's Hosp., U. Mich., Ann Arbor, 1977—, assoc. dir. dept. pediatrics, 1989-92, dir. pediatric cardiology, 1977-97. Served to capt. M.C. USAF, 1962-65. Amnon Rosenthal endowed professorship U. Mich., 1994. Mem. Am. Acad. Pediatrics, Soc. for Pediatric Rsch., Am. Pediatric Soc., Am. Heart Assn., Am. Coll. Cardiology, Am. Bd. Pediatrics, Am. Bd. Pediatric Cardiology (chmn. 1987-88). Office: CS Mott Children's Hosp Ann Arbor MI 48109-0204 E-mail: amnonr@umich.edu.

ROSENTHAL, ARNOLD H. film director, producer, writer, graphic designer, calligrapher; b. Chgo., Jan. 31, 1933; s. Gus and Sara (Ariel) R.; children: Michel, Jason, Anthony. BA, U. Ill., 1954. Graphic designer Whitaker-Guernsey Studios, Chgo., 1954-55; art dir. Edward H. Weiss Advt., 1956-60; owner Arnold H. Rosenthal & Assos., 1960-70; partner, creative dir., pres. Meyer & Rosenthal Inc. (mktg. communications), 1970-75; sr. v.p., creative dir. Garfield-Linn & Co. (Advt.), 1975-81; pres., exec. prodr./dir. Film Chgo., 1981—. TV comml. jury chmn. Chgo. Internat. Film Festival, 1977, 78, 79, 87, mem. governing bd., 1984—; represented at Moscow Film Fest, 1990; TV jury chmn. U.S. Festival, 1980; lectr. Columbia Coll., Purdue U., U. Ill., Ohio State U. Contbr. articles to profl. publs. Bd. dirs. Jewish United Fund. Served with AUS, 1955-56. Recipient creative awards Communication Clubs Chgo., N.Y.C., 1960—, Silver medal N.Y. Film Festival, 1986, Clio award, 1981. Mem. Soc. Typographic Arts (design awards 1958—, pres. 1971-72), Am. Inst. Graphic Arts (spl. award 1974), Dirs. Guild Am., Jazz Inst. Chgo. (charter, jazz drummer), Tau Epsilon Phi, Alpha Delta Sigma.

ROSENTHAL, ARTHUR JESSE, publisher; b. N.Y.C., Sept. 26, 1919; s. Arthur J. and Grace (Ellinger) R.; m. Margaret Ann Roth, Dec. 12, 1975; children: James, Kathryn, Paul. BA, Yale U., 1941; postgrad., Harvard U. Bus. Sch., 1942. Spl. asst. to U.S. ambassador to Israel, Jerusalem, 1948; pres., editor in chief Basic Books, Inc., N.Y.C., 1949-72; dir. Harvard U. Press, Cambridge, 1972-90; pub. Hill and Wang, N.Y.C., 1990—. Founding trustee Bank St. Coll. Edn., 1952-68 Editorial bd.: Pub. Interest, Harvard Bus. Rev, Family Process, Yale U. Press. Trustee Austen Riggs Center, Stockbridge, Mass. Served to capt., M.I. U.S. Army, 1942-46. Mem.: Century Assn. (N.Y.C.); St. Botolph (Boston).

ROSENTHAL, BRIAN DAVID, lawyer; b. Glen Ridge, N.J., May 1, 1952; s. Charles and Dorothy H. (Stanger) R.; m. Joy N. Weisman, Aug. 11, 1974; children: Adam M., Elizabeth J., Alexander H. BA magna cum laude, U. Pa., Phila., 1974; JD, Georgetown U., Washington, 1977. Bar: Pa. 1977, U.S. Dist. Ct. (ea. dist.) Pa. 1983, U.S. Ct. Appeals (3rd cir.) 1984. Asst. dist. atty. Phila. Dist. Attys. Office, 1977-82; assoc. atty. Ominsky Joseph & Welsh PC, Phila., 1982-85; ptnr. Ominsky Welsh & Rosenthal PC, 1986-92; pres., founding ptnr. Rosenthal & Weisberg PC, 1992—; commr. Bd. Commrs., Lower Merion Township, Pa., 1994—. Settlement master Phila. Ct. Common Pleas, 1993—. Author: Medical Malpractice in Pennsylvania, 1993, Insurance Litigation in Pennsylvania, 1993. Pres. Lower Merion Little League, 1991—; dir. baseball Kaiserman J.C.C., Penn Wynne, Pa., 1985; bd. dirs. Nat. Multiple Sclerosis Soc., Phila., 1979-84. Named Outstanding Vol. Kaiserman Jewish Cmty. Ctr., Penn Wynne, 1985, Outstanding Adult Vol. Lower Merion Little League, 1993. Mem. ABA (sects. on litigation, tort and ins. practice, criminal justice), Assn. Trial Lawyers Am., Pa. Trial Lawyers Assn., Pa. Bar Assn., Phila. Bar Assn. (coms. medico legal com., state judiciary com. 1993—), Phi Beta Kappa. Avocations: baseball, reading, travel, coaching. Office: Rosenthal & Weisberg PC 2 Logan Sq Ste 1565 Philadelphia PA 19103-2753

ROSENTHAL, CARLA, medical/surgical nurse; b. Connellsville, Pa., Jan. 6, 1954; d. Charles T. and Christine M. (Dalansky) Freda; m. Lewis Rosenthal, June 30, 1978. Diploma, Uniontown (Pa.) Hosp., 1974. Oper. rm. nurse Allegheny Gen. Hosp., Pitts., 1974-76, Westmoreland Hosp., Greensburg, 1976-78, New York United Hosp. Med. Ctr., Port Chester, NY, 1979—2001, St. John's Riverside Hosp., Yonkers, 2001—. Mem. Assn. Oper. Rm. Nurses (cert. oper. rm. nurse, bd. dirs. 1989-91, treas. 1993—, mem. nominating com. 1992-93), N.Y. State Nurses Assn. E-mail: carlarosenthal@hotmail.com.

ROSENTHAL, CHARLES LOUIS, artist, educator; b. Chgo., Apr. 9, 1917; s. Henry Ditmar and Fredericka (Hoff) R.; m. Joyce Mary La Rocca, Aug. 5, 1944; children: John, James. Student, Central Coll., Chgo., 1937, Art Inst. of Chgo., 1936, Northwestern U., Chgo., 1939, Ariz. State U., 1972, Am. Acad. Art, 1937. Ptnr. Hobbs Rosenthal Studios, Chgo., 1935-40, Metcalf Engravers, Chgo., 1940-53; owner Metcalf Printers, Inc., Itasca, Ill., 1954-68, Pro/Ad Inc., Itasca, 1960-68; pvt. artist/tchr. of papermaking Scottsdale, Ariz., 1968—. Tchr. Shemer Art Ctr., Phoenix, 1980—, Guild Sch. of Art, Phoenix, 1980—; condr. seminars and workshops in field. Writer/artist: The Art World at Your Fingertips, 1991. Founder Inner City Art Program, Phoenix, 1989, Guild Sch. of Art, Phoenix, 1988. Named to Ariz. Artists Guild Hall of Fame, 1995. Mem. Ariz. Artists Guild, Ariz. Watercolor Assn., No. Ariz. Watercolor Assn., Scottsdale Artists League, Itasca Athletic Assn. (founder). Republican. Avocations: family, golf, art, minerals, gardening. Home: 8125 E Gail Rd Scottsdale AZ 85260-6556

ROSENTHAL, CHARLES MICHAEL, financial executive; b. Bklyn., Nov. 21, 1935; s. David B. and Edna (Lefcort) R.; m. Eva F. Sonnenberg, July 7, 1963; children: Andrea (dec.), Nicole. BA, Colgate U., 1957. Rsch. asst. Fed. Res. Bank N.Y., N.Y.C., 1960-62; v.p. L.M. Rosenthal & Co., Inc., 1962-74; ptnr. 1st Manhattan Co., N.Y.C., 1974—. Trustee Brown U., Providence, 1992—; dir. Perlman Music Program, 1998—. Capt. USAF, 1957-60. Mem. East Hampton Tennis Club. Jewish. Home: 784 Park Ave New York NY 10021-3553 Office: 1st Manhattan Co 437 Madison Ave New York NY 10022-7001

ROSENTHAL, DAVID M. philosophy educator, cognitive science professor and administrator; b. New York, Ny, Apr. 10, 1939; s. Morris S. and Helen Cohen Rosenthal; children: Joshua M. PhD, Princeton University, Princeton, Nj, 1961—65; AB, University Of Chicago, Chicago, Il, 1957—61; MA, MA, Princeton University, Princeton, Nj, 1961—65; AB, University Of Chicago, Chicago, Il, 1957—61. Coordinator of cognitive science Graduate Center, City University of New York, New Yorkj, Ny, 1992—now; professor of philosophy City University of New York, Graduate Center and Lehman College, New York, 1971—now; assistant professor Rutgers University, New Brunswick, Nj, 1967—71. Co-chair Columbia University Seminar in History and Philosophy of Science, New York, Ny, 1997—2001; editorial boards Various journals: Philosophical Psychology, Consciousness and Cognition, Journal of Consciousness Studies, Midwest Studies in Philosophy, Psyche, Various, -—2001. Author: (book) Consciousness and Mind, 2002; editor: The Nature of Mind, 1991, Materialism and the Mind-Body Problem, 2nd edition, 2000; author: (journal articles) The Journal of Philosophy, Mind and Language, Philosophical Topics, Consciousnes and Cognition, Philosophical Studies, Philosophical Psychology, Jl of the American Psychoanalytic Assn, Philosophical Perspectives, Social Research , --, Analysis, ----. Mem.: Assn for the Scientific Study of Consciousness, Society for Philosophy and Psychology, American Philosophical Assn. Home: 425 Riverside Drive New York NY 10025 Office: City University Of New York Graduate Cen 365 Fifth Avenue New York NY 10016-4309 Office Fax: (212) 817-1526. Personal E-mail: dro@ruccs.rutgers.edu. Business E-Mail: dro@ruccs.rutgers.edu.

ROSENTHAL, DONNA MYRA, social worker; b. Rochester, N.Y., Feb. 23, 1944; d. Harry Lionel and Leila Estelle (Eber) Rosenthal; m. Thomas Robert Kolar, Aug. 5, 1979. BA, George Washington U., 1965; MS, Columbia U., 1967. Cert. social worker. Community organizer Health & Welfare Coun. Nassau County, Uniondale, N.Y., 1967-68; field rep. N.Y. State Office Aging, N.Y.C., 1968-73; asst. dir. United Neighborhood Houses, 1973-84; exec. dir. Nat. Down Syndrome Soc., 1984-94; exec. vice chmn. CLAL-The Nat. Jewish Ctr. for Learning and Leadership, 1994—. Pres. Exec. Women in Human Svcs., N.Y.C., 1985-89. Pres. Congregation Beth Elohim, Bklyn., 1991-94; pres. Columbia U. Social Work Alumni, N.Y.C., 1989-91; 3rd vice chmn. adv. coun. Columbia U. Sch. Social Work, 1991-2000, co-chair centennial com., 1995-98, chmn. adv. coun. 2000—; treas. Alumni Fedn. Columbia U., 1995-97, sec., 1997-99, v.p., 1999-2001, pres. 2001—. Recipient Alumni medal Columbia U., 1991; NIMH fellow Columbia U., 1966-67, Regents scholar, 1961. Avocation: music. Office: CLAL 440 Park Ave S New York NY 10016-8012

ROSENTHAL, DOUGLAS EURICO, lawyer, author; b. N.Y.C., Feb. 12, 1940; s. Jacob and Edna Louise (Muir) R.; m. Erica Switzen Kremen, Nov. 12, 1967; children: Benjamin Muir, Rachel Elizabeth. BA summa cum laude, Yale U., 1961, LLB, 1966, PhD in Polit. Sci. 1970; postgrad., Oxford (Eng.) U., 1962; MA, Columbia U., 1963. Bar: N.Y. 1968, U.S. Supreme Ct. 1976, D.C. 1980. Project dir. Russell Sage Found., N.Y.C., 1968-70; assoc. Fried, Frank, Harris, Shriver & Jacobson, 1970-74; asst. chief fgn. commerce sect., antitrust div. Dept. Justice, Washington, 1974-77, chief, 1977-80; ptnr. Sutherland, Asbill & Brennan, 1980-88, Coudert Bros., 1989-94, Sonnenschein, Nath & Rosenthal, Washington, 1994—; reporter Am. Law Inst.-Am. Bar Assn. Model Lawyer Peer Rev. System, 1980. Adj. prof. Tokyo U. Law Sch., 1992; spkr. USIA, Australia, France, Eng., Can., Germany, Japan; escrow agt. Boesky settlement funds paid to U.S. Govt.; expert in internat. litigation and U.S. Fgn. rels. law. Author: (with D. Baker and others) Antitrust Guide for International Operations, 1977; author: Lawyer and Client: Who's in Charge?, 1972, 2d rev. edit., (with Knighton) National Law and International Commerce: The Problem of Extraterritoriality, 1982, Competition Policy in Hufbauer, Europe, 1992: An American Perspective, 1990; co-editor (with Carl Green) Competition Regulation in the Pacific Rim, 1996; author (with others) Global Competition Policy, 1997; mem. bd. advisors Antitrust and Trade Regulation Reporter, Am. Antitrust Inst., George Washington Jour. Internat. Law and Econ.; contbr. articles to profl. publs. Committeeman Nassau County (N.Y.) Dem. Com., 1963-65; lifetime mem. corp. Culinary Inst. Am.; mem. Brookings Roundtable on Trade and Investment; mem. trade and competition com. Internat. C. of C. Recipient Edward S. Corwin nat. award Am. Polit. Sci. Assn., 1971; Henry fellow Balliol Coll., Oxford U., 1962, Nobel Internat. and Woodrow Wilson fellow Columbia U., 1963. Mem. ABA (internat. law, litigation and antitrust sect.), Coun. on Fgn. Rels., Am. Law Inst. (life, adv. com. law governing lawyers), Confrerie des Chevaliers du Tastevin, Mory's Assn., Phi Beta Kappa. Jewish. Office: 1301 K St NW Ste 600 Washington DC 20005-3317

ROSENTHAL, EDWARD LEONARD, secondary school educator; b. Chgo., June 15, 1948; s. Irving H. and Nina (Kritchevsky) R.; m. Hilary Rosenberg, June 29, 1969; children: Rachel, Rebecca. BS in Sci. and Letters, U. Ill., 1969; MEd in Earth Sci., Northern Ill. U., 1972. Tchr. St. Joseph Sch., Dyer, Ind., 1969-70; tchr., golf coach Joliet (Ill.) Cath. High Sch., 1970-77; tchr., girls golf coach Naperville (Ill.) N. High Sch., 1977—. Chmn. United Multi Family Homeowners, Bolingbrook, Ill., 1974-75; v.p. Ill. Jr. Miss Program, Bolingbrook, 1985-87; trustee Village of Bolingbrook, 1975-81, mayor, 1981-85; bd. dirs. West Suburban Temple Har Zion, 1988-92. Named one of Outstanding Young men Am., 1975, 82, Ill. Girls' Golf Coach of Yr., 1988-89; elected to Ill. Golf Coaches Hall of Fame, 1995; recipient Disting. Svc. award, 1974. Mem. NEA, (bd. dirs. 1999—) Ill. Edn. Assn. (bd. dirs., 1992-98, 99—, exec. com. 1994-98, chmn. legis. com. 1987-90), Ill. Earth Sci. Assn., Nat. Sci. Tchrs. Assn., Ill. Girls' Golf Coaches Assn. (pres. 1985-88), Naperville Unit Edn. Assn. (1st v.p. 1990-95), Cmty. Assn. Inst. Ill. (bd. dirs. 1980-83), Ill. Jr. Golf Assn. (bd. dirs.). Jewish. Avocation: golf. Home: 508 Clover Ln Bolingbrook IL 60440-1416 Office: Naperville N High Sch 899 N Mill St Naperville IL 60563-2909 E-mail: edrosenthal@hotmail.com.

ROSENTHAL, ELIZABETH ROBBINS, physician; b. Bklyn., Feb. 10, 1943; d. Marc and Ruth Jackson (Oginz) Robbins; m. Samuel Leonard Rosenthal, June 26, 1940; children: Thomas, Benjamin, Marc. AB, Smith Coll., 1963; MD, NYU, 1967. Diplomate Am. Bd. of Dermatology. Intern in pediatrics Upstate Med. Ctr., Syracuse, N.Y., 1967-68; resident in dermatology Henry Ford Hosp., Detroit, 1968-69, Roosevelt Hosp., N.Y.C., 1969-70, Boston U. Med. Ctr., 1972-74; pvt. practice Mamaroneck, N.Y., 1976—; attending United Hosp., Pt. Chester, NY, 1994—. Asst. clin. prof. Albert Einstein Coll. Medicine, Bronx, 1978—. Bd. dirs. Community Counseling Ctr., Mamaroneck, N.Y., 1982—. Fellow Am. Acad. Dermatology; mem. N.Y. State Med. Soc., NOW, Westchester County Med. Soc., Am. Med. Women's Assn. Office: 1600 Harrison Ave Mamaroneck NY 10543-3145 E-mail: drelizrose@aol.com.

ROSENTHAL, FAIGI, librarian; b. Montreal, Que., Can., Sept. 6, 1936; d. Hyman and Anne (Podbere) R.; m. Irwin Rosenthal, Sept. 17, 1964; children: Stephen, Barbara. BA, McGill U., Montreal, 1957, MLS, 1958. Asst. head libr. N.Y. Post, N.Y.C., 1978-86; head libr. N.Y. Daily News, 1986—. Office: NY Daily News 450 W 33rd St New York NY 10001-2603 E-mail: FRosenthal@edit.nydailynews.com.

ROSENTHAL, GERT, economist; b. Amsterdam, The Netherlands, Sept. 11, 1935; arrived in Guatemala, 1937; s. Ludwig and Florence (Koenigsberger) R.; m. Margit Uhlmann, Oct. 18, 1959; children: Caroline, Deborah, Jacqueline, Susan. BA, U. Calif., Berkeley, 1957, MA, 1958. Economist Nat. Planning Office, Guatemala, 1960-65; sr. ofcl. Ministry of Fin., Guatemala, 1966-67; sr. economist Secretariat of Cen. Am. Common Market, Guatemala, 1967-68; min. of planning Nat. Planning Office, Guatemala, 1969-70, 73-74; fellow Adlai Stevenson Inst. for Internat. Affairs, Chgo., 1971; coord. UN Tech. Assistance Project UN Conf. of Trade and Devel., Geneva, 1972; dir. Mex. office Econ. Commn. for Latin Am., Mexico City, 1975-85, dep. exec. sec. Santiago, Chile, 1986—87, exec. sec., 1988—97; rep. of Guatemala to the United Nations, 1999—. Author: Direct Foreign Investment in Central America, 1973; contbr. articles to profl. jours. Home: Residencial Santo Domingo Ste 5 Calle de los Duelos Antigua Guatemala Office: Permanent Mission of Guatemala to UN 57 Park Ave New York NY 10016-3006 E-mail: grosenthal@un.int., grosenthal@guate.net.

ROSENTHAL, GLADYS M. real estate appraiser; b. Westfield, Mass. d. Abraham Milstein and Sarah (Yudman) Milstein; m. Jay S. Rosenthal, Apr. 4, 1954; children: Bruce N., Deborah G. MA in Econs. with honors, Syracuse U.; BS in Econs with honors, Simmons Coll.; cert. in Estates & Trusts, Adelphi U. Cert. appraiser, N.Y. Economist U.S. Govt., Washington; instr. econ. theory U. N.H., Durham, Syracuse (N.Y.) U.; estate and trustee adminstr. Harold King, Esq., Wantagh, N.Y.; estate & truste adminstr. Herrick, Feinstein, N.Y.C., Hess Segal Gutterman Pelz & Steiner P.C., N.Y.C.; mng. ptnr. Rosenthal Appraisers, Great Neck, N.Y. Contbr. articles to profl. jours. Pres. East Williston Schs. PTA, Roslyn Heights, N.Y.; program chmn. Sisterhood Temple Sinai, Roslyn Heights, chmn. Adult Culture and Fun Club; mem. Nassau County Sr. Citizens Com.; patron Met. Opera, N.Y. Philharm., Met. Mus. Art. Established fund in perpetuity for Hilell students Simmons Coll. Mem. Appraisal Inst., L.I. Bd. Realtors (appraisal divsn.), N.Y.C. Bd. Real Estate, Hadassah and Jewish Chatauqua Soc. (life), Heritage Soc. N.Y. Philmarm. Avocations: travel, opera, concerts, ballet, swimming. Office: Rosenthal Appraisers 336 Northern Blvd Great Neck NY 11021-4801

ROSENTHAL, HAROLD LESLIE, biochemistry educator; b. Elizabeth, N.J., Mar. 26, 1922; s. Isadore and Sophia (Shapiro) R.; m. Rose Schwartz, June 7, 1947; children: Jenifer Ann, Pamela Susan. B.Sc., U. N. Mex., 1944; PhD, Rutgers U., 1951. Rsch. asst. Rutgers U., New Brunswick, N.J., 1948-51; instr. Tulane U., New Orleans, 1951-53; chief biochemist Rochester Gen. Hosp., N.Y., 1953-58; prof. biomed. scis. Washington U., St. Louis, 1958-87, prof. emeritus, 1987—. Vis. scientist Minerva Found., Finland, 1966, Nat. Acad. Sci., Hungary, 1974. Served with USN, 1943-46 Fellow AAAS; mem. Am. Chem. Soc. (emeritus), Am. Inst. Nutrition, Am. Soc. for Biochemistry and Molecular Biology, Sigma Xi. Avocations: gardening; oenology. Home: 572 Coeur De Royale Dr Apt 104 Saint Louis MO 63141-6952

ROSENTHAL, HELEN NAGELBERG, county official, advocate; b. N.Y.C., June 6, 1926; d. Alfred and Esther (Teichholz) Nagelberg; m. Albert S. Rosenthal, Apr. 10, 1949 (dec.); children: Lisa Rosenthal Michaels, Apryl Meredith Rosenthal Stuppler. BS, CUNY, 1948; MA, NYU, 1950; postgrad., Adelphia U., L.I. U., Lehman Coll., 1975. Cert. early childhood and gifted edn. tchr., N.Y., N.J., elem. and secondary tchr., Fla. Tchr. gifted students N.Y. Bd Edn., Bklyn., 1949-77, 79-87, Baldwin (N.Y.) Pub. Schs., 1977-79; rep. community affairs County of Dade, Fla., 1988-92; ret., 1992; condo dir. Pembroke Pines, 1999—. Author: Criteria for Selection and Curriculum for the Gifted, 1977, Science Experiments for Young Children, 1982, Music in the Air...and in Our Minds. Dir. Condominium, 1989-91. Recipient Departmental award, 1948. Mem. Concerned Citizens for Educating Gifted and Talented (officer N.Y.C. chpt.), Assn. Gifted and Talented Edn. (N.Y. chpt.), Am. Inst. Cancer Rsch., Bklyn. Coll. Alumni Assn. (pres. Broward-Dade chpt. 1995-96, v.p. membership 1996—).

ROSENTHAL, HOWARD LEWIS, political science educator; b. Wilkinsburg, Pa., Mar. 4, 1939; s. Arnold Sidney R. and Elinor (Kaufman) (Rosenthal) Lewis; m. Annie Regine Lunel, June 30, 1960 (div. Nov., 1967); children: Illia Rebecca, Jean Laurent; m. Margherita Guastoni Spampinato, Feb. 6, 1968; 1 son, Gil Guastoni. BS, MIT, 1960, PhD, 1964. Asst. prof. polit. sci. U. Calif.-Irvine, 1965-66; asst. prof. and assoc. prof. polit. sci. Carnegie-Mellon U., Pitts., 1966-71, prof., 1971-93; Roger Williams Straus prof. social scis. Princeton U, N.J., 1993—. Vis. prof. Hebrew U., Jerusalem, 1968-69, U. Calif., San Diego, 1976-77, MIT, Cambridge, 1989-90, U. Paris I, 1990; Walras-Pareto lectr. U. Lausanne, Switzerland, 1996; vis. grad. lectr. Fondation Nat. des Scis. Politiques, Paris, 1972-73. Author: Prediction Analysis of Cross Classifications, 1977, Analysis of Ordinal Data, 1977, Partisan Politics, Divided Government and the Economy, 1995, Flexible Integration: Towards a More Effective and Democratic Europe, 1995, The Realignment of National Politics and Income Redistribution, 1997, Congress: A Political-Economic History of Roll Call Voting, 1997; mem. editl. bd. Pub. Choice, Economics of Governance. Fellow NSF, 1969-92, 98-2000, Ford Found., 1972-73, Social Sci. Rsch. Coun., 1964-65, nat. fellow Hoover Instn., Stanford U., 1979-80; Sherman Fairchild disting. scholar Calif. Inst. Tech., 1982-83; fellow Internat. Ctr. for Econ. Rsch., Turin, Italy, 1991-93, Ctr. for Advanced Study in Behavioral Scis., 1991-92, 98-99, ECARE U. Libre de Brussels, 1995. Fellow Am. Acad. Arts and Scis.; mem. Pub. Choice Soc. (Duncan Black award 1979), Am. Polit. Sci. Assn. (CQ Press award 1985), French Polit. Sci. Assn. Office: Princeton Univ Politics Dept Princeton NJ 08544-0001

ROSENTHAL, ILENE GOLDSTEIN, lawyer; b. New Haven, Aug. 27, 1952; d. Sidney Leon and Marian (Goodman) Goldstein; m. Steven Siegmund Rosenthal, Oct. 1, 1983; children: Alexandra M., Eliana D. BA, Wesleyan U., 1974; JD, Georgetown U., 1982. Bar: Calif. 1983, U.S. Dist. Ct. (cen. and no. dists.) Calif. 1983, D.C. 1985, U.S. Ct. Appeals (D.C. cir.) 1985, U.S. Dist. Ct. D.C. 1986. Law clk. to Hon. William P. Gray U.S. Dist. Ct. for Cen. Dist. Caif., L.A., 1982-83; assoc. Wyman, Bautzer, Rothman, Kuchel & Silbert, 1983-84; asst. U.S. Atty. D.C., Washington, 1985-88; minority gen. counsel House Gov. Ops. Com., 1989-91; gen. counsel, dir. litigation Software Publs. Assn., 1991-94; gen. counsel and v.p. for govt. affairs Lightspan Partnership, Inc., 1994-97; pres. New Image Media, LLC, 1997—2000, 2002—; chair Everybody Wins!, 1995-99, bd. dirs., 1995—; sr. v.p. Lightspan, Inc., 2000—02. Bd. dirs. Nat. Coalition for Tech. in Edn. and Tng., 1996—; bd. dirs. Aidan Montessori Sch., Washington. 1998-2001. Contbg. editor Tech. and Learning Mag., 1999—. Office: 2619 Woodley Pl NW Ste 201 Washington DC 20008-1525

ROSENTHAL, IRA MAURICE, pediatrician, educator; b. N.Y.C., June 11, 1920; s. Abraham Leon and Jean (Kalotkin) R.; m. Ethel Ginsburg, Oct. 17, 1943 (dec.); children: Anne, Judith; m. Irene Farkis-Conn, Apr. 21, 2001. Student, CCNY, 1936-38; AB, Ind. U., 1940, MD, 1943. Intern Lincoln Hosp., N.Y.C., 1943-44; resident in pathology Albert Einstein Hosp., Phila., 1947-48; resident in pediatrics Fordham Hosp., N.Y.C., 1948-49; practice medicine specializing in pediatrics Bklyn., 1950-52; instr. U. Ill. Coll. Medicine, Chgo., 1953, asst. prof., 1953-55, assoc. prof., 1955-63, prof. pediatrics, 1963-90, prof. emeritus, 1990—, head dept., 1973-82; clin. prof. pediatrics Stritch Sch. Medicine Loyola U., Chgo., 1990-91, lectr., 1991-93; clin. assoc. in pediatrics U. Chgo., 1990-91, clin. prof. pediatrics, 1991—. Mem. med. service adv. com. Nat. Found. March of Dimes, 1975-80 Served to capt. U.S. Army, 1944-46. Mem. Am. Pediatric Soc., Soc. Pediatric Research, Acad. Pediatrics, Lawson Wilkins Pediatric Endocrine Soc., Endocrine Soc. Home: 5490 S South Shore Dr Chicago IL 60615-5984

ROSENTHAL, IRVING, journalism educator; b. N.Y.C., July 31, 1912; s. Max and Rose Rosenthal; m. Ruth M. Rosenthal, May 22, 1943; children: David, Robert, Risa. BSS, CCNY, 1933, MS, 1934. Reporter N.Y. Times, N.Y.C., 1933; fellow to full prof. dept. English CCNY, 1933-77, chmn. comms. and mass media, 1946-77, asst. to pres., 1933-43; coord. broadcasting courses Sta. WCBS-TV, 1969-90, emeritus prof., 1977—. Adj. prof. C.W. Post Coll., Brookville, N.Y., 1967-70; editl. cons. Dance mag., 1983-87, Med. Soc. State of N.Y. Editl. adv. bd. Hadassah mag., 1978-96; co-author: Modern Journalism, 1962, A Contemporary Reader, 1961, Art of Writing Made Simple, 1958, Business English Made Simple, 1955. Mem. Silurians, awards chmn. 1989-91. 1st lt. U.S. Army, 1943-45. Mem. Alpha Phi Gamma, Phi Delta Sigma, Phi Delta Kappa. Home and Office: 62 Hampshire Rd Great Neck NY 11023-1537

ROSENTHAL, JAMES D. retired federal official, former U.S. ambassador; b. San Francisco, Jan. 15, 1932. B.A., Stanford U., 1954; student Fgn. Service Inst., 1960-61, Nat War Coll., 1974-75. With U.S. Fgn. Service, 1956-90, adminstrv. officer, Port of Spain, Trinidad, 1958-60; polit officer, Saigon, Vietnam, 1961-65; faculty U.S. Mil. Acad., 1965-67; internat. relations officer Vietnam affairs Dept. State, 1967-70; mem. U.S. dele. to Vietnam Peace Talks, Paris, 1970-72; dep. chief of mission, Bangui, 1972-74; dir. Vietnam, Laos and Cambodia affairs Dept. State, 1975-77; dep. chief of mission Kuala Lumpur, Malaysia, 1977-79; dep chief mission, Manila, 1979-83; ambassador to Guinea, Conakry, 1983-86, dep. dir. mgmt. ops. Dept. State, Washington, 1986-90; exec. dir. Commonwealth Club of Calif., 1990-96.

ROSENTHAL, JOEL, manufacturing executive; b. Ft. Worth, Oct. 25, 1946; s. Melvin and Jane (Hertzman) R.; m. Susan Ellman, Nov. 15, 1970; children: Jackie Ilene, Harold Joseph. BBA, No. Tex. State U., 1969. V.p. First Street Corp., Ft. Worth, 1969-72; mgr. Edison Jewelers & Distbrs., 1972-73; v.p. Yankton Sioux Industries, Wagner, S.D., 1973-81, pres., 1981-85; cons., Canton, 1985—; pres. Ctrl. Plains Tractor Parts, Sioux Falls, 1986—. Cons. econ. devel. State of S.D., Pierre, 1985-86. Chmn. S.D. Rep. Com., 1995—; mem. Electoral Coll., 1996, 2000; pres. City Coun., Wagner, 1978-83; trustees, Carnegie Libr., Wagner, 1978-83; active Rep. Nat. Com., Washington, 1985—, S.D. Jud. Qualifications Commn., 1983-86, Pvt. Industry Coun., Pierre, 1985-86. Named S.D. Vol. of Yr. Office of Gov., 1983. Republican. Jewish. Home: PO Box 6 Canton SD 57013-0006 Office: PO Box 1818 Sioux Falls SD 57101-1818 Also: SD State Rep Party 401 E Sioux Ave Pierre SD 57501-3162

ROSENTHAL, JUDITH WOLDER, biological sciences educator; b. N.Y.C., May 12, 1945; d. Victor R. Wolder and Ruth Beatrice (Rosenbaum) Lipston. BA in Human Biology, Brown U., 1967, PhD in Physiol. Chemistry, 1971; MA in Biling. Bicultural Edn., Kean Coll of N.J., 1995. Post-doctoral fellow U. Toronto, Ontario, Can., 1971-72, McMaster U., Hamilton, Can., 1972-73; prof. biol. sci. Kean U., Union, 1974—. Author: Teaching Science to Language Minority Students, 1996; editor: Handbook of Undergraduate Second Language Education, 2000. Mem. AAAS, Nat. Assn. for Bilingual Edn., Tchrs. of English to Speakers of Other Langs. Avocation: Spanish language. Office: Kean Univ Morris Ave Union NJ 07083

ROSENTHAL, KATE, lawyer, educator; b. Binghamton, N.Y., May 1, 1954; d. Charles Leopold and Ann Solis-Cohen R. BA in Political Sci., History, Earlham Coll., 1976; JD, Syracuse U., 1981. Bar: N.Y. 1982, U.S. Dist. Ct. (no. dist.) N.Y. 1982, U.S. Ct. Appeals (2nd cir.) 1991. Assoc. Alderman, Samuels, Jerry & Rossi, Syracuse, N.Y., 1981-83; pvt. practice, 1983—. Adv. bd. Thompson Publishing, Rochester, N.Y. Adv. com. Medical Examiner Syracuse, 1990-94; mem. Gender Bias com. 5th Dist. Syracuse, 1990-92, Syracuse City Charter Review commn., 1990. Recipient Mover Shaker in Field of Law award Herald Jour. Newspaper, Syracuse, 1988. Mem. Nat. Conference Criminal Justice Act Panel Attorneys (no. dist. rep. 1995—), N.Y. State Assn. Criminal Defense Lawyers (v.p., bd. mem. 1993—) Syracuse Assn. Criminal Defense Lawyers (co-founder 1990—), N.Y. State Bar Assn. (fifth dist. rep. to exec. com. 1996—). Democrat. Jewish. Avocations: travel, snorkeling, photography. Office: Syracuse City Ct Judge 511 S State St Syracuse NY 13202

ROSENTHAL, LAWRENCE EDWARD, association executive; b. Chgo., Nov. 6, 1938; s. Ben M. and Claire (Hartenstein) R.; m. Ina Rae Brown, Dec. 24, 1961; children: Keith Joseph, Scott Richard. Bachelors in Polit. Sci., DePaul U., 1959, Masters in History, 1963; Masters in Ednl. Adminstrn., Roosevelt U., 1965; Doctorate in Adminstrn., Northern Ill. U., 1974. Tchr. Chgo. (Ill.) Bd. Edn., 1960-66, dir. computer based instructional systems, 1966-76; dir. systems devel. AMA, Chgo., 1976-77; deputy exec. dir. Am. Acad. Dermatology, Evanston, Ill., 1977-95; exec. v.p. Dermotology Svcs., Inc., 1982-95; exec. dir. Am. Soc. for Dermotologic Surgery, Evanston, 1979-95; COO Am. Acad. Orthopaedic Surgeons, 1995—. Pres. Skokie (Ill.) Sch. Dist. 73 1/2, 1978-80 (mem. 1974-80). Fellow Am. Soc. Assn. Execs.; mem. Chgo. Area Health Execs. (former pres.), Chgo. Soc. Assn. Execs., Am. Soc. Assn. Execs., Am. Assn. Med. Soc. Execs. Home: 453 Williamsburg Ln Prospect Heights IL 60070-2593 Office: Am Acad Orthopaedic Surgeons 6300 N River Rd Rosemont IL 60018-4206

ROSENTHAL, LEE H. federal judge; b. Nov. 30, 1952; m. Gary L. Rosenthal; children: Rebecca, Hannah, Jessica, Rachel. BA in Philosophy with honors, U. Chgo., 1974, JD with honors, 1977. Bar: Tex. 1979. Law clk. to Hon. John R. Brown U.S. Ct. Appeals (5th cir.), 1977-78; assoc. Baker & Botts, 1978-86, ptnr., 1986-92; judge U.S. Dist. Ct. (so. dist.) Tex., 1992—. Vis. com. Law Sch. U. Chgo., 1983-86, 94-97, 99—; mem. Fed. Jud. Conf. Adv. Com. for Fed. Rules of Civil Procedure, 1996—; chair 1999 Fifth Cir. Jud. Conf. Mem. bd. editors Manual for Complex Litigation, 1999—. Mem. devel. coun. Tex. Children's Hosp., 1988-92; pres. Epilepsy Assn. Houston/Gulf Coast, 1989-91; trustee Briarwood Sch. Endowment Found., 1991-92; bd. dirs. Epilepsy Found. Am., 1993-98, DePelchin Children's Ctr., 2000—. Fellow Tex. Bar Found.; Mem. ABA, Am. Law Inst. (consultative group for transnat. rules of civil procedure), Texas Bar Assn., Houston Bar Assn. Office: US Dist Ct US Courthouse Rm 11535 515 Rusk St Houston TX 77002-2600

ROSENTHAL, LEIGHTON A. aviation company executive; b. Buffalo, Jan. 27, 1915; s. Samuel and Sadie (Dosberg) R.; m. Honey Rousuck, June 30, 1940; children: Cynthia, Jane. Student, Phila. Textile Sch.; grad. Wharton Sch., U. Pa.; hon. doctorate, Cleve. Coll. Jewish Studies, 1973. Pres. Cleve. Overall Co., 1956-61, Work Wear Corp., 1961-86, The Purity Uniform Service Inc., 1986-89, Lars Mgmt. div. Purity Uniform Service Inc., 1986-89, Lars Aviation Inc., 1990—. Chmn. Architecture Commn., City of Palm Beach, 1988-96. Trustee Jewish Cmty. Fedn. Cleve., Leighton A. Rosenthal Family Found.; bd. dirs. Ohio Motorists Assn. Fellow Am. Assn. Jewish Edn., Oakwood Club, Union Club, Poinciana Club, Marks Club, Annabels Club, Doubles Club, Harmonie Club. Office: Lars Aviation Inc The Halle Bldg 1228 Euclid Ave Ste 310 Cleveland OH 44115-1831

ROSENTHAL, LOUIS AARON, electrical engineer; b. N.Y.C., Aug. 16, 1922; s. Meyer and Sadie (Gersh) R.; wife dec. Sept. 1982; children: Joel I., Bruce D., Amy S. BS, CCNY, 1943; MS, Poly. Inst. Bklyn., 1947. Profl. engr. N.J. Prof. elec. engring. Rutgers U., New Brunswick, N.J., 1944-81; tech. dir. Brunswick Instruments, Cranbury, 1950-90; staff cons. Tel Tech, Mpls., 1988—. Devel. assoc., cons. Union Carbide, Bound Brook, N.J., 1950-85; cons. Naval Surface Weapons Ctr., Silver Spring, Md., 1952-85. Home and Office: 384B Stirling Dr Monroe Township NJ 08831-3922

ROSENTHAL, LUCY GABRIELLE, writer, educator, editor; b. N.Y.C. d. Henry Moses and Rachel (Tchernowitz) R. AB, U. Mich., 1954; MS in Journalism, Columbia U., 1955; MFA, Yale Sch. Drama, 1961; postgrad. Writers Workshop, U. Iowa, 1965-68. Asst. editor Radiology mag., Detroit, 1955-57; free-lance editorial cons. various pub. houses, lit. agts. N.Y.C., 1957-73; mem. admissions staff U. Iowa Writers Workshop, Iowa City, 1965-68; editor Book-of-the-Month Club, N.Y.C., 1973-74, mem. editorial bd. judges, 1974-79, sr. editorial advisor, 1979-87. Mem. biography jury Pulitzer Prize, 1980; mem. bd. Am. Book Awards, 1981-82; adj. prof. English, NYU, 1986—; mem. guest faculty in writing Sarah Lawrence Coll., 1988-96, regular faculty writing, 1996—; lectr., adj. asst. prof. writing program Columbia U., 1990-96, Humanities faculty, 92nd St. YM/YWCA, 1987; fiction workshop The Writer's Voice, West Side YMCA, summer 1991; adj. prof. NYU Sch. Continuing Edn., 1988; mem. faculty Sarah Lawrence Ctr. for Continuing Edn., 1989, 90; instr. fiction writing course Art Workshop Internat., Assisi, Italy, summer 1993. Plays produced at Eugene O'Neill Meml. Theater Ctr., 1966, 67; author: The Ticket Out, 1983; editor: Great American Love Stories, 1988, The World Treasury of Love Stores, 1995; contbr. articles and revs. to various mags. and periodicals including Washington Post and Chgo. Tribune Book World, Saturday Rev., Ms. mag., Mich. Quar. Rev., N.Y. Times Book Rev.; contbr. fiction to Global City Rev., 1995. Pulitzer fellow critical writing, 1968 Mem. Authors Guild, Authors League, Nat. Book Critics Circle, Women's Media Group (bd. mem. 1979-81), PEN, Phi Beta Kappa, Phi Kappa Phi. Office: Sarah Lawrence Coll Bronxville NY 10708 E-mail: lrosenthal@mail.slc.edu.

ROSENTHAL, MARVIN BERNARD, pediatrician, educator; b. Bklyn., Jan. 1, 1930; s. Robert Rosenthal and Elizabeth (Gartner) Rosenthal Dreyfuss; m. Janet H. Swerlick, dec. 31, 1959; 1 child, Robert G. BA, Alfred U., 1951; MD, Leiden U., The Netherlands, 1957. Diplomate Nat. Bd. Med. Examiners, Am. Bd. Pediatrics. Intern Kings County Hosp., Bklyn., 1957-58; resident in pediatrics SUNY Downstate Med. Sch., 1958-60; fellow in hematology Children's Hosp. Phila., 1962; pediatrician Somerset Pediatric Group, Bridgewater, N.J., 1963-84; chief pediatrics Somerset Hosp., Somerville, 1983-84; assoc. dir. family practice residency Warren Hosp., Phillipsburg, 1984—99, chief pediatrics, 1991—99, dir. med. edn., 1989—99, lectr. Mem. cons. staff Morristown (N.J.) Meml. Hosp., 1989—; clin. assoc. prof. Robert W. Johnson Med. Sch., UMDNJ, New Brunswick, N.J., 1980—; mem. adj. faculty U. New Eng. Coll. Osteopathics, Biddeford, Maine, 1988—. Capt. USAF, 1960-62. Recipient Silver medallion Am. Heart Assn., 1976, 78. Fellow Am. Acad. Pediatrics, Am. Acad. Family Practice; mem. N.J. Med. Soc., Acad. Medicine N.J., N.J. Pediatric Soc., Soc. Tchrs. Family Medicine, Ambulatory Pediatric Assn., Assn. Hosp. Med. Educators, Eagle Scout Assn. Home: 500 Spring Valley Rd Easton PA 18042-6872 Office: Warren Hosp Roseberry St Phillipsburg NJ 08865-1628 E-mail: janmar@rcn.com.

ROSENTHAL, MAXINE MACKTEZ, jeweler; b. Woonsocket, R.I., Mar. 28, 1946; d. Philip J. and Shirley Strasmich Macktez; m. Jay Rosenthal, June 25, 1967; 1 child, Fae Elise. BA, Boston U., 1967; MBA, U. Del., 1982. Various profl./analyst positions DuPont, Wilmington, Del., 1967-88, various mgmt. positions, 1988-97. Exhibited jewelry at Polymer Clay Show (1st pl. 1999). Com. mem. Fund for Women, Del., 1994—, chair grants com., 1999; dir. YWCA, Wilmington, 1999—, com. co-chair HR, 2001-02, exec. com.; dir. Delaware Ctr. Contemporary Art, 1986-97, treas., 1996-97. Mem. Mental Health Assn. Del. (dir. 1997—, pres. 2000—, v.p. and acting treas. 2002), Pa. Guild Craftsmen (juried mem.), Phi Beta Kappa, Beta Gamma Sigma. E-mail: maxrosenthal@yahoo.com.

ROSENTHAL, MEYER L(OUIS), lawyer; b. Wilkes-Barre, Pa., May 27, 1944; s. Samuel J. and Lottie G. (Goncher) R.; m. Susan M., Aug. 19, 1967; children: Norman, Bonnie. BA, Rutgers Coll., 1966, JD, 1969. Bar: N.J. 1969, U.S. Dist. Ct. N.J. 1969, Calif. 1975, U.S. Dist. Ct. (cen. dist.) Calif. 1981, U.S. Dist. Ct. (ea. dist.) N.Y. 1980, U.S. Dist. Ct. (so. dist.) N.Y. 1981, U.S. Ct. Appeals (9th cir.) 1981. Law sec. Hon. Leon Milmed N.J. Superior Ct., Newark, 1969-70; assoc. Kaufman & Kaufman, Elizabeth, N.J., 1970-76; ptnr. Trueger & Rosenthal, Morristown, 1976-82; atty. pvt. practice, 1982—. Editor Rutgers Law Rev. Cub scout leader Morris Area Boy Scouts Am., Randolph, N.J., 1980; chmn. Morris City Human Rels. Commn., Morristown, 1992-95, chmn. emeritus, 1999. Recipient Cmty. Hero award Morris County Orgn. Hispanic Affairs, 1996. Mem. Comml. Law League Am., Calif. Bar Assn., N.J. Bar Assn., B'nai B'rith (bd. govs. 1975—, pres. dist. 3 1988-89, Internat. Young Leadership award 1982, Internat. Founders award 1985, nat. commn. anti-defamation league 1992—). Office: 161 Washington St Morristown NJ 07960-3753 E-mail: meyer@therosenthals.net.

ROSENTHAL, MICHAEL BRUCE, lawyer; b. Buffalo, Aug. 16, 1955; s. Jack and Elaine Lois (Brill) R.; m. Tori Johnson; children: Lainey, Haley. BA, Colo. Coll., 1978; JD, U. Wyo., 1981. Bar: Wyo. 1983, U.S. Dist. Ct. Wyo. 1983, U.S. Ct. Appeals (10th cir.) 1986. Landman Mobil Coal Resources, Inc., Denver, 1981-84; pub. defender State of Wyo., Gillette, 1984-86; assoc. Hathaway, Speight, Kunz, Trautwein & Barrett, Cheyenne, Wyo., 1986-90; ptnr. Hathaway, Speight, Kunz, & Trautwein, 1990-94; Hathaway, Speight & Kunz, 1994—. Mem. DePaul Hosp. Health Care Task Force, Cheyenne, 1990-92; chmn. Cheyenne Bd. of Adjustment, 1989-90; pres. Cheyenne Symphony Orch., 1991-92, bd. dirs. 1986-94; bd. dirs. Wyo. chpt. Am. Cancer Soc., Cheyenne, 1990-92, Cheyenne Symphony Found., 1992—, pres., 1992-97; bd. dirs. Laramie County Cmty. Found., 1993—. Mem. ABA, Wyo. Bar Assn., ATLA, Wyo. Trial Lawyers Assn. (bd. dirs. 1988—, sec.-treas. 1993, pres.-elect 1993-94, pres. 1994-95), Laramie County Bar Assn. Republican. Avocations: cycling, tennis, squash, golf. Office: Hathaway Speight & Kunz PO Box 1208 Cheyenne WY 82003-1208

ROSENTHAL, MICHAEL PETER, physician; b. Bklyn., Mar. 31, 1954; s. Paul P. and H. Silvia (Heller) R.; m. Joanne Kurz, July 8, 1984; children: Samuel Jordan, Casey Sarah. BA summa cum laude, U. Pa., 1976; MD, U. Med. and Dentistry N.J., 1980. Diplomate Am. Bd. Family Practice, Geriatrics. Resident in family practice Thomas Jefferson U., Phila., 1980-83, fellow in family practice, 1983-84; instr., clin. asst. prof., clin. assoc. prof. Jefferson Med. Coll., 1983-95, clin. prof., dir. cmty. health sect., 1995—. Com. mem. Nat. Bd. Med. Examiners, Phila., 1985—; med. dir. Equicor Preferred, Phila., 1990-92; mem. quality assurance com. Healthcare Mgmt. Alternates, Phila., 1989—. Contbr. chpt. in book and articles to profl. jours. Bd. dirs. Health Promotion Coun. S.E. Pa., Phila., v.p., 1992—, Outstanding Contbns. to Health Promotion award, 1993. Mem.: Phila. Coll. Physicians, Soc. Tchrs. of Family Medicine, Am. Acad. Family Physicians, Phi Beta Kappa, Alpha Epsilon Delta. Avocations: sports, music. Office: Jefferson Med Coll Dept Family Medicine 1015 Walnut St Ste 401 Philadelphia PA 19107-5005

ROSENTHAL, MICHAEL ROSS, academic administrator, consultant; b. Youngstown, Ohio, Dec. 2, 1939; s. Samuel Herman and Frances Vance (Schlesinger) R.; m. Linda Gabler, Sept. 6, 1963; children: Heidi, Erika, Nicolas Gabler. AB, Case Western Res. U., 1961; MS, U. Ill., 1963, PhD, 1965. Asst. prof. chemistry Bard Coll., Annandale, N.Y., 1965-68, assoc. prof. chemistry, 1968-73, prof. chemistry, 1973-84, assoc. dean acad. affairs, 1980-84; v.p. acad. affairs St. Mary's Coll. of Md., St. Mary's City, 1984-89; provost, dean faculty, prof. chemistry Southwestern U., Georgetown, Tex., 1989-96; dep. sec. Md. Higher Edn. Commn., Annapolis, 1996—99; spl. asst. to provost McDaniel Coll., Westminster, Md., 1999—. Acad. cons., ind. and as rep. of Assn. Am. Colls. Author or co-author of numerous articles in jours. of inorganic chemistry and chem. edn. Chmn. Environ. Mgmt. Coun., Dutchess County, N.Y., 1978-84; founding chmn. Heritage Task Force for Hudson River Valley, 1980-84; pres., bd. dirs. Hudson River Heritage, N.Y., 1978-84; bd. dirs. Hudson River Rsch. Coun., 1976-84; teaching assoc. Danforth Found., 1980. Recipient Outstanding Community Svc. award, Dutchess County (N.Y.) Legislature, 1980. Mem. Am. Chem. Soc., The Royal Society (Chemistry, London), Am. Conf. Acad. Deans, Hudson River Environ. Soc., Sigma Xi, Phi Beta Kappa, Phi Lambda Upsilon Democrat. Office: McDaniel Coll 2 College Hill Westminster MD 21157 Business E-Mail: mrosenth@mcdaniel.edu. *Those of us who spend our professional lives as educators are subject to many pressures and influences - financial influences, political influences, intellectual influences. I try to remember that in the usually chaotic world of education the only really important thing is the welfare of the student.*

ROSENTHAL, MILTON FREDERICK, chemical and minerals company executive; b. N.Y.C., Nov. 24, 1913; s. Jacob C. and Louise (Berger) R.; m. Frieda Bojar, Feb. 28, 1943; 1 child, Anne Rosenthal Mitro. BA, CCNY, 1932; LLB, Columbia U., 1935. Bar: N.Y. 1935. Rsch. asst. N.Y. State Law Revision Commn., 1935-37; law sec. Fed. Judge William Bondy, 1937-40; assoc. atty. Leve, Hecht & Hadfield, 1940-42; sec., treas. Hugo Stinnes Corp., 1946-48, exec. v.p., treas., CEO, 1948-49, pres., dir., CEO, 1949-64, Minerals and Chems. Philipp Corp., N.Y.C., 1964-67; pres., dir., COO Engelhard Minerals & Chem. Corp., 1967-71; chmn., pres., CEO, dir. Engelhard Minerals & Chems. Corp., 1971-81; dir. Salomon, Inc., 1981-88, dir. emeritus, 1988-98; chmn. Engelhard Corp., N.J., 1981-86. Ret. dir. US-USSR Trade and Econ. Coun., 1974-82, Nat. Coun. US-China Trade, 1977-82; chmn., dir. Romanian-Am. Econ. Coun., 1974-89; dir. Fgn. Policy Assn., 1971-91. Life trustee Mt. Sinai Med. Ctr.; bd. dirs. United Cerebral Palsy Rsch. and Ednl. Found., Inc.; ret. trustee Am. Fedn. Arts, Manhattanville Coll., Purchase Coll. Found. 1st lt. JAG dept. U.S. Army, 1942-45. Mem. Assn. of Bar of City of N.Y., Chgo. Bar Assn., Columbia Law Sch. Alumni Assn., Judge Adv. Assn., Phi Beta Kappa. Home: 450 Woodlands Rd Harrison NY 10528-1220 also: 1602 Quartz Valley Dr Carefree AZ 85377 Office: 450 Park Ave Ste 2701 New York NY 10022-2605

ROSENTHAL, MORRIS WILLIAM, pediatrician; b. Houston, July 1, 1926; s. Louis Isaac and Della (Stramer) R.; m. Julien Bliss Epstein, Sept. 11, 1949; children: Laura Ann, Lee Stephen, Sara Jan, Louis Isaac, Martha Bliss. Student, Tex. Tech. U., 1944, Tex. A&M U., 1945, U. Houston, 1946; MD, U. Tex. Med. Br., Galveston, 1951; cert. flight surgeon, USAF Sch. Aerospace Medicine, 1981. Intern Jefferson Davis Hosp., Houston, 1951-52; resident Jefferson Davis Hosp.-Baylor Coll. Medicine, 1953-54, Tex. Children's Hosp., Houston, 1954-55; attending physician Savannah River Project, Aiken, S.C., 1952-53; pvt. practice pediatrics Ashford Pediat. Assocs., Houston, 1955—. Sr. aviation med. examiner FAA, Houston, 1982—. Col. USAFR, ret., 1980-86. Jewish. Office: Ashford Pediat Assocs 14730 Barryknoll Ln Houston TX 77079-2800 E-mail: doctormwr@aol.com.

ROSENTHAL, MURRAY WILFORD, chemical engineer, science administrator; b. Greenville, Miss., Feb. 25, 1926; s. Monnie and Esther (Bernstein) R.; m. Miriam Sylvia Teplit, Aug. 7, 1949; children: Elaine, Douglas I. BSChemE, La. State U., 1949; PhDChemE, MIT, 1953. Devel. engr. heat transfer rsch., reactor exptl. engring. div. Oak Ridge (Tenn.) Nat. Lab., 1953-55, group leader aqueous homogeneous reactor analysis, 1956-59, group leader analysis advanced reactors, reactor div., 1959-61, project engr., 1961-63, chief planning and analysis sect., 1963-65, dir. planning, 1965, dir. molten salt reactor program, 1966-73, acting dep. dir., 1973, assoc. dir. advanced energy systems, 1974-89, dep. dir., 1989-93, lectr. in reactor engring. sch. reactor tech., 1955; cons., 1994—. Vis. prof. chem. engring. MIT, Boston, 1961; tech. asst. to asst. gen. mgr. AEC, Washington, 1966. Vice chmn. Oak Ridge Charter Commn., 1955-56, chmn., 1962-63; mem. Oak Ridge Human Rels. Adv. Bd., 1963-65, Adv. Task Force on Tenn. Energy Future, Oak Ridge, 1978; pres. Oak Ridge Inst. for Continued Learning, 1997-99. Lt. (j.g.) USN, 1943-46. Recipient Disting. Career award Fusion Power Assocs., 1993, Disting. Svc. award Nat. Mgmt. Assn., 1994; inducted into Engring. Hall of Distinction, La. State U., 1982; Humble fellow MIT, 1950, Std. Oil fellow, 1951, Pan Am. fellow, 1952. Fellow Am. Nuclear Soc. (bd. dirs. 1970-73, exec. com. 1971-73); mem. NAE, AAAS, Sigma Xi. Home and Office: 124 Carnegie Dr Oak Ridge TN 37830-7732

ROSENTHAL, NAN, curator, educator, author; b. N.Y.C., Aug. 27, 1937; d. Alan Herman and Lenore (Fry) R.; m. Otto Piene (div.); m. Henry Benning Cortesi, Sept. 5, 1990. BA, Sarah Lawrence Coll., 1959; MA, Harvard U., 1970, PhD, 1976. Asst. prof. art history U. Calif., Santa Cruz, 1971-77, assoc. prof., 1977-84, prof., 1985-86, chair dept. art history, 1976-80; curator 20th-century art Nat. Gallery Art, Washington, 1985-92; cons. dept. modern art Met. Mus. of Art, N.Y.C., 1993—; Lila Acheson Wallace vis. prof. fine arts NYU Inst. Fine Arts, 1996, 2000—. Vis. prof. art history Fordham U., Lincoln Ctr., 1981, 85; vis. scholar N.Y. Inst. for Humanities, NYU, 1982-83; vis. lectr. visual arts Princeton U., 1985, 88, 92. Author: George Rickey, 1977; also exhbn. catalogues, catalogue essays and articles; art editor Show, 1963-64; assoc. editor, then editor at large and contbg. editor Art in Am., 1964-70. Radcliffe Inst. fellow, 1968-69, scholar, 1970-71; travelling fellow Harvard U., 1973-74, rsch. fellow U. Calif., 1978, Ailsa Mellon Bruce curatorial fellow Nat. Gallery of Art, 1988-89; rsch. and travel grantee U. Calif., Santa Cruz, 1974, 77-80, 82-85. Office: Met Mus of Art Dept Modern Art 1000 Fifth Ave New York NY 10028-0113 E-mail: nan.rosenthal@metmuseum.org.

ROSENTHAL, ROBERT, psychology educator; b. Giessen, Germany, Mar. 2, 1933; came to U.S., 1940, naturalized, 1946; s. Julius and Hermine (Kahn) R.; m. Mary Lu Clayton, Apr. 20, 1951; children: Roberta, David C., Virginia. AB, UCLA, 1953, PhD, 1956. Diplomate: clin. psychology Am. Bd. Examiners Profl. Psychology. Clin. psychology trainee Los Angeles Area VA, 1954-57; lectr. U. So. Calif., 1956-57; acting instr. UCLA, 1957; from asst. to assoc. prof., coordinator clin. tng. U. N.D., 1957-62; vis. assoc. prof. Ohio State U., 1960-61; lectr. Boston U., 1965-66; lectr. clin. psychology Harvard U., Cambridge, Mass., 1962-67, prof. social psychology, 1967-95, chmn. dept. psychology, 1992-95, Edgar Pierce prof. psychology, 1995-99, Edgar Pierce prof. emeritus, 1999—; disting. prof. U. Calif., Riverside, 1999—. Author: Experimenter Effects in Behavioral Research, 1966, enlarged edit., 1976; (with Lenore Jacobson) Pygmalion in the Classroom, 1968, expanded edit., 1992, Meta-analytic Procedures for Social Research, 1984, rev. edit., 1991, Judgment Studies, 1987; (with others) New Directions in Psychology 4, 1970, Sensitivity to Nonverbal Communication: The Pons Test, 1979; (with Ralph L. Rosnow) The Volunteer Subject, 1975, Primer of Methods for the Behavioral Sciences, 1975, Essentials of Behavioral Research, 1984, 2d edit., 1991, Understanding Behavioral Science, 1984, Contrast Analysis, 1985, Beginning Behavioral Research, 1993, 4th edit., 2002, People Studying People: Artifact and Ethics in Behavioral Research, 1997, (with Ralph L. Rosnow and Donald B. Rubin) Contrasts and Effect Sizes in Behavioral Research: A Correlational Approach, 2000; (with Brian Mullen) BASIC Meta-analysis, 1985; editor: (with Ralph L. Rosnow) Artifact in Behavioral Research, 1969, Skill in Nonverbal Communication, 1979, Quantitative Assessment of Research Domains, 1980, (with Thomas A. Sebeok) The Clever Hans Phenomenon: Communication With Horses, Whales, Apes and People, 1981; (with Blanck and Buck) Nonverbal Communication in the Clinical Context, 1986; (with Gheorghiu, Netter and Eysenck) Suggestion and Suggestibility: Theory and Research, 1989. Recipient Donald Campbell award Soc. for Personality and Social Psychology, 1988, James McKeen Cattell Sabbatical award, 1995-96; co-recipient Golden Anniversary Monograph award Speech Comm. Assn., 1996; named Watson lectr. U. N.H., Lanzetta Meml. lectr. Dartmouth Coll., Bayer lectr. Yale Sch. Medicine, Foa lectr. Temple U., Disting. Alumni lectr. UCLA; Guggenheim fellow, 1973-74, fellow Ctr. for Advanced Study in Behavioral Scis., 1988-89; sr. Fulbright scholar, 1972. Fellow AAAS (co-recipient Sociopsychol. prize 1960, co-recipient Behavioral Sci. Rsch. prize 1993), APA (co-recipient Cattell Fund award 1967, co-chmn. Task Force on Statis. Inference, Disting. Scientific award for applications of psychology, 2002, Disting. Scientific Contributions award, 2002, divsn. evaluation, measurement and stats., others), Am. Psychol. Soc. (charter, James McKeen Cattell award 2001); mem. Soc. Exptl. Social Psychology (Disting. Scientist award 1996), Ea. Psychol. Assn. (Disting. lectr. 1989), Mid-western Psychol. Assn., Mass. Psychol. Assn. (Disting. Career Contbn. award 1979), Soc. Projective Techniques (past treas.), Phi Beta Kappa, Sigma Xi. Home: 6985 Withers Rd Riverside CA 92506-5621 Office: U Calif LS-p Riverside CA 92521-0001

ROSENTHAL, ROBERT IRWIN, consultant; b. Chgo., Aug. 10, 1928; s. Louis Jack and Esther (Katz) R.; m. Rita Katz, Sept. 16, 1951; children Linda, David, Larry, Debra. BA, U. Chgo., 1950, PhD in Exptl. Psychology, 1955. Mem. tech. staff Rand Corp., Santa Monica, Calif., 1956-60; dept. head Martin/Marietta, Denver, 1960-64; tech. supr. AT&T Bell Labs., Holmdel, N.J., 1964-89; cons. in human factors AT&T, 1991-97. Ops. rsch. adj. instr. NYU, N.Y.C., 1966-67. Patentee in field. Bd. dirs. Jewish Family Svcs., Lakewood, N.J., 1997; lay rabbi Jackson (N.J.) Health Care, 1997. With USN, 1946-48. Mem. Temple Beth El, Phi Beta Kappa, Sigma Xi. Avocations: composing electronic music, racketball. Home: 422 Bowne Rd Asbury Park NJ 07712-3755

ROSENTHAL, ROBERT JON, newspaper editor, journalist; b. N.Y.C., Aug. 5, 1948; s. Irving and Ruth (Moss) R.; m. Inez Katherina von Sternenfels, Nov. 22, 1985; children: Adam, Benjamin, Ariella. BA, U. Vt., 1970. News asst. N.Y. Times, N.Y.C., 1970-73; reporter Boston Globe, 1974-79, Phila. Inquirer, 1979-82, Africa corr., Nairobi, Kenya, 1982-86, fgn. editor, Phila., 1986-91, city editor, 1991-93, asst. mng. editor, daily, 1993-94, assoc. mng. editor, 1994-96, exec. editor, 1996-98, editor, exec. v.p., 1998—2001. Recipient Third World Reporting award Nat. Assn. Black Journalists, 1983, Mag. award Overseas Press Club, 1985, Disting. Fgn. Corr. award Sigma Delta Chi, 1985, Mag. Writing award World Population Inst., 1986. Avocations: ice hockey, gardening, fishing, cooking.*

ROSENTHAL, SOL, lawyer; b. Balt., Oct. 17, 1934; s. Louis and Hattie (Getz) R.; m. Diane Myra Sackler, June 11, 1961; children: Karen Abby, Pamela Margaret, Robert Joel. AB, Princeton U., 1956; JD, Harvard U., 1959. Bar: Md. 1959, Calif. 1961. Law clk. to chief judge U.S. Ct. Appeals, 4th cir., Balt., 1959-60; assoc. Kaplan, Livingston, Goodwin, Berkowitz & Selvin, Beverly Hills, Calif., 1960-66, ptnr., 1966-74, Buchalter, Nemer, Fields & Younger, L.A., 1974-96; of counsel Blanc, Williams, Johnston & Kronstadt, 1996-2000, Arnold & Porter, 2000—. Bd. dirs. Playboy Enterprises, Inc., Chgo.; arbitrator Dirs. Guild Am., L.A., 1976—, Writers Guild Am., L.A., 1976—, Am. Film Mktg. Assn., 1989—, SAG, L.A., 1992—; negotiator Writers Guild-Assn. Talent Agts., L.A., 1978—; mem. entertainment panel and large complex case Am. Arbitration Assn., 1997—. Founder Camp Ronald McDonald for Good Times, L.A., 1985; charter founder Mus. Contemporary Art, L.A., 1988. Fellow: Coll. Comml. Arbitrators, Am. Bar Found.; mem.: ABA, Beverly Hills Bar Assn. (pres. 1982—83), Acad. TV Arts and Scis. (bd.

govs. 1990—92), L.A. Copyright Soc. (pres. 1973—74), Los Angeles County Bar Assn. (trustee 1981—82), Calif. Bar Assn., Phi Beta Kappa. Office: Arnold & Porter 1900 Ave Of Stars Ste 1700 Los Angeles CA 90067-4408

ROSENTHAL, STEVEN SIEGMUND, lawyer; b. Cleve., May 22, 1949; s. Fred Siegel and Natalie Josephine Rosenthal; m. Ilene Edwina Goldstein, Oct. 1, 1983; children: Alexandra M., Eliana D. AB, Dartmouth Coll., 1971; JD, Harvard U., 1974. Bar: Fla. 1974, D.C. 1975, U.S. Supreme Ct. 1978, Calif. 1983. Law clk. judge Malcolm R. Wilkey U.S. Ct. Appeals (D.C. cir.), 1974-75; assoc. Covington & Burling, Washington, 1975-80, Morrison & Foerster, Washington, 1980-81, ptnr., 1981-97, Cooper, Carvin & Rosenthal, PLLC, Washington, 1998-2001, Holland & Knight LLP, Washington, 2001—. Lawyer rep. Jud. Conf. D.C. Cir., 1981-83. Pres. Family and Child Services Washington, 1986-88, trustee, 1978—. Mem. ABA, Am. Law Inst., Phi Beta Kappa. Republican. Office: Holland & Knight LLP 2099 Pennsylvania Ave NW Washington DC 20006-6801

ROSENTHAL, SUSAN BARBARA, retired librarian; b. Elberon Park, N.J., Apr. 7, 1946; d. Joseph and Anna (Warar) Rosenthal. BA, Montclair State Coll., 1967; MEd in Libr. Sci., U. Miami, 1973. Cert. media specialist, tchr., Fla., N.J. Tchr. Manasquan Bd. Edn. (N.J.), 1967-71; tech. svcs. libr. Oakland Park (Fla.) Libr., 1978-92, asst. dir., 1992-93, acting dir., 1993, ret. Author: (mag.) Galumph, 1965-67; contbr. A Micro Handbook for Small Libraries and Media Centers, 1983, 2d edit., 1986, 3d edit., 1991. Mem. Humane Soc., Broward County, Fla., 1981, WPBT-TV PBS sta., 1975-2000, So. Mus. Flight, 1997-2000, Friends of the Oakland Park Libr., 1998—, mem. luncheon com., 1999—, mem. planning com., 1999—; charter mem. Mus. of Discovery and Sci., 1989-96, U.S. Holocaust Meml. Mus., 1994—; donor Miami Book Fair Internat., 1990—, Cats Exclusive, Boca Raton (Fla.) Mus. Art, Survivors of the Shoah Visual History Found., Friends of the Oakland Park Libr.; mem. NFO Rsch. Recipient St. Cloud Tchg. award Sociètè d'Enseignement, St. Cloud, France, 1966, 2 awards Libr. Pub. Rels. Coun., winner, 1983, honorable mention, 1985, cert. appreciation U.S. Holocaust Meml. Mus., 1996, 2000. Mem. ALA, AARP, Fla. Libr. Assn., Fla. Pub. Libr. Assn., Broward County Libr. Assn. (treas. 1981-83, continuing edn. com. 1980), Apple Libr. Users Group, Apple Computer Enjoyment Soc. (chpt. sec. 1984-87, corp. sec. 1985-89), Consumers Union, Wilderness Soc., World Wildlife Fund, Environ. Def. Fund, People for Ethical Treatment of Animals, Nature Conservancy, Mensa, Procrastinators Club Am., Pi Delta Phi. Office: Bibliothéque Lamienne 1522 NE 34th Ct Oakland Park FL 33334-5305

ROSENTHAL, WILLIAM J. lawyer; b. Balt., Nov. 4, 1920; s. Justin J. and Ray Marian (Stern) R.; m. Margaret Irwin Parker, July 4, 1956; children—Adriane Leigh, Jacqueline Rae, John Justin. AB, Johns Hopkins U., 1941; LL.B., U. Balt., 1950. Bar: Md. 1950. Adminstrv. asst. Office Price Adminstrn., Washington, 1941-42; assoc. firm Earle K. Shawe (name changed to Shawe & Rosenthal 1967), Balt., 1951-67; ptnr. Shawe & Rosenthal, 1967—. Lectr. U. Balt., 1952-56; mem. regional adv. council NLRB; vets. rep. Md. Constrn. Adv. Council, 1946-49; lectr. NYU Conf. Labor Relations, Boston U. Labor Law Seminar, 1985; expert witness on labor law, legis. and congl. coms. Contbg. author: The Developing Labor Law; contbr. articles to profl. jours. Served to lt. USNR, 1942-46, ETO. Mem. ABA, Md. Bar Assn., Balt. Bar Assn., Spiked Shoe Soc., Omicron Delta Kappa, Pi Delta Epsilon. Clubs: Suburban of Baltimore County (bd. govs., pres.). Home: 8207 Cranwood Ct Baltimore MD 21208-1823 Office: Shawe & Rosenthal Sun Life Bldg Charles Center Baltimore MD 21201 E-mail: rosenthal@shawe.com.

ROSENZWEIG, CHARLES LEONARD, lawyer; b. N.Y.C., Apr. 12, 1952; s. William and Frieda (Dechner) R.; m. Rya R. Mehler, June 14, 1975; children: Jessica Sara, Erica Danielle. AB cum laude, Princeton U., 1974; JD, NYU, 1977. Bar: N.Y. 1978, U.S. Dist. Ct. (ea. and so. dists.) N.Y. 1978, U.S. Ct. Appeals (7th cir.) 1980, U.S. Ct. Internat. Trade 1981, U.S. Ct. Appeals (2d cir.) 1985. Assoc. Graubard, Moskovitz et al, N.Y.C., 1977-85; ptnr. Rand, Rosenzweig, Smith, Radley, Gordon & Burstein LLP, 1987—. Mem. panel of neutrals comml. divsn. Supreme Ct. State N.Y. Editor NYU Jour. Internat. Law. and Politics. Chmn. of bd. Jewish Cmty. Ctr., Harrison, 1998-2000. Mem. ABA (internat. law sect.), N.Y. State Bar Assn. (co-chair internat. litigation com. 1995-98, mem. exec. com. comml. and fed. litigation sect.), Am. Arbitration Assn., NYU Alumni Assn. (chmn. jour. internat. law and politics alumni 1985-87), Assn. of Commercial Fin. Attys. Avocations: skiing, cycling, tennis, scuba diving. Office: Rand Rosenzweig et al 605 3rd Ave New York NY 10158-0180 Home: 9 Hadley Rd Armonk NY 10504-2417

ROSENZWEIG, KENNETH ERIC, oncologist; b. Bklyn., Apr. 1, 1967; s. Bernard and Lois Rosenzweig; m. Stacey Ann Rosenzweig, Aug. 15, 1993; children: Olivia, Shoshana, Rebecca. MD, Yale U., 1992. Bd. cert. Am. Bd. Radiology. Clin. asst. Meml. Sloan-Kettering Cancer Ctr., N.Y.C., 1997-2000, asst. attending, 2000—. Mem. lung cancer peer rev. group Nat. Cancer Inst., Washington, 2000-01. Recipient Resident Basic Scientist award Am. Soc. Therapeutic Radiation, 1997. Mem. N.Y. Roentgen Soc. (chmn. sect. on radiation oncology 2001-02). Office: Meml Sloan-Kettering Cancer Ctr 1275 York Ave New York NY 10021

ROSENZWEIG, MARK RICHARD, psychology educator; b. Rochester, N.Y., Sept. 12, 1922; s. Jacob and Pearl (Grossman) R.; m. Janine S.A. Chappat, Aug. 1, 1947; children: Anne Janine, Suzanne Jacqueline, Philip Mark. BA, U. Rochester, 1943, MA, 1944; PhD, Harvard U., 1949; hon. doctorate, U. René Descartes, Sorbonne, 1980, U. Louis Pasteur, Strasbourg, France, 1998. Postdoctoral rsch. fellow Harvard U., 1949-51; asst. prof. U. Calif., Berkeley, 1951-56, assoc. prof., 1956-60, prof. psychology, 1960-91, assoc. rsch. prof., 1958-59, rsch. prof., 1965-66, prof. emeritus, 1991—, prof. grad. studies, 1994—. Vis. prof. biology U. Sorbonne, Paris, 1973-74. Author: Biologie de la Mémoire, 1976, (with A.L. Leiman) Physiological Psychology, 1982, 2nd edit., 1989, (with M.J. Renner) Enriched and Impoverished Environments: Effects on Brain and Behavior, 1987, (with D. Sinha) La Recherche en Psychologie Scientifique, 1988, (with W.H. Holtzman, M. Sabourin and D. Bélanger) History of the International Union of Psychological Science, 2000; editor: (with P. Mussen) Psychology: An Introduction, 1973, 2nd edit., 1977, International Psychological Science: Progress, Problems, and Prospects, 1992, (with A.L. Leiman and S.M. Breedlove) Biological Psychology, 1996, 3d edit., 2002; co-editor: (with E.L. Bennett) Neural Mechanisms of Learning and Memory, 1976, (with L. Porter) Ann. Rev. of Psychology, 1968-94, (with K. Pawlik) International Handbook of Psychology, 2000; contbr. articles to profl. jours. Served with USN, 1944-46. Recipient Disting. Alumnus award U. Rochester; Fulbright rsch. fellow; faculty rsch. fellow Social Sci. Rsch. Coun., 1960-61; rsch. grantee NSF, USPHS, Easter Seal Found., Nat. Inst. Drug Abuse. Fellow AAAS, APA (Disting. Sci. Contbn. award 1982, Disting. Contbn. award for Internat. Advancement of Psychology 1997), Am. Psychol. Soc.; mem. NAS, NAACP (life), Am. Physiol. Soc., Internat. Union Psychol. Sci. (hon. life, mem. exec. com. 1996—, v.p. 1980-84, pres. 1988-92, past pres. 1992-96, mem. U.S. nat. com. for Internat. Union Psychol. Sci., NRC and NAS 1984-96), Internat. Brain Rsch. Orgn., Soc. Exptl. Psychologists, Soc. for Neurosci., Société Française de Psychologie, Sierra Club (life), Common Cause, Fulbright Assn. (life), Phi Beta Kappa, Sigma Xi. Office: U Calif Dept Psychology 3210 Tolman Hall Berkeley CA 94720-1650

ROSENZWEIG, MARK RICHARD, economist, educator; b. N.Y.C., Apr. 19, 1947; s. Israel and Bertha (Resnick) R. BA, Columbia Coll., 1969; MA, Columbia U., 1971, PhD with distinction, 1973. Asst. prof. economics Yale U., New Haven, 1973-78, asst. dir. Econ. Growth Ctr., 1978-79, assoc. prof. economics, 1978-79; dir. rsch. Select Commn. on Immigration and Refugee Policy, Washington, 1979-80; vis. fellow Office of Population Rsch. Princeton (N.J.) U., 1976-77; assoc. prof. economics U. Minn., 1979-82, co-dir. Econ. Devel. Ctr., 1982-90, prof. economics, 1982-90; rsch. assoc. Population Studies Ctr. U. Pa., Phila., 1990—, prof. economics, 1990—. Chair Behavioral Medicine Ad Hoc Rev. Panel, NIH, 1987, AIDS Rsch. Ad Hoc Rev. Panel, 1988; lectr. Dvid Horowitz Inst., Tel Aviv U., 1989, Upjohn Inst., We. Mich. U., 1992; Wei Lun vis. prof. Chinese U. Hong Kong, 1995. Author: Contractual Arrangements, Employment and Wages in Rural Labor Markets: A Critical Review, 1982, The New Chosen People: Immigrants in the United States, 1990; editor: The Theory and Experience of Economic Development: Essays in Honor of Sir W. Arthur Lewis, 1982, Contractual Arrangements, Employment and Wages in Rural Labor Markets in South Asia, 1984, Handbook of Population and Family Economics, 1995; contbr. numerous articles and papers to profl. publs. Recipient Herbert H. Lehman fellowship in Social Scis., 1969-72, Columbia U. Faculty fellowship, 1969-73, Woodrow Wilson Dissertation fellowship, 1971-72, NIH Rsch. Svc. award, 1976-77, Social Sci. Rsch. Coun. Rsch. Tng. fellowship, 1976-77; grantee Agy. for Internat. Devel., 1974-75, 76-78, 79-80, 79-82, 82-84, NIH, 1975-77, 78-85, 85-88, 86-88, 87-92, 90-94, 92-95, 93-97, NSF, 79-83, 93-97, Russell Sage Found., 1983-85, Rockefeller Found., 1985-86, 87-89, Ford Found., 1991-92. Fellow Econometric Soc. Office: U Pa Dept Econ 3718 Locust Walk Philadelphia PA 19104-6209

ROSENZWEIG, NORMAN, psychiatry educator; b. N.Y.C., Feb. 28, 1924; s. Jacob Arthur and Edna (Braman) R.; m. Carol Treleaven, Sept. 20, 1945; 1 child, Elizabeth Ann. MB, Chgo. Med. Sch., 1947, MD, 1948; MS, U. Mich., 1954. Diplomate Am. Bd. Psychiatry and Neurology. Asst. prof. psychiatry U. Mich., Ann Arbor, 1957-61; chmn. dept. psychiat. Sinai Hosp., Detroit, 1961-90; assoc. prof. Wayne State U., 1967-73, prof., 1973-98, chmn. dept. psychiat. Sch. Medicine, 1987-90, prof. emeritus, 1998—. Spl. cons., profl. advisor Oakland County Community Mental Health Services Bd., 1964-65; mem. protem med. adv. panel Herman Kiefer Hosp., Detroit, 1970, psychiat. task force N.W. Quadrangle Hosps., Detroit, 1971-78, planning com. mental health adv. council Dept. Mental Health State of Mich., Lansing, 1984-90, tech. adv.rsch. com., 1978-82; psychiat. bed need task force Office Health and Med. Affairs State of Mich., 1980-84; bd. dirs. Alliance for Mental Health, Farmington Hills, Mich., 1986-94; speaker in field. Author: Community Mental Health Programs in England: An American View, 1975; co-editor: Psychopharmacology and Psychotherapy-Synthesis or Antithesis?, 1978, Sex Education for the Health Professional: A Curriculum Guide, 1978; contbr. articles to profl. jours. and chpts. to books. Mem. profl. adv. bd. The Orchards, Livonia, Mich., 1963. Served as capt. USAF, 1955-57. Recipient Appreciation and Merit cert. Mich. Soc. Psychiatry and Neurology, 1970-71, Career Svc. award Assn. Mental Health in Mich., 1994. Fellow Am. Coll. Mental Health Adminstrn., fellow emeritus Am. Coll. Psychiatrists (hon. membership com., com. on regional ednl. programs, liaison officer to The Royal Australian and New Zealand Coll. Psychiatrists 1984-88), Am. Psychiat. Assn. (life fellow, coun. on internat. affairs 1970-79, chmn. 1973-76, assembly liaison to coun. on internat. affairs 1979-80, 82-84, reference com. 1973-76, nominating com. 1978-79, internat. affairs survey team 1973-74, assoc. representing Am. Psychiat. Assn. to Inter-Am. Coun. Psychiat. Assns. 1973-75, chair com. to organize 2nd Pacific Congress Psychiatry, 1978-80, treas. APA lifers 1991-94, v.p. 1994-95, pres. 1995-96, com. on sr. psychiatrists 1993-98, others, Rush Gold Medal award 1974, cert. Commendation, 1973-76, 78-80, Warren Williams award 1986); mem. AAUP, AMA (Physician's Recognition award 1971, 74, 77, 80-81, 84, 87, 90, 92), Am. Assn. Dirs. Psychiat. Residency Tng. (nominating com. 1972-74, task force on core curriculum 1972-74), Am. Assn. Gen. Hosp. Psychiatry, Puerto Rico Med. Assn. (hon., presdl. award 1981), Am. Hosp. Assn. (governing coun. psychiat. svcs. sect. 1977-79, ad hoc com. on uniform mental health definitions, chmn. task force on psychiat. coverage under Nat. Health Ins. 1977-79, others), Brit. Soc. Clin. Psychiatrists (task force on gen. hosp. psychiatry 1969-74), Can. Psychiat. Assn., Mich. Assn. Professions, Mich. Hosp. Assn. (psychiat. and mental health svcs. com. 1979-81), Mich. Psychiat. Soc. (com. on ins. 1965-69, chmn. com. on community mental health svcs. 1967-68, chmn. com. on nominations of fellows 1972-73, 94-98, mem. com. on budget 1973-74, task force on pornography 1973-74, chmn. commn. on health professions and groups 1974-75, pres. elect 1974-75, pres. 1975-76, chmn. com. on liaison with hosp. assns. 1979-81, chmn. subcom. on liaison with Am. Hosp. Assn. 1979-81, numerous others, Past Pres. plaque, 1978, cert. Recognition, 1980, Disting. Service award 1986), Mich. State Med. Soc. (vice chmn. sect. psychiatry 1972-73, chmn. sect. psychiatry 1974-75, mem. com. to improve membership 1977-78, alt. del for Mich. Psychiat. Soc. to Ho. of Dels. 1978-79, del. from Wayne County Med. Soc. to Mich. Med. Soc. Ho. of Dels. 1982-88), N.Y. Acad. Scis., Pan Am. Med. Assn., Wayne County Med. Soc. (com. on hosp. and prof. rels., 1983-84, com. on child health advocacy 1983-87, med. edn. com. 1983-87, mental health com. 1983-87), Royal Australian and New Zealand Coll. Psychiatrists (hon.), Indian Psychiat. Soc. (hon. corr.), World Psychiat. Assn., Sect. Gen. Hosp. Psychiat. Avocations: music, films, reading. Home: 1234 Cedarholm Ln Bloomfield Hills MI 48302-0902 Office: 1234 Cedarholm Ln Bloomfield Hills MI 48302-0902 E-mail: headprof@aol.com.

ROSENZWEIG, RICHARD STUART, publishing company executive; b. Appleton, Wis., Aug. 8, 1935; s. Walter J. and Rose (Bahcall) R. BS, Northwestern U., 1957; Advanced Mgmt. Program, Harvard U., 1975. Credit rep. Dun & Bradstreet, Inc., 1958; with Playboy Enterprises, Inc., 1958—, exec. asst. to pres., 1963-73, sr. v.p., dir., 1973-82, dir. mktg., 1974-82, exec. v.p. publs. group, 1975-77, exec. v.p., head West Coast ops., 1977-80, exec. v.p. corp. affairs, 1980-82, exec. v.p., chmn. emeritus, 1982—; pres. Playboy Jazz Festivals, 1989—. Dir. I. Bahcall Industries, Appleton; exec. v.p. (dir. 1973—) Playboy Enterprises; chmn. Alta Loma Enterment, 2000—. Trustee L.A. Film Expn.; mem. 2d decade coun. Am. Film Inst.; bd. dirs. Mus. Contemporary Art, Chgo., Periodical and Book Assn. Am., Internat. Inst. Kidney Diseases of UCLA, Children of Night, Maple Ctr. Beverly Hills; mem., chmn. bd. UCLA Legis. Network, Town Hall of Calif.; adv. bd. West Hollywood Mktg. Corp., 1985—; bd. dirs. So. Calif. ACLU, 1985—; mem. Los Angeles County Mus.; apptd. to blue ribbon com. project West Coast Gateway. With AUS, 1957; chmn. Modern and Contemporary Art Coun. L.A. County Mus. of Art.; pres. Beverly Hills Cultural Ctr.; exec. com. Henry Mancini Inst.; v.p. Fraternity of Friends music Ctr. Recipient Do-ers award, 1988, Beverly Hills medal Beverly Hills City Coun., 1993. Mem. Am. Mktg. Aslsn., L.A. Pub. Affairs Officers Assn., UCLA Chancellor's Assocs., Pres.'s Cir., Beverly Hills C. of C. (bd. dirs., visitors' bur., v.p.), Beverly Hills Fine Art Commn. (chmn.), Beverly Hills Econ. Devel. Coun., Founders Circle of Music Ctr., Pub. Affairs Coun., Craft and Folk Art Mus., Pres.' Coun. and Contemporary ARts Coun. L.A. Mus. Contemporary Art, The Am. Cinematheque (groundbreaker), Variety Club So. Calif. (bd. dirs.). Office: Playboy Enterprises Inc 9320 Wilshire Blvd #302 Beverly Hills CA 90212

ROSENZWEIG, SAUL, psychologist, educator, administrator; b. Boston, Feb. 7, 1907; s. David and Etta (Tuttle) R.; m. Louise Ritterskamp, Mar. 21, 1941; children: Julia, Ann. AB summa cum laude, Harvard U., 1929, MA, 1930, PhD, 1932. Research assoc. Harvard Psychol. Clinic, 1929-34, Worcester (Mass.) State Hosp., 1934-43; affiliate prof. Clark U., Worcester, 1938-43; chief psychologist Western State Psychiat. Ins. and Clinic, Pitts., 1943-48; lectr. psychology U. Pitts., 1943-48; assoc. prof. psychology and med. psychology Washington U., St. Louis, 1949-51, prof., 1951-75, prof. emeritus, 1975—; chief psychologist Child Guidance Clinic, 1949-59. Cons., mem. life scis. study sect. NIH, 1964-68; mng. dir. Found. for Idiodynamics and the Creative Process, 1972—; adj. prof. psychology St. Louis U., 1996—. Author: (with Kate L. Kogan) Psychodiagnosis, Grune and Stratton, 1949, Rosenzweig Picture-Frustration Study, 1948, Aggressive Behavior and the Rosenzweig Picture-Frustration Study, 1978, Freud and Experimental Psychology: The Emergence of Idiodynamics, 1986, Sally Beauchamp's Career, 1987, Freud, Jung, and Hall the King-Maker, 1992, 2d edit., 1994; assoc. editor: Jour. Abnormal and Social Psychology, 1950-56; cons. editor: Psychol. Monographs, 1948-57, Zeitschrift für Diagnostische Psychologie und Persönlichkeitsforschung, 1953-58, Diagnostica, 1959—; adv. editor: Jour. Cons. Psychology, 1959-64, Jour. Abnormal Psychology, 1965-67; mem. editorial bd. Aggressive Behavior, 1974—; contbr. articles to profl. jours. Fellow Am. Psychol. Assn. (rep. Internat. group for Coordination Psychiatry and Psychol. Methods 1955-61), Am. Psychopathol. Assn.; mem. Internat. Soc. for Research on Aggression (founding pres. 1972-73, archivist 1981-88), Soc. Prof. Emeriti Washington U. (founding pres. 1978), Sigma Xi, Phi Beta Kappa. Home: 8029 Washington Ave Saint Louis MO 63114-6333 Office: Washington U PO Box 1125 Saint Louis MO 63188-1125

ROSER, ROBERT HUTCHINS, JR. systems engineer; b. St. Petersburg, Fla., Nov. 19, 1946; s. Robert Hutchins Roser, Dorothy Gladys Moore; m. Cynthia Lucile Sessions, Feb. 15, 1971; children: Dorothy Jane, Robert Brian, Cynthia Anne. BA, Duke U., 1968; postgrad., George Washington U., 1976—78. Commd. USAF, 1968, advanced through grades to lt. col.; aircraft maint. officer 523 TAC FIRTSQD, Clark AFB, Philippines, 1969—70; aircraft maint. officer pilot tng. wing USAF, Moody AFB, GA., 1970—73; intelligence officer 317 Airlift Wing, Pope AFB, NC, 1973—75; presdl. translator Hot Line, The Pentagon, Washington, 1975—78; ops. officer Air Force Spl. Activities Ctr., Munich, 1978—82, plans officer Ft. Belvoir, Va., 1982—85; ret. USAF, 1985; systems engr. McDonnel Douglas Electronics, Fairfax, Va., 1985—90, BAE Systems, Fairfax, 1990—. Contbr. Editor/writer Plaid Cymru, Cardiff, Wales, 1990—. Mem.: Welsh Soc. of Fredericksburg (pres. 1990—), Cymdeithas Madoo (bd. dirs. 1991—), Sons of Union Vets. of the Civil War, Mary Washington Eagle Pipe Band (piper 1997—). Democrat. Lutheran. Avocations: reading, playing bagpipes. Home: 1203 Harbour Dr Stafford VA 22554 Office: BAE Systems Inc 10400 Eaton Pl Fairfax VA 22030

ROSETT, ANN DOYLE, librarian; b. Valdosta, Ga., Jan. 9, 1955; d. David Spencer Doyle and Lois Annette Gray; m. Robert Allen Richardson, Aug. 1, 1976 (div. June 1981); children: Caitlin Ann, Brendan Wesley; m. John David Rosett, Aug. 6, 1983. Student, Kenyon Coll., 1972-75, U. Dayton, 1974, U. Ala., Birmingham, 1978; BA, Shepherd Coll., 1982; MLS, U. Wash., 1988. Cert. profl. libr., Wash. College libr. Northwest Coll., Kirkland, Wash., 1988—. Mem. ALA, Assn. Christian Librs. (dir.-at-large 1992-93), Assn. Coll. and Rsch. Librs., Am. Theol. Lib. Assn., N.W. Assn. Christian Librs. (treas. 1989-91, pres. 1991-93). Democrat. Office: NW Coll DV Hurst Libr PO Box 579 5520 108th Ave NE Kirkland WA 98033-7523

ROSETT, ARTHUR IRWIN, lawyer, educator; b. N.Y.C., July 5, 1934; s. Milton B. and Bertha (Werner) R.; m. Rhonda K. Lawrence; children: David Benjamin, Martha Jean, Daniel Joseph. AB, Columbia U., 1955, LL.B., 1959. Bar: Calif. 1968, N.Y. State 1960, U.S. Supreme Ct. 1963. Law clk. U.S. Supreme Ct., 1959-60; asst. U.S. atty. So. Dist. N.Y., 1960-63; practice law N.Y.C., 1963-65; assoc. dir. Pres.'s Commn. on Law Enforcement and Adminstrn. Justice, 1965-67; acting prof. law UCLA, 1967-70, prof., 1970—. Author: Contract Law and Its Application, 1971, 6th edit. (with D.J. Bussell), 1999, (with D. Cressey) Justice by Consent, 1976, (with E. Dorff) A Living Tree, 1987. Served with USN, 1956-58. Mem. Am. Law Inst. Home: 641 S Saltair Ave Los Angeles CA 90049-4134 Office: UCLA Law Sch 405 Hilgard Ave Los Angeles CA 90095-1476

ROSETTI, SCOTTY RESTER, lawyer, business owner; b. Gulfport, Miss., Apr. 24, 1941; s. Scotty and Hazel (Rester) R.; married, Oct. 28, 1986; children: Ashley, Raegan, Lindsey, Aaron. BS, U. So. Miss., 1965; JD, U. Miss., Oxford, 1968. Bar: Miss. 1969, U.S. Dist. Ct. Miss. 1969, U.S. Supreme Ct. 1969. Pvt. practice, Gulfport, 1968-78; Computech, Ltd. (formerly Gause Blvd. Moving-Storage) Gause Blvd. Moving-Storage, Slidell, La., 1978—. Home: 124 Reservation Dr Gulfport MS 39503-3044

ROSHEL, JOHN ALBERT, JR. orthodontist; b. Terre Haute, Ind., Apr. 7, 1941; s. John Albert and Mary M. (Griglione) R.; m. Kathy Roshel; children: John Albert III, James Livingston, Angela Kay. BS, Ind. State U., 1963; DDS, Ind. U., 1966; MS, U. Mich., 1968. Individual practice dentistry specializing in orthodontics, Terre Haute, 1968—. Mem. ADA, Am. Assn. Orthodontists, Terre Haute C. of C., Terre Haute Country Club, Lions, Elks, K.C., Lambda Chi Alpha, Delta Sigma Delta, Omicron Kappa Upsilon. Roman Catholic. Home: 15 E Wedgeway Dr Terre Haute IN 47802-4983 Office: 4241 S 7th St Terre Haute IN 47802-4367 E-mail: drjrosh@aol.com.

ROSHKO, ANATOL, aeronautic engineer; b. Bellevue, Alta, July 15, 1923; came to the U.S., 1950; married, 1957; 2 children. BSc, U. Alta, 1945; MS, Calif. Inst. Tech., 1947, PhD in Aero. Engring., 1952. Instr. math. U. Alta, 1945-46, lectr. engring., 1949-50; rsch. fellow Calif. Inst. Tech., Pasadena, 1952-55, asst. prof. to prof., 1955-85; acting. dir. Grad Aero. Labs, 1985-87; Theodore Von Karman prof. aeronautics Calif. Inst. Tech., 1985—, prof. emeritus, 1994—. Sci. liaison officer Office Naval Rsch., London, 1961-62; cons. McDonnell Douglas Corp., 1954-90, Rocketdyne Corp. Divsn., Rockwell Internat., 1984-90; founding dir. Wind Engring. Rsch. Inc., 1970; mem. Aero. & Space Engring. Bd., 1988-93. Recipient Timoshenko medal ASME, 1999; named to U. Alta. Alumni Wall of Recognition, 1998. Fellow AAAS, AIAA (Dryden Rsch. lectr. 1976, Fluid Dynamics award 1998), Am. Phys. Soc. (Fluid Dynamics prize 1987), Indian Acad. Scis. (hon.); mem. ASME, Nat. Acad. Engring. Office: Calif Inst Tech Mail Sta 105-50 1201 E California Blvd Pasadena CA 91125-0001

ROSHON, GEORGE KENNETH, manufacturing company executive; b. July 30, 1942; s. George Washington III and Ellen Eleanor (Knopf) R.; m. Ella Maye Barndt, Nov. 21, 1964; 1 child, Kirsten Renee. BSEE, Pa. State U., 1964; MS, Drexel U., 1974, postgrad., 1974-75. Registered profl. engr., Pa. Sr. engr. Am. Electronics Labs., Inc., Colmar, Pa., 1966-69; v.p. engring. Acrodyne Industries, Inc., Montgomeryville, 1969-74; mgr. electric design W-J divsn. Hayes-Albion Corp., Norristown, 1974-78; mgr. quality assurance PSMBD GE, Phila., 1978-80, mem. exec. com. electronics test coun., 1980-83, mgr. advanced sys. engring., 1983-84, mgr. comm. engring. Malvern, Pa., 1984-86; v.p. quality assurance Hercules Aerospace Display Sys., Inc., Hatfield, 1986-88, v.p. engring., 1988-90; mgr. Electronics Group Westcode, Inc., Malvern, 1991-92; v.p. mfg. Epitaxx, Inc., West Trenton, N.J., 1992-99, v.p. ops. JDSUNIPHASE Divsn., 1999—. Patentee in field. Served to lt. USNR, 1964-66. Mem. NSPE, Am. Soc. Quality Control (cert. quality engr., quality auditor), Pa. Soc. Profl. Engrs., Gen. Electric Mgmt. Assn., Elfun Soc., Drexel U. Alumni Assn., Pa. State U. Alumni Assn., Tri-County Arabian Horse Assn. Home: 454 Eagle Ln Lansdale PA 19446-1547 Office: 7 Graphics Dr Trenton NJ 08628-1547

ROSHONG, DEE ANN DANIELS, dean, educator; b. Kansas City, Mo., Nov. 22, 1936; d. Vernon Edmund and Doradell (Kellogg) Daniels; m. Richard Lee Roshong, Aug. 27, 1960 (div.). BMusEd., U. Kans., 1958; MA in Counseling and Guidance, Stanford U., 1960; postgrad., Fresno State U., U. Calif.; EdD, U. San Francisco, 1980. Counselor, psychometrist Fresno City Coll., 1961-65; counselor, instr. psychology Chabot Coll., Hayward, Calif., 1965-75, coord. counseling svcs. Livermore, 1975-81, asst. dir. student pers. svcs., 1981-89, Las Positas Coll., Livermore, 1989-91, assoc. dean student svcs., 1991-94, dean student svcs., 1991—, life coach, 2000—. Writer, coord. I, A Woman Symposium, 1974, Feeling Free to Be You and Me symposium, 1975, All for the Family Symposium, 1976, I Celebrate Myself Symposium, 1978, Person to Person in Love and Work Symposium, 1978, The Healty Person in Mind and Spirit Symposium, 1980, Change Symposium, 1981, Sources of Strength Symposium, 1982, Love and Friendship Symposium, 1983, Self Esteem Symposium, 1984, Trust Symposium, 1985, Prime Time: Making the Most of This Time in Your Life Symposium, 1986, Symposium in Healing, 1987, How to Live in the World and Still Be Happy Symposium, 1988, Student Success is a Team Effort, Sound Mind, Sound Body Symposium, 1989, Creating Life's Best Symposium, 1990, Choices Symposium, 1991, Minding the Body, Mending the Mind Symposium, 1992, Healing through Love and Laughter Symposium, 1993, Healing Ourselves Changing the World Symposium, 1994, Finding Your Path Symposium, 1995, Build the Life You Want Symposium, 1996, Making Peace With Yourself and Your Relationships Symposium, 1997, Everyday Sacred Symposium, 1998, Wisdom of the Heart Symposium, 1999, Inner Wisdom Symposium, 2000, Second Half of Life Symposium, 2001, others; mem. cast TV prodns. Eve and Co., Best of Our Times, Cowboy; chmn. Calif. C.C. Chancellor's Task Force on Counseling, Statewide Regional Counseling Facilitators, 1993-95, Statewide Conf. Emotionally Disturbed Students in Calif. C.C.s, 1982—, Conf. on the Under Represented Student in Calif. C.C.s, 1986, Conf. on High Risk Students, 1989. Author: Counseling Needs of Comunity College Students, 1980. Bd. dirs. Teleios Sinetar Ctr., Ctr. for Cmty. Dispute Resolution, 1998—, Pleasanton Youth Collaborative Bd., 1997—, Pleasanton Youth Master Plan Bd., 1998—; choir dir., 1996-99; pres. Tri-Valley Unity Ch. bd., 1998, Tri-Valley Haven bd., 2000—, Calif. State U. at Hayward Inst. of Mental Illness and Wellness Edn. bd., 2000—, Ellis Life Coach Tng., 1999—; title III activity dir. Las Positas Coll., 1995-99, dir. pace program, 1999—, dir. quest program, 2000—. Mem.: Calif C.C. Counselors Assn. (svc. award 1986—87, award for Outstanding and Disting. Svc. 1986—87, Pleasanton Mayor's award 2000—01, 2002), Calif. Assn. C. C. (chmn. commn. on students svcs. 1979—84), Assn. Counseling and Devel., Nat. Assn. Women Deans and Counselors, Western Psychol. Assn., Assn. Humanistic Psychologists. Home: 1856 Harvest Rd Pleasanton CA 94566-5456 Office: 3033 Collier Canyon Rd Livermore CA 94550-9797

ROSHWALD, MORDECAI MARCELI, educator, writer; b. Drohobycz, Poland, May 26, 1921; came to U.S., 1955; s. Abraham and Sidonia Feuer R.; m. Miriam Mindla Wyszynski, Aug. 23, 1945 (dec. Nov. 1998); children: Aviel

Isaiah. MA, Hebrew U., 1942, PhD, 1947. Lectr. Hebrew U., Jerusalem, 1951-55; prof. U. Minn., Mpls., 1957-83. Vis. prof. Technion, Haifa, Israel, 1963-64, 78, 88, U. Bath, Eng., 1966, Simon Fraser U., Vancouver, Can., 1972-73, Sun Yat-sen U., Taiwan, 1989-90, U. Guelph, Can., 1983-84. Author: (in Hebrew) Humanism Le-Maasse, 1947, Man and Education, 1954, (rewritten in English) Humanism in Practice, 1955, The Transient and the Absolute: An Interpretation of the Human Condition and of Human Endeavor, 1999, Liberty: Its Meaning and Scope, 2000, Level Seven, 1959, Am. edit., 1960, 13 transls., A Small Armageddon, 1962, Am. edit., 1976, 4 transls.; co-author: (with Miriam Roshwald) Moses: Leader, Prophet, Man: The Story of Moses and His Image Through the Ages, 1969; contbr. articles to profl. publs. Home: 8811 Colesville Rd #502 Silver Spring MD 20910

ROSICA, GABRIEL ADAM, corporate executive, engineer; b. N.Y.C., Jan. 9, 1940; s. Gabriel J. and Elma (P.) R.; m. Bettina R. Nardozzi, Sept. 8, 1962; children: Gregory A., Julie Ann, Mark A. BA in Math. and Physics, Columbia U., 1962, BSEE, 1963; MSEE, Rensselaer Poly. Inst., 1966; MBA, Boston U., 1971. Registered profl. engr., Mass. Rsch. engr. United Aircraft Research Labs., East Hartford, Conn., 1963-67; mgr. electronic devel. The Foxboro (Mass.) Co., 1967-75, gen. mgr. U.S. div., 1975-77, v.p., 1977-80; pres., chief operating officer Modular Computer Systems, Inc., Ft. Lauderdale, Fla., 1980-82, pres., chmn., chief exec. officer, 1982-88; pvt. practice bus. cons. Boca Raton, 1988-91; sr. v.p. Elsag Bailey Corp., Pepper Pike, Ohio, 1991-92; exec. v.p. Bailey Controls Co., Wickliffe, 1993-94; COO Bailey Control Co., 1994-96; sr. v.p. Keithley Instruments, Solon, 1996-2001, exec. v.p., 2001—. Chmn. engring. adv. coun. U. Fla., Gainesville, 1987-90; chmn. hi tech adv. coun. Coll. Boca Raton, Fla., 1987-90. Mem. Pres.'s Coun. Fla. Atlantic U., Boca Raton, 1987-91; trustee Nova U., Ft. Lauderdale, Fla., 1987-94. Recipient Boston U. Chair, 1971, Outstanding Young Engr. of Year award Mass. Soc. Profl. Engrs., 1974. Mem. IEEE (sr. mem.), Am. Electronics Assn. (bd. dirs. 1987, chmn Fla. bd. dirs. 1987-88), Fla. High Tech. and Industry Coun. Home: 35640 Spicebush Ln Solon OH 44139-5063 Office: Keithley Instruments Inc 28775 Aurora Rd Solon OH 44139-1891 E-mail: gabe.rosica@att.net.

ROSICH, RAYNER KARL, physicist; b. Joliet, Ill., Aug. 28, 1940; s. Joseph F. and Gretchen (Cox) R.; m. Judy Louise Jackson, Aug. 20, 1966; children: Heidi Ann, Kimberly Ann, Dawn Ann. BS with Distinction/Honors in Physics, U. Mich., 1962, MS in Physics, 1963; PhD, U. Colo., 1977; MBA, U. Denver, 1982. Teaching fellow and rsch. asst. U. Mich., Ann Arbor, 1962-67; staff Argonne (Ill.) Nat. Lab. Applied Math. Div., summers, 1961-63; physicist, project leader Inst. for Telecommunication Sci. U.S. Dept. Commerce, Boulder, Colo., 1967-80; sr. scientist and program mgr. Electro Magnetic Applications, Inc., Denver, 1980-82; applications mgr. Energy Systems Tech., Inc., 1982-83, mgr. R&D, 1983; prin. scientist, program mgr. Contel Info. Systems, Inc., 1983-84, dir. tech. audits, 1985, dir. basic and applied R&D, 1986; lab. scientist for data systems engring. lab. Hughes Aircraft Co., 1986, lab. scientist for data systems lab., 1986-90, lab. scientist for systems lab., 1990-92; prin. engr. Advanced System Techs., Inc., 1992-95; project mgr. Evolving Systems, Inc., 1995; network planning engr., cons. engr., network arch. Galileo Internat., 1996-99; sr. network arch. Cabletron Sys., Inc., 1999-2000; sr. consulting engr. Time0, Inc., Englewood, Colo., 2000-01; network engring. mgr. CQG, Inc., Denver, 2001—02; lead perf. analyst Tanning Techs. Corp., 2002—. Instr. math. Arapahoe Cmty. Coll., 1987-97. Vol. judo instr., county recreation dist., 1976-77. Recipient Spl. Achievement award U.S. Dept. Commerce, 1974, Outstanding Performance award, 1978, Sustained Superior Performance award, 1979; Libbey-Owens-Ford Glass Co./U. Mich. Phoenix Meml. fellow, 1964-66; NSF Summer fellow, 1965. Mem. AAAS, Am. Phys. Soc., IEEE (sr. mem.), Assn. Computing Machinery, Applied Computational Electromagnetics Soc., Soc. Computer Simulation, Sigma Xi, Phi Kappa Phi. Home: 7932 W Nichols Ave Littleton CO 80128-5558 Office: Tanning Techs Corp Ste 1200 4600 S Syracuse St Denver CO 80237

ROSIELLO, ARTHUR PETER, neurosurgeon; b. N.Y.C., Jan. 13, 1954; s. Arthur and Theresa (Pellegrino) R.; m. Leslie Ann Wessler, Aug. 19, 1995; 1 child, Rachele Ann. BS, MIT, 1975; MD, U. Buffalo, Buffalo, 1979. Postdoctoral assoc. MIT, Cambridge, Mass., 1979; resident Boston U., 1979-80, Harvard-Longwood Area, Boston, 1980-81, NYU, N.Y.C., 1981-87; instr. neurosurgery Boston U. Sch. Medicine, 1988-90, asst. prof. neurosurgery, 1990—. Rsch. assoc. MIT, Cambridge, 1976, 77; acting chief neurosurgery Carney Hosp., 1990-93. Contbr. articles to profl. jours. Spine and cranial base fellow NYU, 1987-88. Mem. AAAS, Am. Assn. Neurol. Surgeons, Mass. Med. Soc., Mass. Neurosurg. Soc., New England Neurosurg. Soc., Boston Soc. Neurology & Psychiatry. Avocations: cycling, baseball, tennis, basketball. Office: Dept Neurol Surgery 720 Harrison Ave Ste 710 Boston MA 02118-2334

ROSIER, DAVID LEWIS, investment banker; b. Sioux City, Iowa, Mar. 22, 1937; s. Orel Lewis and Jewell May (Palmer) R.; m. Jackie Dodd, July 1965 (div. 1973); 1 child, Michele, m. Carol Mary Byre, Nov. 25, 1982 (dec. Sept. 1997); m. Rosemarie Dimino, Sept. 9, 1999. BSBA, U. Denver, 1960. Registered rep. NASD; registered investment assoc. V.p., mgr. mktg. Hertz Internat., Ltd., N.Y., 1970-71; regional v.p. Amtrak, 1971-73; mng. ptnr. Rosier & Assocs., Ltd., San Diego, 1969—; sr. v.p. for strategic mktg. Am. Prins. Holdings, Inc., 1979-84; v.p., registered prin. Am. Diversified Equity Corp., Costa Mesa, Calif., 1984-85; pres. Glen Eagle, Inc., 1986-87; sr. v.p. Western Region Cozad Investment Svcs. Inc., San Diego, 1987-88; dir. corp. fin. Brookstreet Securities Corp., Irvine, Calif., 1993—. Appeared as spkr. on nat. TV, radio and at various industry conferences. Bd. dirs. Nautical Heritage Soc. (Hamburg award 1988). Mem. Oceanside Rotary (Paul Harris fellow, benefactor, pres., founder Rotary Club of Oceanside Found.), Kona Kai Internat. Yacht Club (commodore 1987), Internat. Order of the Blue Gavel (founder, past chmn. bd. trustees Humanities Found.), Phone Charities Internat. (founder, mng. mem. 1996-98), Nat. Investment Banking Assn. (bd. dirs.). Home: 5114 Bella Collina St Oceanside CA 92056-1903 E-mail: daverosier@cox.net.

ROSILE, GRACEANN, finance educator; b. Bessemer, Pa., July 5, 1950; d. Philip Joseph and Carmela Madeline Rosile; m. John Collins Ryan, Mar. 17, 1978 (div. Apr. 15, 1994); m. David Michael Boje, Dec. 30, 1995. BA in English Lit., St. Francis U., 1972; MPH in Hosp. Adminstrn., U. Pitts., 1975, MBA in Bus. Adminstrn., 1978, PhD in Bus. Adminstrn. and Hosp. Adminstrn., 1981. Asst. prof. Indiana U. of Pa., 1980—95; rsch. specialist, adj. faculty bus. adminstrn. N.Mex. State U., Las Cruces, 1996—. Bd. dirs. Jour. Mgmt. Edn.; presenter in field. Contbr. Roman Catholic. Avocation: horseback riding and training. Home: 2831 Buena Vida Ct Las Cruces NM 88011 Office: NMex State U MSC 3DJ Box 3001 Corner Solano and University Las Cruces NM 88003

ROSIN, LINDSAY ZWEIG, clinical psychologist; b. San Antonio, Oct. 28, 1954; s. Morris and Ethel (Rosenberg) R.; m. Susana Aceituno, Sept. 3, 1981; children: Lauren, Melanie. BA, U. Tex., 1975; MA, Xavier U., 1979; PhD, Fla. Inst. Tech., 1985. Lic. psychologist, Tex. Psychology assoc. Dayton (Ohio) Mental Health Ctr., 1980-81, Cin. Neurological Assocs., Cin., 1981-82; intern VA Med. Ctr., Houston, 1982-83; coord. outpatient services Houston Child Guidance Ctr., 1983-84; fellow Med. Ctr. del Oro Hosp., 1984-85; staff psychologist Mid-City Mental Health Mental Retardation, 1985-89; clin. asst. prof. psychology Baylor Coll. Medicine, 1985—; pvt. practice, 1986—; psychologist St. Joseph Hosp., 1987—. Psychologist cons. Mid-City Mental Health Mental Retardation, Houston, 1989—, Tex. Children's Hosp., 1993-96. Contbr. articles to profl. jours. Recipient Outstanding Contbn. to Psychology award, Ohio Assn. Psychologists, 1982. Mem. Am. Psychol. Assn., Tex. Psychol. Assn., Houston Psychol. Assn., Internat. Neuropsychological Soc., Gerontological Soc. Am. Home: PO Box 20671 Houston TX 77225-0671 Office: 3730 Kirby Dr Ste 825 Houston TX 77098-3979 E-mail: lrosin0000@aol.com.

ROSINEK, JEFFREY, judge; b. N.Y.C., Sept. 13, 1941; s. Isidore and Etta (Kramer) R.; m. Sandra Gwen Rosen, Aug. 7, 1977; 1 child, Ian David. BA in History, U. Miami, 1963; postgrad. in polit. sci., JD, 1974. Bar: Fla. 1974. Tchr. Coral Gables (Fla.) High Sch., 1963-78; sole practice Miami, 1974-76; assoc. Tendrich and Todd, 1976-77; ptnr. Todd, Rosinek & Blake, 1984-86; judge Dade County Ct., 1986-89, 11th Jud. Cir., Fla., 1990—, assoc. adminstr. appeal divsn., 1999—; judge Miami Dade County Drug Ct., 1999—. Instr. Boston U., 1975; mem. faculty Fla. Coll. Advanced Jud. Studies, 1992—, Nat. Jud. Coll., 2000—; lectr., presenter in field. Contbr. articles to profl. jours. Chmn. Miami Environ. Rsch. Adv. Com., 1969-73; mem. Miami Beach Tranportation commn., Nat. Bicentennial Competitiion on the Constitution and Bill of Rights com., Dade County Youth Adv. Bd., 1973-75; bd. dirs. U. Miami Law Sch., treas., 1973-75; bd. dirs. U. Miami Law Sch., treas. alumni, jud. dir.; past pres. Dade County Young Dems.; mem. Congl. Civilian Rev. Bd., 1975-90, chmn., 1976-78; bd. dirs., treas. fla. Congl. Com., Legal Svcs. Greater Miami; chmn., 1976-78; chmn. Dade County adv. Coun. Close-Up Found.; Fla. chmn. Porject Concern Internat.; internat. state chmn. Fla. Walk for Mankind, Project Concern, legal adv. com., Kiwanis, 1982-86; v.p. Beth David Congregation, 1982-86; bd. trustees Haven Ctr.; bd. dirs., treas., organizer South Miami-Kendall pro bono project Legal Svc. of Greater Miami, 1983-86; traffic rev. com. Dade County, 1987-92; bd. dirs. Fla. Law Related Edn., 1988—, Adv. Program, 1988—; mem. Miami-Dade County task force for the homeless, 1992-94; active Dade Coalition for the Homeless, 1992—, Dade County Homeless Trust, 1993-2001, chmn. criminal justice com.; chmn. Beck Mus. Judaica, 1988—; ednl. dir. Tempel Judea; jud. cir. rep. Dept. corrections "Boot Camp" program, 1994-98; 11th jud. cir. organizer, rep. Homeless Alt. Rehab. Tracking Program, 1994—, rep. Comprehensive Homeless Integration Program (CHIP), 1992-94, chair Fla. 1st Annual Edn. Seminar/Retreat, 1995, Eugent P. Spellman Am. Inn of Ct., 1996—, South Fla. Super Bowl XXXIII Host Com.; 1st v.p. Coral Gables High Sch. Parent-Tchr.-Students Assn., 1995-96, pres., 1996-98. Recipient award Jewish Theol. Sem., 1978, Outstanding Law Student award Merit award Profl. Law Enforcement Assn., appreciation award Liberty City Christian Assn. Mem.: ABA (task force reduction of litig. cost and delay 1995—), Fla. Assn. Drug Ct. Profls. (inaugural chair), Nat. Ct. Reporters Assn. (strategic com. 1993—), Am. Judges Assn. (bd. govs. 1988—92, domestic violence com. 1990—96, chair 32d Ann. Edn. Conf., Miami Beach 1992, sec. 1992—93, 2d v.p. 1993—94, 1st v.p. 1994—95, chair fed.-state rels. com. 1994—96, pres. 1996—97, exec. com. 1997, chair nominations com. 1997, coord. Close-UP Found. project 1997—, chair 38th Ann. Edn. Conf., Orlando 1998, edn. com. 1998—, exec. com. 2000—01, Image of Judiciary com.), Bar and Gavel Soc., Wig and Robe (chancellor 1973—74), Fla. Conf. Cir. Ct. Judges (criminal justice com. 1995—), Cuban Am. Bar Assn., Miami Beach Bar Assn. (bd. dirs.), Fla. Bar Assn. (rules com. family law sect. 1984—87, jud. nominating procedures com.), Coral Gables Bar Assn., South Miami-Kendall Bar Assn. (past pres.), Dade County Bar Assn. (criminal cts. com. 1994—), Greater Miami C. of C. (v.p. permanent housing 1996—98, pres. 1999—2000, Carrefour Housing Corp. for homeless), U. Miami Law Sch. Alumni Assn. (sec.-treas. 1985—87, jud. dir. 1987—), Chabad of Dade (bd. dirs. 1999—), Dade Ptnrs., Miami-Dade Lions Club (charter), Key Internat. (pres. 1980—81, 1994—95, sec. 1995—, counselor Fla. dist., Key of Honor 1979, honoree 1984), Biscayne Bay Kiwanis (pres. 1994—, disting. past pres., Major Emphasis chmn., lt. gov. Fla. Dist., Kiwanian of Yr. 1983—84), Kiwanis Internat. (life). Home: 535 Bird Rd Coral Gables FL 33146-1307 Office: 1351 NW 12th St Miami FL 33125-1644 E-mail: jefaroz@aol.com.

ROSING, DOUGLAS ROY, cardiologist, educator; b. Buffalo, July 29, 1941; AB, Princeton U., 1963; MD, SUNY, Buffalo, 1967. Diplomate Am. Bd. Internal Medicine, Am. Bd. Cardiovasc. Disease. Intern SUNY Buffalo Gen. Hosp., 1967-68; resident in medicine Peter Bent Brigham Hosp., Boston, 1971-72; assoc. Hosp. U. Pa., 1972-73; co-dir. cardiac catheterization lab. Suburban Hosp., Bethesda, 1985-97, chairperson cardiology, 1995-97; fellow in cardiology NIH, Md., 1968-71, staff assoc., 1976-81, chief cardiovasc. diagnosis, 1981-85; pvt. practice Cardiac Cons. Charter; mem. staff Washington Adventist Hosp., 1995—. Clin. prof. medicine George Washington Med. Sch., 1973—; assoc. clin. prof. Georgetown Med. Sch. and Hosp., 1985-92; with Shady Grove Adventist Hosp., 1985—; Washington Hosp. Ctr., 1986—. Fellow Am. Coll. Cardiology (gov. 1997-2000); mem. Am. Heart Assn. Office: Cardiac Cons Charter 6410 Rockledge Dr Ste 200 Bethesda MD 20817-1830

ROSINSKI, EDWIN FRANCIS, medical educator; b. Buffalo, June 25, 1928; s. Theodore Joseph and Josephine M. (Wolski) R.; m. Jeanne C. Hueniger, Oct. 27, 1951; children: John T., Mary E., Sarah J. BS, SUNY, Buffalo, 1950; EdM, U. Buffalo, 1957, EdD, 1959. Prof. health scis. Med. Coll. Va., Richmond, 1959-66; dep. asst. sec. HEW, Washington, 1966-68; exec. vice chancellor U. Calif., San Francisco, 1968-72, prof., 1972-94; prof. emeritus medicine & pharmacy, 1994—. Adv. Rockefeller Found., N.Y.C., 1962-67, WHO, Geneva, 1962-78, Imperial Com. Health, Tehran, Iran, 1974-77; cons. Stanford Research Inst., Menlo Park, Calif., 1975-79. Author: The Assistant Medical Officer, 1965; contbr. over 100 articles to profl. jours. Served with USAF, 1950-54. Recipient spl. citation HEW, 1968, Merrell Flair award, 1991; named disting. prof. Australian Vice Chancellors Office, 1974, disting. vis. prof. Tulane U., New Orleans, 1983. Fellow AAAS; mem. Assn. Am. Med. Colls. (Merrel Flair award), Am. Ednl. Research Assn., Soc. Health and Human Values (founding mem.), Calif. Pharmacists Assn. (hon.), Phi Delta Kappa. Roman Catholic. Avocation: physical fitness. Home: 80 Sotelo Ave San Francisco CA 94116-1423

ROSITA, ALMA See **DAVIES, ALMA**

ROSKAM, JAN, aerospace engineer; b. The Hague, The Netherlands, Feb. 22, 1930; arrived in U.S., 1957; s. Kommer Jan and Agatha (Bosman) Roskam; m. Janice Louise Thomas-Barron, Dec. 21, 1994. MA in Aerospace Engring., Tech. U. Delft, 1954; PhD in Aeros. and Astronautics, U. Wash., 1965. Asst. chief designer Aviolanda Aircraft Co., Netherlands, 1954-57; sr. aerodynamics engr. Cessna Aircraft Co., Wichita, Kans., 1957-59; sr. group engr. Boeing Co., Wichita and Seattle, 1959-67; Ackers disting. prof. aerospace engring. U. Kans., Lawrence, 1967—; pres. Design, Analysis and Rsch. Corp., 1991—. Cons. to govt. and industry. Author: (book) Airplane Flight Dynamics and Automatic Flight Controls, 2 vols., 1979; co-author: Airplane Aerodynamics and Performance, 1981, Airplane Design, Part I-VIII, 1986. Served to 1st lt. Royal Netherlands Air Force, 1954—56. Fellow: AIAA, Soc. Automotive Engrs.; mem.: Exptl. Aircraft Assn., U.S. Chess Fedn., Koninklijk Instituut van Ingenieurs, Royal Aero. Soc., Am. Def. Preparedness Assn., Air Force Assn., Internat. Wildlife Assn., Aircraft Owners and Pilots Assn., Omicron Delta Kappa, Sigma Gamma Tau, Tau Beta Pi, Sigma Xi. Office: U Kans 2004 Lea Hl Lawrence KS 66045-0001 E-mail: roskam@ku.edn.

ROSKAMP, KARL WILHELM, economics educator; b. Leer, Hannover, Fed. Republic of Germany, Aug. 19, 1923; came to U.S., 1954; s. Jan and Anna Bertha (Witt) R.; m. Jacqueline Odette Labesse, May 25, 1957; children: Eric Jan, Jeannette Anne. BA, U. Frankfurt, 1954; MA, U. Mich., 1955, PhD, 1959; D Honoris Causa (hon.), Pantheon-Assas U., Paris, 1981. Asst. prof. Brandeis U., Waltham, Mass., 1959-60, Wayne State U., Detroit, 1960-62, assoc. prof., 1962-65, prof., 1965-88; assoc. prof. U. Nice (France), 1974, U. Paris 2, 1977-84, 86; prof. emeritus Wayne State U., Detroit, 1988—. Vis. prof. U. Saar, Saarbrucken, 1963; pres. Internat. Inst. Pub. Fin., 1984-87, Acad. Scholars, Wayne State U., 1989-91. Author: Capital Formation in West Germany, 1965; co-author: (with Wolfgang Stolper) Structure of the East German Economy, 1960; contbr. articles to profl. jours. Fulbright grantee, German Economy, 1960; contbr. articles to profl. jours. Fulbright grantee, 1954, 74-75; Ford Found. fellow, 1958-59, 61-62; decorated Officer's Cross of Merit, Fed. Republic of Germany, 1987. Mem. Am. Econ. Assn., Nat. Tax Assn., Verein für Sozialpolitik, Economistes de Langue Francaise, Internat. Inst. Pub. Fin. (hon.).

ROSKENS, RONALD WILLIAM, international business consultant; b. Spencer, Iowa, Dec. 11, 1932; s. William E. and Delores A.L. (Beving) R.; m. Lois Grace Lister, Aug. 22, 1954; children: Elizabeth, Barbara, Brenda, William. BA, U. No. Iowa, 1953, MA, 1955, LHD (hon.), 1985; PhD, U. Iowa, 1958; LLD (hon.), Creighton U., 1978, Huston-Tillotson Coll., 1981, Midland Luth. Coll., 1984, Hastings Coll., 1981; LittD (hon.), Nebr. Wesleyan U., 1981; PhD (hon.), Ataturk U., Turkey, 1987; LHD (hon.), U. Akron, 1987; DSc (hon.), Jayewardenepura U., Sri Lanka, 1991; LHD (hon.), Am. Coll. of Greece, Athens, 1994. Lic. min. United Ch. of Christ (Congl. and E&R). Tchr. Minburn (Iowa) High Sch., 1954, Woodward (Iowa) State Hosp., summer 1954; asst. counselor to men State U. Iowa, 1956-59; dean of men, asst. prof. spl. edn. Kent (Ohio) State U., 1959-63, assoc. prof., then prof., 1963-72, asst. to pres., 1963-66, dean for adminstrn., 1968-71, exec. v.p., prof. ednl. adminstrn., 1971-72; chancellor, prof. ednl. adminstrn. U. Nebr., Omaha, 1972-76; pres. U. Nebr. System, 1977-89, pres. emeritus, 1989; hon. prof. East China Normal U., Shanghai, 1985; adminstr. USAID, Washington, 1990-92; pres. Action Internat., Inc., Omaha, 1993-96, Global Connections, Inc., Omaha, 1996—. Interim exec. officer Omaha Pub. Libr., 1996-98; mem. Bus.-Higher Edn. Forum, 1979-89, exec. com., 1984-87; mem. govtl. relations com. Am. Council Edn., 1979-83, bd. dirs., 1981-86, vice chair, 1983-84, chair, 1984-85; chmn. com. on financing higher edn. Nat. Assn. State Univs. and Land Grant Colls., 1978-83, vice chmn. com. on financing higher edn., 1983-84, chmn. com. on fed. student fin. assistance, 1981-87; mem. nat. adv. com. on accreditation and instl. eligibility U.S. Dept. Edn., 1983-86, chmn., bd. dirs., 1986; exec. bd. North Cen. Assn., 1979-84, chmn. exec. bd., 1982-84, pres., 1989-90; active Environ. Ams. Bd., 1991-92, Strategic Command Consultation Commn., 1993-96, Nat. Exec. Res. Corps, Fed. Office Emergency Preparedness, 1968-88; chmn. Omaha/Douglas Pub. Bldg. Commn., 1996—. Co-editor: Paradox, Process and Progress, 1968; contbr. articles profl. jours. Mem. Kent City Planning Commn., 1962-66; bd. dirs. United Ch. of Christ Bd. Homeland Ministries, 1968-74, Met. YMCA, Omaha, 1973-77, Mid-Am. council Boy Scouts Am., 1973-77, Midlands United Community Services, 1972-77, NCCJ, 1974-77, Omaha Rotary Club, 1974-77, Found. Study Presdl. and Congl. Terms, 1977-89, First Plymouth Congl. Ch., 1989-90, Midland Luth. Coll., 1993—, Coun. Aid to Edn., 1985-89, ConAgra Foods, Inc., 1993—, Russian Farm Cmty. Project, Capitol Fed. Found., Topeka, Kans., 1999—; trustee Huston Tillotson Coll., Austin, Tex., 1968-81, chmn., 1976-78, Joslyn Art Mus., 1973-77, Nebr. Meth. Hosp., 1974-77, 1st Ctrl. Congregational Ch., Brownell-Talbott Sch., 1974-77, Harry S. Truman Inst., 1977-89, Willa Cather Pioneer Meml. and Ednl. Found., 1979-87; pres. Kent Area C. of C., 1966; mem. Met. Commn. Coll. Found., 1993-96. Decorated comdr.'s cross Order of Merit (Germany); recipient Disting. Svc. award for community svc., Kent, Ohio, 1967, Brotherhood award NCCJ, 1977, Americanism citation B'nai B'rith, 1978, Legion of Honor, Order of DeMolay, 1980, gold medal Nat. Interfrat. Coun., 1987, Agri award Triumph Agr. Expn., Omaha, 1989; named Nat. 4-H Alumnus, 1967, Outstanding Alumnus, U. No. Iowa, 1974, Midlander of Yr., Omaha World Herald, 1977, King Ak-Sar-Ben LXXXVI, 1980; named to DeMolay Hall of Fame, 1993; named Hon. Consul Gen. of Japan, 1999. Mem. AAAS, APA, AAUP, Am. Coll. Pers. Assn., Assn. Urban Univs. (pres. 1976-77), Am. Ednl. Rsch. Assn., Coun. on Fgn. Rels., Chief Execs. Orgn., Young Pres. Orgn., Scottish Rite (bd. dirs. Omaha coun. 1999—), Lincoln C. of C. (bd. dirs. 1989-90), Masons (33 deg.), Rotary (bd. dirs. Omaha 1974-77), Phi Delta Kappa, Phi Eta Sigma, Sigma Tau Gamma (pres. grand coun. 1968-70, Disting. Achievement award 1980, Disting. scholar 1981), Omicron Delta Kappa (nat. pres. 1986-90, Found. pres. 1986-96). Home: 10849 N 58th Plz Omaha NE 68152

ROSKI, EDWARD P., JR. professional sports team executive; s. Edward P. Roski, III; m. Gayle Roski. BS in Fin. and Real Estate, U. So. Calif., 1962. Pres. So. Calif.-based Majestic Realty Co.; owner L.A. Kings, 1995—. Dir. Big Bros. of Greater L.A.; bd. govs. Natural History Mus. of L.A. County; bd. dirs. Comerica Bank, Calif. With USMC, 1962-66. Mem. Explorers Club, Soc. Indsl. Realtors. Avocations: cycling, mountain climbing. Office: Los Angeles Kings Staples Center 111 S Figueroa St Los Angeles CA 90012-2465*

ROSKO, KEITH ALLAN, art educator, illustrator; b. Binghamton, N.Y., Jan. 18, 1966; s. Francis James and Barbara Ann R.; m. Lynne Marie Rosko, Dec. 28, 1991; children: Abigail Hannah, Elizabeth Madison. BS in Art Edn., Kutztown (Pa.) U., 1988; MA in Illustration, Marywood U., 1993. Cert. art educator, K-12. Jr. varsity football coach Chenango Forks Sch. Dist., Binghamton, N.Y., 1988-93, art club faculty advisor, 1994-2000, distance learning instr., 1997—, art tchr. 9-12, 1988—. Cons., author Alpha Omega Pub., Chandler, Ariz., 1998-2000; illustrator Wild West mag., Leesburg, Va., 1996, Meridian Mortgage Corp., Phila., 1991, Cath. Charities of Broome County, Binghamton, 1990-93. Author: Elective Art Life Pack, 2000; author/editor (website) The Visual Revolution, 1998-2000; dir. adv. Fine Arts Night, 1996-2000. Recipient Finalist award Photographers Forum mag., 1991, 92, 93. Mem. ACLU, Nat. Art Edn. Assn. Democrat. Roman Catholic. Avocations: science fiction/history reading, stamp collecting. Office: Chenango Forks HS 1 Gordon Dr Binghamton NY 13901

ROSKOSKI, ROBERT, JR. biochemist, educator, author; b. Elyria, Ohio, Dec. 10, 1939; s. Robert and Mary R.; m. Laura Martinsek, Aug. 27, 1974. BS, Bowling Green State U., 1961; MD, U. Chgo., 1964, PhD, 1968. Asst. prof. U. Iowa, Iowa City, 1972-75, assoc. prof., 1975-79, vis. prof., 1993; prof. dept. biochemistry and molecular biology Med. Center, La. State U., New Orleans, 1979—, Fred G. Brazda prof., 1991—. Cons. biochemistry test com. Nat. Bd. Med. Examiners; mem. merit rev. bd. for basic scis. VA; mem. rev. com. biol. scis. U. South Fla., 1992; mem. rev. com. biochemistry St. George's U. Sch. Medicine, 1997. Served with USAF, 1966-69. NIH postdoctoral fellow U. Chgo., 1964-66; NIH spl. fellow Rockefeller U., 1969-71 Mem. Am. Chem. Soc., Am. Soc. Neurochemistry, Soc. for Neurosci., Am. Soc. Biol. Chemists, Am. Soc. Pharmacology and Exptl. Therapeutics, Internat. Soc. Neurochemistry, Assn. Med. and Grad. Depts. Biochemistry (sec. 1994-96, pres. 1997), Coun. Acad. Scos., Assn. Am. Med. Colls. Achievements include condr. research enzymology. Home: 1206 Aline St New Orleans LA 70115-2421 Office: 1100 Florida Ave New Orleans LA 70119-2714 E-mail: biocrr@lsuhsc.edu.

ROSKY, BURTON SEYMOUR, lawyer; b. Chgo., May 28, 1927; s. David T. and Mary W. (Zelkin) R.; m. Leatrice J. Darrow, June 16, 1951; children: David Scott, Bruce Alan. Student, Ill. Inst. Tech., 1944-45; BS, UCLA, 1948; JD, Loyola U., L.A., 1953. Bar: Calif. 1954, U.S. Supreme Ct 1964, U.S. Tax Ct 1964; C.P.A., Calif. Auditor City of L.A., 1948- 51; with Beidner, Temkin & Ziskin (C.P.A.s), L.A., 1951-52; supervising auditor Army Audit Agy., 1952-53; practiced law L.A., Beverly Hills, 1954—; ptnr. Duskin & Rosky, 1972-82, Rosky, Landau & Fox, 1982-93, Rosky, Landau & Stahl, Beverly Hills, 1993-99; pvt. practice, 1999—. Lectr. on tax and bus. problems; judge pro tem Beverly Hills Mcpl. Ct., L.A. Superior Ct.; mem. L.A. Mayor's Community Adv. Council. Contbr. profl. publs. Charter supporting mem. Los Angeles County Mus. Arts; contbg. mem. Assocs. of Smithsonian Instn.; charter mem. Air and Space Mus; mem. Am. Mus. Natural History, L.A. Zoo; supporting mem. L.A. Mus. Natural History; mem. exec. bd. So. Calif. coun. Nat. Fedn. Temple Brotherhoods, mem. nat. exec. bd.; mem. bd. govs. Loyola Sch. Law, L.A. With USNR, 1945-46. Walter Henry Cook fellow Loyola Law Sch. Bd. Govs. Fellow Jewish Chautauqua Soc. (life mem.); mem. Am. Arbitration Assn. (nat. panel arbitrators), Am. Assn. Attys.-CPAs (charter mem. pres. 1968), Calif. Assn. Attys.-CPAs (charter mem., pres. 1963), Calif. Soc. CPAs, Calif., Beverly Hills, Century City, Los Angeles County bar assns., Am. Judicature Soc., Chancellors Assocs. UCLA, Tau Delta Phi, Phi Alpha Delta.; mem. B'nai B'rith. Jewish (mem. exec. bd., pres. temple, pres. brotherhood). Club: Mason. Office: 8383 Wilshire Blvd Beverly Hills CA 90211-2410

ROSKY, THEODORE SAMUEL, insurance company executive; b. Chgo., Apr. 14, 1937; s. Theodore and Lora Marie (O'Connell) R.; m. Jacqueline Reed, Apr. 19, 1958; 1 child, Laura Marie. BA, State U. Iowa, 1959. Various actuarial positions Conn. Gen. Life Ins. Co., Hartford, 1959-66, assoc. actuary, 1967-70, controller, 1970-73, 2d v.p., actuary, 1973, v.p., 1973-78; exec. v.p. Capital Holding Corp., 1978-84, exec. v.p., CFO, 1984-91, exec. v.p., 1991-92; bd. dirs. Legend Funds, 1993-98, SBM Mut. Funds, 1995-97, SBM Certificate Co., 1996-98; fin. svcs. Dory L.P., 1998-99. Instr. State U. Iowa, 1958-59, U. Hartford, 1964-66, U. Conn., 1967-68. Mem. bd. pensions Evang. Luth. Ch. Am., 1974—82, 1984—87, 1989—95; bd. dirs. Hartford Coll. for Women, 1974—78, Macauley Theater, 1983—85, Louisville Fund for the Arts, 1980—97, Louisville Luth. Home, 1983—97, Louisville Orch., 1982—88, 1989—95, Ky. Opera, 1992—2001, Lincoln Found., 1992—2002, Actors Theatre of Louisville, 1995—, New Performing Arts, 1996—98, Oak and Acorn, 1995—2001, Glassworks Found., 2002—. Recipient award Soc. Actuaries, 1958 Fellow Soc. Actuaries; mem. Am. Acad. Actuaries, Southeastern Actuaries Club, Pendennis Club. Republican. Lutheran. Home and Office: 2304 Speed Ave Louisville KY 40205-1642 E-mail: trosky50@hotmail.com.

ROS-LEHTINEN, ILEANA, congresswoman; b. Havana, Cuba, July 15, 1952; d. Enrique Emilio and Amanda (Adato) Ros; m. Dexter Lehtinen; 2 children, 2 stepchildren. AA, Miami (Fla.)-Dade C.C., 1972; BA, Fla. Internat.

U., 1975, MS, 1987. Prin. Ea. Acad., from 1978; mem. Fla. Ho. of Reps., Tallahassee, 1983—87, Fla. Senate, 1986-89, U.S. Congress from 18th Fla. dist., 1989—; mem. govt. reform com., internat. rels. com. Recipient Nat. Legis. award LULACH, 1999. Republican. Roman Catholic. Office: US Ho of Reps 2160 Rayburn Ho Office Bldg Washington DC 20515-0918*

ROSLOW, SYDNEY, marketing educator; b. N.Y.C., July 29, 1910; s. Joseph and Anna (Lipman) R.; m. Irma Sternberg, Oct. 21, 1932; children: Richard Jay, Susan Jane, Peter Dirk. BS, NYU, 1931, MA, 1932, PhD, 1935. Rsch. asst. in market, indsl and pers. rsch. Psychol. Corp., 1931-41; sch. psychologist, mem. Bd. Edn., Hastings on Hudson, N.Y., 1937-48; pub. opinion rsch. program surveys divsn. U.S. Dept. Agr., 1939-43; founder Pulse, Inc., market and audience rsch. in radio, TV, advt., N.Y.C., 1941-78; assoc. prof. Baruch Coll., CUNY, 1967-75; assoc. prof. dept. mktg. Fla. Internat. U., 1976-83, prof. mktg., assoc. dean Coll. Bus. Adminstrn., 1983-90, prof. emeritus, 1990—, acting assoc. dean, 1996. Rschr. in mktg. Contbr. chpts. to books, more than 100 articles to profl. jours. Fellow APA; mem. Am. Mktg. Assn. (pres. Miami chpt. 1980-82), Market Rsch. Coun. (inducted into Hall of Fame, N.Y. 1992), Radio-TV Rsch. Coun. (past pres.), Radio and TV Execs. Soc., Phi Beta Kappa. Office: Fla Internat U North Miami Campus North Miami FL 33181 Home: 1905 Hawaii Ave NE Saint Petersburg FL 33703-3417

ROSMAN, LAWRENCE DAVID, endocrinologist; b. N.Y.C., Apr. 17, 1949; s. Julius and Jennie Rosman; m. Judith Lee Rosman, Mar. 4, 1973; children: Jonathan, Joshua, Michael. BA, Yeshiva U., 1971; HSD, Erna Michael Coll., 1971; MD with honors, NYU Sch. Medicine, 1975. Diplomate Am. Bd. Internal Medicine, Am. Bd. Endocrinologist and Metabolism. Intern, resident, fellow NYU Med. Ctr., 1975—80; clin. asst. prof. medicine NYU Sch. Medicine. Dir., founder Osteoporosis Ctr. of Queens, Forest Hills, N.Y., 1987—; chief of endocrinology The Parkway Hosp., Forest Hills, 1980—. Fellow ACP, Assn. Clin. Endocrinologists; mem. Am. Diabetes Assn. (Cert. of Recognition with distinction 1999), Endocrine Soc., N.Y. Thyroid Club. Avocations: archeology, golf, reading, travel. Office: 11203 Queens Blvd Ste 207 Forest Hills NY 11375-5550

ROSMUS, ANNA ELISABETH, writer; b. Passau, Germany, Mar. 29, 1960; d. Georg Rudolf and Anna Johanna (Friedberger) R.; divorced; children: Dolores Nadine, Beatrice Salome Kassandra M Sociology, German Lit. and Fine Arts, U. Passau, 1994; PhD (hon.), U. S.C., 2000. Spkr. and organizer in field. Author: Resistance and Persecution, 1983 (Geschwister Scholl Preis 1984), Exodus In The Shadow of Mercy, 1988, Robert Klein A German Jew Looks Back, 1991, Wintergreen Suppressed Murders, 1993 (Conscience in Media award 1994), Pocking End and Renewal, 1995, What I Think, 1995, Out of Passau, 1999, Against the Stream, 2002; guest talk shows including Documentaries and Features in Germany, Austria, Great Britain, Denmark, Holland, France, Italy, Sweden, Poland, Can., U.S., South Am., Australia, 1983—. Fundraiser Anne Frank Found., Jewish Cmty. Ctrs., Holocaust Ctrs., others, 1992—. Recipient Immigrant Achievement award Am. Immigration Lawyers Assn., 1998; named Best German Writer, European essay Competition, 1980; Sarnat award Anti Defamation League, 1994; Anna Rosmus Day, City of Santa Cruz, 1994. Mem. PEN Internat., NAFE. Avocations: environment protection, multicultural projects, minority programs. E-mail: researchaer@hotmail.com.

ROSNER, ANN See **SEAMAN, BARBARA**

ROSNER, ANTHONY LEOPOLD, research director, biochemist; b. Greensboro, N.C., Nov. 13, 1943; s. Albert Aaron and Elsie Augustine (Lincoln) R.; m. Ruth Francis Marks, June 19, 1966; 1 child, Rachael. BS, Haverford Coll., 1966; PhD, Harvard U., 1972. Staff fellow NIH-NINDS, Bethesda, Md., 1972-74; gen. dir. Receptor Lab. Beth Israel Hosp., Boston, 1976-83, tech. dir. Chem. Lab., 1981-83; tech. dir. New Eng. Pathology Svcs., Wilmington, Mass., 1983-86, cons., 1986-96; dept. adminstr. Brandeis U., Waltham, 1986-91; rsch. ops. mgr. in newborn medicine Children's Hosp., 1991-92; dir. rsch. and edn. Found. for Chiropractic Edn. and Rsch., Brookline, Mass., 1992—; cons. Ctr. for Alternative Medicine Beth Israel Hosp., Boston, 1996—. Vis. fellow Lab. Molecular Biology, CNRS, Gif-sur-Yvette, France, 1973. Assoc. editor: Jour. Manipulative and Physiol. Therapeutics, mem. editl. bd.: , 1993—, assoc. editor: Jour. Neuromusculoskeletal Sys., —, sect. editor: , 1993—, mem. adv. bd.: Alternative Therapies in Health and Medicine, 1994—; contbr. numerous articles to profl. jours., papers on status of chiropractic rsch. and efficacy, design and interpretive problems in clin. rsch. Testified before various fed. agencies and state legis. regarding status of chiropractic rsch. and efficacy of treatment. Harvard U. fellow, 1966; recipient Humanitarian of Yr. award Am. Chiropractic Assn., 2000. Mem. AAAS, APHA, Am. Chem. Soc. (auditor N.E. chpt. 1990—), Internat. Assn. for Study of Pain, Am. Assn. Integrative Medicine, N.Y. Acad. Scis., Clin. Ligand Assay Soc., Am. Back Soc. Democrat. Jewish. Achievements include identification of meso-diaminopimelic acid for the first time in any organism as an allosteric feedback inhibitor (affecting aspartokinase activity); development of new radioligand assay for measuring estrogen receptor, about 10 times more sensitive and rapid than other methodologies; provision of evidence showing negative cooperativity of binding to estrogen receptor; convened first and second international workshop to develop a chiropractic research agenda; initiated and coordinated research efforts pertaining to chiropractic science and healthcare worldwide. Home: 1443 Beacon St Apt 201 Brookline MA 02446-4709 Office: Found for Chiropractic Edn and Rsch 1330 Beacon St Ste 315 Brookline MA 02446-3202 E-mail: rosnerfcer@aol.com.

ROSNER, FRED, physician, educator; b. Berlin, Oct. 3, 1935; came to U.S., 1949, naturalized, 1955; s. Sidney and Sara (Feingold) R.; m. Saranne Eskolsky, Feb. 24, 1959; children: Mitchel, Miriam, Aviva, Shalom. BA cum laude, Yeshiva Coll., 1955; MD, Albert Einstein Coll., 1959. Diplomate: Am. Bd. Internal Medicine. Intern Maimonides Med. Center, Bklyn., 1959-60, resident in medicine, 1960-62, fellow in hematology, 1962-63, asst. dir. hematology, 1967-70; instr. SUNY Downstate Med. Center, 1968-70, asst. prof. medicine, 1970; asso. prof. SUNY, Stony Brook, 1970-78, prof. medicine, 1978-89; asst. dean, prof. medicine Albert Einstein Coll. Medicine, 1989-93; prof. medicine Mt. Sinai Sch. Medicine, N.Y.C., 1993—; dir. hematology Queens Hosp. Center, Jamaica, N.Y., 1970-78, dir. medicine, 1978—. Author: Modern Medicine and Jewish Law, 1972, Medicine in the Bible and Talmud, 1977, 2d edit., 1995, Biblical and Talmudic Medicine, 1978, 2d edit., 1993, Jewish Bioethics, 1979, 2d edit., 2000, Modern Medicine and Jewish Ethics, 1986, 2d edit., 1991, Practical Medical Halachah, 1990, Medicine and Jewish Law vol. I, 1990, vol. II, 1993, 2001, Encyclopedia of Medicine in the Bible and the Talmud, 2000, Biomedical Ethics and Jewish Law, 2001; translator, editor: many Moses Maimonides' works including Moses Maimonides' Treatise on Hemorrhoids and Responsa, 1969; Medical Aphorisms of Moses Maimonides, 1970, Sex Ethics in the Writings of Moses Maimonides, 1974, 94, Moses Maimonides' Introduction to the Mishnah, 1975, 95, Maimonides Glossary of Drug Names, 1979, Moses Maimonides' Commentary on Sanhedrin, 1981, Maimonides' Treatise on Resurrection, 1982, Medicine in the Mishneh Torah of Maimonides, 1984, Maimonides' Treatises on Poisons, Hemorrhoids and Cohabitation, 1984, Maimonides' Commentary on the Aphorisms of Hippocrates, 1987, Maimonides' Medical Aphorisms, 1990, The Existance and Unity of God: Three Treatises Attributed to Moses Maimonides, 1990, Moses Maimonides' Three Treatises on Health, 1990, Six Treatises Attributed to Maimonides, 1991, Maimonides: Physician, Philosopher and Scientist, 1993, Maimonides' Treatise on Asthma, 1994, Maimonides' Glossary of Drug Names, 1996, Pioneers in Jewish Medical Ethics, 1997, Medical Legacy of Moses Maimonides, 1998, Medical Encyclopedia of Moses Maimonides, 1998, The Wars of the Lord by Abraham Maimonides in Defense of His Father Moses Maimonides, 2000; mem. editl. bd. Cancer Invest, Mt. Sinai Jour. Medicine; contbr.: Ency. Boethics; contbr. articles to tech. lit. Served with USPHS, 1963-65. Recipient Maimonides award Michael Reese Hosp., Chgo., 1969, Bernard Revel Meml. award Yeshiva U., 1971, Maimonides award of Wis., 1977, AMA award leadership in med. ethics and professionalism, 1998. Fellow A.C.P., N.Y. Acad. Medicine; mem. AMA (award for leadership in med. ethics and professionalism 1998), Am. Assn. History Medicine, N.Y. Soc. Study of Blood, Am., Internat. socs. hematology, Am. Fedn. Clin. Research. Home: 750 Elvira Ave Far Rockaway NY 11691-5405 Office: Queens Hosp Ctr 82-68 164th St Jamaica NY 11432-1140

ROSNER, JONATHAN LINCOLN, physicist, educator; b. N.Y.C., July 23, 1941; s. Albert Aaron and Elsie Augustine (Lincoln) R.; m. Joy Elaine Fox, June 13, 1965; children: Hannah, Benjamin. BA, Swarthmore Coll., 1962; MA, Princeton U., 1963, PhD, 1965. Research asst. prof. U. Wash., Seattle, 1965-67; vis. lectr. Tel Aviv U., Ramat Aviv, Israel, 1967-69; asst. prof. physics U. Minn., Mpls., 1969-71, assoc. prof., 1971-75, prof., 1975-82, U. Chgo., 1982—. Contbr. numerous articles to profl. and scholarly jours. Alfred P. Sloan fellow, 1971-73, Guggenheim fellow, 2002. Fellow Am. Phys. Soc. Democrat. Jewish. Avocations: fishing, hiking, skiing, amateur radio. Office: U Chgo Enrico Fermi Inst 5640 S Ellis Ave Chicago IL 60637-1433

ROSNER, LEONARD ALLEN, lawyer; b. N.Y.C., Apr. 13, 1967; s. Arnold and Betty (Zimmerman) R.; m. Rachel Stein, Nov. 19, 1994; 1 child, Andrew N. AB in Polit. Sci., AB in Pub. Rels., Syracuse U., 1989, JD cum laude, 1992. Bar: N.Y. 1993. With Harter, Secrest & Emery LLP, Rochester, NY. Fin. editor Syracuse Jour. Internat. Law and Commerce, 1991-92. Assigned coun. Monroe County Assigned Coun., Rochester, 1993-94. Mem. N.Y. Bar Assn., Monroe County Bar Assn. Avocations: golfing, reading, television sports, nautilus. Office: 1600 Bausch & Lomb Pl Rochester NY 14604-2711

ROSNER, M. NORTON, business systems and financial services company executive; b. Camden, N.J., Aug. 17, 1931; s. Adolph and Anne (Cotler) R.; m. M. Patricia Eskin, Oct. 18, 1953; children— Robert, Susan, Jan BS in Econs., U. Pa., 1953; MBA, U. Mich., 1965. From acct. to mgr. overhead standards RCA Corp., Camden, N.J., 1953-62; supr. methods and programs, then internal cons. forward model planning Ford Motor Co., Dearborn, Mich., 1962-66; asst. controller, then v.p. planning Singer Co., N.Y.C., 1966-70; treas., then v.p. fin. Popular Services, Passaic, N.J., 1970-72; dir. fin. planning, then asst. controller, then gen. mgr. GSD, then v.p. RE/GSD Xerox Corp., Rochester, N.Y., 1972-90; retired, 1990. Bd. dirs., treas. Parcel Post Assn., N.Y.C., 1970-71; dir. Harbinger, Stamford, Conn.; chmn. Xerox Realty Corp., Stamford. Vice chmn. Compeer, Inc., Rochester, N.Y., 1981-87, chmn., 1987-89; chmn. DP2, Rochester, 1985-87; bd. dirs., treas. Rochester Blue Cross-Blue Shield, 1987-89; dir. Palm Beach County Mental Health Assn., 1992, treas., 1993, v.p., 1994-95, pres., 1995-96; dir. JARC, 1992, v.p., 1993, pres., 1994-96. Recipient Nat. Vol. Action award Pres. U.S. Mem.: U. Mich.; U. Pa. Home: 17831 Heather Ridge Ln Boca Raton FL 33498-6423

ROSNER, ROBERT, astrophysicist, educator; b. Garmisch-Partenkirchen, Bavaria, Germany, June 26, 1947; came to U.S., 1959; s. Heinz and Faina (Brodsky) R.; m. Marsha Ellen Rich, Nov. 8, 1950; children: Daniela Karin, Nicole Elise. BA, Brandeis U., 1969; PhD, Harvard U., 1976. Asst. prof. Harvard U., Cambridge, Mass., 1978-83, assoc. prof., 1983-86; astrophysicist Smithsonian Astrophys. Observatory, 1986-87; prof. U. Chgo., 1987—, William E. Wrather prof., 1998—; chief scientist Argonne Nat. Lab., 2002—. Trustee Adler Planetarium, Chgo., 1989-98, chmn. dept. astronomy and astrophysics, 1991-97. Contbr. more than 170 articles to profl. jours. Woodrow Wilson fellow, 1969. Fellow Am. Phys. Soc.; mem. Am. Acad. Arts & Scis., Am. Astron. Soc., Soc. Indsl. and Applied Math., Am. Geophys. Union. Home: 4950 S Greenwood Ave Chicago IL 60615-2816 Office: U Chicago Astrophysics 5640 S Ellis Ave Chicago IL 60637-1433 E-mail: r-rosner@uchicago.edu.

ROSNER, ROBERT ALLAN, advocate; b. Lincoln Park, N.J., Nov. 2, 1956; s. Henry and Katherine (Kravitt) R.; m. Robin Simons, May 20, 1989. BS, U. Puget Sound, 1980; MBA, U. Wash., 1992. Restaurant mgr. Eatery, Phila., 1976-78; pub. rels. mgr. Big Brothers/Sisters, Tacoma, 1979; pub. affairs dir. Sta. KNBQ; exec. dir. Safety Assistance from the Elderly, Seattle, 1981-82, Smoking Policy Inst., Seattle, 1982-93; dep. campaign chair United Way of King County, 1993-94; COO The Sci. Club, 1995. United Features syndicated columnist Working Wounded, 1995; chmn., shop steward Working Wounded-.Com; cons. Seattle Sch. Dist., 1996; bd. dirs., chmn. bd. Giraffe Project, Langley, Wash., 1989, Coming of Age in Am., Seattle, 1989; adj. prof. Heritage Inst./Antioch, Seattle, 1988, Seattle Pacific U. Grad. Sch. Bus., 1993; radio program host KOMO radio; reporter Sta. KOMO-TV, Seattle, 1996. Author: U.S. Environmental Protection, 1990, Guide to Workplace Smoking Policies, 1990, Working Wounded: Advice That Adds Insight to Injury, 1998, Boss's Complete Survival Guide, 2001; contbr. articles to profl. jours. Bd. dirs. Salvation Army, Seattle, 1992, Giraffe Project. Recipient Gen. News Reporting award, Soc. Profl. Journalists, 1980, Emerald award Internat. TV and Video Assn., Seattle, 1986, Surgeon Gen.'s medallion, 1988. Mem. Rotary (Club of Seattle). Avocations: basketball, public relations, tennis. Office: PO Box 10913 Bainbridge Is WA 98110-0913 E-mail: bob@workingwounded.com.

ROSNOW, RALPH LEON, psychology researcher and educator; b. Balt., Jan. 10, 1936; s. Irvin and Rebecca (Faber) R.; m. Mimi Quin Medinger, Aug. 12, 1963. BS, U. Md., 1957; MA, George Washington U., 1958; PhD, Am. U., 1962. Asst. prof. Boston U., 1963-67; assoc. prof. Temple U., Phila., 1967-70, full prof., 1970-2001; vis. prof. London Sch. Econs., 1973, Harvard U., Cambridge, Mass., 1978, 1988-89; Thaddeus Lincoln Bolton prof. Temple U., 1982—2001, Thaddeus Lincoln Bolton prof. emeritus, 2002—, dir. social and orgnl. psychology divsn. psychology, 1988-2000. Cons. editor jours. and encys. in psychology and comm.; cons. on rsch. methods and data analysis, 1976—. Author: Paradigms in Transition, 1981; author: (with Robert Rosenthal) The Volunteer Subject, 1975, Essentials of Behavioral Research, 1984; author: 2d edit., 1991, Contrast Analysis, 1985, Beginning Behavioral Research, 1993, 4th edit., 2002, People Studying People, 1997, Contrasts and Effect Sizes in Behavioral Research, 2000; author: (with Gary Fine) Rumor and Gossip, 1976; author: (with Mimi Rosnow) Writing Papers in Psychology, 1986, Writing Papers in Psychology, 5th edit., 2001; editor (with Robert Rosenthal): Artifact in Behavioral Research, 1969; editor: (with Marianthi Georgoudi) Contextualism and Understanding in Behavioral Science. Recipient George A. Miller award Soc. Gen. Psychology, 1999. Fellow AAAS, APA, Am. Pschol. Soc.; mem. Soc. Exptl. Social Psychology. Avocations: the three R's. Home: 177 Biddulph Rd Radnor PA 19087-4506 E-mail: rosnow@temple.edu.

ROSOFF, WILLIAM A. lawyer, executive; b. Phila., June 21, 1943; s. Herbert and Estelle (Finkel) R.; m. Beverly Rae Rifkin, Feb. 7, 1970; children: Catherine D., Andrew M. BS with honors, Temple U., 1964; LLB magna cum laude, U. Pa., 1967. Bar: Pa. 1968, U.S. Dist. Ct. (ea. dist.) Pa. 1968. Law clk. U.S. Ct. Appeals (3d cir.), 1967-68; instr. U. Pa. Law Sch., Phila., 1968-69; assoc. Wolf, Block, Schorr & Solis-Cohen, 1969-75, ptnr., 1975-96, chmn. exec. com., 1987-88; also vice chmn. bd. dirs. Advanta Corp., Spring House, Pa., 1996—, pres., 1999—. Trustee RPS Realty Trust, 1990-96, Atlantic Realty Trust, 1996—; guest lectr. confs. and seminars on tax law; mem. tax adv. bd. Commerce Clearing House, 1983-94; mem. legal activities policy bd. Tax Analysts, 1978—; mem. Little, Brown Tax Adv. Bd., 1994-96; chmn. bd. dirs. RMH Telesvcs., Inc., 1997-99. Editor U. Pa. Law Rev., 1965-67; mem. bd. contbg. editors and advisors Jour. Partnership Taxation, 1983-2000; contbr. articles to profl. jours. Bd. dirs., past mem. com. on law and social action Phila. coun. Am. Jewish Congress. Fellow Am. Coll. Tax Counsel; mem. Am. Law Inst. (cons. taxation of partnerships 1976-78, assoc. reporter taxation of partnerships, 1978-82, mem. adv. group on fed. income tax project 1982-2000, cons. taxation of pass-through entities 1995-2000, past bd. dirs.), Order of Coif, Beta Gamma Sigma, Beta Alpha Psi. Office: Advanta Corp Welsh and McKean Rd Spring House PA 19477

ROSOVSKY, HENRY, economist, educator; b. Danzig, Sept. 1, 1927; came to U.S., 1940, naturalized, 1949; s. Selig S. and Sophie (Rosovsky) R.; m. Nitza Brown, June 17, 1956; children— Leah, Judith, Michael. AB, Coll. William and Mary, 1949, LL.D., 1976; A.M. (John E. Thayer scholar), Harvard U., 1953, PhD, 1959; L.H.D. (hon.), Yeshiva U., 1977, Hebrew Union Coll., 1978, Colgate U., 1979, Brandeis U., 1984; PhD (hon.), Hebrew U. of Jerusalem, 1982; LL.D. (hon.), Queen's U., Ont., 1984, U. Hartford, 1984, CUNY, 1986, U. Mass., 1986, Harvard U., 1998; DHL (hon.), Hebrew Coll., Brookline, Mass., 1987, NYU, 1993; DL, St. Mary's Coll. Md., 1989, Jewish Theol. Sem., 1995. From asst. prof. to prof. econs. and history U. Calif.-Berkeley, 1958-65; chmn. Center Japanese and Korean Studies, 1962-65; prof. econs. Harvard U., 1965—, Walter S. Barker prof. econs., 1975-84, Geyser univ. prof., 1984-96, Geyser univ. prof. emeritus, 1996—, chmn. dept., 1969-72, dean Faculty Arts and Scis., 1973-84; assoc. dir. East Asia Research Center, 1967-69. Mem. Harvard U. Corp., 1985-97; vis. prof. Hitotsubashi U., Tokyo, 1957, Tokyo U., 1962, Hebrew U., Jerusalem, 1965; hon. dir. Japan Fund.; dir. emeritus Corning, Inc.; hon. prof. Centro U. Francisco, De Vitoria, Madrid, 1996. Author: Capital Formation in Japan, 1868-1940, 1961, Quantitative Japanese Economic History, 1961, (with K. Ohkawa) Japanese Economic Growth, 1973, The University: An Owner's Manual, 1990; editor: Explorations in Entrepreneurial History, 1954-56, Industrialization in Two Systems, 1966, Discord in the Pacific, 1972, (with H. Patrick) Asia's New Giant, 1976, (with P. Higonnet, D. Landes) Favorites of Fortune, 1991, (with S. Kumon) The Political Economy of Japan, Vol. 3: Cultural and Social Dynamics, 1992. Chmn. bd. trustees Am. Jewish Congress, 1975-88. Served to 1st lt. AUS, 1946-47, 50-52. Jr. fellow Soc. Fellows, 1954-57; recipient Schumpeter prize Harvard, 1963, Clark Kerr medal U. Calif., Berkeley, 1992. Fellow Am. Acad. Arts and Scis., Am. Philos. Soc.; mem. Am. Econ. Assn., Econ. History Assn., Assn. Asian Studies, Chevalier, Legion of Honor, Order of Sacred Treasure, Star (Japan). Home: 37 Beechcroft Rd Newton MA 02458-2403 Office: Harvard Univ Loeb House 17 Quincy St Cambridge MA 02138-3805 E-mail: hrosovsky@harvard.edu.

ROSOW, JEROME MORRIS, institute executive; b. Chgo., Dec. 2, 1919; s. Morris and Mary (Cornick) R.; m. Rosalyn Levin, Sept. 28, 1941; children: Michael, Joel. BA cum laude, U. Chgo., 1942. Position classification analyst Dept. Army, Washington, 1942-43, orgn. and methods examiner, asst. mgr. wage and salary div., 1948-51; dir. compensation War Assets Adminstrn., 1946-48; dir. policy, salary stblzn. bd. Econ. Stblzn. Agy., 1952-53; with Creole Petroleum Corp. subs. Standard Oil N.J., Caracas, Venezuela, 1953-55; exec. mem., coord. compensation, indsl. rels. rsch. Standard Oil N.J., N.Y.C., 1955-66; mgr. employee relations dept. ESSO Europe, Inc., London, 1966-69; asst. sec. labor for policy, evaluation and rsch. Dept. Labor, 1969-71; planning mgr. pub. affairs. dept. Exxon Corp., 1971-77; founder, chmn., CEO Work in Am. Inst., 1975—. Cons. fed. pay plans U.S. Bur. Budget and U.S. CSC, 1964; mem. bus. adv. rsch com. Bur. Labor Stats., 1958-65; chmn. coun. of compensation Nat. Indsl. Conf. Bd., 1959-66; assoc. seminar on labor, Columbia U., 1961-91; dir. N.Y.C. Vocat. Adv. Svc., 1961—, chmn. fin. com., 1962-65; mem. White House Working Group on Welfare Reform, 1969-71; chmn. cabinet com. White House Conf. Children and Youth, 1970-71; chmn. subcabinet com. nat. growth policy; U.S. del OECD Ministers Conf., Paris, 1970, 74; vice-chmn. Nat. Productivity Commn., 1971; chmn. tech. experts multinat. indsl. relations OECD, Paris, 1972; chmn. subcom. manpower and social affairs; chmn. Pres.'s Adv. Com. Fed. Pay, 1971-83; adviser Pres. U.S.; chmn. Am. assembly The Changing World at Work. Editor: American Men in Government, 1949, The Worker and the Job: Coping with Change, 1974; (with Clark Kerr) Work in America: The Decade Ahead, 1979, Productivity: Prospects for Growth, 1981, Views from the Top, 1985, Teamwork: Joint Labor-Management Programs in America, 1986, Global Marketplace, 1988, Training-The Competitive Edge, 1988, Allies in Education Reform, 1988; contbr. articles to profl. jours. Bd. dirs. Young Audiences; trustee Nat. Com. Employment of Youth; adviser Com. Econ. Devel., 1972—, Nat. Planning Assn., 1973—; mem. Nat. Commn. Productivity and Quality of Work, 1975; v.p. Population Edn. Inc., 1975—; mem. Study Group Work and Edn. in China, 1978; cons. comptroller gen. U.S., 1972—, Ford Found.; mem. Mayor's Commn. on Gainsharing, N.Y.C., 1993. With AUS, 1943-46. Recipient Comptroller Gen.'s Public Service award, 1980. Mem. Indsl. Relations Rsch. Assn. (life, exec. bd., pres. 1979). Jewish. Home: 117 Fox Meadow Rd Scarsdale NY 10583-2301 Office: 700 White Plains Rd Scarsdale NY 10583-5063

ROSOW, STUART L. lawyer; b. N.Y.C., Mar. 28, 1950; s. Bernard and Lillian (Bonime) R.; m. Amy Berk Kuhn. AB cum laude, Yale U., 1972; JD cum laude, Harvard U., 1975. Law clk. to presiding justice U.S. Ct. Appeals (7th cir.), Chgo., 1975-76; assoc. Paul, Weiss et al, N.Y.C., 1976-79, Kaye, Scholer, Fierman, Hays & Handler, N.Y.C., 1979-84, ptnr., 1984-97, Proskauer Rose LLP, N.Y.C., 1997—. Adj. prof. Columbia Law Sch., N.Y.C., 1998—. Mem. ABA, N.Y. State Bar Assn., Assn. of Bar of City of N.Y. Office: Proskauer Rose LLP 1585 Broadway Fl 27 New York NY 10036-8299

ROSS, ALBERTA BARKLEY, retired chemist; b. Moores Hill, Ind., July 26, 1928; d. Lawrence Houston and Stella Olcott (Wright) Barkley; m. Joseph Hansbro Ross, June 2, 1956; children: Mary Angela, Joseph Hansbro Jr., Robert Barkley, Kathleen Jarrell. BS, Purdue U., 1948, Wash. U., 1951; PhD, U. Md., 1957. Tech. libr. Monsanto Chem. Co., St. Louis, 1948-53; rsch. assoc. U. Mich., Ann Arbor, 1957-58; supr. Radiation Chemistry Data Ctr. U. Notre Dame (Ind.), 1964-95; ret., 1995. Mem. Am. Chem. Soc. (chmn. St. Joseph Valley chpt. 1977-78), Sigma Xi (chpt. pres. 1980-81), Iota Sigma Pi.

ROSS, ALLAN ANDERSON, music educator, university official; b. Amesbury, Mass., Jan. 16, 1939; s. Frank Albert and Ruth Ethel (Anderson) R.; m. Barbara Kay Bedford, Apr. 15, 1962; children: Karen Elizabeth, Judith Carol, Donna Susan, Linda Beth, Jason Andrew. AB, U. Rochester, 1961; MusM, Ind. U., 1962, MusD, 1968. Asst. dir. music U. Rochester, N.Y., 1962-65; instr. music Ind. U., Bloomington, 1967-69, asst. prof. music, 1969-71, assoc. prof., dir. undergrad. studies, 1971-73, prof., 1977-79, asst. to dean, 1973-79; dean Shepherd Sch. Music, Rice U., Houston, 1979-81; prof. music U. Okla., Norman, 1981-99, Regents prof. music, 1999-2001, Regents prof. emeritus, 2001—, dir. music, 1981-92, devel. officer Coll. Fine Arts, 1992-93; condr. U. Okla. Symphony Orch., 1993-2001, interim dir. music, 1997-98. Dir. music Trinity Methodist Ch., Rochester, N.Y., 1963-65, First United Meth. Ch., Bloomington, Ind., 1969-79, 1st Christian Ch., Norman, Okla., 1981-91; bd. dirs. Riemenschneider Bach Inst.; bd. dirs., exec. bd. Okla. Summer Arts Inst. Guest condr. and adjudicator at music festivals throughout, U.S.; Author: Techniques for Beginning Conductors, 1976. Bd. dirs. United Way of Norman, Helpline of Norman, Okla. Arts Inst.; mem. gov.'s commn. for Okla. Symphony Orch. NDEA Title IV fellow, 1965. Mem. Music Educators Nat. Conf., Am. Choral Dirs. Assn., Coll. Music Soc., Nat. Assn. Schs. of Music (grad. commn., evaluator), Okla. Music Educators Assn., Phi Mu Alpha Sinfonia, Pi Kappa Lambda. Home: 1879 Rolling Hills St Norman OK 73072-6707 Office: U Okla Sch Music 500 W Boyd Norman OK 73019-3040

ROSS, ARTHUR J., III, physician; b. N.Y.C., 1949; MD, Case Western Res. U., 1975. Resident Duke U. Med. Ctr., Durham, 1975-83; staff mem. Childrens Hosp., Phila., 1985-93; fellow in pediat. surgery Children's Hosp., 1983-85; with Gundersen/Luth. Med. Ctr., La Crosse, Wis., 1993—; assoc. prof. U. Pa. Sch. Medicine, 1985-93; prof. surgery & pediatrics U. Wis. Med. Sch., 1993—. Fellow ACS, Am. Acad. Pediat.; mem. Am. Pediatric Surg. Assn., Soc. Univ. Surgeons. Office: Gundersen/Luth Med Ctr 1836 South Ave La Crosse WI 54601-5429 E-mail: ajross@facstaff.wisc.edu.

ROSS, AUDREY, theatrical publicist; b. Chgo., Aug. 3, 1938; d. Hyman and Frieda (Tangul) R. Dancer Ballet Russe de Monte Carlo, 1959, Chgo. Opera Ballet, 1963; dancer with Camelot, 1963-64 Lyric Opera Chgo., 1963; dancer with Oklahoma! Lincoln Ctr., 1969; publicist Pentacle Mgmt., N.Y.C., 1980-82, Audrey Ross/Publicity, N.Y.C., 1982—. Cons. dance program N.Y. State Coun. on the Arts, N.Y.C., 1972—, dance program assoc., 1979-80. Jewish. Home: 205 W End Ave Apt 16E New York NY 10023-4811 Office: 130 W 56th St New York NY 10019-3803

ROSS, BARBARA HUSER, real estate company executive; b. Lamar, Colo., Nov. 13, 1943; d. Archie and Mona Belle (Robinson) Huser; m. John T. Ross, Nov. 29, 1971. Student, Drury Coll., Mo., 1982-83. Lic. real estate broker Mo., Ark. Personnel sec. Ford Aeroneutronics, Newport Beach, Calif., 1963-64; mgr. gen. Family Farm, Mt. Vernon, Mo., 1964-65; field sec. Strout Realty Inc., Springfield, Mo., 1965-67, exec. sec., 1967-79, adminstrv. asst., 1979-82, asst. v.p., 1982-85, v.p., 1985— ; seminar speaker/lectr., 1982— . Author-developer: Nat. Listing System, 1983; (manual) Branch Office Computer System Manual, 1984; pub. sales and mktg. newsletters; contbr. articles to profl. jours.; pub. sales and mktg. newsletters. Mem. Nat. Assn. Realtors, Nat. Assn. Female Execs., Mo. Assn. Realtors (bd. dirs. 1986), Springfield Bd. Realtors (chair com. 1985-87), C. of C. (bd. dirs. Springfield, Mo. 1970-74). Lodge: DAR. Avocations: reading; travel; antique collector. Home: 4151 E Tanglewood Rd Rogersville MO 65742-9475

ROSS, BEATRICE BROOK, artist; b. N.Y.C., Mar. 31, 1927; d. Alexander and Ray (Tennenbaum) Brook; m. Alexander Ross, Dec. 23, 1945; children: Robert Alan, Kenneth Jay, Stefani Lynn. Student, Hunter Coll., 1943, CCNY, 1944, Bklyn. Mus. Art Sch., 1959-60, 64-65; pupil of Ruben Tam, Wang Chi Yuan, Leo Manso; scholar, Sch. Chinese Brush Work, 1973. Owner, operator

Jean Rosenthal Bea Ross Gallery, Jericho, 1961-64; represented by Gillary Gallery, N.Y., Patrician Gallery, West Palm Beach, Fla. Founder Birchwood Art League, 1958-63; lectr. bd. edn., Ont., Can., 1972; mem. ad hoc com. with Lucy Lippard Women in Art, 1970-74. Exhbns. include Women in Art, Huntington, N.Y., 1972, C.W. Post Coll., 1972, 73-76, Guild Hall Mus., East Hampton, 1969-72, Lever House, Inc., 1969-72, J. Walter Thompson Loan Show, 1970, Whitehouse Gallery, 1970, Park Ave. Synagogue, 1970, Locust Valley Ann., 1970, Nat. Arts Club, 1970, Loeb Student Ctr., NYU, 1969, Suffolk Mus., Stony Brook, N.Y., 1969, Lynn U., Boca Raton, 1992, Suffolk Mus., Stony Brook, N.Y., 1971, NAD, 1968, Audubon Artists, 1968, 70, Silvermine Guild, 1968, 71, Port Washington (N.Y.) Library, 1968, 70, 76, Profl. Artists Guild L.I., 1968, Bklyn. Coll., 1968, Huntington Twp. Art League, Cold Spring Harbor, N.Y., 1967, Gillary Gallery, Jericho, N.Y., 1966, 68, 70, 72, 79, 83, Hecksher Mus., 1960, 63, 70, Ho. of Reps., 1965, Library of Congress, 1965, Merrick (N.Y.) Gallery, 1963, N. Shore Community Art Ctr. ann., Roslyn, N.Y., 1959, 62, Birchwood Art League, Jericho, N.Y., 1958, 61-62, Hofstra U., 1960, City Ctr., N.Y.C., 1960, Emily Lowe Gallery, 1960, Nassau Democratic County Com. ann., 1958, R.A.A. Gallery, N.Y.C., 1969-70, 77, Roosevelt Field Art Gallery, Garden City, N.Y., 1958, Boca Raton (Fla.) City Hall, 1991, Bryant Library, Roslyn, N.Y., 1973, Women's Interart Ctr., N.Y.C., 1974, Wantagh (N.Y.) Library, 1975, Port Washington Library, 1976, LIU, 1976, N.Y. Tech., 1974, C.W. Post Coll. Schwartz Library, 1976, St. Johns U., 1976, Union Carbide, N.Y.C., 1977, Harley U. Ctr. Gallery, Adelphi U., 1976, 82, Lincoln Ctr., N.Y.C., 1978, 82, Gallery 84, N.Y.C., 1981, Jericho Libr., 1984Donell Libr., N.Y.C., 1991, Am. Properties Inc., Boca Raton, Fla., 1996; represented in pvt. collections, traveling shows in France, Italy and Japan; mus. curated show No. Trust Bank, Boca Mus., Fla., 1992, Nations Bank, Boca Raton Mus., Fla., 1995; contbr. poetry to Nat. Libr. Poetry, anthology Montage of Life. Recipient 1st prize oil Birchwood Art League, 1958; certificate award outstanding contbn. Mid Island Plaza Art League, Hicksville, N.Y., 1961, 2d prize oil, 1962; hon. mention oil Operation Democracy, Inc. ann., Locust Valley, 1967, 1st prize oil, 1970; Benjamin Altman landscape prize N.A.D., 1968; 2d prize Heckscher Mus., Huntington, N.Y., 1970; hon. mention Port Washington Ann., 1971, Benjamin Altman Landscape prize, Nat. award Nat. Acad. Design, N.Y.C., 1969, RAA Gallery, 1967-78, Harbor Gallery, Glen Cove, N.Y., 1983-85, Gillary Gallery Jericho, N.Y., 1984, Judge's Recognition award Boca Raton Mus., 1989, others; named to Nat. Women's Hall of Fame; MacDowell fellow, 1975, 80; selected for Unique and Universal South Fla. Artists Slide and Lctr., 1997. Mem. Profl. Artists Guild L.I. (v.p. admissions 1971-74, exec. v.p. 1975-77, 2d prize for group show 1990), Profl. Artists Guild Fla., Boca Raton Mus. Artist Guild, Easthampton Guild-Women in Arts, N.Y. Artists Equity, Nat. Mus. Women in Arts (charter), Gallery 84 (N.Y. 1979-85). Home: 5253 Bolero Cir Delray Beach FL 33484-1302

ROSS, BENNIE TYRON, music educator; b. Lakeland, Fla., Oct. 31, 1961; s. Eddie L. Ross and Betty J. Davis. BS in Music Edn., Fla. Meml. Coll., 1984. Cert. tchr. Fla. Mgr. Church's Chicken, Broward, Fla., 1984—86; salesperson Kaufman & Roberts, Miami, 1986—88; music tchr. Broward (Fla.) County Schs., 1988—89, Miami Dade Schs., 1990—. Mem.: Music Educators Nat. Conf., United Tchrs. Dade, Alpha Phi Alpha. Avocations: singing, chess, home improvement, learning new musical instruments. Home: 60 NW 171 Terr Miami FL 33169

ROSS, BERNADETTE MARIE-TERESA, librarian; b. New Orleans, Sept. 23, 1948; d. Arnold and Doris Learson. MLS, U. S.C., 1975. Cert. libr., N.C. Instr. Southern U., New Orleans, 1972-74; libr. S.C. State Atty. Gen. Office, Columbia, 1975; head outreach svcs. Forsyth County Pub. Libr. Systems, Winston-Salem, N.C., 1975-77; head libr. Reid Ross Sr. High Sch., Fayetteville, 1977-85; reference libr. Fayetteville State U., 1989—; head libr. Terry Sanford Sr. High Sch., Fayetteville, 1985—, co-chair sch. renewal process, 1992—. Coord. student forum on sch. violence, 1992—; presenter Fayetteville State U. Ednl. Forum, 1999; dist. rep. Cumberland County Schs. Media Adv. Com., 1997—; cons. in field; mem. Supt.'s Roundtable, 1998; participant N.C. State Libr. Leadership Youth Svcs. Project, 1999-00; coord. Black Pearls: African Am. Films in Transition, 2000. Author: Educator's Guide to the Internet, 1995, Vocational Assessment and the Internet: A Beginner's Guide, 1997; editor newsletters From the Shelf, 1980-85, The Media Express, 1985-89; sect. editor N.C. Libr., 1976; book reviewer N.C. Materials and Evaluation Ctr., Raleigh, 1979. Sec. Cumberland County Friends of the Libr., Fayetteville, 1984-86, pres., 1986-88; adv. bd. arts coun. Umoja Cultural Arts Festival, Fayetteville, 1989; creater, organizer First Charles Chesnutt Film Festival, 1991. Fayetteville Jr. League grantee, 1989—, Florence Rogers Trust grantee, Innovation in Edn. grantee, 1999. Mem. ALA, N.C. Libr. Assn., N.C. High Sch. Libr. Assn. (s.e. dist. dir. 1981-82), N.C. Edn. Assn., N.C. Ctr. for Advancement of Tchg., Cumberland County Edn. Assn., Nat. Coun. Negro Women (charter mem. Fayetteville chpt.), Phi Alpha Theta, Delta Sigma Theta. Home: 502 Nottingham Dr Fayetteville NC 28311-1334 Office: Terry Sanford Sr High Sch 2301 Fort Bragg Rd Fayetteville NC 28303-7035

ROSS, BERNARD, engineering consultant, educator; BME, Cornell U., 1957; MSc in Aero. Engrng., Stanford U., 1959, PhD in Aero. and Aerospace Engrng., 1965; Diploma, Ecole Nat. Superieure L'Aero., France, 1960; cert., U. Edinburgh, Scotland, 1961. Registered profl. engr., Calif. Structural test engr. Gen. Dynamics Corp., Montreal, Quebec, Can., 1956; servomechanism and control sys. design engr. Marquardt Corp., Van Nuys, Calif., 1957; stress analyst Douglas Aircraft Co., Santa Monica, 1959; vibration and dynamics engr. ONERA, Paris, 1960; rsch. asst. Stanford U., 1961-63, rsch. assoc., 1963-65; sr. rsch. engr., program mgr. Stanford Rsch. Inst., Menlo Park, Calif., 1965-70; founder, chmn. emeritus Failure Analysis Assocs., San Francisco, 1967—. Vis. prof. U. Santa Clara, Calif., 1970-79; adv. coun. Stanford U., 1991—, cons. prof., 1992—; pres. internat. adv. bd. structural failure, product liability and tech. ins. confs. U. Vienna, 1986—; mem. univ. coun. Cornell U., 1995; reviewer Nat. Acad. Assocs. Program; speaker and lectr. in field. Contbr. articles to Exptl. Mechanics, AIAA Jour., Israel Jour. Tech., Profl. Safety, others. Cons. U.S. Consumer Product Safety Commn., Washington. NATO scholar, 1960. Mem. ASME, NSPE, AIAA, AAAS, Am. Soc. Safety Engrs., Am. Soc. Agrl. Engrs., Calif. Soc. Profl. Engrs., Soc. Automotive Engrs., Soc. Exptl. Mechanics, Internat. Soc. for Law, Technology and Ins. Achievements include research in analysis of structural collapse, mechanics of impact and penetration, accident reconstruction, safety warning design for heavy equipment, mechanical failure of machine parts, transportation system design. Office: Failure Analysis Assocs PO Box 3015 149 Commonwealth Dr Menlo Park CA 94025-1133 E-mail: kng-fruk@fail.com.

ROSS, BEVERLEY LONG, real estate broker; b. Reno, Sept. 1, 1940; d. John Clemons Long and Roma Lucille Barkman; m. Barry L. Ross, Oct. 2, 1959; children: J. Michael Ross, Pamela Jo Ross Snodgrass. BS, Calif. State, Sacramento, 1970; grad., Realtors Inst. Cert. residential specialist, accredited buyer rep. Tchr. Washoe County Schs., Reno, 1961-64; homebound tchr. Prince Georges County, Oxon Hill, Md., 1972-73; kindergarten tchr. Raleigh Pre-Sch., N.C., 1974-75; owner Boise (Idaho) Pre-Sch., 1975-82; realtor United Realty, Boise, 1977-79; assoc. broker, ptnr. Treasure Valley Realty, 1979-92; broker, owner Bev Ross Realty, 1992—. Mem. foothill plans com. City of Boise, 1990-92; mem. source water assessment adv. com. Idaho Dept. Environ. Quality, Boise, 1998; elder Southminster Presbyn. Ch., corp. pres. and treas., 1991-92, 2001—. Recipient Tribute to Women in Industry, Women's and Childrens Alliance, 1999. Mem. Nat. Assn. Realtors, Idaho Assn. Realtors (chair legis. com. 1992, state dir. continuing edn. task force chair 1997-98), Ada County Assn. Realtors (chair legis. com. 1991, Disting. Svc. award 1993, v.p. 2002, dir. Ada County Assn. Realtors Found. 1999-2001), Women's Coun. Realtors (pres. 2000), Soroptimist Internat. Boise (pres. 1988-89). Avocations: singing, reading, walking, traveling. Fax: 208-730-5791. E-mail: bev@bevrossrealty.com.

ROSS, BRENDA MARIE, elementary school educator; b. New Orleans, May 5, 1944; d. Leslie Carl and Dorothy Marie (McElroy) R. BS, La. State U., 1968, cert. in gifted teaching, 1985. With Orleans Parish Schs., New Orleans, 1968-70, 1970—. Mem. Internat. Reading Assn., Nat. Acad. Games, Assn. for Gifted and Talented Students, New Orleans Acad. Games League, Greater New Orleans Tchrs. of Math., La. Assn. Tchrs. of Math., Delta Kappa Gamma (Pi chpt.). Republican. Episcopalian. Office: Claiborne Sch 4617 Mirabeau Ave New Orleans LA 70126-3540

ROSS, CAMILLE, photographer, art educator; b. San Francisco, May 16, 1964; d. Charles Constantin and Julia Ross. BA in Liberal Arts, Goddard Coll., 1989; cert. in photography, Inst. Allende, San Miguel de Alllende, Mex., 1989; MFA in Photography, Cranbrook Acad. Art, Bloomfield Hills, Mich., 1991. Tchr., dir. photography workshops, Paris, 1992-93; instr. photography Acad. Art Coll., San Francisco, 1993-95, U. N.Mex., Taos, 1999—, curriculum developer photography cert. program, 1999—; photography instr. Calif. State U., Northridge, 2002—. Vis. artist, guest lectr. photography dept. Cleve. Inst. Art, 1991; coord. L.Am. film series Mission Cultural Ctr., San Francisco, 1995; lectr. Plan B Evolving Arts, Santa Fe, 1999; tchr. Casa de Corazon Day Treatment Ctr. H.S., 1999-2000. One-woman shows include Santa Fe Mus. Fine Art, 2001, Harwood Mus. and Found., Taos, 2001; represented in permanent collections Paul Kopeikin Gallery, L.A., Oakland (Calif.) Mus. Modern Art, Harwood Mus.; exhibited in group shows, including Cranbrook Art Mus., 1990, 91, Forum Gallery, Bloomfield Hills, 1991, San Jose Civic Ctr., 1991, Atelier Marek, Paris, Belleville Artists, Paris, 1993, Acad. Art Faculty Show, San Francisco, 1994, Mus. N.Mex., Mus. Fine Arts; represented in permanent collections, including Paul Kopeikin Gallery, L.A., Oakland (Calif.) Mus. Modern Art, Harwood Mus., also pvt. collections Recipient award of excellence San Jose Office Cultural Affairs, 1991; Willard Van Dyke Meml grantee N.Mex. Coun., 2000. Mem. Coll. Art Assn., Soc. for Photog. Edn. Democrat. Avocations: equistrian activities, literature, culinary arts, travel, hiking. Office: U NMex 115 Civic Plaza Dr Taos NM 77571

ROSS, CAROLINE ANNE, materials science educator; b. London, June 4, 1964; came to U.S., 1989; d. Sidney David and Rosemary Daphne Ross. BA, Cambridge U., 1985, PhD, 1988. Postdoctoral fellow Harvard U., Cambridge, Mass., 1989-90; rsch. engr. Komag inc., Milpitas, Calif., 1991-96; asst. prof. MIT, Cambridge, 1997-2000, assoc. prof., 2000—. Cons. in field. Contbr. articles to profl. jours.; patentee in field. Grantee NSF, 1988-2002, IBM Corp., 1998, Def. Advanced Rsch. Programs, 1998-2001, Nat. Storage Industries Consortium, 1998, 3M Corp., 1997, 99, TDK, 2000-02. Mem. IEEE, ASME, Materials Rsch. Soc. (councillor 1999-2001), Am. Phys. Soc., Electrochem. Soc. Office: MIT 13-4005 77 Massachusetts Ave Cambridge MA 02139-4307

ROSS, CATHERINE JANE, lawyer, social policy analyst; b. N.Y.C., Dec. 27, 1949; d. Alexander I. and Wilma (Saltzman) R.; m. Jonathan Rieder, Mar. 14, 1981. B.A., Yale Coll., 1971; Ph.D., Yale U., 1977, J.D., 1987. Post doctoral fellow/research assoc. Yale Bush Ctr. in Child Devel. and Social Policy, New Haven, 1977-79; asst. prof. Yale Child Study Ctr., New Haven, 1979-85; assoc. Paul, Weiss, Rifkind, Wharton & Garrison, 1987-94; asst. prof. history and edn. Boston Coll. Law Sch., 1994-96; assoc. prof. George Washington U. Law Sch., 1996—; mem. HHS Expert Working Group Adoption 2002;; cons. Adminstrn. for Children Youth and Families, HEW, 1979, Conn. Dept. Children and Youth Services, 1978-84, ednl. films and radio programs. Joint editor: Child Abuse: An Agenda for Action, 1980. Del., Conn. Task Force on Juvenile Justice, 1979-80; com. mem. Conn. Task Force on Foster Care, 1979-81. Mellon fellow Aspen Inst. for Humanistic Studies, 1983-84. Fellow Am. Bar Found.; mem. ABA (vice-chair working group on unmet legal needs of Am.'s Children and their families 1993-94, steering com. unmet legal needs of children 1993-94, chair 1994-97, co-chair, 1997-98, mem. sect. litigation task force children), Coalition Justice. grantee Edna McConnell Clark Found., 1981-82, Herman and Amelia Ehrmann Found., 1979-82, Ford Found., 1980-82, John and Catherine MacArthur Found., 1981. Jewish.

ROSS, CECIL FITZGERALD, JR. army officer; b. N.Y.C., July 28, 1961; s. Cecil Fitzgerald Sr. and Mary Louise Ross; 1 child, Mavourneen Ann. AAS in Human Svcs., Hudson Valley C.C., 1979; BA in Behavioral Sci., SUNY, Utica, 1985; grad., Sr. Res. Officer Tng. Corps, 1981. Enlisted U.S. Army N.G., 1982, advanced through grades to sgt., 1993, medic Co. A, 1/105 Inf., 1984-85, unit clk. Co. A 1/105 Inf., 1985-87, platoon medic HHC 1/105 Inf., 1987; respiratory care 364th Gen. Hosp. USAR, 1987-90, practical nurse 364th Gen. Hosp., 1990-92; pers. records NCO 444th pers. svc. co. AGR/USAR, 1992-93; pers. records non-commd. officer 98th divsn. (IT) Active Guard Res., 1993-95; pers. records specialist Full Time Mgmt Support Directorate, USAR, St. Louis, 1995—; rehab. asst. Rensselaer Assn. Retarded Citizens, Troy, N.Y., 1985-87, food svc. supr. Wyantskill, 1988-90; nurse Child's Hosp., Albany, 1991-92. Part-time human svcs. profl. Adept Care Health Svc., Troy, 1980-90; music pres., sr. senator SUNY, Utica, N.Y., 1984-85. Author: Collection of Poetry, 1998; composer: Eloquence, 1989, Masks of Existence, 1989, Light Elements, 1990, X-S Time, 1990, Lunar Tick, 1996, Libra Balancing the Sign, 1997. Scoutmaster troop 649 Boy Scouts Am., Valley Falls, N.Y., 1980; mem. Hoosic Valley Vol. Fire Co., Schaghticoke, N.Y., 1979, Knickerbocker Hist. Soc., Schaghticoke, 1979. Recipient Nat. Archive award Libr. of Congress, 1997. Avocations: performing arts, writing, creating musical scores. Office: Full Time Mgmt Support Directorate 1 Reserve Way Saint Louis MO 63132-5299

ROSS, CHARLES, artist; b. Phila., Dec. 17, 1937; s. Fred H. and Gertrude (Hill) R.; m. Elizabeth Ginsberg, 1977. AB in Math, U. Calif., Berkeley, 1960, MA in Sculpture, 1962. Exhibited in one-man shows: Dilexi Gallery, San Francisco, 1961, 65, 66, 68, Dwan Gallery, N.Y.C., 1968, 69, 71, Daytons Gallery 12, Mpls., 1968, John Weber Gallery, N.Y.C., 1972, 77, 79, 81, The Clocktower, N.Y.C., 1974, Utah Mus. Fine Arts, Salt Lake City, 1975, Mus. Contemporary Art, La Jolla, Calif., 1976, Chgo., 1976, Inst. Contemporary Art, Phila., 1977, Susan Caldwell Gallery, N.Y.C., 1977, MIT, 1977, Portland Center for Visual Arts, 1981, Sena Gallery, Santa Fe, 1991, Johnson Gallery U. N.Mex., 1992, Humphrey Gallery, N.Y.C., 1995, Mus. de Arte y Diseno Contemporaneo, San Jose, Costa Rica, 1996; exhibited in group shows: Archtl. League of New York, 1967, Albright Knox Art Gallery, Buffalo, 1967, Finch Coll., N.Y.C., 1967, Aldrich Mus., Ridgefield, Conn., 1967, Nelson Atkins Mus., Kansas City, 1968, Milw. Art Center, 1968, Whitney Mus., N.Y.C., 1969, Art Inst. Chgo., 1969, Art Gallery of Ont., Toronto, 1969, Galeries-pilotes, Lausanne, Switzerland, 1970, Mus. Fine Arts, Boston, 1971, Indpls. Mus. Art, 1974, Neuberger Mus., SUNY, Purchase, 1975, Stadtisches Mus., Leverkusen, Germany, 1975, Phila. Coll. Art, 1977, Hirshhorn Mus., Washington, 1977, Old Customs House, N.Y.C., 1977, Mus. Natural History, N.Y.C., 1977, Leo Castelli Gallery, N.Y.C., 1978, Yale U. Art Gallery, 1978, Dartmouth Coll. Gallery, 1978, Aspen (Colo.) Center for Visual Arts, 1980, Centre Georges Pompidou, Paris, 1980, Renwick Gallery, Smithsonian Instn., Washington, 1980, Mus. Contemporary Art, Chgo., 1981, MIT, Cambridge, 1981, Bard Coll., 1984, Light Gallery, N.Y.C., 1985, Venice Biennale, 1986, Differentes Natures la Defense, Paris, 1992, Anchorage Mus. History & Art, 1994, Richard Humphrey Gallery, N.Y.C., 1995, Kunsthallen Brandts Klaedefabrik, Odense, Denmark, 1996, SITE Santa Fe, 1996, NIT Intercommunication Ctr., Tokyo, Japan, 1997, Biennale de Lyon, France, 2000; commn. include: prism/solar spectrum skylight sculpture for Fed. Bldg, Lincoln, Nebr., 1976, U. Pa., 1977, Dietrich Found., Phila., 1979, Spectrum Bldg, Denver, 1980, Grand Rapids Art Mus., Mich., 1982, Towson State U., Md., 1983, Cumberland Rapid Transit Sta., Chgo., 1983, Linay Corp., Kansas City, Mo., 1985, Plaza of the Americas, Dallas, 1985, Wells Fargo Bldg., San Diego, 1986, San Francisco Internat. Airport, 1987, Anchorage Internat. Airport, 1987, Naugatuck Higher Edn. Ctr., Conn., 1990, Harvard Bus. Sc. Chapel, 1992, French Ministry of Culture Chateau d'Oiron, 1993, Cook Inst., Grand Rapids, Mich., 1996, Dwan Light Sanctuary, United World Coll., Montezuma, N.Mex., 1996, U.S. Fed. Courthouse, Tampa, 1998, Saitama (Japan) U., 1999, Kaufman Found., Kansas City, 2001; represented in permanent collections Nelson Atkins Mus., Whitney Mus. Am. Art, Berkeley Art Mus., Indpls. Mus. Art, Butler Inst. Am. Art, Herbert F. Johnson Mus. Art Cornell U., GSA Art and Architecture Program, U. Pa., Dietrich Found., Grand Rapids Art Mus., Gen. Elec. Corp., City Chgo., Towson State U., Becton Dickinson Corp., Security Pacific Bank, Found. Ctr., N.Y.C., Wynne Jackson Inc., Albuquerque Mus., Linclay Corp., Witco Chem. Corp., City of San Diego, Walker Art Ctr., City of San Francisco, State of Alaska, Koll Co., Los Angeles County Mus. Art, Mus.de Arte y Diseno Contemporaneo, San Jose, Kunsthallen Brandts Klaedefabrik, Odense, Des Moines Art Ctr., French Ministry of Culture, Frederick A. Weisman Mus., Mpls., Harvard Bus. Sch., Mus. Fine Arts, Santa Fe, United World Coll., N.Mex., Saitama U., Japan; works in progress include: Star Axis, monumental sculpture/observatory atop a mesa in N.Mex. Author: Sunlight Convergence Solar Burn (Am. Inst. Graphic Arts award 1976); films Sunlight Dispersion, 1972, Solar Eclipse, 1972. Recipient Art and Architecture Collaborations award Boston Soc. Architects, 1993, Interfaith Forum on Religion, Art and Arch. Design award Harvard Bus. Sch. Chapel, 1993, award for distinction for artistic achievement Nat. Coun. Art Adminstrs., 1997. Office: Joyce Schwartz Ltd 17 W 54th St New York NY 10019-5404 *My work deals with the nature of light, time, and planetary motion.*

ROSS, CHARLES ROBERT, lawyer, consultant; b. Middlebury, Vt., Feb. 24, 1920; s. Jacob Johnson and Hannah Elizabeth (Holmes) R.; m. Charlotte Sells Hoyt, Aug 28, 1948; children— Jacqueline Hoyt, Peter Holmes, Charles Robert. AB, U. Mich., 1941, MBA, LL.B., U. Mich., 1948. Bar: Ky. 1949, Vt. 1954, U.S. Supreme Ct. 1968. Instr. Oreg. State Coll., 1948-49; practice law Louisville and Burlington, Vt., 1949-59; chmn. Vt. Pub. Service Commn., 1959-61; commr. FPC, 1961-68; mem. U.S. sect. Internat. Joint Commn., 1962-81; mem. Nat. Consumers Energy Com., 1973-74; pub. mem. Adminstrv. Conf. U.S., 1971-74; adj. prof. econs. U. Vt., 1969-74. Served to capt. USAAF, 1942-46. Home: 806 Wake Robin Dr Shelburne VT 05482-7582 E-mail: rtaproot@aol.com.

ROSS, CHRISTOPHER THEODORE, lawyer; b. Denver, Oct. 19, 1925; s. Michael Peter and Martha (Stickhausen) R.; m. Luise Maria Reile, June 11, 1952 (div.); children: Mark Alexander, Katherine Luise, Sonya Catherine (dec.). LLB, U. Buffalo, 1950; JD, SUNY, Buffalo, 1968. Bar: N.Y. 1961, U.S. Dist. Ct. (we. dist.) N.Y. 1952, U.S. Ct. Mil. Appeals 1953, U.S. Supreme Ct. 1970, U.S. Ct. Appeals (2d cir.) 1971. Assoc. Lutwak, Parrino & Maurin, Buffalo, 1959-63; atty. pvt. practice, 1963—. Pres. N.Y. State Assn. Bds. Visitors Dept. Mental Hygiene, 1874-78; pres. West Seneca (N.Y.) Devle. Ctr., 1968-70, 72-74; trustee Buffalo Boy's & Girls Clubs. With USN, 1943-46, 52-59; comdr. USNR, ret.; capt. N.Y. NAval Militia, ret. Mem. N.Y. Bar Assn., N.Y. State Assn. Criminal Def. Lawyers, Erie County Bar Assn., Erie County Trial Lawyers Assn., Lawyer-Pilots Assn., Naval Res. Assn. (v.p. legis., v.p. ret. persons), NAval order of U.S., U.S. Navy League, Royual Can. Mil. Inst. (bd. dirs. 1994-97, hon. officer, internat. affairs), Sovereign Mil. Order of Jerusalem, Naval Officers Assn. Can., Buffalo Athletic Club, Quiet Birdmen Club, Saints and Sinners Club, Silver Wings Club, Aero Club, Toronto Naval Club. Republican. Roman Catholic. Office: Ste 233 2330 Maple Rd Williamsville NY 14221-4058 E-mail: ctwross@aol.com.

ROSS, CLARK GRANT, economics educator; b. Gloucester, Mass., June 24, 1950; s. Norman C. and Helen (Blecher) R. B.A., U. Pa., 1971; Ph.D., Boston Coll., 1975. Asst. prof. dept. econs. College of William and Mary, 1975-76; research scientist U. Mich., 1976-79; asst. prof. econs. Davidson Coll., N.C., 1979-83, assoc. prof., 1983— , chmn. dept., 1983— ; cons. in field. Contbr. articles to profl. jours. Mem. Am. Econs. Assn., So. Econs. Assn. Roman Catholic. Home: RR 2 Box 283cc Davidson NC 28036-9802 Office: Dept Economics Davidson Coll Davidson NC 28036

ROSS, COLEMAN DEVANE, accountant, insurance company executive; b. Greensboro, N.C., Mar. 18, 1943; s. Guy Matthews and Nancy McConnell (Coleman) R.; m. Carol Louise Morde, Aug. 26, 1965; children: Coleman, Jonathan, Andrew. BS in Bus. Administrn., U. N.C., 1965; postgrad., Grad. Sch. Banking of South, 1982-84, U. N.C. Advanced Mgmt. Program, 1994, Trinity Coll., 1999—. CPA, CPCU, CLU, ChFC. With Price Waterhouse , 1965—99, ptnr., 1977—99; chmn., mng. ptnr. Nat. Ins. Svcs. Group, 1988-94; exec. v.p., CFO Trenwick Group Ltd., 2000—02, The Phoenix Cos., Inc., 2002—. Bd. dirs. Phoenix Nat. Trust Co., 2001—. Bd. dirs. N.E. Region Boy Scouts Am., 1988—, v.p., 1993-96, 2002--, pres. New England Area, 1988-91; bd. dirs. Greater N.Y. Coun. Boy Scouts Am., 1994—; mem. exec. bd. Conn. Rivers Coun. Boy Scouts Am., 1978—, pres., 1985-88; participant Leadership Greater Hartford, 1977; mem. bd. visitors U. N.C., 2001—. Recipient Silver Beaver award Boy Scouts Am., 1987, Silver Antelope award, 1991. Mem. AICPA (ins. cos. com. 1985-88, reins. auditing and acctg. task force 1979-85, rels. with actuaries com. 1982-85), N.C. Assn. CPAs, Soc. Fin. Svc. Profls., CPCU Soc., Chartered Ins. Inst., Fin. Exec. Internat., Internat. Ins. Soc., Assn. Ins. and Fin. Analysts, Assn. Investment Mgmt. and Rsch., N.Y. Soc. Security Analysts (com. on improved corp. reporting), Hartford Club (bd. govs. 1977-84), Carolina Club. Home: 6 Wild Flower Ln West Simsbury CT 06092-2434 Office: The Phoenix Cos One American Row Hartford CT 06102 E-mail: coleman.ross@phoenixwm.com.

ROSS, DALE GARAND, therapist, programming consultant, speaker, writer; b. Detroit, May 31, 1948; s. Stanley Anthony and Kathleen Mary (Moore) Jamros. BS in Psychology, Mich. State U., 1970; MSW, Wayne State U., 1980. Cert. social worker Nat. Acad. Cert. Social Workers; cert. counselor Nat. Cert. Counselors; cert. social worker, Mich. Ptnr. Unicorns, Detroit, 1970-76; pres. Realities, Ltd., Birmingham, Mich., 1976-78; counselor I univ. counseling Wayne State U., Detroit, 1980-82, counselor II ednl. resources/disabilities, 1982-84, counselor II, univ. counseling, 1984-85; therapist Substance Abuse Ctr., Warren, Mich., 1985; pvt. practice Southfield, 1985—. Founding mem. Wellness Networks, Inc., Detroit, 1983-84; 1t pres., chmn. protem, founding mem. Wellness House Mich., 1985-87; part-time instr., developer grad. courses for Sch. of Social Work, Wayne State U., 1991-96, faculty liaison for student group, 1994-96, AIDS rsch. and edn. program and HIV mental health ednl. series, 1993—; pres. Southeastern Mich. Info. and Referral Alliance, 1992-94; cons. in field; presenter programs. Contbr. articles to profl. jours. Mem. steering com. Venereal Disease Action Coalition, United Cmty. Svcs., 1986-92; mem. steering com. Macomb County AIDS Cmty. Coun., chmn., 1988; mem. Hospice AIDS Task Force, 1986-88, AIDS Spkrs. Bur. and AIDS Phone Network, Mich. State Med. Soc., 1987—; program chmn. Motor City Bus. Forum, 1983-84, chmn. cmty. ctr. com., 1982-83; founding mem. work/worship Wellness Alliance Com., 1998—; group leader Nat. Conf. for Cmty. and Justice, 1999—. Recipient Am. Legion award 1966, Libr. Key award Hazel Park Pub. Schs., 1966; Mich. Bd. Govs. grantee, 1978-79, 79-80. Mem. NASW, Am. Coll. Personnel Assn. (men's task force), Nat. Orgn. for Changing Men (co-chmn. job-work satisfaction task group 1986), Internat. Platform Assn., Mich. Orgn. for Human Rights, World Future Soc., Mich. Alcohol and Addiction Assn. (bd. dirs. 1993-96), Am. Assn. Counseling Devel., Mich. Rainbow Therapist Assn. (co-founder). Avocations: antiques, ceramics. Home: 2366 Earlmont Rd Berkley MI 48072-1838 Office: 206 Americana Plaza 28475 Greenfield Rd Southfield MI 48076-3034 E-mail: realitiesunlimited@home.com.

ROSS, DANIEL R. lawyer; b. Stamford, Conn., Oct. 20, 1941; s. Adrian E. and Ruth (Hill) R.; m. Faye Zerwekh, Aug. 15, 1965; children: Kevin S., Eric D., David W. SB, MIT, 1963; LLB, U. Pa., 1966. Atty. adviser to Hon. Theodore Tannenwald, Jr. U.S. Tax Ct., Washington, 1966-68; assoc. Drinker, Biddle & Reath, Phila., 1970-77, ptnr., 1977-98, Commons & Commons, Phila., 1998—. Presenter in field. Pres. bd. trustees First United Meth. Ch. Germantown, 1984—. Capt. U.S. Army, 1968-70, Vietnam. Mem. ABA (chair com. on income of estates and trusts 1985-87, com. on govt. subcoms. 1988-91, taxation sect.). Avocations: bicycling, skiing, tennis, computers. Office: The Cambridge Ste 1210 2967 W School House Ln Philadelphia PA 19144-5222 E-mail: danrross@aol.com.

ROSS, DANIEL J.J. publishing executive; b. Albany, N.Y., June 2, 1943; AB, Hamilton Coll., 1966; MA, U. Fla., 1969. Prodn. mgr. U. Fla. Press, 1976-80; mktg. mgr. U. Ala. Press, 1980-85; asst. dir. Duke U. Press, 1985-89; editor-in-chief U. Nebr. Press, Lincoln, 1989-95, dir., 1995—. Office: 233 N 8th St Lincoln NE 68508-1305

ROSS, DARIUS ALEXANDER, arbitraguer and commodities trader, philanthropist; b. Laurel, Miss., July 16, 1965; s. Malachi and Alice Audrey (Rodgers) R.; m. Rose Mary Mitchell, Feb. 17, 1995 (div. Dec. 1996); children: Tomika, Alexander, T'mia; m. Linda Johnson, Sept. 17, 1998 (div. Dec. 1999). Student, Chicago State U., 1983-86, Wright Coll., 1984, Internat. Acad. Design, 1985, Lake Forest Coll., 1986, AMA Inst., 1992, World Trade Inst. of N.Y., 1992, U. Pa. Dirs. Inst., 1996-97, Harvard U. Dirs. Inst., 1997, Northwestern U., Evanston, Ill., 1997—, Kennesaw State U., U. Chgo., NYU, Columbia U., N.Y. Inst. Fin., Oxford-Templeton Inst., MIT; cert. divinity & ministry, cert. futurist studies, Abaak Acad., 1999. Cert. bus. broker, merger and acquisition intermediary cons., corp. valuation cons.; lic. real estate comml. broker and appraiser. Pres. Darius Ross Interest Ltd., 1989—, BG III MDW Holdings, 1989—, BG III Ohio Holding, 1989—, BG III Wis., 1989—, BG III Mich., 1989—. Bd. dirs. Rossfinaco, Darfin Holdings, Cacig Group, Creamie Inc., Tamco Holdings, Daril Holdings, Darmac Interest., Ross & Ross Assocs., Altimia Holdings, Tamco Industries, Cacicg Group, Tadar Investments, Rossco Equities, Macross Trading, Ross To Ross Assoc., Daalta

Devels., Nelgui Holdings, Katdad Investments, Soumislau Holdings, The 79th St. Entertainment Group, Albaltal Internat., LLC, Macalicon Multi State Holdings, The Ross 7AM Agrl. Co., Dam 7AM Ross Co. Holdings Group LLC. Bd. dirs. Tilman Cmty. Health Clinic, 1997, N.Y.C. H.S. of Econs. and Fin. Benefit Bd./Bus. Adv. Bd., Chgo. Acad. of Performing Arts Benefit Bd.; active Jobs for Youths, 1991-96, George W. Ross African Am. Studies Award and Found., Target 79th St. Redevel. Group, Kennedy King Coll. Computer Info. Sys. Adv. Bd.; mem. Consolidated Corp. Fund of Lincoln Ctr., N.Y. Trust, Chgo. Symphony Orch. Assn., Rep. Senatorial Trust; bd. dirs. DA 7AM Ross Co. Found., Malalic Inst., NWO-3 Charity Trust, D. Alexamder Ross Ptnrs. Internat. LLC, Alexisal Internat. Edn. Charities. Recipient award Chgo. Directory of Apparel Mfrs., 1989; named Young Leader, S.W. Herald, 1989, N.Y. Times Heir Column, 1989, YEO/The Bridge Wealthy 100, 1990, Ace Young Entrepreneur of Yr., 1989, 90, YEO Entrepreneur Data Directory, 1993. Mem. ABA (assoc. mem.), U.S. Postal Adv. Bd., Chgo. Postal Adv. Bd., Auburn Pk. Postal Adv. Bd., Hyde Pk. Postal Adv. Bd., Urban Bankers Assn., Turnabout Mgmt. Assn., Internat. Assn. Fin. Engrs., Treasury Mgmt. Assn., Chgo. Coun. Fgn. Rels., Nat. Assn. Female Execs., Am. Bus. Women's Assn. Nat. Assn. Women in Edn., Bus. Brokers Assn., Future Industry Assn., World Trade Assn., Nat. Cmty. Econ. Devel. Assn., Nat. Assn. Corp. Dirs. (sec. Chgo. chpt. 1997), N.Y. Stock Exch. Luncheon Club, Mid-Day Club (Chgo.), Met. Club (Chgo.), Chgo. Mercantile Exch. Club, Midam. Club of Chgo., Profl. Security Internat., World Super Projects Fedn., Execs. Club (Chgo.), Mpls. Athletic Club, Univ. Club of Mich. State U., Assn. for Corp. Growth, Nat. Assn. Corp. Treasurers, Coun. Instl. Investors, Nat. Black MBA Assn., Alliance of Bus. Brokers and Intermediaries, Assn. Midwest Bus. Brokers, East Manhattan C. of C., Midwest Assn. Family Bus. Owners, Am. Soc. Corp. Secs., Comml. Fin. Assn., Young Execs. Club, Forest Akers Golf Club, Ohio State U. Faculty Club, Chgo. Athletic Assn., Chgo. Symphony Orch. Assocs., U. R.I. Club, Wellesley Coll. Club, Nat. Bar Assn. Women Lawyers Divsn., Am. Bar Assn., Hispanic Nat. Bar Assn., U. Wash. Faculty Club, World Future Soc., Hispanic Nat. Bar Assoc., Women's Bar Assn., Women's Bar Assn. of DC, Nat. Assn. Women Lawyers, Nat. Assn. Women Execs., Chgo. Social Sports Club, Brown U. Faculty Club, Columbia Faculty HSE Club, U. Del. Faculty Club, U. Pa. Faculty Club, U. Louisville Faculty Club, U. Club Nashville, Hofstra Faculty Club, Texas A&M Faculty Club, U. Texas Faculty Club, U. Wis. Faculty Club, U. Missouri Faculty Club, Harvard Club, Canebrake Golf Club, Polo Club, Powerboat Racing Club, Jai Alai Club, ATV Racing Club, Chariot Racing Club, U. Del. Faculty Club, U. Pa. Faculty Club. Republican. Roman Catholic. Avocations: tennis, soccer, golf, international travel, shooting.

ROSS, DARRIN, composer; Pres. Bad Boi Studios; composer, sound engr. Jam on Prodns., 1984—. Collaborator: with Renee Harris Dance Party USA, : with Renee Harris 1 House Street. Recipient Philly's St. Buzz Producer of Yr. award, 1997. Office: Puremovement PO Box 42009 Philadelphia PA 19101*

ROSS, DAVID A. art museum director; b. Malverne, N.Y., Apr. 26, 1949; s. Joshua and Grayce R.; m. Margaret Gronner; children: Lindsay, Emily. BA, Syracuse U.; postgrad., Grad. Sch. Fine Arts, Syracuse. Curator video art Everson Mus. Art, Syracuse, N.Y., 1971-74; dep. dir. program devel. and TV Long Beach Mus. Art, Calif., 1974-77; chief curator Univ. Art Mus., Berkeley, 1977-82; dir. Inst. of Contemporary Art, Boston, 1982-91; dir., CEO Whitney Mus. Am. Art, 1991-98; dir. San Francisco Mus. Modern Art, 1998—. Active Fed. Adv. Com. om Internat. Exbns., 1990—. Contbr. articles to profl. jours. Mem. Assn. Art Mus. Dirs. Office: San Francisco Mus Modern Art 151 3rd St San Francisco CA 94103-3107*

ROSS, DAVID EDMOND, church official; b. Lewiston, Maine, Oct. 1, 1950; s. Rev. and Mrs. Lorne Arla Collins R.; m. Shirley Evelyn Godin, Aug. 19, 1972. BA in Theology cum laude, Berkshire Coll., 1973; MPA, U. Maine, 1989. Ordained to ministry Advent Christian Ch., 1975. Pastor State Road Advent Christian Ch., Presque Isle, Maine, 1973-91; exec. dir. Advent Christian Ch. Gen. Conf., Charlotte, N.C., 1991—. V.p. Maine State Conf. Advent Christian Chs., 1975-76, pres., 1976-81, 86-91; mem. exec. coun. Advent Christian Ch., 1981-90, long range strategy com., 1986—; seminar leader Am. Festival of Evangelism, Kansas City, 1981; dir. Northern Lights Youth Choir, 1974-90. Exec. dir., CEO Advent Christian Gen. Conf., 1991—. Office: Advent Christian Church PO Box 23152 Charlotte NC 28227-2003 E-mail: execdirect@adventchristian.org.

ROSS, DAVID J. product manager; b. Washington, June 28, 1965; s. Harry E. and Lois Alene (Beaver) R.; m. Keiko Acakaki Ross, Feb. 10, 1989. Student, Presbyn. Coll., Clinton, S.C., 1982, U. Cin., 1984; BS in Design, Ga. Tech. U., 1987. Mech. engr. Comsat, Sterling, Va., 1989-91; product mgr. Am. Mobile Satellite, Washington, 1991-95, dir. of sales Reston, Va., 1995-96; product mgr. Qualcomm, San Diego, 1996—. Patentee in field. Lt. cpl. USMC, 1987-89. Avocations: surfing, oil painting, skiing. Office: Qualcomm 5414 Oberlin Dr Ste 300 San Diego CA 92121-4744

ROSS, DEBRA, interior design executive; b. Bessemer, Ala., Jan. 22, 1952; d. Printis and Fredericka (Swan) B.; div. 1984; children— Ksenia D., Darron L., Erik, Viveca M. Computer cert. U. So. Calif., 1970; B.A., Los Angeles Bus. Coll., 1976. Teller Sumitomo Bank, Los Angeles, 1970-71; fgn. and domestic advisor Bank of Calif., Los Angeles, 1971-73; loan asst., utility exec. Tokai Bank, Inglewood, Calif., 1976-78; asst. mgr. Brunschwig & Fils, Los Angeles, 1979— . Mem. PTA; mem. adv. council World Won For Christ Ministries, also choir group. Mem. Nat. Assn. Female Execs., Single Working Mother Group (pres., founder Hawthorne, Calif. 1986). Democrat. Avocations: reading, cooking, Bible study. Office: Brunschwig & Fils 8687 Melrose Ave Ste 653 West Hollywood CA 90069-5701

ROSS, DEBRA BENITA, jewelry designer, marketing executive; b. Carbondale, Ill., May 1, 1956; d. Bernard Harris and Marian (Frager) R. BS, U. Ill., 1978; MS, U. Wis., 1979. Dir. mktg. Ambion Devel., Inc., Northbrook, Ill., 1983-89, Fitness Horizons, Inc., Northbrook, 1989-91, v.p. mktg., 1991-97; owner Benita Ross Designs, 1992—. Home: 1853 Mission Hills Ln Northbrook IL 60062-5760

ROSS, DELMER GERRARD, historian, educator; b. Los Banos, Calif., Nov. 5, 1942; s. Elmer G. and Orva Beth (Dickinson) R.; m. Karen Ann Gibson, June 17, 1977; children: Michelle, Richard. BA, Pacific Union Coll., 1965; MA, U. Calif., Santa Barbara, 1967, PhD, 1970. Instr. Pacific Union Coll., Angwin, Calif., 1968-69; from asst. to assoc. prof. Oakwood Coll., Huntsville, Ala., 1970-76; from assoc. prof. to prof. history Loma Linda U., Riverside, Calif., 1976-91, chmn. dept. history and polit. sci., 1986-90; prof. history and polit. sci. La Sierra U., 1991—. Author: Visionaries and Swindlers, 1975, Rails Across Costa Rica, 1976, Rails in Paradise, 1991, Gold Road to La Paz, 1992, Development of Railroads in Guatemala and El Salvador, 1849-1929, 2001; mem. editl. bd. Adventist Heritage mag., 1987-90. Bd. dirs. Inst. for Research in Latin Am., Mobile, Ala., 1968-82. Mem. Am. Hist. Assn., Assn. 7th Day Adventist Historians (exec. sec. 1973-74, sec.-treas. 1974-75, pres. 1981-82), Assn. Western Adventist Historians, Nat. Railway Hist. Soc., Colo. Railroad Hist. Found. (life), Railway and Locomotive Hist. Soc. Republican. Office: La Sierra U Dept History Riverside CA 92515 E-mail: dross@lasierra.edu.

ROSS, DIANNA JO, counselor, writer; b. Phoenix, Jan. 13, 1947; d. George William and Verla Robeta Carlile; m. James Author Ross, Aug. 16, 1968; children: Thanyia, Kendra, Allyson, Amber, Micah, Daniel, Holly. Counselor Henry Tech. Svc. Inc., Springfield, Mo., 1994—. Author: STEWARDSHIP-A Commitment to Service, 2001. Mem. Lds Ch. Avocations: reading, gardening, writing. Home: 9070 McRae Ct Manassas VA 20110 Office: Henry Technical Services Inc 4037 South Miranda Ct Springfield MO 65807

ROSS, DONA RUTH, education program director, retired; b. Hot Springs, S.D., June 17, 1930; d. Gordon Richard and Margaret Elizabeth (Emery) Bartell; children: Judy, Barbara, Dale, Peggy, Randall. Student, Aims Jr. Coll., 1968-69; BA, U. No. Colo., 1972, MA, 1973; postgrad., Black Hills State Coll., 1974-75, U. S.D., 1975—, No. State Coll., 1981, U. Ea. N.Mex., 1973, U. Alaska. Speech pathologist Shannon County Schs. Pine Ridge Indian Reservation, Batesland, S.D., 1973-76, Yankton (S.D.) Schs., 1976-77; prin. New Underwood (S.D.) Schs., 1977-80, Pierre (S.D.) Indian Learning Ctr., 1980-81, speech, lang. and hearing specialist coop. svc. unit, 1983-85; speech pathologist Office Indian Edn. Programs Bur. Indian Affairs Schs., Pine Ridge, S.D., 1981-83; edn. program dir. Annette Island Schs., Metlakatla, Alaska; ret. cons. Oglala Sioux Tribe Early Childhood Programs, 1973-80. Sec. Shannon County Dem. Party, 1975-76. Mem. Am. Speech, Lang. and Hearing Assn., Coun. for Exceptional Children. Democrat. Congregationalist. Home: 1218 Georgeson Loop Sitka AK 99835-7013

ROSS, DONALD, JR. English language educator, university administrator; b. N.Y.C., Oct. 18, 1941; s. Donald and Lea (Meyer) R.; m. Sylvia Berger (div.); 1 child, Jessica; m. 2d, Diane Redfern, Aug. 27, 1971; children— Owen, Gillian BA, Lehigh U., 1963, MA, 1964; PhD, U. Mich., 1967. Asst. prof. English U. Pa., Phila., 1967—70; prof. English U. Minn., Mpls., 1970—, dir. composition program, 1982—86, dir. Univ. Coll., 1984—89. Author: American History and Culture from the Explorers to Cable TV, 2000; co-author: Word Processor and Writing Process, 1984, Revising Mythologies: The Composition of Thoreau's Major Works, 1988; co-editor, contbr.: American Travel Writers, 1776-1865, 1997, American Travel Writers, 1850-1915, 1998; contbr. articles to profl. jours. Grantee Am. Coun. Learned Socs., 1976, 90, NSF, 1974, Fund for Improvement of Postsecondary Edn., 1982-85; recipient Disting. Teaching award U. Minn., 1992. Mem. MLA, Assn. for Computers and Humanities (exec. sec. 1978-88). Office: U Minn Dept English 207 Lind Hall 207 Church St SE Minneapolis MN 55455-0152 E-mail: rossj001@umn.edu.

ROSS, DONALD ROE, federal judge; b. Orleans, Nebr., June 8, 1922; s. Roe M. and Leila H. (Reed) Ross; m. Janice S. Cook, Aug. 29, 1943; children: Susan Jane, Sharon Kay, Rebecca Lynn, Joan Christine, Donald Dean. JD, U. Nebr., 1948, LLD (hon.) , 1990. Bar: Nebr. 1948. Practice law, Lexington, Nebr., 1948—53; mayor City of Lexington, 1953; assoc. Swarr, May, Royce, Smith, Andersen & Ross, 1956—70; U.S. atty. Dist. Nebr., 1953—56; gen. counsel Rep. party, Nebr., 1956—58; mem. Rep. Exec. Com. for Nebr., 1952—53; com. mem. Rep. Nat. Com., 1958—70, vice-chmn., 1965—70; sr. judge U.S. Ct. Appeals (8th cir.), 1971—.

ROSS, DONALD EDWARD, engineering company executive; b. N.Y.C., May 2, 1930; m. Jeanne Ellen McKessy, Apr. 4, 1954; children: Susan, Christopher, Carolyn. BA, Columbia Coll., 1952; BS in Mech. Engring., Columbia U., 1953; MBA, NYU, 1960. Registered profl. engr., N.Y., 14 other states. Engr. Carrier Corp., N.Y.C., 1955-70; v.p. Dynadata, 1970-71; with Jaros, Baum & Bolles, N.Y.C., 1971-2000, ptnr., 1977-2000; ret., 2000. Mem. adv. coun. sch. engring. Columbia U. Mem. adv. coun. Columbia U. Sch. Engring. and Applied Sci. Lt. (j.g.) USN, 1953-55. Fellow ASHRAE, Am. Cons. Engrs. Coun.; mem. ASME, NSPE, Nat. Acad. Engrs., Nat. Bur. Engring. Registration, N.Y. Assn. Cons. Engrs. (pres. 1984-86), Coun. on Tall Bldgs. and Urban Habitat (vice chmn. N.Am., mem. steering group), Univ. Club (N.Y.C.), Columbia U. Sch. Engring. Alumni Assn. (pres. 1997-99), Nassau Country Club, Tau Beta Pi. E-mail: Rossd@jbb.com.

ROSS, DONALD HENRY, lawyer; b. Modesto, Calif., Oct. 14, 1923; s. Guy Walden Ross and Dolly Mae Brewer; m. Ruth Lorene Kitching, May 13, 1946; children: Genie Ann Kuehne, Robin Mae. BS in Indsl. Mgmt., U. So. Calif., 1953; MS in Internat. Affairs, George Washington U., 1965; JD, U. Pacific, 1982. Bar: Nev. 1982. Sgt. pilot RAF, 1941-42; commd. 2d. lt. USAF, 1942, advanced through grades to maj. gen., retired, 1974; atty. pvt. practice, Carson City, Nev., 1982—. Republican. Avocations: flying, old car restoration, shooting. Home and Office: 4350 Meadow Wood Rd Carson City NV 89703-9493

ROSS, DONALD MORRIS, retired industrial hygienist, consultant; b. Kenosha, Wis., Aug. 22, 1923; s. Walter Morris and Mame Olive (Fox) R.; m. Martha Jackson, Aug. 10, 1946; children: David, Michael, Katy, Gregory, John, Maria. AA, Edinburg Jr. Coll., 1941; BS, U. Tex., 1943; MPH, U. Pitts., 1953, DSc, 1956. Tech. supr. prodn. divsn. Tenn. Eastman Corp., Oak Ridge, 1943-46, rsch. assoc., 1946-49; indsl. hygienist Carbon and Carbide Corp., 1949-52; rsch. assoc. U. Pitts., 1956-58; indsl. hygienist, chief health prot., occ. health/safety Atomic Energy Com., Energy R&D Adminstrn., Dept. Energy, Washington, 1958-89; cons., sr. scientist Sci. Application Internat. Corp., Germantown, Md., 1989-95. Contbr. chpts. to books and articles to profl. jours. including Health Physics Jour., Applied Indsl. Hygiene. Lector St. Jane de Chantal Cath. Ch., parish coun., 1970-73, 90-93. With U.S. Corps Engring., 1945-46. Recipient Indsl. Hygiene award U.S. Dept. Energy, 1997; U.S. AEC fellow, U. Pitts., 1952-53. Mem. Am. Indsl. Hygiene Assn., Am. Conf. on Govt. Indsl. Hygienists (bd. dirs. 1976-79), Health Physics Soc. Democrat. Avocations: collecting beer cans, tennis, bridge, grandchildren. Home: 6008 Grosvenor Ln Bethesda MD 20814-1852 E-mail: martha.ross@wap.org.

ROSS, DOUGLAS, lawyer; b. L.A., July 12, 1948; s. Mathew and Brenda Butler (Boynton) R.; m. Lynne Rose Maidman, June 14, 1970. AB cum laude, Tufts U., 1970; JD with honors, George Washington U., 1973. Bar: Ohio 1973, D.C. 1980, U.S. Supreme Ct. 1976. Asst. atty. gen., antitrust sect. Office of Ohio Atty. Gen., Columbus, 1973-74; spl. asst. U.S. atty. Ea. Dist. Va., Alexandria, 1977; trial atty. antitrust divsn. U.S. Dept. Justice, Washington, 1975-82; atty. advisor Office of Legis. Affairs, 1984-86, Office of Legal Policy, 1987-89, Office Policy Devel., 1989-92; Supreme Ct. counsel Nat. Assn. Attys. Gen., 1982-91. Ran advocacy project for states to enhance their effectiveness before Supreme Ct., 1982—91; operated clearinghouse on state constl. law, 1987—91; civil divsn. Appellate Staff U.S. Dept. Justice, Washington, 1992—94, Office of Consumer Litigation, 1994—2000, spl. counsel for agr. antitrust divsn. , 2000—. Recipient Meritorious award Dept. Justice, 1979, Spl. Achievement award, 1984, 96, 97. Mem. Supreme Ct. Hist. Soc., D.C. Bar Assn., Supreme Ct. Opinion Network (bd. dirs. 1989-91), Arlington County Sports Commn. (chair subcom. on swimming pools 1995—). Jewish. Home: 3153 19th St N Arlington VA 22201-5103 Office: US Dept Justice 601 D St NW Washington DC 20530-0001

ROSS, DOUGLAS TAYLOR, retired software company executive; b. Canton, Republic of China, Dec. 21, 1929; (parents Am. citizens); s. Robert Malcolm and Margaret (Taylor) R.; m. Patricia Mott, Jan. 24, 1951; children: Jane R. Yoos, Kathryn R. Chow, Margaret R. Thrasher. AB in Math. cum laude, Oberlin Coll., 1951; SM, MIT, 1954, postgrad., 1958; DSc (hon.), Oberlin Coll., 2001. Head computer applications group elec. systems lab. MIT, Cambridge, 1952-69, lectr. dept. elec. engring. and computer sci., 1960-69, 83—, exec. com. MIT Enterprise Forum, 1984-89; pres. SofTech, Inc., Waltham, Mass., 1969-75, chmn. bd., 1975-89, 91-93, chmn. emeritus, 1989-91, 93-94, ret., 1994. Mem. town meeting, Lexington, Mass., 1960-70; trustee, bd. dirs. Charles Babbage Inst., 1984—. Mem. United Ch. of Christ. Home: 33 Dawes Rd Lexington MA 02421-5926 E-mail: dougross@mit.edu.

ROSS, E. EARL, small business owner; b. July 3, 1942; s. Edward Earl and Ruth Randles (Loewen) R.; m. Mary Donna Moore, May 31, 1964; 1 son, Damon Moore. BA in Psychology, Central Mo. State U., 1965; MA in Corrections, Webster U., 1976. Reporter Warrensburg (Mo.) Daily Star-Jour., 1965; social worker St. Louis County Welfare Div., Maplewood, Mo., 1966-68; assoc. dist. scout exec. Boy Scouts Am., St. Louis, 1968; dep. juvenile officer St. Louis County Juvenile Ct., Clayton, Mo., 1969-72; program dir. St. Louis County Detention Ctr., 1972-99, asst. supt., 1978-99; CEO Golf-o-Gram, 1999—. Trainer statewide detention staffs; past pres. Historygram, Inc. Recipient Outstanding Detention Program award Nat. Council Juvenile and Family Ct. Judges, 1982. Mem. St. Louis County Juvenile Justice Assn., Am. Mgmt. Assn. Home: 15333 Appalachian Trl Chesterfield MO 63017-1939

ROSS, E. WAYNE, education educator; b. Greenville, S.C., Apr. 26, 1956; s. Bobby G. and Jean (Clutts) R.; children: Rachel Layne, John Colin Mathison; m. Sandra Mathison. AB, U. N.C., 1978, MA in Teaching, 1979; PhD, Ohio State U., 1986. Cert. secondary social studies tchr., N.C., Ga., Ohio. Secondary social studies tchr. Fulton County Schs., Atlanta, 1979-81; dir. edn. Eastway Ch. of God, Charlotte, N.C., 1981-82; instr. Ohio State U., Columbus, 1982-86; asst. prof. edn. SUNY, Albany, 1986-92, assoc. prof. edn. Binghamton, 1992—. Vis. prof. U. B.C., Vancouver, Can., 1991, U. Victoria, Can., 1994; mem. editl. bd. SUNY Press, Albany, 1988-94, chmn. edtl. bd., 1990-94; pres. N.Y. State Coun. on Social Edn., Rochester, 1988-90; bd. dirs., mem. exec. com. Coll. and Univ. Faculty Assembly of Nat. Coun. for Social Studies, Washington, 1990-94, chmn. exec. com., 1992-93. Author, editor: Teacher Personal Theorizing, 1992, Reflective Practice in Social Studies, 1994, A Casebook for Teaching Ethical Issues in Qualitative Research, 1993, The Social Studies Curriculum, 1997; editor Social Sci. Record, 1990-93, Theory and Rsch. in Soc. Edn., 1996—; contbr. articles to profl. publs., chpts. to books. Bd. dirs. Pierce Hall Day Care Ctr.; vol. Village Soccer Club, Colonie, N.Y.; youth soccer coach Albany Youth Soccer, 1992-95. Mem. John Dewey Soc., Am. Ednl. Rsch. Assn., Nat. Coun. for Social Studies, Social Sci. Edn. Consortium, Am. Fedn. Tchrs. Avocations: baseball, popular and blues music. Office: SUNY Sch Edn and Human Devel PO Box 6000 Binghamton NY 13902-6000

ROSS, EDWARD, cardiologist; b. Fairfield, Ala., Oct. 10, 1937; s. Horace and Carrie Lee (Griggs) R.; m. Catherine I. Webster, Jan. 19, 1974; children: Edward, Ronald, Cheryl, Anthony. BS, Clark Coll., 1959; MD, Ind. U., 1963. Diplomate Am. Bd. Internal Medicine; cert. specialist in clin. hypertension Am. Soc. Hypertension. Intern Marion County Gen. Hosp., Indpls., 1963; resident in internal medicine Ind. U., 1964-66, 68, cardiology rsch. fellow, 1968-70, clin. asst. prof. medicine, 1970; cardiologist Capitol Med. Assn., Indpls., 1970-74; pvt. practice medicine, specializing in cardiology, 1974—. Staff cardiologist Winona Meml. Hosp., Indpls., chief cardiovascular disease, 2000—, med. dir. cardiovascular svcs., 2000—, med. dir. cardiac cath lab, 2000—, chief interventional cardiology, 2000—; staff Meth. Hosp., Indpls., chmn. cardiovasc. sect., 1989-96; chmn. cardiovasc. sect., dir. cardiovasc. ctr. Meth. Hosp., 1990-92; bd. dirs. Meth. Hosp. Heart-Lung Ctr., 1990—, mem. dir. cardiovasc. svcs., 1991-98. Assoc. editor Angiology, Jour. Vascular Disease; sr. editor Jour. Vascular Medicine, 1983—. Mem. Ctrl. Ind. Health Planning Coun., 1972-73; bd. dirs. Ind. chpt. Am. Heart Assn., 1973-74, multiphasic screening East Side Clinic, Flanner Ho. of Indpls., 1968-71; med. dir. Nat. Ctr. for Health Svc. R&D, HEW, 1970; consumer rep. radiologic device panel health FDA, 1988-92; dir. hypertensive screening State of Ind., 1974; J.B. Johnson Cardiovasc. lectr. Nat. Med. Assn., 1991. Capt. MC, USAF, 1966-68. Woodrow Wilson fellow, 1959; Nat. Found. Health scholar, 1955, Gorgas Found. scholar, 1955. Fellow Royal Soc. Promotion of Health (Eng.), Am. Coll. Angiology (v.p. fgn. affairs, sec. 1993—), Internat. Coll. Angiology, Am. Coll. Cardiology, Assn. Black Cardiologists (mem. bd. dirs. 1990-94); mem. NAACP, AMA, Am. Soc. Contemporary Medicine and Surgery, Nat. Med. Assn. (coun. sci. assembly 1985-89), Ind. Med. Soc., Marion County Med. Soc., Am. Soc. Internal Medicine, Am. Heart Assn., Ind. Soc. Internal Medicine (pres. 1987-89), Ind. State Med. Assn. (chmn. internal medicine sect. 1987-89), Ind. Med. Soc., Aesculapean Med. Soc., Hoosier State Med. Assn. (pres. 1980-84, 90-95), Urban League, Alpha Omega Alpha, Alpha Kappa Mu, Beta Kappa Chi, Omega Psi Phi. Baptist. Office: 3231 N Meridian St Ste 700 Indianapolis IN 46208-4668 E-mail: edrossmd@aol.com., rosscath@aol.com.

ROSS, EDWARD JOSEPH, architect; b. Dec. 13, 1934; s. Miriam Ross; m. Gail Tishler, Feb. 2, 1963; children: Linda Joy, Melissa Carol. Student, Boston Archtl. Ctr., 1952-55, 61-62, USAF Surveying Sch., 1955-56, Boston Soc. Civil Engrs., 1956-57, Carl Bolivar Structural Engr., 1962-63. Registered architect, Mass., Calif., N.Y., Fla., N.H., Vt.; cert. Nat. Coun. Archtl. Registration Bds.; lic. constrn. supr., Mass.; expert witness constrn. law. Draftsman, assoc. William W. Drummey, Architect, Boston, 1952-59; job capt., designer Drummey-Rosane-Anderson, 1959-64; projects architect Maginnis & Walsh & Kennedy, 1964-69; v.p. William Nelson Jacobs Assocs., Inc., 1969-73; staff architect Robert Charles Assocs., Inc. Architects, 1973-74; office mgr. Charles F. Jacobs Assocs., Inc., Cambridge, Mass., 1974-76; cons. architect Linenthal, Eisenberg & Anderson, Boston, 1976-77; staff architect Eisenberg Haven Assocs., Inc., 1977-78; chief architect, chief inspector Boston Housing Authority, 1978-83; prin. Edward J. Ross, AIA/FARA, Randolph, Mass., 1983-84; architect, sr. assoc., dir. constrn. adminstrn. Stull and Lee, Inc., Boston, 1984-91; practice architecture Randolph, Stoughton, Mass., 1963—. Mem. FCC Tech Plus. Bd. dirs. Linderhof Property Owners Assn., Knollsbrook Condominium Complex.; mem. Ancient and Hon. Arty. Co. of Mass. Staff sgt. USAF; maj. Mass. Mil. Res. Fellow Soc. Am. Registered Architects; mem. AIA, USO (New Eng. Coun.), Am. Assn. Ret. Persons, Am. Arbitration Assn. (nat. panel 1965—), Mass. State Assn. Architects., Constrn. Specifications Inst., Boston Soc. Architects (housing com. 1982-86), Air Force Assn. (pres. Boston chpt.), Mass. Air Nat. Guard Hist. Assn., Mil. Hist. Soc. Mass., Assn., First Corps Cadets, Ten of Us Club, Oxford 100 Condominium Assn. (pres.), Linderhof Golf Course Site One Assn. (pres. 1980-86), Elks, Knights of Pythias, Am. Legion. Home and Office: 10 Patricia Dr Stoughton MA 02072-1223 also: 100 Oxford Ct # 201 West Palm Beach FL 33411-1535

ROSS, E(DWIN) CLARKE, association executive, educator; b. Balt., Sept. 21, 1948; s. Harry Edwin and Margaret Frances (Turner) R.; m. Elizabeth Christine Shannon, Mar. 26, 1988; 1 child, Andrew Clarke. BA, U. Md., 1970, MA, 1974; D of Pub. Adminstrn., George Washington U., 1981. Vol. VISTA, Washington, 1970-71; legis. asst. Nat. Assn. State Mental Health Program Dirs., 1971-72; from asst. dir. to dir. Govt. Rels. United Cerebral Palsy Assns., 1972-84; asst. prof. European region Troy State U., Weisbaden, Germany, 1984-86; asst. exec. dir. for fed. rels. Nat. Assn. State Mental Health Dirs., Washington, 1986-93, dep. exec. dir., 1993-95; exec. dir. Am. Managed Behavioral Healthcare Assn., 1995-98; dep. exec. dir. pub. policy Nat. Alliance for the Mentally Ill., Arlington, Va., 1998-2000; CEO Children and Adults with Attention Deficit/Hyperactivity Disorder, Landover, Md., 2000—. Adj. grad. faculty, Cen. Mich. U., Washington, 1983-84, 87-93, 99—; adj. assoc. prof. U. Md., College Park, 1992-95. Author: Managed Behavioral Health Care Handbook, 2001; contbr. articles to profl. jours. and chpts. to books; author: Endurance as a Virtue: Army of Northern Virginia Civil War Experiences. Vol. Com. for Legal Svcs., Washington, 1970-71; mem. U.S. Olympic Com. on Winter Sports for Disabled, Colo. Springs, Colo., 1983-84; mem. program com. Dem. Club, Annapolis, Md., 1984. Recipient Maternal and Child Health scholarship to Johns Hopkins U., State of Md., 1975. Mem. SAR, Am. Coll. Mental Health Adminstrn., Am. Soc. Pub. Adminstrn., Am. Polit. Sci. Assn., St. Andrew's Soc., Sovereign Mil. Order of Temple of Jerusalem, Beta Gamma Sigma (life). Presbyterian. Avocations: Scottish country dancing, skiing, Scottish and U.S. history. Home and Office: 1718 Reynolds St Crofton MD 21114-2635 E-mail: clarke_ross@chadd.org.

ROSS, EDWIN WILLIAM, rubber company executive; b. Phila., May 28, 1938; s. Edwin Morrison and Frances Louise (Ort) R.; m. Dorothy Anne Reilly, Sept. 24, 1966; children: E. William Jr., Catherine Ross Conlin, James David. BS, Lehigh U., 1960. Chmn. bd., CEO, Key Chems., Inc., Phila., 1965-87, Ross Enterprises, Inc., Villanova, Pa., 1987—; pres., CEO Pelmor Labs., Inc., Newtown, 1989—; chmn. Pelseal Techs., LLC, 1998—. Mem. adv. bd. Prime Bank, Ft. Washington, Pa., 1995—98; bd. dirs. Baker Industries. Deacon Bryn Mawr (Pa.) Presbyn. Ch., 1977-81, elder, 1985-91, trustee, 1997—, pres. bd. trustees, 2001—; bd. dirs. Main Line Adult Day Care Ctr., 1999. Recipient Alumni award Lehigh U. Alumni Assn., 1985. Mem. SAR, MidAtlantic Employers Assn. (chmn. 1995-96), Metal Finishing Suppliers Assn. (pres. 1986-88, 89-90, Munning award 1992), N.E. Phila. C. of C. (chmn. 1983), Lehigh U. Alumni Assn. (bd. dirs. 1997-2000), Swedish Colonial Soc., Sons. of the Revolution Soc., St. Andrew's Soc., Colonial Soc., Exch. Club (pres. Frankford-Phila. 1972), Phila. Country Club (pres. 1986-89). Republican. Avocations: downhill skiing, hunting, travel, golf. Home: 1514 Willowbrook Ln Villanova PA 19085-1912 Office: Pelmor Labs Inc 401 Lafayette St Newtown PA 18940-2167

ROSS, ERIC ALAN, civil engineer; b. Mineola, N.Y., Sept. 11, 1961; s. Howard Edward and Marjorie Jean (Sheldon) R.; m. Lauren Elizabeth O'Connell, May 31, 1986. BA in Math., Hope Coll., 1983; BE, Hofstra U., 1985. Registered profl. engr., Mich. Asst. civil engr. N.Y.C. Dept. Environ. Protection, 1985-86; project mgr., estimator Angelo Iafrate Constrn., Warren, Mich., 1986-90, purchasing agt., 1990-91; civil engr. McNeely & Lincoln Assocs., Inc., Northville, 1991—. Vol. ARC, Oakland, Mich., 1988—; rep. Northfield Hills Homeowners Assn., Troy, Mich., 1988—, Coun. Troy Homeowners Assn. Mem. ASCE, Nat. Soc. Profl. Engrs., Mich. Soc. Planning Ofcls. Republican. Methodist. Home: 1860 Fordham Dr Troy MI 48098-2542

ROSS, EUNICE LATSHAW, judge; b. Bellevue, Pa., Oct. 13, 1923; d. Richard Kelly and Eunice (Weidner) Latshaw; m. John Anthony Ross, May 29, 1943 (dec. Jan. 1978); 1 child, Geraldine Ross Coleman. BS, U. Pitts., 1945, LLB, 1951. Bar: Pa. 1952. Atty. Pub. Health Law Rsch. Project, Pitts., 1951-52; atty. jud. asst., law clk. Ct. Common Pleas Allegheny County,

1952-70, dir. family divsn., 1970-72, judge, 1972-96, Commonwealth Ct. Pa., 1997—. Adj. law prof. U. Pitts., 1967-73; mem. Bd. Jud. Inquiry and Rev., Commonwealth of Pa., 1984-89, Gov's Justice Commn., 1972-78; mem. orphan's ct. rules com. Supreme Ct. Pa., 1998—. Author: (with others) Survey of Pa. Public Health Laws, 1952; Justice, 1995; co-author: Will Contests, 1992; contbr. articles to law publs. Mem. exec. com. bd. trustees U. Pitts., 1980—86, bd. visitors Law Sch., 1985—, bd. visitors Sch. Health, 1986—98; mem. adv. bd. Animal Friends, Pitts., 1973—; committeewoman for 14th ward, vice chmn. Pitts. Dem. com., 1972; bd. dirs. The Program, Pitts., 1983—87, Pitts. History and Landmarks Found., West Pa. Hist. Soc., West Pa. Conservancy. Named Girls Scouts Woman of Yr., Pitts. coun. Girl Scouts U.S.A., 1975, Alumni of Yr., U. Pitts. Law Sch., 2001; recipient Disting. Alumna award, U. Pitts., 1973, Medal of Recognition, 1987, Alumni award, U. Pitts. Sch. of Law, 2001, Susan B. Anthony award, Women's Bar Assn. Western Pa., 1993, Probate and Trusts award, 1994, cert. of achievement, Pa. Fedn. Women's Clubs, 1975, 1977. Mem.: ABA, Allegheny County Bar Assn. (vice chmn., exec. com. young lawyers sect. 1958—59), Pa. Trial Judges Conf., Scribes, Order of Coif. Home: 1204 Denniston Ave Pittsburgh PA 15217-1329 Office: 402 Frick Bldg 437 Grant St Pittsburgh PA 15219-6002

ROSS, FRANK HOWARD, III, management consultant; b. Charlotte, N.C., Aug. 28, 1946; s. Frank Howard Jr. (dec.) and Alma (Richardson) R. (dec.); m. Beverly Hazel Ross, June 30, 1973 (dec.); children: Martha McCausland, Frank Howard IV. BS in Engring., N.C. State U., 1968. Cons. Fails & Assocs., Inc., Raleigh, N.C., 1968-73; ptnr. Ross-Payne & Assocs., Inc., Barrington, Ill., 1973—. Bd. dirs. Gilldorn Savs., Chgo., 1982-85, Brickman Industries, Inc., Chgo., 1980-90; CFO WRT, Inc., Chgo., 1993-95; pres., chmn. bd. dirs. Emerald Capital Investments, Inc., Barrington, 1993-97; adviser, spkr. on constrn. and fin.; bd. dirs. Sherman Plumbing, 1975-95. Author: More $ Through $ Management, 1975, MIS and You, 1978, Planning and Budgeting, 1979, Profit by Design, 1981, Pricing for Profit, 1983, Wealthbuilding, 1984, Equipment Cost Analysis, 1988, Survivial in a Tight Economy, 1988, Associated Landscape Contractors of America Operating Cost Survey, 1989, 91, Cash Flow, 1989, Dealing with the Competition of the 90's, 1990, Designing Your Accounting System, 1991, Bidding in a Tight Market, 1992, Industry's Wage and Benefit Study, 1992, Financing Your Business, 1993, Pricing, 1994, 2d edit., 1997, How Low Can You Go?, 1995, Valuing Your Business, 1998, Posturing for Growth and Prosperity, 1999. Mem. Presbyn. Ch. Barrington. Mem. Inst. Mgmt. Cons., Barrington Hills Country Club, Haig Point Country Club, Sigma Alpha Epsilon. Home and Office: Ross Payne Assocs Inc 536 Eton Dr Barrington IL 60010-2017

ROSS, FRED MICHAEL, organic chemist; b. N.Y.C., Aug. 26, 1921; s. Albert N. and Shirley (Honig) R.; m. Nee Kilar, May 9, 1954; children: Robin, Bonnie, Richard. BS, Mich. Tech. U., 1943. Sr. gas analyst Pure Oil Co., Chgo., 1943-44; chief chem. engr. Multiplate Glass Corp., Jamaica, N.Y., 1945-51; founder, CEO Diamond Dust Co., Inc., Mineola, 1952-80; chmn. bd. dirs. Portfolio Mgmt., Inc., Rochester, 1976-80; founder, pres. Gemery Corp., Mineola, 1974-80; dir. Indsl. Diamond Assn. of Am., 1977-78; CEO, chmn. Robonard, Inc., Boca Raton, Fla., 1980—. Contbr. over 10 articles to profl. publs. Campaign co-chmn. for R. Shaw for Ariz. Ho. of Reps, 1994. Petty officer USN, 1944-45. Recipient Bd. of Control Silver medal for Outstanding Alumnus Mich. Tech. U., 1978; inducted Mich. Tech. U. Acad. Scis. and Arts, 1997. Fellow Am. Inst. Chemists (life). Achievements include development of process for manufacture of ovate diamonds for use in petroleum bits and geological core drills, process for reclamation and recovery of industrial diamond bearing waste materials. Office: Robonard Inc 10325 Crosswind Rd Boca Raton FL 33498-4757 E-mail: FMR@ATT.NET.

ROSS, GERALD FRED, engineering executive, researcher; b. N.Y.C., Dec. 14, 1930; s. Samuel Henry and Jenny (Saltzman) Rozansky; m. Vivian Ida Turkish, Dec. 24, 1953; children: Jayne T. Ross Kaufman, Steven A., Helene B. Ross Joseph. BEE, CCNY, 1952; MEE, Poly. U., 1955, PhD, 1963. Registered profl. engr., N.Y., Mass., Fla. Rsch. asst. U. Mich., Ann Arbor, 1952-53; sr. engr. W.L. Maxson Corp., N.Y.C., 1954-58; rsch. sect. head Sperry Gyroscope Co., Great Neck, L.I., N.Y., 1958-65; dept. mgr. Sperry Rsch. Ctr., Sudbury, Mass., 1965-81; CEO, chmn. ANRO Engring., Inc., Sarasota, Fla., 1981—. Pres., v.p., treas. Adams Pool Corp., Lexington, Mass., 1968-81. Capt. USAFR, 1953—. Contbg. author 3 books, 1986, 90, 93; contbr. numerous articles to profl. jours.; patentee in field. Fellow Polytechnic U. Fellow IEEE (life, K.C. Black Nerem Best paper award 1974), Nat. Acad. Engring. (life); mem. Electromagnetics Acad., Res. Officers Assn., Lexington Golf Club, Longboat Key Club, Sigma Xi (sr.), Tau Beta Pi, Eta Kappa Nu. Republican. Jewish. Avocations: golf, tennis. Office: ANRO Engring Inc 1800 2d St Ste 730 Sarasota FL 34236-5971 E-mail: drgfr@aol.com.

ROSS, HALLIE RUTH, social worker; b. Orange, Calif., Mar. 10, 1962; d. Terry Allan and Ruth Kibler Ross; m. Robert Edwin Alderman, Dec. 21, 1991 (div. July 15, 2002). BA in Social Work, Calif. State U., Chico, 1986. Lic. social worker, Miss., 1995. Exec. sec. Western Investment Mgmt. Co., Cupertino, Calif., 1986-88; tech. support & sales rep. Oracle Corp., Redwood Shores, 1988-94; 9-1-1 call taker, dispatcher City of Tulsa Dept. Pub. Safety, 1994; transitional care ctr. activities dir. Bapt. Meml. Hosp., New Albany, Miss., 1995-97; family preservation specialist/social worker Miss. Dept. Human Svcs., Tupelo, 1998-99, New Albany, 1999—. Owner Howling Root Music, Belmont, Calif., 1990-94. Artist, songwriter Be There Soon, 1991, Get the Word Out, 1996, Legacy, 1998; artist, co-publ. Logger Rhythms, 1992, After the Lights Go Out, 1994. Mem. New Albany Main St. Assn., Union County Child Abuse Task Force. Named 1st pl. Tupelo GumTree Songwriters Festival, 1997. Mem. Miss. Conf. Social Welfare, Tupelo Gumtree Civitans (newsletter editor 1998-99), New Albany Pilot Club, Civitan Internat., Jr. Auxiliary of New Albany. Methodist. Avocations: singing, guitar, piano, counted cross-stitch, movies. Home: 304 Wilson St New Albany MS 38652-9571 Office: 107A E Bankhead St New Albany MS 38652-3933 E-mail: hallie@datalane.net.

ROSS, HERBERT, physician; b. Bklyn., Oct. 8, 1930; s. Samuel and Etta (Roggen) R.; m. Phyllis Ann Gibralter, June 27, 1965; children: Daniel Jonathan, Lauren Jennifer. BA, NYU, 1950; MD, U. Bern, Switzerland, 1955. Diplomate Am. Bd. Internal Medicine, Am. Bd. Endocrinology and Metabolism. Intern Queens Gen. Hosp., N.Y.C., 1956-57; asst. resident VA Hosp., Bklyn., 1957-59; resident Montefiore Hosp., N.Y.C., 1961-62; fellow in endocrinology and metabolic disease N.Y. Med. Coll., 1962-63; asst. attending physician med. divsn. Montefiore Hosp., 1963-67, adj. attending physician, asst. to the chief of medicine, 1967-74, assoc. attending in medicine, 1974-78, attending in medicine, 1978—; clin. assoc. in medicine N.Y. Med. Coll., 1963-68, adj. asst. prof. medicine, 1968—; pvt. practice White Plains, 1966—; assoc. vis. physician, asst. vis. physician White Plains Hosp., 1966-75, attending physician, 1975—; clin. instr., clin. assoc., asst. clin. prof. Albert Einstein Coll. Medicine, 1967-78, clin. assoc. prof., 1978-93, visiting assoc. prof., 1994—. Chmn. intensive care com. White Plains Hosp., 1975-77; dir. med. edn. White Plains Hosp. Med. Ctr., 1980-89, 94-96; dir. endocrine sect. White Plains Hosp. Ctr. dept. internal medicine, 1987-92; chmn. sect. on internal medicine Westchester Acad. Medicine, 1992—; dir. dept. medicine, chmn. sect. internal medicine White Plains Hosp. Ctr., 1992-98. Contbr. chpts. to books, articles to profl. jours. Fellow ACP, Am. Coll. Endocrinology; mem. Clin. Soc. of N.Y. Diabetes Assn. (chmn. 1990-91), Am. Diabetes Assn. (profl. sect., chmn. profl. edn. com. Downstate NY affiliate 1987-90), Endocrine Soc., Am. Thyroid Assn., Westchester County Med. Soc., N.Y. State Med. Soc. Avocation: hiking. Office: Midwestchester Med Assocs 33 Davis Ave White Plains NY 10605-1015

ROSS, HOWARD PHILIP, lawyer; b. May 10, 1939; s. Bernard and Estelle (Maremont) R.; m. Loretta Teresa Benquil, 1962 (div.); children: Glen Joseph, Cynthia Ann; m. Jennifer Kay Shirley, 1984. BS, U. Ill., 1961; JD, Stetson Coll. Law, 1964. Bar: Fla. 1964, U.S. Ct. Appeals (5th cir.) 1965, U.S. Supreme Ct. 1969, U.S. Ct. Appeals (11th cir.) 1981; cert. civil trial lawyer, bus. litigator. Assoc. Parker & Battaglia and predecessor firm, St. Petersburg, Fla., 1964-67; ptnr. Battaglia, Ross, Dicus & Wein, P.A., 1967-87, 1987—, pres., CEO, 1992-99, chmn. bd. dirs., 2000—. Lectr. Stetson Coll. Law, St. Petersburg, 1971-72, adj. prof., 1987. Author: Florida Corporations, 1979; co-author: Managing Discovery in Commercial and Business Litigation, 1993; contbr. articles to profl. jours. Hon. chair St. Petersburg br. Awards Banquet NAACP, 1995; bd. dirs. St. Petersburg Neighborhood Housing Svcs., Inc., 1997, legal counsel, 1997—, pres., 2000—; bd. dirs. Cmty. Alliance, 1997—. Recipient Woman's Svc. League Best Groomed award, 1979, Fla. Bar Merit citation, 1974, Cmty. Svc. award, NAACP, 1998, Humanitarian award, YMCA of Tampa Bay, 1999, C.W. Bill Young Pinellas Pinnacle award, 2002. Mem. ABA, Fla. Bar Assn. (chmn. civil trial certification com. 1993-94), St. Petersburg Bar Assn., St. Petersburg Area C. of C. (bd. govs. 1990-95, 2000—, v.p. pub. affairs 1992-93, v.p. membership 1993-94, exec. com. 1992-95, counsel 1994-95, dean entrepreneurial acad. 1996—, treas. 2000-02, chair-elect 2002—, Mem. of Yr. 1993-94), Citizen Rev. Com. City of St. Petersburg (chmn. subcom. 1992-94, co-chair 1994-97). Republican. Jewish. Office: Battaglia Ross Dicus & Wein PA PO Box 41100 980 Tyrone Blvd N Saint Petersburg FL 33710-6382 E-mail: hross@brdwlaw.com.

ROSS, HUGH COURTNEY, electrical engineer; b. Dec. 31, 1923; s. Clare W. and Jeanne F. Ross; m. Sarah A. Gordon (dec.); m. Patricia A. Malloy; children: John C., James G., Robert W. Student, Calif. Inst. Tech., 1942, San Jose State U., 1946-47; BSEE, Stanford U., 1950, postgrad., 1954. Registered profl. elec. engr., Calif. Instr. San Benito (Calif.) High Sch. and Jr. Coll., 1950-51; chief engr. vacuum power switches Jennings Radio Mfg. Corp., San Jose, Calif., 1951-62; chief engr. ITT Jennings, 1962-64; pres. Ross Engring. Corp., Campbell, 1964—. Contbr. articles to tech. jours.; patentee in field. Fellow IEEE (life) (chmn. Santa Clara Valley subsect. 1960-61); mem. Am. Vacuum Soc., Am. Soc. Metals. Avocations: electronics, electric autos, camping, ranching, solar power. Office: 540 Westchester Dr Campbell CA 95008-5012

ROSS, IAN BEAUDOIN, neurosurgeon, educator; b. Montreal, Que., Can., Feb. 29, 1960; came to the U.S., 2000; s. Ian Cathcart and Jacqueline Joan Ross; m. Catherine Sylvia Pitfield, June 1, 1985; children: Felicia Lillian, William Leopold. BSc, McGill U., Montreal, 1981; MD, Queen's U., Kingston, Can., 1985; MSc, U. Toronto, Can., 1992. Asst. prof. U. Man., Winnipeg, Can., 1993-99, assoc. prof., 1999-2000, U. Miss., Jackson, 2000—. Vis. fellow Fondation Rothschild, Paris, 1998-99. Contbr. articles to profl. jours. Recipient Penfield McNaughton award Montreal Neurol. Inst., 1992; fellow Fund award Health Sci. Ctr., Winnipeg, 1998. Fellow ACS, Royal Coll. Surgeons Can. (Clin. Traineeship award 1999); mem. Am. Assn. Neurol. Surgeons, Can. Neurol. Soc. (provincial rep. 1998-99). Avocations: reading, skiing, opera. Home: 3605 Old Canton Rd Jackson MS 39216 Office: U Miss Med Ctr 2500 N State St Jackson MS 39216-4505

ROSS, IAN MUNRO, electrical engineer; b. Southport, Eng., Aug. 15, 1927; came to U.S., 1952, naturalized, 1960; m. Christina Leinberg Ross, Aug. 24, 1955; children: Timothy Ian, Nancy Lynn, Stina Marguerite. BA, Gonville and Caius Coll., Cambridge U., 1948, MA in Elec. Engring, PhD, Cambridge U., 1952; DSc (hon.), N.J. Inst. Tech., 1983, Poly. U., 1988; D of Engring. (hon.), Stevens Inst. Tech., 1983; DSc (hon.), Polytech. U., 1988. With AT&T Bell Labs. (and affiliates), 1952-92, exec. dir. network planning div., 1971-73, v.p. network planning and customer svcs., 1973-76, exec. v.p. systems engring. and devel. N.J., 1976-79, pres., 1979-91; pres. emeritus AT&T Bell Labs., 1991—. Bd. dirs. Thomas & Betts Corp., B.F. Goodrich Co., Nacco Industries; chmn. Nat. Adv. Commn. on Semicondrs. Patentee in field. Recipient NASA Pub. Svc. award, 1969, 75, medal Ind. Rsch. Inst., 1987. Fellow IEEE (Founders' medal 1988, Am. Acad. Arts and Scis.; mem. NAS, NAE. Home: 5 Blackpoint Horseshoe Rumson NJ 07760-1500 Office: Lucent Technologies 101 Crawfords Corner Rd Holmdel NJ 07733-1985

ROSS, JAMES ULRIC, lawyer, accountant, educator; b. Del Rio, Tex., Sept. 14, 1941; s. Stephen Mabrey and Beatrice Jessie (Hyslop) R.; m. Janet S. Calabro, Dec. 28, 1986; children: James Ulric Jr., Ashley Meredith. BA, U. Tex., 1963, JD, 1965. Bar: Tex. 1965, U.S. Tax Ct. 1969; CPA, Tex. Estate tax examiner IRS, Houston, 1965-66; tax acct. Holmes, Raquet, Harris & Shaw, San Antonio, 1966-67; pvt. practice law and acctg. Del Rio and San Antonio, Tex., 1968—. Instr. St. Mary's U., San Antonio, 1973-75; assoc. prof. U. Tex., San Antonio, 1975-99, ret. Contbr. articles on U.S. and Internat. Estate Planning and Taxation to legal and profl. jours. Active Am. Cancer Soc., Residential Mgmt., Inc., Am. Heart Assn. Mem. ABA, Tex. Bar Assn., Tex. Soc. CPAs, San Antonion Bar Assn., San Antonio Estate Planners Coun. Home: 3047 Orchard Hl San Antonio TX 78230-3078 Office: 760 Tex Commerce Bank Bldg 7550 IH 10 W San Antonio TX 78229-5803

ROSS, JEFFREY ALAN, research biologist; b. Thayer, Mo., Oct. 19, 1955; s. Ralph and Naomi June (Jacobs) R.; m. Lisa Lynn Pnazek, Apr. 23, 1977; children: Trillian Elise, Jennifer Ariane, Marissa Kerowyn. BS, U. Dallas, 1977; PhD, U. Tex., Dallas, 1982. Predoctoral fellow Robert A. Welch Found., 1979-82; postdoctoral fellow Cancer Ctr. Rsch. div. U. Tex., Smithville, 1982-85; NRC fellow U.S. EPA, Research Triangle Park, N.C., 1985-86, rsch. biologist, 1986-99, chief cancer biology br. NC, 1999—. Contbr. articles to profl. jours. Bd. dirs. 1st Environments Early Learning Ctr., Research Triangle Park, 1989-90, 94-96. John B. O'Hara Found. fellow, 1973-76. Mem. AAAS, Am. Assn. Cancer Rsch., N.Y. Acad. Scis., Genotoxicity and Environ. Mutagen Soc. (bd. dirs. 1991-94, 97-2000). Achievements include research on the formation, repair, and biological consequences of carcinogen DNA adducts.

ROSS, JEFFREY ALLAN, political scientist, educator; b. N.Y.C., Dec. 24, 1947; s. Joseph and Pearl (Epstein) R.; m. Marjorie Appelson, Aug. 30, 1970; children: Craig, Eric, Brian, Allison. BA in Polit. Sci. summa cum laude, SUNY, Binghamton, 1969; PhD in Polit. Sci., U. Minn., 1982. N.Y. State regents' fellow, tchg. asst. U. Minn., Mpls., 1969-71, rsch. asst., 1971-73, instr., 1973, Kirkland Coll., Clinton, N.Y., 1973-78, Huber Found. faculty rsch. grantee, 1973, 74, 77, Mellon Found. grantee, 1974, rsch. prof., 1975-76; instr. govt. Hamilton Coll., 1978-80, asst. prof., 1980-82; vis. prof. polit. sci. Syracuse U., 1984; adj. prof. polit. sci. Queens Coll., CUNY, 1987-88; dir. dept. campus/higher edn. affairs Anti Defamation League, 1984—. V.p., bd. dirs. Rsch. Ctr. for Religion and Human Rights in Closed Socs.; mem. exec. bd. Com. for Pub. Higher Edn., chmn., mem. various profl. panels. Author: (with Ann Cottrell) The Mobilization of Collective Identity: Comparative Perspectives, 1980, Pamyat: Hatred Under Glasnost, 1989, Schooled in Hate: Anti-Semitism on Campus, 1997, Guide for College and University Presidents and Administrators, Responding to Bigotry and Intergroup Strife on Campus, 2001; contbr. articles to profl. jours.; mem. editl. bd. Tchg. Polit. Sci., 1971-81; editor Hamilton Social Sci. Rev., 1977-79; reviewer manuscripts for profl. jours., book pubs. Precinct rep. Dem. Farm Labor Party, Mpls., 1972-73. Mpls. Found., Frances E. Andrews Fund All-Univ. rsch. fellow, surveyor Soviet Jewish emigrants, Israel, 1972. Mem. Am. Polit. Sci. Assn., N.E. Polit. Sci. Assn. (exec coun.), Internat. Polit. Sci. Assn., Internat. Studies Assn., Mongolia Soc., Can.-Mongolia Soc., Comparative Interdisciplinary Studies Soc. (exec. coun.), N.Y. State Polit. Sci. Assn. (v.p. 1982-83, pres. 1983-84), Sound Cyclists Bicycle Club (v.p. 1989-90, 94, pres. 1991-93), Norwalk Ski Club (v.p. 1992-93), River Hills Ski Club (mem. exec. bd., pres. 2002—). Democrat. Note: fax and e-mail may be published if desired). Home: 20 Soundview Loop South Salem NY 10590-2510 Office: Anti-Defamation League 823 United Nations Plz New York NY 10017-3518 Fax: (212) 490-0187. . E-mail: rossj@adl.org. *A satisfying life must be multidimensional. One's community, family and recreation have a necessary place alongside one's career. A fully realized person becomes also a fully realized professional.*

ROSS, JERRY L. astronaut; b. Crown Point, Ind., Jan. 20, 1948; s. Donald J. and Phyllis E. Ross; m. Karen S. Pearson; 2 children. BS in Mech. Engring., Purdue U., West Lafayette, Ind., 1970; MS in Mech. Engring., Purdue U.; Grad. Test Flight Engr., USAF Test Pilot Sch., 1976; DSc (hon.) , Purdue U. Commd. 2d lt. USAF, 1970, retired, 2000; rschr. ramjet engring divsn. Air Force Aeropropulsion Lan, Wright-Patterson AFB, Ohio, 1972—74; lab. exec. officer, chief mgmt. ops. office Wright Patterson AFB Labs., Dayton, 1974—75; flight test engr., supr. crew mem. 6510th; Flight Test Engring. USAF, Edwards AFB, Calif., 1976—79; payload officer, flight controller Lyndon Johnson Space Center, Houston, 1979—80; astronaut NASA, 1980—. Recipient 13 NASA medals, Victor A. Prather award, Am. Astron. Soc., 1985, 1990, 1999. Mem.: Purdue Alumni Assn. (life), Assn. of Space Explorers (life). Achievements include six space flights; over 1133 hours in space, including 44 hours, 9 minutes on seven space walks. Office: Astronaut Ctr NASA Johnson Space Ctr. Houston TX 77058

ROSS, JIMMY DOUGLAS, retired military officer; b. Hosston, La., May 23, 1936; s. Horace Eugene and Lucile Marie (Pontious) R.; m. Patricia L. Cox., Dec. 18, 1955; children: Sabra, DiAnna, Tony. BS, Henderson State U., 1958; MA in Bus. Mgmt., Central Mich. U., 1975. Commd. 2d lt. U.S. Army, 1958, advanced through grades to 4 Star Gen., 1994, served comdr. co., bn., brigade levels, comdg. gen. 2d Support Command (Corps) VII Corps W. Ger., 1980-82; dir. transp., energy and troop support Office Dep. Chief of Staff for Logistics, U.S. Army, Washington, 1982-84; chief staff U.S. Army Materiel Command, Alexandria, Va., 1984-86; comdr. U.S. Army Depot System Command, Chambersburg, Pa., 1986-87; dep. chief of staff for logistics U.S. Army, Washington, 1987-92; commdg. gen. U.S. Army Materiel Command, Alexandria, Va., 1992-94; retired, 1994. Bd. dirs. VSE Engring. Co., Stanley Assoc., Inc.; chmn. Def. Industry Conf. Bd.; pres. bd. dirs. Indsl. Coll. of Armed Forces Assn.; pres., COO Cypress Internat., 2000—. Dist. commr. Alpine dist. Boy Scouts Am., 1980-82; sr. v.p., COO Biomed. Svcs., ARC Nat. Hdqrs., 1994-99; chmn. Army Sci. Bd.; pres. Buffalo Soldiers Meml. Fund Found., 2001; bd. dirs. Buffalo Soldiers Found., 2001. Decorated D.S.M. with oak leaf cluster, Legion of Merit, Bronze Star, Air medal. Fellow Assn. U.S. Army (sr.); mem. Am. Def. Preparedness Assn., Nat. Def. Transp. Assn., Armed Forces Benefit Assn. (bd. dirs.). Methodist. Home: 4981 Maple Glen Pl Lk Forest FL 32771

ROSS, JOHN, physical chemist, educator; b. Vienna, Austria, Oct. 2, 1926; arrived in U.S., 1940; s. Mark and Anna (Krecmar) Ross; m. Virginia Franklin (div.); children: Elizabeth A., Robert K.; m. Eva Madarasz. BS, Queens Coll., 1948; PhD, MIT, 1951; D (hon.) , Weizmann Inst. Sci., Rehovot, Israel, 1984, Queens Coll., SUNY, 1987, U. Bordeaux, France, 1987. Prof. chemistry Brown U., Providence, 1953—66, MIT, Cambridge, 1966—80, chmn. dept., 1966—71, chmn. faculty of Inst., 1975—77; prof. Stanford (Calif.) U., 1980—2001, chmn. dept., 1983—89, prof. emeritus, 2001—. Cons. to industries, 1979—; mem. bd. govs. Weizmann Inst., 1971—. Author: Physical Chemistry, 1980, Physical Chemistry, 2d edit., 2000; editor: Molecular Beams, 1966; contbr. articles to profl. jours. 2nd lt. U.S. Army, 1944—46. Recipient medal, Coll. de France, Paris, Presdl. Nat. Medal of Sci., 1999, Austrian Cross of Honor for Sci. and Art, 1st class, 2002. Fellow: AAAS, Am. Phys. Soc.; mem.: NAS, Am. Chem. Soc. (Irving Langmuir Chem. Physics prize 1992, Peter Debye award in phys. chemistry 2001), Am. Acad. Arts and Scis. Home: 738 Mayfield Ave Palo Alto CA 94305-1044 Office: Stanford U Dept Chemistry Stanford CA 94305-5080 E-mail: john.ross@stanford.edu.

ROSS, JOHN MICHAEL, editor, magazine publisher; b. Bklyn., Oct. 17, 1919; s. Albert Henry and Dorothy Veronica (Murray) R.; m. Kathleen M. Courtney; children: Donna Patricia Ross Easterbrook, Maureen Courtney Ross Fay. Student pub. schs., N.Y.C. Sports writer Bklyn. Eagle, 1937-41, The Newspaper PM, 1946-47; editor Am. Law Tennis mag., 1947-50, Macfadden Publs., 1950-51, 60-61; contbg. editor Am. Weekly, 1952-60; editor-in-chief Golf mag., 1961-67, Golf Bus. mag., 1963-65, Golfdom mag., 1965-67; v.p. Universal Pub. and Distbn. Corp., 1965-67; pres. Golf Promotions, Inc., 1967-70; pub. Golf Bus. Almanac, also Golf TV Guide, 1969; pub. relations dir. Profl. Golfers Assn. Golf Tour, 1970-71; editor-in-chief Golf mag., 1972-79, assoc. pub., 1979-84; publishing dir., v.p. The Golf Link, 1985-87; editorial dir. Am. Golf mag., 1990-94; sr. ptnr. J.M. Ross Assocs., Westport, Conn., 1994—. Bd. dirs. World Golf Hall of Fame, 1974-83, mem. adv. bd. 1993-97; chmn. Women's Golf Scholarship Fund, 1976-82; exec. dir. World Cup Golf Internat. Golf Assn., 1977-84; columnist Paradigm Syndicate, 2000—. Co-author: Nothing But The Truth, 1960; editor: Encyclopedia of Golf, 1977; author: (feature column) Paradigm Syndicate, 1999-; contbr. numerous articles to nat. publs. including Reader's Digest, Life, Sports Illustrated. Justice of peace, Newtown, Conn., 1960-64. Served with AUS, 1942-46. Recipient Christopher award for best mag. story, 1957; recipient Lincoln Werden award for golf journalism, 1991. Mem. U.S. Golf Assn. (nat. com. 1977-99), Lawn Tennis Writers Assn. (sec. 1949-50), Golf Writers Assn. Am. (gov. 1966-67), Met. Golf Writers Assn. (pres. 1975-76), Assn. of Golf Writers (Great Britain), Am. Soc. Mag. Editors, Overseas Press Club (N.Y.C.), Patterson Club (Fairfield, Conn.). Roman Catholic. Home: 19 Riverfield Dr Weston CT 06883-2908 Office: J M Ross Assocs PO Box 774 Westport CT 06881-0774

ROSS, JOHN T. artist, educator; b. N.Y.C., Sept. 25, 1921; s. Ferdinand Joseph and Mary Agnes (Higgins) R.; m. Clare Romano; children: Christopher, Timothy. Student, Cooper Union Art Sch., 1939-48, BFA, 1975. Art dir. Pageant Mag., N.Y.C., 1946-48; mem. faculty New Sch. for Social Rsch., 1957—; prof., chmn. dept. art Manhattanville Coll., Purchase, N.Y., 1964-86. Adj. prof. Yale U., New Haven, 1982; adj. faculty Columbia U., N.Y.C., 1983-85; art dir. Aquarius Press, N.Y.C., 1968-72; chmn. bd. Ctr. for Book Arts, N.Y.C., 1995-99; bd. dirs. Art Ctr. No. N.J., Englewood, 1966-67; fgn. svc. staff officer USIA, Romania and Yugoslavia, 1964-66. Writer-illustrator: Complete Printmaker, 1972-90; exhibited works in 70 one-man shows at various galleries, 1950—; pub. artists books, 1971—; printmaker, artist-designer, 1950—; dir. High Tide Press, N.Y.C., 1991—. Chmn. adv. panel Cooper Union Art Sch., N.Y.C., 1967-69. Sgt. U.S. Army, 1943-46, Italy. Recipient Citation for profl. achievement Cooper Union Art Sch., 1966, Benjamin Clinedinst medal Artists Fellowship, 1992, others; Tiffany Found. grantee, 1954, McDowell Colony fellow, 1978, 82, 87. Mem. NAD, Century Assn. N.Y.C., Soc. Am. Graphic Artists (pres.), Ctr. for Book Arts N.Y.C., Typophiles N.Y.C., Grolier Club. Avocation: swimming. Home: PO Box 1122 New York NY 10159-1122 E-mail: rossromano@aol.com.

ROSS, JOSEPH COMER, physician, educator, academic administrator; b. Tompkinsville, Ky., June 16, 1927; s. Joseph M. and Annie (Pinckley) R.; m. Isabelle Nevins, June 15, 1952; children: Laura Ann, Sharon Lynn, Jennifer Jo, Mary Martha, Jefferson Arthur. BS, U. Ky., 1950; MD, Vanderbilt U., 1954. Diplomate Am. Bd. Internal Medicine (bd. govs. 1975-81), with added qualifications in pulmonary disease. Intern Vanderbilt U. Hosp., Nashville, 1954-55; resident Duke U. Hosp., Durham, N.C., 1955-57, rsch. fellow, 1957-58; from instr. medicine to prof. Ind. U. Sch. Medicine, Indpls., 1958-70; prof., chmn. dept. medicine Med. U. of S.C., Charleston, 1970-80; vis. prof. Vanderbilt U. Sch. Medicine, Nashville, 1979-80, prof. medicine, 1981-99, prof. medicine emeritus, 1999—, assoc. vice chancellor for health affairs, 1982-99, assoc. vice chancellor for health affairs emeritus, 1999—. Mem. cardiovascular study sect. NIH, 1966-70, program project com., 1971-75; mem. adv. coun. Nat. Heart, Lung and Blood Inst., 1982-86; mem. ad hoc coms. NAS, 1966, 67; mem. Pres.'s Nat. Adv. Panel on Heart Disease, 1972; mem. merit rev. bd. in respiration VA Rsch. Svc., 1972-76, chmn., 1974-76. Mem. editorial bd. Jour. Lab. and Clin. Medicine, 1964-70, Chest, 1968-73, Jour. Applied Physiology,1968-73, Archives of Internal Medicine, 1976-82, Heart and Lung, 1977-86; contbr. articles to profl. jours. Bd. dirs., past pres. Nashville Ronald McDonald House; v.p., bd. dirs. Agape, Leadership Nashville; mem. adv. com. Davidson County Cmty. Health Agy.; active Tenn. Lung Assn. With U.S. Army, 1945-47. Fellow ACP, Am. Coll. Chest Physicians (gov. S.C. 1970-76, vice chmn. bd. govs. 1974-75, chmn. bd. govs. 1975-76, exec. council 1974-80, pres.-elect 1976-77, pres. 1978-79, chmn. sci. program com. 1973), Am. Coll. Cardiology; mem. AMA (sect. on med. schs.), Am. Fedn. Clin. Rsch. (chmn. Midwest sect.), Am. Physiol. Soc., Am. Soc. Clin. Investigation, Assn. Am. Physicians, Assn. Profs. Medicine, Cen. Soc. Clin. Rsch., S.C. Med. Soc., Am. Thoracic Soc. (nat. councillor 1972-76), So. Soc. Clin. Rsch., S.C. Lung Assn. (v.p. 1974-75), Am. Soc. Internal Medicine, Phi Beta Kappa, Alpha Omega Alpha. Mem. Ch. of Christ (elder). Office: Vanderbilt U Med Ctr Oxford House Ste 212 Nashville TN 37232-0001 E-mail: joseph.ross@home.com., joseph.ross@vanderbiltmcmail.edu.

ROSS, JULIA, lawyer; b. N.Y.C., Oct. 28, 1940; 1 child, Jennifer. BA, San Francisco State Coll., 1964; MA, Calif. State U., 1971; MPH, U. Calif., Berkeley, 1972; JD, Golden Gate U., 1977. Bar: Calif. 1977, U.S. Dist. Ct. (no. dist.) Calif. 1977. Realtor Mason McDuffee, Berkeley, Calif., 1973-77; educator health Mission Mental Health Svcs., San Francisco, 1973; counselor, coord. teen clinics Planned Parenthood, 1969-71; judge pro tem Berkeley-Albany Mcpl. Ct., 1982—; atty. pvt. practice, Berkeley, 1977—. Contbr. articles to mags. Mem. Calif. State Bar Assn., Alameda County Bar Assn., Berkeley-Albany Bar Assn. (pres. 1991). Office: 1442 Walnut St # 301 Berkeley CA 94709-1405 E-mail: juliar@earthlink.net.

ROSS, JULIE ANNE, social worker; b. Alton, Ill., Feb. 10, 1942; d. Lawrence G. and Lillian L. (Hargis) Whiteside; m. Larry Robert Ross, July 31, 1965; 1 child, Kelly Anne. BA, So. Ill. U., 1964; MSW, Wash. U., 1979. Cert. social worker; lic. clin. social worker, Ill. Social worker Alton (Ill.) State Hosp., 1964-66, Barnes Hosp., St. Louis, 1984-85, Shapiro Devel. Ctr., Kankakee, Ill., 1986-90, Community Unit Sch. Dist. 2, Herscher, 1990—; supr. Neighborhood Youth Corps., Edwardsville, 1966-70; dir. social svcs. St. Joseph's Hosp., Alton, 1979-84, Assn. for Retarded Citizens, Wood River, 1985-86; pvt. practice psychotherapy Kankakee. Coord. Bereavement follow up Hospice Kanakakee Valley, 1987-90; facilitator, co-founder Kids Support Kids, Kankakee, 1989—. Mem. NASW, Ill. Assn. Sch. Social Workers. Mem. United Ch. of Christ. Home: 866 N 1790W Rd Kankakee IL 60901-8206

ROSS, KATHLEEN ANNE, college president; b. Palo Alto, Calif., July 1, 1941; d. William Andrew and Mary Alberta (Wilburn) Ross. BA, Ft. Wright Coll., 1964; MA, Georgetown U., 1971; PhD, Claremont Grad. U., 1979; LLD (hon.), Alverno Coll. Milw., 1990, Dartmouth Coll., 1991, Seattle U., 1992; LHD (hon.), Whitworth Coll., 1992; LLD (hon.), Pomona Coll., 1993; LHD (hon.), Coll. of New Rochelle, 1998; LLD (hon.), U. Notre Dame, 1999, Gonzaga U., 1999. Cert. tchr., Wash. Secondary tchr. Holy Names Acad., Spokane, Wash., 1964-70; dir. rsch. and planning Province Holy Names, Wash. State, 1972-73; v.p. acads. Ft. Wright Coll., Spokane, 1973-81; rsch. asst. to dean Claremont Grad. Sch., Calif., 1977-78; assoc. faculty mem. Harvard U., Cambridge, Mass., 1981; pres. Heritage Coll., Toppenish, Wash., 1981—. Cons. Wash. State Holy Names Schs., 1971-73; coll. accrediting assn. evaluator N.W. Assn. Schs. and Colls., Seattle, 1975—; dir. Holy Names Coll., Oakland, Calif., 1979—; cons. Yakama Indian Nation, Toppenish, 1975—; speaker, cons. in field. Author: (with others) Multicultural Pre-School Curriculum, 1977, A Crucial Agenda: Improving Minority Student Success, 1989; Cultural Factors in Success of American Indian Students in Higher Education, 1978. Chmn. Internat. 5-Yr. Convocation of Sisters of Holy Names, Montreal, Que., Can., 1981, 96; TV Talk show host Spokane Council of Chs., 1974-76. Named Yakima Herald Rep. Person of Yr., 1987, MacArthur fellow, 1997; recipient E.K. and Lillian F. Bishop Founds. Youth Leader of Yr. award, 1986, Disting. Citizenship Alumna award, Claremont Grad. Sch., 1986, Golden Aztec award, Wash. Human Devel., 1989, Harold W. McGraw Edn. prize, 1989, John Carroll awrd, Georgetown U., 1991, Holy Names medal, Ft. Wright Coll., 1981, Pres.'s medal, Estern Wash. U., 1994, First Ann. Leadership award, Region VIII Coun. Advancement and Support Edn., 1993, Wash. State Medal of Merit, 1995, Lifetime Achievement award, Yakima YWCA, 2001, numerous grants for projects in multicultural higher edn., 1974—. Mem. Nat. Assn. Ind. Colls. and Univs., Soc. Intercultural Edn., Tng. and Rsch., Sisters of Holy Names of Jesus and Mary-SNJM. Roman Catholic. Office: Heritage Coll Office of Pres 3240 Fort Rd Toppenish WA 98948-9562

ROSS, KEITH A. electrical engineer; b. Sturgis, S.D., Dec. 19, 1952; s. Floyd I. and Elsie J. Ross; m. June K. Ross, June 20, 1987; children: Samantha J., Kelsi N. BSEE, S.D. Sch. Mines, 1975, MSEE, 1977, PhD, 1983. Assoc. engr. IBM, Rochester, Minn., 1977—79; assoc. prof. ECE S.D. Sch. Mines, Rapid City, 1982—96; staff engr. AMI Semiconductor, Pocatello, Idaho, 1996—. Contbr. articles to profl. jours. Mem.: Am. Vacuum Soc. Republican. Lutheran. Avocation: photography. Home: 1116 Cedar Hollow Dr Pocatello ID 83204 Office: AMI Semiconductors 2300 Buckskin Rd Pocatello ID 83201 Office Fax: 208-234-6740. E-mail: Keith_Ross@amis.com.

ROSS, KENNETH L. lawyer; b. Orange, Tex., Dec. 2, 1944; s. Albert LeVergene Ross and Noreen Belle Welch; m. Lorinda Foltmer Ross, June 4, 1967 (div. 1976); 1 child, Ashley Nicole; m. Linda Cooper, May 27, 1978; children: Dixie Lee, Megan Mae. BA, Southeastern La. U., 1967; JD, La. State U., 1971. Bar: La. 1972, U.S. Dist. Ct. (ea. dist.) La. 1981, U.S. Supreme Ct. 1992, U.S. Dist. Ct. (mid. dist.) La. 1998. Ptnr. Seale Sledge & Ross, Hammond, La., 1972-79, Seale Macaluso Daigle & Ross, Hammond, 1979-96, Seale Daigle & Ross, Hammond, 1997—. Bd. dirs. Ross & Wallace Paper Products, Inc., Hammond, One Mass. Ave. Corp., Washington; chmn. S.E. Region Airspace Conf. for Air Nat. Guard, Washington, 1996-98. Mem. Hammond Airport Bd., 1995; chmn. Leadership Tangipahoa, Hammond, 1996. Brig. gen. USAF Air Nat. Guard, 1969-98. Decorated DSM; recipient Leion of Merit State of La., 1998. Mem. Nat. Guard Assn. of the U.S. (exec. coun. 1992-2000, Disting. Svc. medal 1996, treas. 2000—), Nat. Guard Assn. of La. (pres. 1988), La. Dist. and State Bar Assn., La. Regional Airport Authority. Republican. Southern Baptist. Avocations: flying, boating, scuba diving. Home: 610 W Thomas St Hammond LA 70401-3164 Office: Seale Daigle & Ross APLC 200 N Cate St Hammond LA 70401-3301 E-mail: kross@sdrlawfirm.com.

ROSS, LARRY MICHAEL, county economic development official; b. Williamsport, Pa., Dec. 9, 1954; s. Larry Hoy and Mary Alice (Moyer) R.; m. Donna Jean Barkhymer, Aug. 4, 1979; children: Kira Michelle, Tracy Janelle, Alyssa Danielle. BA in Polit. Sci., Slippery Rock U., 1977; cert. basic edn. devel., Rochester Inst. Tech., 1985; postgrad. in econ. devel., U. Okla., 1987. Statis. analyst Stats., Research and Planning Pa. Dept. Commerce, Harrisburg, 1977-79, procurement specialist Minority Bus. Enterprise, 1979-83; indsl. devel. loan specialist Pa. Dept. Commerce, Pa. Indsl. Devel. Authority, 1983-84; mktg. rep. Bur. Domestic and Internat. Commerce Pa. Dept. Commerce, 1984-86; pres. Franklin County Area Devel. Corp., Chambersburg, Pa., 1986—. Intern Pa. Ho. of Reps., Harrisburg, 1977; houseparent Milton Hersey (Pa.) Sch., 1979-80; mem. employer adv. panel Pa. Job Svc., 1986; mem. adv. panel curriculum devel. Franklin County Career & Tech. Ctr., 1986; bd. dirs. ManTech, 1996; chmn. Punt Commn. on Bus.-Edn. Partnerships; grad. Leadership Pa. Recipient gov.'s letter of recognition State of Pa., 1977, commendation Congressman John P. Murtha, 1977, Disting. Alumni award Slippery Rock U., 1987, Transp. Partnershipping award CSX, Disting. Svc. award Franklin County Farmers Assn., Supporter of Entrepreneurship award Ernst & Young, 1998. Mem. Am. Econ. Devel. Coun. (bd. dirs.), Pa. Econ. Devel. Assn. (past pres.), Ctrl. Pa. Internat. Bus. Assn., Active Corp Execs., Soc. for Human Resource Mgmt., Northeastern Economic Developers Assn. (bd. dirs., pres.). Republican. Lutheran. Avocations: tennis, racquetball, reading. Office: Franklin County Area Devel Corp 1900 Wayne Rd Chambersburg PA 17201-8836 E-mail: mross@pa.net.

ROSS, LEONARD LESTER, anatomist, educator; b. N.Y.C., Sept. 11, 1927; s. Aaron Theodore and Shirley (Smolen) R.; m. Marcella Gamel, June 23, 1951 (dec. Aug. 1995); children: Jane, Jill; m. Frances Robb, Nov. 12, 1998; 1 chld, Jennifer. AB, NYU, 1946, PhD, 1954. Asst. prof. U. Ala. Med. Coll., 1954-57; assoc. prof. Cornell U. Med. Coll., 1957-69, prof., 1969-73; vis. prof. Cambridge U., 1967-68; prof., chmn. dept. anatomy Med. Coll. Pa., Phila., 1973-89, exec. v.p., Annenberg dean, 1989-93, pres. and Annenberg dean, 1993-94, provost and Annenberg dean, 1993-96; provost Allegheny U., 1996-98. Exec. v.p. Allegheny Health, Edn. and Rsch. Found. Assoc. editor: Anat. Record, 1976. Served with M.C., U.S. Army, 1946-47. Recipient Lindback award for teaching, 1976; NIH sr. research fellow, 1967-68 Mem. Am. Assn. Anatomists (exec. com. 1984-88), Soc. Neurosci., Soc. Cell Biology, N.Y. Soc. Electron Microscopists (pres. 1975-76), Assn. Anatomy Chairmen (pres. 1983-84), AAUP (nat. council 1974-77), Sigma Xi. Office: MCP/HU 2900 W Queen Ln Philadelphia PA 19129-1033 E-mail: rossil63@netscape.net.

ROSS, LESA MOORE, quality assurance professional; b. New Orleans, Jan. 25, 1959; d. William Frank and Carolyn West Moore; m. Mark Neal Ross, Nov. 30, 1985; children: Sarah Ann, Jacquelyne Caroline. BS in Engring., U. N.C., Charlotte, 1981; MBA in Quality and Reliability Mgmt., U. North Tex., 1991. Seismic qualification engr. Duke Power Co., Charlotte, N.C., 1981-82; quality assurance engr. Tex. Instruments Inc., Lewisville, Tex., 1982-91; compliance mgr. Am. Med. Electronics, Inc., 1992-93; owner Ross Quality Cons., 1993-95; customer quality assurance sect. mgr. Hitachi Semiconductor (Am.) Inc., 1995-96; v.p. quality Ross Networking Cons. Inc., Flower Mound, Tex., 1996—. Bd. dirs. Greater Lewisville YMCA, 2000—. Recipient Nat. Sci. Found. Rsch. Grant, U. N.C., Charlotte, 1980. Mem. Am. Soc. Quality Control (cert. quality engr., quality auditor, reliability engr., cert. quality technician, cert. quality mgr., sec. Dallas sect. 1994-95, chair-elect Dallas sect. 1995-96, chair 1996-97), Rotary, Zeta Tau Alpha (pres. 1984-85). Avocations: crafts, cross-stitching, reading, travel. Home and Office: 4925 Wolf Creek Trl Flower Mound TX 75028-1955 E-mail: Lross@rnc-inc.com.

ROSS, MADELYN ANN, newspaper editor; b. Pitts., June 26, 1949; d. Mario Charles and Rose Marie (Mangieri) R. BA, Indiana U. of Pa., 1971; MA, SUNY-Albany, 1972. Reporter Pitts. Press, 1972-78, asst. city editor, 1978-82, spl. assignment editor, 1982-83, mng. editor, 1983-93, Pitts. Post-Gazette, 1993—. Bd. dirs. PG Pub. Co.; instr. Community Coll. Allegheny County, 1974-81; Pulitzer Prize juror, 1989, 90. Mem. Task Force Leadership Pitts., 1985-92; v.p. Old Newsboys Charity Fund; bd. dirs. Dapper Dan Charity. Mem. Am. Soc. Newspaper Editors, Women's Press Club, Press Club of Western Pa. (v.p.). Democrat. Roman Catholic. Avocations: tennis; piano; organ. Office: Pitts Post-Gazette 34 Blvd Of The Allies Pittsburgh PA 15222-1204

ROSS, MALCOLM, minerals consultant; b. Washington, Aug. 22, 1929; s. Clarence Samuel and Helen Hall (Frederick) R.; m. Daphne Dee Virginia Riska, Sept. 1, 1956; children: Christopher A., Alexander MacC. BS in Zoology, Utah State U., 1951; MS in Chemistry, U. Md., 1959; PhD in Geology, Harvard U., 1962. Rsch. mineralogist U.S. Geol. Survey, Washington, 1954-5, 61-74, Reston, Va., 1974-95, scientist emeritus, 1996-99; minerals and health cons., 1999—. Prin. investigator lunar sci. program NASA, 1969-74. Author: Asbestos and Other Fibrous Minerals, 1988; contbr. numerous articles to profl. jours. First Lt. U.S. Army, 1952-54. Recipient Disting. Svc. award, U.S. Dept. Interior, 1986; grantee Fulbright Commn., Cyprus, 2000. Fellow Mineral. Soc. Am., Geol. Soc. Am., AAAS; mem. Am. Geophys. Union, Clay Minerals Soc., Mineral Soc. Am. (bd. dirs. treas. 1976-80, v.p. 1990, pres. 1991, Pub. Svc. award, 1990). Home: 1608 44th St NW Washington DC 20007-2025 E-mail: mrdrr@earthlink.net.

ROSS, MARILYN, pediatrician; b. N.Y.C., July 9, 1943; d. Karl F. and Anny Ross; m. Steven Cahn. AB, Barnard Coll., 1965; MD, Woman's Med. Coll. of Pa., Phila., 1969; MS in Health Adminstrn., NYU, 1988. Diplomate Am. Bd. Pediatrics. Intern Lenox Hill Hosp., N.Y.C., 1969-70; resident Mt. Sinai Hosp., 1970-72; staff physician U. Vt., Burlington, 1974-75; med. dir. Winooski (Vt.) Family Health Ctr., 1976; staff Rutgers Cmty. Health Plan, New Brunswick, N.J., 1979-80, Westchester Cmty. Health Plan, White Plains, N.Y., 1980-81; attending pediat. Montefiore Hosp., Bronx, 1986-87; asst. attending pediat. N.Y. Hosp., N.Y.C., 1993-94. Attending ambulatory pediat. Brookdale Hosp. Med. Ctr., Bklyn., 1973-74, 77-79, 81-86, 94-2001; assoc. chief ambulatory pediat. Bklyn. Hosp. Med. Ctr., 1991-93, chief ambulatory pediat. Lutheran Med. Ctr., Bklyn., 1987-91. Fellow Am. Acad. Pediat., Bklyn. Pediatric Soc.

ROSS, MARILYN J. English and communications educator; BA in Am. Studies, U. Miami, Fla., 1969, MA in Am. Studies, 1971, PhD in Higher Edn. Leadership, 1995. Asst. prof. English Fla. Meml. Coll., 1971-84, assoc. prof. English and mass comm. arts, 1985-94, prof. higher edn., 1995—. Founder mass comm. arts program Fla. Meml. Coll., 1980, coord. modern langs., 1999—. Author: Success Factors of Young African American Males at a Historically Black College, 1998; prodr. over 100 hrs. African Am., Caribbean and Hispanic programming, WLRN-TV. Recipient Outstanding Svc. award Vets. Club, 1979, Outstanding and Dedicated Svc. in Behalf of FMC award Miami Cable Access Corp., 1987, award Fla. Meml. Coll./Black Archives History and Rsch. Found. of South Fla., Inc., 1999. Mem. AAUW, Assn. Ednl. Leadership, Nat. Coun. Tchrs. of English, Epsilon Tau Lambda, Kappa Delta Pi, Phi Lambda Pi, Delta Theta Mu, Phi Kappa Phi, Phi Alpha Theta. Address: Unit F-602 1121 Crandon Blvd Apt F602 Key Biscayne FL 33149-2781

ROSS, MARION, actress; b. Albert Lea, Minn. children: Jim, Ellen. Grad., San Diego State U. Performed with Globe Theatre, San Diego, LaJolla Summer Theatre; Broadway debut in Edwin Booth; starred in touring prodns. of Never Too Late, Barefoot in the Park, The Glass Menagerie, Long Days Journey Into Night, Love Letter, Steel Magnolias, Over The River and Throught The Woods, film debut in Forever Female, 1953; on woman show A Lovely Light, 1988—; TV series include Life with Father, 1953-55, Paradise Bay, 1965-66, Happy Days, 1974-84, Love Boat, 1985-86 (2 Emmy nominations), Brooklyn Bridge, 1991-93 (Emmy nomination for lead actress in a comedy 1992, 93), Hidden in Silence, 1995, Evening Star, 1996, The Great War, 1996, The Third Twin, 1997, About Search, 1998, The Lake, 1998, Drew Carey Show, 1998, That 70's Show, 1998, Touched By an Angel, 1999 (Emmy nomination 1999), The Ladies and the Champ, 2001. Office: Dale Olson & Assocs 7420 Mulholland Dr Los Angeles CA 90046-1306

ROSS, MARK SAMUEL, lawyer, educator, funeral director, writer; b. Newark, June 6, 1957; s. Herbert and Selma Ruth (Feldman) R.; m. Robin Liebman, May 19, 1984; children: Adam Micah, Danielle Leah. BA with honors, Rutgers U., 1979; JD, Benjamin Cardozo Law Sch., 1982; diploma, McAllister Inst. Funeral Svc., 1984. Bar: N.J. 1983, U.S. Dist. Ct. N.J. 1983, N.Y. 1989. V.p. Art/Craft Monuments-Shalom Memls., Union, N.J., 1980—; sec., treas., counsel Menorah Chapels at Millburn, NJ, 1983—, funeral dir. N.J., 1984—; atty. pvt. practice, 1983—. Counsel Com. for Consumer Protection, Union, 1985—; adj. prof. law Am. Acad.-McAllister Inst., N.Y.C., 1984-85; instr. Jewish law Emanu-El Religious Sch., Westfield, N.J., 1985. Author: (newspaper column) Through My Father's Eyes, 1995—. V.p. Temple Beth Am, Springfield, N.J., 1986-92, pres., 1992-94; counsel Found. Jewish Arts and Heritage, Inc., Union, 1986—. Named Man of Yr., Springfield B'nai B'rith, 1995, Temple Beth Ahm, Springfield, 2001; recipient Internat. Cmty. Svc. award, B'nai B'rith Internat., 1995. Mem. ABA, N.J. Bar Assn., Union County Bar Assn., B'nai B'rith (pres. 1980-83, Nat. Founders award 1982). Avocations: art, music, photography, golf. Office: 2950 Vauxhall Rd Vauxhall NJ 07088-1246 also: PO Box 641 Millburn NJ 07041-0641

ROSS, MARY ANN, principal; b. Chgo., Aug. 1, 1946; d. Louis and Mary (Zappa) Sirianni. BA, U. Ill., Chgo., 1968; MA, DePaul U., Chgo., 1970, Northeastern U., 1975; PhD, Loyola U., Chgo., 1989. Cert. Engish secondary tchr., guidance and counseling, Type 75 adminstrn., supt. 6th grade tchr. Nettelhorst Elem., Chgo., 1968-69; tchr. English Orr H.S., 1969-70; tchr. English, guidance counselor, adminstr. Steinmetz H.S., 1970-85; adminstrv. intern Rhodes Elem., River Grove, Ill., 1985-86; prin. Sandburg Jr. H.S., Elmhurst, 1986-91, Palatine, 1991—. Trainer Ill. Adminstrn. Acad., Ednl. Svc. Ctr., DuPage, 1997; ednl. cons. Colonial Bank, Chgo., 1978; ednl. advisor in Japan Japanese C. of C., 1996; Lincoln examiner quality Lincoln Found., Chgo., 1999—2001; site examiner Blue Ribbon Award for Excellence U.S. Dept. Edn., 2001—. James scholar U. Ill., 1964, state scholar for women in adminstrn. State of Ill., 1985; recipient Those Who Excel award Ill. State Bd. Edn., 1993; selected blue ribbon examiner U.S. Dept. Edn., 2001, 02. Mem. ASCD, Nat. Mid. Sch. Assn., Nat. Assn. Secondary Prins., Internat. Reading Assn., Palatine Kiwanis (pres., sec., bd. dirs. 1991—, Kiwanian of Yr. 1991), Phi Delta Kappa. Roman Catholic. Avocations: boating, dancing. Office: Walter Sundling Jr HS 1100 N Smith St Palatine IL 60067-2606 E-mail: rossm@ccsd15.k12.il.us.

ROSS, MATHEW, psychiatry educator; b. Boston, July 29, 1917; s. Abraham and Frances (Lampke) R.; m. Brenda Boynton, Dec. 24, 1946; children: Douglas Ross, Gail Ross, Craig Ross, Bruce Ross. BS, Tufts U., 1938, MD, 1942. Diplomate Am. Bd. Psychiatry and Neurology. Intern Kings County Hosp., N.Y.C., 1942-43; resident VA Med. Ctr., L.A., 1946-48, L.A. Psychoanalytic Inst., 1949-53; prof. Sch. Medicine UCLA, 1953-58, George Washington U., Washington, 1958-73; psychiat. adminstrn. U. Chgo., 1959; prof. Sch. Medicine Harvard U., Boston, 1963-73, Brown U., Providence, 1964-65, R.I. U., Providence, 1964-65, U. Calif., Irvine, 1974—; fellow Sch. Alcoholism U. Utah, 1977. Fulbright prof., rsch. scholar U. Gronigen and U. Amsterdam, The Netherlands, 1962-63; med. dir. Am. Psychiat. Assn., Washington, 1958-62. Editor: Newsletter Am. Psychiat. Assn., 1958-62, Mental Hosp. & Community Psychiatry, 1958-62, PDE Scientific Journal, 1975-90. Sr. legislator State of Calif., 1985-86; commr. Newport Beach (Calif.) Arts Commn., 1989-95. Maj. U.S. Army, 1943-46, ETO. Fellow ACP (life), Am. Psychiat. Assn., Am. Assn. Psychiatrists, Am. Pub. Health Assn., So. Calif. Psychiat. Soc. (founding pres. 1953-60); hon. fellow Australia-New Zealand Coll. Psychiatrists. Home: Unit 1162 24055 Paseo Del Lago Laguna Woods CA 92653-2675 E-mail: matross@att.net.

ROSS, MATTHEW, lawyer; b. N.Y.C., Dec. 28, 1953; s. Harvey and Cecile (Shelsky) R.; m. Susan Ruth Goldfarb, Apr. 20, 1986; children: Melissa Danielle, Henry Max, Thomas Frank. BS in Econs., U. Pa., 1975; JD, U. Va., 1978. Bar: N.Y. 1979, U.S. Dist. Ct. (so. dist.) N.Y. 1979. Assoc. Cravath, Swaine & Moore, N.Y.C., 1978-84; prin., assoc. gen. counsel KPMG Peat Marwick LLP, 1984-90; prin., deputy gen. counsel Deloitte & Touche USA, LLP, N.Y.C, 1990—. Mem. ABA (corp. law sect.), N.Y. State Bar Assn. (corp. banking and bus. law sect.), Assn. of Bar of City of N.Y. (corp. law com.), Beta Gamma Sigma. Avocations: basketball, golf, tennis, skiing. Home: 5 Barker Ln Scarsdale NY 10583-7507 Office: Deloitte & Touche USA LLP 1633 Broadway New York NY 10019-6708

ROSS, MATTHEW ALAN, real estate company executive; AB, Harvard U., 1984, JD, MBA, 1989. Ptnr. Hall Properties, Inc., Boston, 1989-98; pres. ValueRealty, Inc., Cambridge, 1998—. Office: Ste 200N 124 Mt Auburn St Cambridge MA 02138-5787

ROSS, MICHAEL JOHN, communications executive; b. Phila., Aug. 30, 1966; s. George Martin and Lyn Merry (Goldberg) R.; m. Michele R. Goldstein, Jan. 4, 1992 (div. June 1995). BA, Tufts U., 1988; MBA, U. Pa., 1993. Budget priority analyst com. on budget U.S. Ho. of Reps., Washington, 1988-89; polit. aide Japanese Diet, Tokyo, 1989-90; summer intern Bechtel Group, San Francisco, 1992; assoc. Goldman Sachs & Co., Mergers and Acquisitions, N.Y.C., 1993-94; mgr. investor rels. Cheyenne Software, Roslyn Heights, N.Y., 1994-95; founder, exec. v.p. bus. devel. JSM Co. LLC, Phila., 1995—. Mem. Am. Jewich Com., U.S.-Japan Soc. Democrat. Avocations: tennis, golf, billiards, music, reading. Home and Office: The Touraine 1520 Spruce St Apt 909 Philadelphia PA 19102-4508

ROSS, MICHAEL NEIL, publishing executive; b. Chgo., Feb. 5, 1952; s. Edward Louis and Muriel (Dlugach) R.; m. Naomi Manaka, Aug. 24, 1983 (dec. 1988); children: Monica Nina, Rachael Erin, Daniel Max; m. Kathleen Schultz, June 14, 1992; children: Rachael Erin, Daniel Max. BA, U. Minn., 1974; MA, Brandeis U., 1977. Editor Time-Life Books, Tokyo, 1979-83; editorial dir. NTC Pub. Group, Lincolnwood, Ill., 1983-92; exec. v.p., pub. World Book, Inc., Chgo., 1992—. Bd. dirs. Internat. Edn. Svcs., Tokyo, Indraweb, Inc.; cons. Ricsher Enterprises, Washington, 1987—; bd, advisers, The Ctr. for Reintegration. Editor: Viva el Español!, 1987, World At Its Best, 1986, Everything Japanese, 1988, Early World of English, 1993, Wonderful World of English, 1994, Say It In English, 1995, Welcome to Reading, 1996, Ency. of Careers, 1997, Discoveries, 1998, Student Discovery Encyclopedia, 1999, Animals of the World, 2000, Tutor Link, 2001, Biographical Encyclopedia of Scientists, 2002. Named to, Print Media Prodn. Execs. Hall of Fame, 2002. Mem. Direct Selling Edn. Found., Am. Coun. Teaching. Fgn. Langs., Chgo. Coun. Fgn. Rels., Chgo. Book Clinic, Ednl. Press Assn. of Am. (elected bd. dirs. 1999—, pres. 2002-). Avocations: photography, squash, tennis, reading, scuba diving. Home: 610 Kincaid St Highland Park IL 60035-5038 Office: World Book Inc 233 N Michigan Ave Chicago IL 60601 E-mail: Michael.Ross@worldbook.com., mrosspub@aol.com.

ROSS, MICHAEL WALLIS, public health educator; b. Palmerston North, New Zealand, Nov. 17, 1951; came to U.S., 1993; s. Wallis Malcolm and Lois Verrell (Stewart) R. BA with honors, Massey U., New Zealand, 1974; BS in Med. Sociology, SUNY, 1976; MA in Social-Clin. Psychology, Victoria U. Wellington, New Zealand, 1975; diploma in Tertiary Edn., U. New England, Australia, 1984; PhD, U. Melbourne, Australia, 1980; MPH, U. Adelaide, Australia, 1989; M Health Personnel Edn., U. NSW, Australia, 1991; diploma in STDs, Prince of Songkla U., Thailand, 1992. Postdoctoral fellow U. Helsinki, 1979; sr. demonstrator psychiatry Flinders U., Adelaide, Australia, 1979-85; dir. STD/HIV Epidemiology and Rsch. South Australian Health Commn., 1985-89; assoc. prof. Sch. Cmty. Medicine U. NSW, Sydney, 1989-93; prof. Sch. Pub. Health, U. Tex., Houston, 1993—. Bd. mem. Kolbe House, Houston, 1994—. Author: The Married Homosexual Man: A Psychological Study, 1983, Psychovenereology: Personality and Lifestyle Factors in Sexually Transmitted Diseases in Homosexual Men, 1986; (with L.C. Channon-Little) Discussing Sexuality: A Guide for Health Practitioners, 1991; (with L.A. Lewis) A Select Body: The Gay Dance Party Subculture and the HIV/AIDS Pandemic, 1995; (with L. Nilsson Schönnesson) Coping With HIV Infection: Psychological and Existential Responses in Gay Men, 1999; (with L.C. Channon-Little and B.R.S. Rosser) Sexual Health Concerns: Interviewing and History Taking for Health Practitioners, 1999; editor: Homosexuality and Social Sex Roles, 1983, Homosexuality, Masculinity and Femininity, 1985, The Treatment of Homosexuals with Mental Health Disorders, 1988, Psychopathology and Psychotherapy in Homosexuality, HIV/AIDS and Sexuality, 1995; (with W.A.W. Walters) Transsexualism and Sex Reassignment, 1986; (with L. Bennett and D. Miller) Health Workers and AIDS: Research, Intervention and Current Issues in Burnout and Response, 1995; co-sci. editor: Surgeon-General's Call to Action on Sexual Health and Responsible Sexual Behavior, 2001; contbr. articles to profl. jours. Fellow APA, Brit. Psychol. Soc., Royal Soc. Health, Royal Inst. Pub. Health and Hygiene, Royal Soc. Arts, New Zealand Psychol. Soc. Roman Catholic. Avocations: aerobatic flying, reading. Home: 401 Anita St Apt 34 Houston TX 77006-3434 Office: Sch Pub Health U Tex PO Box 20036 Houston TX 77225-0186 E-mail: mross@sph.uth.tmc.edu.

ROSS, MIKE, congressman; b. Texarkana, Ark., Sept. 1, 1961; m. Holly Ross; 2 children. BA, U. Ark. Owner Holly's Health Mart and Home Med. Equipment; area mgr. Fox Meyer Drug Co.; mem. Ark. Senate, 1990-2001, chair children and youth com.; mem. 107th Congress from 4th Ark. dist., Washington, 2001—; mem. agr. com., fin. svcs. com., small bus. com.; chief of staff to Lt Gov. of Ark., 1985—89. Democrat. Methodist. Office: 514 Cannon HOB Washington DC 20515-0404*

ROSS, MOLLY OWINGS, gold and silversmith, jewelry designer/sculptor, small business owner; b. Ft. Worth, Feb. 5, 1954; d. James Robertson and Lucy (Owings) R. BFA, Colo. State U., 1976; postgrad., U. Denver, 1978-79. Graphic designer Amber Sky Illustrators and Sta. KCNC TV-Channel 4, Denver, 1977-79; art dir. Mercy Med. Ctr., 1979-83, Molly Ross Design, Denver, 1983-84; co-owner Deltex Royalty Co., Inc., Colorado Springs, Colo., 1981—, LMA Royalties, Ltd., Colorado Springs, 1993—; art dir., account mgr. Schwing/Walsh Advt., Mktg. and Pub. Rels., Denver, 1984-87, prodn. mgr., 1987-88; jewelry designer Molly O. Ross, Gold and Silversmith, 1988—. Coun. mem. feminization of poverty critical needs area coun. Jr. League Denver, 1989—90, chmn. childre in crisis/edn. critical needs area, 1990—91, chmn. project devel., 1991—92, co-chmn. Done in a Day Cmty. Project 75th Anniversary Celebration, 1991—93, bd. dirs., 1993—94, co-chmn. project IMPACT, 1994—95, exec. v.p. external affairs, 1995—96, co-chmn. cmty. coalitions com., 1996—98; mem. steering com. Denver Urban Resources Partnership, 1995—2002; pres.-elect Jr. League Denver, 1989—99, pres., 1999—2000, Four Mile Hist. Park Vol. Bd., 1985—86; bd. dirs. Four Mile Hist. Park Assn., 1985—86, Hist. Denver, Inc., 1986—87, Denver Emergency Housing Coalition, 1989—90; co-founder, bd. dirs. Ctr. Ethics and Social Responsibility/PREP, 1994—2001, pres. bd. dirs., 1997—99, treas. bd. dirs., 1999—2000; bd. dirs. Jr. League Denver Found., 1998—2002, Excelsior Youth Ctr. Found., 2001—, Friends of Warren Village, 2000—01, Art Reach, 2001—. Named Vol. of Month (March), Jr. League Denver, 1990, Vol. of Yr., Four Mile Hist. Pk., 1988; recipient Gold Peak Mktg. award-team design Am. Mktg. Assn., 1986, Silver Peak Mktg. award-team design Am. Mktg. Assn., 1986, Gold Pick award-art dir. Pub. Rels. Soc. Am., 1980-81, cert. Appreciation USDA, 1999, 2001. Mem. Natural Resources Def. Coun., Physicians for Social Responsibility, Am. Farmland Trust, Nat. Trust for Hist. Preservation, Environ. Def. Fund. Avocations: horseback riding, bicycling, hiking, backpacking, pastel drawing.

ROSS, MONTE, electrical engineer, researcher; b. Chgo., May 26, 1932; s. Jacob Henry and Mildred Amelia (Feller) R.; m. Harriet Jean Katz, Feb. 10, 1957; children— Karyn, Dianne, Ethan BS in Elec. Engring., U. Ill., 1953; MS, Northwestern U., 1962. Devel. engr. Chance Vought, Dallas, 1953-54; sr. electronics engr. Motorola, Chgo., 1955-56, project engr., 1957-59, assoc. dir. rsch., 1960-63; dir. rsch. Hallicrafters Co., Chgo., 1964-65; mgr. laser tech. McDonnell Douglas Astronautics Co., St. Louis, 1966-70, dir. laser comms.; program mgr. Laser Space Comms., 1971-87; pres. Ultradata Sys., Inc. (formerly Laser Data Tech.), St. Louis, 1987—2001, CEO, 2001—. Mem. alumni bd. dept. elec. and computer engring. U. Ill., 1985-90; guest lectr. various univs.; cons. NSF. Author: Laser Receivers, 1966; tech. editor Laser Applications Series, vol. 1, 1971, vol. 2, 1974, vol. 3, 1977, vol. 4, 1980; patentee in field. Chmn. Laser Mus. and Space Signal Obs., 1997—. Recipient St. Louis High Tech. Entrepreneur of Yr. award, 1995; McDonnell Douglas

Corp. fellow, 1985. Fellow IEEE; mem. Internat. Laser Comms. Soc. (pres. 1988-89), Sigma Xi. Home: 19 Beaver Dr Saint Louis MO 63141-7901 Office: Ultradata Sys Inc 1240 Dielman Ind Ct Saint Louis MO 63132-2212 E-mail: mross@ultradatasystems.com.

ROSS, NELL TRIPLETT, financial consultant, educator, corporate secretary; b. Winterville, Miss., Feb. 14, 1922; d. Ethel Earl and Myrtie (Harrison) Triplett; m. William Dee Ross, Jr., July 25, 1944; 1 child, William Dee III. BA, Millsaps Coll., 1942. Tchr., Consol. Sch. of Chatham (Miss.), 1942-43, Glen Allan (Miss.) Consol. Sch., 1943-46; sec. econs. dept. Duke U., Durham, N.C., 1946; tchr. Durham High Sch., 1947, E.K. Powe Sch., Durham, 1947-48, Lakewood Elem. Sch., Durham, 1948-49; with purchasing dept. La. State U., Baton Rouge, 1949-50; enrollment officer La. Hosp. Service, Inc., Baton Rouge, 1950-51; owner Mentone Plantation, Erwin and Chatham, Miss., 1961—; owner, dir., v.p., corp. sec. Fin. Cons. Svcs., Inc., 1970—. Methodist. Clubs: Baton Rouge Country, Camelot. Home: 2738 Mcconnell Dr Baton Rouge LA 70809-1113 also: 2763 E Bocage Ct Baton Rouge LA 70809-1143

ROSS, NORMAN ALAN, publisher; b. Bklyn., Nov. 1, 1942; s. Robert E. and Bertha (Cohen) R.; m. Leslie Ann Sandler, Oct. 10, 1969; children: Caroline Beth, Juliet Michelle. BBA, CCNY, 1964, postgrad., 1967-74. Prodn. mgr. Thomas Pub. Co., 1964-67; systems analyst Reuben H. Donnelley Corp., 1968-70; project mgr. Holt Rinehart & Winston, 1971-73; pres. Clearwater Pub. Co., Inc., N.Y.C., 1973-88, Video Strategies USA, Inc., N.Y.C., 1981-84, Broadside Ltd. pub. Broadside Mag., 1983-87, Norman Ross Pub. Inc., 1987—, Acad. Microforms Inc., 1999—. Author: Index to the Decisions of the Indian Claims Commission, 1973, Index to the Expert Testimony Before the Indian Claims Commission, 1973, Guide to Architectural Trade Catalogs from the Avery Library, 1989, Guide to Yiddish Children's Books from the Yivo Inst., 1989. Mem. ALA, Assn. Info. Mgmt. Home: 392 Central Park W Apt 20-c New York NY 10025-5878 Office: Norman Ross Pub Inc 330 W 58th St New York NY 10019-1827 E-mail: norman@nross.com.

ROSS, PATTI JAYNE, obstetrics and gynecology educator; b. Nov. 17, 1946; d. James J. and Mary N. Ross; B.S., DePauw U., 1968; M.D., Tulane, U., 1972; m. Allan Robert Katz, May 23, 1976. Asst. prof. U. Tex. Med. Sch., Houston, 1976-82, assoc. prof., 1982-98, prof., 1998—, dir. adolescent ob-gyn., 1976—, also dir. phys. diagnosis, dir. devel. dept. ob-gyn.; cons. OrthoMcNeil and Wyeth-Pharm.; speaker in field. Bd. dirs. Am. Diabetes Assn., 1982—; mem. Rape Coun. Diplomate Am. Bd. Ob-Gyn, Children's Miracle Network Hermann's Children's Hosp; Olympic torch relay carrier, 1996; founder Women's Med. Rsch. Fund, U. Tex. Med. Sch., Houston; bd. mem. Susan Komen Found. Appeared on Lifetime TV network. Mem. Tex. Med. Assn., Harris County Med. Soc., Houston Ob-Gyn. Soc., Assn. Profs. Ob-Gyn., Soc. Adolescent Medicine, AAAS, Am. Women's Med. Assn., Orgn. Women in Sci., Sigma Xi. Roman Catholic. Clubs: River Oak Breakfast, Profl. Women Execs. Contbr. articles to profl. jours. Office: 6431 Fannin St Houston TX 77030-1501

ROSS, PHILIP ROWLAND, retired library director; b. Indiana, Pa., Apr. 7, 1940; s. David Biddle and Miriam Elizabeth (Hill) R.; m. Elaine Lucille George, July 17, 1965; children: Mary Elizabeth, David Bruce. BA, Pa. State U., 1962; MSLS, U. Md., 1969. Postal fin. officer USAF, Tachikawa AFB Tokyo, 1963-65; chief data control and quality control Hdqrs. Air Force Systems Command, Andrews AFB, Md., 1965-68; asst. libr. acquisitions West Liberty (W.Va.) State Coll., 1969-86; dist. mgr. Wheeling (W.Va.) office First Investors Corp., 1986-89, divs. mgr. State of Ark., 1989-92; dir. Lonoke (Ark.) Prairie County Regional Libr. System, 1992-2000; ret., 2000. Founder, treas.-mgr. West Liberty (W.Va.) State Coll. Fed. Credit Union, 1977-82, chmn. bd., 1984-85; mem. Ark. On Line Network Adv. Com., Little Rock, 1993-96, Libr. Devel. Dist. State Coun., Little Rock, 1993-2000, vice chmn., 1996. Maj. USAF, 1962-68; maj. Res., 1968-84, ret. Decorated various USAF medals and decorations. Mem. ALA, Assn. Ark. Pub. Librs. (treas.-sec. 1993, 94, v.p. pres.-elect 1995, pres. 1996), Ark. Libr. Assn. (com. mem. 1994-95, conv. com. 1996, 97), S.E. Libr. Assn., Lonoke, Ark. C. of C., Am. Legion, Lions. Republican. Methodist. Avocations: reading, gardening, refinishing antique furniture. Home: 691 Wayne Elmore Rd Lonoke AR 72086-9126

ROSS, RANDOLPH ERNEST, management consultant; b. N.Y.C., Mar. 17, 1955; s. David Harvey and Pearl (Frandsen) R.; m. Joan Frances Healey, Apr. 2, 1982. AB in History, Brown U., 1977; MBA in Fin., Columbia U., 1981. CFA; comml. pilot FAA. Nat. editor Sta. WEAN Radio, Providence, 1977-79; rsch. analyst, asst. v.p. Kidder, Peabody & Co., Inc., N.Y.C., 1981-85; rsch. analyst First Manhattan Co., 1985-86; portfolio mgr. Brundage, Story and Rose, 1986-92; sr. portfolio mgr., v.p. Bankers Trust Co., 1992-93; investment strategist, sr. v.p. Kidder, Peabody & Co. Inc., 1993-94; pvt. investor Bklyn., 1994-96; mng. dir. Morgan Hill Corp., N.Y.C., 1996—. Fellow Fin. Analysts Fedn.; mem. Inst. Chartered Fin. Analysts, N.Y. Soc. Security Analysts. Republican. Avocations: commercial pilot, sailing, trap and skeet shooting, architectural and urban history, fiction. Home: 111 Hicks St Ste 4A Brooklyn NY 11201-1638 Office: Morgan Hill Corp 330 E 33rd St New York NY 10016-9466

ROSS, RHODA, artist; b. Boston, Dec. 24, 1941; Student, Skowhegan Sch. Painting; BFA, RISD, 1964; MFA, Yale U., 1966. Tchr. NYU, 1994—, Chautauqua (N.Y.) Sch. Art; participant Art in Embassies Program Dept of State. One-woman shows include Frick Gallery, Belfast, Maine, Yale U., New Haven, Convent of the Sacred Heart, Mcpl. Art Soc., L.I. U., Emma Willard Sch. Dietal Gallery, Marymount Manhattan Coll., N.Y.C., N.Y.C. Landmarks Preservation Commn. 25th Silver Ann., numerous others; groups shows include Walley Findlay Galleries, The Crane Collection, Boston, Michael Ingbar Gallery, N.Y., N.Y. Studio Sch., N.Y.C., Am. U., Washington, Springfield (Mo.) Art Mus., numerous others; permanent collections include The White House, Gracie Mansion, N.Y.C., The Juilliard Sch., N.Y.C., Bankers Trust, Mus. City of N.Y., Chem. Bank Nat. Hqrs., Lehman Coll., Waldorf Astoria Hotel, N.Y.C., Russian Tea Rm., Rose Assocs., Bklyn. Union Gas, numerous other pvt. and pub. collections; artwork appears on New Sch. Social Rsch. catalog cover, Gifts and Decorative Accessories Mag. cover, UNICEF greeting card, The New York Times, The Chronicle, ABC-TV. Treas. R.I. Sch. Design Alumni Exec. Com. Fellow Va. Ctr. for Creative Arts. Mem. RISD Alumni Assn. (treas., mem. alumni exec. com.), Phi Tau Gamma. Home: 473 W End Ave New York NY 10024-4934 E-mail: rr18@nyu.edu.

ROSS, RICHARD STARR, medical school dean emeritus, cardiologist; b. Richmond, Ind., Jan. 18, 1924; s. Louis Francisco and Margaret (Starr) Ross; m. Elizabeth McCracken, July 1, 1950; children: Deborah Starr, Margaret Casad, Richard McCracken. Student, Harvard U., 1942—44, MD cum laude, 1947; ScD (hon.) , Ind. U., 1981; LHD (hon.) , Johns Hopkins U., 1994. Diplomate Nat. Bd. Med. Examiners, Am. Bd. Internal Medicine (subsplty. bd. cardiovasc. disease). Successively intern, asst. resident, chief resident Osler Med. Service, Johns Hopkins Hosp., 1947—54; research fellow physiology Harvard Med. Sch., 1952—53; instr. medicine Johns Hopkins Med. Sch., 1954—56, asst. prof. medicine, 1956—59, assoc. prof., 1959—65, assoc. prof. radiology, 1960—71, prof. medicine, 1965—, Clayton prof. cardiovascular disease, 1969—75; dir. Wellcome Research Lab., Johns Hopkins; physician Johns Hopkins Hosp.; dir. cardiovascular div. dept. medicine, adult cardiac clinic Johns Hopkins Sch. Medicine and Hosp., dir. myocardial infarction research unit, 1967—75; dean med. faculty, v.p. medicine Johns Hopkins U., 1975—90, dean. emeritus, 1990—. Sir Thomas Lewis lectr. Brit. Cardiac Soc., 1969; John Kent Lewis lectr. Stanford U., 1972; bd. dirs. emeritus Johns Hopkins Hosp., Francis Scott Key Med. Ctr.; mem. cardiovasc. study sect. Nat. Heart and Lung Inst., 1965—69, chmn. cardiovasc. study sect., 1966—69, mem. tng. grant com., 1971—73, chmn. heart panel, 1972—73, adv. coun., 1974—78; mem. Inst. Medicine, 1976—; chmn. vis. com. Harvard Med. and Dental Sch., 1979—86; bd. overseers Harvard U., 1980—86. Editor: Modern Concepts Cardiovascular Disease, 1961—65, The Principles and Practice of Medicine, 17th-22nd edits., 1968—88; mem. editl. bd.: Circulation, 1968—74, mem. editl. com.: Jour. Clin. Investigation, 1969—73; contbr. numerous articles to profl. jours. Capt. M.C. U.S. Army, 1949—51. Named hon. fellow, UMDS, Guy's and St. Thomas's Hosps., London, 1996; recipient Flexner award, Assn. Am. Med. Coll., 1994. Master: ACP; fellow: Am. Coll. Cardiology (Convocation medal 1990); mem.: Heart Assn. Md. (pres. 1967—68), Am. Heart Assn. (chmn. sci. sessions program com. 1965—67, chmn. publs. com. 1970—73, pres. 1973—74, dir. 1974—77, Connor lectr. 1979, Gold Heart award 1976, Mames B. Herrick award 1982), Assn. Univ. Cardiologists (councillor 1972—75), Am. Clin. and Climatol. Assn. (pres. 1978—79, councillor 1979—83, Metzger lecture 1986), Am. Soc. Clin. Investigation (councillor 1967—69), Sociedad Peruana de Cardiologie (corr.), Brit. Cardiac Soc. (corr.), Cardiac Soc. Australia and New Zealand (corr.), Assn. Am. Physicians, Am. Physiol. Soc., Am. Fedn. Clin. Rsch., Boylston Med. Soc., Elridge Club, Interurban Club (pres. 1978), Peripatetic Club, Alpha Omega Alpha, Sigma Xi. Home: 830 W 40th St # 851 Baltimore MD 21211-2181 Office: Johns Hopkins U 1830 E Monument St Baltimore MD 21205-2100 E-mail: rross@jhmi.edu.

ROSS, RICHARD CHARLES, music educator; b. Tulsa, Okla., Jan. 1, 1966; s. Charles Ross Thomas and Rosie Ida Ross. BA, Nebr. Wesleyan U., Lincoln, Nebraska, 1984—88; MA, Ariz. State U., Tempe, Arizona, 1988—89. Educational Specialist Nova Southeastern U., 1995. Asst. to alumni dir. Nebr. Wesleyan U., Lincoln, Nebr., 1987—88; adminstrv. asst. Ariz. State U., Tempe, Ariz., 1988—91; choral director-children; music educator Shea and Vista Verde Mid. Schools, Phoenix, 1991—92; choral music educator Greenway Mid. Sch., 1992—2002, Shadow Mountain H.S., Phoenix, 2002—. Dept. chair Greenway Mid. Sch., Phoenix, 1993—2002; negotiations team Paradise Valley Edn. Assn., Phoenix, 1999—; title i parent liaison Paradise Valley Unified Sch. Dist., Phoenix, 1995—. Dir.: (chorus) Thematic Programming. Action co-chair Paradise Valley Edn. Assn., Phoenix, 1998—2002. Recipient Golden Bell award, Ariz. Sch. Bd. Assn., 1996, Mid. Level Educator of the Yr., Ctrl. Ariz. Mid. Level Assn., 1995-1996, Who's Who Among America's Teachers, 1998. Mem.: Ariz. Music Educators Assn., Paradise Valley Edn. Assn. (treas. 1999—2002). Avocations: hiking, reading, travel, music, art. Office: Shadow Mountain High School 2902 E Shea Blvd Phoenix AZ 85028

ROSS, RICHARD FRANCIS, veterinarian, microbiologist, educator, dean; b. Washington, Apr. 30, 1935; s. Milton Edward and Olive Marie (Berggren) R.; m. Karen Mae Paulsen, Sept. 1, 1957; children: Scott, Susan D.V.M., Iowa State U., 1959, MS, 1961, PhD, 1965. Oper. mgr. Vet. Lab. Inc., Remsen, Iowa, 1961—62; rsch. assoc. Iowa State U., Ames, 1959—61, asst. prof., 1962—65, assoc. prof., 1966—72, prof., 1972—, assoc. dir., assoc. dean Coll. Vet. Medicine, 1990—92, interim dean, 1992—93, dean Coll. Vet. Medicine, 1993—2000; interim dean, dean Coll. Agr., dir. Agrl. Expt. Sta. Rocky Mountain Labs., NIAID, Hamilton, 2000—02, postdoctoral fellow Mont., 1965—66. Sr. U.S. scientist Alexander von Humboldt Found., Bonn, Fed. Republic Germany, 1975-76; chmn. Internat. Research Program on Comparative Mycoplasmology, 1982-86; pres. Iowa State U. Research Found., Ames, 1984-86; Howard Dunne meml. lectr. Am. Assn. Swine Practitioners, 1984; mem. adv. bd. Sec. Agr., 1996—, mem. strategic planning task force USDA, 1997-99, mem. safegarding task force, 2001-2002. Contbr. numerous articles to profl. publs., 1963— Named Disting. Prof., Iowa State U., 1982, Hon. Master Pork Producer, Iowa Pork Producers Assn., 1985; recipient faculty citation Iowa State U. Alumni Assn., 1984, Beecham award for rsch. excellence, 1985, Howard Dunne Meml. award Am. Assn. Swine Practitioners, 1988, Am. Feed Mfg. award for rsch., 1995, Sec. of Agr. award for personal and profl. accomplishment, 1996, Gamma Sigma Delta Merit award for disting. achievement in agr. 2002. Mem. Am. Coll. Vet. Microbiologists (diplomate, vice chmn. 1974-75, sec.-treas. 1977-83), Am. Soc. Microbiology (chmn. div. 1985-86), Internat. Orgn. Mycoplasmology (chair 1990-92, Bd. Dirs. award 2002), AVMA, AAAS, Osborn Research Club, Conf. Rsch. Workers in Animal Diseases (coun. mem., pres. 1992), Assn. Am. Vet. Med. Colls. (pres. 1997-98). Republican. Lutheran. Avocations: fishing, gardening, walking, reading. Home: 4022 Stone Brooke Rd Ames IA 50010-2900 Office: Iowa State U Coll Vet Medicine Ames IA 50011-0001

ROSS, RICHARD LEE, lawyer; b. St. Louis, Feb. 26, 1928; s. Julius A. and Minnie B. (Blum) Razovsky; m. Marjorie N. Ross, Apr. 6, 1952; children: Maurice N., Julian E. AB, Washington U., St. Louis, 1948, JD, 1950. Bar: Mo. 1950, U.S. Dist. Ct. (8th cir.) 1950, U.S. Supreme Ct. 1970. V.p., sec. Banner Industries, Inc., St. Louis, 1950-62; ptnr. Slonim & Ross, 1962-77; pvt. practice, 1978—. Bd. dirs. MNR Inc. Contbr. articles to profl. jours. Recipient Outstanding Achievement in Labor Relations award, Automotive Workers of Am., St. Louis, 1967. Mem. ABA, Nat. Acad. Arbitrators (mem. various coms.), Mo. Bar Assn. (mem. various coms.), Met. Bar Assn. (mem. various coms.), Meadow Brook Country Club. (bd. dirs.), Shriners (unit pres.). Home and Office: 451 Conway Meadows Dr Chesterfield MO 63017-9624 E-mail: razov@worldnetatt.net.

ROSS, ROBERT A. lawyer; b. Bklyn., Nov. 27, 1958; s. Victor and Selma Ross; m. Bara Mayo, Sept. 1, 1990; children: Malina, Brielle, Hailey. Bachelor's degree, CCNY, 1980; JD, Hofstra Law Sch., 1983. Bar: (U.S. Supreme Ct.). Pvt. practice, Kew Gardens, NY, 1983—2001. Small claims arbitrator Queens Civil Ct., 1989-2001; village justice Oyster Bay Cove, N.Y., 1998-2001. Recipient Am. Jurist award Lawyers Coop. Pub., 1980. Mem. Queens Bar Assn. (family law com.).

ROSS, ROBERT DONALD, librarian; b. N.Y.C., Mar. 28, 1931; s. William and Cecile (Cross) Rosenfeld. BA, CCNY, 1954; postgrad., NYU, 1960-64, Columbia U., 1968; MLS, Rutgers U., 1966. m. Madeleine Ladner, May 28, 1961; children: Jeffrey Laurence, Jodie Dianne. Ref. libr. Bklyn. Pub. Libr., 1965; reader svcs. libr., asst. prof. Suffolk County (N.Y.) C.C., 1966-69; dir. South Brunswick (N.J.) Pub. Libr., 1969-73, Ridgewood (N.J.) Pub. Libr., 1973-95. Adj. prof. Middlesex County (N.J.) C.C., 1973-76. Mem. exec. bd. South Brunswick Cmty. Coun., 1970-73, Human Rels. Coord. Coun., Ridgewood, 1988-94; mem. adv. com. Nat. Project Ctr. for Films and Humanities, N.Y.C., 1971-75; treas. Bergen-Passaic Regional Libr. Coop., 1987-88, mem. exec. bd., 1986-89; mem. Ridgewood Bicentennial Commn., 1975-76; treas. Temple Emanu-El, Reno, 1998-2000, bd. dirs., 2002-; bd. dirs. For the Love of Jazz, Reno, 1998-2000. Mem. ALA (chmn. discussion group com. fundraising and fin. devel. sect. libr. adminstrn. and mgmt. divsn. 1984-85), N.J. Libr. Assn. (libr. devel. com. 1977-93, chmn. edn. for librarianship com. 1982-83, govt. rels. com. 1982, 100th ann. com. 1988-91), Librs. South Middlesex (chmn. 1970-73), North Bergen Fedn. Librs. (chmn. dirs. coun. 1975), Bergen County Coop. Libr. Sys. (pres., treas. 1982-83, 86-87, exec. bd. computer consortium 1987-89, budget com. 1989-94), Ridgewood C. of C. (bd. dirs. 1983-93, treas. 1988-93), Soc. Valley Hosp., Ridgewood Kiwanis (pres. 1982-83, treas. 1987-88, Disting. Club. Pres. award 1983). Home: 4910 Deer Pass Dr Reno NV 89509-0577 E-mail: RRoss328317@cs.com.

ROSS, ROBERT EVAN, bank executive; b. Alliance, Ohio, Sept. 22, 1947; s. James Jacob Ross and Eva Mae (Forsha) Bodo; m. Susan Margaret Burd, June 20, 1970; children: Margaret Mae, James William. BBA, Kent State U., 1970; MBA, U. Chgo., 1977. Advisor to fraternities, dean of men's office Kent (Ohio) State U., 1970-71; trainee, supr. of trainees Northern Trust Co., Chgo., 1971-73, jr. analyst, 1973-74, trust rep., 1974-77, trust officer, 1977-81, v.p., div. head for personal fin. planning, 1981-85; portfolio mgr., investment rep. Morgan Stanley, 1985-89; pres. Northern Trust Bank in Winnetka, 1989-92; exec. v.p. Northern Trust Bank/Lake Forest, 1992-95, vice chmn., 1995-97, pres., CEO, 1997—2001; pres., CEO Northern Trust Bank-Ohio , 2001—. Bd. dirs. No. Trust Bank, Lake Forest, O'Hare, Ill., DuPage, Ill. Bd. dirs. The Camerata Singers of Lake Forest, Lake Forest Symphony, 1992-2001, Ragdale Found., 1999-2000; bd. govs. Ill. St. Andrew Soc., 1998-2001; suburban chair United Way North Region, 1993—; mem. centennial commn. on identity, values and comm. Kent State U., 1998; trustee DePaul U., Chgo., Barat Coll. Edn. Found. Avocations: sports, reading, stock market, painting. Office: No Trust Bank Lake Forest Deerpath And Bank Ln Lake Forest IL 60045

ROSS, ROBERT JON SANFORD, sociology educator; b. N.Y.C., Feb. 1, 1943; s. Irving Barrett and Marsha (Greenblatt) R.; m. Marion Karyl Levenson, June 13, 1965; children: Gabriel Micah Barrett, Rachel Irene. BA, U. Mich., 1963; postgrad., U. Coll., London, 1963-64; MA, U. Chgo., 1966, PhD, 1975. Exec. dir. New U. Conf., Chgo., 1968-69; rsch. assoc. Inst. for Social Rsch., U. Mich., Ann Arbor, 1969-72; from asst. prof. to prof. sociology Clark U., Worcester, Mass., 1972—, chair dept. sociology, 1975-78, 93-99, dir. internat. studies, chair faculty, 2000—. Vis. prof. U. Mich., Ann Arbor, 1977, MIT, Cambridge, 1981, Harvard U., Cambridge, 1989-92, 94-95; William I. Cole prof. sociology Wheaton Coll., 1999; policy analyst Mass. Senate, Boston, 1983-86; cons. Econ. Devel. Indsl. Corp., Boston, 1988-90. Co-author: Global Capitalism: The New Leviathan, 1990; mem. editorial bd. Socialism and Democracy, 1995-99; contbr. articles to profl. jours. Mem. Dem. Town Com., Southboro, Mass., 1982—99; bd. dirs. Southboro Open Land Found., 1992—2000, Dynamy , Worcester, 1993—. Woodrow Wilson fellow Woodrow Wilson Found., 1963. Mem. Am. Sociol. Assn. Avocations: skiing, running, cycling, hiking. Home: 31 Flagg Rd Southborough MA 01772-1416 Office: Clark Univ Dept Sociology 950 Main St Worcester MA 01610-1477 E-mail: rjsross@clarku.edu.

ROSS, ROBERT JOSEPH, retired professional football coach; b. Richmond, Va., Dec. 23, 1935; s. Leonard Aloysius and Martha Isabelle (MMiller) R.; m. Alice Louise Bucker, June 13, 1959; children: Chris, Mary Catherine, Teresa, Kevin, Robbie. BA, Va. Mil. Inst., 1959. Tchr., head football coach Benedictine High Sch., Richmond, 1959-60; tchr., coach Colonial Heights (Va.) High Sch., 1962-65; asst. football coach Va. Mil. Inst., Lexington, 1965-67, Coll. William and Mary, Williamsburg, Va., 1967-71, Rice U., Houston, 1971-72, U. Md., College Park, 1972-73; head football coach The Citadel, Charleston, S.C., 1973-77; head coach U. Md., College Park, 1982-87; head football coach Ga. Inst. Tech., Atlanta, 1987-91; asst. coach Kansas City (Mo.) Chiefs, 1978-82; head coach San Diego Chargers, 1992-96, Detroit Lions, 1997-2001. 1st lt. U.S. Army, 1960-62. Named Coach of Yr., Washington Touchdown Club, 1982, Kodak Coach of Yr., 1990, Bobby Dodd Coach of Yr., 1990, Bear Bryant Coach of Yr., 1990, Scripps-Howard Coach of Yr., 1990, Nat. Coach of Yr., CBS Sports, 1990, Coach of Yr., Walter Camp Football Found., 1990, NFL Coach of Yr. UPI, 1992, Pro Football Weekly, 1992, Pro Football Writers' Assn., 1992, Football News, 1992, Football Digest, 1992, Maxwell Football Club, 1992, AFC Coach of Yr. Kansas City 101 Banquet. Mem. Am. Football Coaches Assn., Coll. Football Assn. (coaching com. 1988-92). Roman Catholic.

ROSS, ROBERT ROY, JR. urologic surgeon; b. Dearborn, Mich., May 25, 1936; s. Robert Roy and Elizabeth Austin Ross; m. Antoinette Anna Juozunas, June 29, 1963; children: Robert Roy III, Karen Elizabeth, Tracey Austin. BS, U. Mich., 1958; MD, Wayne State U., 1962. Diplomate Am. Bd. Urology. Intern Meml. Hosp., Detroit, 1962-63; resident in gen. surgry Wayne State U. Affiliated Hosp. Program, 1966-67, resident in urolog. surgery, 1967-70; pvt. practice urology Pompano Beach, Fla., 1970-71; asst. prof. urology Wayne State U., Detroit, 1971-72; chief sect. of urology Allen Park (Mich.) VA, 1971-72; urologist RTR Urology, Venice, Fla., 1972—. Chief of staff Venice Hosp., 1978, chief of surgery, 1975; pres., dir. Bon Secour Venice Hosp., Health Park Surg. Ctr. Contbr. articles to profl. jours. Dir. Venice Hosp. Found., 1981-88. Capt. USAF, 1963-66. Fellow ACS; mem. AMA, Fla. Med. Assn., Sarasota County Med. Assn., Am. Urolog. Assn. (southeast sect.), Am. Lithotripsy Soc., Tampa Bay Urolog. Soc., U. Mich. Alumni Assn. (Victors club). Republican. Presbyterian. Avocations: boating, fishing, computing, German shepherd dogs. Hóme: 450 Anchorage Dr Nokomis FL 34275-3102 Office: RTR Urology 530 Nokomis Ave S Venice FL 34285-2819 E-mail: fordson@aol.com.

ROSS, ROBERT THOMAS, neurologist, educator; b. Winnipeg, Man., Can., June 25, 1924; s. John L. and Alberta I. (Gray) R.; m. Margot Joan Ellacott, May 27, 1950; children: Gray T., John L., Mary E.; m. Angela Morrow Brady, Aug. 14, 1970; children: Diana Gray Salter, Drew Garland Salter. MD, U. Manitoba, 1948. Intern Winnipeg Gen. Hosp., 1947-50; resident Nat. Hosp. Queen Sq., London, 1950-52; lectr. dept anatomy U. Manitoba, Winnipeg, 1953-55, asst. prof. dept. medicine, 1955-59, assoc. prof., 1959-77, prof. medicine, 1977-2000, head sect. neurology, 1971-84, emeritus prof. medicine, 2000—. Editor., pub., founder: Can. Jour. Neurol. Scis., 1972-81; author: How to Examine the Nervous System, 3d edit., 1998; Syringobulbia-A Contribution to the Pathophysiology of the Brain Stem, 1986, Syncope, 1988. Trustee Man. Med. Svc., 1958-64; pres. United Health Found., Winnipeg, 1969-71; bd. dirs. Man. Med. Coll. Found., 1983-85, Winnipeg Libr. Found.; mem. senate U. Manitoba, 1988-99; bd. trustees Nat. Gallery of Can.; bd. govs. The Winnipeg Art Gallery, Manitoba Chamber Orch. Recipient E.L. Drewry prize E.L. Drewry Found., 1948; recipient Can. Centennial Medal, 1967, Queen Elizabeth Jubilee Medal, 1977. Fellow Royal Coll. Physicians (Can. and London), Am. Acad. Neurology; mem. Can. Neurol. Soc. (pres. 1971), Coll. Physicians and Surgeons of Man (pres. 1971), Am. Neurol. Assn., Order of Can. Baptist. Home: 312 Park Blvd Winnipeg MB Canada R3P OG7

ROSS, ROBINETTE DAVIS, publisher; b. London, May 16, 1952; d. Raymond Lawrence and Pearl A. (Robinette) Davis; m. William Bradford Ross, III, Mar. 16, 1979; children: Nellie Tayloe, William Bradford IV. Student, Am. U., 1977-78. Asst. to editor The Chronicle of Higher Edn., Washington, 1978, advt. mgr., 1978-82, advt. dir., 1983-88, assoc. pub., 1988-94, The Chronicle of Philanthropy, 1988-94; publ. The Chronicle of Higher Edn., Washington, 1994—; pub. The Chronicle of Philanthropy, 1994—. Mem. Am. News Women's Club, City Tavern Club, Mt. Vernon Club. Episcopalian. Office: The Chronicle of Higher Edn 1255 23rd St NW Ste 700 Washington DC 20037-1146

ROSS, ROSANN MARY, psychotherapist, educator; b. Chgo., May 2, 1956; d. Joseph Charles Ross and Dolores Ann (Horan) Allgaier. BA, U. No. Colo., 1991, MA, 1994. Nat. cert. counselor Nat. Bd. Cert. Counselors; lic. profl. counselor State of Colo. Psychotherapist Counseling Clinic, Greeley, Colo., 1994-96; lectr. U. No. Colo., 1995—; mental health therapist Weld Mental Health, 1996-99. Group facilitator No. Colo. AIDS Project, Ft. Collins, Colo., 1995-96. Vol. therapist Pro Bono of Weld County, Greeley, 1994-96. Avocations: camping, hiking, gardening, reading. Office: Univ Northern Colo Dept Psychology Greeley CO 80639-0001

ROSS, SALLY PRICE, artist, painter; b. Cleve., Oct. 25, 1949; d. Philip E. and Mimi (Einhorn) Price; m. Howard D. Ross, Mar. 3, 1979; children: Sasha, Emily. BFA, Kent State U., 1971; MA, U. Iowa, 1974, MFA, 1975; student, Art Students League, N.Y.C., 1976-78. Art cons. Art Options, Cleve., 1990—94; 1st and only woman artist to paint murals U.S. Capital/Ho. of Reps. corridors, 1978—79. Exhibitions include , Cain Park Art Gallery, Cleve., 1967, Jewish Cmty. Ctr. Cleve., 1967, 1986, Canton (Ohio) Art Inst., 1969, Studio Theatre, Iowa City, 1973, The Cleve. Playhouse Art Gallery, 2000, Fairmount Art Ctr., Russell, Ohio, 2001 (Best in Show), bibl. mural, commd. works, murals. Scholar Edwin Abbey, 1975—77, Fresco, Skowhegan Sch. Painting and Sculpture, 1977. Home: 25 Millcreek Ln Chagrin Falls OH 44022-1265

ROSS, SHEILA MOORE, philanthropic executive; b. Pitts., Apr. 4, 1947; d. John Edward and Alice Regina (Thompson) Moore; m. James D. Ross, Aug. 21, 1969. Student, U. Pitts., 1965-69, Elizabethtown Coll., 1988-89. Dist. asst. Congressman Allen E. Ertel, Harrisburg, Pa., 1977-81; owner Picture Perfect, 1980-82; vol. coord. Ertel for Gov. Campaign, 1982; immigration counselor Migration and Refugee Svcs., 1983-85; investigator, supr. Investigative Cons. Svcs., 1986-90; exec. dir. Cmty. Founds. for Pa., 1991—. Pres. Parents Anonymous of Pa., 2001—. Pres. Greater Harrisburg YWCA, 1988-89, Jr. League Harrisburg, 1989-90; v.p. United Way Pa., Harrisburg, 1994-97; dir. Gaudenzia, Inc., Norristown, Pa., 1994—, Children's Home Found., Harrisburg, 1995—; adv. panel Nat. Iniative to Promote the Growth of Philanthropy, 1998—; nat. mktg. action team Coun. on Found., 2001-. Mem.: Pa. Assn. Non-Profit Orgns. Home: 849 Country Club Rd Camp Hill PA 17011-1616 Office: Cmty Founds for Pa 121 State St Harrisburg PA 17101-1025 E-mail: info@communityfoundations.org.

ROSS, SHERMAN, psychologist, educator; b. N.Y.C., Jan. 1, 1919; s. Max R. and Rachel (Khoutman) R.; m. Jean Goodwin, Aug. 18, 1945; children: Norman Kimball, Claudia Lisbeth (Mrs. Overway), Michael Lachlan. BS, CCNY, 1939; A.M., Columbia U., 1941, PhD, 1943. Asst. psychology, research psychologist Columbia U., 1941-44; asst., then assoc. prof. psychology Bucknell U., 1946-50; research fellow N.Y. Zool. Soc., 1948; guest investigator, sci. asso. Jackson Lab., 1947-77; assoc. prof., then prof. psychology U. Md., 1950-60; spl. cons. Psychopharmacology Svc. Ctr. NIMH, 1956-63; asst. chief NIMH, 1956-57; exec. sec. edn. and tng. bd., sci. affairs officer APA, 1960-68; prof. psychology Howard U., 1968-89, emeritus, 1989—; exec. sec., staff assoc., assembly of behavioral and social scis. Nat. Acad. Scis.-NRC, 1968-76; lectr. Himmelfarb Mobile U., 1994—. Cons. VA, Human Ecology Fund, Stanford Research Inst., Office Naval Research, U.S. Sci. Exhibit, Am. U., HRB-Singer, Inc.; bd. dirs. Interdisciplinary Communications Assocs., Washington; adv. council Woodrow Wilson Rehab. Center Found.; mem. Md. Bd. Examiners Psychology, 1957-58, 84-89; chmn. bd. dirs. Inst. for Research, State Coll., Pa.; mem. Montgomery County Health

Planning Commn.; mem. Md. Statewide Health Coordinating Coun., Met. Washington Area Council of Health Planning Agys., Emergency Med. Svcs. Adv. Council; commr. health emeritus Montgomery County, Md.; v.p. bd. dirs. Mobile Med. Care, Inc., Bethesda, Md. Trustee Carver Research Found., Tuskegee U.; chmn. Coord. Coun. Asbury Meth. Villiage, Gaithersburg, Md. Fellow APA, Am. Coll. Neuropsychopharmacology, Royal Soc. Health, Washington Acad. Scis.; mem. Aerospace Med. Assn., Am. Soc. Zoologists, Ecol. Soc., Ergonomics Rsch. Soc., Md. Psychol. Assn. (pres. 1973-74), D.C. Psychol. Assn. (pres. 1982), Cosmos Club (Washington), Bethesda Naval Club (Md.), Sigma Xi (pres. U. Md. 1957-58, pres. Howard U. 1983-84), Phi Kappa Phi, Psi Chi (nat. pres. 1964-68). Home: 382 Russell Ave Gaithersburg MD 20877-2863 also: 382 Russell Ave Gaithersburg MD 20877-2863 E-mail: Ross197@aol.com.

ROSS, STANFORD G. lawyer, government official; b. St. Louis, Oct. 9, 1931; m. Dorothy Rabin, June 9, 1958; children: John, Ellen. AB with honors, Washington U., 1953; JD magna cum laude, Harvard U., 1956. Bar: D.C. 1969, Calif. 1956, N.Y. 1959. Assoc. Irell & Manella, L.A., 1956-57; tchg. fellow, rsch. asst. Harvard Law Sch., 1957-58; assoc. Dewey, Ballantine, Bushby, Palmer & Wood, N.Y.C., 1958-61; asst. tax legis. counsel U.S. Dept. Treasury, 1961-63; prof. law N.Y. U., 1963-67; White House staff asst. to Pres. Johnson, 1967-68; gen. counsel U.S. Dept. Transp., 1968-69; ptnr. Caplin & Drysdale, Washington, 1969-78; commr. Social Security Adminstrn., 1978-79; ptnr. Califano, Ross & Heineman, 1980-82, Arnold & Porter, Washington, 1983—2002. Pub. trustee Social Security Trust Funds, Washington, 1990-95; chmn. Social Security Adv. Bd., 1997-2002. Editor: Harvard Law Rev, 1954-56. Mem. ABA, Fed. Bar Assn., Internat. Fiscal Assn., Nat. Acad. Social Ins. Office: Arnold & Porter 555 12th St NW Washington DC 20004-1206

ROSS, STEVEN CHARLES, business administration educator, consultant; b. Salem, Oreg., Jan. 14, 1947; s. Charles Reed and Edythe Marie (Calvin) R.; m. Meredith Lynn Buholts, June 15, 1969; children: Kelly Lynn, Shannon Marie. BS, Oreg. State U., 1969; MS, U. Utah, 1976, PhD, 1980. Cons. IRS Tng. Staff, Ogden, Utah, 1977-80; asst. prof. Marquette U., Milw., 1980-88; assoc. prof. Mont. State U., Bozeman, 1988-89; assoc. prof. bus. adminstrn. Western Wash. U., Bellingham, 1989—. Chmn. acad. coord. commn., Western Wash. U., 1997-2002, mem. faculty senate 2000-02; govt. and industry cons.; cons. editor microcomputing series West Pub. Co. Author 35 books and several articles in computer systems field. Mem. adv. com. Milwaukee County Mgmt., 1981-85, Port of Bellingham, 1990-2000; chmn. 1998 U.S. Sailing Jr. Championships. Capt. U.S. Army, 1969-75. Rsch. fellow U. Utah, 1977-79, Marquette U., 1981-84, Western Wash. U., 1998, 2002. Mem. Acad. Mgmt., Decision Scis. Inst., Inst. Mgmt. Scis., Assn. for Computing Machinery, Assn. Computer Educators, Bellingham Yacht Club (trustee 1992-93, sec. 1993-94, rear commodore, 1994-95, vice commodore 1995-96, commodore 1996-97). Office: Western Wash U Coll Bus and Econs Bellingham WA 98225

ROSS, SYDNEY, science educator, researcher; b. Glasgow, Scotland, July 6, 1915; s. Jack C. Ross. B.Sc., McGill Univ., Montreal, Canada, 1936; PhD, Univ. Ill., Urbana, IL, 1940; D.Sc. (hon.) , Heriot-Watt Univ., Edinburgh, Scotland, 2001. Prof., phys. chemistry Rensselaer Polytech Inst., Troy, NY, 1948—90. Author: (book) On Physical Adsorption, Colloidal Systems and Interfaces, Nineteenth-Century Attitudes: Men of Science. Fellow: Royal Soc. of Edinburgh; mem.: History of Sci. Soc., Am. Chem. Soc. Office: Rensselaer Polytech Institute 2194 Tibbits Ave Troy NY 12180-7015 Office Fax: 518-274-6216. E-mail: rosss2@rpi.edu.

ROSS, TERENCE WILLIAM, architect; b. Saginaw, Mich., Sept. 27, 1935; s. Oran Lewis and Drucilla (Chadman) R.; m. Patricia Ann Marshall, Sept. 27, 1974; children by previous marriage: Deborah, David. BArch, U. Mich., 1958. Designer Roger W. Peters Constrn. Co., Fond du Lac, Wis., 1958-62; draftsman Kenneth Clark, Arch., Santa Fe, 1962-63, Holien & Buckley, Archs., Santa Fe, 1963-64; office mgr. Philippe Register, Architect, 1964-68; prin. Register, Ross & Brunets archts./engrs., 1968-71, Luna-Ross & Assocs., 1971-77; staff CNWC Archs., Tucson, until 1981, ADP Archs., 1981-89; sr. arch. U. Calif., 1989-95; arch. ADP Flour Daniel Archs./Engrs., 1995-97, Ross Assocs. Architects, 1997-2000, ret., 2000. Author: Track of the Cats. Vice chmn. N.Mex. R.R. Authority, 1969-74, sec., 1970-72; bd. dirs. colo., N.Mex. Soc. Preservation of Narrow Gauge; v.p. El Dorado Western Narrow Gauge Railway Found. Recipient award for hist. preservation N.Mex. Arts Commn., 1971, award for outstanding svcs. to cmty. Santa Fe Press Club, 1972; named col. aide-de-camp State of N.Mex., 1968, hon. mem. staff atty. gen. Mem. AIA (chpt. pres. 1970, dir.), Constrn. Specifications Inst., N.Mex. Soc. Architects (dir. 1972), Ariz. Soc. Archs., N.Mex. R.R. Authorities (chmn. joint exec. com. 1970-74), Sacto. Valley Garden Ry. Soc. (pres. 1993, dir. 1994-99), San Gabriel Hist. Soc. (hon.), Alpha Rho Chi, Sashay Rounders Sq. Dance Club (pres. 1974), Diamond Squares Sq. Dance Club, Railroad Club (pres. N.Mex. 1969, 70, dir.). E-mail: terry. Home and Office: 2813 57th St Sacramento CA 95817-2403 E-mail: ross@msn.com.

ROSS, TERRY D. lawyer; b. Glendale, Calif., Aug. 12, 1943; BA, U. Calif., Santa Barbara, 1965; JD, Hasting Coll. Law, San Francisco, 1968. Bar: Calif. 1969, U.S. Dist. Ct. (so. dist.) Calif. 1969, U.S. Dist. Ct. (ctrl. dist.) Calif. 1992, U.S. Dist. Ct. (no. dist.) Calif. 1999, U.S. Ct. Appeals (9th cir.) 1977, U.S. Supreme Ct. 1983. Ptnr. Gray, Cary, Ware & Freidenrich, San Diego. Mem. panel arbitrators Am. Arbitration Assn. Note and comment editor Hastings Law Jour., 1967-68. Bd. dirs., mem. exec. bd., 1st v.p. E. San Diego Co. YMCA. Mem. ABA (sect. litigation), State Bar Calif., San Diego County Bar Assn. (mem. arbitration panel, superior ct. com.), S.D. Marlin Club, SDMB Boat and Ski Club, Phi Delta Phi. Office: Gray Cary Ware & Freidenrich 4365 Executive Dr Ste 1100 San Diego CA 92121-4297 E-mail: tross@graycary.com.

ROSS, THOMAS BERNARD, communications company executive; b. N.Y.C., Sept. 2, 1929; s. Henry M. and Evelyn (Timothy) R.; m. Gunilla Ekstrand, Nov. 2, 1963; children: Maria, Anne, Kristina. BA, Yale, 1951. Reporter Internat. News Svc., 1955-58; reporter UPI, 1958; mem. staff Chgo. Sun-Times, 1958-77, mem. staff Washington Bur., 1958-68, fgn. corr., 1968-70, Washington bur. chief, 1970-77; asst. sec. def. for pub. affairs, 1977-81; dir. corp. comm. Celanese Corp., 1981-82; sr. v.p. corp. affairs RCA Corp., 1982-86; sr. v.p. NBC News, 1986-90; sr. v.p., dir. media rels. worldwide Hill and Knowlton, N.Y.C., 1990-94; spl. asst. to pres., sr. dir. pub. affairs NSC, White House, Washington, 1994-95; v.p. govt. rels. Loral, N.Y.C., 1995—. Author: (with David Wise) The U-2 Affair, 1962, The Invisible Government, 1964, The Espionage Establishment, 1967. Lt. (j.g.) USNR, 1951-54. Nieman fellow Harvard U., 1964; recipient Marshall Field award, 1961, 71; decorated Def. Disting. Pub. Svc. medal. Mem. Coun. on Fgn. Rels., Century Assn. (N.Y.), Elizabethan Club (New Haven), Gridiron Club (Washington). Office: Loral 600 3d Ave New York NY 10016

ROSS, THOMAS HUGH, business consultant, retired military officer; b. Pitts., May 18, 1927; s. Thomas Hugh and Anna Marie (Klaiber) R.; m. Ann Carolyn Sipp, Sept. 9, 1950; children: Thomas George, Douglas Alan, James William. BS, U.S. Naval Acad., 1950; BS in Aero. Engring., U.S. Naval Postgrad. Sch., 1957; grad., Command and Staff Naval War Coll., 1962; MS in Internat. Affairs, George Washington U., 1973, postgrad. internat. relations, 1975-78. Enlisted USN, 1945, commd. ensign, 1950, advanced through grades to capt., naval aviator, patrol plane comdr. worldwide, 1952-75, officer in charge 4th Unitas Air Group VP-56, S.Am., 1963, head dept. thermo/fluids U.S. Naval Acad., 1965-67, comdg. officer patrol squadron 16 Naval Air Sta., Jacksonville, Fla., 1968-69; staff SECDEF Pentagon, 1971-74; ret. USN, 1975; cons. Universal Systems, Inc. (Hadron, Inc.), Arlington, Va., 1979-82, Ecosystems, Internat., Inc., Gambrills, Md., 1982-85; cons. then sr. v.p. engring. mgmt. Nat. Bus. Cons., Annapolis, 1982-87. Decorated Air medal, Meritorious Service medal. Mem. DAV (life), Assn. Naval Aviation (life), Ret. Officers Assn. (life), U.S. Naval Acad. Alumni Assn. (life, pres. Annapolis chpt. 1978), Navy League (life), Fleet Res. Assn. Republican. Presbyterian. Avocations: golf, travel, fgn. affairs studies, investments; held world record in turboprop non-stop distance flight 6,857 miles Japan to Md., 1971. Home and Office: 1928 Baltimore Annapolis Blvd Annapolis MD 21401-6248

ROSS, THOMAS MCCALLUM, professional society administrator; b. Hamilton, Ont., Can., May 5, 1931; s. Laverne Robinson and Della Louise (McCallum) R.; m. Marguerite Hilda Ross, Aug. 14, 1954; children: Thomas Wayne, Gregory (dec.), Karyn. Mgr. Sutherland Pharmacy, Hamilton, 1955-60; assoc. sec. Can. Pharm. Assn., Toronto, Ont., 1960-63; mem. research staff Royal Commn. Health Services Govt. Can., Ottawa, 1963-64; exec. dir. Can. Retail Hardware Assn., Toronto, 1964-98; retired. Bd. dirs. People for Sunday Assn., pres. 1987-88. Named to, Can. Hardware-Housewares Hall of Fame, 1999. Founding fellow Hardware Mgmt. Inst.; mem. Internat. Fedn. Ironmongers Assn. (coun. 1970-98), Can. Soc. Assn. Execs. (chmn. edn. com. 1986-88, bd. dirs. 1990-92, Pinnacle award 1989), Am. Soc. Assn. Execs., Can. C. of C. Home: 59 Walby Dr Oakville ON Canada E-mail: tomross@sprint.ca.

ROSS, VALDOR WENDELL, operating room nurse; b. Fayetteville, N.C., Jan. 1, 1956; BSN, Adelphi U., 1978. Cert. operating room nurse. Staff nurse, head nurse Columbia Presbyn. Hosp., N.Y.C., 1978-82; supr., sr. nurse clinician NYU Med. Ctr., 1982-92; staff nurse Northside Hosp., Atlanta, 1992-93; sr. nurse clinician NYU Med. Ctr., 1995-96; staff nurse VA. Med. Ctr., Atlanta, 1993-94, 96—. Capt. Nurse Corps, USAR, 1986. Named Outstanding Perioperative Nurse, Assn. Oper. Room Nurses, 2000. Home: 575 Rockborough Dr Stone Mountain GA 30083-3851 Office: VA Med Ctr Atlanta 1670 Clairmont Rd Decatur GA 30033-4004 E-mail: vwr01@bellsouth.net.

ROSS, WAYNE ANTHONY, lawyer; b. Milw., Feb. 25, 1943; s. Ray E. and Lillian (Steiner) R.; m. Barbara L. Ross, June 22, 1968; children: Gregory, Brian, Timothy, Amy. BA, Marquette U., 1965, JD, 1968. Bar: Wis. 1968, Alaska 1969. Asst. atty. gen. State Alaska, 1968-69; trustee, standing master Superior Ct. Alaska, 1969-73; assoc. Edward J. Reasor & Assocs., Anchorage, 1973-77; prin. Wayne Anthony Ross & Assocs., 1977-83; ptnr. Ross, Gingras & Frenz, Anchorage and Cordova, Alaska, 1983-84, Ross & Gingras, Anchorage and Cordova, 1985; pres. Ross, Gingras and Miner, P.C., Anchorage, 1986-93, Ross and Miner, P.C., Anchorage, 1993—. Col. area def. counsel Alaska State Def. Force; pres. Tyone Mountain Syndicate, Inc. Alaska Rep. Nat. Committeeman, 1992-98; Republican candidate for Gov. of Alaska, 1998, 2002. Decorated knight comdr. Order of Polonia Restituta (Poland), knight Equestrian Order of the Holy Sepulchure of Jerusalem (Vatican). Mem. NRA (bd. dirs. 1980-92, 94—, benefactor), Alaska Bar Assn. (Stanley award), Anchorage Bar Assn., Alaska Gun Collectors Assn. (pres. emeritus), Ohio Gun Colllectors Assn. (hon. life), Smith and Wesson Collectors Assn., 49th Territorial Guard Regiment (pres. 1987-94, 95-96), Alaska Territorial Cavalry (sec. 1991-97, 2001—), Mil. Vehicle Preservation Assn. (v.p. 1994-96), Alaska Peace Officers Assn. Roman Catholic. Home: PO Box 101522 Anchorage AK 99510-1522 Office: Ross & Miner 327 E Fireweed Ln Ste 201 Anchorage AK 99503-2110 E-mail: waralaska@alaska.com.

ROSS, WILBUR LOUIS, JR. investment banker; b. Weehawken, N.J., Nov. 28, 1937; s. Wilbur Louis and Agnes (O'Neill) R.; m. Judith Nodine, May 26, 1961 (div. 1995); children: Jessica, Amanda. AB, Yale U., 1959; MBA with distinction, Harvard U., 1961. Assoc. Wood, Struthers and Winthrop, N.Y.C., 1963-64; pres. Faulkner, Dawkins and Sullivan Securities Corp., 1964-76; sr. mng. dir. Rothschild, Inc., 1976-2000; CEO News Comms., Inc., 1996-98; chmn., chief investment officer Rothschild Recovery Fund, 1997-2000; chmn. Seoul Debt Restructuring Fund, 1998-99; chmn., CEO WL Ross & Co. LLC, N.Y.C., 2000—. Bd. dirs. Biocraft Labs Inc., Rutherford, N.J., FurVault Inc., N.Y.C., Investors Ins. Co., Lawrence Harbor, N.J., Revere Copper and Brass Co., Stamford, Syms Corp., Secaucus, N.J., Am. Bankruptcy Inst., Washington, Allis Chalmers Corp., Milw., Mego Corp., Las Vegas, Nev., KTI Inc., RH Cement Co., Seoul, Korea, Tong Yang Life Ins. Co., Seoul, Kansai Sawayaka Bank, Osaka, Fresca Credit Card Co., Osaka; fin. advisor equity holders com. Texaco Co., A.H. Robins Co., Pub. Service N.H.; hon. econ. amb. from Korea to APEC Investment, Mont., 1999; chmn. Asia Recovery Fund L.P., WL Recovery Fund LP, Asia Co. Investment Ptnrs. L.P., News Comm., Inc., Clarent Hosp. Corp., Internat. Steel Group, Inc., Cleve. Treas. N.Y. State Dem. Com., 1980-83, Am. Fedn. Arts, 1993—, The New Mus., 1993—; vice chmn. Bklyn. Mus., 1981—; chmn. univ. coun. com. on art Yale U., 1983-88; chmn. NAD, N.Y.C., 1985—, Am. Art Forum, Smithsonian Instn., 1987—; trustee, vice chmn. Nat. Mus. Am. Art, Washington, 1986-91, chmn., 1991—; trustee, Mus. Am. Fin. History; trustee Sarah Lawrence Coll., 1986—, chmn. art gallery, 1984—; pres. Parrish Art Mus., 1991-95; chmn. N.Y. Hist. Soc., 1993-94; bd. dirs. Smithsonian Inst. Nat. Bd., 1994—, chmn. bd. 1995; nat. chmn. Smithsonian Bicentennial Celebration, 1996; trustee Gustave Hyde Ctr. Nat. Mus. Am. Indian, 2001—, Nat. Mus. Am. Fin. History; bd. dirs. Turnaround Mgmt. Assn., 2001—; chmn. Absolute Recovery Hedge Fund, Ltd., Hamilton, Bermuda. With U.S. Army, 1961-63. Fellow Jonathan Edward Coll. of Yale U., Met. Mus. Art; mem. Fin. Analysts Fedn. (chartered), Century Assn., Southampton Bath and Tennis Club (chmn. bd. dirs.), Harvard Bus. Sch. Club N.Y. (bd. dirs.). Avocation: collecting art. Office: WL Ross & Co LLC 101 E 52 St 19th fl New York NY 10022 also: WL Ross and Co LLC 101 E 52nd St New York NY 10022

ROSS, WILLIAM DEE, JR. economist; b. Jackson, Miss., May 16, 1921; s. William Dee and Betty (Biggs) R.; m. Nell Triplett, July 25, 1944; 1 child, William Dee III. BA, Millsaps Coll., 1942; MA, Duke U., 1947, PhD, 1951. Economist U.S. Mil. Govt. for Germany, Berlin, 1945—46; instr. econs. Duke U., Durham, NC, 1946—49; assoc. prof. La. State U., Baton Rouge, 1949—54, prof. econs., 1954—56, dean Coll. Bus. Adminstrn., 1956—76; pres. Fin. Cons. Svcs., Inc., 1976—99, Ross Bus. Svcs., Inc., Baton Rouge, 2000—. Bd. dirs. Piccadilly Cafeterias Inc., others; dir. La. Hwy. Fin. Study, La. Legis. Council, 1953-54; cons. Joint House-Senate Hwy. Com., La. Legislature, La. Dept. Hwys., 1955-56; lectr. exec. devel. programs Mich. State U., Ga. Inst. Tech., La. State U.; mem. dept. econs., fin. and adminstrn. Hwy. Research Bd., Nat. Acad. Scis., Washington, 1957-64; mem. adv. council Tax Inst. Am., 1961-63. Author (with B.U. Ratchford) Berlin Reparations Assignment, 1947, Financing Highway Improvements in Louisiana, 1955, Business in a Free Society, 1966; contbr. articles to profl. jours. Bd. dirs. area council Boy Scouts Am. Served to 1st lt. USAAF, 1943-45. Mem. Am. Assn. Collegiate Schs. Bus., Am. Econ. Assn., So. Econ. Assn. (exec. com. 1960-62), Nat. Tax Assn. (exec. com. 1960-63, editorial com. Nat. Tax Jour. 1959-62), Am. Fin. Assn., So. Fin. Assn. (pres. 1962-63), Southwestern Social Sci. Assn., Omicron Delta Kappa, Beta Gamma Sigma. Lodges: Rotary. Methodist. Office Fax: 225-922-5114.

ROSS, WILLIAM JARBOE, lawyer, director; b. Oklahoma City, May 9, 1930; s. Walter John and Bertha (Jarboe) R.; m. Mary Lillian Ryan, May 19, 1962; children: Rebecca Anne Roten, Robert Joseph, Molly Kathleen. BBA, U. Okla., 1952, LLB, 1954. Bar: Okla. 1954. Since practiced in, Oklahoma City; asst. municipal counselor Oklahoma City, 1955-60; mem. firm Rainey, Ross, Rice & Binns, 1960—, ptnr., 1965-99. Mem. admissions and grievences com. U.S. Dist. Ct. (we. dist.) Okla. Bd. visitors Coll. of Law U. Okla., St. Anthony's Hosp. Found., Harn Homestead; dir. Ethics and Excellence in Journalism Found., Inasmuch Found. Mem. Okla. Bar Assn., Okla. Heritage Assn. (vice chmn. edn. com.), The Newcomen Soc., Okla. City Golf and Country Club, Econ. Club, Rotary, Phi Alpha Delta, Beta Theta Pi, KC. Home: 6923 Avondale Ct Oklahoma City OK 73116-5008

ROSS, WILLIAM WARFIELD, lawyer; b. Washington, Oct. 3, 1926; s. W. Warfield and Vera Elfleda (Payne) R.; m. Jennie Fitch, Jan. 30, 1963; children— James, Mary, Billy; m. Nan Robertson, Sept. 25, 1999. AB, St. John's Coll., Annapolis, Md., 1948; LL.B., Yale U., 1951. Bar: D.C. 1951. Legal asst. Exec. Office Pres. Harry S. Truman, 1952-53, Pres. Dwight D. Eisenhower, 1953; atty. appellate sect. civil div. Dept. Justice, Washington, 1954-57; asst. to solicitor FPC, 1957-59; ptnr. Wald, Harkrader & Ross, 1963-87, Pepper, Hamilton & Scheetz, Washington, 1987-91. Adj. prof. Cornell U. Grad. Sch. Bus. and Pub. Adminstrn., 1977-80; chmn. D.C. Council Commn. on Bd. Appeals and Rev. of D.C. Govt., 1972 Chmn. Nat. Capital area ACLU, 1966-68; chmn. audit hearing panel Title I ESEA of 1965, 1976-80. Served with USN, 1945-46 Mem. ABA (chmn. sect. adminstrv. law 1978-79), Bar Assn. D.C. (chmn. adminstrv. law sect. 1968-69, gov. 1969-70), D.C. Bar, Fed. Bar Assn., Fed. Energy Bar Assn. (contbr. articles to jour.). Home: 4978 Sentinel Dr Apt 303 Bethesda MD 20816-3573

ROSSAVIK, IVAR KRISTIAN, obstetrician, gynecologist; b. Stavanger, Rogaland, Norway, Nov. 3, 1936; came to U.S., 1982; s. Andreas and Bergit (Berge) R.; divorced; children: Line, Anne Britt, Kirsten, Solveig; m. Claudia Lagos, May 23, 1987; children: Claudia Kristina, Eevar Benjamin. MD, U. Oslo, 1962, PhD, 1982. Pvt. practice, medicine, Stavanger, 1974; asst. chief, acting chmn. U. Tromsoe, Norway, 1974-76; clin. fellow Nat. Hosp. of Norway, Oslo, 1976-81, Norwegian Radium Hosp./U. Oslo, 1981-82; pvt. practice Oslo, 1977-82; rsch. asst. prof. Baylor Coll. Medicine, Houston, 1983-86; assoc. prof. U. Okla., Oklahoma City, 1987-93, prof., 1993—2001; owner, cons. Clinica Guadalupana, 2001—. Dir. Ultrasound Svcs., Dept. Ob/Gyn., U. Okla. Inventor Rossavik Growth Equation, 1980; author: (textbook) Practical Obstetrical Ultrasound: With and Without A Computer, 1991 (Italian translation 1998). Lt. Royal Norwegian Navy, 1964-65. Mem. Okla. Sheriffs' Assn. (hon.). Lutheran. Avocations: ultrasonography technology, computer technology, fetal growth studies. E-mail: iros@ionet.net.

ROSSBACH, PHILIP EDWARD, civil engineer; b. Omaha, Oct. 6, 1959; s. Joseph James and Mary Carolyn (Clauser) R.; m. Therese Ann La Croix, July 31, 1981; children: Diane, Dan, Lauren. BS, U. Nebr., 1981. Registered profl. engr. Nebr., Kans.; registered structural engr. Mass. Structural engr. Gibbs-Hill, Inc., Omaha, 1981-82, Henningson, Durham and Richardson, Omaha, 1982-83; bridge engr. HDR Engring., Inc., 1983-88, sect. mgr., bridges, 1988—. ASCE rep. Roundtable Profl. Engring. Socs., Omaha, 1991-93. Judge Met. Engring. and Sci. Fair, Omaha, 1987-93. Named Young Engr. of Yr. Nebr. Soc. Profl. Engr., 1990. Mem. Am. Soc. Civil Engrs. (pres. Nebr. sect. 1991, v.p. Nebr. sect. 1989, dir. Nebrs. sect. 1988, treas. Nebr. sect. 1987), Nebr. Chpt. of Am. Concrete Inst., Nat. Soc. Profl. Engrs. Office: HDR Engring Inc 8404 Indian Hills Dr Omaha NE 68114-4098

ROSSBACHER, JOHN ROBERT, retired insurance broker, musician, writer; b. Corry, Pa., Sept. 3, 1929; s. Richard Homer and Ila Lenore (Irwin) R.; m. Nancy Fray, July 28, 1951; children: Paula L. Gordon, Becky A. Morgan. BMus, Mansfield (Pa.) U., 1951. Drummer We Three Trio, Mansfield, 1948-51; tympanist 5th Army Divsn. Band, Ft. Riley, Kans., 1951-53; broker Ins. Svc., Corry, 1953-66; ptnr.er Rossbacher Ins. Svc., 1966-69, owner, 1969-85; drummer 40s Plus Dance Band, 1985-89. Ptnr. Janross Studios, Corry and Erie, Pa., 1972-93; mem. adv. bd. Marine Bank, PNC Bank, Corry, 1970-90; mem. Aetna Life and Casualty Ins. Adv. Coun., Pitts., 1973-81, Aetna Nat. Adv. Coun., Hartford, Conn., 1973. Contbr. articles to profl. and arts jours., 1972—; Tympanist Erie Philharm., 1960-61; drummer 4 Jacks and a Queen, Erie, 1965-69; condr. City Band, Corry, 1954-58, Die Festliche Sanger, Corry, 1955-65, Corry Choral Soc., 1970-82, St. Paul's Luth. Ch. Choir, Corry, 1954-73; composed works for choir and brass, Mansfield U., 1970, 73, 74; author (poetry) in anthologies: Poets on the Park, Collection I, 1997, Collection II, 1998, Collection III, 1999, Florida State Poets Anthology 17, 18, 1999, 2000, 2001, 2002. Chmn. Parking Authority, Corry, 1962-74, United Fund Drive, Corry, 1969, Cancer Fund Drive, Corry, 1970; v.p. Philharm. Bd., Erie, 1972-78, Kiwanis, Corry, 1972-78, Indsl. Devel. Commn., Corry, 1973-74, treas., 1971-73, pres., 1979-81; founder, pres. Fine Arts Coun., Corry, 1971-77; bd. dirs. YMCA, Corry, 1966-72, pres., 1971-72; councilman St. Paul's Luth. Ch., Corry, 1968-74. Sgt. U.S. Army, 1951-53. Named Good Citizen of Yr., Corry Area Life Underwriters, 1975; recipient 3d pl. award Stained Glass Show, Jekyll Island, Ga., 1984. Mem. Masons (3d degree, past high priest), Shriners, Moose, York Rite, Scottish Rite. Episcopalian. Avocations: writing, playing hazz harmonica, boating, conducting sing-a-longs at retirement homes. Home: 9288 SE 178th Delia Pl Lady Lake FL 32162-0830 E-mail: jrossbach1@aol.com.

ROSSBACHER, LISA ANN, university president, geology educator, writer; b. Fredericksburg, Va., Oct. 10, 1952; d. Richard Irwin and Jean Mary (Dearing) R.; m. Dallas D. Rhodes, Aug. 4, 1978. BS, Dickinson Coll., 1975; MA, SUNY, Binghamton, 1978, Princeton U., 1979, PhD, 1983. Cons. Republic Geothermal, Santa Fe Springs, Calif., 1979-81; asst. prof. geology Whittier (Calif.) Coll., 1982-84, Calif. State Poly. U., Pomona, 1984-86, assoc. prof. geol. sci., 1986-91, assoc. v.p. acad. affairs, 1987-93, prof. geol. sci., 1991-93; v.p. acad. affairs, dean faculty Whittier (Calif.) Coll., 1993-95; dean of coll., prof. geology Dickinson Coll., Carlisle, Pa., 1995-98; pres. So. Poly. State U., Marietta, Ga., 1998—. Vis. researcher U. Uppsala, Sweden, 1984. Author: Career Opportunities in Geology and the Earth Sciences, 1983, Recent Revolutions in Geology, 1986; (with Rex Buchanan) Geomedia, 1988; columnist Geotimes, 1988—; contbr. articles to profl. jours. Recipient scholarship Ministry Edn. of Finland, Helsinki, 1984; grantee NASA, 1983-94. Fellow mem. AAAS (geol. nominating com. 1984-87, chair-elect geology and geography sect. 1997-98, chair 1998-99, past chair 1999-2000); mem. Geol. Soc. Am., Sigma Xi (grantee 1976). Office: So Poly State U 1100 S Marietta Pkwy SE Marietta GA 30060-2855

ROSSE, THERESE MARIE, reading and special education educator, curriculum, school improvement and instruction consultant; b. Orleans, Nebr., Dec. 23, 1936; d. Ford Huston and Bertha Therese (Flamming) McCoy; m. John A. Rosse, Apr. 19, 1958 (div. 1979); children: Michelle, John, Robert, David. BS, Coll. St. Mary, Omaha, 1972; MS, U. Nebr., Omaha, 1973; PhD, U. Nebr., Lincoln, 1994. Cert. tchr. reading, spo. edn., history, elem. Tchr., reading clinician Omaha Pub. and Parochial Schs., 1958-72; grad. asst. U. Nebr., Omaha, 1972-73; reading cons. Ralston (Nebr.) Pub. Schs., 1973-75; reading and spl. edn. cons. Area Edn. Agy. 13, Council Bluffs, Iowa, 1975—. Adj. prof. Buena Vista Coll., Storm Lake, Iowa, 1976-79, U. Nebr. Omaha, 1978-79, Marycrest Coll., Danveport, Iowa, 1985—, N.W. Mo. State U., Maryville, 1985—, Met. Cmty. Coll., Omaha, 1990—; tester Ednl. Testing Svcs., Princeton, N.J., 1972-73; cons. Creative Cons., Muncie, Ind., 1973-75, Midlands Ednl. Cons., Omaha, 1974-75; rschr. Iowa Dept. Pub. Instrn., Dept. Edn., Des Moines, 1980-82, advisor, 1987-89; text reviewer Scott Foresman, Glenview, Ill., 1980-82, Zepher Press, Tucson, Ariz.; evaluation team North Ctrl. Accreditation Assn., 1980-82. Author: Viewing Reading Comprehension as a Problem Solving Skill: Approaches to Developing Comprehensive Strategies, 1982, Breaking the Language Barrier of Mathematical Thought Problems, 1982, A Grounded Theory of An Organizaed Learner; A Balanced Ecological System, 1994. Advisor Mayor's Commn. on Status of Women Edn. Divsn., Omaha, 1973-75; trustee Links-for-the-Future. Mem. ASCD, Internat. Reading Assn. (state bd. sec. 1973-75, v.p. local chpt., state co-chairperson, reading chairperson), Am. Ednl. Rsch. Assn. (sec.), The Brain and Edn., Coun. Exceptional Children, Phi Delta Kappa, Phi Delta Gamma (pres. local chpt. 1979-80, mem. nat. bd. 1980-82), Phi Alpha Theta. Avocations: travel, reading, classical music and art, writing/research, tennis. Home: 817 N 131st Plz Omaha NE 68154-4037

ROSSELL, CHRISTINE HAMILTON, political science educator; b. Bklyn., Jan. 22, 1945; d. Robert Hamilton and Ann (Bezold) R.; 1 child, Elise. AB, UCLA, 1967; MA, Calif. State U., Northridge, 1969; PhD, U. So. Calif., 1974. Asst. prof. Pitzer Coll., Claremont, Calif., 1973-74; rsch. assoc. U. Md., College Park, 1974-75; asst. prof. Boston U., 1975-82, assoc. prof., 1982-89, prof., 1989—, chair dept. polit. sci., 1992-95. Vis. asst. prof. Duke U., Durham, N.C., 1977-78, U. Calif., Berkeley, 1981; vis. lectr. Canberra (Australia) Coll., 1985; vis. fellow Pub. Policy Inst. Calif., 1999. Author: (with others) Strategies for Effective Desegregation, 1983, Carrot or Stick for School Desegregation, 1990, Bilingual Education in Massachusetts: The Emperor Has No Clothes, 1996;; co-editor: Consequences of School Desegregation, 1983, Sch. Desegregation in the 21st Century, 2002. Mem. Citywide Coord. Coun., Boston, 1976-77. Home: 44 High St Brookline MA 02445-7707 Office: Boston U Dept Polit Sci 232 Bay State Rd Boston MA 02215-1403 E-mail: crossell@bu.edu.

ROSSEN, JORDAN, lawyer; b. Detroit, June 13, 1934; s. Nathan Paul and Rebecca (Rizy) R.; m. Susan Friebert, Mar. 24, 1963 (div. June 1972); 1 child, Rebecca; m. M. Elizabeth Bunn, Jan. 3, 1981; children— N. Paul, Jordan David BA, U. Mich., 1956; JD, Harvard U., 1959. Bar: Mich. 1960, U.S. Dist. Ct. (ea. dist.) Mich. 1960, U.S. Ct. Appeals (6th cir.) 1966, U.S. Supreme Ct. 1966, U.S. Ct. Appeals (7th cir.) 1974, U.S. Ct. Appeals D.C. cir. 1984, U.S. Ct. Appeals (3rd cir.) 1987, N.Y. 1998, U.S. Dist. Ct. (ea. and so. dists.) N.Y. 1999. Assoc. Sullivan, Elmer, Eames & Moody, Detroit, 1960-62; assoc. Sugar & Schwartz, 1962-64; asst. gen. counsel UAW, 1964-74, assoc. gen. counsel, 1974-83, gen. counsel, 1983-98; of counsel Meyer, Suozzi, English and Klein, N.Y.C., N.Y., 1998—; prof. labor studies Wayne State U., 2000—. Vice pres. N.P. Rossen Agy., Inc., Detroit, 1960-83; gen. counsel Mich. Health & Social Security Research Inst., Inc., Detroit, 1965-83; dir. UAW Job Devel. & Tng. Corp., Detroit, 1984-90. Editor: Mich. Bar Labor Section Publication, 1961-64. Contbr. articles to profl. jours. Pres. Young Democrats, Mich., 1963-65; chmn. Americans for Democratic Action, Mich., 1966-68; chmn. Voter Registration Dem. Party, Mich., 1977. Recipient Human Rights award City of

Detroit, 1978 Mem. ABA, Mich. Bar Assn., Nat. Bar Assn., Fed. Bar Assn., Wolverine Bar Assn., Women Lawyers Assn., Lawyers Guild Jewish. Office: 1350 Broadway Ste 501 New York NY 10018-7705 Fax: 212-239-1311. E-mail: jrossen@msek.com.

ROSSEN, WILLIAM R. engineering educator; b. Washington, June 29, 1954; s. Henry R. and Betty C. Rossen; m. Janice A. Rossen, July 24, 1976. SB in Chem. Engring., MIT, 1976; PhD in Chem. Engring., U. Minn., 1982. Registered profl. engr., Tex. Rsch. engr Chevron Oil Field Rsch., La Habra, Calif., 1982—89; asst. prof. dept. petroleum and geosystems engring. U. Tex., Austin, Tex., 1989—95, assoc. prof. dept. petroleum and geosystem engring., 1995—2001, prof. dept. petroleum and geosystems engring., 2001—. Contbr. articles to profl. jours. Mem.: AIChE, Soc. Petroleum Engrs. (editor, Disting. Achievement award for petroleum engrs. 2002). Office: Dept Petroleum and Geosystems Engring Univ Tex Austin Austin TX 78712-1061

ROSSER, ALVIN RAYMON, artist; b. Port Clinton, Ohio, July 5, 1928; s. Samuel Webster and Reba Della Rosser; m. Barbara Emma Roth, June 10, 1953; children: Rachelle Karen, Jill Allyn. BFA, Ohio U., 1950, MFA, 1953; postgrad., Hans Hofmann Sch. of Art, N.Y.C., 1953—54. Comml. artist Mutual Broadcasting System, N.Y.C., 1954; art tchr. Chagrin Falls H.S., Ohio, 1955; instr. Lehigh U., Bethlehem, Pa., 1956—58; artists' rep. Gerard Agy., N.Y.C., 1958—60; art dir. Topper Toy Co., Elizabeth, NJ, 1961—62; scenic designer Harnick-Adams Prodns., N.Y.C., 1963—66; art tchr. Sparta Bd. of Edn., NJ, 1966—89. Exhibited in group shows at Ward Eggleston Gallery, N.Y.C., 1953, Roko Gallery, 1953, Koltnow Gallery, 1953—57, Cleve. Mus. Art, 1954, N.Y.C. Ctr., 1954, 1955, 1956, 1957, Jersey City Mus., 1959, Montclair Mus., 1967; artist (one-man shows) Ohio U., 1953, Lehigh U., 1955, Paper Mill Playhouse , N.J., 1960, featured artist N.J. State Fair, 2000, Artery Gallery, Milford, Pa., 2000—02. Trustee, v.p. Sussex County Arts Coun., Newton, NJ, 1970—76. Cpl. U.S. Army, 1950—52. Recipient Emerson Poetry award 1st prize, Ohio U., 1954, Skylands Best in Show award, Sussex County Arts Coun., 1989, Skylands Select Best in Show award, 2001. Avocations: fishing, gardening, bee keeping, pool hustling, ventriloquy. Mailing: PO Box 76 Sparta NJ 07871-0076

ROSSER, ANNETTA HAMILTON, composer; b. Jasper, Fla., Aug. 28, 1913; d. Carlos Calvin and Jermai Reuben (Gilbert) Hamilton; m. John Barkley Rosser, Sept. 7, 1935 (dec. Sept. 1989); children: Edwenna Merryday, John Barkley Jr. BM, Fla. State U., 1932. Cert. tchr., Fla. Tchr. music Kirby-Smith Jr. High Sch., Jacksonville, Fla., 1932-35; 1st violinist Santa Monica (Calif.) Symphony, 1949-50; concertmaster Ithaca (N.Y.) Chamber Orch., 1948-56, Cornell Univ. Orch., Ithaca, 1948-56, soloist, 1957; 1st violinist Princeton (N.J.) Symphony, 1959-61; concertmaster Madison (Wis.) Symphony Orch., 1963-66, 1st violinist, 1967-82. Composer of over 100 vocal and instrumental compositions including Meditations on Cross, song cycle for 2 voices, flute and piano, 1976, An Offering of Song, book of 48 songs, 1977, Songs of a Nomad Flute, song cycle for soprano, flute and piano, 1978, Six Songs of the T'ang Dynasty for soprano and violin, 1983, Nocturne for violin and piano, 1989, Trio for flute, violin and piano, 1991, Scherzo for flute ensemble, 1991, (book of 21 songs) Another Offering of Song, 1998. Bd. dirs. Madison Opera Guild, 1972-86, Madison Civic Music Assn., 1983-85; past pres. Madison Symphony Orch. League, Ithaca Federated Music Club, Ithaca Composers Club; bd. dirs. Madison Art Ctr., 1979-83, Madison Woman of Distinction, 1980; bd. dirs. Madison Civics Club, 1976-79, pres., 1977-78; pres. Art League Madison Art Ctr., 1980-82. Recipient Sr. Svc. award Rotary Club, 1994; original music manuscripts and programs were added to archives of U. Wis.-Madison Music Libr., 1996. Mem. AAUW, Internat. Alliance for Women in Music, Wis. Acad. Scis., Arts, and Letters, Univ. League, Univ. League Bird Study Group, Madison Club, Madison Federated Music Club, Wis. Alliance of Composers, Wis. Acad. Scis., Arts, and Letters, PEO, Phi Kappa Phi, Pi Kappa Lambda, Sigma Alpha Iota. Republican. Presbyterian. Avocations: Chinese snuff bottles, English brass rubbings, birding. Home: 4209 Manitou Way Madison WI 53711-3703

ROSSER, DAVID PENDLETON, chemical engineer; b. Bethesda, Md., Sept. 27, 1945; s. John Hodge and Jewel Maxine (Hutchins) R.; m. Patricia Leigh Crabill, Aug. 5, 1967; children: Christopher, Andrew, Amy, Leanna. BSChemE, U. Md., 1967. Devel. engr. Celanese Corp., Cumberland, Md., 1967-71, Shelby, N.C., 1971-73, project engr., 1973-75, product engr., 1975-77, engring. group leader, 1977-78, new product engr., 1978-81, process engr. Summit, N.J., 1981-82, tech. svc. engr., 1982-84, prodn. supr., 1984-86; sr. mfg. engr. Hoechst Celanese Corp., Charlotte, N.C., 1986-92, staff engr., 1992-99, Celgard, Inc., 1999-2001, sect. leader, 2001—. Editor Charlotte Baha'i Nightingale newsletter, 1994-97 Del. Nat. Baha'i Conv., 1981, 82, 89; pres. Assn. Religious Orgns., Plainfield, N.J., 1986; chmn. Spiritual Assembly Baha'is, North Plainfield, N.J., 1984-86, Charlotte, N.C., 1988-89, treas., 1989-99; bd. dirs. Hoechst Celanese-Winterfield Elem. Sch. Partnership, 1995-97. Mem. AIChE (treas. ctrl. Carolinas sect. 1992—), Soc. Plastics Engrs. (sr.), Soc. Mfg. Engrs. (sr., cert. mgr. technologist, cert. mfg. engr.), N.C. Nature Conservancy, Charlotte Area Clergy Assn. Avocations: basketball, stamp collecting. Home: 463 Peaceful Creek Dr York SC 29745-6388 Office: Celgard Inc 13800 S Lakes Dr Charlotte NC 28273-6738

ROSSER, EDWIN MICHAEL, mortgage company executive; b. Denver, Oct. 11, 1940; s. Edwin Michael and Anne (Ratliff) R.; m. Keren Call, July 17, 1969; children: Kevin, William. BS, Colo. State U., 1964; MA, U. No. Colo., 1974. Cert. mortgage banker. Mktg. officer United Bank Mortgage, Denver, 1968-74; dir. nat. accounts PMI Mortgage Ins. Co., 1974-85; v.p. Moore Mortgage Co., 1985-87, Pacific First Mortgage Corp., Englewood, Colo., 1987-89; 1st v.p. 1st Nat. Bank, San Francisco, 1990-93; v.p. nat. accounts United Guaranty Corp., 1993—. Bd. dirs. Rocky Mtn. Women's Inst. Photographer represented in Denver Art Mus., The Buffalo in Winter, (1st place award 1981). Steering com. Blueprint for Colo., Govs. Unified Housing Task Force; mem. Colo. Housing Coun. (chmn. 1986-87); bd. dirs. Colo. State Found.; mem. adv. bd. Arapahoe County Open Space and Trails, 1999—; mem. Colo. Land Use Commn., 1999. Mem. Am. Planning Assn., Soc. of Cert. Mortgage Bankers (chmn.), Mortgage Bankers Assn. Am. (cert., bd. govs. 1986-90, state and local achievement award 1986, Ernest P. Schumacher award 1988, membership achievement award 1995, Burton Wood Legis. Svc. award), Colo. Mortgage Bankers Assn. (bd. dirs. 1979-88, pres. 1986, E.C. Spelman award 1978, Lifetime Achievement award 1998), Colo. Assn. Commerce and Industry, Denver Nat. Soc. Real Estate Fin., Mus. Natural History, Denver C. of C., Rocky Mtn. Mutual Housing Assn. (bd. dirs.), Ctr. of Fin. Real Estate (bd. dirs.), Colo. State U. Alumni Assn. (nat. pres. 1985, bd. dirs. 1979-87, mem. found. bd. 1987-91, 93-2000, Honor Alumnus 1984, ha Sasso award Dept. Athletics 1993), City Club Denver, Commonwealth Club. Calif., Nat. Soc. for Real Estate Fin. (CRF designation 1997), Societas Internat. Real Estate Fin. Found. (adv. bd.), Colo. State U. Henry Alumni (Svc. award 2000), Alpha Sigma Gamma. Republican. Roman Catholic. Avocations: competitive swimming, photography. Home: 12478 E Amherst Cir Aurora CO 80014-3306 Office: United Guaranty Residential Ins Co 6312 S Fiddlers Green Cir Englewood CO 80111-4943 E-mail: emrcmb@aol.com.

ROSSER, JAMES MILTON, academic administrator; b. East St. Louis, Ill., Apr. 16, 1939; s. William M. and Mary E. (Bass) R.; 1 child, Terrence. BA, So. Ill. U., 1962, MA, 1963, PhD, 1969. Diagnostic bacteriologist Holden Hosp., Carbondale, Ill., 1961-63; rsch. bacteriologist Eli Lilly & Co., Indpls., 1963-66; coordinator Black Am. studies, instr. health edn. So. Ill. U., Carbondale, 1968-69, asst. prof. Black Am. studies dir., 1969-70, asst. to chancellor, 1970; assoc. vice chancellor for acad. affairs U. Kans., Lawrence, 1970-74, assoc. prof. edn., pharmacology and toxicology, 1971-74; vice chancellor dept. higher edn. State of N.J., Trenton, 1974-79, acting chancellor, 1977; pres., prof. health care mgmt. Calif. State U., Los Angeles, 1979—. Tech. resource panel Ctr. for Research and Devel. in Higher Edn., U. Calif., Berkeley, 1974-76; health maintenance orgn. com. Health Planning Coun., State of N.J., 1975-79; standing com. on R & D bd. trustees Ednl. Testing Service, 1976-77; steering com. and task force on retention of minorities in engring. Assembly of Engring. NRC, 1975-78; mem. Bd. Med. Examiners, State of N.J., 1978-79; vis. faculty Inst. Mgmt. of Lifelong Edn., Grad. Sch. Edn., Harvard U., 1979; mem. Calif. State U. Trustees Spl. Long Range Fin. Planning Com., 1982-87; mem. Am. Coun. on Edn., 1979—, AFL/CIO Labor Higher Edn. Coun., 1983—, Nat. Commn. Higher Edn. Issues, 1981-82; mem. The Calif. Achievement Coun., 1983-89, strategic adv. counc. Coll. and Univs. Systems Exchange, 1988-91; bd. dirs. Am. Humanities Coun., So. Calif. Am. Humanics, Inc. Coun., United Calif. Bank, Edison Internat., Fedco, Inc.; task force on equality and fairness Texaco, 1999—. Author: An Analysis of Health Care Delivery, 1977. Exec. bd., chmn. varsity scouting program L.A. area coun. Boy Scouts Am., 1980—; bd. dirs. Hispanic Urban Ctr., L.A., 1979—, L.A. Urban League, 1982-95, Cmty. TV of So. Calif., Sta. KCET, 1980-89, 98—, United Way, L.A., 1980-91, Orthopaedic Hosp., 1983-86, L.A. Philharm. Assn., 1986-99, Nat. Health Found., 1990—; mem. Citizen's Adv. Coun. Congl. Caucus Sci. and Tech., 1983—; mem. performing arts coun./edn. coun. Music Ctr., 1984—; minority bus. task force Pacific Bell, 1985-86; bd. govs. Nat. ARC, 1986-91, Mayor's Blue Ribbon Task Force on Drugs, City of L.A., 1988, L.A. Annenberg Met. Project, 1994-2001; Nat. Adv. Coun. on Aging, 1989-93; bd. trustees Woodrow Wilson Nat. Fellowship Found., 1993—; bd. advisors Historically Black Colls. and Univs. and Minority Insts., Dept. Air Force, 1997-2001; bd. dirs. Ams. for the Arts, 1991—; mem. L.A. Adv. Alliance, Pasadena Tournament of Roses, 2000—; mem. Action Forum on Diversity in the Engring. Workforce, Nat. Acad. Engring., 2000—; mem. Calif. Coun. on Sci. and Tech., 1999--; mem. campaign adv. com. The Audubon Ctr. L.A., 2001--. NSF fellow, 1961; NDEA fellow, 1967-68; recipient award of recognition in Edn. Involvement for Young Achievers, 1981, Pioneer of Black Hist. Achievement award Brotherhood Crusade, 1981, Alumni Achievement award So. Ill. U., 1982, Friend of Youth award Am. Humanics, Inc., 1985, Leadership award Dept. Higher Edn. Ednl. Equal Opportunity Fund Program, 1989, Medal of Excellence Gold State Minority Found., 1990, Take Charge of Learning Success award Inst. for Redesign of Learning. Mem. Calif. C. of C. (bd. dirs. 1993—), Alhambra C. of C. (bd. dirs. 1979—), Los Angeles C. of C. (bd. dirs. 1985-90), Am. Assn. State Colls. and Univs., Kappa Delta Pi, Phi Kappa Phi. Roman Catholic. Office: Calif State U Office of Pres 5151 State University Dr Los Angeles CA 90032-4226

ROSSER, JOHN BARKLEY, JR. economics educator; b. Ithaca, N.Y., Apr. 12, 1948; s. John Barkley and Annetta Louise (Hamilton) R.; m. Sue A. Vilhauer, Aug. 31, 1968 (div. 1979); children: Meagan Rebecca, Caitlin Elizabeth; m. Marina R. Vcherashnaya, May 24, 1987; 1 child: Alexandra Ashley. BA, U. Wis., 1969, MA, 1972, PhD, 1976. Project specialist Inst. Environ. Studies, Madison, Wis., 1972-75; planning analyst Dept. Natural Resources, 1975-76; prof. econs. James Madison U., Harrisonburg, Va., 1977—, Kirby L. Kramer Jr. chair of bus. adminstrn., 1996—. Author: From Catastrophe to Chaos: A General Theory of Economic Discontinuities, 1991, (with M.V. Rosser) Comparative Economics in a Transforming World Economu, 1996; editor Jour. Econ. Behavior and Orgn., 2002-; contbr. articles to profl. jours. Mem. Am. Econs. Assn., So. Econs. Assn., N.Y. Acad. Scis. Home: 236 Franklin St Harrisonburg VA 22801-4019 Office: James Madison Univ MSC0204 Dept Economics Harrisonburg VA 22807-0001 E-mail: rosserjb@jmu.edu.

ROSSER, RICHARD FRANKLIN, higher education consultant; b. Arcanum, Ohio, July 16, 1929; s. Harold Arm and Margaret (Whitacre) R.; m. Donna Eyssen., Mar. 21, 1951; children— Eric, Carl, Edward. BA, Ohio Wesleyan U., 1951; M.P.A., Syracuse U., 1952, PhD, 1961. Joined U.S. Air Force, 1952, advanced through grades to col., 1968; prof. polit. sci. U.S. Air Force Acad., Colorado Springs, Colo., 1959-73, head dept., 1967-73, ret., 1973; prof. polit. sci., dean Albion (Mich.) Coll., 1973-77; pres. DePauw U., Greencastle, Ind., 1977-86, chancellor, 1986; pres. Nat. Assn. Ind. Colls. and Univs., Washington, 1986-93; cons. in higher edn. pvt. practice, Racine, Wis., 1993—. Author: An Introduction to Soviet Foreign Policy, 1969; Contbr. articles to profl. jours. Mem. univ. senate United Meth. Ch., 1980-84; mem. spl. commn. of Chief of Staff on Honor Code U.S. Mil. Acad., 1989; bd. visitors Air U., 1991-94; bd. trustees Ohio Wesleyan U., 1991—; mem. nat. adv. com. Instnl. Quality and Integrity, 1994—; co-chair Citizens for Librs., Grand Traverse County, 1995-96. Decorated Legion of Merit with oak leaf cluster. Mem. Phi Beta Kappa, Omicron Delta Kappa. Presbyterian. Home and Office: 31 Sumac Dr Brunswick ME 04011

ROSSET, BARNET LEE, JR. publisher; b. Chgo., May 28, 1922; s. Barnet Lee and Mary (Tansey) R.; m. Joan Mitchell, 1950 (div. 1952); m. Hannelore Eckert, Aug. 1953 (div. 1957); 1 child, Peter; m. Cristine Agnini, Mar. 11, 1965 (div. 1979); children— Tansey, Beckett; m. Elisabeth Krug, 1980 (div. 1991; 1 child, Chantal. Ph.B., U. Chgo., 1947; BA New Sch. Social Research, N.Y.C., 1952. Pub., editor Grove Press, Inc., 1951-86, Evergreen Rev., Rosset and Co., Inc., 1957-73, Blue Moon Books, Inc., N.Y.C., 1987-98, Evergreen Rev. Inc., 1998—, Foxrock, Inc., 1995—. Served to 1st lt. Signal Corps AUS, 1942-46. Recipient Ninth Pub. citation PEN Am. Ctr., 1988, Poor Richard's award Small Press Ctr., 1999, Commandeur De L'Ordre Des Arts et Des Lettres, French Govt., 1999, Nat. Book Critics Cir. Lifetime Achievement award, 2001, Curtis Benjamin award Assn. Am. Pubs., 2001. Mem. PEN, Overseas Press Club. Office: 61 4th Ave New York NY 10003-5204 E-mail: evergreen@nyc.rr.com.

ROSSEY, PAUL WILLIAM, school superintendent, university president; b. Richmond, Ind., July 7, 1926; s. Chris C. and Lela (Longman) R.; m. Adelaide Elizabeth Finnegan; 1 dau., Joanne Rossey Sczubelek. BS, N.J. City Univ., 1952, Litt. D., 1971; MA, NYU, 1953, Ed.D. (Kellogg Found. fellow 1955), 1958. Head jr. sch. Peddie Sch., Hightstown, N.J., 1952-53; cons., elem. sch. instr. West Hempstead, N.Y., 1953-55; prin. elem. sch. Dobbs Ferry, 1955-58; supt. schs. Litchfield, Conn., 1958-60, Scotch Plains-Fanwood, N.J., 1960-67; dist. supt. schs. Nassau County, N.Y., 1967-69; pres. West Chester (Pa.) State U., 1969-74; supt. schs. Millburn-Short Hills, N.J., 1974-92; ret. Lectr. NYU, 1954-67 Contbr. articles to profl. jours. County dir. Boy Scouts Am.; v.p. YMCA; bd. dirs. Garbe Found., Community Fund; trustee NYU, 1970-74, The Peddie Sch., 1974-92; mem. exec. com. N.J. Coun. Edn., 1977-83. With USNR, 1944-46, USMCR, 1972-86; ret. Named Outstanding Alumnus, N.J. City U., 1962; recipient NYU medallion, 1966, Ernest O. Melby award human relations, 1970 Mem. Am. Assn. Sch. Adminstrs. (chmn. N.J. 1965-67), Am. Council Edn., Aircraft Owners and Pilots Assn., N.J. Assn. Sch. Adminstrs. (exec. com. 1964-67, 81-85), Horace Mann League U.S. (nat. pres. 1977-78), Kappa Delta Pi, Phi Delta Kappa. Clubs: Exchange (dir.), N.J. Schoolmasters. Republican. Presbyterian. Home: 219 Summit Ave Summit NJ 07901-2213

ROSSI, ALICE S. sociology educator, author; b. N.Y.C., Sept. 24, 1922; d. William A. and Emma (Winkler) Schaerr; m. Max Kitt, Dec. 1941 (div. Sept. 1951); m. Peter H. Rossi, Sept. 29, 1951; children: Peter Eric, Kristin Alice, Nina Alexis. BA, Bklyn. Coll., 1947; PhD, Columbia U., 1957; 9 hon. degrees. Rsch. assoc. Cornell U., Ithaca, N.Y., 1951-52, Harvard U., Cambridge, Mass., 1952-55, U. Chgo., 1961-67, Johns Hopkins U., Balt., 1967-69; prof. sociology Goucher Coll., 1969-74, U. Mass., Amherst, 1974-91, prof. emerita, 1991—. Author/editor: 11 books; contbr. numerous articles to profl. jours. Founder, bd. mem. NOW, 1966-70; pres. Sociologists for Women in Soc., 1971-72. Career grantee NIMH, 1965-69, rsch. grantee Rockefeller Found., Ford Found., NIH, NSF, others; CommonWealth Disting. Scholarship award, 1988. Mem. Am. Sociol. Assn. (pres. 1983-84), Ea. Sociol. Soc. (pres. 1973-74). Avocations: design, sewing, gardening, creative writing. Home: 34 Stagecoach Rd Amherst MA 01002-3527

ROSSI, ANTHONY GERALD, lawyer; b. Warren, Ohio, July 20, 1935; s. Anthony Gerald and Lena (Guarnieri) R.; m. Marilyn J. Fuller, June 22, 1957; children: Diana L., Maribeth, Anthony Gerald III. BS, John Carroll U., 1957; JD, Cath. U. Am., 1961. Bar: Ohio 1961. Ptnr. Guarnieri & Secrest, Warren, 1961—; former acting judge Warren Municipal Ct. Mem. Mahoning-Shenango Estate Planning Coun., 1968—, past sec.; past pres. Warren Olympic Club; past bd. govs. Cath. U. Am. Law Sch. Coun.; past trustee Trumbull Art Guild, Warren Civic Music Assn. Capt. Transp. Corps, AUS, 1957-65. Mem. ABA, Ohio Bar Assn., Trumbull County Bar Assn. (exec. com. 1975—, pres. 1976-77), Am. Arbitration Assn., Ohio State Bar Found., Ohio Motorist Assn. (corp. mem., trustee 1980-86, 92-98), Wolf's Club, KC, Elks, Ohio Acad. of Trial Lawyers. Home: 2500 Hidden Lakes Dr NE Warren OH 44484-4159 Office: 151 E Market St Warren OH 44481-1102

ROSSI, ENNIO C. physician, educator; b. Madison, Wis., Apr. 3, 1931; s. Joseph and Esther (D'Amelio) R.; m. Anna Maria Bianchi, June 22, 1957; children: Roberta, Marco. BA, U. Wis., 1951, MD, 1954. Diplomate Am. Bd. Internal Medicine. Intern Ohio State U. Hosps., 1954-55; resident medicine U. Wis. Hosps., 1958-61, fellow, 1961-63; instr. medicine Marquette U., Milw., 1963-64, asst. prof. medicine, 1964-66; assoc. prof. medicine Northwestern U., Chgo., 1966-72, prof. medicine, 1972-96, prof. emeritus, 1996—, chief hematology, 1967-84, chief transfusion medicine, 1984-96. V.p. med. affairs Life Source Blood Ctr., Glenview, Ill., 1988-93; vis. scientist Mario Negri Inst., Milan, 1977. Co-editor: Haemostasis and the Kidney, 1989; sr. editor: Principles of Transfusion Medicine, 1991, 2d edit., 1996. Capt. U.S. Army, 1956-58. Fulbright scholar, U.S. Dept. State, U. Rome, 1955; Nat. Heart, Lung Blood Inst. Transfusion Medicine Acad. awardee, 1983; WHO travelling fellow, 1985. Fellow ACP; mem. Am. Soc. Hematology, Am. Soc. Pharmacology and Exptl. Therapeutics, Am. Assn. Blood Banks (chmn. acad. transfusion medicine com. 1988-93), Internat. Soc. Blood Transfusion. Home: 812 Oak St Apt 302 Winnetka IL 60093-2560

ROSSI, FAUST F. lawyer, educator; b. 1932; BA, U. Tornoto, 1953; JD, Cornell U., 1960. Bar: N.Y. 1960. Tax trialy atty. Dept. Justice, Washington, 1960-61; sole practice Rochester, N.Y., 1961-66; assoc. prof. Cornell U., Ithaca, 1966-69, prof., 1970—, assoc. dean, 1973-75, Samuel S. Leibowitz prof. trial techniques, 1982—. Vis. prof. Emory U., 1990; cons. report of fed. class actions Am. Coll. of Trial Lawyers, 1971-72; cons. com. on proposed fed. rules of evidence N.Y. Trial Lawyers Assn., 1970; cons., instr. annual seminar N.Y. State Trial Judges, 1970-78; cons., instr. Nat. Inst. for Trial Advocacy, 1974-75, 80-84, 88; cons. N.Y. Law Revision Commn. Project for N.Y. Code of Evidence, 1978-80. Author: Study of the Proposed Federal Rules of Evidence, 1979, Report on Rule 23 Class Actions, 1972, The Federal Rules of Evidence, 1970, Expert Witnesses, 1991; co-author: New York Evidence, 1997; contbr. articles to profl. jours. Lt. j.g. USN. Recipient Jacobsen prize for tchg. trail advocacy, 1992. Mem. Order of Coif. Office: Cornell U Law Sch Myron Taylor Hall Ithaca NY 14853 E-mail: ffr1@cornell.edu.

ROSSI, JOSEPH ANTHONY, film and television make-up artist, educator; b. Providence, July 10, 1955; s. Michael Thomas and Jennie (Paolucci) R.; m. Christina Elliott; children: Michael Elliott, Sofia Rose. BS, R.I. Coll., 1977. Tchr. film and TV R.I. Coll., Providence, 1983-86, Salve Regina Coll., Newport, R.I., 1983—; owner, prin. Joe Rossi Makeup, Providence, 1977—, 1001 Faces, Providence, 1979—. Make-up artist to Pres. William Clinton and Hillary Rodham Clinton, V.P. Albert Gore; make-up artist Babies in Black, Goodbye, Hello, Shallow Hal, Osmosis Jones, Passionada, Prozac Nation, Me, Myself, and Irene, Bye, Bye, America, David Mamet's State and Main, Thirteen Days, Lift, The Human Stain, Pink Floyd, syndicated show Crimestoppers 800, First Person, Saturday Night Live, Rivera Live, Wide World Sports, Nat. Geographic, 1995 Skating Finals ABC-TV, Unsolved Mysteries, Providence NBC-TV, ABC-TV The Century, Peter Jennings The Century, Access Hollywood, Entertainment Tonight, News Stand, CNN, also key makeup artist on feature film prodn. Outside Providence, Universal feature Meet Joe Black, original design for world premier prodn. Philip Glass Opera, The Fall of the House of Usher, and Genet's The Balcony, at the Bolshoi Theatre, Russia; spl. make-up effects for BBC, PBS, CBS, ABC, NBC CNBC, and several nat. clients. Bd. dirs. R.I. State Coun. on Arts, 1996—. Home and Office: 137 Abbott Run Valley Rd Cumberland RI 02864-3249

ROSSI, JOSEPH O. artist, educator; b. Paterson, N.J. s. Pasquale and Marion (Stampone) R.; m. Joan O'Mara, 1949; children: Robert J., Donald J., Sharon M., Carolyn J. Student, Newark Sch. Fine-Indsl. Art, Columbia U. Instr. watercolor, oil and life drawing Newark Sch. Fine and Indsl. Art, 1946, adminstrv. asst.; instr. watercolor Art Students League, N.Y.C., 1975; instr. advt. illustration du Cret Sch. Art, Plainfield, N.J. Exhibited in group shows Am. Watercolor Soc., NAD, N.Y.C., 1979, Allied Artists, 1979, Audubon Artists, 1979, Royal Acad., London, Rockport (Mass.) Art Assn., 1979; represented in permanent collections Salmagundi Club. Norfolk (Va.) Mus., Newark Hosp.; represented by Grand Central Galleries, N.Y.C.; work reviewed in various publs. Mem. Am. Watercolor Soc. (hon., Lena Newcatle award 1979), Audubon Artists, Salmagundi Club (v.p. Malcolm Tuttle award 1974, Macowin Tuttle Oil award 1995), Allied Artists Am. (former demonstration chmn.), Soc. Illustrators, N.J. Watercolor Soc. (past v.p., award 1978, 94), North Shore Art Assn., Rockport (Mass.) Art Assn., Phila. Watercolor Soc. Home: 45 Lockwood Dr Clifton NJ 07013-1243

ROSSI, KENNETH GERARD, information systems educator; b. Brookline, Mass., Sept. 27, 1951; s. Donald Shepherd Rossi, Mary Foster Rossi; m. Josie Batin Rossi; children: Angela Hughes, Stephaniejoy Alliman, Kenneth, Jr., Jessica Ka'iulani. B Psychology, Chaminae U., 1985; MA Counseling, MS Human Resources Management and Development, Chapman U., 1992; D Edn., U. So. Calif., L.A., 1996. Mgr. career transition svcs. Resource Cons., Inc., Schofield Barracks, Hawaii, 1991—93; coord. satellite program Hawaii Pacific U., Honolulu, 1993—97; career and orgnl. career devel. tng. mgr. Resource Cons., Inc., Mountain View, Calif., 1997—98; transition counselor Right Assocs., Schofield Barracks, 1999—99; asstl prof. info. systems Hawaii Pacific U., 1999—. Vice Chair Our Lady of Perpetual Help School Board, Ewa Beach, HI, 1999—Pres. Vice chair Our Lady of Perpetual Help Sch. Bd., Ewa Beach, 1999—. Sgt. U.S. Army, 1971—91. Mem.: Project Mgmt. Inst., Soc. Info. Mgrs., Am. Acad. Mgmt. Avocations: running, weightlifting. Office: Hawaii Pacific U 1188 Fort St MP 302 Honolulu HI 96813 Business E-Mail: krossi@hpu.edu.

ROSSI, MARIO ALEXANDER, architect; b. Chgo., Apr. 9, 1931; s. Gastone J. and Irma (Giorgi) R.; m. Jo Ann Therese Kneip, Apr. 12, 1958; children: John Vincent, Lyn Ann, Paul Alexander, Mara Ann. BArch, Ill. Inst. Tech., 1955. Architect Omnimetrics, L.A., 1967-78; pvt. practice Seal Beach, Calif., 1975—. Prin. works include fin. models for Calif. Fed. Bank, L.A., First Nat. City Bank, N.Y.C., Glendale (Calif.) Fed. Bank, Wailea, Alexander and Baldwin, Hawaii. Lt. (j.g.) USN, 1955-58. Achievements include research computerized techniques in architecture and economic feasibility land development. Home and Office: 1721 Catalina Ave Seal Beach CA 90740-5710

ROSSI, MARY ANN, classicist, research scholar; b. Torrington, Conn., Jan. 25, 1931; d. George James and Virginia Angelina (Negri) R.; m. John Bruce Brackenridge, June 19, 1954; children: Sandy Rossi (dec.), Lynn, Scot, Rob Brackenridge. BA in Classics, Conn. Coll. for Women, 1952; MA in Classics, Brown U., 1959; PhD in Classics, U. London, 1982. Asst. prof. English and classics Muskingum Coll., New Concord, Ohio, 1955-59; lectr. in classics and freshman studies Lawrence U., Appleton, Wis., 1959-71; lectr. in humanities U. Wis., Green Bay, 1973-76; lectr. in Greek and Latin City Lit. Inst., London, 1973-75, 80-81; asst. prof. classics Ball State U., Muncie, Ind., 1983-86; rsch. fellow Women's Studies Rsch. Ctr. U. Wis., Madison, 1989-95; ind. scholar London and Appleton, Wis., 1995—. Regional dir., reader Latin Exams. for Advancement Placement, 1986-88. Translator articles in field, also Principia. Pres. Fox Valley Human Rights Coun., Appleton, 1976-78; mem. exec. bd. Nat. Assn. Commns. for Women, 1978-80; founder Fox Cities chpt. NOW, 1973. NEH fellow Princeton U., 1979, Am. Acad. in Rome, 1983, Stanford U., 1986; grantee NEH, U. Wis., 1991. Mem. NOW, ACLU, Archaeol. Inst. Am. (founder Appleton chpt.), Am. Classical Assn. (treas. women's classical caucus 1980-85), Amnesty Internat., So. Poverty Law Ctr., Women's Ordination Worldwide. Democrat. Achievements include research on women's ordination. Avocations: choral singing, opera, travel, tennis, research for women in religion and society. Fax: 920-730-1094. E-mail: rossibrack@aol.com.

ROSSI, NORMA J. not-for-profit executive, advocate; b. Melrose, Mass., Dec. 10, 1929; d. Andrew Steven and Marie Eleanor (Nordbo) Scott; m. Bruce A. Rossi (dec. Dec. 1992); children: Robert, Barry, Max. Degree in Nursing, Peter Bent Brigham Hosp., Boston, 1952; grad. mediation skills, S.D. Mediation Ctr., 1992; completion 4-Day Diversity tng., 1998. RN, Mass., Calif. Emergency rm. nurse various hosps., Boston, Modesto, Calif., 1953-75, San Diego, 1962-73. Founder, vol. exec. dir. San Diego Coalition for Homeless, 1988—; mem. Citizens Police Rev. Bd., San Diego, 1994—98; bd. dirs. City of San Diego Human Rels., 1991. Named hon. educator, St. Joseph's Indian Sch., 1997; recipient Leadership award, San Diego Hunger Coalition, 2000, Seahorse award, City of San Diego, 1992, Leadership award, Channel 10, 1999, 2000, Appreciation of Svc. award for serving homeless, poor and needy, Uptown Interfaith, 1995, Spl. Commendation for continued commitment to make San Diego a better place to live, City Coun., 2001, Say award for making a difference in families in San Diego, 2001, Outstanding Citizen of Yr., Iota Chi chpt. Sigma Chi, 1995. Office: San Diego Coalition for Homeless 4101 University Ave San Diego CA 92105-1418 E-mail: Rossinorma@aol.com.

ROSSI, NORMA M. management consultant; b. N.Y.C., July 23, 1947; d. Attilio G. and Laura (Restani) R. BA, CCNY, 1970; Masters, New Sch. Social Rsch., 1988. Dir. corp. quality Met. Life Ins. Co., N.Y.C., 1970—. Sec. Internat. Svc. Quality Assn., 1991—. Co-author: At the Service Quality Frontier, 1993; author: (chpts.) Service Quality Handbook, 1993, Total Quality Management, 1994; contbr. articles to profl. jours. Recipient Cert. of Appreciation, QUIS, 1994. Mem. ASTD, Human Resources Planning Soc. Roman Catholic. Avocations: opera, theater. Home: 260 Garth Rd Apt 8b4 Scarsdale NY 10583-4053 Office: Met Life Ins Co 1 Madison Ave New York NY 10010-3603

ROSSI, PAUL ANDREW, artist, mosaicist; b. Boston, Mar. 13, 1957; s. Roberto Benito and Helen Evengeline Rossi; m. Fabienne Jacqueline Petit, Dec. 6, 1986; children: Rossi, Maxim, Jeremy Rossi. BFA in Painting, U. Conn., 1979. Exhibited in solo shows at Galerie de Lappe, Paris, 1988, Space II XI, N.Y.C., 1991, Greene Gallery, Guilford, Conn., 1992, Adirondack Lakes Ctr. for Arts, Blue Mountain Lake, N.Y., 1995, Hancock House Mus., Ticonderoga, N.Y., 1999; group shows include Salon d'Automne, Grand Palais, Paris, 1989, Museo della Civilta Romana, Rome, 1989, Centre Georges Pompidou, Paris, Lake Placid (N.Y.) Ctr. for the Arts, 1996, others; represented in collections at Sterling and Francine Clark Art Inst., Williamstown, Mass., Homer Babbidge Libr., U. Conn., Storrs, also in France, Germany, Spain, Italy, Eng., Ireland, Switzerland, India, Japan, Can. and other countries. Grantee N.Y. Found. for Arts, 1998. Mem. N.Y. Artists Equity Assn. Mem. Green Party. Home: PO Box 503 Westport NY 12993 E-mail: rossim@westelcom.com.

ROSSI, PETER HENRY, sociology educator; b. N.Y.C., Dec. 27, 1921; s. Peter Maxim and Elizabeth (Porcelli) R.; m. Alice Schaerr, Sept. 29, 1951; children: Peter Eric, Kristin Alice, Nina Alexis. BS, CCNY, 1943; PhD, Columbia, 1951. Research asso. Bur. Applied Social Research, Columbia U., 1947- 51; asst. prof. Harvard U., 1951-55; prof. dept. sociology U. Chgo., 1955-67; dir. Nat. Opinion Research Center, 1960-67; prof. dept. social relations Johns Hopkins, 1967-74, chmn. dept., 1967-70; dir. research Center for Met. Planning and Research, 1972-74; prof. sociology, dir. Social and Demographic Research Inst., U. Mass., Amherst, 1974-92, Stuart A. Rice prof. sociology, dir., 1984-92, prof. emeritus, 1992—; faculty assoc. Chapin Hall U. Chgo., 1994—. Author: Why Families Move, 1956, The Politics of Urban Renewal, 1962, The Education of Catholic Americans, 1966, New Media and Education, 1967, Ghetto Revolts, 1970, Cities Under Siege, 1971, Evaluating Social Programs, 1972, Roots of Urban Discontent, 1974, Reforming Public Welfare, 1976, Prison Reform and State Elites, 1977, Evaluation: A Systematic Approach, 1979, Money, Work & Crime, 1980, After the Clean-up, 1980, Social Science and Natural Hazards, 1981, Measuring Social Judgements, 1982, Natural Hazards and Public Choice, 1982, Under the Gun, 1983, Applied Sociology, 1983, Without Shelter, 1989, Down and Out in America, 1989, Of Human Bonding, 1990, Just Punishments, 1997, Feeding the Poor, 1999; editor: Am. Jour. Sociology, 1957-58; assoc. editor: Am. Sociol. Rev, 1957-60, Am. Sociologist, 1964-66; editor: Social Sci. Research, 1972-89; contbr. articles to profl. and popular jours. Served with AUS, 1942-45. Recipient Alvah and Gunnar Myrdal award for contbns. to evaluation research, 1981; Commonwealth award for contbns. to sociology, 1985; faculty research grantee Social Sci. Research Council, 1959; Carnegie sr. fellow, 1965 Fellow Am. Acad. Arts and Scis.; mem. Am. Sociol. Assn. (sec. 1968-72, pres.-elect 1979-80, pres. 1980-81), Am. Evaluation Assn.

ROSSI, PIERRE MARIE, consultancy company executive; b. Alessandria, Italy, Dec. 30, 1949; s. Vincent Nello and Daisy Desiree (Montmorency) R.; m. Susan Caroline Ellis, Feb. 20, 1990 (div.); children: David, Elissa; m. Salima Mohzar. BSc, Royal Malta U., 1971; MBA, IMEDE, Lausanne, Switzerland, 1974. Cons. Arthur D. Little, Boston, 1975-76; contr. ITT, Brussels; exec. C.G.E.R., 1976-79; dir., ptnr. Deville Petersen & Assocs., 1979-88; exec. I.M.R., Manchester, Eng., v.p. devel. Milan, Italy, 1988-91; v.p. Alexander Proudfoot Productivity Mgmt. Co., Brussels, 1992-95; mng. ptnr. European Inst. Mgmt., London, 1995—. Bd. dirs. P.M.R. Cons. Ltd., London; cons. SAFT (U.K.), SAFT (France) Alcatel Group, Paris, 1990-92; mng. ptnr. European Inst. Mgmt., London, Brussels and Geneva, 1995—; dir. e-consult ltd., 2000—. Author: Une nuit a Pise, 1976, Basic Elements of Europe Accounting, 1991, Total Vision Management, 1995; contbr. articles to profl. publs. Mem. European Acctg. Inst., Inst. Dirs. (London). Avocations: sailing, historic cars, opera, collecting contemporary art. Home: Villa Mara Bierges Belgium Office: EIM 284 Th Decuyper Brussels Belgium also: EIM (Suisse) SA 16 Chemin des Aulx 1228 Geneva Switzerland

ROSSI, RICHARD ROBERT, music educator, composer; b. Oyster Bay, Long Island, NY, July 26, 1962; s. Anthony Francis Rossi and Barbara Anne Rossi (Winfield: maiden). MusB Edn., St. Vincent Coll., 1984; MFA in Music, Carnegie Mellon U.; D Mus. Arts, U. Ill., 1998; ThM, St. Vincent Sem. Dir. of orchestral & choral activities Ea. Ill. U., Charleston, Ill., 2000—. Music dir. St. Vincent Camerata, founder/dir. Camerata Chamber Orch. St. Vincent Coll., Latrobe, Pa., 1986—97; freelance guest condr. & clinician. Composer (singer): (music compositions published through gia) Hodie Christus Natus Est, Coventry Carol, Adoramus Te, Christe, Conditor Alme Siderum . . .more, 2000; counter-tenor Choragos; (music director/conductor): (choir chosen to perform at state conven.) IMEA, 2002; (conductor) (opera) The Barber of Seville, 1999. Grantee, Charleston Area Charitable Found., 2001—02, Ruth & Vaughn Jaenike Acces to the Arts Fund, 2001—02. Mem.: ASCAP, Conductor's Guild, Ill. Coun. of Orchestras, Coll. Music Soc., Am. Choral Directors Assn., Music Educators Nat. Conf., Pi Kappa Lambda. Roman Catholic. Avocations: swimming, fishing, walking, travel, cooking. Home: 21 Woodfield Lane Charleston IL 61920-3099 Office: Ea Ill U 600 Lincoln Ave Charleston IL 61920-3099 Home Fax: 217-581-7137; Office Fax: 217-581-7137. Personal E-mail: cfrrr@eiu.edu. E-mail: cfrrr@eiu.edu.

ROSSI, RONALD ALDO, sports association administrator, Olympic athlete; b. Bronx, N.Y., Dec. 2, 1956; s. Aldo D. and Jeanette (Morretta) R.; m. Susan Veltman, Mar. 26, 1983; children: Scott, Lauren. BEE, Manhattan Coll., 1978. Registered profl. engr., N.Y. Mem. computer ops. staff John Blair and Co., N.Y.C., 1978-83, communications engr., 1984; sports program dir. U.S. Luge Assn., Lake Placid, N.Y., 1984-85, exec. dir., 1985—. Com. mem. U.S. Luge Assn., 1978—, athlete's rep., 1980-83; com. mem. U.S. Olympic Com., Colorado Springs, Colo., 1989-90, 93-96. Mem. U.S. Olympic Luge Team, Sarajevo, Yugoslavia, 1984; mem. Olympic team staff, Calgary, Can., 1988, Albertville, France, 1992, Lillehammer, Norway, 1994, Nagano, Japan, 1998, Salt Lake City, 2002. Avocations: luge, golf, softball, movies, computers. Address: US Luge Association 35 Church St Lake Placid NY 12946-1805

ROSSI, STEPHEN DONALD, pharmaceutical executive; b. Littleton, Colo., Mar. 9, 1971; s. Donald Louis and Suzanne Gerardin Rossi; m. Tiffany Clyte, Sept. 5, 1999 (div. Mar. 8, 2001). BA, Gonzaga U., 1993. With Data Devices, Tulswila, Wash., 1995—96; dist. mgr. Am. Home Products Wyeth-Ayerst Pharms., Phila., 1996—, area account mgr., 1996—, territory specialist, 1996—. Named acad. scholar, Beringer Winery, 1989—92. Mem.: Porsche Club Am. Republican. Roman Catholic. Avocations: team and individual sports, classic automobiles, reading.

ROSSI, WILLIAM MATTHEW, lawyer; b. Coldwater, Ohio, June 11, 1954; s. Hugh Dominic and Patricia Jean (Putts) R.; m. Constance Sue Streacker, July 21, 1973; children: Bryan Thomas, Lauren Michelle, Alexandria Marie. BA cum laude, Miami U., Oxford, Ohio, 1977; JD magna cum laude, U. Dayton, 1981. Bar: Ohio 1981, U.S. Dist. Ct. (so. dist.) Ohio 1982, U.S. Supreme Ct. 1986, U.S. Ct. Appeals (6th cir.) 1987, Fla. 1991, U.S. Dist. Ct. (so. and mid. dists.) Fla. 1992, U.S. Ct. Appeals (11th cir.) 1992. Assoc. Milliken & Fitton, Hamilton, Ohio, 1981-83; dep. law dir., chief city negotiator City of Middletown, 1984-89; pvt. practice, 1989-92; assoc. Jackson, Lewis, Schnitzler and Krupman, Orlando, Fla., 1992-93; dep. county atty. Sarasota County, 1993—. Bd. dirs. Columbia Inst. Bus., Middletown, 1977-78; lectr. Sawyer Coll., Dayton, 1982-83; small claims referee, 1984-92. Asst. coach Knothole Baseball, Middletown, 1981; bd. dirs. Butler County Mental Health Ctr., Hamilton, 1983-85, Summer Youth Theatre, Middletown, 1985-86; mem. bd. rev. Troop 20 Boy Scouts Am., 1986-87; mem. Sch. Adv. Coun., 1996—; mem. adv. bd. St. Joseph's Coll.; chmn. allocations panel United Way, 2001—. Recipient Am. Jurisprudence award Lawyers Coop. Pub. Co., 1979, 81, Internat. Youth Achievement award Internat. Biog. Ctr. and Am. Biog. Inst., 1982. Mem. ABA, Fla. Bar Assn. (co-chmn. labor rels. com. 2002), Nat. Pub. Employer Labor Rels. Assn., Phi Beta Kappa, Phi Delta Phi (bd. dirs., historian 1979-80). Republican. Roman Catholic. Avocations: golf, travel, writing. Home: 6215 Aventura Dr Sarasota FL 34241-9448

ROSSIDES, EUGENE TELEMACHUS, lawyer, writer; b. N.Y.C., Oct. 23, 1927; s. Telemachus and Anna (Maravel) R.; m. Elinor Burcham (div.); 1 child, Gale; m. Aphrodite Macotsin, Dec. 30, 1961; children: Michael, Alexander, Eleni. AB, Columbia U., 1949, JD, 1952. Criminal law investigator Office of Dist. Atty., N.Y.C., 1952; assoc. Rogers & Wells, 1954-56, 61-66, ptnr., 1966-69, 73-92, sr. counsel, 1993—; asst. atty. gen. State of N.Y., 1956-58; asst. to undersec. Dept. Treasury, Washington, 1958-61, asst. sec., 1969-73. Bd. dirs. Sterling Nat. Bank, N.Y.C. Author: U.S. Import Trade Regulation, 2d edit., 1986, Foreign Unfair Competition, 3d edit., 1991, United States Import Trade Law, 1992, also articles; chief import editor Internat. Trade Reporter, Bur. Nat. Affairs, 1980—; editor: The Truman Doctrine of Aid to Greece: A Fifty-Year Retrospective, 1998, Doing Business in Greece, 1996, U.S. Rels. with Greece and Cyprus, 1990—. Mem. Grace Commn., Washington, 1981-82; chmn. nationalities div. Reagan Bush Com., Washington, 1980; campaign mgr. N.Y.C. Nixon for Pres. Com., 1968, Keating for Senator Com., N.Y. State, 1964; bd. dirs. Eisenhower World Affairs Inst., Washington, Am. Hellenic Inst. Inc. Capt. USAF, 1952-60. Recipient Medal for Excellence, Columbia U., 1972, Young Lawyer's award Columbia Law Sch. Alumni Assn., 1972, Silver Anniversary award NCAA, 1974, John Jay award Columbia Coll. Alumni Assn., 1994. Mem. ABA, N.Y. State Bar Assn., Fed. Bar Assn. Republican. Greek Orthodox. Avocations: tennis, photography. Home: 3666 Upton St NW Washington DC 20008-3125 Office: Rogers & Wells 607 14th St NW Ste 900 Washington DC 20005-2000

ROSSING, DAVID ROBERT, internist; b. Detroit, Jan. 8, 1949; s. Robert Grangaard and Dolores (Christenson) R.; m. Ann Marie Tkacz, July 30, 1977; children: Brian, Philip. BA, St. Olaf Coll., 1971; MD, U. Tex. Southwestern, 1975. Diplomate Am. Bd. Internal Medicine, Am. Bd. Pulmonary Disease. Intern Emory U. Affiliated Hosps., Atlanta, 1975-76, resident in internal medicine, 1976-78; fellow in pulmonary diseases U. Tex., 1978-80; pvt. practice specialzing in pulmonary medicine, Sioux Falls, S.D., 1980—. Med. dir. Ctrl. Plains Clinic, 1994—2001; v.p. med. affairs Sioux Valley Hosps. and Health Sys., 2001—; mem. staff McKennan Hosp., Sioux Valley Hosp., Royal C. Johnson VA Hosp.; clin. prof. U. S.D. Sch. Medicine, Sioux Falls. Fellow ACP; mem. AMA, Rotary, Phi Beta Kappa. Lutheran. Home: 7205 E Pine Lake Dr Sioux Falls SD 57110-6236 Office: 1100 S Euclid Ave Sioux Falls SD 57105-0411

ROSSING, THOMAS D. physics educator; b. Madison, S.D., Mar. 27, 1929; s. Torstein H. and Luella E. Rossing; children: Karen, Barbara, Erik, Jane, Mary. BA, Luther Coll., 1950; MS, Iowa State U., 1952, PhD, 1954. Rsch. physicist Univac div. Sperry Rand, 1954-57; prof. physics St. Olaf Coll., 1957-71, chmn. physics dept., 1963-69; prof. physics No. Ill. U., DeKalb, 1971—, disting. rsch. prof., chmn. dept., 1971-73. Rschr. Microwave Lab., Stanford (Calif.) U., 1961-62, Lincoln Lab., MIT, Cambridge, Mass., summer 1963, Clarendon Lab., Oxford (Eng.) U., 1966-67, physics dept. MIT, 1976-77; rsch. assoc. Argonne (Ill.) Nat Lab., 1974-76, scientist-in-residence, 1990—; vis. lectr. U. New Eng., Armidale, Australia, 1980-81; vis. exch. scholar to China, 1988; guest rschr. Royal Inst. Tech., Stockholm, 1983, 84, 85, Inst. Perception Rsch., Eindhoven, The Netherlands, 1984, 85, Physikalisch-Technische Bundesanstalt, Braunschweig, Germany, 1988-89; guest rschr. Ecole Nat. Superiéure des Telecomm., Paris, 1996, Luleå U. Tech., Sweden, 1996, U. Calif., San Diego, 1998, Fraunhofer Inst., Stuttgart, Germany, 1998. Author 12 books in field; contbr. more than 300 articles to profl. publs. Recipient Robert Millikan medal, 2000. Fellow AAAS, Am. Phys. Soc., Acoustical Soc. Am. (Silver medal in mus. acoustics 1992), Acoustical Soc. India (hon.); mem. IEEE, Am. Assn. Physics Tchrs. (pres. 1991, Robert A. Milliken medal 2000), Catgut Acoustical Soc., Sigma Xi (nat. lectr. 1984-87), Sigma Pi Sigma. Achievements include research in musical acoustics, psychoacoustics, speech and singing, vibration analysis, magnetic levitation, environmental noise conrol, surface effects in fusion reactors, spin waves in metals, physics education; 9 U.S. and 11 foreign patents in field. Office: No Ill U Physics Dept Dekalb IL 60115

ROSSING, WILLIAM OSMUND, healthcare administrator; b. Bagley, Minn., June 6, 1934; s. Erling William and Irene Clara R.; m. Ihlene Aubry, Dec. 29, 1958; children: Karen Ihlene, Rebecca Marie, William Robert, Signe Ann. BA, Augustana Coll., 1956; BS, U. S.D., 1957; MD, Northwestern U., 1959. Asst. chief, chief dept. medicine U.S. Army Med. Svc., Nurnberg, Germany, 1963-66; chief of staff Sioux Vly. Hosp., Sioux Falls, S.D., 1974-76; bd. dirs. Sioux Vly. Health Sys., 1978-87; pres., bd. dirs. S.D. Blue Shield Assn., Sioux Falls, 1988-96, also pres. bd. dirs., 1996—; v.p. med. affairs DakotaCare HMO, 1996—. Clin. prof. medicine U. S.D. Med. Sch., Sioux Falls, 1992-98. Bd. dirs. Luth. Social Svcs., Sioux Falls, Sioux Valley Hosp. Found., 1987-2001, S.D. Symphony Orch., 1972-74. Maj. U.S. Army, 1959-66. Fellow ACP; mem. Am. Coll. Phys. Execs., Nat. Assn. Managed Care Physicians, S.D. State Med. Assn. (pres. 1986-87). Republican. Avocations: hunting, fishing, gardening. Home: 2604 S Lyndale Ave Sioux Falls SD 57105-4422 E-mail: wrossing@dakotacare.com.

ROSSINI, JOSEPH, contracting and development corporate executive; b. New Rochelle, N.Y., Nov. 25, 1939; m. Antonia Rossini; children: Katherine, Anthony, Andrew. *Wife, Antonia Rossini, is a nationally recognized American wildlife artist, known for the 1995 Florida State Duck Stamp; she has received numerous awards. She received a BA from Stonybrook State University and an MA from New York University. She is a member of the New Rochelle Council on the Arts. Great-great Uncle Gioachino Rossini was the composer of the "William Tell Overture" and the "Barber of Seville", among other works. Father, Carmelo, was a contractor-builder in the United States and Canada. Brother, Frank, was a deep sea diver and soldier of fortune; he was one of the last Americans to leave Saigon at the end of the war.* Student, Fordham U., 1965-66, Iona Coll., 1972. Pres. Rossini Contracting Corp., Mt. Vernon, N.Y., 1963—; prin. Rossini Devel. Co., Monticello, 1965—. Bd. dirs. Circuit Realty Corp., New Rochelle, 1970-71. Mem. planning bd. City of New Rochelle, 1986-92, mem. bldg. dept. adv. com., 1985; vol. instr. N.Y. State Dept. Environ. Conservation, Albany, 1968-95; vice chmn. New Rochelle Conservative Party, 1984-2001, chmn., 2001—; county committeeman Westchester County Conservative Party; pres., bd. trustees Beechwoods Cemetery, New Rochelle; dir. New Rochelle Neighborhood Revitalization Corp., 1993-96. With USN, 1959-61. Mem. NRA (patron), Gen. Contractors Assn. N.Y., Constrn. Industry Coun. Westchester and Hudson Valley, Bldg. Trades Employers Assn., Soc. Explosives Engrs., Deep Founds. Inst., Young Ams. for Freedom, Am. Lauretana Assn., Mensa, Assoc. Gen. Contractors Am., Caths. in Constrn., Tin Can Sailors, Westchester County Firearm Owners Assn., N.Y. State Rifle and Pistol Assn. Roman Catholic. Office: Rossini Contracting Corp 113 Edison Ave Mount Vernon NY 10550-5005 E-mail: rossinidigs@juno.com.

ROSSIO, JEFFREY L. biologist, educator; b. Cleve., May 22, 1947; s. Maurice and Celia (Smith) R.; m. Susan A. Dunlop, Mar. 19, 1972; children: Sara Dunlop Rossio, Jonathan Dunlop Rossio. BS in Zoology, U. Mich., 1969; MS in Microbiology, Ohio State U., 1971, PhD in Microbiology, 1973; postdoctoral fellow, U. Tex. Med. Br., 1975. Instr. biochemistry dept. U. Tex. Med. Br., Galveston, 1976-78; asst. prof. dept. microbiology and immunology Wright State U. Coll. of Medicine, Dayton, Ohio, 1978-81; numerous sci. positions from scientist II to sr. scientist AIDS prog. Nat. Cancer Inst. at Frederick, Md., 1981—; assoc. prof. biology Hood Coll., Frederick, 1986—. Editor Clin. and Diagnostic Lab. Immunology; contbr. articles to profl. jours. and publs. in field. Named to Outstanding Young Men of Am., 1979-82; recipient Outstanding Svc. to Community award Kiwanis. Mem. Am. Soc. Microbiology, Assn. Med. Lab. Immunologists, Med. Amateur Radio Coun., Sigma Xi. Office: NCI at Frederick AIDS Vaccine Program Bldg 535 Rm 522 Frederick MD 21702 E-mail: rossio@ncifcrf.gov.

ROSSIO, RICHARD DOMINIC, automobile company executive; b. Flint, Mich., May 11, 1933; s. Charles Joseph and Levia Desolina (Peroni) R.; m. Mary Patricia Miller, Aug. 27, 1960; children: Mark, Ronald, Richard, Martin. BME, U. Detroit, 1956; M Automotive Engring., Chrysler Inst., 1958; MBA, U. Detroit, 1961. Registered profl. engr., Mich. Prodn. engr. spl. products Chrysler Corp., Highland Park, Mich., 1958-61, supr. elec. circuits, 1961-65, mgr. elec. sys., 1965-68, asst. chief engr. elec. mechanisms, 1968-71, asst. chief engr. advance engring., 1971-73, asst. chief engr. body elec., 1973-74, chief engr. body elec., 1974-87, dir. elec., 1987-89, gen. mgr. ops., 1989-92, gen. mgr. sci. labs. and proving grounds, 1992-95. Bd. dirs. Engring. Sci. and Devel. Found. Mem. engring. alumni adv. coun. U. Detroit, 1987; mem. motor vehicle safety rsch. adv. coun. NHTSA, Washington, 1989. Named Alumnus of Yr., U. Detroit Engring. Coll., 1981. Fellow Engring. Soc. Detroit; mem. Soc. Automotive Engrs. (mem. tech. rev. bd. 1991-94, chmn. test methods 1965-68), Automotive Mfg. Assn. (chmn. h'lite rsch. 1968-71), Engring. Soc. Detroit (bd. dirs. 1991), Engring. Sci. Devel. Found. (treas., bd. dirs.), Mich. Profl. Engrs. Bd., Great Oaks Country Club, Rochester Hills Tennis Club, Boyne Country Club, Wawashkamo Golf Club. Roman Catholic. Avocations: tennis, skiing, gardening. Home: 852 Peach Tree Ln Rochester MI 48306-3359

ROSSITER, ALEXANDER, JR. news service executive, editor; b. Elmira, N.Y., Mar. 2, 1936; s. Alexander H. and Eleanor (Howell) R.; m. Sylvia Lee Vanlandingham, June 11, 1960; children: Alexander H. III, Jill Jarrell. BA, Rutgers U., 1958; postgrad., Emory U., 1959. With UPI, 1959-92; newsman Atlanta, 1959-61, Richmond, Va., 1961-63; bur. mgr. Cape Canaveral, Fla., 1963-73; sci. editor Washington, 1973-87; exec. editor, 1987-88; exec. editor, sr. v.p., 1988-91; editor, exec. v.p., 1991-92; asst. v.p., dir. news svc. Duke U., Durham, NC, 1992—2001, dir. com. Pratt Sch. Engrs., 2001—. Mem. nat. adv. bd. Knight Ctr. for Specialized Journalism, Colleg Pk., Md., 1988-92; mem. adv. bd. Med. Journalism Program, U. N.C., Chapel Hill, 2000—. Recipient Grady-Stack medal Am. Chem. Soc., 1987, other journalism awards. Mem. Nat. Assn. Sci. Writers, Edn. Writers Assn. Office: Duke U 305 Teer Bldg Box 90271 Durham NC 27708 *Enthusiasm is the key to success. Take on your education, your family responsibilities and your work with enthusiasm and good things will result.*

ROSSITER, BRYANT WILLIAM, chemistry consultant; b. Ogden, Utah, Mar. 10, 1931; s. Bryant B. and Christine (Peterson) R.; m. Betty Jean Anderson, Apr. 16, 1951; children: Bryant, Mark, Diane, Steven, Linda, Karen, Matthew, Gregory. BA, U. Utah, 1954, PhD, 1957. Researcher Eastman-Kodak Co., Rochester, N.Y., 1957-63, head color phys. chem. lab., 1963-70, dir. chemistry div., 1970-84, dir. sci., tech. devel., 1984-86; pres. Viratek Inc., Costa Mesa, Calif., 1986-89; sr. v.p. ICN Pharms., 1989-90; ret., 1990; pres., CEO WRECON, Inc., Laguna Hills, Calif., 1991-96, ret., 1996. Sr. editor John Wiley & Sons, N.Y.C., 1970—; chmn. bd. Nucleic Acid Rsch. Inst., Costa Mesa, 1987-88; trustee Eastman Dental Ctr., Rochester, 1973-93 (bd. pres. 1982-85); bd. dirs. Verax & Corp. Editor: (chem. treatises) Physical Methods of Chemistry (11 vols.), 1970-76, Physical Methods, (12 vols.), 1986—. Chemical Experimentation Under Extreme Conditions, 1979. Mem. rsch. adv. com. U.S. Agy. for Internat. Devel., Washington, chmn. rsch. adv. com., 1989-92; mem. panel on biosci. Pres.' Coun. Advisors on Sci. and Tech., 1991; mem. adv com. Cornell Internat. Inst. for Food, Agr. and Devel., 1991; presiding officer Ch. Jesus Christ Latter Day Saints, Ea. U.S. and Can., 1959-86, counselor presidency San Diego temple, 1998—. 1st lt. USAFR, 1951-58. Named Hon. Alumni Brigham Young U., Provo, Utah, 1982. Fellow AAAS, Am. Inst. Chemists (lectr., Fellows award 1988, Will Judy award Juanita Coll. 1978); mem. Internat. Union Pure and Applied Chemistry (chmn. U.S. nat. com., orignator, chmn. Chemical Rsch. Applied to World Needs com. 1975-87, chmn. Chemical Rsch. Applied to World Needs II The Internat. Conf. on Chemistry and World Food Supplies, 1982), Am. Chem. Soc. (chmn. internat. activities). Avocations: horseback riding, reading, fishing. Home and Office: 25662 Dillon Rd Laguna Hills CA 92653-5800 E-mail: bwr@Ni.Net.

ROSSITER, CHARLES MELVIN, poet; b. Balt., Dec. 11, 1942; s. Charles Melvin Rossiter and Margaret Eleanor Wallace; Linda Wilson, Aug. 1, 1966 (div. Sept. 1972); 1 child, Erika Lynn (dec.); m. Mary Ellen Munley, June 8, 1978; 1 child, Jack Charles. BS, U. Md., 1965, MA, 1968; PhD, Ohio U., 1970; postgrad., Northwestern U., 1975. Prof. U. Wis., Milw., 1969-79, Mt. St. Mary's Coll., Md., 1979-80; freelance writer Washington, 1980-85; sr. rschr. Pacific Inst. Rsch. & Evaluation, 1985-87, Rsch. Found. SUNY, Albany, N.Y., 1987-89; dir. Albany Tng. Program Poetry Therapy, Delmar, 1991-96. Founder, dir. House of Words, Milw., 1975-79; producer, host Poetry Motel TV Program, Delmar, 1990-96. Author: Communicating Personally, 1975, What Men Talk About, 2000, Back Beat, 2001. Founder Chess For Kids, Oak Park, Ill., 2000; cons., bd. dirs. Advs. Acad. Excellence, Frederick, Md., 1982-85. NEH grantee, 1993-95; NEA fellow, 1997. Mem. Nat. Assn. Poetry Therapy (v.p. 1992-93, Outstanding Svc. award 1991). Avocations: photography, travel. Home: 705 S Gunderson Ave Oak Park IL 60304 E-mail: posey@juno.com.

ROSSITER, ROBERT E. interior auto parts manufacturing executive; b. 1946; With Lear Siegler Inc., 1971-87, former pres. seating div.; pres., chief oper. officer Lear Seating Corp., Southfield, Mich., 1987-2000, also bd. dirs.; CEO, pres. Lear Corp., 2000—. Office: Lear Seating Corp 21557 Telegraph Rd Southfield MI 48034*

ROSS-LEE, BARBARA, dean, educator; BS Biology and Chemistry, M Tchr. Spl. Populations, Wayne State U.; grad., Mich. State U., 1973; DSc (hon.) , N.Y. Coll. Osteo. Medicine; degree (hon.) , Wilmington Coll., 2001. Legis. asst. Senator Bill Bradley; chmn. dept. family medicine, assoc. dean health policy Mich. State U. Coll. Medicine; dean Ohio U. Coll. Osteo. Medicine, 1993—2001; dean, v.p. health scis. and med. affairs N.Y. Coll. Osteo. Medicine, 2001—. Lectr. in field; dir. Osteo. Heritage Health Policy Fellowship Program ; exec. dir. Inst. Nat. Health Policy and Rsch., NOMA (the osteo. affiliate NMA) ; mem. bd. dirs. Assn. Acad. Health Ctrs., Nat. Fund Med. Edn., Nat. Health Svs. Corps' Assn. Clinicians Underserved ; trustee Found. Appalachian Ohio; participant confs. Contbr. more than 30 scholarly articles med. and health-care issues. Named to Ohio Women's Hall of Fame, 1998; recipient Magnificent 7 award, Bus. and Profl. Women/USA, 1993, Women's Health award, Blackboard African-Am. Nat. Bestsellers, Disting. Pub. Svc. award, Okla. State U. Coll. Osteo. Medicine, Walter F. Patenge medal pub. svc., Mich. State U. Coll. Osteo. Medicine, 2001. Fellow: Am. Osteo. Bd. Family Physicians; mem.: NIH (adv. com. rsch. on women's health), Future Primary Care (Inst. Medicine's com.), U.S. Dept. Health and Human Svs. (nat. adv. com. rural health), Appalachian Health Policy (Appalachian regional commn.'s adv. coun.), AACOM Bd. Govs. (chair-elect exec. coun.), AOA Bur. Profl. Edn., Trilateral Internat. Med. Workforce Group. Achievements include first to be an osteopathic physician to participate in the prestigious Robert Wood Johnson Health Policy Fellowship. Office: Old Westbury Rd Westbury NY 11568*

ROSSMAN, ROBERT HARRIS, management consultant; b. Phila., Jan. 27, 1932; s. Benjamin Bernard and Vivian (Silnutzer) R.; m. Wanda Ward, Aug. 9, 1980; 1 child, Victoria Anne; children from previous marriage: Rodger Samuel, Robbi Jennifer, Ronni Esther. BS, U.S. Merchant Marine Acad., 1953; MSME with honors, U.S. Naval Postgrad. Sch., 1963; cert. advanced naval architecture, MIT, 1973. Cert. mgr. human resources; cert. value specialist. Commd. ensign USN, 1953, advanced through grades to comdr., 1967, shipboard engr., 1953-55, maintenance and repair officer Reserve Fleet, 1955-57; served as ship supt. Norfolk Naval Shipyard, Portsmouth, Va., 1957-60; maintenance and logistics planning officer Amphibious Squadron Twelve, Little Creek, 1963-65; planning and estimating supt. U.S. Naval Ship Repair Facility, Yokosuka, Japan, 1965-67; design and planning advisor USN, Saigon, Republic Viet Nam, 1967-68; chief prodn. engring. Def. Contract Adminstrn. Svcs., Alexandria, Va., 1968-70; dir. cost reduction Naval Ship Systems Command, Washington, 1970-73; dep. program mgr. new ship class Naval Ship Engring. Ctr., Hyattsville, Md., 1973; ret. USN, 1973; ptnr. Kempter-Rossman Internat., Washington, 1974-91; owner Rossman Assocs. Internat., 1991—. Cons. in cost and time reduction, mgmt. improvement, productivity and competition enhancement. Author: (textbook) Function Based Analysis, 1983, Total Cycle Time Reduction, 1992; editor mag. Performance, 1970-73; contbr. articles to profl. jours. Pres. PTA, Fairfax County, Va., 1969-70, Community Civic Assn., Fairfax County, 1970-71; chmn. Boy Scouts Am. and Weblos troops, 1969-71, del. at large 1st Congl. Dist. Rep. Com., N.C., 1989-90; chmn. Chowan County (N.C.) Rep. Com., 1990-92. Decorated USN Commendation medals, Honor medal-1st Class (Republic of Vietnam Armed Forces), Combat Action medal. Fellow Soc. Am. Value Engrs. (v.p. 1970-73, Disting. Svc. award 1976); mem. U.S. Merchant

Marine Acad. Alumni Assn., Am. Legion, Sigma Xi. Jewish. Avocations: gardening, home remodeling, restoration, writing. Office: Rossman Assocs Internat Speight House 110 Old Hertford Rd Edenton NC 27932-9608 E-mail: bobenviro@inteliport.com.

ROSSMAN, RUTH SCHARFF, artist, educator; b. Bklyn. d. Joseph and Elsie (Frankel) Scharff; m. Phillip Rossman; 1 dau., Joanne. Grad., Cleve. Inst. Art, 1934; BS, Case Western Res. U., 1934; postgrad., Kahn Inst. Art, 1947-50, UCLA, 1960. Art instr. Canton (Ohio) public schs., 1934-39, Canton Art Inst., 1937-45, Rustic Canyon Art Center, Los Angeles, 1978-81. One-woman shows at Heritage Gallery, L.A., 1963, 66, Canton (Ohio) Community Ctr., 1967, Marymount Coll., U. Judaism, 1980, L.A. Fedn. Bldg., 1981, 89, Platt Gallery, 1986, 93, 98, others; exhibited in group shows Mus. Modern Art, N.Y.C., Butler Mus., Washington and Jefferson Coll., Denver Mus., Space Mus., Mt. St. Mary's Coll., L.A., M.H. de Young Mus., San Francisco Mus. Art, Venice Art Walk, ann. 1981-94, 96-2000, Univ. Judaism, 1986, 93, Brand Art Gallery, 1987, Platt Gallery, 1998, others; represented in permanent collections Pa. Acad. Fine Arts, Phila., Brandeis-Bardin Inst., U. Redlands, Calif., Nat. Watercolor Soc., Ahmanson Collection, Rocky Mt. Nat., others; paintings included in book The California Romantics: Harbingers of Watercolor, 1987, Retrospective Art Exhibit U. Judaism Platt Gallery, 1998. Chair selection com. for Platt Gallery, U. Judaism, L.A., 1986—. Recipient purchase-cash awards Los Angeles All-City Art Exhbn. Mem. Nat. Watercolor Soc. (pres. 1974-75, juror 75th Ann. Exhbn. 1995).

ROSSMAN, TOBY GALE, genetic toxicology educator, researcher; b. Weehawken, N.J., June 3, 1942; d. Norman N. and Sylvia Betty (May) Natowitz; m. Neil I. Rossman, Sept. 16, 1962 (div. Sept. 1980); m. Gordon Rauer, Aug. 19, 1990. AB, NYU, 1964, PhD, 1968; postgrad., Brandeis U., 1964-65. Instr. Polytech. Inst. of N.Y., N.Y.C., 1968-69; postdoctoral dept. pathology NYU, 1969-71; from asst. to assoc. prof. Inst. for Environ Medicine NYU Med Ctr, 1974-85; prof. Inst. for Environ. Medicine, 1985—; dir. molecular and genetic toxicology Nelson Inst. Environ. Medicine, NYU Med. Ctr., N.Y.C., 1995—. Mem. editorial bd. Molecular Toxicology, 1989-91, Teratogenesis, Carcinogenesis, Mutagenesis, 1990-91, Environmental and Molecular Mutagenesis, 1994—, Mutation Research, 1994—; contbr. numerous articles to profl. jours. EPA grantee, NIH grantee. Mem. AAAS, Assn. for Women in Sci., Am. Assn. for Cancer Rsch., Am. Soc. for Microbiology, Environ. Mutagen Soc. (councilor 1990-93), Soc. Toxicology. Office: NYU Inst Environ Medicine 57 Old Forge Rd Tuxedo Park NY 10987-5007 E-mail: rossman@env.med.nyu.edu.

ROSSMANN, ANTONIO, lawyer, educator; b. San Francisco, Apr. 25, 1941; s. Herbert Edward and Yolanda (Sonsini) R.; m. Kathryn A. Burns, Oct. 6, 1991; children: Alice Sonsini, Maria McHale. Grad., Harvard U., 1963, JD, 1971. Bar: Calif. 1972, D.C. 1979, N.Y. 1980, U.S. Suprmee Ct. 1980. Law clk. to Justice Mathew Tobriner Calif. Supreme Ct., 1971-72; assoc. Tuttle & Taylor, L.A., 1972-75; pub. advisor Calif. Energy Commn., 1975-76; sole practice San Francisco, 1976-82, 85—; exec. dir. Nat. Ctr. for Preservation Law, 1979-80; mem. McCutchen, Doyule, Brown & Enersen, San Francisco, 1982-85. Adj. prof. law Hastings Coll. Law, 1981-84; vis. prof. UCLA Sch. Law, 1985-88; adj. prof. Stanford Law Sch., 1989-90, U. Calif. Sch. Law, 1991—. Editor Harvard U. Law Rev., 1969-71; contbr. articles to legal jours. Bd. dirs. Planning and Conservation League, 1984—, Calif. Water Protection Coun., 1982-83, San Francisco Marathon, 1982-90; pres. Western State Endurance Run, 1986-96, counselor, 1996—; pres., bd. dirs. Toward Utility Rate Normalization, 1976-79. Served to lt. comdr. USN, 1963-68. Fulbright lectr. U. Tokyo, 1987-88. Mem. Calif. State Bar (chmn. com. on environment 1978-82), Assn. Bar City N.Y., U.S. Rowing Assn., U.S. Soccer Fedn. (state referee) L.A. Athletic Club, Harvard Club (San Francisco, N.Y.C.), Harvard Law Sch. Assn. No. Calif. (pres. 1997—). Office: 380 Hayes St San Francisco CA 94102-4421 E-mail: ar@landwater.com.

ROSSMANN, JACK EUGENE, psychology educator; b. Walnut, Iowa, Dec. 4, 1936; s. Wilbert C. Rossmann and Claire L. (Mickel) Walter; m. Marilyn Martin, June 14, 1958; children: Ann, Charles, Sarah. BS, Iowa State U., 1958, MS, 1960; PhD, U. Minn., 1963. Lic. psychologist, Minn. Asst. prof. Macalester Coll., St. Paul, 1964-68, assoc. prof., 1968-73, prof., 1973—, v.p. acad. affairs, 1978-86, chair dept. psychology, 1990-2000. Cons. Pers. Decisions Internat., Mpls., 1989—2000, Bush Found., 1993—; cons.-evaluator North Ctrl. Assn., 1975—. Author: (with others) Open Admissions at CUNY, 1975; contbr. articles to profl. jours. Bd. dirs. Twin City Inst. for Talented Youth, St. Paul, 1978-91; trustee United Theol. Sem., New Brighton, Minn., 1984-96. 2d lt. U.S. Army, 1959. Mem.: AAUP (pres. Minn. conf. 1993—95), APA, Minn. Psychol. Assn. (treas. 2001, pres.-elect 2002), Am. Assn. Higher Edn., Assn. Instl. Rsch., Am. Psychol. Soc. Home: 99 Cambridge St Saint Paul MN 55105-1947 Office: Macalester Coll 1600 Grand Ave Saint Paul MN 55105-1801 E-mail: rossmann@macalester.edu.

ROSSMANN, MICHAEL GEORGE, biochemist, educator; b. Frankfurt, Germany, July 30, 1930; s. Alexander and Nelly (Schwabacher) R.; m. Audrey Pearson, July 24, 1954; children— Martin, Alice, Heather. BSC with honors, Polytechnic, London, 1951, MSc in Physics, 1953; PhD in Chemistry, U. Glasgow, 1956; PhD (hon.) , U. Uppsala (Sweden), 1983, U. Strasbourg (France), 1984, Vrije U. Brussel, 1990, U. Glasgow (Scotland), 1993, U. York (England), 1994, U. Quebec (Can.), 1998. Fulbright scholar U. Minn., 1956-58; research scientist MRC Lab. Molecular Biology, Cambridge, Eng., 1958-64; asso. prof. biol. scis. Purdue U., West Lafayette, Ind., 1964-67, prof., 1967-78, Hanley Disting. prof. biol. scis., 1978—, prof. biochemistry, 1975—. Editor: The Molecular Replacement Method, 1972; contbr. more than 390 articles to profl. jours. Grantee NIH, NSF; recipient Fankuchen award Am. Crystallographc Assn., 1986, Horwitz prize Columbia U., 1990, Gregori Arminoff prize Royal Swedish Acad. Sci., 1994, Stein & Moore award Protein Soc., 1994, Ewald prize Internat. Union Crystallography, 1996, Cole award Biophysical Soc., 1998, Elion award Internat. Soc. for Antiviral Rsch., 2000, Ehrlich and Darmstaedter prize Paul Erhlich-Fedn., 2001. Mem. Am. Soc. Biol. Chemists, Am. Chem. Soc., Biophys. Soc. (Cole award 1998), Am. Crystallographic Assn. (Fankuchen award 1986), Brit. Biophys. Soc., Inst. Physics, Chem. Soc. (U.K.), AAAS, NAS, Indian Nat. Sci. Acad., Royal Soc., Nat. Sci. Bd., Lafayette Sailing Club. Democrat. Home: 1208 Wiley Dr West Lafayette IN 47906-2434 Office: Dept Biol Scis Purdue Univ West Lafayette IN 47907-1392 E-mail: mgr@indiana.bio.purdue.edu.

ROSSMILLER, GEORGE EDDIE, agricultural economist; b. Great Falls, Mont., June 8, 1935; s. Albert E. and Romaine (Hennford) R.; m. Betty Ann Rinio, Dec. 20, 1955 (dec. Mar. 1990); children: David W., Diane J.; m. Frances Sandiford, May 22, 1996. BS, Mont. State U., 1956, MS, 1962; PhD, Mich. State U., 1965. Rsch. assoc. Mich. State U., East Lansing, 1965-66, asst. prof., 1967-71, assoc. prof., 1972-76, prof. agrl. econs., 1977-80; agrl. attache to OECD, Fgn. Agrl. Service, USDA, Paris, 1978-79; asst. adminstr. internat. trade policy Fgn. Agrl. Svc., USDA, Washington, 1979-81, dir planing and analysis, 1981-85; sr. fellow and dir. Nat. Ctr. Food and Agr. Policy, Resources for the Future, 1986-92; also exec. dir. Internat. Policy Council on Agr. and Trade, 1988-92; chief situation and policy studies svc. Food and Agr. Orgn. of UN, Rome, 1992-97. Author: The Grain-Livestock Economy of West Germany with Projections to 1970 and 1975, 1968, (with others) Korean Agricultural Sector Analysis and Recommended Development Strategies, 1971-1985, 1972; editor: (with others) Agricultural Sector Planning: A General System Simulation Approach, 1978. With U.S. Army, 1956-59. Recipient service citation Korean Ministry of Agrl. and Fisheries, 1973, service citation Office of Prime Minister of Korea, 1977, Superior Service award U.S. Dept. Agr., 1983, Fgn. Agrl. Service merit award, 1984. Mem. Am. Agrl. Econs. Assn. (Disting. Policy Contbn. award 1992), Internat. Assn. Agrl. Economists, Agrl. Econs. Soc. Presbyterian. Home: The Conifers Kennerleigh Devon EX17 4RS England E-mail: gerfsr@globalnet.co.uk.

ROSSOF, ARTHUR HAROLD, internal medicine educator; b. Chgo., Dec. 12, 1943; s. Jack and Libby (Gordon) R.; m. Rebecca Ann, Aug. 11, 1967 (div. 1983); children: Jacob Earl, Lizabeth Eva; m. Kristine Ann, Feb. 14, 1985. Student, Bradley U., 1961-64; MD, U. Ill., 1968. Diplomate Nat. Bd. Med. Examiners, Am. Bd. Internal Medicine, Am. Bd. Oncology, Am. Bd. Hematology. Fellow sect. neurobiology dept. neurology Presbyn.-St. Luke's Hosp., Chgo., 1965-68, intern straight medicine, 1968-69, resident dept. medicine, 1969-71, Eastern Coop. Oncology Group fellow sect. oncology, dept. medicine, 1971-72, asst. attending physician dept. internal medicine, 1976-80, assoc. attending physician, dept. internal medicine, 1980-82, sr. attending physician dept. internal medicine, 1982-90; med. dir. MacNeal Cancer Ctr., Berwyn, Ill., 1985-99; asst. medicine U. Ill. Coll. Medicine, 1969-71; clin. asst. prof. medicine U. Tex. health Sci. Ctr., San Antonio, 1973-76; instr. medicine Rush Med. Coll., 1971-72, asst. prof. medicine, 1976-81, assoc. prof. medicine, 1981-90, Loyola U. Med. Ctr., Chgo., 1990-91, attending physician, 1990-97, prof., 1991-97. Mem. resident selection com. Rush-Presbyn.-St. Luke's Med. Ctr., 1976-88, mem. ethics conf. planning group, 1981-90, tumor com., 1981-90; chmn. med. edn. com., continuing med. edn. subcom., 1982-90; mem. pharmacy and therapeutics com., chmn. instnl. rev. bd., chmn. cancer com. MacNeal Hosp.. chmn. med. edn. com., continuing med. edn. subcom., 1993-97; cons. Cancer Info. Svcv., Ill. Cancer Coun., mem. clin. trials com. 1978-92, credentials rev. com.; mem. adv. com. Lincoln Park Zoo, 1978—; med. advisor Y-ME sci. adv. bd. Chgo. chpt. Israel Cancer Rsch. Found. Author: Lithium Effects on Granulopoiesis and Immune Function, 1980; contbr. articles in field to profl. jours.; patentee in field. Mem. exec. com. prevention com. Cancer Incidence and End Results com. Am. Cancer Soc.; mem. profl. adv. bd. Wellness House, Y-ME, Israel Cancer Rsch. Found. Fellow ACP; mem. AAAS, Internat. Soc. Exptl. Hematology, Am. Soc. Clin. Oncology, Am. Assn. Cancer Research, Am. Soc. Hematology, N.Y. Acad. Scis., Soc. Air Force Physicians, Soc. Med. History Chgo., Chgo. Soc. Internal Medicine, Assn. Community Cancer Ctrs., Sigma Xi, Phi Eta Sigma, Alpha Omega Alpha. Republican. Jewish. Avocation: tennis. Office: Hematology/Oncology Assocs Ill 3245 Grove Ave Berwyn IL 60402-3474 Fax: 708-484-8426. E-mail: krisat@rcnchicago.com., arthur.rossaf@usoncology.com.

ROSSOLIMO, ALEXANDER NICHOLAS, management consultant, business executive, corporate director; b. Paris, June 8, 1939; came to U.S., 1952; naturalized, 1958; s. Nicholas S. and Vera A. (Boudakovitch) R.; m. Meryl Louise Stowbridge, Sept. 10, 1977; children: Gregory, Katherine, Elizabeth. Student, Lycée Français of N.Y., 1955-57; BEE with honors, CUNY, 1962; MA in Applied Math., Harvard U., 1963, PhD in Applied Physics, 1973; MBA, MIT, 1973. Cert. in bus. French. Tchg. fellow Harvard U., 1963-65, rsch. asst., 1966-71; fin. analyst Péchiney, Paris, 1972; brand/advt. mgmt. The Clorox Co., Oakland, Calif., 1973-74; cons. The Boston Consulting Group, 1974-77; dir. planning and fin. analysis United Brands, Boston, 1977-80; sr. dir. Digital Equipment Corp., Maynard, Mass., 1980-92; pres. Internat. Strategy Assocs., Newton, 1992-94, pres., chief exec. officer, 1994—; co-founder, acting CEO, IntellectExchange.com, Inc., 1999—. Vis. fellow Harvard U., Cambridge, Mass., 1991-93; bd. dirs. ACG Internat., Chgo., Newton Consulting Group; founding dir. Forum 128, 1996—; bd. dirs. Ctr. for Security and Social Progress, Inc., chmn., 1998—; dir. Law Enforcement Assistance Found., 1999—. Contbr. numerous articles to bus. and internat. newspapers. Mem. search com. Ecole Bilingue, French-Am. Internat. Sch. of Boston, 1991-93; fund raiser Milton (Mass.) Acad., 1994-97, Phillips Exeter Acad., 1997—, Phillips Andover Acad., 2000—. Recipient award in elec. engring. Blonder-Tongue Co., N.Y.C., 1961, Belden prize, gold medal in math., 1960; NSF postgrad. fellow, 1962-63; ACG Dealmaker Challenge winner, 1995. Mem. Nat. Assn. Corp. Dirs., Bus. Execs. for Nat. Security, Boston Security Analysts Soc., Royal United Svcs. Inst. for Def. Studies (London), French Am. C. of C., Japan Soc. Boston, World Affairs Coun., Assn. for Corp. Growth Boston (chmn. 1995-96), Harvard Club Boston, Harvard Faculty Club, Toastmasters Internat. (pres.), Tau Beta Pi, Eta Kappa Nu. Avocations: jogging, tennis, foreign languages, international organizations, theater. Office: Strategy Assocs Internat PO Box 207 Waban MA 02468-0002 E-mail: a_rossolimo@post.harvard.edu.

ROSSON, GLENN RICHARD, building products and furniture company executive; b. Galveston, Tex., Aug. 17, 1937; s. John Raymond and Elsie Lee R.; m. Edwina Lucille Hart, June 2, 1956; children— Darrell Richard, Alex Mark. BBA, Tex. Tech U., 1959. C.P.A., Tex. Supr., accountant Axelson div. U.S. Industries Inc., Longview, Tex., 1960-67, controller, 1968, group financial v.p., 1969, group chmn., 1969-72, v.p., 1973-74, sr. v.p., 1974, exec. v.p., 1974-80, also dir.; pres. Rosson Investment Co., 1980—; chmn. bd. Yorktowne Inc., 1988—. Chmn. bd. dirs. Quality Product Finishing, Inc., 1998—. Mem. Am. Inst. C.P.A.s, Tex. Soc. C.P.A.s, Nat. Assn. Accts. (past nat. dir., past pres. E. Tex. chpt.), Assn. for Corp. Growth (past pres.). Clubs: Dallas Athletic, TBARM Raquet. Home: 11367 Drummond Dr Dallas TX 75228-1946 Office: 6060 N Central Expy # 560 Dallas TX 75206-5142 E-mail: rosson@gte.net.

ROSSOTTI, BARBARA JILL MARGULIES, lawyer; b. Englewood, N.J., Feb. 28, 1940; d. Albert and Loretta (Jill) Margulies; m. Charles Ossola Rossotti; children: Allegra Jill, Edward Charles. BA magna cum laude, Mount Holyoke Coll., 1961; LLB, Harvard U., 1964. Bar: D.C. 1966. Assoc. Nutter McClennen & Fish, Boston, 1964-65, Covington & Burling, Washington, 1965-72, Shaw, Pittman, Potts & Trowbridge, Washington, 1972-73, ptnr., 1973—. Trustee Mt. Holyoke Coll., South Hadley, Mass., 1984-99, vice chmn., 1989-94, chmn., 1994-99; trustee Legal Aid Soc., D.C., 1979-92, pres. 198-89, mem. pres. coun., 1992—; trustee Choral Arts Soc., Washington, 1989-96, 97—, chair, 1993-95; bd. dirs. Washington Home, 1989—. Fellow Am. Bar Found.; mem. ABA, Am. Soc. Internat. Law, Internat. Law Assn., D.C. Bar, D.C. Bar Found. (adv. com.). Office: Shaw Pittman 2300 N St NW Fl 5 Washington DC 20037-1172

ROSS-SERAKOS, VONIA P. insurance agent, small business owner; b. Taylorville, Ill., Dec. 4, 1942; d. Alvin Clyde and Lois Eva (Weller) Brown; children: Craig Allen Ross, Cayle Allen Ross; m. Leo A. Serakos, May 13, 2000. Student. So. Ill. U., 1962-64, Palomar Coll., 1986-88, San Diego State U., 1988-90. Real estate agt. Joe Foster Agy., Collinsville, Ill., 1964-69; ofice mgr. real estate Bank of St. Louis, 1969-73; real estate agt. Palmer-Stelman, San Diego, 1986-89; office mgr. real estate McMillin Realty, 1989-90; mgr., ins. agt. Calif. Plus Ins., 1990-93; prin. Vonia Ross Ins. Agy., 1993—; owner, pres. Bernardo Flooring, San Diego, 1993—. Mem. Calif. Assn. Real Estate, Sacramento, 1986—, San Diego Bd. Realtors, 1986—, Health Underwriters, 1991—. Mem. adv. com. Rancho Bernardo Libr. Campaign, 1994—; active NOW, San Diego, 1988; mem. activist Barbara Boxer Campaign, San Diego, 1992, Susan Golding Campaign, San Diego, 1992, Barbara Warden Campaign for San Diego City Councilwoman, Barbara Warden Campaign for Mayor of San Diego, 1999—. Scholar Ill. Assembly, 1962; named Philanthropy Coun. Vol. of the Year, 1996; named Hon. Mayor of Rancho Bernardo, Calif., 1999—. Mem. Rancho Bernardo C. of C. (v.p., bd. dirs. 1993-2002, pres.-elect 1996-97, pres. 1997-98), Soroptimists (pres. Rancho Bernardo 1993-94, 95-96), City of San Diego Status of Women Commn. Avocations: walking, reading, golf. Home: 18284 Fernando Way San Diego CA 92128-1213 E-mail: voniap@aol.com.

ROSS-SHERIFF, FARIYAL, social work educator; b. Tabora, Tanzania, Africa, Sept. 1, 1940; came to U.S., 1964; d. Habib K. and Kulsum (Juma) Sheriff; m. Bruce A. Ross, June 24, 1972; children: Tasanee, Ben. BS, Mich. State U., 1967; MA, U. Mich., 1970, PhD, 1972. Tchr. Aga Khan Sch., Tabora, 1961-64; rsch. assoc. High/Scope Ednl. Rsch. Found., Ypsilanti, Mich., 1968-72, U. Mich., Ann Arbor, 1972-74; prof., dir. PhD social work program Howard U., Washington, 1975—; postdoctoral U. Md., Balt., 1983-85. Vis. prof. U. Khan Kaen, Thailand,. 1974-75; dir. Al-Ummah summer program Kalamazoo (Mich.) Coll., 1983—; cons. Latin Am. Youth Ctr., Washington, 1985-89. Co-editor: Mental Health and People of Color, 1983, Social Work Practice with Asian Americans, 1992. Bd. dirs. Family and Child Svcs., Washington, 1989—; mem. Aga Khan Coun. for U.S.A., N.Y., 1991-99; mem. nat. com. Aga Khan Found., Washington, 1991-94; co-dir. Leadership Program for Vols., 1989-92. Mem. NASW (co-chair Asian Am. caucus 1990-95, chair Asian Am. social work educators coun. 1999—). Ismaili Muslim. Avocation: reading. Office: Howard U Howard 6th Pl NW Washington DC 20059-0001

ROSSUM, RALPH ARTHUR, political science educator; b. Alexandria, Minn., Dec. 17, 1946; s. Floyd Arthur and June Marion (Carlson) R.; m. Constance Mary Brazina, Aug. 19, 1972; children: Kristin, Brent, Pierce. BA summa cum laude, Concordia Coll., 1968; MA, U. Chgo., 1971, PhD, 1973. Instr. Grinnell (Iowa) Coll., 1972-73; asst. prof. Memphis State U., 1973-77, assoc. prof., 1977-80, Loyola U., Chgo., 1980-83, assoc. dean grad. sch., 1981-82; dep. dir. bur. justice stats. U.S. Dept. Justice, Washington, 1983-84; Alice Tweed Tuohy prof. govt. Claremont (Calif.) McKenna Coll., 1984-88, v.p. and dean of faculty, 1988-91; pres. Hampden-Sydney (Va.) Coll., 1991-92; Salvatori Vis. prof. Claremont (Calif.) McKenna Coll., 1992-93, Salvatori prof. Am. Constitutionalism, 1994—; Fletcher Jones Prof. of Am. Politics U. Redlands, Redlands, Calif., 1993-94. Mem. adv. bd. Nat. Inst. Corrections, U.S. Dept. Justice, 1988-91; mem. Robert Presley Inst. Corrections Rsch. and Tng., State of Calif., 1988-91; dir. Rose Inst. of State and Local Govt., 2000—. Author: Federalism, the Supreme Court and the Seventeenth Amendment, 2001, others; co-author: The American Founding, 1981, American Constitutional Law, 1983, 1999, 2003—, others; editor (sr.): Benchmark, 1983—86; book rev. editor: , 1986—; contbr. articles to profl. jours. and chpts. to books. Trustee Episcopal Theol. Sch., Claremont, 1987-91. Ford Found. fellow, 1968-72. Mem. Am. Polit. Sci. Assn. Episcopalian. Office: Claremont McKenna Coll Dept Govt 850 Columbia Ave Claremont CA 91711-3901 E-mail: ralph.rossum@claremontmckenna.edu.

ROST, PETER, pharmaceutical company executive; b. Bollebygd, Sweden, May 31, 1959; came to U.S., 1987; s. Siegfrid and Kathie (Zerne) Rost; m. Tina Forssten, Apr. 21, 1984; children: Maximilian Forssten, Sebastian Forssten. MD, U. Gothenburg, Sweden, 1984. Intern anesthesiology dept. Ea. Hosp., Gothenburg, 1984, practice medicine specializing in anesthesiology, 1984; pres., CEO Bus. Lit. Inc., 1985-87; account supr., copywriter Grey Gothenburg, 1985-87; med. dir., account supr. Maher Kaump & Clark, Inc., L.A., 1987-92; assoc. dir. med. edn. Lederle Labs. divsn. Am. Cyanamid Co., Wayne, N.J., 1992, dir. med. edn., 1993; product mgr. Lederle Labs. divsn. Am. Cyanimid Co., 1993-94; mkt. planning mgr. Wyeth-Ayerst Internat., St. Davids, Pa., 1995, dir. mktg internal medicine products, 1995-96, dir. comml. ops. Europe, 1996-98; gen. mgr. Wyeth-Ayerst Global Pharma., Sweden, 1999—2001; v.p. endocrine care, global prescription bus. Pharmacia Corp., Peapack, NJ, 2001—. Chmn., chief exec. officer W. Swedish Model Group, Gothenburg, 1985. Author: Emergency Surgery, 1985, The Art of Driving a Car Free, 1985. Mem. AMA, Am. Coll. Physician Execs., Pharm. Advt. Coun. Office: Pharmacia Corp 100 Rte 206 N Peapack NJ 07977-8616 Home: 29 Great Hills Rd Short Hills NJ 07078

ROST, THOMAS LOWELL, plant biology educator; b. St. Paul, Dec. 28, 1941; s. Lowell Henry Rost and Agnes Marie (Wojtowicz) Jurek; m. Ann Marie Ruhland, Aug. 31, 1963; children: Christopher, Timothy, Jacquelyn. BS, St. John's U., Collegeville, Minn., 1963; MA, Mankato State U., 1965; PhD, Iowa State U., 1971. Postdoctoral fellow Brookhaven Nat. Lab., Upton, N.Y., 1970-72; asst. to full prof. dept. botany U. Calif., Davis, 1972-82, faculty asst. to chancellor, 1982-83, prof., chmn. plant biology sect., 1994-96, assoc. dean divsn. biol. sci., 1996—. Cons. faculty of agronomy U. Uruguay, 1979, 89; vis. fellow Rsch. Soc. Biol. Sci., Canberra, Australia, 1979-80; vis. prof. U. Wroclaw, Poland, 1987, U. Exeter, Eng., 1993. Co-author: Botany: A Brief Introduction to Plant Biology, 1979, Botany: An Introduction on Plant Biology, 1982; co-editor: Mechanisms and Control of Cell Division, 1977, Plant Biology, 1998; also numerous articles to profl. jours. Served to capt. U.S. Army, 1965-67. Fellow Japan Soc. Promotion of Sci.; mem. Bot. Soc. Am., Soc. Exptl. Biology, Am. Inst. Biol. Sci. Democrat. Roman Catholic. Avocation: community theatre. Office: U Calif Sect Plant Biology Davis CA 95616-8537

ROST, WILLIAM JOSEPH, chemist; b. Fargo, N.D., Dec. 8, 1926; s. William Melvin and Christine Ruth (Hamerlik) R.; m. Rita Cincoski, Sept. 15, 1951; children— Kathryn, Patricia, Carol. BS, U. Minn., 1948, PhD, 1952. From asst. prof. to prof. pharm. chemistry Sch. Pharmacy U. Kansas City, Mo., 1952-63; prof. pharm. chemistry Sch. Pharmacy U. Mo., Kansas City, 1963—. Co-author: Principles of Medicinal Chemistry, 1974, 3d rev. edit., 1988; contbr. articles profl. jours. Mem. Am. Pharm. Assn., Am. Chem. Soc., Sigma Xi, Kappa Psi, Rho Chi, Phi Lambda Upsilon. Home: 709 W 115th Ter Kansas City MO 64114-5597 Office: U Mo Sch of Pharmacy Kansas City MO 64110

ROSTAD, LEE B. rancher, writer; b. Roundup, Mont., Oct. 28, 1929; d. Edward and Emma Gail (Haddock) Birkett; m. O. Phillip Rostad, June 29, 1952; children: Phillip, Carl Eric. BA with honors, U. Mont., 1951; LLD (hon.) , Rocky Mountain Coll., Billings, Mont., 1995. Rancher Rostad and Rostad, Martinsdale, Mont., 1952—; tchr. Pub. Sch., Great Falls, 1953-54, White Sulphur Springs, 1967-68, Helena, 1968-72. Bd. dirs., fundraiser Mountainveiw Med. cTr., White Sulphur Springs, 1990—2000. Author: (novels) Honey Wine and Hunger Root, 1985, Fourteen Cents and Seven Green Apples, 1992, Mountains of Gold, Hills of Grass, 1994; illustrator, author Meagher County Sketchbook; newspaper columnist:. Trustee Mont. State Hist. Soc., 1997—, exec. bd.; sec.-treas. Mont. chpt. Nat. Mus. Women in the Arts, 1992—; mem. County Study Commn., Meagher County, 1975; bd. dirs. Mont. Com. Humanities. Recipient Gov.'s Humanities award, 2001; scholar Fulbright, 1952. Mem.: Meathcer County Archives Assn. (charter), Meagher County Hist. Assn. (fundraiser 1960—), Mont. Watercolor Soc. Republican. Avocations: pottery, art, writing. Home and Office: Rostad and Rostad 169 Bozeman Fork Rd Martinsdale MT 59053 E-mail: lrostad@tcc-cmc.net.

ROSTAL, PAMELA MARY, software company executive; b. Chgo., July 17, 1951; d. William George and Helen Mae Cunningham; m. William John Rostal, Oct. 8, 1976; children: Scott Edward, Melinda Kathleen. BA in Chemistry, Coll. of St. Theresa, 1973; BS in Elem. Edn., U. Minn., 1975; MS in Software Engring., U. St. Thomas, 1996; postgrad., Nova Southeastern U. Owner Micro/Com Computer Svcs., St. Paul, 1980-94; tech. specialist Compuware Corp., Mpls., 1994-2000; e-Commerce architect Talent Software Svcs., 2000—. Author: (with others) Business Object Design and Implementation III, 1999. Recipient Chmn.'s Silver award for quality Am. Express Fin. Advisors, 1995. Mem. Assn. for Computing Machinery, Object Tech. User Group (pres.-elect 2000-2001, pres. 2001-2002). Lutheran. Avocations: squash, biking. Office: Talent Software Svcs Inc 5353 Wayzata Blvd Minneapolis MN 55416

ROSTEK, NANCY ELIZABETH, lawyer; b. Plainfield, N.J., June 13, 1970; d. Charles B. and JoAnne M. Longo; m. Thomas G. Rostek, Aug. 13, 1994. BS, Pa. State U., 1992; JD, Villanova U., 1995. Bar: Pa. 1995, N.J. 1996. Law clk. Hon. Rosemary Higgins Cass, Superior Ct. N.J., Newark, 1995-96, Hon. Dickinson R. Debevoise, U.S. Dist. Ct. for N.J., Newark, 1996-97; assoc. Klett Lieber Rooney & Schorling, Pitts., 1997—. Recipient Disting. Svc. award Villanova Law Rev., 1995. Mem. ABA, Pa. Bar Assn., Order of the Coif, Phi Kappa Phi, Potomac Appalachian Trail Club, Eberly Coll. Sci. Office: Klett Rooney Lieber & Schorling One Oxford Ctr 40th Fl Pittsburgh PA 15219 E-mail: nrostek@klettrooney.com.

ROSTEN, IRWIN, writer, producer, director; Writer-producer news, pub. affairs Sta. KNXT-CBS, Los Angeles, 1954-60; dir. news, pub. affairs Sta. KTLA, 1960-63; writer-producer, dir. Wolper Prodns., Inc., 1963-67; chief documentary dept. MGM Studios, Culver City, Calif., 1967-72; pres. Ronox Prodns., Inc., Los Angeles, 1970-87. Writer-prodr.-dir. Nat. Geog. Soc. spls.: Splendid Stones, Elephant, Great Moments with National Geographic, The Thames, Mysteries of the Mind, Gold!, The Legacy of L.S.B. Leakey, The Volga, The Incredible Machine, Grizzly!, The Eerie World of Jacques-Yves Cousteau, National Parks: Playground or Paradise?, numerous other shows including Unsolved Mysteries, The Wolf Men, Ripley's Believe It or Not, Sports Illustrated, Trial by Wilderness, Hollywood: The Dream Factory, Kifaru: The Black Rhinoceros, Birds Do It, Bees Do It, Indestructible People, Journey Into Life, One Man's Noise: Stories of an Adventuresome Oceanographer, Tiger: Lord of the Wild, Celebrate the Century; video prodr. opening ceremonies 1984 Olympic Games, L.A., Interactive Multimedia: Columbus, Evolution/Revolution. Recipient Emmy award Acad. TV Arts and Scis.; recipient Writers Guild Am. award, Peabody award, Am. Med. Writers Assn. award, Christophers award, Ohio State U. award, Saturday Rev. award, CINE Golden Eagle award Mem. Writers Guild Am., Dirs. Guild Am., Acad. TV Arts and Scis., Internat. Documentary Assn. Office: 2217 Chelan Dr Los Angeles CA 90068-2625

ROSTENBERG, LEONA, rare book dealer, writer; b. N.Y.C., Dec. 28, 1908; d. Adolph and Louisa (Dreyfus) R. BA, NYU, N.Y.C., 1930; MA, Columbia U., 1933, PhD, 1973. Founder Leona Rostenberg Rare Books, N.Y.C., 1944—; ptnr. Leona Rostenberg & Madeleine Stern Rare Books, 1945—. Author: English Publishers in the Graphic Arts 1599-1700, 1963, Literary, Political, Scientific, Religious and Legal Publishing, Printing and Bookselling in

England, 1551-1700, 2 vols., 1965, The Minority Press and the English Crown: A Study in Repression 1558-1625, 1971, The Library of Robert Hooke: The Scientific Book Trade of Restoration England, 1989, Bibliately: The History of Books on Postage Stamps, 1977; co-author: Bookman's Quintet: Five Catalogues About Books, 1980, Old and Rare: Forty Years in the Book Business, 1974, 88, Between Boards: New Thoughts on Old Books, 1977, 89, Quest Book - Guest Book: A Biblio-Folly, 1993, Connections: Our Selves - Our Books, 1994, Old Books in the Old World: Reminiscences of Book Buying Abroad, 1996, Old Books, Rare Friends: Two Literary Sleuths and Their Shared Passion, 1997, New Worlds in Old Books, 1999, Books Have Their Fates, 2000, Bookends, 2001, From Revolution to Revolution: Perspectives on Publishing and Bookselling, 2002; contbr. articles to profl. jours. Recipient Alumni Achievement award NYU, N.Y.C., 1998. Mem. Antiquarian Booksellers Assn. Am. (pres. 1972-74), Am. Printing History Assn. (award 1983), Bibliog. Soc. Am., Manuscript Soc. Democrat. Jewish. Achievements include discovery of Louisa May Alcott pseudonym; avocation: dachshunds. Home: 40 E 88th St New York NY 10128-1176 Office: Rostenberg & Stern 40 E 88th St New York NY 10128-1176

ROSTER, MICHAEL, lawyer; b. Chgo., May 7, 1945; AB, Stanford U., 1967, JD, 1973. Bar: Calif. 1973, D.C. 1980. Ptnr. McKenna, Conner & Cuneo, L.A. and Washington, 1973-87, Morrison & Foerster, L.A. and Washington, 1987-93; gen. counsel Stanford (Calif.) U., 1993-2000; exec. v.p., gen. counsel Golden West Fin. Corp., 2000—. Bd. dirs. Silicon Valley Bancshares, vice chmn., 1995—98; chmn. Encirq, 1998—2000, Insert Therapeutics, 2000—, Calif. Bankers Assn., 2001—, Silicon Valley Bancshares, 1998—99. Contbr. articles to profl. jours. Bd. dirs. Pasadena Heritage, 1986-87. Lt. (j.g.) USN, 1969-71. Mem. ABA (chmn. com. on savs. instns. 1985-89, fin. svcs. com. 1981—, banking com. 1989—), Calif. Bar Assn. (chmn. banking com. 1978-79), Am. Corp. Counsel Assn. (chmn. 2000-01), Stanford U. Alumni Assn. (chmn. 1992), L.A. Athletic Club. Home: 1321 Fairlawn Way Pasadena CA 91105-1002 Office: Golden West Fin Corp 1901 Harrison Oakland CA 94612

ROSTOW, CHARLES NICHOLAS, lawyer, educator; b. Geneva, Switzerland, Mar. 3, 1950; s. Eugene Victor and Edna (Greenberg) R.; m. Heyden White, Oct. 31, 1987; children: Theodore Isaac, Celia A.M. BA, Yale U., 1972, PhD, 1979, JD, 1982. Assoc. Shearman & Sterling, N.Y.C., 1982-85; spl. asst. to legal adviser Dept. State, Washington, 1985-87; dep. legal adviser NSC, 1987, spl. asst. to Pres., legal adviser, 1987-93; assoc. prof. Coll. of Law U. Tulsa, Tulsa, 1993—95, disting. rsch. prof. Coll. of Law, 1995—98; exec. dir. Mass. Office Internat. Trade and Investment, 1995-98; dep. staff dir., counsel House Select Comm. on Natl. Sec. & Mil./Comm. Concerns with the PRC, 1998; staff dir. Senate Select Com. on Intelligence, 1999-2000; Charles H. Stockton prof. internat. law U.S. Naval War Coll., Newport, RI, 2001; gen. counsel, sr. policy adviser to U.S. Permanent Rep. to UN, 2001—; gen. counsel & sr. policy adv. to the U.S. Ambassador U.S. Mission to the UN, 2001—. Author: Anglo-French Relations 1934-36, 1984; editor: Akten zur deutschen auswartigen Politik: 1918-1945, vols. XIV-XXI, 1980-83; contbr. articles to prof. jours. Hon. dir. John Goodwin Tower Ctr. for Polit. Studies, So. Meth. U.; nat. adv. bd. Am. Jewish Com. Mem. Royal Inst. Internat. Affairs, Coun. Fgn. Rels., Assn. of Bar of City of N.Y., Phi Beta Kappa, Cosmos Club, Yale Club (N.Y.C.), Elizabethan Club (New Haven). Jewish. Office: US Mission to the UN 799 UN Plaza New York NY 10017

ROSTOW, ELSPETH DAVIES, political science educator; b. N.Y.C. d. Milton Judson and Harriet Elspeth (Vaughan) Davies; m. Walt Whitman Rostow, June 26, 1947; children: Peter Vaughan, Ann Larner. AB, Barnard Coll., 1938; AM, Radcliffe Coll., 1939; MA, Cambridge (Eng.) U., 1949; LHD (hon.), Lebanon Valley Coll.; LLD (hon.), Austin Coll., 1982, Southwestern U., 1988. Mem. faculty various instns. Barnard Coll., N.Y.C. and MIT, Cambridge, 1939-69; mem. faculty U. Tex., Austin, 1969—, dean div. gen. and comparative studies, 1975-77, prof. govt., 1976—, dean Lyndon B. Johnson Sch. Pub. Affairs, 1977-83, Stiles prof. Am. studies, 1985-88, Stiles prof. emerita, 1988—. Mem. Pres.'s Adv. Com. for Trade Negotiations, 1978-82, Pres.'s Commn. for a Nat. Agenda for the Eighties, 1979-81; rsch. assoc. OSS, Washington, 1943-45; Geneva corr. London Economist, 1947-49; lectr. Air War Coll., 1963-81, Army War Coll., 1965, 68, 69, 78, 79, 81, Nat. War Coll., 1962, 68, 74, 75, Indsl. Coll. Armed Forces, 1961-65, Naval War Coll., 1971, Fgn. Svc. Inst., 1974-77, Dept. of State, Europe, 1973; bd. dirs. U.S. Inst. of Peace, vice chmn., 1991, chmn. 1991-92; co-founder The Austin Project, 1991; mem. Gov.'s Task Force on Revenue, Tex., 1991. Author: Europe's Economy After the War, 1948, (with others) American Now, 1968, The Coattailless Landslide, 1974; editor (with Barbara Jordan) The Great Society: A Twenty-Year Critique, 1986; columnist Austin Am. Statesman, 1985-92; contbr. articles to revs., poems to scholarly jours., newspapers, and mags. Trustee Nat. Acad. Pub. Adminstrn., 1989—95, Sarah Lawrence Coll., 1952—59, So. Ctr. for Internat. Studies, 1990—; bd. visitors and govs. St. Johns Coll., 1986—89; bd. dirs. Barnard Coll., 1962—66, Lyndon Baines Johnson Found., 1977—83, Salzburg Seminar, 1981—89, co-chair sr. fellows, 1997—2001; vis. scholar Phi Beta Kappa, 1984—85; bd. adv. to pres. Naval War Coll., Newport, RI, 1995—99; nat. adv Commn. on Deliberative Polling, 1999—. Decorated Order of St. Joan D'Arc; named Fulbright lectr.; recipient Top Hand award, U. Tex. Ex-Students Assn., 1996, Presdl. citation, U. Tex., 1998, Disting. Alumna award, Barnard Coll., 1998; grantee, USIA, 1983—84, 1990. Mem. Tex. Philos. Soc. (trustee 1989-95, 97—), Headliners Found. (vice-chmn. 1996—), Phi Beta Kappa, Phi Nu Epsilon (hon.), Mortar Bd. (hon.), Omicron Delta Kappa. Home: 1 Wildwind Pt Austin TX 78746-2434 Office: U Tex PO Box Y University Station Austin TX 78713 E-mail: elspeth.rostow@mail.utexas.edu.

ROSTOW, WALT WHITMAN, economist, educator; b. N.Y.C., Oct. 7, 1916; s. Victor Aaron and Lillian (Helman) R.; m. Elspeth Vaughan Davies, June 26, 1947; children: Peter Vaughan, Ann Larner. BA, Yale U., 1936, PhD, 1940. Instr. econs. Columbia U., 1940-41; asst. chief German-Austrian econ. div. Dept. State, 1945-46; Harmsworth prof. Am. history Oxford (Eng.) U., 1946-47; asst. to exec. sec. Econ. Commn. for Europe, 1947-49; Pitt. prof. Am. history Cambridge (Eng.) U., 1949-50; prof. econ. history MIT, 1950-60; staff mem. Center Internat. Studies, 1951-60; dep. spl. asst. to Pres. for nat. security affairs, 1961; counselor, chmn. policy planning council Dept. State, 1961-66; spl. asst. to Pres., 1966-69; U.S. rep., ambassador Inter-Am. Com. Alliance for Progress, 1964-66; now Rex G. Baker Jr. prof. polit. economy, depts. econs. and history U. Tex., Austin, prof. emeritus. Mem. Bd. Fgn. Scholarships, 1969-72, Austin Project, 1982—. Author: The American Diplomatic Revolution, 1947, Essays on the British Economy of the Nineteenth Century, 1948, The Process of Economic Growth, 1953, 2d edit., 1960, (with A.D. Gayer, A.J. Schwartz) The Growth and Fluctuation of the British Economy, 1790-1850, 1953, 2d edit., 1975, (with A. Levin, others) The Dynamics of Soviet Society, 1953, (with others) The Prospects for Communist China, 1954, (with R.W. Hatch) An American Policy in Asia, 1955, (with M.F. Millikan) A Proposal: Key to an Effective Foreign Policy, 1957, The United States in the World Arena, 1960, The Stages of Economic Growth, 1960, 2d edit., 1971, 3d edit., 1990, A View from the Seventh Floor, 1964, A Design for Asian Development, 1965, (with William E. Griffith) East-West Relations: Is Detente Possible?, 1969, Politics and the Stages of Growth, 1971, The Diffusion of Power, 1972, How It All Began, 1975, The World Economy: History and Prospect, 1978, Getting From Here to There, 1978, Why the Poor Get Richer and the Rich Slow Down, 1980, Pre-Invasion Bombing Strategy: General Eisenhower's Decision of March 25, 1944, 1981, British Trade Fluctuations, 1868-1896: A Chronicle and a Commentary, 1981, The Division of Europe After World War II: 1946, 1981, Europe After Stalin: Eisenhower's Three Decisions of March 11, 1953, 1982, Open Skies: Eisenhower's Proposal of July 21, 1955, 1982, The Barbaric Counter-Revolution: Cause and Cure, 1983, Eisenhower, Kennedy, and Foreign Aid, 1985, The United States and the Regional Organization of Asia and the Pacific: 1965-1985, 1986, Rich Countries and Poor Countries, 1987, Essays on a Half Century: Ideas, Policies and Action, 1988, History, Policy, and Economic Theory, 1989, Theorists of Economic Growth From David Hume to the Present with a Perspective on the Next Century, 1990, The Great Population Spike, 1998; editor: The Economics of Take-Off Into Sustained Growth, 1963. Maj. OSS, AUS, 1942-45. Decorated Legion of Merit, Hon. Order Brit. Empire (mil.); recipient Presdl. Medal of Freedom with distinction; Rhodes scholar Balliol Coll., 1936-38, Outstanding Work in Social Scis. award Assn. Am. Pubs., 1990. Mem. Am. Acad. Arts and Scis., Am. Philos. Soc., Mass. Hist. Soc., Tex. Philos. Soc., Cosmos Club, Elizabethan Club. Clubs: Cosmos (Washington); Elizabethan (New Haven). Home: 1 Wildwind Pt Austin TX 78746-2434 E-mail: rostow@ecu.utexas.edu.

ROSTROPOVICH, MSTISLAV LEOPOLDOVICH, conductor, music director, musician; b. Baku, USSR, Mar. 27, 1927; s. Leopold and Sofia (Fedotova) R.; m. Galina Pavlovna Vishnevskaya; children: Olga, Elena. Grad., Moscow Conservatory 1948; numerous hon. doctorate degrees. Faculty mem. Moscow Conservatory, 1953, prof., 1960; head cello and double-bass dept., formerly prof. Leningrad Conservatory; music dir., conductor Nat. Symphony Orch., Washington, 1977-94; hon. prof. Cuban Nat. Conservatory, 1960-78. Pres. Evian Internat. Music Festival. Debut as violoncellist, 1940; performer world concert tours, Moscow Philharm. Orch.; recordings include (with various artists) Mstislav Rostropovich Melodiya Recordings, 1949-56, 48-59, The Young Rostropovich: Rare Recordings for the 1950-52 Years, Schnittke's Cello Concerto No. 2, In Memorium, Return to Russia. Decorated Hon. Knight of the Brit. Empire, 1987; Commdr. French Legion of Honor, 1987; Officer's Cross of Merit, Fed. Republic Germany, 1987; recipient Stalin prize, 1951, 53, Lenin prize, 1963, Life in Music prize, 1984, Albert Schweitzer Music award, 1985, Grammy awards, 1970, 77, 80, 84, Presdl. Medal Freedom, 1987, Ditson Condr.'s award, Columbia U., 1990, Four Freedoms award Franklin and Eleanor Roosevelt Inst., 1992; named Musician of Yr., Mus. Am., 1987. Mem. Am. Acad. Arts and Scis., Union Soviet Composers, Brit. Royal Acad. Music (hon.), Acad. Arts of French Inst.-Forty Immortals. Address: c/o CAMI 165 W 57th St New York NY 10019-2201 also: Gazetny per 13 Apt 79 103009 Moscow Russia

ROSVALLY, JENNIFER, psychotherapist; b. N.Y.C., Dec. 8, 1954; d. Sidney R. and Shura Saul; m. William H. Rosvally, Jan. 1984; children: Danielle, Matthew, Amy. BA, Hunter Coll., 1976, MSW, 1978. Diplomate in clin. social workers Am. Bd. Examiners ; cert. social worker N.Y. State Edn. Dept. Pvt. practice psychotherapy, Bedford Hills, NY, 1978—; social worker North Rockland (N.Y.) Sch. Dist., 1980; med. social worker Montefiore Hosp., Bronx, 1980—86. Author: Harmonies/Mother Daughter Duets, 1998; musician: (CD) Harmonies, 1999. Social work family educator Family Resource Network, Westchester County, 1999—. Mem.: NASW (Acad. Cert. Social Workers). Avocations: musician, singer, songwriter, poet, author. Home: PO Box 676 Goldens Bridge NY 10526

ROSWELL, ROBERT H. federal agency administrator; MD, U. Okla., 1975. Diplomate Am. Bd. Internal Medicine. Resident in internal medicine U. Okla. Sch. Medicine; mem. faculty various med. schs.; fellow in endocrinology and metabolism U. Okla. Sch. Medicine; various leadership positions VA facilities, VA Ctrl. Office, Washington; chief of staff VA med. ctrs., Birmingham, Ala., Oklahoma City; dir. Fla. and P.R. VA healthcare network, Bay Pines, Fla., 1995; exec. dir. Fed. Persian Gulf Vets. Coordinating Bd., 1994—99; under sec. health Dept. Vets. Affairs, Washington, 2002—. Served in U.S. Army, 1978—80, col. med. corps USAR. Office: US Dept Vets Affairs Vets Health Adminstrn 810 Vermont Ave NW Washington DC 20420*

ROTARIU, GEORGE JULIAN, retired physical chemist, consultant; b. L.A., Aug. 24, 1917; s. Julian and Anna Rotariu; m. Janet McAuley, June 19, 1948; children: Mark, Ann, William. BS, U. Chgo., 1939, MS in Phys. Chemistry, 1940; PhD in Phys. chemistry, U. Ill., 1950; postgrad., U. Calif., Berkeley, 1950-52. Analytical chemist Toxicity Lab. U. Chgo., 1941-45; asst. prof. phys. chemistry Loyola U., Chgo., 1952-55; dir. Inland Test Labs., dir. nuc. tech. Cook Electric Co., 1955-57; dir. nuc. tech. Booz-Allen Applied Rsch., 1957-62; chief isotope-applied br. U.S. Atomic Energy Commn., Washington, 1962-64, chief divsn. isotopes devel. instruments/radiation br., 1964-70; sr. scientist biology and safety divsn. U.S. Dept. Energy, 1970-85; ret. cons. Bethesda, Md., 1985—. Cons. U.S. Dept. Energy, Washington, 1981-83, Inst. Atomic Physics, Bucharest, Romania, 1992-95; expert cons. Internat. Atomic Energy Agy., Vienna, Austria, 1993. Contbr. articles to profl. jours. Active U.S. Civil Patrol, Berkeley, 1951-53; examiner Boy Scouts Am., Bethesda, Kensington, Md., 1961-65; chmn. judges Internat. Sci. Fair, Kansas City, Mo., 1971; active Men's Club All Saints Episcopal Ch., Chevy Chase, Md., 1975—. Grantee U.S. Atomic Energy Commn., Washington, 1959-61; recipient award Am. Nuclear Soc. Recognition award. Fellow Am. Nuc. Soc. (emeritus, pres. Chgo. chpt. 1960). Achievements include designing and building the world's first large Cobalt-60 Irradiator (62, 500 curies), 1956, precursor to the present gamma irradiators for food sterilization. Avocations: travel, fishing, computers, locksmithing, joke collecting. Home: 4609 Woodfield Rd Bethesda MD 20814-4043 E-mail: g.rotariu@worldnett.att.net.

ROTBERG, EUGENE HARVEY, investment banker, lawyer; b. Phila., Jan. 19, 1930; s. Irving Bernard and Blanche Grace (Levick) R.; m. Iris Sybil Comens; children— Diana Golda, Pamela Lynn. BS, Temple U., 1951; LL.B., U. Pa., 1954; PhD (hon.), Salem-Teikyo U., 1992. Chief counsel Office Policy Research Securities and Exchange Commn., Washington, 1963-66; v.p., treas. World Bank, 1969-87; exec. v.p. Merrill Lynch & Co., N.Y.C., 1987-90. Served with U.S. Army. Decorated King Leopold II medal (Belgium); recipient Disting. Svc. award Securities and Exch. Commn., 1968; named Alumnus of Yr., Temple U. Home: 7211 Brickyard Rd Potomac MD 20854-4808 Office: 1250 24th St NW Ste 350 Washington DC 20037-1124 E-mail: genebanker@aol.com.

ROTBERG, IRIS COMENS, social scientist; b. Phila., Dec. 16, 1932; d. Samuel Nathaniel and Golda (Shuman) Comens; m. Eugene H. Rotberg, Aug. 29, 1954; children: Diana Golda, Pamela Lynn. BA, U. Pa., 1954, MA, 1955; PhD, Johns Hopkins U., Balt., 1958. Research psychologist Pres.'s Commn. on Income Maintenance Programs, Washington, 1968-69, Office Planning, Research and Evaluation, Office Econ. Opportunity, Washington, 1970-73; dep. dir. compensatory edn. study Nat. Inst. Edn., 1974-77, dir. Office Planning and Program Devel., 1978-82; program dir. NSF, Arlington, Va., 1985-87, 89-91, 1993-96; tech. policy fellow Com. on Sci., Space and Tech., U.S. Ho. of Reps., Washington, 1987-89; sr. social scientist RAND, 1991-93; rsch. prof. edn. policy Grad. Sch. Edn. and Human Devel. George Washington U., 1996—. NSF fellow, 1956-58. Home: 7211 Brickyard Rd Potomac MD 20854-4808 E-mail: irotberg@gwu.edu.

ROTBERG, ROBERT IRWIN, historian, political economist, educator, editor; b. Newark, Apr. 11, 1935; s. Louis and Mildred S. R.; m. Joanna H. Henshaw, June 17, 1961; children: Rebecca T.H., Nicola S.D., Fiona J.Y. AB, Oberlin Coll., 1955; MPA, Princeton U., 1957; DPhil, U. Oxford, 1960. Asst. prof. history, rsch. assoc. Ctr. for Internat. Affairs Harvard U., 1961-68, rsch. assoc. Ctr. for Internat. Affairs, 1968-95; rsch. dir. Twentieth Century Fund, 1968-71; prof. polit. sci. and history MIT, 1968-87; acad. v.p. for Arts, Scis. and Tech. Tufts U., Medford, Mass., 1987-90; pres. Lafayette Coll., Easton, Pa., 1990-93, World Peace Found., Cambridge, 1993—; coord. Inst. for Internat. Devel. Harvard U., 1993-99, dir. program on intrastate conflict Kennedy Sch., 1999—. Adj. prof. Kennedy Sch. Govt., Harvard U., 1993—; mem. coun. NEH, 1993—; cons. Dept. State, 1968-78, Commrs. of Middlesex County, Mass., 1976-77. Author: A Political History of Tropical Africa, 1965, The Rise of Nationalism in Central Africa, 1965, Protest and Power in Black Africa, 1970, Joseph Thomson and the Exploration of Africa, 1971, Haiti: The Politics of Squalor, 1971, Africa and Its Explorers, 1971, The Black Homelands of South Africa, 1977, Black Heart: Gore-Browne and the Politics of Multiracial Zambia, 1978, Conflict and Compromise in South Africa, 1980, Suffer the Future: Policy Choices in Southern Africa, 1980, Imperialism, Colonialism and Hunger, 1982, Namibia: Economic and Political Prospects, 1983, South Africa and its Neighbors, 1985, The Founder: Cecil Rhodes and the Pursuit of Power, 1988, Africa in the 1990s and Beyond: Policy Opportunities and Choices, 1988, From Massacres to Genocide: The Media, Public Policy, and Humanitarian Crises, 1996, Vigilance and Vengeance: NGOs Preventing Ethnic Conflict in Divided Societies, 1996, Haiti Renewed: Political and Economic Prospects, 1997, Burma: Prospects for a Democratic Future, 1998, War and Peace in Southern Africa, 1998, Creating Peace in Sri Lanka, 1999, Peacekeeping and Peace Enforcement in Africa, 2000, Truth v. Justice, 2000, Patterns of Social Capital, 2001, Ending Autocracy, Enabling Democracy, 2002; editor Jour. Interdisciplinary History, 1970—. Chmn. Middlesex County Govtl. Rev. Task Force, 1972; v.p. Cambridge Civic Assn., 1969-72; mem. Lexington Town Meeting, 1973-90, 94—, Lexington Sch. Com., 1974-77; mem. Ciskel Commn., 1979-80; trustee World Peace Found., 1980—, Oberlin Coll., 1983—, Coun. Internat. Exch. Scholars, 1991-95. Rhodes scholar U. Oxford, 1960; Guggenheim fellow, 1970-71; Hazen Found. fellow, 1976-77. Fellow Royal Geog. Soc.; mem. Am. Hist. Assn., African Studies Assn., Coun. on Fgn. Rels., Oberlin Coll. Alumni Assn. (pres. 1981-82). Office: World Peace Found Belfer Ctr 79 John F Kennedy St Cambridge MA 02138-5758 E-mail: robert_rotberg@harvard.edu.

ROTCH, JAMES E. lawyer; b. Auburn, Ala., Mar. 26, 1945; s. Elroy B. and Martha (Ellisor) R.; m. Darlene Edwards; children: Jamison B., Susannah R., Amie L. Vaughn. BS, Auburn U., 1967, postgrad., 1967-68; JD, U. Va., 1971. Bar: Ala. 1971, U.S. Dist. Ct. (no. dist.) Ala. 1973. Rsch. asst. Office Instl. Rsch. Auburn (Ala.) U., 1967-68; clk. U.S. Judiciary System, Birmingham, Ala., 1971-72; assoc. Bradley Arant Rose & White LLP, 1971-76; ptnr. Bradley, Arant, Rose & White LLP, 1976—, administrv. ptnr., 1990-93. Mem. adv. com. Bioelastics Rsch. Ltd., Birmingham, 1992—. Gov.'s Task Force on Biotechnology, Ala., 1993. Author: The Birmingham Pledge. Pres. adv. com. Birmingham Mus. Art, 1989-92; bd. dirs. Operation New Birmingham, 1990-91, 95—, co-chmn. cmty. affairs com., mem. exec. com.; Coalition for Better Edn., Birmingham, 1990—; active Boy Scouts Am.; bd. dirs. Birmingham Com. for Olympic Soccer, 1994-96, Ala. Sports Found., 1994-98, Entrepreneurial Ctr. Inc., 1996—, chmn., 2002; mem. adminstrv. bd. Canterbury United Meth. Ch., 1991-93; chmn. Birmingham Pledge Found., 2000—. Capt. USAR, 1972-78. Mem. ALA, Auburn U. Bar Assn., Birmingham Bar Assn., Internat. Bar Assn., Ala. State Bar Assn., Leadership Birmingham, Leadership Ala. (bd. dirs. 1998--), , Auburn Coll. Liberal Arts (adv. coun.), U. Va. Alumni Assn., Newcomen Soc., Birmingham Area C. of C. (bd. dirs. 2001, vice chmn. for tech. devel. 2002), Auburn U. Alumni Assn., Birmingham Venture Club (bd. dirs. 2001), Country Club of Birmingham, Jockey Club, Summit Club (charter), Kiwanis (sec. 1998-99). Methodist. Avocations: horses, bird hunting, cattle farming, golf. Office: Bradley Arant Rose & White LLP One Federal Pl 1819 5th Ave N Birmingham AL 35203

ROTCHFORD, PATRICIA KATHLEEN, lawyer, mediator; b. Chgo., Nov. 17, 1945; d. Charles E. Sr. and Mary (Rodde) R.; 1 child, John. BA with honors, Rosary Coll., River Forest, Ill., 1966; JD, No. Ill. U., 1979. Bar: Ill. 1979; cert. mediator/arbitrator, Mich., Ill. Tchr. pub. schs., Schiller Park, Ill., 1966-76; sole practice Elmhurst, 1977-79; assoc. Shand, Morahan, Evanston, 1979-83; corp. counsel CNA Fin., Chgo., 1983-86; gen. counsel, v.p. and corp. sec. MMI Cos., Bannockburn, Ill., 1986-87; gen. counsel, v.p., corp. sec. Inland Group, Northbrook, 1987-90; pvt. practice fin. and ins. legal counsel, 1990—. Bd. dirs. Notre Dame Corp., Chgo.; U.S. rep. ins. claims Lloyds of London; mediator. Author: (pamphlet) Handle Your Own Claims, 1983, (book) Women's Resource Guide, 1988, Women's Insurance and Financial Resource Guide, 1988. Counselor for battered women. Mem. ABA (mem. dispute resolution sect.), Mich. Bar, Womens Bar Assn. Ill. (active coms. and activities), Corp. Councils Am., Womens Exec. Network, Nat. Assn. for Women in Careers (nat. bd. dirs.), Spider. Office: PO Box 4422 Northbrook IL 60065-4422

ROTE, NELLE FAIRCHILD HEFTY, business consultant; b. Watsontown, Pa., May 23, 1930; d. Edwin Dunkel and Phebe Hill (Fisher) Fairchild; m. John Austin Hefty, Mar. 20, 1948 (div. June 1970); children: Harry E. Hefty, John B. Hefty, Susan E. Hefty DeBartolo; m. Keith Maynard Rote, Dec. 16, 1983 (dec. Aug. 1985). Student, Bucknell U., 1961, Williamsport Sch. of Commerce, 1968-69, Pa. State U., 1971-72, 83, Susquehanna U., 1986. Typesetter, page designer Colonial Printing House, Inc., Lewisburg, Pa., 1970-76; account exec. Sta. WTGC Radio, 1976-78; co-owner Colonial Printing Co., 1978-83; temp. HATS-Temps, 1986-89; artist, editor Create-A-Book, Inc., Milton, Fla., 1980-92; census crew leader, spl. svc. Dept. Commerce, Washington, 1990; cons. Create-A-Book, Inc., Gulf Breeze, Fla., 1991—99, 2002—. Author: McGruff and Me, 1999, My Christmas Wish 1999, School Fun Book, 1999, My Fishing Adventure, 1999; contbg. author: American Nursing: A Biographical Dictionary, 2000; artist: Children's Playmate Mag., 1942; contbr. articles to profl. jours. 1997 proofreader Lewisburg Bicentennial Commn., 1976; editor-poet Holiday Newspaper Bus. Assn., Lewisburg, 1987; charter mem. Women's Art Mus., Washington; charter sponsor Women in Mil. Svc. Meml., Arlington, Va., 1991; founder, donor Nelle Fairchild Rote Book Fund, Union County Libr. Recipient Humanitarian recognition Tri-County Fedn. Women's Clubs, Pa., 1965, Grand Prize in Cooking, Milton Std., 1966, Most Profl. Photo award, Lewisburg Festival of Arts, 1980, Hon. Mention Award Women in Arts, Harrisburg, Pa., 1981, Photo Contest award Congressman Allen Ertel, Washington, 1981, Photo awards 2d and 3d place Union County Fair, Laurelton, Pa., 1981, Hon. Mention Photo award Susquehanna Art Soc., Selinsgrove, Pa., 1981, Silver award for poetry World of Poetry, 1990. Mem.: DAR (nat. def. reporter Shikelimo chpt. 1989—95, sec. 1992—95, regent 1995—2001, vice chmn. Pa. State Soc. DAR women vets com. 1998—2001, vice-regent 2001—, Prize for safety poster 1942), Soc. Profl. Journalists, Warrior Run Heritage Soc., Orgn. United Environment, Marine Corps League Aux. (life), Western Front Assn., Am. Legion Aux. (Unit 182), Civic Club Lewisburg (v.p. 1994—97). Home: 1015 St Paul St Lewisburg PA 17837-1213

ROTENBERG, DON HARRIS, chemist; b. Portland, Oreg., Mar. 31, 1934; s. Morris Hyman and Helen (Harris) R.; m. Barbara Ress, June 29, 1958; children: Laura, Debra. BA, U. Oreg., 1955; AM, Harvard U., 1956; PhD, Cornell U., 1960. Rsch. chemist Enjay Chem. Lab. Exxon Rsch. & Engring. Co., Linden, N.J., 1960-67, sr. rsch. chemist Enjay Polymer Lab., 1967-71; mgr. polymer sci. and engring. Am. Optical Corp., Southbridge, Mass., 1971-75, dir. materials and process lab., 1975-80, v.p. R&D, 1980-85, v.p., gen. mgr. precision products bus., 1985—88; tech. dir. Coburn Optical Industries, Tulsa, 1988-92; cons. Plastics Tech. Assocs., 1992—; v.p. rsch. and devel. Neolens, Inc., Miami, Fla., 1994-96; mgr. process engring. Sola Optical, 1996-99. Contbr. articles to Advances in Chem. Series, Jour. Macromolecular Sci.-Chem. Todd Rsch. fellow Cornell U., Ithaca, N.Y., 1956-59. Mem. Am. Chem. Soc. (plastics, polymer and rubber divns., contbr. to jour.), Soc. Plastics Engrs., Radtech Internat., Phi Beta Kappa, Sigma Xi. Achievements include patents in field; development of first mass-produced coated polycarbonate safety lenses, of first factory-produced coated plastic prescription lenses, of first photochromic plastic prescription lenses. Home: 4507 E 108th St Tulsa OK 74137-6850 Office: Plastics Tech Assocs 4507 E 108th St Tulsa OK 74137-6850 E-mail: donroten@aol.com.

ROTENBERG, SHELDON, violinist; b. Attleboro, Mass., Apr. 11, 1917; s. Joseph and Jennie (Almer) R.; m. Hilde Sussmann, Jan. 25, 1924; children: David, Steffi. AB, Tufts U., 1939, grad. student, 1939-40; violin pupil of, Felix Winternitz, Georges Enesco, Maurice Hewitt. Tchr. violin, 1947—. Music adviser, cons. pub. schs., Brookline, Mass.; archivist, cons. Boston Symphony Orch., 1992-93. Concertized extensively with the Boston String Quartet sponsored by Elizabeth Sprague Coolidge, including concerts and rec. at the Libr. of Congress, 1948-52, occupies endowed Kasdon-Paley chair, 1st violin sect., Boston Symphony Orch., 1948-91, solo performances with Boston Pops Orch., 1939-41; Boston Symphony rep. as soloist, tchr., mem. orch. in State Dept. cultural exch. program with Japan Philharm., Tokyo, 1968-69; mem. faculty Boston U. Tanglewood Inst., 1979—. Served to capt. AUS, 1942-46. Mem. Harvard Mus. Assn., Tufts U. Alumni Assn. Home: 60 Browne St Brookline MA 02446-7050 Office: care Boston Symphony Orch Symphony Hall Boston MA 02115

ROTFELD, ADAM DANIEL, research institute director; b. Przemyslany, Lwow, Poland, Mar. 4, 1938; arrived in Sweden, 1989; s. Leon and Berta Rothfeld; m. Barbara Sikorska, Jan. 15, 1970; 1 child, Alicja. Degree in law and diplomacy, Warsaw U., 1960, postgrad., 1962; PhD in Internat. Law, Jagiellonian U., 1969; habilitation, Inst. Internat. Affairs, Warsaw, 1990. Mem. staff Polish Inst. Internat. Affairs, 1961-89, dep. editor-in-chief monthly, 1963-68, sr. rschr., 1969-77, head European Security Dept., 1978-89; fellow Inst. East-West Security Studies, N.Y., 1984-85; project leader European security Stockholm Internat. Peace Rsch. Inst., 1989—2001, dir., leader security project, 1991—; prof. Warsaw U., 2001—; undersecretary of state Ministry of Fgn. Affairs, Warsaw, 2001—. Negotiator Helsinki Final Act of Conf. for Security and Coop. in Europe, Geneva, 1973-75, Belgrade, 1977-78, Madrid, 1980-83, Vienna, 1986-88; personal rep. chmn.-in-office Trans-Dniester Conflict Region of the Republic of Moldova, 1992-93; mem. numerous internat. coms.; editor, pub. SIPRI Yearbook on Armaments, Disarmament and Internat. Security, 1992—; mem. adv. bd. UNESCO Studies on Peace and Conflict, European Fellowship Programme, Ctr. for European

Securities Studies; co-chmn. ind. working group Future Security Agenda for Europe, 1994-96, Stockholm Agenda for Arms Control, 1999. Author: European Security System In Statu Nascendi, 1990; co-editor: (with Walther Stütze) Germany and Europe in Transition, 1991, (with Armand Clesse) Sources and Areas of Future Possible Crisis in Europe, 1995, (with Ian Anthony) A Future Arms Control Agenda, 2001; editor: Military Security and Confidence Building Measures, 1991, Human Rights-International Obligations of Poland, 1989, Building Security in Europe: CBMs and CSCE, 1986; contbr. articles to profl. jours. Pres. Polish UN Student Assn., 1962-64; sec. gen. Polish UN Assn., 1975-80. Recipient award Polish Acad. Scis., 1988, Polish Inst. Internat. Affairs, 1990. Mem.: Nat. Security Coun. Poland, Sci. Coun. of the Inst. for Peace Rsch. and Security Studies (Hamburg, Germany), Swedish Royal Acad. of War Studies, Internat. Inst. Strategic Studies. Avocations: films, reading, walking. Office: Ministry Fgn Affairs Al J Ch Szucha 23 PL-00580 Warsaw Poland

ROTH, ALEDA VENDER, business educator; b. Cleve., Oct. 8, 1945; d. Joseph Patrick and Beatrice Vender; m. G. Douglas Roth, Sept. 26, 1970; children: G. Brian, Lauren Carter. BS in Psychology with honors, Ohio State U., 1968; MSPH in Biostats., U. N.C., 1970; PhD in Ops. Mgmt., Ohio State U., 1986. Chief statistician Ark. Children's Colony Ark. State Dept. Human Svcs., 1968-69; rsch. assoc., epidemiologist Epidemiologic Field Sta. Greater Kansas City Mental Health Found., 1970-72, statis. cons. Epidemiologic Field Sta., 1972-74; nat. dir. stats. dept. ANA, 1972-79; grad. teaching and rsch. assoc. faculty mgmt. sci. Ohio State U., 1979-83, grad. teaching and rsch. assoc. acctg. dept., 1983, instr. computer and info. sys. Coll. Engring., 1983-84, instr. faculty mgmt. sci. Coll. Adminstrv. Sci., 1984-85; asst. prof. Boston U. Sch. Mgmt., 1985-89, prin. investigator retail banking futures project, 1986-94; co-investigator mfg.'s future rsch. Boston U., 1985-89, prin. co-investigator rsch. DTT-UNC gloal vision in mfg., 1989—2001, rsch. assoc. ctr. health rsch. and edn., 1989-93; assoc. prof. dept. health adminstrn. Duke U. Med. Ctr., Durham, 1989-91; assoc. prof. bus. Duke U., N.C., 1989-93; prof., chair Global Supply Chain Concentration U.N.C. dept. Tech. and Innovation Mgmt., Chapel Hill, 1993—. Prin. rsch. co-investigator Internat. Svc. Study, 1996—; vis. scholar London Business Sch., 2000; Vis. prof. WHU Vallender Germany, 2001; adj. faculty mem. Sch. Pub. Health, U. N.C., Chapel Hill, 1972-74; mem. Coop. Health Stats. Sys. Adv. Com., Nat. Ctr. Health Stats., DHHS, 1974-76; membership svcs. com. Nat. Decision Scis. Inst., 1989-90; adj. rsch. faculty Boston U. Mfg. Roundtable, 1985-90; rsch. adv. com. U. N.C. Ctr. for Mfg. Excellence, 1989-94; exec. com. U. N.C. Cato Ctr. Applied Bus. Rsch., 1994-97, rsch. com. 1997-99. Author (with M. van der Velde): The Future of Retail Banking Delivery Systems, 1988; author: Retail Banking Strategies: Opportunities for the 1990s, 1990, World Class Banking: Benchmarking the Market Leaders, 1992; author: (with C. Giffi and G. Seal) Competing in World Class Manufacturing: America's 21st Century Challenge, 1990; editor: Facts About Nursing, 1972-73 edit., 1974, 1974-75 edit., 1976, 1980-81 edit., 1981; editor: (with J. Jaeger and A. Kaluzny) The Management of Continuous Improvement: Cases in Health Administration, 1993; dep. editor: Manufacturing and Service Operations Management, 1996—, assoc. editor: Decision Sciences, 1993—2002, assoc. editor: Jour. Ops. Mgmt., 1993—2001, assoc. editor: , 2001—, mem. editl. rev. bd.: , 1998—, area editor: Prodn. and Ops. Mgmt. Jour., 1993—, mem. editl. adv. bd.: , 1991—93, assoc. editor: OM Review, 1992—94, assoc. editor: Benchmarking for Quality and Tech. Mgmt., 1993—, mem. editl. bd.: Internat. Jour. Prodn. and Ops. Mgmt., 1995—99, mem. editl. bd.: Jour. Svc. Rsch., 1998—, ad hoc referee: Mgmt. Sci., Jour. Ops. Mgmt., Decisions on Scis., Prodn. and Ops. Mgmt. Jour., IEEE Trans.; contbr. articles to profl. jours., chpts. to books. Recipient Book award of excellence Soc. for Tech. Comm., 1992, Kenan Inst. Faculty Rsch. award, 1994, Outstanding Paper award Literati Club, London, 1995, Kenan-Flagler Bus. Sch. Disting. Rsch. award 1996, Best Paper award Acad. Mgmt., 1996, 2000, Best Paper award XXII Brazilian Assn. Post Grad. Courses in Adminstrn., 1998, 99; winner Decision Scis. Inst.'s Interdisciplinary Paper award, 1996, Best Theoretical/Empirical Rsch. Paper award 1985, Doctoral Dissertation award 1985; Anna Dice scholar Ohio State U., 1985; grantee Performance Excellence Coun. of the Conf. Bd., 1991—; NIMH fellow, 1969-70, U. N.C. Cato Ctr. fellow, 1995, Kenan Inst. fellow, 1995-96, Dalton L. McMichael Sr. Rsch. fellow, 1998; Disting. O'Herron Faculty scholar, 1996. Mem. Prodn. and Ops. Mgmt. Assn. (sec. 1988-91, bd. dirs. 1988-94, planning com. ann. conf. 1990-91, session chair ann. mtg. 1991, pres.-elect 2000-02, pres. 2002-), Decision Scis. Inst. (bd. dirs. 1996-98), Phi Kappa Phi, Delta Omega. Office: U NC Kenan-Flagler Bus Sch Chapel Hill NC 27599-3490

ROTH, ALVIN ELIOT, economics educator; b. N.Y.C., Dec. 18, 1951; s. Ernest and Lillian (Caesar) R.; m. Emilie Matarasso, May 22, 1977; children: Aaron Leon, Benjamin Nathaniel. BS, Columbia U., 1971; MS, Stanford U., 1973, PhD, 1974. Asst. prof. dept. bus. adminstrn. and dept. econs. U. Ill., Urbana, 1974-77, assoc. prof., 1977-79, prof., 1979-82; A.W. Mellon prof. econs. U. Pitts., 1982-98; G. Gund Prof. Econs. and bus. Adminstrn. Harvard U., Boston, 1998—. Author: Axiomatic Models of Bargaining, 1979, Game-Theoretic Models of Bargaining, 1985, Laboratory Experimentation in Economics, 1987, The Shapley Value, 1988; (with M. Sotomayor) Two-Sided Matching: A Study in Game Theoretic Modeling and Analysis, 1990; (with J. Kagel) Handbook of Experimental Economics, 1995. Recipient Founders' prize Tex. Instruments Found., 1980; Guggenheim fellow, 1983; A.P. Sloan research fellow, 1984; 10 Outstanding Young Ams. award, 1984; Lanchester prize Ops. Rsch. Soc. Am., 1991. Fellow Econometric Soc., Am. Acad. Arts and Scis.; mem. AAAS, Am. Econ. Assn. Jewish. Home: 89 Rawson Rd Brookline MA 02445-4509 Office: Harvard U Harvard Bus Sch Dept Econs Boston MA 02163

ROTH, BARBARA EDESON, consultant, speech and language pathologist; b. Pitts., Dec. 29, 1955; d. Samuel and Anne Clare (Opachevsky) Edeson; m. James A. Roth, Jan. 15, 1984; 1 child, Sarah Ann. BS, Pa. State U., 1976; MA, Kent State U., 1978. Speech-lang. pathologist Youngstown (Ohio) Hearing and Speech Ctr., 1979, South Hills Health System, Home Health Agy., Pitts., 1980-83; pvt. practive, cons. Rye, N.Y., 1984—. Mem. Am. Speech, Lang. and Hearing Assn., N.Y. State Speech, Lang. and Hearing Assn., Westchester Speech, Lang. and Hearing Assn., Hadassah. Democrat. Jewish. Home: 3 Mildred Ave Rye NY 10580-2419

ROTH, CAROLYN LOUISE, art educator; b. Buffalo, June 17, 1944; d. Charles Mack and Elizabeth Mary (Hassel) R.; m. Charles Turner Barber, Aug. 4, 1991. Student, Art Student's League N.Y., 1965, Instituto Allende, San Miguel de Allende, Mex., 1966; BFA, Herron Sch. Art, 1967; MFA, Fla. State U., 1969. Asst. prof. art U. Tenn., Chattanooga, 1969-72; lectr. art So. Ill. U., Carbondale, 1973-75; asst. prof. art U. Evansville, Ind., 1975-80; lectr. art U. So. Ind., Evansville, 1984—. Exhbn. coord., gallery dir. Krannert Gallery, U. Evansville, 1977-79; exhbn. coord., conf. advisor Ind. Women in Arts Conf., Ind. Arts Commn., Evansville, 1978; reviewer in field. One-woman shows include Wabash Valley Coll., Mt. Carmel, Ill., 1994, So. Ind. Ctr. for Arts, Seymour, Ind., 1996, Zionsville (Ind.) Muncie Art Ctr., 1997, Oakland City (Ind.) U., 1998; exhibited in group shows Liberty Gallery, Louisville, 1992, Artlink Contemporary Art Gallery, Ft. Wayne, Ind., 1994, S.E. Mo. Coun. on Arts, Cape Girardeau, 1994, Lexington (Ky.) Art League, 1996, Mills Pond Horse Gallery, St. James, N.Y., 1996, SOHO Gallery, Pensacola, Fla., 1996, Indpls. Art Ctr., 1996, Artemesia Gallery, Chgo., 1997, DelMar Coll., Corpus Christi, Tex., 1998, La. State U., Baton Rouge, 1998, Woman Made Gallery, Chgo., 2002; works appeared in various publs.; represented by Gallery Hertz, Louisville. Malone fellow visitor to Morocco and Tunisia, 1996. Mem. Nat. Mus. Women in Arts, Met. Mus. Art, Evansville Mus. Arts and Sci., New Harmony Gallery of Contemporary Art, Golden Key Honor Soc. (hon.). Democrat. Mem. Unity Ch. Avocation: travel to study art works in museums and galleries in Europe and Mex. Home: 10801 S Woodside Dr Evansville IN 47712-8422 Office: U So Ind 8600 University Blvd Evansville IN 47712-3534

ROTH, CHARLES PHILIP, psychotherapist; b. Phila., Mar. 2, 1950; s. Charles Philip and Elizabeth Teresa (Callahan) R.; m. Patricia I. O'Connor, Nov. 9, 1985; 1 child, Caitlin. BA, St. Joseph's U., Phila., 1972; MS, Drexel U., Phila., 1976; MA, PhD, Calif. Sch. Profl. Psychology, Alameda, 1983, 94. Head tech. svcs. LaSalle U., Phila., 1977-79, Phila. Coll. Pharmacy, 1979-81; doctoral intern Fairmont Hosp., San Leandro, Calif., 1982-83, Jung Inst., San Francisco, 1983-85, McAuley Neuropsychiatric, San Francisco, 1984-85; pvt. practice, 1985—; counselor Parent's Place, 1989-92; psychology staff Children's Health Coun., Palo Alto, 1998—; lectr. grad. counseling dept. San Francisco State U., 2001—. Court expert Family Ct., San Francisco, 1993—, Alameda County, 1994—, Marin County, 1997—, San Mateo County, 1996—; assoc. prof. grad. counseling program San Francisco State U., 2001—. Warner grantee Warner Trust, 1984. Mem.: Schwab Learning Found., Epilepsy Found. Am., Learning Disabilities Assn., Internat. Dyslexia Assn., Calif. Assn. Marriage & Family Therapists, APA (divsn. of child psychology). Democrat. Episcopal. Avocations: hiking, writing, travel. Office: 2538 California St San Francisco CA 94115-2616 E-mail: drcproth@aol.com.

ROTH, DANIEL BENJAMIN, lawyer, business executive; b. Youngstown, Ohio, Sept. 17, 1929; s. Benjamin F. and Marion (Benjamin) R.; m. Joann M. Roth; children: William M., Jennifer A., Rochelle. BS in Fin., Miami U., Oxford, Ohio, 1951; JD, Case-Western Res. U., 1956. Bar: Ohio 1956, U.S. Supreme Ct. 1960, D.C. 1983. Pres. Roth, Blair, Roberts, Strasfeld & Lodge, LPA, Youngstown, 1969—; co-founder, vice chmn. Nat. Data Processing Corp., Cin., 1961-69; chmn., pres., CEO Torent, Inc., Youngstown, 1971—, Morrison Metalweld Process Corp., 1979—; vice chmn. McDonald Steel Corp., 1980—, Torent Oil & Gas Co., 1979—, Vaughn Indsl. Car & Equipment Co., 1988—. Bd. dirs. Morrison Metalweld Process Corp., Gasser Chair Co., Hamlin Steel Products, Inc. Profl. singer: appearances including Steve Allen Show, 1952. Bd. dirs. Youngstown Symphony, Stambaugh Auditorium; bd. dirs. Youngstown Playhouse, v.p., 1991-93; pres. Rodef Sholom Temple, Youngstown, 1982-84. 1st lt. USAF, 1951-53, lt. col. Res., ret. Recipient Mgr. of Yr. award Mahoning Valley Mgmt. Assn., 1989, Man of Yr. award Youngstown YWCA, 1995. Mem. ABA, D.C. Bar Assn., Ohio Bar Assn., Mahoning County Bar Assn., Lawyer-Pilots Bar Assn., Soc. Benchers of Case Western Res. U. Law Sch., Youngstown Club, Pelican Marsh Club (Naples, Fla.), Pelican Isle Yacht Club (Naples), Zeta Beta Tau (nat. v.p. 1964-66), Omicron Delta Kappa, Phi Eta Sigma, Tau Epsilon Rho. Jewish. Home: 1699 Persimmon Dr Naples FL 34109 Office: 600 City Centre One Youngstown OH 44503-1514

ROTH, DON, orchestra executive; m. Mary Ellen Roth; children: Florence, Daniel. Gen. mgr. Austin (Tex.) Symphony, 1977-80; mng. dir. Hartford (Conn.) Symphony, 1980-83; exec. dir. Syracuse (N.Y.), 1986; gen. mgr. San Francisco Symphony, 1987-90; exec. dir. Oreg. Symphony, Portland, 1990-98, pres., 1992-98; exec. dir. St. Louis Symphony Orch., 1998—, St Louis Symphony Orch., 1998—2000; pres., CEO Aspen Music Festival, 2002—. Office: 2 Music School Rd Aspen CO 81611*

ROTH, DUANE J. pharmaceutical executive; Grad., Iowa Wesleyan Coll. Chmn., CEO Alliance Pharm. Corp. Chmn. San Diego Regional Econ. Devel. Corp.; mem. bd. dir. Biotechnology Industry Org., CA Healthcare Inst. Chmn. Am. Heart Assn. Heart Walk; co-chair Children's Hosp. Found.'s Ann. Miracles Weekend. Named IFCD Dir. of Yr. for Corp. Citizenship; recipient AT & T Internat. Bus. Leadership award, San Diego Press Club's Headliner of Yr. award, Making a Difference award, San Diego Citizens Against Lawsuit Abuse, Price Waterhouse Svc. to the Biotechnology Cmty. award, James McGraw Disting. Contbn. award for svc. to San Diego biomed. industry. Office: Alliance Pharm Corp 3040 Sci Park Rd San Diego CA 92121*

ROTH, EUGENE, lawyer; b. Wilkes-Barre, Pa., June 28, 1935; s. Max and Rae (Klein) R.; m. Constance D. Smulyan, June 16, 1957; children: Joan Roth Kleinman, Steven P., Jeffrey H., Lawrence W. BS, Wilkes U., 1957; LLB, Pa. State U., 1960. Bar: Pa. 1960, U.S. Dist. Ct. (mid. dist.) Pa. 1961. Assoc. Rosenn, Jenkins & Greenwald LLP, Walkes-Barre, 1960-64, ptnr., 1964—. Mem. Northeastern Pa. Regional bd. 1st Union Bank; bd. dirs. RCN Corp., Commonwealth Telephone Enterprises, Inc.; chmn. Greater Wilkes-Barre Partnership, Inc., 1991-93. Trustee Wilkes U., 1979—, chmn. 1993-98; chmn. United Way of Wyoming Valley, 1983; chmn. annual campaign Osterhout Free Libr. Campaign, 1999; Northeastern Pa. regional bd. dirs. Geiseinger-Wyoming Valley Hosp. Recipient Disting. Pennsylvanian award Phila. C. of C., 1980, Cmty. Svc. award B'nai B'rith, 1994, Disting. Citizen award N.E. Pa. Boy Scouts Am., 1998, Shofar award United Hebrew Inst., 2001; named Outstanding Vol. Fund Raiser Nat. Soc. Fund Raising Exec., 1993. Mem. ABA, Pa. Bar Assn., Luzerne County Law and Libr. Assn., Wilkes-Barre C. of C. (chmn. 1980, vice com. for econ. growth), Wyo. Valley United Jewish Campaign (chmn. 1978 and 1993), B'nai B'rith. Republican. Jewish. Avocations: reading, community svc. Office: Rosenn Jenkins & Greenwald 15 S Franklin St Wilkes Barre PA 18711-0076 E-mail: er@rjglaw.com.

ROTH, GARY NEAL, accountant; b. Santa Monica, Calif., Nov. 30, 1961; s. Lewis David and Beverly Sue (Steel) R.; m. Tiffany Anne Lachtman, Aug. 8, 1998; children: Brandon Steel and Collin Benjamin (twins), Parker Immanuel. BS in Bus. Adminstrn., Calif. State U., Northridge, 1983. CPA, Calif.; cert. tax profl. Clk., field rep. Equifax Svcs., Inc., Santa Monica, Calif., 1979-86; acctg. mgr., contr. OneCard Systems Corp., L.A., 1983-88; sr. tax acct., auditor Pannell Kerr Forster, CPAs, 1989-91; sr. acct., auditor Getz, Krycler & Jakubovits, CPAs, Sherman Oaks, Calif., 1992-96; sr. acct. London & Co LLP, CPAs, L.A., 1996—. Cons. U.S. Resolution Trust Corp., Denver, 1991. Auditor Stop Cancer, L.A., 1992-96; acct. Fair-Taste of L.A., Santa Monica, Calif., 1989-90; venue acct. L.A. Summer Olympics, 1984; tax preparer Vol. Income Tax Assn., L.A., 1983. Mem. AICPA, Calif. Soc. CPAs, Nat. Soc. Tax Profls., Zeta Beta Tau. Avocations: exercise enthusiast, musician, international traveler. Home: 19728 Lull St Winnetka CA 91306-2675 Office: London & Co LLP CPAs 11601 Wilshire Blvd #2040 Los Angeles CA 90025

ROTH, GEORGE STANLEY, research biochemist, physiologist; b. Honolulu, Aug. 5, 1946; s. George Frederick and Laura Ann (Zembrzuski) R.; m. Mary Jane Fletcher, Mar. 11, 1972; children: Susan Marie, George William. BS, Villanova U., 1968; PhD, Temple U., 1971. Fellow Fels Rsch. Inst., Phila., 1971-72; staff fellow Gerontology Rsch. Ctr. NIH, Balt., 1972-76, rsch. chemist, 1976—, chief molecular physiology and genetics sect., 1984-99, sr. guest scientist, 2000—; pres., CEO Gerotech Inc., 2000—. Vis. prof. Mehary Med. Coll., Nashville, 1983; Alpha Omega Alpha prof. U. P.R. Med. Sch., San Juan, 1986; chmn. Gordon Rsch. Conf. on Biology of Aging, Oxnard, Calif., 1985; rsch. cons. George Washington U., 1977-82; Ben Cohen Meml. lectr. U. Mich., 1998; lectr. Med. Sci. Ctr. Student Sci. Program, 1980, Sandoz lectr. gerontology, Basel, Switzerland, 1984, 86, 94, others. Contbr. articles to profl. jours.; editor Exptl. Gerontology, Exptl. Aging Rsch., Proc. Soc. Exptl. Biology and Medicine; co-editor Chem. Rubber Co. Press Series in Aging, 1981—; mem. editl. bd. The Ency. of Aging, 1987—. V.p. Community Coalition Harford County, Bel Air, Md., 1988-90, bd. dirs., 1990-92; co-dir. Ea. Harford County Civic Assn., Bel Air, 1981—. Recipient Rsch. award Am. Aging Assn., 1981, Sandoz prize for gerontol. rsch. Sandoz Ltd., Basel, 1989, Third Age award Internat. Assn. Gerontology, 1989, Spl. award Balt. Longitudinal Study on Aging, 1991; Sigma Chi scholar in residence Miami U., Oxford, Ohio, 1989, Equal Employment Opportunity award NIH, 1995, Merit award, 1996. Fellow Gerontol. Soc. Am. (chair biol. scis. sect. 1975-76, chair rsch. com. 1978-79, chmn. fellowship com. 1986-87); mem. Soc. Exptl. Biology and Medicine. Republican. Roman Catholic. Avocations: basketball, fishing, hiking, canoeing. Office: Gerontology Rsch Ctr Nat Inst on Aging 5600 Nathan Shock Dr Baltimore MD 21224-6825

ROTH, GLADYS THOMPSON, retired early childhood and special education educator; b. N.Y.C., June 24, 1923; d. Meyer and Sarah (Siporin) Thompson; m. Martin Roth, Dec. 25, 1949; children: Jan Roth Hauptman, Lisa. BA, Bklyn. Coll., 1943; postgrad., Queens Coll., 1961-63; M in Spl. Edn., NYU, 1972. Cert. kindergarten tchr., health conservation tchr., tchr. grades K-6, N.Y.C. Bd. Edn. Tchr. Day Care Ctr. Mayor's Com., Bedford & Stuyvesant, N.Y., 1943-45; kindergarten tchr. N.Y.C. Bd. Edn., Red Hook, N.Y., 1945-62; spl. edn. tchr. N.Y.C. Bd. Edn.-St. Francis Hosp., 1962-64, N.Y.C. Bd. Edn.-Queens Gen. Hosp., 1964-65, N.Y.C. Bd. Edn.-St. Mary's Hosp., 1965-79; ednl. evaluator N.Y.C. Bd. Edn. Queens Dist., 1979-90; ret., 1990. Mem. exec. com. Coun. for Exceptional Children, Queens, 1962-64; spl. reading cons. St. Mary's Hosp., Queens, 1964-65. Contbr. articles to profl. jours.; exhibits stone and wood sculpture. Organizer parenting groups Pub. Sch. 84-Queens, Bayside, N.Y., 1979-90; dir. Womanspace in Great Neck, N.Y., 1989-96, dir. of outreach, 1996—; mem. adv. bd. Copay Hispanic Cmty., Inc., Great Neck, 1996—. Recipient Achievement award Soroptomist Soc., Nassau County, N.Y., 1992, Cmty. Achievement award Eleanor Roosevelt chpt. Am. Jewish Congress, Nassau County, 1992, Martin Fisher Post Harvest award Bklyn. Coll., 1997; named Outstanding Woman, Town of North Hempstead, 1994, Disting. Citizen, N.Y. State Assembly, Albany, 1995. Avocations: sculpture, tennis, music. Home: 13 Briar Ln Great Neck NY 11024-1720

ROTH, HADDEN WING, lawyer; b. Oakland, Calif., Feb. 10, 1930; s. Mark and Jane (Haley) R.; m. Alice Becker, Aug., 1987; 1 child, Elizabeth Wing. AA, Coll. Marin, 1949; BA, U. Calif., Berkeley, 1951; JD, U. Calif., San Francisco, 1957. Bar: Calif. 1958, U.S. Dist. Ct. (no. dist.) Calif. 1958, U.S. Ct. Appeals (9th cir.) 1958, U.S. Supreme Ct. 1966. Pvt. practice, San Rafael, 1970—. Judge Marin County Mcpl. Ct., 1966-70; spl. cons. Marin Muni Water Dist., Corte Madera, Calif., County of Marin; atty. Bolinas Pub. Utility Dist., Ross Valley Fire Svc., Tiburon Fire Protection Dist., Town of Ross and San Anselmo, Calif.; hearing officer dist. hosps., 1981—; lectr. law Golden Gate Coll. Law, San Francisco, 1971-73. Chmn. Marin County prison task force, 1973; bd. dirs. Marin Gen. Hosp., 1964-66. Named Outstanding Citizen of Yr., Coll. Marin, 1972. Mem. ABA, Am. Trial Lawyers Assn., Calif. Bar Assn., Marin County Bar Assn., San Francisco Trial Lawyers Assn., Am. Assn. Ind. Investors, Assn. Bus. Trial Lawyers. Avocations: running, weights, reading. Office: Hadden Roth Law Offices 1050 Northgate Dr San Rafael CA 94903-2526

ROTH, HAROLD, architect; b. St. Louis, June 30, 1934; s. Samuel and Dorothy (Yawitz) R.; m. Dvora Feigon, Dec. 6, 1959; children: Elizabeth, David. AB, Washington U., 1956; MArch, Yale U., 1957. Designer Warner Burns Toan & Lunde, N.Y.C., 1957; sr. designer Eero Saarinen & Assocs., Roche Dinkeloo & Assocs., Hamden, Conn., 1959-65; ptnr. Harold Roth—Edward Saad, 1965-72; sr. ptnr. Roth & Moore Architects, New Haven, 1973—; critic archtl. design Yale U. Sch. Architecture, 1964-98. Pres., trustee Perspecta, Yale Archtl. Jour. Trustee Long Wharf Theatre, New Haven, 1972-98, Conn. Trust for Hist. Preservation, 1983-90; pres. bd. trustees Conn. Architecture Found., 1990-93; bd. govs. Bldg. Stone Inst., 1999—; bd. regents Am. Arch. Found., 1999-2001; profl. advisor Western European Architecture Found., 2000—. Officer U.S. Army, 1957-59, Korea. Recipient Design award Nat. Coun. Religious Arch., 1970, 96, Design award New Haven Preservation Trust, 1978, 88, Tucker award Bldg. Stone Inst., 1983, 88, Honor award Concrete Reinforcing Steel Inst., 1983, Design award Portland Cement Assn., 1984, Design award Archtl. Record, 1970, 80, Design award AIA/ALA, 1983, Faculty Design award Assn. Collegiate Schs. of Arch., 1988, Healthcare Facilities Design award Boston Soc. Archs., 1992; fellow Pierson Coll., Yale U., 1978—. Fellow: AIA (chmn. nat. com. on design 1990, bd. dirs. 1992—94, sec. Coll. of Fellows 1998—99, vice-chancellor 2000, chancellor 2001, Design award Conn. 1974, 1978, 1983, 1986, 1988, 1990, 1993, 1997, 1998, Design award New Eng. 1968, 1984, 1992, 2001, N.Y. State Design award of merit 2000). Home: 37 Autumn St New Haven CT 06511-2220 Office: Roth and Moore Architects 65 Audubon St New Haven CT 06510-1205 E-mail: hroth@rothandmoore.com.

ROTH, HARRIET STEINHORN, educator, public speaker; b. Lodz, Poland, Apr. 12, 1929; d. Pinkus Feldman and Brenda Rubinstein; m. Irving Hyman Steinhorn, Apr. 15, 1951 (dec. June 1981); children: Pauline-Sue, Allan Wrenn, Mark Paul; m. Marvin Roth, June 22, 1986; stepchildren: Linda Fern, Steve Howard. B in Hebrew Lit., Balt. Hebrew U., 1974. Tchr. Hebrew Shaare Tefila Hebrew Sch., Silver Spring, Md., 1964-84, ednl. dir., 1984-92. Author: Shadows of the Holocaust, 1983. Publicity chair Jewish Holocaust Survivors & Friends Greater Washington, Rockville, Md., 1990-99. Avocations: gardening, reading, swimming, theater, traveling. Home: 10411 Burnt Ember Dr Silver Spring MD 20903-1337

ROTH, HARVEY PAUL, publisher; b. N.Y.C., Feb. 20, 1933; s. Lewis Theodore and Harriet (Wallow) R.; m. Tanya Cohen; children by previous marriage: Andrea Warriner, Matthew Jay; stepchildren: Laura Meryl Becker, Matthew Robert Turetzky. AB, Bklyn. Coll., 1954; LL.B., N.Y. U., 1957. Bar: N.Y. bar 1959. Editor West Pub. Co., N.Y.C., 1959-61; pres. BFL Communications, Inc., Plainview, N.Y., 1961-76, Roth Pub., Inc., Great Neck, 1976—; chmn. Alcove Press, London, 1970-75, Nash Pub. Corp., Los Angeles, 1971-75. Served with U.S. Army, 1957-58. Office: Roth Pub Inc 175 Great Neck Rd Great Neck NY 11021-3313 E-mail: hroth@poemfinder.com.

ROTH, HOWARD, chemist, engineer, consultant; b. N.Y.C., Oct. 11, 1925; s. Jack Roth and Jean (Welchovsky) Roth-Jaslow; m. Janet Kotlar (dec.); children: Sallyann, Daniel Jack; m. Judith Marcia Gibberman. BS in Chemistry, The City Coll. N.Y., 1952. Chief chemist Loft Candy Corp., N.Y.C., 1945-53; lab. dir. DCA Food Industries, Inc., 1953-75, dir. R&D, 1975-83; assoc. R.F. Schiffmann Assoc., Inc., 1983—; co-chmn. Microwave Concepts, Inc., Yonkers, N.Y., 1990—. Treas., bd. dirs. Internat. Microwave Power Inst., Alberta, Can., 1970-75; mem. industry adv. com. Northeast Regional Lab. USDA, Wooster, Ohio, 1960-63. Inventor in field; contbr. articles to profl. jours. Treas., bd. dirs. Fedn. N.Y. Rifle & Pistol Clubs, Inc., N.Y.C., 1972-92. Mem. Am. Assn. Cereal Chemists (fat & oil chem. com. 1956-57). Avocations: tennis, target shooting, mechanical repair, inventions. Home and Office: 12 Scrimshaw Dr Southampton NY 11968-1103 E-mail: rothhandj@yahoo.com.

ROTH, IRMA DORIS BRUBAKER, editor; b. Lexington, Nebr., Dec. 7, 1914; d. Ralph H. and Hazel Louise (Lincoln) Brubaker; m. George Knox Roth, Dec. 18, 1933; children: Dana Lincoln, Mary Joan, John Knox, Diana Jean. AA, Pasadena City Coll., 1951. Editl. asst., office mgr. New Outlook Mag., L.A., 1955-59; supr. catalog clerical staff J.F.K. Libr., Calif. State Coll., 1960-68; rsch. editor Gen. Rsch. Cons., Las Vegas, San Diego, 1968-75. Editor: Nevada Water Quality, 1969; contbr. articles to popular mag. Mem. Greater L.A. Press Club, 1955-80; assembly candidate Calif. Dem. Party, L.A. County, 1948; press rep. Dem. Nat. Conv., L.A., 1960; bd. dirs. Conf. Christians Jews, Las Vegas, 1968-70; mem. campaign staff Humphrey for Pres., Las Vegas, 1968; rec. sec., Pacific Southwest Dist. Unitarian-Universalist Women's Fedn., 1977-82; treas. San Gabriel Valley Dem. Women, L.A. County, 1982-83, 86-87, pres., 1984-85, 88-94. Named Woman Dem. of Yr., 42nd Assembly Dist. Com., 1991. Mem. Coll. Women Pasadena (publicity chair 1996-98, mem. scholarship com. 1998—), Greater L.A. Press Club. Avocations: reading, knitting, children. Home: 440 N Madison Ave Apt 806 Pasadena CA 91101-1430

ROTH, JAMES ANTHONY, lawyer; b. Kansas City, Dec. 24, 1968; s. Michael Gordon Roth, Marie Kathleen Anthony. BA in Polit. Sci., Kans. State U., 1991; JD, Oklahoma City U., 1994. Bar: Kans. 1994, U.S. Dist. Ct. Kans. 1994, Okla. 1995, U.S. Dist. Ct. (we. dist.) Okla. 1995. Law clk. Hon. Joe Mark Elkouri, Oklahoma City, 1994—95; dep. commr., staff atty. Oklahoma County Dist. One, 1995—99; spl. counsel Oklahoma County, 1999, chief dep. county clk., 1999—. Chmn. AIDS Legal Resource Project, Oklahoma City, 1995—. Mem. Nat. Assn. Civil County Attys. (sec. 1996-98, pres. 1998-99, bd. dirs. 1999), Okla. Bar Assn. (bd. dirs. 1995—), Kans. Bar Assn., ABA. Democrat. Avocations: nature, gardening, politics, reading. Home: 904 NW 40th St Oklahoma City OK 73118 Office: Oklahoma County 320 Robert S Kerr Ave Ste 105 Oklahoma City OK 73102-3441 E-mail: jimrothlaw@cox.net.

ROTH, JAMES FRANK, manufacturing company executive, chemist; b. Rahway, N.J., Dec. 7, 1925; s. Louis and Eleanor R.; m. Sharon E. Mattes, June 20, 1969; children by previous marriage: Lawrence, Edward, Sandra. BA in Chemistry, U. W.Va., 1947; PhD in Phys. Chemistry, U. Md., 1951. Research chemist Franklin Inst., Phila., 1951-53, mgr. chemistry lab., 1958-60; chief chemist Lehigh Paints & Chems. Co., Allentown, Pa., 1953-55; research chemist GAF Corp., Easton, 1955-58; with Monsanto Co., St. Louis, 1960-80, dir. catalysis research, 1973-77, dir. process sci. research, 1977-80; corp. chief scientist Air Products and Chems., Inc., Allentown, 1980-91; indsl. cons., 1991—. Contbr. articles to profl. jours.; mem. editl. bd. Jour. Catalysis, 1976-85, Catalysis Revs., 1973-93, Applied Catalysis, 1981-85; editor for Ams., 1985-88, assoc. editor, 1988-95. With USN, 1943-46. Recipient Richard J. Kokes award Johns Hopkins U., 1977, Chem. Pioneer award Am. Inst. Chemists, 1986, Perkin medal Soc. Chem. Industry, 1988. Mem. NAE, Am. Chem. Soc. (St. Louis sect. St. Louis award 1975, E.V. Murphree nat. award 1976, Indsl. Chemistry award 1991), Catalysis Soc. N.Am. (E.J. Houdry award 1991), Catalysis Club of Phila. (award 1981). Inventor process biodegradable detergents, for acetic acid; U.S., fgn. patents in field. Home: 5440 Eagles Point Cir Apt 205 Sarasota FL 34231-9171

ROTH, JANE RICHARDS, federal judge; b. Philadelphia, Pa., June 16, 1935; d. Robert Henry Jr. and Harriett (Kellond) Richards; m. William V. Roth Jr., Oct. 9, 1965; children: William V. III, Katharine K. BA, Smith Coll., 1956; LLB, Harvard U., 1965; LLD (hon.), Widener U., 1986, U. Del., 1994. Bar: Del. 1965, U.S. Dist. Ct. Del. 1966, U.S. Ct. Appeals (3d cir.) 1974. Adminstrv. asst. various fgn. service posts U.S. State Dept., 1956-62; assoc. Richards, Layton & Finger, Wilmington, Del., 1965-73, ptnr., 1973-85; judge U.S. Dist. Ct. Del., 1985-91, U.S. Ct. Appeals (3d cir.), Wilmington, 1991—. Adj. faculty Villanova U. Sch. Law. Hon. chmn. Del. chpt. Arthritis Found., Wilmington; bd. overseers Widener U. Sch. Law; bd. consultors Villanova U. Sch. Law; trustee Hist. Soc. Del. Recipient Nat. Vol. Service citation Athritis Found., 1982. Fellow Am. Bar Found.; mem. ABA, Fed. Judges Assn., Del. State Bar Assn. Republican. Episcopalian. Office: US Court of Appeals 3rd Circuit 21400 US Courthouse 601 Market St Philadelphia PA 19106-1790*

ROTH, JEFFREY JOSEPH, plastic surgeon; b. L.A., Dec. 28, 1965; s. Marvin and Carol Ann (Shapiro) R. BA, Brandeis U., 1988; MD, u. Nev., 1992. MD, Calif., Nev., Pa.; diplomate Nat. Bd. Med. Examiners. Intern in srugery Med. Coll. of Pa., Phila., 1992-93; resident in surgery Med. Coll. of Pa. and Hahnemann U., 1993-95, resident in surg. rsch., 1995-97, sr. surg. resident, 1997-98, chief surg. resident, 1998-99; resident in plastic and reconstructive surgery U. Calif., San Francisco, 1999—. Contbr. articles to profl. jours., book chpts. Mem. AMA (pres. med. students sect. Nev. 1989-90), ACS (assoc. fellow), AAAS, Am. Soc. Plastic Surgeons, Nev. State Med. Assn. (pres. med. student sect. 1989-90), Am. Fedn. Clin. Rsch., Mensa. Office: U Calif Dept Plastic and Reconstructive Surgery 350 Parnassus Ave Ste 509 San Francisco CA 94143-0001 E-mail: J.J.Roth@Worldnet.att.net.

ROTH, JOHN KING, philosopher, educator; b. Grand Haven, Mich., Sept. 3, 1940; s. Josiah V. and Doris Irene (King) R.; m. Evelyn Lillian Austin, June 25, 1964; children: Andrew Lee, Sarah Austin. BA, Pomona Coll., 1962; student, Yale U., 1962-63, MA, 1965, PhD, 1966; LHD, Ind. U., 1990, Grand Valley State U., 1998, Hebrew Union Coll., 1999, We. U. Health Scis., 1999. Asst. prof. philosophy Claremont McKenna Coll., Calif., 1966-71, assoc. prof., 1971-76, Russell K. Pitzer prof. philosophy, 1976—; vis. prof. philosophy Franklin Coll., Lugano, Switzerland, 1973. Fulbright lectr. in Am. studies U. Innsbruck, Austria, 1973-74, Royal Norwegian Ministry of Edn., Oslo, Norway, 1995-96; vis. prof. philosophy Doshisha U., Kyoto, Japan, 1981-82; vis. prof. Holocaust studies U. Haifa, Israel, 1982. Author: Freedom and the Moral Life, 1969, Problems of the Philosophy of Religion, 1971, American Dreams, 1976, A Consuming Fire, 1979; (with Richard L. Rubenstein) Approaches to Auschwitz, 1987; (with Frederick Sontag) The American Religious Experience, 1972, The Questions of Philosophy, 1988; (with Robert H. Fossum) The American Dream, 1981, American Ground, 1988; (with Rubenstein) The Politics of Latin American Liberation Theology, 1988; (with Michael Berenbaum) Holocaust: Religious and Philosophical Implications, 1989, Ethics, 1991; (with Carol Rittner) Memory Offended, 1991; (with Creighton Peden) Rights, Justice, and Community, 1992; (with Carol Rittner) Different Voices, 1993, American Diversity, American Identity, 1995, Inspiring Teaching, 1997, From the Unthinkable to the Unavoidable, 1997, Encyclopedia of Social Issues, 1997, Private Needs, Public Selves: Talk About Religion in American, 1997, (with Stephen R. Haynes) The Death of God Movement and the Holocaust, 1999, Ethics After the Holocaust, 1999, Holocaust Politics, 2001, Pope Pius XII and the Holocaust, 2002, Will Genocide Ever End?, 2002. Spl. advisor U.S. Holocaust Meml. Coun., Washington, 1980-85, mem., 1995-98. Danforth grad. fellow, 1962-66; Graves fellow, 1970-71; NEH fellow, 1976-77, Koerner fellow Oxford Ctr. for Hebrew and Jewish Studies, Eng.; Faculty Pairing grantee Japan-U.S. Friendship Commn., 1981-83; named U.S. Prof. of Yr. Coun. Advancement and Support of Edn. and Carnegie Found. Advancement of Tchg., 1988. Mem Am. Philos. Assn., Am. Acad. Religion, Am. Studies Assn., Calif. Coun. for Humanities, Phi Beta Kappa. Presbyterian. Home: 1458 Augusta Dr Upland CA 91786-2446 Office: Claremont McKenna Coll 850 Columbia Ave Claremont CA 91711-3901 E-mail: John.Roth@claremontmckenna.edu.

ROTH, J(OHN) REECE, electrical engineer, educator, researcher-inventor; b. Washington, Sept. 19, 1937; s. John Meyer and Ruth Evangeline (Iams) R.; m. Helen Marie DeCrane, Jan. 14, 1972; children: Nancy Ann, John Alexander. *Maternal grandfather George D. Iams, a professional engineer and civil engineer for the Pennsylvania Railroad, consulted as a land surveyor and licenced civil and architectural engineer after his retirement. John's Reece Roth's Iams ancestors arrived in the U.S. in the 17th century, pioneered in Washington County, PA in 1770, and participated in the First Civil War (the "Whisky Rebellion") in 1794. On the paternal side, John is the eighth generation of eldest sons of the Roth family to have the first name of John, (or Johann). Great grandfather Samuel Meyer was a university-trained botanist and first chief gardener for the Heinz Food Company.* S.B. in Physics, MIT, 1959; PhD, Cornell U., 1963. Engring. aide Aerojet-Gen. Corp., Azusa, Calif., 1957, 58; aerospace engr. N.Am. Aviation, Canoga Park, 1959; prin. investigator NASA Lewis Rsch. Ctr., Cleve., 1963-78; prof. elec. engring. U. Tenn., Knoxville, 1978-99, Weston Fulton prof. elec. engring., 1999—; hon. prof. U. Electronic Sci. and Tech. of China, Chengdu, 1992—; prin. investigator Office Naval Rsch., Washington, 1980-89, Air Force Office Sci. Rsch., Washington, 1981-95, 2001—, Army Rsch. Office, 1988-93, NASA Langley Rsch. Ctr., Hampton, Va., 1995-98. 2001—, March Instruments, Inc., Concord, Calif., 1996-98, NSF, 2002—. Cons. TVA, Chattanooga, 1982-84, BDM Corp., 1987-88, Tenn. Eastman, 1989-90, March Instruments, 1995-98; Procter & Gamble, 1996, 2000; Internat. Eco Scis., 1997-98; Environ. Elements Corp., 1997-2000, Tetra Pak Suisse, 1998-2000, Atmospheric Glow Techs., LLC, 1999—; mem. NAS-NRC Com. on Aneutronic Fusion, 1986-87; spkr. at profl. meetings. *Prof. Roth published his first engineering paper in 1957, and maintains an active research and development program which has led to nine patents since 1991, and to proprietary atmospheric plasma technologies which have been licensed for sterilization, deposition, increasing the surface energy of materials, and other uses. Prof. Roth is author of the textbook "Introduction to Fusion Energy," which has been translated into Chinese; and of the three volume reference work "Industrial Plasma Engineering." Volume I of which was published in 1995 and later translated into Chinese. He consults with private industry in the field of industrial plasma applications, and gives minicourses on the subject to in-service professionals.* Author: Industrial Plasma Engineering, Introduction to Fusion Energy; contbr. articles to profl. jours; 9 patents since 1991. Sloan scholar, 1955-59; Ford fellow, 1961-62; recipient B. Otto and Katherine Wheeley award for Excellence in Tech. Transfer, 1999. Fellow IEEE, AIAA (assoc.); mem. Am. Phys. Soc., Am. Nuclear Soc. (exec. com. No. Ohio sect. 1975-78), Nuclear and Plasma Scis. Soc., Am. Soc. Engring. Edn., Knoxville Art Gallery, East Tenn. Soc. of Archaeol. Inst. Am., Sigma Xi (pres. U. Tenn. Knoxville chpt. 1985-86). Clubs: U. Tenn. U. Club (Knoxville). Home: 12359 N Fox Den Dr Knoxville TN 37922-3755 Office: U Tenn Dept Elec Computer Engring 409 Ferris Hall Knoxville TN 37996-2100 E-mail: jrr@utk.edu.

ROTH, JOSHUA S. obstetrician/gynecologist, educator; b. N.Y.C., 1940; s. Joseph D. and Gertrude (Sattinger) R.; m. Isadora Roth, Dec. 22, 1962; children: Andrew, Eric. AB, Princeton U., 1962; MD, SUNY Downstate, 1967. Diplomate Am. Bd. Ob-Gyn. Intern, resident ob-gyn L.I. Jewish Med. Ctr., N.Y.C., 1967-71, attending physician, 1971—, pres. med. staff, 1986-87; ob-gyn Bayside, N.Y., 1971—. Clin. asst. prof. Albert Einstein Coll. Medicine; chief ob-gyn Lyster Army Hosp., Ft. Rucker, Ala., 1972-73. Maj. USMC, 1971-73. Fellow: ACS, Queens Gynecol. Soc., Am. Coll. Ob-Gyn.; mem.: Queens County Med. Soc., N.Y. State Med. Soc. Office: 223-01 Union Tpke Bayside NY 11364-3644

ROTH, JUDITH SHULMAN, lawyer; b. N.Y.C., Apr. 25, 1952; d. Mark Alan and Margaret Ann (Podell) Shulman; m. William Hartley Roth, May 30, 1976; children: Andrew Henry, Caroline Shulman. AB, Cornell U., 1974; JD, Columbia U., 1977. Bar: N.Y. 1978, U.S. Dist. Ct. (ea. dist.) N.Y. 1978, U.S. Dist. Ct. (so. dist.) N.Y. 1978, U.S. Ct. Appeals (2d cir.) 1993. Assoc. Phillips Nizer Benjamin Krim & Ballon, N.Y.C., 1978-87, ptnr., 1988—. Lectr. CLE Fordham Law Sch., N.Y.C., 1990. Mem. Cosmopolitan Club. Jewish. Avocations: reading, tennis, golf, art, gardening. Office: Phillips Nizer Benjamin Krim & Ballon 666 5th Ave New York NY 10103-0001 E-mail: jroth@phillipsnizer.com.

ROTH, LAWRENCE FREDERICK, JR. (LARRY ROTH), writer; b. Bonne Terre, Mo., Mar. 27, 1948; s. Lawrence Frederick and Geneva Maude (Buxton) R. BA in History, Ctrl. State U., Okla., 1970. Tchr. Okla. City Schs., 1970-71; contract negotiator U.S. Govt. and Industry, 1971-95; writer Living Cheap Press, Kansas City, Mo., 1988-95; broker, sales rep. Reece & Nichols, 2001—. Cons. Met. Adult Edn. Program, San Jose, 1990-92, Roth Arnold West, Burbank, Calif., 1982-86; govt. contracting cons., 1997-2001. Author: A Life in the Baby Boom, 1990, Living Cheap, 1990, Living Cheap News: The First Two Years, 1994, Beating the System, 1995, The Best of Living Cheap News, 1996; editor: Living Cheap News, 1992—, The Simple Life, 1998, Living Cheap in the 21st Century, 2000. Named to Million Dollar Club, Lockheed Missiles & Space, Sunnyvale, Calif., 1987; recipient Productivity Improvement award, Austin, Tex., 1986, 87, Sunnyvale, 1988-95. Mem. Mensa. Democrat. Avocations: walking, reading, listening to music, cocooning, travel. Home: 7520 McGee St Kansas City MO 64114-1939 Office: Living Cheap Press 7520 McGee St Kansas City MO 64114-1939 E-mail: livcheap@aol.com.

ROTH, LISA MAE, writer; b. Quakertown, Pa., Apr. 13, 1963; d. Willard Leon Stoneback, Pauline D Stoneback; m. William Andrew Roth; children: Alison, Andrew. BA cum laude, California U. Pa., 1985. Prodn. dir., copywriter WOVU-Radio Sta., Ocean View, Del., 1985—88; pub. rels. coord. Hist. Soc. Talbot County, Easton, Md., 1988—90; home day care provider Lisa Roth Daycare, McDaniel, 1990—2001; tchrs. aide St. Luke's United Meth. Ch. Pre-school, St. Michael's, 1999—2000; writer self-employed, McDaniel, 1998—. Author: (plays) Something to Chew On, 1999, Toying With History, 2000, The Golden Halo Awards, 2001, To Shine Or Not to Shine, 2001; actor: (plays) Women and Children, 1992, Ten Little Indians, 1994, Habitat for Humanity/FOLLIES, 1996, The Man Who Came to Dinner, 1996, The Nerd, 1997, Later Life, 1997, Cat On a Hot Tin Roof, 1998, Neil Simon's Rumors, 2000, (audiotape for hist. ho. tours) St. Mary's Square Museum, 1999; singer: (plays) Habitat for Humanity/Neviaser FOLLIES, 1999, Cabaret, 2000, Habitat for Humanity/Neviaser FOLLIES, 2001; (asst. dir.): (plays) 1776, 1998; (asst. state mgr.) Twelve Angry Men, 2000. Bd. dirs. Tred Avon Players, 2001—02; dir., writer Christmas Pageants St. Luke's United Meth. Ch., St. Michael's, 1996—, comm. coord., 1997—98. Mem.: Ea. Shore Writer's Assn., Alpha Psi Omega (life). Avocations: acting, dancing, swimming, boating, reading, singing. Home: 23387 Sans Souci Dr Mcdaniel MD 21647 Home Fax: 410-745-6359. Personal E-mail: cooldeal@dmv.com.

ROTH, LOREN H. psychiatrist; b. May 9, 1939; m. Ellen A. Roth; children: Jonathan, Alexandra, Elizabeth. BA in Philosophy, Cornell U., 1961; MD cum laude, Harvard U., 1966, MPH, 1972; postgrad., Am. U., 1972-73. Diplomate Am. Bd. Psychiatry and Neurology; lic. physician, Conn., Md., Mass., Pa. Med. intern Univ. Hosps., Western Res. U., Cleve., 1966-67; resident psychiatry Yale U., New Haven, 1969-70, Mass. Gen. Hosp., Boston, 1970-72; staff psychiatrist Ctr. for Studies Crime and Delinquency, NIMH, Rockville, Md., 1972-74; co-dir., dir. law and psychiatry program Western Psychiat. Inst. and Clinic/U. Pitts., 1974—, chief adult clin. svcs., 1983-87, 88-89, chief clin. svcs., 1989-95, co-dir., dir. law and psychiatry program, 1974-94; vice-chmn. dept. psychiatry U. Pitts., 1988-97, asst. prof., 1974-78, assoc. prof., 1978-82, prof., 1982—; v.p. for Managed Care U. Pitt. Med. Ctr., 1993-97; assoc. vice chancellor for edn., health scis. U. Pitts. Sch. Medicine, 1995-97; assoc. sr. vice chancellor health scis. U. Pitts., 1997—; sr. v.p. med. svcs. UPMC Health Sys., 1997—. Med. staff Presbyn.-Univ. Hosp., Pitts., 1983—; gen. med. officer Fed. Penitentiary, Lewisburg, Pa., 1967-69; William E. Schumacher disting. lectr. Maine Dept. Mental Health and Mental Retardation, Portland, 1982; mem. commn. on mentally disabled ABA, Washington, 1987; cons. law and psychiatry Dept. Welfare, Commonwealth Pa., 1974; cons. reviewer, site visitor crime and delinquency sect. NIMH, 1977; examiner Am. Bd. Psychiatry and Neurology, 1985. Author: (with others) Informed Consent: A Study of Decisionmaking in Psychiatry, 1984; editor: (with others) Psychiatry, Social, Epidemiologic and Legal Psychiatry, Vol. 5, 1986; contbr. articles to profl. jours., chpts. to books; editorial bd. Criminology, 1974-78, Law and Human Behavior, 1980-85, Internat. Jour. Law and Psychiatry, 1980-88, Behavioral Scis. and the Law, 1987-95; assoc. editor Am. Jour. Psychiatry, 1982-90; cons. editor Criminal Justice and Behavior, 1982-85. Lt. comrd. USPHS Res., 1967—. Recipient Steve Allen award United Mental Health, Inc., 1990; grantee NIMH, 1979, 80-81, 89, Founds. Fund for Rsch. in Psychiatry, 1980-82. Fellow Am. Psychiat. Assn. (Isaac Ray award 1988), Am. Coll. Utilization Rev. Physicians, Am. Coll. Psychiatrists; mem. AMA, Am. Acad. Psychiatry and Law (pres. 1983-84), Group for Advancement Psychiatry (com. on psychiatry and law 1979-80, chmn. 1981-84), Am. Soc. Criminology, Am. Soc. Law and Medicine (bd. dirs. 1982-85), Internat. Acad. Law and Mental Health (bd. dirs.), Am. Psychopath. Assn., Phi Beta Kappa, Phi Kappa Phi. Home: 6820 Edgerton Ave Pittsburgh PA 15208-2803 Office: UPMC Health System Forbes TWR 200 Lothrop St Ste 11016 Pittsburgh PA 15213-2546

ROTH, LORETTA ELIZABETH, retired educator; b. Chgo., Aug. 28, 1927; d. George Frank and Elizabeth Anna (Herbold) R. BS, St. Xavier U., Chgo., 1956; MS in Edn., No. Ill. U., DeKalb, 1969, cert. of advanced study, 1974. Educator Sisters of Mercy, Chgo., 1948-54, 65-71; registrar St. Xavier U., 1954-65; educator Ill. Dept. Corrections, Springfield, 1976-91; facilitator bereavement seminar Anderson-McQueen Funeral Homes, St. Petersburg, Fla., 1992-97. Bd. dirs., pres. Anna Bixby Women's Ctr., Harrisburg, Ill., 1979-85; vol. Peace Corps, Honduras, 1988-90. Mem. Sisters of Mercy of the Ams. Roman Catholic. Avocation: language study. E-mail: leroth2@juno.com.

ROTH, MARILYN DOROTHY, law library coordinator; b. Camden, N.J., Feb. 22, 1948; d. Robert Miller and Hattie May (Richards) Graeff; m. Walter Henry Roth, Apr. 28, 1973 (div. Aug. 1993); children: Walter Robert, Kara Suzanne. Libr. asst. Phila. Elec. Co., 1966-74, 82-90; coord. law libr. PECO Energy Co., Phila., 1990-99; regional offices libr. mgr. Duane Morris Heckscher LLP, 1999—2001. Mem. Spl. Libr. Assn., Greater Phila. Law Libr. Assn. (bd. dirs. at large 1995-97, chmn. corp. spl. interest sect. 1997-99, membership com.), Am. Assn. Law Librs. Office: Duane Morris Heckscher LLP One Liberty Pl 38th Fl 1650 Market St Fl 38 Philadelphia PA 19103-7302

ROTH, MARILYN GREEN, retired accountant; b. Mitchell, S.D., Nov. 17, 1939; d. Vyron A. and Edna Anna (Ness) G.; m. Wilbert Joseph Roth, Jan. 13, 1958; children: Debra Lynn, Karen Leigh. BA, Dakota Wesleyan U., Mitchell, S.D., 1959; MA, S.D. State U., Brookings, 1967. CPA. Tchr. Mitchell Independent Sch., 1961-80; CPA Hunt & Roth, Mitchell, 1981-82, Warren Stechman, Mitchell, 1981-83; ret., 1984. Recipient Betty Crocker Homemaker of Tomorrow, 1956. Mem. Mitchell Area Ret. Tchrs., Women of the Moose. Avocations: genealogy, bridge. E-mail: wimaroth@santel.net.

ROTH, MARJORY JOAN JARBOE, special education educator; b. Ranger, Tex., May 24, 1934; d. James Aloysius and Dorothy Knight (Taggart) Jarboe; m. Thomas Mosser Roth, Jr., Dec. 22, 1959; children: Thomas Mosser III, James Jarboe. BA in English, Rice U., 1957; MEd in Ednl. Adminstrn., U. N.C., Greensboro, 1981. Cert. tchr.-specific learning disabilities, middle grades lang. arts and social studies, intermediate grades, adminstr.-prin., N.C. Tchr. 4th grade Houston Ind. Sch. Dist., 1957-60; specific lang. disabilities instr. Forsyth Tech. C.C., Winston-Salem, N.C., 1976-77; specific learning disabilities tchr. Forsyth Country Day Sch., 1977-80; tchr. 5th grade Winston-Salem/Forsyth County Schs., 1982-83, specific learning disabilities tchr. Mt. Tabor High Sch., 1983-86; part time instr. English and Learning Disabilities Forsyth Tech. C.C., 1986-90; founding pres., prin. Greenhills Sch., Winston-Salem, 1990—. Co-author, co-editor booklets. Sunday Sch. dir., tchr. Galloway Meml. Episcopal Ch., 1960-70, pres., treas., sec. Churchwomen, 1963-74; treas. Elkin Jr. Woman's Club, 1962; chmn. Elkin Heart Fund Drive, 1968; bd. dirs. Hugh Chatham Hosp. Auxillary, 1968, Friends of the Elkin Pub. Libr., 1968-74, chmn., 1970-72, chmn., exhibits chmn. summer reading program; pres. South Surry Heart Assn., 1969; mem. Churchwomen of St. Paul's Episcopal Ch., Winston-Salem, 1982—, Fiddle and Bow Folk Music Soc., Winston-Salem, 1992—. Recipient June Lyday Orton award for outstanding svc. in the field of dyslexia, 1997; Forsyth fellow NEH, 1985; grantee in field. Fellow Acad. Orton-Gillingham Practitioners and Educators; mem. ASCD, Children with Attention Deficit Disorder (profl. adv. bd. N.C. Triad chpt. 1990-96), Learning Disability Assn. N.C. (sec., bd. dirs. 1981-86), Internat. Dyslexia Assn. (sec., bd. dirs. Carolinas br. 1981-85, founding pres. N.C. br. 1987-91, bd. dirs. 1987-96, nat. nominating com. 1992-94), Internat. Multisensory Structured Lang. Edn. Coun., Inc. (bd.dirs. 2000-). Republican. Avocations: tennis, hiking, folk music. Home: 940 Fox Hall Dr Winston Salem NC 27106-4431 Office: Greenhills Sch 1360 Lyndale Dr Winston Salem NC 27106-9739

ROTH, MICHAEL, lawyer; b. N.Y.C., July 22, 1931; s. Philip Arthur and Mollie (Breitenbach) R.; m. Jeanny Macoir, Nov. 24, 1957; 3 children BA, Yale Coll., 1953; JD, Columbia U., 1956, M. Internat. Affairs, 1964. Bar: N.Y. 1956. Law assoc. Stroock & Stroock & Lavan, N.Y.C., 1956-63; ptnr. Roth, Carlson, Kwit & Spengler, 1964-74; chmn. N.Y. State Liquor Authority, 1974-77; ptnr. Shea & Gould, '1979-89; of counsel Rosenman & Colin, 1989—. Mem. U.S. del. to UN Population Commn., 1969; Rep.-Conservative candidate for N.Y. State atty. gen., 1978; mem. Pres.' Task Force on Internat. Pvt. Enterprise, 1983-84, Pres.' Commn. on Mgmt. AID Programs, 1991-92. Mem. Sunningdale Country Club (Scarsdale, N.Y.). Republican.

ROTH, MICHAEL STEWART, obstetrician-gynecologist; b. Phila., Oct. 27, 1946; s. William Lester and Sara (Freund) R.; m. Bonnie Abrams, Aug. 29, 1971 (div. Feb. 1992); children: Cheryl, Deborah, Howard; m. Adrienne Lee Kahn, Oct. 30, 1993; 1 child, Alexa. BS in Biology, Albright Coll., 1968; MD, Jefferson Med. Coll., 1972. Diplomate Am. Bd. Ob-Gyn. Intern Temple Hosp., Phila., 1972-73, resident in ob-gyn., 1973-76; fellowship in reproductive endocrinology U. Miami/Jackson Meml. Hosp., 1976-78; hosp. staff mem. Pkwy. Regional Med. Ctr., North Miami Beach, Fla.; clin. asst. prof. U. Miami. Fellow: Am. Coll. Ob-Gyn. (mem. vol. rev. quality care divsn. quality care); mem.: Fla. Endocrine Soc., Miami Ob-Gyn. Soc. (pres. 1998—99), Fla. Ob-Gyn. Soc., Am. Soc. Reproductive Medicine. Office: 100 NW 170th St Ste 207 Miami FL 33169-5510

ROTH, OLIVER RALPH, radiologist; b. Culberland, Md., Nov. 30, 1921; s. DeCoursey Andrew and Mabel (Lathrum) R.; m. Virginia McBride, June 2, 1943; 1 child, Tiija. BS, Frostburg State U., 1942; MD, U. Md., 1950; DSc (hon.) , Frostburg State U., 1980. Diplomate Am. Bd. Radiology. Resident Johns Hopkins Hosp., Balt., 1954-57; cancer rsch. fellow Middlesex Hosp., London, 1957-58; founder dept. radiation oncology Presbyn. Hosp., Charlotte, N.C., 1958-62; attending radiologist King's Daus. Hosp., Ashland, Ky., 1962-80; radiologist Our Lady of Bellefonte Hosp., 1981-86; mem. faculty Sch. of Allied Health Shawnee State U., Portsmouth, Ohio, 1986-90; prof. radiology Sch. Medicine Marshall U., Huntington, W.Va., 1990—2001, Pikeville Coll. Sch. of Osteo. Medicine, 2000—; cons. in radiology VA Med. Ctr., Huntington, 2001—. Mem. adv. com. Ky. Cancer Commn., 1978. Book reviewer Radiology, 1954-55. Bd. dirs. Boyd County chpt. Am. Cancer Soc., 1978. With USN, 1942-45. Commanded to Buckingham Palace, June 17, 1958; recipient Disting. Alumni award Frostburg State U., 1979. Mem. AMA, Am. Coll. Radiology, Radiol. Soc. N. Am., Am. Radium Soc., Royal Faculty Radiology, Brit. Inst. Radiology, Shriners (Cumberland, Md. chpt.). Democrat. Lutheran. Home: 2912 Cogan St Ashland KY 41102-5230 E-mail: tiijaranta@aol.com.

ROTH, PAUL B. dean, emergency medicine physician; b. Glen Ridge, N.J., Oct. 7, 1947; s. Jerome M. and Selma (Leitner) R. BS, Fairleigh Dickinson U., 1969, MS, 1972; MD, George Washington U., 1976; postgrad., U. N.Mex., 1976-79. Owner, pres. EMS of N.Mex., Albuquerque, 1978-82; owner, mem. of bd. Heights Urgent Care Ctr., 1980-82; dir. divsn. emergency medicine U. N.Mex. Sch. Medicine, 1982-91, chair dept. emergency medicine, 1991-93; interim chief med. officer U. N.Mex. Med. Ctr., 1992-93, now dean medicine, 1995—; prof. emerg. med. U. N. Mex. Med. Ctr., 1991—. Dir. Ctr. for Disaster Medicine U. N.Mex. Sch. Medicine, Albuquerque, 1990—; co-chair NDMS-Med. Response Steering Com., Rockville, Mass., 1991—; chair sect. on disaster medicine Nat. ACEP, Dallas, 1991—. Contbr. articles to Annals of EM, Current Practice of EM-Disaster Medicine, Jour. of AMA. Recipient Outstanding Individual Svc. award Nat. Disaster Med. System, 1986. Fellow Am. Coll. Emergency Physicians; mem. AMA, Soc. for Acad. Emergency Medicine, Am. Coll. Physician Execs., Am. Acad. Family Physicians. Office: U NMex Sch Medicine Dean Basic Med Scis Bldg Rm 177 Albuquerque NM 87131-0001*

ROTH, PAUL NORMAN, lawyer; b. N.Y.C., May 4, 1939; m. Ellen Joan Lipp, May 24, 1964; children: Stefanie H., Jessica A. AB, Harvard U., 1961, LLB, 1964. Bar: N.Y. 1966, U.S. Ct. Appeals (2d cir.) 1966, U.S. Dist. Ct. (so. and ea. dists.) N.Y. 1967, U.S. Supreme Ct. 1975. Assoc. Cleary, Gottlieb, Steen & Hamilton, N.Y.C., 1965-69; ptnr. Schulte Roth & Zabel LLP, 1969--. Trustee Ctrl. Synagogue, N.Y.C., 1987-95; bd. dirs. Citizens Com. for N.Y.C., 1999—; bd. overseers Weill Med. Coll., Cornell U., 1999-2002. Fulbright fellow, Netherlands, 1965. Mem. ABA (com. on pvt. investment entities, vice chmn.), Nat. Assn. Securities Dealers (legal adv. bd. 1999—), Lawyers Alliance for N.Y. (bd. dirs. 1999-2002), N.Y. State Bar Assn., Assn. of Bar of City of N.Y. (com. on securities regulation 1982-85, chmn. 1989-92), Harvard Law Sch. Assn. N.Y.C. (trustee 1987-90, v.p. 1992-93, pres. 1999—2001), Century Country Club. Office: Schulte Roth & Zabel LLP 919 3rd Ave New York NY 10022-4774

ROTH, PETER, broadcast executive; b. Larchmont, N.Y. m. Andrea Roth; 2 children. Student, U. Pa.; grad., Tufts U., 1972. From mgr. to dir. children's programs ABC TV Network, 1976, dir. current programs, 1979, v.p. current prime-time series, 1981; past pres. Stephen J. Cannell Prodns.; pres. prodn. Twentieth Network TV, 1992, pres., 1993, 20th Century Fox TV, 1994, Fox Entertainment Group, L.A., 1996-98, Warner Bros. TV, Burbank, Calif., 1999—. Office: Warner Bros Television 300 Television Plz Bldg 140 Burbank CA 91522-0001

ROTH, PHILLIP JOSEPH, retired judge; b. Portland, Oreg., Feb. 29, 1920; s. Harry William and Minnie Alice (Segel) R.; m. Ida Lorraine Thomas, Feb. 22, 1957 (div. 1977); children: Phillip Joseph, David Harry; m. Allison Blake Ramsey, Feb. 14, 1978 (div. 1994). BA cum laude, U. Portland, 1943; JD, Lewis and Clark Coll., 1948. Bar: Oreg. 1948, U.S. Dist. Ct. Oreg. 1949, U.S. Ct. Appeals (9th cir.) 1959, U.S. Supreme Ct. 1962. Dep. atty. City of Portland, 1948-50; dep. dist. atty. Multnomah County, Portland, 1950-52; pvt. practice, 1952-64; cir. judge Multnomah County State of Oreg., 1964-94, presiding cir. judge, 1970-71, 76-78. Adj. prof. Lewis & Clark U. Law Sch., Portland, 1978-80, standing com., 1972-90; exec. com. Nat. Conf. State Trial Judges, 1980-91. Author: Sentencing: A View From the Bench, 1973; co-author: The Judicial Immunity Doctrine Today: Between the Bench and a Hard Place, 1984, The Brief Jour.; The Dangerous Erosion of Judicial Immunity, 1989. Mem. Oreg. Legislature, 1952-54; Rep. nominee for Congress, 1956; chmn. Oreg. Rep. Ctrl. Com., 1962-64; adv. bd. Portland Salvation Army, 1976—; mem. bd. overseers Lewis and Clark Coll., 1972-90. Named Alumnus of Yr. U. Portland, 1963, Lewis & Clark Law Sch., 1973. Fellow Am. Bar Found.; mem. ABA (chmn. jud. immunity com. jud. adminstrn. divsn. 1982-90, mem. commn. on standards jud. adminstrn. divsn. 1973-77, chmn. conf. state trial judges 1990-91, HBH Comm. on State Justice Initiatives 1994-98, chmn. jud. adminstrn. divsn. 1994-95), Oreg. Bar Assn. (bd. govs. 1961-64), Multnomah County Bar Assn. (pres. 1959), Am. Judicature Soc., Oreg. Cir. Judges Assn. (pres. 1988-89), U. Portland Alumni Assn. (pres. 1967), Lewis and Clark Coll. Alumni Assn. (prs. 1974-76, 80-81), Multnomah Law Libr. Assn. (bd. dirs.), City Club, Univ. Club, Masons, Shriners, Rotary, B'nai B'rith, Delta Theta Phi. Jewish. Home: 2495 SW 73rd Ave Portland OR 97225-3274

ROTH, RICHARD ALAN, lawyer; b. Endicott, N.Y., Dec. 6, 1958; s. David Manuel and Nelida (Ortner) R.; m. Mara Orentreich, Apr. 11, 1987. BA cum laude, Union Coll., 1981; JD, Hofstra U., 1984. Bar: N.Y. 1985, U.S. Dist. Ct. (so. dist.) N.Y. 1985, U.S. Dist. Ct. (ea. dist.) N.Y. 1985, U.S. Dist. Ct. (no. dist.) N.Y. 1985, U.S. Dist. Ct. (we. dist.) N.Y. 1988, U.S. Ct. Appeals (2d cir.), 1988, U.S. Ct. Appeals (3d cir.) 2000, U.S. Supreme Ct. 2000. Atty. Wilson, Elser Law Firm, N.Y.C., 1984-86, Solin & Breindel Law Firm, N.Y.C., 1986-87, Gordon Hurwitz Law Firm, N.Y.C., 1987-92, Littman, Krooks & Roth, N.Y.C., 1992—. Rep. 20th Century Fox, Warner Bros. Records, Actors Guild, IMG, Nat. Football League,Grad. Sch. N.Y. Acad. Art, City Light Prodns., Giant Records, Azoff Entertainment, Revolution, Robert Edward Auctions, Tin Pan Apple Records, Tomandandy, Eclipse Records, Discart. Contbr. to law revs. Mem. ABA (entertainment sect. 1988—, fed. litigation sect. 1988—), N.Y. State Bar Assn. (litigation sect. 1986—). Office: Littman Krooks & Roth 655 3rd Ave New York NY 10017-5617 also: 81 Main St White Plains NY 10601

ROTH, RICHARD C. marketing executive; b. N.Y.C., July 26, 1937; s. Carl E. and Rose M. Roth; m. Barbara A. Swift, June 13, 1959; children: Steven R., Susan E., Kevin R. BBA, Manhattan Coll., 1959. Account exec. Batten, Barton, Durstine & Osborn, 1959-62; v.p. new products Block Drug Co., Jersey City, 1962-75; sr. v.p. Metaframe Corp., Elmwood Park, N.J., 1975-77; pres. Barich Co., Milltown, 1977-93, Pet Village, Inc., Stroudsburg, Pa., 1980-94; exec. v.p. Maspeth (N.Y.) Mills Ltd., 1983-87; pres. County Village Enterprises, Inc., Milltown, 1986-89; v.p. mktg. and sales C.L.S. & M. Inc., N.Y.C., 1989-95; group v.p. The Coleman Group, 1995-01, FutureBrand Coleman, 2000—01; pres. Axus Inc., Cranbury, NJ, 1998—2001. Lectr. NYU, 1974-75; cons. Assn. for Retarded Citizens, Bergen-Passaic, N.J., 1982-83. Patentee medicinal device. Campaign cons. Middlesex County (N.J.) Rep. Com., 1966-71, pres. Milltown Rep. Club, 1969-71; fund drive chmn. Milltown LIbrary Assn., 1973, trustee, 1974-76. Mem. Assn. Nat. Advertisers (founder and chmn. new products mktg. com. 1971-76), Nat. Acad. TV Arts and Scis. Office: 1246 S River Rd Cranbury NJ 08512-3640

ROTH, ROBERT A. newspaper executive; b. Upper Darby, Pa., Mar. 19, 1947; s. Robert Raymond and Ruth Lorrayne (Jonas) R. BA magna cum laude, Carleton Coll., 1969; postgrad., U. Chgo., 1969-71. Co-founder Chgo. Reader, 1971, pub., 1971-94, editor, 1975-90; pres. Chgo. Reader, Inc., 1975—, Washington Free Weekly, Inc., 1982—. Dir. Inst. for Alternative Journalism, San Francisco, 1983-89, Raw Vision, Inc., London, 1991—. Co-founder Intuit: The Ctr. for Intuitive and Outsider Art, Chgo., 1991, pres., 1991-96, bd. dirs., 1991—; trustee Carleton Coll., Northfield, Minn., 1994-98. Recipient Alumni Disting. Achievement award Carleton Coll., 1989; named to Esquire Register, Esquire mag., 1984; named among Who's Who in Chgo. Bus., Crain's Chgo. Bus., 1990, 91, 92, 93, 94, 95, 96. Mem. Assn. Alternative Newsweeklies (pres. 1983-87). Avocations: folk and outsider art, architecture. Office: Chgo Reader 11 E Illinois St Chicago IL 60611-5652

ROTH, ROBERT EARL, environmental educator; b. Wauseon, Ohio, Mar. 30, 1937; s. Earl Jonas and Florence Lena (Mahler) R.; m. Carol Sue Yackee, Aug. 8, 1959; children: Robin Earl, Bruce Robert. BS, Ohio State U., 1959, BS in Secondary Sci. Edn., MS in Conservation Edn., Ohio State U., 1960; PhD in Environ. Edn., U. Wis., 1969. Supr. conservation edn. Ethical Culture Schs., N.Y.C., 1961-63; naturalist, sci. tchr. Lakeside Sch., Spring Valley, N.Y., 1963-65; instr. No. Ill. U., Oregon, 1965-67; asst. prof. Ohio State U., Columbus, 1969-73, assoc. prof., 1973-78, prof. environ. edn. and sci. edn., 1978-2001, prof. emeritus, 2001—, chmn. divsn., 1973-84, coord. office internat. affairs, 1985-89, asst. dir., sch. sec. Sch. Natural Resources, 1989-93, acting dir. Sch. Natural Resources, 1993-94, assoc. dir., 1994-2001, state extension specialist Environ. Edn., 1993-2001. Rsch. & devel. assoc. Mosely & Assocs., Columbus, 1986-89; project cons. NARMA project, U.S. Agy. internat. Devel., Santo Domingo, Dominican Rep., 1982-87; cons. Richard Trott & Assocs., 1988-90, Kinzelman & Kline, 1990-2001, Midwest consortium Internat. Activity, 1995; evaluator Montclair State U., N.J. Sch. Conservation, 1999; workshop leader Carribean Conservation Assn., Bridgetown, Barbados, 1981-83; vis. scholar Indonesian Second U. Devel. project, Jakarta, 1988; AID lectr., Thesolonika, Greece, 1992. Exec. editor Jour. Environ. Edn., 1974-91 (Pub.'s prize 1970); contbr. articles to profl. jours. Committeeman Boy Scouts Am., 1983-86; adv. coun. McKeever Environ. Learning Ctr., Pa., 1977-83. Named vis. scholar, Uganda Makerere, 1989, Pacific Cultural Found., Taipei, Taiwan, 1989, 1999, 2001; recipient Pomerene Tchg. Enhancement award, Ohio State U., 1986, 1995, Environ. Edn. award, Ohio Alliance for the Enrivon., 1992, Outstanding Advising award, Coll. Food Agrl. and Environ. Scis., 1996. Mem.: Sch. Nat. Resource Alumni Assn. (inducted hon. 100), Nat. Sci. Tchrs. Assn. (life), N.Am. Assn. Environ. Edn. (life; bd. dirs. 1972—82, pres. 1977—78, Walt Jeske award 1988, Outstanding Contbns. to Rsch. award 2000). Avocations: swimming, canoeing, camping, fishing, travel. Home: 570 Morning St Columbus OH 43085-3775 E-mail: roth.3@osu.edu.

ROTH, ROBERT HOWARD, psychologist; b. Newark, Jan. 15, 1933; s. Max and Marion (Gurkewitz) R.; m. Estelle Goldstein, June 16, 1957; children: Lisa C., Neil A. BS, Juilliard Sch., N.Y.C., 1953; MA, Columbia U., 1956, EdD, 1960. Lic. psychologist, N.Y., N.J. Instr. Union Coll., Cranford, N.J., 1959-60, Newark State Coll., Union, 1960-63; asst. prof. Hunter Coll. CUNY, N.Y.C., 1963-65; assoc. prof. Newark State Coll., Union, N.J., 1965-68, chmn. psychology dept., 1967-71; prof. psychology Kean U., 1968—. Cons. Marlboro (N.J.) Psychiat. Hosp., 1982-97; pvt. practice clin. psychology Madison Med. Ctr. Editor: Contemporary Studies in Psychopathology, 1983, Contemporary Studies in Personality, 1986, Explorations in Mental Disorders, 1987, Personality Structures and Functions, 1989, Psychopathologies and Treatments, 1991, Ego, Self, Person, Context, 1992, 2d edit., 1996, Tempest in the Mind, 1994. Fellow Am. Orthopsychiatric Assn.; mem. APA, AAAS, N.Y. Acad. Scis., N.J. Acad. Scis. (chmn. psychology sect. 1971-73). Home: 111 Gallinson Dr New Providence NJ 07974-2723

ROTH, ROBERT SIDNEY, chemist, geologist; b. Chicago, Ill., Aug. 21, 1926; s. Joseph and Clara Schein Roth; m. Audrey Muriel Goldstein, June 13, 1954; children: Stanley Allen, Gail Elen, Diana Lynn. BA, COE Coll., Cedar Rapids, IA, 1947; MS, U. of Ill., Urbana, IL, 1950, PhD, 1951. Rsch. chemist Nat. Inst. of Standards and Tech., Gaithersburg, Md., 1951—91; cons. Victor Idaho Phase Equilibria Rsch. Group, Victor, ID, and Gaithersburg, 1991—. Editor: (books) Phase Diagrams for Ceramists, Vol 4-13; contbr. articles to profl. jours. Recipient Silver and Gold Medals, Dept. of Commerce, 1960-1980, Sosman Lecture, Am. Ceramic Soc., 1990, John Jeppson Award, 1995. Achievements include research in 100 Phase Eqilibria Diagrams Determined. Home: Gaithersburg MD 20878 Office: National Institute of Standards and Tech Amber Tree Ct Gaithersburg MD 20878 Office Fax: 301-975-5334. E-mail: robert-roth@nist.gov.

ROTH, ROBERT WILLIAM, airlines analyst; b. Covington, Ky., Sept. 17, 1953; s. Robert John and Barbara (Model) R.; m. Julie Lavonne Zimmerman, Jan. 29, 1982. BA, Morehead State U., 1978; MBA, U. Ky., 1979; MA, Vision Internat. U., 2000, PhD, 2001. Airport mgr. Am. Airlines, Dallas, 1979-85; sales mgr.-airlines Motorola Inc., 1985-87; maj. accounts exec. Metromedia Inc., 1987-89; field svc. tech. Am. Airlines, 1989-90; telecom. network analyst Tulsa, 1990-91; sr. comm. engr. Am. Airlines, 1991-94, computer field engr. Cin., 1994-97; technology specialist The Sabre Group, 1997-2000; sr. analyst Am. Airlines Inc., 2000—. With U.S. Army, 1972-74, Vietnam. Decorated Silver Star, Bronze Star; named to Hon. Order Ky. Cols., 1975; recipient 1st Pl. award for Best Mktg. campaign KIPA, 1977. Mem. Am. Legion, VFW. Republican. Avocations: hunting, fishing, camping, water sports, guitar. Home: 2144 Branchwood Dr Grapevine TX 76051 Personal E-mail: techguy777@yahoo.com. Business E-Mail: bob.roth@aa.com.

ROTH, ROGER DOUGLAS, small business owner; b. Columbus, Ohio, Nov. 18, 1951; s. Oliver Kenneth and Betty (Isaacs) Roth; m. Rosella Smith, July 16, 1976 (div. Mar. 1980); children: Carmen, Cyan; m. Carol Sue Dillingham, July 7, 1983; children: Caitlyn, Casey. BS in Edn. and Zoology, Miami U., Oxford, Ohio, 1873. Tchr. Sycamore City Schs., Cin., 1973—79; roofing, remodeling contractor Roth Roofing and Remodeling, Inc., 1973—; video and film maker Underwater Film Prodns., 1993—. Cinematographer(and author): (films, underwater) Kiss of Extinction, 1999 (Telly , 1999, from Environmentally Aware Photographic Images Competition (EPIC), 1999), Mahonia Na Dari, 2000 (from Environmentally Aware Photographic Images Competition (EPIC), 2001). Recipient 5 first place awards, Internat. Underwater Video Competition, 1993—2000. Mem.: Nat. Assn. Remodeling Industry (bd. dirs., v.p. 1984—, Contractor of Yr. Cin. chpt. 1990), Ohio Coun. Skin Scuba Diving, Inc. (v.p. and CEO 1995—), Gavia Scuba Club of Cin. (mem. bd. dirs., v.p. 1995—). Home and Office: Roth Roofing & Remodeling Roth Underwater Video Promos 10652 Cinderella Dr Cincinnati OH 45242 E-mail: rroth@gavia.com .

ROTH, SALLYANN, social worker; b. N.Y.C., Mar. 15, 1945; d. Howard Roth and Janet Targove. BA, CCNY, 1967; MSW, Smith Coll., 1969. Lic. social worker, Mass. Clinician Family Svcs. Greater Boston, 1969-75; co-dir. Family Inst. Cambridge, Mass., 1979-95; pvt. practice Medford, 1974—; founding assoc. Pub. Conversations Project, 1989—. Lectr. in treatment methods Sch. Social Work, Smith Coll., Northampton, Mass., 1976-85, 87-88; spl. instr. Simmons Coll., 1976-83, 87; lectr. psychology Harvard Med. Sch./Cambridge (Mass.) Hosp., 1981-97. Contbr. articles to profl. publs. Mem. Am. Family Therapy Acad. Office: 137 Brooks St Medford MA 02155-2243

ROTH, SAMUEL KLEIN, physician assistant; b. Miami, Fla., Apr. 2, 1948; s. David Robert and Miriam Evelyn R.; m. Margart Ray, Feb. 29, 1971 (div. Jun. 1987); children: Chientai, Micah. BA, Lake Coll./Cleve. Clin. Found., 1980. Cert. PA-C by Nat. Commn. on Certification of Physican Asst. Physician asst. U. Mednet, Cleve., 1980-90, Kaiser Permanante, Charlotte, N.C., 1990-97, Urology Specialst of the Carolinas, Charlotte, 1997—. Recipient Charles L. Hudson Award, Ohio Assn. of Physician Assts., 1987. Fellow Am. Acad. of Physician Assts, N.C. Acad. of Physician Assts., Metrolina Acad. Physician Assts. (pres. 1995); mem. N.C. Med. Soc. (assoc.), Ohio Assn. Physician Assts. (pres. 1984-85). Avocations: golf, reading. Home: 1512 Heather Glen Rd Kannapolis NC 28081-6410 Office: Urology Specialist 1918 Randolph Rd Charlotte NC 28207

ROTH, SANFORD HAROLD, rheumatologist, health care administrator, educator; b. Akron, Ohio, June 12, 1934; s. Charles and Rose Marie (Zelman) R.; m. Marcia Ann, June 9, 1957; children: Shana Beth, Sari Luanne B.Sc., Ohio State U., 1955, MD, 1959. Intern Mt. Carmel, Columbus, Ohio, 1959-60; fellow Mayo Grad. Sch. Medicine, 1962-65; pvt. practice medicine specializing in rheumatology Phoenix, 1965—; med dir. Ariz. Rsch. and Edn., 1967—; med. dir. Arthritis Ctr., Ltd., Phoenix, 1983—; dir. Arthritis Program Healthwest Regional Medical Ctr., 1987-89; med. dir. Arthritis/Orthopedic Ctr. for Excellence Humana Hosp., 1989—; dir. arthritis rehab. program St. Luke's Hosp., 1978-87; med. rsch. dir. Harrington Arthritis Research Ctr., 1984-88; prof., dir. aging and arthritis program Coll. Grad. Program, Ariz. State U., Tempe, 1984—; dir. medicine Ariz. Insts., Phoenix, 1985—; sr. med. rheumatologist Arthrocare: Arthritis Care & Rsch.; med. dir. Sr. Health Ctr., Phoenix, 1995—2000. Past state chmn. Gov.'s Conf. on Arthritis in Ariz., 1967; cons., rep. arthritis adv. com. FDA, 1982-97, chmn. anti-rheumatic new drug guidelines, 1984—; cons. Ciba-Geigy, 1983—, Upjohn, 1985-87, Pennwalt, 1985-88, Arthritis Found. Clinics, 3M-Riker Labs, Inc., 1981-89, VA, 1970-87, FTC, 1980—, Boots Pharm. Co., 1980-87, Greenwich Pharm., 1986-87, Hoffman-LaRoche, 1986—, FDA Office Compliance, 1987—, G.D. Searle, 1987—, Cypress Labs, 2000-, Frescuius Labs, 2001-, Elon Pharm, 2000-01, Niucos Pharma GBM, 2000-02; prin. investigator Coop. Systematic Studies of Rheumatic Diseases; vis. scholar in rheumatology Beijing Med. Coll., People's Republic China, 1982; proctor, vis. scholar program U.S.-China Edn. Inst., 1982—; med. research dir., exec. bd., trustee Harrington Arthritis Research Ctr., 1983-88; co-chair PANLAR Collaborative Clin. Epidemiol. Group, 1989—; mem. com. on revision U.S. Pharmacopeial Conv., 1990—; mem. antirheumatic drug task force WHO-Internat. League Against Rheumatism, 1991—; med. dir. columbia ElderCare, 1997—; mem. com. revision U.S. Parmacopia, 1990; med. dir. Ariz. Ctr. Arthritis, 2000-; dean's adv. coun. Grad. Coll. Ariz. State U., 2000-. Author: New Directions in Arthritis Therapy, 1980; Handbook of Drug Therapy in Rheumatoloy, 1985; med. contbg. editor RISS, Hosp. Physician, 1960-68, Current Prescribing, 1976-80; hon. internat. cons. editor Drugs, 1977— ; editor in chief Arthron, 1982-85; editor, contbg. author: Rheumatic Therapeutics, 1985; med. cons. editor Update: Rheumatism, 1985, AMA Drug Evaluations, 6th edit., 1986, 7th edit., 1990; mem. editorial bd. VA Practitioner, 1985—, Comprehensive Therapy, 1987; mem. internat. editorial bd. Jour. Drug Devel., 1988—, Practical Gastroenterology, 1989—; contbr. numerous articles to profl. jours., chpts. to books. Fellow Am. Coll. Rheumatology (founding, liaison com. to regional med. program 1974-76, co-dir. med. info. system ARAMIS, computer com., chmn. antiinflammatory drug study club 1974—, com. on clubs and councils 1977-80, western regional co-chmn. 1977—, therapeutic and drug com. 1979—, glossary com. 1981-83, ad hoc com. on future meeting sites 1983); mem. AMA, ACP (regional program com., ann. Philip S. Hench lectureship chmn. 1978-79), Arthritis Found. (dir. central Ariz. chpt. 1982-83, past chmn. med. and sci. com. 1967-72), Lupus Found. Am. (bd. 1981—), Internat. Soc. Rheumatic Therapy (sec.-gen. 1990—, bd. dirs. 1987—, pres. 1992—), Maricopa County Med. Soc. (rehab. com.), Am. Soc. Clin. Rheumatology (past pres. exec. council), Am. Coll. Clin. Pharmacology, Soc. Internal Medicine, Mayo Clinic Alumni Assn., Mayo Clinic Fellows Assn. (sec. 1964-65), Argentine Rheumatology Soc. (hon.), Mayo Clinic Fellows Rheumatology Soc. (pres. 1964-65), Mayo Clinic Film Soc. (bd. dirs. 1964-65), Pan Am. League Against Rheumatism (chmn. clin. trials com. 1987—), Knights of the Vine (past master comdr. Phoenix chpt.). Office: ArthroCare Arthritis Care and Rsch PC 3330 N 2nd St Ste 601 Phoenix AZ 85012-2395 *To reconcile research of the boundless limits of our restless science with the legacy of our ancient art as to be healer, educator, organizer--all the while blessed by the joys of family love and community service. We create our destiny not alone but with individual dedication.*

ROTH, SANFORD IRWIN, pathologist, educator; b. McAlester, Okla., Oct. 14, 1932; s. Herman Moe and Blanche (Brown) R.; m. Kathryn Ann Corliss, Sept. 3, 1961; children: Jeffrey Franklin, Elisabeth Francyne, Gregory James, Suzannah Joan. Student, Vanderbilt U., 1949-52; MD, Harvard U., 1956. Intern Mass. Gen. Hosp., Boston, 1956-57, resident in pathology, 1957-60, pathologist, 1962-75, Armed Forces Inst. Pathology, 1960-62; asst. prof. Med. Sch. Harvard U., 1962-69, assoc. prof. Med. Sch., 1969-75; pathologist, prof., chmn. dept. Coll. Medicine U. Ark., Little Rock, 1975-81; prof. Med. Sch. Northwestern U., Chgo., 1981—2000, asst. dean admissions, 1998-2000, prof. emeritus, 2000—; chief lab. svc. VA Lakeside Med. Ctr., 1981-86. Attending pathologist Northwestern U. Hosp., 1981-2002; vis. prof. pathology Harvard Med. Sch., 2001—; cons. in pathology Mass. Gen. Hosp., 2001—. With M.C. U.S. Army, 1960-62. Mem. AMA, AAAS, Coll. Am. Pathology, U.S.-Can. Acad. Pathology, Soc. for Investigative Dermatology, Mass. Med. Soc. Home: 169 Tisquantum Rd Chatham MA 02633-2578 Office: Fruit St Boston MA 02114 E-mail: sroth@partners.org.

ROTH, SARAH EVE, quality assurance professional; b. W. Allis, Wis., Mar. 10, 1971; d. Douglas Fred and Rene'e Alice Roth. BS in Edn., U. of Wis., Whitewater, 1994. Sales assoc. K-Mart, Burlington, Wis., 1988—94; safety asst. Velvac, Inc., New Berlin, 1993; safety intern Johnson Controls, Inc, Milw., 1994; corp. safety adminstr. Schweiger Industries, Inc., Jefferson, 1994; tech./product specialist Lab Safety Supply, Janesville, 1994—; tax specialist H & R Block, 1999—; comml. print model, 1997—. Program com. chairperson Jefferson County Area Safety Network, Jefferson, 1994. Author: (book) Moments in Time, 2000. Mem.: Am. Soc. Safety Engrs. (pub. comm. dir. 1992, social chair 1993). Non-Denominational. Avocations: writing, dancing, piano, weightlifting, golf. Home: 1521 Excalibur Dr Janesville WI 53546 Office: Lab Safety Supply 401 South Wright Rd Janesville WI 53546 Home Fax: 608-758-2311; Office Fax: 608-757-4925. Personal E-mail: sarahroth310@hotmail.com. Business E-Mail: s.roth@labsafety.com.

ROTH, SOL, rabbi; b. Rzeszow, Poland, Mar. 8, 1927; came to U.S., 1934, naturalized, 1939; s. Joseph and Miriam (Lamm) R.; m. Debra H. Stitskin, Nov. 26, 1957; children: Steven, Michael (dec.), Sharon. BA, Yeshiva U., 1948, D.D. (hon.), 1977; MA, Columbia U., 1953, PhD, 1966; Rabbi, Yeshiva U. Theol. Sem., 1950; D in Divinity (hon.), Yeshiva U., 1977. Ordained rabbi Orthodox Jewish Congregations, 1950; pres. Rabbinical Council Am., 1980-82, N.Y. Bd. Rabbis, 1976-79; chmn. Israel Commn. Rabbinical Council Am., 1976-78; dean Chaplaincy Sch., N.Y. Bd. Rabbis, 1976-79; Samson R. Hirsch prof. dept. philosophy Yeshiva U., N.Y.C. Rabbi Jewish Ctr. Atlantic Beach, N.Y., 1956-86; Fifth Ave Synagogue, 1986—; pres. Religious Zionists Am., 1991-94. Author: Science and Religion, 1967, The Jewish Idea of Community, 1977, Halakhah and Politics: The Jewish Idea of a State, 1988 (Samuel Belkin Meml. Lit. award 1989), The Jewish Idea of Culture, 1997; editor: Morasha. Recipient award Synagogue Adv. Council United Jewish Appeal, 1975; named Rabbi Dr. Sol Roth Chair in Talmud and Contemporary Halakha established at Yeshiva U., 1989. Home: 30 E 62nd St New York NY 10021-8026 Office: Yeshiva U Dept Philosophy 500 W 185th St Dept New York NY 10033-3299 E-mail: rothsol@aol.com.

ROTH, STANLEY OWEN, federal agency administrator; BA, Brandeis U.; MA, Johns Hopkins U. Legis. asst. Rep. Stephen Solarz, Washington, 1979-82; staff cons. subcom. on Asian and Pacific affairs U.S. House Fgn. Affairs Com., 1983-85, staff dir. subcom. on Asian and Pacific Affairs, 1985-92, dir. com. liaison, 1993; dep. asst. for East Asia and Pacific Affairs Sec. of Def., 1993-94; spl. asst. to pres., sr. dir. Asian affairs Nat. Security Coun., 1994-96; dir. rsch. and studies U.S. Inst. Peace, 1996; asst. sec. of state for East Asia and Pacific Affairs U.S. Dept. State, 1997-2000. Office: US Dept State East Asian and Pacific Affairs 2201 C St NW Washington DC 20520-0001

ROTH, SUSAN AUSTIN, author, photographer; b. Wheeling, W.Va., Oct. 2, 1950; d. Rexford Frazier and Virginia Austin Roth; m. Mark Schneider, June 27, 1986. Student, Mount Holyoke Coll., 1968-70; BS in Horticulture, Cornell U., 1972, MS in Horticulture, 1974; postgrad., SUNY, Stony Brook, 1974-75. Dir. rsch. Valentine Girards Inc., Malvern, N.Y., 1975-77; assoc. editor Gardening Mag., Villanova, Pa., 1977-79; sr. editor Western Pub., N.Y.C., 1979-85; pres. Susan A. Roth & Co., Stony Brook, N.Y., 1984—. Author, photographer: The Weekend Garden Guide, 1991, The Four Season Landscape, 1994, Better Homes and Gardens Complete Guide to Flower Gardening, 1995, Better Homes and Gardens New Complete Guide to Gardening, 1997, Hot Plants for Cool Climates, 2000, Taylor's Guide to Trees, 2001; book packager, photographer Beds and Borders, 1998, Easy-Care Landscapes, 1995, Backyard Landscaper, 1992, Home Landscaper, 1990 Mem. Garden Writers Assn. of Am. (Book Writing award 1992, Mag. Writing award 1991, Photography award 1990), Am. Soc. of Horticulture, Authors Guild, Am. Soc. of Media Photographers. Avocations: hiking, gardening, travel. Office: 3 Lamont Ln Stony Brook NY 11790-1611 E-mail: flowerphotographer@prodigy.net.

ROTH, SUSAN BETSY, artist; b. N.Y.C., May 15, 1950; d. Samuel and Rene Roth; m. Darryl Leo Hughto, June 6, 1976; 1 child, Jeremy Roth Hughto. One-woman shows include Everson Mus. Art, Syracuse, N.Y., 1976, William Edward O'Reilly Gallery, N.Y.C., 1980, Salander-O'Reilly Gallery, N.Y.C., 1981, 82, 84, 86, 87, The Hett Gallery, Ltd., Edmonton, Alta., 1983, Martha White Gallery, Louisville, Ky., 1983, Robert Kidd Gallery, Birmingham, Mich., 1987, Gallery Elca London, Montreal, Quebec, Can., 1987, 88, 90, 91, Sangren Hall Gallery, We. Mich. U., Kalamazoo, 1987, Gallery One, Toronto, Ont., 1988, 90, 96, Rome (N.Y.) Art Ctr., 1995; exhibited in group shows including Everson Mus. Art, 1976, 78, Edmonton Art Gallery, 1977, Boston Mus. Fine Arts, 1977, William Edward O'Reilly, Inc. N.Y.C., 1980, Martha White Gallery, Louisville, Ky., 1981, Nicola Jacobs Gallery, London, 1982, Hirshorn Mus. and Scripture Gallery, Washington, 1982, 83, Rubiner Gallery, Royal Oak, Mich., 1982, Salander-O'Reilly Gallery, N.Y.C., 1984, 86, 90, Richard Brush Art Gallery, Canton, N.Y., 1985, Gallery 53, N.Y.C., 1985, Lowe Art Gallery, Syracusem N.Y., 1985, Picker Art Gallery, Hamilton, N.Y., 1986, Edmonton Art Gallery, 1987, 88, Mus. Art, Ft. Lauderdale, Fla., 1991, Mus. Art. Vero Beach, Fla., 1992, Wendy Hoff Gallery, N.Y.C., 1995, Gallery One, Toronto, 1996; represented in permanent collections including Art Council, Boston, Boston Mus. Fine Arts, Cabot Collection, Portland, Maine, Can. Imperial Bank of Commerce, Toronto, Castillejo Collection, Madrid, Comino Found., Vaduz, Lichtenstein, Corin Internat., Hong Kong, de Menil Family Trust, Paris, Elefant Collection, Montreal, Foley Hoag & Eliot, Boston, Surreal Holding, Inc., Toronto. Home: 8076 N Main St Rd Canastota NY 13032 E-mail: sdstudios@earthlink.net.

ROTH, TERESA ANN, broadcast executive; b. Little Rock, July 13, 1961; d. Carl Henry and Peggy Joann (Hartsell) Habig; m. Paul Gerhardt Roth, July 15, 1989 (div. May 1990). BA in Comm., U. Ark., 1983. Camera operator Sta. KATV-TV, Little Rock, 1983-85, writer, prodr., 1985-87, Sta. WSB-TV, Atlanta, 1987-89; exec. prodr., mgr. St. WSB-TV, 1989—. Prodr., dir. documentary Jo's Town, 1998, Jo's Town Shown at ValleyFest, 2000, The Hot Springs Documentary Film Festival, 2000, The Memphis Film Festival, 2001, The N.Y. Internat. Film Festival, 2001, The Kan Film Festival, 2001. Vol. Habitat for Humanity, Atlanta, 1996—; co-founder NATAS Student Connection, Atlanta, 1997—. Recipient Addy award Ad Club, Little Rock, 1986. Mem. NATAS (bd. dirs. 1991—, sec. 1993-95, v.p. 1995-99, nat. trustee 1999—), Promotion and Mktg. Execs., Atlanta Press Club. Avocations: movies, painting, writing, travel. Office: WSB-TV 1601 W Peachtree St NE Atlanta GA 30309-2641

ROTH, TIM, actor; b. London, 1961; With Glasgow Citizen's Theatre, The Oval House, The Royal Ct. Appeared in play Metamorphosis; films include The Hit, 1985, A World Apart, 1988, The Cook, the Thief, His Wife and Her Lover, 1990, Vincent and Theo, 1990, Rosencrantz and Guildenstern Are Dead, 1991, Jumpin' at the Boneyard, 1992, Reservoir Dogs, 1992, Backsliding, 1993, Bodies, Rest and Motion, 1993, Pulp Fiction, 1994, Rob Roy, 1995 (Acad. award nominee for best supporting actor 1996), Little Odessa, 1995, Four Rooms, 1995, No Way Home, 1996, Everyone Says I Love You, 1996, Hoodlum, 1997, Gridlock'd, 1997, Animals, 1997, Deceiver, 1998, The Legend of the Pianist on the Ocean, 1998, Vatel, 1999, Leggenda del pianista sull'oceano, 1998, Film-Fest DVD: Issue 1-Sundance, 1999, The Million Dollar Hotel, 2000; TV movies include Meantime, Made in Britain, Metamorphosis, Knuckle, Yellow Backs, King of the Ghetto, The Common Pursuit, Murder in the Heartland, 1993; dir.: The War Zone, 1998; TV guest appearance Tales From the Crypt, 1989. Office: Ilene Feldman Agy 8730 W Sunset Blvd Ste 490 Los Angeles CA 90069-2248

ROTH, WILLIAM STANLEY, hospital foundation executive; b. N.Y.C., Jan. 12, 1929; s. Sam Irving and Louise Caroline (Martin) R.; m. Hazel Adcock, May 6, 1963; children: R. Charles, W. Stanley. AA, Asheville-Biltmore Jr. Coll., 1948; BS, U. N.C., 1950. Dep. regional exec. Nat. coun. Boy Scouts Am., 1953-65; exec. v.p. Am. Humanics Found., 1965-67; dir. devel. Bethany Med. Ctr., Kansas City, Kans., 1967-74; exec. v.p. Geisinger Med. Ctr. Found., Danville, Pa., 1974-78; found. pres. Bapt. Med Ctrs., Birmingham, Ala., 1978—. Sec. Western Med. Systems, Cherokee Cmty. Homes, Cullman Sr. Housing, Dekalb Sr. Housing, Limestone Sr. Housing, Oxford Sr. Housing. Editor Torch and Trefoil, 1960-61. Mem.-at-large Nat. coun. Boy Scouts Am., 1972-86; chmn. NAHD Ednl. Fund, 1980-82; ruling elder John Knox Kirk, Kansas City, Mo., Grove Presbyn. Ch., Danville, Pa. Recipient Silver award United Meth. Ch., 1970, Mid-West Health Congress, 1971; Seymour award for outstanding hosp. devel. officer, 1983. Fellow Assn. for Healthcare Philanthropy (life, nat. pres. 1975-76); mem. Nat. Soc. Fund Raising Execs. (pres. Ala. chpt. 1980-82, nat. dir. 1980-84, mem. ethics bd. 1993-2000, advanced cert fund raising exec., Outstanding Fund Raising Exec., Ala. chpt. 1983), Mid-Am. Hosp. Devel. Assn. (pres. 1973-74), Mid-West Health Congress (devel. chmn. 1972-74), Am. Soc. for Healthcare Mktg. and Pub. Rels., Ala. Soc. for Sleep Disorders, Ala. Heart Inst., Ala. Assn. Healthcare Philanthropy (pres. 1991-93, chmn. bd. 1993-94), Ala. Planned Giving Coun. (bd. dirs. 1991-2000, pres. 1994-95), Alpha Phi Omega (nat. pres. 1958-62, dir. 1950—, Nat. Disting. Scv. award 1962), Delta Upsilon (pres. N.C. Alumni 1963-65), Rotary (pres. club 1976-77), Relay House, Summit Club, Green Valley Club (bd. govs.), Elks, Holy Order of the Arrow (Nat. Disting. Svc. award 1958). Home: 341 Laredo Dr Birmingham AL 35226-2325 Office: 3500 Blue Lake Dr Ste 101 Birmingham AL 35243-1908 E-mail: billroth1@aol.com.

ROTH, WILLIAM V., JR. former senator; b. Great Falls, Mont., July 22, 1921; m. Jane K. Richards; children: William V. III, Katharine Kellond. BA, U. Oreg., 1944; MBA, Harvard U., 1947, LLB, 1949. Bar: Del., U.S. Supreme Ct., Calif. Mem. 90th-91st congresses at large from, Del., 1967-71; senator State of Del., 1971-2001; former chmn. senate fin. com., former chmn govt affairs com.; chmn. U.S.-EU-Slovakia Action Comm., Washington. Chmn. Del. Rep. State Com., 1961-64; mem. Rep. Nat. Com., 1961-64; pres. North Atlantic Assembly, 1996-98. Served to capt. AUS, 1943-46. Decorated Bronze Star medal. Mem. ABA, Del. Bar Assn. Episcopalian. Office: US-EU-Slovakia Action Commn Ctr for Strategic & Internat Studies 1800 K St NW Washington DC 20006*

ROTHBAUM, BARBARA OLASOV, psychologist, educator; b. Charleston, S.C., July 4, 1960; d. Sanford Patla and Faye (Rabinowitz) Olasov; m. John Edel Rothbaum, June 19, 1988; children: Alex Olasov, Jake Olasov. BA with highest honors, U. N.C., 1982; MS in Psychology, U. Ga., 1984, PhD in Clin. Psychology, 1986. Gallery asst. Jan Goin Gallery, Charleston, S.C., 1976-82; grad. asst. U. Ga., Athens, 1982-84, 85-86; behavior therapist The Middlesex Hosp. Med. Sch., London, 1984-85; instr. psychiatry Med. Coll. Pa., Phila., 1986-88, asst. prof. psychiatry, 1988-90; asst. prof. Emory U. Sch. Medicine, Atlanta, 1990—. Project coord. Rape and Crime Victim Program, Phila, 1986-90; pvt. practice psychology, Phila., 1986-90, Anxiety Disorders Assocs., Atlanta, 1990-92; mem. DSM-III-R work group on post-traumatic stress disorder. Contbr. articles to profl. jours., chpts. to books. Mem. mental health subcom. Phila. Coalition for Victim Advocacy, 1986-90. Mem. Am. Psychol. Assn., Ga. Psychol. Assn., Assn. for Advancement Behavior Therapy, Soc.

Menstrual Cycle Rsch., Phila. Behavior Therapy Assn. (bd. dirs. 1987-88). Democrat. Jewish. Avocations: art, outdoors, reading. Office: The Emory Clinic Dept Psychiatry 1365 Clifton Rd NE Atlanta GA 30322-1013

ROTHBAUM, DAVID, obstetrician-gynecologist; b. N.Y.C., 1958; BA, N.Y.U., 1978; MD, Boston U., 1982. Intern N. Shore U. Hosp., Manhasset, N.Y., 1982-83, resident ob-gyn., 1983-86, attending physician; clin. instr. Sch. Medicine NYU; pvt. practice. Med. cons. News 12 L.I. Fellow ACOG; mem. Am. Assn. Gynecol. Laparoscopists, Am. Fertility Soc. Office: 233 E Shore Rd Great Neck NY 11023-2433

ROTHBERG, ABRAHAM, author, educator, editor; b. N.Y.C., Jan. 14, 1922; s. Louis and Lottie (Drimmer) R.; m. Esther Conwell, Sept. 30, 1945; 1 son, Lewis Josiah. AB, Bklyn. Coll., 1942; MA, U. Iowa, 1947; PhD, Columbia U., 1952. Chmn. editorial bd. Stateside (mag.), N.Y.C., 1947-49; instr. English, creative writing Columbia U., 1948; instr. English, humanities Hofstra Coll., Hempstead, N. Y., 1947-51; prof. English St. John Fisher Coll., 1973-83, chmn. dept. English, 1981-82; disting. writer-in-residence, vis. prof. Wichita State U., 1985. Ford Found. fellow, N.Y.C., 1951-52; editor-in-chief Free Europe Press, N.Y.C., 1952-59; mng. editor George Braziller, Inc., N.Y.C., 1959, New Leader (mag.), N.Y.C., 1960-61; cons. editor New Jewish Ency., 1960-62; writer, editorial cons.; European corr. Nat. Observer, Washington, Manchester (Eng.) Guardian, 1962-63; sr. editor Bantam Books, Inc., N.Y.C., 1966-67; Cons. editor The New Union Prayer Book, N.Y.C., 1975 (Recipient John H. McGinnis Meml. award for short story 1970, John H. McGinnis Meml. award for essay 1973-74, Lit. award Friends of Rochester Library 1980); Author: Abraham, Eyewitness History of World War II, 1962, The Thousand Doors, 1965, The Heirs of Cain, 1966, The Song of David Freed, 1968, The Other Man's Shoes, 1969, The Boy and the Dolphin, 1969, The Sword of the Golem, 1971, Aleksandr Solzhenitsyn: The Major Novels, 1971, The Heirs of Stalin: Dissidence and the Soviet Regime, 1953-1970, 1972, The Stalking Horse, 1972, The Great Waltz, 1978, The Four Corners of the House, 1981; Editor: U.S. Stories, 1949, Flashes in the Night, 1958, Anatomy of a Moral, 1959, A Bar-Mitzvah Companion, 1959, Great Adventure Stories of Jack London, 1967; Contbr. articles, essays, stories, poems to various publs., anthologies, collections. Served with AUS, 1943-45. Home: 340 Pelham Rd Rochester NY 14610-3355

ROTHBERG, GERALD, editor, publisher, editor-in-chief; b. Bklyn., Oct. 29, 1937; s. Abraham and Pauline Rothberg; m. Glenda Fay Morris, June 18, 1970 (div. 1988); children: Laura, Abigail. BA, Bklyn. Coll., 1960; postgrad., Dickinson Law Sch., 1962. Spl. projects editor Esquire (mag.), 1963-66; owner, editor, pub., founder Circus (mag.), N.Y.C., 1966—; owner, founder, editor Sci. and Living Tomorrow, 1980—, Who's In, 1981; founder, editor Sports Mirror mag., 1983—, MGF mag., 1985—; Country Mirror mag., 1994—. Author: (novels) Composition 36, 1993, The Six-Hour Song, 1994, Redeeming Esau, 1995. Mem. Periodical and Book Assn. Am. (pres.) Office: Circus Mag 6 W 18th St Ste 2C New York NY 10011-4628 E-mail: circusmag@aol.com.

ROTHBERG, GLENDA FAY MORRIS, lawyer; b. Rome, Aug. 7, 1946; d. Glenn Howell and Fay (Givens) Morris; m. Gerald Rothberg, June 18, 1970 (div. Jan. 1989); children: Laura, Abigail. AB, Randolph-Macon Woman's Coll., 1968; JD, Benjamin Cardozo Law Sch., 1985. Bar: N.Y. 1986, U.S. Dist. Ct. (so. and ea. dists.) N.Y. 1987, U.S. Supreme Ct. 1990. Law guardian juvenile rights divsn. Legal Aid Soc., N.Y.C., 1988-91; pvt. practice, 1992—. Faculty dir. Inst. for not-for-profit Mgmt. Columbia Bus. Sch., N.Y.C., 1994-98. Vol. Manhattan Mediation Ctr., N.Y.C., 1996-99; chair legal com. N.Y.C. Comptr. Task Force on Open Adoption, 1999—. Fellow Am. Bar Found.; mem. ABA, Assn. of Bar of City of N.Y. (com. chair 1996-99, mem. coun. on children 1999—). Office: 271 Madison Ave New York NY 10016-1001 E-mail: gmrlaw@aol.com.

ROTHBERG, HARVEY D. retired internist, oncologist; b. Plainfield, N.J., Nov. 17, 1928; s. Harvey Rothberg and Helen Rosenberg; m. Mary Ann Prowell (div. 1973); m. Nancy Mundy; children: Elizabeth, Marjorie, Nancy. BA, Princeton U., 1949; MD, Harvard U., 1953. Diplomate Am. Bd. Internal Medicine, Am. Bd. Med. Oncology, Am. Bd. Hematology. Intern, then resident Mass. Gen. Hosp., Boston, 1953-55; attending physician The Med. Ctr. at Princeton, N.J., 1960—; clin. prof. medicine U. Medicine & Dentistry N.J.-Robert Wood Johnson Sch. of Medicine, Piscataway, 1984—. Pres. Princeton Regional Bd. Edn., 1968; pres. med. staff Med. Ctr. at Princeton, 1975, mem. tumor bd., biomed. ethics com. Author: The First Fifty Years, A History of Princeton Hospital, 1969, The First Seventy-Five Years: A History of the Medical Center at Princeton, 1994; contbr. articles to profl. jours. Docent Princeton U. Art Mus. Capt. U.S. Army, 1957—59. Fellow ACP; mem. AMA, Am. Soc. Clin. Oncology, Oncology Soc. N.J. (pres. 1984). Jewish. Avocations: gardening, golf, reading, art history.

ROTHBERG, JUNE SIMMONDS, retired nursing educator, psychotherapist, psychoanalyst; b. Phila., Sept. 4, 1923; d. David and Rose (Protzel) Simmonds; m. Jacob Rothberg, Sept. 7, 1952 (dec. Feb. 2001); children: Robert, Alan. Diploma in nursing, Lenox Hill Hosp., 1944; BS, N.Y. U., 1950, MA, 1959, PhD (NIH fellow), 1965; Diploma in Psychotherapy and Psychoanalysis, Adelphi U., Inst. for Advanced Psychol. Studies, 1987. USPHS traineeship N.Y. U., 1957-59; sr. public health nurse Bklyn. Vis. Nurse Assn., 1951-53; prin. investigator in nursing, homestead study project Goldwater Hosp. and N.Y. U., 1959-61; instr. N.Y. U., 1964-65, asst. prof., 1965-68, assoc. prof., 1968-69, project dir. grad. program rehab. nursing, 1964-69, prof., 1969-87, prof. emeritus, 1987—; dean Adelphi U., Garden City, N.Y., 1969-85, v.p. acad. adminstrn., 1985-86; pvt. practice West Hempstead, N.Y., 1993-97. Pres. David Simmonds Co. Inc., Med. Supply Co., 1982-89; dir., chmn. compensation com. Quality Care, Inc.; cons. to various ednl. and svc. instns.; cons. region 2 Bur. Health Resources Devel., HHS.; speaker on radio and TV; bd. dirs., mem. audit com. Ipco Corp. (formerly Sterling Optical Corp.), 1991. Contbr. articles to profl. jours. Mem. pres's coun. N.Y. U. Sch. Edn., 1973-75; treas. Nurses for Polit. Action, 1971-73; trustee Nurses Coalition for Action in Politics, 1974-76; bd. visitors Duke Med. Ctr., 1970-74; mem. governing bd. Nassau-Suffolk Health Systems Agy., 1976-79; leader People-to-People Internat. med. rehab. del. to People's Republic of China, 1981; mem. com. for the study pain disability and chronic illness behavior Inst. Medicine, 1985-86, com. on ethics in rehab. Hastings Ctr., 1985-87; trustee Paget's Disease Found., 1987-89. Recipient Disting. Alumna award NYU, 1974, recognition award Am. Assn. Colls. Nursing, 1976, Achievers award Ctr. for Bus. and Profl. Women, 1980 Fellow Am. Acad. Nursing (governing coun. 1980-82); mem. Nat. League Nursing (exec. com. coun. of baccalaureate and higher degree programs 1969-73), Am. Nurses Assn. (joint liaison com. 1970-72), Commn. Accreditation of Rehab. Facilities, Am. Congress Rehab. Medicine (pres. 1977-78, chmn. continuing edn. com. 1979-86, 34th Ann. John Stanley Coulter Meml. lectr. 1984, Gold Key award 1984, Edward W. Lowman award 1990), Am. Assn. Colls. Nursing (pres. 1974-76), L.I. Women's Network (pres. 1980-81), Kappa Delta Pi, Sigma Theta Tau, Pi Lambda Theta. Achievements include having June S. Rothberg collection in Nursing Archives, Mugar Meml. Library, Boston U. Home and Office: 8668 Via Giulia Boca Raton FL 33496-1912

ROTHBLATT, DONALD NOAH, urban and regional planner, educator; b. N.Y.C., Apr. 28, 1935; s. Harry and Sophie (Chernofsky) R.; m. Ann S. Vogel, June 16, 1957; children: Joel Michael, Steven Saul. BCE, CUNY, 1957; MS in Urban Planning, Columbia U., 1963; Diploma in Comprehensive Planning, Inst. Social Studies, The Hague, 1964; PhD in City and Regional Planning, Harvard U., 1969. Cert. Am. Inst. Cert. Planners; registered prof. engr., N.Y. Planner N.Y.C. Planning Commn., 1960-62, N.Y. Housing and Redevel. Bd., 1963-66; research fellow Ctr. for Environ. Design Studies, Harvard U., Cambridge, Mass., 1965-71; teaching fellow, instr., then asst. prof. city and regional planning Harvard U., 1967-71; prof. urban and regional planning, chmn. dept. San Jose State U., Calif., 1971—. Lady Davis vis. prof. urban and regional planning Hebrew U., Jerusalem and Tel Aviv U., 1978; vis. scholar Indian Inst. Architects, 1979, Shandong Province, China, 1996, U. Lodz, Poland, 2000, Paris Regional Transp. Authority, France, 2002; vis. scholar, rsch. assoc. Inst. Govtl. Studies, U. Calif., Berkeley, 1980—; cons. to pvt. industry and govt. agys. Author: Human Needs and Public Housing, 1964, Thailand's Northeast, 1967, Regional Planning: The Appalachian Experience, 1971, Allocation of Resources for Regional Planning, 1972, The Suburban Environment and Women, 1979, Regional-Local Development Policy Making, 1981, Planning the Metropolis: The Multiple Advocacy Approach, 1982, Comparative Suburban Data, 1983, Suburbia: An International Assessment, 1986, Metropolitan Dispute Resolution in Silicon Valley, 1989, Good Practices for the Congestion Management Program, 1994, Activity-Based Travel Survey and Analysis of Responses to Increased Congestion, 1995, An Experiment in Sub-Regional Planning: California's Congestion Management Policy, 1995, Estimating the Origins and Destinations of Transit Passengers from On/Off Counts, 1995, Changes in Property Values Induced by Light Transit, 1996, Comparitive Study of Statewide Transportation Planning Under ISTEA, 1997, North American Metropolitan Planning Reexamined, 1999, Government Performance Measures Linking Urban Mass Transportation With Land Use and Accessibility Factors, 2000, Best Practices in Developing Regional Transportation Plans, 2001; editor: National policy for Urban and Regional Development, 1974, Regional Advocacy Planning: Expanding Air Transport Facilities for the San Jose Metropolitan Area, 1975, Metropolitan-wide Advocacy Planning; Dispersion of Low and Moderate Cost Housing in the San Jose Metropolitan Area, 1976, Multiple Advocacy Planning: Public Surface Transportation in the San Jose Metropolitan Area, 1977, A Multiple Advocacy Approach to Regional Planning: Open Space and Recreational Facilities for the San Jose Metropolitan Area, 1979, Regional Transpotation Planning for the San Jose Metropolitan Area, 1981, Planning for Open Space and Recreational Facilities in the San Jose Metropolitan Area, 1982, Regional Economic Development Planning for the San Jose Metropolitan Area, 1984, Planning for Surface Transportation in the San Jose Metropolitan Area, 1986, Expansion of Air Transportation Facilities in the San Jose Metropolitan Area, 1987, Provision of Economic Development in the San Jose Met. Area, 1988, Metropolitan Governance: American/Canadian Intergovernmental Perspectives, 1993, Metropolitan Governance Revisited, 1998; contbr. numerous articles to profl. jours.; dir.: Pub. TV series Sta. KTEH, 1976. Mem. adv. coun. Bay Area Met. Transp. Commn., 1995—. Served to 1st lt. C.E., U.S. Army, 1957-59. Rsch. fellow John F. Kennedy Sch. Govt. Harvard U., 1967-69; William F. Milton rsch. fellow, 1970-71; faculty rsch. grantee, NSF, 1972-82, Calif. State U., 1977-78; grantee Nat. Inst. Dispute Resolution, 1987-88, Can. Studies Enrichment Program, 1989-90, Can. Studies Rsch. Program, 1992-93, Univ. Rsch. and Tng. Program grantee Calif. Dept. Transp., 1993-97; recipient Innovative Teaching award Calif. State U. and Coll., 1975-79; co-recipient Best of West award Western Ednl. Soc. for Tele-communication, 1976; recipient award Internat. Festival of Films on Architecture and Planning, 1983, Meritorious Performance award San Jose State U., 1986, 88, 90. Mem.: AAUP, Architecture and Urban and Regional Planning (chmn. 1973—75), Calif. Edn. Com. Architecture and Landscape, Internat. Fedn. Housing and Planning, Planners for Equal Opportunity, Am. Planning Assn., Assn. Collegiate Schs. of Planning (pres. 1975—76). Office: San Jose State U Dept Urban & Regional Planni San Jose CA 95192-0185 *My basic view is that we should try to develop ourselves fully and help others do the same, so that we will be able to live in harmony with, and contribute to, our world community.*

ROTHCHILD, DONALD SYLVESTER, political science educator; b. N.Y.C., Aug. 11, 1928; s. Sylvester Edward and Alice Levy Rothchild; m. Edith White, Apr. 23, 1954; children: Derek Edward, Maynard White. BA with high honors, Kenyon Coll., 1949; MA, U. Calif., Berkeley, 1954; PhD, Johns Hopkins U., 1958. From instr. to assoc. prof. Colby Coll., Waterville, Maine, 1957-65; prof. U. Calif., Davis, 1965—, faculty rsch. lectr., 1996-97, fellow Washington Ctr., 2000-01. Vis. Fulbright lectr. Makerere U., Kampala, Uganda, 1962-64; sr. lectr. U. Nairobi, Kenya, 1966-67; vis. Ford prof. U. Zambia, Lusaka, 1970-71; vis. prof. U. Ghana, Legon, 1975-77, 85, U. Calif., Berkeley, 2002; professorial lectr. Johns Hopkins U., Washington, 1993, 95, 2001; internat. adv. bd. mem. Internat. Negotiation, 1995—, 2001; vis. scholar Brookings Instn., 1992-93, Ctr. for Internat. Security and Cooperation, Stanford U., 1998-99. Author: Racial Bargaining in Independent Kenya, 1973, Managing Ethnic Conflict in Africa, 1997; co-author: Sovereignty as Responsibility, 1996; co-editor: The International Spread of Ethnic Conflict, 1998, Ending Civil Wars: The Implementation of Peace Agreements, 2002; editor Jour. Nationalism and Ethnic Politics, 1994—; contbr. articles to profl. jours. Internat. observer mission Carter Ctr., Ghana, 1992; rapporteur Friedrich Ebert Found., Kampala, Uganda, 1993; Hubert H. Humphrey spkr. Alumni Assn. Conf., Accra, Ghana, 1994. Sgt. U.S. Army, 1950-52. Disting. Am. Specialist grantee USIA, Thika, Kenya, 1993; Peace fellow U.S. Inst. Peace, Washington, 1994-95. Mem. Internat. Polit. Sci. Assn. (pres. rsch. com. 1988-94), Am. Polit. Sci. Assn., African Studies Assn. Democrat. Avocations: opera, theatre, ballet. Home: 208 W 8th St Davis CA 95616-3637 Office: Univ Calif Dept Polit Sci 1 Shields Ave Davis CA 95616-5271 E-mail: dsrothchild@ucdavis.edu.

ROTHENBERG, ABRAHAM JOSEPH, architect; b. Bklyn., Jan. 31, 1931; s. Jacob Moshe and Anna (Rothenberg) R.; m. Barbara Ann Henkin, Mar. 12, 1961; children: David Benjamin, Daniel Mark. Cert. in architecture, Ecole des Beaux Arts, Fontainebleau, France, 1958; BArch, Rensselaer Poly. Inst., 1953; MFA in Architecture, Princeton U., 1958. Assoc. Curtis & Davis, N.Y.C., 1959-65, Pomerance & Breines, N.Y.C., 1965-69; prin. Abraham Rothenberg Assocs., Westport, Conn., 1969—. Adj. prof. Fairfield (Conn.) U., CUNY, 1970-80; arbitrator constrn. industry. Prin. works include Sofia Apts., N.Y.C., 1990, Memphis Uptown Apts., N.Y.C., 1991, Temple Israel, Westport, 1990, Hewlett-Woodmere L.I. Pub. Libr., 1996. Mem. Archtl. Rev. Bd., Westport, 1980-92; trustee Silvermine Guild Arts Ctr., New Canaan, Conn., 1991-97, Nature Ctr., Westport, 1985-90. Recipient Merit award Builder Mag., 1987, awards N.Y. State Inst. Architects, 1964. Mem. AIA (mem. design com. 1985—, housing com. 1985—), Conn. Soc. Architects (People's Choice award 1988), Sunrise Rotary (Westport, Conn.). Democrat. Jewish. Avocations: hiking, swimming, travel, reading, music. Home and Office: 303 Bayberry Ln Westport CT 06880-1314 E-mail: araarcht@aol.com.

ROTHENBERG, ADAM LEIGH, lawyer; b. Chgo., Sept. 9, 1963; s. Philip Burton and Roberta Lynn (Keylin) R.; m. Christie Curry, Sept. 23, 1989; children: Alexa Leigh, Zachary Ryan. Student, Tulane U., 1981-83; BABA, U. Wash., 1987; JD cum laude, Seton Hall U., 1993. Bar: N.J. 1993, U.S. Dist. Ct. N.J. 1993. Law clk. Blume Vazquez Goldfaden Berkowitz & Donnelly, Newark, 1992-93; assoc. Levinson Axelrod, Edison, N.J., 1993—. Mem. ATLA, N.J. ATLA (bd. govs. 1996—), Middlesex County Bar Assn., Middlesex County Trial Lawyers, Essex County Bar Assn., N.J. State Bar Assn. Spkrs. Bur. (spkr. 1997—). Avocations: tennis, golf, sailing. Home: 2389 Channing Ave Westfield NJ 07090-4507 Office: Levinson Axelrod 2 Lincoln Ave Edison NJ 08837-3217

ROTHENBERG, ALBERT, psychiatrist, educator; b. N.Y.C., June 2, 1930; s. Gabriel and Rose (Goldberg) R.; m. Julia C. Johnson, June 28, 1970; children: Michael, Mora, Rina. AB, Harvard U., 1952; MD, Tufts U., 1956. Diplomate: Am. Bd. Psychiatry and Neurology. Intern Pa. Hosp., Phila., 1956-57; resident in psychiatry Yale U., West Haven (Conn.) VA Hosp., 1957-58, Grace-New Haven Hosp., 1958-59, Yale Psychiat. Inst., New Haven, 1959-60, chief resident, 1960-61; practice medicine specializing in psychiatry, 1960-61, 1963-75; chief neuropsychiatry Rodriguez U.S. Army Hosp., San Juan, P.R., 1961-63; practice medicine specializing in psychiatry Farmington, Conn., 1975-79, Stockbridge, Mass., 1979-94, Chatham, N.Y., 1994—, Great Barrington, Mass., 1994-98; dir. rsch. Austen Riggs Center, Stockbridge, 1979-94. Asst. dir. Yale Psychiat. Inst., 1963-64, sr. staff mem., 1964-83; mem. staff Yale-New Haven Med. Ctr., West Haven VA Hosp., U. Conn. Health Ctr., Farmington; cons., mem. editorial bd. various jours. in psychiatry and psychology; instr. dept. psychiatry Yale U. Sch. Medicine, 1960-61, 63-64, asst. prof., 1964-68, assoc. prof., 1968-74, clin. prof., 1974-84; prof. psychiatry U. Conn. Sch. Medicine, Farmington, 1975-79, dir. residency tng., 1976-78, dir. clin. svcs., 1975-78; prin. investigator Studies in the Creative Process, 1964— ; vis. prof. Pa. State U., 1971, adj. prof., 1971-78; vis. prof. dept. Am. studies Yale U., 1974-76, U. Capetown Med. Sch., South Africa, 1999, Saltpêtrière Hosp., Paris, 1999; lectr. dept. psychiatry Harvard U. Med. Sch., 1982-86, clin. prof., 1986—; researcher in psychotherapy. Author: (with B. Greenberg) Index of Scientific Writings on Creativity: Creative Men and Women, 1974, Index of Scientific Writings on Creativity: General 1566-1974, 1976; (with C.R. Hausman) The Creativity Question, 1976; The Emerging Goddess: The Creative Process in Art, Science and Other Fields, 1979; The Creative Process of Psychotherapy, 1988; Adolescence: Psychopathology, Normality, and Creativity, 1990; Creativity and Madness: New Findings and Old Stereotypes, 1990, Living Color, 2001; contbr. numerous articles on the creative process, schizophrenia, anorexia nervosa, and psychotherapy to profl. and popular jours. Researcher on creativity in the arts, sci. and tech. Served with M.C. U.S. Army, 1961-63. Recipient Tufts Med. Alumni award 1956, Rsch. Scientist Career Devel. award NIMH 1964, 69, Golestan Found. award 1991, 92, Kovler award MESAB, 1999; Guggenheim Meml. fellow 1974-75, Ctr. Adv. Study in Behavioral Studies fellow 1986-87, Netherlands Inst. for Adv. Study in Humanities and Social Scis. fellow, 1992-93. Fellow Am. Psychiat. Assn. (life), Am. Coll. Psychoanalysts; mem. AAAS, Mass. Psychiat. Soc., Am. Soc. Aesthetics, Rappaport-Klein Group, Sigma Xi. Democrat. Home: PO Box 1002 52 Pine Ridge Rd Canaan NY 12029-3101 E-mail: albert_rothenberg@hms.harvard.edu.

ROTHENBERG, ELLIOT CALVIN, lawyer, author; b. Mpls., Nov. 12, 1939; s. Sam S. and Claire Sylvia (Feller) R.; m. Sally Smalying; children: Sarah, Rebecca, Sam. BA summa cum laude, U. Minn., 1961; JD, Harvard U. (Fulbright fellow), 1964. Bar: Minn. 1966, U.S. Dist. Ct. Minn. 1966, D.C. 1968, U.S. Supreme Ct. 1972, N.Y. 1974, U.S. Ct. Appeals (2d cir.) 1974, U.S. Ct. Appeals (8th cir.) 1975. Assoc. project dir. Brookings Inst., Washington, 1966-67; fgn. svc. officer, legal advisor U.S. Dept. State, 1968-73; Am. Embassy, Saigon; U.S. Mission to the UN; nat. law dir. Anti-Defamation League, N.Y.C., 1973-74; legal dir. Minn. Pub. Interest Rsch. Group, Mpls., 1974-77; pvt. practice law, 1977—. Adj. prof. William Mitchell Coll. Law, St. Paul, 1983—; faculty mem. several nat. comm. law and First Amendment seminars. Author: (with Zelman Cowen) Sir John Latham and Other Papers, 1965, The Taming of the Press: Cohen v. Cowles Media Co., 1999, The Taming of the Press, 1999; contbr. articles to profl. and scholarly jours. and books, newspapers, popular mags. State bd. dirs. YMCA Youth in Govt. Program, 1981-84; v.p. Twin Cities chpt. Am. Jewish Com., 1980-84; mem. Minn. Ho. of Reps., 1978-82, asst. floor leader (whip), 1981-82; pres., dir. North Star Legal Found., 1983—; legal affairs editor Pub. Rsch. Syndicated, 1986—; briefs and oral arguments published in full Landmark Briefs and Arguments of the Supreme Ct. of the U.S., Vol. 200, 1992; mem. citizens adv. com. Voyageurs Nat. Pk., 1979-81. Recipient Legis. Evaluation Assembly Legis. Excellence award, 1980, Vietnam Civilian Svc. medal U.S. Dept. State, 1970, North Star award U. Minn., 1961; Fulbright fellow, 1964-65. Mem. ABA, Minn. Bar Assn., Harvard Law Sch. Assn., Am. Legion, Mensa, Phi Beta Kappa. Jewish. Home and Office: 3901 W 25th St Minneapolis MN 55416-3803 E-mail: srothenbe@aol.com.

ROTHENBERG, HARVEY DAVID, educational administrator; b. May 31, 1937; s. Max and Cecelia Rothenberg; m. Audrey Darlynne Roseman, July 5, 1964; children: David Michael, Mark Daniel. BBA, State U. Iowa, 1960; MA, U. No. Colo., 1961; postgrad., Harris Tchrs. Coll., 1962-63; PhD, Colo. State U., 1972. Distributive edn. tchr. Roosevelt H.S., St. Louis, 1961-63, Proviso West H.S., Hillside, Ill., 1963-64, Longmont (Colo.) Sr. H.S., 1964-69, 70-71; supr. rsch. and spl. programs St. Vrain Valley Sch. Dist., Longmont, 1971-72; chmn. bus. divsn. Arapahoe C.C., Littleton, Colo., 1972-75; dir. vocat., career and adult edn. Arapahoe County Sch. Dist. 6, 1975-96; part-time instr. Met. State Coll., Denver, 1975-85, Arapahoe C.C., Littleton, 1975-80, Regis U., 1980—. Dir. faculty, curriculum Sch. Profl. Studies, Regis U., 1996-98, instr., facilitator, 1998—; owner HDR Bus. and Ednl. Consulting, 1988—; owner Shreveport Bombers Indoor Football Team of Indoor Profl. Football League, 1999—; vis. prof. U . Ala., Tuscaloosa, summer 1972; dir. Chatfield Bank, Littleton, 1974-83, Yaak River Mines Ltd., Amusement Personified Inc.; pres. Kuytia Inc., Littleton, 1975—; co-owner Albuquerque Lasers. Author: Conducting Successful Business Research, 1996. Mem. City of Longmont Long-Range Planning Commn., 1971-72, pres. Homeowners Bd., 1978-80. Recipient Outstanding Young Educator award St. Vrain Valley Sch. Dist., 1967, Outstanding Vocat. Educator, Colo., 1992, Western Region U.S., 1993. Mem. Am. Vocat. Assn., Nat. Assn. Local Sch. Adminstrs., Colo. Vocat. Assn. (mem. exec. com. 1966-68, treas. 1972-73), Littleton C. of C., Colo. Assn. Vocat. Adminstrs., Colo. Educators for and About Bus., Elks, Masons, Delta Sigma Pi, Delta Pi Epsilon. Home: 7461 S Sheridan Ct Littleton CO 80128-7084 E-mail: rothenbergs@msn.com.

ROTHENBERG, JEROME, author, visual arts and literary educator; b. N.Y.C., Dec. 11, 1931; s. Morris and Estelle (Lichtenstein) R.; m. Diane Brodatz, Dec. 25, 1952; 1 son, Matthew. BA, CCNY, 1952; MA, U. Mich., 1953; Doctor of Letters, SUNY, Oneonta, 1997. With Mannes Coll. Music, N.Y.C., 1961-70. Vis. prof. U. Calif., San Diego, 1971, 77-84, U. Wis.-Mils., 1974-75, San Diego State U., 1976-77, U. Calif., Riverside, 1980, U. Okla., Norman, 1984; vis. Aerol Arnold prof. English U.So. Calif., 1983; vis. writer in residence SUNY, Albany, 1986, prof. English SUNY, Binghamton, 1986-88; prof. visual arts and lit. U. Calif., San Diego, 1989—, chmn. visual arts, 1990-93; head, creative writing, 1994-95. Poet, freelance writer, 1956—; author: numerous books of poetry and prose including Between, 1967, Technicians of the Sacred, 1968, Poems for the Game of Silence, 1971, Shaking the Pumpkin, 1972, America a Prophecy, 1973, Revolution of the Word, 1974, Poland/1931, 1974, A Big Jewish Book, 1978, A Seneca Journal, 1978, Vienna Blood, 1980, Pre-Faces, 1981, Symposium of the Whole, 1983, That Dada Strain, 1983, New Selected Poems, 1986, Khurbn, 1989, Exiled in the Word, 1989, The Lorca Variations I-VIII, 1990, Apres le jeu de silence, 1991, The Lorca Variations (complete), 1993, Gematria, 1994, An Oracle for Delfi, 1995, Poems for The Millennium, vol. 1, 1995, Seedings, 1996, The Book, Spiritual Instrument, 1996, Poems for the Millennium, Vol. 2, 1998, A Paradise of Poets, 1999, A Book of The Book, 2000, The Case for Memory, 2001; editor, pub. Hawk's Well Press., N.Y.C., 1958-65, Some/Thing mag., 1966-69, Alcheringa: Ethnopoetics, 1970-76, New Wilderness Letter, 1976-86. Served with AUS, 1953-55. Recipient award in poetry Longview Found., 1960, Am. Book award, 1982, PEN Ctr. USA West award, 1994, 2002 PEN Oakland Josephine Miles award, 1994, 96; Wenner-Gren Found. grantee-in-aide for rsch. in Am. Indian poetry, 1968; Guggenheim fellow in creative writing, 1974; NEA poetry grantee, 1976. Mem. P.E.N. Am. Center, New Wilderness Found., World Poetry Acad. Office: care New Directions 80 8th Ave New York NY 10011-5126 E-mail: jrothenb@ucsd.edu.

ROTHENBERG, JOYCE ANDREA (JOYCE JOYCE ANDREA), composer, poet, writer, singer; b. Bklyn., Oct. 09; d. Norman and Rosie (Alpert) R. BS, SUNY, N.Y.C. Cert. artist Dept. Cultural Affairs. Past owner employment agency; study various holistic health techniques (i.e. polarity); poet Jackie Robinson Forum, 1997; guest annual poetry festival City Coll.; invited guest as poet and songwriter radio, network and cable TV broadcasts; poet Black History Month; invited singer, songwriter, tap dancer on launching of Visual Radio Friction's Digital Art Space", 2nd Annual Winter Tree Festival McCarren Park's Nulty Square; featured poet at Shelly Soc. of N.Y.; featured poet, songwriter, writer, tchrs. and writers collaborative "Poetry in the Morning" radio show; past mem. Pete Seeger Street Singers; appearances include (cable TV) World of Surprises; entertainer at Beaux Arts Soc., N.Y. Author short stories and essays; contbr. poems to lit. anthologies, mags. (various awards). Cert. by Dept. Cultural Affairs as artist. Vol. UNICEF, Sta. WNYC. Contributions given in honor of Outstanding Achievement in Poetry for ongoing projects in Israel. Mem. Internat. Platform Assn. Avocations: classical music, jazz, opera, ballet, interior design, interest in world religions and spirituality, sewing art (crewel), designs clothes and accessories. Home: PO Box 6041 New York NY 10150-6041 E-mail: joyan_us@yahoo.com.

ROTHENBERG, MARC, historian; b. Phila., Oct. 13, 1949; s. William David and Marcella R.; m. Ivy S. Baer, June 23, 1985; children: Sara Jill, Leslie Hannah. BA, Villanova U., 1970; PhD, Bryn Mawr Coll., 1974. Rsch. assoc. Acad. Natural Sci., Phila., 1974-75; staff Joseph Henry Papers, Smithsonian Instn., Washington, 1975-85, editor Joseph Henry Papers, 1985—. Cons. Am. Mus. Natural History, N.Y.C., 1975-78. Editor: History of Science in the U.S.: An Encyclopedia, 2001, Papers of Joseph Henry, vols. 6-9, 2002. Mem. History of Sci. Soc. (exec. com., treas. 1997—). Office: Smithsonian Instn Joseph Henry Papers PO Box 37012 Washington DC 20013-7012

ROTHENBERG, MARC ELLIOT, pediatrics educator; b. N.Y.C., Jan. 17, 1961; s. Leonard Martin and Helen (Weissman) R.; m. Joy Hannah Malka, Aug. 26, 1990; children: Eliana Nitza, Danielle Shoshana, Joelle Adina. BA, Brandeis U., 1983; MD, Harvard U., 1990, PhD. Diplomate Am. Bd. Pediatrics. Intern Children's Hosp., Boston, 1990-91, resident, 1991-92, fellow, 1992-95; instr. Harvard Med. Sch., 1995-96; assoc. prof., sect. chief

Children's Hosp. - U. Cin., 1996—; prof. pediatrics, chief divsn. allergy & immunology clin. childrens Hosp. Med. Ctr. Physician Harvard Med. Sch., Boston, 1990-96, scientist, 1990-96; physician U. Cin., 1996, scientist, 1996. Contbr. articles to profl. jours. Recipient Physician Scientist award Howard Hughes Med. Inst., 1994-96, Damon-Runyon Walton Winchell Cancer Inst. award, N.Y., 1993, NIH-NIAID awards, 1997, 99, Pharmacia Internat. Rsch. Found. award, 1998, Human Frontiers Sci. Program award, 1999. Mem. Am. Acad. Allergy and Immunology (scholar 1993), Am. Acad. of Pediatrics, Am. Assn. Immunology, Am. Soc. Clin. Investigation. Jewish. Achievements include development of first culture system for human eosinophils. Office: Childrens Hosp Med Ctr 3333 Burnet Ave Cincinnati OH 45229-3026 E-mail: rothenberg@chmcc.org.

ROTHENBERG, MICHAEL ANDREW, lawyer, not-for-profit administrator; b. N.Y.C., Apr. 23, 1964; s. Stanley and Eleanore Dubin Rothenberg; m. Zerline Lehman Goodman, Aug. 12, 1990; children: Brice, Garon, Zaya. AB, Hamilton Coll., 1986; JD, NYU, 1991. Bar: N.Y. 1992. Organizer Calif. Pub. Interest Rsch. Group, Berkeley, 1986-87; atty. housing unit South Bklyn. Legal Svcs., 1991-94. Program assoc. Rockefeller Family Fund, N.Y.C., 1994-95; coord. OmbudService, Citizens Jury Project, Vera Inst. Justice, N.Y.C., 1995-97; assoc. dir. N.Y. Lawyers for Pub. Interest, N.Y.C., 1997-2000; exec. dir. N.Y. Lawyers for Pub. Interest, N.Y.C., 2001—. Mem. exec. com. Franklin and Eleanor Roosevelt Inst., N.Y.C., 1998—; treas., bd. dirs. Green Guerillas, 1996—; bd. dirs. Bkly. Cmty. Housong and Svcs., 1998—; chair task force on housing ct. Assn. Bar of City of N.Y., 1997—99; pres. Met. Squash Reacuets Assn., 1993—2002; mem. exec. com. U.S. Squash Racquets Assn., Phila., 1994—2000; pres. Nat. Assn. Pub. Interest Law, Washington, 1989—92, NYU Pub. Interest Law Found., N.Y.C., 1989—93. Arthur Garfield Hays Civil Liberties fellow Arthur Garfield Hays Program, NYU Sch. Law, 1990-91. Mem. Assn. of Bar of City of N.Y., Phi Beta Kappa. Jewish. Avocation: nationally ranked squash player. Home: 15 Clark St Brooklyn NY 11201 Office: N Y Lawyers for Pub Interest 11th Fl 151 W 30th St New York NY 10001-4007 Office Fax: 212-244-4570. E-mail: mar@nylpi.org.

ROTHENBERG, MIRA KOWARSKI, clinical psychologist and psychotherapist; b. Wilno, Poland; came to U.S., 1938; d. Jacob and Rosa (Joffe) Kowarski; m. Tev Goldsman, Dec. 7, 1960 (div. June 1974); 1 child, Akiva. BA, Bklyn. Coll., 1943; MA, Columbia U., 1957, Yeshiva U., 1959, ABD, 1962. Lic. psychologist, N.Y. Therapist, tchr.ir. Hawthorne (N.Y.) Cedar Knolls, 1952-53, League Sch., Bklyn., 1953-58; founder, clin. dir. Blueberry Treatment Ctrs., 1958-90; staff psychologist L.I. Coll. Hosp., 1966—. Pioneer in working with autistic children; cons. Beachbrook Nursery, Bkyn., 1969-70, San Felipe Del Rio, Santa Fe, 1980—, Children's House Montessori Nursery, Bklyn., 1982-89, Austrlia Dept. Edn., Carynia, New South Wales, SOS Village, Vilnius, Lithuania, 1997—; adj. prof. L.I. U., Bklyn., 1976-78; internat. speaker in field; worker, lectr. and cons. with psychotic and autistic children, Croatia, 1994, Lithuania, 1994-99; cons. for movies on foster care, 1990—. Author: Children with Emerald Eyes, 1977, (with others) Pet Oriented Psychotherapy, 1980, The Outsiders, 1989; contbr. to books and articles to profl. jours. and mags.; documentary movie based on work with autistic children, 1962; Lithuanian play based on book, 1999; Children with Emerald Eyes play based on book, 1999. Mem. APA, World Fedn. Mental Health, N.Y. State Psychol. Assn., Inter. Soc. Child Abuse and Neglect (Hamburg, Germany), Physicians for Social Responsibility, N.Y. Acad. Scis., Amnest Internat., ACLU, NOW, Anti Defamation League, Yivo, Nat. Register Svc. Providers in Psychology. Avocations: writing, painting, sculpture, dance. Home and Office: 160 State St Brooklyn NY 11201-5610 E-mail: mirark@oc.s.com.

ROTHENBERG, ROBERT PHILIP, public relations counselor; b. N.Y.C., June 5, 1936; s. Robert Edward and Lillian Babette (Lustig) R. BA, Cornell U., 1956; MS, Boston U., 1958. With publicity dept. Columbia Pictures Corp., N.Y.C., 1959-60; asst. to pres., pub. rels. dir. Harry N. Abrams Pub. Co., 1960-62; press sec. to gubernatorial candidate William R. Anderson Tenn., 1962; with Rowland Co., N.Y.C., 1963-70, v.p., 1965-67, sr. v.p., 1967-70; ptnr., exec. v.p. Robert Marston and Assocs., 1970-88, sr. exec. v.p., 1978-88, also bd. dirs.; ptnr., pres. Marston and Rothenberg Pub. Affairs, Inc., N.Y.C. and Washington, 1977-88; chmn., pres. Rothenberg Pub. Rels. Comms. Counsel, N.Y.C., 1988—; v.p. Medbook Publs., Inc., 1995—; dir. pub. rels. BigChange Networks, LLC, Washington and N.Y.C., 1998—. Sr. cons. The Lund Group, Inc. Trustee Mus. of Holography, N.Y.C.; bd. dirs. Found. to Save African Endangered Wildlife; assoc. Nat. Park Found.; counselor Am. Bus. Cancer Rsch. Found., Southport, Conn.; bd. dirs. World Rehab. Fund, N.Y.C., 1982-98; fellow Met. Mus. of Art, 1990—; pres., chmn., bd. trustees St. Bartholomew's Preservation Found., 1992-95; mem. Blue Hill Troupe, Ltd.; bd. dirs. Amas Musical Theatre, Inc., 2002—. With USAFR, 1959-65. Mem. Internat. Soc. Poets, Pride and Alarm Soc., English-Speaking Union, The Players Club. Unitarian Universalist. Home and Office: 400 E 54th St Apt 29B New York NY 10022-5169

ROTHENBERG, STANLEY, lawyer; b. Bklyn., June 8, 1930; s. Baruch and Lena (Feinman) R.; children: David, Michael, Seth. AB, NYU, 1950; LLB, Harvard U., 1953; LLD, Utrecht (The Netherlands) U., 1954. Bar: N.Y. 1954. Assoc. Margulies & Heit, N.Y.C., 1958-63; ptnr. Heit & Rothenberg, 1964-78, Moses & Singer LLP, N.Y.C., 1979—. Adv. com. on copyright registration and deposit Libr. Congress, 1993-95; adj. prof. law Fordham U., N.Y.C., 1994—, Cardozo Sch. Law, N.Y.C., 1986-89. Author: Copyright & Public Performance of Music, 1954, reissued, 1987, Copyright Law: Basic & Related Materials, 1956, Legal Protection of Literature, Art & Music, 1960, reissued, 1988; contbr. articles to profl. jours. Fulbright scholar U.S. Edn. Found., 1953-54. Mem. ABA (com. chmn.), N.Y. State Bar Assn. (selection del.), Assn. of the Bar of the City of N.Y. (com. chmn.), Copyright Soc. the U.S.A. (pres. 1980-82, hon. trustee 1982—), Harvard Club. Avocations: reading, theatre. Home: 51 Landing Dr Dobbs Ferry NY 10522 Office: Moses & Singer LLP 1301 Avenue Of The Americas New York NY 10019-6022

ROTHENBERGER, DAVID ALBERT, surgeon; b. Sioux Falls, S.D., 1947; MD, Tufts U., 1973. Cert. colon and rectal surgery. Intern St. Paul-Ramsey Med. Ctr., 1973-74, resident gen. surgery, 1974-78; fellow colon rectal surgery U. Minn., Mpls., 1978-79; mem. staff United Hosp., St. Paul; cln. prof. surgery U. Minn., Mpls., chief divsn. colon and rectal surgery; dir. U. Minn. Cancer Ctr.; former pres. Am. Bd. Colon & Rectal Surgery, Taylor, Mich., mem. advisory council. Fellow ACS, Am. Soc. Colon and Rectal Surgeons (exec. coun., immediate past pres. 1997—), Am. Surg. Assn., Soc. for Surgery of the Alimentary Tract, Western Surg. Assn. Address: 2550 University Ave W Ste 313N Saint Paul MN 55114-1903 also: Box 450 Mayo Meml Bldg 420 Delaware St SE Minneapolis MN 55455-0374*

ROTHENBERGER, JACK RENNINGER, clergyman; b. Boyertown, Pa., Oct. 4, 1930; s. Stuart Henry and Beulah (Renninger) R.; m. Jean Delores Schultz, Sept. 8, 1951; children: Susan Marie, Bruce Wayne. BS, Juniata Coll., 1952; MDiv, Hartford Theol. Sem., 1955; STM, Temple U., 1962; D Ministry, Lancaster Theol. Sem., 1977. Ordained to ministry Schwenkfelder Ch., 1955. Pastor Palm and Lansdale (Pa.) Schwenkfelder Ch., 1955-63, 65-66; stated supply, interim pastor Pa. United Ch. of Christ, 1963-69; chaplain, tchr., coach, dir. admissions Perkiomen Sch., Pennsburg, Pa., 1955-56, 62-67, asst. headmaster, headmaster, coach football backfield, basketball, 1967-69; min. Christian edn. Ctrl. Schwenkfelder Ch., Worcester, 1969-74, sr. min., 1974-95, exec. min. emeritus, 2000—; interim supply pastor Wentz United Ch. of Christ, 1997-99. Pres. World Christian Endeavor, 1994-2002, Internat. Christian Endeavor, Columbus, Ohio, 1983-87; v.p. World Christian Endeavor, 1990-94; mem. cabinet and bd. Pa. Coun. Chs., 1957—, sec., 1993-97; mem. Pa. Conf. Interch. Coop.; mem. Schwenckfeld Mission Bd., 1957—, Schwenckfelder Bd. Pubs., 1957—, Schwenckfelder Libr. Bd., 1957—, Schwenckfeldian in Exile Soc., 1955—; chmn. expansion com. Schwenckfelder Libr., 2d Heritage Ctr., also others. Author: Casper Schwenckfeld and the Ecumenical Ideal, 1962; editor The Schwenkfeldian mag., 1964-87; contbr. articles to profl. jours. First v.p. Schwenckfeld Manor, Lansdale, 1973-97, pres., 1997-2002; v.p. Meadowood Total Care Retirement Community, Worcester, Pa., 1983-98. Mem. No. Pa. Assn. United Ch. of Christ Ministerium, No. Pa. Ministerium, Methacton Area Ministerium, Montgomery County Sunday Sch. Assn. (past pres.), also others. Republican. Home: Spruce Run # 73 Meadowood at Worcester Lansdale PA 19446 E-mail: jackrothenberger@cs.com. *I extend the hand of fellowship to all believers in the Living Christ regardless of their specific expression of that faith. In a world of constant rapid change we can find direction through faith in the Living God revealed by Jesus.*

ROTHENHAUS, ROBERT CHARLES, mathematics educator; b. N.Y.C., Nov. 26, 1947; s. Perry and Ada (Goldstein) R.; m. Wendy Baron Rothenhaus, Jan. 13, 1973; children: Amy, Lauren. BS, CCNY, 1968, MA, 1974. Sch. bd. mgmt. chair L.I. City H.S., 1989-92, program chairperson, 1995—; math. tchr. N.Y.C. Bd. of Edn., 1968—. Mem. Assn. of Tchrs. of Math. of N.Y.C., Nat. Coun. of Tchrs. of Math. Avocation: tennis. Office: L I City HS 1430 Broadway Long Island City NY 11106-4530

ROTHERHAM, LARRY CHARLES, insurance executive; b. Council Bluffs, Iowa, Oct. 22, 1940; s. Charles Sylvester and Edna Mary (Sylvanus) R.; m. Florene F. Black, May 29, 1965; children: Christopher Charles, Phillip Larry, Kathleen Florene. Student, Creighton U., 1959-61; BSBA, U. Nebr., 1965; postgrad., Am. Coll., Bryn Mawr, Pa., 1985, 87. CPCU, CLU, ARM. Claims rep. and underwriter Safeco Ins. Co., Albuquerque, 1965-69; br. mgr. Ohio Casualty Group, 1969-99, resident v.p. Denver, 1997-99. Assoc. in risk mgmt. Ins. Inst. Am., 1976—. Mem. PTA Collet Park Elem. Sch., Albuquerque, 1963-82, Freedom H.S., Albuquerque, 1982-86; bd. chmn. N.Mex. Property Ins. Program; mem. N.Mex. Workers compensation Appeals Bd. Mem. New Mex. Soc. Chartered Property & Casualty Underwriters (charter mem., pres. 1975-77), New Mex. Soc. Chartered Life Underwriters, New Mex. Ins. Assn. Democrat. Roman Catholic. Avocations: race walking, swimming, hiking, camping. Home: 10677 W Parkhill Pl Littleton CO 80127-5547

ROTHERMEL, DANIEL KROTT, lawyer, holding company executive; b. West Reading, Pa., Mar. 21, 1938; s. Daniel Grim and Ruth Elizabeth (Krott) R.; m. Sarah Finch, July 9, 1960; children: Anne, Daniel F., K. Melissa. BS, Pa. State U., 1960; JD, Am. U., 1966. Bar: D.C. 1967. Acct. Lukens Steel Co., Coatesville, Pa., 1960-61; pvt. practice Reading, 1966-68; atty. Carpenter Tech. Corp., 1968-70, resident counsel, 1970-78, asst. sec., 1972-73, sec., 1973-88, v.p., gen. counsel, sec., 1978-88; pres., chief exec. officer Cumru Assocs. Inc., Pa., 1989—. Bd. dirs. Sovereign Bank, Sovereign Bancorp, Inc., chmn. exec. com. Mem. Inst. Cmty. Affairs, Pa. State U., 1974-78; bd. dirs. Berks County chpt. ARC, 1983-86; mem., chmn. adv. bd. Berks campus Pa. State U., 1982—; ch. lay leader. Lt. USNR, 1961-66. Mem. ABA, D.C. Bar Assn., Am. Soc. Corp. Secs., U.S. C. of C., Pa. C. of C., Reading-Berks C. of C., Rotary. Republican. Lutheran. Home: 20 Glenbrook Dr Reading PA 19607-9645 Office: Cumru Assocs Inc PO Box 6573 Reading PA 19610-0573

ROTHERMEL, JAMES DOUGLAS, retired finance educator; b. Burton, Tex., Aug. 20, 1918; s. Bailleux Ervin and Nathalie (Ponfick) R.; m. Dorothy Ann Hodde, Aug. 24, 1947; children: James Douglas Jr., Donald Henry. AA, Blinn Coll., 1947; BS, SW Tex. State U., 1949, MEd, 1952; postgrad., U. Houston, 1965-67. Instr. bus. edn. Brenham (Tex.) H.S., 1949-52; prin. Schulenburg (Tex.) H.S., 1952-57, Ganado (Tex.) H.S., 1957-64; instr., chmn. bus. adminstrn. divsn. San Jacinto Coll., Pasadena, Tex., 1964-78, part-time instr., 1978-81; ret., 1981. Councilman City of Brenham (Tex.) High Sch., 1949—52, mayor pro tem, 1988—96; mem. Ret. Sr. Vol. Program (RSVP), 1984—2000, mem. Brazos Valley adv. coun., 1990—97, 2000—, chmn., 1994—97, mem. Washington County adv. coun., 1986—2000, chmn., 1995—2000; organizer, chmn. Washington County Vets. Meml. Plz., 2000—. With 14th Constrn. Bn. USN, 1942—45. Mem. Tex. Ret. Tchrs. Assn., Tex. Bus. Edn. Assn., Brenham Louise Giddings Ret. Tchrs. Assn. (legis. chmn. 1984-00, pres. 1996-98), Am. Assn. Ret. Persons (legis. chmn. 1982-2000, instr. 55/Alive 1985-98, asst. state coord. 55/Alive 1986-88), Am. Legion (comdr. Schulenburg post 143, comdr. 9th dist. 1961-63, vice comdr. 1959-61, comdr. Buddy Wright post 1997-98), Optimists, Rotary. Republican. Lutheran. Avocations: hunting, fishing, travel, gardening, woodworking. Home: 803 Robinhood Rd Brenham TX 77833-2567

ROTHERMEL, JOAN ASHLEY, artist; b. Winchester, Mass., Mar. 10, 1930; d. Mark Braden Ashley and Anne Jorgenson; m. Harold Christian Rothermel, Dec. 30, 1950; children: Lynn Schoenfield, Lawrence. BFA, Miami U., Oxford, Ohio, 1951, MEd in Art, 1970. Art tchr. Middletown (Ohio) Fine Arts Ctr., 1971-77. Sole juror nat. and state watercolor exhbns., including Ohio Watercolor Soc., Cen. Ohio Watercolor Soc., Capital U., Columbus, Beaufort (S.C.) Art Assn., S.C. Watercolor Soc., Toledo Artists Club, 1982-99; instr. watercolor workshops nat. and state exhbns., including Firelands Area Art League, Norwalk, Ohio, Hilton Head Island Workshops, S.C., Wyoming Valley Art League, Wilkes-Barre, Pa., Idaho Watercolor Soc., Boise, St. Louis Artists' Guild, Hawaii Watercolor Soc., Honolulu, 1982— One-person shows include Middletown, Sandusky, Boston Mills Art Festivals, Peninsula, Ohio; exhibited in group shows Am. Watercolor Soc., Nat. Watercolor Soc., Allied Artists of Am., Nat. Acad. Design, Rocky Mountain Nat. Watermedia Exhbn., Knickerbocker Artists, Nat. Arts Club, Ohio Watercolor Soc., San Diego Watercolor Soc., Ga. Watercolor Soc.; represented in corp. collections and galleries Owens-Ill. Corp., Toledo, Soc. Bank, Sandusky, Oglesby-Barnitz Bank, Middletown, 1st Nat. Bank, Middletown, Cen. Bank, Cleve., Livingstine Taylor Gallery, Sandusky; works featured in books Painting the Spirit of Nature, 1984, Exploring Color, 1985, The Creative Artist, 1990, others, also mags., including Am. Artist, The Artist's Mag. Mem. Am. Watercolor So. (treas. 1986—, Dolphin fellow, Gold medal honor, Bronze medal, 8 other awards 1983-99), Nat. Watercolor Soc., Allied Artists of Am., Midwest Watercolor Soc., Ohio Watercolor Soc., Knickerbocker Artists, Salmagundi Club. Home: 221 46th St Sandusky OH 44870-4894 E-mail: johal@kellnet.com.

ROTHERMEL, RODMAN SCHANTZ, manufacturing company executive; b. Norristown, Pa., Apr. 30, 1932; s. Leonard Kehl and Marguerite Hartman (Schantz) R.; m. Paula Cucinotta, Nov. 4, 1961; children: Kristin Rothermel Edwards, Lenore Rothermel Spohn, Megal Julia. BA, Haverford (Pa.) Coll., 1954; postgrad., Drexel U., Phila., 1964, 69. Mgr. mfg. Nuclear Products divsn. Superior Tube Co., Collegeville, Pa., 1957-66; gen. mgr. Buchan Loose Leaf Records Co., Clifton Heights, 1966-71, v.p. ops., 1971-76; pres. Buchan Industries, 1976—; dir., CEO Gen. Bindery Co., Phila., 1993-95; chmn., CEO GH Alliance, Pennsauken, N.J., 1995-97. Bd. dirs. Valley Forge Philharmonic, Norristown, Pa., 1967-69, Muhlenberg Coll., Allentown, Pa., 1979-91, Inter-County Hospitalization Plan, Horsham, Pa., 1977-89, chmn., 1984-85; bd. dirs. Binding Industries Am., Chgo., 1980-94, pres., 1993-94; pres. St. Luke Luth. Ch., Devon, Pa., 1978-79; sch. dir. Marple-Newtown Sch. Dist., Newtown Square, Pa., 1997-02. With U.S. Army, 1955-56. Mem. Union League Phila., Aronimink Golf Club, Right Angle Club (pres. 1986). Republican. Lutheran. Home: 46 Paper Mill Ln Newtown Square PA 19073-1802 Office: Buchan Industries 46 Paper Mill Ln Newtown Square PA 19073-1802

ROTHFELD, MICHAEL B. theatrical productions executive, investor; b. N.Y.C., May 19, 1947; m. Ella M. Foshay, May 22, 1970; 2 children. BA, Columbia U., 1969, MS, MBA, cert. internatl fellows program, Columbia U., 1971. With Time, Inc., 1971-76, assoc. editor Fortune, 1971-74; asst. to chmn. bd. dirs., CEO Time Inc., 1974-76; with Salomon Bros., 1976-83, v.p., 1979-83, The First Boston Corp., N.Y.C., 1983-84, mng. dir., 1985-89; gen. ptnr. Bessemer Ptnrs. and Bessemer Holdings, 1989-97, ltd. ptnr., 1997-98. Chmn. bd. dirs. Graphic Controls Corp., 1995-98; bd. vis. Columbia Coll., 1998—, vice chmn. 2002-, bd. adv. Knight-Bagheot program in fin. journalism Grad. Sch. Journalism, 1998—; chmn. Redfields, LLC, Eagle Prodns., LLC, N.Y.C. Prodr. off-broadway prodn., 1999, Gore Vidal's The Best Man, 2000 (winner Drama Desk award, Outer Critics Circle award, Tony nomination). Office: Eagle Productions LLC 200 E 69th St New York NY 10021

ROTHFIELD, LAWRENCE I. microbiology educator; b. N.Y.C., Dec. 30, 1927; s. Joseph and Henrietta (Brown) R.; m. Naomi Fox, Sept. 18, 1953; children: Susan Anne, Lawrence, Jane, John. BA, Cornell U., 1947; MD, NYU, 1951. Intern, then resident Bellevue, Presbyn. hosps., N.Y.C., 1951-53, 55-57; successively instr., clin. asst. prof., asst. prof. NYU Sch. Medicine, 1957-64; from asst. prof. to assoc. prof. Albert Einstein Coll. Medicine, N.Y.C., 1964-68; prof. U. Conn. Sch. Medicine, Farmington, 1968—, chmn. dept. microbiology, 1968-80. Mem. molecular biology rev. panel NIH, 1970-75, microbiology and immunology adv. com. Pres.'s Biomed. Rsch. Panel, 1975, molecular biology rev. panel NSF, 1979-83; mem. microbial physiology and genetics rev. panel NIH, 1990-94, chairperson, 1991-93. Author: Structure and Function of Biological Membranes, 1972; mem. editorial bd. Jour. Membrane Biology, 1969-83, Jour. Biol. Chemistry, 1974-80. With M.C. U.S. Army, 1953-55. Mem. Am. Soc. Biol. Chemists, Am. Soc. Microbiology (chmn. microbial physiology div. 1975). Home: 540 Deercliff Rd Avon CT 06001-2859 Office: U Conn Health Center Farmington CT 06032 E-mail: lroth@neuron.uchc.edu.

ROTHFIELD, NAOMI FOX, physician; b. Bklyn., Apr. 5, 1929; d. Morris and Violet (Bloomgarden) Fox; m. Lawrence Rothfield, Sept. 18, 1954; children: Susan, Lawrence, John, Jane. BA, Bard Coll., 1950; MD, NYU, 1955. Intern Lenox Hill Hosp., N.Y.C., 1955-56; instr. N.Y. U. Sch. Medicine, 1956-62, asst. prof., 1962-68; assoc. prof. U. Conn. Sch. Medicine, Farmington, 1968-72, prof., 1972—, chief divsn. rheumatic diseases, 1972—99. Contbr. chpts. to books; contbr. articles to med. jours. Bd. dirs., Conn. Choral Artists, 1999—. Mem. Am. Soc. Clin. Investigation, Am. Rheumatism Assn., Assn. Am. Physics. Jewish. Home: 540 Deercliff Rd Avon CT 06001-2859 Office: U Conn Sch Medicine Div Of Rheumatic Diseases Farmington CT 06030-0001 E-mail: rothfield@nso.uchc.edu.

ROTHHAMMER, CRAIG ROBERT, social worker, consultant; b. San Francisco, May 17, 1954; s. Robert Charles and Gloria Lee (Molloy) R.; m. Dawn Alicia Alvarez, 1988. BA, U. Calif., Santa Barbara, 1976; MSW, San Diego State U., 1979. Lic. clin. social worker, Calif. Social work asst. Mercy Hosp., San Diego, 1977; psychiat. social worker Lanterman State Hosp., Pomona, Calif., 1979-83, Sonoma State Hosp., Eldridge, 1983-84; children's social worker County Adoption Service, San Bernardino, 1984-86; psychiat. social worker Patton State Hosp., 1987-88; psychiat. soc. worker II Crisis Outpatient Svcs. Riverside (Calif.) County Mental Health, 1988-90; mental health svcs. supr. Interagy. Svcs. for Families, Riverside County Mental Health, 1990-95; mgr. inpatient psychiatry west/south bay sub-region Kaiser Permanente, Redwood City, Calif., 1995—. Expert examiner Behavioral Sci. Examiners, Calif.; pvt. practice (part time) social work Redlands, Calif., 1986-89; field instr. MSW program Calif. State U., San Bernardino, 1989-95, marriage, family & child counselor program Loma Linda (Calif.) U., 1993. Vol. Social Advs. for Youth, Santa Barbara, Calif., 1974-76, Am. Diabetes Assn., San Diego, 1978-79, San Diego Assn. For Retarded, 1978-80; liason Adoptive Family Assn., San Bernardino, 1986. Mem. NASW, Acad. Cert. Social Workers (diplomate in clin. social work). Democrat. Avocations: scuba diving, bicycling, hiking, writing, ch. related activities. Office: Kaiser Permanente Dept Inpatient Psychiatry 900 Veterans Blvd Redwood City CA 94063-1738

ROTHHOLZ, PETER LUTZ, public relations executive; b. Berlin, June 23, 1929; came to U.S., 1945, naturalized, 1947; s. Alfred and Bertha (Isner) R.; m. Paula Trachtman, Sept. 16, 1951; 1 dau., Amy Elisabeth (dec.); m. Barbara Peters Margules, July 4, 1971; stepchildren: David, Thomas. BA, Queens Coll., 1950; postgrad., N.Y. U., 1956-60; certificates, U. London, 1949, McGill U., 1950. With Lissone-Lindeman U.S., Inc., N.Y.C., 1953-56, KLM Royal Dutch Airlines, N.Y.C., 1956-61; exec. v.p. Simmons Tours, Inc., 1961-62; pres., prin. Peter Rothholz Assocs., Inc., 1962—; mem. faculty div. bus. mgmt. Sch. Continuing Edn. N.Y. U., 1969-70. Mem. faculty Queens Coll., 1992-2000; former mem. exec. com. pacific Asia Travel Assn., Caribbean Tourism Orgn. Contbr. articles to various publs. Bd. dirs. Queens Coll. Found., 1973-94, Nat. Coun. on Aging. With U.S. Army, 1951-52. Fellow Inst. Certified Travel Agts; mem. Pub. Relations Soc. Am., Soc. Am. Travel Writers, Queens Mus. (pres. 1977-78, chmn. 1978-80), Queens Coll. Alumni Assn. (pres. 1973-75), Phi Alpha Theta. Clubs: N.Y. Publicity (past v.p., dir.). Home and Office: 55 Squaw Rd East Hampton NY 11937- E-mail: pr4pr@aol.com.

ROTHING, FRANK JOHN, government official; b. Chgo., July 4, 1924; s. Frank Joseph and Eva A. (Buhl) R.; m. Carita Reiss Corbett, June 16, 1951; children: Frank John, Reginald, Peter, James, Richard, Joseph, Thomas, Carita Ann. BS, U. Notre Dame, 1948. C.P.A., U. Ill., 1954. Pub. accountant Arthur Young & Co., Chgo., 1948-55; v.p. Midwest Stock Exchange, 1955-60, v.p., treas., 1960-66, sr. v.p., 1966-71; exec. v.p., sec., dir. Ill. Co., 1971-74; v.p. 1st Nat. Bank Chgo., 1974-75; exec. v.p. Front St. Securities, Inc., 1975-78; mem. Chgo. Office SEC, 1978, ret., 1989; chmn. bd. Chgo. Bd. Options Exchange Clearing Corp. Mem. Chgo. Bd. Trade. Adviser Jr. Achievement Chgo.; bd. dirs. St. Elizabeth's Hosp., Chgo.; mem. citizens bd. U. Chgo.; Bd. dirs., mem. exec. bd. North Shore Area Boy Scouts Am.; chmn. bd. trustees St. Mary of Woods Coll., Terre Haute, Ind. Served to 1st lt. USAAF, 1943-45. Decorated D.F.C., Air medal. Mem. VFW, Am. Legion, Am. Inst. Accountants, Ill. Soc. C.P.A.s, Am. Accounting Assn., Newcomen Soc., Navy League U.S., Ill. Athletic Club. Clubs: Michigan Shores; Bond of Chicago (dir.), Economic, Chgo. Athletic, Notre Dame (dir.), Attic (Chgo.).

ROTHKIN, MARILYN MAE, psychotherapist; b. Bklyn., Aug. 24, 1940; d. Robert Isadore and Sally Sarah (Perlman) Glazer; m. Richard Murray Rothkin, Jan. 5, 1963; children: Stacey Rothkin Post, Sheryl Rothkin Deppisch. BS, Kent State U., 1961; MA, U. Akron, 1987; cert., Gestalt Inst. Cleve., 1993. Lic. profl. clin. counselor, Ohio; cert. chem. dependency counselor, Ohio. Tchr. Akron, Barberton and Cleve. pub. schs., Ohio, 1961-73; social worker Western Res. Coun. Girl Scouts U.S., Akron, 1974-76, Medina (Ohio) County Dept. Human Svcs., 1987-88; counselor Touchstone Counseling Ctr., 1986-87, YMCA Rape Crisis Ctr., Akron, 1985-89; program dir. Cmty. Drug Bd., 1988-93; psychotherapist N.E. Ohio Psychol. Assocs., Cuyahoga Falls, 1992-2000. Staff writer Village Views/West Side Leader, Akron, 1974-84; spkr., workshop presenter, dir. Rothkin Assocs., Copley, Ohio, 1993—; pres. Intertel, 2001— Co-editor newsletter Alliance for the Mentally Ill, 1992-95. Mem. adolescent comprehensive health care adv. bd. Children's Med. Ctr., Akron, 1991-93; mem. drug free schs. adv. bd. Akron Pub. Schs., 1988-93; mem. edn. alumni bd. U. Akron; mental health disaster svcs. vol. ARC, 1999—. Mem. ACA (pres. 2001), Intertel (bd. dirs., regional dir. 1988-89, 95-99, gen. sec. 1990-95, 99-2000, editor newsletter 1988-89, 95-98, editor Intertel Inquiries column 1999—, Svc. award 1991, pres. 2001—), Am. Soc. Clin. Hypnosis (sec. Akron-Cleve. br. 1995-97), Mensa (exec. com. East Ctrl. Ohio br. 1987-88), Phi Delta Kappa, Chi Sigma Iota. Avocations: gardening, reading. Office: Marilyn Rothkin LPCC Counseling Akron Gen's Wellness Ctr 4125 Medina Rd Akron OH 44333-2483 E-mail: mmg2440@aol.com.

ROTHKOPF, ARTHUR J. college president; b. N.Y.C., May 24, 1935; s. Abraham and Sarah (Mehlman) Rothkopf; m. Barbara Sarnoff, Dec. 25, 1958; children: Jennifer, Katherine. AB, Lafayette Coll., 1955; JD, Harvard U., 1958. Bar: N.Y. 1959, D.C. 1967. Atty. U.S. Dept. Treasury, N.Y.C., 1958—60, SEC, Washington, 1960—63; assoc. tax legis. counsel U.S. Dept. Treasury, 1963—66; ptnr. Hogan & Hartson, 1967—91; gen. counsel U.S. Dept. Transp., 1991—92, dep. sec., 1992—93; pres. Lafayette Coll., Easton, Pa., 1993—. Bd. dirs. Lehigh Valley Econ. Devel. Corp., Ins. Svcs. Office, Inc., Jersey City. Trustee Fed. City Coun., Washington, 1983—91, Lehigh Valley Hosp.; bd. dirs. Coun. Higher Edn. Accreditation; bd. dirs., chmn. Assn. Ind. Colls. and Univs. Pa. Mem.: The Pa. Soc. (treas.), Harvard Club of N.Y.C., Chevy Chase Club, Met. Club of Washington. Jewish. Home: 515 College Ave Easton PA 18042-7623 Office: Lafayette Coll 316 Markle Hall Easton PA 18042

ROTHLEDER, BURTON MARK, nuclear engineer, consultant; b. N.Y.C., Oct. 31, 1931; s. Leo Jules and Elsie Cohen Rothleder; m. Elaine Bialick, June 6, 1954 (div. 1977); children: Mark, Sheila, Dianne. SB, MIT, 1953, SM, 1957. Engr. Bettis Atomic Power Lab. Westinghouse, Idaho Falls, Idaho, 1958—61, Pitts., 1961—63, sr. engr. Astronuc. Lab., 1963—65, fellow engr. nuc. energy sys., 1965—70; supervising engr. Nuc. Fuel Svcs., Rockville, Md., 1970—73; sr. engr. Nuc. Assocs. Internat., 1973—78, Sci. Applications Internat. Corp., McLean, Va., 1978—90; nuc. engr. U.S. Dept. Energy, Germantown, Md., 1990—. Contbr. over 40 articles to profl. jours.; tech. reviewer: Nuc. Sci. and Engring. 1st lt. U.S. Army, 1953—55. Mem.: Am. Nuc. Soc. Achievements include development of fundamental technology for solution of PWR loading pattern combinatorial explosion problem, developed expert systems concepts to solve this for more complex low-leakage designs; fundamental concepts for incorporating burnable gadolinium absorber in PWR fuel and use in to optimize core design; reactivity effect of PWR pellet-cladding contact. Avocations: classical music, musicology. Home: 1131 University Blvd W Apt 203 Silver Spring MD 20902-3306

ROTHLISBERGER, RODNEY JOHN, music educator; b. Bottineau, N.D., May 13, 1940; s. Forrest John and Ellen Rothlisberger; m. Gay Elaine Mohr, Dec. 20, 1975 (div.). BA, St. Olaf Coll., 1962; MA, Eastman Sch. Music, 1967; DMusA, U. Colo., 1978. Anacortes Washington Pub. Schs., 1962-64; organist, choirmaster U.S. Mil. Acad., West Point, N.Y., 1965-67; instr., prof. Bowdoin Coll., Brunswick, Maine, 1967-70; instr. Melbourne (Australia) H.S., 1973-75; prof. Berea (Ky.) Coll., 1976-77; instr. Concordia Coll., Moorhead, Minn., 1979-81, Moorhead Pub. Schs., 1989-95; prof. Minn. State U., Moorhead, 1995—, chmn. music dept., 2002—. Active Civic Opera Bd., 1996—2002; bd. dirs. Red River Boy Choir, Moorhead, 1984—2000, Arts Coun., Moorhead, 1988—. With U.S. Army, 1996—2001. Recipient Achievement award Lake Agassiz Arts Coun., 1987. Mem. Nat. Assn. Tchrs. Singing, Am. Choral Dirs. Assn., Music Educators Nat. Conf., Am. Guild Organists (dean Red River Valley chpt. 1985-87, Minn. state chmn. 1995-2002, chmn. nat. com. on membership, 1994-2000). Presbyterian. Avocation: reading. Home: 1021 River Dr Moorhead MN 56560-3369 Office: Minn State U Moorhead 1104 7th Ave S Moorhead MN 56563-0002 E-mail: rothlisb@mnstate.edu.

ROTHMAN, ADAM ALAN, financial consultant; b. Bklyn., Apr. 5, 1960; s. Bernard and Barbara (Schaeffer) R.; children: Seth Daniel, Joshua David; m. Sharon Gail Winard; children: David Sapolin, Rachael Sapolin. BBA, Am. U., 1982. Acct. exec. Invention Mktg. Co., Washington, 1982-84; sales assoc. Michael Franblau Assoc., Hartsdale, N.Y., 1984-89; exec. v.p. Adam A. Rothman and Assocs., New Rochelle, NY, 1989—2001; sr. v.p. exec. and profl. benefits divsn. USI, 2001—. Author: Wealth Accumulation Strategy for Educators, 1987, Estate Planning for the 21st Century, 1999, How Does the IRA Get Inherited?, 2000, How Does the Defective Insurance Trust Work, 2000, The New IRA Distribution Rules for 2001, 2001, Disability Insurance for High Network Individuals, 2001, Life Insurance Using Yen Based Lending, 2002, High Net Worth Risk Management Solutions and Insurance, 2002; contbg. editor: The Realtor. Chmn. devel. com. The Guidance Ctr. Mem. Interstate Alliance Fin. Planners (founding mem.). Democrat. Jewish. Office: 1086 Teaneck Rd Teaneck NJ 07666-4838 E-mail: adam@sinsernelson.com.

ROTHMAN, BARBARA SCHAEFFER, special education educator; b. Bklyn., Sept. 29, 1934; d. Samuel and Edythe (Manuta) Schaeffer; m. Bernard Rothman, Aug. 23, 1953; children: Brian, Adam, Helene. BS, SUNY, New Paltz, 1955; MS, Coll. New Rochelle, 1979. Cert. sch. adminstrn., supervision, N.Y. State Dept. Edn. Tchr. N.Y.C. Bd. Edn., 1955-75, with child program, 1975-77, placement officer dist. 7, 8, 1978-80, chpt. 53 supr. dist. 8, 1980-83, supr. pupil personnel dist. 8, 1983-85, asst. chairperson Com. of Handicapped dist. 11, 1985-89; educational evaluator N.Y. Bd. Edn., 1977-78; educational dir. Western Queens (N.Y.) Devel. Sch., 1989-98; spl. edn. dir. Alcott Sch., Scarsdale, N.Y., 1998-99; dir. therepeutic nursery New Rochelle (N.Y.) Guidance Ctr., 1999-2000, cons. edn. svcs., 1996—. Adj. faculty Coll. New Rochelle, N.Y., 1980-85, 98, Lehman Coll., Bronx, N.Y., 1982; pre-sch. task force Bd. Edn., 1991-98, Queens regional pre-sch. task force, N.Y.C., 1995-98. Chair LWV, Staten Island, NY, 1968; mem. neighbor adv. com. Group Home, Larchmont, 1985—87; pres. Westchester Symphony Orch., Harrison, 1986—88; past pres. sisterhood B'nai Israel, Staten Island; chmn. Handicapped Boy Scouts Am., White Plains, NY, 1985; corr. sec. NY Coalition Children with Spl. Needs, 1992—96; vol. Hist. Hudson Valley; bd. dirs. Ossining Food Pantry. Avocations: reading, classical music, walking. Home: 69 Hudson Point Ln Ossining NY 10562-5942 E-mail: consulted@worldnet.att.net.

ROTHMAN, BERNARD, lawyer; b. N.Y.C., Aug. 11, 1932; s. Harry and Rebecca (Fritz) R.; m. Barbara Joan Schaeffer, Aug. 1953; children: Brian, Adam, Helene. BA cum laude, CCNY, 1953; JD, NYU, 1959. Bar: N.Y. 1959, U.S. Dist. Ct. (ea. and so. dists.) N.Y. 1962, U.S. Ct. Appeals (2d cir.) 1965, U.S. Supreme Ct. 1966, U.S. Tax Ct. 1971. Assoc. Held, Telchin & Held, 1961-62; asst. U.S. atty. Dept. Justice, 1962-66; assoc. Edward Gettinger & Peter Gettinger, 1966-68; ptnr. Schwartz, Rothman & Abrams, P.C., 1968-78, Ferster, Bruckman, Wohl, Most & Rothman, LLP, N.Y.C., 1978-98, Law Offices of Bernard Rothman, N.Y.C., 1999—. Acting judge Village of Larchmont, 1982-88, dep. Village atty., 1974-81, former arbitrator Civil Ct., N.Y.C., family disputes panel Am. Arbitration Assn.; guest lectr. domestic rels. and family law on radio and TV, also numerous legal and mental health orgns. Author: Loving and Leaving-Winning at the Business of Divorce, 1998; co-author: Family Law Syracuse Law Rev. of N.Y. Law, 1992, Leaving Home, Family Law Review, 1987, Put Your Kids First, 2000; contbr. articles to profl. jours. Mem. exec. bd., past v.p. Westchester Putnam coun. Boy Scouts Am., 1975—; past mem. nat. coun., 1977-81; mem. adv. com. N.Y. State PEACE, 1994—; pres. Congregation B'nai Israel, 1961-63, B'nai Brith, Larchmont chpt., 1981-83. Recipient Silver Beaver award Boy Scouts Am., Wood Badge award. Fellow Am. Acad. Matrimonial Lawyers (bd. govs. N.Y. chpt. 1986-87, 91-93), Interdisciplinary Forum on Mental Health and Family Law (co-chair 1986-97); mem. ABA (family law sect., contbr. Family Advocate Quar.), N.Y. State Bar Assn. (exec. com. family law sect. 1982—, co-chmn. com. on mediation and arbitration 1982-88, 93—, com. on legis. 1978-88, com. on child custody 1985-88, com. alt. dispute resolution), Assn. of Bar of City of N.Y. (women in the cts. com. 1996-99), N.Y. State Magistrate Assn., Westchester Magistrate Assn., N.Y. Rd. Runners Club, Limousine 6 Track Club. Democrat. Office: Law Offices of Bernard Rothman 750 3rd Ave Fl 29 New York NY 10017-2703 E-mail: divorcelawyer@worldnet.att.net.

ROTHMAN, DANIEL HARRIS, geophysics educator; b. N.Y.C., Mar. 25, 1957; s. Eugene Marcus and Sara Rothman; m. Claude Assouline, Oct. 12, 1996; 1 child, Raphael David. AB, Brown U., 1979; PhD, Stanford U., 1986. Rsch. geophysicist Western Geophys. Co., Houston and London, 1979-81; asst. prof. geophysics MIT, Cambridge, Mass., 1986-90, assoc. prof., 1990-96, prof., 1996—. Author: Lattice-gas Cellular Automata, 1997; assoc. editor Phys. Rev. E., 1998—, Jour. Statis. Physics, 1997-2000. Mem. Am. Phys. Soc., Am. Geophys. Union. Avocation: classical guitar. Office: MIT 77 Mass Ave Cambridge MA 02139-4307 E-mail: dan.segovia@mit.edu.

ROTHMAN, DAVID BILL, lawyer; b. N.Y.C., Apr. 25, 1952; s. Julius and Lillian (Halpern) R.; m. Jeanne Marie Hickey, July 7, 1974; children: Jessica Suzanne, Gregory Kozak. BA, U. Fla., 1974, JD, 1977. Bar: Fla. 1977, U.S. Dist. Ct. (so. dist.) Fla. 1980, U.S. Ct. Appeals (5th cir.) 1980, U.S. Supreme Ct. 1981, U.S. Ct. Appeals (11th cir.) 1982, U.S. Dist. Ct. (ea. dist.) Ky. 1985, U.S. Dist. Ct. (mid. dist.) Fla. 1986, cert.: Fla. Bd. , Nat. Bd. Trial Advocacy (criminal trial law). Asst. state atty. Dade County State Atty.'s Office, Miami, Fla., 1977-80; ptnr. Thornton Rothman, P.A., 1980—. Adj. prof. U. Miami Sch. Law, 1995—; com. mem. Fla. Rules Criminal Procedures, 1990-93, metro Dade Ind. Rev. Panel, 1989-97, co-chmn., 1990-91, chmn., 1991-92, 95-97; panel mem. fee arbitration 11th Cir. Ct., 1994-96, co-chair, 1995-96. Mem. ABA, Fla. Bar Assn. (bd. govs. 1999—), Dade County Bar Assn. (criminal ct. com. 1984—, chmn. 1987-90, bd. dirs. 1990-93, treas. 1993-94, sec. 1994-95, v.p. 1995-96, pres. 1997-98), Nat. Assn. Criminal Def. Lawyers, Fla. Assn. Criminal Def. Lawyers (bd. dirs. Miami chpt. 1991—, pres. Miami chpt. 1993-94, statewide sec. 1996-97, treas. 1997-98, v.p. 1998-99, pres.-elect 1999-2000, pres. 2001), Eugene Spellman Inns of Ct. Democrat. Jewish. Avocations: running, weightlifting, reading. Home: 9951 SW 127th Ter Miami FL 33176-4833 Office: Thornton & Rothman PA 200 S Biscayne Blvd Ste 2690 Miami FL 33131-5331 E-mail: DBR@ThorntonRothmanLaw.com.

ROTHMAN, DAVID J. history and medical educator; b. N.Y.C., Apr. 30, 1937; s. Murray and Anne (Beier) R.; m. Sheila Miller, June 26, 1960; children: Matthew, Micol. BA, Columbia U., 1958; MA, Harvard U., 1959, PhD, 1964. Asst. prof. history Columbia U., N.Y.C., 1964-67, assoc. prof., 1967-71, prof., 1971—, Bernard Schoenberg prof. social medicine, dir. Ctr. for Study of Society and Medicine. Fulbright-Hayes prof. Hebrew U., Jerusalem, 1968-69, India, 1982; vis. Pinkerton Prof. Sch. Criminal Justice, State U. N.Y., at Albany, 1973-74; Samuel Paley lectr. Hebrew U., Jerusalem, 1977; Mem. Com. for Study of Incarceration, 1971-74; co-dir. Project on Community Alternatives, 1978-82; chmn. adv. bd. on criminal justice Clark Found., 1978-82; mem. bd. advisors The Project on Death in Am., Open Soc. Inst., 1995-2000, trustee; mem. bd. trustees Open Soc. Inst., 1996—, chmn. bd. advisors Medicine as a Profession program. Author: Politics and Power, 1966, The Discovery of the Asylum, 1971; co-author: Doing Good, 1978, Conscience and Convenience: The Asylum and its Alternatives in Progressive America, 1980; (with Sheila M. Rothman) The Willowbrook Wars, 1984; Strangers at the Bedside, 1991, Beginings Count: The Technological Imperative in American Health Care, 1997; editor: The World of the Adams Chronicles, 1976, (with Sheila M. Rothman) On Their Own: The Poor in Modern America, 1972, The Sources of American Social Tradition, 1975, (with Stanton Wheeler) Social History and Social Policy, 1981, (with Norval Morris) The Oxford History of the Prison, 1995, (with Steven Marcus and Stephanie Kiceluk) Medicine and Western Civilization, 1995. Recipient Albert J. Beveridge prize Am. Hist. Assn., 1971. Mem. Am. Hist. Assn., N.Y. Acad. Medicine, Phi Beta Kappa. Office: Columbia U Coll Physicians and Surgeons Ctr Study Soc and Medicine 630 W 168th St New York NY 10032-3702

ROTHMAN, DEANNA, electroplating company executive; b. Bklyn., Sept. 20, 1938; d. Frank Philip and Elsie (Goldstein) Dukofsky; m. Edward Rothman, Dec. 8, 1956 (div. July 1984); children: Jeffrey Scott, Michele Dawn, Robert Jay; m. Ronald Friedman, Aug. 17, 1986. B.A., Bklyn. Coll., 1968. Exec. Bronzemaster Co., Bklyn., 1969-80, Perma Plating Co. Inc., Bklyn., 1980-84; pres. Duratron Finishing Corp., Bklyn., 1984—, Skillman Metal Corp., Bklyn., 1987—, Deron Holding Corp., Bklyn., 1992—; v.p. Skillman Realty Corp., Bklyn., 1989—. Sec. Tenants Assn., S.I., 1973-77; v.p. Orgn. Rehab. and Tng., Woodmere, N.Y., 1978-80; sponsor Spl. Olympics; mem. East N.Y. Local Devel. Corp. Mem. Masters Electroplating Assn., Am. Metal Finishers, NAFE, NOW, SCORE. Republican. Avocations: painting, collecing art deco, dance, theatre.

ROTHMAN, DENNIS MICHAEL, lawyer; BA, Yale U., 1974; JD, St. John's U., 1977. Bar: N.Y. 1978, N.J. 1997, U.S. Dist. Ct. (ea., so. and no. dists.) N.Y. 1978, U.S. Ct. Appeals (2d cir.) 1978, U.S. Dist. Ct. N.J. 1998, U.S. Tax Ct. 1984, U.S. Supreme Ct. 1986. Ptnr. Lester Schwab Katz & Dwyer LLP, N.Y.C., 1991—. Office: Lester Schwab Katz & Dwyer LLP 120 Broadway Fl 38 New York NY 10271-0071 E-mail: drothman@lskdnylaw.com.

ROTHMAN, FRANK GEORGE, biology educator, biochemical genetics researcher; b. Budapest, Hungary, Feb. 2, 1930; came to U.S., 1938; s. Stephen and Irene Elizabeth (Manheim) R.; m. Joan Therese Kiernan, Aug.22, 1953; children: Michael, Jean, Stephen, Maria. BA, U. Chgo., 1948, MS, 1951; PhD, Harvard U., 1955. Postdoctoral fellow NSF, U. Wis., MIT, 1956-58, Am. Cancer Soc., MIT, Cambridge, 1958-59; postdoctoral assoc. MIT, 1957-61; asst. prof. Brown U., Providence, 1961-65, assoc. prof., 1965-70, prof., 1970-97, dean of biology, 1984-90, provost, 1990-95, prof. emeritus, 1997—. Sr. advisor, Project Kaleidoscope, 1999—. Contbr. articles to profl. jours. Served with U.S. Army, 1954-56. Spl. fellow USPHS, U. Sussex, Eng., 1967-68; NSF grantee, 1961-84. Fellow AAAS; mem. Genetics Soc. Am. Office: Brown U PO Box G-B597 Providence RI 02912-0001 E-mail: frank_rothman@brown.edu.

ROTHMAN, HENRY ISAAC, lawyer; b. Rochester, N.Y., Mar. 29, 1943; s. Maurice M. and Golde (Nusbaum) R.; m. Golda R. Shatz, July 3, 1966; children: Alan, Miriam, Cheryl, Suri. BA, Yeshiva U., 1964; JD, Cornell U., 1967. Bar: N.Y. 1967. Trial atty. SEC, N.Y.C., 1967-69; ptnr. Booth, Lipton & Lipton, 1969-87, Parker, Chapin, Flattau & Klimpl, N.Y.C., 1987-2000, Jenkens & Gilchrist Parker Chapin LLP, N.Y.C., 2001—. Bd. dirs. Camp Morasha, Lake Como, Pa., 1982—, vice chmn., 1992—; bd. dirs. Assn. of Jewish Sponsored Camps, Inc., 1986—; bd. dirs. Yeshiva U. High Schs., N.Y.C., 1984-99, vice chmn. bd., 1990-91, chmn. bd., 1992-95; v.p. Manhattan Day Sch., N.Y.C., 1985-96, bd. dirs.; assoc. v.p. Orthodox Union, N.Y.C., 1990-2000, v.p., 2001—; vice chmn. bd. dirs. Azrieli Grad. Sch. Jewish Edn. and Adminstrn., 2000—. Mem. ABA (com. on fed. regulation of securities), N.Y. State Bar Assn., Assn. of Bar of City of N.Y., Yeshiva U. Alumni Assn. (pres. 1986-88, hon. pres. 1988-90). Office: Jenkens & Gilchrist Parker Chapin LLP The Chrysler Bldg 405 Lexington Ave New York NY 10174-0002 E-mail: hrothman@jenkens.com.

ROTHMAN, HOWARD JOEL, lawyer; b. N.Y.C., July 10, 1945; s. Samuel and Avy (Avrutin) R.; m. Joan Andrea Solomon, July 2, 1967; children: Samantha, Rodney. BA, CCNY, 1967; JD, Bklyn. Law Sch., 1971; LLM, NYU, 1972. Bar: N.Y. 1972. From assoc. to ptnr. Marshall, Bratter, Greene, Allison & Tucker, N.Y.C., 1972-82; ptnr. Rosenman & Colin LLP, 1982-97, Kramer, Levin, Naftalis & Frankel LLP, N.Y.C., 1997—. Mem. adv. panel Commr. Fin. of City of N.Y., 1981-83. Author profl. books and articles. Mem. ABA (corp. tax. com. 1977-87, income from real property com. 1980—), Internat. Bar Assn., N.Y. State Bar Assn. (exec. com. tax sect. 1999-2000, corps. com. 1979-87, partnerships com. 1979—, N.Y.C. tax matters com. 1977—, income from real property com. 1987—), Bur. Nat. Affairs (real estate jour. 1984—, tax mgmt. adv. bd. 1979—), Alliance for Young Artists and Writers (bd. dirs.), Poetry Soc. Am. (bd. dirs.), N.Y. Found. for Arts (bd. dirs.).

ROTHMAN, JOEL HARRY, medical educator, research scientist; b. Walnut Creek, Calif., July 21, 1956; s. Albert and Jeannette Rothman; m. Molly Catherine Baird, June 15, 1980. BS, U. Calif., Davis, 1978; PhD, U. Oreg., 1988; postdoctoral fellow, Med. Rsch. Coun., Cambridge, 1988-91. Asst. prof. U. Calif., Santa Barbara, 1996-97, U. Wis., Madison, 1991-96; grad. rschr. U. Oreg., Eugene, 1983-88; winemaker and prodn. dir. Buena Vista Winery, Sonoma, Calif., 1981-83; chemist Souverain Cellars, Geyserville, 1979-81; grad. rschr. U. Calif., San Francisco, 1978-79, assoc. prof. Santa Barbara, 1997—2001, prof., 2001—. Vis. scientist Med. Rsch. Coun. Lab. of Molecular Biology, Cambridge, U.K., 1988-91; dir., instr. Woods Hole Marine Biol. Lab. Embryology Course, Mass., 1993—; grant rev. panel NIH, 2000-. Mem. editl. bd.: Apoptosis jour., 1995—, Devel. Jour., 2001—, Devel. Biol. Jour., 2002-; contbr. articles to profl. jours. Recipient Searle scholars award Searle Fund./Chgo. Cmty. Trust, 1992-96, Shaw Scientists award Milw. Found., 1993-96; rsch. grantee NIH, 1992—, March of Dimes Birth Defects Found., 1995—. Mem. AAAS, Genetics Soc. Am. Avocations: writing, hiking, photography, travel. E-mail: rothman@lifesci.ucsb.edu.

ROTHMAN, JULIET CASSUTO, social work educator, writer; b. Chgo., Jan. 29, 1942; m. Leonard A. Rothman; children: Susan R. Kolko, Deborah M. Rothman, Daniel M. (dec.). BA, Tufts U., 1962; MSW, CUNY, 1973; MA, St. John's Coll., Annapolis, Md., 1988; PhD, Am. U., 1990. Lic. cert. social worker, Md.; cert. clin. social worker. Geriat. cons. Chesapeake Manor Extended Care Annapolis Convalescent Ctr., 1974-90; social worker Nat. Multiple Sclerosis Soc., Balt., 1980-82; vis. asst. prof. Nat. Cath. Sch. for Social Svc. Cath. U., Washington, 1990—. Tutor Italian, Annapolis, 1974-88; lectr. Anne Arundel C.C., Arnold, Md., 1988-90; chair ethics com. Chesapeake Manor, Annapolis, 1986-90, chair adv. bd., 1987-90; mem. ethics com. Hospice of the Chesapeake, 1992-97; lectr. Sch. Social Welfare, U. Calif., Berkeley, 1998—, Sch. Social Work, San Francisco State U., 1999—; prof. devel. faculty NASW, 1998—. Author: Saying Goodby to Daniel, 1994, A Birthday Present for Daniel, 1995 (award Parent Coun. 1997), The Bereaved Parent's Survival Guide, 1997, German edit., Dutch edit., From the Front Lines: Student Cases in Social Work Ethics, 1998, Contracting in Clinical Social Work, 1998, The Self-Awareness Workbook for Social Workers, 1999, Stepping Out into the Field: A Field Work Manual for Social Workers, 2000; contbr. articles to jours. in field; series editor Internat. Healthcare, Bern, Switzerland, 1990—. Judge Bd . of Elections, Anne Arundel County, Md., 1985-90; sec. Anne Arundel County Cmty. Svcs. Coalition, Annapolis, 1992-93; pres. Friends of Annapolis Chorale, 1992-94; mem. San Francisco City Chorus; vol. Nat. Park Svc. Mem. NASW, Am. Philos. Assn. Avocations: travel, music, photography, arts and crafts, outdoor activities.

ROTHMAN, MARTIN, finance company executive, accountant; b. N.Y.C., June 26, 1946; s. Seymour and Ethel (Swirson) R.; children: Jason David, Heather Michelle. BBA, Pace U., 1968. CPA, N.Y. Sr. acct. Ernst & Young, N.Y.C., 1968-72; audit mgr. Eisner & Lubin, CPAs, 1972-79; exec. v.p., treas., bd. dirs. Orix Comml. Alliance Corp., 1979—. Mem. AICPAs, N.Y. State Soc. CPAs. Avocations: aerobics, reading, theater, antique Corvettes. Office: Orix Comml Alliance Corp 300 Lighting Way Secaucus NJ 07094-3672 E-mail: mrothman@dellmail.com.

ROTHMAN, MELVIN L. judge; b. Montreal, Que., Can., Apr. 6, 1930; s. Charles and Nellie (Rosen) R.; m. Joan Elizabeth Presant, Aug. 4, 1954; children: Ann Elizabeth, Claire Presant, Margot Sneyd. BA, McGill U., 1951, B.C.L., 1954. Bar: Que. 1954. Practice law, Montreal, 1954-71; mem. Phillips, Vineberg, Goodman, Phillips & Rothman; judge Superior Ct., Dist. of Montreal, 1971-83, Ct. Appeal of Que., 1983—; dep. judge Supreme Ct. N.W. Territories, 1977—. Mem. Jr. Bar of Montreal (pres. 1963-64), Bar of Montreal (council 1964-65), Institut Philippe Pinel (sec., dir. 1965-70). Home: 487 Argyle Ave Westmount QC Canada H3Y 3B3 Office: Que Ct of Appeal Court House 10 St Antoine St E Montreal QC Canada E-mail: melvin.rothman@sympatico.ca.

ROTHMAN, MICHAEL JUDAH, lawyer; b. Mpls., June 7, 1962; s. Harvey Michael and Elaine Louise (London) R.; m. Shari Latz, Aug. 1, 1993. BA, Carleton Coll., 1984; JD, U. Minn., 1988. Bar: Minn. 1988, U.S. Dist. Ct. Minn. 1988, Calif. 1993, U.S. Dist. Ct. (ctrl. dist.) Calif. 1993, U.S. Ct. Appeals (9th cir.) 1995, U.S. Supreme Ct. 1995. Law clk. to Hon. J. Gary Crippen Minn. Ct. of Appeals, St. Paul, 1988-89; adminstrv. asst. Minn. State Senate, 1989-92; atty. Rubenstein & Perry, L.A., 1993-95, Loeb & Loeb, L.A., 1995-96; ptnr. Barger & Wolen, LLP, 1996—. Vol. atty. F.A.M.E. Ch. and Temple Isaiah Legal Project, L.A., 1994-96. Recipient Best Brief award Regional Internat. Moot Ct. Competition, Colo., 1988. Mem. ABA, Calif. Bar Assn., L.A. County Bar Assn. Democrat. Avocations: golf, running, reading. Office: Barger & Wolen 515 S Flower St Fl 34 Los Angeles CA 90071-2201

ROTHMAN, PAUL ALAN, publishing executive; b. Bklyn., June 26, 1940; s. Fred B. and Dorothy (Regosin) R.; m. Mary Ann Dalson, July 28, 1966 (div. 1992); m. Carol Ann Liske, Sept. 17, 1999; children: Deborah, Diana. BA, Swarthmore Coll., 1962; JD, U. Mich., 1965; LLM in Taxation, NYU, 1967. Bar: N.Y. 1965. Assoc. Dewey, Ballentine, Busby, Palmer & Wood, N.Y.C., 1965-67; v.p. Fred B. Rothman & Co., Littleton, Colo., 1967-85, pres., 1985-2000; chmn. bd. Colo. Plasticard, 1983-95; owner LoDo Law Books, Denver, 1998—. Editor Mich. Law Rev., 1963-65. Home: 1801 Wynkoop St Apt 708 Denver CO 80202-1196 Office: LoDo Law Books 1701 Wynkoop St Union Sta # 300 Denver CO 80202

ROTHMAN, ROBERT, science educator; b. Bklyn., Mar. 26, 1946; s. R. AB, Lafayette Coll., 1967; MA in Sci. Tchg., Bklyn. Coll., 1991. Sci. tchr. Intermediate Sch. 210, Bklyn., 1968-69, P.S. 161 Elem. Sch., Bklyn., 1969-74; lab. specialist Joan of Arc Jr. H.S., N.Y.C., 1987-89, Beach Channel H.S., N.Y.C., 1988-91, Newtown H.S., Queens, N.Y., 1991—. Chess coach Newtown H.S. Chess Club, Queens, N.Y., 1995—. Mem. Am. Fedn. Tchrs., Kappa Delta Pi. Democrat.

ROTHMAN, STEVEN R. congressman; b. Englewood, N.J., Oct. 14, 1952; divorced; 2 children. BA, Syracuse U., 1974; JD, Washington U., 1977. Pvt. practice law, 1978-93, 96; judge Bergen County's Surrogate's Ct., 1993-96; mem. U.S. Congress from 9th N.J. dist., 1997—; mem. appropriations com. Mayor City of Englewood, 1983-89; Dem. nominee for Bergen County Freeholder, 1989; Dem. candidate for U.S. House 9th dist., N.J., 1996. Jewish. Office: US Ho Reps 1607 Longworth Bldg Washington DC 20515-3009*

ROTHMAN-DENES, LUCIA BEATRIZ, biology educator; b. Buenos Aires, Feb. 17, 1943; came to U.S., 1967; d. Boris and Carmen (Couto) Rothman; m. Pablo Denes, May 24, 1968; children: Christian Andrew, Anne Elizabeth. Lic. in Chemistry, Sch. Scis., U. Buenos Aires, 1964, PhD in Biochemistry, 1967. Vis. fellow NIH, Bethesda, Md., 1967-70; postdoctoral fellow biophysics U. Chgo., 1970-73, rsch. assoc., 1973-74, from asst. prof. to assoc. prof., 1974-83, prof. molecular genetics and cell biology, 1983—. Mem. microbial genetics study sect. NIH, 1980-83, 93-96, chair, 1994-96, mem. genetic basis of disease study sect., 1985-89, mem. coun. Ctr. for Sci. Rev., 2000—; mem. Damon Runyon and Walter Winchell Sci. Adv. Com., N.Y.C., 1989-93; mem. biochemistry panel NSF, 1990-92. Contbr. articles to profl. jours. Fellow AAAS, Am. Acad. Microbiology (bd. govs. 2000—); mem. Am. Acad. Arts and Scis., Am. Soc. Microbiology (divsn. chair 1985, divsn. group II rep. 1990-92, vice chair GMPC 1995-99, chair GMPC 1999-2001), Am. Soc. Virology (councilor 1987-90), Am. Soc. Biochemistry and Molecular Biology. Office: Univ Chgo 920 E 58th St Chicago IL 60637-5415 E-mail: lbrd@midway.uchicago.edu.

ROTHMANN, BRUCE FRANKLIN, pediatric surgeon; b. Akron, Ohio, July 11, 1924; s. Edwin Franklin Rothmann and Mary Madoline Policy; m. Lola May Secor, June 14, 1947; children: Susan Ann, Pamela Jane, Elizabeth Rothmann Rusnak. Student, Case Western Reserve U., 1942-43, Wesleyan U., 1943-44; MD, NYU, 1948. Diplomate Am. Bd. Surgery. Intern Akron City Hosp., 1948-49, from resident in surgery to chief resident surgeon, 1949-55; from resident pediatric surgeon to chief staff Children's Hosp., Akron, 1953-74; pvt. practice in surgery, 1955; pvt. practice in pediatric surgery, 1968—. Clin. instr. Case Western Reserve U., Cleve. 1962-64, asst. clin prof, 1967-83, assoc. clin. prof. pediatric surgery, 1968-99, assoc. clin. prof. emeritus, 1998—; asst. surgeon Univ. Hosp. Cleve. 1962-98; cons. in pediatric surgery Akron City Hosp.; v.p. Nat. Invention Ctr., Inc., 1990-92. Contbr. med. articles to profl. jours. Dir. Med. Outreach Children Hosp. Med. Ctr. of Akron, 1986—; bd. mgmt. Cuyahoga Falls Cmty. YMCA, 1957-63; trustee Akron Symphony Orch., 1959-85, Akron Jr. Achievement, 1980-88, 1st Congl. Ch. Akron, 1960-64; mem. adv. bd. Children's Concert Soc., Akron, 1970—; bd. trustees Children's Family Care, 1984-86, Cuyahoga Falls H.S. Found., 1988—; pres., mem. exec. bd. Gt. Trail coun. Boy Scouts Am., coun. pres., 1997-99; mem. Nat. Inventors Hall of Fame, Cleve. Inst. Music, Nat. Inventors Hall of Fame Found., March of Dimes. With USN, 1942-45, 50-52. Home: 3020 Kent Rd Cuyahoga Falls OH 44224-3044 Office: 330 Locust St Akron OH 44302-1801

ROTHMEIER, STEVEN GEORGE, merchant banker, investment manager; b. Mankato, Minn., Oct. 4, 1946; s. Edwin George and Alice Joan (Johnson) R. BBA, U. Notre Dame, 1968; MBA, U. Chgo., 1972. Corp. fin. analyst Northwest Airlines, Inc., St. Paul, 1973, mgr. econ. analysis, 1973-78, dir. econ. planning, 1978, v.p. fin., treas., 1978-82, exec. v.p., treas., dir., 1982-83, exec. v.p. fin. and adminstrn., treas., dir., 1983, pres., chief operating officer, 1984, pres., chief exec. officer, 1985-86, chmn., chief exec. officer, 1986-89, also bd. dirs.; pres. IAI Capital Group, Mpls., 1989-93; chmn., CEO Great No. Capital, St. Paul, 1993—. Bd. dirs. Gencorp, Precision Castparts, Dept. 56 Inc., Waste Mgmt., Inc., Am. Coun. on Germany, German Marshal Fund. Chmn. St. Agnes Found. Decorated Bronze Star. Mem. Mpls. Club, Chgo. Club. Republican. Roman Catholic. Office: Great Northern Capital 332 Minnesota St Ste W2900 Saint Paul MN 55101-1377 *Success is not an accident; it is a habit. Success is the result of desire, dedication, sacrifice, mental toughness, hard work— and prayer. And you are not successful until you can share your success with others.*

ROTHNER, ARNOLD DAVID, pediatric neurologist; b. Chgo., Nov. 19, 1940; s. Nathan Michael and Shirley R.; m. Sarah Hurwitz, Aug. 25, 1963; childre; Yehuda, Malka. AB, Yeshiva Coll., 1961; MD, U. Ill., 1965. Intern Presbyn.-St. Lukes Hosp., Chgo., 1965-66, resident, 1966-67, Columbia Presbyn, Med. Ctr., N.Y.C., 1967-68; fellow in ped. neurology Neurol. Inst. Columbia Presbyn. Med. Ctr., 1970-73; chief sect. child neurology Cleve. Clinic Found., 1973-2000. Contbr. articles to profl. jours. Maj. U.S. Army, 1968-70. Neurol. Inst. Columbia Presbyn. Med. Ctr. Pediatric Neurology fellow, 1970-73. Fellow Am. Acad. Pediatrics, Am. Acad. Neurology; mem. Am. Assn. Study Headache, Am. Epilepsy Soc., Am. Acad. Cerebral Palsy & Devel. Medicine, Child Neurology Soc., Profs. Child Neurology. Jewish. Avocations: antiques, travel. Office: Cleve Clinic Found S-71 9500 Euclid Ave Cleveland OH 44195-0001 E-mail: rothned@ccf.org.

ROTHROCK, ROBERT WILLIAM, physician assistant; b. Phila., Apr. 21, 1955; s. Arthur Andrew and Margaret (Pilkington) R.; m. Maria Donna Marinelli, May 10, 1980; children: Matthew Robert, Tara Nicole. AS with honors, Cmty. Coll. Phila., 1979; BS, Hahnemann U., 1982. Cert. physician asst.; cert. pain mgmt. specialist. Respiratory therapist Jefferson U. Hops., Phila., 1979-80; physician asst. Pennsbury Family Med. Ctr., Morrisville, Pa., 1982-83, Pennsbury Orthop. Medicine Assocs., Morrisville, 1983-97; physician dept. anesthesia U. Pa. Med. Ctr., Phila., 1997—. Mem. admissions com. Physician Asst. Program, Hahnemann U., 1985; cons. World Boxing Assn. Edo Aragua, Venezuela, 1990—. Author: Chronic Pain, 1991, 2nd edit., 1992; contbg. author: Minor Head Trauma, 1993, Innovations of Pain Management, 1993; contbg. editor Bucks Fortune Mag., 1988-89; peer reviewer Jour. Am. Acad. Physician Assts., 1992—; contbr. articles to profl. jours. Fellow Am. Acad. Physician Assts.; mem. Am. Acad. Pain Mgmt. (site reviewer 1992—), Phila. Pain Soc., Pa. State Soc. Physician Assts., N.J. State Soc. Physician

Assts., Pa. State Soc. Physician Assts., Phi Theta Kappa. Avocations: sports, painting, family activities. Home: 2 Creek Rd Sewell NJ 08080-2720 Office: Presbyn Med Ctr Ste 140 39th and Market Sts Philadelphia PA 19104

ROTHS, BEVERLY OWEN, environmentalist; b. Kansas City, Kans., Aug. 25, 1935; d. Edward Charles and Josephine Mary (Vogel) Owen; m. Robert L. Roths, Sept. 4, 1954; children: Karen Kay, Daniel Owen, Nancy Jo. AA with honors, Antelope Valley Coll., 1975. Sec. McDonnell Aircraft Co., St. Louis, 1955-58; exec. dir. Florissant (Mo.) Valley C. of C., 1976-86; pres. Poppy Reserve/Mojave Desert Interpretive Assn., Lancaster, Calif., 1988-2000. Pres. Soroptomist Internat., North St. Louis County, 1981-82; sec.-treas. St. Louis County League C. of C., Clayton, 1978. Prodr. Small Bus. Profiles, condr. interviews Storer Cable TV, Florissant, 1983-86. Mem. Florissant City Coun., 1968-72; bd. dirs. Mo. Mcpl. League First Woman, Florissant, 1970-71; co-chair Bicentennial, Florissant, 1985-86, Police Bldg. Bond Issue, Florissant, 1980. Recipient Woman of Achievement award Florissant Bus. and Profl. Women, 1979; Inst. Orgn. Mgmt. scholar C. of C., Jefferson City, Mo., 1980; recipient Superior Achievement award State of Calif. Dept. Parks and Recreation, 1999. Mem. Lancaster Woman's Club., Wildflower Preservation Found. (bd. dirs., treas. 1991-2000), League Calif. State Park Non-Profit Orgns. (bd. dirs., sec. 1994-98), Poppy Reserve/Mojave Desert Interpretive Assn. (pres. 1988-2000). Roman Catholic. Avocations: bird watching, gardening, golf, reading, genealogy.

ROTHSCHILD, AMALIE RANDOLPH, filmmaker, producer, director, digital artist, photographer; b. Balt., June 3, 1945; d. Randolph Schamberg and Amalie Getta (Rosenfeld) R. BFA, R.I. Sch. Design, 1967; MFA in Motion Picture Prodn., NYU, 1969. Spl. effects staff in film and photography Joshua Light Show, Fillmore E. Theatre, N.Y.C., 1969-71. Still photographer TWA Airlines Pub. Rels. Dept., Village Voice newspaper, Rolling Stone mag., Newsweek mag., After Dark, N.Y. Daily News, others, 1968-72; co-founder, ptnr. New Day Films, distbn. coop., 1971—; owner operator Anomaly Films Co., N.Y.C., 1971—; mem., co-founder Assn. Ind. Video and Filmmakers, Inc., N.Y.C., 1974; bd. dirs., 1974-78; instr. in film and TV, NYU Inst. of Film and TV, 1976-78; cons. in field to various organizations including Youthgrant Program of Nat. Endowment for Humanities, Washington, 1973-76. Exhibitions include Soho Triad Fine Arts Gallery, 1997, 2000, 2002, Gomez Gallery, 1998, 2000, VH-1 Mus. First Gallery, 1999, Govinda Gallery, 2001; (film): Woo Who? May Wilson, 1969, It Happens to Us, 1972, Nana, Mom and Me, 1974, Radioimmunoassay of Renin, Radioimmunoassay of Aldosterone, 1973, Conversations with Willard Van Dyke, 1981, Richard Haas: Work in Progress, 1984, Painting the Town: The Illusionistic Murals of Richard Haas, 1990 (Emily award Am. Film and Video Festival 1990); editor: Doing It Yourself, Handbook on Independent Film Distribution, 1977; author: Live at the Fillmore East, 1999; licensed photograph collections include Corbis/Bettmann Archive, 1994—, Star File Photo Agy., 1997—. Mem. Cmty. Planning Bd. 1, Borough of Manhattan, N.Y.C., 1974-86. Recipient spl. achievement award Mademoiselle mag., 1972; Ind. filmmaker grant Am. Film Inst. 1973; film grantee N.Y. State Coun. on the Arts, 1977, 85, 87, Nat. Endowment Arts, 1978, 85, 87, Md. Arts Coun., 1977, Ohio Arts and Humanities Couns., 1985. Mem.: AIVF, Ind. Documentary Assn., NY Women in Film, Univ. Film and Video Assn. Democrat. Address: 135 Hudson St New York NY 10013-2102 also: Via delle Mantellate 19 Rome 00165 Italy E-mail: a.rothschild@agora.it.

ROTHSCHILD, ANTHONY JOSEPH, psychiatrist; b. N.Y.C., Dec. 2, 1953; s. Ernest Leo and Edith Margot (Chan) R.; m. Judith Anne Shindul, May 19, 1985; children: Rachel Emma, Amanda Joan. AB, Princeton U., 1975; MD, U. Pa., 1979. Diplomate Am. Bd. Psychiatry and Neurology. Intern medicine/neurology Mass. Gen. Hosp., Mt. Auburn Hosp., Boston, 1979-80; resident psychiatry McLean Hosp., Belmont, Mass., 1980-83; instr. in psychiatry Harvard Med. Sch., Boston, 1983-85, asst. prof. psychiatry, 1985-92, assoc. prof. psychiatry, 1992-96; psychiatrist-in-charge depression rsch. unit McLean Hosp., Belmont, 1983-88, assoc. dir. depression rsch. facility, 1985—, clin. dir. affective disease program, 1988-95, clin. dir. ambulatory svcs., 1995-96, dir. mood and anxiety disorders rsch., 1995-96; prof., dir. clin. rsch. dept. psychiatry U. Mass. Med. Ctr., Worcester, 1996—, Irving S. and Betty Brudnick endowed chair psychiatry, 1997—. Examiner Am. Bd. Psychiatry and Neurology, 1987—; reviewer Am. Jour. Psychiatry, Washington, 1985—, Psychiatry Rsch., 1985—, others. Mem. editl. bd. Depression and Anxiety, 1997—; contbr. articles to profl. publs. Fellow Am. Psychiat. Assn., Am. Psychopath. Assn.; mem. Internat. Soc. Psychoneuroendocrinology, Am. Coll. Neuropsychopharmacology (edn. and tng. com. 1996-98, program com. 2000—), Am. Coll. Psychiatrists, Am. Soc. Clin. Psychopharmacology, Mass. Psychiat. Soc. (nominating com. 1997-98, councillor 2000—), Collegicum Internat. Neuropsychopharmacologie. Office: U Mass Med Ctr Dept Psychiatry 361 Plantation St Worcester MA 01605-2323

ROTHSCHILD, DONALD PHILLIP, lawyer, arbitrator; b. Mar. 31, 1927; s. Leo and Anne (Office) R.; m. Ruth Eckstein, July 7, 1950; children: Nancy Lee, Judy Lynn Hoffman, James Alex. AB, U. Mich., 1950; JD summa cum laude, U. Toledo, 1965; LLM, Harvard U., 1966. Bar: Ohio 1966, D.C. 1970, U.S. Supreme Ct. 1975, R.I. 1989. Tchg. fellow Harvard U. Law Sch., Cambridge, Mass., 1965—66; instr. solicitor's office U.S. Dept. Labor, Washington, 1966—67; prof. law George Washington U. Nat. Law Ctr., 1966—89, prof. emeritus, 1989; prof. law N.Y. Law Sch., 1989—96. Vis. prof. U. Mich. Law Sch., Ann Arbor, 1976; dir. Consumer Protection Ctr., 1971—, Inst. Law and Aging, Washington, 1973—89, Ctr. for Cmty. Justice, Washington, 1974—78, Nat. Consumers League, Washington, 1981—87; v.p. Regulatory Alternatives Devel. Corp., Washington, 1982—; cons. Washington Met. Coun. Govt., 1979—82; counsel Tillinghast, Collins & Graham, Providence, 1989—95, chair human resource group. Author: From the Cockpit of the Rubaiyat, 2002; co-author: Consumer Protection Text and Materials, 1973, Collective Bargaining and Labor Arbitration, 1979, Fundamentals of Administrative Practice and Procedure, 1981; contbr. articles to profl. jours. Chmn. bd. dirs. D.C. Citizens Complaint Ctr., Washington, 1980; mayoral appointee Adv. Com. on Consumer Protection, 1979—80. Recipient Cmty. Svc. award, Television Acad., Washington, 1981. Mem.: ABA, D.C. Bar Assn., Am. Arbitration Assn., Fed. Mediation and Conciliation Svc., Nat. Acad. Arbitrators, Nat. Assn. Coll. and Univ. Attys. (Brown U.), Fed. Trade Commn. Adv. Coun., Phi Kappa Phi. Jewish. Office: Shadow Farm Way Unit 4 Wakefield RI 02879-3631

ROTHSCHILD, JENNIFER ANN, artist, educator; b. Mesa, Ariz., Aug. 16, 1948; d. Joe Dean and Frances Ann (McFarland) Johnston; m. Harry Ronald Rothschild, Feb. 14, 1981. Diploma, El Camino Jr. Coll., 1968; BA in Art Edn., Calif. State U., 1970. Cert. secondary sch. tchr., Calif. Arts and crafts specialist City of Hawthorne (Calif.) Parks and Recreation, 1966-67; portrait artist Disneyland, Anaheim, Calif., 1970-74; secondary sch. art tchr. Orange (Calif.) Unified Schs., 1972-80; freelance custom apparel designer Honolulu, 1982-94; sculptor, artist, 1994—. One woman show at Roy's Honolulu, 2001, Art Centre Gallery, Honolulu, 1997; corp. artist Arts of Paradise Gallery, Honolulu, 1997—; exhibited in show at City of Manhattan Beach, Calif., 1966, Assn. of Hawaii Artists, 1996—, in book Encyclopedia of Living Artists, 10th edit., 1997. Bd. dirs. Hawaii Tennis Patrons, Honolulu, 1996—, Assn. of Hawaii Artists Show chairwoman, 2002. Recipient scholarship Chouinard Sch. Art Inst., 1965-66, 1st Place Stamp Design award Easter Seals, 1995-96, Hokele Artists award Hawaiian Airlines, 1996, Most Unique Art award Assn. of Hawaii Artists Aloha Show, 1997. Fellow Nat. Mus. Women in Arts; mem. AAUW, Honolulu Art Acad., Assn. Hawaii Artists (v.p. 1996-97, pres. 1999-2000), Hawaiian Pacific Tennis Assn. (rules chmn. 1997), mem. Windward Art Guild, 2002, Nat. League of Am. Pen Women, Hon., chapter, Alpha Omicron Pi. Republican. Presbyterian. Avocations: tennis, reading, writing, painting, sculpting.

ROTHSCHILD, LARRY, former professional baseball executive; b. Chgo., Mar. 12, 1954; m. Jane; children: Charlotte, Claire. Grad., Fla. State U. Pitcher Cin. Reds, 1975-81, minor league pitching coach, 1986, bullpen coach, 1990; with Detroit Tigers, 1981; pitching instr. minor league Atlanta Braves; pitching coach Fla. Marlins, 1997; mgr. Tampa Bay Devil Rays, 1997—. Finished 3rd Am. Assn., 1981.*

ROTHSCHILD, STEVEN JAMES, lawyer; b. Worcester, Mass., Mar. 23, 1944; s. Alfred and Ilse (Blumenfeld) R. BA, U. Vt., 1965; JD, Georgetown U., 1968. Bar: D.C. 1968, Del. 1969, N.Y. 1992. Ptnr. Skadden Arps Slate Meagher & Flom, Wilmington. Mem. Del. Bd. Bar Examiners, 1979-83; chmn. Del. Citizens Conf. on Adminstrn. of Justice, 1982; mem. Del. Bd. on Profl. Responsibility, 1992-98, vice chmn., 1993, chmn., 1994-98; vice chmn. rules com. Del. Supreme Ct., 1991-94; chmn. Del. Gov.'s Commn. on Major Comml. Litigation Reform, 1993-94; adj. prof. law Georgetown U. Law Ctr., 2000—. Bd. dirs. United Way Del., 1978-85, 93-99, v.p., 1981-84, chmn. 1994-95; bd. dir s. Milton and Hattie Kutz Home, 1972—, pres., 1982-84; pres., Del. Art Mus., 1990-92; bd. trustees U. Del., 1998—. Mem. ABA, Bar Assn. D.C., Assn. of Bar of City of N.Y., Del. Bar Assn. Office: Skadden Arps Slate Meagher & Flom One Rodney Sq PO Box 636 Wilmington DE 19899-0636 E-mail: srothsch@skadden.com.

ROTHSTADT, GARRY SIGMUND, lawyer; b. Paterson, N.J., Dec. 2, 1958; BA, Rutgers Coll., 1980, JD, 1983. Bar: N.J. 1983, U.S. Dist. Ct. N.J. 1983. Jud. clk. Superior Ct. N.J., Paterson, 1983-84; assoc. Cole Geaney Yamne & Byrne, 1984-88; ptnr. Chiocca Rothstadt & Sweeney, Wayne, 1988-89, Choicca & Rothstadt, Wayne, 1989-90, Bray Chiocca Rappaport & Rothstadt, LLC, Parsippany, N.J., 1990—. Mem. ABA, N.J. State Bar Assn., Passaic County Bar Assn. (sec. 1993-94, treas. 1994-95, v.p. 1995-96, pres.-elect 1996-97, pres. 1997—). Office: Bray Chiocca et al Koll Exec Ctr 100 Misty Ln Parsippany NJ 07054-2710

ROTHSTEIN, ANN LAUREL, clinical social worker, consultant; b. Bronx, N.Y., Dec. 6, 1937; d. Philip and Rachael (Brownstein) Ingegneri; m. Arthur Rothstein; 1 child, Susan Debra. BA, Coll. of New Rochelle, 1976; MSW, NYU, 1980. Cert./ registered social worker, N.Y.; diplomate Am. Bd. Examiners in Clin. Social Work. Clin. social worker Office of Mental Health, Mt. Vernon, N.Y., 1981-90; dir. Westchestr Ctr. for Eating Disorders, New Rochelle, 1986—. Mem. Acad. Cert. Social Workers, N.Y. State Soc. of Clin. Social Work Psychotherapists, Am. Anorexia and Bulimia Assn. (treas.), Westchester Task Force on Eating Disorders. Home and Office: Westchester Ctr for Eating Disorders 14 Rolling Way New Rochelle NY 10804-2406

ROTHSTEIN, ANNE LOUISE, education educator, college official; b. Bklyn., Feb. 15, 1943; d. William and Rose Mary (Smith) R. BS, Bklyn. Coll., 1963; MA, Tchrs. Coll. Columbia, N.Y.C., 1965, EdD, 1970. Tchr. Erasmus Hall High Sch., Bklyn., 1963-64, Fort Hamilton High Sch., Bklyn., 1964-64; lectr. Hunter Coll. in the Bronx, N.Y., 1965-68; instr., prof. Lehman Coll., Bronx, 1968—, dept. chair, 1980-83, assoc. dean, 1983-93, assoc. provost/dir. for sponsored program devel., 1993-98. Dir. Lehman Ctr. for Sch./Coll. Collaboratives, Bronx, 1988—; grant specialist for sch./coll. programs, 1985--; small sch. developer, 1999--. Editor, pub. (jour.) Motor Skills: Theory into Practice, 1976-87; chair editorial bd. (jour.) Strategies, 1986-92; author: Research and Statistics, 1985, Motor Learning: Basic Stuff, 1987. Grantee in field. Fellow Rsch. Consortium Am. Alliance, Am. Alliance for Health, Physical Edn., Recreation and Dance; mem. Nat. Assn. for Sport and Physical Edn., Nat. Assn. for Girls and Women in Sport, Assn. for Supervision and Curriculum Devel., Am. Ednl. Rsch. Assn., Internat. Soc. for Tech. in Edn. Avocations: computers, grants consulting. Home: PO Box 3007 Newtown CT 06470-3007 Office: Lehman Coll Bedford Park Blvd W Bronx NY 10468 E-mail: anner@lehman.cuny.edu., arothstein@yahoo.com.

ROTHSTEIN, BARBARA JACOBS, federal judge; b. Bklyn., Feb. 3, 1939; d. Solomon and Pauline Jacobs; m. Ted L. Rothstein, Dec. 28, 1968; 1 child, Daniel. BA, Cornell U., 1960; LL.B., Harvard U., 1966. Bar: Mass. 1966, Wash. 1969, U.S. Ct. Appeals (9th cir.) 1977, U.S. Dist. Ct. (we. dist.) Wash. 1971, U.S. Supreme Ct. 1975. Pvt. practice law, Boston, 1966-68; asst. atty. gen. State of Wash., 1968-77; judge Superior Ct., Seattle, 1977-80, Fed. Dist. Ct. Western Wash., Seattle, 1980—, chief judge, 1987-94. Faculty Law Sch. U. Wash., 1975-77, Hastings Inst. Trial Advocacy, 1977, N.W. Inst. Trial Advocacy, 1979—; mem. state-fed. com. U.S. Jud. Conf., chair subcom. on health reform. Recipient Matrix Table Women of Yr. award Women in Communication, Judge of the Yr. award Fed. Bar Assn., 1989; King County Wash. Women Lawyers Vanguard Honor, 1995. Mem. ABA (jud. sect.), Am. Judicature Soc., Nat. Assn. Women Judges, Fellows of the Am. Bar, Wash. State Bar Assn., U.S. Jud. Conf. (state-fed. com., health reform subcom.), Phi Beta Kappa, Phi Kappa Phi. Office: US Dist Ct 705 US Courthouse 1010 5th Ave Ste 215 Seattle WA 98104-1189

ROTHSTEIN, GERALD ALAN, investment company executive; b. Bklyn., Oct. 18, 1941; s. Manuel and Gertrude (Buxbaum) R.; m. Cynthia Bea Pincus, June 11, 1967; children: Michael Neil, Lori Pamela, Meryl Patricia. BBA, City Coll. N.Y., 1962; MBA, U. Pa., 1965. 1st v.p. Shearson Hammill & Co., N.Y.C., 1966-74, Shearson Hayden Stone, N.Y.C., 1974-75; v.p. William D. Witter, Inc., 1975-76, Oppenheimer & Co., N.Y.C., 1976-79, sr. v.p., 1979-83, mng. dir., 1983—, dir. rsch., 1986-91, dir. internat. rsch., 1991-95, internat. investment banker, 1995-97; mng. dir. internat. money mgmt. CIBC World Markets, 1998—. Bd. dirs. Indocean, Diamond Tools, Hamilton, Bermuda, India Pvt. Equity Fund, Mauritius. Trustee Ctr. for Social and Emotional Edn., N.Y.C. Mem. N.Y. Soc. Security Analysts, Inst. CFA's, Internat. Soc. Fin. Analysts. Office: CIBC World Markets 425 Lexington Ave New York NY 10017 E-mail: gerald.rothstein@us.cibc.com.

ROTHSTEIN, GLORIA, social worker; b. Bklyn. Student, N.Y. Inst. Tech., Old Westbury, 1974-75, 79; BA in Psychology, SUNY, Oswego, 1978; MSW, UCLA, 1987. LCSW Calif., CSW N.Y. Travel trainer, tchr. Assn. for Help of Retarded Children, Ridgewood, N.Y., 1979-80; supr., treatment worker, tchr. Behavior Rsch. Inst., Northridge, Calif., 1980-81; instr. Work Tng. Program, Inc., Woodland Hills, 1982-84, asst. supr., staff trainer, 1984-85; psychiat. social worker St. John's Hosp. and Health Ctr., The Ross Ctr., Santa Monica, 1987-90; med. social worker Centinela Hosp. and Health Ctr., Inglewood, 1991, 94-99; psychiat. clin. social worker Del Amo Hosp., Torrance, 1994-99; social worker Columbia Presbyn. Med. Ctr., N.Y.C., 2002—. Cons. for phys. therapy chain Health South in So. Calif., 1999; psychotherapist in pvt. practice, Torrance, 1998-99; caregiver for mother with Alzheimer's Disease, Jericho, N.Y., 1999—. Mem. NASW, Soc. for Clin. Social Work, UCLA Grad. Sch. of Social Welfare Alumni Assn.

ROTHSTEIN, MARK ALAN, health law and bioethics educator; b. Phila., May 23, 1949; s. Sidney David and Selma (Rosenfeld) R.; m. Laura Friesen, June 9, 1974; children: Julia, Lisa. BA, U. Pitts., 1970; JD, Georgetown U., 1973. Bar: Pa. 1973, D.C. 1974. Atty., adviser Occupational Safety & Health Rev. Commn., Washington, 1973-75; assoc. prof. law Ohio No. U., Ada, 1975-79; vis. assoc. prof. law U. Pitts., 1979-80; prof. law W.Va. U., Morgantown, 1980-85, Health Law and Policy Inst. U. Houston, 1985-2000; dir. Inst. Bioethics Health Policy and Law U. Louisville, 2000—. Author: Medical Screening of Workers, 1984, Medical Screening and the Employment Health Cost Crisis, 1989, Occupational Safety and Health Law, 1990, Employment Law, 1991, Employment Law Treatise, 1994, Genetic Secrets, 1997. Office: Inst Bioethics Health Policy and Law U Louisville 501 E Broadway # 310 Louisville KY 40292 E-mail: markrothstein@louisville.edu.

ROTHSTEIN, PAULINE MARCUS, library director; BS in English, NYU, 1965; MA in English, Hunter Coll., 1968; MLS, Pratt Inst., 1969; PhD, Fordham U., 1981. Tchr. N.Y.C. Bd. Edn., 1965-69; reference libr. Herbert H. Lehman Coll., 1969-76; coord. libr. svcs. Columbia U., 1977-80; dir. info. svcs. Russell Sage Found., 1982-94; dean libr. svcs. Ramapo Coll. N.J., Mahwah, 1994—. Adj. faculty Baruch Coll., 1981-82, L.I. U., 1988-91, City Coll. Sch. Engring., 1994, Rutgers U. Sch. Comm., 1994; presenter in field. Contbr. articles to profl. jours. Mem. ALA, ACRL, NJLA, N.Y. Acad. Scis. (adv. coun. 1991-92, vice chair 1993-96, chair 1997-98), Internat. Fedn. Libr. Assns. (del. 1989-95, 2001—), Spl. Librs. Assn. (mem. internat. rels. com. 1989-91, sec. N.Y. chpt. 1987-88), mem. long range planning com. 1986-87, other activities). Home: 350 W 24th St Apt 19B New York NY 10011-2236 Fax: 201-684-7628. E-mail: prothste@ramapo.edu.

ROTHSTEIN, SAMUEL, librarian, educator; b. Moscow, Jan. 12, 1921; arrived in Can., 1922, naturalized, 1929; s. Louis Israel and Rose (Checov) R.; m. Miriam Ruth Teitelbaum, Aug. 26, 1951; children: Linda Rose, Sharon Lee. BA, U. B.C., 1939, MA, 1940; grad. student, U. Calif., Berkeley, 1941-42, grad. student, 1946-47, BLS, 1947; postgrad., U. Wash., 1942—43; PhD (Carnegie Corp. fellow 1951-54), U. Ill., 1954; DLitt, York U., 1971. Teaching fellow U. Wash., 1942-43; prin. libr. asst. U. Calif., Berkeley, 1947; mem. staff U. B.C. Libr., Vancouver, 1947-51, 54-62; acting univ. libr. U. B.C., 1961-62, prof. libr. sci., 1961—86, prof. emeritus, 1986—, dir. Sch. Librarianship, 1961-70. Vis. prof. U. Hawaii, 1969, U. Toronto, 1970, 79, Hebrew U., Jerusalem, 1973; mem. Commn. Nat. Plan Libr. Edn., 1963—; mem. assoc. com. sci. info. Nat. Rsch. Coun. Can., 1962-69; councillor B.C. Med. Libr. Svc., 1971; mem. exec. com. Pacific divsn. Can. Jewish Congress, 1962-69, Internat. House Assn. B.C., 1959-60; mem. Can. Adv. Bd. Sci. and Tech. Info.; mem. cabinet Combined Jewish Appeal of Greater Vancouver, 1992-95; pres. Vancouver Pub. Libr. Trust, 1987-88. Author: The Development of Reference Services, 1955, (with others) Training Professional Librarians for Western Canada, 1957, The University-The Library, 1972, Rothstein on Reference..., 1989; also articles.; co-editor: As We Remember It, 1970. Life mem. bd. dirs. Jewish Cmty. Ctr. of Greater Vancouver, pres., 1972-74; bd. dirs. Jewish Fedn. of Greater Vancouver, 1993-2000. Recipient ALISE award Assn. Library Info. Sci. Edn., 1987, Beta Phi Mu award ALA, 1988. Mem. Can. Libr. Assn. (hon. life), Assn. Am. Libr. Schs. (pres. 1968-69), Can. Assn. Libr. Schs. (hon. life, pres. 1982-84), ALA (coun. 1963-69, Beta Phi Mu award 1988), B.C. Libr. Assn. (hon. life, pres. 1959-60, Helen Gordon Stewart award 1970), Pacific N.W. Libr. Assn. (pres. 1963-64, hon. life), Can. Libr. Assn. (hon. life, coun. 1958-60, Outstanding Svc. to Librarianship award 1986), Bibliog. Soc. Can. (coun. 1959-63), Can. Assn. Univ. Tchrs. Home: 1416 W 40th Ave Vancouver BC Canada E-mail: samuelr@interchange.ubc.ca.

ROTHWELL, ELAINE B. artist; b. Mpls., May 8, 1926; d. Frederick Roscoe and Stella Frances (LaVallee) Bartholomew; m. William Stanley Rothwell, May 10, 1946; children: Suzanne, Amy Verrett, Wendy Rothwell-Lopez, Bart. BFA, San Jose State U., 1966; pvt. study, Woodbury Graphic Studio, Los Altos, Calif., 1975-76, Amaranth Intaglio Workshop, Los Altos, 1985. *Rothwell was first known for her series of 14 etchings using chess imagery and chess positions. This series was featured in a cover story in Chess Life Magazine in March 1979. Her 1983 "Spiritus Loci" series of eight etchings forms a cartographical puzzle. Her later series, "Art History Mysteries" 1994, "Mad Meg Amok" 1997, "Inklings" 1999, "Seasons of Romance" 2002 and "Moons" 2002 are online at www.artbyrothwell.com. By means of figure ground ambiguities and enigmatic images, Rothwell's etchings baffle the viewers' eyes with games of visual discovery.* One-woman shows include Triton Mus. Art, Santa Clara, Calif., 1976, Palo Alto (Calif.) Civic Ctr., 1977, Stanford (Calif.) Art Spaces, Stanford U., 1985, 1988, 1989, West Valley Art Mus., Surprise, Ariz., 1996, exhibited in group shows at Carnegie Art Ctr., North Tonawanda, N.Y., 1995, 1996, N.J. Ctr. Visual Arts Internat., Summit, 1997, 1998, Brand Libr. and Art Ctr., Glendale, Calif., 1996, Internat. Exhbn. Art League Manatee County, Fla., 1996, Nat. Soc. Artists, 1997, Am. Color Print Soc., Grand Exhbn. Nat. Competition, Akron, Ohio, 1998, Printwork '98, Barrett Ho., Poughkeepsie, N.Y., 1998, 73d Ann. Internat. Print Competition/Print Ctr., Phila., 1999, Manhattan Arts Internat., 1999, Chautauqua Nat. Exhbn. Am. Art, 1999, No. Colo. Ann. Nat. Exhbns., 1999, 2000, Stage Gallery, Merrick, N.Y., 2000, others, retrospective exhbns., Represented in permanent collections Newberry Libr., Chgo., Triton Mus. Art, Santa Clara, West Valley Art Mus., Brand Libr. Art Ctr., Glendale; contbr. works to publs. Mem.: Am. Color Print Soc. (treas. Loa Altos chpt. 1973—93), Nat. Mus. Women in Arts (charter), Gallery II, Gallery 9, Triton Mus. Art. Home and Office: 3030 Eagles Nest Auburn CA 95603-5918 E-mail: eb.ws.rothwell@prodigy.net.

ROTHWELL, TIMOTHY GORDON, pharmaceutical company executive; b. London, Jan. 8, 1951; came to us., 1966; s. Kenneth Gordon Rothwell and Jean Mary (Stedman) Davey; m. Joanne Claire Fleming; children: Tiffany, Heather. BA, Drew U., 1972; JD, Seton Hall U., 1976; LLM, NYU, 1979, MBA, 1983. With Sandoz Pharms., East Hanover, N.J., 1972—, patent atty., 1974-77, patent and trademark counsel, 1980-82, mng. ops. planning and adminstrn., 1982-84, dir. mktg. ops., 1984-85, exec. dir. field ops., 1985-86, v.p. field ops., 1986-87, pres. profl. bus. ops., 1987-88, corp. v.p., chief oper. officer, 1988-89; sr. v.p. sales and mktg. Squibb, Princeton, 1989; gen. mgr. Squibb U.S. Pharm. divsn. Bristol-Myers Squibb, 1991; sr. v.p. mktg. and sales Burroughs-Wellcome, 1992; pres., CEO Sandoz Pharm. Corp., 1995; pres. pharm. op. Rhone-Poulenc Rorer Inc., 1996, pres., bd. dirs., 1996-97; exec. v.p. Pharmacia Corp., 2000—, pres. global country ops. Exec. v.p., pres. pharm. ops. Pharmacia Upjohn, N.J., 1998—. Mem. N.J. State Bar Assn., N.Y. State Bar Assn., Am. Soc. for Pharmacy Law, Nat. Health Care Quality Coun., Am. Found. for Pharm. Exec. (bd. dirs.), N.J. Patent Law Assn. (pres. 1986). Republican. Episcopalian. Avocations: philately, coaching youth soccer, golf, tennis. Office: Pharmacia Corp 100 Rte 206 North Peapack NJ 07977-0800

ROTI, THOMAS DAVID, judge; b. Evanston, Ill., Jan. 20, 1945; s. Sam N. and Theresa S. (Salerno) R.; m. Donna Sumichrast, July 22, 1972; children: Thomas S., Kyle D., Rebecca D., Gregory J. BS, Loyola U., Chgo., 1967, JD cum laude, 1970. Bar: Ill. 1970, U.S. Dist. Ct. (no. dist.) Ill. 1971, U.S. Ct. Appeals (7th cir.) 1971. Sr. law clk. to Judge Frank McGarr, U.S. Dist. Ct. No. Dist. Ill., 1971-72; assoc. Arnstein, Gluck & Lehr, Chgo., 1972-73, Boodell, Sears et al, Chgo., 1973-75; asst. gen. counsel Dominick's Finer Foods, Inc., Northlake, 1975-77, v.p., gen. counsel, 1977-97; judge Cir. Ct. Cook County, 2000—. Mem. nat. conf. lawyers and econs. com. Food Mktg. Inst., Washington, 1987-97, legis. com. Ill. Retail Mchts. Assn., Chgo., 1987-97; dir. NCCJ. Trustee Joint Civic Com. Italian Ams., Chgo., 1986-95; mem. Chgo. Coun. EDU-CARE Scholarship Program, 1988. Recipient Am. Jurisprudence award, 1970, Alumni Assn. award Loyola U., 1970. Mem. ABA, Ill. Bar Assn., Ill. Judges Assn., Chgo. Bar Assn., Am. Corp. Counsel Assn., Chgo. Zool. Soc., Loyola Alumni Assn., Art Inst. Chgo., Phi Alpha Delta, Alpha Sigma Nu. Roman Catholic. Home and Office: 5002 Sunset Ct Palatine IL 60067-9047 E-mail: tdroti@attbi.net.

ROTMAN, MORRIS BERNARD, public relations consultant; b. Chgo., June 6, 1918; s. Louis and Etta (Harris) R.; m. Sylvia Sugar, Mar. 1, 1944; children: Betty Ruth, Jesse, Richard. Student, Wright Jr. Coll., 1936-37, Northwestern U., 1937-39. Editor Times Neighborhood publs., Chgo., 1938-40; asst. editor City News Bur., 1940-42; mng. editor Scott Field Broadcaster, USAAF, 1942-43; publicity dir. Community and War Fund of Met. Chgo., 1943-45; v.p. William R. Harshe Assocs., 1945-49, pres., 1949-66; chmn. bd., chief exec. officer Harshe-Rotman & Druck, Inc. (formerly William R. Harshe), 1966-81, pres., 1982; ret. Ruder Finn & Rotman, Inc. (merger of Harshe-Rotman & Druck and Ruder & Finn); founder Morris B. Rotman & Assocs., Chgo., 1989—. Former adj. prof. comm. Coll. of the Desert, Palm Desert, Calif. Author: Opportunities in Public Relations Careers, Dear Betty Chronicles. A Memoir of 40 Years in Public Relations. Chmn. solicitations pub. rels. div. Community Fund Chgo., 1948-49, spl. events chmn., 1953; chmn. comms. div. Jewish Fedn. Chgo., 1965, Combined Jewish Appeal, 1966; life dir. Rehab. Inst. Chgo.; U.S. dir. The Shakespeare Globe Centre (N.Am.) Inc.; trustee emeritus Roosevelt U. Recipient Prime Minister Israel medal, 1969 Mem. Pub. Rels. Soc. Am. (past dir.), Chgo. Presidents' Orgn. (pres. 1970-71), Acad. Motion Picture Arts and Scis. (assoc.), Am. Film Inst., World Pres. Orgn., Chief Execs. Orgn., Chgo. Press Vets. Assn., Standard Club, Tamarisk Country Club, Headline Club, Desert Rats (chair), Sigma Delta Chi. Home: 3 Columbia Dr Rancho Mirage CA 92270-3149 also: 2650 N Lakeview Dr Chicago IL 60614 E-mail: mrotman@aol.com.

ROTMENSCH, JACOB, gynecologic oncology; BS, U. Ill., 1971; MS, U. Cin., 1973; MD, Meharry Med. Coll., 1977. Office: U Chgo/Chgo Lying In Hosp Dept Ob-Gyn MC2050 5841 S Maryland Ave Chicago IL 60637-1463

ROTTENBERG, DAVID ALLAN, neurologist; b. Detroit, Jan. 18, 1942; s. Leon and Adeline Rottenberg; m. Rochelle Elaine Cutler, June 16, 1963; children: Elizabeth, Catherine. BA in English, U. Mich., 1963; MSc in Biochemistry, U. Cambridge, 1967; MD, Harvard U., 1969. Diplomate Am. Bd. Psychiatry and Neurology. Intern in surgery Mass. Gen. Hosp., 1969-70; resident in neurology N.Y. Hosp., 1972-74, chief resident, 1974-75; asst. prof. neurology Cornell U. Med. Coll., 1975-79, assoc. prof. of neurology, 1979-89; dir. PET Imaging Ctr., Mpls., 1989—; prof. neurology and radiology U. Minn., 1989—; chief neurology svc. Mpls. VA Med. Ctr., 1990-2000. Asst. attending neurologist N.Y. Hosp., 1975-79, assoc. attending neurologist, 1979-89, asst. attending Meml. Hosp., 1975-79, assoc. attending neurologist, 1979-89; assoc. mem. Meml. Sloan-Kettering Cancer Ctr., 1984-89. Contbr. numerous articles to profl. publs. Harvard Nat. scholarship, 1965-67, Marshall fellowship U. Cambridge, 1963-65; recipient numerous rsch. grants. Fellow Am. Acad. Neurology; mem. AAAS, Am. Neuol. Assn., Soc. for Neurosci., Soc. of Nuclear Medicine, Phi Beta Kappa. Office: VA Med Ctr 123 Minneapolis MN 55417 E-mail: dar@neurovia.umn.edu.

ROTTER, PAUL TALBOTT, retired insurance executive; b. Parsons, Kans., Feb. 21, 1918; s. J. and LaNora (Talbott) R.; m. Virginia Sutherlin Barksdale, July 17, 1943; children: Carolyn Sutherlin, Diane Talbott. BS summa cum laude, Harvard U., 1937. Asst. mathematician Prudential Ins. Co. of Am., Newark, 1938-46; with Mut. Benefit Life Ins. Co., 1946—, successively asst. mathematician, asso. mathematician, mathematician, 1946-59, from v.p. to exec. v.p., 1959-80, ret., 1980. Mem. Madison Bd. Edn., 1958-64, pres., 1959-64; Trustee, mem. budget com. United Campaign of Madison, 1951-55; mem. bd., chmn. advancement com. Robert Treat council Boy Scouts Am., 1959-64. Fellow Soc. Actuaries (bd. govs. 1965-68, gen. chmn. edn. and exam. com. 1963-66, chmn. adv. com. edn. and exam. 1969-72), Phi Beta Kappa Soc.; mem. Brit. Inst. Actuaries (assoc.), Am. Acad. Actuaries (v.p. 1968-70, bd. dirs., chmn. edn. and exam. com. 1965-66, chmn. rev. and evaluation com. 1968-74), Asso. Harvard Alumni (regional dir. 1965-69), Actuaries Club N.Y. (pres. 1967-68), Harvard Alumni Assn. (v.p. 1964-66), Am. Lawn Bowls Assn. (pres. SW divsn.). Clubs: Harvard N.J. (pres. 1956-57); Harvard (N.Y.C.); Morris County Golf (Convent, N.J.); Joslyn-Lake Hodges Lawn Bowling (pres. 1989-90). Home: 18278 Canfield Pl San Diego CA 92128-1002

ROTTER, STEVEN JEFFREY, company executive; b. Bklyn., May 21, 1955; s. Walter and Lillian (Needleman) R.; m. Robin A. Bass, May 3, 1980; children: Marc, Adam, Sara. BS in Acctg., Bklyn. Coll., 1976. CPA, N.Y. Staff acct. Margold, Ersken & Wang, N.Y.C., 1976-78, ptnr., 1980-93; contr. Vanleigh Furniture Co., 1978-80; exec. mng. dir. Jack Resnick & Sons Inc., 1994—. Mem. AICPA, N.Y. State Soc. CPA. Office: Jack Resnick & Sons Inc 110 E 59th St Fl 37 New York NY 10022-1379

ROTTMAN, ELLIS, public information officer; b. Balt., Apr. 5, 1930; s. Abraham Isaac and Sadie (Harris) R.; m. Carol Parker Donovan, May 30, 1965; children— Marcus, Lisa, Jason, Adam. BS, U. Md., 1952. Assoc. editor Army Times Pub. Co., Washington, 1956-59; editor, dir. pub. relations Am. Fedn. Govt. Employees, AFL-CIO, 1959-65; pub. info. officer U.S. Post Office Dept., 1966-69; editor Manpower mag. Dept. Labor, 1969-75; editor, publs. dir. FDA, Rockville, Md., 1975-78; public info. dir. Labor-Mgmt. Services Adminstrn. Dept. Labor, 1978-84; pub. info. officer Office Sec. of Labor, 1984-94. Served with AUS, 1952-54. Recipient Journalism award Internat. Labor Press Assn., AFL-CIO, 1959, 60, 61, 62, 64; award merit Fed. Editors Assn., 1974, 75, 77, 78 Jewish. Home: 901 N Belgrade Rd Silver Spring MD 20902-3247 Office: 2nd St And Constitution Ave NW Washington DC 20210-0001

ROTTMAN, MICHAEL, physician; b. Scranton, PA, July 14, 1954; s. Eugene and Thelma (Cohen) R.; m. Anne Rottman, Mar. 3, 1984; children: Geoffrey, Brandon. BS in Biology magna cum laude, U. Scranton, Pa., 1976; MD, St. George's U., 1981. Diplomate Am. Bd. Internal Medicine. Resident in internal medicine St. John Hosp., Detroit, 1982-85, chief resident, 1984-85; practicing physician internal medicine South Macomb Internists, Warren, Mich., 1985—. Author: (book) The Basic First Aid Deck, 1995. Mem. AMA, ACP, Am. Soc. Internal Medicine, Mich. State Med. Soc., Macomb County Med. Soc., Alpha Epsilon Delta. Avocations: piano, golf, tennis. Office: South Macomb Internists 11900 E 12 Mile Rd Ste 300 Warren MI 48093-3491

ROTUNDA, DONALD THEODORE, public relations consultant; b. Blue Island, Ill., Feb. 14, 1945; s. Nicholas and Frances (Manna) R. BA, Georgetown U., 1967; MA, London Sch. Econs., 1968, PhD, 1972. Analyst NASA, Washington, 1972; lectr. in econs. U. D.C., 1973; legis. asst. Ho. of Reps., Washington, 1974-76, economist budget com., 1977; mgmt. analyst Office Mgmt. and Budget, 1977-81; cons., 1981-82; mgr. editorial svcs. United Technologies Corp., Hartford, Conn., 1982-87, Pepsico, Inc., Purchase, N.Y., 1987-89, Union Carbide Corp., Danbury, Conn., 1989-90; dir. editorial svcs. Martin Marietta, Bethesda, Md., 1990-92; cons. pub. rels., 1992—. Contbr. numerous articles to Washington Post, New Republic, Saturday Rev. Roman Catholic. Home: 4431 Klingle St NW Washington DC 20016-3578 E-mail: donaldrotunda@erols.com.

ROTUNDA, JOSEPH LOUIS, retail and service company executive; b. Washington, Jan. 26, 1947; s. Joseph and Louise (Marchione) R.; m. Patricia Lou Comer, Aug. 27, 1966; 1 child, Joseph. BA in Econs., Washington & Jefferson U., 1969. From mgr. to v.p. customer svc. & new stores Montgomery Ward, Chgo., 1969-91; from divsnl. v.p. to exec. v.p., COO Thorn Americas, Wichita, 1991-98; COO, exec. v.p. G&K Svcs., Inc., Minnetonka, Minn., 1998-2000; pres., CEO EZCorp, Inc, Austin, Tex., 2000—, also bd. dirs. Bd. dirs. RTO Enterprises, Inc., Toronto, Can., Albermarle & Bond, London. Mem. Mensa. Home: 3208 Aztec Fall Cove Austin TX 78746 Office: EZCorp Inc 1901 Capital Pkwy Austin TX 78746 E-mail: joe_rotunda@ezcorp.com.

ROTUNDA, RONALD DANIEL, law educator, consultant; b. Blue Island, Ill., Feb. 14, 1945; s. Nicholas and Frances (Manna) R.; children: Nora, Mark. AB magna cum laude, Harvard U., 1967, JD magna cum laude, 1970. Bar: N.Y. 1971, U.S. Ct. Appeals (2d cir.) 1971, U.S. Ct. Appeals (D.C. cir.) 1971, U.S. Ct. Appeals (7th cir.) 1990, U.S. Supreme Ct. 1974, Ill. 1975. Law clk. U.S. Ct. Appeals (2d cir.), 1970-71; assoc. Wilmer, Cutler & Pickering, Washington, 1971-73; asst. majority counsel Watergate Com., U.S. Senate, 1973-74; spl. cons. Office of Ind. Counsel, 1997-99; asst. prof. U. Ill. Coll. Law, Champaign, 1974-77, assoc. prof., 1977-80, prof., 1980-93, Albert E. Jenner, Jr. prof. of law, 1993—2002; prof. law George Mason U., Arlington, Va., 2002—. Vis. prof. law European U. Inst., Florence, Italy, 1981, U. Ala., 1999; mem. profl. responsibility exam. com. Nat. Conf. Bar Examiners, 1980-87; constl. advisor Supreme Nat. Coun. Cambodia, 1993; cons. Supreme Ct. Moldova, 1996; vis. sr. fellow in constnl. studies Cato Inst., 2000. Author: (with Morgan) Problems and Materials of Professional Responsibility, 1976, 7th edit., 2000; (with Nowak and Young) Constitutional Law, 1978, (with Nowak) 2d edit., 1983, 3d edit., 1986, 4th edit., 1991, 5th edit., 1995, 6th edit., 2000, Modern Constitutional Law: Cases and Materials, 1981, 6th edit., 2000, (with Nowak) Treatise on Constitutional Law, 4 vols., 2d edit., 1992, 5 vols., 3d edit., 1999. Fulbright research scholar, Italy, 1981, Venezuela, 1986. Fellow Am. Bar Found. (life), Ill. Bar Found. (life); mem. Am. Law Inst. Roman Catholic. Office: George Mason Univ Law School 3301 N Fairfax Drive Arlington VA 22201 E-mail: rrotunda@GMU.edu.

ROTUNNO, RON TANK JOSEPH, elementary school educator, writer; b. Sharon, Pa., Dec. 26, 1944; s. Frank A. and Roselyn (Patrone) Rotunno (dec.). BSEd, Kent State U., 1975; MEd, Bowling Green State U., 1979. Cert. 4 year provisional tchrs. cert. Ohio. Writer/pub. Steel Valley Books, New Wilmington, Pa., 1995—; substitute sch. tchr. Howland Local Sch. Dist., Warren, Ohio, 1995—. Asst. baseball/football coach Trumbull County Sch. Dist., Warren, 1975—77; asst. football coach North Baltimore (Ohio) City Sch. Dist., 1977—78; proficiency test tutor Howland Local Sch. Dist., Warren, 2000—. Author: (book) Full Tilt to the NFL-Steel Valley Heroes, 1995, Jack Lambert-Tough As Steel, 1997, Ohio Professional Football: Its First 30 Years, 1999, (technical manual) Auto Cycle Engine, 1979 (Soc. Telecom. Merit award, 1979). Presdl. campaigner Ohio Dem. Party, Kent, 1986—88; polit. campaigner Portage County Dem. Com., Ravenna, 1986—90; presdl. del. Ohio Dem. Party, Columbus, 1987—88. Lance cpl., 1965—65. Recipient Merit award, Soc. Telecom., 1979. Mem.: Marine Corps League. Avocation: political/civic activities. Personal E-mail: tank-71@msn.com.

ROTZ, C. ALAN, agricultural engineer, educator; b. Chambersburg, Pa., Sept. 7, 1951; s. Robert L. and Margret A. Rotz; m. Robin L. McCartney, Nov. 13, 1976; children: Ashley, Dustin. BA, Elizabethtown Coll., 1972; BSME, Pa. State U., 1974, MSAE, 1975, PhD in Agrl. Engring., 1977. Cert. profl. engr., Mich. Asst. prof. Mich. State U., East Lansing, 1978—81; agrl. engr. USDA/Agrl. Rsch. Svc., 1981—97, University Park, Pa., 1997—. Adj. prof. Mich. State U., East Lansing, 1981—97, Pa. State U., University Park, 1997—. Contbr. articles to profl. jours. Recipient award for Excellence, Assn. State Agrl. Expt. Sta. Dirs., 1999, Merit award, Am. Forage and Grassland Coun., 1992. Mem.: Pa. Forage and Grassland Coun., Am. Forage and Grassland Coun. (Merit award 1992), Am. Soc. Agrl. Engrs. (Blue Ribbon award 1981, 1993). Office: USDA Agrl Rsch Svc Bldg 3702 Curtin Rd University Park PA 16802

ROTZIEN, FREDERICK WILLIAM, III, marketing executive; b. Portland, Oreg., Aug. 9, 1944; s. Frederick William Jr. and Vilma E. (Brandon) R.; m. Yvonne Miller, June 12, 1975 (div. Aug. 1979). Student, Clark Coll. Mktg. pres. Rotzien and Assocs., Portland, 1970-85; mktg. exec. Heartland Farms, 1985-88; mfg./mktg. pres. Blue Ribbon Market, 1985-90; mfg. pres. Probe Electronics, 1985-90; mktg. exec. Adventure Mktg., 1990-94, Am. Elec. Motorcycle, Portland, 1994—; pres. Rote-Sun Co. LLC, 1997—. Author, editor: World Chart of History, 1988; author: Step by Step Tobacco Guide, 1988. Pres. Oreg. chpt. Young Am. Freedom Portland, 1962, Portland Young Reps., 1968, Oreg. Young Reps., Portland, 1969. Mem. Am. Mktg. Assn. Lutheran. Avocations: fishing, politics, reading, gardening. Home: 13005 NE Broadway St Portland OR 97230-2262

ROTZOLL, KIM BREWER, advertising and communications educator; b. Altoona, Pa., Aug. 21, 1935; s. Fredrick Charles and Anna (Brewer) R.; m. Nancy Benson, Aug. 26, 1961; children: Keith, Kristine, Amanda, Jason. BA in Advt., Pa. State U., 1957, MA in Journalism, 1965, PhD in Sociology, 1971. Account exec. Ketchum, Macleod and Grove, Pitts., 1957-61; instr. advt. Pa. State U., University Park, 1961-71; asst. prof. advt. U. Ill, Urbana, 1971-72, assoc. prof., 1972-78, prof., 1978—, rsch. prof., head advt. dept., 1983-92; dean Coll. Comms., 1992—. Lectr. in People's Republic of China, Bahrain, Pamplona, Spain Author, co-author, editor: Is There Any Hope for Advertising, 1986, Advertising in Contemporary Society, 1990, 96, Media Ethics, 1995, 97, 2000, The Book of Gossage, 1995, Last Rights: Revisiting Four Theories of the Press, 1995. Named Disting. Advt. Educator of Yr. by Am. Advt. Fedn., 1992. Fellow Am. Acad. Advt. (pres. 1991, Charles Sandage Tchg. award 2000); mem. Ill. Press Assn. Bd., Alpha Kappa Delta, Phi Kappa Phi. Democrat. Presbyterian. Avocations: reading, films, cycling. Office: U Ill 119 Gregory Hall 810 S Wright St Urbana IL 61801-3644 E-mail: krotzoll@uiuc.edu.

ROUB, BRYAN R(OGER), financial executive; b. Berea, Ohio, May 1, 1941; s. Bernard Augustus and Pearl Irene (Koeblitz) R.; m. Judith Elaine Penman, June 19, 1965; children: Paul, Bradley, Michael. Student, Ohio Wesleyan U., 1959-62; BS, Ohio State U., 1966; MBA, U. Pa., 1978. Mem. audit staff Ernst & Ernst, Cleve., 1966-70; asst. contr. Midland-Ross, 1970-73, contr., 1973-81, v.p., 1977-81, sr. v.p., 1981-82, exec. v.p. fin., 1982-84; sr. v.p. fin. Harris Corp., Melbourne, Fla., 1984-93, sr. v.p., CFO, 1993—. Mem. fin. coun. II Machinery and Allied Products Inst., Washington, 1978-84, coun. I, 1984—, vice chmn., 1994-95, chmn., 1996-98; mem. conf. bd. coun. of CFO's, 1993-96. Mem. adv. coun. Coll. Adminstrv. Scis., Ohio State U., 1978-81; mem. citizen's adv. coun. Westlake (Ohio) Schs., 1981-83; trustee Alcoholism Svcs. Cleve., 1982-84; mem. devel. bd. St. John's Hosp., 1983-84; pres. Westridge Homeowners' Assn., 1977; dir., treas. Tortoise Island Homeowners' Assn., 1988-90; bd. dirs. Easter Seal Soc. of Brevard County, 1993-98. Mem. AICPA, Ohio Soc. CPAs, Fin. Execs. Inst. (treas. N.E. Ohio chpt. 1976-78, bd. dirs. 1980-81, 83-84, v.p. 1981-82, pres. 1982-83, bd. dirs. Orlando chpt. 1984—, v.p. 1985-86, pres. 1986-87, nat. bd. dirs. 1987-90, area v.p. 1990-91, chmn. budget and fin. com. 1988-89, chmn. planning com. 1995-97, v.p. at large 1997-99, vice-chmn. 1999-2000, chmn. 2000-01, office of chmn. 1997-2002), Fin. Execs. Rsch. Found. (trustee 1994-97, 1999-2000), Westwood Country Club, Eau Gallie Yacht Club (bd. govs., treas. 1990-92), Suntree Country Club. Office: Harris Corp 1025 W Nasa Blvd Melbourne FL 32919-0002 Address: 10280 S Tropical Trail Merritt Island FL 32952-6919

ROUBIK, SUSANNE EILEEN, architect; b. Milw., Dec. 1, 1959; d. Joseph Rudolph and Gertrude Mae (Brown) R. BS in Architecture, U. Wis., Milw., 1981, MArch summa cum laude, 1984; postgrad., Inst. of Architecture Studies, Paris, Barcelona, 1984, Taller de Architecture:, Ricardo Bofill. Registered architect, Ill. Archtl. photographer U. Wis., Milw., 1983-84, archtl. slide curator, 1983-84; sr. archtl. designer Skidmore, Owings & Merrill, Chgo., 1984-90; prin. S.E. Roubik & Assocs.-Design Cons., 1990—; cons. KMR Group, Inc., 1991-93, World Trade Ctr., Chgo., 1995; pres. Internat. Collaborations Group, Inc., 1997—; sr. project mgr. McClier, 1999-2000, svc. group dir., 2000-01; assoc.-project mgr. Skidmore, Owings & Merrill, 2001. Design critic Notre Dame U., U. Wis. Mil., U. Ill. Chgo., Ill. Inst. Tech., Chgo., U. Ohio, Miami, Andrews U.; com. chairwoman CCAIA V.I.P./Protocol 1993 AIA/UIA World Congress Architects, 1991-93; founder, bd. dirs., exec. v.p. Newhouse Architecture Found., 1989-93, sec., 1987-88, dir. internships, 1984-93. Com. chairwoman CCAIA V.I.P./Protocol, 1991-93; bd. dirs. Rehab. Inst. Chgo., Health Resource Ctr. for Women with Disabilities, 1994-98; mem. program com. Chto. chpt. Urban Land Inst., 1999—; chair English group Internat. Women Assocs., 1998-99, ofcl. photographer, 1998—. Recipient award Nat. Inst. Archtl. Edn., 1984, Piux XI H.S. Alumni award, Milw., 1994. Mem. AIA (program coord. Chgo. chpt. 1987-89, chmn. real estate com. 1989-91, bd. dirs. 1990-95, mem. program com. 1991-93, del. young architects forum 1990-92, steering com. young architects forum 1990-92, Chgo. award 1984, Chgo. chpt.-Chgo. Bar Assn. Young Arch. award 1987, Young Arch. award 1993), Internat. Women Assocs. (chair English group 1998-99, libr. internat. rels., consular ball exec. com., Kent Coll. of Law-Ill. Inst. Tech. 1998—), Am. Mktg. Assn., Graphic Artists Guild, Third Coast Women in Architecture (founder, pres. 1983), Urban Land Inst. (program com. 1999—), Third Coast Design Coop. (v.p. bd. dirs. 1981-84), Mid Day Club Chgo. (assoc. bd. dirs. co-chair 1995-96, chair 1996-97), Women in Planning & Devel. E-mail: icg@mcs.net.

ROUDANE, CHARLES, metal and plastic products company executive; b. L.A., July 16, 1927; s. Rudolph and Irene (Warner) R.; m. Orient Fox, Aug. 20, 1948; children: Mark, Matthew. BSME, Tulane U., 1950. Gen. mgr. Master divsn. Koehring Co., Chgo., 1955-67; gen. sales mgr. Wilton Corp., Schiller Park, Ill., 1967-70; dir. mktg. Flexonics divsn. UOP Inc., Bartlett, 1970-73, v.p., gen. mgr. divsn., 1973-83; pres., CEO, Resistoflex Co. divsn. Crane Co., Marion, N.C., 1983-93; chmn., CEO, ASM Corp., Chgo., 1993—. Bd. dirs. Ctr. Indsl. Mktg. Planning, Inc., PowRhouse Products, Inc. With AUS, 1945-46. Mem. ASME, Am. Mgmt. Assn. (past trustee, chmn. mktg. coun., mem. internat. coun., elected to Inaugural Wall of Fame 1978), Chgo. Pres. Assn., Newcomen Soc. Gt. Britain. Republican. Presbyterian.

ROUECHE, JOHN EDWARD, II, education educator, leadership program director; b. Sept. 3, 1938; s. John Edward and Mary (Harris) R.; m. Suanne Davis; 1 stepchild, Robin Sue Maca; children by previous marriage: Michelle Renee, John Edward III. BA, Lenoir Rhyne Coll., Hickory, N.C., 1960, LittD, 2001; LHD, Lenoir Rhyne Coll., 2001; MA, Appalachian Coll., Boone, N.C., 1961; PhD, Fla. State U., 1964. Dean Gaston Coll., Gastonia, N.C., 1964-67; assoc. rsch. educator UCLA, 1967-69; dir. jr. coll. divsn. Nat. Lab. Higher Edn., 1968-71; assoc. prof. edn. Duke U.; prof. edn., dir. c.c. leadership program U. Tex., Austin, 1971—. Sid W. Richardson regents chair, 1987—. Mem. chancellor's coun. U. Tex. Sys., 1990—, U. Tex. Littlefield Soc., 1992—; lectr. Earl Pullias lectr. U. So. Calif., 1992, Coll. Bd. Disting. Lectr. N.Y.C., 1993, Frances Crain Cook Disting. Lectr. U. Tex., 1994; chmn. nat. ednl. adv. bd. Gt. Am. Res. Ins. Co., 1988-94; co-chair Nat. Adv. Bd. for C.C.s, Invest Learning Corp., 1993-96; chair nat. adv. com. Kaplan Ednl. Partnerships, 1995-98; La Platica Disting. lectr. Ariz. State U., 1999; mem. nat. adv. bd. 3-D Internat. C.C. editor Jossey-Bass Publs., 1971-82; editor Creative Teaching Series, Media Systems Corp., 1980-85; mem. editl. bd. C.C. Times, C.C. Jour., 1990-94, others; author 35 books, including Profiles of Excellence in America's Schools, 1986, Access with Excellence, 1987, Shared Vision, 1989, Teaching as Leading, 1990, Under-representation: A Question of Diversity, 1991, Between a Rock and a Hard Place, 1993, The Company We Keep, 1995, Strangers in Their Own Land: Part Time Faculty, 1995, Embracing the Tiger: The Effectiveness Debate and the Community College, 1997, High Stakes, High Performance: Making Remedial Education Work, 1999, In Pursuit of Excellence: The Community College of Denver, 2001; contbr. over 150 articles and monographs. Pres. Doss Sch. PTA, 1974-75; chmn. bd. N.W. Hills United Meth. Ch., 1973-76. Recipient Disting. Svc. award Nat. Coun. Univs. and Colls., 1990, Disting. Rsch. Publ. award, 1990, 93, 95, 97, Outstanding Alumnus award Appalachian State U., 1979, Disting. Grad. award Fla. State U., 1981, Tchg. Excellence award U. Tex., 1982, Outstanding Rschr. award, 1985, Excellence award for outstanding learned article U.S. Edn. Press Assn., 1983, Disting. Rsch. award Nat. Assn. Devel. Edn., 1984-86, Disting. Rsch. Publ. award Nat. Coun. Student Devel., 1987, Disting. Rsch. award Nat. Coun. Staff, Program, and Orgn. Devel., B. Lamar Johnson Nat. Leadership award League for Innovation in the Cmty. Coll., 1988, Disting. Svc. & Leadership award CCP, INC., 1993, Disting. Faculty award U. Tex., 1994, Disting. Rsch. award Interassn. Student Devel. Orgns., 1995, Chancellor's Leadership award State of Ala., 1995, Career Rsch. Excellence award U. Tex., 1998, Disting. Grad. award Lenoir-Rhyne Coll., 2000; named lifetime amb. for N.C., 1978; Kellogg fellow, 1962-64, Disting. Internat. Leadership award Govt. of South Africa, 2000, 01, Disting. Nat. Svc. award Nat. Coun. Instrnl. Adminstrs., 2001. Mem. Am. Assn. Comty. and Jr. Colls. (bd. dirs. 1989-94, Nat. Leadership award 1986, Disting. Rsch. award coun. colls. and univs. 1990, 94, 96, dist. rsch. sr. scholar award 1994, 96, nat. student devel. inter-assn. rsch. award 1995-96), Am. Assn. Higher Edn., Coun. Univs. and Colls. (past pres., bd. dirs.), Phi Beta Kappa, Phi Delta Kappa. Home: 4700 Lookout Mountain Cv Austin TX 78731-3654 Office: U Tex Austin SZB 348 Austin TX 78712

ROUECHE, SUANNE DAVIS, university administrator; b. Dallas, Aug. 6, 1942; d. Raymond Louis and Edna Sue (Leatherwood) Davis; m. Benjamin Frank Maca, June 12, 1964 (div. Feb. 1975); 1 child, Robin Sue; m. John Edward Roueche, May 22, 1976; children: Michelle, John III. BA in English, North Tex. State U., 1964, MA in English, 1967; PhD, U. Tex., 1976. Tchr. English Sam Houston H.S., Arlington, Tex., 1964-65, MacArthur H.S., Irving, 1966-67; instr. El Centro Coll., Dallas, 1967-74; dir. cmty. coll. internship program U. Tex., Austin, 1976-82, dir. Nat. Inst. for Staff and Orgnl. Devel., 1982—. Cons. in field. Co-author: Between a Rock and a Hard Place, 1993 (Disting. Rsch. award 1993-94), Strangers in Their Own Land, 1995 (Dist. Rsch. award 1995-96), Embracing the Tiger, 1997, The Company We Keep, 1995, High Stakes, High Performance: Making Remedial Education Work, 1998, In Pursuit of Excellence: The Community College of Denver, 2001; contbr. more than 50 articles to profl. jours. Mem. Wildlife Rescue, Austin, 1981—; mem. chancellor's coun. U. Tex. Sys.; mem. Pres.' Assocs., U. Tex., Austin. Named Ky. Col., Ky. State Legis. and Gov., 1979; recipient Disting. Leadership award Fla. State Legis., 1989, Nat. Leadership award Am. Assn. Cmty. Colls., 1997, Disting. Svc. award Nat. Coun. Instrnl. Adminstrn., 2001. Mem. Littlefield Soc., Delta Gamma (pres. alumnae 1979-81). Avocations: needlepoint, reading, gardening. Office: Nat Inst Staff/Orgnl Devel MLK/Speedway SZB 348 Austin TX 78712

ROUGH, HERBERT LOUIS, insurance company executive; b. N.Y.C., Jan. 19, 1935; s. Albert and Jean (Bendeth) R.; m. Fern Sadkin Schultz; children: Lee Michael, Lisa Joi. BS, NYU, 1956. CLU, ChFC, CLTC. From agt. to dist. mgr. Equitable Life Assurance Soc., N.Y.C., 1961-69; brokerage mgr. Bernard Bergen Cos., Inc., 1969-73; pres., gen. agt. Rough Agy. Inc., Great Neck, N.Y., 1973-96, Comprehensive Planning--Goodman, Ltd., Hicksville, 1988—, Rough Agy. Inc. of Fla., Ft. Lauderdale, 1991—. Pres., mem. field adv. coun. Am. Gen. Life Ins. Co. of N.Y., Syracuse, 1978-83, Madison Life Ins. Co., N.Y.C., 1974-77; guest spkr. in field; instr. continuing edn. Broward c.C., Fla. Treasurer Gray Wig Repertory Theatre, Hofstra U., Uniondale, N.Y., 1981-84; pres. Heart Assn. of Great Neck, 1977. Maj. USAF, 1956-59. Mem. Life Underwriters Assn., Gold Coast Assn. of Health Underwriters (pres. 1996-98, Man of Yr. 1998), Nat. Assn. Ind. Life Brokerage Agys., CLU Assn., Fla. Assn. Health Underwriters (membership chmn. 1998-99, Ins. Man of Yr. 1999), Knickerbocker Yacht Club, Kiwanis (pres. Great Neck chpt. 1977-79). Democrat. Jewish. Avocations: racquetball, tennis, singing. Office: Comprehensive Planning Group LLC 1133 S University Dr Ste 200 Fort Lauderdale FL 33324-3303 E-mail: rough@attbi.com.

ROUHANA, WILLIAM JOSEPH, JR. business executive; b. Bklyn., June 23, 1952; s. William Joseph and Anna Freida (Stephan) R.; m. Claudia Caruso, Aug. 27, 1972 (div. 1998); children: Timothy, Rosemary; m. Amy Newmark, Nov. 13, 1999; stepchildren: Michael Damiano, Ella Damiano. BA, Colby Coll., 1972; JD, Georgetown U., 1976. Bar: N.Y. 1977, U.S. Dist. Ct. (so. and ea. dists.) N.Y. 1977. Founding ptnr. Beinhauer, Rouhana & Pike, N.Y.C., 1977-80; pvt. practice, 1980-84; ptnr. Rouhana and Trinko, P.C., 1984-85, Baer, Marks & Upham, N.Y.C., 1985-86; pres. WinStar Corp., 1984-90; CEO WinStar Ptnrs., 1989-90, WinStar Oil Ptnrs., N.Y.C., 1990-91. Chmn. Manson Internat., L.A., 1986-87; vice-chmn. Mgmt. Co. Entertainment Group, Inc., L.A., 1987-90; bd. dirs., chmn., CEO Win Star Comm., Inc., 1993—; bd. dirs. TII Industries, Inc., 1990-93; bd. overseers Colby Coll., 1987-90; bd. dirs., chmn. CEO WinStar Cos., Inc., 1990-94; vice-chmn. UN Assn., 1996-97, bd. govs., 1992-97. Mem. adv. bd. Nassau County Dem. Com., Jericho, N.Y., 1984, Bus. Execs. Nat. Security, 1991—, bd. dirs., 1997—; commr. Ben's Tail to Tooth Commn., 1998—; trustee Cobly Coll., 1999—; co-chmn. Humpty Dumpty Inst., 1999—. Grantee NSF, 1968, Thomas J. Watson Found., 1972-73. Mem. UN Assn. (bd. dirs. 1992-99, vice-chmn. 1996-99), Phi Beta Kappa. Democrat. Roman Catholic. Office: Winstar Comm Inc 685 3rd Ave Fl 31 New York NY 10017-4024

ROUHANI, SHAHROKH, civil engineering/environmental consultant, educator; b. Tehran, Iran, Mar. 28, 1956; came to U.S., 1974; s. Aboutorab and Parirokh (Garakani) R.; m. Firouzeh Yekta, Aug. 18, 1983; children: Nina, Shiva. BSCE, BA in Econs., U. Calif., Berkeley, 1978; SM in Engring., Harvard U., 1980, PhD in Environ. Scis., 1983. Registered profl. engr., Ga. Asst. prof. Ga. Inst. Tech., Atlanta, 1983-90, assoc. prof. civil engring., 1990-96; sr. cons. Dames & Moore, 1990-95; pres. New Fields, Inc., 1995—. NSF vis. scientist Ctr. Geostats., Paris Sch. of Mines, 1987-88; expert mem. ASTM, EPA, U.S. Geol. Survey, Dept. Def. Geostats. Standardization Com., 1991-96. Co-author: Ground Water, 1991; contbr. articles to profl. publs., chpts. to books., also numerous reports, papers in field. Mem. ASCE (award 1991, chmn. nat. ground water hydrology 1991, chmn. task com. on geostatis. techniques in geohydrology 1987-89, sec. water resources com. Ga. sect. 1988, spl. session organizer 1989, 90, contact mem. task com. 1988-90, symposium organizer 1991), Am. Geophys. Union (assoc. editor Water Resources Rsch. 1989-94), Internat. Water Resources Assn., Am. Water Resources Assn., N.Am. Coun. on Geostats., Internat. Geostatis. Assn., Phi Beta Kappa, Tau Beta Pi, Chi Epsilon, Sigma Chi. Office: Newfields Inc 1349 W Peachtree St NW Ste 2000 Atlanta GA 30309-2926

ROUKEMA, MARGARET SCAFATI, congresswoman; b. West Orange, N.J., Sept. 19, 1929; d. Claude Thomas and Margaret (D'Alessio) Scafati; m. Richard W. Roukema, Aug. 23, 1951; children— Margaret, Todd (dec.), Gregory. BA with honors in History and Polit. Sci, Montclair State Coll., 1951, postgrad. in history and guidance, 1951-53; postgrad. program in city and regional planning, Rutgers U., 1975. Tchr. history, govt., public schs., Livingston and Ridgewood, N.J., 1951-55; mem. U.S. Congress from 5th N.J. dist., Washington, 1981—; vice chair fin. svcs. com., chair housing and community opportunity subcom.; mem. banking com., edn. and the workforce com. Vice pres. Ridgewood Bd. Edn., 1970-73; bd. dirs., co-founder Ridgewood Sr. Citizens Housing Corp.; chairwoman Fin. Inst. and Consumer Credit Sub. Com. U.S. Congress; sponcer Family Med. Leave U.S. Congress. Trustee Spring House, Paramus, N.J.; trustee Leukemia Soc. No. N.J., Family Counseling Service for Ridgewood and Vicinity; mem. Bergen County (N.J.) Republican Com.; NW Bergen County campaign mgr. for gubernatorial candidate Tom Kean, 1977. Mem. Bus. and Profl. Women's Orgn. Clubs: Coll. of Ridgewood, Ridgewood Rep. Office: US Ho of Reps 2469 Rayburn Bldg Washington DC 20515-3005 *I have served in several roles in my life. Wife, mother, teacher, public servant. All are personally rewarding; each affords the opportunity to help others in need and to enrich the lives of those around you. As a member of Congress, I find the most rewards are in the knowledge that I can truly make a difference and improve the lives of thousands of people. The challenges are frequently insurmountable, but the rewards are incalculable.**

ROUKES, MICHAEL LEE, science educator; b. Redwood City, Calif., Oct. 9, 1953; s. Nicholas Michael and Glenna Naomi Roukes; m. Anna Gay Del Vescovo, Sept. 19, 1989. PhD, Cornell U., 1978—85. Mem. tech. staff, prin. investigator Bell Commns. Rsch., Red Bank, NJ, 1985—92; assoc. prof. physics Calif. Inst. Tech., Pasadena, Calif., 1992—95, prof. physics. Co-founder, co-dir. Caltech Initiative in Computational Molecular Biology, Pasadena, 1997—. Co-editor: Virtual Jour. of Nanoscale Sci. and Tech. Named Gilbreth lectr., Nat. Acad. Engring., 2002. Fellow: Am. Phys. Soc. Office: Calif Inst of Tech MS 114 36 Pasadena CA 91125 Office Fax: 626-683-9060.

ROULEAU, REYNALD, bishop; b. St.-Jean-de-Dieu, Que., Can., Nov. 30, 1935; Ordained priest, 1963, bishop, 1987. Bishop Churchill-Hudson Bay, 1987—. Home and Office: Diocese Churchill-Hudson Bay PO Box 10 Churchill MB Canada R0B 0E0

ROULET, NORMAN LAWRENCE, psychiatrist, educator; b. Toledo, Mar. 23, 1932; s. Norman Lawrence and Clara Matilda (Whistinghausen) R.; m. Ann Edelen, June 26, 1954; children: Laura, Norman, III. AB, Harvard U., 1954; MD, U. Pa., 1958. Diplomate Am. Bd. Psychiatry and Neurology. Pvt.

practice, Cleve., 1962—; faculty mem. to asst. clin. prof. psychiatry Case Western Res. Sch. Medicine, 1962—; faculty mem. Cleve. Psychoanalytic Inst., 1976—. Author: (book with others) The Specialties in General Practice, 1964, Illegitimacy Today, 1969; contbr. articles to psychiat. jours. Fellow Am. Psychiat. Assn.; mem. Am. Psychoanalytic Assn., various local med., psychiat. and psychoanalytic socs. Republican. Presbyterian. Home: 17400 Shaker Blvd Cleveland OH 44120-1742 Office: Univ Suburban Health Ctr 1611 S Green Rd Cleveland OH 44121-4128

ROULIER, RANDOLPHE G. osteopath; b. Detroit, Nov. 23, 1930; s. Randolphe Edward and Nannie Glenn (Riley) R.; m. Judith A. Corcoran, Sept. 10, 1955; children: Randolphe J., Denise M., Pamela M., David G., Michelle J. BA, Albion Coll., 1952; DO, Chgo. Coll. Osteo. Medicine, 1957. Intern Detroit Osteo. Hosp., Highland Park, Mich., 1957-58, resident general surgery, 1958-61; interim med. dir. med. edn., chmn. nutritional support svc. Mich. Osteo. Med. Ctr., Detroit, 1984-86, acting med. dir., 1985-86; chief of staff (sabbatical) Huron Valley Hosp., 1986-88; chief of staff Parkview Hosp., Toledo, 1986-94; osteopath Toledo (Ohio) Surg. Assocs., Mercy Hosp., Toledo, 1994—, St. Luke's Hosp., Maumee, 1994—, St. Charles Hosp., Oregon, 1995—, St. Vincent's Hosp., Toledo, 1996—, Riverside Mercy hosp., Toledo, 1997—, Flower Hosp., Sylvania, Ohio, 1999—. Chmn. staff, chief surgery Med. Ctr. Hosp., Wayne State U., Huron valley Hosp., 1986; sr. surg. com. Detroit Osteo. Hosp., Bicounty Cmty. Hosp., Mich. Osteo. Med. Ctr., Botsford Gen. Osteo. Hosp., Detroit; mem. med. records com. Mich. Osteopathic Med. Ctr., east unit mgmt. com., tissue com., chmn. house staff training com., 1984-86, exec. com. profl. staff., 1978-86, chief of staff, 1978, vice chief of staff, 1979, chmn. dept. surgery, 1974-84; chmn. dept. surgery Palmer Osteo. Hosp., 1963-68, Sturgis (S.D.) Cmty. Hosp., 1961-63; adj. clin. prof. U. Osteo. Medicine and Health Scis., Des Moines, Iowa, 1997—; clin. prof. surgery Ohio U. Coll. Osteo. Medicine, 1998—, adj. clin. faculty, 1978—; clin. prof. surgery, clin. dir. assoc. hosp., Mich. State U. Coll. Osteo. Medicine, 1972; clin. asst. prof. dept. surgery Med. Coll. Ohio, 1994—; clin. assoc. prof. surgery Coll. Osteo. Medicine Pacific, 1984, N.Y. Coll. Osteo. Medicine, 1980; assoc. clin. prof. surgery Kirksville Coll. Osteopathy and Surgery, 1972; clin. faculty Mercy Family Practice Residency Training Program, 1994—; pres. Wayne County Osteo. Assn., mem., bd. dirs. 1983-86, pres. elect 1983-84, chmn. profl. devel. com. 1978, program chmn. 57th Ann. Clin. Assembly Osteo. Specialists, New Orleans, 1984, Am. Coll. Osteo. Surgeons Review Course, Miami, Fla., 1984, Mich. Osteo. Med. Ctr.-Engring. Soc. Detroit, 1980, Am. Coll. Osteo. Physicians, 1980; vice-chmn. dept. surgery, section chief gen. surgery Mercy Hosp., vice chief surgery, mem. cancer com., 1995; mem. exec. com. Parkview Hosp., Toledo, 1993-94, med. records utilization and review com., 1992, physicians quality assurace com., 1992, hysterectomy/endometriosis support group, 1987; mem. sub.com. intern training, 1982-85, com. postdoctoral training, 1987-89; mem. subcom., surg. expert State of Mich. Ins. Bur., 1976—; mem. Program for Affordable Health Care, Southeastern Mich., 1994—, Mercy St. CharlesJoint Instl. Review Bd., 1996; cancer liaison physician ACS; guest spkr. intern grad. dinner Muslegon Gen. Hosp., 1970; guest lectr. Parkview Hosp., 1984-87, montly lectr. series for staff, 1984-86, Flint Osteo. Hosp., 1991, Tex. Coll. Osteo. Medicine, 1976, 77, Ohio State U. Coll. Medicine, 1975, Saginaw (Mich.) Osteo. Hosp., 1975, Mich. Ctr. Continuing Edn., 1974, Ctrl. States Osteo. Soc. Proctology Conv., 1969, Mich. Assn. Osteo. Physicians and Surgeons 85th Ann. Postgrad. Conf. and Sci. Seminar, Grand Rapids, Mich., 1984, postgrad conv., 1979, ann. conf. Dearborn, Mich., 1986, ann. conv., San Francisco, 1982, Phila. Coll. Osteo. Medicine, 1979, postgrad. seminar, 1979, guest spkr., ann. seminar, 1977, practice seminar, 1984, ACOS Ann. Seminars, San Diego, 1985, clin. assembly, 1978, Toronto, 1983, postgrad. course, 1977, Osteo. Student Orgn., Washington, 1986, 94; mem. ACOS com. Ann. Clin. Assembly Program, 1982-87, chmn., 1982, 83, chmn. awards and exhbts. com., 1986, in-depth review com., 1982-83, clin. examiner bd. surgery, 1978, postgrad. edn. com., 1978, chmn. editl. com., 1977, mem. editl. com., 1973, self-evaluation com. # 8; mem. various coms. 1986—. Guest editor Mich. Osteo. Jour., 1972; participant 1st Internat. Symposium Malignancies of Chest, Head and Neck; guest appearance Update of Breast Cancer, Cmty. Care, 1994; guest spkr. WWJ Radio, Detroit, Close Up program, Nat. Osteo. Week, 1983, Channel 62TV panel discussion, 1977; guest Kelly and Co., WXYZ-TV, 1984; contbr. articles to profl. jours. Pres. N.W. Ohio unit Am. Cancer Soc., 1995-96, chmn. profl. edn. com., 1991-93, bd. dirs., v.p. Ohio Divsn., 1993-95; pres. Health Planning Commn., Lucas County, Ohio, 1995; chmn. Spl. Rev. Com. for Health Delivery, N.W. Ohio, 1994—; mem. Physicians Malpractice Arbitration com., 1978, Comprehensive Health Planning coun., Southeast Mich., 1978, Pub. Edn. Com., 1993—, Northwest Ohio Health Planning Com., v.p., 1995, exec. bd. 1992-95, Lucas County rep., 1991-95; bd. govs. Chgo. Coll. Osteo. Medicine, 1969-71; osteo. rep. Mich. Fedn. Physicians; Mich. Ho. Dels. to Am. Osteo. Assn., 1984; chmn. Lucas County Study Com., 1994; mem. instl. review bd. Sisters of Mercy-Northwest Regional, 1997. Recipient Outstanding Faculty award Ohio U. Coll. Osteo. Medicine, 1995, cert. Appreciation, Mich. Kiwanis Club, 1971; named Outstanding Splty. Physician, Ohio U. Osteo. Medicine, 1998. Fellow Am. Coll. Osteo. Surgeons (cert. in gen. surgery,), Acad. Medicine Lucas County; mem. Am. Osteo. Assn. (hosp. examiner 1975-82, 87—, editl. cons. 1987-89, guest spkr. auxiliary), Toledo Acad. Osteo. Physicians (bd. dirs. 1991—), Assn. Surg. Edrs., Am. Trauma Soc. (founding), Detroit Cancer Club (founding), Ohio Osteo. Assn., Toledo Acad. Osteo. Physicians (bd. dirs. 1991—), Mich. Assn. Osteo. Phsicians and Surgeons (mem. health care liason com. 1982, ho. dels. 1978), Roman Catholic. Office: Toledo Surg Assoc 2200 Jefferson Ave Fl 4 Toledo OH 43624-1120

ROUMAN, JOHN CHRIST, classics educator; b. Tomahawk, Wis., May 1, 1926; s. Christ and Soteria (Dedes) R. BA in Greek, Carleton Coll., 1950; MA in Greek, Columbia U., 1951; student, Rutgers U., 1951-53, U. Kiel, Germany, 1956-57, U. Minn., Mpls., 1959-60; PhD in Classics, U. Wis., 1965. German tchr. Seton Hall Preparatory Sch., South Orange, N.J., 1954-56; ancient history tchr. Malverne (N.Y.) High Sch., 1957-59; tchg. asst. in ancient history U. Wis., Madison, 1960-61, rsch. asst. in ancient history, 1961-65; rsch. asst. in Greek epigraphy Inst. Advanced Study, Princeton, N.J., 1962-63; asst. prof. Classics U. N.H., Durham, 1965-71, assoc. prof., 1971-91, prof., 1991—, prof. classics emeritus, 1999, co-chmn. Spanish and Classics depts., mem. adv. bd. Prof. John C. Rouman classical lectr. series, 1997—. Examiner N.H. State Bd. Edn. in Latin and Greek, 1979-80; judge Warren H. Held Jr. Exam-Contests in Latin and Mythology, 1988—; cons. Nat. Classical Greek Examination, 1980; presenter, lectr. in field; adv. bd. Christos and Mary Papoutsy Disting. Endowed Chair in Bus. Ethics, N.H. Coll./So. N.H. Univ., 2000—; exec. bd. Hellenic Soc. PAIDEIA, NH, 2001. Active Colovos Rd. Com., 1981-82. With USN, 1944-46. Fulbright scholar U. Kiel, 1956-57; recipient Disting. Tchg. award U. N.H. Alumni Assn., 1985, Pericles award Am. Hellenic Edni. Progressive Assn. and Daus. of Penelope, 1993, Profile of Svc. award U. N.H. Aumni Assn., 2000; Prof. John C. Rouman Classical Lecture Series named in his honor. Mem. Am. Classical League (rep. to TCNE at ann. meeting 1978, mem. fin. com. 1981-82, treas. 1982-83), Am. Philol. Assn. (Nat. Excellence in Teaching Classics award, 1991), Archaeol. Inst. Am., Classical Assn. Can., Classical Assn. New Eng. (mem. exec. com. at-large 1981-84, mem. nominating com. 1983-84, 86-87, pres. 1987-88, Barlow-Beach award 1991, mem. ad hoc com. on elections and appointments), Medieval Acad. Am., Modern Greek Studies Assn., Nat. Assn. Advisors for Health Professions, N.H. Classical Assn. (mem. exec. com. 1965—, chair nominating com. 1986—), Strafford County Greco-Roman Found. (pres. 1978—), Vergilian Soc. Am., Carleton Coll. Alumni Assn. (Alumni award for Dist. Achievement 2000), Phi Kappa Theta (faculty advisor, 1982—, chmn. nat. bd., 1993-94, nat. found. mem. 1993—, Man of Achievement award 2000).

ROUMM, PHYLLIS EVELYN GENSBIGLER, English language educator, writer; b. New Alexandria, Pa., Jan. 1, 1927; d. Theodore Roosevelt and Daisy Isabelle (Patterson) Gensbigler; m. Milton Leonard Roumm, Nov. 23, 1946; children: David Lynn, Nikolyn, Dennis Eric, Janna Leigh. BS in English Edn., Indiana U. of Pa., 1945, MEd, 1963; postgrad., Ohio U., 1964, 65; PhD, Kent State U., 1977. Tchr. English Elders Ridge (Pa.) Joint High Sch., 1945-46, Apollo (Pa.) High Sch., 1946-47; tchr. English, speech Indiana Area Jr.-Sr. High Sch., 1959-67; teaching fellow Kent (Ohio) State U., 1970-71; prof. English Indiana U. of Pa., 1967-85, prof. emeritus, 1985—. Freelance writer, 1985—. Bd. dirs. Hist. and Geneal. Soc. of Indiana County, 1984, Indiana Free Libr., 1988-91; mem. strategic planning steering com. Indiana (Pa.) Area Sch. Dist.; mem. health promotion com. Aging Svcs., Inc., Indiana. Mem. AAUW, Coll. English Assn. (life), Ligonier Valley Writers Assn., So. Humanities Conf., Pa. Ret. State Employees (v.p. Indico chpt. 1996-97, pres. 1997-98, bd. dirs. 1998—), Am. Assn. Ret. People, Assn. Pa. State Coll. and Univ. Ret. Faculty (bd. dirs. 1998—), Indiana (Pa.) Wordsmiths, Derry Hist. Soc. (life), Kent State Alumni Assn. (life), New Century Club, Hadassah (life), Alpha Delta Kappa (pres. 1968-70, Silver Sister award 1991), Phi Delta Kappa. Avocations: reading, reviewing books, walking, writing. Home: 310 Poplar Ave Indiana PA 15701-3024

ROUND, ALICE FAYE BRUCE, school psychologist; b. Ironton, Ohio, July 19, 1934; d. Wade Hamilton and Martha Matilda (Toops) Bruce; children: Leonard Bruce, Christopher Frederick. BA, Asbury Coll., 1956; MS in Sch. Psychology, Miami U., Oxford, Ohio, 1975. Cert. tchr., sch. psychologist, supr., Ohio; cert. tchr., Calif. Tchr. Madison County (Ohio) Schs., 1956-58, Columbus (Ohio) Pub. Schs., 1958, San Diego Pub. Schs., 1958-60, Poway (Calif.) Unified Sch. Dist., 1960-64; substitute tchr. Princeton City Schs., Cin., 1969-75; sch. psychologist, intern Greenhills/Forest Park City Schs., 1975-76; sch. psychologist Fulton County Schs., Wauseon, Ohio, 1976-77, Sandusky (Ohio) pub. and Cath. schs., 1977-96, Eric County Ednl. Svc. Ctr., 1996-98; pre-sch. psychologist Huron County Bd. Edn., Norwalk, Ohio, 1998—. Tchr. art cmty. group and pvt. lessons, Sandusky, 1962, Springdale, Ohio, 1962-69; mem. Youth Svcs. Bd., Sandusky, 1978-88; bd. dirs., cons. Sandusky Sch. Practical Nursing, 1983-91; presenter suicide prevention seminars for mental health orgns.; speaker at ch., civic and youth orgns., local radio and TV programs; cons. on teen pregnancy to various schs., health depts. Mem. Huron (Ohio) Boosters Club, 1978-92, Vols. in Action, Sandusky, 1987—. Mem. NAACP, NEA, Nat. Sch. Psychologist Assn., Ohio Sch. Psychologist Assn., Maumee Valley Sch. Psychologist Assn., Ohio Edn. Assn., Sandusky Edn. Assn., Phi Delta Kappa (historian 1984-88, Most Innovative Preservation of History award 1988). Home: 821 Seneca Ave Huron OH 44839-1842 Office: Huron City Schs Cleveland Ave Huron OH 44839 E-mail: AFRound@aol.com.

ROUNDS, GEORGE R. executive coach, organization consultant; b. Providence, Jan. 18, 1934; s. George Irving and Irma Elizabeth Rounds; m. Brenda S. Green, Sept. 28, 1956 (dec. May 1983); m. Jean Gregg Brandner, Apr. 30, 1988; children: Heather Shea, George Robinson, Jon Timothy, Heather Suzanne, Douglas. BA, Williams Coll., 1955. Cert. assn. exec., profl. co-active coach. Sec. Nat. Assn. Engine and Boat Mfrs., N.Y.C., 1960-80; dir. assn. svcs. Nat. Marine Mfrs. Assn., Chgo., 1980-87; pres. Nat. Assn. Marine Products and Svcs., 1987-95; exec. dir. Nat. Assn. Quick Printers, 1995-98; exec. v.p. Am. Soc. Clin. Hypnosis, Roselle, Ill., 1998-2000. Dir. Chgo. Soc. Assn. Execs., 1995-97; bd. dirs. Manking Project, Chgo., 1994-2000. Mem. Am. Soc. Assn. Execs. (cert., Mgmt. Achievement award 1983). Office: Spectrum Assocs 2735 Park Pl Evanston IL 60201

ROUNDS, HOLLIS A. secondary school educator; b. Attleboro, Mass., Feb. 7, 1954; d. Robert Earl and Evelyn Mary Blackburn; m. Russell E. Rounds, Feb. 9, 1979. BA in Psychology, Southeastern Mass. U., Dartmouth, 1977; MEd, U. New Eng., Biddeford, Maine, 2002. Cert. tchr. Mass., travel agt., pub. housing mgr. HUD, pub. mgr. pub. employees Gov. of Mass., hypnotherapist. Social worker Attleboro Housing Authority, Mass., 1976—84; field auditor Mass. Dept. of the State Auditor, Boston, 1984—88; CFO Commonwealth of Mass./Walpole State Prison, 1988—92; tchr. various sch. systems Attleboro, Norton, Foxboro, Mass., 1995—2001; tchr. history and English Walpole Sch. Dist., 2001—. Cons. Attleboro Literacy Ctr., 2001—; cons., curriculum devel. Attleboro Sch. Dist., 1995—2000. Author: poetry in Best Poems and Poets of 2000, Nature's Echoes. Recipient Outstanding Skill and Sportsmanship award, Gov. of Mass., 1974. Mem.: Am. Parapsychol. Assn. (cert.), Mass. Tchrs. Assn., Am. Correctional Assn. Republican. Avocations: art, writing, genealogy research, speech writing, political strategist. Mailing: 28 Rounds Pl Attleboro MA 02703

ROUNDS, LINNEA PAULA, library administrator; b. Gary, Ind., Feb. 12, 1944; d. Paul and S. Dolly (Fudaley) Korpita; m. Keith Rounds, Aug. 17, 1968; children: Daniel K., Paula L. BA in Journalism, Marquette U., 1965. Pub. rels. asst. Wis. Heart Assn., Milw., 1963-66; pub. info. asst. Wyo. Hwy. Dept., Cheyenne, 1966-68; writer, operator AP, 1969; account exec. Media, Inc., 1969-71; comm. specialist Sch. Dist. 1, 1971-73; free-lance writer, 1973-77; pub. programs, publs. and mktg. mgr. Wyo. State Libr., Cheyenne, 1977—. Coord. Wyo. Ctr. for Book, an affiliate of Libr. of Congress' Ctr. for Book, Wyo. Dept. Edn. Family Literacy Consortium. Editor Outrider, 1977—. Den leader Longs Peak coun. Cub Scouts, Boy Scouts Am., 1980, 81, pack liaison, 1982-83; bd. dirs. United Way of Laramie County, Cheyenne, 1981-84, YMCA Writer's Voice Project adv. group, 1999—, Wyo. Tribune Eagle Readers adv. panel, 1999; co-chair Laramie County First Book Adv. Bd., 1999—; mem. Cmty. Action of Laramie County Bd., 2000—, chair 2002; mem. h.s. fundraising subcom. Head Start Devel. Com., 2002--; sec. adv. bd. LC First Book, 2000-2001. Recipient Best of Show award ALA, 1985, 1998, awards Wyo. Press Assn. Assocs. Group Contest, 1997, 98, 99, 2002. Mem. Nat. Fedn. Press Women (sec. 1989-91, 3d v.p. 1991-93, 2d v.p. 1993-95, 1st v.p. 1995-97, pres. 1997-99, pres. edn. fund 2000-2001, Comm. Contest award 1974, 85, 86, 87, 96), Wyo. Press Women (pres. 1983-85, writing contest award 1970-96, Communicator of Achievement 1989, Woman of Achievement 1990 Wyo. Commn. Women), Wyo. Libr. Assn., LWV, Wyo. State Hist. Soc., Wyo. Writers, Inc., Wyo. Info. Officers Coop. (chmn., co-founder 1980-83), Zonta (Cheyenne) (bd. dirs., rec. sec. 1975-76, chmn. scholarship com. 1985, pres. 1988-89, area dir. dist. 12 1988-90, Zontian of Yr. 1991, chmn. literacy com. 1999-2000), Madame Curie Cir., Polish Nat. Alliance. Democrat. Roman Catholic. Home: 7413 Willshire Blvd Cheyenne WY 82009-2090 Office: Wyo State Library 2301 Capitol Ave Cheyenne WY 82002-0001 E-mail: lround@state.wy.us.

ROUNDS, PHILARD LEAON, SR. fundraiser; b. Des Moines, Jan. 9, 1928; s. Clarence Leaon and Alice Rudella (Eitel) R.; m. Shirley Anne Rounds, 1946; children: Rose Ann Rounds Farabough, Philard L. BA, Fla. So. Coll., Lakeland; diploma in Bible, Open Bible Coll., Des Moines. Missionary to Japan, 1950-67; Oral Roberts U., Tulsa, 1967-87; David Livingston Missionary Assn., 1988-89; First United Meth. Ch., 1989—. Regional rep. Oral Roberts U., Tulsa, 1967-87; sr. v.p. planned giving David Livingstone Assn., Tulsa, 1987-88; min. planned giving First United Meth. Ch., tulsa, 1989—. Author: Planned Giving Manual, 1989. Fundraising exec. Nat. Soc. Fundraising, Tulsa, 1988—; active alumnus Nat. Planned Giving Inst., Memphis, 1988. With U.S. Army, 1946-49. Mem. Nat. Inst. Planned Giving, Nat. Soc. Fundraising Execs. (pres. ea. Okla. chpt. 1994), Fla. Acad. Scis., Pi Gamma Mu. Republican. Methodist. Home: 6443 S Sandusky Ave Tulsa OK 74136-1626 Office: First United Methodist Ch 1115 S Boulder Ave Tulsa OK 74119-2492

ROUNDS, WILLIAM C. educator; b. Portland, Maine, Oct. 28, 1942; s. William and Eleanor Rounds; m. Frances L. Lovering, Apr. 1, 1967. PhD, Stanford U., 1968. Asst. prof. Case Western Res. U., Cleveland; prof. U. Mich., Ann Arbor, 1973—; vis. fellow Oxford (Eng.) U., 1980—81; rschr. Xerox PARC, Palo Alto, Calif., 1987—88. Singer: concerts, 2002. Home: 301 Westwood Ave Ann Arbor MI Office: U Mich 1101 Beal Ave Ann Arbor MI 48109

ROUNER, LEROY STEPHENS, religious studies educator, philosophy educator; b. Wolfeboro, N.H., Aug. 5, 1930; s. Arthur Acy and Elizabeth Ward (Stephens) R.; m. Rita Rainsford, May 21, 1955; children: Stephen Rainsford, Timothy Nichols, Jonathan Kerr, Christina Elizabeth. AB in English, Harvard Coll., 1953, postgrad., 1956; MDiv, Union Theol. Sem., 1958; PhD, Columbia U., 1961; LHD (hon.), Lynchburg Coll., 1985. Asst. prof. United Theol. Coll., Bangalore, India, 1961-66; prof. Boston Univ., 1970—, dir. Inst. Philos. & Religion, 1975—. Bd. trustees Jaffna Coll. Funds, Boston, 1975—; bd. trustee endowment fund Am. Coll., Madurai, India, 1975. Author: Within Human Experience, 1969, The Long Way Home, 1989, To Be At Home: Christianity Civil Religion and World Community, 1987; gen. editor: Boston Univ. Studies in Philosophy and Religion, 1981—. Chmn. dem. com. Carroll County, N.H., 1971-73; trustee Ella Lyman Cabot Trust. Mem. APA, Internat. Soc. Metaphysics, Am. Theol. Soc., Soc. Asian & Comparative Philos., Boston Theol. Soc., Soc. Advancement Am. Philos., Phi Beta Kappa. Democrat. Avocations: rowing, hiking. Home: 223 Maple Ridge Rd Center Sandwich NH 03227-3721 Office: Inst Philos & Religion 745 Commonwealth Ave # 523 Boston MA 02215-1401

ROUNICK, JACK A. lawyer, company executive; b. Phila., June 5, 1935; s. Philip and Nettie (Brownstein) R.; m. Noreen A. Garrigan, Sept. 4, 1970; children: Ellen, Eric, Amy, Michelle. BBA, U. Mich., 1956; JD, U. Pa., 1959. Bar: Pa. 1960, U.S. Dist. Ct. (ea. dist.) Pa. 1960; diplomate Am. Coll. Family Trial Lawyers. Spl. asst. atty. gen., 1963-71; ptnr. Israelit & Rounick, 1960-67, Moss & Rounick, 1968-69, Moss, Rounick & Hurowitz, Norristown, Pa., 1969-72, Moss & Rounick, Norristown, 1972-73, Pechner, Dorfman, Wolffe, Rounick and Cabot, Norristown, 1973-87; v.p., gen. counsel Martin Lawrence Ltd. Edits., Inc., 1987-93, dir., 1984-97, Deb Shops, Inc., 1974—; counsel to firm Wolf Block, Schorr & Solis-Cohen LLP, 1997—. Author: Pennsylvania Matrimonial Practice, 6 vols., 1982; editor Pa. Family Lawyer, 1980-87. Fin. chmn. Pa. Young Reps., 1964-66, treas., 1966-68, chmn., 1968-70. Recipient Boss of Yr. award Montgomery County Legal Secs. Assn., 1970, Cert of Appreciation, Pa. Bar Inst., 1980. Fellow: Am. Acad. Matrimonial Lawyers (pres. Pa. chpt. 1982—84, gov. 1983—85, v.p. 1985—87, chmn. bd. rev. 1997—), Internat. Acad. Matrimonial Lawyers; mem.: ABA (coun. family law sect. 1982—87, coun. 2000—), Friends of Hebrew U. (v.p. 1990—91, bd. dirs. 1987—93, nat. coun. trustees 1987—93, pres. Phila. chpt. 1988—91), Montgomery Bar Assn., Pa. Bar Assn. (past chmn. family law sect., Spl. Achievement award 1979—80). Republican. Jewish. Office: 325 Swede St Norristown PA 19401-4801 E-mail: JRounick@WolfBlock.com.

ROUNTREE, ASA, lawyer; b. Birmingham, Ala., Aug. 9, 1927; s. John Asa and Cherokee Jemison (Van de Graaff) R.; m. Elizabeth Rhodes Blue, Aug. 11, 1951 (dec.); children— Robert B., John A.; m. Helen Hill Updike, Oct. 10, 1998. AB, U. Ala., 1949; LL.B., Harvard U., 1954. Bar: Ala. 1954, U.S. Dist. Ct. (no. dist.) Ala. 1954, U.S. Ct. Appeals (5th cir.) 1955, N.Y. 1962, U.S. Dist. Ct. (so. dist.) N.Y. 1963, U.S. Ct. Appeals (2d cir.) 1963, U.S. Supreme Ct. 1972. Assoc. Cabaniss & Johnston, Birmingham, Ala., 1954-60, ptnr., 1960-62; assoc. Debevoise & Plimpton, N.Y.C., 1962-63, ptnr., 1963-91; mem. Maynard, Cooper, & Gale, P.C., Birmingham, 1991—. Bd. dirs. U. Ala. Law Sch. Found. Served with U.S. Army, 1945-46, to lt., 1951-53. Mem. ABA (chmn. litigation sect. 1980-81), Ala. Bar Assn., N.Y. State Bar Assn., Assn. Bar City N.Y., Am. Law Inst., Am. Coll. Trial Lawyers, Am. Bar Found. Clubs: River (N.Y.C.); Mountain Brook (Birmingham). Episcopalian. Office: Maynard Cooper Gale PC 2400 AmSouth/Harbert Plz 1901 6th Ave N Birmingham AL 35203-2618

ROUNTREE, ASHLEY EVERETT, investment banker; b. Pitts., June 14, 1961; s. Benjamin Cox Rountree and Mary Catherine (Martin) Devlin; m. Leslie Linam Dunton-Downer, May 28, 1988; 1 child, Jordan Tucker. AB in History and Lit. cum laude, Harvard U., 1982. Computer cons., Paris, 1982-83; assoc. Downer & Co., 1983-85, v.p. Boston, 1985-88, v.p. Europe Paris, 1988-90; mng. dir. Corp. Fin. Internat., 1989-91; dir. Downer & Co., Paris and Boston, 1988—. Mem. Riverside Players (founding mem., bd. dirs. 1993, Lear award 1994), The Table (founder, pres. 1987-89), Harvard Club Boston. Avocations: music, creative writing. Office: Downer & Co 211 Congress St Boston MA 02110-2410

ROUNTREE, PATRICIA ANN, youth organization administrator; b. Rochester, N.Y., Apr. 2, 1942; d. Robert James and Myrtle Margaret (Cuthbertson) R. AA, Cazenovia Coll., 1961; BA, Parsons Coll., 1965. Gen. clk. Eastman Kodak, Rochester, 1961-63; 6th grade tchr. Wayland (N.Y.) Ctrl. Sch., 1965-67; field dir. Seven Lakes Coun. Girl Scouts U.S.A., Phelps, N.Y., 1967-73, program dir. Palm Glades Coun. Lake Worth, Fla., 1973-76, asst. exec. dir. Seven Lakes Coun., 1976-86, exec. dir. Mich. Trails Coun., 1986-89, exec. dir. Ctrl. N.Y. Coun. Syracuse, 1989—. Pres., bd. dirs. Planned Parenthood of Fingerlakes, Geneva, N.Y., 1982-86. Mem. Rotary Syracuse. Presbyterian. Avocations: needlework, reading, travel. Home: 4 Robinson Dr Baldwinsville NY 13027-2807 Office: Ctrl NY Girl Scout Coun 6724 Thompson Rd # 482 Syracuse NY 13211-2122

ROUNTREE, RUTHANN LOUISE, social worker, lecturer; b. Denver, Mar. 18, 1950; d. Charles Lindy and Marian Louise (Jenkins) R. BSW, U. Nebr., 1972; MSW, Denver U., 1973; MDiv, Fuller Theol. Sem., 1988; postgrad. social work studies, U. So. Calif., 1993—. Lic. clin. social worker, Calif.; ordained minister African Meth. Episcopal Ch. Asst. dir. Denver br. Virginia Neal Blue Resource Ctr. for Colo. Women, Denver, 1973-76; cons, edn. coord. Aurora (Colo.) Community Mental Health Ctr., 1976-78; program evaluator Castle Substance Abuse Program, L.A., 1978-81; program ops. mgr. Nat. Coun. on Aging, 1981-85; program mgr. gerontology out-patient facility Fuller Theol. Sem., Pasadena, Calif., 1985-89; mem. faculty, dir. of admissions, dept. social work Calif. State U., Long Beach, 1989-93, part-time faculty, 1993—; tng. coord. Martin Luther King Jr./Charles R. Drew Med. Ctr., 1997—. Vice chair San Gabriel Valley Elder Abuse Task Force, Pasadena, Calif., 1987-88; bd. dirs. Living at Home Project, Pasadena, 1988-89; mem. Black Aging Network, L.A., 1990-92; patr-time faculty Immaculate Heart Coll. Ctr., L.A., 1997—. Facilitator Diakanas-Inner Healing Workshops, Pasadena, 1987-88; adv. YWCA Rape Hotline, Pasadena, 1987-89; dir. westside counseling and tng. ctr., pastoral counselor Westminster Presbyn. Ch., 1991-93; trainer lay counselor and peer counselor; assoc. min. Grant A.M.E. Ch., Long Beach, 1994—. Recipient Gov.'s award State of Calif., 1987; named Outstanding Young Women of Am., 1987. Mem. NASW, Am. Assn. Christian Counselors, Nat. Assn. Christian Social Workers, Assoc. Gerontology and Human Devel. Council on Social Work Education. Avocations: sewing, crafts, snorkeling, community theatre, art museum.

ROUPE, JAMES PAUL, accountant; b. Havre de Grace, Md., Apr. 20, 1957; s. Paul Clyde and Shirley Louise (Trivette) R. AA, Harford C.C., Bel Air, Md., 1977; BS, Towson State U., 1979. CPA, Md. Mgmt. asst. Loyola Fed. Savings and Loan, Balt., 1979-81; asst. treas. Legum Chevrolet-Nissan, 1983-89; contr. Bob Bell Chevrolet/Nissan, Inc., 1989-92, corp. sec.-treas., 1992—; sr. controller Bob Bell Chevrolet of Bel Air (Md.) Inc., 1991-92; corp. sec.-treas. Bob Bell of Upper Marlboro (Md.), L.C., 1992—. Recipient Bus. Mgmt. Excellence award Nissan Motor Corp., 1990-2001. Mem. AICPA, Md. Assn. CPAs, Inst. Mgmt. Accts., Chevrolet Coun. Bus. Acctg. Mgrs. Republican. Baptist. Office: Bob Bell Chevrolet Nissan 7900 Eastern Blvd Baltimore MD 21224-2125

ROURKE, ARLENE CAROL, publisher; b. N.Y.C. Pres. Rourke Publs., Vero Beach, Fla., 1984—. Author, pub. books for children on Native Am. people, western history, religion, the environment, animal care and personal relationships, science biographies. Active Ctr. for the Arts, 1985—, Riverside Theatre, Vero Beach, 1985—, Humane Soc. Vero Beach; bd. dirs. Dollars for Scholars.

ROURKE, BRADLEY KEVIN, public affairs executive; b. L.A., July 29, 1965; s. Daniel Lee and Sherill Anne (Siebert) Rourke; m. Andrea Kay Jarrell, Sept. 19, 1992; children: Carson Jarrell-Rourke, Daniel Jarrell-Rourke. BA, U. Calif., Berkeley, 1987. Dir. scheduling Contr. Gray Davis, L.A., 1992-93; dist. dir. Congresswoman Jane Harman, 1994; dir. pub. affairs Elec. Bicycle Co., Burbank, Calif., 1995-96; state govt. rels. rep. Northrop Grumman Corp., L.A., 1996-97; prin. Jarrell-Rourke Comm., Pasadena, Calif., 1997; dir. project on campaign conduct Inst. Global Ethics, Camden, Maine, 1997-99, v.p. pub. policy and comms., 1999—2002; sr. project mgr. The Harwood Inst., Bethesda, Md., 2002—. Dep campaign dir Calif Nat Health Care Campaign, Los Angeles, 1993. Episcopalian. Office: The Harwood Inst 4915 Saint Elmo Ave #402 Bethesda MD 20814 E-mail: brourke@theharwoodinstitute.org.

ROURKE, WILLIAM BERNARD, aerospace science educator, consultant; b. Chgo., Sept. 1, 1931; s. William Rourke and Glea Dolores Withers; m. Mary Lee Quirk, June 9, 1956; children: Ellen Ann, William Patrick, Brian David. BA, U. N.Mex., 1955, BS, 1956; MS, U.S. Naval Postgrad., 1965; MBA, Pepperdine U., 1974; EdD, Nova U., 1985. Commd. major USMC, 1956, pilot, 1956-76; prof. Met. State Coll. Denver, 1976-00. Accident prevention counselor FAA, Colo., 1977-00; pres. Sigma Sys., Denver, 1976-00. Author: Aviation Safety, 1976, Aviation Safety, 1986. Bd.d irs. Regional Transp. Dist., Denver, 1982-85, chmn. bd. dirs., 1984-85. Mem. Rotary (pilot

1990-00, Paul Harris fellow 1995). Roman Catholic. Avocation: flying. Home: PO Box 3309 Evergreen CO 80437-3309 Office: Met State Coll Denver PO Box 173362 1006 11th St Denver CO 80217

ROUS, STEPHEN NORMAN, urologist, educator; b. N.Y.C., Nov. 1, 1931; s. David H. and Luba (Margulies) R.; m. Margot Woolfolk, Nov. 12, 1966; children: Benjamin, David. AB, Amherst Coll., 1952; MD, N.Y. Med. Coll., 1956; MS, U. Minn., 1963. Diplomate: Am. Bd. Urology. Intern Phila. Gen. Hosp., 1956-57, resident, 1959-60, Flower-Fifth Ave. and Met. Hosp., N.Y.C., 1957-59, Mayo Clinic, Rochester, Minn., 1960-63; practice medicine specializing in urology San Francisco, 1963-68; assoc. prof. urology N.Y. Med. Coll., N.Y.C., 1968-72, assoc. dean, 1970-72; prof. surgery, chief div. urology Mich. State U., East Lansing, 1972-75; prof., chmn. dept. urology Med. U. S.C., Charleston, 1975-88; urologist-in-chief Med. U. S.C. and County hosps., 1975-88; editorial dir. Norton Med. Books div. W.W. Norton and Co., 1988-94, editorial cons., 1994—; clin. prof. surgery Uniformed Svcs. U. of Health Scis., Bethesda, Md., 1992-2001. Adj. prof. urology Med. U. S.C., 1988-99, prof. emeritus, 1999—; adj. prof. surgery Dartmouth Med. Sch., 1988-91, prof. surgery (urology), 1991-2001, prof. surgery emeritus, 2001—; staff urologist Dartmouth-Hitchcock Med. Ctr., 1991-99; cons. urologist Saginaw VA Hosp., 1971-75, Charleston VA Hosp., 1975-88; hon. cons. St. Peter's Hosp., London, 1981-82; sr. vis. fellow Inst. Urology, London, 1981-82; mil. cons. in urology USAF Surgeon Gen., 1982-85; chmn. alumni devel. com. Mayo Clinic, 1979-82; hon. staff The Exeter Hosp., N.H., 1988—; nat. bd. visitors N.Y. Med. Coll., 1988-97; chief urology VA Med. Ctr., White River Junction, Vt., 1991-2001. Author: Understanding Urology, 1973, Urology in Primary Care, 1976, Spanish edit., 1978, Russian edit., 1979, Urology: A Core Textbook, 1985, 2d edit., 1996, The Prostate Book, 1988, latest rev. edit., 2001, (with Judge Hiller B. Zobel) Doctors and the Law: Defendants and Expert Witnesses, 1993, (with Dr. Pamela Ellsworth) The Little Black Book of Urology, 2001; editor Urology Ann., 1987-97, Stone Disease: Diagnosis and Management, 1987; mem. editl. bd. Mil. Medicine, 1984-94; contbr. articles to med. jours. Mem. East Lansing (Mich.) Planning Commn., 1974-75; vestryman, jr. warden All Saints Episcopal Ch., East Lansing, 1973-75, lay reader, mem. diocesan com. on continuing edn., 1975-86; vestryman St. Michael's Episc. Ch., 1979-82, Charleston, S.C., chmn. every mem. canvas, 1979-80, chmn. lay readers, 1983-86; mem. fin. com., lay reader Christ Episc. Ch., Exeter, N.H., 1989-91; lector St. Thomas Episc. Ch., Hanover, N.H., 1991—, vestryman, 1992-96, stewardship chmn., 1992-94, jr. warden, 1994-96; mem. selectman's alt. Hampton Falls Planning Bd., 1989-91; alt. mem. Zoning Bd. Adjustment, Hanover, 1997-2000; bd. trustees, Nat. Hypertension Assn., N.Y.C., 2001-; bd. dirs. Med. Sci. Techs. Inc., Newport News, Va., 2001-. Col. USAFR, 1981-85, col. USAR, 1985-2000, col. AUS, ret., 2001—. Recipient "A" designator in urology, U.S. Army Surgeon Gen., 1986. Fellow ACS, Am. Acad. Pediatrics; mem. AMA, Soc. Univ. Urologists, Internat. Soc. Urology, Am. Urol. Assn., Nat. Urologic Forum, Soc. Pediatric Urology, Brit. Assn. Urol. Surgeons, German Urol. Assn. (hon.), Mayo Alumni Assn. (v.p. 1979-81, pres. 1983-85), Army and Navy Club (Washington), Lotos Club (N.Y.C.), Dartmouth Club of N.Y.C., Sigma Xi, Alpha Omega Alpha (hon.). Republican. Home: 6 Partridge Rd PO Box 10 Etna NH 03750-0010 E-mail: stephen.n.rous@dartmouth.edu.

ROUSE, CHRISTOPHER CHAPMAN, III, composer, educator; b. Balt., Feb. 15, 1949; s. Christopher Chapman Jr. and Margery (Harper) R.; m. Ann Jensen, Aug. 28, 1983; children: Jillian, Alexandra, Adrian; 1 stepchild, Angela. MusB, Oberlin Conservatory, 1971; MFA, DMA, Cornell U., 1977; DMus (hon.), Oberlin Coll., 1996, SUNY, Geneseo, 2000. Asst. prof. composition U. Mich., Ann Arbor, 1978-81, Eastman Sch. Music, Rochester, N.Y., 1981-85, assoc. prof. composition, 1985-91, prof. composition NY, 1991—2002; faculty Juilliard Sch., 1997—. Composer-in-residence Balt. Symphony Orch., 1986-89, Schleswig Holstein Festival, 1989, Helsinki Biennale, 1997, Tanglewood Music Ctr., 1997, Pacific Music Festival, 1998, Aspen Music Festival, 1999—; writer numerous musical subjects; historian rock music. Composer for numerous renowned soloists and ensembles including Yo-Yo Ma, Evelyn Glennie, Emanuel Ax, Dawn Upshaw, Cho-Liang Lin, Charles Castleman, James VanDemark, Jan de Gaetani, Leslie Guinn, Sharon Isbin, Carol Wincenc, William Albright, Soc. New Music, Blackearth Percussion Group; commd. composer Atlanta Symphony, Phila. Orch., N.Y. Philharm., L.A. Philharm., Balt. Symphony, Houston Symphony, Minn. Orch., London Symphony, Cleve. Orch., Detroit Symphony, St. Louis Symphony, Rochester Philharmonic, Cleve. Quartet, Boston Musica Viva, Aspen Music Festival, Chamber Music Soc. Lincoln Ctr., N.Y. Internat. Festival of Arts, Chamber Music Am., New England Conservatory Music, Nonesuch Records; orchestral works programmed by Berlin, Stockholm, N.Y.C., Buffalo, L.A., Rochester Philharmonics, Orchestre Nat. de France, Residentie, Concertgebouw, Vienna and Zurich Tonhalle, New Zealand, Philharmonia, also Chgo., Boston, St. Louis, Detroit, Balt., Nat., Pitts., Houston, Denver, Milw., Cleve., Minn., Phila., Oakland, Cin., Atlanta, Indpls., Memphis, San Francisco, Dallas Symphony Orchs., also The Netherlands, Finnish, Frankfurt, Moscow, Austrian, and NHK Tokyo Radio Orchs. Recipient awards from Guggenheim Found., League Composers/ISCM, NEA, Rockefeller Found., Am. Music Ctr., Warner Bros. Record Co., Koussevitzky Found., BMI and Pitney Bowes, Friedheim 1st prize Kennedy Ctr., 1988, Pulitzer prize for music, 1993, Acad. award Am. Acad. Arts and Letters, 1993, Grammy award, 2002. Mem.: Am. Acad. Arts and Letters. Office: Juilliard Sch 60 Lincoln Center Plz New York NY 10023

ROUSE, DORIS JANE, physiologist, research administrator; b. Greensboro, N.C., Oct. 3, 1948; d. Welby Corbett and Nadia Elizabeth (Grainger) R.; m. Blake Shaw Wilson, Jan. 6, 1974; children: Nadia Jacqueline, Blair Elizabeth. BA in Chemistry, Duke U., 1970, PhD in Physiology and Pharmacology, 1980. Tchr. sci. Peace Corps, Tugbake, Liberia, 1970-71; research scientist Burroughs Wellcome Co., Research Triangle Park, N.C., 1971-76; sr. physiologist Rsch. Triangle Inst., Durham, 1976-83, ctr. dir., 1980-2000, also dir. NASA tech. application team, 1980-2000, dir. Tuberculosis Tech. Transfer Program, 1999—, dir. Global Health, 2001—. Adminstr. ANSI Tech. Adv. Group for Wheelchairs, N.Y.C., 1982-86; adj. asst. prof. U. N.C. Sch. Medicine, 1983-92; chair Instl. Rev. Bd., Profl. Devel. Award com., chair salary com. Rsch. Triangle Inst.; mem. adv. bd. Assistive Tech. Rsch. Ctr., 1994-96. Mem. adv. bd. Assn. Retarded Citizens, Arlington, Tex., 1981—88, Western Gerontology Soc., San Francisco, 1982—85; bd. dirs. Simon Found., Chgo., 1983—; mem. spl. rev. com. small bus. applications Nat. Forum on Tech. and Aging; mem. fund steering com. Longleaf Venture, 2000—. Recipient Group Achievement award NASA, 1979, 2000. Mem.: Assn. Fed. Tech. Transfer Execs., Licensing Execs. Soc., Rehab. Engring. Soc. N.Am., Rehab. Engring. Soc. N.Am. (chmn. wheelchair com. 1981—86). Home: 2410 Wrightwood Ave Durham NC 27705-5802 Office: Research Triangle Inst PO Box 12194 Durham NC 27709-2194

ROUSE, IRVING, anthropologist, emeritus educator; b. Rochester, N.Y., Aug. 29, 1913; s. Benjamin Irving and Louise Gillespie (Bohachek) R.; m. Mary Uta Mikami, June 24, 1939; children: Peter, David. BS, Yale U., 1934, PhD, 1938; D in Philosophy and Letters (hon.), Centro de Estudios Avanzados de Puerto Rico y el Caribe, 1990. Asst. anthropology Yale Peabody Museum, 1934-38, asst. curator, 1938-47, assoc. curator, 1947-54, research assoc., 1954-62, curator, 1977-85, emeritus curator, 1985—; instr. anthropology Yale U., 1939-43, asst. prof., 1943-48; assoc. prof. Yale, 1948-54; prof. Yale U., 1954-69, Charles J. MacCurdy prof. anthropology, 1969-84, prof. emeritus, 1984—. Author monographs on archaeology of Fla., Cuba, Haiti, P.R., Venezuela, Antigua. Recipient Medalla Commemorativa del Vuelo Panamericano pro Faro de Colon Govt. Cuba, 1945, A. Cressy Morrison prize in natural sci. N.Y. Acad. Sci., 1951, Viking fund medal Wenner-Gren Found., 1960, Wilbur Cross medal Yale U., 1992; Guggenheim fellow, 1963-64; fellow Phi Beta Kappa, 1996. Mem. Am. Anthrop. Assn. (pres. 1967-68), Eastern States Archeol. Fedn. (pres. 1946-50), Assn. Field Archaeology (pres. 1977-78), Soc. Am. Archaeology (editor 1946-50, pres. 1952-53), Nat. Acad. Scis., Am. Acad. Arts and Scis., Internat. Assn. Caribbean Archaeology (hon. mem.), Soc. Antiquaries (London). Office: Yale U Dept Anthropology PO Box 208277 New Haven CT 06520-8277 E-mail: blrouse@aol.com.

ROUSE, LEGRAND ARIAIL, II, retired lawyer, educator; b. Spartanburg, S.C., June 11, 1933; s. LeGrand and Hilda Virginia (Ariail) R.; m. Patricia Adelle White, Aug. 23, 1958; children: LeGrand A. III, Laurie Adelle Rouse-Hazel, Daniel Morris. AB in History and Polit. Sci., Wofford Coll., 1954; LLB, U. S.C., 1959, JD, 1970; MA in Govt., Am. U., 1969. Bar: S.C. 1959, U.S. Dist. Ct. S.C. 1959, U.S. Ct. Appeals (4th cir.) 1964, U.S. Supreme Ct. 1963. Sole practice, Spartanburg, 1959-63, 68-69; assoc. counsel, jud. improvements subcom. U.S. Senate Judiciary Com., Washington, 1963; profl. staff mem. U.S. Senate P.O. and Civil Svc. Com., 1964-68; instructional specialist Office of Instrnl. TV, S.C. Dept. Edn., Columbia, 1970-73; social studies cons. curriculum devel. S.C. Dept. Edn., 1973-79, spl. asst. legal and legis. affairs to State Supt. Edn., 1979-91; spl. asst. to sr. exec. asst. Policy, Rsch. and Leadership, 1991. Cons. S.C. Council for Social Studies, Columbia, 1973-78; dir. S.C. Council Econ. Edn., Columbia. Author: Government-Politics-Citizenship, tchr. lesson guide, 1971-72; creator, on-camera instr. Government-Politics-Citizenship TV series, 1970-72; project dir. econs. edn. kit for tchrs. grades 1-12: People, Production, Profits, 1977. Mem. S.C. Ho. of Reps., Columbia, 1961-64; alt. del. Nat. Dem. Conv., 1964. Served to 1st lt. USAR, 1955-57. Recipient Schoolmens' medal Freedoms Found. at Valley Forge, 1974. Mem. S.C. Bar Assn., S.C. State Employees' Assn. (pres. 1980-82), Masons, Nat. Sojourners (past pres. chpt. 184). Methodist. Home: 1021 Milton Ln Columbia SC 29209-2321

ROUSE, RICHARD HUNTER, historian, educator; b. Boston, Aug. 14, 1933; s. Hunter and Dorothee (Hüsmert) R.; m. Mary L. Ames, Sept. 7, 1959; children: Thomas, Andrew, Jonathan. BA, State U. Iowa, 1955; MA, U. Chgo., 1957; PhD, Cornell U., 1963. Mem. faculty UCLA, 1963—, prof. history, 1975—. Assoc. dir. Ctr. Medieval and Renaissance Studies, 1966-67, acting dir., 1967-68; dir. Summer Inst. in Paleography, 1978, chair grad. coun., 1989-90; adv. bd. Hill Monastic Microfilm Libr., St. John's U., Collegeville, Minn., Ambrosiana Microfilm Library, Notre Dame (Ind.) U., Corpus of Brit. Medieval Libr. Catalogues, Brit. Acad. Author: Serial Bibliographies for Medieval Studies, 1969, (with M.A. Rouse) Preachers, Florilegia and Sermons: Studies on the Manipulus Florum of Thomas of Ireland, 1979; (with others) Texts and Transmission, 1983; (with C.W. Dutschke) Medieval and Renaissance Manuscripts in the Claremont Libraries, 1986; (with M.A. Rouse) Cartolai, Illuminators and Printers in Fifteenth-Century Italy, 1988; (with L. Bataillon and B. Guyot) La Production du livre universitaire au moyen age, exemplar et pecia, 1988, (with others) Guide to Medieval and Renaissance Manuscripts in the Huntington Library, 1989, (with M. Ferrari) Medieval and Renaissance Manuscripts at the University of California, Los Angeles, 1991, (with M.A. Rouse and R.A.B. Mynors) Registrum de libris doctorum et auctorum veterum, 1991, (with M.A. Rouse) Authentic Witnesses: Approaches to Medieval Texts and Manuscripts, 1991, (with M.A. Rouse) Manuscripts and Their Makers: Commercial Book Producers in Medieval Paris 1200-1500, 2 vols., 2000; co-editor: Viator: Medieval and Renaissance Studies, 1970—; mem. editorial bd. Medieval and renaissance manuscripts in Calif. libraries, Medieval Texts, Toronto; Medieval Texts, Binghamton, Library Quar., 1984-88, Speculum, 1981-85, Revue d'histoire des Textes, 1986—, Cambridge Studies in Paleography and Codicology, 1990—, Catalogue of Medieval and Renaissance Manuscripts in the Beinecke Rare Book and Manuscript Library Yale University, 1984—, Filologia MedioLatina, 1994—. Am. Coun. Learned Socs. fellow, 1972-73, vis. fellow All Souls Coll., Oxford, 1978-79, Guggenheim fellow, 1975-76, Rosenbach fellow in bibliography U. Pa., 1976, NEH fellow, 1981-82, 84-85, 94-96, Inst. for Advanced Studies fellow Jerusalem, 1991; J.R. Lyell reader in bibliogrpahy U. Oxford, 1991-92; vis. fellow Pembroke Coll., U. Oxford, 1992, Cambridge, 2000-01. Fellow Royal Hist. Soc., Medieval Acad. Am.; mem. Medieval Assn. Pacific (councillor 1965-68, pres. 1968-70), Medieval Acad. Am. (councillor 1977-80), Comité international de paléographie (treas. 1985-90), Comité international du vocabulaire des institutions et de la communication intellectuelles au moyen age, 1987—, Societa internazionale per lo studio del medioevo latino, 1988—. Home: 11444 Berwick St Los Angeles CA 90049-3416 Office: U Calif Dept History Los Angeles CA 90024 E-mail: rouse@history.ucla.edu.

ROUSE, ROBERT KELLY, JR. judge; b. Lexington, Ky. s. Robert Kelly and Luane (Adams) R.; m. Donna R. Walker, Dec. 21, 1969; children: Kelly B., Erin E. Smith. AA, Daytona Beach (Fla.) C.C., 1966; BS, Fla. State U., 1968; JD, U. Fla., 1974. Bar: Fla. 1975. Ptnr. Regency Talent, Daytona Beach, 1968-69; supr. food divsn. Walt Disney Co., Anaheim, Calif., 1969-70; mgr. restaurants Walt Disney World Co., Orlando, Fla., 1970-71; from assoc. to ptnr. Smalbein, Eubank, Johnson, Rosier & Bussey, P.A., Daytona Beach, 1974-81; ptnr. Smith, Schoder, Rouse & Bouck, P.A., 1981-95; circuit judge State of Fla., 1995—; chief judge Seventh Jud. Cir., 1999—. With USAR, 1969-75. Mem. Am. Bd. Trial Advs., Volusia County Bar Assn. (pres. 1989-90), Volusia Civil Trial Attys. Assn. (pres. 1993-95). Office: Volusia County Courthouse Annex 125 E Orange Ave Ste 307 Daytona Beach FL 32114-4420

ROUSE, ROSCOE, JR. librarian, educator; b. Valdosta, Ga., Nov. 26, 1919; s. Roscoe and Minnie Estelle (Corbett) R.; m. Charlie Lou Miller, June 23, 1945; children: Charles Richard, Robin Lou. BA, U. Okla., 1948, MA, 1952; MALS, U. Mich., 1958, PhD, 1962; student (Grolier Soc. scholar), Rutgers U., 1956. Bookkeeper C & S Nat. Bank, Valdosta, Ga., 1937-41; draftsman R.K. Rouse Co. (heating engrs.), Greenville, S.C., 1941-42; student asst. U. Okla. and Rice U., 1947-48; asst. librarian Northeastern State Coll., Tahlequah, Okla., 1948-49, acting librarian, instr. library sci., 1949-51; circulation librarian Baylor U., 1952-53, acting univ. librarian, 1953-54, univ. librarian, prof., 1954-63, chmn. dept. library sci., 1956-63; dir. libraries State U. N.Y. at Stony Brook, L.I., 1963-67; dean libr. svcs., prof. Okla. State U., Stillwater, 1967-87, univ. libr. historian, 1987-92, chmn. dept. libr. edn., 1967-74. Vis. prof. U. Okla. Sch. Library Sci., summer 1962, N. Tex. State U., summer 1965; acad. library cons.; mem. AIA-Am. Library Assn. Library Bldg. Awards Jury, 1976; bd. dirs. Fellowship Christian Libr. and Info. Specialists. Author: A History of the Baylor University Library, 1845-1919, 1962; editor: Okla. Librarian, 1951-52; co-author: Organization Charts of Selected Libraries, 1973; A History of the Okla. State U. Library, 1992; contbr. articles, book revs., chpts. to publs. in field. Bd. dirs. Okla. Dept. Librs., 1989-92, chmn., 1990-92. 1st lt. USAAF, 1942-45. Decorated Air medal with 4 oak leaf clusters; recipient citation Okla. State Senate, 1987, Rotary Outstanding Achievement award, 1996; named in 150 Prominent Individuals in Baylor's History. Mem. ALA (life, mem. coun. 1971-72, 76-80, 83-84, 84-88, chmn. libr. orgn. and mgmt. sect. 1973-75, planning and budget assembly 1978-79, coun. com. on coms. 1979-80, bldgs. and equipment sect. exec. bd. 1979-80, chmn. bldgs. for coll. and univ. librs. com. 1983-85, chmn. nominating com. libr. history roundtable 1993-94), AARP, (sec. local chpt. 1998-2000), Okla. Libr. Assn. (life, pres. 1971-72, ALA coun. rep. 1976-80, 83-84, OLA Disting. Svc. award 1979, Spl. Merit award 1987), S.W. Libr. Assn. (chmn. coll. and univ. div. 1958-60, chmn. scholarship com. 1968-70), Internat. Fedn. Libr. Assns. (standing com. on libr. bldgs. and equipment 1976-88), Assn. Coll. and Rsch. Librs. (chmn. univ. librs. sect. 1969-70, mem. exec. bd. and rep. to ALA Coun., 1971-72), U. Mich. Sch. Libr. Sci. Alumni Soc. (pres. 1979-80, Alumni Recognition award 1988), mem. Alumni Found. Com., 1992-94, Payne County Ret. Educators Assn. (v.p., pres. elect 1991-92, pres. 1992-93), Okla. State U. Emeriti Assn. (pres. 2000-01), Okla. Hist. Soc. (com. on Okla. Higher Edn. mus. 1985—), Stillwater Rotary Club (pres. 1980-81, Rotarian of Yr. 1999), Beta Phi Mu. Baptist (chmn. bd. deacons 1973). Clubs: Archons of Colophon, Stillwater Rotary (dir. 1978-82, pres. 1980-81). *It is sometimes a hidden influence in our lives which drives us toward a set goal. We ourselves may not recognize the real source of that urge to fulfill a dream. Only after many years was I able to look back and discern the factors in my youth that pushed me toward my goal of attaining a good education. They grew out of the influence that the Great Depression had on my early life. Because of that experience the preparation for a career became my first goal in life, yet the ways and means for achieving it were virtually nonexistent. It was to be, however, and I was fortunate to realize that goal. It causes me to think now that perhaps the degree of determination and endurance one possesses is paced more by adverse condition than by times of comfort and ease.*

ROUSE, TERRIE SUZITTE, performing arts association administrator, museum director, consultant; b. Youngstown, Ohio, Dec. 2, 1952; d. Eurad R. and Florence (Wilcox) R.; 1 child, Malcolm Adam. BA, Trinity Coll., 1974; MS in Profl. Studies, Cornell U., 1977; certificate Internat. Affairs, MA, Columbia U., 1979. Mgr., curator Adam Clayton Powell St. Office Bldg., N.Y.C., 1979-81; sr. curator Studio Mus. Harlem, 1981-86; dir. mus. N.Y.C. Transit Mus., Bklyn., 1986—; artistic dir. Atlanta Ballet, 2002—. Advisor Bellevue Hosp. Art Bd., 1981—. Contbr. articles to profl. jours. Mem. Conf. Mil. Transp. Ofcls. Named Outstanding Young Women Am., 1981-83. Mem. Am. Assn. Museums (assessor 1981—). Avocations: sewing, reading, exploring Harlem, doll collecting. Home: 600 State Dr Los Angeles CA 90037-1267 Office: Atlanta Ballet 1400 W Peachtree St NW Atlanta GA 30309*

ROUSE, WILLIAM BRADFORD, systems engineering executive, researcher, educator; b. Fall River, Mass., Jan. 20, 1947; s. Gaylor Louis Rouse and Barbara (Peirce) Rouse Sherman; m. Sandra Howard Kane, Sept. 8, 1968; children: Rebecca Kane, William Howard. BSME, U. R.I., 1969; SM, MIT, 1970, PhD, 1972. Postdoctoral rsch. assoc. MIT, Cambridge, 1972; asst. prof. Tufts U., Medford, Mass., 1973; prof. U. Ill., Urbana, 1974-81; prof., chair indsl. and systems engring. Ga. Inst. Tech., Atlanta, 1981—; CEO Enterprise Support Sys., Inc., Norcross, 1995—. Author/editor 21 books; also numerous chpts., articles. Recipient O. Hugo Schuck award Am. Automatic Control Council, 1979. Fellow IEEE (Centennial medal 1984, 3d Millennium Medal 2000), Human Factors Soc.; mem. NAE, Systems, Man and Cybernetics Soc. of IEEE (pres. 1982-83, Norbert Wiener award 1986, Joseph Wohl award 2001), Unitarian-Universalist Assn. Home: 2389 Littlebrooke Dr Atlanta GA 30338-3187 Office: Enterprise Support Syss 3295 River Exch Dr Ste 125 Norcross GA 30092-4248 E-mail: rouse@mindspring.com.

ROUSH, DR. CLARK ALAN, music educator, conductor; b. Sioux City, Iowa, Sept. 23, 1958; s. Robert Gene and Barbara Elizabeth Roush; m. Sue Morris Morris, May 7, 1981; children: Matthew Clifton, Mitchell Clark. PhD, U. of Nebr., Lincoln, NE, 1991—95. Chair, music dept. York Coll., York, Nebr., 1986—. Author: (journal article) Teaching Music. Mem. Leadership York, York, Nebr., 1996—2000. Mem.: Nebr. Choral Directors Assn. (treas. 1991—95, Grad. Scholarship Award 1992), Nat. Assn. for Music Edn., Am. Choral Directors Assn. (life). R-Liberal. Church Of Christ. Achievements include Dale R. Larsen Teacher of Achievement. Avocations: golf, reading, viewing sporting events. Home: 525 Ohio Avenue York NE 68467 Office: York College 1125 E 8th St Ste 438 York NE 68467-2699 Office Fax: 402-363-5716. Personal E-mail: cr80947@alltel.net. E-mail: croush@york.edu.

ROUSH, JACK, professional sports team executive; b. Covington, Ky., Apr. 19, 1942; m. Pauline Roush; children: Susan, Patricia, Jack Jr. Math. degree, Berea Coll., 1964; M in Sci. Math., Ea. Mich. U., 1970. Team owner Roush Racing, Concord, NC, 1982—; with processing of car assembling and tooling Ford Motor Co., 1964—69; joined racing group The Fastbacks, 1966—70; engr. Chrysler, 1969—70; ptnr. with Wayne Gapp NHRA, IHRA, AHRA; founder Jack Roush Performance Engring., 1976; formed partnership Zakspeed Racing, 1982. Tchr. math., physics, automotive subjects Monroe (Mich.) C.C., 1971—72; chmn. bd. Roush Enterprises. Recipient winner NHRA championship, 1973, winner IHRA Pro Stock World championship, 1974. Office: Roush Racing 7020 Aviation Blvd Concord NC 28027-8196

ROUSH, WILLIAM R. chemistry educator; BS in Chemistry, UCLA, 1974; PhD in Chemistry, Harvard U., 1977. Disting. prof. chemistry dept. Ind. U., Bloomington; Warner Lambert Park Davis prof. chemistry, chair chemistry U. Mich., Ann Arbor, 1997—. Recipient Arthur C. Cope Scholar award Am. Chem. Soc., 1994, Alan R. Day award Phila. Organic Chemist's Club, 1992. Office: U Mich Dept Chemistry Ann Arbor MI 48109

ROUSSEAU, EUGENE ELLSWORTH, musician, music educator, consultant; b. Blue Island, Ill., Aug. 23, 1932; s. Joseph E. and Laura M. (Schindler) R.; m. Norma J. Rigel, Aug. 15, 1959; children— Lisa-Marie, Joseph. B of Mus Edn., Chgo. Mus. Coll., 1953; MusM, Northwestern U., 1954; student, Paris Conservatory of Music, 1960-61; PhD, U. Iowa, 1962. Instr. Luther Coll., 1956-59; asst. prof. Cen. Mo. State Coll., 1962-64; prof. music Ind. U., Bloomington, 1964-88, disting. prof. music, 1988—; prof. U. Minn., 2000—. Guest prof. U. Iowa, 1964, Hochschule fur Musik, Vienna, Austria, 1981-82, Ariz. State U., 1984, Prague Conservatory Music, 1985, Showa Coll. Music, 1996, 98, Tokyo Coll. Music, 1997, Paris Conservatory, 1997; tchr. U. Wis.-Ext., 1969—; R&D of saxophone mouthpieces; music arranger; svc. on numerous acad. coms.; tchr. 1st course in saxophone Mozarteum in Salzburg, Austria, 1991—; mem. jury Munich Internat. competitions, 1987, 90, 2001, pres. of juries, 1991-92; first solo saxophonist to perform on Prague Spring Festival, 1993; mem. jury Can. Nat. Music competition, 1994; juror Japan Wind and Percussion Competition, 1997; v.p. jury Adolphe Sax Internat. Competition, Belgium, 1998. Worldwide concert saxophonist; Carnegie Hall debut, 1965; author: Marcel Mule: His Life and the Saxophone, 1982, Saxophone High Tones, 1978, Method for Saxophone (2 vols.), 1975; performer 1st solo saxophone recitals, several European cities, 1st Am. solo saxophone performance in Japan, 1984; 1st to record concert saxophone on compact disc (Delos); radio broadcasts in Berlin, Bremen, London, Montreal, Ostrava, Paris, Prague, Toronto, Vienna; saxophone recs. for Deutsche Gramophon, Golden Crest, Coronet, Delos, Liscio, ALM, McGill and RIAX. Instr., asst. band leader 25th Infantry Div. U.S. Army, 1954-56. Named Hon. Prof. Music, Prague Conservatory, 1993, Braga Inst., Italy; recipient Edwin Franko Goldman award, ABA, 1995, Disting. Alumni award, U. Iowa, 1996; grantee, Fulbright Found., 1960—61, Rsch. and Exchange Bd., 1985, NEA, 1986. Mem. N.Am. Saxophone Alliance (pres. 1978-80), Comite Internat. de Saxophone (pres. 1982-85), Coll. Music Soc., Clarinet and Saxophone Soc. (U.K.), Music Tchrs. Nat. Assn. (Tchr. of Yr. award for Ind. 1993), Fulbright Assn. (life), World Saxophone Congress (co-founder 1969, pres. organizing com. 2000--). Office: U Minn Sch Music Minneapolis MN 55455 E-mail: rouss007@tc.umn.edu.

ROUSSEAU, GEORGE SEBASTIAN, eighteenth century studies educator, chamber musician; b. N.Y.C., Feb. 23, 1941; s. Hyman Victoire and Esther (Zacuto) R. BA, Amherst Coll., 1962; diploma, Am. Sch. Classical Studies, Athens, 1963; MA, Princeton U., 1964, PhD, 1966. Instr. English Harvard U., Cambridge, Mass., 1966-68; asst. prof. UCLA, 1968-70, prof. English, 1970-79, prof. 18th Century studies, 1980-94; Regius prof. English U. Aberdeen, Scotland, 1994—; dir. Thomas Reid Inst. Rsch. in Humanities, Scis., Medicine, 1994-98; rsch. prof. English De Montfort U., 1998—. Vis. fellow Magdalen Coll., Oxford U., 1993, Merton Coll., New Coll.,Oxford U., 1999; Fulbright vis. prof. U. Lausanne, 1994; award Leverhulme Trust, 1999—. Author: (with Marjorie Hope Nicolson) This Long Disease, My Life: Alexander Pope and the Sciences, 1968, The Rape of the Lock: Twentieth-Century Interpretations, 1969, The Augustan Milieu: Essays Presented to Louis A. Landa, 1970, (with Neil Rudenstine) English Poetic Satire: Wyatt to Byron, 1972, (with P.G. Boucé) Tobias Smollett: Bicentennial Essays Presented to L.M. Knapp, 1971, Organic Form: The Life of an Idea, 1972, Goldsmith: The Critical Heritage, 1974, (with Roy Porter) The Ferment of Knowledge: Studies in the Historiography of Science, 1980, The Letters and Papers of Sir John Hill, 1982, Tobias Smollett: Essays of Two Decades, 1982, (with Roy Porter) Sexual Underworlds of the Enlightenment, 1987, Exoticism in the Enlightenment, 1989, The Languages of Psyche: Mind and Body in Enlightenment Thought, 1990, Enlightenment Crossings, Perilous Enlightenment, Enlightenment Borders: Pre- and Post-Modern Discourses, 3 vols., 1991 (with others) Hysteria Beyond Freud, 1993 (with Roy Porter) Gout: The Patrician Malady, 1998; mem. editorial bd. The Eighteenth Century, 1974— , History of Psychiatry, 1990—; contbr. The Crisis in Modernism: Bergson and the Vitalist Tradition, 1992. Osgood fellow in lit. Princeton U., 1965-66; Am. Council Learned Socs. fellow, 1970; vis. fellow commoner Trinity Coll., Cambridge U., 1982; sr. Fulbright research prof. Sir Thomas Browne Inst., Leiden, Netherlands, 1983; Clark Library prof. U. Calif., 1985-86; sr. research fellow NEH, 1986-87 Mem. Am. Soc. 18th-Century Studies, MLA, History of Sci. Soc., Am. Hist. Assn. (1972), Am. Assn. History of Medicine, Royal Soc. Arts, Royal Soc. Medicine. Home and Office: Osterley House Wellshead Harwell nr Didcot Oxfordshire OX11 OHD England E-mail: gsr@dmu.ac.uk., george.rousseau@magdalen.oxford.ac.uk.

ROUSSEAU, IRENE VICTORIA, artist, sculptor; children: Douglas, Scott. BA, Hunter Coll., N.Y.C.; MFA, Claremont (Calif.) Grad. Sch., 1969; PhD, N.Y. U., 1977. Tenured prof. William Paterson Coll., Wayne, N.J., 1970-74. Invited spkr. Coll. Art Assn./Women Caucus on Art Conf., L.A., 1985, N.J. Ctr. for Visual Arts, Summit, N.J., 1985, Noyes Mus., 1994, Mus. African Art, 1994, Hillwood Art Mus.-C.W. Post/L.I. U., 2000, AIEMA IX Internat. Conf. on Antique and Medieval Mosaic Rsch., Rome, 2001; guest spkr. Internat. AIEMA Conf., Lausanne, Switzerland, 1997, invited guest spkr. Villeme Colloque Intl. de la Mosaique Antique, Univ. de Lausanne, Switzerland, 1997; spkr. Bridges: Math. Connections in Art, Music and Sci. Exhbns. include Betty

Parsons Gallery, N.Y.C., Claremonte Colls., State Mus. Sci. and Industry, L.A., Morris Mus. Arts and Scis., Morristown, N.J., The Bronx Mus. of Art, Galleri Sci. Agnes, Copenhagen/Roskilde, Denmark, Sculptors 5, Madison, N.J., Edmund Sci. Co., Barrington, N.J., AT&T World Hdqrs., Basking Ridge, N.J., N.J. Ctr. for Visual Arts, The Brotherhood Synagogue Holocaust Meml. Gramercy Pk. (mosaic), N.Y.C., 1986, 1st Internat. Art Biennale, Malta, 1995, U. Lausanne (Switzerland), 1997, Internat. Biennale Malta, 1997 (awards), Am. Inst. Archs., N.Y., 1998, Southwestern Coll., Kans., 1999, Lausanne, Switzerland, 2001; artist in residence Program Greece, 2000. Recipient seven 1st prize awards for creative work in N.J., ER Squibb and Sons Sculpture award, AIA N.J. Presentation Design award, 1995, Internat. Art Biennale Malta Installatin award, 1997, Traveling Exhibit throughout Europe and Middle East and Africa of Winners of the 1997 Biennale in Malta, 1997-99. Mem. AIA (profl. affiliate N.J., N.Y., chmn. architecture dialogue com. Presentation award 1995), Internat. Sculptors Assn., Am. Abstract Artists (exhbn. chmn. 1978-79, pres. 1979-82), Fine Arts Fedn. (bd. dirs.), Coll. Art Assn., Women's Caucus on Art (conf. spkr.), Phi Delta Kappa. Home: 41 Sunset Dr Summit NJ 07901-2322 E-mail: Rousseau1@aol.com.

ROUSSEL, LEE DENNISON, economist; b. N.Y.C., May 15, 1944; d. Ethan Allen and Frances Isabel (Ferry) Dennison; m. Andre Homo Roussel, Sept. 6, 1980; children: Cecilia Frances, Stephanie Anne. AB, Wellesley Coll., 1966; MA, Northeastern U., 1973. Mgmt. intern U.S. Dept. HEW, 1966-68; with Planning Office Commonwealth of Mass., 1968-70; exec. dir. Gov.'s Commn. Citizen Participation, Boston, 1973; with Boston area office U.S. Dept. HUD, 1970-78; fgn. svc. officer USAID, 1978-99, with housing and urban devel. office, 1978-82, chief housing and urban devel. office for C.Am. Honduras, 1982-87, asst. dir. office housing and urban programs, 1987-91, country rep. for Czech and Slovak Fed. Rep., 1991-92, country rep. for Czech Rep., 1993-94; min. counselor, U.S. rep. to devel. assistance com. OECD, Paris, 1994-99; sr. advisor USAID, Panama, 1999—2002. Episcopalian. Office: 25 Appian Way Barrington RI 02806 also: USAID Unit 0949 APO AA 34002 9949 Panama E-mail: leeroussel@hotmail.com.

ROUSSEL, NORMAND LUCIEN, advertising executive; b. Bristol, Conn., July 15, 1934; s. Wilfred and Bernadette (Chaisson) R.; m. Barbara Rund, Dec. 3, 1960; children: Dean, Deena. BS, U. Hartford, 1962; MBA, U. R.I., 1967. Advt. salesman Hartford (Conn.) Courant, 1963; account exec. Bo Bernstein Advt., Providence, 1964-73; pres. Challenge Advt. Inc., 1973-93; dir. comm. City of Providence, 1993-96; pres. ABC Advt., Providence, 1996—. Served with USAF, 1952-56. Mem. R.I. Advt. Club, Epsilon Alpha Zeta. Home: 7 David Dr Johnston RI 02919-2215 Office: ABC Advt 214 Broadway Providence RI 02903-1677 E-mail: norm@home.com.

ROUSSELOT, PETER FRESE, consultant; b. N.Y.C., Jan. 7, 1942; s. Louis Marcel and Evelyn Valdez (Hastrup) R.; m. Mary Dumesnil, Cobb, Nov. 22, 1975; children: Laura Rodman, Richard Frese, Anne Stewart, Louise Dierks. BA summa cum laude, Yale U., 1963; LLB, Harvard U., 1966. Bar: U.S. Dist. Ct. D.C. 1967, U.S. Ct. Appeals (D.C. cir.) 1967, U.S. Ct. Appeals (3d cir.) 1993, U.S. Supreme Ct. 1970. Assoc. Hogan & Hartson, Washington, 1966-74, ptnr., 1975-94, mem. exec. com., 1986-88; mng. dir. corp. affairs So. Pacific Rail Corp., 1994-97; ind. internat. railroad cons., 1997—. Asst. to nat. co-chmn. Citizens for Robert F. Kennedy, Washington, 1968; Arlington (Va.) coord. Bill Bradley for Pres., 2000. Mem. Yale Club Washington, Phi Beta Kappa. Democrat. Episcopalian. Avocations: tennis, hiking, photography. Office: 3182 Key Blvd Arlington VA 22201-5065 E-mail: pfrou@aol.com.

ROUSSEY, ROBERT STANLEY, accountant, educator; b. N.Y.C., July 20, 1935; m. Jeanne Archer, May 8, 1965; children: Robert Scott, John Stephen. BS, Fordham U., 1957. CPA, N.Y., Japan. Staff acct. Arthur Andersen & Co., N.Y.C., 1957-63, mgr. N.Y.C. and Tokyo, 1964-69, ptnr. N.Y.C. and Chgo., 1969-92, dir. auditing procedures, 1977-92; prof. acctg. U. So. Calif., L.A., 1992—. Adj. prof. auditing Northwestern U. Kellogg Grad. Sch. Mgmt., 1990, 91; mem. coll. bus. adminstrn. adv. bd. Fordham U., 1999—. Edit. cons. Handbook of Corporate Finance, 1986, Handbook of Financial Markets and Institutions, 1987; mem. editl. bd. Advances in Accounting, 1987—, Jour. Internat. Acctg. Auditing and Taxation, 1991—, Auditing: A Journal of Theory and Practice, 1994—; mem. adv. bd. Internat. Jour. Acctg., 1998—; contbr. articles to profl. jours. Treas., bd. dirs. Kenilworth (Ill.) Community House, 1979-81, Troop 13 Boy Scouts Am., Kenilworth, 1978-80, St. Joseph's Ch. Men's Club, Bronxville, N.Y., 1971-73. With U.S. Army, 1958, 61-62. Mem. AICPA (chmn. EDP auditing stds. com. 1978-81, auditing stds. bd. 1986-90, MAS practice stds. and adminstrn. com. 1990-93, internat. spl. strategy com. 1997-98, internat. auditing stds. subcom. 1998—, internat. strategy com. 1998—), Am. Acctg. Assn. (v.p. auditing sect. 1987-90, pubs. com. 1993-96), Info. Systems Audit and Control Assn. (stds. bd. 1986-96, v.p., mem. internat. bd. dirs. 1996-2001, mem. audit com. 2000-01, internat. pres. 2001—), Ill. State Soc. CPAs, N.Y. State Soc. CPAs, Inst. Internal Auditors (bd. rsch. advisors 1986-99), Internat. Fedn. Accts. (internat. auditing practices com. 1990-2000, chmn. 1995-2000, EDP audit com. 1980-88), Met. Club (gov. 1977-78), Tokyo-Am. Club (life), Beaver Creek Club, Beta Alpha Psi, Beta Gamma Sigma. Republican. Roman Catholic. Avocations: skiing, sailing, tennis, karate. Office: U So Calif Dept Acctg Los Angeles CA 90089-0441

ROUSSO, DANIEL ELLIOTT, facial plastic surgeon, educator; b. Atlanta, Sept. 15, 1955; s. Morris D. and Corine Rousso; m. Nancy Popkin; children: Emily Beth, Craig Morris. BA, Emory U., 1977; MD, Med. Coll. Ga., 1981. Diplomate Am. Bd. Otolaryngology, Am. Bd. Facial Plastic and Reconstructive Surgery. Intern U. S.C. Sch. Medicine, Charleston, 1981-82; resident in otolaryngology Emory U., Atlanta, 1982-86; fellow in facial and plastic surgery McCollough Plastic Surgery Clinic, Birmingham, Ala., 1986-87; priv. practice. Mem. staff Eye Found. Hosp., Birmingham; clin. asst. prof. otolaryngology, U. Ala., Birmingham. Co-author: Facial Plastic Surgery Clinic, 1994; contbr. articles to profl. jours., chpts. to books. Mem. AMA, Am. Acad. Facial Plastic and Reconstructive Surgery, Am. Bd. Hair Restoration Surgery (bd. dirs.), Am. Acad. Otolaryngology, Head and Neck Surgery, Internat. Soc. Hair Restoration Surgery (pres. 2000). Office: Rousso Facial Plastic Surgery Clinic 2700 Highway 280 Ste 300-W Birmingham AL 35223-2420 E-mail: drousso@aol.com.

ROUSSOS, STEPHEN BERNARD, minister; b. Ft. Wayne, Ind., June 18, 1960; s. James Theodore and Louise Marie (Diller) R.; m. Tina Marie Priest, July 31, 1982; children: Stephanie Marie, Nathaniel David. BA, Diploma in Christian Edn., Taylor U., Ft. Wayne, 1982. Lic. min. Missionary Ch., 1982, ordained to ministry, 1985. Assoc., youth pastor Community Bible Ch., Lomita, Calif., 1982-85, sr. pastor, 1985-91, Freeman (S.D.) Missionary Ch., 1991—. Mem. pastoral com. Luis Palau Crusade, Redondo Beach, Calif., 1990-91; mem. S.E. S.D. Prayer Conf., vice chmn., 1995-97, chmn., 1997—; mem. Midwest Dist. Christian Edn. Com., 1994-97, dir., 1997—; mem. Midwest Dist. Exec. Bd., 1994-95, 97—; mem. bd. dirs. Rushmore/Borglum Ministries, 1993—, Freeman Cmty. Found., 1997-2000. Mem. Lomita/Harbor City Ministerial Assn. (treas. 1988-89, pres. 1989-91), Freeman Min. Assn., sec.-treas., 1992-93, pres., 1993-94). Republican. Office: Freeman Missionary Ch PO Box 460 Freeman SD 57029-0460

ROUSUCK, J. WYNN, theater critic; b. Cleve., Mar. 19, 1951; d. Morton I. and Irene Zelda (Winograd) R. BA summa cum laude, Wellesley Coll., 1972; MS, Columbia U., 1974. Assoc. editor, program guide, Sta. WCLV-FM, Cleve., 1972-73; theater and film reviewer Cleve. Press, 1973; gen. assignment arts reporter Balt. Sun, 1974-84, theater critic, 1984—. Instr. English Goucher Coll., Towson, Md., 1981; master critic O'Neill Critics Inst., Waterford, Conn., 1990—; theater critic Md. Pub. TV., 1986; spkr. in field. Recipient Dog Writers Assn. Am. awards 1977, 79, Md. chpt. 1st Place Arts Reporting award Soc. Profl. Journalists, 1993, Front Page award, Disting. Criticism Washington-Balt. Newspaper Guild, 1997, 99, Bill Pryor Meml. grand prize for writing, 1999; NEH journalism fellow U. Mich., 1979-80, fellow O'Neill Critics Inst., 1982. Mem. Balt. Bibliophiles (bd. dirs. 1982-83), Octavo Plus, Walters Art Gallery, Balt. Wellesley Club (pres. 1978-79). Jewish. Avocations: rare books, art, dogs. Office: The Baltimore Sun 501 N Calvert St Baltimore MD 21278-0001

ROUTH, DONALD K(ENT), psychology educator; b. Oklahoma City, Mar. 3, 1937; s. Ross Holland and Fay (Campbell) R.; m. Marion Starbird Wendler, Sept. 10, 1960; children: Rebecca Ann (dec.), Laura Diane. BA, U. Okla., 1962; PhD, U. Pitts., 1967. Diplomate Am. Bd. Profl. Psychology; lic. psychologist, Fla. Asst. prof. psychology and pediatrics U. Iowa, Iowa City, 1967-70, prof., 1977-85; assoc. prof. psychology Bowling Green State U., Ohio, 1970-71; assoc. prof. U. N.C., Chapel Hill, 1971-77; prof. psychology and pediat. U. Miami, Coral Gables, Fla., 1985—2002, prof. emeritus, 2002—. Chmn. behavioral medicine study sect. NIH, 1983-85 Editor Jour. Pediatric Psychology, 1976-82, Jour. Clin. Child Psychology, 1987-91, Jour. of Abnormal Child Psychology, 1992-98, Am. Jour. on Mental Retardation, 1998-2002; contbr. numerous articles to profl. jours., books Pres. Eno River Unitarian Universalist Fellowship, 1976-77. Recipient award for disting. contbn. Soc. Pediatric Psychology, 1981, Presidential award, 1988; Fla. Psychol. Assn. Research Psychologist of Yr. award, 1987, Reconocimiento, El Colegio Nacional de Psicologis de Mex., 1999. Mem. APA (pres. div. child, youth and family svcs., 1984, pres. div. on mental retardation 1987, pres. divsn. clin. psychol. 1998), Internat. Soc. Clin. Psychology (founder, pres. 1998-99), Disting. Profl. Contbns. to Clin. Psychology (sect. on clin. child psychology 1989, div. clin. psychology, 1992, Nicholas Hobbs award div. child youth and family svcs., 1996, Edgar A. Doll award divsn. mental retardation and devel. disabiities 2001). Democrat. Home: 20131 Seagrove St #402 Estero FL 33928 E-mail: drouth@miami.edu.

ROUTH, JOHN WILLIAM, lawyer; b. Knoxville, Tenn., Dec. 3, 1957; s. John C. and Mary (Parker) R.; m. Martha Carol Carter, Aug. 6, 1983; children: John Carter, Carol Ann. BA, U. Tenn., 1979, JD, 1983. Bar: Tenn. 1983, U.S. Dist. Ct. (ea. dist.) Tenn. 1983. Assoc. Francis W. Headman, Knoxville, 1983-87, Wm. R. Banks and Assocs., Knoxville, 1987-97; judicial commr. Knox County Gen. Sessions Ct., 1992-94; sole practice law, 1997—. Bd. dirs. Cerebral Palsy Ctr. for Handicapped Adults, Knoxville, 1985-88; chmn. adminstv. bd. Emerald Ave. United Meth. Ch., Knoxville, 1988-90, 98—. Mem. Tenn. Bar Assn., Knoxville Bar Assn., Tenn. Assn. Criminal Def. Lawyers, City Salesman Club (v.p. 1988, sec. 1987, pres. 1998). Methodist. Office: 4611 Old Broadway St Knoxville TN 37918-1784

ROUTLEY, LOWELL R. social services administrator, therapist; b. South Milw., Wis., June 7, 1945; s. Raymond W. and Laura S. (Orloff) R.; m. Terry L. Routley, June 3, 1967; children: Ramona S., Paula A. Diploma, Moody Bible Inst., 1966; BA, Greenville Coll., 1968; postgrad., U. Iowa, 1974; PhD, Walden U., 1978. Lic. counselor, Iowa. Dir., counselor Quad City Counseling Svc., Davenport, Iowa; adj. prof. Emmaus Bible Coll., Dubuque; pvt. practice counselor; employee assistance counselor Northwestern Bell, Davenport; assoc. prof. psychology Blackhawk Coll., Moline, Ill. Founder, pres. study group for MPD, Iowa. Mem. AACD, Am. Mental Health Counselors Assn. Home: 16 E 13th St Dubuque IA 52001-5007

ROUTMAN, DANIEL GLENN, business development executive, lawyer; b. Birmingham, Ala., July 26, 1961; s. Stanley and Joyce R.; m. Elizabeth Horchow, Mar. 9, 1991; children: Regen, Emily. BBA, U. Tex., 1983, JD, 1985. Bar: Tex. 1986. Assoc. Liddell, Sapp, Zivley & LaBoon, Austin, 1986-88, Baker & Botts, Dallas, 1989-91; assoc. gen. counsel Perot '92 Campaign/United We Stand Am., 1992-94; prin. Wilson Comms., 1994-95; dir. comms. C/Net: The Computer Network, San Francisco, 1996; v.p. bus. devel. Broadcast.com, Dallas, 1996-99; sr. dir. bus. devel. Yahoo!, Inc., 1999—. Mem. Dallas Assembly; adv. bd. The Family Gateway, Dallas, 1996—; chmn. jr. assocs. Dallas Mus. Art, 1991-92, Friends of the Ctr. for Human Nutrition U. Tex. Southwestern Med. Sch., 1992-96; trustee, exec. com., chmn. devel. com. Dallas Mus. Art, 1998—; bd. dirs. Tex. Bus. Hall of Fame, 2000—, N. Tex. Pub. Broadcasting (KERA Pub. TV), 2001-. Home: 5036 Seneca Dr Dallas TX 75209-2220 Office: Yahoo! Inc 301 N Crowdus St Dallas TX 75226-1436 E-mail: droutman@yahoo.com.

ROUTSON, CLELL DENNIS, manufacturing company executive; b. Elkhart, Ind., Oct. 8, 1946; s. Clell Dean and Olene Maize (Replogle) R.; m. Paula Leone McLallin, Sept. 2, 1967 (div. June 1988); children: Clell Dustin, Courtney Trevor; m. Suzann Kay Bron, 1995. BSBA, Ball State U., Muncie, Ind., 1971. With Proctor & Gamble, Cin., 1971-74; nat. sales mgr. Palmer Instruments, Inc., 1974-76; with Nordson Corp., Amherst, Ohio, 1976-81, MCC Powers, Cleve., Chgo., Singapore, 1981-86; sales mgr., v.p., pres. Burgess, Inc., Freeport, Ill., 1986-89; mgr. mktg. and sales, v.p. sales and mktg. Kloppenberg & Co., Englewood, Colo., 1990-92; v.p. ops., gen. mgr. T.E.I. Engineered Products, 1992-96; pres. (one-yr. contract) Balco Svc. Corp., 1996-97; pres. Composite Tek, Boulder, Colo., 2000—. Mng. dir. Resource Dynamics, Singapore, Chgo., and Denver, 1985-86, 96-99. Contbr. articles to profl. jours. Mem. Met. Club (Denver). Republican. Baptist. Office: Compositetek Mfg Co 6101 Lookout Rd Ste B Boulder CO 80301-3359 E-mail: croutson@compositetek.com.

ROUVILLOIS, PHILIPPE, research and development executive; Gen. adminstr. CEA, Paris, France, 1989-95; chmn. CEA Industrie, France, 1989-99, Institut Pasteur, Paris, France, 1997—; gen. fin. inspector France Ministry Econ., Fin. and Industry, France, 1999—. Office: Min Econ Fin and Industry 139 rue de Bercy 75572 Paris Cedex 12 France

ROUX, KERMIT LOUIS, III, lawyer; b. New Orleans, Aug. 24, 1969; s. Kermit Louis Jr. and Kathryn (Felt) R. BBA, So. Meth. U., 1991; JD, Tulane U., 1994. Bar: La. 1994, U.S. Dist. Ct. (ea., we., and mid. dists.) La. 1994. Atty. Lowe Stein Hoffman Allweiss & Hauver, New Orleans, 1994—. Bd. dirs. Audubon Capital Corp., New Orleans, Paradigm Devel. Corp., New Orleans, Typhon Group, L.L.C. Mem. Federalist Soc., New Orleans, 1994—, Greater New Orleans Republicans, New Orleans, 1994—; pro bono liaison New Orleans Pro Bono Project, 1995—; mem. fin. com. Immaculate Conception Ch., New Orleans, 1996. Mem. ABA, Fed. Bar Assn., La. Bar Assn., New Orleans Bar Assn. Republican. Roman Catholic. Avocation: competitive shooting. Home: 5200 Purdue Dr Metairie LA 70003-1043 Office: 701 Poydras St Ste 3600 New Orleans LA 70139-7735

ROUX, MILDRED ANNA, retired secondary school educator; b. New Castle, Pa., June 1, 1914; d. Louis Henri and Frances Amanda (Gillespie) R. BA, Westminster Coll., 1936, MS in Edn., 1951. Tchr. Farrell (Pa.) Sch. Dist., 1939-55; tchr. Latin, English New Castle (Pa.) Sch. Dist., 1956-76; ret., 1976. Chmn. sr. H.S. fgn. lang. dept. New Castle Sch. Dist., 1968-76, faculty sponsor sch. fgn. lang. newspapers, 1960-76, Jr. Classical League, 1958-76. Mem. Lawrence County Hist. Soc., Am. Classical League, 1958-76. Mem. AAUW (chmn. publicity, chmn. program com. Lawrence County chpt. 1992-96), Am. Assn. Ret. Persons, Nat. Ret. Tchrs. Assn., Pa. Assn. Sch. Retirees (chmn. cmty. participation com. Lawrence County br. 1976-81, telephone com. Lawrence County br. 1990-98), Coll. Club New Castle (chmn. sunshine com. 1989-91, mem. social com. 1991-92), Woman's Club New Castle (chmn. pub. affairs com. 1988-90, internat. affairs com. 1990-92, program com. 1990-92, telephone com. 1992-99). Republican. Roman Catholic. Avocations: church choir, reading, civic interests. Home: 6 E Moody Ave New Castle PA 16101-2356

ROUX, ROBERT JOSEPH, music educator, department chairman, musician; b. New Orleans, Feb. 19, 1949; s. George Joseph and Rachel Ryan Roux. MusB, Loyola U., New Orleans, 1970; MusM, U. Tex., 1978, D in Musical Arts, 1980. Assoc. prof. Wichita (Kans.) State U., Wichita, Kans., 1974—86, prof. Rice U., Houston, 1990—. Vis. lectr. Ariz. State U., Tempe, 1986—90; prof. Rice U., Houston, 1990—. Vis. lectr. U. N.C., Greensboro, NC, 1974; assoc. dir. piano masterclasses Prague (Czech Republic) Internat. , 1997—; chair performance com. World Piano Pedagogy Conf., Orlando, Fla., 2001. Musician piano solo. Artistic amb. U.S. Govt., 1985; advisor Gneissen Inst., Moscow, 2000. Named Steinway artist, Steinway Piano Co., N.Y.C., 1992; recipient 1st place, Nat. Biennial Piano Rec. Festival, 1959, 1st prize, Nina Wideman Competition, Shreveport, La., 1969, Silver medal, Internat. Rec. Competition, Nat. Guild, 1978. Mem.: Music Tchrs. Nat. Assn., Am. Liszt Soc. (bd. dirs. 2000—), Beethoven Soc. (bd. dirs. 1991—). Avocations: chess, stereophile. Home: 4655 Wild Indigo #275 Houston TX 77027 Office: Rice Univ Shepherd Sch Music 2900 Main St Houston TX 77027

ROUZE, JEFFREY ALAN, real estate executive; b. Rockford, Ill., Feb. 5, 1952; s. Robert Lloyd and Ellen Erma (Korpi) R. BBA in Real Estate Fin., U. Wis., 1974, MS in Bus. and Real Estate, 1977. Lic. real estate broker, Wis.; notary pub., Wis. Exec. mgmt. trainee Grootemaat Corp., Milw., 1977-79; real estate cons. CUNA Mut. Ins. Soc., Madison, 1979-84, real property and mortgage mgr., 1984-93, sr. asset mgr., 1994—2001; pres. Hollywood Econ. Alliance, 2002—. Treas. Strollers Theatre, Ltd., Madison, 1985-89; bd. dirs. Hollywood (Calif.) Entertainment Dist., 1998-99, Hollywood Historic Trust, 2000—; treas. St. Paul's Luth. Ch., Santa Monica, Calif., 2002—. Mem. Nat. Assn. Corp. Real Estate Execs. (master corp. real estate), Inst. Real Estate Mgmt. (cert. property mgr.), Mortgage Bankers Assn. Am., Urban Land Inst., Coml. Investment Real Estate Inst., Hollywood C. of C. (treas. 2002). Address: 530 S Barington Ave No 307 Los Angeles CA 90049 E-mail: jarouze@earthlink.net.

ROVE, FRANCES ANN, lawyer; b. Conroe, Tex., Jan. 28, 1960; d. James Vincent and Frances M. (Cashin) R. BS, U. Kans., 1981, JD, 1985. Bar: Kans. 1985, Mo. 1988. Jud. clk. Johnson County Ct., Olathe, Kans., 1984-85; rsch. atty. Nat. Inst. for Child Support Enforcement, Chevy Chase, Md., 1985-86; trust adminstr. United Mo. Bank, N.A., Kansas City, 1986-88; mem. Linde, Thomson, Langworthy, Kohn & Van Dyke, P.C., 1988-90; chief dep., counsel Jackson County Pub. Adminstr., 1990-94, pub. adminstr., 1994—. Mem. ABA, Kans. Bar Assn., Kansas City Met. Bar Assn., Johnson County (Kans.) Bar Assn., Arc of Friends, Mo. Pub. Adminstrn. Assn., Nat. Guardianship Assn. (charter mem., registered guardian), Alliance for Mentally Ill, Midwest Bioethics, Assn. Women Lawyers. Roman Catholic. Office: Pub Adminstr Office 415 E 12th St Kansas City MO 64106-2706

ROVELL, MICHAEL JAY, lawyer; b. Chgo., Mar. 30, 1949; s. Bernard and Charlotte (Schaefer) R.; m. Laurie Strauss, Sept. 2, 1979; children: Brandon, Kendall, Ryan. BA with honors, U. Ill., Chgo., 1969; JD with honors, U. Ill., 1972. Bar: Ill. 1972, U.S. Dist. Ct. (no. and so. dists.) Ill. 1972, U.S. Ct. Appeals (7th cir.) 1973, U.S. Ct. Appeals (8th cir.) 1981, U.S. Supreme Ct. 1983, U.S. Ct. Appeals (5th cir.) 1986, U.S. Ct. Appeals (1st cir.) 1990, U.S. Dist. Ct. P.R. 1992, U.S. Ct. Appeals (10th cir.) 1992, U.S. Ct. Appeals (3rd cir.) 1993, U.S. Ct. Appeals (2nd cir.) 1996, U.S. Ct. Appeals (9th cir.), 1997, Belgium 1997. Assoc. Jenner & Block, Chgo., 1972-78, ptnr., 1979-90; prin. Law Offices of Michael J. Rovell, 1990—. Dir. Cook County Spl. Bail Project, 1972-74; chief exec. officer, bd. dirs. Sunbelt Communications, Colorado Springs, Colo., 1976-78; of counsel Wampler, Buchanan & Breen, Miami, Troncoso & Becker, San Juan, P.R., Law Offices of Robert Bright, Oklahoma City and affiliate offices London, Paris, Brussels; bd. editors U. Ill. Law Forum, 1971-72. Bd. dirs. Steppenwolf Theatre, Chgo., 1979-81. Mem. ABA (coord. litigation seminar on electronic surveillance), Ill. Bar Assn., Hillcrest Country Club (Long Grove, Ill.). Avocations: golf, tennis, bowling. Home: 1516 Christina Ln Lake Forest IL 60045-3848 Office: 20 N Clark St Ste 2450 Chicago IL 60602-5002

ROVELSTAD, GORDON H. dentist, researcher; b. Elgin, Ill., May 19, 1921; s. Henry Randolph and Margot Helen (Greenhill) R.; m. Barbara Jean Johnson, Apr. 8, 1945; children: Craig Gordon, Martha Kay, Andrew Todd. Student, St. Olaf Coll., 1939-41; DDS, Northwestern U., Chgo., 1944, MSD, 1948, PhD, 1960; DSc (hon.), Georgetown U., 1970. Diplomate Am. Bd. Pediatric Dentistry. Asst. prof. pediatric dentistry Northwestern U., Chgo., 1946-53; head dental dept. Children's Meml. Hosp., 1948-53; ensign USNR, 1943, advanced through grades to capt. Va., 1945-46; with USNTC USN, Bainbridge, Md., 1954-59; dir. rsch. U.S. Naval Dental Sch., Bethesda, 1960-65; officer in charge U.S. Naval Dental Rsch. Inst., Gt. Lakes, Ill., 1965-69; dir. rsch. USN Dental Corp., Washington, 1969-74; asst. dean, prof. U. Miss. Sch. Dentist, Jackson, 1974-80; exec. dir. Am. Coll. Dentists, Gaithersburg, Md., 1981-94, exec. dir. emeritus, 1994—; pres. William J. Gies Found., 1982-98, pres. emeritus, 1998—. Contbr. articles to profl. jours. Fellow Am. Coll. Dentists (pres., v.p.), Internat. Coll. Dentists, N.Y. Acad. Sci., N.Y. Acad. Dentists; mem. ADA, Am. Acad. Pediatric Dentistry (pres., v.p.), Internat. Assn. Dental Rsch. (pres., v.p., sec.), Rotary Internat., Sigma Xi. Avocations: miniatures, music, golf, fishing. Home: 11301 Tooks Way Columbia MD 21044-1049

ROVELSTAD, MATHILDE VERNER, library science educator; b. Kempten, Germany, Aug. 12, 1920; came to U.S., 1951, naturalized, 1953; d. George and Therese (Hohl) Hotter; m. Howard Rovelstad, Nov. 23, 1970. PhD, U. Tubingen, 1953; MS in L.S, Catholic U. Am., 1960. Cataloger Mt. St. Mary's Coll., Los Angeles, 1953; sch. librarian Yoyogi Elem. Sch., Tokyo, 1954-56; mem. faculty Cath. U. Am., 1960-90, prof. library sci., 1975-90, prof. emeritus, 1990—. Vis. prof. U. Montreal, 1969 Author: Bibliotheken in den Vereinigten Staaten, 1974; translator Bibliographia, an Inquiry into its Definition and Designations (R. Blum), 1980, Bibliotheken in den Vereinigten Staaten von Amerika und in Kanada, 1988; contbr. articles to profl. jours. Research grantee German Acad. Exch. Svc., 1969, Herzog August Bibliothek Wolfenbüttel, Germany, 1995. Mem. ALA (internat. relations com. 1977-80), Internat. Fedn. Library Assns. and Instns. (standing adv. com. on library schs. 1975-81), Assn. for Library and Info. Sci. Edn. Home: Apt HR-T35 719 Maiden Choice Ln Catonsville MD 21228-6231 Office: Cath U Am Sch Libr & Info Sci Washington DC 20064-0001

ROVER, EDWARD FRANK, lawyer; b. Oct. 4, 1938; s. Frederick James and Wanda (Charkowski) R.; m. Maureen Wyer, June 15, 1968; children: Elizabeth, Emily, William. AB, Fordham U., 1961; JD, Harvard U., 1964. Bar: N.Y. 1964, U.S. Tax Ct. 1968, U.S. Dist. Ct. (so. dist.) N.Y. 1975, U.S. Supreme Ct. 1994. Assoc. White & Case, N.Y.C., 1964-71, ptnr., 1972—. Bd. dirs. Cranshaw Corp., N.Y.C., Harvard-Mahoney Neurosci. Inst., Boston, Waterford Sch., Sandy, Utah, Dana-Farber, Boston, Norton Simon Art Mus., L.A., Rumsey-Carter Found., Geneva, Charles A. Dana Found., N.Y.C.; pres. Dana Found.; sec. Solomon R. Guggenheim Found. Mem. ABA, N.Y. Bar Assn., N.Y. County Lawyers Assn., Assn. Bar City N.Y., Century Assn., Scarsdale Golf Club, Harvard Club, Univ. Club. Avocations: sailing, skiing. Home: 1111 Park Ave New York NY 10128-1234 Office: White & Case Bldg Ll 1155 Avenue Of The Americas New York NY 10036-2787 E-mail: Roveref@usa.net.

ROVIGO, CONNIE BRIGITTA, jewelry and fine arts retailer; b. Bklyn., Oct. 22, 1962; d. Louis and Marta Rovigo. AS in Biology, Queens Coll., 1982; BFA, N.Y. Inst. Tech., 1991. With N.Y.C. Emergency Med. Svcs., 1983-87; tech. illustrator Vantage Art Inc., Massapequa, N.Y., 1987-92; graphic artist Rovigo Graphics, Woodstock, 1992—; jewelry designer, manufacturer Cavallo, Red Hook, 1998—. Instr. riding Silver Springs Ranch, Haines Falls, NY, 1992—97; graphic artist, advt. cons. ; instr. of dressage and hunter, jumpers Green Heron Farm, Woodstock, 1992—2001. Designer fine jewelry 21st Century Fox, 1998, Star of Woodstock, 1998. Avocations: equestrian activities, alternative/herbal medicines, reading, jogging, fitness. Office: Cavallo 4B Tobacco Ln Red Hook NY 12571-1711

ROVIN, ROBERT HARRY, body work practitioner, educator, performer; b. Chgo., May 30, 1941; s. Adolph Isaac and Ruthe (Solomon) Rovin; m. Yvonee Madera Jaffe, June 20, 1988 (div. Jan. 1995); children: Oren Jaffe, Kai Jaffe. BS in Speech, Northwestern U., 1963. Cert. Rosen Method body worker. Practitioner of Rosen Method body work in pvt. practice, Palo Alto and San Rafael, Calif., 1987—; tchr. mindful movement Palo Alto Rsch. Ctr., 1997—. Sec. bd. dirs. Heart of Humanity, Novato, Calif., 1998. Vol. for Marin AIDS Project, San Rafael, 1994-2000, resource counselor for Homeward Bound. Mem. Green Party. Avocations: dancing, storytelling, hiking, swimming, reading. E-mail: gma@greenmanalive.com.

ROVINE, ARTHUR WILLIAM, lawyer; b. Phila., Apr. 29, 1937; s. George Isaac and Rosanna (Lipsitz) R.; m. Phyllis Ellen Hamburger, Apr. 7, 1963; children: Joshua, Deborah. AB, U. Pa., 1958; LLB, Harvard U., 1961; PhD, Columbia U., 1966. Bar: D.C. 1964, N.Y. 1984. Assoc. Curtis, Mallet-Prevost, Colt & Mosle, N.Y.C., 1964-66; asst. prof. Cornell U., Ithaca, N.Y., 1966-72; editor Digest of U.S. Practice in International Law U.S. Dept. State, Washington, 1972-75, asst. legal adviser, 1975-81, agt of U.S. Govt. to Iran-U.S. Claims Tribunal The Hague, Netherlands, 1981-83; of counsel Baker & McKenzie, N.Y.C., 1983-85, ptnr., then sr. ptnr., 1985—. Adj. prof. law Georgetown U., Washington, 1977-81; vis. lectr. law Yale U., 1998. Author: The First Fifty Years: The Secretary-General in World Politics, 1920-1970, 1970; editor: Digest of U.S. Practice in International Law, 1973, 74; co-editor: The Case Law of the International Court of Justice, 1968, 1972, 1974, 1976; contbr. articles Am. Jour. Internat. Law, 1977-87; also articles on internat. law. bd. editors Am. Jour. Internat. Law, 1977-87; also articles on internat. law. Mem. panel on settlement of transnat. bus. disputes, N.Y. panel Ctr. for Pub. Resources; chmn. law subcom. of internat. adv. coun. on profl. edn. Coun. on Internat. Ednl. Exch.; mem. Coun. on Fgn. Rels. Mem. ABA (chmn. internat. law sect. 1985-86, del. to Ho. of Dels. 1988-90), Am. Soc. Internat. Law (cert. of merit 1974, exec. coun. 1975-77, v.p. 1998-99, pres. 2000—), U.S. Coun.

for Internat. Bus. (arbitration com.), Am. Arbitration Assn. (panel of arbitrators), Assn. Bar City N.Y. (coun. on internat. affairs). Home: 215 East 68th St New York NY 10021 Office: Baker & McKenzie 805 3rd Ave New York NY 10022-7513 E-mail: arthur.w.rovine@bakernet.com.

ROVINSKY, JOSEPH JUDAH, obstetrician, gynecologist; b. Phila., Sept. 4, 1927; s. Israel and Sarah (Blackman) R.; m. Judith S. Levin, June 24, 1964; children: Audrey, John, Jill, Michael, Paul, David. BA, U. Pa., 1948, MD, 1952. Diplomate Am. Bd. Ob-Gyn. Intern U. Pa. Hosp., Phila., 1952-53; resident in ob-gyn Mt. Sinai Hosp., N.Y.C., 1953-58; practice medicine specializing in ob-gyn, 1958—; chmn. dept. ob-gyn City Hosp. Center, Elmhurst, N.Y., 1964-74; prof. ob-gyn Mt. Sinai Sch. Medicine, N.Y.C., 1969-74; prof., chmn. dept. ob-gyn Sch. Medicine Health Scis. Center, SUNY, Stony Brook, 1975-79, prof., 1975-89; chmn. dept. ob-gyn L.I. Jewish Med. Center, 1973-92; prof. ob-gyn. Albert Einstein Coll. Medicine, 1989-94; dir. dept. ob/gyn. Sound Shore Med. Ctr. of Westchester, New Rochelle, 1992—. Mem. obstetric adv. com. N.Y.C. Dept. Health, 1964-92. Author: Medical, Surgical and Gynecological Complications of Pregnancy, 1961, 2d edit., 1965; editor: Davis' Gynecology and Obstetrics, 1968-73. Served to capt., M.C. USAF, 1964-66. Mem. ACS, Am. Coll. Obstetricians and Gynecologists, Am. Soc. Reproductive Medicine, Am. Uro-Gynecologic Soc., N.Y. Acad. Medicine, N.Y. Obstetrical Soc., N.Y. Gynecol. Assn., Med. Soc. State N.Y. Jewish. Office: Sound Shore Medical Center of Westchester 16 Guion Pl New Rochelle NY 10801-5500

ROVIRA, LUIS DARIO, state supreme court justice; b. San Juan, P.R., Sept. 8, 1923; s. Peter S. and Mae (Morris) R.; m. Lois Ann Thau, June 25, 1966; children— Douglas, Merilyn. BA, U. Colo., 1948, LL.B., 1950. Bar: Colo. 1950. Justice Colo. Supreme Ct., Denver, 1979-95, chief justice, 1990-95, ret., 1995. Mem. Pres.'s Com. on Mental Retardation, 1970-71; chmn. State Health Facilities Council, 1967-76; arbiter and mediator Jud. Arbiter Group, Denver. Bd. dirs Children's Hosp.; trustee Temple Buell Found. With AUS, 1943-46. Mem. ABA, Colo. Bar Assn., Denver Bar Assn. (pres. 1970-71), Colo. Assn. Retarded Children (pres. 1968-70), Alpha Tau Omega, Phi Alpha Delta. Clubs: Athletic (Denver), Country (Denver). Home: 4810 E 6th Ave Denver CO 80220-5137 Office: Judicial Arbiter Group 1601 Blake St Denver CO 80202

ROVISON, JOHN MICHAEL, JR. chemical engineer; b. North Tonawanda, N.Y., June 15, 1959; s. John Michael and Veronica Marie (Donat) R.; m. Beverly Jean Farinet, Sept. 6, 1986 (div. Oct. 1989); m. Janet Marie Konieczny, Apr. 27, 1991; 1 child, Kevin Michael (dec.). BA in Biology, BSChemE, Washington U., 1982; MS in Cancer Biology, Niagara U., 1986. Physics tchr. North Tonawanda High Sch., 1985; assoc. process engr. Ag Chem. Group FMC Corp., Middleport, N.Y., 1982-83, process engr. Ag Chem. Group, 1983-84, sr. process engr. Ag Chem. Group, 1986-90, sr. process engr. divsn. peroxygen chem. Buffalo, 1990-91, process group leader divsn. peroxygen chem., 1992-93, prod. area supr. divsn. peroxygen chem., 1993-94, prodn. mgr. PXD, 1994-96, plant tech. mgr. AOD, 1996-2000, AOD process tech. and maintenance mgr., 2001—. Mem. new products evaluation bd. Chem. Engring. McGraw Hill, 1983-84; tech. cons. Ag Chem. Group FMC Corp., Middleport, 1985. Contbr. articles to profl. jours. Mem. Resolve through Sharing Parents Group, Williamsville, N.Y., 1992. Recipient FMC Ag Chem Group Tech. award, 1988, FMC Corp. Environ. Achievement award, 1996. Mem. Am. Inst. Chem. Engrs., Am. Chem. Soc. Roman Catholic. Achievements include research in effects of alcohol on S1 endonuclease, reduction of thermal hazards associated with persulfates production; integrated approach to process improvements, risk benefit evaluation to minimize capital expenditures; leading effort to implement first unionized empowered work system within FMC; converted waste stream into usable environmental remediation treatment process; re-designed Brazilian insecticide formulating plant to remediate a dust explosion hazard to keep market profitable. Home: 6066 Ward Rd Sanborn NY 14132-9366 Office: FMC Corp Sawyer Ave And River Rd Tonawanda NY 14150

ROVIT, SAM BRIAN, management consultant; b. Louisville, Jan. 24, 1958; s. Earl Herbert and Honey Weisenfeld Rovit; m. Abigail Caitlin Mackenzie, Feb. 2, 1985; children: Nathaniel, Emma, Eli. BA, Duke U., 1979; MA in Law and Diplomacy, Tufts U., 1987; MBA, Harvard U., 1989. Editor McGraw-Hill, Washington, 1981-82; pub. Dawon-Butwick, 1982-85; dir., v.p. Bain & Co., Chgo., 1989—. Mem. pres's coun. Mus. Sci. & Industry, Chgo., 1998—. Mem. Chgo. Club. Home: 702 W Schubert Ave Chicago IL 60614-1507 Office: Bain & Co Ste 4400 Sears Tower Chicago IL 60606

ROVITO, ANDREW, financial services executive; b. Neptune, N.J., Oct. 28, 1966; s. Joseph P. and Jane W. R. BS, George Washington U., 1989; MBA, Seton Hall U., 1996. With Prudential Investment Corp., Newark, 1989-92; investment analyst Prudential Power Funding, 1992-96; AVP project fin. Ogden Energy Group, Fairfield, N.J., 1996-2000; dir. fin. Intergen North Am., Houston, 2000—. Avocations: cycling, movies, reading, traveling. Office: Intergen North America 909 Fanin Ste 222 Houston TX 77010

ROVNER, ILANA KARA DIAMOND, federal judge; b. Riga, Latvia, 1938; arrived in U.S., 1939; d. Stanley and Ronny (Medalje) Diamond. AB, Bryn Mawr Coll., 1960; postgrad., U. London King's Coll., 1961, Georgetown U., 1961—63; JD, Ill. Inst. Tech., 1966; LittD (hon.) (hon.) , Rosary Coll., 1989, Mundelein Coll., 1989; DHL (hon.) (hon.) , Spertus Coll. of Judaica, 1992. Bar: Ill. 1972, U.S. Dist. . (no. dist.) Ill. 1972, U.S. Ct. Appeals (7th cir.) 1977, U.S. Supreme Ct. 1981, Fed. Trial Bar (no. dist.) Ill. 1982. Jud. clk. U.S. Dist. Ct. (no. dist.) Ill., Chgo., 1972—73; asst. U.S. atty. U.S. Atty.'s Office, 1973—77; dep. chief of pub. protection, 1975—76; chief pub. protection, 1976—77; dep. gov., legal counsel Gov. James R. Thompson, Chgo., 1977—84; dist. judge U.S. Dist. Ct. (no. dist.) Ill., 1984—92; cir. judge U.S. Ct. Appeals (7th cir.), 1992—. Mem. Gannon-Proctor Commn. on the Status of Women in Ill., 1982—84; mem. civil justice reform act adv. com. 7th Cir. Ct., Chgo., 1991—95, mem. race and gender fairness com., 1993—; mem. fairness com. U.S. Ct. Appeals (7th cir.), 1996—, mem. gender study task force, 1995—96; mem. jud. conf. U.S. Com. Ct. Adminstrn. Case Mgmt., 2000—. Ctrl. and East European law initiative vol. ABA, 1997—; trustee Bryn Mawr Coll, Pa., 1983—89; mem. bd. overseers Ill. Inst. Tech./Kent Coll. Law, 1983—; trustee Ill. Inst. Tech., 1989—; mem. adv. coun. Rush Ctr. for Sports Medicine, Chgo., 1991—96; bd. dirs. Rehab. Inst. Chgo., 1998—; bd. visitors No. Ill. U. Coll. Law, 1992—94; vis. com. Northwestern U. Sch. Law, 1993—98, U. Chgo. Law Sch., 1993—96, 2000—; chair Ill. state selection com. Rhodes Scholarship Trust, 1998—2000. Named Today's Chgo. Woman of the Yr., 1985, Woman of Achievement, Chgo. Women's Club, 1986; named one of 15 Chgo. Women of the Century, Chgo. Sun Times, 1999; recipient Spl. Commendation award, U.S. Dept. Justice, 1975, Spl. Achievement award, 1976, Ann. Nat. Law and Social Justice Leadership award, League to Improve the Cmty., 1975, Ann. Guardian Police award, 1977, Profl. Achievement award, Ill. Inst. Tech., 1986, Louis Dembitz Brandeis medal for Disting. Legal Svc., Brandeis U., 1993, 1st Woman award, Valparaiso U. Sch. Law, 1993, ORT Women's Am. Cmty. Svc. award, 1987—88, Svc. award, Spertus Coll. of Judaica, 1987, Ann. award, Chgo. Found. for Women, 1990, Arabella Babb Mansfield award, Nat. Assn. Women Lawyers, 1998, award, Chgo. Attys. Coun. of Hadassah, 1999, 1st Woman award, Georgetown U. Law Ctr., 2001, others, Hebrew Immigrant Aid Soc. Chgo. 85th Anniversary honoree, 1996. Mem.: Decalogue Soc. of Lawyers (citation of honor 1991, Merit award 1997), Chgo. Coun. Lawyers, Chgo. Bar Assn. (commendation def. of prisoners com. 1987), Women's Bar Assn. Ill. (ann. award 1989, 1st Myra Bradwell Woman of Achievement award 1994), Fed. Judges Assn., Fed. Bar Assn. (mem. selection com. Chgo. chpt. 1977—80, treas. 1978—79, sec. 1979—80, 2d v.p. 1980—81, 1st v.p. 1981—82, pres. 1982—83, 2d v.p. 7th cir. 1983—84, v.p. 7th cir. 1984—85), Kappa Beta Pi, Phi Alpha Delta (hon.). Office: 219 S Dearborn St Ste 2774 Chicago IL 60604-1803

ROVNER, LEONARD IRVING, education educator; b. Phila. s. Harry and Fay (Rosenberg) R.; m. Nov. 21, 1970; children: Alisha, Allison. BS in Edn., Temple U., 1953, MS in Edn., 1957; PhD, Tianjin Coll. (China) and U., 1999. Cert. sch. adminstr., supt. schs., prin./supr., N.J.; cert. prin., supt. schs., Pa. Instr. psychology Temple U., Phila., 1960-65; mus. tchr. Acad. Natural Scis., 1960-65; tchr. Sch. Dist. of Phila., 1953-60, prin. at large, 1965-70, asst. to supt., 1970-74; prin. McCall Sch., Phila., 1974-94; adj. prof. edn. Coll. Edn., coord. Sch. Bus. and Mgmt. Temple U., 1994—, prof. edn. Exec. dir., bd. dirs. Prin. Ctr., Phila. Chmn. Prin.'s Ctr., 1991-93; advisor Kasetsart U., Bangkok, Thailand; guest prof. fine arts, Tianjin. Mem. editorial bd. Reflections--Jour. of Nat. Newtork of Prin. Ctrs. at Harvard. Mem. Police Adv. Com., Phila., 1991-95; mem. exec. bd. Phila. Prins.' Ctr. and Nat. Network of Prins.' Ctrs. at Harvard; mem. Mayor's Adv. Coun., Cherry Hill, N.J., 1989-94; chmn. Cherry Hill Hist. Commn., 1989-92, 94, mem., 1995; Sino-Am. Ambassador of Friendship, Tianjin. Citation recipient Phila. City Coun., 1989; recipient Rose Lindenbaum Prin. of Yr. award, 1971, Letter of Commendation, Pres. George H.W. Bush, Washington, 1989; named Hon. Headmaster, Hon. Chancellor of Edn., Hon. Prof., Tianjin. Mem. Ednl. Dynamics Cons. Orgn. (pres.), Assn. for Supervision and Curriculum Devel., Phila. Assn. Sch. Adminstrn., Phi Delta Kappa. Avocations: photography, skiing, scuba diving, history, travel. Home: 26 Greensward Ct Cherry Hill NJ 08002-4702 E-mail: proflenr@aol.com.

ROWAN, C. PATRICK, art educator; b. Milw., Jan. 7, 1937; children: Edward (dec.), Raili, Moira; children from second marriage: Patrick, Annie. BS, U. Wis., 1962, BFA, 1968, MS, 1970; MFA, U. Fla., 1971. Instr. painting U. Wis., Milw., 1969-70; instr. drawing U. Fla., Gainesville, 1970-71; prof. studio art U. Nebr., Lincoln, 1971—. One-man shows include St. John's-St. Benedict's Art Galleries, 1989—99, Carnegie Art Ctr., Kans., 1999, exhibitions include Religious Sculpture 2000 Cath. U., Washington, 2000, exhibitions include N.Am. sculpture, Golden, Colo., 2000, exhibitions include Response to the Holy Mich. St. Gallery, Chgo., 2000, exhibitions include Works in Faith 2000, Portland, Oreg., 2000, one-man shows include Profession, Creighton U., Omaha, 2001, McAuley Gallery, Mt. Mercy Coll., Cedar Rapids, Iowa, 2002. Office: U Nebr Dept Art and Art History Lincoln NE 68588-0114

ROWAN, CAROL BUETTNER, retired art educator; b. Shawno, Wis., Oct. 5, 1938; d. Delmar L. and Erna N. Buettner; children: Elisabeth E., Ellyn Rowan Ruhlmann. BS, U. Wis., Milw., 1961; MFA, Cranbrook Acad. Art, Bloomfield Hills, Mich., 1962. Tchr. of art West Allis (Wis.) Schs., 1969—98; retired, 1998. Exhibitions include Wild Apple Graphics, Woodstock, Vt., 1997—, Guilldmaster, Springfield, Mo., 1997—, Editions Ltd., Emeryville, Calif., 1999—, MCal, San Francisco, 1999—, Enesco, Itasca. Ill., 1999—, Elaine Erickson Gallery, Milw., —, Lakeside Gallery, —, Underwood Gallery, Wauwautosa, Wis., —, Represented in permanent collections Quadgraphics, Northwestern Mutual, Miller Brewing, Milw., Johnson Controls. Home and Studio: 2647 N Maryland Milwaukee WI 53211 E-mail: rowanart@earthlink.net.

ROWAN, JOHN PATRICK, city official; b. N.Y.C., Sept. 18, 1945; s. Patrick Joseph and Dorothy Wynn (McLaughlin) R.; m. Mariann Theresa Onorato, Jan. 1, 1988; children: Chad Hastaba, Keith Hastaba. BA in Polit. Sci., CUNY, 1971, MS in Urban Affairs, 1972. Cmty. liaison to Hon. Ben Rosenthal, U.S. Ho. of Reps., N.Y.C., 1973-77; dist. mgr. Cmty. Bd. 4 of Queens, 1977-86; chief investigator N.Y.C. Coun., 1986-95; adminstrv. staff analyst Office N.Y.C. Comptr., 1995—. Pres. Robert F. Kennedy Dem. Assn., N.Y.C., 1996-97. Sgt. USAF, 1965-67, Vietnam. Mem. Nat. Inst. Govtl. Purchasing (cert. profl. pub. buyer, cert. pub. purchasing officer), Vietnam Vets. Am. (pres. N.Y. State coun. 1995—). Roman Catholic. Avocation: veterans affairs. Home: 82-42 Penelope Ave Middle Village NY 11379 Office: Office NYC Comptroller 1 Centre St New York NY 10007-1602

ROWAN, JOHN ROBERT, retired medical center director; b. Joliet, Ill., Aug. 19, 1919; s. Hugh Hamilton and Elizabeth Margaret (Maloney) R.; m. Ruth Elaine Boyle, June 17, 1944; 1 child, Robert J. Student, Butler U., 1952-53, Ind. U., 1953-54. Personnel specialist VA Br. Office 7, Chgo., 1946; personnel officer VA Hosp., Ft. Benjamin Harrison, Ind., 1946-51, Indpls., 1951-56, asst. dir., 1960-67, asst. mgr. Mich., 1956-60; hosp. adminstrn. specialist VA Central Office, Washington, 1967-69; dir. VA Hosp., Manchester, N.H., 1969-71, Buffalo, 1971-72, VA Med. Center, Lexington, Ky., 1972-88, Montgomery, Ala., 1988-97, VA Med. Dist. 11, 1975-86; ret., 1997. Bd. dirs. Ind. div., 1966-67; bd. dirs. Western N.Y. Regional Med. Program, 1971-72, Eastern Ky. Health Systems Agy., 1976-79, United Way of Bluegrass, 1976-79, 82-85; mem. regional advisory council Ohio Valley Regional Med. Program, 1972-76; mem. State Health Planning Bd., 1982-88; bd. dirs. Hosp. Hospitality House of Lexington, 1981; mem. adv. coun. Cen. Ala. Aging Consortium, 1991; chmn. Montgomery Area Combined Fed. Campaign, 1991. Served in USAAF, 1942-46. Decorated Bronze Star; recipient Meritorious Svc. citations Ind. dept. DAV, 1964, Meritorious Svc. citations Ky. dept. Am. Legion, 1975, Meritorious Svc. citations Ky. dept. VFW, 1976, Meritorious Svc. citations Eastern Ky. U., 1974, Meritorious Svc. citations Ky. dept. DAV 1978, Spl. Recognition award VFW, 1982, cert. of Merit, DAV, 1982; recipient Dedicated Svc. to Vets. award DAV, 1984, Undersec. for Health Exec. Performance award DAV, 1990, Meritorious Svc. to Vets. award, Am. Legion, 1985, Meritorious Svc. award, Chpt. I, Ky. DAV, 1988, Network No 7 Directions Commendation, 1996, VA Performance award, 1990, Joint Fed. Campaign Meritorious Svc. award, 1990, Dedicated Svc. award DAV, 1992, McClusky award Ala. State Nurses Assn., 1993, Outstanding Svc. award U.S. Dept. Vets. Affairs, 1996, Meritorious Svc. award Ala. Vets. Affairs, 1996, commendation Vets. Benifits Regional Office, 1996. Fellow Am. Coll. Healthcare Execs.; mem. Am. Hosp. Assn., Ala. Hosp. Assn. (profl. standards and quality assurance com. 1991-94), Ctrl. Ala. Hosp. Coun., Ala. Assn. Hosp. Execs., Assn. Mil. Surgeons U.S., Fed. Hosp. Inst. Alumni Assn. Roman Catholic. Home: 2213 Walbash Dr Montgomery AL 36116-2220

ROWAN, RICHARD LAMAR, business management educator; b. Guntersville, Ala., July 10, 1931; s. Leon Virgle and Mae (Williamson) R.; m. Marilyn Walker, Aug. 3, 1963; children: John Richard, Jennifer Walker. AB, Birmingham-So. Coll., 1953; postgrad., Auburn U., 1956-57; PhD, U. N.C., 1961. Instr. Auburn (Ala.) U., 1956-57, U. N.C., Chapel Hill, 1958-59, 60-61; lectr. U. Pa., Phila., 1961-62, asst. prof., 1962-66, asso. prof. industry, 1966-73, prof. industry, 1973—. Dir. indsl. research unit, 1989-91; co-dir. Ctr. for Human Resources, 1991—; visitor to Faculty Econs. and Politics Cambridge (Eng.) U., 1972; pvt. sector advisor U.S. State Dept. Com. on Internat. Investment and Multinational Enterprises, OECD, 1982-89; chmn. Labor Relations Council, 1985— . Author: (with H.R. Northrup) The Negro and Employment Opportunity, 1965, Readings in Labor Economics and Labor Relations, 5th edit., 1984, The Negro in the Steel Industry, 1969, The Negro in the Textile Industry, 1970, (with others) Studies of Negro Employment, 1970, Educating the Employed Disadvantaged for Upgrading, 1972, Collective Bargaining: Survival in the 1970's, 1972, Opening the Skilled Construction Trades to Blacks, 1972, The Impact of Government Manpower Programs, 1975, International Enforcement of Union Standards in Ocean Transport, 1977, The Impact of OSHA, 1978, Multinational Bargaining Attempts: The Record, the Cases, and the Prospects, 1980; (with H.R. Northrup) Employee Relations and Regulations in the 80s, 1982; (with others) Multinational Union Organizations in the Manufacturing Industries, (with D.C. Campbell) The Multinational Enterprises and the OECD Industrial Relations Guidelines, 1984, Trade Union Clout Erodes, But For How Long?, 1985, Employee Relations Trends and Practices in the Textile Industry, 1986; contbr. articles to profl. jours. Mem. personnel com. Del. Valley Settlement Alliance, 1966-68. Served with Transp. Corps U.S. Army, 1953-56. Mem. Indsl. Rels. Rsch. Assn. (sec. Phila. 1964-65), Acad. Internat. Bus., The Penn Club. Democrat. Episcopalian. Home: 113 Blackthorn Rd Wallingford PA 19086-6046 Office: U Pa Wharton Sch 3733 Spruce St Philadelphia PA 19104-6301

ROWAN, THOMAS BERNARD, III, political science educator; b. Nashville, Aug. 10, 1964; s. Thomas B. Jr. and Mary A. Rowan. BA with high honors, Vanderbilt U., 1986; MA, U. York, Eng., 1987; PhD, U. Chgo., 1993. Asst. prof. Chgo. State U., 1996-99, assoc. prof., 1999—. Mem. editl. com. New Asia Rsch. Inst., Seoul, 2000—; contbr. articles to profl. jours. Fellow, Rotary, 1986—87, U. Chgo., 1987—90, Korea Found., 2002. Mem. Am. Polit. Sci. Assn., Midwest Polit. Sci. Assn., Phi Beta Kappa. Office: Chgo State U SCI 116A 9501 S King Dr Chicago IL 60628 E-mail: TB-Rowan@csu.edu.

ROWAN, WILLIAM BOYD, parasitologist, author; b. Trenton, N.J., Jan. 27, 1927; s. Henry Madison and Margaret Boyd R.; m. Jeanette West, Aug. 19, 1949 (dec. 1993); children: Mark, Bernard, Kate; m. Effie Bennett, Feb. 19, 1994. BA, Cornell U., 1950, PhD, 1954. Rsch. asst. Cornell U., Ithaca, 1950-54; postdoctoral fellow NIH Okla. State U., Stillwater, 1954-56; sr. asst. scientist USPHS, San Juan, P.R., 1956-58, sr. scientist, 1962-63; asst. prof. Middlebury (Vt.) Coll., 1958-62; assoc. prof. U. Mont., Missoula, 1963-67, prof., 1967. Vis. scientist WHO in South Africa and Tanzania, 1960. Author: On the Spring Tide, 1998, Tales From Towhee Inn, 1999, Incident at Roan High Bluff, 2000; editor: Manila Diary, 1941-45, 2000. With U.S. Army, 1945-46.

ROWARK, MAUREEN, fine arts photographer; b. Edinburgh, Midlothian, Scotland, Feb. 28, 1933; came to U.S., 1960, naturalized, 1970; d. Alexander Pennycook and Margaret (Gorman) Prezdpelski; m. Robert Rowark, May 3, 1952 (div. July 1965). 1 child, Mark Steven. Student, Warmington Bus. Coll., Royal Leamington Spa, Eng., 1950-51, Royal Leamington Spa Art Sch.; diploma, Speedwriting Inst., N.Y.C., 1961; AS in Edn., St. Clair County Community Coll., Port Huron, Mich., 1977, AA, 1978. Supr. proof reading Nevin D. Hirst Advt., Ltd., Leeds, Eng., 1952-55; publicity asst. Alvis Aero Engines, Ltd., Coventry, Eng., 1955-57; adminstrv. asst. Port Huron Motor Inn, 1964-66; adminstrv. asst. pub. rels. dept. Geophysics and Computer Svcs., Inc., New Orleans, 1966-68; sales mgr. Holiday Inn, Port Huron, 1968-70; adminstrv. asst. Howard Corp., 1971-73; sales and systems coord. Am. Wood Products, Ann Arbor, Mich., 1973-74; systems coord. Daniels & Zermack Architects, 1974; systems coord., cataloger fine arts dept. St. Clair County Community Coll., Port Huron, 1976-79; freelance fine arts photographer, 1978—. Photographer Patterns mag. front cover, 1978, Erie Sq. Gazette, 1979, Bluewater Area Tourism Bur. brochure, 1989, 92, 95, 97, 2000, 2001, Corits Castle, Lexington, 2002, Port Huron, Can. Legion, Wyo., Ont. Br., 1987, 88—; Grace Episcopal Ch. Mariner's Day, Port Huron, 1987, 92-2001, Homes mag., 1989. Photographer (one-woman shows) Grace Episcopal Ch., 1995, Port Huron Mus., 1995, St. Clair River Remedial Action Plan, 1995 (Best in Landscape Category), Mich. Waterways Coun. Girl Scouts Exhibit, 1996, exhibited in internat. shows Ann. Ea. Mich. Internat. Juried Exhbn., yearly , 1981—98 (Award of Excellence, 1982, Award of Excellence, 1983, Best Photography award, 1995, Best Photography award, 1996, Best Photography award, 1997), exhibited in group shows Ann. Ea. Mich. Internat. Juried Exhbn. , 2000, exhibited in internat. shows Our Town Juried Exhbn., 1997, St. Clair County C.C., 1983, 1986 (Award of Excellence, 1986), Gallery Lambton Juried Exhbn., Sarnia, Ont., Can., 1983—92 (Best Photography, 1988), 1994, 1996, 1997, 2000, Bluewater Bridge Juried Exhibit, 1988, Kaskilaaksontie Exhibit, Finland, 1991 (Par Excellence award), Swann Gallery, Detroit, 1996, St. Clair (Mich.) Art Gallery, Genesis Gallery, Lexington, Mich., others, represented in permanent exhibit Royal Can. Legion, Wyo. Br. Centaph, Capac State Bank, 1996, Grace Episcopal Ch., 1995, Thomas Edison Inn, Port Huron Hosp., 1996, Front Cover "Good Health News", 1997, costume modelling Bluewater Art Assn., 2000, 01, contbr. short stories to mags., photographer Bluewater Percussion Brochure , 2001. Cons., buyer interior decor Grace Episcopal Ch., 1994; active Port Huron Mus., 1978l; founder Red Hat Soc. Bluewater Les Chapeaux Rouge chpt., 2002. Recipient hon. mention Gallery Lambton, Sarnia, 1981, 2d pl. memoir writing women's history month St. Clair County C.C., 1999; winner 2d and 3d place awards Times Herald Newspaper, 1988, 1st place juried photography award Port Huron Art Festival, 1997. Mem. St. Clair County C.C. Alumni Assn., Phi Theta Kappa, Lambda Mu. Democrat. Episcopalian. Avocations: costumes and interior design, travel, theater, memoir writing. Home and Office: 3512 Walnut St Port Huron MI 48060 E-mail: ha-penerth-of-tar@prodigy.net.

ROWDEN, A(LPHRO) J(OHN), minister; b. Maries County, Mo., Mar. 15, 1906; s. Robert and Clara (Williams) R.; m. Margaret Louise Henderson, Jan. 18, 1936 (dec. July 1982); 1 child, Roberta Louise Rowden Crane; m. Sandra Kay McFadden, Jan. 7, 1985. Student, U. Mo., 1927-28; grad., Evang. United Brethren Corr., Kansas City, Mo., 1946. Lic. to ministry Evang. United Brethren Ch., 1942, ordained itinerant elder, 1947; cert. tchr., Mo. Pastor Evang. United Brethren Ch., Adrian, Mo., 1941-46, Jennings, La., 1947-48; founder, pastor Revival Ch., Houston, 1949-50, Evangelistic Ctr. Ch., Nevada, Mo., 1950-53; founder, sr. pastor, pres. bd. The Evangelistic Ctr. Ch., Kansas City, 1954-94. Daily radio min. The Gospel, 1951-85; founder, trustee Evangelistic Ctr. Ch., Nevada, Mo., 1951-94, Evangelistic Ctr. Ch., Amarillo, Tex., 1965—; co-founder, pres. bd. dirs. Pan Am. Missions, Portland, Oreg., 1959-94; charismatic ch. rep. Ministries of New Life, Prairie Village, Kans., 1986-94; chaplain City Coun. Kansas City, 1987-90; organized chs. in several states and Sidney, Australia; guest speaker in various charismatic chs. and confs. throughout the U.S., Can., Jamaica, Colombia, Mex., 1954-94. Author: (booklets) God's Master Plan, 1970, Kingdom Blessings Now, 1978, Heart of God, 1985. Co-founder, dir. programs using 3d step of Alcoholics Anonymous to minister in 6 secular substance abuse treatment ctrs. throughout the Greater Kansas City Area, 1986-90; vol. Salvation Army, Kansas City, Kans., 1988-90; prayer team minister Bread of Life Ch., Mission, Tex., 1997-99. Home: Parkview Care Center 811 N 1st St Osborne KS 67473 Office: Evangelistic Ctr Ch 1024 E Truman Rd Kansas City MO 64106-3137 *You need to know that you know that you know that He (Christ) lives in your heart and that He (Christ) is able to do exceedingly and abundantly above all that you ask according to the resurrection power that mightily worketh in you who believe.*

ROWDEN, MARCUS AUBREY, lawyer, former government official; b. Detroit, Mar. 13, 1928; s. Louis and Gertrude (Lifsitz) Rosenzweig; m. Justine Leslie Bessman, July 21, 1950; children: Gwen, Stephanie. BA in Econs, U. Mich., Ann Arbor, 1950, JD with distinction, 1953. Bar: Mich. 1953, D.C. 1978. Trial atty. Dept. Justice, 1953-58; legal advisor U.S. Mission to European Communities, 1959-62; solicitor, assoc. gen. counsel, gen. counsel AEC, 1965-74; commr., chmn. U.S. NRC, Washington, 1975-77; 2tnr. Fried, Frank, Harris, Shriver and Jacobson, 1977—. Served with AUS, 1946-47. Decorated officer Order Legion of Honor Republic of France; Recipient Disting. Service award AEC, 1972 Mem. Am., Fed., Mich., D.C. bar assns., Internat. Nuclear Law Assn., Order of Coif. Home: 7937 Deepwell Dr Bethesda MD 20817-1927 Office: Fried Frank Harris Shriver and Jacobson 1001 Pennsylvania Ave NW Washington DC 20004-2505

ROWDEN, WILLIAM HENRY, naval officer; b. Woodsville, N.H., May 12, 1930; s. Henry Thomas and Kathleen M. (Gochey) R.; m. Sarah Sumner, Apr. 14, 1956; children: Sarah Jane, Thomas Sumner, John William. BS, U.S. Naval Acad., 1952, U.S. Naval Postgrad. Sch., 1963. Commd. ensign U.S. Navy, 1952, advanced through grades to vice adm., 1980, comdr. cruiser-destroyer group 3, 1977-79, staff chief naval ops. Washington, 1979-81, comdr. 6th Fleet, 1981-83, comdr. Mil. Sealift Command, 1983-85, comdr. Naval Sea Systems Command, 1985-88, ret., 1988; Disting. fellow Ctr. for Naval Analyses, Alexandria, Va., 1988-97; chmn. bd. dirs. Maersk Line Ltd., 1997—. Decorated D.S.M., Legion of Merit, Bronze Star Mem. Naval Inst. Presbyterian. Avocations: walking, sailing. Home: 55 Pinewood Ct Lancaster VA 22503-2321 E-mail: whrowden@rivnet.net.

ROWE, ALLAN DUNCAN, company executive; b. Corner Brook, Nfld., Can., Feb. 23, 1951; B in Commerce, Dalhousie U., 1974; MBA, U. Western Ont., 1978. V.p. fin. B.F. Goodrich Can. Inc., Kitchener, Ont., 1978-87; chief fin. officer Sobeys Inc., Stellarton, N.S., Can., 1987-96; sr. v.p., chief fin. officer Empire Co. Ltd., Can., 1996-99; exec. v.p., CFO Sobeys Inc., Sellarton, Canada, 1999—2001; CFO, Fishery Products Internat. Ltd., St. John's, Canada, 2001—. Mem. Fin. Execs. Inst. Office: Fishery Products Internat Ltd 70 O'Leary Ave PO Box 550 St Johns NF Canada A1L 5L1

ROWE, AUDREY, paralegal; b. Albuquerque, June 26, 1958; d. James Franklin Ringold and Geneva Doris (Jennings) Robinson. A in Specialized Bus. in Acctg., ICS Ctr. for Degrees, Scranton, Pa., 1988, A in Specialized Bus. in Fin., 1989; BSBA, Century U., 1991, MBA, 1995, cert. paralegal studies, 1996, A in Specialized Bus. in Paralegal Studies, 1999. Svc. rep. Mountain and Southwestern Bell Telephone Co., Albuquerque, Houston, 1978-83; clk., carrier U.S. Postal Svc. PS05, Bellaire, Sugar Land, Tex., 1983-86; supr. mails U.S. Postal Svc. EAS15, Sugar Land, 1986-87; officer-in-charge U.S. Postal Svc. EAS 18, Rosharon, Tex., 1987; from supr. mails EAS 15 to gen. supr. mails EAS 17 U.S. Postal Svc., Houston, 1987-89; relief tour supt. U.S. Postal Svc. EAS 21 (Detail Assignment), 1989; mgr. gen. mail facility U.S. Postal Svc. EAS22 (Detail Assignment), Capitol Heights, Md., 1989-90; mgr. mail processing U.S. Postal Svc. EAS21, Charlottesville, Va., 1990-91; MSC dir. city ops. U.S. Postal Svc. EAS23 (Detail Assignment), Roanoke, 1991; mgr. gen. mail facility U.S. Postal Svc. EAS24, Washington, 1991-96; plant mgr. U.S. Postal Svc. EAS25, Dulles, Va., 1992; pvt. contractor, paralegal, 1996-98; paralegal Lenox, Biddinger & Conrad, P.C., Woodbridge, Va., 1997-99, Wilson Strickland & Benson P.C., Atlanta,

1999-2000, Chamberlain, Hrdlicka, White, Williams & Martin, 2000—. Mem. Am. Soc. Notaries, Nat. Capital Area Paralegal Assn., Nat. Fedn. Paralegal Assn., Nat. Assn. Legal Assts. Avocations: piano, violin, reading. Mailing: PO Box 845 Buford GA 30515-0845

ROWE, B. DAVID, college administrator; b. Dallas, June 23, 1965; s. Ben Duval and Joyce Virginia Rowe; m. Jodi Michelle Hyde, June 27, 1998; 1 child, Carter Harris. BS, Southwestern U., 1987; MDiv., Emory U., 1992; Cert., U. Geneva, Bossey, Switzerland, 1991. Devel. asst. Emory U., Atlanta, 1989-90, assoc. dir. admission Candler Sch. Theology, 1992-93, dir. devel. Oxford Coll., 1993-97, dir. advancement and planning Oxford Coll., 1998; v.p. advancement Wesleyan Coll., Macon, Ga., 1998-99, LaGrange (Ga.) Coll., 2000—. Vol. cons. Ecumenical Inst., Bossey, Switzerland, 1994—. Mem. master planning team City of LaGrange, 2000. Mem. LaGrange-Troup County C. of C. (bd. dirs. 2000—), Lions. Methodist. Avocations: travel, sailing, scuba diving, dancing, foreign languages. Office: LaGrange Coll 601 Broad St Lagrange GA 30240 Fax: (706) 880-8354. E-mail: drowe@lgc.edu.

ROWE, BOBBY LOUISE, art educator; b. Montgomery, Ala., Feb. 15, 1930; d. Herbert and Louise (Barbaree) R. AB, Montevallo U., 1950; MA, Columbia U., 1959; PhD, Fla. State U., 1974. Cert. tchr. K-12 and jr. coll., Fla. Supr. student tchrs. U. Fla. Coll. Edn., Gainesville; assoc. prof. art edn. Mid. Tenn. State U., Murfreesboro; art edn. dir. Cleve. State U.; art curriculum specialist Palm Beach County Sch. Bd., West Palm Beach, Fla. Fiber artist, computer imagist, digital photographer, writer; lectr., presenter in field. Contbr. articles to profl. jours. Mem. Nat. Art Edn. Assn., Am. Edn. Rsch. Assn., Alpha Delta Kappa. E-mail: artrowe711@aol.com.

ROWE, BONNIE GORDON, music company executive; b. Buford, Ga., May 3, 1922; s. Bonnie Gordon and Alma (Poole) R.; m. Mary Wilburta Shidler; 1 child, Sharon Lynn; m. Gloria Lucille Fairfax, Feb. 17, 1962 (div.); 1 child, Susan Rebecca. Student, Ga. Evening Coll., 1939-41, U. Wichita, 1948-49, Ga. State Coll., 1949-52. Traffic mgr. Bonanza Air Lines, Las Vegas, 1946-48, music tchr., 1948-52; owner Rowe Accordion Distbg. Co., Rowe Accordion Ctr., Atlanta, 1952-56, Atlanta Music Pub. Co., 1956—, B. Rowe Music Co., Atlanta, 1957—. Pres.-treas. B. Rowe Enterprises, Inc., 1973—. Bd. dirs. Sandtown Found., Atlanta. Lt. col. USAAF, World War II, ETO. Decorated Air medals with three oak leaf clusters. Mem. 781st Bomb Squadron Assn. (465th bomb group WWII), Southeastern Accordion Assn. (past pres.), Nat. Assn. Music Mchts., Atlanta Fedn. Musicians (life), Travelers Protective Assn., Atlanta C. of C., Res. Officers Assn., Ret. Officers Assn., Air Force Assn., Internat. Platform Assn., Am. Legion, Sandtown Civitan Club (past pres., lt. gov., past pres. Met. Atlanta Coun.), Elks (exalted ruler 1987, 88, 89, past pres. past exalted rulers assn., trustee Union City, state organist Ga. Elks Assn.), Dobbins AFB Officers Club, The Mil. Order of the World Wars (comdr. Atlanta chpt.), Gamma Delta Phi. Home: 5085 Erin Rd SW Atlanta GA 30331-7810 Office: 6102 Mableton Pkwy Mableton GA 30126-4302

ROWE, CARL OSBORN, business consultant; b. Colorado Springs, Colo., Feb. 3, 1944; s. Prentiss Eldon and Jo Ann (Osborn) R.; m. Dale Robin Oren, Apr. 12, 1984; 1 child, Stefanie Osborn. BA in Govt. cum laude, George Mason U., 1972; M Urban Affairs, Va. Poly. Inst. and State U., 1976. Cert. pub. housing mgr.; cert. mgmt. cons. Spl. clk. FBI, Washington, 1968-71; mgmt. analyst ICC, 1972-75; dir. policy and mgmt. U.S. Bur. Reclamation, 1975-82; exec. dir. City of Las Vegas Housing Authority, 1990-94; pres. Rowe Bus. Consulting, Las Vegas, Nev., 1982-90, 94-97; exec. dir. So. Nev. Housing Corp., 1994-95; assoc. Success Strategies, Las Vegas, 1995-96; dir. orgn. and mgmt. devel. Fair, Anderson and Langerman, CPAs, 1997—. Bd. dirs. Flowtronics, Inc., Phoenix, Sportstech, Inc., Scottsdale, Ariz., MSP Sys., Inc., Scottsdale; interim dir. Las Vegas-Clark County Libr. Dist. Columnist Las Vegas Bus. Press, 1989-90, 94-96. Exec. dir. So. Nev. Housing Corp., So. Nev. Reinvestment and Affordable Housing Com.; founding bd. dirs., CEO Family Cabinet of So. Nev., Affordable Housing Inst. So. Nev.; bd. dirs. Opportunity Village, LLV Alumni Found.; mem. exec. bd. Nat. Assn. Housing and Redevel. Ofcls. Pacific S.W. Regional Conf., Oasis So. Nev. Cmty. Svc. Guild, Las Vegas Cmty. Empowerment Comm.; mem. adv. bd. Comty. Food Bank Clark County, Clark County Sch. Dist. CHOICES program. Decorated USAF Commendation medal; named one of Top 50 over 50 in Las Vegas, Prime Mag., Disting. Men in So. Nev. In Bus. Las Vegas Mag.; recipient Cir. of Excellence award Las Vegas C. of C., 2001. Mem.: Leadership Las Vegas, Assn. for Strategic Planning, No. Calif./Nev. Exec. Dirs. Assn., Pub. Housing Authorities Dirs. Assn. (exec. bd.), Inst. Mgmt. Cons., Nat. Assn. Housing and Redevel. Ofcls. (exec. bd.), Am. Soc. Pub. Adminstrn. (governing coun.), Am. Mgmt. Assn., Las Vegas C. of C. (mem. bus. coun. bd. dirs., chmn. bus. a.m. com., chair bus. edn. series, chmn. productivity and partnerships with govt. com., prospectors bd.), LLV Alumni Found. (pres.), Rotary, Phi Theta Kappa. Avocations: reading, home improvement, music, cooking, physical fitness. Office: Fair Anderson and Langerman CPAs 33065 S Jones Blvd Las Vegas NV 89146 E-mail: carl@falcpa.com.

ROWE, CHARLES ALFRED, artist, designer, educator; b. Great Falls, Mont., Feb. 7, 1934; s. Alfred Lewis and Alice Lillian (Ledbetter) R.; m. Eugenia Dean, July 5, 1958; children: Allison Rene, Jon Garner, Dorian Leigh. Student, Mont. State U., 1952-53, So. Meth. U., 1956-57, U. Chgo., 1959-60; BFA, Sch. Art Inst., Chgo., 1960; MFA, Tyler Sch. Art, 1968. Prin. Charles Rowe Advt., Chgo., 1957-60; graphic designer Am. Can Co., Bellwood, Ill., 1960-62, Abrams-Bannister Engraving, Inc., Greenville, S.C., 1962-64; prof. art U. Del., Newark, 1964-97, emeritus prof., 1997—. One-man shows include Tyler Sch. Art, Phila, 1968, C.M. Russell Mus., Gt. Falls, 1972-73, 81, 92, Mickelson Gallery, Washington, 1970, 74, Pleiades Gallery, N.Y.C., 1977, 81, Vision of La Herradura, Almuñecar, Spain, 1988, USAF exhbn. Soc. Illustrators, N.Y.C., 1989, 91, West Chester (Pa.) U., 1992, Soc. Illustrators, N.Y.C., 1993; exhibited in group shows at C.M. Russell Mus., 1974, 76, 78, 80, 82-83, 86-91, Am. Painters in Paris, 1976, Monac-Western Art Exhbt. Spokane, Wash., 1977-78, Easton (Md.) Waterfowl Festival, 1981-82, USAF Nat. Collection, 1989, 91; group shows in Artrium Gallery, N.Y.C., 1995, 96, One Small Step, NASA, U. Del., Newark, 1999, Our Own Show, Soc. Illustrators, N.Y.C., 1990-96, 98-2000, over 200 other exhbns; represented in permanent collections U. Del., Mont. State Collection, Mont. State U., Del. State Collection, Gt. Falls Pub. Schs., Michael Landon Prodns., Calif., Meredith Corp., Des Moines, Collection Knissel, Austria, Archives Victoria and Albert Mus., London, Jacqueline Pierson, Nice, France, 1988; artists USAF Nat. Collection, Washington, 1989, 91, NASA Space Mus., 1992, Hauptman and Greenwood Collections, N.Y.C., 1994, Vera Haas, Dallas, Baker, Honolulu; fabric designer Galleon Fabrics, Inc., N.Y.C., Jones of N.Y., Saks Fifth Ave., Kevin Kilner, Jordan Baker, Hollywood, Calif., 1987, Kevin Kostner Collection, Hollywood, Calif., 1997; designed graphics Mont. State Arts Coun.; designer Del. state duck stamp, 1981. With inf. U.S. Army, 1954-56. Ctr. for Advanced Study fellow, 1981-82; grantee U. Del., 1964-79, Nat. Endowment for Arts and Humanities, 1972-73, U. Del. Bicentennial, 1976 Mem. AAUP, Soc. of Illustrators/N.Y.C. Home: Chapel Hill 133 Aronimink Dr Newark DE 19711-3802 Office: U Delaware Dept Art Newark DE 19711 *In my paintings and other artforms I strive for perfection, uniqueness, and a special inner beauty, but more than that, I try to create art that has a universal quality. This universality makes an artform communicate beyond a specific locale, continent or a limited time reference. All great works of art have this special element regardless of when they were created.*

ROWE, DAVID JOHN, physics educator; b. Totnes, Devonshire, Eng., Feb. 4, 1936; came to Can., 1968; s. Herbert Tyack and Marguerite Ella (Whitehead) R.; m. Una Mary Dawson, Oct. 4, 1959; children: Mark Jørgen Dawson, Jacqueline Amanda. BA, Cambridge (Eng.) U., 1959; MA, DPhil, Oxford (Eng.) U., 1959-62. Research assoc. U. Rochester, N.Y., 1966-68; assoc. prof. U. Toronto, Ont., Can., 1968-74, prof. Can., 1974—. Author: Nuclear Collective Motion, 1970; editor: Dynamic Properties of Nuclear States, 1972; mem. editorial bd. (jour.) Phys. Rev., 1983-86, Jour. Phys. G., 1988-92, assoc. editor, 1992; contbr. articles to profl. jours. Dir. Mont Tremblant Internat. Summer Sch., 1971. Served to cpl. RAF, 1954-56. Ford Found. fellow, 1962-63, U.K. Atomic Energy Authority fellow, 1963-66, Sloan Found. fellow, 1972-74, Isaac Walton Killam rsch. fellow, 1990-92, C.A.P./C.R.M. prize for Theoretical and Mathematical Physics, 1999. Fellow Royal Soc. Can. (Rutherford Meml. medal and prize 1983); mem. Can. Assn. Physicists (chmn. theoretical physics div. 1970-71), Internat. Union Pure and Applied Physics (chmn. C18 commn. on math. physics 1999—2002), Internat. Assn. Math. Physics. Avocations: piano, hiking, travel. Office: U Toronto Physics Dept Toronto ON Canada M5S 1A7 E-mail: rowe@physics.utoronto.ca.

ROWE, DAVID LEE, financial advisor; b. Colorado Springs, Colo., Jan. 30, 1954; s. Prentiss Eldon and Jo Ann (Osborn) R.; m. Elizabeth Webb, June 21, 1986; children: Schuyler Jourdan, Thomas Prentiss. BA, U. Colo., 1976; Master's degree, Johns Hopkins U., 1979; MBA, NYU, 1995. Asst. to undersec. U.S. Dept. Commerce, Washington, 1979-80; analyst Commodities Rsch. Inst., N.Y.C., 1980-81; fin. advisor Merrill Lynch, 1981-83, Prudential Securities, N.Y.C., 1983—, sr. v.p., asst. br. mgr., 1997—. Mem. cmty. ministry coun. St. Bartholomew's Ch., N.Y.C., 1987-96, mem. vestry, 1997—; bd. dirs. 133 E. 80th St. Corp., 1999—. Home: 133 E 80th St New York NY 10021-0317 Office: Prudential Securities 625 Madison Ave New York NY 10022-1801 E-mail: david_rowe@prusec.com.

ROWE, DAVID WINFIELD, lawyer; b. Chgo., Nov. 7, 1954; s. Bernard John and Gertrude Katherine (Johnson) R.; m. Martha Lynn Plott, June 12, 1977; children: Daniel, Peter. BA, Davidson Coll., 1976; PhD in Psychology, U. Tenn., 1981; JD, U. Mich., 1987. Bar: Colo. 1987, U.S. Dist. Ct. Colo. 1987, U.S. Ct. Appeals (10th cir.) 1987, Nebr. 1989, U.S. Dist. Ct. Nebr. 1989. Vis. asst. prof. Davidson (N.C.) Coll., 1981-82; mental health worker Peninsula Psychiat. Hosp., Louisville, 1982-84; asst. prof. dept. psychology U. Tenn., Knoxville, 1982-84; assoc. Gorsuch, Kirgis, Campbell, Walker & Grover, Denver, 1987-89; NIMH postdoctoral fellow in law and psychology U. Nebr., Lincoln, 1989-91; ptnr. Kinsey, Ridenour, Becker & Kistler, Nebr., 1991—. Mem. interim study group on foster care Health and Human Svcs. com. Nebr. State Legislature, 1990-91; adj. prof. psychology U. Nebr., Lincoln, 1992-94; bd. dirs., past treas. Lincoln Attention Ctr. for Youth; mem. The Mediation Ctr. Author: (with others) Dimensions of Child Advocacy: Advocating for the Child in Protection Proceedings, 1990, Children Under Three in Foster Care, 1991. Exec. com. Lancaster County Rep. Com., 1991-97, chmn., 1993-95; bd. dirs. Lincoln-Lancaster Mental Health Found., 1993—, v.p., 1995-96, pres., 1996-97; mem. Ctrl. Com. Nebr. Rep. Com., 1993-97; deacon Westminster Prebyn. Ch., 1996-99. Mem. ABA, Nebr. Bar Assn. (alternative dispute resolution com. 1990—), Kiwanis (pres. Lincoln 1997-98). Office: Kinsey Ridenour Becker & Kistler 121 S 13th St#601 PO Box 85778 Lincoln NE 68501-5778 E-mail: drowe@krbklaw.com.

ROWE, DIANE ELIZABETH, law clerk; b. Grove City, Pa. BS, Ind. U., 1981; M.Pub. Affairs, Ind. U., Gary, 1983; JD, Loyola U. Chgo., 2000. V.p. Ptnrs. in Contracting Corp., Hammond, Ind., 1983-85; energy conservation programs specialist U.S. Dept. Energy, Argonne, Ill., 1985-89, contracting officer Chgo., 1989-97; law clk. U.S. Dist. Ct. (no. dist.) Ill., 2000—. Contbr. articles to profl. jours. Recipient Excellence for the Future award Ctr. for Computer-Assisted Legal Instrn., 1996. Mem.: ABA, Am. Soc. Pub. Adminstrn. (exec. coun. 1985—89, pub. rels. com. chair 1985—89), Fed. Bar Assn., Chgo. Bar Assn., Ill. State Bar Assn. Home: 1313 Azalea Dr Munster IN 46321 Office: US District Court 219 S Dearborn St Chicago IL 60604 E-mail: drowel@att.net., diane_rowe@ind.uscourts.gov.

ROWE, EDWARD LAWRENCE, JR. graphic designer; b. Bridgeport, Conn., Nov. 5, 1940; s. Edward L. Sr. and Elvera Rowe; m. Elayne Bassler, Oct. 24, 1964; children: Heather, Jonathan David. Assoc., U. Bridgeport, 1960, BS, 1963; MFA, Columbia U., 2001; MBA, Babson Coll., 2002. Graphic designer Lester Beall, Brookfield, Conn., 1965-69; graphic design cons. Stead Young & Rowe, New Milford, 1969-87, Rowe Design Group, Brookfield, 1987—. Design cons. Atlas Corp., Allied Signal, Borden, Caterpillar Tractor Co., Com. for Econ. Devel., Honeywell, Internat. Paper, Martin Lockheed, N.Y. Clearing House, Otis Elevator. Design cons. Literacy Vols. N.Y., N.Y.C., 1990, Harlem R.B.I. (Returning Baseball to Inner Cities), N.Y.C., 1993. With U.S. Army, 1963-65. Recipient award Jour. Am. Inst. Graphic Arts, 1967, 68, Indsl. Design Mag., 1969, Packaging Design Mag., 1969, 74, Fin. World Merit award, 1978, Design Excellence award, 1991, Mohawk Paper Merit award, 1993, cert. spl. merit 53d Ann. Graphic Arts Exhbn., 1995, Am. Corp. Identity award Excellence, 1999, 2000, cert. of merit award Printing Industries Am., 2000, Am. Corp. Identity award excellence, 2000. Mem. Conn. Art Dirs. Club. Avocations: scuba diving, photography, architecture, jazz music. Office: Rowe Design Group 8 Galloping Hill Brookfield CT 06804-3611

ROWE, ELIZABETH WEBB, community volunteer; b. Canton, Ohio, Dec. 2, 1957; d. Thomas Dudley Webb and Verity Elizabeth (Voight) O'Brien; m. David Lee Rowe, June 21, 1986; children: Schuyler Jourdan, Thomas Prentiss. AB in History, Mt. Holyoke Coll., 1979. Legal asst. Willkie Farr & Gallagher, N.Y.C., 1979-82, legal asst. supr., 1983-88, adminstrv. asst., 1988-89; outreach dir. St. Bartholomew's Ch., 1989-93, dir. comm., 1991-93; paralegal mgr. Alpha Patterson, Belknap, Webb & Tyler LLP, N.Y.C., 1993-98; office mgr. Alpha N.Am., 1998-2001; co-dir. vols. St. Bartholomew's, 2001—. Legal asst. Cmty. Law Offices, N.Y.C., 1980-82; clerical asst. 17th Precinct Police Detective, N.Y.C., 1981-82. Chair homeless shelter St. Bartholomew's Ch., N.Y.C., 1984-85; vol. Breakfast Feeding Program, 1983-92, mem. Comty. Ministry Coun., 1986-88, 93-96; mem. N.Y. Jr. League, 1979-94; Pres.'s Coun. Mt. Holyoke Coll., 1988-91; rep. Mt. Holyoke Coll. Alumnae Fund, 1986-89, 94—, class officer, 1989-94; bd. dirs. 509 E. 83d St. Corp., E. 67th St. Owners, Inc., Emma J. Adams Meml. Fund, Mid-Manhattan Ctr., Inc. Recipient Mary Lyon award Mt. Holyoke Coll., 1994. Home: 133 E 80th St Apt 2C New York NY 10021-0317 E-mail: ewrowenyc@aol.com.

ROWE, ERNEST RAS, education educator, academic administrator; b. Hot Springs, Ark., July 19, 1933; s. Stephen Paul and Emma Leathia (Martin) R.; m. Carla True Dirk, May 27, 1995. BS with distinction, Ariz. State U., 1955, MEd, 1962, EdD, 1965; postgrad., Gonzaga U., 1975, Dublin City U., Ireland, summer 1989. Tchr. Madison Sch. Dist., Phoenix, 1960-61, Garden Grove (Calif.) Unified Sch. Dist., 1964-66; cons. spl. edn. Ariz. Dept. Pub. Instrn., Phoenix, 1966-67; asst. prof. Idaho State U., Pocatello, 1967-70, assoc. prof., 1970-74, prof. edn., 1974-95, interim chmn. dept. edn., summer 1992; adminstrv. intern Cen. Adminstrn., 1982-83, 94-95. Vis. prof. edn. Calif. State U., Long Beach, summer 1965; adv. mem. Idaho Task Force on Higher Edn., 1982-83; gov. apptd. Idaho commr. to Edn. Commn. of the States, 1979-93, rep. to steering com., 1989-93; elected chmn. Idaho State U. Faculty Senate, 1969, 70, 71-72, 86-87. Contbr. articles to profl. jours. Bd. dirs. Bannock Meml. Hosp., 1975-78; mem. Idaho Bd. Medicine pre-litigation panel for malpractice hearings, 1980-95. 1st lt. U.S. Army, 1955-57. Mem.: AAUP, Am. Inst. Parliamentarians (univ. parliamentarian, gov. N.W. region 1992—94), Nat. Soc. Study Edn., Masons, Chandler Rotary Club (pres. Pocatello 1981—82, bd. dirs. Tempe chpt. 1997—99, asst. dist. gov. 1998—99, pres. elect 2002—), Phi Kappa Phi (pres. 1972—73, 1987—88), Phi Delta Kappa. Episcopalian. Avocations: music, travel, photography, physical fitness. Home: 678 N Poplar Ct Chandler AZ 85226-6801 E-mail: erycyrano@cox.net. *Initiative and responsibility are cornerstones of a meaningful personal and professional life. Sadly they are missing in much of contemporary society. Apathy, the absence of civility and self-indulgence appear most prominently at the turn of the century.*

ROWE, EVELYN KARLA, real estate broker; b. S.I., N.Y., Sept. 27, 1943; d. John Robert and Evelyn Karla (Christiansen) Conger; m. James G. Fitch, July 10, 1965 (div. June 1974); children: Elisabeth Ann Perez, Amy Elaine; m. Richard J. Rowe, Aug. 10, 1982. Grad., St. Petersburg Jr. Coll., 1965. Grad. Resdl. Inst. Ins. rater Allstate Ins. Co., St. Petersburg, Fla., 1961-72, Mut. Ins. Agy., St. Petersburg, 1973-76; sales person Area West Inc., Reno, 1977-78; br. mgr. Real Estate West, Sparks, Nev., 1978-80; sales person Palomino Valley Realty, 1980-83; broker, owner E & R Realty, 1983—. Real estate cons., 1984-89. Rep. dep. registrar, Washoe County, Reno, 1987—. Mem. Reno/Sparks Bd. Realtors (mem. grievance com. 1985-89, chmn. edn. com. 1987, grievance com. 1989, mem. MLS com. vice-chmn. 1992-93), Mensa (mem.-at-large 1985, 89), Pythian Sisters (past chief and grand chief of Nev. 1992-93), Order Eastern Star, Spanish Springs Trap Club, Women's Coun. of Realtors. Home: 2001 Country Cir Sparks NV 89434-6700 Office: E & R Realty PO Box 1864 Sparks NV 89432-1864

ROWE, G. STEVEN, state attorney general; BS, U.S. Mil. Acad.; MBA, U. Utah; JD, U. Maine. Mem. Dist. 30 Maine Ho. of Reps. , 1993-95; mem. Dist. 35 Maine Ho. of Reps., 1995—2001; atty. gen. State of Maine, 2001—. Office: State House Station 6 Augusta ME 04333*

ROWE, HAHN, composer; Composer: (albums) The New Body, performer with Mimi, with Moby, with David Byrne, Foetus, with Syd Straw, with Swans, with True Mori, Michael Brook, with many others; composer: (films) Clean Shaven, The Transformation, Black Kites, Spring Forward.*

ROWE, HARRISON EDWARD, electrical engineer; b. Chgo., Jan. 29, 1927; s. Edward and Joan (Golden) R.; m. Alicia Jane Steeves, Feb. 10, 1951; children: Amy Rogers, Elizabeth Joanne, Edward Steeves, Alison Pickard. BS in Elec. Engring, Mass. Inst. Tech., 1948, MS, 1950, Sc.D., 1952; M of Engring. (hon.), Stevens Inst. Tech., 1988. Mem. tech. staff Radio Research Lab., Bell Labs., Holmdel, N.J., 1952-84; Anson Wood Burchard prof. elec. engring. Stevens Inst. Tech., Hoboken, 1984-93, prof. emeritus, 1993—. Vis. lectr. U. Calif., Berkeley, 1963, Imperial Coll., U. London, 1968; mem. Def. Sci. Bd. Task Force, 1972-74 Author: Signals and Noise in Communication Systems, 1965, Electromagnetic Propagation in Multi-Mode Random Media, 1999; assoc. editor: IEEE Trans. on Communication, 1974-76; contbr. articles to profl. jours.; patentee in field. Served with USN, 1945-46. Co-recipient Microwave prize, 1972, David Sarnoff award, 1977. Fellow IEEE; mem. Monmouth Symphony Soc., Navesink Country Club, Sigma Xi, Tau Beta Pi, Eta Kappa Nu. Clubs: Shrewsbury Sailing and Yacht, Appalachian Mountain. Unitarian Universalist. Home: 9 Buttonwood Ln Rumson NJ 07760-1045 E-mail: harrisonrowe@comcast.net.

ROWE, HENRY THEODORE, JR. (TED ROWE), writer, editor; b. Englewood, N.J., Oct. 8, 1932; s. Henry Theodore and Florence Jane (Bivins) R.; m. Judith Lyttelton Waddell, June 8, 1957 (div. Apr. 1982); children: Henry Theodore III, Lyttelton Waddell, Eliza Ritnour, Virginia Bivins; m. Phyllis Arlene Prevosto, Dec. 26, 1983. Student, Cornell U., 1951-53; BS, St. Lawrence U., 1956; postgrad., Columbia U., 1956-57. Pub. affairs fellow Brookings Instn., Washington, 1961; with IBM Corp., 1957-88, sr. requirements adminstr. N.Y., 1970-76, sr. bus. programs adminstrn. White Plains, also Irving, Tex., 1976-86, cons. mktg. support rep. Roanoke, 1986-88; owner Ted Rowe Assocs., Dallas, El Jebel, Colo. V.p., bd. dirs. West End Post, Dallas. Co-writer, editor weekly food column Food for Thought. 1st lt. U.S. Army, 1956-57. Mem. Am. Film Inst., Am. Fedn. Musicians, Aspen Chamber Resort Assn. Republican. Avocations: photography, music (played in N.Y.C. area 20 yrs.), disk jockey. Office: 1401 Turnberry Way Bel Air MD 21015 E-mail: trafood@juno.com.

ROWE, HERBERT JOSEPH, retired trade association executive; b. Granite City, Ill., Mar. 25, 1924; s. Herbert Bernard and Maude (Klein) R.; m. Ann Muter, Dec. 2, 1950; children: Douglas H., Stephen F., James D., Edith L., Allen. Student, U. Tex., 1942-43, Purdue U., 1943-44; BS in Mgmt.; BS in Mktg., U. Ill., 1948; LittD (hon.), London Inst. for Applied Research, 1975. With Edward Valves, Inc. (subs. Rockwell Mfg. Co.), 1948-50, Muter Co., Chgo., 1952-71, v.p., 1957-64, pres., 1964-71, treas., 1964-67, chmn. bd., 1965-71, also dir., 1957-71; pres., treas., dir. Wescoil Co., 1964-66, Tri-Axial Corp., 1966-67; v.p., treas. Gen. Magnetic Corp., 1965-67, chmn. bd., 1967-70, dir., 1964-70; chmn. bd., dir; Pemcor, Inc., Westchester, Ill., 1971-75; assoc. adminstr. external affairs NASA, 1975-78; sr. v.p. Electronic Industries Assn., 1978-89; chmn. Famro Corp., 1989-90; pres. Internat. Electronics Fedn., 1989-90. Sec.-treas. Englewood Elec. Supply Wis., Inc., 1972-75, Rahr's Inc., 1972-75; pres. Enclave of Naples, Inc., 1992-94, treas., 1994-96; pres. Rowe Corp., 1994-97; treas. Quality wholesale Foods of S.W. Fla., 1994-96. Pres. Pokagon Trails coun. Boy Scouts Am., 1964-66, pres. Calumet coun., 1966-68, region 7 exec. com., 1966-72, vice chmn., 1971-72, bd. dirs. East Ctrl. region, 1972-75, mem. nat. program com., 1970-78, 90-94, nat. Cub Scout com., 1970-80, chmn., 1990-94, S.E. regional exec. com., 1975-78, So. regional exec. bd., 1993—, bd. dirs. Nat. Capital Area coun., 1978-90, adv. bd., 1990-94, mem. exec. bd. S.W. Fla. coun., 1992—, mem. nat. exec. com. and exec. bd., 1990-95, nat. adv. bd., 1995—; membership chmn. Nat. Eagle Scouts Assn., 1976-80; corp. campaign chmn. Chgo. Met. Crusade Mercy, 1964-68; chmn. Bd. Edn. Caucus, Flossmoor, Ill., 1962; mem. bd. Flossmoor United Party, 1963-68; mem. U. Ill. Found., 1967—; mem. adv. com. U. Ill. Coll. Commerce and Bus. Adminstrn., 1968-78, 97—; bd. dirs. Electronic Industries Found., 1974-94; mem. adv. bd. Air and Space Mus., Smithsonian Inst., 1975-78; active Moorings Presbyn. Ch., Naples, Fla. With USMCR, 1942-46, 50-52. Recipient Silver Beaver award Boy Scouts Am., 1966, Silver Antelope award, 1969, Silver Buffalo award, 1994; NASA team award Bicentennial Expo on Sci. and Tech., Exceptional Svc. medal, 1978, Baden-Powell fellow World Scout Found., 1992. Mem. AIAA, AAAS, Electronic Industries Assn. (hon., bd. dirs. 1967-69, bd. govs. 1969-75, exec. com. parts divsn. 1966-75, vice chmn. parts divsn. 1970-74, chmn. 74-75, bd. dirs. consumer electronics divsn. 1972-75, chmn. world trade com. 1968-70, vice chmn. 1970-73, chmn. membership and scope com. 1972-74, Disting. Svc. award 1989), Am. Loudspeaker Mfrs. Assn. (v.p., dir. 1967-68, pres., bd. dirs. 1968-70), Assn. Electronic Mfrs. (bd. dirs. 1970-73), Nat. Space Club, Nat. Space Inst., Am. Acad. Polit. Social Sci., Am. Soc. Assn. Execs. (vice chmn. internat. sect. 1986-87, chmn. 1987-88), U.S. Naval Inst., Field Mus. Natural History, European Soc. of Assn. Execs., Greater Washington Soc. Assn. Execs., Naples Coun. World Affairs, Explorers Club, Chgo. Art Inst., Am. Legion, Chaine des Rôtisseurs, L'Ordre Mondial, Internat. Wine and Food Soc. (pres. Naples br. 2001-), English Speaking Union (pres. Naples chpt. 1996—, nat. dir. 1997—, regional vice chmn. 2000—), Conservancy, S.W. Fla., Forum Club of S.W. Fla. (bd. dirs. 2000—), Naples Press Club (bd. dirs. 1998-2000), Royal Poinciana Golf Club, Naples Yacht Club, Beta Gamma Sigma, Alpha Phi Omega, Sigma Chi (dir. Kappa Kappa corp. 1954-75, sec. 1971-73, pres. 1973-75, Charles J. Kiler award 1975, Grand Consul's citation 1976). Home: 4601 Gulf Shore Blvd N Apt 12 Naples FL 34103-2214 E-mail: hrowe13@comcast.net.

ROWE, HOWARD, JR. composer; b. Rochester, N.Y., June 3, 1942; s. Howard James and Harriett (Rowpp) Rowe; m. Donna Gail Dudley, Aug. 15, 1970; children: Charles James, Lindsay Dudley. BA, Syracuse U., 1965; MA, Ithaca Coll., 1967. Instrumental music tchr. Rush-Henrietta (N.Y.) Ctrl. Sch., 1967—98; ret., 1998. Composer, arranger over 50 band and orch. music publs., 1978—; musician (trumpet): various shoes, including Mel Torme, the Smothers Brothers, 42d St., 1964—. Named Outstanding Educator, Rochester (N.Y.) Philharmonic Orch., 1995, Henrietta Jaycees, 1972. Mem.: ASCAP, Internat. Assn. Jazz Educators, Internat. Trumpet Guild. Avocations: travel, model trains, railroads. Home: 8 Hanford Way Fairport NY 14450

ROWE, JACK FIELD, retired electric utility executive; b. Minn., May 10, 1927; s. William F. and Anna (Stenborg) R.; m. Mary E. Moen, Mar. 26, 1955; 1 child, Lizette Ann. BEE, U. Minn., 1950. Registered profl. engr., Minn., Wis. With Minn. Power and Light Co., Duluth, 1950-89, asst. to pres., 1966-67, v.p., 1967-68, exec. v.p., 1969-74, pres., 1974-84, CEO, 1978-89, chmn., 1969-93, also bd. dirs. Chmn. bd. dirs., CEO FiberCore, Inc., Minn. Paper, Inc., So. States Utilities, Universal Tel., Inc., Topeka Group, Inc., NorLight, Inc.; mem. exec. bd. Nat. Electric Reliability Coun., 1970-73; vice chmn. Mid-Continent Area Reliability Coun., 1970-71, chmn., 1972-73; mem. bus. and econs. adv. bd. U. Minn., Duluth, 1980. Past bd. dirs., v.p. Duluth Jr. C. of C.; mem. exec. bd. Lake Superior coun. Boy Scouts Am., 1967-75, chmn. Explorers, 1968-72; comml. chmn. Duluth United Fund, 1960-61; vice chmn. Duluth United Way, 1975, chmn., 1976, U.S. Savs. Bond chmn., St. Louis County, Minn., 1974-77; chmn. St. Louis County Heritage and Arts Ctr., 1979-81; pres. N.E. Minn. Devel./Assn., 1981-83; mem. Minn. Bus. Partnership, 1979-88; bd. dirs. Minn. Safety Coun., 1979-85, pres., 1983-84, chmn., 1984-85; bd. dirs. Duluth Downtown Devel. Corp., 1979-81, Duluth Growth Co., 1984-85, Greysolon Mall Corp., 1980-86, Duluth Superior Area Cmty. Found., 1984-86, Duluth Clin. Edn. and Rsch. Found., 1985-86, Benedictine Health Sys., 1985-88; mem. adv. bd. exec. program U. Minn., 1979; adv. coun. Inst. Tech., 1979; mem. Minn. High Tech. Coun., 1982-87. With USNR, 1945-46. Recipient Distinguished Svc. award Duluth Jr. C. of C., 1960, Outstanding Leadership award in energy conversion scis. N.Y.C. sect. ASME, 1980, Outstanding Achievement award U. Minn. Alumni Assn., 1986, Bronze CEO of Decade award Fin. World Mag., 1989; named CEO of Yr., Fin. World mag., 1986, 89; Jack F. Rowe Chair of Engring. named in his honor U. Minn., Duluth, 1986. Mem. NAM (dir. 1975-78), IEEE, Electric Info. Coun. (pres. 1978-82), North Cen. Electric Assn., Duluth C. of C. (pres. 1972-73, exec. com., bd. dirs.), Mpls. Club, Engrs. Club (Duluth), Northland Country Club (Duluth), Naples Yacht Club, Kitchi Gammi (Duluth) (dir. 1979-87, pres.

1985-87), Rotary Club (Duluth) (pres. 1974-75), Moorings Country Club, Internat. Mens Club, Royal Poinciana Golf Club, Masons, Shriners, Jesters, Kappa Eta Kappa. Lutheran. Home: 4735 Villa Mare Ln Naples FL 34103-3473

ROWE, JAMES WILLIAM, SR. engineer; b. Richmond, Va., Mar. 10, 1944; s. William Walter and Margaret Lucille (Brauer) R.; m. Janet O'Neal Parker, Mar. 30, 1968; children: James William, Rhett Nelson. BS, Va. Commonwealth U., 1968. Chief operator City of Richmond, 1974-76; supr. Park 500 divsn. Phillip Morris, Richmond, 1976-79; quality control chemist Gen. Metals Tech., 1979-81; process engr. Synertech., 1981-83, FN Mfg., Inc., Columbia, S.C., Genicom Corp., Waynesboro, Va., 1988-93, The Am. Hist. Found., Richmond, 1993—. Republican. Baptist. Office: The Am Hist Found 1142 W Grace St Richmond VA 23220-3613

ROWE, JOHN W. utility company executive; b. Wis. married; 1 son. Grad., U. Wis. Assoc. Isham, Lincoln & Beale, Chgo., 1970-78; ptnr., 1978-80; sr. v.p. law Conrail, 1980-84; pres., CEO Ctrl. Maine Power Co., 1984-89, New Eng. Electric Sys., 1989-98; chmn., pres., CEO Unicom and ComEd, 1998—2000; chmn., CEO Exelon (merger of Unicom and PECO Energy), 2000—. Bd. dirs. UnumProvident Corp., Fleet Boston Fin., Wis. Ctrl. Tranp. Co.; of counsel to trustees Chgo., Milw., St. Paul, Pacific Railroad Co. Bd. trustees Art Inst. Chgo., Chgo. Hist. Soc., Field Mus., Wis. Alumni rsch. Found., Am. Enterprise Inst., Ill. chpt. Nature Conservancy; vice-chmn. Edison Electric Inst.; nat. trustee Northwestern U.; past pres. USS Constitution Mus.; past chmn. Mass. Bus. Roundtable. Mem. Econ. Club. Chgo., Comml. Club Chgo. (civic com.), Order of the Coif, Phi Beta Kappa. Office: Exelon 10 S Dearborn St Chicago IL 60680*

ROWE, JOHN WALLIS, health insurance executive, medical executive; b. Jersey City, June 20, 1944; s. Albert Wallis and Elizabeth (Lynch) R.; m. Valerie Ann DelTufo, Aug. 10, 1968; children: Meredith, Abigail, Rebecca. BS with honors, Canisius Coll., 1966; MD with distinction, U. Rochester, 1970. Diplomate Am. Bd. Internal Medicine, Am. Bd. Nephrology. Resident in internal medicine Harvard Med. Sch., Beth Israel Hosp., Boston, 1970-72; clin. assoc. Nat. Inst. Child Health and Human Devel., Balt., 1972-74; rsch., clin. fellow Harvard Med. Sch., Mass. Gen. Hosp., Boston, 1974-75; from instr. to prof. Harvard Med. Sch., 1976-88; pres. Mt. Sinai Sch. Medicine, N.Y.C., 1988-99, Mt. Sinai Hosp., N.Y.C., 1988-98; prof. geriatrics and medicine Mt. Sinai Sch. Medicine and Mt. Sinai Hosp., 1988—; CEO Mt. Sinai-NYU Med. Ctr. and Health Sys., 1998-2000; pres., CEO, Aetna Inc., Hartford, Conn., 2000—, chmn., 2001—. Trustee N.Y. Acad. Medicine, 1989-98, Buck Ctr. for Rsch. in Aging, Marin, Calif., 1989-99; mem. Medicare Payment Adv. Com., 1997—. Editor: Health and Disease in Old Age, 1982, Geriatric Medicine, 1988, Handbook of the Biology of Aging, 1990, Geriatric Neurology, 1991; author: Successful Aging, 1998; contbr. articles to jours. in field. Lt. comdr. USPHS, 1972-74. MacArthur Found. grantee, 1985-98. Mem. NAS Inst. Med., Gerontol. Soc. Am. (pres. 1988), Am. Fedn. for Aging Rsch. (pres. 1988), N.Y. Yacht Club, Century Assn. Roman Catholic. Avocation: sailing. Home: 300 Central Park W New York NY 10024-1513 Office: Aetna 151 Farmington Ave Hartford CT 06156 E-mail: RoweJW@aetna.com.

ROWE, JOHN WILLIAM, utility executive; b. Dodgeville, Wis., May 18, 1945; s. William J. and Lola (Rule) R.; m. Jeanne M.; 1 son, William John. BS, U. Wis., 1967, JD, 1970. Bar: Wis. 1970, Ill. 1970, U.S. Supreme Ct. 1979, Pa. 1982. Assoc. Isham, Lincoln & Beale, Chgo., 1970-77, ptnr., 1978-80; counsel to trustee Chgo. Milw. St. Paul & Pacific R.R., 1979-80; v.p. law Consol. Rail Corp., Phila., 1980-82, sr. v.p. law, 1982-84; pres., chief exec. officer Cen. Maine Power Co., Augusta, 1984-89; pres., CEO New Eng. Elec. System, Westboro, Mass., 1989-98, former bd. dirs.; chmn., pres., CEO Unicom Corp. & Commonwealth Edison Co., 1998-2000; pres., co-CEO Exelon Corp. Bd. dirs. UNUM Corp., UNUM Provident, Fleet Boston, Bank of Boston Corp. Pres. USS Constitution Mus., 1993-95, Edison Electric Inst., Field Mus. of Natural History; trustee Mechanics Hall, Pioneer Inst. Mem. Chgo. Club, Phi Beta Kappa. Home and Office: Unicom Corp Ten S Dearborn St # 37 Chicago IL 60603

ROWE, JOSEPH CHARLES, elementary school educator, principal; b. Cheyenne, Wyo., June 8, 1953; s. Clyde Joseph and Brunhild W. C. (Bielinski) Rowe. BS, U. Md., 1976; MEd, George Mason U., 1981. Cert. adminstr., supr., elem. tchr., spl. edn. tchr., mid. sch. tchr., jr. gt. books trainer. Case mgr. intermediate EI program Lakewood Elem. Sch., Brown Sta. Elem. Sch.; tchr., dir. wellness program Watkins Mill Elem. Sch.; prin. Stedwick Elem. Sch. Outreach coord. Families of the 90s; chmn., humna rels., prin.'s adv., discipline, mainstreaming, homework and cmty. action team against substance and alcohol abuse PTA, sch. assessment team coord., v.p., quality mgmt. coun. facilitator, comprehensive behavior coord., reading initiative coord. Coord. adult/child programs Reading USA, gifted & talented coord., testing coord., vol. coord. Mem.: ASCD, NEA, Montgomery County Adminstrs. Assn. Elem. Prins., Md. State Tchrs. Assn., Phi Delta Kappa. Home: 2117 Bordly Dr Brookeville MD 20833-2124 E-mail: Heidelbger@aol.com., Joseph_Rowe@fc.mcps.k12.md.us.

ROWE, JOSEPH EVERETT, electrical engineering educator, administrator; b. Highland Park, Mich., June 4, 1927; s. Joseph and Lillian May (Osbourne) R.; m. Margaret Anne Prine, Sept. 1, 1950; children: Jonathan Dale, Carol Kay. BSEE, BS Engring. in Math., U. Mich., 1951, MSEE, 1952, PhD, 1955. Mem. faculty U. Mich., Ann Arbor, 1953-74, prof. elec. engring., 1960-74, dir. electron physics lab., 1958-68, chmn. dept. elec. and computer engring., 1968-74; vice provost, dean engring. Case Western Res. U., Cleve., 1974-76; provost Case Inst. Tech., 1976-78; v.p. tech. Harris Corp., Melbourne, Fla., 1978-81; v.p., gen. mgr. Controls divsn. Harris Corp., 1981-82; exec. v.p. rsch. and def. Gould Inc., 1982, vice chmn., chief tech. officer, 1983-87; sr. v.p., chief technologist Inst. Rsch., Ill. Inst. Tech., Chgo., 1987; v.p. and chief scientist PPG Industries, Inc., Pitts., 1987-92; v.p., dir. Rsch. Inst., U. Dayton, Ohio, 1992-97. Cons. to industry; mem. adv. group electron devices Dept. Def., 1966-78, 93-97; bd. govs. Rsch. inst. of Ill. Inst. Tech.; chmn. Coalition for Advancement of Indsl. Tech., U. Ill.; mem. indsl. adv. bd. U. Ill. at Chgo.; mem. Army Sci. Bd., 1985-91, 93-2001. Author: Nonlinear Electron-Wave Interaction Phenomena, 1965, also articles. Fellow AAAS, IEEE (chmn. adminstrv. com. group electron devices 1968-69, editor procs. 1971-73, Harrell V. Nobel award 1994, Millenium medal 2000); mem. NAE, Am. Phys. Soc., Am. Soc. Engring. Edn. (Curtis McGraw Rsch. award 1964), Am. Mgmt. Assn. (R&D), Sigma Xi, Phi Kappa Phi, Tau Beta Pi, Eta Kappa Nu. also: 81 Governors Club Dr Xenia OH 45385 E-mail: jrowe6427@aol.com.

ROWE, LARRY JORDAN, lawyer; b. Boston, May 24, 1958; s. Benson and Marcia Rowe; m. Nancy Ellen Cardinal; children: Jonathan B., Elizabeth J., David C. AB, Dartmouth Coll., 1980; MPP, JD, Harvard U., 1984. Bar: Mass. 1985, U.S. Dist. Ct. Mass. Assoc. Ropes & Gray, Boston, 1984-93, ptnr., 1993—. Mem. Sudbury (Mass.) Fin. Com., 1998—; pres. Hillel Found. New Eng., 1991-94, bd. dirs., 1986—. Mem. ABA, Mass. Bar Assn., Boston Bar Assn. Home: 10 Spiller Cir Sudbury MA 01776-2681 Office: Ropes & Gray 1 International Pl Fl 4 Boston MA 02110-2624 E-mail: lrowe@ropesgray.com.

ROWE, LISA DAWN, computer programmer/analyst, computer consultant; b. Kenton, Ohio, Feb. 2, 1966; d. Daniel Lee and Frances Elaine (Johnson) Edelblute; m. Jeffrey Mark Rowe, Feb. 13, 1982; children: Anthony David, Samantha Paige Elizabeth, Zane Thomas, Zachary Tyler. Student, Inst. of Lit., 1988-90, Acad. Ct. Reporting, 1988, Marion Tech. Coll., 1991-92; postgrad., Ohio State U., 1993—. Writer, model Newslife, Marion, Ohio, 1982-83; bookkeeper Nat. Ch. Residences, Columbus, 1985, Insty-Prints, Columbus, 1985; asst. editor Columbus Entertainment, 1984-85; book reviewer, writer Columbus Dispatch, 1989-91; writer Consumer News, Delaware, Ohio, 1989-90; computer programmer, supr. Dyserv, Inc., Columbus, 1986-92; bookkeeper, acct., office mgr. Marion Music Ctr., Inc., 1990; computer programmer EBCO Mfg., Columbus, 1992-93; sr. programmer/analyst Borden, Inc., 1993-94; computer cons. System X, 1994-95, LDA Systems, Dublin, 1995-96; pres. Rowe Techs. Inc. , Marion, 1996—. Editor newsletter Assn. System Users, 1989-90; contbr. articles and revs. to profl. jours. Mem. NAFE, MADD, DAV (chaplain 1990), Heart of Ohio ACFA Cat Club (pres. 2002). Republican. Mem. Lds Ch. Avocations: horseback riding, swimming, camping, fishing, reading. Home: 1150 Toulon Ave Marion OH 43302-6610 Office: Rowe Techs Inc 1150 Toulon Ave Marion OH 43302-6610 E-mail: Lisarowe@rowetech.com.

ROWE, MARY ANN GUNDER, education educator; b. Glendale, Calif., Sept. 23, 1937; d. Roger W. and Mary G. (Runyon) Gunder; children: Mary, Tom, Susan. BA, U. Calif., Berkeley, 1959; MPA, Coll. of Notre Dame, Belmont, Calif., 1990; EdD, U. San Francisco, 1996. Cert. tchr., adminstrv. svcs. profl., Calif. Tchr. Lafayette (Calif.) Schs., 1961-62, Castro Valley (Calif.) Schs., 1962-63, Carey Sch., San Mateo, Calif., 1981-86, San Mateo/Foster City Schs., 1986-92; supr. student tchrs. San Francisco State U., 1992-96; lectr., supr. Calif. State U., Hayward, 1996-98; lectr. San Francisco State U., 1999—. Tchr./designer parent-child program Burlinghame Presbyn. Nursery Sch., 1979-81; mem. program quality rev. leadership team Laurel Sch., San Mateo, 1989; P.Q.R. reviewer State of Calif. at Colma Elem. Sch., Daly City, 1990; mem. magnet sch. exploration com. San Mateo-Foster City Schs., 1990. Deacon First Presbyn. Ch., Burlingame, 1978-81. Mem. ACSA, Internat. Reading Assn., P.E.O. Sisterhood (chpt. pres. 1972-73, officer 1978—), Phi Delta Kappa. Avocations: hiking, gardening, reading, travel, arts. Office: San Francisco State U 1600 Holloway Ave San Francisco CA 94132-1722

ROWE, MARY P. organizational ombudsman, management educator; b. Chgo., Feb. 18, 1936; married; children: Katherine, Susannah, Timothy. BA in History, Swarthmore Coll., 1957; PhD in Econs., Columbia U., 1971; LLD (hon.), Regis Coll., 1975. With World Council of Chs./Office of UN High Commr. for Refugees, Salzburg and Vienna, Austria, 1957-58; research asst. Nat. Bur. Econ. Research, N.Y.C., 1961; economist planning bd. Office of Gov., V.I., 1962-63; free-lance cons. Nigeria, 1963-66, Boston, 1967-69; cons., sr. economist with Ctr. for Ednl. Policy Research, Harvard U. Harvard U., Cambridge, Mass., 1970, cons., sr. economist with Abt Assocs., 1970, tech. dir. early edn. project, 1971-72, cons. economist with Abt Assocs., 1971; dir. Carnegie Corp. Grant Radcliffe Inst., Cambridge, 1972; spl. asst. to pres., ombudsperson MIT, 1973—, adj. prof. Sloan Sch. Mgmt., 1985—. Mem. steering com., program on negotiations Harvard U., 1995—. Mem. editorial bd. Negotiation Jour., 1985—, Alternative Dispute Resolution Report, 1987—; contbr. articles to profl. jours. Trustee Cambridge Friends Sch., 1969-75; mem. bd. advisors Brookline Children's Ctr., 1971-76; mem. Cambridge Friends Meeting and Com. on Clearness, 1971-78, New Eng. Concerns Com., 1973—, Mass. Policy Adv. Com. on Child Abuse/Neglect, 1977-79, Mass. State Youth Council, 1978-83; mem. Mass. State Employment and Tng. Council, 1975-83, chair, 1980-83; mem. nat. adv. Com. Black Women's Ednl. Policy and Research Network Project/Wellesley Coll. Ctr. for Research on Women, 1980-83; bd. dirs. Bay State Skills Commn., 1980-81, Wellesley Women's Research Ctr., 1984-87; sec. bd. dirs. Bay State Skills Corp., 1981-90; mem. panel on employment disputes Ctr. for Pub. Resources, 1986—. Recipient Meritorious Civilian Svc. award Dept. of Navy, 1993. Mem. Am. Econs. Assn., Soc. Profls. in Dispute Resolution (chair com. on ombudspersons 1982—, com. law and pub. policy in employment disputes), Calif. Caucus Coll. and Univ. Ombudsmen, Univ. and Coll. Ombudsman Assn., Ombudsman Assn. (pres. 1985-87, program on negotiation steering com. 1995—, Disting. Neutral Ctr. for Pub. Resources 1990—, covenor, presenter confs. 1982, 84, 85, 88, 89, 90-2000). Office: MIT 10-213 77 Massachusetts Ave Cambridge MA 02139

ROWE, MARY SUE, accounting executive; b. Melrose, Kans., Aug. 31, 1940; d. Gene and Carmen (Glidewell) Woffard; m. Edward Rowe, Nov. 27, 1985; children from previous marriage: Denise, Dynell, Dalene, Denette. Student, MTI Bus. Coll., 1968, Calif. State U., Fullerton, 1969, Broome (N.Y.) Community Coll., 1974-76; cert. Sch. Bus. Mgmt., Calif. State U., San Bernardino, 1986. Variou bookkeeping and secretarial, 1968-76; asst. mgr., acct. RM Dean Contracting, Chenango Forks, N.Y., 1976-80; acctg. asst. Hemet (Calif.) Unified Sch. Dist., 1981-86; dir. acctg. Desert Sands Unified Sch. Dist., Indio, Calif., 1986-91; bus. svcs. cons. ednl. div. Vicenti, Lloyd & Stutzman, CPA, La Verne, 1991-97; sch. bus. cons., computer trainer Hemet, 1997—2002; dir. fiscal svcs. San Rafael City Schs., 2002—. Bd. dirs. Family Svcs. Assn., Hemet, 1982-83, PTA Officer, 1993-95. Mem. NAFE, Calif. Assn. Sch. Bus. Ofcls. (acctg. com., R*D com., vice chmn. 1988-90, chmn. 1990-91, state acctg. adv. com. 1990-92), Calif. Assn. Pub. Purchasing Officers, Riverside Assn. Chief Accts. (co-chmn. 1986-88), Coalition for Adequate Sch. Housing. Republican. Home and Office: 4981 Vailwood Dr Hemet CA 92544-7819 Office: San Rafael City Schs 310 Nova Albion Way San Rafael CA 94903 *Personal philosophy: Something good can come of any event no matter how bad it first appears.*

ROWE, MAX L. lawyer, corporate executive, management and political consultant, writer, judge; b. Dallas City, Ill., Aug. 14, 1921; s. Samuel Guy and Nellie (Moyes) R.; m. Maxine Marilyn Gladson, May 23, 1944; children: Melody Ann (Mrs. Gunn), Susan Elaine, Joyce Lynn, Andrew Blair. Student, Knox Coll., Galesburg, Ill., 1939-40; AB, U. Ill., 1943, JD, 1946; MBA, U. Chgo., 1952. Bar: Ill. 1947, Ind. 1954, also U.S. Supreme Ct. 1964. Pvt. practice in, Aurora and Urbana, 1947; asst. to sec., asst. treas. Elgin Nat. Watch Co., 1948-50; gen. atty., asst. to pres.-treas. Rival Packing Co., 1950- 51; gen. counsel, asst. sec.-treas. Victor Mfg. & Gasket Co., Chgo., 1951-54; sec. Mead Johnson & Co., Evansville, Ind., 1954-55; assoc. counsel Caterpillar Tractor Co., 1955-62; assoc. gen. counsel, sec., asst. treas. Thomas J. Lipton, Inc. and subs., 1962-68; v.p., treas. Seeburg Corp., Chgo., 1968-69; v.p. fin., law and adminstrn. Nightingale Conant Corp., 1970-71; pvt. legal practice, also mgmt. and polit. cons., 1968—; v.p. law, sec. Ward Foods, Inc., Wilmette, Ill., 1972-76; mem. firm Kirkland & Ellis, Chgo., 1978-87; pres., CEO Rowe Enterprises, 1987—; atty. Ill. Dept. Profl. Regulation, Chgo. and Springfield, 1987-92; adminstrv. law judge State of Ill., 1993—. Dir. Ward-Johnston, Inc., Ward Internat., Inc., Superior Potato Chips, Inc., Quinlan Pretzel Co., Honiron-Philippines, Inc.; instr. extension div. U. Ill., 1960-61, eve. div. Fairleigh Dickinson U., 1966-68; leader Am. Mgmt. Assn., other corp. seminars, 1966-87. Actor various TV, radio and print commercials, 1992—. Treas. Peoria County (Ill.) Republican Central Com., 1958-62, Rep. precinct committeeman, Peoria County, 1958-62, Bergen County, N.J., 1966-68, del., Rep. Nat. Conv., 1980; elder Presbyterian Ch., 1975—; mem. nat. adv. council SBA, 1976-78; chmn., mem. adv. bd. Ill. Dept. Personnel, 1979-82; mem. Ill. Compensation Rev. Bd., 1984-87; mem. Pres. Reagan's Nat. Commn. for Employment Policy, 1984-88; mem. U. Ill. Found. and Pres.'s Council, 1979—, bd. visitors Coll. of Law, 1993—; dir., mem. exec. com., chmn. Outreach and Devel., World Heritage Mus., 1992-98; dir., Spurlock Mus. of World Culture, 1998—; mem. bd. dirs. Oak Ridge Cemetary, 1994—. Served to 2d lt. AUS, 1943-45, newspaper columnist, 1994—, producer, writer, host of closed circuit TV programs, 1998—. Named Alumni of Month, U. Ill. Coll. Law, 1982; inductee Sr. Illinoisans Hall of Fame, 1995. Mem. Am. Mgmt. Assn., Conf. Bd., Am., Ill, Chgo., Sangamon County bar assns., Am. Soc. Corp. Secs., Phi Gamma Delta. Clubs: Union League (Chgo.), Execs. (Chgo.). Republican. Office: 49 Inverness Rd Springfield IL 62704-3110

ROWE, MELINDA GRACE, public health service officer; b. Decatur, Ala., Aug. 18, 1953; m. Dana Calvin Craig Jr., Jan. 1, 1994. MD, U. Ala., 1978, MPH, 1985, MBA, 1987. Bd. cert. Am. Bd. Pediatrics, Am. Bd. Preventive Medicine. Pediatrics intern U. Ky., Lexington, 1978-79; pediatrics resident Lloyd Nolan Hosp., Fairfield, Ala., 1979-81; physician Columbus (Miss.) Children's Clinic, 1981, pvt. practice, Winfield, Ala., 1982-84; preventive medicine resident U. Ala., Birmingham, 1984-85; asst. state health officer Pub. Health Area III, Pelham, Ala., 1985-95; dir. health Jefferson County Health Dept., Louisville, 1995—. Asst. prof. U. Ala., Birmingham, 1988—, U. Louisville, 1995—. Bd. dirs. Cahaba River Soc., Birmingham, 1988—95, U. Ala.-Birmingham Nat. Alumni Soc., 1988—93, Health Ky., Goodwill Industries. Mem.: Ga. Med. Assn., Ky. Health Depts. Assn. (v.p.), Louisville/Jefferson County Primary Care Assn. (bd. dirs.), Jefferson County Med. Soc., Ky. Pediat. Soc., Ky. Pub. Health Assn. (pres.-elect), Ky. Med. Assn. Methodist. Avocations: reading, walking, travel, music. Office: 2011 Eisenhower Dr Savannah GA 31406

ROWE, MICHAEL DUANE, artist; b. Lykens, Pa., Nov. 5, 1947; m. Kathryn Jean Branoff. Student, Art Inst. Pitts., 1971-72. Exhibited in shows at Art Assn. Harrisburg, Pa., 1985, 86, 87, State Mus. Pa., 1986, 87, Doshi Gallery, Harrisburg, 1987, Cheltenham (Pa.) Art Ctr., 1989, 92, Delaplaine Art Ctr., Frederick, Md., 1989 (1st prize 1989), 90, 91, Immaculata (Pa.) Coll., 1990, U. of the Arts, Phil., 1990, Butler Inst. of Am. Art, Youngstown, Ohio, 1990, 92, Phila. Art Alliance, 1990, Altenative Mus., N.Y.C., 1990, 91, 95, Spaces, Cleve., 1991, Alexandria (La.) Art Mus., 1991, Pa. State U., 1992, Allentown (Pa.) Mus. Art, 1992, Muhlenberg Coll., Allentown, 1992 (award 1992), Michael Stone Gallery, Washington, 1992, Ea. N.Mex. U., 1992, Del. Ctr. for Contemporary Arts, Wilmington, 1993, Laguna Gloria Art Mus., Austin, Tex., 1993, Silvermine Art Guild Exhibit, New Cannan, Conn., 1993, Pa. State U., Univ. Park, 1993, East Tenn. U., Johnson City, 1994, Chrysler Mus., Norfolk, Va., 1994, Davidson (N.C.) Coll. Visual Arts Ctr., 1995, Southern Alleghenies Mus. of Art, 1995, Loretto, Pa., 1996, 97, 99, Susquehanna Art Mus., Harrisburg, Pa., 1998. Whitaker Ctr., Harrisburg, 1999, 2000; represented in permanent collection So. Alleghenies Mus., Loretto, Pa. Grantee Art Matters, Inc., 1988; Pa. Coun. of the Arts fellow, 1993. Episcopalian. Avocations: running, travelling, reading. Home: 814 Meadow Ln Camp Hill PA 17011-1545

ROWE, NEIL CHARLES, science educator; b. Chgo., July 18, 1953; s. Charles Louis Rowe and Bonnie Natalie Parsons; life ptnr. Suzanne Elizabeth Turner. PhD in Computer Sci., Stanford U., 1983. Professor U.S. Naval Postgraduate School, Monterey, CA, 1983—2002. Author: (book) Artificial Intelligence through Prolog, 1988, (website) www.cs.nps.navy.mil/people/faculty/rowe/index.html, 2002; contbr. Mem.: IEEE Computer Soc., ACM, Am. Assn. for Artificial Intelligence. Office: US Naval Postgrad Sch Code CS/Rp 833 Dyer Rd Monterey CA 93943 Business E-Mail: ncrowe@nps.navy.mil.

ROWE, PETER A. newspaper columnist; b. Walnut Creek, Calif., Sept. 7, 1955; s. Raymond Alan and Marion (Green) R.; m. Lynn Hanson, Aug. 13, 1977; children: Kyle, Reid, Alec. BA in History, BA in Journalism, U. Calif., Berkeley, 1977; MSJ, Northwestern U., 1981. Reporter Argus, Fremont, Calif., 1977-80, Va.-Pilot, Norfolk, 1981-84, San Diego Union, 1984-87, asst. features editor, 1987-88, features editor, 1988-92; columnist San Diego Union-Tribune, 1992—. Gannett fellow Northwestern U., 1980-81; Fulbright grantee, 2002—. Mem. Nat. Soc. Newspaper Columnists (pres. 2000-02). Roman Catholic. Office: San Diego Union Tribune PO Box 120191 San Diego CA 92112-0191 E-mail: peter.rowe@uniontrib.com.

ROWE, RICHARD HOLMES, lawyer; b. Waltham, Mass., Jan. 2, 1937; s. Robert C. Rowe and Roberta (Holmes) Hayes; m. Sylvia C. Barrow, Aug. 23, 1963; children: Elizabeth C., Dorothy H., Christopher H. AB, Bates Coll., 1957; JD, Harvard U., 1964. Bar: D.C. 1965, N.Y. 1980. Atty., exec. SEC, Washington, 1964-69, 70-79; v.p. Shareholders Mgmt. Co., L.A., 1969-70; ptnr. Proskauer Rose Goetz & Mendelsohn, Washington, 1979—. 1st lt. USMCR, 1957-60. Mem. ABA, FBA, D.C. Bar Assn., Assn. Bar City of N.Y. Democrat. Office: Proskauer Rose LLP 1233 20th St NW Ste 800 Washington DC 20036-2377

ROWE, SANDRA MIMS, editor; b. Charlotte, N.C., May 26, 1948; d. David Lathan and Shirley (Stovall) Mims; m. Gerard Paul Rowe, June 5, 1971; children: Mims Elizabeth, Sarah Stovall. BA, East Carolina U., Greenville, N.C., 1970; postgrad., Harvard U., 1991. Reporter to asst. mng. editor The Ledger-Star, Norfolk, Va., 1971-80, mng. editor, 1980-82, The Virginian-Pilot and The Ledger Star, Norfolk, 1982-84, exec. editor, 1984-86, v.p., exec. editor, 1986-93; editor The Oregonian, Portland, 1993—. Mem. Pulitzer Prize Bd., 1994—. Bd. visitors James Madison U., Harrisonburg, VA., 1991-95; chmn. adv. bd. The Knight Found.; mem. adv. bd. The Poynter Inst., Medill Sch. Journalism, Northwestern U. Named Woman of Yr. Outstanding Profl. Women of Hampton Rds., 1987; inducted into Va. Journalism Hall of Fame, 2000. Mem. Am. Soc. Newspaper Editors (pres., bd. dirs. 1992-99), Va. Press Assn. (bd. dirs. 1985-93). Episcopalian. Office: The Oregonian 1320 SW Broadway Portland OR 97201-3499*

ROWE, SHERYL ANN, librarian; b. Stephenville, Tex., Sept. 29, 1946; d. Horace Milton and Letha Faye (Hensley) Hughes; m. Darrell Vanoy Rowe, Nov. 27, 1969; children: Jason Burt, Shelley Jean. BA in English, Tarleton State U., Stephenville, 1967; MS in Libr. Sci., Tex. Women's U., Denton, 1986. Cert. tchr. secondary edn. Tchr. Lake Worth (Tex.) H.S., 1967-69, Aledo (Tex.) H.S., 1967-73, 78-84, libr., 1984—. Mem. ALA, Tex. Libr. Assn., Region XI Librs. Assn. (treas. 1984—), Am. Libr. Assn. Office: Aledo HS 1000 Bailey Ranch Rd Aledo TX 76008-4407 E-mail: srowe@aledo.k-12.tx.us.

ROWE, THOMAS DUDLEY, JR. law educator; b. Richmond, Va., Feb. 26, 1942; s. Thomas Dudley and Georgia Rosamond (Stripp) R.; m. Susan Fletcher French, Jan. 5, 2001. BA, Yale U., 1964; MPhil, Oxford U., Eng., 1967; JD, Harvard U., 1970. Bar: D.C. 1971, N.C. 1976. Law clk. to assoc. justice Potter Stewart U.S. Supreme Ct., Washington, 1970-71; asst. counsel adminstrv. practice subcom. U.S. Senate, 1971-73; assoc. Miller, Cassidy, Larroca & Lewin, 1973-75; assoc. prof. Duke U. Sch. Law, Durham, N.C., 1975-79, prof., 1979-96, Elvin R. Latty prof., 1996—, assoc. dean for rsch., 1981-84, sr. assoc. dean acad. affairs, 1995-96. Vis. prof. Georgetown U. Law Ctr., Washington, 1979—80, U. Mich. Law Sch., Ann Arbor, 1985, U. Va. Law Sch., Charlottesville, 1991, UCLA Law Sch., 2002; atty. Munger, Tolles & Solson, L.A., 1991; adv. com. on rules of civil procedure U.S. Jud. Conf., 1993—99; pres. North Ctrl. Legal Assistance Program, Durham, 1998—2001. Author (with others): Constitutional Theory: Arguments and Perspectives, 1993; actor(with others): Constitutional Theory: Arguments and Perspectives, 2000; author: Federal Courts in the 21st Century: Cases and Materials, 1996, 2002; contbr. Fellow U.S. Dept. Justice, Washington, 1980-81; Rhodes scholar, 1964-67; recipient Disting. Teaching award Duke Bar Assn., 1985. Mem. ABA, Am. Law Inst. Democrat. Office: Duke U Sch Law Durham NC 27708-0360

ROWE, WILLIAM DAVIS, financial services company executive; b. Hibbing, Minn., June 5, 1937; s. Richard Lawrence and Alicia (Davis) R.; m. Bobbie Grace Childress, Apr. 20, 1963; children— Lisa, William BA in Psychology, U. Minn, 1959, postgrad. in indsl. relations and bus. adminstrn., 1960; grad. exec. devel. program, Northeastern U., 1975; grad. Advanced Mgmt. Program, Harvard U., 1980. Dir. personnel, adminstrn. EDP Control Data Corp., Mpls., 1964-70; with Comml. Credit Co. subs. Control Data Corp, 1971-84, 85—; sr. v.p. consumer group Balt., 1975-81; sr. v.p. consumer realty services, 1981-83; sr. v.p. consumer banking services, 1983-84; v.p. market devel. Computer Service Co., Control Data Corp., Mpls., 1984; sr. v.p., chief adminstrv. officer Comml. Credit Co., Balt., 1985-87; pres. Enterprise Bank Network Bank Svcs. Co., Atlanta, 1988-91; exec. mng. dir., vice chmn. Foster Ptnrs. Inc., Peat Marwick Alliance Co., 1991—; pres., COO Foster Ptnrs., 1998—. Lectr. in field Mem. Mayor's Vol. Council of Equal Opportunity, Balt.; trustee St. Paul's Sch. for Girls, Brooklandville, Md., 1981— ; bd. dirs. Boy Scouts Am. Served to capt. USMC, 1960-63 Mem. Am. Fin. Services Assn. (bd. dirs. and mem. exec. com. 1980-84, consumer banking adv. com. 1983-84), Am. Mgmt. Assn. (pres.'s roundtable 1976) Republican. Avocations: hunting, skiing, cattle ranching.

ROWE, WILLIAM JOSEPH, internist; b. Cin., Oct. 31, 1927; s. Alvin Harold and Ida Claire (Omansky) R.; m. Mary Elaine Kenkel, Apr. 16, 1955. BS, U. Cin., 1950, MD, 1954. Diplomate Am. Bd. Internal Medicine. Asst. clin. prof. medicine Med. Coll. Ohio, Toledo, 1962-93; chmn. dept. medicine St. Vincent's Hosp., 1979-83; chief adv. com. cardiac rehab. N.W. Ohio Heart Assn., 1981-83. Del. citizen amb. program to China People to People, 1988. Contbr. articles to profl. jours., including Acta Astronautica, Lancet, Circulation. Capt. USAF, 1955-57. Mem. Aerospace Med. Assn., Nat. Space Soc., Brit. Interplanetary Soc. Republican. Achievements include described only the second space-related syndrome-the Apollo 15 space syndrome. Avocations: adventurer, runner, world traveler, author, tennis. Home: 1485 Bremerton Ln Keswick VA 22947 E-mail: rowerun@aol.com.

ROWELL, BARBARA CABALLERO, junior college official; b. New Orleans, Sept. 5, 1922; d. Albert Henry Wischnewske (stepfather) and Antoinette (Angelo) Caballero; m. J.C. Rowell, Dec. 17, 1941; children: Jerrie Carlene, Kerry Gene, Ricky Ray. AA in Bus. Adminstrn., Okaloosa Walton Jr. Coll., Niceville, Fla., 1973; BA in Social Scis., U. West Fla., 1987. Exec. sec. Bishop Enterprises, Ft. Walton Beach; office mgr. and real estate property mgr. Fred Cooke Real Estate, Fla.; adminstrv. sec. to v.p. Okaloosa Walton Jr. Coll., Niceville. Leader brownie scouts Girl Scouts U.S., 1954-56, cub scouts Boy Scouts Am., 1957-59; bd. dirs. U. West Fla. Ctr. for Life Long Learning; chair univ svc. com., pres., began Writing Lab; originator, implementor U. West Fla. Tutor Program, Career Fair, started scholarship program, Proctor Program; presenter S.E. Conf. Insts. of Learning in Retirement, Charleston, S.C.; gov.'s campaign vol.; state legislature campaign vol.; mem. Sr. Ctr. Life Long Learning, U. West Fla. Mem. AAUW, DAV Aux., Order of Ea. Star (past matron). Democrat. Roman Catholic. Avocations: education, travel, reading, gardening, dancing, volunteering.

ROWELL, CHARLES FREDERICK, chemistry educator; b. Lowville, N.Y., May 29, 1935; s. Erwin Charles and Winifred Jane (Manning) R.; m. JoAnn Cowling, June 19, 1955; children: Mark Edward, Jan Ellen. BS, Syracuse U., 1956; MS, Iowa State U., 1959; PhD, Oreg. State U., 1963. From. asst. to assoc. prof. U.S. Naval Postgrad. Sch., Monterey, Calif., 1962-75; field scientist Office Naval Research, Chgo., 1975-76; prof. U.S. Naval Acad., Annapolis, Md., 1976-2000, chmn. dept. chemistry, 1984-88. Scientist Forensic Techs. Internat., Annapolis, 1980—. Mem.: AAAS, Royal Soc. Chemistry, Am. Chem. Soc. (counselor 1980—, sect. chair 1982—83, nat. sec. membership affairs com. 1988—90, chmn. admissions com. 1989—91, chmn. constitution and bylaws com. 1994—96, coun. policy com. 1997—, chmn. coun. policy com. 2000—02), Sigma Xi (sec. chpt. 1972—73, v.p. 1973—74). Presbyterian. Home: 900 Randell Rd Severna Park MD 21146-4726

ROWELL, EDWARD MORGAN, retired foreign service officer, lecturer; b. Oakland, Calif., Oct. 13, 1931; s. Edward Joseph and Mary Helen (Mohler) Rowell; m. Lenora Mary Wood, Aug. 23, 1957; children: Edward Oliver, Karen Elizabeth Schuler, Christopher Douglas. BA in Internat. Relations, Yale U., 1953; postgrad., Stanford U., 1964-65, Stanford Bus. Sch., 1970-71. Fgn. service insp. U.S. Dept. State, Washington, 1971-74; dep. dir., econ. officer Office Iberian Affairs, 1974-75; dep. dir. Office West European Affairs, 1975-76, dir., 1977-78; minister-counselor U.S. Embassy, Lisbon, Portugal, 1978-83; dep. asst. sec. Bur. Consular Affairs, Washington, 1983-85; U.S. amb. to Bolivia La Paz, 1985-88; U.S. amb. to Portugal Lisbon, 1988-90; U.S. amb. to Luxemburg, 1990-94; sr. assoc. Global Bus. Access, Ltd., 1994—. Bd. dirs. Sourcecorp, Dallas, 1995—. Mem. adv. bd. Portuguese-Am. Leadership Coun. U.S., mem., 2000—, Cleveland Park Congregational Ch, Washington, 1956—; bd. dirs. Luso-Am Develop Found., 1988—90. With U.S. Army, 1953—55. Named Disting Vis Lectr, Angelo State Univ, 2000; recipient Bolivian Condor of the Andes, Grand Cross, 1988, Luxembourg Oaken Crown, 1994, Superior Honor Award, 1983, 1991, Predl Honor Award, 1988; fellow, Univ Calif, 1953; grantee, Una Chapman Cox Found, 1984; scholar, Yale Univ, 1949—52. Mem.: Diplomatic & Consular Officers Ret. (gov. 2001—), Arena Stage Assocs., Yale Univ. Alumni Assn., Stanford Univ. Alumni Assn., Wash. Inst. Foreign Affairs (membership com. 1999—), Assn. Diplomatic Studies & Training (pres. 1997—2001), Am. Foreign Svc. Assn. (v.p. 1995—97), Am Acad. Diplomacy (bd. dirs. 2002—), Cosmos Club. Avocations: photography, tennis, music. Home: 5414 Newington Rd Bethesda MD 20816-3316 E-mail: edmrowell@aol.com.

ROWELL, LESTER JOHN, JR. retired insurance company executive; b. Cleve., Apr. 2, 1932; s. Lester John and Francis Laureen (Corbett) R.; m. Patricia Ann Loesch, Jan. 16, 1953 (div. Sept. 1970); children: Deborah, Cynthia, Gregory, Maureen, Diane; m. Carol Ann Jankowski, Sept. 26, 1970. BS, Pa. State U., 1955; grad. Advanced Mgmt. Program, Harvard U. Bus. Sch., 1971. CLU. Second v.p., field mgmt. Mut. Life Ins. Co. N.Y., N.Y.C., 1969-70, v.p. agys., 1970-72, v.p. sales, 1972-78, sr. v.p., 1978-80; exec. v.p. Provident Mut. Life Ins. Co., Phila., 1980-84, pres., 1984-86, pres., chief oper. officer, 1987, pres., chief exec. officer, 1991-93, chmn., pres., chief exec. officer, 1993-96; ret. Bd. dirs. Pa. State U., The PMA Group. Capt. USMC, 1953-62. Recipient Alumni award Pa. State U., 1972, Disting. Alumni award Pa. State U., 1988; Alumni Fellow Pa. State U., 1987. Republican. E-mail: budrowell@aol.com.

ROWELL, LORING BERNARD, music educator, researcher; b. Lynn, Mass., Jan. 27, 1930; s. Ralph Merton and Pearl Davidson Rowell; m. Colleen Crowley, Dec. 26, 1956; children: Thomas John, Kathleen Mary. BS, Springfield Coll., Springfield, MA, 1950—53; PhD, U. Minn., Minneapolis, MN, 1956—62. Instr. Dept Medicine-University Wash., Seattle, 1963—64, rsch. asst. prof., 1964—68; rsch. assoc. prof. U. Wash., 1968—69, assoc. prof., 1970—1072, prof., 1972—97, prof. emeritus, 1997—. Adv. com. Nat. Institutes Health, Bethesda, Md., 1970—74; med. adv. bd. Am. Heart Assn., New York, NY, 1971—74, rsch. study com., Dallas, 1982—85. Contbr. articles to profl. jour.; author: (book) Human Circulation , Human Cardiovascular Control. Recipient Established Investigator, Am. Heart Assn., 1966-1971, Honor Award, Am. Coll. Sports Medicine, 1997, Carl J Wiggers Award, Am. Physiol. Soc., 2002. Fellow: Am. Heart Assn., Am. Physiol. Soc. (chair 1986—87); mem.: Western Soc. for Clin. Rsch. Avocations: skiing, mountaineering, mountain bicycling, oil painting. Office: University Washington School Medicine 1959 NE Pacific St Seattle WA 98195 Office Fax: 206-685-0619.

ROWE-MAAS, BETTY LU, real estate investor; b. Apr. 2, 1925; d. Horace Dewitt and Lucy Belle (Spiker) Rowe; children: Terry Lee, Clifford Lindsay, Craig Harrison, Joan Louise. Real estate investor, Saratoga, Calif., 1968—. Mem. Nat. Trust Hist. Preservation, Smithsonian Instn., Archeol. Inst. Am., San Jose Symphony, San Jose Cleve. Ballet, San Francisco Symphony, San Francisco Ballet, M. H. de Young Meml. Mus., Santa Barbara Mus. Art, Calif. Palice of the Legion of Honor, Loberro Theatre Found., Arlington Theater Restoration Fund, Bishop Mus. Hawaii, Friends of Kawai Mus., Friends of Princeville Libr., others; bd. dirs. Valley Inst. Theatre Arts; mem. Saratoga Good Govt., 1970-89; mem. Rt 85 Task Froce, 1978—, treas., 1984-89; treas. Traffic Relief for Saratoga. Mem. LWV, NOW (mem. world affairs coun. No. Calif. chpt.), Commonwealth Calif. Club (life), Santa Barbara Rep. Club, Toastmasters (past treas. Santa Barbara Rep. club # 5). Home: 5035 Kapiolani Loop Princeville HI 96722

ROWEN, MARSHALL, radiologist; b. Chgo. s. Harry and Dorothy (Kasnow) R.; m. Helen Lee Friedman, Apr. 5, 1952; children: Eric, Scott, Mark. AB in Chemistry with highest honors, U. Ill., Urbana, 1951; MD with honors, MS in Internal Medicine, U. Ill., Chgo., 1954. Diplomate Am. Bd. Radiology. Intern Long Beach (Calif.) VA Hosp., 1955; resident in radiology Los Angeles VA Hosp., 1955-58; practice medicine specializing in radiology Orange, Calif., 1960—. Chmn. bd. dirs. Moran, Rowen and Dorsey, Inc., Radiologists, 1969—; asst. radiologist L.A. Children's Hosp., 1958; assoc. radiologist Valley Presbyn. Hosp., Van Nuys, Calif., 1960; dir. dept. radiology Children's Hosp. Hosp., Orange, 1961—, v.p. staff, 1972; dir. dept. radiology St. Joseph Orange County, 1964—, chief staff, 1977—78, v.p., 1978—83, v.p., trustee, 1990—91, 1992—95; asst. clin. prof. radiology U. Calif., Irvine, 1967—70, assoc. clin. prof., 1979—82, clin. prof. radiology and pediat., 1976—99, pres. clin. faculty assn., 1980—81; trustee Choc. Padrinos; sec. Choco Health Svcs., 1987—89, v.p., 1990—93, trustee, 1995—, Found. Med. Care Orange County, 1972—76, Calif. Comm. Adminstrn. Svcs. Hosp., 1975—79, Profl. Practice Systems, 1990—92, Med. Specialty Mgrs., 1990—, St. Joseph Med. Corp., 1993—98; v.p. Found. Med. Care Children's Hosp., 1988—89; v.p., sr. v.p., bd. dirs. St. Joseph Med. Corp. IPA, 1995—98; bd. dirs. Orange Coast Managed Care Svcs., 1995—98, sr. v.p., 1995—98, Paragon Med. Imaging, 1993—, Calif. Managed Imaging, 1994—, Alliance Premier Hosps., 1995—96; chmn. bd. dirs. Children's Healthcare of Calif., 1995; corp. mem. Blue Shield Calif., 1995—2001; mem. physician's rev. com. Blue Cross Calif., 1996—2001, mem. Blue Shield coun. advisors, 2001—02. Mem. editorial bd. Western Jour. Medicine; contbr. articles to med. jours. Founder Orange County Performing Arts Ctr., mem. Laguna Art Mus., Laguna Festival of Arts, Opera Pacific, S. Coast Reportory, Am. Ballet Theater, World Affairs Council. Served to capt. M.C., U.S. Army, 1958-60. Recipient Rea sr. med. prize U. Ill, 1953; William Cook scholar U. Ill., 1951, Friend of Children award Children's Hosp. Guild, 1995, Charley award Children's Hosp., 1996. Fellow Am. Coll. Radiology; mem. AMA, Am. Heart Assn., Soc. Nuclear Medicine (trustee 1961-62), Orange County Radiol. Soc. (pres. 1968-69), Calif. Radiol. Soc. (pres. 1978-79), Radiol. Soc. So. Calif. (pres. 1976), Pacific Coast Pediatric Radiologists Assn. (pres. 1971), Soc. Pediatric Radiology, Calif. Med. Assn. (chmn. sect. on radiology 1978-79), Orange County Med. Assn. (chmn. UCI liaison com. 1976-78), Cardioradiology Soc. So. Calif., Radiol. Soc. N.Am., Am. Roentgen Ray Soc., Am. Coll. Physician Execs., Soc. Chmn. Radiologists Children Hosp., Center Club, Sports Club (Irvine), Phi Beta Kappa, Phi Eta Sigma, Omega Beta Phi, Alpha Omega Alpha. Office: 1201 W La Veta Ave Orange CA 92868-4213 E-mail: romarsh@aol.com.

ROWEN, RUTH HALLE, musicologist, educator; b. N.Y.C., Apr. 5, 1918; d. Louis and Ethel (Fried) Halle; m. Seymour M. Rowen, Oct. 13, 1940; children: Mary Helen Rowen, Louis Halle Rowen. BA, Barnard Coll., 1939; MA, Columbia U., 1941, PhD, 1948. Mgmt. ednl. dept. Carl Fischer, Inc., N.Y.C., 1954-63; assoc. prof. musicology CUNY, 1967-72, prof., 1972—, mem. doctoral faculty in musicology, 1967—. Author: Early Chamber Music, 1948, reprinted, 1974; (with Adele T. Katz) Hearing-Gateway to Music, 1959, (with William Simon) Jolly Come Sing and Play, 1956, Music Through Sources and Documents, 1979, (with Mary Rowen) Instant Piano, 1979, 80, 83, Symphonic and Chamber Music Score and Parts Bank, 1996; contbr. articles to profl. jours. Mem. ASCAP, Am. Musicol. Soc., Music Library Assn., Coll. Music Soc., Nat. Fedn. Music Clubs (nat. musicianship chmn. 1962-74, nat. young artist auditions com. 1964-74, N.Y. state chmn. Young Artist Auditions 1981, dist. coord. 1983, nat. bd. dirs. 1989-2000, rep. UN 1991-2000), N.Y. Fedn. Music Clubs (pres.), Phi Beta Kappa Home: 115 Central Park West At 25D New York NY 10023-4153 *Opportunity grows with each constructive thought.*

ROWEN, SAMUEL FREDERICK, education educator; b. Phila., Dec. 19, 1933; s. Edward Eugene and Agnes Veronica Rowen; m. Ruth Jean Evans, June 18, 1960; children: Lisa Carol Seay, Pamela Jean, Samuel Frederick Jr. BA in Philosophy, Wheaton (Ill.) Coll., 1960; MDiv in Theology, Westminster Theol. Sem., 1963; PhD in Edn., Mich. State U., 1981. Diplomate Am. Assn. Psychotherapy. Prof. Jamaica Bible Coll., Madeville, Jamaica, W.I., 1965-66; asst. to gen. dir. W.I. Mission, Miami, 1967-70; dir. curriculum Missionary Internship, Farmington, Mich., 1970-90; assoc. prof. mission Reformed Theol. Sem., Jackson, Miss., 1990-92; pres. Ednl. Projects Internat., Farmington, 1992—. Co-editor: Missions: The Education in World Perspective, 1984; co-author: Sojourners: Family on the Move, 1990. With U.S. Army, 1953-55. Mem. Phi Kappa Phi, Delta Epsilon Ch. Presbyterian. Office: Ednl Projects Internat PO Box 216 Farmington MI 48332-0216

ROWLAND, ALLEN R. grocery company executive; With Albertson's, Boise, 1971, various positions to sr. v.p. various cities, 1971-96; pres., COO Smith's Food & Drug Ctrs., 1996-97; pres., CEO, dir. Winn-Dixie Stores, Inc., Jacksonville, Fla., 1999—. Office: Winn-Dixie Stores Inc 5050 Edgewood Ct Jacksonville FL 32254-3699*

ROWLAND, ARTHUR RAY, librarian; b. Hampton, Ga., Jan. 6, 1930; s. Arthur and Jennie (Goodman) R.; m. Jane Thomas, July 1, 1955; children: Dell Ruth, Anna Jane. AB, Mercer U., Macon, Ga., 1951; M. Librarianship, Emory U., 1952; postgrad., Oxford U., 1989. Circulation asst. Ga. State Coll. Library, 1952, circulation librarian, 1952-53; librarian Armstrong Coll., Savannah, Ga., 1954-56; head circulation dept. Auburn U. Library, 1956-58; librarian, assoc. prof. library sci. Jacksonville U., 1958-61, Augusta Coll., 1961-76, prof., libr., 1976-91, libr. emeritus, 1991—. Lectr. libr. edn. U. Ga., 1962-66; trustee Augusta-Richmond County Pub. Libr., 1980-93, pres. bd. trustees, 1983-85, v.p. bd., 1988-91; trustee Augusta Regional Libr., chmn., 1984-85; trustee East Cen. Ga. Regional Libr., 1987-93, chmn., 1988-91; chmn. Gov.'s Conf. on Ga. Librs. and Info. Svcs., 1977; del. White House Conf. on Librs. and Info. Sci., 1979; cons. on libr. mgmt. to Govt. of Indonesia, 1986. Author: Bibliography of the Writings of Georgia History, 1966, A Guide to the Study of Augusta and Richmond County, Georgia, 1967, (with Helen Callahan) Yesterday's Augusta, 1976, (with James E. Dorsey) A Bibliography of the Writings on Georgia History 1900-1970, rev. edit., 1978, (with Marguerite F. Fogleman) Reese Library Genealogical Resources, 1988, supplement, 1990, Goodman Cousins, 1988, Rowland Cousins, 1990, New Guide to the Study of Augusta, 1990, Index to City Directory of Augusta, Georgia, 1841-1879, 1991, More Goodman Cousins, 1993, My Fair Grandmother, 1994, Distant Cousins, The Huguenots Connecting Rowland, Bulloch, de Bourdeaux, DeVeaux and Roosevelt Families of S.C., N.C. and Ga., 1995, The Bessent Family of Georgia, 1995, Reeves Family of Georgia, 1996, Descendants of Wiley Reeves, 1996, Rowland-Huckaby Connections, 1996, Georgia Almanacs, 1996, Rowland Family of Virginia, North Carolina and Georgia and Beyond, 1998, Atkinson Family in Virginia, 1998, Ancestors of David Jackson, 1998, Ancestors of Rachael Hines Lewis, 1998, Ancestors of Elizabeth Proctor in Virginia and England, 1998, Ancestors of Martha Whitehead, 1998, Wiley Reeves, His Descendants and Ancestors, 1999, John Rowland, Immigrant, 2000, Reeves Family in England, Virginia, North Carolina, Georgia and Beyond, 2000, The Mississippi Branch of the Rowland Family, 2000, Ancestors and Connections of Dunbar Rowland, 2000, Printing in Louisville, 2000, Confederate Printing in Augusta, Ga., 2000, Goodman Family of N.C., Ga. and Beyond Their Cherokee Indian Heritage, 2000, Hillhouse Family of Wash., Ga., 2000, Printing in Wash., Ga., 2000, Jacob Martin Hugenot of Charleston, S.C., 2000, John Gensel of Charleston, S.C., 2000, Bessent Family, 2000, Rowland Faimly in Ga., 2000; editor: Reference Services, 1964, Historical Markers of Richmond County, Georgia, rev. edit., 1971, The Catalog and Cataloging, 1969, The Librarian and Reference Service, 1977, Reminiscences of Augusta Marines, 1985; supervising editor (with Heard Robertson) Jour. Archibald Campbell, 1981; contbr. to profl. jours. V.p. Ga. Libr. Assn. Trustees and Friends, 1989-91. With USN, 1948-49. Recipient Nix-Jones award for disting. service Ga. Library Assn., 1981,,Town and Gown award Augusta Coll. Alumni Assn., 1985. Mem. ALA, Am. Assn. State and Local History, Bibliog. Soc. Am., Southeastern Libr. Assn. (hon. life, exec. bd. 1971-72), Ga. Libr. Assn. (hon. life, 2d v.p. 1965-67, 71-73, 1st v.p., pres.-elect 1973-75, pres. 1975-77, chmn. budget com. 1977-79, adv. to pres. 1979-83, 85-92), Ctrl. Savannah River Area Libr. Assn. (past pres., editor union list of serials 1967), Duval County Libr. Assn. (past v.p.), Nat. Geneal. Soc., Ga. Geneal. Soc., N.C. Geneal. Soc., Va. Geneal. Soc., Augusta Geneal. Soc., Richmond County Hist. Soc. (curator 1964-91, pres. 1967-69, founder, editor Richmond County History), Huguenot Soc. S.C., Ga. Hist. Soc. (curator emeritus), Ga. Bapt. Hist. Soc., Nat., Young Men's Libr. Assn. (v.p. 1988-91), Ga. Trusts for Hist. Preservation, Hist. Augusta (trustee emeritus), Soc. Ga. Archivists, Kappa Phi Kappa. Baptist. Address: One Seventh St Ste 1503 Augusta GA 30901 E-mail: RRow999@aol.com.

ROWLAND, CHRISTOPHER LEE, filmmaker, educator, artist; b. Apple Valley, CA, July 15, 1966; s. Ivan Oliver Rowland, Patricia Ann Rowland. BFA; MFA, Otis Coll. Art and Design, L.A., 2000. Indy filmmaker Crimmit Projects, Hermosa Beach, Calif., 1994—2002. Indy Filmmaker Crimmit Projects, Hermosa Beach, 1994—2002; tchr. Otis Coll., L.A., 1996—2002; editor Roy Walford, Venice, Calif., 2000—02. Home: 1022 7th St Hermosa Beach CA 90254 Office: Crimmit Projects 1022 7th St Hermosa Beach CA 90254 Personal E-mail: lrow@hotmail.com.

ROWLAND, ESTHER E(DELMAN), retired college dean; b. N.Y.C., Apr. 12, 1926; d. Abraham Simon and Ida Sarah (Shifrin) Edelman; m. Lewis P. Rowland, Aug. 31, 1952; children: Andrew, Steven, Judith. BA, U. Wis., 1946; MA, Columbia U., 1948, MPhil, 1984; cert. in bioethics, Columbia U./Albert Einstein, 1996. Instr. in polit. sci. CCNY, 1947-51, Mt. Holyoke Coll., South Hadley, Mass., 1948-49; dir. health professions adv. bd. U. Pa., Phila., 1971-73; adviser to pre-profl. students Barnard Coll., N.Y.C., 1974-79, dean for pre-profl. students, 1980-93, assoc. dean studies, 1989-95; ret., 1995—. Proofreader Monthly Review, N.Y.C., 1997—. Mem. exec. com. Nat. Emergency Civil Liberties Com., N.Y.C., 1975-90; mem. exec. com. Women's Counseling Project, 1981-86. Mem. N.E. Assn. Health Professions Advisers (exec. com. 1973-74), N.E. Assn. Pre Law Advisors (exec. com. 1981-83, 85-86), Neurol. Inst. Aux., N.Y.C. Found. Sr. Citizens (ombudsman 1997-99), Aux. Am. Acad. Neurologists (exec. bd. 1999-2001). Home: 404 Riverside Dr New York NY 10025-1861 E-mail: eerowland@aol.com.

ROWLAND, FRANK SHERWOOD, chemistry educator; b. Delaware, Ohio, June 28, 1927; m. Joan Lundberg, 1952; children: Ingrid Drake, Jeffrey Sherwood. AB, Ohio Wesleyan U., 1948; MS, U. Chgo., 1951, PhD, 1952, DSc (hon.), 1989, Duke U., 1989, Whittier Coll., 1989, Princeton U., 1990, Haverford Coll., 1992, Clark U., 1996, U. East Anglia, 1996; LLD (hon.), Ohio Wesleyan U., 1989, Simon Fraser U., 1991, U. Calgary, 1997; laurea honoris causa, U. Urbino (Italy), 1998; DSc, Carleton Coll., 1998, Gustavus Adolphus Coll., 1997, Occidental Coll., 1998, Kanagawa Univ., Japan, 1999, LaTrobe U., Australia, 2000, U. Waterloo, Can., 2001, Ohio State U., 2002. Instr. chemistry Princeton (N.J.) U., 1952—56; asst. prof. chemistry U. Kans., 1956—58, assoc. prof. chemistry, 1958—63, prof. chemistry, 1963—64, U. Calif., Irvine, 1964—, dept. chmn., 1964—70, Aldrich prof. chemistry, 1985—89, Bren prof. chemistry, 1989—94, Bren rsch. prof., 1994—. Humboldt sr. scientist Fed. Republic Germany, 1981; chmn. Dahlem (Germany) Conf. on Changing Atmosphere, 1987; vis. scientist Japan Soc. for Promotion Sci., 1980; co-dir. western region Nat. Inst. Global Environ. Changes, 1989—93; del. Internat. Coun. Sci. Unions, 1993—98; fgn. sec. NAS, 1994—2002, Korean Acad. Sci. Tech.; lectr., cons. in field; mem. ozone commn. Internat. Assn. Meteorology and Atmospheric Physics, 1980—88, hon. life mem., 1996, mem. commn. on atmospheric chemistry and global pollution, 1979—91; mem. acid rain peer rev. panel U.S. Office of Sci. and Tech., Exec. Office of White House, 1982—84; mem. vis. com. Max Planck Inst., Heidelberg and Mainz, Germany, 1982—96; ozone trends panel mem. NASA, 1986—88; chmn. Gordon Conf. Environ. Scis.-Air, 1987; mem. Calif. Coun. Sci. Tech., 1989—95; mem. exec. com. Tyler Prize, 1992—. Contbr. articles. Named to, GTE Acad. All-Am. Hall of Fame, 2000; recipient numerous awards including, John Wiley Jones award, Rochester Inst. Tech., 1975, Disting. Faculty Rsch. award, U. Calif., Irvine, 1976, Profl. Achievement award, U. Chgo., 1977, Billard award, N.Y. Acad. Sci., 1977, Tyler World Prize in Environ. Achievement, 1983, Global 500 Roll of Honor for Environ. Achievement, UN Environment Program, 1988, Dana award for Pioneering Achievements in Health, 1987, Silver medal, Royal Inst. Chemistry U.K., 1989, Wadsworth award, N.Y. State Dept. Health, 1989, medal, U. Calif. Irvine, 1989, Japan prize in Environ. Sci., 1989, Dickson prize, Carnegie-Mellon U., 1991, Albert Einstein prize, World Cultural Coun., 1994, Nobel Prize in chemistry, 1995, Alumni medal, U. Chgo., 1997, Nevada medal, 1997; fellow Guggenheim Found., 1962, 1974. Fellow: Am. Geophys. Union (Roger Revelle medal 1994), Am. Phys. Soc. (Leo Szilard award for physics in pub. interest 1979), AAAS (pres.-elect 1991, pres. 1992, chmn. bd. dirs. 1993); mem.: Korean Acad. Sci. Tech., European Acad. Arts, Scis. and Humanities, Am. Meteorol. Soc. (hon.), Am. Chem. Soc. (chmn. divsn. nuclear sci. and tech. 1973—74, chmn. divsn. phys. chemistry 1974—75, E.F. Smith lectureship 1980, Orange County award 1975, Tolman medal 1976, Zimmerman award 1980, Environ. Sci. and Tech. award 1983, Esselen award 1987, Peter Debye Phys. Chem. award 1993), Am. Acad. Arts and Scis., NAS (co-DATA com. 1977—82, com. atmospheric scis., solar-terrestial com. 1979—83, sci. com. on problems environment 1986—89, bd. environ. studies and toxicology 1986—91, com. on atmospheric chemistry 1987—89, Infinite Voyage film com. 1988—92, Robertson Meml. lectr. 1993, chmn. com. on internat. orgns. and programs 1993—2002, chmn. office of internat. affairs 1994—2002, co-chmn. interacad. panel 1995—2000, mem. exec. com. 2000—02), Sigma Xi, Phi Beta Kappa. Home: 4807 Dorchester Rd Corona Del Mar CA 92625-2718 Office: U Calif Irvine Dept of Chemistry 571 Rowland Hall Irvine CA 92697-2025 Office Fax: 949-824-2905. E-mail: rowland@uci.edu.

ROWLAND, HOWARD RAY, mass communications educator; b. Eddy County, N.Mex., Sept. 9, 1929; s. Lewis Marion and Ursula Lorene (Hunt) R.; m. Meredith June Lee, Apr. 19, 1951; children: Runay Ilene Olson, Rhonda Lee Fisher. B in Journalism, U. Mo., 1950; MS in Journalism, So. Ill. U., 1959; PhD, Mich. State U., 1969. Feature writer Springfield (Mo.) Newspapers, Inc., 1954; newspaper editor Monett (Mo.) Times, 1954-55; editl. writer So. Ill. U., Carbondale, 1955-59; pub. rels. dir. St. Cloud (Minn.) State U., 1959-86, asst. dean, 1986-87, 88-90; dir. Ctr. for British Studies, Alnwick, Eng., 1987-88, 90-91. Emeritus prof. St. Cloud State U., 1991—; cons. Conf. of Campus Ombudsmen, Berkeley, 1971; recorder Seminar on Fund Raising, Washington, 1985; bibliographer Higher Edn. Bibliography Yearbook, 1987. Author: American Students in Alnwick Castle, 1990, St. Cloud State University--125 Years, 1994; editor: Effective Community Relations, 1980; sect. editor: Handbook of Institutional Advancement, 1986; author book revs. Chair All-Am. City Com., St. Cloud, 1973-74. With U.S. Army, 1951-53. NDEA doctoral fellowship Mich. State U., 1967-69; recipient Appreciation award Mayor of St. Cloud, 1974, Disting Svc. award Coun. for Advancement and Support of Edn., 1985. Mem. Soc. of Profl. Journalists (Minn. chpt. pres. 1963-64, dep. dir. 1965-67), Coun. for Advancement and Support of Edn. (dist. 5 chair 1977-79, Leadership award 1979), Rotary Internat., Phi Delta Kappa (Mich. State U. chpt. pres. 1968-69, St. Cloud State Univ. chpt. pres. 1978-79). Presbyterian. Avocations: writing, fishing, travel, photography, antiques. Home: 29467 Kraemer Lake Rd Saint Joseph MN 56374-9646 E-mail: rjrowland@mymailstation.com. *Striving to achieve is more rewarding than striving to succeed. Achievement brings personal satisfaction more fulfilling than recognition and compensation.*

ROWLAND, JAMES RICHARD, electrical engineering educator; b. Muldrow, Okla., Jan. 24, 1940; s. Richard Cleveland and Imogene Beatrice (Angel) R.; m. Jonell Condren, Aug. 24, 1963 (dec. May 1991); children: Jennifer Lynn, Angela Janel; m. Mary Anderson, Jan. 2, 1995. BSEE, Okla. State U., 1962; MSEE, Purdue U., 1964, PhD in Elec. Engring., 1966. Registered profl. engr., Okla. Instr. Purdue U., West Lafayette, Ind., 1964-65; from asst. to assoc. prof. Ga. Inst. Tech., Atlanta, 1966-71; from assoc. to full prof. Okla. State U., Stillwater, 1971-85; prof., chmn. dept. elec. and computer engring. U. Kans., Lawrence, 1985-89, prof., 1985—. Cons. Lockheed-Ga. Co., Marietta, 1966-71, U.S. Army Missile Command, Huntsville, Ala., 1969-79, Sandia Nat. Labs., Albuquerque, 1979, Puritan-Bennett, Lenexa, Kans., 1992. Author: Linear Control Systems, 1986; mem. editorial adv. bd. Computer and Elec. Engring., 1971-98; co-contbr. 50 articles to profl. jours. Fellow IEEE (edn. soc. pres. 1982-83, Centennial medal 1984, edn. soc. Achievement award 1986, edn. conf. award 1988, Region 5 Oustanding Educator award 1995), Am. Soc. Engring. Edn. (dir. grad. div. 1987-89), Eta Kappa Nu (dir. 1989-91), Kiwanis. Republican. Baptist. Avocations: golf, gardening. Home: 2424 Free State Ct Lawrence KS 66047-2831 Office: U Kans Dept Elec Engring & Computer Sci 415 Snow Hall Lawrence KS 66045-7504 E-mail: jrowland@ku.edu.

ROWLAND, JOAN CHARLOTTE, pianist, educator; b. Toronto, Ont., Can., May 7, 1930; came to U.S., 1951; d. Walter Mills and Kathryn Meengs (Bowman) R.; m. John M. Thornton, May 5, 1976; children: Christopher, Fenella, Hugh, Robert. BA in English Lit., Columbia U., 1970. Pianist Columbia Can. Trio, 1951-53, Reginald Kell Players, 1953-55, The Piano Duo Schnabel, 1980—; tchr. piano Manhattan Sch. Music, 1990—. Solo debut with Toronto Symphony, 1942; solo recital, London, 1994, 96; recordings for Sheffield Lab and Town Hall Records. Mem. Internat. Soc. Contemporary Music (bd. dirs. 1993—). Avocations: outdoor sports, collecting antiques, reading. Home: 285 Riverside Dr New York NY 10025-5276

ROWLAND, JOHN G. governor, former congressman; b. Waterbury, Conn., May 24, 1957; s. Sherwood L. and Florence (Jackson) R.; m. Deborah Nabhan; children: Kirsten Elizabeth, Robert John, Julianne Marie. BS in Bus. Adminstrn., Villanova U., 1979. Mem. Conn. Ho. of Reps., 1981—85, 99th-101st Congress from 5th Conn. dist., 1985-91; gov. State of Conn., 1995—. Pres. Rowland Assocs. Ambassador, St. Mary's Hosp., Waterbury; bd. dirs. Am. Cancer Soc., Waterbury; chmn. Rep. Gov.'s Assoc., Washington, D.C., 2001. Recipient Disting. Service award VFW, Holy Cross Alumni Assn. Republican. Home: 990 Prospect Ave Hartford CT 06105-1102 Office: Off of the Governor Exec Chambers 210 Capitol Ave Hartford CT 06106-1535*

ROWLAND, KATHLEEN O'SHEA, accountant; b. Lake Worth, Fla., June 9, 1962; d. Thomas Francis Jr. and Ruth Ann O'Shea; m. Robert Andrew Rowland, Mar. 26, 1994; children: Emily Caitlin, Eric Bradley. AA, U. Fla., 1982, BS, 1984, M in Acctg., 1985. CPA, Fla; CMA. Auditor Price Waterhouse & Co., West Palm Beach, Fla., 1985-91; contr. DeJay Corp., Palm Beach Gardens, 1991-97; adj. prof. Palm Beach C.C., Lake Worth, 1999; temporary contr. Sailfish Point POA, Stuart, 1999. Mem.: AICPA, Inst. Mgmt. Accts. (v.p. profl. edn. Palm Beach Area chpt. 1996—97, v.p. comms. 1997—98, pres. 1998—99, v.p. membership 1999—2000, v.p. adminstrn. 2000—), Moms Offering Moms Support Club (treas. 2000, pres. 2000—01, spkr. 2000—01, publicity coord. 2000—01, newsletter editor 2001—02). E-mail: kathyoshea@bellsouth.net.

ROWLAND, LANDON HILL, diversified holding company executive; b. Fuquay Springs, N.C., May 20, 1937; s. Walter Elton and Elizabeth Carr (Williams) R.; m. Sarah Fidler, Dec. 29, 1959; children: Sarah Elizabeth, Matthew Hill, Joshua Carr. BA, Dartmouth Coll., 1959; LL.B., Harvard U., 1962. Bar: Mo. Assoc. Watson, Ess, Marshall & Enggas, Kansas City, Mo., 1962-70, ptnr., 1970-80; v.p. Kansas City So. Industries, Inc., 1980-83, pres., chief oper. officer, 1983-86, pres., chief exec. officer, 1987—, also bd. dirs.; pres., chief exec. officer Kansas City So. Ry. Co., 1990-91, chmn., 1990—. Lectr. antitrust law U. Mo. Kansas City; chmn. DST Systems, 1983—.

Co-author West's Mo. Practice Series. Trustee Midwest Rsch. Inst., Kansas City, Mo.; chmn. bd. dirs. Swope Ridge Health Care Ctr.; bd. dirs. Lyric Opera of Kansas City, Am. Royal, Jacob L. & Ella C. Loose Found.; chmn. Met. Performing Arts Fund. Mem. ABA, Mo. Bar Assn., Phi Beta Kappa. Clubs: Kansas City Country, Kansas City, River. Home: Ever Glades Farm 12717 NE Mt Olivet Rd Kansas City MO 64166-1236 Office: Stilwell Financial Inc 920 Main St Kansas City MO 64105-2008

ROWLAND, LAWRENCE SANDERS, history educator; b. St. Paul, May 19, 1942; s. Richard Henry and Elizabeth (Sanders) R.; m. Margot Hunter, Jan. 5, 1974; children: Lawrence S., Katherine Hunter, Margaret Waterhouse. BA, Hamilton Coll., 1964; MA, U. S.C., Columbia, 1971, PhD, 1978. Asst. dir. U. S.C., Beaufort, 1971-77, assoc. dean acad. affairs, 1977-83, assoc. prof. history, 1983-86, prof., 1986—, now disting. prof. emeritus. Author: Window on the Atlantic, 1990, History of Beaufort County, S.C., 1996; author articles on S.C. history. Pres. Beaufort County Hist. Soc., 1975-76, S.C. Hist. Soc., Charleston, 1995-96; chmn. Beaufort County Hist. Preservation Bd., 1993—; trustee Beaufort Coll., 1997—, Beaufort Acad., 1991-93, 95-97; conv. chmn. Beaufort County Rep. Party, 1991, 93; bd. dirs. S.C. Policy Coun. and Ednl. Found., vice chair, 1996-97. Lt. U.S. Navy, 1964-68. Recipient Gov.'s award in the humanities State of S.C., 1993; named Outstanding Tchr., U. S.C. at Beaufort, 1972, 76, 78, 83, 95. Mem. Ga. Hist. Soc., Rotary Club of Beaufort. Republican. Roman Catholic. Avocations: boating, sailing. Office: U SC at Beaufort 801 Carteret St Beaufort SC 29902-4601

ROWLAND, LESLIE S. historian, educator; b. Columbia, Mo., Jan. 15, 1947; d. D. Wayne Rowland and Maxine Sipe. Student, Silliman U., Philippines, 1966-67; BA, Tex. Christian U., 1968; MA, U. Rochester, 1970, PhD, 1991. Archivist Nat. Archives of the U.S., Washington, 1974-76; assoc. editor Freedmen & So. Soc. Project, U. Md., College Park, 1976-81, co-editor, 1983-91, dir., 1991—; assoc. prof. U. Md., 1991—; rsch. fellow Carter Woodson Inst., U. Va., Charlottesville, 1981-83. Editor: Freedom: A Documentary History of Emancipation, 1861-1867, 5 vols., 1982—, Free At Last, 1992, Slaves No More, 1992, Families and Freedom, 1997, Freedom's Soldiers, 1998. Recipient J. Franklin Jameson prize Am. Hist. Assn., 1985, Founders award Confederate Meml. Literary Soc., 1985, 95, Thomas Jefferson prize Soc. for History in the Fed. Govt., 1987, 91, 95, Lincoln prize Gettysburg Coll., 1994. Mem. Assn. for Documentary Editing (councilor-at-large 1993-96, pres. 1998-99). Office: Dept History Univ Md College Park MD 20742

ROWLAND, LEWIS PHILLIP, neurology educator, editor, clinical investigator; b. Bklyn., Aug. 3, 1925; s. Henry Alexander and Cecile (Coles) Rowland; m. Esther Edelman Rowland, Aug. 31, 1952; children: Andrew Simon, Steven Samuel, Joy Rosenthal McIntyre. BS, Yale U., 1945, MD, 1948; doctorate (hon.), U. Aix-Marseilles, France, 1986, U. Padua, 1996. Diplomate Am. Bd. Psychiatry and Neurology. Intern New Haven Hosp., 1949-50; asst. resident N.Y. Neurol. Inst., 1950-52, fellow, 1953; clin. assoc. NIH, Bethesda, Md., 1953-54; practice rsch. medicine, specializing in neurology N.Y.C., 1954-67, Phila., 1967-73, N.Y.C., 1973—; asst. neurologist Montefiore Hosp., 1954-57; vis. fellow Nat. Inst. Med. Rsch., London, 1956; from asst. prof. to prof. neurology Columbia Coll. Physicians and Surgeons, 1957-67, prof. dept. neurology, 1973—, chmn. dept. neurology, 1973-98; prof., chmn. dept. neurology U. Pa., Med. Sch., 1967-73; from asst. neurologist to attending neurologist Presbyn. Hosp., 1957-67; co-dir. Neurol. Clin. Rsch. Ctr., 1961-67, dir. neurology service, 1973-98, attending neurologist, 1973—, pres. med. bd., 1991-94. Cons. Harlem Hosp., 1973—; mem. med. adv. bd. Myasthenia Gravis Found., pres., 1971-73; med. adv. bd. Muscular Dystrophy Assocs., Nat. Multiple Sclerosis Soc., Com. to Combat Huntington's Disease; pres. Parkinson's Disease Found., 1979— ; mem. tng. grants com. Nat. Inst. Neurol. Disorders and Stroke, NIH, 1971-73, bd. sci. counselors, 1978-83, chmn., 1981-83, mem. nat. adv. coun., 1986-90, cons. to dir., 2000-01. Mem. editl. bd. Archives of Neurology, 1968-76, Advances in Neurology, 1969—, Italian Jour. Neurol. Sci., 1979—, Handbook of Clin. Neurology, 1982—, New Eng. Jour. Medicine, 1990-2000, Med. Letter, 1990-97, Jour. Neurol. Sci., 1991—, Jour. Neuromuscular Disorders, 1991-97, Clin. Neurosci., 1995-98; editor-in-chief Neurology, 1977-87, Neurology Today, 2001—; assoc. editor Medlink, 1995—. With USNR, 1942-44; with USPHS, 1953-54. Mem. Am. Neurol. Assn. (pres. 1980, hon. mem. 1989—), Am. Acad. Neurology (pres.-elect 1987-89, pres. 1989-91, hon. mem. 1997—), Phila. Neurol. Soc. (pres. 1972), Assn. Research Nervous Mental Disease (pres. 1969, trustee 1976—, v.p. 1980, chmn. bd. trustees 1992-98), Assn. Univ. Profs. Neurology (sec. 1971-74, pres. 1978), Am. Acad. Neurol. Edn. and Rsch. Found. (pres. 1996, chair bd. trustees 1997-99), Eastern Pa. Multiple Sclerosis Soc. (chmn. med. adv. bd. 1969-73); hon. mem. Neurol. Socs. France, Poland, Can., Europe, Italy, Gt. Britain, Spain, Japan; mem. N.Y.C. Multiple Sclerosis Soc. (chmn. med. adv. bd. 1977-92) E-mila. Home: 404 Riverside Dr New York NY 10025-1861 Office: Columbia-Presbyn Med Ctr Neurological Inst 710 W 168th St New York NY 10032-2603 E-mail: lpr1@columbia.edu.

ROWLAND, LUCY MINOGUE, librarian; b. Washington, Jan. 21, 1948; d. James Alexander and Adelaide Lancaster (Emley) Minogue; m. Charles Alden Rowland IV, Nov. 28, 1986; children: William, Eleanor Price. BS, Va. Poly. Inst., 1969; MS, Va. Poly. Inst. & State U., 1972; MLS, U. Md., 1979; postgrad., U. Ga., 1983-88. Microbiologist Va. Poly. Inst. & State U., Blacksburg, 1971-73, U. Ga., Athens, 1973-75; subject specialist U. Ga. Librs., 1975-79; head, sci. collections and br. svcs., 1992—; med. resources libr. U. Ga., Athens, 1980-92. Invited lectr. U. N.C., Chapel Hill, 1984; contract reviewer NIH, Research Triangle Park, 1988, 95—; regional coord. So. Agrl. Documents Microfilming Project, 1970-82, 83-86. Editor New Urban Post, 2001-; contbr. chpt. to book and articles to profl. jours. Mem. Atlanta Kennel Club, 1980—; mem. design com. U. Ga. Student Learning Ctr.; mem. Clarke County Dem. Com., Athens, 1990—, bd. dirs., 1994—; bd. dirs. Athens (Ga.) Area Dem. Women, 1986—; vice chair Athens-Clarke County Planning Commn., 1990-93, chair, 1993-94; mem. Athens-Clarke-Oconee Regional Transp. Study, 1992-98; mem. Ga. State Dem. Com., 1997—; pres. bd. dirs. Jeannette Rankin Found., 2001-. Mem. AMA (nat. patient safety found. comms. com. 1998—), Am. Planning Assn., Am. Soc. for Microbiology, Spl. Librs. Assn. (numerous posts, coms. 1989—), Coun. Planning Librs. (edit. adv. bd.), N.Y. Acad. Scis., Athens C. of C. (Leadership Athens), Am. Shetland Sheepdog Assn., Congress for the New Urbanism, Sigma Xi (recognition award 1983. Mem. Soc. Of Friends. Avocation: political campaign strategist. Home: 475 University Dr Athens GA 30605-1553 Office: U Ga Sci Libr Athens GA 30602

ROWLAND, PAUL MCDONALD, education educator, educator; b. Waverly, N.Y., Oct. 27, 1948; s. Donald Victor and Edith Irene (McDonald) R.; m. Linda S. Wackwitz (div. Dec. 1993); m. Ann G. Batchelder. BA, Rutgers U., 1970, MS, 1979; PhD, N.Mex. State U., 1988. Sci. tchr. South Jefferson Ctrl. Schs., Adams, N.Y., 1973-80; edn. specialist N.Mex. Solar Energy Inst., Las Cruces, 1983-86; asst. prof. sci. edn. East Carolina U., Greenville, N.C., 1988-89; prof. curriculum and instrn. No. Ariz. U., Flagstaff, 1989—. Dir. Ctr. for Environ. Scis. and Edn. No. Ariz. U., Flagstaff, 2000—; dir. No. Ariz. Environ. Edn. Resources Ctr., Flagstaff, 1994—; bd. dirs. Global Network Environ. Edn. Ctrs., Knoxville. Contbr. articles to profl. jours. and books. Dir. Environ. Scis. Day Camp, Flagstaff; bd. dirs. Ariz. Nat. Hist. Assn. Mem. N.Am. Assn. for Environ. Edn., Nat. Assn. for Rsch. in Sci. Teaching, Am. Ednl. Rsch. Assn. Avocations: sea kayaking, landscape design, photography. Home: 6686 E Eagle Crest Dr Flagstaff AZ 86004-7141 Office: No Ariz Univ PO Box 5774 Flagstaff AZ 86011-0001 E-mail: paul.rowland@nau.edu.

ROWLAND, RALPH THOMAS, retired architect; b. Elizabeth, N.J., Oct. 10, 1920; s. Thomas Aloysius and Anna Frances (McQuaid) R.; m. Bernice Barbara Cannizzo, Sept. 7, 1946; children: Glenn Thomas, Mark Louis, Roy Joseph, Lisa Rowland Majewski. Student, Manhattan Coll., 1937-38, Columbia U., 1945-49. Archtl. field supr., specifier Voorhees Walker Foley & Smith, N.Y.C., 1945-50; specifier, project mgr. Sargent Webster Crenshaw & Folley, Watertown, N.Y., 1951-53; pvt. practice Hamden, Conn., 1958-65; field supr. Fletcher Thompson, Inc., Bridgeport, 1954-56, project mgr., 1957, 65-73, asso., 1969-73, v.p., 1973-81, dir. archtl. research, 1981-85, adv. coun., 1994-98. Chmn. Conn. Bldg. Code Standards Com., 1978-82; vice chmn. Conn. State Codes and Standards Com., 1982-86; cons. in field. Editorial chmn.: Conn. Architect Mag., 1966-74; project mgr. design, St. Vincents Med. Center, Bridgeport. Mem. Cheshire Planning Commn., 1966-72, chmn., 1967-68; pres. Hamden C. of C., 1964, New Eng. Bldg. Code Assn., 1989; mem. Cen. Naugatuck Valley Regional Planning Agy., 1966-74, chmn., 1969; mem. Cheshire Democratic Town Com., 1960-70, treas., 1963-69; mem. Conn. Archtl. Sch. Task Force, 1987-88. With USN, 1942-45. Fellow AIA; mem. AIA Conn. (past pres.), AARP (pres. Cheshire chpt. 1995-97), Conn. Bldg. Ofcls. Assn., Cheshire C. of C. Roman Catholic. Home: 201 N Rolling Acres Rd Cheshire CT 06410-2119

ROWLAND, RANDALL G, urologist; b. Springfield, Ill., May 14, 1947; BS, Northwestern U., 1969, PhD, 1971, MD, 1972. Diplomate Am. Bd. Urology. Urology faculty Ind. U. Sch. Med., Indpls., 1978-97; prof., James F. Glenn chair of urology U. Ky. Coll. Med., Lexington, 1997—. Office: U Kentucky Divsn Urology MS 283 800 Rose St Lexington KY 40536-0298 E-mail: rrowlan@uky.edu.

ROWLAND, ROBERT ALEXANDER, III, lawyer; b. McAllen, Tex., Apr. 27, 1943; s. Robert Alexander Jr and Marguerite (Gerry) Rowland; m. Victoria Nalle, Apr. 2, 1977; children: Julia Marie, Emily Nalle. BS, Tex. A&M U., 1966; JD, George Washington U., 1972. Bar: Tex 1972, US Dist Ct (so dist) Tex 1973, US Ct Appeals (5th cir) 1973, US Supreme Ct 1976, US Dist Ct (no dist) Tex 1979, US Dist Ct (we dist) Tex 1982, US Dist Ct (ea dist) Tex 1983. Law clk. U.S. Ct. Appeals (5th cir.), Houston, 1973-74; assoc. Vinson & Elkins, 1975-81; ptnr. susman, Godfrey & McGowan, 1982-88; mng. dir. Johnson and Gibbs, 1988-91; ptnr. Hutcheson & Grundy, LLP, 1992-94; chmn., CEO Associated Counsel of Am., 1995—. Bd. dirs. Vol. Ctr., Houston, 1975—84, pres., 1982—83; founding mem., bd. dirs. Tex. Accts. and Lawyers for Arts, 1979—92, pres., 1989—91; mem. devel. com. Sch. Liberal Arts Tex. A&M U., 1992—; co-chmn. Mayor's Transition Com., City of Houston, 1992—94; mem. mission outreach coun. Christ Ch. Cathedral, 2002—; bd. dirs. Contemporary Art Mus. Houston, 1974—80, 1991—94; bd. dirs. Sarah Campbell Blaffer Gallery of Art U. Houston, 1989—94; bd. dirs. Tex. Opera Theater, 1988—89, Houston Pks. Bd., 1993—, Nat. Recreation and Pk. Assn., 1992—95, Cultural Arts Coun., Houston, 1981—86, Pk. People Inc., 1979—2001, pres., 1991—92. Capt U.S. Army, 1966—69, Vietnam. Fellow: Tex Bar Found., Houston Bar Found.; mem.: Houston Young Lawyers Assn. (bd dirs 1975—79, pres 1978—79), State Bar Tex., Houston Bar Assn. (dir 1979—88, secy 1984—85, 2d vpres 1985—86, chmn law and art comt 1984—85), Coronado Club, River Oaks Country Club, Phi Delta Phi. Episcopalian. Home: 2010 Chilton Rd Houston TX 77019-1502 Office: Associated Counsel Am Inc Ste 125 4605 Post Oak Pl Houston TX 77027-9744 E-mail: wickr@swbell.net., rob@associatedcounsel.com.

ROWLAND, THEODORE JUSTIN, physicist, educator; b. Cleve., May 15, 1927; s. Thurston Justin and Lillian (Nesser) R.; m. Janet Claire Millar, June 28, 1952 (div. 1967); children: Theodore Justin, Dawson Ann, Claire Millar; m. Patsy Marie Beard, Aug. 21, 1968. BS, Western Res. U., 1948; MA, Harvard U., 1949, PhD, 1954. Rsch. physicist Union Carbide Metals Co., Niagara Falls, N.Y., 1954-61; prof. phys. metallurgy U. Ill., 1961-92, asst. dean Coll. Engring., acting assoc. dean Grad. Coll., 1990-91, prof. emeritus, 1992—; pres., dir. Materials Cons., Inc. Cons. physicist, 1961—; cons. metallurgist, 1976—. Editor 2 books; author monograph; contbr. articles to profl. jours. Fellow Am. Phys. Soc.; mem. AIME, AAAS, AAUP, Phi Beta Kappa, Sigma Xi. Achievements include initial verification of charge density waves in dilute alloys; original contributions to theory and experiment in nuclear magnetic resonance in metals. Home: 805 Park Lane Dr Champaign IL 61820-7613 Office: U Ill Dept Materials Sci and Engring 1304 W Green St Urbana IL 61801-2920 E-mail: trowland@staff.uiuc.edu.

ROWLAND, THOMAS C., JR. obstetrician, gynecologist; b. Dawson, Ga., 1934; s. Thomas Clifford and Ethel (Cunningham) R.; m. Isabelle Hall, Aug. 3, 1957; children: Mary Hall Rowland Fagan, Thomas Clifford III. MA, U. S.C., 1955; MD, Med. U. S.C., 1959. Diplomate Am. Bd. Ob-Gyn. Intern Greenville (S.C.) Gen. Hosp., 1959-60; resident in ob-gyn Nat. Naval Med. Ctr., Bethesda, Md., 1962-65; mem. staff Bapt. Med. Ctr., Columbia, S.C., 1968—, chief ob-gyn. svc., 1970, chief staff, 1979; clin. prof. ob-gyn U. S.C. Sch. Medicine, Med. U. S.C., Charleston; pvt. practice ob-gyn Palmetto Ob-Gyn, Columbia. Mem. adv. bd. Nat. Bank S.C. Trustee Med. U. S.C., Charleston, 1981—, chmn. bd., 1990-94, 98-00. Fellow ACOG (treas. 2000—); mem. AMA, So. Gynecol. Soc. (chmn. bd. 1990-94, pres.), Am. Fertility Soc., South Atlantic Assn. Ob-Gyn. (pres.), So. Med. Assn. (pres.), S.C. Ob-Gyn. Soc. (pres.). Office: Palmetto Ob-Gyn 1333 Taylor St Ste 2D Columbia SC 29201-2945

ROWLANDS, DAVID THOMAS, pathology educator; b. Wilkes-Barre, Pa., Mar. 22, 1930; s. David Thomas and Anna Jule (Morgan) R.; m. Gwendolyn Marie York, Mar. 1, 1958; children: Julie Marie, Carolyn Jane. MD, U. Pa., 1955. Diplomate: Am. Bd. Pathology, Am. Bd. Allergy and Immunology. Intern Pa. Hosp., Phila., 1955-56; resident Cin. Gen. Hosp., 1956-60; asst. prof. U. Colo., 1962-64, Rockefeller U., 1964-66; assoc. prof. Duke U., Durham, N.C., 1966-70; prof. pathology U. Pa., Phila., 1970-82, chmn. dept. pathology, 1973-78, prof. medicine, 1979-82; prof., chmn. dept. pathology U. So. Fla., Tampa, 1982-91, assoc. dean, 1983-84, prof. pediatrics, 1986-91; med. dir. Lifelink Tissue Bank, 1991-93. Mem. editorial bd.: Am. Jour. Pathology, 1971-81, Developmental and Comparative Immunology, 1977-79. Served with USNR, 1960-62. Recipient Lederle Med. Faculty award U. Colo., 1964, Jacob Ehrenzeller award Pa. Hosp., 1976 Mem. Am. Assn. Pathologists, Internat. Acad. Pathology, Am. Soc. Clin. Pathology, Am. Assn. Immunologists, Coll. Am. Pathologist, Arthur Purdy Stout Soc. Presbyterian. Home: 13804 Cypress Village Cir Tampa FL 33624-4406

ROWLES, ARLENE BEVERLY, geriatric social program administrator; b. Johnstown, Ohio, July 12, 1935; d. John Wesley and Ruth Margaret (Johnston) Thomas; m. Edward William Rowles, July 21, 1957; children: Kenneth Alan, Keith Thomas, Diane Elizabeth. BS in Home Econs., Ohio State U., 1957. Lic. dietitian, Ohio Bd. Dietetics. Tchr. home econs. Southwestern City Schs., Grove City, Ohio, 1958-59; exec. dir. Meals on Wheels of Fairfield County, Inc., Lancaster, 1975-98. Mem. state and area ext. adv. com. Ohio State U. Ext., 1980—2001, v.p., pres. state adv. com., 1993—97; mem., past officer Fairfield County Ext. Adv. Com., 1971—2001; mem. adv. com. Vis. Nurses Fairfield County, Lancaster, 1983—98, pres., 1993—97; mem., past officer Fairfield County Com. on Aging, Lancaster, 1975—98; mem. adv. com. Ctrl. Ohio Area Agy. on Aging, 1998—, v.p., 2000—01, pres., 2002; mem. Millersport United Meth. Ch. Fellow Nat. Assn. Meal Providers (presenter 1980), Nat. Assn. Nutrition and Svc. Providers, Ohio Assn. Nutrition and Svc. Providers. Republican. Avocations: travel, camping, sewing, cooking.

ROWLETT, KIMBERLY JAYNE, artist, photographer; b. Knoxville, Tenn., Nov. 6, 1963; d. Gary Eugene Rowlett and Glenda Allen Rowlett Sink. Student, Cleveland State C.C., 1982-93. Mem. U.S. Creative Forum for Creative Profls. One-woman shows include Red Clay Hist. Mus., Cleveland, 1995; exhibited in group shows at AVA, Chattanooga, 1994—, Compuserve Fine Art Forum, 1996—, Russian Traveling Group Exhibit, Chattanooga, 1998, Very Spl. Arts Gallery, Washington, 1998—. Pres. Family and Cmty. Ednl. Club, 1994—. Named to Nat. Mus. Women in the Arts. Fellow Assn. Visual Artists, Pets are Lovable Soc., N.Am. Nature Photographers Assn., Cleve. Creative Arts Guild. Avocations: cake decorating, ribbon embroidery, ethnic cooking, animals/pets. E-mail: kimberly@famous.as., kimberlyrowlett@yahoo.com.

ROWLETT, RALPH MORGAN, archaeologist, educator; b. Richmond, Ky., Sept. 11, 1934; s. Robert Kenny and Daisy (Mullikin) R.; m. Elsebet Sander-Jorgensen, Aug. 25, 1963 (div. Jan. 1986); children: Rolf Arvid, Erik Kenneth; m. Elizabeth Helen Dinan, Apr. 21, 1989 (div. Oct. 1995); 1 child, Helen Holly. Student, U. Ky., 1952-53; BA summa cum laude, Marshall U., 1956; postgrad., U. London, 1962-63; PhD, Harvard U., 1968. Instr. anthropology U. Mo., Columbia, 1965-67, asst. prof., 1967-69, assoc. prof., 1969-75, prof., 1975—. Postdoctoral fellow Ghent U., 1969 Co-author: Neolithic Levels on the Titelberg, Luxembourg, 1981, Meeting Anthropology Phase to Phase, 2000; anthropology editor Random House Unabridged Dictionary of English, 1980—; editor: Horizons and Styles, 1993, Horizons and Styles in West Eurasiatic Archaeology; developer thermoluminescence dating of flint, 1972; co-developer electron spin resonance dating of flint, 1981. 1st lt. arty., U.S. Army, 1956-58. Decorated officer Legion de Merit (Luxembourg); named Ky. col., 1976; grantee NSF, 1973-75, 76-79, 82-83, Svc. Archeologique de Neuchatel, 1989, British Coun., 1993, Acad. of Romania, 1996, Internat. Rsch. and Exch. Bd., 1997. Fellow Am. Anthrop. Assn.; mem. AAAS, Archaeol. Inst. Am., Soc. Am. Archaeology, Prehistory Soc., Societe Prehistorique de Luxembourg, Societe Archeologique Champenoise, English Heritage, Palomino Horse Breeders Assn. Democrat. Mem. Christian Ch. (Disciples Of Christ). Home: Hollywell Hill 1197 State Road Ww Fulton MO 65251-5106 Office: Univ Mo Dept Anthropology Columbia MO 65211-0001

ROWLETTE, HENRY ALLEN, JR. social worker; b. Phila., July 8, 1947; s. Henry Allen Sr. and Ophelia Alberta (Kilson) R.; m. Geraldine Lee Stevens, Mar. 1972 (div. Mar. 1986); children: Cessandra N., Deaeon D., Christiene A.; m. Carolyn Rowlette; 1 child, Janetta M.; m. Ann Laura Rowe, Mar. 19, 1989. BA, Cheyney State Coll., 1970; MEd, Boston U., 1981; MSW, Temple U., 1988. Cert. sch. social worker, N.J.; lic. clin. social worker; diplomate Am. Psychotherapy Assn., Nat. Bd. Cognitive Behavioral Therapists; ordained minister Bapt. Ch. Cardiac monitor technician Bapt. Med. Ctr., Little Rock, 1982-83; mental health technician The Horsham Clinic, Ambler, Pa., 1984; psychiat. technician The Lower Bucks Hosp., Bristol, 1984-90; mental health technician The Helene Fuld Med. Ctr., Trenton, N.J., 1988-90, psychiat. social worker, 1988-92; profl. sch. social worker The Willingboro (N.J.) Sch. Dist., 1990—96. Dist. crisis intervention team Willingboro Sch. Dist., 1994-96; therapist The N.J. State Prison, Trenton, 1996-98, The Southwoods State Prison, Bridgeton, N.J.; clinician Kennedy Meml. Health Ctr., Cherry Hill, N.J., 1998—, The Lumberton Schs./Sch. Social Worker, Lumberton, N.J., 1998; behavioral cons. Founds. Behavioral Health, Willow Grove, Pa., 1999; mental health technician The Children's Hosp. Phila., 1999-2000. Clin. social worker Phila. Prison System, 2000; mem. NAACP, Trenton, 1990. With U.S. Army, 1971-79. Mem. NASW, Am. Assn. Christian Counselors, Omega Psi Phi (Delta Upsilon chpt.), Phi Delta Kappa (Trenton chpt.), Am. Psychotherapy Assn., Nat. Bd. Cognitive Behavioral Therapists, Nat. Bd. Addiction Examiners, Nat. Assn. Forensic Counselors. Democrat. Baptist. Avocations: fishing, reading, computer technology/games. Home: 18 Foxchase Dr Burlington NJ 08016-3044 E-mail: rowlettejr161196@msn.com.

ROWLEY, BEVERLEY DAVIES, medical sociologist; b. Antioch, Calif., July 28, 1941; d. George M. and Eloise (DeWitt) Davies; m. Richard B. Rowley, Apr. 1, 1966 (div. 1983). BS, Colo. State U., 1963; MA, U. Nev., 1975; PhD, Union Inst., 1983. Social worker Nev. Dept. Pub. Welfare, Reno, 1963-65, Santa Clara County Dept. Welfare, San Jose, Calif., 1965-66; field dir. Sierra Sage coun. Camp Fire Girls, Sparks, Nev., 1966-70; program coord. div. health scis. sch. medicine U. Nev., 1976-78, program coord., health analyst office rural health, 1978-84, acting dir. office rural health, 1982-84; exec. asst. to pres. Med. Coll. of Hampton Rds., Norfolk, Va., 1984-87; rsch. mgr. Office Med. Edn. Info. AMA, Chgo., 1987-88, dir. dept. data systems, 1988-91; dir. med. edn. Maricopa Med. Ctr., Phoenix, 1991-99; pres. Med. Edn. and Rsch. Assocs., Inc., Phoenix, Chgo., 1999—, Med. Edn. & Rsch. Assocs., Tempe, Ariz., 1999—; vis. prof. Ariz. State U. East, Mesa, 1999-2000. Various positions as adj. prof. and lectr. in health scis. U. Nev. Sch. of Medicine, 1972-75; lectr. dept. family and cmty. medicine U. Nev., 1978-84, asst. dir., evaluator Health Careers for Am. Indians Programs, 1978-84; cons. Nev. Statewide Health Survey, 1979-84; interim dir. Health Max, 1985-86; asst. prof. dept. family and cmty. medicine Med. Coll. of Hampton Rds., Norfolk, Va., 1985-87. Editor of five books; contbr. numerous articles to profl. jours; developer three computer systems including AMA-FREIDA. Mem. Am. Sociol. Assn., Nat. Rural Health Assn. (bd. dirs. 1986-88), Assn. Behavioral Sci. and Med. Edn. (pres. 1986), Assn. Am. Med. Colls. (exec. coun. 1993-95), Coun. Acad. Scis. (adminstrv. bd. 1992-97), Assn. Hosp. Med. Edn. (bd. dirs. 1997—), Delta, Delta, Delta. Avocations: hiking, skiing, gardening, sewing, ceramics. Office: MERA Inc 8850 S Los Feliz Dr Tempe AZ 85284-3430 E-mail: BRowley@MERAInc.com.

ROWLEY, CHARLES KERSHAW, economics educator; b. June 21, 1939; came to U.S., 1984; s. Frank and Ellen (Beal) R.; m. Betty Silverwood, June 19, 1961 (div. 1971); m. Marjorie Isobel Spillets, July 17, 1972; children: Amanda, Sara. Lectr. U. Nottingham, Eng., 1962-65; lectr., then sr. lectr. U. Kent, Canterbury, Eng., 1970-72; prof. econs. U. Newcastle, Eng., 1972-83, George Mason U., Fairfax, Va., 1984—, Duncan Black prof. econs., 2000—. Gen. dir. John Locke Inst., 1989—, sr. rsch. assoc. Ctr. for Study of Pub. Choice, 1987-92; cons. Office Fair Trading, London, 1980-83; rsch. assoc. Wolfson Coll., Oxford, 1984—; program dir. in econs. and the lawa James M. Buchanan Ctr., 2000—. Author numerous books in econ. and law; editor: Pub. Choice, 1990—; contbr. articles to profl. jours. Grantee Bank of Eng., 1965, Social Sci. Rsch. Coun., London, 1970-72, Dept. Environ., London, 1974-80, Bradley Found., 1988—, Liberty Fund, 1990, 93, John M. Olin Found., 1986. Mem. Mont Pelerin Soc., Am. Econ. Assn., Royal Econ. Soc., Pub. Choice Soc. European Pub. Choice Soc. (pres. 1980-82). Home: 5188 Dungannon Rd Fairfax VA 22030-5414 Office: George Mason U Dept Econs 4400 University Dr Fairfax VA 22030-4444 also: The Locke Inst 4084 University Dr Fairfax VA 22030-6803 E-mail: crowley@gmu.edu.

ROWLEY, GEOFFREY HERBERT, management consultant; b. Harrow, Middlesex, Eng., Nov. 10, 1935; came to U.S., 1962; s. Herbert and Muriel Jessie (Nicolls) R. BA, Bristol (Eng.) U., 1958; cert. indsl. adminstrn., Glasgow (Scotland) U., 1962; MBA, Harvard U., 1964. Purchasing officer Pirelli Ltd., London, 1958-61; rsch. assoc. Assn. for Internat. Rsch., Inc., Cambridge, Mass., 1964-68, v.p., dir., 1968—, cons. in expatriate compensation, 1964—. Lectr. in field; dir. U. Bristol Found., Inc. Contbr. articles to profl. jours. Served with Royal Navy, 1953-55. Mem. Am. Compensation Assn., Inst. for Human Resources, Brit. Ins. Mgmt., Harvard Club. Home: 11 Berkeley Pl Cambridge MA 02138-3411 Office: AirInc 1100 Massachusetts Ave Cambridge MA 02138-5241 E-mail: GH.Rowley@verizon.net., GHRowley@aol.com.

ROWLEY, GEORGE HARDY, lawyer; b. Greenville, Pa., May 30, 1923; s. George H. and Susan Mossman (Templeton) R.; m. Rosamond Kahle, Sept. 23, 1950 (dec. July 1997). Student, Thiel Coll., 1941-42; BA, Yale U., 1947; JD, Harvard U., 1949. Bar: Pa. 1950, U.S. Supreme Ct. 1974. Asst. U.S. atty. Western Dist. Pa., 1950-52; of counsel Rowley, Wallace, Keck, Karson & St. John, Greenville, Pa., 1952—. Mem. Greenville adv. bd., 1970-95, dist. trial nominating commn., 1973-75. Sec. bd. trustees Greenville Hosp., 1970-95. Lt. (j.g.) USN, 1943-46. Fellow Am. Coll. Trial Lawyers; mem. ABA, Pa. Bar Assn., Mercer County Bar Assn., Def. Rsch. Inst., Iroquois Boating & Fishing Club, Greenville Country Club. Home: 157 Plum St Greenville PA 16125-1764 Office: Rowley Wallace Keck Karson & St John PO Box 510 Greenville PA 16125-0510 E-mail: growley@neo.rr.com.

ROWLEY, GLENN HARRY, lawyer; b. Hyannis, Mass., May 16, 1948; s. Harold Frederick and Olive Nellie (Jones) R.; 1 child, Brewster Westgate. BBA, U. Mass., 1970; JD with cum laude, Western New Eng. Coll., 1980. Bar: Mass. 1980, U.S. Dist. Ct. Mass. 1981, U.S. Tax Ct. 1981; cert. elder law atty. Nat. Elder Law Found./ABA. Staff mem. Cape Cod Planning and Econ. Devel. Commn., Barnstable, Mass., 1975-76; staff, estate planning tax dept. Coopers and Lybrand, Springfield, 1980-81; legal assoc. Roberts and Farrell, West Chatham, 1982-84; ptnr. Roberts, Farrell & Rowley, 1984-97; pvt. practice Chatham, Mass., 1997—. Cons. Local Citizen Scholarship Trusts, Harwich and Chatham, Mass., 1985—. Contbr. (weekly news column) The Enterprise, others; contbr. articles to profl. jours. Founding mem. Brewster (Mass.) Conservation Trust, 1984; elected mem. Brewster Hist. Dist. Com., 1975; adv. bd. The May Inst., The Cape Cod Writers Ctr., Inc. With USN, 1971-74, Iceland. Recipient Am. Jurisprudence awards Lawyers Co-op. Pub. Co., 1978, 79. Mem. Mass. Bar Assn., Ocean Edge Exec. Club, Profl. Writers of Cape Cod, Cape Cod Estate Planning Coun., Nat. Acad. Elder Law Attys., Phi Delta Phi. Avocations: travel, writing. Home: Annaniases Knoll/Sheep Pond Brewster MA 02631 Office: The Marketplace PO Box 1489 26 George Ryder Rd S West Chatham MA 02669

ROWLEY, HAZEL JOAN, arts educator; b. London, Nov. 16, 1951; arrived in Australia, 1960; d. Derrick and Betty Sewell (Selley) R. PhD, U. Adelaide, South Australia, 1982. Tutor Deakin U., Geelong, Victoria, Australia, 1984-88, lectr. Australia, 1988-94, sr. lectr. Australia, 1995—. Author: Christina Stead: A Biography, 1993. Recipient Nonfiction award Nat. Book Coun. Australia, 1994. Mem. PEN, Australian Soc. Authors. Home: 13/45 Robe St Saint Kilda Victoria 3182 Australia Office: Deakin U Faculty Arts Geelong Victoria 3217 Australia

ROWLEY, JANET DAVISON, physician; b. N.Y.C., Apr. 5, 1925; d. Hurford Henry and Ethel Mary (Ballantyne) Davison; m. Donald A. Rowley, Dec. 18, 1948; children: Donald, David, Robert, Roger. PhB, U. Chgo., 1944, BS, 1946, MD, 1948; DSc (hon.) , U. Ariz., 1989, U. Pa., 1989, Knox Coll., 1991, U. So. Calif., 1992, St. Louis U., 1997, St. Xavier U., 1999, Oxford (Eng.) U., 2000. Diplomate Am. Bd. Med. Genetics. Rsch. asst. U. Chgo., 1949—50; intern Marine Hosp., USPHS, Chgo., 1950—51; attending physician Infant Welfare and Prenatal Clinics Dept. Pub. Health, Montgomery County, Md., 1953—54; rsch. fellow Levinson Found., Cook County Hosp., Chgo., 1955—61; clin. instr. neurology U. Ill., 1957—61; USPHS spl. trainee Radiobiology Lab. The Churchill Hosp., Oxford, England, 1961—62; rsch. assoc. dept. medicine and Argonne Cancer Rsch. Hosp. U. Chgo., 1962—69, assoc. prof. dept. medicine and Argonne Cancer Rsch. Hosp., 1969—77, prof. dept. medicine and Franklin McLean Meml. Rsch. Inst., 1977—84, Blum-Riese Disting. Svc. prof., dept. medicine and dept. molecular genetics and cell biology, 1984—, Blum-Riese Disting. Svc. prof. dept. human genetics, 1997—, interim dep. dean for sci. biol. scis. divsn., 2001—. Bd. sci. counsellors Nat. Inst. Dental Rsch., NIH, 1972—76, chmn., 1974—76; mem. Nat. Cancer Adv. Bd., Nat. Cancer Inst., 1979—84, Nat. Adv. Coun. for Human Genome Rsch. Inst., 1999—; adv. com. Frederick Cancer Rsch. Facility, 1983—84; bd. sci. counsellors Nat. Human Genome Rsch. Inst., NIH, 1994—99, chmn., 1994—97; adv. bd. Howard Hughes Med. Inst., 1989—94, MD Anderson Cancer Ctr., 1998—; vis. com. dept. applied biol. scis. MIT Corp. , 1983—86; bd. sci. cons. Meml. Sloan-Kettering Cancer Ctr., 1988—90; adv. com. Ency. Britannica U. Chgo., 1988—96; Bernard Cohen Meml. lectr. U. Pa., 1993; Katherine D. McCormick Disting. lectr. Stanford U., 1994; Donald D. Van Slyke lectr. Brookhaven Nat. Lab., 1994; Hilary Koprowski lectr. Thomas Jefferson U., 1994; W. Jack Stuckey Jr. lectr. Tulane Career Ctr., 1996; Presdl. Symposium Am. Soc. Pediatric Hematology/Oncology, 1995; Brit. Jour. of Haematology Plenary lectr. Brit. Soc. Haematology, 1997; Peacock Meml. lectr. in pathology U. Tex. Southwestern Med. Sch., 1997; Cosbie lectr. Royal Coll. Physicians and Surgeons Can., 1997; Richard Brunning lectr. U. Minn., 1999; Muriel Verder Millenium lectr. Evanston Hosp., 1999; Disting. Women in Medicine and Sci. lectr. Northwestern Med. Sch., 2000; Edward C. Hill lectr. U. Calif., San Francisco, 2000; Margaret Pitman lectr. NIH, 2000; plenary spkr. Spanish Soc. Hematology, 2000. Co-founder, co-editor: Genes, Chromosomes and Cancer, mem. editl. bd.: Oncology Rsch., mem. editl. bd.: Cancer Genetics and Cytogenetics, mem. editl. bd.: Internat. Jour. Hematology, mem. editl. bd.: Genomics, mem. editl. bd.: Internat. Jour. Cancer, mem. editl. bd.: Leukemia, past. mem. editl. bd.: Blood, past. mem. editl. bd.: Cancer Rsch., past. mem. editl. bd.: Hematol. Oncology, past. mem. editl. bd.: Leukemia Rsch.; contbr. chapters to books, articles to profl. jours. Adv. com. for career awards in biomed. scis. Burroughs Wellcome Fund, 1994—98; selection panel for Clin. Sci. award Doris Duke Charitable Found., 2000—; mem. Pres.'s Adv. Coun. on Bioethics, 2001—; nat. adv. com. McDonnell Found. Program for Molecular Medicine in Cancer Rsch., 1988—98; adv. bd. Leukemia Soc. Am., 1979—84; selection com. scholar award in biomed. sci. Lucille P. Markey Charitable Trust, 1984—87; trustee Adler Planetarium, Chgo.; 1978—; med. adv. bd. G&P Charitable Found., 1999—. Co-recipient Charles Mott prize, GM Cancer Rsch. Found., 1989; named Chicagoan of Yr., Chgo. mag., 1998; recipient First Kuwait Cancer prize, 1984, Esther Langer award, Ann Langer Cancer Rsch. Found., 1983, A. Cressy Morrison award in natural scis., N.Y. Acad. Scis., 1985, Past State Pres. award, Tex. Fedn. Bus. and Profl. Women's Clubs, 1986, Karnofsky award and lecture, Am. Soc. Clin. Oncology, 1987, Antoine Lacassagne Lique prize, Nat. Francaise Contre le Cancer, 1987, King Faisal Internat. prize in medicine (co-recipient), 1988, Katherine Berkan Judd award, Meml. Sloan-Kettering Cancer Ctr., 1989, Steven C. Beering award, U. Ind. Med. Sch, 1992, Robert de Villiers award, Leukemia Soc. Am., 1993, Kaplan Family prize for cancer rsch. excellence, Oncology Soc. Dayton, 1995, Cotlove award and lecture, Acad. Clin. Lab. Physicians and Scientists, 1995, Nilsson-Ehle lecture, Mendelian Soc. and Royal Physiographic Soc., 1995, The Gairdner Found. award, 1996, medal of honor, Basic Sci. Am. Cancer Soc., 1996, Nat. Medal of Sci., 1998, Lasker award for clin. scis., 1998, Woman Extraordinaire award, Internat. Women's Assocs., 1999, Golden Plate award, Am. Acad. Achievement, 1999, Women Achieving Excellence award, YWCA of Met. Chgo., 2000, Philip Levine award, Am. Soc. Clin. Pathology, 2001, Emile M Chamot award, State Microsurg. Soc. Ill., 2001. Fellow: AAAS (nominating com. 1998); mem.: NAS (chmn. sect. 41 1995—99), Inst. Medicine (coun. 1988—90), Am. Assn. Cancer Rsch. (G.H.A. Clowes Meml. award 1989), Am. Soc. Hematology (lectr. Millenium Symposium 1999, Presdl. Symposium 1982, Dameshek prize 1982, Ham-Wasserman award 1995), Genetical Soc., Am. Soc. Human Genetics (pres.-elect 1992, pres. 1993, Allen award and lectr. 1991), Am. Philos. Soc., Am. Acad. Arts and Scis. (nominating com. 1998), Alpha Omega Alpha, Sigma Xi (William Proctor prize for sci. achievement 1989). Episcopalian. Home: 5310 S University Ave Chicago IL 60615-5106 Office: U Chgo 5841 S Maryland Ave Rm 2115 Chicago IL 60637-1463

ROWLEY, MAXINE LEWIS, home economics and consumer educator, writer; b. Provo, Utah, Sept. 23, 1938; d. Max Thomas Lewis and Illa Lewis Sanford; m. Arthur William Rowley, Sept. 23, 1960; children: Anne, Jenefer. BA (Ford Found. scholar), Brigham Young U., 1960, PhD in Edn. Adminstrn., 1989; BS, U. Utah, 1974; MA, Utah State U., 1980. Promotion writer Sta. ABC KCPX-TV, 1960; extension home economist USDA, 1961; mgmt. trainee Deseret Book Co., Salt Lake City, 1969; dept. chair Patricia Stevens Career Coll., 1970; chair consumer and homemaking dept. Sand Ridge Jr. H.S. Weber Sch. Dist., Roy, 1975, learning experience designer, 1976-78; consumer and home econs. faculty Utah State U., Logan, 1978-79; spl. appointee to Utah State U. by the Utah State Bd. Edn., 1978-86; intern Gladys Chalkley/Brannegan Chalkley Am. Home Econ. Assn., 1993; chair dept. family life and home econs. Brigham Young U., 1988—. Cons. Utah Vocat. Bd. Edn.; instrumental writer Utah State U. Found., 1979; faculty Brigham Young U., 1979. Author: Public Policy Handbook, 1997; (filmstrips, texts and tchrs. guide) CHECS, 1979; (curriculum guide) Operation: Free Enterprise, 1982, Curriculum of Food Sci., Nutrition, vol. I, 1990, vol. II, 1992, vol. III, 1993; co-author: Legacy, vol. I, 1998. Active ward, stake and region positions Ch. of Jesus Christ of Latter-day Saints; leader 4-H Club, coun. mem., adv. bd.; leader Girl Scouts U.S.A., Young Homemakers; active State Text Book Evaluation Com., 1978-86, U. Utah Evaluation Com., 1979; edn. and rsch. com. Am. Cancer Soc., State of Utah, 1993-94. Named Outstanding Leader Am. Edn., 1976, Nat. Tchr. of Yr., 1977, Outstanding Tchr. in Dept., Brigham Young U., 1984-94, Outstanding Vocat. Edn. Leader, State of Utah, 1996, Nat. Honor Roll in vocat. edn. Nat. Assn. Vocat. Family and Consumer Scis., 1999. Mem. NEA, Nat. Assn. Vocat. Home Econs. Tchrs., Am. Home Econs. Assn. (contbr., author yearbook 1984, Nat. Leadership award 1993), Am. Assn. Family and Consumer Scis. (nat. v.p., bd. dirs., chair ann. meeting, bd. liaison publs. 1995-97, nat. com. publs. 1999—), Am. Vocat. Assn., Utah Home Econs. Assn., Utah Vocat. Assn., Utah Coun. for Improvement Edn., Utah Nutrition Coun. (chair 1995), Utah Edn. Assn. (award for womens awareness task force project 1976), County Welfare Com., Am. Edn. Rsch. Assn. (nat. chair Home Econs. Related Spl. Interest Group 2000—), Home Econs. Edn. Assn., Vocat. Home Econs. Tchrs. (nat. chmn. public rels. and legis. coms. 1978), Worldwide Orgn. of Women (internat. bd. dirs. 1999—), White Key (pres. 1960), Spurs, Kappa Omicron Nu (advisor 1980—, Nat. award of excellence 1999, nat. endowment honoree 1989, nat. leadership endowment 2001), Phi Kappa Phi, Gamma Phi Omicron. Home: 9801 Lampton Cir South Jordan UT 84095-9211 E-mail: maxine_rowley@byu.edu.

ROWLEY, PETER TEMPLETON, physician, educator; b. Greenville, Pa., Apr. 29, 1929; s. George Hardy and Susan Mossman (Templeton) R.; m. Carol Stone, Mar. 19, 1967; children: Derek Stone, Jason Templeton. AB magna cum laude, Harvard U., 1951; MD, Columbia U., 1955. Diplomate: Am. Bd. Internal Medicine. Intern med. service N.Y. Hosp.-Cornell Med. Center, 1955-56; clin. assoc. Nat. Inst. Neurol. Disease and Blindness, NIH, 1956-58; asst. resident, then resident Harvard Med. Service, Boston City Hosp.; asst. in medicine Harvard U. Med. Sch. and researcher Thorndike Meml. Lab., 1958-60; hon. research asst. dept. eugenics, biometry and genetics Univ. Coll., U. London, 1960-61; postdoctoral fellow dept. microbiology NYU Sch. Medicine, 1961-63; asst. prof. medicine Stanford U., 1963-70; assoc. prof. medicine pediatrics and genetics U. Rochester, 1970-75, prof. medicine, pediatrics, genetics and microbiology, 1975—, prof. oncology, 1991—, chmn. div. genetics, 1990—; physician, pediatrician Strong Meml. Hosp., 1970—. Mem. N.Y. State Exec. and Adv. Coms. on Genetic Disease, 1979—; WHO vis. scholar Inst. Biol. Chemistry, U. Ferrara, Italy, 1970. Editor (with M. Lipkin Jr.): Genetic Responsibility: On Choosing Our Children's Genes, 1974; co-editor: Genetic Testing. With USPHS, 1956-58. Recipient Excellence in Teaching award U. Rochester Class of 1976, 1973; NRC fellow, 1960-63; Buswell research fellow, 1970-71, 71-72 Fellow ACP, Am. Coll. Genetics; mem. Am. Fedn. Clin. Rsch., Am. Soc. Hematology, Am. Soc. Human Genetics (social issues com. 1980-89, program com. 1993-96), N.Y. State Health Rsch. (sci. bd. 1997—). Office: U Rochester Med Sch Div Genetics PO Box 641 601 Elmwood Ave Rochester NY 14642-0001 E-mail: peter_rowley@urmc.rochester.edu.

ROWLEY, ROBERT DEANE, JR. bishop; b. Cumberland, Md., July 6, 1941; s. Robert Deane Sr. and Alice Marquerite (Wilson) W.; m. Nancy Ann Roland, June 27, 1964; children: Karen Gordon Rowley Butler, Robert Deane III. BA, U. Pitts., 1962, LLB, 1965; LLM, George Washington U., 1970; MDiv, Episcopal Sem. of S.W., 1977, DD (hon.), 1989. Ordained deacon Episcopal Ch., 1977; priest, 1978; bishop, 1989. Bar: Pa. 1965, U.S. Supreme Ct. 1970. Dean of students St. Andrew's Priory Sch., Honolulu, 1977-80; canon St. Andrew's Cathedral, 1979-81; rector St. Timothy's Episcopal Ch., Aiea, Hawaii, 1981-83; canon to bishop Diocese of Bethlehem (Pa.), 1983-89; bishop Diocese of Northwestern Pa., Erie, 1989—; pres. 3rd prov., 1993—. Capt. USN, 1966-92. Mem. Erie County Bar Assn., Erie Club, Lake Shore Country Club. Home: 810 Huntington Dr Erie PA 16505-1087 Office: Diocese of Northwestern Pa 145 W 6th St Erie PA 16501-1001 E-mail: rdrowleyjr@aol.com.

ROWLINGSON, JOHN CLYDE, anesthesiologist, educator, physician; b. Syracuse, N.Y., Aug. 3, 1948; s. John Winthrop and Genevieve Estelle (Mahan) R.; m. Rosemary Colette Laney, Oct. 26, 1974 (div. 1992); children: Kristen, Andrew; m. Karen Wheeler, Aug. 4, 2001; stepchild, Isaac. BS, Allegheny Coll., 1970; MD, SUNY, Buffalo, 1974. Intern Millard Fillmore Hosp., Buffalo, 1974-75; resident in anesthesiology U. Va., Charlottesville, 1975-77; fellow in anesthesia pain mgmt. U. Va. Med. Ctr., 1977-78; asst. prof. anesthesiology U. Va. Sch. Medicine, Charlottesville, 1978-82, assoc. prof., 1982-86, prof., 1986—, tenured prof., 1995—. Assoc. dir. Pain Mgmt. Ctr., U. Va. Health Sci. Ctr., 1978-79, dir., 1980-98, dir. acute pain svc., 1987—. Author: Regional Anesthesia, 1984; co-editor: Handbook of Critical Care Pain Management, 1993. Recipient Nils Lofgren award ASTRA, 1999; Nat. Inst. Handicapped Rsch. fellow, 1983-87, Pain fellow 1977-78. Fellow Am. Coll. Anesthesiology; mem. Am. Soc. Anesthesiologists, Am. Soc. Regional Anesthesia (rsch. grantee 1977, pres. 1996-97), Am. Pain Soc., Internat. Assn. Study of Pain, Am. Acad. Pain Medicine (editl. bd. Anesthesia Analg 1996—, Reg. Anesthesia and Pain Medicine, 1997—). Methodist. Avocations: running, tennis, skiing, biking. Home: 5006 Lake Tree Ln Crozet VA 22932 Office: U Va Hlth Sys Health Sci Ctr Anesthesiology PO Box 800710 Charlottesville VA 22908-0710

ROWSON, RICHARD CAVANAGH, publisher; b. Hollywood, Calif., Apr. 7, 1926; s. Louis Cavanagh and Mable Louise (Montney) R.; m. Elena Louisa Costabile, Nov. 22, 1952; children: Peter Cavanagh, John Cummings. AB, U. Calif., Berkeley, 1946; certificate, Sorbonne, 1949; MIA, Columbia U., 1950. Trainee Fgn. Policy Assn., 1950; dir. World Affairs Council R.I., 1951-52; with Fgn. Policy Assn., 1951-62, dir. finance and devel. n.e. region, 1960-62; with Radio Free Europe, 1962-69, dir. policy and planning, 1964-69; dir. spl. studies Praeger Pubs., Inc., N.Y.C., 1969-77, pres., 1975-77, Pergamon Press, 1977-80, R.R. Bowker, 1980. Info. and pub. cons., 1981; dir. Duke U. Press, 1981-90, sr. cons. editor, 1990-91; dir. Am. U. Press, 1989-91, cons. acquisitions, 1992-94, cons. pub., dir., 1994-97; pub. Woodrow Wilson Ctr. Press, 1992-93; v.p. Nat. Exec. Svc. Corps, 1999-2000; dir. Exec. Svc. Corps. of Washington, 2000—; pub. cons., lectr., condr. workshops in field. Contbr. articles to profl. jours. Served to lt. (j.g.) USNR, 1944-47. Mem. Am. Assn. Advancement Slavic Studies, N.Y. Acad. Scis., U. Calif. Alumni Assn., Columbia U. Alumni Assn., Pomona Coll. Alumni Assn., Overseas Press Club. Democrat. Home: Apt 503 4701 Connecticut Ave NW Washington DC 20008-5633 E-mail: rcrowson2@aol.com., drowson@thecil.org.

ROXIN, EMILIO OSCAR, mathematics educator; b. Buenos Aires, Apr. 6, 1922; came to U.S., 1960; s. Emil Karl and Ullranda Hildegard (Loebel) R.; m. Gudrun D. Kappus, 1962 (div. 1983); children: Ursula R., Walter E. Diploma in engring., U. Buenos Aires, 1947, PhD in Math., 1958. Mem. faculty U. Buenos Aires, 1947-62; researcher Rsch. Inst. Advanced Study, Balt., 1960-64; prof. math. U. R.I., Kingston, 1960-92, prof. emeritus, 1992—. Researcher, AEC of Argentina, Buenos Aires, 1956-59. Author: Differential Equations, 1972, Control Theory and its Applications, 1996; contbr. to sci. publs. Mem. Am. Math. Soc., Math. Assn. Am., Soc. Indsl. and Applied Math., Union Math. Argentina, AAAS. Home: 31 Nichols Rd Kingston RI 02881-1803 Office: U RI Dept Math Kingston RI 02881 E-mail: eroxin@etal.uri.edu.

ROY, ARTHUR PUTNAM, lawyer; b. Baton Rouge, Nov. 23, 1940; s. Chalmer John and Elizabeth Putnam (Richards) R.; m. Sara Hinrichsen, Mar. 16, 1963; children: Mary Louise Manchadi, Christine Elizabeth Roy Yoder, Sara Katherine Allex. BS, Iowa State U., 1962; JD, U. Colo., 1969. Bar: Colo. 1969, U.S. Dist. Ct. Colo. 1969, U.S. Ct. Appeals (10th cir.) 1972, U.S. Supreme Ct. 1973. Pvt. practice, Ft. Collins, Colo., 1969-70; assoc. counsel State Bd. Agriculture, 1970-73; dep. dist. atty. Office of Dist. Atty., Greeley, 1973-74; pvt. practice, 1974-94; judge Colo. Ct. Appeals, Denver, 1994—. Capt. USAR, 1963-74, Vietnam, 1965-66. Mem. ABA, Colo. Bar Assn. (v.p. 1984-85), Denver Bar Assn. Republican. Presbyterian. Home: 2800 S University Blvd Denver CO 80210-6070 Office: Colo Ct Appeals 2 E 14th Ave Denver CO 80203-2115

ROY, ASIM, business educator; b. Calcutta, India, May 5, 1948; came to U.S., 1975; s. Samarendra Nath and Chhaya (Mukherjee) R.; m. Suchandra Mukherjee, Feb. 10, 1974; 1 child, Sion Roy. BE, Calcutta U., 1971; MS (scholar), Case Western Res. U., 1977; PhD, U. Tex., 1979. Foreman, supr. Guest, Keen, Williams, Calcutta, 1972—74; mgr. optimization group Execucom Systems Corp., Austin, 1980-82; asst. prof. U. Nebr., Omaha, 1983, Ariz. State U., Tempe, 1983-89, assoc. prof., 1989-99, prof., 1999—. Vis. prof. Stanford (Calif.) U., 1991; cons. Mid-Am. Steel Corp., 1976-77, Fabri-Centre, Inc., Cleve., 1976; pres., chief exec. officer Decision Support Software, Inc., 1984-98. Author software: IFPS/Optimum and Maxima; contbr. articles to profl. jours.; patentee brain-like computer (neural network device); pub. new theory for brain-like learning. Calcutta U. Merit scholar, 1967, U. Tex. Rsch. scholar, 1978-80; grantee NSF. Mem. Inst. Mgmt. Sci. (program chmn. 1990), Ops. Rsch. Soc. Am. (gen. chmn. 1993), Internat. Neural Network Soc. Hindu. Home: 5771 W Gail Dr Chandler AZ 85226-1232 Office: Ariz State U Sch of Business Tempe AZ 85287

ROY, CHUNILAL, psychiatrist; b. Digboi, India, Jan. 1, 1935; came to Can., 1967, naturalized, 1975; s. Atikay Bandhu and Nirupama (Devi) R.; m. Elizabeth Ainscow, Apr. 15, 1967; children: Nicholas, Phillip, Charles. MB, BS, Calcutta Med. Coll., India, 1959; diploma in psychol. medicine, Kings Coll., Newcastle-upon-Tyne, Eng., 1963. Intern Middlesborough Gen. Hosp., Eng., 1960-61; jr. hosp. officer St. Luke's Hosp., Middlesborough, Eng., 1961-64, sr. registrar Eng., 1964; sr. hosp. med. officer Parkside Hosp., Macclesfield, Eng., 1964-66; sr. registrar Moorehaven Hosp., Ivybridge, Eng., 1966; reader, head dept. psychiatry Maulana Azad Med. Coll., New Delhi, 1966; sr. med. officer Republic of Ireland, County Louth, 1966; sr. psychiatrist Sask. Dept. Psychiat. Services, Can., 1967-68; regional dir. Swift Current, Can., 1968-71; practice medicine specializing in psychiatry Regina, Sask., Can., 1971-72; founding dir., med. dir. Regional Psychiat. Ctr., Abbotsford, B.C., Can., 1972-82. With dept. psychiatry Vancouver Gen. Hosp., 1983—; cons. to prison adminstrs.; hon. lectr. psychology and clin. prof. dept. psychiatry U. B.C., clin. prof. emeritus, 2000; ex-officio mem. Nat. Adv. Com. on Health Care of Prisoners in Can.; cons. (hon.) psychiatrist Vancouver Hosp.; advisor Asian chpt. Psychosomatic Medicine, World Congress of Law and Medicine, New Delhi, 1985; appointed hon. consul for Burkina Faso, 1997; appointed auditor Med. Svcs. Com. B.C., 1997; appointed advisor mental health Govt. West Bengal, India, 1999; pres. organizing com. World Mental Health Assembly, 1999, clinical prof. emeritus, Dept. of Psychiatry, UBC, 2000-. Author: (with D.J. West and F.L. Nichols) Understanding Sexual Attacks, 1978, Hospital or Prison Memories; co-author: Oath of Athens, 1979; ; assoc. editor Internat. Jour. Offender Therapy and Comparative Criminology, 1978—; field editor Jour. of Medicine and Law; corr. editor Internat. Jour. Medicine; mem. bd. Internat. Law Medicine, 1979—; mem. editl. rev. bd. Evaluation, 1977—; contbr. articles to profl. jours. Recipient merit awards Dept. Health, Republic of Ireland, 1966, Can. Penitentiary Svc., 1974, Correctional Svcs. Can., 1983, citation by pres. U. B.C., 1983, Letten Saugstad Found. prize, Holland, 1995; knighted by Order of St. John Ecumenical Found., 1993, Awarded Order of Francisco Fajardo Gov. of Caracas, 1998, Legacy award Vancouver Travel and Conv. Ctr., 1998. Fellow: Pacific Rim Coll. Psychiatrists (founder), Royal Coll. Psychiatry (Eng.), Royal Coll. Psychiatry (Can.); mem.: B.C. Psychiat. Assn. (pres. 1995—96), U. Calcutta Med. Assn. of Am. (pres. 2000), World Assembly for Mental Health (pres. 2001), World Assn. Health, Culture and Environ. (sec.-gen. 1995, award 1995), Internat. Conf. on Health, Culture and Contemporaray Soc. (chief advisor Bombay 1989), Internat. Coll. Psychosomatic Medicine (adv. Asian chpt.), Can. Physicians Interested in South Asia (v.p. 1989, pres. 1990), Internat. Found. for Tng. in Penitentiary Medicine and Forensic Psychiatry (founding pres. 1980), Indian Psychiat. Assn. (life), Australian Acad. Forensic Sci. (corr.), Assn. Physicians and Surgeons Who Work in Can. Prisons (founding pres. 1974), Internat. Acad. Legal Medicine and Social Medicine, Can. Psychiat. Assn., Can. Med. Assn., Internat. Coun. Prison Med. Svcs. (founding sec.-gen. 1977), World Fedn. Mental Health, World Psychiat. Assn. (sec., vice chmn. forensic psychiatry 1983), Vancouver Multicultural Soc. (bd. dirs. 1992—93), Order of St. John (knight 1992). Home: 2439 Trinity St Vancouver BC Canada V5K 1C9 Office: 1417-750 W Broadway Vancouver BC Canada V5Z 1J4 Fax: (604) 872-0302.

ROY, DAVID TOD, Chinese literature educator; b. Nanking, China, Apr. 5, 1933; s. Andrew Tod and Margaret (Crutchfield) R.; m. Barbara Jean Chew, Feb. 4, 1967. AB, Harvard U., 1958, AM, 1960, PhD, 1965. Asst. prof. Princeton U., 1963-67; assoc. prof. U. Chgo., 1967-73, prof., 1973—99, prof. emeritus, 1999—, chmn. com. on Far Eastern Studies, 1968-70, chmn. dept. Far Eastern Langs. and Civilizations, 1972-75. Author: Kuo Mo-jo: The Early Years, 1971; contbr.: How to Read the Chinese Novel, 1990, Minds and Mentalities in Traditional Chinese Literature, 1999; co-editor: Ancient China: Studies in Early Civilization, 1978; translator: The Plum in the Golden Vase or Chin P'ing Mei, vol. 1, 1993, vol. 2, 2001. Served with U.S. Army, 1954-56. Ford Found. fellow, 1958-60, Jr. fellow Harvard Soc. Fellows, 1960-63, fellow Fulbright-Hays Commn., 1967, Chgo. Humanities Inst. fellow, 1994-95; grantee Am. Coun. Learned Socs., 1976-77, NEH, 1983-86, 95-96. Mem. Am. Oriental Soc., Assn. for Asian Studies. Clubs: Quadrangle (Chgo.). Democrat. Home: 5443 S Cornell Ave Chicago IL 60615-5603 Office: U Chgo 1050 E 59th St Chicago IL 60637-1559 E-mail: davidroy@midway.uchicago.edu.

ROY, DONALD, artist, poet; b. Lafayette, La., Aug. 2, 1950; s. Albert and Geraldine Roy. Chaplain PTO, 1992-98; with Gumbeaux Mag., 1994—. Motivational spkr., 1995—. Editor: Creative Consultant (Editors Choice award 2000); author bi-mo. Perimeter, 2001; author: (book) Aesthetics Reflection, 2001; author poetry. Co-founder S.W. La. Black Mus., Lake Charles, La., 1999; asst. dir. The Langston Hughes Poetry Contest, Lake Charles, 2000; co-dir. The Zora Neal Hurston Writers Award, Lake Charles, 2000, The Play God's Trombones, Lake Charles, 2001; co-founder Gathering of Artist Spring Festival, Lake Charles, 2001; vol. voter registration Lake Charles, 1997—; activist for civil rights; advocate for human rels. Recipient Recognition in Achievement U.S. and La. State senates, 2000, Poet of the Yr. award Gumbeaux Mag., 1997, Dr. Nancy Shephard Arts Ensemble Writers award, 2000, Outstanding Achievement award Dist. 3, Ward I, Police Juror, Opelousas, La., 2001, Exceptional Leadership award Ladies of Focus, 2001. Avocations: drama, modern dance, theater, youth activities. Home: 932 N Division St Lake Charles LA 70601

ROY, ELMON HAROLD, minister; b. Russell Springs, Ky., Dec. 17, 1924; s. Leslie C. and Olza (Gosser) R.; m. Retha Adkins; children: Joel, Michael. BA in Theology, So. Missionary Coll., 1953; MA, Belin U., 1958, Spalding U., 1970; PhD in Theology, Pacific We. U., 1966; postgrad., Andrews Theol. Seminary, 1974; LLD, Coll. St. Thomas, 1982. Ordained to ministry, 1959. Assoc. pastor, Bucyrus, Ohio, 1955-56, Akron, 1956-57; pastor East Liverpool, 1957-60, Coudersport, Pa., 1960-64, Huntsville, Ala., 1964-65, Louisville, 1965-71; chaplain Pleasant Grove Hosp., 1965-71; pastor Springfield, Ohio, 1975-85, Wooster, 1985-88; chaplain Louisville, 1989—. Cons. religious liberty, 1983-88; chaplain Jefferson County Ct. Author: In Remembrance of Redemption, 1996, Courage for Hospital Days 1973, Earth's Coming Events, 1968, Israel's Early Leaders, 1984, Moments of Meditation, 1975, The Word for These Times, 1988, Morning is Coming, 1989, Something to Live By, 1958, Prescription for Personal Peace, 1995, Decisions Determine Destiny, 1994; contbr. numerous articles to mags. Pres. South Oldham Ch. Coun., 1971-72; mem. Ohio conf. bd. edn., 1985-88. With USN, 1943-46. Recipient Outstanding Cmty. Svc. award Pleasant Grove Hosp., Commrs. Commendation award Wayne County, Ohio Senate Commendation award, Gov.'s Outstanding Kentuckian award; decorated six battle stars, knight Sovereign Order of St. John of Jerusalem, Knights of Malta, Hospitallers, comdr. Star of Peace Fedn. des Combattants En Europe, Tenn. Col., Ky. Adm., Croix De Guerre, Cross of Valor, Royal Afghanistan Order of Crown of Amanullah, Order of Polonia Restituta; named hon. citizen of Tenn., hon. sheriff Clark County, Ohio, hon. Ky. Sec. of State, Ky. Amb.; named to Order Ky. Cols. Fellow Philos. Soc. Gt. Britain, Huguenot Soc., Royal Soc. Arts; mem. SAR (chaplain Louisville-Thruston chpt. 1974-75), Am. Acad. Religion, Ky. Hist. Soc., Order Founders and Patriots of Am., East Liverpool Ministerial Assn. (sec., treas. 1960), Coudersport Ministerial Assn. (v.p. 1971-72), Soc. Ky. Pioneers. Address: 2417 W Highway 22 Crestwood KY 40014-9481

ROY, HERBERT CLARENCE, research scientist; b. Lakewood, N.J., Nov. 5, 1947; s. Morris and Reba (Stern) R. BS, Monmouth U., West Long Branch, N.J., 1969; MS, Drexel U., Phila., 1972, MS, 1977; PhD, Rutgers U., 1989. Electronics aide Naval Air Test Facility, Lakehurst, N.J., 1968; engring. aide Ocean County Engring. Dept., Toms River, 1970; grad. teaching asst. dept. physics Drexel U., Phila., 1972-74, computer programmer, 1974-78, adj. instr. dept. math., 1978-80; cons. instr. Satinsky Inst., 1979-80; rsch. scientist radon sect. N.J. Dept. Environ. Protection, Trenton, 1989—. Computer cons. Rutgers U., Piscataway, N.J., 1984-89; rsch. fellow radiation sci. program Rutgers U., Piscataway, 1983-85. Mem. Soc. Physics Students (pres. Monmouth U. chpt. 1968-69), Monmouth U. Honor Soc. Lambda Sigma Tau (life), Sigma Xi (assoc.), Pi Mu Epsilon. Home: PO Box 501 Cranbury NJ 08512-0501 Office: NJ Dept Environ Protection Radon Sect CN415 Trenton NJ 08625

ROY, LAWRENCE (JUDE), JR. English literature educator, writer; b. Chatagnier, La., June 29, 1949; s. Lawrence Roy Sr. and Ola Marie Ogea; m. Pamela Jane Woodside, May 29, 1984; children: Jessie, Lawrence III. BA in English, U. Southwestern La., 1979, MA in English, 1985; MFA in Creative Writing (Fiction), George Mason U., 1989. English instr. Clemson (S.C.) U., 1989-93, Gov.'s Schs. of Tenn., Martin, 1993, Southwest Mo. State U., Springfield, 1993-98; asst. prof. English Madisonville (Ky.) C.C., 1998—. Contbr. short stories, poems, essays to profl. jours. and mags.; co-editor The Gadfly (lit. mag.), 1998—. With USN, 1970-76. Mem. Ky. Philol. Soc., Assoc. Writers Programs. Avocations: carpentry, tennis, basketball, reading, computers. Office: Madisonville C C 2000 College Dr Madisonville KY 42431 E-mail: jude.roy@kctcs.edu.

ROY, MATTHEW LANSING, lawyer; b. Gainesville, Fla., May 5, 1968; s. Lansing John and JoAnn Ruth R.; m. Melinda Iresta Leaver, Aug. 15, 1993. BS in Acctg., Oral Roberts U., 1990; JD, U. Fla., 1993. Bar: S.C. 1994, Oreg. 1994. Atty. Drose, Davidson & Bennett, Greenville, S.C., 1993-94, Vick & Conroyd, Salem, Oreg., 1994—. Recipient Family Law Book award, U. Fla., 1993. Mem. ABA, Oreg. State Bar Assn. (mem. exec. com. workers' compensation sect., mem. exec. com. new lawyers div., med. legal com.), Marion County Bar Assn. Republican. Avocations: hunting, fishing, skiing, golf, basketball. Home: 1340 Roseway Ct SE Salem OR 97302-1818 Office: Vick & Conroyd 698 12th St SE Ste 200 Salem OR 97301-4010 E-mail: mroy@vickronroydlaw.com.

ROY, MICHAEL JOSEPH, higher education administrator; b. Kankakee, Ill., Aug. 15, 1945; s. Raymond Joseph and Barbara Elizabeth (Gulczynski) R.; m. Joanne Lee Isley, June 5, 1971; 1 child, Amanda. BS, Mont. State U., 1967; MBA, Ctrl. Mich. U., 1970; EdD, Western Mich. U., 1994. Acct. Mont. State

U., Billings, 1967-70; acct., asst. contr. Ctrl. Mich. U., Mt. Pleasant, 1971-75, contr., 1975-78; chief acct. No. Mich. U., Marquette, 1978-81, asst. v.p. fin., contr., 1981-91, interim v.p. fin. and adminstrn., treas., 1991-93, v.p. fin. and adminstrn. and treas., 1993—. Trustee No. Mich. U. Devel. Fund, 1991—; bd. dirs. Mich. Univs. Self-Ins. Corp., Detroit, 1985-97; bd. dirs., treas. No. Initiatives, Marquette, 1992—; allocation com. mem. United Way of Marquette, 1980-91; pres., dir. Marquette Area Cath. Edn. Fund, Marquette, 1988-90; chair fin. coun. St. Louis the King Parish, Marquette, 1985—. Mem. rotary Club of Marquette (treas. 1997—). Roman Catholic. Avocations: woodworking, skiing. Office: Northern Michigan Univ 1401 Presque Isle Ave Marquette MI 49855-5305

ROY, PATRICK, professional hockey player; b. Quebec City, Que., Can., Oct. 5, 1965; Goaltender Montreal Canadiens, 1984-95, Colo. Avalanche, 1995—. Mem. Stanley Cup Championship teams, 1986, 93, 96, 2001. Recipient Conn Smythe trophy as playoff MVP, 1986, William M. Jennings trophy 1986-89, 91-92, Trico Goaltender award, 1988-89, 89-90, Georges Vezina trophy, 1988-89, 89-90, 91-92; named to NHL All-Rookie Team, 1985-86, NHL All-Star Second Team, 1987-88, 90-91, NHL All-Star First Team, 1988-89, 89-90, 91-92., Sporting News All-Star Team, 1988-89, 89-90, 91-92. Office: Colo Avalanche 100 Chopper Pl Denver CO 80204*

ROY, PAUL EMILE, JR. county official; b. Sumter, S.C., Dec. 18, 1942; s. Paul Emile and Harriette Orvilla (Sorenson) R.; m. Patricia Jane Stariha, July 2, 1977; 1 child, Jennifer Jo. AA, Grand Rapids Jr. Coll., 1963; student, Universidad de las Americas, Mexico City, 1963-64, Instituto Mexicano-Norteamericano de Relaciones Culturales, 1964-65; BA, Aquinas Coll., Grand Rapids, 1967; MA, U. Americas Escuela de Graduados, Mexico City, 1968; postgrad., U. Mich., 1977-79; MBA, Calif. Coast U., 1994. Asst. prin., instr. Spanish Muskegon (Mich.) Cath. Cen. High Sch., 1971-75; govt. offcl. County of Muskegon, 1975—, dir. employment and tng. Muskegon/Oceana Consortium, 1975-87, dir. employment and tng., 1988-95, dir. employment and tng. and facilities mgmt., 1995—. Mem. Mich. Com. for Devel. of Romance Lang. Performance Objectives; adult edn. adv. com. Muskegon Pub. Schs.; appointee Mich. Youth Employment Coun.; v.p. regional adv. coun. U.S. Dept. Labor, 1981; mem. City of Muskegon Local Devel. Funding Authority, 1988—, Downtown Devel. Authority, 1988—, City of Whitehall (Mich.) Local Devel. Funding Authority, 1988—, Muskegon Econ. Growth Alliance Edn. Com.; bd. dirs. United Way, 1998—, YMCA, 1999-01; cons. U.S. Dept. Labor, Washington, Mich. Dept. Labor, Lansing, Gov.'s Office Manpower, Ind., U. Mich., Ann Arbor, various pvt. cos., non-profit orgns. Campaign chmn. Muskegon County United Way, 1986-88, Pacesetter award, 1987; bd. dirs. United Way, 1998—, YMCA, 1999-2001. Mem. Am. Assn. Tchrs. Spanish and Portuguese, Mich. Assn. Tchrs. English as Second Lang., Mich. Assn. Employment and Tng. Dirs. (pres. 1980-81), Mich. Employment and Tng. Inst. (founding bd. dirs. 1980-81), Nat. Assn. Counties (employment steering com.), Nat. Assn. County Employment and Tng. Adminstrs. (nat. bd. dirs. 1979-80, nat. chmn. organizational resources com. 1981). Avocations: golf, travel, reading, theater. Office: Muskegon Cty Dept Employment & Tng 1611 Oak Ave Muskegon MI 49442-2405

ROY, RALPH LORD, clergyman; b. St. Albans, Vt., Sept. 30, 1928; s. Howard Allen and Olive Lydia (Corliss) R.; m. Margaret Ellen Finlay, Feb. 12, 1960 (dec.); 1 child, Joyce Victoria. BA, Swarthmore Coll., 1950; MA, Columbia U. and Union, Theol. Seminary, 1952. Ordained to ministry United Meth. Ch. as deacon, 1952, as elder, 1961. Asst. minister Met. Community United. Meth. Ch., N.Y.C., 1957-60; minister Grace United Meth. Ch., 1960-63, Greene Ave./Knickerbocker United Meth. Ch., Bklyn., 1964-68, Cuyler Warren St. Community Ch., Bklyn., 1968-70, United Meth. Ch., Clinton, Conn., 1970-74, Mary Taylor United Meth. Ch., Milford, 1974-79, First United Meth. Ch., Meriden, 1979-94, pastor Thomaston, 1994-99, United Meth. Ch., East Berlin, 2000—01, First and Summerfield United Meth. Ch., New Haven, 2001—02. Author: Apostles of Discord, 1953, Communism and the Churches, 1960; contbr. articles to profl. jours. Chaplain Meriden (Conn.) Police Dept., 1981-92; radio ministry, 1983-2002; newspaper columnist, 1999-. Home: 697 S End Rd Unit 37 Plantsville CT 06479-1843 E-mail: ralphlroy@aol.com. *When I consider the magnificence and vastness of the universe, I can be overwhelmed by childlike marvel. That's one key aspect of God's creation. Another is the almost infinite variety, complexity, and beauty of life on our planet, all of it interdependent, making it urgent that we dwell together in harmony, mutual respect and peace.*

ROY, RANJIT KUMAR, mechanical engineer; b. Barisal, E. Bengal, India, Jan. 1, 1947; came to U.S., 1968; s. Rajani and Kumundini (Baral) R.; m. Krishna Majumder, Apr. 25, 1970; children: Purba, Paula. Student, Khulna U., East Bengal, India, 1963; BSME, Regional Engring. Coll., Durgapur, India, 1968; MSME, U. Mo., Rolla, 1970, PhD, 1972. Registered profl. engr., Mich. Sr. engr. Burroughs Corp., Detroit, 1972-76; sr. project engr. GM, Warren, Mich., 1976-79, staff engr. Chevrolet Motors Mcih., 1979-82, mgr. reliability CPC engring., 1982-87; pres. Nutek Inc., Birmingham, Mich., 1987—. Adj. prof. Oakland U., Rochester, Mich., 1976—. Author: A Primer On The Taguchi Method, 1990, Design of Experiments Using the Taguchi Approach, 2001; author computer software Qualitek-4, 1991. Pres. Bichitra Inc., Troy, 1980-82. Fellow Am. Soc. Quality Control (sr., v.p. profl. devel. 1987-88); mem. Soc. Automotive Engrs. Democrat. Hindu. Avocations: photography, computer programming, music, chess. Home: 3829 Quarton Rd Bloomfield Hills MI 48302-4059 Office: Nutek Inc 3829 Quarton Rd Ste 102 Bloomfield Hills MI 48302-4059 E-mail: rkroy@rkroy.com.

ROY, ROB J. biomedical engineer, anesthesiologist; b. Bklyn., Jan. 2, 1933; m. Carole Ann Apmann, Aug. 1, 1959 (div.); children: Robert Bruce, David John, Bruce Glenn; m. Judith Anne Webb, Oct. 6, 1996. BSEE, Cooper Union, N.Y.C., 1954; MSEE, Columbia U., 1956; DEngSc, Rensselaer Poly. Inst., 1962; MD, Albany (N.Y.) Med. Coll., 1976. Profl. engr., N.Y.; diplomate Am. Bd. Anesthesiology. Prof. elec. engrin. dept. Rensselaer Poly. Inst., Troy, N.Y., 1962, prof. elec. engring. dept., 1980—, head biomed. engring. dept., 1985-94; prof. anesthesiology Albany (N.Y.) Med. Ctr., 1979—. Author: State Variables for Engineers, 1965, 2d edit., 1998; author over 200 papers in field. Mem.: IEEE (life), Am. Soc. Anesthesiologists, Sigma Xi. Home: 565 Highwood Cir Albany NY 12203-5037 Office: Albany Med Ctr Dept Anesthesiology 47 New Scotland Ave Albany NY 12208-3412 E-mail: royr@rpi.edu, robjroy@worldnet.att.net.

ROY, ROBERT RUSSELL, toxicologist; b. Mpls., Sept. 14, 1957; s. Rudolph Russell and Arlene Charlotte (Miller) R.; m. Barbara Jane Richie, Oct. 10, 1987; children: Andrew, Katherine. BA cum laude, Augsburg Coll., 1980; MS, U. Minn., 1986, PhD, 1989. Bd. cert. in toxicology. Toxicologist, project mgr. Pace Labs., Inc., Mpls., 1989-90; toxicologist Minn. Dept. Health, 1990-93, Minn. Regional Poison Ctr., St. Paul, 1990-97; team leader, toxicology specialist 3M, 1997—, sr. toxicology specialist, 2000—. Lectr. U. Minn., Mpls., 1986-90, Midwest Ctr. Occupl. Health and Safety, St. Paul, 1990—, instr., 1989; adj. assoc. prof. U. Minn., 1993—; mem. grad. faculty in toxicology and pub. health U. Minn.; adj. asst. prof. emergency medicine Oreg. Health Sci. U., Portland. Mem. Mt. Carmel Luth. Ch. Coun., Mpls., 1983-85. Mem. Soc. Toxicology, Am. Indsl. Hygiene Assn., Delta Omega. Home: 6201 Near Mountain Blvd Chanhassen MN 55317-9117 Office: Corp Toxicology 3 M Ctr Bldg 220-2E-02 Saint Paul MN 55144-1000 E-mail: rroy@mmm.com.

ROY, ROBERT WILLIAM, artist, educator; b. Worcester, Mass., Oct. 7, 1945; s. Vincent Charles and Rita Marie R.; m. Laurie Jean Zephir, Aug. 1, 1981; children: Patrick Zephir, Roy. BFA magna cum laude, U. Mass., 1969; MFA, Yale U., 1971. Instr. Sch. of the Worcester Art Mus., 1972-81; prof., chair painting dept. Montserrat Coll. of Art, Beverly, Mass., 1988—. Adj. instr. Mount Wachusett C.C., Gardner, Mass., 1982-98, mem. adv. bd., 1997—; vis. lectr. U. Lowell., Mass., 1982-83, Worcester State Coll., 1986-87; vis. critic Smith Coll., Northampton, Mass., 1983. Exhibited in group shows at Rose Art Mus., Brandeis U., 1977, Williams Coll. Mus. Art, 1977, Danforth Mus. Art, 1981, Hudson River Mus., 1984, Worcester Art Mus., 1984, Berkshire Mus., 1986, Brainerd Art Gallery, State Univ. Coll. at Potsdam, N.Y., 1986, Siegfried Gallery/Ohio U., 1987, John Szoke Gallery, N.Y.C., 1988, Fitchburg Art Mus., 1988, Laguna Gloria Art Mus., 1989-90, DeCordova Mus., 1991, Danforth Mus. Art, 1994, Cragin Fife Gallery, Brookline, Mass., 1995, U. Ariz., 1996, Butler Inst. Am. Art, 1998, Boston U., 1999, 2001, Fed. Res. Bank, Boston, 1999, Montserrat Coll. Art, 2000, Danforth Mus. Art, 2001, Ben Shahn Galleries, William Paterson U., Wayne, N.J., 2002, The European Biennial of Contemporary Art, Frankfurt, Germany, 2002; represented in permanent collections at Mus. Modern Art N.Y.C., The Danforth Mus. Art, Trenton State Coll. Fellow Yale U., Norfolk, Conn., 1968, Mass. Artists Found., Boston, 1977. Mem. L.A. Printmaking Soc., Coll. Art Assn. N.Y.C., Boston Printmakers. Home: 95 Regan St Gardner MA 01440-4015 Office: Montserrat College of Art 23 Essex St # Beverly MA 01915-4508

ROY, ROBIN JENNIFER, landscape designer, retired education fundraiser; b. N.Y.C., June 3, 1953; d. George Robert and Margaret (Snow) R.; m. Michael Katz, July 19, 1986; 1 child, Edward. AB, Smith Coll., 1975, MA, 1978; MBA, Columbia U., 1988. Dir. devel. and alumni affairs, Sch. Nursing Columbia U., N.Y.C., 1989-92, dir. devel. Spence Sch., 1992-93, devel. specialist Coll. Physicians & Surgeons, 1993-95, assoc. dean devel. Sch. Pub. Health, 1995-97; founder, prin. Epione Health Sci. Assocs., 1997-2001; landscape designer N.Y. Botanical Garden, 2001—. Mem. Am. Horticultural Soc., Assn. Profl. Landscape Designers. E-mail: robinroy@att.net.

ROY, RUSTUM, interdisciplinary educator, materials researcher; b. Ranchi, India, July 3, 1924; came to U.S., 1945, naturalized, 1961; s. Narendra Kumar and Rajkumari (Mukherjee) R.; m. Della M. Martin, June 8, 1948; children: Neill, Ronnen, Jeremy. BSc with honors, Patna (India) U., 1942; MSc, Patna (India) U., India, 1944; PhD, Pa. State U., 1948; DSc (hon.), Tokyo Inst. Tech., 1987, Alfred U, 1993. Research asst. Pa. State U., 1948-49, mem. faculty, 1950—, prof. geochemistry, 1957—, prof. solid state, 1968—, chmn. solid state tech. program, 1960-67, chmn. sci. tech. and soc. program, 1977-84, dir., 1984-89, dir. materials research lab., 1962-85, Evan Pugh prof., 1981—; sr. sci. officer Nat. Ceramic Lab., India, 1950; mem. com. mineral sci. tech. Nat. Acad. Scis., 1967-69, com. survey materials sci. tech., 1970-74; exec. com. chem. div. NRC, 1967-70, nat. materials adv. bd., 1970-77, mem. com. radioactive waste mgmt., 1974-80, chmn. panel waste solidification, 1976-80, chmn. com. USSR and Eastern Europe, 1976-81. Mem. com. material sci. and engring. NRC, 1986-89; mem. Pa. Gov.'s Sci. Adv. Com.; chmn. materials adv. panel Gov.'s Sci. Adv. Com., 1965-80; mem. adv. com. on engring. NSF, 1968-72, adv. com. to ethical and human value implications sci. and tech., 1974-76, adv. com. div. materials rsch., 1974-77; Hibbert lectr. U. London, 1979; cons. to industry; mem. adv. com. Coll. Engring., Stanford U., 1984-86; internat. sci. lectr. NRC, 1991-92. Author: Honest Sex, 1968, Crystal Chemistry of Non-metallic Materials, 1974, Experimenting with Truth, 1981, Radioactive Waste Disposal, Vol. 1, the Waste Package, 1983, Lost at the Frontier, 1985; founding editor-in-chief: Materials Rsch. Bull., 1966—, Jour. Materials Edn., 1980-2000, Bull. Sci. Tech. and Soc, 1981-2000, Materials Rsch. Innovations, 1997—; contbr. over 1000 articles to profl. jours., 25 patents in field. Chmn. bd. Dag Hammarskjold Coll., 1973-75; chmn. ad hoc com. sci., tech. and ch. Nat. Council Chs., 1966-68. Sci. policy fellow Brookings Instn., 1982-83; recipient Ellis Island medal of hon., 1996. Fellow: AAAS (Orton lectr. 1984, chmn. chemistry sect. 1985), U.S. Nat. Acad. Engring., Mineral. Soc. Am. (award 1957), Am. Ceramic Soc. (Sosman lectr. 1975, disting. life, Educator of Yr. 1993), Am. Phys. Soc., Indian Acad. Scis. (hon.); mem.: Materials Rsch. Soc. (founder, pres. 1976), Am. Soc. Engring. Educators (Centennial medal 1993, Hall of Fame 1993), Am. Chem. Soc. (Petroleum Rsch. Fund award 1960, Dupont award for Chem. of Materials 1993), Fine Ceramics Assn. Japan (Internat. award), Ceramic Soc.Japan (hon. Centennial award 1991), Mineral Soc. Am., Fedn. Materials Socs. (Nat. Materials Advancement award 1991), Russian Acad. Scis. (elected fgn.), Engring. Acad. Japan (elected fgn.), Indian Nat. Sci. Acad. (fgn.), Royal Swedish Acad. Engring. Scis. (elected fgn.). Home: 528 S Pugh St State College PA 16801-5312 Office: 102 Materials Research Lab University Park PA 16802-4800 E-mail: rroy@psu.edu. *My major responsibility to the increasingly unified world culture, as a scientist supported largely by the public, is to integrate into its emerging radically pluralist yet globally unifying Religion, the insights from Science and the impact of Technology on the human condition. As a Christian Radical Pluralist, I am committed to presenting to my fellow humans—expecially all non-scientists, from Presidents and CEOs to the person in the street—an accurate picture of the whole truth about my scientific "advances" and those of others—their limited and ambivalent nature and their relatively minor position in the sum total of human concerns.*

ROY, THOMAS DAVID, accountant; b. Hartford, Conn., Nov. 5, 1964; s. Raymond and Jacqueline (Leonard) R.; m. Dawn Butler, May 14, 1988; children: Zachary Raymond, Olivia Anna, Jared Thomas. BS in Acctg., Ctrl. Conn. State U., 1996. CPA, Conn. Owner Carney, Roy & Gerrol, PC, West Hartford, 1995—; mgr. Kostin, Ruffkess & Co., LLC, 1996. Lectr. in field. Mem. town com. East Hartford (Conn.) Rep. Party, 1995—, chmn. 1998—; treas. bd. dirs. Big Bros./Big Sisters, Hartford, 1989-94; host family Spl. Olympics World Games, East Hartford, 1996; mem. parish coun. Blessed Sacrament Ch., 1995—. Recipient Mayor's Recognition award Town of East Hartford, 1995. Mem. AICPA, Conn. Soc. CPAs, East Hartford C. of C. Roman Catholic. Avocations: hockey and baseball coaching, boating, swimming, fishing. Home: 64 Winding Ln East Hartford CT 06118-3229 Office: Carney Roy & Gerrol PC 35 Cold Spring Rd Ste 412 Rocky Hill CT 06067-3169

ROY, WILLIAM ROBERT, physician, lawyer, former congressman; b. Bloomington, Ill., Feb. 23, 1926; s. Elmer Javan and Edna Blanche (Foley) R.; m. Jane Twining Osterhoudt, Sept. 1947; children: Robin Jo, Randall Jay, Richelle Jane, William Robert, Renee Jan, Rise Javan. BS, Ill. Wesleyan U., 1946; MD, Northwestern U., 1949; JD with honors, Washburn U., 1970. Pvt. practice medicine, 1955-70, 79-89; mem. 92d-93d congresses from 2d Dist. Kans., 1971-75; exec. dir. Kans. Med. Edn. Found., 1976-94; newspaper columnist, 1989-2001. Former dir. Sentry Ins.; Democratic candidate for U.S. Senate, 1974, 78. Mem. Inst. Medicine of Nat. Acad. Scis. Democrat. Methodist. Home: 6137 SW 38th Ter Topeka KS 66610-1307

ROYAL, DARRELL K. university official, former football coach; b. Hollis, Okla., July 6, 1924; s. Burley Ray and Katy Elizabeth (Harmon) R.; m. Edith Marie Thomason, July 26, 1944; children: Marian (Mrs. Abraham Kazen III) (dec.), Mack, David (dec.). BS in Bus, U. Okla., 1950. Former head football coach, then dir. athletics U. Tex., now asst. to univ. pres. Author: Darrell Royal Talks Football, 1963. Named Coach of Yr., Football Coaches Assn., 1963, 70, Tex. Sports Writers, 1961, 63, 69, 70, Southwesterner of Yr., 1961, 62, 63; named to U. Tex. Longhorn Hall of Fame, 1976, Tex. Sports Hall of Fame, 1976, Jim Thorpe Okla. Hall of Fame, 1977, Nat. Football Hall of Fame, 1983, Coach of Decade for 1960's, ABC; recipient Horatio Alger award, 1996; Darrell K. Royal Meml. Football Stadium, U. Tex. named in his honor, 1996; inducted into Southwestern Bell Cotton Bowl Hall of Fame, 1998, Okla. Heritage Soc. Hall of Fame, 2000. Mem. Delta Upsilon. Presbyterian. Office: U Tex SRH2.101 Austin TX 78712

ROYAL, DOROTHY PATRICIA, retired library media specialist; b. Washington, Oct. 13, 1935; d. Frederick James and Willie Nora (Levister) Constantine; m. H.B. Royal, Feb. 16, 1957; children: Duane Alan, Brett Ashley, Craig Stephen. BA, U. Md., 1977, MLS, 1982. Cert. advanced profl. in ednl. media, Md. Libr. media specialist Charles Carroll Middle Sch., New Carrollton, Md., 1977-83, Crossland H.S., Temple Hills, 1983-95. Editor film festivals, 1977-83; book reviewer Sch. Libr. Jour., 1985-99, Kliatt Paperbacks, Wellesley, Mass., 1990-99. Pres. Friends of Sampson County Pub. Libr., 1998—; exec. bd. Sampson County Arts Coun., 1996; master gardener vol. N.C. Coop. Extension Svc., 1998—. Mem. AAUW, NOW, Md. State Tchrs. Assn., Md. Ednl. Media Orgn., Ednl. Media Assn. Prince Georges County (v.p. 1983-84), Smithsonian Assocs., Nat. Mus. Women in Arts, Clinton Women's Club, Sampson County Garden Club. Avocations: reading, gardening, exercise, travel. Home: 11500 Keener Rd Faison NC 28341-5724

ROYAL, HENRY DUVAL, nuclear medicine physician; b. Norwich, Conn., May 14, 1948; MD, St. Louis U., 1974. Diplomate Am. Bd. Internal Medicine; Am. Bd. Nuclear Medicine. Intern R.I. Hosp., Providence, 1974, resident in internal medicine, 1975-76; resident in nuclear medicine Harvard Med. Sch., Boston, 1977-79; from assoc. to staff physician Barnes Hosp., St. Louis, 1987—; from assoc. to cons. staff physician Children's Hosp., 1987—; prof. Washington U., 1993—. Co-team leader health effects sect. Internat. Atomic Energy Agy. Internat. Chernobyl Project, 1990; mem. Am. Bd. Nuclear Medicine, 1993-99; mem. com. on assessment of CDC radiation studies NRC/NAS, 1993-98; mem. sci. com. 1 and 4 Nat. Coun. on Radiation Protection and Measurements, 1993—; mem. coun. Nat. Coun. on Radiation Protection, 1996—, bd. dirs., 2000—; Vets. Adv. Com. on Environ. Hazards, 1997—. Contbr. articles to profl. jours. Mem. Soc. Nuc. Medicine (v.p. 2002), Alpha Omega Alpha. Office: Acad Faculty Mallinckrodt Inst Radiology 510 S Kingshighway Blvd Saint Louis MO 63110-1016

ROYAL, SUSAN, classical musician, music educator; b. Phila., July 21, 1955; d. Douglas David and Bette (Caum) Royal; m. Wayne Arthur Jones, Aug. 13, 1988; children: Daria Jones, Ethan Jones. BMusic, Ithaca Coll., 1977; MMusic, Yale U., 1981; DMusical Arts, SUNY, Stony Brook, 1989. Instr. flute Tenn. Technol. U., Cookeville, 1981-83; flutist Erie (Pa.) Philharm., 1983—, Fredonia Chamber Players, 1983—; substitute flutist Buffalo Philharm., 1984—; prof. flute SUNY Coll., Fredonia, 1983—. Performer/clinician Fredonia Woodwind Quintet Summer Camp, 1994—, Fredonia Woodwind Quintet, 1983—; artist performer Armstrong/Artley Flutes, 1991—. Concert soloist; performances on CD include Opera Sacra, 1994, Piorkowski, 1998. Elder First United Presbyn. Ch., Dunkirk, N.Y., 1987—. Mem. Nat. Flute Assn. (performer/adjudicator/panelist 1977—), Niagara Frontier Flute Assn. Democrat. Avocations: sailing, running, gardening. Office: SUNY Coll at Fredonia Sch Music Fredonia NY 14063

ROYAL, WILLIAM HENRY, real estate developer, architect; b. Jackson, Tenn., Dec. 16, 1924; s. Joe Henry and Millie Earline (Anderson) R.; m. Odell Peebles, June 16, 1943; children: William H. Jr., Frederick E., Diana, Carolyn M., Wanda H. Diploma, Chicago Tech. Coll., 1959; student, MIT, 1969, '73, U. Neb., 1971-76, U. Minn., 1974-76. Reg. architect, Ill., Mo. Architect, engr. U.S. Army Engr. Dist., Detroit, 1957-61, gen. architect St. Paul, 1959-62, supr. architect Chgo., 1962-70, gen. architect Omaha, 1970-73; architect, job captain Ellerbe & Co., St Paul, 1962; cons. FREBO, U.S. Postal Svc., St. Paul, 1973-77; constr. mgr. H.Q. U.S. Postal Svc., Washington, 1977-80; pres. William H. Royal & Assocs., Inc., Lake St. Louis, Mo., 1987—, Chgo., 1995-97, St. Louis Airport Devel. Corp., 1988-89; v.p. Steelgrade Corp., Clayton, Mo., 1991-93; sec.-treas. Am. Community Telecomms. System, Inc., Ferguson, 1992-97; pres. Royal King Constrn. Co., St. John, 1995-97. Author: (tng. manual) Architect Engineer Contracts, 1970; editor: Master Planning, Kinloch Redevelopment, 1987. Steward, United Meth. Ch., Omaha, 1970-73; urban cons. United Meth. Ministries, Omaha, 1970-73, Youth Coord., United Meth. Ch., Omaha, 1971-73; mem. Douglas County Parole Bd., Omaha, 1971-72. Recipient Commendation U.S. Postal Svc., Washington, 1976, Svc. award, 1980, letter of Appreciation, 1982; nominee Rockefeller Pub. Svc. award, U.S. Postal Svc., St. Paul, 1976. Avocations: computer programming, fishing, travel. Home: 1 Berry Ct Lake Saint Louis MO 63367-1921 Office: William H Royal & Assocs 1 Berry Ct Lake Saint Louis MO 63367-1921

ROYBAL-ALLARD, LUCILLE, congresswoman; b. Boyle Heights, Calif., June 12, 1941; d. Edward Roybal; m. Edward T. Allard; 4 children. BA, Calif. State U., L.A. Former mem. Calif. State Assembly; mem. U.S. Congress from 33rd Calif. dist., 1993—; mem. appropriationscom. Democrat. Office: Ho of Reps 2435 Rayburn Bldg Washington DC 20515-0533*

ROY-BURMAN, PRADIP, molecular biology and virology educator; b. Comilla, Bengal, India, Nov. 12, 1938; came to U.S., 1963; s. Prafulla Nath and Mrinalini (Barman) Roy-Burman; m. Sumitra Ghosh, Nov. 26, 1963. BSc. with honors, Calcutta (India) U., 1956, MSc., 1958, PhD, 1963. Rsch. assoc. dept. biochemistry Sch. of Medicine U. So. Calif., L.A., 1963-66, Dernham sr. rsch. fellow in oncology Am. Cancer Soc., 1966-71, asst. prof. dept. biochemistry, 1967-72, assoc. prof. dept. pathology and biochemistry, 1972-78, prof. dept. pathology and biochemistry, 1978—, vice chmn. dept. pathology, 1987—. Interim chmn. dept. molecular microbiology and immunology, U. So. Calif., L.A., 1995-97; mem. pathology B study sect., NIH, 1990-94, reviewers res., 1994-98, ad hoc mem. sci. tech. rev. bd. for biomed. behavioral rsch. facilities NCRR, NIH, 1997—, prostate cancer rsch. program review panel, Dept. of Defense, 2001—; chmn. symposium internat. congress biochem. molecular biology, 1994, co-chmn. symposium internat. cancer congess, 1994, chmn. workshop on pathogenesis of animal retrovirus, session immune interaction, 1996; spkr. in field. Author (with others) books; contbr. articles to profl. jours.; book reviewer; inventor novel transcription regulatory elements for gene transfer vectors; mem. editorial bd. Hematological Oncology, 1987—97, Cancer Biology and Therapy, 2001—. Rsch. grantee Am. Cancer Soc., NIH, Am. Diabetes Assn., Wright Found., Martell Found. Mem. Am. Soc. for Microbiology, Am. Soc. for Biol. Chemists and Molecular Biology, Am. Assn. Cancer Rsch., Am. Soc. Investigative Pathology, Internat. Assn. for Comparative Rsch. on Leukemia and Related Diseases. Democrat. Hindu. Avocations: writing, hiking, golf. Office: Keck Sch Of Medicine Hmr 209 2011 Zonal Ave Los Angeles CA 90033

ROYCE, BARRIE SAUNDERS HART, physicist, educator; b. Eng., Jan. 10, 1933; came to U.S., 1957, naturalized, 1978; s. Vincent Pateman Hart and Kathlene (Saunders) R.; m. Dominique J.M. Vallee, May 7, 1964; children: Vincent Rene Hart, Marc Edward Hart. BSc in Physics, King's Coll., U. London, 1954, PhD, 1957. Rsch. assoc. Carnegie Inst. Tech., 1957-60, Princeton U., 1960-61, mem. faculty, 1961—, prof. applied physics and materials scis., 1978—; master of Dean Mathey Coll. Dean Mathey Coll., 1986-94. Editorial adv. bd. Jour. Photoacoustics, to 1984. Mem. Princeton Borough Zoning Bd. Adjustment, 1980-93, chair, 1993—. Grantee NSF; Grantee Air Force Office Sci. and Rsch.; Grantee Army Rsch. Office. Mem. Am. Phys. Soc., Sigma Xi. Office: Princeton U D416 Duffield Hall Eq Princeton NJ 08544-0001

ROYCE, EDWARD R. (ED ROYCE), congressman; b. Los Angeles, Oct. 12, 1951; m. Marie Porter. BA, Calif. State U., Fullerton. Tax mgr. Southwestern Portland Cement Co.; mem. Calif. Senate, 1983-93, U.S. Congress from 39th Calif. dist., 1993—; mem. banking and fin. svcs. com., internat. rels. com. Vice chmn. Public Employment and Retirement Com.; mem. Bus. and Profs. com., Indsl. Rels. com.; legis. author, campaign co-chmn. Proposition 15 Crime Victims/Speedy Trial Initiative; author nation's 1st felony stalking law, bill creating Foster Family Home Ins. Fund, legis. creating foster parent recruitment and tng. program; mem. Banking and Fin. Svcs. Com., Internat. Rels. Com. Named Legis. of Yr. Orange County Rep. Com., 1986, Child Adv. of Yr. Calif. Assn. Svc. for Children, 1987. Mem. Anaheim C. of C. Republican. Office: US Ho Reps 2202 Rayburn Ho Office Bldg Washington DC 20515*

ROYCE, PAUL CHADWICK, medical administrator; b. Mpls., July 2, 1928; BA, U. Minn., 1948, MD, 1952; PhD, Case Western Res. U., 1959. Diplomate Am. Bd. of Internal Medicine. Intern U. Chgo. Clinics, 1952-53; fellow NSF Case Western Res. U., Cleve., 1953-54, 56-58, Upjohn fellow, 1958-59; resident internal medicine Bronx Mcpl. Hosp., N.Y., 1959-61; asst. prof. of medicine Albert Einstein Coll. of Med., N.Y.C., 1961-69; sr. staff endocrinologist Guthrie Clinic, Sayre, Pa., 1970-81; assoc. prof. of medicine Hahnemann Med. Sch., Phila., 1973-81; emeritus prof. medicine Med. Coll. Pa./Hahnemann U., 1996—; dean and prof. clin. sci. and physiology Sch. Medicine U. Minn., Duluth, 1981-87; sr. v.p., clin. dir. Monmouth Med. Ctr., Long Branch, N.J., 1987-94; med. dir. The Segal Co. N.Y., 1995-98; prin. Royce Assocs., Atlantic Highlands, N.J., 1995—; lectr. Writing Ctr., Monmouth U., NJ, 2001—. Producer, host TV prgram Doctors on Call, 1983-87 (Nat. Friends of Pub. Broadcasting Hill award 1987). Lt. USNR, 1954-56. Mem. Harvey Soc., Am. Physiol. Soc., Fedn. Am. Scientists, Physicians for Social Responsibility, Am. Coll. Physician Execs., Sigma Xi, Alpha Omega Alpha. Avocations: skiing, cycling, canoeing. Office: Royce Associates 9 Prospect Rd Atlantic Highlands NJ 07716-1721

ROYCE, ROBERT KILLIAN, retired physician; b. Greenville, Miss., Mar. 18, 1917; s. Owen and Eda (Luhm) R.; widowed; children: Corinne Elizabeth Royce Ulbright, Margaret Anne Royce Chida. BS, U. Miss., 1939; MD, Washington U., 1942. Diplomate Am. Bd. Urology. Rotating intern U. Chgo. Clinics, 1942-43; intern, asst. resident in gen. surgery Barnes Hosp.-Wash. U. Sch. Medicine, St. Louis, 1945-47, resident in urology, 1947-49; asst. prof. Washington U., 1949-55, assoc. prof., 1955-70, prof. surgery, 1970—, chmn. divsn. urology, 1975-78. Cons. U.S. Vet.'s Hosp., St. Louis, 1953—. Maj. Med. Corps, 1943-46, ETO. Decorated Bronze Star. Fellow Am. Coll. Surgeons; mem. Am. Urol. Assn., Soc. Univ. Urologists, Univ. Club, Old Warson Country Club, Alpha Omega Alpha. Republican. Roman Catholic.

Avocations: golf, forestry, farming. Home: 766 High Hampton Rd Saint Louis MO 63124-1018 Office: Washington Univ Divsn Urology 4960 Childrens Pl Saint Louis MO 63110-1002 E-mail: robkroy@aol.com.

ROYCE, STANTON, motivational speaker, consultant; b. Steubenville, Ohio, June 1, 1950; m. Melanie Viray Espinosa, Mar. 23, 1984; children: Mason, Angela. Student, Franciscan U., Steubenville, 1973; AS in Elec. Engring., Jefferson C.C., Steubenville, 1983; BS in Psychology, U. Cin., 1991; MBA, U. Phoenix, 1994. Night club entertainer, hypnotist, Wintersville, Ohio, 1970-73; mgr. Liberty Fin. Corp., Columbus, 1973-76, Bally Mfg., Steubenville, 1976-79; pres., clergyman Cmty. Interfaith Svcs., 1979-83; dir. engring. May Co., Youngstown, Ohio, 1983-84; ops. mgr., dir. ops. LaSalle Ptnrs., Chgo., 1984-93; mgr. Core Resources, Inc., Cin., 1993-94; pres. Royce Personal Devel., Hamden, Conn., 1994-97; dir. The Royce Bus. Inst., Houston, 1997—. Author: The Salesman's Quick & Easy Success System, 1993, Million Dollar Persuasion, 1994, Encyclopedia of Sales Techniques, 1995, Billion Dollar Success Secrets, 1996, Billion Dollar Power Persuasion, 1996, Creating Commitment Throughout the Organization, 1997, How to Prevent Escalating Wages and Employee Turnover in a Tight Labor Market, 1998. Founder, 1st pres. Alternatives to Living in Violent Environments, Jefferson County, 1980-81; victims asst. counselor Jefferson County Cmty. Mental Health Ctr., Steubenville, 1977-79; mem. disaster comms. ARC, Jefferson County, 1965-77. Mem. Nat. Spkrs. Assn., Nat. C. of C., Alpha Sigma Kappa Honor Soc. Avocations: family, hiking, mountain biking, travel. Office: One Royce Plz Houston TX 77230-0089 E-mail: millionairescoach@mycoach.org.www.mycoach.orgn.

ROYCHOUDHURI, CHANDRASEKHAR, physicist; b. Barisal, Bengal, India, Apr. 7, 1942; s. Hiralal and Amiyabala (Sengupta) Roychoudhuri; m. Suzanne Cas; children: Asim, Onnesha. BS in Physics, Jadavpur U., India, 1963; MS in Physics, Jadavpur U., 1965; PhD in Optics, U. Rochester, 1973. Asst. prof. U. Kalyani, India, 1965—68; sr. scientist Nat. Inst. Astrophysics, Puebla, Maine, Mexico, 1974—78; sr. staff scientist TRW Inc., Redondo Beach, 1978—86; mgr. laser sys. Perkin-Elmer, Danbury, Conn., 1986—89; chief scientist Optics & Applied Tech. Lab. United Technologies Optical Sys., West Palm Beach, Fla., 1990—92; dir. Photonics Rsch. Ctr. U. Conn., Storrs, 1992—2000; rsch. prof. dept. physics Photonics Lab., U. Conn., 2001—. Mem sci adv bd All Optical Network, 2001—; bd. dirs. Aptus Inc. Contbr. chapters to books, articles to profl jours. Scholar Fulbright, Univ Vt, 1968. Fellow: Soc Photo-Optical Instrumentationi (bd dirs 2000—), Optical Soc Am, Conn Acad Sci and Eng; mem.: IEEE, Am Physical Soc (life). Achievements include research in on applications of diode lasers in spectrometry, laser radar and desk-top manufacturing; interference, diffraction and dispersion phenomena with ultrashort light pulses. E-mail: chandra@phys.uconn.edu.

ROYCHOUDHURY, SIDDHARTHA, research scientist; b. Shillong, Meghalaya, India, May 10, 1964; came to the U.S., 1984; s. Saurendra and Binapani (Bhattacharya) R.; m. Monica S. Chakravorty, Jan. 31, 1991. B in Chem. Engring., Jadavpur U., Calcutta, India, 1984; MSChemE, Ill. Inst. Tech., 1986; PhD in Microbiology, U. Ill., Chgo., 1992. Postdoctoral scientist Eli Lilly & Co., Indpls., 1993-94; rsch. scientist Procter & Gamble, Cin., 1994-98, sr. scientist, 1998—. Contbr. articles to profl. jours. Recipient Pre-doctoral Trainee award Cystic Fibrosis Found., 1990; Nat. Merit scholar Govt. of India, 1978. Mem. AAAS, Am. Soc. for Microbiology. Achievements include discovery of bacterial signal tranduction inhibition and non-fluorinated quinolones. Avocation: percussionist. Home: 6483 Jayfield Dr Hamilton OH 45011-7119 Office: Procter & Gamble Pharms 8700 S Mason Montgomery Rd Mason OH 45040-9462 E-mail: roychoudhury.s@pg.com.

ROYCROFT, CHERYL, secondary education educator; b. Buffalo, Mar. 11, 1961; d. Edward Stanley and Delphine Theresa Janusz; m. Henry Phillip Roycroft, Oct. 14, 1983. BS, Daemen Coll., 1993; MEd, Cambridge Coll., 2002. Cert. tchr. Payroll clerk Sellmore Industries, Buffalo, 1984-85; acct. clerk Desiderio Produce, 1985-87, Fisher-Price, E. Aurora, 1987-90, Acme Electric, E. Aurora, 1993-94; tchr. Bryant & Stratton, Buffalo, 1994-96, Lake City H.S., S.C., 1996-97, Mt. Pleasant H.S., Elliott, 1997-2000, Lee Ctrl. H.S., Bishopville, 2000—. Mem. Assn. Career and Tech. Educators, S.C. Bus. Educators Assn., Coun. for Exceptional Children, Kappa Delta Pi (pres. 1992-95, historian 1991-92), Delta Mu Delta (v.p. 1991-92, pres. 1992-93), ASCD. Avocations: reading, swimming, dancing. Office: Lee Ctrl HS 1800 Wisacky Hwy Bishopville SC 29010 E-mail: keyteacher77@hotmail.com.

ROYCROFT, HOWARD FRANCIS, lawyer; b. Balt., Sept. 9, 1930; s. Howard F. and Bessie (Weaver) R.; m. Barbara Lee Seal, Mar. 20, 1954; children: Suzanne Carol Roycroft Soderberg, Nancy Lee Roycroft Branigan. BA, U. Md., 1953; LLB, Georgetown U., 1958. Bar: D.C. 1958. Mem. firm Hogan & Hartson, Washington, 1958, ptnr., 1965-87, exec. com., 1970-73, counsel, 1987—. Dir. United TV, Inc., 1982—2001, U TV San Francisco, Inc., 1983; mng. ptnr., dir. WIJY, Inc., Hilton Head, SC, 1989—97; lectr. Howard U. Sch. Law, 1973—74; guest lectr. U. Tex., 1980; mem. Met. Washington Bd. Trade. Bd. dirs. YMCA Met. Washington, 1974-76. 1st lt. USMC, 1953-55. Mem. ABA, Va. Bar Assn., Fed. Comm. Bar Assn., Bar Assn. D.C., Nat. Broadcasters Club, Barristers, Aircraft Owners and Pilots Assn., Nat. Acad. TV Arts & Scis., Broadcast Pioneers, Alexandria Rotary Club, Bryce Mountain Ski and Country Club (dir., pres. 1974-87), Mt. Vernon Country Club, Old Dominion Boat Club, Washington Tennis Patrons Club, Army-Navy Club, Chaine des Rotisseurs Gastronome Club, Skull Creek Yacht Club, Kappa Alpha, Beta Kappa, Delta Theta Phi. Republican. Methodist. Office: Hogan & Hartson 555 13th St NW Ste 800E Washington DC 20004-1161 E-mail: HRoycroft@aol.com.

ROYDS, ROBERT BRUCE, physician; b. Harrogate, England, Oct. 3, 1944; came to U.S., 1974; s. John Edmund and Ailsa Dorothea (Williams) R.; m. Marilyn Maria Valerio, Apr. 28, 1948; children: Elizabeth Caroline, Leslie Alexandra. MB, BS, U. London, 1967, MRCP, 1970. Sr. house officer Royal Northern Hosp., London, 1968; sr. house officer Luton and Dunstable Hosp., Beds, England, 1968-69; registrar St. Albans City Hosp., Herts, England, 1969-70; research fellow clin. pharmacology dept. St. Bartholomew's Hosp., U. London, London, 1970-72, chief asst., sr. registrar med. professorial unit, 1972-74; assoc. dir. Merck, Sharp & Dohme, Inc., Rahway, N.J., 1974-75; sr. research physician Hoffmann-La Roche Inc., Nutley, 1976-78; v.p. Besselaar Assocs., Princeton, 1979-82; pres. Theradex Sys., Inc., 1982-94, chmn. bd. dirs., 1994—. Cons. Ctr. for Rsch. Mothers/Infants Nat. Inst. Child Health & Human Devel., Washington, 1983; prin. investigator Clin. Trials Monitoring Svc. Nat. Cancer Inst., 1982—, Bd. trustees Chapin Sch., Princeton, 1984-89, pres. bd. trustees, 1986-89; pres. Riverside Condominium Assn., Cranford, N.J., 1978-79. Fellow Royal Soc. Medicine; mem. Royal Coll. Physicians, Am. Coll. Clin. Pharmacology Therapeutics, Am. Soc. for Clin. Research (sr. mem.), Am. Soc. Microbiology. Home: 5 Quick Ln Plainsboro NJ 08536-1424 Office: Theradex Systems Inc CN5257 Theradex CN5257 Princeton NJ 08540 E-mail: rroyds@theradex.com.

ROYER, DIANA AMELIA, educator; b. Camden, N.J., Aug. 2, 1959; m. Carl G. Royer. BA, Mary Washington Coll., 1981; MA, Temple U., 1986, PhD, 1989. Vis. instr. Am. U., Cairo, 1989-90, Widener U., Chester, Pa., 1991, Temple U., 1990-91; assoc. prof. Miami U., Oxford, Ohio, 1991—. Vol. docent McGuffey Museum, Oxford, Ohio, 1997—. Mem. Virginia Woolf Soc., Popular Culture Assn., Nat. Coun. Tchrs. English. Avocations: ballet, modern dance, gardening. Office: Miami U Bachelor Hall Oxford OH 45056 E-mail: royerda@muohio.edu.

ROYER, LINDA BATES, medical case manager; b. Quantico, Va., Mar. 11, 1954; BSN, McNeese State U., 1977. Cert. casemgr., cert. disability mgmt. specialist. ICU/CCU cardiovascular surgery nurse Lake Charles (La.) Meml. Hosp., Christus St. Patrick Hosp., 1977-86; chem. dependency and psychiat. staff, nurse mgr. Charter Behavioral Health unit Charter Hosp., Lake Charles, 1986-94; med. casemgmt. cons. Crawford & Co., 1994—. Mem. Casemgmt. Soc. Am., Am. Assn. Legal Nurse Cons., Sigma Theta Tau. Home: 6808 E Calcasieu Dr Lake Charles LA 70605-0451 Office: Crawford and Co PO Box 958 Lake Charles LA 70602-0958

ROYER, MARILYN ANN, accountant, educator; b. Buffalo, Sept. 25, 1948; d. William S. and Eugenia (Lorenc) R. BA, SUNY, Buffalo, 1970, MBA, 1980; MEd, Niagara U., 1975. CPA, N.Y. Acct. Conway Porter, Buffalo, 1979-81, Seidman & Seidman, Buffalo, 1981-84; ptnr. Rader & Royer, Tonawanda, N.Y., 1985-88; pvt. practice, 1988—. Instr. part-time Niagara (N.Y.) U., 1991; commr. Niagara Frontier Transp. Authority, Buffalo, 1988—. Dir.-treas. Buffalo Area Coun. Alcoholism, 1982-84; prior sec. Zonta, North Tonawanda, N.Y., 1989. Recipient cert. Appreciation Daemen Coll., 1985. Mem. AICPA, Am. Soc. Women Accts., Nat. Assn. Accts. (dir. socioecon. projects 1984, dir. CMA affairs 1985, Disting. Svc. award 1984), N.Y. State Soc. CPA's. Home: 1328 Belling Pl North Tonawanda NY 14120-3101 Office: 305 Delaware St Tonawanda NY 14150-3511

ROYER, RICHARD BRIAN, industrial engineer, educator; b. Los Angeles, Calif., Sept. 8, 1955; s. Roderick L. and Mary C. Royer; m. Lucy Royer, May 8, 1992; children: Michael, Nehl. BS Indsl. Tech., So. Ill. Univ., Carbondale, IL, 1981; MBA, Univ. Phoenix, Phoenix, AZ, 1994. Flight simulation technologist USAF, Fayetteville, NC; indsl. engr. WACBAR, Chandler; sr. indsl. engr. AUNET. Prof. Western Internat. Univ., Phoenix. E-4 USAF, 1977—81, Fayetteville, NC. Home: 248 S Rush Circle West Chandler AZ 85226 Personal E-mail: royerc2u@earthlink.net.

ROYER, ROBERT LEWIS, retired utility company executive; b. Louisville, Jan. 2, 1928; s. Carl Brown and Martha Helen (Garrett) R.; m. Carol Jean Pierce, June 24, 1950; children: Jenifer Lea, Todd Pierce, Robert Douglas. BS in Elec. Engring., Rose Hulman Inst. Tech., 1949. Registered profl. engr., Ky. With Louisville Gas and Electric Co., 1949-91, asst. v.p. ops., 1962-63, asst. v.p., asst. gen. supt., 1963-64, v.p., gen. supt., 1964-69, v.p. ops., 1969-78, exec. v.p., 1978, pres., chief exec. officer, 1978-89; chmn., 1989-91; dir. Louisville Gas and Electric Co., 1972-91, chmn. emeritus, 1991—; dir. LG8E Energy Corp., 1990-91. Mem. exec. bd. East Cen. Area Reliability Coun., 1978-89; mem. Ky. Energy Resources Commn., 1975-79; mem. energy task force Gov.'s Econ. Devel. Commn., 1976-79; mem. Ky. Energy Rsch. Bd., 1978-88; v.p. Ind.-Ky. Electric Corp., 1979-89; dir. Ohio Valley Transmission Corp., 1978-90, Ohio Valley Electric Corp., 1979-89, Citizens Fidelity Corp. & Citizens Fidelity Bank and Trust Co., 1976-90. Mem. exec. bd. Old Ky. Home Coun. Boy Scouts Am., v.p. dist. ops., 1970-75, 79-80, 1st v.p., 1981-82, pres., 1982-84, commr., 1975-79, rep. to nat. coun., 1975-84, 95—, mem. regional bd., 1985—, S.E. region area pres., 1988-93; bd. dirs. East End Boys Club, 1975-78, Louisville Indsl. Found., 1980-86, Ky. Coun. Sci. and Tech., 1987-92; trustee Spirit of Louisville Found., 1978-90, J. Graham, Brown Found., 1980—; bd. mgrs. Rose Hulman Inst. Tech., 1979—; bd. dirs. Ky. Derby Mus., 1991-93, Leadership Louisville Found., 1985-91, Alliant Health Sys., 1989-94; mem. Louisville Devel. Com., 1979-83. Served with U.S. Army, 1953-55. Recipient Silver Beaver award Boy Scouts Am., 1975, Disting. Eagle award, 1989, Silver Antelope award, 1990. Mem. IEEE, Am. Radio and Relay League, Execs. Club Louisville (dir. 1980-83), Louisville Automobile Club (dir. 1974-96, treas. 1977-79, v.p. 1979-81, pres. 1981-83, nat. adv. coun. 1982-86), Louisville Area C. of C. (dir. 1978-80), Hurstbourne Country Club, Pendennis Club, Rotary. Methodist. Home and Office: 4014 Norbourne Blvd Louisville KY 40207-3806

ROYER, THOMAS JERRY, financial planner; b. Coshocton, Ohio, June 17, 1943; s. Walter H. Sr. and Francis (Guerke) R.; m. Felipa T. Pagal, Dec. 24, 1965; children: Matthew Vincent, Brian Eugene, Nicholas Alexander. Student, Xavier U., 1979, Coll. for Fin. Planning, Denver, 1986. Cert. fin. planner. Agt. Met. Life Ins. Co., N.Y.C., 1966-68, mgr., 1968-70; gen. agt. Summit Nat. Life Ins. Co., Akron, Ohio, 1970—, Community Nat., Worthington, 1989, Life USA, 1990, Am. Life & Casualty, 1997; prin. Royer & Co., Fairfield, Ohio, 1985-88; founder, pres. Group-10 Fin., 1988—; founder, CEO United Group Mktg., Cin., 1993, Altamonte Springs, Fla., 1996. Mem. Inst. Cert. Fin. Planners, Nat. Exchange Club. Republican. Roman Catholic. Avocations: golf, swimming, physical fitness. Office: Group-10 Fin 2790 Mack Rd Fairfield OH 45014-5129 also: United Group Mktg 921 Douglas Ave Ste 208 Altamonte Springs FL 32714-5202

ROYERE, WILLIAM RANDOLPH, III, computer company executive; b. N.Y.C., Nov. 24, 1964; s. William Randolph Royere Jr. and Rose Marie Polisi; children: Alexander Constable-Maxwell, Stevin Tyler Wilkins; m. Michelle Anne Wagner, May 12, 2000. Chief sci. officer TradeRights, Isle of Man, England, 1997—99, Global Network Security Sys., Oxnard, Calif., 1997—99; chief info. officer MPM Pub., 1997—99; chief tech. officer CoreCPA, N.Y.C., 1999—2000; chief network security ResolveNet Devel. Corp., 1999—2000; chief tech. officer Resolvement Devel., Inc., Agoura, Calif., 2001, E-Bullion, Camarillo, 2001—, Eisner Data Security Svcs., N.Y.C., 2001—; CEO Villeneuve, McElwee, Roberts & Royere, Newbury Park, Calif., 2001—; chief of devel. Electronic Commerce Code Mgmt. ASsn., Bethlehem, Pa.; chief tech. officer Midlersoft, Prague, Czech Republic, 2001—. Dir. adv. bd. Open Bus. Reporting Consotium, 1999—; chief tech. officer Silicon Valley Rsch., LLC, 1999—; tech. advisor UN Products and Svcs. Classification. Author, series editor Macmillan, Indpls., 1997—; author: Maximum Security: A Hacker's Guide to Protecting Your Internet Site and Network, 1998, The American Institue of Certified Public Accountants Web and Internet Security Education, Vols. I and II, 1998, Maximum Linux Security: A Hacker's Guide to Protecting Your Linux Server and Workstation, 1999, Maximum Windows 2000 Security, 2000, Maximum Apache Security, 2002, Maximum Security 4, 2002, others; editor Environ. Protection Jour.--Calif.; columnist Newsmax. Mem. Federalist Soc., Jud. Watch, St. George's Anglican. Mem. NRA, Soc. Study Social Biology, Nat. Orgn. for European-Am. Rights, Nat. Assn. Advancement of White People. Republican. Anglican. Avocations: astronomy, history, ancient religions, artificial intelligence, human network analysis. Home: 6 N Madrid Ave Newbury Park CA 91320-3315 Office: ResolveNet 2111 Norma St Oxnard CA 93030-2259 E-mail: william@royere.net.

ROYHAB, RONALD, journalist, newspaper editor; b. Lorain, Ohio, Oct. 6, 1942; s. Halim Farah and Elizabeth Della (Naiser) R.; m. Roberta Lee Libb, Apr. 20, 1969; children: David Libb, Aaron Nicholas. Student, Lorain County (Ohio) Coll., Kent State U.; student grad. program, Am. U., Washington. Reporter Lorain Jour., 1966-69; reporter spl. assignment Scripps Howard Cin. Post, 1971-72; investigative reporter Scripps Howard Cleve. Press, 1972-75; chief bur. Scripps Howard Ohio Bur., Columbus, 1975-78; asst. mng. editor Scripps Howard News Svc., Washington, 1978-81; mng. editor Scripps Howard El Paso (Tex.) Herald Post, 1981-83; asst. mng. editor Scripps Howard Pitts. Press, 1983-92; assoc. editor Pitts. Post Gazette, 1992-93; mng. editor Toledo Blade, 1993-97, exec. editor, 1997—. Bd. dirs. Am. Lebanese Congress; mem. Knight in Order of St. Ignatius of Antioch, 1997. With USAR, 1964-70. Recipient 7 awards for Excellence Cleve. Newspaper Guild, 1972-75, Spl. Sect. awards Pa. Newspaper Pubs. Assn., 1985, 86, 88; named to DeMolay Legion of Honor, 1997; fellow Am. Polit. Sci. Assn., 1970-71. Mem. Am. Soc. Newspaper Editors, AP Soc. Ohio (past pres.), Ohio Newspaper Assn., Toledo Press Club (pres.). Eastern Orthodox. Home: 27262 Fort Meigs Rd Perrysburg OH 43551-1230 Office: Toledo Blade 541 N Superior St Toledo OH 43660-0002 E-mail: royhab@theblade.com.

ROYLE, ANTHONY WILLIAM, accountant; b. Corona, Calif., Dec. 22, 1956; s. William Lloyd Royle and Patricia Rae (McGahan) Magda; m. Patricia Jean Blaylcok, Aug. 13, 1977 (div. Nov. 1983); children: Nicholas Anthony, Elizabeth Marie, Michael George. BS in Acctg., Weber State U., 1979. CPA, N.Mex. Sr. tax acct. Fox & Co. CPA, Farmington, N.Mex., 1981-83; tax mgr. Cox & Co. CPA, 1983-85; tax supr. Arthur Young, Albuquerque, 1985-87; tax supr., tax mgr. Neff & Co., 1987-95, tax ptnr., 1995—. Advisor for Sound Advice C. of C., Albuquerque, 1996—. With U.S. Army, 1974-76. Mem. AICPA (tax divsn.), N.Mex. Soc. CPA, Constrn. Fin. Mgmt. Assn. (Albuquerque chpt.). Avocations: reading, weight lifting, snow skiing. Office: Neff & Co LLP 6100 Uptown Blvd NE #400 Albuquerque NM 87110

ROYLE, DAVID BRIAN LAYTON, television producer, journalist; b. Claygate, Surrey, England, Jan. 29, 1955; came to U.S., 1974; s. John Hardy Layton and Jessie Monica (Pringle) R.; m. Cornelia Boardman Service; children: William Brian Layton, Richard John Boardman. BA cum laude, U. N.C., 1978; MA, U. Minn., 1985. Journalist Northcliffe Newspapers, Stoke-on-Trent, England, 1979-82; news producer Ctrl. Ind. TV, Birmingham, England, 1982-83; producer Inside Story, N.Y.C., 1984-86; pres. New Atlantic Prodns., 1986-89, David Royle Prodns., N.Y.C., 1989—. Field prodr. Am. Detective in Russia, ABC, L.A., 1992; exec. prodr. Target: Mafia, A&E, CBS, 1993; prodr. TV Nation, NBC, BBC, 1994, Wall St. Jour. TV, 1995; pres. Pub. Media Inc., N.Y.C., 1992-97; dir. The Russian Archive, 1992—; sr. prodr. Nat. Geog. TV, Washington, 1996-98, exec. prodr., 1998—, sr. v.p. prodn., 2000—. Prodr.: (tv shows) Rupert Murdoch: Press Baron Who Would Be King, PBS, 1985 (Emmy nomination), Assignment Africa, PBS, 1986 (Emmy nomination), Senator Sam, PBS, 1988 (Ohio State award, Cine Golden Eagle), Inside Gorbachev's USSR, PBS, 1989 (George Polk award, DuPont-Columbia U. Gold Baton); (TV series) The Eagle and The Bear, ABC/A&E, 1993 (Cine Golden Eagle), Dr. Frank, PBS, 1994 (Cine Golden Eagle, Regional Emmy award), TV Nation, NBC/BBC, 1994 (Prime Time Emmy award), Emerging Powers: Brazil, PBS/NHK Japan, 1996, Trauma: Life and Death in the E.R., The Learning Channel, 1996, National Geographic Explorer, TBS, 1999—2001 (5 Emmy awards, Emmy nominations). Pres. Brit. Morehead Scholarship Fund, 1993—; gov. Clifton Coll., Bristol, Eng., 1997—. Morehead scholar, 1974-78, scholar Rotary Internat., 1983, N.J. Arts Fellowship, 1995; named Hon. Citizen, Mpls., 1983; recipient excellence award U. Minn. Sch. Journalism & Mass Comm., 2000. Mem. NATAS, Soc. Profl. Journalists, Writers Guild of Am. Avocations: running, sailing, photography, reading. Office: Nat Geog TV 1145 17th St NW Washington DC 20036-4701

ROYSE, BROOKE SARNO, editor, writer; b. Columbia, Mo., Nov. 8, 1962; d. Donald A. and Wendy Elizabeth (Gooder) Sarno; divorced; children: Jack, Elizabeth. BA, Northwestern U., 1984; PhD, U. Calif., Santa Barbara, 1992. Instr. U. Calif., Santa Barbara, 1985-87, 89-91; dir. info. svcs. McCann-Erickson, Oslo, 1987-88; ednl. writer and cons. Evanston, Ill., 1992—; freelance editor, writer, 1994—. Cross-cultural ednl. cons. various schs., Chgo., 1992-94. Author: Windows to the World: Themes for Cross-Cultural Understanding, 1996. Charlotte Newcombe fellow Woodrow Wilson Nat. Fellowship Found., 1990-91, Humanities Grad. Rsch. fellow U. Calif., 1989-90, Regents fellow, 1985-86, 91-92. Fellow Soc. for Values in Higher Edn.; mem. MLA, Henry James Soc., Assn. for Practical and Profl. Ethics, Phi Beta Kappa. Democrat. Avocations: making jewelry, travel, geology. E-mail: bsroyse@aol.com.

ROYSE, SUE MARION, special education educator; b. Ironton, Ohio, Oct. 28, 1944; d. Paul Hurt and Clyda (Forson) Marion; m. David T. Royse, May 20, 1972. BS in Edn., Concord Coll., Athens, W.Va., 1971; MS in Edn., Ind. U., 1977. Tchr. Greater Clark County Schs., Jeffersonville, Ind., 1977-88, Phoenix (Ariz.) Union Dist. 210, 1989-91, Warren Achievement Ctr., 1991-93, State of Ill. Dept., Corrections Hill Correction Ctr., 1993-94, Ind. Sch. Dist. # 196, Rosemount, Minn., 1994-96, Knox County Sch. Transition Program, 1996—. Recipient Olin Davis award State of Ind., 1982. Mem. Coun. for Exceptional Children, Correction Edn. Assn., Beta Sigma Phi. Home: 2700 Ed Stallings Ln Knoxville TN 37931-4135

ROZARTO, DENISE, nurse; b. Phila., Dec. 23, 1958; d. Francis John and Ercolina Marie (Madotto) R. BSN, Widener U., 1980. Cert. CNOR, ACLS. Staff nurse ICU/CCU stepdown unit Met. Hosp., Phila., 1981-83; ICU staff RN Phila. Coll. Osteopathic Medicine, 1983; staff RN parenteral therapy Methodist Hosp., 1983-88; staff RN oper. rm. Misericodia Hosp., 1988-90, Pa. Hosp., Phila., 1990-97, Thomas Jefferson U. Hosp., Phila., 1997—. Mem. Am. Found. for AIDS Rsch., 1989—. Widener U. grantee, 1976. Mem. AORN. Avocations: playing classical guitar, travel, astronomy, cooking. Home: 515 Country Club Pkwy # A Mount Laurel NJ 08054-2708 Office: Thomas Jefferson U Hosp Philadelphia PA 19107

ROZEL, SAMUEL JOSEPH, lawyer; b. Louisville, Apr. 22, 1935; s. Sam and Anna (Sessmer) R.; m. Jeanne Frances Foulkes, July 3, 1965; children: Brooke Jane, John Samuel. BSL, U. Louisville, 1955, LLB, 1957; grad., Advanced Mgmt. Program, Harvard U., 1979. Bar: Ky. 1958, D.C. 1962, Minn. 1968, Ind. 1970, N.Y. 1983. Atty. FTC, Washington, 1962-67; antitrust counsel Honeywell, Inc., Mpls., 1967-69; atty. Magnavox Corp., Ft. Wayne, Ind., 1969-71, gen. counsel, 1971, v.p., 1972-75, sec., 1973-75; v.p. U.S. Philips Corp., N.Y.C., 1975-77, sr. v.p., 1977—; assoc. gen. counsel Philips Electronics N.Am. Corp., sec. exec. mgmt. com., 1980—; v.p., sec., gen. counsel, dir. Phillips Electronics N.Am. Corp., 1987-91, sr. v.p., sec., gen. counsel, mem. exec. com. bd. dirs., 1991—. Bd. dirs. Philips Electronics N.Am. Corp., Philips Electronics N.Am. Region, Std. Communications Corp. Served to capt. JAGC, AUS, 1957-62. Mem. ABA, Fed. Bar Assn., Ky. Bar Assn., Ind. Bar Assn., N.Y. Bar Assn., Harvard Club (N.Y.C.), Met. Club (Washington). Home: 215 S Bald Hill Rd New Canaan CT 06840-2908 Office: Philips Electronics N Am 125 Park Ave New York NY 10017-5529

ROZELL, JOSEPH GERARD, accountant; b. Kansas City, Kans., Mar. 20, 1959; s. Joseph Frank and Frances Elizabeth (Gojmeric) R. BSBA, Rockhurst Coll., 1981; MBA, U. Mo., Kansas City, 1992. Staff acct. Donnelly, Meiners & Jordan, Kansas City, Mo., 1981-82, Francis A. Wright & Co., Kansas City, 1982-88, Libby Corp., Kansas City, 1988-90, Sprint Corp., Overland Park, Kans., 1990—. Mem. Greater Kansas City Young Reps., pres. 1988-89; treas. Jackson County Rep. Com., 1989-97. Mem. AICPAs, Mo. Soc. CPAs (legis. com., liaison com.), Greater Kans. Jaycees (treas. 1988-89). Republican. Roman Catholic. Avocations: basketball, soccer, volleyball. Home: 12112 Madison Ct Kansas City MO 64145-1023

ROZELLE, LEE THEODORE, physical chemist, researcher; b. Rhinelander, Wis., Mar. 9, 1933; s. Theodore and Alice (Omholt) R.; m. Barbara J. Ingli, June 21, 1955; children— David, Steven, Carolyn, Ann, Kenneth BS, U. Wis., 1955, PhD, 1960. Rsch. chemist DuPont Corp., Circleville, Ohio, 1960-63; prin. scientist-tech. coord. Honeywell Corp., Mpls., 1963-67; dir. chemistry div. North Star Rsch. Inst., 1967-74; v.p. R&D USCI div. C.R. Bard, Billerica, Mass., 1974-77; dir. engring. tech. div. Mellon Inst., Pitts., 1977-78; dir. rsch. and devel. Permutit Co., Monmouth Junction, N.J., 1978-80; v.p. rsch. and devel. Gelman Scis., Inc., Ann Arbor, Mich., 1980-82; v.p. sci. and tech. Culligan Internat. Co., Northbrook, Ill., 1982-87; assoc. dir. rsch. Olin Chems. Rsch. div. Olin Corp., Cheshire, Conn., 1987-92; cons. in water treatment tech., mktg. and mgmt., 1992—; pres., cons. Water Solutions, Inc., 1995—; exec. v.p. Puraq Water Systems, Inc., 1996—. Cons. in field; mem. Nat. Drinking Water Adv. Council EPA, 1987-90; mem. small bus. inovative rsch. com. U.S. EPA, 1999—. Contbr. chpts. to books, numerous articles to profl. jours. Bd. dirs. Unitarian Ch., Andover, Mass., 1974-77 NIH fellow, 1958-60; recipient Spl. Hominum award Nat. Sanitation Found., 1988. Fellow Am. Inst. Chemists; mem. AAAS, Am. Chem. Soc., Am. Soc. Artificial Internal Organs, Health Industry Mfrs. Assn. (chmn. spl. activities com.), Water Pollution Control Fedn., Water Quality Assn. (chmn. sci. adv. com., Award of Merit 1989), Am. Water Works Assn., Assn. Met. Water Agencies, Filtration Soc., Pacific Water Quality Assn. (bd. dirs. 1987-90, Robert Gans award 1988), Am. Soc. Agrl. Engring., Internat. Water Supply Assn., European Membrane Soc., N.Am. Membrane Soc., Asociacion Interamericano De Ingenieria Sanaitaria y Ambiental, Sigma Xi, Phi Alpha, Phi Lambda Upsilon. Home and Office: 626 23rd St N La Crosse WI 54601-3825 *My professional goal has always been to make significant contributions to the well being of our society through science. Goals have been accomplished from contributions to water purification to health care.*

ROZEN, BARBARA LEE LINDNER, enterostomal therapist; b. Weehawken, N.J., June 16, 1928; d. George Hugo and Marjorie Pierce (Morehouse) Lindner; m. Jerome George Rozen Jr., Dec. 18, 1948; children: Steven G., Kenneth C., James R. BA, U. Kans., 1951; BSN, U. of the State of N.Y., 1972; M in Pub. Adminstrn., NYU, 1986. RN, N.J., N.Y.; cert. secondary tchr., N.J. Med.-surg. clin. specialist, various units Pascack Valley Hosp., Westwood, N.J., 1970-85; clin. coord. St. Luke's Hosp., N.Y.C., 1986-87, clin. adminstrv. liaison nurse, 1987-90; clin. nurse specialist enterostomal therapy Meml. Sloan Kettering Cancer Ctr., 1990—. Tchr. Dumont (N.J.) H.S. Contbr. articles to profl. jours. Mem. AAUW (program chair), Nat. Nurses in Bus. Assn., Urol. Assn. Ltd., Soc. of Ostomy, Wound and Continence Nurses, Am. Assn. of Diabetes Educators, United Ostomy Assn., Sigma Theta Tau. Presbyterian. Avocations: swimming, bicycling, reading, listening to music, traveling with husband doing field work in entomology. Home: 55 Haring St Closter NJ 07624-1709 Office: Meml Sloan Kettering Cancer Ctr 160 E 53rd St New York NY 10022

ROZEN, JEROME GEORGE , JR. research entomologist, museum curator and research administrator; b. Evanston, Ill., Mar. 19, 1928; s. Jerome George and Della (Kretchmar) R.; m. Barbara L. Lindner, Dec. 18, 1948; children—Steven George, Kenneth Charles, James Robert Student, U. Pa., 1946-48; BA, U. Kans., 1950; PhD, U. Calif.-Berkeley, 1955. Entomologist in taxonomy U.S. Dept. Agr., 1956-58; asst. prof. entomology Ohio State U., 1958-60; assoc. curator divsn. invertebrate zoology Am. Mus. Natural History, N.Y.C.,

1960-65, curator hymenoptera, 1965—, chmn. dept. entomology, 1960-71, dep. dir. research, 1972-86. Field expdns. in U.S., Europe, Mex., Trinidad, Argentina, Chile, Brazil, Peru, Venezuela, Morocco, Pakistan, Republic of South Africa, Namibia, Israel, Egypt, Kyrgyzstan, Turkey; adj. prof. CUNY, 1968—. Contbr. numerous sci. articles on bees (Apoidea) and beetles (Coleoptera). Fellow AAAS; mem. Am. Inst. Biol. Scis., Entomol. Soc. Am. (editor misc. publs. 1959-60), Soc. Study of Evolution, Soc. Systematic Biology, N.Y. Entomol Soc. (pres. 1964-65), Washington Entomol. Soc., Pacific Coast Entomol. Soc., Kans. Entomol. Soc., Orgn. Biol. Field Stas. (pres. 1990), Internat. Soc. Hymenopterists. Home: 55 Haring St Closter NJ 07624-1709 Office: Am Mus Natural History Central Park West New York NY 10024-5192

ROZENBLAT, ANATOLY ISAACOVICH, manufacturing engineer, inventor; b. Moscow, Aug. 25, 1938; came to the U.S., 1990; s. Isaac Saimolovich Rozenblat and Natalie Ivanovna Fedorisheva; m. June 27, 1964 (div. 1979) children: Inna, Moshe. BS in Mech. Engring., Inst. Marine Engrs., Odessa, Ukraine, 1967; BS in Computer Sci., East-West U., 1997. Cert. mech. and mfg. engring. Adminstrv. staff Ship Repair and Shipbldg. Plant, Odessa, 1970-80; project engr. Sci. Prodn. Assn., 1980-89; pvt. practice scientist and inventor Chgo., 1990—. Mem. Internat. Biog. Ctr., Eng., 1995, adv. bd. Am. Biog. Inst., N.C., 1996; presenter 26th Israel Conf., 1996, 27th Israel Conf., 1998. Author: Regression Analysis of Ship Speed in Waves and The Tropics, 1997, Rozenblat's Innovations For The Twenty-First Century, 1998; contbr. articles to profl. jours.; patentee in field. With Russian Air Force, 1964. Mem. ASME, Soc. Mfg. Engrs., Soc. Naval Architects and Marine Engrs., Nat. Congress Inventors Orgns. Avocations: chess, literature, music, travel, nature. Home: Apt 2606 10 E Ontario St Chicago IL 60611-4770

ROZMAN, GILBERT FRIEDELL, sociologist, educator; b. Mpls., Feb. 18, 1943; s. David and Celia (Friedell) R.; m. Masha Dwosh, Jan. 25, 1945; children: Thea Dwosh, Noah Dwosh. BA, Carleton Coll., Northfield, Minn., 1965; PhD (Woodrow Wilson fellow 1965-66), Princeton U., 1971. Mem. faculty Princeton U., 1970—, prof. sociology, 1979—, Musgrave prof. sociology, 1992—. Mem. com. studies Chinese civilization Am. Council Learned Socs., 1975-80; mem. U.S.-USSR Bi-Nat. Commn. Humanities and Social Scis., 1978-86, IREX Univ. Coun., 1998—. Author: Urban Networks in Ch'ing China and Tokugawa Japan, 1973, Urban Networks in Russia, 1750-1800, and Premodern Periodization, 1976, Population and Marketing Settlements in Ch'ing China, 1982, A Mirror for Socialism: Soviet Criticisms of China, 1985, The Chinese Debate About Soviet Socialism 1978-85, 1987, Japan's Response to the Gorbachev Era, 1985-1991: A Rising Superpower Views a Declining One, 1992; co-author: The Modernization of Japan and Russia, 1975; editor: The Modernization of China, 1981, Soviet Studies of Premodern China: Assessments of Recent Scholarship, 1984, Japan in Transition: From Tokugawa to Meiji, 1986, The East Asian Region: Confucian Heritage and Its Modern Adaptation, 1991, Dismantling Communism: Common Causes and Regional Variations, 1992, Russia and East Asia: The 21st Century Security Environment, 1999, Japan and Russia: The Tortuous Path to Normalization, 1949-1999, 2000. Guggenheim fellow, 1979-80; grantee NSF, NEH, Social Sci. Rsch. Coun., Nat. Coun. for Soviet and E. European Studies, U.S. Inst. Peace, Woodrow Wilson Internat. Ctr. Mem. Assn. Asian Studies, Am. Sociol. Assn., Am. Assn. Advancement Slavic Studies. Home: 20 Springwood Dr Trenton NJ 08648-1048 Office: Princeton U 149 Wallace Hill Princeton NJ 08544-0001 E-mail: grozman@princeton.edu.

ROZMAN, JAMES D. military chaplain; b. Lynwood, Calif., Sept. 5, 1950; s. Clyde A. and Mae A. Rozman. AA, Coll. San Mateo, 1970; BS, We. Bapt. Coll., Salem, Oreg., 1977; MDiv, Talbot Theol. Sem., La Mirada, Calif., 1981; D in Ministry, Biola U., La Mirada, Calif., 1989; grad., USAF Acad. Instr. Sch., 1984, USAF Squadron Officer Sch., 1988, Air Command and Staff Coll., 1994, USAF Air War Coll., 1996; cert. wing chaplain course, Air U., Maxwell AFB, 2001. Cert. in clin. pastoral edn., 1998. Commd. USAF, 1980, advanced through ranks to lt. col., installation chaplain N.Mex., 1981-84, installation staff chaplain Sondrestrom Air Base, Greenland, 1984-85, protestant chaplain Travis AFB, Calif., 1985-87, Tactical Air Command site chaplain Griffiss AFB, N.Y., 1987-89, sr. protestant chaplain San Vito dei Normanni, Italy, 1989-91, protestant chaplain Langley AFB, Va., 1991-94, sr. protestant chaplain Tinker AFB, Okla., 1994-97; clin. pastoral edn. resident Walter Reed Army Med. Ctr., Washington, 1997-98; sr. parish chaplain USAF, Travis AFB, 1998—, wing chaplain L.A. AFB, Calif., 2001—. Acting sr. chaplain, USAF Chapel Team, Apr. 1995 Oklahoma City Bombing Rescue Effort, Tinker AFB, Okla. Mem. Mil. Chaplains Assn. (life), Air Force Assn. (life), Air Force Sgts. Ass.n (life), Assn. Clin. Pastoral Edn., Biola U. Alumni Assn., We. Bapt. Coll. Alumni Assn. Republican. Baptist. Avocations: walking, travel, swimming, reading. Home: 55 E Old Fort Rd San Pedro CA 90731-7212 Office: 61 ABG/HC 325 Challenger Way Ste 1901 El Segundo CA 90245-4677 Office Fax: 310-363-0693. E-mail: james.rozman@losangeles.af.mil., TheRozman@juno.com.

ROZOF, PHYLLIS CLAIRE, lawyer; b. Flint, Mich., Aug. 3, 1948; d. Eugene Robert and Loveta Lucille Greenwood; m. Robert James Rozof, July 17, 1970 (dec. Oct. 1995); children: Nathan, Zachary. AB with high distinction, U. Mich., 1970, JD magna cum laude, 1977. Bar: Mich. 1977, Fla. 1978. Assoc. Hönigman Miller Schwartz and Cohn, Detroit, 1977-81, ptnr., 1982—. Mem. Comml. Real Estate Women Detroit (pres. 1992-93). Office: Honigman Miller Schwartz & Cohn 2290 1st National Bldg Detroit MI 48226

ROZRAN, JACK LOUIS, courier service executive; b. Chgo., Mar. 4, 1939; s. Philip Reuben and Rose (Rosenberg) R.; m. Dawn Faulkner, May 25, 1986; children: Justin Grant, Claire Ashley, Ryan Bjur. BA, Northwestern U., 1960; JD, Harvard U., 1963. Bar: Ill. 1963. Law clk. to judge U.S. Dist. Ct. Ill., 1963-64; v.p. Cannonball, Inc., Chgo., 1964-66, pres., 1966-92, chmn., 1992-98. Trustee Hull House Assn., 1972-90, v.p., 1987; sec. Erikson Inst., 1982, trustee, 1971-92; mem. vis. com. Northwestern U., Evanston, Ill.; bd. dirs. Crohn's and Colitis Found. Am., 1997—, Cove Sch.. Mem. ABA, Messenger Svc. Assn. Ill. (pres. 1987-89, v.p. 1990-92, bd. dirs. 1987-98), Chicagoland C. of C. (bd. dirs. 1997—), Air Courier Conf. Am. (treas. 1980-82, pres. 1982-84, bd. dirs. 1976-98, adv. bd. dirs. 1998—), Expedited Package Ind. Contractors Coun. (co-chair 1992-95), Chgo. Bar Assn., Chgo. C. of C. (downtown traffic study), Econ. Club, Beta Alpha Psi. Home: 579 W Hawthorne Pl Chicago IL 60657-2922 Office: 875 W Huron St Chicago IL 60622-5960 E-mail: jlrozran@aol.com.

RÓZSA, GYÖRGY, academy library foundation president; b. Oradea, Romania, Oct. 13, 1922; s. Rezső and Jolán (Zuckerman) R.; m. Borbála Robitsek (dec. 1967); children: Gábor, Mihály. Cert., Hungarian Inst. Internat. Rel., Budapest, 1947; Dipl. Libr. Ship, Inst. Pedagogy, Budapest, 1953; Dr. Econ., U. Econs., Budapest, 1964; DS in Econs., High Comm. Sci. Qualification, Budapest, 1988. Sec. Ministry for Fgn. Affairs, Hungary, 1947-50; libr. Ctr. for Pub. Librs., Hungary, 1952-55; chief libr. and sci. sec. Inst. Econs. Acad. Scis., Hungary, 1955-60; dir. gen. Libr. Hungarian Acad. Sci., Hungary, 1960-96; chief libr. UN Libr. at Geneva, Switzerland, 1969-75. Field cons. UNESCO-UNDP, Asia, Africa. Author: Scientific Information and Society, 1973, Information from Claims to Needs, 1988, 7 other books; contbr. over 470 articles to profl. jours. Recipient medal Internat. Coun. of Archives, 1977, Librarianship Meml. medal, 1982, Pro Scientia Hungarica medal Hungarian Acad. Scis., 1996. Avocations: reading, tennis, fine arts. Home: XIII Csanády u. 4/B Budapest Hungary Office: Libr Hungarian Acad Scis V Arany Janos u 1 Budapest Hungary E-mail: probib@vax.mtak.hu.

ROZUMNYJ, JAROSLAV, literature educator, researcher; b. Honcharivka, Ukraine, Sept. 6, 1925; s. Hryhory and Anna (Parubocha) R.; m. Oksana Olha Hrycenko, Mar. 10, 1938; children: Larysa, Roman, Istan, Ruslan. BA with honors, Theol. Sem., Culemborg, Netherlands, 1950; MA, U. Ottawa, Ont., Can., 1958, PhD, 1968. Lectr. Laurentian U., Sudbury, Ont., 1960-63; asst. prof. Western Mich. U., Kalamazoo, 1963-64, U. Man., Winnipeg, Can., 1964-71, head dept. Can., 1976-89, prof. lit. Can., 1989—, sr. scholar Can., 1997. Vis. prof. U. Ottawa, 1972, Ukrainian Cath. U., Rome, 1987; dean Faculty of Philosophy, Ukrainian Free U., Munich, Germany, 1995-96; vis. rsch. scholar Macquarie U., Sydney, 1989; mem. internat. adv. bd. U. Kiev-Mohyla Acad., 1992—, hon. prof., 1996. Editor: New Soil--Old Roots: The Ukrainian Experience in Canada, 1983, I Was Nineteen... KM Academia, 2001; ; co-editor: Jubilee Collection of the Ukrainian Academy of Arts and Sciences, 1976; lit. editor: Anthology of Musical Compositions on the Poems of M. Shashkewych, 1992; editor Can. vol. Ency. of Ukrainian Diaspora, 7 vols.; editor-in-chief: Collection of Scholarly Papers, 1996; mem. editl. bd. Suchasnist, 1984-91. Pres. Ukrainian Cultural and Ednl. Ctr., Winnipeg, 1970-73; pres. Can. Friends of Rukh in Ukraine, Winnipeg, 1990-92; Can. rep. U. Kiev-Mohyla-Acad., 1992—; bd. govs. Man. Mus. Man and Nature, Winnipeg, 1976-80; pres. Markian Shashkevych Inst., Winnipeg, 1999—. Recipient Outreach Activities award U. Man., 1986, Order of the Eternal Flame in Silver World Conf. Ukrainian Scouts, 1994, Taras Shevchenko medal Ukrainian Can. Congress, 1995. Mem. Ukrainian Acad. Arts and Scis. in Can. (pres. 1977-80, v.p. 1995—), Schevchenko Sci. Soc. U.S., Internat. Assn. Ukrainian Studies. Home: 801 Cambridge St Winnipeg MB R3M 3G3 Canada E-mail: rozumnyj@ms.umanitoba.ca.

ROZWAT, CHARLES, information technology executive; B in Fin. and Info. Sys., Marquette U. Mgmt. staff Digital Equipment Corp.; v.p. Oracle New Eng. Devel. Ctr.; exec. v.p. server tech. divsn. Oracle Corp., Redwood City, Calif. Office: Oracle Corp 500 Oracle Pkwy Redwood City CA 94085*

ROZYCKI, EDWARD GEORGE, education educator; b. Phila., June 30, 1943; s. Edward George and Marguerite Marie (Zuschmidt) R.; m. Carole Jean Carpey, Apr. 21, 1964; children: Sara Beth, David Michael. AB in Philosophy, U. Pa., 1964; MEd, Temple U., 1971, EdD, 1974. Cert. German and math. tchr., prin., fgn. lang. supr., Pa. Counselor Coll. Settlement Camps, Horsham, Pa., 1961-63; substitute tchr. math. Sch. Dist. of Phila., 1964-66, tchr. ESL J.P. Jones Jr. H.S., 1972-86, tchr. ESL Cooke Mid. Sch., 1987-92; German tchr. George Washington H.S., Phila., 1966-71; headmaster Swarthmore (Pa.) Acad., 1986-87; assoc. prof. edn. Widener U., Chester, Pa., 1992—. Adj. prof. German Phila. Coll. Art, 1968-72; adj. prof. philosophy of edn. Temple U., Phila., 1977-83. Pres., treas. Germantown Children's Cmty., Phila., 1974-76; bd. dirs. Phila. Consumer's Coop., Phila., 1967-69. Fellow Philosophy of Edn. Soc. (pres. Mid. Atlantic States chpt. 1991-93); mem. AAUP, Ea. Pa. Assn. Tchrs. English to Spkrs. Other Langs. (founder 1980, pres. 1983), Pi Lambda Theta (pres. Phila. chpt. 1993-94), Phi Delta Kappa (McComb award 1973). Home: 534 General Patterson Dr Glenside PA 19038-3202 Office: Widener U Ctr for Edn Chester PA 19013

ROZYCKI, PAUL ANDREW, political science educator; b. Dekalb, Ill., July 18, 1944; s. Gene Conrad and Frieda Cecile (Lojewski); m. Nancy Ann Lenz, Dec. 16, 1967. BA, No. Ill. U., 1966; MA, Ind. U., 1967. Instr. polit. sci. Ball State U., Muncie, Ind., 1967-69; prof. Mott Community Coll., Flint, Mich., 1969—. Photography instr. U. Mich., Flint, 1980-92, Flint Art Inst., 1994-98. Author: Introduction to Genesee County Legal System, 1977, Study Guide to American Government, 1984; co-author: Politics and Government in Michigan, 1983, 3d edit., 2000, A Clearer Image, 1998; polit. commentator ABC TV-12. Dem. precinct del., Flint, 1972—, exec. com., 1999—; mem. Genesee County Jury Bd., 1997—. Mem. Mich. Polit. Sci. Assn. (bd. dirs. 1982-85, 90—), Coll. Media Advisers, Community Coll. Journalism Assn. Roman Catholic. Avocations: photography, writing, travel. Home: 135 Commonwealth Ave Flint MI 48503-2151 Office: Mott Community Coll 1401 E Court St Flint MI 48503-6208 E-mail: prozycki@mcc.edu.

ROZZELL, SCOTT ELLIS, lawyer; b. Texarkana, Tex., Apr. 12, 1949; s. George M. and Dora Mae (Boyett) R.; m. Michelle Miller; children by previous marriage: Stacey Elizabeth, Kimberly Marie. BA, So. Meth. U., 1971; JD, U. Tex., 1975. Bar: Tex. 1975, U.S. Dist. Ct. (so. dist.) Tex. 1975, U.S. Dist. Ct. (no. dist.) Tex. 1977, U.S. Ct. Appeals (1st, 3d, 9th cirs.) 1977, U.S. Ct. Appeals (5th and D.C. cirs.) 1976. Assoc. BakerBotts, LLP, Houston, 1975-82, ptnr., 1983-94, sr. ptnr., 1995-2000; exec. v.p., gen. counsel CenterPoint Energy, Inc., 2001—. Mem. State of Tex. Aircraft Pooling Bd., 1997-2002; devel. bd. U. of Tex. Health Sci. Ctr. Houston, 1992—; chair Tex. Commn. for Lawyer Discipline, 2001—. Bd. dirs. Manned Space Flight Edn. Found., Inc., 1997—, vice chair 2000-, Tex. Aviation Hall of Fame, 2001—; vice-chmn. Cancer Counseling Inc., Houston, 1991-92; mem. so. regional adv. bd. Inst. Internat. Edn. Fellow Tex. Bar Found. (sustaining life), Houston Bar Found. (sustaining life, bd. dirs. 1991-93, chair 1993), Am. Bar Found.; mem. ABA, State Bar Tex. (bd. dirs. 1997-2000), Houston Bar Assn. (bd. dirs. 1991-95, pres. 1996-97), Fed. Energy Bar Assn., Houston Young Lawyers Assn. (bd. dirs. 1978-82, pres. 1983-84), Coronado Club, Houstonian. Republican. Presbyterian. Avocation: flying vintage airplanes. Home: 1229 Post Oak Park Houston TX 77027 Office: CenterPoint Energy Inc PO Box 4567 Houston TX 77210-4567 E-mail: scott.rozzell@centerpointenergy.com.

RUB, TIMOTHY F. museum director; BA in Art History, Middlebury Coll., 1974; MA in Art History, NYU, 1979; MBA, Yale U., 1987; postgrad., Harvard U., 1998. Curatorial intern Met. Mus. Art, 1983; lectr. art and archtl. history Cooper-Hewitt Mus./Parsons Sch. Design, Stevens Inst. Tech., 1979-84; guest curator Bronx Mus. Arts, N.Y., 1985-86; curator Cooper-Hewitt Mus., N.Y.C., 1983-87; assoc. dir. Hood Mus. Dartmouth Coll., Hanover, N.H., 1987-91, dir., COO, 1991-2000; dir. Cin. Art Mus., 2000—. Office: Cin Art Mus 953 Eden Park Dr Cincinnati OH 45202-1596

RUBACK, ALAN STEVEN, lawyer; b. Bklyn., June 9, 1949; s. Isidore and Shirley Ruback; m. Carol Maselli, Jan. 24, 1976; children: Joshua, Jenna. BA, SUNY, Stony Brook, 1971; JD, New Eng. Sch. of Law, 1974. Bar: Mass. 1974, Fla. 1978, U.S. Dist. Ct. (so. dist.) Fla. 1978. Staff atty. Office of Hearings and Appeals Social Security Adminstrn., Raleigh, N.C., 1976-77, Miami, Fla., 1977-82, Ft. Lauderdale, 1982-83; ptnr. Connors Ruback & Koster P.A., 1983-96; sole practice, 1996—. Mem. Nat. Orgn. Social Security Claimant's Reps. (sustaining), Mem. Fla. Bar Assn., Fla. Bar Assn., B'nai B'rith Justice League. Office: PO Box 1659 440 S Andrews Ave Fort Lauderdale FL 33302-1659 E-mail: aruback171@aol.com.

RUBACK, RICHARD BARRY, psychologist, educator; b. Omaha, Mar. 29, 1950; s. Norman and Mary (Piha) R. BA, Yale U., 1972; JD, U. Tex., 1975; MS, U. Pitts., 1977, PhD, 1979. Bar: Tex. 1975, Ga. 1981, U.S. Supreme Ct. 1995. Asst. prof., assoc. prof. psychology Ga. State U., Atlanta, 1979-88, prof., 1988-96; prof. dept. sociology Pa. State U., University Park, 1996—, dir. Ctr. for Rsch. on Crime and Justice, 1997—. Co-author: Social Psychology of the Criminal Justice System, 1982, After the Crime: Victim Decision Making, 1992; co-editor: Interpersonal Violent Behaviors, 1995; editor Criminal Justice Rev., 1992—. Fulbright fellow Coun. Internat. Exch. Scholars, 1985-86, 93-94, Fulbright-Hays fellow U.S. Dept. Edn., 1991, vis. fellow Nat. Inst. Justice U.S. Dept. Justice, 1986-87, jud. fellow U.S. Supreme Ct., 1995-96; recipient Justice Tom C. Clark award Supreme Ct. Hist. Soc., 1996. Fellow APA; mem. Am. Psychology-Law Soc., Soc. Exptl. Social Psychology. Democrat. Jewish.

RUBARDT, PETER CRAIG, conductor, educator; b. Oakland, Calif., Aug. 7, 1958; s. Kenneth and Betty (Maspero) R.; m. Hedi Salanki; children, Daniel, Vivienna. BA, U. Calif., Berkeley, 1981; M of Music, SUNY, Stony Brook, 1984; student, Hochschule fur Musik, Vienna, 1984-86; D Mus. Arts, Julliard Sch., 1989. Prof., conductor SUNY, Purchase, 1989-90, Rutgers U., New Brunswick, N.J., 1991-96; resident conductor N.J. Symphony, Newark, 1990-93; assoc. conductor Syracuse (N.Y.) Symphony, 1993-97; music dir., condr. Greater Pensacola (Fla.) Symphony Orch., 1997—. Guest conductor various orchs. Condr. rec. Bach Concerti, 1988. Fullbright fellow USIA, 1984-86; Bruno Walter scholar, Julliard Sch., 1986-88. Mem. Am. Symphony Orch. League, Condrs. Guild. Democrat. Home: 8774 Thunderbird Dr Pensacola FL 32514 Office: Pensacola Symphony Orch PO Box 1752 Pensacola FL 32598-1752

RUBELLO, DAVID JEROME, artist; b. Detroit, Sept. 3, 1935; s. Ludovico and Girolama (Trupiano) R.; m. Mary Anne Keithan, Oct. 14, 1978. BFA, Am. Acad. Art, Rome, 1961; MFA, U. Mich., 1972; cert., Acad. Fine Art, Copenhagen, 1966. Lect. art U. Mich., Ann Arbor, 1973-74; asst. prof. art Pa. State U., University Park, 1974-80; assoc. prof. art Towson (Md.) State U., 1980-81; assoc. prof. U. Mich., Ann Arbor, 1988-90. One man shows include Cade Gallery, Royal Oak, Mich., 1987; exhibited in group shows at Detroit Inst. Art, 1987, GMB Gallery Internat., Bloomfield Hills, Mich., 1991, Kresge Art Inst., 1989, Kalamazoo Art Inst., 1990, 91, Photo Nat. 2, Ella Sharp Mus., Jackson, Mich., BBAA, Birmingham, Mich., Arts Coun., Traverse City, Mich., 1995-96, Patrimonio Invitational Wayne State U., Detroit, 1996, Ann. Celebrate Mich. Artists P.C. Art Ctr., Rochester, 1994, 95, 96, Art Ctr., Mt. Clemens, Mich., 1997, Crative Art Ctr., Pontiac, Mich., 1997; exhibited Null Dimension, Fulda, Germany, 1988, Systematica Constructive Art, Madrid, 1989, B4 Pub. Invitational, London, 1990, Archive 90s, Amsterdam and London, Konkrete Miniatures Invitational, Amsterdam, 1991, Planet Art Gallery, Capetown, South Africa, 1999; contbr. articles to profl. jours. including the Structurist. Recipient awards for art work; featured professional artist profile B&W Fine Art Photography Mag., June 2001.

RUBEN, ALAN MILES, law educator; b. Phila., May 13, 1931; s. Maurice Robert and Ruth (Blatt) R.; m. Betty Jane Willis, May 23, 1965. AB, U. Pa., 1953, MA, JD, U. Pa., 1956. Bar: Pa. 1957, Ohio 1972. Law clk. Supreme Ct. Pa., 1956-58; pvt. practice Phila., 1958-65; assoc. counsel Aetna Life & Casualty Co., Hartford, Conn., 1965-69; corp. counsel Lubrizol Corp., Cleve., 1969-70; prof. Cleve.-Marshall Coll. Law, Cleve. State U., 1970—; adv. prof. law Fudan U., Shanghai, People's Republic of China, 1993—; dep. to city solicitor Phila., 1958-61; dep. atty. gen. State of Pa., 1961-65; spl. counsel to U.S. Senate Subcom. on Nat. Stockpile, 1962; commentator Higher Edn. Issues Sta. WCLV-FM, Cleve., 1975-87. Mem. nat. panel labor arbitrators Nat. Acad. Arbitrators, Fed. Mediation and Conciliation Svc. and Am. Arbitration Assn., Ohio State Employment Rels. Bd.; lectr. law U. Conn. Law Sch., 1968; vis. prof. law FuDan U., Shanghai, Peoples Republic of China, 1988-89; cons. Shanghai Law Office for Fgn. Economy and Trade, Peoples Republic of China, 1991-94. Author: The Constitutionality of Basic Protection for the Automobile Accident Victim, 1968, Unauthorized Insurance: The Regulation of the Unregulated, 1968, Arbitration in Public Employee Labor Disputes: Myth, Shibboleth and Reality, 1971, Illicit Sex of Campus: Federal Remedies for Employment Discrimination, 1971, Model Public Employees Labor Relations Act, 1972, Sentencing the Corporate Criminal, 1972, Modern Corporation Law, supp. edit., 1978, An American Lawyer's Observations on the Inauguration of the Shanghai Stock Exchange, 1989, Ohio Limited Partnership Law, 1992—, Practice Guides, Ohio Limited Liability Company, Law, 1995—; co-editor: How Arbitration Works, 1997; contbr.: With an Eye to Tomorrow: The Future Outlook of the Life Insurance Industry, 1968, The Urban Transportation Crisis: The Philadelphia Plan, 1961, Philadelphia's Union Shop Contract, 1961, The Administrative Agency Law: Reform of Adjudicative Procedure and the Revised Model Act, 1963, The Computer in Court: Computer Simulation and the robinson Patman Act, 1964. Bd. dirs. U.S. Olympic Com., 1968-73; chmn. U.S. Olympic Fencing Sport Com., 1969-73; pres. U.S. Fencing Assn., 1968-73; capt. U.S. Pan-Am. Fencing Team, 1971, U.S. Olympic Fencing Team, 1972; bd. dirs. Legal Aid Soc. Cleve., 1973-77; trustee Cleve.-San Jose Ballet, 1999-2001. Winner Internat. Inst. Edn. Internat. Debate Championship, 1953; recipient Harrison Tweed Bowl and Am. Law Inst. prizes Nat. Moot Ct. Competition, 1955; named Guggenheim scholar, 1949-53, Fulbright scholar FuDan U., Shanghai, 1993-94. Mem. ABA, Ohio Bar Assn. (corp. law and profl. responsibility com.), Cleve. Bar Assn. (Securities Law Inst.), Assn. Am. Law Schs. (chmn. sect. law and edn. 1976-78), Internat. Indsl. Rels. Rsch. Assn., Internat. Soc. Labor Law, Internat. Bar Assn., Union Internat. Des Avocats, Internat. Law Assn., AAUP (pres. Ohio conf. 1974-75), Rowfant Club, Phi Beta Kappa, Pi Gamma Mu. Home: 9925 Lake Shore Blvd Bratenahl OH 44108-1052 Office: Cleve State U 18th St And Euclid Ave Cleveland OH 44115

RUBEN, AUDREY H. ZWEIG, lawyer, arbitrator, actress; b. Union City, N.J. m. Robert J. Ruben; children: Pamela J. Ruben Golum, James B. BA, NYU, 1948; MA, Columbia U., 1953; JD, St. John's U., 1976. Bar: N.Y. 1977, U.S. Dist. Ct. (so. and ea. dists.) N.Y. 1977, U.S. Supreme Ct. 1982. Law intern Westchester Dist. Atty.'s Office, White Plains, N.Y., summer 1975, Westchester Legal Svcs., White Plains, 1976-77; assoc. Granik, Silverman, New City, N.Y., 1977-79, Pierro, Colangelo & Killea, Port Chester, 1979-84; legal adminstr. Poloron Products, Harrison, 1984-86; pvt. practice Rye, 1986-90. Arbitrator N.Y. State Office of Ct. Adminstrn., 1979-90, Am. Arbitration Assn., 1980—, Better Bus. Bur., 1980—, N.Y. Stock Exch., 1991—, Nat. Assn. Securities Dealers, 1991—, Pacific Stock Exch., 1993—; mediator Westchester Med. Ctr. Cluster-Westchester County, N.Y., 1984-90; law guardian Family Ct., Westchester County, 1979-84; guardian ad litem Surrogates Ct., Westchester, 1978-84. Theatre critic (newspaper) L.I. Herald; movie reviewer Saddleback Valley News; freelance children's book reviewer; actress cmty. and summer theatre; actress Readers Repertory Theatre. Commr. Human Rights Commn., Rye, 1984-89, Rye Cable TV Commn., 1989-90; pres. LWV of Rye, 1971-73; bd. dirs. pub. rels. com. Community Media Orgns.; bd. dirs. Rye Youth Coun., 1974-80; mem. Mission Viejo Cultural Arts com.; MME Modjeska chpt. Orange County Performing Arts Ctr. Mem. ABA, Am. Arbitration Assn., N.Y. State Bar Assn., N.Y. Women's Bar Assn. (legis. and real property com.), Westchester County Bar Assn. (corp. law com.), Portchester/Rye Bar Assn., Internat. Fedn. Women Lawyers, Am. Judges Assn., Columbia U. Club of So. Calif., Mission Viejo Am. Assn. of Univ. Women (pub. policy chmn.), Woman's Club (bd. dirs. 1966-90). Avocations: theatre, swimming, aerobics, skiing, dancing. Home and Office: 21285 Amora Mission Viejo CA 92692-4930

RUBEN, GARY A. marketing and communications consultant; b. Cochem, Germany, Jan. 1, 1924; came to U.S., 1939, naturalized, 1943; s. Jules and Erna (Hirsch) R.; m. Irene Jehle, Aug. 12, 1962; 1 child, Monique L. Student, Acad. Comml. Art, Indpls., 1940-41. With advt. dept. Indpls. News, 1940-41; advt. mgr. Greater Indpls. Amusement Corp., 1941-42; pres. Ruben Advt. Agy., Indpls., 1948-68; chmn. bd. Ruben, Montgomery & Assos., 1968-76; pres. Prestige Program Sales Inc., 1973-76, Gary A. Ruben Inc. (advt. and mktg. cons.), Indpls., 1976—. Past lectr. advt. and bd. fellows Northwood Inst.; past pres. Nat. Fedn. Advt. Agys., 1971. Hon. trustee Indpls. Children's Mus. With Combat Engrs. AUS, 1943-46. Paul Harris fellow Rotary Internat. Home: 7370 Lions Head Dr Indianapolis IN 46260-3460 Office: 931 E 86th St Ste 206 Indianapolis IN 46240-1852 *It was years ago, in the late 30's in Vienna, that the cry "Lebensraum" echoed across yet another land. And, a family, judged comfortable by most standards, scattered to the four winds, leaving behind all things material, but salvaging the will to survive and to commence once again in a new land. To a boy in his teens and still dressed in European-style short pants upon arrival in this country, the emotion, the sights, the sounds, and the smells were overwhelming and exciting to say the least. . .so began another chapter in my life. In the ensuing years, I learned the true meaning of individual freedom. And while the echoes of Vienna have become dim, that dim sound will continue to remind me that all worthwhile things in life are earned—not given, and even in adversity, there is opportunity.*

RUBEN, IDA GASS, state senator; b. Washington, Jan. 07; d. Sol and Sonia E. (Darman) Gass; m. L. Leonard Ruben, Aug. 29, 1948; children: Garry, Michael, Scott, Stephen. Del. Md. Ho. of Dels., Annapolis, 1974-86; mem. Md. Senate, 1986—, majority whip, 1995-99, pres. pro-tem, 2000—. Chair Montgomery County House Delegation, 1981-86, Montgomery County Senate Delegation, 1987—; mem. house econ. matters com., 1974-85, house ways and means com., 1985-86, legis. policy com., 1991—, vice-chair senate budget and taxation com., 1997-99, joint budget and audit com., 1991—, exec. nominations com., 1991—, joint protocol com., 1991—, chair, senate budget and tax., subcom. on pub. safety, transp., econ. devel. and natural resources, 1995-99, mem. joint com. on spending affordability, 1995—, mem. capital budget subcom., 1995—; mem. Gov.'s Motor Carrier Task Force, 1989—; conv. chair Nat. Order Women Legislators, 1980. Chair Women Legislators Caucus Md., 1982-84; trustee Adventist Health Care Mid-Atlantic, Takoma Park, Md.; bd. dirs. Ctrs. for Handicapped, Silver Spring, Md.; former internat. v.p. B'nai Brith Women. Recipient Cert. Appreciation Ctrs. for Handicapped, 1987, Meritorious Svc. award Safety and Survival, 1989, Cover Those Trucks award AAA Potomac, 1989, Leadership Laurel award Safety First Club Md., 1989, Woman of Valor award B'nai B'rith Women, 1991, Pub. Affairs award Planned Parenthood Md., 1992, ESOL support recognition Montgomery County Pub. Schs., 1992, Appreciation award Fraternal Order Police, 1992, John Dewey award Montgomery County Fedn. Tchrs., 1992, ARC of Md., 1992, Safety Leader award Advocates for Hwy. and Auto Safety, 1993, Disting. Svc. award Gov.'s Commn. Employment of People with Disabilities, 1993, award Faculty Guild U. Md. for support of faculty and univ., 1993, Sincere Appreciation award for commitment to Md.'s youth Md. Underage Drinking Prevention Coalition, 1994, Faithful Svc. to citizens Montgomery County award Montgomery County Assn. of Realtors, 1994; named Most Effective Pub. Ofcl. by residents of Silver Spring, 1990, one of 100 Most Powerful Women in Washington Metro Area by Washingtonian Mag., 1994, 97, Legislator of Yr. award Nat. Commn. Against Drunk Driving, 1995,

Legislator of Yr. award Montgomery County Med. Soc., 1995, Carmen S. Turner Achievement in Cmty. Svc. award Montgomery County Dept. Transp., 1995, Safety Leader award Advocates for Hwy. and Auto Safety, 1996, Legislator of Yr. award AAA, Potomac, Md., 1997, Vince and Larry award Md. Com. for Safety Belt Use, 1997, Legislative Leadership award Montgomery County, 1998, Leadership award Olney Theater Ctr., 1998, Legislator of Yr. award Greater Montgomery County C. of C., 1999, Hwy. Safety Herd award Advocates for Hwy. and Auto Safety, 1999, One of Md.'s Top 100 Women, The Daily Record, 1994, 97, 2001, Am. Lung Assn. Appreciation award in protecting youth from tobacco industry, 2000, Olney Theater honoree contbns. Olney Theatre and arts in Md., 2000, Pub. Policy Leadership award Am. Cancer Soc., 2002; M.A.D.D. Award of Exellence, 2002, named to Washington, Md., Del., Pa. Svc. Sta. Assn. Hall of Fame, 1994, Suburban Md. Transp. Priorities outstanding leadership in transp. pub. policy adminstrn., 2000, Md. Coll. Art and Design honoree contbns. arts in Md., 2000. Mem. Coun. State Govts. (com. on suggested legislation), Hadassah. Democrat. Jewish. Home: 11 Schindler Ct Silver Spring MD 20903-1329 Office: Md State Senate 143 Miller Senate Office Bldg 110 College Ave Annapolis MD 21401-8012

RUBEN, LAWRENCE, real estate developer, building company executive, lawyer; b. Bklyn., Sept. 28, 1926; s. Irving and Minnie (Sruelif) R.; m. Selma Belfer, Dec. 20, 1952; children: Richard Gordon, Lenore Denise, Rochelle Gail Ruben Kivell. BA, NYU, 1949; LLB, Bklyn. Law Sch., 1951. Bar: N.Y. 1952. Gen. practice law, N.Y.C., 1952-53; pres. Ru-Min Constrn. Co., 1953-54; exec. v.p. Belco Petroleum Corp., 1954-64, dir., 1954-85; v.p. Fundamental Bldg. Corp., 1952—; pres. Randall Devel. Co., Aragon Devel. Corp., Lawrence Ruben Co., Inc.; ptnr. Lexington Madison Co., Tower Plaza Assocs., Devonshire Assocs., Boylston Ptnrs., Devonshire Constrn. Co. Inc., Lawrence Assocs., Granite Ptnrs., Inc., Harper-Lawrence; pres. Washington Mgmt. Corp. Mem. adv. bd. NYU Real Estate Inst.; mem. med. ctr. adv. bd. N.Y. Hosp. Cornell Med. Ctr. Chmn. N.Y. Builders and Realtors Fellowship Fund; trustee Nat. Jewish Ctr. for Immunology and Respiratory Medicine, Denver; patron Albert Einstein Coll. Medicine; sponsor Grad. Sch. Sci.; bd. dirs. Cardoza Sch. Law at Yeshiva U.; chmn. United Jewish Appeal, Scarsdale, N.Y., 1974-75; mem. pres.'s coun. Meml. Sloan Kettering Cancer Ctr. With AUS, 1945-46. Mem. ABA, Fenway Golf Club, Boca Rio Golf Club, Harmonie Club. Office: 600 Madison Ave New York NY 10022-1615

RUBEN, LEONARD, retired art educator; b. St. Paul, June 3, 1921; s. Theodore and Elizabeth (Hauchman) R.; m. Sue Levey; children: James M., Elizabeth A., Nancy L., Thomas C. Diploma with hon., Pratt Inst., 1948, BFA, 1952; MA, Columbia Tchrs. Coll., 1961; PhD, NYU, 1970. Designer L.W. Frolich, N.Y.C., 1949-52; art dir. Young & Rubicam, 1952-60; art group head North Advt., 1960-62; instr. Columbia U. Tchrs. Coll., 1962-63; assoc. creative dir. Compton Advt., 1962-64; v.p. assoc. creative dir. J.M. Mathes, 1964-68; exec. creative dir. Lake Spiro Shurman, Memphis, 1968-69; asst. prof. art Northeast La. U., Monroe, 1969-71, U. Tex., Austin, 1971-74, assoc. prof., 1974-79, prof. art, 1979-82, F.J. Heyne Centennial Prof. in Communication, 1983-87. Design cons. B.B. Martin Pub. Co., Austin, 1978; creative dir. Heart Assn., Austin, 1973. Precinct chmn. Dems., Lake Travis, Tex., 1979; chmn. advt. com. Austin Community Coll., 1980-84. 1st lt. U.S. Army, 1940-46, ETO, PTO. Decorated Bronze Arrowhead, Presdl. Unit emblem; recipient numerous awards including Advt. Appreciation award City of Houston, 1980, Thomas McCartin Tchg. Excellence award, 1983, Founders Day award NYU, 1971; Leo Burnet Creative Excellence Endowment, 1986, Frank Rizzo Meml. Creative grant Tracy-Locke, 1986. Mem. 27th Infantry Div. Assn., 105th (226th) Field Arty Assn., Dallas Soc. Visual Communication. Jewish. Home: 2033 Dolina Dr Virginia Beach VA 23464-8210

RUBEN, ROBERT JOEL, physician, educator; b. N.Y.C., Aug. 2, 1933; s. Julian Carl and Sadie (Weiss) R.; children: Ann, Emily, Karin, Arthur. AB, Princeton U., 1955; MD, Johns Hopkins U., 1959. Intern Johns Hopkins Hosp., Balt., 1959-60, resident, 1960-64, dir. neurophysiology lab., div. otolaryngology, 1958-64; practice specializing in pediatric otorhinolaryngology N.Y.C., 1964—; asst. prof. otorhinolaryngology N.Y. U. Sch. Medicine, 1966-68; mem. staff hosps. Montefiore Med. Ctr., Bronx Med. Hosp. Ctr., N. Cen. Bronx Hosp., Montefiore Med.; prof., chmn. Montefiore Med. Ctr., Bronx Mcpl. Hosp. Ctr., N. Cen. Bronx, Bronx, N.Y., 1979-99; prof. Montefiore Med. Ctr., Bronze Mcpl. Hosp. Ctr., N. Cen. Bronx, 1999—; prof. pediatrics Albert Einstein Coll. Medicine, 1983—, assoc. prof. otorhinolaryngology N.Y.C., 1968-70, prof., chmn. dept. otolaryngology, 1970-98, prof. dept. otolaryngology, 1970—, chmn. emeritus dept. otolaryngology, 1998—, disting. univ. prof., 1998—; prof. pediatrics Albert Einstein Coll. Medicine and Montefiore Med. Ctr., 1983—. Chmn. Nat. Com. for Rsch. and Neurol. and Communicative Disorders, pres., 1982-84; bd. dirs. Am. Bd. Otolaryngology-Head and Neck Surgery, 1989—; chmn. ENT devices com. FDA, 1993-96. Editor-in-chief: Internat. Jour. Pediatric Otorhinolaryngology, 1979—. Bd. dirs. N.Y. League Hard of Hearing, 1969-75, 76-85, Friends of the Liber. Princeton U. Libr. Served to surgeon USPHS, 1964-66. Recipient Rsch. award Am. Acad. Ophthalmology and Otolaryngology, 1962, Edmund Prince Fowler award Am. Rhinological-Laryngological-Otological Assn., 1973, Gold medal Best Didactic Film, IX World Congress Otorhinolaryngology, 1977, Pres.'s award Am. Acad. Otolaryngology-Head and Neck Surgery, 1992, Johns Hopkins U. Soc. of Scholars, 1993, George E. Schambaugh Otology prize, 1996. Fellow ACS, N.Y. Acad. Medicine; mem. AMA, Am. Assn. Anatomists, Audiology Study Group N.Y. (pres. 1964-66), Acoustical Soc. Am., Am. Acad. Ophthalmology and Otolaryngology, Soc. Univ. Otolaryngologists, Am. Otol. Soc. (sec.-treas. rsch. fund 1979—), Soc. for Ear, Nose and Throat Advances in Children (pres. 1973), Assn. for Rsch. in Otolaryngology (pres. 1985-86), Am. Acad. Pediat. (chmn. otol. bronchoesphology 1983-85), Am. Soc. Pediat. Otolaryngology (historian 1986-95), Am. Soc. Pediat. Otolaryngologists (historian 1986-93, pres.-elect 1993-94, pres. 1994-95), Nat. Inst. Deafness and Other Comm. Disorders (adv. coun. 1989-93), Am. Laryngol. Soc., Grolier Club. Home: 1025 5th Ave Apt 12C S New York NY 10028-0134 Office: Montefiore Med Ctr 111 E 210th St Bronx NY 10467-2401

RUBEN, ROBERT JOSEPH, lawyer; b. N.Y.C., Apr. 9, 1923; s. Ira Herbert and Kathleen Marie (Murphy) R.; m. Audrey H. Zweig, Nov. 20, 1949; children: Pamela Joan, James Bradford. BS, Columbia U., 1943; MA, Harvard U., 1948; LL.B., Fordham U., 1953. Bar: N.Y. 1954. Exec. trainee Chase Nat. Bank, N.Y.C., 1948-49; economist, 1949-53; assoc. Milbank, Tweed, Hope & Hadley, N.Y.C., 1953-55; assoc., then ptnr. Shea & Gould, 1955-90; sec. Gen. Battery Corp., Reading, Pa., 1963-73, Fiat Metal Mfg. Co., Inc., Plainview, N.Y., 1961-64, Filtors, Inc., East Northport, 1961-64, Trans-Industries, Inc., 1969-2001; asst. sec. Elgin Nat. Industries, 1975-88. Asst. judge City Ct., Rye, N.Y., 1977-90; arbitrator Nat. Assn. Securities Dealers, 1990—, Pacific Stock Exch., 1992—, Am. Arbitration Assn., 1990—, N.Y. Stock Exch., 1994—. Trustee Rye Hist. Soc.; bd. dirs. Carver Center, Port Chester, N.Y., 1972-90. Served with AUS, 1943-46. Decorated Combat Inf. medal. Mem. ABA, N.Y. State Bar Assn., Assn. Bar of City of N.Y., Harvard Club (N.Y.C.), Harvard-Radcliffe Club So. Calif., Columbia U. Club So. Calif., Beta Gamma Sigma, Zeta Beta Tau. Home: 21285 Amora Mission Viejo CA 92692-4930

RUBENDALL, RICHARD ARTHUR, civil engineer; b. Pierre, S.D., Sept. 24, 1957; s. Quentin Theodore and Doris (Noe) R.; m. Susi M. Conley, Nov. 7, 1998; children: Amy Rose, Logan, Bailey Marie. BSCE, S.D. Sch. Mines & Tech., 1979; postgrad., U. N. Mex. Registered profl. engr., Mont., Ariz. Commd. officer USPHS, 1979; field engr. USPHS/Indian Health Svc., Lame Deer, Mont., 1979-86, sr. field engr. Many Farms, Ariz., 1986-89, Sells, 1989-90, dist. engr., 1990-93, Tucson, 1993—; advanced through ranks to capt. USPHS, 2000. Recipient Isolated Hardship award USPHS, 1980, 84, 88, 91, Hazardous Duty award 1984, Citation with plaque, 1990, USPHS Achievement medal, 1985, 97, USPHS Crisis Response award, 1998; named Indian Health Svc. Engr. of Yr., Tucson area, 1990. Mem. ASCE, Am. Water Works Assn., Water Environment Fedn., USPHS Commd. Officers Assn. (pres. Tucson chpt. 1993-95, nat. recorder 1995-96, pres.-elect 1996-97, pres. 1997-98, bd. dirs. 1998—), Res. Officers Assn., Assn. Mil. Surgeons U.S. Home: 3421 N Tonto Pl Tucson AZ 85750 Office: USPHS 7900 S J Stock Rd Tucson AZ 85746-7012 E-mail: rsrubendall@msn.com., richard.rubendall@mail.ihs.gov.

RUBENFELD, SHELDON, thyroidologist; b. Bklyn., Jan. 9, 1946; s. Irving and Mia (Silber) R.; m. Linda Rose Steele, Nov. 28, 1971; children: Jesse, Sarah. B in Chem. Engring., The Cooper Union, 1966; MS in Environ. Health Engring., Northwestern U., 1967; MD, Georgetown U., 1971. Diplomate Am. Bd. Internal Medicine. Intern Boston City Hosp., 1971-72; assoc. in medicine Georgetown U., Washington, 1972-74; resident Baylor Affiliated Hosps., Houston, 1974-76, fellow in endocrinology, 1976-78; cons. endocrinologist Med. Clinic Houston, 1978-90; pvt. practice Houston, 1990—. From instr. to clin. assoc. prof. Baylor Coll. Medicine, Houston, 1979—. Author: Could It Be My Thyroid?, 1996; contbr. articles to profl. jours. Mem. AMA, Am. Coll. Physicians, Harris County Med. Soc., Tex. Med. Asn., Am. Thyroid Assn., Endocrine Soc., Am. Fertility Soc., Am. Assn. Clin. Endocrinologists, Am. Diabetes Assn., Tex. Soc. Internal Medicine, Am. Soc. Internal Medicine. Jewish. Avocations: reading, swimming, biking. Office: 7515 Main St Ste 690 Houston TX 77030-4599

RUBENFELD, STANLEY IRWIN, lawyer, director; b. N.Y.C., Dec. 7, 1930; s. George and Mildred (Rose) R.; children: Leslie Ann, Lise Susan, Kenneth Michael; m. Madeleine Conway, Nov. 5, 2000. BA, Columbia U., 1952, JD, 1956. Bar: N.Y. 1956. Practice law, N.Y.C., 1956-65, 68—, 1965-68; assoc. Shearman & Sterling, 1956-65, ptnr., 1965-68, N.Y.C., 1968-93, of counsel, 1994—. Arbitrator and mediator NASD; mediator U.S. Fed. Ct., IRS Panel, CPR Panel; arbitrator NYSE, Internat. C. of C.; bd. dirs. Brit. Gas US Holdings, Inc., BG Energy Fin. Inc., Brit. Transco Fin., Inc., BGLNG Svcs., Inc. Editor-in-chief Columbia Law Rev., 1955-56; contbr. articles to profl. jours. Bd. dirs., past pres. Port Washington (N.Y.) Cmty. Chest; former bd. dirs. Residents for a More Beautiful Port Washington. Lt. (j.g.) USNR, 1952-54. Stone scholar, 1951-52, 54-55, 55-56; Rockefeller Found. grantee, 1955 Mem. ABA, N.Y. State Bar Assn. (tax sec., past chmn. fgn. activities com., reorgn. corp.), Assn. Bar City N.Y. (past chmn. com. on recruitment lawyers), Nat. Assn. Law Placement (past bd. dirs., exec. com.), Columbia U. Law Sch. Alumni Assn. (bd. visitors, adviser past bd. dirs.), Columbia Coll. Alumni Assn., Tax Club (past chmn.), Phi Delta Phi, Tau Epsilon Phi (past pres.). Office: 599 Lexington Ave Ste 728 New York NY 10022-6030

RUBENS, LINDA MARCIA, home health services administrator; d. Harry and Ruth Slutzah; m. Robert A. Rubens; children: Scott, Mark. AS, Fla. Jr. Coll., Jacksonville. Lic. nursing home adminstr. RN U. Hosp. of Jacksonville, 1976-82; dir. nursing Mandarin Manor Nursing Home and Retirement Village, 1982-85, asst. adminstr., 1985-87; dir. nursing P.H.E.O. Med. Ctr., 1987-88; dir. clin. and profl. svcs. Kimberly Quality Care, 1988-90, br. mgr., 1990-93; adminstr. Health Care Mgmt. Cons., Jacksonville, 1993-95; exec. dir. Mount Carmel Gardens Retirement Cmty., 1995—. Past mem. Gerontol. Search Team for Cathedral Found.; past treas. Mayor's Orgn. for Vol. Effort, past bd. dirs.; chairperson State-Wide Human Rights Advocacy Com., State of Fla., 1996-97, chairperson consumer rels. subcom., 1990—; apptd. to Dist. IV Ombudsman Com., 1982-90, Dist. IV Human Rights Advocacy Com., 1989-90, Dist. IV Human Rights Advocacy Com. for Mental Health; bd. dirs. Mt. Carmel Retirement Cmty., State Mental Health Planning Coun.; mem. Dist. Human Rights Adv. Commn. Mem.: Fla. Assn. of Homes for the Aging (dist. coord. 2001), Dirs. of Nursing Assn., Rehab. Nurses Assn. Home: 13116 Mandarin Rd Jacksonville FL 32223-1748

RUBENS, PHILIP, communications educator, technical writer; b. Washington, Jan. 13, 1943; s. Maurice and Anna Mae (Kindilien) R.; m. Brenda Knowles, May 4, 1969; children: Theresa Marie, Alesia Laure Chavez. BA, U. Tex., Arlington, 1970; MA, U. Tex., 1972; PhD, No. Ill. U., 1976. Instr. Braniff Airways, Santiago, Chile, 1966-67; teaching asst. U. Tex. at Arlington, 1970-71, No. Ill. U., DeKalb, 1972-74; asst. prof. William Rainey Harper Coll., Chgo., 1975-76; assoc. prof. Mich. Tech. U., Houghton, 1976-80; prof. visual & tech. comm. Rensselaer Poly. Inst., Troy, N.Y., 1980-98, East Carolina U., Greenville, N.C., 1998—. Tech. writer Washington Gas Light Co., Washington; sr. tech. writer, cons. Gas Dynamics Lab., City of Arlington; dir. comm. Braniff Airways, LTV Aerospace, Gas Dynamics Lab., City of Arlington; sr. rsch. assoc. TechWriting Affiliates, Inc.; cons. in field including Software Group, 1984, N.Y. Edn. Assn., 1981-84, IBM Corp., 1984, 85, 87, TechWriting Affiliates Inc., 1985, 86, 88—, Short Bros., Inc., Belfast, Ireland, 1985, Info. Assocs., 1985, DuPont Corp., 1985, Bell Labs., 1985, U. Leeds, 1986, High Tech., Inc., Tokyo, 1987. Editor: (book) Science and Technical Writing: A Manual of Style, 1993; mem. editorial bd. Mohawk Monitor, 1980—, Roxbury Press, 1986, Iowa Jour. Bus. and Tech. Comm., 1987—, Computers and Composition, 1987—, MIT Press, 1988—. Mem. Smithsonian Inst., Washington, 1976—; faculty advisor Keweenaw Chpt. Soc. for Tech. Comm., 1976-80; mem. Sierra Club, 1980—; dept. rep. Hudson-Mohawk Consortium, 1980-81; sustaining mem. No. Ill. U. Exec. Alumni Assn., 1980—; chair, membership com. Mohawk Chpt. Soc. for Tech. Comm., 1980-81, vice chair, 1981-82; exec. alumni U. Tex. at Arlington, 1981—; mem. Saratoga Sailing Club, 1981—, Saratoga Performing Arts Ctr., 1981—; mem. Westport (Conn.) Hist. Soc., 1985—; charter mem. Nat. Mus. Women in Arts, 1992—. Recipient Chgo. Poetry Soc. Award for Outstanding Religious Poetry, Award for Outstanding Children's Poetry, Award for Most Outstanding Poem for Yr., 1975, Writer's Key for Outstanding Writing Ability, Sigma Tau Delta, 1976, Chpt. Achievement award Soc. for Tech. Comm., 1979, Outstanding Article award, 1982, Tchr. of Excellence award N.Y. State English Coun., 1984, Award of Merit for Softbridge Online Tutorial, 1986; MIT Sloan Sch. Mgmt. Rsch. fellow, 1990, Soc. for Tech. Comm. fellow, 1992. Mem. AAAS (edn. com. 1982—, MLA, Am. Bus. Comm. Assn. (chair undergrad. studies com. 1977), Coun. for Programs in Tech. and Sci. Comm. (charter mem., judge CPTSC Logo Competition 1982), IEEE Profl. Comm. Soc. (edn. com. 1986, co-program chair of 1989 conf.), Midwest MLA, Nat. Coun. Tchrs. English (mem. tech. writing com. 1976—), Popular Culture Assn., Sci. Fiction Rsch. Assn., Sci. Writing Educators Group, Soc. for Tech. Comm. (judge internat. audio-visual competition 1985— and others. Home: 303 Bebington Dr Cary NC 27513-1750 Office: East Carolona U GCB Greenville NC 27858

RUBENS, SIDNEY MICHEL, physicist, technical advisor; b. Spokane, Wash., Mar. 21, 1910; s. Max Zvoln and Jennie Golda (Rubinovich) R.; m. Julienne Rose Fridner, May 11, 1944; 1 child, Deborah Janet. BS, U. Wash., 1934, PhD, 1939. Instr. U. So. Calif., L.A., 1939—40; rsch. assoc. UCLA, 1940—41; physicist Naval Ordnance Lab., Washington, 1941—46, Engring. Rsch. Assocs., St. Paul, 1946—52; mgr. physics Univac divsn. Sperry Rand, 1958—61, dir. rsch., 1961-66, staff scientist, 1969—71, dir. spl. projects, 1971—75, cons., 1975—81; tech. advisor Vertimag Sys. Corp., 1981—, Advanced Rsch. Corp., Mpls., 1986—. Lectr. U. Pa., 1960-61; mem. adv. subcom. on instrumentation and data processing NASA, 1967-69; mem. panel on computer tech. NAS, 1969. Author: Amplifier and Memory Devices, 1965; contbg. author: Magnetic Recording—The First Hundred Years, 1999. Hon. fellow U. Minn., 1977—. Fellow IEEE (Magnetic Soc. info. storage award 1987, Millennium medal 2000); mem. AAAS, N.Y. Acad. Scis., Am. Phys. Soc., Am. Geophys. Union, Acad. Applied Sci., Minn. Acad. Sci., Am. Optical Soc., Phi Beta Kappa, Sigma Xi, Pi Mu Esilon. Achievements include patents in magnetic material and devices. Home: 1077 Sibley Hwy Apt 506 Saint Paul MN 55118-3616 Office: Advanced Rsch Corp 815 14th Ave SE Minneapolis MN 55414-1515

RUBENSTEIN, ALAN MORRIS, county judge; b. Phila., Mar. 13, 1946; s. Philip and Lilyian Ruth (Eveloff) R.; m. Marilynn Z. Rubenstein, Mar. 31, 1973; children: Samuel Alex, Justin Simon. BA in History, Temple U., 1967; JD, U. Toledo, 1970. Bar: Pa. 1971, U.S. Dist. Ct. (ea. dist.) Pa. 1971, U.S. Ct. Appeals (3d cir.) 1985, U.S. Supreme Ct. 1980. Pvt. practice, Phila., 1970-73; asst. dist. atty. Bucks County Dist. Atty.'s Office, Doylestown, Pa., 1973-75, dep. dist. atty., 1975-79, chief dep. dist. atty., chief trials, 1979-83, 1st asst. dist. atty., 1983-86, dist. atty., 1986-2000; judge Ct. of Common Pleas of Bucks County, 2000—. Law enforcement coordinating com. for ea. dist. Pa., U.S. Dept. Justice Drug task force adv. com. Office Atty. Gen., Commonwealth of Pa.; mem. Bucks County Prison Adv. Bd.; bd. dirs. Bucks County Hero Scholarship Fund; advisor, bd. dirs. for Southea. Pa., Joe Frazier's Golden Gloves; judge Pa. Athletic Commn., Del. Boxing Commn., N.J. Athletic Control Bd., Conn. State Athletic Commn. Recipient award for outstanding performance and svc. to cmty. Fraternal Order Police, Phila., 1987, Disting. Pub. Svc. award County and State Detectives Assn. Pa., 1989, award for outstanding svc. in field law enforcement Delaware Valley Assn. Profl. Police Ofcls., 1991, Law Enforcement commendation medal Valley Forge chpt. Nat. Soc. SAR, 1992, award in appreciation for svc. for drug and alcohol prevention through edn. Nat. Awareness Found., 1996, N.E. Cmty. Svc. award, 1996, Diamond Achievement award in social scis. Temple U. Coll. Arts and Scis., 1997 Mem. ATLA, Am. Coll. Pros. Attys., Assn. Govt. Attys. in Capital-Death Penalty Litigation, Am. Judicature Soc., Pa. Dist. Attys. Assn. (mem. exec. com. 1985-97, sec.-treas. 1989-90, v.p. 1990-91, pres. 1991-92, Pa. Dist. Attys. Inst. (bd. dirs. 1986-97, pres. 1993-94, 96-97), Order Ky. Cols., Phi Alpha Delta. Republican. Jewish. Office: Ct of Common Pleas Bucks County Main and Court Sts Doylestown PA 18901

RUBENSTEIN, ALBERT HAROLD, industrial engineering and management sciences educator; b. Phila., Nov. 11, 1923; s. Leo and Jean (Kaplan) R.; m. Hildette Grossman, Sept. 11, 1949; children: Michael Stephen, Lisa Joan. BS in Indsl. Engring. magna cum laude (Sr. prize econs.), Lehigh U., 1949; MS in Indsl. Engring, Columbia, 1950, PhD in Indsl. Engring. and Mgmt, 1954; DEng (hon.), Lehigh U., 1993. Asst. to pres. Perry Equipment Corp., 1940-43; rsch. assoc. Columbia U., 1950-53; asst. prof. indsl. mgmt. MIT, 1954-59; prof. indsl. engring. and mgmt. scis. Northwestern U., 1959-97; emeritus prof., 1997—; Walter P. Murphy prof. Northwestern U., 1986—, dir. Ctr. for Info. Tech., 1986-97; pres. Internat. Applied Sci. and Tech. Assos., 1977—; vis. prof. U. Calif., Berkeley; pres. Sr. Strategy Group, 1995—. Adj. prof. U. Calif., San Diego, 1997—; cons. to govt. and industry. Dir. Narragansett Capital Corp. Author books and articles in field. Served with inf. AUS, World War II. Decorated Purple Heart, Combat Inf. badge.; Recipient Lincoln Arc Welding Found. prize paper, 1948, Pioneer in Innovation Mgmt. award Ctr. Innovation Mgmt., 1992; Omicron Delta Kappa annual fellow, 1949-50; Fulbright research fellow, 1955 Fellow IEEE (editor trans. 1959—, 1975-80, Engring. Mgr. of Yr. award 1992), Soc. Applied Anthropology; mem. AAAS (chmn. indsl. sci. and tech. sect. 1997—), Inst. Mgmt. Scis. (sr. mem., dir. studies for coll. on R & D 1960—, v.p. rsch. and edn. 1966-68) Home and Office: 1630 Chicago Ave Apt 2010 Evanston IL 60201-6025

RUBENSTEIN, ANDREA FICHMAN, lawyer; b. Hartford, Conn., Dec. 6, 1947; d. Milton and Sara (Bronstein) Fichman; m. James Arthur Rubenstein, Aug. 23, 1970; children: Daniel H.F., Rebecca C.F. BA, Wheaton Coll., 1969; JD, U. Minn., 1977. Bar: Minn. 1978, U.S. Dist. Ct. Minn. 1986, U.S. Ct. Appeals (8th cir.) 1995. Atty. Law Offices of Cooper et al, Mpls., 1978-80; assoc. atty. Arthur, Chapman & Michaelson, P.A., 1980-83; atty., of counsel Hedin & Goldberg, P.A., 1985—. Pres., bd. dirs. Mpls. Legal Aid Soc., 1985—; pres., chair pers. com. Minn. Women's Fund, Mpls., 1995-99. Dir. Alternatives for People with Autism, Brooklyn Park, Minn., 1981—; bd. dirs. Mpls. YWCA, 1983-89. Mem. Nat. Employment Lawyers Assn. (Mpls. chpt. 1993—), Hennepin County Bar Assn. (dist. ethics com. 1983-88, 90-97, 98—). Office: Hedin & Goldberg PA 2100 Stevens Ave S Minneapolis MN 55404-2533 Fax: 612-871-1312. E-mail: arubenstein@isd.net.

RUBENSTEIN, ARTHUR HAROLD, medical school official and dean, physician; b. Johannesburg, South Africa, Dec. 28, 1937; came to U.S., 1967; s. Montague and Isabel (Nathanson) R.; m. Denise Hack, Aug. 19, 1962; children: Jeffrey Lawrence, Errol Charles. MB BCh, U. Witwatersrand, 1960. Diplomate Am. Bd. Internal Medicine. Intern, then resident Johannesburg Gen. Hosp., 1961, 63-65, 66-67; fellow in endocrinology Postgrad. Med. Sch., London, 1965-66; fellow in medicine U. Chgo., 1967-68, from asst. prof. to assoc. prof., 1968-74, prof., 1974-97, Lowell T. Coggeshall prof. med. sci., 1981-97, assoc. chmn. dept. medicine, 1975-81, chmn., 1981-97; attending physician Mitchell Hosp., U. Chgo., 1968-97; dean, CEO, Gustave L. Levy disting. prof. Mt. Sinai Sch. Medicine, N.Y.C., 1997—2001; exec. v.p., dean U. of Penn. Health System, School of Med., Phila., 2001—. Mem. study sect. NIH, 1973-77, Hadassah Med. Adv. Bd., 1986-95, adv. council Nat. Inst. Arthritis, Metabolism and Digestive Diseases, 1978-80; chmn. Nat. Diabetes Adv. Bd., 1982, mem., 1981-83. Mem. editorial bd. Diabetes, 1973-77, Endocrinology, 1973-77, Jour. Clin. Investigation, 1976-81, Am. Jour. Medicine, 1978-81, Diabetologia, 1982-86, Diabetes Medicine, 1987-91, Annals of Internal Medicine, 1991-96, Medicine, 1992—; contbr. articles to profl. jours. Mem. Gov.'s Sci. Adv. Coun. State of Ill., 1989-96. Recipient David Rumbough Meml. award Juvenile Diabetes Found., 1978 Master ACP (John Phillips Meml. award 1995); fellow South African Coll. Physicians, Royal Coll. Physicians (London), N.Y. Acad. Medicine; mem. Am. Soc. for Clin. Investigation, Am. Diabetes Assn. (Eli Lilly award 1973, Banting medal 1983, Solomon Berson Meml. lectr. 1985), Brit. Diabetes Assn. (Banting lectr. 1987), Endocrine Soc., Am. Fedn. Clin. Rsch., Ctrl. Soc. Clin. Rsch. (v.p. 1988, pres. 1989), Assn. Am. Physicians (treas. 1984-89, councillor 1989-94, v.p. 1994-95, pres. 1995-96), Am. Bd. Internal Medicine (bd. govs. 1985-93, exec. com. 1990-93, chmn. 1992-93), Residency Rev. Com., Am. Acad. Arts and Scis., Inst. Medicine (coun. 1991-96), Assn. Profs. Medicine (councillor 1991-94, v.p. 1994-95, pres. 1995-96, Robert Williams award 1997). Office: U of Penn School of Med 295 John Morgan Bldg, 3620 Hamilton Walk Philadelphia PA 19104*

RUBENSTEIN, BARBARA AILENE, music educator; b. Gettysburg, Pa., June 23, 1955; d. John Henry and Ruth Ailene (Robert) Riley; m. Todd Ira Rubenstein, May 15, 1977; children: Brendan, Veronica, Valerie. B in Music Edn., Ithaca Coll., 1977; MEd, SUNY, Brockport, 1981. Cert. tchr. music K-12. Band dir. elem. & mid. sch. Dallas Ind. Sch. Dist., 1977-79; elem. band dir. Rush-Henrietta Cen. Schs., Rochester, N.Y., 1980-81; jr. high band dir. Victor (N.Y.) Cen. Schs., 1981—. Mem. Music Educators Nat. Conf., N.Y. State Sch. Music Assn., N.Y. State Band Dirs. Assn., N.Y. State Coords. & Adminstrs. Music Edn., Ontario County Music Educators Assn., Sigma Alpha Iota (sword of honor 1976, chaplain 1981-83). Republican. Jewish. Avocations: travel, sewing, aerobics, baking. Office: Victor Cen Sch Dist High St Victor NY 14564

RUBENSTEIN, BERNARD, orchestra conductor; b. Springfield, Mo., Oct. 30, 1937; s. Milton and Evelyn Marion (Friedman) R.; m. Ann Warren Little, Aug. 28, 1961; children: Tanya, Stefan Alexei. B.Mus. with distinction, Eastman Sch. Music, U. Rochester, 1958; M.Mus., Yale U., 1961. Assoc. prof. conducting, dir. orch. orgns. Northwestern U., Evanston, Ill., 1968-80; music dir. San Juan Symphony, Durango, Colo., 1997—, Farmington, N.Mex., 1997—. Asst. condr. R.I. Philharm. Orch., 1961-62; condr. music dir. Santa Fe Symphony Orch., 1962-64; condr. Greenwood Chamber Orch., Cummington, Mass., 1968-79; asst. condr. Stuttgart Opera, 1966-68; condr., music dir. Music for Youth, Milw., 1970-80; assoc. condr. Cin. Symphony Orch., 1980-86; music dir. Tulsa Philharm., 1984-96, condr. laureate, 1996—, condr. laureate, 1996—; music dir. San Juan Symphony, 1997—; guest condr. numerous orchs. including Milw. Symphony Orch., St. Paul Chamber Orch., Guadalajara Symphony Orch., Berlin Radio Orch., Frankfurt Radio Orch., Grant Park Orch., Chgo., die reihe, Vienna, Austrian Radio Orch., Eastman Philharm., Halle Symphony Orch., E. Ger., Warsaw Philharm., St. Louis Little Symphony, W. German Radio Orch., Palazzo Pitti Orch. Florence, Italy, Frankfurt Opera, Tonkuenstler Orch., Vienna, S.W. German Radio Orch., Baden-Baden, Jerusalem Symphony, Anchorage, Hamilton, Ont., Hartford Conn., L.A. Chamber Orch., Austin (Tex.) Symphony, Am. Composers Orch. N.Y.C., Nat. Opera of Mongolia. Winner internat. conducting competition Serate Musicale Fiorentine, 1965; Fulbright scholar, 1964-66; recipient Charles Ditson award Yale U., 1961, Martha Baird Rockefeller award, 1966-68 Mem. Am. Symphony Orch. League, Condrs. Guild. Office: 1070 Governor Dempsey Dr Santa Fe NM 87501-1078 E-mail: baton@ix.netcom.com.

RUBENSTEIN, DAVID AARON, military officer, health care administrator; b. Rockville Centre, N.Y., Nov. 23, 1954; s. Robert R. and Mona Sydney (Feder) R.; m. Patricia Barrier, Mar. 18, 1978; children: Sarah Elizabeth, William Robert. BS in Health Edn., Tex. A & M U., 1977; MHA, Baylor U., 1989; M of Mil. Arts and Sci., Command and Gen. Staff Coll., 1990. Commd. 2d lt. U.S. Army, 1977, advanced through grades to col., 1999, med. platoon leader 3d inf. div. Fed. Republic Germany, 1977-79, ops. officer 3d med. battalion Fed. Republic Germany, 1979-80, pers. officer 307th med. battalion N.C., 1981-82, co. comdr., 1982-83, mil. instr. Acad. of Health Scis. Ft. Sam Houston, Tex., 1984-87, grad. student, 1987-88, adminstrv. resident William Beaumont Army Med. Ctr. Ft. Bliss, 1988-89, grad. student Command and Gen. Staff Coll. Ft. Leavenworth, Kans., 1989-90; adminstrv. asst. Office of the Army Surgeon Gen. Army Med. Svc. Corps, Washington, 1990-92; chief coordinated care Army Hosp., Ft. Belvoir, Va., 1992-93; hosp. comdr. 18th Mobile Army Surg. Hosp., Ft. Lewis, Wash., 1994-96; grad. student Army War Coll., Carlisle Barracks, Pa., 1996-97; dep. comdr. Eisenhower Army Med. Ctr., Ft. Gordon, Ga., 1997-99; hosp. comdr. 21st Combat Support Hosp., Ft.

Hood, Tex., 1999-2001, Bosnia-Herzegovina, 1999-2000; cmdr. Landstuhl Regional Med. Ctr., Germany, 2001. Pres. Health Orgn. Network, El Paso, Tex., 1989, Healthcare Execs. Ctrl. Savannah River Area, 1998-99; participant U.S. Army seminar Baylor U., Ft. Sam Houston, 1989. *Colonel David A. Rubenstein has over 25 years of Military Service in progressively complex positions culminating as commander (CEO) of Landstuhl Regional Medical care to Landstuhl, Germany. He is responsible for tertiary- level referral medical care to 300,000 beneficiaries in Europe, Northern Africa, and Southwest Asia. He serves as a Governor of the American College of Healthcare executives, the world's premier professional Society for healthcare executives.* Author leadership seminar; reviewer books Lehigh U. Press, 1990, Mil. Rev. Jour., Mil. Medicine; contbr. articles to profl. jours. Religious lay leader Office of the Jewish Chapel, Ft. Bragg, 1982-83, Ft. Bliss, 1988-89, Ft. Leavenworth, 1989-90, Bosnia-Herzegovina, 1999-2000; fund drive coord. United Fund, Ft. Leavenworth, 1989; vol. Muscular Dystrophy Assn., Washington, 1990-91. Decorated Legion of Merit; recipient Award of Excellence Chief of Med. Svc. Corps, 1984. Fellow: Am. Coll. Healthcare Execs. (regent 2000—02, gov. 2002—, Regent's award 1993); mem.: VFW, Assn. of U.S. Army, Am. Hosp. Assn., Assn. Mil. Surgeons of U.S. Republican. Jewish. Avocations: private flying, running, civil war medical support research, reading.

RUBENSTEIN, EDWARD, physician, educator; b. Cin., Dec. 5, 1924; s. Louis and Nettie Rubenstein; m. Nancy Ellen Millman, June 20, 1954; children: John, William, James. MD, U. Cin., 1947. House staff Cin. Gen. Hosp., 1947—50; fellow May Inst., Cin., 1950; sr. asst. resident Ward Med. Svc., Barnes Hosp., St. Louis, 1953—54; chief of medicine San Mateo County Hosp., Calif., 1960—70; assoc. dean postgrad. med. edn., prof. medicine Stanford (Calif.) U., 1971—, emeritus, active. Faculty Stanford Photon Rsch. Lab.; affiliated faculty Stanford Synchortron Radiation Lab., 1971—; maj. materials facilities com. NRC, 1984—85, Nat. Steering Com. 6 GeV Electron Storage Ring, 1986—. Author (textbook): Intensive Medical Care; editor: Synchotron Radiation Handbook, 1988, vol. 4, 1991, Synchotron Radiation in the Biosciences, Molecular Medicine; mem. editorial bd. : Sci. Am., Inc., 1991—94; editor (textbook): Sci. Am. Medicine, 1978—94; editor: (series) Molecular Cardiovascular Disease, 1995, Molecular Oncology, 1996, Molecular Neuroscience, 1998. With USAF, 1950—52. Recipient Kaiser award for outstanding and innovative contbns. to med. edn., 1989, Albion Walter Hewlett award, 1993. Master: ACP; fellow: AAAS, Royal Soc. Medicine; mem.: Am. Clin. and Climatol. Assn., Soc. Photo-Optical Engrs., Western Assn. Physicians, Calif. Acad. Medicine, Inst. Medicine, APS, Alpha Omega Alpha. Achievements include research in mechanisms of autoimmunity, dysfunction of the choroid plexus and cerebrospinal fluid circulatory system, snychrotron radiation, and molecular chirality. Office: Stanford Med Ctr Dept of Medicine Stanford CA 94305

RUBENSTEIN, ERIC DAVIS, real estate executive; b. Chgo., Oct. 21, 1952; s. Leonard S. and Ruth B. R.; m. Chaya Michelle Cohen, 1985; children: Rebecca, Renee. BA, Drake U., Des Moines, 1971; student percussion, A. Conservatory of Music, Chgo., 1963-67. Media rels. dir. Ill. Inst. Tech., Chgo., 1972-78; owner Alpine Communications, 1975—; pres. Alpine Realty and Management Co., 1977—, Single Rm. Operators Assn., Chgo., 1985—; also bd. dirs.; pres. Carter Realty & Devel. Co., 1984—. Bd. dirs. Single Rm. Housing Assistance Corp.; mem. ad hoc strategic planning com. City of Chgo. Dept. Human Svcs., 1996-2000; lectr. in field. Contbr. articles to profl. jours. Bd. dirs., pres. Job Resources for Disabled, Chgo., 1982-84, 90-92, treas., 1987-90; mem. Chgo. Task Force on Homelessness, 1987-90, 1998-2000, Task Force on SRO's, 1993-94; mem. forcible entry and retainer com. Cook County Cir. Ct., 1987-91, mem. housing and eviction ct. merger com., 1989-91; mem. Chgo. Single Room Occupancy Adv. Com., 1985-86, Evanston (Ill.) Bldg. Code Appeals Bd., 1982-92; mem. Nat. Alliance to End Homelessness, Skokie (Ill.) Bd. Health, 1992-94, Cook County State's Atty. Criminal Housing Task Force, 1994-95; bd. dirs. Piven Theatre Workshop, 1998—, Defiant Theater Co., 2000—. Recipient Disting. Svc. award Job Resources for Disabled, 1989, Cert. of Merit, Iowa Daily Press Assn., 1971, others. Mem. Chgo. Property Owners Assn., Ill. Coalition for the Homeless, Single Rm. Operators Assn., Edgewater Community Coun., Ill. Inst. Tech. Parents Assn. (exec. sec. 1972-78), Drake U. Journalism Alumni Coun. of Chgo., Zeta Beta Tau. Jewish. Avocation: percussion instruments. Office: Alpine Realty & Mgmt Co 4917 N Kenmore Ave Chicago IL 60640-3709

RUBENSTEIN, HARVEY ALLAN, physician, educator; b. N.Y.C., July 4, 1941; s. Jack and Beatrice (Bedell) R.; m. Lisa J. Stark; children: Jeffrey, Barry, Todd. BA with honors, NYU, 1963; MD, SUNY, Syracuse, 1967. Diplomate Am. Bd. Internal Medicine, Am. Bd. Endocrinology. Intern Roosevelt Hosp., N.Y.C., 1967-68, resident, 1968-69, Columbia-Presbyn. Med. Ctr., N.Y.C., 1969-70, clin. and rsch. fellow in endocrinology and diabetes, 1970-71, asst. physician med. svcs., 1971-72; chief endocrinology svc. Malcolm Grow USAF Med. Ctr., Andrews AFB, 1972-73; attending physician Georgetown U. Hosp., Washington, 1974—, Arlington (Va.) Hosp., 1973—, Reston (Va.) Hosp., 1988—, Fairfax (Va.) Hosp., 1973—, mem. utilization rev. com., quality accountability com., 1982-83, mem. endocrine subsect. com. and endocrine lectr., 1973—, attending tchg. rounds, 1973—, mem. patient care com., 1987-90; from clin. instr. to clin. assoc. prof. medicine Georgetown U. Med. Ctr., Washington, 1972—. Interviewed on numerous radio and TV shows, including CNN, 1989, Channel 8 News, 1993, 94, and Channel 7, 1994. Author:The Endocrine System in Guides to the Evaluation of Permanent Impairment, 5th edit., 2000; contbr. articles to profl. jours. Pres. Washington chpt. Am. Diabetes Assn., 1993-95, bd. dirs., 1987—, v.p. profls., 1989-91, ctrl. coun. del. Atlanta, 1990, task force to recruit and instruct instrs. for patient edn. chmn. 1985-86, profl. edn. com. chmn. 1985-90, diabetes screening task force, 1985-86, lectrs. to interested citizen groups, 1985—, chmn. clin. edn. program, 1989-90, fund devel. com., 1990-92, govt. rels. com. chmn., 1990-91, ctrl. coun. del. Washington, 1991, budget and fin. com., 1991-93, long-range planning com. chmn. 1991-93, pres.-elect 1991-93, pres. 1993-95, immediate past pres., 1995—; pres. Potomac (Md.) Station Homeowners Assn., 1984-95. Maj. USAF, 1971-73. Recipient Vol. of Yr. award Am. Diabetes Assn., 1985-86, Physician's Recognition award AMA, 1974-77, 77-81, 83-87, 87-91, 91-94, 94-97, 97-2000. Fellow ACP, Am. Coll. Endocrinology; mem. Endocrine Soc., Thyroid Found. Am., Am. Assn. Clin. Endocrinologists (charter, chmn. clin. practice stds. com.), Internat. Diabetes Fedn., Am. Fedn. for Clin. Rsch., AMA, Am. Soc. Internal Medicine, D.C. Endocrine Club, Fairfax County Med. Soc. (credentials com. 1974-76, utilization rev. com. 1979-81, mediation com. 1986-88, 93—, med.-legal com. 1991-93, legis. com. 1995—), No. Va. Acad. Internal Medicine, Va. State Med. Soc., Am. Diabetes Assn. (master faculty for clin. edn. program 1989-90), Juvenile Diabetes Found. Internat. (bd. dirs. 1986-88). Avocations: skiing, hiking, gardening, travel, woodworking.

RUBENSTEIN, HOWARD JOSEPH, public relations executive; b. N.Y.C., Feb. 3, 1932; s. Samuel and Ada (Sall) R.; m. Amy Forman, Dec. 17, 1959; children: Roni, Richard, Steven. AB, U. Pa., 1953; student law, Harvard, 1953; LL.B. (Dean's scholar), St. Johns Sch. Law, 1959, LLD (hon.), 1990. Bar: N.Y. State bar 1960. Pres. Rubenstein Assocs., Inc. pub. rels. cons., N.Y.C., 1954—; asst. counsel judiciary com. U.S. Ho. of Reps., 1960; cons. U.S. Fgn. Claims Commn., 1961-62; cons. joint legis. com. child care needs N.Y., 1965-66; adviser SBA, 1965-66. Mem. Gov.'s Com. on Sale of World Trade Ctr., 1981, Mayor's Com. on Holocaust Commemoration, 1981—, N.Y. State Task Force on Energy Conservation, Dept. Housing, 1981-83, Mayor's Coun. Econ. Bus. Advisors, 1991-93; co-chmn. Holocaust Commn., 1993—; v.p. Jewish Cmty. Rels. Coun., 1988-94, advisor, 1995—; past dir. Brownsville Boys Club; bd. dirs. Provide Addict Care Today, Police Athletic League, N.Y. chpt. March of Dimes; mem. U.S. Internat. Coun., 1977-81, Commn. on Status of Women, 1982-89, N.Y.C. Commn. Operation Welcom Home, 1991-92; trustee Ctrl. Park Conservancy; mem. Mayor's Bus. Adv. Coun., 1996—; advisor N.Y. Commn. on Status of Women, 1995—; comm. advisor Gov.'s Com. Jerusalem 3000, 1996—; bd. dirs. Albert Einstein Coll. Medicine, 1997—; bd. govs. Jewish Cmty. Rels. Coun., 1999—. Mem. Assn. Better N.Y. (mem. exec. com. 1972—), Phi Beta Kappa, Beta Sigma Rho. Jewish (dir. congregation). Home: 993 5th Ave New York NY 10028-0105 Office: Rubenstein Assoc Inc 1345 Avenue Of The Americas New York NY 10105-0302

RUBENSTEIN, IRA SAUL, retired physician, pediatrician; b. Orange, N.J., Apr. 14, 1924; s. Ellis and Ada (Blum) R.; m. Babette Wattel, Apr. 11, 1948; children: Daniel, Roy, Beth Rubenstein Mitchell. BA, NYU, 1944, MD, 1947. Diplomate Am. Bd. Pediats. Intern Mt. Sinai Hosp., N.Y.C., 1947-48; pediat. intern Bellevue Hosp., 1948-49; asst. resident in pediats. N.Y. Hosp.-Cornell U., N.Y.C., 1949-50; resident Willard Parkers Hosp., 1950; pvt. practice Franklin Square and Valley Stream, N.Y., 1951, 53-88; ret., 1988. Capt. USAF, 1952-53. Fellow Am. Acad. Pediats. Home: 1 Bay Club Dr # 17 0 Bayside NY 11360-2915 E-mail: docira@webtv.net.

RUBENSTEIN, JACOB SAMUEL, rabbi; b. Rosenheim, Germany, July 17, 1949; came to U.S., 1951; s. David and Eva (Bergman) R.; m. Deborah Powell, Sept. 1, 1969; children: Shira, Daniel, Jonathan, Yoheved. BA, Hebrew U., Jerusalem, 1972; MA, Harvard U., 1976. Ordained rabbi, 1972. Chief justices Ashkenazic and Sephardic Rabbinic Cts., Jerusalem, 1972; rabbi Congregation Beth Sholom, Milford, Mass., 1975-77, Providence, 1977-84, Young Israel of Scarsdale, N.Y., 1984—. Trustee Westchester Jewish Conf., White Plains, 1986-98; vice chmn. rabbinic adv. bd. N.Y. United Jewish Appeal Fedn., 1990-92, exec. officer Westchester Rabbinical Coun., 1986—; vice chmn. Nat. Rabbinic Cabinet of United Jewish Appeal, N.Y.C., 1990-93; pres. Westchester (N.Y.) Bd. Rabbis, 1990-93; nat. chmn. United Jewish Appeal-Rabbinic Cabinet, 1993-95, pres., 1995-96; pres. Rabbinical Coun. of Am., 1997-99, hon. pres. 1999-2000. Contbr. to: Rabbinical Council of America Sermon Manual, 1982, 84, 85, 87-88, 91-92, HaDarom, Torah for Today, 1990, Theological and Halaknic Reflections on the Holocaust; mem. Congl. Acad. Rev. Bd., 1986-89. Mem. Blue Ribbon Panel on Anti-Bias Crime, Westchester County-White Plains, N.Y., 1988; mem. adv. bd. Washington Inst. for Jewish Leadership and Values, 1988—. Recipient City of Peace award Israel Bonds, 1978, Dr. and Mrs. Abraham Stern Svc. award Yeshiva U., 1983, Rabbinical Leadership award Ohr Hameir Theol. Sem., 1985, Rabbinic Svc. award United Jewish Appeal, 1987, Samuel W. and Rose Hurowitz award United Jewish Appeal Fedn., 1993, Ohev Torah award Ariel Am. Friends of Midrasha, 1995, award Nat. United Jewish Appeal, 1993, Orthodox Union Nat. Rabbinical Leadership Centennial medallion, 1999. Mem. Rabbinical Coun. Am. (exec. bd., chmn. legis. and pub. affairs coms. 1985-97), Religious Zionists Am., Inst. for Pub. Affairs (chmn. rabbinical adv. com. 1990-93), Bet Din of Am., The Orthodox Jewish Caucus. Office: Young Israel of Scarsdale 1313 Weaver St PO Box 103H Scarsdale NY 10583-8603 *Physical and social forces govern my life. But in the area of moral freedom, no matter how strong and overwhelming the limitations and mysteries, I can be sovereign, and under the burden of conditioning and conflict motivate my life.*

RUBENSTEIN, JAY D. b. Paterson, N.J., Aug. 8, 1947; s. Julius and Sylvia D. (Krieger) R.; m. Gena I. Connolly Fischer, May 21, 1989. BA, Rutgers Coll., 1969; JD, Rutgers Sch. of Law, 1973. Bar: N.J. 1973, Idaho 1974; N.Y. 1983; U.S. Dist. Ct. N.J. 1973, U.S. Dist. Ct. Idaho 1974; U.S. Ct. Appeals (3rd cir.) 1982; U.S. Supreme Ct. 1982. Atty. VISTA Western Idaho Legal Aid Svcs., Caldwell, Idaho, 1973-74; atty. assoc. Rubenstein & Sherwood, Esqs., Totowa, N.J., 1975-81; atty. shareholder Stern Steiger Croland, P.A., Parmus, 1981-95; ptnr. Shapiro & Croland, Esqs., Hackensack, 1995—. Trustee and gen. counsel The Milton Schamach Found., Inc., N. Haledon, N.J., 1982—. Mem. ABA, N.J. State Bar Assn., Bergen County Bar Assn., Idaho State Bar Assn. Office: Shapiro & Croland Esqs 411 Hackensack Ave 6th Fl Hackensack NJ 07601-6365 E-mail: jayr@shapiro-croland.com.

RUBENSTEIN, JEROME MAX, lawyer; b. St. Louis, Feb. 16, 1927; s. Jacob J. and Anne (Frankel) R.; m. Judith Hope Grand, July 31, 1954; children— Edward J., Emily Rubenstein Muslin, Daniel H. AB, Harvard U., 1950, LLB, 1955. Bar: Mo. 1956, U.S. Dist. Ct. (ea. dist.) Mo. 1956, U.S. Ct. Appeals (8th cir.) 1956. Mem. English lit. faculty U. So. Philippines, Cebu, 1950-51; law clk U.S. Dist. Ct., St. Louis, 1955-56; assoc. Lewis, Rice, Tucker, Allen & Chubb, 1956-64, Grand, Peper & Martin, St. Louis, 1964-65, ptnr., 1965-66; jr. ptnr. Bryan Cave, 1966-67, ptnr., 1968-97, of counsel, 1998—. Dir. Commerce Bank, N.A. Bd. dirs. Independence Ctr., St. Louis, 1985-88, The Arts and Edn. Coun. Greater St. Louis, 1991-99. Served with USN, 1945-46. Bd. dirs. Independence Ctr., St. Louis, 1985. Served with USN, 1945-46 Mem. ABA, Mo. Bar Assn., St. Louis Bar Assn., Mo. Athletic Club, Harvard Club of St. Louis (pres. 1982-83, bd. dirs. 1983-90). Jewish. Avocations: jogging; tennis. Home: 7394 Westmoreland Dr Saint Louis MO 63130-4240 Office: Bryan Cave 1 Metropolitan Sq Ste 3600 Saint Louis MO 63102-2750

RUBENSTEIN, JOSHUA SETH, lawyer; b. Bklyn., Aug. 5, 1954; s. Seth and Elaine (Freedman) R.; children: Mary-Jane, Kenan, Rebecca, Marlena. BA magna cum laude, Columbia U., 1976, JD, 1979. Bar: N.Y. 1980, N.J. 1980, U.S. Dist. Ct. (ea. dist.) N.Y. 1980, U.S. Dist. Ct. (so. dist.) N.Y. 1980, U.S. Dist. Ct. N.J. 1980, U.S. Tax Ct. 1986. Assoc. Fried, Frank, Harris, Shriver & Jacobson, N.Y.C., 1979-82, Rosenman & Colin LLP, N.Y.C., 1982-88, ptnr., 1988—, mgmt. com., 1994—. Chmn. trusts and estates dept. Rosenman & Colin, N.Y.C., 1995—, mgmt. com., 1994—, adv. bd. TE/DEC Systems, Inc., Jour. N.Y. Taxation; lectr. in field; adv. com. on surrogate's cts. Office of Ct. Adminstrn., 1997—; adv. coun. Columbia Law Sch. Trusts, Wills and Estate Planning, 1997—. Contbr. articles to legal publs. Dir., sec. Irvington Inst. Med. Rsch., 1991, treas., 1991-92, sec., 1992-93, co-pres., 1993-94, pres., 1994-2000, vice-chmn., 2000—; chmn. estates and trust spIty. group, chmn. splty. group; task force, mem. exec. com. lawyers divsn. United Jewish Appeal-Fedn., 1989-99; mem. legis. com., devel. com., bd. governance com., Madeleine Borg com., chmn., mem. exec. com., 1994—; trustee Jewish Bd. Family and Children's Svcs., 1991—. Recipient James H. Fogelson award Lawyer's divsn. United Jewish Appeal-Fedn., 1993; named to Best Lawyers in N.Y., N.Y. Mag. Fellow Am. Coll. Trusts and Estate Counsel (state laws com.), N.Y. State Bar Found.; mem. ABA (real property and probate sect.), Internat. Acad. Estate and Trust Law (academician 1997—), Practising Law Inst. (estate adv. com., lectr. 1984—, Hadassah estate planning seminar faculty and adv. bd. 1993—), N.Y. State Bar Assn. (trust and estate law sect., treas. 1997-98, sec. 1998-99, chair elect 1999—, vice chmn. legis. com. 1988, chmn. 1988-91, co-chmn. ad hoc com. to rev. proposals of EPTL adv. com. of N.Y. State 1991—, mem.-at-large exec. com. 1992-95, liaison to legis. policy com. 1995—, Pres.'s Pro Bono Svc. award 1991, Exec. Com. award, 1992, 95, 96, treas. 1997), N.J. Bar Assn. adv. com. rels. with legis. and exec. brs., real property and probate sect.), Assn. Bar City N.Y, Phi Beta Kappa. Democrat. Jewish. Office: Rosenman & Colin 575 Madison Ave Fl 22D New York NY 10022-2511

RUBENSTEIN, LEONARD, engineering company executive; b. N.Y.C., June 18, 1931; s. William and Sylvia (Jaffe) R.; m. Reva Scharf, Jan. 1951 (div. 1960); m. Geraldine Marilyn Porper, Aug. 14, 1965 (dec. Sept. 2000); children: Alan, Elaine, Philip, Ruth, Jennie. BS in Physics, Poly. Inst. N.Y., 1964. Registered profl. engr. N.Y., N.J., Del., Ga. Equipment engr. We. Elec., N.Y.C., 1957-66; elec. engr. Gibbs & Hill, 1966-69; chief engr. Kiegl Lighting, 1969-72; project mgr. Stone & Webster, 1972-87; v.p. engrng. Laramore Douglas & Popham, 1988-90; v.p., dir. engring. Gibbs & Hill, 1990-92; mktr. NPS, Florham Park, N.J., 1992-95; pres., prin. Rubenstein Engrng. PC, N.Y.C., 1975—. Pres., CEO David Internat. Enterprise Corp., N.Y.C.; chmn. bd. HLP, N.Y.C. Contbr. articles to profl. publs.; designer of largest air cooled power plant; first commercial utility size power plant using compressed air stored in salt mines. Chmn. Walt Whitman Ind. Dems., Bklyn., 1966-68, chmn. West Bklyn. Ind. Dems., 1964-66; bd. dirs. N.Y. Gilbert & Sullivan Players, N.Y.C., 1993—, 450 West End Corp, 1984-88; mem. bd. mgrs. McBurney YMCA, 1988-97. With U.S. Army, 1951-53. Mem. IEEE (sr., chmn. N.Y. sect. 1995-96, asst. editor Today's Engr. 1997-98, Region I award 1985, 94, 96), NSPE, Soc. Mfg. Engrs. (charter mem. Vision Soc., sr. mem. Robotics Internat.), Power Engrng. Soc. (chmn. N.Y./L.I. chpt. 1984-85). Avocations: handball, music. Home and Office: 8 W 65th St New York NY 10023

RUBENSTEIN, LEONARD SAMUEL, communications executive, ceramist, painter, sculptor, photographer; b. Rochester, N.Y., Sept. 22, 1918; s. Jacob S. and Zelda H. (Gordon) R.; m. (dec. 1983); children: Carolinda, Eric, Harley. Student, Case Western Res. U., 1938; BFA cum laude, Alfred U., 1939; postgrad., U. Rochester, 1940-41. Creative dir. Henry Hempstead Advt. Agy., Chgo., 1949-55; v.p., exec. art dir. Clinton E. Frank Advt. Agy., 1955-63; v.p., nat. creative dir. Foster & Kleiser divsn. Metromedia, Inc., L.A., 1967-73; ret. Metromedia, Inc., 1984, v.p. corp. creative cons., 1984-88. Guest lectr. U. Chgo.; instr. Columbia Coll., Chgo., Fashion Inst., L.A.; creator Smithsonian exhibition Images of China: East and West, 1982; lectr. in field. Author: (with Charles Hardison) Outdoor Advertising, 1967; contbr. articles to profl. jours.; one-man show at Calif. Mus. Sci. and Industry, 1970; two-person shows at Palos Verdes Art Ctr., 1987, one-man show, 1998; exhibited in group shows; writer, prodr.: (video) Paul Soldner, Thoughts on Creativity, 1989, High-Tech/Low-Tech: The Sci. and Art of Ceramics, 1994; represented in permenant collections Smithsonian Instn. Renwick Gallery, Am. Ceramic Soc. Ross C. Purdy Ceramic Mus., Internat. Mus. Ceramic Art Alfred U., Laguna Mus. Art, Calif. Past pres. Art Dirs. Club Chgo. Recipient Spl. Citation, Art Dirs. Club Chgo. Mem. Soc. Typog. Arts (past dir.), Am. Ceramic Soc. (bd. dirs. So. Calif. design chpt. 1998), Am. Craft Coun., Inst. Outdoor Advt. (past plans bd.), L.A. County Mus. Art, Mus. Contemporary Art L.A. (charter), Palos Verdes (Calif.) Art Ctr., B'nai B'rith, Phi Epsilon Pi. Home and Office: 30616 Ganado Dr Palos Verdes Estates CA 90275 *Personal philosophy: I have a disdain for the trendy, the superficial and the transient.*

RUBENSTEIN, MICHAEL REID, artist, writer; b. Chgo., Jan. 5, 1949; s. Jean Rhoda Rubenstein. BFA, U. Hartford, 1974. Cert. tchr. Sch. Art Inst. Chgo. Painer, writer Deson Saunders Gallery, Chgo., 1990—91, Oskar Friedl Gallery, Chgo., 1999—. Author: (book) Spit & Uno Mas, 2002;exhibitions include 10th Juried Exhbns. Ill. Artists, N.A.M.E. Gallery, Chgo., 1984. Grantee Ill. Arts Coun. Fellowship grant, 1987. Business E-Mail: mrrupainter@yahoo.com.

RUBENSTEIN, PAMELA SILVER, b. Lansing, Mich., May 12, 1953; d. Neil M. and Leah Rebecca (Coffman) Silver; m. Alec Robert Rubenstein. BA in Linguistics, U. Mich., 1974; MA in teaching English to spkrs. of other langs., Columbia U. Tchrs. Coll., 1976; MA in Linguistics, U. Ill., 1978, doctoral studies in linguistics, 1978-80. Instr. Columbia U. Tchrs. Coll., N.Y.C., 1976, U. Ill., Urbana, 1978, libr. Linguistic Dept., 1978-79; asst. libr. Ill. State Geol. Survey, 1979-80; tchr. Congregation Temple Israel, Springfield, Ill., 1980-81; adminstr., tchr. Springfield Bd. Jewish Edn., 1981-82; instr. Comm. Divsn. Lincoln Land C.C., Springfield, 1981-82; tchr. Cmty. Hebrew Sch., Charleston, S.C., 1982-83; instr. The Citadel and Coll. of Charleston, 1983; legal sec. Gibbs & Holmes, Charleston, 1984, May, Oberfell & Lorber, South Bend, Ind., 1984-88; instr. U. Notre Dame, 1987; tchr. Triton Sch. Corp., Bourbon, 1988-89; v.p. Allied Screw Products, Inc., Mishawaka, 1989—. Contbr. articles to profl. jours. Mem. Temple Beth-El Sisterhood, South Bend, 1987—, Hadassah (life mem.). Mem. Michiana Gem and Mineral Soc. (treas. 1995-98). Office: Allied Screw Products Inc 815 E Lowell Ave Mishawaka IN 46545-6480

RUBENSTEIN, RICHARD LOWELL, theologian, educator; b. N.Y.C., Jan. 8, 1924; s. Jesse George and Sara (Fine) R.; m. Betty Rogers Alschuler, Aug. 21, 1966; children by previous marriage: Aaron, Nathaniel (dec.), Hannah Rachel, Jeremy. Student, Hebrew Union Coll., Cin., 1942-45; AB, U. Cin., 1946; MHL rabbi, Jewish Theol. Sem., N.Y.C., 1952; DHL (honoris causa), Jewish Theol. Sem., 1987; STM, Harvard U., 1955, PhD, 1960; LHD (hon.), Grand Valley State U., 1999. Rabbi in, Brockton, Mass., 1952-54, Natick, 1954-56; chaplain to Jewish students Harvard U., 1956-68; univ. chaplain to Jewish students U. Pitts. and Carnegie Inst. Tech., 1958-70; adj. prof. humanities U. Pitts., 1969-70; prof. religion Fla. State U., Tallahassee, 1970-77, Disting. prof. religion, 1977-81, Robert O. Lawton Disting. prof. religion, 1981-95, prof. emeritus religion $D, 1995—, co-dir. Inst. for Humanities, 1980-95; pres. Washington Inst. for Values in Pub. Policy, 1982-95, U. Bridgeport, 1995-99, pres. emeritus, 2000—, disting. prof. religion, 2000—. Edgar M. Bronfman vis. prof. U. Va., 1985; adv. bd. Washington Times, 1982-91, chmn. editl. adv. bd., 1991-96; exec. adv. bd. The World and I mag., 1986—; exec. com. Internat. Jour. of the Unity of Scis., 1987-95; mem. presiding coun. Internat. Religious Fedn. for World Peace, 1991—; chmn. bd. trustees U. Bridgeport, 1994; dir., exec. com. Aegis Trust, U.K. Author: After Auschwitz: Radical Theology and Contemporary Judaism, 1966, The Religious Imagination, 1968 (Portico d'Ottavia lit. prize for Italian transl. 1977), Morality and Eros, 1970, My Brother Paul, 1972, Power Struggle: An Autobiographical Confession, 1974, The Cunning of History, 1975, The Age of Triage, 1983, (with John K. Roth) Approaches to Auschwitz, 1986, After Auschwitz: History, Theology and Contemporary Judaism, Johns Hopkins U. Press, 1992; editor: Modernization: The Humanist Response to Its Promise and Problems, 1982, Spirit Matters: The Worldwide Impact of Religion on Contemporary Politics, 1987, The Dissolving Alliance: The United States and the Future of the NATO Alliance, 1987, In Depth: A Journal of Values in Public Policy, 1991-94; regular columnist Sekai Nippo, Tokyo, 1987-94. Trustee Greater Bridgeport Regional Bus. Coun., 1996-99; trustee United Way of Ea. Fairfield County, Conn., 1998, chmn. acad. divsn., 1997-98, bd. trustees, 1998; trustee Bridgeport Pub. Edn. Fund, 1997—; life bd. trustees U. Bridgeport, 2000—; dir., exec. com. Ctr. for Humanity, Beth Shalom Holocause Ctr., U.K. Recipient Portico d' Ottavia lit. prize Rome, 1977; John Phillips fellow Phillips Exeter Acad., 1970; postdoctoral fellow Soc. Religion in Higher Edn.; Nat. Humanities Inst. fellow Yale U., 1976-77; Rockefeller Found. fellow Aspen Inst. for Humanistic Studies, 1979 Mem. Rabbinical Assembly Am., Am. Acad. Religion, Soc. Sci. Study Religion, Profs. World Peace Acad. (exec. com. 1980—, pres. 1981-82), Internat. House of Japan, Harvard Club (N.Y.C.), Cosmos Club, Rotary. Office: Univ Bridgeport Office of Pres Bridgeport CT 06601 E-mail: rlr@bridgeport.edu.

RUBENSTEIN, STEVEN PAUL, newspaper columnist; b. L.A., Oct. 31, 1951; s. Victor Gerald and Florence (Fox) R.; m. Caroline Moira Grannan, Jan. 1, 1989; children: William Laurence, Anna Katherine. BA, U. Calif., Berkeley, 1977. Reporter L.A. Herald Examiner, 1974-76, San Francisco Chronicle, 1976-81, columnist, 1981—. Office: San Francisco Chronicle 901 Mission St San Francisco CA 94103-2905

RUBERG, ROBERT LIONEL, surgery educator; b. Phila., July 22, 1941; s. Norman and Yetta (Wolfman) R.; m. Cynthia Lief, June 26, 1966; children: Frederick, Mark, Joshua. BA, Haverford (Pa.) Coll., 1963; MD, Harvard U., 1967. Diplomate Am. Bd. Surgery, Am. Bd. Plastic Surgery. Instr. surgery U. Pa., Phila., 1972-75; asst. prof. Ohio State U., Columbus, 1975-81, assoc. prof., 1981-88, prof., 1988—. Bd. dirs. Am. Bd. Plastic Surgery, 1991-97, vice-chair, 1996-97; chmn. curriculum com. Coll. Medicine, Ohio State U., 1984-97; chief plastic surgery Ohio State U. Hosps., 1985—. Plastic Surgery Ednl. Found. research grantee, 1976, 78. Fellow ACS; mem. Am. Assn. Plastic Surgeons, Assn. Acad. Chairmen of Plastic Surgery (pres. 1994-95), Plastic Surgery Edn. Found. (pres. 2000-01, chair residency rev. com. for plastic surgery 2000—). Avocation: bicycling. Home: 100 Walnut Woods Ct Gahanna OH 43230-6200 Office: N325-B Means Hall 1654 Upham Dr Columbus OH 43210

RUBERTI, KATHRYN, social worker, psychotherapist; b. Chgo., Jan. 3, 1951; d. Wilbert Roy and Mary Louise (Gingrich) Franz; m. Richard Elvio Ruberti, Apr. 30, 1988; children: Jeffrey Richard, Mark Nicholas. BSW, Ind. U., 1973; MSW, Smith Coll., 1976. Lic. social worker, Mass. Psychiat. social worker Westboro (Mass.) State Hosp., 1976-78; clin. social worker Martha Eliot Health Ctr., Jamaica Plain, Mass., 1978-81; head social worker Children's Hosp., Boston, 1981-86; psychotherapist Fallon Clinic, Worcester, Mass., 1986-89; pvt. practice psychotherapy Westminster, 1990—. Tchr. Simmons Coll., other ednl. instns., Boston, 1978-89; cons. day care orgns., pediatricians, others, 1978-89; rsch. coord. Evaluation of Diagnostic Svc. of Sexual Abuse, 1988, 89; guest various local TV programs. Mem. NASW, Alpha Lambda Delta. Democrat. Avocations: swimming, skiing, bicycling, writing poetry, reading. Home and Office: 24 S Shore Rd Westminster MA 01473-1610

RUBIN, ALAN, physician; b. Phila., 1923; s. Hyman and Miriam (Magil) R.; m. Helen Metz, May 1, 1947; children: Alan, Stephen, Blake. MD, U. Pa., 1947. Diplomate Am. Bd. Ob-Gyn. Intern Hosp. Pa., Phila., 1947-48, resident in ob-gyn., 1949-52; trainee Nat. Cancer Inst., 1950-51; fellow in pharm. U. Pa., 1948-49; mem. staff Grad. Hosp.; clin. prof. ob-gyn. Temple U. Contbr. more than 150 articles to profl. jours. Fellow ACS, Royal Soc. for the Promotion of Health; mem. Am. Coll. Ob-Gyn., Sigma Xi, Alpha Omega Alpha.

RUBIN, ALAN A. pharmaceutical and biotechnology consultant; b. N.Y.C., July 10, 1926; s. Harry and Gertrude R.; m. Helen M. Feinstein; children: Jeffrey, Ronald, Howard. BS, NYU, 1950, MS, 1953, PhD, 1959. Pharmacologist Schering Corp., Bloomfield, N.J., 1954-64; dir. pharmacology Endo Labs., Garden City, N.Y., 1964-70, v.p. rsch., 1970-74; dir. rsch. DuPont Pharms., Wilmington, Del., 1974-82, dir. sci. info. and tech., 1982-87; dir. licensing tech. DuPont Merck Pharms., 1987-91; cons. ARA Assoc., Rockland, 1991—. Bd. dirs. Redox Pharms., Greenvale, N.Y. Editor: Search for New Drugs, 1972, New Drugs: Discovery and Development, 1978; contbr. articles to profl. jours. With U.S. Army, 1944-46. Mem. AAAS, Am. Soc. Pharmacology and Exptl. Therapeutics, Soc. Exptl. and Biol. Medicine, Am. Heart Assn. Home: 207 Hitching Post Dr Wilmington DE 19803-1914 Office: ARA Assoc PO Box 244 Rockland DE 19732-0244 E-mail: alannar@msn.com.

RUBIN, ALAN EDWARD, meteorite researcher, science popularizer; b. Chgo., Feb. 3, 1953; s. David Bernard and Florence (Fine) R.; m. Dorene Janet Hamerman, Aug. 3, 1980; children: David, Joshua, Jeremiah. BS in Astronomy, U. Ill., 1974; MS in Geol. Sci., U. Ill., Chgo., 1979; PhD in Geology, U. N.Mex., 1982. Postdoctoral fellow Smithsonian Instn., Washington, 1982-83; staff rsch. assoc. UCLA, 1983-89, asst. rsch. geochemist, 1989-91, assoc. rsch. geochemist, 1991-99, rsch. geochemist, 1999—. Contbr. over 100 articles to profl. jours.; author: Disturbing the Solar System, 2002. Recipient Nininger Meteorite award Ariz. State U., 1982. Fellow Meteoritical Soc. Avocation: philosophy of religion. Home: 13161 Ortley Pl Van Nuys CA 91401-1329 Office: Inst Geophys & Planetary UCLA 405 Hilgard Ave Los Angeles CA 90095-1567 Fax: 310-206-3051. E-mail: rubinx5@msn.com., aerubin@ucla.edu.

RUBIN, ALAN J. environmental engineer, chemist, photgrapher; b. Yonkers, N.Y., Mar. 20, 1934; s. Jerome and Lydia R.; m. Ann Kopyt, June 17, 1962; 1 dau., Sara. BS in Civil Engring, U. Miami (Fla.), 1959; MS in San. Engring, U. N.C., Chapel Hill, 1962, PhD in Environ. Chemistry, 1966. Civil engr. FAA, Ft. Worth, 1959-60; asst. prof. U. Cin., 1965-68; prof. civil engring. Ohio State U., Columbus, 1968-91, prof. emeritus, 1991—; with U.S. Geol. Survey, 1991-93. Vis. prof. Technion, Haifa, 1984. Editor 4 books on environ. chemistry; contbr. articles profl. jours. Served with AUS, 1953-55. Mem. Am. Water Works Assn., Water Pollution Control Fedn., Internat. Assn. Water Pollution Research. Achievements include research on giardia cysts, metal ion chemistry, flotation techniques, disinfection, flocculation, coagulation, adsorption, and other physical-chemical treatment processes. Home: 1438 Sherbrooke Pl Columbus OH 43209-3113 Office: Ohio State Univ Dept Civil and Environtl Engring Columbus OH 43210-1058 E-mail: arubin@columbus.rr.com.

RUBIN, ALBERT LOUIS, physician, educator; b. Memphis, May 9, 1927; s. Malcolm M. and Sarah Anne (Bryan) R.; m. Carolyn M. Diehl, Sept. 28, 1953; 1 child, Marc. Student, Williams College, 1944-45, MIT, 1945-46; MD, Cornell U., 1950. Diplomate Am. Bd. Internal Medicine. Intern Bellevue Hosp., N.Y.C., 1950-51, resident internal medicine, 1951-54, fellow nephrology, 1954-55, physician-in-charge, 1953-61; established investigator Am. Heart Assn., N.Y.C., 1958-63; dir. Rogosin Labs., Cornell U. Med. Coll., 1963—, The Rogosin Kidney Ctr., N.Y.C., 1971—, The Rogosin Inst., N.Y.C., 1983—; prof. biochemistry, surgery, medicine Cornell U. Med. Coll., 1969—; surgeon The N.Y. Hosp., 1969—. Mem. com. on sci. and tech. aspects of processing materials in space NRC, N.Y.C.; dir. affiliations and patient referrals N.Y. Hosp.-Cornell Med. Ctr., 1977-80; bd. dirs., bd. incorporators neuroscis. rsch. program MIT. Author: Physical Diagnosis: A Textbook and Workbook in Methods of Clinical Examination, 1972, Humoral Aspects of Transplantation, 1976, Manual of Clinical Nephrology, 1980; cons. editor Am. Jour. Medicine; med. editl. cons. Time mag., 1983-94. With USN, 1944-45. Recipient Hoeing award Nat. Kidney Found., 1982. Mem. ACP, AAAS, Am. Soc. for Artificial Internal Organs, Transplantation Soc., Sigma XI. Home: 220 Allison Ct Englewood NJ 07631-4301 Office: The Rogosin Inst 505 E 70th St 2d Fl Rm 230 New York NY 10021-9809

RUBIN, ALLAN B. radiologist, consultant; b. N.Y.C., July 16, 1939; BS cum laude, CCNY, 1961; MD, Einstein Coll. Medicine, N.Y.C., 1965. Diplomate Am. Bd. Radiology, Am. Bd. Med. Examiners, Am. Bd. Forensic Medicine, cert. in neuropsychology and psychotherapy Am. Bd. Psychol. Spltys. Intern Cornell Med. Ctr.; resident in psychiatry, resident in radiology Mt. Sinai Hosp., N.Y.C.; pvt. practice, Spring Valley, N.Y.; asst. prof. radiology Mt. Sinai Sch. Medicine, N.Y.C., 1977-87, N.Y. Med. Coll., Valhalla, 2000—. Contbr. articles to profl. jours. Mem. Am. Coll. Radiology, Radiologic Soc. N.Am., Am. Roentgen Ray Soc., Clin. Magnetic Resonance Soc., Internat. Soc. Magnetic Resonance Imaging in Medicine, Phi Beta Kappa. Avocation: reading. Office: 21st Century Open & Closed MRI 2 Perlman Dr Spring Valley NY 10977

RUBIN, ALLAN MAIER, physician, surgeon; b. Bavaria, Germany, Aug. 4, 1947; s. Benjamin Rubin and Ida Spiegle; children: Alanna T., Marissa D., Sarina D.; m. Jean Tellander, Mar. 5, 1989. BS, McGill U., Montreal, Que., Can., 1968, MS, 1970; PhD, MD, U. Toronto, Ont., Can., 1979. Diplomate Am. Bd. Otolaryngology. Demonstrator neuroanatomy U. Toronto, 1971-73, resident, 1979-84; investigator Toronto Gen. Hosp., 1976-78; fellow otolaryngology Toronto East Gen. Hosp., 1985; asst. prof. dept. otolaryngology Creighton U., Omaha, 1986-87; assoc. prof. dept. surgery Med. Coll. Ohio, Toledo, 1987-88, chmn., prof. dept. otolaryngology, 1988—. Mem. resident edn. com. Blue Cross N.W. Ohio, Toledo, 1992-93, HMO/Toledo Health Plan, 1989-93; pres. Acad. Senate Med. Coll. Ohio, Toledo, 1991-92; chmn. search for urology chair Med. Coll. Ohio, 1991-92, presdl. search com., 1991-93. Mem. internat. editl. adv. bd. Jour. Otolaryngology, 1991—, editl. rev. bd. Am. Jour. Otolaryngology, 1989-94. Rsch. grantee Biomed. Rsch. Support Grant, 1984, NIH, 1986, 87. Fellow ACS, Royal Soc. Medicine, Am. Neurotology Soc., Am. Acad. Otolaryngology-Head and Neck Surgery (subcom. on equilibrium 1988—, subcom. on med. aspects of noise, editl. rev. bd. 1993—); mem. Soc. Univ. Otolaryngologists (resident edn. com., membership com.), Barany Soc., Triological Soc., Sigma Xi, Alpha Omega Alpha (v.p. Delta of Ohio chpt. 1996—, chmn. search com. for orthopaedic surgery chmn.). Achievements include management and treatment of vestibular dysfunction and dizziness in children; correlation and transcranial doppler (TCD) and brain single photon emission computed tomography (SPECT) in patients with dizziness. Office: Med Coll Ohio 3000 Arlington Ave Toledo OH 43614-2595

RUBIN, ARNOLD JESSE, aeronautical engineer; b. Bklyn., Sept. 30, 1924; s. Jack and Birdie (Reiss) R.; m. Gloria Form, June 19, 1949 (dec. Sept. 1994); children: Jacqueline Sue Rubin Grob, Mitchell Myles. B in Aero. Engring., NYU, 1949; postgrad., U. Va., 1950, Poly. Inst. Bklyn., 1960-62. Aero. rsch. scientist Langley Rsch. Ctr., NASA, Hampton, Va., 1949-51; with Fairchild Republic Co., Fairchild Industries, Inc., Farmingdale, N.Y., 1951-87, prin. aerodyn. engr., 1979-82, chief aerodyns., T-46A, 1982-87. Served with USAAF, 1943-45. Fellow AIAA (assoc.); mem. Soc. Flight Test Engrs., NYU Alumni Assn., Huron Club. Home: 1710 John St Merrick NY 11566-4837

RUBIN, ARTHUR HERMAN, retired university official, consultant; b. N.Y.C., Aug. 14, 1927; s. Samuel and Bessie (Moritt) R.; m. Janice Levy, Apr. 9, 1950 (div. 1965); children: Renee Ellen, Linda Joy; m. Audrey M. Schmidt, July 1, 1973. BS, NYU, 1950, MA, 1951. Adminstrv. asst. to asst. dean Sch. Edn. NYU, 1947-54, lab. asst. bus. edn. dept., 1950-54, instr., 1954-56, program dir. grad. students orgn., 1954-63, dir. tours, 1955-58, coord. summer sessions activities, 1959-64, dir. Bur. Pub. Occasions, 1963-74, asst. v.p. pub. occasions, 1974-75, dir. extramural affairs Coll. Dentistry, 1976, assoc. dean adminstrn., 1976-80, adj. asst. prof. behavioral scis. and cmty. health, 1976-80, dir. alumni rels. Sch. of Med., 1980-95, dir. spl. events med. ctr., 1988-95; cons. to Office Alumni Rels. NYU Sch. Medicine, 1995-2000; cons. to Office Spl. Events, NYU Med. Ctr., 1995-2000; ret., 2000. Tchr. Patrick Henry Jr. High Sch., N.Y.C., 1949-58; acting asst. prin. Robert F. Wagner Jr. High Sch., N.Y.C., 1958-63; cons. in field. Trustee Agnew Found., 1967—. Recipient NYU Presdl. citation, 1971, GSO award, 1980, Ernest O. Melby award Sch. Edn. Alumni Assn., 1976, citation Bus. Edn. Assn. Met. N.Y., 1976, Sesquicentennial award NYU Alumni Fedn., 1982, Meritorious Svc. award, 1985, dir. Emeritus citation, 1992. Mem. Ea. Bus. Tchrs. Assn. (chmn. exhibits 1953-74, exec. bd. 1969-71, pres. 1972-73, award 1974), Bus. Edn. Assn. Met. N.Y. (exec. bd. 1962-83), Nat. Bus. Edn. Assn. (exec. bd. 1972-74, conv. mgr. 1974-92, Disting. Svc. award 1992, Cert. of Appreciation 1992), N.Y. Acad. Pub. Edn. (bd. dirs. 1979-98, pres. 1992-94), NYU Edn. Alumni Assn. (v.p. 1961-62, 64-67), NYU Club (bd. govs. 1972-78, 79-89, v.p. 1983-86, chmn. bd. 1986-87), Princeton Club N.Y., Delta Pi Epsilon Rsch. Found. Inc. (bd. dirs. 1990-92), Delta Pi Epsilon (Svc. awards Alpha chpt. 1971, 81). Home: 2605 Houghton Lean Macungie PA 18062-9506

RUBIN, CATHY ANN, retired educator; b. Denver, July 17, 1948; d. Harry Phillip and Charlotte Ruth (Brinig) R. BA, Colo. State U., 1970; MA, U. No. Colo., 1971. Cert. tchr., Colo. Tchr. Adams County Dist. 50 Schs., Westminster, Colo., 1971-72; tchr. educationally handicapped Jefferson County Pub. Schs., Golden, 1972-98. Typist, bookkeeper Kenmark-Shaw's Jewelers, Denver, 1966—. Sec.-treas. Hillel Found., Denver, 1979-81; fundraiser Women's Am. Orgn. for Rehab. through Tng., Denver, 1979—; bookkeeper Religious Coalition for Abortion Rights, Denver, 1982-90; vol. TV PBS sta., Denver, 1978, Muscular Dystrophy Assn., Colo. AIDS Project; vol. usher DCTC, 1999—. Democrat. Jewish. Avocations: music, reading, sailing, knitting, needlepoint. Home: 3500 S Ivanhoe St Denver CO 80237-1123

RUBIN, CHANDA, professional tennis player; b. Lafayette, La., Feb. 18, 1976; d. Edward and Bernadette Rubin. Grad., Episcopal Sch. Acadiana, 1993. Mem. USTA Jr. Devel. Team, 1989, USTA Nat. Team, 1990; prof. tennis player, 1991—. Player 20 tournaments and Fed. Cup with 43 wins, 19 losses, 1995, named to Olympic Team, Atlanta, 1996. Ranked 25th, 1999; recipient 3 U.S. Jr. Titles, 12 Singles, 1988, 14 Singles, 1989, 16 Indoor Doubles, 1989, Silver and Bronze medal 1995 Pan Am Games, 1995; winner U.S. nat. title and Rolex Orange Bowl 12s crown, 1988, 14 Nat., 1989, 16 Indoor Doubles, 1989, U.S. Tennis Assn. Challenge of Midland Mich.; named Most Improved Female Player, Tennis Mag., 1995, Female Athlete of Yr., U.S. Tennis Assn., 1995, Most Caring Athlete, USA Weekend Mag., 1997; singles winner Hobart, 1999, finalist, Quebec City, 1999, semifinalist, Indian Wells, 1999, Madrid, 1999; winner Doubles (with Testud) Filderstadt, 1999, finalist (with Testud) U.S. Open, 1999, winner Bell Challenge at Quebec City, 2000. Office: USTA 70 W Red Oak Ln White Plains NY 10604-3602 also: Advantage International 1751 Pinnacle Dr Ste 1500 Mc Lean VA 22102-3833*

RUBIN, CHARLES ALEXIS, writer; b. L.A., Dec. 4, 1953; s. Herbert Bernard and Jacqueline (Bashor) R.; m. Doris Sara Villalobos, July, 23, 1978; 1 child, Daniel Charles. BA in English magna cum laude, San Francisco State U., 1978, MA in English, 1980. Communications supr. Am. Protective Services, Oakland, Calif., 1982-83; assoc. editor Personal Computing mag., San Jose, 1983-84; free-lance writer Oakland, 1984—; sr. assoc. Waterside Assocs., Fremont, Calif., 1986-87; sr. analyst Internet Rsch. Group, Los Altos, 1999-2000; sr. strategist Gallagher Pub. Rels., Alameda, 2000—02; ptnr. Gallagher Group Pub. Rels., 2002—. Editorial cons. Televisual Market Strategies, Saratoga, 1985-86. Author: The Endless Apple, 1984, Thinking Small: The Buyer's Guide to Portable Computers, 1984, Appleworks: Boosting Your Business with Integrated Software, 1985, Command Performance: Appleworks, 1986, Microsoft Works, 1986, Macintosh Hard Disk Management, 1988, Running Microsoft Works, 1990, The Macintosh Bible (What Do I Do Now?), 1990, The Macintosh Bible Guide to System 7, 1991, The Macintosh Bible Guide to File Maker Pro, 1991, The Macintosh Bible Guide to Clarisworks, 1993, The Little Book of Computer Wisdom, 1994, Guerrilla Marketing Online Weapons, 1996, Guerrilla Marketing Online, 1997, Managing Your Business with Quickbooks, 1998, Running Microsoft Word 2000, 1999. Democrat. Jewish.

RUBIN, DAVID LEE, humanities educator, publisher; b. Indpls., Sept. 30, 1939; s. Ira Bertram and Jeanne Iva (Gamso) R.; m. Carolyn Dettman, June 12, 1965; 1 child, Timothy Craig. BA, U. Tenn., 1962; cert., U. Paris, 1963; MA, U. Ill., 1964, PhD, 1967. Instr. French U. Ill., Urbana, 1966-67; asst. prof. U. Chgo., 1967-69, U. Va., Charlottesville, 1969-74, assoc. prof., 1974-82, prof. French, 1982-2001, mem. com. on comparative lit., 1997-2001, prof. emeritus, assoc. univ. seminar program, 2001—; seminar dir. Folger Inst., 1989. Assoc. ctr. advanced studies U. Va., 1979, 80-81, 87, 93, 99-2000; founder Rookwood Press, 1992—; cons. Can. Coun., Etudes littéraires françaises, NEH, numerous univ. presses; lectr., spkr. in field. Author: Higher Hidden Order, 1972, The Knot of Artifice, 1981, A Pact with Silence, 1991; editor: The Selected Poetry and Prose of John T. Napier, 1972, La poésie française du premier 17e siècle, 1986, Sun King, 1991; co-editor: La Cohérence Intérieure, 1977, Convergences, 1989, The Ladder of High Designs, 1991, The Fulbright Difference, 1993; founding editor Continuum, 1989-93, EMF: Studies in Early Modern France, 1994-2002, EMF Critiques, 1994-2002, Rookwood Texts, 1997—, Rookwood Reprints, 2002—; mem. editl. bd. Purdue Studies in Romance Literatures, 1975-2001, Oeuvres et Critiques, 1976-2001, French Rev., 1986-94; Am. corr. Cahiers Maynard, 1973-2001, Cahiers Tristan L'Hermite, 1989-2001; contbr. articles to profl. jours., chpts. to books. U.S. State Dept. Fulbright fellow, 1962-63, Woodrow Wilson Found. fellow, 1963-64, Guggenheim Found. fellow, 1980-81, Hewlett fellow, summer 1997. Mem. MLA, ACLU, Farmington Club, Boar's Head Club, Phi Beta Kappa. Avocations: reading, travel, fitness. Home: 520 Rookwood Pl Charlottesville VA 22903-4734

RUBIN, DEBORAH JEAN, social worker; b. Pitts., June 13, 1949; m. Fred Howard Rubin, June 20, 1971; 1 child Matthew David. BA, Chatham Coll., 1972; B Social Work, McGill U., 1977, MSW, 1978; PhD, Univ. Pittsburgh, 1999. Bd. cert. diplomate social work; lic. social worker, Mass., Pa. Clin. social worker Judge Baker Guidance Ctr., Boston, 1978-81; clin. fellow McLean Hosp., Belmont, Mass., 1981-82, clin. social worker, 1983-84, sr. clin. social worker, 1984-87; social worker Western Psychiatric Inst. & Clinic, Pitts., 1989, chief social worker, 1989-91; dir. social work prog. Chatham Coll., Pittsburgh, 1999—. Mem. NASW. Office: Chatham Coll Woodland Rd Pittsburgh PA 15232

RUBIN, DONALD BRUCE, statistician, educator, research company executive; b. Washington, Dec. 22, 1943; s. Allan A. and Harriet Rubin; m. Kathryn M. Kazarow; children: Scott Wilk, Paul Stuart. AB magna cum laude, Princeton U., 1965; MS, Harvard U., 1966, PhD, 1970. Rsch. statistician Ednl. Testing Svc., Princeton, N.J., 1971-75, chmn. stats., 1975-79, sr. statis. advisor, 1979-81; pres. Datametrics Rsch. Inc., Waban, Mass., 1981—; prof. U. Chgo., 1982-84, Harvard U., Cambridge, Mass., 1984—, chmn. stats., 1985-94, 2000—. Author: Handling Nonresponse in Sample Surveys by Multiple Imputation, 1980, Multiple Imputation for Nonresponse in Surveys, 1987; author: (with others) Incomplete Data in Sample Surveys (Vol. 2): Theory and Bibliography, 1983; co-author: (with R.J.A. Little) Statistical Analysis With Missing Data, 1987, (with A. Gelman, J. Carlin. H. Stern) Bayasian Data Analysis, 1995, (with R. Rosenthal and R. Rosnow) Contrasts and Effect Sites in Behavioral Research: A Correlational Approach, 2000; co-editor: (with P.W. Holland) Test Equating, 1982; contbr. over 250 articles to profl. jours. Recipient Parzen prize for statis. innovation, 1996; Woodrow Wilson Grad. fellow, 1965; NSF Grad. fellow, 1965, 68, John Simon Guggenheim fellow, 1977-78. Fellow AAAS (chmn. stats. 1992), Am. Statis. Assn. (editor jour. 1980-82, dir. 1980-82, statistician of yr. Boston chpt. 1995, Chgo. chpt. 2000, S.S. Wilks medal 1995), Inst. Math. Stats. (coun. mem. 1990-92, 99-2001); mem. NAS (com. on nat. stats. 1989-92, mem. panel on confidentiality data 1989-92, panel on bilingual edn. 1990-92, working group on statis. analysis of com. on basic rsch. in behavioral and social scis. 1985-86, panel statis. in 21st century 1995, other coms.), AAAS, Am. Acad. Arts and Sci., Biometric Soc., Internat. Assn. Survey Statisticians, Internat. Statis. Inst., Psychometric Soc., Royal Statis. Soc. Office: Harvard U Dept Statistics Cambridge MA 02138 E-mail: rubin@stat.harvard.edu.

RUBIN, ELIZABETH D. health insurance company official; b. Gloversville, N.Y., Mar. 28, 1970; d. Lewis and Barbara Gayle Vant; m. Dana Fredric Rubin, May 23, 1999. BA, Emory U., 1992; MPA, Columbia U., 1995. Cert. profl. Acad. Healthcare Mgmt.. Mktg. coord. Thomas Jefferson U. Hosp., Phila., 1992-93; sr. fin. analyst NYLCare Health Plans, 1995-98; dir. fin. control Empire Blue Cross Blue Shield, N.Y.C., 1998—. Fellow Columbia U. Sch. Internat. and Pub. Affairs, 1994-95. Mem. Healthcare Fin. Mgmt. Assn, Hadassah Women's Orgn. (life). Avocations: fitness walking, tennis. E-mail: elizabeth.rubin@empirehealthcare.com.

RUBIN, EMANUEL, pathologist, educator; b. N.Y.C., Dec. 5, 1928; s. Jacob and Sophie R.; m. Barbara Kurn, Mar. 27, 1955 (div. 1985); children: Raphael, Jonathan, Daniel, Rebecca; m. Linda A. Haegele, Oct. 13, 1985; children: Ariel, Ethan. BS, Villanova U., 1950; MD, Harvard U., 1954. Intern Boston City Hosp., 1954-55; resident Children's Hosp. of Phila., 1957-58; research fellow in pathology Mt. Sinai Hosp., N.Y.C., 1958-62, asst. attending pathologist, 1962-64, assoc. attending pathologist, 1964-68, attending pathologist, dir. hosp. pathology services, 1968-72, pathologist-in-chief, 1972-76; dir. labs. Hahnemann Hosp., Phila., 1977-86; physician-in-chief pathology Thomas Jefferson U. Hosp., 1986—. Prof. pathology Mr. Sinai Sch. Medicine, CUNY, 1966-72, Irene Heinz and John LaPorte Givien prof. pathology, chmn. dept., 1972-76; prof., chmn. dept. pathology and lab. medicine Hahnemann U. Sch. Medicine, Phila., 1977-86; Gonzalo Aponte prof. pathology, chmn. dept. pathology and cell biology Thomas Jefferson U. Coll. Medicine, Phila., 1986-94, chmn. dept. pathology, anatomy and cell biology, 1994—; adj. prof. biochemistry and biophysics U. Pa. Sch. Medicine, Phila., 1977-88. Author: (with J.L. Farber) Pathology, 1988, 94, 98; (with K.W. Miller and S.H. Roth) Cellular and Molecular Mechanisms of Alcohol and Anesthetics, 1991; editor-in-chief Lab. Investigation, 1982-96; pathology editor: Fedn. Proc., 1982-86, Jour. Studies in Alcoholism, 1982-94, Alcoholism: Clin. Exptl. Rsch., 1999—. Served with USN, 1955-57. Mem. ACP, Am. Soc. Investigative Pathology, Internat. Acad. Pathology, U.S.-Can. Acad. Pathology, Am. Soc. Biol. Chemists and Molecular Biology, Am. Assn. Study of Liver Diseases, Am. Gastroent. Assn., Internat. Assn. Study of the Liver, Am. Coll. Toxicology. Home: 1505 Monk Rd Gladwyne PA 19035-1316 Office: 1020 Locust St Philadelphia PA 19107-6731 E-mail: emanuel.rubin@mail.TJU.edu.

RUBIN, E(RWIN) LEONARD, lawyer; b. Chgo., Jan. 11, 1933; s. Samuel and Frances Birdie (Rabin) R.; m. Stephanie Siegel, Mar. 4, 1961 (div. Dec. 1981); children: Matthew, Suzanne; m. Audrey Gay Holzer, May 8, 1983; children: Margot, Bette. Student, U. Ill., Urbana, 1948-51; AB, U. Miami, 1956, JD, 1959. s. N.Y. 1960, Ill. 1962, U.S. Dist. Ct. (no. dist.) Ill. 1962, U.S. Ct. Appeals (7th cir.) 1990. Assoc. Hays, St. John A&H, N.Y.C., 1960-62, Devoe, Shadur, Mikva & P., Chgo., 1962-65; gen. counsel Playboy Enterprises, Inc., 1965-78; ptnr. E. Leonard Rubin Law Offices, 1978-81, Epton, Mullin & Druth Ltd., Chgo., 1981-86, Brinks, Hofer, Gilson & Lione, Chgo., 1986-96, Gordon & Glickson, LLC, Chgo., 1996—. Adj. prof. U. Ill., Northwestern U. Law Sch., Loyola U. Sch. Law, John Marshall Law Sch. Pres. Lawyers for Creative Arts, Chgo., 1983-85; chmn. bd. dirs. Mus. Holography; bd. dirs. Wisdom Bridge Theatre, Chgo., 1983-85; mem., bd. dirs. Appletree Theater of Highland Park. Cpl. U.S. Army, 1953-5, ETO. Mem. ABA, Ill. Bar Assn., Chgo. Bar Assn. (bd. mgrs. 1983-85, chmn. various coms., dir. Christmas Spirits Satire Show 1965-99), Union Internat. Des Avocats (pres. intellectual property commn. 1997-2000), Copyright Soc. Am. (trustee, past pres. midwest chpt.). Jewish. Home: 270 Sunset Dr Northfield IL 60093-1047 Office: Gordon & Glickson LLC 444 N Michigan Ave Ste 3600 Chicago IL 60611-3901 E-mail: elrubin@ggtech.com.

RUBIN, HANAN, retired insurance company executive, mathematician, auditor; b. N.Y.C., Mar. 9, 1927; s. Hyman and Esta (Greenberg) R.; m. Mona Klein, June 29, 1958; children: Eric Stuart, Karen Jill Rubin Dauber, Wendy Risa Rubin Axelrod. AB magna cum laude, NYU, 1948, PhD in Math., 1953. Cert. internal auditor, information systems auditor. Teaching asst. math. NYU, 1946-48, instr. math., asst. rsch. scientist Courant Inst. Math. Scis., 1948-51, instr. math., assoc. rsch. scientist, 1951-53, asst. prof. math., rsch. scientist, 1954-58, instr. Bell Telephone Labs., 1954-56; staff mathematician, cons. IBM, 1958-59, cons. analytical svcs. dept., 1959-60, asst. mgr., 1960, mgr., 1960-62; head computer group, sr. supervisory scientist TRG, 1962-64; tech. asst. to pres. Gen. Applied Sci. Labs., 1964-67; corp. staff mem., dir. edn. & tng. Computer Applications Inc., 1967-69; exec. asst. Met. Life Ins. Co., 1972-75, asst. v.p., 1975-77, v.p., 1977-91. Vis. asst. prof. math. U. Tenn., 1953-54; cons. Union Carbide Nuc. Co., Oak Ridge, Tenn., 1953-66; vis. mathematician Brookhaven Nat. Lab., Upton, N.Y., 1957; co-chair Stony Brook Conf. Advances Computing SUNY, 1966; mem. bi-county task force com. computer applications medicine Nassau Heart Assn., Mineola, N.Y., 1971-72; chair ad hoc EFT com. Life Office Mgmt. Assn., 1978. Contbr. numerous articles to profl. jours. Bd. dirs. South Nassau Cmtys. Hosp., Oceanside, 1980-2002, dir. emeritus, 2002, treas. bd. dirs., 1985-89, 1st v.p. bd. dirs., 1989-90; bd. dirs. Winthrop South Nassau U. Health Sys., Mineola, Oceanside, 1996-2001. With USN, 1945-46. Rockefeller fellow NYU, 1948. Mem. Phi Beta Kappa, Tau Kappa Alpha, Sigma Xi. Avocations: computing, golf, music. Home: 359 Green Ct Oceanside NY 11572-5615

RUBIN, HARRY MEYER, entertainment industry executive; b. N.Y.C., Dec. 21, 1952; s. Martin J. and Helene Rubin; m. Cathy Hemery, May 26, 1990; children: Gabriella, James. BA, Stanford U., 1974; MBA, Harvard U., 1976. Investment banker Wertheim & Co., Inc., N.Y.C., 1976-77; fin. mgr. Am. Airlines, Inc., 1977-79; dir. fin. planning-entertainment, electronics groups RCA Corp., 1979-81; CFO RCA Videodiscs, RCA Home Video, RCA Cable RCA Entertainment Group; v.p. strategic planning RCA Corp., group fin. exec. RCA entertainment ops., 1981-86; gen. mgr. Home Video Gen. Electric Co., 1986-87; v.p., gen. mgr. home video ops. NBC, Inc., 1988-93; exec. v.p. GT Interactive Software Corp., 1994-98; pres. GT Interactive Internat., 1998-2000; pres. internat. Infogrames, Inc., 2000-01, sr. exec. v.p., 2001—. Dir., co-head exec. com. RCA/Columbia Pictures Worldwide Video; founding ptnr. Samuel Adams Beer; founding dir. Arts & Entertainment Network. Mem. Phi Beta Kappa, 22 Club. Avocations: travel, foreign languages. Home: 784 Park Ave New York NY 10021-3553

RUBIN, HAYA RAHEL, physician, researcher; b. Pitts., May 20, 1957; d. Israel and Anna (Halberstam) Rubin; m. Jerome Karsh; 1 child Miriam Rebecca Rubin Karsh. MD, PhD, Case Western Res. U., 1982; MSP.H., UCLA, 1989. Cert. Am. Bd. Internal Medicine. Assoc. prof. medicine, Hehlth Popicy and mgmt. and epidemiology The Johns Hopkins U., Balt., 1995—2002, asst. prof. medicine and health policy and mgmt.; asst. prof. medicine The University of California, San Francisco, San Francisco, 1990—90; instr. medicine U. Calif., 1988—90, Mount Sinai Med. Ctr., N.Y., NY; resident in medicine Mount Sinai Sch. Medicine, New York, 1982—85; Robert Wood Johnson Clin. Scholar UCLA, L.A., Calif., 1986—88. Assoc. editor Jour. General Internal Medicine, Balt., 1999—2002; mem. editl. bd. Internat. Jour. for Quality in Health Care, Boston, 1996—2002; cons. Delmarva Found. Med. Care, Easton, 2000—02. Contbr. over 50 articles healthcare quality peer-reviewed sci. jour. Mem. coun. leadership United Way, Johns Hopkins U. Chpt., Balt., 2002—02. Named to Unusual accomplishment, Case Western Res. U. Sch. Medicine, 1982; recipient Harry Goldblatt award excellence in expl. rsch., 1982, Shirley Sohmer award excellence in nursing rsch., Johns Hopkins Sch. Nursing, 1992. Fellow: ACP, Acad. Health Svcs. Rsch.; mem.: Soc. General Internal Medicine (pres. Mid-Atlantic region 1992—93, Excellent Original Investigation 1991), Delta Omega, Alpha Omega Alpha. Achievements include research in patient satisfaction with medical care, medical peer review, improving physician adherence to clinical practical guidelines; measuring patients' quality of life as an outcome of medical care and treatment. Office: The Johns Hopkins U 1830 East Monument St #8015 Baltimore MD 21205

RUBIN, HERBERT, lawyer; b. Lisbon, Conn., June 4, 1918; s. Simon and Rose (Berko) R.; m. Rose Luttan, July 6, 1941; children: Barbara, Caroline, Donald. AB, CCNY, 1938; JD, NYU, 1942. Bar: N.Y. 1942, U.S. Dist. Ct. (so. and ea. dists.) N.Y. 1951, U.S. Supreme Ct. 1956, U.S. Ct. Appeals (2d, 3d, 4th, 6th, 9th, 10th, D.C. cirs.). Assoc. Newman & Bisco, 1942; faculty NYU Law Sch., 1946-50, 57-62; prof. creditors' rights Rutgers U. Law Sch., 1949-57; pvt. practice, 1946-56; ptnr. Sereni, Herzfeld & Rubin, and successor Herzfeld & Rubin, N.Y.C., 1956—, sr. ptnr., 1968—. Instr. mil. law, 1944-46; prof. constl. law L.I. U., 1963-68; trustee North Shore L.I. Jewish Hosp. Editor-in-chief NYU Law Rev., 1940-41; bd. editors N.Y. Law Jour., 1971—; contbr. articles to profl. jours. Mem. N.Y. State Banking Bd., 1975-85, N.Y. State Jud. Selection Com., 1975-83, Sen. Moynihan's Jud. Selection Com., 1982—, Sen. Schumer's Jud. Selection Com., 1999—, City Charter Revision Commn., 1998—. 1st lt. Signal Corps, AUS, 1942-46. Recipient award NCCJ, 1967, United Jewish Appeal, 1968, 97, Israel Bonds, 1973, NYU Law Assn. award 1987, Judge Weinfeld award, 1992. Fellow Am. Bar Found.; mem. ABA (mem. coun. N.Y. state), N.Y. State Bar Assn., Queens County Bar Assn. (pres. 1970), Assn. Bar City Of N.Y., Fed. Bar Coun., Jewish Lawyers Guild (award 2001). Jewish. Office: Herzfeld & Rubin 40 Wall St Fl 54 New York NY 10005-2301

RUBIN, IRVIN I. plastics company executive; b. Bklyn., Feb. 27, 1919; children: Jesse, Julie. BS in Chemistry, CCNY, 1938; postgrad., Bklyn. Coll., 1939-40. Pres. Robinson Plastics Corp., Bklyn., 1940-42, 44—; engr. Montrose Chem., Newark, 1942-45; prin. Robinson, Lewis & Rubin, Inc., N.Y.C., 1957-70. Adj. prof. plastics N.Y. Inst. Tech., 1960-63; mem. Plastics Ednl. Commn., Adv. Bd. Vocat. and Extension Edn., Bd. Edn. N.Y.C., 1960-71; cons. Dupont, Am. Optical, Kodex. Author: Injection Molding Theory and Practice, 1973; editor: Handbook of Plastic Materials and Processes, 1990. Named to Plastics Hall of Fame. Fellow Soc. Plastic Engrs. (pres. N.Y. sect.).

RUBIN, JACOB CARL, mechanical research engineer; b. N.Y.C., Nov. 22, 1926; s. Abraham and Bessie (Tockman) R.; m. Nancy Jean Weinstein, Aug. 2, 1952; children: Sara Lee, Jeffrey Daniel. BSME, CUNY, 1945; MMechE, NYU, 1947; MS of Applied Statistics, Rochester (N.Y.) Inst. Tech., 1969, MSEE, 1971, MS in Imaging Sci., 1975. Registered profl. engr., N.Y., D.C. Design group leader MacDonnell Aircraft Corp., St. Louis, 1955-56; mem. research staff U. Mich., Ann Arbor, 1956-57; staff engr. IBM, Vestal, N.Y., 1957-58; engr. advance design GE, Johnson City, 1958-60, program engr. Phila., 1960-62; mgr. standards engring. Martin-Marietta Corp., Balt., 1962-63; mgr. product design dept. Am. Car & Foundry Co., Rockville, Md., 1963-64; cons. reliability NASA, Greenbelt, 1964-65; project engr. Eastman Kodak Co., Rochester, 1965-75, sr. rsch. assoc., 1975-90; staff mech. engr. Med. Lab. Automation, Inc., Pleasantville, N.Y., 1990-91; prin. engr. instrument div. Dresser Industries, Stratford, Conn., 1992; sr. mech. engr. Materials Rsch. Corp., Congers, N.Y., 1993; sr. mech. design engr. Electronics Retailing Sys. Inc., Wilton, Conn., 1993-94; mfg. engr. Contact Sys. Inc., Danbury, 1995; sr. mech. engr. Barnes engring. divsn. EDO Corp., Shelton, 1995-96; mech. engr. Screen Tech, Oakville, 1996-97, Premier Microwave Corp., Port Chester, N.Y., 1997-98; prin. mech. engr. Microphase Corp., Norwalk, Conn., 1998; cons. product engr. Walboro Automotive, Meriden, 1998; cons. project engr. Ingersoll-Rand Corp., Watertown, 1999-2000; sr. mech. engr. Electro Energy, Inc., Danbury, 2000-01. Course dir. Ctr. Profl. Advancement, East Brunswick, N.J., 1975—; adj. faculty Rochester Inst. Tech., 1965-90; assoc. prof. mech. engring. Bridgeport Engring. Inst., 1991-94, Fairfield U., 1994—. Patentee artificial kidney, piezo-electric generator. Pres. Grove Place Neighborhood Assn., Rochester, 1984. Mem. NSPE (life), N.Y. State Soc. Profl. Engrs. Republican. Jewish. Avocations: teaching Sunday sch., music appreciation, theater, travel. Home: 161B Heritage Vlg Southbury CT 06488-1433 E-mail: jcrubinpe@aol.com.

RUBIN, JAMES P. international affairs analyst, public affairs administrator; b. N.Y.C., 1960; BA in Polit. Sci., Columbia U., 1982, M in Internat. Affairs, 1984. Rsch. dir. Arms Control Assn., Washington, 1985-89; profl. staff mem. U.S. Senate Com. on Fgn. Rels.; sr. fgn. policy advisor to Sen. Joseph R. Biden, Jr.; sr. advisor, spokesman for U.S. Rep. to UN, Madeleine K. Albright; dir. fgn. policy, spokesman for Clinton/Gore '96 Campaign; asst. sec., chief spokesman Pub. Affairs Bur., Washington, 1997-2000; pub. spkr., commentator, author, London, 2000—. Cons. on nuclear arms control issues Senate Fgn. Rels. Com., 1985-89. Recipient John Jay award for disting. profl. achievement Columbia Coll., Columbia U., 1998, Disting. Svc. award Sec. State, 2000. Office: 43 Brunswick Gardens London W8 4AW England E-mail: jamesprubin@aol.com.

RUBIN, JEAN ESTELLE, mathematics educator; b. Bklyn., Oct. 29, 1926; d. Leonard Lewis and Phyllis Irma (Mann) Hirsh; m. Herman Rubin, Mar. 23, 1952; children: Arthur Leonard, Leonore Anne Rubin Findsen. BS, Queens Coll., 1948; MA, Columbia U., 1949; PhD, Stanford U., 1955. Instr. Queens Coll., 1949-51, Stanford U., 1953-55; lectr. U. Oreg., 1955-59; asst. prof. Mich. State U., 1960-67; asso. prof. math. Purdue U., West Lafayette, Ind., 1968-75, prof., 1975—. Author: Set Theory for the Mathematician, 1967, Mathematical Logic: Applications and Theory, 1990; co-author: (with H. Rubin) Equivalents of the Axiom of Choice, 1963, Equivalents of the Axiom of Choice II, 1985, (with P. Howard) Consequences of the Axiom of Choice, 1998. Vol. West Lafayette Libr., 1981—; bd. dirs. Lafayette Symphony Orch., Inc., 1987-93, Friends of West Lafayette Libr., 1993—. Mem. Am. Math. Soc., Assn. Symbolic Logic, Math. Assn. Am. (vis. lectr. 1976-86), Purdue Staff Aero Club Inc. (bd. dirs. 1975-90). Home: 1214 W Sunset Ln West Lafayette IN 47906-2429 Office: Purdue U Math Dept West Lafayette IN 47907-1395

RUBIN, JEFFREY MARK, lawyer, insurance company executive; b. N.Y.C., Apr. 26, 1956; s. Irwin S. and Tamara (Benenson) R.; m. Susan L. Rubin, Aug. 4, 1990; children: Leigh, Kate. BA in Polit. Sci., SUNY, Oneonta, 1978; JD, Cornell U., 1981. Bar: Ill. 1981. Assoc. Abramson & Fox, Chgo., 1981-84; from assoc. to ptnr. Phelan, Pope & John, Ltd., 1984-96; of counsel Lovell White Durrant, 1996-97; sr. v.p., gen. counsel, bd. dirs. Internat. Ins. Co., 1997-99, v.p., dir. claims litigation, 1999-2001; v.p. reins. work-out, 2001—. Mem. ABA (chair tort and ins. sect. corporate counsel com. 1995-96), Chgo. Bar Assn. (chair jud. evaluation com. 1995-96, bd. mgrs. 1997-99), Law Club of Chgo., Abraham Marovitz Inn of Ct. Office: Internat Ins Co 250 Commercial St Ste 5000 Manchester NH 03101-1143 E-mail: JeffRubinNH@attbi.com., Jeff_Rubin@trg.com.

RUBIN, JOEL EDWARD, consulting company executive; b. Cleve., Sept. 5, 1928; s. Morris and Pearl (Jacobs) R.; m. Lucille Schutmaat, Dec. 18, 1953; children: Brian G., Jennifer L., Rebecca R. BS, Case Inst. of Tech., 1949; MFA, Yale U., 1951; PhD, Stanford U., 1960. Exec. v.p. Kliegl Bros. Lighting, N.Y.C., 1954-85; prin. cons. Joel E. Rubin & Assocs., 1985-93; sr. adv. theater planning, v.p. Artec Cons. Inc., 1993—. Sr. advisor theater planning. Co-author: Theatrical Lighting Practice 1954; author: Technological Development of Stage Lighting 1960. Member Coll. of Fellows of Am. Theatre, John F. Kennedy Ctr. for the Performing Arts, Washington. Recipient Golden Triaga, Prague Quadrennial, 1987, Zlatou medal, 1991, 1st time award Bus. Com. for the Arts, Forbes Mag., 1987, Founders' award U.S. Inst. for Theatre Tech., 1972, 79, U.S. Inst. Tech. Nat. award, 1990, U.S. Inst. for Theatre Tech. lifetime hon. membership award, 1996, Spl. citation, 1996; Dr. Joel E. Rubin Founder's award named in his honor U.S. Inst. Theatre Tchrs., 2000, Internat. Student Rsch. Grants established in his honor U.S. Inst. Theatre Tchrs., 2000. Fellow Am. Theatre Assn. (v.p. 1961-63), U.S. Inst. of Theatre Technology (pres. 1963-64); mem. Am. Nat. Theatre Acad. (bd. dirs. 1971-75), Internat. Theatre Inst. of the U.S. (bd. dirs. 1975-79), Nat. Coun. of Arts and Govt. (bd. dirs. 1975-79), Internat. Orgn. Theatre Architects and Scenographers (U.S. chmn., rep. 1968-98, pres. 1971-79, Gold medal award 1996), Illuminating Engring. Soc. Avocations: collecting books, stage design, Lincolniana. Home: 24 Edgewood Ave Hastings On Hudson NY 10706-2024 Office: Artec Cons 114 W 26th St New York NY 10001-6812

RUBIN, KAREN BETH, publishing, marketing executive; b. N.Y.C., Aug. 30, 1951; d. Samuel M. and Eleanor (Spiegel) Rubin; m. Neil Leiberman, Dec. 29, 1983; children: David, Eric. BA magna cum laude, SUNY, Binghamton, 1972. Sr. editor Travel Agt. mag., N.Y.C., 1973-86, Tour & Travel News, Manhasset, N.Y., 1986-89; pres. Workstyles, Inc., Great Neck, 1989—; founder, pub., editor Making It! Careers Newsmag., 1981—, Family Travel Letter, Great Neck, 1995—; editor, pub. Travel Features Syndicate, 1995—; editor Great Neck News, 1995—. Adj. prof. NYU, 1992-98. Author: Flying High in Travel, 1986, 92, Inside Secrets to Finding a Career in Travel, 2001. Recipient Neal Cert. of Merit, Am. Bus. Press, 1984. Avocations: travel, photography, tennis, running, biking. Office: Workstyles Inc 5 Rose Ave Great Neck NY 11021-1530

RUBIN, KENNETH ALLEN, lawyer; b. Rockville Centre, N.Y., Nov. 24, 1947; s. Albert Alton and Marion (Osterweis) R.; m. Susan Kurman, Sept. 14, 1980; children: Jennifer, Kelly. BS, Cornell U., 1969, MS, 1971, JD, 1973. Bar: D.C. 1974, N.Y. 1974, U.S. Ct. Appeals (D.C. crct.) 1974, U.S. Ct. Appeals (5th crct. 1975, U.S. Ct. Appeals (4th, 9th and 10th crct.) 1976, U.S. Ct. Appeals (3d, 8th and 11th crcts.) 1986, U.S. Supreme Ct. 1992. Trial atty. Dept. Justice, Washington, 1973-74; sr. ptnr. Morgan, Lewis & Bockius LLP, 1974—. Mem. pol. USDA Grad. Sch., Washington, 1977-85, U. Ala., Huntsville, 1978-91, Antioch U., Washington, 1978; lectr. Cornell U., Ithaca, N.Y., 1979—. Author: What the Business Executive Needs To Know about U.S. Environmental Laws and Liabilities, 1991, (manual) A Tidal Wave of Lawsuits and Regulations Flood the Once-Placid Waters of Drinking Water Utilities, 2000. Mem. adv. com. Cornell Ctr. for Environment. Mem. ABA, Am. Water Works Assn., Swiss Club Washington, Cornell Club Washington. Office: Morgan Lewis & Bockius 1800 M St NW Washington DC 20036-5802 E-mail: karwaterlawyer@aol.com.

RUBIN, LAWRENCE GILBERT, physicist, laboratory manager; b. Bklyn., Sept. 17, 1925; s. Harry E. and Ruth (Feirberg) R.; m. Florence Ruth Kagan, Feb. 11, 1951; children: Michael G., Richard D., Jeffrey N. Student, Cooper Union, N.Y.C., 1943, 46-47; BS in Physics, U. Chgo., 1949; MA in Physics, Columbia U., 1950. Staff mem., physicist research div. Raytheon Co., Waltham, Mass., 1950-64; group leader Nat. Magnet Lab., MIT, Cambridge, 1964-78, divsn. head high magnetic field facility, 1978-93; advisor to high magnetic field facility, 1994-95; vis. scientist MIT, 1996—. Mem. NAS adv. panel Nat. Bur. Standards, 1976-82, 85-90; bd. dirs. Lake Shore Cryotronics, Inc., Columbus, Ohio; gen. chmn. 6th Internat. Temperature Symposium, Washington, 1982, 7th Internat. Temperature Symposium, Toronto, Ont., Can., 1992, 8th Internat. Temperature Symposium, Chgo.; chmn. adv. com. Physics Today Buyers' Guide; contbg. editor Physics Today; organizer Am. Physical Soc. Tutorial program. Mem. editorial bd. Rev. Sci. Instruments, 1968-70, 79-81; contbr. articles to physics jours. With U.S. Army, 1943-46, ETO. Fellow IEEE (life), Am. Phys. Soc. (organizer and 1st chmn. instrument and measurement sci. group 1985); mem. Instrument Soc. Am. (sr.), Am. Vacuum Soc. Jewish. Home: 1504 Centre St Newton Center MA 02459-2447 Office: MIT Bldg NW14 1209 170 Albany St Cambridge MA 02139-4208 E-mail: lrubin@mit.edu.

RUBIN, LEONARD SIDNEY, physiologist, educator, researcher; b. New York, Ny, Aug. 27, 1922; s. Hyman Hersh and Toba Rubin; m. Blanche Rubin, Mar. 30, 1950; children: Beth S., Joshua T., Matthew M. BS Chemistry, CUNY, New York, NY, 1943; PhD Neuroscience, NY Univ., New York, NY, 1950. Instr. NY Univ., New York, NY, 1943—44, rsch. assoc., 1950—53; chief psychophysiology br. Med. Labs, Army Chem. Corps., Edgewood, 1953—57; assoc. prof. Univ. Pa. Sch. of Medicine, Philadelphia, 1960—81; rsch. cons. Childrens Hosp. of Phila., 1960—65; prof. Temple Univ. Med. Coll., 1970—75; rsch. cons. St. Christopher's Hosp. for Children, 1964—67; cons., behavioral toxicology FDA, 1976—81; prof. Phila. Coll. of Med., Philadelphia, 1982—92; cons., biostatistics Cellcor Corp., Boston, 1988—92; prof., physiology/pharmacology Phila. Coll. of Osteo. Med., Philadelphia, 1981—. Armed forces nrc com. on vision, Washington, 1956—57; armed forces nrc com. on bioacoustics, Washington, 1956—57. Editl. cons. Jour. Studies on Alcohol, Jour. Nervous and Mental Disease, Psychophysiology, Psychopharmacologia, Am. Jour. Psychiatry. Gen. US Army, 1944—46. Recipient Social Sci. Rsch. Award, Inst. of Math., Stanford, CT, 1955, A.E. Bennet Award, Soc. of Biol. Psychiatry, 1961; scholar Fgn. Exch. Scholar, NAS, Yugoslavia, 1974. Fellow: Am. Psychol. Soc., Soc. of Biol. Psychiatry, Am. Psychol. Assn.; mem.: Soc. for Psychophysiological Rsch., Acad. of Psychosomatic Medicine, Sigma Xi. Jewish. Achievements include Author, In Numerous Research Journals, 1952-1996. Avocation: studying philosophy, art, and music. Home: 706 Powder Mill Lane Wynnewood PA 19096-4035

RUBIN, LORRY GLEN, physician; b. Chgo., Aug. 30, 1953; s. Harry and Beverly (Ivener) R.; m. Leonie Rice, June 27, 1976; children: Marcie, Craig, Lindsay. BA, Northwestern U., Evanston, Ill., 1974; MD, Rush Med. Coll., Chgo., 1978; Fellow in Pediat. Infectious Diseases, Johns Hopkins U., 1982. Diplomate Nat. Bd. Med. Examiners, Am. Bd. Pediatrics, Am. Bd. Pediat. Infectious Diseases. Instr. dept. pediatrics Johns Hopkins Hosp., Balt., 1982-83; asst. prof. pediatrics SUNY, Stony Brook, 1983-89; chief Divns. of Pediat. Infectious Disease Schneider Children's Hosp. - L.I. Jewish Med. Ctr., New Hyde Park, N.Y., 1983—; asst. prof. pediatrics Albert Einstein Coll. of Medicine, Bronx, 1989-90, assoc. prof. pediatrics, 1990-95, prof. pediatrics, 1995—; dir. pediatric infectious diseases North Shore-L.I. Jewish Healt System, 2001—. Mem. editl. bd. Jour. of Clin. Microbiology, Washington, 1988—; reviewer jours. in fields; contbr. articles to profl. jours., chpts. to books in field; author abstracts in field. Fellow IDSA; mem. Am. Acad. Pediatrics, L.I. Infectious Disease Soc. (pres. 1988-90), Nassau County Pediatric Soc. (exec. bd. 1992-94), Am. Soc. for Microbiology, Alpha Omega Alpha, Phi Beta Kappa. Democrat. Jewish. Avocation: tennis. Office: Schneider Childrens Hosp 26901 76th Ave New Hyde Park NY 11040-1434 E-mail: lrubin@lij.edu.

RUBIN, MARK RICHARD, French language educator; b. N.Y.C., Mar. 14, 1944; s. Barnet and Rose (Lazar) R. AB, Rutgers U., 1966; AM, Princeton (N.J.) U., 1968, PhD, 1978. Instr. French, Kent (Ohio) State U., 1972-79, asst. prof., 1979-88, assoc. prof., 1988—, assoc. dir. Lemnitzer Ctr. NATO and European Union Studies, dir. Ctr. for Internat. and Comparative Programs. Co-editor: Europe's Neutral and Nonaligned States: Between NATO and the Warsaw Pact, 1989, Dien Bien Phu and Crisis of Franco-American Relations, 1990, NATO After Forty Years, 1990, NATO after 50 Years, 2001; author, translator chpts. in books. Capt. U.S. Army, 1970-72. Rutgers U. scholar, 1965-66; Soc. des Prof. Francais grantee, 1969. Mem. Am. Soc. for 18th Century Studies, Am. Assn. Tchrs. of French, Soc. Retif de la Bretonne, Societe francaise d'etude du XVIIIeme siecle, Societe des professeurs francais et francophones en Amerique. Avocations: travel, music. Office: Kent State U PO Box 5190 Ctr Internat Programs Kent OH 44242-0001 E-mail: mrubin@kent.edu.

RUBIN, MARK JONATHAN, anesthesiologist; b. N.Y.C., Nov. 16, 1965; s. Harold Joseph and Toby Lee Rubin. BA, Tulane U., 1987; MD, U. South Fla., 1991. Intern Allegheny Gen. Hosp., Pitts., 1991-92; resident Mt. Sinai Med. Ctr., N.Y.C., 1992-95; attending physician Boston U. Med. Ctr., 1995-96, Wayne Gen. Hosp., Waynesboro, Miss., 1996—. Pres. Sun-Lite, Inc.-Wellness Ctr., Waynesboro, 1997—. Dep. sheriff Wayne County (Miss.) Sheriff's Office, 1996—. Home: PO Box 1049 Waynesboro MS 39367-1049

RUBIN, MARK STEPHEN, ophthalmic surgeon; b. Syracuse, N.Y., Dec. 22, 1946; s. Max Leon and Ruth (Dworski) R.; m. Patrizia Silvestri, May 1, 1994; 1 child, Jonathan C. BA, SUNY, Buffalo, 1968; MD summa cum laude, U. Bologna, Italy, 1974. Diplomate Am. Bd. Ophthalmology, cert. authorized aviation med. examiner FAA, U.K., Cayman Is. Civil Aviation Authority. Intern Deaconess Hosp., Buffalo, 1976; resident in ophthalmology Wettlauffer Eye Clinic, 1979; chief ophthalmology Augsburg (Fed. Republic Germany) Army Hosp., 1979-80; pvt. practice Modena, Italy, 1980-88; head dept. ophthalmology Fla. Health Care Plan, Daytona Beach, 1988-90; pvt. practice Daytona and Ormond Beach, Fla., 1990—; asst. prof. U. South Fla., Tampa, 1997—. Cons. USAF, Aviano Air Base, Italy, 1982-88; cons. surgeon Hesperia Hosp., Modena, 1980-88. Author: (with others) Extracapsular Cataract Surgery, 1988; translator: Lasers and Microsurgery, 1986, Ophthalmic Lasers, 1986. Pres., bd. dirs. Ctr. for Visually Impaired, Daytona Beach; cons. Volusia County Health Dept. Fellow Am. Coll. Internat. Physicians, ACS; mem. Italian Order Physicians and Surgeons, Internat. Assn. Ocular Surgeons, Am. Acad. Ophthalmology, Am. Soc. Cataract and Refractive Surgery, Fla. Med. Soc., European Soc. Refractive Surgery, Italian Ophthalmologic Soc., Italian Soc. Profl. Ophthalmologists, Volusia County Med. Soc., Internat. Eye Assn. (pres.), Ctrl. Fla. Soc. Ophthalmology, Volusia County Reef Rsch. Dive Team, Cayman Islands Med. Soc. Jewish. Avocations: research scuba diving, ultralight and fixed wing piloting, horseback riding, cooking, enology. Home: 891 N Beach St Ormond Beach FL 32174-4002 Office: 550 Memorial Cir Ste N Ormond Beach FL 32174-5055 also: Cayman Med and Surg Ctr PO Box 11728-APO Georgetown FL 32118-4016 also: 7 Old Kings Rd N Palm Coast FL 32137-8248

RUBIN, MARTIN N. meeting planner, consultant; b. N.Y.C., Aug. 9, 1928; s. Max and Esther (Chernow) R.; m. Shirley Anne Rubin, Aug. 22, 1954 (div. Aug. 1964); m. Karen Anne O'Brien, Sept. 21, 1981. AB, U. Mich.; AM, Miami U., Oxford, Ohio; PhD., Sussex U., Eng. Lic. psychologist. With Dayton (Ohio) Sch. System, 1951-60, West Alexandria (Ohio) Sch. System, 1961-63; instr. Wright State U., Dayton, 1961-63; with Devereux Found., Pa., N.Y. Dept. Corrections, Bklyn., 1971-73, Council for Retarded Children, Albany, N.Y., 1973-75; prin. M. Rubin & Co., Inc., Mount Vernon, 1975—. Author: Developmentally Disabled, 1965. Candidate Dem. State Legis., 1982; adv. bd. Mt. Vernon Mental Health Bd., 1985. Master's degree scholar Miami U., 1958; Guidance Inst. grantee Miami U., 1959. Fellow Am. Assn. Mental Deficiency (pres. 1967); mem. Soc. Assn. Execs. (bd. dirs. 1985—). Lodges: Masons (sr. warden 1983). Avocations: dancing, singing.

RUBIN, MELVIN LYNNE, ophthalmologist, educator; b. San Francisco, May 10, 1932; s. Morris and May (Gelman) R.; m. Lorna Isen, June 21, 1953; children: Gabrielle, Daniel, Michael. AA, U. Calif., Berkeley, 1951, BS, 1953; MD, U. Calif., San Francisco, 1957; MS, State U. Iowa, 1961. Diplomate Am. Bd. Ophthalmology (bd. dirs. 1977-83, chmn. 1984). Intern U. Calif. Hosp., San Francisco, 1957-58; resident in ophthalmology State U. Iowa, 1958-61; attending surgeon Georgetown U., Washington, 1961-63; asst. prof. surgery U. Fla. Med. Sch., Gainesville, 1963-66, assoc. prof. ophthalmology, 1966-67, prof. ophthalmology, 1967—, chmn. dept. ophthalmology, 1978-95, eminent scholar, 1989-97, eminent scholar emeritus, 1997. Author: Studies in Physiological Optics, 1965, Fundamentals of Visual Science, 1969, Optics for Clinicians, 1971, 2d edit., 1974, 25th ann. edit., 1995, The Fine Art of Prescribing Glasses, 1978, 2d edit., 1991; editor: Dictionary of Eye Terminology, 1984, 4th edit., 2001, Eye Care Notes, 1989, revised edit., 2001; cons. editl. bd. Survey Ophthalmology; contbr. more than 100 articles to profl. jours. Co-founder Gainesville Assn. Creative Arts, Citizens for Pub. Schs., Inc., ProArteMusica Gainesville, Inc., 1969, pres., 1971-73; mem. Thomas Ctr. Adv. Bd. for the Arts, 1978-84, nat. sci. adv. bd. Helen Keller Eye Rsch. Found., 1989-96; bd. dirs. Hippodrome State Theater, 1981-87; Friends of Photography Ansel Adams Ctr., 1991-97; trustee U. Fla. Performing Arts Ctr., 1995—. With USPHS, 1961-63. Recipient Best Med. Book for 1978 award Am. Med. Writers Assn., 1979, Shaler Richardson award for svc. to medicine Fla. Soc. Ophthalmology, 1995; M.L. Rubin Ann. Lectureship established in his honor by Fla. Soc. of Ophthalmology, 1993. Fellow ACS, Am. Acad. Ophthalmology (sec., dir. 1978-92, pres. 1988, Sr. Honor award 1987, Guest of Honor 1992), Found. Am. Acad. Ophthalmology (bd. trustees, 1988-95, chmn., 1992-94), Joint Commn. on Allied Health Pers. in Ophthalmology (Statesman of Yr. award 1987); mem. Assn. Rsch. in Vision and Ophthalmology (trustee 1973-78, pres. 1979), Retina Soc., Macula Soc., Club Jules Gonin, N.Y. Acad. Sci., Fla. Soc. Ophthalmology, Am. Ophthal. Soc. (coun. 1998-2002), Pan Am. Soc. Ophthalmology, Ophthalmic Photographers Soc., Alachua County Med. Soc., Fla. Med. Assn., AMA (editorial bd. Archives of Ophthalmology 1975-85), Sigma Xi, Alpha Omega Alpha., Phi Kappa Phi. Office: U Fla Med Ctr PO Box 100284 Gainesville FL 32610-0284 E-mail: mrubin@eye1.eye.ufl.edu.

RUBIN, MICHAEL, lawyer; b. Boston, July 19, 1952; m. Andrea L. Peterson, May 29, 1983; children: Peter, Eric, Emily. AB, Brandeis U., 1973; JD, Georgetown U., 1977. Bar: Calif. 1978, U.S. Dist. Ct. (no. dist.) Calif. 1978, U.S. Ct. Appeals (9th cir.) 1978, U.S. Ct. Appeals (5th, 7th, 10th cirs.) 1982, U.S. Supreme Ct. 1984, U.S. Ct. Appeals (D.C. cir.) 1984, U.S. Ct. Appeals (11th cir.) 1987. Teaching fellow Law Sch. Stanford (Calif.) U., 1977-78; law clerk to Hon. Charles B. Renfrew U.S. Dist. Ct. (no. dist.) Calif., San Francisco, 1978-79; law clerk to Hon. James R. Browning U.S. Ct. Appeals (9th cir.), 1979-80; law clerk to Hon. William J. Brennan, Jr. U.S. Supreme Ct., Washington, 1980-81; assoc. Altshuler & Berzon, San Francisco, 1981-85, ptnr., 1985-89, Altshuler, Berzon, Nussbaum, Berzon & Rubin, San Francisco, 1989-2000, Altshuler, Berzon, Nussbaum, Rubin & Demain, San Francisco, 2000—. Office: Altshuler Berzon Nussbaum Rubin & Demain 177 Post St Ste 300 San Francisco CA 94108-4700 E-mail: mrubin@altshulerberzon.com.

RUBIN, MICHELE S. radiologist; b. Bklyn., Aug. 7, 1962; d. Philip L. and Charlotte (Susskind) R.; m. Floyd Martin, May 26, 1996; 1 child, Shane Perry. BA summa cum laude, NYU, 1983, MD, 1987. Diplomate in radiology and in neuroradiology Am. Bd. Radiology. Resident in pathology North Shore Univ. Hosp., Manhasset, N.Y., 1987-88; resident in radiology Nassau County Med. Ctr., East Meadow, 1988-92; fellow in neuroradiology Montefiore Med. Ctr., Bronx, 1992-94; neuroradiologist, asst. prof. radiology Jacobi Med. Ctr., 1994-97; owner, med. dir. Broadway Open MRI, Amityville, N.Y., 1997—. Mem. AMA, Am. Soc. Neuroradiology, Am. Soc. Spine Radiology, Radiol. Soc. N.Am., Am. Roentgen Ray Soc., Phi Beta Kappa. Office: Broadway Open MRI 355 Broadway Ste 3 Amityville NY 11701-2715

RUBIN, PAUL HAROLD, economist; b. Boston, Aug. 9, 1942; s. Joseph and Freda (Goldhagen) R.; m. Marcia Ann Claybon, June 15, 1964 (dec. Feb. 1973); children: Joseph Saul, Rachel Beth; m. Mariam Hope Moss, July 26, 1985. BA, U. Cin., 1963; PhD in Econs., Purdue U., 1970. Prof. econs. U. Ga., Athens, 1968-82; sr. staff economist Pres. Coun. Economic Advisers, Washington, 1981-82; prof. econs. Baruch Coll. and the Grad. Ctr., N.Y.C., 1982-83; head, consumer protection Bur. Econs., FTC, Washington, 1983-85; chief economist Consumer Product Safety Commn., 1985-87; v.p. Glassman-Oliver Economic Cons., Inc., Washington, 1987-91; prof. econs. Emory U., Atlanta, 1991—, prof. econs. and law, 1999—. Adj. prof. George Washington U. Law Ctr., Washington, 1985-89. Author: Congressmen, Constituents and Contributors, 1982, Business Firms and the Common Law, 1983, Managing Business Transactions, 1990, Tort Reform by Contract, 1993; editor-in-chief Managerial and Decision Economics; contbr. articles to profl. jours. Mem. Am. Econ. Assn., So. Econ. Assn. (v.p. 1994-96), Am. Law and Econs. Assn., Pub. Choice Soc. Republican. Office: Emory U Dept Econs Atlanta GA 30322-0001

RUBIN, RICHARD ALLAN, lawyer; b. N.Y.C., June 19, 1942; s. Louis Max and Ruth Ann (Goldman) R.; m. Susan Deborah Levitt, June 18, 1966; children: Karen, Jill. BS, Queens Coll., 1964; JD, Bklyn. Law Sch., 1967; LLM, NYU, 1968. Bar: N.Y. 1967. Assoc. Schwartz and Frank, N.Y.C., 1968-69, Javits and Javits, N.Y.C., 1969-71; ptnr. Wolf Haldenstein Adler Freeman Herz & Frank, 1972-76, Parker Chapin LLP, N.Y.C., 1977-2000, Jenkens & Gilchrist, Parker Chapin LLP, N.Y.C., 2001—. Lectr. Am. Mgmt. Assn., N.Y. Bar Assn. Mem. ABA. Office: Jenkens & Gilchrist Parker Chapin LLP Chrysler Bldg 405 Lexington Ave New York NY 10174-0002

RUBIN, ROBERT SAMUEL, investment banker; b. Boston, Sept. 22, 1931; s. Jesse Abraham and Rose (Solomon) R.; m. Martha Lucy Adams, Dec. 15, 1956; children: Rebecca, David, James, Nathaniel. BA, Yale U., 1953; MBA, Harvard Coll., 1955. With Lehman Bros., 1958-70, ptnr., 1967-70; mng. dir., bd. dirs. Lehman Bros. Kuhn Loeb, Inc., N.Y.C., 1970-84; mng. dir. Salomon Smith Barney, Inc., 1989—2001; sr. v.p. Bank One, 2002—. Trustee Bklyn. Hosp.; chmn. Bklyn. Mus.; bd. dirs. St. Ann's Sch. 2nd lt. AUS, 1955-58. Home: 218 Columbia Hts Brooklyn NY 11201-2105 Office: Bank One 320 Park Ave New York NY 10022

RUBIN, ROBERT E. former secretary of treasury; b. N.Y.C., Aug. 29, 1938; s. Alexander and Sylvia (Seiderman) R.; m. Judith Leah Oxenberg, Mar. 27, 1963; children: James Samuel, Philip Matthew. AB summa cum laude, Harvard U., 1960; postgrad., London Sch. Econs., 1960-61; LLB, Yale U., 1964; DHL (hon.), Yeshiva U., 1996. Bar: N.Y. 1965. Assoc. Cleary, Gottlieb, Steen & Hamilton, N.Y.C., 1964-66, Goldman Sachs & Co., N.Y.C., 1966-70, ptnr., 1971, mem. mgmt. com., 1980, vice chmn., co-chief oper. officer, 1987-90, co-sr. ptnr., co-chmn., 1990-92; asst. to Pres. for econ. policy, head nat. econ. coun. Exec. Office of Pres., The White House, Washington, 1993-95; sec. U.S. Dept. of the Treasury, 1995-99; chmn. exec. com. Citigroup, 1999—. Mem. Pres.'s Adv. Com. for Trade Negotiations, Washington, 1980-82, mem. adv. com. on tender offers SEC, Washington, 1983, Gov.'s Commn. on Trade Competitiveness, 1987, regulatory adv. com. N.Y. Stock Exch., 1988-90, adv. com. internat. capital markets Fed. Res. Bank N.Y., 1989-93, Securities and Exch. Commn. Market Oversight and Fin. Svcs. Adv. Com., 1991-93, Gov.'s Adv. Panel on Fin. Svcs., 1988-89; ptnr., bd. dirs. N.Y.C. Partnership Inc., 1991-93; bd. dirs. Ctr. for Nat. Policy, 1982-93, vice chmn., 1984; bd. dirs. N.Y. Futures Exch., N.Y.C., 1979-85, Chgo. Bd. Options Exch. Inc., 1972-76; trustee Mt. Sinai Hosp., 1977, vice chmn., 1986; trustee Sta. WNET-TV, 1985-93; mem., trustee Carnegie Corp. of N.Y., 1990-93; mem. Mayor's Coun. Econ. Advisors, 1990, Gov.'s Coun. on Fiscal and Econ. Priorities, 1990-92. Trustee Am. Ballet Theatre Found., Inc., N.Y.C., 1969-93, trustee Collegiate Sch., 1978-84; mem. bd. overseers' com. to visit econs. dept. Harvard U., 1981-87, com. on univ. resources, 1987-92; mem. fin. com. N.Y. campaign Mondale for Pres., 1983-84; mem. investment adv. coun. N.Y.C. Pension Fund, 1980-89; chmn. Dem. Congl. Dinner, Washington, 1982; Dems. for the 80s, 1985-89, Dems. for the 90s, 1989-90; chmn. N.Y.C. host com. 1992 Dem. Conv., 1989-92; mem. Commn. Nat. Elections. Recipient award Nat. Assn. Christians and Jews, N.Y.C., 1977, Disting. Leadership in Govt. award Columbia Bus. Sch., 1996, Euromoney Mag. award Fin. Min. Yr., 1996, Medal for High Civic Svc. award Citizens' Budget Com., 1997, Fgn. Policy Assn. medal, 1998, "Chmn." award Washington Greater Boys/Girls Clubs, 1998, Intrepid Sea Air Space Mus. award, 1998, Jefferson award Am. Inst. Pub. Svc., 1998, Award of Merit Yale U., 1998, Global Leadership award UN Assn., 1998, Paul Tsongas award, 1998. Mem. Phi Beta Kappa, Harvard Club (N.Y.C.), Century Country Club (Purchase, N.Y.). Jewish.

RUBIN, ROBERT JAY, toxicologist; b. Boston, Mar. 25, 1932; s. Edward and Ruth (Lichter) R.; m. Frances Stone, Sept. 5, 1954 (dec. Nov. 1981); children: Ellen Joyce, Howard Scott, Steven Glen; m. Idalea Kofsky, Aug. 28, 1983; stepchildren: David Wolfe, Jennifer Sirota, Aaron Wolfe. BA, U. Mass., 1953; MS, Boston U., 1955, PhD, 1960. Diplomate Am. Bd. Toxicology. Postdoctoral fellow Yale U. Sch. of Medicine, New Haven, 1960-64; asst. prof. pharmacology Kans. U. Med. Ctr., Kansas City, 1964; asst. prof. toxicology Johns Hopkins Sch. of Pub. Health, Balt., 1964-67, assoc. prof. toxicology, 1967-73, prof. toxicology, 1973-98, prof. emeritus, 1998—. Cons. in toxicology, 1978—; adv. bd. Johns Hopkins Sch. of Pub. Health, Balt., 1985-86. Contbr. articles to profl. jours. including Toxicology and Applied Pharmacology, Jour. Toxicology and Environ. Health, Environ. Health Perspectives, many others. Pres. Stevenswood Community Assn., Balt., 1970-71; treas. Canton Square Community Assn., Balt., 1993-94. Postdoctoral fellowship NIH, Yale U., 1960-64, Career Devel. award NIH, Johns Hopkins U., 1969-74. Mem. Soc. of Toxicology (pres. Nat. Capital Area chpt. 1994-95, pres. risk assessment specialty sect. 1999-2000), Am. Soc. Pharmacology and Exptl. Therapeutics, Delta Omega (chmn. membership com. 1990-92). Avocation: travel to foreign countries. Home: 1201 S Linwood Ave Baltimore MD 21224-4869 Office: Johns Hopkins Sch Hygiene and Pub Health 615 N Wolfe St Baltimore MD 21205-2103 E-mail: rrubin@jhsph.edu.

RUBIN, ROBERT JOSEPH, physician, health care consultant; b. Bklyn., Feb. 7, 1946; s. B. Norman and Suzanne (Fried) R.; m. Fran Auerbach, June 14, 1970; children: Elyse Beth, David Jon. AB, Williams Coll., 1966; MD, Cornell U., 1970. Diplomate Am. Bd. Internal Medicine. Intern New England Med. Ctr. Hosps., Boston, 1970-71, resident, 1971-72, 74-76; epidemic intelligence officer, respiratory disease and spl. pathogens, divsn. viral diseases Ctr. for Disease Control, 1972-74; asst. dean govt. affairs Tufts U., 1979-84, assoc. prof. medicine, 1981-84. Chief renal divsn. Lemuel Shattuck Hosp., Boston, 1979-81; asst. sec. planning and evaluation U.S. HHS, Washington, 1981-84; clin. assoc. prof. Georgetown U., Washington, 1984-95, clin. prof., 1995—; exec. v.p. ICF, Inc., 1984-88; pres. Health and Scis. Internat., 1988-92, Lewin ICF Inc., 1992, Lewin-VHI, Inc., 1992-96, Lewin Group, 1996-99, CEO, 1999-2001. Contbr. articles to profl. jours. With USPHS, 1972-74, asst. surgeon gen., 1981-84. Robert Wood Johnson Health Policy fellow, 1977 Mem. ACP, AMA, Am. Soc. Nephrology, Internat. Soc. Nephrology, Mass. Med. Soc., Kenwood Club, Potomac Club, Williams Club, Phi Beta Kappa. Republican. Jewish.

RUBIN, ROBERT SAMUEL, lawyer; b. Cin., Apr. 25, 1954; s. Carl B. and Gloria W. R.; m. Virginia K. Carson, May 14, 1983; children: John C., Claire W., Elizabeth K. LLB, U. Wales, Aberystwyth, Eng., 1976; JD, U. Cin., 1979. Bar: Ohio 1979, U.S. Dist. Ct. (so. dist.) Ohio 1979. Assoc. Brown, Cummins & Brown, Cin., 1979-82, Porter, Wright, Morris & Arthur, Cin., 1982-88, partner, 1988-92; ptnr. Cohen Todd Kite & Stanford, 1992—. Mem. arbitration rules com. U.S. Dist. Ct. (so. dist.) Ohio 1984, fed. mediation panel, 1990—; lectr. Nat. Bus. Inst., 1994, 99; mem. oversight adv. bd. Lunken Airport, 2000—, chmn. bd. dirs., 2001—. Author: Fundamentals of Commercial Lending Law. Mem. cmty. initiatives com., cert. com. United Way and Cmty. Chest, 1995—. Mem. Ohio Bar Assn. (banking law com. documentation chmn.), Cin. Bar Assn., U. Cin. Coll. Law Alumni Assn. (trustee 1988-90), Univ. Club. Home: 3693 Kroger Ave Cincinnati OH 45226-1931 Office: Cohen Todd Kite & Stanford 1200 Chiquita Ctr 250 East 5th St Cincinnati OH 45202-3176

RUBIN, ROBERT TERRY, physician, researcher, educator; b. Los Angeles, Aug. 26, 1936; s. Joseph Salem and Lorraine Grace (Baum) R.; m. Lynne Esther Mathews, Mar. 10, 1962 (div. Dec. 1980); children: Deborah, Sharon, Rachel; m. Ada Joan Mickas, Jan. 18, 1985. AB, UCLA, 1958; MD, U. Calif., San Francisco, 1961; PhD, U. So. Calif., 1977. Diplomate Am. Bd. Psychiatry and Neurology. Intern Phila. Gen. Hosp., 1961-62; resident in psychiatry Sch. Medicine UCLA, 1962-65, asst. prof. psychiatry, 1965-71, prof. psychiatry, 1972; prof. Pa. State U., Hershey, 1972-93; Highmark Blue Cross Blue Shield prof. neuroscis. MCP Hahnemann U. Sch. Medicine, Pitts., 1992—, prof. psychiatry, dir. Ctr. Neurosci. RSch. Allegheny Campus, 1992—. Cons. Naval Health Rsch. Ctr., San Diego, 1969-70; mem. Brain Rsch. Inst. UCLA, 1969—; assoc. dir. Pitts. Tissue Engring. Initiative, 1994—; trustee Kinsey Inst. Sex Rsch., Ind. U., 1986-90. Contbr. articles to profl. jours. With USNR, 1967-69. Recipient Rsch. Sci. Devel. awards NIMH, 1972-77, Rsch. Scientist award, 1982, 87, 93. Fellow AAAS, Am. Psychiat. Assn., Am. Coll. Psychiatrists; mem. World Psychiat. Assn. (sec. sect. biol. psychiatry 1983-88, chmn. sect. biol. psychiatry 1988-93), Internat. Soc. Psychoneuroendocrinology (pres. 1984-87). Avocations: swimming, bagpiping. Office: Allegheny Gen Hosp Ctr Neurosci Rsch 320 E North Ave Pittsburgh PA 15212-4756 E-mail: rubin@wpahs.org.

RUBIN, ROBERTA GAIL, pathologist; b. Bklyn., Apr. 2, 1934; d. Victor and Pearl Berger Rubin; m. Walter D'Ull; children: Leon Jesse, Victoria Roslyn. MD, SUNY, Bklyn., 1958. Pathologist Chilton Meml. Hosp., Pompton Plains, N.J., 1968-98; dir. lab. Livingston (N.J.) Cmyt. Hosp., 1987-88; assoc. pathologist Bronx Lebanon Hosp. Ctr., 1967-68; staff pathologist Maimonides-Coney Island Med. Ctr., Bklyn., 1964-67; dir. MDS Lab., Wayne, N.J., 1973-89. Clin. instr. pathology SUNY, Bklyn., 1964-67, Albert Einstein Sch. Medicine, Bronx, 1967-68. Sec., treas. bd. Morris Area Cmty. Fedn., Whippany, N.J., 1989—. Fellow: Coll. Am. Pathologists; mem.: N.J. Soc. Pathologists (bd. dirs. 1989—2001), Found. Am. Med. Women's Assn. (treas. 2001—), Nat. Coun. Women's Health (pres. 1999—2001), Am. Women's Hosp. Assn. (chmn. 1993—), Am. Med. Women's Assn. (v.p. fin. 1993, Camille Mermod award 1995). Avocations: doll art collector, cosmology, reading. Home: 10 Woodland Ave Glen Ridge NJ 07028

RUBIN, ROSE MOHR, economics educator; b. Montgomery, Ala., Nov. 20, 1939; d. Michael and Bernice (Solomon) Mohr; m. Richard M. Rubin, June 20, 1963; children: Mark, Debra. BS, Wellesley Coll., 1961; MA, Emory U., 1966; PhD, Kans. State U., 1968. Economist OEA, State of Kans., Manhattan, 1969-70; asst. prof. Miss. State U., Starkville, 1970-77; resident in pub. svc. NSF, Fort Worth, 1980-81; asst. prof. econs. U. North Tex., Denton, 1977-84, assoc. prof., 1984-90, prof., 1990-94; chair dept. econs. U. Memphis, 1994-96, prof. econs., 1996—. Faculty fellow Johns Hopkins U., Balt., 1986-87; vis. fellow Brookings Inst., Washington, 1987 Bd. dirs. Vis. Nurses Assn., Ft. Worth, 1987-90, Temple Beth El, Ft. Worth, 1988-91, Plough Towers, Memphis, 1998—. Assoc. Danforth Found., 1981-87; grantee Robert Wood Johnson Found., 1987-88, Andrus Found. grantee Am. Assn. Ret. Persons, 1990-94. Mem. Southwestern Econs. Assn. (treas. 1981-89, v.p. 1989-90, pres.-elect 1990-91, pres. 1991-92), Southwestern Social Sci. Assn. (treas. 1990-93, v.p. 1998—), Assn. for Social Econs. (exec. coun. 1988-90), Midsouth Acad. Econs. and Fin. (exec. bd. 1983-87, v.p. 1991-92), Mo. Valley Econs. Assn. (bd. dirs. 1998—), Omicron Delta Epsilon, Phi Kappa Phi, Phi Chi Theta (hon.), Golden Key (hon.). Office: U Memphis Fogel Coll Bus and Econs Dept Econs Memphis TN 38152-0001

RUBIN, SAMUEL HAROLD, physician, consultant; b. N.Y.C., July 24, 1916; s. Joseph and Esther (Goldfarb) R.; m. Audrey Arndt, Nov. 20, 1943; children: James E., David A. AB, Brown U., 1938; MD, St. Louis U., 1943; MS, U. Chgo., 1957; DSc (hon.), N.Y. Med. Coll., 1997. Diplomate: Am. Bd. Internal Medicine. Intern Jewish Hosp., St. Louis, 1943-44; resident St. Louis U. Group Hosp., 1944-45, St. Mary's Hosp., Kansas City, Mo., 1945-46; practice medicine Asbury Park, N.J., 1948-61; vol. faculty mem. N.Y. Med. Coll., 1948-61, assoc. prof. dept. medicine, 1962-65, prof., 1965—, dir. Inst. Human Values in Med. Ethics, 1984-86; chief med. service N.Y. Med. Coll.-Met. Hosp. Center, 1966-71, assoc. dean, 1971-72, exec. dean, 1972-74, dean, v.p. acad. affairs, 1975, provost, dean, 1977-83, provost, dean emeritus, 1983—, cons., 1983—. Mem. bd. trustees St. Clares' Hosp., N.Y.C., 1985-2000, N.Y. Med. Coll., 1988-94. Contbr. articles to med. jours. With M.C. AUS, 1946-48. NIH program dir. grantee, 1966-71 Fellow A.C.P.; mem. N.Y. Acad. Sci. Home: 425E Heritage Hills Dr Somers NY 10589-1912

RUBIN, SANDRA MENDELSOHN, artist; b. Santa Monica, Calif., Nov. 7, 1947; d. Murry and Freda (Atliss) Mendelsohn; m. Stephen Edward Rubin, Aug. 6, 1966. BA, UCLA, 1976, MFA, 1979. Instr. Art Ctr. Coll. Design, Pasadena, Calif., 1980, UCLA, 1981. One-woman exhbns. include L.A. County Mus. Art, 1985, Fischer Fine Arts, London, 1985, Claude Bernard Gallery, N.Y.C., 1987, L.A. Louver Gallery, L.A., 1992; group exhbns. include L.A. County Mus. Artm 1977, 82, 83, L.A. Mcpl. Art Gallery, 1977, 83, 93, L.A. Contemporary Exhbns., 1978, L.A. Inst. Contemporary Arts, 1978, Newport Harbor Art Mus., Newport Beach, Calif., 1981, Odyssia Gallery, N.Y.C., 1981, Nagoya (Japan) City Mus., 1982, Long Beach (Calif.) Mus. Art, 1982, Brooke Alexander Gallery, N.Y.C., 1982, Laguna Beach (Calif.) Mus. Art, 1982, Jan Baum Gallery, L.A., 1984, San Francisco Mus. Art, 1986, Claude Bernard Gallery, 1986, Struve Gallery, Chgo., 1987, Boise (Idaho) Mus., 1988, Judy Youen's Gallery, London, 1988, Tatistscheff Gallery, Inc., Santa Monica, Calif., 1989, Tortue Gallery, Santa Monica, 1990, Contemporary Arts Forum, Santa Barbara, Calif., 1990, San Diego Mus. Art, 1991, Fresno (Calif.) Met. Mus., 1992, Jack Rutberg Fine Arts, L.A., 1993. Recipient Young Talent Purchase award L.A. County Mus. Art, 1980; Artist's Fellowship grant NEA, 1981, 91. Avocations: gardening, exercise, reading, singing.

RUBIN, SAUL, producer, writer, labor and civil rights organizer; b. N.Y.C., Feb. 8, 1921; m. Gloria Stone, Dec. 8, 1942; children: Jonathan, Susan, Raymond. Grad., Coll. of William and Mary. Exec. v.p. U. Judaism, L.A., 1959; pres. Tantalus Inc., Nat. Comm. Found., 1978-80; media cons. dept. humanities U. So. Calif., L.A.; creator Beyond Sound, deaf prodn. co. Prodr., author more that 1000 TV programs, many documentaries. Capt. USAF, 1941—46, ETO. Decorated Silver Star, Purple Heart, D.F.C., 9 Air Medals, 5 Oak Leaf Clusters and Silver Cluster, Battle Ribbons for European Theatre of War and Anti-Submarine Svc.; recipient over 120 awards, 2 Emmy awards, Ace awardfor pioneering in prodn. of sign lang. news programs, 2001. Office: 3876 Carpenter Ave Studio City CA 91604-3729 E-mail: srubin1@flash.net.

RUBIN, SETH ISAIAH, psychologist; b. Alexandria, LA, Mar. 6, 1945; BA, Northwestern U., 1966, MA, 1968, PhD in Psychology, 1971. Diplomate in psychoanalysis and analytical psychology; cert. profl. qualification in psychology; lic. psychologist, Pa., Calif., Ariz., Mass. Outpatient psychology fellow Hosp. U. Pa., 1978-80; tng. candidate, diploma candidate C.G. Jung Inst., Zurich, 1982-87; instr. dept. psychology Northwestern U., 1969-70; asst. prof. dept. psychology U. Ill. at Chgo. Circle, 1970-72; asst. rsch. prof. dept. psychiatry Med. Coll. Pa., 1974-75; asst. prof. dept. cmty. medicine U. Pa., 1975-76, asst. prof. dept. rsch. medicine, 1976-77, asst. prof. dept. ob-gyn., 1976-83, clin. assoc. dpet. psychiatry, 1987-88, clin. asst. prof./clin. assoc prof. psychology in psychiatry, 1987-92; allied health prof. Phila. Psychiat. Ctr., 1988-92; allied health affiliate, clin. psychologist Calif. Pacific Med. Ctr., 1994—. Adj. prof. Union Grad. Sch., 1989-96, Calif. Sch. Profl. Psychology, Berkeley/Alameda, 1992—; vis. prof. psychology Saybrook Inst., 1994-95; lectr. in field. Contbr. numerous articles to profl. jours. Fellow Am. Coll. Advanced Practice Psychologists, Internat. Coll. Prescribing Psychologists; mem. APA, Internat. Assn. for Analytical Psychology, Am. Soc. Clin. Psychopharmacology, Assn. Grad. Analytical Psychologists of the C.G. Jung Inst., San Francisco Jung Inst., Soc. for Psychotherapy Rsch., othrs. Office: 2019 A Webster St San Francisco CA 94115-2329 E-mail: sirseth@well.com.

RUBIN, STANLEY CREAMER, producer; b. N.Y.C., Oct. 8, 1917; s. Michael Isaac and Anne (Creamer) R.; m. Elizabeth Margaret von Gerkan (actress Kathleen Hughes), July 25, 1954; children: John, Chris, Angela, Michael. Student, UCLA, 1933-37. Writer Universal Studios, Universal City, Calif., 1940-42, Columbia Pictures, Los Angeles, 1946-47; writer, producer NBC-TV, Burbank, Calif., 1948-49; theatrical film producer various studios, 1949-55, Rastar Prodns., Columbia Pictures, 1988-91; TV producer CBS-TV, Los Angeles, 1956-59, Universal Studios, Universal City, 1960-63, 20th Century-Fox, Los Angeles, 1967-71, MGM Studios, Culver City, Calif., 1972-77; pres. TBA Prodns., Los Angeles, 1978—. Producer theatrical films including The Narrow Margin, 1950, My Pal Gus, 1950, Destination Gobi, 1951, River of No Return, 1952, Promise Her Anything, 1966, The President's Analyst, 1967, Revenge, 1989; co-producer White Hunter, Black Heart, 1990; TV prodns. include G.E. Theatre, 1959-63, Ghost and Mrs. Muir, 1968-69, Bracken's World, 1969-71; writer, producer TV film The Diamond Necklace, 1948 (Emmy award 1949); producer TV films including Babe, 1975 (Hollywood Fgn. Press Golden Globe award, Christopher medal), And Your Name is Jonah, 1978 (Christopher medal 1979), The Story of Satchel Paige, 1980 (Image award 1981); exec. producer TV prodn. Escape from Iran: The Canadian Caper, 1981. Producer spl. programming Dem. Nat. Conv., San Francisco, 1984, Columbia Pictures and Rastar Prodns., 1988-91. 1st lt. USAAF, 1942-46. Mem. Writers Guild Am. (dir. 1941-42), Producers Guild Am. (bd. dirs. 1968-74, pres. 1974-79, v.p. 1987-94, bd. dirs. 1994-2000), Acad. Motion Picture Arts and Scis., Acad. TV Arts and Scis. (bd. govs. 1971, 73), Phi Beta Kappa. Home and Office: 8818 Rising Glen Pl Los Angeles CA 90069-1222 *I'm still too young to sum up my life, but here's a thought in progress: Stay curious.*

RUBIN, STANLEY GERALD, aerospace engineering educator; b. Bklyn., May 11, 1938; s. Harry Jack and Cele (Sake) R.; m. Carol Ruth Kalvin, Sept. 29, 1963; children— Stephany, Elizabeth, Barbara B.Ae.E., Poly Inst. Bklyn., 1959; PhD, Cornell U., 1963. Asst. prof. to prof. dept. aerospace engring. Poly. Inst. N.Y., Farmingdale, 1964-79, Assoc. dir. aerodynamic labs., 1977-79; prof. aerospace engring. and engring. mechanics U. Cin., 1979—2000, head dept., 1979-89, dir. NASA Univ. Space Engring. Ctr. on Health Monitoring Space Propulsion Systems, U. Cin., 1988-91, prof. emeritus, 2000—; sci. coun. Inst. for Computer Application in Sci./Engring. NASA Langley Rsch. Ctr., Hampton, Va., 1998—. Cons. Aerospace Corp., NASA AAC/ARTS, Allison (GM), others; mem. adv. com. Inst. for Computational Methods in Propulsion, NASA; keynote spkr. 9th Internat. Conf. Numerical Methods in Fluid Mechanics, Saclay, France Editor-in-chief Internat. Jour. Computers and Fluids, Elsevier Sci. Ltd., 1978—; contbr. articles to profl. jours. and Ann. Rev. Fluid Mechanics, 1992. NSF fellow, 1963-64; grantee Office Naval Research, 1978-88, AFOSR 1968-92, NASA, 1973—96, others Fellow AIAA (assoc.), ASME; mem. Am. Soc. Engring. Edn., Sigma Xi, Sigma Gamma Tau, Tau Beta Pi Home: 10695 Deershadow Ln Cincinnati OH 45242-0070 E-mail: U Cin ML 070 509 Old Chem Hall Cincinnati OH 45221-0070 E-mail: srubin@uceng.uc.edu.

RUBIN, STEPHEN CURTIS, gynecologic oncologist, educator; b. Phila., May 24, 1951; s. Alan and Helen (Metz) R.; m. Anne Loughran, May 30, 1985; children: Michael, Elisabeth. BS, Franklin & Marshall U., 1972; MD, U. Pa., 1976. Diplomate Am. Bd. Ob-Gyn. (mem. divsn. gynecol. oncology), Nat. Bd. Med. Examiners. Intern in ob.-gyn. Hosp. of Univ. of Pa., Phila., 1976-77, residency in ob.-gyn., 1977-80, fellow in gynecologic oncology, 1980-82; asst. prof. of ob-gyn Med. Coll. of Pa., 1982-85, dir. surg. gynecology, 1982-85, chief gynecol. oncology, 1984-85; asst. mem. gynecol. staff Meml. Sloan-Kettering Hosp., N.Y.C., 1985-90, assoc. mem., 1990-93; asst. prof. ob-gyn Cornell U. Med. Coll., 1985-90, assoc. prof., 1990-93; prof. ob-gyn., dir. gynecologic oncology U. Pa., Phila., 1993—. Editor: Ovarian Cancer, Cervical Cancer, Chemotherapy of Gynecologic Cancer; contbr. over 200 articles to profl. publs. Recipient Career Devel. award Am. Cancer Soc., 1987, Boyer award Meml. Sloan-Kettering; grantee Nat. Cancer Inst., 1991, 96, 98, 99. Mem. ACS, ACOG, Am. Soc. Clin. Oncology, Soc. Gynecol. Oncologists (Pres.'s award 1993), Am. Gyn. and Obstet. Soc., Soc. Gynecologic Investigation, Soc. Pelvic Surgeons, Gynecol. Cancer Found. (Karin Smith award 1996). Office: U Pa Med Ctr 3400 Spruce St Philadelphia PA 19104-4206

RUBIN, STUART HARVEY, computer science educator, researcher; b. N.Y.C., Mar. 18, 1954; s. Jack and Rhoda Rochelle (Lentz) R. BS, U. R.I., 1975; MS in Indsl. and Systems Engring., Ohio U., 1977; MS, Rutgers U., 1980; PhD, Lehigh U., 1988. Lectr. U. Cin., 1977-78; electronic engr. U.S. Army Rsch. Labs., Ft. Monmouth, N.J., 1980-83; assoc. prof. computer sci. Ctrl. Mich. U., Mt. Pleasant, 1988—2002, assoc. prof., 1996—, founder, dir. Ctr. for Intelligent Systems, 1990—2002. Tech. cons. RCA, Princeton, N.J., 1982-83, Babcock and Wilcox Corp., Alliance, Ohio, 1990, Booz-Allen and Hamilton, Inc., San Diego, 1990-91, Adept Tech., San Jose, Calif., 1990-91; mem. rsch. coun. Scripps Clin.; cons. USAF, 1995. Contbr. articles to profl. jours.; inventor in field. Agt. United Fund Isabella County, Mt. Pleasant, 1988; supporting coach Mich. Spl. Olympics, Mt. Pleasant, 1990; event capt. San Diego Regional Sci. Olympic Competition, 1990, 92; judge 37th, 38th, 39th, 40th, 41st, 42nd, 43d, 44th, 45th, 46th, 47th, 48th, Ann. Greater San Diego Sci. and Engring. Fair, 1991-2002. Recipient Am. Chem. Soc. award, 1972, U.S. Govt. Cert. of Merit, Washington, 1987, Letter of Appreciation, Gen. Charles C. McDonald, 1990; grantee NSF, Office Naval Tech., State of Mich., others, 1988—. Mem. IEEE, Am. Assn. Artificial Intelligence, Am. Soc. Engring. Edn. (ONT postdoctoral fellow 1990-93), N.Y. Acad. Scis., Internat. Assn. Knowledge Engrs., Assn. for Computer Machinery. Avocations: boating, skiing, hiking and nature. Home: 1542 La Playa Ave # 4-208 San Diego CA 92109-6328 E-mail: srubin@spawar.navy.mil.

RUBIN, THEODORE ISAAC, psychiatrist, writer; b. Bklyn., Apr. 11, 1923; s. Nathan and Esther (Marcus) R.; m. Eleanor Katz, June 16, 1946; children: Jeffrey, Trudy, Eugene. BA, Bklyn. Coll., 1946; MD, U. Lausanne, Switzerland, 1951; grad., Am. Inst. Psychoanalysis, 1964. Resident psychiatrist Los Angeles VA Hosp., 1953, Rockland (N.Y.) State Hosp., 1954, Bklyn. State Hosp., 1955, Kings County (N.Y.) Hosp., 1956; chief psychiatrist Women's House of Detention, N.Y.C., 1957; mem. faculty Downstate Med. Sch., N.Y. State U., 1957-59; pvt. practice N.Y.C., 1956—. Tng. and supervising psychoanalyst Am. Inst. for Psychoanalysis of Karen Horney Clinic and Ctr.; mem. faculty Am. Inst. Psychoanalysis, 1962—; pres. emeritus bd. trustees Am. Inst. Psychoanalysis. Author: Jordi, 1960, Lisa and David, 1961, Sweet Daddy, 1963, In The Life, 1964, Platzo and the Mexican Pony Rider, 1965, The Thin Book by a Formerly Fat Psychiatrist, 1966, The 29th Summer, 1966, Cat, 1966, Coming Out, 1967, The Winner's Note Book, 1967, The Angry Book, 1969, Forever Thin, 1970, Emergency Room Diary, 1972, Doctor Rubin Please Make Me Happy, 1974, Shrink, 1974, Compassion and Self-Hate, An Alternative to Despair, 1975, Love Me, Love My Fool, 1976, Reflections in a Goldfish Tank, 1977, Alive and Fat and Thinning in America, 1978, Reconciliations, 1980, Through My Own Eyes, 1982, One to One, Understanding Personal Relationships, 1983, Not to Worry, The American Family Book of Mental Health, 1984, Overcoming Indecisiveness, 1985, Lisa and David, The Story Continues, 1986, Miracle at Bellevue, 1986, Real Love, 1990, Child Potential, 1990, Anti-Semitism: A Disease of the Mind, 1990, Little Ralphie and The Creature, 1998; mem. editl. bd. Am. Jour. Psychoanalysis; also articles, columns.; co-writer (TV movie) Lisa and David, 1998. Served as officer USNR, World War II. Recipient Adolf Meyer award Assn. Improvement Mental Health, 1963 Fellow Am. Acad. Psychoanalysis; mem. N.Y. County Med. Soc., Am. Psychiat. Assn., Assn. Advancement Psychoanalysis, Authors Guild, Contemporary Authors, Writers Guild East. Office: 113 1/2 E 62nd St New York NY 10021-7301

RUBIN, VERA COOPER, astronomer, researcher; b. Phila., July 23, 1928; d. Philip and Rose (Applebaum) Cooper; m. Robert J. Rubin, June 25, 1948; children: David M., Judith S. Young, Karl C. Allan. BA, Vassar Coll., 1948; MA, Cornell U., 1951; PhD, Georgetown U., 1954, DHL (hon.), 1997; DSc (hon.), Creighton U., 1978, Harvard U., 1988, Yale U., 1990, Williams Coll., 1993, U. Mich., 1996, Ohio State U., 1998; DSC (hon.), Smith Coll., 2001, Grinnell Coll., 2001. From rsch. assoc. to asst. prof. Georgetown U., Washington, 1955-65; physicist U. Calif., LaJolla, 1963-64; astronomer Carnegie Inst., Washington, 1965—2001, sr. fellow, 2001—. Chancellor's Disting. prof. U. Calif., Berkeley, 1981; vis. com. Harvard Coll. Obs., Cambridge, Mass., 1976—82, 1992—, Space Telescope Sci. Ins., 1990—92; Beatrice Tinsley vis. prof. U. Tex., 1988; Commonwealth lectr. U. Mass., 1991; Yunker lectr. Oreg. State U., 1991; Bernhard vis. fellow Williams Coll., 1993; Oort vis. prof. U. Leiden, The Netherlands, 1995; Halley lectr. Oxford U., 1998; lectr. in field, Chile, Russia, China, Armenia, India, Japan, Europe; trustee Assoc. Univs., Inc., 1993—96; mem. Pres. Commn. to Select U.S. Nat. Medal Sci. Awardees, 1995—98, chair, 1997—98; Pres.'s disting. visitor Vassar Coll., 1987; Halley lctr. Oxford Univ., 1997; bd. dir. Sci. Service, 2002—. Assoc. editor: Astrophys. Jour. Letters, 1977—82, mem. editl. bd.: Sci. Mag., 1979—87, mem. sr. editl. bd.: , 2001—. Named to Nat. Sci. Bd., 1996; recipient U.S. medal of Sci., 1993, Gold medal, Royal. Astorn. Soc. London, 1996, Weizmann Women and Sci. award, 1996, Helen Hogg prize, Can. Astron. Soc., 1997, John Scott Award, City Of Phila., 2001. Mem.: NAS (space sci. bd. 1974—77, chair sect. on astronomy 1992—95), Am. Acad. Arts and Scis., AAAS, Am. Philos. Soc., Assn. Univ. Rsch. in Astronomy (trustee 1973—76, 1994—96), Pontifical Acad. Scis., Internat. Astron. Union (pres. commn. on galaxies 1982—85, chair U.S. nat. commn. 1999—2001), Am. Astron. Soc. (coun. 1977—80, Russell prize lectr. 1994), Phi Beta Kappa (scholar 1982—83). Democrat. Jewish. *As an observational astronomer, it is my aim to obtain data of highest quality in order to answer questions concerning the universe in which we live. In spite of our enormous ignorance, each day offers exciting opportunities to learn a little more. This is the real joy of doing science.*

RUBIN, WILLIAM, editor; b. N.Y.C., Jan. 10, 1928; s. Herman and Molly (Goodman) R.; m. Claire Levine, Aug. 30, 1953; children: Deborah E., Joan S., Howard I. BA, Bklyn. Coll., 1953. Tech. editor Drug Trade News, N.Y.C., 1952-63; dir. pub. info. Nat. Vitamin Found., 1958-61; editorial dir. FDC Reports & Drug Rsch. Reports, Washington, 1963-64; proprietor Sci. Reports and Projects, Bethesda, MD., 1964-67; editor Internat. Med. News Group, Rockville, Md., 1967-91; editorial cons., 1992—. Editor Clin. Psychiatry News, Family Practice News, Internal Medicine News, Ob-Gyn. News, Pediatric News, Skin & Allergy News, Internat. Med. News Group. Bd. dirs. Washington chpt. Am. Found. for Suicide Prevention; chmn. Md. Adv. Coun. on Arthritis and Related Diseases; bd. dirs. Reginald Lourie Ctr. for Infants and Young Children; mem. spkrs' bur. Met. Washington chpt. Arthritis Found.; vice chmn. Montgomery County (Md.) Libr. Bd. With USAAF, 1946-47. Mem. Nat. Assn. Sci. Writers (life), Am. Med. Writers Assn., N.Y. Acad. Scis., Nat. Press Club. Avocations: book accumulating, reading history, woodworking. Office: 6808 Greyswood Rd Bethesda MD 20817-1541

RUBIN, ZICK, psychology educator, lawyer, writer; b. N.Y.C., Apr. 29, 1944; s. Eli and Adena (Lipschitz) R.; m. Carol Moses, June 21, 1969; children— Elihu James, Noam Moses BA, Yale U., 1965; PhD, U. Mich., 1969; JD, Harvard U., 1988. Bar: Mass., 1988. Asst. to assoc. prof. Harvard U., Cambridge, Mass., 1969—76; Louis and Frances Salvage prof. social psychology Brandeis U., Waltham, 1976—89, adj. prof. psychology, 1989—96; law clk. chief judge U.S. Ct. Appeals (1st cir.), 1988—89; assoc. Palmer & Dodge, Boston, 1990—93, counsel, 1994—2001, Hill & Barlow Agy., Boston, 2001—. Chmn. com. behavioral scis. Yale U. Coun., New Haven, 1981-86; mem. Adams papers adminstrv. com. Mass. Hist. Soc., 2001—. Author: Liking and Loving, 1973, Children's Friendships, 1980; co-author: Psychology, 1993; editor: Doing Unto Others, 1974, Relationships and Development, 1986; contbg. editor: Psychology Today, 1980-85; editorial bd.: Harvard Law Rev., 1986-88. Recipient Socio-Psychol. prize AAAS, 1969, Nat. Media award Am. Psychol. Found., 1980; grantee NSF, NIMH, Ford Found., Social Sci. Research Council, Found. Child Devel. Mem. ABA, Mass. Bar Assn., Boston Bar Assn., Am. Psychology-Law Soc., Authors Guild, Text and Acad. Authors Assn. (mem. coun. 1994-95), Phi Beta Kappa. Clubs: Elihu (New Haven). Jewish. E-mail: zrubin@attbi.com., zrubin@hillbarlow.com.

RUBINE, ROBERT SAMUEL, lawyer; b. Rockaway, N.Y., Feb. 28, 1947; s. George and Beatrice (Simon) R.; m. Marilyn Goldberg Rubine, Aug. 15, 1970; children: Seth B., Marisa H. BA, Queens Coll., 1968; JD, Syracuse U., 1971. Bar: N.Y. 1972, Fla. 1975; U.S. Dist. Ct. (ea. and so. dists.) N.Y., 1976; U.S. Supreme Ct. 1976. Trial atty. Legal Aid Soc. Nassau County, Mineola, N.Y., 1971-77; atty. Reifman and Rubine, Jericho, 1977-79; ptnr. Stein, Rubine and Stein, Mineola, 1979-94, Rubine and Rubine, Mineola, 1995—. Adj. prof. C.W. Post Coll., Greenvale, N.Y., 1979-82. Author: (chpt.) Criminal and Civil Investigation Handbook, 1981. Dir. Legal Aid Soc. Nassau County, 1989—, pres., 1994-95, treas., 1996—. Mem. N.Y. State Bar Assn., N.Y. State Assn. Criminal Def. Lawyers, N.Y. State Defenders Assn., Nassau County Bar Assn. Avocation: golf. Home: 5 Woodland Rd Oyster Bay NY 11771-3910 Office: Rubine and Rubine PLLC 114 Old Country Rd Mineola NY 11501-4400

RUBINFIEN, LEO H. photographer, filmmaker; b. Chgo., Aug. 16, 1953; Student, Reed Coll.; BFA, Calif. Inst. Arts, 1974; MFA, Yale U., 1976. Instr. in photography Swarthmore Coll., 1977, Sch. Visual Arts, N.Y.C., 1978-87; assoc. prof. art Fordham U., 1981-87; represented by Robert Mann Gallery, N.Y.C.; mem. faculty Gallatin Sch., NYU, 2001—. Vis. lectr. Cooper Union, 1982. One man shows include Castelli Gallery, N.Y., 1981, Fraenkel Gallery, San Francisco, 1982, 86, Robert Mann Gallery, N.Y.C., 1994, 2001, Met. Mus.

Art, N.Y.C., 1992, Seibu Art Forum, Tokyo, 1993, Cleve. Mus. Art, 1994, Seattle Art Mus., 1994, Robert Mann Gallery, N.Y.C.; exhibited in group shows at Internat. Ctr. Photography, N.Y., 1981, Inst. Contemporary Arts, London, 1981, San Francisco Mus. Modern Art, 1981, George Eastman House, Rochester, N.Y., 1981, Corcoran Gallery, Washington, 1981, Mus. Modern Art, N.Y., 1984; dir., co-author (film) The Money Juggler, 1988, My Bed in the Leaves, 1990; author: (books) A Map of the East, 1992, 10 Takeoffs 5 Landings, 1994, (essays) A Love-Hate Relations, Artforum, 1978, Investigations of a Dog, 1999, Guesses About the Work of Wu Yiming, 1999, The Poetry of Plain Seeing, 2000, Perfect Uncertainty, 2001. Fellow Guggenheim Found., 1982-83, Asian Cult Coun., 1984, Internat. Ctr. Advanced Studies, 1998—, Japan Found., 2002. Home: 1 Furnace Dock Rd Croton On Hudson NY 10520-1406 Personal E-mail: oscawana@earthlink.net.

RUBIN-KATZ, BARBARA, sculptor, human services administrator; b. Springfield, Mass., May 3, 1931; d. Samuel and Jane (Freeman) Kurn; m. Emanuel Rubin, Mar. 27, 1955 (div. Dec. 1984); children: Raphael, Jonathan, Daniel, Rebecca; m. Robert Nathan Katz, June 15, 1986. BA, U. Ariz., 1952; MSW, Simmons Coll., 1955; MPH, Columbia U., 1977; postgrad. in Sculpture Studies, Phila. Coll. Art, 1981-85. Rschr. Bellevue Hosp., N.Y.C., 1970-75; health svcs. coord. Fedn. Jewish Agencies, 1977-79, assoc. dir. planning Phila., 1979-84; sculptor Brookline, Mass., 1985—. Prin. works include sculpture at Mass. Gen. Hosp., Villa Campana, Tucson, Worcester Poly. Inst., Regency Park, Brookline, Mass; exhibited in group shows at Copley Soc. Boston shows, 1990—, New Eng. Sculptors Assn. shows, 1987—, The Roxbury Latin Sch., 1991, Jr. League Boston Decorator's Showhouse, Walpole, Mass., 1994, Fanuiel Hall, Boston, 1994, Prestige Gallery, Danvers, Mass., 1995, Michael Allen Gallery, Brookline, Mass., 1996, Curtis Gallery Lenox, Mass., 1996—, Festival Arts, Newton, 1997, Curtis Gallery, Lenox, Mass., 1997, 98, Worcester Poly. Inst., 1997-98, Bradford (Mass.) Coll., 1999; contbr. articles to profl. jours. Mem. Copley Soc. Boston (Copley Artist award 1992), New Eng. Sculptor's Assn. (bd. dirs. 1993), Brookline Coun. for Arts and Humanities. Home: 1731 Beacon St Apt 1403 Brookline MA 02445-5329

RUBINO, JOHN ANTHONY, management and human resources consultant; b. Port Chester, N.Y., Nov. 22, 1956; s. Angelo J. and Ann (Posillipo) R.; m. Cynthia C. Corica, Nov. 9, 1980; 1 child, Sean Anthony. BA in Psychology magna cum laude, Wagner Coll., 1978; MBA with distinction, Pace U., 1985. Cert. compensation profl. Convention svc. mgr. Waldorf-Astoria Hotel, N.Y.C., 1978-80; compensation analyst County of Westchester, White Plains, N.Y., 1980-82; sr. compensation analyst Anaconda-Ericsson, Inc., Greenwich, Conn., 1982-83; compensation mgr. ASEA, Inc., White Plains, N.Y., 1983-84, Sterling Drug, Inc., N.Y.C., 1984-87; dir. exec. compensation The Equitable Life Insur. Co., 1987-93; sr. mgr. human resources cons. Ernst & Young, 1993-96; pres. Rubino Cons. Svcs., Pound Ridge, N.Y., 1996—. Author: Developing Compensation Programs, 1990, Communicating Compensation Programs, 1992; contbr. articles to profl. jours. Mem. Am. Compensation Assn. (course developer, instr., course leader, guest speaker 1988—), Am. Mgmt. Assn. (course developer, instr., course leader, guest speaker 1988—), Soc. for Human Resource Mgmt. (guest spkr. 1999—). Avocations: performing renaissance music, writing poetry, golf. Home and Office: Rubino Cons Svcs 29 Conant Valley Rd Pound Ridge NY 10576-1815 E-mail: RuBinoConsulting@aol.com.

RUBINO, MARY ANN, interior decorator, writer; b. Chgo., Nov. 24, 1965; d. Paul Joseph and Ann Marie (Freborg) R. BA in Econs., Brown U., 1987; MA in Social Scis., U. Chgo., 1993. Freelance writer, Chgo., 1988, 90; ind. researcher Bari, Italy, 1989-90; pvt. practice interior decoration Evanston, Ill., 1996—. Author: Extracting the Essence, 1987-89, Houses of Strangers, 1990-91, Thinking with the Heart, 1993. Mem. Brown U. Recent Alumni Group (founder, chmn. 1987-89). Roman Catholic.

RUBINO, VICTOR JOSEPH, academic administrator, lawyer; b. N.Y.C., Dec. 25, 1940; s. Joseph V. and Olympia (Gayda) R.; 1 child, Victor Gayda. BA in Govt., Cornell U., 1962, LLB, 1965. Bar: N.Y. 1965, U.S. Dist. Ct. (so. dist.) N.Y. 1969. Staff atty. Westchester Legal Svcs., White Plains, N.Y., 1968-71; assoc. Squadron Ellenoff Plesent & Lehrer, N.Y.C., 1971; treas., program officer Council on Legal Edn., 1971-79; assoc. dir. Practising Law Inst., 1979-83, exec. dir., 1983—. Democratic candidate for N.Y. State Assembly, 1970; chmn. Rye (N.Y.) Human Rights Commn., 1975-76. Served to capt. U.S. Army, 1966-68. Mem. ABA, Assn. Bar City N.Y. Office: Practising Law Inst 810 7th Ave Fl 26 New York NY 10019-5818

RUBINOVITZ, SAMUEL, diversified manufacturing company executive; b. Boston, Dec. 26, 1929; s. Benjamin Ephraim and Pauline (Kaufman) R.; m. Phyllis Ann Silverstein; children: David Jay, Robert Neal. BS, MIT, 1951, MS, 1952. Sales engr. Clevite Transistor Products, Waltham, Mass., 1954-63; sales mgr. EG&G Inc., Wellesley, 1963-72, divsn. mgr., 1972-79, v.p., 1979-86, sr. v.p., 1986-89, exec. v.p., 1989-94; ret., 1994. Bd. dirs. Richardson Electronics Ltd., Chgo., Kronos Inc., Waltham, KLA Tencor Techs. Inc., LTX Corp. 1st lt. USAF, 1952-54. Democrat. Jewish. E-mail: Srubinovitz@Kronos.com.

RUBINSON, HOWARD ALAN, physician; b. Bklyn., Aug. 24, 1949; s. Samuel and Hilda (Cohen) R.; m. Carol Berman, May 16, 1976; children: Roger, Abby. AB, Cornell U., 1971; MD, Hahnemann Med. Coll., Phila., 1975. Diplomate Am. Bd. Radiology. Radiology instr. Sch. Medicine U. Miami, Fla., 1979-81, asst. prof. radiology, 1981-84; mem. attending staff North Beach Hosp., Ft. Lauderdale, 1984-89, North Ridge Med. Ctr., Ft. Lauderdale, 1989—, Pkwy. Regional Med. Ctr., 2001—. Contbr. articles to profl. jours. Mem. Am. Coll. Radiology, Am. Soc. Emergency Radiology, Soc. Breast Imaging, Radiol. Soc. N.Am., Am. Roentgen Ray Soc., Soc. Thoracic Radiology, South Fla. Radiol. Soc. (pres. 1996-97), Fla. Radiol. Soc., Fla. Med. Assn., Broward County Med. Assn. Office: North Ridge Med Ctr Dept Radiology 5757 N Dixie Hwy Fort Lauderdale FL 33334-4135

RUBINSTEIN, ARYE, pediatrician, microbiology and immunology educator; b. Tel Aviv , Oct. 02; came to U.S., 1971; s. Reuven and Kathe (Samson) R.; m. Orna Eisenstein, Dec. 7, 1965 (div. 1982); children: Ran, Yair, Avner, Noam; m. Charline Nezri, Dec. 27, 1983; children: Reuven, Rena, Rachel. MD, U. Berne, Switzerland, 1962. Diplomate Am. Bd. Pediatrics; bd. cert. in pediatrics, Israel, Switzerland; Am. Bd. Allergy and Immunology cert. in allergy and immunology. Intern, pediatrics resident, fellow U. Tel Aviv, 1962-67; rsch. assoc. divsn. immunology Med. Sch. Harvard Coll., 1971-73; dir. divsn. immunology and bone marrow transplantation U. Berne, 1969-71; asst. prof. cell biology Albert Einstein Coll. Medicine, Bronx, 1973-80, asst. prof. pediatrics, 1973-77, assoc. prof., 1977-82, assoc. prof. microbiology and immunology, 1981-85, prof. pediatrics, 1982—, prof. microbiology and immunology, 1985—. Dir. divsn. clin. allergy and immunology Albert Einstein Coll. Medicine, dir. tng. program for allergy and immunology; dir. divsn. clin. allergy and immunology Albert Einstein Coll. Medicine, Montefiore Med. Ctr.; attending pediatrician Bronx Mcpl. Med. Ctr., Hosp. Albert Einstein Coll. Medicine; mem. study sect. on AIDS rsch. NIH. Mem. editl. bd. Annals of Allergy; reviewer New England Jour. Medicine, Jour. for Clin. Investigation, Jour. Pediatrics, Jour. Clin. Allergy and Immunology; contbr. over 175 articles to profl. publs. Lt. armed svcs., Israel, 1955-57. Recipient Lifetime award in Immunology, Humanitarian award DIFFA, Birch Svcs. for Children, Annual award U.S. Asst. Sec. of Health for excellence in AIDS rsch. and treatment, 1990, Bela Shick award for Pediatric Rsch., 1993, Ackerman award for Sci. and Humanity, 1995, Heroes in Medicine Internat. award, 2000; AIDS Rsch. Program grantee NIH, Bronx. Fellow Am. Acad. Allergy and Immunology, Am. Coll. Allergy & Immunology; mem. N.Y. Acad. Scis., Soc. Pediatric Rsch., The Harvey Soc., Am. Coll. Allergy, Clin. Immunology Soc., Clin. Immunology Soc. Office: Albert Einstein Coll Medicine 1300 Morris Park Ave Bronx NY 10461-1926

RUBINSTEIN, ERNEST, librarian, educator; b. Queens, N.Y., July 11, 1952; s. Jack and Jeanne Rubinstein; life ptnr. Paul Glassman. BA, Brandeis U., 1974; AMLS, U. Mich., 1977; MTS, Harvard U., 1979; MA, Hebrew Union Coll., 1985; PhD, Northwestern U., Evanston, Ill., 1995. Indexer H.W. Wilson Co., Bronx, NY, 1984—88; editor Am. Theological Libr. Assn., Chgo., 1988—90; reference libr. North Park Coll., 1990—94; libr. Interchurch Ctr., N.Y.C., 1994—; book rev. Publs. Weekly, 1999—. Asst. adj. prof. humanities NYU, N.Y.C., 1995—; adj. faculty New Sch., N.Y.C., 2001—. Author: (novels) Episode of Jewish Romanticism, 1999. Vol. peer counselor Horizons, Chgo., 1992—94, Aids Pastoral Care Network, Chgo., 1992—94. Mem.: Am. Acad. Religion. Jewish. Home: 200 Cabrini Blvd Apt 42 New York NY 10033 Office: Interchurch Ctr 475 Riverside Dr Rm 900 New York NY 10115 Personal E-mail: ehr3@nyu.edu.

RUBINSTEIN, EVA (ANNA RUBINSTEIN), photographer; b. Buenos Aires, Argentina, 1933; d. Arthur and Aniela (Mlynarska) R.; m. William Sloane Coffin Jr., 1956 (div. 1968); children: Amy, Alexander (dec.), David. Ballet tng., Paris, N.Y.C., Calif., 1938-53; student, Scripps Coll., 1950-51, UCLA, 1952-53; student in photography, Lisette Model, 1969, Jim Hughes, 1971, Ken Heyman, 1970, Diane Arbus, 1971. Lectr. numerous workshops, seminars, confs.; instr. photo seminars Lodz Film Sch., Poland, 1986, 86-87. Dancer, actress: off-Broadway and Broadway, including original prodn. The Diary of Anne Frank, 1955-56; European dance tour, 1955; one-person shows of photographs include Underground Gallery, N.Y.C., 1972, Dayton Art Inst., Ohio, 1973, Arles Festival, France, 1975, Canon Photo Gallery, Amsterdam, 1975, Neikrug Gallery, N.Y.C., 1975, 79, 81, 82, 85, La Photogalerie, Paris, 1975, Friends of Photography, Carmel, Calif., 1975, Galerie 5.6, Ghent, Belgium, 1976, Gallery Trochenpresse, Berlin, 1977, Frumkin Gallery, Chgo., 1977, Galeria Sinisca, Rome, 1979, Hermitage Found. Mus., Norfolk, Va., 1982, Photographers Gallery, London, 1983, Galerie Forum Labo, Arles, France, 1983, Galerie Nicephore, Lyon, France, 1983, Image Gallery, Madrid, 1984, Muzeum Sztuki, Lodz, Poland, 1984, Il Diaframma/Canon Gallery, Milan, 1984, A.R.P.A. Gallery, Bordeaux, 1984, Chateau d'Eau, Toulouse, France, 1985, Galerie Demi-Teinte, Paris, 1985, Associated Artist Photographers galleries in Warsaw, Krakow, Lodz, Katowice and Gdansk, Poland, 1985-86, Foto/Medium/Art Gallery, Wroclaw, Poland, 1986, Visions Gallery, San Francisco, 1986, Canon Galerie, Paris, 1986, Salone Internat. SICOF, Milan, 1987, St. Krzysztof Gallery, Lodz, 1987, L'Image Fixe, Lyon, 1988, Artotheque, Grenoble, 1988, Neikrug Photographica, N.Y.C., 1989, Heuser Art Ctr. Gallery, Bradley U., Peoria, Ill., 1989, 3-os Encontros da Imagem, Braga, Portugal, 1989, Bibliotheque Nat. Galerie Colbert, Paris, 1989, Galerie Picto-Bastille, Paris, 1989-90, Portfolio Gallery, London, 1990, Vaison-La-Romaine, France, 1990, Hist. Mus. of City of Lodz, 1990, Galerie Artem, Quimper, France, 1993, Galerie F.N.A.C. Etoile, Paris, 1994, other F.N.A.C. galleries (France, Belgium, Spain), 1994-97, Galerie Augustus, Berlin, 1995, L'Imagerie, Lannion, France, 1995, Zacheta Gallery, Warsaw, 1996, Salon of Modern Art B.W.A., Bydgoszcz, Poland, 1997, Galleries of Polish Insts., Sofia, Bulgaria, Berlin, Moscow, Bratislava, Slovakia, I. Beszkova Gallery, Plewen, Bulgaria, 1997, Hungarian Mus. Photographic Art, Budapest, 1997, LTF Gallery, Lodz, Poland, 1998, Konfrontacje Fotograficzne, Gorzow Wielopolski, Poland, 1998, Centrum Kultury Zamek, Poznan, Poland, 1998, Mus. Regionalny, Wrzesnia, Poland, 1998, Galeria Korytarz, Jelenia Gora, Poland, 1998, Galeria Foto-Medium-Art, Wroclaw, Poland, 1998, Galeria Pusta, Centrum Kultury, Katowice, Poland, 1998, Teatr Wielki, Lodz, Poland, 2000; group shows include, Internat. Salon, Krakow, Poland, 1971, Delgado Mus., New Orleans, 1972, Neikrug Gallery, 1972, 73, 75, Salone Internationale, Milan, Italy, 1973, Photo-OVO, Montreal, Que., Can., 1974, Nat. Portrait Gallery, London, 1976, Hera Gallery, R.I., 1977, Musee National d'Art Moderne Georges Pompidou, Paris, 1977, Centre Culturel de l'ouest Aquitain, Bordeaux, France, 1978, Fotografiska Museet, Stockholm, 1978, Nat. Arts Club, N.Y.C., 1979, Chrysler Mus., Norfolk, 1979, Maine Photog. Gallery, 1981, Floating Found. Photography, N.Y.C., 1970, 71, 72, 73, 79, 82, Ffoto Gallery, Cardiff, Wales, 1983, Musée d'Art Moderne de la Ville de Paris, 1987-88, Boca Raton (Fla.) Mus., 1989, Galerie PICTO Bastille, Paris, 1989, Galerie Arena, Arles, 1989-90, Settimana della Fotografia, Palermo, 1990, Festival de l'Image, Le Mans, France, 1993, Quimper (France), 1995, Galerie Camera Obscura, Paris, 1996, Zacheta Gallery, Warsaw, 2002, Lodz Photographic Soc., 2002; represented: in permanent collections Library of Congress, Washington, Met. Mus. Art, N.Y.C., Bibliotheque Nationale, Paris, Musee Reattu, Arles, France, Kalamazoo Inst. Arts, Israel Mus., Jerusalem, Fotografiska Museet, Stockholm, Muzeum Sztuki, Lodz, Poland, Histo Mus. of City of Lodz, others; author: (monographs) 2 ltd. edit. portfolios with introductions by John Vachon and André Kertész, Lodz: Brief Encounters, 1998; contbr. photographs in various books, mags., profl. jours. *Making photographs is my way of exploring the questions that keep me alive by ever leading to further questions.*

RUBINSTEIN, FREDERIC ARMAND, lawyer; b. Antwerp, Belgium, Apr. 20, 1931; came to U.S., 1942; s. Samuel N. and Steffa (Warrenreich) R.; m. Susan August, Dec. 24, 1968; 1 child, Nicolas Eric August Rubinstein. BA, Cornell U., 1953, JD, 1955. Bar: N.Y. 1955. Assoc. Law Offices of I. Robert Feinberg, N.Y.C., 1955-60, Guggenheimer & Untermyer, N.Y.C., 1960-65, ptnr., 1965-85, Kelley Drye & Warren LLP, N.Y.C., 1985—. Vice chmn. zoning & planning com. Local Community Bd. # 6, N.Y.C., 1980-86. Mem. ABA (bus. law sect., emerging growth ventures subcom., chmn. 1988-96), Cornell Club of N.Y. Office: Kelley Drye & Warren LLP 101 Park Ave New York NY 10178-0002

RUBINSTEIN, MARK ISAAC, physician; b. Havana, Cuba, 1957; MD, Jefferson Med. Coll., 1983. Diplomate Am. Bd. Otolaryngology, Am. Bd. Facial Plastic and Reconstructive Surgery. Intern Pa. Hosp., Phila., 1983-84, resident in surgery, 1984-85; resident in otolaryngology, head and neck surgery U. Mich., Ann Arbor, 1985-89; mem. staff Fairfax (Va.) Hosp., 1989—, Fair Oaks (Va.) Hosp., 1989—; mem. courtesy staff Reston (Va.) Hosp., 1989—; clin. asst. prof. Georgetown U. Hosp., Washington; chief otolaryngology Fairfax Hosp., 2000—. Mem. AMA, Am. Acad. Otolaryngology-Head and Neck Surgery, Am. Acad. Facial Plastic and Reconstructive Surgery, Med. Soc. Va., Wash. Met. Ear, Nose and Throat Soc. (pres. 1996-97), Va. Soc. Otolargyngology Head and Neck Surgery, Fairfax County Med. Soc. Office: 8316 Arlington Blvd Ste 300 Fairfax VA 22031-5216

RUBINSTEIN, MOSHE FAJWEL, engineering educator; b. Miechow, Poland, Aug. 13, 1930; came to U.S., 1950, naturalized, 1965; s. Shlomo and Sarah (Rosen) R.; m. Zafrira Gorstein, Feb. 3, 1953; children: Iris, Dorit. BS, UCLA, 1954, MS, 1957, PhD, 1961. Designer Murray Erick Assos. (engrs. and archs.), L.A., 1954-56; structural designer Victor Gruen Assos., 1956-61; asst. prof. UCLA, 1961-64, assoc. prof. dept. engring., 1964-69, prof., 1969—, chmn. engring. sys. dept., 1970-75, program dir. modern engring. for execs. program, 1965-70. Cons. Pacific Power & Light Co., Portland, Oreg., Northrop Corp., U.S. Army, NASA Rsch. Ctr., Langley, Tex. Instruments Co., Hughes Space System Divsn., U.S. Army Sci. Adv. Com., Kaiser Aluminum and Chem. Corp., IBM Corp., TRW. Author: (with W.C. Hurty) Dynamics of Structures, 1964 (Yugoslavian transl. 1973), Matrix Computer Analysis of Structures, 1966 (Japanese transl. 1974), Structural Systems, Statics Dynamics and Stability, 1970 (Japanese transl. 1979), Patterns of Problem Solving, 1975, (with K. Pfeiffer) Concepts in Problem Solving, 1980, Tools for Thinking and Problem Solving, 1986; IEEE Press Videotapes; Models for People Driven Quality, 1991, Quality through Innovation, 1991, Creativity for Ongoing Total Quality, 1993, Relentless Improvement, 1993, (with I.R. Firstenberg) Patterns of Problem Solving, 2d edit., 1995, (with I.R. Firstenberg) The Minding Organization, 1999 (Portuguese/Japanese transl. 2000, Spanish/Chinese/Russian transls. 2001). Recipient Disting. Tchr. award UCLA Acad. Senate, 1964, Western Electric Fund award Am. Soc. Engring. Edn., 1965, Disting. Tchr. trophy Engring. Student Soc., UCLA, 1966; Sussman prof. for disting. visitor Technion-Israel Inst. Tech., 1967-68; named Outstanding Faculty Mem., UCLA Engring. Alumni award, 1979, Outstanding UCLA Civil Engring. Alumni award, 1990, Outstanding Faculty Mem., State of Calif. Command Coll., 1987, 88, 89, 94, 95; Fulbright-Hays fellow, Yugoslavia and Eng., 1975-76; voted one of UCLA's Top 20 Profs. of the Century. Mem. ASCE, Am. Soc. Engring. Edn., Seismol. Soc. Am., Sigma Xi, Tau Beta Phi. Achievements include research in use of computers in structural systems, analysis and synthesis; problem solving and decision theory; creativity and innovation in the organization. Home: 10488 Charing Cross Rd Los Angeles CA 90024-2646 Office: UCLA Sch Engring & Applied Sci Los Angeles CA 90024 E-mail: mrubinst@ucla.edu.

RUBINSTEIN, NANCY G. social worker, consultant; b. New Haven, June 23, 1945; d. Louis and Florence (BLumenthal) Goodwin; m. Joel Franklin Rubinstein, June 18, 1967 (div. Mar. 1991); children: Sally Goodwin Rubinstein, Ann Goodwin Rubinstein. BA, Smith Coll., 1967; MSW, Boston U., 1973. LCSW Lic. ind. clin. social worker. Pub. health adminstrv. asst. Conn. State Dept. Health, New Haven, 1967-70; designer, rschr. cardiac care program study Maine Med. Ctr., Portland, 1970-71; clin. case worker depression study Mass. Gen. Hosp., Boston, 1973-74; dir. clin. svcs. Emmaus Inc., Haverhill, Mass., 1987—; psychotherapist North Essex Mental Health Ctr., 1990-95. Mem. med. rev. team, cons. social worker Mass. Dept. Pub. Health, Boston, 1998-2000. Mem. Newburyport (Mass.) Sch. Health and Safety Task Force, 1998-2000, Seacoast Affordable Housing Coalition, 2001—; bd. dirs. Merrimack Valley Watershed Coun., 1979-90, now mem.; mem. Acad. of Women/Haverhill YWCA, 1997—. Recipient Mass. Common Works award State of Mass. Dept. Welfare, 1991. Mem. NASW, Smith Coll. Aumni ASsn., Andover Merrimack Valley Smith Coll. Club (pres. 1986-88). Jewish. Avocations: choral singing, ski touring, gardening, bicycling. Home: 29 Collins St Newburyport MA 01950-2138 Office: Emmaus Inc 127 How St Haverhill MA 01830-5615

RUBINSTEIN, ROSALINDA, allergist, medical association administrator; b. Buenos Aires, Jan. 3, 1942; came to U.S., 1967; MD, U. Buenos Aires, 1965. Residence Beth Israel Hosp., 1968-70; fellow in allergy-asthma Harvard Med. Sch., Boston, 1970-71; allergy-asthma asst. pediatrician Columbia Presbyn., N.Y.C., 1971—, Mt. Sinai Med. Ctr., N.Y.C., 1972—. Bd. dirs. N.Y. Women's Agenda, Argentina Am. Med. Soc.; pres. elect Nat. Coun. Women's Health, 1998—; pres. Women's Med. Assn., N.Y.C., 1995-97. Recipient Recognition award N.Y. Women's Agenda, 1997, Women's Med. Assn., N.Y.C., 1996, Community award Am. Med. Women's Assn., 1998. Mem. AMA, Am. Coll. Allergy-Asthma, Am. Acad. Allergy-Asthma, N.Y. County Med. Soc., Columbia Presbyn. Club, N.Y. Harvard Club. Avocation: women's health issues. Home and Office: 1016 5th Ave New York NY 10028-0132

RUBIO, PEDRO A. cardiovascular surgeon; b. Mexico City, Dec. 17, 1944; came to U.S., 1970; s. Isaac and Esther; m. Debra Rubio; children: Sandra, Edward. MD, U. Nat. Autónoma Mexico, 1968; MS in Surg. Tech., Pacific Western U., 1981, PhD in Biomed. Tech., 1982. Diplomate Am. Bd. Surgery, Am. Bd. Abdominal Surgery, Am. Bd. Laser Surgery, Am. Bd. Quality Assurance and Utilization Rev. Physicians, Am. Acad. Pain Mgmt., Am. Bd. Forensic Medicine, Am. Bd. Forensic Examiners, Mexican Bd. Angiology and Vascular Surgery, Infectious Diseases and Gen. Surgery; profl. cert. law enforcement sci. Nat. Com. Profl. Law Enforcement Stds., 1972. Prof. neurology Escuela Normal de Especialización Secretaria de Educación Publica, Mexico City, 1968-69; asst. instr. dept. surgery Baylor Coll. Medicine, Houston, 1971-76; clin. instr. dept. surgery U. Tex. Med. Sch., 1978-91, clin. assoc. prof. surgery dept. surgery, 1991—. Profl. vascular surgery Nat. U. Mexico Med. Sch., clin. supr. psychiatry residency tng. program Tex. Rsch. Inst. Mental Scis., Houston, 1979-85; surgeon, dir. Cardiovasc. Surg. Ctr., Houston, 1976-85, Houston Cardiovasc. Inst., 1985-89, Laser Gallbladder Surgery Ctr. Houston, 1990-94; course dir. Laser Tng. Inst., 1919-96, Houston Laser Inst., 1989-91; chmn. surgery dept. Med. Ctr. Hosp., Houston, 1978-94, chmn. emeritus dept. surgery Med. Ctr. Hosp., Houston, 1994—; nat. med. dir. Nat. Assn. Preferred Providers, Houston, 1995-96, pres., CEO, chmn. bd., 1996—; chmn., pres., CEO Henley Healthcare, Inc.; cons. Tex. Med. Liability Trust; rsch. projects with FDA, NCI, HEW, VA.; pres. exec. com. Houston Chamber Singers, 1982-83. Author: Atlas of Angioaccess Surgery,1 983, Atlas of Stapling Techniques, 1986; contbr. 260 articles to publs.; patentee med. instrumentation. Decorated Palms Honor Cross (hon.), Mex. Army; recipient Recognition diploma bachelor's class U. Nat. Autonoma Mexico, 1961, Faculty Medicine, 1966; named Outstanding Surg. Intern, Baylor Coll. Medicine, 1970-71, Doctor of Humane Letters Loudou Inst. Applied Rsch. FEllow Acad. de Ciencias Medicas del Inst. Mexicana de Cultura, Acad. Mexicana de Cirugia, ACS (Best Paper award South Tex. chpt. 1976), Am. Coll. Angiology, Am. Coll. Chest Physicians, Assn. Surgeons India (hon.), Soc. Surgeons Nepal (hon.), Internat. Coll. Surgeons (hon.), Knight Grand Cross, The Sovereign and Mil. Order of Saint John of Jerusalem, Houston Acad. Medicine, Internat. Coll. Angiology, Internat. Coll. Surgeons (N.Am. fedn. sec. 1991-92, pres. U.S. sect. 1988-89, pres. Tex. divsn. 1983-85, world pres.-elect 1993-94, world pres. 1995, historian 1985-94, chmn. membership com. U.S. sect. 1984-86, 3d pl. sci. motion picture 1980), Israel Med. Assn. USA, Royal Soc. Medicine, Am. Heart Assn. (stroke coun.), Am. Geriatrics Soc., AMA (Recognition award 1972-95), Am. Trauma Soc., Denton A. Coooley Cardiovasc. Soc., Harris County (Tex.) Med. Soc., Houston Surg. Soc. (1st pl. essay 1973, 75), Internat. Assn. Study Lung Cancer, Internat. Cardiovasc. Soc., Internat. Soc. Laser Medicine and Surgery, Soc. Mexicana de Angiologia (1st pl. nat. essay contest 1974), Soc. Internat. Chirurgie, Soc. Am. Gastrointestinal Endoscopic Surgeons, Soc. Laparoendoscopic Surgeons, Soc. for Minimally Invasive Surgery, Southwestern Surg. Congress, Tex. Med. Assn., World Med. Assn., Internat. Coll. Surgeons (world pres.), Phi Beta Delta, Rosicrucian Lodge. Office: 20682 Sweetglen Dr Porter TX 77365-6385

RUBLEY, CAROLE A. state legislator; b. Bethel, Conn., Jan. 18, 1939; d. George B. and Evelyn M. (Maloney) Drumm; m. C. Ronald Rubley, Aug. 25, 1962; children: Lauren M. Rubley Simpson, Stephen R., Kristin Rubley Vaughan. BA in Biology, Albertus Magnus Coll., 1960; MS in Environ. Health, West Chester U., 1988. Tchr. biology Danbury (Conn.) High Sch., 1960-62, Waltham (Mass.) High Sch., 1962-63; real estate salesperson Henderson-Dewey, Wayne, Pa., 1976-81; solid waste coord. Chester County Health Dept., West Chester, 1981-88; environ. cons. Environ. Resources Mgmt., Exton, 1988-92; mem. Pa. Ho. Reps., Valley Forge, 1992—. Mem. environ. resources, energy, consumer affairs, fin. and children and youth com. House of Reps.; mem. Pa. 21st Century Environ. Commn.; vice-chair environ. com. NCSL, task force on protecting Democracy, chair environ. and natural resources com. Author: (with others) Leading Pennsylvania into 21st Century, 1990. Chmn. Ea. Chester County Regional Planning Commn., 1976-85; vice chmn. planning commn. Tredyffrin Twp., Berwyn, Pa., 1976-86, mem. bd. suprs., 1987-92; bd. dirs. Pa. Resources Coun., exec. v.p., 1988-92. Mem. LWV (pres. Upper Main Line chpt. 1976-78, Involved Voter of Yr. award 1993), Pa. Environ. Coun., Green Valleys Assn., Open Land Conservancy. Republican. Roman Catholic. Avocations: aerobics, tennis, hiking, reading, traveling. Home: 621 Vassar Rd Wayne PA 19087-5312

RUBNER, MICHAEL, international relations educator, university administrator; b. Tel Aviv, Israel, Aug. 3, 1940; came to U.S., 1956; s. Maurice and Eva Edith (Katz) R.; m. Audrey Ann Pfingst, Feb. 16, 1969; children: Daniel, Jessica. BA, Rockford (Ill.) Coll., 1962; MA, Marquette U., 1964; PhD, U. Calif., Berkeley, 1975. Instr. James Madison Coll. Mich. State U., East Lansing, 1970-75, asst. prof., 1975-80, assoc. prof., 1980-85, prof., 1985—. Univ. faculty grievance official Mich. State U., 1989—. Co-author: The Palestinian Problem and U.S. Policy, 1986; contbr. articles to profl. jours. Pres. Jacob Schiff B'nai B'rith Lodge 694, Lansing, 1980-93; pres. Congregation Shaarey Zedek, East Lansing. Mem. Acad. Polit. Sci., Internat. Studies Assn. (governing coun. Midwest divsn. 1986-92), U.S. Arms Control Assn., Midwest Consortium for Internat. Security Studies, Phi Beta Kappa (pres. Epsilon of Mich. 1983-84), Alpha Sigma Nu, Phi Beta Delta. Democrat. Jewish. Office: Mich State U 113 Auditorium East Lansing MI 48824-1120

RUBNITZ, MYRON ETHAN, pathologist, educator; b. Omaha, Mar. 2, 1924; s. Abraham Srol and Esther Molly (Jonich) R.; m. Susan Belle Block, Feb. 9, 1952; children: Mary Lu Rubnitz Roffe, Peter, Thomas (dec.), Robert. BSc, U. Nebr., 1945; MD, U. Nebr., Omaha, 1947. Diplomate Am. Bd. Pathology. Intern Mt. Sinai Hosp., Cleve., 1947-48; fellow Mt. Sinai Hosp., N.Y.C., 1948-49; resident in pathology Michael Reese Hosp., Chgo., 1949-51; pathologist VA Hosp., Hines, 1953-56, chief labs., 1956-93, cons., 1993—; assoc. prof. pathology Loyola U. Med. Sch., Maywood, 1963-70, prof., 1970-99, prof. emeritus, 1999—. Adj. prof. Ill. State U., Normal, 1979-96, U. St. Francis, Joliet, Ill., 1989—, Ea. Ill. U. Charleston, 1991—, Western Ill. U., Macomb, 1991—; clin. instr. Augustana Coll., Rock Island, Ill., 1991—. Chmn. candidates com. Village Caucus, Winnteka, Ill., 1969-70; bd. dirs. Chgo. Commons Assn., 1968—, North Shore Sr. Ctr., 1998—; mem. New Trier High Sch. Caucus, Winnetka, 1972-74. With AUS, 1943-46, PTO; 1st lt. M.C., U.S. Army, 1951-53. Fellow Am. Soc. Clin. Pathologists, Coll. Am. Pathologists; mem. Internat. Acad. Pathology, Assn. VA Pathologists (pres. 1982-84), Chgo. Pathology Soc., Lake Shore Country Club (Glencoe, Ill.), North Shore Racquet Club, Mich. Shores Club (Wilmette, Ill.). Republican. Jewish. Avocations: electronics, tennis, travel. Home: 979 Sheridan Rd Winnetka IL 60093

RUBOTTOM, ROY RICHARD, JR. retired diplomat and educator, consultant; b. Brownwood, Tex., Feb. 13, 1912; s. Roy Richard and Jennie Eleanor (Watkins) R.; m. Billy Ruth Young, Dec. 23, 1938; children: Eleanor Ann Rubottom Odden, Frank, John. BS, So. Meth. U., 1932, MA, 1933; postgrad., U. Tex.; LLD, Southwestern Coll., Winfield, Kans., 1968, Cen. Meth. Coll., Fayette, Mo., 1985. Asst. dean student life U. Tex., 1937-41; apptd. fgn. service officer, 1947; sec. of embassy and consul Bogota, Colombia, 1947-49; officer-in-charge Mex. affairs State Dept., 1950, dep. dir. Middle Am. Affairs, 1951, dir., 1952-53; 1st sec. embassy Madrid, 1953; counselor of embassy, 1954; dir. U.S. Ops. Mission, 1954-56; asst. sec. of state for inter-Am. affairs, 1957-60; U.S. Ambassador to Argentina, 1960-62; advisor Naval War Coll., Newport, R.I., 1962-64; v.p. So. Meth. U., Dallas, 1964-71, prof. polit. sci. emeritus, 1975—; dir. Ctr. of Ibero-Am. Civilization, 1975-77; pres. U. Americas, Puebla, Mex., 1971-73; dir. Office Internat. Affairs, Dallas, 1985-87. Co-author: Spain and the U.S. Since W.W. II, 1984. Active Scouting U.S.A. Served with USNR, 1941-46. Recipient Silver Beaver award Boy Scouts Am., 1975, Inter-Am. award Boy Scouts Am., Silver Buffalo, 1993. Mem. Lambda Chi Alpha, Pi Sigma Alpha. Lodges: Rotary. Methodist. Home: 7831 Park Ln Apt 51B Dallas TX 75225-2039

RUBRIGHT, JAMES ALFRED, paper and packaging company executive, lawyer; b. Phila., Dec. 17, 1946; s. James Alfred and Helen Lucille (Evans) R. (deceased); m. Mary Elizabeth Angelich, Dec. 30, 1987; children: Noah Michael, Benjamin James, Jami Anne, Nathaniel Drew, James McCurdy, William Angelich. BA, Yale U., 1969; JD, U. Va., 1972. Bar: Ga. 1972. Ptnr. King & Spalding, Atlanta, 1972-94; sr. v.p., gen. counsel Sonat Inc., Birmingham, 1994-97; pres. So. Natural Gas Co. subs. Sonat Inc., 1997-98; exec. v.p. Sonat Inc., 1998-99; CEO Rock-Tenn Co., Norcross, Ga., 1999—. Office: Rock-Tenn Co 504 Thrasher St Norcross GA 30071-1914

RUCH, CHARLES P. academic administrator; b. Longbranch, N.J., Mar. 25, 1938; s. Claud C. and Marcella (Pierce) R.; m. Sally Joan Brandenburg, June 18, 1960; children: Cheryl, Charles, Christopher, Cathleen. BA, Coll. of Wooster, 1959; MA, Northwestern U., 1960, PhD, 1966. Counselor, tchr. Evanston (Ill.) Twp. High Sch., 1960-66; asst. prof. U. Pitts., 1966-70, assoc. prof., dept. chmn., 1970-74; assoc. dean sch. edn. Va. Commonwealth U., Richmond, 1974-76, dean sch. edn., 1976-85, interim provost, v.p., 1985-86, provost, v.p., 1986-93; pres. Boise (Idaho) State U., 1993—. Cons. various univs., govtl. agys., ednl. founds. Author or co-author over 50 articles, revs., tech. reports. Mem. Am. Psychol. Assn., Am. Ednl. Research Assn., Phi Delta Kappa. Office: Boise State U 1910 University Dr Boise ID 83725-0399 E-mail: cruch@boisestate.edu.

RUCH, MARCELLA JOYCE, retired educator, biographer; b. Brutus, Mich., Sept. 20, 1937; d. Virgil Murray and Grace Milbry (Collier) Wallace; m. Robert Kirkman McMain, Aug. 29, 1956 (div. Aug. 1970); children: Melodie McMain, Kirk McMain, Nancy Hedges, Elizabeth Curran; m. Peter Jerome Ruch, Dec. 22, 1973; children: David, Dan, Michael and Justin Moore Ruch. BS, Western Mich. U., 1964; MA, U. Colo., Colorado Springs, 1973; PhD, U. Colo., Boulder, 1980. Cert. tchr., prin., counselor, Colo. Tchr. Colorado Springs Pub. Schs., 1964-69; supr. child care El Paso County Social Svcs., Colorado Springs, 1970-73; exec. dir. Antlers Day Care Ctr., 1973-77, Green Shade Schs., Colorado Springs, 1977-81, Pueblo (Colo.) Toddler Ctr., 1981-83; tchr. Penrose (Colo.) Elem. Sch., 1983-86; adminstrv. intern Cottonwood Elem. Sch., Denver, 1986-87; elem. prin. Simla (Colo.) Pub. Schs., 1987-89; tchr. Colorado Springs Pub. Schs., 1989-97. Adv. bd. for early childhood edn. Pikes Peak C.C., Colorado Springs, 1970-75; child care specialist Cmty. Agencies Working Together, Colorado Springs, 1970-75; humanitarian and med. aid mission trips to Russia with Unitred Meth. Ch. Author: The Gang of One, 1998, Pablita Velarde: Painting Her People, 2001, Just Doing My Job, 2002. Founder Green Shade Schs., 1977; campaign chair United Way, Canon City, Colo., 1983—84, pres., 1984—85; chair adult edn. St. Paul's United Meth. Ch., 1994—96, participant mission trips to Russia, 1997, 1999; lay evangelist. Mem. Delta Kappa Gamma (v.p. membership 1994-96), Phi Delta Kappa. Methodist. Avocations: gardening, hiking, reading, camping. Home and Office: 1111 Modes St Colorado Springs CO 80904-3242

RUCHELMAN, LEONARD ISADORE, urban studies and public administration educator; b. Bklyn., June 28, 1933; s. Jacob and Sarah (Rosenblum) R.; m. Diana G. Hoffberger, Feb.11, 1961; children: Lauren, Charles. BA, Bklyn. Coll., 1954; PhD in Polit. Sci., Columbia U., 1965. Vis. asst. prof. dept. polit. sci. W.Va. U., Morgantown, 1962-64; assoc. prof., chair polit. sci. Alfred (N.Y.) U., 1964-69; assoc. prof., dir. urban studies Lehigh U., Bethlehem, Pa., 1969-75; prof., chmn. dept. urban studies and pub. adminstrn. Old Dominion U., Norfolk, Va., 1975-92, dir. Ctr. for Regional Studies, 1986-90, Eminent Scholar of Pub. Adminstrn., 1992—2002. Mem. editorial com. on socio-polit. influences Coun. on Tall Bldgs. and Urban Habitat, Bethlehem, 1975—. Author: Big City Mayors, 1969, Police Politics, 1974, The World Trade Center, 1977, A Workbook in Program Design for Public Managers, 1985, A Workbook in Redesigning Public Services, 1989. Cities in the Third Wave, 2000. With U.S. Army, 1954-56. Mem. AAUP, Am. Soc. Pub. Adminstrn. (pres. Tidewater chpt. 1977-78), Urban Affairs Assn., Am. Polit. Sci. Assn. E-mail: lruchelm@odu.edu.

RUCHLIN, HIRSCH S. educator, consultant; b. New York, Feb. 25, 1942; s. Ben Z. Ruchlin, Freida Ruchlin; m. Eleanor Seltzer; children: Ari, Deena Traum. PhD, Columbia U., 1968. Prof. Weill Med. Coll. Cornell U., New York, 1972—. Contractor, cons. Merck Rsch. Lab., Blue Bell, Pa. Office: Weill Med Coll of Cornell Univ 411 East 69th Street - KB 319 New York NY 10021

RUCKENSTEIN, ELI, chemical engineering educator; b. Botosani, Romania, Aug. 13, 1925; arrived in U.S., 1969; m. Velina Rothstein, May 15, 1948; children: Andrei, Lelia. BSChemE, Poly. Inst., Bucharest, Romania, 1949, PhD , 1967; PhD (hon.), Tech. U., Bucharest, Romania, 1993. Prof. Poly. Inst., Bucharest, 1949—69; vis. prof. U. London, 1969; NSF sr. scientist Clarkson Coll. Tech., Potsdam, NY, 1969—70; prof. U. Del., Newark, 1970—73, SUNY, Buffalo, 1973—81, disting. prof., 1981—. Vis. Humbolt prof. Bayreuth U., Germany, 1986; Gulf vis. prof. Carnegie Mellon U., Pitts., 1988—89; disting. lectr. U. Waterloo, 1985, U. Mo., 1983; Fair Meml. lectr. U. Okla., 1987; Colburn Symposium lectr. U. Del., 1988, Robert L. Pigford meml. lectr., 99; Van Winkle lectr. U. Tex., 1989; Berkeley lectr., 97; Robert A. Welch Found. lectr., 97; Barnett F. Dodge disting. lectr. Yale U., 1998; Merk disting. lectr. Rutgers U., 1992. Contbr. articles to profl. jours. Named Merk Disting. Lectr., Rutgers U., 1992; recipient Nat. award, Romanian Dept. Edn., 1958, 1964, Tchg. award, 1961, George Spacu award, Romanian Acad. Sci., 1963, Sr. Humbolt award, Alexander von Humbolt Found., 1985, Creativity award, NSF, 1985, Nat. Medal of Sci., 1998. Mem.: AIChE (Alpha Chi Sigma award 1977, Walker award 1988, Founders award 2002), NAE, Am. Chem. Soc. (Kendall award 1986, Jacob F. Schoellkopf medal 1986, Langmuir Disting. Lectr. award 1994, E.V. Murphree award 1996, Nat. Medal of Sci. 1998). Office: SUNY Dept Chem Engring 303 Furnas Hall Buffalo NY 14260-4200

RUCKER, DONALD W. emergency physician, educator, consultant; b. Montreal, Que., Can. came to U.S., 1960; s. Klaus G. and Daisy Rucker. AB, Harvard U., 1977; MD, U. Pa., 1981; MBA, Stanford U., 1987, MS, 1988. Diplomate Am. Bd. Internal Medicine, Am. Bd. Emergency Medicine. Product mgr. Datamedic, Waltham, Mass., 1988-93; emergency physician Beth Israel Hosp., Boston, 1990—2000; instr. Med. Sch. Harvard U., 1992—2000; v.p., chief med. officer Siemens Health Svcs., 2000—. Fellow Am. Coll. Emergency Physicians. also: 51 Valley Stream Pkwy Malvern PA 19355-1406

RUCKER, DOUGLAS PENDLETON, JR. lawyer; b. Richmond, Va., Dec. 26, 1945; s. Douglas Pendleton and Margaret (Williams) R.; m. Marian F. Copeland; 1 child, Louise Meredith. BA, Hampden-Sydney Coll., 1968; JD, U. Va., 1972. Bar: Va. 1972, D.C. 1986, U.S. Dist. Ct. (ea. and we. dists.) Va. 1972, U.S. Ct. Appeals (4th cir.) 1982, U.S. Supreme Ct. 1982, U.S. Ct. Claims 1995. Assoc. Sands, Anderson, Marks & Miller, Richmond, Va., 1972-76, mem., 1977—, also bd. dirs. Active Lewis Ginter Bot. Garden; mem. adv. com. Richmond Renaissance; active St. John's Episcopal Ch., mem. vestry, 1994—98, register, 1996, jr. warden, 1997, sr. warden, 1998, trustee, 1994—; bd. dirs. Va. Ctr. for the Book Capital chpt. ARC; bd. dirs., vice chmn. James River Devel. Corp. With Va. Army N.G., 1968—74. Fellow: SAR, ABA, Met. Richmond C. of C., Bar Assn. D.C., Soc. Colonial Wars in the State of Va. (dep. gov. gen.), Richmond Bar Assn. (real estate sect., bd. dirs. 1994—97), Va. Bar Assn. (constrn. law chmn. 1992, real estate and bus. law sects., exec. com. 1992—97, pres. 1996), Va. Law Found. (bd. dirs. 1998—), Am. Bar Found., The Twenty-Three Hundred Club, Country Club Va., Commonwealth Club. Office: Sands Anderson Marks & Miller PO Box 1998 Richmond VA 23218-1998 E-mail: DRucker@sandsanderson.com.

RUCKER, KENNETH LAMAR, law enforcement officer, educator; b. Atlanta, July 16, 1961; s. Jack Lamar and Priscilla Anne (Anderson) R.; m. Kerri Lynn Hairston; children: Kenneth Lamar II, Kerbi Lynn. BSBA, Brenau U., 1991; MPA in Pub. Mgmt., Ga. State U., 1993; postgrad., U. Ga., 1993—. Cert. peace officer, supr., Ga., field tng. officer, law enforcement exec.; cert. supply corps, Navy Supply Corps Sch., 1997. Law enforcement officer Met. Atlanta Rapid Transit Authority, 1984-93; sch. resource officer Fulton County Bd. Edn., Atlanta, 1993-95; field facilitator Cmtys. in Schs. of Ga., Inc., 1995-97, field facilitator Cross Roads program, 1995-97; chief of police Fulton County Schs. Police Dept., 1997—. Bd. dirs. Benefactors of Edn., Inc., Atlanta; cons. pub. security Fulton County Bd. Edn., Atlanta, 1993-95; supply corps officer Navy Supply Corps Sch. USNR, Athens, 1997; bd. advisors Fulton County Pub. Safety Tng. Ctr., 2000—. Sunday sch. tchr. Simpson St. Ch. of Christ, Atlanta, 1991—; youth motivator Atlanta Pub. Schs., 1988—. Commd. officer Supply Corps, USNR, 1995—. Doctoral fellow U. Ga. Mem. Am. Soc. Pub. Adminstrn., Internat. Assn. Chiefs of Police, Nat. Orgn. Black Law Enforcement Execs., Nat. Forum Black Pub. Adminstrs., Ga. Assn. Chiefs of Police, Benefactors of Edn., Inc. (bd. dirs. 1996-99), Brenau U. Alumni Club (bd. dirs. 1999—), Ga. State U. Alumni Club, U.S. Naval Inst., Naval Res. Assn., Res. Officer's Assn., Navy Supply Corps Assn., Pi Alpha Alpha, Pi Sigma Alpha, Omicron Delta Kappa (cir. pres. 1992-93). Avocations: computer tech., reading, photography, classical music, fitness. Home: 1835 Jenny Ln Lithia Springs GA 30122-2857 Office: Fulton County Schs Police Fulton County Bd Education 786 Cleveland Ave SW Atlanta GA 30315-7239 E-mail: rucker.kenneth.l@fulton.k12.ga.us.

RUCKER, R.D. lawyer; b. Swifton, Ark., Jan. 14, 1950; s. Curtis and Demora (Tidwell) R. BA, U. Ark., 1971; MA, U. Iowa, 1972, PhD, 1981; JD, U. Tex., 1985. Bar: Tex. 1985, U.S. Dist. Ct. (no. dist.) Tex. 1988, U.S. Ct. Appeals (5th cir.) 1989. Asst. atty. gen. Atty. Gen.'s Office, Austin, Tex., 1985-86; asst. dist. atty. Dist. Atty.'s Office, Waco, 1986-87; 1st asst. pub. defender Pub. Defender's Office, Wichita Falls, 1987-88; atty. R.D. Rucker's Law Office, Dallas, 1988—. Author: Eros and the Sexual Revolution: Studies in the Psychology of the Human Mind, 1991, Drugs, Drug Addiction and Drug Dealing: The Origin and Nature of, and the Solution to, the American Drug Problem, 1991, Abraham Lincoln's Social and Political Thought, 1992, Jesus Christ and the Origin of Christianity, 1993, Marriage, Love, and the Family: An Investigation into the Role of the Black Woman in the African-American Family, 1998, Sweet Land of Liberty: A Poetical Journey Through America, 1996-1998, 1998, The Nature, Evolution and Structure of the Universe: A Twenty First Century Theory, 1999. Avocations: poetry, track, calisthenics. Office: PO Box 222167 Dallas TX 75222-2167 E-mail: RDRUCK@aol.com.

RUCKER, RICHARD S. information systems executive; b. Dayton, Ohio, Sept. 4, 1947; s. Wilbert Hunter and Estelle Janet Rucker. BBA, Wright State U., Dayton, 1976; MBA, Cen. Mich. U., 1987; PhD in Mgmt. Info. Systems, Kennedy-Western U., 1990. Asst. program mgr. Synergy, Inc., Dayton, 1968-78; mgr. data processing Ledex, Inc., Vandalia, Ohio, 1978-83; cons. analyst NCR Corp., Dayton, 1983-85; mgr. info. systems SelectTech Corp., 1985; dir. computing and tech. svcs. Dayton Bd. Edn., 1985-91, asst. supt. bus. and tech. svcs., 1991-92; v.p. Midwest region Metters Industries, Inc., 1992-97; CEO, pres. The Rucker Group, Dayton, 1997—. Pres. Richard S. Rucker & Assocs., Dayton, 1982-97. Bd. dirs. Dakota Youth Ctr., Dayton, 1983, Dayton Urban League, 1986—; mem. exec. council Congl. Adv. Council to U.S. Congressman Tony Hall, 1986. Named one of Outstanding Young Men Am., 1984, Man of Achievement, 1988. Mem. Kappa Alpha Psi. Democrat. Avocations: painting, reading, swimming, astro-physics, basketball. Home: 2914 Forest Grove Ave Dayton OH 45406-4039

RUCKER, ROBERT D. judge; b. Canton, Ga. married; 3 children. BA, Ind. U.; JD, Valparaiso Sch. of Law; LLM, U. Va. Dep. prosecuting atty., Lake County, Ind.; city atty. City of Gary; pvt. practice East Chicago; justice Ind. State Supreme Ct., Indpls., 1999—. Former vice chmn. Ind. Commn. for Continuing Legal Edn. Bd. dirs. Legal Svcs. of N.W. Ind. Decorated Vietnam Vet. Office: State House Rm 312 200 W Washington St Indianapolis IN 46204-2798*

RUCKER, SUE C. psychiatric nurse practitioner; b. Anacortes, Wash., Nov. 9, 1948; d. William Eugene and Maldetta Mae Compton; m. Richard Warren Rucker, Mar. 23, 1979; children: Linda Marie, Shannon Kathleen. BSN, U. Cin., 1971; MSN, Vanderbilt U., 1974. Cert. in adult psychiatry and mental health. Instr. in nursing edn. Alvin C. York VA Med. Ctr., Murfreesboro, Tenn., 1974-75, assoc. chief nursing svc. for edn., 1975-79, staff nurse, 1979-83, nurse mgr., 1983-86, clin. nurse specialist, 1986-94, nurse mgr., 1994-98, nurse practitioner, 1998—. Test exam. reviewer Ednl. Testing Orgn., Princeton, NJ, 1997. Asst. blood drives ARC, Murfreesboro, 1978—; camp nurse North Blvd. Ch. of Christ, Murfreesboro, 1979-97. Mem. Sigma Theta Tau. Democrat. Mem. Ch. of Christ. Avocations: needlework, crochet, sewing, reading, cooking. Home: 3437 Red Oak Trl Murfreesboro TN 37130-6853 Office: Alvin C York VA Med Ctr 3400 Lebanon Rd Murfreesboro TN 37129-1237

RUCKERT, ANN JOHNS, musician, singer; b. N.Y.C., Mar. 12, 1945; d. G. Wallace and Elizabeth (Johns) R. Student, Julliard Sch., 1961-69, NYU, 1969-70, Royal Acad. Music, London, 1972; studies in composition with Nadia Boulanger, Paris, 1972-73; studies with Helen Hobbs Jordon, N.Y.C., 1973-75; studies with David Sorin Collyer, 1975-78. Profl. musician over 3,000 commercially released records, 1960—; owner, pres. Ann Ruckert Music, N.Y.C. and Los Angeles, 1980—. Cons., spkr. Platinum Record Industry seminars; chairperson N.Y. Jazz Mus., N.Y.C., 1977-79; bd. dirs. Jazzmobile, N.Y.C., 1983-89, 92—; TV com. Grammy awards, 1985-87; mem. creative staff Lifetime Achievement awards show, 1987; adv. Universal Jazz Coalition, N.Y.C., 1979-87; cons. rec. industry including: Zero House Records, Warner Group, bd. dirs. ASCAP; also individual artists: Roberta Flack, Diane Schnur, Morgan Ames, over 300 clients; performance Ann Ruckert Choir, Macy's 4th of July Show, 1996; lectr. NYU, SUNY, Harvard, 1996-97. Musician, singer: (recs.) Strawbs, Greatest Hits (Gold Record award, 1975); music contractor: (film) Housesitter, 1993, Boys on the Side, 1994; performed at Hudson Theatre, 1994, Shea Stadium, 1994, Lincoln Ct., 1994; producer albums: Jane Jarvis, Jazz, Mike Longo, Jazz, 1996-97. Commr. Deed, N.Y., 1986—, Schomberg Collection N.Y.C. Pub. Library; mem. county com. Westside Manhattan, 1980-89; co-chair and chair edn. com. Grammys in the Schs., N.Y.C. Mem. NARAS (Named Most Valuable Player 1982, 89, trustee, gov., v.p. N.Y. chpt., bd. trustees 1989—, bd. dirs. World Hunger Yr.), Soc. Singers (bd. dirs. N.Y.C. chpt.), Songwriters Guild Am. (bd. dirs., concert, Pres.'s award 1997). Democrat. Episcopalian. Avocations: arts, music, visual arts. Home and Office: 119 W 71st St New York NY 10023-3876

RUCKMAN, MARK WARREN, physicist; b. Rolla, Mo., Dec. 26, 1954; s. Homer Leslie and Audrey (Warren) R. BS in Physics, Pa. State U., 1977; PhD in Physics, Rensselaer Polytechnic Inst., 1984. Asst. physicist Brookhaven Nat. Lab., Upton, N.Y., 1985-87, assoc. physicist, 1987-91, physicist, 1991-93, physics assoc. I, 1993-2000; physicist Fusion UV Sys., Inc., Gaithersburg, Md., 2000—. Contbr. articles to profl. jours. Mem. Am. Phys. Soc., Am. Vacuum Soc., Am. Chem. Soc., Materials Rsch. Soc., Phi Beta Kappa, Phi Kappa Phi. Republican. Baptist. Office: Fusion UV Sys Inc 910 Copper Rd Gaithersburg MD 20878-1357 Fax: 301-527-2661.

RUCKMAN, PETER STURGES, JR. political science educator; b. Pensacola, Fla., Sept. 29, 1959; s. Peter S. and Janie Bess (May) R. BA in Theology, Pensacola Bible Inst., 1980, ThM, 1982; BA in Philosophy and Polit. Sci., U. West Fla., 1986; MS in Polit. Sci., Fla. State U., 1988, PhD in Polit. Sci., 1991. Vis. asst. prof. Memphis State U., 1991-92; asst. prof. No. Ill. U., DeKalb, Ill., 1992—. Faculty advisor Model Ill. Govt. Orgn., DeKalb, 1992—, Kappa Sigma, 1992—. Contbr. articles to profl. jours. Mem. Am. Polit. Sci. Assn., Am. Judicature Soc., Midwest Polit. Sci. Assn., Law and Soc. Assn., So. Polit. Sci. Assn. Avocations: reading, music, sports. Home: # 513 1305 N Annie Glidden Rd Apt 513 Dekalb IL 60115-1249 Office: No Ill U Dept Polit Sci Dekalb IL 60115

RUCKMAN, ROGER NORRIS, pediatric cardiologist; b. Washington, Dec. 15, 1944; s. Norris Elliott and Eugenia (Campbell) R.; m. Kathleen Anne Smith; children: Robert, Karen, Stephen, Jonathan. BA in Chemistry, Williams Coll., Williamstown, Mass., 1966; MD, U. Va., 1970. Intern Peter Bent Brigham Hosp., 1970-71; resident Med. Ctr. Hosp. of Vermont, 1973-75; fellow in cardiology Children's Hosp., Boston, 1975-77; asst. prof. pediatrics U. Nebr., Omaha, 1977-79, George Washington U., Washington, 1980-82, assoc. prof. pediatrics, 1982-90, prof. pediatrics, 1990—; pediatric cardiologist Children's Hosp. Nat. Med. Ctr., 1980—, chmn. cardiology, 1986-89. Contbr. articles to profl. jours. Served to capt. U.S. Army, 1971-73. Recipient Disting. Service award, Am.-Korea Found., 1972; NIH grantee, 1982—. Fellow Am. Acad. Pediatrics, Am. Coll. Cardiology; mem. Am. Heart Assn., Teratology Soc., Soc. Pediatric Research, Columbia Country Club (Chevy Chase, Md.). Republican. Presbyterian. Avocations: tennis, golf. Office: CNMC Dept Cardiology 111 Michigan Ave NW Washington DC 20010-2916 E-mail: rruckman@cnmc.org.

RUDA, HOWARD, lawyer, finance company executive; b. N.Y.C., Sept. 7, 1932; s. Menahem and Lucy (Gillenson) R.; m. Leah E. Zeliger, Sept. 22, 1963; 1 child, Amy. BA, CCNY, 1954; JD, Columbia U., 1959. Bar: N.Y. 1959, U.S. Dist. Ct. (so. and ea. dists.) N.Y. 1959. Assoc., then ptnr. Laporte & Meyers, N.Y.C., 1959-63; staff atty., then gen. counsel Meinhard Comml. Corp., 1963-68; with C.I.T. Group Holdings, Inc., 1968-87, asst. gen. counsel, 1968—; gen. counsel, v.p., dir. C.I.T. Corp., C.I.T. Leasing Corp., 1973-84; counsel Hahn & Hessen, 1987—. Lectr. Practicing Law Inst., Banking Law Inst.; dir. Am. Bankruptcy Inst., 1982-91; arbitrator Am. Arbitration Assn. Editor: Asset Based Financing, Jour. of Bankruptcy Law and Practice. Served with U.S. Army, 1954-56. Fellow Am. Bar Found., Am. Coll. Comml. Fin. Lawyers (regent 1992-95); mem. ABA (chmn. equipment financing com. 1982-85, chmn. ad hoc bulk sales com. 1987-90), Am. Law Inst., Phi Beta Kappa. Jewish. Avocations. Home: 8 Mirrielees Rd Great Neck NY 11021-2928 Office: Hahn & Hessen 350 5th Ave Ste 3700 New York NY 10118-0075 E-mail: hruda@hahnhessen.com.

RUDACILLE, SHARON VICTORIA, medical technologist; b. Ranson, W. Va., Sept. 11, 1950; d. Albert William and Roberta Mae (Anderson) R.; BS cum laude, Shepherd Coll., 1972. Med. technologist VA Ctr., Martinsburg, W.Va., 1972—, instr. Sch. Med. Tech., 1972-76, assoc. coord. edn., 1976-77, edn. coord., 1977-78, quality assurance officer clin. chemistry, 1978-80, lab. svc. quality assurance and edn. officer, 1980-84, clin. chemistry sect. leader, 1984-86, staff med. technologist, 1986-94, suprvisory med. technologist, 1994-95, sr. med. technologist, 1995—; adj. faculty mem. Shippensburg (Pa.) State Coll., 1977-78, Shepherd Coll., 1977-78. Mem. Am. Soc. Med. Tech., Am. Soc. Clin. Pathologists, W.Va. Soc. Med. Technologists, Shepherd Coll. Alumni Assn., Sigma Pi Epsilon. Baptist. Home: PO Box 14 Ranson WV 25438-0014

RUDCZYNSKI, ANDREW B. academic administrator, medical researcher; b. Nottingham, England, Sept. 7, 1947; came to U.S., 1951; s. Richard B. and Krystyna Z. R.; m. Andrea Skalny, Oct. 16, 1976 (div. Oct. 1990); children: Christina, Thomas. BSc in Biology/Biochemistry, McGill U., 1969; PhD in Immunology, Syracuse U., 1974; MBA in Adminstrn., So. Ill. U., 1984. Prin. investigator scrub typhus project divsn. Rickettsiology U.S. Army Med. Rsch. Infectious Diseases, Ft. Detrick, Md., 1974-76; rsch. assoc. dept. Biology Mich. Cancer Found., Detroit, 1976-77, rsch. scientist dept. Immunology, unit chief immunology unit Breast Cancer Prognostic Study, 1977-80; asst. dir. Office Rsch. and Grants U. Md. Ea. Shore, Princess Anne, 1980-83; extramural assoc. Office Extramural Rsch. and Tng., Office of Dir. NIH, 1981-82; asst. dir. Office Rsch. & Sponsored Programs Rutgers U., Piscataway, N.J., 1983-84, dir., 1984-99, asst. v.p. rsch. adminstrn., 1985-93, assoc. v.p. rsch. policy and adminstrn., 1993-99; assoc. v.p. fin., exec. dir. rsch. svcs. U. Pa., Phila., 1999—. Field reader strengthening devel. instns. program U.S. Dept. Edn., 1990; mem. Chancellor's task force instrn. and rsch. infrastructure support N.J. Dept. Higher Edn., 1992. Contbr. articles, abstracts to profl. jours. Capt. U.S. Army Med. Svc. Corps, 1974-76. Recipient traineeship award NSF, 1969-71; predoctoral fellow NIH, 1973-74. Mem. AAAS, Nat. Coun. Univ. Rsch. Adminstrs. (profl. devel. com. 1988-90, region II program com. 1989-90, chmn. region II 1990-92, nat. program com. 1994-95), Coun. Govtl. Rels. (fed. mgmt. devel. com. 1989-90, bd. dirs. 1998, tech. transfer and ethics com. 1998-2002, rsch. compliance and adminstrn. com.), Beta Gamma Sigma, Sigma Xi. Roman Catholic. Home: 2033 Rodman St Philadelphia PA 19146-1359 Office: Univ Pa Office Rsch Svcs 3451 Walnut St Ste P-221 Philadelphia PA 19104-6205

RUDD, D(ALE) F(REDERICK), chemical engineering educator; b. Mpls., Mar. 2, 1935; m. 1964; 2 children. BS, U. Minn., 1956, PhD in Chem. Engring., 1960. Asst. prof. chem. engring. U. Mich., Ann Arbor, 1960-61; from asst. prof. to prof. U. Wis., Madison, 1961-94, Schlicter emeritus prof. chem. engring., 1994—. Named J.S. Guggenheim fellow, 1970; recipient Allan P. Colburn award, 1971. Mem. Nat. Acad. Engring., 1978. Achievements include contributions to the knowlege of process engineering.

RUDD, DAVID WILLIAM, management consultant, engineering consultant; b. Floral Park, N.Y., Dec. 31, 1931; s. Edward Lynn and Joanna (McSorley) R. m. Harriet Fay Sart, Aug. 8, 1953; children: Rebecca, Rachel. BA in Chemistry, Colby Coll., 1953; MS in Phys. Chemistry, Northeastern U., 1962. Rsch. chemist Monsanto Chem. Co., Everett, Mass., 1956-58, Kendall Co., Walpole, 1958-60, Metal Hydrides, Beverly, 1960-62; sr. staff engr. Western Electric Co., North Andover, 1969-78; mem. rsch. staff Engring. Rsch. Ctr., Princeton, NJ, 1978-80; co-founder, dir. David W. Rudd Assocs., mfg. cons., 1985—. Iso-9000 auditor, 1993. Vol. Tutor program Lawrence, Mass. Pub. Sch., 1991; active Bernard McLaughlin Found.; pres. Western Electric Engring Soc., 1977-78, 82-83. With U.S. Army, 1953-55. Recipient Western Electric Co. Engring. Excellence award, 1969, C.B. Sawyer Meml. award, 1974, Vol. Tutoring program award, AT&T, 1991, patent award for growth of synthetic quartz Lucent Techs., 1999. Mem.: Svc. Corp Ret. Execs., Telephone Pioneers of Am. (life). Achievements include research in surface chemistry, permeability of metals to hydrogen, rocket propellant synthesis infrared method of Q evaluation synthetic quartz, crystal growth, printed circuit tech., metal joining; computer-integrated mfg. techniques, statis. quality control, soldering tech., environ. modifications of mfg. processes, ISO 9,000 auditor. Home: 489 Valley Rd Sumner ME 04292-3402 E-mail: davhar@megalink.net.

RUDD, ELDON, retired congressman, political consultant; b. Camp Verde, Ariz. m. Ann Merritt. BA, Ariz. State U., 1947; JD, U. Ariz., 1950. Bar: Ariz. 1949, U.S. Supreme Ct. 1953. Pvt. practice, Tucson, 1950; spl. agt.-diplomatic assignment principally Latin Am. FBI, 1950-70; mem. Maricopa County (Ariz.) Bd. Suprs., 1972-76; bd. dirs. Ariz.-Mex. Commn., 1972-92; with U.S.-Mex. Interparliamentary Com., 1976-84; mem. 95th-99th Congresses from 4th Dist. Ariz., 1976-87; of counsel Shimmel, Hill, Bishop & Gruender, P.C., Phoenix, 1987-93; pres. Eldon Rudd Consultancy, Scottsdale, Ariz., from 1993. Chmn. Phoenix chpt. Soc. Former Spl. Agts. FBI, 1995-96, western regional v.p., 1974. Author: World Communism-Threat to Freedom, 1987. Mem. numerous pub. svc. orgns., including energy and water, mil. and internat. affairs. Fighter pilot USMCR, 1942-46. Mem. Fed. Bar Assn. (chpt. pres. 1976), Ariz. Bar Assn., Maricopa County Bar Assn., Scottsdale Bar Assn., Paradise Valley Country Club (bd. dirs. 1989-92), Phi Delta Phi, Blue Key. Republican. Roman Catholic. Home: Scottsdale, Ariz. Died Feb. 8, 2002.

RUDD, GERALD PATRICK, ophthalmologist; b. Larned, Kans., Oct. 27, 1947; s. Gerald Vern and Olive Irene (Montgomery) Rudd; children: Samuel Patrick McArthur, Sarita Rohani. BA in Chemistry, Ottawa (Kans.) U., 1969; DO, Kirksville Coll. Osteo. Med., 1976; cert. in leprology, Schieffelin Leprosy Rsch. Ctr., Kirigiri, India, 1976; postgrad., Stanford U., 1981. Diplomate in Osteo. Medicine and Surgery Nat. Bd. Examiners. Intern Riverside Osteo. Hosp., Trenton, Mich., 1976-77; commd. lt. USPHS, 1977, advanced through grades to comdr., 1985; resident in ophthalmology USPHS Hosp., San Francisco, 1980; resident in ophthalmology, then chief resident Walter Reed Army Med. Ctr., Washington, 1981-83, fellow in vitro-retinal disease and surgery, 1983-85; gen. med. officer Winslow (Ariz.) Indian Health Ctr.,

1977-79, clin. dir., 1979-80; asst. chief ophthalmology, chief vitreo-retinal surgery Ophthalmology Svc., Gallup (N.Mex.) Indian Med. Ctr., 1985-88; vitreo-reginal surgery and gen. ophthalmology practice Omni Eye Svc., Phoenix, 1988-89, Santa Fe, 1990-91, Eye Clinic, Las Vegas, 1990-91; asst. chief ophthalmology, chief vitreo-retinal surgery Trippler Army Med. Ctr., Honolulu, 1991-94, chief ophthalmology, 1994-96, chief vitreo-retinal surgery ophthalmology svc., 1996-97. Chief EENT clinic, chief ophthalmology svc., chief cons. in ophthalmology to comdg. gen. for S.E. regional med. command Dwight D. Eisenhower Army Med. Ctr., Ft. Gordon, Ga., 1997—2000; instr. dept. surgery F. Edward Hebert Sch. Medicine Uniformed Svcs. U. of Health Scis., Bethesda, Md., 1984—2000; instr. U. Hawaii Sch. Medicine, Honolulu, 1992—97; chief of vitreo-retinal surgery Phoenix Indian Med. Ctr., 2001—. Contbr. articles to profl. jours. Life mem. Rep. Nat. Com. Named Rep. of the Yr., Rep. Nat. Com., 2000; fellow Med. Assistance Programs Internat., Reader's Digest, 1976; scholar Citizens Honors, Ottawa U., 1965—69. Mem.: Confederate Air Force, SAR. Avocations: hunting, fishing. Office: Phoenix Indian Med Ctr Ophthalmology Dept Phoenix AZ 85016

RUDD, NICHOLAS, investor, consultant; b. N.Y.C., Mar. 18, 1943; s. Emmanuel and Lucie Lia Rudd; m. Judith Carol Anderson, 1995; children: Alexis Henry, Kenneth Charles. BA, Columbia U., 1964, MBA, 1967. Mem. staff Ford Motor Co., N.Y.C., 1964-65, Young & Rubicam Inc., N.Y.C., 1968-99, sr. v.p. mgmt. svcs., 1980-90, chief info. officer, 1990-95; chief knowledge officer Wunderman Cato Johnson, 1996-99; prin. Venture Mgmt. Svcs., Inc., 1999—. Bd. dirs. Nat. Choral Coun., chmn., 1993-95, Veritas Therapeutic Cmty. Found. Mem. Beta Gamma Sigma. Office: 20 Sea Spray Rd Westport CT 06437

RUDDEN, JANE FRANCES, education educator; b. St. Louis, Apr. 22, 1945; d. Francis Edward and Julia Margaret (Chartrand) R. BA, Fontbonne Coll., 1968; MA, W.Va. U., 1992, EdD, 1994. Cert. reading specialist, K-12 multi-subject tchr., 7th-8th grade remedial reading tchr. 5th-8th grade lang. arts tchr. Our Lady of the Ams., Kansas City, Mo., 1968-71; 7th-8th grade lang. arts tchr. St. Anthony's Jr.-Sr. H.S., Wailuku Maui, Hawaii, 1971-75; 7th-8th lang. arts tchr. St. Margaret of Scotland, St. Louis, 1977-78; unit supr., 3d-4th grade tchr. St. Joseph's Child Care Ctr., Chgo., 1975-77; dir. meetings and convs. Smith, Bucklin and Assocs., Washington, 1978-80; mgr. data processing tng. Riggs Nat. Bank, 1980-82; edn. cons., mktg. rep. Deltak, Inc., Fairfax, Va., 1982-89; 8th grade lang arts tchr. Berkeley Springs (W.Va.) Jr.-Sr. H.S., 1990-92; asst. prof. elem. edn. Millersville (Pa.) U., 1995—; adj. prof. reading W.Va. U., Morgantown, 1995. Guest lectr., cons. W.Va. Writing Project, Morgantown, 1993-94; mem. pedagogy team W.Va. U., 1993-94; liaison to pub. sch. Benudum Project, Morgantown, 1994; grad. asst. W.Va. U., 1992-94; presenter in field. Accreditation coord. Nat. Coun. Accreditation Tchr. Edn., 1999—, Millersville U., 1999—. Recipient Golden Apple Achiever award Ashland Oil Corp., 1991; W.Va. U. Fellow, 1992-94, Millersville U. Sch. Edn. fellow, 1999—; W.Va. U. grantee, 1993-94. Mem. Coll. Reading Assn. (session chair 1994), Pa. Reading Tchr. Edn., Coll. Reading Improvement (treas., mem. chair), Internat. Reading Assn., Lancaster Lebanon Reading Coun. (co-chair), Keystone State Reading Assn., Phi Delta Kappa, Phi Delta Phi. Avocations: writing children's books, reading, stitchery, gardening, karate. E-mail: jane.rudden@millersville.edu.

RUDDER, ERIC, information technology executive; married; 2 children. Grad. with honors, Brown U., 1988. Gen. mgr. Visual Studio Microsoft, Redmond, Wash., v.p. tech. strategy, sr. v.p. Developer and Platform Evangelism. Office: Microsoft One Microsoft Way Redmond WA 98052-6399*

RUDDOCK, ELLEN SYLVES, business consultant; b. Pitts., May 9, 1944; d. Clyde Lysle and Margaret Beck (Tilley) Sylves; m. Rodney David Ruddock, Apr. 2, 1966; children: Dana William, Darin Willis. BS, Indiana U. Pa., 1966; cert. in entrepreneurial mgmt., Carnegie Mellon U., 1995. Lic. real estate agt., Pa.; cert. facilitator, Leadership Mgmt. Inc. Tchr. Penn Hills H.S., Pitts., 1966; adminstrv. asst. Utah-Martin-Day, Bangkok, 1967-68, Comusmachthai, Bangkok, 1968-69; tchr. United H.S., Armagh, Pa., 1969-70; owner Swing Set Children's Store, Indiana, 1975-80; radio cons. RMS Media Mgmt., 1980-89; owner Career Dynamics, Pitts., 1989—. Bd. dirs. PowerLink, Pitts., pres., 2000-01; initiator partnership between PowerLink and Athena Found. to aid women-owned businesses. Initiator 100-mem. vol. strategic planning group Indiana County for 2020, revitalization program Indiana for the 80s, also fundraisers; chairperson New Growth Arts Festival, Indiana, 1984—85, 1995—, Greater Indiana Strategic Planning Commn.; bd. dirs. PNC Adv. Bd., Indiana, 1986—2000, Nat. Athena Found., Lansing, Mich., 1996—; bd. dirs., now emeritus Downtown Indiana, 1975—, pres., 1979—81. Named World Sales Leader of Assessments, Leadership Mgmt. Inc., 2000, 2001, Retailer of Yr., Kids Mag., N.Y.C., 1978, Ind. County Civic Leader of Yr., 2000; named one of Pa. 50 Best Women in Bus., 1999; recipient Athena award, Nat. Athena Found., 1987, Svc. award, Alice Paul Ho., Ind., Pres.'s Club award, Leadership Mgmt., Inc., Waco, Tex., 1997, Golden Eagle award, 1997, Distbr. of Yr. award, Leadership Mgmt. Inc., 2000, Outstanding Civilian Svc. award, USAR, Pitts., 1997, 2000, Distbr. of Yr. award, Leadership Mgmt. Inc., 2001. Mem. Indiana County C. of C. (chairperson task force 1975-97, bd. dirs. 1997—), Quota Club (pres. 1986-88, Svc. award 1986). Republican. Methodist. Avocations: reading, walking, community service. Home: 465 Edgewood Ave Indiana PA 15701 Office: 1830 Monroe St Pittsburgh PA 15218-2350 E-mail: eruddock@adelphia.net.

RUDDY, FRANK, lawyer, former ambassador; b. N.Y.C., Sept. 15, 1937; s. Francis Stephen and Teresa (O'Neil) Ruddy; children: Neil, David, Stephen. AB, Holy Cross Coll., 1959; MA, NYU, 1962, LLM, 1967; LLB, Loyola U., New Orleans, 1965; PhD, Cambridge U., Eng., 1969. Bar: D.C., N.Y., Tex., U.S. Supreme Ct. Faculty Cambridge U., 1967-69; asst. gen. counsel USIA, Washington, 1969-72; sr. atty. Office of Telecomm. Policy, White House, 1972-73; dep. gen. counsel USIA, 1973-74; counsel Exxon Corp., Houston, 1974-81; asst. adminstr. AID (with rank asst. sec. state) Dept. State, Washington, 1981-84; U.S. ambassador to Equatorial Guinea, 1984-88; gen. counsel U.S. Dept. Energy, Washington, 1988-89; v.p. Sierra Blanca Devel. Corp., 1989-92; pvt. practice Law Offices of Frank Ruddy, 1992-94; ptnr. Ruddy & Muir. Vis. scholar Johns Hopkins Sch. Advanced Internat. Studies, 1990—94; dep. chmn. UN Referendum for Western Sahara, 1994. Author: International Law in the Enlightenment, 1975; editor: American International Law Cases (series); editor in chief Internat. Lawyer; contbr. articles to legal jours. Bd. dirs. African Devel. Found., Washington, 1983-84, Human Life Internat., 1999—; mem. Coun. of Am. Ambs., Washington, 1988—. Served with USMCR, 1956-61 Mem.: ABA (chmn. treaty compliance sect. 1991—93), Hague Acad. Internat. Law Alumni Assn., Internat. Law Assn., Am. Soc. Internat. Law, Dacor House, Cosmos Club (Washington). Republican. Roman Catholic. Home: 5600 Western Ave Chevy Chase MD 20815-3406 Office: Ruddy and Muir 1717 K Street NW Ste 600 Washington DC 20036 E-mail: global@globalltd.com.

RUDDY, JAMES VINCENT, JR. tax advocate; b. N.Y.C., June 15, 1941; s. James Vincent Ruddy and Stella Rotas; m. Judy Anne Garland, Mar.21, 1964 (div. Feb. 1998); children: David George, James Vincent, Jason Nicholas; m. Gwyn Goettig, Nov. 2000. BS Elec. Engring., U.S. Missile Warfare Sch., 1964; JD, LaSalle U., 1966; BS in Aeronautical/Astron. Engring., AET in Indsl. Engring., Embry Riddle Aeronautical U., 1968; diploma in securities law, ITT Hartford Group, 1969, diploma in life, health and accident insurance law, diploma in property and casualty insurance law, ITT Hartford Group, 1972; BS, MS, PhD emphasis in human nutrition, Am. Coll. Nutrition, 1995; D of Naturopathy, Clayton Sch. of Medicine, 1996; diploma in real estate, real estate appraisal law, U. Conn., 1972; MS in Computer Sci., Inst. of Computer Sci.; LLM, Washington Law Sch. Lic. real estate broker; cert. gen. appraiser. Embalmer Rhee Lowe Funeral Home, Miami, 1960-63; instr. Embry-Riddle Aero Inst., Daytona Beach, Fla., 1966-68; rsch. engr. Avco Lycoming, Stratford, Conn., 1968-72; cons., pres. Cons. Assocs., Milford, 1979-97; tax advocate Sleepy Eye, Minn., 1994—, Goettig Erickson, 1997—; adminstr. Profl. Arbitration Assn., 1999—. Author: Jet and Rocket Propulsion, 1967; six patents in electro-mechanical design. With U.S. Army, 1963-69. Mem. AAIS, N.Y. Acad. Scis. Roman Catholic. Avocations: oceanography, flying, computers, preventative medicine. Office: Goettig Ruddy Ltd 128 Main St W Sleepy Eye MN 56085-1328

RUDDY, RICHARD M. physician; b. N.Y.C., Aug. 7, 1950; s. Walter R. and Juliana Ruddy; m. Barbara Wriston; children: Charlotte, Amanda, Meg. BS, U. Notre Dame, 1972; MD, Georgetown U., 1976. Asst. prof. pediatrics Children's Hosp. of Phila./U. Pa., 1980-85; assoc. prof. N.Y. Med. Coll., Westchester, 1985-91; assoc. prof. pediatrics U. Cin. Coll. Medicine, 1991-96, prof. pediatrics, 1996—; dir. emergency medicine Children's Hosp. Med. Ctr., Cin., 1991—. Assoc. editor: Textbook of Pediatric Emergency Medicine, 1983. Fellow Am. Acad. Pediatrics (exec. com. 1997—), Am. Coll. Emergency Physicians; mem. Ambulatory Pediatric Assn. Office: Children's Hosp Med Ctr 3333 Burnet Ave Cincinnati OH 45229-3026 E-mail: richard.ruddy@chmcc.org.

RUDE, BRIAN DAVID, utilities company executive; b. Viroqua, Wis., Aug. 25, 1955; s. Raymond and Conelee (Johnson) R.; m. Karen Thulin; children: Erik, Nels. BA magna cum laude, Luther Coll., 1977; MA, U. Wis., Madison, 1994. Mem. Wis. Assembly, Madison, 1982-84, Wis. Senate, Madison, 1984-2000; pres. Wis. State Sen., 1993-96, 98. With corp. communications The Trane Co., La Crosse, Wis., 1981-85; dir. external rels. Dairyland Power Cooperative; chmn. Midwestern Higher Edn. Commn. Mem. Evang. Luth. Ch. Am. Coun. Mem. Lions, Sons of Norway, Norwegian-Am. Hist. Assn. (bd. dirs.), Rotary. Republican. Lutheran. Avocations: reading, gardening, traveling, fishing. Home: 307 Babcock St PO Box 367 Coon Valley WI 54623-0367 Office: 3400 East Ave S PO Box 817 La Crosse WI 54602 E-mail: bdr@dairynet.com.

RUDEBUSCH, ALICE ANN, lawyer; b. Milw., July 9, 1966; d. Leroy George and Maryann Grace (Carlson) Rudebusch; m. Todd William Nejedlo, May 25, 1991 (div. 1999). BA, Northwestern U., 1988; JD, U. Wis., 1991; Certificat De Langue, Université De Paris, 1986. Bar: Wis. 1991, U.S. Dist. Ct. (we. dist.) Wis. 1991, U.S. Dist. Ct. (ea. dist.) Wis. 1995, U.S. Dist. Ct. (no. dist.) Ill. 1995. Assoc. Hanson Gasiorkiewicz & Weber, S.C., Racine, Wis., 1991-96; ptnr. Hanson & Gasiorkiewicz, S.C., 1997—. Alderperson City of Oak Creek Common Coun.; bd. dirs. YWCA, Racine, 1995—2001, sec., 1996—98, pres., 1999—2001; vol. Legal Action of Wis., Kenosha, 1996—97. Mem. State Bar Wis., Wis. Acad. Trial Lawyers, Racine County Bar Assn. Office: Hanson & Gasiorkiewicz SC 2932 Northwestern Ave Racine WI 53404-2249 E-mail: hglawofc@execpc.com.

RUDEE, MERVYN LEA, engineering educator, researcher; b. Palo Alto, Calif., Oct. 4, 1935; s. Mervyn C. and Hannah Rudee; m. Elizabeth Eager, June 20, 1958; children: Elizabeth Diane, David Benjamin. BS, Stanford U., 1958, MS, 1962, PhD, 1965. Asst. prof. materials sci. Rice U., Houston, 1964-68, assoc. prof., 1968-72, prof. materials sci., 1972-74; prof. U. Calif. San Diego, La Jolla, 1974—, founding provost Warren Coll., 1974-82, founding dean Sch. Engring., 1982-93, coord. grad. program on materials sci., 1994-99, faculty athletic rep., 1999—; interim dean engring. U. Calif., Riverside, 1995-97. Vis. scholar Corpus Christi Coll., Cambridge, Eng., 1971-72; CFO, prin. Univ. Planning Assocs., Inc.; vis. scientist IBM Thomas J. Watson Rsch. Ctr., Yorktown Heights, N.Y., 1987; dir. fellows program Calif. Coun. on Sci. and Tech., 1999-2000. Pres., bd. trustees Mus. Photographic Art, San Diego, 1995-96; trustee The Burnham Inst., 1998—, The Glen Canyon Inst., 1999—. Lt. (j.g.) USN, 1958-61. Guggenheim fellow, 1971-72 Fellow AAAS; mem. Microscopy Soc. Am., Materials Rsch. Soc., Tex. Soc. Electron Microscopy (hon., pres. 1966), Sigma Xi, Tau Beta Pi. Home: 1745 Kearsarge Rd La Jolla CA 92037-3829 Office: U Calif San Diego Dept Elec & Cptr Engring La Jolla CA 92093-0407 E-mail: rudee@ucsd.edu.

RUDEL, JULIUS, conductor; b. Vienna, Austria, Mar. 6, 1921; came to U.S., 1938, naturalized, 1944; s. Jakob and Josephine (Sonnenblum) R.; m. Rita Gillis, June 24, 1942 (dec. May 1984); children: Joan, Madeleine, Anthony Jason. Student, Acad. Music, Vienna; diploma in conducting, Mannes Coll. Music, 1942; diploma hon. doctorates, U. Vt., 1961, U. Mich., 1971; doctorates hon. causa, Pace Coll., Manhattan Coll., 1994, Mannes Coll. Music, 1994, Manhattanville Coll., 1994, Manhattan Sch. Music, 1996. With N.Y. City Opera, 1943-79, debut, 1944, gen. dir., 1957-79, 3rd St. Music Sch. Settlement, 1945-52, mus. dir. Chautauqua Opera Assn., 1958-59, Caramoor Festival, Katonah, N.Y., 1964-76, Cin. May Festival, 1971-72, Kennedy Ctr. Performing Arts, 1971-75; music advisor Wolf Trap Farm Pk., 1971, Phila. Opera, 1978-81; condr. Spoleto (Italy) Festival, 1962-63; music dir. Buffalo Philarm. Orch., 1979-85, debut as condr. Met. Opera, 1978, San Franciso Opera, 1979, Vienna State Opera, 1976, Royal Opera, Covent Garden, 1984, Rome Opera, 1987, Opera de la Bastille, 1992, Teatro Colon, Buenos Aires, 1992, Royal Danish Opera, Copenhagen, 1993, L.A. Opera, 1995; dir. prodn.: Kiss Me Kate, Vienna Volksoper Opera, 1956; guest condr. Chgo. Symphony, Phila. Orch., N.Y. Philharm., Boston Symphony, Detroit Symphony, Israel Philharm., Paris Opera, Munich Opera, Hamburg State Opera, Vienna State Opera, other symphonic, operatic orgns. in U.S. and Europe. Decorated Croix du Chevalier in arts and letters France; recipient gold medal Nat. Arts Club, 1958, citation Nat. Assn. Am. Composers and Conductors, 1958, citation Nat. Fedn. Music Clubs, 1959, Ditson award Columbia, 1959, Page One award in music Newspaper Guild, 1959, hon. insignia for arts and sci. Govt. of Austria, 1961, Handel medallion for music City N.Y., 1965, citation Nat. Assn. Negro Musicians, 1965, citation Nat. Opera Assn., 1971, comdr.'s Cross German Order Merit, 1967, hon. lt. Israeli Army, 1969, Julius Rudel award for young condrs., Pan Am./Pan African award for humanism, 1981, Peabody award, 1985, Disting. Achievement award Kurt Weill Found., 2000. Office: c/o Shuman Assocs 120 W 58th St Apt 8D New York NY 10019-2126

RUDELIUS, WILLIAM, marketing educator; b. Rockford, Ill., Sept. 2, 1931; s. Carl William and Clarissa Euclid (Davis) R.; m. Jacqueline Urch Dunham, July 3, 1954; children: Robert, Jeanne, Katherine, Kristi. BS in Mech. Engring., U. Wis., 1953; MBA, U. Pa., 1959, PhD in Econs., 1964. Program engr., missile and space vehicle dept. Gen. Electric Co., Phila., 1956-57, 59-61; sr. research economist North Star Research Inst., Mpls., 1964-66; lectr. U. Minn., 1961-64, asst. prof. mktg. Coll. Bus. Adminstrn., 1964, assoc. prof., 1966-72, prof., 1972—. Co-author: (with W. Bruce Erickson) An Introduction to Contemporary Business, 1973, rev. 4th edit., 1985, (with Eric N. Berkowitz, Roger A. Kerin and Steven W. Hartley) Marketing, 1986, rev. 7th edit., 20030, (with Krzysztof Przybytowski, Roger A. Kerin and Steven W. Hartley) Marketing na Przykładach, 1998, (with others) Mapketkht, 1st Russian edit., 2001; contbr. articles to profl. jours. Served with USAF, 1954-55. Home: 1425 Alpine Pass Minneapolis MN 55416-3560 Office: U St Thomas Grad Sch Bus MPL 331 1000 LaSalle Ave Minneapolis MN 55403-2005 E-mail: wrudelius@stthomas.edu.

RUDENSTINE, NEIL LEON, academic administrator, educator; b. Ossining, N.Y., Jan. 21, 1935; s. Harry and Mae (Esperito) R.; m. Angelica Zander, Aug. 27, 1960; children: Antonia Margaret, Nicholas David, Sonya. BA, Princeton U., 1956; BA (Rhodes Scholar), Oxford U., 1959, MA, 1963; PhD, Harvard U., 1964. Instr. dept. English Harvard U., Cambridge, Mass., 1964-66, asst. prof., 1966-68; assoc. prof. English Princeton (N.J.) U., 1968-73, prof. English, 1973-88, dean of students, 1968-72, dean of Coll., 1972-77, provost, 1977-88, provost emeritus, 1988—; exec. v.p. Andrew W. Mellon Found., N.Y.C., 1988-91; pres. Harvard U., Cambridge, Mass., 1991-2001, prof. English, 1991-2001, pres. emeritus, 2001—. Chair adv. bd. ArtStor, A.W. Mellon Found., 2001—. Author: Sidney's Poetic Development, 1967, Pointing Our Thoughts, 2001; (with George Rousseau) English Poetic Satire, 1972; (with William Bowen) In Pursuit of the PhD, 1992. Served to 1st lt. arty. AUS, 1959-60. Hon. fellow New Coll./Oxford U., Emmanuel Coll./Cambridge U., 1991. Fellow Am. Acad. Arts and Scis.; mem. Am. Philos. Soc., Coun. on Fgn. Rels., Com. for Econ. Devel. Office: AW Mellon Found 140 E 62d St New York NY 10021

RUDER, DAVID STURTEVANT, lawyer, educator, government official; b. Wausau, Wis., May 25, 1929; s. George Louis and Josephine (Sturtevant) R.; m. Susan M. Small; children: Victoria Chesley, Julia Larson, David Sturtevant II, John Coulter; m stepchildren: Elizabeth Frankel, Rebecca Wilkinson. BA cum laude, Williams Coll., 1951; JD with honors, U. Wis., 1957. Bar: Wis. 1957, Ill. 1962. Of counsel Schiff Hardin & Waite, Chgo., 1971-76; assoc. Quarles & Brady, Milw., 1957-61; asst. prof. law Northwestern U., Chgo., 1961-63, assoc. prof., 1963-65, prof., 1965—, William W. Gurley meml. prof. of law, 1994—, assoc. dean Law Sch., 1965-66, dean Law Sch., 1977-85; chmn. Securities and Exch. Commn., Washington, 1987-89; ptnr. Baker & McKenzie, Chgo., 1990-94, sr. counsel, 1994-99. Cons. Am. Law Inst. Fed. Securities Code; planning dir. Corp. Counsel Inst., 1962-66, 76-77, com. mem., 1962-87, 90—; adv. bd. Ray Garrett Jr. Corp. and Securities Law Inst., 1980-87, 90—; vis. lectr. U. de Liege, 1967; vis. prof. law U. Pa., Phila., 1971; faculty Salzburg Seminar, 1976; mem. legal adv. com. bd. dirs. N.Y. Stock Exch., 1978-82; mem. com. profl. responsibility Ill. Supreme Ct., 1978-87; adv. bd. Securities Regulation Inst., 1978—, chmn., 1994-97; bd. govs. Nat. Assn. Securities Dealers, 1990-93, chmn. Legal Adv. Bd., 1993-96, Arbitration Policy Task Force, 1994-97; trustee Fin. Acctg. Found., 1996—, Internat. Acctg. Stds. Found., 2000—; mem. Internat. Acctg. Stds. Com. Strategy Working Party, 1997-99; chmn. Securities and Exch. Commn. Hist. Soc., 1999—; chmn. Mut. Fund Dirs. Forum, 1999—. Editor-in-chief: Williams Coll. Record, 1950-51, U. Wis. Law Rev, 1957; editor: Proc. Corp. Counsel Inst, 1962-66; contbr. articles to legal periodicals. 1st lt. AUS, 1951-54. Fellow Am. Bar Found.; mem., com. chmn. ABA (coun. sect. corp. banking and bus. law 1970-74), Chgo. Bar Assn., Wis. Bar Assn., Am. Law Inst., Order of Coif, Comml. Club of Chgo., Econ. Club of Chgo., Gargoyle Soc., Phi Beta Kappa, Phi Delta Pi, Zeta Psi. Home: 325 Orchard Ln Highland Park IL 60035-1939 E-mail: d-ruder@law.northwestern.edu.

RUDER, WILLIAM, public relations executive; b. N.Y.C., Oct. 17, 1921; s. Jacob L. and Rose (Rosenberg) R.; m. Betty Cott, May 23, 1980; children: Robin Ann, Abby, Brian, Michal Ellen, Eric. BSS., City Coll., N.Y., 1942. With Samuel Goldwyn Prodns., 1946-48; pres. Ruder & Finn, Inc., N.Y.C., 1948-80, William Ruder Inc., 1981—. Asst. sec. commerce, 1961-62; Tobe lectr. Harvard Grad. Sch. Bus., 1962; mem. grad. adv. bd. City Coll. N.Y., Baruch Sch. Bus., N.Y.C.; cons. State Dept.; bd. dirs. W.P. Carey & Co., Inc. Author: The Businessman's Guide to Washington. Bd. dirs. Bus. Com. for Arts, Jewish Bd. Guardians, Chamber Music Soc. Lincoln Ctr., Fund for Peace, Project Return Found.; exec. com. United Way Am.; trustee, chmn. Manhattanville Coll., Purchase, N.Y., 1974-75; trustee Com. for Econ. Devel.; bd. overseers Wharton Sch. U. Pa.; mem. pres.'s coun. Meml. Sloan-Kettering Cancer Ctr.; chmn. bd. ACCESS. Capt. USAAF, 1941-45. Mem. UN Assn. U.S.A. (nat. policy panel dir., trustee com. for econ. devel.). Home: PO Box 230 East Hampton NY 11937 Office: Ruder Finn Inc 301 E 57th St New York NY 10022-2900

RUDERMAN, ARMAND PETER, health economics educator, consultant, volunteer; b. Bklyn., Nov. 19, 1923; s. Louis and Lillian (Prigozhy) R.; m. Alice Helen Holton, June 17, 1948; children: Ann, Mary, William, John. SB, Harvard U., 1943; MA, 1946, PhD, 1947; MBA, U. Chgo., 1944. Instr. econs. various U.S. univs., 1946-50; statistician, economist ILO, Pan.-Am. Health Orgn., WHO, 1950-67; chmn. sci. working group on social and econ. aspects of tropical disease research WHO/TDR, 1979-83; prof. health adminstrn. U. Toronto, Ont., Can., 1967-75; founding dean adminstrv. studies Dalhousie U., N.S., Can., 1975-80, prof. health adminstrn. Can., 1981-89, prof. emeritus Can., 1989—. Vis. prof. Nat. U. Singapore, 1982-83, adj. prof. Health Adminstrn. U.S.Carolina, 1983—; cons. in field. Contbr. articles to profl. jours. Bd. dirs. Northwood Manor, 1987-89, Northwestern Gen. Hosp., Toronto, 1991-96, Baker Ctr., 2000—; mem. Etobicoke Bd. Health, 1991-95; cmty. adv. com. Toronto Hosp., 1992-95, 97—; region 3 exec. com. Ont. Hosp. Assn., 1994-96. Mem. Royal Econ. Soc. E-mail: apeterr@idirect.com.

RUDERMAN, WARREN, chemist; b. N.Y.C., Jan. 7, 1920; s. Jack and Mollie (Ettin) R.; m. Carol Carver Schmied, June 15, 1945; children: Barbara, Clifford, William, Genevieve. PhD, Columbia U., 1949. Rsch. scientist, lectr. in chemistry Columbia U., N.Y.C., 1947-54; pres., founder Isomet Corp., Oakland, N.J., 1954-73; chmn., CEO, pres. INRAD Inc., Northvale, 1973—. Fellow N.Y. Acad. Scis.; mem. Am. Chem. Soc., Am. Phys. Soc., Optical Soc. Am. Republican. Baptist. Office: INRAD Inc 181 Legrand Ave Northvale NJ 07647-2498

RUDERT, CYNTHIA SUE, gastroenterologist; b. Cin., Mar. 17, 1955; d. John Wayne and Hilda Wanda (Loftus) R.; children: Ronald Lamar Hilley II, Henry Byron Hilley. BS with honors, U. Ky., 1975; MD, U. Louisville, 1979. Diplomate Am. Bd. Internal Medicine, Am. Bd. Gastroenterology. Intern internal medicine Emory U., Atlanta, 1979-80, resident, 1980-82, fellow in gastroenterology, 1982-84, asst. prof. medicine, 1984-91; med. dir. Gluten Sensitive Support Group, 1997—. Guest spkr. Alcoholism Conf., Kanasawa, Japan, 1987; founding mem. Celiac Standardization Group, 1999; med. advisor Gluten Intolerance Group N.Am., 1999, Celiac Disease Found.; nat. and internat. spkr. in gastroenterology; med. dir. Gluten Sensitive Support Group Atlanta. Author: Medicine for the Practicing Physician, 3d rev. edit., 1991, (chpts.) Acute Pancreatitis, Chronic Pancreatitis, Ischaemic Hepatitis, Rudert, C.X. Alcohol Related Symptoms; editl. cons. Life in Medicine mag.; med. advisor Women in Medicine mag. Fellow ACP; mem. AMA, Am. Med. Women's Assn., Am. Assn. for Study of Liver Disease, Am. Gastroent. Assn., So. Med. Assn., Am. Liver Found., Am. Acad. Scis., Ga. Gastroent. Soc., Med. Assn. Ga., Med. Assn. Atlanta, Atlanta Women's Med. Alliance (founder).

RUDGERS, DAVID FRANK, writer; b. Washington, Feb. 12, 1941; s. Anthony Joseph and Frances Marie Rudgers; m. Kathleen Dunlap, Oct. 12, 1968 (dec. Dec. 1978); children: Kyle David, Eric Michael; m. Bette Faye Pascoe, Sept. 29, 1979. BA with honors, U. Md., 1963; MA, George Washington U., 1966, PhD, 1972. Archivist Nat. Archives, Washington, 1968—76; intelligence officer CIA, 1976—98; ret., 1998. Author: Creating the Secret State, 2000 (Henry Adams award of Soc. for History in Govt., 2001). With U.S. Army, 1963—69. Presbyterian. Home: a610 S Irving St Arlington VA 22204

RUDIE, ALAN WILLIAM, pulp and paper research and development educator; b. Sheboygan, Wis., Nov. 17, 1950; s. Lawrence Gilbert and Elaine Lillian Rudie; m. Cynthia Nivert, June 8, 1977; children: Ian, Gwen. BA, Wartburg Coll., 1973; PhD, MIT, 1978. Sr. rsch. assoc. II Internat. Paper Co., Tuxedo Park, NY, 1978—89; assoc. prof., chemistry Inst. of Paper Sci. and Tech., Atlanta, 1989—2002. Faculty chair Inst. of Paper Sci. and Tech., Atlanta, 1998—, chmn. of the inst. self study, 1999—2002; tech. program chmn. TAPPI Mech. Pulping Com., Atlanta, 1997—98. Contbr. tech. papers to profl. jours. Pres. Jackson Creek Homeowners Assn., Marietta, 1994—95. Mem.: Am. Chem. Soc., Tech. Assn. of the Pulp and Paper Industry. Office: Inst Paper Sci and Tech 500 10th St NW Atlanta GA 30318 Business E-Mail: alan.rudie@ipst.edu.

RUDIGER, LANCE WADE, secondary school educator; b. Bklyn., Mar. 27, 1948; s. H.F. and Muriel Marie (Staudermann) R.; 1 child, Heidi. BS in Chemistry, SUNY, Albany, 1976; MEd, St. Lawrence U., 1982. Cert. tchr., N.Y. Tchr. chemistry Potsdam H.S., 1982—, sci. dept. chmn., 1992-97. Adj. prof. Canton (N.Y.) Coll. Tech., Mater Dei Coll., Ogdensburg, N.Y., Empire Coll., Albany, 1986—; tchr. Inst. Chem. Edn.-Sci. demonstration; bd. dirs., treas. St. Lawrence Valley Tchrs. Learning Ctr., Canton; sci. coord. Upward Bound St. Lawrence U.; program com., bd. dirs. N.Y. Assn. State Computers & Tech. in Edn.; writer for N.Y. State Regents chemistry core curriculum; mem. N.Y. State Part D Performance Regents Test Devel. Com.; mem. SED Regents Benchmark Commn.; item writer NYS Chem. Regents; mem. NYSED-McGraw Hill Chemistry Regents Anchor Com. Co-author: Chemistry Environment, 1990. Bd. dirs. March of Dimes N.Y. State, Syracuse, N.Y. State chemistry regional and state coord. mentor; mem. environ. mgmt. bd. St. Lawrence County, 1997-2001, edn. com. chair, 1999; mem. bd. examiners Nat. Coun. Accreditation Tchr. Edn., 2001—. Recipient Newmast award NASA, 1987, Dreyfus Master Tchr. award, 1989, Fulbright Symposium award Australia, 2002; grantee Am. Chem Soc., Woodrow Wilson Found., Binghamton U. Step Program, St. Lawrence Valley Tchrs. Ctr., 1991-98, Sweetwater Found., Miami U. (Ohio), 1995, Johns Hopkins Space Grant Consortium, Wright Ctr. for Aerospace and Space Engring., Reynolds Metals Excellence in Edn., 1990-94, Cornell U. Sch. Workshop, IRIS; named solar sys. amb. Jet Propulsion Lab., NASA. Mem. Nat. Sci. Tchrs. Assn. (local leader, manuscript review adv. panel The Sci. Tchr., sci. safety com. 2000, webwatchers 2001, Exxon BaP key leader and North Country liaison), Nat. Radio Astronomy Obs. (assoc., mentor astronomy workshop), Am. Astron. Soc. (tchr. resource agent 1996-98, Leadership Workshop award 1998), Sci. Tchrs. Assn. N.Y. State (bd. dirs. 1990—, chmn. sect. 1992—, fin. com. 2000—, presenter at convs. 1988—, hospitality chair ann. conf. 1996, 98, 2000), North Country Conservation Edn. Assn. (life), USCG Acad. Nat. Parents Assn. (bd. dirs. 1997-98), Canton Club, Lions (past pres. Waddington, N.Y., Pres.'s award, bd. dirs. Canton, pres. 1997-98, treas. 1998-99, dir. 1999—), Potsdam Kiwanis (charter, bd. dirs. 1989-91), Phi Delta Kappa (rsch. dir., v.p. program 1999, v.p. membership, pres. 2001—). Home: 54 Court St Canton NY 13617-1159 Office: Potsdam High School Leroy St Potsdam NY 13676-1798

RUDIGIER, ROBERTA LYNN, librarian; b. Honolulu, HI, June 3, 1947; d. James Philip Carbaugh and Doris Ida Clements; m. Gregory Charles Rudigier, Jun. 8, 1968; children: Darcy, Holly. BA, St. Mary's Coll. of Md., 1972. Art tchr., 1973-74; home sch. pioneer, 1977-84; reference libr. St. Mary's Meml. Libr., Leonardtown, Md., 1997—. Editor: Where Maryland Began, 2000. Mem. Md. Libr. Assn. Avocation: travel. Office: St Marys County Meml Library 23250 Hollywood Rd Leonardtown MD 20650 E-mail: lrudigier@somd.lib.md.us.

RUDIN, ANNE, former mayor, nurse; b. Passaic, N.J., Jan. 27, 1924; m. Edward Rudin, June 6, 1948; 4 children BS in Edn., Temple U., 1945, RN, 1946; MPA, U. So. Calif., 1983; LLD (hon.), Golden Gate U., 1990. RN, Calif. Mem. faculty Temple U. Sch. Nursing, Phila., 1946-48; mem. nursing faculty Mt. Zion Hosp., San Francisco, 1948-49; mem. Sacramento City Council, 1971-83; mayor City of Sacramento, 1983-92; ind. pub. policy cons. Pres. LWV, Riverside, 1957, Sacramento, 1961, Calif., 1969-71, Calif. Elected Women's Assn., 1973—; trustee Golden Gate U., 1993-96; mem. adv. bd. U. So. Calif., Army Depot Reuse Commn., 1992-94; bd. dirs. Sacramento Theatre Co., 1992-99, Japan Soc. No. Calif., Sacramento Symphony, 1993-96, Calif. Common Cause, 1993 -96, Sacramento Edn. Found., 1993-2002; v.p. Sacramento Traditional Jazz Soc. Found.; pres. bd. dirs. Natomas Basin Conservancy; foreman Sacramento County Grand Jury, 2000-01. Recipient Women in Govt. award U.S. Jaycee Women, 1984, Woman of Distinction award Sacramento Area Soroptimist Clubs, 1985, Civic Contbn. award LWV Sacramento, 1989, Woman of Courage award Sacramento History Ctr., 1989, Peacemaker of Yr. award Sacramento Mediation Ctr., 1992, Regional Pride award Sacramento Mag., 1993, Humanitarian award Japanese Am. Citizen's League, 1993, Outstanding Pub. Svc. award Am. Soc. Pub. Adminstrn., 1994; named Girl Scouts Am. Role model, 1989, Cmty. Svc. Recognition award, Japanese Am. Citizens League, 1999, Sacramento Traditional Jazz Soc. Hall of Fame, 2000.

RUDIN, DONALD OLIVER, physician, scientist; b. Honolulu, Mar. 31, 1923; married. MD, Harvard U., 1948. Rsch. fellow Harvard U., 1949-51, rsch. assoc. Mass., 1951-56; dir. dept. of molecular biology Ea. Pa. Psychiatric Inst., Phila., 1956-80; scientist, author, 1980—. Mem. psychopharmacological study sect. NIH, 1958-80, grants referee 1958-80. Editl. referee Nature, Sci., Jour. Theoretical Biology, Biochimica Biophysica Acta, IEEE Trans. SCM; contbr. numerous articles to profl. jours. Capt. U.S. Army, 1952-54. Greene Scholarship , 1944-46. Mem. IEEE (Disting. Prof. Internat. Inst. for Advanced Studies), Internat. Inst. for Advanced Studies Achievements include discovery of electrically variable channel-forming peptides, ion selective carrier peptides and syntheis of ion ultraselective bilayer membranes; pioneering patent in ultraselective ion electrodes. Home and Office: 208 Victor Pky #3G Annapolis MD 21403

RUDIN, MAX ALLEN, publishing executive; b. Phila., Feb. 11, 1953; s. Norman and Elinor Ruth (Klass) R.; m. Amy Lyn Schatz, Oct. 9, 1999. BA summa cum laude, Princeton U., 1975; MA, Columbia U., 1980, MPhil, 1982. Editl. cons. Libr. Am., N.Y.C., 1980-84, editor, 1984-86, dir. mktg. and sales, 1986-90, assoc. pub., 1990-94, pub., 1994—. Curator N.Y. Pub. Libr., 1982, N.Y. Hist. Soc., 1983. Bd. dirs. N.Y. Festival of Song, Great Books Found. Mem. Century Assn., The Coffee House, Phi Beta Kappa. Home: 526 W 111th St Apt 6D New York NY 10025-1949 Office: The Libr Am 14 E 60th St New York NY 10022-1006 E-mail: mrudin@loa.org.

RUDIS, GARY KEITH, medical equipment company executive; b. Lawrence, Mass., May 2, 1952; s. Alphonse and Norma Irene (Hines) R.; m. Linda Denise Martel, July 24, 1971; children: Keith, Todd, Glen, Alex. AS with high honors, No. Essex Coll., Haverhill, Mass., 1974; BS with high honors, Franklin Pierce Coll., Rindge, N.H., 1990. Registered respiratory therapist, Mass. Regional mgr. Inhalation Therapy Svcs., Lexington, Mass., 1974-83; pres., owner Home Care Specialists, Inc., Haverhill, 1979—. Bd. dirs. No. Essex Respiratory Adv. Com., Haverhill, 1986—; mem. Nat. Bd. Respiratory Therapy, 1974-90. Grantee Mass. Soc. Respiratory Therapists, 1976; recipient Innovator award Greater Haverhill C. of C. Mem. Nat. Assn. Med. Equipment Suppliers, New Eng. Med. Equipment Dealers, Alpha Sigma Lambda. Democrat. Avocations: jogging, reading, fishing. Home: 21 Singing Wood Dr Haverhill MA 01830-1452

RUDLIN, DAVID ALAN, lawyer; b. Richmond, Va., Nov. 4, 1947; s. Herbert and Dorothy Jean (Durham) R.; m. Judith Bond Faulkner, Oct. 4, 1975; 1 child, Sara Elizabeth. BA with high distinction, U. Va., 1969, JD with honors, 1973. Bar: Va. 1973, U.S. Dist. Ct. (ea. dist.) Va. 1975, U.S. Ct. Appeals (4th cir.) 1975, U.S. Ct. Appeals (10th cir.) 1980, U.S. Ct. Appeals (2d cir.) 1983, U.S. Supreme Ct. 1979. Assoc. gen. counsel U.S. Commn. on Orgn. of Govt. for Conduct Fgn. Policy, Washington, 1973-75; assoc. Hunton & Williams, Richmond, 1975-82, ptnr., 1982—. Adj. faculty civil litigation, appellate practice, libel litigation Duke Univ. Law Sch., Univ. Richmond, T.C. Williams Sch. of Law, Washington and Lee Sch. of Law, William and Mary Sch. of Law, U. Va. Sch. of Law; faculty mem. Boulder and S.E. Regional programs Nat. Inst. Trial Advocacy; faculty mem. Am. Law Inst. ABA. Author: (book chpts.) Toxic Torts: Litigation of Hazardous Substances Cases, 1983, 2d edit., 1992, Federal Litigation Guide, 1989, Corporate Counselor's Guide to Environmental Law, 1989, Sanctions: Rule 11 and Other Powers, 1992, Business and Commercial Litigation in Federal Courts, 1997, Corp. Counsel's Guide to ADR Techniques, 1999, Successful Partnering Between Inside and Outside COunsel, 1999; contbr. articles to profl. jours. and mags., chpts. to books; mem. bd. editl. advisors The Environ. Counselor, Chesterland, Ohio, 1989—, The Toxics Law Reporter, Washington, 1988—. Alumni Metro Leadership Richmond, 1988-89. Mem. ABA (chmn. litig. sect. environ. litig. com. 1985-88, co-chmn. litig. sect. liaison with jud. com. 1988-91, vice-chmn. toxic and hazardous substances and environ. law com. tort and ins. practice sect. 1988-91, co-liaison to standing com. on environ. law from environ. litig. com. litig. sect. 1988-92, dir. div. IV litig. sect. 1991-95, litig. sect. co-chair programs subcom. first amendment and media litig. com. 1993—, mem. litig. sect. task force on specialization 1994—, co-chair litigation sect., 1997, specialization 1994—, mem. litigation sect. task foce on justice sys. 1994—, litigation sect. liaison to ABA jud. adminstrn. divsn. task force on reducion of litigation cost and delay 1995—, co-chair litigation sect. 1997 ann. meeting Washington 1995-97, chair toxic torts and environ. litigation committee sect. of Environment, Energy and Resources 1997-2000; council mem. litigation sect. 1997-2000, co-chair report card on the litigation section, 2000), Am. Arbitration Assn. (Va. mediation panel 1996—), Va. Bar Assn. (chair joint com. on alt. dispute resolution with Va. State Bar 1991-97, exec. com. mem.), Richmond Bar Assn. (chmn. mem. com. 1988-91, mem. judiciary com. 1991-94, mem. continuing legal edn. com. 1994-96), Va. Assn. Def. Attys., CPR Inst. Dispute Resolution (products liability com. 1988, 97—, judge Ann. Awards in Alt. Dispute Resolution 1990—, mem. panels disting. neutrals Va. 1997—), Va. Bar Assn. (mem. exec. com. 2001), Internat. Assn. Def. Counsel. Office: Hunton & Williams Riverfront Pla E Tower 951 E Byrd St Ste 200 Richmond VA 23219-4074 Fax: 804-788-8218. E-mail: arudlin@hunton.com.

RUDLOFF, WILLIAM JOSEPH, lawyer; b. Bonne Terre, Mo., Feb. 19, 1941; s. Leslie W. and Alta M. (Hogenmiller) R.; m. Rita Howton, Aug. 5, 1965; children: Daniel, Andrea, Leslie, Susan. AB, Western Ky. U., 1961; JD, Vanderbilt U., 1965. Bar: Ky. 1965, Tenn. 1965, U.S. Supreme Ct. 1975, U.S. Ct. Appeals (sixth cir.) 1981. U.S. magistrate Western Dist. Ky., 1971-75. NDEA fellow U. Nebr., 1961-62, U. Ky. fellow. Fellow: Ky. Bar Found. (life; charter); mem.: Internat. Acad. Litigators (diplomate), Ky. Acad. Trial Attys., Am. Coll. Legal Medicine, Trial Attys. Am., Def. Rsch. Inst., Am. Counsel Assn., Am. Bd. Trial Advocates. Home: 126 Broadway St Smiths Grove KY 42171-8258 Office: 553 E Main St Bowling Green KY 42101-2256 E-mail: rudloff@aol.com.

RUDMAN, JOAN ELEANOR, artist, educator; b. Owensburg, Ind., Oct. 7, 1927; d. William Hobart and Elizabeth Joaquin (Edington) Combs; m. William Rudman, June 9, 1951; children: Mary Beth, Pamela Ann. BA, Mich. State U., 1949, MA, 1951. Tchr. Arlington Jr. and H.S., Poughkeepsie, NY, Rippowam H.S., Stamford, Conn., North Branch Club, West Dover, Vt.; artist, demonstrator Round Hill Cmty. House, Greenwich; artist-in-residence So. Vt. Art Ctr., Manchester, Peony Festival at Hildene, Manchester, 2000; jurist of selection Hudson Valley Art Assn., 1971—, pres., 2000; selection and awards jurish 2d Bergen County Mus. Open Mems. Juried Awards-Allied Artist, NY; dir. Watercolor Workshops, Greenwich; liaison to Metro Mus. Catharine Lorillard Wolfe Art Club; watercolor lectr. and demonstrator tri-state area.; chair Millennium-Larry Rivers Show, Art Soc. of Old Greenwich benefit, 1999—; juried show, 1996, 97, 98, 99, 2000, 01, 02; agt. Larry River's Band; guest spkr., guest tchr. 2-day workshop Vt. Watercolor Soc., Chester; watercolor juror Walter Brooks Meml. Watercolor Show, Rowaton, Conn. One-woman shows include Burning Tree Country Club, Greenwich, Town and Country Club, Hartford, Conn., U. Conn., Stamford, Conn. Valley Art Gallery, New Milford, So. Vt. Art Ctr., Manchester, The Nathaniel Witherall Gallery, Greenwich, Burke Rehab. Ctr., White Plains, N.Y.; exhibited in group shows at Wadsworth Antheneum, 1970, Mus. of Am. Art, New Britain, Conn., So. Vt. Art Ctr., Manchester, 1980-81, Nature Ctr., Westport, Conn., 1979-80, Mus. Fine Arts, Springfield, Mass., 1977, Wadsworth Antheneum, 1970, Mus. Am. Art, New Britain, Conn., Nat. Arts Club Open Show, 1969, 78, 79, 81, 82, Salmagundi Club, N.Y.C., 1978, 79, 80, 82, Am. Watercolor Soc., N.Y.C., 1974, 77, 82, Nat. Acad. Design, 1986, 94, W.C. Founder's Show, Art Soc. Old Greenwich, 1999, Walter Brooks Meml. Catercolor Show, Rowayton, Conn., 2000; represented in permanent collection Kresge Mus., East Lansing, Mich., numerous others; contbr. chpts. to books. Mam, art dir. Round Hill Cmty. Guild; active North Stamford Congl. Ch., asst. assoc. curator of healing through Art at Christ Ch., (artisic interpretations of Spet. 11, 2002, N.Y.C.) Grennwich. Recipient Nat. Art League awards, 1969, 71, 72, 73, Art Soc. Old Greenwich award, 1989, 94, 99, Windsor Newton award, 1982, YWCA Greenwich Contemporary Women's Art Exhibit award, 1985, Best in Show award Art Soc. Old Greenwich, 1991, 1st Prize Graphics award Art Soc. Old Greenwich, 1994, 2nd Prize award Watercolor, Vol. of Yr. plaque, 1997. Mem. AAUW (New Canaan chpt.), Am. Watercolor Soc. (bd. dirs., asst. editor newsletter), Acad. Artists, Inc., Hoosier Salon (awards 1975, 76), Am. Artists Profl. League (50th Nat. Exhbn. award 1978), Hudson Valley Art Assn. (pres. 2000—, bd. dirs., publ. rels. editor, designer catalog and brochure, awards 1970, 80—, pres.), Conn. Watercolor Soc. (award 1978), Conn. Artists 33, Whiskey Painters Am. (award 1978), Conn. Women Artists, Catharine Lorillard Wolfe Art Club (awards 1989, 90, chmn. 1989-90, co-chair 1994, v.p. 1992-94), Pen and Brush (award 1977-78, 97), Nat. League Am. Pen Women (awards 1967, 69, 76-87, treas. 1990—), Nat. Press Club, Columbia U. Alumni Club (hon.), Nat. Soc. DAR (mem. Stamford chpt., historian, good citizens chair), Mich. State Alumni Club, Delta Phi Delta (hon.), Phi Kappa Phi (hon.), Alpha Xi Delta. Republican. Home: 274 Quarry Rd Stamford CT 06903-5004

RUDMAN, SOLOMON KAL, magazine publisher; b. Phila., Mar. 6, 1930; s. Benjamin and Lena (Holtzman) R.; m. Lucille Steinhauer, June 29, 1958; 1 child, Mitchell. BS in Edn., U. Pa., 1951; MS in Edn., Temple U., 1957. Chmn. dept. spl. edn. Franklin D. Roosevelt Sch., Bristol Twp., Pa., 1960-68; pub. premier record/ radio trade Fri. Morning Quarterback, Cherry Hill, 1968—. Bd. dirs. Variety Club, NARAS, Crime Commn., Pa., N.J., Del.; co-host Merv Griffin TV Show, 1981-82; music expert Today Show, 1981-82, Tomorrow Show, 1981-82, Tom Snyder TV Show; creator-sponsor high sch. jazz piano competition, Phila. and suburbs of Pa., with Univ. of the Arts, Phila.; sponsor-host Phila. Franklin Inst. of Sci. and Fels Planetarium mobile sci. programs, top-level entertainment shows to most Phila.-N.J. Sr. Citizens' homes, children's and vets. hosps.; co-host, talent booker Easter Seals Telethon; sponsor 47 scholarships for h.s. jazz musicians at Univ. of the Arts; created "e-hooks" for the recording industry; bought bullet proof vests and 2 police dogs for Montgomery Co. Pa.; funded 60 college scholarships for Camden Co., N.J. police, Phila. Middle Sch. Programs with the Harold Prince Theatre; sponsored authors E.L. Doctorow, Norman Mailor and Ed Koch, Jewish Book Week. Pub.: (mag.) MQB (Modern QB) for Modern Rock Music; prodr. CD's of advance hits N.Am. radio stas.; launched music trade mag. Pro QB, launched Q-Beatl created e-books for rec. industry. Bd. dirs. Phila. Broadcast Pioneers; sponsor carillon bells Ave. of Arts, Phila., Franklin Inst. Travelling Sci. Show to Phila. elem. schs., 100th Anniversary Jewish Fedn. Phila.; bd. dirs. Citizens' Crime Commn.; sponsor 1st ann. classical piano H.S. competition, Chestnut Hill Coll.; co-sponsor purchase and distbn. of dictionaries to Phila. Elem. Sch. pupils (in memory of Ennis Cosby), Robotics Competition Phila. h.s., N.J. United Cerebral palsy Marathon Dance, Rutgers U.; sponsor Franklin Inst. Time Capsule, Phila., Jewish Fedn. Atrium, Phila.; co-sponsor Succeeding By Reading Program; contbr. numerous civic orgns. including: Phila. Middle Schs., Jewish Book week, Phila. Ave. of Arts., others. Recipient Lifetime Achievement award in music Phila. Music Conf., Lifetime Music Achievement award Delaware Valley Music Poll., Presdl. Citation, Citizens Crime Com., Plaque on Walk of Fame, Ave. of the Arts; named to Broadcast Pioneers Hall of Fame Phila.; named Penndelphia Humanitarian of Yr. Mem. Phila. Music Alliance (bd. dirs.), Nat. Arthritis Found. (bd. dirs.), NARAS (bd. dirs.), Masons, Phila. Police Commrs. Club. Office: Friday Morning Quarterback 1930 Marlton Pike E Cherry Hill NJ 08003-2150

RUDNER, SARA, dancer, choreographer; b. Bklyn., Feb. 16, 1944; d. Henry Nathaniel and Jeannette (Smolensky) R.; 1 child, Eli Rudner Marschner. AB in Russian Studies, Barnard Coll., 1964; MFA in Choreography, Bennington Coll., 1999. Dancer Sansardo Dance Co., N.Y.C., 1964-65, Am. Dance Co. at Lincoln Ctr., N.Y.C., 1965, Shakespeare Festival Touring Children's Show, N.Y.C., 1966; featured dancer Twyla Tharp Dance Found., 1966-85; artistic dir., dancer 18th St. Dance Found., 1977—; guest dancer Joffrey Ballet, 1973, Pilobolus Dance Theatre, N.Y.C., 1975, Lar Lubovitch Dance Co., N.Y.C., 1975-76; guest lectr., choreographer grad. dance dept. UCLA, 1975. Dir. dance Sarah Lawrence Coll.; tchr. master workshop NYU Theater Program, 1988-90. Choreographer: Palm Trees and Flamingoes, 1980, Dancing for an Hour or So, 1981, Minute by Minute, 1982, Eight Solos, 1991, Heartbeats, Inside Out, 1993; (with Jennifer Tipton and Dana Reitz) Necessary Weather, 1994; (with Rona Pondick, Robert Feintuch and Jennifer Tipton) Mine, 1996, Alley Theater-The Greeks part I and II, 1997, Heartbeat/mb with Christopher Janney and Mikhail Barysnikov, 1998. Choreographer Dancing-on-View St. Mark's Ch., N.Y.C., 1999, Santa Fe Opera. Grantee Creative Artists Pub. Svc. Program, N.Y., 1975-76, N.Y. State Coun. on Arts, 1975-78, Nat. Endowment for Arts, 1979-81, 91-92, 94-97; Guggenheim fellow, 1981-82; recipient N.Y. Dance and Performance award, 1984.

RUDNEY, BERNICE SNIDER, social worker, psychotherapist; b. London, Can., May 17, 1924; came to U.S., 1948; D. I. Leonard and Rebecca (Freeman) Snider; m. Harry Rudney, June 25, 1946; children: Joel D., Robert. BA, U. Toronto, Ont., Can., 1946, BSW, 1947, MSW, 1949. Caseworker Jewish Family Svc., Cleve., 1948-51, 60-67; sr. caseworker Family Svc. of Greater Cin., 1968-92; assoc. R. Kravetz, M.D., Cin., 1977—. Mem. Women's City Club. Mem. Ohio Soc. for Clin. Social Work, U. Cin. Woman's Club, Contemporary Club. Avocations: hiking, swimming, cooking. Office: 3131 Harvey Ave Ste 101 Cincinnati OH 45229-3006

RUDNICK, ALAN A. retired management company executive, corporate lawyer; b. Cleve., 1947; BA, U. Chgo., 1969; JD, Case Western Res. U., 1973. Bar: Ohio 1973, Md. 1984, Va. 1988. With Chessie Systems, Inc., 1976-86, asst. treas., 1980-82, asst. v.p. taxation, 1982-84, asst. v.p., treas. taxation, 1984-85; gen. counsel CSX Corp., Richmond, Va., 1985-91, v.p., gen. counsel, corp. sec., 1991—2002. Adj. prof. Sch. Law, Coll. William and Mary. Mem. ABA, Ohio Bar Assn., Md. Bar Assn., Va. Bar Assn. Office: CSX Corp PO Box 85629 Richmond VA 23285-5629

RUDNICK, BEN, software professional, retail automotive executive; b. Minerva, N.Y., July 11, 1976; s. Joseph Y. and Patricia Rudnick. BS in Biomed. Engring., Boston U., 1998. Cons. DataSage, Inc., Reading, Mass., 1998-99, project mgr., 1999-2000; CEO, Automotive Anything, Harrisburg, N.C., 2000—; product mgr. Vignette, Inc., Waltham, Mass., 2000—. Fax: 781-487-2800.

RUDNICK, ELLEN AVA, health care executive; b. New Haven; d. Harold and C. Vivian (Soybel) R.; children from previous marriage: Sarah, Noah; m. Paul W. Earle. BA, Vassar Coll., 1972; MBA, U. Chgo., 1973. Sr. fin. analyst Quaker Oats, Chgo., 1973-75; various positions Baxter Internat., Deerfield, Ill., 1975-80, dir. planning, 1980-83, corp. v.p., 1985-1990; pres. Baxter Mgmt. Svcs., 1983-1990, HCIA, Balt., 1990-92, CEO Advs., Northbrook, Ill., 1992—; prin., chmn. Pacific Biometrics, Lake Forest, Calif., 1993-99; exec. dir., clin. prof. Entrepreneurship Program Sch. Bus. U. Chgo., 1999—. Bd. dirs. Liberty Mut. Ins., Oxford Health Plans, 2001—. Chief crusader Met. Chgo. United Way, 1982—85; mem. cir. friends Chgo. YMCA, 1985—89; bd. dirs. Evanston Northwestern-Highland Park Hosp., 1990—99, Health Mgmt. Sys., Evanston-Northwestern Hosp., 2000—; pres. coun. Nat. Coll. Edn., Evanston, Ill., 1983—93. Office: Univ Chgo Grad Sch Bus 1101 E 58th St Chicago IL 60637-1511

RUDNICK, HOLLY LYNN, lawyer; b. Wright-Paterson AFB, Ohio, Apr. 1, 1971; d. Terry I. and Jennifer C. Phillips; m. Phillip M. Rudnick, Mar. 16, 1996. BS in Physics, U. Tex., Dallas, 1993; JD, U. Tex., Austin, 1996. Bar: Tex. 1996, U.S. Patent and Trademark Office 1998. Assoc. Groover & Assocs., Dallas, 1996-97, Jenkens & Gilchrist, Dallas, 1997—. Mem. Am. Intellectual Property Law Assn., Dallas-Ft. Worth Intellectual Property Law Assn. Avocations: reading, movies. Office: Jenkens & Gilchrist 1445 Ross Ave Ste 3200 Dallas TX 75202-2785

RUDNICK, IRENE KRUGMAN, lawyer, former state legislator, educator; b. Columbia, S.C., Dec. 27, 1929; d. Jack and Jean (Getter) Krugman; m. Harold Rudnick, Nov. 7, 1954 (dec.); children: Morris, Helen Gail. AB cum laude, U. S.C., 1949, JD, 1952. Bar: S.C. 1952. Individual practice law, Aiken, S.C., 1952—; now ptnr. Rudnick & Rudnick; instr. bus. law, criminal law U. S.C., Aiken, 1962—; tchr. Warrenville Elem. Sch., 1965-70; supt. edn. Aiken County, 1970-72; mem. S.C. Ho. of Reps., 1972-78, 80-84, 86-94. Pres. Adath Yeshurun Synagogue; active Aiken County Dem. Party, S.C. Dem. Party; hon. mem. Aiken Able-Disabled. Recipient Citizen of Yr. award, 1976-77, Bus. and Profl. Women's Career Woman of Yr., 1978, 94, Aiken County Friend of Edn. award, 1985, 93, Outstanding Legis. award Disabled Vets., 1991, Citizen of the Yr. award Planned Parenthood, 1994, Sertoma Svc. to Mankind award, 1996. Mem. NEA, S.C. Tchrs. Assn., Aiken County Tchrs. Assn., Am. Bar Assn., Aiken County Bar Assn., Nat. Order Women Legislators, AAUW, Aiken Able-Disabled (hon.), Aiken Hist. Soc., Alpha Delta Kappa, Order Eastern Star, Hadassah Sisterhood, Am. Legion Aux. Office: PO Box 544 135 Pendleton St NW Aiken SC 29801-3859

RUDNICK, REBECCA SOPHIE, lawyer, educator; b. Bakersfield, Calif., Nov. 26, 1952; d. Oscar and Sophie Mary (Loven) R.; m. Robert Anthoine, Dec. 2, 1990. BA, Willamette U., Salem, Oreg., 1974; JD, U. Tex., 1978; LLM, NYU, 1984. Bar: Tex. 1978, La. 1979, N.Y. 1980, Calif. 1980. Law clk. to Hon. Charles Schwartz, Jr. U.S. Dist. Ct., New Orleans, 1978-79; assoc. Winthrop, Stimson, Putnam & Roberts, N.Y.C., 1979-85; spl. counsel N.Y. Legis. Tax Study Commn., 1983-84; asst. prof. law Ind. U., Bloomington, 1985-90; assoc. prof. Ind. U. Sch. Law, 1990-94; assoc. prof. law London Law Consortium, Eng., 1994. Vis. assoc. prof. law U. Conn., Hartford, 1984-85; vis. asst. prof. law U. Tex., Austin, 1988; vis. assoc. prof. law U. N.C., Chapel Hill, 1991, Boston U., 1994-95, U. Pa., Phila., 1995-96; prof.-in-residence, IRS, 1991-92; vis. scholar NSW, Australia, 1994, U. Sydney, Australia, 1994; vis. prof. law Seattle U., 1996-97, Wayne State U., 1997, U. Ky., 1998, U. Houston, 1998, Tulane U., 1999, Northwestern Sch. Law, Lewis and Clark Coll., 1999-2000, Boston Coll., 2001, Vt. Law Sch., 2001—. Contbr. articles to profl. jours. Dir., gen. counsel Project GreenHope: Svcs. for Women, N.Y.C., 1980-83; advisor, tech. asst. Internat. Monetary Fund, Washington, 1994. Mem. ABA (tax sect. 1982—, sec. tax sect. passthrough entities task force 1986-88, subcom. chairs for incorps. and CLE/important devel. tax sect., 1989—, corp. tax com. 1989—, tax sect. task force on integration 1990—), Am. Assn. Law Schs. (editor tax sect. newsletter 1987-97), Assn. Bar of City of N.Y. (admiralty com. 1982-85), Internat. Fiscal Assn., Internat. Bar Assn. Office: Vermont Law Sch PO Box 96 Chelsea St S South Royalton VT 05068 E-mail: rrudnick@vermontlaw.edu.

RUDNICKI, MAREK, surgeon; b. Łańcut, Poland, Jan. 2, 1948; came to U.S., 1987; s. Stanisław Rudnicki and Aniela Wawrzkiewicz; m. Joanna, May 27, 1972; children; Anna Maria, Jacek Damian. MD, Silesian Sch. of Medicine, Katowice, Poland, 1972, PhD, 1980, DSc, 1993. Lic. MD, Poland, N.Y., Ill. Intern, then resident in surgery Univ. Hosp., Silesian Sch. Medicine, 1972-79; asst. prof., surgeon Silesian Sch. Medicine, 1980-1987; fellow U. Cin., 1987-1990; attending surgeon Mary Imogene Bassett Hosp., Cooperstown, N.Y., 1990-98; assoc. prof. clin. surgery Columbia U., 1992-98; prof. surgery U. Ill., Chgo., 1999—. Dir. surg. rsch. Mary Imogene Basset Hosp., 1990—98; advisor to Min. of Health Republic of Poland, 2001—02. Author: (with others) General Surgery Board Review, 1992, 98; contbr. articles to profl. jours. Co-founder Solidarity, Silesian Sch. Medicine, 1980. Recipient 1st prize European Assn. for Gastroenterology and Endoscopy, 1987, Polish Assn. for Gastroenterology, 1985; grantee Steven C. Clark Found., 1992-95. Fellow ACS; mem. AMA, Assn. for Acad. Surgery, Soc. for Surgery of Alimentary Tract, Collegium Internat. Chirurgiae Digestivae, European Soc. for Surg. Rsch., Plish Assn. for Surgery, Fedn. Polish Med. Soc. Abroad (v.p.). Roman Catholic. Avocations: skiing, mountaineering, travel. Home: 195 N Harbor Dr Apt 5002 Chicago IL 60601-7540 Office: U Ill 840 S Wood St Rm 439 Chicago IL 60612-7317 also: Ill Masonic Med Ctr 836 W Wellington Chicago IL 60657

RUDO, MILTON, retired manufacturing company executive, consultant; b. Balt., Jan. 17, 1919; s. Saul E. and Bertha (Berkowitz) R.; m. Roslind Mandel, Mar. 27, 1943; children: Stephanie Ellen, Neil Dennis. BA, Johns Hopkins U., 1940; AMP, Harvard U., 1964. Various positions Brunswick Corp., Skokie, Ill., 1940-66, corp. v.p., pres. Bowling divsn. Chgo., 1966-74, group v.p. recreation bus., 1974-84, ret., 1984, cons. to the CEO, 1984-87; dir., cons. to the CEO Donlen Leasing Corp., Skokie, 1986-90. Pres. Nat. Bowling Hall of Fame and Mus., 1979. Capt. AUS, 1942-45, ETO. Recipient ann. award N.Y. Mktg. Club, 1960, Industry Svc. award, 1973; named to Bowling Hall of Fame, 1984. Mem. Nat. Bowling Coun. (pres. 1972), Briarwood Country Club, Hamlet Country Club (Delray Beach Fla.). Home: 1777 Balsam Rd Highland Park IL 60035-4343

RUDO, SAUL E. tax lawyer; b. Balt., Aug. 2, 1958; m. Gail Rudo, June 12; children: Victor, Sarah. BS in Acctg., U. Ill., 1980; JD, Harvard U., 1983. Bar: Ill. 1983. Ptnr. Katten Muchin & Zavis, Chgo., 1983—. Spkr. in field. Bd. dirs. Bernard Weinger Jewish Cmty. Ctr., Deerfield, Ill., 1997-2002. Mem. Chgo. Bar Assn. (mem. partnership tax com., internat. tax com.), U. Ill. Commerce Alumni Assn. (bd. dirs.). Home: 510 Susan Ln Deerfield IL 60015-3951 Office: Katten Muchin Zavis Rosenman 525 W Monroe St Ste 1600 Chicago IL 60661-3693 E-mail: saul.rudo@kmzr.com.

RUDOFF, SHELDON, lawyer; b. Bklyn., May 29, 1933; s. Raphael and Goldie (Gorelick) R.; m. Hedda Muller, Nov. 22, 1964; children: Shaindy, Sara, Simone. BA cum laude, Yeshiva Coll., 1954; JSD cum laude, NYU, 1958; ordination, RIETS, 1957. Bar: N.Y. 1958, U.S. Dist. Ct. (so. and ea. dists.) N.Y. 1958, U.S. Supreme Ct. 1978. Ptnr. Shatzkin, Cooper & Rudoff, N.Y.C., 1970-84, Goodkind, Labaton, Rudoff & Sucharow, N.Y.C., 1984—; pres. Union Orthodox Jewish Congregation Am., 1990-94, hon. pres., 1994—; pres. Beth Din Am., 1996—. V.p. Yeshiva Coll. Alumni, N.Y.C., 1962-64; pres. Young Israel West Side, N.Y.C., 1969-72; sec. Orthodox Union, 1972-76, v.p., 1976-78, sr. v.p., 1978-84, chmn. bd., 1984-90, pres. 1990-94, mem. exec. com. World Zionist Orgn.; trustee Fedn. Jewish Philanthropies, 1980-91, United Jewish Appeal. Recipient Pres.'s award Orthodox Union, N.Y.C., 1972, Nat. Leadership award Nat. Conf. Synagogue Youth, N.Y.C., 1974, Kesser Shem Tov award Ortohdox Union, 1995. Mem. ABA, N.Y. State Bar Assn., Assn. Bar City N.Y. (transp. com. 1976—). Office: Goodkind Labaton Rudoff & Sucharow 100 Park Ave New York NY 10017-5516 E-mail: sradoff@glrslaw.com.

RUDOLPH, ABRAHAM MORRIS, pediatrician, educator; b. Johannesburg, Republic of South Africa, Feb. 3, 1924; s. Chone and Sarah (Feinstein) Rudolph; m. Rhona Sax, Nov. 2, 1949; children: Linda, Colin, Jeffrey. MBBCh summa cum laude, U. Witwatersrand, Johannesburg, 1946, MD, 1951; D (hon.) , Rene Descartes U., Paris, 1996. Instr. Harvard Med. Sch., 1955—57, assoc. pediat., 1957—60; assoc. cardiologist in charge cardiopulmonary lab. Children's Hosp., Boston, 1955—60; dir. pediatric cardiology Albert Einstein Coll. Medicine, 1960—66, prof. pediat., assoc. prof. physiology, 1962—66; vis. pediatrician Bronx Mcpl. Hosp. Ctr., 1960—66; prof. pediat. U. Calif., San Francisco, 1966—94, prof. physiology, 1974—88, Neider prof. pediatric cardiology, prof. ob-gyn and reproductive scis., 1974—94, chmn. dept. pediat., 1987—91, prof. pediatr. emeritus, 1994—; practice medicine, specializing in pediatric cardiology San Francisco. Mem. cardiovasc. study sect. NIH, 1961—65; mem. nat. adv. heart coun., 1968—72;

established investigator Am. Heart Assn., 1958—62; career scientist Health Rsch. Coun., N.Y.C., 1962—66; Harvey lectr. Oxford (Eng.) U., 1984; inaugural lectr. 1st Nat. Congress Italian Soc. Perinatal Medicine, 1985. Editl. bd. Pediat., 1964—70, Circulation, 1966—74, 1983—88, assoc. editor Circulation Rsch., 1970, Pediatric Rsch., 1970—77; editor: Rudolph's Pediatrics, Rudolph's Fundamentals of Pediatrics; contbr. articles to profl. jours. Recipient Merit award, Nat. Heart, Lung and Blood Inst., 1986, Arvo Yllpo medal, Helsinki (Finland) U., 1987, Jonxis medal, Children's Hosp. Groningen, 1993, Nils Rosen von Rosenstein award, Swedish Pediat. Soc., 1999. Fellow: AAAS, Am. Assn. Adv. Sci., Royal Coll. Physicians (London), Royal Coll. Physicians (Edinburgh); mem.: Am. Heart Assn. (Rsch. Achievement award 1991), Am. Pediatric Soc. (coun. 1985—92, v.p. 1992—93, pres. 1993—94, Howland award 1999), Soc. for Pediatric Rsch. (coun. 1961—64), Soc. for Clin. Investigation, Am. Phys. Soc., Am. Acad. Pediat. (past chmn. sect. on cardiology, E. Mead Johnson award for rsch. in pediat. 1964, Borden award 1979, Lifetime Med. Edn. award 1992, Joseph St. Geme leadership award Pediat. 1993, Founder award, cardiology sect. 2001), NAS Inst. Medicine. Office: U Calif Cardiovascular Rsch Inst Calif Rm M1331 San Francisco CA 94143-0001

RUDOLPH, ANDREW HENRY, dermatologist, educator; b. Detroit, Jan. 30, 1943; s. John J. and Mary M. Rudolph; children: Kristen Ann, Kevin Andrew. MD cum laude, U. Mich., 1966. Diplomate Am. Bd. Dermatology. Intern Univ. Hosp., U. Mich. Med. Ctr., Ann Arbor, 1966-67, resident dept. dermatology, 1967-70; pvt. practice medicine specializing in dermatology, 1972—. Asst. prof. dermatology Baylor Coll. Medicine, Houston, 1972-75, assoc. prof., 1975-83, clin. prof., 1983—; chief dermatology svc. VA Hosp., Houston, 1977-82; mem. staff Meth. Hosp., Tex. Children's Hosp., St. Luke's Episcopal Hosp. Mem. editl. bd. Jour. Sexually Transmitted Diseases, 1977-85; contbr. to med. publs. Served as surgeon USPHS, 1970-72. Regent's scholar U. Mich., 1966. Fellow Am. Acad. Dermatology; mem. AMA, Am. Dermatol. Assn., So. Med. Assn., Tex. Med. Assn., Harris County Med. Soc., Houston Dermatol. Soc. (past pres.), Tex. Dermatol. Soc., Internat. Soc. Tropical Dermatology, Dermatology Found., Skin Cancre Found., Am. Venereal Disease Assn. (past pres.), Am. Soc. Dermatol. Surgery, Soc. Investigative Dermatology, S. Ctrl. Dermatol. Congress, Mich. Alumni Assn. (life), Alpha Omega Alpha, Phi Kappa Phi, Phi Rho Sigma, Theta Xi. Office: 6560 Fannin St Ste 724 Houston TX 77030-2768

RUDOLPH, ANDREW J. lawyer; b. Camden, N.J., Jan. 16, 1957; s. Richard M. and Selma (Weiner) R.; m. Melinda Jean Pearlman, Dec. 21, 1980; children: Joshua Aaron, Julia Rose. BA cum laude, U. Pa., 1978, JD magna cum laude, 1982. Bar: Pa. 1982, U.S. Dist. Ct. (ea. dist.) Pa. 1982, U.S. Tax Ct. 1983. Assoc. Dechert Price & Rhoads, Phila., 1982-88; cons. Hewitt Assocs., Bedminster, N.J., 1989-90; ptnr. Wolf, Block, Schorr and Solis-Cohen, Phila., 1990-91, Ballard Spahr Andrews & Ingersoll, Phila., 1991-95, Pepper Hamilton LLP (and predecessor firm), Phila., 1996—. Lectr. Temple U. Sch. Law, Phila., 1991—98. Mem. ABA, Phila. Bar Assn., Order of Coif, Haddon Field Club. Democrat. Jewish. Home: 667 Washington Ave Haddonfield NJ 08033-3435 Office: Pepper Hamilton LLP 3000 Two Logan Sq Philadelphia PA 19103-2799

RUDOLPH, FREDERICK, history educator; b. Balt., June 19, 1920; s. Charles Frederick and Jennie Hill (Swope) R.; m. Dorothy Dannenbaum, June 18, 1949; children: Marta R. MacDonald, Lisa R. Cushman. BA, Williams Coll., 1942, Litt.D., 1985; MA, Yale U., 1949, PhD, 1953; LHD, U. Rochester, 1994, Wilkes U., 1998. Instr. history Williams Coll., 1946-47; asst. instr. Yale, 1949-50; mem. faculty Williams Coll., 1951—, prof., 1961—, Mark Hopkins prof. history, 1964-82, emeritus, 1982—, chmn. Am. civilization program, 1971-80. Williams Coll. marshal, 1978-87; vis. lectr. history and edn. Harvard U., 1960, 61; vis. prof. Sch. Edn., U. Calif.-Berkeley, 1983; mem. commn. plans and objectives Am. Council Edn., 1963-66; mem. study group on postsecondary edn. Nat. Inst. Edn., 1980-83; mem. com. on baccalaureate degrees Assn. Am. Colls., 1981-85; vis. assoc. Ctr. Studies in Higher Edn., U. Calif.-Berkeley, 1983 Author: Mark Hopkins and the Log, 1956, rev. edit. 1996, The American College and University: A History, 1962, rev. edit., 1990, Curriculum: A History of the American Undergraduate Course of Study Since 1636, 1977, rev. edit., 1993; editor: Essays on Education in the Early Republic, 1965, Perspectives: A Williams Anthology, 1983; exec. editor: Change, 1980-84, cons. editor, 1985-92. Founding mem. Berkshire County Hist. Soc., 1962, v.p., 1962-66, pres., 1966-68, bd. dirs., 1974-76; trustee Hancock-Shaker Cmty. Inc., 1974-91, Wyoming Sem., 1976-79, Bennington Mus., 1985-95; bd. dirs. Armand Hammer United World Coll. Am. West, 1993—. Capt. AUS, 1942-46. Guggenheim fellow, 1958-59, 68-69; recipient Frederic W. Ness award Assn. Am. Colls., 1980, Rogerson cup Williams Coll., 1982, Disting. Svc. award Wyo. Seminary, 1986. Mem. Nat. Acad. Edn., Mass. Hist. Soc. (fellow), Am. Hist. Assn., Am. Studies Assn., Orgn. Am. Historians, AAUP, Phi Beta Kappa. Democrat. Home: PO Box 515 Williamstown MA 01267-2800

RUDOLPH, FREDERICK BYRON, biochemistry educator; b. St. Joseph, Mo., Oct. 17, 1944; s. John Max and Maxine Leah (Wood) R.; m. Glenda M. Myers, June 18, 1971; children: Anna Dorine, William K. BS in Chemistry, U. Mo., Rolla, 1966; PhD in Biochemistry, Iowa State U., 1971. Prof. biochemistry Rice U., Houston, 1972—, chair biochemistry and cell biology, 1995—, dir. Lab. for Biochem. and Genetic Engring., 1986—, exec. dir. Inst. Bioscience and Bioengineering, 1993—. Cons. World Book, Chgo., 1972—; mem. biochemistry study sect. NIH, Bethesda, Md., 1983-87; bd. dirs. Coun. Biotech. Ctrs., Tex. Healthcare & Bioscis. Inst. Contbr. over 160 articles to profl. jours. including Jour. Biol. Chemistry, Biochemistry, Transplantation, Exptl. Hematology, Jour. Parenteral and Enteral Nutrition, Jour. Molecular Biology, Applied and Environ. Microbiology, Life Scis., Archives Biochem. Biophysics, Critical Care Medicine, Archives Surgery, Sci.; also chpts. in books. Recipient Disting. Alumnus award Iowa State U., 1980, 99, 2000. Fellow AAAS; mem. Am. Chem. Soc., Am. Soc. for Biochemistry and Molecular Biology, Am. Soc. Nutritional Scis. Achievements include research on dietary requirements for immune function, new enteral feeding formulas and infant formulas, new techniques for protein purification, new methods for kinetic analysis of enzymes, structure and function of various enzymes. Office: Rice U Dept Biochemistry and Cell Biology MS 140 6100 Main St Houston TX 77005-1827

RUDOLPH, GILBERT LAWRENCE, lawyer; b. L.A., Aug. 23, 1946; s. Martin Muttel and Marion (Perlman) R.; Susan Ilene Fellenbaum, Sept. 18, 1983; children: Samara Lisa, Felicia Beth. BA, Ariz. State U., 1967; postgrad., Am. U., Washington, 1967-69; JD, U. Cin., 1973. Bar: D.C. 1973, U.S. Dist. Ct. D.C. 1974, U.S. Ct. Appeals (D.C. cir.) 1974, Ariz. 1975, U.S. Dist. Ct. Ariz. 1975, Calif. 1979. Assoc. Streich, Lang, Weeks & Cardon, P.A., Phoenix, 1975-78; ptnr. Gilbert L. Rudolph, P.C., 1978-87; sr. mem. O'Connor, Cavanagh, Anderson, Killingsworth & Beshears, P.A., 1987-99; shareholder Greenberg Traurig LLP, 1999—. Lectr. on lending issues. Bd. dirs. Make-A-Wish Found. of Am., 1984-89, Aid to Adoption of Spl. Kids, Ariz., 1995—, Temple Chai, 2002—. Fellow Am. Coll. Consumer Fin. Svcs. Lawyers; mem. ABA (com. on consumer fin. svcs. bus. law sect. 1981—, com. on comml. fin. svcs. 1989—, mem. com. on uniform comml. code 1992—), Conf. on Consumer Fin. Law (governing com. 1986—). Republican. Jewish. Office: Greenberg Traurig LLP Ste 700 2375 E Camelback Rd Phoenix AZ 85016 E-mail: RudolphG@gtlaw.com.

RUDOLPH, KATHLEEN ANN, insurance company executive; b. Minnetonka, Minn., Feb. 22, 1962; d. Russell Edward and Joan Lou Schaub; m. Stephen Mark Rudolph, May 26, 1991. BA, DePauw U., 1984. Underwriter The Hartford, Brea, Calif., 1985-88, sales supr. Southington, Conn., 1988-93, underwriting mgr., 1993-96, strategic underwriting dir., 1996-98, dir. outsourcing, 1998-99, v.p. ops. ea. divsn., 1999-2000, underwriting v.p., 2000—. Mem. Delta Delta Delta. Avocations: traveling, interior designing, reading, gardening. Office: The Hartford 200 Executive Blvd Southington CT 06489 E-mail: krudolph@thehartford.com.

RUDOLPH, LAVERE CHRISTIAN, library director; b. Jasper, Ind., Dec. 24, 1921; s. Joseph Frank and Rose (Stradtner) R. AB, DePauw U., 1948; B.D., Louisville Presbyn. Sem., 1951; PhD, Yale, 1958; student, U. Zurich, Switzerland, 1960; M.L.S., Ind. U., 1968. Ordained to Ministry Presbyn. Ch., 1950; pastor in Ind. and Conn., 1950-54; mem. faculty Louisville Presbyn. Sem., 1954-69, prof. ch. history, 1960-69; lectr. history U. Louisville, 1965-69; rare books bibliographer Van Pelt Library U. Pa.; head tech. services Lilly Library, Ind. U., 1970-78, curator of books, 1978-86, librarian emeritus, 1987—. Author: Hoosier Zion, 1963 (Thomas Kuch award Ind. U. Writers Conf. 1964), Story of the Church, 1966, Francis Asbury, 1966, Indiana Letters, 1979, Religion in Indiana, 1986, Hoosier Faiths, 1995. Served to capt. USAAF, 1940-46. Mem.: Presbyn. Hist. Soc., Am. Soc. Ch. History, Phi Beta Kappa. Democrat. Home: 1021 Sassafras Cir Bloomington IN 47408-1280 Office: Ind U Library Bloomington IN 47405

RUDOLPH, LINDA LOUISE, social worker, legal advocate; b. Henderson, N.C., Aug. 22, 1947; d. Frank and Belle (Milton) Sicurella (div. Oct. 1999); children: Gregory, Stefanie. Cert. social worker, N.J., domestic violence specialist. Facilitator Child Abuse Prevention, Ocean County, N.J., 1986-89; caseworker children's program Cath. Charities, Toms River, 1989-94, legal advocate, 1995-97; transitional housing coord. State N.J., 1992-94; sr. program coord. Counseling & Referral of Ocean Inc., Brick, NJ, 1998—2001, program supr. transitional housing program of Ocean County N.J., 1998—; outreach dir. Legal Advocate Carteret County Domestic Violence Program, 2002—. Cons., presenter Lacey Twp. H.S., Lanoka Twp., N.J., 1986; advisor gited & talented program Millstone Twp. Schs., Perrineville, N.J., 1982-84. Mem. ACA, Am. Counseling Specialists in Group Work, N.J. Counseling Assn., N.J. Coalition Battered Women, Soroptimists (v.p. 1997-99, pres. 1999—). Avocations: boating, volunteering. Home: 131 Silver Creek Dr Swansboro NC 28584-9438

RUDOLPH, RONALD ALVIN, human resources executive; b. Berwyn, Ill., May 12, 1949; s. Alvin J. and Gloria S. (Nicoletti) R. BA, U. Calif., Santa Cruz, 1971. Sr. cons. De Anza Assocs., San Jose, Calif., 1971-73; pers. adminstr. McDonnell Douglas Corp., Cupertino, 1974-75; employment rep. Fairchild Semiconductor, Mountain View, 1973-74, 75; compensation analyst Sperry Univac, Santa Clara, 1975-78; mgr. exempt compensation div. Intel Corp., 1978-79, compensation mgr., 1979-82, dir. corp. compensation, 1982-85; v.p. human resources UNISYS Corp., San Jose, 1985-91, ASK Group Inc., Mountain View, Calif., 1991-94, 3 Com Corp., Santa Clara, 1994-98; v.p. adminstrn. Wyse Tech. Inc., San Jose, Calif., 1999—. Cons. Rudolph Assocs., Cupertino, 1982—; bd. dirs. Dynamic Temp. Svcs., Sunnyvale, Calif. Mem. Spl. Com. for Parolee Employment, Sacramento, 1973-75; bd. dirs. Jr. Achievement, San Jose, 1987-88. Mem. Am. Soc. Pers. Adminstrs., Am. Compensation Assn., No. Calif. Human Resources Coun. Avocations: sailing, reading, running, camping. Office: 3 Com Corp Santa Clara CA 95050

RUDOLPH, WALLACE MORTON, law educator; b. Chgo., Sept. 11, 1930; s. Norman Charles and Bertha (Margolin) R.; m. Janet L. Gordon, Feb. 14, 1964 (div. Jan. 1998); children: Alexey, Rebecca, Sarah; m. Mimi Longworth, Mar. 22, 1998; children: Haille, Bryon. BA, U. Chgo., 1950, JD, 1953. Bar: Ill. 1953, U.S. Ct. Mil. Appeals 1954, U.S. Supreme Ct. 1954, Nebr. 1962, Wash. 1978. Rsch. assoc. Ford Found., 1953-54, Ford Found. (Project in Law and Behavior Sci.), 1954-55; instr. U. Chgo. Law Sch., 1959; assoc. Antonow & Fink, Chgo., 1960-61; asst. prof. law U. Nebr., Lincoln, 1961-63, assoc. prof., 1963-64, prof., 1965-76, U. Puget Sound Sch. Law, 1976-94, dean, 1976-80; prof. Seattle U. Sch. Law, 1994—. Vis. prof. law U. Wis., 1980-81, U. Ill., 1984; chair excellence in law Memphis State U. Law Sch., 1991; mem. Commrs. Uniform State Law, 1973-77; judge Ct. Indsl. Rels., Nebr., 1975-77; mem. Wash. Jud. Coun. and COm. II, 1976-80, Pub. Employment Rels. Commn., Wash., 1977-97; dean U. Orlando, 1997-98. Author: Handbook for Correctional Law; contbr. articles to profl. jours.; author: Model Criminal Procedure Code, 1975, Model Sentencing and Corrections Act, 1978, Amicus Curiae Brief, Wash. State Supreme Ct, 1979. Bd. dirs. LIMIT, 1992-94, Nebr. chpt. ACLU, 1965-72; mem. Nebr. Dem. Contact Com., 1973-74, 75-76; chmn. Firt Congl. Dist. Dem. Party, 1975-76; mem. exec. com. Unitarian Ch., Lincoln, 1965-67. With JAGC, U.S. Army, 1954-57. Mem. AAUP, ABA, Soc. Criminology, Am. Law Inst., Am. Arbitration Assn. E-mail: wallace.rudolph@celebration.fl.us.

RUDOLPH, WALTER PAUL, engineering research company executive; b. Binghamton, N.Y., Aug. 17, 1937; s. Walter Paul and Frieda Lena (Hennemann) R.; m. Leila Ortencia Romero, Dec. 18, 1960; children: Jonathan, Jana, Catherine. BEE, Rensselaer Poly. Inst., 1959; MSBA, San Diego State U., 1964. Elec. engr. Gen. Dynamics/Astronautics, San Diego, 1959-62; ops. research analyst Navy Electronics Lab., 1962-64; mem. profl. staff Gen. Electric Tempo, Honolulu, 1964-70, Ctr. for Naval Analysis, Arlington, Va., 1970-77; pres. La Jolla (Calif.) Rsch. Corp., 1977—. Served to Capt. USNR, 1959-92. Republican. Presbyterian. Home: 1559 El Paso Real La Jolla CA 92037-6303 Office: La Jolla Rsch Corp PO Box 1207 La Jolla CA 92038-1207

RUDRAPATNA, ASHOK N. research manager; b. Bombay, India, Dec. 28, 1949; s. Narasimhaiya and Padmavathi Narasimhaiya R.; m. Roopa Ashok Basavapatna, Apr. 19, 1958; children: Vivek, Tara. B in Technology, Indian Inst. Tech., Bombay, 1971; MS in Engring., U. Va., Charlottesville, 1973, PhD in Engring., 1977. Postdoc. fellow Rsch. Labs. for Engring. Sci., Charlottesville, Va., 1976—77; mem. tech. staff Bell Labs, Holmdel, NJ, 1978—83; supr. AT&T Bell Labs./AT&T Labs., Holmdel and Whippany, 1984—98; tech. mgr. Bell Labs Lucent Techs., Whippany, 1998—. Contbr. articles. Mem. election com. Hindu Temple & Cultural Soc., Bridgewater, NJ, 1999—2000; mem. pres.'s internat. student adv. bd. U. Va., Charlottesville, 1972—75; mem. Athi Rudra planning com. Sringeri Vidya Bharathi Found., Stroudsburg, 1997. Mem.: IEEE (sr.; mem. conf. organizing com. 1998—99), North Am. Sankethi Assn. (bd. dirs. 1992—96, sec. 1998—2000). Hindu. Achievements include patents for 11 patents in telecomms; invention of. Avocations: philosophy, genealogy, bicycling. Office: Wireless Advanced Technologies Lab 67 Whippany Rd Room 15H222 Whippany NJ 07981

RUDY, DAVID ROBERT, physician, educator; b. Columbus, Ohio, Oct. 19, 1934; s. Robert Sale and Lois May (Arthur) R.; m. Rose Mary Sims; children by previous marriage: Douglas D., Steven W., Katharine L. Rudy Hoffer, Hunter A. Elam. BSc, Ohio State U., 1956, MD, 1960; MPH, Med. Coll. Wis., 1995. Diplomate Am. Bd. Family Practice, Am. Bd. Preventive Medicine. Intern Northwestern Meml. Hosp., Chgo., 1960-61; resident in internal medicine Ohio State U. Hosp., 1963-64; resident in pediatrics Children's Hosp., Columbus, Ohio, 1964; pvt. family practice, 1964-75; dir. residency program Riverside Meth. Hosp., 1975-85; dir. family practice residency Monsour Med. Ctr., Jeannette, Pa., 1985-88; dir. residency Bon Secours Hosp., Grosse Pointe, Mich., 1988-91; prof., dept. chmn. Finch U. Health Scis., Chgo. Med. Sch., 1991-95, 97—; prof. Pomerene chair family medicine Ohio State U., 1995-97. Editor, contbr. (textbook) Family Medicine for the House Officer; author: Family Medicine Q & A: NMS Series; contbr. articles to profl. jours. Capt. flight surgeon MC. USAF, 1961—63; col. USAFR (ret.). Recipient USAF Commendation medal. Fellow Am. Acad. Family Physicians; mem. AMA, Ill. State Med. Assn. Republican. Office: Chgo Med Sch Finch U Clinic 3333 Green Bay Rd North Chicago IL 60064-3037 also: 540 Ambria Dr Mundelein IL 60060-4806

RUDY, FRANK R. pathologist; b. Harrisburg, Pa., Jan. 23, 1949; s. Burton B. and Blanch T. (Rhoads) R.; m. Debra R. Bromberg, Dec. 27, 1970; children: Allison, Nicole. BA, Franklin & Marshall Coll., 1970; MD, U. Pitts., 1974. From assoc. pathologist to chmn. lab. Polyclinic Hosp., Harrisburg, 1979-95; chmn. Pinnacle Health Lab., 1996-99, vice-chmn., 2000—. Pres. Pathology Assocs. Ctrl. Pa., Harrisburg, 1997—. Author: Uropathology, 1989, Principles and Practices of Surgical Pathology; contbr. articles to profl. jours. Fellow Coll. Am. Pathology, Am. Soc. Clin. Pathologists; mem. Internat. Acad. Pathology, Am. Pathology Found., U.S. Acad. Pathology, Canadian Acad. Pathology. Avocation: scuba diving. Office: Polyclinic Hosp 2601 N 3rd St Harrisburg PA 17110-2098 E-mail: frudy@pinnaclehealth.org.

RUDY, JOEL S. association administrator; b. Bklyn., Jan. 20, 1941; s. Sidney T. and Selma Rudy; m. Marlene Yourga, Nov. 24, 1965; children: Lisa Michele, Brian Scott, Julia. BS in Biology, Bethany Coll., 1962; MA in Sociology, Kent State U., 1964; cert. in Edni. Mgmt., Harvard U., 1985. Instr. sociology, asst. dean students Hunter Coll., CUNY, Bronx, N.Y., 1964-67; assoc. dir. housing, dir. resident student devel. U. Miami, Coral Gables, 1967-71; dean student resident life, asst. v.p. Kent (Ohio) State U., 1971-76; dir. residence life U. Ohio, Athens, 1976-78, assoc. dean students, then dean of students, 1978-95, v.p., dean, 1995-98, v.p. and dean emeritus, 1999—; exec. dir. Phi Kappa Tau Nat. Fraternity, Oxford, Ohio, 1998—2001, exec. v.p., COO, 2001—. Sr. fellow Acad. Leadership U. Md., College Park, 1999—. Pres. Athens City Sch. Bd., 1987-91; vice chmn. Athens County Red Cross, 1997-99, Athens County Heart Fund, 1980-81; trustee Phi Kappa Tau Nat. Found., 2002—. Recipient Phil Tripp Outstanding award Ohio Coll. Pers. Assn., Gerald Saddlemire award Ohio Coll. Pers. Assn. Mem. Ohio Assn. Student Pers. Adminstrn. (pres. 1983-84), Rotary, Golden Key Nat. Honor Soc., Phi Kappa Phi, Phi Delta Kappa, Omicron Delta Kappa. Democrat. Jewish. Avocations: boating, volunteer work. Home: 19 Roxbury Dr Athens OH 45701 E-mail: rudyhome@aol.com.

RUDY, KATHLEEN VERMEULEN, small business owner; b. Grand Rapids, Mich., Dec. 29, 1931; d. John Weston and Geneva (Swiet) Vermeulen; m. Fredrick Albers Yonkman, June 9, 1953 (div. Sept. 1980); children: Sara Yonkman Davis, Margriet Yonkman Finnegan, Nina Tower; m. Raymond Bruce Rudy, Nov. 14, 1981. BA, Hope Coll., Holland, Mich., 1953. Owner Kate's Antiques, 1974-2000. Editor mag. Jr. League of Boston, 1960's, Scarsdale Jr. League, 1960's. Bd. dirs. Jr. League of Boston, 1960s, Greenwich Cmty. for Human Svcs., 1970s-80s, Neighbor to Neighbor, Greenwich, 1980-98; trustee Hope Coll., Holland, 1986-96; chmn. Mary Fund com. Ladies Golf Tournament, 1985; mem. Women's Nat. Rep. Club, N.Y.C., 1995—, bd. govs., 1997—; mem. Hope Coll. Pres.'s Task Force, 1997-99; treas. Women's Nat. Rep. Club, 2000-2002, chmn. nominating com. 2000—, 2d v.p., 2002-. Mem. Greenwich Jr. League, Greenwich Country Club, Dorset Field Club, Kappa Alpha Theta. Republican. Congregationalist. Avocations: tennis, golf, antiques, travel. Home and Office: 37 Lismore Ln Greenwich CT 06831-3741 E-mail: RayRudy@worldnet.att.net.

RUDY, LESTER HOWARD, psychiatrist, educator; b. Chgo., Mar. 6, 1918; s. Sol and Mildred (Weinzimmer) R.; m. Ruth Jean Schmidt, Nov. 25, 1950; 1 dau., Sharon Ruth. BS, U. Ill., 1939, MD, 1941; MS in Hosp. Adminstrn, Northwestern U., 1957. Diplomate: Am. Bd. Psychiatry and Neurology (exec. dir. 1972-86). Intern Cedars of Lebanon Hosp., Los Angeles, 1941-42; resident in psychiatry VA Hosp., Downey, Ill., 1946-48, staff psychiatrist, 1948-52, chief service, 1952-54; supt. Galesburg (Ill.) State Research Hosp., 1954-58; practice medicine specializing in psychiatry Chgo.; supt. Ill. State Psychiat. Inst., 1958-61, dir., 1961—, Ill. Mental Health Insts., Chgo., 1967-75; prof. psychiatry U. Ill. Coll. Medicine, 1971-88, emeritus, 1988—, head dept. psychiatry, 1975-88, pres. hosp. staff, 1979-80; dir. U. Ill. Hosp., 1981-82; sr. med. dir. Health Care Compare, 1988—. Chmn. research rev. com. mental health services NIMH, 1972-73; AMA commr. Joint Commn. on Accreditation of Hosps., 1967-75; sr. cons. VA; cons. adv. bd. Chgo., Police Dept.; lectr. dept. psychiatry and neurology Loyola U., 1968-75; mem. Ill. Gov.'s Com. Competency to Stand Trial, 1968; cons. psychiatry Blue Cross/Blue Shield of Ill., 1996—, Cir. Ct. of Winnebago County (Ill.), 1995—. Contbr. articles to profl. jours. Served to col. AUS, 1942-46. Decorated Bronze Star with two oak leaf clusters Fellow Am. Psychiat. Assn. (chmn. ethics com. 1963, Simon Bolivar award 1985), Am. Coll. Psychiatrists (charter, Bowis award 1979); mem. Am. Acad. Psychoanalysis (sci. asso.), Ill. Psychiat. Soc. (pres. 1962-63), U. Ill. Med. Alumni Assn. (ann. outstanding achievement award 1980) Home: 6343 Collingswood Ct Rockford IL 61103-8961 Office: 912 S Wood St Chicago IL 60612-7325 E-mail: rjandlhr@aol.com.

RUDY, RAYMOND BRUCE, JR. retired food company executive; b. L.A., Apr. 24, 1931; s. Raymond Bruce and Wrena Margaret (Higgins) R.; m. Kathleen Vermeulen; children: Bruce Rudy, Alice M.R. Price, Barbara R. Frith. BS, UCLA, 1953; MBA, Xavier U., Cin., 1960. Brand mgr. Procter & Gamble, Cin., 1956-62; product mgr. Hunt-Wesson Foods, Fullerton, Calif., 1962-63; group v.p. Gen. Foods Corp., White Plains, N.Y., 1963-79; pres. Oroweat Foods Co. subs. Continental Grain Co., N.Y.C., 1979-83; chmn., pres. Arnold Foods Co., Inc., Greenwich, Conn., 1984-86; pres. Affiliates of Best Foods subs. CPC Internat., Englewood Cliffs, N.J., 1987-89; ret., 1989; chmn., CEO, New Hampton, Inc., 1993-94; dep. chmn. Snapple Natural Beverages, Inc., 1992-94; mng. dir. J.W. Childs Assoc., 1995—; chmn. Personal Care Group, Inc., 1996-98. Chmn. Beltone Electronics Corp., 1997-2000, Internat. Diverse Foods, 1998-99, Empire Kosher Poultry, Inc., 1997-2000, DESA Internat., 1999-2001, Am. Safety Razor, 2000—, Hartz Mountain Corp., 2001—, The Meow Mix Co., 2002—; bd. dirs. Widmer Brothers Brewing, Inc. With U.S. Army, 1954-56. Mem. Greenwich Country Club, Dorset Field Club, The Links, The Boulders. Congregationalist.

RUDY, RUTH CORMAN, former state legislator; b. Millheim, Pa., Jan. 3, 1938; d. Orvis E. and Mabel Jan (Stover) Corman; m. C. Guy Rudy, Nov. 21, 1956; children: Douglas G., Donita Rudy Koval, Dianna F. Degree in x-ray tech., Carnegie Inst., 1956; student, Pa. State U., 1968-71. Clk. of cts. County of Centre (Pa.), Bellefonte, 1976-82; rep. Pa. Gen. Assembly, Harrisburg, 1982-96. Mem. Dem. Nat. Com., 1980—, chair women's caucus, 1989-91; past pres. Pa. Fedn. Dem. Women, Harrisburg; pres. Nat. Fedn. Dem. Women, 1987-89; mem. exec. com. Dem. Nat. Com., 1987-89; candidate U.S. Congress, 5th Dist., 1995-96; rep. Nat. Dem. Inst. for Internat. Affairs, Centre Hall, Pa., 1997—. Granted U.S. Patent on hair spray face shield 1995. Named Woman of Yr. Pa. Fedn. dem. Women, 1982, Centre County Living Legend, 2000. Methodist.

RUDY, WILLIS, historian; b. N.Y.C., Jan. 25, 1920; s. Philip and Rose (Handman) R.; m. Dorothy L. Richardson, Jan. 31, 1948; children: Dee Dee, Willis Philip, Willa. BSS, CCNY, 1939; MA, Columbia U., 1940, PhD, 1948. Instr. CCNY, 1939-49; instr., lectr. Harvard U., 1949-53, 57-58; prof. Mass. State Coll., Worcester, 1953-63; prof. history Fairleigh Dickinson U., Teaneck, N.J., 1963-82, prof. emeritus, 1982—. Mem. editorial bd. Fairleigh Dickinson U. Press, 1966-77. Author: The College of the City of New York, A History, 1847-1947, 1949, 1977; The American Liberal Arts College Curriculum, 1960; Higher Education in Transition, 1958, 68, 76, 97; Schools in an Age of Mass Culture, 1965; The Universities of Europe: A History, 1984; Total War and Twentieth Century Higher Learning, 1991, The Campus and a Nation in Crisis: From the Revolution to Vietnam, 1996. Mem. Orgn. Am. Historians, Phi Beta Kappa. Home: 161 W Clinton Ave Tenafly NJ 07670-1916 Office: Fairleigh Dickinson U Dept Of Hist Teaneck NJ 07666 *As a teacher, my greatest reward has been to see people get involved in the sheer joy of learning new things and seeking answers to the big questions that life proposes. As a writer, my enduring satisfaction has come from the opportunity to explore the seemingly chaotic events of human history in the hope of finding a meaningful and instructive pattern.*

RUDY, YORAM, biomedical engineer, biophysicist, educator; b. Tel Aviv, Israel, Feb. 12, 1946; came to U.S., 1973; s. Nahum and Yaffa (Krinkin) R. BSc, Technion/Israel Inst. Tech., Haifa, 1971, MSc in Physics, 1973; PhD in Biomed. Engring., Case Western Res. U., 1978. Asst. prof. dept. biomed. engring. Case Western Res. U., Cleve., 1981-86, assoc. prof., 1986-89, prof., 1989—, prof. dept. of physiology and biophysics, 1991—, prof. dept. medicine, 1992—. Dir. cardiac bioelectricity rsch. and tng. ctr., vis. prof. Technion/Israel Inst. Tech., 1982-83, U. Parma, Italy, 1986, 87, U. Utah, Salt Lake City, 1990, Tel-Aviv (Israel) U., 1991, Russian Acad. of Scis., St. Petersburg, 1997, U. Berne, Switzerland, 1998; mem. cardiovascular and pulmonary study sect. NIH, 1984-88; Rijlant lectr. Internat. Congress on Electrocardiology, 2000. Mem. editorial bd. Jour. Electrocardiology, Jour. Cardiovascular Electrophysiology, Cardiovasc. Rsch., Cardiac Electrophysiology Rev.; contbr. articles to profl. jours. Grantee NIH, 1985—, Am. Heart Assn., 1990-95, NSF, 1987-94; recipient Gordon K. Moe Prof. award, 1997, NIH-Nat. Heart, Lung and Blood Inst. Merit award, 1998. Fellow IEEE, Am. Physiol. Soc., Am. Inst. Med. and Biol. Engring.; mem. Am. Heart Assn., Biophys. Soc., Biomed. Engring. Soc. (sr., Disting. Lectr. award 2001). Achievements include development of a novel imaging modality for noninvasive imaging of cardiac electrical events from electrical potentials measured on the body surface (electrocardiographic imaging, ECGI), of theoretical models of cardiac excitation at the cellular, sub-cellular and tissue levels; elucidation of the cellular mechanisms of cardiac arrhythmias and the role of tissue architecture in arrhythmogenesis. Office: Case Western Res U Dept Biomed Engring Cleveland OH 44106-7207

RUDZKI, ROBERT A. steel company executive; b. West Bromwich, Eng., Oct. 11, 1953; m. Nancy Eleanor Boylston. BS in Indsl. Engring., Lehigh U., 1975; MBA, U. Pa., Wharton, 1977. Cert. cash mgr. Credit asst. Bethlehem (Pa.) Steel Corp., 1977-79, sr. credit asst., 1979, fin. analyst, 1979-80, adminstrv. mgr. credit, 1980-82, dir. bus. devel., 1982-86, mgr. banking,

1986-88, asst. treas., 1988-93, asst. contr., 1993-94, gen. mgr. purchasing and transp., 1994-96, v.p. purchasing and transp., chief procurement officer, 1996—. Trustee Pension Trust of Bethlehem Steel Corp., 1988-94. Bd. dirs. Lehigh Valley Mental Health Mental Retardation, Allentown, Pa., 1979; v.p., bd. dirs. Homemaker Health-Aide Svc., Inc., Bethlehem, 1982-83. Mem. Treasury Mgmt. Assn., Treasury Mgmt. Assn. Ctrl. Pa. (v.p., co-foudner 1989-90, pres. 1990-91), Nat. Assn. Purchasing Mgmt. Office: Bethlehem Steel Corp 8th And Eaton Ave Bethlehem PA 18016

RUE, DOUGLAS MICHAEL, technical application consultant; b. Pensacola, Fla., Apr. 9, 1964; s. Barbara J. Rue; m. Andra O'Neal, 1995; 1 child, Christian Michael Rue. AA in Bus., AA in Computer Sci., Pensacola (Fla.) Jr. Coll., 1984; BS in Computer Sci. cum laude, St. Augustine's Coll., 1988; MS in Telecomms., DePaul U., 1990. Data sys. analyst Internat. Paper, Memphis, 1990-91, project analyst, 1991-94; tech. cons. Sprint, L.A., 1994—, sr. tech. applications cons. Universal City, Calif., 1998—, Jacksonville, Fla., 1999—. Instr. DeVry Inst., Pomona, Calif., 1994. With U.S. Army Res., 1985-91.

RUE, NELSON B. nursing administrator; b. Dayton, Ohio, Nov. 8, 1956; s. Nelson B. Jr. and Martha Sue R.; m. Carol Ann Wear, July 1, 1978; children: Laura, Suzanne. AS in Nursing, Western Ky. U., 1977, BA, 1980; MBA, Thomas More Coll., 1999. RN. Acct. mgr. Regent Hosp. Products, Ltd., Cin., 1988-91; v.p. Commonwealth, Inc., 1991-95; sr. v.p. MedComm Fulfillment, Inc., 1995-97; sr. v.p., chief oper. officer Pinnacle Packaging & Fulfillment, Inc., 1997-2000; surg. nurse St. Elizabeth Hosp., Edgewood, Ky., 2000—01; dir. adminstrn. Advanced Surg. Care, PSC, 2001—. Squad comdr. Civil air Patrol, 2000—. Mem. Coun. Logistics Mgmt. (v.p. exec. com. 1994-95, pres. exec. com. 1995-96), Rotary (v.p. 1985). Republican. Presbyterian. Avocations: search & rescue, boating, scuba diving. Home: 2843 Fraternity Ct Crestview Hills KY 41017-2512 Office: Advanced Surg Care PSC 20 Medical Village Dr Edgewood KY 41017

RUEB, SHEREE A. social services administrator; b. Lincoln, Nebr., Aug. 23, 1960; d. Larry Hawkins, Annette Hawkins; m. Brent G. Rueb, July 7, 1985. BA, Hastings Coll., 1979—83; MA, Witchita State U., 1989—91. V.p. Mental Health Assn. South Ctrl. Kans., Wichita, 1991—95; state dir. Green Thumb, In.c, Arlington, Va., 1995—97; dir. sr. work experience ARC, Wichita, 1997—. Adv. bd. Reno County Workforce, Hutchinson, Kans., 1998—; bd. dirs. Kans. Workforce Investment, Hays, 1997—; adv. bd. Sedgwick County Workforce Partnership, Wichita, 1998—. Vice chair Older Workers Task Force State of Kans., 1997—. Mem.: Harvey County Archl. Assn. (sec., treas. 1995—, pres. 1996—98). Avocation: historic architecture, historic preservation. Office: ARC Midway KS Chpt 707 N Main Wichita KS 67203*

RUEBE, BAMBI LYNN, interior, environmental designer; b. Huntington Park, Calif., Nov. 13, 1957; d. Leonard John Ruebe and Vaudis Marie Powell. BS, UCLA, 1988. Millwright asst. Kaiser Steel Corp., Fontana, Calif., 1976-79; electrician Fleetwood Enterprises, Riverside, 1977; fashion model internat., 1977-85; free-lance draftsman, 1982-83; project coord. Philip J. Sicola Inc., Culver City, Calif., 1982-83; prin. designer Ruebe Inclusive Design, Highland, 1983-89, Ventura, 1990—; part time instr. Fillmore H.S., 1995-96. Cons. mfg. design Burlington Homes New Eng. Inc., Oxford, Maine, 1987-90, DeRose Industries, Chambersburg, Pa., 1984, Skyline Corp., Redlands, Calif., 1982-84; cons. lighting Lightways Corp., L.A., 1984-87; mem. design rev. bd. San Bernardino (Calif.) Downtown Main St. Redevel. Com., 1987-89. Motion picture project designer, lighting design, archtl. design for the movie Deceptions, 1990. Mem. World Affairs Coun., Inland So. Calif., 1986-90; mem. Citizens adv. com. Highland Calif. Gen. Plan, 1988-90; co-chmn. civil rights com. AFL-CIO, Fontana, 1978-79. Recipient Cert. Merit Scholastic Art award Scholastic Mags. Inc., Southeastern Calif., 1974, Dirs. Incentive award for Archtl. Design City of Ventura, Calif., 1990, Calif.'s Best Spl. Event award for Rte 66 Rendezvous Calif. State Dept. Tourism. Mem. Nat. Trust for Hist. Preservation. Democrat. Achievements include design and specification of the first drywall system for use in the manufactured housing industry; design of first hot sea water oxygen therapy spa for people. Avocations: research in alternative energies, aromatherapy, marine and exotic animals, horseback riding, antique sportscar restoration. Office: Ruebe Inclusive Design 50 N Oak St Ventura CA 93001-5625 E-mail: ancientaromatics@juno.com.

RUEBEL, MARION A. university president; b. Manson, Iowa; B in Biol. Scis., U. No. Iowa, 1958, M in Sch. Adminstrn., 1962; PhD in Ednl. Adminstrn., Iowa State U., 1969. Asst. prof. secondary edn. U. Akron, 1970-73, dept. chmn., assoc. prof., 1973, asst. dean Coll. Edn., dean Univ. Coll., exec. asst. to pres., interim sr. v.p., dir. alumni affairs and govtl. rels., prof. edn.; pres. St. Vincent-St. Mary H.S., Akron, 1994-96, U. Akron, 1996-99, trustee prof., 1999—. Bd. dirs. Ohio Aerospace Inst., Northeastern Ohio Univs. Coll. of Medicine; mem. Ohio Scis. and Tech. Coun. Contbr. numerous papers, reports, and articles to profl. publs. Office: Univ of Akron Stitzleis Alumni Ctr Buchtel Common Akron OH 44325-2602

RUEBHAUSEN, OSCAR MELICK, retired lawyer; b. N.Y.C., Aug. 28, 1912; s. Oscar and Eleonora J. (Melick) R.; m. Zelia Krumbhaar Peet, Oct. 31, 1942. AB summa cum laude, Dartmouth Coll., 1934; LLB cum laude, Yale U., 1937. Bar: N.Y. 1938, U.S. Supreme Ct. 1945. Assoc. Debevoise, Stevenson, Plimpton & Page, N.Y.C., 1937-42, Lend-Lease Adminstrn., Washington, 1942-44; gen. counsel Office Sci. Rsch. and Devel., 1944-46; ptnr. Debevoise and Plimpton, 1946-84, presiding ptnr., 1972-81, of counsel, 1984-87; counselor to ednl. instn., 1988-99; retired. Editor: Pension and Retirement Policies in Colleges and Universities, 1990; contbr. articles to profl. jours. Chmn. Commn. on Coll. Retirement, 1984-93; spl. adviser atomic energy to gov. N.Y. State, 1959; vice chmn. N.Y. State adv. com. on atomic energy, 1959-62; chmn. N.Y. State Gov.'s Task Force on protection from radioactive fallout, 1959; mem. Pres.'s Task Force on Sci. Policy, 1969-70, Pres.'s Sci. Adv. Com. Panel on Chems. and Health, 1970-72, Commn. on Critical Choices for Am., 1973-77, adv. com. Carnegie Commn. on Sci., Tech. and Govt., 1988-93; chmn. UN Day, N.Y. State, 1962, chmn. Spl. N.Y. Com. on Ins. Holding Cos., 1967-68; mem. U.S. govt. panel on Privacy and Behavioral Rsch., 1965-66; mem. presdl. panel Chronic Renal Disease, 1966-67; sec., dir. Fund Peaceful Atomic Devel., Inc., 1954-72; dir. Carrie Chapman Catt Meml. Fund, 1948-58; chmn. bd. Bennington Coll., 1957-61, 62-67; trustee Hudson Inst., Inc., 1961-71; trustee Russell Sage Found., chmn. bd., 1965-80; vice-chmn. N.Y.C. Univ. Constrn. Fund, 1966-69; mem. Coun. on Fgn. Rels., Nat. Com. on U.S.-China Rels.; mem. New Sch. Univ. Instl. Policy Com., 1991-2000; bd. dirs. Greenwall Found., 1956-95, chmn., 1982-91, chmn. emeritus, 1991—; bd. dirs. Scripps Clinic and Rsch. Found, 1983-89. Recipient U.S. Presdl. Cert. of Merit, 1948. Mem. ABA, N.Y. State Bar Assn., Yale Law Sch. Assn. (exec. com. and pres. 1960-62, chmn. 1962-64), Assn. of Bar of City of N.Y. (pres. 1980-82, pres. and bd. dirs. fund 1980-82), Order of Coif, Rancho Santa Fe Assn., Century Club (N.Y.C.), River Club (N.Y.C.), Phi Beta Kappa, Sigma Phi Epsilon, Sigma Xi (hon.). Clubs: Century (N.Y.C.), River (N.Y.C.); Rancho Santa Fe Assn. (Calif.). Home: 450 E 52nd St New York NY 10022-6448

RUEBNER, BORIS HENRY, pathologist, educator; b. Düsseldorf, Germany, Aug. 30, 1923; came to U.S., 1959, naturalized, 1965; s. Fred and Martha (Klein) R.; m. Susan Mautner, Sept. 20, 1957; children: Sally, Anthony. MB, Edinburgh (Scotland) U., 1946, MD, 1956. Diplomate Am. Bd. Anatomic Pathology, Am. Bd. Clin Pathology. Intern Royal Infirmary, Edinburgh, 1946-47; resident Royal Bristol (Eng.) Infirmary, 1947—50, Hammersmith Hosp., London, 1950-56; asst. prof. pathology Dalhousie U., Halifax, N.S., Can., 1957-59; assoc. prof. Johns Hopkins U., Balt., 1959-68; prof. U. Calif., Davis, 1968—94, prof. emeritus, 1994—. Author: Diagnostic Pathology of the Liver, 1982, 2d edit., 1991, The Gastrointestinal System, 1983. Served to capt. M.C., Brit. Army, 1947-49. Recipient Career Devel. award NIH, 1962-68. Fellow Coll. Am. Pathologists; mem. Assn. Am. Pathologists, Internat. Acad. Pathologists. Office: U Calif Sch Medicine Dept Med Pathology Davis CA 95616

RUECKER, MARTHA ENGELS, retired special education educator; b. South Gate, Calif., Sept. 22, 1931; d. Eugene and Minna (Wilhelm) Engels; m. Geert Frank Ruecker, Aug. 10, 1959 (div. 1964); 1 child, Ann. MusB, U. So. Calif., 1954, Calif. tchr. credential, 1955. Cert. tchr. for non-English speaking students, Calif. Tchr. educationally handicapped Downey (Calif.) Unified Schs., 1964-92; tchr. 2d grade Lynwood (Calif.) Unified Schs., 1992-97, 1997—2001. Recipient award for work with mentally gifted Johns Hopkins U., 1992; South Gate Kiwanis scholar U. So. Calif., 1949-54. Mem. NEA (life), Los Angeles County Art Mus. Republican. Methodist. Avocations: interior design, gardening, music, travel. Home: PO Box 630 Downey CA 90241-0630

RUECKERT, FREDERIC, plastic, reconstructive and hand surgeon; b. Boston, Oct. 24, 1921; s. Frederic and Elizabeth (Howe) R.; m. Joan Dodge, May 31, 1947; children: Nancy Lee, Patricia, William Dodge, Carolyn. AB, Hamilton Coll., 1945; MD, Columbia U., 1947. Diplomate Am. Bd. Plastic Surgery, Nat. Bd. Med. Examiners; lic. physician, N.Y., N.H. Intern internal medicine Bellevue Hosp., N.Y.C., 1947-48; resident gen. surgery Am. U. Hosp., Beirut, 1948-50; fellow surg. pathology Columbia-Presbyn. Hosp., N.Y.C., 1950-51; resident gen. surgery Dartmouth-Hitchcock Med. Ctr., Hanover, N.H., 1953-54, staff surgeon, 1956-86; resident plastic surgery, teaching fellow plastic surgery U. Pitts. Med. Ctr., 1954-56; mem. faculty Dartmouth Med. Sch., Hanover, 1956—, prof. plastic surgery, 1974-86, prof. plastic surgery emeritus, 1986—; cons. plastic surgery VA Hosp., White River Junction, Vt., 1956—2001. Contbr. articles to profl. jours., chpts. to books. Mem. Sch. Bd. Edn., Hanover, N.H., 1964-67; trustee Northfield (Mass.) Mt. Hermon Sch., 1969-71, 80-90. With USNR, 1943-45; flight surgeon USAF, 1951-53. Recipient Lamplighter award Northfield Mt. Herman Sch., 1991. Mem. AMA, ACS, Am. Assn. Plastic Surgeons, Am. Assn. Med. Colls., Am. Soc. Plastic Surgeons (bd. dirs. 1980-83, 84-86), Plastic Surgery Ednl. Found. (bd. dirs. 1978-87, pres. 1985-86), Plastic Surgeons Assn. Am. (pres. 1984-85), Internat. Confederation Plastic, Reconstructive and Aesthetic Surgeons, Am. Soc. Aesthetic Plastic Surgeons, New Eng. Surg. Soc., Northeastern Soc. Plastic Surgeons, New Eng. Soc. Plastic and Reconstructive Surgeons (pres. 1969-71), N.H. State Med. Soc., Grafton County Med. Soc. (pres. 1974-75), Univ. Club (N.Y.C.). Republican. Presbyterian. Avocations: swimming, tennis, skiing, photography, wood carving. Home: 18 Berrill Farms Ln Hanover NH 03755-3213 E-mail: frjd@dartmouth.edu.

RUECKERT, ROLAND RUDYARD, retired virologist, educator; b. Rhinelander, Wis., Nov. 24, 1931; s. George Leonard and Monica Amelia (Seiberlich) R.; m. Ruth Helen Ullrich, Sept. 5, 1959; 1 child, Wanda Lynne. BS in Chemistry, U. Wis., 1953, PhD in Oncology, 1960. Fellow Max Planck Inst. for Biochemistry, Munich, 1960-61, Tübingen, Fed. Republic Germany, 1961-62; asst. rsch. virologist virus lab. U. Calif., Berkeley, 1962-65; asst. prof. biophysics lab. U. Wis., Madison, 1965-69, assoc. prof. biophysics lab., 1969-73; prof. Inst. for Molecular Virology, Madison, 1973-85, dist. rsch. prof., 1985-96, prof. emeritus, 1996-97. Mem. viology study sect. NIH, Bethesda, Md., 1981-85; pres. Am. Soc. Virology, 1989-90. With U.S. Army, 1953-55. Quent William D. Stovall award U. Wis., 1953, Marie Christine Kohler award U Achievements include research in dodecahedral model for picornavirus structure and assembly, molecular biology of picornaviruses (polio 8 common cold), structure 8 biology of small insect viruses, mechanism of neutralization by antibodies and antivirals. Avocations: forest management and ecology. Home: 2234 W Lawn Ave Madison WI 53711-1952 E-mail: rrruecke@facstaff.wisc.edu.

RUEDEN, HENRY ANTHONY, accountant; b. Green Bay, Wis., Dec. 25, 1949; s. Bernard M. and Audrey Virgin R. BS, U. Wis., Green Bay, 1971; MBA, U. Wis., Oshkosh, 1973; postgrad., Internat. Grad. Sch., St. Louis, 1984—. CPA, Ill., Wis.; cert. mgmt. acct.; cert. internal auditor; cert. info. systems auditor; cert. cost analyst. Auditor U.S. Customs Svc., Chgo., 1974-86; systems acct. U.S. R.R. Retirement Bd., 1986—. With USAR, 1972-2000 (ret.), Desert Storm, 1991, Operation Joint Endeavor, Bosnia, 1996. Mem. CPAs For The Pub. Interest, Nat. Wildlife Fedn., Nat. Audubon Soc., Wis. Farm Bur., Wis. State Hist. Soc., Wis. Farm Bur. Fedn., Future Farmers Am., Am. Inst. CPAs, Wis. Inst. CPAs, Nat. Assn. Accts., Assn. Govt. Accts. Roman Catholic. Achievements include completed marathons in all 50 states and D.C. twice. Home: 2661 S Pine Tree Rd De Pere WI 54115-9028

RUEDENBERG, KLAUS, theoretical chemist, educator; b. Bielefeld, Germany, Aug. 25, 1920; came to U.S., 1948, naturalized, 1955; s. Otto and Meta (Wertheimer) R.; m. Veronika Kutter, Apr. 8, 1948; children: Lucia Meta, Ursula Hedwig, Annette Veronika, Emanuel Klaus. Student, Montana Coll., Zugerberg, Switzerland, 1938-39; licence es Scis., U. Fribourg, Switzerland, 1944; postgrad., U. Chgo., 1948-50; PhD, U. Zurich, Switzerland, 1950; PhD (hon.), U. Basel, Switzerland, 1975, U. Bielefeld, Germany, 1991, U. Siegen, 1994. Research assoc. physics U. Chgo., 1950-55; asst. prof. chemistry, physics Iowa State U., Ames, 1955-60, assoc. prof., 1960-62, prof., 1964-78, disting. prof. in sci. and humanities, 1978-91, disting. prof. emeritus, 1991—, sr. chemist Ames Lab., U.S. Dept. Energy, 1964-91, assoc., 1991—. Prof. chemistry Johns Hopkins U., Balt., 1962-64; vis. prof. U. Naples, Italy, 1961, Fed. Inst. Tech., Zurich, 1966-67, Wash State U. at Pullman, 1970, U. Calif. at Santa Cruz, 1973, U. Bonn (Germany), 1974, Monash U. and CSIRO, Clayton, Victoria, Australia, 1982, U. Kaiserlautern, Germany, 1987; lectr. univs., rsch. instns. and sci. symposia, 1953—. Author articles in field; assoc. editor: Jour. Chem. Physics, 1964-67, Internat. Jour. Quantum Chemistry; Chem. Physics Letters, 1967-81, Lecture Notes in Chemistry, 1976—, Advances in Quantum Chemistry, 1987—; editor-in-chief Theoretica Chimica Acta, 1985-97; hon. editor Theoretical Chemistry Accounts, 1997—. Co-founder Octagon Center for the Arts, Ames, 1966, treas., 1966-71, also bd. dirs. Guggenheim fellow, 1966-67; Fulbright sr. scholar, 1982 Fellow: AAAS, Internat. Acad. Quantum Molecular Scis., Am. Inst. Chemists, Am. Phys. Soc.; mem.: AAUP, Am. Chem. Soc. (Midwest award 1982, nat. award in theoretical chemistry 2002), Phi Lambda Upsilon, Sigma Xi. Office: Dept Chemistry Iowa State Univ Ames IA 50011-0001

RUEDRICH, RANDY, political party official; Chmn. Alaska Rep. Party, 2000—. Office: 1515 W 13th Ave Anchorage AK 99501 Office Fax: 907-276-0425.*

RUEGER, DANIEL SCOTT, horticulture educator; b. Flint, Mich., May 16, 1957; s. William John and Barbara Jane (Ledford) R.; m. Michel Sharon Holzbach, July 22, 1989; children: Danielle Sharon, Christina Anne, Michael Scott. BS in Agr., MS in Agr. Edn., Ohio State U., 1980. Cert. profl. vocational, horticulture teacher, Ohio. Mgr. Idle R's Farms, Plain City, Ohio, 1973-77; research services worker O.M. Scott & Sons Co., Marysville, 1977; tng. counselor Cen. Ohio Rural Consortium, Delaware, 1978; supt. parks grounds City of Delaware, 1979; tchr. horticulture Ashland (Ohio) City Schs., 1980—. Co-author: Success Handbook, 1980. Sustaining mem. Rep. Nat. Com., 1980-92; lay leader Emmanuel Meth. Ch., 1988-94; chmn. adminstrv. bd., 1990-91. Named Citizen of Yr. Citizens Commn. for the Right to Keep and Bear Arms, 1986, 87, 88, Disting. Patriot Concil for Inter-Am. Security. Mem. NEA, Nat. Assn. Agrl. Educators, Inc., Ohio Edn. Assn. (state coun. ednl. polit. action com. 1988-91, profl. devel. com. 1990-98), North Cen. Ohio Edn. Assn. (exec. com. 1986—), Ohio Assn. Agrl. Educators (hort. state chmn. 1988-92, Outstanding Agrl. Edn. Program 1992), Assn. for Career and Tech. Edn., Ohio Assn. for Career and Tech. Edn., Ashland City Tchrs. Assn. (pres. 1988-89), Ohio State U. Alumni Assn., Air Force Assn., Future Farmers Am. Alumni Assn., Orgn. for Secondary Students Enrolled in Agrl. Edn., Ohio Forestry Assn., Gamma Sigma Delta, Phi Delta Kappa. Avocations: reading, aviation, swimming, fishing, philately. Office: Ashland High Sch 1440 King Rd Ashland OH 44805-3635 E-mail: darueger@ashland-city.k12.oh.us.

RUEGG, DONALD GEORGE, retired railway company executive; b. LaJunta, Colo., Sept. 11, 1924; s. George Albert and Cecilia Corrine (Decker) R.; m. Ruth Carson, June 27, 1946 (dec. 1963); m. Mary Ann Eichelberger, June 24, 1964. BA, Dartmouth Coll., 1947; MBA, U. Chgo., 1972. Stenographer Atchison, Topeka & Santa Fe Ry. Co., Pueblo, Colo., 1942-51, supr., trainmaster various locations, 1951-68, asst. to v.p. info. systems Topeka, 1968-69; asst. to v.p. ops. Atchison Topeka & Santa Fe Ry. Co., Chgo., 1969-72, gen. mgr. Los Angeles, 1972-73; asst. v.p. ops. Atchison, Topeka & Santa Fe Ry. Co., Chgo., 1973-78, v.p. ops., 1978-83, exec. v.p., 1983-86. Served with USN, 1943-46. Republican. Roman Catholic.

RUEGGER, PHILIP T., III, lawyer; b. Plainfield, N.J., Oct. 14, 1949; s. Philip T. Jr. and Gloria Marie (McLaughlin) R.; m. Rebecca Lee Huffman, Aug. 3, 1974; children: Sarah, Britt, Michael. AB, Dartmouth Coll., 1971; JD, U. Va., 1974. Bar: N.Y. 1975. Assoc. Simpson Thacher & Bartlett, N.Y.C., 1974-81, ptnr., head corp. dept., 1981—. Mem. Assn. Bar City N.Y., Phi Beta Kappa. Clubs: Manursing Island (Rye, N.Y.), Apawamis (Rye). Home: 275 Grace Church St Rye NY 10580-4201 Office: Simpson Thacher & Bartlett 425 Lexington Ave Fl 15 New York NY 10017-3954 E-mail: pruegger@stblaw.com.

RUEGSEGGER, DONALD RAY, JR. radiological physicist, educator; b. Detroit, May 29, 1942; s. Donald Ray and Margaret Arlene (Elliot) R.; m. Judith Ann Merrill, Aug. 20, 1965 (div.); children: Steven, Susan, Mark, Ann; m. Patricia Ann Mitchell, Oct. 16, 1999. BS, Wheaton Coll., 1964; MS, Ariz. State U., 1966, PhD (NDEA fellow), 1969. Diplomate Am. Bd. Radiology. Radiol. physicist Miami Valley Hosp., Dayton, Ohio, 1969—, chief med. physics sect., 1983—. Physics cons. X-ray dept. VA Hosp., Dayton, 1970—; adj. asst. prof. physics Wright State U., Fairborn, Ohio, 1973—, clin. asst. prof. radiology, 1976-81, clin. assoc. prof. radiology, 1981—, group leader in med. physics, dept. radiol. scis. Med. Sch., 1978—. Mem. AAAS, Am. Assn. Physicists in Medicine (pres. Ohio River Valley chpt. 1982-83, co-chmn. local summer sch. arrangements com. 1986), Am. Coll. Radiology, Am. Coll. Med. Physics (founding chancellor), Am. Phys. Soc., Ohio Radiol. Soc., Health Physics Soc. Baptist. Home: 6252 Donnybrook Dr Centerville OH 45459-1837 Office: Radiation Therapy Miami Valley Hosp 1 Wyoming St Dayton OH 45409-2722

RUEHLE, CHARLES JOSEPH, pathologist, military officer; b. May 26, 1943; s. John Donald and Alta (Brown) R.; m. Nellie Backus, Aug. 5, 1972. DVM, Iowa State U., 1967; MD, U. Iowa, 1973; MS, 1973. Diplomate Am. Bd. Preventive Medicine, Am. Bd. Pathology. Commd. 2d lt. USAF, 1964; advanced through grades to col., sr. flight surgeon, 1984; chief flight surgeon, 1987; chief Vet. Svcs., Grissom AFB, Ind., 1967-69; resident in aerospace medicine Brook AFB, Tex., 1973-75; resident in pathology Wilford Hall USAF Med. Ctr., Lackland AFB, 1975-79; with div. aerospace pathology Armed Forces Inst. Pathology, Washington, 1979-88; chief div. aerospace pathology, 1982-85; chmn. dept. forensic scis., 1985-88; sec. Joint COm. Aviation Pathology, 1984-88; exec. asst. to fed. air surgeon FAA, Washington, 1988—; sr. aviation med. examiner, 1989—. Adj. asst. prof. prevetive medicine Uniformed Services U. Health Scis. lectr. aerospace pathology; cons. USAF Sugeon Gen., 1987. Fellow Am. Soc. Clin Pathologists, Aerospace Med. Assn.; mem. Am. Acad. Forensic Scis. AMA, USAF Flight Surgeons, Nat. Sojourners, Assn. Mil. Surgeons U.S., Internat. Soc. Air Safety Investigators, Air Force Assn., Alpha Zeta, Gamma Sigma Delta, Omega Tau Sigma (gov. 1967-75), Cosmos Club. Republican. Presbyterian. Home: 1000 Lower Pindell Rd Lothian MD 20711-2704 Office: Fed Air Surgeon FAA 800 Independence Ave SW Washington DC 20591-0001

RUEHLMANN, VIRGINIA JUERGENS, foundation creativity director, writer; b. Cin., Dec. 31, 1924; d. Arthur Henry and Florence Johanna (Doogan) Juergens; m. Eugene Peter Ruehlmann, Aug. 30, 1947; children: Virginia Wiltse, E Peter, Margaret Straus, Andrea Cornett, Gregory, James, Mark, Rick. BS in Edn., U. Cin., 1946, M in Adminstrn., 1948. Swimming instr. Williams YMCA, Cin., 1942-43; recreation leader City of Cin., 1942-43; camp dir. U. Cin. Girls Summer Camp, 1943-45; instr. U. Cin., 1946-47, Wellesley Coll., Wellesley, Mass., 1947-48; homemaker Cin., 1948-84; dir., rschr., editor, writer, creativity dir. Helen Steiner Rice Found., 1984—. Controller Revell Pub. Baker Book House, Grand Rapids, Mich., 1984—; consult Gibson Greeting, Cincinnati, Ohio, 1989—. Ed, compiler: devotional and inspirational books, author (of prayers) ; researcher: ; co-author: (activity book) Making Family Memories, 1994, From the Heart Daily Devotional, 1992, Joy for the Heart, 1992, Gifts of Love, 1992, Blossoms of Friendship, 1992, A Book of Thanks, 1993, A Book of Comfort, 1994, Wings of Encouragement, 1995, A Book of Prayer, 1995, A Book of Hope, 1996, A Book of Courage, 1996, Eyes of Tenderness, 1997, An Old Time Christmas, 1997, Celebrating the Golden Years, 1998, Our Family Treasury, 1998, God's Promises from A to Z, 1999, Mother, I Love You, 1999, Gift's of Love, 2d ed, 2000; compiler 50 vol. themed Helen Steiner Rice books An Instrument of Your Peace, 2001. Chair Spec Olympics Greater Cincinnati, Ohio, 1974, Ind., 1974, Ky., 1974; pres Freedom Found Valley Forge, Cincinnati, Ohio, 1974—76; mem Western Hamilton County Econ Coun, Nat Fedn Rep Women, Rep Women's Club Hamilton County; pres Cath Social Serv SW Ohio, 1984—86; trustee Glenmary Missions, 1989—91; mem nat adv bd United Theological Sem; Athenaeum Ohio. Named Woman of the Yr, Cincinnati Enquirer, 1977, Lady Equestrian Order Holy Sepulchre Jerusalem, 1989; named to Ohio Women's Hall of Fame, 1991. Mem.: Guideposts Nat. Adv., Mortar Bd, Donors Forum Ohio, Coun Founds, Argus Club, Queen City Club, Cincinnati Women's Club. Roman Catholic. Avocations: golf, activities with 24 granchildren. Home: 1523 Anderson Ferry Rd Cincinnati OH 45238-3632 Office: Helen Steiner Rice Found 221 E Fourth St Atrium 2 # 2100 Cincinnati OH 45202-4122 E-mail: hsrice@fuse.net.

RUEHLMANN, WILLIAM JOHN, communications educator; b. Cin., Apr. 27, 1946; s. William E. and Margaret T. (Smith) R.; m. Lynn Elise Klausli, Sept. 6, 1969; children: Benjamin Derek, Martha Jill. BA, Am. U., 1968; MA, U. Ariz., 1970; PhD, U. Cin., 1974. Tchr. Elder H.S., Cin., 1970-71; reporter The Ky. Post, Covington, 1974-75; ast. prof. journalism Suffolk U., Boston, 1975-77; feature writer The Virginian-Pilot, Norfolk, Va., 1977-93; from assoc. prof. to prof. journalism and comm. Va. Wesleyan Coll., 1993—. Adv. bd. Crippen & Landru Publs., Norfolk, 1994—, Blackwater Rev., Virginia Beach, 1995—. Author: Saint With a Gun, 1974, Stalking the Feature Story, 1977; series editor: International Polygonics, 1988-91; book columnist The Virginian-Pilot, 1992—; columnist Port Folio Weekly, 1999—. Bd, dirs. Williamsburg (Va.) Film Festival, 1996—, Family Svcs. Tidewater, Norfolk, 1984-92. Staff sgt. USANG, 1970-75. Recipient exemplary tchg. award United Meth. Ch., 1997, award Endependence Ctr., 1989, 93, writing awards Va. Press Assn., 1986, 87, 89, 90, journalism award Gallaudet U., 1989, Slover award The Virginian-Pilot, The Ledger-Star, 1977, 83, 84, Herbert Bayard Swope award Nat. Editl. Workshop Svcs., 1981. Mem. AAUP, Nat. Book Critics Cir., Soc. Collegiate Journalists (pres. 2002-, Advisor of Yr. 2001), Coll. Media Advisers, So. Book Critics Cir., Omicron Delta Kappa, Sigma Tau Delta. Presbyterian. Avocation: reading. Office: Va Wesleyan Coll 1584 Wesleyan Dr Norfolk VA 23502-5599 E-mail: wjruehlmann@vwc.edu.

RUELLAN, ANDREE, artist; b. N.Y.C., Apr. 6, 1905; d. André and Louise (Lambert) R.; m. John W. Taylor, May 28, 1929. Student, Art Students League, 1920-22; art schs., France and Italy. Guest instr. Pa. State Coll., summer 1957 One-man shows include Paris, 1925, Weyhe Galleries, N.Y.C., 1928, 31, Maynard Walker Galleries, 1937, 40, Kraushaar Galleries, 1945, 52, 56, 63, 80-81, Phila. Art Alliance, 1955, S.I. Mus., 1958, nat. exhbns., Carnegie Inst., Whitney Mus., Art Inst. Chgo., Corcoran Gallery, Internat. Expn., San Francisco, Artists for Victory Exhbn., N.Y.C., other cities U.S.; retrospective exhbns., Storm King Art Ctr., Mountainville, N.Y., 1966, Lehigh U., 1965, Woodstock Artists Assn., 1977, Ga. Mus. of Art, 1993, Hyde Collection, Glens Falls, N.Y., 1993, Gibbs Mus of Art, Charleston, S.C., 1993, Prints Gallery at Parkbest, Kingston, N.Y., 1995; drawing retrospective Kaushaar Galleries, 1990, 93, Ga. Mus. Art, Athens, 1993, The Hyde Collection, Glen Falls, N.Y., 1993, Gibbs Mus. Art, Charleston, S.C., 1993, Butler Inst., 1996, Grolier Club, 1996-97; executed murals in Emporia, Va., Lawrenceville, Ga.; represented in permanent collections at Met. Mus. Art, Whitney Mus. Am. Art, N.Y.C., Fogg Mus., Harvard U., Phila. Mus., Storm King Art Ctr., William Rockhill Nelson Mus., Kansas City, Mo., Duncan Phillips Gallery, Washington, Springfield Mus., Norton Gallery, Art Mus., New Britain, Conn., Libr. of Congress, Ency. Brit., IBM Collections, Art Inst., Zanesville, Ohio, U. Ga., S.I. Mus., Butler Inst., Pa. State U., Lehigh U., Columbia (S.C.) Mus. Art, The Whatcom Mus., Washington, Springville (Utah) Mus. Art, S.C. State Mus., Wichita Art Mus., Telfair Mus., Savannah, Ga., drawing retrospective Butler Inst. Am. Art, 1996; also numerous pvt. collections. Recipient 3d prize for painting Charleston Worcester Mus. Biennial, Jan. 1938; 1,000 grant in arts Am. Acad. and Inst. Arts and Letters, 1945; Pennell medal Pa. Acad., 1945; medal of Honor and purchase Pepsi-Cola Paintings of Year, 1948; Dawson Meml. medal Pa. Acad., 1950; Purchase award N.Y. State Fair, 1951; Drawing award Ball State Tchrs. Coll.; Guggenheim fellow, 1950-51; recipient Kuniyoshi award, 1994. Mem. Woodstock Artists Assn. (Sally Jacobs award 1981); Art Students League (life), Nat. Mus. Women in Arts Home: 54 Garrison Rd Bearsville NY 12409-9510

RUESCHEMEYER, MARILYN SCHATTNER, sociology educator; b. N.Y.C., June 3, 1938; d. Julius Schattner and Bela Wax; m. Dietrich Rueschemeyer, June 14, 1962; children: Julia Yael, Simone Margalit. BA in Sociology, Queens Coll., 1959; MA in Sociology, U. Toronto, Can., 1965; PhD in Sociology, Brandeis U., 1978. Asst. prof. RISD, Providence, 1981-87, assoc. prof., 1987-93, prof. sociology, 1994—. Fellow Russian Rsch. Ctr., Harvard U., Cambridge, Mass., 1986—; adj. prof. sociology Brown U., Providence, 1987—; adj. prof. internat. rels. Brown U. Watson Inst., Providence, 1996—; adv. bd. Sociol. Analysis, 1998-2000; sr. assoc., mem. St. Anthony's Coll., Oxford U., 1979, 82, 97; vis. fellow dept. sociology Hebrew U. of Jerusalem, 1990. Author: Professional Work and Marriage: An East West Comparison, 1981; co-author (with Golomshtok and Kennedy): Soviet Emigré Artists, 1985; editor: Women in the Politics of Post Communist Eastern Europe, 1994, 1998; co-editor (with D. Rueschemeyer and B. Wittrock): Participation and Democracy East and West, 1998. Founding mem. Women's Polit. Caucus R.I.; active Reform Dems. R.I.; founder Friday Group, Providence, 1971—; bd. mem. RISD-Brown Hillel, 1990-2002. Rsch. grantee Internat. Rsch. and Exchs. Bd., Washington, 1984, 86, 91, 92, 97, Am. Coun. Learned Socs., 1987, 88. Fellow: Swedish Colloquium for Advanced Study in Social Scis.; mem.: Women East and West, German Studies Assn., Am. Sociol. Assn. (chair com. on internat. sociology 1993—96, rep. to Am. Assn. Advancement Slavic Studies), Am. Assn. for Advancement Slavic Studies (bd. dirs. 1996—99, 2001—). Office: Watson Inst for Internat Studies Brown Univ Providence RI 02912-9042 E-mail: marilyn_rueschemeyer@brown.edu.

RUESINK, ALBERT WILLIAM, biologist, plant sciences educator; b. Adrian, Mich., Apr. 16, 1940; s. Lloyd William and Alberta May (Foltz) R.; m. Kathleen Joy Cramer, June 8, 1963; children: Jennifer Li, Adriana Eleanor. BA, U. Mich., 1962; MA, Harvard U., 1965, PhD, 1966. Postdoctoral fellow Swiss Fed. Inst. Tech., Zurich, 1966-67; prof. biology Ind. U., Bloomington, 1967—, spl. asst. to Pres. for Faculty Rels., 1999—. Recipient Amoco Teaching award Ind. U., 1980 Mem. AAUP (pres. chpt. 1978-79, 90-91), Am. Soc. Plant Physiologists, Bot. Soc. Am. Democrat. Mem. United Ch. of Christ. Home: 2605 E 5th St Bloomington IN 47408-4286 Office: Ind U Dept Biology 1001 E 3d St Bloomington IN 47405 E-mail: ruesink@indiana.edu.

RUETER, THOMAS JAMES, federal judge; b. 1955; BA, U. Scranton, 1977; JD, Dickinson U., 1980. Bar: Pa. 1980. Law clk. to Hon. Joseph L. McGlynn, Jr., U.S. Dist. Ct. for Ea. Dist. Pa., Phila., 1980-82; assoc. White & Williams, 1982-85; asst. U.S. atty. for ea. dist. Pa., U.S. Dept. Justice, 1985-90, chief narcotics sect., 1990-94. Notes editor Dickinson Law Rev., 1979-80; contbr. articles to law jours. Office: 601 Market St Rm 3038 Philadelphia PA 19106-1714

RUF, DONNIE LEE, delivery service provider, fashion model, designer; b. Ardmore, Ala., Aug. 23, 1954; s. David Eberhardt Sr. and Thelma Mae (Callahan) R.; m. Cathy Marie Paulk, Aug. 20, 1977 (div. 1986); children: Katie Leigh, Bonnie Brook. BS in Mktg., BS in Edn., Auburn U., 1976. Salesman Burroughs Corp., Huntsville, Ala., 1977; farmer, mgr. Ruf Farms, Athens, 1977-80; salesman Limestone Farmer's Coop., 1980; driver United Parcel Svc., Huntsville, 1981-2001; coord. United Way, 1981-98; model United Way Brochure, 1996; sec. Huntsville Driver Relief Fund, 1990-95; cover model Big Idea (UPS), 1989, 94. Contbg. designer, Sew Beautiful, 1993, 94, Internat., Needle Arts, 1994, nat. Cover model consumer Savs. Group brochure, 1989; mem. cast (mus. prodn.) Oliver at Athens State U., 1991, contbr. article to profl. jour., contbr. designer to profl. orgns. Big bro. Big-Bros.-Big-Sisters King's Acres, Auburn, 1975-76; vol. Limestone Health Facility; model spokesperson United Way, chmn. Huntsville chpt., 1983-91; sec.-treas. Huntsville Driver Relief Fund, 1988-91; mem. United Parcel Safety Com., Huntsville, 1985-90; leadership giver United Way, 2000. Named Mr. Ala. Male Am., Kansas City, Mo., 1989, Mr. Ala. N. Am., Scottsdale, Az., 1992, N.J., 1989-90, Faces Internatl., feature model, 1992, 93, Mr. Man Premiere Finalist, 1998, Person of Yr. Boys and Girls Club Limestone county, 1997, Outstanding Citizen award Jaycees, 1995, rep. to Congress Outstanding Young Alabamians, 1994; recipient Nat. Interpretaton Design Winner, Embroiders Guild of Amer., 1994, Natl. Adaption Design Winner, Embroiders Guild of Amer., 1994; Ala. United Way/UPS Leadership pin design winner, 2000. Mem. Rotary, Limestone County 4-H Club, Delta Sigma Pi. Mem. Ch. of Christ. Avocations: travel, interior design, antiques. Home: 26528 South Rd Athens AL 35613-3744 Fax: 1-256-859-1380.

RUF, H(AROLD) WILLIAM, JR. retired lawyer, corporation executive; b. Madison, Wis., July 1, 1934; s. Harold W. and Margaret (Dottridge) R.; m. Suzanne Williams, Aug. 25, 1962 (div. Jan. 1978); m. Jocelyn C. Ruf, Nov. 21, 1981; children: David W., Margaret E., Katharine S. BS, U. Wis., 1960, JD, 1962. Bar: Wis. 1962, Ohio 1963. Field atty. N.L.R.B., Cleve., 1962-65; counsel Oglebay Norton Co., 1965-74, dir. indsl. rels., 1974-78, v.p., 1978-94; v.p. adminstrn. and legal affairs Oblebay Norton Co., 1994-97; ret. Pres. bd. trustees Moreland Ct. Condo. Assn. Mem.: Cleve. Skating, Cleve. Union. Home: 13515 Shaker Blvd Cleveland OH 44120-5602

RUFE, CYNTHIA MARIE, judge; b. Phila., Oct. 30, 1948; d. Lucien Russell and Antoinette Marie (Galizia) Favata; m. John J. Rufe, Jan. 2, 1999; children: Tiffany Marie, Meredith Anne. BA, Adelphi U., 1970; secondary edn. cert., Bloomsburg State Coll., 1972; JD, SUNY, Buffalo, 1977. Bar: Pa. 1977, U.S. Dist. Ct. (ea. dist.) Pa. 1983, U.S. Ct. Appeals (3d cir.) 1987, U.S. Supreme Ct. 1984. Tchr. Bristol (Pa.) Jr./Sr. H.S., 1970-72; law clk. Div. of Claims, State of N.Y., Buffalo, 1976; asst. pub. defender Bucks County, Doylestown, Pa., 1977-79, dep. pub. defender, 1979-81; pvt. practice Newtown, 1982-93; judge Ct. of Common Pleas, Bucks County, 1994—. Mem. appellate ct. rules com. Supreme Ct. of Pa. Appellate Ct., 1999—; solicitor Children and Youth Agy., Bucks County, 1984-88; spkr., panelist on various law related issues, Bucks County; mem. Conf. State Trial Judges, 1994—, mem. jud. edn., correction and nominating com. juvenile ct. sect. Pres. bd. dirs. Preventive Rehab. Youth and Devel., Bristol, 1978-81; bd. dirs. Reaching-at-Problems Group Home, Chalfont, Pa., 1981-84, Three Arches, Inc., Falls Twp., Pa., 1985, Orgn. to Prevent Teenage Suicide, 1984-93, Youth Svcs., Inc., 1984-93, Today, Inc., 1987-93, Schofield Ford Bridge Reconstrn. Com., 1990-93. Recipient Trial Lawyer's award Erie County Bar Assn., 1977, Four Chaplains Legion of Honor, 1987, M.J. Kirkpatrick Leadership award A Woman's Place, 1999, award Commn. for Social Justice, Sons of Italy, 2000. Mem. Nat. Coun. Juvenile and Family Ct. Judges, Bucks County Bar Assn. (dir. 1983-85, chair criminal law sect. 1987-88, chair bench-bar com. 1988-89, chair membership com. 1983-85, lawyer reaching lawyer com. 1996—), Pa. Bar Assn., Pa. Trial Lawyers Assn., Pa. Coll. Criminal Def. Lawyers, Ill. Bar Assn., Soroptimists (past pres.). Republican. Roman Catholic. Office: Judges Chambers Courthouse Doylestown PA 18901

RUFENACHT, ROGER ALLEN, accounting educator; b. Waldron, Mich., Dec. 17, 1933; s. Alphus Leroy and Frieda (Aschliman) R.; m. Carol Carnahan, June 13, 1965; children: Jeffrey, Jonathan. BS, Mich. State U., 1959, MS, 1965. Cert. tchr., Fla. Tchr. Madison High Sch., Adrian, Mich., 1959-61; bus. edn. instr. Charlotte High Sch., Rochester, N.Y., 1961-62, Edgewater High Sch., Orlando, Fla., 1962-68, chmn. bus. dept., 1965-68; instr. in acctg. Orlando Vo Tech. Ctr. (formerly Orlando Vocat. Sch.), 1968-94, chmn. bus. dept., 1980-85; ret., 1994. Bd. dirs., v.p. Winter Park Jaycees, 1963-68; asst. coach, scorekeeper N.W. Little League; chmn. adv. com. local PTA, 1973-83; pres. Bandboosters 1985-86; cub scout den leader, com. chmn., mem. dist. com., mem. coms. Boy Scouts Am.; adminstrv. bd. local Meth. Ch., 1965—. Recipient Scouters Tng. award, Fifteen Yr. Vet. award Boy Scouts Am., 1996. Mem. NEA, Am. Vocat. Assn., Fla. Vocat. Assn. (registration com. ann. conf., pres.'s reception planning com.), Orange County Classroom Tchrs. Assn. (bd. dirs., bldg. rep.), Orange County Credit Union (rep.), Orange County Vocat. Assn. (bd. dirs., Pres.'s award 1988-89, Outstanding Vocat. Educator Bus. Edn. award 1988-89), Fla. Bus. Edn. Assn. (chmn., mem. various coms.), Orange County Bus. Edn. Assn. (pres. 1968, 76, chmn., mem. various coms.). Republican. Avocations: reading, gardening, golf, swimming. Home: 9510 Bear Lake Rd Apopka FL 32703-1917

RUFF, CAROLYN K. retired real estate agent, accountant; b. Tonkawa, Okla., July 29, 1934; d. Virgil E. and Viola E. McWilliams; m. Jack W. Ruff; children: Jack, Jill Barton. Grad., Fairfax (Okla.) HS, 1952. Lic. real estate broker 1982. Acct. Conoco, Inc., Ponca City, Okla., 1968—85; realtor Carolyn K. Ruff Real Estate, 1983—98; ret., 1998. Women's county coord. Dem. Party, Ponca City, 1968—75. Avocation: rebuilding computers . Home: 1112 N 14th St Ponca City OK 74601

RUFF, DUREEN ANNE, small business owner, operater; b. Grand Forks, N.D., Feb. 27, 1931; d. Conrad and Margaret (Johnson) A.; m. R. William Ruff, June 23, 1956; children: Susan Lynne, Kristine Louise, Steven William, Anne Marie. BS, U. N.D., 1953. Cert. tchr., N.D., Minn., Calif. Tchr. Roosevelt Elem. Sch., Grand Forks, 1953-56, San Miguel Elem. Sch., Sunny Vale, Calif., 1956-57, Regent Jr. High Sch., Robbinsdale, Minn., 1957-59, Carl Sandburg Jr. High Sch., Golden Valley, 1959-60; designer, mfr. Anne Ruff Miniatures, Plymouth, 1970—. Mem. Abbott Hosp. Aux., Mpls., 1966-78, Abbott Northwestern Aux., 1978—; elder Westminister Presbyn. Ch., 1981-87. Mem. Nat. Assn. Miniature Enthusiasts (Acad. Honor 1986—), Miniatures Industry Assn. Am., Cottage Industry Miniatures Trade Assn., Miniature Guild of Minn, Internat. Guild of Miniature Artisans (artisan status 1989—). Republican. Avocations: painting, sculpture, hiking, canoeing, travel. Home and Office: 1100 Vagabond Ln N Minneapolis MN 55447-2560

RUFF, EDWARD JOSEPH, retired lawyer; b. Sewickley, Pa., Aug. 14, 1915; s. Edward John and Mary Edna (Hegner) R.; m. Marjorie Elizabeth Warner, Dec. 16, 1938. AB, U. Mich., 1936, JD, 1938. Lawyer Enos, Sherman & Morrato, Denver, 1938-40, Davis & Wallbank, Denver, 1940-42, 46, Brobeck, Phleger & Harrison, San Francisco, 1946-47, Thelen, Marrin, Johnson & Bridges, San Francisco, 1947-53, partner, 1953-91; retired, 1991. Lt. USCG, 1943-46. Fellow Am. Coll. Trial Lawyers; mem. ABA, Calif. Bar Assn., World Trade Club. Republican. Roman Catholic. Avocations: travel, photography.

RUFF, LORRAINE MARIE, technology management consultant; b. Washington, Feb. 13, 1947; d. William Stanley and Jeanne Ann (Murray) Charlton; m. R. Eugene Ruff, July 17, 1968; 1 child, David Michael. BS in Liberal Arts, Oreg. State U., 1976. Reporter The Oregonian, Corvallis, Oreg., 1976-79, Union-Bull., Walla Walla, Wash., 1979-80; dir. pub. rels. Strategic Mktg., Corvallis, 1980-82; gen. mgr. Campaigns Northwest, 1982-84; account supr. Arthur D. Little, Inc., Cambridge, Mass., 1985-87, mgr. corp. ID, 1988-89; dir. biotechnology New Eng. Hill and Knowlton, Waltham, 1989, v.p., dir. biotechnology, 1990, sr. v.p., mng. dir. internat. biotechnology practice, 1990-91, sr. v.p., gen. mgr., 1991-93; sr. v.p., mng. dir. divsn. biosci. comm. Stoorza, Ziegaus & Metzger, San Diego, 1993-94, dir. life scis. practice, 1993-94; owner Charlton Ruff Comm., Puyallup, Wash., 1994—; co-founder Chromos Molecular Sys., Vancouver, B.C., Can., 1996—; pres., founder Milestones-The Critical Thinking Co., Seattle, 1997—. Bd. dirs. Civic Light Opera, Seattle. Mem. Wash. State Biotech. and Biomed. Assn. Avocations: collecting antique ivories, international cuisine, gardening, writing. Office: Milestones-The Critical Thinking Co Ste 250 16300 Christensen Rd Seattle WA 98188

RUFF, ROBERT LOUIS, neurologist, physiology researcher; b. Bklyn., Dec. 16, 1950; s. John Joseph and Rhoda (Alpert) R. BS summa cum laude, Cooper Union, 1971; MD summa cum laude, PhD in Physiology, U. Wash., 1976. Diplomate Am. Bd. Neurology and Psychiatry. Asst. neurologist N.Y. Hosp., Cornell Med. Sch., N.Y.C., 1977-80; asst. prof. physiology and medicine U. Wash., Seattle, 1980-84; assoc. prof. neurology Case Western Res. Med. Sch., Cleve., 1984-92, prof. neurology and neuroscis., 1993—, residency dir., neurology dept., 1994—, vice chair neurology dept., 1995—; chief dept. neurology Cleve. VA Med. Ctr., 1984—, chief phys. medicine and rehab. svc., 1998—2000, mgr. rehab. and spinal cord injury and disorder product line, 1999—; med. dir. Functional Elec. Stimulation Ctr., Cleve., 2000—. Adv. Child Devel. and Mental Retardation Ctr., Seattle, 1980-84, Burien Devel. Disability Ctr., Wash., 1982-84; mem. med. adv. bd. Muscular Dystrophy Assn., Seattle, 1984, NE Ohio chpt. Multiple Sclerosis Soc., 1986—; mem. adv. bd. for Neurology Dept. Vets. Affairs, 1989—, mem. study sect. for rehab. career devel. awards; chmn. med. adv. bd. N.E. Ohio chpt. Myasthenia Gravis Found., 1987—, trustee, 1993—, nat. med. adv. bd., 1988—, grant and fellowship com., 1990—. Assoc. editor: Neurology, 1994—96, mem. editl. bd. , 1996—97, assoc. editor: Jour. Rehab. Rsch. and Devel., 2000—, ad hoc reviewer: various profl. and sci. jours., mem. editl. bd.: Jour. Rehab. and Devel., 1999—; contbr. articles to profl. jours., chapters to books. Nat. bd. dirs. Myasthenia Gravis Found., 1994—, Doctor's award, 2002. Recipient Tchr. Investigator award NIH; NSF fellow, 1971; NIH grantee, Muscular Dystrophy Assn. grantee, Dept. Vets. Affairs, Rsch. Enhancement Advanced Ctr. awards, 1999—, Drs. award Myasthenia Gravis Found. Am., 2002; N.Y. State Regents med. scholar, 1971. Fellow Am. Heart Assn. (stroke coun.), Am. Acad. Neurology (scientific issues com., legis. action com.); mem. AMA, IEEE, Am. Paraplegia Soc., Am. Soc. Neuro-Rehab., Am. Physics Soc., Neurosci. Soc., Biophys. Soc., Am. Neurol. Assn., N.Y. Acad. Sci., Am. Geriatrics Soc., Am. Physiol. Soc., Sigma Pi Sigma (v.p. 1970-71), Alpha Omega Alpha (v.p. 1975-76). Home: 4026 Princeton Blvd South Euclid OH 44121 Office: VA Med Ctr 10701 East Blvd Ste 127W Cleveland OH 44106-1702 E-mail: robert.ruff@med.va.gov.

RUFFER, DAVID GRAY, retired museum director, former college president; b. Archbold, Ohio, Aug. 25, 1937; s. Lawrence A. and Florence A. (Newcomer) R.; m. Marilyn Elaine Taylor, Aug. 23, 1958; children: Rochelle Lynne, Robyn Lynne, David Geoffrey. BS, Defiance Coll., 1959; MA, Bowling Green State U., 1960; PhD, U. Okla., 1964. Spl. instr. U. Okla., 1963-64; asst. prof. biology Defiance Coll., 1964-68, asso. prof., 1968-73, faculty dean, 1969-73; provost Elmira (N.Y.) Coll., 1973-78; pres. Albright Coll., Reading, Pa., 1978-91, U. Tampa, Fla., 1991-94; exec. dir. Dayton (Ohio) Soc. Natural History, 1995-99, ret., 2000—. Author: Exploring and Understanding Mammals, 1971; contbr. articles to profl. jours. NSF grantee, 1965, 67; Ohio Biol. Survey grantee, 1968-69 Fellow AAAS; mem. Am. Assn. Higher Edn., Animal Behavior Soc., Am. Soc. Mammalogists, Sigma Xi. Clubs: Rotary. Methodist. Home: 167 Mill Creek Rd Youngstown OH 44512-1402 E-mail: mdruffer@aol.com.

RUFFER, JOYCE SELLARS, poet, artist; b. Cairo; children: Charles Scott Mason, Jeffrey Dewayne Mason. Artist, all mediums. Author: (poetry) Rose Moon. Named Best Poet 1994, Nat. Libr. Poetry, Poet of Yr., Internat. Soc. Poets, 1996; recipient Editor's Choice award Nat. Libr. Poetry, Poetic Achievement award, Am. Poetry Soc. Avocations: spiritual enhancement, birding, nature photography, marine ecology, feline appreciation. Home: Sea Lily 2426 Maher Ave Crescent City CA 95531-9137 Fax: 707 464-7557. E-mail: Jpolli@cc.northcoast.com.

RUFFIER, JOAN DIAL, small business owner, accountant; b. Orlando, Fla., June 15, 1939; d. William Henry and Grace (Franklin) Dial; m. Eugene Daniel Ruffier, Mar. 18, 1961; children: William Eugene, Margaret Ruffier Farris, John Daniel. BA, U. Fla., 1961; MBA, Rollins Coll., 1982. CPA, Fla.; cert. fin. planner. Mgmt. cons. Nat. Orgn. Bank Women, Chgo., 1978-82; acct. Colley, Trumbower & Howell, Orlando, 1982-86; v.p., co-owner Vista Landscaping, Inc., 1988-91; gen. ptnr. Sunshine Cafes, airport food and beverage concessions, 1986-91, Jacksonville, Fla., 1990-99; chmn. bd. dirs. Human Svcs. Tech. Inc., 1999—2001. Mem. adminstrv. bd. Sun Bank N.A., Orlando; bd. dirs., chmn., Jacksonville br., Fed. Res. Bank, Atlanta; bd. dirs. Fed. Res., 1989-96, chmn., 1993-96; bd. dirs., chair fin. com. Fla. Progress Corp., St. Petersburg, chmn. compliance, fin. and audit coms., 1990-2000; bd. dirs. Cypress Equity Fund, Fla., Invest, Inc., Fla.Winter Park Health Found., 2002-; bd. dirs., chair fin. and investments com. Shands Healthcare, Inc., 1996—; bd. overseers Cummer Grad. Sch. Bus., Rollins Coll., 1998—. Elder Presby. Ch.; chmn. redistricting advc. com. City of Orlando, 2001; mem. exec. com., bd. dirs. Econ. Devel. Commn. Mid Fla. Inc., Orlando, 1990-93; bd. regents State U. Sys. of Fla., 1986-91, chmn., 1988-90; trustee Winter Park Meml. Hosp., 1983-91, chmn. bd. trustees, 1990-91; chair Cmty. Svcs. Network, Orlando; bd. dirs. U. Fla. Found., Gainesville, 1985—, pres. 1998-2000; bd. overseers Crummer Grad. Sch. of Bus., Rollins Coll., 1998—; bd. dirs. U. Ctrl. Fla. Found., Orlando, 1985—, Collins Ctr. Pub. Policy, Tallahassee, Fla. Children's Coalition, Tallahassee, 1988, NCCJ, 1989-91, Fla. Coun. Econ. Edn., Tampa, 1988, Orange County Pub. Sch. Found., Orlando, 1986-87, United Way Orange, Seminole and Osceola Counties, 1985-86, Astronauts Meml. Found., 1989; pres. Jr. League Orlando, 1970-71, Coun. Arts & Scis. for Ctrl. Fla., 1971-73, Orange County Sch. Vol. Program, 1974, Ctrl. Fla. Kidney Ctr., 1983-85; mem. Fla. Coun. of 100, 1988-89; mem. downtown devel. bd. City of Orlando, 1980-82; bd. trustees Edyth Bush Charitable Found., 2000—. Recipient Outstanding Community Svc. award Hadassah, Orlando, 1978, Downtown Orlando Woman of Yr. award, 1982, Svc. to Mankind award Sertoma, Orlando, 1983, Outstanding Achievement award U. North Fla., 1989, Pegasus award U. Cen. Fla., 1989, Woman of Yr. award Midtown Bus. and Profl. WWomen's Club, 1989, Summit award Orlando Women's Resource Ctr., 1990, Spirit of Achievement award Jr. Achievement, 1998, Disting. Alumna award U. Fla., 1994, Alumna of Outstanding Svc., U. Fla., 1997, Disting. Svc. award U. Fla. Coll. Liberal Arts and Scis; Paul Harris fellow Rotary Internat., 1997. Mem. AICPA, Fla. Bue Key (hon.), Citrus Club (bd. govs. 1987—), Beta Alpha Psi (hon.), Beta Gamma Sigma (hon.), Phi Delta Kappa. Methodist. Home and Office: 722 Alba Dr Orlando FL 32804-7207 E-mail: jruffier@bellsouth.net.

RUFFIN, EDMUND M. biotechnologist; BA, U. Va.; MA in Internat. Rels./Econs., Johns Hopkins Sch. for Advanced Internat. Studies. Rsch. assoc. Ctr. for Strategic and Internat. Studies; policy analyst Systems Planning Corp., Arlington, Va.; sr. legis. asst. to Sen. Arlen Specter; v.p. bus. devel. and emerging companies Biotechnology Industry Orgn., Washington. Office: Biotechnology Industry Orgn 1225 Eye St NW Ste 400 Washington DC 20005*

RUFFING, ANNE ELIZABETH, artist; b. Bklyn. d. John Paul and Ruth Elizabeth (Price) Frampton; m. George W. Ruffing, Mar. 29, 1967; 1 dau., Elizabeth Anne. BS, Cornell U., 1964; postgrad., Drexel Inst. Tech., 1966. One-woman exhbns. include, IBM, 1966, Hall of Fame, Goshen, N.Y., 1971, group exhbns. include, Internat. Women's Arts Festival, World Trade Center, N.Y.C., 1975-76, Berkshire Mus., Pittsfield, Mass., 1965, 76, Cooperstown (N.Y.) Mus., 1969; represented in permanent collections, Met. Mus. Art, Bklyn. Mus., Library of Congress, Harvard U., Smithsonian Instn., N.Y. Hist. Soc. Johnston Hist. Mus., Atwater Kent Mus., Albany Inst. History and Art, Whitney Mus. Am. Art, Boston Public Library. Recipient 1st place Eric Sloane award, 1974; Internat. Women's Year award Internat. Women's Art Festival, 1976 Address: 1031 Lewis Farm Rd Zebulon NC 27597

RUFFING, JANET KATHRYN, spirituality educator; b. Spokane, Wash., July 17, 1945; d. George Benjamin and Dorothy Edith (Folsom) R. BA, Russell Coll., 1968; M of Applied Spirituality, U. San Francisco, 1978; lic. in Sacred Theology, Jesuit Sch. Theology, 1984; PhD in Christian Spirituality, Grad. Theol. Union, 1986. Joined Sisters of Mercy Congregation, Roman Cath. Ch., 1963. Tchr. reading and English Mercy High Sch., Burlingame, Calif., 1968-72, 75-77, San Francisco, 1972-75; tchr., dept. head Marian High Sch., San Diego, 1978-80; faculty and originating team mem. Fully Alive, Burlingame, 1980-86; faculty, facilitator Permanent Diaconate Formation Program, Oakland, Calif., 1984-86; faculty Internship in Art of Spiritual Direction, Burlingame, 1984, 85, 87; assoc. prof. spirituality and spiritual direction Fordham U., Bronx, N.Y., 1986—, prof., 2000—. Spkr. Villanova Theol. Inst., 1995, Roger Williams Symposium, Pullman, Wash., 1985; vis. faculty Australian Cath. U., Brisbane, summer 1994, San Francisco Theol. Sem., summer 1993, U. San Francisco, summer 1991, St. Michael's Coll., Vt., summer 1990, Fordham at Limerick, Ireland, 1996-97, Colston Symposium, Bristol, Eng., 2000, San Francisco Theol. Sem., 2001, Gettysburg Luth. Sem., 2001; presenter in field. Author: Uncovering Stories of Faith, 1989, Spiritual Direction: Beyond the Beginnings, 2000; contbg. author, editor: Mysticism and Social Transformation, 2001; assoc. editor The Way; contbr. articles to profl. jours. Mem. Cath. Theol. Soc. Am. (seminar moderator 1987-90), Am. Acad. Religion (chairperson mysticism group 1994-98), Mercy Assn. in Scripture and Theology (treas. 1987-96, mem. editorial bd. MAST jour.), Spiritual Drs. Internat. (founding coord. com. mem. 1990-93, coord. of regions 1990-93), Women's Ordination Conf. Democrat. Avocations: cooking, hiking, swimming. Office: Fordham U Grad Sch Religion and Religious Bronx NY 10458

RUFFNER, CHARLES LOUIS, lawyer; b. Cin., Nov. 7, 1936; s. Joseph H. and Edith (Solomon) R.; m. Mary Ann Kaufman, Jan. 30, 1966 (div. 1993); children: Robin Sue, David Robert; m. Nanette Diemer, Feb. 26, 1995. BSBA in Acctg., U. Fla., 1958; JD cum laude, U. Miami, 1964. Bar: Fla. 1964, U.S. Dist. Ct. (so. and Mid. dists.) Fla. 1964, U.S. Ct. Appeals (5th cir.) 1964, U. S. Ct. Appeals (11th cir.) 1984, U.S. Claims Ct. 1966, U.S. Tax Ct. 1966, U.S. Supreme Ct. 1969; cert. in taxation. Trial atty. tax divsn. Dept. Justice, Washington, 1964-67; pres. Forrest, Ruffner, Traum & Hagen, P.A., Miami, Fla., 1967-78, Ruffner, Hagen & Rifkin, P.A., Miami, 1978-81; tax ptnr. Myers, Kenin, Levinson, Ruffner, Frank & Richards, 1982-84; pres. Charles L. Ruffner, P.A., 1984—. Lectr. Fla. Internat. U., Miami. Author: A Practical Approach to Professional Corporations and Associations, 4 edits., 1970, (column) Tax Talk, Miami Law Rev.; editor Miami Law Rev., 1963-64; contbr. numerous articles on taxation to law jours. Named One of Best Lawyers in Am., 1999-2001. Mem. ABA, Fed. Bar Assn., Fla. Bar (exec. coun. tax sect. 1967-92, 95—, amicus curiae in test case of validity profl. corps.), Dade County Bar Assn., South Fla. Tax Litigation Assn. (chmn. 1986-00), Phi Alpha Delta, Phi Kappa Phi. Office: Pinecrest A 8830 SW 67th Ct Miami FL 33156-1700 E-mail: cruff7117@aol.com.

RUFFNER, FREDERICK G., JR. book publisher; b. Akron, Ohio, Aug. 6, 1926; s. Frederick G. and Olive Mae (Taylor) R.; m. Mary Ann Evans, Oct. 8, 1954; children: Frederic G. III, Peter Evans. BS, Ohio State U., 1950. Advt. mgr. Jim Robbins Co., Royal Oak, Mich., 1950-52; research mgr. Gen. Detroit Corp., 1953-54; pres. Gale Research Co., Detroit, 1954-87, Omnigraphics, Inc., 1987—. Editor: Ency. of Assns, 1956-68, Code Names Dictionary, 1963, Acronyms and Initialisms Dictionary, 1965, Allusions Dictionary, 1985; pub. Gold Coast Mag., 1992—; patentee in field. Bd. dirs. Friends of Detroit Pub. Libr., pres., 1975-76; mem. exec. bd. Detroit coun. Boy Scouts Am., 1974—, v.p., 1976-82; pres. Coun. for Fla. Librs., 1979—; trustee Bon Secours Hosp., Grosse Pointe, Mich., 1980-81; v.p. Etruscan Found., Florence, Italy, 1980—; pres. Mich. Ctr. for the Book, 1990, Literary Landmarks Assn., Gold Coast Jazz Soc., Ft. Lauderdale, 1992—; bd. dirs., v.p. Ohio State U. Found., Bonnet House, Ft. Lauderdale, 1992. 1st lt. AUS, 1944-46. Decorated Bronze Star, Combat Inf. award; recipient Centennial award Ohio State U., 1970, Benjamin Creativity award Assn. Am. Pubs., 1985, Career medal Ohioana Libr. Assn., 1988, Lifetime Achievement award Am. Libr. Trustees Assn., 1992; named to Entrepreneurs Hall of Fame, Nova U. Mem. Am. Antiquarian Soc., ALA (hon. life), Am. Mgmt. Assn., Am. Assn. Mus., Detroit Hist. Soc., Am. Hist. Print Collectors Soc., Bibliog. Soc. Am., Sierra Club, Pres. Assn., Audubon Soc., Am. Name Soc., Early Am. Industries Assn., Nat. Press Club (Washington), Ephemera Soc., Johnny Appleseed Soc., Navy League, Newcomen Soc., Cen. Bus. Dist. Assn. Detroit (vice-chmn. 1985-87), Jazz Forum (Grosse Pointe Farms, Mich.), Nat. Trust Hist. Preservation, Fairfield Heritage Soc., Archives Am. Art, Pvt. Librs. Assn., Friends Ft. Lauderdale Pub. Libr. (pres. 1974-78), Phileas Soc. (pres. 1985—), Ohio State U. Club (pres. Detroit club 1958, nat. chmn. Ohio State U. campaign, 1985-88), Masons, Shriners, Book Club, Detroit Athletic Club, Econ. Club, Prismatic Club (pres. 1990), Fontenada Soc. (pres. 1990-91), Detroit Club, Country Club Detroit, Ocean Reef Club, Grosse Pointe Yacht Club, Coral Ridge Yacht Club, Lauderdale Yacht Club, Princeton Club, Salmagundi Club, Grolier Club, Century Assn., Marco Polo Club, Faculty Club Ohio State U., Old Club, Commonwealth Club (San Francisco), Gross Pointe Club, Wawetonong Club, Tau Kappa Epsilon. Republican. Presbyterian. Home: 221 Lewiston Rd Grosse Pointe MI 48236-3519 also: 1000 Flamingo Isle Dr Fort Lauderdale FL 33301-2670 also: 901 E Las Olas Blvd Fort Lauderdale FL 33301-2320 Address: Omnigraphics Inc 615 Griswold St Detroit MI 48226-3415

RUFFO, MICHAEL, painter; b. Staten Island, N.Y., Mar. 9, 1954; s. Thomas Anthony and Marie (Papa) R.; m. Lorelei Ann Perez, July 5, 1995. BFA, Sch. Visual Arts, N.Y.C., 1991. Exhibited in group shows at Salmagundi Club, 1992-93, 95-99, Agora Gallery, 1998-99, World Fine Art, 1999, Knickerbocker Gallery, 1999, Hiram Blauvelt Mus., 1999, Nexus Gallery, 1999, 2000, 2001, Greene County Coun. on the Arts, 2002, NYU, 2000; represented in permanent collections U.S. Dept. State; patentee lockable lid support; work pub. in New Art Internat., 1999. Recipient Excellence award Manhattan Arts Internat. Competition, 1997-98, 99. Mem.: Nurture Art (registry artist), NY Artists Circle, Orgn. Ind. Artists, NY Artists Equity Assn. Roman Catholic.

RUFOLO, ANTHONY MICHAEL, economics educator; b. Newark, Aug. 9, 1948; s. Philip and Marie Antoinette (Petrillo) R.; m. Patricia Jeanne Lickorai, Aug. 29, 1970; children: Amy, Laura, Christine. BS in Econs., MIT, 1970; PhD in Econs., UCLA, 1975. Cons. Appraisal Rsch. Assocs., Thousand Oaks, Calif., 1971-72; adj. asst. prof. Temple U., Phila., 1976-79; economist Fed. Res. Bank Phila., 1974-78, sr. economist, 1978-80; adj. assoc. prof. U. Pa., Phila., 1978-80; assoc. prof. Portland (Oreg.) State U., 1980-85, prof. urban studies and planning, 1985—. Vis. prof. Jilin U. Tech., People's Republic of China, 1984, UCLA, 1984, 85, 88. Co-author: Public Finance and Expenditure In A Federal System, 1990; co-editor: Economics of Municipal Labor, 1983. Mem. Pub. Works Adv. Coun., Washington County, Oreg., 1981-84; mem. budget com. City of Beaverton, Oreg., 1989—, chair, 1992-94; mem. Gov.'s Coun. Econ. Adv., Oreg., 1983-94; mem. Citizen's Adv. Coun. on Budget, Tri-Met, 1991—; mem. investment adv. coun. City of Portland, 1992—. Rsch. grantee Urban Mass Transp. Adminstrn., 1984, Portland State U., 1986, 87, Ford Found., 1988, U.S. Dept. Transp., 1991, 92, 94, Oreg. Dept. Transp., 1994, Urban Mass Transp. Adminstrn. tng. grantee, 1986. Mem. Am. Econ. Assn., Nat. Tax Assn., Soc. Oreg. Economists. Avocations: racquetball, bridge, reading. Home: 13255 SW Saratoga Ln Beaverton OR 97008-7607 Office: Portland State U PO Box 751 Portland OR 97207-0751

RUGABER, WALTER FEUCHT, JR. interim university president, newspaper executive; b. Macon, Ga., Nov. 29, 1938; s. Walter Feucht and Edith Almeda (Maynard) R.; m. Sally Sanford, Oct. 6, 1962; children— Leslie, Christopher, Mark BS, Northwestern U., 1960. Corr., editor N.Y. Times, 1965—78; v.p., exec. editor Greensboro Daily News & Record, NC, 1978—82; pres., pub. The Roanoke Times, Va., 1982—2000; pres. Landmark Pub. Group, 1995—99; interim pres. Hollins U., Roanoke, Va., 2001—02. Mem. Pulitzer Prize Bd., 1990-99. Bd. dirs. United Way of Roanoke Valley, Va., 1982—88, Roanoke Symphony Soc., 1985—91, pres., 1986—88; trustee Hollins U., 1993—2002. Mem. Am. Newspaper Pubs. Assn., Am. Soc. Newspaper Editors, So. Newspaper Pubs. Assn. E-mail: wrugaber@swva.net.

RUGALA, KAREN FRANCIS (KAREN FRANCIS), painter, television producer; b. Memphis, Apr. 27, 1950; d. Ben Porter Francis and Marguerite K. Higginbotham; children: Sarah Helfinstein, Ben Helfinstein. BA in Communication Arts, Rhodes Coll., 1971; MA, U. Mo., 1973. Cert. tchr., Tenn. Secondary sch. tchr. Memphis City Schs., 1971-72; speech tchr. U. Ga., Athens, 1973-75; dir. computer systems installations Planning Rsch. Corp., McLean, Va., 1976-78; dir. account mgmt. TDX Systems, Cable & Wireless, Vienna, 1978-80; cons. telecommunications MCI, Washington, 1985-87; producer Fairfax Cable Access, Merrifield, Va., 1991-96. Owner Art Promotions, McLean, 1989—. Exhibited paintings in numerous group and one-woman shows and in cyberspace including McLean Project for Arts, 1992, Hospice of No. Va. Auction Gala, 1992, Capitol Hill Art League, Washington, 1995, Mus. Contemporary Art, Washington, 1996, Arts Coun. Fairfax County, Va., 1999, many others; paintings numerous pvt. collections. Active Family AIDS Housing Found., 1992, Hospice No. Va., 1991, 92, Friends of Vietnam Vets. Meml., 1992; founding bd. mem. Jobs for Homeless People, 1988-90; founder Non-Violence Award Program, 1998. Avocations: tennis, dancing, bridge, reading. Office: Art Promotions PO Box 3104 Mc Lean VA 22103-3104 E-mail: karen@artpro.com.

RUGE, CHRISTOPHER WAYNE, music educator; s. Kenneth Wayne and Melody Lynn Ruge; m. Emily Ann Henderson. MusB, U. of Wis., Madison, 1998. Cert. Music Education Ill., 1998. Vocal music tchr. Morrison H.S., Morrison, Ill., 1998—. Mem.: Ill. Music Educators' Assn., Am. Choral Dirs.' Assn.

RUGE, DANIEL AUGUST, retired neurosurgeon, educator; b. Murdock, Nebr., May 13, 1917; s. August Daniel and Mary Louise R.; m. Greta Piper, June 12, 1942; children: Charlotte, Thomas. BA, N. Central Coll., Naperville, Ill., 1939, Sc.D., 1971; MD, Northwestern U., 1945, PhD, 1961. Intern Wesley Meml. Hosp., Chgo., 1945-46, resident, 1949-50, Passavant Meml. Hosp., Chgo., 1946-49, VA Hosp., Hines, Ill., 1950-52; practice medicine specializing in neurosurgery Chgo., 1952-76; prof. surgery Northwestern U., 1973-76; professorial lectr. George Washington U., Washington, 1976-86, ret., 1986; dep. dir. spinal cord injury service VA Central Office, 1976-80, dir., 1980-81, 85-86, ret., 1986; physician to pres. U.S., White House, 1981-85. Author: Spinal Cord Injuries, 1969, Spinal Disorders: Diagnosis and Treatment, 1977; editor: Jour. Am. Paraplegia Soc., 1976-88. Trustee North Cen. Coll., 1960—, chmn. bd., 1974-77. Lt comdr. USN, 1954-56. Recipient Service award Northwestern U., 1966, Merit award Northwestern U., 1983; Outstanding Alumnus award N. Central Coll., 1978, Meritorious Service award VA, 1986. Fellow A.C.S.; mem. AMA, Am. Assn. Neurol. Surgeons, Central Surg. Assn., James IV Assn. Surgeons. Republican. Presbyterian. Home: 240 S High St Denver CO 80209-2628

RUGE, MICHAEL HELMUTH, research scientist, consultant, mathematician; b. Hagen, Germany, Mar. 13, 1962; s. Helmuth and Ruth Ruge. MS, La. State U., 1986, PhD, 1989; Diplom, U. Kaiserslautern, Germany, 1988. Tchg. asst. U. Kaiserslautern, 1983-84, Fla. State U., Tallahassee, 1984, La. State U., Baton Rouge, 1984-89; sys. engr. EDS/GM, Detroit, 1990-91, rsch. sys. engr. Plano, Tex., 1991; rsch. engr. tech. assessment R&D Siemens AG, Munich, 1991-94, rsch. sci. pub. comm. networks group, 1994-96, mgr. innovation field healthcare R&D, 1996-98; sr. cons. task force Y2K/Euro Siemens Bus. Svcs., 1998-99, sr. cons. mgmt. cons. Frankfurt, Munich, Germany, 1999—. Cons. Delgu Schuh- und Textilhandels GmbH, Kaiserslautern, 1993-95. Co-author: Neue Techniken in der Informationsverarbeitung, 1994; co-referee: Calculus with Analytic Geometry, 1988, Procs. Modellierung und Simulation im Umweltbereich, 1992, Procs. European Simulation Multiconf., 1993, Systems Analysis, Modelling and Simulation, Vols. 18-19, 1995; contbr. articles to profl. jours. Recipient award Studienstiftung des Deutschen Volkes, 1980; Fulbright scholar, 1984-86. Mem. Am. Math. Soc., German Math. Soc., Burschenschaft Markomannia, Phi Kappa Phi. Home: PO Box 1311 D-82003 U'haching Germany Fax: 603-947-7242. E-mail: mhr@e-math.ams.org.

RUGGERI, ROBERT EDWARD, lawyer; b. N.Y.C., Sept. 16, 1952; s. Mario Philip and Margaret Gloria (Pascale) R.; m. Mary Beth Thackeray, June 6, 1981. BA, Union Coll., 1974; JD, Antioch U., 1980. Bar: D.C. 1981, N.Y. 1993, U.S. Dist. Ct. D.C. 1982, U.S. Ct. Internat. Trade 1982, U.S. Ct. Appeals (fed. and D.C. cirs.) 1982, U.S. Supreme Ct. 1984. Trainee Commn. European Communities, Brussels, Belgium, 1980-81; legal cons. Secretariat, OECD, Paris, France, 1981-82; assoc. Stewart & Stewart, Washington, 1982-83, Graham and James, Washington, 1984-85, Rogers & Wells, Washington, 1985-92; dep. dir. legal affairs N.Y. State Dept. Environ. Conservation, 1993-94; assoc. counsel SUNY System, Albany, 1994—. Arbitrator NAFTA panels apptd. by U.S., Can., and Mex. govts., 1992—; adj. prof. Georgetown U. Law Ctr., 1988-92. Editor comments Antioch Law Jour., 1979-80. Trustee Schenectady County C.C., 1999—. Fulbright scholar, 1980-81. Mem. ABA, D.C. Bar Assn., Washington Fgn. Law Soc. (sec., treas. 1985-87, bd. govs. 1987-88), Am. Soc. Internat. Law. Roman Catholic. Home: 1846 Union St Niskayuna NY 12309-4502 Office: SUNY Office U Counsel Univ Plz Rm S315 Albany NY 12246-0001

RUGGERO, MARIO ALFREDO, physiologist, educator; b. Resistencia, Argentina, Nov. 7, 1943; came to U.S., 1961; s. Juan M. and Carolina F. (Volpe) R.; m. Elsa L. Statzner, Apr. 2, 1973. BA, Cath. U. Am., 1965; PhD, U. Chgo., 1972. Rsch. assoc. U. Wis., Madison, 1975; asst. prof. otolaryngology U. Minn., Mpls., 1975-87, assoc. prof., 1987-92, prof., 1992-93; Hugh Knowles prof. hearing sci. dept. comm. scis. and disorders Northwestern U., Evanston, Ill., 1993—, head Audiology & Hearing Scis. Program, 1996-2000. Mem. comm. disorders rev. com. Nat. Inst. on Deafness and Other Comm. Disorders, NIH, Bethesda, Md., 1990-94. Assoc. editor Jour. of Neurosci., 1989-95; mem. editl. bd. of Audiology and Neuro-Otology, 1998—; co-editor: The Mechanics and Biophysics of Hearing; contbr. articles to profl. jours. including Nature, Sci., J. Neurosci., Jour. Neurophysiology, Jour Acoustical Soc. Am., Procs. Nat. Acad. Sci. USA. Grantee NIH, 1975—, NSF, 1983-87. Fellow AAAS, Acoustical Soc. Am.; mem. Soc. for Neurosci., Assn. for Rsch. in Otolaryngology. Achievements include research in relationship between submicroscopic vibrations of the inner ear and the excitation of the auditory nerve. Home: 1209 Central St # A Evanston IL 60201-1611 Office: Northwestern U Dept Comm Scis and Disorders 2240 Campus Dr Evanston IL 60208-3550 E-mail: mruggero@northwestern.edu.

RUGGIE, JOHN GERARD, political science educator, diplomat; b. Graz, Austria, Oct. 18, 1944; came to U.S., 1967; s. Josef and Margaret (Macic) R.; m. Mary Zacharuk, May 21, 1965; 1 child, Andreas John. BA, McMaster U., 1967; MA, U. Calif., Berkeley, 1968; PhD, U. Calif., 1974; LLD (hon.), McMaster U., 2000. Asst. prof. polit. sci. U. Calif., Berkeley, 1974-78, prof. internat. rels. San Diego, 1987-91, dir. inst. global conflict and cooperation, 1989-91; prof. polit. sci. Columbia U., N.Y.C., 1978-87, prof. polit. sci., internat. affairs, 1991-97, dean Sch. Internat. and Pub. Affairs, 1991-96; Kirkpatrick prof. internat. affairs Harvard U., 2001—. Asst. sec. gen. UN, N.Y.C., 1997-2001. Author: Winning the Peace, 1996, Constructing the World Polity, 1998; editor: 4 books; contbr. over 50 articles to profl. jours. Recipient Hubert H. Humphrey award Notable Pub. Svc., Am. Polit. Sci. Assn., 2000; Internat. Studies Assn. Disting. scholar, 1999. Fellow Am. Acad. Arts Sci.; mem. UN Assn. (bd. dirs. 1985—), Fgn. Policy Assn. (bd. govs. 1992-95), Coun. Fgn. Rels. Avocations: skiing, scuba, tennis. Office: Kennedy School of Govt Harvard University Cambridge MA 02138 E-mail: john_ruggie@harvard.edu.

RUGGIERO, ALESSANDRO G. physicist, researcher; b. Rome, Apr. 10, 1940; came to the U.S., 1970; s. Ettore Antonio Ruggiero and Irma Zuppa; m. Amalia Lucia Comis, Feb. 7, 1965; children: Sara, Filippo. PhD in Physics, U. Rome, 1964. Physicist CERN, Geneva, 1966-69, Fermilab, Batavia, Ill., 1970-84; sr. physicist Argonne (Ill.) Nat. Lab., 1985-86; divsn. head Brookhaven Nat. Lab., Upton, N.Y., 1987-92, sr. physicist, 1993—. Cons. Dept. Energy, 1985—. Author, editor: Crystalline Beams, 1995, Hadron Colliders, 1996; editor: Stability of Particle Motion, 1992. Fellow Am. Phys. Soc.; mem. N.Y. Acad. Scis. Republican. Roman Catholic. Avocations: history, phylosophy. Home: 33 Inlet View Path W East Moriches NY 11940 Office: Brookhaven Nat Lab PO Box 5000 Upton NY 11973 E-mail: agr@bnl.gov.

RUGGIERO, MATTHEW JOHN, bassoonist; b. Phila., Sept. 18, 1932; s. Pompeo and Theresa (Ciampa) R.; m. Nancy Cirillo, Apr. 2, 1961; children: Eleanor, Claudia, Lisa. Diploma, Curtis Inst. Music, 1957; AA, Harvard U., 1982, BA cum laude, 1984, MA, 1987; PhD, Boston U., 1993. Second bassoonist Nat. Symphony Orch., Washington, 1957-60; asst. prin. bassoonist Boston Symphony Orch., 1961-89; prin. bassoonist Boston Pops Orch., 1974-89; ret., 1989. Mem. faculty Boston U., 1963— , New Eng. Conservatory Music, 1963— Served with U.S. Army, 1954-57. Boston U. Profs. Program scholar and fellow, 1989.

RUGGLES, JOANNE BEAULE, artist, educator; b. N.Y.C., May 19, 1946; d. Robert H. and Evelyn (Corzin) Beaule; m. Philip Kent Ruggles, Aug. 31, 1968; 1 child, Lauren. BFA, Ohio State U., 1968, MFA, 1970. Lectr. art Ohio State U., Columbus, 1970-71, Allan Hancock Coll., Santa Maria, Calif., 1971-76, Cuesta Coll., San Luis Obispo, 1977-79; lectr. arch. and art Calif. Poly. State U., 1973-80, assoc. prof. art, 1984-88, prof., 1988—. Reviewer Dorland Mountain Arts Cmty. Artists Residency Grants, 1988—; adv. bd. San Luis Obispo County Arts Coun., 2000—. Author: (with others) Darkroom Graphics, 1975. Mem. San Luis Obispo City Promotional Coordinating Com., 1978-82, chmn., 1980-82; bd. dirs. San Luis Obispo Art Assn., 1993-95, v.p., 1994-95. Recipient jurors spl. mention Cabo Frio Internat. Print Biennal, Brazil, 1983, Univ. purchase award Wesleyan 2d Internat. Print and Drawing Exhbn., Macon, Ga., 1983, Purchase award Artists World, Somerville, N.J., 1984, Purchase award Minot State U., 1996, Jurors award Gallery Contemporary Art U. Colo., 1997, John McKee Meml. award 45th Annual Internat. San Diego Art Inst., 2001; selected artist Art in Embassies program U.S. Dept. State, Washington, 1997, U.S. Embassy in Luanda, Angola, 1999—. Mem. Nat. Assn. Women Artists, Nat. Mus. Women in Arts (founding mem.), Nat. Acrylic Painters Assn. (signature mem., Am. Artist award 1997), Am. Soc. Contemporary Artists (signature), Calif. Soc. Printmakers, L.A. Printmaking Soc., Boston Printmakers, Women Painters West. Home: PO Box 46 San Luis Obispo CA 93406-0046 E-mail: jruggles@calpoly.edu.

RUGGLES, RUDY LAMONT, JR. international security advisor, consultant; b. Evanston, Ill., Nov. 11, 1938; s. Rudy Lamont and Ruth (Cain) R.; m. Cecelia Ann Consorte, July 20, 1974 (div. 1996); m. Sara Joyce Silbernagel, Feb. 3, 1998; children— Rudy, Christopher, Daniel, Andrew BA, Harvard U., 1960, MBA, 1966. Sr. assoc. physicist IBM Labs., Poughkeepsie, N.Y., 1960-64; corp. planning cons. corp. hdqrs. IBM, Armonk, 1966-71; sr. mem. profl. staff Hudson Inst., Croton-on-Hudson, 1971-75, pres., 1975-79, also dir.; prin. Cresap, McCormick & Paget, Inc., 1979-82; ptnr. The Phila. Mgmt. Cons. Group, Inc., 1982—; mng. dir. New China Group, Inc., 1982—. Chmn. residential solicitation United Fund, Pound Ridge, N.Y., 1969; mem. parents com. St. Paul's Sch., Concord, N.H.; dir. Danbury Hosp. and Danbury Hosp. Devel. Fund, Conn., 1978—, med. affairs com.; chmn. fin. com. Pound Ridge Community Ch., 1969-70; bd. dirs. Harry Frank Guggenheim Found., 1982—, Mid-Western Conn. Coun. Alcoholism; bd. visitors Sch. Langs. and Linguistics Georgetown U.; trustee New Canaan Country Sch., The Newberry Libr.; mem. Ridgefield (Conn.) Drug and Alcohol Commn.; treas., bd. dirs. Nat. Coun. Alcoholism and Drug Dependence, Midwestern Conn. Coun. on Alcoholism. With C.E., U.S. Army, 1962 Fellow Explorers Club; mem. Hudson Inst. (hon.), N. Am. Soc. Corp. Planning (dir. 1966-72), Internat. Inst. Strategic Studies, Internat. Map Collectors Soc., James Caird Soc., Ends of the Earth (hon.), U.S.-China Bus. Coun., Harvard Club of N.Y.C., Sigma Xi.

RUGGLES, RUSTY L, music educator; b. Aledo, Ill., Feb. 5, 1972; s. Gary E and Nancy S Ruggles; m. Julene W Dellitt, June 7, 1997; children: Anthony J. Bachelor in Music Edn., Augustana Coll., Rock Island, IL, 1990—94; Masters in Music Edn., Vandercook Coll. of Music, Chicago, IL, 1995—99. Music dir. MVK Mid. Sch., Mazon, IL, Ill., 1994—99; band dir. Aledo H.S., Aledo, IL, 1999—. Mem.: MENC. Achievements include development of Mercer County Community Band. Office: Aledo High School 1500 South College Ave Aledo IL 61231 Personal E-mail: ruggles30@yahoo.com.

RUGLAND, WALTER S. fraternal benefit society executive; b. Appleton, Wis. BA, Luther Coll., 1959; MBA, U. Mich., 1961. With Conn. Gen. Life Ins. Co., until 1975; cons. actuary, equity prin. Milliman & Robertson, Inc., Hartford, Conn., 1975—98; exec. v.p., chief operating officer Aid Assn. Lutherans, Appleton, Wis., 1998—2001; exec. v.p Thrivent Fin. Luths., 2002—. Fellow Conf. Cons. Actuaries, Soc. Actuaries; mem. Inst. Actuaries. Office: Thrivent Fin Luths 4321 N Ballard Rd Appleton WI 54919-0001 E-mail: walt_rugland@aal.org.

RUGMAN, ALAN MICHAEL, international business educator; b. Bristol, Eng., June 9, 1945; arrived in Can., 1968; naturalized, 1973; s. Kenneth M. and Dorothy Irene Rugman; m. Helen Scruton, 1970; 1 child, Andrew. BA in Econs. with honors, U. Leeds (Eng.), 1966; MSc in Econs., U. London, 1967; PhD in Econs., Simon Fraser U., Can., 1974. Lectr. econs. U. Winnipeg, Man., Can., 1970-73, asst. prof., 1973-78, assoc. prof., 1978-79; assoc. prof. fin. Concordia U., Montreal, 1979-80; assoc. prof. bus. adminstrn. Dalhousie U., Halifax, N.S., Can., 1980-82, prof., 1982-87, dir. Ctr. Internat. Bus. Studies, 1980-87; prof. mgmt. U. Toronto, 1987—, rsch. dir. Ont. (Can.) Internat. Bus. Ctr., 1988-92; vis. assoc. prof. internat. bus. Columbia U., 1978-79, vis. prof., 1982; vis. scholar Ctr. for Internat. Affairs, Harvard U., 1984; vis. prof. London Bus. Sch., 1985, U. Hawaii, 1985, U Alberta, 1988; mem. internat. trade adv. com. Govt. of Can., 1986-88; sr. Fellow, Massey Coll. Author: International Diversification and the Multinational Enterprise, 1979, Multinationals in Canada: Theory, Performance and Economic Impact, 1980, Inside the Multinationals: The Economics of Internal Markets, 1981, Outward Bound: Canadian Direct Investment in the United States, 1987, Multinationals and Canada: United States Free Trade, 1990; co-author: International Business: Firm and Environment, 1985, Megafirms: Strategies for Canada's Multinationals, 1985, Administered Protection in America, 1987, Global Corporate Strategy And Trade Policy, 1990; editor: New Theories of the Multinational Enterprise, 1982, Multinationals and Technology Transfer: The Canadian Experience, 1983, International Business in Canada, 1989, Research In Global Strategic Management, 1990, 91; co-editor: Multinationals and Transfer Pricing, 1985, Business Strategies and Free Trade, 1988; referee manuscripts for numerous profl. jours.; reviewer manuscripts for numerous pubs.; contbr. articles, book revs. to profl. jours.; lectr. to profl. confs.; contbr. chpts. to books. Soc. Scis. and Humanities Rsch. Coun. Can. grantee, 1983, 84. Fellow Acad. Internat. Bus. (v.p. 1989-90); mem. North Am. Econ. and Fin. Assn. (bd. dirs. 1979-91, pres. 1984), Acad. Mgmt., Am. Econ. Assn. Office: U Toronto Faculty Mgmt 246 Bloor St W Toronto ON Canada M5S 1V4

RUH, ROBERT, materials scientist; b. Plainfield, N.J., Aug. 2, 1930; s. Harry John and Martha Agusta Ruh; m. Sally Ivins Burnside, Dec. 27, 1952; children: Robert jr., Susan D., William N. BSc, Rutgers U., New Brunswick, N.J., 1952; MSc, Rutgers U., 1953, PhD, 1960. Task scientist USAF Aerospace Rsch. Labs., Wright-Patterson AFB, Ohio, 1955—58, rsch. ceramist, 1958—67; post-doctoral fellow Chem. Rsch. Labs. Commonwealth Sci. and Indusl. Rsch. Orgn., Melbourne, Australia, 1965—66; sr. project scientist Air Force Materials Lab., Wright-Patterson AFB, 1967—86; materials rsch. engr. Signature Tech. Office, Wright Lab., 1986—93; materials cons. Universal Tech. Corp., Beavercreek, Ohio, 1993—. Adj. assoc. prof. U. Dayton, Ohio, 1987. Contbg. and assoc. editor Jour. Am. Ceramic Soc., 1965—95; contbr. articles to profl. jours. Treas. BSA Troop 215, Kettering, Ohio, 1972—78; Sunday sch. tchr. Fairmont Presbyn. Ch., 1972—76, deacon, elder, 1980—2000. Recipient Edward Orton Ceramic Found. fellowship, Rutgers U., 1952, The Ian Potter Found. fellowship, CRL, 1965. Fellow: Am. Ceramic Soc. (numerous offices including vice-chmn., sec., chmn. Basic Scis. divsn. 1970—78, Hon. mention Ceramographic Exhibit 1974, 1st pl. Ceramographic Exhibit 1995); mem.: Am. Soc. Metals, Ceramic Edn. Coun., Nat. Inst. Ceramic Engrs. Achievements include research in the mullite-silicon carbide whisker composites, the silicon carbide-aluminum nitride system, the boron carbide-boron nitride system, a number of phase diagrams wih zirconia. Home: 4225 Murrell Dr Kettering OH 45429 Office: Universal Tech Corp 1270 N Fairfield Rd Beavercreek OH 45432

RUHE, GUENTHER HARRY, mathematician; b. Leipzig, Germany, May 29, 1952; s. Harry Ruhe and Erika (Wahl) Noack; children: Melanie, Stella. Diploma in Math., U. Leipzig, Germany, 1975; D of Natural Scis., Bergakademie Freiberg, Germany, 1981; D of Habilitation, TH Leipzig, 1987. Asst. prof. Tech. Hochschule, 1986-90; vis. prof. U. Bayreuth, Germany, 1991-92; vis. scientist IBM Info. Systems GmbH, Heidelberg, Germany, 1993; sr. scientist Software Tech. Transfer Initiative, Kaiserslautern, Germany, 1993-95; dep. dir. Fraunhofer Inst. for Exptl. Software Engring., Germany, 1996—2001; iCORE prof., indsl. rsch. chair in software engring. U. Calgary, 2001—. Author: Algorithmic Aspects of Flows in Networks, 1991, Learning Software Organizations, 2000. Recipient Rsch. Excellence award, iCore Alberta Informatics Cir., 2001. Mem. IEEE, Assn. Computing Machinery, Assn. for Informatik, Assn. for Ops. Rsch. Avocations: tennis, jogging, jazz, literature. Office: U Calgary Calgary AB T2N 1N4 Canada

RUHLIN, PEGGY MILLER, investment adviser, financial planner; b. Dayton, Ohio, May 20, 1949; d. Charles Raymond and Shirlee E. (Menke) Miller; m. John B. Ruhlin Jr., June 19, 1982; 1 child, Megan R. Kolb. BA magna cum laude, Otterbein Coll., 1979. CPA, Ohio; Cert. fin. planner. Acct. Borden, Inc., Columbus, Ohio, 1971-72; mgr. Intraspace Planning Group, Inc., 1972-74; v.p. Mgmt. Media, Inc., 1974-80, pres., 1980-87; prin. Budros & Ruhlin, Inc., 1987—. Adj. prof. Franklin U., Columbus, Ohio, 2000—01; mem. nat. adv. bd./coun. Schwab Instl., 1994—95; mem. Vanguard Group Investment Adv. Coun., 1996—97. Columnist: Bus. First of Greater Columbus, 1986, columnist: Jour. of Retirement Planning, 2001; commentator Sta. WCBE-FM, 1989—91, 1995, Sta. WOSU-AM, 1992—; contbr. articles to profl. jours. Trustee Otterbein Coll., 2001—. Found. for Fin. Planning, 2001—. Named One of Best Fin. Advisors in U.S. Worth mag., 1996—, One of Best Fin. Advisors for Drs., Med. Econs. mag., 1998, 2000, One of 100 Great Fin. Planners, Mut. Funds Mag., 2001. Mem. AICPA, Assn. for Investment Mgmt. and Rsch., Fin. Planning Assn. (chpt. pres. 1989-91, nat. bd. dirs. 1992-98, pres. 96-97, chair 1997-98), Nat. Assn . Personal Fin. Advisers (Fin. Planner of Yr. award 1988), Internat. Women's Forum. Office: Budros & Ruhlin Inc 1650 Lake Shore Dr Ste 150 Columbus OH 43204-4942

RUHLMAN, HERMAN C(LOYD), JR. manufacturing company executive; b. Warren, Pa., Jan. 17, 1949; s. Herman Cloyd and Virginia Lee (Wimer) R.; divorced; children: Brian, Jason, Chad; m. Lorraine; stepchildren: Bethany, Michelle, Randy. BS in Indsl. Tech., Calif. (Pa.) State Coll., 1974. Gen. mgr. Rand Machine Products, Inc., Falconer, N.Y., 1974-80, pres., chmn. bd. dirs., 1980—; pres. Spartan Tool Co., Gerry, 1986—. Active Boy Scouts Am. With USAF, 1968-72. Mem. Epsilon Pi Tau. Republican. Home: PO Box 284 15 Annis St Frewsburg NY 14738-9564 Office: PO Box 72 Allen St Extension Falconer NY 14733 E-mail: rand@madbbs.com.

RUHLMANN, WILLIAM JAMES, music critic; b. Newark, May 13, 1955; s. William Edwin and Margaret Mary (Neagle) R. BA, Columbia U., 1977. Editl. asst. Rsch. Inst. of Am., N.Y.C., 1977-79; asst. treas. Chase Manhattan Bank, 1979-89; music critic N.Y.C. Tribune, 1983-91; contbr. Goldmine Mag., Iola, Wis., 1984—; assoc. editor Relix Mag., N.Y.C., 1987-91; writer, editor The All-Music Guide, Ann Arbor, Mich., 1991—. Author: The Rolling Stones, 1993, Barbra Streisand, 1995; co-author, contbr.: Scribner Ency. Am. Lives; co-author, editor: Baker's Biographical Dictionary. Mem. NARAS. Democrat. Home: 315 W 105th St Apt 4F New York NY 10025 E-mail: wruhlmann@aol.com.

RUHM, CHRISTOPHER JOHN, economics educator; b. San Francisco, Apr. 26, 1955; s. John Felix and Maria Bertha (Kirs) R.; m. Maryanna Robin Williams, May 6, 1989; children: William Christopher, Peter Thomas. BA, U. Calif., Davis, 1978; MA, U. Calif., Berkeley, 1981, PhD, 1984. Teaching and rsch. assoc. U. Calif., Berkeley, 1980-84; asst. prof. Boston U., 1984-91; assoc. prof. U. N.C., Greensboro, 1991-94, prof., 1994—, sr. staff economist coun. econ. advisors, 1996—97. Rsch. assoc. Nat. Bur. Econ. Rsch., 1994—; rsch. fellow Brandeis U., Waltham, Mass., 1988—90. Contbr. articles to profl. jours. Mem. Am. Econ. Assn., Internat. Health Econs. Assn., Soc. Labor Economists. Avocations: running, biking, yoga, meditation. Office: U NC Dept Econs Greensboro NC 27402-6165

RUHM, THOMAS FRANCIS, retired lawyer, investor; b. Bridgeport, Conn., June 8, 1935; s. Herman David and Martica (Sturges) R.; m. Michele Wood, Oct. 5, 1974; children: Wendy Sturges, Thomas Wood. BA, Yale U., 1957; JD, Havard U., 1962. Bar: N.Y. 1963, U.S. Dist. Ct. (so. and ea. dists.) N.Y. 1964, U.S. Ct. Appeals (2d cir.) 1969. Assoc. Shearman & Sterling, N.Y.C., 1962-70; asst. gen. counsel Bessemer Securities Corp., 1970-96, v.p., 1981-96; ret., 1996. Chmn. legal aspects venture capital investing Practicing Law Inst., N.Y. and San Francisco, 1979-81; lectr. on venture capital NYU Grad. Sch., 1986-90, Concordia Coll., Bronxville, N.Y., 1999-2001; expert on fed. securities law, venture capital legal matters, investment tax policy, Fed. Res. monetary policy; witness during 1980s fed. tax hearings; adj. prof. fin. St. John's U., 2000—. Contbg. author: Technology and Economic Policy, 1986; contbr. articles to profl. jours. Commr. upper divsn. Eastchester (N.Y.) Youth Soccer League, 1990-91, coach, 1985-91, dir. coaching 1995-96; sr. warden Christ Ch., Bronxville, N.Y., 1991-94; past v.p. and treas. Bronxville Sch. PTA; treas., bd. dirs. Friends of Bronxville Pub. Libr., 1997-2000; mem. Quogue (N.Y.) Cultural Com., 1998—; mem. Blue Hill Troupe, Ltd., 1972—. Lt. (j.g.) USNR, 1957-59, mem council 2001 -. Mem. Univ. Club, Bronxville Field Club, Quogue Field Club, Quogue Beach Club. Republican.

RUI, HALLGEIR, cancer researcher; b. Rissa, Norway, Dec. 13, 1961; came to U.S., 1989; s. Tarald Martin and Gerd (Neverlien) R. MD, U. Oslo, 1987, PhD in Pathology, 1988. Lic. med. doctor, Norway. Clin. resident in surgery and internal medicine Notodden (Norway) Hosp., 1987-89; postdoctoral fellow Lee Moffitt Cancer Ctr. and Rsch. Inst., Tampa, 1989-91; scientist Nat. Cancer Inst., Frederick, Md., 1991-95; asst. prof. Uniformed Svcs. U. Health Scis. Sch. Medicine, Bethesda, 1995-2001, assoc. prof., 2001—02; assoc. prof. oncology Georgetown U. Lombardi Cancer Ctr., Washington, 2002—. Assoc. prof.. Georgetown U., Lombardi Cancer Ctr, Washington, 2002—. Contbr. over 80 articles to profl. jours. Norwegian Sci. Coun. fellow, 1983-87, Fulbright fellow, 1989, Fogarty fellow, 1989-95. Mem. AAAS, Internat. Cytokine Soc. Achievements include cloning of rat Jak2 tyrosine kinase and demonstrating that prolactin activates Jak-Stat and Shc-Ras signaling pathways. E-mail: hrui@usuhs.mil.

RUINA, JACK PHILIP, electrical engineer, educator; b. Rypin, Poland, Aug. 19, 1923; came to U.S., 1927; naturalized, 1932; s. Michael and Nechuma (Warshaw) R.; m. Edith Elster, Oct. 26, 1947; children: Ellen, Andrew, Rachel.

BEE, CCNY, 1944; MEE, Poly. Inst. Bklyn., 1949, DEE, 1951. Rsch. fellow Microwave Rsch. Inst., Poly. Inst. Bklyn., 1948-50; from instr. to assoc. prof. elec. engring. Brown U., 1950-54; rsch. assoc. prof. coordinated sci. lab. U. Ill., 1954-59, rsch. prof., prof. elec. engring., 1959-63; prof. elec. engring. MIT, 1963—, v.p. for spl. labs., 1966-70. U.S. observer Antarctica, 1964; on leave to U.S. Govt., 1959-63, pres. Inst. Def. Analysis, 1964-66; dep. for rsch. to asst. sec. air force, 1959-60; asst. dir. for def. rsch. and engring. Office Sec. Def., 1960-61; dir. Advanced Rsch. Projects Agy., Dept. Def., 1961-63; mem. panel Presdl. Sci. Adv. Commn., 1963-72, sci. adv. bd. USAF, 1964-67, adv. bd. and panels for Dept. Def., HEW, Dept. Transp., ACDA, Office Tech. Assessment, NSF, NSC, 1963—; mem. gen. adv. com. ACDA, 1969-74; sr. cons. Office Sci. and Tech. Policy, The White House, 1977-80; chmn. com. on environ. decision making NAS, 1974-77; bd. dirs. Mitre Corp. Recipient Fleming award, 1962, Disting. Alumnus award Poly. Inst. Bklyn., 1970, One Hundred and Twenty Fifth Anniversary medal CCNY, 1973. Fellow IEEE, AAAS, Am. Acad. Arts and Scis.; mem. Internat. Sci. Radio Union. Office: MIT Dept Elec Engring 292 Main St Cambridge MA 02142-1014 Home: PO Box 91 Wellfleet MA 02667-0091 E-mail: ruina@mitre.org.

RUIZ, COOKIE, performing company executive; Pres. Jr. League, Austin, Tex.; dir. fund devel. Ballet Austin, 1996-97, exec. dir., 1997—. Office: Ballet Austin 3002 Guadalupe St Austin TX 78705-2818*

RUIZ, LILLIAN, English language educator; b. Bronx, N.Y., July 10, 1967; d. John and Nereida (Acosta) Ruiz. BA magna cum laude, U. Rochester, 1989; MA, UCLA, 1991. English instr. Palomar C.C., San Maros, Calif., 1992-93, Miracosta C.C., Oceanside, 1992-93, Greenfield (Mass.) C.C., 1993-96, asst. prof. English, 1996-99, assoc. prof. English, 1999-2001, chmn. dept. English, 1999—, prof. English, 2001—. Alumnia interviewer U. Rochester, N.Y., 1994—. Mem. MLA, Nat. Coun. Tchrs. English, Phi Theta Kappa (hon.). Home: 42A Thayer Rd Greenfield MA 01301-9664 Office: Greenfield Cmty Coll 1 College Dr Greenfield MA 01301-9755 E-mail: ruiz@gcc.mass.edu.

RUIZ, MICHELE ILENE, lawyer; b. Washington, Nov. 3, 1969; BS, Cornell U., 1991; JD, U. Chgo., 1994. Bar: U.S. Dist. Ct. (no. dist.) Ill. 1994. Assoc. McDermott, Will & Emery, Chgo., 1994—96, Sidley Austin Brown & Wood, Chgo., 1996—. Office: Sidley Austin Brown & Wood Bank One Plz 10 S Dearborn Chicago IL 60603 Office Fax: 312-853-7036. E-mail: mruiz@sidley.com.

RUIZ, PEDRO, psychiatrist; b. Cuba, Dec. 31, 1936; MD, U. Paris VI, 1964. Intern Jackson Meml. Hosp., Miami, Fla., 1965, resident in psychiatry, 1966-68; prof. psychiatry U. Tex./Houston Health Sci. Ctr.; pres. American Board of Psychiatry and Neurology, 2002—. Office: U Tex-Houston Health Sci Ct Mental Sci Inst 1300 Moursund St Houston TX 77030-3406*

RUIZ, RAMON EDUARDO, history educator; b. La Jolla, Calif., Sept. 9, 1921; s. Ramon and Dolores (Urueta) R.; m. Natalia Marrujo, Oct. 14, 1944; children— Olivia, Maura. BA, San Diego State Coll., 1947; MA, Claremont Grad. Sch., 1948; PhD, U. Calif., Berkeley, 1954. Asst. prof. U. Oreg., Eugene, 1955-57, So. Meth. U., Dallas, 1957-58; prof. Smith Coll., Northampton, Mass., 1958-69; prof. Latin Am. history U. Calif. at San Diego, 1969-91, prof. emeritus, 1991—, chmn. dept. history, 1971-76, chmn. divsn. humanities, 1972-74; mem. project grant com. NEH, 1972-73, 75-77, dir. public programs div., 1979-80; Ralph Chase lectr. San Angelo State U, 2000. Vis. prof. Facultad de Economia, Univ. de Nuevo Leon, Mexico, 1965-66, Coll. de Sonora, Mexico, summer 1983, Pomona Coll., 1983-84, Coll. de Michoacan, Mexico, summer 1986, 87, Univ. Nacional Autonoma de Mexico, fall 1992; scholar-in-residence Colegio de la Frontero Norte, Mexico, 1994-96; MacArthur Found. nominator, 1981-82; mem. project grant com. Ford Found. Author: Cuba: The Making of A Revolution, 1968 (One of Best History Books, Book World Washington Post 1968), Mexico: The Challenge of Poverty and Illiteracy, 1963, An American in Maximillians's Mexico, 1865-1866, 1959; (with James D. Atwater) Out From Under; Benito Juarez and Mexico's Struggle for Independence, 1969; (with John Tebbel) South by Southwest: The Mexican-American and His Heritage, 1969, Interpreting Latin American History, 1970, Labor and the Ambivalent Revolutionaries: Mexico, 1911-23, 1975, The Mexican War: Was it Manifest Destiny?, 1963, The Great Rebellion: Mexico, 1905-1924, 1980 (Hubert C. Herring prize), The People of Sonora and Yanqui Capitalists, 1988, Triumphs and Tragedy: A History of the Mexican People, 1992 (named One of Five Best History Books 1991-92, L.A. Times, Gold Medal award Commonwealth Club San Francisco 1993); (with Olivia Teresa Ruiz) Reflexiones Sobre la Identidad de los Pueblos, 1996, On the Rim of Mexico: Encounters of the Rich and Poor, 1998. Served to lt. USAAF, 1943-46. William Harrison Mills traveling fellow in internat. relations, 1950; John Hay Whitney Found. fellow, 1950; Fulbright fellow Mex., 1965-66; fellow Ctr. for Advanced Study in Behavioral Scis., 1984-85, Ena H. Thompson lectureship, Pomona Coll., 1995; recipient Am. Philos. Soc. grant in aid, 1959, Nat. medal Humanities Pres. U.S., 1998. Mem. Am. Hist. Assn. (Beveridge prize com. 1974-76), Conf. Latin Am. History, Chicano-Latino Faculty Assn. U. Calif. (pres. 1989-91), Phi Beta Kappa, Sigma Delta Pi. Home: PO Box 1775 Rancho Santa Fe CA 92067-1775 E-mail: reruiz@ucsd.edu.

RUIZ, VANESSA, state supreme court justice; b. San Jaun, P.R., Mar. 22, 1950; d. Fernando and Irma (Bosch) Ruiz-Suria; married; m. David E. Birenbaum, Oct. 22, 1983; stepchildren: Tracy, Matthew. BA, Wellesley Coll., 1972; JD, Georgetown U., 1975. Bar: D.C. 1972, U.S. Supreme Ct. 1981. Assoc. Fried, Frank, Harris, Shrives & Kampelman, Washington, 1975—83; sr. mgr., counsel Sears World Trade Inc., 1983—94; assoc. judge D.C. Ct. of Appeals, 1994—. Spkr. in field. Mem.: ABA, Inter-Am. Bar Assn. Office: DC Ct of Appeals 500 Indiana Ave NW Fl 6 Washington DC 20001-2131*

RUIZ-FORNELLS, ENRIQUE, history and Spanish educator; b. Madrid, Dec. 6, 1925; came to U.S., 1963; s. Camilo Ruiz-Fornells and Teresa Silverde; m. Cynthia Young, Mar. 21, 1959. Degree, U. Madrid, 1951, MA, 1953, PhD, 1958. Prof. U. Madrid, 1956-59; lectr. McGill U., Montreal, Can., 1959-61; asst. prof. U. S.C., Columbia, 1961-63; assoc. prof. U. Ala., Tuscaloosa, 1963-69, prof., 1970-86, tech. prof., 1987-90, rsch. prof. emeritus, 1991—. Vis. prof. Washington U., St. Louis, 1967, Miss. State U., Mississippi State, 1968-75 Author: Estudiantes españoles en los Estados Unidos, 1956, A Concordance to Gustavo Adolfo Bequer's Poetry, 1970, Las concordancias de El Ingenioso Hidalgo Don Quijote de la Mancha, 1980, A Concordance to the Poetry of Leopoldo Panero, 1978, La muralla, 1980, Concordancias del Quijote de Avellaneda, 1984, (with others) La muralla, 1962, The United States and Spanish World, 1979, United States Dissertations in Hispanic Languages and Literatures, 1967-1977, 1981; editor: Revista de estudios hispánicos, 1965-84; asst. editor: Mundo Hispánico, 1954-55, Cuadernos Hispanoamericanos, 1958-59, Ediciones Cultura Hispánica, 1958-59; contbr. numerous articles and papers to profl. publs. Recipient Medalla al Mérito Turístico, 1968, Encomienda al Mérito Civil, 1972, Comendador de Numero de la Orden del Mérito Civil, 1977, Encomienda de la Orden de Isabel La Católica, 1984, Encomienda de la Orden Civil de Alfonso X el Sabio, 1998; scholar Seminar of Ibero-Am. Studies, 1948, Internat. U. Menéndez Pelayo, 1950, French Govt., 1952, Internat. Inst. Edn., 1953-54; grantee U. Ala. Rsch. Com., 1966, 67, 74, 77, Program of Cultural Coop. between U.S. and Spain, summer 1978, 79, 81. Mem. AAUP, MLA, Internat. Assn. Hispanistas, Am. Assn. Tchrs. of Spanish and Portuguese (nat. v.p. 1975, nat. pres. 1976, pres. Ala. chpt. 1967, Disting. Svc. award 1986), Am. Assn. Spanish and Portuguese Hist. Studies, South Atlantic Modern Lang. Assn. (v.p. 1989, pres. 1990), Real Academia de la Lengua Española (corr. mem.), Sigma Delta Pi. Office: U Ala PO Box 864931 Tuscaloosa AL 35486-0044 Fax: 205-556-3529. E-mail: erfs@msn.com.

RUIZ SACRISTÁN, CARLOS, Mexican government official; b. Mexico City, Oct. 27, 1949; BA in Bus. Adminstrn., Anahuac U., 1972; MA in Fin., Northwestern U., Chgo., 1974. From chief of currency exch. to mgr. internat. ops. Bank of Mex., 1974-86; dir. Commn. on Exch. Rate Risk Ins., 1986-88; gen. dir. pub. credit Secretarian of Fin. and Pub. Credit, 1988-92, dep. sec. expenditures, 1992-94; dir. Gen. Mex. Petroleum "Pemex", 1994; sec. comm. and transport Govt. Mex., 1994—. Office: Xola esq Av Universidad Cuerpo c 1er piso 03028 Mexico City Mexico

RUIZ-SURIA, FERNANDO, lawyer; b. San Juan, P.R., May 18, 1916; s. Abelardo and Teresa (Suria) R.; m. Irma Bosch, Aug. 18, 1946; children: Fernando, Vanessa, Ivan, Mimi. BA, U. P.R., 1938, LLB, 1940. Bar: P.R. 1941, U.S. Dist. Ct. P.R. 1941, U.S. Ct. Appeals (1st cir.) 1959, U.S. Supreme Ct. 1963, U.S. Ct. Appeals D.C. 1977, Temporary Emergency Ct. Appeals 1980. House counsel Shell Co. Ltd., San Juan, 1942-53; sr. ptnr. Sifre & Ruiz-Suria, San Juan, 1953-67, McConnell Valdes Kelley Sifre Griggs & Ruiz-Suria, San Juan, 1967-81; of counsel McConnell Valdes et al; dir. corps.; mem. jud. confs.; former mem. P.R. Bar Examiners; former mem. Evidence Rules Com. Fellow Am. Coll. Trial Lawyers; mem. Colegio de Abogados de P.R., Sara Bay C. of C., Meadows C. of C., Bird Key Yacht Club (Sarasota, Fla.), Bankers Club (San Juan, P.R.). Roman Catholic. Home: 888 Blvd Of The Arts Apt 1104 Sarasota FL 34236-4832

RUKEYSER, LOUIS RICHARD, economic commentator; b. N.Y.C., Jan. 30, 1933; s. Merryle Stanley and Berenice Helene (Simon) R.; m. Alexandra Gill, Mar. 3, 1962; children: Beverley Jane, Susan Athena, Stacy Alexandra. AB, Princeton U., 1954; LittD (hon.), N.H. Coll., 1975; LLD (hon.), Moravian Coll., 1978, Mercy Coll., 1984, Am. U., 1991; DBA (hon.), Southeastern Mass. U., 1979; LHD (hon.), Loyola Coll., 1982, Johns Hopkins U., 1986, Western Md. Coll., 1992; D of Fin. (hon.), Roger Williams U., 1997. Reporter Balt. Sun newspapers, 1954-65; chief polit. corr. Evening Sun, 1957-59; chief London bur. The Sun, 1959-63, chief Asian corr., 1963-65; sr. corr., commentator ABC News, 1965-73, Paris corr., 1965-66, chief London bur., 1966-68, econ. editor, commentator, 1968-73; econ. columnist McNaught Syndicate, 1976—86, Tribune Media Services, 1986—93. Lectr. in field. Author: How to Make Money in Wall Street, 1974, 2d edit., 1976 (Literary Guild selection 1974, 76), What's Ahead for the Economy: The Challenge and the Chance, 1983, 2d edit., 1985 (Literary Guild selection 1984), Louis Rukeyser's Business Almanac, 1988, 2d edit., 1991, Louis Rukeyser's Book of Lists, 1997, Right on the Money, 1998; editor-in-chief (newsletter) Louis Rukeyser's Wall Street, 1992—, Louis Rukeyser's Mutual Funds, 1994—; TV host Wall St. Week With Louis Rukeyser, 1970-2002, Louis Rukeyser's Wall Street, 2002-. With U.S. Army, 1954-56. Recipient Overseas Press Club award, 1963, Overseas Press Club citation, 1964, G.M. Loeb award U. Conn., 1972, Janus award for excellence in fin. news programming, 1975, George Washington Honor medal Freedoms Found., 1972, 78, N.Y. Fin. Writers Assn. award, 1980, Free Enterprise Man of the Yr. award Tex. A&M U. Ctr. for Edn. and Research in Free Enterprise, 1987, Women's Econ. Round Table award, 1990, 1st Hero of Wall Street award The Mus. of Am. Fin. History, 1998, Malcolm S. Forbes award for Excellence in Advancing Fin. Understanding, Fin. Planning Assn., 2000. Office: 586 Round Hill Rd Greenwich CT 06831-2724

RUKEYSER, M.S., JR. television consultant, writer; b. N.Y.C., Apr. 15, 1931; s. Merryle Stanley and Berenice (Simon) R.; children: Jill Victoria, Patricia Bern; m. Susan Gardiner Chopin, Mar. 10, 1997. Student, U. Va., 1948-52. Reporter Albany (N.Y.) Times-Union, 1949, Internat. News Service, N.Y.C., 1951; TV publicist Young & Rubicam, Inc., 1952-57; with NBC, 1958-80, 81-88, dir. news info., 1962, v.p. press and publicity N.Y.C., 1963-72, v.p. corp. info., 1972-74, v.p. pub. info., 1974-77, exec. v.p. pub. info., 1977-80, 81-84, exec. v.p. corp. communications, 1984-88; v.p. comm. Newsweek Inc., 1980-81; sr. v.p. GTG Entertainment, N.Y.C., 1988-90; pres. Rukeyser Communications, 1990—. Sr. fellow Freedom Forum Media Ctr., 1991-92. Author (with Grant Tinker): Tinker in Television: From General Sarnoff to General Electric, 1994. With U.S. Army, 1953—54. Home and Office: 216 Bahama Ln Palm Beach FL 33480-3308 E-mail: budruk@aol.com.

RUKEYSER, ROBERT JAMES, manufacturing executive, management consultant; b. New Rochelle, N.Y., June 26, 1942; s. Merryle Stanley and Berenice Helene (Simon) R.; m. Leah A. Spiro, July 26, 1964; children: David Bern, Peter Lloyd. BA, Cornell U., 1964; MBA with distinction, N.Y.U., 1969. Bond analyst Dun & Bradstreet, N.Y.C., 1964-65, Standard & Poors, N.Y.C., 1965-66; mktg. rep. data processing div. IBM, 1967-72, regional mktg. staff, 1973-74, mktg. mgr., 1974-76, corp. mgr. internal communications and editl. programs Armonk, N.Y., 1976-79, mgr. communication ops. Franklin Lakes, N.J., 1979-81; pub. affairs dir., asst. to chmn. Fortune Brands, Inc. (formerly Am. Brands, Inc.), N.Y.C., 1981-83, v.p. pub. affairs, asst. to chmn., 1983-85, v.p. office products Old Greenwich, Conn., 1986-87, v.p. ops., 1987-89, sr. v.p. corp. affairs, 1990-99. Bd. dirs. Fortune Brands (formerly Am. Brands Inc.); mgmt. cons. and author, 2000--. Bd. dirs., chair fin. com., mem. exec. com. The Hole in the Wall Gang Camp.; bd. dirs., mem. exec. com. Stamford Ctr. for Arts. Mem. Bus. Products Industry Assn.

RUKEYSER, WILLIAM SIMON, journalist; b. N.Y.C., June 8, 1939; s. Merryle Stanley and Berenice (Simon) R.; m. Elisabeth Mary Garnett, Nov. 21, 1963; children: Lisa Rukeyser Burn, James William. AB, Princeton U., 1961; rsch. student, Cambridge (Eng.) U., 1962—63; LittD (hon.) , Maryville Coll., 2002. Copyreader Wall St. Jour., 1961-62, staff reporter Europe, 1963-67; assoc. editor Fortune mag., 1967-71, mem. bd. editors, 1971-72; mng. editor Money mag., N.Y.C., 1972-80, Fortune mag., 1980-86; dir. internat. bus. devel. Time Inc., 1986-88; editor in chief, exec. v.p. Whittle Communications, Knoxville, Tenn., 1988-91; chmn., CEO, Whittle Books, 1991-94; pres. William Rukeyser, Inc., 1994—; editl. dir. Corporate Board Member mag., 1998—; contbg. editor CNN, 1995-97. Commentator Good Morning America, ABC-TV, 1978-85, CBS Radio Stas. News Svc., 1979-86; mem. nat. adv. coun. Maryville (Tenn.) Coll., 1998—; mem. adv. bd. Ctr. of Inquiry in Liberal Arts Wabash Coll., Crawfordsville, Ind., 2001—. Mem. jud. com. Union County (N.J.) Med. Soc., 1977-80; co-chair capital campaign Nat. Mental Health Assn., 1984-85; mem. liaison com. U. Tenn. Med. Ctr., 1992-99; vice chmn. U. Health Sys. Inc., 1999—; chmn. bd. dirs. Knoxville Jazz Orch. Office: 1001 First Tennessee Plz Knoxville TN 37929 E-mail: wsr@finehand.com.

RULAND, MIDLRED ARDELIA, retail executive, retail buyer; b. Draketown, Ga., Aug. 11, 1918; m. Harry Morse Ruland, Aug. 19, 1947; children: Hal Morse, Judy Lee Ruland Rigas. BS, West Ga. Coll., 1966. Elem. tchr., New London, Conn., 1947-48, Atlanta, 1948-51, Rome, 1951-81; mgr. McBrayer Bros. Furniture Co., 1981—. Rosenwald Found. scholar, 1941-42. Mem. NEA, Nat. Fedn. Ind. Bus. (corr. sec. 1975—), Ga. Edn. Assn. (del. 1964-74), Ga. Home Furnishings Assn., Twickham Garden Club, Rome Pride Assn., Rome C. of C., Alfa Delta Kappa. Republican. Baptist. Avocations: dancing, swimming, bowling, hiking, singing.

RULAND, RICHARD EUGENE, English and American literature educator, critic, literary historian; b. Detroit, May 1, 1932; s. Eugene John and Irene (Janette) R.; m. Mary Ann Monaghan; children: Joseph, Michael, Paul, Susan; m. Birgit Noll. BA, Assumption Coll. U. Western Ont., Can., 1953; MA, U. Detroit, 1955; PhD, U. Mich., 1960. Instr., then asst. prof. English and Am. studies Yale U., New Haven, 1960-67, Morse rsch. fellow, 1966-67; prof. English and Am. lit. Washington U., St. Louis, 1967—, chmn. dept. English, 1969-74; chmn. comparative lit. program, 1993-94. Vis. Bruern prof. Am. lit. Leeds (Eng.) U., 1964-65; vis. Fulbright prof. U. Groningen, The Netherlands, 1975, Sch. of English and Am. Studies U. East Anglia, Eng., 1978-79; vis. disting. prof. Am. lit. Coll. of William and Mary, 1980-81. Author: The Rediscovery of American Literature: Premises of Critical Taste, 1900-1940, 1967, America in Modern European Literature: From Image to Metaphor, 1976, (with Malcolm Bradbury) From Puritanism to Postmodernism: A History of American Literature, 1991 (paperback 1992), translation into Czech and Hungarian, 1997; editor: Walden: A Collection of Critical Essays, 1967, The Native Muse: Theories of American Literature, Vol. I, 1972, 76, A Storied Land: Theories of American Literature, Vol. II, 1976; contbr. articles to profl. jours. Guggenheim Rsch. fellow, 1982-83. Mem. Assn. Depts. English (pres. 1974). Avocation: jazz musician. Office: Washington U Dept English Saint Louis MO 63130 E-mail: rruland@artsi.wustl.edu.

RULAU, RUSSELL, numismatist, author, consultant; b. Chgo., Sept. 21, 1926; s. Alphonse and Ruth (Thorsen) R.; m. Hazel Darlene Grizzell, Feb. 1, 1968; children by a previous marriage: Lance Eric, Carla Rae, Russell A.W., Marsha June, Scott Quentin, Roberta Ann, Kyle Christopher. Student, U. Wis., 1946-48. Enlisted U.S. Army, 1944-50; transferred to USAF, 1950-62; master sgt. USAFR, 1963-73; asst. editor Coin World newspaper, Sidney, Ohio, 1962-74; editor World Coins mag., 1964-74, Numis. Scrapbook mag., 1968-74; editl. coord. How to Order Fgn. Coins guidebook, 1966-74; editor-in-chief World Coin News newspaper, 1974-84, Bank Note Reporter, 1983-84; fgn. editor Numis News newspaper, 1974-77; cons. editor Std. Catalog of World Paper Money, 1975-83; contbg. editor Std. Catalog of World Coins, 1974-81; pres. House of Rulau, 1984—, Alpha Enterprises Inc., 1989—. V.p. Keogh-Rulau Galleries, Dallas, 1984-85, Pobjoy Mint, Ltd., Iola, Wis., 1985-97, cons., 1997-98; U.S. agent Christie's Pty. Ltd., 1992-95; chmn. bd. dirs. Thorsen Estates, Inc., 1998—; apptd. mem. U.S. Assay Commn., 1973. Author: (with George Fuld) Spiel Marken, 1962-65, American Game Counters, 1972, World Mint Marks, 1966, Modern World Mint Marks, 1970, (with J.U. Rixen and Frovin Sieg) Seddelkatalog Slesvig Plebiscit Zone Iog II, 1970, Numismatics of Old Alabama, 1971-73, Hard Times Tokens, 1980, 96, 2001, Early American Tokens, 1981, U.S. Merchant Tokens 1845-1860, 1982, U.S. Trade Tokens 1866-1889, 1983, Tokens of the Gay Nineties, 1987, Discovering America: The Coin Collecting Connection, 1989, Latin American Tokens, 1992, 2000, (with George Fuld) Medallic Portraits of Washington, 1985, 99, Standard Catalog of U.S. Tokens 1700-1900, 1994, 97, 99, Tokens of Spain since 1800, 2002; contbr. articles to profl. jours. Sec. Numismatic Terms Standardization Com., 1966-74; vice-chmn. Waupaca County Rep. Party, 1977-79, 88-89, chmn., 1979-82; chmn. county chairmen, 3d vice chmn. Wis. Rep. Party, 1981-83; del. Rep. Nat. Conv., 1980; exec. com. 6th Wis. Dist. Rep. Com., 1984-87. Recipient Clemy Literary award, 1993, Smedley Lifetime Achievement award, 1994, Numismatic Ambassador award, 1995; elector Numismatic Hall of Fame, 1995—; inductee Numismatic Hall of Fame, 2000. Fellow Royal Numis Soc., Am. Numis Soc.; mem. Token and Medal Soc. (editor 1962-63, gold cataloging medals 1982, 83, 92), Am. Numis Assn. (merit medal 1995, Lifetime Achievement award 2000), Canadian Numis Assn., Am.-Israel Numis. Assn., Md. Token & Medal Soc., Numis Lit. Guild (dir. 1974-78, editor 1984-86. Best Specialized Book awards 1985, 89, 92, 94, 97, 99), VFW (post commdr. 1985-89. 96-2001), Am. Legion (11th Airborne Divsn. Assn.). Lutheran. Home: N7747 County J Iola WI 54945-9710 Office: Thorsen Estates Inc PO Box 153 Iola WI 54945-0153 E-mail: rviking@athenet.net.

RULE, CHARLES FREDERICK (RICK RULE), lawyer; b. Nashville, Apr. 28, 1955; s. Frederick Charles and Mary Elizabeth (Malone) R.; m. Ellen Friedland, May 13, 1976 BA, Vanderbilt U., 1978; JD, U. Chgo., 1981. Bar: U.S. Ct. Appeals. (D.C. cir.) 1983. Law clk. U.S. Ct. Appeals (fed. cir.), Washington, 1981-82; spl. asst. to asst. atty. gen. Antitrust div. Dept. Justice, 1982-83, dep. asst. atty. gen. policy planning, 1984-85, acting asst. atty. gen., then dep. asst. atty. gen. regulatory affairs, 1985-86, asst. atty. gen., 1986-89; ptnr. Covington & Burling, 1989-2001, Fried, Frank, Harris, Shriver & Jacobson, Washington, 2001—. Legal, econ. analyst Lexecon, Inc., Chgo., 1979-80 Mem. Bar of D.C. Ct. Appeals, Phi Beta Kappa, Phi Eta Sigma. Republican. Presbyterian. Office: Fried Frank Harris Shriver & Jacobson 1001 Pennsylvania Ave Nw Washington DC 20004-2505

RULE, JOHN CORWIN, history educator; b. Evanston, Ill., Mar. 2, 1929; s. Corwin V. and Elaine (Simons) R. AB, Stanford U., 1951, MA, 1952, Harvard U., 1955, PhD, 1958. Tutor and fellow Harvard U., Cambridge, Mass., 1956-58; instr. Northeastern U., Boston, 1955-56; from instr. to prof. history Ohio State U., Columbus, 1958—; vis. asst. prof. Western Res. U., Cleve., 1961; vis. prof. Johns Hopkins U., Balt., 1968. Editor and contbg. author: Louis XIV and the Craft of Kingship, 1970; editor: Louis XIV, 1974, Letters from the Hague and Utrecht, 1711-1712, 1979, The Reign of Louis XIV, 1990. Folger Shakespeare Library fellow, 1968,, 1970; Huntington Library fellow, 1978; Am. Council Learned Socs. fellow, 1981 Fellow Royal Hist. Soc. (London); mem. Soc. for French Hist. Studies (sec. 1963-70, assoc. editor jour. 1975-86, co-pres. 1989-91), Signet Soc., Crichton Club. Democrat. Home: 118 E Beck St Columbus OH 43206-1110 Office: Dept History Ohio State U 230 W 17th Ave Rm 106 Columbus OH 43210-1367

RULEY, STANLEY EUGENE, cost analyst; b. Akron, Ohio, Jan. 24, 1934; s. Royal Lovell and Opal Lenora (McDougall) R.; m. Annie Adam Patterson, Dec. 15, 1962; children: Cheryl Ann, Janice Lynn. Student, Kent State U., 1951-53; BSBA, Ohio State U., 1955. Registered profl. engr., Calif. Indsl. engr. Gaffers & Satler Inc., Hawthorne, Calif., 1961-62; mfg. engr. data systems div. Litton Industries Inc., Van Nuys, 1962-65; contract price analyst Naval Plant Rep. Office Lockheed, Burbank, 1966-72; contract negotiator Naval Regional Procurement, Long Beach, 1972-75; cost/price analyst Def. Contract Adminstrn. Services, Van Nuys, 1975-82; chief of contract pricing, dir. contracting Air Force Flight Test Ctr., Edwards AFB, Calif., 1982-89. Cons. engr., Northridge, Calif., 1971—. Served as sgt. U.S. Army, 1956-59. Recipient Sustained Superior Performance award Air Force Flight Test Ctr., 1984, Excellent Performance award Air Force Flight Test Ctr., 1982-83, Outstanding Performance award NAVPRO Lockheed, 1970. Mem. Am. Inst. Indsl. Engrs., IBM Computer User Group (Madison, Wis., Conn., San Fernando Valley), Air Force Assn. (life), Nat. Contract Mgmt. Assn. Clubs: Lockheed Employee Recreation (treas. Gem and Mineral 1976, pres. 1976), Camper (Burbank) (pres. 1974). Lodges: Masons (past master, 1992). Republican. Presbyterian. Avocations: flying, golf, camping, travel, computers. Home: 18751 Vintage St Northridge CA 91324-1529

RULIS, RAYMOND JOSEPH, manufacturing company executive, consultant; b. New Britain, Conn., June 2, 1924; s. James Alexander and Eva (Ragauskas) R.; m. Thelma Pelchat, June 16, 1949 (dec.); children: Elaine, Jeffery, Catherine, Elizabeth, Amy, Daniel, Jean; m. Virginia Kleene, Oct. 9, 1999. BSME, U. Conn., 1949; postgrad., U. Conn., Ohio State U., Northeastern U., 1949-58; student, Fed. Exec. Inst., Charlottesville, Va., 1976. Devel. engr. Hamilton Standard, U.T.C., Windsorlocks, Conn., 1951-55; mgr. fuel controls Lycoming Textron, Stratford, 1955-59; mgr. controls and accessories GE, Lynn, Mass., 1959-62; successively program mgr. sert spacecraft, chief spacecraft engr., chief launch vehicle engr., chief engring design, program mgr. QCSEE program NASA Lewis Rsch. Ctr., Cleve., 1962-81; v.p. rsch. and. devel. Textron Turbocomponents Group, Walled Lake, Mich., 1981-92; cons., 1992—. Cons. Joint FAA/NASA Civil Aero Rsch. Document Study, 1972, Cruise Missile PRogram, 1977-78, C-17 Aircraft Source Selection Bd., 1978, Tri-Svcs. Propulsion Group, 1976-78; chmn. Conf. on Short Haul Systems, NASA, 1976; mem. exec. coun. Aerospace Industries Tech. Coun., 1988-89. Contbr. articles to profl. jours.; patentee in field. Chmn. Boy Scouts Am. Fund Drives, Cleve., 1976-78; mem. Coun. on World Affairs, Cleve., 1976-81. Mem. Am. Helicopter Soc. (chmn. tech. session 1970), AIAA (chmn. tech. session 1965), Detroit Engring Soc., KC. Roman Catholic. Avocation: golf. Office: RJR Cons 9 Outpost Ln Hilton Head Island SC 29928-3820

RULISON, JOSEPH RICHARD, investment advisor; b. Syracuse, N.Y., May 14, 1956; s. Laurence M. and Catherine (Fox) R.; m. Karen Richards, Sept. 6, 1980; children: Elizabeth, Mallorie, Morgan, Abigail. BA, St. John Fisher Coll., 1978. Account exec. Prudential-Bache Securities, Rochester, 1982-84; investment exec. Tucker Anthony & R.L. Day, Inc., 1984-89; ptnr., ex v.p. Marsh Capital Mgmt., 1989-96; pres., CEO Rulison & Co., Inc., 1996—2001; founder, gen. mgr. Muniflow, 2001—. Trustee, past chmn. bd. trustees, past pres., hon. trustee Geva Theatre; vice chmn. St. John Fisher Coll.; treas. Monroe County Rep. Com.; chmn. County Monroe Indsl. Devel. Agy., Monroe County Greater Outdoor Sports Facility-Frontier Field, Monroe County Mid-Sized Arts Com.; past councilman Brighton Town Bd.; past mem. Brighton Planning Bd., Master Plan Com., Archtl. Rev. Bd.; bd. dirs. Rochester Cmty. Baseball, Camp Good Days and Spl. Times; trustee Rochester Mus. and Sci. Ctr. Mem. Genesee Valley Club (gov., house chmn.). Roman Catholic. Avocations: politics, theatre, art, wine. Office: Muniflow NY-UT-37602C 1 East Ave Rochester NY 14638 E-mail: Joseph_R_Rulison@fleet.com.

RUMAKER, MICHAEL, writer, English educator; b. Phila., Mar. 5, 1932; s. Michael Joseph and Winifred Marvel Rumaker. Honors degree in writing, Black Mountain Coll., 1955; MFA, Columbia U., 1970. Lectr. writing New Sch. for Social Rsch., N.Y.C., 1967-71; tchr. writer, mem. intellectual resources pool Tappan Zee H.S., Orangeburg, N.Y., 1965-69; instr. writing workshops Rockland Ctr. for Arts, West Nyack, 1975-78; adj. lectr. Rockland C.C., Suffern, 1978-87; writer-in-residence CCNY, CUNY, 1969-71, adj. prof., 1985—. Author: (novels) The Butterfly, 1962 (English edit., 1968, Russian edit., 2002), A Day and a Night at the Baths, 1979 (German edit. 1997), My First Satyrnalia, 1981, To Kill a Cardinal, 1992, Pagan Days, 2000, (short stories) Gringos and Other Stories, 1967, 2nd edit., 1991 (German edit. 1968, English edit. (Exit 3) 1966), (memoir) Robert Duncan in San Francisco, 1996, (memoir) Black Mountain Days, 2001. Mem. Nat. Writers Union. Literary Agent: Harold Ober Assocs 425 Madison Ave Rm 1001 New York NY 10017-1183 E-mail: mr6213@tco.com.

RUMBAUGH, CHARLES EARL, arbitrator, mediator, educator, lawyer, speaker, judge; b. San Bernardino, Calif., Mar. 11, 1943; s. Max Elden and Gertrude Maude (Gulker) R.; m. Christina Carol Pinder, Mar. 2, 1968; children: Eckwood, Cynthia, Aaron, Heather. BS, UCLA, 1966; JD, Calif. Western Sch. Law, 1971; cert. in advanced mgmt., U. So. Calif., 1993. Bar: Calif. 1972, U.S. Dist. Ct. (cen. dist.) Calif. U.S. Ct. Appeals (9th cir.), U.S. Supreme Ct. Engr. Westinghouse Electric Corp., Balt., 1966-68; legal counsel Calif. Dept. of Corps., L.A., 1971-77, Hughes Aircraft Co., L.A., 1977-84, asst. to corp. dir. contracts, 1984-89, asst. to corp. v.p. contracts, 1989-95; corp. dir. contracts/pricing Lear Astronics Corp., 1995-97; pres. Ctr. for Conflict Resolution, 1998-99. Arbitrator, mediator, comml., govt. contracts, internat. law, franchise, securities, torts, personal injury, real estate and constrn. panels Am. Arbitration Assn., L.A., San Francisco; former EEOC mediator, adminstrv. law judge; mem. arbitration and mediation panels ArbitrationWorks, 1994—, Nat. Assn. Security Dealers, Franchise Arbitration & Mediation, Inc., L.A. County Superior Ct., Santa Barbara County Superior Ct.; mem. panel pvt. alt. dispute resolution neutrals U.S. Ct. Fed. Claims; armed svcs. bd. of contract appeals panel of pvt. alt. dispute resolution neutrals, DLA panel of dispute neutrals, also settlement officer U.S. Dist. Ct.; alternative dispute resolution panel World Bank; faculty Calif. State U.; spkr. in field. Mem. editl. bd. Nat. Contract Mgmt. Jour., 1996-00; contbr. articles to profl. jours. Counselor Boy Scouts Am., L.A., 1976—; mem. City of Palos Verdes Estates (Calif.) Citizen's Planning Com., 1986—90; judge pro tem L.A. County Superior Ct. , L.A., 1991—2000. Fellow: Nat. Contract Mgmt. Assn. (pres. L.A./South Bay chpt. 1991—92, nat. dir. 1992—93, nat. v.p. southwestern region 1993—95, founder, chmn. alt. dispute resolution com., cert. profl. contracts mgr., nat. bd. advisors, Fellow of Yr. award 1994); mem.: FBA (pres. Beverly Hills chpt. 1992—93), ABA (founder fed. contracts dispute resolution com. dispute resolution sect, forum on franchising, forum on constrn. industry, pub. contract law sect., vice chair strategic alliance com.), Christian Legal Soc., Aerospace Industries Assn. (chmn. procurement techniques com. 1987—88, 1993—94), Soc. Profls. in Dispute Resolution (chmn. internat. sector com. 1996—2000, past bd. dirs. L.A. chpt.), State Bar Calif. (chmn. franchise law com. 2002—, Wiley W. Manual pro bono award 1992), Nat. Def. Indsl. Assn. (vice-chmn. west coast legal subcom. 1994—2000, procurement planning com. 1994—), Calif. Dispute Resolution Coun. (cons. to qualifications com. 1997—99), Nat. Assn. Purchasing Mgmt. (chair acquisition info.). Avocations: camping, skiing, jogging, equestrian. Office: PO Box 2636 Rolling Hills Estates CA 90274 E-mail: adroffice@ieee.org.

RUMBAUGH, MAX ELDEN, JR. professional society administrator; b. Ada, Okla., Dec. 11, 1937; s. Max E. and Gertrude (Gulker) R.; m. Joan E. Brockway; children: Maria Rumbaugh Gross, Max E. III. BS in Engring., U.S. Mil. Acad., 1960; MS in Engring. Scis., Purdue U., 1965, MBA, 1972. Instr. Purdue U., West Lafayette, Ind., 1964-65; corp. officer Midwest Applied Sci. Corp., 1965-72; chief engr. advanced tech. Schwitzer div. Wallace-Murray Corp., Indpls., 1972-77, dir. research, 1977-81; mgr. engring. activities div. Soc. Automotive Engrs., Warrendale, Pa., 1981-84, v.p., asst. gen. mgr., 1984-86, exec. v.p., 1986—; pres. Performance Rev. Inst., 1991—2001. Pres. Soc. Rsch. Adminstrs. Internat., 1973-74; chmn. Ind. sect. Soc. Automotive Engrs., 1978-79; bd. dirs., exec. com. Am. Nat. Standards Inst., N.Y.C., 1986—; bd. dirs. Intelligent Transp. Soc. of Am., 1992—, mem. exec. com., 1998—. Author mag. column Focus, 1986—. Bd. dirs. Jr. Achievement Western Pa., Pitts., 1986-98, YMCA, North Hills, Pitts., 1985-94; sec. Intelligent Transp. Soc. Am. Bd. Dirs., 2000—. 1st lt. U.S. Army, 1960-63. Mem. ASME, Am. Soc. Assn. Execs., Coun. Engring. and Sci. Soc. Execs. (bd. dirs. 1990-97, sec. 1993-94, v.p. 1994-95, pres. 1995-96), Russian Internat. Acad. Engring., Intelligent Transp. Soc. Am. (bd. dirs. 1992—, sec., chmn. fin. com. 2000—), Russian Acad. Quality Problems, Rotary (bd. dirs. 1982-84, 93-97, v.p. 1994-95, pres. 1995-96). Avocations: skiing, photography. Home: 320 Fort Duquesne Blvd Apt 25L Pittsburgh PA 15222-1141 Office: Soc of Automotive Engrs Inc 400 Commonwealth Dr Warrendale PA 15086-7511

RUMBERGER, JOHN ARTHUR, cardiologist; b. East Liverpool, Ohio, Dec. 16, 1948; s. John Arthur and Mary Alice (Duffy) R.; m. Susan L. Panzing, Dec. 15, 1973 (div. Aug. 1979); m. Suzanne Marie Rumberger, June 14, 1980; children: Meagan, Andrew. B in Aerospace/Astro Engring., MSc in Engring., Ohio State U., 1972, PhD in Engring., 1976; MD, U. Miami, 1978. Diplomate Am. Bd. Internal Medicine, Am. Bd. Cardiovascular Diseases. Rsch. assoc. Ohio State U., Columbus, 1969-76; instr. medicine Ohio State U. Hosp., 1978-81; instr., fellow U. Iowa Sch. Medicine, Iowa City, 1981-84, asst. prof., 1984-87; prof. medicine Mayo Clinic and Found., Rochester, Minn., 1987-98; dir. cardiac rehab. Grant Hosp., Columbus, Ohio, 1998—; med. dir. Ohio Heart, LLC, 1998—; assoc. Heartcare, Inc., 1998—; prof. dept. internal medicine Ohio State U., 1998—; nat. med. dir. Lifetest Imaging, 2000—01. Cons. Mayo Clnic and Found., Rochester, 1987—98. Contbr. numerous articles to profl. jours. Vice chair Am. Heart Assn., Dallas, 1995-99. Fellow: Am. Coll. Cardiology; mem.: Am. Heart Assn. (coun. on cardiovascular radiology, chair 2000—), Tau Beta Pi. Avocations: martial arts (2nd degree black belt). Office: Heartcare Inc/Ohio Heart 765 N Hamilton Rd Columbus OH 43230-1758 also: Ohio Heart 765 N Hamilton Rd Columbus OH 43230-1758 E-mail: rumbj@attglobal.net.

RUMBERGER, REGINA, retired English language educator; b. Pitts., Aug. 6, 1921; d. Edward T. and Margaret (Berry) Flynn; m. Wilson A. Rumberger, July 31, 1943 (div. 1974); children: Edward, Wilson J., Susan A., Gerard, Paul, Nancy, Joe. BEd, Duquesne U., 1942; MEd, U. Pitts., 1950; grad., State Office Div. Blind Svcs., Ft. Myers, Fla., 1984. Professed Lay Carmelite, 1990. Primary tchr. Allegheny County Pub. Sch., Pa., 1942-43, Sharpsburg (Pa.) Schs., 1943-50; instr. English, Edison C.C., Ft. Myers, 1964-78; ret., 1978. Media cons., Lee County and Ft. Myers, 1956; cons., evaluator State of Fla. and Lee County, 1987-88; cons., evaluator Lee County Dept. Transp., Ft. Myers, 1988-90. Chmn. water and safety ARC, Ft. Myers, 1960-65, first aid adminstr., 1965-68; pres. Lee County Med. Aux., 1965-66; consumer rep. Lee County Dept. Transp.; adv. bd. Met. Planning Orgn., Ft. Myers, 1990—; v.p. S.W. Fla. Curia, 1988—; asst. tour guide to Fr. Stanislaw Pierog, tour dir. Andrew's Pilgrimages, Stockbridge, Mass., 1990—; cons. on accessibility for handicapped Mayor's Alliance, mem. Coun. Disabled, 1991-92; cons., citizen adv. Divsn. Blind Svcs., State of Fla., 1990-91; vol. Lee Mem. Hosp., 1992, Caloosa Retirement Ctr., 1988-96; mem. coun. Lee County Bd. Parks and Recreation, 1994—; mem. citizen's adv. com. Metro. Planning Orgn., 1996—; amb. of Mass. Trans., State of Fla.; spokesperson for disabled Lee County Citizen Adv. Coun., mem.-at-large met. planning orgn., 1992—. Recipient award Boy Scouts Am., Ft. Myers, 1967, State of Fla., 1984, Ft. Myers Care Ctr./Lee Convalescence, 1990, Vol. of Yr., State of Fla., 1994, award Caloosa Retirement Ctr., 1996. Mem. AAUW (pub. rels. com. Ft. Myers 1987-90), Met. Planning Orgn. (mem.-at-large citizen adv. coun. 1992—, Ch. spkrs. bur., Mayors Alliance, 1999-01). Roman Catholic. Avocations: swimming, walking. Home: 2140 Cottage St Apt 109 Fort Myers FL 33901-3666

RUMBOUGH, STANLEY MADDOX, JR. industrialist; b. N.Y.C., Apr. 25, 1920; s. Stanley Maddox and Elizabeth (Colgate) R.; m. Nedenia Hutton, Mar. 23, 1946 (div. 1966); children: Stanley H., David P. (dec.), Nedenia Colgate; m. Margaretha Wagstrom, Dec. 21, 1967 (div. 1990); m. Janna Herlow, Mar. 8, 1990. AB, Yale U., 1942; postgrad. in bus. adminstrn., NYU, 1947-51. Vice pres., dir. Willis Air Service, Teterboro, N.J., 1946-47; v.p., dir. White Metal Mfg. Co., Hoboken, 1945-61, pres., 1960-61; pres., dir. Metal Container Corp., 1950-59, Am. Totalisator, Balt., 1956-58; chmn. bd. Extrusion Devel. Corp., 1959-61; co-founder, chmn. bd. Elec. Engring. Ltd., 1960-69; chmn. bd. Wallace Clark & Co., 1962-69; co-founder, dir. Trinidad Flour Mills, 1961-72, Jamaica Flour Mills, 1963-66; dir. Telemedia Inc., 1980-89. Spl. asst. to sec. Dept. Commerce, 1953; spl. asst. White House charge exec. br. liaison, 1953-55; founder Washington D.C. Tennis Patrons Found. Chmn. U.S. Com. for UN, 1957-58; co-founder Citizens for Eisenhower, 1951; vice chmn. Citizens for Eisenhower-Nixon Com., 1952; trustee Young Pres. Found., 1957-70, pres., 1962-65; bd. dirs. N.Y. World's Fair Corp., 1961-70, Nat. Conf. on Citizenship, 1973—, Population Resource Ctr., 1978-92, Planned Parenthood of Palm Beach Area, 1979-95, Planned Parenthood Fedn. Am., 1981-84, Kravis Ctr. Performing Arts; co-chmn., bd. dirs. Palm Beach Civic Assn.; trustee Libr. for Presdl. Papers, 1966-70, Internat. House, 1959—, Fgn. Policy Assn., 1961-70, Am. Health Found., 1972-76; Capt. USMCR, 1942-46. Decorated Air medal (8), D.F.C. (2). Mem. Chief Execs. Orgn., World Pres.'s Orgn., Young Pres.'s Orgn. (founding), Def. Orientation Conf. Assn., Racquet and Tennis Club, Internat. Lawn Tennis Club, Maidstone Club, Seminole Club, Bath and Tennis Club, Everglades Club, Nat. Golf Links Am. Club, Zeta Psi. Republican. Home: 655 Island Dr Palm Beach FL 33480-4744 Office: 44 Cocoanut Row Ste B103 Palm Beach FL 33480-4069

RUMFOLO, MARILU, financial analyst, non-profit corporation executive; b. Houston, July 19, 1953; d. Walter John and Lucille (Jones) R. Grad., Arrons Sch. Real Estate, 1978; student, U. Houston, 1979. Lic. real estate agt. Jr. acct. Gen. Leisure Corp., Houston, 1973-75; security cons. Burns Internat. Security, 1975-77; founder, dir. govt. affairs Time Energy Systems, Inc., 1977-83; founder, exec. dir., chmn. bd. trustees The Children's Drug Abuse Network, 1983—; founder, pres. Sun Am. Fin., LLC, 2000; general securities, principal, pres. founder Rumfolo & Assocs., Securities, LP, 2000—; founder, pres. Tex. Capital Securities, LLC, 2002. Bd. dirs. Eliza Johnston Home for Aging, Houston, 1981-82; chmn. bd. Citizens United for Pub. Edn., Houston, 1980-82; candidate city council, Houston, 1981, 83; team capt. Am. Heart Assn. Houston, 1982. Recipient Drugbuster award Children's Drug Abuse Network, 1985; honoree ann. appreciation breakfast for outstanding work in community, County Commr. Houston, 1986; named Rep. of Yr., Tex., 2001. Mem.: Order Eastern Star (officer 1986-87). Republican. Avocations: swimming, reading, writing poetry, walking. Office: Rumfolo & Assocs Securities LP 4708 Tamarisk Bellaire TX 77401

RUML, TREADWELL, English language educator; b. N.Y.C., Mar. 22, 1952; s. Alvin and Zona Ruml; m. Laura Susan Funkhouser, Dec. 30, 1990; children: James Alvin Treadwell, John Jordan Beardsley. AB, Harvard Coll., 1974, JD, 1977; PhD, U. Va., 1989. Assoc. Nutter, McClennan & Fish, Boston, 1977-80; lectr. in English U. Va., Charlottesville, 1989-90; asst. prof. Calif. State U., San Bernardino, 1990-94, assoc. prof., 1994—. Contbr. articles to profl. jours. Sec. faculty senate Calif. State U., San Bernardino, 1998-99. Mem. Am. Soc. for Eighteenth-Century Studies, Western Soc. for Eighteenth-Century Studies (pres. 1998-99, sec.-treas. 1999—) Samuel Johnson Soc. So. Calif. (newsletter editor 1999—). Office: Calif State U Dept English 5500 University Pkwy San Bernardino CA 92407-2318

RUMLER, DIANA GALE, geriatrics nurse; b. Manchester, Tenn., Feb. 23, 1943; d. Donald Yale and Thelma Irene (Beach) Miller; m. Herschel Hinkle, Aug. 1961 (div. Jan. 1978); children: David, John, Jody Hinkle West; m. Lester Rumler, Jr. (div. June 1984). AA in Nursing, Ind. U.-Purdue U., Indpls., 1974; BS in Pub. Health-Journalism-Psychology, Ball State U., 1983. RN, Ariz. Psychiat. nurse Meth. Hosp., Indpls., 1974-78; women's infant and children's coord. Cmty. & Family Svcs. Inc., Portland, 1978-81, Ball Meml. Hosp., Muncie, 1981-84; pub. health nurse Health & Rehab. Svcs., Ft. Lauderdale, Fla., 1984; med.-surg. nurse Holy Cross Hosp., 1985; pre-op-post-op nurse VA Med. Ctr., Nashville, 1986-89, nurse vascular, orthopedics, intensive care, telemetry, tchr. geriat. hospice chart auditing and rsch. data collector, relief staff coord. Tucson, 1990—. WIC advocate hearings/radio show, Ind., 1978-81; health vol. outreach clinic St. Mary's Hosp., Tucson, 1993-94; vol. Hospice Family Care, Tucson, Shalom House, Tucson, 1996-98. Contbr. articles to profl. jours. Vol. Hospice Family Care, Tucson, Shalom Ho., Tucson, 1996—98; health vol. outreach clinic St. Mary's Hosp., 1993—94. Mem. Nurses of Vet. Affairs, Ladies' Hermitage Assn. Democrat. Roman Catholic. Avocations: ceramics, crossstitch, health club activities, travel. Home: PO Box 11053 Chandler AZ 85248 Office: VA Med Ctr S 6th Ave Tucson AZ 85723-0001

RUMLER, ROBERT HOKE, agricultural consultant, retired association executive; b. Chambersburg, Pa., Apr. 4, 1915; s. Daniel Webster and Jennie (Sellers) R.; m. Frances Jeannette Montgomery, June 7, 1939 (dec. 1983); children: Craig M., Karen A. Loden; m. Hazel Miller-Karper, Aug. 23, 1986 (dec. 1998). BS, Pa. State U., 1936. Asst. county agt. U. Mo., 1936-37; county agrl. agt. Pa. State U., 1937-45; asst. mgr., editor agrl. promotion div. E. I. duPont de Nemours & Co., Inc., Wilmington, Del., 1945-48; asst. exec. sec. Holstein-Friesian Assn. Am., 1948-53, 53-75, exec. sec., chief exec. officer, 1975-81, exec. chmn., 1981-82, chmn. emeritus, 1982—. Pres. Holstein-Friesian Svcs., Inc., 1968-81; agribus. cons., 1982—; hon. mem. Holstein-Firesian de Mex. (C.A.); bd. dirs., chmn. Vt. Nat. Bank, Vt. Fin. Svcs., Inc., 1957-88; mem. U.S./USSR Joint Com. Agrl. Cooperation; past chmn. U.S. Agrl. Export Devel. Coun., FAS-USDA; mem. coordinating group Nat. Coop. Dairy Herd Improvement program USDA, 1964-80; mem. agrl. policy adv. com. USTR/USDA Multilateral Trade Negotiations, 1973-87, mem. agrl. tech. adv. com., 1987-95. Contbg. editorial writer Holstein World Trustee Ea. States Expn., trustee emeritus, 1993—; trustee Assoc. Industries Vt.; past bd. dirs. Internat. Stockmans Ednl. Found.; chmn. adv. bd. Pa. State U., Mont Alto, 1988-98, chmn. 1990-94, emeritus 1998; bd. advisors Pa. State U., Harrisburg, 1990-94. Recipient Disting. award Nat. Dairy Herd Improvement Assn., 1974, Disting. Svc. award Nat. Agrl. Mktg. Orgn., 1977, Cert. of Appreciation, USDA, 1982, Disting. Svc. award Holstein Assn., 1985; named Dist. Alumnus Pa. State U. Coll. Agr., 1978, 2000, Dairy Industry Man of Yr., World Dairy Expo, 1979, Headliner-of-Yr. Livestock Publs. Coun., 1995, Internat. Person of Yr. World Dairy Expo, 1996, 1st Disting. Alumnus AZ Fraternity Penn State, 1996, Disting. Alumnus, Pa. State U. Coll. Agrl., 2000; named to Internat. Livestock Hall of Fame, 1987; Robert H. Rumler scholar. Fellow Agr. Adventures; mem. Purebred Dairy Cattle Assn. (dir., exec. com.), Nat. Soc. Livestock Record Assns. (past pres., dir., Disting. Svcs. award 1981), Am. Dairy Sci. Assn. (Disting. Svc. award 1977), Agri-Bus. Found. (All-Time Gt. award 1981), Nat. Dairy Shrine (Dairy Hall of Fame 1976), N.E. Master Farmers Assn. (hon. master farmer 1999, Pa. Farm Bureau Disting. Svc. to Agr. award 1999), U.S. Animal Health Assn., Kiwanis, Masons, Elks, Alpha Zeta (hon. roll 1997), Gamma Sigma Delta. Mem. United Ch. of Christ. Home: 937 Wallace Ave Chambersburg PA 17201-3884 E-mail: bobrumler@pa.net.

RUMMAGE, STEPHEN MICHAEL, lawyer; b. Massillon, Ohio, Dec. 27, 1955; s. Robert Everett and Kathleen Patricia (Newman) R.; m. Elizabeth Anne Seivert, Mar. 24, 1979; children: Everett Martin, Carter Kevin. BA in History and English, Stanford U., 1977; JD, U. Calif., Berkeley, 1980. Bar: Wash. 1980, U.S. Dist. Ct. (we. dist.) 1980, U.S. Ct. Appeals (9th cir.) 1983, U.S. Supreme Ct. 1985. Assoc. Davis, Wright et al, Seattle, 1980-85; ptnr. Davis Wright Tremaine, 1986—. Co-author: Employer's Guide to Strike Planning and Prevention, 1985. Mem. Wash. Athletic Club. Democrat. Roman Catholic. Office: Davis Wright Tremaine 1501 4th Ave Ste 2600 Seattle WA 98101-1688 E-mail: steverummage@dwt.com.

RUMMAN, WADI (SALIBA RUMMAN), civil engineer, consultant; b. Beit-Jala, Palestine, Sept. 7, 1926; came to U.S., 1948, naturalized, 1959; s. Saliba Y. and Miladeh (Nasrallah) R.; m. Doris E. Reed, Sept. 6, 1955; children— Mary Elaine, Linda Jean. BSE, U. Mich., 1949, MSE, 1953, PhD, 1959. Field engr. Finkbeiner Pettis and Strout, Toledo, 1949; structural engr. Vogt, Ivers, Seaman and Assos., Cin., 1950-51, Giffels and Vallet, Inc., Detroit, 1951-52; instr. U. Mich., 1952-59, asst. prof. civil engring., 1959-64, assoc. prof., 1964-75, prof., 1975-88, prof. emeritus, 1988—. Cons. on design of reinforced concrete chimneys and other tower structures to industry and other agys. Author: Engineering, 1974, 3d edit., 1991. Fellow Am. Concrete Inst.; mem. ASCE (life), Am. Soc. Engring. Edn. (life), Internat. Assn. Bridge and Structural Engring., Sigma Xi, Chi Epsilon, Phi Kappa Phi. Home: 4648 Bayberry Cir Ann Arbor MI 48105-9762 Office: U Mich Dept Civil Engring Ann Arbor MI 48109 E-mail: wsrumman@umich.edu.

RUMMEL, EDGAR FERRAND, retired lawyer; b. New Bern, N.C., June 29, 1929; s. Robert French and Reba Jeanette (Burgess) R.; m. Lillian Hildebrandt, Dec. 28, 1954. BA, Ohio State U., 1955; JD, DePaul U., 1965; LLB, U. London, Eng., 1973; LLM, George Washington U., 1978. Bar: U.S. Dist. Ct. D.C. 1967, U.S. Ct. Appeals (D.C. cir.) 1968, U.S. Supreme Ct. 1971, Md. 1980. Atty.-adviser Dept. Army, Washington, 1971-74, 78, counsel U.S. Army Real Estate Agy., Frankfurt, W.Ger., 1975-77, supervisory atty.-adviser, asst. div. chief Office of Chief of Engrs., Dept. Army, Washington, 1977-83; sr. atty. advisor Office of Judge Advocate Gen., Dept. Army, Washington, 1983-85, trial atty., 1987; spl. asst. U.S. Atty. Dist. Colo., 1985-87, ret. 1987; chmn. mineral leasing com. Dept. Def., 1981-84; mem. Oreg. Nat. Trial Adv. Council, 1983-84. With AUS, 1947-51. Mem. Md. State Bar Assn. Democrat. Episcopalian (vestryman 1981-84). Home: 7812 Adelphi Ct Hyattsville MD 20783-1848

RUMMEL, HAROLD EDWIN, real estate development and retail sales executive; b. Youngstown, Ohio, Oct. 4, 1940; s. Harold Edward and Florence Louise (Hill) R.; children: Timothy B., Jonathan S., Briana. BS, U. Fla., 1963. Writer, editor various newspapers, Fla., 1958-70; polit. campaign mgr. various state campaigns, Tallahassee, 1971-79; sr. v.p. Fla. Fed. Sav. Bank, St. Petersburg, 1979-86; pres., CEO Rummel Cos. including The Rummel Real Estate Group, Inc., HardwareUSA.net, 1986—, Woodland Bay Group Inc., Mobile, Ala., 1986—. Pres., CEO Rummel Group Inc., Summer Court Inc., Azalea Apts. Inc., Dauphin Place Inc., Oak Knoll Inc., Bay Vista Inc. Active in civic and polit. orgns. Democrat. Avocations: nature, wildlife photography. Home: 1682 Oceanview Dr Tierra Verde FL 33715-2500 Office: Rummel Cos 1641 1st Ave N Saint Petersburg FL 33713-8935 E-mail: rumgroup@aol.com.

RUMMEL, ROBERT WILAND, aeronautical engineer, writer; b. Dakota, Ill., Aug. 4, 1915; s. William Howard and Dora (Ely) R.; m. Marjorie B. Cox, Sept. 30, 1939; children— Linda Kay, Sharon Lee, Marjorie Susan, Robert Wiland, Diana Beth. Diploma aeronautical engring., Curtiss Wright Tech. Inst. Aeros., 1935. Stress analyst Hughes Aircraft Co., Burbank, Calif., 1935-36, Lockheed Aircraft Corp., Burbank, 1936; draftsman Aero Engring. Corp., Long Beach, Calif., 1936, Nat. Aircraft Co., Alhambra, 1936-37; chief engr. Rearwin A/C & Engines, Inc., Kansas City, Kans., 1937-42; chief design engr. Commonwealth A/C, Inc., 1942-43; v.p. engring. Trans World Airlines, Inc., Mo., 1943-59, v.p. planning and research, 1959-69, v.p. tech. devel., 1969-78; pres. Robert W. Rummel Assos., Inc., Mesa, Ariz., 1978-87; aerospace cons., 1987—. Commnr. Presdl. Commn. Space Shuttle Challenger Accident, 1986; chmn. nat. rsch. coun. Aero Space Engring. Bd. Fellow Inst. Aero. Scis., Soc. Automotive Engrs.; mem. NAE, Masons (32 deg.), Shriners. Home and Office: 1189 Leisure World Mesa AZ 85206-3067 E-mail: RWRummel@aol.com.

RUMMELL, HELEN MARY, critical care and pediatrics nurse; b. Detroit, Dec. 5, 1942; d. William John and Helen (Robbins) Mohn; m. Larry L. Rummell, Aug. 1, 1964; children: Robin Renee, Richard William, Christopher Lee, Kathryn Elizabeth. BSN, U. Mich., 1964; MSN, UCLA, 1984; PNP, U. Cin., 1995. Cert. Brazelton newborn assessment examiner; cert. clin. nurse specialist; cert. PNP; cert. instr. pediat. advanced life support. Nurse specialist, neonatal intensive care Northridge (Calif.) Med. Ctr.; instr. pediat. Ohio State U., Columbus, 1985—87; neonatal nurse practitioner Riverside Meth. Hosp., 1987—88; clin. nurse specialist, cardiac care coord. cardiology-cardio vascular surgery Children's Hosp., 1988—2001; clin. nurse specialist pediatric cardiology Legacy Emanuel Children's Hosp., Portland, Oreg., 2001—. Contbr. articles to profl. jours. Mem. Am. Heart Assn., Soc. Pediat. Cardiovasc. Nurses, Sigma Theta Tau (chpt. pres.). Home: 12535 NW Lilywood Dr Portland OR 97229

RUMMER, KENNETH DALE, pastor; b. Lawrence, Kans., Feb. 2, 1951; s. Dale Ivan and Patricia Ann (Burnham) R.; m. Myrna Belle Hooper, Aug. 10, 1974; children: Timothy James, Tricia Marie. BSEE, Mich. State U., 1973; MDiv, U. Dubuque Theol. Sem., Dubuque, Iowa, 1976. Ordination to Ministry of Word and Sacrament, Presbyn. Ch., 1976. Asst. pastor Douglas Ave Presbyn Ch., Des Moines, 1976-80; pastor First Presbyn. Ch., Corning, Iowa, 1980—. Den leader, cubmaster Cub Scout Pack #124, Corning, Iowa, 1987-96; chair Ctrl. Pk. Com., Corning, 1990—; chair Main St. Design Com., Corning, 1990-95, pres., 1996-98; moderator Presbytery of Des Moines Presbyn. Ch., 1988; mem. Permanent Jud. Commn. Synod of Lakes & Prairies Presbyn. Ch. (USA), 1990-98. Avocations: playing violin, reading sci. fiction, woodworking. Home: 905 Grove Ave Corning IA 50841-1343 Office: 1st Presbyn Ch 907 Grove Ave Corning IA 50841-1343

RUMNEY, LYNNE S. musician, educator; b. Omaha, Mar. 17, 1968; d. Wallace Gale and Marcia (Shaffer) Haggard; m. Jon Marc Rumney, Dec. 23, 1992. AB in English, Princeton U., 1990; MusM in Violin Performance, Eastman Sch. Music, 1992. Violin instr. in pvt. practice, Minot, N.D., 1993—; freelance violinist, freelance editor, 1994—; lectr. of humanities Minot State U., 1995—; concertmaster Bismarck (N.D.)/Mandan Symphony, 1996-99; adminstrv. dir. Dakota Chamber Music, Minot, 1996—. U.S. Presdl. scholar, 1986; recipient Isidore and Helen Sacks prize Princeton U. Dept. Music, 1990. Mem. Phi Beta Kappa. Democrat. Methodist. Home: 628 24th Ave NW Minot ND 58703-0938 Office: Minot State U 500 University Ave W Minot ND 58707-0002

RUMPEL, PETER LOYD, architect, educator, artist; b. Hamilton, Ont., Can., Mar. 25, 1939; s. George Hilburn and Reine (Loyd) R.; children: Hillary, Reine. BArch, U. Fla., 1961. Registered architect. Architect Clements, Rumpel, Assocs., Jacksonville, Fla., 1976-84; architect Clements, Rumpel, Goodwin, d'Avi, 1984—, CRG Archs./Planners, Inc., 1992; assoc. prof. U. Fla., Gainesville, 1984-92. Adj. prof. U. Fla., 1982-84; disting. lectr. 1984-92; chmn. Hist. Archtl. Rev. Bd., St. Augustine, Fla., 1999. Prin. works include Fla. Jr. Coll. Jacksonville-N. Campus (honor award Fla. Assn. AIA 1979, merit award Jacksonville chpt. AIA 1972), River Garden Hebrew Home for Aged (Modern Nursing Home of Month award 1971, hon. mention Fla. Assn. AIA 1971, merit award Jacksonville chpt. AIA 1972), Fla. Christian Home Apts. (award merit Fla. Assn. AIA 1973, merit award Jacksonville chpt. AIA 1974, 4th ann. award Outstanding Concrete Structure in Fla. 1974), St. Mary's Episcopal Ch. Renovation (honor award Jacksonville chpt. AIA 1974, award merit Fla. Assn. AIA 1974), Rumpel Residence (first award Jacksonville chpt. Am. Plywood Assn. 1974, honor award Jacksonville chpt. AIA 1974, award merit AIA Homes for Better Living Program 1975), Higginson Residence (merit award Jacksonville chpt. AIA 1974), Sawgrass Harbor Condominiums (award merit Jacksonville chpt. AIA 1975), Sawgrass Golf Club (citation Jacksonville chpt. AIA 1975), Jacksonville Jewish Ctr. (honor award Fla. Assn. AIA 1976, citation Jacksonville chpt. AIA 1977), U. N. Fla. Lab.-Office Bldg. (merit award Jacksonville chpt. AIA 1977), Fla. Jr. Coll., S. Campus, Phase II (honor award Jacksonville chpt. AIA 1977), Drew Bldg. Renovation (merit award Jacksonville chpt. AIA 1978), Mayport Jr. High Sch. (merit award Jacksonville chpt. AIA 1978, award merit Fla. Assn. AIA 1978, First Ann. Gov.'s Design award 1981), T.R.E.E.O. U. Fla. (honor award Jacksonville chpt. AIA 1979, honor award Fla. Assn. AIA 1979), Officer's Conf. Ctr., Camp Keystone (merit award Jacksonville chpt. AIA 1980), St. James Community Life Ctr. (honor award Jacksonville chpt. AIA 1981), U. N. Fla. student activity ctr. (honor award Jacksonville chpt. AIA 1982, award excellence Fla. Assn. AIA 1982), Unenlisted Personnel Housing (award merit ASID 1983), Hurley Manor Elderly Housing (award excellence Jacksonville chpt. AIA 1984), Arlington By the River (honor award Jacksonville chpt. AIA 1984, award excellence Jacksonville chpt. AIA 1984), 120-Bed Nursing Home Care Unit (honor award Jacksonville chpt. AIA 1984, award excellence Concrete Inst. Fla. 1984), Fla. A&M U. Sch. Architecture Bldg. (honor award Jacksonville chpt. AIA 1985), Drew Bldg. (design recognition award Jacksonville area C. of C. 1984, preservation award City of Jacksonville and Jacksonville Hist. Landmarks Com. 1985), Cypress Village Apts. (award for excellence Jacksonville chpt. AIA 1991), Drew Bldg. Renovation (Merit award Jacksonville chpt. AIA. 1989), Bachelor Enlisted Quarters and Enlisted Men's Dining Facility (Significant Concrete Structure Fla. First Coast chpt. ACI 1994), Additions and remodeling Pine Forest Elem. Sch. (award for excellence Jacksonville chpt. AIA 1995). Pres. Jacksonville Community Design Ctr.; mem. Jacksonville Hist. Landmarks Com., 1981-84; chmn. Hist. Archtl. Rev. Bd., 1998. Served with USMC. Recipient First award to design new sch. architecture at Fla. A&M U., 1980, Dist. Alumni award U. Fla., 1995, Millennium award of honor Design Fla. Assn., 2000. Fellow AIA (Honor award Fla. chpt. 1981, John Dyal award Jacksonville chpt. 1985, Honors award Jacksonville chpt. 2002). Democrat. Episcopalian. E-mail: duoarch.aol.com. Home: 133 Marine St Saint Augustine FL 32084-5003 Office: CRG Architects Planners Inc 2111 Corporate Square Blvd Jacksonville FL 32216-1919 E-mail: crgarch@aol.com.

RUMSCHITZKI, DAVID SHELDON, chemical engineering educator; BS in Chem. Engring. and Math., Cooper Union, 1978; MS in Chem. Engring., U. Calif., Berkeley, 1979, PhD in Chem. Engring., 1984. Process engr. Stauffer Che. Co., Dobbs Ferry, N.Y., summer 1978; rsch. engr. Mobil R&D Corp., Paulsboro, N.J., summer 1984; asst. prof. dept. chem. engring. CCNY,

1983-84, 85-89, assoc. prof., 1990-96, prof., 1997—. Vis. scientist Max Planck Inst. fur Biophys. Chemistry, Gottingen, Germany, 1985, dept. molecular biology Rsch. Inst. Scripps Clinic, La Jolla, Calif., 1988-89, dept. biophysics Rohr U. Bochum, Germany, 1996-97. Alexander von Humboldt fellow, 1996-97; recipient Frederick Urban Meml. scholarship for excellence in chem. engring., 1978, Harry W. Reddick Fund prize and medal for math., 1978, Standard Oil Co. fellowship, 1978, 79, Presdl. Young Investigator award NSF, 1987-93, Best Papter award ASME Bioengring. Divsn., 1995-96, Melville medal ASME, 1996. Mem. Sigma Pi Sigma, Tau Beta Pi, Sigma Xi. Office: Dept Chem City Coll NY 140th St Convent Ave New York NY 10031 E-mail: David@che.ccny.cuny.edu.

RUMSEY, VICTOR HENRY, electrical engineering educator emeritus; b. Devizes, Eng., Nov. 22, 1919; s. Albert Victor and Susan Mary (Norman) R.; m. Doris Herring, Apr. 2, 1942; children: John David, Peter Alan, Catherine Anne. BA, Cambridge U., 1941, DSc in Physics, 1972; DEng, Tohoku U., Japan, 1962. With U.K. Sci. Civil Service, 1941-48; asst. to asso. prof. Ohio State U., 1948-54; prof. U. Ill., 1954-57, U. Calif., Berkeley, 1957-66, prof. elec. engring. and computer scis. San Diego, 1966-87, prof. emeritus, 1987—, dept. chmn., 1977-81. Author 1 book in field; contbr. articles to profl. jours.; patentee in field. Guggenheim fellow.; recipient George Sinclair award Ohio State U., 1982 Fellow IEEE (Morris Liebman prize), Union Radio Scientifique Internationale, Internat. Astron. Union; mem. Nat. Acad. Engring. Home: 1171 Bohemian Ln Occidental CA 95465-9115

RUMSFELD, DONALD HENRY, federal official, former corporate executive; b. Chgo., July 9, 1932; s. George Donald and Jeannette (Husted) R.; m. Joyce Pierson, Dec. 27, 1954; 3 children. AB, Princeton U., 1954; hon. degree, De Paul U. Coll. Commerce, Ill. Coll., Lake Forest Coll., Park Coll., Tuskegee Inst., Nat. Coll. Edn., Bryant Coll., Claremont (Calif.) Grad. Sch., Ill. Wesleyan U., RAND Grad. Sch., Hampden-Sydney Coll. Adminstrv. asst. U.S. Ho. of Reps., 1957-59; with A.G. Becker & Co., Chgo., 1960-62; mem. 88th-91st Congresses from 13th Ill. dist., Pres. Richard Nixon's Cabinet, 1969-73; dir. OEO, asst. to pres., 1969-70; counsellor to Pres., dir. econ. stabilization program, 1971-72; U.S. ambassador and permanent rep. to NATO, 1973-74; chief of staff for Pres. Gerald Ford, mem. Cabinet, 1974-75; sec. Dept. Def., 1975-77; pres., chief exec. officer, then chmn. G.D. Searle & Co., Skokie, Ill., 1977-85; spl. envoy of Pres. Ronald Reagan to Mid. East, 1983-84; sr. advisor William Blair & Co., Chgo., 1985-90; chmn., chief exec. officer General Instrument Corp., 1990-93; chmn. bd. dirs. Gilead Scis., Inc., Foster City, Calif., 1997—2001; sec. of def., 2001—. Bd. dirs. Amylin Pharms., Inc., Asea Brown Boveri, Ltd., Tribune Co.; bd. trustees RAND Corp., 1977—; chmn. U.S. Commn. to Assess the Ballistic Missile Threat to the U.S., 1998; commr. U.S. Fed. Trade Deficit Rev. Commn., 1999, U.S. Commn. to Assess Nat. Security Space Mgmt. and Orgn., 2000—. Naval Aviator USN, 1954-57. Recipient Presdl. Medal of Freedom, 1977, George Catlett Marshall award, Woodrow Wilson award, Dwight David Eisenhower medal. Office: Department of Defense 1000 Defense Pentagon Washington DC 20301-1000*

RUMSFELD, HERBERT WILLIAM, JR. retired obstetrician, gynecologist; b. Oak Park, Ill., Dec. 24, 1925; MS in Biochemistry, U. Wis., 1952, PhD in Biochemistry, 1953; MD, U. Tex. SW, 1962. Diplomate Am. Bd. Ob-gyn. Intern Parkland Meml. Hosp., Dallas, 1962-63, resident in ob-gyn., 1963-66; ret., 1994. Instr., assoc. prof. biochemistry U. Tex. Southwestern Med. Sch., 1953-62; clin.asst. prof., clin. prof. U. Tex. Southwestern Med. Sch., 1966-94. Fellow Am. Coll. Ob-gyn., Am. Coll. Surgeons; mem. AMA, Alpha Omega Alpha. E-mail: grie@worldnet.att.net.

RUMYANTSEV, SERGEY L. research scientist, educator; b. St.Petersburg, Russia, June 26, 1954; arrived in U.S., 1998; s. Lev Rumyantsev, Galina S. Rumyantseva; m. Irina D. Shurygina, Apr. 29, 1952; 1 child Vladimir 1 child Irina 1 child Alexandra Rumyantseva. Master, Inst. Elec. Tech., St. Petersburg, 1977; PhD, State Tech. U., St. Petersburg, Russia, 1987; DSc, Ioffe Inst., St. Petersburg, Russia, 1997. Sr. engr. "Svetlana" Corp., St. Petersburg, Russia, 1980—88; leading scientist Ioffe Inst. of Russian Acad. Scis., Russia, 1989—; rsch. prof. Rensselaer Poly. Inst., Troy, NY, 1998—. Vis. rschr. Simon Frazer U., Vancouver, Canada, 1996—98. Editor: (book) "Handbook Series of Semiconductor Parameters, v.1: Elementary Semiconductors and A3B5 Compounds, Si, Ge, C, GaAs,GaP,GaSb, InAs,InP,InSb., 1996, Handbook Series of Semiconductor Parameters, v.2: Ternary and Quarternary A3B5 Compounds, AlGaAs, GaInP, GaInAs, GaInSb, GaAsSb, InAsSb, GaInAsP, GaInAsSb., 1999; author: (book) Properties of Advanced Semiconductor Materials: GaN, AlN, InN, BN, SiC, SiGe , 2001; contbr. articles to profl. jours., chapters to books. Recipient prize for the best paper, Ioffe Inst., 1989, 1995, prize for the best paper of Solid State Electronics Divsn., 1999, 2000. Achievements include research in physics of semiconductors and semiconductor devices; microwav devices; wide band gap semiconductors (SiC, GaN, CdS); noise in microwave and optical devices; power Si, SiC, GaN devices; Si bipolar and Field Effect Transistors; organic semiconductors. Office: Rensselaer Polytech Inst CII 9015 110 8th St Troy NY 12180 Office Fax: 518-276-2990. Business E-Mail: roumis2@rpi.edu.

RUNCK, ROBERT RIDGWAY, publishing executive; b. Lincoln, Nebr., June 4, 1935; s. Roger John and Theodora May (Ridgway) R.; m. Sallie Ann Rowe, June 2, 1962; 1 child, Brian Christian. BA, Ohio State U., 1958. Sr. editor Holt, Rinehart & Winston, N.Y.C., 1962-67; exec. editor Scott, Foresman & Co., Glenview, Ill., 1967-79; editorial dir. D.C. Heath & Co., Lexington, Mass., 1979-82; pres., pub. Ballinger Pub. Co., Cambridge, 1982-84, Brick House Pub. Co., Amherst, N.H., 1984-90; dir. prod. devel. Am. Mgmt. Assn., Watertown, Mass., 1991-94; exec. dir. Nat. Assn. Desktop Pubs., Topsfield, 1995-97; editor-in-chief Desktop Pubs. Jour., 1995-97; sr. v.p., pub. Victory, Inc., Worcester, Mass., 1998—2001. Chmn. faculty rels. com. higher edn. divsn. Assn. Am. Pubs., N.Y.C., 1982-83. With USAR, 1959-62. Avocations: community theater, acting, producing, directing. Office: Prentice Hall 160 Gould St Needham MA 02494 E-mail: rrunck@macconnect.com.

RUNCO, MARIO, JR. astronaut; b. Bronx, N.Y., Jan. 26, 1952; s. Mario and Filomena (Ragusa) Runco; m. Susan Kay Friess; 2 children. BS in Meteorology and Physical Oceanography, CCNY, 1974; MS in Meteorology, Rutgers U., New Brunswick, N.J., 1976; DSc (hon.) , NYU, N.Y.C., 1999. Rsch. hydrologist U.S. Geol. Survey, Long Island, NY, 1976—77; state trooper N.J. State Police, 1977—78; commd. ensign USN, 1978; rsch. meteorologist Navy Oceanogrphic and Atmospheric Rsch. Lab., Monterey, Calif., 1978—81; meteorol. officer USS Nassau, 1981—83; lab. instr. Naval Postgrad. Sch., Monterey, 1984—85; comdg. officer USNS Chauvenet , 1985—86; fleet environ. svcs. officer USN, Pearl Harbor, Hawaii, 1986—87; astronaut NASA Johnson Space Ctr., Houston, 1987—. Decorated 3 Space Flight medals NASA; recipient Townsend Harris medal, CCNY, 1993. Achievements include 3 space flights, 551 hours in space and one of 48 astronauts to take a space walk. Avocations: baseball, camping, hockey, astronomy, model building. Office: Astronauts Office Johnson Space Ctr Houston TX 77058

RUND, DOUGLAS ANDREW, emergency physician; b. Columbus, Ohio, July 20, 1945; s. Carl Andrew and Caroline Amelia (Row) Rund; m. Sue E. Padavana, 1980; children: Carie, Emily, Ashley. BA, Yale U., 1967; MD, Stanford U., 1971. Lic. physician Ohio, diplomate Nat. Bd. Med. Examiners, Am. Bd. Family Practice, Am. Bd. Emergency Medicine . Intern U. Calif. San Francisco-Moffett Hosp., 1971—72; resident in gen. surgery Stanford U., 1972—74, Robert Wood Johnson Found. clin. scholar in medicine, 1974—76; med. dir. Mid-Peninsula Health Svc., Palo Alto, Calif., 1975—76; clin. instr. dept. medicine and preventive medicine Stanford U. Med. Sch., 1975—76; assoc. prof., dir. divsn. emergency medicine Ohio State Coll. Medicine, 1982—87, dir. emergency medicine residency program, assoc. prof. dept, 1976—87, prof., chmn. dept. preventive medicine, 1988—90, prof., chmn. dept. emergency medicine, 1990—, prof., interim chmn. dept. family medicine, 1994—95, assoc. dean, 2001—. Attending staff Ohio State U. Hosps., 1976—; med. dir. CSCC, Emergency Med. Svcs. Dept.; pres. Internat. Rsch. Inst. Emergency Medicine; sr. rsch. fellow NATO: Health and Med. Aspects of Disaster Preparedness, 1985—87; mem. Residency Rev. Com. for Emergency Medicine, 1997—; vis. epidemiology and injury control U. Edinburgh, Scotland, 1987; working group, emergency and critical care in space NASA, 2001—; bd. dirs. Am. Bd. Emergency Medicine , 1988—97, sr. editor in tng. exam. , 1989—, pres., 1995—. Author: Triage, 1981, Essentials of Emergency Medicine, 1982, 2d edit., 1986, Emergency Radiology, 1982, Emergency Psychiatry, 1983, Environmental Emergencies, 1985; editor: Emergency Medicine Ann., 1983—84, Emergency Medicine Survey, Annals of Emergency Medicine, Annals of Emergency Medicine Symposium, 1986; editor: (in chief) Ohio State Series on Emergency Medicine, Emergency Medicine Observer, 1986—87; mem. editl. bd. : Physician, Sports Medicine, Emergency Med. Svcs.; co-author: Family Medicine Priciples and Practice, 1978, 2d edit., 1983; contbr. articles to profl. jours. Recipient Faculty Tchg. award, Ohio State U. Coll. Medicine Alumni Assn., 1999. Fellow: Am. Coll. Emergency Physicians (task force on substance abuse and injury control); mem.: IAAA, Internat. Soc. for Emergency Med. Svcs. (med. dir.), Columbus Med. Forum (pres. 1993—), Soc. Acad. Emergency Medicine (chmn. internat. com. 1991—), Assn. Acad. Chairs Emergency Medicine (pres. 1992—93), Nat. Inst. on Alcohol Abuse and Alcoholism, Alpha Omega Alpha. Office: Ohio State U HSL 016 376 W 10th Ave Columbus OH 43210-1240

RUNDE, CRAIG ERIC, academic director; b. St. Petersburg, Fla., Apr. 12, 1951; s. Harold Edward and Geraldine Major Runde; m. Kathleen Bridget Fenn, July 9, 1978; 1 child, Matthew Ehren. BA, Harvard U., 1973; JD, Duke U., 1978; M in Law Librarianship, U. Denver, 1979. Bar: Colo. 1978, U.S. Dist. Ct. Colo. 1978. Pvt. practice law, Denver, 1979-82; mgr. West Pub. Co., St. Paul, 1982-97; dir. Internat. Ctr. for Computer Enhanced Learning Wake Forest U., Winston-Salem, N.C., 1997-2000; dir. new program devel. Eckerd Coll., St. Petersburg, Fla., 2000—. Com. chair Winston-Net, Winston-Salem, 1997. Contbr. to book: The Learning Revolution, 1997. Pres. Minn. Youth Symphonies, St. Paul, 1995; bd. dirs. Triad Info. Reading Svc., Winston-Salem, 1999; tutor Forest Park Elem. Sch., Winston-Salem, 1998; mem. Crossing 52, Winston-Salem, 1998. Harvard Nat. scholar, 1969. Mem. Educause. Avocation: social service. Office: Eckerd Coll 4200 54th Avenue S Saint Petersburg FL 33711 E-mail: rundece@eckerd.edu.

RUNDEL, PHILIP WILSON, environmentalist, consultant, science educator; b. Palo Alto, Calif., Aug. 7, 1943; s. Morton Stanley and Marion Dean Rundel; children: Alexandra Saxon, Colin Witter, Tyler Wilson. PhD, MA, Duke U., Durham, North Carolina, 1965—69; BA, Pomona Coll., Claremont, california, 1961—65. Prof. U. of Calif., Irvine, Irvine, Calif., 1969—82, U. of Calif., LA (UCLA), Los Angeles, 1983—. Dir. Stunt Ranch Santa Monica Mountain Res., Calabasas, Calif., 1994—; cons. WWF, Hanoi, Vietnam, 1998—2000; exec. bd. Internat. Soc. for Mediterranean Ecology, 1991—98; dir. of the mus. of systematic biology U. of Calif., Irvine, Calif., 1980—82. Author: (scholarly book) Ecological communities and processes in a Mojave Desert ecosystem.; editor: Landscape disturbance in mediterranean-type ecosystems., Tropical alpine ecosystems: plant form and function., Physiological plant ecology: field methods and instrumentation., Stable isotope ratios in ecological research. Recipient Disting. Tchg. Aeward, UCLA, 2000-2001; fellow fellowship, Alexander von Humboldt Found., 1976, Vis. Fellow, East-West Ctr., Honolulu, 1978, Environ. Fellow, U.S. Asia Found., 1995. Mem.: Soc. for Conservation Biology (assoc.), Orgn. for Tropical Studies (assoc.; rsch. com. mem. 2001—02), Assn. for Tropical Biology (assoc.), Brit. Ecol. Soc. (assoc.), Ecol. Soc. of Am. (assoc.; pres. of the physiol. ecology sect. 1980—82). Avocations: travel, gardening, reading. Office: University of California Los Angeles Los Angeles CA 90095 Home Fax: 310-825-9433; Office Fax: 31- 825-9433. Personal E-mail: rundel@biology.ucla.edu. E-mail: rundel@biology.ucla.edu.

RUNDELL, ORVIS HERMAN, JR. psychologist, educator; b. Oklahoma City, June 16, 1940; s. Orvis Herman and Virginia Reid (George) R.; m. Jane Shannon Brians, June 25, 1966; children: Leslie Jane, Anne Reid. BS, U. Okla., 1962, MS, 1972, PhD, 1976. Lab. mgr. Okla. Ctr. Alcohol and Drug-Related Studies, Oklahoma City, 1969-76, staff scientist, 1974—. Asst. prof. psychiatry and behavioral scis. U. Okla. Health Sci. Center, 1976—; dir. clin. physiology and sleep disorders ctr. Columbia Presbyterian Hosp., Oklahoma City, 1982-2001; clin. dir. Diagnostic Sleep Ctr. of Dallas, 1989-93; ptnr. Sleep Medicine Assocs., 1994—, Sleep Assocs., 2000—; dir. Columbia Sleep Ptnrs. Program, 1996-2001; clin. dir. The Sleep Clinic, Oklahoma City, 2000—, Sleep Labs PRN, 2001—; cons. in field; instl. rev. bd. U. Okla. Health Sci. Ctr., 1989-2001. Contbr. articles to profl. jours., chpts. in books; asst. editor Alcohol Tech. Reports, 1976-90; cons. editor Psychophysiology, 1974-2001. Bd. dirs. Hist. Preservation, Inc., Oklahoma City, 1978-90. With USAR, 1963-69. Grantee Nat. Inst. Drug Abuse, Nat. Inst. Alcohol Abuse and Alcoholism. Fellow Am. Acad. of Sleep Medicine; mem. N.Y. Acad. Scis., Psi Chi, Phi Gamma Delta. Home: 431 NW 20th St Oklahoma City OK 73103-1918 Office: 5530 N Francis Oklahoma City OK 73118 Fax: 405-879-2476. E-mail: zzzs@cox.net.

RUNDHAUG, JOYCE ELIZABETH, biochemist, former nurse; b. Seattle, Sept. 8, 1952; d. Robert Norman and Elsie Elizabeth (Ohm) Ball; m. William George Rundhaug, July 16, 1977. BSN, U. Md., Balt., 1974; PhD, U. Hawaii, 1989. Teaching asst. S.W. Tex. State U., San Marcos, 1978-80, U. Hawaii, Honolulu, 1980-81, rsch. asst., 1982-89; staff fellow Nat. Inst. Environ. Health Sci., Research Triangle Park, N.C., 1989-92; rsch. assoc. M.D. Anderson Cancer Ctr. Sci. Park, U. Tex., Smithville, 1992—2000, asst. prof. M.D. Anderson Cancer Ctr. Sci. Park, 2000—. Contbr. articles to jours. Cancer Rsch., Carcinogenesis, Jour. Cellular Physiology, Molecular Carcinogenesis. Capt. U.S. Army, 1970-77. Walter Reed Army Inst. Nursing scholar, 1970-74, Achievement Rewards for Coll. Scientists scholar, 1987. Mem. AAAS, Am. Assn. Cancer Rsch., N.Y. Acad. Scis., Phi Kappa Phi. Office: MD Anderson Cancer Ctr Sci Park-Rsch Divsn PO Box 389 Smithville TX 78957-0389 E-mail: jerundhaug@sprd1.mdacc.tmc.edu.

RUNDIO, JOAN PETERS (JO RUNDIO), public administrator; b. Dearborn, Mich., Mar. 17, 1941; d. Joe and Donna (Sells) Peters; m. Florian (Pug) Frank Rundio Jr., Sept. 8., 1971; children: Jeffrey Daniel, David Eric. Diploma, Bronson Meth. Sch. Nursing, 1962; BA, U. Redlands, 1978; MPA, U. South Ala., 1987. RN, Mich. Emergency nurse Bronson Meth. Hosp., Kalamazoo, 1962-63, The Queen's Med. Ctr., Honolulu, 1963-65; orthopaedic nurse The Honolulu Med. Group, 1965-72; sch. nurse Corpus Christi (Tex.) Sch. Dist., 1979-81; pub. health nurse Tri-County Health Dept., Traverse City, Mich., 1983-85; adminstrv. intern City of Troy (Mich.), 1987-88; acting econ. devel. dir. City of Traverse City, 1988-89; mgr. personal health svcs. Tri-County Health Dept., Traverse City, 1989; asst. city mgr. City of Traverse City, 1990-98. Mediator Conflict Resolution Svc., 1998—, pres., 2000—02, exec. com., 2002—. V.p. Women's Econ. Devel. Orgn., Traverse City, 1993-95, mem., 1984—; mem. Traverse City Planning Commn., 1995-97; rep. Traverse City Schs. Adv. Com., 1982-85, 88-89; trustee Nat. Cherry Festival, 1996-98; bd. mem. Conflict Resolution Svc., 1999—. Recipient James H. Boyd award U. South Ala., Mobile, 1987. Mem. AAUW (sec. Traverse City br. 2000—), NOW (founding mem. Meridian, Miss. chpt. 1973), Michigan City. Mgmt. Assn. (bd. dirs. 1996-98), Internat. City Mgmt. Assn., Cherryland Humane Soc., Pi Sigma Alpha. Avocations: travel, reading, canoeing, cross-country skiing.

RUNDIO, LOUIS MICHAEL, JR. lawyer; b. Chgo., Sept. 13, 1943; s. Louis Michael Sr. and Germaine Matilda (Pasternack) R.; m. Ann Marie Bartlett, July 10, 1971; children: Matthew, Melissa. BS in Physics, Loyola U., Chgo., 1965, JD, 1972. Bar: Ill. 1972, U.S. Dist. Ct. (no. dist.) Ill. 1972, U.S. Ct. Appeals (7th cir.) 1974, U.S. Dist. Ct. (ea. dist.) Mich. 1983. Assoc. McDermott, Will & Emery, Chgo., 1972-77, ptnr., 1978—. Served to 1st lt. U.S. Army, 1965-68, Vietnam. Mem. ABA, Chgo. Bar Assn. Home: 676 Skye Ln Barrington IL 60010-5506 Office: McDermott Will & Emery 227 W Monroe St Ste 3100 Chicago IL 60606-5096

RUNDLE, MARGARET, literary arts educator; b. Staten Island, N.Y., Mar. 18, 1955; d. James Urvin and Marjorie (Arnold) R. BA magna cum laude, U. Hartford, 1976, MA with honors, 1979; DPhil, U. Oxford, Eng., 1993; cert., U. Grenoble, France, 1973, Sorbonne, Paris, 1975. Mem. adj. faculty U. Hartford, West Hartford, Conn., 1979-84, 1993-2000, co-dir. Creative Writing Workshop, 1995—2000, reader, judge English dept. ann. writing contest, 1995—, vis. asst. prof., 2000—01, vis. asst. prof. Pres.'s Coll., 2001—. Mem. U. Hartford Introduction to Lit. Com., 1993—, Western Heritage Com., 1994—. Asst. editor: Hartford Studies in Literature, 1977-79; bd. adv. editors, 1979-84; editor: (Norman and Charlotte Strouse edit., German vol.) The Writings of Thomas Carlyle; contbr. articles to profl. jours. Mem. Nat. Coun. Women, Oxford, 1988, Nuclear Freeze, McGovern campaign, 1972; area organizer Muskie campaign, Keene, N.H., 1969. Recipient grant St. Hugh's Coll., Oxford, 1986, Social Scis. and Humanities Rsch. Coun. Can., 1995; Armstrong Browning Libr. vis. fellowship Baylor U., 1999, 2002. Mem. MLA, Carlyle Soc., Northeast Victorian Studies Assn., Midwest Victorian Studies Assn. Democrat. Avocations: singing (Hartford Chorale 1979-84), hiking, swimming, dance, drama. Home: 2 Edwards Rd Portland CT 06480-1522 E-mail: rundle@earthlink.net.

RUNDLETT, ELLSWORTH TURNER, III, lawyer; b. Portland, Maine, Jan. 12, 1946; s. Ellsworth Turner II and Esther (Stevens) R.; m. Lisa Warren, Oct. 25, 1964 (div. June 1967); 1 child, Ellsworth Turner IV; m. Jamie Donnelly, June 7, 1982 (div. 1986); m. Marilyn DeJenzano, Aug. 17, 1994. AB cum laude, Bowdoin Coll., 1968; JD, U. Maine, 1973. Bar: Maine 1973, U.S. Dist. Ct. Maine 1973, U.S. Ct. Appeals (1st cir.) 1973; cert. civil trial specialist, Nat. Bd. Trial Advocacy; diplomate Nat. Coll. Advocacy. Bodwoin Coll. intern U.S. Senate, Washington, 1967; law clk. Superior Ct. Maine, Portland, 1972-73; asst. corp. counsel City of Portland, 1973-76; ptnr. Childs, Rundlett, Fifield & Childs, Portland, 1980—. Author: Maximizing Damages in Small Personal Injury Cases, 1991; contbr. legal articles to Maine Bus. Digest, 1978-84. Pres. Pine Tree Alcohol Treatment Ctr., Windham, Maine, 1978-80; trustee Portland Players, Inc., South Portland, Maine, 1977-84, pres., 1985-87. Mem. ATLA, Cumberland County Bar (trustee 1983-84, 86-87, v.p. 1988-90, pres. 1990), Maine Bar Assn. (bd. govs. 1991—), Maine Trial Lawyers Assn. (pres. 2000-01), U. Maine Law Alumni (bd. dirs. 1984-87, v.p. 1988, pres. 1989, bd. govs. 1991—), Cumberland Club, Portland Club (gov. 1983-86), Bowdoin Club of Portland (pres. 1978). E-mai;l. Office: Childs Rundlett & Fifield 257 Deering Ave Portland ME 04103-4858 E-mail: derry@maine.rr.com.

RUNDQUIST, BARRY S. political science educator; b. Yakima, Wash., June 5, 1941; s. Cecil Bond Spencer and Alice (Barry) R.; m. Susan Dorothy Ebner, Sept. 20, 1962 (div. July 1977); children: Carolyn, Johanna, Alicia; m. Andrea E. Friedman, Sept. 13, 1981; children: Abigail, Matthew, Bridget. Student, St. Martin's Coll., 1959-60; BS, U. Oreg., 1963; PhD, Stanford U., 1973. Congl. fellow Am. Polit. Sci. Assn., Washington, 1969-70; instr. U. Ill., Urbana, 1970-73, asst. prof., 1973-77, assoc. prof., 1978-99, prof., 2000—, mem. campus rsch. bd., 1996-99, dir. grad. studies, 1981-84, 92-95, 2000—. Vis. prof. Am. U., Washington, 1979-80; fellow Great Cities Inst., U. Ill., Chgo., 1995-96. Co-author: Congress and Military Procurement, 2001; editor: Political Benefits, 1980; contbr. articles to profl. jours. Co-dir. Ill. Voter Proejct, 1994-95, Chgo. Budget Project, 1989-91. Grantee NSF, 1984-85, 98-99, MacArthur Found., Chgo. Cmty. Trust, among others. Mem. Am. Polit. Sci. Assn., Midwest Polit. Sci. Assn., Legis. Studies Assn. Office: U Ill at Chicago Harrison St Chicago IL 60607 E-mail: barryr@uic.edu.

RUNDQUIST, HOWARD IRVING, investment banker; b. Winona, Minn., Mar. 21, 1929; s. Howard Wadsworth and Delilah Jeanette (Erickson) R.; m. Nancy Evelyn Hood, July 30, 1960; children: Sarah Louise, Beth Anne, Peter Hood, Susan Jenniffer, Rebecca Jane. AB, Gustavus Adolphus Coll., 1951; MBA, Harvard U., 1958. Mem. staff MIT Lincoln Lab., Lexington, Mass., 1954-56, 58-60; sr. v.p. Aubrey G. Lanston Co. Inc., N.Y.C., 1960-92; ret., 1992. Lt. USNR, 1951-54. Mem. Webhanet Golf Club, Edgcomb Tennis Club (Kennebunk, Maine). Republican. Lutheran.

RUNES, KENNETH ALAN, lawyer; b. Chicago Heights, Ill., Jan. 23, 1959; s. Eugene and Helen Lee (Hersh) R. BSW, U. Ill., 1981; JD, Northeastern U., 1991. Bar: Ill. 1991, U.S. Ct. Appeals (7th cir.) 1994, U.S. Dist. Ct. (no. dist.) Ill. 1997. Foster care case worker Ctrl. Bapt. Family Svcs., Chgo., 1981-84, family counselor Elgin, 1984-86; case worker Ill. Dept. Children and Family, DeKalb, 1986-88; assoc. Tucker, Pavesich & Assocs., Oak Lawn, 1991-94, Thill, Favaro, Buzek & Gorman, Ltd., Palatine, 1994—2001; ptnr. Runes Law Offices, P.C., Mount Prospect, 2001—. Candidate for sch. bd. Sch. Dist. # 206, Chicago Heights, 1977. Mem.: N.W. Suburban Bar Assn. Avocations: music, sports, strategy games. Office: Runes Law Offices PC Ste 104 800 W Central Rd Mount Prospect IL 60056

RUNFOLA, ROSS THOMAS, lawyer, educator, writer, journalist, poet; b. Buffalo, Aug. 30, 1943; s. Joseph Paul and Isabelle Louise (Santi) R.; children: Jennifer, Ross Thomas; m. Nancy S. Cox, Aug. 10, 1993. BA summa cum laude, SUNY, Buffalo, 1965, MA, 1968, PhD, 1973, JD, 1981. Bar: N.Y. 1982. Prof. social scis. Medaille Coll., Buffalo, 1969—; asst. prof. SUNY, 1970-73; sports columnist Buffalo New Times, 1973-74; co-anchor Sta. WUTV, 1974; reporter Buffalo Courier Express, 1975-76; columnist Spree mag., 1979-82; asst. Erie County Pub. Adminstr., 1981; ptnr. Fiorella, Leiter & Runfola, 1982-86; spl. matrimonial counsel Matusick, Spadafora & Verrastro, 1986-87; ptnr. Siegel, Kelleher & Kahn, 1987—. Dir. Matrimonial Mediation Ctr. Author: Jock: Sports and Male Identity, 1980; contbr. numerous articles to profl. jours.; chief film scriptwriter: Organized Sports: Are They Good for Young People, 1975. Active Mayor's Energy Task Force City of Buffalo, 1973, commn. Human Rights and Cmty. Relations, 2000, Minority task group for 8th judicial dist., 2000, Attica Prison Task Force, N.Y., 1973, Western N.Y. Consortium on Higher Edn., 1974, Erie County (N.Y.) Task Force on Physical Edn. and Recreation for Meeting the needs of the Handicapped, 1974, Instl. Task Force Pvt. Colls. Western N.Y., 1974, Western N.Y. Higher Edn. Task Force, 1975, Legis. Adv. Com. N.Y. State Assembly, 1976, Children's Hosp. Adolescence Program, 1978, Western N.Y. Heart Assn., 1978, Southern Poverty Law Ctr., 1978—, Erie County Dem. Com., 1978—, Step Family Assn. Western N.Y., 1983—, Frontier Dem. Club, 1983—; mem. adv. com. United Way Buffalo, 1991—; bd. dirs. Monsignor Carr Inst., Just Buffalo Lit. Ctr., 1996. Named One of Ten Best Coll. Profs. Western N.Y. Buffalo News, 1987, Prof. of Yr. Medaille Coll., 1998, Leadership Buffalo for Outstanding Leadership and Cmty. Commmitment, 1999; recipient 1st pl. award oral competition Greater Buffalo Poetry Slam, 1998, Social Svcs. award Nat. Conf. for Community and Justice, 1998. Mem. ABA, AAUP, N.Y. State Bar Assn., Erie County Bar Assn. (vice chmn. matrimonnial and family law com. 1992—), N.Y. State United Tchrs., N.Y. State Coun. Divorce Mediation, Am. Acad. Family Mediators (designated cons.), Am. Trial Lawyers Assn. Roman Catholic. Avocations: writing, reading, bicycling, cross country skiing. Home: 96 Cleveland Ave Buffalo NY 14222-1610 Office: Siegel Kelleher & Kahn 420 Franklin St Buffalo NY 14202-1302 also: 18 Agassiz Cir Buffalo NY 14214-2601

RUNFOLA, SHEILA KAY, nurse; b. Canton, Ohio, Feb. 8, 1944; d. Benjamin and M. Suzanne (deBord) Suarez; m. Steven Joseph Runfola, Aug. 17, 1968; children: Michael, Janine, Christine; stepchildren: Stephanie Bufalini, Darlene Teran. BS in Nursing, St. John Coll. Cleve., 1966; teaching credential jr. coll. nursing, UCLA Ext., San Diego, 1973. RN, Calif.; cert. occupational health nurse, cert. pub. health nurse. Staff nurse emergency rm. Leland Meml. Hosp., Riverdale, Md., 1966-67; staff nurse/team leader med./surg. Mercy Hosp., San Diego, 1967-68; staff nurse, charge nurse emergency dept., dept. radiology U. Calif.-San Diego Med.Ctr., 1968-76; staff devel./asst. dir. nurses TLC Nursing Home, El Cajon, Calif., 1978-80; staff nurse/charge nurse emergency dept. Kaiser Permanente Hosp., San Diego, 1980-89, staff nurse emergency dept. Sacramento, 1989-90, house supr., 1992-94, case mgr. occupational medicine, 1995—; health svcs. nurse U.S. Automobile Assn., 1990-95. Contbr. articles to profl. jours. Leader Girls Scouts Am., San Diego and Sacramento, 1982-91, treas., local svc. team, 1986-89, 90; parent rep. Elk Grove (Calif.) Sch. Bd. for Elk Grove H.s., 1994, co-chair Sober Grad. Night, 1993-95. Mem. Sacramento Valley Occupational Health Nurses (v.p. 1992-95, sec. 1998—, election chair 1998), Newcomers Club, Calif. State Assn. Occupl. Health Nurse (bd. dirs. 1998—, newsletter editor). Democrat. Roman Catholic. Avocations: crafts (quilting), piano, reading, cooking, boating. Office: Kaiser Permanente Dept Occupl Med 6600 Bruceville Rd Sacramento CA 95823-4671

RUNG, GEORGE W. physician; b. Altoona, Pa., Dec. 18, 1957; s. Wilbur Karl and Emma May (Peterson) R.; m. Catherine Ann Kline, June 9, 1979; children: Katrina, Allison, Jonathan, Christopher. BS, Juniata Coll., 1978; MD, Pa. State U., 1982. Diplomate Am. Bd. Anesthesiology; cert. in pain mgmt. Intern Pa. State U. Hosp., Hershey, 1983, anesthesia resident, 1984-85; asst. prof. Pa. State U., 1986, assoc. prof., 1993—; anesthesia/crit. care fellow U. Western Australia, Perth, 1985-86. Vis. scientist and univ. sabbatical, U. Copenhagen, Denmark, 1995; fellow Project Hope, Guayaqil, Equador, 1992. Author: A Practice of Cardiac Anesthesia, 1991, 95, Anesthesia for Vascular

Surgery, 1993; contbr. articles to profl. jours. Vis. scientist, Pa. State U., Denmark, 1995. Mem. Am. Soc. Anesthesiologists, Am. Soc. Regional Anesthesiologists, Internat. Anesthesia Rsch. Soc. Home: 222 E Granada Ave Hershey PA 17033-1343 Office: Anesthesia Assocs Lancaster 133 E Frederick St Lancaster PA 17602-2222 E-mail: georgerung@earthlink.net.

RUNGE, DONALD EDWARD, food wholesale company executive; b. Milw., Mar. 20, 1938; s. Adam and Helen Teresa (Voss) R.; divorced; children: Roland, Richard, Lori. Grad., Spencerian Coll., Milw., 1960. Fin. v.p. Milw. Cheese Co., Waukesha, Wis., 1962-69; dir. Farm House Foods Corp., Milw., 1966-89, pres., 1966-89, CEO, treas., 1984-89, chmn., pres., 1985-89; chmn., CEO Retailing Corp. Am., 1982-89; CEO, treas. Drug Sys. Inc., 1984-89; chmn. Drug Sys. Inc. (now Retailing Corp. of Am.), 1985-89; pres. TDC, 1987-89; chmn., pres. Runge Industries, Gen. Growth, Inc., 1989—. Bd. dirs. Convenient Food Mart, CasaBlanca Industries, Inc., City of Industry, Calif., Palm Beach Opera, 1992—; sec. The Diana Corp., Milw., 1985-86, treas. 1986—, pres. 1987-96; chmn. Economy Dry Goods Co. Inc.; treas. Fairbanks Farms Inc.; adv. bd. Honors Coll., 2000—, bd. trustees, Highland Acad., 2002—. Adventist. *I believe there is very little in life that cannot be accomplished if a person truly wants to attain the goal.*

RUNGE, JEFFREY WILLIAM, federal agency administrator; m. Ginny Runge; children: Emily, Will. B. U. of South; MD, U. S.C., 1981. Diplomate Am. Bd. Emergency Medicine. Resident Charlotte Meml. Hosp. and Med. Ctr. , 1984; faculty emergency medicine residency Carolinas Med. Ctr., Charlotte, NC, 1984; dir. Carolinas Ctr. Injury Prevention and Control; nat. hwy. traffic safety adminstr. U.S. Dept. Transp., Washington, 2001—. Mem.: N.C. Med. Soc. (spkr.), N.C. Coll. Emerency Physicians (past pres.), Am. Coll. Emergency Physicians (trauma care and injury control com., rsch. com.). Office: US Dept Transp Nat Hwy Traffic Safety Adminstr 400 7th St SW Washington DC 20590 Office Fax: 202-366-2106.*

RUNGE, KAY KRETSCHMAR, library director; b. Davenport, Iowa, Dec. 9, 1946; d. Alfred Edwin and Ina (Paul) Kretschmar; children: Peter Jr., Katherine. BS in History Edn., Iowa State U., 1969; MLS, U. Iowa, 1970. Pub. svc. libr. Anoka County Libr., Blaine, Minn., 1971-72; cataloger Augustana Coll., Rock Island, Ill., 1972-74; dir. Scott County Libr. Sys., Eldridge, Iowa, 1974-85, Davenport (Iowa) Pub. Libr., 1985—2001, Pub. Libr. Des Moines, 2001—. V.p. Quad-Cities Conv. and Visitors Bur., 1992—97, Quad-Cities Grad. Study Ctr., 1992—2001, Downtown Davenport Devel. Corp., 1992—2000, Hall of Honor Bd., Davenport Ctrl. H.S., 1992—95, Brenton Bank Bd., 1995—2001, Wells Fargo Bank Bd., 2001; steering com. Quad-Cities Visions for the Future, 1987—91, Humanities Iowa, 1993—2000, chair, 1998—99; bd. govs. Iowa State U. Found., 1991—; citizens adv. coun. Iowa State U., 1998—2000, Leadership Iowa, 1998—99; adv. bd. mem. U. Iowa Sch. Libr. Sci., 1999—, adj. prof., 2000—01; mem. Iowa State U. Found. Devel. Bd., 2000—; bd. dirs. Wells Fargo Bank, 2000—, River Ctr. for Performing Arts, Davenport, 1983—97, Iowa State U. Rsch. Pk., 1998—2000; chmn. bd. dirs. Am. Inst. Commerce, 1989—98; bd. dirs. Quest Ednl. Corp., 1999—, Davenport One, Downtown Devel., 2000—01. Recipient Svc. Key award Iowa State U. Alumni Assn., 1979, ALA/ALTA Nat. Advocacy Honor Roll award, 2000; named Quad City Panhellenic Woman of Yr., 1998. Mem. ALA (chmn. library adminstrs. and mgrs. div., fundraising section 1988), Iowa Library Assn. (pres. 1983, Mem. of Yr. award 2000), Pub. Library Assn. (bd. dirs. 1990-99, pres. 2000-2001), Iowa Edn. Media Assn. (Intellectual Freedom award 1984), Alpha Delta Pi (alumni state pres. 1978). Lutheran. Office: Pub Libr of Des Moines 100 Locust St Des Moines IA 50309-1791

RUNGE, PATRICK RICHARD, lawyer; b. Iowa City, Oct. 25, 1969; s. Richard Gary and Sally Louise (Cozzolino) R. BSBA in Econs., U. Nebr., Omaha, 1991; JD, Creighton U., 1994. Bar: Nebr. 1994, U.S. Dist. Ct. Nebr. 1994. Prodn. editor U.N.O. Gateway, Omaha, 1990-91; graphic designer Omaha Pub. Power Dist., 1991-97; intern U.S. Dist. Ct., Omaha, 1993; rsch. asst. Creighton U., 1993; sr. cert. law student Creighton Legal Clinic, 1994; atty. Runge Law Office, 1994-95, Runge & Chase, Omaha, 1995—. Pub. defender Winnebago Tribe Nebr., 1996—, Omaha Tribe Nebr., 2000-01. Disting. scholar Omaha (Nebr.) World-Herald, 1987-91; Merit scholar Creighton Law Sch., Omaha, 1991-94. Mem. ABA, Winnebago Bar Assn., Omaha Tribal Bar Assn. Democrat. Lutheran. Office: Runge & Chase 7701 Pacific St Ste 323 Omaha NE 68114-5480 E-mail: patricrunge@hotmail.com.

RUNKLE, MARTIN DAVEY, library director; b. Cin., Oct. 18, 1937; s. Newton and Ilo (Neal) R.; m. Nancy Force, Aug. 7, 1965; children: Seth, Elizabeth. BA, Muskingum Coll., 1959; MA, U. Pitts., 1964, U. Chgo., 1973. Library systems analyst U. Chgo., 1970-75, head cataloging librarian, 1975-79, asst. dir. tech. services, 1979-80, dir. library, 1980—. Sr. lectr. grad. library sch. U. Chgo., 1977-90. Fulbright grantee, 1965. Mem. ALA, Univ. Club Chgo. Office: U Chgo 1100 E 57th St Chicago IL 60637-1596 E-mail: maru@midway.uchicago.edu.

RUNNALLS, OLIVER JOHN CLYVE (JOHN RUNNALLS), nuclear engineering educator; b. Barrie Island, Ont., Can., June 26, 1924; s. John Lawrence and Ethel May (Arnold) Runnalls; m. Vivian Constance Stowe, Sept. 13, 1947; children: David John, Catherine Ruth. BA in Sci., U. Toronto, 1948, MA in Sci., 1949, PhD, 1951. Registered profl. engr., Ont. R & D scientist Atomic Energy of Can., Ltd., Chalk River, Ont. and Paris, 1951-71; sr. adviser uranium and nuclear energy Energy, Mines and Resources Can., Ottawa, Ont., 1971-79; prof. energy studies U. Toronto, 1979-89, chmn. Ctr. Nuclear Engring., 1983-89; prof. emeritus nuclear engring. and energy studies, 1989—; chmn. bd. Inst. Hydrogen Systems, 1983-89. Pres. O.J.C. Runnalls & Assocs., Ltd. Contbr. Decorated Queen's Silver Jubilee medal; named Hall of Distinction, U. Toronto, 2001; recipient B.T.A. Bell Commemorative medal, Can. Mining Jour., 1979. Fellow: Can. Acad. Engring., Royal Soc. Can.; mem.: Can. Nuclear Soc., Can. Nuclear Assn. (bd. dirs., past chmn., Ian F. McRae award 1980), Assn. Profl. Engrs. Achievements include patents for in field. Home and Office: 170 Lytton Blvd Toronto ON Canada M4R 1L4

RUNNELS, VINCENT BRIAN, neurosurgeon; b. Hot Springs, Ark., July 11, 1943; s. Lon Earl Reed and Ruby Spencer Runnels; m. Bonnie Szoke; children: Meredith, Ted, Jennifer, Katie. BS, Purdue U.; MD, Ind. U. Resident in neurology Ind. U., Lafayette; pvt. practice neurosurgery Fayetteville, Ark., 1974—. Republican. Avocations: gardening, fishing, pottery, hunting. Office: NW Ark Neurosurgery Clinic 1706 E Joyce Blvd Fayetteville AR 72703-5238

RUNNION, CINDIE J. elementary school educator; b. Knoxville, Tenn., Mar. 8, 1958; d. James B. and Josephine Marie (Sykes) Runnion. BS, East Tenn. State U., 1979, MEd, 1989; postgrad., U. Madrid. Sec. Runnion Ent., Newport, Tenn.; tchr. 3rd grade Cocke County Bd. Edn., 1980—. First Bapt. Ch. meml. scholar. Mem. NEA, ASCD, Tenn. Edn. Assn., Cocke County Edn. Assn. (faculty rep., v.p. 1991-92, accreditation com. for sch.). Home: 146 New Cave Church Rd Newport TN 37821-7404 E-mail: runnionj@planetc.com.

RUNNION, HOWARD J., JR. banker; b. Hot Spring, N.C., May 23, 1930; s. Howard Jackson and Blanche Mae (Elam) R.; m. Betty Ann Bishop, June 30, 1951; children: Debra Joy Sizemore, Jill Marie Glenn. BS, U. N.C., 1952. Various postions Wachovia Bank and Trust Co.-Wachovia Corp., Winston-Salem, N.C., 1952—; ret. vice chmn., former dir. Depository Trust Co., N.Y.C., 1985-95; chmn. bd. PSA Treasury Com, 1984-85. Ret. vice-chmn, CFO Wachovia Corp.; bd. dirs. SI Corp. Chmn. bd. trustees Coll. Found. Raleigh, 1978-95. Mem. Res. City Bankers Assn., Pub. Securities Assn. (dir. 1976-79, 84-85) Clubs: Forsyth Country, Roaring Gap. Lodges: Elk. Republican. Presbyterian. Avocation: golf. Home: 3521 York Rd Winston Salem NC 27104-1346 Office: Wachovia Corp PO Box 3099 Winston Salem NC 27102-3099

RUNQUIST, LISA A. lawyer; b. Mpls., Sept. 22, 1952; d. Ralf E. and Violet R. BA, Hamline U., 1973; JD, U. Minn., 1976. Bar: Minn. 1977, Calif. 1978, U.S. Dist. Ct. (ctrl. dist.) Calif. 1985, U.S. Supreme Ct. 1995. Assoc. Caldwell & Toms, L.A., 1978-82; ptnr. Runquist & Flagg, 1982-85; pvt. practice Runquist & Assocs., 1985-99, Runquist & Zybach LLP, L.A., 1999—. Mem. adv. bd. Exempt Orgn. Tax Rev., 1990—, Calif. State U. L.A. Continuing Edn. Acctg. and Tax Program, 1995—. Mem. editl. bd.: ABA Bus. Law Today, 1994—2002. Mem. ABA (bus. law sect. coun. 1995-99, com. on nonprofit corps. 1986—, chair 1991-95, subcom. current devels. in nonprofit corp. law 1989—, chair 1989-91, subcom. rels. orgns. 1989—, chair 1987-91, 95-98, subcom. legal guidebook for dirs. 1986—, ad hoc com. on info. tech., 1997—, chair 1997-98, co-chair, 1998—2002, sect. liaison to ABA tech. coun. 1997-2000, subcom. model nonprofit corp. act, partnerships and unincorp. bus. orgns. com. 1987—, state regulation of securities com. 1988-99, exempt orgns. com. 1987—, subcom. religious orgns. 1989—, co-chair 1995-97, subcom. non (c) (3) orgns. 1997—, co-chair 1997—, corp. laws com. 1999-, subcom. guidebook for dirs. of closely held corps. chair 2000—), Calif. Bar Assn. (bus. law sect., nonprofit and unincorp. orgns. com. 1985-92, 93-96, 97—, chair 1989-91), Christian Legal Soc., Ctr. Law and Religious Freedom, Christian Mgmt. Assn. (dir. 1983-89). Office: 10618 Woodbridge St Toluca Lake CA 91602-2717 E-mail: lisa@runquist.com.

RUNSER, DIANNE STRONG, music educator, music director; b. Atlanta, Jan. 30, 1953; d. Daniel Kline and Mary Anne (Logan) Strong; m. Frederic William Runser, June 24, 1978; children: Heather Dianne, Megan Danielle. B in Music Edn. cum laude, W.Va. Wesleyan Coll., 1974; M in Music Edn., Duquesne U., 1977. Cert. tchr. vocal and instrumental grades K-12, Pa. Tchr. vocal music K-12 Edgewood (Pa.) Sch. Dist., 1974-78; pvt. practice Trafford, Pa., 1978—. Substitute tchr. Penn-Trafford Sch. Dist., Penn. Twp., Pa., Pa., 1978—94; dir. music Monroeville (Pa.) Cmty. Chorus, 1984—, 1st United Meth. Ch., Irwin, Pa., 1986—; music tchr. Level Green Pres. Pre-Sch., Trafford, 1987—, Murrysville United Meth. Pre-Sch., 2001—; plays organ for weddings; accompanist soloists and ensembles, Pitts. Co-author: Strong Family History Update, Vol. IV, 1995. Bd. dirs., corr. sec. Strong Family Association Am., Inc., 1977-2002, charter and life mem.; mem. Fellowship of United Meths. in Music and Worship Arts. Mem. Order Ea. Star (Pa. Grand Chpt. Worthy Matron 1981-82, Dist. Dep. Grand Matron 1984-85, Grand Choir Dir. 1987-88, Grand Chor Accompanist 1983-84, 86, 94, 95-97, 99, 2000, Grand Organist Page, 1998), Am. Guild English Handbell Ringers, Mortar Board, Sigma Alpha Iota, Zeta Tau Alpha. Avocations: geneology, needlework, reading, computers. Home: 201 Maple Dr Trafford PA 15085-1401 Office: 1st United Meth Ch 310 Oak St Irwin PA 15642-3558 E-mail: dsrunser@aol.com.

RUNTE, ROSEANN, academic administrator; b. Kingston, N.Y., Jan. 31, 1948; arrived in Can., 1971, naturalized, 1983; d. Robert B. and Anna Lorreta (Schorkopf) O'Reilly; m. Hans-Rainer Runte, Aug. 9, 1969. BA summa cum laude, SUNY, New Paltz, 1968; MA, U. Kans., 1969, PhD, 1974; DLitt (hon.) , Acadia U., 1989, Meml. U., 1990, U. Vest Timisoara, 1996, U. Arad, 2001. Lectr. Bethany Coll., W.Va., 1970—71; lectr. adult studies St. Mary's U., Halifax, Canada, 1971—72; from lectr. to assoc. prof. Dalhousie U., Canada, 1972—83, asst. dean Canada, 1980—82, chmn. dept. French Canada, 1980—83; pres. U. Sainte-Anne, Pointe-de-l'Eglise, Canada, 1983—88; prin. Glendon Coll., Toronto, Canada, 1988—94; pres. Victoria U., 1994—2001, Old Dominion U., 2001—. Bd. dirs. Banque Nationale, Va. Advanced Carrier and Shipbldg. Integration Ctr. Author: Brumes Bleues, 1982, Faux-Soleils, 1984, Birmanie Blues, 1993; editor: Studies in 18th Century Culture, 1977—79, A Canadian in Love, 2000, The Passionate Mind, 2000, French Rev., 1988—94, Lit. Rsch., 1994—97; co-editor: Man and Nature, 1982, Le Development Regional, 1986—87, From Orality to Literature, 1991, Lectures Canadiennes, 1993, Visions of Beauty, 1995, The Foundation for International Training: 25 Years of International Development, 2001; co-translator: Local Development, 1987; mem. editl. bd., 2001—. V.p. Can. commn. UNESCO, 1991—92, pres., 1992—96; vice-chair exec. bd. Found. for Internat. Tng., 1994—95, chair bd., 1995—2000; internat. adv. bd. Expo 2000, 1995—2000; v.p. Assn. Internat. des études québecoises, 1999—2001; active Internat. Women's Forum, 1998—; chair Gottschalk Prize Com., 1994; chair publs. com. Hannah Found., 1989—92; vice-chair bd. Gardiner Mus., 1994—; active Commn. Langs. Instrn., Ontario, Canada, 1999—2001; chair prix du salon Livre Com., 1998; bd. dirs. Assn. Med. Svcs., 1989—92; adv. bd. Nat. Libr., 1984—91. Decorated Ordre du Mérite Can.; recipient Acad. Palmes, 1986, Fr. Coppée award, French Acad., 1989; grantee Title IV grant, NDEA, 1968; scholar Regents scholar, SUNY, 1965. Fellow: Royal Soc. Can., Soc. Study Values in Edn., World Acad. Arts & Sci.; mem.: Royal Coll. Physicians and Surgeons, Soc. for Study Higher Edn. (bd. dirs. 1988—90), Can. Soc. 18th Century Studies (pres. 1975—76), Atlantic Soc. 18th Century Studies (pres. 1972—76), Can. Fedn. Humanities (pres. 1982—84), Internat. Assn. of Comparative Lit. (treas. 1985—91, sec. 1991—94), Internat. Soc. 18th Century Studies (assoc. treas. 1983—87), Club of Rome (exec. com. 1999—), Knights of Malta (grande dame 1991—), Phi Delta Kappa, Delta Kappa Gamma. Home: 5000 Edgewater Dr Norfolk VA 23508 Office: Old Dominion U Norfolk VA 23529 E-mail: r.runte@odu.edu.

RUNTSCH, CLARENCE FREDERICK, artist, sculptor; b. Verdigre, Nebr., Mar. 13, 1923; s. Albert and Anna Marie (Czekay) R.; m. Alice Jean McCabe, Aug. 2, 1947 (div. Mar. 1977); 1 child, Teresa Ann Runtsch Duffett. Student, Texas A&M, 1942, Cumming Sch. of Art, Des Moines, 1946-48, Drake U., 1947, Kansas City Art Inst., 1948-50; BFA, U. Kansas City, 1950; student, Kansas City Art Inst., 1950-51; MFA, Univ. Tennessee, 1956. Artist/designer Mus. Natural History, Kansas City, 1951-52; illustrator Civil Svc., U.S. Army, 1952-54; chief designer Am. Mus. Atomic Energy, Oak Ridge, Tenn., 1954-76. Artist/sculptor ltd. edits. and commns., 1951—; principal works include collections at Smithsonian Inst., 1961, U.S. Marine Corps. Mus., 1993, Buffalo Bill Hist. Ctr., 2000, art in corp. and pvt. collections, U.S., Switzerland, Germany. Tech. Sgt. USMC, 1942-46. Recipient 5 Combat Stars USMC, Presdl. Unit Citation. Mem. Am. Soc. Arms Collectors, Smoky Mountain Gun Collectors (charter life mem., pres. 1964), Oak Ridge Art Ctr. (dir. 1956-59), Sertoma (charter pres. 1966—), Southeastern Antique Arms Collectors (charter life mem., dir. 1977—), Free and Accepted Masons (life mem.), Elks. Avocations: collecting and researching antique weapons, collecting Indian beadwork. Home: 131 E Vanderbilt Dr Oak Ridge TN 37830-6182

RUNYAN, DESMOND KIMO, medical educator, researcher; b. Pasadena, Calif., Aug. 27, 1950; s. Raymond Albert and Patricia Alona (Collins) R.; m. Carol Sue Wolf, Dec. 23, 1972; 1 child, Alexander. BA, Macalester Coll., 1972; MD, U. Minn., 1976; DPH, U. N.C., 1983. Diplomate Am Bd. Pediat., Am. Bd. Preventive Medicine. Resident in pediat. U. Minn. Health Scis. Ctr., Mpls., 1976-79; Robert Wood Johnson clin. scholar U. N.C., Chapel Hill, 1979-81, from asst. to assoc. prof. social medicine and pediat., 1981-95, dir. preventive medicine residency, 1989-98, prof. social medicine and pediat., 1995—, chmn. dept. social medicine, 1999—. Mem. faculty Internat. Clin. Epidemiology Network, 1987—; mem. exec. com. Nat. Adv. Coun. Family Violence, Chgo., 1994—; med. dir. N.C. Child Med. Evaluation Program, Chapel Hill, 1986-98, Ctr. for Child and Family Health-N.C., Durham, 1996—; prin. investigator rsch. study of child abuse and neglect, Nat. Ctr. Child Abuse and Neglect, 1990—; co-prin. investigator nat. study child and adolescent well-being, U.S. Congress, 1997—. Mem. editl. bd. Internat. Jour. Child Abuse and Neglect, 1994—; bd. govs. Am. Journ. Preventive Medicine, 1996—. Soc. for Pediatric Rsch. fellow. Fellow Am. Coll. Preventive Medicine; mem. Internat. Soc. Prevention Child Abuse and Neglect, Ambulatory Pediat. Assn. Avocations: skiing, sailing. Office: U NC Dept Social Medicine PO Box 7240 Chapel Hill NC 27599-0001 Fax: 919-966-7499. E-mail: drunyan@med.unc.edu.

RUNYAN, TIMOTHY JACK, historian, educator; b. Gary, Ind., Aug. 9, 1941; s. Jack Elmore and Mavis Lydia (Lewis) R.; m. Laurie Ann Blackmore, July 25, 1964; children: Christopher T., Michael A. BS, Capital U., 1963; MA, U. Md., 1965; postgrad., U. Md. fellow, U. London, 1967-69; PhD, U. Md., 1972. Instr. U. Md., College Park, 1969, Cleve. State U., 1969-71, asst. prof., 1971-74, assoc. prof., 1974-87, prof. dept. history, 1987-97, asst. dean Coll. Arts and Scis., 1976-79, dir. classical and medieval studies, 1978-86, chmn. dept. art, 1981-82, chmn. dept. modern langs., 1982-86; chmn. dept. history, 1991-94. Vis. prof. Oberlin (Ohio) Coll., 1989; vis. prof., dir. Program in Maritime History and Nautical Archaeology East Carolina U., N.C., 1994-96, prof., program dir., 1997—; editor Am. Neptune, Jour. of Maritime History, Peabody Essex Mus., Salem, Mass., 1990-95. Author: European Naval and Maritime History, 300-1500, 1985; editor: Ships, Seafaring and Society, 1987 (John Lyman Book award 1988), To Die Gallantly: The Battle of the Atlantic, 1994 (selection of Mil. Book Club); contbr. articles to scholarly publs. Mgr. Cleve. Commn. on Higher Edn., 1976-79; pres. Gt. Lakes Mus. Sci., Tech. and Environment, Cleve., 1987-91, vice chair bd. trustees, 1991-94; gov.'s appointee to Ohio 1992 Commn., Columbus, 1989-92; chmn. sect. interior Nat. Maritime Heritage Grants Com., 1997—. Recipient Award of Achievement for Mus. N. Ohio Live, 1991; Am. Philos. Soc. grantee, 1973, 76; NOAA Ocean Exploration grantee, 2002--; NC Sea grantee. Fellow Royal Hist. Soc. (London); mem. Internat. Commn. Maritime History (exec. coun. 1985—, treas. 1990-95, v.p. 1995—), N.Am. Soc. Oceanic History (pres. 1980-84), Nat. Maritime Alliance Bd. (treas. 1992-97, chair 1997—), Nat. Maritime Hist. Soc. (adv bd. 1989—), Gt. Lakes Hist. Soc. (pres. 1985-95), Medieval Acad. Am. (nominating com. 1985-87, chair 1990-91, endowment campaign com. 1990-95), Midwest Medieval Hist. Conf. (pres. 1981-82), Assn. Gt. Lakes Maritime History (v.p. 1984-87). Episcopalian. Avocations: sports, travel. Home: 101 Wesley Rd Greenville NC 27858-6532 Office: East Carolina Univ Maritime Studies Eller House Greenville NC 27858-4353

RUNYON, BRETT L. lawyer; b. Fresno, Calif., Oct. 20, 1959; AA, Fresno City Coll., 1981; BS, Calif. State U., Fresno, 1982; JD, San Joaquin Coll. Law, 1986; MS, Syracuse U. Bar: Calif. 1988, D.C., U.S. Dist. Ct. (ea. dist.), U.S. Ct. Appeals (Fed. cir.) 1998. Arbitrator Fresno County Superior Ct., Fresno County Farm Bur. Mem. ABA, ATLA, Fed. Bar Assn., No. Calif. Assn. Def. Counsel, Fresno County Bar Assn., Delta Theta Phi (meritorious svc. award 1986). Office: Marderosian Runyon Cercone & Lehman 1260 Fulton Mall Fresno CA 93721-1916

RUNYON, KEITH LESLIE, lawyer, newspaper editor; b. Louisville, Oct. 3, 1950; s. Leslie Thomas and Marjorie Fillmore (Fisher) R.; M. Amelia Payne Sweets, Dec. 29, 1979; children; Amelia Brown Payne, Keith Leslie Jr. Student, U. London, 1971; BA cum laude, U. Louisville, 1972, JD, 1982. Staff writer Courier-Jour., Louisville, 1972-77, staff atty., 1984-86; staff atty., assoc. editor Louisville Times and Courier Jour., 1977-86, forum editor, 1986-90; editl. page editor, 1990-92; editor opinion pages, 1992-96; opinion editor, 1996—. Moderator Ky. Author Forum, 1996-2001. Editor: (novels) The Forum and Book Editor, 2001—. Nat. bd. dirs. English-Speaking Union U.S., N.Y., 1976-79, pres. Ky. br., Louisville, 1986-87; pres., dir. U. Louisville Alumni Assn., 1987-93; mem. exec. com. Louisville com. on fgn. rels., 1985-87, Leadership Louisville, 1990-91; clk. Session Calvin Presbyn. Ch., Louisville, 1986-88; mem. St. Francis in the Fields Ch., Harrods Creek, Ky.; bd. dirs. Walden Theatre, Louisville, 1999-2001; alumni council, Brandeis Sch. of Law, 2001—. Recipient William E. Leidt award The Episc. Ch. of U.S., 1975, Roy Howard award (shared) Scripps Howard Journalists Nat. for Pub. Svc., 1976; named Alumnus of Yr., U. Louisville, 1991, disting. alumnus U. Louisville Sch. Law, 1996; Ctr. Fgn. Journalists fellow, 1993, Bingham fellow, 1995-96. Mem. ABA, Ky. Bar Assn., Louisville Bar Assn., Nat. Conf. Edit. Writers (editor The masthead, 1994-96), Soc. Profl. Jours. (Outstanding Editl. Writing award, 1983, 84, 85, Outstanding Criticism award 1997, 98). Home: Nitta Yuma Harrods Creek KY 40027 Office: Courier-Jour and Louisville Times Co 525 W Broadway Louisville KY 40202-2206

RUNYON, MARIE MORGAN, not-for-profit administrator; b. Brevard, N.C., Mar. 20, 1915; d. Ralph Siler and Louise McIntosh) M.; m. Richard Bailey Runyon, Jan. 11, 1947 (div. Mar. 1952); 1 child, Louise Runyon Barth. BA, Berea (Ky.) Coll., 1937. Membership dir. ACLU, N.Y.C., 1954-63; dir. devel. Nat. Conf. for Sane Nuclear Policy, 1964-67, Nat. Conf. New Politics, N.Y.C., 1967-69; owner Marie Runyon Assocs., 1969-75; assemblywoman N.Y. State Assembly, 1975-77; exec. dir., founder Harlem Restoration Project, N.Y.C., 1977—. Housing activist/organizer, Harlem, N.Y.C., 1960—. Democrat. Episcopalian. Home: 130 Morningside Dr New York NY 10027-6055 Office: Harlem Restoration Project 461 W 125th St New York NY 10027-4201

RUOF, RICHARD ALAN, clergyman; b. Lancaster, Pa., Oct. 11, 1932; s. Robert Jacob and Geneva May (Devers) Ruof; m. Anne Margaret Demos; children: Mark Alan Demos Ruof, Anne Tracy Demos Ruof, Richard James Demos Ruof. AB, Franklin and Marshall Coll., 1954; MDiv, Lancaster (Pa.) Theol. Sem., Union Theol. Sem., Richmond, Va., 1960; STM, Luth. Theol. Sem., Gettysburg, Pa., 1974; DMin, McCormick Theol. Sem., 1981. Ordained to ministry United Ch. Christ, 1960. Pastor Harrisville (Va.) Charge of United Ch. Christ, 1959-62, Thurmont (Md.) Charge, 1962-67, First Congl. Ch., Cortland, N.Y., 1967-77, St. Paul's United Ch. Christ of Hamlin, Fredericksburg, Pa., 1977-82, St. John's United Ch. Christ, Egg Harbor City, N.J., 1982-87, Friedensburg, Pa., 1987-94, pastor emeritus, 1994. Registrar-treas. Susquehanna Assn., N.Y. Conf., United Ch. Christ, 1968-74; mem. Egg HArbor City Bd. Edn., 1984. With USNR, 1954-56.

RUOFF, A. LAVONNE BROWN, English language educator; b. Charleston, Ill., Apr. 10, 1930; d. Oscar and Laura Alice (Witters) Brown; m. Milford Anthony Prasher, Aug. 19, 1950 (div. 1964); m. Gene W. Ruoff, Jan. 10, 1967; children: Stephen Charles, Sharon Louise(dec.). Student, U. Ill., Chgo., 1948-50; BS in Edn., Northwestern U., 1953, MA in English, 1954, PhD in English, 1966. From instr. to asst. prof. Roosevelt U., Chgo., 1961-66; asst. prof. English U. Ill., 1966-69, assoc. prof., 1969-81, prof., 1981-94, prof. emerita, 1994—. Interim dir. D'Arcy McNickle Ctr. for Am. Indian History, Newberry Libr., 1999-2000; editor Am. Indian Lives series U. Nebr. Press, Lincoln, 1985—; mem. Am. lit. com. Internat. Exch. of Scholars, Washington, 1987-90, chair, 1989-90; NEH dir. Sumer Seminars for Coll. Tchrs. on Am. Indian Lit., 1979, 83, 89, 94. Author: American Indian Literature, 1990, Literatures of the American Indian, 1990; editor: The Moccasin Maker, 1987, 2d edit., 1998, Wynema, 1997, From the Deep Woods to Civilization and Indian Boyhood, 2001; (with Jerry W. Ward, Jr.) Redefining American Literary History, 1990; (with Donald Smith) Life, Letters and Speeches of George Copway, 1997. Bd. dirs. Am. Indian Coun. Fire, Chgo., 1980-88. Recipient Lifetime Achievement award Before Columbus Found., 1998, Lit., MLA and Assn. for Study of Am. Indian Lits. award for outstanding contbns., 1993, MELUS award for outstanding contbns. to multiethnic lit., 1986; named Writer of Yr. for Annotation/Bibliography, Wordcraft Circle of Native Writers and Storytellers, 1997; NEH fellow, 1992-93, U. Ill.-Chgo. Inst. for Humanities fellow, 1990-91; NEH Rsch. Divsn. grantee, 1981. Mem.: MLA (chair discussion group Am. Indian lit., co-chair lit. of people of color com. 2000—01, exec. coun. 2002—), Assn. for Study of Am. Indian Lits., Multi-ethnic Lit. in the U.S., Am. Studies Assn. E-mail: lruoff@uic.edu.

RUOFF, CYNTHIA OSOWIEC, foreign language educator; b. Chgo., Mar. 1, 1943; d. Stephen R. and Estelle (Wozniak) O.; m. Gary Edward Ruoff, June 5, 1965; children: Gary S., Laura A. AB, Loyola U., 1965; MA, Western Mich. U., 1973; PhD in French Lang. and Lit., Mich. State U., 1992. Tchr. Kalamazoo (Mic.) Pub. Schs., 1965-68; asst. prof. Western Mich. U., Kalamazoo, 1980—. Nat. and internat. spkr. in field; asst. prof. Western Mich. U. Contbr. articles to profl. jours. Mem. MLA, N.Am. Soc. Seventeenth-Century French Lit., Am. Assn. Tchrs. of French, Mich. Fgn. Lang. Assn., Internat. Soc. Phenomenology and Lit., L'Alliance Française, Soc. Interdisciplinary French Seventeenth-Century Studies, Phi Sigma Iota, Pi Delta Phi. Avocations: piano, skiing. Office: Dept Fgn Langs & Lit Western Mich Univ Kalamazoo MI 49008 *Reach beyond intelligence and reason by experiencing the beauty, harmony, grandeur, and mystery of the cosmos..to achieve a higher understanding and truth.*

RUOTSALA, JAMES ALFRED, historian, writer; b. Juneau, Alaska, Feb. 17, 1934; s. Bert Alfred and Eva (Karppi) E.; m. Janet Ann Whelan, July 31, 1987; stepchildren: Theresa Cowden, Douglas Whelan, Peggy MacInnis, Michael Whelan, Bruce Whelan. Student, U. Md., 1960-61, Basic Officers Sch., Maxwell AFB, 1964, Air U., 1985; AA, U. Alaska, Kenai, 1990. Asst. div. mgr. Macmillan Pub. Co., 1964-80; mgr. Denny's Restaurants, 1980-82; dir. mktg. and sales Air Alaska, 1982-89; state security supr., lt. Knightwatch Security, Juneau, Alaska, 1990-96; ret., 1996. Archival dir. Alaska Aviation Heritage Mus., 1987-90. Author: Lockheed Vegas in Southeast Alaska, 1980, We Stand Ready, 1986, Eielson, Father of Alaskan Aviation, 1986, Pilots of the Panhandle, The Early Years 1920-1935, 1997; Alaska's Aviation Heritage Air Alaska newspaper; contbr. articles to profl. jours. Journalist 1st cl. USN, 1951-56; sgt. U.S. Army, 1958-64; 1st sgt. USAR, 1983-94; ret. USAR, 1994; col. Alaska State Defense Force, 1985-98, ret. Decorated Korean Svc. medal with 2 combat stars, Korean Presdl. unit citation, UN Svc. medal, Nat. Def. Svc. medal, Vietnam Svc. medal, Meritorious Svc. medal with 2 oak leaf clusters, Army Commendation medal with 4 oak leaf clusters; recipient USAF Brewer Aerospace award, Grover Leoning award, Paul E. Garber award, 1984-85, State of Alaska Gov.'s Cert. Appreciation, 1983, Mayor's Pub. Svc. award, Anchorage, 1985, Commendation from Gov. of Alaska, 1993, 94, 18th Session Alaska Legis. Cert. Recognition, 1993, 94, Cert. of Appreciation, Pres. Bill Clinton, 1994. Mem. VFW (sr. vice comdr. 1995, post quartermaster 1996-99, sr. vice comdr. 2000), Res. Officers Assn. (pub. affairs officer

1985—), U.S. Naval Inst., Aviation and Space Writers Assn., Am. Aviation Hist. Soc., Am. Legion (historian), Pioneers of Alaska (sec. 1988, v.p. 1989, pres. 1990, Igloo 33, treas. 1994-95, Igloo 6, Cert. Appreciation 1988, Alaskan of Yr. award 2000). Lutheran. Home: 2723 John St Juneau AK 99801-2020

RUPCICH, MATTHEW WILLIAM, music educator; b. Chgo., Jan. 31, 1968; s. Lawrence P. and Marceline Marie Rupcich; life ptnr. Patrick Roy Field, Aug. 1, 1995. Bachelors of Music, Johns Hopkins U., 1990; Master's in Music, U. Md., 1996. Tchr. gen. music Dasher Green Elem. and St. John's Ln. Elem. Schs., Columbia, Md., 1990—91; choral dir. Atholton H.S., 1991—93; asst. dir. music ministries Bradley Hills Presbyn. Ch., Bethesda, 1991—98; choral music dir. The Madeira Sch., McLean, Va., 1993—98; dir. vocal music grades 5-12 Trinity Sch., N.Y.C., 1998—. Actor: (musical theater) Forever Plaid, 2002; dir.: (musical) Damn Yankees, 2001, The Baker's Wife, 2000, (musical/cabaret) Side by Side by Sondheim, 2000, (musical) Pippin, 1999, A Grand Night For Singing, 1999. Mem. Johns Hopkins U. Alumni Coun., Balt., 1999; mem. steering com. Peabody Conservatory, 1993—98. Recipient Superior, First Pl., and Best Overall awards for Choral Groups, Music Competitions, 1992—98; scholar All-Am. scholar, 1989. Mem.: Music Educator's Nat. Conf., Am. Choral Director's Assn., Bloomfield Third Riverbank Assn., Chorus Am., Johns Hopkins U. Alumni Assn. (mem. N.Y. chpt.), Pi Kappa Lambda. Office: Trinity Sch 139 West 91st St New York NY 10024 Office Fax: 212-932-6845. Personal E-mail: mrupcich@trinity.nyc.ny.us. Business E-Mail: mrupcich@trinity.nyc.ny.us.

RUPE, MEREDITH, minister; b. Noblesville, Ind., Aug. 3, 1941; s. Robert A. and Margaret E. Rupe; m. Pauline E. Wirt, Mar. 16, 1963; 3 children. BS, Ball State U., 1963; MDiv, Drew U., 1966; DD, McCormick Theol. Sem., Chgo., 1973. Cert. Ordained deacon, elder Meth. Ch. Min. Hillcrest United Meth. Ch., Elkhart, Ind., 1966—68, Keeler and Silver Creek United Meth. Chc., Powagian, Mich., 1968—70, Three Oaks (Mich.) United Meth. Ch., 1970—75; chaplain Marquette (Mich.) Br. Prison, 1975—79; chaplain/dir. Wesley Found. , Ferris State U., Big Rapids, 1979—98; sr. pastor Trinity United Meth. Ch., Iron Mountain, 1998—; adj. prof. Ferris State U., Big Rapids, 1979—98. Com. sec. Gen. Bd. Global Ministries, N.Y.C., 1972—76. Contbr. articles. Mem. planning bd., Big Rapids, 1985—90; v.p. Menominee River Habitat for Humanity, Dickinson City, Mich., 1998—; mem. Dickinson County Salvation Army Bd., 2001—. Named to Outstanding Young Men of Am., Washington, 1975. Avocation: Indpls. 500, gardening, reading.

RUPEKA, ROBERT W. court administrator; b. Youngstown, Ohio; s. Robert E. and Donna J. Rupeka. BA in Polit. Sci./Mgmt., Case Western Res. U., 1993. Cons. Prodigal Media Co., Youngstown, Ohio, 1993-94; adminstr. Mahoning County Clk. of Cts., 1994-2000; ct. adminstr. Mahoning County Common Pleas Cts., 2000—. Media/polit. cons., Youngstown, 1993-99. Mem., v.p. Mahoning County Alcohol and Drug Addiction Svcs. Bd., Youngstown, 1998-2001. Mem. Ohio Assn. for Ct. Adminstrn., Mahoning/Shenango Case Western Res. U. Alumni Assn. (pres. 1999-2000). Office: Mahoning County Common Pleas Ct 120 Market St Youngstown OH 44503 Office Fax: (330) 740-2088.

RUPEL, DANIEL PATRICK, retail and consulting excutive; b. Long Beach, Calif., July 19, 1955; s. Edgar Lee and Bobetta (Quantrell) R.; m. Karen Marie Connair, Sept. 26, 1973; 1 child, Danielle Patricia. Grad., Goldenwest Coll., 1978; PhD, Columbia State U., 1997. Cert. tchr., Calif. Ops. mgr. Treasury Stores, Orange, Calif., 1976-78; mdse. mgr. Sav-On Drugs, Anaheim, 1978-81; divisional mgr. HRT Corp., L.A., 1981-83; gen. mgr. Ross Stores, Norwalk, Calif., 1983-88; exec. v.p. New China Emporia, Huntington Beach, 1988—; sr. officer Huntington Beach Police Dept., 1996—. Educator Woodbury U., L.A., 1986—, Fashion Inst. Design and Mdse., 1987—, Brooks Coll., 1988—; pres., CEO, Kujawa Entertainment Corp., Huntington Beach, 1977—, Danco Cons. Group, 1998—, Retail Cons. Internat., 1999—. Author: A Song for You, 1979; columnist: Fashion Facts mag., 1987—; songwriter musical scores; published poet. Mem. adv. bd., Woodbury U., 1986—, chmn. 1987—; vol. Am. Diabetes Assn., Orange, 1984, Ocean View Little League, Huntington Beach, 1986—, Girl Scouts of U.S., Huntington Beach, 1984. With U.S. Army, 1973-76. Recipient award of honor and Golden State award State of Calif. Mem. Am. Songwriters Assn. (hon. mention 1977), Am. Poetry Writers Assn. (hon. mention 1988, Golden Poet award 1988), Norwalk C. of C., Norwalk Mchts. Assn. (pres. 1988), Meadowlark Country Club. Republican. Roman Catholic. Avocations: golf, tennis, racquetball, skiing. Home and Office: 13622 Olive St Westminster CA 92683-2644 E-mail: dancoconsulting.resourcez.com., retailconsultants.resourcez.com., rupel@webtv.net.

RUPEL, DIMITRIJ, diplomat; b. Apr. 7, 1946; Degree in Comparative Lit. and Sociology, U. Ljubljana, Slovenia, 1970; PhD in Sociology, Brandeis U., 1976. Lectr., asst., assoc. prof. U. Ljubljana, 1970-92, prof., 1992—; min. Ministry Fgn. Affairs, Slovenia, 1990-93; mem. Nat. Assembly, Rep. of Slovenia, 1993-95; mayor City of Ljubljana, 1995-97; ambassador to U.S., Mex. Washington, 19972000; min. of fgn. affairs Republic of Slovenia, 2000—. Office: Ministry Foreign Affairs Gregorciceva 25 SI-1000 Ljubljana Slovenia also: Ministry of Foreign Affairs Presernova 25 1000 Ljubljana Slovenia

RUPERD, THERESA, music educator; b. Kansas City, Kans., Nov. 1, 1972; d. Walter Raymond and Karen Lorene R. BA, U. Mo., 1995. Freelance musician, ind. music tchr., Prairie Village, Kans., 1991—. Singer Madrigalia Bar Nonne, Overland Park, Kans., 1996—; mgr. W.J. Music & Gifts, Overland Park, 1996—, Independence, Mo., 1999—2001; mem. U. Mo.-Kansas City Conservatory Women's Com., 1998—. Author: (newsletter) KCFA Newsletter, 1991-96; editor: (newsletter) Pieces of Pi, 1996-97; contbr. articles to profl. jours. Mem. Fedn. Music Tchrs., Music Tchrs. Nat. Assn., Kansas City Music Tchrs. Assn., Kansas City Flute Assn., Nat. Flute Assn., Sigma Alpha Iota, Mortar Board, Omicron Delta Kappa, Golden Key. Avocations: gardening, cooking, travel, reading. Office: WJ Music & Gifts 7316 W 119th St Overland Park KS 66213-1112

RUPERT, DANIEL LEO, education and educational technology consultant; b. Waynoka, Okla., Nov. 12, 1953; s. Robert Anthony and Georgia Yvonne (Lewis) R.; m. Emily Carol Lummus, June 12, 1977; 1 child, Joshua Daniel. AA, Miss. County C.C., 1979; BA in Social Psychology, Park Coll., 1981; MDiv, New Orleans Bapt. Theol. Sem., 1985; EdS, Miss. State U., Starkville, 1991. Chaplain East Miss. State Hosp., Meridian, 1985-87; dir. of rsch. Am. Family Assn., Tupelo, Miss., 1988-89; cons. Rupert & Assocs., 1989-93; guidance counselor Okolona (Miss.) Elem. Sch., 1993-94, guidance counselor, asst. prin., chpt. 1 coord., 1994-96, prin., 1996-97; edn. and ednl. tech. cons. Rupert Cons., 1997—. Computer cons. Lee County Schs., Tupelo, 1990. Author: Selected Poems by Author, 1990; co-author: (state core objectives) Health Education Core Objectives for the State of Mississippi, 1991. Prt-time pastor Koinonia Bapt. Mission, Mooreville, Miss., 1992-96; mem. Christian Bus. Men's Com., Tupelo, 1989-94. With USAF, 1976-82; capt. USAFR, 1983-91, ret., 1995. Mem. ASCD, Am. Assn. Christian Counselors, United Am. Karate Assn., Christian Martial Arts Instrs. Assn. (bd. dirs.), Miss. Counseling Assn. (bd. dirs.), Miss. Spiritual, Ethical and Religious Values in Counseling (pres.), Tupelo Martial Arts Acad., Luncheon Civitan Club, Chi Sigma Iota. Republican. Southern Baptist. Avocations: Karate, writing, singing, playing guitar, spending time with family. Home: 1931 E Main St PO Box 495 Tupelo MS 38802-0495 Office: 1933 E Main St Tupelo MS 38804-2972

RUPERT, DONALD WILLIAM, lawyer; b. Clearfield, Pa., Oct. 15, 1946; s. Donald Lee and Dorothy Mae (Bonsall) R.; m. Patricia A. Rupert, June 21, 1969. BS in Chemistry, Miami U., Ohio, 1968; JD, Washburn U., Topeka, 1976. Bar: Tex. 1976, Ill. 1978, U.S. Ct. Appeals (Fed. cir.) 1978, U.S. Dist. Ct. (so. dist.) Tex. 1977, U.S. Ct. Appeals (7th cir.) 1981, U.S. Dist. Ct. (no. dist.) Ill. 1979, U.S. Supreme Ct., 1992. Assoc. Arnold, White & Durkee, Houston, 1976-78, Kirkland & Ellis, Chgo., 1978-83, ptnr., 1983-86; ptnr. Neuman, Williams, Anderson & Olson, Chgo., 1986-90; founding ptnr. Roper & Quigg, 1990-93; ptnr. Keck, Mahin & Cate, Chgo., 1993-96; ptnr. Mayer, Brown, Rowe & Maw, Chgo., 1996—; cons. USAF, Dayton, Ohio, 1974-81. Contbr. articles to profl. jours. Served to capt. USAF, 1968-74. Miami U. Undergrad. Rsch. fellow, 1967, Grad. Rsch. fellow, 1968. Mem. ABA, Am. Intellectual Property Law Assn., Tex. Bar Assn., Phi Kappa Phi. Democrat. Presbyterian. Home: 2519 Park Pl Evanston IL 60201-1315 Office: Mayer Brown Rowe & Maw 190 S La Salle St Ste 3100 Chicago IL 60603-3441

RUPERT, ELIZABETH ANASTASIA, retired university dean; b. Emlenton, Pa., July 12, 1918; d. John Hamilton and Eva Blanche (Elliott) R. Diploma, Altoona Sch. Commerce, 1936; BS in Edn., Clarion State Coll., 1959; MSLS, Syracuse U., 1962; PhD, U. Pitts., 1970. Sec. Quaker State Oil Refining Corp., 1939-56; tchr., libr. Oil City Area Schs., 1959-61; libr. Venango campus Clarion (Pa.) U., 1961-62, prof. Coll. Libr. Sci., 1962-70, dean Sch. Libr. Sci., Coll. Libr. Sci., 1971-85; prof. emeritus, 1994. Interim pres. Clarion U., spring 1977; acct. William Rupert Mortuary, Inc., 1948-88. Author: Pennsylvania Practicum Program for School Librarians: An Appraisal, 1970; mem. ad hoc edit. com. Pa. Media Guidelines, Pa. Dept. Edn., 1976, author (with others) Encyclopedia of Library and Information Science, 1984. Bd. dirs. Knox Pub. Libr., 1991-97; mem. Abscurf, Sec. Ch. Orgns. Recipient Disting. Faculty award Clarion U. Alumni Assn., 1976, Disting. Alumni award, 1987, Zonta Internat. Women of Achievement award, 1987. Mem. Beta Phi Mu, Pi Gamma Mu. Republican. Home: PO Box H Knox PA 16232-0608

RUPERT, HOOVER (LYNN HOOVER RUPERT), minister; b. Madison, N.J., Nov. 3, 1917; s. Lynn Hoover and Hazel L. (Linabary) R.; m. Hazel Pearl Senti, June 22, 1941; children— Susan (Mrs. Max Unland), Elizabeth (Mrs. Warren W. Wright). AB, Baker U., 1938; A.M., Boston U., 1940, M.Div. cum laude, 1941; student (summers), Garrett Bibl. Inst. and Northwestern U., 1942, Union Theol. Sem., 1943; D.D., Adrian Coll., 1952, Baker U., 1966; L.H.D., Milliken U., 1974. Ordained to ministry Methodist Ch., 1940; asst. pastor First Meth. Ch., Baldwin, Kans., 1936-38, St. Mark's Meth. Ch., Brookline, Mass., 1938-41; pastor Thayer-St. Paul, Kans., 1941-43, First Ch., Olathe, 1943-45; dir. youth dept. Gen. Bd. Edn. Meth. Ch., Nashville, 1945-50; pastor 1st Meth. Ch., Jackson, Mich., 1950-59, 1st United Meth. Ch., Ann Arbor, 1959-72, Kalamazoo, 1972-83; faculty dept. religion Fla. So. Coll., Lakeland, 1983-89; adj. faculty Wesley Theol. Sem., Washington, 1989-93. Dean Mich. Meth. Pastors Sch., 1959-65; mem. Jud. Council United Meth. Ch., 1968-88 , sec., 1976-88, sec. emeritus, 1988. Author: Prayer Poems on the Prayer Perfect, 1943, Christ Above All (editor), 1948, Youth and Evangelism, 1948, Youth and Stewardship, rev. edit., 1960, Your Life Counts (editor), 1950, What Methodists Believe, rev. edit., 1959, John Wesley and People Called Methodists, 1953, I Belong, 1954, And Jesus Said, 1960, Enjoy Your Teen-Ager, 1962, A Sense of What is Vital, 1964, The Church in Renewal, 1965, My People are Your People, 1968, Where is thy Sting?, Christian Perspectives on Death, 1969, What's Good About God?, 1975 God Will See You Through, 1976, An Instrument of Thy Peace, 1982, The High Cost of Being Human, 1986, Why Didn't Noah Swat Both Mosquitoes, 1993, Up to Your Armpits in Alligators, 1996; writer, syndicated weekly mag. column Accent on Living; newspaper feature Talking to Teens; other publs., periodicals, and newspapers. Trustee Bronson Hosp., 1972-88, Adrian Coll., 1952-67, Asbury Meth. Village, 1996-2000; pres., bd. dirs. Youth for Understanding, 1970-83, Ann Arbor United Fund, YMCA-YWCA. Recipient Distinguished Alumnus award Boston U., 1969; Lucinda Bidwell Beebe fellow Boston U., 1941 Mem. World Meth. Council, Nat. Council Chs., Mark Twain Soc., Nat. Forensic League, Pi Kappa Delta, Alpha Psi Omega. Lodges: Mason, Rotary (Paul Harris fellow 1983). Home: 403 Russell Ave Gaithersburg MD 20877-2811

RUPERT, JOHN EDWARD, retired savings and loan executive, business and civic affairs consultant; b. Cleve., Oct. 19, 1927; s. Edward J. and Emma (Levegood) R.; m. Virginia Carlson, Oct. 27, 1951; children: Kristen, Karen Rupert Keating, David. BA, Cornell U., 1949, LL.B., 1951; certificate, Grad. Sch. Savs. & Loan, Ind. U., 1958. With Broadview Savs. & Loan Co., Cleve., 1953-86, v.p., 1964-74, mng. officer, 1965-86, pres., chief exec. officer, 1974-86, chmn., 1979-86. Mem. Cleve. Real Estate Bd., 1955-86; mem. Lakewood (Ohio) Bd. Edn., 1971-77, pres., 1975-77; v.p., trustee Lakewood Hosp., 1966-71; trustee exec. com. of Cleve. Zool. Soc., 1980—, pres., 1987-92, chmn., 1992—; trustee Cleve. Orch., WVIZ Ednl. TV; trustee, exec. com. Greater Cleve. Reads, 1991—; mem. Cornell U. Coun., 1971—, pres., 1977; mem. adv. bd. Cornell Coll. Arts and Scis., 1980—; trustee Med. Ctr. Corp., 1987-96, chair, 1990-96; trustee Internat. Ctr. for Preservation of Wild Animals, 1991—. With USAF, 1951-53. Mem. Cleve. Interfaith Housing Corp. (pres. 1971—), Inst. Fin. Edn. (pres. 1970), Cleve. Real Property Inventory (pres. 1976—), Ohio Motorists Assn. (corp. bd.), Delta Kappa Epsilon, Phi Delta Phi, Sphinx Head Soc. Clubs: Cleve. Yachting, Cornell (Cleve.) (trustee); Cornell (N.Y.C.). Home and Office: 18129 W Clifton Rd Cleveland OH 44107-1037 E-mail: rup18129@aol.com.

RUPERT, WAYNE RICHARD, protective services official; b. Jersey City, June 18, 1943; s. Arthur Barr and Mary (Garner) R.; m. Beverly Jean LaVance, June 8, 1968; children: Susan, Jennifer, Mark. Student, Rutgers U., 1962. Sheriff's officer Ocean County Sheriff's Dept., Toms River, N.J., 1967-71, sgt., 1971-74, lt., 1974-85, capt., 1985-95, chief, 1995-2000, undersheriff, 2000—. Mem. Ocean County Emergency Planning Coun., Toms River, 1992—, N.J. Radiol. Emergency Response Planning Com., Trenton, N.J., 1992—, N.J. Emergency Comm. Planning Com., Trenton, 1995—. Contbr. articles to profl. jours. Life mem., past capt. Comty. First Aid Squad, Brick, N.J., 1961-89; elder Faith Bible Ch., Brick, 1985—; com. chmn. troop 38 Boy Scouts of Am., Brick, 1996-2000, mem. dist. com., Toms River, 1996—2001, mem. Order of Arrow, 1991—, mem. Jersey Shore Coun. Recipient Running Water Dist. Svc. award Boy Scouts Am., 1996, Jersey Shore Coun. Svc. award, 1997, 99, Vigil Honor, 1996, Order Arrow Founders award, 1999. Mem. Internat. Assn. Emergency Mgrs., Nat. Sheriff's Assn. Presbyterian. Avocations: camping, reading, hunting, fishing. Office: Ocean County Sheriff's Dept PO Box 2191 Toms River NJ 08754-2191

RUPORT, SCOTT HENDRICKS, lawyer; b. Nov. 22, 1949; s. Fred Hendricks and Juyne (Kennedy) R.; m. Linda Darlene Smith, Sept. 12, 1970; children: Brittany Lyle, Courtney Kennedy. BSBA, Bowling Green U., 1971; JD, U. Akron, 1974. Bar: Ohio 1974, Pa. 1984, U.S. Dist. Ct. (no. dist.) Ohio 1974, U.S. Ct. Appeals (6th cir.) 1975, U.S. Supreme Ct. 1978; cert. civil trial specialist Nat. Bd. Trial Advocacy. Assoc. Schwab, Sager, Growenburgh, Rothal, Fort, Skidmore & Nukes, Akron, Ohio, 1974-76, Skidmore & George Co. LPA, Akron, 1976-79, Skidmore, Ruport & Haskings, Akron, 1979-83; ptnr. Roderick, Myers & Linton, 1983-85, Ruport Co. LPA, Akron, 1985—. Instr. real estate law U. Akron, 1976-77, adj. asst. prof. constrn. tech. Coll. Engring., 1983—. Capt. Fin. Corps. USAR, 1971-79. Mem. ABA, ATLA, Ohio Bar Assn., Ohio Acad. Trial Lawyers (chmn. civil and bus. litigation sect. 1989), Akron Bar Assn., Beta Gamma Sigma, Sigma Chi. Republican. Presbyterian. Office: Ruport Co LPA 3700 Embassy Pkwy Ste 440 Akron OH 44333-8367

RUPP, GEORGE ERIK, former academic administrator; b. Summit, N.J., Sept. 22, 1942; s. Gustav Wilhelm and Erika (Braunoehler) R.; m. Nancy Katherine Farrar, Aug. 22, 1964; children: Katherine Heather, Stephanie Karin. Student, Ludwig Maximilians U., Munich, Germany, 1962-63; AB, Princeton U., 1964; B.D., Yale U., 1967; postgrad., U. Sri Lanka, Peradeniya, 1969-70; PhD, Harvard U., 1972. Ordained to ministry Presbyn. Ch. U.S.A., 1971; faculty fellow in religion, vice chancellor Johnston College, U. Redlands, Redlands, Calif., 1971-74; asst. prof. Harvard Divinity School, Harvard U., Cambridge, Mass., 1974-76, assoc. prof., 1976-77, prof., dean, 1979-85; prof., dean acad. affairs U. Wis., Green Bay, 1977-79; prof., pres. Rice U., Houston, 1985-93, Columbia U., N.Y.C., 1993—2002; pres. Int. Rescue Committee, NY, 2002—. Bd. dirs. Com. for Econ. Devel., Inst. Internat. Edn., InterAction. Author: Christologies and Cultures: Toward a Typology of Religious Worldviews, 1974, Culture Protestantism: German Liberal Theology at the Turn of the Twentieth Century, 1977, Beyond Existentialism and Zen: Religion in a Pluralistic World, 1979, Commitment and Community, 1989; contbr. articles to profl. jours. Danforth Grad. fellow, 1964-71 Mem. AAAS, Am. Acad. Religion, Coun. on Fgn. Rels., Soc. for Values in Higher Edn. Office: International Rescue Committee 122 East 42nd Street New York NY 10168

RUPP, MONICA CECILIA, nursing administrator; b. Washington, July 20, 1956; d. Francis Aloysius and Cecilia Evangeline (Wilkinson) R.; 1 child, Mary Elizabeth. BSN, U. Md., 1979, postgrad., 1980-83, Tex. Christian U., 1989-90, U. Tex., Arlington, 1992-94; MBA, City U., Washington, 2000. Cert. oper. rm. nurse, nurse adminstr. Staff nurse Washington Adventist Hosp., Takoma Pk., Md., 1979-80; charge nurse Washington Hosp. Ctr., Washington, 1980-86; staff nurse surg. svcs. NIH, Bethesda, Md., 1983-86; nurse clinician cardiovascular thoracic Washington Hosp. Ctr., Washington, 1986-88; edn. coord. surgery Harris Meth., Ft. Worth, 1988-90; cons. Higman Healthcare, 1991; unit mgr. day surgery Harris Meth., Ft. Worth, 1992-93; adminstrv. asst. Ctr. for Neurol. Disorders, 1993-94; quality assessment coord. Children's Nat. Med. Ctr., Washington, 1995-96, clin. mgr. 2 Perioperative Svcs., CHAI project coord., 1996-97, mgr. sterile processing and distbn. dept., 1997-99, project coord. children's health accountability initiative, 1999—; dir. clin. svcs. Ctr. for Ambulatory Surgery, Inc. Contbr. to Textbook of Perioperative Nursing; contbr. articless to profl. jours. Mem. ANA, Am. Assn. Oper. Rm. Nurses (nat. legis. contract 1988-90, Ft. Worth chpt. legis. com. chair 1988-90, edn./program chair 1988-90, bd. dirs. 1989-90), Nat. Assn. for Healthcare Quality (nat. lectr. Perioperative Nursing Rev. 1990-91, recommended practices coord. com. 1992-94, co-author Preparing for Certification 1991, reviewer core curriculum), Tex. Nurses Assn. (legis. liaison 1988-90, govt. affairs com. 1988-89, edn. com. 1989-90, membership com. 1991-92), Alpha Phi. Avocations: horsebackriding, swimming, tennis, running. Home: 11220 Cherry Hill Rd # 2 Beltsville MD 20705-3825

RUPP, RALPH RUSSELL, audiologist, educator, author; b. Saginaw, Mich., Apr. 12, 1929; s. Martin Carl and Veronica Marie (Riethmeier) R. BA, U. Mich., 1951, MA, 1952; PhD, Wayne State U., 1964. Speech and hearing cons. Detroit Pub. Schs., 1955-60; exec. dir. Detroit Hearing and Speech Center, 1960-62; assoc. in audiology Henry Ford Hosp., Detroit, 1962-65; prof. audiology U. Mich., Ann Arbor, 1965-89; coord. audiology Eastern Mich. U., 1985-93, cons. in audiology, 1994—, U. Mich., 1994—. Cons. St. Joseph Mercy Hosp., Ann Arbor, Ann Arbor VA Hosp., Mott Children's Health Ctr., Flint, Mich., Pontiac (Mich.) Gen. Hosp., U. Mich. Health Svcs.; pres. Detroit Hearing Ctr., 1966. Author: (with James Maurer) Hearing and Aging: Tactics for Intervention, 1979, (with Kenneth Stockdell) Speech Protocols in Audiology, 1980; contbr. articles to profl. jours. Served with Med. Service Corps, U.S. Army, 1953-55. Named Disting. Alumnus, Saginaw High Sch., 1981, Outstanding Grad., Wayne State U. Fellow Am. Speech, Lang. and Hearing Assn. (Editor's award); mem. Acad. Rehab. Audiology (past editor Jour.), Mich. Speech and Hearing Assn. (pres. 1954, Disting. Service award, past editor Jour, honor award). Home: 3163 Plymouth Rd Ann Arbor MI 48105-3203

RUPP, SHARON KAY, sculptor; b. Deer-Lodge, Mont., Feb. 15, 1955; d. Ben and Larada Sinerius; children: Amity, Jason, Aaron, Matthew, Brian. BA, U. Great Falls, 1995. Author: The Baby Maker. Mem.: Wash. State Arts Alliance (bd. legis. affairs 2000—, arts wrangler 2002), Artist Trust (grant 1998), Women's Caucus for Art (v.p. N.W. chpt.). Avocations: painting, sculpting, photography, drawing. Home: 1613 W 9th Ave Kennewick WA 99336

RUPP, SHERON ADELINE, photographer, educator; b. Mansfield, Ohio, Jan. 14, 1943; d. Warren Edmund Rupp and Frances Adeline (Hanson) Christian. BA in Sociology and Psychology, Denison U., 1965; MFA in Photography, U. Mass., 1982. Teaching asst. in photography Hampshire Coll., Amherst, Mass., 1981; instr. photography Northfield (Mass.) Mt. Hermon Sch., 1982-83, U. Mass., Amherst, 1984, Holyoke (Mass.) Community Coll., 1986, 87-88; vis. asst. prof. photography Hampshire Coll., 1985, 87; vis. lectr. photography Amherst (Mass.) Coll., 1994. Guest artist, lectr. Boston Mus. Sch., Portland (Maine) Sch. Art, NYU, U. Mass., Deerfield (Mass.) Acad., Hartford Sch. Art/U. Hartford-Conn., Springfield Mus. Fine Arts, Mass., Bard Coll, N.Y., Mass. Coll. Art, Boston, others; guest lectr. Carpenter Ctr., Harvard U., Cambridge, Mass., 2000. Exhibited in one-person shows at Tisch Sch. Arts NYU, 1987, Portland Sch. Art, 1989, Hart Gallery, Northampton, Mass., 1992, O.K. Harris Gallery, N.Y.C., 1992, Cleve. Mus. Art, 2000; exhibited in 2-person shows at Columbus (Ohio) Mus. Art, 1997-98, Springfield (Mass) Tech. C.C., 2000; exhibited in group shows at DeCordova Mus., Lincoln, 2000—, Zone Art Ctr., N.Y.C., 1987, Mus. Modern Art, N.Y.C., 1991, 99—, Springfield Mus. Fine Art, 1993, U. Mass., Amherst, 1993, Dirs. Guild, L.A., 1994, Manchester (N.H.) Inst. Arts and Scis., 1995, Weber State U., Utah, 1995, Grand Ctrl. Terminal, N.Y.C., 1995, Photographic Resource Ctr. 3d Biennial, Boston, 1995, Smithsonian Arts and Scis., Washington, 2001; represented in collections at DeCordova Mus., Lincoln, Mass., Mus. Modern Art, N.Y.C., Fogg Art Mus. at Harvard U., Hallmark Collection of Photography, Kansas City, Columbus (Ohio) Mus. Art, Mus. Fine Arts, Boston, Rose Art Mus. Brandeis U., Mead Art Mus. Amherst Coll., Smith Coll. Mus. Art, Danforth Mus. Art, Springfield Tech. C.C. Found., Carpenter Ctr. for Visual Arts Harvard U., The Smithsonian; photographs (including cover photo) in Double-Take Mag., winter 1998. Bd. dirs. Zone Art Ctr., 1987-94. Recipient Mass. Fellowship award in photography Artist Found., 1984, 87; visual artist fellow Nat. Endowment for the Arts, 1986, 94, Guggenheim fellow, 1990. Avocations: hiking, bicycling, writing. Home and Office: 364 Hatfield St Apt C Northampton MA 01060-1541 E-mail: sheron@crocker.com.

RUPP, THEODORE HANNA, retired French language educator; b. Windham, N.Y., Oct. 22, 1915; s. Theodore Franklin and Mary Zelia (Hanna) R.; m. Earla Mary Roberts, Aug. 11, 1940; children: Carol Roberts Rupp Licastro, Patricia Hanna Rupp Solomon. BA, Franklin and Marshall Coll., 1935; MA, Pa. State U., 1942; PhD, U. Pa., 1954; postgrad., Sorbonne, U. de Montpellier, France, 1952-53, U. de Besançon, 1964-65. Cert. tchr., Pa. Tchr., coach Franklin & Marshall Acad., Lancaster, Pa., 1935-43, Solebury Sch., New Hope, 1943, Shady Side Acad., Pitts., 1943-44; tchr., coach, dept. chmn. Millersville (Pa.) U. of Pa., 1946-82; tchr. Lancaster (Pa.) Area Coll., 1946-48, York Coll. of Pa., 1982-87, Elizabethtown (Pa.) Coll., 1987-88, Millersville U. French Summer Sch., 1967—99. Resident dir. West Chester Jr. Yr. Abroad, Besançon, France, 1964-65; founder, dir. Millersville (Pa.) Grad. Fgn. Lang. Summer Sch., 1967-79; assoc. adv. coach wrestling Millersville U., 1993—; cons. devel. office Franklin & Marshall Coll., Lancaster, 1978—. Editor: A Collection of Recollections, 1993, rev. edit., 1998; contbr. articles to profl. jours. Lt. comdr. USNR, ret. Decorated Chevalier dans l'ordre des Palmes Académiques; recipient Outstanding Svc. award Pa. State Dept. Edn., 1990, Alumni medal Franklin and Marshall Coll., 1994; named to Millersville U. Athletics Hall of Fame, 1995, Nat. Wrestling Hall of Fame in Class of 1999 for Lifetime Svc. to Wrestling; named Ea. Intercollegiate Wrestling Assn. Man of Yr., 2002; Fulbright scholar, 1952-53. Mem. MLA, Pa. State MLA (pres. 1964-67, editor The Bull. 1970-90, Educator of Yr. 1975), Am. Assn. Tchrs. French, Am. Assn. Coll. and Univ. Profs. (pres. local chpt. 1954), Internat. Arthurian Soc., Internat. Courtly Lit. Soc., The Res. Officers Assn., Lancaster Rd. Runners Club (hon. life), Phi Beta Kappa, Phi Sigma Kappa, Phi Kappa Phi (hon.), VFW. Republican. United Ch. of Christ. Avocations: road running, French slang, French and English proverbs, fgn. travel, fund raising for scholarships. Home: 17 Bentley Ln Lancaster PA 17603-6203 Office: Franklin & Marshall Acad PO Box 3003 Lancaster PA 17604-3003

RUPPE, ARTHUR MAXWELL, lawyer; b. Boone, N.C., Dec. 15, 1928; s. Arthur Monroe and Floye (Robinson) R.; m. Ruth Marie Ledford; children: Ruth Carol, Sharon Marie, Arthur Maxwell Jr., Susan Lunette. AA, Gardner Webb Coll., 1947; AB, U. N.C., 1950, JD, 1952. Bar: N.C. 1952, U.S. Dist. Ct. (ea. dist.) N.C. 1955, U.S. Ct. Mil. Appeals 1968; cert mediator. Asst. staff, judge advocate U.S. Army, Ft. Bragg, N.C., 1952-55; sole practice Fayetteville, 1955-98; mediator, 1997—. Served to 1st lt. U.S. Army, 1952-55. Mem. ABA, N.C. Bar Assn. (patron), N.C. State Bar Assn., 12 Jud. Dist. Bar Assn., Cumberland County Bar Assn. (pres. 1982-83), K.P. Democrat. Baptist. Avocations: snow ski, tennis. Home: 336 Summertime Rd Fayetteville NC 28303-4658

RUPPEL, HOWARD JAMES, JR. sociologist, sexologist, educator; b. Orange, N.J., July 22, 1941; s. Howard J. and Lillian M. (Wordley) R.; m. Barbara Margaret Wiedemann, June 3, 1967. BA, St. Joseph's Coll., Ind., 1963; MA, No. Ill. U., 1968; postgrad., U. Iowa, 1968-76; EdD, Inst. for Advanced Study Human Sexuality, 1993, PhD, 1994. Diplomate Am. Bd. Sexology; cert. sexologist Am. Coll. Sexologists. Instr. social sci., debate coach St. Francis H.S., Wheaton, Ill., 1963-65; instr. sociology St. Dominic Coll., St. Charles, 1966-67, Cornell Coll., Mt. Vernon, Iowa, 1969-70, asst. prof., 1970-72, lectr., 1972-73; rsch. dir. Social Sci. Rsch. Assocs., Cedar Rapids, Iowa, 1973-80; founder, co-dir. Ctr. for Sexual Growth and Devel., Mt. Vernon, 1980-95; instr. Sch. Social Work, U. Iowa, 1976-78, adj. asst. prof., 1979-81, adj. assoc. prof., 1981-96, prof., 1997—. Exec. dir. Soc. for Sci. Study of Sexuality, 1988—, Found. for the Sci. Study of Sexuality, 1989-98, Am. Assn. Sex Educators, Counselors and Therapists, 1996—; prof. Inst. Advanced Study Human Sexuality, 1996—; cons. Iowa Dept. Social Svcs., Families Inc., West Branch, A&E Network (Biography); bd. dirs. The

Human Outreach and Achievement Inst., Boston, 1988-90, Inst. Advanced Study Human Sexuality, 1995—. Co-editor: Sexuality and the Family Life Span, 1983; assoc. editor Ann. Rev. of Sex Rsch., 1992, 93, 94, 95, 96, 97, 98, 99; contbr. articles on complex orgns., marriage and the family, sexual attitudes and behavior, childhood and preadolescent sexuality, methodology and child care theory to profl. publs. NSF fellow, 1968. Fellow Am. Acad. Clin. Sexologists; mem. Am. Sociol. Assn., Nat. Coun. Family Rels., Iowa Coun. Family Rels. (sec. 1983-84, treas. 1985), Changing Family Conf. (bd. dirs. 1983-87), Soc. Sci. Study of Sex Inc. (bd. dirs. 1983-88, pres. Midcontinent Region 1984-85, treas. 1986-88, chmn. membership com. 1983-85, chmn. exhibits com. 1983-88, ann. meeting chmn. 1986), Am. Assn. Sex Educators, Counselors and Therapists (exec. dir. 1996—, cert. sex educator), Harry Benjamin Internat. Gender Dysphoria Assn., Coun. Assns. for Sexual Sci., Health and Edn. (del.), Inst. for the Advanced Study of Human Sexuality Alumni Assn., Alpha Kappa Delta, Alpha Sigma Lambda (hon.). Democrat. Home: 608 5th Ave N Mount Vernon IA 52314-1107 Office: 103 A Ave S Ste 2-b Mount Vernon IA 52314-1400

RUPPERT, CONRAD JACK, JR. civil engineer, technology manager; b. Flushing, N.Y., Mar. 29, 1955; s. Conrad Jack and Elsie Ann (August) R.; m. Joann Nussbaumer, Aug. 6, 1977; children: Jessica, Abigail, Matthew. BS in Civil Engring., Princeton U., 1977; postgrad., U. Pa., 1998—. Jr. engr. Amtrak, N.Y.C., 1977-78, project engr., 1978-80, staff engr., 1980-83, engr. spl. projects Phila., 1983-86, mgr. field engring., 1986-95, tech. dir. engring., 1995—. Pastor, New Jerusalem Christian Ch., Hightstown, N.J., 1989—. Mem. Am. Ry. Engring. Assn. (sec. com. 1998), Transp. Rsch. Bd. (mem. com.). Christian. Avocations: reading, hiking, fishing. Office: Amtrak PO Box 24 Philadelphia PA 19105-0024

RUPPERT, JOHN HUTCHINS, sculptor; b. Winchester, Mass., May 8, 1951; s. C. Farrell and June (Hutchins) R.; m. Sally Price, Mar. 20, 1952; children: June, Kimberly. BA in Art Edn., Miami U., Oxford, Ohio, 1974; MFA, Rochester Inst. Technology, 1977. Resident artist Wildcliff Mus., New Rochelle, N.Y., 1977-79; lectr. U. Wyo., Laramie, 1979; instr. Webster U., St. Louis, 1980-85; resident artist Liberty Foundry, 1985-87; asst. prof. U. Md., College Park, 1987-92, assoc. prof., 1992—, chair dept. art, 1998—. Chair dept. art U. Md., 1998—. One-man shows include Elliot Smith Gallery, St. Louis, 1984, George Ciscle Gallery, Balt., 1985, 87, Southeastern Ctr. for Contemporary Art, Open Air Gallery, Winston-Salem, N.C., 1988, Barbara Fendrick Gallery, N.Y.C., 1989, Franz Bader Gallery, Washington, 1991, 95, Va. Beach Ctr. for Arts, 1996, Cleve. Ctr. for Contemporary Art, 1996, Chgo. Cultural Ctr., 1996, C. Grimaldis Gallery, Balt., 1997, Art et Industrie, N.Y.C., 1997, Evanston (Ill.) Art Ctr., 1999, Contemporary Art Mus., Raleigh, N.C., 2000-01, Weatherspoon Gallery, Greensboro, N.C., Montavo Sculpture Park, Sarasota, Calif.; group shows include Corcoran Sch. of Art, Washington, 1994, Luminy-Marseille, France, 1995, Delaware Mus., Wilmington, 1996, C. Grimaldis Gallery, Balt., 1991-92, 94-96, 2000, Art Scape, Balt., 1992, 94, 96, others; work collected at Grounds for Sculpture, N.J., Balt./Washington Airport, Md., Am. Visionary Art Mus., Balt., Xerox Corp., Rochester, Contemporary Art Found., Marseille, Suwa Mcpl. Art Mus., Japan, Art Mus. We. Va., Roanoke, Stone Quarry Hill, Cazenovia, N.Y., 1998-2000, Yawkey Woodson Art Mus., Wausau, Wis., DeCordova Mus. and Sculpture Park, Boston, Kreeger Mus., Washington. Trustee Md. Art Place, 1956. Artist grantee Md. State Arts Coun., 1991, 95, 97, Baltimore City, 1991; Creative and Performing Arts award, U. Md., 1987, 89, 91, 97. Home: 532 Allegheny Ave Towson MD 21204-4232 E-mail: jr59@umail.umdiedu.

RUPPERT, JOHN LAWRENCE, lawyer; b. Chgo., Oct. 7, 1953; s. Merle Arvin and Loretta Marie (Ford) R.; m. Katharine Marie Tarbox, June 5, 1976. BA, Northwestern U., 1975; JD, U. Denver, 1978; LLM in Taxation, NYU, 1979. Bar: Colo. 1978, U.S. Dist. Ct. Colo. 1978, Ill. 1979, U.S. Tax Ct. 1981. Assoc. Kirkland & Ellis, Denver, 1979-84, ptnr., 1984-88, Ballard, Spahr, Andrews & Ingersoll, Denver, 1988-96; shareholder Brownstein Hyatt Farber & Strickland, P.C., 1996—. Lectr. U. Denver Coll. Law, fall 1984-92; adj. prof. law grad. tax program, 1993-94; sec. Capital Assocs., Inc., 1989-96; sec. Brothers Gourmet Coffees, Inc., 1995-2000; asst. sec. Renaissance Cosmetics, Inc., 1996-98; sec. Skillset Software, Inc., 2000-01; asst. sec. Rhythms NetConnections Inc., 2000-01. Contbr. articles to profl. jours. Mem. ABA, Colo. Bar Assn. (mem. exec. coun. tax sect. 1985-89), Denver Bar Assn. Office: Brownstein Hyatt Farber & Strickland PC 410 17th St Fl 22D Denver CO 80202-4402 E-mail: jruppert@bhfs.com., jruppert53@aol.com.

RUPPERT, SUSAN DONNA, critical care nursing educator, family and adult nurse practitioner; b. LaSalle, Ill., Aug. 17, 1953; d. Joseph J. and Phyllis A. (Koontz) Stachowicz; m. Robert M. Ruppert; children: Sarah E., Michael R. AAS in Nursing, Ill. Valley C.C., Oglesby, 1974, AS in Sci., 1975; BSN, No. Ill. U., 1976; MSN, U. Tex. Health Sci. Ctr., San Antonio, 1979; PhD in Nursing, Tex. Woman's U., 1992; FNP, U. Tex. Med. Br., 1995. CCRN; NP-C (FNP), CS (ANP). Evening supr. Met. Gen. Hosp., San Antonio, 1978-79; instr. U. Iowa Coll. Nursing, Iowa City, 1979-81; program coord. continuing edn. Meth. Hosp., Houston, 1981-89; assoc. prof. U. Tex. Health Sci. Ctr., 1989—. Editor: Critical Care Nursing: Clinical Management Through the Nursing Process, 2d edit.; editor-in-chief Internet Jour. Advanced Practice Nursing; contbr. articles to profl. jours. and books. Recipient Outstanding Young Alumni award, No. Ill. U., 1992, Outstanding Houston Nurse award, Tex. Nurses Assn., 1995, Great 100 Nursing Alumni awrd, Tex. Woman's U., 2001. Fellow: Am. Coll. Critical Care Medicine; mem.: Nat. Orgn. Nurse Practitioner Faculties, Houston Area Nurse Practitioners, Greater Houston Soc. Critical Care, Soc. Critical Care Medicine (FCCS com. 1998—), Tex. Nurse Practitioners, Tex. Nurses Assn., Am. Acad. Nurse Practitioners, ANA, AACN (past bd. dirs., Excellence in Critical Care Edn. award 1995), Sigma Theta Tau (Region 3 coord. 1997—99, Regional Dissertation award 1992, Info. Tech. award 1999). Avocations: foreign travel, reading. Home: 4602 Springfield Lakes St Sugar Land TX 77479-2051 Office: U Tex Houston Hlth Sci Ctr 1100 Holcombe Blvd Rm 6250 Houston TX 77030-3906

RUPPRECHT, HERBERT HARALD, pharmaceutical technologist; b. Nuernberg, Germany, Nov. 10, 1936; s. Philipp and Berta R.; m. Ilse Hohloch, Mar. 24, 1966; children: Schneider Birgit, Adam Ursula. Grad. in Pharmacy, Ludwigs-Maximilian U., Munich, 1963; Apotheker, Bayerische Staatsregierung, Munich, 1965; D of Natural Scis., Ludwigs-Maximilian U., 1968. Sci. asst. Ludwigs-Maximilian U., 1964-74, docent, 1974-76; prof. U. Regensburg, Germany, 1976-97; ret., 1997. Dir. Inst. Pharmacy, U. Regensburg, 1977-79, 88-90, dean faculty chemistry, 1981-83. Co-editor: Arbeitsgemeinschaft für Pharmazuetische Verfahrensterhnik (Assn. Pharmaceutical Technologist), (10 vols.) 1982-85; contbr. over 130 articles to profl. jours.; patentee in field. Lifeguard Red Cross, Munich, 1955-60. Mem. Pharm. Soc. Slovenia (hon.), German Colloidal Soc., Assn. of Pharm. Technologists. Avocations: video, music. Home: Machthildstrasse 47 93053 Regensburg Germany

RUPPRECHT, NANCY ELLEN, historian, educator; b. Coeur d'Alene, Idaho, Sept. 23, 1948; d. George John and Nancy Berneeda (Baird) R. BA with honors, U. Mo., 1967, MA, 1969; PhD, U. Mich., 1982. Acad. dir. pilot program U. Mich., Ann Arbor, 1971-73, lectr. in women studies, 1973-75; vis. lectr. history U. Mo., St. Louis, 1976-77; vis. instr. of history Wash. U., 1977-79, Grinnell (Iowa) Coll., 1979-81; asst. prof. Oakland U., Rochester, Mich., 1981-83; asst. prof. of history Mid. Tenn. State U., Murfreesboro, 1985-91, assoc. prof., 1991-97, prof. history, 1997—. Dir. women's studies program Middle Tenn. State U., 1988—, publicity dir. women's history month, 1989-92, mem. faculty senate, 1992-95. Mem. editl. bd. German Studies Rev., 1999—; contbr. articles to profl. jours. Mem.: NOW, AAUW, AAUP (chpt. v.p. 1988—89, pres. 1989—93), Assn. Faculty and Adminstrv. Women (chpt. pres. 1995—), Concerned Faculty and Adminstrv. Women (chpt. v.p. 1993—95, chpt. pres. 1995—96), Women in Higher Edn. in Tenn., German Studies Assn., Mid Tenn. Women's Studies Assn., Holocaust Studies Assn., So. Humanities Assn., So. Hist. Assn. (chair nominating com. European divsn. 1996—97, mem. exec. com. 1996—, mem. program com. 1997—, chmn. program com. 2001—02, vice chair European divsn. 2002—), S.E. Women's Studies Assn., Am. Hist. Assn. Home: 1106 Jones Blvd Murfreesboro TN 37129-2310 Office: Middle Tenn State U 275 Peck Hall Murfreesboro TN 37132-0001

RUPRACHT, WILLIAM GEORGE, chaplain; b. Central Square, N.Y., Apr. 18, 1945; s. William S. and Neva Mae House Rupracht; 1 child, Kimberly Coker. BA, Carson-Newman Coll., 1971; grad., Air Command and Staff Coll.; MDiv, New Orleans Bapt. Theol., 1974; D of Ministry, San Francisco Theol. Sem., 1982. Cert. clin. chaplain Coll. Chaplains, 1978. Pastor 1st Bapt. Ch., White Castle, La., 1971-74; staff chaplain Audie L. Murphy VA Hosp., San Antonio, 1975-77; instr. USAF Chaplain Sch., Maxwell AFB, Ala., 1978-91; sr. IMA to command chaplain Air Force Materiel Command, Wright-Patterson AFB, Ohio, 1991-94, Air Force Space Command, Peterson AFB, 1991-94; chief chaplain svc. VA Med. Ctr., Tuscaloosa, Ala., 1997; IMA to directorate of chaplain svcs. Wilford Hall Med. Ctr., Lackland AFB, Tex., 1997—. Mem. writer's bd. CAP, Maxwell AFB; mem. USAF Chaplain Recruiting Team, USAFR, Denver; pastoral cons. Ala. Coll. Cmty. Health Scis., Tuscaloosa, U. Ala. Sch. Dentistry, Tuscaloosa; lectr. CAP Chaplain Svc. Writer's Study Guide. Author: (book) Pastoral Care to Huntington Patients and Families, 1982; editor: (book) Department of Veteran Affairs Chaplain Service Manual M-2, Part II, 1993. State pk. vol. Mt. San Jacinto, Palm Springs, Calif.; past comdr. Am. Legion, Northport, Ala., 1980; founding bd. dirs. West Ala. AIDS Bd., Tuscaloosa; past pres. West Ala. AIDS Edn. Com., Tuscaloosa; devel. mem. Hospice of West Ala., Tuscaloosa; state chaplain Nat. Huntington's Disease Assn., Birmingham, Ala. Col. USAFR, 1978. Decorated Meritorious Svc. medal; recipient 4 Chaplains Legion of Merit, Am. Legion; named Pub. Citizen of Yr., NASW. Mem.: Mil. Chaplains Assn., Mins. in Med. Edn. (nat. sec., treas., comdr.), Coll. Chaplains, Leadership VA Alumni Assn. (life; founding mem.), Am. Legion (post 208). Southern Baptist. Avocation: traveling. Home: 145 Sage Dr Palm Springs CA 92264-6461 Home Fax: 760-322-4602. E-mail: billybama@aol.com.

RURAK, ZBIGNIEW TADEUSZ, executive search consultant; b. Sept. 25, 1947; BA, Harvard U., 1969; MSc, London Sch. Econs., 1976. Cons. McKinsey & Co., Inc., Duesseldorf, Germany, 1979-82; dir. internat. mktg. Comsat Telesys., Washington, 1982-85; v.p. Leon A. Farley Assoc., 1985-87; pres. Rurak & Assocs., Inc., 1987—. Home: 3818 1/2 Huntington St NW Washington DC 20015-1928 Office: Rurak & Assocs Inc Ste 300 1776 Massachusetts Ave NW Washington DC 20036-1915

RURY, JOHN LESLIE, education educator; b. Syracuse, N.Y., Apr. 6, 1951; s. John and Virginia (Gould) R.; m. Ellen Kennedy, June 18, 1981 (div. Oct. 1992); children: Aaron, Derek; m. Aida Alaka, May 12, 1995. AB, Fordham U., 1973; MS in Edn., CUNY, 1975; PhD, U. Wis., 1982. Instr. history Wayne State U., Detroit, 1980-83; asst. prof. history Antioch Coll., Yellow Springs, Ohio, 1983-84; asst. prof. edn. Ohio State U., Columbus, 1984-87; from assoc. to prof. DePaul U., Chgo., 1987—; sr. program officer Spencer Found., 1999—2002, sr. advisor, 2002—. Program chmn. Midwest History of Edn. Soc., Chgo., 1989-90; core group mem. Policy Rsch. Action Group, Chgo., 1993-99; mem. pub. policy coun. Harris Sch., U. Chgo., 1997. Author: Education and Women's Work, 1991; editor: Seeds of Crisis, 1993 (Cambrnus prize 1993), DePaul University, 1998; editor Am. Edn. Rsch. Jour., 1992-96; mem. editl. bd. History of Education Quarterly, 1985-89. Rsch. grantee Nat. Inst. Edn., Washington, 1979-80, Spencer Found., Chgo., 1985, Radcliffe Coll., Cambridge, Mass., 1987; Spencer fellow Nat. Acad. Edn., Stanford, Calif., 1986-87. Mem. Am. Hist. Assn., Am. Ednl. Rsch. Assn. (v.p. 1997-99), History of Edn. Soc. (v.p. 1996-97, pres. 1997-98), John Dewey Soc. Office: Sch Edn DePaul Univ 2320 N Kenmore Ave Chicago IL 60614-3210 E-mail: jrury@condor.depaul.edu.

RUS, JAN, III, anthropologist; b. Ithaca, N.Y., Jan. 9, 1948; arrived in Mex., 1985; s. Jan and Mary Jean (Hayes) R.; m. Diane Louise Crow, June 15, 1968; children: Jan IV, Jacob R. AB summa cum laude, Harvard U., 1969, MA, 1976. Tutor in anthropology and Latin Am. studies Harvard U., Cambridge, Mass., 1972-74; field dir. Harvard-Chiapas Project, San Cristobal, Mex., 1975-76; prof. Autonomous U. Chiapas an Cristobal, 1976-77; investigator U.S.-Mex. Border Task Force, Pasadena, Calif., 1978-81; dir. native lang. project Maya Region Applied Anthropology Inst., San Cristobal, 1985—. Lectr. Latin Am. studies Stanford U., 1988; editor, 1985—. Author: Guerra de Castas de Quien, 1988; contbr. numerous articles to profl. jours. Vol. Peace Corps, 1969-71, Cath. Com. Against Hunger, 1985—. Doherty Found. fellow 1975; grantee Wenner-Glen Found., 1981-82, EEC, 1989. Mem. Latin Am. Studies Assn., Soc. Mexican Anthropologists, Phi Beta Kappa. Avocation: cycling. Home: Belisario Dominguez 43 San Cristobal de Las Casas 29200 Chiapas Mexico Office: INAREMAC AP San Cristobal 29200 Chiapas Mexico

RUSAN, TIBERIUS, materials science researcher; b. Periam, Timis, Romania, June 23, 1968; s. Vintilă and Agripina Rusan; m. Marcela Elena Balaban, Aug. 18, 1998. Mech. engr., U. Aurel Vlaicu, Arad, Romania, 1995; European welding engr., Schweisstechnische Lehr-und Versuchsanstalt-Munich, Germany, 1996; MSc in Advanced Tech. and New Materials, U. Poly., Timisoara, Romania, 1998. Cert. in engring. and materials sci. Engr. Nat. Inst. for R&D in Welding and Material Testing Timisoara, 1995-96, sr. engr., 1996-98, sr. rschr., 1998—. Contbr. articles to profl. jours. Mem. Trade Union, Timisoara, 1995—. Soldier Romanian Army, 1986-88. Mem. Internat. Metallographic Soc., Am. Soc. for Materials, Multidisciplinary Rsch. Soc. (founder). Avocations: swimming, culture, art history, opera, orchestra. Home: Nr 808 1963 Periam Romania Home (Summer): 2170 Sherobee Rd apt 603 Mississauga ON Canada L5A 3P8 E-mail: rtiberius@hotmail.com.

RUSAW, SALLY ELLEN, librarian; b. Potsdam, N.Y., Apr. 24, 1939; d. Ralph Clinton and Marion Ellen (Jenack) R. BS in Edn., Potsdam Coll., 1964; MLS, SUNY, Albany, 1975. Cert. libr. media specialist, pub. libr., permanent tchr. N-6, N.Y. Tchr. grade 7th-9th Diocese of Ogdensburg, N.Y., 1960-74, cons. office edn., 1975-78; assoc. libr. Mater Dei Coll., Ogdensburg, 1974-89, head libr., 1989-99, SUNY, Potsdam, 2000—. Vol. Ogdensburg Correctional Facility, 1982-95, Riverview Correctional Facility, Ogdensburg, 1987—; lector, Eucharistic min. Rite for Christian Initiation of Adults catechist St. Mary's Cathedral; vol. Ogdensburg Cath. Ctrl. Sch., sch. bd., 1995-2000. Named Vol. of Yr. Ogdensburg Correctional Facility, 1985, Outstanding Vol. Riverview Correctional Facility, 1991; Nat. Def. Edn. Act grantee, 1965. Mem. ALA, N.Y. Libr. Assn., North Country 3Rs Coun., North Country Ref. and Rsch. Resources Coun. (trustee 1994-99). Roman Catholic. Avocations: music, reading, berrying, outdoor activities, swimming.

RUSCH, GEORGE MICHAEL, toxicology and risk assessment director; b. N.Y.C., Dec. 19, 1947; s. George Warren and Emma Ellen (Whitford) R.; children: Heather Lynn, Michael. BS, Hobart Coll., Geneva, N.Y., 1963; MS, CUNY, 1967; PhD, Adelphi U., Garden City, N.Y., 1971. Rsch. assoc. NYU Med. Ctr., 1972-77; dir. inhalation toxicology Huntingdon Life Sci., East Millstone, N.J., 1977-80; mgr. inhalation toxicology Allied Signal Corp., Morristown, 1980-84, mgr. gen. toxicology, 1984-89; dir. toxicology and risk assessment Honeywell Internat., 1989—. Mem. com. of toxicology Nat. Rsch. Coun., Washington, 1997—; chair nat. adv. com. on acute exposure guidance levels, U.S. Environ. Protection Agy., Washington, 1996—. Contbr. articles to profl. jours. Adjunct prof. Rutgers U., Piscatawy, N.J., 1997—. Recipient Herbert Stockinger award Am. Conf. of Govt. Indsl. Hygienes, Cin., 2000, Hammer award Vice Pres. Gore, 2001. Mem. Soc. Toxicology, Am. Indsl. Hygiene Assn., Emergency Response Planning Guideline Commn. Home: 870 Dow Rd Bridgewater NJ 08807-1179 Office: Honeywell International 101 Columbia Rd Morristown NJ 07960-4658 E-mail: george.rusch@honeywell.com.

RUSCH, GERALD ALLEN, financial representative; b. Milw., July 8, 1937; s. Herman A. and Martha H. (Gebauer) R.; m. Joan R. Ruehlman, Dec. 29, 1961; children: Susan, Heidi. BA, U. Wis., 1960. Area rep. Wis. Heart Assn., Milw., 1960-61, Tex. Heart Assn., Austin, 1961-63; comms. cons. Wis. Telephone, Milw., 1963-74; sole proprietor Rusch Ins., Eau Claire, Wis., 1974—. Contbr. articles to mags. 1st lt. USAR, 1960-67. Named Agent of Yr. Eau Claire Gen. Agents and Mgrs. Assn., 1980. Mem. Nat. Assn. Fin. Profls., Million Dollar Roundtable, Phi Sigma Epsilon. Avocations: photography, walking, reading, classical music. Office: Northwestern Mut Fin Network 4330 Golf Ter Ste 209 Eau Claire WI 54701-4688 Home (Winter): 14071 Brandt Point Cir #621 Fort Myers FL 33919 Home (Summer): 4224 W Robin Meadows Ln Eau Claire WI 54701

RUSCH, JONATHAN JAY, lawyer; b. Nyack, N.Y., Oct. 16, 1952; s. Thaddeus David and Alice Marjorie (Lewis) R.; m. Doreen Evelyn Lacovara, Aug. 10, 1974; children: Rachel Madeline, Catherine Elizabeth. AB in Pub. Affairs with honors, Princeton U., 1974; MA, U. Va., 1978, JD, 1980. Bar: D.C. 1981, U.S. Dist. Ct. D.C. 1981, U.S. Ct. Appeals (D.C. cir.) 1981, U.S. Ct. Appeals (7th cir.) 1985, U.S. Ct. Appeals (9th cir.) 1990, U.S. Ct. Appeals (5th cir.) 1992, U.S. Supreme Ct. 1992. Assoc. Cleary, Gottlieb, Steen & Hamilton, Washington, 1980-83; spl. asst. to atty. gen. U.S. Dept. Justice, 1983-84; counsel Pres. Commn. on Organized Crime, 1984-86; acting dir., then dir. office of fin. enforcement U.S. Dept. Treasury, 1986-88; trial atty. fraud sect., criminal divsn. U.S. Dept. Justice, 1988-93, asst. spl. counsel House banking facility, 1992, sr. litigation counsel fraud sect., criminal divsn., 1993—, spl. counsel for fraud prevention, criminal divsn., 1998—. Adj. prof. Georgetown U. Law Ctr., 1996—. Recipient Atty. Gen.'s Disting. Svc. award, 1995. Mem. ABA (coun. mem. adminstrv. law sect. 1990-93, chmn. criminal process com. 1987-90, 93-98, chmn. regulatory initiatives com. 1998—), Assn. Am. Law Schs., Tower Club. Home: 4600 Connecticut Ave NW Apt 207 Washington DC 20008-5702 Office: US Dept Justice 1400 New York Ave NW Washington DC 20530 E-mail: jonathan.rusch@worldnet.att.net., Jonathan.Rusch2@usdoj.gov.

RUSCH, THOMAS WILLIAM, manufacturing executive; b. Alliance, Nebr., Oct. 3, 1946; s. Oscar William and Gwen Falerne (Middleswart) R.; m. Gloria Ann Sutton, June 20, 1968 (div. Oct. 1979); children: Alicia Catherine, Colin William; m. Lynn Biebighauser, Jan. 17, 1981. BEE, U. of Minn., 1968, MSEE, 1970, PhD, 1973; MS in Mgmt. of Tech., U. Minn., 1993. Sr. physicist cen. rsch. 3M Co., St. Paul, 1973-77, rsch. specialist cen. rsch., 1977-79; project scientist phys. electronics div. Perkin Elmer Corp., Eden Prairie, Minn., 1979-83, sr. project scientist phys. electronics div., 1983-85, lab mgr. phys. electronics div., 1985-87, product mgr. phys. electronics div., 1987-88, sr. product mgr. phys. electronics div., 1988-93; v.p. product devel. Chorus Corp., St. Paul, 1993-94; pres. Creekside Techs. Corp., Plymouth, Minn., 1994—; v.p. Xoft microTube, Inc., 1998—; chief tech. officer Xoft MicroTube, INc., Fremont, Calif., 2001—. Editor: X-rays in Materials Analysis, 1986; co-author: Oscillatory Ion Yields, 1977; patentee in field. Recipient IR100 award for transfer vessel Rsch. and Devel. mag., 1981, IR100 award for energy analyser, 1985. Office: 49000 Milmont Dr Fremont CA 94538

RUSCH, WILLIAM GRAHAM, religious organization administrator; b. Buffalo, Dec. 23, 1937; s. William Godfrey and Hope (French) R.; m. Thora Joan Ellefsen, Sept. 2, 1967. BA, SUNY, Buffalo, 1959, MA in Classical Langs., 1960; MDiv, Luth. Theol. Sem., Phila., 1963; PhD, Oxford (Eng.) U., 1965; DD (hon.), Yale U., 1995. Ordained to ministry Evang. Luth. Ch., 1966. Assoc. pastor Evang. Luth. Ch. of the Holy Trinity, N.Y.C., 1966-68; asst. prof., chmn. dept. classical langs. Augsburg Coll., Mpls., 1968-71; assoc. exec. dir. div. Theol. Studies Luth. Coun. in the USA, 1971-78; adj. prof. The Gen. Theol. Sem., N.Y.C., 1978-82, 95; exec. dir., asst. to Bishop Evang. Luth. Ch. in Am., Chgo., 1987-96; dir. Commn. on Faith and Order Nat. Coun. of Chs. of Christ USA, N.Y.C., 1996-2001; exec. dir. Found. for Faith and Order, 2001—. Adj. prof. Luth. Theol. Sem., Philadelphia., 1998—; vis. lectr. Waterloo Luth. Theol. Sem., 1969; adj. prof. theology Fordham U., N.Y.C., 1984-86; mem. cen. com. World Coun. Chs., 1991-98, mem. standing com. faith and order commn., 1991—; adj. faculty Yale Div. Sch., 1999—. Author: The Trinitarian Controversy, Ecumenism: A Movement Toward Church Unity; contbr. articles to profl. jours. Samuel Trexler fellow of N.Y. Synod Luth. Ch. in Am., 1964, 65. Mem. Am. Acad. Religion, Am. Soc. Christian Ethics, Am. Soc. Ch. History, Internat. Assn. Coptic Studies. Avocations: book collecting, chess, tennis. Office: Found for Faith and Order 99 Park Ave 298A New York NY 10016 E-mail: ruschgrif@worldnet.att.net.

RUSCIANO, FRANK LOUIS, political science educator, consultant; b. Elizabeth, N.J., Oct. 4, 1954; s. Francis Joseph and Philomena (Martucci) R.; m. Roberta Louise Fiske, Sept. 8, 1979; 1 child, Francesco Fiske Rusciano. BA, Cornell U., 1976; MA, U. Chgo., 1978, PhD, 1983. Rsch. asst. Nat. Opinion Rsch. Ctr., Chgo., 1978-80; rsch. assoc. Upsala Coll., East Orange, N.J., 1980-82; asst. prof. Rider Coll., Lawrenceville, 1982-89; methodology cons. Total Rsch. Corp., 1995—; prof. polit. sci. Rider U., 1996—, chair polit. sci. dept., 1998—. Guest lectr. Columbia U., N.Y.C., 1984; vis. prof. U. Mainz, Germany, 1985-86; cons. Ednl. Testing Svc., 1995, Total Rsch. Corp. Author: Isolation and Paradox: Defining the Public in Modern Political Analysis, 1989, World Opinion and the Emerging International Order, 1998; contbr. Magill's History of Europe, 1991, Great Events from History: Human Rights, 1992, Media and the Persian Gulf War, 1993, Ready Reference: Ethics, 1994, Cyberimperialism; editor Adminstrn. and Policy Jour., 1983-85. Survey cons. Planned Parenthood Assn., 1990. NSF grantee, 1980-82; Alexander von Humboldt Found. fellow, 1985-86, 87, 95, 99. Mem. Am. Polit. Sci. Assn., Am. Assn. for Pub. Opinion Rsch., Phi Beta Kappa. Avocations: running. Office: Rider U Polit Sci Dept 2083 Lawrenceville Rd Trenton NJ 08648-3099

RUSCONI, LOUIS JOSEPH, marine engineer; b. San Diego, Oct. 10, 1926; s. Louis Edward and Laura Ethelyn (Salazar) R.; m. Virginia Caroline Bruce, Jan. 1, 1972. BA in Engring. Tech., Pacific Western U., 1981, MA in Marine Engring. Tech., 1982; PhD in Marine Engring. Mgmt., Clayton U., 1986. Cert. nuclear ship propulsion plant operator, surface and submarine; diplomate naval ship nuclear propulsion system. Enlisted USN, 1944, electrician's mate chief, 1944-65, retired, 1965; marine electrician planner U.S. Naval Shipyard, Vallejo, Calif., 1965-72; marine elec. technician Imperial Iranian Navy, Bandar Abbas, Iran, 1974-79; marine shipyard planner Royal Saudi Navy, Al-Jubail, Saudi Arabia, 1980-86. Cons. in marine engring., 1986—. Author: Shipyards Operations manual, 1980, poetry (Golden Poet award 1989, Silver Poet award 1990). Mem. Rep. Presdl. Task Force, Washington, 1989-90, trustee, 1991. Mem. IEEE, U.S. Naval Inst., Soc. of Naval Architects and Marine Engrs. (assoc. mem.), Fleet Res., Nat. Geographic Soc. Avocations: creative writing, poetry, martial arts. Home: 949 Myra Ave Chula Vista CA 91911-2315

RUSEN, THEODORE, JR. civil engineer, city official; b. Steubenville, Ohio, Sept. 4, 1947; s. Theodore and Mary H Rusen; m. Anne Marie Smith Rusen, June 10, 1972; children: Rebecca, Christina, Marybeth. BSCE, U. Cin., 1970; postgrad., Xavier U., Cin., 1971-75. Registered profl. engr., Ohio, 1974. Engr.-in-tng., engr. co-op. Ohio Dept. Transp., Lebanon, 1966-70; city engr. City of Norward, Ohio, 1970-78; dir. pub. svc., city engr. City of Vandalia, 1978—. Transp. tech. adv. com. mem. Miami Valley Regional Planning Commn., Dayton, Ohio, 1980—; tech. adv. com. mem. Tri-Cities North Regional Wastewater Authority, Dayton, Ohio, 1986—. Mem. Vandalia (Ohio) Kiwanis Club (pres. 1985-86, 1994-95, 1997-99), Vandalia Pres.'s Club, 1985-86, Cmty. Drug Intervention Com., Vandalia, Ohio, 1985-86, Norwood (Ohio) Kiwanis Club, 1974-78. Recipient cert. of appreciationI 70/I-75 Reconstruction Study Steering com. Ohio Dept. Transp. and Miami Valley Regional Planning Comm., 1997, award for outstanding svc. ASCE, 1975, 76. Mem. Am. Pub. Works Assn., Street Maint. and Sanitation Officials Ohio, Pub. Works Officials of Southwest Ohio. Avocations: golf, pool, home renovation and design. Office: City of Vandalia 333 James E Bohanan Dr Vandalia OH 45377 Fax: 937-415-2319. E-mail: trusen@ci.vandalia.oh.us.

RUSER, JOHN WILLIAM, economist; b. Medford, Mass., Sept. 11, 1955; s. Claus William and Beverly Jeanne (Baughman) R.; m. Vera Konovodoff, Feb. 21, 1982. AB, Princeton U., 1977; MA, U. Chgo., 1980, PhD, 1983. Asst. prof. econs. U. N.C., Chapel Hill, 1982—83; economist U.S. Bur. Labor Stats., Washington, 1984—95, Chief, Comp. Res. and Prog. Devel. Group, 1995—2002; Assoc. Dir. for Reg. Econ. U.S. Bur. Econ. Analysis, 2002—. Prog. chmn., bd. dirs. Washington Stats. Soc., 1989—91; Mem., Study Panel Workers Comp. Data, Nat. Acad. Social Ins., 1999—. Contbr. articles to profl. jours. Mem. Washington Mayor's Adv. Commn. on Fin. and Revenue, 1989-91. Mem.: Soc. Labor Economists, Am. Econ. Assn. Office: US Bur Econ Analysis BE-5 1441 L St NW Washington DC 20230

RUSH, ANDREW WILSON, artist; b. Detroit, Sept. 24, 1931; s. Harvey Ditman and Mary Louise (Stalker) R.; m. Jean Cochran, Apr., 1957; children: Benjamin, Samuel, Joseph, Margaret; m. Ann Woodin, Oct., 1978. B.F.A. with honors, U. Ill., 1953; M.F.A., U. Iowa, 1958. Asso. prof. art U. Ariz., 1959-69; co-dir. Rockefeller Found. Indian Arts Project, 1960-64; vis. artist, artist-in-residence Ohio State U., 1970, U. Ark., 1972, Colo. Coll., 1973-74; resident mem. Rancho Linda Vista, Community of the Arts, Oracle, Ariz., 1969—;

founder, dir. The Drawing Studio, Tucson, 1992—; 1998—. One-man shows include Carlin Galleries, Ft. Worth, 1973, Graphics Gallery, Tucson, 1972, 75, Tucson Art Inst., 1984, Cruzitas Gallery, San Antonio, 1996; exhibited in group shows at World's Fair, N.Y.C., 1964, USIS exhbns., Europe, Latin Am., 1960-65; represented in permanent collections Libr. of Congress, Uffizzi Mus., Dallas Mus., Ft. Worth Mus., Seattle Mus., Free Libr., Phila.; illustrator: Andrew Rush on Oliver Wendell Holmes, 1973, Rule of Two (Ann Woodin), 1984, Voice Crying in the Wilderness (Edward Abbey), 1990, Ask Marilyn, 1992 (pub. art winner 1995); designer The Tucson Gateway Project, 1998. Served with USMC, 1953-55. Fulbright grantee, 1958-59 Address: Rancho Linda Vista O M Star Rte 2360 Oracle AZ 85623

RUSH, BOBBY L. congressman; b. Ga., Nov. 23, 1946; m. Carolyn Rush; 5 children. BA in Polit. Sci., Roosevelt U., 1974; MA in Polit. Sci., U. Ill., 1992. Fin. planner Sanmar Fin. Planning Corp.; assoc. dean Daniel Hale Williams U.; ins. agent Prudential Ins. Co.; city alderman Chgo., 1984-93; democratic committeeman Chgo. 2nd ward, 1984, 88, Central Ill., 1990; dep. chmn. Ill. Democratic Party, 1990; mem. U.S. Congresses from 1st Ill. Dist., 1993—. Chmn. Environ. Protection, Energy and Pub. Utilities com., Budget and Govt. Operations com., Capitol Devel. com., Hist. Landmark Preservation Com.; mem. Commerce com. Former mem. Student Non-Violent Coordinating com.; founder Ill. Black Panther Party; past coord. Free Breakfast for Children, Free Med. Clinic. With US Army, 1963-68. Recipient Ill. Enterprise Zone award Dept. Commerce and Community, Operation PUSH Outstanding Young Man award, Henry Booth House Outstanding Community Svc. award, Outstanding Bus. and Profl. Achievement award South End Jaycees, Chgo. Black United Communities Disting. Polit. Leadership award. Office: US Ho of Reps 2416 Rayburn House Office Bldg Washington DC 20515-1301*

RUSH, DOMENICA MARIE, health facilities administrator; b. Gallup, N.Mex., Apr. 10, 1937; d. Bernardo G. and Guadalupe (Milan) Iorio; m. W. E. Rush, Jan. 5, 1967. Diploma, Regina Sch. Nursing, Albuquerque, 1958. RN N.Mex.; lic. nursing home adminstr. Charge nurse, house supr. St. Joseph Hosp., Albuquerque, 1958-63; dir. nursing Cibola Hosp., Grants, 1960-64; supr. operating room, dir. med. seminars Carrie Tingley Crippled Children's Hosp., Truth or Consequences, N.Mex., 1964-73; adminstr. Sierra Vista Hosp., 1974-88, pres., 1980-89; clin. nursing mgr. U. N.Mex. Hosp., 1989-90; adminstr. Nor-Lea Hosp., Lovington, N.Mex., 1990-94; with regional ops. divsn. Presbyn. Healthcare Svcs., Albuquerque, 1994—, regional ops., 1994—; adminstr. Sierra Vista Hosp., Truth or Consequences, N.Mex., 1995—. Bd. dirs. N.Mex. Blue Cross/Blue Shield, 1977-88, chmn. hosp. relations com., 1983-85, exec. com. 1983—; bd. dirs. Region II Emergency Med. Svcs. Originating bd. SW Mental Health Ctr., Sierra County, N.Mex., 1975; chmn. Sierra County Personnel Bd., 1983—. Named Lea County Outstanding Woman, N.Mex. Commn. on Status of Women; Woman of Yr. for Lea County, N.Mex., 1993. Mem. Am. Coll. Health Care Adminstrs., Sierra County C. of C. (bd. dirs. 1972, 75-76, svc. award 1973, Businesswoman of the Yr. 1973-74), N.Mex. Hosp. Assn. (bd. dirs., sec.-treas., pres.-elect, com. chmn., 1977-88, pres. 1980-81, exec. com., 1980-83, 84-85, recipient meritorius svc. award 1988), N.Mex. So. Hosp. Coun. (sec. 1980-81, pres. 1981-82), Am. Hosp. Assn. (N.Mex. del. 1984-88, regional adv. bd. 1984-88). Republican. Roman Catholic. Avocations: raising thoroughbred horses, cooking. Home: 1100 N Riverside Dr Truth Or Consequences NM 87901-9789 Office: 800 E 9th Ave Truth Or Consequences NM 87901-1954

RUSH, HERMAN E. television executive; b. Phila., June 20, 1929; s. Eugene and Bella (Sacks) R.; m. Joan Silberman, Mar. 18, 1951; children: James Harrison, Mandie Susan. BBA, Temple U., 1950. With Ofcl. Films, 1951-57; owner Flamingo Films, 1957-60; with Creative Mgmt. Assos., N.Y.C., 1960-71, pres. TV divsn., 1964-71, exec. v.p. parent co., dir., 1964-71; ind. prodr., 1971-75; prodr. Wolper Orgn., 1975-76; pres. Herman Rush Assos., Inc. (Rush-Flaherty Agy. subs.), 1977-78, Marble Arch TV, Los Angeles, 1979-80, Columbia Pictures TV, Burbank, Calif., 1980-87; chmn., CEO, Coca-Cola Telecom., 1987-88, Rush Assocs., Inc., Burbank, 1988—, Katz/Rush Entertainment, Beverly Hills, Calif., 1990-96, New Tech Entertainment, LLC, Beverly Hills, 1996—; chmn., CEO internet content provider Entertainment Internat., Inc. CEO Infotainment Internat., Inc.; chmn. Entertainment Industries Coun.; pres., chmn. Royal Animated Art, Inc.; chmn. bd. dirs. E Capital Fin. Corp.; bd. dirs. High Speed Network Solutions, Inc. Trustee Sugar Ray Robinson Youth Found., 1967-75; pres. Retarded Infant Services, N.Y.C., 1957-63; bd. dirs. U.S. Marshall's Service Found., Just Say No Found.; conferee White House Conf. for a Drug Free America, 1987, 88. Mem. Acad. TV Arts and Scis., Hollywood Radio and TV Soc., Producers Caucus. Clubs: Friars, Filmex. Office: Rush Entertainment Group # 3045 3340 Ocean Park Blvd Santa Monica CA 90405 E-mail: hermanrush@aol.com.

RUSH, JEFFREY, JR. federal agency administrator; b. Kansas City, Kans. m. Dawn Rush; 2 children. B, Baker U.; JD, George Mason U. Criminal investigator USDA, Hyattsville, Md., 1971—75, with supervisory criminal investigation Kansas City, Mo., 1975—78, asst. regional inspector gen. Chgo., 1978—80, regional inspector gen., 1980—83, dep. asst. inspector gen., 1983—94; acting inspector gen. Peace Corp, 1993; inspector gen. USAID, 1994—99, Dept. Treasury, Washington, 1999—. With U.S. Army, 1968—71. Mem.: ABA, DC Bar Assn., Va. State Bar Assn. Office: Dept of the Treasury Inspector General 1500 Pennsylvania Ave Washington DC 20220

RUSH, JULIA ANN HALLORAN (MRS. RICHARD HENRY RUSH), artist, writer; b. St. Louis, Oct. 25, 1927; d. Edward Roosevelt and Flavia Hadley (Griffin) Halloran; m. Richard Henry Rush, Aug. 15, 1956; 1 child, Sallie Haywood. Student Washington U., St. Louis, 1945-47; B.A., George Washington U., 1949. One-woman shows: Fort Amador Officers Club, Panama Canal Zone, El Panama Hotel, Panama, George Washington U., Statler Hotel, Roosevelt Hotel, Washington, Newspaper Women's Club, Washington, Waukegan Library, Ill., Epworth Heights Hotel, Ludington, Mich.; exhibited in group shows: Panama Art League, Corcoran Gallery; represented in permanent collections: U. Panama; also pvt. collections; model John Robert Powers Agy., 1950; sec.-treas., dir. N.Am. Acceptance Corp., 1956-58; v.p. Rush and Halloran, Inc., 1957-58, ptnr., 1954-57; research asst. to husband's bi-weekly newsletter Art/Antiques Investment Report, 1973—, articles in Wall St. transcript, 1971—. Illustrator: Antiques As An Investment (author Richard H. Rush), 1968; research asst.: Investments You Can Live With and Enjoy (author: Richard H. Rush), 1974, 2d, edit., 1975, 3d edit., 1976; Photographer: Automobiles as an Investment, 1982; Investing in Classic Cars, 1984. Recipient 1st prize (Panama) Newspaper Women's Club, 1953; First Prize Panama Art League, 1953. Mem. DAR, Nat. League Am. Penwomen, Florence Crittenton Circle (rec. sec. 1968-69), Kappa Kappa Gamma. Club: Washington, Royal Palm Yacht (No. Ft. Myers, Fla.), Boca West Golf and Country (Boca Raton, Fla.)

RUSH, NORMAN, author; b. San Francisco, Oct. 24, 1933; s. Roger and Leslie (Chessé) R.; m. Elsa Scheidt; children: Jason, Liza. BA, Swarthmore Coll., 1956. Dealer antiquarian books, 1960-78; instr. English, history Rockland C.C., Suffern, N.Y., 1973-78; co-dir. Peace Corps, Botswana, 1978-83; freelance writer, 1983—. Author: Whites, 1986, Mating, 1991 (Nat. Book award for fiction 1991, Internat. Fiction prize Irish Times and Aer Lingus 1992). Mem. lit. com. War Resisters League, N.Y.C., 1985—; bd. dirs. A.J. Muste Inst., N.Y.C., 1988-92; sec. Rockland County, N.Y. chpt. Amnesty Internat., 1990—. Recipient Rosenthal award Nat. Acad. and Inst. Arts and Letters, 1987; fellow Nat. Endowment for Arts, 1986, Guggenheim fellow, 1987, Bellagio residency fellow Rockeller Found., 1990. Mem. PEN Am. Ctr.

RUSH, RICHARD HENRY, financial executive, writer, lecturer; b. N.Y.C., Mar. 6, 1915; s. Henry Frederick and Bessie (Vreeland) R.; m. Julia Ann Halloran, Aug. 15, 1956; 1 dau., Sallie Haywood. *Dr. Rush is the great grandson of Philip Freneau, "The Poet of the American Revolution" who is credited as having saved the country from "monarchy" through his publication of the "National Gazette". He is the great grandnephew of General Phil Kearny, Civil War general and New Jersey's most prominent soldier. The grandnephew of America's first Consul General and Minister to Japan, Townsend Harris, who through his determined negotiating of the American Japanese trade treaty, signed in 1858, opened Japan to trade with the west. Harris, before going to Japan, founded the free College of the City of New York as President of the New York Board of Education.* BA summa cum laude, Dartmouth Coll., 1937, MCS, 1938; MBA with highest distinction, Harvard U., 1941, DCS (Littauer fellow), 1942. Dir. aviation U.S. Bur. Fgn. and Domestic Commerce, 1945-46; chief economist, chmn. planning com. All Am. Aviation (U.S. Air), 1943-45; dir. aircraft divsn. Nat. Security Resources Bd., 1948-51; Washington rep. to J. Paul Getty, 1951-52; ptnr. Rush & Halloran, 1953-58; pres., chmn. bd. N.Am. Acceptance Corp., Atlanta, also Washington, 1956-59; owner Richard H. Rush Enterprises, Greenwich, Conn., also Washington, 1953-73; prof., chmn. dept. finance and investments Sch. Bus. Adminstrn., Am. U., Washington, 1967-70, 77-79. Author: Art as an Investment, 1961, A Strategy of Investing for Higher Return, 1962, The Techniques of Becoming Wealthy, 1963, Antiques as an Investment, 1968, The Wrecking Operation: Phase One, 1972, Investments You Can Live With and Enjoy, 1976, Techniques of Becoming Wealthy, 1977, Automobiles as an Investment, 1982, Selling Collectibles, 1982, Collecting Classic Cars for Profit and Capital Gain, 1984, Collector Cars: Classics for the New Century, 2001; contbr. over 700 articles to newspapers, mags. and profl. jours.; editor series of books on starting businesses for U.S. Dept. Commerce; contbg. editor Wall St. Transcript, 1971-97, Art/Antiques Investment Report, 1972-97. Trustee, exec. com. Finch Coll., 1968-72. Recipient Pres.'s med., CCNY, 1997. Mem. Am. Mktg. Assn. (chmn. nat. com.), Am. Econ. Assn., Am. Statis. Assn., Internat. Platform Assn., AAUP, Harvard Club (N.Y.C.), Royal Palm Yacht Club (Ft. Myers), Phi Beta Kappa, Phi Kappa Phi, Omicron Delta Kappa. Episcopalian.

RUSH, RICHARD R. academic administrator; Pres. Calif. State U. Channel Islands, Camarillo. Office: Calif State U Channel Islands 1 University Dr Camarillo CA 93012 Fax: 805-437-8414. E-mail: richard.rush@csuci.edu.

RUSH, STEPHEN C. radiation oncologist; b. N.Y.C., May 9, 1959; BS, Howard U., 1981, MD, 1983. Intern in surgery Lenox Hill Hosp., N.Y.C., 1983-84; attending emergency medicine Westside Hosp., L.A., 1984-86; resident in radiation oncology NYU Med. Ctr., N.Y.C., 1986-89; attending radiation oncology North Shore Hosp., Manhasset, N.Y., 1989-91, Long Island Radiation Therapy, Manhasset, 1991—; clin. assoc. prof. NYU Med. Ctr. Med. advisor cancer working group U.S. Ho. of Reps., Washington. Recipient Young Oncologist Essay award Am. Radium Soc., 1988. E-mail: StephenCRush2aol.com. Office: Long Island Radiation Therapy 1129 Northern Blvd Manhasset NY 11030-3022

RUSHBOLDT, RAYMOND JUDE, political science educator; b. Dunkirk, N.Y., Sept. 5, 1966; s. Richard Paul Rushboldt and Patricia Mae Tworek BA, SUNY, Fredonia, 1988; MA, SUNY, Buffalo, 1992. Lectr. in polit. sci. SUNY, Fredonia, 1994—. Mem. polit. sci. faculty St. Bonaventure U., Allegany, N.Y., 1993; mem. adj. faculty Jamestown (N.Y.) C.C., 1996, 98; acad. advisor Pi Sigma Alpha Honor Soc., Fredonia, 1998—. Alpha Phi Omega Svc. Fraternity, Fredonia, 1999—; mem. adv. com. Social Work program, Fredonia, 1999—. Reviewer (book) Public Policy Practice, 2000. Mem. Chautaugua County Youth Bd., Mayville, N.Y., 1996—; mem. com. State Employees Federated Appeal, Fredonia, 2000—. Mem. Polish Lit. Soc. (bd. dirs. 1999—), Am. Polit. Sci. Assn., Acad. Polit. Sci., Polish Falcons, No. Chautagua Conservation Club. Roman Catholic. Avocations: reading, gardening. Home: 3719 Middle Rd Dunkirk NY 14048 E-mail: rushbold@netsync.net.

RUSHER, WILLIAM ALLEN, writer, commentator; b. Chgo., July 19, 1923; s. Evan Singleton and Verna (Self) R. AB, Princeton, 1943; JD, Harvard U., 1948; DLitt (hon.), Nathaniel Hawthorne Coll., 1973. Bar: N.Y. bar 1949. Assoc. Shearman & Sterling & Wright, N.Y.C., 1948-56; spl. counsel fin. com. N.Y. Senate, 1955; assoc. counsel internal security subcom. U.S. Senate, 1956-57; pub., v.p. Nat. Review mag., N.Y.C., 1957-88, also bd. dirs.; Disting. fellow The Claremont Inst, 1989—. Mem. Adv. Task Force on Civil Disorders, 1972 Author: Special Counsel, 1968, (with Mark Hatfield and Arlie Schardt) Amnesty?, 1973, The Making of the New Majority Party, 1975, How to Win Arguments, 1981, The Rise of the Right, 1984, The Coming Battle for the Media, 1988; editor: The Ambiguous Legacy of the Enlightenment, 1995; columnist Universal Press Syndicate, 1973-82, Newspaper Enterprise Assn., 1982—; played role of Advocate in TV program The Advocates, 1970-74. Chmn., bd. dirs. Media Rsch. Ctr., Washington, 2001—, Nat. Rev. Bd., 1957-88, 90—; bd. advisors Ashbrook Ctr., Ashland, Ohio, past chmn.; past vice chmn. Am. Conservative Union; past trustee Pacific Legal Found., Sacramento. Served as 2d lt. to capt., USAAF, 1943-45, India-Burma Theater. Recipient Disting. Citizen award NYU Sch. Law, 1973. Mem. ABA, U. Club (N.Y.C. and San Francisco), Met. Club (Washington). Anglican. Home and Office: 850 Powell St San Francisco CA 94108

RUSHFELT, GERALD LLOYD, magistrate judge; b. Kansas City, Kans., Aug. 4, 1929; s. Henry Lawrence and Marie Ernestine (Heinrich) R.; m. Joy Marie Jungferman, May 28, 1960. AA, Graceland Coll., 1949; BA, U. Kans., 1953, LLB, 1958. Bar: Kans. 1958, U.S. Dist. Ct. Kans. 1958, U.S. Ct. Appeals (10th cir.) 1969. From assoc. to ptnr. Sullivant and Smith and successor firms, Kans. City, Overland Park, Kans., 1958-75; sr. ptnr. Rushfelt, Mueller, Lamar and Druten and successors, Overland Park, 1975-85; U.S. magistrate judge U.S. Dist. Ct. Kans., Kansas City, 1985—. Mcpl. judge pro tem City of Leawood (Kans.) 1977-85; critique instr. U. Kans. Law Sch., Lawrence, 1981-92. Active Roeland Park (Kans.) City Council, 1964-69. With U.S. Army, 1953-55. Fellow Am. Coll. Trial Lawyers, Internat. Soc. Barristers; mem. ABA, Kans. Bar Assn., Johnson County Bar Assn. (pres. 1986-87), Am. Bd. Trial Advocates, Earl E. O'Connor Am. Inn of Ct. Democrat. Mem. Cmty. Of Christ. Avocations: swimming, baseball, philately. Office: 500 State Ave Rm 628 Kansas City KS 66101-2400

RUSHING, DAVID WAYNE, poet, language educator; b. Gainesville, Ga., Aug. 12, 1959; s. Leslie Wayne and Thelma Eunice Rushing; m. Susan Rebecca Burland, Apr. 17, 1982 (div. 1986); 1 child Rebecca Anne. BA in History, Calif. Poly. Inst., 1999. Actor Don Schwarz Agy., West Hollywood, Calif., 1988—94; tutor English, Calif. Poly. Inst., Pomona, 1999; tchr. 7th grade Duarte Unified Sch. Dist., 1999—2000; tchr. spl. edn. L.A. Unified Sch. Dist., L.A., 2000—01; instr. ESL, Pacific Rim Lang. Inst., Rowland Heights, 2002—. Contbr. poetry to profl. jours.; actor: (commls.) , 1991—93. Scholar, Calif. Poly. Inst., 1999. Republican. Roman Catholic. Home: Apt 129 311 W Foothill Blvd Monrovia CA 91016-2148 Office: Pacific Rim Lang Inst 1719 F ullerton Rd La Puente CA 91748 Personal E-mail: davidwrushing@yahoo.com.

RUSHING, DOROTHY M. retired historian, writer; b. Bonham, Tex., Aug. 28, 1925; d. Van Bain and Ada (Price) Hawkins; m. J. E. Rushing, Aug. 6, 1960 (dec. 1985); children: Charles Maret, Bill Maret, Bob Maret, Charles Rushing, Martha Rushing Sosebee. BA, Tex. Woman's U., 1972; MA, Tex. A&M Commerce, 1974; PhD, U. North Tex., Denton, 1981. Instr. Tex. A&M Commerce, Commerce, 1972-74, 80-81, U. North Tex., Denton, 1975-76; prof. Richland Coll., Dallas, 1975-98, Collin County Community Coll., McKinney, 1985-88; historian-archivist J.C. Penney, Inc., Dallas, 1988-95. Vis. prof. Johns Hopkins U., 1985, U. Va., 1989; statis. analyst Dallas County C.C., 1982; lay rep. N.E. Tex. Libr. System, 1982-90. Contbg. author: Handbook of Texas, 1996. Named Outstanding Instr., Richland Coll., 1987, Disting. Alumni, Denison H.S., 2001; postdoctoral fellow NEH, 1985, 89. Mem. Phi Kappa Phi, Sigma Tau Delta, Phi Alpha Theta. Avocations: genealogy, literacy, history. Home: 516 Lockloma Ct Denison TX 75020-3667

RUSHING, PHILIP DALE, retired social worker; b. Carbondale, Ill., Mar. 15, 1932; S. Paul and Beulah Myrl (Benton) R.; m. Linda North, July 5, 1958 (div. July 1964); 1 child, Lisa Anne Rushing Burrow; m. Rosalie Anne Sturm, Aug. 20, 1966. BA, So. Ill. U., 1958; MSW, Washington U., St. Louis, 1960. Bd. cert. diplomate, ACSW; lic. social worker, Ill. Child welfare worker Ill. Dept. Pub. Welfare, Salem, East St. Louis, 1958-60, child welfare supr. East St. Louis, 1960-63; field rep. Nat. Assn. for Retarded Children, Dallas, Denver, 1963-65; dir. social svcs. A.L. Bowen Children's Ctr., Harrisburg, Ill., 1965-68; asst. zone dir. for mentally retarded Ill. Dept. of Mental Health, 1968-74; regional coord. for devel. disabilities Ill. Dept. of Mental Health & Devel. Disabilities, Marion, 1974-83; social work adminstr. Choate Mental Health & Devel. Ctr., Anna, Ill., 1983-95; ret., 1995. Adj. asst. prof. So. Ill. U. Rehab. Inst., Carbondale, Ill., 1968-78; bd. dirs. Southeastern Ill. Pastoral Counseling Ctrs., chmn. pers. com., 1996-98. Bd. cert. diplomate ACSW; lic. clin. social worker. Bd. deacons First Presbyn. Ch., Harrisburg, 1974-77, bd. trustees, 1978-80, bd. elders, 1980-83, 96-98. With USN, 1951-55, Korea. Fellow Am. Assn. on Mental Retardation (life, chmn. social work divsn. Ill. chpt. 1973-74); mem. NASW (chmn. East St. Louis br. 1962). Home: 6542 Hwy 13 W Harrisburg IL 62946-4142 E-mail: prrushing@juno.com.

RUSHMER, ESTELLA VIRGINIA DIX (DIXIE RUSHMER), artist; b. Sullivan, Ind., Oct. 17, 1919; d. William Porter Jessop and Roxie Gertrude (Johnson) Dix; m. Robert Frazer Rushmer, Apr. 5, 1942; children: Donald Scott, Anne, Elizabeth. BS, Purdue U., 1940. cert. Am. Dietetic Assn. Diatetic intern St. Mary's Hosp. Mayo Clinic, Rochester, Minn., 1941-42. Docent Wash. State Burke Mus., 1963-78. Author, artist: Whidbey Island Sketchbook, 1985; one-woman shows include Good Years Gallery, Edmonds, Wash., 1975, 75, 77, Stillwater Gallery, Seattle, 1979, Artists Gallery Northwest, 1979, 82, 83, Stonington Gallery, Seattle, 1985, Port Angeles (Wash.) Fine Arts Ctr., 1988; group shows include Bellevue (Wash.) Art Mus., 1979, 82, 84, 86-90, Peter Kirk Gallery, Kirkland, Wash., 1985-90, Frye Mus., Seattle, 1979, Frederick and Nelson Gallery, Seattle, 1980, 82, Fremont Fine Art Gallery, Seattle, 1987, Black Swan Gallery, Seattle, 1989, Portico Gallery, Kobe, Japan, 1987, Meguro Mus., Tokyo, Japan, 1987, Columbia Art Ctr., Vancouver, Wash., 1990, Nat. Watercolor Soc. Show, Muckenthaler Cultural Ctr., Fullerton, Calif., 1990; represented in permanent collections at Rainier Bank, Samotomo Bank, Alpac Corp., Honeywell, Seattle; represented in pvt. collections. Pres. U. Wash. Med. Sch. Aux., Seattle, 1948; leader Girl Scouts U.S.A., Lake Forest Park, Wash., 1958-63. Mem. Northwest Watercolor Soc., U. Wash. Auxiliary, U. Wash. Med. Auxiliary, U. Wash. Retiree Assn., Women Painters of Wash. Avocations: gardening, travel, reading, genealogy, grandparenting. Home: 10901 176th Cir NE # 3526 Redmond WA 98052-7248

RUSHNELL, SQUIRE DERRICK, television executive; b. Adams Center, N.Y., Oct. 31, 1938; s. Reginald Grant and Erica Mifanwy Redwood Sedgemore (Squire) R.; children: Robin Tracy, Hilary Adair, Squire Grant Sedgemore. Ed., Syracuse U., 1956-60. Disc jockey Stas. WOLF, WHEN and WFBL, Syracuse, N.Y., 1958-61, Sta. WTRL, Bradenton, Fla., 1961-62; exec. prodr. Sta. WBZ AM-TV, Boston, 1962-67; program dir. KYW News-Radio, Phila., 1968; exec. prodr. Kennedy & Co. Sta. WLS-TV, Chgo., 1969-71, program dir., 1971-73; v.p. programs ABC-owned TV stas., N.Y.C., 1973-74; v.p. children's TV ABC Entertainment Network, 1974-78; v.p. Good Morning Am. and children's programs ABC-TV Network, 1978-81, v.p. long range planning and children's TV, 1981-87; v.p. late night and children's TV ABC Entertainment, 1987-89; pres. Rushnell Comm. & Pub., Inc., 1990-96; pres., CEO GoodLife TV Network, Washington, 1996—2001; motivational spkr., 2001—. Author: The Kingdom Chums Greatest Stories, 1986, When God Winks: How the Power of Coincidence Guides Your Life, 2001; co-author: Broadcast Programming, 1981, Broadcast/Cable Programming, 1985, rev. edit., 1989, 1993. Recipient Emmy awards, 1975-88, TV Critics Circle award, 1976, all for outstanding children's TV programming, Am. Children's TV Festival award, 1985, 87. Mem. NATAS, Nat. Acad. Arts and Scis., Internat. Radio and TV Soc., Action for Children's TV (award for outstanding children's TV programming). E-mail: squire@whengodwinks.com.

RUSHO, KAREN G. critical care and community health nurse, educator; b. Albany, N.Y., Sept. 18, 1955; d. Joseph R. and Ann E. (Cline) Gabriels; m. Michael E. Rusho, Dec. 18, 1976; 1 child, Elizabeth Ann. BSN, Mt. St. Mary Coll., Newburgh, N.Y., 1977; MS in Nursing, Boston U., 1984. Cert. emergency nurse. Staff and charge nurse, emergency dept. Jennie Stuart Med. Ctr., Hopkinsville, Ky., 1977-80, Commanche County Hosp., Lawton, Okla., 1980; staff and charge nurse ICU 97th Gen. Army Hosp., Frankfurt Am Main, West Germany, 1981-82; sch. nurse Enterprise (Ala.) City Sch. System, 1989-91; clin. instr. Quinnipiac Coll., Hamden, Conn., 1991-94; client care coord. Vis. Nurse Assn. Hospice, Inc., Waterbury, 1993-94; dir. nursing Brian Ctr., Concord, N.C., 1994-2000; regional clin. dir. Mariner Post Acute Network, 2000—. Active Girl Scouts Am. Mem. ANA, Assn. Profl. Infection Control. Home: 1023 Reverdy Ln Matthews NC 28105-6803

RUSHTON, ALAN R. physician, medical historian; b. Oak Park, Ill., Mar. 10, 1949; s. Raymond H. and D. Loree (Swan) R.; m. Nancy Spencer, May 5, 1973; children: Andrew, Daniel. AB in Chemistry, Earlham Coll., 1971; PhD in Genetics, U. Chgo., 1975, MD, 1977. Diplomate Am. Bd. Pediatrics, Am. Bd. Med. Genetics. Resident Yale U.-New Haven (Conn.) Hosp., 1977-80; physician Hunterdon Med. Ctr., Flemington, N.J., 1980—; assoc. clin. prof. pediatrics Robert Wood Johnson Med. Sch., New Brunswick, 1980—. Lectr. genetics Princeton (N.J.) U., 1980-84. Author: Genetics and Medicine in the United States 1800-1922, 1994. Fellow Am. Acad. Pediatrics, Am. Coll. Med. Genetics, N.Y. Acad. Medicine, Royal Soc. Medicine; mem. Am. Assn. History Medicine, History Sci. Soc. Office: Hunterdon Pediatric Assocs 1100 Wescott Dr Ste G-3 Flemington NJ 08822-4600

RUSHTON, BRIAN MANDEL, chemical company executive; b. Sale, Cheshire, Eng., Nov. 16, 1933; came to U.S., 1957; s. Ronald Henry and Edith (Slater) Riley; m. Jean Wrigley, Apr. 1, 1958; children: Jacqueline, Lisa, Amy. A.R.I.C. in Chemistry, U. Salford, Eng., 1957; MS in Phys. Organic Chemistry, U. Minn., 1959; PhD in Phys. Organic Chemistry, U. Leicester, Eng., 1963; postgrad. Sr. Exec. program, MIT, 1972. Prodn. mgr. trainee 3M Co. U.K., 1959-60; sr. research chemist Petrolite Corp., 1963-65, group leader, 1965-66; sect. mgr. Ashland Chem. Co., 1966-69; corp. research mgr. Hooker Chem. Corp. subs. Occidental Petroleum, 1969-72, dir. polymer and plastics research and devel., 1972-74, v.p. research and devel. chem. and plastics div., 1974-75; pres. Celanese Research Corp., 1975-80; corp. v.p. tech. Celanese Corp.; also pres. Celanese Research Corp., 1980-81; v.p. research and devel. Air Products & Chem., Inc., Allentown, Pa., 1981-92, sr. v.p. rsch. and devel., 1992-94. Pres., mem. exec. com., bd. dirs. Indsl. Rsch. Inst., 1990-94, chmn. plans and policies com., 1988-90; bd. dirs. Mallinckrodt Corp., Inc.; mem. chem. vis. com. Lehigh U., 1992-96; mem. exec. master sci.-in-engring. adv. coun. U. Pa., 1992-94. Contbr. articles to profl. jours.; patentee in field. Mem. life scis., vis. com. Lehigh U., chmn. surface sci. vis. com., 1983-86; bd. dirs. WLVT Channel 39, Bethlehem, Pa., 1992-95; trustee Summit YMCA, N.J., 1976-79; mem. nat. materials bd. NRC, 1980-84. Mem. Coun. Chem. Rsch. (dir., treas.), Am. Chem. Soc. (pres.-elect 1994, pres. 1995), Soc. Chem. Industry, Saucon Valley Country Club. Episcopalian. Home: 3366 Bingen Rd Bethlehem PA 18015-5715

RUSHTON, HARRY GIL, pediatric urologist, educator; b. Greenville, S.C., July 20, 1952; BA, Clemson U., 1974; MD, Med. U. S.C., 1978. Diplomate Am. Bd. Urology. Intern U. Ky. Med. Ctr; residency Med. U. S.C.; fellow Emory U., Atlanta; chmn. dept. pediatric urology Children's Nat. Med. Ctr., Washington, 1996—; prof. urology and pediat. George Washington U. Sch. Medicine, 1996—. Exec. sec. pediat. urology adv. coun. Am. Bd. Urology, 2001—. Mem. Am. Acad. Pediat. (sec., treas. sect. on urology 1996-99, chair elect 1999-2000, chmn. urology sect. 2000-2001), Am. Urol. Assn. (program & pubs. coms.). Office: Children's Hosp 111 Michigan Ave NW Washington DC 20010-2970 E-mail: hrushton@cnmc.org.

RUSHTON, LYNN NOELLE, artist; b. Dallas, Dec. 28, 1967; d. Harold R. and Mary Ann (Wagliardo) Hawkins; m. James Edward Rushton III, June 11, 1994; children: James Edward Burne-Jones, Charles Laurent Cosley-Daubigny. BA in Comm. and Fine Art, Vanderbilt U., 1990; postgrad., Tulane U., 1990-92. Intern (devel.) Kenndy Ctr., Washington, 1990; intern Nat. Mus. Am. Art, 1990. Guest lectr. Austin Peay State U., Tenn., 1998. Gallery representation includes Estelle Stair Gallery, Rockport, Tex., 1996-97, Pace Collection, 1996-97, Beaux Arts, Dallas, 1996, Visual Effects, Dallas, 1996-99, Wally Workman Gallery, Austin, 1997—, Continental Gallery, 2001; one-woman shows Celebrity Cafe, Dallas, 1996, Sarratt Gallery, Nashville, 1998, Deep Ellum Ctr. for Arts, Dallas, 1999, Plano (Tex.) Art Ctr., 1999, Quadrangle, 2000, Wally Workman Gallery, Austin, 2001; two-person show at Annarella Gallery, Georgetown, 2002; group shows Aardvark Gallery, Garland, Tex., 1996, Dallas Visual Art Ctr., 1996, 98, Richardson Civic Arts Co., Richardson Pub. Libr., 1997, Irving (Tex.) Art Ctr., 1997, Visual Art League, Lewisville, Tex., 1997 (merit award), Associated Creative Artists Awards Show, 1999, Slidell Cultural Ctr., 1999, Assemblage, L.A., 1999, Soc. Outdoor Painters 1997-2000; represented in permanent private collections. Mem. Oil Painters Am., Associated Creative Artists (bd. dirs. 1999—), Tex. Visual Arts Assn., Soc. Outdoor Painters, Jr. League Dallas, Dallas Vanderbilt Alumni (pres. 1997-98), Lakewood Svc. League (bd. dirs. 1997—). Home: 8350 Santa Clara Dr Dallas TX 75218-4342

RUSIE, BARRY LEE, songwriter, poet; b. Indpls., June 4, 1965; s. Roland Cecil Rusie and Norma Jean Wooley; m. Carrie Ann Rusie, Aug. 6, 1994; children: Barry Martin, Sarah Elizabeth. Grad., Broadway Christian H.S., Indpls., 1983. Christian songwriter Ind. Gospel Music Assn., Indpls., 1983—.

Author: (poem in) 2001 Poetic Odyssey, 2000 (Poet of Yr. award 2000), Nature's Ehoes, 2000, Time After Time, 2000, Poetry's Elite, 2000. Song leader Lawrence Bapt. Ch., Indpls., 1999—, usher, 1995—. Avocations: reading, writing, exercise, walking.

RUSIE, RUTH LOUISE, literacy educator; b. Russiaville, Ind., Oct. 13, 1918; d. Volna Ernest and Mamie Audrey (Gallion) Ritz; m. Horace Robert Rusie, June 28, 1941; children: James Frederick, David Robert, John Lindley. BA, DePauw U., 1940; MS, Ind. U., 1972. Elem. sch. tchr. Met. Sch. Dist. Martinsville (Ind.), 1958-72, spl. reading tchr., 1972-80; coord. Martinsville Literacy Coalition, 1982—. Mem. Ind. Right-to-Read Com., 1975-78; mem. adv. bd., participant Reading is Fundamental, Martinsville, 1992-96. Composer music for elementary students The Stupid Thief, 1972. Bd. dirs. Martinsville Edn. Found., 1991—, Cmty. Found. of Morgan County, 2001–; bd. dirs., treas. Morgan County Pub. Libr., Martinsville, 1984-2001; mem. com. on food Habitat for Humanity, Martinsville, 1997—; mem. Martinsville Arts Coun., 1981—, dir., 1981—; driver cancer patients ARC, Martinsville, 1981-2000, dir., 1986-92; dir. vol. desk Morgan County Meml. Hosp., Martinsville, 1982-94; driver Meals-On-Wheels, Martinsville, 1985—; grand marshall Morgan County Fall Foliage Festival Parade, Martinsville, 1993; bd. dirs. People Respecting Individuality and Diversity in Everyone (P.R.I.D.E.), 1997—; bd. dirs. Cmty. Concerts N.Y.C., 1994—, initial contact. Recipient Citizen of the Yr. Kiwanis, 1990, Cmty. Spirit award High Sch. Nat. Honor Soc., 1992, Mayor's award for literacy Mayor and City Officials, 1993, Citizen of the Yr. award Rotary, 1993, Excellence of Cmty. Svc. award DAR, 1995, Ind. Jefferson award Am. Inst. Pub. Svc./Indpls. Star, 1996. Mem. Martinsville Woman's Club (pres. 1957-59), Martinsville Literary Club, Coterie (pres. 1986-88), Monday Afternoon Art Club, Foxcliff Golf Club (pres. 1981-82), Kappa Kappa Kappa (pres. 1956-57, province officer 1957-59). Presbyterian. Avocations: reading, bell and singing ch. choirs, bridge, opera, theater.

RUSINKO, FRANK, JR. fuels and materials scientist; b. Nanticoke, Pa., Oct. 12, 1930; s. Frank Sr. and Eva (Ruduski) R.; m. Lucy Geryak, June 1, 1957; children: Nancy, Lawrence. BS, Pa. State U., 1952, MS, 1954, PhD, 1958. Vice-pres., tech. dir. Airco Carbon, St. Mary's, Pa., 1959-76; pres. Electrotools Inc., Broadview, Ill., 1976-89, Intech EDM Electrotools, Broadview, 1989-91; sr. scientist, dir. Carbon Rsch. Ctr. Pa. State U., University Park, 1991—, dir.Consortium Premium Carbon Products from Coal, 1998—. Bd. dirs., bd. chmn. transor Filter USA, Elk Grove Village, Ill., C-Cor Electronics State Coll., Pa.; cons. in field., 1996—. Contbr. articles to profl. jours. Mem. Hinsdale (Ill.) Plan Commn., 1986; mem. Region Campaign Pa. State U., 1989; pres. Sch. Bd. Edn., St. Marys, Pa., 1965-76. Fellow Pa. State Alumni Assn. (indsl. cons.); mem. Am. Chem. Soc., Am. Carbon Soc., N.Y. Acad. Sci., Sigma Xi. Orthodox. Home: 2392 Pine Hurst Dr State College PA 16803-3385 Office: The Energy Inst Carbon Rsch Ctr 407 Academic Activities Bld University Park PA 16802-2308 Fax: 814-863-8892. E-mail: fjr4@psu.edu.

RUSK, KARLA MARIE, nurse practitioner; b. Zanesville, Ohio, Sept. 7, 1956; d. Willard E. Jr. and Charlotte M. (Basford) King; m. Jason T. Rusk, Aug. 30, 1980; 1 child, Whitney Malone. AS Nursing, Ohio U., 1977, BSN, 1985; MS, Ohio State U., 1987; postgrad. cert. adult nurse practitioner, Otterbein Coll., 1997. Cert. specialist adult nurse practitioner, ANCC; cert. specialist acute care nurse practitioner. Staff nurse Bethesda Hosp., Zanesville, Ohio, 1977—80; team leader ICU-recovery rm. Providence Hosp., Cin., 1980—81; staff nurse Bethesda Hosp., Zanesville, 1981—82; staff nurse open heart ICU Grant Med. Ctr., 1982—83, edn. coord., critical care, 1984—88; critical care educator Lancaster, 1985—90; staff nurse III CCU Riverside Meth. Hosp., Columbus, 1988—92, staff nurse invasive recovery unit, 1992—96; clin. rsch. coord., mgr., adminstrv. dir. Mid-West Cardiology Rsch. Found., 1990—98; adminstrv. clin. dir. Midohio Cardiology Cons., Inc., Columbus, 1993—96; acute care nurse practitioner Mid. Ohio Cardiology and Vascular Cons., Inc., 1998—. Contbr. articles to profl. jours. Mem. AACN (cert.), Am. Heart Assn. (mem. coun. cardiovasc. nursing), Am. Acad. Nurse Practitioners, Internat. Soc. Cardiovascular Interventionalists, Phi Kappa Phi, Sigma Theta Tau, Lambda Omega (pres., chmn. fin., internat. del.). Home: 1050 Creswell Cir New Albany OH 43054-9596

RUSKAUP, CALVIN, therapist, history professor; b. St. Louis, Feb. 5, 1939; s. Henry and Viola (Vogt) R.; m. Chandricka Maharaj, Apr. 1, 1991. BSc, U. Mo., St. Louis, 1967; PhD, Ohio State U., 1979. Diplomate Am. Psychotherapy Assn., Am. Assn. Integrative Medicine. Co-founder Cmty. Broadcasting-Sta. WFAC, Columbus, Ohio, 1975-77; lectr. Ohio State U., 1975-79; designer Trimobile Safety Car, Aspen, Colo., 1980-81; pastoral counselor United Luth. Ch., Knoxville, Tenn., 1982—85, pres. Hilo, Hawaii, 1986—. Spkr. World Parliament Scientists, 2000. Chmn. Commn. to Stop Violence, 1999-2000; editor Patriot Press, 1997-98; Patriot and Libertarian parties U.S. presdl. candidate, 1996. Mem. AAAS Sr. Scientists Engrs. (emeritus), Am. Anthropol. Assn., Acad. Polit. Sci., Orgn. Am. Historians, Assn. Transpersonal Psychology, N.Y. Acad. Scis., Am. Psychoanalytic Assn., Pub. Rels. Soc. Am., Nat. Press Club, Circumnavigators Club.

RUSKIN, ARNOLD MILTON, engineer, educator; b. Bay City, Mich., Jan. 4, 1937; s. Dave Burnard and Florence Shirley (Ruttenberg) R. BSChemE, BS in Materials Engring., U. Mich., 1958, MS in Engring. Materials, 1959, PhD, 1962; M of Bus. Econs., Claremont Grad. U., 1970. Registered profl. engr., Calif., Colo.; chartered engr., Eng. Lectr. Rugby (Eng.) Coll. Engring. Tech., 1962-63; asst. prof. engring. Harvey Mudd Coll., Claremont, Calif., 1963-66, assoc. prof., 1966-72, prof., 1972-73; assoc. prof. bus. and econs. Claremont Grad. U., 1970-72; prof. Claremont Grad. Sch., 1972-73; engring. mgr. Everett/Charles, Inc., Pomona, Calif., 1973-74; v.p., program mgr. Claremont Engring. Co., 1974-78; system engr. Jet Propulsion Lab., Pasadena, Calif., 1978-80, mgr. network strategy devel., 1980-86, dep. mgr. system engring. resource ctr., 1986-90, mgr. Cassini project planning, 1990—94; founder, ptnr. Claremont Cons. Group, 1979—; project mgr., adminstrv. processes reengring. initiative Calif. Inst. Tech., Pasadana, 1996—98. Lectr. UCLA, 1974-77, adj. prof. engring., 1977-84, dir. engring. exec. program, 1978-84; lectr. Indsl. Relations Ctr., Calif. Inst. Tech., Pasadena, 1985-2001; Zambelli fellow in sys. engring. and project mgmt. Royal Melbourne Inst. Tech., Australia, 1990. Author: Materials Considerations in Design, 1967, What Every Engineer Should Know About Project Management, 1982, 85; patent thermally metamorphosing oil shale to inhibit leaching, 1980; book rev. editor Engring. Mgmt. Internat., 1981-84, mem. editorial bd. 1984-87, mem. editorial rev. bd. Project Mgmt. Jour., 1988—; mem. editorial bd. Engring. Mgmt. Jour., 1989—; contbr. papers to profl. publs. Mem. Archtl. Commn., Claremont, 1974-76, chmn. 1976; mem. Profl. Adv. Group, Claremont, 1968; bd. dirs. ARC, Claremont, 1970-72. Fellow AIAA (assoc., tech. com. on mgmt. 1986-90); mem. AICE, Am. Soc. Engring. Edn. (founding chmn., engring. mgmt. com. 1972-73, vice chmn. materials divsn. 1972-73, sec. materials divsn. 1963-67, editor Pacific S.W. sect. 1965-66, editorial com. Engring. Edn. 1970-71), Project Mgmt. Inst. (cert.), Inst. Mgmt. Cons. (cert.), Am. Soc. Engring. Mgmt., Internat. Coun. on Sys. Engring., Sigma Xi, Tau Beta Pi, Phi Lambda Upsilon, Omicron Delta Epsilon, Phi Kappa Phi. Office: Claremont Cons Group 4525 Castle Ln La Canada CA 91011-1436

RUSKIN, JOSEPH RICHARD, actor, director; b. Haverhill, Mass., Apr. 14, 1924; s. Ely and Betty Edith (Chaimson) Schlafman; m. Barbara Greene; 1 child, Alicia. Grad., Carnegie Inst. Tech., 1949. Founder Rochester (N.Y.) Arena Theatre, 1949-52. Actor N.Y. stage plays, 1952-58, Theatre Group, UCLA, Mark Taper Forum, 1959—, (films) Fall of Legs Diamond, 1959, Magnificient Seven, 1960, Escape from Zahrein, 1963, Robin and the Seven Hoods, 1965, Prizzi's Honor, 1985, Longshot, 1987, Indecent Proposal, 1992, regular appearances various TV programs, 1952—; dir. Houston Alley, 1965-69; freelance dir., 1969—. Served with USNR, 1943-46. Mem. AFTRA, SAG, Actors Equity Assn. (nat. coun.). Home: 1326 Devon Ave Los Angeles CA 90024-5346

RUSKIN, RICHARD A. obstetrician-gynecologist; b. New Rochelle, N.Y., Oct. 1, 1919; MD, Duke U., 1944. Intern Kings County Hosp., Bklyn., 1944; resident in ob.-gyn. N.Y. Polyclinic Hosp., N.Y.C., 1947-49, 51-52, N.Y. Lying-In Hosp., N.Y.C., 1949-51; sr. attending ob.-gyn. N.Y. Hosp., 1952—, St. Lukes-Roosevelt Hosp. Ctr., N.Y.C., 1973—. Clin. prof. ob.-gyn. Cornell U. Med. Sch., 1970—. Fellow Am. Coll. Ob.-Gyn., ACS; mem. AMA, N.Y. Gynecol. Soc. Home: 415 E 52nd St New York NY 10022-6424

RUSKIN, ROBERT STERLING, association executive; b. Washington, Nov. 27, 1945; s. Robert Edward and Thelma (Gipe) R.; m. Rebecca Lynne Wilson, Aug. 11, 1967; 1 child, Brant Edward. BA, Washington Coll., Chestertown, Md., 1967; MA, W.Va. U., 1969, PhD, 1971. Lic. psychologist Va., D.C. Prof. dept. psychology Georgetown U., Washington, 1971-86, chmn. dept. psychology, 1976-85, dir. Ctr. for Personalized Instrn., 1977-80, dir. Teaching Resource Ctr., 1985-86; chief psychol. assessor leadership devel. U. Md., College Park, 1984—; prin. investigator and project dir., consortium univs. rsch fellows program U.S. Army Rsch. Inst., Washington, Alexandria, 1985—; nat. rsch. fellow U.S. Dept. Edn., Washington, 1986-87; affiliate prof. psychology George Mason U., 1989—; prin. investigator Consortium & Office of Substance Abuse Prevention, 1990-93; dir. programs and rsch. Consortium of Univs. of Washington Metro. Area, 1987-88, v.p., 1989—. Psychol. cons. DuPont Corp., Seaford, Del., 1986-88; psychol. cons. Consortium of Univs. of D.C., 1984—; cons. in field; rep. of U.S. to UNESCO Planning Meeting, Paris, 1979. Co-author: Behavioral Instruction: An Evaluative Review, 1977; editor manuscript: Consortium Research Fellows Program; editor The Jour. of Personalized Instrn., 1975-81, Revista a Tecnologia Educativa, 1976-83. Battelle Inst. Disting. Acad. Rsch. fellow U.S. Army Rsch. Inst., 1984-86. Fellow APA, Am. Psychol. Soc. (charter); mem. AAAS, D.C. Psychol. Assn., Va. Psychol. Assn., Psi Chi. Methodist. Avocations: golf, fishing. Home: 309 W Alex Ave Alexandria VA 22302 Office: Consortium of Univs of Wash 1 Dupont Cir NW Washington DC 20036-1110

RUSKIN, RUTH ZAFREN, social worker; b. Washington, May 23, 1953; d. Frank and Rose (Charkin) Zafren; m. Jonathan S. Ruskin, June 12, 1976; children: David Frank, Diana Beth. BA cum laude, Cornell U., 1975; MSW, Cath. U. Am., 1977. Lic. clin. social workers, Va. Social worker Arlington (Va.) County Dept. Social Svcs., 1977-85; clin. social worker, supr., dir. hypnotherapy program Roundhouse Sq. Psychiat. Ctr., Alexandria, Va., 1985—. Mem. NASW. Home: 5905 6th St Falls Church VA 22041-2535

RUSKIN, RYAN SCOTT, packaging company executive; b. Pitts., Jan. 31, 1968; s. Stanley C. and Judith Anne (Blitzstein) R. BA, Princeton U., 1990; MBA, Northwestern U., 1994. Dir. tng. and devel. The Princeton Rev., 1987-90, nat. tng. dir., 1987-92; mgr. Vail (Colo.) Assocs., 1990-92; dir. strategic planning Sterling Lebanon Packaging Corp., Jeannette, Pa., 1992-94; assoc. A.T. Kearney, Chgo., 1994-96, sr. mgr., 1996-98; exec. v.p. Sterling Packaging Corp., Pitts., 1998-2000, pres., 2000—. Advisor Coro Ctr. for Civi Leadership, Pitts., 1999—, J.L. Kellogg Sch. Northwestern U., 1994—. Mem. alumni coun. Shady Side Acad., Pitts., 1998; speech writing team, media coord. Rep. Nat. Conv., 1988; dir. Open Hand Chgo., 1999—; nat. faculty U.S. Sailing, Newport, 1990-94. Mem. Am. Soc. for Quality Control, Union League Club of Chgo., Chgo. Yacht Club, Inst. of Packaging Profls. Avocations: sailing, skiing, tennis, golf. Home: 823 W Junior Ter Chicago IL 60613-1607 Office: Ste 301 201 Penn Center Blvd Pittsburgh PA 15235 Office Fax: 412-317-8010. E-mail: rruskin@ruskingroup.com.

RUSS, JAMES MATTHIAS, lawyer; b. Duluth, Minn., Sept. 20, 1929; s. Matthias James and Agnes Margaret (Jerina) R.; m. Nanelle Davis, June 27, 1953; children: Tanya, Robin, Sarah, Claudia, Janine, Monica, Matthias James, Kateri. AB cum laude, Spring Hill Coll., 1955; JD, Georgetown U., 1957. Bar: D.C., 1957, Fla., 1958, U.S. Dist. Ct. (no., so. and mid. dists.) Fla., U.S. Ct. Appeals (5th and 11th cirs.), U.S. Supreme Ct.; cert. criminal trial lawyer 1987, criminal appellate lawyer 1992. County solicitor Orange County, Fla., 1961-65. Lectr. criminal law and legal ethics seminars. Contbr. articles to profl. jours. Trustee Orange County Legal Aid Soc.; chmn. The Chester Bedell Meml. Found., 1997-98. Recipient Tobias Simon Pro Bono Svc. award Fla. Supreme Ct., 1997. Master, Am. Inns of Ct.; fellow Am. Coll. Trial Lawyers, Am. Bd. Criminal Lawyers; mem. ABA (criminal justice sect.-speedy trial com. 1976-77, com. on privacy 1982-83, def. function com. 1983-89, chmn. 1987-89), The Fla. Bar (chmn. criminal law com. 1964-65, 66-67, exec. coun. trial lawyers sect., 1967-68, mem. criminal law cert. com. 1988-91, recipient President's Pro Bono Svc. award, 9th jud. cir. 1993), Orange County Bar Assn. (exec. coun. 1967-70, sec. 1984-88), Nat. Assn. Criminal Def. Lawyers (2d v.p. 1992-93, 1st v.p. 1993-94, dir. 1984—, chmn. Lawyers' Assistance Strike Force 1987-89, Robert C. Heeney Meml. award 1988), Fla. Assn. Criminal Def. Lawyers (chmn. Lawyers' Assistance Strike Force 1988-89, Steven M. Goldstein Criminal Justice award 2002), Nat. Bd. Trial Advocacy (cert. 1982). Office: Tinker Bldg 18 W Pine St Orlando FL 32801-2612

RUSS, JOANNA, author; b. N.Y.C., Feb. 22, 1937; d. Evarett and Bertha (Zinner) R. BA in English with high honors, Cornell, U., 1957; M.F.A. in Playwriting and Dramatic Lit, Yale U., 1960. Lectr. in English Cornell U., 1967-70, asst. prof., 1970-72; asst. prof. English, Harpur Coll., State U. N.Y. at Binghamton, 1972-75, U. Colo., 1975-77; asso. prof. English, U. Wash., 1977-90, prof., 1984-90. Author: Picnic on Paradise, 1968, And Chaos Died, 1970, The Female Man, 1975, We Who Are About To, 1977, Kittatinny: A Tale of Magic, 1978, The Two of Them, 1978, On Strike Against God, 1980, The Adventures of Alyx, 1983, The Zanzibar Cat, 1983, How To Suppress Women's Writing, 1983, Extra (Ordinary) People, 1984, Magic Mommas, Trembling Sisters, Puritans and Perverts: Feminist Essays, 1985, The Hidden Side of the Moon, 1987, To Write Like a Woman, 1995, (nonfiction) What Are We Fighting For, 1998; also numerous short stories. Mem. Sci. Fiction Writers Am. (Nebula award for best short story 1972, Hugo award for best novella 1983). Address: 8961 E Lester St Tucson AZ 85715-5568

RUSSE, CONRAD THOMAS CAMPBELL, accountant; b. Bethesda, Md., July 15, 1954; s. Frederick William Jr. and Constance Oakman (Fagan) R.; m. Deborah Joyce Thompson, June 14, 1980; children: Thomas Campbell, Catherine Alexandra, Caroline Saunders. BS, Duke U., 1977; MBA, Ga. State U., 1982. CPA, Ga., Tenn., N.C. Estimator Advance Builders, Inc., Smyrna, Ga., 1978; contractor B&B Drywalls, Marietta, 1979-81; acct. Evans, Snyder & Co., Atlanta, 1981-82; tax acct. Peat Marwick Mitchell & Co., Charlotte, N.C., 1982-85, Ernst & Whinney & Co., Chattanooga, 1985-86; tax mgr. Costello, Strain & Co, CPAs, 1986-89; prin. Thomas C. Russe, CPAs, 1989—. Bd. dirs., treas. Visually Impaired Tng. and Learning Ctr., Chattanooga, 1988-93, Chattanooga Tax Practitioners, 1987-95. Membership chmn. Cherokee Area coun. Boy Scouts Am., Chattanooga, 1987, 88; bd. dirs. Allegro Dance Theater, 1990-92; bd. dirs. Small Bus. Devel. Ctr., 1995—. English Speaking Union scholar, 1972-73. Mem. N.C. Assn. CPAs, Ga. Soc. CPAs (mem. taxation com. 1993—, tax forum com. 1995—), Tenn. Soc. CPAs (taxation com. 1990, 92, tax liaison com. 1992-95, small bus. com. 1999), Chattanooga Estate Planning Coun., Chattanooga Area C. of C. (seminars chmn. small bus. coun. 1987, 88, steering com. small bus. coun. 1986-95), CPA Club (bd. dirs. 1991-92), CPA-Atty. Forum (pres. 1992-94), Chattanooga Golf and Country Club. Episcopalian. Avocations: reading, antique refinishing, biking. Home: PO Box 4322 Chattanooga TN 37405-0322 Office: PO Box 4322 Chattanooga TN 37405-0322

RUSSEL, RICHARD ALLEN, telecommunications consultant, aerospace engineer, nuclear engineer, electrical engineer, computer scientist, retired naval officer; b. Shreveport, La., Jan. 24, 1958; s. Robert Lee and Gloria Jeanette (Gile) R.; m. Kathryn Joy Koehler, Dec. 30, 1983; children: Richard Allen Russel Jr., Kammie Joyce Jeanette, Jonathan Mark, Katie Jacqueline Keala, Stephen Sungmin. BSEE, U. N.Mex., 1980; AeE in Aeros. and Astronautics, MSc in Astron. Engring., Naval Postgrad. Sch., Monterey, Calif., 1994; postgrad., Colo. Tech. U., 2000—. Commd. ensign, nuclear submarine officer USN, 1980, advanced through grades to lt. comdr., 1990; main propulsion asst. USS Puffer, Pearl Harbor, Hawaii, 1981-85; antisubmarine analyst, nuclear engr., comdr. 3d fleet USN, 1985-87; combat systems officer USS TAUTUG, 1987-89; navigator, ops. officer USS Indpls., 1989-92; UHF/EHF satellite navy rep. PEO-SCS, USN, El Segundo, Calif., 1994-96; project mgr. for spacecraft comms. Booz-Allen and Hamilton, Inc., San Diego, 1996-97; dir. Space and Comm. Predicate Logic Inc., Colorado Springs, Colo., 1997-2000; dir. sys. engring. Maxim Systems Inc., 2000—. Chief engr. Ctr. Y2K Strategic Stability; core systems engr. SPACE Battle Mgmt.; chief sys. engr. worldwide shared early warning program USSPACE Command. Contbr. articles to profl. jours. Pres. congregation Christ the Cornerstone Luth. Ch.; mem. sch. bd. Our Savior Luth. Sch., Aiea, Hawaii, 1986; den leader webelos Boy Scouts Am., 1995-97; bd. dirs. Children's Angelcare Aid Internat., 1998-99; chmn. bd. dirs. Christ the Cornerstone Luth. Ch.; h.s. wrestling coach; mem. telecomm. policy adv. com. Colorado Springs City Coun., 2000—; mem. telecomms. policy advisory com., Colorado Springs, 2000—, e-commerce advisory com., 2000—. Fellow Inst. for the Advancement of Engrng.; assoc. fellow AIAA (vice-chair edn. L.A. sect. 1991—, dep. dir. edn. region VI 1994-97, Spl. Svc. Citation for developing internet capability 1996); mem. Space Nuclear Thermal Propulsion, Adventurers Club of L.A., Eta Kappa Nu. Republican. Lutheran. Achievements include design of predictive control system for thermoacoutic refrigerator; 3D laser range and orientation measuring system; navy satellite/computer secure communications systems; asynchronous transfer mode (ATM) networks; satellite and ground system design on SYBERSTAR, EHF Communications Satellite, Global Broadcase Service, Navy UHF Follow-on Satellite; GEOSAT Follow-on satellite; digital modular radio design; submarine communications support system; wireless ethernet design and installation; U.S.-Russia Center for Y2K strategic stability; U.S. space command space-based Blue Force Tracking Project; Mobile User Objective System satellite. Home: 1450 Branding Iron Dr Colorado Springs CO 80915-2413 E-mail: rrussel@maximsys.com.

RUSSEL, WILLIAM BAILEY, engineering educator; b. Corpus Christi, Tex., Nov. 17, 1945; m. 1972; 2 children. BA, MS in Chem. Engring., Rice U., 1969; PhD in Chem. Engring., Stanford U., 1973. NATO fellow applied math. Cambridge U., 1973-74; from asst. prof. to assoc. prof. chem. engring. Princeton U., N.J., 1974-83, prof., 1983—, chmn. dept. chem. engring., 1987-96, dir. Materials Scis. Inst., 1996-98. Olaf A. Hougen prof. U. Wis., 1984. Mem. AIChE (William H. Walker award 1992), NAE, Soc. Rheology, Am. Chem. Soc., Math. Rsch. Soc. Office: Princeton U Dept Chem Engring Princeton NJ 08540 E-mail: cobrussel@pucc.princeton.edu.

RUSSELL, ALAN HAROLD, computer specialist, educator; b. Waterbury, Conn., Aug. 15, 1948; s. Vernon Harold and Sylvia Louise (Pierpont) R.; m. Donna Ruth Van De Car, July 17, 1971; children: Christopher, Kimberly. BS in Computer Sci., Mich. State U., 1969, MS in Computer Sci., MBA, 1971; PhD, Kennedy Western U., 1989. Cert. computer profl. V.p. Toar Assocs., East Lansing, Mich., 1970-71; systems analyst Uniroyal, Inc., Oxford, Conn., 1971-72, Olin Corp., New Haven, 1972-75, Air Products and Chems., Allentown, Pa., 1975-80, systems assurance mgr., 1980-85, info. tech. specialist, 1985-2000, sr. bus. analyst, 2000—. Instr. DeSales U., 1980—; mem. assoc. faculty US Open U., 2001—02, U. Md., Balt., 2002—; commr. Computer Sci. Accreditation Commn., N.Y.C., 1985—91, Computing Accreditation Commn., N.Y.C., 2001—. Vice-chmn. Lehigh Christian Acad., Allentown, 1991-94; chmn. bd. Lehigh Valley Christian H.S., Allentown, 1992—. Mem. IEEE, IEEE Computer Soc. (cert. of appreciation 1990), Assn. for computing Machinery (recognition of svc. award 1985), Am. Sci. Affiliation, Computer Profls. for Social Responsibility. Avocations: teaching, reading. Home: 6601 Crown Ln Zionsville PA 18092-2327 Office: Air Products & Chems Inc 7201 Hamilton Blvd Allentown PA 18195-1526 E-mail: russelah@apci.com., ahrussell@aol.com.

RUSSELL, ALAN JAMES, chemical engineering and biotechnology educator; b. Salford, Lancashire, Eng., Aug. 8, 1962; came to U.S., 1987; s. Francis Anthony and Yvonne (Heilbrunn) R.; m. Janice Elaine Quoresimo, Sept. 19, 1987; children: Hannah Justine Serena, Vincent Anthony Alexander, Christian Sebastian, Trevor Alan James. BSc with honors, U. Manchester, U.K., 1984; PhD, Imperial Coll., London, 1987. NATO rsch. fellow MIT, Cambridge, 1987-89; chmn., Nickolas DeCecco prof. dept. chem. engring. U. Pitts., 1989-2001, assoc. dir. Ctr. for Biotech., 1991-2001, dir. program in advanced biomaterials, prof. surgery; dir., prof. surgery McGowan Inst. for Regenerative Medicine. Prof. biochemistry and molecular genetics U. Pitts. Med. Ctr.; exec. dir. Pitts. Tissue Engring. Initiative; founder Alerhan Techs., Inc., Agentase, LLC; cons. to chem. and pharm. industries, 1988—. Contbr. articles to profl. jours. Recipient Presdl. Young Investigator award NSF, 1990, Chancellor's Disting. Rsch. award U. Pitts., 1993; NATO fellow, 1988, Am. Inst. Med. and Biol. Engrs. fellow, 1998. Mem. Am. Chem. Soc. (session chmn. 1990-91, awards 1989, 93), Biochemistry Soc., Am. Inst. Chem. Engrs. Lutheran. Achievements include pioneering use of protein engineering to alter rationally the pH dependence of enzymes; discovery of the phenomenon of enzyme memory in organic solvents, biotechnological destruction of chemical weapons. Office: McGowan Inst 401 Scaife Pittsburgh PA 15261

RUSSELL, ALLAN DAVID, lawyer; b. Cleve., May 6, 1924; s. Allan MacGillivray and Marvel (Codling) R.; m. Lois Anne Robinson, June 12, 1947; children: Lisa Anne, Robinson David, Martha Leslie. BA, Yale U., 1945, LLB, 1951. Bar: N.Y. 1952, Conn. 1956, Mass. 1969, U.S. Supreme Ct. 1977. Atty. Sylvania Electric Products, Inc., N.Y.C., 1951-56, div. counsel Batavia, N.Y., 1956-65, sr. counsel, 1965-71; sec., sr. counsel GTE Sylvania Inc., Stamford, Conn., 1971-76; asst. gen. counsel GTE Service Corp., 1976-80, v.p., assoc. gen. counsel staff, 1980-83; pvt. practice Redding, Conn., 1983—. Sec., dir. mktg. subs. Sylvania Entertainment Products Corp., 1961-67; sec. Wilbur B. Driver Co. Dist. leader Rep. Party, New Canaan, Conn., 1955-56; sec. bd. dirs. Youth Found., Inc., 1981-83, bd. dirs., 1985-2001, pres., 2000-01; mem. planning commn., Redding, Conn., 1987-89; mem. Redding Bd. Ethics, 1990-96, chmn., 1992-96; warden Christ Ch. Parish, Redding, 1987-89; bd. dirs. Mark Twain Libr., 1988-94, v.p., 1988-89, pres., 1990-92. With USAAF, 1943-46. With USAAF, 1943—46. Mem. SAR, Assn. of Bar of City of N.Y., Conn. Bar Assn. (exec. com. corp. counsel sect. 1986-90), Am. Soc. Corp. Secs., St. Nicholas Soc., Collie Club Am. Found., Inc. (v.p., dir. 1986-89, pres. 1989-90), Soc. Colonial Wars, Yale Alumni Assn. (sec. local chpt. 1953-56), Yale Club of Danbury (pres. 1990—), Phi Delta Phi. Home: 9 Little River Ln Redding CT 06896-2018 E-mail: adavidfancy14184@aol.com.

RUSSELL, ALLEN STEVENSON, retired aluminum company executive; b. Bedford, Pa., May 27, 1915; s. Arthur Stainton and Ruth (Stevenson) R.; m. Judith Pauline Sexauer, Apr. 5, 1941. BS, Pa. State U., 1936, MS, 1937, PhD, 1941. With Aluminum Co. Am., 1940-82, assoc. dir. research, 1973-74; v.p. Alcoa, Pa., 1974-78; v.p. sci. and tech. Pitts., 1978-81; v.p., chief scientist, 1981-82. Adj. prof. U. Pitts., 1981-86 Contbr. articles to profl. jours.; patentee in field. Named IR-100 Scientist of Yr., 1979; Pa. State U. alumni fellow, 1980; K.J. Bayer medalist, 1981; recipient chem. Pioneer award Am. Inst. Chemists, 1983 Fellow Am. Soc. Metals (Gold medal 1982), AIME (James Douglas gold medal 1987), Am. Inst. Chemists; mem. NAE (coun. 1978-84), Am. Chem. Soc., Sigma Xi. Republican. Presbyterian. Home: 20 Wild Laurel Ln Hilton Head Plantation Hilton Head Island SC 29926 E-mail: alsrus@aol.com.

RUSSELL, ANDREW JAMES, government agency official; b. Kingston, Ont., Can., Apr. 19, 1964; arrived in U.S., 1987; s. Kenneth Edwin and Esther Marjorie Russell; m. Judith Kallick, Aug. 14, 1993; children: Joshua Kallick, Sarah Kallick. B.Econs. and Polit. Sci., Queen's U., Kingston, Ont., 1986; M.Internat. Affairs, Columbia U., 1989. Program officer youth initiatives Can. Internat. Devel. Agy., Ottawa, 1989—90; program officer UNDP, El Salvador, 1990—93, L.Am. program officer, 1993—95, asst. rep. Guatemala, 1995—98, Ctrl. Am. desk officer, 1998—2000, 2000—, advisor to the Regional Dir., Latin Am. Adj. prof. Haverford Coll., Pa., 2000, Columbia U., N.Y.C., 2001. Co-author: Lessons From Below, 2000. Democrat. Mailing: 160 W 95th St #8C New York NY 10025

RUSSELL, BEVERLY ANN, librarian, writer; b. Riverside, Calif., Jan. 15, 1947; d. James and Hazel M. Russell. BA in Polit. Sci., Calif. State U., 1971, MLS, 1973. Libr. asst. Riverside Pub. Libr., 1974—75; asst. libr. U. Calif., 1975—76; office asst. Calif. State Dept. Rehab., L.A., 1976—77; libr. technician Magnavox Rsch. Labs., Torrance, 1976—83; libr. asst. Burbank (Calif.) Unified Sch. Dist., 1985—86; office technician Social Svcs. Dept., Van Nuys, 1988—92; libr. Pleasant Valley State Prison, Coalinga, 1994—. Co-author (poetry): Roots & Wings, 1986, Three Women Black, 1988. Mem.: Alpha Kappa Alpha. Avocations: writing, poetry. Home: 250 Truman St #250 Coalinga CA 93210 Office: Pleasant Valley State Prison 24863 W Jayne St Coalinga CA 93210

RUSSELL, BRENDA SUE, critical care nurse; b. Painesville, Ohio, Oct. 30, 1958; d. Manfred Emil and Dorothea M. (McClintock) Klann; m. Mark A. Russell, Sept. 5, 1982; children: Brendan S., Christopher A., Emily Brooke. AAS, Lakeland Community Coll., Mentor, Ohio, 1980, 1984. RN, Ohio; cert. med.-surg. nurse; registered dental hygienist. Surg. step-down St. Luke's Hosp., Cleve., 1984-85, nurse intensive care nursery, surg. ICU, 1986-87; nurse; RN, high-risk newborns Meridia Euclid (Ohio) Hosp., 1987-89; nurse cardiac cath. lab. St. Luke's Hosp., Cleve., 1989-90; nurse cardiac cath lab. Meridia Hillcrest Hosp., Mayfield, 1990-92; charge nurse electrophysiology lab., study coord. M.U.S.T.T., Huron Hosp., Cleve., 1992-96; staff nurse stepdown unit Meridia Hillcrest Hosp., Mayfield, 1996-97; patient care coord. cardiac catheterization labs. Hillcrest-High Risk and Radiology Nurses, Euclid and Huron, 1997—2001. Prepaid legal cons.; Creative Memories ind. cons. Mem. Am. Heart Assn.. Home: 9524 Graystone Ln Mentor OH 44060-4538 E-mail: brendastar10@hotmail.com.

RUSSELL, BYRON EDWARD, physical therapy educator; b. Louisiana, Mo., Apr. 27, 1949; s. John Franklin and Nellie Mae (Bryant) R.; m. Anna Jean Talkington, Mar. 25, 1972 (div. Dec. 19, 1979); children: Brad Michael, Audrey Lynn; m. Roberta Louise Snover, May 22, 1982. BS in Microbiology, Colo. State U., 1975; BS in Phys. Therapy, Tex. Tech. Health Sci. Ctr., 1988; MHS in Phys. Therapy, U. Indpls., 1994; PhD, Tex. Woman's U., 1999. Diplomate Am. Acad. Pain Mgmt. Staff therapist Lubbock (Tex.) Gen. Hosp., 1988-89, S.W. Gen. Hosp., San Antonio, 1989-90; dir. phys. therapy Brady/Green Health Ctr., 1990-92; asst. prof. phys. therapy U. Tex. Health Sci. Ctr., 1992-95, Hardin-Simmons U., Abilene, 1995-2000, Ea. Wash. U., Spokane, 2000—, chmn. dept. phys. therapy, 2002—. Item writer Profl. Exam Svc., N.Y.C., 1996—; editor PT Series, Del-Mar Pubs., 1993-94. Editl. bd. Indsl. Rehab. Jour., 1996. Maj. USAR, 1989—. Mem. Am. Phys. Therapy Assn., Wash. Phys. Therapy Assn., Am. Coll. Sports Medicine, Sigma Xi. Baptist. Avocations: golf, hiking, fishing, horseback riding. Office: Ea Wash U Health Scis Bldg 310 N Riverpoint Blvd Box T Spokane WA 99202-1675 E-mail: byron.russell@ewu.edu.

RUSSELL, C. EDWARD, JR. lawyer; b. Portsmouth, Va., Aug. 19, 1942; BA, Hampden-Sydney Coll., 1964; LLB, Washington & Lee U., 1967. Bar: Va. 1967. Law clk. to Hon. John A. MacKenzie U.S. Dist. Ct. (ea. dist.) Va., 1967-68; atty. Kaufman & Canoles, Norfolk. Mem. ABA (bus. law sect., real property, probate and trust law sect.), Va. State Bar (bus. law sect., real property sect., health law sect.), Va. Bar Assn. (bus. law sect., real estate sect., chmn. young lawyers sect. 1977), Omicron Delta Kappa, Phi Alpha Delta. Office: PO Box 13368 Norfolk VA 23506-0368 E-mail: cerussell@kaufcan.com.

RUSSELL, CAROL ANN, personnel service company executive; b. Detroit, Dec. 14, 1943; d. Billy and Iris Koud; m. Victor Rojas (div.). BA in English, CUNY-Hunter Coll., 1993. Registered employment cons. Various positions in temp. help cos., N.Y.C., 1964-74; v.p. Wollborg-Michelson, San Francisco, 1974-82; co-owner, pres. Russell Staffing Resources, Inc., San Francisco and Sonoma, 1983-98; ret.; co-founder Workplacecentral.com, 1999—. Media guest, spkr., workshop and seminar leader in field; host/cmty. prodr. Job Net program for TCI Cable T.V. Pub. Checkpoint Newsletter; feature writer/columnist The Slant; contbr. articles to profl. publs. Founding v.p. The Friends of the Frank Lloyd Wright Civic Ctr. Libr. Marin County. Named to the Inc. 500, 1989, 90. Mem. Am. Women in Radio and TV, Soc. to Preserve and Encourage Radio Drama Variety and Comedy, No. Calif. Human Resources Coun., Soc. Human Resource Mgmt., Calif. Assn. Pers. Cons. (pres. Golden State chpt. 1984-85), Calif. Assn. Temp. Svcs., Bay Area Pers. Assn. (pres. 1983-84), Pers. Assn. Sonoma County, Scrowers and Molly Maguires, Sherlock Holmes Soc. London, Nat. Women's Polit. Caucus (comms. chair Marin chpt. 2002), Am. Jewish Congress. E-mail: carolrussell@ix.netcom.com.

RUSSELL, CATHY ANN, furniture company manager; b. Chgo., Apr. 3, 1953; d. Paul Eugene and Gaycina Elizabeth (Trager) R. B.A. in Mktg., U. Fla., 1975. Asst. buyer, mgr. Burdines Dept. Stores, Miami, Fla., 1976-81; dir. pub. relations Intro Prodns., Inc., North Miami, Fla., 1981; funding chmn. Miami Design Preservation League, Miami Beach, Fla., 1981-82; adminstrv. asst. ops. Montgomery Ward Co., Hialeah, Fla., 1982-83; standard procedures mgr. Levitz Furniture Corp., Boca Raton, Fla., 1983— ; mem. Employment Relocation Council, Washington, 1984-85. Mem. cultural arts bd. Miami Beach C. of C., 1981-82. Recipient Outstanding Service award Miami Design Preservation League, 1982. Mem. Nat. Assn. Female Execs., Miami Design Preservation League. Club: Bus. Unit Group-Boca Raton Mus. Art. Office: Levitz Furniture Corp Ste 101 14000 Military Trl Delray Beach FL 33484-2600

RUSSELL, CHARLES HARRY, music educator, restaurant manager; b. Flint, Mich., Oct. 7, 1962; s. Harry Charles and Sandra Kay Russell; m. Pamela Rene Flewelling, Aug. 20, 1983; children: Alena, Angela, Charles. BA, U. Michigan, Flint, Michigan, 1992; MusB in Edn., U. Michigan, Flint, 2002. Sr. asst. restaurant mgr. Taco Bell, Flint, 1987—; trumpet tchr. Herter Music Ctr., 1997—. Composer: (music) Your Memory Will Live, 1991, If Only, 1990. Recipient Eagle Scout, Boy Scouts of Am., 1980. Mem.: Mich. Band and Orch. Assn., Music Educator Nat. Conf. Home: 4379 Regency Rd Swartz Creek MI 48473 Personal E-mail: cruss9299@aol.com.

RUSSELL, CHARLES ROBERTS, chemical engineer; b. Spokane, Wash., July 13, 1914; s. Marvin Alvin and Dessie Corselia (Price) R.; m. Dolores Kopriva, May 17, 1943; children: Ann E., John C., David F., Thomas R. BS in Chem. Engring, Wash. State U., 1936; PhD in Chem. Engring. (Procter and Gamble Co. fellow 1940-41), U. Wis., 1941. Egr. div. reactor devel. AEC, Washington, 1950-56; engr. Gen. Motors Tech. Center, Warren, Mich. and Santa Barbara, Calif., 1956-68; assoc. dean engring. Calif. Poly. State U., San Luis Obispo, 1968-73, prof. mech. engring., 1973-80. Mem. nuclear standards bd. Am. Nat. Standards Inst., 1956-78; cons., 1980—; sec. adv. com. reactor safeguards AEC, 1950-55 Author: Reactor Safeguards, 1962, Elements of Energy Conversion, 1967, Energy Sources, Ency. Britannica. Served with USNR, 1944-46. Mem. Am. Chem. Soc. Clubs: Channel City (Santa Barbara). Republican. Roman Catholic. Home and Office: 3071 Marilyn Way Santa Barbara CA 93105-2040 E-mail: crrus1@aol.com.

RUSSELL, CHARLIE L. writer; b. Monroe, La., Mar. 10, 1932; s. Charlie L. and Katie O. Russell; children: Katheryn K., Joshua E. BS in English, U. San Francisco, 1959; MSW, NYU, 1966; MFA, U. Calif., San Diego, 1986. Author: (play) Five on the Black Hand Side, 1969, (film script) Five on the Black Hand Side, 1972 (Image award, NAACP, 1972), The Worthy Ones, 2002. Pvt. U.S. Army, 1953—55, Korea. Home: 1413 Neilson St Berkeley CA 94702 E-mail: charlierussell@attbi.com.

RUSSELL, CLIFFORD SPRINGER, economics and public policy educator; b. Holyoke, Mass., Feb. 11, 1938; s. Kenneth Clifford and Helen Alwilda (Springer) R.; m. Louise Pancoast Bennett, Feb. 3, 1965 (div. June 1985); m. Susan Vanston Reid, Sept. 7, 1985; stepchildren: Timothy Taylor Greene, Elizabeth Claussen Greene (dec.). BA, Dartmouth Coll., 1960; PhD, Harvard U., 1968. Sr. rsch. assoc. Resources for the Future, Washington, 1968-70, fellow, 1970-73, sr. fellow, 1973-85, div. dir., 1981-85; prof. econs. and pub. policy Vanderbilt U., Nashville, 1986—, dir. Vanderbilt Inst. for Pub. Policy Studies, 1986—. Valfrid Paulsson vis. prof. environ. econs. Beijer Inst., Royal Swedish Acad. Scis., Stockholm, 1997. Author: Drought and Water Supply: Implications of the Massachusetts Experience for Municipal Planning, 1970, Residuals Management in Industry: A Case Study of Petroleum Refining, 1973, Steel Production: Processes, Products and Residuals, 1976, Environment Quality Management: An Application to the Lower Delaware Valley, 1976, Freshwater Recreational Fishing: The National Benefits of Water Pollution Control, 1982, Enforcing Pollution Control Laws, 1986, Applying Economics to the Environment, 2001; contbr. articles to profl. jours. Trustee, treas. Environ. Def. Fund, N.Y.C., and Washington, 1973-85; mem. Tenn. Gov.'s Energy Adv. Bd., Nashville, 1989-94; trustee Tenn. Environ. Coun., Nashville, 1989-96; pres. 1992-95. Lt. USN, 1960-63. Mem. Assn. Environ. and Resource Econs. (bd. dirs. 1983-85, chmn. workshop com., pres. 1993-94). Avocations: tennis, fly fishing, sailing, boat building. Home: 1222 Clifftee Dr Brentwood TN 37027-4105 Office: Vanderbilt Inst Pub Policy Studies 1207 18th Ave S Nashville TN 37212-2807 E-mail: cliff.russell@vanderbilt.edu.

RUSSELL, CYNTHIA PINCUS, social worker, educator; b. N.Y.C., May 30, 1935; BA magna cum laude, Radcliffe Coll., 1957; MSW, Columbia U., 1959; postgrad., Hebrew U., Jerusalem, 1974-75; PhD, Union Rsch. Inst., 1978. Med. social worker Neurol. Inst.-Columbia-Presbyn. Med. Ctr., N.Y.C., 1958; caseworker Edwin Gould found. for Children, 1958-61; med. social worker Yale-New Haven Hosp., 1961, instr., 1961-62; rsch. asst. Yale Child Study Ctr. Nursery Sch., 1962-65; psychiat. social worker, rsch. asst. Regional Ctr. for Mental Retardation U. Conn. Sch. Social Work, 1966; psychiat. social worker Clifford Beers Guild Guidance Clinic, New Haven, 1966; dir. Info. and Counseling Svc. for Women Yale U., 1969-77, asst. clin. prof. dept. psychiatry, 1969—; mem. dept. student counseling Hebrew U., Jerusalem, 1974-75; pvt. practice New Haven and Stratford, Conn., 1977—. Lectr. Albertus Magnus Coll., 1975; supr. social and counseling U. Bridgeport, So. Conn. State U., 1975—77; psychosynthesis trainer Temenos Inst., Westport, 1987; founder Conn. Inst. for Psychosynthesis, 1990, trainer, supr., 1990—; adj. prof. Union Doctoral Program, 1990; supr. Yale Dept. Clin. Psychiatry; cons. Davenport Residence, Hamden, Conn., 2002. Author: Double Duties, 1978 (Book of Yr. New Haven Pub. Libr., Woman Today Book Club); author: (with others) At Grandmother's Table, 2000; editor: Psychosynthesis Lifeline, 1984—; contbr. chapters to books, articles to profl. jours. Nat. adv. bd. Vital Active Life After Trauma, Cambridge, Mass., 1990—99; mem. regional manpower coun. New Haven, 1975—76; mem. New Haven YWCA Women in Leadership, 1977—78, 1989—91; pres. Except. Cancer Patients, 1990—91, health profl. trainer, 1995—98; mem. Mayor's com. on volunteerism, 1975—76; bd. dirs. Connection for Health, 1990. Mem. NASW, Acad. Cert. Social Workers (diplomate), Address: PO Box 1183 Stratford CT 06615-8683 also: 2225 Main St Stratford CT 06615-5920

RUSSELL, DAN M., JR. federal judge; b. Magee, Miss., Mar. 15, 1913; s. Dan M. and Beulah (Watkins) R.; m. Dorothy Tudury, Dec. 27, 1942; children— Ronald Truett, Dorothy Dale, Richard Brian. BA, U. Miss., 1935, LL.B., 1937. Bar: Miss. bar 1937. Practice in, Gulfport and Bay St. Louis, Miss.; U.S. judge So. Dist. Miss., 1965—; now sr. judge. Lt. comdr. U.S. Naval Intelligence, 1941-45. Recipient U.S. Supreme Ct. Justice Scalia award, 2000. Founder's Day award Gulfport Rotary Club, 2001. Mem. Miss. Bar Assn., Hancock County Bar Assn., Hancock and Harrison Counties Bar Assn., Bay St. Louis Rotary Club (hon.), Gulfport Rotary Club (hon.), Am. Inns Ct. (hon. Russell-Blass-Walker chpt.), Federalist Soc. (adv. bd. Miss. chpt.), Hancock County C. of C., Tau Kappa Alpha. Clubs: Rotarian (pres. Bay St. Louis, Miss. 1946). Office: US Dist Ct PO Box 1930 Gulfport MS 39502-1930

RUSSELL, DAVE, information technology executive; b. Sioux City, Iowa, Nov. 5, 1963; Inventory mgr. Gateway, 1988, now sr. v.p. supply chain mgmt. Calif. Office: Gateway 14303 Gateway Pl Poway CA 92064 Office Fax: 858-848-3402.*

RUSSELL, DAVID E. judge; b. Chicago Heights, Ill., Mar. 19, 1935; s. Robert W. and Nellie Russell; m. Denise A. Hurst, Apr. 1, 1968 (div. 1978); children: Dirk, Kent, Laura, Rachel; m. Sandra M. Niemeyer, Oct. 31, 1982. BS in Acctg., U. Calif., Berkeley, 1957, LLB, 1960. Bar: Calif. 1961, U.S. Dist. Ct. (no. dist.) Calif. 1961, U.S. Tax Ct. 1967; CPA, Calif. Staff acct. Lybrand, Ross Bros. & Montgomery, San Francisco, 1960-64; assoc. Robert C. Burnstein, Esquire, Oakland, Calif., 1964-65; ptnr. Russell & Humphreys, Sacramento, 1965, Russell, Humphreys & Estabrook, Sacramento, 1966-70, prin., 1971-73; shareholder Russell, Jarvis, Estabrook & Dashiell, 1974-86; bankruptcy judge U.S. Bankruptcy Ct. for Ea. Dist. Calif., 1986—. Office: US Bankruptcy Ct 501 I St Sacramento CA 95814-7300

RUSSELL, DAVID EMERSON, mechanical engineer, consultant; b. Jacksonville, Fla., Dec. 20, 1922; s. David Herbert and Wilhelmina Russell. BMech Engring., U. Fla., 1948; postgrad., Oxford (Eng.) U. Registered profl. engr., Fla., Ga. Mech. engr. United Fruit Co., N.Y.C., 1948-50; civilian mech. engr. U.S. Army C.E., Jacksonville, 1950-54; mech. engr. Aramco, Saudi Arabia, 1954-55; v.p. Beiswenger Hoch and Assocs., Inc., Jacksonville, Fla., 1955-57; owner, operator David E. Russell and Assocs., Cons. Engrs., 1957-98; cons. engr., 1998—. Contbr. articles to profl. jours. Chmn. Jacksonville Water Quality Control Bd., 1969-73; bd. dirs. Jacksonville Hist. Soc., 1981-82; mem. Jacksonville Bicentennial Commn., 1973-79. 2d lt. AUS, 1943-46, PTO. Recipient Outstanding Svs. award City of Jacksonville, 1974. Mem. ASME (chmn. N.E. Fla. 1967-68), Nat. Soc. Profl. Engrs., ASHRAE, Fla. Engring. Soc. Univ. Club (Jacksonville), Jacksonville Humane Soc. (life). Episcopalian. Achievements include 5 patents including the ability to detect the arrival of important mail at a remote location. Avocations: world travel, boating, classical music. Home and Office: 4720 Timuquana Rd Jacksonville FL 32210-8231

RUSSELL, DAVID L. federal judge; b. Sapulpa, Okla., July 7, 1942; s. Lynn and Florence E. (Brown) R.; m. Dana J. Wilson, Apr. 16, 1971; 1 child, Sarah Elizabeth BS, Okla. Bapt. U., 1963; JD, Okla. U., 1965. Bar: Okla. 1965. Asst. atty. gen. State of Okla., Oklahoma City, 1968-69, legal adviser to gov., 1969-70; legal adviser Senator Dewey Bartlett, Washington, 1973-75; U.S. atty. for Western dist. Okla. Dept. Justice, 1975-77, 81-82; ptnr. Benefield & Russell, Oklahoma City, 1977-81; judge U.S. Dist. Ct. (we. dist.) Okla., 1982—, chief judge, 1994—2002. Lt. comdr. JAGC, USN, 1965-68. Selected Outstanding Fed. Ct. Trial judge Okla. Trial Lawyers Assn., 1988. Mem. Okla. Bar Assn., Fed. Bar Assn. (pres. Oklahoma City chpt. 1981), Order of Coif (alumnus mem.). Republican. Methodist. Office: US Dist Ct US Courthouse 200 NW 4th St Oklahoma City OK 73102-3026

RUSSELL, DAVID WILLIAMS, lawyer; b. Lockport, N.Y., Apr. 5, 1945; s. David Lawson and Jean Graves (Williams) R.; m. Frances Yung Chung Chen, May 23, 1970; children: Bayard Chen, Ming Rennick. AB, Dartmouth Coll., 1967, MBA, 1969; JD cum laude, Northwestern U., 1976. Bar: Ill. 1976, Ind. 1983. English tchr. Talledega (Ala.) Coll., summer 1967; math. tchr. Lyndon Inst., Lyndonville, Vt., 1967-68; asst. to pres. for planning Tougaloo (Miss.) Coll., 1969-71, bus. mgr., 1971-73; law clk. Montgomery, McCracken, Walker & Rhoads, Phila., summer 1975; with Winston & Strawn, Chgo., 1976-83; ptnr. Klineman, Rose, Wolf & Wallack, Indpls., 1983-87, Johnson, Smith, Pence, Densborn, Wright & Heath, Indpls., 1987-99, Bose McKinney & Evans, Indpls., 1999—. Cons. Alfred P. Sloan Found., 1972-73; dir. Forum for Internat. Profl. Svcs., 1985—, sec., 1985-88, pres. 1988-89; U.S. Dept. Justice del. to U.S. China Joint Session on Trade, Investment & Econ. Law, Beijing, 1987; leader Ind. Products Trade Fair, Kawachinagano, Japan, 1996; lectr. Ind. law Ind. Gov.'s Trade Mission to Japan, 1986, internat. law Ind. Continuing Legal Edn. Forum, 1986-96, 2000, 2001, chmn., 1987, 89, 91, 2001; adj. prof. internat. bus. law Ind. U., 1993-95; bd. dirs. Ind. ASEAN Coun., Inc., 1988-93; nat. selection com. Woodrow Wilson Found. Adminstrv. Fellowship Program, 1973-76; vol. Lawyers for Creative Arts, Chgo., 1977-83; dir. World Trade Club of Ind., 1987-93, v.p., 1987-91, pres., 1991-92; dir. Ind. Swiss Found., 1991—; dir. Writer's Ctr., Indpls., 1999—, treas., 2001-; dir. Asian Am. Alliance, 1999—, Friends of Taiwan Assn., Inc., 2001-; dir. Ind. Soviet Trade Consortium, 1991-99, sec., 1991-92; v.p., bd. dirs. Ind. Sister Cities, 1988—; dir. Internat. Ctr. Indpls., 1988-92, v.p. 1988-89; Ind. dist. enrollment dir. Dartmouth Coll., 1990-99; dir. Carmel Sister Cities, 1993—, v.p. 1995-96, pres. 1997-99, chmn., 1999—; v.p., gen. coun. Lawrence Durrell Soc., 1993—; mem. internat. affairs adv. bd. Kelley Sch. Bus., Ind. U., 2001-; mem. bd. advisors Ctr. for Internat. Bus. Edn. and Rsch. Krannert Grad. Sch. Mgmt. Purdue U., 1995—; dir., v.p., gen. coun. Global Crossroads Found., Inc., 1995—; mem. bd. arbitrators NASD, 1999—; mem. Ind. Dist. Export Coun., 1999—. Named Internat. Bus. Person of Yr., World Trade Club of Ind., 2002, Person of Yr., Sagamore of the Wabash, 2002, Jan. 15, 2002 declared "David Williams Russell Day", Indpls., hon. fellow, Ctr. for Internat. Legal Studies, 2002; fellow Woodrow Wilson Found adminstrv. fellow, 1969—72. Mem. ABA, ACLU, Ill. Bar Assn., Ind. Bar Assn. (vice chmn. internat. law sect., 1988-90, chmn. 1990-92, co-chmn. written publs. com. 1997-99, treas. 2002—), Indpls. Bar Assn., Dartmouth Lawyers Assn., Indpls. Assn. Chinese Ams., Chinese Music Soc., Dartmouth Club of Ind. (sec. 1986-87, pres. 1987-88), Internat. Bar Assn., Zeta Psi. Presbyterian. Home: 10926 Lakeview Dr Carmel IN 46033-3937 Office: Bose McKinney & Evans LLP 2700 First Ind Plz 135 N Pennsylvania St Indianapolis IN 46204-2400

RUSSELL, DIANE ELIZABETH HENRIKSON, career counselor; b. Chgo., July 18, 1952; d. Arthur Allen and Lois Elizabeth (Wessling) H.; m. Darrell Lee Slider, May 31, 1975 (div. Dec. 1992); m. Thomas Lee Russell, July 27, 1999. BA in Spanish, U. Ill., 1974; MA in Counselor Edn., U. South Fla., 1996. Employment counselor Crown Personnel Inc., Mt. Prospect, Ill., 1974-75; bilingual tchr.'s aide Sch. Dist. #21, Wheeling, 1975; sec., asst. registrar Yale U., New Haven, 1975-77; asst. to personnel dir., personnel coord. Housing Authority New Haven, 1977-79; benefits specialist Profl. Pensions Inc., New Haven, 1980-81, Chloride Inc., Tampa, Fla., 1981-83; personnel technician II human resources dept. U. South Fla., 1984-86, personnel technician III, personnel svcs. specialist, 1986-90, coord. human resources dept., 1990-96, career specialist career ctr., 1996—2002, counselor, advisor honors coll., 2002—. Mem. choirs St. Mark United Ch., Valrico, Fla., 1987-99, dir. Cregivers, 2001-02; mem. chorus U. South Fla., 1986-88, women's chorale, 1993-95. Mem. AAUW (treas. 1976-78, 80-81), Am. Assn. Employment in Edn., Fla. Coop. Edn. and Placement Assn., Phi Kappa Phi, Phi Beta Kappa, Alpha Lambda Delta. Avocations: singing, theater, going to theme parks, traveling. Home: 723 Herlong Ct Brandon FL 33511-7920 Office: U South Fla Honors Coll 4202 E Fowler Ave Stop Svc FA0274 Tampa FL 33620-6930 E-mail: trussel5@tampabay.rr.com.

RUSSELL, DICK, journalist; b. Mpls., Aug. 19, 1947; s. Clarence H. and Olive Nelson Russell; 1 child, Frank. BA in Humanities, U. Kans., 1969. Staff reporter Sports Illustrated Mag., N.Y.C., 1969-70; staff writer TV Guide Mag., L.A., 1977-79. Author: The Man Who Knew Too Much, 1992, Black Genius, 1998, Eye of the Whale, 2001. Recipient Golden Swordfish award Nat. Coalition for Marine Conservation, 1984, Chevron Conservation award Chevron, 1988. Mem. Soc. Environ. Journalists. Avocations: fishing, music.

RUSSELL, DOUGLAS CAMPBELL, cardiologist; b. Oxford, Eng., July 26, 1945; came to U.S., 1989; s. David Syme and Marion Hamilton (Campbell) R.; m. Mercedes Dumas, Nov. 16, 1975; 1 child, Georgina Mercedes. BA with 1st class honors, Cambridge U., 1966, MB, BChir, 1969, MD, 1981; PhD, Edinburgh (Scotland) U., 1979. House officer Charing Cross Hosp. Med. Sch., London, 1970-71, sr. house officer, 1971-73, Hammersmith Hosp., London, 1973; registrar cardiology London Chest Hosp., 1973-75; rsch. asst. Med. Rsch. Coun. Edinburgh U., 1975-77, Brit. Heart Found. fellow, 1977-79, lectr. medicine, 1979-83, sr. lectr., sr. rsch. fellow cardiovascular rsch. unit, 1983-89; prof. medicine, chief cardiology U. Va. Sch. Medicine, Salem (Va.) VA Med. Ctr., Roanoke, 1989-97; prof. medicine U. Wis., Madison, 1997—; chief cardiology VA Hosp., 1997—. Cons. cardiologist Royal Infirmary Edinburgh, 1983-89. Contbr. articles to med. jours. Rsch. grantee British Heart Found., Chest Heart and Stroke Assn., Thyssen Found., Scottish Home & Health, Pharm. Cos., 1976-89; John French Meml. lectr. Arteriosclerosis Discussion Grop, Oxford, 1979. Fellow Am. Coll. Cardiology, Royal Coll. Physicians; mem. British Cardiac Soc., British Soc. Cardiovascular Rsch. (treas. 1984-87), Internat. Soc. Heart Rsch., British Med. Assn. Baptist. Avocation: orchid culture.

RUSSELL, ELBERT WINSLOW, neuropsychologist; b. Las Vegas, N.Mex., June 4, 1929; s. Josiah Cox and Ruth Winslow Russell; children from previous marriage: Gwendolyn Marie Harvey, Franklin Winslow, Kirsten Nash, Jonathan Nash; m. Sally Lynn Kolitz, Apr. 2, 1989. BA, Earlham Coll., Richmond, Ind., 1951; MA, U. Ill., 1953; MS, Pa. State U., 1958; PhD, U. Kans., 1968. Clin. psychologist Warnersville (Pa.) State Hosp., 1959-61; clin. neuropsychologist VA Med. Ctr., Cin., 1968-71, dir. neuropsychology lab. Miami, Fla., 1971-89, rsch. psychologist, 1989—. Adj. prof. Nova U., Ft. Lauderdale, 1980-87, U. Miami Med. Sch., 1980-94, U. Miami, 1979—. Author: (with C. Neuringer and G. Goldstein) Assessment of Brain Damage, 1970; (with R.I. Starkey) Halstead Russell Neuropsychology Evaluation System (manual and computer program), 1993; contbr. articles to profl. jours. Fellow APA, Am. Psychol. Soc., Nat. Acad. Neuropsychology; mem. Sigma Xi. Democrat. Mem. Soc. Of Friends. Home: 6091 SW 79th St Miami FL 33143-5030 Office: 9350 S Dixie Hwy Ph 3 Miami FL 33156-2944

RUSSELL, EUGENE ROBERT, SR. engineering educator, administrator; b. Cromwell, Conn., Aug. 24, 1932; s. Arland William and Annie Margaret (LeBlanc) R.; m. Mary Lou Conner, June 29, 1957; children: Theresa, Janice, Eugene Jr., Anna, Ruth, Julie, Susan, Paul, Carol, Cecilia. BSCE, U. Mo., Rolla, 1958; MS in Civil Engring., Iowa State U., 1965; PhD, Purdue U., West Lafayette, Ind., 1974. Registered profl. engr., Iowa, Ind. Asst. bridge engr. State of Calif. Pub. Works, Sacramento, 1958-62; asst. area constrn. engr. Iowa Hwy. Commn., Grinnell, 1962-63; rsch. asst. soils Iowa State U., Ames, 1963-65; asst. prof. Ind. Inst. Tech., Ft. Wayne, 1965-69; rsch. assoc. Purdue U., West Lafayette, 1969-74; assoc. prof. Kans. State U., Manhattan, 1974-80, prof. civil engring., 1980—, dir. Ctr. for Transp. Rsch. and Tng., 1990—, assoc. dir. Mid-Am. Transp. Ctr., 1995-99, Mark and Margaret Hulings prof. civil engring., 1997—. Contbr. more than 60 articles to profl. jours. With USN, 1951-53. Fellow ASCE (life mem., br. pres.), Inst. Transp. Engrs.; mem. Am. R.R. Engring. & Maintenance Assn., Transp. Rsch. Bd. (univ. rep., mem. emeritus com. A3AO5), Transp. Rsch. Forum, Am. Soc. Engring. Edn., Nat. Assn. Railroad Passengers, Roadway Safety Found., Nat. Assn. County Engrs., Am. Pub. Works Assn., Sigma Xi, Chi Epsilon. Home: 3424 Dickens Ave Manhattan KS 66503-2413 Office: Kansas State Univ Dept Civil Engring 2118 Fiedler Hall Manhattan KS 66506

RUSSELL, FRANCIA, ballet director, educator; b. Los Angeles, Jan. 10, 1938; d. W. Frank and Marion (Whitney) R.; m. Kent Stowell, Nov. 19, 1965; children: Christopher, Darren, Ethan. Studies with, George Balanchine, Vera Volkova, Felia Doubrouska, Antonina Tumkovsky, Benjamin Harkarvy; student, NYU, Columbia U. Dancer, soloist N.Y.C. Ballet, 1956-62, ballet mistress, 1965-70; dancer Ballets USA/Jerome Robbins, N.Y.C., 1962; tchr. ballet Sch. Am. Ballet, 1963-64; co-dir. Frankfurt (Fed. Republic Germany) Opera Ballet, 1976-77; dir., co-artistic dir. Pacific N.W. Ballet, Seattle, 1977—; dir. Pacific N.W. Ballet Sch. Affiliate prof. of dance U. Wash. Dir. staging over 100 George Balanchine ballet prodns. throughout world, including Russia and China, 1964—. Named Woman of Achievement, Matrix Table, Women in Comm., Seattle, 1987, Gov.'s Arts award, 1989, Dance Mag. award, 1996. Mem. Internat. Women's Forum. Home: 2833 Broadway E Seattle WA 98102-3935 Office: Pacific NW Ballet 301 Mercer St Seattle WA 98109-4600

RUSSELL, FRANK ELI, retired newspaper publishing executive; b. Kokomo, Ind., Dec. 6, 1920; s. Frank E. and Maude (Wiggins) R.; children: Linda Carole Russell Atkins, Richard Lee, Frank E. III, Rita Jane Russell Eagle, Julie Beth Russell; m. Nancy M. Shover, Oct. 5, 1991. AB, Evansville Coll., 1942; JD, Ind. U., 1951; LLD (hon.), U. Evansville, 1985; HHD (hon.), Franklin Coll., 1989. Bar: Ind. 1951; CPA, Ind. Ptnr. George S. Olive & Co., Indpls., 1947-53; exec. v.p. Spickelmier Industries, Inc., 1953-59; bus. mgr. Indpls. Star & News, 1959-77; v.p., gen. mgr. Ctrl. Newspapers, Inc., Indpls., 1977-79, pres., 1979-95, chmn., bd. dirs., 1996-98; ret., 1998; also bd. dirs. Ctrl. Newsprint; pres. Bradley Paper Co., also bd. dirs. Past chmn. adv. bd. Met. Indpls. TV Assn., Inc.; trustee retirement trust Ctrl. Newspapers, Inc.; chmn. retirement com. Hoosier State Press. Bd. dirs. Ariz. Cmty. Found., 1992-96, Eiteljorg Mus., 1994—; trustee, chmn. bd. Nina Mason Pulliam Charitable Trust, 1997—. Recipient Life Salvation award Salvation Army, 1989, Disting. Alumni award Ind. U. Sch. Law, 1989, Life Trustee award U. Evansville, 1991, Ralph D. Casey award, 1997. Mem. ABA, AICPA, Ind. Bar. Assn., Indpls. Bar Assn. (past bd. dirs., past treas.), Ind. Assn. CPAs (past dir.), Tax Execs. Inst. (past pres.), Ind. Assn. Credit Mgmt. (dir., v.p.), Inst. Newspaper Controllers and Fin. Officers (dir., past pres.), Ind. Acad. Ind. Assn. Colls., Midwest Pension Conf. (Ind. chpt.), Newspaper Advt. Bur. (bd. dirs.), Salvation Army (life mem. award), Columbia Club, Meridian Hills Country Club, Masons, Shriners, Order of Coif, Phi Delta Phi, Sigma Alpha Epsilon. Methodist. Office: Nina Mason Pulliam Charitable Trust 135 N Pennsylvania St Ste 1200 Indianapolis IN 46204-1956

RUSSELL, GEORGE ALLEN, composer, theoritician, author, conductor; b. Cin., June 23, 1923; s. Joseph and Bessie (Sledge) R.; 1 son, Jock Millgardh; m. Alice Norbury, Aug. 4, 1981. Grad. h.s.; ed. in pupil composition, Stephan Volpe, 1949. Apptd. mem. faculty New England Conservatory Music, 1969. Also tchr. in Sweden, Norway, Finland, U.K., Italy, Austria, Germany, France and Japan; mem. panel Nat. Endowment of Arts, 1975-76 Composer (with Dizzy Gillespie); 1st composition featuring jazz and Latin influences Cubana-Be, Cubana Bop; presented Carnegie Hall, 1947; performed John F. Kennedy's People to People Music Festival, Washington, 1962, Philharmonic Hall, Lincoln Center, 1963, tours of Europe with Newport Jazz Festival, 1964, jazz orchestras 1970—; performed original compostions with large and small European ensembles for radio, TV and new music socs., in Scandinavia, Italy, Sweden, W.Ger., also other parts Europe, 1964-70; Carnegie Hall performance, 1975; participant 1st White House Jazz Festival, 1978; recs. for RCA Records, Decca, Prestige, Capitol, Atlantic, Columbia, Contemporary, Blue Note, Soul Note, numerous others.; commd. composer maj. jazz work, Brandeis U., 1957, Norwegian TV; other commns. include original music for ballet Othello, 1967, Norwegian Cultural Fund, 1st choral work Listen to the Silence, 1971, Columbia Recs., Living Time for big band featuring Bill Evans,

1975, Swedish Radio for orch., 1977, 81, 83, Mass. Council on the Arts, 1983, Boston Musica Viva, 1987, work for orch. New Eng. Presentors, 1988, work for Relache New Music Ensemble, 1989; sponsor Am. Music Week, 1985, 86; artist-in-residence Glasgow Internat. Festival, 1990, Ezz-thetics with Don Ellis, Dave Baker, et al, N.Y. Big Band, New York, N.Y., Electronic Sonata for Souls Loved By Nature, The Essence of George Russell; tours of U.K., Europe, Japan with George Russell Living Time Orch., 1986—; co-commn. Swedish Concert Inst. and Brit. Coun., 1995; recordings Label Bleu, 1989, 96; seminars: Paris Conservatoire Nat. Superier, Royal Coll. Music, Stockholm, Huddersfield Contemporary Music Festival, Guildhall, others, 1986-96; author: Lydian Chromatic Concept of Tonal Organization, 1953, 59, 98. Recipient Outstanding Composer award Metronome mag., 1958, New Star Composer award Downbeat mag., 1961, Nat. Endowment for the Arts award, 1969, 76, 80, 81, Jazz Masters fellow, 1989; recipient Nat. Music award Am. Music Conf., 1976, numerous awards for recs.; Guggenheim fellow, 1969, 72; Nat. Endowment for Arts grantee, 1979; MacArthur Found. fellow, 1989. Mem. Internat. Soc. Contemporary Music, Norwegian Soc. New Music, Am. Fedn. Musicians, Royal Coll. Music (fgn. mem.). Address: care Concept 1770 Massachusetts Ave Ste 182 Cambridge MA 02140-2808 E-mail: lydconcept@aol.com.

RUSSELL, GEORGE HAW, video production company executive; b. Neosho, Mo., May 22, 1945; s. Kenneth L. and Marjorie (Haw) R.; m. Suzanne Bennett, June 1, 1967; children: Margaret Anne, Marjorie Jane, Karen Lee, George Andrew. BA, La. State U., 1967. Ednl. Video Network, Huntsville, 1990—; ptnr. The Sam Houston Group Ltd. Liability Partnership, 1991—. Producer ednl. videos Nombres et Couleurs, 1988 (Silver Apple award 1988), Napoleon, 1989 (Silver Apple award 1989), Bullfight, 1990, The French Revolution, 1990; exec. producer Spain's Historic Cities, 1992, Munich's Oktoberfest, 1992, The New Nutriton Pyramid, 1992, The Visual Language of Design, 1992, Florence, 1993, Joan of Arc, 1993, New Food Guide Pyramid, 1993, Cleaning and Maintaining Your VCR, 1993, Arts and Crafts of Mexico, 1993, Understanding Geysers and Hot Springs, 1993, Thoreau at Walden Pond, 1993, French Markets, 1993, Great Zimbabwe, 1993. Bd. govs. Tex. Com. on Natural Resources, Dallas, 1979—; bd. dirs. Gibbs-Powell House Mus., Huntsville, 1984—, Natural Area Preservation Assn., Dallas, 1986—; chmn. forest practices Lone Star Sierra Club, Austin, Tex., 1984—; chmn. Fed. Forest Reform, Washington, D.C., 1991—. 1st lt. U.S. Army, 1971-74. Recipient spl. achievement award Sierra Club, San Francisco 1985, chpt. conservation award 1987, environ. heroes for centennial 1991; named Citizen of Month, Huntsville Item 1988. Democrat. Methodist. Avocations: environmental advocacy, historic building restoration, collecting antiques and folk art. Home: 1409 19th St Huntsville TX 77340-5056 Office: Ednl Video Network 1401 19th St Huntsville TX 77340-5057

RUSSELL, HARRIET SHAW, social worker; b. Detroit, Apr. 12, 1952; d. Louis Thomas and Lureleen (Hughes) Shaw; m. Donald Edward Russell, June 27, 1980; children: Lachante Tyree, Krystal Lanae. BS, Mich. State U., 1974; AB, Detroit Bus. Inst., 1976; BA in Pub. Adminstrn., Mercy Coll., Detroit, 1988; MSW, Wayne State U., 1992. Factory staff Gen. Motors Corp., Lansing, Mich., 1973; student supr. tour guides State of Mich., 1974; mgr. Ky. Fried Chicken, Detroit, 1974-75; unemployment claims examiner State of Mich. Dept. Labor, 1975-77, asst. payment worker, 1977-84, social svcs. specialist, 1984-90; pres. Victory Enterprises, 1991; social worker Detroit Bd. Edn., 1992—. Ind. contractor Detroit Compact; moderator Mich. Opportunity Skills and Tng. Program, 1985-86. Vol. Mich. Cancer Soc., East Lansing, 1970-72, Big Sisters/Big Bros., Lansing, 1972-73; elected rep. Mich. Coun. Social Svcs. Workers; spkr. Triumphant Bapt. Ch., Detroit, 1976-80; chief union steward Mich. Employees Assn., Lincoln Park, 1982-83; leader Girl Scouts U.S.; area capt. Life Worker Project Program; bd. dirs. Neighborhood Found., 1995-97. Wayne State U. scholar, 1990-91, Deans scholar, 1991-92; recipient Outstanding Work Performace Merit award Mich. Dept. Social Svcs., 1979, Unsung Hero award Neighborhood Found., 1995; elected to Wayne State Sch. Social Work Bd., 1992-98. Mem. NAFE, Am. Soc. Profl. and Exec. Women, Assn. Internat. Platform Spkrs., Mich. Coun. Social Svcs. Workers, Nat. fedn. Bus. and Profl. Womens Clubs Inc. U.S.A. (elected del. to China), Nat. Assn. Black Social Workers, Wayne State U. Social Work Alumni Assn. (bd. dirs. 1992-98), Delta Sigma Theta. Democrat. Baptist. Office: PO Box 361 Lincoln Park MI 48146-0361

RUSSELL, HELEN DIANE, retired museum curator, educator; b. Kansas City, Mo., Apr. 8, 1936; d. Harry Fay Russell and Georgia Mae (Canfield) Haeberle. AB, Vassar Coll., 1958; PhD, Johns Hopkins U., 1970; postgrad., Inst. for Advanced Study, Princeton, N.J., 1980-81. Mus. curator Nat. Gallery Art, Washington, 1964-90, curator of Old Master Prints, 1990-98. Professorial lectr. The Am. U., Washington, 1966-82, adj. prof. Art History, 1982—. Author: Rare Etchings of G.B. and G.D. Tiepolo, 1972, Jacques Callot, 1975, Claude Lorrain, 1982 (Barr award 1984), EVA/AVE: Woman in Renaissance and Baroque Prints, 1990. Woodrow Wilson Foun. fellow, 1958-59; Univ. fellow, Johns Hopkins U., 1961-63; Kress Found. fellow, 1973; Nat. Endowment for Arts fellow, 1980-81. Mem. Coll. Art Assn., Renaissance Soc. Am., Print Coun. Am., Vassar Club. Avocations: poodles, photography.

RUSSELL, HELEN ROSS, environmental consultant, author; b. Myerstown, Pa., Feb. 21, 1915; d. George Smith and Helen Louise (Boyd) Ross; m. Robert S. Russell, Sept. 24, 1960. Cert. teaching, West Chester State Tchrs. Coll., 1934; BA, Lebanon Valley Coll., 1943, DHL (hon.), 1973; MA, Cornell U., 1947, PhD, 1949; DSc, Fitchburg State Coll., 1992. Tchr. Jackson (Pa.) Twp., 1934-35; tchr. 3d grade Bethel Twp. Consolidated Sch., Pa., 1935-42; tchr. art and sci. Lebanon (Pa.) City Schs., 1942-46; assoc. prof. biology Fitchburg (Mass.) State Tchrs. Coll., 1949-52, chmn. sci. dept., 1952-56, acad. dean, 1956-66; environ. edn. cons., Jersey City, 1968—. Author: City Critters, 1969, Clarion the Killdeer, 1970, Earth the Great Recycler, 1973, Ten Minute Field Trips, Using the School Grounds for Environmental Studies, 1973, 90, Translated into Russian, 1997; editor Nature Study, 1973-99; lectr. in field. Recipient Eva L. Gordon award Children's Sci. Lit., 1976, Outdoor Edn. Literary award N.Y. State Outdoor Edn. Assn., 1982, US/UNEP 500 Environ. Achievement U.S. Com. UN Environ. Program, 1991, Lifetime Achievement award Urban Environ. Edn. City Club N.Y.C., 1992, Taft Campus award No. Ill. U., 1995, N.J. State Outstanding Environ. Educator award, 1996, Roger Tory Peterson Inst. award Nat. Leadership in Environ. Edn., 1997, Harlan Gold Metcalf award for leadership in environ. edn. N.Y. State Outdoor Edn. Assn., 1998, alumni citation Lebanon Valley Coll., 1999; named to Hall of Fame Eastern Lebanon County, 1997. Fellow: AAAS (sect. E); mem.: Am. Nature Study Soc. (pres. 1974, editor 1980—97, Liberty Hyde Bailey award 1995). Methodist. Avocations: travel, skiing, photography, cooking. Home: 44 College Dr Jersey City NJ 07305-1003 Office: Tulpehocken Creek Trails 51 S Ramona Rd Myerstown PA 17067-2348

RUSSELL, HILARY FRANCIS, secondary education educator; b. Mt. Kisco, N.Y., Feb. 6, 1943; s. Hilary Francis and Mary Elizabeth R.; m. Jane Peabody, Aug. 22, 1970; children: Lydia Slocum, Caitlin Peabody. BS in Edn., English, Villanova U., 1966; MA in Liberal Studies, Wesleyan U., 1971. Tchr., coach St. Paul's Sch., Garden City, N.Y., 1966-68, Berkshire Sch., Sheffield, Mass., 1968-72, 85—, chair dept. English, 1985—; tchr., coach chair dept. English Tower Hill Sch., Wilmington, Del., 1972-85. Evaluator English dept. Albuquerque Acad., 1989; spkr. in field. Author: The Portable Writer, 1989, 1998, The Anthology of American Poetry, 1992, Giving Up the House; contbr. Founding bd. dirs. Sheffield Land Trust, 1997-98. Grantee Nat. Endowment Arts, 1974, Strom Fund, 1997; Ind. Study Humanities fellow Coun. Basic Edn., 1996. Avocations: boat building, hiking, canoeing, gardening. Home: PO Box 578 Sheffield MA 01257 Office: Berkshire Sch 245 N Undermountain Rd Sheffield MA 01257

RUSSELL, HORACE ORLANDO, theology studies educator; b. Clarendon, Jamaica, Nov. 3, 1929; Came to the U.S., 1988; s. Cleveland Augustus and Rowena Nerissa (Gordon) R.; m. Beryl Joyce Redman, Aug. 31, 1957; children: Elisabeth Jennifer, Jonathan Paul Carey, Heather Dawn Marie. BD, Calabar Theological Coll., London, 1954; BA, St. Catherine Coll., Oxford, 1957; PhD, Regent's Park Coll., Oxford, 1972. Ordained Baptist min. Febr. 10, 1958. Prof. church history United Theol. Coll. W.I., U. W.I., Jamaica, 1958-76, pres. Jamaica, 1972-76; sr. pastor East Queen, Kingston Jamaica Bapt. Union, 1976-89; dean of chapel, prof. hist. theology Ea. Bapt. Theol. Sem., Phila., 1989—. Mem. faith and order commn. World Coun. of Chs., Geneva, Switzerland, 1968-90, world assoc. of Christian commn., London, 1969—; v.p. Jamaica Baptist Union, 1980; vice moderator Faith and Order O, 1986-90. Author: Five Words of Love, 1982, The Baptist Witness, 1983, Foundations and Anticipations-The Baptist Story in Jamaica 1783-1892, 1993, Jamaica Mission W.I. to West Africa, 1999; founder, editor: Carribean Jour. of Religious Studies, 1966. Mem. nat. commn. on unemployment Govt. of Jamaica, 1969, mem. pub. svc. commn., 1980-88, mem. nat. commn. on drug abuse, 1984-89, chair nat. heritage trust, 1988-89, cultural devel. commn. 1987-88. Recipient Jamaica Prime Minister's medal Jamaican Govt., 1984, Marcus Garvey medal Marcus Garvey Internat., 1984, Jamaica Council of Churches award Churches of Jamaica, 1986. Mem. Am. Soc. of Ch. History, West Indies Group of Univ. Tchrs., Soc. for the Study of Black Religion, Hist. Soc. of Great Britain, Univ. Lodge English Masons (chaplain 1970), Oxford Soc. Baptist. Avocations: photography, creative writing. Home: 1030 E Lancaster Ave Bryn Mawr PA 19010 Office: Ea Baptist Theological Seminary 6 E Lancaster Ave Wynnewood PA 19096-3430 E-mail: horussell@aol.com., horussell@ebts.edu.

RUSSELL, IRWIN EMANUEL, lawyer; b. N.Y.C., Jan. 24, 1926; m. Suzanne Russell, Nov. 15, 1968. BS in Econs., U. Pa., 1947; JD, Harvard U., 1949. Bar: N.Y. 1949, Calif. 1971. Atty. office chief counsel Wage Stabilization Bd., Washington, 1951-53; pvt. practice N.Y.C., 1954-71; founder, chmn., dir. RAI Rsch. Corp., Hauppage, N.Y., 1954-91; exec. v.p., treas., dir. The Wolper Orgn., Inc., L.A., 1971-76; pvt. practice Beverly Hills, Calif., 1977—. With USAAF, 1944-45. Home: 10590 Wilshire Blvd Apt 1402 Los Angeles CA 90024-4563 Office: 9401 Wilshire Blvd Ste 760 Beverly Hills CA 90212-2933

RUSSELL, JAMES ALVIN, JR. college administrator; b. Lawrenceville, Va., Dec. 25, 1917; s. Dr. James Alvin and Nellie M. (Pratt) R.; m. Lottye J. Washington, Dec. 25, 1943; children: Charlotte Justyne, James Alvin III. BA, Oberlin Coll., 1940; BS, Bradley U., 1941, MS, 1950, spl. insts.; EdD, U. Md., 1967; spl. insts., Wayne U., U. Mich., U. Ill., NSF. Prof., dir. div. engring., also prof. edn. div. grad. studies Hampton Inst., 1950-71; pres. St. Paul's Coll., Lawrenceville, 1971-81; dir. instructional programs and student services Va. C.C. System, 1981-82; chmn. div. profl. studies W.Va. State Coll., 1982-86, acting pres., 1986-87, exec. asst. to pres., 1987-88; pres. So. W.Va. C.C., 1988-89, ret., 1989. Pres. Peninsula Council Human Relations, 1961-65. United Negro Coll. Fund fellow, 1966-67. Mem. IEEE, Am. Soc. Engring. Edn., Am. Assn. Univ. Adminstrs., Am. Vocat. Assn., Am. Tech. Edn. Assn., Nat. Assn. Indsl. Tech., Am. Assn. for Higher Edn., Nat. Assn. for Equal Opportunity in Edn., Brunswick C. of C., Sigma Pi Phi, Alpha Kappa Mu, Iota Lambda Sigma, Omega Psi Phi. Home: 811 Grandview Dr Dunbar WV 25064-1175

RUSSELL, JAMES BRIAN, broadcast executive, media consultant; b. Hartford, Conn., Jan. 30, 1946; s. Seymour and Marian (Kamins) R.; m. Kathleen Anne Schardt, Dec. 28, 1968; children: Theodore, Jennifer, Kimberly. BA in Journalism, Am. U., 1968; postgrad. Wharton Sch. Bus., U. Pa.; postgrad., Stanford U. News dir. Sta. WPIK-AM, Arlington, Va., 1965-66; editor, anchorman Sta. WAVA-AM/FM, Washington, 1966-68; editor, corr. UPI, Washington, Cambodia and, Vietnam, 1968-71; from reporter to exec. prodr. All Things Considered Nat. Pub. Radio, Washington, 1971-78; sta. dir., sr. v.p. programming Stas. KTCA/KTCI-TV, Mpls./St. Paul, 1978-88; v.p. nat. prodns., exec. prodr. Marketplace U. So. Calif., L.A., 1988-97; v.p. USC Radio and GM Marketplace Prodns., 1997-99; sr. v.p. Minn. Pub. Radio & GM Marketplace Prodns., 2000—. Cons. Corp. Pub. Broadcasting, Nat. Endowment Arts, Sta. WNET-TV, N.Y.C., Sta. WGBH-TV, Boston, Nat. Pub. Radio, Am. Pub. Radio, Pub. Radio Internat., Am. Documentary Consortium, The Learning Channel, The Pacific Rim Consortium, Internat. Pub. TV Conf., Audible, Inc.; adv. bd. Assoc. Press Broadcasters, 2002-. Columnist pub. broadcasting's Current newspaper. Mem. prison visitor program AMICUS, St. Paul, 1984-85. Postgrad. fellow in journalism U. Mich.; recipient Nat. Headliner award 1972, 74, Ohio State award, 1973, 75, duPont Columbia awards Columbia U., 1979, 81, 97, Peabody award 2001, Nat. TV Emmy award Acad. TV Arts and Scis., 1989, William Kling award for Innovation and Entrepreneurship, 1998, Mo. Honor medal for disting. svc. in journalism, 2000. Home: 671 W Orange Grove Ave Sierra Madre CA 91024 Office: Marketplace Prodns 261 S Figueroa Ave #200 Los Angeles CA 90012 E-mail: jrussell@marketplace.org.

RUSSELL, JAMES T. research scientist; b. Nagercoil, Tamilnadu, India, Oct. 26, 1944; arrived in U.S., 1976; s. James and Lizzie Russell; m. Arulini M. Jacobs, July 1970 (div. June 1981); children: Ivan Gould, Kamala R.; m. Andra E. Miller, Jan. 12, 1990. B of Vet. Sci., Madras (India) Vet. Coll., 1966; MS, Postgrad. Inst. Med. Edn., Chandigarh, India, 1971; PhD, Copenhagen U., 1974. Adj. lectr. Copenhagen U., 1974—76; rsch. assoc. St. Louis U., 1976; sr. investigator NIH, Bethesda, Md., 1982—. Contbr. over 90 articles to profl. jours. Bd. dirs. Barrie Sch., Silver Spring, Md., 1994—97. Office: NIH 49 Convent Dr Bethesda MD 20892

RUSSELL, JAMES WEBSTER, JR. newspaper editor, columnist; b. Shreveport, La., Nov. 30, 1921; s. James Webster and Aline (Faulk) R.; m. Jean Buck, June 29, 1949; children: Nancy Russell Dearr, Eileen Russell Goure. BA, La. State U., 1942. Fla. mgr. Internat. News Service, 1946-51; bur. chief UPI, Tallahassee, 1951-52; regional editor U.P.I., Atlanta, 1953-57; asst. city editor Miami (Fla.) Herald, 1957-58, bus.-fin. editor, 1958-74, fin.-econ. columnist, 1974—. Guest lectr. U. Miami, Fla. Internat. U., Miami-Dade Community Coll., La. State U. Contbr. articles to: Fla. Trend, Times of London, N.Y. Times, Gentlemen's Quar. Trustee Fla. So. Coll. Served with USAAF, 1942-45. Recipient Eagle award Invest-in-Am. Nat. Council, 1976; Decorated Air medal with eleven oak leaf clusters; inducted La. State U. Sch. of Mass Comms. Hall of Fame, 1998. Mem. Soc. Am. Bus. Writers, Lambda Chi Alpha, Sigma Delta Chi. Republican. Methodist (chmn. ch. council on ministries 1971-72). Home: 4800 SW 64th Ct Miami FL 33155-6133

RUSSELL, JAMES WILLIAM, neurologist, neuroscientist, electrophysiologist; b. Salisbury, Rhodesia, Jan. 1, 1960; s. William and Olive Russell; m. Jane, Nov. 3, 1990; 3 children. Student, U. Oxford, Eng., 1982-83; MB, ChB, U. Rhodesia, 1984; postgrad., Mayo Clinic, Rochester, Minn., 1991-93; MS, U. Mich., 2001. Diplomate in neurology and electrodiagnostic medicine Am. Bd. Am. Bd. Psychiatry and Neurology; diplomate Am. Bd. Electrodiagnostic Medicine; lic. physician, Iowa, Mich. Intern in medicine and surgery U. Hosps. and Coll. Medicine U. Rhodesia, Salisbury, 1984-85; resident in internal medicine U. Hosps. and Coll. Medicine U. Zimbabwe, 1985-86; resident in internal medicine Pembury and Lewisham Hosps., London, 1986-88, S.E. Thames Regional Neurology Ctr., Brook Hosp., London, 1986-88; resident in neurology U. Iowa Coll. Medicine and Univ. Hosps., Iowa City, 1988-91; rsch. fellow in neuroscis. Mayo Postgrad. Med. Sch., Rochester, Minn., 1991-92; clin. peripheral nerve fellow Mayo Clinic, 1992-93; clin. assoc. in electrophysiology and neuromuscular disease Nat. Insts. Neurologic Diseases and Stroke/NIH, Bethesda, Md., 1993-95; instr. residents and fellow dept. neurology U. Mich., Ann Arbor, 1995—; assoc. chief neurology Ann Arbor VA Med. Ctr., 1997-2000. Lectr. med. student neurology rotation U. Iowa Coll. Medicine, 1989—91, lectr., organizer neurology residents' confs., 1988—91, lectr. phys. therapists grad. courses, 1989—91, mem. quality assurance com., 1989—91; organizer, presenter confs. Peripheral Nerve Ctr., electromyography residents and fellows Mayo Clinic, 1991—93, lectr. neurology grand rounds and postgrad. neurosci., 1991—93; lectr. electrophysiology and neuromuscular confs. Nat. Inst. Neurologic Diseases and Stroke, NIH, 1993—95, assoc., 1993—95, instr. electrophysiology and neuromuscular disease fellows and residents, 1994—2001; spkr. numerous confs. in field; cons. NIH Intramural Program, 1996; grant reviewer FDA Orphan Products Divsn., 1996—97, Am. Diabetes Assn., 2001—02, Juvenile Diabetes Rsch. Found., 2001. Contbr. numerous articles to profl. publs., confs.; ad hoc reviewer for neurology Jour. AMA., diabetes jours. Grantee NIH, Juvenile Diabetes Rsch. Found., VA. Mem. Royal Colls. Physicians (Edinburgh and Glasgow), Royal Coll. Physicians (London), Am. Acad. Neurology, Am. Diabetes Assn., Juvenile Diabetes Rsch. Found., Am. Autonomic Soc., Peripheral Nerve Soc., Am. Acad. Electrodiagnostic Medicine, Soc. Neurosci., Am. Soc. for Cell Biology, Endocrine Soc. Avocations: golf, equestrian activities. Office: U Mich 4422 Kresge III 200 Zina Pitcher Pl Ann Arbor MI 48109-2205 E-mail: jruss@umich.edu.

RUSSELL, JANE DEXTER, retired librarian; b. Teaneck, N.J., Dec. 17, 1928; d. William Henry and Jane (Dexter) Gerolstein; m. William Albert Braun, (div. Mar. 1960); children: Richard Alan Braun, William Albert Braun Jr.; m. Thomas Lee Russell, June 27, 1980. AA with honors, Daytona Beach (Fla.) Jr. Coll., 1967; BAE summa cum laude, U. Fla., 1969, MEd, 1970; advanced MLS, Fla. State U., 1974. cert. law libr. Assoc. dir. Learning Resources Ctr. Lake City (Fla.) C.C., 1970-72; instr. U. Fla., Gainesville, 1973, asst. law libr., 1974-78, U. Mo., Kansas City, 1978-79, U. N.C., Chapel Hill, 1980-82; asst. dir. N.C. Japan Ctr. N.C. State U., Raleigh, 1983-86; CEO Russell Ventures Internat., 1984—. Adj. N.C. Japan Ctr., Raleigh, 1986—. Fellow Inst. Applied Lang. Sci. Libr. and Culture Ctr. (Mysore, India); Mem. Phi Theta Kappa, Pi Lambda Theta, Beta Phi Mu, Phi Kappa Phi. Republican. Episcopalian. Avocation: world travel. Home and Office: 2861 Rue Sans Famille Raleigh NC 27607-3048 E-mail: tjrussell@mindspring.com.

RUSSELL, JEAN ELIZABETH, biomedical endocrinologist, researcher; b. Chgo., Feb. 24, 1943; d. James Robert and Helen Jeanne (Dunham) R. BA, Cornell Coll., 1965; PhD, Rice U., 1970. Postdoctoral fellow in endocrinology Washington U., St. Louis, 1970-73, rsch. assoc., 1973-76, asst. prof. oral biology, 1977-79, rsch. instr. surgery, 1980-83, rsch. asst. prof. surgery, 1983-90, rsch. assoc. prof. surgery, 1990—. Sci. reviewer Calcified Tissue Internat. Jour., 1983—, Am. Inst. Biol. Scis. Jour., 1988—. Contbr. articles to profl. jours. Trustee pvt. neighborhood subdivision govt., Olivette, Mos., 1985-88. Mem. AAAS, Am. Physiol. Soc., Am. Fedn. Clin. Rsch., Am. Soc. Bone and Mineral Rsch., Am. Isnt. Biol. Sci., Am. Diabetes Assn., N.Y. Acad. Scis., Orthopedic Rsch. Soc., Internat. Congress Calcium Regulating Hormones, Endocrine Soc. Home: 5715 Wayne Ave Pentwater MI 49449-9514 Office: Washington U 660 S Euclid Ave # 8109 Saint Louis MO 63110-1093

RUSSELL, JEFFREY BURTON, historian, educator; b. Fresno, Calif., Aug. 1, 1934; s. Lewis Henry and Ieda Velma (Ogborn) R.; m. Diana Emily Mansfield, June 30, 1956; children: Jennifer, Mark, William, Penelope. AB, U. Calif., Berkeley, 1955, A.M., 1957; PhD, Emory U., 1960. Asst. prof. U. N.Mex., Albuquerque, 1960-61; jr. fellow Soc. of Fellows, Harvard U., Cambridge, Mass., 1961-62; mem. faculty U. Calif., Riverside, 1962-75, prof. dept. history, 1969-75, assoc. dean grad. div., 1967-72; dir. Medieval Inst.; Michael P. Grace prof. medieval studies U. Notre Dame, South Bend, Ind., 1975-77; dean grad. studies Calif. State U., Sacramento, 1977-79; prof. history U. Calif., Santa Barbara, 1979—, prof. religious studies, 1994—. Author: Dissent and Reform in the Early Middle Ages, 1965, Medieval Civilization, 1968, A History of Medieval Christianity: Prophecy and Order, 1968, Religious Dissent in the Middle Ages, 1971, Witchcraft in the Middle Ages, 1972, The Devil: Perceptions of Evil from Antiquity to Primitive Christianity, 1977, A History of Witchcraft: Sorcerers, Heretics, and Pagans, 1980, Medieval Heresies: a Bibliography, 1981, Satan: The Early Christian Tradition, 1981, Lucifer: The Devil in the Middle Ages, 1984, Mephistopheles: The Devil in the Modern World, 1986, The Prince of Darkness, 1988, Ruga in Aevis, 1990, Inventing the Flat Earth: Columbus and the Historians, 1991, Dissent and Order in the Middle Ages, 1992, A History of Heaven: The Singing Silence, 1997, Essays in Honor of Jeffrey B. Russell, 1998; contbr. articles in field to profl. jours. Fulbright fellow, 1959-60; Am. Council Learned Socs. grantee, 1965, 70; Social Sci. Research Council grantee, 1968; Guggenheim fellow, 1968-69; Nat. Endowment for Humanities sr. fellow, 1972-73 Fellow Medieval Acad. Am.; mem. Medieval Assn. Pacific, Am. Soc. Ch. Histor Am. Acad. Religion, Astron. Soc. Pacific, Sierra Club. Home: 4798 Calle Camarada Santa Barbara CA 93110-2053 Office: U Calif Dept History Santa Barbara CA 93106 E-mail: russell@history.ucsb.edu.

RUSSELL, JHE, ballet dancer; b. Boston; arrived in Can., 1991; Student, Boston Ballet Sch., Sch. Am. Ballet, Nat. Ballet Sch., Can., 1991. Dancer Dance Theatre Harlem, Boston Ballet; apprentice Nat. Ballet Can., Toronto, Canada, mem. corps de ballet, 1995—99, second soloist Canada, 1999—. Dancer (ballets) Cinderella, Swan Lake, Taming of the Shrew, Septet, the weight of absence. Recipient Erik Bruhn prize, 1999. Office: Walter Carsen Ctr for Nat Ballet Can 470 Queens Quay W Toronto ON Canada M5V 3K4*

RUSSELL, JOHN FINTAN, theology educator, editor; b. Springfield, Mass., July 19, 1934; s. David Joseph and Ellen Teresa (Shea) R. BA, St. Bonaventure U., 1957; STL, Lateran U., Rome, Italy, 1962; MA, Roosevelt U., 1968; STD, Cath. U., 1979. Dean of boys Carmel High Sch., Mundelein, Ill., 1962-67; dir. counseling Carmel Sem., Hamilton, Mass., 1967-70; dir. Whitefriars Hall, Washington, 1972-77; asst. prof. theology I.C.S. Sem., Mahwah, N.J., 1977-83; assoc. prof. theology Seton Hall U., South Orange, 1983-91, prof. theology, 1991—. Theology cons. Nat. Office of Renew, Plainfield, N.J., 1988—. Author: (with others) Experiencing St. Therese Today, 1990; editor: Sword Mag., 1990-96; contbr. articles to profl. jours. Mem. Com. for Ednl. Excellence, Cresskill, N.J., 1983-84. Faculty rsch. grantee Seton Hall U., 1989, 94. Mem. Cath. Theol. Soc. Am. Roman Catholic. Avocations: sports, reading, travel. Home: Lewis Hall Seton U South Orange NJ 07079 Office: Seton Hall U 400 W South Orange Ave South Orange NJ 07079-1478

RUSSELL, JOHN FRANCIS, retired librarian; b. Mt. Carmel, Ind., Apr. 30, 1929; s. David Freeman and Bertha (Major) R.; m. Edith Raymond Hyde, June 27, 1953; 1 child, Anne Marie. BA, DePauw U., 1951; postgrad., Ind. U., 1951-52; MA, Johns Hopkins U., 1954; student, Cath. U. Am., summer 1955; MS, Grad. Sch. Libr. Sci./Drexel, U., 1977. Tchr. English Park Sch. Balt., 1954-75, chmn. dept., 1957-75; tchr. speech, dir. Ira Aldridge Players Morgan State Coll., fall 1965-66; tchr. drama Loyola Coll., 1964, 66. Editor: The Secondary School Theatre, 1972-74. Pres. Tchrs.'s Assn. Ind. Sch. Balt. Area, 1960-62, adv. bd., 1966-67, chmn. com. on English, 1966-68; exec. com. Assn. Ind. Md. Sch., 1967-68; dir., costumer Johns Hopkins U. Playshop, 1963-64; lectr. Lecture Group, Woman's Club Roland Park, others, 1964—; bd. dirs. Balt. area coun. World Federalists U.S.A., 1961-67, vice chmn., 1964-67, nat. exec. coun., 1963-65; bd. dirs. Ctr. Stage, 1964-77; dir. Blvd. Players, pres., 1960-67; dir. Pasadena Little Theatre, v.p., 1979-83, pres., 1983-85, 2d v.p., 1990—; dir. Center Stage Players, New Image Theatre, Theatre Network of Houston, U.S.A. Theatre, Actors Conservatory Tex., v.p., 1990-91, Glenbrook United Meth. Ch. Drama Ministry; bd. dirs. Unicorn Sch. Acting, 1996—, v.p., 1997—; adv. com. Am. H.S. Theatre Festival, 1975; mem. adminstrv. bd. St. Mark's United Meth. Ch., 1957-67, Towson United Meth. Ch., 1967-77, First United Meth. Ch., Houston, 1980-89; adminstrv. coun., vice-chmn. Glenbrook United Meth. Ch., 1997, chmn. pastor-parish rels. com., 1998, lay del., 1999, 2000, lay leader 1999—; sec. Festival Angels, 1982-2001 (Outstanding Svc. award 1991); cmty. vol. svcs. com., ARC, 1985-90; comprehensive volunteerism adv. com., Sheltering Arms, 1986-89. Recipient Nat. Citation of Merit Am. Shakespeare Festival, 1961, Theatre Goddess award U.S.A. Theatre, 1998, Critics Choice award Houston Post, 1984; certs. of appreciation Sheltering Arms, 1986-89, cert. of recognition, 1988. Mem. Am. Assn. Cmty. Theatre, Harris County Heritage Soc., Am. Film Inst., Drama League, Am. Theatre Assn. (v.p. Mid-Atlantic dist. 1967-68, pres. 1968-69, nat. dir. 1970-73, Mid-Atlantic chpt. award for achievement and contbn. to theatre 1973), Secondary Sch. Theatre Assn. (v.p. devel. 1974-75), Tex. Non-Profit Theatre, Nat. (bd. dirs. 1969), Md. Coun. Tchrs. English (pres. 1969-70), Capital Area Media Educators Orgn. (exec. com. 1970-73, screening chmn. 1971-73), ALA, Tex. Libr. Assn. (audiovisual chmn. conv. planning com. 1981), Coun. Info. and Referral Svcs. (newsletter editor 1984-86), Tex. Alliance Info. and Referral Svcs. (conv. speaker 1981, 83, 84, 85), Alliance of Info. and Referral Svcs. (conv. speaker 1985), Houston Pub. Libr. Staff Assn. (pres. 1981-82), Literacy Vols. Am. (sec. Houston 1984-87, adv. bd. 1989-91, 95-96, bd. dirs. 1992-95, chmn. program com. 1991-93), Reading, Edn. and Devel. Coun. (recruitment chmn., exec. com. 1984-86), Cultural Arts Coun. of Houston/Harris County, Park Pl. Civic Club (exemplary svc. award 1991), AARP (bd. dirs. chpt. 1172 1998—, v.p. 1999-2000, 01-02), Phi Beta Kappa, Phi Eta Sigma, Beta Phi Mu. Home: 7817 Grove Ridge Dr Houston TX 77061-1405 E-mail: jrussell10@houston.rr.com.

RUSSELL, JOHN ROBERT, neurosurgeon; b. Bloomington, Ind., Mar. 17, 1922; s. John Dale and Elsie Violet Russell; m. Jane Elizabeth Bureau, Aug. 21, 1943; children: Thomas William, John Bureau, Ann Elizabeth, Amy Catherine. BS, U. Chgo., 1941, MS, 1942, MD, 1945. Diplomate Am. Bd. Neurol. Surgery. Intern Chgo. Meml. Hosp., 1945-46, resident, 1948-50, Bapt. Meml. Hosp, Memphis, 1950-51; mem. faculty Ind. U. Sch. Medicine, Indpls., 1951-59; ptnr. pvt. practice neurosurgery, 1959-71; pres. pvt. practice neurosurgery Indpls. Neurosurg. Group, 1971-84; neurosurg. cons. forensic medicine Chiron/EMC, Madison, Wis., 1991-97. V.p. Neurosurg. Soc. Ind., 1976-77. Fellow ACS; mem. Am. Assn. Neurol. Surgeons (bd. dirs. 1967-70), Congress Neurol. Surgeons (sec. 1962-65, pres. 1967). Avocations: woodworking, swimming. Home: PO Box 197 Boulder Junction WI 54512-0197

RUSSELL, JOHN WILLIAM, insurance executive; b. Springfield, Mass., May 24, 1952; s. John Jacob Jr. and Helen (Mullaly) R.; m. Beronica N. Trevino, Feb. 19, 1987. BS in Indsl. Engring., Western New Eng. Coll., 1975. Registered profl. engr., Mass; cert. profl. ergonomist. Rep. loss prevention Liberty Mut. Ins. Co., Hamden, Conn., 1975-76, Norwich, 1976-78, sr. loss prevention rep., 1978-80, cons. loss prevention, 1980-81, cons. indsl. loss prevention, 1981, sr. cons. indsl. loss prevention East Hartford, 1981-85, tech. cons. indsl. Glastonbury, 1985-88, div. tech. dir. indsl. Weston, Mass., 1988-91; mgr. mfg. tech. Liberty Mutual Ins. Co., Boston, 1991—. Tchr. evening div. Hartford (Conn.) State Tech. Coll., 1982-87. Contr.: Material Handling Handbook, 1985. Mem. planning com. City of Manchester, Conn., 1986-87; fin. bd. United Way, Groton, Conn., 1979; VIP com. Leukemia Soc., Hartford, 1984-85; mem. parish devel. team All Saints Episcopal Ch., East Hartford, 1987-88; mem., chmn. B11 parent com., B7, B24.1, B11.1, B11.2535 coms. ANSI. Mem. Inst. Indsl. Engrs., Am. Soc. Safety Engrs., Internat. Material Mgmt. Soc. (cert.), Cert. Safety Profls., Nat. Fire Protection Assn., Nat. Welding Soc., Mass. Soc. Profl. Engrs. (bd. dirs.), Western New Eng. Coll. Alumni Assn. (v.p. 1987, pres. 1988), Indsl. Engring. Club (pres. 1973-74), Electronics Club (pres. 1969-70). Avocations: electronics, photography, golf, exercising, reading. Home: 40 Connolly St Randolph MA 02368-1511 Office: Liberty Mut Ins Co 13 Riverside Rd Weston MA 02493

RUSSELL, JOSEPH ALLEN, instrumentation and controls engineer, consultant; b. Lompoc, Calif. s. Clark Earl and Nanice Mercedis (Poett) Russell; m. Nancy Bolson, July 3, 1971 (div. 1981); children: Elizabeth, Rosalind; m. Reevah Simon, July 18, 1999. Student, Allen Hancoc Coll., Santa Maria, Calif., 1968-70, Calif. Polytechnic Inst., San Luis Obispo, Calif., 1970-71. Registered profl. engr., Calif. Electro optical engr. Electro Optical Industries, Santa Barbara, Calif., 1971-73; designer, field engr. Stearns/Roger, Denver, 1973-74; instrumentation and controls engr. C.F. Braun, Alhambra, Calif., 1974-76; technician, supr. S.C.E., Rosemead, 1976-84, constrn. supt., 1984-85; project mgr. De La Guerra Power, Santa Barbara, 1985-87; sys. engr. Fairfield Energy, Ft. Fairfield, 1988; project engr. G.W.F. Power Sys., Walnut Creek, Calif., 1989-92; chief telescope engr. Mt. Wilson Observatory, Pasadena, 1992—. Tech. expert for profl. engring. test Price & Assocs., Pomona, Calif., 1991. Candidate state sen. Libertarian Party, West L.A., 1985. Achievements include patent for storage ring fusion energy generator. Office: De La Guerra Power Inc PO Box 41955 Los Angeles CA 90041-0955

RUSSELL, JOSETTE RENEE, industrial engineer; b. Defiance, Ohio, June 14, 1964; d. Eugene Alvin and Carole Josette (Galusha) R. BS in Indsl. Engring., GMI Engring. and Mgmt. Inst., 1988. Electronics engr. aero. systems divsn. USAF, Wright Patterson AFB, Ohio, 1985-90; process engr. Masland Industries, Carlisle, Pa., 1990-91, prodn. supr., 1991-92, prodn. tech. dir., 1992-93; mgr. quality McCord Winn Textron, Cookeville, Tenn., Cookeville, 1993; tech. sales rep. Deezee Chem. Co., Camden, N.J., 1994; dyehouse tech. cons. Downs Carpet Co., Willow Grove, Pa., 1995; dir. power sports & comml. mkts. Holley Performance Products, Bowling Green, Ky., 1995—; in bus. devel. and mktg. Eaton Corp., Galesburg, Mich., 1999—. Appeared on cover of Woman Engr. Mag., 1988. Mem. Mensa. Republican. Avocation: reading. Home: 92 Garrison Ave Battle Creek MI 49017 Office: 13100 Michigan Ave Galesburg MI 49053

RUSSELL, JOYCE ANNE ROGERS, librarian; b. Chgo., Nov. 6, 1920; d. Truman Allen and Mary Louise (Hoelzle) Rogers; m. John VanCleve Russell, Dec. 24, 1942; children: Malcolm David, John VanCleve. Student, Adelphi Coll., 1937; BS in Chemistry, U. Ky., 1942; M.L.S., Rosary Coll., 1967; postgrad., Rutgers U., 1970-71. Research chemist Sherwin Williams Paint Co., Chgo., 1942-45; reference librarian Chicago Heights (Ill.) Pub. Library, 1959-61; librarian Victor Chem. Works, Chicago Heights, 1961-62; lit. chemist Velsicol Chem. Corp., Chgo., 1964-67; chemistry librarian U. Fla., Gainesville, 1967-69, interim assoc. prof., 1967-69; librarian Thiokol Chem. Corp., Trenton, N.J., 1969-73; supr. library operations E.R. Squibb Co., Princeton, 1973-80, sr. research info scientist, 1980-91. Mem. library adv. commn. Mercer Community Coll., 1979— ; adv. asso. Rutgers U. Grad. Sch. Library and Info. Scis., 1978— Editor: Bibliofile, 1967-69; contbr. articles to profl. jours. Mem. PTA, 1950-66; den mother Cub Scouts, 1952-59. Mem. Spl. Libraries Assn. (sec., dir., v.p., pres. Princeton-Trenton 1971, 75-80), Am. Chem. Soc. (bus. mgr., sec., dir. Trenton sect. 1969-78), AAUW, Mortar Board, Beta Phi Mu, Sigma Pi Sigma, Chi Delta Phi, Pi Sigma Alpha. Home: 1189 Parkside Ave Trenton NJ 08618-2625

RUSSELL, KENNETH CALVIN, metallurgical engineer, educator; b. Greeley, Colo., Feb. 4, 1936; s. Doyle James and Jennie Frances (Smith) R.; m. Charlotte Louise Wolf, Apr. 13, 1963 (div. 1978); children: David Allan, Doyle John, Mattias. Met.E., Colo. Sch. Mines, 1959; PhD, Carnegie Inst. Tec., 1963. Engr. Westinghouse Research and Devel. Center, 1959-61; NSF postdoctoral fellow Physics Inst., U. Oslo, 1963-64; asst. prof. metallurgy M.I.T., Cambridge, 1964-69, assoc. prof., 1969-78, prof. metallurgy, 1978—, prof. nuclear engring., 1979—. Contbr. articles to profl. publs. Served as 2d lt. U.S. Army, 1959-60. DuPont fellow, 1961-62; NSF grad. fellow, 1962-63 Mem.: Internat. Soc. Electrophys. Kinesiology, Internat. Soc. Biomechanics, Scandinavian Physiol. Soc. Office: MIT Rm 13-5050 Cambridge MA 02139

RUSSELL, KURT VON VOGEL, actor; b. Springfield, Mass., Mar. 17, 1951; s. Bing Oliver and Louise Julia (Crone) R.; m. Season Hubley, Mar. 17, 1979 (div.), 1 son, Boston; 1 son (with Goldie Hawn), Wyatt Russell. Student, pub. schs. Profl. baseball player, 1971-73. Actor in numerous films including The Absent Minded Professor, 1961, It Happened at the World's Fair, 1963, Follow Me Boys, 1966, The One and Only Genuine Original Family Band, 1968, The Horse in the Grey Flannel Suit, 1968, The Computer Wore Tennis Shoes, 1970, The Barefoot Executive, 1971, Fools' Parade, 1971, Now You See Him Now You Don't, 1972, Charley and the Angel, 1972, Superdad, 1974, The Strongest Man in the World, 1975, Used Cars, 1980, Escape from New York, 1981, The Thing, 1982, Silkwood, 1983, Swing Shift, 1984, The Mean Season, 1985, The Best of Times, 1986, Big Trouble in Little China, 1986, Overboard, 1987, The Winter People, 1988, Tequila Sunrise, 1988, Winter People, 1989, Tango and Cash, 1989, Backdraft, 1991, Unlawful Entry, 1992, Captain Ron, 1992, Tombstone, 1993, Stargate, 1994, Executive Decision, 1996, Escape from L.A., 1996 (also writer, producer) , Breakdown, 1997, Soldier, 1998, 3000 Miles To Graceland, 2001, Vanilla Sky, 2001, Dark Blue, 2002; TV series include Travels with Jamie McPheeters, 1963-64, The New Land, 1974, The Quest, 1976; TV movies include Search for the Gods, 1975, The Deadly Tower, The Quest (pilot), 1975, Christmas Miracle in Caulfield USA, 1977, Elvis, 1979, Amber Waves, 1988; TV guest appearences include The Fugitive, Daniel Boone, Gilligan's Island, Lost in Space, The FBI, Love American Style, Gunsmoke, Hawaii Five-O. Served with Calif. Air N.G. Recipient numerous auto racing trophies, 10 baseball awards, 5 acting awards, 1 golf championship. Mem. Profl. Baseball Players Assn., Stuntman's Assn. Achievements include being the World championship Class Modified Stock, 1959 Race of Champions, Las Vegas. Office: Creative Artists Agy 9830 Wilshire Blvd Beverly Hills CA 90212-1825*

RUSSELL, LIANE BRAUCH, geneticist; b. Vienna, Austria, Aug. 27, 1923; came to U.S., 1941; d. Arthur and Clara (Starer) Brauch; m. William Lawson Russell, Sept. 23, 1947; children: David Lawson, Evelyn Ruth. AB, Hunter Coll., 1945; PhD, U. Chgo., 1949; ScD (hon.), Hunter Coll., N.Y.C., 1999. Fellow U. Chgo., 1945-46, teaching asst., 1946-47; rsch. asst. Jackson Lab., Bar Harbor, Maine, 1945, 46; rsch. staff mem. Oak Ridge (Tenn.) Nat. Lab., 1947-75, sect. head., 1975-95, sr. rsch. fellow, 1988—2001. Sci. advisor U.S. Del. at 1st Atoms for Peace Conf., Geneva, Switzerland, 1955; mem. numerous sci. bds. including Nat. Research Council com. on energy and environment, 1975-77, com. on biol. effects of ionizing radiation, 1977-80, bd. on environ. studies and toxicology, 1981-90, Nat. Council on Radiation Protection and Measurement Task Group, Washington, 1975-77, Genetox Program EPA, Washington, 1979—, Internat. Com. for Protection Against Environ. Mutagens and Carcinogens, Lausanne, Switzerland, 1977-83, Internat. com. on standardized genetic nomenclature for mice, 1977-91, office of tech. assessment, scientific adv. panel, 1985-86; mem. task group Internat. Agy. for Research on Cancer, Hanover, Fed. Republic of Germany, 1979, EPA review panel on mutagenicity guidelines, 1985-86; adj. faculty U. Tenn., 1980-. Assoc. editor Mutation Rsch., 1976-96, Environ. Mutagenesis, 1980-83; editor TCWP Newsletter, 1966—; editor: (book) Genetic Mosaics and Chimeras, 1979; contbr. more than 165 articles to profl. jours. Founder Tenn. Citizens for Wilderness Planning, Oak Ridge, 1966, pres. 1967-70, 86-87; active numerous environ. groups. Corp. fellow Union Carbide, 1983; corp. fellow Martin Marietta, 1985, sr. corp. fellow, 1988; recipient Merit award Mademoiselle, 1955, Roentgen medal City of Remscheid-Lennep, 1973, Disting. Assoc. award U.S. Dept. Energy, 1987; named to Hall of Fame Hunter Coll., 1979, Sol Feinstone Environ. Achievement award SUNY, 1987, Tenn. Environ. Coun. Lifetime Achievement award, 1990, Oak Ridge Rotary Club Vocational Svc. award, 1992, Marjorie Stoneman Douglas award Nat. Parks & Conservation Assn., 1993, Enrico Fermi award U.S. Dept. Energy, 1993, Lifetime Environ. Conservation award Tenn. Dept. Environ. & Conservation, 2000. Fellow AAAS, Environ. Health Inst.; mem. Nat. Acad. Scis. (elected 1986), Environ. Mutagen Soc. (EMs award 1993, pres. 1984-85), Genetics Soc. Am. (presdl. nominee 1979), Tenn. Environ. Honor Soc. Avocation: environ. acitivism. Office: Oak Ridge Nat Lab Divsn Life Sci PO Box 2009 Oak Ridge TN 37831-8077

RUSSELL, LOUISE BENNETT, economist, educator; b. Exeter, N.H., May 12, 1942; d. Frederick Dewey and Esther (Smith) B.; m. Robert Hardy Cosgriff, May 3, 1987; 1 child, Benjamin Smith Cosgriff. BA, U. Mich., 1964; PhD, Harvard U., 1971. Economist Social Security Adminstrn., Washington, 1968-71, Nat. Commn. on State Workmen's Compensation Laws, Washington, 1971-72, Dept. Labor, Washington, 1972-73; sr. economist Nat. Planning Assn., 1973-75; sr. fellow Brookings Instn., 1975-87; rsch. prof. Inst. for Health, Health Care Policy and Aging Rsch. Rutgers U., New Brunswick, N.J., 1987—, prof. econs., 1987—. Chmn. health care policy divsn. Rutgers U., 1988—. Author: Technology in Hospitals, 1979, The Baby Boom Generation and the Economy, 1982, Is Prevention Better Than Cure, 1986, Evaluating Preventive Care: Report on a Workshop, 1987, Medicare's New Hospital Payment System: Is It Working, 1989, Educated Guesses: Making Policy About Medical Screening Tests, 1994, (with MR Gold, JE Siegel and MC Weinstein) Cost-Effectiveness in Health and Medicine, 1996; also numerous articles. Mem. U.S. Preventive Svcs. Task Force, 1984-88; co-chair Panel on Cost Effectiveness in Health and Medicine DHHS, USPHS, 1993-96; mem. tech. bd. Milbank Fund, 1993-95. Mem. Inst. Medicine of NAS (com. to study future pub. health 1986-87, bd. on health scis. policy 1989-91, com. on clin. practice guidelines 1990-91, com. on setting priorities for practice guidelines 1994, mem. nat. cancer policy bd. 2001-). Office: Rutgers U Inst for Health Care Policy 30 College Ave New Brunswick NJ 08901-1283

RUSSELL, MARGARET JONES (PEG RUSSELL), secondary school educator, retired writer; b. Durham, N.C., Apr. 25, 1938; d. Roderic O. and Margaret (Moore) Jones; m. Michael Morgan Russell; children: Lauren Skinner, Carol Martin, Seth Russell, Jay Russell. BA, Muskingum Coll., 1961. Ordained deacon Presbyn. Ch., 1970. Tchr. Sarasota (Fla.) County Sch. Bd., 1962-97, Sarasota H.S., 1982-96, ret., 1997. Sponsor literary mag. Quest, 1988—. Editor: (newsletter) The Mainsail, 1992-95; contbr. poems to profl. pubs. ARC vol. Sarasota Meml. Hosp., 1966-83, aux. vol., 1994—; reader Fla. Studio Theatre, Sarasota, 1980—. Sarasota Herald Tribune scholar, 1993; Fla. Writing Project fellow, 1990. Mem. Nat. Coun. Tchrs. English, Fla. Coun. Tchrs. English, Light Verse Workshop (co-chair 1995, chair 1998—), Sarasota Fiction Writers, Selby Poets, Sarasota Genealogical Soc., Alpha Gamma Delta. Republican. Presbyterian. Home: 1150 Willis Ave Sarasota FL 34232-2148

RUSSELL, MARJORIE ROSE, manufacturing company executive; b. Welcome, Minn., Sept. 3, 1925; d. Emil Frederick and Ella Magdalene (Sothman) Wohlenhaus; m. Kenneth Kollmann Russell, Sept. 15, 1947 (div. May 1973); children: Jennie Rose, Richard Lowell, Laura Eloise, James Wesley. Student, Northwestern Sch., Mpls., 1944-45, St. Paul Bible Inst., 1946-47. Cook U. Minn., Mpls., 1943-45; maintenance person U. Farm Campus/N.W. Schs., St. Paul, 1945-46; clk. Kresge Corp., Mpls., 1945; cook, waitress, mgr. Union City Mission Bible Camp, 1944-47; caterer for v.p. Gt. No. R.R., St. Paul, 1947; custodian Old Soldiers Home, 1946; nurse Sister Elizabeth Kenney Polio Hosp., 1946; seamstress Hirsch, Weis, White Stag, Pendleton, Mayfair, Portland, Oreg., 1960-72; owner, operator, contract mgr., creative designer The Brass Needle, 1972—. Contractor Forrester's Sanderson Safety, Scotsco, Nero & Assocs., Gara Gear, Portland, 1972—, Columbia Sportswear; tchr. Indo Chinese Cultural Ctr., Portland, 1982; mfr. of protective chaps and vests for the Pacific Northwest hogging industry. Designer, producer Kisn Bridal Fair, 1969; composer: He Liveth in Me, 1968; prodr. Safety Chaps for Loggers. Sec. Model Cities Com., Portland, 1969; com. mem. Neighborhood Black Christmas Parade, Portland, 1970; custume designer Local Miss Jr. Black Beauty Contest, Portland, 1973; nominating com. Nat. Contract Mgmt. Assn., Portland, 1978; mem. nominating com. Multi-Cultural Sr. Adv. Com., 1988-91. Mem. NAFE, Urban League, Urban League Guild (historian 1991-92), Am. Assn. Ret. Persons, Nat. Contract Mgmt. Assn. Democrat. Mem. United Ch. of Christ. Avocations: music, swimming, painting, gardening, arts. Home and Office: The Brass Needle 2809 NE 12th Ave Portland OR 97212-3219

RUSSELL, MARK, comedian; b. Buffalo, Aug. 23, 1932; s. Marcus Joseph and Marie Elizabeth (Perry) Ruslander; m. Alison Kaplan, Dec. 17, 1978; children: Monica, John, Matthew. Student, George Washington U., 1952; LittD, Union Coll., 1987; LHD, Canisius Coll., 1988; LHD (hon.), Goucher Coll., 1990. Lectr., public speaker. Polit. comedian, featured performer Shoreham Hotel, Washington, 1961-81; prin. Mark Russell Comedy Spls., Pub. Broadcasting Svc., 1975—. Mark Russell's 25th Anniversary Special, 2000 (Silver Telly award 2000); host Mark Russell's England, PBS-TV, 1988, Mark Russell's Irish Fling, 1993, Mark Russell's Great Ala. Trek, 1994, Mark Russell's Tour de France, 1995, Mark Russell's Viva Italia, 1996; co-host NBC's Real People, 1979-84; regular contbr. Good Morning Am., ABC-TV, Inside Politics Weekend, CNN; author: Presenting Mark Russell, 1980; syndicated columnist via L.A. Times Syndicate, 1975. Served with USMC, 1953-56. Recipient Mark Twain award Internat. Platform Assn., 1980, 86, 4th Ann. Lucy award Shea's Buffalo, 1992, Nat. Humor Treasure award Nat. Humor Conf., 1995, SOAR St. Elizabeth Ann Seton award Washington, 1995, Washingtonian of the Yr. Washingtonian Mag., 1996, Disting. Washingtonian award Univ. Club, 2001. Mem. AFTRA, Am. Fedn. Musicians. Office: PO Box 9904 Washington DC 20016-8904 E-mail: mail@markrussell.net.

RUSSELL, MARLOU, psychologist; b. June 2, 1956; d. William Herman and Carole Eleanor (Musgrove) McBratney; m. Jan Christopher Russell, Sept. 9, 1989. BA, U. Ariz., 1981; MA, Calif. Grad. Inst., 1983, PhD, 1987. Lic. psychologist, marriage, family and child counselor. Asst. to pres. Western Psychol. Svcs., L.A., 1978-81; crisis counselor Cedars-Sinai Med. Ctr., 1980-84; psychotherapist PMC Treatment Sys., 1984-85, Beverly Hills Counseling Ctr., 1984-85, Comprehensive Care Corp., L.A., 1985-86; pvt. practice, 1986—. Counselor Brotman Med. Ctr., L.A., 1982-83, Julia Ann Singer Ctr., L.A., 1984; bd. dirs. Los Angeles Commn. Assaults Against Women, 1987-89. Author: Adoption Wisdom: A Guide to the Issues and Feelings of Adoption, 1996; adoptee, reunion expert www.adopting.org, 1999—. Mem. Internat. Assn. Eating Disorders Profls., Women in Health (bd. dirs. 1993-94), Women's Referral Svc., Calif. State Psychol. Assn., Calif. Assn. Marriage & Family Therapists (bd. dirs. 1993-94), Am. Adoption Congress, Westside Bus. Womens Assn. (bd. dirs. 1993-94). Democrat. Office: 1452 26th St Ste 103 Santa Monica CA 90404-3042 E-mail: marlourussell@hotmail.com.

RUSSELL, MARTIN JOHN, minister; b. San Jose, Calif., Dec. 12, 1963; s. John Douglas and Colleen Bonderson Russell. BA in Bus. Adminstrn., Midland Luth. Coll., 1986; MDiv, Luth. Theol. Sem., Gettysburg, Pa., 1990. Ordained pastor Evang. Luth. Ch. Am. Pastor Eben-Ezer Luth. Ch., Brenham, Tex., 1990-93; pastor, redeveloper Faith Luth. Ch., Phila., 1993-96; sr. pastor Our Savior Luth. Ch., Wayne, Nebr., 1996-2000; asst. to Bishop of Nebr. Synod (ELCA), 2000—. Trustee Midland Luth. Coll., Wayne, 1998—; pastoral exch. program participant Evang. Luth. Ch. Tanzania, Maragu, 1999. Bd. mem. Luth. Campus Ministry Bd., Wayne State Coll., 1996—, Providence Med. Ctr. Found. Bd., Wayne, 1998—. Recipient Outstanding Young Alumni award Midland Luth. Coll., Fremont, Nebr., 1995. Mem. Wayne Ministerial Assn. Avocations: swimming, reading, traveling. Home: 7129 S 176th Ave Omaha NE 68136-2036 Office: Nebr Synod ELCA Ste D 4980 S 118th St Omaha NE 68137-2220

RUSSELL, MARY WENDELL VANDER POEL, non-profit organization executive, interior; b. N.Y.C., Feb. 6, 1919; d. William Halsted and Blanche Pauline (Billings) Vander Poel; m. George Montagu Miller, Apr. 5, 1940 (div. 1974); children: Wendell Miller Steavenson, Gretchen Miller Elkus; m. Sinclair Hatch, May 14, 1977 (dec. July 1989); m. William F. Russell, June 24, 1995 (dec. Apr. 1996). Pres. Miller Richard, Inc., Interior Decorators, Oyster Bay, N.Y., 1972—; bd. dirs. Eye Bank Sight Restoration, N.Y.C., pres., 1980-88, hon. chair, 1988—; v.p. Manhattan Eye Ear and Throat Hosp., 1978-90; sec. Cold Spring Harbor Lab., N.Y., 1985-89, 92-97; mem. DNA Learning Ctr. Bd., 1991-97; bd. dirs. DNA Learning Ctr., 1997-2000; sec. Cold Spring Harbor Lab, 1992-97, hon. trustee, 1998—. V.p. North Country Garden Club, Nassau County, N.Y., 1979-81, 1983-85; dir. Planned Parenthood Nassau County, Mineola, N.Y., 1982-84, Hutton House C.W.Post Coll.,Greenvale, N.Y., 1982—; chair Hutton House, 1992-94. Recipient Disting. Trustee award United Hosp. Fund, 1992. Mem. Colony Club (N.Y.C.), Church Club (N.Y.C.), Piping Rock Club (Long Island), Order St. John Jerusalem (N.Y.C.). Republican. Episcopalian. Home: Mill River Rd # 330 Oyster Bay NY 11771-2733 E-mail: ydnewr@aol.com.

RUSSELL, MASON WEBSTER, healthcare economist, educator; b. Beverly, Mass., July 28, 1956; s. Gordon Arthur and Elizabeth Mason (Webster) R.; m. Susanne Rachel Nadeau, Oct. 22, 1982. BA in Econs., Salem State Coll., 1978; MA in Polit. Economy, Boston U., 1981, postgrad., 1981-87. Lectr. econs. Boston U., 1979-82; asst. prof. econs. Bentley Coll., Waltham, Mass., 1982-85; sr. economist Policy Analysis Inc., Brookline, 1985-88, 94; exec. dir. White Mountain Health Svcs., Gorham, N.H., 1988-91; dir. corp. devel. North Care Corp., Berlin, 1991-92; dir., COO Mountain Health Svcs., 1991-92; sr. economist Piedmont Group, Richmond, Va., 1992-94; sr. health economist Med. Rsch. Internat., Burlington, Mass., also London, 1994-98; dir. health econs. ICSL Healthcare Rsch., also London, 1998-2000, v.p. outcomes rsch. Waltham, 2000—02; dir. global health econ. Biogen, Inc., Cambridge, 2002—. Faculty assoc. Sch. for Lifelong Learning, Univ. System N.H., Berlin, 1990-92; sec., dir. Gorham Devel. Corp., 1990-92; adj. instr. Salem (Mass.) State Coll., 1995—. Contbr. articles to profl. jours. Pres., dir. United Way No. N.H., Berlin, 1990-92; vice chmn. gt. no. dist. Daniel Webster coun. Boy Scouts Am., 1990-92. Mem. Am. Coll. Healthcare Execs., Internat. Soc. Pharmacoecons. and Outcomes Rsch., Am. Coll. Clin. Pharmacy, Masons, Phi Kappa Phi. Democrat. Roman Catholic. Office: Biogen Inc 10 Cambridge Ctr Cambridge MA 02138 E-mail: mason_russell@biogen.com., masonwr@aol.com.

RUSSELL, MAURICE LLOYD, judge; b. Caldwell, Idaho, Aug. 6, 1950; s. Maurice Lloyd and Betty M. (Pledger) R.; m. Hilary Higginson, May 19, 1984. BA, U. Calif., Santa Cruz, 1972; MA, U. Calif., Santa Barbara, 1975; JD, UCLA, 1978. Bar: Oreg. 1978, U.S. Dist. Ct. Oreg. 1980. Gen. counsel Mid-Columbia Cmty. Action Coun., The Dalles, Oreg., 1978-79; assoc. Stephen H. Miller, Atty., Reedsport, 1979-80; city atty., planner, asst. city m gr. City of Independence, 1980-82; assoc. Chester Scott, P.C., Independence, 1982-83; pres. M.L. Russell, P.C., 1983-85; v.p., gen. counsel Citizens Savings & Loan Assn., Salem, 1985-88; assoc. Churchill, Leonard et al, 1988-93, Tarlow, Jordan & Schrader, Beaverton, 1993-94; adminstrv. law judge State of Oreg. Dept. Transp., Salem, 1995—. Screenwriter, dir. (continuing legal edn. videotapes) Limits of Zealous Representation, 1995 (Inns of Ct. award 1995), Oregon Jury System, 1996, DUI—Recent Cases, 1996. Chair budget com. Chemekata Cmty. Coll., Salem, 1996-97; pres., bd. dirs. Mid-Vlley Arts Coun., Salem, 1991-93, chmn. bd. dirs. Salem Pastoral Counselling Ctr., 1993-95. Mem. Oreg. State Bar Assn. (bd. mem. debtor-creditor sect. 1992-93, legis. subcom. 1990-92, 93-96), Masons (Master), Willamette Valley Am. Inns of Ct. Democrat. Episcopalian. Avocations: writing, flytying, fishing, blacksmithing, music. Office: Oregon Dept Transportation DMV 1905 Lana Ave NE Salem OR 97314-5000

RUSSELL, MICHAEL JAMES, lawyer; b. Northampton, Mass., May 19, 1958; Cert. in German, U. Vienna, 1979; BA summa cum laude, Gettysburg Coll., 1980; MA, JD, Vanderbilt U., 1984. Bar: Pa. 1984, D.C. 1985, U.S. Supreme Ct. 1995. Rsch. asst. Vanderbilt U., Nashville, 1982-84; legal intern U.S. State Dept., Washington, 1982; law clk. Stewart, Estes & Donnell, Nashville, 1983; atty. U.S. Dept. Agr., Washington, 1984-85; majority counsel subcom. on juvenile justice senate judiciary com. U.S. Senate, 1985-86, minority gen. counsel subcom. on constn., 1987, legis. dir. to Senator Arlen Specter, 1987-90; senate staff mem. Congrl. Crime Caucus, 1987-90; dep. dir. Nat. Inst. Justice U.S. Dept. Justice, Washington, 1990-93, acting dir., 1993-94; pres. Russell & Assocs., 1994-96; sr. pub. safety advisor Corp. Nat. Svc., 1994-96; dep. chief of staff to Senator Ben Nighthorse Campbell, 1996—2001; dep. asst. sec. for policy and budget (enforcement) U.S. Dept. Treasury, 2001—. Editorial staff Vanderbilt Jour. Transnat. Law, Nashville, 1982-83, contbr., 1983, rsch. editor, 1983-84 (editor award 1984). Mem. senate staff club, 1985-90, Bush/Quayle Campaign's Crime Adv. Com., 1988, Friends of the Nat. Parks at Gettysburg, Pa., 1989-98; bd. fellows Gettysburg Coll., 1990—; vol. Nat. Constrn. Ctr., Phila., 1990; mem. Bush/Quayle Adminstrn. S.E.S. Assn., 1990-92; Eisenhower Leadership Prize Dinner Com., Eisenhower World Affairs Inst., 1992, 93, mem. com. to celebrate bicentennial of constn., Northampton, Mass., 1987; mem. Bush/Quayle Alumni Assn., 1993—. Recipient Voluntary Svc. award VA, Northampton, 1978, Trustees award Forbes Libr., Northampton, 1989, cert. of appreciation Correctional Edn. Assn., 1991, Phi Alpha Delta, 1989, Fed. Bur. Alcohol, Tobacco and Firearms, 1989, Gettysburg Coll. Career Svcs. Office, 1992, Young Alumni Achievement award Gettysburg Coll., 1992, Wasserstein Fellowship Harvard Law Sch. Office of Pub. Interest Adv., 1995-96. Mem. Am. Soc. Internat. Law, Pa. Soc. of Washington, Phi Beta Kappa, Psi Chi (jr. award 1979). Avocations: racquetball, politics, volunteer svc. Office: Treasury Dept Rm 4308 1500 Pennsylvania Ave NW Washington DC 20220

RUSSELL, NAS'NAGA ROGER, illustrator; b. Dayton, Ohio, Apr. 13, 1941; s. Willard Dudly and Kathryn Louise (Pangborn) R.; m. Harriet Ann Russell, June 1967 (div. 1973); 1 child, Jamie Noelle; m. Barbara Jane Mullins, Sept. 14, 1983. Grad. h.s. Mgr. AAAirlines, Ft. Worth, 1970-74; writer Harper & Rowe, N.Y.C., 1974-75; owner, dir. Art Gallery, Kettering, Ohio, 1979-83. Dir., owner Nas'Naga Enterprises, Inc. Pro., Centerville, Ohio, 1980-83; lectr., spkr. in field. Author, illustrator: Indians' Summer, 1975, Faces Beneith The Grass, 1979, Darker Side of Glory, 2000; columnist Nishnabe Mag., Oslo, Norway, 1976-79. Airlines rep. Okla. for Indian Opportunity, Tex., 1970—74; steering com. Newark state mound project Ohio Hist. Soc., 2000. Recipient Humanitarian Svc. award Oklahomians for Indian Opportunity, Norman, Okla., 1973, United Cerebeal Palsy, Dayton, 1984, Outstanding Artistic Achievement award Green County Ohio, Xenia, 1975. Avocations: archery, painting, research. Home: 3000 B E Main St #359 Columbus OH 43209

RUSSELL, NEWTON REQUA, retired state legislator; b. L.A., June 25, 1927; s. John Henry and Amy (Requa) R.; m. Diane Henderson, Feb. 12, 1953; children: Stephen, Sharon, Julia. BS, U. So. Calif., 1951; postgrad., UCLA, Georgetown U. Spl. agt. Northwestern Mut. Life Ins. Co., Calif., 1954-64; mem. Calif. State Assembly, 1964-74, Calif. Senate, 1974-96, ret., 1996. Vice-chmn. com. on energy, utilities and comm., mem. com. on local govt., mem. com. on fin. and investment, internat. trade, mem. com. on transp., com. ins., joint com. on rules, select com. on Calif.'s wine industry, mem. Com. on Legis. Ethics, Joint Oversight Com. on Lowering the Cost of Electric Svcs, chmn. senate select com. mediation. Mem. Rep. State Ctrl. Com. Served with USN, 1945-46. Recipient Outstanding Legislator award Calif. Rep. Assembly, 1968, 76, 81, Mayor's commendation City of Burbank, 1978, Disting. Svc. awrad County Suprs. Assn. Calif., 1980, Nat. Rep. Legislator of Yr., 1981, Legislator of Yr. award Los Angeles County Fedn. Rep. Women, 1982, Legislator of Yr. award Calif. Credit Union League, 1983, Paul Harris Fellow award Rotary Found. Rotary Internat., numerous honors from cmty. orgns. and instns. Mem. Rotary Internat., Am. Legion, Delta Tau Delta, Alpha Kappa Phi. Mem. Church on the Way.

RUSSELL, PAMELA REDFORD, writer, film documentarian; b. Long Beach, Calif., June 11, 1950; d. George Martin and Helen Glyn (Brewen) R.; children: Caitlin, Maggie, Tess. Student, UCLA, 1970-74. Field prodr. Santa Fe Comm., L.A., 1983-84; exec. prodr. Guiding Star Prodns., 1994-96. Author: The Woman Who Loved John Wilkes Booth, 1978, Wild Flowers, 1982, (screenplay) Am American Woman, 1993; writer for Mary Tyler Moore Show, 1974, Touched By An Angel, 1997, also 14 scripts for Sears and Mut. Radio Theater, 1980-81, (TV show) Touched by An Angel, 1997, (teleplay) Have You Seen Me, 1998. Mem. Nat. Trust for Hist. Preservation, Civil War Trust., Pacific Grove Heritage Soc. Mem. PEN, Authors Guild, Writers Guild Am. West, PEN Ctr. USA West. Avocation: historic preservation.

RUSSELL, PATRICK JAMES, priest; b. Boise, Idaho, May 10, 1959; s. Glenn Edward and Doralea (Trumble) R. BA, Boise U., 1982; MDiv, St. Patrick's Sem., 1986. Ordained priest Roman Catholic Ch., 1986. Assoc. pastor St. Marks Cath. Ch., Boise, 1986-91; chaplain Chateau de Boise, 1991—, Bishop Kelly H.S., 1993—. Active Nat. Cath. Office for Persons With Disabilities, 1991—, Idaho Vocations Bd., 1992-95; founder, dir. Father Russell Charity Golf Scramble for Persons with Chronic Illnesses, 1986—; apptd. tribunal advocate Office of Canonical Affairs, Idaho, 1996—; apptd. priest mem. bioethics com. St. Alphonsus Regional Med. Ctr., 1999. Named Idaho Handicapped Student of Yr., 1974, Best Actor, Boise Little Theatre, 1979-80, Outstanding Young Man of Am., 1983, 84, 86, 87, Outstanding Youth in Achievement, Cambridge, U.K., Internat. Man of Yr., Cambridge, 1995. Mem. Osteogenesis Imperfecta Fdn., Am. Film Inst., Amnesty Internat., Nat. Theatre Comm. Group (charter), Internat. Soc. Poets (life, award), Right to Life/Spl. Olympics, Sigma Phi Epsilon. Democrat. Avocations: writing, painting, music, public speaking, acting. E-mail: patrick7e@mindspring.com.

RUSSELL, PAUL EDGAR, electrical engineering educator; b. Roswell, N.Mex., Oct. 10, 1924; s. Rueben Matthias and Mary (Parsons) R.; m. Lorna Margaret Clayshulte, Aug. 29, 1943; children: Carol Potter, Janice Russell Cook, Gregory. BSEE, N.Mex. State U., 1946, BSME, 1947; MSEE, U. Wis., 1950, PhDEE, 1951. Registered elec. engr., Ariz. From instr. to asst. prof. elec. engring. U. Wis., Madison, 1947-52; sr. engr., design specialist Gen. Dynamics Corp., San Diego, 1952-54; from prof. to chmn. elec. engring. dept. U. Ariz., Tucson, 1954-63; dean engring. Kans. State U., Manhattan, 1963-67; prof. Ariz. State U., Tempe, 1967-90; dir. engring. Ariz. State U. West, Phoenix, 1985-88; dir. Sch. Constrn. and Tech. Ariz. State U., Tempe, 1988-90. Cons. in field, 1954—; programs evaluator, mem. engring. commn. Accreditation Bd. for Engring. and Tech., N.Y.C., 1968-81. Contbr. articles to jours. and chpts. to books. Served as sgt. U.S. Army, 1944-46. Recipient Disting. Service award N.Mex. State U., 1965. Fellow IEEE (life, chmn. Ariz. sect. 1960), Accreditation Bd. Engring. and Tech.; mem. Am. Soc. Engring. Educators. Home: 5902 E Caballo Ln Paradise Valley AZ 85253

RUSSELL, PAUL FREDERICK, lawyer; b. Kansas City, Mo., Feb. 3, 1948; s. Walter Edward and Dorothy Marie (Sickels) R.; m. Kerry Diann Anderson, June 2, 1973; children: Philip, Erin, Shannon, Kelsey, Scott. BA, Northwestern, 1970; JD, U. Mich., 1973. Bar: Ill. 1973, U.S. Dist. Ct. (no. dist.) Ill. 1973. Assoc. Vedder, Price, Kaufman & Kammholz, Chgo., 1973-79, ptnr., 1980—. Mem. ABA, Chgo. Bar Assn., Ill. State Bar Assn., Univ. Club (Chgo.), Mich. Shores Club. Office: Vedder Price 222 N La Salle St Chicago IL 60601-1003 E-mail: prussell@vedderprice.com.

RUSSELL, PAUL SNOWDEN, surgeon, educator; b. Chgo., Jan. 22, 1925; s. Paul Snowden and Carroll (Mason) R.; m. Allene Lummis, Sept. 24, 1952; children— Katherine Swift, Paul Snowden, Allene, Laura Rice. Student, Groton (Mass.) Sch., 1939-41; PhB, U. Chgo., 1944, BS, 1945, MD, 1947; MA (hon.), Harvard U., 1962. Diplomate Am. Bd. Surgery, Am. Bd. Thoracic Surgery. From surg. intern, to resident Mass. Gen. Hosp., 1948-56, asst. surgery, 1957-60, chief gen. surg. svcs., 1962-69, chmn. com. on rsch., 1973-76; postdoctoral fellow USPHS, 1954-55; from tchg. fellow to clin. assoc. surgery Harvard Med. Sch., 1956-60, John Homans prof. surgery, 1962-98, John Homans Disting. prof. surgery, 1998—; assoc. prof. surgery Columbia Coll. Phys. and Surg., 1960-62; assoc. attending surgeon Presbyn. Hosp., N.Y.C., 1960-62; assoc. vis. surgeon Francis Delafield Hosp., 1960-62, 74-94. Mem. com. tissue transplantation NRC-Nat. Acad. Scis., 1963-71, com. trauma, 1963-68; ad hoc com. to study clin. investigation and edn. in USN, 1971-73; allergy and immunology study sect. USPHS, 1963-65, chmn. allergy and immunology study sect. B, 1965-67; mem. transplantation and immunology com. Nat. Inst. Allergy and Infectious Diseases, 1967-69, chmn., 1970; mem. com. on cancer immunotherapy Nat. Cancer Inst., 1974-79. Contbr. papers in field.; Editorial bd.: Archives Surgery, 1963-72, Surgery, 1963-71, Transplantation, 1965-79, Annals of Surgery, 1966— , Transplantation Procs, 1966— , Jour. Immunology, 1977-80. Trustee Pine Manor Coll., Chestnut Hill, Mass., 1963-76, Groton Sch., 1964-79, The Conservation Law Found., 1997—; bd. dirs. Boston Fulbright Com., 1968, pres., 1980—; bd. governing trustees Jackson Lab., vice chmn., 2000; bd. trustees Worcester Found. for Biomed. Rsch. With USAF, 1951-53. Fellow ACS, Royal Soc. Medicine; mem. AAAS, Am. Acad. Arts and Scis., Assn. Immunologists, N.Y. Acad. Scis., Mass. Med. Soc., New Eng. Surg. Soc., Boston Surg. Soc. (pres. 1994), Soc. Univ. Surgeons, Soc. Exptl. Biology and Medicine, Halsted Soc., Whipple Soc., Internat. Soc. Surgery, Am. Surg. Assn., Transplantation Soc. (pres. 1970), Polish Acad. Sci. (fgn.), Sigma Xi. Home: 32 Lawrence Rd Chestnut Hill MA 02467-1230 Office: Dept Surgery Mass Gen Hosp Boston MA 02114

RUSSELL, RALPH TIMOTHY, insurance company executive, mayor; b. Foley, Ala., May 26, 1948; s. Ralph Joseph and Dorothy Eleanor (Peterson) R.; m. Sandra Earle Schultz, May 30, 1970; children: Karen, Kevin, Kenton. BS in Acctg., U. Ala., 1970; MBA, U. South Ala., 1975. Chartered property casualty underwriter. Pres. Baldwin Mutual Ins. Co., Foley, Ala., 1972—; mayor City of Foley, 1996—. Bd. dirs. Baldwin Mutual Ins. Co., 1976—, Riviera Utilities, Foley, 1976—, Gulf Coast Title Ins. Co., Foley, 1978—, Colonial Bank, Foley, 1991—. Pres. South Baldwin United Way, 1981-82; nat. v.p. U. Ala. Alumni Assn., Tuscaloosa, 1978-79; chmn. Foley Pub. Libr., 1975-84, St. Margaret's Ch. Bd., Foley, 1989-90, Baldwin County Econ. Devel. Alliance, South Ala. Regional Planning Commn.; treas. South Baldwin Hosp.; mayor City of Foley, 1996—; bd. dirs. Bus. Coun. Ala. Paul Harris fellow, 1986. Mem. Nat. Assn. Mut. Ins. Cos. (chmn. bd. dirs. 1986-94), Ala. Ins. Planning Com. (bd. dirs.), Ins. Edn. Found. (bd. dirs. 1991-94), Soc. CPCU (pres. 1982), South Baldwin C. of C. (past pres.), Ala. League Municipalities (ecec. com.). Roman Catholic. Home: 117 W Rosetta Ave Foley AL 36535-2223 Office: Baldwin Mutual Ins Co 315 E Laurel Ave Foley AL 36535-2617

RUSSELL, RHONDA CHERYL, piano educator, musician; b. Ada, Okla., May 19, 1947; d. Joe Roy and Vina Olive (McEntire) Sammons; m. James Michael Davis, June 1, 1973 (div. Mar. 1986); m. Joel Reed Russell, Apr. 2, 1989; 1 child, Christopher Nathaniel. BFA in Music, U. Okla., 1969, postgrad., 1970-71; M of Ch. Music, Performance, Golden Gate Bapt. Theol. Sem., 1984; postgrad., U. Ariz., 1986. Piano tchr., various states, 1969—; music evangelist So. Bapt. Conv., nationwide, 1969—; asst. choral dept. Elk City (Okla.) H.S. Elk City Pub. Schs., 1975-78; supr. banking ops. Alaska Statebank, Anchorage, 1978-82; tchg. asst. to piano prof. Golden Gate Bapt. Theol. Sem., Mill Valley, Calif., 1982-83, mem. adj. faculty, 1984-85, mem. music adv. coun., 1998-01; touring accompanist, ednl. tutor Tucson Ariz. Boys Chorus, 1985; choral dir., program founder fine arts dept. Buckingham Charter Sch., Vacaville, Calif., 1994-2001. State music cons. Calif. Bapt. Conv., Fresno, 1984-01; music dir., artistic dir. Solano Childrens Chorus, Fairfield, Calif., 1993-94; music dir. Playground Prodns. Theatre, Vacaville, 1994-96; music conf. clinician Nev. Bapt. Conv., Reno and Las Vegas, 1995, 96; con. pianist N.Am. Mission Bd., So. Bapt. Conv., Santa Clara, Calif., 1995; accompanist Anchorage Civic Opera, 1979-81, So. Ariz. Light Opera Co., 1985; minister of music Internat. Bapt. Ch., 1999-2000, Garland Rd. Bapt. Ch., Enid, Okla., 2001-. Contbr. poetry to anthologies. Pres. Decent Lit. Coun., Ponca City, Okla., 1977-78; campaign office helper Dem. Party of Okla., Oklahoma City, 1968; music dir. nursing home; beauty pageant coach, cons. Miss Am. Pageant Scholarships, Okla. and Calif., 1969—. Scholar Calif. Singing Churchwomen and Calif. Bapt. Conv., 1983. Mem. Nat. Guild Piano Tchrs., Music Ednl. Nat. Conf., Music Tchr. Assn. of Calif. (past treas. 1987-89), Calif. Profl. Music Tchrs. Assn. (program chair 1996), Tau Beta Sigma (life mem., treas., v.p., pres. 1965-69, Outstanding Mem. 1965). Democrat. Southern Baptist. Avocations: writing, composing, traveling, reading. Home and Office: 3012 Bluebird Ln Enid OK 73703-1555

RUSSELL, RICHARD DONCASTER, geophysicist, educator, geoscientist; b. Toronto, Ont., Can., Feb. 27, 1929; s. Richard Douglas and Ada Gwennola (Doncaster) R.; m. Virginia Ann Reid Clippingdale, Aug. 11, 1951; children: Linda Jean, Morna Ann, Mary Joyce. BA, U. Toronto, 1951, MA, 1952, PhD, 1954. Asst. prof. physics U. Toronto, 1956-58, prof., 1962-63; asso. prof. physics U. B.C., Vancouver, 1958-62, profl. geophysics, 1963-91, prof. emeritus, 1991—, head dept. geophysics, 1968-72, head dept. geophysics and astronomy, 1972-79, bd. govs., 1978-81, assoc. dean sci., 1980-83, assoc. v.p. acad., 1983-86. Sec.-gen. Inter-Union Commn. on Geodynamics, 1976-80; profl. geoscientist. Author textbooks.; Contbr. articles to profl. jours. Fellow Royal Soc. Can.; mem. Am. Geophys. Union, Can. Geophys. Union (J. Tuzo Wilson medal 1992). Home: 226-4955 River Rd Delta BC Canada V4K 4V9 Office: U BC Dept Earth & Ocean Scis Vancouver BC Canada V6T 1Z4 E-mail: russell@geop.ubc.ca.

RUSSELL, RICHARD M. federal agency administrator; Grad., Yale U. Staff mem. subcom. on oceanography, Gulf of Mexico and Outer Continental Shelf U.S. Ho. of Reps. Com. on Merchant Marine and Fisheres, 1993—94; from profl. staff for the subcom. on energy and environment, staff dir. for subcom. on tech. to dep. chief of staff for sci. com. U.S. Ho. Reps. Com. on Sci., 1995—2001; chief of staff Office Sci. and tech. Policy Exec. Office of the Pres., Washington, assoc. dir. Office Sci. and Tech. Policy, 2001—. Office: Exec Office of the Pres Sci and Tech Policy EEOB 17th & Pennsylvania Ave NW Washington DC 20502*

RUSSELL, RICHARD OLNEY, JR. cardiologist, educator; b. Birmingham, Ala., July 9, 1932; s. Richard Olney and Louise (Taylor) R.; m. Phyllis Hutchinson, June 15, 1963; children: Scott Richard, Katherine Hutchinson, Meredith Cooper, Stephen Wilbon. AB cum laude, Vanderbilt U., 1953, MD, 1956. Diplomate Am. Bd. Internal Medicine, Am. Bd. Cardiovascular Disease. Intern Peter Bent Brigham Hosp., Boston, 1956-57, resident, 1959-60, 63-64; fellow in cardiology Med. Coll. Ala., Birmingham, 1960-62, instr., 1962-63; instr. medicine U. Ala., Birmingham, 1964-65, asst. prof., 1965-70, assoc. prof., 1970-73, prof., 1973-81, clin. prof., 1981—; pvt. practice medicine specializing in cardiology Birmingham, 1981—. Mem. Jefferson County Bd. Health, 1977-81, chmn., 1979 Author: (with Charles Edward Rackley) Hemodynamic Monitoring in a Coronary Intensive Care Unit, 1974, 2d rev. and enlarged edit., 1981, Coronary Artery Disease: Recognition and Management, 1979, (with others) Radiographic Anatomy of the Coronary Arteries: An Atlas, 1976, Acute Ischemic Syndromes in American College of Cardiology Self Assessment Program, 1993; mem. editorial bd. Circulation, 1976-80, Am. Jour. Cardiology, 1977-82, Heart and Lung, 1978-83, Chest, 1978-83, Ala. Jour. Med. Scis, 1977-80, Jour. Am. Coll. Cardiology, 1987-90; contbr. articles to profl. jours. Distbn. com. Greater Birmingham Found., 1984-90; exec. bd. Birmingham area coun. Boy Scouts Am., 1987—, v.p., 1990-96, coun. commr., 1996-98; vice chmn. Vulcan dist., 1988-89, chmn., 1989-91, bd. dirs. S.E. region, 1990-92, bd. dirs. southern region, 1992—; bd. dirs. Ctrl. Ala. United Way, 1988-92; mem. Newcomen Soc., 1988—; chmn. exec. com. Birmingham Bapt. Med. Ctr., Montclair, 1995, pres.-elect med. staff, 1998-99, pres. 1999-00, Nat. Eagle Scout Assn. Scholarship Com. So. Region, 2001-; asst. coun. cmmr. Greater Ala. Coun., 1998-2000, coun. commr., 2001—. Capt. U.S. Army. Decorated Commendation medal; recipient Dist. Award of Merit, Boy Scouts Am., 1991, Silver Beaver award, 1990, Disting. Eagle Scout, 1999, Silver Antelope award 2001; NIH rsch. fellow, 1966-67. Fellow: ACP, Am. Coll. Cardiology (bd. govs. 1979—81, trustee 1984—85, 1989—94, ann. sci. session program chmn. 1994, disting. fellowship 2001); mem.: Med. Assn. State Ala. (spkr. house counselors dels. 1989—94, Laureate award 1999), Birmingham Soc. Internists (pres. 2001—03), Birmingham Cardiovascular Soc. (pres. 1981), Jefferson County Med. Soc. (v.p. 1982, pres. 1984), So. Soc. Clin. Investigation, Am. Fedn. Clin. Rsch., Am. Coll. Chest Physicians (bd. regents 1985—91), Am. Heart Assn. (pres. Ala. affiliate 1975—76, v.p. so. region 1986—87, task force on practice guidelines 1998—2000), Royal Soc. Medicine, NY Acad. Scis., Kiwanis (Brimingham sec. 1984—85, pres. 1994—95), Leadership Birmingham, Omicron Delta Kappa, Alpha Omega Alpha, Phi Beta Kappa. Home: 4408 Kennesaw Dr Birmingham AL 35213-1826 Office: Ala Heart Inst 880 Montclair Rd 1st Fl Birmingham AL 35213 E-mail: rrussell@cvapc.com.

RUSSELL, ROBERT LEONARD, professional association executive; b. July 18, 1916; s. Charles Arthur and Edna Mabel (Yearwood) R.; m. Jeanne Lucille Tackenberg, May 21, 1942 (dec. Feb. 1990). Student, St. Petersburg C.C., 1971-72; BS, U. Mid. Fla., 1973, MS, 1974. Reporter Peoria (Ill.) Jour., 1939-42, 46-47, Chgo. Daily News, 1947-57; asst. exec. dir. Profl. Golfers Assn., Dunedin, Fla., 1957-65; exec. dir. United Vol. Svcs., San Mateo, Calif., 1965-66; reporter St. Petersburg (Fla.) Evening Ind., 1967-70; exec. v.p. Fla. Health Care Assn. (formerly Fla. Nursing Home Assn.), Orlando, 1970-77, Mortgage Bankers Assn. Fla., Orlando, 1977-90, Mortgage Bankers Assn. Cen. Fla., Orlando, 1978-94, Mortgage Bankers Ednl. Found. Fla., Orlando, 1986-90; CEO B. & B. Trust, Ltd., 1994—. Adminstr. Fla. Health Care Self Insurers Fund, 1972-78; sec.-treas. Mortgage Bankers Fla. Polit. Action Com., 1977-85, treas., 1987-90; pres. Profl. Assn. Svcs., Inc., 1977-81, 90-94, chmn. bd., 1981-90; CEO B. & B. Trust, Ltd., 1994—. Editor: Profl. Golfer mag., 1957-65, Nat. Golfer mag., 1965-66, Communicator, 1977-80, Bull., 1980-81, The Messenger, 1981-90, the newsletter, 1980-94, The Knightly News, 1996—; exec. editor Rx Sports and Travel mag., 1966-67. Elder Park Lake Presbyn. Ch., Orlando, 1979-83, St. Paul's Presbyn. Ch., Orlando, 1983-87, Presbyn. Ch. of Lakes, 1987-93; mem. coord. coun. Presbytery of Cen. Fla., 1989-90; active Holy Family Cath. Ch., Orlando, 1993—; fin. sec. Holy Family Dr. Phillips Coun., KC, 1994—; mem. Holy Family Parish Planning Forum, Orlando, 1996—, mem. liturgy com.; mem. core com. SW FallFest, 1997—. With USAAF, 1942-46. Mem. NRA (life), KC, Am. Soc. Assn. Execs. (cert.), Fla. Soc. Assn. Execs., Cen. Fla. Soc. Assn. Exec., Am. Coll. Health Care Adminstrs. (fellow emeritus), Fla. Sheriffs Assn. (hon.), Mortgage Bankers Assn. Fla. (hon. life), Mortgage Bankers Assn. Cen. Fla. (hon. life), U.S. Basketball Writers Assn. (life, pres. 1956-57), Am. Legion (life). Republican. Home: 7316 Lismore Ct Orlando FL 32835-6150 Office: PO Box 916 Windermere FL 34786-0916

RUSSELL, ROBERT HILTON, Romance languages and literature educator; b. Oak Park, Ill., Dec. 26, 1927; s. Melvin Alvord and Gladys (Hilton) R.; m. June Adele Thayer, Oct. 27, 1956. AB, Knox Coll., 1949; A.M., Harvard U., 1950, PhD, 1963; A.M., Dartmouth Coll., 1968. Instr. Romance langs. and lits. Dartmouth Coll., 1957-61, asst. prof., 1961-63, assoc. prof., 1963-67, prof., 1967-91, prof. emeritus, 1991—. Vis. prof. Spanish, U. San Diego, 1989, 90, 91, Knox Coll., 1993; guest lectr. Trinity Coll., Dublin, 1967, U. Salamanca, 1977, U. Leeds, 1978, Oxford U., 1978, U. P.R., 1987. Author: The Christ Figure in Misericordia, 1968; translator: Our Friend Manso, 1987. Corporate mem. United Ch. Bd. Homeland Ministries, 1963-69; N.H. del. Gen. Synod, United Ch. Christ, 1973, 75; corporator Internat. Inst. in Spain. Mem. MLA, Asociación Internacional de Hispanistas, Asociación Internacional de Galdosistas, Phi Beta Kappa. Democrat. Home: 17 Willow Spring Cir Hanover NH 03755-2901 Office: 6072 Dartmouth Hall Hanover NH 03755-3511

RUSSELL, ROBIE GEORGE, lawyer; b. Moscow, July 7, 1948; s. George Robie Russell and Jean Ray (Atkinson) O'Reilly; m. Nancy Kay Olson, May 31, 1975; children: George Robie, Erin Kay. BS in Polit. Sci., Pub. Adminstrn., U. Idaho, 1972, cert. in Pub. Adminstrn., 1974, JD, 1978. Bar: Idaho 1979, U.S. Dist. Ct. Idaho 1979, U.S. Ct. Claims 1980, U.S. Ct. Appeals (9th cir.) 1980, U.S. Tax Ct. 1981, U.S. Ct. Appeals (fed. cir.) 1985, U.S. Supreme Ct. 1985, Wash. 1991. Dep. atty. gen. State of Idaho, Boise, 1979-81, sr. dep. atty. gen., div. chief, 1981-86; regional adminstr. region 10 U.S. EPA, Alaska, Idaho, Oregon, Wash., 1986-90; pres. Environ. Property Mgmt., Inc., Bainbridge Island, Wash., 1991-93; of counsel Ryan Swanson & Cleveland, Seattle, 1993-94; atty. Russell & Assocs., 1995—. Counsel Idaho Sec. of State, Boise, 1982-86. Contbg. author: Idaho Media Law Handbook, 1986; editor: Idaho Cities Mag., 1974-75, (newsletter) Local Govt. Legal News, 1981-86; contbr. articles to profl. jours. Pres., treas. Lincoln Day Assn., Boise, 1979-86; vice-chmn. Selective Svc. Bd., Boise, 1983-86; chmn., vice-chmn. Ada County Reps., Boise, 1984-86; chmn. Combined Fed. Campaign, 1988; mem. Puget Sound Fed. Exec. Bd., 1986-90; mem. Am. Ctr. Internat. Leadership, Soviet Union/Poland delegation, 1989; active Boy Scouts Am. Named one of Outstanding Young Men in Am., 1980—. Mem. ABA, Idaho State Bar Assn., Wash. State Bar Assn. (CLE com.), Boise Bar Assn., King County Bar Assn., Nat. Inst. Mcpl. Law Officers, Assn. Idaho City Attys. (sec., treas. 1981-86, founder), Assn. Idaho Cities (advisor 1981—, Boyd Martin award 1985), Phi Alpha Delta, U. Idaho Alumni Assn. (bd. dirs. 1973-74), Sons and Daus. Idaho Pioneers, U. Idaho Vandal Boosters (Moscow, Idaho) (chpt. pres., bd. dirs. 1975—, nat. v.p. 1987-89, nat. pres. 1989-90, Vandal Booster of Yr. 1985). Republican. Avocations: stamp collecting, fishing, gardening, music, lit. Home: PO Box 10667 Bainbridge Island WA 98110-0667 Office: Russell & Assocs 76 S Main St Seattle WA 98104-2514

RUSSELL, STEPHEN SPEH, lawyer; b. Pitts., June 4, 1943; s. Peyton S. and Jane (Speh) R.; children: Amanda, Katie. AA, Hershey (Pa.) Jr. Coll., 1963; BA, Pa. State U., 1968; JD, Dickinson Sch. Law, Carlisle, Pa., 1971. Bar: Pa. 1971. Assoc. Rhoads Simon & Reader, Harrisburg, Pa., 1971-72; tax counsel Bd. Fin. and Revenue Commonwealth of Pa., 1972-73; chief counsel Pa. Sch. Bds. Assn. Inc., New Cumberland, 1973-98; shareholder Stock & Leader, P.C., York, Pa., 1998—. Contbr. articles to profl. jours. Vestryman Mt. Calvary Episc. Ch., Camp Hill, Pa., 1983-86. With U.S. Army, 1965-67. Mem. ABA, Pa. Bar Assn., Nat. Coun. Sch. Attys. (bd. dirs. 1989-93, 97—). Republican. Avocations: swimming, walking, golf, reading. Home: 226 Ore Bank Rd Dillsburg PA 17019-9335 Office: Stock & Leader PC PO Box 5167 35 S Duke St York PA 17405-5167

RUSSELL, SUE ANN, clinical psychologist; b. Connersville, Ind., Apr. 14, 1949; d. Hugh B. Russell and Martha Jane Meyer. BS, U. Colo., 1971; MDiv, Abilene Christian U., 1981; PhD in Clin. Psychology, U. N.D., 1992. Intern Psychol. Svcs. Ctr. U. N.D., Grand Forks, 1986-92; intern Stone Ctr. Wellesley Coll., 1991-92; rsch. psychologist women's drinking project U. N.D., 1986-92; pvt. practice, 1993—. Founding fellow Jean Baker Miller Tng. Inst. of Wellesley Coll., 1996. Contbr. articles to profl. jours. Fellowship Nat. Inst. on Alcohol Abuse and Alcoholism Nat. Inst. of Mental Health, 1991-92, Nat. Rsch. Svc. award 1988-91; pre-doctoral rsch. fellow Stone Ctr. of Wellesley Coll., 1991-92. Mem. Am. Psychol. Assn. (clin. psychology of women), N.D. Psychol. Assn., Assn. of Prevention and Cruelty to Animals. Avocations: American Eskimo dogs, creating wildlife sanctuary and natural prairie habitat on 290 acres. Office: 628 7th Ave S Ste B Grand Forks ND 58201-4854

RUSSELL, SUE ELLEN, lawyer; b. Centre, Pa., Aug. 17, 1959; d. Richard Basil and Patricia Ann Glazer; m. David Tyler Russell, Oct. 6, 1990. BA with distinction, U. Va., 1981; JD, Am. U., Washington, 1987. Bar: Va. 1987, D.C. 1988, U.S. Ct. Appeals (D.C. cir.), U.S. Dist. Ct. (ea. and we. dists.) Va., Tex. Bankruptcy Ct. (cir. no. dist.). Staff asst. Rep. Stanley Lundine, Washington, 1981-84, Senator Gary Hart, Washington, 1984-85; law clk. Legal Aid Soc., Prince Georges County, Md., 1985; appellate clk. U.S. Atty's. Office, Appellate, Washington, 1986-87; jud. clk. to Chief Judge William C. Pryor, 1987-88; assoc. Brand & Lowell, 1988-94, ptnr., 1994-95; founding and mng. ptnr. Russell & Russell, PC, Falls Church, Va., 1995—. Del. Jud. Conf., Washington, 1988-90. Mem. ABA (trustee Coun. on Law in Higher Edn, v.p. for student affiars), Nat. Health Lawyers Assn., Nat. Assn. Coll. and Univ. Attys., Va. State Bar, D.C. Bar., No. Va. Tech. Coun. Democrat. Avocations: sailing, hiking, swimming. Home: 1613 N Danville St Arlington VA 22201-3903

RUSSELL, THEODORE EMERY, diplomat; b. Madras, India, Nov. 21, 1936; s. Paul Farr and Phyllis Hope (Additon) R.; m. Sara Mather (Stedman) Russell, Sept. 3, 1960; children: Douglas Richmond Russell, Richard Mather Russell. BA, Yale U., 1958; MA, Fletcher Sch. Law & Diplomacy, 1960, MALD, 1961; sr. tng., Nat. War Coll., 1980-81. Fgn. svc. officer Dept. State, Italy, Czechoslovakia, Washington, 1963-80, dep. office dir. (EUR/RPE) Washington, 1981-83; dep. chief mission Copenhagen, 1983-87, Prague, Czechoslovakia, 1988-91; dep. asst. adminstr. for internat. activities EPA, Washington, 1992-93; ambassador to Slovak Republic Bratislava, Slovakia, 1993-96; dep. comdt. internat. affairs Army War Coll., Carlisle, Pa., 1996-99; dir. internat. relations MHz Networks, 2001—. Adj. fellow CSIS. Councillor Atlantic Coun.; mem. Army-Navy Club, Fgn. Svc. Assn., Nat. War Coll. Alumni Assn. Avocations: hiking, fishing, history, numismatics, philately. Home and Office: 1833 Briar Ridge Ct Mc Lean VA 22101-4233

RUSSELL, THOMAS, retired British government official; b. Melrose, Scotland, May 27, 1920; s. Thomas and Margaret Thomson (Wilkie) R.; m. Andrée Irma Désfossés, Jan. 2, 1951 (dec. May 1989). MA, St. Andrews U., Scotland, 1941; diploma in anthropology, Cambridge (Eng.) U., 1947. Dist. commr. Colonial Adminstrv. Svc., Solomon Islands, 1948-51, 54-56, asst. sec. Western Pacific high commn., 1951-54; adminstrv. officer on secondment to col. Office, London, 1956-57; dep. fin. sec. Western Pacific high commn. Colonial Adminstrv. Svc., Solomon Islands, 1956-65, fin. sec. Solomon Islands, 1965-70, chief sec. Solomon Islands, 1970-74; gov. Cayman Islands, 1974-81; Cayman Islands govt. rep. U.K., 1982-2000; ret., 2000. Capt. Brit. armed forces, 1940-46, North Africa and Italy, prisoner of war, Germany. Named Comdr. of Order of Brit. Empire, The Queen of England, 1970, Companion of the Order of St. Michael and St. George, The Queen of England, 1980. Fellow Royal Anthropol. Inst.; mem. Commonwealth Parliamentary Assn. (Cayman Islands br. pres. 1974-81, hon.), Brit. Commonwealth Ex-Svcs. League (mem. coun. 1982—, chmn. welfare com. 1993—), Pacific Islands Soc. (mem. coun. 1989—, past chmn.), U.K. Overseas Territories Assn. (chmn. 1997-98), Caledonian Club, Royal Commonwealth Soc. Mem. Ch. of Scotland. Avocations: archaeology, anthropology. Home: Hassendean, Gattonside Melrose TD6 9NA Scotland

RUSSELL, THOMAS JAMES, critical care supervisor; b. Meriden, Conn., July 30, 1954; s. Joseph George and Anna M. (Ruszcek) R. BS in Immunology, Kans. State U., 1977; BS in Microbiology, U. New Haven, 1981; MS, Yale U., 1984; postgrad., 1999—; cert. EMT-P, Norwalk C.C. Instr. in biology U. New Haven, West Haven, Conn., So. Conn. State U., New Haven; PALS instr, ACLS instr., PHTLS instr. Yale U.; ops. supr. New Eng. Ambulance, Shelton, Conn., New Haven Ambulance. Instr. EMS, Conn.; EMS coord. Bradley Meml. Hosp., Southington, Conn.; mem. pre-hosp. pediatric task force State of Conn.; clin. coord. EMT-P Program, Yale U. Sch. Medicine. Mem. Nat. Assn. EMT's, Nat. Paramedic Assn., N.Y. Acad. Scis., Nat. Acad. Scis., Am. Soc. Microbiology, Am. Acad. Pediats. (prehosp. emergency pediatric program coord.), Am. Soc. Immunology, Conn. Soc. Paramedics, Conn. CISD Team, Conn. EMS-C Com., Conn. Spl. Olympics World Games Med. Team Leader, Narcotic Enforcement Officers Assn., Phi Beta Kappa, Tau Kappa Epsilon (Teke of Yr.), Beta Beta Beta. Home: 129 Tuttle Rd Durham CT 06422-2208 E-mail: Tom.j.russell@worldnet.att.net.

RUSSELL, TIMOTHY, poet; b. Steubenville, Ohio, May 25, 1951; s. Charles William and Ruth Louise Russell; m. Josephine Dolan, July 17, 1971; children: Shane, Ivan, Violet, Laurel. BA, West Liberty State Coll., 1977; MA, U. Pitts., 1979. Author: (poetry collections) The Possibility of Turning to Salt, 1987 (Golden Webb award, 1987), In Dubio, 1988 (State Street Press award, 1988), In Medias Res, 1991, Adversaria, 1993 (Terrence des Pres prize in Poetry, 1993), What We Don't Know Hurts, 1995 (Talent House Press award, 1995), In Lacrimae, 1997 (White Eagle Coffee House Press award, 1996). Sgt. U.S. Army, 1970—72. Recipient 4th Shiki Internet Haiku award, Shiki Team, Ehime Prefecture, Japan, 1999. Home and Office: Poets Anonymous 202 Daniels St Toronto OH 43964 Personal E-mail: timothyrussell@earthlink.net.

RUSSELL, TIMOTHY WELLS, music educator, researcher; b. Wilmington, Del., Aug. 3, 1955; s. Robert McWatty and Ruth Mackay Russell; m. Jill Susan Williams, June 25, 1977; children: Geoffrey Stuart, Kathryn Ellen. BME, Northwestern U., Evanston, Illinois, 1977; MA, The Ohio State U., Columbus, Ohio, 1977, Ph. D., 1980. Educator The Ohio State U., Colombus, Ohio, 1980—83, U. of Rochester, Rochester, NY, 1983—89; music dir. Naples Philharm., Naples, Fla., 1983—89; educator Ariz. State Universirty, Tempe, Ariz., 1993—; music dir. Pro Musica, Columbus, Ohio, 1980—. V.p. USTA SW Sect., Pheonix, Ariz., 2002—02. Recipient Svc. to Contemporary Music, ASCAP, eight awards. Avocation: tennis. Home: 14032 South 36th Place Phoenix AZ 85044 Office: Arizona State University Tempe AZ 85287 Office Fax: 480-759-6026. E-mail: timothy.russell@asu.edu.

RUSSELL, WILLIAM STEVEN, finance executive; b. Evanston, Ill., Aug. 5, 1948; s. John W. and Lillian H. Russell; m. Susan M. Hanson, Aug. 20, 1972. BS, So. Ill. U., 1970. CPA, Ill. Sr. staff auditor Arthur Andersen & Co., Chgo., 1972-76; acctg. mgr., controller, asst. sec. and treas. Lawter Internat., Inc., Northbrook, Ill., 1976-86, treas., sec., 1986-87, v.p. fin., treas. and sec., 1987-96, pvt. investor, 1996—. Served with U.S. Army, 1970-72. Mem. Am. Inst. CPA's, Beta Alpha Psi, Beta Gamma Sigma. Roman Catholic. Home and Office: 51 Park Lane Park Ridge IL 60068-2834

RUSSELL, WILLIAM ALEXANDER, JR. environmental scientist; b. Havre de Grace, Md., Nov. 12, 1946; s. William Alexander Sr. and Margaret Adams Webster (Scott) R.; m. Nancy Dion Stacey, Jan. 4, 1965 (div. June 1971); 1 child, Angela Dion; m. Lynne Allison Ertle, July 10, 1971; children: Sara Lynne, Brent William. AA, Harford Community Coll., 1973; BS, Towson State U., 1983, MA, 1991; grad., Army Mgmt. Staff Coll., 1991; PhD in Commn. Sci., Boy Scouts Am. Commrs. Coll., 2001. Cert. EMT level III firefighter. Environ. coord. U.S. Army Aberdeen Proving Ground (Md.), 1976-81; environmental protection specialist Hdqrs. Dept. Army Nat. Guard Bur., Washington, 1981-85, U.S. Army Environ. Hygiene Agy., Aberdeen Proving Ground, 1985-94, U.S. Army Ctr. Health Promotion & Preventive Medicine, Aberdeen Proving Ground, 1995—. Master cons. U.S.A. Ctr. Health Promotion and Preventive Medicine, Aberdeen Proving Ground, 1997. Author and contbr. tech. papers. Vol., asst. chief, dir., others Aberdeen (Md.) Fire Dept., 1962—; asst. scout master Boy Scouts Am., 1989—91, troop com. chmn., 1992—96, mem. Order of the Arrow Advisor, 1996—, asst. dist. commr., 1995—99, dist. commr., 1999—; bd. dirs. Md. Ornithol. Soc., Balt., 1982—92, Harford Glen Found., Bel Air, 1989—92; chmn. Harford County Environ. Adv. Bd., 1985—96. Mem.: Inst. Noise Control Engring., Acoustical Soc. Am., Nat. Assn. Environ. Profls., Nat. Wildlife Fedn. (life), Nature Conservancy, Nat. Audubon Soc., Raptor Rsch. Found., Md. Conservation Fedn. (charter), Internat. Geographical Honor Soc. Democrat. Avocations: birding, hiking, environ. conservation. Home: 318 Willow Way Havre De Grace MD 21078-4150 E-mail: William.Russell@amedd.army.mil., k.falcon2@home.com.

RUSSELL, WILLIAM JOSEPH, educational association administrator; b. Boston, Sept. 23, 1941; s. Stanley Whiteside and Helen Rita R.; m. Frances Marie Chapdelaine, June 25, 1967; 1 son, Scott David. BS, Boston Coll., 1963; M.Ed., Northeastern U., 1966; PhD, U. Calif., Berkeley, 1971. Head math. dept. Oceana, Pacifica, Calif., 1966-71; asst. for fed. and profl. affairs Am. Ednl. Research Assn., Washington, 1971-73, dep. exec. dir., 1973-74, exec. dir., 1974—. Adv. bd. Edn. Resource Info. Center Ednl. Testing Center, Princeton, N.J., 1975-87; exec. officer Nat. Council on Measurement in Edn., Internat. Assn. Computing in Edn., 1987-89. Editor: Ednl. Researcher, 1979-90. Mem. Am. Ednl. Research Assn., Phi Delta Kappa. Roman Catholic. Home: 1443 Creekside Ct Vienna VA 22182-1701 Office: AERA 1230 17th St NW Washington DC 20036-3078

RUSSELL, WILLIAM LEE, surgeon; b. Memphis, June 4, 1942; MD, U. Ark. Sch. Medicine, 1968. Diplomate Am. Bd. Surgery. Intern U. Tenn.-Memphis City Hosps., 1968-69, resident in surgery, 1972-76; fellow in cardiovasc. surgery Baylor Hosp., Houston, 1979-80; staff Erlanger Med. Ctr., Chattanooga, 1980—. Prof. surgery, vice chmn. dept. surgery U. Tenn. Coll. Medicine. Mem. Am. Acad. Surgery, DeBakey Internat. Cardiovasc. Soc., Internat. Soc. Cardiovasc. Surgery, So. Assn. Vasc. Surgeons, So. Surg. Assn. Office: Dept Surgery 979 E 3rd St Ste 401 Chattanooga TN 37403-2139 E-mail: russellwl@erlanger.org.

RUSSELL HARRSCH, PATRICIA EILEEN, former healthcare rules writer; b. Niagara Falls, N.Y., Sept. 14, 1951; d. William Joseph and Jane Marie (Taylor) R.; m. Keith Alan Harrsch, Aug. 13, 1988. ADN, Madison Area Tech. Coll., Wis., 1985; BSN, Edgewood Coll., 1987; MSN, U. Wis., 1994. Nurse clin. II Mendota Mental Health Inst., Madison, Wis., 1986-91, U. Wis. Hosp. and Clinics, Madison, 1991-94, diabetes support group leader, 1992-95; nurse cons. I, facilities surveyor Dept. Health and Family Svcs., 1994-97, healthcare rules writer, 1997-98. Mem. Am. Coll. Legal Medicine (Hirsch award 1993), ANA, Am. Diabetes Assn., Alliance for the Mentally Ill, Sigma Theta Tau (rsch. award 1992). Democrat. Unitarian Universalist. Avocations: performing arts, gardening, cooking, camping. Home: 1151 Jenifer St Madison WI 53703-3744

RUSSELL JR. JOHN WALLACE, composer, educator; b. Norfolk, Va., Feb. 7, 1952; s. John Wallace Russell Sr. and Melinda Farrar Russell; m. Melinda Farrar Russell, July 9, 1977; children: John Russell, Charles Russell, Elizabeth Russell. BM, W.Va. U., Morgantown, WV, 1974; MME, Shenandoah Conservatory Music, Winchester, VA, 1990. Band and choral dir. Warren County Schools, Front Royal, Va., 1974—90; dir. bands Clarke County Schools, Berryville, 1990—92, Frederick County Schools, Winchester, 1992—. Trumpeter For Dancers Only, Winchester, Va., 1993—; brass player Tuscarora Civil War Band, Winchester, Va., 1996—; dir. and co-founder Warren County / Giles B. Cook Am. Legion Cmty. Band, Fort Royal, Va., 1986—89; trumpeter The Couriers Swing Band, Winchester, Va., 1996—. Composer: works for bands and precussion ensembles. Handbell choir, various instruments for worship services First United Meth. Ch., numerous churches, 1974—2002. Recipient Fifteen Yr. Tchg. Recognition, VMEA, 1988, Twenty-five Yr. Tchg. Recognition, 1998. Mem.: MENC, VBODA, VMEA. United Methodist. Home: 820 Parishville Road Gore VA 22637 Office: James Wood Middle School Amherst Street Winchester VA 22637

RUSSELL-RADER, KATHLEEN, secondary school educator; b. Dayton, Ohio, Jan. 23, 1954; d. Reid Jerome and Margie (Miller) Russell; m. Donald Mark Rader, July 9, 1977. BS, Bowling Green (Ohio) State U., 1975; MS, U. Dayton, 1987. Cert. tchr., Ohio. English tchr. Fairborn (Ohio) City Schs., 1976—, Sinclair C. C., Dayton, 1991—. Dir., choreographer Fairborn High Sch. Flyerette Dance Corps, 1976-81; adv. Nat. Jr. Honor Soc., Fairborn, 1985—, student leadership, 1990—, mem. acad. coun., 1988—; adv./dir. Drama Club, Fairborn, 1991—; coach Power of the Pen Writing Team, Fairborn, 1987—. Recipient Golden Apple Tchr. Achiever award Ashland Oil Corp., 1996; named Tchr. of Yr. Fairborn City Schs., 1989-90, Tchr. Honor Roll, Ohio Interscholastic Writing League, Cleve., 1990; Vera Schneider Teaching grantee Fairborn City Schs., 1988-92. Mem. Nat. Coun. Tchrs. English (judge Promising Young Writers Program 1991-93), Western Ohio Coun. Tchrs. English, Ohio Coun. Tchrs. English, Ohio Coun. English and Lang. Arts (judge writing contest 1989-93), Dayton Area Coun. Internat. Reading Assn. (pres. 1991-92), Ohio Coun. Internat. Reading Assn., Internat. Reading Assn., Nat. Assn. Student Activity Advisers, Phi Delta Kappa. Republican. Roman Catholic. Avocations: dancing, travel. Home: 1701 Provincetown Rd Dayton OH 45459-3452 Office: Fairborn City Schs 200 Lincoln Dr Fairborn OH 45324-5349

RUSSELL-WOOD, ANTHONY JOHN R. history educator; b. Corbridge-on-Tyne, Northumberland, Eng., Oct. 11, 1939; came to U.S., 1971; s. James and Ethel Kate (Roberts) R.-W.; m. Hannelore Elisabeth Schmidt, May 19, 1972; children: Christopher James Owen, Karsten Anthony Alexander. Diploma in Portuguese studies, Lisbon U., Portugal, 1960; BA with honors, Oxford (Eng.) U., 1963, MA, DPhil., 1967. Lectr. Portuguese lang. and lit. Oxford U., 1963-64; rsch. fellow St. Antony's Coll., Oxford, 1967-70; vis. assoc. prof. Johns Hopkins U., Balt., 1971-72, assoc. prof., 1972-76, prof., 1976—, chmn. dept. history, 1984-90, 96-99, chmn. dept. Hispanic and Italian studies, 1996-97, Herbert Baxter Adams prof., 2001—. Mem. U.S. Commn. Maritime History, 1977—; disting. vis. prof. U. Mass.-Dartmouth, 2000; vis. prof. Portuguese and Brazilian studies and history Brown U., 2001. Author: Manuel Francisco Lisboa: A Craftsman of the Golden Age of Brazil, 1968, Fidalgos and Philanthropists: The Santa Casa da Misericordia of Bahia, 1550-1755, 1968, The Black Man in Slavery and Freedom in Colonial Brazil, 1982, Society and Government in Colonial Brazil, 1500-1822, 1992, A World on the Move: The Portuguese in Africa, Asia and America 1415-1808, 1992, Portugal and the Sea: A World Embraced, 1997, The Portuguese Empire, 1415-1808, 1998;, Slavery and Freedom in Colonial Brazil, 2002; co-author: From Colony to Nation: Essays on the Independence of Brazil, 1975; editor: Local Government in European Overseas Empires, 1450-1800, 1999, Government and Governance of Empires, 1415-1800, 2000; gen. editor: An Expanding World: The European Impact on World History, 1450-1800, 1995-2000; mem. editl. com. L.Am. Studies, Tsukuba, Japan, 1989—. Chmn. CLAH Columbus Quincentennial Com., 1987-90, Md. State Humanities Coun., 1980-82; mem. Md. Heritage Com., 1982-85, Balt. County Commn. Arts and Scis., 1982-84. Decorated comendador Order of Prince Henry (Portugal); recipient Bolton Meml. prize Conf. Latin Am. Hist., 1969, Whitaker prize Middle-Atlantic Coun. Latin Am. Studies, 1983, Dom João de Castro prize Portuguese Nat. Commn. for Commemoration of Discoveries, 1993, Benemérito, Santa Casa da Misericordia, Bahia, 1999, comdr. Internat. Order of Merit of Misericórdias, 2000. Fellow: European Acad. Scis. & Arts, Royal Hist. Soc., Academia de Letras da Bahia (corr.), Instituto Geografico e Historico da Bahia (corr.), Royal Geog. Soc. (life), Instituto Historico e Geografico Brasileiro (corr.); mem.: Conf. on Latin Am. History, Forum on European Expansion and Global Interaction. Avocations: hiking, cycling. Home: 113 Belmore Rd Lutherville Timonium MD 21093-6111 Office: Johns Hopkins Univ Dept Of History Baltimore MD 21218

RUSSERT, TIMOTHY JOHN, broadcast journalist, executive; b. Buffalo, May 7, 1950; m. Maureen Orth; 1 child, Luke. BA, John Carroll U., 1972; JD, Cleve. State U., 1976; LHD (hon.), Canisius Coll., 1993; LLD (hon.), Albany Law Sch., 1993; LHD (hon.), Marist Coll., 1994; LLD (hon.), D'Youville Coll., 1995; LHD (hon.), Merrimack Coll., 1996, Seton Hall U., 1997, Loyola Coll., 1997; LLD (hon.), John Carroll U., 1997; LHD (hon.), U. Scranton, 1997, Cath. U., 1998, Manhattan Coll., 1998; DPS, St. Louis U., 1998, Providence Coll., 1999; LLD, St. Johns U., 1999; DPolSci, Monmouth U., 1999. Bar: N.Y., D.C. Spl. counsel U.S. Senate, 1977-82; counselor N.Y. Gov.'s Office, 1983-84; with NBC News, 1984—; moderator, mng. editor Meet the Press, 1991—; anchor The Tim Russert Show CNBC, 1994—; sr. v.p., Washington bureau chief NBC News. Nat. polit. analyst Today program and NBC Nightly News with Tom Brokaw; supr. NBC News Today program live broadcasts from Rome, 1985; overseer prodn. prime time spl. A Day in the Life of President Bush, 1990, A Day in the Life of President Clinton, 1993; has covered 8 U.S./Russian Summits, Geneva, Malta, Washington, Moscow, Vancouver; lectr. at more than 30 univs. Recipient Alumni Spl. Achievement award Cleve.-Marshall Coll. Law, Pres.'s medal Trocaire Coll., Dean's award Cleve.-Marshall Coll. Law, John Peter Zenger award N.Y. State Bar Assn., 1992, Disting. Grad. award Nat. Cath. Educator's Assn., 1995, Spl. Achievement Alumni medal John Carroll U. Fellow Commn. European Communities. Office: NBC News Meet the Press 4001 Nebraska Ave NW Washington DC 20016-2733

RUSSETT, BRUCE MARTIN, political science educator; b. North Adams, Mass., Jan. 26, 1935; s. Raymond Edgar and Ruth Marian (Martin) R.; m. Cynthia Margaret Eagle, June 18, 1960; children: Margaret Ellen, Mark David, Lucia Elizabeth, Daniel Alden. BA magna cum laude, Williams Coll., 1956; diploma in econs., Cambridge (Eng.) U., 1957; MA, Yale U., 1958, PhD, 1961, Uppsala U., 2002. Instr. MIT, Cambridge, 1961-62; asst. prof., then assoc. prof. Yale U., New Haven, 1961-68, prof., 1968—, Dean Acheson prof. internat. rels. and polit. sci., 1985—, chair dept. polit. sci., 1990-96, dir. UN studies, 1993—. Vis. prof. Columbia U., 1965, U. Mich., 1965-66, U. Libre Brussels, 1969-70, U. N.C., 1979-80, Richardson Inst., London, 1973-74, Netherlands Inst. Advanced Study, 1984, Tel Aviv U., 1989, U. Tokyo, 1996, Harvard U., 2001; prin. cons. pastoral letter on peace Nat. Conf. Cath. Bishops, Washington, 1981-83; co-dir., secretariat ind. working group Future of the UN, 1993-96. Author: World Handbook of Political and Social Indicators, 1964, What Price Vigilance?, 1970 (Kammerer award Amn. Polit. Sci. Assn. 1971), Interest and Ideology (with E. Hanson), 1975, Controlling the Sword, 1990, Grasping the Democratic Peace, 1993, The Once and Future Security Council, 1997, (with John Oneal) Triangulating Peace, 2001, others; editor: Jour. Conflict Resolution, 1972—; contbr. articles to profl. jours. Grantee NSF, 1964, 65, 69, 77, 79, 85, 88, 89, 90, 95, 98, Ford Found., 1993, 94, 97, John and Catherine MacArthur Found., 1988, 91; Fulbright-Hays fellow, Belgium and Israel, 1969, 89; John Simon Guggenheim Found. fellow, 1969, 77; German Marshall Fund fellow, 1977. Fellow Am. Acad. Arts and Scis.; mem. AAUP, Am. Polit. Sci. Assn. (coun. 1984-86), Internat. Studies Assn. (pres. 1983-84), Peace Sci. Soc. Internat. (pres. 1977-79). Avocations: tennis, classical music, hiking. Home: 70 Martin Ter Hamden CT 06517-2333 Office: Yale U Dept Polit Sci PO Box 208301 New Haven CT 06520-8301 E-mail: bruce.russett@yale.edu.

RUSSIANO, JOHN See MILES, JACK

RUSSILLO, ALFRED GEORGE, retired military officer, military officer, educator; b. New Rochelle, N.Y., Nov. 26, 1920; s. Joseph and Teresa Russillo; m. Catherine Ann O'Donnell, Dec. 8, 1945; 8 children. BS in Engring., U.S. Naval Acad., 1943; MBA, George Washington U., 1963, DPA, 1978. Advanced through grades to capt., 1964; commd. ensign USN, 1943; instr. U.S. Naval Acad., Annapolis, Md., 1950-52; dir. Seminar Sch., Indsl. Coll. Armed Forces, Washington, 1971—73; ret. U.S. Navy, 1973; engr., analyst Vitro Labs., Silver Spring, Md., 1973-74; asst. prof. Ctrl. Mich. U., Mount Pleasant, 1978-82, assoc. prof., 1982-87. V.p. Woods Homeowners Assn., Hedgesville, W.Va., 1993—2002. Decorated three Legion of Merit, Bronze Star. Mem. U.S. Naval Acad. Found., Am. Soc. Pub. Adminstrn. (pres. W.Va. chpt. 1991-92), Acad. Polit. Sci., Ret. Officers Assn. Republican.

RUSSIN, JONATHAN, lawyer, consultant; b. Wilkes-Barre, Pa., Oct. 30, 1937; s. Jacob S. and Anne (Wartella) R.; m. Antoinette Stackpole, Oct. 6, 1962; children: Alexander, Andrew, Benjamin, Jacob. BA, Yale U., 1959, LLB, 1963. Bar: D.C. 1963. Guide interpreter Am. Nat. Exhibit, Moscow, 1959; rsch. asst. Law Faculty U. East Africa, Dar es Salaam, Tanganyika, 1961-62; regional legal adviser for Caribbean AID, 1967-69; ptnr. Kirkwood, Kaplan, Russin & Vecchi, Santo Domingo, Dominican Republic, 1969-74, Washington, 1974-78, Kaplan Russin & Vecchi, Madrid, 1978-81, Washington, 1981-92; ptnr., dir. Russian practice group Russin & Vecchi, Moscow, 1992—. Washington rep. for Moscow Patriarchate of Russian Orthodox Ch.; convener adv. coun. Inst. for European, Russian and Eurasian Studies, George Washington U.; mem. adv. bd. Caribbean Am. Directory; trustee St. Nicholas Cathedral, Washington, St. Vladimir's Orthodox Theol. Sem., Crestwood, N.Y., 1985-93; legal adviser Orthodox Ch. in Am. Contbr. articles to profl. jours. Bd. dirs. Nat. Coun. Internat. Visitors, Washington, 1987—93, Fund for Democracy and Devel., Washington, 1993—, MUCIA Global Edn. Group, Inc., 1996—2000, Delphi Internat., Washington, 1988—2000, Dominican Am. Cultural Inst., Santo Domingo, 1988—92. Recipient Order of St. Vladimir, Moscow Patriarchate, Russian Orthodox Ch., 1991. Mem. ABA, L.Am. Studies Assn., Caribbean Studies Assn., Inter-Am. Bar Assn., Yale Club N.Y., Yale Club Washington. Republican. Office: 815 Connecticut Ave NW Ste 650 Washington DC 20006-4004

RUSSIN, ROBERT ISAIAH, sculptor, educator; b. N.Y.C., Aug. 26, 1914; s. Uriel and Olga (Winnett) R.; m. Adele Mutchnick, May 21, 1937; children: Joseph Mark, Lincoln David, Uriel Robin. BA, CCNY, 1933, MS, 1935; postgrad. (Inst. fellow), Beaux Arts Inst. Design, 1935-36. Tchr. sculpture Copper Union Art Inst., N.Y.C., 1944-47; prof. art U. Wyo., Laramie, 1947-86, prof., artist-in-residence, 1976-85, Disting. prof. emeritus, 1985—. One-man shows Tucson Fine Arts Ctr., 1966, Colorado Springs (Colo.) Fine Arts Ctr., 1967, Palm Springs (Calif.) Desert Mus., Chas. G. Bowers Meml. Mus., Judah L. Magnes Meml. Mus., Berkeley, Calif.; retrospective one-man exhbn. Nat. Gallery Modern Art, Santo Domingo, Dominican Republic, 1976, Tubac Ctr. of the Arts, Ariz., 1987, Old Town Gallery-Park City, Ut., Riggins Gallery, Scottsdale, Ariz., 1989, Fine Arts Mus., U. Wyo., 1991; sculpture commns. include 2 8-foot metal figures, Evanston (Ill.) Post Office, 1939, three life-size carved figures, Conshohocken (Pa.) Post Office, 1940, Benjamin Franklin Monument, U. Wyo., 1957, Bust of Lincoln, Lincoln Mus., Washington, (now in Gettysburg Mus.), 1959, Lincoln Monument atop summit Lincoln Hwy., (now U.S. Interstate 80), Wyo, 1959, monumental bas-relief bronze Cheyenne (Wyo.) Fed. Bldg, 1966, two carved wood walls, Denver Fed. Bldg., 1966, monumental fountain, City of Hope Med. Ctr., Los Angeles, 1966-67, statue, Brookhaven (N.Y.) Nat. Lab., 1968, life-size bronze sculpture fountain, City of Hope, 1969, Pomona Coll., 1973, monumental bronze sculpture Prometheus Natrona County (Wyo.) Pub. Library, 1974, Man and Energy, Casper (Wyo.) C. of C., 1974, 12-foot marble carving Menorah Med. Ctr., Kansas City, Mo., 1975, Einstein and Gershwin medals Magnes Meml. Mus, Berkeley, Nat. Mus. Art, Santo Domingo, Dominican Republic, 1975, monumental fountain, Galleria d'Arte Moderna, Santo Domingo, 1977, Duarte Monument, Santo Domingo, 1977, 30 foot steel and water fountain monument City Hall, Casper, 1980, marble and bronze monument, Lincoln Centre, Dallas, 1982, acrylic steel and bronze monument, Herschler State Office Bldg., Cheyenne, 1984, marble monument, U. Wyo., Laramie, 1985, portrait head Charles Bluhdorn, chmn. Gulf & Western, 1975, portrait bust Pres. J. Balaguer of Dominican Republic, 1975, portrait head G. Wilson Knight, Shakespearean actor and scholar, 1975, 2 12-foot bronze figures The Greeting and the Gift for Bicentennial Commn., Cheyenne, 1976, monumental marble head of Juan Pablo Duarte liberator Dominican Republic, Santo Domingo, 1976, monumental marble, Pan Am. Family, Dominican Republic, 1977, marble sculpture Trio, U. Wyo., 1985, Isaac B. Singer medal for Magnes Mus., 1983, monumental Holocaust Figure Tucson Jewish Community Ctr., 1989, granite monument Chthonodynamis, Dept. Energy Bldg., Washington, 1992, bust Hon. Milward Simpson, 1993, bust James Forest U. Wyo., 1993, bronze statue Univ. Med. Ctr., Tuscon, Head, Gov. Stanley Hathway, Cheyenne, Wy. 1995; Head, Pres. Franklin D. Roosevelt, Rotunda (pres.hosp. Bethesda, Md.), monuments and sculpture, Nat. Jewish Rsch. and Med. Ctr., Denver, Colo., Denver Med. and Rsch. Ctr.; contbr. articles to profl. jours. Recipient awards sec. fine arts U.S. Treasury, 1939, 40, Lincoln medal U.S. Congress, 1959, Alfred G.B. Steel award Pa. Acad. Fine Arts, 1961, medal of Order of Duarte Sanchez y Mella, Dominican Republic, 1977; Ford Found. fellow, 1953. Mem. Nat. Sculpture Conf. (exec. bd.), Sculptors Guild, Nat. Sculpture Soc., AIA, AAUP, Coll. Art Internat. Inst. Arts and Letters, Phi Beta Kappa (hon.) Home: 61 N Fork Rd Centennial WY 82055 also: 1160 W Placita Salubre Green Valley AZ 85614-1334 E-mail: adbo@webtv.net.

RUSSMAN, IRENE KAREN, artist; b. Chgo., Mar. 10, 1942; d. Andrew Earl and Irene Margaret Kane (Barthley) James; m. James Ora Duffy, Jan. 24, 1963 (div. Oct. 20, 1993); children: Dawn Ann, James Sean, Maureen Marie; m. Stephen George Russman, Aug. 10, 2002. BA, Wash. State U., 1985, MFA, 1989; student, Pilchuck Glass Sch., 2001, Red Deer Coll., 2001. Juried invitational exhbns. include Gallery X "Out of the Box", Art Inst. Chgo., 1995, Wash. State U./U. Ill., 1994, Virginia Inn, Seattle, 1993, Chase Gallery, Spokane, 1992, Union Gallery, Pullman, 1991, Acad. Arts, Riga, Latvia, 1990, Galeria 5, Caracas, Venezuela, 1989; collections include Johanna Bur. for the Handicapped, Chgo., Gordon Gilkey Collection, Portland Art Mus., Modern Art Gallery, Leningrad, Russia, Neill Pub. Libr., Vetreria 2001, S.R.L., Murano, Italy; juried summer workshop Pulchuk Glass Sch., 2001. Bd. dirs. Pullman/Moscow Regional Airport, 1981-84; mem. Global Vols. Project, Ostuni, Italy, 1998, Passport in Time Forest Svc., 2000. Recipient Civic Appreciation award City of Pullman (Mayor Pete Butkus), 1984. Mem. Palouse Folklore Soc., Lions Club Internat. Avocations: folk dancing, flying, travel, gardening. Home: PO Box 215 Palouse WA 99161-0215 Studio: Artspace 114 E 525 Church PO Box 247 Palouse WA 99161-0247 E-mail: ireneduffy@hotmail.com.

RUSSO, ALEXANDER PETER, artist, educator; b. Atlantic City, June 11, 1922; s. Peter Joseph and Lillian Mary (Soma) R.; 1 child, Eugenie. Student, Pratt Inst., 1940-42, Swarthmore Coll., 1946-47; S.S., Bard Coll., 1947; B.F.A. (Breevort-Eickenmeyer fellow), Columbia U., 1952; postgrad., Acad. Fine Arts, Rome, 1952-54, Inst. Advanced Fine Arts, 1977-79. Instr. New Orleans Acad. Art, 1948-49; asst. prof. art U. Buffalo, 1955-58; instr. in graphic design Parsons Sch. Design, 1958-60; chmn. dept. drawing and painting Corcoran Sch. Art, 1961-70, chmn. faculty, acting dean, 1967-70; lectr., thesis adv. George Washington U., 1961-70; prof. Hood Coll., Frederick, Md., 1970-90, prof. emeritus, 1990—, chmn. dept. art, 1970-87. Vis. guest prof. art Instituto Allende, San Miguel de Allende, Mexico, 1993-94; panelist Md. State Coun. Arts, Balt., 1981-82; reviewer art programs Md State Bd. Edn., 1981—; guest art critic Southampton Press, N.Y., 1989, 91; cons. in field. One-man shows include Corcoran Gallery Art, Washington, 1946, 64, Chiurazzi Gallery, Rome, 1953, Cavallino Gallery, Venice, Italy, 1954, U. So. Ill., 1955, Frank Rehn Gallery, N.Y.C., periodic exhbns., 1954-74, Phoenix II Gallery, Washington, 1983, Ingber Gallery, N.Y.C., 1983, Washington Gallery Art, 1963, Franz Bader Gallery, Washington, 1967, Internat. Monetary Fund, Washington, 1968, 79, Agra Gallery, Washington, 1971, Benson Gallery, Bridgehampton, L.I., 1976, Phoenix Fine Arts, Frederick, 1981, Benton Gallery, Southampton, N.Y., 1985, 86, 88, 90, 91, Arlene Bujese Gallery, East Hampton, N.Y., 1994, 95, 97, 98, Hood Coll., Frederick, Md., 1991, Western Md. Coll., Westminster, 1991, Bell Gallery, Seattle, 1991, 92, Gettysburg (Pa.) Coll., 1989; group exhbns. include Salon de la Marne, Paris, 1945, Met. Mus. Art, N.Y.C., 1948, Bordighera Internat., Italy, 1953-54 (hon. mention), Mus. Modern Art, Madrid, 1953, Sala di Esposizione delle Biblioteca Americano, Rome, 1953, Whitney Mus. Am. Art, N.Y.C., 1960, Mus. Modern Art, N.Y.C., 1969, Guild Hall, East Hampton, N.Y., 1976, East Hampton Avant-Garde, A Salute to the Signa Gallery, 1990, NAS, Washington, 1984, Bell Gallery, Seattle, 1990, Illustrator's Club, N.Y.C., 1991, Armory Exhbn., N.Y.C., 1991, Instituto Alleude, San Niguel de Allende, Mex., 1994, Fulbright Assoc. 20th Anniv. Art Exhibition, 1997, Josh Kligerman Gallery, San Miguel de Allende, Mex., 1994; represented in permanent collections Albright-Know Gallery, Buffalo, Columbia U., N.Y.C., Delgado Mus. Art, New Orleans, Corcoran Gallery Art, Fiat Automobile Co., Rome, Nat. Collection Smithsonian Inst., Washington, Fed. Ins. Deposit Corp., Washington, Gettysburg Coll. of Pa.; author: Profiles on Women Artists, 1985, The Challenge of Drawing, 1986, (poetry) Vignettes, 1996. Served with USNR, 1942-46. Fellow Guggenheim Found., 1947-48, 49-50,Edward McDowell Found., 1956, Hood Coll. Hodson teaching fellow, 1983; Fulbright grantee for painting and research, Rome, 1952-54, U.S.-Indo Subcommn. on Edn. and Culture grantee, India, 1984. Office: PO Box 1377 Wainscott NY 11975-1377 also: Arlene Bujese Gallery 66 Newtown Ln East Hampton NY 11937-2400 *Success is an equivocal matter. "Outward success", no doubt, is meaningful and necessary to most people in terms of fulfilling goals or for some similar reason. "Interior success" is more difficult to achieve, for it means the labor of a developing soul, and, more often than not, the relinquishing of what most would consider to be "material success." Whatever I have achieved in the way of outward or material success, therefore, is but a minute reflection of that which I would wish to achieve on the spiritual level. There is a long way to go.*

RUSSO, ANTHONY JOSEPH, public relations professional; b. N.Y.C., Oct. 23, 1953; s. Lucio and Tina (Iarossi) R. BA cum laude, Alfred U., 1974; MA, Columbia U., 1975; PhD, Claremont Grad. Sch., 1982. Asst. to chmn. Mocatta Metals, N.Y.C., 1982-83; account exec. Gavin Anderson and Co., 1983-85; sr. account exec. Adams and Reinhart, 1985; dir. corp. rels. Geto and DeMilly, 1985-86; v.p. Cameron Assocs., 1986-88; CEO Noonan/Russo Presence Euro RSCG, 1988—, chmn. London, 1995—. Mem. APA, Pub. Rels. Soc. Am., Psi Chi. Democrat. Office: Noonan/Russo Presence EURO RSCG 220 Fifth Ave New York NY 10001-7708 also: 240 Stockton St San Francisco CA 94108-5306 Office: Noonan/Russo Ltd 15 Basinghall St London EC2V 5BR England also: 10509 Vista Sorrento Pkwy San Diego CA 92121

RUSSO, ANTHONY SEBASTIAN, telecommunications industry executive; b. Woodbury, N.J., Sept. 9, 1947; s. Anthony Joseph and Rose (Leonardi) Russo; m. Carmen Sanchez, July 1970; children: A. Scott, Thomas Allen, Darryl Alexander. BS, Belknap Coll., 1969. Sales and sys. engr. IBM, Balt., Washington, 1969-78, regional staff Washington, 1978-80; mgr. data and teleconferencing svc. SBS, McLean, Va., 1980-82, mktg. mgr., 1982-83, dir. shared network products, 1983-86; v.p. mktg. and sales Lightnet, Rockville, Md., 1986-87; pres. CEI, 1987-88; v.p. mktg. and sales TCom Sys., Washington, 1988-89; dir. data mktg. MCI, 1990-95, v.p. global mktg., 1995-96, v.p. data and global bus. solutions, 1997-99; sr. v.p. Global Bus Solutions, 1999-2001; pres., COO InPhonics, Washington, 2001—02; CEO PLSGLOBAL, 2002—. Sgt. U.S. Army, 1969—71. Mem.: IEEE, Train Collectors Assn., KC. Roman Catholic. Avocations: model trains, classic cars collection. Home: 16200 Whitehaven Rd Silver Spring MD 20906-1128

RUSSO, DONNA LEE, social worker; b. Suffern, N.Y., Sept. 9, 1963; d. Donald Ernest and Kathleen Helen (Killacky) D.; m. Kevin Frank Russo, Nov. 3, 1990. BS in Psychology, St. Lawrence U., 1985; MSW, Columbia U., 1987. Child care relief worker St. Agatha's Home of N.Y. State Foundling Hosp., Nanuet, 1981-85; med. social worker Burke Rehab. Hosp., White Plains, N.Y., 1987—. Founder, leader support group traumatic brain injured and families. Mem. Assn. Cert. Social Workers (cert.), N.Y. State Head Injury Assn. (support group founder/leader 1988—). Office: Burke Rehab Hosp 785 Mamaroneck Ave White Plains NY 10605-2523

RUSSO, GILBERTO, engineering educator; b. Rome, Aug. 23, 1954; s. Guido and Maria (Mazzoni) R. Laurea, Poly. Inst. Turin, Italy, 1975; ScD, MIT, 1980; MD, U. Chgo. Pritaker Sch. of Medicine. Pres. Studio Russo, Inc. Engrng. Cons., Turin, 1970; asst. prof. Poly. Inst. Turin, 1975-80; lectr. MIT, Cambridge, Mass., 1985-91; dr. dept. plastic and reconstructive surgery U. Chgo., 1992-95; mem. dept. surgery U. Calif., San Francisco, 1995—. Mem. designer selection bd. State of Mass., Boston, 1989. Contbr. articles to profl. publs., chpts. to books. Pres. Dante Alisheri Soc., Cambridge, 1986-88; treas. MIT/Poly. Alumni Assn., Turin, 1970. Fulbright fellow, 1978. Fellow Nat. Coun. Engrng. Examiners; mem. Mass. Soc. Profl. Engrs. (v.p. 1991—), Tau Beta Pi (chpt. advisor 1985, Eminent Engr. 1985). Achievements include patents in solar energy collectors, development of computer aided therodynamics, computer methods for engineering, optimization of non-steady-state systems, compressible fluid flow with heat transfer, thermal dynamics models, diagnostics and surgical repair of electric/burn injuries. Address: Dept Surgery LIJ Med Ctr New Hyde Park NY 11004 Office: U Chgo Dept Plastic-Reconstrv Surg Chicago IL 60637 also: U Calif Dept Surgery Rm S-343 Box 0470 513 Parnassus Ave San Francisco CA 94122-2722

RUSSO, GREGORY THOMAS, lawyer; b. Bellerose, N.Y., Dec. 19, 1949; s. Albert Thomas and Geraldine Ann (Norton) R.; m. Helen Mary Shannon, Dec. 29, 1973; children: Deirdre Leslie, Nicholas Shannon, Barbara Celeste. AB, Georgetown U., 1971; JD, Cath. U. Am., 1974. Bar: N.Y. 1975, D.C. 1978, U.S. Supreme Ct. 1979. Gen. counsel Broadcort divsn. Merrill Lynch Profl. Clearing Corp., N.Y.C., 1974. Capt. USAR, 1975. Mem. ABA. Republican. Roman Catholic. Avocation: golf. Office: Broadcort divsn Merrill Lynch 222 Broadway Fl 6 New York NY 10038-2510

RUSSO, IRMA HAYDEE ALVAREZ DE, pathologist; b. San Rafael, Mendoza, Argentina, Feb. 28, 1942; came to U.S, 1972; d. Jose Maria and Maria Carmen (Martinez) de Alvarez; m. Jose Russo, Feb. 8, 1969; 1 child, Patricia Alexandra. BA, Escuela Normal MTSM de Balcarce, 1959; MD, U. Nat. of Cuyo, Mendoza, 1970. Diplomate Am. Bd. Pathology. Intern Sch. Medicine Hosps., Argentina, 1969-70; resident in pathology Wayne State U. Sch. Medicine, Detroit, 1976-80. Rsch. asst., instr. Inst. Histology and Embryology Sch. Medicine U. Nat. of Cuyo , 1963-71, assoc. prof. histology Faculty Phys., Chem. and Math. Scis., 1970-72; rsch. assoc. Inst. Molecular and Cellular Evolution U. Miami, Fla., 1972-73; rsch. assoc. exptl. pathology lab. divsn. biol. scis. Mich. Cancer Foun., Detroit, 1973-75, rsch. scientist, 1975-76, vis. rsch. scientist, 1976-82, asst. mem., pathologist, 1982-89, assoc. rsch. mem., 1989-91, co-dir. pathology reference lab., 1982-86, chief exptl. pathology lab., 1989-91; co-dir. Mich. Cancer Found. Lab. Svcs., 1986-91; mem. Fox Chase Cancer Ctr., 1991—; dir. anatomic pathology Am. Oncologic Hosp. Dept. Pathology, 1991-92; dir. Lab. Svcs., 1992-94; chief molecular endocrinology sect. Breast Cancer Rsch. Lab. Fox Chase Cancer Ctr., 1994—; chief resident physician dept. pathology Wayne State U. Sch. Medicine, 1978-80, asst. prof., 1980-82; mem. staff Harper-Grace Hosps., Detroit, 1980-82; adj. prof. Pathology and Cell Biology Jefferson Sch. Medicine/Thomas Jefferson U., 1992—, chairperson Basic Breast Biology Study Sect. U. Calif. Breast Cancer Program, 1997, mem. endocrinology panel peer rev. com. breast cancer rsch. program U.S. Army R & D Command, 1994, 95, 96, 2002, chairperson endocrinology peer rev. com., 1996; ad-hoc mem. biochem. endocrinology study sect. NIH, DHHS, 1994, metabolic pathology study sect., 1996-97; mem. European Commn. Cancer Prevention, 1994—; mem. bd. sci. counselor, sec. health and human svcs. Nat. Toxicology Program Bd., 1994-98; mem. Internat. Life Scis. Inst.-Risk Sci. Inst. Mammary Working Group, 1992—; pres., founder League of Women Against Cancer, Rydal, Pa., 1994—; guest lectr. dept. obstetrics Sch. Medicine U. Nat. of Cuyo, 1965-71; mem. resource devel. subcommittee of the profl. advisory com., Latinas Living Beyond Breast Cancer, 2000—; mem. Breast Cancer Res. Sci. Review Panel, N.J.commr. on cancer rsch., Trenton, N.J., 1997, 2000. Editor-in-chief Jour. Women's Cancer, 1997—; contbr. articles to profl. jours. Rockefeller grantee, 1972-73; Nat. Cancer Inst. grantee, 1978-81, 84-87, 94-99, Am. Cancer Soc. grantee 1988-89, 91-94, U.S. Army Med. R & D Command grantee, 1994-99; recipient Shannon award Nat. Cancer Inst./NHHSS, 1992-94, Gold medal Inst. U. Dexeus, Barcelona, Spain, 2000. Mem. AAAS, Soc. Española Senología y PAtología Mamaria, Nat. Cancer Inst. (breast cancer working group, breast cancer program 1984-88), Nat. Alliance Breast Cancer Orgns. (med. adv. bd. N.Y.C. chpt. 1986—), Ea. Coop. Oncology Group, Coll. Am. Pathologists, Am. Soc. Clin. Pathologists, Am. Assn. Cancer Rsch., Am. Assn. Clin. Chemistry, Internat. Coll. Physicians and Surgeons, Women in Cancer Rsch., The Endocrine Soc., Internat. Assn. Against Cancer, Sigma Xi, Food Quality Protection Act, Sci. Review Bd., Fed. Insecticide Fungi and Rodenticide Act, Adivsory Panel, EPA. Roman Catholic. Office: Fox Chase Cancer Ctr 7701 Burholme Ave Philadelphia PA 19111-2497 E-mail: I_Russo@fccc.edu, Lowac@msn.com.

RUSSO, JOSE, pathologist; b. Mendoza, Argentina, Mar. 24, 1942; came to U.S., 1971; s. Felipe and Teresa (Pagano) R.; m. Irma Haydee, Feb. 8, 1969; 1 child, Patricia Alexandra. BS, Agustin Alvarez Nat. Coll., 1959; MD, U. Nat. Cuyo, 1967. Instr. Inst. Gen. and Exptl. Pathology Med. Sch., Mendoza, 1961-66; asst. prof. Inst. Histology and Embryology, 1967-71; Rockefeller Found. postdoctoral fellow Inst. Molecular and Cellular Evolution U. Miami, 1971-73; chief exptl. pathology lab. Mich. Cancer Found., Detroit, 1973-81; assoc. clin. prof. pathology Wayne State U., 1979-91, chmn. dept. pathology, 1981-91; chmn. dept. pathology, sr. mem. Fox Chase Cancer Ctr., Phila., 1991-94, sr. mem., dir. Breast Cancer Rsch. Lab., 1994—; sci. dir. League of Women Against Cancer. Mem. Mich. Cancer Found., 1982-91; adj. prof. pathology Jefferson Sch. Medicine, Univ. Penn. Sch. Medicine, Phila. Author: Tumor Diagnosis by Electron Microscopy, vol. 1, 1986, vol. 2, 1988, vol. 3, 1990, Immunocytochemistry in Tumor Diagnosis, 1985; editor-in-chief Jour. of Women's Cancer; contbr. over 380 articles to profl. jours. USPHS grantee, 1978, 80, 84, 88, 90, 93, 94, 95, 98, 2000, grantee Am. Cancer Soc., 1982, Dept. of Def., 1999-2002; NRC Argentina fellow, 1967-71. Mem. Am. Assn. Cancer Rsch., Am. Soc. Cell Biology, Soc. Exptl. Biology and Medicine, Tissue Culture Assn., Am. Soc. Clin. Pathology, Internat. Acad. Pathology, Am. Coll. Pathology, Sigma Xi Roman Catholic.

RUSSO, JOSEPH MARIA, public affairs executive; b. Cheverly, Md., Aug. 13, 1950; s. Frank N. Russo and Theresa E. McIntyre; m. Nancy E. Meier, Apr. 4, 1992; children: Emily E., Amy M. Student, Ohio U., 1968-69; BA, Fordham U., 1972; postgrad., New Sch. Social Rsch., 1972-73. Spl. projects writer Prentice-Hall Inc., Englewood Cliffs, N.J., 1972-73; writer, editor Peat Marwick Mitchell & Co., N.Y.C., 1973-76; publs. officer U.S. Trust Co., 1976-79; acct. supr. Harshe-Rotman & Druck, 1979-80; v.p. Norstar Bank, Newburgh, N.Y., 1981-83, First Jersey Nat. Corp., Jersey City, 1983-84, The Hertz Corp., Park Ridge, N.J., 1984-2000; v.p. pub. affairs and corp. comm. Niagara Mohawk, Syracuse, N.Y., 2000—. Recipient Joseph Meddill Patterson award NY Daily News, 1971. Mem. Pub. Rels. Soc. Am. (Silver Anvil 1988), Commerce and Industry Assn. N.J. (bd. dirs. 1998-2000), The Wisemen, The Princeton Club N.Y. (assoc.). Republican. Presbyterian. Avocations: golf, fishing, painting. Home: PO Box 922 354 Sarah Wells Trl Goshen NY 10924-5107 Office: Niagara Mohawk 300 Erie Blvd W Syracuse NY 13202-4250 also: 293 Westbrook Hills Dr Syracuse NY 13215

RUSSO, PATRICIA F. communications executive; BA, Georgetown U.; postgrad. in advanced mgmt., Harvard U., 1989. Sales and mktg. mgmt. exec. IBM, 1973-81; with AT&T (now Lucent Techs. Inc.), 1981—; pres. bus. unit Bus Comm. Sys., 1992-96; exec. v.p. strategy bus. devel. and corp. ops. Lucent Techs., Inc., Murray Hill, NJ, 1997-99; exec. v.p., CEO svc. provider networks Lucent Techs, Inc., Warren, 1999—2000; pres., CEO Lucent Technologies, Murray Hill, 2002—; pres., COO Eastman Kodak, 2000—02. Bd. dirs. Xerox Corp., Schering-Plough Corp., N.J. Mfrs. Ins. Co., Georgetown U. Office: Lucent Techs 600 Mountain Ave New Providence NJ 07974*

RUSSO, PEGGY ANNE, English language educator; b. Sturgis, Mich., Sept. 7, 1940; d. Dale Miller and Virginia (Rifenburg) B.; m. Jerry Russo (dec.); children: Daniel Carleton, Christopher Sanford. AA with honors, Jackson C.C., 1967; BA in English Lang. and Lit., U. Mich., 1972, MA in English Lang. and Lit., 1979, PhD in English Lang. and Lit., 1988. Teaching asst. English dept. U. Mich., Ann Arbor, 1979-83; lectr. Pa. State U., University Park, 1985-88, asst. prof. English Mont Alto, 1988—. Part-time instr. Jackson (Mich.) C.C., 1979; adj. instr. Wayne C.C., Detroit, 1979-83; adj. lectr. U. Mich., 1984-85; participant workshops in field; presenter in field. Sr. editor: The Adelphi Theater Calendar, Part II, 1993; asst. editor RaJah, 1981-83; contbr. articles to profl. jours. Recipient Avery Hopwood award in drama U. Mich., 1979; Roy W. Cowden Meml. fellow U. Mich., 1983, Rackham Thesis grantee, 1982, Dorothy Guies McGuigan scholar, 1983; Cranbrook Writers Conf. scholar Cranbrook Acad., 1979, 80. Mem. MLA, Am. Soc. Theatre Rsch., Internat. Fedn. Theatre Rsch., Pa. Coll. English Assn., Shakespeare Assn. Am. Office: Pa State U Dept English Mont Alto PA 17237 E-mail: u7k@psu.edu.

RUSSO, PIERANTONIO, pediatric cardiac surgeon; b. Bergamo, Italy, Apr. 5, 1954; came to U.S., 1988; s. Vincenzo and Bianca (Raneri) R. Classic Liceum, Collegio San Luigi, Bologna, Italy, 1972; MD cum laude, Bologna U., 1978. Lic. physician, Italy, Pa., Eng. Intern in gen. surgery Castel-San Pietro Hosp., Bologna, 1979-80; intern in emergency medicine Univ. Hosp., 1980-81; asst. dept. surgery Bologna Med. Sch., 1981-82; surg. fellow Cardiothoracic Inst., U. London, 1982-84; rsch. fellow dept. pediatrics Cardiothoracic Inst., Brompton Hosp., London, 1982-84; fellow cardiothoracic and cardiovascular surgery Mayo Clinic and Mayo Found., Rochester, Minn., 1984-86; surg. sr. registrar Cardiothoracic Unit Hosp. for Sick Children, London, 1986-87; dir. CICU and dir. heart transplant program St. Christopher's Hosp. for Children, Phila., 1988—; dir. surg. divsn. Pediatric Heart Inst. Temple U., 1988—, chief pediatric cardiothoracic surgery and assoc. prof., 1988—; surgical dir.heart ctr. for children St. Christopher Hosp. for Children. Dir. fetal rsch. lab. Temple U., 1989—; attending surgeon cardiothoracic surgery Temple U. Hosp.; hon. mem. acad. staff dept. physiology U. Reading, U.K., 1987-88; hon. fellow pediatric cardiology Inst. of Child Health, U. London, 1987-88; vis. prof. cardiothoracic surgery U. Ark., Little Rock, 1992, Bologna Med. Sch., 1992; vis. prof. Baltic Soc. of Cardiac Surgery, Riga, Latvia, 1993; vis. surgeon cardiothoracic surgery, Riga, 1993; lectr. in field; assoc. prof. Cardiothoracic Surgery Med. Coll. Hahnemann U., 1995. Contbr. numerous articles, abstracts to profl. jours., chpts. to books. Recipient Princeps Studiorium aaward in Classic Studies, Bologna, Italy, 1972, Award Gran Croce Al Merito della Sanita, Acad. Internat. Sci. Econ. Sociali, and others, 1986; grantee Brit. Heart Found., 1987, Temple U., 1982. Fellow Internat. Coll. Surgeons, Soc. Acad. Surgeons, Am. Coll. Angiology; mem. AAAS, AMA, Internat. Soc. Heart and Lung Transplantation, Greater Delaware Valley Soc. Transplant Surgeons, N.Y. Acad. Sci., STS, Mayo Alumni Assn., Italian Med. Soc. Roman Catholic. Avocations: music, reading, tennis. Office: St Christophers Hosp Front St and Eric Ave Philadelphia PA 19134-1095

RUSSO, RICHARD, writer; Writer, Camden, Maine. Author: Mohawk, The Risk Pool, Nobody's Fool, Straight Man. Home: 3 High St Camden ME 04843*

RUSSO, ROY LAWRENCE, retired electronic design automation engineer; b. Kelayres, Pa., Nov. 6, 1935; s. Peter John and Mary (Fudge) R.; m. Elizabeth Jean Tautkus, Dec. 26, 1959; children: Mark, Keith, Aileen, Linda. BSE.E., Pa. State U., 1957, MSE.E., 1959, PhDE.E., 1964. Asst. prof. elec. engrng. Pa. State U., University Park, 1964-65; mgr., staff mem. IBM Research, Yorktown Heights, N.Y., 1965-77, mem. research staff, 1983-85, mgr. design automation lab., 1985-94; sr. engr. Gen. Tech. div. IBM, Hopewell Junction, 1977-81, mgr. strategy, 1981-82; cons. prof. elec. engrng Stanford U., 1982-83; retired, 1994. Editor-in-chief IEEE Computer Soc., 1983-85; co-inventor ink jet printer correction system. Treas. St. Patrick's Ch., Yorktown Heights, 1975-77. Recipient Invention Achievement award IBM, 1978, Outstanding Contbn. award IBM, 1968, 89, Outstanding Writing award Pa. State U., 1967 Fellow IEEE (dir. computer disvn. 1989); mem. IEEE Computer Soc. (pres. 1986-87, Svc. award, Centennial medal 1984, Richard E. Merwin award 1992), Eta Kappa Nu.

RUSSO, ROY R. lawyer; b. Utica, N.Y., July 26, 1936; BA, Columbia U., 1956; LLB cum laude, Syracuse U., 1959. Bar: N.Y. 1959, D.C. 1967, U.S. Supreme Ct. 1969. Atty. FCC, 1959—66; ptnr. Cohn and Marks, LLP, Washington, 1966—; spl. counsel Nat. Cath. Conf. for Interracial Justice, 1984—. Mem. Order of Coif, Phi Alpha Delta. Democrat. Home: 6528 Bowie Dr Springfield VA 22150-1309 Office: Cohn and Marks LLP 1920 N St NW Ste 300 Washington DC 20036-1622

RUSSO, STEVEN P. television producer, actor; b. Providence, Oct. 1, 1967; s. Carl F. Russo, Lucille Russo. BS, Emerson Coll., 1993. Quality control staff Todd-AO Video Svcs., Hollywood, Calif., 1994—95; pres. Stricom Prodns., North Attleboro, Mass., 1996—; pub. access coord. AT&T Broadband, Franklin, 1996—; v.p. Ipacs Solar Energy Corp., 2001—. Tchr. Franklin Adult Edn., 2001—01; technician Sprocketman Computer & Web Design, North Attleboro, 1996—. Prodr.: (TV) Strictly Comedy, 2000—01 (First Pl. Alliance For Cmty. Media Awards, 2000, First Pl. Alliance For Cmty. Media Awards, 2001); actor: (comml.) Speedway Heat, 2001; prodr.: Franklin Access Pub. Svc. Announcement, 2002; , author numerous poems and short stories. Video cons. Oasis of Grace Christian Fellowship, Providence, 1990—2002. Pentecostal. Home: Apt 1 22 North Washington St North Attleboro MA 02760 Office: Stricom Prodns Apt 1 22 North Washington St North Attleboro MA 02760 Personal E-mail: steve.russo@juno.com.

RUSSO, THOMAS ANTHONY, lawyer; b. N.Y.C., Nov. 6, 1943; s. Lucio F. and Tina (Iarossi) R.: m. Nancy Felipe, June 18, 1966 (div. 1974); m. Janice Davis, June 10, 1977 (div. 1979); m. Marcy C. Appelbaum, June 16, 1985; children: Morgan Danielle and Alexa Anne (twins), Tyler James. BA, Fordham U., 1965; MBA, JD, Cornell U., 1969. Bar: N.Y., 1970, U.S. Ct. Appeals (2d cir.) 1971, U.S. Dist. Ct. (so. and ea. dists.) N.Y. 1971, U.S. Ct. Appeals (7th cir.) 1982. Staff atty. SEC, Washington, 1969-71; assoc. Cadwalader, Wickersham & Taft, N.Y.C., 1971-75; dir. div. trading and markets Commodity Futures Trading Commn., Washington, 1975-77; ptnr. Cadwalader, Wickersham & Taft, N.Y.C., 1977-92, mgmt. com. vice chmn., chief legal officer; mng. dir., mem. op. com. Lehman Bros., 1993—. Vice chmn. bd. trustees, mem. exec. com. Inst. for Fin. Markets; bd. dirs. Rev. Securities and Commodities Regulation, N.Y.C., Women's Interart Ctr.; trustee, mem. exec. com., chmn. devel. com. Inst. Internat. Edn.; trustee, chmn. audit com. NYU Downtown Hosp., SEC Hist. Soc.; mem. nat. bd. trustees, mem. exec. com. and nominating com., chmn. pension investments com., vice chmn. fin. and audit com. March of Dimes. Author: Regulation of the Commodities Futures and Options Markets; co-author: Regulation of Brokers, Dealers and Securities Markets, Supplement Markets; editorial bd. mem. Internat. Jour. Regulatory Law and Practice; practitioner bd. advisors Stanford Jour. of Law.; mem. editl. bd. Futures and Derivatives Law Report. Mem. ABA (mem. subcom. on exec. coun., fed. regulation of securities, derivative instruments subcom., regulation of futures and derivative instruments), Assn. of Bar of City of N.Y. (chmn. internat. law sub com. of the com. on commodities regulation 1984-85, chmn. com. commodities regulations 1981-82), D.C. Bar Assn., Econ. Club N.Y., Fgn. Policy Assn. Office: Lehman Bros Inc 745 7th Ave 31st Fl New York NY 10018-6801 E-mail: trusso1@lehman.com.

RUSSO, VINCENT BARNEY, music educator; b. Carmel, Calif., Oct. 19, 1944; s. Salvatore Dody and Betty Lou (Posey) R. BA, San Francisco State U., 1967, MA, 1969; lic. de concert, Ecole Normale de Musique, Paris, 1973; PhD, U. Calif., San Diego, 1978. Assoc. in voice U.S. Internat. U., San Diego, 1976-83; assoc. in music Internat. U., London, 1979-80; adj. prof. Tex. Christian U., Ft. Worth, 1986-88, asst. prof. vocal performance pedagogy, 1988-95; faculty Coll of the Redwoods, Mendocino, Calif., 1996—. Apprentice artist Santa Fe Opera Co., 1971; tching. asst., rsch. asst. U. Calif., San Diego, 1974-78; baritone San Diego Opera Co., 1976-82; asst. editor, editor Jour. Rsch. in Singing, Ft. Worth, 1978-95; music coach, dir. Inst. Vocal Studies, Ft. Worth, 1981-88. Baritone soloist French Radio TV, 1971; performer The Merry Widow, PBS, 1977; editor: Jour. Rsch. in Singing and Applied Vocal Pedagog, 1987-95; vocal dir. Gloriana Opera Co., 1995—, Opera Fresca, 1996—; appeared at Mendocino Music Festival, 1996, 97, 98, 99. Recipient Alexander Saunderson award Met. Opera San Francisco, 1969, Young Artist award Nat. Fedn. Music Clubs, 1969, 77, Harriet H. Wooley and Frank Huntington Beebe award, 1972, 73, William M. Sullivan Music Found. award for European audition, 1974. Mem. Internat. Assn. Rsch. in Singing (gen. sec. 1987-95), Nat. Assn. Tchrs. Singing (Singing Artist award 1971), Coll. Music Soc. Avocations: bicycling, hiking, movies, theater.

RUSSO, VINCENT JOSEPH, surgeon; b. Phila., Apr. 15, 1939; s. Joseph Vincent Russo and Yolanda Italia D'Ambrosio; m. Sheila Kay Roos, June 8, 1963; children: Teresa, Joseph, Katrina, Anita. AB, Columbia U., 1960; MD, Boston U., 1964, MPH, 1983. Diplomate Am. Bd. Surgery. Staff surgeon Anna Jaques Hosp., Newburyport, Mass., 1971-88; clin. instr. surgery Harvard Med. Sch., Boston, 1984-98; med. dir. Blue Cross/Blue Shield, Methuen, 1990-98; sr. staff surgeon Lawrence (Mass.) Gen. Hosp., 1990-2000; med. dir. Ea. Mass. Health Ctrs., 1997-2000; clin. instr. Sch. Medicine Boston U., 2001—, 2001—; seaterm ship's physician Mass. Maritime Acad., 2001—. Cons. surgeon Manchester (N.H.) VA Med. Ctr., 1985-98; pres. Essex North Med. Soc., Newburyport, 1988-89; dist. 3 med. examiner Essex County, 1986—; ship's doctor Mass. Maritime Acad., 2001—. Bd. trustees, corporator, mem. auditing com. Newburyport Savings Bank, 1987—; mem. UNICO, Andover, Mass., 1994-97. Lt. cmdr. USN, 1969-71, Vietnam; lt. col. U.S. Army, 1990-91, Desert Storm. Fellow ACS (councillor Mass. chpt. 1995-98); mem. AMA, Soc. Am. Gastrointestinal Endoscopic Surgeons, Mass. Med. Soc. (legis. com. 1990—, del. 2000—), Boston Surg. Soc., Essex North Dist. Med. Soc. (exec. com. 1986—), Rotary (sr. active), Mass. Med. Soc. (reference com. 2002—). Roman Catholic. Avocations: downhill skiing, automobiles, boating, swimming. E-mail: vjrusso@massmed.org.

RUSSON, LEONARD H. state supreme court justice; b. Salt Lake City, May 15, 1933; JD, Utah Coll., 1962. Pvt. practice, Salt Lake City, 1962-84; judge Utah Dist. Ct. (3d dist.), Utah Ct. Appeals; justice Utah Supreme Ct., Salt Lake City, 1995—. Vice chair Utah Bd. Dist. Ct. Judges; mem. Jud. Conduct Commn., Utah Supreme Ct. Adv. Com. on Code of Profl. Conduct. Office: Utah Supreme Ct PO Box 140210 450 S State St Salt Lake City UT 84114-0210*

RUSSOTTI, BETTY JAYNE, shipping company administrator; b. Dayton, Ohio, Dec. 14, 1949; d. Harry William and Marion Jayne (Bold) Trigg; m. Thomas G. Russotti, Feb. 14, 1976 (div. Apr. 1992); children: Stephanie, David. Grad., Orlanda (Fla.) Jr. Coll., 1968, Parks Sch. of Bus., Denver, 1970. Mgr. United Parcel Svc ., Commerce City, Colo., 1972-84; v.p., co-founder Shipping Connection, Golden, 1982-91, pres., 1991-95, dir. tng. West Palm Beach, Fla., 1995—. Republican. Home: 555 Foresteria Dr West Palm Beach FL 33403-3309

RUSSOTTI, PHILIP ANTHONY, lawyer; b. N.Y.C., Mar. 24, 1948; s. Philip Armond and Yolanda (Morelli) R.; m. Mary Wolfe, Jan. 20, 1973 (div. Mar., 1996); children: Thomas, Matthew, Peter; m. Kathleen Kettles, May 25, 1996. BA, Columbia U., 1970; JD, St. John's U., Queens, N.Y., 1973. Bar: N.Y. 1974, U.S. Dist. Ct. (so. dist.) N.Y. 1974, U.S. Dist. Ct. (ea. dist.) N.Y., 1980, U.S. Ct. Appeals (2nd cir.) 1982, U.S. Ct. Appeals (D.C. cir.) 1989, U.S. Ct. Internat. Trade 1986, U.S. Ct. Fed. Claims, 2000, U.S. Supreme Ct., 1997; bd. cert. civil trial atty. Nat. Bd. Trial Advocacy, 1997, U.S. Ct. Fed. Claims, 2000. Bur. chief, Supreme Ct. trial bur. asst. dist. atty. N.Y. County Dist. Atty.'s Office, N.Y.C., 1973-80; pvt. practice, 1980-84; partner Russotti & Barrison, 1985-89, Wingate, Russotti & Shapiro, N.Y.C., 1990—. Lectr. in the field. Gen. counsel Italian Am. Repertory Theatre, N.Y., 1985-90; mem. Prospect Park Alliance, Bklyn., 1996—. Recipient Am. Jurisprudence awards Bancroft Whitney & Lawyers Co-op, 1971, 73. Mem. ABA, ATLA, N.Y. State Bar Assn., N.Y. State Trial Lawyers Assn. Roman Catholic. Home: 433 3rd St Brooklyn NY 11215-2949 Office: Wingate Russotti Shapiro 420 Lexington Ave Rm 2750 New York NY 10170-2793 E-mail: prussotti@yahoo.com.

RUSSOTTO, PAUL, artist, educator; b. N.Y.C., May 28, 1944; s. John and Margaret Russotto; m. Ellen Russotto, Aug. 30, 1969; children: Vita, Luca. Student, Art Students League, N.Y.C., 1962-63. Painting and drawing instr., MFA program Parsons Sch. Design, N.Y.C., 1978-80, N.Y. Studio Sch. Drawing, Painting and Sculpture, N.Y.C., 1980-82, Vt. Studio Ctr., Johnson, 1985—, Internat. Sch. Art, Montecastello di Vibio, Italy, 1993, 94, Pa. Acad. Fine Arts, Phila., 1997, SUNY, Binghamton, 1997, Nat. Acad. Design, N.Y.C., 1999-2000. One-man shows include Forty-year Drawing Survey 1960-2000, traveling to U.N.C. and Italy, exhibited in group shows at Mus. Chateau de Rochefort-en-Terre, Brittany, France, 1995, Omaggio a Marino Marini, Venice, Florence, Rome, Paris, 2000, Heckscher Mus. Fine Art, Huntington, N.Y., 2000, 8 Artisti da New York, Florence, Rome, Montecatini Terme, Italy, 2001, Angeli, Rome, Florence, Montecatini Terme, Venice, Romania, 2001—02, numerous others, Represented in permanent collections Met. Mus. Art, N.Y.C., Heckscher Mus. Fine Art, GE Corp., Novartis Corp., East Hanover, N.J. Recipient Purchase award, AAAL, N.Y.C., 1997, Found. award, Rochefort-en-Terre Found., 1995. Mem.: Nat. Acad. Design (cert. of merit 1996, Palmer Meml. prize 2000, Henry Ward Ranger award 2001). Office: P O Box 385 Canal St Sta New York NY 10013-0385

RUST, EDWARD BARRY, JR. insurance company executive, lawyer; b. Chgo., Aug. 3, 1950; s. Edward Barry Sr. and Harriett B. (Fuller) R.; m. Sally Buckler, Feb. 28, 1976; 1 child, Edward Barry III. Student, Lawrence U., 1968-69; BS, Ill. Wesleyan U., 1972; JD, MBA, So. Meth. U., 1975. Bar: Tex. 1975, Ill. 1976. Mgmt. trainee State Farm Ins. Cos., Dallas, 1975-76, atty. Bloomington, 1976, sr. atty., 1976-78, asst. v.p., 1978-81, v.p., 1981-83, exec. v.p., 1983-85; pres., CEO State Farm Life Ins. Cos., 1985—87; CEO, chmn. State Farm Mutual Auto Ins. Co., 1987—. Pres. and bd. dirs. State Farm Investment Mgmt. Corp., State Farm Internat. Services, Inc., State Farm Cos. Found.; bd. dirs. exec. and investment coms. State Farm Annuity and Life Ins. Co., State Farm Mut. Automobile Ins. Co., State Farm Life Ins. Co., State Farm Fire and Casualty, State Farm Gen. Trustee Ill. Wesleyan U., 1985—; mem. adv. coun. Grad. Sch. Bus. Stanford U., 1987-94; mem. bus. adv. coun. Coll. Commerce and Bus. Adminstrn. U. Ill. Mem. Am. Enterprise Inst., Bus. Roundtable (chmn. edn. task force), Tex. State Bar Assn., Ill. Bar Assn., Am. Inst. Property and Liability Underwriters (trustee 1986-96), Ins. Inst. Am. (trustee 1986-96), Ins. Inst. for Highway Safety (vice chmn.), Nat. Alliance of Bus. (chmn. 1998—), Ill. Bus. Roundtable (chmn. 1998—). Office: State Farm Ins Cos 1 State Farm Plz E-12 Bloomington IL 61710-0001*

RUST, LIBBY KAREN, fundraising and public relations counsel; b. York, Maine, Feb. 8, 1951; d. Myron Davis and Meta Mildred (Libby) R. BA, Wheaton Coll., 1973; MS, Columbia U., 1977. Day care field asst. Childhood Ednl. Enrichment Program, Waterville, Maine, 1974-75; cons. Ctr. for Cmty. Planning and Cons., N.Y.C., 1975-76; intern Morgan Guaranty Trust Co., 1976; staff asst. subcom. on mental health Task Force on N.Y.C. Fiscal Crisis, 1976-77; auditor AT&T, N.Y.C., 1977; budget examiner Legis. Office of Budget Rev., 1977-78; exec. dir. Strafford County Human Svcs., Dover, N.H., 1978-79; dir. allocations and agy. rels. United Way, Inc., Portland, Maine, 1979-82, planning and allocations divsn. dir., 1982-84; exec. dir. Seacoast United Way, Portsmouth, N.H., 1984-87; dir. devel. Am. Cancer Soc., L.A., 1987-88; assoc. dir. St. Vincent Med. Ctr., 1988-89; dir. ann. giving St. Joseph Hosp. Found., Orange, Calif., 1989-91, asst. dir. devel., 1991-93; dir. devel. Cmty. Health Svcs., Inc., Portland, Maine, 1993-94; exec. dir. York County Tech. Coll. Found., 1994-99; founder Rust Comm. Group, 1999—. Mem. budget com. Town of York, 1979-80; trustee Kents Hill Sch., 1991-93, York Pub. Libr., 1999-2002, Mercy Hosp. VNA-Homecare, Pine Tree Soc., Maine. Mem. Assn. Fundraising Profls. No. New Eng. (pres.-elect 2002), Pine Tree Soc., Jr. League Portland. Republican. Office: PO Box 1227 York Harbor ME 03911-1227

RUST, PATRICIA JOAN, television production company executive, writer, producer; b. L.A., Sept. 24, 1958; d. William Evans Jr. and Jacquelyn (Knox) R. BA, UCLA, 1978, postgrad., 1978-80, 87-89; student, Am. Film Inst. Writer, producer PBS, L.A., 1978-79, creator, host On Cue; corr. ABC-TV, L.A., 1979-82; pres. Patricia Rust Prodns., 1982—. Host, writer, creator, producer numerous syndicated spls., 1982-89; writer, producer comedy shows and spls. ABC, NBC, CBS and PBS. Film and TV writer, story editor: including network comedy spls., TV movies, episodes; author: (children's picture book) The King of Skittledeedoo, 1999, 3d edit., 2001 (Parents' Choice award winning literacy book); assoc. editor: Prodrs. Guild Mag., 1990—; contbr. Pres., founder, The Rust Found. for Literacy, 1999—; founder JackietheAngel.com, 1999, PowerforKids.com, 2000. Recipient Golden Mike award Radio and TV News Assn., Hollywood, 1984; named Best Network Comedy Writer NBC, 1990; winner comedy writing competition Am. Film

Inst., 1989. Mem. NATAS, Hollywood Radio and TV Soc., Producers Guild, Writers Guild Am., Am. Film Inst., Daily Bruin Alumni Assn. Office: Patricia Rust Prodns # 924 12021 Wilshire Blvd # 924 Los Angeles CA 90025-1206 E-mail: patricia@powerforkids.com.

RUST, ROBERT FRANCIS, retired publishing executive; b. Herrick, S.D., Oct. 26, 1927; s. Charles William and Agatha Susan R.; m. Wilma Lorraine LeBeau, Oct. 18, 1948; children: Randal, Roberta, Ann, Mary. Student, U. Houston, 1950-53. Billing clk. Armour Fertilizer Works, Houston, 1950-53; v.p. Gulf Pub. Co., 1953-98. With USAF, 1948-49.

RUST, ROBERT WARREN, retired lawyer; b. Jamaica, N.Y., Aug. 16, 1928; s. Adolf Harry and Helen Margaret (Dauth) R.; m. Mary Ruth Duncan, Jan. 28, 1953 (dec. Aug. 1981); children: Benjamin, Lani, Debra, Bonnie, Randall, Wendy; m. Theresa Maria Nagymihaly, Dec. 18, 1982; 1 stepchild, Brandon. Student, St. Lawrence U., 1946-48; JD, U. Miami, Coral Gables, Fla., 1954; postgrad., Naval War Coll., 1975. Bar: Fla. 1954, U.S. Ct. Appeals (5th cir.) 1959, U.S. Supreme Ct. 1960, U.S. Customs Ct. 1960. Police officer City of Miami (Fla.) Police Dept., 1953-54; asst. auditor First Nat. Bank, Miami, 1954-56; assoc. Smathers, Thompson & Dyer, 1956-57; asst. U.S. atty. Dept. of Justice, 1957-61; assoc. Shutts & Bowen, 1961-63; chief asst. county solicitor Palm Beach County, West Palm Beach, Fla., 1963-66; state rep. Fla. Legislature, Palm Beach, Martin County, Fla., 1966-68; chief counsel House Crime Com., Tallahassee, 1968-69; U.S. atty. So. Dist. Fla., Miami, 1969-77; ptnr. Rust & Rust, 1977-89; ret., 1989;. 1989. Col. USMCR, 1947-88, Ret. Recipient award of merit for assisting in preventing assassination Pres. of U.S., Sec. of Treasury and Chief U.S. Secret Svc., 1964, Outstanding Legislator award St. Petersburg Times, 1967, Fla. lodge Fraternal Order Police, 1967, So. Fla. Law Enforcement Comty. award for Honesty, Integrity and Leadership as U.S. Atty., 1977, Outstanding Svc. award Nat. Exec. Bd. of Fed. Criminal Investigators, 1977, Outstanding Svc. award Secret Svc., 1977. Mem. NRA, Fla. Bar, Navy League, Marine Corps Res. Officers Assn. (pres. West Palm Beach chpt. 1964-65), Am. Legion, Mil. Order World Wars, Res. Officers Assn., Key Biscayne Yacht Club, Capitol Hill Club, Audobon Soc., Nat. Wildlife Fedn., Defenders of Wildlife, Rock Mt. Elk Found., Ducks Unlimited, Sierra Club, Rotary. Republican. Presbyterian. Avocations: sailing, shooting, skiing, dog sledding. Office: 1700 S Bayshore Ln Apt 2A Miami FL 33133-4041 Home: PO Box 7339 0251 Gold Nugget Dr Breckenridge CO 80424

RUST, S. MURRAY, III, builder, real estate developer; b. Pitts., Oct. 31, 1939; s. S. Murray and Gladys (Over) R.; m. Shirley Irene Bone, Dec. 22, 1964; children: Robert Bruce, Richard Mark. BA in Applied Sci., Lehigh U., 1961, BSME, 1962. With Rust Engring. Co., Pitts., 1962-72; pres. Montgomery and Rust, 1972—. Trustee Chatham Coll.; chmn. Builder Svcs. Inc., 2000—. Pres. The Rust Found., 1997— Mem. Builders Assn. Met. Pitts. (pres. 1980, Builder of the Yr. 1977), Pa. Builders Assn. Harrisburg (bd. dirs., v.p., treas., pres. 1990, Builder of the Yr. 1991), Nat. Assn. Home Builders, Washington (bd. dirs.). Avocations: tennis, skiing. Office: Montgomery & Rust Inc Castle Town Sq S 4284 Route 8 Allison Park PA 15101-1439

RUST, WILLIAM DAVID, JR. retired structural engineer; b. Washington, Oct. 11, 1931; s. William David and Anna Mae (Lyles) R.; m. Eunice Charles Williams, Oct. 24, 1953; children: Diann Yvonne Rust-Tierney, Cheryl Frances, William Douglas. BS in Civil Engring., Howard U., 1954; postgrad., Cath. U. Am., 1956-57; MS in Engring., George Washington U., 1962; postgrad., U. Va., 1973-74. Registered profl. engr., Mass. Naval architect Phila. Naval Shipyard, 1954; structural engr. U.S. Gen. Svcs. Adminstrn., Washington, 1956-92; ret. 1992. Lectr. civil engring. Fed. City Coll. (now U. D.C.), Washington, 1973; mem. com.Interagency Seismic Safety, Washington, 1978-90, ASCE, Found. and Excavation Stds., N.Y.C., 1978-95, AISC, Steel Specification Simplification, Chgo., 1980-81; mem. coms. Fed. Constrn. Coun., Washington, 1978-90. Chmn. cub pack no. 24 Boy Scouts Am., Washington, 1968; clk. session Northminster Presbyn. Ch., Washington, 1972; commr. genn. assembly Presbyn. Ch. U.S., Ft. Worth, 1973. Lt. C.E., U.S. Army, 1954-56. Fellow ASCE; mem., NSPE, Structural Stability Rsch. Coun. (mem.-at-large), Tau Beta Pi (life). Achievements include administration of development of first nationwide microfilming of design and construction drawings system for the U.S. General Services Adminstration. Home: 7600 Alaska Ave NW Washington DC 20012-1469 E-mail: w.rustjr@worldnet.att.net.

RUST, WILLIAM JAMES, retired steel company executive; b. Newark, Mar. 21, 1929; s. William G. and Anna (Glavin) R.; m. Adele M. Laubner, July 29, 1950; 1 dau., Rita Marie. BS in Math. magna cum laude, Boston Coll., 1953; MBA with high distinction, Harvard, 1955. With Nat. Cash Register Co., 1955-68, dir. distbn. and material, 1964-68; v.p., treas. Indian Head, Inc., 1968-72, v.p. planning and fin., 1972-77; v.p. fin. Nat. Steel Co., Pitts., 1977-84, ret., 1984. Pres. Social Health Agy., Dayton, Ohio, 1966-68; chmn. United Fund campaigns, Dayton, 1962-68; Bd. dirs. Good Samaritan Hosp., 1965-68. Served with USAAF, 1946-49. Mem. Nat. Assn. Accountants (bd. dirs. Dayton 1960-63), Fin. Execs. Inst. Clubs: Duquesne, Fox Chapel Golf. Home: 4729 Tahiti Dr Bonita Springs FL 34134-7172

RUSTEN, JON E. financial planner, risk management executive; b. Bagley, Minn., Feb. 14, 1943; s. Elmer R. and Doris Olga (Hudspeth) R.; m. Kay Diane Dale, Dec. 27, 1968; children: Chad, Kyle, Shanna. BS in Bus., Moorhead State U., 1966; MS in Bus., Bemidji State U., 1985; postgrad., Drake U., 1969-70. CFP. Bus. instr. Gen. Learning Corp., Clinton, Iowa, 1968-69, Des Moines Pub. Schs., 1969-71, N.W. Tech. Coll., Minn., 1971-72; owner, mgr. Ben Franklin Store, Park Rapids, 1972-81; dist. rep. Luth. Brotherhood, Bemidji, 1981-88, advanced mktg. specialist Grand Forks, N.D., 1988-96; region v.p. Fin. Instsn. Group Am. Express Fin. Advisors, Mpls., 1996—. Mem. planning coun. Red River Valley Estate Planning Coun., Fargo, N.D., 1989-96; bd. dirs. North Valley Underwriters, Grand Forks, 1989-91; pres. Northwest Minn. Life Underwriters, Bemidji, 1985-86; pub. rels. dir. N.D. Life Underwriters, Bismark, 1992-96. Regional dir. Girl Scouts U.S., Grand Forks, 1993-96; mem. sml. bus. advisory, Grand Forks C. of C., 1990-93; bd. dirs. Sharon Luth., Grand Forks, 1992-96; mem. govtl. affairs coun. Grand Forks Chamber, 1991-93; bd. dirs. Willow Bible Camp, 1990-96. Named to White House Sml. Bus. Conf., U.S. Govt., Washington, 1980. Mem. Jaycees (named one of 10 Outstanding Minnesotans 1978), Rotary 9bd. dirs. 1971-92, Outstanding Project award 1979), Million Dollar Round Table. Republican. Avocations: winter skiing, tennis, sailing, golf, restore automobiles. Office: American Express Fin Advisors 3520 Prairie Lake Rd Grand Rapids MN 55744-9213

RUSTIN, RUDOLPH BYRD, III, surgeon, educator; b. Charleston, S.C., May 14, 1957; s. Rudolph Byrd and Mary Pringle (Herrin) R.; m. Sandra Lee Talbott, Nov. 28, 1985; children: Jonathan, Jeffrey. BS in Chemistry cum laude, Hampden Sydney Coll., 1979; MD, Med. U. S.C., 1983. Diplomate Am. Bd. Surgery, Am. Bd. Colon and Rectal Surgery. Intern Cleve. Clinic Found., 1983-84, resident, 1984-88, chief resident gen. surgery, 1987-88, fellow, 1988-89; private practice colon rectal surgery Charleston, 1989—; clin. assoc. surgery Med. U. S.C., 1989—. Active staff Roper Hosp., Charleston, St. Francis Xavier Hosp., Trident Med. Ctr., AMI East Cooper Community Hosp., Mt. Pleasant, S.C.; presenter in field. Fellow ACS, Am. Soc. Colon Rectal Surgeons, Southeastern Surgical Congress; mem. Med. Soc. S.C., S.C. State Med. Assn., S.C. Med. Assn. (del.), So. Med. Assn., Charleston County Med. Soc., Phi Beta Kappa. Office: 125 Doughty St Ste 770 Charleston SC 29403-5764

RUSTIN, VARIE BEATRICE, community volunteer; b. Hawkinsville, Ga., Dec. 29, 1955; d. Jessie Lewis Rustin and Janis Marie Jones Rustin Stewart; m. Nick Pierce Pollett, Nov. 25, 1978 (div. May 1992); m. John Gerald Klayer, Feb. 24, 1996. BBA in Acctg. and Mgmt., Ga. Coll. and State U., 1988; Diploma in Gen. Banking, Am. Inst. Banking, Atlanta, 1994. Fundraiser, chair AAUW, Warner Robins, Ga., 1993-94, membership v.p., 1994-96, edn. chair, 1996-97, Reading Is Fundamental chair, 1997-98; v.p. bd. dirs. Houston Arts Alliance, 1998-99, pres. bd. dirs., 1999-2000, county assessment chair, 2000—01; spl. articles chair Officers' Spouses Club OSC, Robins AFB, 2002—. Judge Relay for Life events Am. Cancer Soc., Warner Robins, 1999; judge state competitive events Ga. Tech. Student Assn., 2000, 2001, 2002; mentor Houston County Assn. Exceptional Children; mem. fine Arts Soc. Mid. Ga., Hawkinsville-Pulaski County Arts Alliance. Named Cmty. Leader/C. of C., Houston Arts Alliance, 2000. Mem. AAUW (rec. sec. 1990-91, chair nominating com. 1992, 94, chair cmty. vols. award com. 1992), Nat. Speleological Soc. (local rep. 1992—, mid. Ga. grotto trip coord. 2001-), Ga. Coll. and State U. Alumni Soc., Ga. Assn. Cmty. Arts Agencies, Ga. Coll. & State Univ. Acctg. Assn., Mid. Ga. Grotto (sec. 1992—), Nat. Vocat. Tech. Honor Soc. Avocations: spelunking/caving, reading, writing, horses, travel. Home: PO Box 350 Bonaire GA 31005 E-mail: cavecrab@hom.net.

RUSU, SIR ANDREW PETER (SIR ANDREW RUSU BARON ROCHEFORT), ambassador, lawyer; b. Arad, Romania, Mar. 24, 1949; s. Andrew and Yank Rusu. Eötvoös Jorant, Law Sch., Budapest, Hungary, 1981; BA, Trinity Coll., 1997. Consul gen., amb. Holy See of Antioch, N.Y.C., 1991—; amb. at large Diplomatic Mission of Liberia, 1997—. Internat. law cons. Rep. senatorial Innter Cir., Washington, 1993, Round Table, 1996. Mem. N.Y. Acad. Scis., Am. Inst. of Sci. and Tech., Knight of Malta (chevaliers). Avocations: reading, tennis, travel, swimming. Office: Diplomatic Mission of Liberia 95-09 43rd Ave Flushing NY 11373 E-mail: andrewrusu@aol.com.

RUSUNEN, ROBERT LEE, purchasing consultant; b. Missoula, Mont., Mar. 16, 1946; m. Sherry M. Rusunen, June 16, 1972. BS in Bus., U. Mont., 1971; MBA in Bus., Wash. State U., 1977. Cert. purchasing mgr.; cert. prodn. inventory mgmt. Buyer, merchandise mgr. Hart-Aldin Co., Billings, Mont., 1971-75; region materials mgr. GE Supply, Seattle, 1976-79; dir. purchasing Riedel Internat., Portland, Oreg., 1979-82, v.p. purchasing and support svcs., 1982-84; mgr. corp. purchasing Pacific Telecom, Inc., Vancouver, Wash., 1985-97; materials team mgr. Pacificorp, Portland, 1997-98; prin. cons. Price Waterhouse Coopers, 1998-2001; dir. procurement Kelly Group, LLC, Vancouver, Washington, 2001—. V.p. Wishing Wells Home Owners Assn., Ridgefield, Wash., 1996-97. Staff sgt., USAF, 1964-68. Me. Inst. for Supply Mgmt., Am. Prodn. and Inventory Control Soc., Constrn. Owners Assn. Am., Nat. Contract Mgmt. Assn., VFW. Home: 2730 S Cornett Dr Ridgefield WA 98642-8558 Office: Kelly Group LLC 200 Grand Blvd Vancouver WA 98661 E-mail: rrusunen@attbi.com.

RUTA, SUZANNE, writer; b. N.Y.C., June 11, 1940; d. Nelson and Tillie Frank; m. Peter Paul Ruta, Sept. 26, 1969; children: Sebastian, Garance, Vanessa. BA, Barnard Coll., 1961; postgrad., U. Grenoble (France), 1961-62, NYU, 1967-69. Tchg. asst. in French NYU, 1967-69; asst. fiction editor Esquire mag., N.Y.C., 1969-70; freelance writer, editor, translator, 1970—. Author: Stalin in the Bronx, 1987 (N.Y. Times Notable Book of Yr. 1987); social satire columnist Wig Wag mag., Working Mother mag.; contbr., reviewer N.Y. Times, The Village Voice, Newsday, others. Bd. dirs. Somos un Pueblo Unido, Santa Fe, N.Mex., 1995-99. Fulbright grantee, France, 1961-62.

RUTA, THOMAS V. professional sports team executive, accounting executive; married. BS summa cum laude, Fordham U., 1966; MBA with distinction, Pace U.; postgrad. in law, Fordham U. CPA, N.Y., N.J., Minn. Founding ptnr. Behan, Ling & Ruta, N.Y.C., now chmn., pres.; ltd. ptnr. Pitts. Penguins. Ltd. ptnr. Manchester Hockey Group. Office: 358 5th Ave 9th Fl New York NY 10001 E-mail: truta@blrcpaspc.com.

RUTAN, CHARLES R. musician; b. May 10, 1966; s. Frank and Peggy (Hendry) Rutan; m. Catherine Mayer, May 29, 1999; 1 child Gwendolyn. MusB in Composition summa cumlaude, Univ. of Arts, Phila., 1992; postgrad. in music instrn., Chestnut Hill Coll., 1994; postgrad., Pierce Ctr., Glasgow, Scotland, 1998. Cert. tchr. Pa. CEO, founder Bagpipes FAO, Phila.; mgr., prin. oboist Chestnut Hill Orch. Performed for Pres. George Bush, First Lady of Pa., Phila. Police Commr.; opened for Rod Stewart Trump Taj Majal, Atlantic City; piper MiGaea Yacht; featured on various TV programs, mags., newspapers, including Phila. Weddings, Modern Bride mags., WKY, WPVI, WPHL, Finnish Nat. TV, Irish Am. Newspaper, others; ceremonial piper retirement ball for Phila. Episcopal Bishop; poper installation ceremonies Phila. Archdiocesan parishes, Presbytery ofcls., organ dedication ceremonies; performer Irish Uilleann (Union) Pipes, Renaissance Bagpipes. Composer (symphonic music). Mem.: ASCAP (spl. composer award 1994), Music Educators Nat. Conf., Eastern U.S. Pipeband Assn., Am. Fedn. Musicians, Internat. Double Reed Soc. E-mail: bagpipesfao@worldned.att.net.

RUTANEN, ROY STEWART, producer, television personality; b. Putnam, Conn., July 1, 1947; s. Phyllis Morse Rutanen; children: Rene, Jade Babey, Jessica Smith, Sarah. BA, U. Mass., 1998. TV reporter, anchor Sta. KENS-TV, San Antonio, 1982-87; TV reporter Sta. KMOL-TV, Tex., 1987-88; anchor, reporter Sta. XTRA-TV, San Diego, 1988-89; writer, prodr., dir. Electronic Scribe, Southbridge, Mass., 1990-2000; talk-show host Sta. WESO-TV, 1998-99, Sta. 13-10 WORC-TV, Worcester, Mass., 1999—. Author, narrator (documentary) Holy Ground, 1996; (video) Welcome to Strubridge, 1999; author, prodr. (documentary) Reflections of Belchertown, 2000; Writer, prodr. Rehabilitative Resources, Inc., 2000 (Telly award 2001). Active Am. Cancer Soc., Southbridge, 1999. With U.S. Army, 1966-69. Recipient 2d pl. Tex. AP, 1982, Best Feature award Soc. Profl. Journalists, 1984, award of Honor Tex. Safety Assn., 1984, Media award of the Yr., 1986, 2 Golden Mike awards, 1988, 2 Telly awards, 1996. Home and Office: 901 N Woodstock Rd Southbridge MA 01550 Fax: 508-764-3572. E-mail: royr2000@juno.com.

RUTENBERG-ROSENBERG, SHARON LESLIE, retired journalist; b. Chgo., May 23, 1951; d. Arthur and Bernice (Berman) Rutenberg; m. Michael J. Rosenberg, Feb. 3, 1980; children: David Kaifel and Jonathan Reuben (twins), Emily Mara. Student, Harvard U., 1972; BA, Northwestern U., 1973, MSJ., 1975; cert. student pilot. Reporter-photographer Lerner Home Newspapers, Chgo., 1973-74; corr. Medill News Service, Washington, 1975; reporter-newsperson, sci. writer UPI, Chgo., 1975-84; ret., 1984. Interviewer: exclusives White House chief of staff, nation's only mother and son on death row; others. Vol. Chgo.-Read Mental Health Ctr. Recipient Peter Lisagor award for exemplary journalism in features category, 1980, 81; Golden Key Nat. Adv. Bd. of Children's Oncology Service Inc., 1981; Media awards for wire service feature stories, 1983, 84, wire service news stories, 1983, 84, all from Chgo. Hosp. Pub. Relations Soc. Mem. Profl. Assn. Diving Instrs., Nat. Assn. Underwater Instrs., Hon. Order Ky. Cols., Hadassah, Sigma Delta Chi, Sigma Delta Tau Home: 745 Marion Ave Highland Park IL 60035-5123

RUTFORD, ROBERT HOXIE, geologist, educator; b. Duluth, Minn., Jan. 26, 1933; s. Skuli and Ruth (Hoxie) R.; m. Marjorie Ann, June 19, 1954; children: Gregory, Kristian, Barbara. BA, U. Minn., 1954, MA, 1963, PhD, 1969; DSc (hon.), St Petersburg State Tech U., Russia, 1994. Football and track coach Hamline U., 1958-62; rsch. fellow U. Minn., 1963-66; asst. prof. geology U. S.D., 1967-70, assoc. prof., 1970-72, chmn. dept. geology, 1968-72, chmn. dept. physics, 1971-72; dir. Ross Ice Shelf Project U. Nebr., Lincoln, 1972-75; dir. divsn. Polar Programs NSF, Washington, 1975-77; vice chancellor for research and grad. studies, prof. geology U. Nebr., 1977-82, interim chancellor, 1980-81; pres., prof. geoscis. U. Tex., Dallas, 1982-94, Excellence in Edn. Found. prof. of geoscis., 1994—. U.S. del. to Sci. Com. on Antarctic Rsch., 1986-2002, v.p., 1996-98, pres., 1998-2002; chmn. NRC Polar Rsch. Bd., 1991-95. Mem. editl. bd. Issues in Sci. and Tech., 1991-94. Trustee Baylor Coll. Dentistry, 1989—. 1st lt. U.S. Army, 1954-56. Recipient Antarctic Svc. medal, 1964, Disting. Svc. award NSF, 1977, Ernie Gunderson award for svc. to amateur athletics S.D. AAU, 1972, Outstanding Achievement award U. Minn., 1993, "M" Club Lifetime Achievement award, 1995. Fellow Geol. Soc. Am.; mem. Antarctican Soc. (pres. 1988-90), Arctic Inst. N.Am., Explorers Club, Am. Polar Soc. (hon.), Philos. Soc. Tex., St. Petersburg Acad. Engring. (Russia), Tex. Acad. Sci., Nebr. Acad. Sci., Cosmos Club, Sigma Xi. Lutheran. Home: 1882 Quail Ln Richardson TX 75080-3456 Office: Univ Tex Dallas Geosciences Program Richardson TX 75083-0688

RUTH, BRYCE CLINTON, JR. lawyer; b. Greenwood, Miss., Dec. 19, 1948; s. Bryce Clinton and Kathryn (Arant) R.; m. Martha M. Ruth; children: Lauren Elizabeth, Bryce Clinton III. BS, Delta State U., 1970; JD, Memphis State U., 1979. Bar: Tenn., 1979, U.S. Dist. Ct. (mid. dist.) Tenn. 1979, U.S. Ct. Mil. Appeals 1991, U.S. Ct. Appeals (6th cir.), 1994. Criminal investigation spl. agt. IRS, Memphis and Nashville, 1971-82; asst. dist. atty. Dist. Atty. Office, Gallatin, Tenn., 1982-89; asst. pub. defender Pub. Defender's Office, 1989-90; pvt. practice White House, 1989—; judge City of Cross Plains, Tenn., 1992—; juvenile ct. referee judge Robertson County, 1995-98. Mem. dist. investigating com. dist. VI Tenn. Bd. Law Examiners, 1989—; mem. child enforcement steering com. Asst. Dist. Atty. Office, 1983-84, chmn. legis. subcom., 1985; lectr. in field. Chmn. fin. com. White House First United Meth. Ch., 1983-88, trustee, 1988-90, chmn., 1990; trustee Vol. State Coll. Found., 1993-2000, chmn., 1998-99; bd. dirs. Crime Stoppers of Sumner County, 1989-94; bd. dirs. White House Youth Soccer, 1992-93, coach, 1987-91; bd. dirs. White House Soccer Booster Club, 1996-2000, pres., 1998; bd. dirs. Sumner County CASA, 1992-93; coach Jr. Pro Football, 1980-85; video cameraman for football team White House H.S., 1991—; mem. Leadership Sumner, 1989; bd. dirs. White House Men's Club, 1981-83, 85-88, v.p., 1984, 88, pres., 1985. Lt. col. JAGC, USAR, 1983—. Recipient Disting. Expert award for pistol marksmanship U.S. Treasury, Disting. Svc. award City of White House. Mem. NRA, Tenn. Bar Assn. (del. 1993—, mem. family law code revision commn. 1996—), Sumner County Bar Assn. (chmn. domestic rels. com. 1984-85, v.p. 1998-99, pres. 1999-2000), White House Area C. of C. (bd. dirs. 1990-95, pres. 1993-94), United C. of C. of Sumner County (pres. 1995). Avocations: scuba diving, skiing, golf, hunting, pistol shooting. Office: 3210 Hwy 31W PO Box 68 White House TN 37188-0068 E-mail: bcruthjr@aol.com.

RUTH, BYRON EDWARD, civil engineering educator; b. Chgo., Mar. 25, 1931; s. Edward Luther and Evelyn Pearl (Wells) R.; m. Margarete Rohweder, Sept. 10, 1960; children: Boyd Owen, Toni Karen. BS, Mont. State U., 1955; MS, Purdue U., 1959; PhD, W.Va. U., 1967. Registered profl. engr., Ind., W.Va., Fla. Field engr. Walter H. Knapp, Drummond Island, Mich., 1959; asst. dir. R & D, Symons Mfg. Co., Des Plaines, Ill., 1960-61; instr. civil engring. W.Va. U., Morgantown, 1961-67, asst. prof., 1967-70; assoc. prof. civil engring. U. Fla., Gainesville, 1970-77, prof., 1977-2000, prof. emeritus, 2000—. Cons. transp., materials and design. Contbr. numerous articles to profl. jours. With U.S. Army, 1956-58. Recipient Ronald D. Kenyon rsch. award, 1996. Mem. ASCE, ASTM (chmn. D04 exec. com. 1993-94), Assn. Asphalt Paving Technologists (pres. 1986), Transp. Rsch. Bd. (chmn. com. A2D05 1994-99, mem. SuperPave com.), Can. Tech. Asphalt Assn. (hon.), Sigma Xi, Tau Beta Pi. Achievements include patents for concrete forming equipment. Office: U Fla Dept. Civil and Coastal Engring Gainesville FL 32611-6580

RUTH, DAVID ALLEN, accountant; b. St. Louis, Apr. 7, 1956; s. Donald Avery and Eugenia Elizabeth (Heep) R. BS in Bus. Adminstrn., Drake U., 1978; MBA, St. Louis U., 1988; MS in Taxation, Fontbonne Coll., 1997. CPA, Mo. Jr. acct. Mueller & Herring CPA's, St. Louis, 1978, Meriwether, Wilson & Sitrick, Des Moines, 1978-79, Denman & Co CPA's, Des Moines, 1979-80; acct. Accountemps of St. Louis, 1981-83; sr. tax acct. ITT Fin. Corp., St. Louis, 1983-96; state and local tax specialist Arthur Andersen LLP, 1996-2000, Thermadyne Holdings Corp., St. Louis, 2000—01. Fund raiser Drake U. Alumni St. Louis; mem. Mo. Hist. Soc., St. Louis. Fellow Life Mgmt. Inst.; mem. AICPA, Mo. Soc. CPAs (co-chair tax com. St. Louis chpt., chair legis. subcom. state tax com.). Roman Catholic. Home: 7500 Hillsdale Dr Saint Louis MO 63121-4748 E-mail: davidallenruth@cs.com.

RUTH, EDWARD B. principal; b. Lancaster, Pa., Aug. 23, 1943; s. Edward B. and Jeanne L. (Schaeffer) R.; m. Betsy A. Lorenz, Aug. 28, 1965; 1 child, Heather L. BS in Biology, Lebanon Valley Coll., Annville, Pa., 1965; MEd, Millersville (Pa.) U., 1970; cert. secondary prin., Temple U., 1990. Cert. secondary prin., secondary tchr. gen. sci., biology. Sci. tchr. Milton Hershey (Pa.) Sch., 1965-87, mid. sch. asst. prin., 1987-92, mid. sch. prin., 1992-99; coord. pre-svc. and in-svc. tng., 1999—; asst. athletic dir. Milton Hershey (Pa.) Sch., 1983-87. Recreation supr. Milton Hershey Sch.; mgr. Palmyra Swimming Pool; evaluation team Pa. Assn. Pvt. Acad. Schs., 1991; planning com. Pa. Commonwealth Partnership, F&M Coll., Lancaster, Pa., 1987; biol. safety and recombinant DNA com. Hershey Med. Ctr., 1987—; union negotiations team Milton Hershey Sch., 1994, 2002; judge regional and state meetings Pa. Jr. Acad. Sci., Capital Area Sci. and Engring. Fairs, Pa. Coll. Energy Debates; bd. dirs. Pa. Staff Devel. Coun.; mem. Nat. Staff Devel. Coun. Author, editor: Energy Teaching Units Energy Concepts, 1982; tech. writer Harrisburg Energy Edn. Adv. Coun.; author: (flow chart) Summary: Modern Interpretation of the Central Dogma (Watson & Crick's DNA Model), 1983; reviewer pre-publ. articles, books, audio-visual materials Am. Biology Tchr. Mem. camping program com. Keystone Area Boy Scouts, Harrisburg, Pa., 1994; chmn. Derry Twp. Environ. Adv. Coun., Hershey, Pa., 1993-94. Mem. Nat. Assn. Biology Tchrs. (Outstanding Pa. Biology Tchr. 1984), Nat. Assn. Secondary Sch. Prins., Pa. Assn. Secondary Sch. Prins., Nat. Eagle Scout Assn., Lancaster County Conservancy. Avocation: walking. Home: 356 William Dr Hershey PA 17033-1859 Office: Milton Hershey Sch PO Box 830 Hershey PA 17033-0830 E-mail: ruthe@mhs-pa.org.

RUTH, EDWARD KEITH, information systems specialist, management consultant; b. Louisville, June 28, 1960; s. William Edward and Lillian Loretta (Wyatt) R. BS in Bus. Data Processing, BA in Econs., William Carey Coll., 1982; MBA, Oklahoma City U., 1990; EdD in Adult Edn., Okla. State U., 1997. Cert. data processor, computer prof., project mgmt., profl., Inst. Certification Computing Profls., Ill., PMP Project Mgmt. Inst., Pa. Sr. sys. analyst IV Miss. State Tax Commn., Jackson, 1982-96; sr. sys. programmer Cooper Industries, Vicksburg, Miss., 1985-86, Hertz Corp., Oklahoma City, 1986-90; applications platform mgr. Acxiom Corp., Conway, Ark., 1991-92; sr. product developer Teubner & Assocs., Stillwater, Okla., 1992-93; sr. software developer BMC Software, Austin, Tex., 1996-98; sr. info. tech. specialist IBM, Lexington, Ky., 1998-2000. Contbr. articles to profl. jours. Mem. Project Mgmt. Inst., Nat. Sys. Programmers Assn., Am. Vocat. Ednl. Rsch. Assn., Mgmt. Sci. Inst. Republican. Baptist. Avocations: art, travel, reading, music. E-mail: edruthfax@yahoo.com.

RUTH, GAIL, artist; b. Mansura, La., Jan. 15, 1951; d. Dallas D. Strong, Jeanette M. Strong; m. James M. Ruth; children: Darrel, Jimmy. Grad., Simmesport (La.) H.S., 1967. Artist, New Roads, La., 1987—. Art instr., New Roads, 1994—. Exhibitions include G.A. Ruth Fine Arts, 1998; author: (instrnl. book) North And South Reflections Oil Painting, 2002; prodr.: (instrnl. video) Designer of Ruth Old Master Oil Mediums And Varnishes, A Special Blend of Oils Designed to My Own Specifications, 1998. Recipient One of the flags designed for the city of New Roads, Louisiana, Granted by City of New Roads, La. for winning drawing design of city flag, 1997. Mem.: Soc. Decorative Painters (Magnolia chpt.). Home: 10310 Belle View Dr New Roads LA 70760 Personal E-mail: gruthart@bellsouth.net.

RUTH, HENRY SWARTLEY, retired lawyer; b. Phila., Apr. 16, 1931; s. Henry Swartley and Lola Althouse (Zendt) R.; m. Christine Mallet-Prevost Polk, Dec. 4, 1955 (div. Oct. 1989); children: Laura Ruth-Davis, Diana, Tenley; m. Deborah Ruth Mathieu, Feb. 28, 1991. BA, Yale U., 1952; LLB, U. Pa., 1955. Bar: Pa. 1957, U.S. Dist. Ct. Pa. 1957, U.S. Ct. Appeals (3rd cir.) 1957, D.C. 1964, U.S. Dist. Ct. D.C. 1975, U.S. Supreme Ct. 1975, U.S. Ct. Appeals (4th cir.) 1978. Watergate dep. spl. prosecutor, 1973-74; spl. prosecutor, 1974-75; chief criminal justice rsch. Urban Inst., Washington, 1975-76; gen. counsel UMWA Health and Retirement Funds, 1976-79; litigation ptnr. Shea & Gardner, 1979-81; chief litigation divsn. Saul, Ewing, Remick & Saul, Phila., 1981-87; ethics and spl. litigation counsel Unisys Corp., Blue Bell, Pa., 1987-91; of counsel Crowell & Moring, Washington, 1991-94; ret., 1994. Cons. Joint Legis. Com. on Crime, Trenton, N.J., 1967-68, Violence Commn., Washington, 1968, Nat. Legal Svcs. Orgn., Washington, 1975; Waco ind. reviewer Office Sec. Treasury, Washington, 1993. Contbr. articles to profl. jours. With U.S. Army, 1955-57. Avocations: hiking, piano, golf. E-kmail. Home: 6251 N Camino Santa Valera Tucson AZ 85718 E-mail: hruth@dakotacom.net.

RUTH, JAMES PERRY, financial planning executive; b. Washington, Feb. 27, 1946; s. Robert Walker and Virginia Null Ruth; m. Kathleen McHugh, Aug. 10, 1968; children: Heather Lynn, Michael James. BS in Bus. and Public Adminstrn., U. Md., 1970; postgrad., Am. Coll., Bryn Mawr, 1971-83. CLU, CFP, chartered fin. cons. agt., Northwestern Mutual Life Ins. Co., Washington, 1967-74. Gen. agt. Indpls. Life, Rockville, Md., 1974-82; partner Fox, Ruth & Middledorf, 1975-82; mgr. Mfrs. Fin. Svcs., Rosslyn, Va., 1982-84; pres. Potomac Fin. Group, 1984—. Contbr. articles to profl. publs.; quoted in N.Y. Times, U.S. News and World Report, USA Today, others. Past pres. Jelleff Boys' Club; past pres. Montgomery County Police Boys' and Girls' Club; bd. dirs. Asbury Meth. Village Found. Named Outstanding Young Man Am., U.S. Jaycees, 1979. Mem. Nat. Assn. Insurance & Fin. Advisors (pres. Md. chpt. 1995-96), Nat. Assn. Securities Dealers, Suburban Md. Life Underwriters

Assn. (past pres., H.L. Meyer Meml. award 1980), Fin. Planning Assn., Suburban Md. Estate Planning Coun. (past pres.), Million Dollar Round Table. Lutheran. Home: 508 Lawson Way Rockville MD 20850 Office: Ste 420 18310 Montgomery Village Ave Gaithersburg MD 20879-3553 E-mail: jruth@pfgroup.org.

RUTH, RODNEY, musician, music consultant, contractor, educator; b. Robesonia, Pa., Sept. 12, 1934; s. Herbert J. and Pearl (Rentz) R.; m. Gloria Mae Kauffman, Nov. 14, 1953; 1 child, Tiffany Tunisia. MusB, Manhattan Sch. Music, 1960; MA, Columbia U., 1964. Freelance musician; music cons., contractor Meadowlands Sports Complex, various theaters and performing arts ctrs., individual conductors and performers, bands, orchs., festivals, N.J., N.Y., Pa., 1957—; tchr. Paterson (N.J.) Bd. Edn., 1961-98. Performed with USAF Band, 1953-57; music contractor for world premiers (musicals) Lucifer, Laugh a Little, Cry a Little, Shoemakers Holiday, Love Games, Las Vegas Laugh-In '75. Scholar Manhattan Sch. Music, N.Y.C., 1958-60. Mem. Nat. Edn. Assn., Music Educators Nat. Conf., Am. Fedn. Musicians. Avocations: travel, gardening, golf. Home and Office: Rod Ruth Music 129 Schuyler Rd Allendale NJ 07401-1836 E-mail: rodruthmusic@aol.com.

RUTH, SHIELA GRANT, music educator; b. Sagamiono, Japan, May 12, 1955; came to U.S., 1957; d. Allan Francis and Eiko (Nagasawa) Grant; m. Terrence Allan Ruth, Sept. 8, 1979. BA, Frostburg State Coll., 1977. Health care asst. Deaton Med. Ctr., Balt., summer 1974, 75, Nursing Staff, Annapolis, Md., 1977; sub. tchr. Anne Arundel County Schs., 1977-78; tchr. piano/organ Jordan Kitts, Glen Burnie, 1978-79; music asst. Lindale Jr. H.S., Ferndale, 1986-90, Harundale Presbyn. Ch., Glen Burnie, 1990—; tchr. piano/organ Severn, Md., 1977—. Mem. Md. State Music Tchrs. Assn., Music Tchrs. Nat. Assn., Anne Arundel Music Tchrs. Assn. (corr. sec. 1997—), Delta Omicron (warden 1975-77), Sigma Delta Pi. Republican. Presbyterian. Avocations: playing piano, touring Civil War battlefields, ice skating. Home: 753 Rosewood Rd Severn MD 21144-2069 Office: Harundale Presbyn Ch 1020 Eastway Glen Burnie MD 21060-7303

RUTHCHILD, GERALDINE QUIETLAKE, training and development consultant, writer, poet; d. Nathan and Ruth (Feldman) Stein; m. Neil Wolinsky, Dec. 31, 1993; 1 child, Nathaniel Gideon Wolinsky. BA summa cum laude, Queens Coll., 1977; MA in Am. Lit., Johns Hopkins U., 1980, PhD in Am. Lit., 1983. Asst. prof. Albion (Mich.) Coll., 1982-84; assoc. Investor Access Corp., N.Y.C., 1984-85; program dir. Exec. Enterprises, Inc., 1985-86; pres. Ruthchild Assocs., 1987-90, Exemplar, N.Y.C., 1991-95, Exemplar, Ltd., N.Y.C., 1995—. Cons. J.P. Morgan & Co., Inc., MetLife, Bankers Trust Co., MasterCard Internat., Koch Industries, Inc., Chase Manhattan Bank N.A., Merrill Lynch, TIAA-CREF, Drake Beam Morin, Trans Union Corp, NatWest Bank, U.S.A., Citibank N.A., Robert Morris Assocs., Goldman, Sachs & Co., Dean Witter Reynolds, Inc., also others, 1987—. Contbr. articles, poems to profl. and lit. jours. Vol. handicapped children N.Y. Foundling Hosp., N.Y.C., 1988-90, Fgn. Visitors Desk, Met. Mus. Art, N.Y.C., 1989-97. Hopkins fellow Johns Hopkins U., 1979-80, Andrew Mellon Found. fellow, 1980-81, 81-82. Mem. ASTD, Internat. Soc. Philos. Enquiry, Phi Beta Kappa. Avocations: foreign languages, needlework, gardening. Office: Exemplar Ltd 366 N Broadway Ste 410 Jericho NY 11753-2000 E-mail: GQR@exemplar-ltd.com.

RUTHCHILD, ROCHELLE GOLDBERG, education educator; b. Jersey City, Nov. 30, 1940; d. Samuel A. and Ruth (Raichelson) Goldberg; 1 child, Rafael A. BA, Hofstra U., 1962; MA, U. Rochester, 1964, PhD, 1976. Instr. Cardinal Cushing Coll., Brookline, Mass., 1969-72, Goddard-Cambridge Grad. Program, Cambridge, 1971-74, core faculty, 1974-79, Plainfield, Vt., 1979-81; asst. prof. Vt. Coll. of Norwich U., Montpelier, 1981-82, prof. grad. studies, 1988—; dir. Russian Sch. Norwich U., Northfield, Vt., 1988-94; assoc. Davis Ctr. for Russian Studies Harvard U., 1980—; prof. grad. studies Vt. Coll. of Union Inst. and U., Montpelier, 2001—. Author: (book) Women in Russian and the Soviet Union: An Annotated Bibliography, 1994; contbr. articles to profl. jours. Jewish Women's Archive mem. Temple Israel, Boston, 1996—. N.Y. State Regents scholar, 1958-62; grantee Internat. Rsch. and Exchs., Leningrad, Moscow, 1966-67, 78-79, 95, NEH, 1996, Dana Grant, 1997-98, others. Mem. Assn. for Women in Slavic Studies (bd. dirs. 1990—, pres./co-founder, 1988-90). Jewish. Office: Grad Program Regional Offic 137 Coolidge St Brookline MA 02446-5807

RUTHERFOORD, REBECCA HUDSON, computer science educator; b. Elkhart, Ind., Feb. 24, 1948; d. Charles Melvin Hudson and Eunice Klaire (Lund) Edmonds; m. James Kincanon Rutherfoord, Aug. 31, 1968; children: James Kincanon Jr., Charles Penn. BS, Ind. State U., 1971, MS, 1972, EdD, 1975; MS in Computer Sci., So. Poly State U., Marietta, Ga., 1995. Cert. data processor. Staff asst. Ind. State U., Terre Haute, 1969-71; vocal music tchr. S.W. Parke Schs., Rockville, Ind., 1971-73; fellowship asst. Ind. State U., Terre Haute, 1974-75; vocal music tchr. Slidell (La.) H.S., 1977-78; programmer, analyst La. State U., Baton Rouge, 1978-79, dir. computer rehab. program, 1979-80; programmer, analyst Hanes Corp., Atlanta, 1980-81; asst. prof. Devry Inst., 1981-83; acting dept. chair So. Poly. State U., Marietta, Ga., 1989-92, prof. computer sci., 1983—, computer sci. grad. program coord., 1996-97, asst. to pres., 1997-98, interim dean arts and scis., 1998-99, chair MSIT program, 1999—, acting head dept. computer sci., 2000-01, program head, info. tech., 2001—. Cons. The Assocs. Group, Inc., Roswell, Ga., 1986-88, Crawford Comm., Atlanta, 1987; adj. prof. Cobb County Bd. Edn., Marietta, 1985-87, Joseph T. Walker Sch., Marietta, 1985-86; vis. prof. Leicester (U.K.) Poly., 1990. Choir dir. St. Peter and Paul Episcopal Ch., Marietta, 1981-85, choir mem., 1992—, bd. dirs. preschool 1998—; Christian edn. dir. St. Francis Episcopal Ch., Denham Springs, La., 1978-80; choir mem. St. David's Episcopal Ch., Roswell, 1985-92, Ch. of the Messiah, 1992-2001; bd. dirs., mem. Cherokee Cmty. Habitat for Humanity, 1994-98. Mem. Data Processing Mgmt. Assn., Assn. Computing Machinery, Nat. Assn. Women in Edn., Computer Sci. Edn. (spl. interest group), Nat. Assn. Women Edn., Delta Kappa Gamma, Sigma Alpha Iota. Republican. Avocations: boating, reading. Office: So Poly State Univ 1100 S Marietta Pky Marietta GA 30060-2855

RUTHERFORD, DIANE C. mechanical engineer; b. Columbus, Ga., Dec. 12, 1964; d. Martin R. and Marjorie V. Vissers; m. Robert Greg Rutherford. BSME, U. Tex., Arlington, 1998. EIT 1998. Design engr. Retractable Technologies, Inc., Little Elm, Tex., 1999—. Mem.: ASME (assoc.; minority leadership intern 2001—02, fin. mgr. W. Tex. sect. 2000—01, vice chair W. Tex. sect. 2001—, sec. 1999—2000, region X rep. to bd. minorities and women 2001—). Office: Retractable Technologies, Inc. 511 Lobo Le Little Elm TX 75068

RUTHERFORD, DOREEN, artist, excavating company executive; b. Newton, N.J., Dec. 12, 1966; m. Daniel Grey Rutherford, Aug. 30, 1986; children: Lillian, Julia. Diploma in computer programming, Warren Vocat. Sch., N.J., 1986; pvt. studies in art, with Howard Carr and Charles Slovek. CEO, Rutherford's Excavating, Bend, Oreg., 1992—. Art cons. Gallery Haleiwa, Hawaii, 1988-89, Fettiq Gallery, Haleiwa, 1989-90, Where Eagles Soar Gallery, Sun River, Oreg., 1991-92; mem. adv. bd. Humane Soc. Art Show, Bend, 1992; distbr. lit. Living Waters, Beijing and Canton, 1987, Taipei, Taiwan, 1987. Illustrator: (book) Bend Business Woman's Association, 1994; one-woman shows Rix of Hawaii, Haleiwa, Oahu, 1987, Sun River (Oreg.) Coffee Co., 1999, Wind River Gallery, Bend, Oreg., 1997, Charlotts Fine Art Gallery, 2001. Contbr. Sara Fisher Cancer Rsch. Auction, Bend, Oreg.; sole contbr. SunRiverDance Acad. Ann. Presentation, 2002. Mem. Oreg. C. of C. Avocations: skiing, equestrian sports, antiquing, writing, plein air painting.

RUTHERFORD, HAROLD PHILLIP, educational association administrator; b. N.Y.C., Sept. 3, 1951; s. Steve and Ethel Leona (Hollinger) R.; married, July 30, 1980; 1 child, Paitra Denise. AB, John Carroll U., 1974; MA, Kent State U., 1977, PhD, 1988; cert. in mgmt. proficiency, U. Pa., 1986. Spl. asst. to dean Kent (Ohio) State U., 1976-78, dir. ednl. rsch., 1978-80; vice-city mgr. City of East Cleve., 1980-84; dir. spl. univ. programs U. Akron (Ohio), 1984-85; spl. asst. to pres., dir. devel. Ft. Valley (Ga.) State Found., 1985—; chmn., pres. adv. bd. Ft. Valley State Coll., 1986. Contbr. articles to profl. jours. Chmn. C.W. Pettigrew Endowment Fund Drive, Ft. Valley, 1985—; co-convener Nat. Issues Forum, 1987—; presenter, speaker Nat. Assn. Equal Opportunity in Higher Edn., 1987; presenter, Woodrow Wilson Found. Regents fellow SUNY, 1988-90, Woodrow Wilson fellow, 1985-87, Mgmt. Devel. Program fellow Harvard U., 1986; named One of Best Black Instl. Advancement Officers, 1987; recipient Disting. Service and Recognition award U. Akron, 1984, award Domestic Planning and Policy Assn., 1987, 25 best award CASE, 1987. Mem. Council for Adv. and Support of Edn., Omicron Delta Kappa, Sigma Pi Phi. Democrat. Roman Catholic. Office: Ft Valley State Coll 805 State College Dr Fort Valley GA 31030-4310

RUTHERFORD, JEFFREY ALLEN, music educator; b. Fremont, Ohio, July 20, 1969; s. Robert Donald and Susan Marie Rutherford. B in Music Edn., Bowling Green State U., 1991. Provisional tchg. cert. music K-12 Va. Instr. Vanlue (Ohio) Local Sch., 1991—93; dir. bands Clyde (Ohio) H.S., 1993—96, James Wood H.S., Winchester, Va., 1996—. Mem.: Va. Band And Orch. Dirs Assn., Va. Music Edn. Assn., Internat. Trombone Assn., Music Educators Nat. Conf., Nat. Band Assn. Methodist. Home: 2334 Roosevelt Blvd Winchester VA 22601 Office: James Wood HS 161 Apple Pie Ridge Rd Winchester VA 22603 Personal E-mail: musicman@jaruth.net. Business E-Mail: rutherfj@frederick.k12.va.us.

RUTHERFORD, JOHN SHERMAN, III (JOHNNY RUTHERFORD), professional race car driver; b. Coffeyville, Kans., Mar. 12, 1938; s. John Sherman and Mary Henrietta (Brooks) R.; m. Betty Rose Hoyer, July 7, 1963; children: John Sherman, Angela Ann. Student, Tex. Christian U., 1956. Profl. race car driver, 1959-94; ret., 1994; driver super-modified race cars, sprint cars, stock cars, midgets, sports cars, Indy cars, Trans-Am cars and formula 5000. Mem. Indy Car Racing Inc.; dir. spl. events Indy Racing League, 1995—; pace car driver for Championship Auto Racing Teams, 1992-95; auto racing cons. Pennzoil Products-Racing Divsn.; lectr. in field. Author: (autobiography) Lone Star J.R., 2000; host: TV show The Racers; race commentator TV show, NBC, ESPN, CBS, ABC; appeared in numerous TV commercials; art work included in traveling exhbn. Art and Athletes; TV and radio pub. services messages for Nat. Safety Council, Calif. Hwy. Patrol, U.S. Marines, Muscular Dystrophy Assn., Cystic Fibrosis Assn., Boy Scouts, Camp Fire, Shriner's Hosp., Tex. Soc. to Prevent Blindness, Air N.G. Hon. state chmn. Am. Cancer Soc., Tex., Tarrant County Soc. to Prevent Blindness, Emergency Medicine Found., Ft. Worth Kidney Assn., Ft. Worth Burn Ctr.; Ind. chmn. Am. Heart Assn.; hon. mem. bd. dirs. Tex. chpt. Speedway Children's Charities, 1998—; bd. dirs. Indy HOF and Oldtimers, 2002—. Named Ft. Worth Newsmaker of Yr., 1974, Driver of Yr. Sport Mag., 1976, Driver of Yr. Auto Race Writers and Broadcasters Am., 1974, 80, Olsonite Driver of Yr., 1980, Corvette Challenge's Sportsman of Yr., 1988, Motorsports amb., 1993; recipient Jim Clark award, 1969, Extra Mile award, 1973, Jim Malloy award, 1974, Eddie Sachs award, 1975, Louie Meyer award, 1992; chosen for Internat. Race of Champions, 1974, 76, 77, 78, 79, 84, chosen Fast Masters, 1993; elected to Tex. Sports Hall of Fame, 1981, Indy 500 Hall of Fame, 1987, Boys Clubs Am.'s Celebrity Hall of Fame, 1987, Tex. Auto Racing Hall of Fame, 1988, Nat. Sprint Car Hall of Fame, 1995, Internat. Motorsports Hall of Fame, 1996. Mem. Fedn. Internat. Automobile, Internat. Motors Sports Assn., Exptl. Aircraft Assn., Warbirds of Am., Confederate Air Force, Internat. Aerobatic Club, League Auto Racing (sec., bd. dirs.), Championship Drivers Assn. (bd. dirs.), Nat. Rifle Assn., Air Force Assn., Air Power Coun., Blue Angels Assn., Ft. Worth Boat Club, Shady Oaks Country Club, Lions. Achievements include winning 27 championship car races; winner Indianapolis 500, 1974, 76, 80, second place, 1975; set new world's record for stock cars, Daytona Beach, Fla., 1963; set record at Indpls. 500, 1973; at Mich. Internat. Raceway, 1984; U.S. Auto Club Nat. Sprint Car champion, 1965; Nat. Driving champion USAC and CART, 1980; oldest driver (48) to win a 500 mile Indy Car Race, 1986. E-mail: lonestarjr@hotmail.com. *I am a firm believer in the fact that a person can do anything in this world he or she wants to as long as you have desire. People have to set goals, things to achieve. No one ever remembers who finished second. Luck is where preparation meets opportunity.*

RUTHERFORD, MARY JEAN, laboratory administrator, science educator; b. Webb City, Mo., Apr. 23, 1935; d. John Edward and Martha Rose (Hare) R. AA, Joplin Jr. Coll., 1955; BS, Northwestern U., 1957; MEd, Drury Coll., 1984. Cert. med. technologist, specialist in chemistry. Med. technologist Northwestern U., Chgo., 1957-60; lab. supr., instr. St. Louis U. Hosp.-Med. Tech., 1961-67; supr. in chemistry, instr. U. Ill. Rsch. and Edn. Hosp., Chgo., 1967-68; teaching supr. in chemistry L.E. Cox Med. Ctr. Sch. of Med. Tech., Springfield, Mo., 1968-86; asst. prof., mem. faculty Ark. State U., Jonesboro, 1986-90, program dir. clin. lab. scis., asst. prof., 1990-98, assoc. prof., 1998—, chmn. faculty senate, 1999-2000. Mem. adv. bd. Springhouse (Pa.) Pub., 1992—; mem. rev. com. Nat. Accrediting Agy. for Clin. Lab. Scis., Chgo., 1993-94, 95—. Author: Inorganic Chemistry-Applied Science Review, 1992. Pres. LWV, Jonesboro, 1991-92. Mem. Am. Soc. Clin. Lab. Scis., Ark. Soc. Clin. Lab. Scis. (editor 1997-99, bd. dirs. 1996-99, pres. 2001—), Ark. Clin. Lab. Educator's Forum (chair 1993-94), Ark. Coalition of Lab. Profls. (treas. 1992—), Ark. State U. Faculty Assn. (pres. 1999-2000). Avocations: travel, photography, needlecrafts. Office: Ark State U PO Box 910 State University AR 72467-0910 E-mail: mjruth@crow.astate.edu.

RUTHERFORD, PAUL HARDING, physicist; b. Shipley, Yorkshire, Eng., Jan. 22, 1938; came to U.S., 1965, naturalized, 1976; s. Joseph William and Annie (Harding) R.; m. Audrey Jones Irvine, Oct. 31, 1959; children— Andrea Christine, Julia Irvine. BA, Cambridge (Eng.) U., 1959, MA, PhD, Cambridge (Eng.) U., 1963. Research asso. Princeton (N.J.) U. Plasma Physics Lab., 1962-63, mem. research staff, 1965-68, research physicist, 1968-71, sr. research physicist, 1971-99, head theoretical div., 1972-80, dep. asso. dir. for research, 1978-80, asso. dir. research, 1980-95. Chair tech. adv. com. Internat. Thermonuclear Exptl. Reactor, 1992-99; research asso. U.K. Atomic Energy Authority Culham (Berkshire, Eng.) Lab., 1963-65; lectr. astrophys. scis. Princeton U. Co-author: (with R.J. Goldston) Introduction to Plasma Physics, 1995; mem. bd. assoc. editors Physics of Fluids, 1973-75; mem. editl. bd. Nuclear Fusion, 1980099. Recipient E.O. Lawrence award U.S. Dept. Energy, 1983, Disting. Career award Fusion Power Assocs., 1998. Fellow Am. Phys. Soc. Home: 10 Burr Dr Princeton NJ 08540-1950 Office: Plasma Physics Lab PO Box 451 Princeton NJ 08543-0451 E-mail: rutherfo@pppl.gov.

RUTHERFORD, REID, finance company executive; b. Morristown, N.J., Dec. 30, 1952; s. Clinton Homer and Bonnie Beth (Bergner) R.; m. Beth Ann Husak, Apr. 3, 1977; children: Ian Michael, Laurel Bryce, Corinne Leigh, Alyse Allyne. BA, Pepperdine U., 1975; MBA, Stanford U., 1981. Exec. v.p. Analytics, Inc., N.Y.C., 1976-79; pres. Softlink Corp., Santa Clara, Calif., 1981-83, Rsch. Applications for Mgmt., Menlo Park, 1984-85; pres., bd. dirs. Concord Growth Corp., San Mateo, 1985—; chmn. EFin. Corp., 1998—2002; prin. R2 Co., Los Altos, 2002—. Contbr. articles to profl. jours. Disting. alumnus, bd. vis. Stanford U.

RUTHERFORD, THOMAS TRUXTUN, II, former state senator, county commissioner; b. Columbus, Ohio, Mar. 3, 1947; s. James William and Elizabeth Whiting (Colby) R.; m. Linda Sue Rogers, Aug. 28, 1965 (div.); 1 child, Jeremy Todd. BBA, U. N.Mex., 1970, JD, 1982. Page, reading clk. N.Mex. State Legislature, 1960-65; mem. N.Mex. Atty. Gen. Environ. Adv. Commn., 1972; radio broadcaster Sta. KOB Radio and TV, 1963-72; mem. N.Mex. Senate, Albuquerque, 1972-96, majority whip, 1978-88. Chmn. rules com. N.Mex. State Senate, chmn. econ. devel. and new tech. interim. com., mem. sci. and new tech. oversight com., majority fl. leader, 1996; pres. Rutherford & Assocs., Albuquerque, 1978—83; pvt. practice, Albuquerque, 1983—; gen. counsel Nat. Fraternal Order of Police, 1996—2001; commr., chair Bernalillo County Commn., 1996—; lobbyist, 1996—; bd. dirs. Hispano C. of C., Kirtland Partnership Com., Camp Sierra Blanca Youth Detention Ctr.; past chmn. Albuquerque Cable TV Adv. Bd.; mem. S.W. Regional Energy Coun., N.Mex. Gov.'s Commn. on Pub. Broadcasting; bd. dirs., v.p. Rocky Mountain Corp. for Pub. Broadcasting; mem. Am. Coun. Young Polit. Leaders; del. mission to Hungary, Austria, Greece, 1983; mem. Fgn. Trade Adv. Com. Bd. Econ. Devel. and Tourism; trade del. People's Republic of China, 1985. N.Mex. Broadcasting Assn. scholar, 1970. Home: 1910 Ridgecrest Dr SE Albuquerque NM 87108-4530 also: PO Box 81256 Albuquerque NM 87198

RUTHERFORD, VICKY LYNN, special education educator; b. Florence, S.C., Sept. 12, 1947; BS, Hampton U., 1969, MA, 1971; PhD, Mich. State U., 1991. Cert. tchr. French, spl. edn., reading specialist, Va., tchr. spl. edn., S.C. Social worker day care Hampton (Va.) Dept. Social Svc., 1970-72; reading therapist, asst. dir., dir. Bayberry Reading Clinic, Hampton, 1973-77; tchr. reading, English, counselor York County Schs., Yorktown, Va., 1977-85; staff advisor, asst. to course coord. Mich. State U., East Lansing, 1985-90; tchr. autism Florence (S.C.) Dist. 1 Sch. Sys., 1992-96, tchr. emotionally impaired, 1996—. Instrnl. designer: Addiction Severity Index #1, 1987, #2, 1988, Managing a Diverse Workforce, 1990; designer, trainer: Project Teach, 1991; designer, developer: (video) Camp Takona Summer Experience, 1992. Bass guitarist, Sun. sch. sec., youth worker, Sun. sch. supt. Progressive Ch. of Jesus, Florence, 1992-98, Greater Zion Tabernacle Apostolic Ch., Florence, 1998—. Fellow Mich. Dept. Edn., 1987-89. Mem. Internat. Reading Assn. Office: Delmae Heights Elem Sch 1211 S Cashua Dr Florence SC 29501-6399

RUTHERFORD, WILLIAM DRAKE, investment executive; b. Marshalltown, Iowa, Jan. 14, 1939; s. William Donald and Lois Esther (Drake) R.; m. Janice W. Rutherford, Feb. 4, 1965 (div. Mar. 1982); children: Wayne Donald, Melissa Drake; m. Karen Anderegg, Jan. 2, 1994. BS, U. Oreg., 1961; LLB, Harvard U., 1964. Bar: Oreg. 1964, U.S. Dist. Ct. Oreg. 1966. Assoc. Maguire, Kester & Cosgrave, Portland, Oreg., 1966-69; house counsel May & Co., 1969-70, pvt. practice, 1970-71, McMinnville, Oreg., 1971-84; mem. Oreg. Ho. of Reps., Salem, 1977-84; state treas. State of Oreg., 1984-87; chmn. Oreg. Investment Coun., 1986-87; exec. v.p., dir. U.S. and Australia ops. ABD Internat. Mgmt. Corp., N.Y.C., 1987-88, pres., chief exec. officer, bd. dirs., 1988-89; pres., bd. dirs. Societé Gen. Touche Remnant, 1990-93; dir. spl. projects Metallgesellschaft Corp., N.Y.C., 1994-95; mng. dir. Macadam Capital Ptnrs., Portland, 1995-96; CEO Fiberboard Asbestos Compensation Trust, 1997; prin. Rutherford Investment Mgmt. LLC, 1998—. Chmn. bd. dirs. Metro One Telecomms. Bd. dirs. Portland Opera Assn., 1995-99. Recipient Contbn. to Individual Freedom award ACLU, 1981 Mem. Nat. Assn. State Treas. (exec. v.p. 1985, 86, pres. western region 1985, 86), Nat. Assn. State Auditors, Comptr. and Treas. (exec. com. 1987), Nat. Assn. Corp. Dirs. Republican. E-mail: WRutherford@rutherfordinvestment.com. Home: 6978 SW Foxfield Ct Portland OR 97225-6054 Office: 10300 S W Greenburg Rd Ste 115 Portland OR 97223

RUTHMAN, THOMAS ROBERT, manufacturing executive; b. Cin., May 24, 1933; s. Alois H. and Catherine (Gies) R.; m. Audrey J. Schumaker, Mar. 17, 1979; children: Thomas G., Julia C., Theresa K. Grad., LaSalle U., 1970. With Ruthman Pump and Engring. Inc. (formerly Ruthman Machinery Co.), Cin., 1953—, gen. mgr., 1964-70, v.p., 1970-74, pres., 1974—, pres., owner, 1981—. Pres. Gusher Pumps, Inc., Fulflo Spltys. Co., Gusher Pumps of New Castle, Cin., Williamstown (Ky.), Dry Ridge, Calif.; pres., owner, dir.Great Lakes Pump & Supply, Mich.; owner BSM Pump Corp, North Kingston, R.I.; pres., owner Birmingham (Eng.) Pump Supply, Ruthmann Pumpen, GMBH, Germany. Home: Princess del Mar Unit 1202 174 S Collier Blvd Marco Island FL 34145-4333 Office: 1212 Streng St Cincinnati OH 45223-2643

RUTHSATZ, RANDALL A. accountant; b. Sandusky, Ohio, Apr. 1, 1964; s. Kenneth Harold and Sylvia Ruth (Poeschl) R. BA, Heidelberg Coll., 1986; MBA, Case Western Res. U., 1988. CPA, Ohio. Tax cons. Deloitte & Touche, Cleve., 1988-93; sr. tax cons. Howard, Wershbale & Co., Beachwood, Ohio, 1994-95; pvt. practice Sandusky, 1995—. Mem. Ohio Soc. CPAs. Republican. Episcopalian. Avocations: church organist, travel, American Impressionist art. Home: 402 E Washington St Sandusky OH 44870-2821 E-mail: rruthsatz@aol.com.

RUTKIN, PHILIP, chemist; s. Benjamin and Anna Rutkin; m. Marlene Joan Rutkin, Apr. 13, 1957; children: Alan, Robin, Melissa, Bruce. Bachelor Sci. Chemistry, CCNY, New York, New York, 1951—55; Phd Organic Chemistry, NYU, New York, New York, 1955—60. V.p. rsch. devel. Faberge, New York, NY, 1960—; sr. v.p. quality control Estee Lauder, 1975—; v.p. rsch. devel. Bath Body Works, 1996—. Contbr. Home: 6 Henhawk Road Great Neck NY 11024-2107 Office Fax: 212-904-8280. E-mail: prutkin@bbw.com.

RUTKOFF, ALAN STUART, lawyer; b. Chgo., May 31, 1952; s. Roy and Harriet (Ruskin) R.; m. Mally Zoberman, Dec. 22, 1974; children: Aaron Samuel, Jordana Michal, Robert Nathaniel. BA with high distinction, U. Mich., 1973; JD magna cum laude, Northwestern U., 1976. Bar: Ill. 1976, U.S. Dist. Ct. (no. dist.) Ill. 1976, U.S. Ct. Appeals (7th cir.) 1977, U.S. Ct. Appeals (3d cir.) 1978, U.S. Supreme Ct. 1981, U.S. Ct. Appeals (5th cir.) 1983, U.S. Ct. Appeals (8th cir.) 1990, U.S. Dist. Ct. (we. dist.) Wis. 1996. Assoc. Altheimer & Gray, Chgo., 1976-80; ptnr. Kastel & Rutkoff, 1980-83, Holleb & Coff Ltd., Chgo., 1983-84, McDermott, Will & Emery, Chgo., 1984—. Pres. N. Suburban Synagogue Beth El, Highland Pk., Ill., 1999-2001.. Mem. ABA, Chgo. Bar Assn., Order of Coif. Home: 801 Timberhill Rd Highland Park IL 60035-5148 Office: McDermott Will & Emery 227 W Monroe St Ste 4400 Chicago IL 60606-5096 E-mail: arutkoff@mwe.com.

RUTKOWSKI, THADDEUS, author; b. Kingston, Pa., Oct. 23, 1954; s. B. Richard Rutkowski and Chia In Wang; m. Randi Hoffman, Feb. 7, 1999; 1 child, Shay Eve Hoffman. BA in English, BFA, Cornell U., 1976; MA in Creative Writing, Johns Hopkins U., 1977. Copy editor Crain's NY Bus., N.Y.C. Fiction-writing instr. The Writer's Voice of the West Side YMCA, 1999—, Asian Am. Writers workshop, 2001. Author: Roughhouse, 1999 (Finalist Asian Am. Book award 2000), Basic Training, 1996; copy editor NY Times Book Rev., 1982; editl. staffer Adweek, 1985-97. Mem. PEN, The Author's Guild, The Nat. Book Critics Circle.

RUTLAND, DAVID LEE, lawyer; b. East Chicago, Ind., July 11, 1958; s. Marshall Edgar and Margaret (Powers) R.; m. Catherine Dorrian; children: Christopher, Michael, Steven, Brian. BS, Mt. St. Mary's Coll., 1980; JD, U. Md., 1983. Bar: Md. 1983, U.S. Dist. Ct. Md. 1984, D.C. 1985, U.S. Dist. Ct. D.C. 1985, U.S. Ct. Appeals (4th and D.C. cirs.) 1986, U.S. Supreme Ct. 1987, Va. 1993, U.S. Dist. Ct. (ea. dist.) Va. 1993. Law clk. to presiding judge Montgomery County (Md.) Cir. Ct., 1983-84; assoc. McCarthy, Wilson & Ethridge, Rockville, Md., 1984-85, Digges, Wharton & Levin, Annapolis, 1985-89; ptnr. Wharton, Levin & Ehrmantraut, 1989-91, Wharton, Levin, Ehrmantraut, Klein & Nash, Annapolis, 1991—. Mem. ABA, Md. Bar Assn., D.C. Bar Assn., Md. Def. Counsel, Def. Rsch. Inst., Va. State Bar Assn. Office: Wharton Levin & Ehrmantraut PO Box 551 104 West St Annapolis MD 21404-0551

RUTLAND-AMAGLIANI, CAROL ELAINE, music director, educator; b. Memphis, Aug. 11, 1952; d. Charles Wesson and Evelyn (Matthew) Rutland; m. Malcolm Brown Futhey (div. Mar. 1986); children: Malcolm Brown III, Meredith Elaine; m. Michael Lewis Amagliani, July 1993; 1 child, Christopher Ian Amagliani. Cert. in theory teaching/piano pedagogy, St. Louis Inst. Music, 1970, 71; BS in Edn., Memphis State U., 1989. Cert. in theory and piano, Tenn. Pvt. tchr. piano, voice and keyboard, Memphis, 1970—; lower sch. music coord. Evangelical Christian Sch., 1983—. Judge piano competitions, drama tchr. and choreographer; fgn. study culture and music and missions trip, Papua, New Guinea, 1990. Keyboard accompanist, voice tchr. various chs., Memphis; mem. King's Daughter Women's Fellowship. Mem. Tenn. Counseling Assn., Women's Fellowship, Kings Daus., Pi Mu Beta. Avocations: gardening, music groups.

RUTLEDGE, CHARLES OZWIN, pharmacologist, educator; b. Topeka, Oct. 1, 1937; s. Charles Ozwin and Alta (Seaman) R.; m. Jane Ellen Crow, Aug. 13, 1961; children: David Ozwin, Susan Harriett, Elizabeth Jane, Karen Ann. BS in Pharmacy, U. Kans., 1959, MS in Pharmacology, 1961; PhD in Pharmacology, Harvard U., 1966. NATO postdoctoral fellow Gothenburg (Sweden) U., 1966-67; asst. prof. U. Colo. Med. Ctr., Denver, 1967-74, assoc. prof., 1974-75; prof., chmn. dept. pharmacology U. Kans., Lawrence, 1975-87; dean, prof. pharmacology Purdue U., West Lafayette, Ind., 1987—2002, program dir. Discovery Park, 2001—. Contbr. articles on neuropharmacology to profl. jours. Grantee NIH, 1970-87. Mem. AAAS, Am. Soc. Pharmacology and Exptl. Therapeutics (councillor 1982 84, sec.-treas. 1990-93, pres. 1996-97), Am. Assn. Coll. Pharmacy (chmn. biol. scis. sect. 1983-84, chmn. coun. faculties 1986-87, chmn. coun. deans 1993-94, commn. implement change pharm. edn. 1989-92, pres. 1996-97), Soc. for Neurosci., Am. Pharm. Assn. Avocations: gardening, skiing. Home: 40 Brynteg Est West Lafayette IN 47906-5643 Office: Purdue U Discovery Park 1210 Houde Hall Rm 232 West Lafayette IN 47907-1210 E-mail: chipr@purdue.edu.

RUTLEDGE, JOANNE, artist, consultant; b. Indpls., Dec. 17, 1941; d. Edward John and Dorothy Louise (Bachelor) Underwood; m. Kenneth Clay Smith, Sept. 7, 1963 (div. May 1990); children: Elizabeth, Kenneth Clay, Jr., Andrew; m. Mark Alan Rutledge, July 31, 1993. RN, St. Vincent's Sch.

Nursing, Indpls., 1962; BSN, Ind. U., 1979. Staff RN Children's Hosp., Washington, 1962—63, St. Vincent's Hosp., Indpls., 1963—64, Women's Hosp. Spl. Care Nursery, Indpls., 1990—97; nurse cons. Hosp. Care for Indigent Ind. State Program, 1995—. Exhibitions include Ind. State Fair, Ind. Heritage Arts, Southside Art League Regional Show. Docent Indpls. Mus. Art, 1983—; tutor reading Kiwanis Project, 2002; active various coms. Children's Mus. Guild, 1975—; v.p. Indpls. Athletic Club Art Bd. Found., 1990—. Recipient Billy Cothran Landscape award, Indpls. Art Ctr., 1985. Mem.: Ind. Plein Art Painters Assn., Stutz Artist's Assn., Ind. Artist's Club (assoc.), Proctor Club (pres. 1994—95). Roman Catholic. Avocations: travel, photography, hiking, canoeing, attending concerts and theater. Home: 1019 W 75th St Indianapolis IN 46260-3408 Office: Ind Hosp Care for the Indigent 402 W Washington St Indianapolis IN 46204

RUTLEDGE, JOE, pathologist, scientist; b. Lewisburg, Tenn., Aug. 18, 1950; s. Edward and Geraldine Rutledge; m. Ellen Armistead, May 15, 1976; children: Jack, Rosemary. BS, Rhodes Coll., 1972; MD, Vanderbilt U., 1976. Diplomate Am. Bd. Pediatric Pathology, Am. Bd. Anatomic and Clin. Pathology. Asst. prof. pathology Univ. Tex. Southwestern Medical Sch., Dallas, 1980-88; assoc. prof. lab. medicine U. Washington, Seattle, 1988—91, prof. lab. medicine, 1991—. Mem. adv. bd. Human Developmental Anatomy Ctr., Washington, 1992—; collaborative rschr. Oak Ridge (Tenn.) Nat. Lab., 1982—; mem. test coms. Am. Bd. Pathology and Nat. Bd. Med. Examiners. Contbr. chpts. to books; contbr. articles to profl. jours. Adv. bd. Healthcare Profl. West Washington, Seattle, 1992-96, March of Dimes. Fellow Coll. Am. Pathology (practice com. 1990-95); mem. Soc. for Pediatric Pathology (coun. 1988-94, pres. 1999), Am. Assn. Clin. Chemistry (pediatric com. 1980-94), Am. Soc. Clin. Pathology, Am. Soc. Human Genetics. Avocations: ham radio, photography, hiking, camping, skiing. Office: Childrens Hosp & Med Ctr Lab Ch 37 4800 Sand Point Way NE Seattle WA 98105-3901

RUTLEDGE, PETER J. federal agency administrator; BSME, Rutgers U.; M Indsl. Engring., Tex. A&M U.; M Sci. Reliability Engring., U. Md., PhD in Reliability Engring., 1997. Mech. engr. Delaval Steam Turbine Co., Trenton, NJ, 1972; safety engr. Army Materiel Command Intern Tng. Ctr., Texarkana, Tex., 1972—74, Picatinny Arsenal, Dover, NY, 1974—75; chief engring. br. safety office Army Materiel Command, Alexandria, Va., 1975—83; tech. advisor Dir. Army Safety, the Pentagon, Washington, 1983—85; dep. dir. occupl. safety and health Safety and Occupl. Health POlice Directorate Office of Sec. of Def., 1985—88; with NASA, 1988—, dir. OSMA, 1996—97, dir. enterprise safety and mission assurance divsn. Office Safety and Mission Assurance, 1997—. Office: NASA Hdqrs Mail Code Q 300 E St NW Washington DC 20546

RUTMAN, ROBERT J. medical researcher; b. N.Y.C., June 23, 1919; s. Leon and Anna Porringer; m. Julia Zubroff, Dec. 1942 (div. 1969); children: Rose, Randi; m. Geraldine Burell, Jan. 15, 1980; children: Steven, David, Ellen. BS, Pa. State U., 1940; postgrad., U. Idaho, 1941-42; PhD, U. Calif., Berkeley, 1950; MS, U. Pa., 1976. Asst. prof. biochem. Thomas Jefferson U., Phila., 1950-54; sr. scientist U. Pa., 1954-61, assoc. prof. chemistry, 1961-68, prof. biochem. & molecular biology, 1968-88, chmn. biochem., 1971-73, 76-78; ret. Vis. prof. U. Ibaden, Nigeria, 1973—74, U. North, South Africa, 1998. Editor: Women and Cancer, 1999—2001, Nat. Black Leadership Initiative on Cancer, 2001—02; contbr. articles to profl. jours. Founder, v.p. M.L. King Jr. Ctr., Phila., 1984-89; chmn. Ile-Ife Humanitarian Ctr., Phila., 1986-88; fin. dir. Campaign Orgn. Polit. Office, Phila., 1965-86; pres. Home and Sch. Assn., Phila., 1962-63, Citizens Commn. Pub Edn., 1963. Capt. AUS, 1943-46. Named Man of Yr., Phila. Tribune, 1985. Fellow AAAS; mem. Nat. Assn. Environ. Profls., Am. Assn. Cancer Rsch. Achievements include patents for in field. Avocations: tennis, swimming, dancing, music. Home: 3900 Ford Rd Apt PH-P Philadelphia PA 19131

RUTSALA, VERN A. poet, English language educator, writer; b. Feb. 5, 1934; s. Ray Edwin and Virginia Mae (Brady) R.; m. Joan Merle Colby, Apr. 6, 1957; children: Matthew, David, Kirsten. BA, Reed Coll., 1956; MFA, U. Iowa, 1960. Instr. Lewis and Clark Coll., Portland, 1961-64, asst. prof., 1964-69, assoc. prof., 1969-76, prof., 1976—. Vis. prof. U. Minn., Mpls., 1968-69, Bowling Green (Ohio) State U., 1970; writer-in-residence U. Idaho, Moscow, 1988, Redlands (Calif.) U., 1979; chair English dept. Lewis and Clark, Portland, 1986-89. Author: The Window, 1964, Laments, 1975, The Journey Begins, 1976, Paragraphs, 1978, Walking Home from the Icehouse, 1981, Backtracking, 1985, Ruined Cities, 1987, Selected Poems, 1991, Little-Known Sports, 1994. With U.S. Army, 1956-58. Guggenheim Found. fellow, 1982-83, NEA fellow, 1975, 79, Masters fellow Oreg. Arts Commn., 1990; recipient Carolyn Kizer prize Western Oreg. State Coll., 1988, N.W. Poets prize N.W. Rev., 1975, Hazel Hall award Oreg. Inst. Lit. Arts, 1992, Juniper prize U. Mass. Press, 1993, Duncan Lawrie prize Arvon Found., 1994, Carolyn Kizer prize, 1997. Mem. AAUP, AWP, PEN, Poetry Soc. Am. Avocations: drawing, painting, watching the ocean, sports. Office: Lewis & Clark Coll Dept English Portland OR 97219

RUTSCHKE, ANNAMARIE, artist; b. Santa Barbara, Calif., June 29, 1965; d. Benjamin Wiley Jordan and Jeannette Irene Rutschke; m. Robert Allan Bryant, July 31, 1988 (div. 1996). File clk. San Luis Welding Supply, San Luis Obispo, Calif., 1983; customer svc. clk. The Living Picture, Alameda, 1984, 7-11, Alameda, 1985-86; clk. Def. Subs. Reg. Pacific, 1987-88; pers. clk. Def. Depot Tracy, 1988-90; adminstrv. clk. Gen. Svcs. Adminstrn., San Francisco, 1990, purchasing agt., 1990-96, adminstrv. technician, 1996-99; legal clk. IRS Dist. Counsel, 1999-2000. Freelance artist. Co-coord. Fed. Recycling Coun., 1992, 93; operator Muscular Dystrophy Assn., Arroyo Grande, Calif., 1980. Republican. Lutheran. Avocations: art, writing, computer programming, web design, cooking. E-mail: ldrsnewswolfe@aol.com.

RUTSKY, LESTER, textiles executive, writer; b. N.Y.C., May 23, 1924; s. Samuel and Bess (Millman) Rutsky; m. Elaine Selesnik, Aug. 30, 1959. Student viola, Stuyvesant House, 1935—37, Christadora House, 1937—38. Co-writer (songs) You're Gonna be Sorry; contbr. articles to profl. jours.; author: numerous poems. Recipient Paul Elliot Meml. award, Poetry Soc. Mich., 1982, 1st pl., Ind. State Poetry Soc., Poetry Clubs Ind. Democrat. Avocations: painting, violin, piano. Home: 2930 W 5th St Brooklyn NY 11224

RUTSTEIN, DAVID W. lawyer, food products executive; b. N.Y.C., July 7, 1944; s. David and Mazie (Weissman) R.; m. Rena E. Bergsmann, July 19, 1967; children: Sara E., Charles B. BA, U. Pa., 1966; JD with honors, George Washington U., 1969. Bar: Pa. 1969, D.C. 1969. Dep. atty. gen., Pa., 1969-70; ptnr. firm Danzansky, Dickey, Tydings, Quint & Gordon, Washington, 1970-78; sr. v.p., gen. counsel Giant Food, Inc., 1978—; of counsel Venable Law Firm, 2001—. Bd. dirs., chmn., treas. Washington Met. Bd. Trade, Fed. City Coun. Bd. dirs., pres. Washington Hebrew Home for Aged, 1989-91; mem. exec. com. Fed. City Coun.; chmn. Agnes and Eugene Meyer Found., Wash. Met. Bd. Trade; trustee Greater Washington Rsch. Ctr. Mem. D.C. Bar Assn., Washington Met. Area Corp. Counsel Assn. (pres. 1986). Jewish. Home: 9 Greentree Ct Bethesda MD 20817-1440 Office: Giant Food Inc Dept 593 PO Box 1804 Washington DC 20013-1804

RUTSTEIN, SEDMARA ZAKARIAN, piano educator, musician; b. Kazan, Russia, Oct. 18, 1937; came to U.S., 1974; d. Suren and Ekaterina (Todorovskaya) Zakarian; m. Alexander Rutstein, Aug. 29, 1958; 1 child, Alla. D in Music, Leningrad State Conservatory, USSR, 1961, diploma (hon.), 1959. Prof. Leningrad State Conservatory, 1961-73; artist-in-residence Grinnell (Iowa) Coll., 1974-78; prof. Oberlin (Ohio) Conservatory, 1976—. Recording artist, classical piano music XVIII through XX centuries, 1972-98. Grantee Oberlin Coll., 1984-98. Mem. Am. Music Tchrs. Assn. Avocations: reading, music, travel. Home: 226 N Prospect St Oberlin OH 44074-1035 Office: Oberlin Coll Conservatory of Music Oberlin OH 44074

RUTSTEIN, STANLEY HAROLD, apparel retailing company executive; b. Wilkes-Barre, Pa., July 1, 1941; s. Sydney D. and Bessie H. (Cohen) R.; m. Jo Ella Rutstein; children— Wendy Sue, Michael Scott, Lynne Elizabeth. Student, Wilkes Coll., 1959-61; grad., Advanced Mgmt. Program, Harvard U., 1975. Buyer Barbara Lynn Stores, Inc., N.Y.C., 1961-63; buyer, then mdsg. mgr. Casual Corner div. U.S. Shoe Corp., Enfield, Conn., 1963-71, pres., 1971-76; pres., cons., dir. U.S. Shoe Corp., Cin., 1976-79; pres. Commonwealth Trading, Inc., Stoughton, Mass., 1979-85, Chadwick's of Boston Ltd., 1983-85; cons. Commonwealth Trading, Inc., 1985—; pres. Trim Trends, Inc., Boston, 1986-87, chmn., 1987-91; chmn., chief exec. officer, pres. Narragansett Clothing Co., Tiverton, R.I., 1987-90, also bd. dirs.; bd. dirs. Reynolds Bros. Inc., 1989-95; pres., chief exec. officer S/J Designs Inc.;, 1989—; pres., chief exec. officer DBA, Northeast Knitters. Bd. dirs. The Icing, Inc., Sycamore Shops, Inc. Bd. dirs. Ptnrs. for Disabled Youth, 1992. Mem. Young Pres. Orgn. Home: 18 Charles River Sq Boston MA 02114-3266 Office: 560 Harrison Ave Boston MA 02118-2436 E-mail: nekbos@aol.com.

RUTTAN, VERNON WESLEY, agricultural economist; b. Alden, Mich., Aug. 16, 1924; s. Ward W. and Marjorie Ann (Chaney) R.; m. Marilyn M. Barone, July 30, 1945; children: Lia Marie, Christopher, Alison Elaine, Lore Megan. BA, Yale U., 1948; MA, U. Chgo., 1950, PhD, 1952; LLD (hon.), Rutgers U., 1978; D Agrl. Sci. ((hon.), U. Kiel, Germany, 1986, Purdue U., 1991. Economist TVA, 1951-54; prof. agrl. econs. Purdue U., 1954-63; staff economist President's Council Econ. Advisers, 1961-63; economist Rockefeller Found., 1963-65; head dept. agrl. econs. U. Minn., St. Paul, 1965-70, Regent's prof., 1986-99, Regent's prof. emeritus, 2000—. Pres. Agrl. Devel. Council, N.Y.C., 1973-77 Author: (with Y. Hayami) Agricultural Development: An International Perspective, 1971, 85, Agricultural Research Policy, 1982, Aid and Development, 1989, U.S. Development Assistance Policy, 1996, Technology, Growth and Development, 2001. Recipient Alexander von Humboldt award, 1985. Fellow AAAS, Am. Acad. Arts and Scis., Am. Agrl. Econs. Assn. (pres. 1971-72, Publ. award 1956, 57, 62, 66, 67, 71, 79, 85, 97); mem. NAS. Home: 1666 Coffman St Apt 112 Saint Paul MN 55108-1326 Office: Dept Applied Econs U Minn Saint Paul MN 55108

RUTTENBERG, CHARLES BYRON, lawyer; b. Reading, Pa., Nov. 16, 1922; s. Abraham David and Mollie Belle (Rabinowitz) Ruttenberg; m. Arden Honore Suk, July 29, 1955; children: Victoria Arden, Valerie Honore, Alexandra Anne. BA, U. Va., 1946; LLB, U. Pa., 1949. Bar: D.C. With Covington & Burling, Washington; gen. counsel NSF, Nat. Found. Arts and Humanities, Washington, 1949-69; dptnr. Arent, Fox, Kintner, Plotkin & Kahn, 1969—; fed. mediator U.S. Dist. Ct., 1998—, D.C. Superior Ct., 2000—. Chmn. legis. bur., mem. exec. com., bd. dirs., gen. counsel Greater Washington Bd. Trade, 1983—92, Nat. Assn. Recording Merchandisers, Video Software Dealers Assn., 1980—95. Editor, mem. mng. bd.: U. Pa. Law Rev., 1947—49. Co-chmn. U. Pa. Law Sch. Alumni Fund, Washington, 1983—91; chmn. lawyers com. D.C. Commn. Arts, 1972—75; gen. counsel People to People Music Program, 1970—91; trustee, gen. counsel Wolf Trap Found. Performing Arts, Vienna, 1981—91, Nat. Inst. Music Theatre, Washington, 1969—90; gen. counsel, bd. dirs. Am. Film Inst., 1969—91; trustee U. D.C., 1990—94; bd. dirs., pres. Cosmos Club Hist. Preservation Found., 1987—; bd. dirs., v.p., exec. com. Iona Sr. Svcs., 1997—; bd. dirs. Washington Area Lawyers for Arts, 1984—95, Greater Washington Rsch. Ctr., 1980—95. With USAAF, 1942—46, capt. USAFR, 1946—55. Recipient Outstanding Svc. awards, U.S. Govt., 1967, 1968. Mem.: ABA, Arts Internat. (gen. counsel), U. Pa. Law Alumni Assn. (pres. 1967—71, bd. dirs. 1967—78), Washington Athletic Club (bd. govs. 1969—74), Mitchell Law Club, St. Alban's Club, Cosmos Club (bd. mgmt. 2000—), Phi Beta Kappa. Home: 4735 Butterworth Pl NW Washington DC 20016-4459 Office: Arent Fox Kintner Plotkin & Kahn 1050 Connecticut Ave NW Ste 500 Washington DC 20036-5303 E-mail: ruttenbc@arentfox.com., cbruttenberg@aol.com.

RUTTENBERG, RUTH A. economist; b. Washington, Feb. 16, 1948; d. Stanley Harvey and Gertrude Leah Bernstein Ruttenberg; children: Estye Ross, Jack Ross. BA in Econs. with honors, U. Wis., 1969; M in City Planning, U. Pa., 1971, PhD in City Planning, 1981. Prof. Bradford Coll., 1972-73; sr. assoc. Ruttenberg, Kilgallon & Assocs., Inc., Washington, 1973-86; pres. Ruth Ruttenberg & Assocs., Bethesda, Md., 1986—; sr. staff assoc. George Meany Ctr. for Labor Studies, Nat. Labor Coll., 2001—. Sr. lectr. Am. U., Washington, 1973—75; asst. prof. Howard U., Washington, 1975—82; adj. faculty U. Md., College Park, Md., 1974—; bd. mem. Be. Equalization and Rev., Washington, 1981—82; sr. economist Occupl. Safety and Health Adminstrn., Washington, 1979—80; dir. Nat. Clearinghouse for Worker Safety and Health Tng., Bethesda, 1995—2000; co-chair Instnl. Rev. Bd. Ctr. to Protect Workers Rights, Washington, 1996—; peer rev. mem. U.S. Dept. Energy, Washington, 1996, 97. Author: Occupational Safety and Health in the Chemical Industry, 1981. Bd. dirs. Group Health Assn., Washington, 1982-88, 90-94; bd. dirs., sec.-treas. Consumer Health Found., Washington, 1994—; bd. dirs. Children's Internat. Summer Villages, Washington, 1994—. Woodrow Wilson fellow Woodrow Wilson Found., 1969-70; Bicentennial grantee Govt. Sweden, 1978. Democrat. Avocations: reading, kayaking, traveling. Office: Ruth Ruttenberg & Assocs Inc 5107 Benton Ave Bethesda MD 20814-2807 E-mail: rra@rrainc.com., rruttenberg@georgemeany.org.

RUTTENBERG, SUSANN I. health sciences administrator; b. Chgo., Apr. 7, 1943; d. William and Audrey A. Kray; m. Harold Seymour Ruttenberg, Aug. 11, 1963 (div. Oct. 1977); children: Adam, Michael, Leslie. BS, Northwestern U., 1964; MBA, U. Calif., Irvine, 1993. Wrtier, prodr. Kragie Newell & Assocs., Des Moines, 1977-80; writer, prodr. Nat. Cable Prodns. and Teleshopper, 1980-81; owner, mgr. Rib Joint, Des Moines, 1978-81; gen. mgr. Stuart Anderson's Black Angus, Ariz. and Calif., 1982-87; various adminstr. positions in pediats. U. Calif., Irvine, 1988-93, adminstr. child devel. ctr., 1997-98, adminstr. dermatology, 1996—, adminstr. phys. medicine and rehab., 1999—. V.p. U. Calif. Irvine GSM Healthcare Alumni, 1995—, bd. dirs., 1999—; mem. exec. bd. Acad. Bus. Officers Group, 2000—, chair exec. bd., 2000—01, bd. dirs., 2000—. Editor, contbr.: (cookbook) Child's Play, 1989; editor, writer newsletter UCInsights on Pediatrics, 1995; contbr. Executive Decisions in Dermatology, 2000—. Women's chair United Jewish Appeal, Des Moines, 1975; bd. dirs. Child Guidance Ctr., Des Moines, 1976-77, Cmty. Telephone Coun., Des Moines, 1978-81; mem. dir.'s coun. U. Calif. Irvine Chao Family Comprehensive Cancer Ctr., 1998—; vol. rep., sec. bd. dirs. Rancho Mirage, Calif. C. of C., 1984-86. Northwestern U. scholar, 1963-64; U. Calif. Irvine Coll. Medicine Career Devel. award, 1992-93. Mem.: Assn. Dermatology Adminstrs./Mgrs. (chair newsletter com. 2001, chair comms. com. 2002—, bd. dirs. 2002—), Assn. Profs. Dermatology, Med. Group Mgmt. Assn. Avocations: cooking, reading, literacy tutoring, dancing, travel. Office: U Calif Irvine C340 Med Scis I Irvine CA 92697-0001

RUTTENCUTTER, BRIAN BOYLE, manufacturing company executive; b. Long Beach, Calif., June 15, 1953; s. Wayne Andrew and Florence Mae (Heckman) F.; m. Marilyn Ruth Grubb, Sept. 9, 1978; children: Christi Anne (dec.), Melissa Lyn. BS in Bus. Adminstrn. and Acctg., Biola U., 1976; MBA, Calif. State U., Long Beach, 1983. Cert. mgmt. acct. Controller Fuller Theol. Sem., Pasadena, Calif., 1976-80; dir. gen. acctg. Air Calif., Newport Beach, 1980-84; corp. controller PBS Bldg. Systems, Inc., Anaheim, Calif., 1984-88, v.p. fin. and adminstrn., 1988-93; CFO, v.p. fin. For Better Living, Inc., and The Quikset Orgn., Auburn and Irvine, 1993-95; v.p. fin., CFO, bd. dirs. Phillips Industries Inc., Commerce, 1996—; chmn., vice chmn., fin. commn. City of Irvine (Calif.), 1990-94, vice-chmn. cmty. svcs. commn., 1996-98. Mem. Drivers for Hwy. Safety, Irvine, Calif., 1986; bd. dirs. Grace Brethren Ch., Long Beach, 1978-80; bd. dirs. Woodbridge Cmty. Ch., Irvine, 1986-88, 91-92, vice chmn., 1991, chmn., 1992; v.p. Greater Irvine Rep. Assembly, 1990, treas., 1991. Mem. Inst. Cert. Mgmt. Accts., Inst. Mgmt. Accts., Fin. Execs. Internat. (past pres., chpt. bd. dirs., nat. bd. dirs., nat. v.p.), Assn. Corp. Growth (chpt. bd. dirs., v.p., treas.). Republican. Avocations: tennis, golf, flying stunt kites, performing contemporary Christian music. Home: 1071 Castlerock Ln Cowan Heights CA 92705-6110

RUTTER, ALAN, federal agency administrator; m. Melanie Rutter; children: Sarah, Elizabeth. BA, MPA, U. Tex. Fed. R.R. adminstr. U.S. Dept. Transp., Washington, 2001—; dep. exec. dir. Tex. High-Speed Rail Authority, 1995; dir. transp. policy State of Tex.; served Tex. Govs. Bill Clements and Mark White, 1984—90. Office: US Dept Transp Fed RR Adminstrn 1120 Vermont Ave NW 7th Flr Washington DC 20005 Office Fax: 202-493-6009.

RUTTER, ELIZABETH JANE, consulting firm executive; b. Lansing, Mich., June 27, 1955; d. Robert Emmett and Anna Lou (Edwards) Martin; m. David Bruce Rutter, June 25, 1988; children: Robert Corey Myers, Jacob Martin Myers, Laura June Rutter. Student, Harrisburg Area C.C., Pa., 1975-76, U. Mo., 1990-91, Stephens Coll., 1995—. Exec. sec. Timeter Instrument, Inc., Lancaster, Pa., 1983-85; editorial asst. U. Extension, Columbia, Mo., 1985-88; grants/contracts specialist U. Mo. Office of Sponsored Programs, 1988-91; pres. Grants Link, Inc., 1991—. Mem. Econ. Devel. Com. Ashland (Mo.) C. of C., 1991-93; chair Adminstrn. Commn. Sacred Heart Cath. Ch., Columbia, Mo., 1996; officer Exec. Bd. Advent Enterprises, Inc., Columbia, Mo.. 1992-95; bd. dirs. Ctrl. Mo. Sheltered Enterprises, Author: The Self-Sustaining Nonprofit: Planning for Success, 1997; editor: Corporate Funders Operating in Missouri, 1992, 3d edit., 1996, The Funding Connection Newsletter, 1994, Right on The Money Newsletter, 1994, Corporate Funders Operating in Texas, 1996, Corporate Funders Operating in Illinois, 1996. Named Small Svc. Bus. of Yr. Columbia C. of C., 1994, Vol. of Yr., Advent Enterprises, Inc., 1997. Mem. Nat. Soc. Fund Raising Execs. (chair ctrl. Mo. chpt. 1996), Columbia C. of C. Roman Catholic. Avocations: reading, fishing, camping, children's sports. Office: Grants Link Inc 601 W Nifong Blvd Columbia MO 65203-6804

RUTTER, FRANCES TOMPSON, publisher; b. Arlington, Mass., Apr. 12, 1920; d. Harold F. and Mildred F. (Wheeler) Tompson; m. John H. Ottemiller, Mar. 24, 1943; children: Joan Tompson Gillum, John Tompson; m. William D. Rutter, Oct. 26, 1970. AB magna cum laude, Pembroke Coll., Brown U., 1941; postgrad., Mt. Holyoke Coll., 1942-43. Res. book librarian Brown U., 1941-42; annotator ship's papers John Carter Brown Library, Providence, 1943-44; librarian Sci. Service, Washington, 1944-45; ptnr. Shoe String Press, Hamden, Conn., 1952-58; sec., treas. Shoe String Press, Inc., 1958-68, pres., treas., 1968-80, also bd. dirs.; sec.-treas., dir. Tompson-Malone, Inc., book mfrs., 1967-80; pres., treas., dir. Tompson & Rutter, Inc., 1980-89. V.p. class 1941 Pembroke Coll., 1967-73, 76-91, pres., 1973-76, head class agt., 1979-85, bequests and trust chmn., 1979-90, 40th reunion gift com., 1980, co-chair 50th reunion gift com., 1990-91, 55th reunion gift com., 1995-96; spl. projects adv. panel N.H. Commn. on Arts, 1980-84; mem. natural resources com. Grantham, 1980; mem. Grantham Planning Bd., 1981-87, sec., 1981-83, chmn., 1985-87; chmn. Grantham Recycling Com., 1988-89, Grantham Hist. Soc., 1992-96, Habitat for Humanity-Kearsarge/Sunapee chpt., 1989-94; mem. Diocesan Altar Guild Bd., 1990-93, sec., 1991-92; vol. Mary Hitchcock Meml. Hosp. Aux., 1991—; mem. vestry St. Paul's Episc. Ch., 1997-2000, jr. warden, 1998-2000; assoc. Holy Cross Monastery, West Park, N.Y. Mem. Friends of Fernald Libr. of Colby-Sawyer Coll., ACLU (life), LWV (editor newsletter 1987-89), Assoc. Alumni Brown U. (bd. dirs. 1981-83), Nicholas Brown Soc., Pembroke Ctr. Assocs. (coun. 1984-86), Soc. for Preservation N.H. Forests, Episcopal Peace Fellowship, Phi Beta Kappa. Episcopalian. Home: 80 Azalea Cir # 19 White River Junction VT 05001 E-mail: franbill@valley.net.

RUTTER, JEREMY BENTHAM, archaeologist, educator; b. Boston, June 23, 1946; s. Peter and Nancy Kendall (Comstock) R.; m. Sarah Robbins Herndon, Jan. 31, 1970; children: Benjamin Ryerson, Nicholas Kendall. BA Classics with honors, Haverford Coll., 1967; PhD Classical Archaeology, U. Pa., 1974; MA, Dartmouth Coll., 1993. Vis. asst. prof. dept. classics UCLA, 1975-76, from asst. prof. to prof. dept. classics, 1976—, chmn. dept. classics, 1992-98, prof. humanities, 2001—. Participant excavations West Germany, 1966, Italy, 1968-69, Greece, 1972, 73-74, 75, 77, 78, 80-81, 84-86, 88-89, 91—; mem. numerous coms. Am. Sch. Classical Studies, Athens. Author: Lerna III: The Pottery of Lerna IV, 1995; exec. com. Am. Sch. Classical Studies at Athens; contbr. numerous articles, reviews to profl. jours. With U.S. Army, 1969-71, Vietnam. Woodrow Wilson fellow, 1967-68; NDEA fellow U. Pa., 1968-69, 71-73; Olivia James Traveling fellow Archeol. Inst. Am., 1974-75; NEH rsch. grantee, 1979-81; travel grantee Am. Coun. Learned Socs., 1982; sr. faculty grantee, 1985-86, 91-92, 2001-02. Mem. Am. Schs. Oriental Rsch., Archaeol. Inst. Am. (numerous coms.), Classical Assn. New England, Phi Beta Kappa. Home: 47 Eagle Rdg Lebanon NH 03766-1900 Office: Dept Classics Dartmouth College Hanover NH 03755 E-mail: jeremy.rutter@dartmouth.edu.

RUTTER, MARIE E. music educator; b. Bklyn., Nov. 6, 1939; d. Edward George de Beaumont and Lela Dean Graham; m. Stuart Mishler Rutter, Aug. 26, 1961; children: Deborah Gulliver, Jeanne Meister, Suzanne Cook, Caryn. BA, Albion Coll., 1961. Profl. cert. in piano Music Tchrs. Nat. Assn. Pub. sch. music tchr. Mona Shores Sch. Dist., Muskegon, Mich., 1961-63; pvt. piano tchr., 1962-63, Ft. Wayne, Ind., 1963-73, Lincoln, Nebr., 1973-74, Elk Grove Village, Ill., 1974-76, Hickory, N.C., 1976-84, Schaumburg, Ill., 1984—. Elder Ch. of the Cross, Hoffman Estates, Ill., 1995—96, mem. Christian edn. com., 1996—2000. Mem. Ill. State Music Tchrs. Assn. (profl. cert. in piano, state syllabus performance chair 1994—), N.W. Suburban Music Tchrs. Assn. (syllabus chair, 2nd v.p., 1st v.p., pres.). Presbyterian. Avocations: quilting, reading, sewing, gardening.

RUTTER, MARSHALL ANTHONY, lawyer; b. Pottstown, Pa., Oct. 18, 1931; s. Carroll Lennox and Dorothy (Tagert) R.; m. Winifred Hitz, June 6, 1953 (div. 1970); m. Virginia Ann Hardy, Jan. 30, 1971 (div. 1992); children: Deborah Frances, Gregory Russell, Theodore Thomas; m. Terry Susan Knowles, Dec. 19, 1992. BA, Amherst (Mass.) Coll., 1954; JD, U. Pa., 1959. Bar: Calif 1960. Assoc. O'Melveny & Myers, Los Angeles, 1959-64, Flint & MacKay, Los Angeles, 1964-67, ptnr., 1967-72, Rutter, Hobbs & Davidoff, Los Angeles, 1973—. Bd. dirs. Ojai Festivals Ltd., 2001. Gov. The Music Ctr. of L.A. County, 1978-86, 89-92; bd. dirs. Music Ctr. Operating Co., 1992-96; bd. dirs. Chorus Am., Washington, 1987-96, pres., 1993-95; bd. dirs. L.A. Master Chorale Assn., 1964—, pres., 1980-92, chmn. 1992-96, vice chmn., 1996-2001; vestryman All Saints Ch., Beverly Hills, Calif., 1983-86, 88-90. Mem. ABA, Assn. Bus. Trial Lawyers (bd. dirs. 1980-82), L.A. County Bar Assn., Beverly Hills Bar Assn., Century City Bar Assn., English-Speaking Union (various offices L.A. chpt. 1963-91), L.A. Jr. C. of C. (bd. dirs. 1964-67). Democrat. Episcopalian. Avocations: classical and choral music, golf. Home: 1045 S Orange Grove Blvd Apt 10 Pasadena CA 91105-1795 Office: Rutter Hobbs & Davidoff Ste 2700 1900 Ave of Stars Los Angeles CA 90067-4508 Fax: 310-286-1728. E-mail: mrutter@rutterhobbs.com.

RUTTER, MICHAEL LLEWELLYN, child psychiatry educator; b. Brummanna, Lebanon, Aug. 15, 1933; arrived in Eng., 1936; s. Llewellyn Charles and Winifred Olive (Barber) R.; m. Marjorie Heys, Dec. 27, 1958; children: Sheila Carol, Stephen Michael, Christine Anne. MB, BChir, U. Birmingham, Eng., 1955, MD with honors, 1963; diploma in psychol. medicine, U. London, 1961; degree (hon.), U. Leiden, 1985, Cath. U., 1990, U. Birmingham, 1990, U. Edinburgh, 1990, U. Chgo., 1993, U. Minn., 1993, U. Ghent, 1994; degree, U. Warwick, 1999, U. East Anglia, 2000, U. North London, 2000. Various tchg. positions in pediat., neurology, internal, 1955-58; registrar then sr. registrar Maudsley Hosp., London, 1958-62; mem. sci. staff MRC Social Psychiatry Rsch. Unit, 1962-65; sr. lectr. then reader U. London Inst. Psychiatry, 1966-73, prof. child psychiatry, 1973-98, hon. dir. MRC Child Psychiatry unit, 1984-98, Social Genetic and Devel. Psychiatry Rsch. Ctr., 1994; prof. devel. psychopathology Inst. Psychiatry, 1998—. Nuffield med. traveling fellow Albert Einstein Coll. Medicine, N.Y.C., 1961-62; fellow Ctr. for Advanced Study in Behavioral Scis., Stanford, Calif., 1979-80; hon. prof. U. Amsterdam, 2001. Author: Helping Troubled Children, 1975, Maternal Deprivation Reassessed, 2nd edit., 1981, (with H. Giller) Juvenile Delinquency: Trends & Perspectives, 1983, (with M. Rutter) Developing Minds: Challenge and Continuity Accross the Lifespan, 1993, (with H. Giller, A. Hagell) Antisocial Behavior by Young People, 1998, (with T. Moffitt, A. Caspi and P. Silva) Sex Differences in Antisocial Behavior: Conduct Disorder, Delinquency and Violence in the Dunedin Longitudinal Study, 2001; co-editor: Child and Adolescent Psychiatry, 4th edit., 2002, Stress, Risk and Resilience In Children and Adolescents: Processes, Mechanisms and Interventions, 1994, Psychosocial Disorders in Young People: Time Trends & Their Causes, 1995, Antisocial Behavior by Young People, 1998, Autism: A Reappraisal of Concepts and Treatment, 1978, Development Through Life: A Handbook For Clinicians, 1994; editor: Scientific Foundations of Developmental Psychiatry, 1980, Developmental Neuropsychiatry, 1983. Recipient Am. Assn. Mental Deficiency rsch. award, 1975, C. Anderson Aldrich award Am. Acad. Pediat., 1981, Disting. Sci. Contbn. award APA, 1995, Castilla del Pino prize for achievement in psychiatry, Spain, 1995; named Goulstonian lectr. Royal Coll. Physicians, 1973, Salmon lectr. N.Y. Acad. Medicine, 1979, Adolf Meyer ward lectr. APA, 1985; Belding travelling scholar, 1963; Rock Carling fellow, 1979, Royal Soc. fellow, 1987. Fellow Royal Soc. Medicine (London, hon.), Royal Coll. Pediat. and Child Health (hon. founding fellow 1996), Royal Coll. Psychiatrists (London, hon.), Kings Coll. London, Brit. Acad.; mem. AAAS (fgn. hon.), Internat. Soc. Rsch. in Child and Adolescent Psychiatry (pres. 1997-99), U.S. Nat. Acad. Edn. (fgn. assoc.), Brit. Pediat. Assn. (hon.), Assn. Child Psychology and Psychiatry (chmn. 1973-74), Brit.

Psychol. Soc. (hon. fellow), Am. Acad. Child Psychiatry (hon. membership), NAS (fgn. assoc. Inst. Medicine), Soc. Rsch. in Adolescence (John P. Hill award for excellence in theory devel. and rsch. 1992), Soc. Rsch. Child Devel. (pres. 1999-2001), Inst. Child Health (London, hon. fellow 1996), Internat. Acad. Rsch. in Learning Disabilities, Academia Europaea (founding mem.), Acad. Med. Scis. (founder). Home: 190 Court Ln London SE21 7ED England Office: Inst Psychiatry DeCrespigny Park London SE5 8AF England E-mail: j.wickham@iop.kcl.ac.uk.

RUTTER, NATHANIEL WESTLUND, geologist, educator; b. Omaha, Nov. 22, 1932; s. John Elliot and Karleen (Ludden) R.; m. Mary Marie Munson, Sept. 11, 1961; children: Todd, Christopher. BS, Tufts U., 1955; MS, U. Alaska, 1962; PhD, U. Alta., 1965, DSc honoris causa, 2001. Geologist Venezuelan Atlantic Refining Co., 1955-58; research scientist Geol. Survey Can., Calgary, Alta., 1965-74, head urban projects sect Ottawa, Ont., 1974; environ. advisor Nat. Energy Bd., 1974-75; assoc. prof. dept. geology U. Alta., Edmonton, 1975-77, 77-80, prof., chmn. dept., 1980-89, 77-96; pres. Can. nat. com. Internat. Geol. Correlation Program, UNESCO, 1996-97; prof. dept. atmospheric scis. U. Alta. (Can.), Edmonton, 1996-97, univ. prof., 1997—, assoc. dean. faculty sci. Pres. Internat. Union Quaternary Rsch. Congress, 1982-87; mem. Internat. Geosphere-Biosphere Program: A Study of Global Change, 1988-94; mem. rsch. com. Can. Global Change Program, 1992-94; chmn. global change com. INUQA, 1991-95; hon. prof. Chinese Acad. Sci., Beijing, 1994—; disting. lectr. Sigma Xi, 1995-97; mem. scientific bd. Internat. Union of Geol. Scis.-UNESCO, 1997—. Contbr. numerous articles to profl. jours.; assoc. editor Arctic, Geosci. Can. Quaternary Rsch.; mem. editorial bd. Quaternary Sci. Revs., Quaternary Rsch., Estonia Jour. Sci., Arctic; editor in chief Quaternary Internat. Grantee Natural Scis. and Engring. Research Council of Can.; grantee Energy, Mines and Resources; named Officer Order of Can., 2001. Fellow Royal Soc. Can.; mem. Assn. Profl. Engrs., Geologists and Geophysicists of Alta., Internat. Union Quaternary Rsch. (v.p. 1982-87, pres. 1987-91, hon. 1999), Can. Quaternary Assn. (v.p. 1981-82, Johnston medal 1997), Geol. Soc. Am. (mgmt. bd. dirs. quaternary geol. and geomorphology div. 1982-84), Geol. Assn. of Can. (J. Willis Ambrose medal 1998), Internat. Assn. Quaternary Rsch. (hon.). Clubs: Explorer's, Cosmos. Home: Rural Route 3 Stony Plain AB Canada T7Z 1X3 Office: U Alta Dept Earth & Atmospheric Scis Edmonton AB Canada T6G 2E3 E-mail: nat.rutter@ualberta.ca.

RUTTINGER, GEORGE DAVID, lawyer; b. Detroit, Jan. 17, 1948; s. George Jacob and Margaret Mary (Smith) R.; m. Camille Ann Larson, Oct. 4, 1975; children: Jacob Charles, David Hayes, Philip George. AB with high distinction and honors, U. Mich., 1970, JD magna cum laude, 1973. Bar: Calif. 1975, D.C. 1975, U.S. Dist. Ct. D.C. 1975, U.S. Dist. Ct. Md. 1987, U.S. Ct. Appeals (D.C. and 4th cirs.) 1984, U.S. Ct. Appeals (1st cir.) 1988, U.S. Supreme Ct. 1984, U.S. Dist. Ct. (ea. dist.) Mich. 1995, U.S. Ct. Appeals (6th cir.) 1996, U.S. Ct. Appeals (3d cir.) 1999. Law clk. to Hon. Malcolm R. Wilkey U.S. Ct. Appeals, Washington, 1973-74; assoc. Latham & Watkins, L.A., 1974, Crowell & Moring (formerly Jones, Day, Reavis & Pogue), Washington, 1975-79, ptnr., 1980—. Author: (with others) Containing Legal Costs: ADR Strategies for Corporations, Law Firms and Government, 1988; contbr. articles to profl. jours. Fellow Am. Bar Found. Office: Crowell & Moring 1001 Pennsylvania Ave NW Fl 10 Washington DC 20004-2595 E-mail: gruttinger@crowell.com.

RUTYNA, RICHARD ALBERT, history educator; b. San Diego, Apr. 10, 1937; s. Micszlav and Mary Elizabeth (Sawyer) R. BA in History, Coll. of William and Mary, Norfolk, Va., 1959; MA in History, Coll. of William and Mary, Williamsburg, Va., 1961; postgrad., U. Va., 1963-66. Tchr. history Granby H.S., Norfolk, 1960-61; instr. history Old Dominion U., 1961-63, asst. prof., 1966-78, assoc. prof., 1978-92, assoc. prof. emeritus, 1992—. Author: Heritage and Horizons: Old Dominion University, 1987, The History of Freemasonry in Virginia, 1998; editor: (anthologies) Virginia in The American Revolution I, 1977, Virginia in The American Revolution II, 1983, Conceived in Conscience, 1983; contbr. articles to profl. and other publs. Sec. 2nd Congl. Dist. Dem. Com., Va., 1968-72, chmn., 1972-75; mem. Dem. State Cen. Com., 1968-75; mem. steering com. Dem. Party, 1972-75. Sgt. USMCR, 1954-62. Mem. Phi Alpha Theta. Roman Catholic. Avocation: church-state relations. Home: 1228 Lowery Ct Norfolk VA 23502-2209

RUTZ, RICHARD FREDERICK, physicist, researcher; b. Alton, Ill., Feb. 9, 1919; s. Erwin William and Esther Norma (Brooks) R.; m. Mary Lamsom Lambert, June 10, 1945; children— Frederick R., Carl R., William L. BA, Shurtleff Coll., Alton, Ill., 1941; MS, State U. Iowa, 1947. Staff mem. Sandia Corp., Albuquerque, 1948-51; mem. staff, mgr. IBM T.J. Watson Sr. Rsch. Ctr., Yorktown Heights, N.Y., 1951-87. Contbr. articles to profl. jours.; patentee numerous semicond. devices With U.S. Maritime Svc., 1941-42, USAAF, 1942-46. Fellow IEEE; mem. Am. Phys. Soc. Home: 9 Burgundy Ct Grand Junction CO 81503-1212 E-mail: rfrutz@frontier.net.

RUUD, CLAYTON OLAF, engineering educator; b. Glassgow, Mont., July 31, 1934; s. Asle and Myrtle (Bleken) R.; children: Kelley Astrid, Kirsten Anne; m. Paula Kay Mannino, Feb. 24, 1990. BS in Metallurgy, Wash. State U., 1957; MS in Materials Sci., San Jose State U., 1967; PhD in Materials Sci., U. Denver, 1970. Registered profl. engr., Calif., Colo. Asst. remelt metallurgist Kaiser Aluminum & Chem. Corp., Trentwood, Wash., 1957-58; devel. engr. Boeing Airplane Co., Seattle, 1958-60; mfg. rsch. engr. Lockheed Missiles & Space Corp., Sunnyvale, Calif., 1960-63; rsch. engr. FMC Corp., San Jose, 1963-67; sr. rsch. scientist U. Denver, 1967-79; prof. indsl. engring. Pa. State U., University Park, 1979—. Cons. in field; bd. dirs. Denver X-Ray Inst. Inc., Altoona, Pa. Editor series of books: Advances in X-Ray Analysis, Vol. 12-22, 1970-80, Nondestructive Character of Materials, Vol. 1-6, 1983—; editor X-Ray Spectometry, 1975-87; editl. com. Nondestructive Testing and Evaluation, 1991—. Mem., chmn. Nat. Acad. Sci. Safe Drinking Water Com., Washington, 1976-78. Recipient IR 100 award, 1983, Gov.'s New Product Award, Pa. Soc. Profl. Engrs., 1988. Fellow ASM Internat. (chmn. Resid. Stress Conf. 1989-91); mem. Internat. Ctr. for Diffraction Data, Soc. Mfg. Engrs., Metall. Soc. of AIME. Achievements include patent on Method for Determining Internal Stresses in Polycrystalline Solids; patent on Stress-Unstressed Standard for X-Ray Stress Analysis; invention of a Fiber Optic Based Position Sensitive Scintillation X-Ray Detector; invention of an instrument for simultaneous stress and phase composition measurement; development of an X-ray diffraction instrument for manufacturing process quality control; founder, developer, and co-director of Pa. State U. quality and manufacturing management masters degree. Office: 310 Leonhard University Park PA 16802 E-mail: cor1@psu.edu.

RUUD, JAY WESLEY, dean; b. Racine, Wis., Nov. 3, 1950; s. Wesley J. and Alyce R.; m. Cynthia Lee Krsitopeit, Sept. 4, 1971 (div. Nov. 29, 1993); m. Stacey Margaret Jones, Mar. 2, 2001. BA, U. Wis.-Parkside, Kenosha, Wis., 1972; MA, U. Wis.-Milw., 1974, PhD, 1981. Instr. English U. Wis.-Parkside, Kenosha, 1978-83, testing coord., 1983-84; instr. English U. Wis.-Marathon County, Wausau, Wis., 1984-85; prof. English Northern State U., Aberdeen, S.D., 1985-96, asst. dean coll. arts and scis., 1996-97, dean coll. arts and scis., 1997—. Dir. NEH Inst. on Lit. of Plains Indians, Aberdeen, S.D., 1994, NEH Inst. on Chaucer's Canterbury Tales, Aberdeen, S.D., 1989. Author: Many a Song and Many a Leccherous Lay: Tradition and Individuality in Chaucer's Lyric Poetry, 1992; editor: Proceedings of the First Dakotas Conference on Earlier British Literature, 1992, Proceedings of the Seventh Northern Plains Conference on Early British, 1999; contbr. articles to profl. jours. Named Outstanding Faculty Mem. Northern State U., 1989; recipient Burlington Northern Faculty Achievement award Burlington Northern Faound. and Northern State U., 1989. Mem. New Chaucer Soc., Medieval Assn. of the Midwest. Avocation: acting in local community theater. E-mail address. Office: Northern State U 1200 S Jay St Aberdeen SD 57401-7155 Fax: 605-626-2635. E-mail: ruudj@northern.edu.

RUWE, ROBERT P. federal judge; b. 1941; Grad., Xavier U., 1963; JD, No. Ky. U., 1970. Chief counsel IRS Dept. Treasury, 1970-87; judge U.S. Tax Ct., Washington, 1987—. Office: US Tax Ct 400 2nd St NW Washington DC 20217-0002

RUWWE, WILLIAM OTTO, retired automotive engineer; b. Cuba, Mo., July 25, 1930; s. Otto Albert and Maude May (Hines) R.; m. Helen Leona Haynes, Jan. 1, 1958; children: Teresa Lynn, Nancy Jean. BS, Cen. Mo. State U., 1959. Engring. clk. Wagner Brake div. Cooper Industries, St. Louis, 1959-64, engr., 1964-67, quality control chemist, 1967-68, mfg. mgr., 1968-82, plant mgr., 1982-93; ret., 1993. Inventor electroless nickle plating process for cast iron, 1964, dissolution of crystal formation in brake fluid, 1971. With U.S. Army, 1951-53. Mem. Soc. Automotive Engrs. (cert., product bus. com.1985-90), St. Louis Geneal. Soc. Avocations: genealogy, history. Home: 540 Innsbrook Estates Dr Innsbrook MO 63390-5325

RUX, PAUL PHILIP, management consultant, educator; b. Ripon, Wis., Mar. 29, 1944; s. Emil Richard and Irene Theresa (Menge) R.; m. Parry Bee Parkinson, Nov. 11, 1967 (div. Oct. 1983). BA, U. Wis., 1967, MALS, 1977, PhD, 1994; MA, U. Toronto, Ont., Can., 1971. Cert. sch. dist. adminstr., N.Y.; K-12 libr., Ill.; 7-12 tchr., Ont., Can. Tchr. Loyalist Collegiate, Kingston, Ont., 1975-76, Wayland Acad., Beaver Dam, Wis., 1977-80; dist. libr. Warren (Ill.) Schs., 1981-88; libr. dir. The Masters Sch., Dobbs Ferry, N.Y., 1988-90, South H.S., Valley Stream, 1990-91; author/columnist/editor Linworth Pub., Worthington, Ohio, 1981-97; automation cons. S.W. Wis. Libr. Sys., Fennimore, 1992-98; mgmt. prof. Upper Iowa U. Ctr., Madison, Wis., 1996—; pres., cons. Quality Plus Sys., Inc., Middleton, 1997—; prof. tech. Keller Grad. Sch. Mgmt. Ctr., Milw., 1998—. Prof. tech. Kellert Grad. Sch. Mgmt. Ctr., Milw., 1998—; prof. mgmt. Marquette U., 2000—, Cardinal Stritch U., 2001—, Lakeland Coll. Online, 2001—; mem. accreditation team Johnstown (Ill.) Schs., 1987, The Spence Sch., N.Y.C., 1991; cons. Port Byron (Ill.) Schs., 1995; pres. planning panel Ill. Rural Devel. Ctr., 1998; cons. mng. info. Kellogg Found., 1998—; keynote spkr. ann. conf. Assn. Instl. Rschrs. Upper Midwest, 1999. Editor: Skills for Life, 1993; contbr. articles to profl. jours. Mem. Universal Svc. Fund Coun., Wis. State Pub. Svc. Commn., Madison, Wis., 1996—; pres. Youth Care, Inc., Middleton, 1999—. Recipient Svc. citation Wis. State Telecom. Assn., 1993, Wis. State Senate, 1997 Winner Top 10 Rural Devel. award Gov. Wis., 1998; U. Toronto Grad. fellow, 1969-70; Internat. Engring. Consortium faculty scholar, 1995—. Mem. Nat. Fedn. Ind. Bus., Meiklejohn Integrated Liberal Studies Assn. (v.p. 1998-2000), U. Toronto Alumni Assn., World Future Soc., Harbor Athletic Club, Univ. Club, Hoofers Sailing Club. Lutheran. Avocations: sailing, skiing, folk dancing, personal fitness, reading. Office: Quality Plus Systems Inc 7229 University Ave # 2 Middleton WI 53562-2759 E-mail: PRux@badger.alumni.wisc.edu.

RUXIN, PAUL THEODORE, lawyer; b. Cleve., Apr. 14, 1943; s. Charles and Olyn Judith (Koller) R.; m. Joanne Camy, May 25, 1965; children; Marc J., Sarah. BA, Amherst Coll., 1965; LLB, U. Va., 1968. Bar: Ill. 1968, U.S. Dist. Ct. (no. dist.) Ill. 1968, U.S. Ct. Appeals D.C. 1972. Assoc. Isham, Lincoln & Beale, Chgo., 1968-73, ptnr., 1974-77; ptnr., chmn. energy utilities sect. Jones, Day, Reavis & Pogue, Cleve., 1977—. Mem. Hudson Archtl. and Hist. Bd. Rev., 1981-81; mem. Folger Shakespeare Libr. Com., 1999—; exec. bd. Greater Cleve. Boy Scouts Am., 1978-90; bd. dirs. Cleve. chpt. ARC, 1991-97. Mem. ABA, Ohio State Bar Assn. (pub. utilities sect.), Bar Assn. Greater Cleve., Fed. Energy Bar Assn. (com. chmn. 1981), Chgo. Bar Assn., Club at Soc. Ctr., Rowfant Club, Chgo. Club, Caxton Club, Grolier Club. Office: Jones Day Reavis & Pogue 77 W Wacker Dr Fl 35 Chicago IL 60601-1662 also: 901 Lakeside Ave Cleveland OH 44114-1116 E-mail: paultruxin@jonesday.com.

RUYBALID, LOUIS ARTHUR, social worker, community development consultant; b. Allison, Colo., Apr. 6, 1925; s. Mike Joseph and Helen Mary (Rodriguez) R.; m. Seraphima Alexander, June 12, 1949; children: Mariana, John. BA, U. Denver, 1946-49, MSW, 1951; PhD, U. Calif., Berkeley, 1970; Professor Ad-Honorem (hon.), Nat. U., Caracas, Venezuela, 1964. Social worker, Ariz., Calif., Colo., 1951-62; advisor community devel. Unitarian Service Com., Caracas, 1962-64, U.S. Agy. for Internat. Devel., Rio de Janeiro, Brazil, 1964-66; area coordinator U.S. Office Econ. Opportunity, San Francisco, 1966-68; prof., dept. head U. So. Colo., Pueblo, 1974-80; licensing analyst State of Calif., Campbell, 1984—; prof. sch. of social work Highlands U., Las Vegas, N.Mex., 1988-89. Cons. UN, Caracas, 1978, Brazilian Govt., Brazilia, 1964-66, Venezuelan Govt., Caracas, 1962-64. Author: (books) Favela, 1970, Glossary for Hominology, 1978, (research instrument) The Conglomerate Hom., 1976. Mem. exec. com. Pueblo (Colo.) Regional Planning Com., 1974-79, Nat. Advisory com. The Program Agy. United Presbyn. Ch., 1978-79. Served with USN, 1944-46. Recipient Pro Mundo Beneficio medal Brazilian Acad. Human Sci., Sao Paulo, 1976; United Def. Fund fellow U. Calif., Berkeley, 1961-62, Cert. World Leadership Internat. Leaders of Achievement, 1988-89. Mem. NASW (cert.), Ethnic Minority Commn., IMAGE (nat. edn. chair), Am. Hominol. Assn. (nat. pres. 1975-79), U. Calif. Alumni Assn., AARP (minority spokesperson), Phi Beta Kappa, Phi Sigma Iota. Democrat. Avocations: tennis, boxing history. Home and Office: Ruybalid Assoc Inc 129 Calle Don Jose Santa Fe NM 87501-2364 *Personal philosophy: As a personal credo, I have adopted the philosophy of the Pueblo Indians of New Mexico which is: Amity, not conquest, stability, not strife, conservation, not waste, restraint, not aggression, I embrace the conviction that human energy should be used to care for the primal needs of people!.*

RUYECHAN, MICHAEL J., JR. writer; b. Aug. 3, 1966; Assocs., ICM Sch. of Bus., Pitts., 1986. Author: From the Pillow and Through a Dream, 1997.

RUZICKA, CHARLES EDWARD, music educator, director; b. Grafton, N.D., Mar. 15, 1941; m. Barbara Jean Finney, Oct. 8, 1945; children: Todd, Tami, Amy. MA in Vocal Music, U. N.D., 1974; D in Musical Arts, U. Iowa, 1983. Music tchr. pub. and parochial sch., N.D., Minn., and Iowa, 1963—76; choral music dir. Dakota Wesleyan U., SD, 1979—80, Bemidji (Minn.) State U., 1980—83, Mayville (N.D.) State University, 1983—92; dir. choral activities Minn. State U., Moorhead, 1992—. Singer, chorister: Norman Luboff Choir, 1967; composer: (choral arrangement) Swing Low, Sweet Chariot-SSATB , 1987, Bound For The Promised Land-SATB, 1989, (choral arrangement) Alleluia! Sing To Jesus-SATB/piano/flute, 1988, Loch Lomond-SATB, 1992, Numerous arrangements for the Catholic Church Service, (songs) Come To Me and Rest-SATB, 1996, Flow Gently, Sweet Afton-TTBB, 2002, (choral edit.) Te Deum in C, 1994. Mem.: N.D. Am. Choral Dirs. Assn. (pres. 1990—91), Nat. Assn. Tchrs. Singing, Music Educators Nat. Conf., Am. Choral Dirs. Assn., Pi Kappa Lambda. Avocations: photography, choral music composing and arranging. Home: 2855 Edgewood Dr Fargo ND 58102 Office: Minn State U Moorhead 1104 7th Ave S Moorhead MN 56563 Office Fax: 218-236-4097. Personal E-mail: ruzicka@mnstate.edu. Business E-Mail: ruzicka@mnstate.edu.

RUZOW, DANIEL ARTHUR, lawyer; b. Bronx, N.Y., Apr. 27, 1951; s. Theodore Morton and Renee Rhoda Ruzow; m. Meris Francie Entin, June 16, 1974; children; Jenny, Benjamin. BA, Franklin & Marshall Coll., 1973; JD, Fordham U., 1976. Bar: N.Y. 1977, U.S. Ct. Appeals (2d cir.) 1977, U.S. Dist. Ct. (so. and ea. dists.) N.Y. 1977, U.S. Dist. Ct. (no. and we. dists.) N.Y. 1985. Assoc. Arum, Friedman & Katz, N.Y.C., 1976-79; asst. counsel N.Y. State Dept. Environ. Conservation, Albany, 1979-80, hearings counsel, 1980-84, asst. commr., commr.'s counsel, 1984-85; assoc. Whiteman, Osterman & Hanna, 1985-86, ptnr., 1986—, mng. ptnr., 1993—. Co-author: Environmental Impact Review in New York, 1990-01. Mem. bioethics com. St. Margaret's House and Hosp. for Babies, Albany, 1984—. Mem. ABA, N.Y. State Bar Assn. (chmn. environ. law sect. 2001-02, co-chmn. environ. impact assessment com. of environ. law 1983-97, mem. bd. of editors, editor environ. jour. 1984—), Assn. Bar City N.Y., Albany Bar Assn. Jewish. Home: 34 Via Da Vinci Clifton Park NY 12065-2907 Office: Whiteman Osterman & Hanna One Commerce Pla Albany NY 12260 E-mail: dar@woh.com.

RYALL, MARTY, state official; Campaign mgr. U.S. Senator Paul Coverell , Ga., 1998; nat. dep. polit. dir. Elizabeth Dole for Pres., 1999; campaign mgr. Tom Gallagher for U.S. Senate , Fla., 2000; exec. dir. Republican Party Del., 2000; with Bush/Cheney Recount Team, Fla., 2000; exec. dir. Republican Party of Ark., state chmn., 2002. Republican. Office: 1201 west 6th St Little Rock AR 72201*

RYAN, ALLAN JAMES, publishing executive, editor; b. Bklyn., Dec. 9, 1915; s. Lorne McDonnell and Valerie (Britton) R.; m. Agnes Louise Nelson, July 4, 1942; children: Brendan Michael, James Allan, Robert Edward. BA, Yale U., 1936; MD, Columbia U., 1940; D in Sports Sci., U.S. Sports Acad., 1983. Diplomate Am. Bd. Gen. Surgery. Intern in gen. surgery Kings County Hosp., Bklyn., 1940-42, research fellow surgery, 1942-43; asst. resident surgery Grace New Haven (Conn.) Hosp., 1943-45; chief resident surgery Long Island (N.Y.) Coll. Hosp., Bklyn., 1945-46; attending surgeon Meriden (Conn.) Hosp., 1947-1965; assoc. prof. U. Wis., Madison, 1965-70, prof., 1970-76; editor-in-chief Postgrad. Medicine, Mpls., 1976-79, The Physician & Sports Medicine, Mpls., 1973-85; dir. Sports Medicine Enterprise, Edina, Minn., 1985-95; editor-in-chief Fitness in Bus. mag., 1986-90. Athletic teams physician U. Wis., Madison, 1965-76. Author: Medical Care of Athlete, 1962, Guide to Running, 1980; co-author: The Healthy Dancer's Complete Guide to Health Care, 1989; editor: Sports Medicine, 1974, Dance Medicine, 1986; co-editor: Sports Medicine, 2d edit., 1989, The Healthy Dancer, 1989. Mem. Commn. Mil. Accidents, Washington, 1964-69; med. examiner City of Meriden, 1947-65; trustee U.S. Sports Academy, Mobile, 1985-87; mem. Minn. Gov.'s Coun. on Phys. Fitness and Sports, 1986—. Recipient Silver Medal award City of Paris, 1983, Nat. Phys. Fitness Leadership award Jr. C. of C., 1971. Fellow Am. Coll. Sports Medicine (pres. 1963—), Am. Orthopaedic Soc. Sports Medicine (assoc.); mem. Am. Alliance Health, Phys. Edn. Recreation and Dance, Council Phys. Fitness and Sports (cons., pres. 1960—), AMA (commn. on med. aspects of athletics), Internat. Fedn. Sports Medicine (sec. gen. 1980-86), Phi Beta Kappa, Sigma Xi. Republican. Roman Catholic. Avocations: racing bicycles, attending veterans classification.

RYAN, ALLYN CAUAGAS, writer, educator; b. Larena, The Philippines, June 2, 1938; came to U.S., 1957; d. Ignacio Fallorina Cauagas and Ignacia (Prudencia) Padayhag; m. James Edward Ryan, June 13, 1964; children: Monica Lynn Ryan-Border, Colleen Marie Ryan-Spence. BA in English, UCLA, 1959, MFA in Theater, 1964. Cert. tchr. lang. arts, lit., comm. arts, theater arts, basic edn., Calif. Adj. faculty Saddleback Coll., Mission Viejo, Calif., 1983-90, Orange Coast Coll., Costa Mesa, 1986-87, Chapman U., Orange, 1987-88, Rancho Santiago Coll., Santa Ana, 1986-98. Author: Salt Mines, 2001, Phantom of Alabat, 2002, Ulan, the Rain Maiden, 2002; contbr. poetry, short stories to profl. jours. Mem. legis. adv. com. Rancho Santiago Coll., 1996-97, instructional calendar group mem., 1996-97. UCI Writing Project fellow, 1989. Mem. NEA, Calif. Tchrs. Assn., C.C. Assn. (WHO award 1997), Continuing Edn. Faculty Assn. (Rancho Santiago Coll. chpt. pres. 1996-97, negotiations chmn. 1995-96). Avocations: oil painting, gourmet cooking. Home: 37261 Mojave Sage St Palm Desert CA 92211-1389

RYAN, ARTHUR FREDERICK, insurance company executive; b. Bklyn., Sept. 14, 1942; s. Arthur Vincent and Gertrude (Wingert) R.; m. Patricia Elizabeth Kelly; children: Arthur, Kelly Ann, Kevin, Kathleen. BA in Math., Providence Coll., 1963. Area mgr. Data Corp., Washington, 1965-72; project mgr. Chase Manhattan Corp. and Bank, N.Y.C., 1972-73, 2d v.p., 1973-74, v.p., 1974-75, ops. exec., 1978-82, exec. v.p., from 1982, vice-chmn., then pres., chief operating officer, 1990-94; chmn., CEO Prudential Ins. Co. Am., Newark, 1994—. Mem. policy and planning com.; bd. dirs., chmn. audit com. Depository Trust Co.; past mem. exec. com., Cedel (European Depository); past chmn. steering com., program mgr. CHIPS Same Day Settlement, N.Y. Clearing House. Past bd. dirs. Urban Acad. N.Y.C. Lt. U.S. Army, 1963-65. Mem. Am. Bankers Assn. (vice chmn. ops. and automation div. and govt. rels. coun., past chmn. internat. ops. com.). Office: Prudential Ins Co Am Prudential Plaza 24th Fl 751 Broad St Newark NJ 07102-3714*

RYAN, BARBARA DIANE, management information systems director; b. Phila., Nov. 3, 1950; d. Joseph Wayne and Elsie Elaine (Schafer) Hart; m. Dennis M. Ryan, Mar. 20, 1976; 1 child, Christine Susan. BA in Math., Eastern Coll., St. Davids, Pa., 1972. Computer programmer H. F. Michel, King of Prussia, Pa., 1972-73, L. P. Muller, King of Prussia, 1973-77, Hajoca Corp., Ardmore, Pa., 1977-78, MIS dir., 1978—. Vol. installing, setting up and tng. for home personal computers, 1991—. Vol. chmn. publicity com. Trinity Luth. Ch., 1985-87, supt. Sunday sch., 1986-88, vol. Sunday sch. tchr., 1988-91, chmn. staff support Cong. Coun. 1988-91, v.p. Congl. Coun., 1991-92, sec. Congl. Coun., 1992-94, chmn. Evangelism, 1992-94, mem. 1995-96, co-chmn. fall holiday bazaar, 1994, fin. rec. sec., 1995—, intern com. mem., 1996-97, ch. fin. com., 2001—; mem. Haverford Band & Orch. Parents, 1994-98, treas., 1994-98, band festival program, book chmn., 1996-98; mem. Haverford Parent's Assn. of Women's Sports, 1994-98; mem. prom com. Haverford PTO, 1996-98. Mem. NAFE, Llanerch Civic Assn., Coll. Alumni Assn. Republican. Avocations: cooking, gardening, traveling, walking on the beach. Office: Hajoca Corp 127 Coulter Ave Ardmore PA 19003-2473

RYAN, BARRY THOMAS, university administrator, lawyer; b. Palo Alto, Calif., Feb. 12, 1955; BA in History, Westmont Coll., Santa Barbara, Calif., 1977; PhD in History, U. Calif., Santa Barbara, 1987; JD, U. Calif., Berkeley, 1992. Bar: Calif. Asst. prof. history Westmont Coll., 1987-89; atty. Farella, Braun and Martel, San Francisco, 1992-93; asst. prof. history Northwestern Coll., Orange City, Iowa, 1993-94; prof. history Point Loma Nazarene U., San Diego, 1995-98, v.p., 1998-2000; judicial fellow U.S. Supreme Ct., Washington, 2000—. Vis. asst. prof. history U. Calif., Santa Barbara, 1987-89; adj. prof. law Thomas Jefferson Sch. Law, San Diego, 1996—; vice chmn. bd. trustees Tyndale Soc., Oxford (Eng.) U., 1998—. Office: Supreme Court Room 5 1 First Street NE Washington DC 20543

RYAN, CAROL ANDERSON, systems analyst; b. Milw., Dec. 14, 1942; d. George Walter and Juanita June (Albers) A.; m. Frederick C. Haberland, May 4, 1963 (div. Apr. 1973); children: Christina Louise Haberland, Heather Noel Haberland; m. Kenneth James Ryan, Oct. 5, 1984. Student, Ripon Coll., 1962-63, Boston Coll., 1973-74; BA in Applied Behav. Scis., Nat. Coll. Edn., McLean, Va., 1987. Sec. Corning Med., Medfield, Mass., 1972-76, supr. word processing, 1976-77; customer support rep. Itek Graphic Products, Waltham, 1977-78; sr. market support rep. Micom Data Systems, Inc., Boston, 1978-79, sales rep., 1979-80; supr. word processing Fidelity Data Systems, Inc., 1981-82; methods analyst Arkwright-Boston Ins. Co., Waltham, 1982-83; gen. mgr. WordSystems, Inc., Washington, 1983-84; sr. analyst ASI Systems Internat., Falls Church, Va., 1984-88; cons. TEM Assocs., Inc., Washington, 1988-89; sr. systems analyst Integrated MicroComputer Systems, Inc., Rockville, Md., 1989-91, Advanced Technology Systems, Inc., Vienna, 1991—. Guest lectr. Johnston-Wales Coll., Providence, 1975; instr. Needham (Mass.) Adult Edn., 1981-83; mem. adv. com. Occupational Career Edn., Needham, 1982-83. Bd. dirs. Needham Theater Group, 1981-83. Mem. Assn. Info. Systems Profls. (bd. dirs. 1981-83), Women in Info. Processing, DAR. Avocations: theater, needlework, sailing. Office: Advanced Technology Systems Inc Vienna VA 22180 Address: 4830 E Altadena Ave Scottsdale AZ 85254-4625

RYAN, CLARENCE AUGUSTINE, JR. biochemistry educator; b. Butte, Mont., Sept. 29, 1931; s. Clarence A. Sr. and Agnes L. (Duckham) R.; m. Patricia Louise Meunier, Feb. 8, 1936; children: Jamie Arlette, Steven Michael (dec.), Janice Marie, Joseph Patrick (dec.). BA in Chemistry, Carroll Coll., 1953; MS in Chemistry, Mont. State U., 1956, PhD in Chemistry, 1959. Postdoctoral fellow in biochemistry Oreg. State U., Corvallis, 1959-61, U.S. Western Regional Lab., Albany, Calif., 1961-63, chemist Berkeley, 1963-64; asst. prof. biochemistry Wash. State U., Pullman, 1964-68, assoc. prof., 1968-72, prof., 1972—, Charlotte Y. Martin disting. prof., 1991—, chmn. dept. agrl. chemistry, 1977-80, fellow Inst. Biol. Chemistry, 1980—. Faculty athletics rep. to PAC-10 & NCAA Wash. State U., 1991-94, 96-97; vis. scientist dept. biochemistry U. Wash., 1981, Harvard U. Med. Sch., 1982, Bert and Natalie Vallee vis. prof., 1997; res. adv. bd. Kemin Industries, Des Moines, 1981—, Plant Genetics, Davis, Calif., 1987-89; research adv. bd. Frito-Lay, Inc., Dallas, 1982, Plant Genetic Engring. Lab., N.M. State U., Las Cruces, 1986-89, Noble Found., 1996—; mem. NRC rev. bd. Plant Gene Exptl. Ctr., Albany, Calif., 1990-93; mgr. biol. stress program USDA Competitve Grants Program, Washington, 1983-84; former mem. adv. panels for H. McKnight Found., Internat. Potato Ctr., Lima, Peru, Internat. Ctr. Genetic Engring. and Biotech., New Delhi, Internat. Ctr. Tropical Agr., Cali, Columbia, Internat. Tropical Agr., Ibandan, Africa; mem. grant rev. panels NSF, USDA, DOE, NIH; co-organizer Internat. Telecomms. Symposium on Plant Biotech.; mem. adv. bd. Bert and Natalie Vallee Found., Harvard Med. Sch., 1997-2000. Mem. editl. bd. several biochem. and plant physiology jours.; contbr. articles to profl. publs., chpts. to books; co-editor 2 books. Trustee Carroll Coll., Helena, Mont., 1998—; mem. rsch. bd. Danforth Plant Sci. Ctr., Washington U., 1998—. Grantee USDA, NSF, NIH, Rockefeller Found., McKnight Found.; recipient Merck award for grad. rsch. Mont. State U., 1959, career devel. awards NIH, 1964-74, Alumni Achievement award Carroll Coll., 1986, Pres.'s Faculty Excellence award in rsch. Wash. State U., 1986; named to Carroll Coll. Alumni Hall of Fame, 1981, Carroll Coll. Basketball Hall of Fame, 1982; named 1 of 100 centennial disting. alumni Mont. State U., 1993;

non-resident fellow Noble Found., 1996—, 151 Highlycited Rschr., 2002. Mem. AAAS, Nat. Acad. Scis. (elected 1986), Am. Chem. Soc. (Kenneth A. Spencer award 1992), Am. Soc. Plant Physiologists (Steven Hales Prize 1992), Am. Soc. Exptl. Biology, Biochem. Soc., Am. Peptide Soc., Internat. Soc. Chem. Ecology (Silverstein-Simione award 1997), Internat. Soc. Plant Molecular Biology (bd. dirs.), Phytochem. Soc. N.Am., Nat. U. Continuing Assn. (Creative Programming award 1991), Phi Kappa Phi (Recognition award 1976, ISI Most Cited Recognition award 2002). Democrat. Avocations: fishing, basketball, golf. Office: Wash State Univ Inst Biol Chemistry Pullman WA 99164-0001

RYAN, D. JAY, lawyer; b. N.Y.C., May 19, 1943; s. Dudley F. and Maud (Delaney) R.; m. Janeen L. Bausch, Aug. 12, 1979 (div. Jan. 1991); 1 child, Erin Delaney. AB in Am. Govt., Georgetown U., 1965; JD, U. Ariz., 1968. Bar: Ariz. 1968, U.S. Dist. Ct. Ariz. 1968, U.S. Ct. Appeals (9th cir.) 1972, U.S. Supreme Ct. 1972. Asst. atty. gen. Ariz. Atty. Gen.'s Office, Phoenix, 1970-72; sole practitioner, 1968-70, 72-77; atty. Wilson, McConnell & Kahn, 1977-80; sole practitioner, 1980—. Mem. Ariz. State Bd. Accountancy, Phoenix, 1974-79. Bd. dirs. Ariz. Recreational Ctr. for the Handicapped, Phoenix, 1981—. Mem. State Bar Ariz. (adminstrv. law sect. 1975—, constrn. law sect. 1989—), Jaguar Club Ctrl. Ariz. (v.p. 1998—). Republican. Roman Catholic. Avocations: weight lifting, jogging, water skiing, jet skiing. Office: 4150 W Northern Ave Phoenix AZ 85051-5765

RYAN, DABERATH, chemistry educator; b. Sacramento, May 3, 1946; d. Clarence Arthur and Ernestine H. (Croy) Kouts; divorced. BS in Chemistry, So. Oreg. U., 1968; MS in Chemistry, Oreg. State U., 1971; MS in Food Sci. and Tech., 1987. Instr. So. Oreg. U., Ashland, 1971-72; prof., dept. chair Rogue Community Coll., Grants Pass, Oreg., 1971-76; chemist State of Alaska, Juneau, 1978; chem. cons. Appleby Sailplanes, Albuquerque, 1978-79; prof. U. Alaska-S.E., Juneau, 1981-82, Mt. Hood Community Coll., Graham, Oreg., 1987, Coll. of Siskiyous, Weed, Calif., 1987—. Mem. Am. Chem. Soc., Coll. of Siskiyous Faculty Assn, Two Yr. Coll. Chemistry Conf., Calif. Tchrs. Assn., Calif. Sci. Tchrs., No. Calif. Sci. Tchrs., Oreg. State U. Alumni Assn., So. Oreg. U. Alumni Assn. Avocations: outdoor recreation, fishing, camping, hunting. Home: PO Box 381 Montague CA 96064-0381 Office: Coll of the Siskiyous 800 College Ave Weed CA 96094-2806

RYAN, DANIEL JOHN, university administrator; b. Buffalo, June 5, 1960; s. Michael E. and Joan F. R.; m. Sandra Suffoleto, Aug. 19, 1989. BA in Pol. Sci., Canisius Coll., Buffalo, 1982, MS in Edn., 1992; PhD in Edn., SUNY, Buffalo, 1997. Fin. cons. First Albany Corp., Buffalo, 1982-84; confidential investigator County of Erie, 1984-87; econ. mkt. analyst City of Buffalo, 1987-90; asst. dir. career planning Canisius Coll., 1990-97, asst. dean students svcs., 1997—; dir. career planning and placement SUNY. Lectr. Buffalo and Erie County Pub. Libr., Buffalo, 1990—; dir. career planning and placement SUNY Buffalo. Author: A Job Search Handbook for People with Disabilities. Pres. Univ. Dist. N. Buffalo Civic Assn., Buffalo, 1990-91; v.p. Kiwanis Club of N. Buffalo, 1987-88; vice chmn. City of Buffalo rep. Com., 1989-91, sec. 1993-95; chmn. Delaware Ward Rep. Com., 1985-91. Recipient Edward A. Parish award, Ea. Assn. Colls. and Employers. Mem. Nat. Assn. Student Personnel Admininstrn.(region II Outstanding New Profl.), N. Buffalo Community Devel. Corp., Assn. for Higher Edn. and Disabilities. Republican. Avocations: reading, raquetball. E-mail: dryan@buffalo.edu.

RYAN, DANIEL LEO, bishop; b. Mankato, Minn., Sept. 28, 1930; s. Leonard Bennett and Irene Ruth (Larson) R. BA, Ill. Benedictine Coll., 1952; JCL, Pontificia Università Lateranense, Rome, 1960. Ordained priest Roman Cath. Ch., 1956, consecrated bishop, 1981. Parish priest Roman Cath. Diocese, Joliet, Ill, 1956-82, chancellor, 1965-78, vicar gen., 1977-79, aux. bishop, 1981-84, bishop Springfield, Ill., 1984-99. Office: Diocese of Springfield PO Box 3187 1615 W Washington St Springfield IL 62702-4757 E-mail: dlryan@dio.org.

RYAN, DAVID ALAN, computer specialist; b. Cin., Nov. 13, 1961; s. James Patrick and Virginia Ann (Stewart) R. BS, Wright State U., 1983; MS, Tex. A&M U., 1988. Statistician U.S. Bur. of Census, Washington, 1988-92, computer specialist, 1992—. Vol. math. modeling Soil Conservation Svc., Washington, 1991—; math. and. probability vol. Washington Opera, 1992—; data entry/programming vol. Opera Am., Washington, 1990-91; hist. rschr. Gasby's Tavern Mus., Alexandria, Va., 1991—; mem. Bravo! for the Washington Opera, 1991-95. Recipient Vol. Svc. award Soil Conservation Svc., 1992, 93. Mem. Am. Statis. Assn., Capitol PC Users Group, Ballston-Va. Square Civic Assn. (exec. com. 1995—, sec. 1996—, NCAC rep. 1997-98), The Washington Opera Guild, The Washington Opera Camerata. Avocations: classical music, ethnomusicology, history, geography, travel. Personal achievements include built a supercomputer at home, 2000. Office: Bur of Census/CES Ste 208 Washington Plz II Washington DC 20233-6300

RYAN, DAVID THOMAS, lawyer; b. Torrington, Conn., Apr. 18, 1939; s. Edward John and Margaret (Murphy) R.; m. Dale Anderson, Aug. 21, 1965; children: Rachael Anderson, Conor Anne. BS, U. Md., 1961; LLB, Georgetown U., 1965. Bar: Conn. 1966, U.S. Dist. Ct. Conn. 1967, U.S. Ct. Appeals (2d cir.) 1969, U.S. Ct. Appeals (fed. cir.) 1982, U.S. Claims Ct. 1983, U.S. Supreme Ct. 1992. Ptnr. Cooney, Scully & Dowling, Hartford, Conn., 1966-77, Robinson & Cole, Hartford, 1977—. Fellow Am. Coll. Trial Lawyers; mem. Am. Bd. Trial Advs. Home: 126 Westerly Ter Hartford CT 06105-1117 Office: Robinson & Cole 280 Trumbull St Ste 26 Hartford CT 06103-3509

RYAN, DIANE PHYLLIS, nurse; b. Buffalo, June 19, 1954; d. Edward John and Helen (Pasko) Vnuk; m. Terrance Patrick Ryan, May 14, 1977; children: Kevin Daniel, Jaclyn Nicole, Amanda Leigh, Scott Michael. BSN, D'Youville Coll., 1976; MS in Nursing, SUNY, 1980. Cert. adult nurse practitioner, gerontol. nurse practitioner, cmty. health nurse splst. Staff nurse Buffalo VA Med. Ctr., 1976-79, nurse practitioner, 1980-83, community referral nurse coordinator, 1983-92, nurse practitioner, 1992—2001. Contbr. articles to profl. jours. Recipient continuing edn. award Homemaker's Upjohn, Buffalo, 1976, Carol Sinicki manuscript award Am. Diabetes Educators, 1984, 1st place award 11th Ann. Discharge Planning Symposium, Soc. Hosp. Social Work Dirs., Am. Hosp. Assn. Mem. Western N.Y. Nurse Practitioners, Sigma Theta Tau. Office: St John Fisher Coll 3690 East Ave Rochester NY 14618-3597 Office Fax: 716-385-8466. E-mail: ryan@sjfc.edu., dryan91660@AOL.com.

RYAN, EDWARD W. economics educator; b. Plainfield, N.J., Aug. 23, 1932; s. Edward A. and Helen R. (Shannon) R.; m. Georgian Hurley, Dec. 17, 1966; children: Sarah, Jennifer. BS, U. Pa., 1955; MA, Duke U., 1957. Lectr. Fordham U., N.Y.C., 1956-57; instr. Iona Coll., New Rochelle, N.Y., 1958-60; Ryan-Bacardi prof. econs. Manhattanville Coll., Purchase, 1958—. Dir. Econ. Freedom Inst. Author: In the Words of Adam Smith: The First Consumer Advocate, 1990, Liberty, Virtue and Happiness: The Story of Economic Freedom in America, 2000. Mem. Am. Econ. Assn., Assn. Pvt. Enterprise Edn., Econ. History Assn. Roman Catholic. Home: 25 Jefferson Rd Scarsdale NY 10583-6411 Office: Manhattanville College 2900 Purchase St Purchase NY 10577-2132 E-mail: edwryan1@aol.com.

RYAN, ELLEN BOUCHARD, psychology educator, gerontologist; b. Holyoke, Mass., Jan. 11, 1947; emigrated to Can., 1982; d. Raoul Rosario and Etiennette Marie (Morin) Bouchard; m. Patrick J. Ryan, July 12, 1969; children: Lorraine Yvette, Dennis Patrick, Kevin Myles. BA, MA, Brown U., 1968; PhD, U. Mich., 1970. Asst. prof. psychology U. Notre Dame, 1970-76, assoc. prof., 1976-81, prof., 1981-82, chmn. dept., 1978-82; prof. psychiatry McMaster U., Hamilton, Ont., Can., 1982—, dir. Ctr. for Gerontol. Studies Can., 1985-95, prof. gerontology Can., 1987—. Editor: Attitudes Toward Language Variation, 1982, Language Communication and The Elderly, 1986, Intergenerational Communication, 1994, Language Attitudes, 1994, Communication, Aging and Health, 1996. Grantee NICHD, 1972-75, NSF, 1976-79, Nat. Inst. Edn., 1979-82, Natural Scis. and Engring. Rsch., 1983-89, Gerontol. Rsch. Coun. of Ont., 1983-85, Ont. Ministry Health, 1986-89, Soc. Sci. and Humanities Rsch. Coun., 1986—. Fellow APA, Gerontol. Soc. Am., Can. Psychol. Assn.; mem. Internat. Assn. of Lang. and Social Psychology, Can. Assn. Gerontology. Roman Catholic. Home: 346 Brookview Ct Ancaster ON Canada L9G 4C2 Office: McMaster U Dept Psychiatry 1200 Main St W Hamilton ON Canada L8N 3Z5 E-mail: ryaneb@mcmaster.ca.

RYAN, EVONNE IANACONE, capital management company executive; b. Buffalo, Aug. 30, 1949; d. Raphael and Mary (Silvaroli) Ianacone; m. Thomas William Ryan, July 11, 1981; children: Christine Irving, Thomas William IV. Student, U. Buffalo, 1970-72; BS in Edn., So. Ill. U., 1974, postgrad., 1975-78, U. Mo., 1989-91; MBA, Harrington U., 1993. Registered securities prin.; cert. estate planner; cert. sr. adv. Spl edn. tchr. Belleville (Ill.) Pub. Sch., 1974-78; rsch. dir. Mo. Pub. Interest Rsch. Group, St. Louis, 1978-79, exec. co-dir., 1979-83; corp. trainer, producer, dir. cmty. access coordination Storer Cable Comms., Florissant, Mo., 1983-85, prodn. mgr., 1985-86; employee devel. and cmty. rels. dir. Cencom Cable TV, St. Louis, 1987-88; stockbroker Edward D. Jones & Co., Littleton, Colo., 1989-93, SunAmerica Securities, Littleton, 1993-97, ProEquities, Inc., Littleton, 1997—; co-founder Fin. & Tax Strategies, Inc., 1994; CEO FTS Capital Mgmt., 1997—, NFP Securities, Inc., 2000—. Co-founder Life Transition Planners, Inc., 2000, Fin. and Tax Strategies, 1994. Contbr. articles to profl. publs. Recipient ACE award for cable excellence Nat. Acad. Cable Programming, 1988, Emmy award, 1988. Home: 144 Willowleaf Dr Littleton CO 80127-3572 Office: 5944 S Kipling St Ste 350 Littleton CO 80127-5557 E-mail: proadvisor@msn.com.

RYAN, FRANK THOMAS, tire company executive; b. N.Y.C., Aug. 27, 1939; s. Harry Matthew and Dorothy Joan (Kolson) R.; m. Devote M. Ryan, Feb. 14, 1970. BA, Providence Coll., 1962; MA, St. Stephen's Coll., 1965; B of Sacred Theology, Dominican House of Studies, Washington, 1965, Lic. of Sacred Theology, 1967; PhD, Georgetown U., 1970. Editor World Pub., Washington, 1969-70; asst. mng. dir. Truck Trailer Mfrs. Assn., 1970-71; govt. rels. assoc. Rubber Mfrs. Assn., 1971-74, dir. environ. health and safety affairs, 1974-81, v.p. govt. rels., 1981-89; dir. state and regulatory affairs The Goodyear Tire & Rubber Co., 1989-95, dir. fed. and state affairs, 1995-2000, sr. govt. rels. counselor, 2000-01, govt. rels. cons., 2001—. Bd. dirs. State Govt. Affairs Coun., Washington, 1997-99; adv. mem. Bus. Rsch. Adv. Coun., Washington, 1985-95; v.p., mem. Nat. Energy Resources Orgn., Washington, 1983-91. Author: The Body as Symbol, 1970; contbg. editor Sports in the Modern World, 1972, Encyclopedic Dictionary of Religion, 1979. Bd. dirs. Zen Cmty. of Balt. Mem. Nat. Press Club, Washington Indsl. Roundtable, Woodstock Bus. Conf. Roman Catholic. Avocations: hiking, photography, study of comparative religion. Home: 10824 Larkmeade Ln Potomac MD 20854-2742

RYAN, FREDERICK JOSEPH, JR. lawyer, retired federal official; b. Tampa, Fla., Apr. 12, 1955; s. Frederick Joseph and Cordelia Beth (Hartman) Ryan; m. Genevieve Ann McSweeney, Dec. 28, 1985; children: Genevieve Madeline, Madeline Elizabeth, Caroline Elizabeth. BA, U. So. Calif., 1977, JD, 1980. Bar: Calif. 1980, D.C. 1986. Assoc. Hill, Farrer and Burrill, L.A., 1980-82; dep. dir. then dir. presdl. appointments and scheduling The White House, Washington, 1982-87, dir. pvt. sector initiatives, 1985-87, asst. to the Pres., 1987-89; chief of staff Office of Ronald Reagan, L.A., 1989-95; vice-chmn. Allbritton Comm. Co., Washington, 1995—; pres., COO Allbritton Comm. Co., 1998—. Staff Reagan-Bush Campaign, L.A., 1980; dir. Internat. Conf. Pvt Sector Initiatives, Paris, 1986, Italian-Am. Conf. Pvt. Sector Initiatives, 1987, Brit. Am. Conf. Pvt. Sector Initiatives, 1988; bd. dirs. Riggs Bank Europe Ltd., Riggs Bank Washington. Columnist: Legal Briefs, 1980—82; editor: (book) Ronald Reagan: The Wisdom and Humor of the Great Communicator, 1995, Ronald Reagan: The Great Communicator, 2001. Chmn. Monterey Park (Calif.) Cmty. Rels. Commn., 1977—78; chmn. bd. trustees Ronald Reagan Presdl. Found.; bd. advisors Ronald Reagan Inst. Emergency Medicine, George Washington U. Med. Ctr.; bd. dirs. Ford's Theater, Washington, Town Hall of Calif., L.A., Nancy Reagan Found. Decorated comdr. Order Merit Republic of Italy, Ouissam Alaouite of Morocco; recipient Presdl. commendation for pvt. sector initiatives, Pres. Ronald Reagan, 1986, medal Arts and Letters, Govt. of France, 1986, Golden Ambrosiana medal, Milan, Italy, 1987, Lion of Venice medal, Italy, 1987, Ronald Reagan Disting. Svc. award, 1999. Mem.: ABA, White House Hist. Assn. (bd. dirs.), Chevy Chase Club, Confrérie des Chaveliers du Tasevin, Alfalfa Club, Met. Club (Washington). Presbyterian. Avocations: tennis, skiing. Office: Allbritton Comm Co 808 17th St NW Washington DC 20006-3910

RYAN, GEORGE H. governor, pharmacist; b. Maquoketa, Iowa, Feb. 24, 1934; s. Thomas J. and Jeanette (Bowman) R.; m. Lura Lynn Lowe, June 10, 1956; children: Nancy, Lynda, Julie, Joanne, Jeanette, George. BS in Pharmacy, Ferris State Coll., Big Rapids, Mich. Mem. Ill. Ho. of Reps., 1973-82, minority leader, 1977-80, speaker, 1981-82; lt. gov. State of Ill., 1983-91, sec. of state, 1991-98, gov., 1999—. Mem. Kankakee County Bd., 1966-72, chmn., 1971-72; chmn. Ill. Literacy Coun., 1991—. With U.S. Army, Korea. Recipient Humphrey award Am. Pharm. Assn., 1980, Top award Ill. chpt. DARE, 1989, Govt. Leadership award Nat. Commn. Against Drunk Driving and MADD Govt. Leader Against Drunk Driving award, 1994-95, City Club of Chgo. Man of Yr. award, 1995. Mem. Am. Pharm. Assn., Ill. Pharm. Assn., One Hundred Club, Masons (33d degree). Lodges: Elks, Moose, Shriners. Republican. Methodist. E-mail: governor@state.il.us.*

RYAN, HALFORD ROSS, speech educator; b. Anderson, Ind., Dec. 29, 1943; AB, Wabash Coll., 1966; MA, U. Ill., 1968, PhD, 1972. Prof. Washington and Lee U., Lexington, Va., 1970—. Author: FDR's Rhetorical Presidency, 1988, Harry Emerson Fosdick, 1989, Henry Ward Beecher, 1990, Classical Communication for the Contemporary Communicator, 1992, Harry S. Truman, 1993; editor: Oratorial Encounters, 1988, Inaugural Addresses of Twentieth-Century American Presidents, 1993, U.S. Presidents as Orators, 1995; also articles. Recipient awards Eleanor Roosevelt Inst., 1979, Herbert Hoover Inst., 1986, Maurice Mednick Found., 1991; Rockefeller Theol. fellow, 1967. Mem. Speech Communication Assn. Office: Washington and Lee U Robinson Hall Lexington VA 24450

RYAN, HAROLD MARTIN, judge; b. Detroit, Feb. 6, 1911; s. Martin and Ida Ryan; m. Lilliana Wargnier, Sept. 4, 1944; children: Kathleen, Nancy, Harold Jr., John, Theresa. Student, Mich. State U., 1930-31; JD, U. Detroit, 1935. Bar: Mich. 1935, U.S. Supreme Ct. 1935. Atty., 1935—; asst. pros. atty. Wayne County, Detroit, 1942-45; state senator Mich. 1st Dist., Lansing, 1948-61; U.S. congressman 14th Congrl. Dist. Mich., Washington, 1961-65; cir. ct. judge Wayne County, Detroit, 1978-85. With USAFR, 1961-66. Democrat. Roman Catholic. Avocations: golf, football, history. Home: 28601 Little Mack Ave Saint Clair Shores MI 48081-3012

RYAN, IONE JEAN ALOHILANI, retired educator, counselor; b. Honolulu, Oct. 18, 1926; d. William Alexander and Lilia (Nainoa) Rathburn; m. Edward Parsons Ryan, June 23, 1962 (dec.); children: Ralph M., Lilia K. BEd, U. Hawaii, 1948; MS in Pub. Health, U. Minn., 1950; EdD, Stanford U., 1960. Lic. marital and family therapist, N.C. Tchr. W.R. Farrington High Sch., Honolulu, 1948; instr. to asst. prof. U. Hawaii, 1950-66; assoc. prof. to prof. East Carolina U., Greenville, 1966-90, prof. emerita N.C., 1990—. Contbr. articles to profl. publs. Recipient first scholarship Honolulu C. of C., 1948-50. Mem. APA.

RYAN, J. BRUCE, healthcare management consulting executive; b. Southbridge, Mass., Mar. 28, 1944; s. Charles J. and Doris (Olney) R.; m. Sarah E. Pattison, Aug. 16, 1993. BSBA in Fin., U. Mass., 1972, MSBA, 1975; MA in Econs., U. Wash., 1976. Regional v.p. Amherst Assocs. Inc., Atlanta, 1976-85; exec. v.p. Jennings Ryan & Kolb, Inc., 1985—. Mem. managed care adv. bd. St. Anthony Pub.; bd. advs. Managed Care Contract Negotiation. Mem. editl. rev. bd. Healthcare Fin. Mgmt., Managed Care Reimbursment Advisory; contbr. articles to profl. jours. With U.S. Army, 1968-70. Mem. Healthcare Fin. Mgmt. Assn. (Helen M. Yerger/L. Van Seawell best article award 1990), Soc. for Healthcare Planning & Mktg., Fin. Mgmt. Assn. Avocation: sailing. Home: 1060 Kentucky Ave NE Atlanta GA 30306-3534 Office: Jennings Ryan & Kolb Inc 17 Executive Park Dr NE Ste 500 Atlanta GA 30329-2225

RYAN, JACK, physician, retired hospital corporation executive; b. Benton Harbor, Mich., Aug. 26, 1925; s. Leonard Joseph and Beulah (Southworth) R.; m. Lois Patricia Patterson; children: Michele, Kevin, Timothy, Sarah, Daniel. AB, Western Mich. U., 1948; postgrad., U. Mich. Law Sch., 1949-50, Emory U., 1950-51; MD, Wayne State U., 1955. Intern St. Luke's Hosp., Saginaw, Mich., 1955-56; pres. Meml. Med. Ctr., Warren, 1956-77; v.p. med. affairs Detroit-Macomb Hosps. Corp., 1976-77, pres. and chief exec. officer, 1977-96; ret., 1996. Assoc. prof. medicine Wayne State U., Detroit, 1974—; bd. chmn. Mich. Hosp. Ins. Co., 1990—. Recipient Disting. Alumnus award Wayne State U. Med. Sch., 1974, Wayne State U., 1979, Western Mich. U., 1989, Disting. Key award Mich. Hosp. Assn., 1986, Tree of Life award Jewish Nat. Fund, 1996. Fellow Am. Coll. Family Physicians, Am. Coll. Physician Execs., Detroit Acad. Medicine; mem. Internat. Health Econs. and Mgmt. Inst. (charter), Econ. Club Detroit, Detroit Athletic Club, Renaissance Club, Red Run Club. Avocations: Civil War, history, golf, tennis. Home: 175 Hendrie Blvd Royal Oak MI 48067-2412

RYAN, JACK LEWIS, chemist, researcher, consultant, educator; b. Dallas, May 14, 1933; s. Charles William and Cornie Alice (Lewis) R.; m. JoAnne Mrgarette Ryan, Mar. 18, 1986 (div. Aug. 1998); 1 child, Rex Charles. BS, Oreg. State Coll., 1953, MS, 1956. Sr. rsch. scientist Hanford Atomic Products Opn., Richland, Wash., 1955-65, Pacific N.W. Nat. Lab., Richland, 1965-93, part-time 1993—. Cons. PDI Tech. Contbr. articles to sci. jours., chpts. to books. Recipient Glenn T. Seaborg Actinide Separation award Actinide Separations Conf., 1998. Mem. AAAS, Am. Chem. Soc. (sect. chmn. 1974, Outstanding Chemist award Richland sect. 1991), Sigma Xi, Phi Lambda Upsilon. Achievements include patents in field. Avocations: mountain climbing, wilderness backpacking, hunting, fishing, gardening. Home: 1326 Broadview Dr West Richland WA 99353

RYAN, JAMES, insurance company executive; b. Pitts., Jan. 21, 1937; s. Martin Charles and Lucy Elizabeth (Misklow) r.; m. Marlene Sullivan Ryan, Jan. 27, 1973. BA, U. Pitts., U. Louisville. Cert. ins. wholesaler. Chmn. Market Finders Ins. Corp., Louisville, 1972—. Com. chmn. Am. Assn. Mng. Gen. Agts., 1988-89; pres. Ky. Lloyd's Agts. Assn., 1985—; bd. dirs. Nat. Assn. Profl. Surplus Lines Office, Inc., 1983-86; pres. Ky. Surplus Lines Assn., Louisville, 1988-89; mem. adv. coun. Essex Ins. Co., 1991-93, Am. Equity Ins. Co., Scottsdale, Ariz., 1999. Pub. in Best Rev., 1995. Mem. Ky. Thoroughbred Owners & Breeders, Inc., Hon. Order of Blue Goose Internat., Kosair Shrine Temple, Hon. Order of Ky. Col. Named Adv. Coun. Colony Ins. Co., Glen Allen, Va., 1991-93, Hamilton Ins. Co., 1993, Cardinal Ins. Co., 1991-93. Mem. Profl. Ins. Agts., Ind. Ins. Agts. Assn., Am. Assn. Mng. Gen. Agts. (cert., chmn. adv. com. 1991-92, bd. dirs. 1994-96, v.p. zone 2 1995-96, pres.-elect 1996-97, pres. 1997-98), Nat. Assn. Profl. Surplus Lines Offices (chmn. legis. com. 1988-89, Published Best Rev. 1995), Am. Assn. of Gen. Agts. Republican. Roman Catholic. Avocations: breeding and racing Thoroughbred horses, golf.

RYAN, JAMES LEO, federal judge; b. Detroit, Nov. 19, 1932; s. Leo Francis and Irene Agnes Ryan; m. Mary Elizabeth Rogers, Oct. 12, 1957; children: Daniel P., James R., Colleen M. Hansen, Kathleen A. LLB, U. Detroit, 1956, LLD (hon.) , 1986, BA, 1992; LLD (hon.) , Madonna Coll., 1976, Detroit Coll., 1978, Thomas M. Cooley Law Sch., Lansing, Mich., 1986. Justice of peace, Redford Twp., Mich., 1963—66; judge 3d Cir. Ct. of Mich., 1966—75; justice Mich. Supreme Ct., 1975—86; judge U.S. Ct. Appeals (6th cir.), 1986—. Faculty Nat. Jud. Coll., Reno; adj. faculty U. Detroit Sch. Law, Thomas M. Colley Law Sch.; adj. faculty, bd. dirs. Ave Maria Sch. Law. Contbr. articles to profl. jours. Capt. JAGC USNR, 1957—92, ret. mil. judge USNR. Mem.: Fed. Bar Assn., State Bar Mich., Fed. Judges Assn., KM, KC. Office: US Ct Appeals US Courthouse 231 W Lafayette Blvd Detroit MI 48226-2700

RYAN, JAMES DANIEL, history educator; b. Buffalo, Nov. 29, 1938; s. James Daniel Ryan and Antoinette Marie La Teer; m. Jeanne Anne Ryan, Apr. 15, 1963; children: James Daniel III, Julia Regina, Matthew George. BA in Philosophy, St. Bonaventure U., 1960; MS in Edn., Canisius Coll., 1962; PhD in History, NYU, 1972. Prof., dept. chair dept. history CUNY, Bronx C.C., 1970—2002; dir. spl. projects Bronx C.C., 1985—, coord. humanities divsn., 1995—2001. Author: (book) U.N. Under Kurt Waldheim, 2001; contbr. articles to profl. jours. Pres., bd. dirs. Columbus Park Corp., N.Y.C., 1973—. Grantee NEH, 1981, 96, travel grantee Am. Coun. Learned Socs., 1990. Mem. Medieval Acad. Am., Am. Hist. Assn., Soc. for Study of Crusades, Am. Cath. Hist. Assn., Ea. C.C. Social Scis. Assn. (Disting. Svc. award 1992, bd. dirs. 1986-92), Medieval Club. N.Y. (pres. 1994-96). Democrat. Roman Catholic. Avocations: fishing, woodworking, music. Home: 100 W 94th St New York NY 10025 Office: CUNY Bronx C C University Ave and W 181st Bronx NY 10453

RYAN, JAMES E. state attorney general; b. Chgo., Feb. 21, 1946; m. Marie Ryan; children: John, Jim, Matt, Amy, Patrick, Anne Marie(dec.). BA in Polit. Sci., Ill. Benedictine Coll., 1968; JD, Ill. Inst. Tech., 1971. Bar: Ill. 1971. Asst. state's atty. criminal divsn. DuPage County State's Atty.'s Office, 1971—74, 1st. asst. state's atty., 1974—76; founder Ryan & Darrah; state's atty. DuPage County State's Atty.'s Office, 1984—94; atty. gen. State of Ill., 1994—. Named Lawyer of Yr., DuPage County Bar Assn., 1997; recipient numerous awards from various orgns. including, Nat. Assn. Counties, Alliance Against Intoxicated Motorists. Mem.: Ill. State's Attys. Assn. (past pres., Ezzard Charles award). Republican. Roman Catholic. Office: James R Thompson Ctr 100 W Randolph St Chicago IL 60601*

RYAN, JAMES FRANKLIN, retail executive; b. London, Can., July 21, 1948; s. Patrick and Helen Anne (Wenechuk) R.; m. Dora Lee Ballan, Mar. 17, 1979 ; children: Christine, Carol. BS, U. Western Ont., London, 1970; MBA, York U., Toronto, Ont., 1972. Various mgmt. positions Shell Can. Ltd., Toronto, 1972-84, mgr. retail Calgary, 1984-85; dir. mktg. svcs. Petro-Can., Inc., Toronto, 1985-86; pres. Pyne Mgmt., Inc., 1986-88, Can. Tire Petroleum, Toronto, 1988-92; sr. v.p. dealer rels. Can. Tire Corp., 1992-99; ret., 1999. Bd. dirs. Soroc Tech., Inc., Brantford Energy Inc., Niagara-on-the-Lake Hydro. Bd. dirs. Niagara Coll. Found. also: 3 Christopher Ct. Niagara-on-the-Lake ON Canada L0S 1J0

RYAN, JAMES GILBERT, historian, educator, writer; b. Wilmington, Del., Jan. 31, 1947; s. James A. and Audrey May (Davis) Urian; m. Anita Louise Noble, Jan. 20, 1973 (div. Sept. 1978). BA, U. Del., 1970, MA, 1973, U. Notre Dame, 1975, PhD, 1981. Vis. instr. dept. history Purdue U., 1976, 77, 78; lectr. dept. history Pa. State U., Delaware County campus, 1978-79; instr. dept. history U. Notre Dame, summers 1979-80; adj. asst. prof. dept. history Ind. U. at South Bend, 1980-81; adj. asst. prof. dept. polit. sci. Temple U., 1982-84, 85-87; adj. asst. prof. dept. history and politics Drexel U., Phila., 1982-85, 85-87, vis. asst. prof. dept. history and politics, 1985; vis. asst. prof. dept. polit. sci. Muhlenberg Coll., Allentown, Pa., 1987-90; asst. prof. history dept. gen. acad. Tex. A&M U., Galveston, 1990-96, assoc. prof., 1996—. Faculty senate Tex. A&M U., 1997-99; vis. researcher Russian Ctr. for Preservation and Study of Documents of Recent History, Moscow, 1993; vis. researcher Mexico City program Tex. A&M U., 1998; presenter in field. Author: Earl Browder: The Failure of American Communism, 1997; contbr. chapters to books, articles to profl. jours. and encys. Grantee Muhlenberg Coll., 1988, 90, Tex. A&M U., 1990-99, 2001-02, Manchester (Eng.) U., 2001. Mem. NEA, The History Soc., Am. Hist. Assn., Orgn. Am. Historians, Historians of Am. Communism (ctrl. com. 1995—), Tex. Faculty Assn. (exec. com. 1997—, v.p. gulf coast chpt. 1998-2000), Nat. Writers Union. Democrat. Avocations: weightlifting, skiing. Home: Apt 315 7302 Heards Ln Galveston TX 77551-1152 Office: Tex A&M U Dept Gen Acad PO Box 1675 Galveston TX 77553-1675 E-mail: ryanj@tamug.tamu.edu.

RYAN, JAMES HERBERT, retired security and retail services company executive; b. Petersburg, Va., Feb. 1, 1931; s. Richard Hillsdon and Mary Orgain (Mann) R.; m. Patricia Louise Abbott, June 7, 1955; 1 child, Pamela Louise. BS, U.S. Mil. Acad., 1955; MA, U. Pa., 1962; MS, George Washington U., 1972; grad. Program for Mgmt. Devel., Harvard U., 1972; PhD, Walden U., 1984. Commd. 2d lt. U.S. Army, 1955, advanced through grades to lt. col., 1968, ret., 1972; gen. mgr. U.S. ops. Ryan Enterprises, Washington, 1970-73; pres. Ford Enterprises, Ltd., Mt. Rainier, Md., 1973-87; James H. Ryan Assocs., Inc., Petersburg, 1987-97. Gen. mgr. U.S. ops. Ryan Enterprises, Washington, 1970-73; pres. Ford Enterprises, Ltd., Mt. Rainier, Md., 1973-87; pres. James H. Ryan Assocs., Inc., Petersburg, Va., 1987-97; advisor to Sec. of Army, 1975, chief of naval material, 1980-82. Mem. Pres.'s Pvt. Sector Survey on Cost Control (Grace Commn.), 1982; bd. govs. USO, 1977-86; pres. Hist. Petersburg Found,. 1991-93; vestryman St. Paul's Episcopal Ch., 1994-96, 98—. Decorated Legion of Merit, Soldiers medal, Bronze Star, Air medal, Vietnamese Gallantry Cross. Mem. Am. Mgmt. Assn., Nat. Retail Fedn., Am. Soc. Indsl. Security, Internat. Assn. Profl. Security Cons. (pres. 1993-95), Ret. Officers Assn., West Point Soc. Ctrl. Va., Rotary

Club of Petersburg (pres. 1993-94), Petersburg Area Art League (pres. 1997-2000, treas. 2000—). Episcopalian. Home: 1221 Woodland Rd Petersburg VA 23805-1911 Office: PO Box 2126 Petersburg VA 23804-1426

RYAN, JAMES THOMAS, organizational consultant, business owner; b. Auburn, N.Y., Aug. 28, 1947; s. Thomas Francis and Gertrude Helen (Whalen) R.; m. Anne Peduto, June 15, 1974; children: Thomas Michael, Jennifer Lynn, Kathleen Meghan. AA, Auburn C.C., 1967; BA, Ohio State U., 1972; MBA, Gannon U., 1979. Cert. sr. profl. in human resources Human Resource Cert. Inst. Sales rep. Gallery of Homes, Rochester, N.Y., 1974-75, Johnson & Johnson, Erie, Pa., 1975-77; pers. mgr. Singer, 1977-80; employee rels. mgr. Frito-Lay, Vancouver, Wash., 1980-85; corp. dir. human resources Welch's, Westfield, N.Y., 1985-94; pres. The North Coast Consulting Group, Erie, 1994—; owner Express Personnel Svcs., 2001—. Mem. adv. coun. Gannon U., Erie, 1990-95; mem. human resources coun. Am. Mgmt. Assn., N.Y.C., 1989-95. Mem. Pres. Club, Republican Party, Washington, 1995, Senatorial Inner Cir., 1992-95. With USAF, 1968-72, Vietnam. Mem. ASTD, Soc. Human Resources Mgmt., Kahkwa Club, Erie Club, Aviation Club. Roman Catholic. Avocations: golf, reading, travel. Home: 5410 Mintwood Ct Erie PA 16506-3935 Office: Express Personnel Svcs 2503 W 15th St Erie PA 16505 E-mail: jryan@northcoastconsulting.com.

RYAN, JAMES WALTER, physician, medical researcher; b. Amarillo, Tex., June 8, 1935; s. Lee W. and Emma E. (Haddox) R.; children: James P.A., Alexandra L.E., Amy J.S. AB in Polit. Sci., Dartmouth Coll., 1957; MD, Cornell U., 1961; D.Phil., Oxford U. (Eng.), 1967. Diplomate: Nat. Bd. Med. Examiners. Intern, Montreal (Que.) Gen. Hosp., McGill U., Can., 1961-62, asst. resident in medicine, 1962-63; USPHS research asso. NIMH, NIH, 1963-65; guest investigator Rockefeller U., N.Y.C., 1967-68, asst. prof. biochemistry, 1968; assoc. prof. medicine U. Miami (Fla.) Sch. Medicine, 1968-79, prof. medicine, 1979-95, mem. vasc. biology ctr., 1995-00; prof. anesthesiology, pharmacology and toxicology Med. Coll. Ga., Augusta, 1995-00; sr. cons. ntGen, 2000—. Sr. scientist Papanicolaou Cancer Rsch. Inst., Miami, 1972-77; hon. med. officer to Regius prof. medicine Oxford U., 1965-67; vis. prof. Clin. Rsch. Inst. Montreal, 1974; mem. vis. faculty thoracic disease divsn., dept. internal medicine Mayo Clinic, 1974; vis. prof. Montreal Gen. Hosp./McGill U., 1985. Contbr. numerous articles on biochem. research and pathology to sci. jours.; patentee in field. Rockefeller Found. travel awardee, 1962; William Waldorf Astor travelling fellow, 1966; USPHS spl. fellow, 1967-68; Pfizer travelling fellow, 1972; recipient Louis and Artur Luciano award for research of circulatory diseases McGill U., 1984-85 Fellow Am. Inst. Chemists; mem. AAAS, Am. Physiol. Soc., Am. Chem. Soc., Biochem. Soc., Am. Soc. Biochemist, Am. Heart Assn. (mem. coun. cardiopulmonary diseases 1972—, Coun. for High Blood Pressure Research 1976—), Microcirculatory Soc., So. Soc. Clin. Investigation, N.Y. Acad. Scis., Club: United Oxford and Cambridge U. (London), Sigma Xi. Baptist. Home: 3047 Lake Forest Dr Augusta GA 30909-3027 Office: ntGen 3047 Lake Forest Dr Augusta GA 30909 E-mail: jasryan@bellsouth.net.

RYAN, JANE FRANCES, corporate communications executive; b. Bronxville, N.Y., Nov. 1, 1950; d. Bernard M. and Margaret M. (Griffith) R.; m. Kevin Horan, Dec. 26, 1982; 1 child, Kevin. BS in Journalism, Ohio U., 1972; MBA in Mktg., Golden Gate U., 1990. Asst. promotion mgr. Fawcett Publs., Greenwich, Conn., 1972-75; mktg. coordinator Fawcett Mktg. Services div. CBS, 1975-78; dist. sales mgr. CBS Publs., San Francisco, 1978; prodn. mgr. Cato Inst., 1979-81; account supr. Bus. Media Resources, Mill Valley, Calif., 1981-90, dir. mktg. svcs., 1990-93; dir. publs. RAND Corp., Santa Monica, 1993—. Office: RAND 1700 Main St Santa Monica CA 90401-3297

RYAN, JEROME FRANCIS, artist; b. St. Paul, Mar. 11, 1929; s. Bernie and Esther Louise (Francis) R.; m. Virginia May Horrigan, May 17, 1952 (div.); children: Matthew John, Kevin Francis, Kathleen Ann, Timothy Michael; m. Muriel Alexandra Bohush, Sept. 12, 1987. BFA, Mpls. Sch. Art, 1951. Artist Fenne-Vaughan Illustrators, Dallas, 1952; studio artist Merlin Krupp Studio, Mpls., 1955-56; agy. art dir. Kerker & Assocs., 1956-61; freelance studio artist Ryan Studio, St. Paul, 1961-74, freelance painter, tchr., 1974-84, Crisfield, Md., 1984—. Executed numerous portraits, landscapes, and figure works; portraits include a Minn. Gov., a Senator, Minn. Supreme Ct. Chief Justices, also deans, bishops, others. Cpl. U.S. Army, 1953-55. Avocations: sailing, fly tying and trout fishing. Studio: Bayside Studio 3417 Lawsonia Rd Crisfield MD 21817-2213

RYAN, JOHN DUNCAN, lawyer; b. Portland, Oreg., Dec. 20, 1920; s. Thomas Gough and Virgian Abigail (Hadley) R.; m. Florence A. Ryan, Jan. 30, 1970 (dec. 1987); m. Virginia Kane Wilson, June 15, 1996. BS, Fordham U., 1943; JD, Lewis & Clark Coll., Portland, 1950. Bar: Oreg. 1950. Pvt. practice, Portland, 1950—. Adj. instr. Northwestern Sch. Law Lewis & Clark Coll., 1953-70. Author: (poems) Expressions, 1993, Expressions II, 1995, (book) Cooking with John Ryan, 2002. Sgt. Air Corps, U.S. Army, 1942-46, ETO. Recipient St. Thomas More award Catholic Lawyers for Social Justice, 1993. Mem. ABA (Oreg. delegate 1985-93, chmn. spl. com. on law & literacy 1991-93), Am. Coll. Trial Lawyers, Am. Trial Lawyers Assn., Oreg. State Bar (bd. govs. 1963-67), Oreg. Trial Lawyers Assn. (Trial Lawyer of Yr. 1993), Multnomah County Bar Assn. (Professionalism award 1997), Washington County Bar Assn. Home and Office: 1206 Circulo Aguilar Rio Rico AZ 85648-3355 and: 503 SW Colony Dr Portland OR 97219-7763 E-mail: ryan98@theriver.com.

RYAN, JOHN M. lawyer; b. Glen Ridge, N.J., May 18, 1936; AB, Dartmouth Coll., 1958; LLB, U. Va., 1963. Bar: Va. 1964. Lectr. at law Marshall-Wythe Sch. Law Coll. William and Mary, 1976-86; ptnr. Vandeventer Black LLP, Norfolk, Va.; gen. counsel Va. Internat. Terminals, Inc. Trustee John Marshall Found., Contemporary Art Ctr. Va.; commr. Arts and Humanities Commn., City of Virginia Beach; bd. dirs. Children's Health Sys., Inc., Greater Norfolk Corp. Fellow: Va. Law Found., Am. Bar Found., Am. Coll. Trial Lawyers; mem.: ABA (labor rels., litigation sect.), So. Conf. Bar Pres., Nat. Conf. Bar Pres., Va. State Bar, Norfolk-Portsmouth Bar Assn., Maritime Law Assn. U.S. (chmn. stevedore and maritime terminals com.), Va. Bar Assn. (pres. 1988), S.E. Admiralty Law Inst., James Kent Am. Inn of Ct. (past pres.), 4th Cir. Jud. Conf. Office: Vandeventer Black LLP 500 World Trade Ctr Norfolk VA 23510-1679 E-mail: jryan@vanblk.com.

RYAN, JOHN MICHAEL, landscape architect; b. Chgo., Sept. 27, 1946; s. Terrance Joseph and Norma (Morris) R.; m. Victoria Jean Wheetley, June 26, 1986; children: Micheline Giannasi-Mennecke, Tony Giannasi, Nick Giannasi, Andrew Morris Jennings, Melissa Contance Victoria, Cameron Michael Montgomery. B in Landscape Architecture, U. Ill., 1969. Registered landscape architect, Ill., cert. Mich., registered Ariz., Ind., Wis., Tenn., cert. CLARB. Assoc. landscape architect Carl Garnder & Assocs., Inc., Chgo., 1969-71; sr. landscape architect Collaborative Rsch. & Planning, 1971-73; v.p. Michael L. Ives & Assocs., Inc., Downers Grove, Ill., 1973-84; pres. Ives/Ryan Group, Inc., Naperville, 1984—. Prin. works include renovation of Old Orchard Shopping Ctr., Skokie, Ill., Lake Katherine Nature Preserve, Palos Heights, Ill., Crystal Tree Residential Golf Course Cmty., Orland Park, Ill., Corporetum Office Campus, Lisle, Ill., Maravilla Rainforest Atrium, Vernon Hills, Ill. Trustee Wheaton Evangelical Free Ch., 2000—. Recipient Nat. Landscape award Am. Assn. Nurserymen, 1988, 92, Key award in landscape arch. Home Bldrs. Assn. Greater Chgo., 1981, 84, 90, Best Project Grand award Interiorscape mag., 2001. Mem. Am. Soc. Landscape Archs. (Merit award 1991, 94, 96), Assoc. Landscape Contractors Am. (Environ. Improvement Grand award 1997, 2000, Environ. Improvement honor award 2000), Ill. Landscape Contractors Assn. (Gold award 1991, 96, 2001, Silver award 1986, 90, 93, 2001, Merit award 1988, 91), Chgo. Hort. Soc., Perennial Plant Assn. (Nat. Honor award 1993), Morton Arboretum. Avocations: gardening, travel. *My life is committed to raising my dear children to the best of my ability in a loving christian atmosphere, which I believe to be my true purpose for being here. As a professional landscape architect, if I can enhance or imporve the environment for my children and their children, I have made a worthwhile professional contribution to my perceived purpose in life.*

RYAN, JOHN WILLIAM, academic administrator; b. Chgo., Aug. 12, 1929; s. Leonard John and Maxine (Mitchell) R.; m. D. Patricia Goodday, June 20, 1949; children: Kathleen Elynne Ryan Acker, Kevin Dennis Mitchell, Kerrick Charles Casey. BA, U. Utah, 1951; MA, Ind. U., 1958, PhD, 1959, LLD (hon.), 1988, U. Notre Dame, 1978, Oakland City Coll., 1981, St. Joseph Coll., 1981, Hanover Coll., 1982, DePauw U., 1983, U. Ma., 1983, Manchester Coll., 1983, U. Evansville, 1985, Wabash Coll., 1986, Ind. U., 1988; DLitt (hon.), U. St. Thomas, 1977; D Pub. Adminstrn., Nat. Inst. Devel. Adminstrn., Thailand, 1991; LLD (hon.), U. Md., 1994. Rsch. analyst Ky. Dept. Revenue, Frankfort, 1954-55; vis. rsch. prof. U. Thammasat, Bangkok, Thailand, 1955-57; asst. dir. Inst. Tng. for Pub. Svc. Ind. U., 1957-58; successively asst. prof., assoc. prof. polit. sci., assoc. dir., Bur. Govt. U. Wis., 1958-62; exec. asst. to pres., sec. of univ. U. Mass., Amherst, 1962-63, chancellor Boston, 1965-68; v.p. acad. affairs Ariz. State U., 1963-65; v.p., chancellor regional campuses Ind. U., Bloomington, 1968-71, pres., 1971-87, pres. emeritus, 1987—, prof. polit. sci., 1968-95, prof. pub. and environ. affairs, 1981-95, prof. emeritus, 1995—; cons. AID, 1991-92; chancellor SUNY, Albany, 1997-99, chancellor emeritus, 2000—; hon. prof. Moscow State U., 1999. Interim pres. Fla. Atlantic U., 1989, U. Md., Balt., 1994; bd. dirs. Ind. U. Found., chmn. 1972-87; chmn. Nat. Adv. Bd. on Internat. Edn. Programs, 1985-89; chancellor SUNY System, 1996-2000. Contbr. articles to profl. jours. Bd. govs. Pub. Broadcasting Svc., 1973-82; bd. visitors Air U., 1974-81; chmn. Air Force Inst. Tech Subcom., 1976-81; mem. univ. adv. com. Am. Coun. Life Ins.; bd. dirs. Corp. Community Coun., 1976; mem. nat. adv. coun. Pan Am. Games, 1985; mem. adv. bd. Assocs. for Religious and Intellectual Life, 1984—; active United Way Ind. Centennial Commn. Mem. Am. Soc. Pub. Adminstrn. (pres. Ind. chpt. 1969-70, nat. chpt. 1972-73, nat. coun. from 1970, Ind. Soc. Chgo. (non-resident v.p. from 1976, Am. Polit. Sci. Assn., Assn. Asian Studies, Am. Coun. Edn., Assn. Am. Univs. (chmn. 1981-82), Nat. Acad. Public Adminstrn., Ind. Acad., Explorers Club, Adelphia (hon.), Columbia Club (Indpls.), Skyline Club, Cosmos Club (Washington), Athenaeum (London), KC, Equestrian Order of Holy Sepulchre, Elks, Phi Kappa Phi, Phi Alpha Theta, Pi Sigma Alpha, Beta Gamma Sigma, Kappa Sigma (worthy grand master 1985-87). Office: Ind U SPEA 415 1315 E 10th St Bloomington IN 47405-1701 E-mail: chancem123@aol.com., ryan@indiana.edu.

RYAN, JOHN WILLIAM, association executive; b. Manchester, N.H., Sept. 16, 1937; s. William Charles and Mary Ann (Marcoux) R.; m. Carol Jean Battaglia, Sept. 17, 1960; children: James, Kathleen, John, Michael. AB, St. Anselm Coll., 1959; MA, Niagara U., 1960; PhD, St. John's U., 1965. Asst. prof. history Gannon U., Erie, Pa., 1965-66; edn. specialist, div. grad. programs U.S. Office Edn., Washington, 1966-68, regional coordinator, grad. acad. programs, 1968-70; dir. univ. programs Univ. Assocs., Inc., Washington, 1970-72; asst. to pres., sec. Council of Grad. Schs. in U.S., 1972-80; exec. v.p. Renewables Research Inst., Annandale, Va., 1980-81; exec. dir. Worcester (Mass.) Consortium Higher Edn., 1981-89, N.H. Coll. and Univ. Coun., Manchester, 1989-93; cons.; exec. dir. Mass. Vet. Med. Assn., Marlborough, Mass., 1995-98; cons., 1998—. Contbr. articles to profl. jours. Bd. dirs. No. Va. C.C., 1999—, Loudoun Healthcare, Inc., 2000—, Loudoun County Econ. Devel. Commn., 2000.

RYAN, JOSEPH F. educator; b. N.Y.C., Jan. 27, 1949; s. Henry Martin and Anita (Vanderburg) R.; married; children: Robert M., Daniel J., Nora Jean. BA in Criminal Justice, John Jay Coll., MA in Criminal Justice, 1978; PhD in Sociology, Fordham U., 1984. Detective N.Y.C. Police Dept., 1968-91; assoc. prof. Pace U., N.Y.C., 1991—, chmn. dept. pub. adminstrn./criminal justice, 1995—. Cons. Urban Inst., Washington, 1995—; peer rev. Nat. Inst. Justice, Washington, 1990—; lectr. Indian Health Svc., Albuquerque, 1991-96. Co-author 1 book; mem. editl. rev. bd. Am. Jour. Police, 1995—. Vis. fellow Nat. Inst. Justice, Washington, 1991-93. Mem. Am. Soc. Criminology. Avocations: reading, canoeing, hiking, biking, museums.

RYAN, JOSEPH W., JR. lawyer; b. Phila., June 24, 1948; s. Joseph W. Sr. and Marie R. (Hillgrube) R.; m. Mary Pat Law, Sept. 11, 1971; children: Caitlin, Joseph W. III. BA, St. Joseph's U., Phila., 1970; MA, Villanova U., 1971; JD, U. Va., 1978. Bar: Ohio 1978, U.S. Supreme Ct. 1982. Ptnr. Porter, Wright, Morris & Arthur, Columbus, Ohio, 1978—. Lectr. Sch. Dentistry Ohio State U., Columbus, 1982-89, Continuing Legal Edn. Inst., 1984—; mem. trial acad. faculty Internat. Assn. Def. Counsel, Boulder, Colo., 1994. Author: Use of Demonstrative Evidence, 1985; assoc. editor Litigation News, 1986—, editor in chief, 2000—. Trustee Columbus Zool. Assn., 1980-90; bd. dirs. Columbus Speech and Hearing Ctr., 1988-99, pres., 1995-96. Mem. ABA, Ohio State Bar Assn., Columbus Bar Assn., Internat. Assn. Def. Counsel, Am. Arbitration Assn. (panel of arbitrators). Republican. Roman Catholic. Office: Porter Wright Morris & Arthur 41 S High St Ste 30 Columbus OH 43215-6101 E-mail: jryan@porterwright.com.

RYAN, JOYCE ETHEL, artist, author; b. Atlanta, Aug. 29, 1949; m. Jim Cyril Klar, Apr. 5, 1975. BFA, U. Ga., 1972. Instr. Marsh Draughon Coll., Atlanta, 1972-73; retail store mgr. Army & Air Force Exch. Svc., Dallas, 1974; illustrator U.S. Army Logistics Ctr., Ft. Lee, Va., 1975-77; graphics mgr. Ecosystems Internat., Millersville, Md., 1980-82; freelance art studio dir. Seoul, 1983-85; pres. Butterfly Books, Ariz., 1985—. Instr. Cochise Coll., Sierra Vista, 1986. Illustrator, author: Seoul Sketches, 1985, Scenes of Southern Arizona, 1986, Seoul Travel Guide, 1987, Traveling with Your Sketchbook, 1990, The Happy Camper's Gourmet Cookbook, 1992, Calligraphy: Elegant and Easy, 1994, Drawing at Home, 1996, America's Best Cheesecakes, 1998, Fifty Years of Excellence: Texas Watercolor Society, 1999. Mem. Tex. Watercolor Soc. Avocations: drawing, painting. E-mail: wavelady@artistsnetwork.com.

RYAN, JUDITH W. geriatrics consultant, adult nurse practitioner, educator, researcher; b. Waterbury, Conn., Dec. 8, 1943; d. James Patrick Ryan and Edna (Swanson) Billings. BS, U. Conn., 1965; MS, Boston U., 1967; PhD, U. Md., 1984. RN, Md., Conn.; cert. adult nurse practitioner ANCC. Instr. U. Conn., Storrs, 1967-69; asst. prof. Ind. U., Purdue U., Indpls., 1969-73, U. Md., Balt., 1973-82, dir. primary care adult nurse pracitioner cert. program, dept. medicine, supportive care project, 1985-87, asst. prof. sch. nursing, 1987-95, asst. prof., 1976-82; clin. dir. EverCare, 1995-99; pres. Nurse Practitioners and Cons., P.C. of Prime Health Group, 2000—. Arbitrator Health Claims Arbitration Program, Md., 1976—; bd. mem. Md. Bd. Nursing, Balt., 1991-98, pres., 1993-96; trustee Md. Nurses Assn. Polit. Action Com., Balt., treas., 1989-91. Contbr. articles to profl. jours. Named Distinguished Practitioner Nursing, Nat. Acad. Practice, 1984-99. Mem. Am. Coll. Nurse Practitioners, Md. Nurses Assn. (2d v.p. 1986-88), Nurse Practitioner Assn. Md., Sigma Theta Tau, Phi Kappa Phi. Home: 622 Lucia Ave Baltimore MD 21229-4516 Office: 20 New Plant Ct Ste 204 Owings Mills MD 21117 E-mail: jwryan@starpower.net.

RYAN, KAY PEDERSEN, poet; b. San Jose, Calif., Sept. 21, 1945; d. Kay Richard and Bessie Margaret (Barrett) Pedersen. BA, UCLA, 1967, MA, 1968. Reader poetry Libr. of Congress, 2001. Author: (poetry) Flamingo Watching, 1994, Elephant Rocks, 1996, Say Uncle, 2000; contbr. 23 poems to New Yorker mag., numerous poems to lit. publs. Recipient Poetry award, Ingram Merrill Found., 1995, Maurice English award, 2001; grantee, Nat. Endowment for Arts, 2001. Home: 60 Taylor Dr Fairfax CA 94930

RYAN, KENNETH, research scientist; b. Bay Shore, N.Y., Jan. 20, 1960; s. Harry Joseph Ryan Jr. and Edith Muriel Kent. BS, SUNY, Stony Brook, 1982; PhD in Biol. Chemistry, Johns Hopkins U., 1992. Postdoctoral fellow, rsch. scientist U. Cambridge, Eng., 1993-96, rsch. assoc., 1996-99; asst. mem. Joseph Stokes Jr. Rsch. Inst., U. Penn. Sch. Medicine, 2000—, rsch. asst. prof. pediatric cardiology, 2001—. Contbr. sci. rsch. articles to profl. jours. Grad. Sch. studentship NIH, 1985; Cancer Rsch. Campaign postdoctoral fellow, 1993, Florence R.C. Murray fellow, 2000. Mem.: N.Y. Acad. Scis., Am. Soc. Biochemistry and Molecular Biology. Roman Catholic. Office: Children's Hosp of Phila/U Pa Sch Medicine Abramson Rsch Bldg Ste 710 34th St and Civic Ctr Blvd Philadelphia PA 19104 Fax: 215-590-5454. E-mail: ryank@chop.email.edu.

RYAN, KENNETH EUGENE, engineer; b. Guilford, N.Y., Apr. 3, 1936; s. Julian Nichols and Irene M. Ryan; m. Nancy Race, Aug. 29, 1959; children: Patrick, Kathleen, Timothy, Maureen. BS, Cornell U., 1958, MS, 1959. Registered profl. engr., N.Y. With various mobile equipment mfrs., 1959-66; rsch. assoc. Cornell U., Ithaca, N.Y., 1966-69; sr. project engr. Raymond Corp., Greene, 1969—. Chmn. Zoning Bd. Appeals, Oxford, N.Y., 1973-83; chmn. com. North Guilford (N.Y.) Ch., 1989-91; mem. Oxford Planning Bd., 1970—. Mem. Nat. Soc. Profl. Engrs., Soc. Exptl. Stress Analysis. Avocation: photography. Home: 221 Ryan Rd Oxford NY 13830-9801

RYAN, KENNETH J. academic administrator, educator; MD, U. Wash., 1966. Cert. pathologist. Mem. staff Univ. Med. Ctr., Tuscon; dean acad. affairs, medicine U. Ariz., prof. pathology, microbiology, immunology. Avocations: golf, tennis. Office: U Ariz Sch Medicine 1501 N Cambell Ave # C 206 Tucson AZ 85724-0002*

RYAN, KEVIN WILLIAM, virologist, researcher, science educator, health facility administrator; b. Ft. Dodge, Iowa, Dec. 8, 1952; s. Joseph Michael Ryan and Etoile Evelyn Werth; m. Mary Ellen Lyman, June 1, 1974; children: Matthew Lyman, Mark Joseph. BS, U. Iowa, 1978; PhD, U. Mich., 1984. Staff fellow Nat. Inst. Allergy and Infectious Diseases, NIH, Bethesda, Md., 1984-86; rsch. asst. dept. virology and molecular biology St. Jude Children's Rsch. Hosp., Memphis, 1986-89, asst. mem., 1989-98; asst. prof. pathology U. Tenn. Coll. Medicine, 1994-98; sci. rev. adminstr. Nat. Inst. Allergy and Infectious Diseases, NIH, Rockville, Md., 1998-2000; program officer virology vaccine and prevention rsch. prog. divsn. AIDS, Nat. Inst. Allergy and Infectious Diseases, NIH, Bethesda, 2000—; NIAID program ofcl., HIV prevention trials network coop. agreements, 2000—; NIAID program ofcl. HIV prevention trials in injecting drug users ctrl. lab. coop. agreement, 2000—; deputy chief Prevention Scis. Br., 2001—; acting chief Prevetnion Scis. Br., 2002—; deputy chief NIAID, working group, comprehensive Internat. Program for Rsch. in AIDS (CIPRA), 2001—. Prin. investigator Nat. Inst. Allergy and Infectious Diseases, 1992—98. Contbr. . Fellow postdoctoral Mich. Cancer Rsch. Inst., U. Mich., 1982. Mem.: Am. Soc. for Microbiology. Roman Catholic. Avocation: woodworking. Office: Nat Inst Allergy and Infectious Diseases Divsn AIDS 6700-b Rockledge Dr Bethesda MD 20892-0001

RYAN, LEO VINCENT, business educator; b. Waukon, Iowa, Apr. 6, 1927; s. John Joseph and Mary Irene (O'Brien) Ryan. BS, Marquette U., 1949; MBA, DePaul U., 1954; PhD, St. Louis U., 1958; postgrad., Catholic U. Am., 1951-52, Bradley U., 1952-54, Northwestern U., 1950; LLD, Seton Hall U., 1988; DHL, Ill. Benedictine U., 1997. Joined Order Clerics of St. Viator, Roman Cath. Ch., 1950. Faculty Marquette U., Milw., 1957-65, dir. continuing edn. summer sessions, coord. evening divsns., 1959-65, prof. indsl. mgmt., 1964; prof., chmn. dept. mgmt. Loyola U., Chgo., 1965-66, adj. prof. mgmt., 1967-69; dep. dir. Peace Corps, Lagos, Nigeria, 1966-67, dir. Western Nigeria Ibadan, 1967-68; asst. superior gen. and treas. gen. Clerics of St. Viator, Rome, 1968-69, dir. edn. Am. province Arlington Heights, Ill., 1969-74; pres. St. Viator H.S., 1972-74; dean, prof. mgmt. U. Notre Dame Coll. Bus. Adminstrn., Ind., 1975-80; dean DePaul U. Coll. Commerce, 1980-88, prof. mgmt., 1980-99; Wicklander prof. profl. ethics DePaul U., 1993-94; prof. emeritus, 1999. Dir. Peace Corps tng. programs Marquette U., 1962-65; adj. prof. human devel. St. Mary's Coll., Winona, Minn., 1972-74; mem. sch. bd. Archdiocese Chgo., 1972-75, vice-chmn., 1973-75, nat. edn. com. U.S. Cath. Conf., 1971-75, exec. com., 1973-75; nat. adv. bd. Benedictine Sisters of Nauvoo, 1973-83; nat. adv. coun. SBA, 1982-85, vice-chmn. minority bus., 1982-85, exec. com. Chgo. chpt., 1982-84; vis. prof. U. Ife, Ibadan, 1967-68,; chmn. trust audit com. First Bank-Milw., 1980-85, chmn. audit and examination com., 1985-90, adv. coun., 1991-93; bd. dirs. Henricksen & Co., Inc.; fin. commn. Clerics of St. Viator, 1978-, provincial chpt., 1985-97, 2001-, devel. adv. bd. 1996-2001, new foundations com. 1996-98, alt. mem., 1997-, provincial coun., 2001-; Fulbright prof. Adam Mickiewicz U., Poland, 1993-99; vis. prof. Helsinki Sch. Econs., 1992—, Polish-Am. Ctr., U. Lodz, 1998, Poznan Acad. Econs., 1991, 1999-2002; co-chair bus. and profl. com. Archdiocese of Chgo. Sesquetennial Com. Out Reach Divsn. Ctrl. Planning Group, 1993-94; vis. prof. Notre Dame, 2000, Helsinki Sch. Econs., 2000; adv. bd. Sch. of Bus. Univ. Kieve, Ukraine, 2001-. Author: Human Action in Business, 1996, Etyka Biznesu, 1997, 4th edit., 2000, From Autarcy to Market: Polish Economics and Politics, 1945-1995, 1998, 2d edit., 1999, Students Focus on Business Ethics, 2000, Praxiology and Pragmatism, 2002; mem. editl. bd. Internat. Jour. Value Based Mgmt., European Bus. Jour., Bus. Ethics Quar., Mid Atlantic Jour. of Bus. Mem. Pres.'s Com. on Employment Handicapped, 1959-65, Wis. Gov.'s Com. on Employment Handicapped, 1959-65, Wis. Gov.'s Com. on UN, 1961-64, Burnham Park Planning Commn., 1982-88; bd. dirs. Ctr. Pastoral Liturgy U. Notre Dame, 1976-79; trustee Lake Forest Grad. Sch. Mgmt., 1989-91, St. Mary of Woods Coll., 1978-81, Cath. Theol. Union, U. Chgo., 1992-95, Divine Word Coll., 1997—; regent Seton Hall U., 1981-87, mem. acad. affairs com., 1981-87, chmn., 1983-87; dir. Ctr. for Enterprise Devel., 1992-95; elected fellow St. Edmonds Coll. Cambridge U., 1992—; mem. Cath. Commn. Intellectual and Cultural Affairs, 1992—, Cath. Campaign for Am., 1994-98; bd. dirs. Internat. Bus. Ethics Inst., Am. Grad. Sch. Internat. Mgmt., 1995-97, Assn. Profl. Ethics, 1995-96; mem. adv. com. Mgmt. Edn. in Poland, U. Md., College Park, 1995-2000. Recipient Freedom award Berlin Commn., 1961, chieftancy title Asoju Atoaja of Oshogbo Oba Adenle I, Yorubaland, Nigeria, 1967, B'nai B'rith Interfaith award, Milw., 1963, Disting. Alumnus award Marquette U., 1974, DePaul U., 1976, Tchr. of Yr. award Beta Alpha Psi, 1980, Centennial Alumni Achievement award Marquette U., 1981, Boland Meml. Disting. Alumni award, St. Louis, 1989, Disting. Alumni and Bicentennial awards Jesuit Bus. Schs., 1989, Pres.' award St. Viator H.S., 1992, Medal of Merit Adam Mickiewicz U., 1995, Excellence in Tchg. award Adam Mickiewicz U., 1997, Ill. Ernst and Young Entrepreneur Supporter award, 1999, Vincentian U. Ethics Scholar award, 2000, Centennial award Dominican U. Sch. Bus., 2002, Centennial award for lifetime leadership and bus. ethics Dominican U.; Brother Leo V. Ryan award named in his honor Cath. Bus. Edn. Assn., 1962; Ryan Scholars in Mgmt. established in his honor DePaul U., 1989, Outstanding Svc. award, 1991-93, Commerce Alumni award of merit, 1997; DePaul Creativity Ctr. named in his honor, 1997, trustee; named hon. life chmn. Nat. Adv. Com., Ryan Creativity Ctr., Creative Cutting Edge award, 1999; Ryan Scholarship named in his honor St. Viator H.S., 1992, Lion award, 1997, trustee, 2000-01, gov., 2001-; named Man of Yr. Jr. C. of C., Milw., 1959, Marquette U. Bus. Adminstrn. Alumni Man of Yr., 1974; named Disting. Vis. Term Prof. Seton Hall U., 2001; Milw. Bd. Realtors traveling fellow, 1964, Nat. Assn. Purchasing Agts. faculty fellow, 1958, German Am. Acad. Exch. Coun. fellow, summer 1983, Presdl. fellow Am. Grad. Sch. Internat. Mgmt., 1989, vis. scholar, 1995, Malone fellow in Islamic studies, 1990, fellow Kosciuszko Found. Adam Mickiewicz U., 1990; scholar-in-residence Mgmt. Sch. Imperial Coll. Sci. and Tech. U. London, 1988; vis. scholar U. Calif., Berkeley, 1989; USIA Acad. Specialists grantee, Poland, 1991-93; fellow St. Edmund's Coll. Cambridge U., 1992; named vis. rsch. fellow Von Hugel Inst., 1992-93; scholar-in-residence Am. Grad. Sch. Internat. Mgmt., 1995; guest scholar Kellogg Inst. Internat. Studies U. Notre Dame, 1997; named disting. vis. term prof. Seton Hall U., 2001. Mem. Cath. Bus. Edn. Assn. (nat. pres. 1960-62, nat. exec. bd. 1960-64), Assn. Sch. Bus. Ofcls. (nat. com. chmn. 1965-67), Am. Assembly Collegiate Schs. Bus. (com. internat. affairs 1977-84, chmn. 1981-84, bd. dirs. 1981-87, program chmn. 1979-80, exec. com., chmn. projects/svc. mgmt. com. 1984-86), Am. Fgn. Svc. Assn., Am. Assn. Profl. Ethics (bd. dirs. 1996-98), Allamakee County Hist. Soc. (charter life), Acad. Internat. Bus., Acad. Mgmt. (social issues div., chmn. membership com. 1990-91), Ancient Order of Hibernians, Nat. Returned Peace Corps Assn., Atomic Vets. Assn., August Derleth Soc., Chgo. Area Return Peace Corps Vols., Econ. Club Chgo., Chgo. Coun. Fgn. Rels., Coun. Fgn. Rels. (Chgo. com., diplomat cir. 1998), European Bus. Ethics Network Poland (hon. 1998), Soc. Bus. Ethics (mem. exec. com. 1991—, pres. 1993-94, adv. bd. 1995-97), Assn. Social Econs. (life), Assn. Christian Economists, Dubuque County Hist. Soc., Iowa Hist. Soc., Iowa Postal History Soc., Fulbright Assn. (life), Internat. Assn. for Bus. and Soc. (founder), Internat. Soc. for Bus., Econs. and Ethics (charter), Internat. Trade and Fin. Assn. (founder, bd. dirs. 1989-92, 96-98, v.p. membership 1991-92, 96-97), Internat. Learned Soc. Praxiology, (hon. life, internat. adv. bd. praxiology ann.), Polish Inst. Arts and Scis. in Am., DePaul Inst. Bus. and Profl. Ethics (founder 1984, adv. bd. 1984-94, Founders award 1999), USS Mt. McKinley Reunion Assn. (hon. chaplain AGC-7 1989-96, Disting. Svc. award 1991, 96), Alpha Sigma Nu, Alpha Kappa Psi (bd. dirs. found. 1985-91, vice-chmn. 1987-91, chmn. scholarship com. 1987-91, chmn. devel. com. 1987, exec. com. 1990-91, Bronze Disting. Svc. award 1949, Silver Disting. Svc. award 1958, Recognition medal, 2001), Beta Alpha Psi, Beta Gamma Sigma (co-chair 75th Anniversary com. Ill., faculty advisor DePaul chpt. 1986-92), Century Travel Club (Silver award), Delta Mu Delta, Pi Gamma Mu, Tau Kappa Epsilon. Home and Office: 1212 E Euclid Ave Arlington Heights IL 60004-5747 E-mail: LeovRyan@aol.com.

RYAN, LEONARD EAMES, judge; b. Albion, N.Y., July 8, 1930; s. Bernard and Harriet Earle (Fitts) R.; m. Ann Allen, June 18, 1973; 1 child, Thomas Eames Allen-Ryan. Grad., Kent Sch., 1948; AB, U. Pa., 1954; JD, NYU, 1962. Bar: D.C. 1963, N.Y. 1963, U.S. Ct. Appeals (D.C. cir.) 1963, U.S. Dist. Ct. (so. and ea. dists.) N.Y. 1965, U.S. Ct. Appeals (2nd cir.) 1966, U.S. Supreme Ct. 1967. Field engr. constrn. U.S. Steel Fairless Works, Morrisville, Pa., 1951-52; reporter Upper Darby (Pa.) News, 1954; newsman AP, Pitts., Phila., Harrisburg, N.Y.C., 1955-62; reporter, spl. writer on law N.Y. Times, 1962-63; info. adviser corp. hdqrs. IBM, N.Y.C., 1963; trial atty. firm Perrell, Nielsen & Stephens, 1964-66; trial atty. civil rights div. Dept. Justice, Washington, 1966-68; asst. to dir. bus. affairs CBS News, N.Y.C., 1968; program officer Office Govt. and Law, Ford Found., 1968-74; pvt. practice law, cons. pub. affairs, 1974-91; v.p., sec. W. P. Carey & Co., Inc., 1977-83; impartial hearing officer Edn. for All Handicapped Children Act of 1975, 1976-91; per diem adminstrv. law judge N.Y. State Agys., 1976-91; hearing examiner N.Y. State Family Ct., 1980-81; apptd. U.S. adminstv. law judge, 1991; adminstv. law judge Office Hearings and Appeals, San Rafael, Calif., 1991-93, Phila., 1993-94, N.Y.C., 1994—. Arbitrator Small Claims Ct., N.Y.C., 1974-84; bd. dirs. Community Action for Legal Svcs. Inc., N.Y.C., 1971-77, vice-chmn., 1975-77; co-chmn. Citizens Com. to Save Legal Svcs., N.Y.C., 1975-76; bd. dirs. Lower East Side Svc. Ctr., N.Y.C., 1977-89. Author: (with Bernard Ryan Jr.) So You Want to Go Into Journalism, 1963; contbr. articles to profl. jours. Served with USAR, 1950-57. Mem. Am. Judicature Soc., Assn. of Bar of City of N.Y., N.Y. State Bar Assn., St. Elmo Club (Phila.), Heights Casino (Bklyn.). Home: 32 Orange St Brooklyn NY 11201-1634 Office: 111 Livingston St Brooklyn NY 11201-5078

RYAN, LINDA LEE, sculptor, art educator; b. Bartlesville, Okla., Mar. 12, 1952; d. Howard Allen and Mary Ardis Ryan; m. Louie Kistler III, July 6, 1997. BA, Mont. State U., 1974; MA, Ctrl. Wash. U., 1979; MFA, W.Va. U., 1981; postgrad., Internat. Acad. Bilden deKunst, Salzburg, Austria, 1986. Ceramics instr. Ketterer Art Ctr., Bozeman, Mont., 1972; jewelry instr. Coll. of Great Falls, 1975; tchg. asst. Ctrl. Wash. U., Ellensburg, 1976-79, W.Va. U., Morgantown, 1979-80; art prof. Casper (Wyo.) Coll., 1982—. Trustee, chair exhbns. and collections com. Nicolaysen Art Mus., Casper, 1994-2000; mem. com. task force Western States Arts Fedn., Santa Fe, N.Mex., 1991; co-chair Arts 500 Wyo. Arts Alliance, 1985-88; guest artist Idaho State U., Pocatello, 1987, 90, 10th Ann. Dunconnor Jewelry Workshop, Taos, N.Mex., 1987, U. Mont., Missoula, 1989, Western Wyo. Coll., Rock Springs, 1989, 94, 99, CC Theatre, Casper, 1994, N.W. C.C., Powell, Wyo., 1995, others; panelist, juror in field. One woman shows at St. Katherine's Women's Coll., St. Paul, 1984, Sarah Spurgeon Gallery Ctrl. Wash. U., 1978, Crew Gallery, Seattle, 1979, Alderson-Broddus Coll., Philippi, W.Va., 1980, Creative Arts Ctr., W.Va. U., 1981, Transition Gallery Idaho State U., 1987, Visual Arts Ctr. Gallery Casper Coll., 1989, Davis Gallery Idaho Satte U., 1990, WW Coll. Art Springs, 1991, 94, Goodstein Gallery Casper Coll., 1996; exhibited in group shows at Meadows Gallery, Denton, Tex., 1992, Paris Gibson Sq. Mus. Art, Great Falls, Mont., 1992, Nichlaysen Art Mus., 1992, 93, 99, CC Visual Arts Gallery, 1993, 94, 95, 96, 97, 98, 2000, Wyo. Arts Coun. Traveling Artbox Project, 1994-95, 1999-2000, Sarah Spurgeon Gallery, 1995, Wyo. Arts Coun. Gallery, 1995, U. N.D., 1995, West Wyo. Coll., others; represented in permanent collections at Wyo. State Mus., Casper Coll., Inkfish Gallery, Denver, Scottish Arts Coun., Edinburgh, Crew Gallery; contbr. to books, periodicals and newspapers. Visual arts fellow Wyo. Arts Coun., 1990, 2001; grantee Wyo. Arts Coun., 1995. Mem. Wyo. Alliance for Art Edn., Nicolaysen Art Mus. (trustee 1994-2000), Denver Art Mus., Internat. Sculpture Ctr., Soc. N.Am. Goldsmiths, Delta Phi Delta. Avocations: cross country skiing, weightlifting. Office: Casper Coll 125 College Dr Casper WY 82601-4612 E-mail: lryan@caspercollege.edu.

RYAN, MARIANNE ELIZABETH, lawyer; b. Ft. Knox, Ky., Nov. 15, 1964; d. John L. and Frances J. (McIntosh) R. BA, Trinity Coll., 1986; JD, Yale U., 1991. Bar: Ill. 1991, U.S. Dist. Ct. (no. dist.) Ill. 1991. Assoc. Pattishall, McAuliffe, Newbury, Hilliard & Geraldson, Chgo., 1991-93; internet editor Law Jour. EXTRA! The N.Y. Law Pub. Co., N.Y.C., 1994-95; rsch. scholar Nat. Ctr. for Philanthropy and the Law NYU Sch. Law, 1996-99; tech. coord. Americorps/Project F.I.R.S.T., N.Y.C., 1999-2000; VISTA svc. leader Americorps/Ohio Campus Compact, Yellow Springs, Ohio, 2000—01; resident fellow Lloyd Hall Scholars Program, U. Mich., Ann Arbor, 2002—, Cmty. Info. fellow Alliance for Cmty. Tech., 2002—. Adj. prof. trademark and copyright law John Marshall Law Sch., Chgo., 1993. Exec. editor Yale Jour. on Regulation. Mem. Computer Profls. for Social Responsibility, Internet Soc., Internet Corp. for Assigned Names and Numbers, Phi Beta Kappa. Home: PO Box 4455 Ann Arbor MI 48106-4455 E-mail: marianne@aya.yale.edu.

RYAN, MARK ANTHONY, architect; b. Council Bluffs, Iowa, Sept. 6, 1964; s. Paul Elmer and Darreline Kay (Wyland) R.; m. Shelli Ann Hagerbaumer, Sept. 26, 1992. BA in Architecture with distinction, Iowa State U., 1987; postgrad. Sch. of Law, Creighton U., 2000—. Registered profl. architect, Wis. Project architect U.S. Army C.E., Omaha, 1987-90, architect, security engr., 1990-91, environ. project mgr., 1991-96; owner, architect Ryan Designs, 1987—; project mgr. Bovis Constrn. Corp., 1997-2000; CEO, Ad Hoc Comm. Resources, LLC, 1999—. Owner The Ryan Co., Omaha, 1994-96; bd. adv. Fitness Plus, Council Bluffs, Iowa, 1990-92; expert witness, Iowa and Nebr., 1991—. Chmn. City Devel. Commn., Council Bluffs, 1992; trustee San. and Improvement Dist. No. 142, Douglas County, Nebr., 1995-96. Scholar, State of Iowa, 1982, Valentino scholar, 2001. Mem. AIA (sec. S.W. Iowa sect. 1991, treas. 1992, v.p. 1993, pres. 1994-96), Am. Mil. Engrs., Nat. Trust for Hist. Preservation, Downtown Omaha Inc., Golden Key, Phi Kappa Phi, Tau Sigma Delta, Phi Delta Phi. Avocations: archl. restoration, biking, freshwater aquatics. Home and Office: Ad Hoc Communication Resources 9030 Raven Oaks Dr Omaha NE 68152-1759 E-mail: ryandesigns@nfinity.com.

RYAN, MARLEIGH GRAYER, Japanese language educator; b. N.Y.C., May 1, 1930; d. Harry and Betty (Hurwick) Grayer; m. Edward Ryan, June 4, 1950; 1 child, David Patrick. BA, NYU, 1951; MA, Columbia U., 1956, PhD, 1965; Cert., East Asian Inst., 1956; postgrad., Kyoto U., 1958-59. Research assoc. Columbia U., N.Y.C., 1960-61, lectr. Japanese, 1961-65, asst. prof., 1965-70, assoc. prof., 1970-72; vis. asst. prof. Yale U., New Haven, 1966-67; assoc. prof. U. Iowa, Iowa City, 1972-75, prof., 1975-81, chmn. dept., 1972-81; prof. Japanese SUNY, New Paltz, 1981-98, dean liberal arts and scis., 1981-90, prof. emeritus, 1999—; assoc. in rsch. Reischauer Inst. for Japanese Studies, Harvard U., Cambridge, Mass., 1999—, chair study group on Asian Am. Lit., 2000—02. Vice chmn. seminar on modern Japan, Columbia U., 1984-85, chmn., 1985-86; co-chmn. N.Y. State Conf. on Asian Studies, 1986, editor, 1993-99, mem. exec. com., 1993-96, sec., 1993-99, co-chmn., 1998. Co-author: (with Herschel Webb) Research in Japanese Sources, 1965; author: Japan's First Modern Novel, 1967, The Development of Realism in the Fiction of Tsubouchi Shoyo, 1975; assoc. editor: Jour. Assn. Tchrs. Japanese, 1962-71, editor, 1971-75. East Asian Inst. fellow Columbia U., 1955; Ford Found. fellow, 1958-60; Japan Found. fellow, 1973, Woodrow Wilson Ctr. Internat. Scholars fellow, 1988-89; recipient Van. Am. Disting. Book award Columbia, 1968 Mem. MLA (sec. com. on teaching Japanese Lang. 1962-68, mem. del. assembly 1979-87, mem. exec. com. div. Asian lit. 1981-86), Assn. Tchrs. Japanese (exec. com. 1969-72, 74-77), Assn. Asian Studies (bd. dirs. 1975-78, N.E. asian coun. 1975-78, coun. of confs., 1993-96), Midwest Conf. Asian Studies (pres. 1980-81) *Studying the most difficult language in the world has taught me patience and tact. One learns what it is to sit completely still at the Japanese No theatre and absorb wondrous sights and sounds in an atmosphere of absolute peace. Discovering the stillness in movement is perhaps the most important lesson we in the West can derive from our Asian experience.*

RYAN, MARY A. diplomat; b. New York, N.Y., Oct. 1, 1940; BA, St. John's Univ., 1963, MA, 1965. With Foreign Service, Dept. of State, 1966—; consular and adminstrv. officer Naples, Italy, 1966-69; personnel officer Am. Embassy, Tegucigalpa, Honduras, 1970-71; consular officer Am. Consulate Gen., Monterrey, Mexico, 1971-73; adminstrv. officer Bur. of African Affairs, Dept. of State, Washington, 1973-75, post mgmt. officer, 1975-77; career devel. officer Bur. of Personnel, Dept. of State, 1977-80; adminstrv. counselor Abidjan, Ivory Coast, 1980-81, Khartoum, Sudan, 1981-82; inspector, Office of Insp. Gen. Dept. of State, Washington, 1982-83, exec. dir. Bur. of European and Can. Affairs, 1983-85, exec. asst. to Under Sec. of State for Mgmt., 1985-88; ambassador to Swaziland, 1988-90; dep. asst. sec. Bur. of Consular Affairs, Washington, 1990; dir. Kuwait task force, 1990-91; ops. dir. UN spl. commn. on elimination of Iraqi weapons, 1991; dep. asst. sec. Bur. European & Can. Affairs, Washington, 1991-93; asst. sec. Bur. of Consular Affairs, 1993—, career amb., 1999. Office: Dept State Bureau of Consular Affairs 2201 C St NW Washington DC 20520-0001*

RYAN, MEG, actress, producer; b. Fairfield, Conn., Nov. 19, 1961; m. Dennis Quaid, 1991 (div. 2001); 1 child, Jack Henry. Student, NYU. Appearences include (TV) One of the Boys, 1982, As The World Turns, 1982-84, Wild Side, 1985, (films) Rich and Famous, 1981, Amityville 3-D, 1983, Top Gun, 1986, Armed and Dangerous, 1986, Innerspace, 1987, Promised Land, 1987, D.O.A., 1988, The Presidio, 1988, When Harry Met Sally, 1989, Joe Versus the Volcano, 1990, The Doors, 1991, Prelude to a Kiss, 1992, Sleepless in Seattle, 1993, Flesh and Bone, 1993, When a Man Loves a Woman, 1994, Restoration, 1994, I.Q., 1994, French Kiss, 1995, Two for the Road, 1996, Courage Under Fire, 1996, Addicted to Love, 1997, Anastasia (voice), 1997, City of Angels, 1998, Hurlyburly, 1998, You've Got Mail, 1998, Hanging Up, 1999, Proof of Life, 2000, Kate & Leopold, 2001; owner Prufrock Pictures movie prodn. co.; prodr.: French Kiss/Paris Match, 1995, Two for the Road, 1997, Northern Lights, 1997 (TV, exec. prodr.), Lost Souls, 1999. Recipient Golden Apple award Hollywood Women's Press Club, 1989, Woman of Yr. award Hasty Pudding Theatricals, 1994, ShoWest Conv. Actress of Yr. award, 1999, Am. Comedy Award, 1990, 1994, Women in Film Crystal Award, 1995. Office: care ICM c/o Steve Dontanville 8942 Wilshire Blvd Beverly Hills CA 90211-1934*

RYAN, MELBAGENE T. retired food and nutrition service director; b. Arkadelphia, Ark., Jan. 6, 1927; d. Horace Samuel and Eunice Bridges (Moorman) Tull; m. Wayne Stuart Ryan, Dec. 26, 1954. BS in Edn., Henderson U., 1948; M in Edn., Tex. Women's U., 1951. Registered dietitian. Tchr. Eudora (Ark.) Pub. Schs., 1948-52; dir. food services Tex. Christian U., Ft. Worth, 1952-53, Tex. Women's U., 1953-58; dir. food and nutriton service Irving (Tex.) Ind. Sch. Dist., 1958-85. Project dir. to develop standards excellence with a self study and evaluation Tex. Sch. Food Service Assn., 1985-88; cons. in field. Co-author and project dir.: (with others) Youth Advisory Council Resource Manual, 1978-79, Effective Food Service Management Using Computers, 1982. With child nutrition Tex. Sch. Food Service Assn., Washington, 1974-79; with legis. Am. Sch. Food Service Assn., Irving, 1980-85; mem. Denton Co. Historical Commn., 1997—, Denton Co. Courthouse-on-the Square Mus., chmn. 1998—, Lake Forest good Samaritan Village, adv. bd., 1998—, Tex. Woman's U. Centennial Celebration, 2001, planning com., 1998-99. Recipient Food Facilities Design award Instns. Volume Feeding Awards Program, New Orleans, 1977, Trend Setter award, North Tex. Brokers Assn., Dallas, 1978; Melbagene Ryan Scholarship named in her honor by Dallas Profl. Friends, 1985. Mem. Denton Dietetic Assn. (pres. 1977-78), Tex. Dietetic Assn., Am. Dietetic Assn. (chmn. joint com. 1979-82), Tex. Sch. Food Service Assn. (pres. 1975-76, nutrition edn. 1975), Am. Sch. Food Service Assn. (conf. com. 1977-78, 1982-83), Tex. Women's U. Alumni Assn. Methodist. Home and Office: 1121 Ryan Rd Denton TX 76210-5539

RYAN, MICHAEL See BAVOTA, MICHAEL FRANCIS

RYAN, MICHAEL BEECHER, lawyer, former government official; b. Chgo., Aug. 20, 1936; s. Walter Joseph and Mary Agnes (Beecher) R.; m. Maria Chantal Wiesman, June 1, 1963; children— Mary, Catherine, Matthew. BS in Labor Relations, Manhattan Coll., 1957; JD, U. Notre Dame, 1964. Bar: N.Y. 1964, Ill. 1991. With NLRB, 1964-91, sr. trial atty. Ill. region, 1968-74, dep. officer in charge, 1974-78, regional atty., 1978-91; exec. v.p. NLRB Union, 1968-69, pres., 1969-71; mem. Peoria Planning Commn., 1977-89, chmn., 1979-89; sole practice Peoria. Adj. prof. labor relations Bradley U., 1972-74 Mem. Tri-County Land Use Adv. Com., 1978-82; Pres. Catholic Interracial Council Peoria, 1971-72, North Sterling Homeowners Assn., 1973-77. Served with AUS, 1958-61, Korea. Mem. Regional Attys. Guild (chmn. 1982-88), Wedgewood Country Club. Roman Catholic. Home: 3438 W Villa Rdg Apt A Peoria IL 61604-1739 also: E-9 Plantation Hale Kapaa Kauai HI 96746

RYAN, MICHAEL D. state supreme court justice; BA, St. John's U., Collegeville, Minn., 1967; JD, Ariz. State U., 1977. Dep. county atty. Maricopa County Atty.'s Office, 1977—85; judge pro tempore Superior Ct. State of Ariz., 1985—86, judge, 1986—96; vice chief judge Ariz. Ct. Appeals, Divsn. 1, 2001—02, judge, 1996—2002; justice Ariz. Supreme Ct., 2002—. Chair Ariz. Supreme Ct. Com. Appointment Counsel for Indigent Defendants in Capital Cases; mem. Ariz. Atty. Gen. Capital Case Commn. Mem. Maricopa County Resource Site Team Ctr. for Sex Offender Mgmt., 1995—; mem. x-tattoo adv. com. At Risk Youth Divsn. City of Phoenix Parks, Recreation and Libr. Dept., 1996—. Infantry platoon comdr. USMC, 1968, Vietnam. Mem.: Maricopa County Bar Assn. (bd. dirs. 1987—91, 1998—, chair task force recruitment & retention of women and minority lawyers, Bd. Mem. of Yr. 1999—2000). Office: Ariz Supreme Ct 1501 W Washington Phoenix AZ 85007-3231*

RYAN, MICHAEL LOUIS, controller; b. Corning, Iowa, Feb. 22, 1945; s. Leo Vincent and Elda May (Lawrence) R. AAS in Constrn. Tech., Iowa State U., 1965; BS in Acctg., Drake U., 1972. CPA, Iowa, Wyo. Acct. Ernst & Ernst, Des Moines, 1972-75, Becker, Herrick & Co., Pueblo, Colo., 1975-78; pvt. practice acctg. Gillette, Wyo., 1978-81; acct. Karen M. Moody, CPAs, Sheridan, 1981-85; contr. T-C Investments, Inc., 1985—; ptnr. WHG Partnership, 1991—; v.p. Bosley-Ryan Constrn., Inc., 1993—. With spl. forces U.S. Army, 1966-68, Vietnam. Mem. AICPA (tax div.), Wyo. Soc. CPAs, Am. Legion (fin. officer 1977-81), Lodge (sec. Sheridan club 1982-90, pres. 1989), Phi Kappa Phi, Beta Alpha Psi, Beta Gamma Sigma. Democrat. Roman Catholic. Home: 735 Canby St Sheridan WY 82801-4907 Office: T-C Investments Inc 1566 Terra Ave Sheridan WY 82801-6125 E-mail: mryan@warecom.net.

RYAN, MICHAEL TIMOTHY, sociology educator; b. Mpls., Mar. 22, 1947; s. Martin Fremont and Kathleen Lucille (Shaughnessy) Ryan; 1 child Sean Martin. BA, U. Minn., 1975; MA, SUNY, Stony Brook, 1977. Vis. asst. prof. sociology Susquehanna U., Selingsgrove, Pa., 1980-81; asst. prof. sociology Va. Wesleyan Coll., Virginia Beach, 1981-89, Upper Iowa U., Fayette, 1989-2000; prof. sociology Dodge City (Kans.) C.C., 2000—. Cons. Pine Forge Press, N.Y.C., 1994—, Roxbury Press, L.A., 2000. Chair bd. adjustment, Fayette, 1994-2000; advisor Coll. Reps., Upper Iowa U., 1992-98, Coll. Dems., 1998-2000. Mem. Midwest Sociol. Soc. Democrat. Avocations: swimming, body surfing, mountain biking, writing poetry, movies. Home: 1111C Wright Ave Dodge City KS 67801 Office: Dodge City C C 2501 N 14th Ave Dodge City KS 67801 E-mail: mryan@dccc.rc.ks.us.

RYAN, MICHELE KING, marketing professional; b. Connellsville, Pa., Nov. 25, 1939; d. Francis Joseph and Ella Elizabeth (Hoffman) King; m. Charles Joseph Ryan Jr. (dec Jan. 1994); children: Charles J. Ryan III, Kimberly Ryan Winchester; m. Ernest Bayard Crofoot, Jan. 6, 1996; 6 stepchildren. Student, Georgetown U., 1958. Lic. real estate broker, Md. Adminstr. Corridor Info. Ctrs., Laurel, Md., 1977; devel. dir. Resource Realty, Inc., 1977-81, v.p., 1981-88; exec. v.p. Resource Enterprises LLC, 1988-95; dir. mkgt. Balt./Washington Corridor C. of C., 1997-2000; pres. The Ryan Group, Annapolis, Md., 2000—. Bd. dirs. Citizens Nat. Bank, Laurel; commr. Md. Aviation Commn., Annapolis, 1995—, Md. Commn. on Transp. Investment, Annapolis, 1999; v.p. Gtr. Laurel Nursing Home, 1980-93 Author, co-editor: Travel Patterns in Baltimore/Washington Corridor, 1977. Bd. dirs. Balt./Wash. Internat. Airport Devel. Coun. Named Bus. Woman of Yr. Bowie Crofton BPW, 1981. Mem.: Balt.-Washington C. of C. (chmn. bd. 1991—92), Soroptimist Internat. (treas. 1976), Bowie Women's Club (pres. 1966—68), Bowie Bus. Profl. Women's Club (pres. 1976). Roman Catholic. Avocations: music, reading, travel. Home: 910 Boom Way Annapolis MD 21401-6889 Office: The Ryan Group 910 Boom Way Annapolis MD 21401

RYAN, MIKE, investment advisor, consultant; b. Evansville, Ind., Oct. 5, 1951; s. Mike and Mabel (Mason) R.; m. Pamela Marie Bogdalik, Aug. 19, 1973; children: Dylan Michael, Devin Michael. BA, Ind. U., 1974, MA, 1978. Cert. fin. planner; cert. investment mgmt. analyst. Filmmaker Image Makers, Bloomington, Ind., 1978-79; travel cons. Am. Express Co., Chgo., 1979; pvt. investor Wilmette, 1979-82; pres. Ryan Fin. Advisors, Ltd., 1983-92, Paragon Asset Mgmt., Wilmette, 1983—; regional mgr. Hewins Fin. Advisors, LLC, 2000—01; chmn. fin. svcs. Mut. Ins. Co., 1995-98. Mem. adj. faculty Coll. of Fin. Planning, Denver, 1984-90. Chmn. endowment com. N.E. Ill. coun. Boy Scouts Am., 1998-2002; chmn. Leadership Resource Coun., 1998-99. Named One of Am's. Best Fin. Planners Money Mag., 1987. Mem. Investment Mgmt. Cons. Assn., Inst. Cert. Fin. Planners (v.p. greater Chgo. Soc. 1985-86, pres. 1986-87, chmn. 1987-88, nat. bd. dirs. 1989, 90, Svc. award 1988, 90, 97, Ann. Retreat dean 1991, bd. dirs. 1996-97), Internat. Assn. Fin. Planners (bd. dirs. Greater O'Hare chpt. 1984-86, North Shore chpt. 1987-88, Svc. award 1986), Am. Assn. Ind. Investors (life). Avocations: conservation, art, writing, wilderness canoeing. Office: Paragon Asset Mgmt Ltd 120 Launderle Wilmette IL 60091

RYAN, MILES FRANCIS, III, lawyer; b. Washington, July 31, 1963; s. Miles Francis Jr. and Vernance Dolores (Beste) R. AB cum laude, Harvard U., 1986; JD, Columbia U., 1990. Bar: Pa. 1991, U.S. Ct. Fed. Claims 1995, U.S. Tax Ct. 1995, U.S. Ct. Appeals for Armed Forces 1995, U.S. Ct. Vets. Appeals 1995, U.S. Supreme Ct. 1995. Staff mem. U.S. Senator William Proxmire, Washington, 1980, 82, 83; intern U.S. Senator Tom Harkin, 1989; law clerk U.S. Dept. Commerce Office of Gen. Counsel's Honors Program, 1990-91, atty.-advisor, 1991-92, U.S. Dept. Commerce Office Gen. Counsel's Office of Chief Counsel for Econ. Affairs, Washington, 1992-96. Mem. U.S. Dept. Commerce Office of Gen. Counsel's Law Libr. Com., Washington, 1992, 93; key worker U.S. Dept. Commerce's Combined Fed. Campaign, Washington, 1992, 93. Mem. Harvard-Radcliffe Dem. Club, Cambridge, Mass., 1983-86; vol. Joe Kennedy for Congress Campaign, Cambridge, 1986, Don Mooers for Congress Campaign, Wheaton, Md., 1996; at-large mem., treas. Columbia U. Law Sch. Student Senate, N.Y.C., 1987-90, 89-90. Jaffin Pub. Interest and Student Funded Fellowship grantee Columbia U. Sch. Law, 1989, John Harvard scholar Harvard U., 1983-86; recipient Gold Medal award U.S. Dept. Commerce, 1995. Mem. ABA, FBA (D.C. chpt., bd. dirs., alt. nat. del., sec., pres.- elect, nat. coun. del., nat. membership com., younger lawyers divsn. bd. dirs., chair nat. admissions com.), Columbia U. Law Sch. Alumni Assn., Columbia U. Club, Harvard U. Club Washington, KC (local coun. co-comty. activities dir. 1982). Democrat. Roman Catholic. Avocations: reading historical, political and current affairs books and articles, attending public policy and historical lectures, visiting museums, attending the theater and concerts, travel. Home: 12502 Two Farm Dr Silver Spring MD 20904-2931

RYAN, NOEL, librarian, consultant; b. Saint John, N.B., Canada, May 27, 1925; s. Fergus James and Evelyn Grace (Hayes) R.; m. Doreen Lillian Allison, Dec. 19, 1950; children: Colin Allison, Karen Jennifer. BA, Sir George Williams U., Montreal, 1964; M.L.S., McGill U., 1967; MBA, Northland U., Toronto, 1983. Vice-pres. Temco Electric Mfg. Co., Montreal, 1949-57; owner, operator photo finishing co. Local Photo, 1957-67; chief libr. Dorval (Que.) Pub. Libr., 1967-69, Brampton (Ont.) Pub. Libr., 1969-71, Mississauga (Ont). Libr. Sys., 1971-87; bldg. projects mgr. Noel Ryan Auditorium Missauga Ctrl. Libr., 1987-89. Joint author: Juxtaposied, 1974. Served with Can. Army, 1944-46, ETO. Mem. Toronto Black Watch Assn. Avocations: painting, making pots, writing poetry. Home and Office: 55 Falconer Dr Apt 35 Mississauga ON Canada L5N 1B3 Address: 35-55 Falconer Dr Mississauga ON Canada L5N 1B3 E-mail: noel@alumni.concordia.ca.

RYAN, PATRICIA ELLEN, healthcare executive; b. Lincoln, Nebr., Apr. 3, 1953; d. Leo Joseph Ryan and Margaret Mary Casson; m. Kevin Donald Procida, Nov. 8, 1997; stepchildren: Matt Procida, Chad Procida. BA, San Francisco State U., 1975; MPA, George Washington U., 1987. Merchandise mgr. J.C. Penney Co., San Bruno, Calif., 1975-81; dir. constituent svcs. Congressman Tom Lantos, San Mateo, 1981-83, legis. asst. Washington, 1983-84, Congressman Richard Ottinger, Washington, 1984; asst. dir. govt. rels. Am. Psychiat. Assn., 1985-87; assoc. dir. govt. rels. Nat. Assn. Psychiat. Health Sys., 1987-92; v.p. behavioral health and governance Calif. Healthcare Assn., Sacramento, 1992—2001; exec. dir. Calif. Mental Health Dirs. Assn., 2001—. Bd. dirs. Cult Awareness Network, Barrington, Ill., 1985-93, pres. bd., 1989-92; mem. adv. bd. Leo J. Ryan Edn. Found., 1999—; vol. Robert F. Kennedy for Pres., San Francisco, 1968, Leo J. Ryan for Congress, 1972-78, Jackie Speier for Congress, San Mateo, 1979; mem. steering com. Calif. Women's Mental Health Policy Coun., 2000—. Recipient Leo J. Ryan award Cult Awareness Network, 1993. Mem. Calif. Coalition for Mental Health, FactNet (mem. adv. bd. 1991—). Avocations: home decorating, wine tasting, walking. Office: Calif Mental Health Dirs Assn 2030 J St Sacramento CA 95814-2030 Fax: 916-446-4519. E-mail: pryan@cmhda.org.

RYAN, PATRICK G. diversified financial services company executive, director; b. Milw., May 15, 1937; m. Shirley Welsh, Apr. 16, 1966; children: Patrick Jr., Robert J., Corbett M. BS, Northwestern U., 1959. Sales agt. Penn Mut., 1959-64, Pat Ryan & Assocs., 1964-71; chmn., pres. Ryan Ins. Group Inc., 1971-82; pres., chief exec. officer Combined Internat. Corp. (now Aon Corp.), Northbrook, Ill., 1982—, bd. dirs., 1982—; chmn., pres., CEO Aon Corp., Chgo., 1990—. Bd. dirs. Sears Roebuck and Co., Chgo., Tribune Co., Chgo. Trustee Rush-Presbyterian-St. Luke's Med. Ctr., Chgo., chmn. bd. trustees; trustee Northwestern U., Field Mus. Natural History, Chgo. Office: Aon Corp 123 N Wacker Dr Chicago IL 60606-1700*

RYAN, PATRICK MICHAEL, lawyer; b. Chgo., May 26, 1944; s. Edward Michael and Kathleen Teresa (Crimmins) R.; m. Holly Ann Daleske, Aug. 31, 1968; children: Rebecca Eileen, Brendan Patrick, Abigail Christine, Lucas Christopher. BA, St. Mary's Coll., Winona, Minn., 1966; JD, Marquette U., 1969. Bar: Wis. 1969. Law clk. Wis. Supreme Ct., Madison, 1969-70; ptnr. Quarles & Brady, Milw., 1970—. Dir. and officer several pvt. bus. corps. Mem. ABA, Wis. Bar Assn., Milw. Bar Assn., University Club. Avocations: reading, sports. Home: 363 Huntington Dr Cedarburg WI 53012-9507 Office: Quarles & Brady LLP 411 E Wisconsin Ave Ste 2550 Milwaukee WI 53202-4497 E-mail: pmr@quarles.com.

RYAN, PAUL, congressman; b. Janesville, Wis., 1970; son. Paul and Betty R. BS in Econs. and Polit. Sci., Miami (Ohio) U., 1992. Aide to Sen. Bob Kasten (R-Wis.), Washington; legis. dir. U.S. Senate; economic advisor, speechwriter Empower Am., Jack Kemp, Bill Bennett; mktg. cons. Ryan Inc., Central, Janesville; mem. U.S. Congress from 1st Wis. dist., 1999—; mem. ways and means com.; mem. joint econ. com. Defeated former Kenosha City Coun. Pres. Lydia Spottswood in 1998 to succeed two-term Rep. Mark Neumann, who ran unsuccessfully for the Senate. Mem. Janesville YMCA, Janesville Bowmen Inc. and Ducks Unlimited. Republican. Roman Catholic. Office: 1217 Longworth Ho Office Bldg Washington DC 20515-4901*

RYAN, PAUL RYDER, writer, journalist; b. Mineola, N.Y., Jan. 5, 1932; s. Paul Ryder Ryan and Lillian Roos; m. Ruthann Tobin, Nov. 8, 1958; children: Liane, Beth, Paul, Michael. Student, Mexico City Coll., 1955-58; BA, Harvard U., 1981. Editor Reuters, London, 1950-65, The N.Y. Times, N.Y.C. and Paris, 1965-68; asst. to new dir. RFE, Munich, 1968-69; editor The Drama Rev. NYU, 1970-75; editor Oceanus, Woods Hole (Mass.) Oceanographic Inst., 1975-92; dir. comm. Inst. for Sci. Info., Phila., 1990—. Mem. adv. bd. Bangladesh Ctr. for Devel. Journalism and Comm., Dhaka, 1999-2000. Author: (non-fiction) China Daily, 1995, Bangladesh 2000, 2000, (novel) Khmer Rouge End Game, 1998. Sgt. USAF, 1950-54. Knight Internat. Press fellow, Bangladesh, 1999; Fulbright fellow, Japan, 1988-89, Indochina, 1995-96. Mem. VFW, Am. Legion. Democrat. Avocation: chess. Home: Apt 6 37 Main St Cummington MA 01026-9652

RYAN, PAULINE JEN, biomedical company executive; b. Oakland, Calif., June 1, 1967; d. Joseph Jwu-Shen Jen and Salina Shing-Wei; m. Terrence Keane Ryan, Aug. 31, 1991; children: Alexandra Jen, Colby Jen. BA, Northwestern U., 1988, MBA, 1992. Bus. analyst ZS Assocs., Evanston, Ill., 1988-89, sr. analyst, 1989-90; cons. The Alexander Group, Wellesley, Mass., 1992-93; mgr. bus. devel. ImmunoGen, Inc., Cambridge, 1993-94; assoc. dir. bus. devel. Organogenesis Inc., Canton, 1994-97; v.p. Capital Mgmt. Cons., Cambridge, 1998-99; sr. dir. bus. devel. ImmunoGen, Inc., 1999-00, v.p. bus. devel., 2000—. Sec. exec. bd. Mass. Com. for Children & Youth, Boston, 1994-96; pres. Young Chicagoans for Prevention of Child Abuse, 1989-92. Home: 9 Whistler Ln Southborough MA 01772-1131 Office: ImmunoGen Inc 128 Sidney St Cambridge MA 02139 E-mail: pauline.jen.ryan@immunogen.com.

RYAN, PERRY T. assistant attorney general, author; b. Owensboro, Ky., Nov. 26, 1962; s. Thomas Lawrence and Lula Yvonne (Miller) R. BA, U. Ky., 1984, BA in Edn., 1985, JD, 1988. Bar: Ky. 1988, U.S. Ct. Appeals (6th cir.) 1989, U.S. Supreme Ct. 1991. Dep. county clerk Breckinridge County, Hardinsburg, Ky., 1980-88; asst. atty. gen. Office of Ky. Atty. Gen., Frankfort, 1988—. Author: (Books) The Ryan Family of Breckinridge County, Kentucky, 1983, The Criminal Justice System of Kentucky, 1984, Legal Lynching: The Plight of Sam Jennings, 1989, The Last Public Execution in America, 1992, A History of New Clover Creek Baptist Church: Founded on Failure, Built on Faith, 1994, A Biography of Maurice F. O'Connell: The Story of an American Hero, 1996, The Keenan Family of Breckenridge County, Kentucky, 2002. Advisor Ky. Archives and Records Commn., Frankfort, 1991—96; advisor Breckenridge County Archives Commn., Hardinsburg, Ky., 1985—88; pres. Breckenridge County Hist. Soc., 1984—85, 1990—92. Named Historian of Yr., Breckenridge County Hist. Soc., 1998. Mem. Ky. Bar Assn., Ky. State Govt. Bar Assn. (v.p., 1994-95, pres., 1995-96), Frankfort Rotary Club (Outstanding Svc. award, 1996), Phi Beta Kappa. Dem. Southern Baptist. Avocations: genealogy, photography, ancient coin collecting. Office: Office of the Atty Gen 1024 Capital Center Dr Frankfort KY 40601-8204

RYAN, RAYMOND D. retired steel company executive, insurance and marketing firm executive; b. Big Timber, Mont., Feb. 7, 1922; s. Robert Allen and Elsie (Beery) R.; m. Eunice Dale Burnett, Jan. 17, 1943; children: Raymond Brant, Brenda Ruth, Ronald Dale. BA, U. Mont., 1948, JD (hon.), 1970; LLM, NYU, 1949. Bar: Mont. 1948. Various fin. officer positions U.S. Steel and subsidiaries in U.S. and Venezuela, 1949-75; v.p., treas. U.S. Steel, 1975-83; pres. The Evergreen Group Inc., Stamford, Conn., 1984-94, chmn., 1995-96, Evergreen Benefits Inc., 1996-99, The Money Suite Co., Missoula, Mont., 1999—. With mil. police AUS, 1943-45, ETO. Mem. ABA, Met. Club (N.Y.C.), Phi Sigma Kappa, Phi Delta Phi. Home: PO Box 160601 Big Sky MT 59716-0601 *Although luck and ambition are the basis of many apparently successful careers, true success comes from hard work, ethical relationships, dedication, and a willingness to accept responsibility.*

RYAN, RICHARD J. emergency medicine physician; b. Tarrytown, N.Y., Apr. 28, 1964; MD, N.Y. Med. Coll., 1990. Diplomate Am. Bd. Emergency Medicine. Intern U. Cin., 1990-91, resident in emergency medicine, 1991-94; v.p. Vanguard Med. Inc., Cin., 1997—; asst. prof. U. Cin., 1994—. Dir. emergency medicine The Jewish Hosps., Cin., 1997—. Office: U Cin Dept Emergency Medicine 231 Albert Sabin Way Cincinnati OH 45267-0769 E-mail: Richard.Ryan@uc.edu.

RYAN, ROBERT, consulting company executive; b. Columbus, Ohio, July 25, 1922; s. Howard L. and Jannie Gertrude (McComis) R.; m. Esther Lee Moore, Mar. 15, 1947; children: Phillip Craig, Lynda Joyce, Lois Jean. BS in Indsl. Engring, Ohio State U., 1947. Registered profl. engr., Ohio, Ind. Maintenance foreman Internat. Harvester Co., Richmond, Ind., 1947-52; prin. welding engr. Battelle Meml. Inst., Columbus, 1952-55; dir. engring. Columbia Gas System, 1955-67, sr. v.p. Pitts., 1967-73; sr. v.p., dir. Columbia Gas Cos. in Pa., W.Va., Md., N.Y., 1973-75; dir. Columbia Gas Distbn. Cos., N.Y., Md., Ky., Ohio, W.Va., Va., Ohio Energy and Resource Devel. Agy., 1975-76, Ohio Dept. Energy, 1977-80; mem. Gov.'s Cabinet; pres. Robert S. Ryan & Assocs., 1981—; chmn. bd. dirs. Resource Gen. Corp., Columbus, 1995-96. Contbr. articles profl. jours. Pres. USA Fibromyalgia Assn., 1994-2001. Capt. U.S. Army, 1943—46, Japan. Recipient Disting. Alumnus award Ohio State U. Coll. Engring., 1970. Mem. NSPE, Am. Gas Assn., Pa. Gas Assn. (pres. 1974), Capital Club (Columbus). Republican. Methodist. Avocation: golf. Home: 1675 Becket Ave Columbus OH 43235-7309 Fax: (614) 457-9659. E-mail: robertsryanl@compuserve.com.

RYAN, ROBERT COLLINS, lawyer; b. Evanston, Ill., Sept. 15, 1953; s. Donald Thomas and Patricia J. (Collins) R.; m. Joanne Kay Holata, Nov. 5, 1983. BA in Econs., BS in Indsl. Engring. with high honors, U. Ill., 1976; JD, Northwestern U., 1979. Bar: Ill. 1979, U.S. Dist. Ct. (no. dist.) Ill. 1980, U.S. Ct. Appeals (Fed. cir.) 1982, U.S. Supreme Ct. 1984, Nev. 1999. Assoc. Allegretti, Newitt, Witcoff & McAndrews, Ltd., Chgo., 1979-83, ptnr., 1983-88; founding ptnr. McAndrews, Held & Malloy, Ltd., 1988-96, of counsel, 1996—2000; v.p. digital gen. sys., Inc. CNASDAQ DGIT, 2001—. Chief legal and intellectual property officer, exec. v.p. StarGuide Digital Networks, Inc., Reno, 1996-; ; mem. Ian Burns & Assocs., P.C., Reno, 1998—; of counsel Pauley, Petersen, Kinne & Fejer, Hoffman Estates, Ill., 1998—; lectr. engring. law Northwestern U. Tech. Inst., Evanston, Ill., 1981-85, adj. prof. engring. law, 1985-90; lectr. patent law and appellate practice John Marshall Law Sch., 1991-93, adj. prof. patent law and appellate advocacy, 1993—; mem. faculty Nat. Jud. Coll., Reno, Nev., 1998-2000; mem. alumni bd. mech. and indsl. engring. dept. U. Ill., Urbana, 1996—. Exec. editor Northwestern Jour. Internat. Law & Bus., 1978-79; contbr. articles to profl. jours. Dir. Washoe Assn. Retarded Citizens, Reno, 1997—, sec., 2001—, v.p. 2002. James scholar U. Ill., 1976. Mem. ABA, Fed. Cir. Bar Assn., Intellectual Property Law Assn. Chgo., Licensing Execs. Soc., Tau Beta Pi, Phi Eta Sigma, Alpha Pi Mu, Phi Kappa Phi. Home: 95 Rimfire Cir Reno NV 89509-2989 Office: StarGuide Digital Networks 300 E 2nd St Ste 1510 Reno NV 89501-1591

RYAN, ROBERT DAVIS, lawyer; b. Lynbrook, N.Y., Aug. 14, 1941; s. Thomas Francis and Agnes Frances (Davis) R.; children: John, Daniel, Carolyn. BBA, St. John's U., 1962; JD, Fordham U., 1972. Bar: N.Y. 1973, U.S. Dist. Ct. (so. and ea. dists.) N.Y. 1973, U.S. Ct. Appeals (2d cir.) 1975, U.S. Supreme Ct. 1984. Asst. dist. atty. Westchester County, White Plains, N.Y., 1972-77; assoc. Clark, Gagliardi & Miller, 1977-82; ptnr. Rende, Ryan & Downes, 1982—. Adj. prof. law St. John's U., 1992-95, 99—. Chmn. Cable TV Adv. Com., Lewisboro, N.Y., 1983-99. Mem. Assn. Trial Lawyers Am., N.Y. State Trial Lawyers Assn., Westchester County Bar Assn., N.Y. State Bar Assn. (continuing legal edn. com. trial lawyers sect.), No. Westchester Bar Assn. (bd. govs. 1987-92, pres. 1986-87), White Plains Bar Assn. Republican. Roman Catholic. Home: PO Box 113 Bedford NY 10506-0113 Office: Rende Ryan & Downes 202 Mamaroneck Ave Ste 600 White Plains NY 10601-5312

RYAN, ROBERT JEFFERS, lawyer; b. Evanston, Ill., Dec. 26, 1947; BBA in Fin., U. Notre Dame, 1970; JD, Loyola U., Chgo., 1973. Bar: Ill. 1973, U.S. Dist. Ct. (no. dist.) Ill. 1973. Pvt. practice, Winnetka, Ill., 1979—. Office: 560 Green Bay Rd Ste 303 Winnetka IL 60093-2242

RYAN, ROBERT JOHN, endocrinology educator and researcher; b. Cin., July 18, 1927; s. Robert M. and Marian J. (Hoffman) R.; m. Elizabeth E. Kennedy, Apr. 18, 1954 (div. Jan. 1980); children: Kathleen, Michel, Robert, Thomas, James, Barbara; m. Gloria A. Patton, May 15, 1981 (div.); m. Diane E. Casper, Sept. 12, 1986. Student, Xavier U., 1945, 47-48; MD, U. Cin., 1952. Resident U. Ill., Chgo., 1953-57, asst. prof., 1959-63, assoc. prof., 1963-67; rsch. fellow Tufts U., Boston, 1957-59; assoc. prof. Mayo Clinic, Rochester, Minn., 1967-71; prof. medicine Mayo Med. Sch., 1971-81, Bartells prof., 1983, prof. biochemistry and molecular biology, 1981-90, prof. emeritus, 1990—. Mem. study sect. NIH, 1970-73, chmn., 1972-73; mem. population ctrs. com. NICHD, 1974-78, 81-85, chmn., 1982-85. Contbr. articles to profl. jours. SErved with U.S. Army, 1945-46. NIH grantee, 1960-90; recipient Daniel Drake medal U. Cin., 1990. Mem. AAAS, Endocrine Soc. (coun. 1974-77, , v.p. 1977-78, Robert H. Williams award 1984), Soc. Study Reprodn. (v.p. 1986-87, pres. 1987-88, Carl Hartman award 1991), Am. Soc. Biol. Chemistry, N.Y. Acad. Sci., Am. Sco. Clin. Investigation. Republican. Avocations: stamp collecting.

RYAN, SHEILA A. nursing educator, former dean; Former dean Sch. Nursing, U. Rochester, NY, dir. Med. Ctr. Nursing; prof. U. Nebr. Med. Sch. of Nursing, Omaha. Mem.: Institute of Medicine (IOM), American International Health Alliance (AIHA) (bd. dirs. 1999—). Office: Amer Int Hlth Alliance 1212 NY Ave, NW, Ste 750 Washington DC 20005*

RYAN, STEPHEN COLLISTER, funeral director; b. Salina, Kans., Jan. 10, 1942; s. Kenneth Richard and Janys (Collister) R.; m. Lynne Katheryn Slease, June 18, 1966; children: Scott Richard, Carrie Anne. BS in Bus. Adminstrn., U. Kans., 1964; Cert. in Mortuary Sci., Kans. U. Med. Ctr., 1965. Cert. funeral svc. practitioner; lic. funeral dir. and embalmer. Sec.-treas. Ryan Mortuary, Inc., Salina, 1969-80, pres., COO, 1980—. Contbr. articles to profl. jours. Mem., chmn. City Planning Commn., Salina, 1981-85; mem. Salina City Commn., 1985-93, 95, mayor, 1987-88, 91-92; mem. Kans. State Bd. Mortuary Arts, 1996—, pres., 1997-99; trustee Kans. Wesleyan U., 1998—, vice chmn. instnl. advancement com., 1999—. Capt. USAF, 1965-69. Mem. Selected Ind. Funeral Homes (bd. dirs. 1993-96, pres. 1995-96), Nat. Funeral Dirs. Assn. (Spl. Recognition award 1991), Ind. Funeral Dirs. Cooperative (bd. dirs. 1998—), Kans. Funeral Dirs. Assn. (bd. dirs. 1984-92, pres. 1990-91), Morticians of the S.W. (Kans. Funeral Dir. of Yr. 1991), Salina Area C. of C. (bd. dirs. 1982-84, 94-97, vice chair 1984-85, sec./treas. 1994-95, chmn. 1996-97), Salina Country Club (bd. dirs. 1998—, pres. 2000-01), Lions, Masons (33d degree Scottish Rite), Shriners (ct. no. 94, Royal Order of Jesters), Phi Gamma Delta. Republican. Lutheran. Avocations: golf, nautilus exercise. Home: 405 E Park Ln Salina KS 67401-3552 Office: Ryan Mortuary Inc 137 N 8th St Salina KS 67401-2686 E-mail: ryan67401@aol.com.

RYAN, STEPHEN JOSEPH, JR. ophthalmology educator, university dean; b. Honolulu, Mar. 20, 1940; s. S.J. and Mildred Elizabeth (Farrer) Ryan; m. Anne Christine Mullady, Sept. 25, 1965; 1 child Patricia Anne. AB, Providence Coll., 1961; MD, Johns Hopkins U., 1965. Intern Bellevue Hosp., N.Y.C., 1965—66; resident Wilmer Inst. Ophthalmology, Johns Hopkins Hosp., Balt., 1966—69, chief resident, 1969—70; fellow Armed Force Inst. Pathology, Washington, 1970—71; instr. ophthalmology Johns Hopkins U., Balt., 1970—71, asst. prof., 1971—72, assoc. prof., 1972—74; prof. ophthalmology Keck Sch. Medicine U. So. Calif., L.A., 1974—, chmn. dept. ophthalmology Sch. Medicine, 1974—95, dean Keck Sch. Medicine, 1991—; acting head ophthalmology div., dept. surgery Children's Hosp., 1975—77; med. dir. Doheny Eye Inst. (formerly Estelle Doheny Eye Found.), 1977—86; chief of staff Doheny Eye Hosp., 1985—88. Mem. adv. panel Calif. Med. Assn., 1975—. Editor (with M.D. Andrews): A Survey of Ophthalmology--Manual for Medical Students, 1970; editor: (with R.E. Smith) Selected Topics on the Eye in Systemic Disease, 1974; editor: (with Dawson and Little) Retinal Diseases, 1985; editor: (with others) Retina, 1989; exec. prodr.(with others): Retina, 2000; assoc. editor: Ophthalmol. Surgery, 1974—85, mem. editl. bd.: Am. Jour. Ophthalmology, 1981—, mem. editl. bd.: Internat. Ophthalmology, 1982—, mem. editl. bd.: Retina, 1983—, mem. editl. bd.: Graefes Archives, 1984—; contbr. articles to med. jours. Recipient cert. of merit, AMA, 1971, Louis B. Mayer Scholar award, Rsch. to Prevent Blindness, 1973, Rear Adm. William Campbell Chambliss USN award, 1982. Mem.: AMA, Jules Gonin Club, Rsch. Study Club, Nat. Eye Care Project, Retina Soc., Macula Soc., Pan-Am. Assn. Microsurgery, L.A. Acad. Medicine, Pacific Coast Oto-Ophthal. Soc., Los Angeles County Med. Assn., Calif. Med. Assn., L.A. Soc. Ophthalmology, Assn. Univ. Profs. of Ophthalmology, Pan-Am. Assn. Ophthalmology, Am. Ophthal. Soc., Am. Acad. Ophthalmology and Otolaryngology (award of Merit 1975), Wilmer Ophthal. Inst. Residents Assn., Soc. Scholars of Johns Hopkins U. (life). Office: 1450 San Pablo St Los Angeles CA 90089-0106

RYAN, SUZANNE IRENE, nursing educator; b. Yonkers, N.Y., Mar. 13, 1939; d. Edward Vincent and Winifred E. (Goemann) R. BA in Biology, Mt. St. Agnes Coll., Balt., 1962; BSN, Columbia U., 1967, MA in Nursing Svc., 1973, MEd in Nursing Edn., 1975, MS in Oncology, 1982, EdD in Nursing Edn., 1997. RN, N.Y.; cert. AIDS educator, N.Y. Prof. nursing Molloy Coll., Rockville Centre, N.Y., 1970—, co-dir. health svcs., dir. ednl. programs, 1987-94, dir. health svcs., 1994—, health educator, 1992—, co-dir. mobile health van, adminstr. health edn., 1992—; pres., CEO SIR Enterprises, Inc., 1982—; photographer Molloy Coll. Pubs., 1991—. Photographic dir. Bali-Art, Inc., 1992—; mem. N.Y. State AIDS Coun., 1987—, L.I. Alcohol Consortium, 1987—; educator Nassau County Dept. Sr. Citizens Health, 1991—; photographer-in-residence Molloy Coll., 1992—; lectr. on landscape, wildlife and flower photography, L.I., N.H., Can., 1993—. Represented in permanent collections in photographic galleries in Carmel, Calif., Laconia, Wolfboro and Moultonboro, N.H., 1963—; one-woman shows include Mollay Coll., Rockville Ctr. Library; photographer 4 books on Monterey Peninulsa, New Eng. and N.H.; writer, editor Health News Letter Molloy Coll., 1990—. Health educator Nassau County Dept. of Sr. Citizens Outreach Program, Molloy Coll., AIDS educator, 1991—; adminstr., chief AIDS counselor Interaction AIDS Counseling, Babylon, N.Y., 1992—; lic. AIDS educator N.Y. Metro Area; chairperson of grants com. in higher edn. Nassau U.; dir. AIDS Outreach Program, Episcopal Diocese of L.I., 1997—; dir. photography Visual Graphics N.H., 1997—; co-chair AIDS Outreach Cathedral of the Incarnation, 1998—. USPHS fellow, 1962, Nat. Cancer Inst. fellow, l981-82. Mem. AAUP, AAUW, Nat. Congress Oncology Nurses, N.Y. State Fedn. Health Educators, Inc., Nurses Assn. Counties L.I. Dist. 14, N.Y. State Nurses Assn., World Wildlife Orgn., Audubon Soc., Internat. Ctr. Photography, Nature Conservancy, Sierra Club, Cathedral Womens Club, Alter Guild, Sigma Theta Tau (Epsilon Kappa chpt., rsch. grantee 1985, 87), Zeta Epsilon Gamma. Roman Catholic. Avocation: writing, photography. Home: 16 Walker St Malverne NY 11565

RYAN, THERESA ANN JULIA, accountant; b. N.Y.C., Mar. 1, 1962; d. John Patrick and Diane Elizabeth Ryan. BA in Math. and Econs., Fordham U., 1984, MBA in Profl. Acctg., 1989. CPA, N.Y., F.L.M.I. With sales dept. Abraham & Straus, White Plains, N.Y., 1980-84; adminstrv. asst. Companion of N.Y., Rye, 1984-86, asst. fin. analyst, 1986-87; with tech. ctr. Fordham U., N.Y.C., 1987-88; staff acct. Konigsberg Wolf & Co., 1989-91; sr. audit assoc. Coopers & Lybrand, L.L.P., 1992-95; internal auditor N.Y. Power Authority, White Plains, 1996-99; circulation acctg. analyst Gannett Corp., 2000-2001; sr. accountant Time Warner Cable, 2001—. Mem. Inst. Internal Auditors (cert.), Beta Gamma Sigma. Avocations: music, biking, writing, travel, psychology. Home: 5 Clare Ter Yonkers NY 10707-3201 Office: Time Warner Cable 290 Harbor Drive Stamford CT 06902-7441

RYAN, THOMAS M. drug store chain executive; b. 1953; Pharmacist CVS Corp., Woonsocket, R.I., from 1975, numerous managerial positions v.p. pharmacy ops., sr. v.p. pharmacy, exec. v.p. pharmacy, exec. v.p. stores, unti. 1993; pres., CEO CVS Pharmacy, Inc. (then part of Melville Corp.), from 1993; vice chmn., COO, CVS Corp., until 1998, pres., CEO, chmn., 1998—. Bd. dirs. Fleet Fin. Group, Reebok Internat. Ltd. Office: CVS Corp One CVS Dr Woonsocket RI 02895*

RYAN, THOMAS WILLIAM, lawyer; b. Tulsa, Feb. 16, 1953; s. Dean Lawrence and Helen Ladeen (Steinkierchner) R.; m. Mary Ellen Poxon, Jan. 30, 1973; children: Matthew Alan, Jennifer Erin. BA, U. Houston, 1975, JD, 1978. Bar: Tex. 1978. Ptnr. Hart, Ryan & Pfeffer, Houston, 1978-80; contracts adminstr. Texaco Inc., 1980-85; asst. gen. counsel Total Minatome Corp., 1985-99; gen. counsel, corp. sec. Total Exploration Prodn. USA, Inc., 1999-2001; v.p., gen. counsel, corp. sec. TotalFinaElf E&P USA, Inc., 2001—. Adv. bd. Inst. for Energy Law. Coach youth sports YMCA, Houston, 1990-94. Mem. KC (adv. 1985-87), State Bar Tex. Avocations: golf, bowling. Office: TotalFinaElf E&P USA Inc One Memorial City Plz 800 Gessner Ste 700 Houston TX 77024

RYAN, TRACY TUTEN, marketing and managemnt educator; b. Washington, Aug. 31, 1967; d. Terry Lee T. and Linda Ward Cochran; m. Michael Kerin Ryan. BS in Bus. Adminstrn., E. Carolina U., Greenville, N.C., 1988, MBA, 1990; DPhil, Va. Commonwealth U., Richmond, 1996. Asst. prof. bus. Randolph-Macon Coll., Ashland, Va., 1995—99; asst. prof. mktg. and mgmt. Longwood Coll., Farmville, 1999—. Contbr. articles. Scholar Fulbright Scholar, Coun. Internat. Exch. Scholars, 2001. Mem.: Am. Mktg. Assn., Soc. Mktg. Advances, Acad. Mgmt. Office: Longwood Coll 201 High St Farmville VA 23909

RYAN, UNA SCULLY, health sciences professional, medical educator; b. Kuala Lumpur, Malaysia, Dec. 18, 1941; d. Henry and Amy (Yee) Scully; m. Allan Dana Callow, May 26, 1989; children: Tamsin Spencer Smith, Amy Jean Susan Ryan. BSc in Zoology, Chemistry & Microbiology, Bristol (Eng.) U., 1963; PhD in Cell Biology, Cambridge (Eng.) U., 1968. Fellow dept. biology U. Va., Charlottesville, 1964-66; fellow dept. medicine U. Miami, Fla., 1966-67, adj. asst. prof. biology, 1968-71; dir. lab. for ultrastructure studies Howard Hughes Med. Inst., Miami, 1967-71; from instr. to assoc. prof. medicine U. Miami Sch. Medicine, 1967-80, prof. medicine, 1980-89; sr. scientist Papanicolaou Cancer Rsch. Inst., Miami, 1972-77; rsch. prof. surgery Washington U. Sch. Medicine, St. Louis, 1990—; dir. health scis. Monsanto Co., 1990-93; pres., CEO T Cell Scis., Needham, Mass., 1993-98; rsch. prof. medicine Boston U. Sch. Medicine, 1993—; pres., CEO AVANT Immunotherapeutics, Needham, Mass., 1998—. Dir. course W. Alton Jones Cell Sci. Ctr., 1979-81; dir. Hybridoma Facility, U. Miami, 1986-89; chair local organizing com. Internat. Coun. on Thrombosis and Hemostasis, 1984; chair Rev. Com. for Extracellular Matrix Interactions in Lung, 1983; chair various revs. NHLBI; mem. various rev. and adv. coms. Author: J. Tissue Culture Methods, 1987, Pulmonary Endothelium in Health Disease, 1987, Endothelial Cells, 1988, Vascular Endothelium: Receptors and Transduction Mechanisms, 1989; editor: Tissue & Cell, 1981-87; rev. editor: In Vitro, 1986; reviewer profl. jours.; contbr. articles to profl. jours. UK state scholar, 1960, Country Major scholar, 1960; D.S.I.R. rsch. fellow, 1964, 65, Ethel Sargant Rsch. fellow, 1964-65, Sci. Rsch. Coun. fellow, 1966; recipient Louis and Artur Lucian award for rsch. in circulatory diseases, 1984, Merit award Nat. Heart, Lung and Blood Inst., 1986, Lillie award Woods Hole, Marine Bill, Lab., 1989. Mem. Am. Soc. Cell Biology, Soc. Neurosci., Tissue Culture Assn., Internat. Soc. Heart Rsch., Am. Heart Assn. (coun. on basic rsch., coun. on circulation, cardiopulmonary coun.), Am. Physiol. Soc., Am. Microcirculatory Soc., European Soc. Microcirculation, Am. Thoracic Soc. (dir. course on culture of pulmonary endothelial cells), Internat. Soc. Applied Cardiovascular Biology, N.Y. Acad. Scis., Fla. Soc. Electron Microscopy, Sigma Xi. Office: AVANT Immunotherapeutics 119 4th Ave Needham MA 02494-2725

RYAN, VINCE, lawyer; b. Houston, Aug. 12, 1947; m. Teresa Pamela Rodriguez; 2 children. BA in English, U. Houston, 1969, JD, 1974; MA in History, Rice U., 1979. Bar: Tex. 1974. Assoc. James Patrick Smith, 1974—75, Thomas P. Duncan, Houston, 1975-76, Smith and Conner, Houston, 1976-79, Watrous, Joyce and Ryan, Houston, 1980-81; divsn. chief commrs. ct. divsn. Office of the Harris County Atty., 1981-83, first asst., 1983-88; of counsel Sinex & Stephenson, Houston, 1988—; regional mng. atty. Clame Linebarger, 1996-98; of counsel Linebarger Goggan, 1998—. Dir. legal rsch. svc. U. Houston; adj. faculty U.S. Army Command and Gen. Staff Coll., 1988—. Mem. Dist. C Houston City Coun., 1988—94; alt. City of Houston rep. Houston-Galveston Area Coun., 1989—94; bd. dirs. S.W. YMCA, 1988—94, Panama Canal Commn., 1995—99. With U.S. Army, 1969—72, Vietnam, with U.S. Army, 1991, lt. col. USAR. Fellow Grad., 1977—78, Rsch., 1978—79; scholar Undergrad Cullen Tuition, 1968—69. Office: Linebarger Heard Goggan et al LLP 1021 Main St Ste 1500 Houston TX 77002-6602 Home Fax: 713-661-2337; Office Fax: 713-844-3504. E-mail: vincer@publicans.com.

RYAN, WARREN SCOTT, physician assistant; b. Hutchinson, Kans., June 9, 1957; s. Leo Jackson and Mary Elizabeth Ryan; m. Karen Sue Plank, Dec. 29, 1979; children: Alissa Renee, Lindsey Ann, Megan Joy, Gabriel Scott, Emily Dawn, Katie Abigail, Hannah Michelle. BS in Health Sci., Wichita State U., 1981; M of Physician Asst. Studies, U. Nebr., 1998. Cert. Nat. Commn. on Certification of Physician Assts. Physician asst. Scott City (Kans.) Clinic, 1981-85, Kans. Cardiology Assocs., Wichita, 1985—. Avocations: computers, reading, following and serving the Lord Jesus Christ. Office: # 102 9350 E 35th St N Wichita KS 67226-2016 E-mail: wryan@dnamail.com.

RYAN, WILLIAM FRANCIS, priest; b. Renfrew, Ont., Can., Apr. 4, 1925; s. William Patrick Ryan and Helen Mary Doneg BA, Montreal U., 1951; MA in Labor Rels., St. Louis U., 1953; postgrad., Heythrop Coll., Oxon, Eng.; STL, St. Albert Coll., Louvain, 1958; PhD in Econs., Harvard U., 1964. Ordained priest Roman Catholic Ch., 1957. Asst. prof. econs. Loyola Coll., Montreal, Que., Can., 1963-65; nat. dir. Social Justice Office Can. Conf. Cath. Bishops, Ottawa, Ont., 1964-70, gen. sec., 1984-90; founding dir. Ctr. of Concern, Washington, 1970-78; nat. supr. Jesuit Order, Toronto, Ont., Can., 1978-84; chancellor Sch. Theology Regis Coll., 1978-84; vis. sr. rsch. fellow Can. Inst. for Internat. Peace and Security, Ottawa, 1990-91; chair on Cath. social thought St. Paul U., 1991-92; dir. Jesuit Project on Ethics in Politics, 1992—. Exec. sec. Inter-religious Peace Colloquium, Washington, 1975-78; bd. dirs. Roncalli Internat. Found., Montreal, 1979-83, North/South Inst., Ottawa, 1979-91; spl. advisor to Internat. Devel. Rsch. Ctr., Ottawa, 1993—; coord. Jesuit Ctr. for Social Faith and Justice, 1997—; lectr. in field. Author: The Clergy and Economic Growth in Quebec, 1966, Culture, Spirituality and Economic Development—Opening a Dialogue, 1995, Our Way of Proceeding, in the Lab, The Temple and The Market: Reflections at the Intersection of Science, Religion and Development, 2000; co-author: Religious as Contemplatives in the 80's, 1984; translator: The Primacy of Charity in Moral Theology, 1961; contbr. articles to profl. jours. Mem. Am. Econs. Assn. Avocations: hiking; skiing. Office: 169 Sunnyside Ave Ottawa ON Canada K1S 0R2

RYAN, WILLIAM JOSEPH, multimedia and distance education designer, information technology executive; b. Amsterdam, N.Y., Aug. 12, 1958; s. William John and Joann Gail (Birmingham) R.; m. Amy Diane Friedberg, Aug. 31, 1997; children: Rachel Erin, Haley Ann. BS, SUNY, Brockport, 1979; MS, Ithaca Coll., 1987; PhD, Nova Southeastern U., 2001. Prodn. coord., disc jockey WWBK, Brockport, N.Y., 1979; video prodn. asst. Nat. Tech. Inst for Deaf at Rochester Inst. of Tech., Rochester, 1979-80; media specialist Coll. of St. Rose, Albany, 1980-85; video developer Sci. Rsch. Assocs., Chgo., 1987-89; sr. tng. comms. specialist Westinghouse Savannah River Co., Aiken, S.C., 1989-97; dir. instrnl. techs. Lakeland C.C., Kirtland, Ohio, 1997-98, v.p. tech., 1998—. Mem. adv. com. on tng. and learning Educause, 2002--; cons. Infocomm, Internat. Comms. Industries Assn., Internat. TV Assn. Transition Team, 1991-94; mem. nat. stds. com. for. curriculum devel. for multimedia developers and producers/dirs. Contbr. articles to profl. jours.; presenter at tng. and ednl. workshops. Recipient Total Quality Achievement award Environ. Safety, Health and Quality Assurance divsn. Westinghouse Savannah River Co., 1991; grantee Am. Speech-Hearing Assn. and Dept. Edn., 1986; multiple tech. grant Ohio Bd. of Regents, 1997-2001. Mem. Internat. TV Assn. (chair electronic com. commn. 1995-96, bd. dirs. Augusta chpt. 1990-97, chmn. tech. support svcs. 1989-95, judge and panel host ann. video festival interactive category, 1991-99, Nat. Svc. award 1993, 95), Assn. for Applied Interactive Multimedia (bd. dirs. 1993-95), Soc. Motion Picture and TV Engrs., U.S. Sailing Assn., Phi Kappa Phi. Avocations: sailing, music, computers, skiing. Home: 1325 Avondale Rd South Euclid OH 44121-2527 Office: Lakeland CC Tech Divsn 7700 Clocktower Dr Kirtland OH 44094-5198 E-mail: WJRyan@lakeland.cc.oh.us.

RYAN-HALLEY, CHARLOTTE MURIEL, oncology clinical specialist, family nurse practitioner, family practice nurse practitioner; b. Beedeville, Ark., Sept. 2, 1939; d. Eugene Sanford and Edith Elizabeth (Goforth) Breckenridge; m. Alexander Halley; children: Russell Kenth Ryan, Cary Randall Ryan, Molly Reneé Ryan Nankervis. BSN cum laude, Calif. State U., Fresno, 1991, MSN, clin. specialist, 1997. RN, Calif.; nat. cert. oncology nurse; cert. pub. health nurse, sch. nurse. Psychiat. technician Porterville (Calif.) State Hosp., 1959-67; tchr. developmentally disabled Ariz. Tng. Ctr., Coolidge, 1967-71; Montessori tchr. Tucson, 1972-77; tchr. developmentally disabled Heartland Opportunity Ctr., Madera, Calif., 1977-79; med. office mgr. office of orthopedic surgeon, 1979-83, office mgr., x-ray technician, 1983-87; staff nurse in oncology St. Agnes Med. Ctr., Fresno, 1991—99. Instr. nursing dept. Calif. State U., Fresno, 1992-93, 95-98. Treas. Hospice of Madera County, 1990-92, bd. dirs., 1992; peer counselor Calif. State U., Fresno, 1989-91; pres. bd. dirs. Easter Seals Soc., Madera, 1981. Mem. Nat. Oncology Nursing Soc. (on-line forum moderator, item writer cert. test 1998), Nightingale Soc., Golden Key, Sigma Theta Tau (chmn. pub. com., editor MUNEWS newsletter 1994-95). Republican. Avocations: reading, improving quality of life for cancer patients. Home: 2235 S Virmargo St Visalia CA 93292-1311

RYANT, CHARLES JOSEPH, JR. environment executive; b. Chgo., Apr. 1, 1920; BS in Chem. Engring., Armour Inst. Tech., 1940; MS in Chem. Engring., Ill. Inst. Tech., 1941, PhD in Chem. Engring., 1947. Pres. C.J. Ryant, Jr. & Assocs., Chicago, 1959—70; exec. dir. Midwest Legislative Coun. on the Environment, 1970—80; pres. C.J. Ryant, Maple City, Mich., 1980—. Home: 504 W. Ryant Rd PO Box 250 Maple City MI 49664

RYBAK, JAMES PATRICK, engineering educator; b. Cleve., Mar. 16, 1941; s. John Anthony and Irene Marcella (Kovar) R.; m. Linda Louise Watkins, Oct. 12, 1968. BSEE, Case Western Res. U., 1963; MS, U. N.Mex., 1965; PhD, Colo. State U., 1970. Registered profl. engr., Colo. Mem. tech. staff Sandia Nat. Labs., Albuquerque, 1963-66; rsch. asst., NDEA fellow Colo. State U., Ft. Collins, 1966-70, postdoctoral fellow, 1970-72; prof. engring. and math. Mesa State Coll., Grand Junction, Colo., 1972—, asst. v.p. acad. affairs, 1986-88, v.p. acad. affairs, 1988-98. Contbr. articles to profl. publs. including IEEE Transactions, Engring. Edn., Popular Electronics, Elektrosvyaz (Russia),

Radio (Russia). Mem. adv. bd. Grand Mesa Youth Svcs., Grand Junction, 1986-88; bd. dirs. Hilltop Rehab. Hosp., Grand Junction, 1989-93, Salvation Army, Grand Junction, 1993—. NEDA fellow, 1968-70, THEMIS fellow, 1970-72. Mem. IEEE, Am. Soc. Engring. Edn. (vice chmn. Rocky Mountain sect. 1974-75, chmn. 1975-76). Avocation: amateur radio. Home: 314 Quail Dr Grand Junction CO 81503-2527 Office: Mesa State Coll 1175 Texas Ave Grand Junction CO 81501-7605

RYBAK, R.T. mayor; m. Megan O'Hara; 2 children. Mayor City of Minneapolis, Minn.; cons. various orgn.; gen. mgr. WCCO TV & WCCO Radio; v.p. Internet Broadcast Sys.; pub., mgr., bus. ops. Twin Cities Reader. Founder, mem. bd. Save the Water in Mpls.; served Minn. Soc. Architects, Night of the Penguin, Hennepin Ave. Adv. Com., Adv. Fedn. Minn., Eiji Oue Inaugural Com.; coach Little League Baseball, Youth Soccer; vol. reader Minn. Pub. Sch.; co-coord. Bill Bradley for Pres. , 2000; co-chair Tony Bouza for Gov., 1994. Office: 350 S Fifth St 331 City Hall Minneapolis MN 55415*

RYBCZYNSKI, WITOLD MARIAN, architect, educator, writer; b. Edinburgh, Scotland, Mar. 1, 1943; emigrated to Can., 1953; s. Witold Kasimir and Anna Jadwiga (Hofman) R.; m. Shirley Hallam, Nov. 15, 1974. Diploma, Loyola Coll., Montreal, 1960; B.Arch., McGill U., 1966, M.Arch., 1972. Pvt. practice architecture, Montreal, 1970-82; research assoc. McGill U., 1972-75, asst. prof. architecture, 1975-80, assoc. prof., 1980-86, prof., 1986-93; Meyerson prof. of Urbanism U. Pa., 1994—. Cons. UN, Manila, 1976, Internat. Devel. Research Ctr., Ottawa, 1977, Banco de Mex., 1979-80 Author: Paper Heroes: A Review of Appropriate Technology, 1980, Taming the Tiger: The Struggle to Control Technology, 1983, Home: A Short History of an Idea, 1986, The Most Beautiful House in the World, 1989, Waiting for the Weekend, 1991, Looking Around: A Journey Through Architecture, 1992, A Place for Art, 1993, City Life, 1995, A Clearing in the Distance, 1999, One Good Turn, 2000, The Look of Architecture, 2001, The Perfect House, 2002; contbg. editor Saturday Night, 1990—2001; adv. bd. Ency. Americana; founding editor Wharton Real Estate Rev., 1996—. Recipient QSPELL lit. prize for nonfiction, 1988, 89, Prix Paul-Henri Lapointe, 1988, Progressive Architecture Design award, 1991, Alfred Jurzykowski Found. award, 1993, Athanaeum Lit. prize, 1997, 2001, Christopher award, 2000, J. Anthony Lukas prize, 2000; Ballard real estate scholar, 1994-95. Fellow AIA (hon.). Office: Grad Sch Fine Arts U Pa Meyerson Hall Philadelphia PA 19104 E-mail: rybczyns@pobox.upenn.edu.

RYBERG, WILLIAM A. orchestra executive; BMus, Western Wash. State U.; MMus, Ind. U. Teller, loan officer, br. mgr., regional mgr. Ranier Nat. Bank; v.p., area mgr. West One Bank, Tacoma; v.p., dist. mgr. Key Bank, Wash., 1993-96; exec. dir. Bellingham (Wash.) Festival of Music, 1996-98; pres. Grand Rapids (Mich.) Symphony, 1998—. Office: Grand Rapids Symphony Ste 1 169 Louis Campau Promenade NW 1 Grand Rapids MI 49503-2629*

RYBICKI, CLARICE ANNETTE, former restaurant professional; b. Cleve., Sept. 10, 1959; d. Paul Eugene and Maryellen (Ross) Craven; m. James Edmund Rybicki, Aug. 25, 1984. Student, Greenville (S.C.) Tech. Coll., 1984-85; AA cum laude in Applied Bus., Hospitality Mgmt., Cuyahoga Community Coll., 1987; student, Auburn Career Ctr., 1998. Mem. staff various restaurants in Cleve. area, 1977-83; full-menu cook, cook trainer Denny's Restaurant, Greenville, 1984; breakfast-lunch cook Holiday Inn Haywood, 1984-85; relief mgr. Arthur Treacher's Seafood, Cleve., 1985; now ind. caterer Auburn Corners; kitchen mgr. Post House Restaurant, Parkman, 1990; kitchen supr. Manor House Punderson State Pk., Newbury, 1990-91, asst. food & beverage dir. Manor House, 1991—, del. safety com., 1992—; asst. dietary mgr. HCR/Manorcare, Mentor, 1994-2000; ind. rep. ACN Global Network, 2002—. Coord. meal functions, Fraternal Order Eagles, Chagrin Falls, Ohio, 1979—. Outreach dir. Free Meth. Ch., Burton, Ohio, 1990—, soc. mem., 1989, dir. adult ministries, 1991; troop co-leader Girl Scouts Am., 1991—; co-coord. Hwys. of the Heart women's support group, 1991—. Mem. Fraternal Order of Eagles, Women's Ministries Internat. (outreach dir. 1989, v.p. women's ministries 1991-92). Avocations: reading, crafts, music, swimming, bicycling.

RYBIN, VITALYI OLEGOVICH, research scientist; b. Moscow, Dec. 6, 1957; came to U.S., 1992; s. Oleg Aleksandrovich and Valentina Alekseevna R.; m. Irina Victorovna, Jan. 12, 1979; 1 child: Andrew Vitalevich. MS in Biochemistry, Moscow State U., 1980; PhD in Enzymology, USSR Cardiology Rsch. Ctr., Moscow, 1986. Jr. investigator Cardiology Rsch. Ctr., Moscow, 1983-87, rsch. assoc., 1987-89, sr. investigator, 1989-92; vis. assoc. rsch. scientist Columbia U., N.Y.C., 1992-95, assoc. rsch. scientist, 1995—. Author: (book chpts.) Lung Biology in Health and Disease, vol. 65, 1993, G Proteins, 1996; contbr. articles to profl. jours. Mem. Am. Soc. Pharmacology and Exptl. Therapeutics. Avocation: philately. Home: 138 Panorama Dr Edgewater NJ 07020 Office: Columbia U 630W 168 St New York NY 10032 E-mail: vrybin4609@aol.com.

RYCE, DONALD THEODORE, lawyer; b. New Orleans, Dec. 15, 1943; s. Donald Theodore and Martha (Herndon) R.; m. Claudine Dianne Walker, July 8, 1984; children: Ted, Martha, Jimmy. BA, U. Fla., 1966, JD, 1968. Bar: Fla. 1968, U.S. Dist. Ct. (so. dist.) Fla. 1972, U.S. Ct. Appeals (5th and 11th cirs.) 1973. Jud. law clk. Fla. Dist. Ct. Appeals (4th cir.), West Palm Beach, 1968-70; ptnr. Hogg, Allen, Ryce, Norton & Blue, Miami, Fla., 1970-89, Donald T. Ryce, P.A., Miami, 1989-96, Hogg, Ryce & Hudson, Miami, 1997—99, Hogg, Ryce & Spencer, Miami, 2000—. Co-chmn. liaison com. labor and employment sect. NLRB, Fla., 1990-92, mem. publs. com., 1990-91, exec. coun. labor and employment sect., 1994-98; apptd. missing children adv. bd. Fla. Dept. Law Enforcement, 1996—. Active Fla. Police Chiefs Edn. Rsch. Found.; dir. Jimmy Ryce Ctr. for Victims of Predatory Abduction. Named to Policeman Hall of Fame, 1996, Grand Knight of Order of Michael the Archangel; recipient Leadership award Fla. Police Chiefs Edn. Rsch. Found., 1993. Mem. ABA, Microcomputer Edn. for Employment of the Disabled (bus. adv. coun.), Winter Haven C. of C. (Cmty. Leadership award 1994), Miami Rotary. Episcopalian. Avocations: tennis, gourmet cooking, biking. Office: Ste 305 1111 Kane Concourse Bay Harbor Islands FL 33145-2041 Fax: 305-864-7008. E-mail: employerlawyer@yahoo.com.

RYCHLAK, JOSEPH FRANK, psychology educator, theoretician; b. Cudahy, Wis., Dec. 17, 1928; s. Joseph Walter and Helen Mary (Bieniek) R.; m. Lenora Pearl Smith, June 16, 1956; children: Ronald, Stephanie. BS, U. Wis., 1953; MA, Ohio State U., 1954, PhD, 1957. Diplomate Am. Bd. Examiners in Profl. Psychology. Asst. prof. psychology Fla. State U., Tallahassee, 1957-58, Washington State U., Pullman, 1958-61; assoc. prof., then prof. psychology St. Louis U., 1961-69; prof. psychology Purdue U., West Lafayette, Ind., 1969-83, interim dept. head, 1979-80; prof. Loyola U. Chgo., 1983-99, Maude C. Clarke prof. humanistic psychology, 1983—, prof. emeritus, 1999—. Dir. Human Relations Ctr., Pullman, Wash., 1958-61; research cons. AT&T, 1957-82. Author: The Psychology of Rigorous Humanism, 1977, 2d edit., 1988, Discovering Free Will and Personal Responsibility, 1979, A Philosophy of Science for Personality Theory, 2d edit., 1981, Personality and Life Style of Young Male Managers, 1982, (with N. Cameron) Personality Development and Psychopathology, 2d edit., 1985, Artificial Intelligence and Human Reason: A Teleological Critique, 1991; assoc. editor Psychotherapy: Theory, Research and Practice, 1965-76, Jour. Mind and Behavior, 1985-94, Logical Learning Theory: A Human Teleology and Its Empirical Support, 1994, In Defense of Human Consciousness, 1997. With USAF, 1946-49. Named Outstanding Contbr. to Human Understanding, Internat. Assn. Social Psychiatry, 1971. Fellow Am. Psychol. Assn. (div. 24 pres. 1977-78, 86-87), Am. Psychol. Soc.; mem. Soc. Personality Assessment, Phi Beta Kappa Roman Catholic. Home: 916 Michigan Ave Apt 2 Evanston IL 60202-5416 *From my father I learned to have a sense of purpose, work hard, and assume responsibility. From my mother I learned not to take myself too seriously, and to realize that my achievements are never entirely up to me.*

RYCHWA, JEFFREY NATHAN, wildlife specialist; b. Peterboro, N.H., Sept. 2, 1971; s. James Wilbur Potter; m. Tara Anne Sabino, Sept. 10, 1994; children: Dakota James-Paul, Quinn Evan, Aaron Douglas. Student, Keene (N.H.) State Coll., Air Force Fire Tng. Fire/rescue specialist USAF, Torrejon, Spain, 1990—92; instr./owner Zanshinkan Martial Arts, Peterboro, 1994—98; nature and martial arts instr. The Well Sch., 1997—98; LPG technician/driver Suburban Propane, Milford, 1998—99; trimmer/operator Lewis Tree Svc., 1999—2001; wildlife technician Critter Control of N.H., Merrimack, 2001; wildlife mgmt. technician Total Wild!, Keene, 2001—. Author: (novels) Puppeteer, 2000, The Fifth, 2001, (albums) Prophecy of the Bones, 2000. With USAF, 1990—92. Pantheist. Avocations: tracking, writing, primitive living, philosophy. Home: 14 Schult St Keene NH 03431

RYDALCH, ANN, state senator; m. Vernal Rydalch. Mem. Idaho Senate, 1985— . Past mem. Idaho Bicentennial Commn.; former vice chmn. Idaho Republican Com. Home: 3824 E 17th St Idaho Falls ID 83406-6869*

RYDELEK, THEODORE FRANCIS, priest; b. Kearny, NJ, Apr. 8, 1942; s. Joseph Vincent Fydelek and Bertha Agnes Stanislawczyk. BA in Spanish Lit., Seton Hall U., 1983; MA in Scripture, Holy Apostles Sem., 1988, MDiv, 1989. Ordained priest Roman Cath. Ch., 89. Priest Cath. Ch., Tyler, Tex., 1989—. Substitute tchr. Newark Bd. Edn., 1984—89; chaplain Latin Mass Group, Buffalo, 1993—. Mem.: K.C. (4th degree). Home: 220 N Merrill St Buffalo TX 75831 Office: Blessed Kateri Tekakwitha 208 N Merrill St Buffalo TX 75831 Fax: 903-322-3155. E-mail: bkateri@ezmailbox.net.

RYDÉN, BENGT GUNNAR, stock exchange executive; b. Stockholm, Oct. 30, 1936; s. Gunnar H. and Ragnhild L. (Soederbaum) Rydén; m. Monica I.H. Tillberg, May 18, 1961. MBA, Stockholm Sch. Econs., 1960, PhD, 1972. Dep. chief economist Fedn. Swedish Industries, Stockholm, 1965-66; editor-in chief Swedish "Veckans Affärer", 1971-73; chief exec. Ctr. Bus. and Policy Studies, 1974-84, Stockholm Stock Exch., 1985-98, exec. chmn., 1998-99; vice chmn. The Swedish Acctg. Stds. Coun., 1989—. Chmn. Internat. Fedn. Stock Exchs., 1995—97, Mus. Nat. Antiquities, Sweden, 1998—, Hallvarsson & Halvarsson AB, Sweden, 1999—, Seventh Swedish Nat. Pension Fund, 1999—; bd. dirs. OM AB, Sweden, Capital Market Group, Sweden, Stockholmsborsen AB, The Acctg. Standards Bd. of Sweden; mem. Com. of Wise Men on the Regulation of European Securities Mkts., 2000—01. Fellow, Indsl. Inst. Econ. and Social Rsch., 1966—70. Fellow: Royal Swedish Acad. Engring. Scis.

RYDEN, JOHN GRAHAM, publishing executive; b. N.Y.C., Dec. 19, 1939; s. Albert Graham and Margaret Keating (Bastable) R.; m. Barbara Dee Kelly, June 19, 1962; children: Linda, Patricia. AB, Harvard U., 1961. Sales rep. McGraw-Hill Book Co., 1965-68; editor coll. dept. Harper & Row, 1968-71, editor in chief coll. dept., 1971-74; editor in chief, asst. dir. U. Chgo. Press, 1974-78, assoc. dir., 1978-79; dir. Yale U. Press, New Haven, 1979—; chmn. bd. trustees Yale Univ. Press, London, 1981—. Mem. adminstr. bd. The Papers of Benjamin Franklin, 1979— ; chmn. adv. bd. Beacon Press, 1983—. Mem. editl. bd. Public Historian, 1980-86, Scholarly Publishing, 1992-95, The Yale Editions of the Private Papers of James Boswell, 1993—; adv. bd. The Yale Review, 1992—. Trustee Orch. New Eng., 1980-2000, pres., 1983-86, chmn., 1995-2000; bd. dirs. Fund for Free Expression, 1990-96; mem. Helsinki Watch Com., 1992-96. With USNR, 1962-65. Berkeley Coll. fellow Yale U. Mem. Assn. Am. Publs. (bd. dirs. 1990-94), Assn. Am. U. Presses (bd. dirs. 1980-83, 87-90, pres. 1988-89), Conn. Acad. Arts and Scis., Internat. Assn. Scholarly Pubs., Grads. Club, New Haven Lawn Club, Hasty Pudding Club (Cambridge, Mass.), Yale Club (N.Y.C.), Century Assn. (N.Y.C.). Office: Yale Univ Press PO Box 209040 New Haven CT 06520-9040 also: Yale U Press 302 Temple St New Haven CT 06511-6601

RYDER, EDWARD FRANCIS, secondary education educator; b. Lynn, Mass., Mar. 25, 1931; s. Edward W. and Theresa (Callahan) R. BSBA, Salem State U., 1954, EdM in Edn., 1973; EdM in Bus. Edn., Boston U., 1956. Cert. tchr., Mass. Bus. tchr. North Quincy (Mass.) High Sch., 1968—. Owner, pub. Sunnyside Pub. Co., 1975—. Author: The Art of Playing Bingo and Winning Consistently, 1980, The Art of Entering Sweepstakes and Winning Consistently, 1981, How To Save a Fortune Using Refunds and Coupons, 1983, How to Unlock the Secrets of Winning and Good Luck, 1983, How You Can Achieve Total Success Through Self-Hypnosis, 1984, Where to Buy Everything Wholesale--A Book of Lifetime Savings, 1984, A Guide to Over 1,000 Things You Can Get--For Free!, 1984, The Art of Betting Horses and Winning Consistently, 1985, Blackjack: How to Play and Win Like an Expert, 1985, Hot Dice! How to Leave the Table a Winner, 1986, Winning Secrets of a Poker Master, 1986, Picking Winners at the Harness Races, 1987, Winning Consistently at the Greyhound Races, 1987, Lucky Slots!! How to Beat the Casino Bandits, 1988, Secrets of Winning at Casino Roulette, 1988, Keno: The Art of Playing and Winning, 1989, How to Play and Win at Casino Baccarat, 1989, Secrets of Winning at Video Poker, 1990, Winning Secrets of a Master Sports Bettor--Football, 1991, Winning Secrets of a Master Sports Bettor--Basketball, 1992, Winning Secrets of a Master Sports Bettor--Baseball, 1992; all publs. updated, 1997. Roman Catholic. Home: 28 Sunnyside Rd Lynn MA 01905-1105 Office: Sunnyside Pubs 51 Willow St # 29 Lynn MA 01901-1108 E-mail: hardwoodhoudini@aol.com.

RYDER, HAL, theater educator, director; b. Evanston, Ill., Aug. 21, 1950; s. Lee Sigmund and Katherine (Philipsborn) Rosenblatt; m. Caroline Margaret Ogden, Nov. 17, 1976 (div. 1991) Student, U. Ariz., 1968-72, U. Miami, summer 1971; cert. in drama, Drama Studio London, 1973; BA in Drama, U. Wash., 1987. Drama specialist Rough Rock (Ariz.) Demonstration Sch., 1971-72; artistic dir. Mercury Theatre, London, 1973-75, Fringe Theatre, Orlando, Fla., 1976-79; dir. Drama Studio London, 1980-82, interim adminstrv. dir., 1985; artistic dir. Alaska Arts Fine Arts Camp, Sitka, 1987, Shakespeare Plus, Seattle, 1983-92; full prof. Cornish Coll. Arts, 1982-98; prof., 1998—; producer theatre Cornish Coll. Arts, Seattle, 1987-97, acting-chmn. theatre dept., 1990, 2001, pres. faculty senate, 1999-2001; artistic dir., exec. dir. Open Door Theatre, 1992-98, exec. dir., 1998-00; artistic dir. Snoqualmie Falls Forest Theatre, 1992-94; founder, v.p., CEO Ednl. Arts Resource Svcs., Inc., 1996—; producing artistic dir. Seattle Pub. Theatre, 2001—. Creative cons. Sea World Fla., Orlando, 1979; lit. mgr. Pioneer Square Theatre, Seattle, 1983; space mgr. Seattle Mime Theatre, 1986-87. Author: Carmilla, 1976, (with others) Marvelous Christmas Mystery, 1978; editor: Will Noble Blood Die, 1987, The New Emperor's New Clothes, 1990, Hamlet & Juliet, 1997, Yeoman of the Guard, 2000, Two Errors of Vernona, 2001; dir. over 150 stage plays; appeared in over 40 prodns. Artistic dir. Seattle Pub. Theater, 2001—. Recipient Faculty Excellence award Seafirst Bank, Seattle, 1988. Mem. SAG, AFTRA, Am. Fedn. Tchrs. (pres. faculty senate Cornish chpt. 1999—), Alpha Kappa Lamda. Democrat. Jewish. Avocations: writing, cooking, gardening, travel, scuba diving. Home: 1012 NE 62nd St Seattle WA 98115-6604 Office: Cornish Coll Arts 710 E Roy St Seattle WA 98102-4604

RYDER, HENRY C(LAY), lawyer; b. Lafayette, Ind., Feb. 18, 1928; s. Raymond Robert and Mina Elizabeth (Arnold) R.; m. Ann Sater Clay, Nov. 29, 1952 (dec.); children: David C., Sarah Paige Hugon, Anne M.; m. Velma Iris Dean, Aug. 27, 1976 BS, Purdue U., 1948; LLB, U. Mich., 1951; LLD, Hanover Coll., 1998. Bar: Mich. 1951, Ind. 1952, U.S. Dist. Ct. (so. dist.) Ind. 1953, U.S. Ct. Appeals (7th cir.) 1957, U.S. Supreme Ct. 1981. Assoc. Buschmann, Krieg, DeVault & Alexander, Indpls., 1953-57, ptnr., 1957-60, Roberts & Ryder and successor firms, Indpls., 1960-86, Barnes & Thornburg (merger), Indpls., 1987-95, of counsel, 1996—. Pres. Ind. State Symphony Soc. Inc., 1979-82, bd. dirs., 1972-91, trustee, 1991—; chmn. United Way of Greater Indpls., 1984; vice chmn. Greater Indpls. Progress Com., 1979-86, chmn., 1987-89, mem. exec. com., 1979-2000; trustee Purdue U., 1983-89, Hanover Coll., 1979—, chmn., 1988-98; bd. dirs. Hist. Landmark Found. of Ind., 1985-96, chmn., 1992-95; bd. dirs. Purdue Rsch. Found., 1992—; hon. v.p. Ind. Soc. Chgo.; bd. govs. Heartland Film Festival, 2000—. Lt. U.S. Army, 1951-53. Recipient Jefferson award Indpls. Star, 1983, Whistler award Greater Indpls. Progress Com., 1989; Sagamore of the Wabash, 1984; named Man of Yr., B'nai B'rith Soc., 1984, Ind. Acad., 1992, Lifetime Achievement award Nat. Soc. Fund Raising Execs., 1999. Fellow: Ind. Bar Found., Am. Bar Found.; mem.: ABA, Indpls. Bar Assn., Ind. Bar Assn., Ind. C. of C. (bd. dirs. 1991—94), Purdue U. Alumni Assn. (pres. 1975—77, Alumni Svc. award 1982, Citizenship award 1989), Indpls. Lit. Club, Kiwanis (pres. Indpls. 1983, Civic award 1981), Columbia Club (bd. dirs. 1987—90, sec. 1988, trustee 1990—, pres. Found. 1990—95, Benjamin Harrison award 1983, Columbian Student of Yr. award 2002), USAC Benevolent Found. (bd. dirs., pres. 1999—), USAC Properties (sec., bd. dirs.), U.S. Auto Club (sec., bd. dirs., Pres.'s award 1989, Eddie Edenburn award 2000), Lawyers Club (pres. Indpls. 1966). Republican. Presbyterian. Office: Barnes & Thornburg 11 S Meridian St Ste 1313 Indianapolis IN 46204-3535

RYDER, JAMES LEE, missionary, community-based agency official; b. Detroit, June 21, 1963; s. Paul Joseph and Louise Joan Ryder; m. Louise K. Ntaganda, Mar. 26, 2000. BA, Boston Coll., Chestnut Hill, Mass., 1986; MRE, Loyola U., Chgo., 1999. Camp counsellor Glenmary Home Missioners, Aberdeen, Miss., 1988; tchr. theology St. Martin de Porres H.S., Chgo., 1988-89; direct care worker Link Crisis Intervention Ctr., St. Joseph, Mich., 1992-94; grad. asst. Loyola U., 1996; site coord. Life Directions Inc., Chgo., 1997-2000, dir. Detroit, 2000—. Roman Catholic. Avocations: oil painting, creative writing, camping, reading. Home: 1367 Beaconsfield Unit A Grosse Pointe Park MI 48230 Office: Life Directions Inc-Detroit 3000 Gratiot Ste 107 Detroit MI 48207 E-mail: jimmylee7000@aol.com.

RYDER, KENNETH WILLIAM, pathologist, educator; b. Mobile, Ala., May 1, 1945; BA, Knox Coll., 1967; PhD, Ind. U., 1972; MD, U. Ill., Chgo., 1975. Asst. prof. Ind. U. Sch. Medicine, Indpls., 1978-83, assoc. prof., 1983-88, prof., assoc. chair, 1986—; chief of svc. Wishard Meml. Hosp., 1986-99; med. dir. Vencor Hosp. Lab., 1995-2001; dir. chemistry labs., outreach svcs./point of care testing Clarian Health Ptnrs., 2000—; chief pathologist VA Med. Ctr., 2000-01. Author: Interferographs, 1987, 2nd Edit., 1991; (with others) Difficult Diagnoses, 1991; contbr. articles to profl. jours. Fellow Coll. Am. Pathologists, 1979, Nat. Acad. Clin. Biochemistry, 1989. Office: Ind U Sch Medicine Meth Hosp Pathology Svc 1701 N Senate Ave Rm AG002A Indianapolis IN 46202-5306 E-mail: kryder@iupui.edu.

RYDER, MARY RUTH, English language educator; b. Bloomington, Ill., Apr. 1, 1950; d. Bernard Leroy and Ruth Marie (Blacker) R. BA, Monmouth Coll., 1972; MA, Ill. State U., 1981; PhD, U. Ill., 1987. Tchr. English and Latin, Monmouth (Ill.) H.S., 1972, Normal (Ill.) Cmty. H.S., 1972-85; asst. prof. English, Ill. State U., Normal, 1985-89; prof. English, S.D. State U., Brookings, 1989—, Disting. prof. English, 2002—, coord. grad. studies in English, 1993—. Author: Willa Cather and Classical Myth, 1990 (Mildred Bennett Prize for Disting. Cather Scholarship, Classical and Modern Lit. Quar. Incentive award). Mem. MLA, Willa Cather Pioneer Meml. and Ednl. Found., Phi Kappa Phi, Alpha Xi Delta. Methodist. Office: SD State U Dept English Brookings SD 57007-0001

RYDER, RONALD ARCH, science educator; b. Feb. 3, 1928; s. Wendell Martin Ryder and Florence Ball; m. Audry Teele Ryder, Sept. 5, 1955; children: Raymond, Helen. BS, Colo. State U., Fort Collins, CO, 1949, MS, 1951; PhD, Utah State U., Logan, UT, 1958. Rsch. assoc. Colo. Wildlife Rescue Unit, Fort Collins, Colo., 1949—51, Utah Wildlife Rescue Unit, Logan, Utah, 1954—58; instr. Wartburg Coll., Waverly, Iowa, 1958—59; from asst. prof. to prof. Colo. State U., Fort Collins, 1959—85, emeritus prof. Colo., 1985—. Lcdr USN, 1951—54, Korea. Fellow: Am. Ornithology Union (fellowship 1994). Avocations: birding, birding, bird banding. Home: 748 Eastdale Drive Fort Collins CO 80524 Office: Department Fishery and Wildlife Biology Colorado State University Fort Collins CO 80523

RYDER, STEPHEN WILLIS, newspaper publisher; b. Kurume, Kyushu, Japan, May 10, 1923; came to U.S., 1929; s. Stephen Willis and Reba Catherine (Snapp) R.; m. Mary Irene Knappenberger, Dec. 7, 1946; 1 dau., Lynne Ryder Moke. BA in Journalism, Liberal Arts., Syracuse U., 1946. Sta. mgr. WENE, Endicott, N.Y., 1947-58; asst. to pub. News-Times, Danbury, Conn., 1958; pub. Press-Republican, Plattsburgh, N.Y., 1959-64; v.p. Ottaway Newspapers, Inc. (subs. Dow Jones & Co.), Campbell Hall, 1964-89; pub. Mail Tribune, Medford, Oreg., 1973-82. Bd. dirs. N.Y. State Pubs. Assn., 1968-73, pres. 1972-73; bd. dirs. Oreg. Newspaper Pubs. Assn., 1974-82, pres. 1980-81; bd. dirs. Endicott Girls Club; former chmn. Broome County (N.Y.) Tri-cities Aviation Coun.; pres. Greater Endicott C. of C., 1956-57; bd. dirs. Plattsburgh Physicians/Champlain Med. Ctr.; pres. Clinton County (N.Y.) Indsl. Devel. Commn.; bd. dirs. Rogue Valley Med. Ctr., 1974-92, chmn. health svcs., 1988-92; dir. Oreg. Shakespeare Festival Assn., 1975-83, pres., 1980-82; bd. dirs. Oreg. Ind. Coll. Found., 1983-89; mem. Syracuse U. Journalism Adv. Coun., 1970-73, U. Oreg. Journalism adv. coun, 1992—; chmn. we. adv. bd. Am. Press Inst., 1980-85; bd. dirs. Craterian Ginger Rogers Theatre bd., Medford, 1993-2001; elder Presbyn. Ch., 1956—. With USAF, 1943-45, China-Burma-India Theatre. Ops. Ruhl fellow U. Oreg. Journalism Sch., 1980; inducted Oreg. Newspaper Hall of Fame, 1994. Home: 2964 Fairview Dr Medford OR 97504-7743

RYDER, TIMOTHY THOMAS, classics educator; b. Claygate, Surrey, Eng., Jan. 11, 1930; s. Thomas Alfred and Enid Mary (Sanger) R.; m. Jean Temple, Apr. 12, 1955; children: Penelope Anne Burnham, Philippa Kathryn Lea. BA, Cambridge (Eng.) U., 1952, MA, PhD, Cambridge (Eng.) U., 1956. Asst. lectr. classics U. Hull (Eng.), 1955-57, lectr. classics, 1957-66, sr. lectr. classics, 1966-71, reader classics, 1971-90, dean Sch. Humanities, 1987-90; reader classics U. Reading (Eng.), 1990-95, vis. fellow, 1995—. Vis. prof. history Mich. State U., East Lansing, 1966-67, vis. prof. history, 1981. Author: Koine Eirene, 1965; editor: Dictionary of World History, 1972. Mem. Soc. for Promotion of Hellenic Studies, Soc. for Promotion Roman Studies, Classical Assn. Gt. Britain. Mem. Ch. Of Eng. Avocations: cricket, travel. Office: U Reading Dept Classics Whiteknights PO Box 218 RG6 2AA Reading England

RYDHOLM, RALPH WILLIAMS, advertising agency executive; b. Chgo., June 1, 1937; s. Thor Gabriel and Vivian Constance (Williams) R.; m. Jo Anne Beechler, Oct. 5, 1963; children: Kristin, Erik, Julia. BA, Northwestern U., 1958, postgrad. in bus. adminstrn, 1958-59; postgrad. Advanced Mgmt. Program, Harvard U., 1982. Acct. trainee, copywriter Young & Rubicam Advt., Chgo., 1960-63; copywriter Post-Keyes-Gardner Advt., 1963, E. H. Weiss Advt., Chgo., 1963-65; copy group head BBDO Advt., 1965-66; with J. Walter Thompson Advt., 1966-86, creative dir., v.p., 1969-76, exec. creative dir., 1976-86, sr. v.p., 1972-80, exec. v.p., dir., 1980-86; exec. v.p., chief creative officer, dir. Ted Bates Worldwide, N.Y.C., 1986-87; mng. ptnr., chmn. mgmt. com., chief creative officer, chmn., CEO EURO RSCG Tatham Advt., Chgo., 1987-98; pres. R2 Cons., 1999—; spl. counsel J. Walter Thompson, 1999-2000. Bd. dirs., ops. com., chmn. creative com., vice chmn., 1996, chmn., 1997-98; Am. Assn. Advt. Agys. guest spkr. Ad Age Workshop, 1969, 77, 86, Adweek Seminar, 1993, CLIO awards, 1995; keynote spkr. Stephen B. Kelly Awards, 1993, CEBA Awards, 1997; dir. Euro RSCG, USA.; chmn. CEBA Awards, 1997. Mem. assoc. bd. Newberry Libr. Assn., Friends com. Northwetern U.; adv. coun. Chgo. Pub. Edn. Fund; Prin. for a Day Chgo. Pub. Schs., 1998, 1999, 2000, 2001; chmn. bd. dirs. Am. Scandinavian Coun.; dir. Am. Assn. Advt. Agys. Found., 1997—99. Staff sgt. USAF, 1959—65. Recipient Clio awards, Internat. Broadcast award, Lion awards, Cannes Film Festival, Addy awards; named one of Top 100 Creative Ad People Ad Daily, 1972, Advt. Exec. of Yr. Adweek, 1991, Best Man in Advt. McCalls and Adweek, 1992; named to Creative Leader Hall of Fame, Wall St. Jour., 1994. Mem. ASCAP, Am. Advt. Fedn. (Silver medal Lifetime Svc. 1997), Chgo. Advt. Fedn., Chgo. Coun. on Fgn. Rels., Saddle and Cycle Club, Econ. Club Chgo. (bd. dirs. 1996-98), Northwestern Club Chgo., Harvard Club Chgo., Harvard Club Boston, Execs. Club Chgo., Tavern Club, Carlton Club, Chikaming Country Club (Mich.), Dunes Club (Mich.), Lost Dunes Club (Mich.), Internat. Club, Hon. Order Ky. Cols., Openlands, Friends of the Parks, Friends of Chgo. River, Fernwood, Art Inst. Chgo., Phi Delta Theta. E-mail: rydholm@aol.com.

RYDSTROM, CARLTON LIONEL, chemist, chemicals consultant; b. Indpls., Dec. 4, 1928; s. Carlton Lionel and Sara Ann (McNeese) R.; m. Kathleen O'Leary, Oct. 21, 1954 (dec.); children: Carlton L. III, Michael, Mary (dec.), Leslie, Patricia, Timothy, Molly. BS in Polymer Chemistry, N.D. State U., 1951; MS in Phys. Chemistry, U. Puerto Rico, Rio, Piedras, 1953. Chemist Am. Marietta Co., Kankakee, Ill., 1951-52; chemist, plant mgr. Chinamel Paints, Hato Rey, Puerto Rico, 1952-53; tech. mgr. Midwest Synthetics (Valspar), Rockford, Ill., 1953-55; mng. ptnr. Norcote Co., St. Petersburg, Fla., 1955-71; pres. C.M. Industries, Inc., 1971-74, Tuf-top/Norcote Coatings, Inc., St. Petersburg, 1974-80; owner Rydstrom Lab., Inc., 1980—. Bd. dirs. Stacote Finishes, Ltd., W.I.; cons. Sch. Bds. State of Fla., 1981—, paint and adhesive industries. Pres. parish coun. St. Jude Cath. Cathedral Parish, 1977-78, 78-79, 97—, St. Vincent de Paul Pinellas Dist., St. Petersburg, 1988-91; nat. secretariat Cursillo Movement, Roman Cath. Ch., Dallas, 1985-88; dir. Cursillo Movement, Diocese of St. Petersburg, 1995—; dir. St. Vincent de Paul Food Ctr., St. Petersburg, 1988—; chmn. Waterfront Planning Com., St. Petersburg, 1959; mem. bd. dirs. St. Petersburg Cath. H.S., 1977-80; trustee N.D. State U. Devel. Found., 1998—. Fellow N.Y. Acad. Sci.,

Am. Inst. Chemists; mem. Nat. Assn. Corrosion Engrs., Soc. Coatings Tech. (chmn./pres. 1958-59, Disting. Svc. award 1975), Fla. Paint and Coating Assn. (treas., dir. 1959-75), St. Vincent dePaul Soc. (Top Hat award 1991), Jr. C. of C. (DSA 1960). Republican. Roman Catholic. Avocations: golf, gardening, travel, public speaking, working with elderly. Home and Office: 6300 25th Ave N Saint Petersburg FL 33710-4128 E-mail: Bud-rydstrom@msn.com.

RYE, SCOTT CAIRNEY, advertising executive, author; b. Florence, Ala., Aug. 10, 1961; s. Tommy Gary and Betty Jean (Anderson) R.; m. Ruth Melissa Metcalfe, Aug. 11, 1984; children: Lauren Victoria, Colin Metcalfe. BA, Rhodes Coll., Memphis, 1983. Copywriter, prodr. Timbes & Yeager, Mobile, Ala., 1983-99; assoc. creative dir. Sullivan-St. Clair Advt., 1999-2001, v.p. pub. rels. and govt. affairs, 2001—. Dir. Benchmark Polit. and Image Cons., Mobile, 2000—. Author: Of Men and Ships, 1993, Men and Ships of the Civil War, 1995; contbr. articles to Civil War Times. Chmn. cmty. watch Historic Murphy Dist. Assn., Mobile, 1996-97, 99—, chmn. beautification com., 1997-98; bd. dirs. CSS Ala. Assn., 1999—, Ala. Advt. Edn. Found., 1989-90; bd. dirs., mem. pub. affairs com. Mobile Bay Area Vets. Day Commn., 1988-94. Lt. comdr. USNR, 1990—. Recipient Disting. Svc. award Arthritis Found., 1994; named to Outstanding Young Men of Am., 1989, 96, 97. Mem. Advt. Fedn. Greater Mobile (pres. 1993-94), Am. Advt. Fedn. (Silver medal 1998). Avocations: wing shooting, scuba diving. Office: Sullivan-St Clair Advt 2610 Dauphin St Mobile AL 36606-4802 E-mail: scott@sullivanstclair.com.

RYERSON, GENE GROVE, internist; b. Glen Ridge, N.J., Jan. 8, 1945; s. Wilbur Doremus and Frances R.; m. Beverly Smith, June 29, 1969; children: Krister, Anders, Britt, Kjell. BS, Bucknell U., 1967; MD, N.J. Coll. Medicine, 1971. Intern, then resident N.J. Med. Sch., Newark, 1971-73; resident U. Fla. Gainesville, 1973-74, 76, fellow in pulmonary diseases, 1977-79; mem. faculty U. Fla. Coll. Medicine, 1979—. Major USAF, 1974-76. Fellow ACP, Am. Coll Chest Physicians; mem. Am. Thoracic Soc. Office: Univ Fla Coll Medicine PO Box 100225 Gainesville FL 32610-0225

RYERSON, MARJORIE GILMOUR, journalist, educator, poet, photographer; b. Germantown, Pa., Mar. 28, 1943; d. William Newton and Jean (Hamilton) R.; children: Nicholas, Emily. BA, Beloit Coll., 1965; MFA, U. Iowa, 1976. Assoc. editor, reporter, photographer White River Valley Herald, Randolph, Vt., 1981-85; dir. pub. rels. and fund devel. Gifford Meml. Hosp., 1986; editor Country Courier mag., Barre, Vt., 1986-90; features editor Burlington (Vt.) Free Press, 1990; asst. prof. English dept. Johnson (Vt.) State Coll., 1990-91; assoc. prof. Comm. Dept. Castleton (Vt.) State Coll., 1991—, chair comm. dept., 1996-98. New England Young Writers Conf. faculty, Middlebury Coll., 1991—; dir. Vt. Network Cmty. Newspapers, 1996—; journalism tchr. Dorothy Canfield Fisher Writing Conf., Burlington, 1993; mem. faculty Vt. Coun. on Arts, 1992, lit. advisor; mem. state poet adv. com. for Vt.; faculty fellow Vt. State Colls., 2000-2001. Selectman, Town of Randolph, 1995; mem. Randolph Cmty. Devel. Corp. Bd.; corporator Gifford Meml. Hosp.; justice of the peace County of Orange; bd. dirs. Vt. Mozart Festival; vol. Big Bros./Big Sisters Program. Mem. Am. Med. Writers Assn., Image Co-op (pres. bd. dirs.), Vt. League of Writers (hon.), Physicians for Social Responsibility. Avocations: playing saxophone and piano, hiking, canoeing, opera. Home: 36 Randolph Ave Randolph VT 05060

RYERSON, PAUL SOMMER, lawyer; b. Newark, Oct. 2, 1946; s. Robert Paul and Audrey Mae (Sommer) R.; m. Susan Jean Duckrow, Aug. 7, 1971 (div. Apr. 1995); children: James Sommer, Jill Carin. BA, Wesleyan U., 1968; JD, Columbia U., 1971. Bar: N.Y. 1972, D.C. 1972, U.S. Ct. Appeals (D.C. cir.) 1973, U.S. Dist. Ct. D.C. 1973, U.S. Supreme Ct. 1976, U.S. Ct. Appeals (5th cir.) 1979, U.S. Ct. Appeals (4th cir.) 1980. Law clk. to judge Jack B. Weinstein U.S. Dist. Ct. ea. dist. N.Y., 1971-72; assoc. Arnold & Porter, Washington, 1972-79, ptnr., 1980-89, Jones, Day, Reavis & Pogue, Washington, 1989—. Contbr. articles to profl. publs. Mem. ABA, D.C. Bar Assn. Home: 5809 Nicholson Ln North Bethesda MD 20852-5719 Office: Jones Day Reavis & Pogue 51 Louisiana Ave NW Washington DC 20001-2113

RYERSON, RICHARD ALAN, historian, editor; b. Boston, May 6, 1942; s. Wendell Egerton and Susan Isabel (Souther) R.; m. Marla Diane Eby, Nov. 2, 1991; children: Anna Magdalena Eby. AB, Harvard Coll., 1964; MA, Johns Hopkins U., 1969, PhD, 1972. Instr. Hebron (Me.) Acad., 1965-67, U. Tex., Austin, 1971-73, asst. prof., 1973-78; assoc. editor Papers of William Penn, Phila., 1979-83; editor in chief Adams Papers, Boston, 1983-2001; acad. dir. David Libr. of the Am. Revolution, Washington Crossing, Pa., 2002—. Author: The Revolution Is Now Begun, 1977; editor: Adams Family Correspondence (2 vols.), 1994. Recipient J. Franklin Jameson prize Am. Hist. Assn., 1995; U. Pa. fellow, 1975-76, Harvard U. fellow, 1978-79. Mem. Assn. Documentary Editing, Soc. Historians Early Republic (adv. coun. 1993-95), Mass. Hist. Soc., Colonial Soc. Mass., Harvard Musical Assn. Democrat. Avocation: classical music. Home: 8 Trotting Horse Dr Lexington MA 02421-6339 E-mail: rryerson@earthlink.net.

RYERSON, WILLIAM NEWTON, non profit organization executive; b. Phila., Mar. 9, 1945; s. W. Newton and Jean (Hamilton) R.; m. Leta C. Finch, Dec. 6, 1975. BA, Amherst Coll., 1967; M.Phil., Yale U., 1971. Dir. student intern program Population Inst., Washington, 1971-73, dir. youth and student div., 1973-79; dir. devel. Planned Parenthood Southeastern Pa., Phila., 1979-81; assoc. dir. Planned Parenthood No. New Eng., Burlington, Vt., 1981-86; pres. Ryerson & Assocs., fundraising counsel, Shelburne, 1986-2000; exec. v.p. Population Comm. Internat., N.Y.C., 1986-98; pres. Population Media Ctr., Shelburne, Vt., 1998—. Co-author: Population Activist's Handbook, 1974. NASA trainee in biology, Yale U., 1967-70. Mem.: Phi Beta Kappa, Sigma Xi (assoc.). Home: PO Box 580 Shelburne VT 05482-0580 Office: PO Box 547 Shelburne VT 05482-0547 E-mail: wryerson@earthlink.net.

RYESKY, KENNETH H. lawyer; b. Phila., July 30, 1954; s. A. and Helene (Silbermann) R.; m. Tamara E. Weiss, Mar. 11, 1983; children: H.Z., Damilola. BBA, Temple U., 1977, JD, 1986; MBA, La Salle U., 1982; MLS, CUNY, 1999. Bar: Pa. 1986, N.J. 1987, N.Y. 1988, U.S. Supreme Ct. 1996. Procurement specialist Def. Logistics Agy., Phila., 1979-87; atty. IRS, N.Y.C., 1987-91; pvt. practice East Northport, N.Y., 1991—. Adj. asst. prof. Queens Coll./CUNY, Flushing, N.Y., 1993—. Co-author: Federal Government Intelligence Property Guide, 1995; contbr. articles to profl. jours. Jewish. Avocations: cooking, gardening, collecting. E-mail: 'khresq@sprintmail.com. Office: PO Box 926 East Northport NY 11731-0529 Fax: 631-266-3198.

RYGIEL, EDWARD K. chemical engineer; BSChemE, U. Toronto. Pres., CEO MDS Capital Corp., Toronto, Canada; exec. v.p. MDS Inc. Chmn. bd. Henosol Inc., Mississauga, Ont., Canada; bd. dirs. NPS Pharm., Inc., MDS Nordion, Can. NeuroSci. Can. Partnership. Office: Henosol Inc 2585 Meadowpine Blvd Mississauga ON L5N 8H9 Canada also: MDS CapitalCorp 100 International Blvd Toronto ON M9W 6J6 Canada Office Fax: 905-286-6300., 416-213-4232. E-mail: info@mdscapital.com.*

RYGIEWICZ, PAUL THADDEUS, plant ecologist; b. Chgo., Feb. 19, 1952; s. Sigismund Thaddeus and Regina (Korpalski) R. BS in Forestry, U. Ill., 1974; MS in Wood Sci., U. Calif., Berkeley, 1976; PhD in Forest Resources, U. Wash., 1983. Research wood technologist ITT Rayonier, Inc., Shelton, Wash., 1977; research assoc. Centre National de Recherches Forestières, Nancy, France, 1983-84; research soil microbiologist U. Calif., Berkeley, 1984-85; rsch. ecologist, global climate change project leader EPA, Corvallis, Oreg., 1985—. Asst. prof. dept. forest sci. Oreg. State U., 1987—. Contbr. articles to profl. jours.; rsch. on reforestation of tropical forests in Brazil, global climate changes on forests, health and function of forest ecosystems. Vol. Big Bros. of Am., Urbana, Ill., 1972-74. Fellow Regents U. Calif., Berkeley, 1973-74, Weyerhaeuser U. Calif., Berkeley, 1978-79, Inst. Nat. de la Recherche Agronomique, France, 1983-84, French Ministry of Fgn. Affairs, 1983-84. Mem. Ecol. Soc. Am., Soil Ecology Soc., Forestry Club, Sigma Xi, Gamma Sigma Delta, Xi Sigma Pi (officer 1973-74). Avocations: bicycling, skiing, mountain climbing, camping, hiking. Office: EPA 200 SW 35th St Corvallis OR 97333-4996 E-mail: rags@mail.coriepa.gov.

RYK, MARY A. retired chaplain; b. Chgo., Dec. 12, 1943; d. Anthony and Helen (Dankowski) Mishur; m. Jan Ryk, Apr. 20, 1963; seven children. BA, DePaul U., 1990. Chaplain Bethlehem Woods Retirement Living Ctr., La Grange Park, Ill., 1990—96, cons. chaplain, 1996—97. Author, illustrator, pub.: Poetry of the Soul, vol. I, 1993, vol. II, 1993, vol. III, 1996, Poetry Night Songs, 3 vols., 2002. Mem. Downers Grove Choral Soc. and Chamber Chorus, 1998—2001, Chamber Chorus, 1998—2000.

RYKEN, PHILIP GRAHAM, minister, theologian; b. Eugene, Oreg., Sept. 29, 1966; s. Leland and Mary Alice (Graham) R.; m. Elisabeth Kristen Maxwell, June 6, 1987; children: Joshua, Kirsten, James, Kathryn. BA summa cum laude, Wheaton (Ill.) Coll., 1988; MDiv with honors, Westminster Theol. Sem., Phila., 1992; PhD, U. Oxford, Eng., 1995. Ordained minister, Presbyn. Ch. in Am., 1996. Lectr. Ctr. for Medieval and Renaissance Studies, Oxford, Eng., 1993-95; assoc. min. preaching 10th Presbyn. Ch., Phila., 1995-2000, sr. min., 2001—. Author: Courage to Stand, 1998, The Heart of the Cross, 1999, Discovering God in Stories From the Bible, 1999, Thomas Boston as Preacher of the Fourfold State, 1999, When You Pray, 2000, Jeremiah and Lamentations, 2001, The Communion of Saints, 2001, The Message of Salvation, 2001; contbr. articles to books; author: Jesus on Trial, 2002, The Doctrines of Grace, 2002, My Father's World, 2002, The Prayer of Our Lord, 0200. Recipient Overseas Rsch. Student award Com. of Vice-Chancellors and Prins. of the Univs. of the U.K., Oxford, 1992-95. Mem. Evang. Theol. Soc., Alliance of Confessing Evangelicals (coun. mem.). Avocation: basketball. Office: 10th Presbyn Ch 1701 Delancey St Philadelphia PA 19103-6714

RYKWERT, JOSEPH, architecture and art history educator; b. Warsaw, Poland, Apr. 5, 1926; arrived in Eng., 1939; s. Szymon Mieczyslaw and Elizabeth (Melup) R.; m. Anne-Marie Sandersley, Feb. 14, 1972; 1 child from previous marriage, Simon Sebastian; 1 stepchild, Marina Joanna Engel. Student, Archtl. Assn., London, 1944-47; MA, U. Cambridge, London; PhD, Royal Coll. Art, London, 1970; MA (hon.), U. Pa., 1988; DSc (hon.), U. Edinburgh, Scotland, 1995; D (hon.), U. Cordoba, 1998, U. Bath, Eng., 2000. Libr., tutor Royal Coll. Art, 1960-67; prof. art, chmn. dept. U. Essex, Colchester, Eng., 1967-81; Slade prof. fine arts U. Cambridge, 1980, reader in architecture, 1981-87; Paul Philippe Cret prof. architecture, prof. art history U. Pa., Phila., 1988-98, prof. emeritus, also chmn. PhD program in architecture. Andrew Mellon prof. Cooper Union, N.Y.C., 1977; George Lurcy prof. Columbia U., N.Y.C., 1986; commr. Venice (Italy) Biennale, 1974-77; mem. jury Parc de la Villette Competition, Paris, 1982, Wolf Found. Prize, Jerusalem, 1983; trustee Cubitt Trust, London, 1986-98; sr. scholar Getty Ctr. for History Art and Humanities, 1 992, 93; co-editor catalogue, curator Alberti Exhbn., Mantua, Italy, 1994. Author: The Golden House, 1947, The Idea of a Town, 1963, 76, 88, Church Building, 1966, On Adam's House in Paradise, 1972, 82, The First Moderns, 1980, 84, The Necessity of Artifice, 1982, (with Anne-Marie Rykwert) The Brothers Adam, 1985; editl. transl.: On the Art of Building (L.B. Alberti), 1989, 91, The Dancing Column, 1996, The Seduction of Place, 2000; editor Res. jour., Peabody Mus., Cambridge, Mass., 1979—. Mem. steering com. UNESCO Conf. on Urbanism, 1989—. Decorated Chevalier des Arts et des Lettres, Govt. of France, 1985; recipient Alfred Jurzykowski Found. award, 1990, Accademia di San Luca, 1993. Mem. Polish Acad. of Arts and Scis., Coll. Art Assn., Comite Internat. des Critiques d'Arch. (pres.), Savile Club (London). Office: U Pa Dept Architecture 210 S 34th St 207 Meyerson Hall Philadelphia PA 19104-6311 E-mail: rykwert@pobox.upenn.edu.

RYLAND, V. WALLACE, business developer; b. Alexandria, Va., July 30, 1969; s. Virgil Wallace Ryland and Ann Louise Sedberry. BA in Liberal Arts, U. Tex., 1991. Instr. English Fork Union (Va.) Mil. Acad., 1991-93; receiver/sales NCH Corp., Irving, Tex., 1994-96; account exec. Contractor's Register, Jefferson Valley, N.Y., 1996-98; pub., v.p. Marcoa Pub., Houston, 1998-2000; dir. bus. devel. blue-silicon, San Jose, Calif., 2000—. Pub., mem. Greater Houston Partnership, 1998—. Mem. Tex. Ex-Students Assn. Mem. Masons (grand lodge # 127, Marshal 1991-92), Fork Union Mil. Acad. Alumni Assn., Woodlands C. of C. (pub.), Sugar Creek Country Club, Chi Phi (alumni chmn. 1991). Republican. Avocations: writing, golf, sailing. Home: E 311 Everett Palo Alto CA 94301 Office: blue-silicon 70 Bonaventura Dr San Jose CA 95134 E-mail: vwr3@yahoo.com.

RYLANDER, HENRY GRADY, JR. mechanical engineering educator; b. Pearsall, Tex., Aug. 23, 1921; married; 4 children. BS, U. Tex., 1943, MS, 1952; PhD in Mech. Engring., Ga. Inst. Tech., 1965. Design engr. Steam Div., Aviation Gas Turbine Div., Westinghouse Elec. Corp., 1943-47; from asst. to assoc. prof. mech. engring. U. Tex., Austin, 1947-68, research scientist, 1950, prof. mech. engring., 1968—, Joe J. King prof. engring., 1980—. Cons. engr. TRACOR, Inc., 1964-69; founding dir. Ctr. for Electromechanics, U. Tex., 1977-85, chmn., mech. engring. dept., 1976-86. Named Disting. Grad. Coll. Engring., U. Tex., Austin, 1989. Fellow ASME (Leonardo da Vinci award 1985); mem. ASME. Office: U Tex Coll Engring C2200 Austin TX 78712 E-mail: hgr@mail.utexar.edu.

RYLANDER, ROBERT ALLAN, financial service executive; b. Bremerton, Wash., Apr. 8, 1947; s. Richard Algot and Marian Ethelyn (Peterson) R.; children: Kate, Erik, Meagan. BA in Fin., U. Wash., 1969; postgrad., U. Alaska, 1972-74. Controller Alaska USA Fed. Credit Union, Anchorage, 1974-77, mgr. ops., 1977-80, asst. gen. mgr., 1980-83, exec. v.p., COO, 1983—; pres., CEO Alaska Option Svcs. Corp., 1983—97. Chmn. Alaska USA Mortgage, Inc., Anchorage, 1992—, Alaska Option Svcs. Corp., Anchorage, 1997—, Alaska USA Trust Co., Anchorage, 1997—. Served to capt. USAF, 1969-74. Avocations: audio electronics, music, home theater. Home: PO Box 220587 Anchorage AK 99522-0587 Office: Alaska USA Fed Credit Union PO Box 196613 Anchorage AK 99519-6613

RYLANT, CYNTHIA, author; b. Hopewell, Va., June 6, 1954; d. John Tune and Leatrel (Rylant) Smith; 1 child, Nathaniel. BA, U. Charleston, 1975; MA, Marshall U., 1976; MLS, Kent State U., 1981. English instr. Marshall U., Huntington, W.Va., 1979-80, U. Akron, Ohio, 1983-84; children's libr. Akron (Ohio) Pub. Libr., 1983. Part-time lectr. Northeast Ohio Univs. Coll. Medicine, Rootstown, Ohio, 1991—. Author: (picture books) When I Was Young in the Mountains, 1982 (Caldecott Honor book 1983, English Speaking Union Book-Across-the-Sea Amb. of Honor award 1984, Am. Book award nomination 1983), Miss Maggie, 1983, This Year's Garden, 1984, The Relatives Came, 1985 (Horn Book Honor book 1985, Children's Book of Yr. Child Study Assn. Am. 1985, Caldecott Honor Book 1986), Night in the Country, 1986, Birthday Presents, 1987, All I See, 1988, Mr. Grigg's Work, 1989, An Angel for Solomon Singer, 1992, The Everyday Town, 1993, The Everyday School, 1993, The Everyday House, 1993, The Everyday Garden, 1993, The Everyday Children, 1993, The Everyday Pets, 1993, Mr. Putter and Tabby Pour the Tea, 1994, Mr. Putter and Tabby Walk the Dog, 1994, The Old Woman Who Named Things, 1994, The Blue Hill Meadows and the Much Loved Dog, 1994, Gooseberry Park, 1995, A Story of E.B. White, 1996, A Story of Margaret Wise, 1996; (Henry and Mudge series) Henry and Mudge: The First Book of Their Adventures, 1987, Henry and Mudge in Puddle Trouble, 1987, Henry and Mudge in the Green Time, 1987, Henry and Mudge Under the Yellow Moon, 1987, Henry and Mudge in the Sparkle Days, 1988, Henry and Mudge and the Forever Sea, 1989, Henry and Mudge Get the Cold Shivers, 1989, Henry and Mudge and the Happy Cat, 1990, Henry and Mudge and the Bedtime Thumps, 1991, Henry and Mudge Take the Big Test, 1991, Henry and Mudge and the Long Weekend, 1992, Henry and Mudge and the Wild Wind, 1993, Henry and Mudge and the Careful Cousin, 1994, Henry and Mudge and the Best Day Ever, 1995; (poetry) Waiting to Waltz ... a Childhood, 1984 (Nat. Coun. for Social Studies Best Book 1984), Soda Jerk, 1990, Something Permanent, 1994; (novels) A Blue-Eyed Daisy, 1985 (Children's Book of Yr. Child Study Assn. Am. 1985), A Fine White Dust, 1986 (Newbery Honor Book 1987), A Kindness, 1988; (stories) Every Living Thing, 1985, Children of Christmas: Stories for the Season, 1987, A Couple of Kooks: And Other Stories About Love, 1990; (autobiography) But I'll Be Back Again: An Album, 1989, Best Wishes, 1992; (other) Appalachia: The Voices of Sleeping Birds, 1991 (Boston Globe/Horn Book Honor book for nonfiction 1991), Missing May, 1992 (John Newbery medal 1992), I Have Seen Castles, 1993, The Dreamer, 1993, The Cobble Street Cousins: A Little Shopping, 1998. Office: Simon & Schuster Children's 4th Floor 1230 Ave of The Americas New York NY 10020*

RYLEE, GLORIA GENELLE, educator; b. Commerce, Ga., Nov. 26, 1947; d. John Otis Sr. and Genelle Byrd Rylee. BS in Edn., Ga. So. Coll., 1969; MusM, Southwestern Bapt. Theol. Sem., 1973. Tchr. Banks County Bd. Edn., Homer, Ga., 1969-71; piano tchr. Ft. Worth, 1972-73; min. music, ch. sec. Mt. Olive Bapt. Ch., Commerce, Ga., 1974-81; sec. Ga. Bapt. Conv., Atlanta, 1981-86; parapro Banks County Bd. Edn., Homer, 1986-87, tchr. music, 1987—. Tchr. piano, Homer, 1975-81, 89-96; staff mem. Youth II Music Camp, Norman Park, Ga., 1996-98. Pianist Webbs Creek Bapt. Ch., Commerce, 1991—. Mem. Grassroots Arts Coun., Gainesville, Ga., 1994—; team mem. Vol. Missions-Ga. Bapt. Conv., Seoul, Korea, 1998-2000; active State Bapt. Women's Choral Group, 1979-86, 96—. Mem. Nat. Mus. Educators Assn., Music. Tchrs. Nat. Assn., Ga. Music Educators Assn., Profl. Assn. Ga. Educators. Home: 1785 Wilson Bridge Rd Homer GA 30547-2911 Office: Banks County Elem Sch 335 Evans St Homer GA 30547

RYLES, GERALD FAY, private investor, business executive; b. Walla Walla, Wash., Apr. 3, 1936; s. L. F. and Janie Geraldine (Bassett) R.; m. Ann Jane Birkenmeyer, June 12, 1959; children— Grant, Mark, Kelly. BA, U. Wash., 1958; MBA, Harvard U., 1962. With Gen. Foods Corp., White Plains, N.Y., 1962-65, Purex Corp., Ltd., Lakewood, Calif., 1966-68; cons. McKinsey & Co., Inc., Los Angeles, 1968-71; with Fibreboard Corp., San Francisco, 1971-79, v.p., 1973-75, group v.p., 1975-79; with Consol. Fibres, Inc., 1979-88, exec. v.p., 1979-81, pres., dir., 1981-86, chief exec. officer, 1986-88; cons. Orinda, 1988-90; with Interchecks Inc., 1990-92, pres., CEO, 1990-92; bus. exec., pvt. investor, 1992-94; chmn. bd., CEO Microserv, Inc., Kirkland, Wash., 1994—2001, chmn. bd., 2001—. Mem. adv. com. entrepreneur and innovation program U. Wash. Bus. Sch. Served to capt. U.S. Army, 1958-66. Mem.: Harvard Bus. Sch. Assn., U. Wash. Alumni Assn., Harbor Club (Bellevue and Seattle. Republican. Episcopalian. Home: 127 3rd Ave Apt 301 Kirkland WA 98033-6177 E-mail: geraldr@msvinc.com.

RYMAN, ROBERT TRACY, artist; b. Nashville, May 30, 1930; s. William Tracy and Nora (Boston) R.; m. Lucy Lippard, 1961 (div. 1966); children: Ethan, Ryman; m. Merrill Wagner, Jan. 31, 1969; children: William Tracy, George Corydon. Exhibited one man shows: Paul Bianchini Gallery, 1967, Solomon R. Guggenheim Mus., N.Y.C., 1972, Kunsthalle, Basel, Switzerland, 1975, Palais des Beaux-Arts, Brussels, 1974, Stedelijk Mus., Amsterdam, Netherlands, 1974, Whitechapel Gallery, London, 1977, Centre Pompidou, Paris, 1981, Sidney Janis Gallery, N.Y.C., 1981, Kunsthalle, Dusseldorf, Germay, 1982, Bonnier Gallery, N.Y.C., 1983, Daniel Weinberg Gallery, L.A., 1983, Galerie Maeght LeLong, Paris, 1984, Rhona Hoffman Gallery, Chgo., 1985, Leo Castelli Gallery, N.Y.C., 1986, Galerie Maeght LeLong, N.Y.C., 1986, Pace Gallery, N.Y.C., 1990, DIA Art Found., N.Y.C., 1988-89, Konrad Fischer Gallery, Dusseldorf, Fed. Republic Germany, 1987, Pace Gallery, N.Y., Tate Gallery, London, MMA, N.Y., San Francisco Mus. Modern Art, Walker Arts Ctr., Mpls.; group shows: Biennal Whitney Mus. Am. Art, N.Y.C., 1977, Stedelijk Mus., Amsterdam, 1978, Art of the 70's, Venice Bernnale, Italy, 1980, Haus der Kunst, Munich, 1981, Stedelijk Mus., Amsterdam, 1983, Whitney Mus. Am. Art, 1983, Skowhegan Sch. of Painting and Sculpture Medal, 1987, Whitney Biennal Exhbn, 1987; Mus. Modern Art, N.Y.C., 1985, Carnegie International, 1985; represented permanent collections: Mus. Modern Art, N.Y.C., Milw. Art Center, Stedelijk Mus., Amsterdam, Whitney Mus. Am. Art, pvt. collections; apptd. commr. City of N.Y. Art Commn. Mem. AAAL, Am. Acad. Arts and Scis., Mcpl. Art Soc. N.Y. (bd. dirs. 1991—). Home: 17 W 16th St New York NY 10011-6301 Studio: 637 Greenwich St New York NY 10014-3306 *There is never a question of what to paint, but only how to paint. The "how" of painting is the image, the end product.*

RYMAR, JULIAN W. manufacturing company executive; b. Grand Rapids, Mich., June 29, 1919; student Grand Rapids Jr. Coll., 1937-39, U. Mich., 1939-41, Am. Sch. Dramatic Arts, 1946-47, Wayne U., 1948-52, Rockhurst Coll., 1952-53; Naval War Coll., 1954-58; m. Margaret Macon Van Brunt, Dec. 11, 1954; children: Margaret Gibson, Gracen Macon, Ann Mackall. Entered USN as aviation cadet, 1942, advanced through grades to capt., 1964; chmn. bd., chief exec. officer, dir. Grace Co., Belton, Mo., 1955-90; chmn. bd. dirs. Shock & Vibration Research, Inc., 1956-66; chmn. bd., CEO Bedtime Story Fashions; bd. dirs. Am. Bank & Trust; comdg. officer Naval Air Res. Squadron, 1957-60, staff air bn. comdr., 1960-64. Mem. Kansas City Hist. Soc.; bd. dirs. Bros. of Mercy, St. Lukes Hosp.; adv. bd. dirs. St. Joseph Hosp.; trustee Missouri Valley Coll., 1969-74; pres. Rymar Found. Active Sch. Am. Rsch., Inst. Am. Arts, Mus. N.Mex. Found., Spanish Colonial Art Soc. Mem. Mil. Order World Wars, Navy League U.S. (pres. 1959-60, dir. 1960-70), Rockhill Homes Assn. (v.p.) Friends of Art (pres., chmn. bd. govs. 1969-70, exec. bd. 1971-74), Soc. of Fellows of Nelson Gallery Found. (exec. bd. 1972-77), Soc. Profl. Journalists, Press Club, Univ. of Mich. Club, Arts Club of Washington, Sch. of Am. Rsch., Santa Fe Symphony, Inst. Am. Indian Art, Mus. NMex. Found., Mus. Indian Arts & Culture, Mus. Internat. Folk Art, Mus. Fine Arts, Spanish Colonial Arts Soc., Quiet Birdman Club, Sigma Delta Chi. Episcopalian (dir., lay reader, lay chalice, vestryman, jr. warden, sr. warden, diocesan fin. bd., parish investment bd.).

RYMARCSUK, JIM ARTHUR, aerospace industry executive, consultant; b. Chgo., July 2, 1964; s. Louis Arthur and Hazel Annabelle (Oas) R.; m. Jennifer Ann Field, Aug. 26, 1989. BSME, Stanford U., 1986, MS in Astronautical Engring., 1987; MBA in Mgmt., Golden Gate U., 1989; MS in Tech. and Policy, MIT, 1993; grad., Internat. Space U., Toulouse, France, 1992. Rsch. technician Stanford Linear Accelerator Ctr., 1983-84; engring. technician U.S. Army Corps of Engrs., Warsaw, 1983-85; well test engr. Schlumberger Internat., Aberdeen, Scotland, 1985; rsch. fellow NASA-Lewis Rsch. Ctr., Cleve., 1986; internat. advisor Russian Space Enterprises MIT/Moscow Aviation Inst., Cambridge, MAss., 1992-93; engagement mgr., cons. McKinsey & Co., Washington, 1993-97; dir. mktg. and investment planning Lockheed Martin Corp., Bethesda, Md., 1997—. Advisor, cons. Nat. Ctr. for Therapeutic Riding, Washington, 1994-96; organizer, presenter NASAs Space Grant Program, Cambridge, 1991-92; pro bono cons. MIT Aerospace Engring. Dept., Cambridge, 1996. Contbr. articles to profl. jours. 1st lt. USAF, 1987-90. Fellow Smithsonian Inst., 1996—, NSF, 1990-93, Stanford U., 1987; nat. finalist White House Fellows, 1997. Mem. Stanford Engring. Assn. (bd. dirs. 1984-85), Nat. Geog. Soc., Nat. Trust for Hist. Preservation. Avocations: English riding, sailing, hiking, international travel. Office: Lockheed Martin Corp 6801 Rockledge Dr Bethesda MD 20817-1877

RYMER, ILONA SUTO, artist, retired art educator; b. N.Y.C., Dec. 1, 1921; d. Alexander and Elizabeth (Komaromy) Suto; m. Robert Hamilton Rymer, Mar. 27, 1944 (dec. Dec. 1999); children: Thomas Parker, Shelley Ilona. BA, Long Beach State U., 1953, MA, 1954. Tchr., cons. Long Beach (Calif.) Sch. Dist., 1953-56; tchr. Orange (Calif.) Sch. Dist., 1956-58; tchr., cons. Brea (Calif.)-Olinda Sch. Dist., 1958-80; ind. artist, designer Graphic Ho. Studio, Santa Ynez, 1980—, Stampa-Barbara, Santa Barbara, 1990—. Lectr. folk art Brea Sch. Dist., 1975—80. Author: (instrn. book) Folk Art U.S.A., 1975 (Proclamation City of Brea, 1975); art editor, feature writer, illustrator: Arabian Conneciton mag., 1985—86; needlepoint designer Backstitch Store, Solvang, Calif., 1982—83; one-woman shows include Liberty Bell Race Track, Pa., exhibited in group shows, 1970—, exhibitions include Dennas Mus. Ctr., Northwestern Mich. Coll., 2001, exhibited in group shows at Nat. Exhbn. Am. Watercolor, 2002, Adirondack's Nat. Exhbn. of Am. Watercolors, Old Forge, N.Y., 2002—, commission. Co-founder, mem. Gallery Los Olivos, pres., 1993—. Recipient 1st pl. Seminar award, Rex Brandt, 1961, Affiliate award, Laguna Art Mus., 1967, Best of Watercolor award, Orange County Fair, 1969, Bicentennial trip to France, Air France, 1975, Proclamation for Tchg., City of Brea, 1980, Theme award, Santa Barbara County Fair, 1991. Mem.: Artist Guild Santa Ynez Valley, Ctrl. Coast Art Assn., Santa Barbara ARt Assn., Calif. Gold Coast Watercolor Soc. (signature). Presbyterian. Studio: PO Box 822 Santa Ynez CA 93460-0822 E-mail: ilonarymer@aol.com.

RYMER, JEANNE STOCKDALE, interior design educator; b. Morgantown, W.Va., Mar. 30, 1928; d. Charles E. and Bly (Schaffer) Stockdale. AB, W. Va. U., 1949, MS in Interior Design, 1970-72; postgrad., U. N.H., 1986, Ea. Ky. U., 1977. Instr. housing and design Fairmont State Coll., W.Va., 1972-76; asst. prof. interior design Ea. Ky. U., Richmond, 1976-77; dir. McAlpin's Design Studio, Lexington, Ky., 1977-79; assoc. prof. interior design U. Del., Newark, 1979-94; prin. Lighting Design Assocs., Wilmington, Del., 1994—. Cons. in interior design, W.Va. and Ky., 1970-76; cons. in interior and lighting design Wilmington, Del., 1980—; lectr. in field. Contbr. articles to profl. jurs. Bd. dirs. Rymer Stakgold Mus., Wilmington, Del., 2001—. U. Del. Innovative Instrn. grantee, 1982, rsch. grantee for energy efficient window treatments, 1983; recipient Gov.'s award for energy innovation State of Del., 1985, Nat.

Dept. of Energy award for energy innovation, 1985, Environ. Design award Am. Soc. Interior Design, 1986; Energy Power Ptnrs. rsch. grantee, 1988. Mem.: Rymer Stakgold Mus. (dir.), Interior Design Educators Coun., Illuminating Engring. Soc., Internat. Assn. Lighting Designers (bd. dirs.), Am. Soc. Interior Designers.

RYMER, PAMELA ANN, judge; b. Knoxville, Tenn., Jan. 6, 1941; AB, Vassar Coll., 1961; LLB, Stanford U., 1964; LLD (hon.) , Pepperdine U., 1988. Bar: Calif. 1966, U.S. Ct. Appeals (9th cir.) 1966, U.S. Ct. Appeals (10th cir.), U.S. Supreme Ct. V.p. Rus Walton & Assoc., Los Altos, Calif., 1965—66; assoc. Lillick McHose & Charles, L.A., 1966—75, ptnr., 1973—75, Toy and Rymer, L.A., 1975—83; judge U.S. Dist. Ct. (cen. dist.) Calif., 1983—89, U.S. Ct. Appeals (9th cir.), L.A., 1989—. Faculty The Nat. Jud. Coll., 1986-88; mem. com. summer ednl. programs Fed. Jud. Ctr., 1987-88, mem. com. appellate judge edn., 1996-99; chair exec. com. 9th Cir. Jud. Conf., 1990; mem. com. criminal law Jud. Conf. U.S., 1988-93, Ad Hoc com. gender-based violence, 1991-94, fed.-state jurisdiction com., 1993-96; mem. commn. on structural alternatives Fed. Cts. Appeals, 1997-98. Mem. editorial bd. The Judges' jour., 1989-91; contbr. articles to profl. jours. and newsletters. Mem. Calif. Postsecondary Edn. Commn., 1974-84, chmn., 1980-84; mem. L.A. Olympic Citizens Adv. Commn.; bd. visitors Stanford U. Law Sch., 1986-99, trustee, 1991-2001, chair, 1993-96, exec. com., chmn. bd. trustees com. acad. policy, planning and mgmt. and its ad. hoc. com. athletics., chmn. bd. visitors Sch. Law, 1987—; bd. visitors Pepperdine U. Law Sch., 1987—; mem. Edn. Commn. of States Task Force on State Policy and Ind. Higher Edn., 1987-89, Carnegie Commn. Task Force Sci. and Tech. Jud. and Regulatory Decision-making, 1990-93, Commn. Substance Abuse Coll. and Univ. Campuses, 1992-94, commn. substance abuse high schs. Ctr. Addiction and Substance Abube Columbia U.; bd. dirs. Constnl. Rights Found., 1985-97, Pacific Coun. Internat. Policy, 1995—, Calif. Higher Edn. Policy Ctr., 1992-97; Jud. Conf. U.S. Com. Fed.-State Jurisdiction, 1993, Com. Criminal Law, 1988-93, ad hoc com. gender based violence, 1991-94; chair exec. com. 9th cir. jud. conf., 1990-94. Recipient Outstanding Trial Jurist award L.A. County Bar Assn., 1988; named David T. Lewis Disting. Jurist-in-Residence U. Utah, 1992. Mem. ABA (task force on civil justice reform 1991-93, mem. coord. com. agenda civil justice reform in Am. 1991), State Bar Calif. (antitrust and trade regulation sect., exec. com. 1990-92), L.A. County Bar Assn. (chmn. antitrust sect. 1981-82, mem. editl. bd. The Judges Jour. 1989-91, mem. com. professionalism 1988—, numerous other coms.), Assn. of Bus. Trial Lawyers (bd. govs. 1990-92), Stanford Alumni Assn., Stanford Law Soc. Soc. Calif., Vassar Club So. Calif. (past pres.). Office: US Ct Appeals 9th Cir US Court of Appeals Bldg 125 S Grand Ave Rm 600 Pasadena CA 91105-1621

RYMER, S. BRADFORD, JR. retired appliance manufacturing company executive; b. Cleveland, Tenn., May 30, 1915; s. S. Bradford and Clara Ladosky (Gee) R.; m. Anne Roddye Caudle, Nov. 7, 1942; children: Anita Elise, S. Bradford III. Grad., Fishburne Mil. Sch., 1933; BS in Indsl. Mgmt, Ga. Inst. Tech., 1937; D of Bus. Adminstration (hon.), Tenn. Wesleyan Coll. Indsl. engr. Dixie Foundry Co., Inc., Cleveland, Tenn., 1937-40, sec.-treas., dir. prodn., 1940-50; pres. Dixie Foundry Co., Inc. (name changed to Magic Chef Inc. 1961), 1950-61; pres., chmn. Magic Chef Inc., 1961-87; chmn. Magic Chef Inc. div. Maytag Corp., 1986-87, ret., 1987. Past chmn. Dixie-Narco, Inc., Ranson, W. Va.; forum dir. Munford Co.; former dir. Provident Life and Accident Ins. Co., Citizens & So. Nat. Bank, Atlanta. Past pres. Cleveland Asso. Industries; past trustee Tenn. Wesleyan Coll., Ga. Tech. Found.; past bd. dirs. Bradley County Meml. Hosp., Allied Arts of Chattanooga; past nat. dir. Jr. Achievement; trustee Fishburne Mil. Sch.; trustee Hiwassee Coll., John Templeton Found., 1993-99. War Tng. Svc. flight instr. World War II. Recipient Palm Beach Atlantic Colleges Am. Free Enterprise medal. Mem. Am. Gas Assn. (past exec. com., dir.), NAM (past dir.), Chief Execs. Orgn. (pres. 1971, dir.), Gas Appliance Mfrs. Assn. (pres. 1965), Young Pres. Orgn. (past dir., area v.p., chmn. Rebel chpt.), Ga. Tech. Nat. Alumni Assn. (past trustee), Toastmasters (bd. dirs. 1992-99), Phi Gamma Delta. Methodist (past chmn. bd. trustees). Home: 28 Stonedge 100 Scenic Hwy Lookout Mountain TN 37350-1267 also: Apt 28 100 Scenic Hwy Lookout Mountain TN 37350-1267 *No man is a success unto himself; for his success has been wrought with the help and talents of many associates.*

RYMER, THÉRÈSE ELIZABETH, family practice nurse practitioner; b. New London, Conn., Dec. 5, 1947; d. Kenneth Frank and Ursula Kathleen (O'Reilly) Gmeiner; m. Timothy Charles Rymer, Dec. 29, 1973; children: Gerard, Andrew, Deirdre. Diploma, St. Joseph's Coll. Nursing, 1969; cert. nurse practitioner, U. Calif., San Diego, 1976, cert. occupational health nurse, 1990, M in Advanced Studies, Leadership of Healthcare Orgns., 2002. RN, Calif.; cert. Am. Bd. Occupational Health Nurses. Staff nurse ICU Marin Gen. Hosp., San Rafael, Calif., 1969-70, Pacific Med. Ctr., San Francisco, 1970-71; staff nurse, charge nurse Mercy Hosp., San Diego, 1972-75; family practice nurse practitioner U. Calif. San Diego Med. Ctr., 1976-83, employee health nurse, coord., then dir. employee health, 1983-91; dir. clin. svc. U. Calif. San Diego Ctr. Occupational and Environ. Medicine, 1991—. Exec. steering com., mem. med. planning bd. St. Vincent de Paul/Joan Kroc Med. Clinic, San Diego; cons., lectr. Mem. editl. bd. Jour. Hosp. Occupational Health, 1993-2000; contbr. articles to profl. jours.; coord. video prodn. Mem., dep. team leader disaster med. assistance team Nat. Disaster Med. Sys., 1995—. Mem. Calif. State Assn. Occupational Health Nurses (bd. dirs. 1992-94, membership chair San Diego chpt. 1991-92), Assn. Hosp. Employee Health Profls. (pres. San Diego chpt. 1988-89). Roman Catholic. Avocations: camping, outdoor activities. Office: U Calif Ctr Occupational & Environ Med 200 W Arbor Dr San Diego CA 92103 E-mail: trymer@ucsd.edu.

RYN, CLAES GÖSTA, political science educator, author, research institute administrator; b. Norrköping, Sweden, June 12, 1943; permanent resident of U.S., 1979; s. Gösta Karl and Cecilia Edit (Blom) R.; m. Marianne Carin Tedhagen, Aug. 30, 1969; children: Charlotte, Viveka, Elisabet. Fil.kand. (MA), Uppsala (Sweden) U., 1967, postgrad., 1969-71, Syracuse U., 1968-69; PhD, La. State U., 1974. Asst. prof. politics Cath. U. Am., Washington, 1974-78, assoc. prof. politics, 1978-82, prof. politics, 1982—; asst. dean Sch. Arts and Scis., Catholic U. Am., 1977-79; chmn. dept. politics Catholic U. Am., 1979-85. Adj. prof. govt. Georgetown U.; vis. assoc. prof. U. Va., Charlottesville, 1981; co-founder, chmn. Nat. Humanities Inst., Washington, 1984—; referee, evaluator NEH, Dept. Edn., USIA, pubs., jours., others; dir. numerous scholarly confs. and lecture series; mem. Richard M. Weaver fellowship selection com., 1980—; faculty sponsor Earhart Found., 1989—; mem. awards com. Ingersoll Prizes, 1990; mem. Salvatori doctoral fellowship selection com. Intercollegiate Studies Inst., 1990—; lectr. series Peking U., May 2000; numerous appearances on TV and radio, U.S., internat. Author: (with Bertil Häggman) Nykonservatismen i USA, 1971, Democracy and the Ethical Life, 1978, 2nd expanded edit., 1990, Will, Imagination and Reason, 1986, 2nd expanded edit., 1997, Individualism och Gemenskap, 1986, The New Jacobinism, 1991, Unity Through Diversity (in Chinese), 2001, In the Name of Democracy, 2003; editor: Humanitas, 1992—; co-editor (with George Panichas), author (with others): Irving Babbitt in Our Time, 1986; editor, author introduction for other volumes; contbr. numerous articles to profl. jours. and collective vols.; mem. editl. adv. bd. Modern Age, 1981—; editl. advisor Marknadsekonomisk Tidskrift, Sweden, 1986-92; mem. editl. bd. This World, 1992—; editl. columnist Svenska Dagbladet, Sweden, 1996—. Mem. vestry St. Francis Episcopal Ch., Potomac, Md., 1986-88. Served with Swedish Army, Royal Life Company I 4 Regt., 1963, Signal Corps, 1967-68. Rsch. fellow various orgns., including Earhart Found., 1980-81, 87-88, Wilbur Found., 1980-81, 90, 93-94; Disting. Fgn. scholar Peking U., 2000; recipient award King of Sweden, 1983; named Outstanding Grad. Prof., Cath. U. Am., 1992. Mem. Phila. Soc. (trustee 1999, 2d v.p. 2000-01, pres. 2001—). Episcopalian. Home: 10008 Crestleigh Ln Potomac MD 20854-1820 Office: Cath Univ Am Dept Politics Washington DC 20064-0001

RYNEAR, NINA COX, retired registered nurse, author, artist; b. Cochranville, Pa., July 11, 1916; d. Fredrick Allen and Nina Natalie (Drane) Cox; m. Charles Spencer Rynear, Aug. 22, 1934 (dec. May 1941); children: Charles Joseph, Stanley Spencer. RN, Coatesville Hosp. Sch. Nursing, 1945; BS in Nursing Edn., U. Pa., 1954. Interviewer Nat. Opinion Rsch. Ctr., U. Denver, Colo., 1942-47; sch. nurse West Goshen Elem. Sch., West Chester, Pa., 1946-47; pub. health nurse Pa. Dept. Health Bur. Pub. Health Nursing, Harrisburg, 1947-51; staff nurse V.A. Hosp., Coatesville, Pa., 1951-54, staff nurse, asst. head nurse Menlo Park, Calif., 1954-56; asst. chief nursing svc. Palo Alto and Menlo Park VA Hosps., Palo Alto, Menlo Park, 1956-76; self employed Reno, 1976—. Author: (poems, musical compositions) Old Glory and the U.S.A., 1989, Mister Snowman, 1988, Dawn Shadow of Lenape, 1988; (poem and song compilation) This Side of Forever, 1990; (musical compositions) Blessed Are Those Who Listen, The Hobo's Promise, What Can I Leave, 1998, Visit with Santa, 2000, Glad Tidings, 2000, The Summer of the Church School Class; (children's stories) Wilyum of Orange 1st, Lady Harley and Pepper, 1995; composer: Visit With Santa, Hilltop Records; other works include Pathways (in Tracing Shadows/Nat. Libr. Poetry), 1997, In Remembrance of Diana, Princess of Wales, 1998 (poem), Athanasia (poem), 1998, Legend of the Goose Boy, 1999; contbr. sonnets to Newsletter of N.Am. Acad. Esoteric Studies; paintings represented in numerous pvt. collections. Pres. Chester County Pub. Health Nurses Assn., 1950. Staff nurse Cadet Corps, 1944-45. Mem. VFW Aux. (patriotic instr. 1989-90, chmn. safety div. Silver State #3396 chpt. 1990-91), New Century Rebekah Lodge #244. Methodist. Home and Office: 3476 Harbor Beach Dr Lake Wales FL 33859-8059

RYNEVELD, EDNA LYNN COPELAND, small business owner; b. San Antonio, Sept. 12, 1943; d. L.D. and Mary Edna (Smith) Copeland; m. Mariuus Ryneveld, Dec. 16, 1969 (div. Feb. 1994). BA, Tex. Womens U., 1967. Various sec. jobs, Dallas, 1962-67; sec. high-energy physics lab., math. dept. Stanford U., Palo Alto, Calif., 1967-76; sec. Kaiser Aerospace, 1967-76; copy writer Sta. KYOO Radio, Bolivar, Mo., 1978-82; owner New Life Natural Foods, 1981—. Spkr., workshop leader in field. Author: Transits in Reverse, 1988, Secrets of A Natural Menopause, 1994, Menopause, A Gentle, Natural Approach, 2d edit., 1998; contbr. (book) Sacred Sites in America, 1992. Mem. AAUW, NOW, NAFE. Avocations: photography, water color painting, reading, carpentry, alternative healing. Office: New Life Natural Foods 451B S Springfield Ave Bolivar MO 65613-2147 E-mail: andes43@cs.com.

RYNKIEWICZ, STEPHEN MICHAEL, journalist; b. Sheboygan, Wis., Oct. 20, 1955; s. Walter Paul and Ruth Catherine (Van Hercke) R.; m. Brenda Gail Russell, Sept. 27, 1986. BA, U. Wis., 1976. Various staff assignments Chgo. Sun-Times, 1979-97, real estate editor, 1990-97; Internet prodr. Chgo. Tribune, 1997-2000. Pres. Ill. Freedom of Info. Coun., 1991-93; mem. profl. faculty Columbia Coll., Chgo., 1998; dir. Nat. Assn. Real Estate Editors, 1999—. Pres. Chgo. Headline Club, 1991-92, treas., 2001—. Mem. Soc. Profl. Journalists (regional dir. 1992-95, sec. treas. 1995-96, membership chair 1997-98, diversity chair 1996-97), Nat. Soc. Real Estate Editors (bd. dirs. 1999—), Sigma Delta Chi Found. (bd. dirs. 1995-96). Office: Ste 400 435 N Michigan Ave Chicago IL 60611-4001

RYNN, NATHAN, physics educator, consultant; b. N.Y.C., Dec. 2, 1923; s. Meyer and Rose (Wolkerwiczer) Rynkowsky; m. Glenda Brown, June 24, 1989; children by previous marriage: Jonathan, Margaret, David. BSEE, CCNY, 1944; MS, U. Ill., 1947; PhD, Stanford U., 1956. Rsch. engr. RCA Labs., Princeton, N.J., 1947-52; rsch. asst. Stanford U., Palo Alto, Calif., 1952-56, rsch. assoc., 1958; mem. tech. staff Ramo-Woolridge, L.A., 1956-57; supr. Huggins Labs., Menlo Park, Calif., 1957-58; rsch. staff physicist Princeton U., 1958-65; prof. physics U. Calif.-Irvine, 1965-94, prof. physics emeritus, rsch. prof. physics, 1994—. Vis. prof. Ecole Polytechnique Fed. of Lausanne, Switzerland, 1984-90, Ecole Polytechnique, Paris, and other European univs. and labs., 1973-80; indsl. sci. advisor/cons., 1964—; com. mem. Plasma Sci. Com. Nat. Rsch. Coun.; founder and leader plasma physics rsch. facility. Contbr. articles and revs. to profl. jours. With USN, 1944-46. Grantee NSF, U.S. Dept. Energy, Air Force Geophys. Lab.; Fulbright sr. fellow, 1978. Fellow Am. Phys. Soc., IEEE, AAAS; mem. Am. Geophys. Union, Sigma Xi. Office: U Calif Dept Physics & Astronomy Irvine CA 92697-4575 E-mail: nrynn@uci.edu.

RYPCZYK, CANDICE LEIGH, employee relations executive; b. Norman, Okla., Apr. 24, 1949; d. John Anthony and Lee (Brunswick) Wirth; m. Peter Charles Rypczyk, Nov. 27, 1976. BA, Kalamazoo Coll., 1971; cert. labor studies extension program, Cornell U., N.Y. Sch. Indsl., Labor Relations, Middletown, 1985. Personnel asst. PFW divsn. Hercules Inc., Middletown, N.Y., 1973-77, asst. personnel mgr., 1977-79, mgr. employee relations, 1979-92; mgr. human resources Huck Internat., Kingston, 1992-2000. Mem. DAR, Soc. for Human Resource Mgmt. (v.p. Mid-Hudson Valley chpt. 1985, pres. 1986, treas. N.Y. State coun. 1986, dist. bd. dirs. 1988-90, cert.), Orange County C. of C. (Vol. of the Yr. 1986, program com., treas., exec. com.). Avocations: photography, reading, genealogy.

RYPKA, EUGENE WESTON, microbiologist; b. Owatonna, Minn., May 6, 1925; s. Charles Frederick and Ethel Marie (Ellerman) R.; m. Rosemary Speeker, June 1, 1967. Student, Carleton Coll., 1946-47; BA, Stanford U., 1950, PhD, 1958. Prof. microbiology, systems, cybernetics U. N.Mex., Albuquerque, 1957-62; bacteriologist Leonard Wood Meml. Lab. Johns Hopkins U., Balt., 1962-63; sr. scientist Lovelace Med. Ctr., Albuquerque, 1963-71, chief microbiologist, 1971-93. Adj. prof. U. N.Mex., 1973—; cons. Hoffmann-LaRoche Inc., 1974—. Airline Pilots Assn., Washington, 1976, Pasco Lab., Denver, 1983—; advisor Nat. Com. Clinic Lab. Standards, Pa., 1980-84. Contbr. articles to profl. jours. and chpts. in books. Served with USNR, USMC 1943-46. Fellow AAAS. Republican. Presbyterian. Avocations: martial arts, bicycle racing, pets. Home: PO Box 1637 Cedar Crest NM 87008-1637 E-mail: gryba@mindspring.com.

RYSAVY, RICHARD LUDWIG, physician; b. Owatonna, Minn., Apr. 20, 1949; s. Ludwig John and Lula (Ressler) R.; m. Wendy Storch, Sept. 4, 1971; children: Erin, Michael, Timothy, Meghan. BA, St. Mary's U., 1971; MD, U. Minn., 1976. Diplomate Am. Bd. Family Practice. Resident Duluth (Minn.) Family Practice, 1976-79; family physician St. Cloud (Minn.) Med. Group, 1979—. Fellow Am. Acad. Family Practice; mem. Minn. Acad. Family Practice, Minn. Med. Assn. Office: St Cloud Med Group NW 4544 County Road 134 Saint Cloud MN 56303-9546

RYSER, HUGUES JEAN-PAUL, pharmacologist, medical educator, cell biologist; b. Chaux-de-Fonds, Switzerland, June 11, 1926; came to U.S., 1958, naturalized, 1972; s. Ernest Jacob and Marthe Alice (Zimmermann) R.; m. Carol Leigh Pierson, June 10, 1961; children: Marc Alain, Jeannine, Eve. MD, U. Berne, Switzerland, 1953, Dr. Med., 1955. Instr. pharmacology Harvard U. Med. Sch., Boston, 1960-62, assoc. in pharmacology, 1962-64, asst. prof. pharmacology, 1964-69; assoc. prof. cell biology and pharmacology U. Md. Med. Sch., Balt., 1969-70, prof., 1970-72; prof. pathology and pharmacology Sch. Medicine, Boston U., 1972—, prof. biochemistry, 1981—; prof. pub. health Sch. Pub. Health, Boston U., 1980—. Contbr. numerous articles to sci. jours. Bd. dirs. Am. Cancer Soc., Mass. div., 1983-97. Recipient Lederle Med. Faculty award, 1964-67; Nat. Cancer Inst. Rsch. Career Devel. awardee, 1968-69, grantee, 1972-97; NIH rsch. grantee, 1961-69, 97-2000, Am. Cancer Soc. Instl. Rsch. grantee, 1975-2000, Pediat. Aids Found. grantee, 1997-99. Fellow AAAS; mem. Am. Assn. Cancer Rsch., Am. Soc. Cell Biology, Am. Soc. Exptl. Pharmacology and Therapeutics. Home: 503 Annursnac Hill Rd Concord MA 01742-5414 Office: Boston U 715 Albany St Boston MA 02118-2526 E-mail: hryser@bu.edu. *My purpose as an educator is to engage in the creative process of making important knowledge exciting. As a scientist, I am driven by curiosity and derive pleasure from being at the cutting edge of a field, however narrow it may be.*

RYSKAMP, CARROLL JOSEPH, retired chemical engineer; b. Grand Rapids, Mich., Dec. 25, 1930; s. Henry C. and Edna E. (Robinson) R.; m. Joanne Ruth Winter, Nov. 17, 1951; children: Jan C., John M., Julie K., Jay A. BS in Chem. Engring., Wayne State U., 1953. Registered profl. control systems engr. Chem. engr. Reichhold Chem. Co., Ferndale, Mich., 1953-55; process supv. and specialist Marathon Oil Co., Detroit, 1955-65, process control coordinator Findlay, Ohio, 1965-70; control cons. Foxboro (Mass.) Co., 1970-85; owner Process Performance Co., Foxboro, 1986; ret. Contbr. articles to profl. jours.; patentee in field. Bristol fellow, The Foxboro Co., 1985. Mem. Instrument Soc. Am. (sr., Philip T. Sprague award, 1981). Republican. Avocations: electronics, travel. Home and Office: 48 Prospect St Foxboro MA 02035-1724

RYSKAMP, CHARLES ANDREW, museum executive, educator; b. East Grand Rapids, Mich., Oct. 21, 1928; s. Henry Jacob and Flora (DeGraaf) R. AB, Calvin Coll., 1950; MA, Yale U., 1951, PhD, 1956; postgrad., Pembroke Coll., Cambridge U., 1953-54; Litt.D., Trinity Coll., Hartford, 1975; L.H.D., Union Coll., 1977. Nathan Hale fellow Yale U., 1954-55; instr. English Princeton U., 1955-59, asst. prof., 1959-63, assoc. prof., 1963-69; curator English and Am. lit. Univ. Library, 1967-69, prof., 1969—. Procter & Gamble faculty fellow, 1958-59; jr. fellow Council of Humanities, 1960-61, John E. Annan preceptor, 1961-64; dir. Pierpont Morgan Library, N.Y.C., 1969-87, dir. emeritus, fellow (hon.), 1997—; dir. Frick Collection, N.Y.C., 1987-97, dir. emeritus, fellow (hon.), 1997—; dir. vis. Inst. Advanced Study, Princeton, 1997-99; exhbn. of drawings, Pierpont Morgan Libr., 2001; mem. adv. bd. Skowhegan Sch. Painting and Sculpture, Pvt. Papers of James Boswell, Yale U. Author: William Cowper of the Inner Temple, Esq. 1959, William Blake, Engraver, 1969; editor: (with F.A. Pottle) Boswell: The Ominous Years, 1963, The Cast-Away, 1963, Wilde and the Nineties, 1966, William Blake: The Pickering Manuscript, 1972, (with J. King) The Letters and Prose Writings of William Cowper, vol. I, 1979, vol. II, 1981, vol. III, 1982, Vol. IV, 1984, Vol. V, 1986, (with R. Wendorf) The Works of William Collins, 1979, (with J. Baird) The Poetical Works of William Cowper, vol. I, 1980, vols. II-III, 1995, (with J. King) William Cowper: Selected Letters, 1989, Report to the Fellows of the Pierpont Morgan Library, vols. 16-21, 1969-89, Charles Ryskamp and Friends, 1999, (with Scott Westrem) The Works of John Chalkhill, 1999. Trustee, mem. exec. com. Mus. Broadcasting, 1977-87; trustee John Simon Guggenheim Meml. Found., Libr. of Am., Amon Carter Mus., trustee emeritus; past mem. vis. com. dept. paintings conservation Met. Mus. Art; patron William Blake Trust; mem. bd. mgrs. Lewis Walpole Libr., Yale U.; bd. dirs., v.p. Gerard B. Lambert Found.; v.p. Frederick R. Koch Found.; mem. Venetian Heritage. Decorated Order St. John of Jerusalem, comdr. Order Orange Nassau, The Netherlands, officer Order Leopold II, Belgium, comdr. Order of Falcon, Iceland; recipient Peter Stuyvesant award Dutch Am. West-India Co., 1987, Gold medal Holland Soc., 1991. Mem. Am. Acad. Arts and Scis., Am. Philos. Soc., Museums Coun. N.Y.C. (past v.p.), Keats-Shelley Assn. Am. (past v.p.), Master Drawings Assn. (past pres.), Met. Opera Assn. (bd. advisors), Drawing Soc. (nat. com.), Bibliog. Soc. Am., Acad. Am. Poets, Am. Antiquarian Soc., Assn. Art Mus. Dirs. (past pres.), N.Y. Geneal. and Biog. Soc. (spl. corr.), Neuropathy Assn. (nat. adv. coun.), Cowper Soc., Assn. Internationale de Bibliophilie (com. of Honor), Found. French Mus. (adv. bd.), Wordsworth Rydel Mount Trust, Pilgrims, Grolier Club, Century Assn., Lotos Club, Knickerbocker Club, Elizabethan Club (New Haven), Roxburghe Club (London).

RYSKAMP, KENNETH LEE, federal judge; b. 1932; m. Karyl Sonja Ryskamp; 1 child, Cara Leigh. AB, Calvin Coll., 1954; JD, U. Miami, 1956. Bar: Fla. 1956, Mich. 1957, U.S. Supreme Ct. 1970. Law clk. to presiding judge Fla. Ct. Appeals 3d Dist., 1957-59; pvt. practice Miami, Fla., 1959-61; ptnr. Goodwin, Ryskamp, Welcher & Carrier, 1961-84; mng. ptnr. Squire, Sanders & Dempsey, 1984-86; judge U.S. Dist. Ct. (so. dist.) Fla., 1986—. Office: US Dist Ct 701 Clematis St Rm 416 West Palm Beach FL 33401-5112

RYTI, RANDALL TODD, scientist; b. Chgo., Mar. 12, 1958; s. Warren Douglas and June Elizabeth R.; m. Wendy Lee Swanson, July 15, 1993; children: Lora Whitmore, Ben Whitmore. BA, U. Calif., L.A., 1979; PhD, U. Calif., San Diego, 1986. Rsch. scientist Mont. State U., Bozeman, 1987-92; scientist Neptune and Co., Inc., Los Alamos, N.Mex., 1992—. Contbr. articles to profl. jours. Mem. Am. Soc. Naturalists, Am. Statis. Assn., Ecol. Soc. Am., Soc. Risk Analysis, Soc. Environ. Toxicology and Chemistry. Avocation: basketball. Office: Neptune and Co Inc 1505 15th St Ste B Los Alamos NM 87544 Fax: 505-662-0500. E-mail: rryti@neptuneinc.org.

RYU, JAY H. physician, educator, researcher; b. May 25, 1951; BA, Johns Hopkins U., 1974, MD, 1978. Cons. divsn. pulmonary and critical care medicine Mayo Clinic, Rochester, 1989; dir. tng. program divsn. pulmonary & critical care medicine Mayo Grad. Sch. Medicine, 1990—95; assoc. prof. medicine Mayo Med. Sch., Minn., 1993—2002, prof. medicine, 2002—. Author: Comprehensive Respiratory Medicine, 1999; co-editor: Year Book of Pulmonary Medicine, 1998—2002. Office: Mayo Clinc and Mayo Found Div Pulm and Crit Care Med 200 1st St SW Rochester MN 55905-0001

RYU, KYOO-HAI LEE, physiologist; b. Seoul, Republic of Korea, Sept. 5, 1948; came to U.S., 1972; d. Hee Soon and Jung Ock Lee; m. David Tai-Hyung Ryu, May 13, 1978; children: Eugenia, Christina, John. BS, Yonsei U., Seoul, 1971; PhD, U. Minn., 1981. Postdoctoral fellow U. Minn., Mpls., 1980-81, staff scientist, 1981-82; sr. rsch. assoc. Wright State U., Dayton, Ohio, 1985-91; adminstr. Ohio Ctr. of Cosmetic Surgery, Bellefontaine, 1991—. Home: 15 Bexley Ave Springfield OH 45503-1103

RYUN, JIM, congressman; b. Wichita, Kans. m. Anne Ryun; children: Ned, Drew, Catharine, Heather. Founder, pres. Jim Ryun Sports, Inc.; mem. Congress from 2d Kans. dist., 1996—, comm. on armed services, comm. on the budget, comm. on financial services. Participant Olympic Games, 1964, 68, 72. Recipient Silver medal 1500 meter run Olympic Games, 1968; held world record in the mile, 1500 meters, 800 yards. Office: 330 Cannon Ho Office Bldg Washington DC 20515-0001 : 800 SW Jackson Ste 100 Topeka KS 66612*

RYUZD, HIGUCHI, medical educator; b. Wakayama, Japan, Sept. 28, 1948; s. Kiyoshi and Toyoko Higuchi; m. Kimi Imotani; children: Yuichi, Hisako, Ryoko. MD, Wakayama (Japan) Med. U., 1974, PhD, 1989. Head divsn. pediat. Hidaka Hosp., Japan, 1980—82; chief instr. neonatal ICU Wakayama Med. Coll., 1985—99, assoc. prof., 1999—. Pres. Kinakuni Co-op Union, Wakayama, 1983—99. Home: 89-4 Fiuchu Wakayama 649-6338 Japan Office: Wakayama Med Univ Wakayama 641-0012 Japan

SA, LILY, artist, educator; b. St. Petersbourg, Russia, Sept. 26, 1909; came to the U.S., 1970; d. Yin-Tu Sa and Lan-Hsing Wang; m. Tan-Chi Sang, June 6, 1945 (dec. Aug. 1987); children: Barbara Liang Sang, Rebecca Liang Sang, Mildred Liang Sang. BS, Coll. S.I., 1984; MFA, CUNY, 1991; postgrad., NYU, 1993—. Recipient Women of Excellence award CUNY Women's Coalition, N.Y.C., 1992. Mem. Pi Lambda Theta (Rho chpt.), Golden Key Nat. Honor Soc. Home: 36 Hamilton Ave Staten Island NY 10301-1816

SAAB, DEANNE KELTUM, real estate appraiser, real estate broker; b. Allentown, Pa., Jan. 27, 1945; d. James A. and Agnes G. (Hanzlik) S. BA, Cedar Crest Coll., 1966; MS, U. Calif., Santa Barbara, 1973; realtors cert., Pa. State U., 1978. Cert. appraiser Assoc. Appraisal Inst., Pa., 1991; cert. sales profl. Nat. Assn. Home Builders, 1994. Tchr. Ojai (Calif.) Unified Sch. Dist., 1966-74; pvt. practice Allentown, Pa., 1978—; pres./treas. DeAnne & Assoc., Inc., 1987—; owner Heritage Gardens, 1981—. Co-founder, treas. performance group Lehigh Valley Folk Music Soc., 1996. Mem. AAUW (various offices, Best State Newsletter award 1987), Nat. Assn. Realtors, Pa. Assn. Realtors, Allentown Lehigh Valley Assn. Realtors, Cedar Crest Coll. Alumnae Assn. (class rep., various offices), Lehigh Valley Guild Craftsmen (various offices). Avocations: gourd, herbal crafting, painting, folk music performance. Home and Office: 1360 Dorney Ave Allentown PA 18103-9731

SAAD, BARBARA T. occupational health nurse, administrator; b. Takoma Park, Md., Apr. 9, 1942; d. Ernest Leroy and Jean Marie (Oliver) Thompson; m. John R. Saad, May 28, 1961; children: John R., Daniel Lewis. AA, Palomar Coll., San Marcos, Calif., 1971; BSNS, Nat. U., San Diego, 1982. Pres. Saad Enterprises, Escondido, Calif.; Nurse in emergency room, med.-surg., ICU, telemetry Palomar Meml. Hosp.; nursing mgr. Doctors Care Med. Ctr., Carlsbad, Escondido and Oceanside, Calif.; occupational health nurse Hewlett Packard Co., San Diego. Mem. San Diego Assn. Occupational Health Nurses.

SAAD, EDWARD THEODORE, architect; b. Jan. 25, 1923; s. Theodore and Kafa (Ghandour) S.; m. Alice Ruth Harms, May 24, 1954; children: Roxana, Theodore, Lydia, Mark. BA in Archtl. Engring., U. Nebr., 1953. Project mgr. Eero Saarinen & Assocs., Bloomfield Hills, Mich., 1955-65; ptnr. Harold Roth & Edward Saad, Hamden, Conn., 1965-72; prin. Edward Saad & Assocs. Architects, Cheshire, 1973—. Cons. Upjohn Co., North Haven, Conn., 1966-67, Cheshire Acad., The Apostles of Sacred Heart Acad., 1990, Meml. Sch., Middlefield, Conn., 1996, John Lyman Sch., Middlefield, 1996, Sacred Heart Acad., Hamden, 1996, Village Sch., A.C.E.S., N. Haven, Conn., 1997, St. Peter's Episcopal Ch. Parish Addition, Cheshire, Conn., 2000. Important archtl. works include Mack House, Cheshire, 1966; Surf Club West, Milford, Conn., 1967; Trinity Ch., Orange, Conn., 1967; No. Br. YMCA, Hamden, 1968; West Rock Nature Ctr., New Haven, 1968; Ridge Hill Sch., Hamden, 1970; Ernsestine Stodelle Dance Studio, Cheshire, 1973; Cheshire Pub. Libr.,

1974; Cheshire Acad. Place Profl. Ctr., 1976; Conn. 7-Up Bottling Co. Hdqrs., Meriden, 1979; R.T. Barba Hdqrs. Office Bldg., Greenwich, Conn., 1982, Cheshire Acad. Girl's Dormitory, 1984, Marshall Fisco Offices and Gymnastic Ctr., Cheshire, Conn., 1985, Dowling Ford Offices and Comml. Complex, Cheshire, 1986, A.C.E.S. Staff Devel. Ctr., Hamden, Conn., 1987, Church St. Sch., Hamden, 1987, Circuit-Wise Mfg. Facilities, Chihuahua, Mexico, 1988, Dunbar Hill Sch., Hamden, 1995, Sacred Heart Academy, Hamden, 1996, Durham Schs., Middlefield, 1997, Village Spl. Edn. Sch., North Haven, 1998, William Douglas Spl. Edn. Sch., North Bramnord, 1999, St. Peter's Episcopal Ch., Cheshire, 2000, Ednl. Ctr. Arts Magnet Sch., New Haven, 2000. Mem. AIA (corp. mem., Honor award New Eng. chpt. 1968, Honor award nat. council religious architecture div. 1970). Club: Rotary (bd. dirs. Hamden, pres. 1972-73). Address: 608 S Brooksvale Rd Cheshire CT 06410-3517 E-mail: esanda@worldnet.att.net.

SAAD, GERMAINE H. finance educator, researcher; b. Bany-Suef, Egypt, Nov. 26, 1944; d. Hozayen and Helpis Saad; m. Ayoub Barsoum Ayoub, Feb. 5, 1972; children: Mariane Ayoub; m. Makram Ragheb, Apr. 10, 1966 (dec. Feb. 9, 1968); children: Sameh Ragheb. PhD, Wharton Sch., U. of Pa, Philadelphia, PA, 1980, MA, 1978; MBA, Cairo U., Guiza, Egypt, 1970, BCom, 1964. Educator Widener U., Chester, Pa., 1986—, CUNY, New York, NY, 1982—84, Ain-Shams U., Cairo, Egypt, 1980—86, U. of Pa, Philadelphia, Pa., 1978—80, grad. asst., 1975—78; demonstrator and educator Cairo U., Guiza, Egypt, 1964—74. Editl. bd. mem. Bus. Jour., New Haven, 1991—, Jour. of Mgmt. Systems, Arlington, Va., 1989—95; cons. Ctrl. Agy. for Organizations and Administrations, Cairo, 1984—86. Contbr. articles to profl. jours. Fund raising participant Am. Soc. for Cancer, Philadelphia, Pa., 1999—2001; vol. Abington Meml. Hosp., Abington, 1999; bd. mem. St. George Orthodox Ch., Norristown, 1997—2002. Christian-Orthodox. Avocations: painting, travel, artwork. Home: 1847 Watson Road Abington PA 19001 Office: Widener University One University Place Chester PA 19013 Office Fax: 610-499-4644. E-mail: germain.h.saad@widener.edu.

SAAD, VALERIE ANN, nursing administrator, naval officer; b. Easton, Pa., Oct. 12, 1954; d. Samuel and Josephine (Badway) S. BSN, Seton Hall U., 1976. RN, Pa., N.J.; cert. advanced trauma life support, BCLS instr., Lamaze instr. Nurse ob-gyn, operating room, newborn nursery med.-surg. ICU Easton (Pa.) Hosp., 1976-77; commd. ensign Nurse Corps, USN, 1977, advanced through grades to lt. comdr., 1989; staff nurse Naval Regional Med. Ctr., Orlando, Fla., 1977-80; intern operating rm. nursing program Mass. Gen. Hosp., Boston, 1980-81; nurse Allentown (Pa.)-Sacred Heart Hosp. Ctr., 1981-82; staff nurse MOR, charge nurse, clin. instr. Naval Hosp., Bethesda, Md., 1983-87, relief supr. ambulatory care Portsmouth, Va., 1987-89, staff nurse main operating rm. Phila., 1989-91, staff nurse perioperative nursing San Diego, 1991-97; dir. surg. svcs. Riverview Med. Ctr., Red Bank, N.J., 1997-00; dir. ambulatory surg. ctr. Holy Redeemer Healthcare Sys., Meadowbrook, Pa., 2000—. Contbr. articles to nursing jours. Mem. Phi Delta Kappa, Sigma Theta Tau. Avocations: cooking, sewing, needle point. Home: 164 Linden Ave Highlands NJ 07732-1328

SAADA, ADEL SELIM, civil engineer, educator; b. Heliopolis, Egypt, Oct. 24, 1934; came to U.S., 1959, naturalized, 1965; s. Selim N. and Marie (Chahyne) S.; m. Nancy Helen Hernan, June 5, 1960; children: Christiane Mona, Richard Adel. Ingénieur des Arts et Manufactures, École Centrale, Paris, 1958; MS, U. Grenoble, France, 1959; PhD in Civil Engring, Princeton U., 1961. Registered profl. engr., Ohio. Engr. Société Dumez, Paris, 1959; research assoc. dept. civil engring. Princeton (N.J.) U., 1961-62; asst. prof. civil engring. Case Western Reserve U., Cleve., 1962-67, asso. prof., 1967-72, prof., 1973—, chmn. dept. civil engring., 1978-98, Frank H. Neff prof. civil engring., 1987. R.J. Carroll Meml. lectr. Johns Hopkins U., 1990; cons., lectr. soil testing and properties Waterways Expt. Sta. (C.E.), Vicksburg, Miss., 1974-79; cons. to various firms, 1962— . Author: Elasticity Theory and Applications, 1974, 2d edit., 1993; contbr. numerous articles on soil mechanics and foundation engring. to profl. jours. Recipient Telford Prize Instn. of Civil Engrs., U.K., 1995, Disting. Leadership award Cleve. Tech. Socs., 2001. Fellow ASCE (named Outstanding Civil Engr. of Yr. Cleve. sect. 1992); mem. Internat. Soc. Soil Mechanics, ASTM, One Two One Athletic Club. Achievements include invention of pneumatic analog computer and loading frame. Home: 3342 Braemar Rd Shaker Heights OH 44120-3332 Office: Case Western Res U Dept Civil Engring Case Sch Engring Cleveland OH 44106 E-mail: axs31@po.cwru.edu.

SAADE, GEORGE ROBERT, physician; b. Paris, Oct. 05; MD, Am. Univ. Beirut, Beirut, Lebanon, 1985. Diplomate Am. Bd. Obstetrics and Gynecology. Asst. prof. Baylor Coll. Medicine, Houston, 1994-95; assoc. prof. U. Tex. Med. Br., Galveston, 1995—2002, prof., 2002—. Co-dir. Maternal-Fetal Medicine fellowship Univ. Tex. Medical Br., Galveston, 1998—. Contbr. articles to profl. jours. Recipient Outstanding Individual Contributions Soc. Perinatal Obstetricians, 1998. Mem. Alpha Omega Alpha, Tau Beta Pi. Office: The Univ Tex Medical Br 301 University Blvd Galveston TX 77555-5302

SAADIAN, JAVID, cultural organization administrator, consultant; b. Tehran, Iran, Dec. 25, 1953; came to U.S., 1971; s. Avshalom and Akhtar (Barookhian) S.; m. Janet Elissa Salins, Dec. 30, 1978 (div.); children: Jason, Sarah, Susan. Student, Montgomery Coll., spring 1972; BS in Acctg., U. Md., 1976. CPA, Md., Va. Acct. Lewis Kest and Co., Washington, 1977-78; auditor, sr. acct. Aronson, Greene, Fisher & Co., Bethesda, Md., 1978-80; auditor Price Waterhouse, Washington, 1980-81, contr., 1981-83; dir. fin. Mt. Vernon Estate and Gardens and subs., 1983-94, assoc. dir. for fin. and adminstrn., 1994-2000; CFO, COO Bermuda Biol. Sta. for Rsch., St. George, 2000—. Cons. various orgns. Washington met. area, 1979—; mem. U.S. Taxation, Acctg. and Bus. Del. to China and Hong Kong, 1989. Fin. advisor Ft. Hunt Coop. Presch., Alexandria, 1986-89; treas. Collingwood on Potomac Homeowners Assn., Alexandria, 1987-89; mem. budget and fin. com. Mt. Vernon Coun. of Citizens Assns., 1988, treas., 1988-89; treas., mem. fin. com., bd. dirs. Adat Reyim Congregation, 1991, fin. v.p., 1996-99. Recipient cert. of merit SBA, Washington, 1976. Mem. AICPA, Va. Soc. CPA's, Am. Soc. Assn. Execs., Fairfax C of C, Mt. Vernon-Lee C. of C. (1982-91), Beta Alpha Psi (chmn. tutoring com. 1976). Jewish. Avocations: volleyball, physical fitness, backgammon, swimming, philately. Office: Bermuda Biol Station 31 Biological Ln Saint George GE01 Bermuda E-mail: jay@bbsr.edu.

SAAKVITNE, KAREN WINSLOW, psychologist; b. Chappaqua, N.Y., Aug. 13, 1957; BA, Yale U., 1979; MA, U. Mich., 1984, PhD, 1986. Lic. psychologist, Conn., Mass. Post doctoral fellow Austen Riggs Ctr., Stockbridge, Mass., 1986-90; clin. dir. Traumatic Stress Inst., South Windsor, Conn., 1990—. Author: Trauma and the Therapist, 1995, Transforming the Pain, 1996, Risking Connection, 2000, Relational Teaching, Experiential Learning: The Teaching Manual for Risking Connection, 2001. Mem.: APA (sec. divsn. psychoanalysis 1998—2000, bd. profl. affairs adv. com. colleague assistance 1998—2001), Internat. Soc. for Traumatic Stress Studies. Office: TSI/CAAP 22 Morgan Farms Dr South Windsor CT 06074-1385 E-mail: kwstsi@snet.net.

SAAL, HOWARD MAX, clinical geneticist, pediatrician, educator; b. N.Y.C., Aug. 20, 1951; s. Josef and Ester (Morgenstern) S.; m. Cara Tina Schweitzer, May 3, 1987; 1 child, Rebecca. BS, U. Mass., Amherst, 1973, MS, 1975; MD, Wayne State U., 1979. Intern pediatrics U. Conn. Med. Ctr., 1979-80; resident pediatrics U. Conn. Health Ctr., 1980-82; fellow med. genetics U. Wash. Sch. Medicine, 1982-84; dir. cytogenetics U. Conn. Health Ctr., Farmington, 1984-87; vice chmn. med. genetics Children's Nat. Med. Ctr., Washington, 1987-93, head clin. genetics Cin., 1993—. Asst. prof. pediats. George Washington U., Washington, 1987-93, assoc. prof. pediats., 1993; assoc. prof. clin. pediats. U. Cin. Sch. Medicine, 1993—, prof. pediats., 2000—. Contbr. articles to profl. jours. Mem. med. adv. com. Nat. Neurofibromatosis Found., N.Y.C., 1987—; mem. health profl. adv. com. March of Dimes, Arlington, Va., 1991-93; bd. dirs. Capital Area March of Dimes, 1993. Tng. grantee NIH, 1979-82. Fellow Am. Acad. Pediats. (chmn. exec. com. for sect. on genetics and birth defects 1999—), Am. Coll. Med. Genetics; mem. Am. Soc. Human Genetics, Soc. Craniofacial Genetics (sec.-treas. 1990-96). Avocation: photography. Home: 3715 Monets Ln Cincinnati OH 45241-3847 Office: Childrens Hosp Med Ctr 3333 Burnet Ave Cincinnati OH 45229-3026

SAALFELD, FRED ERICH, retired, naval researcher; b. Joplin, Mo., Apr. 9, 1935; s. Eric Arthur and Milla (Kessler) S.; m. Elizabeth Renner, Nov. 22, 1958; 1 child, Fred E. Jr. (dec.). BS cum laude, So. East Mo. State U., 1957; MS in Phys. Chemistry, Iowa State U., 1959, PhD in Phys. Chem., 1961. Instr. Iowa State U., Ames, 1961-62; chemist Naval Rsch. Lab, Washington, 1962-63, head mass spectrometry sect., 1963-74, head physical chm. br., 1974-76, supt. chem. divsn., 1976-82; chief scientist Office Naval Rsch., London, 1979-80, dir. rsch. Arlington, Va., 1982-87, dir., 1987-93, dep. chief naval rsch., tech. dir., 1993-98, exec. dir., tech. dir., 1998—2002, ret., 2002. Author more than 500 publications, reports, presentations on applications of mass spectrometry to fields of combustion, laser, environ. analysis. Recipient Disting. Rank awards U.S. Pres., Washington, 1989, 96, Meritorious Rank award U.S. Pres., Washington, 1986, Robert Conrad award Sec. USN, Washington, 1988, Disting. Civilian Svc. award Sec. of Def./Dept. Def., 1999; named Fed. Exec. of Yr., Fed. Exec. Inst., Washington, 1991. Fellow AAAS; mem. Am. Chem. Soc. (councilor 1973-89), Am. Soc. Mass Spectrometry (sec. 1970-74), Combustion Inst., Chem. Soc. Washington (pres. 1972). Achievements include provision for science base for life support systems used in enclosed environments; development of educational programs used by USN for scientist training. Avocations: history, woodworking, sports.

SAAM, ROBERT HARRY, human resources consultant; b. Toledo, Mar. 7, 1947; s. Robert J. and Dorothy H. (Kinney) S.; m. Pamela Soder, Oct. 30, 1982; children: Robert C., Cara B., Stacia J. BA, U. Toledo, 1970; MS in Ednl. Psychology, U. Wis., 1993. Investigative supr. Ohio Civil Rights Commn., Cleve., 1973-76; councillator U.S. EEO Commn., Cin., 1976-79; mgr. labor rels. Internat. Minerals and Chems., Mundelein, Ill., 1979-85; dir. human resources svcs. Rexnord, Inc., Brookfield, Wis., 1985-87; v.p., owner Thompson Cons. Ltd., 1987-2000; sr. v.p. Wisc. ops. Lee Hecht Harrison, 2000—. Contbr. articles to profl. jours. Mem. Am. Assn. Counseling and Devel. Home: 646 N 77th St Milwaukee WI 53213-3512 Office: 17700 W Capitol Dr Brookfield WI 53045-2006

SAARI, DONALD GENE, mathematician, economist; b. Ironwood, Mich., Mar. 9, 1940; s. Gene August and Martha Mary (Jackson) S.; m. Lillian Joy Kalinen, June 11, 1966; children: Katri, Anneli. BS, Mich. Technol. U., 1962; PhD, Purdue U., 1967, DSc (hon.), 1989, U. Caen, France, 1998, Mich. Tech. U., 1999. Research astronomer Yale U., New Haven, 1967-68; prof. dept. math. Northwestern U., Evanston, Ill., 1968-2000, prof. econs., 1988-2000, Pancoe prof. math., 1995-2000, chmn. dept., 1981-84; prof. U. Nanjing (China), 1995; disting. prof. econ., prof. math., dir. ctr. for decision analysis U. Calif., Irvine, 2000—. Cons. Nat. Bur. Standards, Gaithersburg, Md., 1979-86, Commn. 9, Internat. Astron. Union, 1985-91; mem. nat. com. math. Nat. Rsch. Coun., 1997—, chair 2001—, math./sci. edn. bd., 2001—, Bd. Internat. Sci. Orgns., 2001—. Assoc. editor Jour. Econ. Behavior and Orgn., 1988-94, Celestial Mechanics and Dynamical Astronomy. 1989-97, Econ. Theory, 1990—, Social Choice and Welfare, 1997—, Qualitative Theory of Dynamical Sys., 1999—, Positivity, 2000—. Recipient Duncan Black award, Pub. Choice Soc., 1991, Chauvenet prize Mathematical Assn. of Am., 1995; Guggenheim fellow, 1988-89. Mem. NAS, Am. Math. Soc. (chief editor bull. 1999—, mem. coun. 1999-2002), Am. Astron. Soc., Soc. Indsl. and Applied Math. (editor jour. 1981-88), Econometric Soc. Office: U Calif Dept Econs Dept Math Irvine CA 92697-0001 E-mail: dsaari@uci.edu.

SAARI, JOHN WILLIAM, JR. lawyer; b. Jersey City, Oct. 12, 1937; s. John William Sr. and Ina Marie (Bain) S.; m. Susan Jo Olson, Aug. 27, 1967 (div. June 1971); m. Marjorie Ann Palm, Nov. 16, 1973. Student, Duke U., 1955-58, U. N.C., 1962-63; JD with honors, Ill. Inst. Tech., Chgo., 1972. Bar: Ill. 1972, U.S. Dist. Ct. (no. dist.) Ill. 1972, Wis. 1980, U.S. Dist. Ct. (ea. and we. dists.) Wis. 1980, U.S. Ct. Appeals (7th cir.) 1972, U.S. Supreme Ct. 1997. Assoc. Yates, Goff, Gustafson & Been, Chgo., 1972-76, Hubbard, Hubbard, O'Brien & Hall, Chgo., 1976-78; atty. Ill. Bell Telephone Co., 1978-79; assoc. Cirilli Law Office, Rhinelander, Wis., 1979-83; pvt. practice, 1983-90; ptnr. Mouw, Saari, Krueger, Paulson & Smith, 1990—. Bd. dirs. Northwoods United Way, 1980-88, pres., 1983-84. With U.S. Army, 1958-61, ETO. Mem. ABA, Ill. Bar Assn., Wis. Bar Assn., Oneida-Vilas-Forest Bar Assn. (pres. 1996-97), Lions (pres. Sugarcamp 1983-84). Avocations: hunting, fishing, baseball, reading, golf. Home: 7279 Arbutus Dr Eagle River WI 54521-9249 Office: Mouw Saari Krueger Paulson Smith 8A W Davenport St Rhinelander WI 54501-3467

SAARI, JOY ANN, family nurse practitioner, geriatrics medical and surgical nurse; b. Chippewa Falls, Wis., July 14, 1953; d. Harry R. and Hilda R. (Christianson) Harwood; m. Allan A. Saari, Dec. 31, 1973 (dec.); children: Christopher, Erik. BSN summa cum laude, U. Wis., Eau Claire, 1978; postgrad., Blue Ridge Community Coll., Verona, Va., 1987; MSN, FNP, George Mason U., 1995; MSN. RN, Mich., Wis., Va.; FNP, Va.; cert. BLS instr., ACLS. Staff nurse Portage View Hosp., Hancock, Mich., 1979-80; evening supr., asst. dir. nursing Chippewa Manor, Chippewa Falls, 1980-86; staff nurse Bridgewater (Va.) Home, Inc., 1986-90; p.m. charge nurse Medicalodge Leavenworth, Kans., 1990-91; outdoor edn. nurse Montgomery County (Md.) Schs., 1991-93; FNP Leesburg/Sterling Family Practice, 1995—. Maj. USAR Nurse Corps, 1995—. Mem. Am. Acad. Nurse Practitioners, Nat. League of Nursing, No. Va. Nurse Practitioner Assn., Res. Officer Assn., Am. Legion Aux., Phi Kappa Phi. E-mail: saarin@aol.com.

SAARIO, TERRY NATALIE TINSON, foundation executive; b. McKeesport, Pa., Nov. 16, 1941; d. John Thomas and Margaret Louise (Kanyusik) Tinson; m. Leland Theodore Lynch, Jan. 22, 1983. BA, U. Calif., Riverside, 1963, MA, 1966; PhD, Claremont (Calif.) Grad. Sch., 1970. Lectr. Claremont Grad. Sch., 1969-70; mem. rsch. team S.W. Regional Lab., Inglewood, Calif., 1969-70; asst. in fed. affairs A.E.R.A., Washington, 1970-71; mem. rsch. staff Rand Corp., Santa Monica, Calif., 1971-72; sr. program officer Ford Found., N.Y.C., 1971-80; dep. asst. sec. Edn. Dept. Carter Adminstrn., Washington, 1980-81; dir. corp. cont. Standard Oil Co., Cleve., 1981-83; v.p. Pillsbury Co., Mpls., 1983-84; pres. N.W. Area Found., St. Paul, 1984-96. Bd. dirs. Cowles Media Co., Mpls., Minn. Mut. Life Ins. Co., St. Paul, Employee Benefit Life (now named 1st Data Card), Musicland Group, Inc. Contbr. articles to profl. jours. Mem. Gov.'s Commn. on Univs., Mpls., 1988; chair, bd. dirs. St. Paul Chamber Orch., Minn. Women's Campaign Fund. Recipient One of 5 Best Found. Mgrs. award Bus. Week Mag., 1990; European Cmty. Brussels fellow, 1982, U.S.-Japan Leadership fellow Japan Soc., 1990. Mem. Minn. Women's Econ. Roundtable (pres. 1988), Tomas Rivera Ctr. (trustee emeritus). Democrat. Episcopalian. Avocations: tennis, race walking, skiing, classical music, opera.

SAAVEDRA, CHARLES JAMES, banker; b. Denver, Nov. 2, 1941; s. Charles James and Evangeline Cecilia (Aragon) S.; m. Ann Helen Taylor, 1967; children: Michael, Kevin, Sarah. BSBA, Regis U., Denver, 1963; postgrad., U. Calif., San Francisco, 1964-66. V.p. Western States Bankcard Assn., San Francisco, 1969-77; dir. info. systems World Airways, Inc., Oakland, Calif., 1977-79; v.p. computer svcs. First Nationwide Bank, San Francisco, 1979-83; sr. v.p. Wells Fargo Bank, 1983-92, Union Bank Calif., San Francisco, 1992—. Instr. Programming & Systems Inst., San Francisco, 1968-69; lectr. Am. Mgmt. Assn., 1984—. Pres. Richt Direction Project Contra Costa County; bd. dirs. No. Calif. Family Ctr. With USNR, 1963-64. Mem. Data Processing Mgrs. Assn. (bd. dirs., chmn. program com. 1981), Am. Nat. Stds. Inst., Am. Bankers Assn., San Francisco Jaycees, Commonwealth Club Calif., Lake Lakewood Assn., Alpha Delta Gamma. Home: 210 Lakewood Rd Walnut Creek CA 94598-4826 Office: Union Bank Calif 350 California St San Francisco CA 94104-1476

SAAVEDRA GARCIA, KATHERINE ANDREWS, health group executive director; b. Auckland, New Zealand, Feb. 16, 1956; d. Selwyn Edward and Judith Andrews; m. Boyd Thornton McCleary, Feb. 19, 1977 (div. July 1995); children: Jessica Rachel, Dane Thornton; m. Francisco Paulino Saavedra Garcia, Mar. 13, 1999; 1 child, Diego Edward. RN, Canberra Sch. Nursing, Australia, 1977. Emergency RN Saline (Mich.) Hosp., 1986-90, Foothills Hosp., Calgary, Can., 1990-91, Castle Med. Ctr., Kailua, Hawaii, 1991—, account analyst, 1995-96, dir. med. svcs. staff, 1996—, exec. dir., 1998—. Mem. Windward Soccer Club (bd. dirs., treas. 1997-99), MGMA. Democrat. Avocations: soccer, biking, travel. Office: Castle Health Group 640 Ulukahiki St Kailua HI 96734-4454 E-mail: saavedka@ah.org.

SABA, SHOICHI, manufacturing company executive; b. Tokyo, Feb. 28, 1919; s. Wataru and Sumie (Uemura) S.; m. Fujiko Saito, 1945 (dec.); children: Hiroko, Kazuhisa (dec.), Shunji. Grad., Imperial U., Tokyo, 1941. With Toshiba Corp., Tokyo, 1942-87, mng. dir., 1972-74, exec. v.p., 1974-76, sr. exec. v.p., 1976-80, pres., CEO, 1980-86, chmn., exec. officer, 1986-87, adviser to bd., 1987—; pres. Japanese Indsl. Stds. Com., 1994—2001. Dir. numerous cos.; adviser Japan Fedn. Econ. Orgns., 1994—. Chmn. nat. bd. govs. Nat. Assn. Boy Scouts of Nippon, 1994—; chmn., bd. trustees Internat. Christian U., 1994—. Office: Toshiba Corp 1-1 Shibaura 1-chome Minato-ku Tokyo 105-8001 Japan

SABA, WALTER PEDRO, health education communications executive; b. Lima, Peru, Apr. 29, 1955; came to U.S., 1991; s. Elias S. and Gabriela E. (Salomon) S.; m. Flor D. Giusti, Dec. 4, 1980; children: Elias G., Paulina T. *Walter Saba, a Health Communication executive with Johns Hopkins University / Center for Communications Programs (JHU/CCP), is the son of Elias Saba and Gabriela Salomon. He was born in Peru on 1955 and moved to the United States in 1991. He married Flor Giusti in 1980 and they have one son, Elias Gabriel, and one daughter, Paulina Teresa. Walter completed a Diploma in Film Studies, Conservatoire Libre de Cinema, Paris, 1977; masters in Health Science, at Johns Hopkins University, Baltimore, 1993. Walter received the Global Media Award on Population Communication form The Population Institute, 1996; the Silver Apple Award from the National Education Media Network, 1996.* Diploma in Film Studies, Conservatoire Libre de Cinema, Paris, 1977; M in Health Sci., Johns Hopkins U., 1993. Video producer Cath. U. of Peru, Lima, 1978-88; inf. coord. Nat. Program on AIDS, 1988-91; program officer Johns Hopkins U., Balt., 1993-97, sr. program officer, 1997—2000, chief Latin Am. divsn., 2002—. Recipient Global Media award The Population Inst., Washington, 1996, Silver Apple award Nat. Ednl. Media Network, Oakland, Calif. 1996. Mem. Am. Pub. Health Assn. Office: Johns Hopkins U 111 Market Pl Ste 310 Baltimore MD 21202-7112 E-mail: wsaba@jhuccp.org.

SABACKY, JEROME (JERRY SABACKY), retired research chemist; b. Cedar Rapids, Iowa, June 22, 1939; s. Milton and Emma Sabacky; m. Jane Bourbon, June 17, 1967; children: Kevin, Alisa Sommer. MS and PhD, Universtiy of Ill., Champaign/Urbana,Illinois, 1961—66; BA, Coe Coll., Cedar Rapids, 1957—61. Fellow Monsanto Co., St. Louis, 1985—99; rsch. chemist Monsanto, 1966—85. Home: 324 Holloway Road Ballwin MO 63011 Personal E-mail: mjsaba@aol.com.

SABADIE, FRANCISCA ALEJANDRA, lawyer, interpreter, translator; b. New Orleans, July 7, 1947; d. Alfonso and Margaret Gibbons (Burke) S.; m. Robert Thomas Dwyer, Jan. 6, 1973. BA, Newton Coll., 1968; JD, Loyola U., 1975. Bar: N.Y. 1976, U.S. Dist. Ct. (so. and ea. dists.) N.Y. 1976, U.S. Ct. Appeals (2nd cir.) 1977. Clk. Sessions, Fishman, Rosenson, Snelling, Boisfontaine, New Orleans, 1973-75; assoc. Shearman-Sterling, N.Y.C. and Paris, 1975-84; real estate developer London, 1985-87; pvt. practice Scarsdale, N.Y., 1987—. Mem. pub. affairs com. Jr. League Ctrl. Westchester (N.Y.); freedom writer Amnesty Internat.; bd. trustees Nativity Mission Ctr. Mem. Assn. Bar City of N.Y. (mem. entertainment com. 1998—). Roman Catholic. Avocations: music, cycling, cooking, reading, theatre. Office: One Walworth Ave Scarsdale NY 10583-1417 Fax: 914-723-6679.

SABALJA, LORRAINE, development marketing consultant; b. Smithtown, N.Y., Mar. 14, 1969; d. Philip Anthony and Lorraine Agatha Sabalja. BBA, Loyola Coll., Balt., 1991; JD, Quinnipiac Coll., 1996. Bar: N.Y. 1997, Conn. 1997. Assoc. Law Office of Steven I. Hilsenrath, N.Y.C., 1997-98; asst. counsel Hadassah The Women's Zionist Orgn. Am., 1998-2000; devel. mktg. cons. Girl Scouts of the USA, 2000—. Mem. N.Y. State Bar Assn., Conn. Bar Assn., City Bar Assn. N.Y. Avocations: hiking, biking, running, tennis, horsemanship. Office: Girls Scouts USA Inc 420 Fifth Ave New York NY 10018 E-mail: lsabalja@girlscouts.org.

SABAROFF, ROSE EPSTEIN, retired education educator; b. Cleve., Sept. 4, 1918; d. Hyman Israel and Bertha (Glaser) Epstein; m. Bernard Joseph Sabaroff, Dec. 28, 1940; children: Ronald Asher, Katya Nina. BA, U. Ariz., 1941; MA, San Francisco State U., 1954; EdD, Stanford U., 1957. Tchr. Presidio Hill Elem. Sch., San Francisco, 1951-55; asst. prof. edn. Oreg. State U., Corvallis, 1958-61; asst. dir., then dir. elem. edn. Harvard Grad. Sch. Edn., Cambridge, Mass., 1961-66; prof. edn., head elem. edn., head reading program Va. Poly. Inst. and State U., Blacksburg, 1967-82; dir. Grad. Edn. Ctr. Calif. Luth. Coll., North Hollywood, 1982-84; reading specialist How to Learn, Inc., West Los Angeles, Calif., 1983-88. Author: (with Hanna, Davies, Farrar) Geography in the Teaching of Social Studies, 1966, (with Mary Ann Hanna) The Open Classroom, 1974, Teaching Reading with a Linguistic Approach, 1980, Developing Linguistic Awareness, 1981; contbr. articles to profl. jours. Recipient Disting. Research award Va. Edn. Research Assn., 1977; Phi Delta Kappa grantee, 1980 Mem. AAUP, Internat. Reading Assn., NEA, Va. Edn. Assn., Va. Coll. Reading Educators (pres. 1976-77), Va. Reading Assn., Phi Delta Kappa, Pi Lambda Theta, Gamma Theta Upsilon. Democrat. Jewish. Achievements include conducting 15 month study abroad comparing ednl. sys. in 4 European countries with differing social-econ. sys. Home: 23826 Villena Mission Viejo CA 92692-1818

SABAT, ROBERT HARTMAN, magazine editor; b. Newark, Aug. 28, 1957; s. Charles and Marilyn Ruth (Hartman) S.; m. Jessica Schilling Fine, Oct. 15, 1989; children: Nathaniel, Olivia. BA, Brandeis U., 1980. Mng. editor Penthouse mag., N.Y.C., 1986-91, Connoisseur mag., N.Y.C., 1991-92, Lear's mag., N.Y.C., 1992-94, Interview mag., N.Y.C., 1994-95, Smart Money mag., N.Y.C., 1995-99, exec. editor, 1999—. Mem. Am. Soc. Mag. Editors. Office: Smart Money 1755 Broadway Fl 2 New York NY 10019-3798 E-mail: rsabat@hearst.com.

SABATELLA, ELIZABETH MARIA, clinical therapist, educator, mental health facility administrator; b. Mineola, N.Y., Nov. 9, 1940; d. D. F. and Blanche M. (Schmetzle) S; 1 child, Kevin Woog. BS, SUNY, Brockport, 1961; MA, SUNY, Stony Brook, 1971, MSW, 1983; postgrad., Univ. Calif., San Diego, 1999. Lic. social worker N.Y., N.Mex., Oreg.; tchr., sch. counselor Oreg., N.Y., cert. pupil pers. credential, sch. counselor, registered clin. social worker Calif., Oreg. Tchr. physical edn. Comseqogue Sch. Dist., Port Jefferson, N.Y., 1968-73, 84-87, 88-91; sch. counselor, 1975—84; clin. therapist Cibola Counseling Svcs., Grants, N.Mex., 1991-95, regional dir., 1993-95; clin. therapist Family Growth Counseling Ctr., Encinitos, Calif., 1995-96; clin. social worker Family Advocacy, San Diego, 1995-99; sch. counselor, 1999-2000; counselor Navy Coll., 2000—01; sch. counselor Redmond (Oreg.) Sch. Dist., 2001—, 2001—. Therapist for abused children Farmingville Mental Health Clinic; therapist for adolescents Comsewogue Sch. Dist.; therapist for alcoholics Lighthouse Ctr.; mem. Family Systems Network for Continuing Edn., Calif., Colo., 1978-80; mem. biofeedback and mediation com. McLean Hosp., Boston, 1978; mem. therapeutic touch team East and West Ctr., N.Y.C., 1980-84, sexual abuse treatment coord., 1992-95. Art and photographs exhibited at group show N.Mex. Art League, 1991; author: Stop Before You Blow Your Top, 1998, We Want You To Stop. Children Who Witness Domestic Violence, 1998, Children at Play: Tales of Gang Boys in Treatment, 1999; contbr. poetry and children's story to various publs. Recipient Editor's Choice award and Best New Poet award Nat. Libr. Poetry, 1988, Merit award and Place Winner for Poetry, Iliad Press, 1993. Mem.: NASW, Oregon Ed. Assn., Writers Assn., Oreg. Tchrs. Assn., Acad. Cert. Social Workers, N.Y. State United Tchrs., Sierra Club. Avocations: travel, cycling, yoga, dance, photography. Home: 826 NE Providence Dr Bend OR 97701 E-mail: LIZSABOR@MSN.com.

SABATES, FELIX S., JR. professional sports team executive; b. Cuba; arrived in U.S., 1959; m. Carolyn Pearce Sabates; children: Mimi, Mario, Chany. Doctorate(hon.) , Elon Coll. Team owner Chip Ganassi Racing, Mooresville, NC, 1987—; car salesman City Chevrolet; salesman Top Sales Co., Inc., 1967, owner, chmn., CEO, 1974; owner, pres. Victory Ln. Enterprises; co-owner Team SABCO, 1987. Part-owner Charlotte Hornets, 1988—91; founder Charlotte Profl. Sports Team, Inc., 1990; bd. dirs. Windmere Corp. Mem. Dream Makers Soc. of Boys and Girls Club Broward County, Fla.; bd. dirs. Carolinas Health Care Sys., U. N.C., Charlotte.

Recipient Belmont Abbey's dining hall named in his honor, Spl. Blessing, the Pope, Felix and Carolyn Sabates Athletic Ctr. dedicated in their honor, 2000. Mem.: Charlotte C. of C. (bd. dirs.). Office: Chip Ganassi Racing 114 Meadow Hill Cir Mooresville NC 28115

SABATINI, DAVID DOMINGO, cell biologist, biochemist; b. Bolivar, Argentina, May 10, 1931; came to U.S., 1961; m. Zulema Lena Sabatini, 1960; children: Bernardo L., David M. MD, U. Litoral, Rosario, Argentina, 1954; PhD in Cell Biology, Rockefeller U., 1966. Instr., lectr., assoc. prof. cell biology Inst. Gen. Anatomy and Embryology, U. Buenos Aires, 1957-60; dir. admissions Sch. Medicine U. Buenos Aires, 1957-60; Rockefeller Found. fellow Sch. Medicine Yale U., 1961; rsch. assoc. cell biol. lab Rockefeller U., N.Y.C., 1961-63, from asst. prof. to assoc. prof. cell biology, 1966-72; prof., chmn. dept. cell biology Sch. Medicine NYU, 1972-74, Frederick L. Ehrman prof., chmn. dept. cell biol. Sch. Med., 1975—, dir. MD-PhD program, 1987-97. Wendell Griffith Meml. lectr. St. Louis U., 1977; Mary Peterman Meml. lectr. Meml.-Sloan Kettering Inst., N.Y., 1977; 25th Robert J. Terry lectr. Wash. U., 1978; 3d ann. Keith R. Porter lectr. cell biology, 1994; vis. prof. Coll. France, Paris, 1986, George Washington U., 1986; 7th Ann. Kenneth F. Naidorff Meml. lectr. Columbia U., 1989; fellow Nat. Acad. Medicine, Argentina, 1956; UNESCO fellow Biophysics Inst., Rio de Janeiro, 1957; Pfizer traveling fellow, 1972; mem. molecular biology study sect. NIH, 1973-77, chmn., 1976-77; mem. bd. basic biology Nat. Rsch. Coun., 1986-89. Editor Jour. Cell Biology, 1971—, Jour. Cellular Biochemistry, 1980-84, Molecular & Cellular Biology, 1980-82, Procs. NAS USA, 1985—, Biol. Cell, 1986—, Current Opinions Cell Biology, 1990—; mem. editl. bd. Procs. NAS, 1993-96. Mem. sci. adv. com. Irma T. Hirshcl Charitable Trust, 1979-85; bd. dirs. Pub. Health Rsch. Inst., 1980-88; bd. sci. dirs. Jane Coffin Childs Meml. Fund, 1980-86, Nat. Inst. Diabetes Digest Kidney Disease, 1982-86; sci. adv. com. Robert Wood Johnson Found. Minority Med. Faculty Devel. Program, 1987—, Human Frontier Sci. Program, 1991—, chair molecular grants, 1994—; mem. sci. rev. com. Pew Internat. Fellows Program, 1990—, med. adv. bd., 1989-93, internat. program, 1994—; mem. sci. adv. com. Inst. d'Embryologie Cellular Mol., Coll. France, 1994—;, Ctr. Adv. Biotech. and Medicine, 1996—; mem. Alfred P. Sloan Jr. award selection com. GM Cancer Rsch. Found., 1996—. Recipient Samuel Roberts Noble Rsch. Recognition award, 1980. Fellow AAAS, Am. Acad. Microbiology, N.Y. Acad. Sci.; mem. NAS (chmn. cell and devel. biology sect. 1994-96), Am. Soc. Cell Biology (pres. 1978-79, coun. mem. 1974-77, E. B. Wilson award 1986), Harvey Soc. (v.p. 1985-86, pres. 1986-87), Argentine Med. Assn. (hon.), French Acad. Sci. (fgn. assoc., Charles Leopold Mayer prize 1988), Am. Soc. Biol. Chemistry, Am. Soc. Microbiology, N.Y. Soc. Electron Microbiology ((pres. 1971), Am. Assn. Anatomy (chair cell biology, neurobiology, exec. coun. 1992—), Inst. Medicine. Office: NYU Sch Medicine 550 1st Ave Rm 659 New York NY 10016-6481*

SABATINI, NELSON JOHN, government official; b. Rochester, N.Y., Jan. 20, 1940; s. John R. and Ida M. (Ceconi) S.; m. Marilyn Jean Gromala, Jan. 19, 1963; children— John Nelson, Michael Christopher Student, Lewis Coll., Lockport, Ill., 1958-62; BA in Psychology, George Washington U., 1971, postgrad. Claims rep. Social Security Adminstrn., Chgo., 1962-65, various positions Balt., 1965-79, dep. dir. disability programs, 1979-81, exec. asst. to commr., 1981-82, assoc. commr., 1982—, dep. commr., 1983-88; dep. sec. health and mental hygiene State of Md., 1988, sec. health and mental hygiene, 1991-95; exec. v.p. Univ. Md. Medical Systems, 1995—. V.p. U. Md. Med. System, 1995—. Named Disting. Marylander of Yr. 1993; recipient Sec.'s cert. HHS, 1975; Commr.'s citation Social Security Adminstrn., 1977, 81; Presdl. Merit Rank award Pres. of U.S., 1984 Roman Catholic. Avocations: sailing; tennis.

SABATINI, SANDRA, physician; b. N.Y.C., Dec. 1, 1940; BS in Chemistry, Millsaps Coll., 1962; MS in Pharmacology, Marquette U., 1966; PhD in Pharmacology, U. Miss., 1968; MD in Internal Medicine, Tex. Med. Sch., 1974. Lic. physician, Ill., Tex. Intern in medicine U. Ill. Hosp., Chgo., 1974-75; asst. prof. U. Tex. Med. Sch., San Antonio, 1968-70; assoc. dir. U. Ill. Hosp., Chgo., 1977-78; asst. prof. U. Ill. Coll. of Medicine, 1977-83, assoc. prof. medicine and physiology, 1983-84; attending physician in nephrology VA, 1977-84; med. dir. Dialysis Unit U. Ill., 1978-84; prof. internal medicine and physiology Tex. Tech. U. Health Sci. Ctr., Lubbock, 1985—, chmn. dept. physiology, 1993-96; attending physician in nephrology U. Med. Ctr., 1985—. Lab. instr. Millsaps Coll., Jackson, Miss., 1961-62; instr. pharmacology Bapt. Hosp. Sch. Nursing, Jackson, 1966-68; merit rev. mem. NSF, 1987, 91, 92; rev. mem. several orgns. including Chgo. Heart Assn., 1984, NIH, 1983, 86, 89-93, 96, Nat. Kidney Found., 1987, 89—, Am. Heart Assn., 1981-84, others; cons. U.S. Med. Licensing Exam/Nat. Bd. Med. Examiners, Step 1 Physiology Test Com., 1996-99. Editl. referee Am. Jour. Kidney Disease, Am. Jour. Physiology, Am. Jour. Nephrology, Annals of Internal Medicine, others; mem. editl. bd. Am. Jour. Nephrology, 1989-93, Seminars in Nephrology, 1984—; co-editor Am. Jour. Kidney Diseases, 1997—; author numerous publs. and abstracts in field; contbr. articles to profl. jours. Bd. dirs. YWCA of Lubbock, 1994-99; mem. Leadership Tex., 1994. Predoctoral fellowship grantee Marquette U., 1963-66; pub. health predoctoral fellow U. Miss. Med. Sch., 1967-69, gen. medicine sci. rsch. grantee U. Tex. Med. Sch., 1968-70, post-grad. fellow Karolinska Inst., Swedish Med. Coun., 1971, 73, NIH grantee, 1979-82, 84-99, Chgo. Heart Assn. grantee-in-aid, 1979-85, 99; grantee Nat. Eye Inst., 1979-80; recipient Banes Charitable trust award U. Ill., 1984-85, U.S. Olympic com. Rsch. Foudn., 1986-87; recipient Outstanding Alumnus award Tex. Med. Sch., 1994, numerous other awards in field. Fellow: ACP; mem.: AAUP, AAAS, ADA (hon.), Nat. Kidney Found. West Tex. (bd. dirs. 1993—99, Outstanding Vol. 1995, 2001, Disting. Svc. award 1996), Nat. Kidney Found. (numerous offices including chmn. several coms.), Italian-Am. Nephrologists, Inc., Internat. Soc. Nephrology, Ill. Kidney Found., Ctrl. Soc. Clin. Rsch., So. Soc. Clin. Rsch. (councillor 1997—99, pres.-elect 1999, pres. 2000), Assn. Chairs Dept. Physiology (councillor 1995—97), Am. Soc. Renal Biochemistry and Metabolism (pres.-elect 1994), Am. Soc. Pharmacology and Exptl. Therapeutics, Am. Soc. Nephrology, Am. Physiol. Soc., Am. Heart Assn., Am. Fedn. Med. Rsch. Office: Tex Tech U Health Sci Ctr 3601 4th St Lubbock TX 79430-0001

SABATINO, CARL DANIEL, music educator; b. Bklyn., June 28, 1967; s. Aniello Daniel and Nina Sabatino; m. Lisa Russoniello, July 19, 1966; children: Alec. MusB, William Paterson U., 1989. Cert. K-12 instrumental/vocal music tchr. NJ. Band dir. Whippany (NJ) Park H.S., 1989—. Band dir. Mt. Tabor Summer Band, Parsippany, NJ, 1998—. Musician: (pit orchestra) Carnival, 2000, You're a Good Man Charlie Brown, 2001, Once on this Island, 2001, Most Happy Fella, 2002. Named condr., North Jersey Area Band, 2002. Mem.: North Jersey Area Band (wind ensemble mgr. 2000—02), Nat. Band Assn., North Am. Saxophone Alliance, Music Educators Nat. Conf. Home: 252 Garden Rd Pompton Lakes NJ 07442 Office: Whippany Park HS 165 Whippany Rd Whippany NJ 07981

SABATINO, CARMEN, mayor; Former tchr. Modesto City Sch. Dist., Calif.; restaurant owner; mayor City of Modesto, Calif., 1999—. Founder Modesto Basketball Assn.; chair Audit Com. Office: City Hall PO Box 642 Modesto CA 95353-0642 E-mail: csabatino@ci.modesto.ca.us.*

SABATO, LARRY JOSEPH, political science educator; b. Norfolk, Va., Aug. 7, 1952; s. N.J. and Margaret F. (Simmons) S. BA, U. Va., 1974; postgrad., Princeton U., 1974-75; DPhil, Oxford U., 1977. Lectr. politics New Coll. Oxford U., 1977-78; dir. U. Va. Ctr. for Governmental Studies; Robert Kent Gooch prof. Govt. and Foreign Affairs U. Va., Charlottesville, 1978—. Guest scholar Brookings Instn., 1980; Thomas Jefferson vis. prof. Downing Coll., Cambridge U., 1982. Author: The Rise of Political Consultants: New Ways of Winning Elections, 1981, Goodbye to Goodtime Charlie: The American Governorship Transformed, 1983, PAC Power: Inside the World of Political Action Committees, 1984, The Party's Just Begun: Shaping Political Parties for America's Future, 1988, Feeding Frenzy: How Attack Journalism Has Transformed American Politics, 1991, American Government: Roots and Reform, 1992, Dirty Little Secrets: The Persistence of Corruption in American Politics, 1996, Toward the Millennium: The Elections of 1996, Overtime! The Election 2000 Thriller. Danforth fellow, 1975; Kellog fellow, 1983; Rhodes scholar; recipient Thomas Jefferson award U. Va., 2001. Mem. Am. Polit. Sci. Assn., Phi Beta Kappa. Office: U Va Dept Govt 240 Cabell Charlottesville VA 22901

SABAU, CARMEN SYBILE, chemist; b. Cluj, Romania, Apr. 24, 1933; naturalized U.S. citizen; d. George and Antoinette Marie (Chiriac) Grigorescu; m. Mircea Nicolae Sabau, July 11, 1956; 1 child, Isabelle Carmen. MS in Inorganic and Analytical Chemistry, U. C.I. Parhon, Bucharest, Romania, 1955; PhD in Radiochemistry, U. Fridericiana, Karlsruhe, Fed. Republic of Germany, 1972. Chemist Inst. Atomic Physics, Bucharest, Romania, 1956—74, Argonne (Ill.) Nat. Lab., 1976-98; ret., 1998. Author: Ion-exchange Theory and Applications in Analytical Chemistry, 1967; contbr. articles to profl. jours. Internat. Atomic Energy Agy. fellow, 1967-68, Humboldt fellow, 1970-72. Mem. Am. Romanian Acad. Arts and Sci., Internat. Soc. Intercomm. of New Ideas, Alexander von Humboldt Assn. Am., Alpha Friends Antiquity. Home: 689 Banbury Way Bolingbrook IL 60440-1057 Office: Argonne Nat Lab 9700 Cass Ave Bldg 205 Argonne IL 60439-4837 E-mail: Carmen_Sabau@hotmail.com.

SABBAGHA, RUDY E. obstetrician, gynecologist, educator; b. Oct. 29, 1931; arrived in U.S., 1965, naturalized; s. Elias C. and Sonia B.S.; m. Asma E. Sahyouny, Oct. 5, 1957; children: Elias, Randa. BA, Am. U., Beirut, 1952, MD, 1958. Diplomate Am. Bd. Ob-Gyn. Sr. physician Tapline, Saudi Arabia, 1958-64; resident Northwestern Meml. Hosp./Prentice Women's Pavilion, Chgo., U. Pitts./Magee Women's Hosp., 1965—68; ob-gyn specialist Tapline, Saudi Arabia, 1969-70; tchg. fellow U. Pitts, 1965-68, asst. prof. ob-gyn, 1970-75; prof. Northwestern U., Chgo., 1975-94; med. dir. Obstet. and Gynecol. Ultrasound S.C., 1994—; clin. prof. U. Chgo. Pritzker Sch. Medicine, 1995-2000, prof., 1995—. Obstetrician, gynecologist Prentice Women's Hosp., Chgo., 1995—. Editor: Ultrasound Applied to Obstetrics and Gynecology, 1980, 3d edit., 1994; co-editor: Fetal Anomalies: Ultrasound Diagnosis and Postnatal Management, 2001; contbr. Fellow Am. Coll. Obstetricians and Gynecologists, Am. Inst. Ultrasound in Medicine; mem. Soc. Gynecol. Investigation, Am. Gynecol. and Obstet. Soc., Ctrl. Assn. Obstetricians and Gynecologists. Research on diagnostic ultrasound, obstetrics and gynecology. Office: 680 N Lake Shore Dr Ste 1430 Chicago IL 60611-8702 Fax: 312-656-9202.

SABBAJ, JACOBO, internist; b. Guatemala, Guatemala, Oct. 20, 1939; came to U.S., 1965; s. Alfredo and Jeannette (Kleff) S.; m. Perla Tenenbaum, Feb. 16, 1963; children: Steffanie, Alfredo. MD, U. San Carlos, Guatemala, 1965. Diplomate Am. Bd. Internal Medicine. Intern Newton Wellesley Hosp., Boston, 1965-66; resident in medicine Lemuel Shattuck Hosp., 1966-69; rsch. fellow Tufts U., 1967-69, Wadsworth VA Hosp., L.A., 1969-71; from staff physician to chief infectious diseases unit Roosevelt Hosp., Guatemala, 1971-81; dir. infectious diseases Merck Rsch. Lab., Rahway, N.J., 1981-86, sr. dir., 1986-91, exec. dir., 1991-97, v.p. clin. ops. worldwide, 1997—. Contbr. articles to profl. jours. Decorated knight St. Sylvester (Vatican City); recipient Gold medal Guatemalan Congress Medicine, 1981. Fellow ACP, Infectious Diseases Soc. Am.; mem. Pan Am. Soc. Infectious Diseases (treas. 1985-86), Coll. Physicians and Surgeons, Guatemala. Achievements include research on anaerobic pyogenic liver abscess, clinical spectrum anaerobic infections, norfloxacin in chronic typhoid carriers and norfloxacin in UTI. Office: Merck Rsch Lab PO Box 2000 Rahway NJ 07065-0900 Address: 195 Crystal Springs Ct Holmdel NJ 07733-2528

SABEL, BRADLEY KENT, lawyer; b. Charleston, Ill., Oct. 6, 1948; s. Walter Bernard and Charlotte (Ahlstrom) S.; m. Nancy Jean Parker, Apr. 4, 1984 BA, Vanderbilt U., 1970; JD, Cornell U., 1975; MS in Bus. Policy, Columbia U., 1983. Bar: N.Y. 1976. Atty. Fed. Reserve Bank of N.Y., N.Y.C., 1975-80, asst. counsel, 1980, sec., asst. counsel, 1981-85, assoc. counsel, 1985-87, counsel, 1988-93, counsel, v.p., 1993-94; counsel Shearman & Sterling, N.Y.C., 1994-97, ptnr., 1997—. Contbr. numerous articles to profl. jours. Bd. dirs., treas. N.Y. Chamber Orch., N.Y.C., 1985-87; Served with U.S. Army, 1970-72 Home: 2 Midland Gdns Apt 4E Bronxville NY 10708-4727 Office: 599 Lexington Ave Fl C2 New York NY 10022-6030 E-mail: bsabel@shearman.com.

SABELIS, HUIBERT, artist; b. The Netherlands, 1942; One-person shows include Shute Inst., London, Ont., Can., 1967, 71, Philippine Nat. Mus., Manila, 1972, Isetan Gallery, Tokyo, 1974, Can. Consulate Gen., L.A., 1977, Woodstock (Can.) Pub. Art Gallery, 1980, Gallery 3, Kampen, The Netherlands, 1981, Upcake Gallery, Fairfield, NSW, Australia, 1983, Karney-Daniels Gallery, Toronto, Ont., 1986, Galerie Jan J. Albers, Apeldoorn, The Netherlands, 1989, Kasteel Groeneveld, Baarn, The Netherlands, 1991, Gallery En Suite, Apeldoorn, 1995, Vispoort, Harderwijk, The Netherlands, 1997, Galerie Peter Bax, Sneek, The Netherlands, 2000; group exhbns. include Royal Ont. Mus., Toronto, 1971, Scan '74, Vancouver, B.C., Can., 1974, 1st Fgn. Artist in Japan Exhbn., Tokyo, 1977, DF Galeria Polyforum, Mexico City, 1980, Grimsby (Can.) Pub. Art Gallery, 1982, 34th Ann. Color and Miniature Print Biennale, Seoul, 1986, Collioure Gallerie des Editions Universelles, Toulouse, France, 1988, Philippine Centre Gallery, N.Y.C., 1990, Ariel Croft Studio Gallery, Mansfield, Can., 1993, Shakai Kyouiki Ctr., Kariya, Japan, 1994, Galerie Kasteel de Essenburgh, Harderwijk, 1998, M&A Gallery, The Hague, The Netherlands, 1999, Mississauga Art Gallery, Can., 2000. Studio: Atelier Symphony 1136 Bancroft Dr Mississauga ON Canada L5V 1B9 Fax: (905) 567-0880., 905-567-0880. E-mail: sabelis@hotmail.com.

SABERS, RICHARD WAYNE, state supreme court justice; b. Salem, S.D., Feb. 12, 1938; s. Emil William and Elrena Veronica (Godfrey) S.; m. Colleen D. Kelley, Aug. 28, 1965 (dec. Feb., 1998); children: Steven Richard, Susan Michelle, Michael Kelley; m. Ellie Schmitz, June 9, 2000. BA in English, St. John's U., Collegeville, Minn., 1960; JD, U. S.D., 1966. Bar: S.D. 1966, U.S. Dist. Ct. S.D. 1966, U.S. Ct. Appeals (8th cir.) 1983. From assoc. to ptnr. Moore, Rasmussen, Sabers & Kading, Sioux Falls, S.D., 1966-86; justice Supreme Ct. S.D., Pierre and Sioux Falls, 1986—. Mem. editorial bd. U. S.D. Law Rev., 1965-66. State rep. March of Dimes, Bismarck, N.D., 1963; bd. dirs. St. Joseph Cathedral, Sioux Falls, 1971-86; trustee, bd. dirs. O'Gorman Found., Sioux Falls, 1978-86; active sch. bd. O'Gorman High Sch., Sioux Falls, 1985-86. Lt. U.S. Army, 1960-63. Named Outstanding Young Religious Leader, Jaycees, Sioux Falls, 1971. Mem. ABA, S.D. Bar Assn., Inst. Jud. Adminstrn., St. John's Alumni Assn. (pres. Sioux Falls chpt. 1975-91). Republican. Roman Catholic. Avocations: tennis, skiing, sailing, sports, wood carving. Office: SD Supreme Ct 500 E Capitol Ave Pierre SD 57501-5070 Home: 5218 S Sweetbriar Ct Sioux Falls SD 57108-2855

SABERSKY, ROLF HEINRICH, mechanical engineer; b. Berlin, Germany, Oct. 20, 1920; came to U.S., 1938, naturalized, 1944; s. Fritz and Berta (Eisner) S.; m. Bettina Sofie Schuster, June 16, 1946; children— Carol, Sandra. BS, Calif. Inst. Tech., 1942, MS, 1943, PhD, 1949. Devel. engr. Aerojet Gen. Co., 1943-46, regular cons., 1949-70; asst. prof. Calif. Inst. Tech., Pasadena, 1949-55, assoc. prof., 1955-61, prof. mech. engring., 1961-88, prof. emeritus, 1988—. Cons. various indsl. orgns. Author: Engineering Thermodynamics, 1957, Fluid Flow, 4th edit., 1999; contbr. articles to profl. jours. Fellow ASME (Heat Transfer Meml. award 1977, 50th anniversary award Heat Transfer Div 1988); mem. Sigma Xi, Tau Beta Pi. Home: Valle Verde EG 117 900 Calle De Los Amigos Santa Barbara CA 93105-4435 Office: Calif Inst Tech Divsn Engring & Applied Sci Pasadena CA 91125-0001 E-mail: sabersky@silcom.com.

SABET, HORMOZ, entrepreneur; b. Tehran, Iran, Aug. 10, 1936; came to U.S., 1941; s. Habib and Bahereh (Khamsi) S.; children: Reja, Aram, Karim. BS in Econs., U. Pa.; Econs., Wharton, 1958. Chmn, chief exec. officer Firooz Corp., Tehran, Iran, 1958-78, Gulf Assocs., Inc., N.Y., 1960—; chmn. Summit Filter Corp., Union, N.J., 1975—; chmn., CEO, Sabet Group, N.Y.C., 1978-95; v.p. Bear Stearns & Co., 1982-83; vice chmn. Stella Meuble S.A., Bassecourt, Switzerland, 1983—; chmn. Shaffer Products, Inc., Middlesex, N.J., 1983—; vice chmn. BGS Holdings, Glen Cove, N.Y., 1989—; chmn. Gulf Assocs. Comm., Ltd., Switzerland, British V.I., 1990—; vice chmn. FLAG (Fiberoptic Link Around the Globe), Bermuda, British Virgin Islands, 1990—. MideastonLine.com, 1999—. Chmn. Radio TV Corp. of Iran, Tehran, 1961-78, Johnson & Johnson Iran Ltd., Tehran, 1974-78; vice chmn. TRRC (Exxon) Iran, Tehran, 1965-78. Mem. Iran C. of C., Tehran, 1959-78, Internat. C. of C., Paris, 1962-78, Iran-U.S. C. of C., N.Y., 1971-75. Named Woman of Yr., N.Y. League Bus. and Profl. Women, 2002. Avocations: art collector, travel, philanthropist. Office: Gulf Assoc Inc 30 Rockefeller Plz Ste 2829 New York NY 10112-0184 Fax: 212-246-5870. E-mail: gulfny@aol.com.

SABEY, J(OHN) WAYNE, academic administrator, consultant; b. Murray, Utah, Dec. 10, 1939; s. Alfred John and Bertha (Lind) S.; m. Marie Bringhurst, Sept. 10, 1964; children: Clark Wayne, Colleen, Carolyn, Natasha Lynne. BA in Asian Studies, Brigham Young U., 1964, MA in Asian History, 1965; PhD in East Asian History, U. Mich., 1972. Teaching asst. Brigham Young U., Provo, 1964-65, rsch. asst., 1965, adj. prof. history, 1988-89; rsch. asst. U. Mich., Ann Arbor, 1966; from instr. to asst. prof. history U. Utah, Salt Lake City, 1970-80; v.p. Western Am. Lang. Inst., 1980-84, dir., 1984-86, pres., 1986—; exec. v.p. Pacific Rim Bus. Coords., 1993—, also bd. dirs., 1993—; dir. Japan Ops. E'OLA Products, Inc., St. George, 1996-99; MBA program dir. Walden U., Mpls., 1999—2001. Assoc. dir. exch. program between U. Utah and Nagoya Broadcasting Network of Japan, 1973-79; lectr. in field, Superior award in extemporaneous speaking, 1956. Author essay, contbr. articles to ency. Chmn. bd. trustees Western Am. Lang. Inst., 1986—, sec. to bd. trustees, 1980-86; chmn. bd. trustees Found. for Internat. Understanding, 1982—; mem. internat. adv. coun. Salt Lake C.C., 1988-94; mem. bd. advisors Consortium for Internat. Edn., 1972-77. Horace H. Rackham Sch. grad. studies fellow, 1969-70, Fulbright-Hays rsch. fellow (Japan), 1968-69, U.S. Nat. Def. fgn. lang. fellow, 1965-68. Mem. Assn. for Asian Studies (gen. chairperson, chairperson local arrangements western conf. 1970-72), Phi Kappa Phi. Avocations: piano, hiking, basketball, stamp collecting, tennis. Home and Office: 8710 Oakwood Park Cir Sandy UT 84094-1800 E-mail: wmnsabey@aros.net.

SABHARWAL, RANJIT SINGH, mathematician; b. Dhudial, India, Dec. 11, 1925; came to U.S., 1958, naturalized, 1981; s. Krishan Ch and Devti (An) S.; m. Pritam Kaur Chadha, Mar. 5, 1948; children— Rajinderpal, Amarjit, Jasbir. BA with honors, Punjab U., 1944, MA, 1948; MA U. Calif, Berkeley, 1962; PhD, Wash. State U., 1966. Lectr. math. Khalsa Coll., Bombay, India, 1951-58; teaching asst. U. Calif., Berkeley, 1958-62; instr. math. Portland (Oreg.) State U., 1962-62, Wash. State U., 1963-66; asst. prof. Kans. State U., 1966-68; assoc. prof. math. Calif. State U., Hayward, 1968-74, prof. math., 1974-92, prof. emeritus math., 1992—. Author papers on non-Desarguesian planes. Mem. Am. Math. Soc., Math. Assn. Am., Sigma Xi. Address: 25179 Old Fairview Ave Hayward CA 94542-1355

SABHERWAL, RAJIV, information scientist, educator; b. Bhopal, India, Dec. 16, 1960; s. Kailash Chander and Premlata Sabherwal; m. Komal Sabherwal; children: Pulkit, Eesha. B of Engring., Maulana Azad Coll. of Tech., Bhopal, India, 1976—81; postgrad. in mgmt., Indian Inst. of Mgmt., Calcutta, India, 1981—83; PhD, U. Pitts., 1985—89. Asst. prof. Fla. Internat. U., Miami, Fla., 1988—94, assoc. prof., 1994—99, Fla. State U., Tallahassee, 1999—2000; Emery C. Turner prof. of Information Systems U. Mo., St. Louis, 2000—. Dir. PhD program U. Mo., St. Louis, 2000—. Contbr. articles. Recipient Tchg. Incentive award, Fla. Internat. U., 1996, Coll. of Bus. award for Outstanding Rsch., 1998; grantee Rsch. grant, David D. Lattanze Ctr., Balt., 1995, Doctoral fellow, Soc. Info. Mgmt., 1987. Mem.: Assn. for Info. Sys. Office: Univ of Mo St Louis CCB 206 8001 Natural Bridge Rd Saint Louis MO 63121 Business E-Mail: sabherwal@umsl.edu.

SABIK, JOSEPH ANDREW, psychometrist, counselor; b. Uniontown, Pa., Dec. 28, 1943; s. Joseph Andrew and Dorothy G. (Maycheck) S. AB in Philosophy, St. Vincent Coll., 1966; MDiv, St. Vincent Sem., 1969; postgrad., John Carroll U., 1982-84, MA in Counseling and Human Svcs., 1991. Ordained priest Roman Cath. Ch., 1970; profl. clin. counselor, Ohio. Assoc. pastor, Pa., 1970-80, St. Paul Parish, Euclid, Ohio, 1982, St. Peter & Paul Parish, Garfield Heights, 1982-85; psychometrist John Carroll U., Cleve., 1986-91; cons., 1991—; counselor family svcs. dept. Cleve. Christian Home, 1998—. Counselor CAEL/Ohio Bell, Cleve., 1989-91; instr. John Carroll U., 1989, 92. Mem. ACA, Assn. for Religious Values in Counseling, Assn. for Assessment in Counseling. Roman Catholic. Avocations: sculpting, Ukrainian Easter eggs, computers. Home: 19508 Meadowlark Ln Cleveland OH 44128-2743 Office: Cleve Christian Home Family Svcs Dept 1700 Denison Ave Ste 205 Cleveland OH 44109-2926 E-mail: jsabik@cchome.org.

SABILI, ERLINDA ASA, internist, psychiatrist, pastoral care minister; b. San Juan, Batangas, The Philippines, Sept. 27, 1959; came to U.S., 1991; d. Marciano Acorda and Rita Lalvces (Asa) S. BS in Med. Tech., U. Santo Tomas, Manila, 1976, MD, 1982. Registered med. technician, The Philippines. Intern U. Santo Tomas Hosp., 1982-83, pre-resident and resident dept. internal medicine, 1987-90; physician Antipolo (Rizal, The Philippines) Rural Health Clinic, 1983; missionary physician Sister of St. Paul, Manila, 1984-87; physician-in-charge Patronato de Sra. de Lourdes Free Clinic, 1984-95, 90-91; pastoral care vol. St. Elizabeth's Hosp., Elizabeth, N.J., 1991-93; sr. resident in internal medicine and psychiatry Albert Einstein Med. Ctr., Phila., 1993—. Presenter in field. Contbr. articles to med. jours. Vol. physician Archdiocese of Bulacan, The Philippines, 1985-86, San Antonio Feeding Ctr. for Malnourished Children, Manila, 1989-91; vol. Homeless Shelter Dwelling Place, N.Y.C., 1991-93; pastoral care vol. Albert Einstein Healthcare Network, Phila., 1993—; choir leader, pastoral care vol. to Filipino cmty. St. Mary's Cath. Ch., Elizabeth, 1991-93. Recipient young investigator's award Philippine Coll. Cardiology, 1990; Laughlin fellow Faughlin Found., 1997. Mem. AMA, ACP, Am. Psychiat. Assn., Am. Assn. Medicine and Psychiatry, Philippine Med. Assn., U. Santo Tomas Med. Alumni Assn., U. Santo Tomas Med. Mission. Avocations: playing guitar, writing poetry, singing, cooking, gardening. Home: 3207 Friendship St Philadelphia PA 19149-1516 Office: Albert Einstein Med Ctr 5501 Old York Rd Philadelphia PA 19141-3018

SABIN, JACK CHARLES, engineering and construction firm executive; b. Phoenix, June 29, 1921; s. Jack Byron and Rena (Lewis) S.; BS, U. Ariz., 1943; BSChemE, U. Minn., 1947; m. Frances Jane McIntyre, Mar. 27, 1950; children— Karen Lee, Robert William, Dorothy Ann, Tracy Ellen. With Standard Oil Co. of Calif., 1947-66, sr. engr., 1966— ; pres., dir. Indsl. Control & Engring., Inc., Redondo Beach, Calif., 1966— ; owner/mgr. Jack C. Sabin, Engr.-Contractor, Redondo Beach, 1968— ; staff engr. Pacific Molasses Co., San Francisco, 1975-77; project mgr. E & L Assocs., Long Beach, Calif., 1977-79; dir. Alaska Pacific Petroleum, Inc., 1968— , Marlex Petroleum, Inc., 1970, 71— , Served with U.S. Army, 1942-46; capt. Chem. Corps, Res., 1949-56. Registered profl. engr., Calif., Alaska; lic. gen. engring. contractor, Ariz., Calif. Mem. Nat. Soc. Profl. Engrs., Ind. Liquid Terminals Assn., Conservative Caucus, Calif. Tax Reduction Com., Tau Beta Pi, Phi Lambda Upsilon, Phi Sigma Kappa. Republican. Clubs: Elks; Town Hall of Calif. Address: 151 Camino De Las Colinas Redondo Beach CA 90277-5828

SABIN, JOHN ROGERS, physics educator; b. Springfield, Mass., Apr. 29, 1940; s. Henry Bowman and Elizabeth (Rogers) S.; m. Claudia Ball, 1963 (div. 1978); children: Peter Bowman, Amanda Ball; m. Birgit Horn, Aug. 8, 1987; children: Lene Elizabeth Horn, Niels Kristian Horn. AB, Williams Coll., 1962; PhD, U. N.H., 1966. Asst. prof. chemistry U. Mo., Columbia, 1968-71; assoc. prof. physics U. Fla., Gainesville, 1971-77, prof., 1977—, dir. IT, Coll. Liberal Arts and Scis., 1998—, interim chmn. dept. physics, 2002—; adjungeret prof. U. So. Denmark, 1992—. Guest prof. Odense (Denmark) U., 1980-92, Nordita prof., Odense, 1982-83, Fulbright prof., 1986, 91. Editor Advances in Quantum Chemistry; assoc. editor Internat. Jour. Quantum Chemistry; mem. editl. bd. Croatia Chemica Acta, 2000—. Fellow Am. Phys. Soc.; mem. Am. Chem. Soc., Danish Phys. Soc. Home: 415 NW 23rd St Gainesville FL 32607-2618 Office: U Florida Dept Physics PO Box 118435 Gainesville FL 32611-8435 E-mail: sabin@qtp.ufl.edu.

SABIN, PAUL EDGAR, developer; b. Rochester, N.Y. s. Edgar and Mabelle S.; m. Onalee Rae Barton, 1962 (div. Dec. 1978); m. Linda Emerson, 1979; children: Craig Alan, Laural Ann, Todd Aaron. BA in Psychology, Lycoming Coll., 1962; MDiv, Pacific Sch. Religion, 1966; MSW, Barry U., 1981. Pastor Ontario St. Meth. Ch., Buffalo, 1966-70; exec. sec. Meth. Metro, 1970-74; exec. dir. Man-to-Man Assoc., Columbus, Ohio, 1974-75, Watson Homestead Found., Painted Post, N.Y., 1975-79; dir. social svcs. Meth. Hosp., Jacksonville, Fla., 1981-89; pres., CEO Meth. Children's Home, Jackson, Miss., 1989-94; dir. devel. La. Meth. Children's Home, Ruston, 1994—. Exec. dir. Watson Homestead Found. Elizabeth Hay Bechtel fellow Pacific Sch. Religion, 1965. Mem. NASW (La. bd. dirs. 1997), Academy Cert. Social Workers, People to People Internat., Rotary. Democrat. Avocations: golfing, photography. Home: 2702 Huntington St Monroe LA 71201-2520 Office: La Meth Childrens Home 901 S Vienna St Ruston LA 71270-5829

SABIN, WILLIAM ALBERT, writer; b. Paterson, N.J., May 29, 1931; s. David and Esther (Goodman) S.; m. Marie Frances Noonan, May 31, 1958; children— Margaret, John, Katherine, Christopher, James BA in English, Yale U., 1952, MA in English, 1956. Pub. bus. and office edn. McGraw Hill Book Co., N.Y.C., 1973-78, editor in chief bus. books, 1979-86, pub. bus. books, 1987-90. Author: The Gregg Reference Manual, 9th edit., 2000; co-author: College English: Grammar and Style, 1967. Served as cpl. U.S. Army, 1952-54, ETO Home: 540 Fogler Rd Bristol ME 04539-3101

SABINE, GORDON ARTHUR, educator, writer; b. Brockton, Mass., Feb. 10, 1917; s. Charles Arthur and Esther (Carey) S.; m. Lois Eleanor Freiburg, June 26, 1941 (div. 1973); children: Ellen Jean, Gordon Arthur, Robert Allan, Roger Malcolm; m. Patricia Lundblade Williams, May 15, 1980; children: Patricia Glyn Williams Rhodes, John Paul, Nina Lynn Williams Keenan, Janet Anne Williams Maxim. AB, U. Wis., 1939, MA, 1941; PhD, U. Minn., 1949. Reporter, Lynchburg (Va.) News, 1931-35; reporter, copy editor Wis. State Jour., 1939-42; corr. UP, 1946-47; grad. asst. journalism U. Wis., 1939-41; instr., later asst. prof. journalism U. Kans., 1945-47; lectr. journalism U. Minn., 1947-48; asst. prof. U. Oreg., 1948-50, assoc. prof., 1950-52, prof. journalism, 1952-55, dean Sch. Journalism, 1950-55; prof., dean Coll. Communication Arts, Mich. State U., 1955-60, v.p. spl. projects, 1960-71; spl. asst. to pres. Ill. State U., 1971-72; dir. Sch. Journalism, U. Iowa, 1972-75; prof. journalism Va. Poly. Inst. and State U., 1975-84, Ariz. State U., 1985, spl. asst. for oral history to univ. libr. dean, 1986-93. Dir. Nat. Project in Agrl. Communication, 1960-62, GI Project MEMO, 1969-70; prof.-in-residence Time, Inc., 1951; Bd. dirs. Oregon Newspaper Pubs. Assn., 1950-55 Contbr. articles to nat. mags. and newspapers, 1938—; writer syndicated newspaper column Youthpoll America, 1976-77, Books That Made the Difference project Ctr. for the Book, Libr. of Congress, 1980-81; author: Quiz for College Presidents, 1970, When You Listen, This Is What You Can Hear, 1971, How Students Rate Their Schools and Teachers, 1971, Teachers Tell It Like It Is, Like It Should Be, 1972, The Folks in the Newsroom, 1977, Broadcasting in Virginia: Benchmark '79, 1980; (with Patricia L. Sabine) Books That Made the Difference: What People Told Us, 1983, Monsignor Donohoe, 1988; (with Donald Riggs) Libraries in the '90s: What the Leaders Expect, 1988, Tom Chauncey, A Memoir, 1989, Rabbi Plotkin, A Memoir, 1992, G. Homer, A Biography of Arizona State University President G. Homer Durham, 1992, Culver Bill Nelson, 1992, Phyllis B. Steckler and the Oryx Press, 1993, "... a damn beautiful butterfly": The Memoir of the Rev. William Lee Burkhardt, 1993, Nan Pyle: Payson's Unhappy Millionaire, 1993, Father Jack: Physician to the Soul, 1993, The Memoir of a Book: The Norton Reader of Expository Prose, 1993, The Evolution of a Dream, 1996, The Life and Times of Robert Lytle, 1999, The Wonderful World of Norman C. Crewfoot, 2000; cons. editor One Step From Heaven, 2001, Footprints on My Heart, 2002. Mem. Gov.'s Commn. on Employment of Handicapped, 1958-59; mem. rsch. com. Am. Coun. Edn. for Journalism, 1951-53; founder (with Patricia L. Sabine) FRIENDS of the AZ Talking Book Libr., 1995. 1st lt. AUS, 1942-45, Iceland. Carnegie Corp. fellow, 1953; FAE-NAEB scholar TV, 1954; sr. postdoctoral research fellow Am. Coll. Testing Program, 1970-71 Mem. Assn. Edn. in Journalism, Assn. Accredited Schs. and Depts. Journalism (pres. 1954-55), Am. Polit. Sci. Assn., Sigma Delta Chi (nat. research com. 1949-51), Omicron Delta Kappa. Home: 2625 E Southern Ave C-102 Tempe AZ 85282

SABINO, CATHERINE ANN, magazine editor; b. N.Y.C., May 6, 1952; d. Joseph A. and Frances (Phelan) S. AB, Barnard Coll., 1973. Beauty editor, editor-at-large Harper's Bazaar, Italia, Men's Bazaar, 1976-79; beauty editor Seventeen mag. Triangle Comms., 1979-83; N.Y. editor Linea Italiana Mondadori, 1983-85; N.Y. editor Moda RAI, 1985-86; editor in chief Worldstyle The Aegis Venture Group, 1987-88; editor in chief In Fashion Murdoch Mags., 1988-89; editor mag. devel. European Home, 1989-91; cons. Hachette Mags., 1992; editor in chief Woman's Day Beauty Hachette Mags., 1993; editor-in-chief, group editor N.Y. Times Custom Pub., N.Y.C., 1993-97; editor-in-chief, group editor, v.p. Forbes Spl. Interest Publs. Group, 1997—; v.p., editor-in-chief Brit. Living and Style, 2000—. Author: Italian Style, 1985, Italian Country, 1988. Recipient Folio award 1994, Clarion award 1998-2000, 2002. Mem. Am. Soc. Mag. Editors, Barnard-Columbia Club N.Y. (dir. at large 1991-93), Yale Club. Office: 28 W 23d St New York NY 10010-7629

SABINO, WILLIAM, lawyer, consultant; b. N.Y.C., Apr. 22, 1955; s. Albert Joseph and Mildred (Smoll) S. BA, CCNY, 1976; JD, U. N.C., 1979; LLM, Washington U., St. Louis, 1984. Bar: Ill. 1980, U.S. Tax Ct. 1984. Cons. tax. atty., Bloomfield, N.J., 1985—. Capt. U.S. Army, 1980-85. Mem. Phi Beta Kappa, Phi Alpha Theta. Republican. Avocations: sports, exercise, travel, reading, museums.

SABINSON, HARVEY BARNETT, theatrical organization administrator; b. N.Y.C., Oct. 24, 1924; s. Samuel and Sarah Sabinson; m. Sarah S. Sabinson, Aug. 15, 1944; children: Eric, Allen. BS, Queens Coll., 1947. Freelance publicist, N.Y., 1946-73; dir. spl. projects League Am. Theatres & Prodrs., N.Y.C., 1976-82, exec. dir., 1982-95. Vis. prof. theatre adminstrn. Yale U. Sch. of Drama, New Haven, 1966-70. Author: Darling, You Were Wonderful, 1977. Recipient Lifetime Achievement award United Jewish Appeal Fedn., 1990, Lifetime Achievement Tony award, 1995, Theatre Hall of Fame Founder's award, 1996. Mem. Actor's Fund of Am. (trustee 1990—), Broadway Assn. (bd. dirs. 1977—), Theater Devel. Fund (bd. dirs. 1992-96), Berkshire Theatre Festival (trustee 1995-2001), Mayor's Midtown Citizens Com., Coll. Fellows of Am. Theatre. Avocation: theatre.

SABISTON, DAVID COSTON, JR. surgeon, educator; b. Onslow County, N.C., Oct. 4, 1924; s. David Coston and Marie (Jackson) S.; m. Agnes Foy Barden, Sept. 24, 1955; children: Anne Sabiston Leggett, Agnes Sabiston Butler, Sarah Coston. BS, U. N.C., 1944; MD, Johns Hopkins U., 1947; DSc (hon.) (hon.) , U. Madrid. Successively intern, asst. resident, chief resident surgery Johns Hopkins Hosp., Balt., 1947—53; successively asst. prof., assoc. prof., prof. surgery Johns Hopkins U. Med. Sch., 1955—64; Howard Hughes investigator Johns Hopkins Med. Sch., 1955—61; Fulbright research scholar U. Oxford, England, 1960; research assoc. Hosp. Sick Children, U. London, England, 1961; James B. Duke prof. surgery, chmn. dept. Duke Med. Sch., Durham, NC, 1964—, chmn. dept. thoracic surgery, 1064—1994; chief of staff Duke U. Med. Ctr., 1994—96, dir. internat. programs, 1996—96, 1996—. Chmn. Accreditation Council for Grad. Med. Edn., 1985—86. Editor: Textbook of Surgery, Essentials of Surgery, Atlas of General Surgery, Atlas of Cardiothoracic Surgery, A Review of Surgery; co-editor: Gibbon's Surgery of the Chest, Companion Handbook to Textbook of Surgery; chmn. editl. bd.: Annals of Surgery, mem. editl. bd.: Annals Clin. Rsch., mem. editl. bd.: ISI Atlas of Sci.: The Classics of Surgery Libr., mem. editl. bd.: Surgery, Gynecology and Obsetrics, mem. editl. bd.: Jour. Applied Cardiology, mem. editl. bd.: Jour. Cardiac Surgery, mem. editl. bd.: World Jour. Surgery. Capt. M.C., AUS, 1953—55. Named named Disting. Physician, U.S. Va., 1995; recipient Career Rsch. award, NIH, 1962—64, N.C. award in Sci., 1978, Disting. Achievement award, Am. Heart Assn. Sci. Coun., 1983, Michael E. DeBakey award for Outstanding Achievement, 1984, Significant Sigma Chi award, 1987, Coll. medalist, Am. Coll. Chest Physicians, 1987, Disting. Tchr. award, Alpha Omega Alpha, 1992. Mem.: ACS (chmn. bd. govs. 1974—75, regent 1975—82, chmn. bd. regents 1982—84, pres. 1985—86), James IV Assn. Surgeons (bd. dirs. U.S. chpt.), Soc. Internat. De Chirurgie, Soc. Thoracic Surgeons Great Britain and Ireland, Soc. Surg. Chairmen (pres. 1974—76), Johns Hopkins U. Soc. Scholars, Soc. Surgery Alimentary Tract, Soc. Thoracic Surgery, Surg. Biology Club II, Halsted Soc., Soc. Univ. Surgeons (pres. 1968—69), Soc. Vascular Surgery (v.p. 1967—68), Internat. Soc. Cardiovascular Surgery, Soc. Clin. Surgery, Am. Assn. Thoracic Surgery (pres. 1984—85), So. Surg. Assn., Am. Surg. Assn. (pres. 1977—78, sec. 1969—73, pres. 1973—74), NAS Inst. Medicine, Am. Bd. Surgery (chmn. 1971—72, diplomate), Philippine Coll. Surgeons (hon.), Surg. Congress Assn. Espanola de Cirujanos (hon.), French Surg. Assn. (hon.), Japanese Coll. Surgeons (hon.), Brazilian Coll. Surgeons (hon.), Colombian Surg. Soc. (hon.), German Surgical Soc. (hon.), Royal Australasian Coll. Surgeons (hon.), Royal Coll. Surgeons Ireland (hon.), Royal Coll. Physicians and Surgeons Can. (hon.), Asociación de Cirugía del Litoral (Argentina) (hon.), Royal Coll. Surgeons Eng. (hon.), Royal Coll. Surgeons Edinburgh (hon.; editl. bd. jour.), Phila. Acad. Surgery (hon.), Ill. Surg. Soc. (hon.), Hope Valley Country Club, University Club, Cosmos Club (Washington), Alpha Omega Alpha, Phi Beta Kappa. Home: 1528 Pinecrest Rd Durham NC 27705-5817 Office: Duke U Med Ctr PO Box 2600 Durham NC 27715-2600

SABL, ANDREW, political scientist, educator; b. Santa Monica, Calif., Mar. 17, 1969; s. Bedrich Max Sabl, Verena Frymann Sabl, Verena F. Sabl; m. Miriam Jane Laugesen, Aug. 2, 1998. PhD, Harvard U., 1997, BA, 1990. Asst. prof. Policy Studies UCLA, 2000—; asst. prof. Polit. Sci. Vanderbilt U., Nashville, 1998—2000. Author: Ruling Passions: Political Offices and Democratic Ethics, 2002. Recipient Leo Strauss award for Best Dissertation in Polit. Theory, Am. Polit. Sci. Assn., 1997—98. Office: UCLA Sch Pub Policy 3250 Public Policy Bldg Los Angeles CA 90095-1656 Business E-Mail: sabl@ucla.edu.

SABLE, BARBARA KINSEY, former music educator; b. Astoria, L.I., N.Y., Oct. 6, 1927; d. Albert and Verna (Rowe) Kinsey; m. Arthur J. Sable, Nov. 3, 1973. BA, Coll. Wooster, 1949; MA, Tchrs. Coll. Columbia U., N.Y.C., 1950; DMus, U. Ind., 1966. Office mgr., music dir. Sta. WCAX, Burlington, Vt., 1954; instr. Cottey Coll., 1959-60; asst. prof. N.E. Mo. State U., Kirksville, 1962-64, U. Calif., Santa Barbara, 1964-69; prof. music U. Colo., Boulder, 1969—, prof. emeritus, 1992—. Author: (novels) The Vocal Sound, 1982; contbr. poetry and short stories. Mem.: Colo. Music Tchrs. Assn., AAUP, Nat. Assn. Tchrs. Singing (past state gov., assoc. editor bull.). Democrat. Avocation: poetry. Home: 3430 Ash Ave Boulder CO 80305-3432 Office: U Colo PO Box 301 Boulder CO 80309-0301 E-mail: bks@sable-boulder.com.

SABLE, MORRIS HERBERT, retired obstetrician-gynecologist; b. Pitts., Nov. 6, 1930; s. Louis David and Sarah (Glantz) S.; m. Barbara Sue Glazer, July 3, 1955; children: Jeffrey Howard, Pamela Joy. BA, W.Va. U., 1952, MS, 1953; MD, Chgo. Med. Sch., 1957. Diplomate Am. Bd. Ob-gyn. Intern Mt. Sinai Hosp., Cleve., 1957-58, resident, 1958-61; pvt. practice ob-gyn. Milw., 1961—2001; assoc. chmn. dept. ob-gyn. Mt. Sinai Med. Ctr., 1977-81, vice chief med. staff, 1981-83, chief med. staff, 1983-87; assoc. clin. prof. ob-gyn. U. Wis. Med. Sch., Madison, Milw., 1977—; ret., 2001, 2002. Lt. comdr. USN, 1961-63. Fellow ACS, ACOG. Democrat. Jewish.

SABLE, ROBERT ALLEN, gastroenterologist; b. Bklyn., June 21, 1948; s. Benjamin and Sara (Dickstein) S.; m. Valerie P. Kubie Kopelman, July 1, 1969 (div. Mar. 1982); 1 child, Jesse; m. Ellen Sue Finer, May 29, 1982; children: Scott, Eric. BS, MIT, 1969; MD, Albert Einstein U., 1973. Bd. cert. in internal medicine, gastroenterology and geriatrics Am. Bd. Internal Medicine. Staff physician N.Y. Telephone Co. Mid Manhattan Med. Dept., N.Y.C., 1978-81; physician Riverdale Gastroenterology Cons., Bronx, N.Y., 1981—. Chief gastroenterology St. Barnabas Hosp., Bronx, 1982—, pres. med. bd., 1985-90. Contbr. articles, reports, revs. to profl. jours. Fellow ACP, Am. Coll. Gastroenterology; mem. AMA, Am. Gastroenterologic Assn., Am. Soc. for Gastrointestinal Endoscopy. Avocations: philately, numismatics. Office: Riverdale Gastroenterol Con 3765 Riverdale Ave Bronx NY 10463-1845 E-mail: rasable@prodigy.net.

SABLEMAN, LYNN, educator; b. Niagara Falls, N.Y., Nov. 10, 1956; d. Arne and Marie Melby; m. Mark Stephen Sableman, Jan. 26, 1985; children: Paul, Charlotte, Brian. BA, Mercy Coll., 1981, MA, 1985. Tchr. Esperanza, Chgo., 1982-86, Springboard for Learning, St. Louis, 1991, Shining Rivers Sch., St. Louis, 1992—. Mem. St. Louis Waldorf Assn. (pres. 1989-91, bd. dirs. 1991—). Avocations: knitting, spinning, gardening, weaving, skiing. Office: Shining Rivers Sch 5000 Washington Pl Saint Louis MO 63108

SABLIK, MARTIN JOHN, research physicist; b. Bklyn., Oct. 21, 1939; s. Martin C. and Elsie M. (Fuzia) S.; m. Beverly Ann Shively, Nov. 26,1965; children: Jeanne, Karen, Marjorie, Larry. BA in Physics, Cornell U., 1960; MS in Physics, U. Ky., 1965; PhD, Fordham U., 1972. Jr. engr. The Martin Co., Orlando, Fla., 1962-63; instr. half-time U. Ky., Lexington, 1963-65; rsch. assoc. Fairleigh Dickinson U., Teaneck, N.J., 1965-67, instr. physics, 1967-72, asst. prof., 1972-76, assoc. prof., 1976-80; sr. rsch. scientist Southwest Rsch. Inst., San Antonio, 1980-87, staff scientist, 1987—. Local chmn. Intermag. Conf., San Antonio, 1995; mem. adv. bd. Conf. on Properties and Applications of Magnetic Materials, 1990—, Workshop on advances in Measurement Techniques and Instrumentation for Magnetic Properties Determination, 1994, Magnetic Materials, Measurements and Modeling Symposium, 1996, Magnetic Materials, Measurements and Microstructure Symposium, 1998, Symposium Magnetic Materials for Magnetoelectronic Devices, 2000; mem. exec. bd. Topical Group on Magnetism and Its Applications, 1996-97; mem. program com., assoc. editor Intermag 2000, Toronto. Mem. editl. bd.: Nondestructive Testing and Evaluation, 1989—, mem. editl. bd.: IEEE Transactions on Magnetics, 2002—; contbr. articles to profl. jours. Recipient Imagineer award Mind Sci. Found., 1989. Mem. IEEE (sr.), Am. Phys. Soc., Am. Geophys. Union, Am. Soc. Nondestructive Testing (chmn.So. Tex. sect. 1983-84, 2001—), Am. Assn. Physics Tchrs. Roman Catholic. Office: SW Rsch Inst PO Box 28510 San Antonio TX 78228-0510 E-mail: msablik@swri.edu.

SABLOFF, JEREMY ARAC, archaeologist; b. N.Y.C., Apr. 16, 1944; s. Louis and Helen (Arac) S.; m. Paula Lynne Weinberg, May 26, 1968; children: Joshua, Saralinda. AB, U. Pa., 1964; MA, PhD, Harvard U., 1969. Asst. prof., asso. prof. Harvard U., Cambridge, Mass., 1969-76; asso. prof. anthropology U. Utah, Salt Lake City, 1976-77; curator anthropology Utah Mus. Natural History, 1976-77; prof. anthropology U. N.Mex., Albuquerque, 1978-86, chmn. dept., 1980-83; Univ. prof. anthropology and the history and philosphy of sci. U. Pitts., 1986-94, chmn. dept. anthropology, 1990-92; Charles K. Williams II dir. U. Mus., U. Mus. Term prof. anthropology, curator Mesoamerican archaeology U. Pa., Phila., 1994—. Sr. fellow for Pre-Columbian Studies, Dumbarton Oaks, 1986-92, chmn. 1989-92. Author: (with G.R. Willey) A History of American Archaeology, 1974, 2d edit., 1980, 3d edit., 1993, Excavations at Seibal: Ceramics, 1975, (with C.C. Lamberg-Karlovsky) Ancient Civilizations: The Near East and Mesoamerica, 1979, 2nd edit., 1995, (with D. A. Freidel) Cozumel: Late Maya Settlement Patterns, 1984, The Cities of Ancient Mexico, 1989, rev. edit., 1997, The New Archaeology and the Ancient Maya, 1990, (with G. Tourtellot) The Ancient Maya City of Sayil: The Mapping of a Puuc Region Center, 1991; editor(with C.C. Lamberg-Karlovsky) The Rise and Fall of Civilizations, 1974, (with C.C. Lamberg-Karlovsky) Ancient Civilization and Trade, 1975, (with W.L. Rathje) A Study of Changing Pre-Columbian Commercial Systems, 1975, American Antiquity, 1977-81, (with G.R. Willey) Scientific American Readings in Pre-Columbian Archaeology, 1980, Simulations in Archaeology, 1981, Supplement to the Handbook of Middle American Indians: Archaeology, 1981, Archaeology: Myth and Reality: A Scientific American Reader, 1982, Analyses of Fine Paste Ceramics, 1982, (with D. Meltzer and D. Fowler) American Archaeology: Past and Future, 1986, (with E.W. Andrews V) Late Lowland Maya Civilization: Classic to Postclassic, 1986, (with J.S. Henderson) Lowland Maya Civilization in the Eighth Century A.D., 1993. Pres. Kolb Found., 1995—; chair Smithsonian Coun., 1999-2001, chair sci. adv. commn., 2001—. Nat. Geog. Soc. grantee, 1972-74; NSF grantee, 1983-88; NEH grantee, 1990-91 Fellow Am. Anthrop. Assn., AAAS (sec. H. chair 1994-95), Royal Anthrop. Inst., Soc. Antiquaries London; mem. Nat. Acad. Sci., Am. Philos. Soc., Soc. Am. Archaeology (pres. 1989-91), Am. Acad. Arts and Sci., Internat. Soc., Comparative Study of Civilizations, Sigma Xi. Office: U Pa Mus Archaeology and Anthropology 33d and Spruce Sts Philadelphia PA 19104-6324

SABNIS, RAM WASUDEO, research chemist; b. Bombay, June 21, 1961; s. Wasudeo Shridhar and Suhasini (Kulkarni) S.; m. Seema Ram, Oct. 19, 1994. BS in Chemistry, U. Bombay, 1982, MS in Organic Chemistry, 1984, PhD in Organic Chemistry, 1990. Rsch. fellow dept. chem. tech. U. Bombay, 1985-90; indsl. postdoctoral fellow, supr. Molecular Probes Inc., Eugene, Oreg., 1990-91; scientist N.C. State U., Raleigh, 1991-93; chief chemist U.S. Textile Corp., Lancaster, S.C., 1993-94; sr. rsch. chemist Brewer Sci., Inc., Rolla, Mo., 1994—. Adj. asst. prof. U. Mo., Rolla, 1999—; reviewer Biotechnic and Histochemistry, Sulfur Reports, Biochemistry and Cell Biology, and Bioorganic Chemistry; symposia presenter and spkr. Author: (with others) Methods in Cell Biology; contbr. more than 70 articles to profl. jours.; mem. editl. bd. Textile Chemists and Colorists, 1996—, Jour. Textile Assn., 1996—, Colourage, 1996—. Fellow Ciba-Geigy, 1991-93, Dianippon Ink and Chems., 1991-93, NIH, 1990-91, U. Grants Commn., 1985-90. Fellow AIC, Am. Assn. of Textile Chemists and Colorists, Soc. of Dyers & Colourists (CCol cert.); mem. Am. Chem. Soc. Achievements include patents for ultra thin organic black matrix, use of haloalkyl derivative of reporter molecules to analyse metabolic activity in cells, fluorescent haloalkyl derivates of reporter molecules well retained in cells; rschr. dyestuff, heterocyclic, polymer, medicinal chemistry, and biochemistry. Office: Brewer Sci Inc 2401 Brewer Dr Rolla MO 65401-7003

SABO, MARTIN OLAV, congressman; b. Crosby, N.D., Feb. 28, 1938; s. Bjorn O. and Klara (Haga) S.; m. Sylvia Ann Lee, June 30, 1963; children: Karin, Julie. BA cum laude, Augsburg Coll., Mpls., 1959; postgrad., U. Minn., 1961-62. Mem. Minn. Ho. of Reps. from 57B Dist., 1960-78, minority leader Dem.-Farmer-Labor party, 1969-72, speaker, 1973-78; mem. U.S. Congress from 5th Minn. Dist., 1979—; chmn. Dem. Study Group; dep. majority whip 96th to 103rd Congresses; mem. permanent select com. on intelligence 102d Congress; chmn. Ho. Budget Com. 103d Congress; ranking minority mem. house budget com. 104th-106th Congress, mem. standards of official conduct com., appropriations com., ranking minority mem. transp. subcom. Former mem. Nat. Adv. Commn. on Intergovtl. Rels.; past pres. Nat. Legis. Conf.; bd. regents Augsburg Coll. Mgr., player Dem. Congl. Baseball Team, 1987—. Recipient Disting. Alumni citation Augsburg Coll., Arms Control Leadership award Employees Union, Local 113, SEIU, AFL-CIO; named One of 200 Rising Young Leaders in Am. Time mag., 1974; Man of Yr. Mpls. Jr. C. of C., 1973-74, One of Ten Outstanding Young Men of Yr. Minn. Jr. C. of C., 1974; inducted Scandinavian Am. Hall of Fame, 1994. Mem. Nat. Conf. State Legis. Leaders (past pres.) Office: 2336 Rayburn Bldg Washington DC 20515-2305

SABO, RICHARD STEVEN, electrical company executive; b. Walkertown, Pa., Jan. 1, 1934; s. Alex S. and Elizabeth (Haluska) S.; m. Gail P. Digon, Feb. 15, 1954; children: Gailyn J., Richard A., Kerry S., Dale A. BS in Edn., California (Pa.) U., 1955; MS in Edn., Edinboro (Pa.) U., 1965. Tchr. Northwestern Sch. Dist., Albion, Pa., 1955-65; prodn. technician The Lincoln Electric Co., Cleve., 1965-66, staff asst. mktg., 1966-70, mgr. pub. rels., 1971-86, asst. to chmn., 1986-96, dir. cop. comms. and investor rels.; also exec. dir. James F. Lincoln Arc Welding Found.; ret., 1999. Editor: The Procedure Handbook of Arc Welding, 1994, 10 other books on arc welding; contbr. numerous articles to profl. jours. Chmn. Area Recreation Bd., Chesterland, Ohio, 1970, West Geauga Boosters, Chesterland, 1973-77; mem., bd. dirs. Profit Sharing Coun. Am., 1991-99. Recipient Svc. award Future Farmers Am., 1970—, Svc. award U.S. Skill Olympics, 1980, Lakeland Community Coll. award, 1990, Ohio State U. Hon. Welding Engring. Alumni award, 1990, Calif. U. (Pa.) medallion of Distinction, 1990, Internat. Bus. Exec. of Yr. Internat. Acad. of Bus. Disciplines, 1997. Mem. Am. Welding Soc. (vice chmn. edn. and fin. com., mem. fin. com. 1988-94, speaker, various awards, Plummer lectr. 1992), Am. Soc. for Engring. Edn., Am. Inst. Steel Cons. (mem. edn. com. 1986—), Steel Plate Fabricators Assn. (past chmn. promotions com., mem. bd. dirs. profit sharing coun. 1991-99—), California U. Alumni Assn. (trustee 1983-99—). Lodges: Masons. Republican. Presbyterian. Avocations: golf, hunting, fishing, classical music.

SABOT, RICHARD HENRY, economics educator, researcher, investor, entrepreneur; b. N.Y.C., Feb. 16, 1944; s. Arnold G. and Victoria (Gomberg) S.; m. Judith A. Plunkett, Sept. 9, 1969; children: Diana, Christopher, Oliver, Julia. BA, U. Pa., 1966, Oxford U., 1968, MA, 1970, DPhil, 1973. Rsch. officer Inst. Econs. and Stats. Oxford (Eng.) U., 1972-74; rsch. economist World Bank, Washington, 1974-84; John J. Gibson prof. econs. Williams Coll., Williamstown, Mass., 1984-99, John J. Gibson prof. econs. emeritus, 1999—. Chmn., co-founder Tripod Inc., 1992-2000 (now Terra Lycos, Inc.); also bd. dirs.; econ. advisor Office of the Exec. V.P., Interam. Devel. Bank, Washington, 1994-98; sr. rsch. fellow Internat. Food Policy Rsch. Inst., Washington, 1987-92; sr. rsch. fellow policy rsch. dept. World Bank, 1992-94; cons. OECD Devel. Ctr., Paris, 1971-74, Internat. Inst. Applied Sys. Analysis, Vienna, Austria, 1982-83, Harvard Inst. Internat. Devel., Cambridge, Mass., 1985-88, World Bank, 1985—; co-founder, chmn. eZiba.com; ptnr. Peabody-Sabot Ventures; bd. mgrs. Old Westbury Venture Fund II, Village Venture Svcs., New Forum Inc., Old Westbury Global Pvt. Equity Fund.; chmn. bd. Geek Corps. Author: Economic Development and Urban Migration, 1979, Education Productivity and Inequality, 1990, The East Asian Miracle, 1993, Making Schools Work, 1995; editor: Migration and the Labor Market in Developing Countries, 1982, Unfair Advantage, 1991, Opportunity Foregone: Education in Brazil, 1996, Development Strategy and Management of the Market Economy, 1997, Beyond Tradeoffs, 1998; contbr. numerous articles to scholarly jours. Mem. Nat. Panel on the Econ. of Ednl. Reform, Pew Found., 1991-95; trustee Nat. Child Rsch. Ctr., Washington, 1978-81; mem. nat. bd. Fund for Improvement Post-Secondary Edn., Washington, 1987-91; mem. bd. overseers Coll. Arts and Scis., U. Pa. Rsch. grantee Ford Found., Mellon Found., Rockefeller Found., MacArthur Found., World Bank; Fulbright fellow, Thouron fellow, Danforth fellow; Hon. fellow Pembroke Coll., Oxford U. Mem. Am. Econ. Assn., Royal Econ. Soc., United Oxford and Cambridge U. Club (London), Williams Club (N.Y.C.), Mt. Greylook Ski Club (bd. dirs. 1984-85). Avocations: hiking, yoga, flyfishing, cross country skiing, swimming. Home: Birch Hollow Oblong Rd Williamstown MA 01267 Office: eZiba 90 Marshall St North Adams MA 01247-2454 E-mail: dick@eziba.com.

SABRA, STEVEN PETER, lawyer; b. Fall River, Mass., Dec. 1, 1951; s. Peter B. and Eliza J. Sabra; m. Bernadette L. Brown, Sept. 24, 1977. BA in Polit. Sci., Fairfield U., 1973; JD, Duquesne U., 1976. Bar: Mass. 1977, U.S. Dist. Ct. Mass. 1977, U.S. Supreme Ct. 1985. Assoc. Law Offices of Richard N. LaSalle, Fall River, Mass., 1977-80; owner Law Offices of Steven P. Sabra, Somerset, 1980-87, Sabra Law Offices, Somerset, 1987-93, Law Offices Sabra & Aspden. P.A., Somerset, 1993—. Arbitrator accident claims Am. Arbitration Assn., Boston, 1988—; mem. hearing com. Bd. Bar Overseers, Mass., 1988-93; mem. Southeastern Regional Com. of Jud. Nominating Coun., 1995—; corporator Fall River Five Cents Savs. Bank, 1987—; mem. Bd. of Bar Overseers, Mass., 1998-2001. Chmn., pres. Fall River Port Authority/Fall River Line Pier, Inc., 1992-95. Mem. ABA, ATLA (Pres.'s Club 1998—), Mass. Bar Assn. (bd. delegates 1997-2000), Mass. Acad. Trial Attys., Bristol County Bar Assn. (pres. 1994-95), Fall River Bar Assn. (pres. 1985-87), Mass. Bar Found. Avocation: sports. Office: Law Offices Sabra & Aspden 1026 County St Somerset MA 02726-5138 E-mail: stevensabra@aol.com.

SABSAY, DAVID, library consultant; b. Waltham, Mass., Sept. 12, 1931; s. Wiegard Isaac and Ruth (Weinstein) S.; m. Helen Glenna Tolliver, Sept. 24,1 966. AB, Harvard U., 1953; BLS, U. Calif., Berkeley, 1955. Circulation dept. supr. Richmond (Calif.) Pub. Library, 1955-56; city libr. Santa Rosa (Calif.) Pub. Library, 1956-65; dir. Sonoma County Library, Santa Rosa, 1965-92; libr. cons., 1992—. Coordinator North Bay Coop. Library System, Santa Rosa, 1960-64; cons. in field, Sebastopol, Calif., 1968—. Contbr. articles to profl. jours. Commendation, Calif. Assn. Library Trustees and Commrs., 1984. Mem. Calif. Library Assn. (pres. 1971, cert. appreciation 1971, 80), ALA. Clubs: Harvard (San Francisco). Home and Office: 667 Montgomery Rd Sebastopol CA 95472-3020 E-mail: dsabsay@sonic.net.

SABY, JOHN SANFORD, physicist, consultant; b. Ithaca, N.Y., Mar. 21, 1921; s. Rasmus S. and Maude Emily (Sanford) S.; m. Mary Elizabeth Long, June 9, 1945; children: Arthur D., Thomas S., Joseph A., Jean E. BA, Gettysburg (Pa.) Coll., 1942, Sc.D. (hon.), 1969; MS, Pa. State U., 1944, PhD, 1947. Lab. instr. Gettysburg Coll., 1940-42; instr. Cornell U., 1947-50; with Gen. Electric Co., 1951-82, mgr. semicondr./solid state N.Y., 1954-56, mgr. lamp phenomena research Cleve., 1956-82; cons., 1982—; mem. vis. com. biol. and phys. scis. Case Western Res. U., chmn., 1969. Co-author: Principles of Transistor Circuits, 1953; patentee in field. Fellow IEEE (past com. officer); mem. Am. Phys. Soc., Cleve. Assn. Research Dirs. (pres. 1963-64), Am. Watchmakers Inst., Nat. Assn. Watch and Clock Collectors, Phi Beta Kappa, Sigma Xi, Phi Kappa Phi, Phi Sigma Kappa. Home: 10 Quail Trl Hendersonville NC 28792-3900

SACACCIO, MARGARET MARY, critical care, geriatrics nurse; b. S.I., N.Y., Sept. 20, 1960; d. Michael and Helen M. (Moritz) Quagliano; m. Joseph Sacaccio, Sept. 15, 1984; children: Christopher, Lisa. BSN, Wagner Coll., 1981, MS in Nursing, 1987. Cert. critical care nurse, nurse mgr., ACLS, CPR. Staff nurse, charge nurse Clove Lakes Nursing Home/H.R.F., S.I., N.Y., 1981-82, charge nurse, staff nurse, float head nurse, 1982-83; grad. nurse S.I. Hosp., 1982; staff nurse, charge nurse Bklyn. Vets. Med. Ctr., 1983, staff nurse, charge nurse ICU, CCU, 1984, nurse care coord. neurology, 1984-85, per diem charge nurse, float nurse critical care units, 1985-86, float charge, staff nurse to med./surg. units, 1986-87, nurse hematology, oncology chemotherapy,

1987-88; charge nurse, staff nurse, float perdiem nurse on call Eger Home, Inc., S.I., 1986-87; staff nurse ICU, CCU-perdiem/casual S.I. U. Hosp.-South, 1988—; adj. nursing instr. med.-surg. and pediatrics nurse Coll. of S.I./CUNY, S.I., N.Y., 1991-94, substitute lectr. pediatrics, 1995; substitute tchr. N.Y.C. Bd. Edn., 2001—02; instr. med.-surg. St. Vincent's Cath. Med. Ctr., Sch. Nursing, S.I., 2002—. Adj. instr. nursing med.-surg., pediatrics, 1995—2001.

SACCA, HARRIET WANDS, music educator; b. Pittsfield, Mass; d. Harry J. and Anna F. (Mara) Wands; BS, Coll. St. Rose, 1939, MA, 1962; student SUNY, Albany, Oneonta. Tchr. pub. schs., Albany, N.Y., 1942-66; instr. Coll. St. Rose, 1962-63; dir. music edn. Albany (N.Y.) Bd. Edn., 1966—; bur. assoc. examiner personnel N.Y. State Dept. Edn. Past pres. Soroptimist Internat., 1969-70, City Club Albany, Inc., 1974-75; active Albany County Dem. Com., 1962—; jud. del. 3d Jud. Dist. N.Y. State, 1975-96; mem. Albany Local Devel. Corp.; bd. dirs. St. Joseph's Housing Corp., Albany Tulip Festival; mem. adv. bd. capital Region Ctr. Arts in Edn., 1983—, Albany County Alteratives to Incarceration, 1983-96, chair sub com., 1985—; bd. dirs. Coop. Extension Community Resources Devel., 7 County Youth Symphony Orch., 1970-84; project dir. N.Y. Council on Arts; chair festival N.Y. Sch. Music, 1988; mem. com. of 5 appointed select name for 16,000 seat Civic Arena; trustee assoc. Coll. of St. Rose, 1996—; mem. exec. bd. N.Y.S. Coun. Music Adminstrs., 1996—; area 3 rep. N.Y. State Coun. Music Adminstrs., 1995—. Recipient Citizen of Yr. award Ford Motor Co., 1971; Women Helping Women award Soroptimist, 1975; Disting. Service award N.Y. State PTA, 1985. Fellow Harry Truman Library; mem. Nat. Coun. Music Adminstrs., Music Educators Nat. Conf., N.Y. State Sch. Music Assn., Capitol Hill Choral Soc. (dir.), N.Y. St. Council Arts Award Childrens Opera (dir. project), Albany Adminstrs. Assn., Albany Civic Auditorium (dir.), Delta Kappa Gamma, Delta Epsilon. Democrat. Roman Catholic. Clubs: Bus. and Profl. Women's, Soroptimist, Club of Albany, Cath. Women's Service League, Coll. St. Rose Alumni, Pres.'s Soc. Home: 10 Birch Hill Rd Albany NY 12211-2003 Office: Albany Bd Edn Acad Park Albany NY 12207

SACCHET, EDWARD MICHAEL, foreign service officer; b. Bklyn., Sept. 28, 1936; m. Elizabeth Priore. BA in Internat. Affairs, George Washington U., 1958; postgrad., Sch. Advanced Internat. Studies, Johns Hopkins U., Bologna, Italy, 1958-59; MA in Internat. Affairs, Sch. Advanced Internat. Studies, Johns Hopkins U., 1960; postgrad., U. Oslo, Norway, 1959. Labor economist U.S. Dept. of Labor, Washington, 1961-63; mem. U.S. Fgn. Service-Dept. of State, 1963—; internat. economist White House Office of Spl. Trade Rep., Washington and Geneva, 1964-67; sec., econ. comml. officer Am. Embassy, Tananarive, Madagascar, 1967-69; consul, econ. comml. officer Am. Consulate Gen., Naples, Italy, 1969-72; 1st sec., fin. economist Am. Embassy, Rome, Italy, 1972-75; congl. fellow U.S. House of Reps and U.S. Senate, 1975-76; econ. officer Bur. Econ. and Bus. Affairs-U.S. Dept. State, 1976-78; career devel. and assignments officer Bur. of Personnel-U.S. Dept. State, 1978-80; consul gen. Am. Consulate Gen., Marseille, France, 1980-84; Pearson fellow, spl. advisor to Gov. of Fla. for Internat. Issues Tallahassee, 1984-85; fgn. svc. inspector Office Inspector Gen. Fgn. Svc.-U.S. Dept. State, Washington, 1985-87; U.S. consul gen. Am. Consulate Gen., Martinique, French W. Indies, 1987-88; spl. asst. Office Exec. Dir., Bur. Econ. and Bus. Affairs-Dept. State, 1987; acting ambassador U.S. Embassy, Antigua, W.I., 1988; cons. Bur. Adminstrn., info. mgmt. system and diplomatic security U.S. Dept. State, 1989-95; dir. state dept. ops. br. U.S. Archives, College Park, Md., 1996-98; information mgmt. State Dept., Washington, 1998—. Mem. IL CIRCOLO, Palm Beach, Fla. George Washington U. scholar, 1954-58, Johns Hopkins Sch. Internat. Studies scholar, Washington and Bologna, Italy, 1958-60; State Dept. fellow, 1980, Pearson fellow Office of Gov. Fla., 1984, Congl. fellow Am. Polit. Sci. Assn., 1980. Mem. Am. Fgn. Svc. Assn., Johns Hopkins U. Alumni Assn., Army-Navy Club of Washington. Home: 118 Monroe St Apt 907 Rockville MD 20850-2513 also: 13167 La Lique Ct Palm Beach Gardens FL 33410-1417

SACCHETTI, KAREN, creative arts educator; b. Phila., Sept. 15, 1964; d. Anthony Robert Sacchetti and Eleanor Joanne Crissman. BA, Lesley U., 1998. Yoga/creative movement tchr. All That Matters, Wakefield, R.I., 1998—; yoga/movement tchr. Jamestown (R.I.) Early Learning Ctr., 1999—, Wickford (R.I.) Elem. Sch., 1999—, R.I. State Task Force, Narragansett, 1999—, South County Montessori Sch., North Kingstown, R.I., 2000—. Actress, dancer Riverside Theatre, Boston, 1993, 94; actress Landsdowne St. Playhouse, Boston, 1995. Author: (poetry) Passage, 1983, (short stories) Once Upon An Archetype, 1996. Mem.: People for Ethical Treatment of Animals. Avocations: piano, dancing, theater, reading, travel. E-mail: creativeyoga@msn.com.

SACCO, ALBERT, JR. astronaut; b. Boston, May 3, 1949; s. Albert and Sarah Kathleen Sacco; m. Teran Lee Gardner, Nov. 1971; 4 children. BS in Chem. Engring., Northeastern U., 1973; PhD in Chem. Engring., MIT, 1977. Cert. scuba instr. Faculty, to prof. chem. engring. Worcester (Mass.) Poly. Ins., 1977—, head dept. chem. engring., 1989—; astronaut, payload specialist NASA STS-73, 1995. Prin. investigator Zeolite Crystal Growth experiments, STS-73; cons., fields of catalysis, solid/gas contacting, and equipment design for space applications; former co-owner restaurant bus., Boston; invited expert joint U.S./European NATO Advanced Study Inst., 1989. Contbr. articles profl. jours., chapters to books. Recipient Adm. Earl award, Worcester Engring. Soc., 1984; grantee NSF, 1978. Mem.: AIAA (tech. com. on space processing 1990—95), AIChE (treas. We. sect. 1979—82), Assn. Space Explorers-USA, Am. Carbon Soc. (adv. bd.), N.Am. Catalysis Soc. (New Eng. rep. 1985—89), New Eng. Catalysis Soc. (pres. 1983—85). Avocations: jogging, reading, walking, scuba diving. Office: Astronaut Office/CB NASA Johnson Space Ctr Houston TX 77058*

SACCO, JOHN MICHAEL, accountant; b. N.Y.C., Oct. 17, 1952; s. Anthony Carmine and Angelina (Pellegrino) Sacco. BS, St. John's U., 1974. CPA CPA. Staff acct. Price Waterhouse & Co., N.Y.C., 1974-75; semi-sr. acct. Seidman & Seidman, CPAs, White Plains, N.Y., 1976-77; sr. acct. Diamond Internat. Corp., N.Y.C., 1977-79, Burns Internat. Security Svcs., Inc., Briarcliff Manor, N.Y., 1979-81; acctg. mgr. Burns Integrated Sys., Inc., NY, 1981-83; pvt. practice White Plains, N.Y., 1978—. Mem.: AICPA, N.Y. Soc. CPA. Republican. Roman Catholic. Home: 197 Upper Shad Rd Pound Ridge NY 10576-2237 Office: 3010 Westchester Ave Purchase NY 10577-2535

SACCO, RUDOLPH AUGUSTINE, retired judge; b. Pittsfield, Mass., May 2, 1927; s. Domenico S. and Carmella (Pinyone) S.; m. Katherine M. Turschmann, June 21, 1953; children: Cami, Domenick, Carolyn, Robert, Judi, Catherine, Dianne, Alycia, Rudolph A., Virginia. BS, Boston Coll., 1951; LLB, Suffolk U., 1956. Bar: Mass. 1957. Asst. atty. gen. Commonwealth of Mass.; commr. Dept. Pub. Utilities, Commonwealth of Mass.; judge, trial divsn. Probate and Family Ct. of Mass., 1973-97; ret., 1997. Bd. dirs. Boy Scouts Am., United Cerebral Palsy, Big Sisters, Make A Wish, Italian Cultural Com. of Springfield. Served with USN, 1945-46. Mem. Mass. Bar Assn., Berkshire Bar Assn. (sec.), Am. Acad. Matrimonial Lawyers (bd. of mgrs.). Republican. Roman Catholic. Home: 885 Washington Mt Rd Washington MA 01223

SACERDOTE, ALAN SCOTT, endocrinologist; b. Mount Vernon, N.Y., Mar. 11, 1948; s. Paul Emil and Pearl Rita (Quittel) Sacerdote; m. Nancy R. Sacerdote, Feb. 7, 1971; children: Derek, Allison. BA, NYU, 1970; MD, N.Y. Med. Coll., 1974. Dir. diabetes/endocrine ctr. The Bklyn. Hosp. Ctr., 1979-83; chief adult endocrinology sect. Woodhull Med. and Mental Health Ctr., Bklyn., 1983—; asst. prof. medicine SUNY Health Scis. Ctr., 1979-92, clin. assoc. prof. medicine, 1992—. Adj. prof. endocrinology Pa. Program L.I. U., Bklyn., 1980—; endocrine cons. Bklyn. VA Med. Ctr., 1979—; adv. bd. mem. Juvenile Diabetes Found., Bklyn., 1979—. Mem., spkrs. panel Physicians Com. for Responsible Medicine, Washington, 1990—. Grantee travel, Westwood-Squibb Pharms., 1996, Merck Pharms., 1994, Hoechst-Celanese Pharms. (now Arentis Pharms.), 1994, multi-ctr. clin. rsch., 1993. Fellow: ACP; mem.: Am. Diabetes Assn. (clin. soc., govt. rels. com.), The Endocrine Soc., Rosicrucian Order. Democrat. Jewish. Avocation: Avocations: underwater photography, antiquing. E-mail: WalrusA@netscape.net.

SACERDOTE, PETER M. investment banker; b. Turin, Italy, Oct. 15, 1937; came to U.S., 1940; s. Giorgio S. and Luciana (Levi) S.; m. Bonnie Lee Johnson, June 18, 1967; children: Alisa, Alexander, Laurence. B.E.E., Cornell U., 1960; MBA, Harvard U., 1964. Assoc. investment banking div. Goldman, Sachs & Co., N.Y.C., 1964-69, v.p. investment banking div., 1969-73, gen. ptnr., 1973-90, ltd. ptnr., 1990-99; advisory dir., 1999—. Bd. dirs. AMF Corp., Richmond, Va., Qualcomm, Inc., San Diego, Franklin Resource, San Mateo, Calif.; in charge Pvt. Fin. Dept., 1974-80, The Corp. Fin. Dept., 1980-87, Merch Bank, 1987-90; chmn. Committments, Credit and Investment Cons., 1987-90, GS Capital Partnership; adj. prof. Columbia Grad. Sch. Bus., 1984-86; nat. chmn. HBSFD, Milton (Mass.) Acad. Trustee Day Sch., N.Y.C., 1980-85; chmn. Alumni Bd. Harvard Bus. Sch., 1990-92; bd. visitors Fuqua Sch. Duke U., 1990-96; bd. overseers Cornell Med. Coll.; bd. dirs. Nantucket Conservation Found. Served to lt. (j.g.) USNR, 1960-62. Mem. Harvard Club N.Y.C., River Club N.Y.C., Downtown Assn., Nantucket Yacht Club, Stanwich Golf Club, Country Club of the Rockies, Sankaty Head Golf Club, Nantucket Golf Club, Eagle Springs Golf Club. Office: Goldman Sachs & Co 85 Broad St Fl 10 New York NY 10004-2434

SACHA, ROBERT FRANK, osteopathic physician; b. Each Chicago, Ind., Dec. 29, 1946; s. S. Frank John and Ann Theresa S.; m. Linda T. LePage, 1988; children: Joshua Jude, Josiah Gerard, Anastasia Levon, Jonah Bradley. BS, Purdue U., 1969; DO, Chgo. Coll. Osteo. Medicine, 1975. Diplomate Am. Bd. Pediatrics, Am. Bd. Allery and Immunology. Pharmacist, asst. mgr. Walgreens Drug Store, East Chicago, Ind., 1969-75; intern David Grant Med. Ctr., San Francisco, 1975-76, resident in pediatrics, 1976-78; fellow in allergy and immunology Wilford Hall Med. Ctr., 1978-80; staff pediatrician, allergist Scott AFB (Ill.), 1980-83; practice medicine specializing in allergy and immunology Cape Girardeau, Mo., 1983—. Assoc. clin. instr. St. Louis U., 1980—; clin. instr. Purdue U., 1971-72, Pepperdine U., 1975-76, U. Tex.-San Antonio, 1978-80, assoc. clin. instr. So. Ill. U. Pres., Parent Tchrs. League; bd. gov. Chgo. Coll. Osteopathic Medicine. Maj. M.C. USAF, 1975-83, comdr. USNR. Named one of Top Pediatricians 2002-2003, Pediatric Allergy, Immunology. Fellow Am. Coll. Allergy, Am. Coll. Chest Physicians, Am. Acad. Pediatrics, Am. Acad. Allergy-Immunology, Am. Assn. Cert. Allergists; mem. ACP, AMA, Am. Acad. Allergy, Assn. Mil. Allergists, Am. Coll. Emergency Physicians, Mil. Surgeons and Physicians. Republican. Lutheran. E-mail: lsacha@ldd.net.

SACHAR, DAVID BERNARD, gastroenterologist, medical educator; b. Urbana, Ill., Mar. 2, 1940; s. Abram Leon and Thelma (Horwitz) S.; m. Joanna Maud Belford Silver, Aug. 29, 1961; children: Mark Benson, Kenneth Hulbert Belford (dec.). AB magna cum laude, Harvard U., 1959, MD cum laude, 1963. Diplomate Am. Bd. Gastroenterology, Am. Bd. Internal Medicine. Intern Beth Israel Hosp., Boston, 1963-65, resident in internal medicine, 1967-68; asst. chief clin. rsch. Pakistan-SEATO Cholera Rsch. Lab., Dhaka, Bangladesh, 1965-67; resident in gastroenterology Mt. Sinai Hosp., N.Y.C., 1968-70; from instr. to prof. medicine Mt. Sinai Sch. Medicine, CUNY, 1970-92, 1st Burrill B. Crohn prof. medicine, 1992-99; dir. div. gastroenterology Mt. Sinai Hosp., 1983-99, vice-chmn. dept. medicine, 1992-99, dir. emeritus, 1999—. Co-chmn. work group on inflammatory bowel disease NIH, 1973-75; expert adv. panel on gastroenterology and nutrition U.S. Pharmacopeial Conf., 1980-85; chmn. rsch. devel. com. Nat. Found. for Ileitis and Colitis, 1984-89; co-founder, sec.-treas. Burrill B. Crohn Rsch. Found., N.Y.C., 1984—; chmn. GI adv. bd. Solway Pharm., Inc., 2000—; K.H. Koster meml. lectr. Danish Soc. of Gastroenterology, 1992; Internat. State of the Art lectr. Falk Symposia, Germany, 1996, 2000, Belgium, 1998, Italy, 2001, Brit. Soc. Gastroenterology, 1998, World Congresses Gastroenterology, Austria, 1998, Italy, 1999, Turkish Soc. Gastroenterology, 1998, Hungarian Soc. Gastroenterology, 1999, Hellenic Soc. Gastroenterology, 1999; 20th ann. Norman Tanner Meml. lectr. St. George's Hosp. Med. Sch., London, 1997, 25th ann. Nana Svartz Meml. lectr., Örebro, Sweden, 2000; mem. Gastroenterology Leadership Coun. Task Force on Fellowship Curriculum, 1994; co-chmn. 40th ann. postgrad. course Portuguese Soc. Gastroenterology, 2000. Author over 200 articles and chpts. on natural history and treatment of inflammatory bowel disease; editor 7 books and monographs on gastroenterology. Trustee Bangladesh Coun. of the Asia Soc., N.Y.C., 1972-75, Bd. Edn., Englewood Cliffs, N.J., 1973-75. Sr. surgeon, comdr. USPHS,1965-67. Recipient Jacobi medallion for Disting. Achievement, Mt. Sinai Alumni Assn., 1994, Alexander Richman Commemorative award for humanism in medicine, 1996, Norman Tanner medal St. George's Hosp. Med. Sch., 1997, Gold Headed Cane award, 1997. Fellow ACP, Am. Coll. Gastroenterolotgy (program dirs. com. 1991—, Henry Baker Presdl. lectr. 1989); mem. Am. Gastroent. Assn. (chmn. subcom. on cert. 1987, 1st chmn. clin. tchg. project 1984-90, mem. 1990-93, 98—, nominating com. 1993-94, chmn. immuno-inflammatory disorders sectional nominating com. 1995, Disting. Educator award 1996), Crohn's and Colitis Found. Am. (grants rev. com. and coun. 1990-94, Disting. Svc. award 1991, N.Y. Govs. medal 1992, chmn. clin. rsch. subcom. Disease Classification and Measurement 1994), Internat. Orgn. for Study of Inflammatory Bowel Disease (1st Am. elected chmn. 1989-92), Phi Beta Kappa, Alpha Omega Alpha. Achievements include co-development of oral rehydration therapy for diarrhea; development of resources and standards for clinical teaching in gastroenterology. Office: Mt Sinai Med Ctr One Gustave L Levy Pl New York NY 10029

SACHAR, LOUIS, writer prose; b. East Meadow, N.Y., Mar. 20, 1954; married, 1985; 1 child. Student, Antioch Coll.; BA, U. Calif., Berkeley, 1976; JD, Hastings Coll. Law, San Francisco, 1980. Part-time atty. Author: (children's books) Sideways Stories From Wayside School, 1978 (1979 Children's Choice Book), Johnny's in the Basement, 1981, Someday Angeline, 1983, Sixth Grade Secrets, 1987, There's A Boy in the Girls' Bathroom, 1987, The Boy Who Lost His Face, 1989, Wayside School is Falling Down, 1989, Dogs Don't Tell Jokes, 1991, Marvin Redpost: Kidnapped at Birth?, 1992, Marvin Redpost: Is He a Girl?, 1993, Marvine Redpost: Why Pick on Me?, 1993, Alone in His Teachers' House, 1994, Wayside School Gets a Little Stranger, 1995. Winner 1999 Newberry medal for Holes. Mem. Soc. Children's Book Writers and Illustrators, Authors Guild. Office: c/o Farrar Straus & Giroux 19 Union Sq W New York NY 10003-3304

SACHAROW, BEVERLY LYNN, gerontologist; b. N.Y.C. d. Jules and Mary (Trupine) Levy; m. Stanley Sacharow, June 18, 1961; children: Scott Hunter, Brian Evan. BA, Rutgers U., 1980, M in Gerontology Edn., cert. ednl. gerontology, Rutgers U., 1983. Rschr. U. Pa., Robert W. Johnson Hosp., New Brunswick, N.J., 1976-81; dir. Gerontology Inst. N.J., Milltown, 1983—, Gerontology Inst. N.J., Pa., N.Y., Milltown, 1996—. Tour guide, rsch. leader, del. on tour of geriatric facilities, Moscow, Kiev and St. Petersburg, Russia, 1992; invited reporter White House Conf. on Aging, Washington, 1996; conf. planner in gerontology and health; cons. assisted living industry, long term care nursing homes, start-up divsn. of social work practice. Editor (newsletter) Update on Aging, 1983; video prodr. over 300 gerontology vide tapes, 1985—. Adv. com. mem. Gov. Conf. on Aging, Trenton State Coll., 1981; mem. adv. bd. East Brunswick (N.J.) Office on Aging, 1982; planner Brandeis U. Women Study Group. Mem. Am. Soc. on Aging, Nat. Coun. on Aging (mem. press for nat. conf.), Sigma Phi Omega. Avocations: travel, golf. Office: Gerontology Inst PO Box 345 Milltown NJ 08850-0345 E-mail: geronusa@aol.com.

SACHAROW, STANLEY, chemist, consultant, writer; b. N.Y.C., Oct. 8, 1935; s. Max and Fannie (Rosenberg) S.; m. Beverly Lynn Levy, June 18, 1961; children: Scott Hunter, Brian Evan. AB, Hunter Coll., 1957, MA, 1965. Engr. Standard Packaging Corp., Clifton, N.J., 1960-65; sales engr. Archer Aluminum, Winston-Salem, N.C., 1965-67; tech. svc. mgr. Reynolds Metals Co., Richmond, Va., 1967-84; exec. dir. The Packaging Group Inc., 1984—. Author: Food packaging, 1970; Principles of Packaging Development, 1972; A Packaging Primer, 1979; Packaging Regulations, 1979. Contbr. articles to profl. jours. Recipient Golden Keys award Club Printing N.Y., 1969, Best Tech. Article award Chilton Press, 1974. Mem. Packaging Inst., Am. Chem. Soc., Coblentz Soc., Inst. Dirs. (U.K.), Inst. Packaging (U.K.), Napoleonic Soc. (Clearwater, Fla.), Victorian Soc. (Phila.). Republican. Avocations: antiques, writing, Napoleonic battles. Home: 70 Valley Forge Dr East Brunswick NJ 08816-3278 Office: Packaging Group Inc PO Box 345 Milltown NJ 08850-0345

SACHDEV, OM PRAKASH, biochemist; b. Allahabad, India, May 15, 1949; s. Jhangi Ram and Thakuri Devi (Keswani) S.; m. Chander Prabha Lulla, Nov. 5, 1984; children: Bindu, Nina. MS, Alahabad U., 1971; PhD, Howard U., 1980; MBA, Fairleigh Dickinson U., 2000. Lectr. biochemistry Med. Coll., Jabalpur, India, 1971-74; postdoctoral fellow Coll. of Physics and Surgery Columbia U., N.Y.C., 1981-82, assoc. Coll. of Physics and Surgery, 1983-84; biochemist Lederle Labs., Pearl River, N.Y., 1984-88; clin. rsch. assoc. med. rsch. div. Am. Cyanamid Co., 1989-92, dir. R&D, 1992-95; assoc. dir. clin. pharmacy Chemex Pharms., Inc., 1995-96; trial ctr. mgr. Janssen Rsch. Found., Titusville, N.J., 1996—; dir. project mgmt. Kyowa Pharms., Inc., 2001—; global clin. trial mgr. pharm. R&D divsn. Johnson & Johnson, 1996—2001. Chmn. Lederle Sci. Lect. Com., Pearl River, 1988—. Contbr. articles to profl. jours. Soc. sec. City Delegacy, Allahabad U. Student Union, 1967-69. Mem. Am. Assn. Pharm. Soc. (moderator biotech. sect. 1989), Am. Chem. Soc., Am. Soc. for Microbiology. Achievements include invention of cellular and molecular models to study lipoprotein metabolism in humans. Home: 14 Crestwood Dr Piscataway NJ 08854-7502

SACHER, BARTON STUART, lawyer; b. Birmingham, Ala., Apr. 9, 1948; s. Martin R. and Inez (Joseph Alan) S.; 1 child, Joseph Alan; m. Susan Angela Anton, Sept. 30, 1976. BS, U. Ala., 1970, JD, 1973. Law clk. to judge S. Pointer U.S. Dist. Ct., Birmingham, 1973-74; assoc. Berkowitz, Lefkowitz & Patrick, 1974-77; atty. investigations, trial counsel SEC, Washington, 1977-79, chief of investigations and enforcement Atlanta Region, 1979-85; ptnr. Tew, Jorden, Schulte & Beasley, Miami, 1986-90; pres., dir., ptnr. Sacher, Zelman, Van Sant, Paul, Beiley, Hartman, Terzo & Waldman PA, 1990—. V.p., trustee Temple Israel of Greater Miami, Inc.; v.p., dir. Alex Muss H.S., Israel; regional dir. ADL, Nat. Fin. Com., Dem. Party, Dem. Leadership Coun.; mem. S.E. regional coun. Union Am. Hebrew Congregations. Mem. ABA, Fed. Bar Assn., Fla. Bar Assn., D.C. Bar Assn., Ala. State Bar Assn., Greater Miami C. of C. (trustee), Grove Isle Club. Jewish. Office: Sacher Zelman Van Sant Paul Beiley Hartman Terzo & Waldman P 1401 Brickell Ave 7th Fl Miami FL 33131-3506

SACHER, RONALD ALAN, hematologist; b. Johannesburg, South Africa, Feb. 6, 1946; s. Barney and Doris S.; m. Heather, Feb. 3, 1970; children: Gregory Neill, Samantha Anne. BSc, Witwatersrand U., 1965, MBBCh, 1969. Intern in medicine, surgery Baragwanath Hosp., Johannesburg, 1970; sr. house office pediat. Johannesburg Children's Hosp., 1972; registrar hematology South African Inst. Med. Rsch., Johannesburg, 1974-75; from asst. prof. to prof., head dept. lab. medicine Georgetown U. Sch. Medicine, Washington, 1980-2000; prof., dir. Hoxworth Blood Ctr. U. Cin. Med. Ctr., 2000—. Chmn. med. adv. bd. Chesapeak chpt. ARC, 1992-2000, scientific review com. for blood transfusion scis., 1981-87, med. adv. com. Washington chpt., 1980-2000. Fellow Royal Coll. Physicians and Surgeons of Can.; mem. AAAS, Am. Assn. Blood Banks (chmn. several nat. & internat. meetings 1982, nat. co-chmn. pediat. hemotherapy com. 1982-83, chmn. 1983-87, tech. & scientific workshop com. 1987-94, chmn. 1991-94, chmn. continuing edn. com. 1994), Coll. Am. Pathology, Internat. Soc. Thrombosis and Hemostasis, Am. Soc. for Clin. Pathology, Am. Fedn. Clin. Rsch., Am. Soc. Hematology, Am. Assn. of Blood Banks, Am. Clin. Climate Soc. Office: U Cin Med Ctr Hoxworth Blood Ctr 3130 Highland Ave Cincinnati OH 45267-0055

SACHER, SETH BARRY, economist; b. Bklyn., Oct. 12, 1962; s. Herbert Jerome and Eunice Sacher; m. Barbara Helene Glickstein, Dec. 21, 1991; children: Elana, Sara, Max. BA, SUNY, Binghamton, 1984; MA, U. Md., 1989, PhD, 1990. Economist FTC, Washington, 1990-98, Charles River Assocs., Washington, 1998—. Contbr. articles to profl. jours. N.Y. State regents scholar, 1980-84. Avocation: reading. Home: 2975 Emerald Chase Dr Oak Hill VA 20171-2324 Office: Charles River Assocs Ste 700 1201 F St Washington DC 20004-1204 E-mail: sbs@crai.com.

SACHER, STEVEN JAY, lawyer; b. Cleve., Jan. 28, 1942; s. Albert N. and Cecil P. (Chessin) S.; m. Colleen Marie Gibbons, Nov. 28, 1970; children—Alexander Jerome, Barry Elizabeth, William Paul BS, U. Wis., 1964; JD, U. Chgo., 1967. Bar: D.C. 1968. Assoc. solicitor Employee Retirement Income Security Act U.S. Dept. Labor, Washington, 1974-77; spl. counsel com. on labor and human resources U.S. Senate, 1977-79, gen. counsel, 1980-81; ptnr. Pepper, Hamilton & Scheetz, 1982-88; shareholder Johnson & Gibbs, 1988-94; ptnr. Kilpatrick Stockton LLP, 1994—. Adj. prof. law Georgetown U. Law Ctr., 1977; co-chair sr. editors Employee Benefits Law and Annual Supplements, Bur. Nat. Affairs, Washington, 1991-2000. Mem. adv. bd. BNA Pension and Benefits Reporter; mem. editorial bd. Benefits Law Jour., Jour. Pension Planning and Compliance. Founding mem. ERISA Roundtable, Washington. Fellow Coll. Labor and Employment Lawyers, Am. Coll. Employee Benefits Counsel (charter); mem. ABA (mgmt. co-chmn. com. on employee benefits, sect. on labor and employment law 1988-91, chmn. prohibited trans. subcom., com. on employee benefits, sect. on taxation 1986-91), D.C. Bar Assn. Office: Kilpatrick Stockton LLP 607 14th St NW Ste 900 Washington DC 20005 E-mail: ssacher@kilpatrickstockton.com.

SACHINIS, HARRY (GEORGE SACHINIS), information industry executive; b. Athens, Greece, Sept. 26, 1958; came to U.S., 1982; s. George Pericles and Athanassia (Spyropoulos) S. Diploma in engring., Nat. Tech. U., Athens, 1982; MBA, Harvard U., 1984. Cons. DRI/McGraw-Hill, Houston, 1984-85; cons. mgr. Platts/McGraw-Hill, 1985-88; v.p. Standard & Poor's ComStock, Harrison, N.Y., 1988-92; group v.p. Standard & Poor's, N.Y.C., 1992-97; pres. Platts, 1997—. Avocations: windsurfing, tennis, car racing.

SACHITANO, SHEILA MARIE, secondary school educator, small business owner; b. Austin, Tex., July 25, 1948; d. Marvin Valery and Dorthy Marie (Gunn) Louviere; m. Bennett Meigs Jenkins, Jr. June, 1973 (div. Sept. 1975); m. Fred Clarke Sachitano, May 8, 1979; 1 child, Derek Alexander. BA, U. Tex., 1970; MA, Lamar U., 1975. Cert. tchr., supr., Tex. Tchr. Anahuac (Tex.) H.S., 1970-75; sales mgr. Jarad's Inc., Beaumont, Tex., 1976-78; tchr. Hamshire (Tex.) Fannett H.S., 1978—. Mng. agt. Young Estate Farm, Port Arthur, Tex.; sec. campus site base Hamshire Fammett H.S., 1994-96, 98-99; pres. dist. site base, Hamshire-Fannet Ind. Sch. Dist., 1996-2000; presenter New Tchr. Orientation, Hamshire-Fannett H.S., 1994—, VIL coord., 1999--; owner Modern Electric Co. of Beaumont, Inc. Compiler Genealogical Books: The D'Amours de Louvieres in France, Canada, Louisiana, (3 vols.). Pres. Twin County Babe Ruth League, Winnie, Tex., 1994, 95; team organizer Twin County Baseball, Sour Lake, Tex., 1996-97. Mem NEA, Am. Assn. Tchrs. French (v.p. East Tex. chpt. 1998—), Nat. Coun. Tchrs. of English, Tex. State Tchrs. Assn. (pres. 1986-88), Pi Delta Phi. Roman Catholic.

SACHS, DAVID, lawyer; b. N.Y.C., Aug. 4, 1933; s. Morris and Fannie R. (Sachs; m. Frumet P. Lome, July 7, 1957; children: Diane R., Daniel L., Francine E. BS, U. Pa., 1954; JD, Harvard U., 1957. Bar: N.Y. 1958, U.S. Tax Ct. 1959, U.S. Ct. Fed. Claims 1960, U.S. Ct. Appeals (2d cir.) 1960, U.S. Supreme Ct. 1967. Assoc. White & Case, N.Y.C., 1957-68, ptnr., 1968-88, ret. ptnr., 1988—. Fellow Am Coll. Tax Counsel, N.Y. Bar Found.; mem. N.Y. Bar Assn. (chmn. tax sect. 1980, ho. dels. 1981-82, tax sect. exec. com.), N.Y.C. Bar Assn. (chmn. com. on taxation 1986-89, mem. coun. on taxation 1990-96). Office: White & Case 1155 Avenue Of The Americas New York NY 10036-2787

SACHS, DAVID HOWARD, surgery and immunology educator, researcher; b. N.Y.C., Jan. 10, 1942; s. Elliot and Elsie (Hurvitz) S.; m. Kristina Olsson, Mar. 15, 1969; children: Michelle, Jessica, Karin, Teviah. AB, Harvard U., 1963; DES, U. Paris, 1964; MD, Harvard U., Boston, 1968. Intern in surgery Mass. Gen. Hosp., Boston, 1968-69, resident in surgery, 1969-70, dir. transplantation biology rsch. ctr. surgery dept., 1991—; chief immunology br. Nat. Cancer Inst., Bethesda, Md., 1982-90; prof. surgery and immunology Harvard U. Med. Sch., 1991—. Capt. PHS, 1970-91. Avocations: gardening, fishing, windsurfing, skiing. Office: Mass Gen Hosp East Bldg 149-9019 13th St Boston MA 02129 E-mail: sachs@helix.mgh.harvard.edu.

SACHS, FREEMAN, retired management consultant, volunteer; b. Omaha, Nov. 28, 1921; s. Charles and Anna Behrendt Sachs; m. Auguste Erika Sachs, Sept. 26, 1947; children: Michael Eduard, Martin Gregor (dec.). Grad. h.s., 1939; student, U. San Francisco, 1961, 77, U. Calif., Berkeley, 1962, 75, San Jose (Calif.) State U., 1975. With U.S. Mil., 1942-78, Internat. Exec. Svc. Corps., Stamford, Conn., 1978-88; ind. rschr., exec. vol., 1988-98. Mgmt. cons. Nat. Port Authority, Liberia, 1978, Cidade U., São Paulo, 1981, Guatemala, 1982, Empressa Nat. Portuaria, Honduras, 1983, Transp. Navieros Ecuatorianos, Ecuador, 1984, Intraship Kenya Ltd., Mombasa, Kenya, 1987, Sierra Leone Nat. Petroleum Co., Ltd., 1988. Recipient 9 Outstanding Performance and Achievement awards U.S. Army, 1964-78, 24 acknowledgments Dept. Def., U.S. industry. Lutheran. Avocations: shortwave radio, gardening, parrots. Home: 772 Montecillo Rd San Rafael CA 94903-3136

SACHS, HOWARD F(REDERIC), federal judge; b. Kansas City, Mo., Sept. 13, 1925; s. Alex F. and Rose (Lyon) S.; m. Susanne Wilson, 1960; children: Alex Wilson, Adam Phinney. BA summa cum laude, Williams Coll., 1947; JD, Harvard U., 1950. Bar: Mo. 1950. Law clk. U.S. Dist. Ct., Kansas City, Mo., 1950-51; pvt. practice law Phineas Rosenberg, 1951-56; with Spencer, Fane, Britt & Browne, 1956-79; U.S. dist. judge Western Dist. Mo., Kansas City, 1979—, chief dist. judge, 1990-92, now sr. judge. Contbr. articles to various publs.; contbr. chpt. to Mid-America's Promise, 1982. Mem. Kansas City Commn. Human Rels., 1967-73; chmn. Jewish Community Rels. Bur., 1968-71, Kansas City chpt. Am. Jewish Com., 1963-65; mem. exec. com. Nat. Jewish Community Rels. Adv. Coun., 1968-71; pres. Urban League Kansas City, 1957-58, Kansas City chpt. Am. Jewish Congress, 1974-77; co-chmn. Kansas City chpt. NCCJ, 1958-60; mem. Kansas City Sch. Dist. Desegregation Task Force, 1976-77; pres. Jackson County Young Democrats, 1959-60; treas. Kennedy-Johnson Club, Jackson County, 1960. Served with USNR, 1944-46. Mem. ABA, Mo. Bar, Kansas City Bar Assn., Am. Judicature Soc., Lawyers Assn. Kansas City, Dist. Judges Assn. (8th cir., pres. 1992-94), Phi Beta Kappa. Office: US Dist Ct US Courthouse 400 E 9th St Kansas City MO 64106-2607

SACHS, JOHN PETER, carbon company executive; b. Duesseldorf, Germany, 1926; married. BAChemE, Ill. Inst. Tech., 1948, MAChemE, 1950, PhDChemE, 1952. Various mgmt. positions in research and devel., engring. and ops. Union Carbide Corp., 1951-66; v.p. ops. then group v.p. Great Lakes Carbon Corp., N.Y.C., 1966-78; pres., chief exec. officer Gt. Lakes Carbon Corp., 1978-86; chmn. bd., dir. Gen. Refractories Co., 1978-85; mng. ptnr. J.P. Sachs Assocs., Mgmt. Cons., New Canaan, Conn., 1987—99. Trustee Fairfield U., 1978-92; bd. dirs. Kneissl-Dachstein 1992—, Peridot, 1989-98. Mem. Am. Inst. Chem. Engrs. (pres. 1985) Home and Office: JP Sachs Assocs 67 Dunning Rd New Canaan CT 06840-4009

SACHS, JONATHAN RICHARD, gastroenterologist; b. Phila., Apr. 9, 1957; s. Robert and Marcia Sachs; m. Susan Sachs, OCt. 15, 1983; 2 children. BA, Amherst Coll., 1980; MD, Med. Coll. Pa., 1984. Diplomate in internal medicine and gastroenterology Am. Bd. Internal Medicine. Intern in internal medicine Temple U. Hosp., Phila., 1984-85, resident in internal medicine, 1985-87; fellow in gastroenterology Grad. Hosp., 1987-89; physician Princeton (N.J.) Med. Group, 1989-93, Princeton Gastroenterology Assocs., PA, 1993—; chief sect. gastroenterology Med. Ctr. at Princeton, 1992-97; clin. isntr. medicine Robert Wood Johnson Med. Sch., New Brunswick, N.J., 1992—. Trustee at large Unitarian Ch. of Princeton, 1995-98. Fellow ACP, Am. Coll. Gastroenterology, Phi Beta Kappa. Avocations: biking, hiking, skiing. Office: 281 Witherspoon St Ste 230 Princeton NJ 08540-3210

SACHS, LEO, geneticist, educator; b. Leipzig, Germany, Oct. 14, 1924; s. Elijah and Louise (Lichtblau) S.; m. Pnina Salkind; 4 children. PhD, Cambridge U., 1951; Dr h.c., Bordeaux U., 1985; Dr.Med. h.c., Lund U., 1997. Rsch. scientist John Innes Inst., 1951-52; mem. sci. staff Weizmann Inst. Sci., Rehovot, Israel, 1952—, prof., chmn. genetics dept. Israel, 1962—. Mem. Israeli Acad. Sci. and Humanities, 1975; hon. fellow U. Wales, Bangor, 1999. Contbr. articles to sci. jours. Recipient Israel prize for natural sci., 1972; named Fogarty Internat. scholar NIH, 1972, Harvey Lecture, 1972; recipient Rothschild prize in biol. scis., 1977, Wolf prize in medicine, 1980, Bristol-Myers award for disting. achievement in cancer rsch., 1983, Royal Soc. Wellcome Found. prize, 1986, Sloan prize GM Cancer Rsch. Found., 1989, Warren Alpert prize Harvard Med. Sch., 1997. Fellow Royal Soc., 1997; mem. U.S. Nat. Acad. Scis. (fgn. assoc. 1995), Academia Europaea (fgn.), 1998. Office: Weizmann Inst Sci Dept Molecular Genetics Rehovot 76100 Israel Business E-Mail: leo.sachs@weizmann.ac.il.

SACHS, MARGARET V. law educator; b. Washington, Nov. 10, 1951; d. Jeremiah and Thelma S. AB, Harvard U., 1973, JD, 1977. Bar: N.Y. 1978. Law clk. U.S. Ct. Appeals, 2d cir., N.Y.C., 1977-79; assoc. Simpson Thacher & Bartlett, 1979-81; from asst. to assoc. prof. Sch. Law U. Bridgeport, Conn., 1982-86; assoc. prof. Sch. Law Widener U., Wilmington, Del., 1986-90, U. Ga., Athens, 1990-95, prof. Sch. Law, 1995-97, Robert Cotten Alston prof. Sch. Law, 1997—. Mem. exec. coun. Am. Assn. Law Schs. Sect. on Bus. Assns., 1993-96. Mem. editl. bd. Jour. Legal Edn., 1995-98; contbr. articles to profl. jours. Mem. Am. Law Inst., Phi Beta Kappa. Presbyterian. Home: 458 Highland Ave Athens GA 30606-4316 Office: U Ga Sch Law Herty Dr Athens GA 30602 E-mail: mvs@uga.edu.

SACHS, MARILYN STICKLE, author, lecturer, editor; b. N.Y.C., Dec. 18, 1927; d. Samuel and Anna (Smith) Stickle; m. Morris Sachs, Jan. 26, 1947; children: Anne, Paul. BA, Hunter Coll., 1949; MSLS, Columbia U., 1953. Children's libr. Bklyn. Pub. Libr., 1949-60, San Francisco Pub. Libr., 1961-67. Author: Amy Moves In, 1964, Laura's Luck, 1965, Amy and Laura, 1966, Veronica Ganz, 1968, Peter and Veronica, 1969, Marv, 1970, The Bears' House, 1971 (Austrian Children's Book prize 1977, Recognition of Merit award George C. Stone Ctr. for Children's Books 1989), The Truth About Mary Rose, 1973 (Silver Slate Pencil award 1974), A Pocket Full of Seeds, 1973 (Jane Addams Children's Book Honor award 1974), Matt's Mitt, 1975, Dorrie's Book, 1975 (Silver State Pencil award 1977, Garden State Children's Book award 1978), A December Tale, 1976, A Secret Friends, 1978, A Summer's Lease, 1979, Bus Ride, 1980, Class Pictures, 1980, Fleet Footed Florence, 1981, Hello...Wrong Number, 1981, Call Me Ruth, 1982 (Assn. Jewish Librs. award 1983), Beach Towels, 1982, Fourteen, 1983, The Fat Girl, 1984, Thunderbird, 1985, Underdog, 1985 (Christopher 1986), Baby Sister 1986, Almost Fifteen, 1987, Fran Ellen's House, 1987 (award Bay Area Book Reviewers Assn. 1988, Recognition of Merit award George C. Stone Ctr. for Children's Books 1989), Just Like A Friend, 1989, At the Sound of the Beep, 1990, Circles, 1991, What My Sister Remembered, 1992, Thirteen, 1993, Ghosts in the Family, 1995, Another Day, 1997, Suprise Party, 1998, Jo Jo & Winnie, 1999, Jo Jo & Winnie Again, 2000, The Four Ugly Cats in Apartment 3D, 2002; co-editor: (with Ann Durell) Big Book for Peace, 1990 (Calif. Children's Book award 1991, Jane Addams Children's Book prize 1991); reviewer books N.Y. Times, San Francisco Chronicle, 1970—. Mem. PEN, ACLU, Sierra Club, Authors' Guild. Democrat. Jewish. Avocations: reading, walking, baseball. Home: 733 31st Ave San Francisco CA 94121-3523

SACHS, SAMUEL, II, museum director; b. N.Y.C., Nov. 30, 1935; s. James Henry and Margery Sachs; m. Susan McAllen (div.); children: Katherine, Eleanor; m. Jerre S. Hollander (div.); 1 child, Alexander; m. Elizabeth M. Gordon; 1 child, Hadley Elizabeth. BA cum laude, Harvard U., 1957; MA, NYU Inst. Fine Arts, 1962. With Mpls. Inst. Arts, 1958-60; asst. dir. U. Mich. Mus. of Art, Ann Arbor, 1963-64; chief curator Mpls. Inst. Arts, 1964-73, dir., 1973-85, Detroit Inst. Arts, 1985-97; dir., CEO Frick Collection, N.Y.C., 1997—. Bd. dirs. Internat. Com. on Fine Arts, Art Mus. Image Consortium, IFAR, NINCH, Japan Soc. Decorated knight 1st class Order North Star (Sweden); Order of Dannebrog (Denmark). Mem. Am. Assn. Museums, Assn. Art Mus. Dirs. Clubs: Century Assn, Harvard, Grosse Pointe. Home: 1112 Park Ave # 16B New York NY 10128-1235 Office: Frick Collection 1 E 70th St New York NY 10021-4907 E-mail: sachs@frick.org.

SACHS, WILLIAM, film director, producer, screenwriter, distributer; b. N.Y.C., Oct. 16, 1942; s. Milton Irving and Ann (Shuman) S.; children: Brandon Michael, Alexandra Roma. Student, U. Md., 1963-67, London Film Sch., 1967-68. Ind. dir., screenwriter, 1968—; pres. William Sachs Prodns., Inc. Head prodn. Heritage Entertainment, N.Y.C. and L.A., 1971-72; guest lectr. film UCLA, 1987. Dir., screenwriter: (film shorts) Breakfast, This is Ford, Dear Mrs. Smith, (feature films) The Force Beyond, 1976, The Incredible Melting Man, 1978, Van Nuys Blvd., 1980, Galaxina, 1982, Hot Chili, 1987, Hitz, 1988, dir. Concrete War, 1990, producer Servants of the Twilight, 1990, Leprechaun, 1992; dir., screenwriter, exec. producer: (feature films) Exterminator 2, 1986; writer, co-prodr. They Slew the Dreamer; dir., prodr., co-writer: (feature film) Spooky House; also numerous motion picture trailers, 1970-76. Served as sgt. USAF, 1962-65. Recipient numerous awards from various internat. film festivals, films included in permanenet collection Brit. Film Inst., Best of Fest award for Spooky House, Chgo. Internat. Children's Film Festival, 2000, 1st prize Children's Jury award for Spooky House, 2000. Mem.: ASCAP, Entertainment Hwy. Inc. (pres., CEO), Writers Guild Am. (screen credits com. 1977—88), Dirs. Guild Am. (creative rights com. 1987). E-mail: bill@entertainmenthighway.net.

SACHSMAN, DAVID BERNARD, communications educator; b. N.Y.C., Aug. 16, 1945; s. Edgar and Susan (Sassower) S.; m. Judith Mittleman, Mar. 15, 1967; children: Jonathan William, Susanne Elizabeth. BA in English, U. Pa., 1967; AM in Comm., Stanford U., 1968, PhD in Comm., 1973. Asst. prof., lectr. Calif. State U., Hayward, 1969-71; asst. prof. Rutgers U., New Brunswick, N.J., 1971-76; spl. corr., copy editor The Home News, 1974-77; assoc. prof. Rutgers U., 1976-88; sr. Fulbright-Hays scholar U. Nigeria, Nsukka, 1978-79; chairperson dept. journalism Rutgers U., New Brunswick, 1983-88; adj. assoc. prof. U. Medicine and Dentistry of N.J., Piscataway, 1987-89; dean, prof. Calif. State U., Fullerton, 1988-91; west chair of excellence in comm., pub. affairs U. Tenn., Chattanooga, 1991—. News cons., writing coach Sta WRCB-TV , Chattanooga, 1996—98; mem. editl. bd. Mass. Comm. Rev., 1976—; prin. investigator externally funded rsch. New Brunswick, N.J., Fullerton, Calif., 1977—91; cons. in field. Co-editor: (jour.) Media Casebook, 1996—98; co-author: Media: An Introductory Analysis of American Mass Communications, 1972, 3d rev. edit., 1982, The Press and the Suburbs: The Daily Newspapers of New Jersey, 1985, Environmental Risk and the Press, 1987; editor (assoc.): Advances in Telematics, 1983—86, Mass Comm. Rev., 1984—87; contbr. articles to profl. jours. Trustee The Daily Pennsylvania, Inc., Phila., 1985-88; bd. dirs. Girl Scout Coun. of Orange County, 1989-91, Moccasin Bend Girl Scout Coun., Chattanooga, Tenn., 1992—; bd. dirs., v.p. Girls Inc. of Chattanooga, 1991-94. Recipient award for Rsch. and Journalism, N.J. Chpt. Soc. for Profl. Journalists, 1984, 86, 88, 89; grantee Hazardous Substance Mgmt. Rsch. Ctr., 1985-89, 1985-90, Calif. Dept. Transp., 1990. Mem. Assn. for Edn. in Journalism and Mass Comm., Internat. Comm. Assn., Soc. of Environ. Journalists, Nat. Speech Comm. Assn., Investigative Reporters and Editors, Radio-TV News Dirs. Assn., N.J. Profl. Chpt. Soc. Profl. Journalists (pres. 1981-83, bd. dirs. 1984-88), Alpha Phi Gamma. Avocations: reading, film, TV, walking, music. Home: 1002 Centennial Dr Chattanooga TN 37405-4256 Office: U Tenn at Chattanooga 210 Frist Hall Chattanooga TN 37403

SACHTLER, WOLFGANG MAX HUGO, chemistry educator; b. Delitzsch, Germany, Nov. 8, 1924; came to U.S., 1983; s. Gottfried Hugo and Johanna Elisabeth (Bollmann) S.; m. Anne-Lore Luise Adrian, Dec. 9, 1953; children: Johann Wolfgang Adriaan, Heike Kathleen Julia, Yvonne Rhea Valeska. Diplomchemiker, Tech. U., Braunschweig, Ger., 1949; Dr.rer.nat. (Ph.D), 1952. Research chemist Kon-Shell Lab., Amsterdam, Netherlands, 1952-71, dept. head Netherlands, 1972-83; extraordinary prof. chemistry U. Leiden, Netherlands, 1963-83; V.N. Ipatieff prof. Northwestern U., Evanston, Ill., 1983-96; chmn. Gordon Research Conf. Catalysis, N.H., 1985. Rideal lectr. Faraday div. Royal Soc. Chemistry, 1981; F. Gault lectr., 1991. Mem. editl. bd. Jour. Catalysis, 1976-88, Applied Catalysis, 1983-87, Catalysis Letters, 1987—, Advances in Catalysis, 1987—, Catalysis Today, 1996—, Catalysis Reviews, 1997—; contbr. numerous articles to sci. jours. Recipient Deutsche Gesellschaft Mineraloel und Kohle Kolleg, 1991. Fellow AAAS; mem. Royal Netherlands Acad. Scis., Internat. Congress Catalysis (pres. coun. 1992-96), Royal Dutch Chem. Soc. (hon. mem. catalysis divsn.), Am. Chem. Soc. (E.V. Murphee award 1987, Petroleum Chemistry award 1992), Catalysis Soc. N.Am. (Robert L. Burwell award 1985, E. Houdry award 1993). Home: 2141 Ridge Ave Apt 2D Evanston IL 60201-2788 Office: Northwestern U 2137 Sheridan Rd Evanston IL 60208-0001 E-mail: wmhs@northwestern.edu.

SACK, EDGAR ALBERT, electronics company executive; b. Pitts., Jan. 31, 1930; s. Edgar Albert and Margaret Valentine (Engelmohr) S.; m. Eugenia Ferris, June 7, 1952; children: Elaine Kimberley, Richard Warren. BS, Carnegie-Mellon U., 1951, MS, 1952, PhD, 1954. Dept. mgr. Westinghouse Research Lab., Pitts., 1960-63; engring. mgr. Westinghouse Microelectronics, Balt., 1963-65, operations mgr., 1965-67, div. mgr., 1967-69; div. v.p. Gen. Instrument Corp., Hicksville, N.Y., 1969-73, group v.p., 1973-77, sr. v.p., 1977-84; pres., chief exec. officer Zilog Inc., Campbell, Calif., 1984-98, also chmn. bd. dirs.; pres. Productivity Assocs., Coronado; founder, chmn. CDT, Inc., San Jose, 1998-99. Bd. dirs. Enfo-Web, Inc., Mountainview, Calif., LXi, Inc., Mountainview; vis. com. elec. engring. dept. Carnegie-Mellon U., 1969-74; mem. indsl. adv. coun. SUNY, Stony Brook, 1979-83; mem. adv. com. on solid state electronics Poly. Inst. Tech., 1981-83. Author: Forward Controllership Business Management System, 1989, 2nd edit., 1993; patentee in field. Mem. Action Com. Long Island, 1982-84; bd. dirs. Coronado Shores Assn. # 7, landscaping and recreational com., 2000—, chair, 2002; mem. Sharp Coronado Hosp. Aux.; sec. San Diego Imperial Coun. of Vols., 2002. Recipient 2nd Ann. Hammerschlag Disting. Lectr. award Carnegie Mellon U., 1995. Fellow IEEE, Poly. Inst. Tech.; mem. Semicondr. Industry Assn. (dir. 1982-85); mem. Carnegie Mellon Alumni Assn. (Merit award 1981), Eta Kappa Nu (Outstanding Young Elec. Engr. 1959), Huntington Yacht Club (vice comdr. 1977), Tau Beta Pi (finalist San Francisco Entrepreneur of Yr. award 1991), Phi Kappa Phi. Home and Office: 1780 Avenida Del Mundo Unit 404 Coronado CA 92118-4011 E-mail: esack@pacbell.net.

SACK, EDWARD J. retired lawyer; b. N.Y.C., Apr. 7, 1930; AB, Harvard U., 1951, LLB, 1954; LLM, NYU, 1959. Bar: N.Y. 1954, U.S. Dist. Ct. (so. dist.) N.Y. 1959, U.S. Ct. Appeals (4th cir.) 1975, U.S. Ct. Appeals (2nd cir.) 1979, U.S. Supreme Ct. 1982. Assoc. Simpson Thacher & Bartlett, N.Y.C., 1954—66; atty. Am. Electric Power Svc. Corp., 1966—69; sr. atty. Consol. Edison Co., 1969—79; gen. counsel Internat. Coun. Shoppings Ctrs., 1979—2002; ret., 2002. Mem. Bar Assn. City of N.Y.

SACK, JAMES MCDONALD, JR. radio and television producer, marketing executive; b. London, Oct. 11, 1948; s. James McDonald and Ruth Elmore (Bryant) S.; m. Cheryl S. Gremaux, July 13, 1969 (div. June 1974); 1 child, Graehm McDonald; m. Svetlana Antsoulevich, Oct. 14, 1999. BA in History, Ind. U., 1975, MS in Telecomm., 1976. Coord. Latin Am. Ednl. Ctr., Ft. Wayne, Ind., 1979-81, Mayor's Office, Ft. Wayne, 1981-83; producer WMEE-WQHK Radio, 1983-85; owner, operator Festival Mgmt. and Devel., 1984—; owner Lily Co., 1991—2001; region sales mgr. Plan Mgmt., 1995-96; v.p. comm., mktg. United Way of Allen County, 1989-96; owner The Sack Co., 1996—. Pub. affairs prodr. WBYR/WFWA, Ft. Wayne; co-founder, treas. Vurpar Project (aid to Romania), 1999—. Producer radio documentary, 1985 (First Pl. award Ind. Broadcasters Assn., 1985), producer WFWA-PBS Eye on the Arts, 1987-89. Founder, pres. Germanfest of Ft. Wayne, 1981-92; pres. cable TV program adv. coun. City of Ft. Wayne; founder Ft. Wayne-Gera (Germany) Sister City Affilation; commr. Ind. Hoosier Celebration, 1988; dir. Ind. Highland Games, 1992, cons., 1993-99; mktg. dir. Germanfest of Ft. Wayne, 1996-98; cmn. adv. bd. Ft. Wayne Cable Fund, 2000-; bd. dirs. Ft. Wayne Sister Cities Com., 2000—. Named Ky. Col., 1991. Mem. German Heritage Soc. (founder, bd. dirs. 1986-99), Ind. German Heritage Soc. (founder, bd. dirs. 1986-92, Gov.'s Commendation award 1983), N.Am. Sängerbund (sec. 1985-86), Männerchor Club (Ft. Wayne), Ft. Wayne Sport Club (sec. 1985-86, trustee 1987-89). Lutheran. Avocations: flying, politics, linguistics, travel. Home and Office: 902 West Rudisill Fort Wayne IN 46807 E-mail: jimsack@yahoo.com.

SACK, ROBERT DAVID, judge, educator; b. Phila., Oct. 4, 1939; s. Eugene J. and Sylvia I. (Rivlin) Sack; children: Deborah Gail, Suzanne Michelle, David Rivlin. BA, U. Rochester, 1960; LLB, Columbia U., 1963. Bar: N.Y. 1963. Law clk. to judge Fed. Dist. Ct. of N.J., 1963—64; assoc. Patterson, Belknap & Webb, N.Y.C., 1964—70; ptnr. Patterson, Belknap, Webb & Tyler, 1970—86, Gibson, Dunn & Crutcher, N.Y.C., 1986-98; sr. assoc. spl. counsel U.S. Ho. of Reps. Impeachment Inquiry, 1974; judge U.S. Ct. Appeals (2d cir.), 1998—. Lectr. Practising Law Inst., 1973—97, Columbia U. Law Sch., 2001—02, bd. vis., adv.; adv. bd. Media Law Reporter. Author: Libel, Slander, and Related Problems, 1980, 2d edit., 1994, CD-ROM edit., 1995, Sack on Defamation-Libel, Slander, and Related Problems, 3d edit., 1999; co-author: Advertising and Commercial Speech, a First Amendment Guide, 1999; contbr. articles to profl. jours. Chmn. bd. dirs. Nat. Council on Crime and Delinquency, 1982—83; trustee seminars on media and society Columbia U. Sch. Journalism, 1985—92, N.Y.C. Commn. on Pub. Info. and Comm., 1995—98; v.p., bd. dirs. William F. Kerby and Robert S. Potter Fund. Fellow: Am. Bar Found.; mem.: ABA (bd. govs. forum com. on comm. law 1980—88), Assn. Bar City N.Y. (chmn. comm. law com. 1986—89). Office: US Circuit Ct for 2d Circuit 40 Foley Sq New York NY 10007-1502

SACKETT, DAVID HARRISON, electrical engineer; b. Syosset, N.Y., June 2, 1971; s. Robert H. Sackett and Bonnie-Jean Rohner; m. Hien Dieu Phan, Aug. 6, 1994; children: Tiffany Holly, Brendan Harrison. BS, Rochester Inst. Tech., 1994, MS, 1996. Devel. engr. Eastman Kodak, Rochester, 1995—. Owner Pro Nails and Tan. Mem. IEEE, Soc. Profl. Engring., Lasers and Electro-Optics Soc., Internat. Soc. Optical Engring., Optical Soc. Am. Achievements include 1 U.S. patent. Home: 52 Angels Path Webster NY 14580-2299 Office: Eastman Kodak 6-81-rl Mc 02008 Rochester NY 14650-0001 E-mail: dsackett@ieee.org.

SACKETT, JOYCE WILHELMINA, hospitality coordinator; b. Balt., Jan. 27, 1941; d. Gordon William and Frances Theresa (Chetelat) Clark; m. John Wesley Sackett, June 22, 1963; children: Julie Shields, John, Jeanine, Joyella Mischke. BS, Towson (Md.) State Tchrs.Coll., 1962. Art tchr. Prince Georges County Pub. Schs., Adelphi, Md., 1962-63, St. Mary's County Pub. Schs., Leonardtown, 1963-64; missionary to univ. students The Navigators, Amsterdam, 1965-69, Quezon City, Los Banos, The Philippines, 1970-74, area rep. Balt., 1974—. Author: In God's Garden, 1998; author (devotional perpetual calendar): Finding God in the Garden, 1997; contbr. articles to profl. jours. Republican. Presbyterian. Avocations: gardening, writing. Home: Blessing Hill 231 W Timonium Rd Lutherville Timonium MD 21093

SACKIN, CLAIRE, retired social work educator; b. N.Y.C., Oct. 1, 1925; d. Harry and Diana (Mednick) Gershfeld; m. Milton Sackin, Feb. 4, 1955; children: William, Daniel, David. BA, Hunter Coll., 1946; MEd, U. Pitts., 1968, MSW, 1972, PhD, 1976. Tenured tchr. jr. high sch., Bronx, N.Y., 1947-57; rsch. asst. U. Pitts., 1973, instr. dept. urban mgmt., 1974; rsch. assoc. U. Pitts. Sch. of Social Work, 1975-76, Health & Welfare Planning Assn., 1974; prof. social work, dir. social work program St. Francis U., Loretto, Pa., 1976-97, prof. emerita, 1997—. Registered trainer alcoholism specialists cert. program; mem. adv. bd. Cedar Manor Treatment Ctr., Cresson, Pa., 1994-95; mem. Pa. Gov.'s Coun. Alcoholism, 1980, Nat. Assn. People with AIDS; presenter in field. Contbr. articles to jours. Mem. NASW (social action com. Pa. chpt. 1983-85, mem. Del. Assembly 1984, eastern regional coalition liaison 1984), Coun. on Social Work Edn., Amyotrophic Lateral Sclerosis Assn., Alpha Delta Mu (nat. bd. dirs.). Avocations: reading, crossword puzzles, opera, gardening, travel. Home: 531 Sandrae Dr Pittsburgh PA 15243-1727 Office: St Francis U Loretto PA 15940 E-mail: sackin@worldnet.att.net.

SACKLOW, STEWART IRWIN, advertising executive; b. Albany, N.Y., July 29, 1942; s. Jacob David and Freda Ruth (Pearlman) S.; m. Harriette Lynn Cooperman, July 2, 1967; 1 son, Ian Marc. AAS, N.Y.C. C.C., 1962; BS, We. Mich. U., 1965. Asst. dist. office Humble Oil & Refining Co., Inc., Albany, 1963-65; dir. advtsg. and sales promotion Albany Pub. Markets divsn. Weiss Foods, 1965-68, Golub Corp.; v.p., dir. advtsg. Price Chopper Discount Foods, Schenectady, N.Y., 1968-78; pres., creative dir. Wolkcas Advtsg., Inc., 1978-93; pres., CEO, 1993-95; pres., creative dir. Wolkcas Comms. Group, 1995—. Exec. dir. Ski the Catskills, 1982-84; pres. Broadcast Creations, 1985—; pres. testimonials, Inc., 1991-93; chmn. N.Y. State Arbor Day Com., 1988—. Mem. Dist. Atty.'s readiness team; active Albany County Cerebral Palsy telethons, 1966-68; mem. fund drive com. Sta. WMHT-TV ednl. TV, 1967-74; bd. dris. N.e. Cystic Fibrosis Found., Video Spirit; bd. dirs., mem. exec. com. Upstate Leukemia Assn.; mem. bd. Gov. Clinton coun. Boy Scouts Am., leader Voorheesville, N.Y.; pres. Takundewide Home Owners Assn., 1991-92; key market coord. Partnership Drug Free Am.; coord. Drug Free N.Y. State; bd. dirs. Daughter of Sarah Found., 1997-99; instr. skindiving program YMCA; bd. dirs. Internat. Snorkeling Soc., 2002—, housing B'nai B'rith, 1992-93. Recipient cert. merit Nat. Rsch. Bur., 1966, Freedoms Found., 1966, Amsterdam Recorder, 1968, Retail Advtsg. Conf., 1969, 70, Woman's Day Mag., 1971, 72, 73, 74, 75, 76, Grand Nat. award Am. Dairy Assn., 1969, Hunt Wesson Foods, 1970, 4 1st Place awards Am. Advtsg. Fedn., 1973, Addy award Internat. Newspaper Advtsg. execs, 1972, Gold Leaf award Internat. Arborist Soc., 1993, Disting. Svc. award Albany Ad Club, 1976. Mem. Ad Club N.Y. (bd. dirs. 1974-79, 93-94, pres. 1976-77, chmn. ednl. com. 1996—, Disting. Svc. award 1976), Am. Advt. Fedn. (bd. govs. 1975, Crystal Prism award 1978), N.Y. Art Dirs. Club, K.P., Elec. Boat Assn. Am., Lake George Assn. Home: 716 St Marks Ln Niskayuna NY 12309-4843 E-mail: ssacklow@wolkcas.com.

SACKMANN, INGE-JULIANA, astrophysicist; b. Schönau, Germany, Feb. 8, 1942; came to U.S., 1971; d. Emil Sackmann and Lilly Stelter; m. Robert Frederick Christy, Aug. 4, 1973; children: Ilia Juliana Lilly Christy, Alexandra Roberta Christy. BA, U. Toronto, Ont., Can., 1963, MA, 1965, PhD, 1968. Postdoctoral fellow U. Göttingen, Germany, 1968-69, Max-Planck-Inst. for Physics and Astrophysics, Munich, 1969-71; rsch. assoc. U. Hamburg Obs., Germany, 1971, Jet Propulsion Labs., Pasadena, 1974-76; rsch. fellow Calif. Inst. Tech., 1971-74, sr. rsch. fellow, 1976-81, faculty assoc., 1981—. Recipient Zonta Club award in math. and physics, 1961-62, Math. and Physics Soc. prize, 1962-63, AAAS award in math. and physics, 1962-63, McLennan prize in math. and physics, 1963-64, Loudon Gold medal in math. and physics, 1963-64, Chant award, 1963-64, Alexander von Humboldt award, 1970-71; co-recipient B'nai B'rith award, 1961-62; 1st alumni scholar U. Toronto, 1959-60, 60-61, Ont. scholar, 1959-60, 1st Alumni scholar, 1962-63, Gamma Phi Beta scholar, 1963-64, Nat. Rsch. Coun. Can. scholar, 1963-64, 64-65, 66-67, 68-69, 69-70; U. Toronto Open fellow, 1965-66. Mem. Internat. Astron. Union, Am. Astron. Soc., Orgn. of Women in Sci. Achievements include scientific findings in carbon creation, preditions of lively future of the sun. Avocations: children, flower arranging, growing organic garden, horseback riding, hiking. Home: 1230 Arden Rd Pasadena CA 91106-4146 Office: U Calif Inst Tech 1201 E California Blvd Pasadena CA 91125-0001 E-mail: ijsekrl@caltech.edu.

SACKMANN, MARGARET E. geriatric nurse practitioner; b. Adak, Alaska, July 20, 1956; d. Duane St. Clare and Elizabeth Ashley (King) Lee; m. Paul Timothy Sackmann, May 26, 1979; children: Christina Maria, Elizabeth Ann, Ruth Sarai. BSN, Pacific Luth. U., 1978; cert. nurse practitioner, U. Wash., 1986. Onocology, hospice charge nurse Tacoma Gen. Hosp., 1979-84; office nurse Munoz, Regimbal & Assocs., Tacoma; geriatric nurse practitioner Internal Medicine, N.W., 1984—. Mem. clin. faculty U. Washi. and Pacific Luth. U. Mem.: ANA, Nat. Conf. Gerontol. Practitioners, Wash. State Nurses Assn. Home: 5115 Beverly Ave NE Tacoma WA 98422-1823 E-mail: msackmann@imnw.org.

SACKS, CHARLES BERNARD, physician, educator; b. Cleve., May 14, 1939; s. Jerry and Frances (Shifrin) S.; m. Lora Jane Glickman, May 2, 1993; children: Eliza, Aaron. BA, Ohio State U., 1961, MD, 1965. Staff psychiatrist Washington Vets. Hosp., 1971-77; asst. clin. prof. Georgetown U., Washington, 1971—; staff psychiatrist Reston Clinic, Fairfax City, Md., 1976-77, Drug Treatment Adminstrn., Washington, 1971-72, Washington Free Clinic, 1971-73, Arlington & Fairfax City Hosp., 1977-88, Group Health Assocs., Washington, 1984-86; psychiatrist pvt. practice, McLean, Va., 1977—, Greenbelt, Md., 1977—; dir. Chevy Chase Psychiat. Clinic, Washington, 1987-89; Mt. Vernon Mental Health Ctr., 1994—. Maj. U.S. Army, 1969-71. Decorated Bronze medal with Oak Leaf Cluster. Mem. Am. Psychiat. Assn. Avocations: sailing, photography, music, reading, sports. Office: 6201 Greenbelt Rd College Park MD 20740-2354 also: 1313 Vincent Pl Mc Lean VA 22101-3615

SACKS, DAVID HARRIS, historian, humanities educator; b. Bklyn., Dec. 14, 1942; s. Fred and Lillian Pearl (Levy) S.; m. Eleanor Darby Woodward, July 25, 1971. BA magna cum laude, Bklyn. Coll., 1963; AM in History, Harvard U., 1965, PhD in History, 1977. Lectr. history U. Mass., Boston, 1977-79; preceptor in expository writing Harvard U., Cambridge, Mass., 1979-80, lectr. in history and lit., 1980-83, rsch. affiliate Ctr. for European Studies, 1983-86; asst. prof. history and humanities Reed Coll., Portland, Oreg., 1986-89, assoc. prof., 1989-93, prof., 1993—. Vis. prof. history Yale U., 1998—99; vis. fellow Clare Hall, Cambridge U., 2001—02; mem. bd. advisors Yale Ctr. for Parliamentary History. Author: Trade Society and Politics in Bristol, 1500-1640, 1985, The Widening Gate: Bristol and the Atlantic Economy, 1450-1700, 1991; editor: Thomas More, Utopia, 1999, (with Donald R. Kelley) The Historical Imagination in Early Modern Britain: History, Rhetoric, and Fiction, 1500-1800, 1997; mem. bd. editors Jour. of History of Ideas; contbr. articles to profl. jours. Recipient fellowships Folger Shakespeare Libr., Washington, 1989-90, Woodrow Wilson Internat. Ctr. for Scholars, 1992-93, John Simon Guggenheim Meml. Found., 1992-93, NEH, 2001-02, ACLS, 2001-02, John Carter Brown Libr., 2002--. Fellow Royal Hist. Soc.; mem. N.Am. Conf. Brit. Studies (chair nominating com. 1993-95, exec. sec. 1995-98), Am. Hist. Assn. (program com. 1993-95, Leo Gershey prize com. 1992-95, mem. coun. 2001—). Office: Reed Coll 3203 SE Woodstock Blvd Portland OR 97202-8138 Home: John Carter Brown Libr. Box 1894 Providence RI 02912

SACKS, HERBERT SIMEON, psychiatrist, educator, consultant; b. N.Y.C., Nov. 29, 1926; s. Maxwell Lawrence and Anne (Edelstein) S.; m. Helen Margery Levin, Dec. 26, 1948; children— Eric Livingston, Katharine Bird, Douglas Lowell, Russell Avery AB magna cum laude, Dickinson Coll., 1948; MD, Cornell U., 1952. Diplomate Am. Bd. Psychiatry and Neurology and subspecialty Child and Adolescent Psychiatry. Clin. assoc. Western New Eng. Psychoanalytic Inst., New Haven, 1955-63; intern in pediatrics Yale-New Haven Med. Ctr., 1952-53; jr. asst. resident in psychiatry Yale Psychiat. Inst., 1953-54; sr. asst. resident in psychiatry, USPHS fellow Yale-New Haven Med. Ctr., psychiat. out patient dept., 1954-55; USPHS fellow in child psychiatry Yale U. Child Study Ctr., 1955-57; clin. dir. Mid-Fairfield Child Guidance Ctr., Norwalk, Conn., 1957-59; cons. Expt. in Internat. Living, Putney, Vt., 1962-69; sr. cons. U.S. Peace Corps, Washington, 1962-69; cons. AID, U.S. Dept. State, Office of Sahel, West Africa, 1974-84, Neurosci. Consultation Group, Grosse Point Farms, Mich., 1984-94; clin. prof. child and adolescent psychiatry Child Study Ctr., Yale U. Sch. Medicine, New Haven. Co-investigator, co-dir. Senegal River pilot health research program, New Haven and West Africa, 1976-78, co-investigator, co-dir. health sector, design team Senegal River integrated devel. project, 1981-83; vis. lectr. Yale Coll., 1969-71; mem. com. reviewers Dept. Commerce Nat. Bur. Standards, Inst. for Computer Scis. and Tech., Washington, 1975-77; mem. exec. com. Nat. Commn. on Confidentiality of Health Records, 1975-80 Author: Hurdles: The Admissions Dilemma in American Higher Education, 1978; contbg. author chpts. in books, articles on confidentiality, juvenile justice, higher edn., issues of youth in transition, other topics; author monographs Mem. Conn. Juvenile Justice Commn., Hartford, 1975-80; bd. advisors Dickinson Coll., Carlisle, Pa., 1980-85. Served to lt. (j.g.) U.S. Navy, 1944-46; PTO Fellow AMA, ACPO, Am. Psychiat. Assn. (trustee 1988-94, v.p. 1994-96, pres. 1997-98), Am. Acad. Child and Adolescent Psychiatry, Am. Orthopsychiat. Assn., Am. Coll. Psychiatrists; mem. Conn. Psychiat. Soc. (pres. 1976-77), Conn. Coun. Child and Adolescent Psychiatrists (pres. 1972-73), World Fedn. for Mental Health, Phi Beta Kappa. Avocations: farming, photography, fishing, lawn bowling. Home: 110 Laurel Rd New Haven CT 06515-2426 Office: 260 Riverside Ave Westport CT 06880-4804 also: Yale U Child Study Ctr PO Box 207900 New Haven CT 06520-7900

SACKS, JEFFREY HOWARD, psychiatrist, psychoanalyst; b. Bklyn., Sept. 11, 1946; s. Sam and Anne (Beichman) S.; m. Jill Schehr, June 29, 1979; children: Alexandra, Liza. BA, CUNY, 1968; DO, Coll. Osteo. Medicine-Surgery, Des Moines, 1972; cert. in psychoanalysis, William Alanson White Inst., 1983. Diplomate Am. Bd. Psychiatry and Neurology, Am. Bd. Child Psychiatry. Intern, resident in psychiatry, asst. clin. instr. SUNY, Buffalo, 1972-74; resident in psychiatry, postgrad. fellow Yale U., New Haven, 1974-76; chief resident brief treatment and evaluation unit West Haven (Conn.) VA Hosp., 1974-76; fellow in child psychiatry, clin. instr. SUNY Downstate Med. Ctr., Bklyn., 1976-78; pvt. practice, 1976-78, N.Y.C., 1978—, Mt. Kisco, N.Y., 1979—; clin. dir. foster care divsn. Jewish Child Care Assn., N.Y.C., 1994—. Emergency room physician Cmty. Mental Health Ctr., Buffalo, 1973-74; clin. instr. Albert Einstein Coll. Medicine, Bronx, N.Y., 1978-79; psychiat. cons. Westchester Jewish Cmty. Svcs., Chappaqua, Yorktown Heights, New Rochelle, N.Y.; chief psychiatrist Children's Day Treatment Ctr. and Sch., N.Y.C., 1982-92; assoc. in clin. psychiatry Coll. Physicians and Surgeons, Columbia U., 1993—; dir. tng. and edn. dept. child psychiatry St Luke's Roosevelt Hosp. Ctr., N.Y.C., 1978-94, acting asst. dir. 1980-89; clin. dir. foster care divsn. Jewish Child Care Assn., N.Y.C.; asst. clin. prof. psychiatry Mt. Sinai Med. Sch., N.Y.C., 1996—. Mem. Am. Psychiat. Assn. (chmn. com. on continuing med. edn. Bklyn. div. 1977-78, course instr. 1976-78), Am. Acad. Child and Adolescent Psychiatry, Am. Assn. Dirs. Psychiatry Residency Tng. Home: 15 Woodland Rd Mount Kisco NY 10549-3842 Office: 230 Central Park W New York NY 10024-6029

SACKS, MICHAEL ALAN, educational consultant, educator; b. Philadelphia, PA, Aug. 3, 1970; PhD, Northwestern University, Evanston, IL, 1994—2000. Asistant Professor Goizueta Business School, Emory University, Atlanta, 2000—02; Lecturer Kellogg School of Management, Northwestern University, Evanston, IL, 1998—2000. Consultant, Atlanta, 2000—02. Author: (Newspaper) Turning Disputes Into Corporate Advantage, 2002 (*, 0), (Journal) The Social Structure of Entrepreneurial Financing: Stratification and the Differential Liability of Newness in U.S. Venture Capital, 2002, (journal) Global Institutions and Networks: Contingent Change in The Structure of World Trade Advantage, 1965-1980, 2001, Broadening the Evaluation of Dispute Resolution: Context and Relationships Over Time, 1999. Diversity consultant Anti-Defamation League, Chicago, IL, 1995—2000. Office: Goizueta Business School, Emory Univ. 1300 Clifton Road Atlanta GA 30322 Office Fax: 404-727-6663. Business E-Mail: Michael_Sacks@bus.emory.edu.

SACKS, PATRICIA ANN, librarian, consultant; b. Allentown, Pa., Nov. 6, 1939; d. Lloyd Alva and Dorothy Estelle (Stoneback) Stahl; m. Kenneth LeRoy Sacks, June 27, 1959. AB, Cedar Crest Coll., 1959; MS in Libr. Sci., Drexel U., 1965. News reporter Call-Chronicle, Allentown, 1956-59, 61-63; reference libr. Cedar Crest Coll., 1964-66, head libr., 1966-73; dir. librs. Muhlenberg and Cedar Crest Colls., 1973-94; dir. libr. svcs. Cedar Crest Coll., 1994; sr. fellow Lehigh Valley Assn. Ind. Colls., 1994-97, Ctr. Agile Ptnrs. in Edn., 1997-98; info. svcs. cons., 1998—. Del. On Line Computer Library Ctr. Users Council, Columbus, Ohio, 1977-84; cons. colls./health care orgns., libr. orgns. 1981—. Author: (with Whildin Sara Lou) Preparing for Accreditation: A Handbook for Academic Librarians, 1993; mem. editl. bd. Jour. Acad. Librarianship, 1982-84. Mem. United Way Lehigh Valley Coms., 1993—97; trustee Cedar Crest Coll., 1985—89; bd. dirs. John and Dorothy Morgan Cancer Ctr., 1994—96. Named Outstanding Acad. Woman, Lehigh Valley Assn. for Acad. Women, 1984, Muhlenberg Coll. Outstanding Adminstr., 1987, Alumni Tricorn awrd Muhlenberg Coll., 1989, Alumnae Achievement award Cedar Crest Coll., 1994. Mem. ALA (chmn. copyright com. 1985-87), Assn. Coll. and Rsch. Librs. (chmn. stds. and accreditation com. 1976-78, 81-84), Lehigh Valley Assn. Ind. Colls. (chmn. librs. sect. 1967-81, 88-92), AAUW, LWV Lehigh Valley Conservancy, Appalachian Mountain Club, Phi Alpha Theta, Phi Kappa Phi, Beta Phi Mu. Democrat. Home: 2997 Fairfield Dr Allentown PA 18103-5413 E-mail: sackspa@ptd.net.

SACKS, ROBERT D. educational administrator, fund raiser; b. N.Y.C., Oct. 29, 1931; s. Robert and Hortense (Saperstein) S.; divorced; children: David Robert (dec.), Michael Alan. BA, Amherst Coll., 1953; MS, Juilliard Sch., 1956; postgrad., Columbia U., 1951, 52, NYU, 1959-62, U. Paris (Sorbonne), 1962-63. Instr. SUNY, Buffalo, 1963-65; asst. prof. Antioch Coll., Yellow Springs, Ohio, 1965-69; assoc. prof. Temple U., Phila., 1969-73; dean of faculty Phila. Musical Acad., 1973-75; assoc. dir. Transactional Dynamics inst., Glenside, Pa., 1976-82; exec. dir. Keswick Theatre, 1982-84, Delaware Valley Coun. of Am. Youth Hostels, Inc., Phila., 1993-99. Commn. on Higher Edn. of the Mid. States Assn. Colls. and Schs. rep. in evaluation of colls. for accreditation/renewal of accreditation, 1974-75. Vol. Hoeffel for Congress, Montgomery County, Pa., 1996, 98, 99—, U.S. Senator Harris Wofford for Re-election, 1995; chmn. Amherst Coll. Vols. for Stevenson, 1952. With U.S. Army, 1957-59. Fulbright scholar, 1962-63; grantee Danforth Found., 1966-67, Ford Found., 1966-67, N.Y. State Regents fellow, 1960-61, Millicent James scholar and Univ. fellow NYU, 1961-62. Mem. Nat. Trust for Hist. Preservation, Preservation Pa. Avocations: gardening, woodworking, water sports. Home: 627 Twickenham Rd Glenside PA 19038-2034

SACKS, SUSAN BENDERSKY, mental health clinical specialist, educator; b. San Antonio, June 1, 1957; d. Gordon and Renée (Freedman) Bendersky; m. Stephen Sacks, Sept. 18, 1988. BSN, U. Pa., 1981, MS in Nursing. Cert. psychiat. clin. nurse specialist, cognitive behavioral therapist and trauma response clinician. Faculty U. Pa. Sch. Nursing, Phila.; pvt. practice psychotherapy cons. Spkr. in field. Home: 650 Malin Rd Newtown Square PA 19073-2613 E-mail: sacksfamily@yahoo.com.

SACKS, TEMI J. public relations executive; b. Phila. d. Jule and Adeline (Levin) S. BA, Temple U. Pubs. editor Del. Valley Regional Planning Commn., Phila.; comms. assoc. Fedn. Jewish Agys.; exec. v.p., mng. dir. healthcare div. Lobsenz-Stevens Inc., N.Y.C.; sr. v.p., dir. nat. healthcare practice Shandwick; pres. T.J. Sacks & Assocs. Inc. Mem. Healthcare Businesswomen's Assn., Healtcare Mktg. Assn., Women Execs. in Pub. Rels. Avocations: painting, skiing, Americana antiques, jewelry design.

SACKSTEDER, FREDERICK HENRY, former foreign service officer; b. N.Y.C., July 12, 1924; s. Frederick H. and Denise (Dorin) S.; m. Evelyn M. Blickensderfer, Oct. 14, 1977; children by previous marriage: Frederick Henry, III, Timothy W. BA, Amherst Coll., 1947; postgrad., Sch. Advanced Internat. Studies, Washington, 1947. Asst. to exec. v.p. Internat. Standard Electric Corp., N.Y.C., 1948-49; joined U.S. Fgn. Service, 1950; Kreis resident officer U.S. High Commn. for Germany, 1950-52; vice consul, consul, sec. Am. embassy, Lyon, France, 1952-55, Madrid, 1959-61, Barcelona, Spain, 1962-65, Tunis, Tunisia, 1967-69; internat. relations officer Dept. State, 1955-59; 65-67; mem. U.S. Mission to UN, 1969-72, Internat. Boundary and Water Com., El Paso, Tex., 1972-75; consul gen. Hermosillo, Sonora, Mexico, 1975-79; bd. examiners Fgn. Service, Dept. State, 1979-81, expert cons. Bur. Personnel, 1981-86. Mem. U.S. del. to UN Gen. Assembly, N.Y.C., 1969-71. Mem. UN Trusteeship Coun., 1970-71, U.S. rep., 1971; pres. El Paso chpt. UN Assn., 1973-75. Lt. (j.g.) USNR, 1943-46. Mem. Fgn. Service Assn., Diplomatic and Consular Officers Ret., Council Fgn. Relations (chmn. Charlottesville com.). Lodges: Rotary (local club pres. 1988-89). Home: The Westchester Apt 344 4000 Cathedral Ave NW Washington DC 20016-5280

SACKSTEDER, THOMAS MICHAEL, corporate executive, entrepreneur, writer; b. Dayton, Ohio, July 27, 1950; s. Harry Pius and Mary Kay (Liebhardt) S.; m. Teresa Ann Nevius, Oct. 12, 1968 (div. Sept. 1980); children: Lori Ann, Kristi Marie, Julie Kay. Student, Sinclair Community Coll., 1968-72, Wright State U., 1972-73, Grand Valley State Coll., 1978-79, Lourdes Coll., 1994-95. Installer Western Electric, Dayton, 1968-69; sales rep. Smith Corona Mcht., 1969-70; office mgr. Indsl. Machinery, 1970-71; advisor Bell Pub. Rels., 1972-73; sales mgr. Washington Nat. Ins., 1974-81, Am. Fidelity Assurance Co., 1981-95; gen. ptnr. Innovative Benefits Resource Ltd., 1995—. Gen. ptnr., Annuity Compliance Specilaists, ptnr., Christopher Blake Family Wellness Assn., benefits cons. Ind. State Tchrs. Assn. Ins. Trust, Indpls., 1986-91. Bd. dirs. Mental Health Assn., Dayton, 1971-75, Good Samaritan Mental Health Ctr., 1972-75; campaign mgmt. for polit. candidates and issue oriented policies, 1972—. Mem. Ohio Assn. Sch. Bus. Ofcls. (legis. com. 1993-95), Assn. of Sch. Bus. Ofcls., Natl. Tax Shelter Annuity Assn., Employers Counc. on Flexible Compensation, Natl. Assn. of Life Underwriters, Buckeye Assn. Sch. Adminstrs., Jaycees, Kiwanis. Roman Catholic. Avocations: golf, swimming, writing, research. Address: Innovative Benefits Resource Ltd Annuity Compliance Specialists PO Box 70 Holland OH 43528-0070 E-mail: tom.sacksteder@lbracs.com

SACKSTEIN, ROSALINA GUERRERO, music educator, consultant; b. Camaguey, Cuba, Mar. 5, 1923; came to U.S., 1948; d. Luis and Rosalina (Santana) Guerrero; m. Louis Aguirre, Jan. 1, 1939 (div. June 1946); 1 child, Louis Aguirre Jr.; m. Harold C. Sackstein, Apr. 19, 1952; children: Rosalin R., Robert. B in Arts and Scis., Inst. Camaguey, 1941; prof. piano, violin theory, solfege, Conservatory of Music, Camaguey, 1944; D in Pedagogy, U. Havana, Cuba, 1947; M in Secondary Edn., U. Miami, Coral Gables, 1964. Music tchr. Abraham Lincoln Jr. H.S., Havana, 1944-47; psychology of music tchr. Tchrs. Coll., 1953-59; tchr. music theory, ear tng., solfege U. Miami Sch. Music, Coral Gables, 1963-65, asst. prof. to assoc. prof., 1963-78, prof. music, 1978—. Faculty advisor Sigma Chi chpt. U. Miami, 1970-90; founding mem. women's adv. com. acad. affairs, U. Miami, 1972—. Concert pianist, Cuba, 1944-48, U.S., 1952—; various solo recitals and orch. solos, U.S. and abroad; also appearances on radio and T.V. Chair of judges, Fla. Fedn. Music Clubs, Royal Poinciana, 1980—; mem. bd. Chopin Found. Miami, 1998. Recipient Gold medal, concerto competition, Havana, 1947; recipient Baldwin Keyboard award, 1977-78, 83-84; recipient Cmty. Svc. award B'nai B'rith, 1992. Mem. Am. Coll. Musicians (judge 1964—), Nat. Music Tchrs. Assn., Fla. State Music Tchrs. Assn. (pres. dist. 6 1969-71, pub. sch. liaison dist. 1971-73), Miami Music Tchrs. Assn. (pres. 1991-93, bd. dirs. 1993—), Young Performers Music Club (advisor 1970—), Miami Civic Music Assn. (v.p. 1981-83, pres. 1983—), Sigma Alpha Iota (advisor, v.p. 1964—, sword of honor 1975), Pi Kappa Lambda. Avocations: sports, games. Office: U Miami Sch Music PO Box 248165 Coral Gables FL 33124-8165

SACKTON, FRANK JOSEPH, public affairs educator; b. Chgo., Aug. 11, 1912; m. June Dorothy Raymond, Sept. 21, 1940. Student, Northwestern U., 1936, Yale, 1946, U. Md., 1951-52, BS, 1970; grad., Army Inf. Sch., 1941, Command and Gen. Staff Coll., 1942, Armed Forces Staff Coll., 1949, Nat. War Coll., 1954; MPA, Ariz. State U., 1976, DHL (hon.), 1996. Mem. 131st Inf. Regt., Ill. N.G., 1929-40; commd. 2d lt. U.S. Army, 1934, advanced through grades to lt. gen., 1967; brigade plans and ops. officer (33d Inf. Div.), 1941, PTO, 1943-45; div. signal officer, 1942-43; div. intelligence officer, 1944; div. plans and ops. officer, 1945; sec. to gen. staff for Gen. MacArthur Tokyo, 1947-48; bn. comdr. 30th Inf. Regt., 1949-50; mem. spl. staff Dept. Army, 1951; plans and ops. officer Joint Task Force 132, PTO, 1952; comdr. Joint Task Force 7, Marshall Islands, 1953; mem. gen. staff Dept. Army, 1954-55; with Office Sec. Def., 1956; comdr. 18th Inf. Regt., 1957-58; chief staff 1st Inf. Div., 1959; chief army Mil. Mission to Turkey, 1960-62; comdr. XIV Army Corps, 1963; dep. dir. plans Joint Chiefs Staff, 1964-66; army general staff mil. ops., 1966-67; comptroller of the army, 1967-70; ret., 1970; spl. asst. for fed./state relations Gov. Ariz., 1971-75; chmn. Ariz. Programming and Coordinating Com. for Fed. Programs, 1971-75; lectr. Am. Grad. Sch. Internat. Mgmt., 1973-77; vis. asst. prof., lectr. public affairs Ariz. State U., Tempe, 1976-78; founding dean Ariz. State U. Coll. Public Programs, 1979-80; prof. public affairs Ariz. State U., 1980—, finance educator, v.p. bus. affairs, 1981-83, dep. dir. intercollegiate athletics, 1984-85, dir. strategic planning, 1987-88. Contbr. articles to public affairs and mil. jours. Mem. Ariz. Steering Com. for Restoration of the State Capitol, 1974-75, Ariz. State Personnel Bd., 1978-83, Ariz. Regulatory Coun., 1981-93. Decorated D.S.M., Silver Star, also Legion of Merit with 4 oak leaf clusters, Bronze Star with 2 oak leaf clusters, Air medal, Army Commendation medal with 1 oak leaf cluster, Combat Inf. badge. Mem. Ariz. Acad. Public Adminstn., Pi Alpha Alpha (pres. chpt. 1976-82) Clubs: Army-Navy (Washington); Arizona Country (Phoenix). Home: 12000 N 90th St Unit 3072 Scottsdale AZ 85260-8643 Office: Ariz State U Sch Pub Affairs Tempe AZ 85287-0603 E-mail: frank.sackton@asu.edu.

SADAO, SHOJI, architect; b. Los Angeles, Jan. 2, 1927; s. Riichi and Otatsu (Kodama) S.; m. Tsuneko Sawada, Apr. 8, 1972. B.Arch., Cornell U., 1954; Fulbright scholar, Waseda U., Tokyo, 1956-57. Designer Geodesics, Inc., Raleigh, N.C., 1954-56; job capt. Edison Price, Inc., N.Y.C., 1959-64; v.p. Fuller & Sadao (P.C.), Long Island City, N.Y., 1965—. Assoc. prof. archtl. design Sch. Architecture and Environ. Design, SUNY, Buffalo, 1976-77. Works include Dymaxion World Map, 1954; co-designer works include, U.S. Pavilion at Montreal Expo 67. Trustee and exec. dir. Isamu Noguchi Found., Long Island City, N.Y., 1989—. With AUS, 1945-49. Mem.: The Century Assn., Japan Soc. Address: Fuller & Sadao 32-37 Vernon Blvd Long Island City NY 11106-4926

SADDLEMYER, ANN (ELEANOR SADDLEMYER), educator, critic, theater historian; b. Prince Albert, Sask., Can., Nov. 28, 1932; d. Orrin Angus and Elsie Sarah (Ellis) S. BA, U. Sask., 1953, DLitt, 1991; MA, Queen's U., 1956, LLD (hon.), 1977; PhD, U. London, 1961; DLitt (hon.), U. Victoria, 1989, McGill U., 1989, Windsor U., 1990, U. Toronto, 1999, Concordia U., 2000. Lectr. Victoria (B.C.) Coll., 1956-57, instr., 1960-62, asst. prof., 1962-65; assoc. prof. U. Victoria, 1965-68, prof. English, 1968-71, Victoria Coll. U. Toronto, 1971-95; prof., dir. Grad. Ctr. for Study of Drama, U. Toronto, 1972-77, 85-86; prof. emerita Dept. English, Comparative Lit. Grad Ctr. for Study of Drama, U. Toronto, 1995—; sr. fellow Massey Coll., 1975-88, master, 1988-95, master emerita, 1995—; Berg prof. NYU, 1975. Adj. prof. U. Victoria. Dir. Theatre Plus, 1972-84; dir. Colin Smythe Pubs.; author: (with Robin Skelton) The World of W.B. Yeats, 1965, In Defence of Lady Gregory, Playwright, 1966, Synge and Modern Comedy, 1968, J.M. Synge Plays Books One and Two, 1968, Lady Gregory Plays, 4 vols., 1970, Letters to Molly: Synge to Maire O'Neill, 1971, Letters from Synge to W.B. Yeats and Lady Gregory, 1971, Collected Letters of John Millington Synge, Vol. 1, 1983, vol. II, 1984, Theatre Business, The Correspondence of the First Abbey Theatre Directors, 1982, (with Colin Smythe) Lady Gregory Fifty Years After, 1987, Early Stages: Theatre in Ontario, 1980-1914, 1990, J.M. Synge: The Playboy of the Western World and Other Plays, 1995; (with Richard Plant) Later Stages: Theatre in Ontario, 1914-1970s, 1997, Becoming George--The Life of Mrs. W.B. Yeats, 2002; co-editor Theatre History in Canada, 1980-86; editorial bds. Modern Drama, 1972-82, English Studies in Can., 1973-83, Themes in Drama, 1974-93, Shaw Rev., 1977—, Research in the Humanities, 1976-90; Irish Univ. Rev., 1970—, Yeats Ann., 1982-86; Studies in Contemporary Irish Lit., 1986—, Irish Studies Rev., 1997; contbr. articles to profl. jours. Recipient Brit. Acad. Rose Mary Crawshay award, 1986, Disting. Svc. award Province of Ont., 1985, U. Toronto Alumni award of excellence, 1991, award yeats Soc. N.Y. 2001; named Disting. Dau. of Pa., 1992, Woman of Distinction in Letters, Toronto, YWCA, 1994; Officer of Order of Can., 1995; Can. Coun. scholar, 1958-59, fellow, 1968, Guggenheim fellow, 1968, 77, sr. rsch. fellow Connaught, 1985. Fellow Royal Soc. Can., Royal Soc. Arts; mem. Internat. Assn. Study Anglo-Irish Lit. (chmn. 1973-76), Assn. Can. Theatre Rsch. (pres. 1976-77), Can. Assn. Irish Studies, Assn. Can. Univ. Tchrs. English. Home: 10876 Madrona Dr Sidney BC Canada V8L 5N9 E-mail: saddlemy@uvic.ca.

SADDLER, GARY L. government official; b. Colby, Kans., June 17, 1941; s. Guy M. and Berta M. Saddler; m. Nancy C. Saddler, Sept. 2, 1967; children: Lara L. Perrin, Garlyn B., Brian L. BS in BA, Ft. Hays (Kans.) State U., 1964. Territory mgr. Burroughs Corp., Denver, 1968-70, sys. rep. Englewood, Colo., 1970-72, sys. supr., 1972-78, mgr. program applications, 1978-83; dist. software svc. mgr. Unisys Corp., 1983-87, br. customer tech. svc. mgr., 1987-90, mgr. major products, 1990-93; prin. sys. analyst Colo. Dept. Corrections, Colorado Springs, 1993-97, dir. info. tech. divsn., 1997—. Cons. in field. Dist. coord. Rep. Party, Denver, 1979, 80, 81, committeeman, 1980, 81. Lt. USN, 1964-67. Baptist. Home: 2201 S Corona St Denver CO 80210 Office: Colorado Dept Corrections 2862 S Circle Dr Colorado Springs CO 80906 E-mail: gary.nanc@netzero.net.

SADDLER, GEORGE FLOYD, government economic adviser; b. Memphis, Sept. 27, 1925; s. Henry Rutherford and Ludorn Myrtle (Woods) S.; m. Pauline Evelyn McKissack, Jan. 3, 1944 (dec. Aug. 1988); children: Paula Frederica, Paulette Yvonne. BS, NYU, 1950; postgrad., Northwestern U., Chgo., 1954, U. Chgo., 1961-62. Supr. acctg. dept. Aldens, Inc., Chgo., 1950-57; sr. acct. City of Chgo., 1957-65; internat. adminstrn. officer U.S. Dept. State, Washington, 1965-68; chief budget sect. UN, N.Y.C., 1968-74; dir. fin. UN Devel. Program, 1974-78; minister-counselor U.S. Mission to UN, 1978-81; asst. dir. gen. UNESCO, Paris, 1981-86; sr. econ. adviser U.S. Mission to UN, N.Y.C., 1986-89; sr. advisor, cons. UN Orgns., 1989-96. Pres. Assn. Former Internat. Civil Servants in N.Y., 1994—2002, Riverdale chpt. of the UN Assn. of the U.S., 1995—99; chmn. Fedn. Assns. of Former Internat. Civil Servants, 1999—. Treas. The Hague Appeal for Peace, 2000—. E-mail: saddlerg@un.org., gfsaddler@mindspring.com.

SADDLETON, MICHAEL JOHN, emergency physician; b. U.K., June 21, 1943; MD, U. Sask., Can., 1974. Diplomate Am. Bd. Emergency Medicine. Intern St. Paul's Hosp., Saskatoon, Sask., 1974-75; resident in gen. surgery U. Hosp., 1975-76; mem. staff Summa Health Sys., Akron, Parma Cmty. Gen. Hosp.; pvt. practice occupational health Akron, Cleve. Mem. AMA, Am. Coll. Emergency Physicians, Am. Coll. Occupl. and Environ. Medicine, Wilderness Med. Soc. Office: Parma Cmty Gen Hosp Employers Health Source 6681 Ridge Rd Ste 300 Parma OH 44129-5705

SADE, DONALD STONE, anthropology educator; b. Charleston, W.Va., July 17, 1937; s. Samuel and Charlotte Tracy (Stone) S.; m. Bonita Diane Chepko, Dec. 24, 1971 (div. Feb. 1994); children: Irony Cuervo del Norte, Omen Ondatra; m. Kerry L. Knox, Nov. 24, 1994. Grad., N.Y. State Ranger Sch., 1957; student, Hamilton Coll., 1957-60; AB, U. Calif., Berkeley, 1963, PhD, 1966. Instr. anthropology Northwestern U., Evanston, Ill., 1965-66, asst. prof., 1966-70, assoc. prof., 1970-75, prof., 1975-95, sr. lectr., 1995—; scientist-in-charge Cayo Santiago, U. P.R., 1970-77; prof. emeritus Northwestern U., 1997—. Founder, pres. North Country Inst. for Natural Philosophy, Inc., Mexico, N.Y., 1980— Sr. author: Basic Demographic Observations on Free-Ranging Rhesus Monkeys, 3 vols., 1985; editor: The North Country Naturalist, Vol. 1, 1987. NSF grantee, 1967— Mem. Animal Behavior Soc., Guild Am. Luthiers, The Nature Conservancy, The Adirondack Mountain Club, The Adirondack Coun. Office: North Country Inst for Natural Philosophy Inc 18 Emery Rd Mexico NY 13114-3311 *...and all I've done for want of wit, to memory now I can't recall. (Irish ballad).*

SADE, ROBERT MILES, physician, bioethicist, educator; b. Malden, Mass., Sept. 23, 1938; BA, Wesleyan U., 1959; MD, Columbia U., 1963. Diplomate Am. Bd. Surgery, Am. Bd. Thoracic Surgery. Intern Boston City Hosp., MA, 1963-64, resident, 1964-68, New England Deaconess Hosp., 1971, Peter Bent Brigham Hosp., 1972, Childrens Hosp., 1972-73; asst. prof. surgery Harvard U., Boston, 1973-75; prof. surgery U. S.C. Sch. Medicine, Charleston, 1975—. Med. dir., bd. dirs. LifePoint, Inc., Charleston, 1998—. Assoc. editor Annals Thoracic Surgery, 2001—. Lt. Comdr. USNR, 1969-70, Vietnam. Avocations: squash, golf. Office: 96 Jonathan Lucas St Charleston SC 29425-8900

SADEGH, ALI M. mechanical engineering educator, researcher, consultant; b. Tehran, Iran, Sept. 1, 1950; came to U.S., 1974; s. Saleh S. Mir-Mohamad-Sadegh and Asam Lotfi; m. Guita Miremadi, July 10, 1980; children: Mietra, Cameron, Mona, Jasmin, David. BSME, Arya-Mehr U. Tech., Tehran, 1972; MSME, Mich. State U., 1975, PhD in Mechanics, 1978; postgrad., U. Mich., 1979. Registered profl. engr., Mich.; cert. mfg. engr. Design engr. Nat. Radio engrng. sect., Tehran, 1972-74; rsch. and teaching asst. Mich. State U., East Lansing, 1975-78; asst. prof. Arya-Mehr U. Tech., 1979-81; vis. asst. prof. Mich. State U., 1981-82; asst. prof. CUNY, N.Y.C., 1982-87, assoc. prof., 1987-91, prof., 1991—, chmn. dept. mech. engrng., 1992-96, tchr. courses in solid mechanics, design and CAD/CAM. Cons. Devel. Iranian Heavy Industries, Tehran, 1979-81; tech. cons. AC Rochester Gen. Motors Co., 1986-92; forensic engr., 1990—; cons. and presenter in field. Contbr. over 100 articles to profl. jours.; 7 patents in field. U. Mich. scholar, Ann Arbor, 1978-79; recipient 36 Rsch. awards NSF, AT&T Found ., PSC-CUNY, others. Fellow ASME (Best Paper award 1992, Melville medal 1993), Soc. Mfg. Engrs. (chmn. chpt. 320); mem. Am. Acad. Mechanics, Biomed. Engrs. Soc., Sigma Xi. Achievements include patents in field. Avocations: tennis, swimming, soccer. Home: 787 Oneida Trl Franklin Lakes NJ 07417-2216 Office: CUNY Dept Mech Engring 140th St and Convent Ave New York NY 10031

SADEGHI-NEJAD, ABDOLLAH, pediatrician, educator; b. Meshed, Iran, Apr. 29, 1938; s. Abdolhossein and Azizeh (Jabbari) S.-N.; m. Marion M. Marquardt, Jan. 26, 1974; children; Nathan R., Adrienne R. BA, Beloit Coll., 1960; MS in Pathology, MD, U. Chgo., 1964. Diplomate Am. Bd. Pediatrics. Intern then resident U. Chgo., 1964-67; fellow pediatric endocrinology New Eng. Med. Ctr., Boston, 1967-69, U. Calif., San Francisco, 1969-70; from asst. prof. to prof. pediatrics Tufts U., Boston, 1970—; chief pediatric endocrinology and metabolism divsn. New Eng. Med. Ctr., 1989—. Author and co-author books and articles. Mem. town meeting Town of Brookline, Mass., 1987-2001, mem. adv. com., 1993-99; founder, mem. Friends of Lost Pond. Fellow Am. Acad. Pediatrics; mem. Am. Pediatric Soc., Am. Diabetes Assn., Endocrine Soc., European Soc. Pediatric Rsch., Lawson Wilkins Pediat. Endocrine Soc., Soc. Pediat. Rsch. Office: New Eng Med Ctr 750 Washington St Boston MA 02111-1526

SADEK, ADEL, engineering educator; b. Alexandria, Egypt; m. Marianne Sadek, July 23, 2000. PhD, U. Va., 1998. Cert. engr. intern. Asst. prof. U. Vt., Burlington, 1998—. Contbr. Recipient NSF Career award, NSF, 2002, Milton Pikarsky award for best dissertation in field of transp. sci. and tech., 1998. Mem.: ASCE (mem. computing in transp. com. 2000—), Transp. Rsch. Bd. (mem. artificial intelligence com. 2002—). Christian. Avocations: reading, travel. Office: U Vt Dept Civil and Environ Engring Burlington VT 05405 Office Fax: 802-656-8446. Business E-Mail: asadek@emba.uvm.edu.

SADER, ALAN, actor, children's advocate; b. Durham, N.C., Sept. 9, 1940; s. Julius and Barbara Muellerschoen; m. Ann Chenoweth, Apr. 18, 1987; children: Julianna, Mary. BA, Duke U., 1962. Appeared in numerous roles on TV, film stage. Mem. Screen Actors Guild (life).

SADER, CAROL HOPE, former state legislator; b. Bklyn., July 19, 1935; d. Nathan and Mollie (Farkas) Shimkin; m. Harold M. Sader, June 9, 1957; children: Neil, Randi Sader Friedlander, Elisa Sader Waldman. BA, Barnard Coll., Columbia U., 1957. Sch. tchr. Bd. Edn., Morris, Conn., 1957-58; legal editor W. H. Anderson Co., Cin., 1974-78; freelance legal editor Shawnee Mission, Kans., 1978-87; mem. Kans. Ho. of Reps., 1987-94. Chair Ho. Pub. Health and Welfare Com., 1991-92; chair Joint Ho. and Senate Com. on Health Care Decisions for the 90's, 1992; vice chair Ho. Econ. Devel. Com., 1991-92; policy chair Ho. Dem. Caucus, 1993-94; appointee Kans. jud. qualifications commn. Kans. Supreme Ct., 1995—. Pres. LWV, Johnson County, 1983—85; mem. State of Kans. LWV Bd., 1986—87; pres. Johnson County Found. Aging, 2002—; mem. Johnson County Charter Commn., 1999; mem. exec. bd. Johnson County C.C. Found., 2000—; dem. candidate for Kans. Lt. Gov., 1994; chmn. bd. trustees Johnson County C.C., Overland Park, Kans., 1984—86, trustee, 1981—86; bd. dirs. United Cmty. Svcs. of Johnson County, Shawnee Mission, 1984—92, Jewish Vocat. Svc. Bd., 1983—92, House of Menuha, 1998—99, Midwest Ctr. Holocaust Edn., 1999—, Appleseed Found. Kans., 1999—2001; chmn. Kans. State Holocaust Commn., 1991—94; pres. MAINstream Coalition, 1995—97, vice chair, 1998—; v.p. Kans. Advocates for Better Care, 1998—2001. Recipient Trustee award Assn. of Women in Jr. and C.C., 1985, awards Kans. Pub. Transit Assn., 1990, AARP, 1992, Assn. Kans. Theater, 1992, Nat. Coun. Jewish Women, 1992, Kans. Assn. Osteo. Medicine, 1992, Kans. Chiropractic Assn., 1992, United Com. Svcs. Johnson County, 1992, Disting. Pub. Svcs. award Johnson County, 1993, Hallpac Kans. Pub. Svc. award Hallmark Cards, Inc., 1993, Eddie Jacobsen award B'nai B'rith, 1994, Cmty. Svc. award House of Menuha, 1998. Mem. Coun. Women Legislators, Phi Delta Kappa. Democrat. Avocations: grandparenting, lakehouse, theatre, travel. Home: 8612 Linden Dr Shawnee Mission KS 66207-1807 E-mail: hcsader@aol.com.

SADER, NEIL STEVEN, lawyer; b. Torrington, Conn., Oct. 10, 1958; s. Harold M. and Carol Hope (Shimkin) S.; m. Elizabeth Napshin, Jan. 3, 1988; children: Samantha Isabel, Daniel Scott, Lani Eden. AB, Columbia U., 1980; JD, U. Kans., 1984. Bar: Mo. 1984, U.S. Ct. Appeals (10th cir.) 1988, U.S. Supreme Ct. 1993, Kans. 1994, U.S. Dist. Ct. (ea. dist.) Mich. 1995; bd. cert. consumer bankruptcy law Am. Bd. Certification, 2000. Asst. White House Domestic Policy Staff, Washington, 1980-81; assoc. Wasserstrom & Wasserstrom, 1984-86, Brown, Nachman & Sader, P.C., Kansas City, Mo., 1986-90, shareholder, 1990-97; mng. mem. Sader & Garvin LLC, 1997—. Planning commr. Johnson County, Kans., 1983-85, Overland Park, Kans., 1985-90; mem. Overland Park City Coun., 1990—, pres., 1995-96, 2000-01; bd. dirs. Mid-Am. Regional Coun., 1993—; precinct committeeman Johnson County Dem. Party, 1983—, mem. exec. com., 1984-90, vice chmn., 1988-90; bd. dirs. Jewish Family and Children's Svcs. Kansas City, 1986-90; bd. dirs. Overland Park Conv. and Visitors Bur., 1995-98; del. Dem. Nat. Conv., 1996. Mem. Am. Bankruptcy Inst., Mo. Bar Assn., Columbia U. Club Kansas City (bd. dirs.), Kansas City Met. Bar Assn. Jewish. Avocations: travel, sports, coaching youth baseball. Home: 11736 W 102nd St Overland Park KS 66214-2686 Office: Sader & Garvin LLC Ste 300 4739 Belleview Avenue Kansas City MO 64112-1364 E-mail: nsader@sadergarvin.com., nbsader@aol.com.

SADIK, MARVIN SHERWOOD, art consultant, former museum director; b. Springfield, Mass., June 27, 1932; s. Harry Benjamin and Florence (Askinas) S. AB magna cum laude, Harvard U., 1954, A.M., 1960; D.F.A. (hon.), Bowdoin Coll., Brunswick, Maine, 1978. Curatorial asst. Worcester (Mass.) Art Mus., 1955-57; curator Mus. Art Bowdoin Coll., 1961-64, dir., 1964-67, Mus. Art U. Conn. at Storrs, 1967-69, Nat. Portrait Gallery, Washington, 1969-81. Author: Colonial and Federal Portraits at Bowdoin College, 1966, The Drawings of Hyman Bloom, 1968, The Paintings of Charles Hawthorne, 1968, Edith Halpert and the Downtown Gallery, 1968, The Life Portraits of John Quincy Adams, 1970, Christian Gullager: Portrait Painter to Federal America, 1976, Portraits of George Bellows, 1981; co-author: American Portrait Drawings, 1980. Decorated knight Order Dannebrog Denmark; recipient Detur prize Harvard Coll., 1952, Maine State Art award, 1975, gold medal for exceptional svc. Smithsonian Instn., 1981; Harris fellow, 1957-61; Barr fellow, 1957-61; fellow Belgian Art Seminar, 1956. Fellow Pierpont Morgan Library; mem. Am. Antiquarian Soc., Colonial Soc. Mass. (corr.) Clubs: Century Assn, Grolier. Home: PO Box 6360 Scarborough ME 04070-6360

SADILEK, VLADIMIR, architect; b. Czechoslovakia, June 27, 1933; came to U.S., 1967, naturalized, 1973; s. Oldrich and Antoine (Zlamal) S.; m. Jana Kadlec, Mar. 25, 1960; 1 child, Vladimir. PhD in City Planning summa cum laude, Tech. U. Prague, 1957. Lic. architect, 28 states. Chief architect State Office for City Planning, Prague, 1958-67; architect, designer Bank Bldg. Corp., St. Louis, 1967-70, assoc. architect San Francisco, 1970-74; owner, CEO Bank Design Cons., San Mateo, Calif., 1974-81, West Coast Devel. Co., San mateo, 1975—; pres., CEO Orbis Devel. Corp., 1981—. Served with Inf. of Czechoslovakia, 1958. Recipient awards of excellence Bank Bldg. Corp. and AIA for planning and Design of fin. instns. in Hawaii and Calif., 1971, Ariz., N.Mex. and Tex., 1972, Colo. and Wyo., 1973, Idaho, Oreg., Wash., 1974. Republican. Roman Catholic. Home: 80 Orange Ct Burlingame CA 94010-6516 Office: 1777 Borel Pl San Mateo CA 94402-3509

SADLER, CHARLES BENJAMIN, JR. pharmacist, real estate associate, marketing professional; b. Petersburg, Va., Feb. 2, 1939; s. Charlie Benjamin and Ellen Elizabeth (Rathine) S.; m. Nancy Marie Newton, June, 1960 (div. Mar. 1979); children: Charles Benjamin III, Tracy Lynn; m. Linda Lee Puryear, Apr. 14, 1979. BS in pharmacy, Med. Coll. of Va., 1960; postgrad., Richard Bland Coll., 1971-72, 76, Va.Commonwealth U., 1972-73; cert. in real estate, Moseley-Flint Coll., Richmond, Va., 1977. Registered pharmacist, Va.; lic. real estate. Pharmacist, instr. John Randolph Hosp., Hopewell, Va., 1960-61; pharmacist Peoples Drugs, Richmond, 1961-63, O.P. Hare Drugs, Petersburg, 1963-65; mgr., pharmacist supr. Super X Drugs, Covington, Danville, Clipton Forge, 1965-68; pharmacist mgr. Gray Drug Fair, Hopewell, Col. Hts., Richmond, 1968-88; mgr. pharmacy Standard Drug Store, Petersburg, 1988-91, Phar-Mor Drugs, Colonial Heights, Va., 1991-92, Farmco Drug, 1992-95, Revco/Eckerd, Petersburg, Va., 1996—. Pres. CBS Assocs. Internat. Active mem. Smithsonian Inst., Washington, 1965—, Met. Guild Pharmacists, Citizens Choice, Washington, 1984—. Mem. Am. Pharm. Assn., Va. Pharm. Assn. (4th dist.), Va. Commonwealth U. Alumni Assn., Cousteau Soc., Kappa Psi. Republican. Baptist. Avocations: computers, woodworking, reading, swimming, fishing. Home: 4104 Birchleaf Ct Chester VA 23831-4618

SADLER, DAVID GARY, management executive; b. Iowa City, Mar. 14, 1939; s. Edward Anthony and Elsie June (Sherman) S.; m. Karen Sadler. Student, St. Ambrose Coll., 1957-59; BS in Indsl. Adminstrn. and Prodn., Kent State U., 1961. Various mgmt. positions Ford Motor Co., Lorain, Ohio, 1962-67, Sperry-New Holland, Lebanon, 1967-71; mgr. mfg. Allis Chalmer, Springfield, Ill., 1971-72; dir. mfg. Purolator, Inc., Fayetteville, N.C., 1972-73; v.p. mfg. farm equipment and ops. truck div. White Motor Co., Eastlake, Ohio and Chgo., 1973-78; corp. v.p. mfg. Massey Ferguson Ltd., Toronto, Ont., Can., 1978-80, Internat. Harvester, Chgo., 1980-81, sr. v.p. ops. staff, 1981-82, v.p. bus. devel., 1982, pres. diversified group, 1982-83, pres. internat. group, 1983-85; pres. AMI, Inc., 1985-86; vice chmn., chief exec. officer Savin Corp., Stamford, Conn., 1986, chmn., chief exec. officer, 1986-89, also bd. dirs.; pres. Asset Mgmt. Internat., Westport, 1989-95; chmn., CEO, Rowe Internat., Grand Rapids, Mich., 1995-2000, also bd. dirs., 2000—01; CEO Merisel, Inc., El Segundo, Calif., also bd. dirs.; chmn., CEO, bd. dirs. Global Motorsport Group, Inc., Morgan Hill, 2002. Bd. dirs. greater Chgo. Safety Coun., 1981-84; mem. adb. bd. Hellmond Assocs. Opportunity Fund II. Roman Catholic. Home: 751 Bradford Farms Ln NE Grand Rapids MI 49525-3348 E-mail: davidgsadler@aol.com.

SADLER, ELLIOTT, race car driver; b. Emporia, Va., Apr. 30, 1975; s. Herman and Bell Sadler. Student, James Madison U. Named winner, Late Model Stock Cars Winston Racing Series, 1994, South Boston Speedway Track, 1995, Core States Advantage 200, 1997, Myrtle Beach, 1997, Gateway Internat. Raceway, 1997, Bristol, 1998, Winston Cup, 2001; recipient Busch Pole award, 1997, 2d pl., Kroger 250, 1998. Avocations: golf, basketball, hunting. Office: c/o Wood Bros Racing 21 Performance Dr Stuart VA 24171*

SADLER, JAMES BERTRAM, psychologist, clergyman; b. Albuquerque, Mar. 29, 1911; s. James Monroe and Mary Agnes (English) S.; m. Vera Ellen Ahrendt, Apr. 10, 1938. AB, U. N.Mex., 1938; BD, Crozer Theol. Sem., 1941, ThM, 1948; MA, U. Pa., 1941, EdD, 1959. Lic. psychologist, S.D.; ordained to ministry Bapt. Ch., 1941. Pastor First Bapt. Ch., Mt. Union, Pa., 1941-42; chaplain USAF, 1943-48; pastor Hatboro (Pa.) Bapt. Ch., 1948-61; chmn. dept. psychology Sioux Falls (S.D.) Coll., 1961-75; pvt. practice psychology Sioux Falls, 1975—. Cons. in psychology and religion. Contbr. articles to profl. jours. Mem. mins. coun. Am. Bapt. Conv. Mem. APA, Soc. for Sci. Study Religion, Masons, Rotary (pres. 1960). Home and Office: 4312 Glenview Rd Sioux Falls SD 57103-4935

SADLER, SALLIE INGLIS, psychotherapist; b. Phila., Nov. 16, 1941; d. H. Barton Off and Janet (Miller) Nelson; m. William A. Sadler, Jr., Apr. 23, 1977; children: Lisa, Nelson, Ashley, Kirsten. BA, Rollins Coll., Winter Park, Fla., 1964; MSW with high acad. achievement, Rutgers U., 1979; postgrad., Pa. State U., 1986-89; PhD in Clin. Psychology, Ctr. for Psychol. Studies, 1998. Cert. social worker. Caseworker II, dir. group work Family and Children's Svc. West Essex, Caldwell, N.J., 1979-81; dir. Single Parent Ctr. West Essex, Montclair, 1981-85; pvt. practice Upper Montclair, 1981-85; chief clin. svcs. Family Svc. Ctr., U.S. Naval Air Base, Alameda, Calif., 1990-95; sr. psychiat. social worker dept. psychiatry Kaiser Permanente Med. Ctr., San Francisco, 1995—2001; pvt. practice, 2001—. Oral license examiner Calif. Bd. Behavioral Sci. Examiners; adj. instr. div. social scis. Bloomfield (N.J.) Coll., 1979-81, N.J. Inst. Tech., 1984-85; instr. psychology dept. Lock Haven (Pa.) U., 1985-90. Mem. NASW, APA, Assn. Women Faculty in Higher Edn. Avocations: skiing, sailing, hiking, cooking.

SADLER, WILLIAM JACQUES, psychiatric social worker; b. Tomah, Wis., Apr. 21, 1959; s. John Weldon and Maureen (Sullivan) S.; m. Danna Bustamante, June 22, 1990; 1 child, Jordan Wyatt. BSW, U. Tex., El Paso, 1986, postgrad., 1986-87; MA in Counseling, Webster U., 1989, cert., 1990; MSW, U. Tex., 1994. Children's protective svcs. specialist Tex. Dept. Human Svcs., El Paso, 1989, social worker children's protective svcs., 1989—. Psychotherapist Jewish Family Svcs., 1992-93, Family Sci. of El Paso, 1993-94, Alliance Hosp. of Santa Teresa, N.Mex., 1994. Vol. Tex. Dept. Human Svcs., 1989. Mem. NASW, Tex. Soc. Clin. Social Work, Am. Assn. Marriage and Family Therapists (El Paso chpt.). Democrat. Roman Catholic. Avocations: rugby, reading, research.

SADLO, KENNETH LOUIS, poet, writer; b. St. Louis, Oct. 16, 1969; s. Kenneth Edward Sadlo, Mary Ann Cherrick. Student, St. Louis U., 1988—89, Lincolnland C.C., Springfield, Ill., 1991—92. Author: (CD compilation of various authors) The Sound of Poetry, 2001, The Silence Within, 2001, The Best Poems and Poets of 2001, 2001. Liaison Quincy U. "The Falcon", Ill., 1992—93. Scholar John J. McDaniel scholar, 1984—88. Home: 11733 Lindemere Des Peres MO 63131

SADOCK, BENJAMIN JAMES, psychiatrist, educator; b. N.Y.C., Dec. 22, 1933; s. Samuel William and Gertrude S.; m. Virginia Alcott, Oct. 20, 1963; children: James William, Victoria Anne. AB, Union Coll., 1955; MD, N.Y. Med. Coll., 1959. Rotating intern Albany (N.Y.) Hosp., 1959-60; resident Bellevue Psychiat. Hosp., N.Y.C., 1960-63; instr. psychiatry Southwestern Med. Sch., Dallas, 1964-65, N.Y. Med. Coll., N.Y.C., 1965-67, asst. prof., 1967-71, assoc. prof., 1972-74, prof., 1975-80, dir. student health psychiatry, 1980—; prof. psychiatry NYU Sch Medicine, 1981-99, Menas S. prof. psychiatry, 2000—, vice chmn. dept. psychiatry, 1984—, faculty scholar, 2000—. Attending physician Lenox Hill Hosp.; attending psychiatrist Tisch Univ. Hosp. of NYU Med. Ctr., Bellevue Hosp.; cons. psychiatrist Franklin Delano Roosevelt VA Hosp., 1970-78, U.S. Dept. State, 1980-81, P.R. Inst. Psychiatry, 1976-80; examiner Am. Bd. Psychiatry and Neurology, 1970-80; mem. conf. on recert. Am. Bd. Med. Spltys.-Am. Psychiat. Assn., 1974; mem. Commn. on Continuing Edn. in Psychiatry, NIMH-Am. Psychiat. Assn., 1974-75. Co-author: Comprehensive Group Psychotherapy, 1971, 3d edit., 1993, Synopsis of Psychiatry, 1972, 8th edit., 1998, The Sexual Experience, 1976, Study Guide Modern Synopsis of Psychiatry, 1983, 6th edit., 1998, Comprehensive Textbook of Psychiatry, 7th edit., 2000, Pocket Handbook of Clinical Psychiatry, 1991, 3d edit., 2001, Comprehensive Glossary of Psychiatry and Psychology, 1991, Pocket Handbook of Drug Treatment in Psychiatry, 1992, 3d edit., 2000, Pocket Handbook of Psychiatric Emergency Medicine, 1993, Pocket Handbook of Primary Care Psychiatry, 1996; contbr. articles on psychiat. edn., individual and group psychotherapy, diagnosis and treatment psychiat. and sexual disorders to med. jours.; contbr. to Ency. Americana. Fellow Am. Psychiat. Assn. (treas. N.Y. County dist. br. 1973-76, mem. conf. on psychiatry and med. edn. 1967), N.Y. Acad. Medicine, A.C.P.; mem. AMA, Med. Soc. County and State N.Y., Am. Group Psychotherapy Assn., World Psychiat. Assn., Royal Soc. Medicine (London), Psychiat. Soc. N.Y. Med. Coll. (founder, pres. 1975-79), N.Y. Med. Coll. Alumni Assn. (gov. 1965-90), NYU-Bellevue Psychiat. Soc. (pres. 1981—), Alpha Omega Alpha. Office: 4 E 89th St New York NY 10128-0636 also: NYU Med Ctr 550 1st Ave New York NY 10016-6402 E-mail: bjs6@nyu.edu.

SADOCK, KAREN, editor, writer; b. Detroit, Feb. 12, 1943; d. Warren Siebren and Daisy Annie (Taylor) Nauta; m. Geoffrey Johnston Sadock, Sept. 4, 1971; 1 child, Katharine Cordelia Johnston Sadock. AB, U. Mich., 1965; MDiv, Gen. Theol. Sem., N.Y.C., 1975. Assoc. editor Wards Automotive Reports, Detroit, 1966-68; tech. editor Freuhauf Corp., 1968-71; author's editor Mt. Sinai Med. Ctr., N.Y.C., 1975-97, spl. projects mgr., Dean's Office, 1997—, asst. dir. sci. integrity, 1999—. Editor med. scholarly articles New Eng. Jour. Medicine, Circulation, others; author articles on Christian spirituality. Mem. Am. Med. Writers Assn., Cavalier King Charles Spaniel Clubs U.S.A. Republican. Roman Catholic. Avocations: figure skating, quilting. Home: 67 W Shore Ave Dumont NJ 07628-2332 E-mail: karen.sadock@mssm.edu.

SADOFF, ROBERT LESLIE, psychiatrist, educator; b. Mpls., Feb. 8, 1936; s. Max and Rose C. (Karroll) S.; m. Joan A Handleman, June 21, 1959; children: Debra, David, Julie, Sherry. BA, U. Minn., 1956, BS, 1957, MD, 1959; MS, UCLA, 1963. Intern L.A. VA Hosp., 1959—60; resident in psychiatry UCLA, 1960—63; asst. prof. psychiatry Temple U., Phila., 1966—72; clin. prof. U. Pa., 1972—; pvt. practice Jenkintown, 1965—. Lectr. law Villanova U., 1972-85. Author: (with Marvin Lewis) Psychic Injuries, 1975, Forensic Psychiatry, 1975, 2d edit., 1988, Legal Issues in the Care of Psychiatric Patients, 1982, Violence and Responsibility, 1988, (with Robert I. Simon) Psychiatric Malpractice, 1992; editor: Psychiatric Clinics of North America, 1984. Bd. dirs. Joseph T. Peters Inst., Phila., 1980-92. Capt. M.C., U.S. Army, 1963-65. Recipient Earl Bond award U. Pa., 1979, VII ann. Nathaniel Winkelman award Phila. Psychiat. Ctr., 1988. Fellow: Am. Coll. Legal Medicine, Am. Psychiat. Assn. (Manfred Guttmacher award 1993); mem.: Internat. Acad. Law and Mental Health (Philippe Pinel award 1995), Internat. Soc. for Philos. Enquiry (mentor 1987—), Am. Acad. Psychiatry and Law (pres. 1971—73), Am. Coll. Psychiatrists, Am. Red Magen David for Israel (nat. pres. 1986—2001). Avocation: collecting antique books in law and medicine. Office: The Pavilion Ste 326 261 Old York Rd Jenkintown PA 19046

SADOSKI, MARK CHRISTIAN, education educator; b. Bristol, Conn., June 2, 1945; s. Waldmyr John Sadoski and Ruth Elaine (Gustafson) Kantorski; m. Carol Ann Bove, June 28, 1969; 1 child, Thomas Christian. BS, So. Conn. State U., 1968, MS, 1973; PhD, U. Conn., 1981. Cert. reading, English, social studies tchr. Tchr., reading cons. Milford (Conn.) Pub. Schs., 1968-81; assoc. faculty So. Conn. State U., New Haven, 1978-81; prof. edn. Tex. A&M Univ., College Station, 1981—. Author: (with Allan Paivio) Imagery and Text: A Dual Coding Theory of Reading and Writing, 2001; mem. editl. bd. Reading Rsch. Quar., 1989—, Jour. Reading Behavior, 1990-95, Reading Psychology, 1990—, Jour. Literacy Rsch., 1995—, Document Design, 1998—, Reading and Writing, 2001; contbr. over 70 articles to profl. jours. and books. Accident prevention counselor S.W. region FAA, 1989-91. Recipient Disting. Alumnus award So. Conn. State U., 1994. Mem. Internat. Reading Assn. (outstanding dissertation award com. 1983-85, finalist Outstanding Dissertation award 1982), Nat. Reading Conf. (Outstanding Book award com. 1994-99), Am. Ednl. Rsch. Assn. (outstanding book award com. 1994-2000), Soc. for Sci. Study of Reading (chair pubs. com. 1996-97), Phi Kappa Phi. Avocations: reading, cinema. Office: Tex A&M Univ Dept TLAC College Station TX 77843-4232 E-mail: msadoski@tamu.edu.

SADOVE, STEPHEN IRVING, retail executive; b. Washington, July 25, 1951; s. A. Robert and Harriet (Tenenbaum) S.; m. Sandra Rozenberg, Feb. 24, 1982; children: Stacy, David, Laurie. BA, Hamilton Coll., 1973; MBA, Harvard U., 1975. Asst. product mgr. desserts divsn. Gen. Foods Corp., White Plains, N.Y., 1975-76, assoc. product mgr., 1976-77, product mgr., 1977-80, group product mgr., 1980-82, category mgr., 1982-84, mktg. mgr., 1984-86; bus. unit mgr. meals divsn. Gen. Foods Corp., 1986-88; v.p., gen. mgr. Gen. Foods Corp., 1988-89, exec. v.p., gen. mgr. desserts divsn., 1989-91; pres. Clairol, Inc., Stamford, Conn., 1991-96, Bristol-Myers Squibb Beauty Care, Stamford, 1996-97, Bristol-Myers Squibb Beauty Care and Nutritionals, Stamford, 1998—2001; vice-chmn. Saks Inc., N.Y.C., 2002—. Bd. dirs. Saks Inc., Ruby Tuesday Inc. Trustee Hamilton Coll., Caramoor, Hazelden. Avocations: tennis, golf, reading, arts. Office: Saks Inc 12 E 49th St New York NY 10017 Home: 7 Hickory Pine Ct Purchase NY 10577

SADOW, HARVEY S. health care company executive; b. N.Y.C., Oct. 6, 1922; s. Nat. and Frances Donna (Saveth) S.; m. Sylvia June Riber, Dec. 22, 1944 (div. 1966); children: Harvey Jr., Suzanne Gail, Todd Forrest, Gay Summer; m. Jacqueline Lucille Clavel, Jan. 24, 1969 (div. 1993); 1 adopted child, Daniel Jean Marie; m. Mary Morrissey McSwiggan, July 13, 1995. BS, Va. Mil. Inst., Lexington, 1947; MS, U. Kans., 1949; PhD, U. Conn., 1953, DSc (hon.), 2000. Intelligence officer CIA, Washington, 1951-53; assoc. dir. rsch. Lakeside Labs., Inc., Milw., 1953-56; med. rsch. cons., 1956; dir. clin. rsch. U.S. Vitamin & Pharm. Corp., N.Y.C., 1957-64, v.p. R & D, 1964-68; sr. v.p. scientific affairs USV Pharm./Revlon Corp., 1969-71; pres., CEO Boehringer Ingelheim, Ltd. (named changed to Boehringer Ingelheim Pharms., Inc. 1984), Ridgefield, Conn., 1971-88, Boehringer Ingelheim Corp., Ridgefield, 1984-88, chmn. bd., 1988-90. Chmn. bd. Roxane Labs., Inc., Columbus, Ohio, 1981-88, Boehringer Ingelheim Animal Health, Inc., St. Joseph, Mo., 1981-88, Henley Co., N.Y.C., 1986-88, U. Conn. Rsch. and Devel. Corp., Storrs, 1984-87; bd. dirs. Anika Therapeutics, Inc., Trega Bioscis., Inc., chmn. 2000-01, Cortex Pharms., Inc., Irvine, Calif., chmn. bd., 1991-99; bd. dirs. Cholestech Corp., Hayward, Calif., chmn. bd. 1992-2000; adv. bd. Salk Inst. Biotechnology-Indsl. Assocs., Inc., La Jolla, 1988-90; chmn. bd. dirs. Acacia Bioscis. Inc., 1996-99, Rosetta Inpharmatics, Inc., 1999-2001. Co-author: Oral Treatment of Diabetes, 1967; contbr. articles to profl. jours. Bd. dirs. Pharm. Mfrs. Assn., 1983-90; chmn. Pharm. Mfrs. Assn. Found., 1988-90; bd. dirs. Conn. Bd. Higher Edn., Hartford, 1977-83, Govs. Tech. Adv. Bd., Hartford, 1984-87; mem. Conn. Commn. on Bus. Opportunity, Def. Diversification and Indsl. Policy, 1991-93; mem. bd. visitors Va. Mil. Inst., Lexington, 1987—, pres. bd., 1991-95; chmn. bd. Conn. Law Enforcement Found., Hartford, 1981-86, 92-97, U. Conn. Found., Storrs, 1984-87; chmn., pres.' coun. Am. Lung Assn., N.Y.C., 1986-87, York Sch., Monterey, Calif., 1988-89; trustee Conn. Coll., Groton, 1991-96, Aldrich Mus. Contemporary Art, Ridgefield, Conn., 1991-98. Decorated Disting. Svc. Cross, Fed. Republic of Germany, 1987; recipient Univ. medal U. Conn., 1987, Recognition award Nat. Hypertension Assn., 1990, Humanitarian award Am. Lung Assn. Conn., 1993, Disting. Svc. award Conn. Innovations, Inc., 1996, Va. Mil. Inst. Found., 1998. Mem. Am. Soc. for Clin. Pharmacology and Therapeutics, Am. Fedn. for Clin. Rsch., Am. Diabetes Assn., Danbury C. of C. (Abraham Ribicoff Community Svc. award City of Danbury 1987, bd. dirs. 1978-81), Union League (N.Y.C.), Landmark Club (Stamford, Conn.), Masons, Sigma Xi, Sigma Pi Sigma, Phi Lambda Upsilon. Avocations: art collecting, photography, music, writing, golfing. Home and Office: 120-36 Prospect St Ridgefield CT 06877-4648 E-mail: hssadow@aol.com.

SADOWSKI, CAROL JOHNSON, artist; b. Chgo., Mar. 20, 1929; d. Carl Valdamar Johnson and Elizabeth Hilma (Booth) Johnson-Chellberg; m. Edmund Sadowski, July 9, 1949; children: Lynn Carol Mahoney, Christie Sadowski Cortez. AAS, Wright-Ill. Coll., 1949. Tchr. art Malverne (N.Y.) H.S., 1968-69; artist Valley Stream, N.Y., 1968-76, Hollywood, Fla., 1976—. Guest spkr. Mus. Art Ft. Lauderdale, Fla., 1991, Libr. League, Oakland Park, 1985, Boca Raton (Fla.) Mus., others; TV appearances on WCGB, Gainesville, WSVN, Miami, Storer and Hollywood Cable, Artist Guild, Boca Raton Mus., Broward C.C., Hollywood, Fla. One-woman shows include Mus. Fla. History, Tallahassee, 1984-85, 87, Hist. Mus. South Fla., Miami, 1986, Thomas Ctr. Arts, Gainesville, Fla., 1985, 87, Elliott Mus., Stuart, Fla., 1987, Hemingway Mus. & Home, Key West, Fla., 1986, I.G.F.A. Fishing Hall of Fame Mus., Dania, Fla., 1999, Alliance Francaise de Miami, 1995; commd. painting St. Agustin Antigua Found., St. Augustine, Fla., 1985, Atlantic Bank, Ft. Lauderdale, Fla., Bonnet House Fla. Trust, Ft. Lauderdale, Hollywood Art & Culture Ctr., Hemingway Mus., San Francisco de Paula, Cuba, Presdl. Palace, Havana, Tropical Art Gallery, Naples, Fla., 1981-83, Tequesta (Fla.) Art Gallery, 1985-89, Gingerbread Square Gallery, Key West, 1990—, Wally Findlay Galleries, Inc., Palm Beach and N.Y.C., 1996-99, DeBruyne Fine Arts Gallery, Naples, 1998—, Patricia Cloutier Gallery, Tequesta, Fla., 1992—. Mem. Ft. Lauderdale Mus. Art, Hollywood Art and Culture Ctr. Recipient Hemingway medal Ernest Hemingway Mus., Cuba, 1990, appreciation award City of Hollywood; Art Inst. Chgo. scholar; Salmagundi Club N.Y. scholar. Mem. Internat. Platform Assn., Broward Art Guild, Fla. Hist. Assn., Ernest Hemingway Soc., Chopin Found., Am. Inst. for Polish Culture, Alliance Francaise de Miami, Women in the Arts Nat. Mus. (charter mem.). Avocations: travel, biking, swimming, reading. Home: 1480 Sheridan St Apt B-17 Hollywood FL 33020-2295 *I try to do my best at what I love to do, not for money or fame, but for self satisfaction.*

SADOWSKI, CHESTER PHILIP, JR. real estate executive; b. Pensacola, Fla., May 28, 1946; s. Chester P. and Florence Edna (Perry)S.; m. Jerriann Gibson Steller, Oct. 4, 1975; children: Julie K., Charles P., Robert T., David A. BSBA, U. Fla., 1968. CPA, Fla. Sr. auditor Arthur Andersen & Co., Tampa, Fla., 1969-74, U.S. Home Corp., Clearwater, Fla. and Houston, 1974-77, audit mgr., 1977-81, sr. audit mgr., 1981-82, audit dir., 1982-85, controller, 1985-87, v.p., controller, chief acctg. officer, 1987—. Mem.: AICPA (real estate com. N.Y.C. 1986—89), Inst. Mgmt. Accts., Fla. Inst. CPA's. Office: US Home Corp 10707 Clay Rd Houston TX 77041-5497

SADOWSKI, RICHARD J. former publishing executive; b. Mar. 26, 1947; Publ. Press-Telegram, Long Beach, Calif., 1992—97; pres., publ. St. Paul Pioneer Press, 1997—2001. Office: St Paul Pioneer Press 345 Cedar St Saint Paul MN 55101-1057*

SADRUDIN, MOE, humanitarian organization executive; b. Hyderabad, India, Mar. 3, 1943; came to U.S., 1964; m. Azmath Qureshi, 1964; 3 children. BSME, Osmania U., Hyderabad, 1964; MS in Indsl. Engring., NYU, 1966; IE, MBA, Columbia U., 1970. Cons. project engr. Ford, Bacon & Davis, N.Y.C., 1966; staff indsl. engr. J.C. Penney, 1966-68; sr. cons. Drake, Sheahan, Stewart & Dougall, 1968-70, Beech-Nut Inc. subs. Squibb Corp., N.Y.C., 1970-72; founder, pres. Azmath Constrn. Co., Englewood, N.J., 1972-77; crude oil cons., fgn. govt. rep., 1977—89; pres. A-One Petroleum Co., Fullerton, Calif., 1985—95; chmn., CEO, Azhar Found., 1989—. Govt. advisor Puerto Rico, 1980-82, Dominica, 1983-84, St. Vincent, 1981-82, Kenya, 1983-84, Belize 1984-85, Costa Rica 1983-86, Paraguay 1984-87. Chmn. Azhar Found., 1989—; involved in bldg. 50 charitable hosps. and 9000 schools for the poor in India and 25 charitable hosps. and 5000 schools for the poor in Bangladesh; mem. L.A. World Affairs Coun. Mem. Internat. Platform Assn. Address: Azhar Foundation 2656 Camino Del Sol Fullerton CA 92833-4806 E-mail: Azherfound@aol.com. *Personal philosophy: I learned from a young age that acquisition of knowledge, developing honesty and integrity and service to humanity in the form of charity, love and struggle to help the poor and needy, are the main foundation stones of a successful life. I believe that acquisition of wealth is only a means to an end and not an end in itself. With accumulation of wealth, one has to care for the underprivileged and try to improve their lot.*

SADUN, ALBERTO CARLO, astrophysicist, educator; b. Atlanta, Apr. 28, 1955; s. Elvio Herbert and Lina (Ottolenghi) S.; m. Erica Liebman. BS in Physics, Mass. Inst. Tech., 1977; PhD in Physics, MIT, 1984. Asst. prof. Agnes Scott Coll., Decatur, Ga., 1984-90, assoc. prof., 1990—, dir. Bradley Obs., 1987-97; chmn. dept. physics U. Colo., Denver, 1997—. Adj. prof. Ga. State U., Atlanta, 1986-97; rsch. affiliate NASA/Caltech Jet Propulsion Lab., Pasadena, Calif., 1988-90, summer faculty fellow, 1987, 88. Contbr. articles to Nature, Astrophys. Jour., Astron. Jour., Publ. Aston. Soc. of the Pacific, Astrophys. Letters and Communications. Mem. Am. Jewish Com., Atlanta, 1984—. Fellow Royal Astron. Soc.; mem. Internat. Astron. Union, Am.

Astron. Soc., N.Y. Acad. Scis. Achievements include relocation of Agnes Scott College's telescope to Hard Labor Creek Observatory. Home: 90 S Ivy St Denver CO 80224-1023 Office: U Colo-Denver Dept Physics PO Box 173364 Denver CO 80217-3364

SADUN, ALFREDO ARRIGO, neuro-ophthalmologist, scientist, educator; b. New Orleans, Oct. 23, 1950; s. Elvio H. and Lina (Ottoleghi) S.; m. Debra Leigh Rice, Mar. 18, 1978; children: Rebecca Eli, Elvio Aaron, Benjamin Maxwell. BS, MIT, 1972; PhD, Albert Einstein Med. Sch., Bronx, N.Y., 1976, MD, 1978. Intern Huntington Meml. Hosp. U. So. Calif., Pasadena, 1978—79; resident Harvard U. Med. Sch., Boston, 1979—82, HEED Found. fellow in neuro-ophthalmology Mass. Eye and Ear Inst., 1982—83, instr. ophthalmology, 1983, asst. prof. ophthalmology, 1984; dir. residential tng. U. So. Calif. Dept. Ophthalmology, L.A., 1984-85, 90—; asst. prof. ophthalmology and neurosurgery U. So. Calif., 1984—87, assoc. prof., 1987—90, full prof., 1990—, mem. internal review bd., F. Thornton endowed chair, prof. vision rsch., 2000—. Prin. investigator Howe Lab. Harvard U., Boston, 1981-84, E. Doheny Eye Inst., L.A., 1984—; examiner Am. Bd. Ophthalmology; mem. Nat. Residency Rev. Com. for Accreditations, 1993—, chmn., 1998—; mem. internal rev. bd. U. So. Calif.; mem. sci. exec. bd. K. Rasmussen Found.; mem. sci. adv. bd. Internat. Found. for Optic Nerve Diseases. Author: Optics for Ophthalmologists, 1988, New Methods of Sensory Visual Testing, 1989, 3 books; editor: Ophthalmology, 2000; contbr. 160 articles to profl. jours., 40 chpts. to books. Recipient Pecan D. award, 1988—92, Rsch. to Prevent Blindness Sr. Investigator award, 1996—97, 1996, Lighthouse Internat. Pizart award, 1999, James Adams scholar, 1990—91, sr. investigator award, 1999—2000, Decade medal, Cuban Nat. Acad. Scis. Fellow Am. Acad. Ophthalmology Neuro-Ophthalmologists; mem. NIH (Med. Scientists Tng. award 1972-78), Am. Assn. Anatomists, Assn. Univ. Prof. Ophthalmology (assoc.), Am. Bd. Ophthalmology (rep. to residency rev. com. 1994—), Soc. to Prevent Blindness, Nat. Eye Inst. (New Investigator Rsch. award 1983-86, rsch. grants 1988-91, 93—), Soc. Neuroscis., Assn. Rsch. in Vision and Ophthalmology, N.Am. Neuro-Ophthal. Soc. (chmn. membership com. 1990—, v.p. 1994—). Avocation: writing. Home: 2478 Adair St San Marino CA 91108-2610

SADYKOVA, VERA PHILIPPOVNA, librarian, educator; b. Dneprostroy, Zaporozhie, Ukraine, Mar. 4, 1933; arrived in Kazakhstan, 1947; d. Yabtchenko and (Phesik) Philipp; m. Albert Sadykov, May, 13, 1956; children: Aleksey, Gennady. Grad., Kazakh State U., Alma-Ata, 1957, Inst. Culture, Leningrad, Russia, 1966. Cert. libr., philologist. Libr. Sci. and Tech. Libr. Kazakhstan, Almaty, 1960-62, asst. dir., 1964-65, dir., 1965-88, chief libr., 1988-94, mgr. sci.-methodical dept., 1962-64, 94—, instr. advanced courses, 1962—, head sci. rsch. sector, 1998. Instr. advanced courses Kazakh State Inst. Sci. and Tech. Info., Almaty, 1962—. Author brochures; mem. editl. bd. Nautchnie i Technitcheskie Biblioteki, 1990-91; contbr. articles to profl. jours. Mem. presidium Trade Unions Com. of State Instns. Ofcls., Almaty, 1971-86. Recipient medals and hon. degree Honoured Worker of Kazakh Soviet Socialist Republic, Presidium of Supreme Soviet USSR, 1970, 83, 84, bronze medals Exhbn. Econ. Achievements of USSR, 1969, 74, 81. Avocations: collecting books, gardening. Office: Sci & Tech Libr Kazakhstan S Mukanov 223B 480077 Almaty Kazakhstan E-mail: mtbb@nursat.kz.

SAEED, ATHAR, civil engineer; b. Faisalabad, Pakistan, July 14, 1965; came to U.S., 1991; BS, U. Engring. & Tech., Lahore, Pakistan, 1991; MS, U. Tex., 1993, PhD, 1996. Rsch. engr., scientist asst. Ctr. Transp. Rsch., Austin, 1993-96; sr. pavement engr. ERES divsn. Applied Rsch. Assocs., Vicksburg, Miss., 1998—. Postdoctoral rsch. fellow Ctr. Transp. Rsch., 1996-98. Mem. ASCE, Inst. Transp. Engrs., Am. Soc. Engring. Educators. Avocations: photography, technology. Office: Applied Rsch Assocs 112 Monument Pl Vicksburg MS 39180-5160 E-mail: asaeed@ara.com.

SAEED, GOHAR, interventional cardiologist; b. Lahore, Punjab, Pakistan, Sept. 19, 1969; s. Athar Saeed and Parveen Nargis; m. Ayesha Mansoor; children: Tehreem Gohar. MBBS, King Edward Med. Coll., Lahore , Pakistan., 1993. Fellow U. Fla., Jacksonville, 1998—2001, fellow interventional cardiology, 2001—. Mem.: Am. Coll. Cardiology. Avocations: swimming, running, travel, reading.

SAEED, SY ATEZAZ, psychiatrist, physician; b. Karachi, Pakistan, Nov. 15, 1956; came to U.S., 1985; s. Syed M. Laiq and Tanwira Begum; m. Janel Rene Saeed, June 29, 1991; children: Zack Allen, Karen Kelsey, Sophia Marie. MD, Dow Med. Coll., 1982; MS, St. Francis U., 1987. Diplomate Am. Bd. Psychiatry and Neurology, Am. Bd. Med. Psychotherapists; cert. in psychiat. adminstrn. mgmt. Dir. edn. in psychiatry U. Ill. Coll. Medicine, Peoria, 1993-95, chmn. dept. psychiatry, 1995—. Clin. dir. North Cen. Network of Ill., Peoria, 1998—; advisor Regional D&MDA of Am., Peoria, 1993—. Contbr. articles to profl. jours. Mem. Am. Assn. Psychiat. Adminstrs. (coun. mem., editor Psychiat. Adminstr.), Am. Coll. Psychiatrists, Am. Psychiat. Assn., Cen. Ill. Psychiat. Soc. (pres. 1995-97) Office: U of Ill Dept Psychiatry 5407 N University Peoria IL 61614 E-mail: sasaeed@uic.edu.

SAEGESSER, MARGUERITE M. artist; b. Bern, Switzerland, May 27, 1922; came to U.S., 1974; d. Wilhelm and Fanny (Kuepfer) Ruefenacht; m. Max Saegesser, May 27, 1952; 1 child, Francisca Marguerite; stepchildren: Anne-Marie Logan, Elisabeth, Barbara, Ursula L'Eplattenier. Solo exhbns. include De Saisset Mus., Santa Clara, Calif., 1995, Smith Andersen Gallery, Palo Alto, Calif., 1981, 85, 89, 91, 92, 95, Galerie Schindler, Bern, 1968, 90, Art Fair, Basel, Switzerland, 1990, many others; group exhbns. include Long Beach, Calif., 1971, Bienne Open Air Sculpture Show, Switzerland, 1958, 62, 66, Soc. Painters & Sculptors, Bern, 1945-46, 52, 56. Grantee Swiss Endowment Arts, 1995. Mem. South Bay Area Women's Caucus for Arts. Democrat. Home: 840 Mesa Ave Palo Alto CA 94306-3709

SAEKS, ALLEN IRVING, lawyer; b. Bemidji, Minn., July 14, 1932; m. Linda J. Levin; 1 child, Adam Charles. BS in Law, U. Minn., 1954, JD, 1956. Bar: Minn. 1956, U.S. Dist. Ct. Minn. 1956, U.S. Ct. Appeals (8th cir.) 1957, U.S. Ct. Appeals (fed. cir.) 1959, U.S. Supreme Ct. 1959, U.S. Ct. Appeals (11th cir.) 1997; cert. civil trial specialist. Asst. U.S. atty. Dept. Justice, St. Paul, 1956-57; assoc. Leonard Street and Deinard, Mpls., 1960-63, ptnr., 1964—. Adj. prof. law U. Minn. Law Sch., 1960-65; chmn. Lawyer Trust Account Bd., Interest on Lawyers Trust Accounts, 1984-87. Nat. bd. dirs. Equal Justice Works; chmn. Property Tax Com., 1986—87; bd. dirs. Citizens League, Mpls., 1984—87; pres. Jewish Cmty. Rels. Coun of Minn. and the Dakotas, 1994—96. 1st lt. JAGC U.S. Army, 1957—60. Recipient City of Mpls. award, 1996, Lifetime Commitment award Cardozo Soc., 2001. Fellow Am. Bar Found. (life); mem. ABA (commn. on interest on lawyers trust accts. 1990-93), Minn. State Bar Assn., Fund for the Legal Aid Soc. (chmn. 1997-98, Law Day Testimonial award 1996), Hennepin County Bar Assn. (pres. 1983-84), Order of Coif, Phi Delta Phi. Office: Leonard Street and Deinard 150 S 5th St Ste 2300 Minneapolis MN 55402-4238

SAEKS, RICHARD EPHRAIM, engineering executive; b. Chgo., Nov. 30, 1941; s. Morris G. and Elsie E. S. BS, Northwestern U., 1964; MS, Colo. State U., 1965; PhD, Cornell U., 1967. Elec. engr. Warwick Mfg. Co., Niles, Ill., 1961-63; asst. prof. dept. elec. engring. U. Notre Dame, 1967-71, assoc. prof., 1971-73; assoc. prof. depts. elec. engring., math. Tex. Tech U., Lubbock, 1973-77, prof., 1977-79, Paul Whitfield Horn prof. elec. engring., math. computer sci, 1979-83; prof., chmn. elec. engring. Ariz. State U., 1983-88; dean Armour Coll. Engring. Ill. Inst. Tech., 1988-91, Motorola prof., 1991-92; v.p. engring. Accurate Automation Corp., 1992-2000, CTO, 2000—. Cons. Research Triangle Inst., 1978-80, Marcel Dekker Inc., 1978-80. Author: Generalized Networks, 1972, Resolution Space Operators and Systems, 1973, Interconnected Dynamical Systems, 1981, System Theory: A Hilbert Space Approach, 1982; contbr. articles to profl. jours.; Editor: Large-Scale Dynamical Systems, 1976, Rational Fault Analysis, 1977, The World of Large Scale Systems, 1982. Recipient Disting. Faculty Research award Tex. Tech U., 1978 Fellow IEEE, AIAA (assoc.).

SAENGER, BRUCE WALTER, consulting firm executive; b. Hanover, N.H., July 16, 1943; s. Werner Hugo and Natalie Bertha (Brown) S.; m. Cheryl Jeanne Bouchard, Nov. 6, 1976. BA, Pa. State U., 1969; postgrad., Am. Coll., Bryn Mawr, Pa., 1979, Coll. Fin. Planning, Denver, 1980. CPCU; ChFC; CLU. Agt. Nationwide Ins., Lansdale, Pa., 1969-73, dist. sales mgr. Springfield, Mass., 1973-75, Am. Mut., Braintree, 1975-77; dir. mktg. Bankers LIfe & Casualty, Chgo., 1977-78; pres., founder Sales Tng. Techniques, Southboro, Mass., 1979-81, The Saenger Orgn., Medway, 1981—. Mem. faculty Notre Dame U., South Bend, Ind., 1977-78, Northeastern U., Boston, 1984-92; mem. RHU Commn., Washington, 1979-81; dir. Northeastern U. Inst. Inst., Boston, 1985-93; mem. Mass. Ins. Dept. Continuing Edn. Rev. Com., 1985—; program dir. U. Del. Ins. Program, 1989-91; acad. cons. Mass. Soc. Lic. Ins. Advisers, 1995—; cons. in field. Author: Series 6 Study Book, 1983, Series 22 Study Book, 1984, Tax Shelter Market Guide, 1985, Marketing Mutual Funds, 1985, also articles. Bd. dirs. Lansdale Gen. Hosp., 1971-73, New Directions Theater Co., 1988-91; mem. Medway Bus. Couhn., 1989-94, pres., 1990-92. With U.S. Army, 1960-66. Recipient Ednl. Achievement award Profl. Ins. Agts. Assn., 1983; named Outstanding Fin. Exec. of Yr., Fin. Mgmt. Assn., 1993. Fellow Soc. CLUs (ednl. adv., bd. dirs. 1987-91), Soc. CPCUs (ednl. adv.), Life Mgmt. Inst. (Outstanding Lectr. award 1984); mem. Internat. Assn. Fin. Planners (ednl. adv., bd. dirs. 1986-92, pres. 1989-91), Internat. Assn. for Fin. Planning (chmn. bd. dirs. 1990-92), Soc. Cert. Ins. Counselors, Life Underwriters Assn., Inst. CFP (v.p. edn., bd. dirs. 1990-91), Mass. Assn. Health Underwriters (pres. 1992-93, Boston Bus. Ethics award 2001). Republican. Roman Catholic. Avocation: skiing. Home: 68 Orchard St Millis MA 02054-1018 Office: The Saenger Orgn 77 Main St Medway MA 02053-1812

SAENGER, ELIZABETH BAIRD, elementary school educator, writer; b. Boston, May 20, 1942; d. Raleigh William and Elizabeth Hill Baird; m. Robert Mark Saenger, Oct. 11, 1965; children: David Robert, Michael Baird. BA, Rice U., 1964; MEd, Tufts U., 1965. Cert. secondary sch. social studies tchr. Mass., Calif., N.Y. Tchr. Jr. H.S. East, Arlington, Mass., 1965—66; job coord. Nepparhan Cmty. Ctr., Yonkers, NY, 1975—76; coord. Momarmeck Law Edn., Mamoroneck, 1976—81; tchr. Hommocles Mid. Sch., 1981—83; tchr. ethics Fieldston Lower Sch., Riverdale, 1983—. Presenter in field. Author: (novels) Exploring Ethics Through Children's Literature, 1993. Active Moral Edn. Seminar Columbia U., 1983—; bd. dirs. ACLU Westchester Chpt., 1999—, Washingtonville Housing Alliance, Mamoroneck, NY, 1990—96, Larchmont (N.Y.) Temple, 1990—93; bd. dirs., founder, pres. Youth Shelter Program of Westchester, 1974—99. Mem.: Assn. for Moral Edn. Democrat. Jewish. Avocations: walking, reading, Torah study, jazz, travel. Home: 702 Hall St Mamaroneck NY 10543 Office: Ethical Culture Fieldston Sch Manhattan Coll Pkwy Bronx NY 10471 Personal E-mail: rsaenger@aol.com. Business E-Mail: esaenger@ecfs.org.

SÁENZ, ALBERT WILLIAM, theoretical physicist, researcher, consultant; b. Medellín, Colombia, Aug. 27, 1923; came to U.S., 1941; s. Alberto Sáenz Moreno and Agnes (Williams) Sáenz; m. Pilar González García-Suelto, Sept. 7, 1957. BS, U. Mich., 1944, MA, 1945, PhD, 1949. From rsch. physicist to br. head Naval Rsch. Lab., Washington, 1950-66, br. head, 1966-76, divsn. cons., 1976-89, ret., 1989; rsch. prof. Cath. U., 1981—. Vis. fellow Ind. U., Bloomington, Ind., 1951-52; vis. prof. Johns Hopkins U., Balt., 1964; vis. sr. scientist Princeton (N.J.) U., 1976-77, Max Planck Inst., Stuttgart, Germany, 1990-91, Budker Inst. Nuclear Physics, Novosibirsk, Russia, 1996; cons. Naval Rsch. Lab., Washington, 1990—. Author: (with others) Long Distance Neutrino Detection, 1979, Mathematical Methods and Applications of Scattering Theory, 1980, Coherent Radiation Sources, 1985, Relativistic Channeling, 1987, Synergetics, Order and Chaos, 1988, Essays in Classical and Quantum Dynamics, 1991, Asymptotics Beyond All Orders, 1991, others; editor numerous books; contbr. 55 articles to profl. jours. Fellow Am. Physical Soc., Washington Acad. Scis.; mem. Am. Math. Soc., N.Y. Acad. Scis., Cosmos Club. Democrat. Roman Catholic. Achievements include symmetry and degeneracy in quantum mechanics, general relativity, spin-wave theory of complex magnetic structures and spin-wave scattering of polarized neutrons, coherent radiation from electrons traversing crystals or quasicrystals, rigorous quantum mechanical scattering theory, averaging theory of periodic and nonperiodic classical dynamical systems and its quantum analogues, channeling stability studies, nonintegrability and chaos. Home: 6338 Old Town Ct Alexandria VA 22307-1227 Office: Naval Research Lab 4555 Overlook Ave SW Washington DC 20375-0001

SAENZ, GILBERT, computer programmer and analyst, poet; b. Detroit, Oct. 17, 1941; s. Valentine and Lena (Mireles) S. BA in English Lit., Wayne State U., 1968, postgrad., 1979-81. U.S. diplomatic courier Dept. State, Washington, 1969-70; computer programmer/analyst Detroit IRS Computing Ctr., 1974—. Mem. Fed. Exec. Bd./Hispanic Employment Program Com., Detroit, 1988—, also past chair. Author: (poetry) Where Love Is, 1988, Colorful Impressions, 1993, Moments in Time, 1995, Dreaming of Love, 1999; (co-author) (with Jacqueline Sanchez) Lavender & Lace, 1998, Poems of Life/Poemas de la Vida, 2001. Mem. IMAGE, Detroit, 1995; v.p., bd. dirs. Manic Depressive and Depressive Assn. Met. Detroit, 1983—. Mem. U.S. Diplomatic Courier Assn. Democrat. Roman Catholic. Avocation: poetry and other writings. Home: 19211 Wall St Melvindale MI 48122-1876

SAENZ, L. ARNOLDO, judge; b. Premont, Tex., Apr. 30, 1952; s. Leonel S. and Belia (Perez) S.; m. Gretchen Arlene Shoots, Apr. 25, 1987; children: Bryan Tinsley, Meagan, Brianna. BBA, Tex. A&I U., 1977. City sec. City of Premont, Tex., 1976-77; asst. county auditor Jim Wells County, Alice, 1978-89, county auditor, 1989-95, county judge, 1995—. Chmn. Alice/Jim Wells County Econ. Devel. Bd., Alice, 1996; dir. I-69 Hwy. Alliance, 1996; treas. Coastal Bend Coun. Govts., Corpus Christi, Tex., 1997-98. Sec., treas. Real, Inc., Alice, 1994; chmn. Jim Wells County United Way, Alice, 1996-97, Coastal Bend Coun. Govts., Corpus Christi, Tex., 2001-2002, Coastal Plains MHMR, 2000—. Mem.: Nat. Assn. Counties (bd. dirs.). Avocations: photography, golfing. Office: Jim Wells County 200 N Almond St Alice TX 78332-4845 E-mail: lasaenz@thei.net.

SAENZ, MICHAEL, college president; b. Laredo, Tex., Oct. 25, 1925; s. C.A. and Pola R. Saenz; m. Nancy Elizabeth King; children: Michael King, Cynthia Elizabeth. BS in Acctg. with honors, Tex. Christian U., 1949, MEd, 1952; PhD in Econs., U. Pa., 1961. Dep. collector IRS, Ft. Worth, Dallas, 1949-52; adminstr. United Christian Missionary Soc., Bayamon, P.R., 1954-57, 59-65, exec. sec. Indpls., 1965-71; acad. dean Laredo (Tex.) Jr. Coll., 1971-74; pres. N.W. campus Tarrant County Jr. Coll., 1975—. Founder Nat. Comm. Coll. Hispanic Coun., 1985, bd. dirs., 1985—, pres., 1989-91; founder, co-dir. Nat. Hispanic Leadership Inst., 1989—; trustee Tex. Christian U., Brite Div. Sch., 1973—. Bd. dirs. Civic Ballet of Laredo, Ft. Worth chpt. NCCJ, Juliette Fowler Homes, Dallas; chmn. Aztec dist., dir. Gulf Coast coun. Boy Scouts Am., 1971-75; gov. Career Devel. Ctr., Arlington, Tex.; chmn. Laredo's Bicentennial Com., 1973-76; trustee, bd. dirs. United Way Ft. Worth, 1979—; mem., vice moderator gen. bd. Christian Ch. (Disciples of Christ), 1991-93. Mem. Am. Assn. Cmty. Colls. (bd. dirs. 1991-94), Commn. Internat. Edn. Am. Coun. Edn., Tex. Jr. Coll. Tchrs. Assn., Tex. Assn. Jr. Coll. Instructional Adminstrs., Am. Acad. Polit. and Social Scis., Urban Ministries in Higher Edn., Civic Music Assn. Laredo, No. Ft. Worth C. of C. (dir. 1978-97), Rotary. Home: 4427 Tamworth Rd Fort Worth TX 76116-8127 Office: Tarrant County Jr Coll NW Capmus 4801 Marine Pkwy Fort Worth TX 76179

SAENZ, REBECCA BUCHANAN, family physician; b. Vicksburg, Miss., June 30, 1964; d. Sam Henry and Laura Alsworth Buchanan; m. Joseph M. Saenz Jr., June 6, 1987; children: Janette Marie, Larissa Leigh. BS, Belhaven Coll., 1984; MD, U. Miss., 1990. Diplomate Am. Bd. Family Practice; internat. bd. cert. lactation cons. Intern dept. family medicine U. Miss. Sch. Medicine, 1990-91; residency in family medicine U. Tenn. Health Scis. Ctr./St. Francis Hosp., 1991-93; pvt. practice Peabody Med. Group, Memphis, 1993-94; locum tenens family physician Ch. Health Ctr., 1994; asst. prof. dept. family medicine U. Miss. Med. Ctr., Jackson, 1994-00, assoc. prof., 01—. Locum tenens family physician Ch. Health Ctr., Memphis, 1994. Reviewer Am. Family Physician, 1999; curriculum reviewer Jour. Human Lactation, 1999; contbr. articles to profl. jours. Fellow Am. Acad. Family Practice/Assn. Family Practice Residency Dirs., 1999; recipient cert. appreciation Ch. Health Ctr., Memphis, 1994, Miss. State Dept. Health, 1997. Mem. Am. Acad. Family Physicians, Miss. Acad. Family physicians, Soc. Tchrs. Family Medicine, Christian Med. Dental Soc., Am. Soc. Colposcopy and Cervical Pathology, Acad. Breastfeeding Medicine, Internat. Lactation Cons. Assn., Miss. Breastfeeding Coalition, La Leche League Internat. Med. Assocs. Presbyterian. Avocation: photography. Office: U Miss Med Ctr 2500 N State St Jackson MS 39216-4500 E-mail: litldoc@netdoor.com.

SAENZ, RUTH E. missionary; b. Columbus, Ind., Nov. 26, 1952; d. A. Allen and Eunice J. McVey; m. Leon Saenz, Jan. 31, 1989; children: E. Rose, Jonathan A. BA in Religious Edn., Carolina Christian Coll., 1981. Tchr., Bermudian Springs, Pa., 1971—74, Immanual Missionary Christian Sch., Spring Grove, 1975—78; pastor Immanuel Missionary Christian Ch., Spencer, Ind., 1974—75; missionary Latin Holiness Mission, San Ildefonso, Mexico, 1983, Immanuel Missionary Church Bolivian Mission, Sucre, 1974—97; mission fund raiser Emmanuel Mission of Bolivia, Shoals, Ind., 1997—. Dist. sec. Immanuel Missionary Ch., Shoals, 1974—82, Shoals, 1997—99; founding missionary, sec. Iglesia Evangelica Emanuel, Sucre, 1984—97. Contbr. articles, poems. Avocations: writing, health and nutrition, music, sewing. Home: Rte 2 Box 280 Shoals IN 47581-9673 E-mail: ruthmcveydesaenz@hotmail.com.

SAEZ GUILLERMO, FRANCISCO EDUARDO, photographer; b. Montevideo, Uruguay, Mar. 24, 1950; s. Francisco Alberto Saez and Rosa Gershanik; m. Carlota Pascual, Dec. 3, 1999. Student cinematography, U. La Plata (Argentina), 1971—. Film prodr., dir. photography films, 1972—75; video prodr. for tv N.Y.C., Washington, 1990. Creator Photographic Expressionism, N.Y.C., 1999. Commercial, advtsg., film prodn., fine art and portrait photography, 1974—; work appeared in World Poetry, 1994, The Dominican Times, 1995. Recipient 2nd prize 1st Nat. Competition for Thematic Photography, Zaragoza, Spain, 1979. Avocations: sculpture, reading, poetry, music, biking. Home: 431 W 204th St #2F New York NY 10034

SAFA, AFSHIN AKHAVAN, oncologist, researcher; came to the U.S., 1984; s. Mansour Safa. BS, UCLA, 1991; MD, U. Calif., San Diego, 1995. Diplomate Am. Bd. Radiology. Intern U. Calif., San Diego, resident Los Angeles; radiation oncologist UCLA, 1992—. Radiologicol Soc. N.Am. rsch. grantee Am. Bd. Radiology, 1998. Mem. Radiol. Soc. N.Am., Am. Radium Soc., Am. Soc. Therapeutic Radiology. Avocations: skiing, scuba, tennis. Office: San Monica Cancer Treatment Ctr 2428 Santa Monica Blvd 200 UCLA Medical Plaza Santa Monica CA 90404 E-mail: safa@radonc.ucla.edu.

SAFAI, BIJAN, physician, investigator; b. Ardestan, Iran, Mar. 26, 1940; came to U.S., 1968; s. Abdol-Khalegh Safai and Kanom-Sadat Sadjaddi; m. Vera Plaskon, Sept. 16, 1978; 1 child: Matthew. MD, Tehran U., Iran, 1965; DSc, U. Gutenburg, Sweden, 1981. Diplomate Am. Bd. Dermatology, Am. Bd. Internal Medicine. Intern Nassau County Med. Ctr., East Meadow, N.Y., 1968-69; resident N.Y.U. Med. Coll. VA Hosp., N.Y.C., 1969-70; resident in dermatology N.Y.U. Med. Coll., 1971-73; fellow in immunology Sloan-Kettering Inst. for Cancer & Allied Diseases, 1973-74; from asst. attending physician to chief dermatology svc. Meml. Hosp., 1974-93; from assoc. to attending physician in dermatology N.Y. Hosp., 1980-93; dir. dermatology Westchester County Med. Ctr., Valhalla, N.Y., 1993—; from asst. prof. to prof. in medicine/dermatology Cornell U. Med. Coll., N.Y.C., 1974-93; prof., chmn. dept. dermatology N.Y. Med. Coll., 1993—, prof. dept. microbiology and immunology, 1994—. Teaching clin. asst. in dermatology NYU Med. Coll, N.Y.C., 1973-74; adj. mem. Rockefeller U., N.Y.C., 1982-84; rsch. assoc. Sloan-Kettering Inst. for Cancer and Allied Diseases, N.Y.C., 1977-79, asst. mem., 1979-83, assoc. mem., 1983-88; assoc. mem. Memorial Sloan-Kettering Cancer Ctr., N.Y.C., 1983-88, mem. 1988-93; mem. grad. sch. med. scis. N.Y. Med. Coll., Valhalla, 1994—; mem. adv. bd. Skin Cancer Found., 1982—; sec. dermatology sect. N.Y. Acad Medicine, 1988-89, chmn. 1989-90; mem. med. adv. bd. Cancer Rsch Instn., 1997—. Mem. editl. bd. Cancer Investigation, 1984-88, AIDS Rsch. and Human Retroviruses, 1986-90, Jour. of Acquired Immune Deficiency Syndromes, 1988—; contbr. numerous articles on immunodermatology to profl. jours. Mem. AIDS adv. task force, NCI/NIH, 1982-85; mem. AIDS Etiology task force, NCI, 1982-85; mem. ad hoc study sect. for AIDS, NIH, 1982-88; mem. spl. dermatology rev. group, GM2 study sect., NIH, 1990-96; mem. spl. rev. team NCI Intramural Rev., Lab. of Tumor cell Biology, 1987, 92, Medicine br., NCI, 1996; mem. study sect. on HIV, NCI, 1996; mem. spl. rev. group FDA Intramural Rev., 1995. Mem. AMA, Internat. Soc. Tropical Dermatology, Am. Fedn. for Clin. Rsch., Am. Acad. Dermatology (mem. AIDS com. 1989-91, task force on cutaneous oncology 1988-9, mem. adv. coun. 1988-91), Am. Dermatol. Soc. for Allery and Immunology, Soc. for Investigative Dermatology, Med. Soc. of State of N.Y., Med. Soc. of County of N.Y., N.Y. State Soc. Dermatology, Dermatol. Soc. of Greater N.Y., N.Y. County Health Svs. Rev. Orgn., N.Y. Acad. Scis., N.Y. Dermatol. Soc. (pres 1990-91, sec., treas. 1989-90), Dermatology Found., Z & E Fisher Med. Found. (pres. 1993—). Home: 340 E 64th St New York NY 10021-7503 Office: NY Med Coll Dept Dermatology Valhalla NY 10595 also: 625 Park Ave New York NY 10021-6545 E-mail: safai@aol.com.

SAFARS, BERTA See FISZER-SZAFARZ, BERTA

SAFAVI, HADI AKBAR, tranportation planner; b. Shamsabad, India, June 17, 1935; came to U.S., 1971; s. S. M. Akbar Husain and Bilquis Jahan Begum; m. Razia Sultana, Apr. 26, 1965; children: Syed Kaiwan, Sumbula Rabaab. BS in Engring., Aligarh U., India, 1956; diploma in town planning, Durham U., Newcastle-on-Tyne, Eng., 1958. Retired, 2000. UN advisor Ministry Mcpl. and Rural Affairs Govt. Saudi Arabia, Riyadh, 1978-83, Ministry of Works, Govt. Bangladesh, 1984-85. Treas. UN Assn., Riyadh, 1982-83. Fellow Royal Town Planning Inst. Gt. Britain, Inst. Town Planners India; mem. Am. Inst. Cert. Planners. Avocations: reading. bridge, cycling, travel. Home: 5129 Sterling Manor Dr Tampa FL 33647-2010 E-mail: hadisafavi@juno.com.

SAFE, KENNETH SHAW, JR. fiduciary firm executive; b. Providence, Oct. 13, 1929; s. Kenneth Shaw and Louise (King) S.; m. Elizabeth Kelley, Dec. 20, 1952; children: Hope, Elizabeth, Kenneth (dec.), Thorn and Edith (triplets). AB, Harvard U., 1951. Intelligence officer CIA, Washington, 1954-56; with trust dept. Old Colony Trust Co., Bank of Boston, 1956-59; registered rep. Tucker, Anthony & R.L. Day, Boston, 1959-68; ptnr. Welch & Forbes, 1968—, mng. ptnr., 1983—. Pres. Travelers Aid Soc. Boston, 1980-82, Cmty. Workshops, Inc., Boston, 1968-72; asst. treas. Wellesley (Mass.) Coll., 1970-80; trustee Georgiana Goddard Eaton Meml. Trust, Boston, 1975—, G. Howland Shaw Found., Boston, 1977—; treas. Woods Hole (Mass.) Oceanographic Inst., 1981-92, Mass. Soc. Cin.; bd. dirs. Beverly Land Co., Providence, 1982—; trustee R.I. Hosp., Providence; trustee Crossroads for Kids, Inc., Boston; bd. dirs. Boston Port and Seaman's Aid Soc. With CIC, U.S. Army, 1952-54. Mem. Boston Security Analysts Soc., Somerset Club, Duxbury Yacht Club, Marshall St. Hist. Soc., Mason, Country Club. Republican. Episcopalian. Avocations: sailing, skiing, hunting, snorkeling. Home: 207 King Caesar Rd Duxbury MA 02332-3912 Office: Welch & Forbes 45 School St Fl 5 Boston MA 02108-3297 E-mail: ksafe@welchforbes.com.

SAFER, DANIEL J. psychiatrist; b. Milw., June 29, 1934; s. Mendel and Belle (Rottman) S.; children: Debra, Alan, Judith. BS, U. Wis., 1956, MD, 1959. Diplomate in psychiatry and child psychiatry Am. Bd. Psychiatry and Neurology. Rotating intern D.C. Gen. Hosp., Washington, 1959-60; resident psychiatry Cleve. Psychiat. Inst., 1960-63; fellow in child psychiatry Inst. for Juvenile Rsch., 1963-64; asst. attending psychiatrist Children's Meml. Hosp., Chgo., 1964-66; fellow in child psychiatry Johns Hopkins Hosp., Balt., 1968-69; pychiat. cons. Balt. City Hosps., 1966-68; co-dir. sch. child mental health scs. Balt. County Dept. Health, 1969-72, dir. child pschiatry svcs., ea. region, 1972-95, med. dir. Ea. Community Mental Health Ctr. Md., 1983-92; staff psychiatrist Southeastern Cmty. Mental Health Ctr., Balt., 1995—. Psychiat. cons. Franklin Sq. Hosp., Rosedale, 1970-73, Delaware Guidance Svcs. for Children, 1981-82; instr. psychiatry dept. neurology and psychiatry Northwestern U. Sch. Medicine, 1964-66; instr. dept. psychiatry and pediatrics Johns Hopkins Hosp., 1969-70; asst. prof. dept. psychiatry and pediatrics Johns Hopkins U. Sch. Medicine, 1970-79, assoc. prof., 1979—. Co-author: Hyperactive Children: Diagnosis and Management, 1976, School Programs for Disruptive Adolescents, 1982, numerous other chpts.; contbr. articles to profl. jours. Capt. med. corps U.S. Army, 1966-68. NIH fellow in pharmacology U. Wis. Med. Sch., 1956; grantee CIBA Labs, 1970-72, Merrell Lab., 1971-74, NIMH, 1974-77, Law Enforcement Assistance Adminstrn., 1977-80. Fellow Am. Psychiat. Assn. (life); mem. Md. Psychiat. Soc., Am. Orthopsychiat. Assn., Am. Acad. Child Adolescent Psychiatry. Avocation: tennis. Home: 6 Hadley Sq N Baltimore MD 21218-1810 Office: 7702 Dunmanway Baltimore MD 21222-5436 Fax: 410-366-3876. E-mail: dsafer@jhmi.edu.

SAFER, JOHN, artist, lecturer, banker, real estate developer; b. Washington, Sept. 6, 1922; s. John M. and Rebecca (Herzmark) S.; m. Joy Scott; children: Janine Whitney, Thomas. AB, George Washington U., 1947; LLB, Harvard, 1949. Chmn. NationsBank/D.C., 1980-92; chmn. exec. com. Fin. Gen. Bankshares, 1977-80; bd. dirs. Scripps Rsch. Inst., Nat. Air and Space Mus., The Shakespeare Guild, Materia. Represented in permanent collections at Balt. Mus. Art, Corocoran Gallery Art, Frederik Meijer Sculpture Gardens, Folger Shakespeare Libr., Nat. Air and Space Mus., Washington Tennis Ctr., High Mus. Art, Atlanta, Milw. Mus. Art, Harvard Law Sch., Harvard Bus. Sch., Hofstra U., Phila. Mus. Art, San Francisco Mus. Art, Duke U. Med. Ctr., Embry-Riddle Aeronautical U., Georgetown U., George Washington U., Williams Coll., Scripps Rsch. Inst., Daniel Webster Coll., Am. Hosp., Paris, Embassy of U.S., London, Nassau, Beijing, New Delhi, Fayetteville Mus. Art, N.C.., Nat. Jewish Mus., Nat. Peace Inst., Ponce Mus. of Art, P.R., UN, N.Y.C., corps. including Celanese Corp., N.Y., Crown Equip. Corp., New Bremen, Ohio, First Union Bank of M.d, Bank of Am. Ctr., Norfolk, Va., Gen. Mills Corp., Mpls Rosemont Co., Atlanta, West Chase Corp., Houston, numerous others. 1st lt. USAAF, 1942-46. Mem.: Cosmos, Burning Tree, Harvard, Woodmont (Washington), Lyford Cay (Nassau), Linville Ridge (N.C.). Office: PO Box 6720 Mc Lean VA 22106-6720 Office Fax: 703-276-7770.

SAFER, MARTIN A. psychologist, educator; b. Milw., Oct. 26, 1946; s.Joseph and Rita Safer; m. Carolyn H. Lichtenstein, Jan. 3, 1987; children: Aaron, Jonathan. PhD, U. Wis., 1978. Prof. psychology Cath. U. Am., Washington, 1979—. Contbr. articles to profl. jours. Office: Catholic Univ of America Dept Psychology Washington DC 20064

SAFER, MORLEY, journalist; b. Toronto, Ont., Can., Nov. 8, 1931; came to U.S., 1964; s. Max and Anna (Cohn) Safer; m. Jane Fearer; 1 child Sarah. Student, U. Western Ont., 1952. With Reuters, London, Eng., 1955; corr., producer Canadian Broadcasting Corp., 1955-60, writer, London corr., 1961-64; corr., producer BBC, 1961; corr. CBS, London bureau , 1964; Vietnam corr. CBS, 1965—70; London bureau chief, 1967—70; corr. & co-editor 60 Minutes news program CBS-TV , 1970—. Writer-corr. news documentary "The Second Battle of Britain", 1976; host "One for the Road: A Conversation with Charles Kuralt and Morley Safer", 1994; prin. reporter "CBS Reports". Author: Flashbacks: On Returning to Vietnam, 1990. Recipient Polk award L.I.U., 1965, Sigma Delta Chi award, 1965, Paul White award Radio and TV, News Dirs. Assn., 1966, Emmy for "Lenell Geter's in Jail", 60 Minutes broadcast, 1984, three Overseas Press Club awards, 11 Emmy awards, three George Foster Peabody awards, two Alfred I. duPont-Columbia U. awards, Robert F. Kennedy Journalism first prize for "School for the Homeless" report, 2002; named Chévalier dans l'Ordre des Arts et des Lettres, French Government, 1995. Fellow Royal Coll. Bloviation (Edinburgh). Office: c/o 60 Minutes 524 W 57th St New York NY 10019-2902*

SAFFELL, JOHN EDGAR, retired history educator; b. North Georgetown, Ohio, July 22, 1916; s. Byron Edgar and Athalia Isabel (Anderson) S.; m. Helen Weaver, Oct. 8, 1955. AB, Mount Union Coll., 1937; AM, Western Res. U., Cleve., 1938, PhD, 1965; LHD, Mount Union Coll., 1996. Elem. sch. prin. Bd. Edn., Stark County, Ohio, 1939-41; tchr. Harvey Sr. H.S., Painesville, 1941-43; rsch. analyst U.S. Army, Tokyo, 1945-47; faculty mem. history Mt. Union Coll., Alliance, Ohio, 1948-82; ret., 1982—. Owner cattle farm, Homeworth, Ohio, 1955-89. Author: Sesquicentennial History of Mount Union College, 1996, Title: Wake the Echoes. With U.S. Army, 1943-45. Mem. Am. Hist. Assn., Orgn. Am. Historians, Ohio Acad. History, Free and Accepted Masons, Alliance Country Club. Republican. Presbyterian. Home: Copeland Oaks 7-314 800 S 15th St Sebring OH 44672

SAFFELL, WILLIAM JOSEPH, language educator; b. Front Royal, Va., July 5, 1947; s. Richard James and Mabel Lee Saffell; m. Krisnajanti Supardi; children: Jessie Lin, Megan, Michael. BA, Mary Wash. Coll., 1988; MA, George Mason U., 1999. Cert. ESL tchr. Author: (novel) Kyushu Blues, 2001. Sp/4 US Army, 1967—71, Vietnam, Japan, Germany. Avocation: music. Personal E-mail: wsaffell@infi.net.

SAFFELS, DALE EMERSON, federal judge; b. Moline, Kans., Aug. 13, 1921; s. Edwin Clayton and Lillian May (Cook) S.; m. Margaret Elaine Nieman, Apr. 2, 1976; children by previous marriage: Suzanne Saffels Gravitt, Deborah Saffels Godowns, James B.; stepchildren: Lynda Cowger Harris, Christopher Cowger. AB, Emporia State U., 1947; JD cum laude, LLB cum laude, Washburn U., 1949. Bar: Kans. 1949. Pvt. practice law, Garden City, Kans., 1949-71, Topeka, 1971-75, Wichita, Kans., 1975-79; U.S. dist. judge Dist. of Kans., Topeka, 1979—. County atty. Finney County, Kans., 1951-55; chmn. bd. Fed. Home Loan Bank Topeka, 1978-79; mem. Jud. Conf. Com. on Fin. Disclosure, 1993-99. Mem. bd. govs. Sch. Law Washburn U., 1973-85; pres. Kans. Dem. Club, 1957; Dem. nominee Gov. of Kans., 1962; mem. Kans. Ho. of Reps., 1955-63, minority leader, 1961-63; mem. Kans. Corp. Commn., 1967-75, chmn., 1968-75; mem. Kans. Legis. Coun., 1957-63; Kans. rep. Interstate Oil Compact Commn., 1967-75, 1st vice chmn., 1971-72; pres. Midwest Assn. Regulatory Commn., 1972-73, Midwest Assn. R.R. and Utilities Commrs., 1972-73; trustee Emporia State U. Endowment Assn.; bd. dirs. Nat. Assn. Regulatory Utility Commrs., 1972-75. Maj. Signal Corps U.S. Army, 1942-46. Fellow Am. Bar Found., Kans. Bar Found.; mem. ABA, Kans. Bar Assn., Wichita Bar assn., Am. Judicture Soc., Delta Theta Phi. Lutheran. Office: US Dist Ct 420 Federal Bldg 444 SE Quincy St Topeka KS 66683 Fax: (785) 295-2809.

SAFFER, ALFRED, retired chemical company executive; b. N.Y.C., Dec. 3, 1918; s. Louis and Ruth (Mirkis) S.; m. Ruth Lillian Rudow, Jan. 31, 1942 (dec. Dec. 1983); children: Anita Carolyn Horowitz, Martin Kenneth; m. Doris Barbara Graubard, June 18, 1985 (dec. 1999). AB in Chemistry, NYU, 1939, MS in Chemistry, 1941, PhD, 1943. Research chemist Princeton (N.J.) U., 1943-46; sr. research assoc. Firestone Tire and Rubber Co., Akron, Ohio, 1946-48; dir. research Sci. Design Co., Inc., N.Y.C., 1948-57, v.p. mfg.; pres. Catalyst Devel. Corp., Little Ferry, N.J., 1957-69; exec. v.p. Halcon Internat., Inc., N.Y.C., 1963-69; vice chmn. ret. Halcon SD Group, Inc., 1978-81; exec. v.p. Oxirane Corp, Princeton, 1969-76; pres. Oxirane Internat., 1976-78. Bd. dirs. Norwood Venture Co., N.Y.C. Contbr. articles to profl. jours.; patentee in field. Trustee Internat. Ctr. for Disabled, N.Y.C., 1978—; assoc. trustee North Shore U. Hosp., Manhasset, N.Y., 1981—; active instl. rev. bd. Boca Raton (Fla.) Community Hosp., 1992—. Fellow Am. Inst. Chemists (Chem. Pioneer award, 1982); mem. Nat. Acad. Engring., Am. Chem. Soc., Soc. Chem. Industry. Clubs: Glen Oaks (Old Westbury, N.Y.); Delaire Country (Delray Beach, Fla.). Avocation: golf. Home: 16629 Ironwood Dr Delray Beach FL 33445-7050 E-mail: fredsaffer@aol.com.

SAFFER, AMY BETH, foreign language educator; b. N.Y.C., Apr. 19, 1950; d. William and Evelyn (Yankowitz) S. BA, Fairleigh Dickinson U., 1972, MA, 1983; postgrad., Jersey City State Coll., 1983-84. Cert. tchr. Spanish K-12, N.J. Tchr. Madison (N.J.) High Sch., 1973, Livingston (N.J.) High Sch., 1973—. Mem. faculty and dist. coms. Livingston Sch. Dist., 1975—; advisor to class of 1977, Livingston High Sch., 1975-77, chair mid. states subcom., 1990. Inducted Livington H.S. Alumni Hall of Fame, 1993. Mem. NEA, Am. Assn. Tchrs. of Spanish and Portuguese, N.J. Edn. Assn., Fgn. Lang. Educators of N.J., Livingston Edn. Assn. (negotiations rep. 1980—), Essex County Edn. Assn. Office: Livingston High Sch Livingston NJ 07039

SAFFIOTTI, UMBERTO, pathologist; b. Milan, Jan. 22, 1928; came to U.S., 1960, naturalized, 1966; s. Francesco Umberto and Maddalena (Valenzano) S.; m. Paola Amman, June 21, 1958; children: Luisa M., Maria Francesca. MD cum laude, U. Milan, 1951, splty. diploma occupational medicine cum laude, 1957. Intern Inst. Pathol. Anatomy U. Milan, 1951-52, asst. to chmn. occupational medicine, chief lab. pathology, Inst. Occupational Medicine, 1956-60, fellow Inst. Gen. Pathology, 1957-60; rsch. asst. oncology, rsch. assoc. Chgo. Med. Sch., 1952-55, from asst. prof. to prof. oncology, 1960-68; mem. staff Nat. Cancer Inst., NIH, Bethesda, Md., 1968—, assoc. dir. carcinogenesis, 1968-76, chief lab. exptl. pathology, 1974-98, acting head Registry of Exptl. Cancers, 1988-98; scientist emeritus, 1998—; adj. prof., Environ. & Occ. Hlth. The George Washington U., Washington, 2000—. Mem. pathology B study sect., NIH, 1964-68; former mem. various adv. coms. govt. agys.; mem. cancer prevention com. Internat. Union Against Cancer, 1959-66, panel on carcinogenicity, 1963-66; chmn. ad hoc com. evaluation low levels environ. carcinogens HEW, 1969-70. Co-editor books; contbr. articles to profl. jours. Bd. dirs. Rachel Carson Trust, 1976-79. Recipient Career Devel. award NIH, 1965-68, Superior Svc. Honor award HEW, 1971, Pub. Interest Sci. award Environ. Def. Fund, 1977, Spl. Recognition award USPHS, 1980 Fellow NYAS; mem. AAAS, Am. Assn. Cancer Rsch. (pres. Chgo. chpt. 1966-67), Am. Soc. Investigative Pathology, Internat. Commn. Occupational Health, Soc. Occupational and Environ. Health (councillor 1972-76, v.p. 1976-78, pres. 1978-82), Soc. Toxicology, Mineralogical Soc. of Am., Sigma Xi. Democrat. Home: 5114 Wissioming Rd Bethesda MD 20816-2259 Office: NIH Nat Cancer Inst 6116 Executive Blvd Rm 7064 Bethesda MD 20892-8314 E-mail: saffiotti@nih.gov.

SAFFIR, HERBERT SEYMOUR, structural engineer, consultant; b. N.Y.C., Mar. 29, 1917; s. A.L. and Gertrude (Samuels) S.; m. Sarah Young, May 9, 1941; children: Richard Young, Barbara Joan. BS in Civil Engring. cum laude, Ga. Inst. Tech., 1940. Registered profl. engr., Fla., N.Y., Tex., P.R., Miss. Civil engr. TVA, Chattanooga, 1940, NACA, Langley Field, Va., 1940-41; structural engr. Ebasco Services, N.Y.C., 1941-43, York & Sawyer & Fred Severud, N.Y.C., 1945; engr. Waddell & Hardesty, Cons. Engrs., 1945-47; asst. county engr. Dade County, Miami, Fla., 1947-59; cons. engr. Herbert S. Saffir, Coral Gables, 1959—. Adj. prof. civil engring. Coll. Engring., U. Miami, 1964—; adviser civil engring. Fla. Internat. U., 1975-80; cons. on bldg. codes Govt. Bahamas; cons. on engring. in housing to UN; mem., chmn. Met. Dade County Unsafe Structures Bd., 1977-92; mem. Bldg. Code Evaluation Task Force after Hurricane Andrew; mem. Am. Nat. Stds. Inst. Commn. Bldg. Design Loads, Nat. Adv. Group on Glass Design, Dade County Bldg. Code Com. 1993-96; mem. U. Miami/Coral Gables Community Rels. Com., 1993-96; cons. to govt. and industry, condr. seminars, Australia and Ga. Tech.; reviewer for NSF; mem. bd. adjustment City of Coral Gables, 1994-97, mem. budget bd., 1997-2001; presenter seminars in field. Author: Housing Construction in Hurricane Prone Areas, 1971, Nature and Extent of Damage by Hurricane Camille, 1972, Evaluation of Structural Damage Caused by Hurricanes, 1993; contbg. author: Wind Effects on Structures, 1976; editor: Wind Engr., 1986-92; editor Manual of Wind Damage Investigation; contbr. articles to profl. jours.; designer Saffir/Simpson hurricane scale. With N.Y. Guard, 1942-43, AUS, 1943-44, WWII. Recipient Outstanding Service award Fla. Profl. Engrs., 1954, Pub. Service award Nat. Weather Service, 1975, Disting. Service award Nat. Hurricane Conf., 1987; named Miami Engr. of Year, 1978, 94, Gov.'s Design award, 1986, Gov. Gilchrist award for Profl. Excellence, 1988, Albert H. Friedman Community Svc. award, 1992, Engring. award Nat. Hurricane Conf., 1997; named to Ga. Tech. Engring. Hall of Fame, 1995. Fellow Fla. Engring. Soc. (award for outstanding tech. achievement 1973, Cmty. Svc. award 1980); mem. ASCE (hon., past pres., sec., aerodynamics com. 1983—, mem. mitigation of wind damage com. 1985—, chmn. com. on damage investigation 1989—, mem. com. A7 on design loads for bldgs. 1972—), Soc. Am. Mil. Engrs., Am. Concrete Inst., ASTM (mem. com. performance bldg. constrn.), Internat. Assn. for Bridge and Structural Engring., Colegio de Ingenieros P.R., Am. Meterol. Soc., Am. Arbitration Assn., Wind Engring. Rsch. Coun. (past bd. dirs., Svc. award 1990), Am. Assn. for Wind Engring., Coral Gables C. of C. (bd. dirs., past pres., past chmn.), Tau Beta Pi, Chi Epsilon (hon.). Clubs: Country of Coral Gables. Office: 350 Sevilla Ave Ste 108 Coral Gables FL 33134-6617

SAFFIR, LEONARD, public relations executive; b. N.Y.C., Apr. 19, 1930; s. Abraham and Gertrude S.; m. Patricia Roemer (div. 1980); children: Andrew, Michelle; m. Wendy McConaughy (div. 1992); 1 child, Samantha; m. Eleanor Unger, 1997. Student, Syracuse U., 1948-51. Editor, bur. chief Internat. News Service, Dallas, Tokyo, 1953-58; producer Eng., Australia, Asia, 1958-60; ptnr. Haft, Saffir, Siegel Polit. Pub. Relations & Advt., N.Y.C., 1960-62; asst. pub. N.Y. Standard, 1962-63; cons. Ferdinand Marcos, 1964; pub. Latin Am. Times, N.Y.C., 1965; exec. v.p. Franchises Internat., 1965-69; press sec., chief of staff to Senator James Buckley U.S. Senate, Washington, 1970-76; pub., editor The Trib, N.Y.C., 1977-78, The Sun, Bridgehampton, N.Y., 1978-84; exec. v.p. Porter/Novelli, N.Y.C., 1984-90; pres. Jay DeBow & Ptnrs., Fla., 1989-90, Leonard Saffir & Assocs. Pub. Rels., 2000—. CEO Adventures One, 1998-2000, Celebrity Stores.com, 1998-2000. Author: Power Public Relations, 1992, Power Public Relations: How to Master the New PR, 2000. Campaign mgr. Marchi for Mayor, N.Y.C., 1973, Buckley for Senator, N.Y., 1976. Served as sgt. USMC, 1951-53. Recipient Silver Anvil and Big Apple awards Pub. Rels. Soc. Am., Mayor's award City of N.Y.; others. Mem. Authors Guild, Overseas Press Club (pres. 1988-89). Home: 6137 Rainbow Circle Lake Worth FL 33463 E-mail: lenpr@bellsouth.net.

SAFFMAN, PHILIP G. mathematician, educator; b. Leeds, Eng., Mar. 19, 1931; s. Sam Ralph and Sarah (Rebecca) S.; m. Ruth Arion, Sept. 2, 1954; children: Louise J., Mark E., Emma E. BA, Trinity Coll., Cambridge U., 1953, MA, PhD, Cambridge U., 1956. Asst. lectr. applied math. Cambridge U., 1958-60; reader in applied math. Kings Coll., London U., 1960-64; prof. fluid mechanics Calif. Inst. Tech., Pasadena, 1964-69, prof. applied math., 1969-95, Theodore von Kármán prof. applied math. and aeros., 1995—. Contbr. articles to profl. jours. Trinity Coll. fellow, 1955-59; recipient Otto Laporte award, Am. Physical Soc., 1994, Fluid Dynamics Award, Am. Inst. Aeronautics and Astronautics, 1995. Fellow Am. Acad. Arts and Scis., Royal Soc. London. Office: 217-50 Firestone Calif Inst Tech Pasadena CA 91125

SAFFRAN, KALMAN, venture capitalist, entrepreneur; b. Boston, Dec. 28, 1947; s. Max and Marion (Patick) S. BA, Northeastern U., 1971; postgrad., MIT, 1971-72. Lic. real estate broker, Mass. Mgr. sys. MIT, 1972-76; corp. cons. United Brands Co., Boston, 1977-78; CEO Monitrex Corp., 1977-82; pres. Kalman Saffran Assocs., Inc., Newton, 1978—2000; bd. advisers Prism Venture Ptnrs. Bd. advisors Blackstone Bank and Trust Col, Boston; mem. network implementation panel U.S. Energy Research and Devel. Adminstrn., Washington, 1975-76; mem. computer com. MIT Lab. for Nuclear Sci., 1975-76. Mem. Data Processing Mgmt. Assn., Assn. Computing Machinery, Soc. for Info. Mgmt., IEEE, Mensa. Republican. Jewish. Home: 1564 Commonwealth Ave Newton MA 02465-2806 Office: Kalman Saffran Assocs Inc PO Box 66033 Auburndale MA 02466-0001

SAFFURI, KHALED AHMAD, cultural organization executive; b. Beirut, July 28, 1956; came to U.S., 1981; s. Ahmad Hasan Saffouri and Siham Sihani; m. Jeniffer Ann Hall, Aug. 28, 1994 (div. Aug. 1997). BA in Bus. Adminstrn., USIA, Calif., 1985; MA in Mgmt., U. Redlands, Calif., 1987. Dir. Mid. East affairs Am.-Arab Anti-Discrimination Com., Washington, 1987-90; asst. exec. dir. Nat. Assn. Arab-Americans, 1990-93, Am. Muslim Coun., Washington, 1994-97; exec. dir. Am. Task Force for Bosnia, 1992-98, Islamic Inst., Washington, 1998—. Co-author: (book) Islam and Free Market, 1998. Moslem. Office: Islamic Inst Found 1920 L St NW Ste 200 Washington DC 20036-5036

SAFI, ARSHAD MAHMOOD, physician, researcher; b. Bahawalnagar, Punjab, Pakistan, Oct. 26, 1965; came to US, 1992; s. Dost Muhammed and Khadeeja. BS, Punjab U., Lahore, Pakistan, 1986; M.B.BS, King Edward Med. Coll., Lahore, Pakistan, 1988. Diplomate Am. Bd. Internal Medicine, Am. Bd. Cardiovascular Medicine, Am. Bd. Interventional Cardiology. Asst. clin. instr. Health Sci. Ctr. Bklyn. SUNY, 1992-99; dir. cardiac catheterization lab./interventional cardiology Bklyn. Hosp. Ctr., 1999—, in charge initiation Chest Pain Ctr. project, 1999—; clin. asst. prof. medicine Health Sci. Ctr. Bklyn., SUNY, 2000—, Weill Med. Coll. of Cornell U., 2000—. Contbr. articles to med. jours. Mem. ACP, Am. Coll. Cardiology, Am. Coll. Chest Physicians. Moslem. Avocations: travel, sports, music. Office: The Bklyn Hosp Ctr 121 Dekalb Ave Brooklyn NY 11201-5425

SAFIAN, GAIL ROBYN, public relations executive; b. Bklyn., Dec. 12, 1947; d. Jack I. and Harriet S.; m. Jay Mark Eisenberg, Jan. 6, 1979; children: Julia, Eric. BA, SUNY, Albany, 1968; MBA, NYU, 1982. Reporter Albany (N.Y.)-Knickerbocker News/Times-Union, 1969, Athens (Ohio) Messenger, 1969-71; pub. relations asst. Mountainside Hosp., Montclair, N.J., 1971-74; dir. pub. relations Riverside Hosp., Boonton, 1974-78; consumer affairs coordinator Johnson & Johnson Personal Products Div., Milltown, 1978-79; v.p., group mgr. Harshe Rotman & Druck, N.Y.C., 1979-82; exec. v.p., dir. Health Care Div. Ruder Finn & Rotman, 1982-84; v.p., mgr. client services Burson-Marsteller, 1984-86; v.p., group mgr. health care Cohn & Wolfe, 1986-90; exec. v.p., gen. mgr. MCS, Summit, N.J., 1990-94; pres. Safian Comm. Inc., Maplewood, 1994—. Mem. devel. com. Cancer Care, N.Y.C., 1985—. Recipient MacEachern award Am. Hosp. Assn., 1974, Communications Award Internat. Assn. Bus. Communicators, 1976, Creativity in Pub. Rels. award Inside PR, 1992, 93. Mem. Healthcare Businesswomen's Assn. (mem. bd. dirs.), N.Y. Acad. Scis., Women in Comm. (Clarion award 1974). Jewish. Home and Office: Safian Comm Inc 31 Hickory Dr Maplewood NJ 07040-2107 E-mail: gsafian@safianhealth.com.

SAFIAN, HARRIET SARA, social worker; b. N.Y.C., Jan. 7, 1921; d. Simon and Pauline (Posner) Cohen; m. Jack I. Safian, Apr. 7, 1946; children: Gail Robyn Safian Eisenberg, Keith Franklin, Shelley Carole. BA, Bklyn. Coll., 1941; M Social Sci., Smith Coll., 1943. Lic. social worker, N.Y. Social worker mil. hosp. ARC, Utica and St. Albans, N.Y., 1943-46; med. social worker Coney Island Hosp., Bklyn., 1962-65, supr. social svc. dept., 1965-75; dir. social svc. dept. Kings Hwy. Hosp., 1975-77; dir. dept. social work Caledonian Hosp., 1977-86; social work cons., community liaison specialist Greater Sheepshead Bay Devel. Corp., 1987—. Adj. assoc. prof. NYU Sch. Social Wk., N.Y.C., 1966-75; lectr. The Bklyn. Hosp., 1988, 89, 90, Caledonian Hosp., 1988, 89, 90. Mem. Dept. Social Svcs. adv. bd. Human Resources Adminstrn., N.Y.C., 1984—; coord. sr. citizen's outreach prog. Bklyn. Philharmonic Orch., 1987-93; chair adv. coun. HRA, Bklyn., 1980-95; chair svc. and rehab. com. Am. Cancer Soc., Bklyn., 1986-90, chair bd. dirs. Brooklyn, 1994-96; chair adv. com. JASA, Bklyn., 1986-95; vol. oncology nursing dept. TBH/Caledonian Hosp., 1986-2001; vol. Info. and Referral Svc. of Jewish Ctr. Kings Hwy., Bklyn., 1986—. Mem. NASW, Acad. Cert. Social Workers. Democrat. Avocations: travel, needlepoint, volunteer work. Home: 4592 Bedford Ave Brooklyn NY 11235-2527

SAFIAN, KEITH FRANKLIN, hospital administrator; b. Bklyn., June 22, 1950; s. Jack I. and Harriet S. (Cohen) S.; m. Ellen Rita Babat, May 18, 1974; children: Elizabeth Anne, Alexander William. BS in EE and Indsl. Engring., SUNY, Buffalo, 1972; MBA, U. Pa., 1974. Asst. dir. Kings County Hosp. Ctr., Bklyn., 1974-76; asst. adminstr. NYU Med. Ctr., N.Y.C., 1977-80, assoc. adminstr., 1981-84, sr. assoc. adminstr., 1984-85; adminstr. St. John's Episcopal Hosp., Far Rockaway, N.Y., 1985-89; pres., CEO Phelps Meml. Hosp. Ctr., Sleepy Hollow, 1989—. Bd. dirs. Addabbo Family Health Ctr., Arverne, N.Y., 1987-89, Rockaway Devel. and Revitalization Corp., Far Rockaway, 1988-89; bd. dirs. The ExcelCare Sys., Bronxville, N.Y., 1993-99, chmn. 1995-98; bd. dirs. No. Met. Hosp. Assn., Newburgh, N.Y., 1989—, mem. exec. com., 1993-98, 2000, chmn., 1996, treas., 2001, vice chmn. 2002 Fellow Am. Coll. Healthcare Execs.; mem. Hosp. Adminstrs. Club of N.Y., Health Assn. N.Y. State (trustee 1996-98). Home: 16 Brokaw Ln Great Neck NY 11023-1160 Office: Phelps Memorial Hosp 701 N Broadway Tarrytown NY 10591-1096

SAFIAN, LEROY SCHELLER, radiologist; b. N.Y.C., Dec. 15, 1916; s. Harry Markus and Frances (Scheller) S.; m. Renée Morgenstern Bonis, June 15, 1946 (div. Feb. 1952); m. Helen Hoffman, Jan. 25, 1953 (div. Nov. 1962). BS, NYU, 1938; MD, Med. Coll. Va., 1943. Diplomate Am. Bd. Radiology. Instr. radiology N.Y. Med. Coll., N.Y.C., 1962-64; asst. radiologist Coney Island Hosp., Bklyn., 1965-69, assoc. radiologist, 1969-70; asst. radiologist Maimonides Med. Ctr., N.Y.C., 1966-70; attending radiologist Golden Isles Hosp., Hallendale, Fla., 1970-71; instr. radiology Columbia Coll. Physicians & Surgeons, 1972-75, Montefiore Med. Ctr., Bronx, 1975-87; asst. prof. radiology Albert Einstein Coll. Medicine, 1975-88; asst. attending radiologist North Cen. Hosp., 1975-84, assoc. attending radiologist, 1984-86. Hon. radiologist North Cen. Hosp., Bronx, 1986—. Author articles on radiology and plastic surgery; cons. editor Urban & Schwarzenberg Med. Pubs. Recipient Cert. of Merit, Mallinckrodt Pharms., 1981; Overseas fellow. Fellow Royal Soc. Medicine; mem. Am. Coll. Legal Medicine (assoc.), N.Y. Acad. Sci., N.Y. Med. Soc. (grievance com.), Fla. Med. Soc., Univ. Club, various radiol. socs. Home: 301 E 66th St New York NY 10021-6205

SAFIRE, WILLIAM, journalist, author; b. N.Y.C., Dec. 17, 1929; s. Oliver C. and Ida (Panish) S.; m. Helene Belmar Julius, Dec. 16, 1962; children: Mark Lindsey, Annabel Victoria. Student, Syracuse U., 1947-49. Reporter N.Y. Herald Tribune Syndicate, 1949-51; corr. WNBC-WNBT, Europe and Middle East, 1951; radio-TV producer WNBC, N.Y.C., 1954-55; v.p. Tex McCrary, Inc., 1955-60; pres. Safire Pub. Relations, Inc., 1960-68; spl. asst. to Pres. Nixon, Washington, 1969-73; columnist N.Y. Times, 1973—. Trustee Syracuse U.; dir. Charles W. Dana Found. Author: The Relations Explosion, 1963, Plunging into Politics, 1964, Safire's Political Dictionary, 1968, rev. edit., 1972-78, Before the Fall, 1975, Full Disclosure, 1977, Safire's Washington, 1980, On Language, 1980, What's the Good Word?, 1982, (with Leonard Safir) Good Advice on Writing, 1982, I Stand Corrected, 1984, Take My Word for It, 1986, Freedom, 1987, You Could Look It Up, 1988, Words of Wisdom, 1989, (with Leonard Safir) Leadership, 1990, Language Maven Strikes Again, 1990, Fumblerules, 1990, Coming to Terms, 1991, The First Dissident, 1992, Lend Me Your Ears, 1992, Good Advice on Writing, 1992, Quoth the Maven, 1993, Safire's New Political Dictionary, 1993, In Love with Norma Loquendi, 1994, Sleeper Spy, 1995, Watching My Language, 1997, Spread the Word, 1999, Scandalmonger, 1999, Let A Simile Be Your Umbrella, 2001. Served with AUS, 1952-54. Recipient Pulitzer prize for Disting. Commentary, 1978 Mem. Pulitzer Bd. Republican. Office: NY Times 1627 I St NW Washington DC 20006-4007

SAFLEY, JAMES ROBERT, lawyer; b. Cedar Rapids, Iowa, Sept. 19, 1943; s. Robert Starr and Jean (Engelman) S.; m. Dianne Lee McInnis; children: Anne Michele, Jamie Leigh. BA, U. Iowa, 1965; JD, Duke U., 1968. Bar: Minn. 1968, U.S. Ct. Appeals (4th, 5th, 6th, 8th, 9th and 11th cirs.), U.S. Supreme Ct. Law clk. U.S. Dist. Ct. Minn., Mpls., 1968-69; assoc. Robins, Kaplan, Miller & Ciresi, 1969-74, ptnr., 1974—. Mem. adv. coun. Women's Intercollegiate Athletics, U. Minn., 1988-94; mem. Minn. Fed. Bar Assn. Commn. on ADR, 1995—. Mem. ABA, Minn. State Bar Assn. (antitrust sect. chmn. 1985-87), Hennepin County Bar Assn., Duke Law Alumni Assn. (bd. dirs. 2001--), Phi Beta Kappa. Office: Robins Kaplan Miller & Ciresi 2800 LaSalle Pla 800 Lasalle Ave Ste 2800 Minneapolis MN 55402-2015

SAFONOV, ALEXANDRE ANATOLEVICH, artist; b. Maikop, Krasnodarski Adgeya, Russia, Mar. 25, 1959; s. Anatoly Alexandrovich Safonov and Lubov Ivanovna Safonova; m. Charlene Avanel Hartsell, Sept. 20, 1995; m. Elena Fiodorovna Yakovleva, June 9, 1979 (div. July 25, 1995); children: Valdimir Alexandrovich, Andre Alexandrovich. BA, Maikop Sch. Art, Maikop, Russia, 1976—80; MA, Krasnodarski Inst. Art, Krasnodar, Russia, 1980—86. Prin. works include Sacred Heart, Daughter of the Sea, Madonna and Child, Fisherman's Memorial, one-man shows include Moscow; St. Petersburg, Russia; Paris; Brandenburg, Germany. Iconographer Russian Orthodox Ch., Russia, 2002—02. Home: 351 NE 163 Street Seattle WA 98155 Home Fax: 206-368-0137. Personal E-mail: safonov@foxinternet.net.

SAFONOV, MICHAEL GEORGE, electrical engineering educator, consultant; b. Pasadena, Calif., Nov. 1, 1948; s. George Michael and Ruth Garnet (Ware) S.; m. Nancy Kelshaw Schorn, Aug. 31, 1968 (div. Oct. 1983); 1 child, Alexander; m. Janet Sunderland, Feb. 25, 1985; 1 child, Peter. BSEE, MSEE, MIT, 1971, EE, 1976, PhDEE, 1977. Electronic engr. Air Force Cambridge Rsch. Lab., Hanscom AFB, Mass., 1968-71; rsch. asst. MIT, Cambridge, 1975-77; prof. elec. engring. U. So. Calif., L.A., 1977—, assoc. chmn. dept., 1989-93, vice chmn. engring. faculty coun., 2001—. Vis. scholar Cambridge (Eng.) U., 1983-84, Imperial Coll., London, 1987, Calif. Inst. Tech., Pasadena, 1990-91; cons. Honeywell Systems and Rsch. Ctr., Mpls., 1978-83, Space Systems div. TRW, Redondo Beach, Calif., 1984, Northrop Aircraft, Hawthorne, Calif., 1985-91, also numerous others. Author: Stability and Robustness of Multivariable Feedback Systems (hon. mention Phi Beta Kappa 1981); co-author: (book and software) Robust-Control Toolbox, 1988; assoc. editor IEEE Trans. on Automatic Control, 1985-87, Internat. Jour. Robust and Nonlinear Control, 1989-93, Sys. and Control Letters, 1995—. Awards com. chair Am. Automatic Control Coun., 1993-95. Lt. (j.g.) USNR, 1972-75. Rsch. grantee Air Force Office Sci. Rsch., 1978—, NSF, 1982-84. Fellow IEEE; mem. AIAA (sr.), Common Cause. Republican. Office: U So Calif Dept EE Sys MC 2563 3740 McClintock Ave # 310 Los Angeles CA 90089-2563 E-mail: msafonov@usc.edu. *Consider first only the very simplest problem--but strive for a representation of the simplest problem that generalizes.*

SAFRAN, EDWARD MYRON, financial consultant, banking executive; b. Boston, Oct. 9, 1937; s. Morris and Sophie (Radin) S.; m. Harriet Reva Podolsky, Jan. 15, 1966; children: Steven, Rebecca. BS in Metall., MIT, 1959; MBA, Harvard U., 1961. Pres. Suncrest Corp., Worcester, Mass., 1962-65;

exec. asst. Am. Metal Climax, N.Y.C., 1966; sr. auditor Gen. Electric Co., Lynn, Mass., 1966-68; fin. analyst Polaroid Corp., Cambridge, 1968-70, mgr. banking and investments, 1970-84, asst. treas., 1984-87; pres. Merganser Capital Mgmt. Corp., 1984-2000. Chmn. Direct Fed. Credit Union, Needham, Mass., 1986—. Gleason Works fellow Harvard U., 1959-60. Mem. Harvard Club of Boston Home: 37 Barney Hill Rd Wayland MA 01778-3601 Office: Direct Fed Credit Union PO Box 9123 50 Cabot St Needham MA 02494

SAFRAN, LINDA JACQUELINE, fundraiser; b. Buffalo, Oct. 1, 1946; d. Nathaniel and Dorothy Louise (Luce) S.; m. Eliel G. Redstone, 1967 (div., 1970); m. James K. Smolev (div. 1983); children: Jennifer Smolev, Melanie Smolev. BA, U. Mich., 1968; mgmt. cert., Goucher Coll., 1983. Cert. Fundraising Exec., Am. Fundraising profl. Program dir., dir. libr. devel. Johns Hopkins U., Balt., 1984-90; assoc. dir. resource devel. Enterprise Edn., Columbia, Md., 1990-92; v.p. devel. and pub. rels. Children's Hosp., Balt., 1993-94; pres. Devel. Collaborative, 1994—. Bd. dirs. Chesapeake Planned Giving Coun., Balt. Vol. Peace Corps, Brazil, 1968-70; mem. Balt. Presbytery Planned Giving Coun., Tri-Presbytery Planned Giving Commn.; deacon 2d Presbyn. Ch., Balt. Mem. Assn. Fundraising Profls. (cert. fundraising exec.), U. Mich. Alumni Assn. (bd. dirs. 1989-92), Md. Assn. Non-Profit Orgns. Task Force on Ethics (peer reviewer), Johns Hopkins Club, Hamilton St. Club. Democrat. Avocations: genealogy, oral history, flag collecting. Office: Devel Collaborative 221 Ridgemede Rd Baltimore MD 21210-3040

SAFRASTYAN, RUBEN, historian, political scientist; b. Yerevan, Yerevan, Armenia, Oct. 5, 1955; s. Aram and Susanna Safrastyan; m. Lilit Arakelyan; children: Aram Safrastyan ; m. Karine Ter-Gazaryantz (div. Mar. 7, 1992); children: Artashes. MD, Ios, Anas, Yerevan, Armenia, 1980. Deputy dir., dept. polit. analysis Office of the Pres. of Armenia, Yerevan, Armenia, 1991—96; counselor of embassy Armenian Embassy in Germany, Bonn, Germany, 1996—97; director Turkish studies program IOS, ANAS, Yerevan, Armenia, 1998—. Senior expert Parlament of Armenia, Yerevan, Armenia, 1991—92. Author: Doctrine of Ottomanism, 1985; editor: Genocide of 1915, 1995, Armenian-Turkish Relations, 1987. Scholar, Fulbright, 2001—, Humboldt, Germany, 1999—2000. Mem.: German Mid. East Studies Assn., Ctrl.Eurasian Studies Soc., Mid. East Studies Assn. N.Am., Am. Polit. Sci. Assn., Am. Hist. Assn. (assoc.). Avocation: travel. Home: 1222 Talbot #A Berkeley CA 94706 Office: U Calif Isees 260 Stephens Hall Berkeley CA 94720-2304 E-mail: rsafrast@uclink.berkeley.edu.

SAFT, STUART MARK, lawyer; b. N.Y.C., Feb. 17, 1947; s. Stanley and Dorothy (Ligerman) S.; m. Stephanie C. Optekman, June 6, 1970; children: Bradley S., Gordon D. BA, Hofstra U., 1968; JD, Columbia U., 1971. Bar: N.Y. 1972, Fla. 1975, U.S. Dist. Ct. (so. dist.) N.Y. 1975, U.S. Supreme Ct. 1990. Ptnr. Wolf Haldenstein Adler Freeman & Herz, N.Y.C., 1988—. Chmn., bd. dirs. Coun. of N.Y. Coops., N.Y.C., 1981—, N.Y.C. Workforce Investment Bd.; chmn. bd. dirs., CEO Pvt. Industry Coun. of N.Y.C., 1994-2000; bd. dirs. Am. Women's Econ. Devel. Corp., Nat. Assn. Housing Coops., Nat. Coop. Bank, S.L.E. Lupus Found.; adj. asst. prof. NYU, Real Estate Inst. Author: Commercial Real Estate Forms, 3 vols., 1987, Commercial Real Estate Transactions, 1989, Commercial Real Estate Workouts, 1991, Real Estate Development: Strategies for a Changing Market, 1990, Commercial Real Estate Leasing, 1992, Real Estate Investor's Survival Guide, 1992, Commercial Real Estate Financing, 1993, Commercial Real Estate Forms, 3d edit., 8 vols., 2001, Commercial Real Estate Transactions, 2d edit., 1995, Commercial Real Estate Workouts, 2d edit., 1996; contbg. editor: The Real Estate Finance Jour., 1989—; contbr. articles to profl. jours. Served to capt. USAR, 1968-76. Mem. ABA, Am. Coll. Real Estate Lawyers, N.Y. Bar Assn., Fla. Bar Assn. Office: Wolf Haldenstein Adler Freeman & Herz 270 Madison Ave New York NY 10016-0601

SAFYER, STEVEN M. chief medical officer; MD, Albert Einstein Coll. of Med., 1982. Cert. internal medicine . Chief med. officer Montefiore Med. Ctr., resident, 1983—85, intern, 1978—82. Office: MMC Centennial Bldg 111 E 210 St 4th Fl Bronx NY 10467*

SAG, JEROME E. internist; b. N.Y.C., Nov. 30, 1946; s. David and Marcelle Sag; m. Marna L. Sag, May 23, 1971 (div. Nov. 2000); children: Jessica L., Michael A. BS in Chemistry, Queens Coll., N.Y.C., 1968; MD, N.Y. Med. Coll., 1972. Diplomate Am. Bd. Internal Medicine. Intern M.S. Hershey (Pa.) Med. Ctr., 1972-73, resident, 1975-77; internist Lansdale (Pa.) Med. Group, 1977—, pres., 1998-2000. Pres. med. staff N. Penn Hosp., Lansdale, 1986-88, mem. bd. dirs., 1996—. With USPHS, 1973-75. Mem. ACP. Avocations: hiking, gardening, music. Office: Lansdale Internal Medicine 1025 S Broad St Lansdale PA 19446 E-mail: jeromesag@msn.com.

SAGAFI-NEJAD, TAGI, business educator; b. Bainabaj, Khorasan, Iran, Dec. 19, 1941; came to U.S., 1968; s. Mir Gholam-Reza and Tayebeh Sagafi; m. Nancy Gail Black Sagafi-nejad, Nov. 22, 1967; children: Jahan Crawford Reza, David Joseph Hossein. MA, U. Pa., 1971, PhD, 1979. Lectr. U. Pa., Phila., 1974-76; asst. prof. U. Wash., Seattle, 1976-80, U. Tex., Austin, 1980-84; assoc. prof. Loyola Coll., Balt., 1984-93, prof., 1993—, dept. chair, 1995-96, prof. emeritus, 2002—. Cons. UN Indsl. Devel. Orgn., 1982-84, UN Ctr. on Transnational Corp., 1985—, Office of Tech. Assessment, U.S. Congress, 1983-84; lectr., spkr. in field. Author: Technology Transfer Trilogy, 1980, 1981, The United Nations and Transnational Corporations, 2002; editl. bd. Transnational Corp., 1993—, Competitiveness Rev., 1995—. Recipient Best Paper award Acad. of Mgmt., 1994, Pacific Asia Mgmt. Inst., U. Hawaii, 1988. Mem. Am. Competitiveness Soc. (adv. bd. 1996-2000), Acad. of Internat. Bus. (chair N.E. chpt. 1988-93), Iranian Scholars Assn. (founding mem., v.p. 1989-90), Middle East Studies Assn., Middle East Inst., Strategic Mgmt. Soc. Democrat. Avocations: gardening, golf, painting, walking. Office: Sellinger Sch Loyola Coll 4501 N Charles St Baltimore MD 21210-2601

SAGALKIN, SANFORD, lawyer; b. N.Y.C., June 24, 1942; s. Nathan and Blanche (Hoffner) S.; m. Monda E. Fifield, Aug. 25, 1969; children: Nicholas, Amy. BA, Queens Coll., 1964; LLB, Columbia U., 1967. Bar: N.Y. 1967, Alaska 1969, D.C. 1980, Md., 1986. Staff atty. N.Y. Mental Health Info. Service, N.Y.C., 1967-69; mem. firm Faulkner, Banfield, Doogan, Gross and Holmes, Juneau, Alaska, 1969-74; firm Ely, Guess & Rudd, Juneau, 1974-75; asst. atty. gen. Atty. Gen.'s Office, State of Alaska, 1975-77; dep. asst. atty. gen. Dept. Justice, Washington, 1977-80; mem. firm Ely, Guess & Rudd, 1980-82; pvt. practice Sharpsburg, Md., 1982-86; assoc. gen. counsel CIA, Washington, 1986—. Mem. Juneau Parks and Recreation Com., 1972—74; bd. dirs. Defenders of Wildlife, 1986—90, Tifereth Israel Congregation, 2000—01. Mem. D.C. Bar Assn., Md. Bar Assn. Democrat. Jewish. Office: Cia Washington DC 20505-0001

SAGANICH, BONNIE SUE, medical/surgical nurse; b. Lancaster, Pa., Apr. 30, 1956; d. Gerald Charles and Reta Ruth (Rupp) Hake; m. David Anthony Saganich, Aug. 30, 1980. BSN, Temple U., 1988; MSN, U. Pa., 1991. RN, Pa.; bd.cert. med.-surg. nurse. Med.-surg. nurse Lancaster Gen. Hosp., 1988-90, renal dialysis nurse, 1991-93; med.-surg. nurse York (Pa.) Hosp., 1993-94; staff nurse Vis. Nurse Assn., Lancaster, 1994-95, nurse long term care, 1996; neurology and step-down trauma nurse Lancaster Gen. Hosp., 1997-2000, step-down nurse open heart surgical unit, 2000—. Contbr. profl. jours. Mem. Sigma Theta Tau. Avocations: vegetable gardening, photography, country walks, travel. Home: 75 Silver Mine Rd Conestoga PA 17516-9732 Office: Lancaster Gen Hosp 555 N Duke St Lancaster PA 17602

SAGAR, AMBUJ D. environmental and technology policy professional; b. Delhi, India, July 27, 1963; came to U.S., 1985; s. Daya and Nirmal Sagar. BTech in Mech. Engring., Indian Inst. Tech., Delhi, 1985; MS in Aerospace Engring., U. Mich., 1986; MS in Materials Sci., MIT, 1989, MS in Tech. and Policy, PhD in Materials Sci., MIT, 1994. Rsch. assoc. Belfer Ctr. for Sci. and Internat. Affairs John F. Kennedy Sch. Govt., Harvard U., Cambridge, Mass., 1995—. Patentee in field. Mem. Sigma Xi. Office: Harvard U Kennedy Sch Govt 79 John F Kennedy St Cambridge MA 02138 E-mail: ambuj_sagar@harvard.edu.

SAGAR, MICHAL BASS, art educator, artist; b. Cin., June 29, 1953; d. Herbert and Helen Bass; m. Gregory Sagar, June 2, 1979; 1 child, Simone. BFA, San Francisco Art Inst., 1975; MFA, Mpls. Coll. Art and Design, 1996. Instr. painting/drawing Mpls. Coll. Art and Design, 1994-96; head dept. visual arts Breck Sch., Mpls., 1996—. One-woman shows include Shepard Ctr. Gallery, St. Paul, 1998; exhibited in group shows at Thomas Barry Fine Art, Mpls., 1997, A.I.R. Gallery, N.Y.C., 1997, 2002, Plains Art Mus., Fargo, N.D., 1999 (Juror's Choice award 1999), Minn. Biennial, 2000, Minn. Mus. Art, St. Paul, 2000, Soap Factory, 2002. Mem.: NEA. Democrat. Jewish. Home: 3704 Twenty-fourth Ave S Minneapolis MN 55406 Office: Breck Sch 123 Ottawa Ave N Minneapolis MN 55422-5189 E-mail: michal.sagar@breckschool.org.

SAGARIN, JAMES LEON, rabbi, author, editor, publisher; b. Oceanside, N.Y., Dec. 31, 1951; s. Lawrence and Ethel (Wallace) S.; m. Lori Beth Baumblatt, Aug. 31, 1986. BA, SUNY, Albany, 1974; MA in Hebrew Letters, Hebrew U. Coll. Jewish Inst. Religion, 1978. Ordained rabbi, 1979, Reform Jewish educator, 1992. Hillel dir., congl. rabbi So. Ill. U., Carbondale, 1979-80; dir. Young Judaea Jewish Community Ctrs. Assn., St. Louis, 1980-82; sr. adult coord., chaplain, dir. contg. edn. Cen. Agy. for Jewish Edn., 1982-88; prof. Hebrew langs. and lit. Washington U., 1985-88; assoc. rabbi Temple Beth-El, Chgo., 1988-91; rabbi Temple Menorah, 1991-99, Temple B'nai Israel, Kankakee, 2000—01, Temple Shir Shalom, Buffalo Grove, 2001—. Fgn. lang. tchr. Niles North H.S., Skokie, Ill., 1994-2001. Author: Hebrew Noun Patterns, 1987; co-author: Oseh Shalom, 1990; author, editor: First Harvest: Jewish Writings in St. Louis, 1991-97, 1997; pub., youth editor Sagarin Rev., 1991-97, contbr., 1992-97; asst. editor Pastoral Outreach Newsletter, 1992, 93; contbr. to Chgo. Jewish Star, 1991-93, Chgo. Jewish News, 1995. Mem. Cen. Conf. Am. Rabbis, Nat. Assn. Profs. Hebrew, Nat. Assn. Temple Educators, B'nai Brith. Avocations: running, swimming, writing. Home and Office: 200 Valley Vw Wilmette IL 60091

SAGAWA, SHIRLEY SACHI, lawyer; b. Rochester, N.Y., Aug. 25, 1961; d. Hidetaka H. and Patricia (Ford) S.; m. Gregory A. Baer; children: Jackson Ford Baer, Matthew Sagawa Baer, Thomas Arthur Baer. AB, Smith Coll., 1983; MSc, London Sch. Econs., 1984; JD, Harvard U., 1987. Bar: Md. 1988. Chief counsel youth policy, labor and human resources com. U.S. Senate, Washington, 1987-91; sr. counsel and dir. family and youth policy Nat. Women's Law Ctr., 1991-93; spl. asst. to Pres. Clinton for domestic policy, 1993; exec. dir., mng. dir., exec. v.p. Corp. for Nat. and Comty. Svc., Washington, 1993-97; exec. dir. Learning First Alliance, 1997-98; dep. asst. Pres. Clinton, dep. chief staff First Lady The White House, 1998-2001; ptnr. sagawa/jospin, 2001—. Co-author: Common Interest, Common Good, Creating Value Through Business and Social Sector Partnership, 1999. Mem. exec. bd. Orgn. for Pan-Asian Am. Women, Washington, 1987-89; mem. Women of Color Leadership Coun., 1991-92; vice chair, bd. dirs. Nat. Community Svc. Commn., 1991-93; trustee Am. Folklife Ctr., Libr. Congress, 1996-97; commr. Head Start Fellowships Commn., 1996-97; bd. dirs. My Sister's Place, 1996-98, Jumpstart, 1998, Campus Outreach Opportunity League, 1997-98, Nat. Inst. Dispute Resolution, 1997-98. Recipient Philip V. McGance award Coun. for Advancement of Citizenship, 1991, cert. of recognition Nat. Coun. Jewish Women, 1989, Alexandrine medal Coll. St. Catherine, St. Paul, 1995, Alec Dickson Servant Leader award Nat. Youth Leadership Coun., 2002; named one of 25 most influential working women Working Mother Mag., 1999; recipient Alec Dickson Servant Leader award, National Youth Leadership Council, 2002; Harry S. Truman scholar, 1981; Smith Coll. Alumnae Assn. fellow, 1983, AAUW fellow, 1986. Mem. Md. Bar Assn. Democrat. Episcopalian. E-mail: ssagawa@sagawajospin.com.

SAGAWA, YONEO, horticulturist, educator; b. Olaa, Hawaii, Oct. 11, 1926; s. Chikatada and Mume (Kuno) S.; m. Masayo Yamamoto, May 24, 1962 (dec. Apr. 1988); children: Penelope Toshiko, Irene Teruko. AB, Washington U., St. Louis, 1950, MS, 1952; PhD, U. Conn., 1956. Postdoctoral research assoc. biology Brookhaven Nat. Lab., Upton, NY, 1955—57, guest in biology, 1958; asst. prof., then assoc. prof. U. Fla., 1957—64; dir. undergrad. sci. ednl. research participation program NSF, 1964; cons. biosatellite project NASA, 1966—67; prof. horticulture U. Hawaii, 1964—; dir. Lyon Arboretum, 1967—91; assoc. dir. Hawaiian Sci. Fair, 1966—67, dir., 1967—68; research assoc. in biology U. Calif., Berkeley, 1970—71; rsch. assoc. Bishop Mus., Honolulu, 1992—, Botanical Rsch. Inst. of Tex., 1993—, Hawaii Tropical Botanical Garden, 1995—; external assessor U. Pertanian, Malaysia, 1994—. Mem. Internat. Orchid Commn. on Classification, Nomenclature and Registration; fellow Inst. voor Toepassing van Atoomengerie in de Landbouw, U. Agr., Wageningen, The Netherlands, 1979-80; mem. sci. adv. bd. Nat. Tropical Bot. Garden, Kauai, Hawaii; councilor Las Cruces Bot. Garden, Costa Rica; cons. FAO, Singapore, 1971, USAID-Agribus. Assistance Program, Vols. in Overseas Coop. Assistance, UN Devel. Program-UN Internat. Short Term Adv. Resources; dir. Hawaii Tropical Bot. Garden; hon. scientist Rural Devel. Adminstrn., Republic of Korea, 1998—; cons. Fiji-N.Z. Bus. Coun., 1996, 97, 98, 99, 2000; cons. IRETA, Western Samoa, 1997, 98; cons. Nat. Hort. Rsch. Inst., Suwon, Republic of Korea, 1998, 2000. Editor: Hawaii Orchid Jour., 1972-99, Pacific Orchid Soc. Bull., 1966-71; mem. editl. bd.: Allertonia, 1976; contbr. numerous articles to profl. jours. Trustee Friends of Honolulu Bot. Gardens, 1973-99 Recipient Disting. Svc. award South Fla. Orchid Soc., 1968, Cert. of Achievement Garden Club Am., 1995, Gold award Hawaii Orchid Growers Assn., 1996; grantee Am. Orchid Soc., Atomic Energy Commn., NIH, HEW, Inst. Mus. Svcs., Stanley Smith Hort. Trust, Honolulu Orchid Soc. Fellow Am. Orchid Soc. (hon. life, Gold medal for outstanding contbns. and svcs. 1999); mem. AAAS, Internat. Assn. Hort. Sci., Am. Assn. Hort. Sci., Am. Inst. for Biol. Scis., Bot. Soc. Am., Hawn Bot. Soc. (past v.p.), Internat. Assn. Plant Tissue Culture, Internat. Palm Soc., Am. Anthurium Soc. (hon. life), Pacific Orchid Soc. (trustee 1994), Kaimuki Orchid Soc. (hon. life), Honolulu Orchid Soc. (hon., life), Lyon Arboretum Assn. (trustee 1974-91), Garden Club Honolulu (hon., life), Aloha Bonsai Club, Sigma Xi, Gamma Sigma Delta, Phi Kappa Phi (past pres., v.p., councillor U. Hawaii chpt.). Democrat. Office: U Hawaii TPSS St John Rm 102 3190 Maile Way Honolulu HI 96822-2279 Fax: 808-956-3894. E-mail: yoneo@hawaii.edu.

SAGE, ANDREW GREGG CURTIN, II, corporate investor, manager; b. Bryn Mawr, Pa., Mar. 11, 1926; s. Henry W. and Eleanor (Purviance) S.; m. Sara Wakefield, Sept. 29, 1956; children: Andrew Gregg Curtin III, Sally. Mem. staff DeCoppet & Doremus (odd lot stock house), N.Y.C., 1946-47, Sage & Co., N.Y. Stock Exchange Specialists, N.Y.C., 1947-48; assoc. Lehman Bros., 1948-60, gen. partner, 1960-68, pres., 1970-73, vice chmn., 1973-77, mng. dir., 1977-82, Lehman Bros. Kuhn Loeb, Inc., 1977-82, Shearson Lehman Bros., Inc., 1982-87, sr. cons., 1987-90; pres., CEO, dir. Robertson CECO Corp., Boston, 1992-93, chmn. bd. dirs., 1994—, San Ramon, Calif. Bd. dirs. Tom's Foods, Am. Superconductor Corp.Worldport Comm.Corp.; pres., treas. Sage Land Devel. Co.; pres., dir. Sage Capital Corp. Served with USAAF, 1944-46. Home: PO Box 937 Wilson WY 83014-0937

SAGE, ANDREW PATRICK, JR. systems engineer, management educator; b. Charleston, S.C., Aug. 27, 1933; s. Andrew Patrick and Pearl Louise (Britt) S.; m. LaVerne Galhouse, Mar. 3, 1962; children: Theresa Annette, Karen Margaret, Philip Andrew. BS in Elec. Engring, The Citadel, 1955; SM, MIT, 1956; PhD, Purdue U., 1960; DEng (hon.), U. Waterloo, Can., 1987, Dalhousie U., Halifax, Nova Scotia, Can., 1997. Registered profl. engr., Tex. Instr. elec. engring. Purdue U., 1956-60; assoc. prof. U. Ariz., 1960-63; mem. tech. staff Aerospace Corp., Los Angeles, 1963-64; prof. elec. engring. and nuclear engring. scis. U. Fla., 1964-67; prof., dir. Info. and Control Scis. Center, So. Methodist U., Dallas, 1967-74; head elec. engring. dept. So. Meth. U., 1973-74; Quarles prof. engring. sci. and systems U. Va., Charlottesville, 1974-84, chmn. dept. chem. engring., 1974-75, chmn. dept. engring. sci. and systems, 1977-84, assoc. dean, 1974-80; First Am. Bank prof. info. tech. George Mason U., Fairfax, Va., 1984—, assoc. v.p. for acad. affairs, 1984-85, dean Sch. Info. Tech. and Engring., 1985-96, univ. prof., founding dean emeritus, 1996—. Cons. Martin Marietta, Collins Radio, Atlantic Richfield, Tex. Instruments, LTV Aerospace, Battelle Meml. Inst., TRW Sys., NSF, Inst. Def. Analyses, Planning Rsch. Corp., MITRE, Engring. Rsch. Assocs., Software Productivity Consortium; gen. chmn. Internat. Conf. on Sys., Man and Cybernetics, 1974, 87; mem. spl. program panel on sys. sci. NATO, 1981-82; trustee, cons. Ctr. Naval Analysis, 1990-94. Author: Optimum Systems Control, 1968, 2d edit., 1977, Estimation Theory with Applications to Communications and Control, 1971, System Identification, 1971, An Introduction to Probability and Stochastic Processes, 1973, Methodology for Large Scale Systems, 1977, Systems Engineering: Methodology and Applications, 1977, Linear Systems Control, 1978, Economic Systems Analysis, 1983, System Design for Human Interaction, 1987, Information Processing in Systems and Organizations, 1990, Introduction to Computer Systems Analysis, Design, and Applications, 1989, Software Systems Engineering, 1990, Decision Support Systems Engineering, 1991, Systems Engineering, 1992, Systems Management for Information Technology and Software Engineering, 1995, Handbook of Systems Engineering and Management, 1999, Introduction to Systems Engineering, 2000; assoc. editor IEEE Transactions on Systems Sci. and Cybernetics, 1968-72; editor: IEEE Transactions on Systems, Man and Cybernetics, 1972-98; assoc. editor: Automatica, 1968-81; editor, 1981-96; mem. editl. bd. Systems Engring, 1968-72, IEEE Spectrum, 1972-73, Computers and Elec. Engring., 1972, Jour. Interdisciplinary Modeling and Simulation, 1976-80, Internat. Jour. Intelligent Sys., 1986—, Orgn. Sci., 1994—; editor Elsevier North Holland textbook series in sys. sci. and engring., 1970-88, John Wiley textbook series on sys. engring. and mgmt., 1989—; co-editor-in-chief Jour. Large Scale Sys.: Theory and Applications, 1978-88, Info. and Decision Technologies, 1988-94, Info. and Sys. Engring., 1995-96; editor in chief Sys. Engring., 1998—; co-editor in chief Info., Knowledge and Sys. Mgmt., 1999—; contbr. articles to profl. jours. Recipient Norbert Wiener award, 1980, Joseph G. Wohl career award, 1991, Superior Pub. Svc. award Sec. of the Navy, 1994; Case Centennial scholar, 1980, Award Washington Soc. of Engrs., 1996. Master: IEEE Sys./Man and Cybernetics Soc. (pres. 1984—85); fellow: AAAS (chmn. sect. M 1990), IEEE (life M. Barry Carlton award 1970, Centennial medal 1984, Outstanding Contbn. award 1986, Donald G. Fink prize 1994, Simon Ramo medal 2000); mem.: Inst. for Ops. Rsch. and Mgmt. Sci., Washington Soc. Engrs. (award 1996), Am. Soc. Engring. Edn. (Frederick Emmonds Terman award 1970, Centennial cert. for exceptional contbn. 1993), Internat. Fedn. Automatic Control (Oustanding Svc. award), Inst. Mgmt. Scis., Tau Beta Pi, Eta Kappa Nu (eminent mem. award 2002), Sigma Xi. Home: 8011 Woodland Hills Ln Fairfax VA 22039-2433 Office: George Mason U Sch Info Tech Fairfax VA 22030-4444

SAGE, ELDERIA FRANCKLING, social worker; b. Hartford, Conn., Feb. 9, 1942; BA, Beaver Coll., 1964; MSW, U. Conn., 1968. Lic. clin. social worker, Conn. Program dir. YWCA of Wilkes-Barre, Pa., 1964-66; sch. social workers Hartford Bd. of Edn., 1968-72; social work cons. Chesterfield Convalescent Home, Chester, Conn., 1977-85; social worker Colchester (Conn.) Convalescent Home, 1985-89; clin. social worker Middlesex Meml. Hosp., Middletown, Conn., 1989—. Sec., bd. dirs. Vis. Nurses of the Lower Valley, Centerbrook, Conn., 1978-80; bd. dirs. Nat. Kidney Found. Conn., 1993-95. Mem.: NASW, Conn. Social Work Oncology Group, Assn. Oncology Social Workers, Conn. Coun. Nephrology Social Workers (sec. 1989—90, chairperson 1990—92, 1997—98), Acad. Cert. Social Workers. Office: Middlesex Meml Hosp Cancer Ctr 28 Crescent St Middletown CT 06457-3650

SAGE, JACOB I. neurologist, educator; b. Sept. 26, 1946; s. Joseph and Fern (Ginsburg) S.; m. Cynthia Fox; children: Naomi, Rebecca, Abigail. AB, U. Chgo., 1968; MD, U. Pitts., 1972. Intern Yale-New Haven Hosp., 1972-73; resident in neurology U. Pitts., 1976-78; fellow in neurochemistry Cornell Med. Coll., N.Y.C., 1978-80; asst. prof. neurology U. Medicine and Dentistry of N.J., New Brunswick, 1980-86, assoc. prof., 1986-90, prof. neurology, 1990—, dir. movement disorders divsn., 1995—. Mem. sci. adv. bd. Am. Parkinsons Disease Assn., N.Y.C., 1995—. Author: Parkinson's Disease: A Guide for Patients, 1996; editor: Practical Neurology of the Elderly, 1996; contbr. articles to profl. jours. Fellow Am. Neurol. Assn.; mem. Acad. of Neurology. Avocations: skiing, gardening. Office: UMDNJ Robert Wood Johnson Med Sch Dept Neurology New Brunswick NJ 08903 E-mail: sage@umdnj.edu.

SAGE, MARTIN LEE, chemistry educator; b. N.Y.C., Mar. 4, 1935; s. Joseph and Fannie Sage; m. Gloria Arline Welt, June 15, 1958; 1 child, Daniel Simon. AB, Cornell U., 1955; MA, Harvard U., 1958, PhD, 1959. Postdoctoral fellow Brandeis U., Waltham, Mass., 1959-61; asst. prof. U. Oreg., Eugene, 1961-67; assoc. prof. Syracuse (N.Y.) U., 1967-82, prof. chemistry, 1982—, dir. sci., tech. and society program, 1991—. Vis. assoc. prof. Tel Aviv U., 1977-78; visitor Oxford (Eng.) U., 1985-86. Mem. AAAS, AAUP (pres. Syracuse U. chpt. 1988-89), Am. Phys. Soc., Am. Chem. Soc., Nat. Assn. for Sci., Tech., and Soc., Sierra Club. Office: Syracuse U CST 1-014 Syracuse NY 13244

SAGE, ROBERT EPHRAM, social service agency administrator; b. N.Y.C., Oct. 1, 1945; s. Aaron and Sylvia (Buiar) S.; m. Elaine Francis Zahnstecher, Aug. 17, 1968; children: Holly, Jeremy. BA, CUNY, 1967; PhD, St. John's U., Jamaica, N.Y., 1976. Cert. alcohol and substance abuse counselor, N.Y. Tchr. N.Y.C. Bd. Edn., 1968-73; psychol. counselor, dir. peer counseling Bklyn. Coll., 1973-76; dir. Jamaica Hosp. MMTP, 1976-77; mental health cons., coord. mental health svcs. Addiction Rsch. and Treatment Corp., Bklyn., 1977-79; v.p. treatment svcs. Urban Resource Inst./Addiction Rsch. and Treatment Corp., 1979-2000, sr. v.p., 2000—. Co-dir., cons. Urban Adv. Group, Bklyn., 1988—; bd. dirs. N.Y. State Com. Methadone Program Adminstrs., 2001—. Author rsch. studies. Mem. APA, ACA. Home: 21411 Richland Ave Flushing NY 11364-3547 Office: Urban Resource Inst 22 Chapel St Brooklyn NY 11201-1996

SAGE, WEBSTER LEGENE, JR. ophthalmologist; b. St. Louis, Oct. 22, 1925; s. Webster LeGene and Alice Virginia (Gollehon) S.; m. Claudine New, May 20, 1952 (dec. June 1986); children: Bryan LeGene, Evan Webster; m. Shirley Barr, Jan. 2, 1988. BS, U. Ariz., 1949; MD, Baylor U., 1953. Diplomate Am. Bd. Ophthalmology. Inter Good Samaritan Hosp., Phoenix; resident Loma Linda (Calif.) U.; pvt. practice in medicine Phoenix, 1956—. Chmn. dept. ophthalmology Good Samaritan Hosp., Phoenix, 1960-62, St. Joseph's Hosp., Phoenix, 1971-72; cons. Ariz. Bd. Med. Examiners, Phoenix; owner Surg. Eye Ctr. Ariz., Phoenix, 1985—. Chmn. bd. of elders and deacons Camelback Christian Ch., Scottsdale, Ariz. Maj. U.S. Army, 1962-64. Fellow ACS (life), Am. Acad. Ophthalmology, Internat. Coll. Surgeons; mem. Ariz. Ophthalmological Soc. (pres. 1963-64), Phoenix Ophthalmological Soc. (pres. 1967-68), Kiwanis Club, Paradise Valley Country Club, Phoenix Country Club. Avocations: traveling, photography. Home: 8210 N Charles Dr Paradise Valley AZ 85253-2405 Office: 5133 N Central Ave Ste 100 Phoenix AZ 85012-1438

SAGER, CLIFFORD J. psychiatrist, educator; b. N.Y.C. s. Max and Lena (Lipman) S.; m. Anne Scheinman; children by previous marriage: Barbara L., Philip T., Rebecca J., Anthony F. BS, Pa. State U., 1937; MD, NYU, 1941; cert. in psychoanalysis, N.Y. Med. Coll., 1949. Diplomate: Am. Bd. Psychiatry and Neurology. Rotating intern Montefiore Hosp., N.Y.C., 1941-42; resident in psychiatry Bellevue Hosp., 1946—48; practice medicine specializing in psychiatry N.Y.C. and East Hampton, N.Y., 1946—; dir. therapeutic services, assoc. dean, dir. tng. Postgrad. Ctr. Mental Health, 1948-60; vis. psychiatrist, med. bd. Flower and Fifth Ave Hosp., 1960-71, Met. Hosp., 1960-71; dir. psychiat. tng. and edn. N.Y. Med. Coll., 1960-71; attending psychiatrist Bird S. Coler Hosp., 1960-71; clin. dir. N.Y. Med. Coll., 1960-63, assoc. prof. psychiatry, 1960-65, prof., 1966-71, dir. partial hosp. programs and family treatment and study unit, 1964-71; clin. prof. psychiatry Mt. Sinai Sch. Medicine, 1971-80; assoc. dir. psychiatry Beth Israel Hosp. for Family and Mental Therapy; chief of psychiatry Gov.'s Hosp., 1970-74; dir. family therapy Mt. Sinai Sch. Medicine, 1974-80; clin. prof. psychiatry N.Y. Hosp.-Cornell Univ. Med. Ctr., 1980—; attending psychiatrist N.Y. Hosp.-Payne Whitney Clinic, 1980—98; dir. marital and family clinic N.Y. Hosp., 1991—. Attending psychiatrist Mt. Sinai Hosp., 1971-80; chief behavioral scis. Gouverneur Hosp.; chief family treatment unit Beth Israel Med. Ctr., 1970-74, assoc. dir. psychiatry family and group therapy, 1971-74; psychiat. dir. Jewish Family Svc., 1974-77; dir. family psychiatry Jewish Bd. Family and Childrens Svcs., 1978-90; dir. Remarried Consultation Svc., 1976-90; dir. Tng. and Sex Therapy Clinic, 1974-90; psychiat. dir. Employee Consultation and Corp. Health Programs, 1980-83; faculty , supr. Contemporary Ctr. Advanced Psychoanalytic Studies; chief neuropsychiatry 42d and 312th Gen. Hosp.; psychiat. cons. Employee Consultation Svc. and Corp. Health Svcs., 1983-1992. Author: Marriage Contracts and Couple Therapy, 1976, Intimate Partners, 1979, Treating the Remarried Family, 1983; 4 other books; mem. editorial bd. Am. Jour. Orthopsychiatry, 1960-69, Internat. Jour. Group Psychotherapy, 1968—, Family Process, 1969-92, Divorce and Remarriage, 1977—, Comprehensive Rev. Jour. Family and Marriage, 1978—; cons. Sexual Medicine, 1974-82; co-editor, founder Jour. Sex and Marital Therapy, 1974—; mem. editorial bd.: Jour. Marriage and Family Counseling, 1977—, Internat. Jour. Family Counseling, 1977—; author or contbr. numerous sci.

articles to jours. Capt. M.C. U.S. Army, 1942—46. Recipient Am. Family Therapy Assn. award for Outstanding Contribution to Family Therapy 1983, Assn. Marriage and Family Therapists award for Outstanding Contributions to the field of Marital and Family Therapy, 1984. Fellow Am. Psychiat. Assn. (life), Am. Orthopsychiat. Assn. (life), Acad. Psychoanalysis (charter), Am. Group Psychotherapy Assn. (pres. 1968-70, dir. 1962-74), Soc. Med. Psychoanalysts (pres. 1960-61, dir. 1958-62, pres.-elect 1997-99), Am. Assn. Marital and Famiy Therapists; mem. AMA (life), Am. Soc. Advancement Psychotherapy (dir. 1954-67), N.Y. Soc. Clin. Psychiatry, Soc. for Sex Therapy and Rsch. (pres. 1976-77, bd. dirs. 1953-58) PAIRS Found. (bd. dirs. 1985—). Office: 35 E 75th St New York NY 10021-2761 also: 33 Breeze Hill Rd East Hampton NY 11937-4505

SAGER, DONALD JACK, librarian, consultant, former publisher; b. Milw., Mar. 3, 1938; s. Alfred Herman and Sophia (Sagan) Sager; m. Sarah Ann Long, May 23, 1987; children: Geoffrey, Andrew. BS, U. Wis., Milw., 1963; MSLS, U. Wis., 1964. Sr. documentalist AC Electronics divsn. GM, Milw., 1958-63; teaching asst. U. Wis., Madison, 1963-64; dir. Kingston (N.Y.) Pub. Libr., 1964-66, Elyria (Ohio) Pub. Libr., 1966-71, Mobile Pub. Libr., 1971-75, Pub. Libr. Columbus and Franklin County, Ohio, 1975-78; commr. Chgo. Pub. Libr., 1978-81; dir. Elmhurst Pub. Libr., Ill., 1982-83, Milw. Pub. Libr., 1983-91; pub. Highsmith Press, Ft. Atkinson, Wis., 1991-2000; pres., CEO Gossage Sager Assocs. LLC, N.Y.C., 2000—. Secy Online Computer Library Ctr, 1977—78, disting vis scholar, 1982; chmn investment comt PLA Pub Library, 1985—89, chmn mus comt, 1989—91, mem hist comt, 1993—95, chmn PLA nat conf comt, 1986—88; bd dirs Coun Wis Libraries, 1982—91, Urban Libraries Coun, 1985—93, secy, 1991—93; adj faculty Univ Wis, Milwaukee, 1984—91; consult in field. Author: (book) Reference: A Programmed Instruction, 1970, Binders, Books and Budgets, 1971, Participatory Management, 1981, The American Public Library, 1982, Public Library Administrators Planning Guide to Automation, 1983, Managing the Public Library, 1984, Small Libraries, 1992, Small Libraries, 3d rev ed, 2000; co-editor: Urban Library Management Trends, 1989; contbg. editor: Public Libraries, 1990—; contbr. articles to profl jours. Pres Milwaukee Civic Alliance, 1990—91; chmn Milwaukee United Way Campaign, 1984; pres Milwaukee Westown Asn, 1987—90; bd dirs Goethe House, 1985—91. With AUS, 1956—58. Mem.: ALA (coun mem 1995—, policy monitoring comt, awards comt, chmn core values task force), Library Admin Asn Wis (chmn 1987—88), Wis Library Asn Found (chmn 1986—88), Wis Library Asn, Chicago Book Clin, Ill Library Asn, Pub Library Asn (bd dirs, vpres, pres-elect, pres 1982—83), Exchange Club Milwaukee (pres 1988—89). Home: 590 Wilmot Rd Deerfield IL 60015-3955 Office: Gossage Sager Assocs LLC 25 W 43d St Ste 812 New York NY 10036 E-mail: dsager@gossagesager.com.

SAGER, GILBERT LANDIS, investment company executive; b. Harrisonburg, Va., June 28, 1947; s. Roy Franklin and Beatrice (Bradfield) S.; m. Esther Kendrick Brown, Nov. 8, 1969. BA in History, George Mason Coll., 1969; MBA in Fin., Fairleigh Dickinson U., 1978. Mgmt. trainee Chem. Bank, N.Y.C., 1969-73, 69-81, asst. v.p. internat. human resources, 1980-81; v.p. human resources Midlantic Nat. Bank, Edison, N.J., 1981-90; sr. v.p. human resources Trust Co. N.J., 1990-93; investment rep. Edward Jones, Ephrata, Pa., 1993—. Bd. dirs. Jr. Achievment Ctrl. Pa., 1996-98, Ephrata Pub. Libr., 1997—, TRACK, 1996-99, Ephrata Cmty. Hosp., 1997—. With USMC, 1969-71. Mem. Ephrata Area C. of C. (bd. dirs. 1996-98). Avocations: golf, reading, basketball. Home: 984 Martin Ave Ephrata PA 17522-1322

SAGER, LAWRENCE COOPER, psychologist; b. Manhattan, Kans., Jan. 15, 1952; s. Roderick Cooper and Ruth Regina (Ross) S.; m. Lynn Whaley, Apr. 29, 1978 (div. Feb. 1994); children: Lauren M., MacKenzie M.; m. Stephanie Kulak, Jan. 8, 1999. BA, Hamilton Coll., Clinton, N.Y., 1974; MA, Johns Hopkins U., 1976, PhD, 1978. Mem. tech. staff AT&T Bell Labs., Holmdel, N.J., 1978-84, disting. mem. tech. staff, 1984-91; prin. tech. staff mem. AT&T Comms. Svcs., 1991-98; dir. project mgmt. VocalTec Comms., Inc., Ft. Lee, N.J., 1998-2001; dir. sys. engring. Vonage Holdings, Inc., Edison, NJ, 2001—02; dir. bus. devel. Masterson Tech., Inc., N.Y.C., NY, 2002—; tech. cons. CGS Tech. Assoc., Inselin, NJ, 2002—. Contbr. articles to profl. jours. and symposia. Vestryman, St. John's Ch., Little Silver, N.J., 1992-94, Lincroft (N.J.) Ch., 1999--. NIMH grad. fellow, 1974-78. Mem. ACM, Project Mgmt. Inst., Human Factors/Ergonomic Soc., Sigma Xi. Achievements include research on speech recognition, computer graphics and video telephony, management of large-scale telecommunications projects; leadership of startup activities for new business ventures; design of bus. processes and infrastructure for start-up ventures. Avocations: sailing, skiing, music. Home: 11 Yale Ct Eatontown NJ 07724-9727 E-mail: lsager@comcast.net.

SAGER, PHILIP TRAVIS, academic physician, cardiac electrophysiologist; b. N.Y.C., Jan. 23, 1956; s. Clifford Julius nad Ruth (Levy) S. BS in Chemistry and Biology, MIT, Cambridge, Mass., 1977; MD, Yale U., New Haven, Conn., 1982, resident, cardiology fellow, 1982-88. Diplomate Am. Bd. Internal Medicine, Am. Bd. Cardiology, AM. Bd. Cardiac Electrophysiology. Asst. prof. medicine Sch. Medicine, U. So. Calif., L.A., 1988-90, asst. dir. electrophysiology, 1988-90, dir. Pacemaker Ctr., 1988-90; asst. prof. medicine Sch. Medicine, UCLA, 1990-96, assoc. prof. of medicine, 1996—; dir. cardiac electrophysiology West L.A. VA Med. Ctr., 1990-96. Mem. cardiology adv. com. VA Adminstrn., Washington, 1990-94; cons. electrophysiology ACGME, Chgo., 1995—; vis. prof. Kern Med. Ctr., Bakersfield, Calif., 1991, 94, U. Iowa Sch. Medicine, 1994, Northwestern U. Sch. Medicine, 1994, Yale U. Sch. Medicine, 1995, U. Calif., San Francisco, 1996; co-chair NASPE EPS Fellowship Dirs. com., 1997—; invited lectr. major med. instns. and symposiums; cons. pharm. cos. Contbr. chpts. to books, numerous rsch. articles to profl. jours. of innovative rsch.; reviewer many scientific jours. Recipient many rsch. grants, including Am. Heart Assn., 1996. Fellow Am. Heart Assn. (coun. on clin. cardiology 1997—), Am. Coll. Cardiology, Am. Coll. Physicians; mem. Am. Fedn. Clin. Rsch., Nat. Assn. Pacing and Electrophysiology (program dirs. com. 1992—, govt. com. 1994—, assoc. chair program dirs. com. 1997—), Phi Beta Kappa, Alpha Omega Alpha. Avocations: bicycling, scuba diving, reading history, movies. Office: W LA VAMC-UCLA Dept 111E 11301 Wilshire Blvd Dept 111E Los Angeles CA 90073-1003 Fax: 310-470-0954. E-mail: PSAGER@UCLA.edu.

SAGER, ROBERT WENDELL, retired social work administrator; b. Schenectady, N.Y., Nov. 8, 1927; s. Clinton White and Cora Ethel (Cullings) S.; m. Clare June Sussdorff, June 16, 1956; children: Clinton White II, Susan Joy Sager Moody. BA, Colgate U., 1951; MSW, Columbia U., 1966. ACSW. Probation officer Schenectady County Probation Dept., 1955-57; psychiat. social worker Ellis Hosp., Schenectady, 1957-59; supr. psychiat. social worker Mohawk Valley Psychiat. Ctr., Utica, N.Y., 1959-90. Organist Trinity Temple of Albany; sec. World Federalist Assn., Capital Dist., 1994—; pres. Schenectady County Hist. Soc., 1995-99; treas., bd. dirs. Meml. Soc. of Mohawk Hodson Rgion, Albany, 1996—; treas., bd. dirs. NAACP, Schenectady, 1954-66, mem. 1966—; mem. Friends of Schenectady County Pub. Libr., 1987—. With U.S. Army, 1946-47. Mem. NASW, Holland Soc. of N.Y. (life), Soc. of Mayflower Descendants, Capital Dist. Geneol. Soc., Heritage Soc. of Montgomery County (bd. dirs.), Am. Legion, Lambda Chi Alpha. Republican. Unitarian Universalist. Avocations: history, music, motorcycling, antique cars, the occult. Home: 1033 Waverly Pl Schenectady NY 12308-3014

SAGER, RODERICK COOPER, retired life insurance company executive; b. Washington, May 25, 1923; s. Theron Parker and Rebecca (Ward) S.; m. Ruth Regina Ross, Sept. 2, 1947; children: Lawrence Cooper, Jonathan Ward, Timothy Charles. AB, Syracuse U., 1948, JD, 1950. Bar: N.Y. 1951, U.S. Supreme Ct. 1958; C.L.U., 1969; chartered fin. cons. Assoc. Mackenzie, Smith, Lewis, Michell and Hughes, Syracuse, 1950-62; gen. counsel Farmers and Traders Life Ins. Co., 1962-66, v.p., gen. counsel, 1966-69, sr. v.p., gen. counsel, 1969-74, exec. v.p., gen. counsel, 1974-79, pres., chief exec. officer, 1979-89, also bd. dirs., ret., 1989. Chmn. Life Ins. Council, N.Y., 1984 Trustee Jamesville-DeWitt Cen. Sch. Dist., 1956-69, Onondaga Community Coll., 1971-75; bd. dirs. N.Y. State Tchrs. Retirement System, 1977-92, Onondaga Indsl. Devel. Corp., 1984-89, Lit. Vols. of Greater Syracuse, Inc., 1990-91; trustee Rescue Mission Alliance, Syracuse, 1980-96, pres., 1985-86. 1st lt. U.S. Army, 1943-46, 51-52. Mem. Onondaga County Bar Assn., Assn. Life Ins. Counsel. Clubs: Century (Syracuse); Onondaga Golf and Country (Fayetteville, N.Y.). Lodges: Rotary. Home: 3 Wynnridge Rd Fayetteville NY 13066-2532 E-mail: rsager@twcny.rr.com.

SAGER, STEVEN TRAVIS, lawyer; b. Boston, June 3, 1957; AB, Allegheny Coll., 1979; JD cum laude, Western New Eng. Coll., 1986. Bar: Mass. 1986, N.Y. 1987, U.S. Dist. Ct. Mass. 1987, U.S. Ct. Appeals (1st cir.) 1987. Mem. staff Office of Marc Redlich, Boston, 1990—. Active Putterman Civic Assn., 1988-93, Brookline Civic Assn., 1988-93, Anti-Defamation League, Moot Ct., Friends of Beth Israel Hosp.; chmn. Young Profls. Com., 1988-90; bd. dirs. Newton Symphony Orch., v.p., 1992-93, pres., 1993-97. Mem. ABA (bus. law sect.), Mass. Bar Assn., N.Y. State Bar Assn., Boston Bar Assn., Smaller Bus. Assn. of New Eng., Metrowe St C. of C., Theta Chi. Home: 5 Janlyn Cir Westborough MA 01581-1558

SAGER, WILLIAM FREDERICK, retired chemistry educator; b. Glencoe, Ill., Jan. 22, 1918; s. Fred Anson and Alta (Stansbury) S.; m. Marilyn Olga Williams, Dec. 26, 1941; children: Karen Louise Sager Dickinson, Judith Lynn SagerPeyton), Kathryn Gwen Sager Potts. BS in Chemistry, George Washington U., 1939, MA in Organic Chemistry, 1941; PhD in Organic Chemistry, Harvard U., 1948. Research chemist The Texas Co., 1941-45; prof. chemistry George Washington U., 1948-65, U. Ill.-Chgo., 1965-86, prof. emeritus, 1986—, chmn., 1965-80. Cons. to govt. and industry, 1952—. Founder, pres. Sager Innovations, Inc. Patentee (U.S. patents on evergy saving devices.). Recipient Disting. Service award U. Ill. Alumni Assn., 1985; Guggenheim fellow, 1954-55. Mem. Am. Chem. Soc., Sigma Xi, Alpha Chi Sigma. Home: 1552 John Anderson Dr Ormond Beach FL 32176-3567 Office: Dept Chemistry U Ill-Chicago Chicago IL 60680

SAGERHOLM, JAMES ALVIN, retired naval officer; b. Uniontown, Pa., Dec. 23, 1927; s. Frithiof Norris and Margaret Blocher S.; m. Margaret Ann Herrlich, June 7, 1952; children— Lisa Marie, Ann Denise, Jeannine Louise, Mark Christian *Son, Mark Christian Sagerholm, BS, U.S. Naval Academy 1983, commissioned 2nd LT US Marine Corps, Artillery. 1985, qualified as Aerial Observer, assigned to VMO-2, Camp Pendleton, CA, flying aircrafts, light attack reconnaissance jet aircraft, deployed with VMO-2 to Okinawa 1986-87. Advanced through grades to captain killed in OV-10 training accident in California on 30 Dec 1987.* BS, U.S. Naval Acad., 1952. Commd. ensign U.S. Navy, 1952, advanced through grades to vice admiral, navigator USS Seadragon, 1965, exec. officer blue crew USS Mariano G. Vallejo, 1966-67, comdg. officer gold crew USS Kamehameha, 1968-71, head gen. purpose warfare forces group Office of Chief Naval Ops., 1971, dep. exec. dir. Chief Naval Ops. Exec. Panel, 1972, exec. sec. Chief Naval Ops. Exec. Bd., 1973, comdr. Naval Intelligence Support Ctr., 1974-75, dep. dir. naval intelligence Chief Naval Ops., 1975-76, comdr. South Atlantic Force, U.S. Atlantic Fleet, 1976-78, dir. Office of Program Appraisal, Office of Sec. Navy, 1978-81, chief naval edn. and tng. Fla., 1983-85; exec. dir. Pres. Fgn. Intelligence Adv. Bd. White House, Washington, 1981-82; ret., 1985. Chmn. bd. dirs. Piedmont Environ. Coun., 1987-89; v.p. for nat. affairs Gen. George C. Marshall Home Found., 1990-91. Bd. trustees Balt. Polytech. Inst. Found., 2000—. Decorated D.S.M., Legion of Merit, Meritorious Service medal; named Disting. Alumnus, Balt. Poly. Inst. Mem. Naval Submarine League, U.S. Naval Inst., K.C. Roman Catholic. Avocations: golf, Civil War history. Home: 414 Rockfleet Rd Unit 102 Lutherville Timonium MD 21093-7582

SAGERMAN, ROBERT HOWARD, radiation oncologist; b. N.Y.C., Jan. 23, 1930; s. Irving R. and Ethel Sagerman; m. Malyne Sagerman, Dec. 23, 1954; children: Jason E., Eric S., Evan C., Roger F. BS, NYU, 1951, MD, 1955. Diplomate Am. Bd. Radiology. Intern Meadowbrook Hosp., Mineola, N.Y., 1955-56; resident Charity Hosp., New Orleans, 1956-57; instr. Tulane U., 1956-57; resident Montefiore Hosp., Bronx, N.Y., 1959-61; asst. prof. Stanford (Calif.) U., 1961-64, Columbia U., N.Y.C., 1964-68; prof. SUNY Health Sci. Ctr., Syracuse, 1968—. Cons. radiologist Crouse Irving Meml. Hosp., Syracuse, St. Joseph's Hosp., Syracuse, Community Gen. Hosp., Syracuse, VA Hosp., Syracuse, 1968—. Author, co-editor: Radiotherapy of Intraocular and Orbital Tumors, 1993. Capt. USAF, 1957-59. Mem. Radiol. Soc. N.Am. (Erskine lectr. 1992). Office: SUNY Health Sci Ctr 750 E Adams St Syracuse NY 13210-1834 E-mail: sagermar@upstate.edu.

SAGESER, KENDALL WAYNE, mineral exploration executive; b. El Reno, Okla. s. Albert John and Louise Pauline Sageser; m. Jane E. Conrad, Mar. 28, 1959; children: Janice Lucy Runnels, Daniel Scot, David Mark. BS in Mining Engring., S.D. Sch. Mines & Tech., Rapid City, 1962, BS in Geol. Engring., 1963; MS in Geology, Stanford U., Palo Alto, Calif., 1964. Exploration geologist Shell Oil Co., Oklahoma City, 1964-65; geologist, sr. geologist U.S. Steel Corp., Pitts., 1965-72; exploration mgr. Asia Essex Minerals Co., Singapore, 1972-76; exploration mgr. U.S.A. U.S. Steel Corp., Salt Lake City, 1976-81; v.p. Essex Minerals Co., Pitts., 1981-83; v.p., sr. v.p. Santa Fe Pacific Gold Corp., Albuquerque, 1985-96; sr. assoc. Behre Dolbear & Co. Inc., Corrales, N.Mex., 1996—. Mem. Pres. Club, Rep. Party, Corrales, N.Mex., 1997-99, Rep. Senatorial Inner Cir., Corrales, 1997-99; life mem. Rep. Nat. Com., Corrales, 1995-99. Fellow Geol. Soc. Am., Soc. Econ. Geologists; mem. AIME (dir. Ctrl. N.Mex. sect. 1986-90, pres. local sect. 1988-89), Geol. Soc. Nev. Avocations: classical history, astronomy, mountain climbing, white-water canoeing, skiing. Home and Office: Behre Dolbear & Co Inc 490 Manierre Rd Corrales NM 87048-8338 E-mail: ksageser@aol.com.

SAGET, BOB, director, actor, comedian, writer; Grad. film studies, Temple U., 1978. Host 2002 Winter Olympics. Appeared at Carnegie Hall, Las Vegas, Atlantic City, The Comedy Store, The Improv, Calif.; actor (films) Critical Condition, 1986, 1998, Half Baked, 1998; (TV) Full House, 1987-95; actor, exec. prodr. Father and Scout, 1994, Jitters, 1997; dir., exec. prodr. For Hope, 1997; co-host The Morning Program, 1986; host, writer: America's Funniest Home Videos, 1989-97; dir., actor, writer: HBO Comedy Hour: In The Dream State; dir. Dirty Work, 1998, Mind of the Married Man, 2001; dir., actor Becoming Dick, 2000; actor WB series Raising Dad, 2001—. Address: Brillstein/Grey Entertainment 9150 Wilshire Blvd Ste 350 Beverly Hills CA 90212-3453

SAGHIR, ADEL JAMIL, artist, painter, sculptor; b. Beirut, Lebanon, May 27, 1930; came to U.S., 1973; s. Jamil Khalil and Aisha Rachid (Mirii) S.; m. Jindriska Antonin Moucka, Aug. 24, 1968; children: Jamil, Ryan. BA, Am. U., Beirut, 1968, diploma in tchg., 1973; MFA, Pratt Inst., 1975; postgrad., NYU, 1976-79. Asst. prof. Fine Arts Inst., Lebanese U., Beirut, 1963-73; lectr. Am. Beirut U. Coll., 1972-73; adj. prof. Western Conn. State U., Danbury, 1988—; instr. sculpture, mural painting, art history Silvermine Sch. Art, New Canaan, Conn., 1989-98. Artist various murals and tapestries. Recipient 4th prize Alexandria Biennale, Egyptian Govt., 1963, 1st prize silk tapestries Nat. Contest Lebanon, 1965, 1st prize major sculpture monuments, 1966, 1st prize City Ctr. Sculpture Contest, 1969; Fine Arts scholar, Germany, Munic Acad., 1958-60; Fulbright-Hayes fellow NYU, N.Y.C., 1973-79. Mem. Internat. Soc. Advancement of Living Traditions in Art, Washington Pl. Artists Assn. (pres. 1977-80), Lebanese Artists Assn. (v.p. 1964-73). Avocations: gardening, fishing, upland hunting. Home: 20 Newfane Rd New Fairfield CT 06812-4721 Office: Western Conn State U 181 White St Danbury CT 06810-6826 E-mail: ajsaghir@snet.net.

SAGINOR, SIDNEY V. management consultant; b. London, May 28, 1909; s. Phillip Saginor Sr. and Polly Miller; m. Ruth K. Saginor, Dec. 13, 1935; children: Mark L., Gail J. Slater. BSME, Case Res. U., 1933. Registered profl. engr.; lic. real estate broker. Estimator, engr. Johns-Manville Corp., Cleve., 1928-35; mech. engr., heat transfer specialist Carbide & Carbon Chems. Corp., 1935-39; prodn. mgr. Davey Compressor Co., 1939-41, gen. mgr., 1941-46; 1st v.p., dir. Robinson Clay Products Co., Akron, Ohio, 1946-53; v.p. tech. svcs. Gladding, McBean & Co., L.A., 1953-57, v.p. corp. tech. planning & overseas assignments, 1958-61, v.p., gen. mgr. tech. ceramics divsn., 1961-64; exec. v.p., dir. Ilco Corp. (formerly Ind. Lock Co.), Fitchburg, Mass., 1964-67, pres., CEO, 1969-73; mgmt. cons., 1967-69, 73—. Fin. advisor Federally Registered Investment Advisor, Washington, 1975—; bd. dirs., CFO San Fernando Valley Mental Health Assn., Van Nuys, Calif., 1983-93, advisor, 1983—. Bd. dirs. Fitchburg C. of C., 1964-73; chmn. indsl. comm. Fitchburg Red Cross, 1966. Lt. U.S. Army Corps Engrs., 1939-43. Recipient Cert. Merit Office Sci. R&D Com., 1945. Mem. ASME (life, award), Nat. Soc. Profl. Journalists (life), Nat. Soc. Ceramic Engrs., Am. Ceramic Soc. (Emeritus award), Indsl. Rsch. Inst., Inc., Am. Mgmt. Assn., Nat. Clay Pipe Rsch. Corp., Masons, Rotary, Jonathan Club, Sigma Delta Chi. Home and Office: 5333 Zelzah Ave # 304 Encino CA 91316

SAGMEISTER, EDWARD FRANK, retired military officer, business owner; b. N.Y.C., Dec. 10, 1939; s. Frank and Anna (Unger) S.; m. Anne Marie Ducker, Aug. 18, 1962; children: Cynthia Anne, Laura Marie, Cheryl Suzanne, Eric Edward. BS, U. San Francisco, 1962; MBA, Syracuse U., 1968; postgrad., Air Command and Staff Coll., 1977, Air War Coll., 1981. Commd. 2d lt. USAF, 1963, advanced through grades to lt. col., pers. officer, 1963, aide-de-camp, 1965; dir. pers. sys. Alaskan Air Command, 1968; sys. design and program analysis officer HQ USAF, The Pentagon, 1971; spl. asst. sec. Air Force Pers. Coun., USAF, 1975; dir. pers. programs and assignments HQUSAF Europe, 1979; Air Force dep. asst. inspector gen., 1982; ret. USAF, 1984; dir. devel. Am. Cancer Soc., Riverside, Calif., 1984-87; cons. Redlands, 1987-92; chmn. of bd., pres., CEO Hospitality Pub and Grub, Inc., San Bernardino, 1992—2002. Instr. Am. Internat. U., L.A., 1987; program dir. Am. Radio Network, L.A., 1987; ptnr., owner Midway Med. Ctr., San Bernardino, 1990-91. Foreman pro-tem San Bernardino County Grand Jury, 1990-91; mem. Redlands 2000 Com., 1988; campaign cabinet mem. Arrowhead United Way, San Bernardino, 1986-87, loaned exec., 1985; exec. dir. Crafton hills Coll. Found., Yucaipa, Calif., 1988; vol. San Bernardino County Dept. Probation, 1985-88; mem. Redlands Cmty., Chorus, 1988-90; vice-chmn., charter mem. Redlands Human Rels. Commn., 1994-97, chmn., 1996-97; mem. Redlands Youth Accountability Bd., San Bernardino County, 1994-97, treas. 1996; mem. supt.'s human rels. adv. com., Redlands Unified Sch. Dist., 1996-97; vol. Loma Linda U. Med. Ctr., 2002-; mem. Inland Master Chorale, 2001-. Mem. Ret. Officers Assn., Nat. Soc. Fundraising Execs., (dir., charter mem. Inland Empire chpt. 1987-88), Empire Singers (v.p. 1987). Republican. Roman Catholic. Avocations: travel, music, singing, tennis, reading. Home: 503 Sunnyside Ave Redlands CA 92373-5629

SAGO, JANIS LYNN, photography educator; b. St. Louis, Nov. 27, 1948; d. Bernard William and Eunice Alberta (Henry) Osthof; m. William Leo Sago Jr., Feb. 18, 1967 (dec. Mar. 1989); children: Brian William, Shelley Lynn, Carrie Renee. AA, St. Louis C.C., 1990; BA cum laude, Webster U., 1993. Office mgr. C.B. Smith Co., St. Louis, 1989—; free-lance photographer, 1990—; adj. faculty photography St. Louis C.C., 1993—, St. Charles County C.C., 1998—. Interim staff photographer St. Louis C.C., 1990; gallery asst. Webster U., St. Louis, 1993; adj. faculty photography St. Louis C.C., 1993—, St. Charles County C.C., 1998—; photography instr. Mo. Bot. Gardens, 1999—. Photographer The Webster Jour., 1992-93; photo's exhibited at May Gallery, 1993, Campus Gallery, 1996—, Martin Schweig Gallery, 1996, St. Charles County C.C., 1998—, St. Peters Cultural Art Ctr., 2002—. Mem. St. Louis Art Mus., 1994—, St. Louis Sci. Ctr., 1996-97, Mo. Bot. Gardens, 1997—; officer, asst. chief YMCA Indian Guides, St. Louis, 1989-97; vol./chair Mothers' Club, Lindbergh Schs., St. Louis, 1974-90, PTO, 1974-90. Mem. AAUW, Greater St. Louis Orchid Soc., Phi Theta Kappa. Avocations: gardening, reading, travel, music. Office: St Louis C C 11333 Big Bend Rd Saint Louis MO 63122-5720

SAH, CHIH-TANG, electrical and computer engineering educator; b. Beijing, Nov. 10, 1932; s. Adam Peng-tung and Shu-shen Huang; m. Linda Chang, Nov. 29, 1959; children: Dinah W.Y., Robert L.Y. BS Physics, BSEE, U. Ill., 1953; MSEE, Stanford U., 1954, PhD, 1956; D honoris causa, U. Leuven, Belgium, 1975. Research assoc. Stanford Electronics Lab., Palo Alto, Calif., 1956; sr. mem. tech. staff Shockley Transistor Corp., 1957-59; head, mgr. physics dept. Fairchild Semiconductor Lab., 1959-64; prof. physics and elec. engring. U. Ill., Urbana, 1962-88, dir. Ill. Solid State Electronics Lab.; Pittman Eminent Scholar chair, grad. research prof., chief scientist Coll. Engring. U. Fla., Gainesville, 1988—. Cons. Jet Propulsion Lab., Dept. Energy, Pasadena, Calif., 1976-85, Harry Diamond Lab., Washington, 1974-75, IBM Corp., N.Y, numerous other electronics firms 1964-88; advisor Intel Corp., Oreg., Calif., other semicondr. mfrs., 1988—; program dir. 1st generation Si VLSI tech. Fairchild Corp., 1959-64. Author: Fundamentals of Solid-State Electronics, 1991, Transistor Reliability in Fundamentals of Solid-State Electronics—Solution Manual, 1996; co-developer Complementary Metal-Oxide Semiconductor circuit, 1962, other tech. discoveries and inventions; co-discoverer Si P-N junction diode phenomena (Sah-Noyce-Shockley Theory), 1957; co-inventor deep-level transient spectroscopy (Sah, Tasch, Yau), 1966-71, and DVIC diagnosis for deep-submicron transistor design and reliability (Sah, Neugroschel), 1996; contbr. 250 articles to profl. jours. Recipient first high tech. award Asian American Mfg. Assn., 1982; named 1 of 1000 World's Most Cited Scientists, 1965-78. Fellow IEEE (life, IRE Browder J. Thompson prize 1963, J.J. Ebers award 1980, Jack Morton award 1989), AAAS, Am. Physical Soc., Franklin Inst. (life mem., Cert. of Merit award 1975); mem. Nat. Acad. Engring., Academia Sinica (academician). Office: U Fla 216 Larsen Hall Gainesville FL 32611-6200

SAH, RAAJ KUMAR, economist, consultant, educator; b. Muzaffarpur, Bihar, India, Oct. 18, 1952; came to U.S., 1976; m. Cynthia Serina Tabios, June 22, 1983; 1 child, Jaya T. MBA, Indian Inst. Mgmt., Ahmedabad, India, 1975; PhD in Econs., U. Pa., 1980. Ford asst. prof. MIT, Cambridge, 1980-82; vis. asst. prof. U. Pa., Phila., 1982-84; from asst. to assoc. prof. Yale U., New Haven, 1984-91; prof. U. Chgo., 1990—. John M. Olin vis. prof. Princeton (N.J.) U., 1987-88; vis. assoc. prof. U. Chgo., 1989-90; advisor and cons. to numerous corps. and fin. instns. Contbr. numerous articles in field to scholarly and profl. jours. Office: U Chgo Sch Pub Policy 1155 E 60th St Chicago IL 60637-2745

SAHA, ARUN KUMAR, engineering educator, researcher; b. Gauripur, Assam, India, May 7, 1967; s. Ramani Mohan and Arati Saha; m. Mira Saha, Apr. 26, 1970. B Mech. Engring., Gauhati U., Assam, India, 1990; M Mech. Tech. , Indian Inst. Tech. , Kanpur, India, 1994; PhD , Indian Inst. of Tech. Kanpur, India, 1999. Lectr. Jorhat Engring. Coll., Jorhat, India, 1992; asst. exec. engr. Oil & Natural Gas Corp., Sibsagar, India, 1993; post doctoral rsch. assoc. SUNY, Stony Brook, NY, 1999—2000, La. State U., Baton Rouge, 2000—. Contbr. chapters to books, articles to profl. jours. and confs. (Best Paper Award, 2000). Avocations: painting, art, gardening.

SAHA, BADAL CHANDRA, biochemist; b. Jamurki, Tangail, Bangladesh, July 1, 1949; came to U.S., 1984, naturalized; s. Kalachand and Milan (Deshmukhya) S.; m. Sarabi Roychowdhury, June 7, 1976; children: Susmita, Saroj. BS with honors, Dhaka U., Bangladesh, 1969, MS, 1970, Kyushu U., Fukuoka, Japan, 1981, PhD, 1984. Biochemist Dhaka (Bangladesh) Med. Coll. Hosp., 1972-73; rsch. scholar Dhaka U., 1973-74; lectr. Bangladesh Agrl. U., Mymensingh, 1974-75, asst. prof., 1975-79; rsch. assoc. U. Md., College Park, 1984-85, Mich. State U., East Lansing, 1985-86; rsch. scientist Mich. Biotech. Inst., Lansing, 1986-92; vis. scientist, rsch. chemist USDA Agrl. Rsch. Svc., Peoria, Ill., 1992—. Asst. adj. prof. Mich. State U., East Lansing, 1988-92. Author: Clostridia, 1989, Biocatalysis, 1990, (with others) Mixed Cultures in Biotechnology, 1991; editor: Fuels and Chemicals from Biomass, 1997, Applied Biocatalysis in Specialty Chemicals and Pharmaceuticals, 2000; mem. editl. bd. Jour. Indsl. Microbiology and Biotech.; asst. editor World Jour. Microbiology and Biotech.; contbr. some 100 articles to profl. jours. including Trends in Biotech., Biochem. Jour., Applied Environ. Microbiology, others; patentee in field. Recipient UNESCO fellowship Japanese Nat. Commn. for UNESCO, 1977-78, Rsch. scholarship Japanese Govt., 1979-84, Grad. scholarship Dhaka U., 1969-70, Dhaka Bd. scholarships, 1962-69. Mem. AAAS, Am. Chem. Soc. (chmn. Peoria sect.), Am. Soc. for Microbiology, Soc. for Indsl. Microbiology (chmn. awards com.), Japan Soc. for Biosci., Biotech. and Agrochemistry. Hindu. Home: 1519 W Queens Court Rd Peoria IL 61614-1705 Office: USDA-ARS Nat Ctr. for Agrl Utilization Rsch 1815 N University St Peoria IL 61604-3902

SAHA, BIDHAN CHANDRA, physics educator; b. Rangunia, Chittagong, Bangladesh, Sept. 29, 1946; came to U.S., 1981; s. Chinta Haran and Charu Bala S.; m. Krishna Chakraborty, June 29, 1979; 1 child, Paban. BS, Dhaka U., Bangladesh, 1966; MS, Rajshahi U., Bangladesh, 1969; PhD, Kolkata U., India, 1976. Postdoctoral fellow Indian Assn. Cultivation Sci., 1976-78; rsch. assoc. Flinders U., Adelaide, Australia, 1979-80, Yale U., New Haven, 1981; rsch. scientist U. Okla., Norman, 1982-88; asst. prof. Fla. A&M U., Tallahassee, 1994-2000, assoc. prof., 2000—01, prof., 2002—. Pres. Bangladesh Assn. Tallahassee, 1998. Fellow, Indian Assn. for the Cultivation of Sci., 1976—78,

Welch Found. fellow, Rice U., 1989—93; grantee, NASA, 1997, 2000, Rsch. Corp., Tucson, 1998, NSF-CREST, 1998, Army HPCRC, 2000. Mem. Am. Phys. Soc., Indian Assn. for the Cultivation of Sci. (life), Sigma Xi. Avocations: gardening, fishing, outdoor sports. Office: Fla A&M U Dept Physics 301B FSH Rsch Bldg Tallahassee FL 32307 E-mail: saha@cennas.nhmfl.gov.

SAHA, PAUL SANTOSH, physician; b. Khulna, Bangladesh, June 21, 1941; came to U.S., 1969; s. Matilal and Gurudasi Saha; m. Dipika Saha, Feb. 3, 1967; children: Charles, Edward, Daniel. MB BS, Dacca Med. Coll., 1964; MS in Nutrition, Columbia U., 1969. Diplomate Am. Bd. Internal Medicine. Intern in internal medicine Beekman Downtown Hosp., N.Y.C., 1970-71, resident in medicine, 1971-74; fellow in hematology St. Vincent's Hosp. and Med. Ctr., 1974-76; vol. assoc. attending physician, cons. hematology NYU Downtown Hosp., 1976-92; attending cons. hematology L.I. Coll. Hosp., Bklyn., 1982-92, hon. attending cons.hematology, 1999—; pvt. practice, 1976—; HMO physician in internal medicine N.Y. Hotel Trade Coun. and Hotel Trade Assn. N.Y., N.Y.C., 1979—. Fellow ACP. Republican. Avocations: attending professional meetings, travel, reading medical journals. Home: 510 Mountainview Ave Staten Island NY 10314-6483

SAHAI, HARDEO, medical statistics educator; b. Bahraich, India, Jan. 10, 1942; m. Lillian Sahai, Dec. 28, 1973; 3 children. BS in Math., Stats. and Physics, Lucknow U., India, 1962; MS in Math., Banaras U., Varanasi, India, 1964; MS in Math. Stats., U. Chgo., 1968; PhD in Stats., U. Ky., 1971. Lectr. in math. and stats. Banaras U., Varanasi, India, 1964-65; asst. stats. officer Durgapur Steel Plant, Durgapur West Bengal, India, 1965; statistician Rsch. and Planning div. Blue Cross Assn., Chgo., 1966; statis. programmer Cleft Palate Ctr., U. Ill., 1967, Chgo. Health Rsch. Found., 1968; mgmt. scientist Mgmt. Systems Devel. Dept. Burroughs Corp., Detroit, 1971-72; from asst. prof. to prof. dept. math. U. P.R., Mayaguez, 1972-82; vis. research prof. Dept. Stats. and Applied Math. Fed. U. of Ceara, Brazil, 1978-79; sr. research statistician Travenol Labs., Inc., Round Lake, Ill., 1982-83; chief statistician U.S. Army Hqrs., Ft. Sheridan, 1983-84; sr. math. statistician U.S. Bur. of Census Dept. of Commerce, Washington, 1984-85; sr. ops. rsch. analyst Def. Logistics Agy. Dept. Def., Chgo., 1985-86; prof. Dept. Biostats. and Epidemiology U. P.R. Med. Scis., San Juan, 1986—. Cons. P.R. Univ Cons., P.R. Driving Safety Evaluation Project, Water Resources Rsch. Inst., Travenol Labs., Campo Rico, P.R., U.S. Bur. Census, Washington, Lawrence Livermore Nat. Lab., Calif., others; vis. prof. U. Granada, Spain, U. Veracruzana, Mex., patrimonial prof. stats., 1997—; vis. prof. U. Nacional de Colombia, U. Nacional de Trujillo, Peru, 1993-94, hon. prof. stats., 1994—; adj. prof. dept. math. U. P.R. Natural Scis. Faculty, 1995—; Patrimonial prof. stafs U. Veracruzana, 1997—. Author: Statistics and Probability: Learning Module, 1984; author: (with Jose Berrios) A Dictionary of Statistical Scientific and Technical Terms: English-Spanish and Spanish-English, 1981, (with Wilfredo Martinez) Statistical Tables and Formulas for the Biological Social and Physical Sciences, 1996, (with Anwer Khurshid) Statistics in Epidemiology: Methods, Techniques and Applications, 1996, (with Satish C. Misra and Michael Graham) Quotations on Probability and Statistics with Illustrations, 2000, (with Anwer Khurshid) A Pocket Dictionary of Statistics, 2000, (with Mohammad I. Ageel) The Analysis of Variance: Fixed, Random and Mixed Models, 2000, (with Wilfredo Martnez) Statistical Glossary: English-Spanish, 2000, (with Hector W. Colon) Statistics Vocabulary for Health Professionals, 2000, (with Mario M. Ojeda) Un Manual de Distribuciones t, x2y F Centrales Y No Centrales, 2000, (with Mario M. Ojeda) A Glossary of Computer and Management Terms: English/Spanish, 2000, (with Mario M. Ojeda) Comparisons of Approximations to the Percentiles of Noncentral t, x2 and F Distributions, 2001, (with A. Khurshid) Pocket Dictionary of Statistics, 2001, Noncentral t, x2y and F Distributions, 1998, Analysis of Variance for Random Models, Vol. 1: Balanced Data and Vol. 2: Unbalanced Data; mem. editl. bd. Sociedad Colombiana de Matematicas, P.R. Health Scis. Jour.; contbr. editor Current Index to Stats.; reviewer Collegiate Microcomputer, Comm. in Statistics, Indian Jour. Stats., Jour. Royal Statis. Soc. (series D, The Statistician), New Zealand Statistician, Biometrics, Can. Jour. Stats., Technometrics, Problems, Resources and Issues in Math. Undergrad. Studies; contbr. more than 150 articles and papers to profl. and sci. jours., numerous articles to tech. mags. Active Dept. Consumer Affairs Svcs. Commonwealth of P.R., San Juan, Dept. Anti-Addiction Svcs., Commonwealth of P.R., San Juan., Inst. of AIDS, Municipality of San Juan, VA Med. Ctr. of San Juan, Caribbean Primate Rsch. Ctr., Ctr. Addiction Studies Caribbean Ctrl. U. Recipient Dept. Army Cert. Achievement award, 1984, U. Ky. Outstanding Alumnus award, 1993, medal of honor U. Granada, 1994, plaque of honor U. Nacional de Trujillo, 1994; fellow Coun. Sci. and Indsl. Rsch., 1964-65, U. Chgo., 1965-68, Harvard U., 1979, Fulbright Found., 1982; U.P. Bd. Merit scholar, 1957-59, Govt. India Merit scholar, 1959-64; grantee NSF, 1974-77, NIMH, 1987-90, 91—, NIDA, 1991—. Fellow AAAS, Am. Coll. Epidemiology, Inst. Statisticians (charter statistician), Inst. Math. and Its Applications (charter mathematician), N.Y. Acad. Scis., Royal Statis. Soc.; mem. Internat. Statis. Inst., Internat. Assn. Tchg. Stats., Soc. Epidemiol. Rsch., Inst. Math. Stats., Bernouilli Soc. for Math. Stats. and Probability, Internat. Biometric Soc., Am. Soc. for Quality Control, Am. Stats. Assn., Japan Statis. Soc., Can. Statis. Soc., Inter-Am. Statis. Inst., Internat. Assn. Statis. Computing, Sch. Sci. and Math. Assn., Sigma Xi. Avocations: religious studies, philosophy, reading, gardening. Home: Urb Mayaguez Terrace 7083 Calle B Gaudier Texidor Mayaguez PR 00682-6617 E-mail: hsahai@centennialpr.net.

SAHAKIAN, ALAN VARTERES, electrical engineer, educator; b. L.I., N.Y., Oct. 21, 1954; s. Harold and Mariam Varteres (Garoukian) S.; m. Jill M. Morrison, Aug. 14, 1982. B.S. in Applied Sci. and Physics, U. Wis.-Parkside, 1976; M.S. in Elec. Engring., U. Wis.-Madison, 1979, Ph.D. in Elec. Engring., 1984. Research asst. elec. and computer engring. U. Wis.-Madison, 1978-79, 80-84; sr. elec. engr. Medtronic, Inc., Mpls., 1979-80; cons. Applied Electronics Cons., Madison, 1982-84; assoc. prof. elec. engring. and computer sci. Northwestern U., Evanston, Ill., 1984— . Co-author: Design of Microcomputer-Based Medical Instruments, 1981, Russian edit., 1983. Contbr. articles to profl. jours. Vol. life saver-water safety instr. ARC, Madison, 1973. Mem. IEEE, Sigma Xi. Avocations: ham radio, watchmaking, microscopy, photography. Office: Northwestern Univ Dept Elec Engring Computer Scis Tech Inst Sheridan Rd Evanston IL 60201

SAHANEK, TATANA, librarian, editor; b. Nov. 2, 1922; naturalized, 1969; d. Emanuel and Frances (Blovsky) S. JUDr, Masaryk U., Brno, Czechoslovakia, 1947; BLS, U. Toronto, Ont., Can., 1953; PhD, U. Tex., 1973. Cataloger Toronto Pub. Libr., 1953-55; law libr., gen. reference libr. Ont. Legis. Libr., Toronto, 1956-61; head catalog and classification divsn. Harvard Law Sch. Libr., Cambridge, Mass., 1962-65; head catalog dept. Law Libr. U. Mich., Ann Arbor, 1965-66; translator, interpreter Dow Chem. Internat., Midland, Mich., 1967-68; libr.-translator Dow Chem. Co., Freeport, Tex., 1968-70; asst. libr. Antioch Sch. Law, Washington, 1972-74; editor index legal periodicals H. W. Wilson Co., Bronx, N.Y., 1974-78; coord. Saginaw (Mich.) Med. Ctr., 1978-79; acquisitions libr. Exec. Office of Pres. Info. Ctr., Washington, 1980—. Author: Entries for Provincial Publications, Province of Ontario, 1867-1960, 1960. Recipient Subvention Fund award U. Tex. Grad. Sch., 1972. Mem. ALA, Assn. Am. Law Librs., Spl. Librs. Assn., Can. Libr. Assn., Ont. Libr. Assn., Czechoslovak Soc. Arts and Scis, Worldwide Sportsmen's Club. Home: 205 S Yoakum Pky Apt 1602 Alexandria VA 22304-3840 Office: New Exec Office Bldg Washington DC 20503-0001

SAHATJIAN, MANIK, nurse, psychologist; b. Tabris, Iran, July 24, 1921; came to U.S., 1951; d. Dicran and Shushanig (Der-Galustian) Mnatzaganian; m. George Sahatjian, Jan. 21, 1954; children: Robert, Edwin. Nursing Cert., Am. Mission Hosps.-Boston U., 1954; BA in Psychology, San Jose State U., 1974, MA in Psychology, 1979. RN, Calif. Head nurse Am. Mission Hosp., Tabris, 1945-46; charge nurse Banke-Melli Hosp., Tehran, 1946-51; vis. nurse Vis. Nurse Assn., Oakland, Calif., 1956-57; research asst. Stanford U., 1979-81, Palo Alto (Calif.) Med. Research Found., 1981-84; documentation supr. Bethesda Convalescent Ctr., Los Gatos, Calif., 1985-86; sr. outreach worker City of Fremont (Calif.) Human Svcs., 1987-90, case mgr., 1990-97; ret., 1997. Guest rsch. asst. NASA Ames Lab., Mountain View, Calif., summers 1978, 79. Author (with others) psychol. research reports. Mentor elem. sch. children., pro bono tchg./counseling for srs. who are home bound, Bay Area, Calif., 1999—; pro bono tchr. peer counseling trainers for srs. Armenian Cmty. Santa Clara, Calif., St. Andrew Ch. Fulbright scholar, 1951; Iran Found. scholar, 1953. Mem. AAUW, Western Psychol. Assn., Am. Assn. Sr. Counseling. Democrat. Mem. St. Andrew Armenian Church. Avocations: oil painting, classic dance. Home: 339 Starlite Way Fremont CA 94539-7642

SAHATJIAN, RONALD ALEXANDER, science foundation executive; b. Cambridge, Mass., Oct. 1, 1942; s. Vartan and Roxy (Abrahamian) S.; m. Jean Khachadoorian, July 15, 1966; 1 child, Jennifer. BS in Chemistry, Tufts U., 1964; MS in Chemistry, U. Mass., 1968, PhD in Chemistry, 1969. Scientist color photographic rsch. lab. Polaroid Corp., Cambridge, 1971-73, sr. scientist color photograhic rsch. lab., 1973-75, sr. rsch. group leader photographic/optical materials, 1976-79, program mgr. polacolor transparency projects, 1979-81, mgr. applications rsch. lab., 1980-84; dir. R & D Chem. Fabrics Corp., Merrimack, N.H., 1984-87; v.p. corp. tech. Boston Sci. Corp., Watertown, Mass., 1987—. Mem. adv. bd. Franklin Inst., Boston, 1989—. Contbr. articles to Jour. Polymer Sci., Macromolecules, Radiology. Fellow Am. Inst. Chemists; mem. ASTM, Radiol. Soc. N.Am., Watertown C. of C. (bd. dirs. 1991—). Achievements include 58 U.S. and internat. patents. Home: 29 Saddle Club Rd Lexington MA 02420-2121 Office: Boston Sci Corp 1 Boston Scientific Pl Natick MA 01760-1536 E-mail: sahatjian@bsci.com.

SAHGAL, RANJIT, financial executive; b. Allahabad, India, Nov. 22, 1951; came to U.S., 1974; s. Gautam and Nayantara (Pandit) S.; m. Franca Dal Bianco, June 10, 1975; children: Gautam Giorgio, Giorgio Gautam. BA with honors in Econs., U. Bombay (India), 1974. With Ciba-Geigy Corp., 1974—, cost adminstr. controller's dept. N.Y., 1980-81, mgr. fin. controls treas. dept., 1981-84, mgr. treasury planning and analysis, 1984-85, mgr. fin. acctg. and control support, 1985-87, dir. mgmt. acctg. systems and devel., controller's dept., 1987-90, dir. spl. situation analysis Saronno, Italy, 1990-91, project mgr. Basle, Switzerland, 1991-92, head fin. and control, Europe Switzerland, 1992—; head of fin. Novartis (Italy) Spa, 1996-2001; head group fin. planning Syngenta AG, Basle, 2001—. Mem. Inst. Mgmt. Acctg. E-mail. E-mail: ranjit.sahgal@syngenta.com.

SAHID, JOSEPH ROBERT, lawyer; b. Paterson, N.J., Feb. 14, 1944; s. Joseph James and Helen (Vitale) Sahid; m. Serra Yavuz; children: Annunziata, Joseph, Olivia. BS, Rutgers U., 1965; LLB, U. Va., 1968. Bar: N.Y. 1973, U.S. Dist. Ct. N.Y., U.S. Ct. Appeals (2d and 3d cirs.), U.S. Supreme Ct. Staff mem. Nat. Commn. on Causes and Prevention of Violence, Washington, 1968-69; cons. Pres.'s Commn. on Campus Unrest, 1970; assoc. Cravath, Swaine & Moore, N.Y.C., 1972-77, ptnr., 1977-93, cons., 1994-97; ptnr. Barrack, Rodos & Bacine, 1994-96; pvt. practice, 1996—. Mediator U.S. Dist. Ct. (so. dist.) N.Y., N.Y. Civil Ct.; arbitrator N.Y. cts. Author: (book) Rights in Concord, 1969; co-author: Law and Order Reconsidered, 1969; contbr. articles to profl. jours. Lt. USCG, 1968—72. Mem.: ABA, Assn. of the Bar of the City of N.Y. (profl. discipline com.), N.Y. State Bar Assn. (profl. discipline com.). Address: 845 3rd Ave Fl 20 New York NY 10022-6601 E-mail: sahid@att.net.

SAHIM, SOLEIMAN, artist; b. Hamedan, Iran, Dec. 24, 1931; s. Habib and Rohangiz Sahim; children: David, Jonathan, Susannah. BS in Accounting, Golden Gate U., San Francisco, 1968—74; art student, Tehran Acad. Art, Iran. Cost accountant Peplinski Electronic, San Jose, Calif., 1999—2000; sr accountant Pemstar, 2000—01. Cost/schedule analyst Westinghouse, Sunnyvale, Calif. (Award for the best oil painting, 1964). Mem.: Villages Art Club. Home: 4152 Loganberry Drive San Jose CA 95121-1133 Personal E-mail: solsahim@earthlink.net. Business E-Mail: solsahim@earthlink.net.

SAHLFELD BUNGER, KIMBERLY KATHERINE, speech language pathologist; b. Big Spring, Tex., Sept. 23, 1965; d. Robert F. and Janice M. (Miller) Sahlfeld; m. Robert Lee Bunger, July 15, 1989; children: Cory L., Cody L. B of Gen. Studies, U. Kans., 1987; MS in Comm. Disorders, U. Vt., 1988. Speech lang. pathologist Des Moines Public Schs., 1989-91, Devereaux Hosp., Melbourne, Fla., 1991-92, Brevard County Sch. System, Viera, 1992-95; PRN, speech lang. pathologist St. Francis Hosp., Cape Girardeau, Mo., 1995-96; pvt. practice Whitewater, 1996—. Cons., speech lang. pathologist Chaffee (Mo.) Public Schs., 1997; chmn. devel. dirs. com. Fla. SLHA, 1992-94. Mem. St. Ambrose Cath. Ch., Chaffee, 1995-97, St. Ambrose Ladies Orgn., 1995-97, Immaculate Conception Cath. Ch., 1997—. Fellowship U. Vt., 1987-88; Nancy Miller Martin scholarship U. Kans., 1988, Harbaugh scholarship Harbaugh Found., 1984, Loyd E. Emery scholarship, 1984. Mem. Am. Speech Lang. and Hearing Assn. Avocations: reading, attending sporting events, family. Home and Office: 262 County Road 377 Whitewater MO 63785-5965

SAHLIN, ANNIE MALORY, bookkeeping professional, photographer; b. Princeton, N.J., June 14, 1948; d. John C. and Malory (Campbell) Ausland; m. Richard Sahlin, Sept. 1977 (div. Dec. 1985). BA in Anthropology, U. Md., 1971; MA in Guidance and Counseling, U. N.Mex., 1977; postgrad., Gallaudet U., 1987. Counselor various youth agys., Albuquerque, Santa Fe, 1976-80; bookkeeper Agua Fria Nursery, Santa Fe, 1980-83, James Reid Ltd., Santa Fe, 1984-88; prin. Annie's In Bus., 1989—; photographer Nat. Mus. Am. History-Smithsonian Instn., Washington, 1991—. Photographs appear in Am. Encounters exhibit Smithsonian Instn., 1992—, numerous books and articles; participant group exhbns., Santa Fe, 1988—. Big sister N.Mex. Sch. for Deaf, Santa Fe, 1986-92. Mem. Phi Beta Kappa. Avocations: fishing, crafts, dogs.

SAHLSTROM, E(LMER) B(ERARD), retired lawyer; b. Seattle, Feb. 25, 1918; s. August Waldimer and Alma Carolyn (Ostrom) S.; m. Phyllis May Horstman, June 18, 1946; children: Gary Bernard, Cheryl Linn Sahlstrom Monohan, Gregory Lane. BS, U. Oreg., 1945, JD, 1947. Bar: Oreg. 1947, U.S. Dist. Ct. Oreg. 1948, U.S. Dist. Ct. Hawaii, 1961, U.S. Ct. Appeals (9th cir.), 1950, U.S. Supreme Ct. 1977; CPA, Oreg. Acct. Haskins & Sells, N.Y.C., 1941-44; mem. Thompson & Sahlstrom, Eugene, Oreg., 1947-57, Sahlstrom, Lombard, Starr & Vinson, and predecessor, Eugene, 1957-76, Sahlstrom & Lombard, Eugene, 1976-78; sole practice, 1978-80; ptnr. Sahlstrom & Dugdale, 1980—. Bd. visitors U. Oreg. Law Sch., 1977-79, 92—. Mem. ATLA (1st v.p. western regional conf. 1954, 4th v.p. conf. 1956, dir. 1955-56, v.p. Oreg. chpt. 1970-71, pres. So. Oreg. chpt. 1972-74), ABA, Oreg. State Bar (com. taxations, unauthorized practice of law, procedure and practice, CLE, coun. on ct. procedures), Am. Judicature Soc., Assn. Attys. and CPA's, U. Oreg. Sch. Law Alumni Assn. (bd. dirs., pres.), C. of C., Country Club, Town Club (dir. 1970-71, pres. 1978) (Eugene), Multnomah Club (Portland), Elks, Sister Theodore Marie Soc., Order of the Antelope, Order of the Buggy Ride, Phi Alpha Delta, Beta Alpha Psi. Home: 745 Sand Ave Eugene OR 97401-6032

SAHOO, RAMENDRA KUMAR, engineer, researcher; b. Nayagarh, Orissa, India; PhD, SUNY, Stony Brook, 1998. Asst. mgr. Tata Engring., Pune, India, 1992-95; cons. IBM, Poughkeepsie, NY, 1998—99, scientist T.J. Watson Rsch. Ctr. Yorktown, N.Y., 1999—. Mem. IEEE Computer Soc., ASME (assoc.).

SAHOTA, GURCHARN SINGH, mechanical engineer; b. Talwandi Jattan, Punjab, India, Jan. 4, 1940; came to U.S., 1971; naturalized, 1980; s. Karam Singh and Amar Kaur (Nijjar) S.; m. Gurvindar Kaur Johal, May 4, 1966 (dec. Mar. 1978); 1 child, Saryadvinder Singh; m. Kamaljit Kaur Grewal, Jan. 10, 1979; children: Parmeet Kaur, Sonia K. BSME, Punjab U., 1957-61; MSME, N.J. Inst. Tech., 1975-77. Engr. Heavy Elecs., Bhopal, India, 1962-70; mfg. engr. Engelhard Industries, Union, N.J., 1974-76; from sr. plant engr. to supr. plant engring. group Am. Cyanamid Co., Stamford, Conn., 1976-93; mgr. plant engring. Cytec Industries Inc., 1994—. Home: 34 Duke Dr Stamford CT 06905-1017 Office: Cytec Industries Inc 1937 W Main St Stamford CT 06902-4516 E-mail: gurcharn_s._sahota@st.cytec.com.

SAHR, MORRIS GALLUP, financial planner; b. Schenectady, Nov. 28, 1928; s. Nathan and Esther (Gallup) S.; m. Sarah Diane Eisenberg, Dec. 23, 1956; children: Evelyn, David, Janet. AB, U. Oreg., 1951, MA, 1953; PhD, Calif. Open U., Oakland, 1978. CFP. Pres. Deposit Mgmt. Svc., Inc., Palmyra, Va., 1978—. Pres. Am. Coll. Funding. Author: Nine Ways to Beat the High Cost of College, 1999; co-author: Your Book of Financial Planning, 1983, Encyclopedia of Financial Planning, 1984, The Financial Planner, 1986, Financial Planning Can Make You Rich, 1987. Chmn. Fairfax County Planning Commn., 1964-68; del. White House Conf. on Aging, 1980, U.S. Congl. Adv. Bd., 1984-87; bd. dirs. Fairfax Indsl. Devel. Authority, 1985-95; adjudicator Am. Arbitration Assn., 1988-99; del to China, People to People Amb. Program, 2000. Recipient award Danforth Found.; named 1 of Top 200 Planners in U.S., Money Mag.; hon. fellow Kennedy Libr., 1985; Paul Harris fellow, 1989. Mem. Internat. Assn. Fin. Planning (founder, 1st pres. Metro Washington chpt.), Inst. Cert. Fin. Planners (nat. govt. affairs com.), Am. Assn. Practicing Fin. Planners (past pres.), Rotary (pres. Fairfax 1984-85, Srs. Project Internat. award). Home and Office: DMS Inc ACF 61 Wildwood Dr Palmyra VA 22963-2225

SAIA, DIANE PLEVOCK DIPIERO, nutritionist, educator, legal association administrator; b. Oct. 2, 1941; d. Charles and Monica (Alexandravich) Plevock; married; 1 child David. BS, Framingham (Mass.) State Coll., 1962; MS, Simmons Coll., Boston, 1969; doctoral candidate, U. Mass., 1974—75. Field nutritionist Mass. Dept. Edn., Boston, 1962—64; field cons., sch. program coord. New Eng. Dairy and Food Coun., 1964—67, sr. staff and nutrition edn. cons., program coord. Springfield, 1970—83; pres. Food/Nutrition Consignments, 1967—70; tchr. Weymouth (Mass.) Schs., 1967—70; mem. faculty Springfield Coll., 1970—, assoc. prof. nutrition, 1970—; pres. Food and Nutrition Consignments, 1979—. Mem. faculty, cons. Baystate Med. Ctr., Springfield; mem. faculty Western N.E. Coll., 1982—84; legal adminstr. SAIA Law Offices, 1984—; host radio show Law Talk, 1997—; prodr. TV shows, radio and consumer edn. programs. Mem.: ATLA, Assn. Legal Adminstrs., Sales and Mktg. Execs., Mass. Home Econs. Assn. (exec. bd. 1972—, pres. 1978—79), New Eng. Pub. Health Assn., Mass. Bar Assn., Am. Assn. Famly and Consumer Scis., Valley Press Club (assoc. dir. 1976—79, chmn. scholarship ball 1977—79). Roman Catholic. Home: 502 Frank Smith Rd Longmeadow MA 01106-2928 Office: 106 State St Springfield MA 01103-2034

SAIAH, EDDINE MK, SR. research scientist; b. Ain Temouchent, Apr. 12, 1967; came to U.S., 1993; M. Pierre and Marie Curie U., 1989, PhD, 1992. Rsch. asst. Cancer Rsch. Inst., Paris, 1989-93; rsch. fellow Mayo Clinic, Jacksonville, Fla., 1993-94, Merck-Sigma Italy, Rome, 1994-95; rsch. scientist U. Miss., Oxford, 1995-96, Helios Pharm., Louisville, 1996-98, CombiChem Inc., San Diego, 1998—. Contbr. articles to Jour. Medicinal Chem., Jour. Organic Chem. Fellow Elso Univ. Pardee Found., 1995. Mem. Am. Chem. Soc., Am. Assn. Advancement Sci., Mayo Alumni Assn., Rho Chi, Sigma Xi. Achievements include new findings in the field of cocaine addication, using robotics to prepare new drugs for healing, and estrogen mimics for the treatment of cancer. Office: CombiChem Inc 4570 Executive Dr Ste 400 San Diego CA 92121-3074 E-mail: esaiah@aol.com.

SAIAKHOV, ROUSTEM DAMIROVICH, chemist, consultant; b. Kazan, Tatarstan, Russia, Aug. 20, 1965; s. Lev Pavlovich Spiridonov (Stepfather) and Asija Vildanovna Spiridonova; m. Natalia Michailovna Makarova; 1 child Alina. PhD, Kazan (Russia) State U., 1990; MSc in Chemistry, Kazan (Russia) State University, 1987. Rsch. asst. Organoelement Compounds Lab., Kazan State U., 1990—91, rsch. assoc., 1991—95; scientist Organoelement Compounds Lab., Kazan State U., 1996—97; organic chemist Ctr. Molecular and Macromolecular Studies of the Polish Acad. Scis., Lodz, Poland, 1995—96; postdoctoral rsch. assoc. Case Western Res. U., Cleve., 1997—2000; computational chemist Multicase Inc., Beachwood, 2000—. Recipient NIH SBIR award, 2001, 2002. Mem.: AAAS, N.Y. Acad. Scis., Am. Chem. Soc. Avocation: martial arts. Home: #330A 446 Richmond Park E Dr Cleveland OH 44143 Office: Multicase Inc 23811 Chagrin Blvd Ste 305 Beachwood OH 44122 Home Fax: 216-831-3742; Office Fax: 216-831-3742. Personal E-mail: saiakhov@multicase.com. Business E-Mail: saiakhov@multicase.com.

SAID, CHRISTINE, city official; b. L.A., Sept. 29, 1975; d. Nader Armia and Mona (Marcos) Said. BS in Urban Planning, Calif. Poly., Pomona, 1997. Redevel. project mgr. City of Moreno Valley, Calif., 1998-99; intern City of Alhambra, 1997-98, redevel. project mgr., 1999—2001, asst. to city mgr., 2001—. Advisor Better Moreno Valley, 1998-99. Mem., exhibitor San Gabriel Cities Econ. Partnership, 1999—. Mem. Internat. Coun. Shopping Ctrs. (exhibitor 1999—), Calif. Redevel. Assn. Office: City of Alhambra 111 S 1st St Alhambra CA 91801

SAID, CLIFFORD EVERETT, seminar company executive, speaker, author; b. Dedham, Iowa, Dec. 6, 1937; s. Clifford William and Marjorie Lucille (Homrighouse) S.; m. Mildred Ann Hoyt, Apr. 13, 1958; children: Cynthia L. Said Mason, Tammara J. Said Schuett. Grad. high sch., Scranton, Iowa. Salesman Matt Furniture Co., Ft. Dodge, Iowa, 1960-66, Koos Bros. Carpet, Rahway, N.J., 1966-68; sales mgr. Matt Furniture Co., Ft. Dodge, 1968-70, gen. mgr. Sioux City, Iowa, 1970-73; chief exec. officr Wayne Jones Furniture, LeMars, 1973-75; chief exec. officer, owner Cliff & Millies Furniture, Jefferson, 1975-79; account exec. Herrigan Distbrs., Des Moines, 1979-85; pres. Cliff Said Seminars, Jefferson, Iowa, 1985—. Chmn. Retail Bur., Jefferson, 1976-78; continuing edn. provider Iowa Bd. Nursing, Des Moines, 1989-93. Actor, mem. reading com. Community Theatre, Jefferson, 1975-79; co-chmn. Greene County Compensation Bd., 1987—; chmn. membership com. Iowa Elks Assn., 1993—; bd. dirs. Creative Arts Coun.; ordained deacon and elder, lay pastor and Sunday sch. tchr. Recipient Disting. Svc. award Iowa Sheriffs Assn., 1987. Mem. Iowa Hawkeye Floor Covering Assn. (pres. 1981-85, editor newsletter 1981-85), Jefferson C. of C. (assoc.), Elks (Elk of Yr. 1991, chmn. mem. com.). Presbyterian. Avocations: golf, fishing, singing, acting. Office: PO Box 388 Jefferson IA 50129-0388 Fax: (515) 386-3894. E-mail: csuccess@netins.net.

SAID, EDWARD W. English language and literature educator; b. Jerusalem, Palestine, Nov. 1, 1935; s. Wadie A. and Hilda (Musa) S.; m. Mariam Cortas, Dec. 15, 1970; children: Wadie, Najla. AB, Princeton U., 1957; A.M., Harvard U., 1960, PhD, 1964; degree (hon.), U. Chicago, Bir Zeit U., Jawaharlal Nehru U., U. Michigan, U. Edinburgh, Nat. U. Ireland. Tutor history and lit. Harvard U., 1961-63; instr. Columbia U., 1963-65, asst. prof. English, 1965-67, assoc. prof., 1968-70, prof., 1970-77, Parr prof. English and comparative lit., 1977-89, Old Dominion Found. prof. humanities, 1989—; univ. prof., 1992—. Vis. prof. Harvard U., 1974, Johns Hopkins, spring 1979, Yale U., fall 1985; fellow Ctr. for Advanced Study in Behavioral Scis., Palo Alto, Calif., 1975-76; Christian Gauss lectr. in criticism Princeton U., spring 1977, T.S. Eliot lectr. U. Kent, Canterbury, U.K., 1985, Messenger lectr. Cornell U., 1986, Little lectr. Princeton U., 1988, Raymond Williams Meml. lectr., London, 1989, Wilson lectr. Wellesley Coll., 1991, Amnesty lectr. Oxford U., 1992, Lord Northcliffe lectr., U. Coll., London, 1993, Reith lectr. BBC, London, 1993, others; Carpenter prof. U. Chgo., 1983; Northrop Frye chair U. Toronto, fall 1986. Author: Joseph Conrad and the Fiction of autobiography, 1966, Beginnings: Intention and Method, 1975, Orientalism, 1978, The Question of Palestine, 1979, Covering Islam, 1980, The World, The Text and the Critic, 1983, After the Last Sky, 1986, Blaming the Victims, 01988, Musical Elaborations, 1991, Culture and Imperialism, 1993, Representations of the Intellectual, 1994, Politics of Dispossession, 1994, Peace and Its Discontents, 1996, Out of Place, 1999, The End of the Peace Process, 2000, Reflections on Exile, 2000; editor: Literature and Society, 1979, Ghazzah-Arihah: Salam Amriki, 1994, Henry James' Completed Stories 1884-1891, 1999. Social Sci. Research fellow, 1975; Guggenheim fellow, 1972-73; Recipient Lionel Trilling award Columbia U., 1976, 94, Sultan Owais Prize, 1998, Spinoza Prize, 1999, New Yorker Book Award for Non-Fiction, 1999, Year 2000 Anisfeld-Wolf Book Award for Non-Fiction, Morton Dauwen Zabel Award in Literature, 2000. Mem. AAAS, MLA, Assn. Arab Am. U. Grads. (past v.p.), N.Y. Coun. Fgn. Rels., Am. Comparative Lit. Assn. (René Wellek award 1985), PEN (exec. bd. 1989—), Am. Acad. Arts and Scis., Royal Soc. Literature, Am. Philosophical Soc., Modern Language Assn. (pres. 1999). Office: Columbia U Dept English 602 Philosophy Hall New York NY 10027

SAIDA, TOYOYASU, chemical and biochemical engineer; b. Tokyo, Jan. 18, 1935; came to U.S., 1985; s. Tameo and Fukiko Saida; m. Mariko Itano, Jan. 16, 1961; children; Tetsuo, Miyoko Asahi, Takashi Saida. BS, U. Tokyo, 1958. Registered profl. engr., Japan. Ops. engr. Toyo Gas Chems. Corp., Niigata, Japan, 1958-59; rschr. Tokyo Inst. of Tech., 1959-61; rsch. engr. Mitsui-Toatsu Chems. Ltd., Yokohama, Japan, 1961-69, chief rsch. engr. Japan, 1969-78; mgr. process rsch. divsn. Toyo Engring. Corp., Mobara, Japan, 1978-84, adv. bd. mem. Chiba, Japan, 1984-85; sr. v.p. BW Biotec, Inc., Chgo., 1985-86; gen. mgr. Hazarmacorp Rsch. Ctr., Tsukuba, Japan, 1987-95; mng. dir. Saida & Assocs., Deerfield, Ill., 1997—. Author: Handbook of Membrane Technology, 1978, Handbook of Bioprocess, 1985, Cellulose, 1986. Recipient Excellent Invention of Yr. Sci. and Tech. Agy., 1965. Mem. Am. Chem. Soc., Soc. of Chem. Engrs. Japan. Achievements include invention of new synthetic method of urea, large scale manufacturing process of single cell protein from n-paraffin, fuel alcohol manufacturing process from lignocellulosics, volume reduction method of radioactive wastes with liquid phase oxidation. Avocations: working with metallic materials, movies, computers. Home and Office: 431 Kelburn Rd Apt 315 Deerfield IL 60015-4367 E-mail: tomsaida@aol.com.

SAIDI, PARVIN, hematologist, medical educator; b. Teheran, Iran, Mar. 21, 1932; came to U.S., 1946; d. Ahmad and Fatemeh (Ashouri) S.; m. Allahverdi Farmanfarmaian, May 27, 1958; children: Dellara Farmanfarmaian Terry, Kimya Farmanfarmaian Harris. BS, Smith Coll., Northampton, Mass., 1952; MD, Harvard U., 1956. Diplomate Am. Bd. Internal Medicine, subspecialty hematology and med. oncology. Intern medicine UCLA Med. Ctr., 1956-57; resident internal medicine U. Calif., San Francisco, 1957-59; NIH rsch. fellow hematology U. Calif. Hosps. and Children's Med. Ctr., 1959-61, 63-64; asst. prof. medicine U. Medicine & Dentistry N.J.-Rutgers Med. Sch., New Brunswick, 1968-71, assoc. prof., 1971-74; prof. U. Medicine & Dentistry N.J.-Robert Wood Johnson Med. Sch., 1974—, chief divsn. hematology and oncology, dept. medicine, 1972—, Robert Wood Johnson U. Hosp., New Brunswick, 1981—. Cons. internist, hematologist, oncologist St. Peter's Med. Ctr., New Brunswick, Douglass Coll., Rutgers U., New Brunswick, VA Hosp., Lyons, N.J., Muhlenberg Hosp., Plainfield, N.J., Princeton (N.J.) Med. Ctr.; dir. Melvyn H. Motolinsky Lab. Hematology Rsch., N.J. Regional Comprehensive Hemophilia Care Program; mem. Gov.'s Adv. Coun. on AIDS; chmn. N.J. Regional Comprhensive Hemophilia Care Program Adv. Bd.; chmn. HHS region II Comprehensive Hemophilia Diagnostic and Treatment Ctrs., 1984-85, 89-90, 94-95, 99-2000; chmn. med. adv. bd. Hemophilia Found. N.J.; mem. med. adv. exec. com. N.J. Blood Svcs. Cons. editor Am. Jour. Medicine; contbr. articles to profl. jours. Recipient disting. svc. award for rsch. in leukemia Melvyn H. Motolinsky Rsch. Found., 1977, Humanitarian award Hemophilia Assn. No. N.J., 1978. Fellow ACP (mem. sci. program com. N.J. region), Acad. Medicine N.J.; mem. Am. Soc. Hematology (edn. com.), N.J. Hemophilia Assn. (chmn. med. adv. com., spl. award, Dr. L. Michael Kuhn Meml. award 1996), Coop. Oncology Group N.J. (exec. com., chairperson subcom. on lymphoma), Am. Heart Assn. (coun. on thrombosis), Am. Fedn. Clin. Rsch., Royal Soc. Medicine (affiliate), Am. Soc. Clin. Oncology, World Fedn. Hemophilia, Alpha Omega Alpha, Phi Beta Kappa, Sigma Xi. Office: Robert Wood Johnson Med Sch 1 Robert Wood Johnson Pl New Brunswick NJ 08901-1928

SAIED, JAMES GUY, conductor, consultant; b. Wirt, Okla., June 14, 1915; s. Oscar and Minnie (Adwan) S.; m. Helen Louella Ricker, Feb. 14, 1943; children: James Robert, Delia Ann Pierson. Ba, East Cen. U., Ada., Okla., 1936; postgrad., Vandercook Sch. Music. Cert. pub. sch. tchr. Band dir. Stroud (Okla.) Pub. Schs., 1936, Guthrie (Okla.) Pub. Schs., 1937-40, El Reno (Okla.) Pub. Schs. and Jr. Colls., 1940-42; ret. Music industry exec.; condr. of Univ., profl., mil. and community bands nationwide; cons., condr. John Sousa Concerts, 1981—. Found, condr. Oil Capitol Concert Band, Tulsa, 1959-62; condr. Tulsa Starlight Profl. Band, 1967-70; bd. dirs. Okla. Soc. Crippled Children, 1980—, Jr. Achievement, 1982-84. With U.S. Army, 1942-45, ETO. Decorated Bronze Star; named Disting. Alumnus East Cen. U., 1990; recipient Honor medal DAR, 1988, Order of Merit, John Philip Sousa Found., 1991, Nat. Good Citizen award SAR, 1992, Phi Beta Mu Internat. Outstanding award, 1990, George Washington Honor medal Freedoms Found., 1992, Will Rogers Ann. Spirit award, 1999, Outstanding Contbn. to Music Edn. award Okla. Bandmasters Assn., 1999, Okla. Gov.'s Arts Cmty. award, 2000. Mem. Nat. Assn. Music Merchants (bd. dirs. 1962-65, 71-74), Am. Bandmasters Assn. (hon. award 1988), Nat. Band Assn. (Citation of Excellence 1984, 86), Associated Concert Bands of Am., Rotary (pres. 1976-77, Outstanding Rotarian of Yr. dist. 6110 1981), Masons, Knife & Fork Club (pres. 1977-78), Kappa Kappa Psi (Disting. Svc. to Music award 1989). Democrat. Methodist. Home: 5832 S Florence Ave Tulsa OK 74105-7424 Office: PO Box 4684 Tulsa OK 74159-0684 E-mail: jsaied@cox.net.

SAIFER, MARK GARY PIERCE, pharmaceutical executive; b. Phila., Sept. 16, 1938; s. Albert and Sylvia (Jolles) S.; m. Phyllis Lynne Trommer, Jan. 28, 1961 (dec.); children: Scott David, Alandria Gail; m. Merry R. Sherman, June 26, 1994. AB, U. Pa., 1960; PhD, U. Calif., Berkeley, 1966. Acting asst. prof. zoology U. Calif., Berkeley, 1966, fellow, 1967-68; sr. cancer rsch. scientist Roswell Park Meml. Inst., Buffalo, 1968-70; lab. dir. Diagnostic Data Inc., Palo Alto, Calif., 1970-78; v.p. DDI Pharms., Inc., Mountain View, 1978-94, Oxis Internat., Inc., 1994-95; sci. dir. Mountain View Pharms., Inc., Menlo Park, Calif., 1996—, also bd. dirs. Author, patentee: in field, mem. editl. bd.: Current Pharm. Biotechnology Jour. Mem. AAAS (life), Am. Assn. Pharm. Scientists, Parenteral Drug Assn. Home: 1114 Royal Ln San Carlos CA 94070-4277 Office: Mountain View Pharms Inc 3475 Edison Way Ste S Menlo Park CA 94025-1821 E-mail: saifer@mvpharm.com.

SAIFF, JOSHUA M. mechanical engineer; b. Ridgewood, N.J., May 8, 1975; s. Edward I. and Roberta I. (Lichter) S. BSME, Rutgers U., 1997; MSME, Rensselaer Poly. Inst., 2002. Engr. Electric Boat Corp., Groton, Conn., 1997—. Mem. AIAA, ASME. E-mail: jsaiff@yahoo.com.

SAIGO, ROY HIROFUMI, university chancellor; b. Aug. 6, 1940; BA, U. Calif., Davis, 1962; PhD, Oreg. State U., 1969. Mem. faculty U. Wis., Eau Claire, 1967-84; intern acad. affairs U. Wis. Sys., Madison, 1976-77, dir. rsch. projects, summer 1976; asst. to dean Coll. Arts and Scis. U. Wis., Eau Claire, 1976-80; asst. dean, 1981-84; dean Coll. Natural Scis. U. No. Iowa, Cedar Falls, 1984-90; provost, v.p. acad. and student affairs Southeastern La. U., Hammond, 1990-94; chancellor Auburn U., Montgomery, Ala., 1994—. Bd. dirs. Children's Trust Fund, Ala. Shakespeare Festival, Montgomery Mus. Fine Arts, United Way; mem. alumni bd. Auburn U., Montgomery; mem. bd. dirs. Columbia East Med. Ctr., mem. Com. of 100. Recipient Charles E. Bessey award Bot. Soc. Am., svc. and contbn. award Am. Inst. Biol. Scis., Disting. Alumni award U. Calif., Davis, 1994; named to Alpha Gamma Rho Hall of Fame, Phi chpt., 1996. Fellow AAAS (life); mem. Am. Assn. Higher Edn., Am. Assn. State Colls. and Univs., Montgomery C. of C. (bd. dirs.), Phi Delta Kappa, Pi Kappa Phi, Omicron Delta Kappa. Office: St Cloud U 720 Fourth Ave S Saint Cloud MN 56301

SAIGUSA, MAKATO, oral and maxillofacial surgeon; b. Tokyo, July 12, 1961; s. Naoto and Tomoko Saigusa; m. JillR. Saigusa, June 2, 1991. BS, Samford U., 1985; DMD, U. Ala., 1991; MD, U. Tex., San Antonio, 1995. Diplomate Am. Bd. Oral and Maxillofacial Surgery. Resident U. Tex. Health Sci. Ctr., San Antonio, 1991-97, clin. instr., 1992-98, asst. prof., 1999—; pvt. practice Tyler, Tex., 1997—. Contbr. articles to profl. jours. Vol. surgeon Cleft Lip and Palate Surg. Team Med. Mission Trip, Mexico, 1995, Belize, 1999. Fellow Am. Assn. of Oral and Maxillofacial Surgery (award 1991), Am. Coll. of Oral and Maxillofacial Surgery; mem. AMA, Am. Dental Assn., Tex. Med. Assn. (mem. polit. action com. 1998—), Tex. Dental Assn., Smith County Med. and Dental Soc., Alpha Omega Alpha, Omicron Delta Kappa. Avocations: weight lifting, water skiing, music. Office: 1110 Medical Dr Tyler TX 75701-2109 E-mail: MSaigusa@Tyler.com.

SAIIDI, MEHDI, engineering educator; b. Tehran, Iran, May 24, 1950; s. Ramezan Saeedi and Mansoureh Karmbay; m. Sohila Bemanian, Aug. 12, 1977; children: Dustin, Uptin. PhD, U. Ill., 1979. Profl. civil engr. , Calif., Nev. Prof. civil engring. U. Nev., Reno, 1988—, chmn. civil engring. dept., 1988—94. Structrual and earthquake engring. cons., Reno, 1979—; dir. NSF Natural Hazard Mitigation Workshops, 1995. Editor: (book) Council on Tall Buildings and Urban Habitat, 1992. Recipient various awards, NSF, MCEER, Caltrans, Nev. Dept. Transp., and others, 1980—2002. Fellow: Am. Concrete Inst. (aci 341 com. chair 1990—97); mem.: ASCE (pres. Nev. sect. 1995—2000, pres. Truckee Meadows br. 1986—89, officer Truckee Meadows br. 1986—89), Earthquake Engring. Rsch. Inst. Avocations: painting, hiking, camping, travel. Office: Civil Engring 258 U Nev Reno NV 89557 Home Fax: 775-784-1390; Office Fax: 775-784-1390. Business E-Mail: saiidi@unr.edu.

SAIKI, PATRICIA (MRS. STANLEY MITSUO SAIKI), former federal agency administrator, former congresswoman; b. Hilo, Hawaii, May 28, 1930; d. Kazuo and Shizue (Inoue) Fukuda; m. Stanley Mitsuo Saiki, June 19, 1954; children: Stanley Mitsuo, Sandra Saiki Williams, Margaret C., Stuart K., Laura H. BA, U. Hawaii, 1952. Tchr. U.S. history Punahou Sch., Kaimuki Intermediate Sch., Kalani High Sch., Honolulu, 1952-64; sec. Rep. Party Hawaii, 1964-66, vice chmn., 1966-68, 82-83, chmn., 1983-85; rsch. asst. Hawaii State Senate, 1966-68; mem. Hawaii Ho. of Reps., 1968-74, Hawaii State Senate, 1974-82, 100th-101st Congresses from 1st Hawaii dist., Washington, 1987-91; adminstr. SBA, 1991-93. Mem. Pres.'s Adv. Coun. on Status of Women, 1969-76; mem. Nat. Commn. Internat. Women's Yr., 1969-70; commr. We. Interstate Commn. on Higher Edn.; fellow Eagleton Inst., Rutgers U., 1970; fellow Inst. of Politics, Kennedy Sch. Govt., Harvard U., 1993; bd. dirs. Bank of Am.-Hawaii, Landmark Systems Corp., Internat. Asset Recovery Corp.; mem. nat. selection com. Innovations in Am. Govt., Ford Found., Harvard U., 1999—. Mem. Kapiolano Hosp. Aux.; sec. Hawaii Rep. Com., 1964-66, vice chmn., 1966-68, chmn., 1983-85; del. Hawaii Constl. Conv., 1968; alt. del. Rep. Nat. Conv., 1968, del., 1984, Rep. nominee for lt. gov. Hawaii, 1982, for U.S. Senate, 1990, for. gov. Hawaii, 1994; mem. Fedn. Rep. Women; trustee Hawaii Pacific Coll.; past bd. govs. Boys and Girls Clubs Hawaii; mem. adv. coun. ARC; bd. dirs. Nat. Fund for Improvement of Post-Secondary Edn., 1982-85; past bd. dirs. Straub Med. Rsch. Found., Honolulu, Hawaii's Visitors Bur., Honolulu, Edn. Commn. of States, Honolulu, Hawaii Visitors Bur., 1983-85; trustee U. Hawaii Found., 1984-86, Hawaii Pacific Coll., Honolulu. Episcopalian. Avocation: golf. Home: 784 Elepaio St Honolulu HI 96816-4710

SAIKOWSKI, RONALD ALEXANDER, consulting engineer; b. Wichita Falls, Tex., May 15, 1950; s. Alexander Edward and Marie (Balazs) S.; m. Martha Elizabeth Dixon, July 21, 1973; children: Natalie, Emery, Denise. BCE, Tex. Tech. U., 1973. Registered profl. engr., Tex. Design engr. Lockwood-Greene Engring., Atlanta, 1973-75; environ. engr. Champion Internat., 1975-77; project mgr. Greiner Engring., Houston, 1977-82; mgr. engring. Montgomery Engring., 1982-83; owner, pres., bd. dirs. Sitech Engring. Corp., Woodlands, Tex., 1983—. Mem. adv. bd. Lower Lake Creek Reservoir Com., Conroe, Tex., 1985-89; pres., bd. dirs. Montgomery County Flood Control Corp., Conroe, 1987-89; pres. Comml. Real Estate Assn., Montgomery County, 1989, bd. dirs. Editor newsletter. Precinct chmn. Montgomery County Reps., 1982-96, chmn. candidates com., 1985—, mem. exec. com., 1982-96, del. Nat. Rep. Conv., 1992; mem. adv. com. Congressman Joe Barton, Concoe, 1984-92, chmn. steering com. Richard Smith for State Senate; v.p., bd. dirs. Montgomery County Mcpl. Utility Dist. 46, 1987-89; election judge Montgomery County, 1983-96; mem. steering com. CROP Walk; chmn. mktg. bd. Jr. Achievement, Montgomery County; adv. bd. Child Advocacy Support Assn.; bd. dirs. McCullough H.S., 1993-95, band booster, 1995—. Mem., South Montgomery County C. of C. (chmn. numerous coms., Small Bus. Man of Yr. 1992), Conroe C. of C., Tex. Tech. Civil Engrs. dv. coun. 1996—, chmn. 2000—), Montgomery County Comml. Real Estate Assn. (bd. dirs. 1987-90, 99—, pres. 1989), Edn. for Tomorrow Alliance, Women Helping Women, Tex. Tech. Civil Engring. Acad. (chmn. 2000—), Toastmasters, Kiwanis (bd. dirs. Montgomery County 1986-87), Rotary, Tau Beta Pi, Chi Epsilon. Methodist. Avocations: pioneer camping, water skiing, woodworking, living history. Home: 62 N Misty Morning Trce The Woodlands TX 77381-3862 Office: Sitech Engring Corp Ste 100 1544 Sandust Rd The Woodlands TX 77380 E-mail: rons@sitecheng.com.

SAIL, JOHN, data processing executive; Co-founder, exec. v.p. SAS Inst. Inc., Cary, NC, 1976—. Office: SAS Inst Inc 100 SAS Cmpus Dr Cary NC 27513-2414 Office Fax: 919-677-4444.

SAILER, RUTH LUCKENBILL, retired women's health nurse; b. Port Carbon, Pa., Jan. 28, 1925; d. Oscar I. and Kathryn (Sanders) Luckenbill; m. Donald Stanley Sailer, June 21, 1952. Diploma, Reading Hosp. Sch. Nursing, West Reading, Pa., 1946. Asst. head nurse newborn nursery Reading Hosp., 1946-52; obstet. staff nurse Chambersburg (Pa.) Hosp., 1952-61, head nurse labor and delivery, 1961-73, charge nurse labor and delivery, 1973-87; ret., 1987. Mem. Alumni Assn. of Reading Hosp. Sch. Nursing (life), Am. Assn. Ret. Persons. Avocations: horseback riding, reading, crossword puzzles, theatre, collecting Hummel figurines.

SAIN, CHARLES (HACK), civil engineer, surveyor; b. New Market, Ala., Jan. 20, 1923; s. Will Oris and Clayta (Speck) Sain; m. Marie Myers, Aug. 8, 1942; children: Charles R., Elizabeth Lester Stockdale, Ann Marie Hays; m. Helen Weil, Mar. 18, 2000. BSCE, U. Fla., 1949. Registered profl. engr., Ala., Ariz., Colo., Conn., Fla., Ga., Ill., Ind., Iowa, Kans., Ky., La., Minn., Miss., N.J., N.Y., N.C., Okla., Pa., S.C., S.D., Tenn., Vt., Va., W.Va., Wis. V.p. engring. Moss-Thornton Co., Inc., Leeds, Ala., 1946-59; gen. mgr. Vecellio & Grogan, Beckley, W.Va., 1960-64; v.p. engring. A.E. Burgess Co., Inc., Birmingham, Ala., 1964-67; pres. Charles H. Sain Assocs., 1968-89, Sain South Engring., Birmingham, 1978-89; CEO, chmn. bd. dirs. Sain Assocs., Inc., 1989—. Bd. visitors civil engring. dept. Coll. Engring. U. Ala., Birmingham; lectr. Auburn U., 1971, 72. Author: (with others) Standard Handbook for Civil Engineers, 1968, 4th edit., 1996; contbr. articles to profl. jours. Bd. dirs. State of Ala. Toll Bridge Authority, 1970-74; city engr. City of Vestavia Hilla, Ala., 1976-88, City of Homewood, Ala., 1976-80; vice chmn., bd. dirs. Ala. Bapt. Retirement Ctrs., Montgomery, 1986-93; mem. Vestavia Hills, Ala. Bd. Zoning Adjustment, 1986-90; vice chmn. Jefferson County Bd. Zoning Adjustment, 1986—; mem. Vestavia Hills Bapt. Ch., 1991—, deacon. Lt. U.S. Army, 1944-46. Named Engr. of Yr. Ala., Engring. Found. Coun. U. Ala.-Birmingham, 1999. Mem. NSPE, ASCE (program chmn. Ala. chpt. 1966, equipment maintenance com. 1958-78, Life Achievement award), Am. Soc. Mil. Engrs., Internat. Platform Assn., Internat. Coun. Shopping Ctrs. (water quality com., environ. site assessment com., lectr., Disting. Svc. award 1996), Birmingham C. of C. (environ. ethicc com., lectr.), Tau Beta Phi, Sigma Tau. Avocations: golf, reading. Office: Sain Assocs Inc 244 W Valley Ave Ste 200 Birmingham AL 35209-3616 E-mail: hsain@sain.com.

SAINANI, RAM HARIRAM, civil engineer; b. Ratodero, Sind, India, Feb. 22, 1925; came to U.S., 1981; s. Hariram Gurdasmal and Radha Hariram (Ahuja) S.; m. Usha Ram (Devkaran-Nanjee), Jan. 16, 1956; 1 child, Devkumar Ram. BA in Math. with honors, U. Bombay, 1943, BA in Physics and Chemistry with honors, 1944, BS in Math. and Physics, 1945, BCE, 1948; MCE, U. Colo., 1958. Registered profl. engr., Ont., Can., Mass., Maine, N.H. Dep. dir. designs Cen. Water & Power Commn. Govt. India, New Delhi, 1951-59; sr. hydraulic engr. SNC Group, Montreal, Que., Can., 1959-65; asst. chief hydraulic engr. Tecsult Internat., 1965-79; staff engr. Acres Internat., Niagara Falls, Ont., Can., 1979-81; prin. engr. Internat. Engring. Co. Inc., Norwalk, Conn., 1981-85; v.p. engring. Consol. Hydro Inc., Greenwich, 1985-94; ind. cons. engr., London, Can., 1994—. Pres. India Can. Assn., Montreal, 1974-77. Mem. ASCE (life), Rotary. Democrat. Hindu. E-mail: rsainani@home.com.

SAINE, BETTY BOSTON, elementary school educator; b. Newton, N.C., Dec. 1, 1932; d. Glenn and Carrie Queen Boston; m. Thomas Paul Saine, Aug. 3, 1968; 1 child, Carrie Ann. BA, Lenoir Rhyne Coll., 1956. Tchr. grade 4 High Point (N.C.) City Schs., 1956-59, Charlotte City Schs./Charlotte-Mecklenburg Schs., 1959-66; art tchr. grades 1-8 Newton-Conover City Schs., 1966-67; tchr. grade 4 Charlotte-Mecklenburg Schs., 1967-68; tchr. grade 6 Lincolnton (N.C.) City Schs., 1968-70; tchr. grades 5 and 6 Lincolnton City Schs./Lincoln County Schs., 1972-90; ret. Historian, publicity chair beautification com. Sunflower Garden Club, Lincolnton, 1976-87. Mem. Alpha Delta Kappa (various offices and coms.). Methodist. Avocations: painting, creative embroidery, horticulture, calligraphy, children's books. Home: 2492 Pickwick Pl Lincolnton NC 28092-7748

SAINER, ARTHUR, writer, theater educator; b. N.Y.C., Sept. 12, 1924; s. Louis and Sadie (Roth) S.; m. Maryjane Treloar, Apr. 18, 1981; children: Douglas M., Stephanie M., Jane M., Ross M. BA, Washington Sq. Coll., N.Y.C., 1946; MA, Columbia U., 1948. Tchr. C.W. Post Coll., Bennington Coll., Vt., 1967-69, Adelphi U., Garden City, N.Y., 1974-75, S.I. Community Coll., 1974-75; faculty Wesleyan U., Middletown, Conn., 1977-80, Hunter Coll., N.Y.C., 1980-81; assoc. prof. theatre Middlebury Coll., Vt., 1981-83; theater faculty New Sch. for Social Rsch., N.Y.C., 1985—, Sarah Lawrence Coll., Bronxville, N.Y., 1990—; play dir. Boat Sun Cavern Middlebury Coll., Vt., 1983; drama critic Village Voice, N.Y.C., 1961—; play dir. Lord Tom Goldsmith at Theatre for New City, 1979, Witnesses at Open Space, N.Y.C., 1977, Poor Man Rich Man, Theatre for the New City, 1992. Editor: Village Voice, 1962; author: (plays) Jews and Christians in the End Zone, 2000 (Nat. Found. for Jewish Culture award), The Burning Out of 82, 1997, The Celebration Reclaimed, 1993-95, Images of the Coming Dead, 1980, After the Baal-Shem Tov, 1979, Carol in Winter Sunlight, 1977, The Children's Army Is Late, 1974, Cruising Angel, 1984, Sunday Childhood Journeys to Nobody at Home (Berman award), 1984, (criticisms), The New Radical Theatre Notebook, 1975, 97, The Sleepwalker and the Assassin, 1964, Zero Dances, 1998, The Burning Out of 82, 1997; reporter: Nat. Endowment for Arts, Washington, 1979-82. Panelist Vt. Council on the Arts, Montpelier, 1982, 83; panelist N.Y. State Council on the Arts, 1976-78. Ford Found. grantee, 1979, 80; recipient grant Office for Advanced Drama Research, U. Minn., 1967, award for Grab Your Hat John Golden Found., 1946 Address: 462 1st St Brooklyn NY 11215-2606 *From the Burning Out of 82: Francis: But finally, who is going to do my work? No one is going to do it. Lev: Each will do his work. But in the end only God's work amounts to anything. Francis: And does that make you happy? Lev: It makes me useful.*

SAINI, GULSHAN RAI, soil physicist, agricultural hydrologist; b. Oct. 1, 1924; s. Ram Saran and Parmeshri Devi (Bhondi) S.; m. Veena Chaudhri, Jan. 14, 1950; 1 child, Vikas. BSc, Panjab U., 1945, MSc, 1956; PhD, Ohio State U., 1960. soil and water conservation cert. USDA Tng. Ctr., 1959. Rsch. asst. Govt. Agrl. Coll., Ludhiana, India, 1945-57; rsch. assoc. Ohio State U., Columbus, 1957-60; asst. prof. Punjab Agrl. U., Ludhiana, 1960-61; rsch. scientist Can. Dept. Agriculture, Fredericton, N.B., 1962-84. Adj. prof. Faculty of Forestry, U. N.B., Fredericton, 1968-76; founding bd. dirs. U. Human Rights Group, Inc.; vis. prof. Rutgers U., 1984-85; mem. hydrology subcom. Atlantic Provinces Inter-Univ. Com. on Scis., 1966-76, Atlantic Provinces Soil & Water Engring. Com., 1972-82; mem. Restore Olmsted's Waterway Coalition, 1986—, treas. 1990-93, chair 1994-96; CSO tech. adv. com. Commonwealth of Mass., 1995-99; chmn. Saini Found. for Edn. and Human Progress. Contbr. articles to profl. jours. Bd. dirs. Coalition for a Strong UN, 1994-99; treas. Fredericton br. Can. Inst. Internat. Affairs, 1975-80. Fellow Internat. Inst. Land Reclamation and Improvement; mem. Indian Sci. Congress Assn. (life), Profl. Inst. Pub. Svcs. Can. (nat. v.p. 1980, 81, chmn. Atlantic regional coun. 1978, 79), Union Concerned Scientists, Fredericton Rotary Club (dir. internat. svc. 1967-68), 3d World Scholars Consortium (treas. 1995—). Home: 24 Brook St Brookline MA 02445-6914 E-mail: gulshansaini@rcn.com.

SAINI, KULVINDER SINGH, molecular biologist, biochemistry educator; b. Ludhiana, Punjab, India, Aug. 5, 1956; arrived in Australia, 1991; s. Parkash Singh and Harkishan Kaur (Bola) S.; m. Ranjit Kaur Sahni, Aug. 7, 1991; 1 child, Anmol Simran Kaur. BS, Punjab Agrl. U., 1977, MS, 1980; PhD, Sydney (Australia) U., 1987. Rsch. fellow Punjab Agrl. U., 1980-81; postdoctoral Case Western Res. U., Cleve., 1986-87; rsch. fellow Harvard U., Boston, 1988-91; rsch. scientist Commonwealth Sci. and Indsl. Rsch. Orgn., Sydney, 1991-94; sr. scientist Princess Alexandra Hosp., Brisbane, Australia, 1994-97, Lahey Clinic, Burlington, Mass., 1998-2000; sr. scientist neurobiology divsn. Alphagene Inc., Woburn, 2000—, assoc. dir. oncology, 2001—. Rsch. grant assessor Diabetes Australia Rsch. Trust; cons. FMC BioProducts, Maine, 1989-91. Contbr. articles to profl. jours. Cashier Animal Sci. Club, Punjab Agrl. U., 1977, Australian Sikh Assn., Sydney, 1984; sec. Punjabi Folk Dance Gp, Sydney, 1982-84; v.p. Punjabi Cultural Assn., Sydney, 1992. Recipient Postgrad. Rsch. award U. Sydney, 1981, Postdoctoral fellowship NIH, 1989, Sr. Rsch. fellow Princess Alexandra Hosp. Rsch. Found., 1994-97. Fellow Animal Nutrition Soc. India; mem. Am. Soc. Biochemistry, Am. Assn. Cancer Rsch. Sikh. Avocations: soccer, tennis, cricket, classical music (Indian), movies. Home: 62 Mill St Apt 6 Woburn MA 01801-2753 Office: Alphagene Inc Oncology Divsn 260 W Cummings Pk Woburn MA 01801 E-mail: ksaini@alphagene.com.

SAINI, VASANT DURGADAS, computer software company executive; b. Mumbai, Jan. 31, 1952; came to U.S., 1974; s. Durgadas D. and Pushpa (Sethi) S.; m. Sonia Juneja, May 20, 1983; children: Isha Seyjal, Kaasha Priyal. B Tech. Electronics, Ind. Inst. Tech., Kharagpur, 1974; MSEE, U. Rochester, 1975, PhD in Elec. Engring., 1979. Asst. prof. elec. engring. U. Rochester (N.Y.), 1980-88; pres., CEO Advanced Computer Innovations, Inc., Pittsford, N.Y., 1988—. Cons. All-Pro Printers, Rochester, 1986, W. Main Ultrasound Group, Rochester, 1986; software developer Dantec Electronics, Denmark, 1987-89, Brother Industries Ltd., Japan, 1992-93, 95-2001, Manpower Internat., USA, 1993-94, 95-96, DataEase Internat., USA, 1992-94, Wholly Genes, Inc., 1994—, Automated Legal Sys., Inc., 1996—, The Technology Group, 1996-2000, Nota Bene, 1994—, Expert Ease, Inc., 1997-2000, Info Access, Inc., 1997, Duxbury Sys., 1997—, McDonnell Douglas Helicopter Sys., 1997, U. of Rochester Med. Ctr., 1998-99, Sungard Planning Solutions, 1999—, TenDotZero (U.K.) Ltd., 2000-01, Boss Info. Sys., Switzerland, 2001, Brit. Aerospace, U.K., 1999—. Co-author: Doppler Echocardiography, 1985, 2d edit., 1992; also articles. Mae Stone Goode Found. grantee, 1979-81. Avocations: Indo-jazz music, mathematics of music, squash. Home: 19 Roxbury Ln Pittsford NY 14534-4202 E-mail: vsaini@rochester.rr.com.

SAINT, EVA MARIE, actress; b. Newark, July 4, 1924; d. John Merle and Eva Marie (Rice) S.; m. Jeffrey Hayden, Oct. 28, 1951; children: Darrell, Laurette. BA, DFA, Bowling Green State U., 1946; student, Actors Studio, after 1950. Appeared in various radio and TV dramatic shows, N.Y.C., 1947—; theater roles include The Trip to Bountiful, 1953 (Outer Circle Critics award, N.Y. Drama Critics award 1953), The Rainmaker, 1953, Winesburg, Ohio, 1970, The Lincoln Mask, 1972, Summer and Smoke, 1973, Desire Under the Elms, 1974, The Fatal Weakness, 1976, Candida, 1977, Mr. Roberts, First Monday in October, 1979, Duet for One, 1982-83, The Country Girl, 1986 (L.A. Dramalogue award 1986), Death of a Salesman, 1994, Love Letters, 1994-2002, On the Divide, 1994-2002; appeared in films On the Waterfront, 1954 (Acad. Award for best supporting actress 1955), That Certain Feeling, 1956, Raintree Country, 1957, A Hatful of Rain, 1957, North by Northwest, 1959, Exodus, 1961, All Fall Down, 1962, 36 Hours, 1963, The Sandpiper, 1964, The Russians are Coming, The Russians are Coming!, 1965, Grand Prix, 1966, The Stalking Moon, 1969, Loving, 1970, Cancel My Reservation, 1972, Nothing in Common, 1986, Mariette in Ecstacy, 1995, I Dreamed of Africa, 2000; TV dramas include The Macahans, 1976 (Emmy nom.), The Fatal Weakness, 1976, Taxi!!, 1978 (Emmy nom.), A Christmas to Remember, 1978, When Hell Was in Season, 1980, The Curse of King Tut's Tomb, The Best Little Girl in the World, 1981, Splendor in the Grass, 1981, Love Leads the Way, 1983, Jane Doe, 1983, Fatal Vision, 1984, The Last Days of Patton, 1986, A Year in the Life, 1986, Breaking Home Times, 1987, I'll Be Home for Christmas, 1988, Voyage of Terror: The Achille Lauro Affair, 1990, People Like Us, 1990 (Emmy award 1990), Palomino, 1991, Kiss of the Killer, ABC, 1992, My Antonia, 1994, After Jimmy, 1996, Time to Say Goodbye, 1997, Titanic, 1997; (documentary) Primary Colors: The Story of Corita, 1991; (with Bill Moyers) Children in America's Schools, 1997, Papa's Angels, 2000.

SAINT, JOHN GARDNER, obstetrician; b. Erie, Pa., 1952; MD, Washington U., 1980. Diplomate Am. Bd. Ob-Gyn. Resident in ob-gyn. Barnes Hosp., St. Louis, 1980-84; staff St. John's Hosp., Springfield, Ill.; clin. assoc. prof. Sch. Medicine So. Ill. U. Mem. AMA, Am. Coll. Ob-Gyn., Ill. State Med. Soc. Home: 415 N 9th St Ste 600 Springfield IL 62702-5366

ST. AMAND, JANET G. government relations lawyer; b. N.Y.C., Feb. 27, 1953; d. Leonard Marsh and Glenda Weaver St. A.; children: Nikolai, Peter. BA, Arcadia U., 1975; JD, Georgetown U., 1980. Bar: D.C. 1981, N.Y. 1989. Legis. counsel Congressman Jim Coyne, Washington, 1981-83, Congressman Tom Carper, Washington, 1983-85, Sen. John Heinz, Washington, 1985-86, Am. Bankers Assn., Washington, 1986-87; asst. resident counsel J.P. Morgan, N.Y.C., 1987-90; counsel Fin. Svcs. Coun., Washington, 1990-93; fed. dir., counsel Household Internat., 1993—. Mem. Leadership Coun., Salvation Army, 1994—; trustee Arcadia U. (formerly Beaver Coll.), Glenside, Pa., 1999—, alumni bd. dirs., 1995—; mem. Tax Coalition, 1999—. Recipient Mary Armstrong Wolf award Arcadia U., 1999. Mem. Women in Housing & Fin. (bd. dirs. 1991-95, mem. of yr. 1993), Univ. Club, Columbia Country Club, Exchequer Club, Tax Coalition. Presbyterian. Avocations: reading, traveling, jogging, politics. Home: 5423 33rd St NW Washington DC 20015 Office: Household Internat 1730 K St NW Ste 1106 Washington DC 20006-3830 E-mail: jgst.amand@household.com.

SAINT-AMAND, PIERRE NEMOURS, humanities educator; b. Port-Au-Prince, Haiti, Feb. 22, 1957; came to U.S., 1978; s. Nemours and Carmen (Clerveaux) Saint-A. BA, U. Montreal, 1978; MA, Johns Hopkins U., 1980, PhD, 1981. Asst. prof. Yale U., New Haven, 1981-82, Stanford (Calif.) U., 1982-86; assoc. prof. Brown U., Providence, 1986-90, prof., 1990—, Francis

Wayland prof., 1996—. Vis. prof. Harvard U., Cambridge, Mass., 1992, U. Iowa, Iowa City, 2001. Author: Diderot, Le Labyrinthe de La Relation, 1984, Séduire Ou La Passion des Lumières, 1986, Les Lois de L'Hostilité, 1992, The Libertine's Progress, 1994, The Laws of Hostility, 1996; editor: Diderot, 1984, Le Roman au Dix-huitième siécle, 1987, Autonomy in the Age of the Enlightenment, 1993, Thérèse philosophe, 2000. Fellow Stanford Humanities Ctr., 1985-86, John Simon Guggenheim Meml. Found., 1989; recipient Chevalier dans l'Ordre des Palmes académiques, 2001. Office: Brown U PO Box 1961 Providence RI 02912-1961

ST. AUBYN, RONALD ANTHONY, pediatrics nurse; b. Vineland, N.J., Nov. 30, 1954; s. Richard Francis and Rita Margaret (DeFeo) St. A. BSN, Northwestern State U., Natchitoches, La., 1980. RN, La. High-risk infant homecare nurse Physicians Prescription Svcs., Shreveport, La., 1982-86; nursing dir., neonatal cons. Quality Care, Inc., 1985-86; poison info. specialist La. Poison Control Ctr., 1987; pediatric clin. supr. La. State U. Med. Ctr., 1988-92, pediatric edn. nurse, 1993—. Mem. ANA, La. State Nursing Assn., Soc. of Pediatric Nurses of La., Krewe Club of Aesclepius, Royalty Club, Beta Beta Beta. Home: 865 Sewanee Pl Shreveport LA 71105-2245

ST. CLAIR, DONALD DAVID, lawyer; b. Hammond, Ind., Dec. 30, 1932; s. Victor Peter and Wanda (Rubinska) Small; m. Sergine Anne Oliver, June 6, 1970 (dec. June 1974); m. Beverly Joyce Tipton, Dec. 28, 1987. BS, Ind. U., 1955, MS, 1963, EdD, 1967; JD, U. Toledo, 1992. Bar: Ohio 1992, U.S. Dist. Ct. (no. dist.) Ohio 1993, U.S. Supreme Ct., 1996. Assoc. prof. Western Ky. U. Coll. Edn., Bowling Green, 1967-68, U. Toledo, 1968-77, prof., 1977-92; atty., ptnr. Garand, Bollinger, & St. Clair, Oregon, Ohio, 1992-97; pvt. practice Law Offices Donald D. St. Clair, Toledo, 1997—. Mem. Ohio Coun. Mental Health Ctrs., Columbus, 1978-79; dir. honors programs U. Toledo. Author: (poetry) Daymarks and Beacons, 1983, Impressions from an Afternoon in a Paris Courtroom, 1998; contbr. articles to profl. jours. Organizer Students Toledo Organized for Peace, 1970-71; mem. Lucas County Dem. Party, 1990—. With U.S. Army, 1955-57. Mem. ABA, AAU (nat. bd. dirs. 1973-74), Am. Inns of Ct., Ohio Bar Assn., Toledo Bar Assn., Ohio Acad. Trial Lawyers, Toledo Power Squadron (comdg. officer 1981), Bay View Yacht Club, Ohio Criminal Def. Lawyers Assn., Lucas County Bar Assn., Maumee Valley Criminal Def. Lawyers Assn., Ottawa County Bar Assn., Masons (32 degree), Shriners, Ancient Order Friars, Phi Alpha Delta. Home: 3353 Christie Blvd Toledo OH 43606-2862 Office: 5415 Monroe St Toledo OH 43623-2800 E-mail: stclairlaw@attglobal.net.

ST. CLAIR, HAL KAY, electrical engineer; b. L.A., Oct. 11, 1925; s. Millard T. and Ruth (McGrew) St. C.; m. Jane Creely, June 24, 1949; children: Gregory, Russell, Elizabeth; m. Bereniece Langham, Mar. 6, 1998. Student, U. So. Calif., 1943-44; BS, U. Calif.-Berkeley, 1946, MS, 1948. Research engr. Marchant Calculators, Emeryville, Calif., 1948-52; project engr. RCA, Camden, N.J., 1953-54; program mgr. IBM, San Jose, Calif., 1954-69, tech. staff Boca Raton, Fla., 1969-72, mgr. input/output devel., 1972-75, mgr. gen. lab. devel., 1975-81, mgr. small comml. systems engring., 1981-83, ergonomics adviser div. hdqrs. staff White Plains, N.Y., 1983-85, devel. edn. mgr., 1986-88, ret., 1988. Instr. U. Calif. Extension Div., 1951-52; tech. adv. U.S. Nat. Com. Internat. Electrotechnical Commn., 1967-69. Mem. Republican Central Com. of Calif., 1962-66. Served to lt. (j.g.) USNR, 1943-46. Mem. IEEE, SAR, Mensa, Phi Beta Kappa, Sigma Xi, Tau Beta Pi, Eta Kappa Nu. Home: 17187 Prado Pl San Diego CA 92128-2163 E-mail: stclair@san.rr.com.

ST. CLAIR, JAMES EARL, music educator; b. Cincinnati, Ohio, Dec. 22, 1944; s. Harold L. St. Clair and Alma Ester Kuhn; m. Jean Marie Schnabel, July 1, 1988; children: Jennifer Leigh, Todd Christopher; m. Joanne Elizabeth Coulter, June 9, 1968 (div.); children: Matthew Justin Ciesielski. Bachelor's Music Edn., Fla. State U., Tallahassee, FL, 1966. Teaching Certificate Fla. Dept. Edn. Tchr. Stuart Mid. Sch., Stuart, Fla., 1966—71, Crystal Lake Mid. Sch., Pompano Beach, 1971—89, Ramblewood Mid. Sch., Coral Springs, 1989—. Asst. dir. Symphonic Band Palm Beaches, Lake Worth, Fla., solo clarinetist, Fla. Recipient 25 Years Award, Fla. Music Edn. Assn., 1992, Hon. Life Membership, Fla. Bandmaster Assn., 1992. Mem.: Internat. Mil. Music Soc., Music Educators Nat. Conf., Nat. Band Assn., Am. Sch. Band Directors Assn. (rsch. chmn. 1985—2002). R-Consevative. Christian. Achievements include design of Produced a compact disc saluting Colonel Albert Schoepper, U.S. Marine Band; Produced a variety of cello and string bass stops to be put on slick floors. Avocations: collecting march music or recordings, collecting coins, deep-sea fishing, visiting air museums and historical sites. Home: 661 SW 18th Street Boca Raton FL 33486-7028 Personal E-mail: jmstc@yahoo.com.

ST. CLAIR, JANE ELIZABETH, management executive; b. Concord, Mass., Aug. 15, 1944; d. James F. and Mary E. (Clyne) Connell. BA, Salem State Coll., 1969; MPH, Columbia U., N.Y.C., 1990. Field rep., safety program Am. Red Cross of Greater N.Y., 1971-72; program dir. Bronx Community Coll., N.Y., 1973-75; dir. edn. Council N.Y.C., Inc., 1975-77, asst. exec. dir., 1978; exec. dir. Regional Emergency Med. Services, N.Y., 1979-91; dir. Peace Corps, Kenya, 1991-94, Gulfcoast South Area Health Edn. Ctr., Sarasota, Fla., 1995—96; cons. Dept. Anesthesiology Boston Med. Ctr., 1996—99; exec. dir. Mid/Upper Cape Cmty. Health Ctr., Hyannis, 2000—. Adjunt asst. prof., Hunter Coll. N.Y., 1973-91. Contbr. articles to profl. jours. Mem. Emergency Cardic Care Com. N.Y., Heart Assn., Am. Soc. Safety Engrs., Profl. Edn. Com., Am. Red Cross, First Aid Com. Address: 182 Thacher Shore Dr Yarmouth Port MA 02675

ST. CLAIR, JESSE WALTON, JR. retired savings and loan executive; b. Phila., Jan. 15, 1930; s. Jesse Walton and Susan Elizabeth (Leath) St. C.; m. Elizabeth Anne Bartlett, Oct. 6, 1951; children: Jesse Walton III, Susan Elizabeth, Bruce Bartlett, Anne Leath. BA, Coll. of William and Mary, 1951; MBA, U. Pa., 1958; postgrad., Harvard U., 1968. Trainee Fed. Res. Bank, Phila., 1955-57; with Girard Trust Bank, 1957-78, asst. treas., 1960-64, asst. v.p., 1964-67, v.p., 1967-70, sr. v.p., 1970-75, exec. v.p., 1976-78; pres., chief exec. officer First Nat. Bank of Allentown (Pa.), 1978-82; chmn., chief exec. officer Wilmington Savs. Fund Soc., 1982-90, ret., 1990. Trustee emeritus endowment fund Coll. William and Mary; dir. Del. Am. Ins. Co.; former mem. exec. bd. Delmarva coun. Boy Scouts Am.; past trustee Wesley Coll. With USN, 1951-55. Mem. Wilmington Country Club, Theta Delta Chi. Republican. Methodist. Home: 4011 Springfield Ln Greenville Wilmington DE 19807

ST. CLAIR, PHILIP ROLAND, humanities educator, poet; b. Warren, Ohio, Apr. 30, 1944; s. Harvey Lee St. Clair and Ruth A. Sutton; m. Christina St. Clair, Aug. 24, 1996. BA, Kent State U., 1970, MA, 1972, MLS, 1974; MFA in Poetry, Bowling Green State U., 1985. Instr. Bowling Green (Ohio) State U., 1985-86; lectr. So. Ill. U., Carbondale, 1986-91; prof. composition and creative writing Ashland (Ky.) C.C., 1991—, chair humanities divsn., 1998—. Dir. Jesse Stuart Writers' Conf., Ashland, 1992—. Author (books of poetry): In the Thirty-Nine Steps, 1980, At the Tent of Heaven, 1984, Little-Dog-of-Iron, 1985, Acid Creek, 1997. With USAF, 1961-65. NEA Creative Writing fellow, 1994, Al Smith fellow, Ky. Arts Coun., 1999; recipient Hellen Bullis prize, Poetry Northwest Mag., 1986. Mem. Christian Ch. (Disciples Of Christ). Avocations: travel, philately, postal history. Office: Ashland Cmty Coll 1400 College Dr Ashland KY 41101 E-mail: philip.stclair@kctcs.edu.

ST. CLAIR, THOMAS MCBRYAR, mining and manufacturing company executive; b. Wilkinsburg, Pa., Sept. 26, 1935; s. Fred C. and Dorothy (Renner) St. C.; m. Sarah K. Stewart, Aug. 1, 1959; children— Janet, Susan, Carol. AB, Allegheny Coll., 1957; MS, MIT, 1958; grad. advanced mgmt. program, Harvard U. With Koppers Co., Inc., Pitts., 1958-88, asst. to gen. mgr. engring. and constrn. div., 1966-69, comptroller, asst. treas., 1969-78, pres. Engineered Metal Products Group, 1978-83, v.p., asst. to chmn., 1983-84, v.p., treas., chief fin. officer, 1984-88; sr. v.p., chief fin. officer Phelps Dodge Corp., Phoenix, 1989-99; retired, 1999. Trustee Allegheny Coll.; bd. dirs. Pitts. Theol. Sem. Mem. Fin. Execs. Inst., Duquesne Club (Pitts.), Allegheny Country Club (Sewickley, Pa.). Presbyterian.

ST. CLAIRE, FRANK ARTHUR, lawyer; b. Charlotte, N.C., June 16, 1949; BS, MIT, 1972; JD, NYU, 1975. Bar: Tex. 1975, U.S. Dist. Ct. (no. dist.) Tex. 1985; bd. cert. in comml. real estate law. Assoc. James H. Wallenstein, Dallas, 1975-78; v.p. Wallenstein & St. Claire, 1978-81; pres. Frank A. St. Claire, P.C., 1981-84; ptnr. St. Claire & Case, P.C., 1984-88, pres., 1988-93; chmn. bd. Sunbelt Empire Title Co., 1983-88; pres. St. Claire & Assocs., 1993—; chmn. real estate section Godwin & Carlton, P.C., 1994-96; ptnr., chmn. real estate sect. Strasburger & Price, L.L.P., 1996-2000; CEO EnsureLink, 2001—; pres. StClaireNet, 2001—. Author: Texas Condominium Law, 1986; co-author: Texas Real Estate Guide, 2000; contbr. articles to profl. jours. Ofcl. del. Dallas to Baltic Legal Conf., Riga, Latvia, 1990. Mem. Am. Coll. Mortgage Attys. (chmn. pubs. com. 1998—, mem. programs com. 1998—), Tex. Bar Assn. (study of uniform condominium act com., legis. liaison com. 1981-85, vice chmn. 1981-82, chmn. 1982-85, chmn. condominium and coop. housing com. 1985-89, title ins. com., mem. coun. real estate, probate and trust coun. 1991-95, treas. 1996-97, sec., chair-elect 1997-98, chair 1998-99), Dallas Bar Assn., Cmty. Assn. Inst. (bd. dirs. Dallas-Ft. Worth chpt. 1984-85, 87-89, pres.-elect 1989-90), Real Estate Fin. Exec. Assn. (asst. sec. 1996-97), Real Estate Coun., Am. Coll. Real Estate Lawyers (planning com. 1990-98, chmn. practice tech. com. 1993-96, mem. common interest ownership com. 1986-98, alternative dispute resolution com. 1993-95), Tex. Coll. Real Estate Attys. (chmn. projects com. 1991-92, bd. dirs. 1994—), Internat. Assn. of Attys. and Execs. in Corp. Real Estate (website com. 1997—). Episcopalian.

ST. CYR, JOHN ALBERT, II, cardiovascular and thoracic surgeon; b. Mpls., Nov. 26, 1949; s. John Albert and Myrtle Lavira (Jensen) St. C.; m. Mary Helen Malinoski, Oct. 29, 1977. BA summa cum laude, U. Minn., 1973, BS, 1975, MS, 1977, MD, 1980, PhD, 1988. Teaching asst. dept. biochemistry U. Minn., Mpls., 1973, rsch. asst. dept. surgery, 1977-78, intern surgery dept. surgery, 1980-81, resident surgery, 1981-88, cardiovascular rsch. fellow dept. surgery, 1983-86, with dept. surgery, 1991-92; rsch. assoc. fellow Cardiovasular Pathology, United Hosp., St. Paul, 1987-88; cardiovascular surg. resident U. Colo., Dept. Cardiovascular Surgery, Denver, 1988-91; med. advisor Organetics, Ltd., Mpls., 1992, med. dir., 1992. Med. advisor Aor Tech., Inc., St. Paul, 1992; bd. dirs. Minn. Acad. Sci.; pres. Virotech, Inc., 1993-94; med./surg. cons. Medtronic, Inc., 1993—; ind. rsch., 1992—; dir. R&D Medcorp Internat., 1996, Jacqmar, Inc., 1996—; med. dir. IHI, 1996, First Circle Med., Inc., 1997-99; med. dir. Bioenergy Inc., 1998—. Contbr. Recipient NIH Rsch./Fellowship award, 1983-86, Grant in Aid Rsch. award Minn. Heart Assn., 1983-85, Med. Student Rsch. award Minn. Med. Found., 1980, Acad. Excellence award Merck Found., 1980. Mem. AAAS, AMA, Assn. Acad. Surgeons, Minn. Acad. for Scis., Am. Physiol. Soc., Am. Fedn. and Clin. Rsch., N.Y. Acad. Scis., Am. Heart Assn., Am. Med. Writers Assn., Internat. Soc. Heart Rsch., So. Med. Assn., Phi Kappa Phi. Republican. Achievements include patents for Achievements include patents in field with subsequent clinical studies.

ST. DAVID, EILEEN, music educator, stage director; b. Cleve., Oct. 16, 1942; BA, Barnard Coll./Columbia U., 1965; degree in vocal performance, MMusic/Vocal Pedagogy, Holy Names Coll., Oakland, Calif., 1983. Prin. pvt. voice studio, Oakland, 1979-94; voice educator Early Music Night at East Bay Ctr. for Performing Arts, Richmond, Calif., 1982-84; adj. instr. in vocal music Holy Names Coll., 1985-94; prin. St. David Studio, Boston, 1994—; music tchr./referral Harvard-Radcliffe Office for the Arts, Cambridge, 1994—. Adjudicator various song festivals, San Francisco Bay area, Boston, 1984—; career advisor Alumnae Resources, San Francisco, 1984—94; master classes New Eng. Gilbert and Sullivan Soc., 2000—01. Translator: (song cycle) Weihnachtslieder, 1980; author: Case Studies in Vocal Pedagogy, 1983; stage dir. Harvard-Radcliffe Gilbert and Sullivan Players; dir. opera scenes, Three's A Charm. Mem. Nat. Assn. Tchrs. Singing (NATS) (bd. dirs. Boston chpt. 1995-2000). Avocation: sea otter spotting.

ST. DENIS, BRENT, member of parliament; b. Blind River, ON, Canada, May 27, 1950; B of Applied Sci. in Indsl. Engring., U. Toronto. Indsl. engr. Internat. Harvester, Hamilton; math. and physics tchr. Jamaica, 1973-75; acctg., math., fin. tchr. Cambrian Coll. Applied Arts and Tech., Sudbury; mcpl. adminstr., clk.-treas., sec.-treas. Town of Massey, 1977-83, mgr. Pub. Utilities Commn.; parliamentary exec. asst. to Dr. Maurice Foster House of Commons, Ottawa, 1983-93, M.P. for Algoma, 1993-97, mem. standing com. on fin., chair fin. com. internat. fin., M.P. for Algoma-Manitoulin, 1997—, chmn. standing com. on natural resources and govt. ops., 1997-99; parliamentary sec. Ministry Natural Resources, 1999-2000, Minister for Transport, 2000—01; mem. standing com. on industry, sci., and tech., 2001—. Mem. No. Ont. Liberal Caucus (past chair). Office: House of Commons 584 Confederation Ottawa ON Canada K1A 0A6

SAINT-DONAT, BERNARD JACQUES, finance company executive; b. Avignon, France, May 22, 1946; came to U.S., 1971; s. Jean Eugene and Paule Louise (Chastan) S.; m. Ingrid Claire Armstrong, June 6, 1986. PhD in Sci., U. Paris, 1973. Research fellow Harvard U., 1971-74; asst. prof. Columbia U., N.Y.C., 1974-76; assoc. prof. Yale U., New Haven, 1976-81; assoc. Lehman Bros., N.Y.C., 1981-84; v.p. Shearson Lehman Bros., 1984-86, sr. v.p., 1986-89; mng. gen. ptnr. Knox Parthers, 1989-93; mng. dir. CCF, 1993-95, Credit Agricole Lazard Fin. Products, N.Y.C., 1995-96, Lazard Frères & Co. LLC, N.Y.C., 1996—2001, Lehman Bros., N.Y.C., 2001—. Bd. dirs. New Haven Sister Cities, Inc.; mem. overseas vis. com. for maths. Harvard U. Author: Toroidal Embeddings, 1975; contbr. articles to profl. jours. Fellow Berkeley Coll., Yale U. Mem. Elizabethan Club (New Haven), Yale Club. Roman Catholic. Home: 1755 York Ave New York NY 10128 Office: 399 Park Ave New York NY 10022 E-mail: bernard@saint-donat.com.

ST. GEORGE, JOYCE, conflict and crisis management educator, writer; b. N.Y.C., June 19, 1951; d. Salvatore and Gloria (Munoz) St. G.; m. Francis Patrick Canavan, Dec. 11, 1982; 1 child, Kathleen. B, John Jay Coll., 1974; grad., NYU, 1980. Diplomate Am. Acad. Experts in Traumatic Stress. Spl. anti corruption investigator N.Y. State Atty. Gen.'s Office Criminal Justice, N.Y.C., 1973-79; pres. Pact Tng., New Kingston, N.Y., 1980—; rape crisis counselor, cons. St. Vincent's Hosp. Rape Crisis Program, N.Y.C., 1976-87; expert witness in sexual assault Queens County Dist. Atty.'s Office Spl. Victims Divsn., 1985-90; instr. New Sch. Social Rsch., 1984-86; instr., writer Columbia U., 1988-89; expert witness rape trauma syndrome Queens County Dist. Atty.'s Office, 1985-90; co-founder, dir. pact tng. and drama based tng. Cons., instr. U.S. Dept. Justice, N.Y.C., 1990-94; dir. Ctr. Theater Techniques in Edn., New Haven, Conn., 1985—. Author: Conflict Management in Hospital Settings, 1988, Perfect Cover, 1994. Recipient Disting. Alumna award John Jay Coll. Criminal Justice, 1994. Office: Pact Tng LLC PO Box 106 New Kingston NY 12459 Fax: 845-586-4277. E-mail: pactrain@catskill.net.

ST. GEORGE, JUDITH ALEXANDER, author; b. Westfield, N.J., Feb. 26, 1931; d. John Heald and Edna (Perkins) Alexander; m. David St. George, June 5, 1954; children: Peter, James, Philip, Sarah Anne. BA, Smith Coll., 1952. Author: Turncoat Winter, Rebel Spring, 1970, The Girl with Spunk, 1975, By George, Bloomers!, 1976, The Chinese Puzzle of Shag Island, 1976, The Shad Are Running, 1977, The Shadow of the Shaman, 1977, The Halo Wind, 1978, The Halloween Pumpkin Smasher, 1978, Mystery at St. Martin's, 1979, The Amazing Voyage of the New Orleans, 1980, Haunted, 1980, Call Me Margo, 1981, The Mysterious Girl in the Garden, 1981, The Brooklyn Bridge: They Said It Couldn't Be Built, 1982 (Am. Book award, N.Y. Acad. of Sci. award), Do You See What I See?, 1982, In The Shadow of the Bear, 1983, What's Happening to My Junior Year?, 1983, Who's Scared? Not Me!, 1984, The Mount Rushmore, 1985 (Christopher award), Panama Canal: Gateway to the World, 1989 (Golden Kite award), The White House, 1990, Mason and Dixon's Line of Fire, 1991, Dear Dr. Bell...Your Friend Helen Keller, 1992, Crazy Horse, 1994, To See With the Heart: The Life of Sitting Bull, 1996, Betsy Ross: Patriot of Philadelphia, 1997 (N.Y. Sons of the Am. Revolution award), Sacagawea, 1997, In the Line of Fire: President's Lives at Stake, 1999, So You Want To Be President?, 2001 (Caldecott medal, 2001), John and Abigail Adams: An American Love Story, 2001, So You Want to be an Inventor?, 2002. Adv. coun. on children's lit. Rutgers U., 1977-94; chmn. ednl. com. Bklyn. Bridge Centennial Commn., 1981-83; tchr. creative writing York Correctional Instn., Niantic, Conn. Mem. Soc. Children's Book Writers, Author's Guild. Episcopalian. Avocations: tennis, hiking, travel. Home: 8 Binney Rd Old Lyme CT 06371-1445

ST. GEORGE, LAURA MAE, retired middle school educator; b. Yakima, Wash., Apr. 4, 1935; d. Clarence C. and Bertha E. (Roy) S. BA, Cen. Wash. Coll., 1957; MEd, Seattle U., 1969. Tchr., staff devel. Bellevue (Wash.) Sch. Dist., 1958-90; adj. faculty Seattle Pacific U., 1981-90; tchg. assoc., instr. edn. U. Wash., Seattle, 1989-91; tchr. Forest Ridge Mid. Sch., Bellevue, Wash., 1990-99, ret., 1999. Mem. Nat. Bd. for Profl. Tchg. Stds. Vol. Habitat for Humanity. Mem. NEA, ASCD, Nat. Mid. Sch. Assn., Wash. Edn. Assn., Alpha Delta Kappa. Home: 795 E Chesapeake Dr Shelton WA 98584-9411 E-mail: stgeorge@hctc.com.

ST. GERMAIN, FERNAND JOSEPH, retired congressman; b. Blackstone, Mass. s. Andrew Joseph and Pearl (Talaby) St. Germain; m. Rachel O'Neill, Aug. 20, 1953 (dec.); children: Laurene, Lisette. PhB in Social Sci, Providence Coll., 1948, LLD, 1965; LLB, Boston U., 1955; JSD (hon.), Suffolk U., 1976; DCL (hon.), Our Lady of Providence Sem., 1968; DBA (hon.), Bryant Coll., 1981; D in Pub. Svc. (hon.), Roger Williams Coll., 1981; LLB, Brown U., 1985. Bar: R.I. 1956, Fed. 1957, U.S. Supreme Ct. 1983. Mem. R.I. Ho. of Reps., 1952-60, 87th to 100th Congresses from 1st R.I. Dist., 1961-1989, chmn. house com. on banking fin. and urban affairs, 1980-88; ret., 1988. Served with AUS, 1949-52. Recipient Silver Shingle award for disting. public service Boston U. Sch. Law Alumni Assn., 1981, Alumni award disting. pub. service Boston U. Sch. Law, 1982 Mem. ABA, R.I., Bar Assn. Fed. Bar Assn., alumni assns. Our Lady of Providence Sem., Providence Coll., Boston U. Law Sch., Am. Legion.

ST. GERMAIN, SHERYL A. humanities educator, writer; b. New Orleans, July 28, 1954; d. Jules Francois and Myrl Marie (Frank) St. G.; m. Charles Henry Gideon, Aug. 9, 1983 (div.); 1 child, Gray. BA in English, Southeastern La. U., 1979; MA in Arts and Humanities, U. Tex., Dallas, 1982, PhD, 1986. Asst. prof. English U. La., Lafayette, 1991-94, Knox Coll., Ill., 1994-98; assoc. prof. English Iowa State U., Ames, 1998—. Author: (poetry) The Mask of Medusa, 1987, Making Bread at Midnight, 1991, How Heavy the Breath of God, 1994, The Journals of Scheherazade, 1996. Fellow NEA, 1992, 96. Avocations: cooking, gardening, music. Office: Iowa State U Dept English Rose Hall 203 Ames IA 50011 E-mail: sgermain@iastate.edu.

ST. GERMAINE-LATTIG, CHARLES EDWIN, political writer; b. Rhinelander, Wis., Feb. 12, 1949; s. William St. Germaine and Ina Margaret (Lobermier) Valliere; children: Spencer Charles, Aimy Dixon. Student, SUNY, Buffalo, 1967-68, Syracuse U., 1969. Polit. writer Am. Indian Movement, 1972-79, Mpls., 1979—. Free-lance photographer, 1976—; co-hose, prodr. radio program: Living on Indian Time, KPFA, Berkeley, Calif., 1976-77; founder, editor Bay Area Indian News, Oakland, 1976-77; contbr. articles to profl. jours. Cadre mem. Am. Indian Movement, 1972-79; mem. Met. Opera Guild; tribal mem. Lac du Flambeau Band of Lake Superior Chippewa, Wis. With U.S. Army, 1971-72, Korea. Mem. Acad. Polical Sci., Nat. Audobon Soc., Nature Conservancy. Avocations: wildlife and environmental preservation, astronomy, classical music, Shakespearean drama, N.E. Asian political history. Home: 2447 16th Ave S Minneapolis MN 55404-3905 E-mail: nativerealist@aol.com.

SAINT-GIRARD, CHRISTIAN, theatre director, choreographer, actor, educator, theater producer; b. N.Y.C., May 29, 1954; s. Victoria J. Walter. Student, U. Oslo, 1972, Fordham U., 1972-74, Stella Adler Conservatory, N.Y.C.; studied with Uta Hagen and H. Berghof, HB Studios, N.Y.C.; studied dance, Joffrey Ballet; student dance, Am. Ballet Theatre; also others. Dir. Merry-Go-Round Playhouse, Auburn, N.Y., 1990-92; dir. edn. Polka Dot Playhouse, Bridgeport, Conn., 2002; artistic dir. Playhouse-on-the-Green, 2002. Mem. bd. advisors Actor's Outlet Theatre Ctr., N.Y.C., 1981-85, chmn. steering com., 1982-83; pres., producing artistic dir. Prodrs.' Assn. Real Theatre for Youth, Darien, Ct., 1986-87; tchr. workshops and classes; guest instr. acting and auditioning for mus. theatre and dance at profl. studios, including Actor's Outlet Theatre, Manhattan Theatre Workshop, N.Y.C., Studio at Once Upon a Time Prodns., Inc., N.Y.C., Phil Black's Dance Studio, N.Y.C., Darien Dance Ctr., Darien Arts Coun., Conn. Conservatory for Performing Arts, Workshop Prodns., Inc., Stratford (Conn.) Acad. Dance, Conn. Dance, Newtown (Conn.) Ctr. for Performing Arts, Showbiz Kids, Conn.; performer on Broadway in A Chorus Line, Grease, Shenandoah; on nat. tours in Camelot, A Light Night Music, Oliver!, title role in Pippin; performer in stock and dinner theatre in Funny Girl, Hello Dolly!, The King & I, Cabaret; also appeared in TV pilots, feature films, commls. and operas. Author: (with Viveca Lindfors) (play) Three Boards and A Passion, 1981; librettist (mus. play) Alice in Wonderland, 1985, (ballet) The Red Shoes, 1987; dir., choreographer Singin' in the Rain, She Loves Me, 42d Street, Cabaret, Mame, Into the Woods, Camelot, Applause, My Fair Lady, Unsinkable Molly Brown, Hello, Dolly!, Shenandoah, Music Man, Gypsy, Forty Carats, Chicago, On the Town, Twelfth Night, Cinderella, A Touch of Spring, West Side Story, Annie, Snow White, Pinocchio, Hansel and Gretel, Sleeping Beauty, The Magic Flute, also others; choreographer Paint Your Wagon, Oklahoma, South Pacific, Fame Mem. SAG, AFTRA, Actors Equity Assn., Cath. Actors Guild. Republican. Roman Catholic. Avocations: painting, sketching, tennis. E-mail: CSGDirchor@aol.com.

ST. GOAR, HERBERT, retired food corporation executive; b. Hamburg, Germany, Apr. 7, 1916; came to U.S., 1938, naturalized, 1943; s. Otto and Thekla St.G.; m. Maria Karsch, Sept. 3, 1954; children: Edward, Elisabeth. Student schs., Hamburg, Germany; LL.B., Chattanooga Coll. Law, 1943. With Internat. Harvester Co., Hamburg, Germany, 1936-38; with Dixie Saving Stores, Inc., Chattanooga, 1938—, pres., 1969-98, chief exec. officer, 1969-98, pres. emeritus, 1998-99; ret., 1999. Author: Autobiography: Taking Stock of My Life, 2000. Bd. dirs. Chattanooga Opera Assn., Jr. C. of C., 1945-54; mem. Hamilton County Juvenile Ct. Commn. Served with Intelligence Sect., U.S. Army, World War II. Decorated Bronze Star, Legion of Merit.; Named Disting. Citizen Chattanooga, 1979 Mem. Southeastern Food Coop. Assn. (past pres.), Tenn. Wholesale Grocers Assn. (bd. dirs. 1988-91), Retailer-Owned Food Distrbrs. Assn. (bd. dirs. 1988-98), NGA Retailer-Owned Exec. Coun., Asparagus Club. Home: 1502 Hixson Pike Chattanooga TN 37405-2431

ST. GODARD, EDWARD G. Roman Catholic priest; b. Pawtucket, RI, Apr. 24, 1939; s. David Benson and Antoinette M. St-Godard. BA, Our Lady of Providence Seminary, RI, 1960; M. Div, St. Bernard Seminar, NY, 1970. Assoc. pastor St. John the Baptist Church, W. Warwick, RI, 1964—68, St. Joan of Arc, Cumberland, 1968—71, Our Lady of Consolation, Pawtucket, 1971—76, St. John the Baptist, Pawtucket, 1976—82, St. Joseph Church, Pawtucket, 1982—91; pastor Holy Family Church, Woonsocket, 1991—. Mem. Ecumenical Comn., Diocese of Providence, 1975—, Priests-Rabris Dialogue, 1990—; assoc. mem. Sisters of Mercy, 1985—. Co-author: (book) The French in Rhode Island, 1978; author: St. John's Parish in Pawtucket RI, 1979, History of Holy Family Parish, 1991. Trustee Pawtucket Pub. Libr., 1984—; bd. mem. Pawtucket Redevelopment Bd., 1982—84; Chaplain Woonsocket Fire Dept., 1992—. Roman Catholic. Avocations: Genealogy, Counselling, Hiking. Home: 99 Clyde St Pawtucket RI 02860 Office: Holy Family Church 414 S Main St Woonsocket RI 02895

ST. HILAIRE, CAROLINE, member of parliament; b. Longueuil, Can., Nov. 16, 1969; 1 child, Etienne. BA in Adminstrn., U. Quebec, 1993. With Soc. du droit de reproduction des auteurs, compositeurs et éditeurs du Can.; M.P. for Bloc Quebecois House of Commons, asst. house leader. Founder Soc. de Promotion Pour La Releve Musicale de l'espace Francophone. Avocation competitive figure skating. Office: House of Commons 647-S Centre Block Ottawa ON Canada K1A 0A6

ST. HILAIRE, CHERIE ANN, pharmacist; b. Yakima, WA, Feb. 22, 1968; d. Thomas Charles and Rose Marie St. Hilaire. Student, Yakima C.C., 1986-87, U. Wash., 1987-89; BS, Wash. State U., 1993. Registered pharmacist. Staff pharmacist Payless Drug Store, Spokane, Wash., 1993-97; clin. pharmacist Virginia Mason Hosp., Seattle, 1997-2000; agy. pharmacist Cameron & Co., 2000—. Mem. Am. Pharm. Assn., Wash. State Pharmacists Assn. Avocations: travel, reading, house remodeling, spending time with friends. Home: 15328 SE 179th St Renton WA 98058-9043 E-mail: Pharmerc@hotmail.com.

ST. HILAIRE, DAVID WILLIAM, county official, financial manager; b. Bennington, Vt., Jan. 5, 1964; s. Donald Wilfred Sr. and Gudrun Albertine St. Hilaire; m. Julie Diane Prebble, Nov. 6, 1992; children: Jonathan Mathieu, Shania Albertine. BS in Bus. Econs., SUNY, Oneonta, 1986; MBA in Fin., SUNY, Binghamton, 1989; MS in Acctg., SUNY, Albany, 1995, MS in Taxation, 2001. Loan originator Bennington Savs. and Loan, 1987; fin. analyst Unisys Corp., Flemington, N.J., 1988-89; lead sr. fin. analyst Shearson Smith Barney, N.Y.C., 1990-93; sales agt. Northwestern Mut. Life, Latham, N.Y.,

1993-95; dept. chief fiscal officer Rensselaer County, Troy, 1996—. Town supr. Town of Hoosick, Hoosick Falls, N.Y., 1996-99; chmn. bd. dirs., fin. com. Hoosick Falls Ctrl. Sch. Dist., 1994-95; bd. dirs. Rensselaer County Sr. Citizen Adv. Bd., 1996-2001, Buskirk's Bridge Preservation Assn., 1998-99, Rev. Edith Craig Reynolds Found., 1996-99; mem. fin. com. St. Francis deSales, 2001—; active ARC, 2001—. Recipient Citizenship award Hoosick Falls Ctrl. Sch. Dist., 1982, Am. Hometown Leadership award Nat. Assn. Towns and Twps./Walmart, Washington, 1998, highest achievement award Dale Carnegie Course, Colonie, N.Y., 1999. Mem. Rensselaer County Suprs. Assn. (founder, organizer, chmn. 1998-99), Kiwanis (v.p. Hoosick Falls chpt. 1999), Inst. of Mgmt. Accts., Nat. Soc. Tax Profls., Elks, St. Stansilaw Soc., Beta Gamma Sigma, Alpha Phi Omega. Roman Catholic. Avocations: travel, outdoor activities, gardening, family. Office: Rensselaer County 1600 7th Ave Troy NY 12180-3410 Home: 125 Main St Hoosick Falls NY 12090-2006

SAINT-JACQUES, BERNARD, linguistics educator; b. Montreal, Que., Can., Apr. 26, 1928; s. Albert and Germaine (Lefebvre) Saint-J.; m. Marguerite Fauquenoy. MA, Sophia U., Tokyo, 1962; MS, Georgetown U., 1964; Doctorat es Lettres and Scis. Humaines, Paris U., 1975. Asst. prof. linguistics U. B.C., Vancouver, 1967-69, assoc. prof., 1969-78, prof., 1978-90, prof. emeritus, 1991—; prof. Aichi U., Japan, 1990—. Mem. U.S. Citizen Amb. Program. Author: Structural Analysis of Modern Japanese, 1971, Aspects sociolinguistiques du bilinguisme canadien, 1976, Language and Ethnic Relations, 1979, Japanese Studies in Canada, 1985, Studies in Language and Culture, 1995; editor: Intercultural Communication Studies, 1998; co-editor: Contrasting Political Institutions, 1997, (with M. Iwasaki) Democratic Viability in Politics, 2000. Leave fellow Can. Council, 1974; profl. fellow Japan Found., 1981; research fellow French Govt., 1982, Ohira Programme, Japan, 1983 Fellow Royal Soc. Can. Acad., Internat. Acad. Intercultural Rsch.; mem. Linguistic Soc. Am., Can. Soc. Asian Studies, Can. Linguistics Assn., Sietar Japan. Office: U BC Dept Linguistics Vancouver BC Canada V6T 1Z1 also: Aichi ShuKutoKu U Katahira NagaKute NagaKute-cho Aichi-gun 480-1197 Japan E-mail: saintj@asu.aasa.ac.jp.

ST. JEAN, JOSEPH, JR. micropaleontologist, educator; b. Tacoma, July 24, 1923; s. Joseph Leger and Ruby Pearl (Burg) St. J.; m. Elena Mikhailovna Melnikova, Sept. 22, 1971. BS, Coll. Puget Sound, 1949; MA, Ind. U., 1953, PhD, 1956. Field asst., party chief Ind. Geol. Survey, summers 1950-53; instr. Kans. State U., Manhattan, 1951-52; instr., asst. prof. Trinity Coll., Hartford, Conn., 1955-57; faculty U. N.C., Chapel Hill, 1957-90, prof. geology, 1966-90, gen. coll. advisor, 1979-90, ret., 1990. Peer reviewer NSF, 1966-92, profl. jours., 1960— 2d violinist, Durham (N.C.) Symphony Orch., 1977-84; Contbr. sects. to McGraw-Hill Ency. Sci. and Tech; papers to paleontol., biol. jours. Served as Q.M. USNR, 1942-45. Grantee Geol. Soc. Am., 1956-58; Grantee AEC, 1958-60; Grantee NSF, 1960-62; Grantee U. N.C. Faculty Research Council, 1960-62; Grantee Soc. Sigma Xi, 1954-56 Mem. Paleontol. Soc., Soc. Econ. Paleontologists and Mineralogists, Carolina Geol. Soc., Paleontol. Rsch. Instn., N.C. Acad. Scis., Paleontol. Assn. London, Sigma Xi. Home: 1212 Hillsborough Rd Chapel Hill NC 27516-8712 Office: U NC Dept Geol Scis Cb 3315 Mitchell Hall Chapel Hill NC 27599-3315 E-mail: jstjean@email.unc.edu.

ST. JOHN, ADRIAN, II, retired army officer; b. Ft. Leavenworth, Kans., Nov. 16, 1921; s. Adrian and Marie (McMahon) St John; m. Petronella Elizabeth Durham, Jan. 19, 1943 (dec. 1982); children: Adrian III, Brian; m. Florence Tucker Parrish, Jan. 29, 1998. BS, U.S. Mil. Acad., 1943; MA, U. Va., 1951; MPA, Am. U., 1981; postgrad., Army War Coll., 1960, U. Hawaii, 1963, Am. U., 1977-82. Commd. 2d lt. U.S. Army, 1943, advanced through grades to maj. gen., 1969, co. comdg. officer 15th Cav., 1943-45, intelligence staff officer, 1945—47, China desk officer gen. staff Washington, 1951-53, bn. comdg. officer 3d Bn., 31st Inf. Regt. Korea, 1954, comdr. 73d Tank Bn. Korea, 1955; mem. faculty Command and Gen. Staff Coll., Ft. Leavenworth, 1956-59; faculty adviser Iranian Def. Coll., 1959; S.E. Asia plans officer G3, U.S. Army-Pacific, 1960-64; long range plans br. Strategic Div., Orgn. Joint Chiefs of Staff, Washington, 1964-66; chief Surface P & O Div. J3, USMACV, Vietnam, 1966-67; comdg. officer 14th Armored Cav. Regt., Europe, 1967-69; asst. div. comdr. 4th Armored Div., Europe, 1969-70; chief Strategic Plans and Policy Div. J5, Orgn. Joint Chiefs of Staff, Washington, 1970-71; dir. plans gen. staff U.S. Army, 1971-72; comdg. gen. 1st Armored Div., Europe, 1972-74; vice dir. joint staff Joint Chiefs of Staff, 1974-76; ret., 1976; mem. adv. council on internat. security affairs Republican Nat. Com., 1977-80; del. Va. State Rep. Conv., 1980, 81; sr. mil. adv. U.S. Negotiating Del. Mut. Balanced Force Reductions, Vienna, 1982-88; Joint Chiefs of Staff rep. U.S. Del. Conventional Stability Talks, 1987-88, negotiations on Conventional Armed Forces, Europe, 1989-92. Del., presenter Congress Arms Control Mid. East, Delphi, Greece, 1994; U.S. del. World Helicopter Championships, Moscow, 1994, Oreg., 1996; chmn. operational working group internat. conf. on arms control in Mid. East, Jordan, 1994; mem. advance party OSCE to prepare for elections, Bosnia, 1997; presenter plaques signed by Sec. of Def. to Australian authorities in 6 cities during ceremonies commemorating VJ Day, 1995; supr. parliamentary elections, Bosnia, 1997; participant Conf. on Reshaping European Security Rels., Eng., 2001. Co-chmn. orchestral benefit ball Austrian Embassy, 1993, 1994; supr. Mcpl. Election Commn., Bosnia, 2000; participant in Conf. on Application European Arms Control Negotiations to Pakistan-India Situation, U.K., 2001; election supr. Kosovo, 2001. Decorated D.S.M. with oak leaf cluster, Silver Star, Legion of Merit with 3 oak leaf clusters, Bronze Star with V device, Joint Svc. Commendation medal, Army Commendation medal with oak leaf cluster, Joint Meritorious Unit award, French Croix de Guerre with silver star, Vietnamese Gallantry Cross with palm; recipient European Comdr. in Chief's Individual Project partnership award, 1968, Presdl. award Disting. Citizen, 1993, Dept. State Superior honor award, 1989, 91, Sec. of Def. medal for disting. pub. svc., 1992, medal as disting. grad. U.S. Mil. Acad., 1998. Mem. Am. Security Coun., Am. Fgn. Affairs Coun., Heritage Found., World Affairs Coun. Roman Catholic. Office: 9110 Belvoir Woods Pkwy Apt 118 Fort Belvoir VA 22060-2717 E-mail: sinjenii@att.net. *There are no limits to the heights man can reach so long as he cares not who gets the credit.*

ST. JOHN, BILL DEAN, diversified equipment and services company executive; b. Wewoka, Okla., 1931; BBA, So. Meth. U., 1952. Asst. treas. Seaboard Oil Co., 1954-58; auditor Alford Merony & Co., 1958-60; v.p. fin. Can. Refractories Ltd., 1968; with Dresser Industries Inc., Dallas, 1960-96; treas. Ideco div. Dresser Industries, 1961-63; fin. contr. Dresser Industries Inc., 1970-73, staff v.p. fin. svcs., 1975-76, v.p. acctg., 1976-80; exec. v.p. adminstrn. Dresser Industries, Inc., 1980-92, vice chmn., 1992-96, vice chmn., CFO, 1993-96; mng. dir. SMG Mgmt. L.L.C., 1997-2000; ret., 2000. With U.S. Army, 1952-54. Mem. AICPA.

ST. JOHN, CHARLES VIRGIL, retired pharmaceutical company executive; b. Bryan, Ohio, Dec. 18, 1922; s. Clyde W. and Elsie (Kintner) St. J.; m. Ruth Ilene Wilson, Oct. 27, 1946; children: Janet Sue St. John Amy, Debra Ann St. John Mishler. AB, Manchester Coll., 1943; MS, Purdue U., 1946; DSc honoris causa, Manchester Coll., 1999. Asst. gen. mgr., dir. ops. Eli Lilly and Co., Clinton, Ind., 1971-75, gen. mgr. Lafayette, 1975-77, v.p. prodn. ops. divsn., 1977-89. Bd. dirs. Bank One of Lafayette, Lafayette Life Ins. Co., Lafayette Cmty. Found., Bioanalytical Sys., Inc., West Lafayette, Ind. Past pres. bd. dirs. United Way Greater Lafayette and Tippecanoe County; bd. trustees Lafayette Symphony Found.; past chmn. lay adv. coun. St. Elizabeth Hosp.; mem. pres.'s coun. Purdue U.; trustee Manchester (Ind.) Coll.; bd. dirs. Lafayette Cmty. Found., Jr. Achievement of Greater Lafayette, Vols. in Probation, Long Ctr. for Performing Arts, Sagamore of the Wabash, 2001. Recipient Elizabethan award, St. Elizabeth Hosp., Lafayette, 1985, Sagamore of the Wabash award, 2001; named Cmty. Hero Olympic Torch Bearer, 1996. Mem. Am. Chem. Soc., Purdue Rsch. Found., Greater Lafayette C. of C. (past bd. dirs., Grand Marquis de Lafayette award Cmty. Svc. 1996), Lafayette Country Club, Rotary. Republican. Methodist. Home: 3627 Senior Pl West Lafayette IN 47906

ST. JOHN, EVERT EUGENE, insurance company executive; b. Ft. Worth, Nov. 20, 1926; s. Warren Evert and Madeline Emily (Mount) St. J.; m. Mary Frances Wilson, June 23, 1953; children: Mary Madeline Whittinghill, James Warren, Paul Eugene. BA with hons., U. Tex., 1947. CFP, CLU, ChFC. Dir. agys. Prudential, Houston, 1960-69; v.p., founding dir. Sysco Corp., 1969-75; gen. agent Prin. Life, Des Moines, 1975—. Pres. bd. dirs. Goodwill Industries, Ft. Worth, 1998-2001, immediate past pres., bd. dirs., 2001—. Lt. USNR, 1944-69. Mem. Rotary. Republican. Baptist. Avocations: creative writing, golfing. Office: St John Rigg Inc Carter Burgess Plz 777 Main St Ste 760 Fort Worth TX 76102-5353

ST. JOHN, HENRY SEWELL, JR. utility company executive; b. Birmingham, Ala., Aug. 18, 1938; s. H. Sewell and Carrie M. (Bond) St. J.; m. J. Ann Morris, Mar. 7, 1959; children: Sherri Ann, Brian Lee, Teresa Lynn, Cynthia Faye. Student, David Lipscomb Coll., 1956-58, U. Tenn., 1958-59, U. Ala., 1962-64. Engring. aide Ala. Power Co., Enterprise , 1960-62, Birmingham, 1962-66; asst. chief engr. Riviera Utilities, Foley, Ala., 1966-71, sec.-treas., gen. mgr., 1972—2001. Deacon Foley Ch. of Christ, 1975-82, elder, 1983-; chmn. Baldwin County unit Am. Cancer Soc. , 1977; treas. Christian Care Ctr. Inc., 1981—; bd. dirs. AGAPE of Mobile , 1977—80; bd. dirs. South Baldwin Civic Chorus, pres., 1979-82; bd. dirs. Baldwin County Econ. Devel. Alliance2000-2001 , 1997—2001; exec. com. Baldwin County Econ. Devel. Alliance, 1999—2001, sec., 1998—99, treas., 1999—2000, chmn., 2000—01. Mem.: IEEE, Chevrolet Nomad Assn. (bd. dirs. 1991—2002, v.p. 1993—2002), South Baldwin C. of C. (dir. 1972—75, pres. 1974, dir. 1981—90, 1992—95), Pub. Gas Assn. Ala. (bd. dirs. 1987—88), Am. Pub. Power Assn. (com. legis. and resolutions 1972—2001, chmn. State of Ala. mem. com. 1982—2001, com. on coms. 1997—2000, bd. dirs. 1997—2001, exec. com. 1999—2000, chmn. nat. membership com. 1999—2000, chmn. bylaws com. 2000—01), United Mcpl. Distbrs. Group (bd. dirs. 1972—2001), Electric Cities Ala. (bd. dirs., exec. com. 1989—2001, vice chmn. 2000—01, chmn. 2001), Ala. Mcpl. Electric Authority (vice chmn. 1981—83, bd. dirs. 1981—2001, chmn. 1984—2001), Mcpl. Electric Utility Assn. Ala. (exec. com., dir. 1971—85), Ala. Consumer-Owned Power Distbrs. Assn. (chmn. 1974—75, sec.-treas. 1980, vice chmn. 1981, chmn. 1982—83), South Ala. Power Distbrs. Assn. (chmn. 1973—74), S.E. Electric Reliability Coun. (assoc.), Azalea City Classic Chevy (bd. dirs., exec. com. 1989—99, v.p. 1991—92, v.p. 1996—99), Gulf Shores Golf (dir. 1974—75), Foley Quarterback (sec.-treas. 1984—85), Classic Chevy, Internat. (life). Home: PO Box 1817 Foley AL 36536-1817 E-mail: stjohn@gulftel.com.

ST. JOHN, MARIA ANN, nurse anesthetist; b. Rochester, Pa., Dec. 15, 1953; d. James Edward and Evelyn Marie (Sayers) St. J.; m. Paul David Dworsky, Aug. 19, 1978 (div. Dec. 13, 1991); children: Lauren Marie Dworsky, Michael David Dworsky. BSN, U. Pitts., 1975; cert. reg. nurse anesthetist, U. Health Ctr. Pitts. Sch. Anesthesia for Nurses, 1984. Advanced RN practitioner Fla., Ohio; cert. RN anesthetist, Pa., Ohio, N.C., Ky. Nurse Presbyn. U. Hosp., Pitts., 1975-77, VA Hosp., Pitts., 1977-82; nurse anesthetist Anesthesia Assocs. of Hollywood, Fla., 1984-87, North Hills Anesthesia Assocs., Pitts., 1987-98, Queen City Anesthesiologists, Inc., Cin., 1998—. Vol. tchr. art history, fundraiser St. Alexis Sch., Wexford, Pa., 1991-97, recording sec. PT6 Bd., 1996-97, v.p. PT6 Bd., 1997-98; mem. Cranberry Twp. Athletic Assn., 1991-98, Oak Hills PTA, Cin., 1998-99, Oak Hills Athletic Boosters, 1999, PTG Springmeyer Sch. and Bridgetown Jr. H.S., Cinn., 1998-99, PTG and Athletic Boosters, Bridgetown Middle Sch., 1999—. Recipient scholarship March of Dimes, Beaver County, Pa., 1971, Pitt. scholarship, 1971-75. Mem. DAR, Am. Assn. Nurse Anesthetists, Pa. Assn. Nurse Anesthetists, Ohio Assn. Nurse Anesthetists, Fla. Assn. Nurse Anesthetists, Ky. Nurse Anesthetists, N.C. Nurse Anesthetists. Avocations: playing piano, reading, traveling, school volunteering, swimming. Home: 6073 Werk Rd Cincinnati OH 45248-4043

ST. JOHN, SHAY, fundraising executive; b. Roanoke, Va., June 17, 1944; d. Stuart Dexter and Reba Claudine (Summers) Bancroft; m. Robert Bryan Ellsworth, July 10, 1973 (div. Dec. 1978); m. Neble Allen Sears, Aug. 30, 1985; children: Megan Nau, Deborah Fifer. BA, Va. Poly. Inst., 1969; postgrad., Hollins Coll., 1973-75. Cert. fundraising exec.; ordained to ministry, 1982. Tchr. German and Spanish Roanoke County Schs., 1969-74; tchr. German Va. Western Coll., Roanoke, 1974-75; min. Unity Ch. Savannah, Ga., 1977-84, Unity Christ Ch., San Francisco, 1984-89; v.p. devel. Assn. Unity Chs., Lees Summit, Mo., 1990—. Chaplain for women police San Francisco Police Dept., 1985-88; regional rep. West Ctrl. Chs., Calif., Nev., eastern Conn., 1986-89. Author: Incredible Journey, 1993, Gift Planning Manual, 1997, Development Resource Manual, 1993, Ministry Leadership Manual, 1993; contbr. articles to mags. Vol. AIDS Found., San Francisco, 1985-90; pres. bd. dirs. Kairos House, San Francisco, 1986-87, vol., 1986—; vol., tchr. Unity Sch. Religious Studies, Unity Village, Mo., 1988— Mem. Nat. Soc. Fundraising Execs., Greater Kansas City Coun. of Philanthropy, Phi Kappa Phi. Avocations: writing, photography. Office: Assn Unity Chs PO Box 610 Lees Summit MO 64063-0610

ST. JOHN, WILLIAM CHARLES, JR. business educator, administrator; b. N.Y.C., Mar. 28, 1944; s. William Charles and Marie Ellen St. John; m. Katrin A. Wesner, Dec. 7, 1996. BS in Econs., Siena Coll., 1966; MS in Indsl. Mgmt. Adminstrn., Union Coll., 1972; PhD in Urban Environ. Studies, Rensselaer Poly. Inst., 1989. Cert. govt. fin. mgr. Contr., treas. Cap. Dist. Transp. Authority, Albany, N.Y., 1970-82; chief fiscal officer Rensselaer County, Troy, 1982-85; prof. Rensselaer Poly. Inst., 1990—; exec. dir. Market Block Incubator, 1997-98. Pres. Econ. Devel. Agy., Troy, 1984-88; chmn. Indsl. Devel. Agy., Troy, 1986-90, Greater Troy C. of C., 1985. Office: PO Box 785 Troy NY 12181-0785

ST. JUDE, F. M. actor, writer, artist; b. Pottsville, Pa., Jan. 14, 1950; s. Fred G. and Martha L. Dengler; m. Suzanne Stutz Dengler, Dec. 28, 1969; 1 child Shannon Dengler. Student, Immaculate Heart Acad., Ford Sch. Bus. Lead singer, musician various bands; entrepreneur internet sites Fla. Author: Insidious, 1999, Visions in Deep Sleep, 1999; musician: (CD) Gang War, 1997; author: (screenplays) Deacon Blues, 1999, Space Dog, 2000, (compilation of 1 act plays) Space Plays, 2000; prodr.: (videos); publisher: magazine Zazz Magazine. Mem.: SAG, Bone Valley Fossil Soc. Avocations: sculptor, paleontology , archaeology.

ST. LANDAU, NORMAN, lawyer; b. Vienna, Austria, Apr. 14, 1925; s. Henry M. and Anka (Nemirovska) St. L.; m. Maisie Dennis, July 18, 1942; children— Lorraine, Jon L., Norman D. BS, AB with honors, U. Ill., 1941; LL.B., Rutgers U., 1948; LL.M., NYU, 1951. Bar: D.C. 1948, U.S. Supreme Ct. 1952, N.J. 1958. With Pitts. Plate Glass Co., Ohio, 1941-42; with Johnson & Johnson, New Brunswick, N.J., 1942-84, internat. counsel, 1957-84, chief trademark counsel, 1961-84; dir., officer numerous affiliates Johnson & Johnson Internat.; of counsel Lalos, Leeds, Keegan & Marsh, Washington, 1983-85, Durand, Gorman, Heher, Imbriaco & Morrice, Princeton, N.J., 1984-86, Brylawski, Cleary & Leeds, 1985-90; ptnr. Heher, Clarke & St. Landau, Princeton, 1987-97; counsel Tucker, Flyer, Lewis, Washington, 1990—; chmn. bd. Action Law Systems, Inc., 1987-90; of counsel Tucker Flyer & Lewis, Washington, 1989—; prin. Law Offices of Norman St. Landau, Princeton, 1990—. Mem. adv. com. Sec. State and Commr. Patents, 1975—; bd. dirs. Nika Ltd., Pulsair Ltd., BP Johnson. Co-author: Trademark Management, 1977, Guide to Patent Arbitration, 1987; fgn. editor Les Nouvelles, 1965—. Exec. com., gen. counsel N.J. State Opera, 1958—. Mem. N.J. State Bar Assn. (v.p. patent, trademark and unfair competition sect. 1980-82, vice-chmn. immigration and nationality sect. 1988—), Nat. Fgn. Trade Council (chmn. indsl. property com.), N.J. Patent Law Assn. (past pres.), Nat. Council Patent Law Assns. (sec.-gen.), Nat. Panel Arbitrators, Am. Arbitration Assn., ABA, Am. Chem. Soc. (nat. councillor), Am. Patent Law Assn. (bd. mgrs.), Am. Immigration Lawyers Assn., Inter-Am. Assn. Indsl. Property (exec. com.), Internat. Patent and Trademark Assn., Lic. Execs. Lawyers, Nassau Club, Rotary, Hershey's Hill Club. Home: 200 Sunrise Blvd Exton PA 19341-2337

ST. LIFER, JANE M. art dealer, curator; b. N.Y.C., Apr. 19, 1956; d. Martin R. and Marcia (Simon) St. L. BFA, Syracuse U., 1978; MA, N.J. City U., 1996. Dir. print dept. Trail Side Galleries, Jackson, Wyo., 1978—79, Scottsdale, Ariz., 1978—79; gallery dir., Phoenix Art Press, 1980-81; dir. print dept. Hammer Galleries, N.Y.C., 1981-86; sales mgr. Gallery Urban, 1986-88; dir., owner Jane St. Lifer Fine Art, Inc., 1988—; asst. dir. Grand Ctrl. Art Galleries, 1991-92. Mem. Am. Soc. Appraisers, Auctioneers Assn. (sec., v.p. 1990—), Avocations: culinary arts, dog fancier, theater. Office: Jane St Lifer Fine Art Inc 11 Hanover Sq # 703 New York NY 10005-2819

ST. LOUIS, NENA, artist, performance artist; b. St. Louis, Sept. 17, 1951; d. Hughes Hannibal and Lela Nuna (Knox) Shanks; m. Michael Barton Lewis, July 30, 1987. Student, Macalester Coll., 1972-73; BA, U. Nebr., 1974; postgrad., U. Calif., Berkeley, 1988-90, Lorraine Hansberry Theatre, San Francisco, 1991-93. Playwright Lorraine Hansberry Theatre, San Francisco, 1991-93; s. Artist in residence Univ. Nebr. Artist Diversity Program. One woman plays performed at Solo Mio, San Francisco, 1993, The Marsh Theatre, 1993, 94, 97, 98, Lorraine Hansberry Theatre, San Francisco, 1994, African-Am. Performance Art Festival, 1994, 97, Afro Solo Festival, 1994-95, 97, 99, Sneak Previews at the Marsh Theatre, 1997, 98, Cafe Voltaire, Chgo., 1998; exhibited in group shows at Bomani Gallery, San Francisco, 1992—; playwright: Indigo Lady, 1993, Essays on Anger and Custard Pie, 1994, Alan Klasky Never Loved Me, 1996, 2000, Schools!, 1997, 2000, JUMP, 2001; program dir. Monday Night Marsh, Marsh Theatre. Bd. dirs. 11th St. Gallery, Lincoln, Nebr., 1985. Nat. Achievement scholar, 1969. Mem. Theatre Bay Area. Democrat. Office: 547 Hayes St Apt 1 San Francisco CA 94102-4288 E-mail: lewishan@aol.com.

ST. LOUIS, PAUL MICHAEL, foreign language educator; b. Vernon, Conn., Aug. 30, 1946; s. Wilfred Henry and Alice Agnes (Brennan) St. L. Spl. cert. Jr. Yr. Abroad program, U. Louvain, Belgium, 1967; BA, Boston Coll., 1968; MA, Trinity Coll., 1975. Cert. tchr. secondary French, Conn. Tchr. French East Hartford (Conn.) H.S., 1968-96, head dept. fgn. lang., 1984-85; retired, 1996. Advisor to French club East Hartford H.S., 1969-85, jr. class advisor, 1985, 87, 89-90, 92, sr. class advisor, 1986, 88, 90-92, bus. mgr. grades 9-12, 1993—. Vis. com. New England Assn. Schs. and Colls., Milford, Conn., 1980, steering com. for sch. evaluation, 1978, 88. Mem. Am. Coun. Tchg. of Fgn. Lang., Mass. Fgn. Lang. Assn., Conn. Coun. Lang. Tchrs. (treas. bd. dirs. 1992—, chairperson registration fall conf. 1989—, co-chairperson fall conf. 1991, cons. poetry recitation contest 1992—, Disting. Svc. award 1999), Am. Assn. Tchrs. of French (cons. regional conf. 1990), Mass. Fgn. Lang. Assn., East Hartford Edn. Assn. Avocation: computer technology. Home and Office: 275 Cedar Swamp Rd Monson MA 01057-9303

ST. ONGE, DENIS ALDERIC, geologist, research scientist; b. Ste-Agathe, Man., Can., May 11, 1929; s. Adolphe and Jeanne M (Ritchot) St-Onge; m. Jeanne Marie Behaegel, Jan. 7, 1955; children: Marc R St-Onge, Nicole J M St-Onge. BA, Coll. St-Boniface, 1951; Lic. Sci., U. Louvain, Belgium, 1957, D.Sc., 1962; D.Sc. honoris causa, U. Man., 1990. Research scientist Geol. Survey, Ottawa, Ont., Can., 1958-68, sect. head Can., 1982-85; chief sub. div. Quaternary Geology, 1985-87, dir. terrain scis. div., 1987-91, sci. advisor Polar Continental Shelf Project, 1991-97; prof. geography U. Ottawa, 1968-82, chmn. geography, 1974-77, vice dean grad. studies, 1977-80, prof. emeritus, 1998—, bd. govs., 2000—; scientist emeritus Geol. Survey Can., 1997—. Author: (book) Geomorphologie Ellef-Ringes Island, 1965, Quaternary Geology, Inman River Region, N.W.T. Canada, 1995; contbr. articles to profl jours. Pres Ont Francophone PTA, 1967—69. Decorated Officer Order of Can; recipient Commemorative medal, Govt. of Can., 1992, Medal, Queen Elizabeth II, 1979, Medal of Honor, Univ Liege, Belgium, 1980, Medal, A Cailleux, 1991, Can 125, 1992, Royal Scottish Geograhic Soc, 1994. Fellow: Arctic Inst N Am, Royal Can Geographic Soc (bd dirs 1980—2001, pres 1992—98, chmn Partnership Group Sci Eng 1999—2001), Geological Asn Can (pres 1984—85, J W Ambrose Medal 2001); mem.: Can Geoscience Coun (pres 1996—97), Asn Quebecoise pour l'etude du Quaternaire (hon.), Int Union Quaternary Research (hon.), Can Quaternary Asn, Can Asn Geographers (pres 1979—80, Award for Serv to the Profession 2000). Avocations: swimming, skiing, photography. Home: 1115 Sherman Dr Ottawa ON Canada K2C 2M3 Office: Geolog Survey of Canada 601 Booth St Ottawa ON Canada K1A OE8 E-mail: dstonge@nrcan.gc.ca.

ST. PIERRE, CATHY M. family nurse practitioner; b. Manchester, N.H., Mar. 23, 1954; d. Roland J. and Beatrice A. (Devine) St. P. BS in Nursing, Northeastern U., Boston, 1977; MS in Nursing, U. Pa., Phila., 1981; PhD, Boston Coll., 1995. Cert. family nurse practitioner. Staff nurse St. Elizabeth's Hosp., Brighton, Mass., 1977-78, VA Med. Ctr., Manchester, N.H., 1978-79, Boston Vis. Nurse Assn., 1979-80, Grad. Hosp., Phila., 1980-82; family nurse practitioner Dorchester (Mass.) House Health Ctr., 1982-85; instr., lectr. U. Lowell (Mass.), 1985-88; adolescent nurse practitioner Child Health Svcs., Manchester, 1988-89; family nurse practitioner Valley Med. Assocs. HMO, Methuen, Mass., 1989-97; assoc. prof. Rivier Coll., Nashua, N.H., 1994—. Instr., lectr. U. Pa., Phila., 1981-82; clin. instr. Northeastern U., Boston, 1984-85, U. Mass., Boston, 1982-84; mem. nurse practitioner liaison com. Bd. Nursing in N.H., 1986-88. Bd. mem. Family Svcs. Greater Lowell, 1987-88; apptd. mem. Joint Health Coun. for N.H., 2000-2002; faculty senate chair Rivier Coll., 2002—. Named Nurse Practitioner of Yr., N.H., 2001; recipient Appreciation award Lawrence, Mass., 1997. Mem.: So. N.H. AHEC (bd. dirs. 1998—), N.H. Nurse Practitioner Assn. (co-pres. 1986—88, v.p. 1992—94, mem. edn. com. 1996—).

ST. PIERRE, CHERYL ANN, retired art educator; b. Buffalo, Apr. 26, 1945; d. Guy Thomas and Madeline (Duncan) St. P. BS in Art Edn., SUNY, Buffalo, 1967, MS in Art Edn., 1970; MA in Italian, Middlebury Coll., 1976; PhD in Humanities, NYU, 1992. K-12 art tchr. Kenmore-Town of Tonawanda (N.Y.) Union Free Sch. Dist., 1967-2000; mentor to new tchrs., 1995-98. Cooperating tchr. for art student tchrs. SUNY, Buffalo, 1972-2000; advisor on original multi-media prodn. N.Y. State Coun. for Arts, Tonawanda, 1990-95; coord., tchr. Parents As Reading Ptnrs. Artwork, Tonawanda, 1990-98; grad. asst. NYU, N.Y.C., 1987-88, adj. prof. grad. sch., Medaille Coll., 1999—; coll. supr. for student tchrs. in art SUNY Coll. Buffalo, 2000—; sr. ptnr. for the arts N.Y. State Acad. Tchg. and Learning, 2000—. Illustrator jour. Italian Americana, 1971-81; designer greeting cards for State of N.Y. and Maine, Am. Lung Assn., 1978-79. Earthwatch vol. Identity through Native Costume, Macedonia, 1995. Mem.: AAUW, ASCD, Kenmore Tchrs.' Assn., Am. Fedn. Tchrs., N.Y. State Art Tchrs. Assn. (Outstanding Svc. award 2001), N.Y. State Tchrs. Assn., Nat. Art Edn. Assn., N.Y. State United Tchrs. (sec. 1999—2001, Outstanding Svc. award 2001), Internat. Mentor Assn., Alpha Delta Kappa. Avocations: travel, photography, film studies, animal rights, reading. Home: 3881 N Bailey Ave Buffalo NY 14226-3202 Office: Buffalo State Coll Dept Art Edn Bishop Hall 1300 Elmwood Ave Buffalo NY 14222 E-mail: cherie_stpierre@kenton.k12.ny.us.

ST. PIERRE, GEORGE ROLAND, JR. materials science and engineering administrator, educator; b. Cambridge, Mass., June 2, 1930; s. George Rol and Rose Ann (Levesque) St. P.; m. Roberta Ann Hansen, July 20, 1956; children: Anne Renee, Jeanne Louise, John David, Thomas George; m. Mary Elizabeth Adams, Dec. 11, 1976; m. Gretchen Ann Butrick, June 29, 2001. BS, MIT, 1951, ScD, 1954; DSc (hon.), Ohio State U., 1998. Rsch. metallurgist Inland Steel Co., 1954-56; faculty Ohio State U., 1956—, prof. metall. engring., 1957-88, assoc. dean Grad. Sch., 1964-66, chmn. metall. engring., 1983-88, chmn. mining engring., 1985-92; dir. Ohio Mineral Rsch. Inst., 1984-92, prof., chmn. material sci. and engring., 1988-92, Presdl. prof., 1988-92, chmn., disting. u. prof. emeritus, 1992—; chief scientist Materials Directorate, Wright-Patterson AFB, 1995-96. Cons. in field; vis. prof. U. Newcastle, NSW, Australia, 1975; adv. com. materials sci. MIT, 1990-97; adv. bd. Argonne Nat. Lab., 1994—. Editor: Physical Chemistry of Process Metallurgy, Vols. 7 and 8, 1961, Advances in Transport Processes in Metallurgical Systems, 1992, Transactions Iron and Steel Soc., 1994—; contbr. articles to profl. jours. Bd. dirs. Edward Orton Jr. Ceramic Found., 1989-92. With USAF, 1956-57. Recipient Milton (Mass.) Clarence Boylston Sci. prize, 1947; MacQuigg award, 1971; Alumni Disting. Tchr. award, 1978; named Disting. scholar Ohio State U., 1988, Presdl. prof. Ohio State U., 1988. Fellow Minerals, Metals & Materials Soc., AIME (bd. dirs. 1988-91, 93-96, Educator award 1996), Am. Soc. Materials Intern. (Bradley Stoughton Outstanding Tchr. award 1961, Gold medal 1987, Albert E. White award 1997); mem. Am. Inst. Mining Metall. and Petroleum Engrs. (Mineral Industry Edn. award 1987), Iron and Steel Soc. (Elliott lectr. 1994), Am. Contract Bridge League (gold life master), Faculty Club (pres. 1990-92), Sigma Xi. Home: 4091 Chevy Chase Ave Columbus OH 43220 Office: Ohio State U Dept Materials Sci/Enging 2041 N College Rd Columbus OH 43210-1124 E-mail: st-pierre.2@osu.edu.

SAINT-PIERRE, GUY, engineering executive; b. Windsor Mills, Que., Can., Aug. 3, 1934; s. Arm and Alice (Perra) Saint-P.; m. Francine Garneau, May 4, 1957; children: Marc, Guylaine, Nathalie. B in Applied Sci. in Civil Enging, Laval U., 1957; diploma, Imperial Coll., London, 1958; MSc, U. London, 1959; LLD (hon.), Concordia U., 1992; hon. degree, le Coll. militaire Royal de Saint-Jean, 1993; DSc (hon.), Laval U., 1992; hon. degree Applied Sci., Sherbrooke, 1994; DSc (hon.), Montreal U. Registrar, Corp. Engrs. Que.,

1964-66. Dir. Irnes Inc., 1966-67; v.p. Acres Que., 1967-70; minister of edn. Govt. Que., 1970-72, of industry and commerce, 1972-76; asst. to pres. John Labatt Ltd., Montreal, 1977-80, sr. v.p.; pres., chief operating officer Ogilvie Mills Ltd., Montreal, 1977-80; pres., chief exec. officer, bd. dirs. The SNC-Lavalin Group Inc., 1989-96; chmn. bd. The SNC-Lavalin Group, Inc., 1996—. Dir. GM of Can., Royal Bank, BCE Inc., Bell Can., Alcan Aluminum; chmn. Bus. Coun. Nat. Issues, 1995-97; chmn. bd. Royal Bank Fin. Group. Gov. Conseil de Patronat de Que. Served as officer C.E. Can. Army, 1959-64. Decorated officer Order of Can.; named Canada's CEO of Yr., 1994, Canada's Internat. Exec. of Yr., 1996; recipient Sir John Medal, 1993, Can. Engrs. Gold Medal award Can. Coun. Profl. Engrs., 1996; Engring. Inst. of Can.; inducted into Can. Bus. Hall of Fame, 2001. Mem. Engring. Inst. Can., Can. Mfrs. Assn. (chmn. bd., pres. 1987), Order Engrs. Que., Coun. Can. Unity (v.p.), Mt. Montreal C. of C., Can. Club Montreal (adv. com.), Mt. Royal Club, Mt. Bruno Club, Forest and Streams Club, Hermitage Club. Liberal. Roman Catholic. Office: Royal Bank of Canada 1 Pl Ville Marie PO Box 6001 Montreal PQ H3C 3A9 Canada E-mail: saing@snc-lavalin.com.

ST. PIERRE, JOYCE BOURRÉ, art educator; b. Sanford, Maine, Nov. 22, 1951; d. Marcel and Josephine Bourré; m. Michael Rene St. Pierre, Feb. 4, 1953; 1 child, Daniel. BA in Humanities, Nasson Coll., 1974; MA in Edn., U. Maine, 1985. Lectr. U. Miane, Farmington, 1978-81; tchr. Farmington Schs., 1979-81; art specialist Sanford Sch. System, Maine, 1980—. Tchr. adult edn. programs Sanford and Waterboro, Maine, 1981-86; lectr. U. New England, Biddeford, Maine, 1992-94; presenter in field. Contbr. articles to profl. jours. Publicity campaigner worker Jan Tockman to Sch. Bd., Sanford, Maine, 1979; vol. St. Thomas Sch., Sanford, 1998—; mediator Youth Alt., 1990-92. Scholar Nasson scholar, Nasson Coll., 1970—74. Mem. Berwick Libr. Assn. (sec. 1992-2000), Jaycees (state pres. 1986-87, editor photographer Jaycettes In Action, 1982-83), Maine Jaycee Women (v.p., program mgr. 1980-85, Outstanding Mem. award 1982). Roman Catholic. Avocations: cross-country skiing, hockey, travel, speaking.

SAINT-PIERRE, MICHAEL ROBERT, funeral director, consultant; b. Indpls., July 12, 1947; s. Robert Ross and Gaile Russell (Cousins) S.; m. Betty Carolyn Wilhoit, Jan. 14, 1967; children: Michelle René, Paul Christopher. Student, Milligan Coll., 1965-67, Butler U., 1966; BS, East Tenn. State U., 1969; diploma, Ind. Coll. Mortuary Sci., 1970; postgrad., Nat. Found. Funeral Svc., Ind. U., Indpls., 1977; DLitt, Cin. Coll. Mortuary Sci., 1994. Cert. funeral svc. practitioner. Intern Hamlett-Dobson, Kingsport, Tenn., 1967-69; pres. J.C. Wilson & Co., Inc., Indpls., 1969—; evaluator, practitioner rep. Am. Bd. Funeral Svc. Edn., 1980—; prof., trustee Ind. Coll. Mortuary Sci., 1971-76; prof. Nat. Found. Funeral Svc., 1987—2000, trustee, chmn., 1995-96. Bd. advisors Nat. Bank Greenwood, Inc., 1978-80. Contbr. articles to profl. jours. Mem. Johnson County (Ind.) Sheriff's Merit Bd., 1989—; bd. dirs. Ctrl. Ind. Better Bus. Bur., Indpls., 1982-86, Adult/Child Mental Health Ctr., Indpls., 1982-85, Allied Meml. Coun., Indpls., 1979—; bd. dirs. Greater Johnson County Cmty. Found., chmn., 1996-99, 2002-; elder Greenwood Presbyn. Ch., 1976; mem. coun. commn. Crossroads of Am. coun. Boy Scouts Am.; past mem., treas., bd. dirs. Consumer Info. Bur., Inc.; past mem. bd. dirs. Ctr. for Life/Death Edn., Indpls. Recipient Disting. Svc. awards Ind. Coll. Mortuary Sci., 1978, Mid Am. Coll. Funeral Svc., 1982. Fellow: Ind. Funeral Dirs. Assn. (former bd. dirs., pres.), Acad. Profl. Funeral Svc. Practice, Nat. Funeral Dirs. Assn. (exec. bd. 2001—03), Associated Funeral Dirs. Internat. (pres. 1981), Nat. Found. Funeral Svc., Nat. Selected Morticians (bd. dirs. 1988—93, pres. 1991—92); mem.: Marion County Funeral Dirs. Assn., Skyline Club, Rotary (Paul Harris fellow), Shriner (past potentate), Scottish Rite (33d degree), York Rite, Masons (past master), Order Eastern Star, Nat. Eagle Scout Assn. Republican. Presbyterian. Office: Wilson St Pierre Funeral Svc PO Box 147 Greenwood IN 46142-0147 E-mail: mrs@wilsonstpierre.com.

ST. PIERRE, RONALD LESLIE, medical and public health educator, university administrator; b. Dayton, Ohio, Feb. 2, 1938; s. Leslie Frank and Ruth Eleanor (Rhoten) St.P.; m. Joyce A. Guilford, Apr. 1, 1961; children: Michele Christine, David Bryan. BS, Ohio U., 1961; M.Sc., Ohio State U., 1962, PhD, 1965. Instr. anatomy Ohio State U., Columbus, 1965-67, asst. prof., 1967-69, assoc. prof., 1969-72, prof., 1972—, chmn. dept. anatomy, 1972-81, assoc. v.p. health scis., 1981-83, sr. assoc. v.p. health scis. and acad. affairs, 1983-2000, 2000—, assoc. dean Coll. Medicine and Pub. Health, 1987-96, vice dean Coll. of Medicine and Pub. Health, 1996-2000, exec. vice dean, 2000—, interim dean pub. health, 1999—; assoc. dir. Cancer Rsch. Ctr., 1974-78. Vis. research asso. Duke U., 1966-67; cons. Battelle Meml. Inst., Columbus. Contbr. articles to profl. jours. Chmn. Ohio Gov.'s Com. on Employment of Handicapped, 1970-78; mem. state exec. com. Presdl. Commn. Employment of Handicapped, 1970-78, chmn., 1971-72; mem. planning and adv. council White House Conf. on Handicapped Individuals, 1975-78; mem. Columbus Mayor's Com. on Internat. Yr. of Disabled. Recipient Lederle Med. Faculty award, 1968-71; prize for basic research South Atlantic Assn. Obstetricians and Gynecologists, 1968; Outstanding Individual award Ohio Rehab. Assn., 1969; Gov.'s award for community service, 1973 Mem. Am. Assn. Anatomists, Am. Assn. Immunologists, Soc. Exptl. Biology and Medicine, Sigma Xi (pres. Ohio State chpt. 1979-80) Republican. Presbyterian. Home: 8586 Button Bush Ln Westerville OH 43082-8675 Office: Ohio State U 218 Meiling Hall 370 W 9th Ave Columbus OH 43210-1238

SAISSELIN, REMY GILBERT, fine arts educator; b. Moutier, Bern, Switzerland, Aug. 17, 1925; came to U.S., 1938, naturalized, 1944; s. Paul A. and Jeanne (Nydegger) S.; m. Nicole M. Fischer, May 31, 1955; children: Anne, Juliet, Peter. BA, Queens Coll., 1951; MA, U. Wis., Madison, 1952, MA in French, 1953, PhD, 1957. Asst. prof. French Western Res. U., Cleve., 1956-59; asst. curator publs. Cleve. Mus. Art, 1959-65; prof. French lit. U. Rochester, N.Y., 1965-70, prof. fine arts, 1970-87; prof. humanities Hobart & William Smith Coll., 1987-90. Asst. editor: Jour. Aesthetics and Art Criticism, 1959-62; author: Taste in Eighteenth Centruy France, 1965, Rule of Reason and Ruses of the Heart, 1970, Literary Enterprise in XVIII Century France, 1979, The Bourgeois and the Bibelot, 1984, The Enlightenment Against the Baroque, 1992; exhbns. landscapes, still lifes, and abstractions in France, 1997. Served with U.S. Army, 1944-46. Guggenheim fellow, 1972-73 Mem. Phi Beta Kappa. Home: Route de Sancerre 18220 Saint Ceols France

SAITO, FRANK KIYOJI, import and export firm executive; b. Tokyo, Feb. 28, 1945; s. Kaoru and Chiyoko S.; m. Elaine Tamami Karasawa, Feb. 22, 1975; children: Roderic Kouki, Lorine Erika. LLB, Kokugakuin U., 1967. With import dept. Trois Co. Ltd., Tokyo, 1967-68; founder import/export dept. Three Bond Co., Ltd., 1968-71; sales mgr. Kobe Mercantile, Inc., San Diego, 1971-76; pres. K&S Internat. Corp., 1976-97, K&S Techs., Inc., San Diego, 1997—. Office: 9710 Scranton Rd Ste 150 San Diego CA 92121-1771

SAITO, REISUKE, pathologist, researcher; b. Shimizu, Japan, July 4, 1933; came to U.S., 1966; s. Kenji and Fuji (Kobayashi) S.; m. Ayako Watanabe, July 10, 1966; children: Hiroshi H., Yuri A., Emi K. MD, Nihon U., Tokyo, 1959, DMS, 1966. Diplomate Am. Bd. Pathology; lic. physician, Japan, Pa. Intern Japan Red Cross Cen. Hosp., Tokyo, 1959-60; resident USAF Hosp. Tachikawa, 1960-62, Jefferson Davis Hosp. and Ben Taub Gen. Hosp., Houston, 1962-64; pathologist Nat. Sagamihara Hosp., Kanagawa, Japan, 1964-66; resident Cleve. Met. Gen. Hosp., 1966-68; fellow Magee-Womens Hosp., Pitts., 1968-70; clin. asst. prof. U. Pitts., 1971-86, assoc. prof., 1986—; staff pathologist VA Med. Ctr., Pitts., 1970—, chief cytology svc., chief anatomic pathology, 1990—. Mem. Japan Assn. Greater Pitts., 1991—; bd. dirs. Japan-Am. Culture Ctr., Pitts., 1992—. Mem. Internat. Acad. Pathology, Coll. Am. Pathologists. Achievements include electron microscopic documentation of anaplastic small cell carcinoma of thyroid, demonstration that phospholipids are essential for enzyme induction in rat liver, documentation of atypical fibrous histiocytoma of bone, documentation of adenosquamous carcinoma of prostate; avocations: reading, classical music appreciation, photography, model railroad. Office: VA Med Ctr University Dr C Pittsburgh PA 15240

SAITO, ROBERT SHUNICHI, writer, poet; b. Alameda, Calif., Sept. 9, 1933; s. Sam Shunji Saito and Yayeko Umegawa; m. Naida Cervantes, Dec. 7, 1966. Cert., Coronado Sch. Fine Arts, 1980. Enlisted USN, 1955, advanced through grades to chief petty officer, 1971, pers. officer USS Camden, 1972-75, ret., 1975. Pres. Mega Travel Inc., La Mesa, Calif., 1983-84. Author of poetry, short stories. Recipient 1st Pl. award for Batik, Coronado Art Assn., 1977. Roman Catholic. Avocations: Batik art, photography, fishing, walking, Tai-Chi.

SAITO, SHUZO, electrical engineering educator; b. Nagoya, Aichi, Japan, Jan. 12, 1924; s. Sukesaburo and Masa Saito; m. Yoko Nakane, Mar. 26, 1953; children: Jun'ichiro, Ken'jiro. BSEE, Nagoya U., 1948, MSEE, 1953, PhD, 1962. Mem. tech. staff Elec. Com. Lab. NT&T, Tokyo, 1953-64, chief rsch. sect., 1964-75, dir. rsch. dept., 1975-79; prof. speech sci. U. Tokyo, 1979-84; prof. elec. engring. Kogakuin U., 1984-92; prof. info. sci. Hokkaido Info. U., 1992-98. Mem. tech. staff Japanese Patent Agy., Tokyo, 1963; tech. specialist Japanese Ministry Transp., Tokyo, 1982. Author: Fundamental Speech Signal Processing, 1979; contbr. articles to profl. publs.; inventor PARCOR speech synthesis. Recipient Meritorious award Min. Sci. & Tech., Japan, 1977, Promotion award Asahi Newspaper Co., 1981, Nat. Rising Sun medal of 4th Grade of merit, 2000. Fellow: The Inst. of Electronics, Info. and Comm. Engrs. Japan (adviser speech rsch. com., pattern recognition com. 1983, paper award 1970, 1971, 1979, achievement award 1973), Acoustical Soc. Am., IEEE (chmn. acoustics, speech and signal processing Tokyo chpt. 1986—88, chmn. tech. program com. internat. conf. on acoustics, speech 1986); mem.: Acoustical Soc. Japan (exec. coun. 1969—83, Sato paper award 1972, meritorious award 1994), Audio and Visual Rsch. Group (hon.; pres. 1985—88). Avocations: golf, photography. Home: 2-40-3 Sakuragaoka Tama Tokyo 206-0013 Japan E-mail: ssaito@pep.ne.jp.

SAITOU, KAZUHIRO, engineering educator; b. Tokyo, Dec. 12, 1966; PhD, MIT, 1996. Asst. prof. U. Mich., Ann Arbor, 1997—. Recipient Career award, NSF, 1999. Mem.: ASME (assoc.). Office: U Mich Mech Engring Dept 2350 Hayward St Ann Arbor MI 48109-2125 Office Fax: 734-647-3170. Business E-Mail: kazu@umich.edu.

SAIZ, LEONOR, physicist, researcher; b. Barcelona, Spain, Jan. 17, 1969; d. Jesus Saiz and Leonor Ardanaz. BSc in Physics, U. Barcelona, 1992, PhD in Physics, 1998. Postgrad. rsch. asst. U. Barcelona and SOCIMAG S.A. , Barcelona, 1992—93; postdoctoral Fellow U. Manchester Inst. Sci. and Tech. , England, 1998; postdoctoral fellow U. Pa., Phila., 1999—. Reviewer European Phys. Jour.-E Soft Matter, Biophys. Jour., Chem. Physics Letters; contbr. articles to profl. jours. Fellow, DGICYT (Spanish Govt.), 1993. Mem.: Am. Phys. Soc. Avocations: hiking, music, dancing, reading, travel. Office: U Pa 231 S 34th St Philadelphia PA 19107

SAIZAN, PAULA THERESA, oil company executive; b. New Orleans, Sept. 12, 1947; d. Paul Morine and Hattie Mae (Hayes) Saizan; m. George H. Smith, May 26, 1973 (div. July 1976). BS in Accts. summa cum laude, Xavier U., 1969. CPA, Tex.; notary pub. Systems engr. IBM, New Orleans, 1969-71; acct., then sr. acct. Shell Oil Co., Houston, 1971-76, sr. fin. analyst, 1976-77, fin. rep., 1977-79, corp. auditor, 1979-81, treasury rep., 1981-82, sr. treasury rep., 1982-86; asst. treas. Shell Credit Inc., Shell Leasing Co., Shell Fin. Co., 1986-88, sr. pub. affairs rep., 1988-89, sr. staff pub. affairs rep., 1990-91, program mgr., 1991-96, sr. program mgr., 1996-97, mgr. constituent rels. and edn. support, 1997-2000, mgr. nat. and cmty. outreach, 2000—. Bd. dirs. Houston Downtown Mgmt. Dist., Greater Houston Conv. and Visitors Bur., St. Joseph Hosp. Found., NAACP Spl. Contbn. Fund, United Negro Coll. Fund; mem. found. adv. coun. Links, Inc.; mem. adv. bd. Sch. Engring, Tex. So. U.; del. White House Conf. on small bus., 1995. Mem. AICPA, NAACP (life) , Tex. Soc. CPAs, Leadership Houston, Greater Inwood Partnership, LWV of Houston, Xavier U. Alumni Assn., Nat. Assn. Black Accts., Links Inc., Nat. Coun. Garden Clubs (life), Nat. Coun. Negro Women, Inc., Nat. Congress of Black Women, Alpha Kappa Alpha, Phi Gamma Nu, Kappa Gamma Pi. Roman Catholic. Home: 5426 Long Creek Ln Houston TX 77088-4407 Office: Shell Oil Co PO Box 2463 Houston TX 77252-2463 E-mail; paulusinv@aol.com.

SAJJADI, SHAHRDAD GHOTB, theoretical physicist, mathematician, fluid dynamicist, educator; b. Tehran, Iran, Feb. 1, 1961; s. Shamseddin and Parirokh (Badie) S. BSc, Coventry (Eng.) U., 1984, PhD, 1988, ScD, 1991, DSc, 1998. Rsch. officer Rutherford Appleton Lab., Didcot, Eng., 1982-84; lectr. math. Coventry U., 1984-85, rsch. asst., 1985-88; rsch. fellow Cranfield Inst. Tech., 1988-89; rsch. assoc. Manchester Inst. Sci. Tech., 1989-91; dir. Ctr. for Computational Fluid Dynamics and Turbulence U. Salford, 1991-2000; sec. ERCOFTAC (WOW) SIG, 1994—; mem. ERCOFTAC SPC, 1995—; prof. applied math. Stennis Space Ctr., NASA, Miss., 2001—. Rsch. cons. Rutherford Appleton Lab., Didcot, 1984-99; vis. acad. DAMTP, U. Cambridge, U. Manchester Inst. Sci. and Tech., Scripps Inst. Oceanography, La Jolla, Calif., Proudman Oceanographic Lab., Merseyside, Eng., Med. U. Pécs, Hungary, othrs. Editor: Air-Sea Interfaces, 1987, Wind-over-Waves Couplings, 1997; contbr. articles to profl. jours. Fellow Inst. Math. and its Applications; mem. Soc. Indsl. Applied Math., Am. Math. Soc., London Math. Soc. Avocations: classical music, cinematography, squash. E-mail: sgsajjadi@hotmail.com., sajjadi@ssc.usm.edu.

SAKAGUCHI, TAKEHIRO, health educator, researcher; b. Tokyo, July 1, 1947; s. Takeichi and Kimiko (Aota) Sakaguchi; m. Sanae Sakaguchi, Mar. 21, 1974. M of Hygiene, Kitasato U., Tokyo, 1972; D Med. Sci., St. Marianna U. Sch. Medicine, Kawasaki, Japan, 1985. Lectr. dept. pub. health Kitasato U., 1972-80; asst. prof. dept. hygiene St. Marianna U. Sch. Medicine, 1980-96, assoc. prof. dept. hygiene, 1996-97; prof. dept. life sci. Kawamura Coll., Tokyo, 1997-2000; prof. dept. human environment Kawamura Gakuen Woman's U., Abiko, Japan, 2000—. Lectr. Chuo U., Tokyo, 1988-97, Shizuoka (Japan) U., 1997-99, Nippon Dental U., Tokyo, 1998—. Contbr. articles Toxicology & Environmental Health and others. Mem. AAAS, Japanese Soc. Hygiene (councilor 1987—), Japan Soc. Occupl. Health (councilor 1990-96), Japanese Soc. Pub. Health (councilor 1993-96, 2002--), Japanese Assn. Infectious Diseases (councilor 1997—), Japanese Soc. Bacteriology, N.Y. Acad. Scis. Avocation: travel. Office: Kawamura Gakuen Woman's Univ 1133 Sageto Abiko Chiba 270-1138 Japan E-mail: t.sakagu@kgwu.ac.jp.

SAKAI, HIROKO, trading company executive; b. Nishiharu, Aichi-ken, Japan, Jan. 9, 1939; came to U.S., 1956; d. Kichiya and Saki (Shiraishi) S. BA, Wellesley Coll., 1963; MA, Columbia U., 1967, PhD, 1972. Journalist Asahi Evening News, Tokyo, 1963-65; escort interpreter Dept. State, Washington, 1967-68; econ. analyst Port Authority N.Y. and N.J., N.Y.C., 1968-69; sr. cons. Harbridge House, Inc., Boston, 1970-84, Quantum Sci. Corp., White Plains, N.Y., 1984-87; corp. planner ITOCHU Internat. Inc., N.Y.C., 1988-92, dir. bus. devel., 1993-94, dir. venture and investment, 1995—. Interpreter Govt. Mass., Boston, 1974. Wellesley Coll. fellow, 1960-63, Columbia U. fellow, 1965-68; Columbia U. grantee, 1969. Mem. Regional Sci. Assn., Assn. Am. Geographers. Buddist. Avocations: piano, oil painting, tennis. Office: ITOCHU Internat Inc 335 Madison Ave New York NY 10017-4605 Home: Apt 5 163 Beacon St Boston MA 02116-1413

SAKAI, KIYOKO, artist; b. Oct. 24, 1938; Osaka, Japan, m. Keizo Sakai, Nov. 7, 1965; children: Miyako, Alisa *Sakai's father, Bunichiro Sakai, came to the U.S. from Japan in1951 to expand the family business. Her Husband, Keizo Sakai, succeeded his business in N.J. Keizo's grandfather started the Oriental Department of the Boston Museum with Okakura Kakuzo, the author of the "Book of Tea," an ancestor of his mother. Sakai's daughter, Miyako, is a piano teacher in CA after having studied at the Liszt Academy in Budapest. Her younger daughter, Alisa, is researcher of intellectual property at the Japan External Trade Organization, NYC after having graduated from the divinity school at Harvard University.* BA, Doshisha U., Kyoto, Japan, 1961; postgrad., Art Students League, N.Y.C., 1973-78. *Kiyoko Sakai, an abstract expressionist, paints with oil and acrylic on canvas and paper. Her recent focus has been on the celestial theme. An installation based on her imagination of the cosmos exhibited in 1998 at the Myung Sook Lee Gallery, NYC and was also reviewed by Angela Moore in Cover Magazine. Solo Show titled 'the Realm of High Altitude, inspirations from Tibet' was at the Cottage Gallery in Ridgewood, N.J., 2002. At the solo show in Osaka Contemporary Art Center in 1993, she presented the marriage of East and West by combining her Japanese traditional hand dyed materials with abstract paintings.* Exhibited in one woman shows at Cottage Gallery, N.J., Move 21, Osaka, Japan, Kanner Kurzan Mus., N.Y., Myung Sook Lee Gallery, N.Y., Osaka Prefecture Comtemporary Art Ctr., Japan, Drew U., N.J., Permanent Collection: Deloitte, Haskins and Sells, N.J., The Zen Studies Soc., N.Y., The New York Stock Exchange, N.Y.; group exhbn. Bergen Mus. of Art and Sci., N.J., Instituto Superiore Per Industrio Artistiche, Urbino, Italy, Newark Mus. Recipient award Bergen Mus. Juried Show, Ramapo Coll. Juried Show, Art Showcase award, Manhattan Art Internat. Life mem. Art Student League of N.Y. Avocations: Music, Dance, Literature.

SAKAI, PETER A. lawyer; b. McAllen, Tex., Oct. 21, 1954; s. Pete Y. and Rose Marie (Kawahata) S.; m. Raquel M. Dias, Mar. 10, 1982; children: George Y., Elizabeth K. BA, U. Tex., Austin, 1976, JD, 1979. Bar: Tex. 1979. Asst. dist. atty. County of Bexar, San Antonio, 1980-82; pvt. practice, 1983-94; assoc. judge Bexar County Dist. Ct., 1994—. Hearings arbitrator City of San Antonio, 1983-93; judge Mcpl. Ct., City of Elmendorf, Tex., 1985; juvenile assoc. judge 289th Dist. Ct., San Antonio, 1989-94; city atty. City of Leon Valley, Tex., 1986-90. Contbr. to profl. publs. Bd. dirs. Bexar County Juvenile Vols. in Probation, San Antonio, 1983-93; Japan Am. Soc. San Antonio, 1987-89, Cmty. Cultural Arts Orgn., San Antonio, 1987-92, Bexar County Local Devel. Corp., San Antonio, 1989-94. Mem. ABA, State Bar Tex., San Antonio Bar Assn. Avocation: sports. Office: Bexar County Courthouse 100 Dolorosa Rm 205 San Antonio TX 78205-3038

SAKAI, RICHARD, motion picture and television executive, producer; b. San Francisco, Jan. 28, 1954; s. Hisasi Quintus and Jean Misako S.; childern; Benjamin, Timothy, Reilly. BA, UCLA, 1977, MFA, 1980. Pres. Gracie Films, Culver City, Calif., 1984—. Prodr. (film) Jerry Maguire, Bottle Rocket, As Good As It Gets, (TV) Simpsons. Mem. Acad. TV Arts and Scis. (6 Emmys), Acad. Motion Picture Arts and Scis. (nomination), PGA, ACLU. Office: Gracie Films 10202 Washington Blvd Culver City CA 90232-3119

SAKAOKA, YASUE, artist, educator; b. Himeji-City, Hyogo-Ken, Japan, Nov. 12, 1933; came to U.S., 1953; naturalized, 1980; s. Naoshi and Sachie Sakaoka. BA, Reed Coll., 1959; Artists' Cert., Portland Mus. Sch., 1959; MFA, U. Oreg., 1963. Instr. U. Oreg., Eugene, 1961-63, Md. Coll. Art, Balt., 1963-65; asst. prof. art St. Paul's Coll., Lawrenceville, Va., 1965-77; asst. prof. sculpture and art history Mansfield State U., 1977-78; adj. prof. Ohio U., Athens, 1979-80; lectr. Ohio State U., Columbus, 1980—. Vis. artist Stivers Sch. for the Arts, Dayton, Ohio, 1989—; mem. minority adv. com. Ohio Arts Coun., Columbus, 1992—; mem. adv. bd. Internat. Biog. Ctr., Cambridge, Eng., 1998-2000; cons. in field of Japanese art and culture. (Curator): Dublin (Ohio) Arts Coun., 1988—2002; Fitton Ctr., 1999; Sandusky Cultural Ctr., 1999; Pub. Arts Coun. Mem. choir St. Stephen's Episcopal Ch., Columbus, 1993—; bd. mem. Asian Am. Cmty. Svc. Orgn., 1993—. Recipient fellowship NEH, 1976, Devel. grant Ohio Arts Coun., 1987-88, Pollock-Krasner Found. award, 1967-88, Traditional Art Apprenticeship award Ohio Arts Coun., 1990-91, 91-92, 94-95, 97-98, 2001-02. Mem.: Ctrl. Ohio Japan Am. Assn., Coll. Art Assn. Am., Internat. Sculpture Ctr., Dayton Visual Arts Ctr. Avocations: gardening, music.

SAKARA, MARILYN JUDITH, social worker; b. Youngstown, Ohio, Nov. 21, 1949; d. Michael Joseph and Mary Jane (Makar) S. AB, Youngstown State, 1967-71; MSW, La. State, 1973. Lic. ind. social worker. Social worker Los Lunas (N.Mex.) Hosp. and Tng. Sch., 1977-78, Dept. Human Services, Albuquerque, 1978-79, Santa Fe, 1979-80, Child Devel. Ctr., Santa Fe, 1980-83; social worker supr. Children's Med. Svcs., 1983-89, program mgr., 1989-99, chief Family Health Bur., 1999—. Pres. Field Rsch., Inc., Santa Fe, 1978—; clin. co-dir. N.Mex. Critical Incident Stress Debriefing Team, 1988-90. Mem. NASW, Acad. Cert. Social Workers. Democrat. Avocations: gardening, cooking. Home: 251 Plaza Canada Santa Fe NM 87501-2374 Office: Dept of Health Pub Health Divsn Family Health Bur 1190 S Saint Francis Dr Santa Fe NM 87505-4182

SAKER, JAMES ROBERT, music educator; b. Sharon, Pa., Apr. 13, 1945; s. James W. and Florence A. (Wray) S.; m. Cheryl Ann Mayer, Dec. 26, 1966; children: James R. Jr., Robert David. MusB, Bowling Green State U., 1967; MusM, Youngstown State U., 1975; PhD, U. Iowa, 1982. Dir. instrumental music Hillsdale Schs., Jeromesville, Ohio, 1967-70; chmn. music dept., dir. h.s. bands Champion Schs., Warren, 1970-76; grad. teaching asst., band staff U. Iowa, Iowa City, 1976-78; dir. bands U. Nebr., Omaha, 1978—, prof., chmn. dept. music, 1992-99, 2001—, Isaacson Disting. Prof. Music, 1997—. Regional dir. Music Bowl, Inc., Chgo., 1986-92; music dir. Nebr. Ambs. of Music, Omaha, 1986-93; mem. Nebr. Consortium on Discipline Based Music Edn., Lincoln, 1988-92; pres. Windthyme, Inc., Omaha, 1984—; music dir. Plam Springs (Calif.) Internat. Children's Festival, 1989, Bluffs Run Iowa Charity Jazz Festival, 1991; coord. City of Paris Nat. Ambassadors of Music Programs, 1994—. Founding pres. Tiburon Home Owners Assn., 1996—99; bd. dirs. Omaha Area Youth Orch., 1981—84; mem. adv. bd. KVNO Pub. Radio, 1997—; mem. parade com. River City Roundup, Inc., Omaha, 1983—. Recipient Chancellors medal U. Nebr., Omaha, 1999. Mem.: Omaha Jazz Soc. (v.p. 1981—86), Coll. Music Soc., Coll. Band Dirs. Nat. Assn. (state chmn. 1981—), Nebr. Bandmasters Assn. (pres. 1983—84, Donald A. Lentz Outstanding Bandmaster award 1993), Nebr. Music Educators Assn. (pres. 1987—89, Disting. Svc. award 1989, Outstanding Svc. award 2001, Award of Recognition 2001), Ohio Music Educators Assn. (pres.-elect local dist. 1974—76), Nat. Band Assn. (exec. bd. 1983—86, 1990—, Citation of Excellence 1986, 1999), Rotary (chmn. Rotaract 1988—90), Golden Key Honor Soc., Phi Beta Mu (hon.), Omicron Delta Kappa (hon.). Episcopalian. Avocations: woodworking, camping, travel, sports. Home: 17509 Riviera Dr Omaha NE 68136-1951 Office: Univ Nebr Dept Of Music Omaha NE 68182-0245 E-mail: jimsaker@unomaha.edu.

SAKIC, JOSEPH STEVE, professional hockey player; b. Burnaby, B.C., Canada, July 7, 1969; Capt. Quebec Nordiques, 1991-95; with Colo. Avalanche, 1995—. Won WHL East Most Valuable Player Trophy, 1986-87, WHL Stewart (Butch) Paul Meml. Trophy, 1986-87, Four Broncos Meml. Trophy, 1987-88, Bob Clarke Trophy, 1987-88, Conn Smythe Trophy NHL, 1996; named to WHL All-Star Second Team, 1986-87, Can. Hockey League Player of Yr., 1987-88, WHL Player of Yr., 1987-88; played in NHL All-Star Game, 1990-94, 96. Office: c/o Colo Avalanche 1000 Chopper Cir Denver CO 80204-5809*

SAKIMOTO, SUSAN ELIZABETH HUBBARD, research scientist; b. Peoria, Ill., Dec. 30, 1966; d. Charles Franklin and Elizabeth Ann (Wickstrom) H.; m. Philip Jon Sakimoto, Dec. 31, 1988. BA, Whitman Coll., 1989; MA, Johns Hopkins Univ., 1991, PhD, 1995. NRC resident rsch. assoc. NASA/Goddard Space Flight Ctr., Greenbelt, Md., 1995—. Earth and planetary scis. instr. The Johns Hopkins Space Grant Consortium, Balt., 1995. Contbr. articles to profl. jours. including Jour. of Volcanology and Geothermal Rsch., Jour. of Fluid Mechanics. Planetary geology and geophysics rsch. grantee NASA, 1994; recipient Rsch. Associateship award Nat. Rsch. Coun., 1995, Grad. student rschrs. fellowship NASA/Goddard, 1989. Mem. Am. Geophys. Union, Geol. Soc. of Am., Am. Astronomical Soc., Sigma Xi. Office: Goddard Space Flight Ctr Nasa Code 921 Greenbelt MD 20771-0001

SAKITA, BUNJI, physicist, retired educator; b. Inami, Toyama-ken, Japan, June 6, 1930; came to U.S., 1956; s. Eiichi and Fumi (Morimatsu) S.; children— Mariko, Taro. BS, Kanazawa U., 1953; MS, Nagoya U., 1956; PhD, U. Rochester, 1959. Rsch. assoc. U. Wis., Madison, 1959-62, asst. prof., 1962-64, prof., 1966-70; assoc. physicist Argonne (Ill.) Nat. Lab., 1964-66; disting. prof. City Coll. CUNY, N.Y.C., 1970-99, disting. prof. emeritus, 1999—. Vis. prof. IHES, Bures-sur-Yvette, France, 1970-71, Ecole Normale Superieur, Paris, 1979-80, 88, U. Tokyo, 1987; Pandit Jawaharlal Nehru chair U. Hyderabad, India, 2000. Recipient Nishina prize, 1974; Guggenheim fellow, 1970-71, Japan Soc. Promotion Sci. fellow, 1975, 80, 87, 95. Fellow Am. Phys. Soc. Home: 5 Horizon Rd Apt 2406 Fort Lee NJ 07024-6646 Office: CUNY City College Convent Ave at 138th St New York NY 10031 E-mail: sakita@scisun.sci.ccny.cuny.edu.

SAKKAL, MAMOUN, architect, interior designer; b. Damascus, Syria, Dec. 31, 1950; came to U.S., 1978; s. Lutfi Sakkal and Dourieh Khatib; m. Seta K. Sakkal, Mar. 13, 1980; children: Aida, Kindah. BArch with honors, U. Aleppo, Syria, 1974; MArch, cert. urban design, U. Wash., 1982. Registered architect, Wash., Syria; lic. interior designer, U.S. Archtl. designer MCE, Damascus, 1974-75, dir. design Aleppo, 1975-76; prin. Sakkal & Assocs., 1976-78; archtl. designer Arch. Assocs., Seattle, 1978-82; sr. designer RD&S, Bellevue, Wash., 1982-84; prin. Restaurant/Hotel Design, Seattle, 1984—, Sakkal Design, Bothell, 1991—. Lectr. U. Aleppo, 1974-75, Applied Arts Inst., 1977-78, affiliate instr. U. Wash., 1990—. Author: Geometry of Muquarnas in Islamic Architecture, 1981; designer Oct. Mus., Damascus, Syria, 1977 (1st prize Syrian Ministry Dev.); one man shows include Nat. Mus. Aleppo, Syria, 1969, U. Aleppo, 1984, U. Wash., 1979, 80, 90, 91, U. Cambridge, Eng., 1990, Islamic Soc. N.Am. Conv., Chgo., 1994, U. Tex., Austin, 1997; contbr. articles to profl. jours.; produced Islami Clip Collection clip art software, 1991. Recipient Best Logo Design award Arab Union Sports, 1976, Best Project Design award Aleppo Ministry of Culture, 1975, Best Modernization Project award Holiday Inns System, 1986, Best Lounge Renovation award Bowlers Jour. Ann. Design Contest, 1987, 1st award in Kufi style 3d Internat. Calligraphy Competition, Rsch. Ctr. for Islamic History, Art and Culture, Istanbul, Turkey, 1993. Avocations: typeface design, illustration. Office: Sakkal Design 1523 175th Pl SE Bothell WA 98012-6460

SAKODA, ROBIN (SAK SAKODA), security professional, consultant; b. Chgo., Apr. 3, 1956; s. Tom K. and Harumi Sakoda; m. Hannah Sakoda; children: David, Elliott, Leah, Thomas. BA, The Citadel, 1978; MA, U.S. Naval Postgrad. Sch., 1988. Sr. dir. for Japan Office of the Sec. of Def., Washington, 1994—98; pres. Sakoda Assocs., Arlington, Va., 1999—; sr. assoc. AALC, Ltd. Co., 1999—. Sr. assoc. Pacific Forum, Ctr. for Strategic Internat. Studies, 1999—; assoc. Ctr. for Strategic and Internat. Studies, 2001—; adj. faculty U.S. Naval Postgrad. Sch., Monterey, Calif., 2000—. Lt. col. U.S. Army, 1978-99. Avocations: judo, fishing. Office: AALC Ltd Co Ste 701 1550 Wilson Blvd Arlington VA 22209

SAKOWICA, JOHN, protective services official, writer; b. Mt. Vernon, N.Y., June 3, 1952; s. John and Rita (Avallone) Sakowicz; m. Shannon Morris; children: Kitty Sakowicz, Marithea Sakowicz, Vanessa Sakowicz, Arianna Sakowicz, Ryan Sakowicz, Austin Sakowicz. BA, Johns Hopkins U., 1977, MA, 1979; JD, U. Md., Balt., 1983. Bar: N.Y. 1984. With Mendocino County Sheriff's Office, Ukiah, Calif., Morgan Stanley Dean Witter, N.Y.C., Spear Leeds Kellogg, N.Y.C. Lt. USMC, 1970—73. Home: 1201 El Dorado Rd Ukiah CA 95482

SAKS, ERIC MAURICE, film producer, film director; Prodr., dir. Wipe Out, 1981, Insomnia, 1982, Suddenly I Burst into Another: The Life of Henry Tanner, 1983, Automatic, 1984, 4 Songs, 1986, Designated Shooting Area, 1987, Forevermore: Biography of Leach Lord, 1989, Don From Lakewood, 1989, You Talk/I Buy, 1990, Hide, 1990, Big Pixel Theory, 1990, I Will Testify: The Porter Wagoner Story, 1991, Gun Talk, part 1, 1991, part 2, 1995, Vote PSA, 1991, Cappy Peeper Trailers, 1991, This Summer PSA, 1991, KNBR, 1993, Copper Connection, 1993, Straight Talk About Deserts, 1994, Encrypts PSA, 1994, Friar-fr-kinds, 1994, Like I, Media Bust, 1994, Oceania: 10 years of lounge, tiki and exotica wanderings, 1995, Neglectosphere, 1995, Touch Tone, 1995, Fax Attack, Creosote, 1996, Smooth Warming, 2000, Love Machine, 2001, Dust, 2001. Annenberg grantee, Guggenheim fellow, 1997.*

SAKS, GENE, theater and film director, actor; b. N.Y.C. Began career as an actor off-Broadway at Provincetown Playhouse and the Cherry Lane Theatre; played in: Auden's Dog Beneath the Skin, E.E. Cummings' Him, Molière's The Bourgeois Gentilhomme; appeared on Broadway in Mr. Roberts, South Pacific, Middle of the Night, The Tenth Man, A Shot in the Dark, Love and Libel, A Thousand Clowns; debut as dir. on Broadway Enter Laughing, 1963; dir. stage plays Nobody Loves an Albatross, 1964, Half a Sixpense, 1964 (Tony nominee Best Dir. Musical), Generation, 1965, Mame, 1966 (Tony nominee Best Dir. Musical), Same Time, Next Year, 1975 (Tony nominee Best Dir. Play), California Suite, 1972, I Love My Wife (best dir. of Musical award Drama Desk, Tony), 1977, Brighton Beach Memoirs (best dir. award, Tony), 1983, Biloxi Blues (best dir. of play award, Tony), 1985, The Odd Couple (female version), 1985, Broadway Bound, 1986, A Month of Sundays, 1987, Rumors, 1988, Lost in Yonkers, 1991 (Tony nominee Best Dir., Outer Critics Cir. award), Jake's Women, 1992, Barrymore, 1997; dir. films Barefoot in the Park, The Odd Couple, Cactus Flower, Last of the Red Hot Lovers, Mame, Brighton Beach Memoirs, A Fine Romance; dir. TV movie Bye, Bye Birdie, 1995; appeared in films including a Thousand Clowns, Prisoner of Second Aveneue, Lovesick, The One and Only, The Goodbye People, 1986, Nobody's Fool, 1994, IQ, 1994. Recipient George Abbott award for lifetime achievement in the theatre, 1990; elected to Theatre Hall of Fame, 1991. Mem. Stage Dirs. and Choreographers (pres.).

SAKS, JUDITH-ANN, artist; b. Anniston, Ala., Dec. 20, 1943; d. Julien David and Lucy-Jane (Watson) S.; m. Haskell Irvin Rosenthal, Dec. 22, 1974; 1 child, Brian Julien. Student, Tex. Acad. Art, 1957-58, Mus. Fine Arts, Houston, 1962, Rice U., 1962; BFA, Tulane U., 1966; postgrad., U. Houston, 1967. Curator student art collection U. Houston, 1968-72; artist Am. Revolution Bicentennial project Port of Houston Authority, 1975-76. Solo shows include Alley Gallery, Houston, 1969, 2131 Gallery, Houston, 1969; group shows include Birmingham (Ala.) Mus., 1967, Meinhard Galleries, Houston, 1977, Galeire Barbizon, Houston, 1980, Park Crest Gallery, Austin, 1981; represented in permanent collections including L.B. Johnson Manned Space Mus., Clear Lake City, Tex., Harris County Heritage Mus., Windsor Castle, Smithsonian Instn.; commns. include Pin Oak Charity Horse Show Assn., Roberts S.S. Agy., New Orleans, Cruiser Houston Meml. Rm., U. Houston. Recipient art awards including 1st prize for water color Art League Houston, 1969, 1st prize for graphics, 1969, 1st prize for sculpture, 1968, Nat. 1st place award for original print DAR/Am. Heritage Com., 1987, Nat. 1st place award for acrylic painting, DAR, 2000, Nat. 3rd place award for painting, 2001, Tex. State 1st prize for drawing DAR, 2002, Outstaind Svc. awrd Boy Scout Troop 806, 2002. Mem. Art League Houston, Houston Mus. Fine Arts, DAR (Lady Washington chap., curator 1983-85, 93-95, contbr. Tex. sesquicentennial drawing for DAR mag., recording sec. 2001—), Daus. Republic of Tex. Home: 2215 Briar Branch Dr Houston TX 77042-2959

SAKS, WILLIAM JOSEPH, JR. osteopathic physician, educator; b. Allentown, Pa., Feb. 3, 1943; s. William J. and Josephine (Sorrentino) S.; m. Valerie E. Nacinovich, June 17, 1967; children: William, Stephen, Damian, Jessica, Benjamin, Erika. BS in Biology, King's Coll., Wilkes-Barre, Pa., 1964; postgrad., Cath. U. Am., 1964-65; DO, Phila. Coll. Osteo. Medicine, 1969. Intern Brentwood Hosp., Warrensville Heights, Ohio, 1969-70, resident in gen. surgery and ob-gyn. Warensville Heights, 1970-72; resident in ob-gyn. surgery Allentown Osteo. Med. Ctr., 1972-74, mem. staff, 1972-90, chmn. ob-gyn. dept., 1979-80, 85-90, vice chmn., 1982-85; pvt. practice, Wescosville, Pa., 1974-90, Montour Falls, N.Y., 1990-92; pvt. practice Guthrie Clinic, Inc., Watkins Glen, 1992—. Asst. clin. prof. Phila. Coll. Osteo. Medicine, 1980—; chmn. ob-gyn. dept. Schuyler Hosp., Montour Falls, 1990—. Bd. dirs. CONFRONT, drug and alcohol rehab. ctr., past mem. adv. bd.; mem. med. adv. bd. Allentown-Bethlehem Midwifery Ctr., 1983—; former lectr. pre-marriage confs. and religious ednl. program on natural family planning Dioceses of Allentown and Rochester, Roman Cath. Ch. Fellow Am. Coll. Osteo. Obstetricians and Gynecologists (diplomate); mem. Am. Osteo. Assn. (insp. intern and residency tng. programs), Pa. Osteo. Med. Assn. (bd. dirs. dist. III 1984-90, chmn. com. on ob-gyn., com. on constn. and bylaws, com. on orgn. policy, com. on publs., com. on property), Lehigh Valley Osteo. Soc. (treas. 1975-80, chmn. 1982-90). Avocations: music, hunting, fishing, boating, archery.

SAKSON, ROBERT GEORGE, artist; b. Trenton, N.J., Feb. 13, 1938; s. George Anthony and Teresa Margaret (Schwarz) S.; m. Carla Ann Hagberg, Oct. 29, 1977. AA, Trenton Jr. Coll., 1958. Instr. in field. One-man shows include Moonmouth Mus., 1991, Historic New Jersey, Bristol-Myers Squibb Galleries, Princeton, 1991, Coryell Gallery, 1996, Ednl. Testing Svc., 1997, Forestal Ctr., 1997, Ellarslie-Trenton City Mus., NJ, 2002; exhibited in group shows at Am. Watercolor Soc. Annuals, Nat. Acad. Design, Allied Artists Am., Pastel Soc. of Am.- Nat. Arts Club N.Y., Phila. Art Alliance, Woodmere Art Gallery, Hunterdon State Exhibits, N.J. State Mus., Nat. Mus. Sport, Mercer County C.C., Phillips Mill Annual, Trenton State Coll., Monmouth Coll., Am. Artists Profl. League, Salmagundi Club, Assoc. Artists N.J. 50th anniversary, Audubon Artists, Best Foods Corp.-Calendar, 1986, Painting With the White of Your Paper, 1995, Best of Watercolor, 1996, Splash 4-The Splendor of Light, 1996, Painting with the White of Your Paper, 1996, People in Watercolor, 1996, Best of Watercolor 2, 1997, Painting Light and Shadow, 1997, Painting Texture, 1997, Watercolor Expressions, 1999, Artists of the River Towns, 2002. Recipient numerous exhibition awards including Memory of Walter E. Martin award, 1991, Lenox award, 1991, A Friend's award Nummie Warga, 1991, Coryell Gallery award, 1993, Gold medal at Allied Artists Am., 1983, 3 Silver medals N.J. Watercolor Soc., 1976, 83, 92, Cert. Merit, NAD, 1973; grantee Yellowstone Art Ctr., Frye Mus., Williamette U., Mansfield Fine Arts Guild, Brooks Meml. Art Gallery, Columbia Mus. Art, Sarasota Art Assn., McMurray Coll., Okla. Art Ctr., Gibbes Art Gallery, Bay Region Groups, Anchorage Fine Arts Mus. Mem. Am. Watercolor Soc.. (Helen Gapen Ohler award 1970, Paul B. Remmey award 1977, Elizabeth Callan Meml. medal 1993, Dolphin fellow 1993), Allied Artists Am., Pastel Soc. Am., Phila. Watercolor Soc. (Isa Barnett Meml. award 2001), N.J. Watercolor Soc. (Peter Thomas Jones award 1991, Continental Airlines award 2001), Garden State Watercolor Soc. (Commodities Corp. award 1994, bd. govts. award Phila. Watercolor Club Annual Exhbn. 1998, Friends award 33d ann. exhbn. 2002), Trenton Artists Workshop Assn., Assoc. Artists N.J., Audubon Artists, Knickerbocker Artists, U.S. Coast Guard Art Program, Salmagundi Club.

SAKURADA, YUTAKA, chemist; b. Kyoto, Japan, Jan. 1, 1933; s. Ichiro and Chiyoko (Okumura) S.; m. Keiko Sugimoto, May 10, 1960; children: Kazuhiro, Akihiro. BS, Kyoto U., 1956, MS, 1958, PhD, 1966. Rsch. fellow Cen. Rsch. Lab. Kuraray Co. Ltd., Kurashiki, Japan, 1958-62, 64-66; internat. fellow Stanford Rsch. Inst., Menlo Pk., Calif., 1962-64; tech. rep. N.Y. Office Kuraray Co. Ltd., N.Y.C., 1968-71; mgr. Med. Bus. Devel. Div. Kuraray, Osaka, Japan, 1974-77, gen. mgr. Med. Products Div., 1977-88, gen. mgr. Corp. Rand D Div., 1988-89; mng. dir. Kuraray Plastics Co. Ltd., 1989-91. Bd. dirs. Haemonetics Corp., USA, 1991—; vice chmn. Japanese Soc. for Biomaterials, Tokyo, 1987—96; pres. Haemonetics, Japan, 1991—2001, chmn., CEO, Japan, 2001—. Recipient Technology award The Soc. Polymers, 1984, Japanese Chem. Soc., 1985. Achievements include development of ethylene vinyl alcohol copolymer hollow fiber for hemo-dialyzer; development of dental adhesives. Home: YGT2-420 4-20-2 Ebisu Shibuya-ku Tokyo 150-0013 Japan

SAKUTA, MANABU, neurologist, educator; b. Ichikawa, Japan, Oct. 31, 1947; s. Jun and Shizuko (Tsuji) Sakuta; m. Yuko Fukushi, June 17, 1973; children: Akiko, Junko, Ken-Ichi. MD, U. Tokyo, 1973, PhD, 1978; MS in Neurology, U. Minn., 1981. Diplomate Japanese Bd. Neurology, Japanese Bd. Internal Medicine. Asst. dept. neurology U. Tokyo, 1980, lectr. dept. neurology, 1984—; rsch. fellow dept. neurology U. Minn., Mpls., 1980-81, asst. prof., 1981-82; head dept. neurology Japanese Red Cross Med. Ctr., Tokyo, 1982-2000; prof. Japanese Red Cross Women's Coll. Sch. Nursing, 1983-85, instr., 1986-88; lectr. dept. medicine U. Kobe, 1990—; prof. dept. neurology Kyorin U., Tokyo, 2000—, chmn., 2000—. Cons. Nakayama Hosp., Ichikawa, Japan, 1980—. Contbr. articles to profl. jours. Fellow: Royal Soc. Medicine (London); mem.: AAAS, Am. Acad. Neurology, Japanese Soc. Autonomic Nervous Sys. (coun.), Japanese Soc. Sarcoidosis (coun.), Japanese Soc. Cerebrovascular Disease (coun.), Japanese Soc. Clin. Neurophysiology, Japanese Soc. Diabetology, Japanese Soc. Neurology (mem. coun. 1985—, mem. coun. Kanto br. 1984—, pres. Kanto br. 1984, mem. editl. bd. 1988—), Japanese Soc. Internal Medicine (pres. Kanto br. 1992), N.Y. Acad. Sci., Tetsumon Club, U. Minn. Alumni Club, Chevalier du Tastevin (Burgundy), Chevalier Club (pres. internat. com. 1995—), Clin. Neurology Club. Democrat. Buddhist. Office: Kyorin U Dept Neurology 6-20-2 Shinkawa Mitaka Tokyo 181-8611 Japan Fax: 0422 47 5931., 0422-47-5931. E-mail: manabu.sakuta@nifty.ne.jp.

SAKUTA, MASAAKI, engineering educator, consultant; b. Kagoshima, Japan, Feb. 16, 1929; s. Masanori and Haruko (Oozato) S.; m. Akiko Shimomura, Nov. 4, 1956; children: Shigeru, Mitsuru. B of Engring., Tokyo Inst. Tech., 1952; postgrad, MIT, 1959-60; DEng, Tokyo Inst. Tech., 1966. Cert. oceanic architect, architect-engr., Japan. Rschr. Taisei Constrn. Co. Ltd., Tokyo, 1956-58, chief rschr., 1960-69; mng. dir. Fuyo Ocean Devel. and Engring. Co. Ltd., 1969-77; advisor Taisei Corp. Co. Ltd., 1978-79; prof. Nihon U., 1977-99, prof. emeritus, 1999—; pres. Tsuruga Jr. Coll., Fukui, Japan, 2002—. Councilor Archtl. Inst. Japan, Tokyo, 1975-76, dir., 1989-91; vice dean Coll. Sci. and Tech., Nihon U., 1978-94; vice chmn., life mem. Pacific Congress on Marine Sci. and Tech., Japan, 1990—. Author: Transportation in Ocean Space, 1975, Construction Method of Marine Structures, 1976, Introduction of Ocean Development, 1977; patentee in field of Marine structure system with soft-touched basement. Mem. Visualization Soc. Japan, Inc. (hon., pres. 1991-92, Merit award 1992), Rotary (sr., charter). Mem. Liberal Dem. Party. Buddhist. Avocations: hiking, tennis, table tennis, painting, reading. Home: 39-723 2chome2 Jingumae Shibuya-ku Tokyo 150-0001 Japan Office: 9-1004 1 chome 43 Kameido koutou-ku Tokyo 136-0071 Japan

SALA, MARTIN ANDREW, biophysicist, inventor; b. Buffalo, Sept. 6, 1957; s. Paul and Adrienne (Williams) Zahm; m. Erie Anne Wagner-Sala, Nov. 23, 1986; 1 child, Rebeckah. BA in Biophysics, SUNY, Buffalo, 1981. Dir. clin. engring. Buffalo Columbus Hosp., 1982-85; lab. inst. designer Roswell Park Cancer Inst., Buffalo, 1985-89; v.p. for R&D MBS Foundry, Brook's Grove, N.Y., 1989-96; pressetter applications engr. Nationwide Precision Prods., Henrietta, 1996-97; sr. measurements engr. sci. and tech. disvn. Corning (N.Y.), 1997—. Cons. Lotus Link Found., Buffalo, 1990—, West N.Y. Clin. Engring. Assn., Buffalo, 1989—. Author: Theory & Design of Core Memory, 1979, Purely Natural Causes, 1999; editor various periodicals, 1970—; inventor, developer Retrospex Sys. for large vehicles. With USN, 1976-81. Grantee NIH, 1990. Mem. Am. Inst. Physics, Instrument Soc. Am., AAAS, Internat. Soc. Magnetic Resonance in Medicine, Soc. for Advancement Med. Instrument Design, SPIE. Mem. Anglican Ch. Achievements include patents pending for new surgical measuring tool, facsimile design, canine surgical tool; invention of various novel scientific instruments, Retrospex Rear Vision System, patented vehicular safety devices, microscopic MRI analysis. Office: Corning Sp Td 01 Corning NY 14831-0001

SALABERRY, MÁXIMO RAFAEL, language educator, researcher; b. San Carlos, Uruguay, Apr. 12, 1963; s. Omar Salaberry and Dora Perez; m. María Jose Tort, Sept. 20, 1990. MA in Tchg., U. Maine; PhD, Cornell U., 1997. Tchg. asst. Cornell U., Ithaca, N.Y.; asst. prof. U. Minn., Mpls., 1997-98, Pa. State U., State College, 1998-2000, Rice U., Houston, 2000—. Author: The Development of Spanish Past Tense Morphology in a Classroom Environment, 2000; co-editor (with Yasuhiro Shibi) The L2 Acquisition of Tense-Aspect Morphology, (with Barbara Lafford) Studies in Spanish Second Language Acquisition: The State of Science; contbr. articles to profl. jours. Sage grad. fellow Cornell U., 1993-97; Nat. Fgn. Lang. Resource Ctr., 1995. Mem. MLA (exec. com. applied linguistics 1997—), Am. Assn. Tchrs. Spanish and Portuguese, Am. Assn. Applied Linguistics. Home: 4235 Law St Houston TX 77005 Office: Rice U 6100 Main St Houston TX 77005-1892 E-mail: salaberry@rice.edu.

SALACUSE, JESWALD WILLIAM, lawyer, educator; b. Niagara Falls, N.Y., Jan. 28, 1938; s. William L. and Bessie B. (Buzzelli) S.; m. Donna Booth, Oct. 1, 1966; children: William, Maria. Diploma, U. Paris, 1959; AB, Hamilton Coll., 1960; JD, Harvard U., 1963. Bar: N.Y. 1965, Tex. 1980. Lectr. law Ahmadu Bello U., Nigeria, 1963-65; assoc. Conboy, Hewitt, O'Brien & Boardman, N.Y.C., 1965-67; assoc. dir. African Law Ctr., Columbia U., 1967-68; prof., dir. Rsch. Ctr., Nat. Sch. Adminstrn., Zaire, 1968-71; Mid. East regional advisor on law and devel. Ford Found., Beirut, 1971-74, rep. in Sudan, 1974-77; vis. prof. U. Khartoum, Sudan, 1974-77; vis. scholar Harvard Law Sch., 1977-78; prof. law So. Meth. U., Dallas, 1978-86, dean, 1980-86; dean, prof. internat. law Fletcher Sch. Law and Diplomacy, Tufts U., Medford, Mass., 1986-94, Henry J. Braker prof. comml. law, 1994—. Fellow Inst. Advanced Legal Studies, U. London, 1995; vis. prof. Ecole Nat. Ponts et Chaussées, Paris, 1990-95, Inst. Empressa, Madrid, 1995, U. Bristol, U. London Sch. Oriental and African Studies, 1995—; cons. Ford Found., 1978-82, 93, U.S. Dept. State, 1978-80, UN Ctr. on Transnat. Corps., 1988—, Harvard Inst. Internat. Devel., 1990—, Asia Found., 1992, Harvard Law Sch./World Bank Laos Project, 1991-93; with Sri Lanka fin. sector project ISTI/U.S. AID, 1993-94; lectr. Georgetown U. Internat. Law Inst., 1978-94, Panam. U., Mexico City, 1981; chmn. com. on Mid. Ea. law Social Sci. Rsch. Coun., 1978-84; chmn. Coun. Internat. Exch. Scholars, 1987-91; bd. dirs. Boston World Affairs Coun., 1988-95, Emerging Markets Income Funds. I & II, Inc., Global Ptnrs. Income Fund, Inc., Salomon Bros. Worldwide Income Fund, Inc., Asia Tigers Fund, Inc., India Fund, Inc., Emerging Markets Floating Rate Fund, Inc., Mcpl. Advantage Fund, Inc., Mcpl. Ptnrs. Funds I & II, Salomon Bros. High Income Funds I & II, Salomon Bros. 2008 Worldwide Dollar Govt. Term Trust, Mcpl. Ptnrs. Funds I & II; trustee Southwestern Legal Found., 1992—, Am. U. Paris, 1993-97; pres. Internat. Third World Legal Studies Assn., 1987-91; chmn. Inst. Transnat. Arbitration, 1991-93; pres. Assn. Profl. Schs. Internat. Affairs, 1988-89; Fulbright disting. chair in comparative law, Italy, 2000. Author: (with Kasunmu) Nigerian Family Law, 1966, An Introduction to Law in French-Speaking Africa, Vol. I, 1969, Vol. II, 1976, (with Steng) International Business Planning, 1982, Making Global Deals-Negotiating in the International Marketplace, 1991, The Art of Advice, 1994, (video course) Negotiating in Today's World, 1995, The Wise Advisor, 2000; contbr. articles to profl. jours. Mem. ABA, Dallas Bar Found. (trustee 1983-86), Coun. on Fgn. Rels., Am. Law Inst., Am. Soc. Internat. Law, Cosmos Club (Washington). Home: 220 Stone Root Ln Concord MA 01742-4755 Office: Tufts U Fletcher Sch Law-Diplomacy Medford MA 02155 E-mail: jeswald.salacuse@tufts.edu.

SALAFSKY, BERNARD, medical educator, scientist; b. Chgo., Dec. 27, 1935; s. Mandel and Jeanette (Pritikin) S.; m. Marilyn Ann Ritchie, June 18, 1961; children— Joshua, Daniel, David. B.S. in Pharmacy, Phila. Coll. Pharmacy and Sci., 1958; M.S. in Pharmacology, U. Wash., 1961, Ph.D. in Pharmacology, 1962. Instr. U. Wash., Seattle, 1962-64; from asst. prof. to assoc. prof. U. Ill.-Chgo., 1964-70; adj. assoc. prof. U. Pa., Phila., 1970-72; prof. WHO, Geneva, Switzerland, 1973-75; prof. U. Ill.-Rockford, 1977— , dir., 1983— ; cons. Biomed. Health Cons., Hong Kong, 1976; external examiner U. Malaya, Malaysia, 1982— . Contbr. articles to profl. jours. Bd. dirs. local devel. corp., Rockford, 1983— . Muscular Dystrophy Assn. spl. fellow, 1972; recipient NIH Prin. Investigator award, 1965-71, 80-83, 84— . Fellow Royal Soc. Tropical Medicine and Hygiene; mem. AAAS, Am. Soc. Pharmacology and Exptl. Therapeutics, Am. Soc. Tropical Medicine and Hygiene. Home: 5730 Clarendon Dr Rockford IL 61114-5506

SALAGI, DORIS, educational administrator, retired; b. Perth Amboy, N.J., July 30, 1947; d. Joseph William and Anna Salagi. BA, Trenton State Coll. (name now Coll. of N.J.), 1969, MA, 1973. Cert. elem. sch. tchr., supr., tchr. of the handicapped. 3d grade tchr. Willingboro (N.J.) Bd. Edn., 1969-79, basic skills math. tchr., 1979-83, resource rm. tchr., 1983-87, tchr. of the handicapped, 1987-92, 95-98, individualized ednl. plan facilitator, 1992-95; Homebound instr. Woodbridge (N.J.) Twp. Sch. Dist., 1999—. Curriculum writer Willingboro Bd. Edn., 1973, 77, 79-83, 88-89, 98. Co-author: (composition curriculum) The Care and Handling of Compositions, 1973. Vol. Rancocas Hosp., Willingboro, 1978-98. Named for Outstanding Achievement in Edn., Trenton State Coll. Alumni Assn., 1991. Mem.: NEA, Burlington County Edn. Assn., N.J. Ret. Educators Assn., Willingboro Edn. Assn. (rep. 1974—76), Burlington County Ret. Edn. Assn., N.J. Educators Assn., Rancocas Hosp. Aux. (scholarship chair 1978—81, bazaar chair 1981—85, rec. sec. 1983—87, pres. 1987—89), Alpha Zeta (World Fellowship chair 1985—87, 1st v.p. 1988—90, pres. 1990—92, Eta chpt. treas. 1992—, State rec. sec. 1995—99, chmn. social 1997—2001, chmn. nominations 1999—2001, chmn. rsch. 2001—), Delta Kappa Gamma (internat. rep. to UN dept. pub. info. 1998—2000). Avocations: reading, travel, walking, theatre, gardening.

SALAH, JOSEPH ELIAS, research scientist, educator; b. Jerusalem, Feb. 27, 1944; came to U.S., 1961; s. Elias and Souraya (Nesnas) S.; m. Marie Shintani, Jan. 30, 1965; 1 child, Anthony. BSEE, U. Ill., 1965, MSEE, 1966; PhD, MIT, 1972. Staff mem. Lincoln Lab., MIT, Lexington, 1966-76, group leader, 1977-83, sr. lectr. dept. earth, atmospheric and planetary scis. Cambridge, 1983—, prin. rsch. scientist, 1983—, dir. Haystack Obs. Westford, 1983—. Mem. adv. com. for astron. scis. NSF, Washington, 1985-88, mem. steering com. Coupling, Energetics and Dynamics of Atmospheric Regions, 1987-90, 96—; mem. com. on solar terrestrial rsch. NRC-NAS, Washington, 1986-89. Contbr. articles on physics of earth's upper atmosphere and ionosphere to sci. jours. Mem. Am. Geophys. Union, Am. Astron. Soc., Am. Meteorol. Soc., Internat. Union Radio and Sci., Internat. Assn. for Geomagnetism and Aeronomy. Office: MIT Haystack Obs RR 40 Westford MA 01886

SALAH, SAGID, retired nuclear engineer; b. Seoul, Sept. 2, 1932; came to U.S., 1954; s. Galim and Faiza (Sultan) Salahutdin; m. Ravile Almakay, Apr. 2, 1966; children: Shamil, Kamil, Safiye. BChemE, U. Fla., 1958, MS in Nuclear Engring., 1960, PhD in Nuclear Engring., 1964. Nuclear engr. AEC, Bethesda, Md., 1964-66; sr. design engr. Westinghouse Astronuclear Lab., Large, Pa., 1966-70; sr. sys. engr. Westinghouse Nuclear Energy Sys., Pitts., 1970-73; mem. sys. safety engring. staff U.S. Nuclear Regulatory Commn., Bethesda, 1973-93; ret., 1993. Nuclear engring. cons. Oak Ridge (Tenn.) Inst. Nuclear Studies, 1963, 64; instr. U. Md., College Park, 1973-76. Contbr. articles to Nuclear Sci. and Engring. Youth coach Nat. Capital Soccer League, Vienna, Va., 1975-85. Mem. Am. Nuclear Soc. (emeritus, reviewer trans. papers 1972), Sigma Tau. Moslem. Achievements include measurements of neutron energy spectra in heterogeneous media using differential and integral methods, neutron energy spectra measurements and analysis in intermediate spectra reactors, three-dimensional transient analysis of boron dilution in PWR reactors. Avocations: astronomy, neurology, financial analysis, tennis, swimming. Home: 9302 Kilport Ct Vienna VA 22182-3426 E-mail: srsalah@ix.netcom.com.

SALAHUDDIN, AHMAD, civil engineer, educator; b. Anbala, India, Sept. 19, 1941; arrived in Zimbabwe, 1987; s. Ahmad Chaudhary Shamsuddin and Sultanta Mahmuda. BSCE, Panjab U., Lahore, Pakistan, 1961; MSc in Civil Engring., Columbia U., 1967; PhD in Structural Engring., Concordia U., Montreal, Can., 1971. Design engr. cons. industry, Pakistan, 1961-65; rsch. assoc., asst. prof. Concordia U., Montreal, 1971-73, 77-81; specialist cons. Can., 1973-76, 81-83; assoc. prof. U. Bahrain, 1983-85; dir. Can. Inst. Tech. Edn., 1985-87; prof. engring. U. Zimbabwe, Harare, 1987—. Editor specifications draft Standards Assn. Zimbabwe, 1993—; coord. Indsl. cons. Civil Engring. U. Zimbabwe, 1994—; mem. sci. com. Internat. Symposium Design of Structures, Germany, 1996; mem. African Structural Engring. Edn. Forum, Johannesburg, South Africa, 1996. Contbr. numerous articles to profl. jours. Fulbright-Hays fellow, Washington, 1965-67. Mem. ASCE, Internat. Assn. Shell and Spatial Sturctures, Internat. Assn. Bridge and Structural Engring. Avocations: scientific reading and writing, listening to music, computer technology. Home: 6 Montagu Ct 142 Josiah Chinamano Ave Harare Zimbabwe Office: U Zimbabwe Civil Engring Dept PO Box MP167 Harare Zimbabwe E-mail: salahuddin@eng.uz.ac.zw., ahmadzw@yahoo.com.

SALAMA, C. ANDRE TEWFIK, electrical engineering educator; b. Heliopolis, Egypt, Sept. 27, 1938; arrived in Can., 1957; s. Tewfik and Sarine (Bigio) S.; m. Rhoda R. Kurtz, Dec. 19, 1974. BASc with honours, U. B.C., Vancouver, Can., 1961, MASc, 1963, PhD, 1966. Registered profl. engr., Ont. Mem. sci. staff Bell No. Rsch., Ottawa, Ont., Can., 1966-67; asst. prof. elec. engring. U. Toronto, 1967-70, assoc. prof., 1970-77, prof., 1977-92, univ. prof., 1992—. Chmn., bd. dirs. Can. Microelectronics Corp., Kingston, Ont., 1984—; program leader, bd. dirs. Micronet, Toronto, 1990—. Mem. editorial bd. Solid State Electronics, 1982—; contbr. over 200 articles to sci. jours. Recipient Izaak Walton Killam Meml. prize, 1994; Info. Tech. Assn. Can. and Natural Scis. and Engring. Rsch. Coun. fellow U. Toronto, 1989-90. Fellow IEEE (assoc. editor Trans. on Cirs. and Systems 1987-89, Millenium medal 2000), Royal Soc. Can.; mem. Electrochem. Soc., Assn. Profl. Engrs. Ont. Avocations: swimming, sailing, scuba diving, horseback riding, reading. Office: U Toronto Dept Elec Engring Toronto ON Canada M5S 1A4

SALAMA, FARID, astrophysicist, spectroscopist, research scientist; b. Paris, Jan. 28, 1957; s. Aly and Marie Rose (Garroux) S.; m. Josie Bove, July 5, 1986; 1 child, Maissa. BS in Chem. Physics, U. Paris, Orsay, France, 1981; MS in Chem. Physics, U. Pierre & Marie Curie, 1983; PhD in Physical Chemistry, U. Pierre & Marie Curie, France, 1986. Postdoctoral rsch. fellow Lawrence Berkeley Lab., Berkeley, Calif., 1987-88; rsch. assoc. Nat. Rsch. Coun./NASA, Moffett Field, 1988-90; from vis. rsch. astronomer to rsch. physicist U. Calif./NASA, Berkeley, 1990-94; prin. investigator SETI Rsch. Inst./NASA, Moffett Field, Calif., 1994-99; astrophysicist NASA, 1999—. Fellow Gen. Delegation Sci. Tech. Rsch., France, 1983-85; fellow NRC, 1988-90; panelist, reviewer NASA Astrophysics Rsch. & Analysis Program, 1994, 98, 2001; spkr. symposium German-Am. Frontiers Sci., 1995; reviewer Petrol. Rsch. Fund, 1996, 99, NSF, 2000-2002; NAS fellow German-Am. Acad. Coun., 1996-98 Contbr. articles to profl. jours., chpts. to books. Fellow Found. France, 1986. Mem. Internat. Soc. for Origin of Life, Astron. Soc. Pacific, Am. Phys. Soc., Am. Astron. Soc., Internat. Astron. Union. Achievements include pioneering research in laboratory astrophysics in which the techniques of low temperature spectroscopy are applied to the study of interstellar and planetary material analogs. Avocations: reading, hiking, music, movies. Office: NASA-Ames Rsch Ctr Space Science Divn Mail Stop 245-6 Mountain View CA 94035-1000 E-mail: fsalama@mail.arc.nasa.gov.

SALAMACK, LAURICE SULLIVAN, city planner; b. Oakland, Calif., Jan. 28, 1959; d. William Joseph and Helen Ryan Sullivan; m. Joseph George Salamack, III, June 29, 1985; children: Kelly Kathleen, Allison Cecelia. BA with distinction, U. Calif., Berkeley, 1981; MS, Rensselaer Poly. Inst., 1989. Acquisition specialist Properities of Am., Williamstown, Mass., 1986-88; intern dept. econ. devel. City of Troy, N.Y., 1989; cons. Rensselaer Tech. Pk., North Greenbush, 1989; city planner City of Piedmont, Calif., 1990—. Mem. Am. Planning Assn., Omicron Delta Epsilon. Avocation: travel. Home: 1115 Clarendon Cres Oakland CA 94610-1807 Office: Town of Moraga 350 Rheem Blvd Moraga CA 94556- E-mail: lori@moraga.ca.us., salamack@earthlink.net.

SALAMON, GEORGES M. radiologist; b. Montpellier, France, Mar. 20, 1931; s. Nathan M. Salamon and Hena Eizemberg; m. Noriko Murayama; children: Christopher, Marie Helene, Ivan. MD, Univ., Marseille, 1956. Cert. Neuroradiologist. Asst. prof. U. Marseille, 1964, assoc. prof., 1968, prof., 1972; chmn. Neuroradio, 1974; cons. French Atomic Commn., 1986. Author: (textbook) Radiologic Anatomy Brain, 1968 (prize Francfort Fair), An Atlas of Brain Arteries, 1970 (prize Acad. Medicine), numerous others. Pres. Assn. Museums Marseille; sec. rsch. group of neuroradiology World Fedn. Neurology, Marseille, 1995. Capt. French Army. Mem. RSNA (hon. Chgo.), Am. Coll. Radio (hon. San Diego), Sailing Club, Nautical Soc. Marseille. Avocations: skiing, sailing, history, art, literature. Home: 11628 Montana Ave Unit 107 Los Angeles CA 90049 Office: UCLA-Dept Radiological Sci #BL-428 CHS Box 951721 10833 Le Comte Ave Los Angeles CA 90095-1721

SALAMON, LESTER MILTON, political science educator; b. Pitts., Jan. 11, 1943; s. Victor William Salamon and Helen (Sanders) Weiss; m. Lynda Anne Brown, June 27, 1965; children: Noah, Matthew. BA in Econs. and Pub. Policy, Princeton U., 1964; PhD in Govt., Harvard U., 1971. Instr. dept. polit. sci. Tougaloo (Miss.) Coll., 1966-67; asst. prof. Vanderbilt U., Nashville, 1970-73; assoc. prof. policy scis. and polit. sci. Duke U., Durham, N.C., 1973-80, dir. Ctr. for Urban and Regional Devel., 1973—77; dep. assoc. dir. U.S. Office Mgmt. and Budget, Washington, 1977-79; dir. Ctr. for Governance and Mgmt. Rsch., Urban Inst., 1980-86; prof., dir. Inst. for Policy Studies, Johns Hopkins U., Balt., 1987-97, dir. Ctr. Civil Soc. Studies, 1997—. Author: America's Nonprofit Sector: A Primer, 1992, The Emerging Sector: Nonprofit Organizations in Comparative Perspective, 1994, Partners in Public Service: Government Nonprofit Relations in the Modern Welfare State, 1995, Defining the Nonprofit Sector: A Cross-National Analysis, 1996, International Guide to Nonprofit Law, 1997; editor: Beyond Privaitzation, 1989, Human Capital and America's Future, 1991, Global Civil Society, 1998, The Tools of Government, A Guide to The New Governance, 2002; mem. editl. bd. Adminstrn. and Soc., 1985—, Voluntas, 1988—, Nonprofit and Voluntary Sector Quar., 1990—, Pub. Adminstrn. Rev., 2000—. Mem. Balt. City Planning Commn., 1987-95; mem. Chesapeake Cmty. Found.; mem. adv. com on voluntary fgn. aid USAID. Recipient Laverne Burchfield award Am. Soc. Pub. Adminstrn., 1977, Disting. Book award Assn. of Rschrs. on Nonprofit Orgns. and Vol. Action. Mem. Internat. Soc. Third Sector Rsch. (vice chmn. 1991-95), Nat. Acad. Pub. Adminstrn., Social Sci. Rsch. Coun. (nonprofit field com.), Md. Assn. Nonprofit Orgns. (bd. dirs.). Avocations: tennis, swimming, carpentry, sailing. Home: 903 Lynch Dr Arnold MD 21012-1504 Office: Johns Hopkins U Inst Policy Studies 3400 N Charles St Baltimore MD 21218-2680 E-mail: lsalamon@jhu.edu.

SALAMON, LINDA BRADLEY, English literature educator; b. Elmira, N.Y., Nov. 20, 1941; d. Grant Ellsworth and Evelyn E. (Ward) Bradley; divorced; children: Michael Lawrence, Timothy Martin. BA, Radcliffe Coll., 1963; MA, Bryn Mawr Coll., 1964, PhD, 1971; Advanced Mgmt. Cert., Harvard U. Bus. Sch., 1978; D.H.L., St. Louis Coll. Pharmacy, 1993. Lectr., adj. asst. prof. Eng., Dartmouth Coll., Hanover, N.H., 1967-72; mem. faculty lit. Bennington Coll., Vt., 1974-75; dean students Wells Coll., Aurora, N.Y., 1975-77; exec. asst. to pres. U. Pa., Phila., 1977-79; assoc. prof. English, Washington U., St. Louis, 1979-88, prof., 1988-92, dean Coll. Arts and Scis., 1979-92; prof. English, George Washington U., Washington, 1992—, dean Columbia Sch. Arts and Scis., 1992-95, interim v.p. for acad. affairs, 1995-96. Mem. faculty Bryn Mawr Summer Inst. for Women, 1979-99. Author, co-editor: Nicholas Hilliard's Art of Limning, 1983; co-author: Integrity in the College Curriculum, 1985; contbr. numerous articles to literary and ednl. jours. Bd. dirs. Assn. Am. Colls., vice chmn., 1985, chmn., 1986; bd. dirs. Greater St. Louis council Girl Scouts U.S.A.; trustee Coll. Bd., St. Louis Coll. Pharmacy. Fellow Radcliffe Coll. Bunting Inst., 1973-74; Am. Philos. Soc. Penrose grantee, 1974; fellow Folger Shakespeare Library, 1986, NEH Montaigne Inst., 1988. Mem. MLA, Renaissance Soc. Am., Cosmos Club, Phi Beta Kappa. Office: George Washington U Dept of Eng Rome Hall 760 801 22D St NW Washington DC 20052-0001

SALAMON, MICHAEL JACOB, psychologist, health care and psychology educator, media consultant; b. Bklyn., Oct. 18, 1951; s. Milton and Bessie (Kessler) S. BA, Queens Coll., 1974, MA, 1977, Hofstra U., 1981, PhD, 1983. Project dir. Nat. Coun. Sr. League, Far Rockaway, N.Y., 1974-78; dir., founder Adult Devel. Ctr., Hewlett, 1978—; dir. rsch. Gustave Hartman YM-YWHA, Far Rockaway, 1978-82; asst. prof. psychology L.I. U., 1981-83; gerontology cons. St. Johns Hosp., Far Rockaway, 1980-83; adult devel. cons. CSE, 1980-83, N.Y. State Dept. of Labor, Far Rockaway, 1978-80; dir. rsch. divsn. Hebrew Home for Aged at Riverdale, 1983-85; dir. psychology St. John's Home and Hosp., 1986-88; dir. rsch., clin. supr. New Hope Guild Ctrs., Bklyn., 1989—. Vis. scholar Brookdale Found., Jerusalem, 1985; TV, radio, print media cons. on psych. issues. Author: Adult Assessment Scale, 1982; textbooks on gerontology, nursing homes, marriage and family, child and adolescent develop.; editor: Jour. Clin. Gerontology; reviewer Jour. Cons. and Clin. Psychology; contbr. articles to profl. jours. Assoc. bd. dirs. Dem. Club of Rockaways, 1981; bd. dirs. Young Israel of Woodmere, 1982; mem. bd. edn., exec. bd. Hebrew Acad. of the Five Towns and Rockaways, 1991, chmn., 1995-97; mem. bd. edn. PTACH Ctrs. for Learning Disabilities, 1991, chmn. 2000—. Bruner Found. grant, 1979, N.Y. State Dept. Social Svcs. grant, 1982. Fellow: APA, Prescribing Psychologists Register, Gerontol. Soc. Am. (rsch. fellow 1983, fellow behavior and soc. scis. sect. 1998); mem.: Am. Psychiat. Assn., Assn. Jewish Scientists, Psychologists in Long-Term Care Network (bd. dirs., chair steering com. 1993—98), Northeastern Gerontol. Soc. Democrat. Jewish. Office: Adult Devel Ctr 1728 Broadway Hewlett NY 11557-1601

SALAMON, MIKLOS DEZSO GYORGY, mining engineer, educator; b. Balkany, Hungary, May 20, 1933; came to U.S., 1986; naturalized, 1993; s. Miklos and Sarolta (Obetko) S.; m. Agota Maria Meszaros, July 11, 1953; children: Miklos, Gabor. Diploma in Engring., Polytech U., Sopron, Hungary, 1956; PhD, U. Durham, Newcastle, England, 1962; doctorem honoris causa, U. Miskolc, Hungary, 1990. Rsch. asst. dept. mining engring. U. Durham, 1959-63; dir. rsch. Coal Mining Rsch. Controlling Coun., Johannesburg, South Africa, 1963-66; dir. collieries rsch. lab. Chamber of Mines of South Africa, 1966-74, dir. gen. rsch. orgn., 1974-86; disting. prof. Colo. Sch. Mines, Golden, 1986-98, disting. prof. emeritus, 1998—, head dept. mining engring., 1986-90; dir. Colo. Mining and Mineral Resources Rsch. Inst., 1990-94; pres. Salamon Cons. Inc., Arvada, Colo., 1995—. 22d Sir Julius Wernher Meml. lectr., 1988; hon. prof. U. Witwatersrand, Johannesburg, 1979-86; vis. prof. U. Minn., Mpls., 1981, U. Tex., Austin, 1982, U. NSW, Sydney, Australia, 1990, 91-96; mem. Presdl. Commn. of Inquiry into Safety and Health in South African Mining Industry, 1994-95. Co-author: Rock Mechanics Applied to the Study of Rockbursts, 1966, Rock Mechanics in Coal Mining, 1976; contbr. articles to profl. jours. Mem. Pres.'s Sci. Adv. Council, Cape Town, South Africa, 1984-86, Nat. Sci. Priorities Com., Pretoria, South Africa, 1984-86. Recipient Nat. award Assn. Scis. and Tech. Socs., South Africa, 1971. Fellow South African Inst. Mining and Metallurgy (hon. life, v.p. 1974-76, pres. 1976-77, gold medal 1964, 85, Stokes award 1986, silver medal 1991, 99), Inst. Mining and Metallurgy (London), Hungarian Acad. Scis. (external), 1998; mem. AIME, Internat. Soc. Rock Mechanics. Roman Catholic. E-mail: mdg_salamon@msn.com.

SALAMON, MYRON BEN, physicist, educator, dean; b. Pitts., June 4, 1939; s. Victor William and Helen (Sanders) S.; m. Sonya Maxine Blank, June 12, 1960; children— David, Aaron. BS, Carnegie-Mellon U., 1961; PhD, U. Calif., Berkeley, 1966. Asst. prof. physics U. Ill., Urbana, 1966-72, assoc. prof., 1972-74, prof., 1974—, program dir. Materials Research Lab., 1984-91, assoc. dean. Coll. Engring., 2000—. Vis. scientist U. Tokyo, 1966, 71, Tech. U. Munich, Fed. Republic Germany, 1974-75; cons. NSF; Disting. Vis. Prof. Tsukuba (Japan) U., 1995-96. Editor: Physics of Superionic Conductors, 1979; co-editor: Modulated Structures, 1979; divisional assoc. editor: Phys. Rev. Letters, 1992-96; contbr. sci. papers to profl. jours. Recipient Alexander von Humboldt Sr. U.S. Scientist award, 1974-75; NSF coop. fellow, 1964-66; postdoctoral fellow, 1966; A.P. Sloan fellow, 1972-73; Berndt Matthias scholar Los Alamos Nat. Lab., 1995-96; visiting scientist CNRS and Inst. Laue-Langevin Grenoble, France, 1981-82. Fellow Am. Phys. Soc. Office: U Ill Dept Physics 1110 W Green St Urbana IL 61801-9013

SALAMON, RENAY, real estate broker; b. N.Y.C., May 13, 1948; d. Solomon and Mollie (Friedman) Langman; m. Maier Salamon, Aug. 10, 1968; children: Mollie, Jean, Leah, Sharon, Eugene. BA, Hunter Coll., 1969. Licensed real estate borker, N.J. Mgr. office Customode Designs Inc., N.Y.C., 1966-68; co-owner Salamon Dairy Farms, Three Bridges, N.J., 1968-86; assoc. realtor Max. D. Shuman Realty Inc., Flemington, 1983-85; pres., chief exec. officer Liberty Hill Realty Inc., 1985—. Cons. Illva Saronna Inc. (Illva Group), Edison, N.J. 1985—; real estate devel. joint venture with M.R.F.S. Realty Inc. (Illva Group), 1986—; bd. dirs. Anderson House. Mem. Readington twp. Environ. Commn., Whitehouse Sta., N.J., 1978-87, N.J. Assn. Environ. Commrs., Trenton, 1978—; fundraiser Rutgers Prep. Sch., Somerset, N.J., 1984-95; bd. dirs. Hunterdon County YMCA, 1987-95, Anderson House, 2000-; mem. N.J.-Israel Commn., 1998—; bd. trustees Rutgers Prep. Sch., 2000—; chair Hunterdon County Bd. Social Svc., 2002-; vice-chair Hunterdon County Health and Human Svcs. Commn., 2002-. Named N.J. Broker Record, Forbes Inc., N.Y.C. 1987. Mem.: Realtors Land Inst. Republican. Jewish. Office: Liberty Hill Realty Inc 415 US Highway 202 Flemington NJ 08822-6021

SALAMON, SAMUEL M. surgeon; b. N.Y.C., June 8, 1953; s. David and Toby Salamon; m. Ruthie Gelb, Sept. 4, 1977; children: Rachel, Yosef, Yehuda. BA, Columbia U., 1974; MD, Albert Einstein Med. Sch., 1977. Diplomate Am. Bd. Ophthalmology, Nat. Bd. Med. Examiners. Asst. prof. ophthalmology U. Ala. Sch. of Medicine, Birmingham, 1982—85; dir. divsn. ophthalmology St. Vincent Charity Hosp., Cleve., 1985—; pres. Cataract Eye Ctr. of Cleve., 1987—; med. dir. Cleve. Surg. Suites, Richmond Heights, Ohio. Contbr. articles to profl. jours. Fellow: ACS, rgeons, Am. Acad. Ophthalmology. Avocation: guitar. Office: Euclid Med Plaza 26300 Euclid Ave Ste 312 Euclid OH 44132-3703 also: 6701 Rockside Rd Independence OH 44131-2316 also: Ste 307 2322 E 22d St Cleveland OH 44115

SALAMONE, JOSEPH CHARLES, polymer chemistry educator; b. Bklyn., Dec. 27, 1939; s. Joseph John and Angela (Barbagallo) S.; children: Robert, Alicia, Christopher. BS in Chemistry, Hofstra U., 1961; PhD in Chemistry, Poly. Inst. N.Y., 1967. NIH postdoctoral fellow U. Liverpool, Eng., 1966-67; rsch. assoc., Horace H. Rackham postdoctoral fellow U. Mich., Ann Arbor, 1967-70, adminstrv. sec., 1968-70; asst. prof., then assoc. prof. chemistry U. Mass., Lowell, 1970-76, prof., 1976-90, prof. emeritus, 1990—, dean Coll Sci., 1978-84, Disting. Rsch. fellow, 1984-90, chmn. dept. chemistry, 1975-78. Pres. Optimers Inc., Lowell, 1985-99; bd. dirs. Rochal Industries, Inc., Boca Raton, Fla.; cons. editor CRC Press, Inc., Boca Raton, 1992-97; v.p. chem. rsch. Bausch and Lomb, 1997-2000, v.p. rsch., 2000—. Author 2 books, 2 encys. in polymeric materials; mem. editl. bd. Polymer, 1976-94, Jour. Macromolecular Sci.-Chemistry, 1985—, Progress of Polymer Sci., 1987—, ChemTech, 1995-99; mem. adv. bd. Jour. Polymer Sci., 1974—; editor-in-chief Polymeric Materials Ency., 1993-97; contbr. more than 160 articles to profl. jours.; holder 25 U.S. and internat. patents. Recipient Disting Alumnus award, Poly. Inst. N.Y., 1984. Mem. Am. Chem. Soc. (chmn. div. polymer chemistry 1982), Polymer Sci., Am. Acad. Ophthalmology (assoc.), Pacific Polymer Fedn. (sec., treas. 1988-90, dep. v.p. 1991-92, v.p., 1993, pres. 1994-95). Office: Bausch & Lomb 1400 N Goodman St PO Box 30450 Rochester NY 14603-0450 E-mail: joe_salamone@bausch.com.

SALAMONE-KOCHOWICZ, JEAN GLORIA, retired banker; b. White Deer, Pa., Dec. 28, 1929; d. Dewey and Pearl Viola (Bastian) Smith; m. Daniel W. Salamone, Nov. 2, 1946 (div. 1977); children: Daryl Joseph, John Daniel; m. John T. Kochowicz, Feb. 10, 1990 (dec. 1993). Student, Bloomsburg State Coll., 1946, Am. Inst. Banking, 1974-85. Sec. Chef Boy-ar-Dee Foods, Milton, Pa., 1946-48, Arthur Andersen & Co., Washington, 1948-58; exec. sec. Citizens Bank and Trust Co., Riverdale, Md., 1970-74, asst. treas., 1974-77, asst. v.p., 1977-84; v.p. Citizens Bank, Laurel, 1984-97; corp. sec. Citizens Bancorp (holding corp. for Citizens Bank), 1982-96; ret. CRESTAR, 1997. Trustee Prince George's Arts Coun., Riverdale, 1983-98, treas., 1983-89, pres. 1990-91. Mem. Fin. Women Internat. (pres. met. Md. group 1977-78). Roman Catholic. Avocations: travel, photography, art collecting, volunteering. E-mail: salakoch@aol.com.

SALAMOUN, PETER V. retired manufacturing executive; b. Jirice, Czechoslovakia, Sept. 6, 1926; came to U.S., 1956; s. Charles and Helen Salamoun; m. Mildred B. Bohac, June 3, 1950; children: Dashie Schouten, Peter C. Diploma in Bus., Acad. of Commerce, Czechoslovakia, 1946; Diploma in Indsl. Engring., Indsl. Engring. Coll., Chgo., 1959; Diploma in Bus., Al Hamilton Exec. GRP Program, Chgo., 1964. Cert. mfg. engr. Supt. plastics, castings Bell & Howell Co., Chgo., 1959-66, mgr. mfg., 1966-78, divsn. mgr. mfg., 1978-81, ops. mgr., 1981-85, internat. project mgr., 1985-87, ops. mgr., v.p. ops. Documail Systems, 1987-92. V.p., team leader total quality mgmt. Bell & Howell Documail Systems Comp., Chgo., 1992-93; internat. mfg. cons. Bell & Howell, Brazil, Australia, 1985-87, Internat. Exec. Svc. Corps, Stamford, Conn., 1992—. Author productivity and quality tech. papers in field. Chmn. referendum Niles (Ill.) Park Dist.; planning com. Save Open Space Referendum Project, Niles, 1974. Mem. Czechoslovak Nat. Coun. (chpt. chmn. 1988), Soc. Plastic Engrs. (sr. mem.) Republican. Roman Catholic. Avocations: snowskiing, traveling, langs., tree planting. Home: 2826 Pawnee Cir Glenview IL 60025-7301

SALAND, DEBORAH, psychotherapist, educator; b. Val Dosta, Ga., July 25, 1954; d. Charles and Audrey (Horan) Gianniny. B in Profl. Studies, Barry U., 1990, MSW, 1992; D in Psychology, So. Calif. Sch. Profl. Studies, 1996. Lic. clin. social worker, Fla. Substance abuse counselor Spectrum Programs, Ft. Lauderdale, Fla., 1974-79; owner Obsession in Time, Miami, 1984-88; asst. clin. dir. Interphase Recovery, 1988-89; substance abuse counselor Transitions Recovery, 1989-91; clin. dir. level II Pathways Treatment; pvt. practice Inst. Human Potential, 1993—; founder Eating Disorder Tex. Program, 1997—. Lectr. Addiction Traingin Inst. U. Miami, 1992, mem. faculty, 1993—; clin. supr. Transitions Recovery, Miami, 1993—, Treatment Resources, Miami, 1993-94; adj. faculty N.Y. Inst. Tech., Boca Raton, Fla., 1997—; dir. Am. Family Eating Disorder Tract, 1997-98. Contbr. articles to profl. jours. Named Spl. Alumni Barry U., 1996. Mem. NASW, APA, Am. Group Psychotherapy Assn. (clin.), Med. Psychotherapist Am. (assoc. clin.) Nat. Bd. Cert. Counselors (counselor), Broward County Mental Health Assn. Office: Inst Human Potential 19501 NE 10th Ave Ste 305 Miami FL 33179-3502

SALAND, LINDA CAROL, anatomy educator, neuroscience researcher; b. N.Y.C., Oct. 24, 1942; d. Charles and Esther (Weingarten) Gewirtz; m. Joel S. Saland, Aug. 16, 1964; children: Kenneth, Jeffrey. BS, CCNY, 1963, PhD in Biology, 1968; MA in Zoology, Columbia U., 1965. Rsch. assoc. dept. anatomy Columbia U. Coll. Physicians and Surgeons, N.Y.C., 1968-69; sr. rsch. assoc. dept. anatomy Sch. Medicine U. N.Mex., Albuquerque, 1971-78, asst. prof. anatomy, 1978-83, assoc. prof., 1983-89, prof., 1989-97, prof. dept. neuroscis., 1997—. Ad hoc reviewer study sect. NIH, 1994, 95, 97, 2000, mem. site visit team. Mem. editl. bd. Anat. Record, 1980-98; contbr. articles to profl. jours. Recipient Khatali Tchg. Excellence award, U. N.Mex. Med. Class of 2001; fellow NDEA, 1966—68. Mem. AAAS, Am. Assn. Anatomists, Soc. for Neurosci., Women in Neurosci. (chmn. steering com. 1991-93), Am. Soc. Cell Biology. Office: U NMex Sch Medicine Dept Neuroscis Basic Med Sci Bldg Albuquerque NM 87131-0001 E-mail: lsaland@salud.unm.edu.

SALANDRA, HELEN E. volunteer, retired nurse; b. Niles, Ohio, Mar. 6, 1922; d. Joe A. and Annette (Cantisano) S. RN, St. Luke's Hosp. Sch. Nursing, 1942; postgrad., Margaret Hague Maternity Hosp., Jersey City, N.J., 1943; BSN summa cum laude, Youngstown U., 1955; MA in Health and Safety summa cum laude, Calif. State U., 1958. General duty nurse to asst. head nurse St. Luke's Hosp., Cleve., 1942-43, 44; supr. ob-gyn. dept. Youngstown (Ohio) Hosp., 1944-46, obstet. clin. instr., 1946-48; lead nurse labor and delivery Huntington Meml. Hosp., Pasadena, Calif., 1948-51, asst. dir. nursing svcs., 1951-53; med. clin. instr., 1953-55; med. clin. instr., sch. nurse L.A. Unified Sch. Dist., 1955-65; supr. and asst. dir. L.A. Sch. Dist., 1965-85. Presenter in field of nursing; field coord. sch. nursing, L.A. Unified Sch. Dist. Contbr. articles to profl. jours. Tchr. classes ARC; bd. dirs. Pasadena Symphony, 1985-95; named hon. life mem. 10th Dist. PTA, Pasadena, 1986. Named VIP Hostess 1984 Olympics; recipient Outstanding Vol. Svc. award Vol. Ctr. of San Gabriel, 1988, Vol. Svc. award Coun. of Women's Club, Pasadena, 1991, Woman of Achievement award Arcadia Br. AAUW, Calif., 1991, Disting. Alumni award St. Luke's Hosp., Cleve., 1997, Pres. Coll. Women's Club/Scholarship Found., 1990-91, others; Helen E. Salandra Eye Clin. dedicated in her honor, L.A., 1985. Mem. AAUW (pres. Arcadia br. steering com. 1992, mem. state mem. and nominating coms. 1998), NEA, Coun. of Women's Clubs, Coll. Women's Clubs (nom. chair 1999), Pi Lambda Theta, Phi Delta Kappa, Delta Kappa Gamma (pres. Omicron chpt. Area XIII, dir. state nominating com.), others. Roman Catholic. Avocations: Bridge, water aerobics, symphony, L.A. Dodgers, UCLA football team. Home: 1039 N Holliston Ave Pasadena CA 91104-3015

SALANS, CARL FREDRIC, lawyer; b. Chicago Heights, Ill., Mar. 13, 1933; s. Leon and Jean (Rudnick) Salans; m. Edith Motel, Sept. 26, 1956; children: Eric Lee, Marc Robert, Christopher John. AB, Harvard U., 1954; BA, Cambridge (Eng.) U., 1956, MA, 1958, LLB, 1958; JD, U. Chgo., 1957. Bar: Ill. 1958, D.C. 1973, U.S. Supreme Ct. 1972, (admitted in France as conseil juridique) 1972, (admitted in France as avocat) 1992. With State Dept., 1959-72, dep. legal adviser, 1966-72; practice law Paris, 1972—; ptnr. Salans Hertzfeld & Heilbronn, 1978—. Legal adviser U.S. del. Vietnam Peace Talk, Paris, 1968—71; mem. ICC Internat. Ct. Arbitration; arbitrator internat. cases; arbitrator U.S.-Iran Claims Tribunal, The Hague. Mem.: ABA (chmn. com. East-West trade and investment 1975—82), Am. Arbitration Assn. (panel arbitrators), Am. Soc. Internat. Law, Am. C. of C. in France (bd. dirs. 1977—87, chmn. laws and pub. affairs com. 1980—85). Home: 18 Ave Raphael 75016 Paris France Office: Salans Hertzfeld & Heilbronn 9 Rue Boissy d'Anglas 75008 Paris France E-mail: csalans@salans.com.

SALANS, LESTER BARRY, physician, scientist, educator; b. Chicago Heights, Ill., Jan. 25, 1936; s. Leon K. and Jean (Rudnick) S.; m. Lois Audrey Kapp, Dec. 21, 1958; children: Laurence Eliot, Andrea Eileen. BA, U. Mich., 1957; MD with honors, U. Ill., 1961. Internal medicine intern Stanford U. Med. Ctr., 1961, resident, 1962-64; USPHS postdoctoral and spl. fellow Rockefeller U., 1964-67, asst. prof., 1967-68, adj. prof., 1984—; asst. prof. medicine Dartmouth Coll., 1968-70, assoc. prof., 1970-77, adj. prof., 1978-79; assoc. dir. diabetes, endocrinology, metabolism, also chief lab. cellular metabolism and obesity Nat. Inst. Arthritis, Metabolism and Digestive Diseases, NIH, Bethesda, 1976-81; dir. Nat. Inst. Arthritis, Diabetes, Digestive and Kidney Diseases, NIH, 1981-84; v.p., head preclin. rsch. Sandoz Rsch. Inst., 1985-92, v.p. scientific and acad. affairs, 1993-97; pres. LBS Advisors, Inc., 1997—; dean Mt. Sinai Sch. Medicine, 1984, prof. internal medicine, 1984-85, clin. prof. medicine, 1987—; ptnr. BioPharmAnalysis LLC, 2001—. Adj. prof. Rockefeller U., 1985—2001; vis. prof. U. Geneva (Switzerland), 1974—75; dir. Forest Labs., 1998—; mem. adv. bd. Columbia-Presbyn. Hosp. Naomi Berrie Diabetes Ctr., 1999—. Contbr. articles on insulin, diabetes mellitus, obesity to profl. jours., textbooks. Recipient NIH Research Career Devel. award, 1972-76, NIH Dirs. award, 1980, Juvenile Diabetes Fedn Pub. Service award, 1979 Fellow ACP; mem. AAAS, Am. Soc. Clin. Investigation, Am. Fed. Clin. Rsch., Am. Diabetes Soc., Am. Diabetes Assn. (Charles H. Best award 1985), Endocrine Soc., Assn. Am. Physicians, Am. Soc. Clin. Nutrition. Office: LBS Advisors inc 21 E 90th St # 6C New York NY 10128-0654

SALANT, DAVID JOHN, medical educator, nephrologist; b. Johannesburg, May 8, 1944; m. Anne Salant; children: Alon, Talya, Nira. MB BCh, U. of Witwatersrand, Johannesburg, 1969. Diplomate Am. Bd. Internal Medicine (chmn., bd. examiners in nephrology 1998—), Am. Bd. Nephrology. Cons. nephrologist Johannesburg Gen. Hosp., 1974-77; rsch. fellow Boston U. Med. Ctr., 1977-78, asst. prof. medicine, 1979-83, assoc. prof. medicine, 1983-88, prof. medicine, 1988—, chief renal sect., 1997—; prof. pathology and lab. medicine Boston U. Sch. Medicine, 1992—. Vis. prof. Stanford U., Calif., 1995; mem. study sect. NIH, Bethesda, Md., 1989-93. Contbr. articles to profl. jours., chpts. to books. Mem. sci. adv. bd. Nat. Kidney Found., N.Y.C., 1996—. Recipient Established Investigator award Am. Heart Assn., 1985-90. Mem. Am. Soc. Clin. Investigation, Am. Assn. Physicians, Am. Bd. Internal Medicine (chmn. 1992-2002, bd. dirs. 1998-2002). Office: Boston U Med Ctr Evans Biomed Rsch Ctr 650 Albany St Fl 5 Boston MA 02118-2518 Fax: 617-638-7326. E-mail: djsalant@acs.bu.edu.

SALANT, JONATHAN D. reporter; b. N.Y.C., Feb. 15, 1954; s. Harry and Claire Leatrice (Weinstock) S.; m. Joan Friedenberg; 1 child, Isaac. BA in Polit. Sci., SUNY, Stony Brook, 1976; MS in Journalism, Columbia U., 1978. Reporter Bergen Record, Hackensack, N.J., 1976-78, Miami Herald, 1978-81; st. capitol reporter Albany (N.Y.) Times Union, 1981-84, Syracuse Herald Jour., 1984-87; Washington reporter Syracuse Newspapers, 1987-94; reporter Congressional Quar., 1994-97, AP, 1997—. Contbg. editor: Capital Region mag., 1986—89; Washington editor: Empire State Report, 1997—2001. Contbr. U.S. Holocaust Mus., Washington, 1994—, United Jewish Appeal Fedn. Greater Washington, 1988—; sec. Standing Com. of Corr., Washington, 1991-92. Recipient Reporting awards AP, 1984-85, 89-91, Syracuse Press Club, 1984-87, 89, 91; Paul Miller fellowship Freedom Forum, 1988-89. Mem. Nat. Press Club (speakers com. chair 1992-93, profl. affairs com. chair 1993-95, reporting awards 1990, 92, chair Freedom of Press com. 1995-96; forums com. vice-chmn. 1996-97, bd. govs. 1998—, v. chmn. 2000—), Soc. Profl. Journalists (sec. of chpt. 1991-92, v.p. 1992-93, pres. D.C. chpt. 1994-95), Am. Polit. Items Collectors. Jewish. Avocations: political button collector, softball coach, collector of road maps. Home: 11430 Hollowstone Dr Rockville MD 20852 Office: AP 2021 K St NW Washington DC 20006 E-mail: jds15@aol.com.

SALANT, RICHARD FRANK, mechanical engineer, educator; b. N.Y.C., Sept. 4, 1941; s. Joseph and Augusta (Dick) S.; m. Barbel Lang, Sept. 9, 1962; children: Scott M., Stephanie. BS, MS, MIT, 1963, DSc, 1967. Registered profl. engr., Ga. Asst. prof. U. Calif. Berkeley, 1966-68; asst. prof., assoc. prof. MIT, Cambridge, 1968-72; mgr. fluid mech. and heat transfer Borg-Warner Rsch. Ctr., Des Plaines, Ill., 1972-87; prof., chair tribology rsch. group Ga. Inst. Tech., Atlanta, 1987—, Ga. Power Disting. prof., 2001—. Cons. fluid sealing tech., Atlanta, 1987—. Assoc. editor Jour. Tribology, 1993-99, Jour. Fluids Engring., 1984-87; contbr. articles to profl. jours.; patentee in field. Fellow ASME (Henry R. Worthington medal 1996), Soc. Tribologists and Lubrication Engrs. (Edmond E. Bisson award 2000, Frank P. Bussick award 2002). Home: 1138 Manning Farms Ct Dunwoody GA 30338-2648 Office: Ga Inst Tech Sch Mech Engring Atlanta GA 30332-0405 E-mail: richard.salant@me.gatech.edu.

SALAS, HENRY JOSEPH, environmental engineer; b. N.Y.C., Jan. 30, 1947; s. Alberto and Orestes (Martinez) S.; m. Mirna Delicia Bardalez, Oct. 22, 1991; 1 child, Henry Joseph Jr. B in Civil Enging., Manhattan Coll., 1969, M in Environ. Engring., 1970. Registered profl. engr., N.Y. Project engr. Hydrosci., Inc., Westwood, N.J., 1970-73, project mgr., 1973-79; cons. Environ. Quality Bd. P.R., San Juan, 1979-82; regional adviser in water pollution control Panamerican Ctr. Sanitary Engring. and Environ. Scis., Lima, Peru, 1982-97, regional adv. environ. impact and health, 1997-2001; regional advisor in environ. protection Pan Am. Health Orgn., Washington, 2001—. Cons. Pan Am. Health Orgn., Brazil, Peru, Cuba, Uruguay, 1975-81; lectr. in field. Author: History and Application of Microbiological Water Quality Standards in the Marine Environment, 1998; co-author Manual for the Evaluation and Management of Toxic Substances in Surface Waters, 1988-94; contbr. articles to profl. jours. Mem. ASCE, Water Environ. Fedn., Chi Epsilon. Roman Catholic. Achievements include simplified mathematical model for the evaluation of eutrophication in warm-water tropical lakes/resevoirs. Home: 7476 Westlake Ter Bethesda MD 20817-6502 Office: Pan Am Health Orgn 525 23rd St NW Washington DC 20037 E-mail: salashen@paho.org.

SALAS, JE-AN, ballerina; b. Ilolio City, The Philippines; arrived in Can., 1990; Student, Philippine HS for Performing Arts, Nat. Ballet Sch., Can., 1990. Mem. corps de ballet Nat. Ballet Can., Toronto, 1994—2001, second soloist, 2001—. Dancer (ballets) The Merry Widow, The Sleeping Beauty, Cinderella, The Four Seasons, The Nutcracker, soloist Paquita, (world premieres) Perreault's The Comforts of Solitude, Dumais' one hundred words for snow, the weight of absence. Office: Walter Carsen Ctr for Nat Ballet Can 470 Queens Quay W Toronto ON Canada M5V 3K4 Office Fax: 416-345-8323.*

SALAS, JOAQUIN LEON GUERRERO, protective services official; b. Tamuning, Guam, Jan. 31, 1956; m. Ramona Sablan, June 21, 1975; 4 children. Student, Archdiocese Agana, Guam, 1971; AA in Police Sci., U. Guam Police Acad., 1983; BS in Criminal Justice magna cum laude. Traffic comdr. Guam Police, 1974-87; chief program adminstr., motor vehicle Govt. of Guam, 1987-88; investigator CNMI Workman Compensation Commn., 1989-90; deputy U.S. marshal U.S. Marshals Svc., 1988-97, U.S. marshal, 1997—. Instr. Guam C.C., 1985-88, No. Mariana Coll., 1992. With U.S. Army Res., 1977-83, U.S. Army NG, 1988-90. Mem. KC. Roman Catholic. Avocations: gardening, fishing, guitar, family, basketball. E-mail: joaquin.salas.usdoj.gov. Office: US Courthouse 520 W Soledad Ave Hagatna GU 96910-5206 Fax: 671-473-9195.

SALAS, RANDALL NOUEL, automotive company executive; b. Willemstad, Curazao, Venezuela, Oct. 20, 1945; s. Herbert and Claire (Nouel) S.; m. Silvia M. Mago, Feb. 16, 1974; children: Maria Silvia, Claudia Isabella. Student, Santiago de León, Caracas, Venezuela, 1965; BS in Indsl. Engring., Cath. U., Caracas, 1971, BA in Journalism, 1976. Pilots coordinating engr. Gen. Motors de Venezuela, Caracas, 1971-73, methods engr., 1973-76, gen. supply products facilitator, 1976-78, products facility mgr., 1978-80, prodn. mgr., 1980-81, dir. personnel, 1981-86, dir. personnel and pub. govtl. relations, v.p., 1987-97; human resources and pub. rels. v.p. Orinoco Iron-Sivensa, 1997—. Bd. dirs. Camara Automotriz de Venezuela, Caracas. Named to Labor Merit Order 1st Degree, Ministry of Labor, 1987. Mem. Coll. Engrs. Venezuela, Assn. Venezolana de Ejecutivos, Nat. Assn. Indsl. Relations Execs. Clubs: Lagunita Country (Caracas). Roman Catholic. Avocation: reading. Office: Sivensa Av Venezuela Torre America Piso 14 Bello Monte Caracas 1060 Venezuela Address: c/o SDP (OI) 14505 Commerce Way Ste 700 Miami Lakes FL 33016-1514

SALATA, ROBERT ANDREW, physician, researcher; b. Youngstown, Ohio, Feb. 14, 1952; s. Joseph Andrew and Margaret (Yanek) S.; m. Mary Jo Hummer, July 5, 1975; children: R. Christopher, Michael J., Andrew J., Matthew J. BA summa cum laude, U. Notre Dame, 1975; MD, Case Western Res. U., 1979. Diplomate Am. Bd. Internal Medicine, Am. Bd. Infectious Diseases; lic. physician, Ohio. Intern U. Hosps. Cleve., 1979-80, resident in internal medicine, 1980-82; fellow in infectious diseases U. Va. Med. Ctr., Charlottesville, 1982-85; from asst. prof. to assoc. prof. medicine Case Western Res. U., Cleve., 1986-98, prof. medicine, internat. health and epidemiology/biostatis., 1998—. Chief divsn. infectious diseases Case Western Res. U., Cleve., 1988-91, dir. ann. course in internat. health, 1990-92, dir. infectious diseases area concentration, 1991—; profl. adv. com. U. Hosps. Cleve., 1994-95, chmn. infection control com., 1994—, performance improvement coun., 1995—; rschr. and presenter in field. Co-editor: Amebiasis: Human Infection, 1998, Tropical and Geographical Medicine Companion Handbook, 1993; contbr. articles to profl. jours. Grantee NIH-NIAID, 1996—, Rhone-Poulenc Rorer, 1995—, Parke-Davis, 1995—, Wallace Labs, 1996—, AMGEN, 1996—, Aronex Pharm., 1996—, Collaborative Exch. Antifungal Rsch., 1996—, Janssen Pharm., 1996—, Merck, 1996—, Mycoses Study Group, 1996—, Hoffman-La Roche, Inc., 1996-97, Chiron, 1997-98, Family Health Internat., 1997-98; named Tchr. of Yr., Case Western Res. U. and U. Hosps., 1990; recipient Lubrizol award, 1979, Elton Hoyt III award U. Hosps. Cleve., 1982. Fellow ACP; mem. AMA, AAAS, Am. Fedn. for Clin. Rsch., Ctrl. Soc. for Clin. Rsch., Infectious Disease Soc. Am., Am. Soc. Tropical Medicine and Hygiene, Am. Assn. Immunologists, Internat. Soc. Travel Medicine, Am. Soc. for Microiology, Ohio State Med. Assn., Soc. for Healthcare Epidemiology Am., Phi Beta Kappa, Alpha Omega Alpha. Avocations: reading, coaching basketball, cooking. Home: 20828 Colby Rd Cleveland OH 44122-1904 Office: Univ Hosps Cleve 11100 Euclid Ave Cleveland OH 44106-1736

SALATHE, JOHN, JR. manufacturing company executive; b. Montreal, Sept. 25, 1928; s. John and Ida (Schenk) S.; m. Harriet Edith Styles; children: Linda Paul, Craig. BSME, San Jose State U., 1950. Gen. mgr. Indsl. Steel Tank & Body Co., Berkeley, Calif., 1958-62; project mgr. Pacific Foundry div. PACCAR Inc., Renton, Wash., 1962-66, prodn. mgr., 1966-70, asst. gen. mgr., 1970-71, gen. mgr., 1971-79; asst. v.p. PACCAR Inc., Bellevue, 1979-81, v.p., 1981-90; ret., 1991. Bd. dirs. Jr. Achievement, Seattle, 1979-85; mem. adv. bd. Seattle Pacific U., 1985-95. Sloan fellow Stanford U., 1970. Mem. Soc. Mfg. Engrs. (sr.), Am. Soc. Quality Control (sr.). Avocations: gardening, boating, reading.

SALATICH, JOHN SMYTH, retired cardiologist, internist; b. New Orleans, Nov. 28, 1926; s. Peter B. and Gladys (Malter) S.; m. Patricia L. Mattison, Sept. 26, 1959; children: John Smyth, Elizabeth, Allison, Stephanie. BS cum laude, Loyola U., New Orleans, 1946; MD, La. State U., 1950. Diplomate Am. Bd. Internal Medicine. Intern Charity Hosp., New Orleans, 1950-51, resident, 1951-54; practice medicine specializing in cardiology and internal medicine, 1954-92, Gen. Internal Med. Clinic, Tulane Med. Sch., 1992-99; dir. EKG dept. Southeastern La. Hosp., Mandeville, 1972-99; ret., 1999—. Prof. clin. medicine La. State U., 1994; mem. staff Touro Infirmary, St. Charles Gen. Hosp.; chmn. dept. medicine Hotel Dieu, 1974-86; pres., New Orleans Emergency Room Corp., Physician Supplemental Services; adv. bd. Bank La., 1960-89; mem. Pres.'s Coun. Loyola U., 1990-92. Contbr. articles to profl. and bus. jours. Bd. dirs. La. Regional Med. Program, 1972. Served to capt. M.C., AUS, 1954-56; Korea. Decorated Medallion of Greek Army. Fellow Am. Coll. Chest Physicians, ACP; mem. Am. Heart Assn., La. Heart Assn., New Orleans Acad. Internal Medicine, La. Soc. Internal Medicine, AMA, La. Med. Soc., Orleans Parish Med. Soc., New Orleans Country Club, Theta Beta, Alpha Sigma Nu, Delta Epsilon Sigma. Home: 6458 Fleur de Lis Dr New Orleans LA 70124

SALATINO, DAVID, critical care nurse; b. Kingston, Pa., Apr. 9, 1954; s. Leo P. and Margaret S.; m. Lucinda K. Salatino, July 9, 1996. Diploma, Mercy Hosp., Wilkes-Barre, Pa., 1975; BSN, Wilkes Coll., 1984. RN, Pa.; CEN, ACLS and BCLS instr. ICU-CCU supr. Mercy Hosp., Wilkes-Barre, 1979-84, mobile ICU Nurse Scranton, Pa., 1984-86, emergency rm. nurse, critical care nurse, open heart nurse, 1984-86; head nurse emergency rm. Lehigh Valley Hosp., Allentown, 1986-90, nurse cardiac catheterization lab., 1990—. Mem. Am. Heart Assn.

SALATKA, CHARLES ALEXANDER, retired archbishop; b. Grand Rapids, Mich., Feb. 26, 1918; s. Charles and Mary (Balun) S. Student, St. Joseph's Sem., Grand Rapids, 1932-38; MA, Cath. U. Am., 1941; J.C.L., Inst. Civil and Canon Law, Rome, 1948. Instr. St. Joseph's Sem., Grand Rapids, Mich., 1945; ordained priest Roman Catholic Ch., 1945; assigned chancery office Diocese of Grand Rapids, 1948-54, vice chancellor, 1954-61; aux. bishop, 1961; vicar gen., 1961; consecrated bishop, 1962; pastor St. James Parish, Grand Rapids, 1962-68; titular bishop of Cariana and aux. bishop of Grand Rapids, 1962-68; bishop of Marquette, 1968-77; archbishop of Okla. City, 1977-92; ret., 1992. Mem. Canon Law Soc. Am.

SALAVERRIA, HELENA CLARA, language educator; b. May 19, 1923; d. Blas Saturnino and Eugenia Irene (Loyarte) S. AB, U. Calif., Berkeley, 1945, secondary tchg. cert., 1946; MA, Stanford U., 1962. H.s. tchr., 1946-57; asst. prof. Luther Coll., Decorah, Iowa, 1959-60; prof. Spanish Bakersfield (Calif.) Coll., 1961-84, chmn. dept., 1973-80. Mem. srs. adv. group edn. Cuesta Coll. Cmty. Svcs. Mem. AAUW (edn. com.), NEA, Calif. Fgn. Lang. Tchrs. Assn. (dir. 1976-77), Kern County Fgn. Lang. Tchrs. Assn. (pres. 1975-77), Union Concerned Scientists, Natural Resources Def. Coun., Calif. Tchrs. Assn. (chpt. sec. 1951-52), Yolo County Coun. Retarded, Soc. Basque Studies in Am., RSVP, Amnesty Internat., Common Cause, Sierra Club, Prytanean Alumnae, U. Women of Cambria, U. Calif. Alumni Assn., Stanford U. Alumni Assn., Friends of the Cambria Libr. Democrat. Address: PO Box 63 Cambria CA 93428-0063

SALAY, CINDY ROLSTON, technical advisor, registered nurse; b. Roanoke, Va., July 18, 1955; d. Gilbert Wilson and Elinor Patterson (Sandridge) Rolston; m. John Matthew, July 7, 1988; 1 child, David. AAS, Va. Western Community Coll., 1976; AS, J. Sargeant Reynolds Community Coll., 1982; BS, Va. Commonwealth U., 1984. RN. Operating room RN Henrico Doctors Hosp., Richmond, Va., 1979-80; nursing supr. Johnston Willis Hosp., 1980-87; systems analyst, coord. Health Corp Va., 1983-87, sr. project leader, 1987-88; sr. systems analyst Hosp. Corp. Am., Nashville, 1987; sr. systems cons. IBAX Healthcare Systems, Reston, Va., 1988-94; sys. analyst MCV Hosps. Info. Sys., Richmond, 1994-95; advisor McKesson, Atlanta, 1995—. Methodist. Avocations: reading, plants, pets, exercising. Home: 13800 Sunrise Bluff Rd Midlothian VA 23112-2512 Office: McKesson 5995 Windward Pkwy Alpharetta GA 30005-4184 E-mail: cindy.salay@mckesson.com.

SALAYMEH, MUHAMMAD TAWFIK, surgeon; b. Hebron, Palestine, June 10, 1929; came to U.S., 1960; s. Tawfik Abdulfattah Salaymeh and Alamiyeh Ahmad Abu-Sabbah; m. Maha Minkarah, Jan. 13, 1959; children: Basil, Raja, Rima. MD, Am. U., Beirut, 1958. Diplomate Am. Bd. Surgery, Am. Bd. Thoracic Surgery. Intern Am. U. Beirut Hosp., 1957-58; resident in pathology Peter Bent Brigham Hosp./Harvard Med. Sch., Boston, 1960-61; surgery I and II Worcester (Mass.) City Hosp., 1961-63; surgery III and IV Creighton U. Hosp., Omaha, 1963-65; thoracic and cardiovasc. surgery I and II LDS Hosp., Salt Lake City, 1965-77; chief of surgery Ash-Sarg Hosp., Al-Khobar, Saudi Arabia, 1967-69; fellow in thoracic and cardiovasc. surgery Jewish Hosp. St. Louis, 1969-71; chief surgeon Christian County Med. Clinic, Taylorville, Ill., 1971-85; thoracic and vascular surgeon 22nd Strategic Hosp. March AFB, Riverside, Calif., 1985-88; chief surgeon FHP Charter Cmty. Hosp., Hawiian Garden, 1988-93. Republican. Avocations: tennis, golf. Home: 15891 Bowie St Westminster CA 92683-7250

SALAZAR, KENNETH L. state attorney general; b. Mar. 2, 1955; s. Henry and Emma Salazar; m. Hope Hernandez; children: Melinda, Andrea. BA in Polit. Sci., Colo. Coll., 1977, LLD (hon.) , 1993; JD, U. Mich., 1981. Bar: Colo. 1981, U.S. Dist. Ct. Colo. 1981, U.S. Ct. Appeals (10th cir.) 1981, U.S. Supreme Ct. 1999. Farmer, rancher, Conejos County, Colo.; law clk. Colo. Atty. Gen., 1979; assoc. Sherman & Howard, Denver, 1981—86; chief legal counsel Office of Gov., 1986—90; exec. dir. Colo. Dept. Natural Resources, 1990—94; dir. Parcel, Mauro, Hultin & Spaanstra, 1994—98; atty. gen. State of Colo., 1999—. Gov.'s rep. State Bd. Equalization, Denver, 1990. Mem. Israel Friendship League, 1986—89; chair Great Outdoors Colo., Denver, 1993—94, Rio Grande Compact Commn., 1995—97, Sangre de Cristo Land Grant Commn., 1993—95; mem. Colo. Water Conservation Bd., Denver, 1990—, City and County of Denver Ethics Panel, 1993; gov.'s rep. State Bd. on Property Tax Equalization, 1987—91; del. Soviet-Am. Young Leadership Dialogue, 1984; mem. adv. com. Colo. U. Sch. Law Natural Resources Law Ctr., 1989—92; mem. Western Water Policy Rev. Adv. Commn., 1995—97; bd. dirs. Denver Cmty. Leadership Forum, 1988, Servicios de la Raza HUD 202 Project, 1985—89, chair, 1986. Scholar Juan Tienda. Mem.: ABA, Am. Judicature Soc., Hispanic Bar Assn. (ABA task force on opportunities for minorities in legal profession, bd. dirs. 1986—87), Denver Bar Assn. (2d v.p. 1989, chair policy-cmty. rels. subcoms. 1982—84), Colo. Bar Assn. (bd. govs. 1989—90, task force to assess the legal profession 1986). Avocations: basketball, outdoor activities, politics. Office: State Colo Dept Law 1525 Sherman St 7th Floor Denver CO 80203-1700 E-mail: attorney.general@state.co.us.*

SALAZAR, LUIS ADOLFO, architect; b. New Orleans, Sept. 17, 1944; s. Gustavo Adolfo and Luz Maria (Florez) S.; m. Sandra Kay Bucklew, May 30, 1969 (div. Jan. 1984); 1 chld, Staci Dahnal. AA, Harbor Coll., 1966; BArch, Ariz. State U., 1971. Registered architect, Ariz., Calif. Area architect Peace Corps, Sierra Leone, 1971-73; project architect Van Sittert Assocs., Phoenix, 1973-77; pres., owner Salazar Assoc. Architects, Ltd., 1977—. Bd. dirs. Terraco Properties. Prin. works include bldg. design Kenema (Sierra Leone) Cathedral, 1980, U.S. West Foothills Switching Ctr., Phoenix, Celebration Luth. Ch., Peoria, Ariz.; mem. Subcom. on Bond Election, Phoenix, 1984; mem. Visual Improvement Awards Com., City of Phoenix, 1985-88. Bd. dirs. Cmty. Behavioral Svcs., Phoenix, 1983-85. Mem. AIA (chmn. program com., Honor award Ariz. chpt. 1984, Visual Improvement award 1985, 86, Internat. Illumination Design award 1998).

SALAZAR, RAMIRO S. library administrator; b. Del Rio, Tex., Mar. 3, 1954; s. Jesus and Juanita (Suarez) S.; m. Cynthia Castillo, Dec. 19, 1976 (div. 1990); children: Ramiro Orlando, Selinda Yvette. BA, Tex. A&I U., 1978; MLS, Tex. Woman's U., 1979. Asst. libr. dir. Val Verde County Libr., Del Rio, 1975-76; libr. Robert J. Kleberg Libr., Kingsville, Tex., 1977-78; libr. dir. Eagle Pass (Tex.) Pub. Libr., 1980-84; dir. Main Libr. San Antonio Pub. Libr., 1984-90; dir. librs. El Paso Pub. Libr., 1991-93, Dallas Pub. Libr., 1993—. Chmn. Tex. State Libr. Planning Task Force, 1991-92; active Tex. Women's U. Sch. Libr. and Info. Studies Adv. Bd., 1993—, Alliance for Higher Edn. Libr. Dirs. Coun., 1993—. Trustee AMIGOS Bibliographic Coun.; bd. advs. U. N. Tex. Sch. Lib. and Info. Scis., 1993, Booker T. Washington H.S. of Performing and Visual Arts, 1995-96. Chair customer svc. steering com. City of Dallas, 1993—; chair coupon book/resident privilege card task force City of Dallas, 1995-96; active home instrn. program for presch. children Nat. Coun. Jewish Women, 1996—. Recipient H.W. Wilson Staff Devel. award jury, 1995-96. Mem. ALA, Coun., 1996-2000 (mem. nominations com. 1997—), Libr. Adminstrn. and Mgmt. Assn. (bldg. and equipment sect., arch. for pub. libr. com. 1993-95, cultural diversity com. 1995—, pres.'s programs com. 1996—), Tex. Mcpl. League (resolutions com. 1995—), Tex. Mcpl. Libr. Dirs. Assn. (Libr. Dir. of the Yr. 1996), Pub. Libr. Adminstrs. North Tex., Reforma (exec. bd. dirs.), Tex. Libr. Assn. (chmn. pubs. com. 1992-93, legis. com. 1993-95, ad hoc com. value of pub. librs. 1995—, awards com. 1995—), Jaycees. Democrat. Roman Catholic. Home: PO Box 15031 Dallas TX 75201-0031 Office: Dallas Pub Libr 1515 Young St Dallas TX 75201-5499

SALAZAR-CARRILLO, JORGE, economics educator; b. Jan. 17, 1938; came to U.S., 1960; s. Jose Salazar and Ana Maria Carrillo; m. Maria Eugenia Winthrop, Aug. 30, 1959; children: Jorge, Manning, Mario, Maria Eugenia. BBA, U. Miami, 1958; MA in Econs., U. Calif., Berkeley, 1964; cert. in econ. planning, U. Calif., 1964, PhD in Econs., 1967. Sr. fellow, non-resident staff mem. Brookings Instn., Washington, 1965—. Dir., mission chief UN, Rio de Janeiro, Brazil, 1974-80; prof. econs. Fla. Internat. U., Miami, 1980—, chmn. dept. econs., 1980-89; dir. Ctr. Econ. Rsch. & Edn.; mem. coun. econ. advisors State of Fla.; advisor U.S. Info. Agy., advisor, contbg. editor Library of Congress, Washington, 1972—; chmn. program com. Hispanic Profs. of Econs. and Bus.; cons. econs. Agy. for Internat. Devel., Washington, 1979—; coun. mem. Internat. Assn. Housing, Vienna, 1981—; exec. bd. Cuban Am. Nat. Coun., Miami, 1982—; bd. dirs, pres. Fla. chpt. Insts. of Econ. and Social Rsch. of Caribbean Basin, Dominican Republic and Costa Rica, 1983—, U.S.-Chile Coun., Miami, 1984—, Fla.-Brazil Inst. Co-author: Trade, Debt and Growth in Latin America, 1984; Prices for Estimation in Cuba, 1985, The Foreign Debt and Latin America, 1983, External Debt and Strategy of Development in Latin America, 1985, The Brazilian Economy in the Eighties, 1987, Foreign Investment, Debt and Growth in Latin America, 1988, World Comparisons of Incomes, Prices, and Product, 1988, Comparisons of Prices and Real Products in Latin America, 1990, The Latin American Debt, 1992, International Comparisons of Prices, Output and Productivity, 1996, Capital Markets, Growth and Economic Policy in Latin America, 1999, Growth in Latin America in the 1990s, 2000; author: Wage Structure in Lating America, 1982, Oil and Development of Venezuela During the Twentieth century, 1994. Fellow Brit. Coun., London, 1960, Georgetown U., Washington, 1961-62, OAS, Washington, 1962-64, Brookings Instn., Washington, 1964-65. Mem. Am. Econ. Assn., Internat. Assn. Rsch. in Income and Wealth, Econometric Soc. Latin Am., N.Am. Econs. and Fin. Assn., Nat. Assn. Cuban Am. Educators (pres. exec. com.), Internat. Assn. Energy Economists (pres. Fla. chpt.), Nat. Assn. Forensic Economists, Assn. for Study Cuban Economy (exec. com., dir. Cuban banking study group), Collegium of Cuban Economists (1st v.p.), Latin Am. Studies Assn., Knights of Malta. Roman Catholic. Home: 1105 Almeria Ave Coral Gables FL 33134-5503 Office: Fla Internat U Tamiami Campus Dm 347 Miami FL 33199-0001 E-mail: salazar@fin.edu.

SALCEDO-DOVI, HECTOR EDUARDO, anatomist, educator, surgeon; b. Cordoba, Argentina, Nov. 9, 1958; s. Domingo and Rosa (Dovi) Salcedo; m. Adriana Gomez, Apr. 3, 1993; 1 child, Camila. MD, U. Nat. Cordoba, 1984; DO, N.Y. Coll. Osteopathic Medicine, 1995. Asst. prof. anatomy, histology N.Y. Coll. Osteopathic Medicine, Old Westbury, 1990-93, prof. anatomy, physiology, 1993; chief intern Good Samaritan Hosp., 1996—, chief resident surgery, 2000. Fellow critical care/trauma. Mem.: ACS, Soc. CCM, Am. Coll. Chest Physicians, Am. Osteopathic Assn., Am. Med. Student Assn. Roman Catholic. Avocations: soccer, bicycling, tennis. Home: 2 Manchester Rd Huntington NY 11743-5532

SALCH, STEVEN CHARLES, lawyer; b. Palm Beach, Fla., Oct. 25, 1943; s. Charles Henry and Helen Louise (Alverson) S.; m. Mary Ann Prim, Oct. 7, 1967; children— Susan Elizabeth, Stuart Trenton BBA, So. Meth. U., 1965, JD, 1968. Bar: Tex. 1968, U.S. Tax Ct. 1969, U.S. Dist. Ct. (so. dist.) Tex. 1969, U.S. Dist. Ct. (ea. dist.) Tex. 1972, U.S. Ct. Appeals (5th cir.) 1969, U.S. Ct. Appeals (fed. cir.) 1982, U.S. Ct. Fed. Claims, 1982. Assoc. Fulbright & Jaworski, Houston, 1968-71, participating assoc., 1971-75, ptnr., 1975—. Co-author: Tax Practice Before the IRS, 1994; contbr. articles to legal jours. Pres. Tealwood Owners Assn., 1982—83, Meml. H.S. PTA, 1985—86; hon. life mem. Tex. PTA, 1986—; mem. devel. bd. U. Tex. Med. Br., Galveston, 2002—; adv. dir. 1894 Grand Opera House Soc., 2002—. Mem.: ABA (coun. dir. 1985—88, vice chair tax sect. 1988—91, chair tax sect. 1996—97), Houston Bar Found., Am. Bar Found., Internat. Fiscal Assn., Am. Coll. Tax Counsel (regent 5th cir. 1999—), Am. Law Inst., Fed. Bar Assn., Houston Bar Assn., State Bar Tex., Colonial Williamsburg Found., Menard Soc., Galveston Hist. Found., Galveston Artillery, Houston Ctr. Club, Galveston Country Club, Galveston Arty. Club, Yacht Club, Pelican Club of Galveston, Order of Coif, Phi Delta Phi, Phi Eta Sigma, Beta Alpha Psi. Presbyterian. Office: Fulbright & Jaworski 1301 Mckinney St Fl 51 Houston TX 77010-3031 Home: 4600 Caduceus Pl Galveston TX 77551-5719 E-mail: ssalch@fulbright.com. *Set goals for yourself. Unless you know where you are and where you want to be in life, you will not be able to map a plan to accomplish your goals.*

SALCUDEAN, MARTHA EVA, mechanical engineer, educator; b. Cluj, Romania, Feb. 26, 1934; arrived in Can., 1976, naturalized, 1979; d. Edmund and Sarolta (Hirsch) Abel; m. George Salcudean, May 28, 1955; 1 child, Septimiu E. BEng, U. Cluj, 1956, postgrad., 1962; PhD, U. Brasov, Romania, 1969; DSc (hon.) , U. Ottawa, Ont., Can., 1992, U. B.C., 2001. Mech. engr. Armatura, Cluj, 1956-63; sr. rsch. officer Nat. Rsch. Inst. Metallurgy, Bucharest, 1963-75; part-time lectr. Inst. Poly., 1967-75; sessional lectr. U. Ottawa, 1976-77, from asst. prof. to assoc. prof. to prof., 1977-85; prof., head dept. mech. engring. U. B.C., Vancouver, Can., 1985-93, assoc. v.p. rsch. Can., 1993-96, acting v.p. rsch. pro-tem Can., 1995, Weyerhausen Indsl. Rsch. chair computational fluid dynamics Can., 1996—. Mem. grant selection com. for mech. engring. Natural Scis. and Engring. Rsch. Coun. Can.; mem. Nat. Adv. Panel to Min. Sci. and Tech. on advanced indsl. materials, Can., 1990; mem. governing coun. Nat. Rsch. Coun.; mem. defense science adv. bd. Dept. Nat. Def.; chair Sci. Coun. B.C. Contbr. numerous articles to profl. jours. Decorated Order of B.C., 1998; recipient Gold medal B.C. Sci. Coun., Killam Rsch. prize U. B.C. Rsch. Coun. Can. grantee, 1978—, Commemorative medal 125th anniversary Can. Confederation, 1993, Julian C. Smith medal Engring. Inst. Can., 1994-95, Meritorious Achievement award Assn. Profl. Engrs. & Geoscientists B.C., 1996, Killam Meml. prize engring., 1998, Order of B.C., 1998. Fellow CSME, Can. Acad. Engring., Royal Soc. Can.; mem. ASME, Assn. Profl. Engrs. Ont. Home: 1938 Western Pkwy Vancouver BC Canada V6T 1W5

SALDIN, DILANO KERZAMAN, physicist, educator; b. Colombo, Sri Lanka, Aug. 26, 1949; s. Hamlin Mesrur and Muzeena Saldin. BA, U. Oxford, 1971, DPhil, 1975. Jr. rsch. fellow Wolfson Coll., Oxford, England, 1976—81; lectr. Brasenose Coll., 1979—81; rsch. fellow Imperial Coll., London, 1981—88; from asst. prof. to prof. U. of Wis., Milw., 1988—96, prof., 1996—. Contbr. articles over 100 to profl. jours. Grantee, Petroleum Rsch. Fund, 1990—94, NSF, 1994—, U.S. Dept. of Energy, 2001—; scholar Alice and Edith Hamer Major scholarship, U. of Manchester, Eng., 1968. Mem.: Am. Physical Soc. Office: University of Wisconsin Milwaukee Physics Dept PO Box 413 Milwaukee WI 53201 Personal E-mail: dksaldin@uwm.edu. Business E-Mail: dksaldin@uwm.edu.

SALE, DAVID TODD, lawyer; b. L.I., N.Y., July 3, 1968; s. Jon A. and Beth K. Sale. B of Polit. Sci., Gettysburg Coll., 1990; JD, Nova Southeastern U., 1993. Bar: Fla. 1994, U.S. Dist. Ct. (so. dist.) Fla. 1994. Intern to spkr of house U.S. Ho. of Reps., Washington, 1988; asst. atty. gen. Fla. Atty. Gen.'s Office, Hollywood, 1994-95; asst. state atty. Broward County State Atty., Ft. Lauderdale, Fla., 1994-97; sole practitioner, 1997—. Mem. Com. to Re-elect Atty. Gen. Butterworth, 1992, Com. to Re-elect Judge Gary Cowart, 1997. Mem. Broward County Bar Assn., Broward Assn. Criminal Def. Lawyers (treas. 2001—). Avocations: politics, history, basketball, golf, tennis. Office: 400 SE 9th St Fort Lauderdale FL 33316 E-mail: DefendingD@aol.com.

SALE, GEORGE EDGAR, pathologist; b. Missoula, Mont., Apr. 18, 1941; s. George Goble and Ruth Edna (Polleys) S.; m. Joan M. Sutliff, 1989; children: George Gregory Colby, Teo Marie Jonsson. AB, Harvard U., 1963; MD, Stanford U., 1968. Intern U. Oreg., Portland, 1968-69; sr. asst. surgeon USPHS, Albuquerque, 1969-71; resident in pathology U. Wash., Seattle, 1971-75, instr. pathology, 1975-78, asst. prof., 1978-81, assoc. prof., 1981-88, prof., 1988—. Asst. mem. faculty clin. divsn. Hutchinson Cancer Ctr., Seattle, 1975-88, assoc. mem., 1988-91, mem., 1991—. Author, editor: Pathology of Bone Marrow Transplantation, 1984, Pathology of Transplantation, 1990. Mem. AAAS, Internat. Acad. Pathology, Coll. Am. Pathologists, Am. Assn. Investigative Pathologists, Physicians for Social Responsibility. Office: Fred Hutchinson Cancer Rsh Ctr G1-309 1100 Fairview Ave N Seattle WA 98109-4417 E-mail: gsale@fhcrc.org.

SALE, LLEWELLYN, III, lawyer; b. St. Louis, May 19, 1942; s. Llewellyn Jr. and Kathleen (Rice) S.; m. Cynthia Jean Bricker, Aug. 17, 1968 (div. Apr. 1995); children: Allyson J., Eryn E. AB cum laude, Yale U., 1964; LLB cum laude, Harvard U., 1967. Bar: Mo. 1967, U.S. Dist. Ct. (ea. dist.) Mo. 1967, U.S. Tax Ct. 1982, U.S. Ct. Claims 1985. From assoc. to ptnr. to mng. ptnr. Husch & Eppenberger, St. Louis, 1967-88; ptnr. Bryan Cave LLP, 1988—. Bd. dirs. Washington U. Child Guidance Clinic, St. Louis, 1978-80, Mental Health Assn. St. Louis, 1988-89. Mem. ABA, Bar Assn. Met. St. Louis (chmn. law econs. subcom. 1982), Media Club, Noonday Club. Avocations: spectator sports, jogging. Office: Bryan Cave 211 N Broadway Ste 3600 Saint Louis MO 63102-2733 E-mail: lsale@bryancavellp.com.

SALE, MERRITT, classicist, comparatist, educator; b. New Haven, Nov. 27, 1929; s. William Merritt and Helen (Stearns) S.; m. Marilyn Mills, June 13, 1953 (div. Oct. 1967); children: Elizabeth, David; m. Anne Perkins, May 18, 1991. BA, Cornell U., 1951, MA, 1954, PhD, 1958. Engr. U.S. Metals Co., Carteret, N.J., 1951-52; instr. in classics Yale U., New Haven, 1957-58; asst. prof., assoc. prof. Washington U., St. Louis, 1958-75, chmn. classics dept., 1961-69, prof. classics and comparative lit., 1975—, chmn. comparative lit. dept., 1981-90. Author: Sophocles' Electra: Commentary with Introduction and Translation, 1970, Existentialism and Euripides, 1977, Homer and the Roland, 1993, The Government of Troy, 1995. Recipient Founder's Day award for Excellence in Teaching Washington U., 1978 Mem. Am. Philol. Assn., London Inst. for Classical Studies Home: 2342 Albion Pl Saint Louis MO 63104-2524 E-mail: aperkins@midwest.net.

SALE, TOM S., III, financial economist; b. Haynesville, La., July 27, 1942; s. Thomas and Mary Belle (Fagg) S.; divorced; children: Jennifer Elizabeth, Sarah Elaine. BA, Tulane U., 1964; MA, Duke U., 1965; PhD, La. State U., 1972. CFA. Faculty La. Tech. U., Ruston, 1965-75, prof. econs., 1975-98, ret., 1998. Head dept. econs. and fin. La. Tech. U., 1974-86, 90-95, dir. grad. studies Coll. Adminstrn and Bus., 1988-89; fin. cons. Contbr. articles to profl. jours. Mem. Southwestern Fin. Assn. (pres. 1985-86), Assn. Investment Mgmt. and Rsch. (exam. com. 1983-92, curriculum com. 1993—), SW Fedn.

Adminstrv. Disciplines (v.p. 1988-89, pres. 1989-90), Dallas Assn. Fin. Analysts, Omicron Delta Kappa, Omicron Delta Epsilon. Episcopalian. Home: PO Box 1365 Ruston LA 71273-1365 E-mail: tomsale3@tcainternet.com.

SALEEBA, DAVID A. federal agency administrator; b. Hazleton, PA. BA in History, Pa. State U., 1971. Police officer, detective organized crime bur. Metro-Dade County Police Dept., Miami, Fla., 1972—75; with U.S. Secret Svc., Washington, N.Y.C., Miami, N.Mex., 1975—2001, spl. agt. in charge of district Albuquerque, 1990—95; asst. adminstr. for security mgmt. and safeguards NASA, Washington, 2001—. Office: NASA Hdqrs Mail Code X 300 E St SW Washington DC 20546

SALEEBY, ELI RICHARD, dermatologist; b. Phila., Dec. 14, 1949; s. Eli Richard and Eleanor Deegan Saleeby; m. Cherie Lee, Aug. 6, 1977; 1 child, Eli Reid. BA, U. N.C., 1971; MD, Jefferson Med. Coll., 1981. Intern in internal medicine U. Miami, Fla., 1981-82; resident in dermatology Henry Ford Hosp., Detroit, 1982-85; fellow in Mohs surgery U. Wis., Madison, 1985-86; ptnr. Dermatology Cons. of South Fla., Coral Springs, 1986—. Fellow Am. Acad. Dermatology, Am. Soc. Dermatol. Surgery, Am. Soc. Mohs Micrographic Surgery, Am. Soc. Lasers in Medicine and Surgery; mem. Broward County Dermatology Soc. (pres. 1997), Palm Beach County Dermatology Soc. Avocations: boating, fishing, golf. Home: 3000 N University Dr Coral Springs FL 33065-5055

SALEH, ALI-ABDULLAH, state official; b. Beit al-Ahmer, Sanhan, Yemen, 1942; married; several children. Student, NCO Sch. Armed Forces, 1960; grad., Armor Sch., 1964; M in Mil. Sci. (hon.), 1989. With Yemen Armed Forces, 1958, advanced through ranks to marshal, 1997, dir. Armor Corps Arsenal, sgt., promoted to warrant officer, then to second lt., colonel, 1963, commandant various squadrons, battalions, brigades; commandant Taiz Governorate; mem. provisional Republican Coun.; dep.-in-chief, chief of staff Armed Forces, 1978; pres. Republic of Yemen, 1978—, 83, 94, lt. gen., 1990, chmn. Presdl. Coun., 1990, 93; pres. Armed Forces, 1978, 83, comdr.-in-chief, 1978, 88; dir. Armor Corps Arsenal; comdt. Armor Squadron, Armor Co., Armor battalion; comdt. armor brigade, mil gov. Bab El-Mandab region. Founder modern state of Yemen based on Dem. basis, polit. pluralism and freedom of the press, respect for Human Rights and the peaceful transfer of power; sec.-gen. People's Gen. Congress, 1982; chmn. Presdl. Coun. of Republic of Yemen, 1990—; ofcl. rep. to country both alone and as leader of dels. to several friendly and brotherly countries. Republican award People's Constituent Assembly for efforts and sacrifices in serving the country, 1979. Achievements include the rebuilding of Mareb great dam, extraction of oil and gas, and the establishment of the free-zone in Aden. Office: Embassy of Republic Yemen 2600 Virginia Ave NW Ste 705 Washington DC 20037-1905 Fax: 202-337-2017.

SALEH, BRIAN BEHROOZ, aerospace executive; b. Tehran, Iran, Apr. 25, 1939; came to U.S., 1959; m. Farideh Navidi, May 12, 1983. BSEE, Northrop U., Ingelwood, Calif., 1967; MBA, Golden Gate U., San Francisco, 1973; instr. credential, Calif. Design engr. radio frequency cirs. Space Systems/Loral, Palo Alto, Calif., 1970—, mgr. GOES Comm. Subsys., 1974-76, program engr. NATO-III Satellite, 1976-79, mgr. Insat Program Engrng., 1979-85; mgr. GOES Spacecraft Engrng., 1985-91; mgr. GOES Spacecraft, 1991-92; dir. GOES Prodn. Program Space Systems/Loral, 1992-95, dir. Telstar Program, 1995-97, sr. dir. Fixed Svc. Satellite Programs, 1997-98, sr. dir. common products and planning, 1998, sr. exec. dir. CD Radio Program, 1998-99, v.p. program mgmt., 1999—2002. Republican.

SALEH, DAVID JOHN, lawyer; b. Buffalo, Apr. 24, 1953; s. Donald Thomas and Joan Barbara (Labaki) S.; m. Elizabeth Catherine Abdella, July 2, 1976; children: Anthony Donald, Amy Madeline, Anne Teresa, Andrew David. BA, SUNY, Buffalo, 1975, JD, 1978. Bar: N.Y. 1979, U.S. Dist. Ct. (we. dist.) N.Y. 1980. Assoc. Jeffrey D. Oshlag, Esq., Batavia, N.Y., 1978-82; ptnr. Oshlag, Saleh & Earl, L.L.P., 1982—; chief counsel, sec. Am. Real Time Svcs., Inc., N.Y.C., 1988-91; atty. Town of Stafford, N.Y., 1994—; town atty. Town of Darien, 2000—, Town of Batavia, NY, 2002—. Prosecutor Village of Corfu, N.Y., 1997—; legal counsel City of Batavia Housing Authority, 1982—; atty. Village of Corfu, N.Y., 1981—, Pembroke Ctrl. Sch. Dist., 1985-90; town atty. Town of Batavia, N.Y., 2002—; chief counsel Intelligent Quotation Sys. Inc., Norwalk, Conn., 1987-93; prosecutor Town of Pembroke, 1988—; chief counsel, dir., treas. GB's Country Corners Inc., 1991-93; v.p., chief counsel Marine Ptnrs. Funding, Inc., 1994—; counsel Corfu Fire Dist., 1995—; chief counsel Network Two Comm. Group, Inc., 1997-99; counsel Weston Info. Techs. Inc., others. Mem. staff Buffalo Law Rev., 1976-78. Mem. Pembroke Vol. Fire Dept., 1976-79, Corfu Vol. Fire Dept., 1979—; bd. dirs. Corfu Area Bus. Assn., 1986-87; del. Rep. Caucus; trustee Corfu Free Libr. Assn., 1991—, pres., 1993-96; bd. dirs. St. Jerome Hosp. Found., 1992-98, treas., 1994-98; treas. Genesee Mercy Healthcare Found., Inc., 1996-98; parliamentarian Genesee County Rep. Com., 2000—. Mem. ABA, ATLA, N.Y. Defenders Assn., N.Y. State Bar Assn., Genesee County Bar Assn. (mem. jud. nominations com. for 8th jud. dist. N.Y., chmn. criminal def. com. 1995—), Erie County Bar Assn., N.Y. State Housing Renewal Ofcls., U. Buffalo Alumni Assn. (bd. dirs., v.p. fin. 1997-99, exec. v.p., pres.-elect 1999-2000, pres. 2000—), Lions. Republican. Roman Catholic. Home: 54 E Main St Corfu NY 14036-9601 Office: Oshlag Saleh & Earl LLP 432 E Main St Batavia NY 14020-2519 E-mail: dsaleh@rochester.rr.com.

SALEH, FARIDA YOUSRY, chemistry educator; b. Cairo, Egypt, June 17, 1939; came to U.S., 1968; d. Michael Yousry and Fakiha Yousef (Badawy) Wassif; m. Hosny Gabra Saleh, Oct. 8, 1959; children: Magda, Nagwa. BS, Ain Shams U., 1959; MS, Alexandrial U., Egypt, 1967; PhD, U. Tex., 1976. Postdoctoral rsch. assoc. Tex. A&M U., College Station, 1977-78; rsch. scientist II U. North Tex., Denton, 1978-83, asst. prof. chemistry, 1980-83, assoc. prof., 1985-94, prof., 1994—. Cons. Stanford Rsch. Inst., Menlo Park, Calif., 1983-84, Allied Chems. Co., Hackettstown, N.J., 1985-86, Am. Chrome Chems., Corpus Christi, Tex., 1988-89, USEPA Rev. Panel, Washington, 1986—. Contbg. author book chpts. in field; contbr. more than 60 articles to profl. jours. Recipient Svc. award U.S. EPA, Washington, 1993; recipient numerous grants in field. Mem. Am. Chem. Soc., Internat. Union of Pure and Applied Chemistry, Internat. Humic Substances Soc., Assn. Women in Sci. Avocations: music, swimming, tennis. Office: Univ North Tex PO Box 310559 Denton TX 76203-0559 E-mail: saleh@unt.edu.

SALEH, JOHN, lawyer; b. O'Donnell, Tex., June 29, 1928; s. Nahum and Arslie S. BBA, U. Tex., 1950, JD with honors, 1952; cert. U.S. Army Judge Advocate Sch., U. Va., 1953. Bar: Tex. 1952, U.S. Ct. Mil. Appeals, 1953, U.S. Tax Ct. 1954, U.S. Dist. Ct. (no. dist.) Tex. 1956, U.S. Ct. Appeals (5th cir.) 1960, U.S. Supreme Ct. 1961, D.C. 1982. Pvt. practice, Lamesa, Tex., 1954—. Tchg. instr. legal rsch. writing U. Tex. Sch. Law, 1950-52. Mem. editl. bd. Tex. Law Rev., 1951-52. Mem. ABA, ATLA, Tex. Law Rev. Assn. (life), Tex. Bar Assn. (spl. com. to study rev. code criminal procedure 1969-71), D.C. Bar Assn., Tex. Trial Lawyers Assn., Tex. Bar Found., Order of the Coif, The Million Dollar Advocates Forum, Phi Delta Phi. Home: 605 Doak Odonnell TX 79351 Office: 502 N 1st St Lamesa TX 79331-5406 E-mail: bigjohn@pics.net.

SALEH, KHALED J. orthopaedic surgeon, educator; b. Can., Sept. 24, 1964; s. Joinal N. and Fathi Saleh; m. Lena Saleh, July 24, 1984; children: Jasmine, Jamal, Jenine. BSc, U. Western Ont., London, Ont., Can., 1987; MD, U. Western Ont., 1991; MS, U. McMaster, Hamilton, Ont., 1995. Lic. Med. Coun. Can., Coll. Physicians and Surgeons, Commonwealth Pa. Rotating intern U. Western Ont., Victoria Hosp., 1991-92; jr. resident gen. orthopaedics and trauma U. Toronto-Toronto Western Hosp., 1992; jr. resident ICU U. Toronto-Wellesley Hosp., 1993; jr. resident gen. surgery U. Toronto-St. Joseph's Hosp., 1993; jr. resident vascular surgery, sr. resident ICU U. Toronto-Wellesley Hosp., 1993, sr. resident arthritis and gen. orthopaedics, 1993; jr. resident hand surgery U. Toronot-Toronto Western Hosp., 1994, sr. resident sports medicine, 1996-97; jr. resident orthopaedic oncology U. Toronto-Mt. Sinai Hosp., 1994; chief resident trauma orthopaedics U. Toronto-Sunnybrook Health Sci. Ctr., 1996; sr. resident pediat. orthopaedics U. Toronto-Hosp. for Sick Children, 1997; Outcome and Health Related Rsch. fellow Med. Rsch. Coun. Can., 1997-98; postgrad. fellow U. Toronto-Mt. Sinai Hosp., 1997-98; Orthopaedic Rsch. and Edn. Found. Health Svcs. fellow Am. Acad. Orthopaedic Surgeons, 1998-99; postgrad. fellow U. Cornell Med. Coll., Hosp. for Spl. Surgery, N.Y.C., 1998-99. Clin. instr. Hosp. for Spl. Surgery, Cornell U. Med. Coll., N.Y.C., 1998-99; asst. prof. dept. orthopaedic surgery U. Minn., Mpls., 1999—; with Hosp. for Spl. Surgery, Osteoporosis Ctr., 1998-99; with dept. orthopaedic surgery VA Med. Ctr., Mpls., 1999—; assoc. staff South Huron Hosp., Exeter, Ont., 1992-95, Alexander Marine Hosp., Goderich, Ont., 1992-98, Mt. Sinai Hosp., Toronto, 1997-98, N.Y. Hosp., N.Y.C., 1998-99, Meml. Hosp. for Cancer and Allied Disease, 1998-99, Hosp. for Spl. Surgery, N.Y.C., 1998-99; attending physician Fairview U. Med. Ctr. VA Med. Ctr., 1999—; resident team physician Can. Nat. Ballet, 1992-97, NHL Toronto Maple Leafs, 1992-97; presenter in field. Reviewer Jour. Bone and Joint Surgery, 1999—; contbr. chpts. to books and articles to profl. jours. Grantee Am. Acad. Orthopaedic Surgery Knee Soc., 1998-99, 98-99, Arthritis Soc., 1998—, Am. Acad. Orthopaedic Surgeons and Orthopaedic Rsch. and Edn. Found., 1998-2000; scholar Nat. Sci. and Engrng. Coun., 1986, 87, Med. Rsch. Coun. Can., 1997-98. Fellow Royal Coll. Surgeons Can.; mem. Am. Acad. Orthopaedic Surgeons (rsch. com. Knee Soc. 1998—, outcomes rsch. com. 1998—), Can. Orthopaedic Assn., Coll. Physicians and Surgeons Ont., Ont. Med. Assn. Office: Dept Orthopaedic Surgey UHMC #492 420 Delaware St SE Minneapolis MN 55455-0374 Fax: (612) 626-6032.

SALEH, MOHAMMED, diplomat; b. Manama, Bahrain, Oct. 2, 1967; s. Saleh Mohammed Saleh and Fatima Abdulla (Syed) Hussain; m. Khatoon Adbulla A. Salman, Aug. 11, 1995; children: Jaffer Salman, Ali Salman. BA in Polit. Sci., Law, Kuwait U., 1992; hon., Oxford, 1996. Third sec. Ministry Foreign Affairs, Manama, Bahrain, 1993-99; second sec. Bahrain Mission to UN, N.Y.C., 1999—. Cons. UN Security Coun., N.Y.C., 1998—99, UN Econ. and Social Coun. Recipient Hist. award, Bahrain Hist. Archeol. Soc., 1998. Avocation: collection of Polioldi Polit. and religious books. Office: Bahrain Mission to the UN 866 E Second Ave New York NY 10017

SALEM, GEORGE RICHARD, lawyer; b. Jacksonville, Fla., Dec. 24, 1953; s. Kamel Abraham and Margaret Virginia (Bateh) S.; m. Rhonda M. Ziadeh, June 28, 1980; children: James George, Jihan Camille, Laila Suad, Sarah Rose. BA, Emory U., 1975, JD, 1977; LLM, Georgetown U., 1984. Bar: Ga. 1978, Fla. 1979, D.C. 1981. Ptnr. Thompson, Mann & Hutson, Washington, 1977-85; dep. solicitor U.S. Dept. Labor, 1985-86, solicitor of labor, 1986-89; ptnr. Akin, Gump, Strauss, Hauer & Feld, 1990—. Bd. dirs. Overseas Pvt. Investment Corp. Contbr. articles to profl. jours. Nat. exec. dir. ethnic voters div. Reagan Bush '84; bd. dirs. United Palestinian Appeal, Inc., 1981-85, 86—; mem. Arab Am. Inst., Jan.-Mar., 1985, Dec. 1986—, chmn. bd. dirs., 1999—; chmn. Arab-Ams. for Bush-Cheney, 2000; mem. Am. Arab Anti-Discrimination Com.; chmn. Arab-Ams. for Bush-Quayle '88, '92; adv. bd. Search for Common Ground in the Mid. East, 2001—; exec. adv. bd. Mid. East Inst., 2002—; bd. dirs. Am. Com. on Jerusalem, 1995—, Emory Law Sch. Coun., 2000-2002, Emory Bd. Govs., 1997-2001. Recipient Ellis Island Medal of Honor, 1992. Mem. ABA (labor and employment law sect.), Ga. Bar Assn. (labor rels. div.), Fla. Bar Assn. (labor rels. div.), D.C. Bar Assn. (labor rels. div.), Nat. Assn. Arab Ams. (bd. dirs. 1987, pres. 1992-94), Am. Ramallah Club (pres. D.C. chpt. 1984, Wash. rep. 1982-84), Am. Ramallah Fedn. (chmn. human rights com., Washington rep. 1982-84), Arab Am. Rep. Fedn. (chmn. 1985), Century Club Nat. Rep. Heritage Groups Coun., Delta Theta Phi, Omicron Delta Kappa. Mem. Eastern Orthodox Christian Ch. Office: Akin Gump Strauss Hauer & Feld 1333 New Hampshire Ave NW Washington DC 20036-1511

SALEM, HADI, thoracic surgeon; b. Cairo, Feb. 22, 1929; came to U.S., 1951; s. Mohamed Salem and Alyea Ismail; m. Maha Hammad, June 5, 1953; children: Hadi, Alyea, Djamila, Gihan, Ramsey. Diplomate Am. Bd. Thoracic Surgeons, Am. Bd. Surgery. Thoracic surgeon Queen of Angels/Hollywood Presbyn. Med. Ctr., L.A., chmn. thoracic cardiovascular surgery dept.; vice chmn. dept. surgery Hollywood Presbyn. Med. Ctr. Mem. staff St. Vincent Med. Ctr., L.A.; vis. lectr., thoracic surgeon U. Alexandria (Egypt) Med. Sch., Inst. Heart and Lung, Cairo; vis. thoracic surgeon, San Pedro Sula, Honduras; tchg. fellow cardiac surgery N.Y. Med. Coll.; vis. surgeon Ministry of Health, Kuwait; asst. clin. prof. L.A. County-U. So. Calif. Med. Sch.; tchg. fellow cardiac surgery N.Y. Med. Coll.; instr., asst. assoc., rsch. assoc. surgery Duke U. Med. Ctr. Contbr. articles to profl. jours. Chmn. L.A.-Giza Sister City Assn.; bd. dirs., founder Friends of Wafaa Wal-Amal, Rehab. City, Cairo; bd. dirs. mem. West Coast com. Am. Near East Refugee Aid; chmn. adv. bd. Am. Mid. East Rehab.; founder U.S. Orgns. for Med. and Ednl. Needs, Ctr. for Islamic Studies; chmn., former mem. adv. bd. Islamic Ctr. So. Calif.; mem. Am. Found. for Blind. Scholar Govt. of Egypt, Fulbright Found.; fellow Smith-Mundt, Hanes Found., Am. Cyanamid. Fellow Internat. Coll. Surgeons (pres., chmn. postgrad. thoracic surgery 5th western congress); mem. Am. Coll. Chest Physicians, Am. Trudeau Soc., Calif. Med. Assn., Egyptian Med. Assn., European Thoracic Soc. (hon.), United Arab Republic TV Assn. (hon.), Hollywood Acad. Medicine, Deryl Hart Surg. Soc. Office: 1300 N Vermont Ave Los Angeles CA 90027-6005

SALEM, RICHARD ALLEN, mediator; b. N.Y.C., Aug. 15, 1930; s. Louis H. and Catherine (Levy) S.; m. Greta Waldinger, June 26, 1955; children: Susanne, Peter, Erica. BA in Sociology, Antioch Coll., 1953; MS in Journalism, Columbia U., 1957. Reporter Washington Post, 1957-59; editor, publ. Washington SBIC Newsletter, 1960-62; spl. asst. to dep. dir. for investment Small Bus. Adminstrn., Washington, 1963-64, assoc. dir. Office of Equal Opportunity, 1964-67, regional dir., 1967-68; Midwest dir. Cmty. Rels. Svc. U.S. Dept. Justice, Chgo., 1968-82; pres. Conflict Mgmt. Initiatives, Evanston, Ill., 1982—. Adj. prof. Loyola U., Chgo., 1986-90; mediator Wounded Knee Takeover, 1972, Skokie-Nazi Conflict, 1980. Co-author: Students Guide to Mediation and Law, 1987, Ctr. for Pub. Resources award, 1987; mem. editl. bd. Chgo. Reporter, 1996—; editor: Witness to Genocide - the Children of Rwanda, 2000; contbr. articles to profl. jours. Bd. dirs. Housing Options for Mentally Ill, Evanston, 1997—, Found. Self-Sufficiency Ctrl. Am., 2000—. With U.S. Army, 1953-55. Recipient Outstanding Performance award U.S. Sr. Exec. Svc., 1980. Mem. Soc. Profls. in Dispute Resolution (2d v.p. 1988, bd. dirs. 1982-89, Cmty. Mediation Tng. in South Africa award 1993). Home and Office: 1225 Oak Ave Evanston IL 60202-1220

SALEM, SUSANNE FRANCES, consulting executive; b. San Francisco, Mar. 25, 1945; d. Edward L. and Mary F. (Adams) Ledinski; m. Lee C. Salem, July 14, 1979. BS, Ariz. State U., 1979. Ins. agt. Atlantic Mut. Ins. Co. and Harris & Assocs., Los Angeles, 1964-73; ptnr. Acero Enterprises, Sierra Vista, Ariz., 1973-77; lease account mgr. Truck Leasing, Phoenix, 1979-80; sales and cons. Internat. Transp., 1980; owner Corp. Directions Cons. & Recruiting, 1980-86; v.p., bd. dirs. The Prism Group, Inc., Cons., Tempe, 1987-94; human resource leader W.L. Gore & Assocs., 1994-95; cons. Salem & Assoc., 1986—99, Silterra, 1999—. Guest speaker. Bd. dirs. Southeastern Ariz. Drug Abuse Coun., 1975-77, The Ariz. Partnership, 1989-90, adv. bd. dirs. Maricopa Skill Ctr., 1989-91. Contbr. articles to profl. jours. Mem. Am. Trucking Assns. (bd. dirs., scholar 1977-79, outstanding transp. grad. 1979), Ariz. C. of C. E-mail: ssalem@sprintmail.com.

SALEMBIER, VALERIE BIRNBAUM, publishing executive; b. Teaneck, N.J. d. Jack and Sara (Gordon) Birnbaum; m. Paul J. Block, Dec. 9, 1990. BA, Coll. of New Rochelle, 1973. Advt. dir. Ms. Mag., N.Y.C., 1976-79, assoc. pub., 1979-81; pub. Inside Sports Mag., 1982; sr. v.p. advt. USA Today, 1983-88; pub. TV Guide, Radnor, PA, 1988-89; pres. N.Y. Post, N.Y.C., 1989-90; pub. Family Circle Mag., 1991-93; v.p. advt. The N.Y. Times, 1993-95; pub. Esquire Mag., 1996—. Lectr. in field. Author: Rotisserie League Baseball, 1982; freelance mag. writer. Former trustee Coll. of New Rochelle; trustee, exec. com. N.Y.C. Police Found.; trustee N.Y.C. Sports Devel. Corp.; former trustee Ctrl. Synagogue; bd. dirs., past pres. Nat. Alliance Breast Cancer Orgns., BOX (Beneficial Orgn. to Aid Ex-Fighters); former bd. dirs. Nat. Alliance Breast Cancer Orgns. Mem.: Womens Forum, Women in Comm., C200. Home: 1075 Park Ave New York NY 10128-1003 Office: Esquire 250 W 55th St New York NY 10019-5201

SALEMI, JOSEPH SALVATORE, classics and humanities educator, poet, writer; b. N.Y.C., Feb. 1, 1948; s. Salvatore Joseph and Liberty Luce (Previti) S.; m. Helen Louise Palma, June 1, 1991. BA, Fordham U., 1968; MA, NYU, 1970, PhD, 1986. Permanent cert. English tchr., N.Y. Prof. composition and lit. Pace U., N.Y.C., 1977-84; prof. English, Nassau C.C., Westbury, N.Y., 1984-86, Fordham U., Bronx, 1988-89; prof. classics Bklyn. Coll., CUNY, 1993-2000, Hunter Coll., CUNY, N.Y.C., 1989—; prof. humanities NYU, 1983—. Author: Formal Complaints, 1997, Nonsense Couplets, 1999, Masquerade, 2003; poems and translations published in over sixty jours.: , book reviewer, essayist: Expansive Poetry and Music Online, assoc. editor: Iambs and Trochees; contbr. Recipient award Classical and Modern Lit. Jour., 1993; Musurillo scholar CUNY Grad. Ctr., 1975; sr. fellow NEH, 1982, Lane Cooper fellow NYU, 1983-84. Mem. Nat. Assn. Scholars, Am. Lit. Translators Assn., Renaissance Soc. Am. Roman Catholic. Avocation: military research. Home: 220 9th St Brooklyn NY 11215 Office: CUNY Hunter Coll Classics Dept 695 Park Ave New York NY 10021

SALEMI, MICHAEL KERRY, economist, educator; b. Chgo., Mar. 30, 1946; s. Michael and Helen Hill S.; m. Carrie Frances Benoit, Dec. 27, 1967 (div. July 1989); children: Benjamin, Caitlin; m. Ariana Pancaldo, Aug. 18, 1990; 1 child, Chiara. BA, St. Mary's Coll., Winona, Minn., 1968; MS, Purdue U., 1969; PhD, U. Minn., 1976. Asst. dir. Ctr. for Econ. Edn./U. Minn., Mpls., 1973-76; asst. prof. econs. U. N.C., Chapel Hill, 1976-82, assoc. prof. econs., 1982-87, prof. econs., 1987—; rsch. assoc./vis. prof. Grad. Inst. Internat. Studies, Geneva, 1982-83. Chair com. econ. edn. Am. Econ. Assn., 1995-2000. Bd. editors Jour. of Econ. Edn., 1995—; contbr. articles to profl. jours. Adv. bd. The Econ. Literacy Project of Fed. Res. Bank, Mpls., 1999; bd. dirs. N.C. Coun. Econ. Edn., Raleigh, N.C., 1999-2000; chair rev. com. Vol. Nat. Content Stds. in Econs. Project, N.Y., 1996-97; bd. founders Nat. Coun. on Econ. Edn., N.Y., 1995—. Recipient Bower medal in econ. edn. Nat. Coun. Econ. Edn., N.Y., 1998, Erskine fellowship Canterbury U., Christchurch, New Zealand, 1998, Zachary Smith Professorship U. N.C., Chapel Hill, 1993-96, Bowman and Gordon Gray Professorship for Excellence in Undergrad. Tchg., 1987-90, Villard award for rsch. in econ. edn. Am. Assn. Econ. Educators, 2001. Mem. Am. Econ. Assn., Econometric Soc. Avocations: squash, photography, fishing. Office: Dept Econs Cb 3305 Gardner Hl Chapel Hill NC 27599-3305 E-mail: Michael_Salemi@unc.edu.

SALEN, WAYNE LOUIS, insurance agency official, consultant; b. Hornell, N.Y., Oct. 18, 1954; s. Louis Delbert and Roselyn Ann (Muscarella) S.; children: Wesley Louis, Janelle Ashley. Cert. internat. study, Lycée Rouget de Lisle, Lons-Le-Saunier, France, 1973; BA, SUNY, Buffalo, 1977; MBA, Canisius Coll., 1986. Lic. ins. broker, N.Y.; cert. hazard control mgr., product safety mgr.; assoc. in risk mgmt. Exec. trainee Jones Chem. Co., Inc., Caledonia, N.Y., 1977-78; asst. to prodn. dir. FMC Corp., Middleport, 1978-79; risk mgr. Twin Fair, Inc., West Seneca, 1979-82, Peter J. Schmitt Co., Inc., West Seneca, 1987-90, Empire Soils Investigations, Inc., Middleport, 1990-91; loss control cons. Lansing B. Warner, Inc., Chgo., 1982-84; mgr., asst. to pres. Laverack & Haines, Inc., Buffalo, 1984-87; account exec. Teach, Ryan & Cable, Inc., 1991; risk mgr. County of Niagara, Lockport, N.Y., 1991-95, The Park Assoc., Inc., 1995-2001; dir. risk mgmt. First Niagara Fin. Group, Inc., 2001—. Dir. risk mgmt., mem. steering com. Food Mktg. Inst., Washington, 1988-90; cons. on risk mgmt. Mem. Royalton Hartland Cen. Sch. Bd., Middleport, 1984-89. Recipient Ron Judd Heart of RIMS award, 2001—02. Mem. Am. Soc. Safety Engrs. (profl.), Nat. Fire Protection Assn., Risk and Ins. Mgmt. Soc. (bd. dirs.), N.Y. State Assn. Self-Insured Counties. Republican. Methodist. Avocations: Buffalo Bills, Buffalo Bisons, Buffalo Sabres. Office: 170 Northpointe Pkwy Amherst NY 14228-1884 E-mail: wsalen@warren-hoffman.com.

SALENIUS, SYLVIA MARJA, environmental planner; b. Mineola, N.Y., Nov. 7, 1948; d. Aimo George and Florence (Jones) Salenius; m. Kevin Robert Bracken, Aug., 1980 (div. Aug. 1984); 1 child, Saara Liisa. BA in Polit. Sci. with distinction, BA in Studio Arts with distinction, U. Rochester, N.Y., 1969; M. City and Regional Planning, IIT, Chgo., 1974. Relocation aide 3d Ward Urban Renewal Project City of Rochester, 1996-70; grad. tchg. asst. IIT, Chgo., 1973-74; project planner Deleuw, Cather & Co., Washington, 1974-76, P&D Cons., Inc., Orange, Calif., 1977, environ. specialist, 1977-78, project mgr., 1978-89, sr. project mgr., 1989, assoc. v.p., 1986-90, v.p., 1990—. Bd. dirs. Heritage Orange County, Santa Ana, Calif., 1997—; mobile registration unit campaign coord. Port Washington (N.Y.) Dem. Orgn., 1963-68. Mem. Am. Inst. Cert. Planners (cert.), Am. Planning Assn. (profl. devel. dir. Orange sect. 1982-84, newsletter editor 1980-82, state conf. co-chair 1990), Phi Beta Kappa. Avocations: auto racing, sport motorcycling, cooking, baking, reading. Office: P&D Consultants Inc 999 Town & Country Rd Orange CA 92868 E-mail: saleniuss@pdconsultants.com.

SALENTINE, THOMAS JAMES, pharmaceutical company executive; b. Milw., Aug. 8, 1939; s. James Edward and Loretta Marie (Burg) S.; m. Susan Anne Sisk, Apr. 16, 1966; children: Anne Elizabeth, Thomas James Jr. BS in Acctg., Marquette U., Milw., 1961. CPA, Ind., Wis. Sr. audit mgr. Price Waterhouse, Milw., 1961-74; dir. corp. acctg. Ward Foods Inc., Wilmette, Ill., 1974-78; corp. contr. Johnson Controls Inc., Milw., 1984-85; v.p., contr. Stokely Van Camp Inc., Indpls., 1978-87; exec. v.p., chief fin. officer Bindley Western Industries Inc., 1987—, also bd. dirs. Bd. dirs. Priority Healthcare Corp., Nat. Refrigeration Svcs. Inc. Chmn. com. United Way, Indpls., 1989-90. Lt. USN, 1962-65. Mem. AICPA, Fin. Execs. Inst. Republican. Roman Catholic. Home: 13540 Brentwood Ln Carmel IN 46033-9488 Office: Bindley Western Industries 8909 Purdue Rd Indianapolis IN 46268-3146

SALER, MICHAEL THEODORE, history educator; b. Phila., Aug. 13, 1960; s. Benson and Joyce Saler. BA, Brandeis U., 1985; PhD, Stanford U., 1992. Assoc. prof. dept. history U. Calif., Davis, 1992—. Author: The Avant-Garde in Interwar England: 'Medieval Modernism' and the London Underground, 1999. Mem. Phi Beta Kappa. Home: 288 Fairlawn Dr Berkeley CA 94708 Office: Univ Calif Dept History 1 Shields Ave Davis CA 95616 E-mail: mtsaler@aol.com., mtsaler@ucdavis.edu.

SALERNO, CHERIE ANN (C. S. MAU), artist; b. Chgo., Nov. 21, 1948; d. Henry Jasper and Helen (Polyak) Mau; m. Kenneth Daniel Salerno; children: Nick Anthony, Brittney Ann. AAS in Advertising, Triton Coll., 1985; BFA, Art Inst. Chgo., 1999. Freelance comml. artist, Chgo., 1986-90, 2000—; artist Chgo. Fine Arts Exch., 1994-98; artist, owner C.S. Mau Studio, River Grove, Ill., 1992—; art dir., bd. dirs. Harrison St. Coop. Gallery, Oak Park, 2000—02; art tchr., 1998—. Designer Centennial Quilt, River Grove Libr., 1988; logo designer, River Grove Sch., 1984. Designer stained glass window Bethlehem Luth. Ch., River Grove, Ill., 1999; cover designer Louie Records, Corvallis, Oreg., 1998-99, MSS Pub., Jefferson, Oreg., 2002. Vol. tchr. art Bethlehem Luth. Sch., River Grove, Ill., 1996-99; vol. ElderCare, 1990-94. Fellow: West Suburban Art League (excellences honor 1991—93), Glenview Art League (Excellence award 1996), Chgo. Artist Coalition; mem.: Oak Park Art League (juror of artist stds., bd. dirs. 1989—, sch. bd. 1993—94, arts and stds. judge 1991—93, active fundraising 1994, stds. judge 2000—, excellences merit 1990—94). Lutheran. Avocations: patio gardening, reading, aerobics and weight-lifting, sewing, gourmet cooking. E-mail: cheriesart@salerno.com.

SALERNO, LOUIS J. research scientist; b. San Mateo, Calif., Mar. 5, 1949; s. Louis Samuel Salerno and Bettina Marion Giordano; m. Imelda Terrazas, Jan. 28, 1994. BSME, San Jose State U., 1979; MSME, Stanford U., 1982. Rsch. scientist NASA-Ames Rsch. Ctr., Moffett Field, Calif., 1979—; lectr. San Jose (Calif.) State U., 1980—. Contbr. chpt. to book: Handbook of Cryogenic Engineering, 1998. Mem. Cryogenic Soc. Am. (life mem., bd. dirs., chmn. No. Calif. chpt. 1998—). Roman Catholic. Avocations: amateur radio, photography, audio. Office: NASA Ames Rsch Ctr Mail Stpo 234-1 Moffett Field CA 94035

SALERNO, SISTER MARIA, nursing educator, adult and gerontological nurse; b. Syracuse, N.Y. d. Joseph and Josephine (Ostrowski) S. Diploma in nursing, St. Joseph's Hosp., Syracuse, 1962; BSN summa cum laude, Cath. U. Am., 1974, MS in Nursing, 1976, D of Nursing Sci., 1981; cert. nurse practitioner, U. Rochester, 1984. RN, N.Y., Md., Washington; cert. adult, geriatric nurse practitioner ANCC; joined Sisters of Third Franciscan Order, Roman Cath. Ch., 1963. Staff nurse St. Joseph Hosp. Health Ctr., Syracuse, 1962-63; sr. charge nurse ICU, gen. med. and surg. units St. Elizabeth Hosp., Utica, N.Y., 1965-66, head nurse pediatrics unit, 1966-69; head nurse ECF Loretto Geriatric Ctr., Syracuse, 1969-72; lectr. Cath. U. Am., Washington, 1979—81, asst. prof. nursing, 1978-79, 81-92, assoc. prof., 1992—, dir. primary care adult/geriatric nurse practitioner programs, 1984—, co-dir. FNP program, 1994-97. Contbr. chpts. to books; contbr. articles to profl. jours. Vol. nurse practitioner Cmty. of Hope, Washington; instl. animal care and use com. George Washington U., 1996—; mem. scholarship com. Franciscan Holy Land Found., 1996—. Grantee NIH, 1984-89, Cath. U. Am., 1989-90. Mem.: AAUP, ANA, D.C. League for Nursing (bd. dirs. 1995—97, 1999—), D.C.

Nurse Practitioners Assn., N.Y. Acad. Scis., Nat. League for Nursing, Nat. Orgn. Nurse Practitioner Facilities, Nat. Gerontol. Nurses Assn., Am. Coll. Nurse Practitioners, Am. Acad. Nurse Practitioners, Am. Assn. for History of Nursing, Cath. U. Am. Nursing Alumni Assn. (pres. 1986—87, chpt. exec. bd. 1992—, treas. 1998—2002), Nat. Italian Am. Found. (assoc.), Sigma Theta Tau (grad. counselor Kappa chpt. 1985—87, eligibility com. 1985—87, awards com. 1987—89, grad. counselor Kappa chpt. 1991—97, eligibility com. 1991—97). Fax: 202-319-6485. E-mail: salerno@cua.edu.

SALERNO, PHILIP ADAMS, information systems specialist; b. Harrisburg, Pa., Oct. 25, 1953; s. Lewis Gabriel S. and Barbara Ellen (Garlinger) Hardisty. AS, Baylor U., 1975; BS in Med. Tech., Our Lady of the Lake U., 1979. Cert. med. technologist, lab. technologist. Lab. technician U.S. Army, Stuttgart, West Germany, 1971-74, instr., Acad. Health Scis. Ft. Sam Houston, 1976-80; asst. instr. Baylor U., 1976-78; staff med. technologist M.D. Anderson Hosp., Houston, 1980; lab. supv. Twelve Oaks Hosp., 1980-83; clin. lab. instr., Acad. Health Scis. U.S. Army, Ft. Sam Houston, 1982-90; dir. current product engrng. Cmty. Health Computing, Houston, 1983-94; owner Salerno Systems Group, 1985-95; sr. project mgr. Systems Xcellence, Dallas, 1995-96; dir. engrng. svcs. HealthCor, 1996-98; IT dir. TRS (CIT Group), DFW Airport, Tex., 1998-2000; owner Sheersox.com, South San Francisco, Calif., 2000—; sr. mgr. clin. sys. svcs. ViroLogic Inc., 2001—. Co-author: Basic Med. Parasitology, 1977. Del. Rep. State Conv., 1986, 88, 90; precinct chmn. Rep. Party of Harris County, Houston, 1988-92; vol. fireman Kentland, Md., 1969-73; bd. dirs. Belmont Park Townhomes, 1993-95. Named Soldier of the Year, U.S. Army Baden Wurtemburg Support Dist., Federal Republic of Germany, 1974. Mem. Soc. Armed Forces Med. Lab. Scientists; assoc. mem. Am. Soc. Clin. Pathologists. Lutheran. Avocations: stamp collecting, animals. Home: 1000 Holloway Ave San Francisco CA 94132 Office: PO Box 2641 South San Francisco CA 94083-2641 E-mail: philip@earthlink.net.

SALERNO-SONNENBERG, NADJA, violinist; b. Rome, Jan. 10, 1961; came to U.S., 1969; d. Josephine Salerno-Sonnenberg. Grad., Curtis Inst. Music, 1975, Juilliard Sch., 1982; doctorate (hon.), N.Mex. State U., 1999. Profl. debut with Phila. Orch., 1971; appearances include Am. Symphony Orch., Balt., Chgo., Cin., Detroit, Houston, Indpls., Milw., Montreal, N.J., Pitts. symphonys, Cleve., L.A. Chamber, Phila., Minn. orchs., New Orleans, N.Y., L.A. philharms.; festival appearances include Mostly Mozart Festival, Ravinia, Blossom, Meadow Brook, Gt. Woods, Caramoor, Aspen, Hollywood Bowl; internat. orchestral appearances include Vienna, Munich, Stuttgart, Frankfurt, Geneva, Rotterdam, Lisbon, Tokyo; featured on 60 Minutes, CBS, CBS Sunday Morning, NBC Nat. News, PBS Live from Lincoln Ctr., CNN Newsstand, Charlie Rose Show, Sesame Street; numerous appearances on The Tonight Show with Johnny Carson; rec. artist Angel, 1987—, Nonesuch, 1996—; subject of documentary: Speaking in Strings, 1999 (film nominated for Oscar 2000). Recipient 1st prize Naumburg Violin Competition, N.Y.C., 1981; Avery Fisher Career grantee., N.Y.C., 1983, Avery Fisher prize, N.Y.C., 1999. Mem. AFTRA, Screen Actors Guild. Office: care M L Falcone Pub Rels 155 W 68th St Ste 114 New York NY 10023-5808

SALES, ANGEL RODOLFO, financial executive; b. Holguin, Oriente, Cuba, Sept. 20, 1948; came to U.S., 1961; s. Angel Alberto and Adeina Rosa (Paneque) S.; m. Barbara Cornell Felix, Aug. 26, 1972; children: Ashley Lynden, Alison Lane. BS, Ind. U., 1972, MBA, 1977. Mgmt. trainee Lincoln Nat. Bank, Ft. Wayne, Ind., 1972-73; asst. v.p. Am. Fletcher Nat. Bank, Indpls., 1973-77; treasury mgr. The Upjohn Co., Kalamazoo, 1977-82, v.p., treas., 1985-90; asst. treas. Midland-Ross Corp., Cleve., 1982-85; treas. Arvin Industries, Inc., Columbus, Ind., 1990-98, v.p. fin. planning and rels., 1998—; exec. v.p., CFO Arvin Roll Coater subs. Arvin Industries, Inc., Indpls., 1999-2000; pres. Roll Coater Subs. Arvin Meritor, Inc., 2000—01; v.p., CFO, COO Best Access Sys., Indpls., 2001—. Bd. dirs. C. Brown Speech and Hearing Ctr., Kalamazoo, 1987-90, treas., 1989; bd. dirs. Columbus Econ. Devel. Bd., Columbus Regional Hosp. Found., Bartholomew Co. United Way, chmn. 1997—; adv. bd. Ind. U.-Purdue U., Columbus. Mem. Fin. Execs. Inst., Nat. Assn. Corp. Treas., Beta Gamma Sigma. United Methodist. Avocations: tennis, golf, art. Office: Best Access Sys 8900 Keystone Crossing Ste 1100 Indianapolis IN 46250 E-mail: salesA@bestaccess.com.

SALES, CLIFFORD M. surgeon; b. N.Y.C., Jan. 29, 1961; MD, Mt. Sinai Sch. Medicine, N.Y.C., 1986. Diplomate Am. Bd. Surgery with added qualifications in vascular surgery. Intern Montefiore Med. Ctr., Bronx, N.Y., 1986-87, res. gen. surgery, 1987-91, fellow vascular surgery, 1991-93; chief vascular surgeon Union Hosp. Mem. Am. Coll. Surgeons, Am. Venous Forum, East Vascular Surgery, Internat. Soc. Cardiovasc. Surgery, Internat. Soc. Endosurgery, N.J. Vascular Soc., Per. Vascular Surgery Soc., Soc. Clin. Vascular Surgery, Am. Assn. Vascular Surgery. Office: 5 Franklin Ave Ste 310 Belleville NJ 07109-3522

SALES, EUGENIO DE ARAUJO CARDINAL, emeritus archbishop; b. Acari, Brazil, Nov. 8, 1920; s. Celso Dantas and Josefa de A. Sales Student, Sem. Fortaleza City. Ordained priest Roman Cath. Ch., 1943, consecrated bishop, 1954, elevated to cardinal, 1969. Sede Plana apostolic adminstr., Natal, 1962, Salvador, 1964; archbishop Sao Salvador, 1968-71, Rio de Janeiro, 1971—. Editor: The Pastors Voice. Address: Rua Visconde de Piraja 339 22410-003 Rio de Janeiro Brazil

SALES, JAMES BOHUS, lawyer; b. Weimar, Tex., Aug. 24, 1934; s. Henry B. and Agnes Mary (Pesek) Sales; m. Beuna M. Vornsand, June 3, 1956; children: Mark Keith, Debra Lynn, Travis James. BS, U. Tex., 1956, LLB with honors, 1960. Bar: Tex. 1960. Practiced in, Houston, 1960—; sr. ptnr. Fulbright & Jaworski, 1960—2000, head litig. dept., 1979—99; ret., 2000. Author: Products Liability in Texas, 1985; co-author: Texas Torts and Remedies, 6 vols., 1986; assoc. editor: Tex. Law Rev., 1960; contbr. articles to profl. jours. Trustee South Tex. Coll. Law, 1982—88, 1990—, A.A. White Dispute Resolution Ctr., 1991—94; cir. chair for membership The Supreme Ct. Hist. Soc., 1998—2001; bd. dirs. Tex. Resource Ctr., 1990—97, Tex. Bar Hist. Found., 1990—2001. Named among Best Lawyers in Am., 1989—. Fellow: Houston Bar Found. (chmn. bd. 1982—83, sustaining life), Tex. Bar Found. (trustee 1991—95, vice-chmn. 1992—93, chmn. 1993—94, chair adv. bd. for planned giving 1994—, sustaining life mem.), Am. Bd. Trial Advocates, Am. Bar Found. (state chmn. 1993—98, sustaining life), Internat. Acad. Trial Lawyers, Am. Coll. Trial Lawyers (state chmn. 1993—96); mem.: FBA, ABA (ho. of dels. 1984—, mem. Commn. on IOLTA 1995—97), Bar Assn. 5th Fed. Cir., Gulf Coast Legal Found. (bd. dirs. 1982—85), Houston Bar Assn. (bd. dirs. 1970—79, pres.-elect 1979—80, pres. 1980—81), Tex. Law Rev. Assn. (bd. dirs. 1996—, pres. 1999—2000), Tex. Assn. Def. Counsel (v.p. 1977—79), State Bar Tex. (bd. dirs. 1983—88, chmn. bd. 1985—86, pres. 1988—89), So. Tex. Coll. Trial Advocacy (dir. 1983—87), So. Conf. Bar, Nat. Conf. Bar Pres. (coun. 1989—92), Internat. Assn. Def. Counsel, The Forum, Order of Coif, Inns of Ct. (bd. dirs. 1981—84), Westlake Club (bd. govs. 1980—85). Roman Catholic. Home: 10803 Oak Creek St Houston TX 77024-3016 Office: Fulbright & Jaworski 1301 Mckinney St Houston TX 77010-3031 E-mail: jsales@fulbright.com.

SALES, JAMES WILLIAM, chemical engineer; b. Mobile, Ala., May 1, 1958; s. John Wesley and Willean (Bondurant) S.; m. Cynthia Lynn Griffis, Feb. 23, 1980; children: James William Jr., Christopher Brandon, Kimberly Nicole, Rebecca Lynn. AS, Patrick Henry Jr. Coll., 1977; BSChemE, U. Ala., 1979. Registered profl. engr., Tenn., Ohio, N.Y., Ala., Colo. Design engr. Eastman Chem. Co., Kingsport, Tenn., 1979-85, project engr. Ectona polyethylene terethalate project London, 1985-88, engrng. mgr. filtrate purge project Columbia, S.C., 1989-90, engrng. mgr. Ectona polyethylene terethalate project London, 1990-93, engrng. mgr. Mex. polyethylene terethalate project Mexico City, 1993-94, bus. devel. mgr. fine chems. bus. orgn. Kingsport, 1994-97; bus. mgr. imaging and photographic bus. unit Fine Chems. Bus. Orgn., Eastman Chem. Co., 1997-99; pres., chief op. officer A.M. Kinney, Inc., 1999—2002; pres., CEO Walter Kidda Constructors, 2000—02; market segment mgr. Mitsubishi Chem. Am., 2002—. Chmn. deacons First Bapt. Ch., Kingsport, 1995-96, Sunday sch. dir., 1994-95; pres. Tellico Hills Home Owners Assn., Kingsport, 1988-89. Mem. AIChE, Kiwanis (sec. 1981-86), Phi Kappa Sigma (treas. 1978-79), Tau Beta Pi, Alpha Chi Omega, Chi Omega Epsilon. Avocations: golf, tennis. Office: Mitsubishi Chem Am 401 Volvo Pkwy Chesapeake VA 23320 E-mail: jameswsales1@cs.com., Jim_sales@m-chem.com.

SALESKY, WILLIAM JEFFREY, corporate executive; b. Boston, June 12, 1957; s. Harry Michael Salesky and Eleanor Faith (Stutman) Spater; m. Cherri Lynne DeGreek, Nov. 27, 1982; 1 child, Joshua Steven. BS, U. Calif., Davis, 1978; MS, U. Calif., Berkeley, 1980, PhD, 1982. Co-op engr. Bechtel Corp. Inc., San Francisco, 1977-78; engr. U. Calif., Davis, 1978-79; rsch. assoc. Lawrence Berkeley Lab., 1979-82; project mgr. Smith Internat., Irvine, Calif., 1982-89; dir. engrng. & quality assurance Mark Controls, Long Beach, 1989-94; v.p. engring. Stamet Inc., Gardena, 1994-97; pres., founder Skytron Corp., Irvine, 1997—; founder Skytron Mall TV Network, 1999—. Cons. Printnonix Corp., Irvine, Calif., 1988, Metal Alloys Inc., Irvine, 1986-88, Ceracon Inc., Irvine, 1984-86; chmn. L.A. Conf. on Fugitive Emissions from Valves, 1993. Patentee in field. Mgr. Irvine Baseball Assn., 1990; grad. asssembly rep. U. Calif., Berkeley, 1980-81; mem. race com. Internat. Am.'s Cup Class World Championship; mem. San Diego Crew Classic Race Com., 1992—; mem. Am.'s Cup Race Com., 1992, 95. Recipient Meritorious award Petroleum Engr. mag., 1988, award for outstanding contbns. Valve Mfrs. Assn. Am., 1993. Mem. ASTM, Am. Soc. Metals Internat. (bd. dirs. 1988-90, Earl Parker fellow 1981), Soc. Petroleum Engrs., Am. Petroleum Inst., South Shore Yacht Club (CFO 1989-91, bd. dirs. 1991-93). Avocation: yacht racing, golf. Office: Skytron Corp 16 Technology Dr Ste 134 Irvine CA 92618-2328 E-mail: bill@skytron.com.

SALETTA, MARY ELIZABETH (BETTY SALETTA), sculptor, rancher; b. Miami, Fla., Sept. 30, 1941; d. Earl Robert and Alta Florence Cotner; m. Albert Michael Saletta, July 1, 1959; children: Tia Suzanne, Kamber Ann. Graphic artist Moore Bus. Forms Inc., Modesto, Calif., 1960-67, Live Oak Pub. Co., Oakdale, 1977-80; freelance artist U.S. Forest Svc., Modesto Irrigation Dist., Stanislaus Schs., New Don Pedro Dam Project, Calif., 1967-77; sculptor Saletta Sculpture, Oakdale, 1980—. Mem. adv. bd. Calif. State U. Coll. Arts, Letters and Sci., Turlock, 1999-2002; charter mem., dir. Downtown Arts Project, Modesto, 1992-96. One-woman shows City of Oakdale Redevel. Agy., 1990, Modesto C. of C., 1996; group shows include Calif. State U. Stanislaus, Turlock, 1986, Cowboy Artist Am. Mus., Kerrville, Tex., 1988, Benson Park Sculpture Garden, Loveland, Colo., 1989, 90, 93, Danada Sculpture Garden, Chgo., 1991, 93, Tucson Mus. Art, 1995; represented in permanent collections Tucson Mus. Art, Buckaroo Hall of Fame, cities of Modesto, Oakdale, Ripon, Calif., Stockton, Calif.; sculptures include life-size pub. sculptures Yesterday Is Tomorrow, 1991, Am. Graffiti, 1997, Stockton Firefighters Meml., 1998, World War II Meml., 1999, Nursing, the Finest Art, 2001, Chief Estanislao, 2001. Recipient Excellence in Fine Art award Bank Am., Stockton, Calif., 1959, Best of Show award Western Art Roundup, Winnamucca, Nev., 1987, 88, Excellence in Visual Arts award Stanislaus Arts Coun., Modesto, 1999. Mem. Nat. League Am. Pen Women, Ctrl. Calif. Art League (advisor 1991, Best of Show award 1987), Rotary (bd. dirs. Oakdale 1997-99). Democrat. Avocations: horses, skiing, mountain climbing, fishing. Home: 4255 Wellsford Rd Oakdale CA 95361-7930 Fax: 209-572-4089. E-mail: salettasculpture@aol.com.

SALEWSKI, RUBY MARIE GRAF, nursing educator; b. Vernon, Tex., Feb. 22, 1932; d. Albert Carl and Olga Emma (Mertink) Graf; children: Stephen, Elizabeth, Matthew, Rebecca, Deborah. Diploma in nursing, Meth. Hosp. Sch. Nursing, Dallas, 1952; BSN, U. Tex., Galveston, 1956; postgrad., U. Tex., Austin, 1979-82, 87, St. Louis U., 1960-61; MEd in Nursing, U. Minn., 1967, postgrad., 1982. Lic. nurse, Minn., Tex. Mem. nursing faculty U. Tex., Galveston, 1956-59, Luth. Hosp., St. Louis, 1959-60, Anoka-Ramsey Community Coll., Coon Rapids, Minn., 1968-69; faculty pre-nursing advisor U. Minn., Mpls., 1970, 72, 73-74; mem. nursing faculty Austin (Minn.) C.C., 1975-76; mem. faculty Rochester (Minn) C.C., 1976-90, coord. continuing edn. in nursing, 1981-82; asst. prof. Tex. Tech U. Health Scis. Ctr. Sch. Nursing, Lubbock, 1991-95, U. Tex. Coll. Nursing and Health Scis., El Paso, 1995—. Bd. dirs., coord. Family Edn. Ctr., 1985;; vol. Contact Ministries, 1984-89; mem. organized caring and sharing ministry Good Shepherd Luth. Ch., 1990; parish nurse Hope Luth. Ch., Lubbock, 1991-92, Manhattan Presbyn. Ch., El Paso, 1998-2000. Mem.: NEA, LWV (bd. dirs. local chpt. 1985—88), ANA, Tex. Nurses Assn. (GAC com. 1997—99, bd. dirs. TNA dist. 1 1999—), Alderian Soc., Minn. League Nursing (v.p. 1985—87, founding com. mem. educators coun.), Nat. League Nursing, Minn. Nurses Assn. (govtl. affairs com. 1987—89, chmn. dist. 13 1988), Phi Lambda Theta, Sigma Theta Tau. Home: 1601 Mcrae Blvd Apt H6 El Paso TX 79925-7536 Office: U Tex Coll Health Scis Sch Nursing 1101 N Campbell St El Paso TX 79902-4238 E-mail: rubysalewski@aol.com.

SALGADO, ELIZABETH M. R. lawyer; b. Lynchburg, Va., July 19, 1966; d. Morton Spitz and Josephine Taylor Roberts; m. R. Anthony Salgado. BA in History and Women's Studies, Ind. U, 1988; MEd in Counselor Edn., U. Va., 1991, JD, 1998. Counselor Salem Elem. Sch., Spotsylvania County, Va., 1991-95; assoc. Dow, Lohnes & Albertson, PLLC, Washington, 1998—. Tax cite editor, mng. bd. Va. Tax Rev., 1996-98. Contbr. articles to profl. jours. Mem. ABA, Phi Beta Kappa. Democrat. Lutheran. Office: Dow Lohnes & Albertson PLLC Ste 800 1200 New Hampshire Ave NW Washington DC 20036-6800 E-mail: esalgado@dlalaw.com.

SALGADO, LYNN ENZA GRANT, educator; b. Columbus, Ga., Oct. 21, 1950; d. Ninan Edward and Bessie Enza (Martin) Grant; m. Sal Salgado, July 3, 1999; children: Thomas Grant, Matthew Edward. BS, Vanderbilt U., 1973; MEd, Columbus U., 1984. Cert. tchr., spl. educator, speech pathologist, Ga. Tchr. Dodson Elem. Sch., Hermitage, Tenn., 1973-75, Milford (Ohio) Village, 1975-77, Winterfield Elem. Sch., Columbus, Ga., 1980-81; spl. edn. tchr. Shaw H.S., 1981-83; behavior specialist Lincoln Jr. H.S., Naperville, Ill., 1984-87; behavior specialist, dept. chair Severely Emotionally Disturbed, Broward County, Fla., 1987-97; behavior specialist Stoneman Zone, 1998—. Creator, implementer spl. edn. program Forest Acad., Margate, Fla., 1988; facilitator Coop. Learning Insvc. for Tchrs., Broward County, 1989; tchr., trainer Broward Schs., 1998, North Area Broward Schs., 1998; lectr. in field; chair Sch. Improvement Team Goal #3 student performance, 1994; dept. chair, Cross Creek, Broward County Schs., 1994. Co-author: (trainer's manual) N. Area Broward County Functional Behavioral Assesment. Mgr. Coral Springs boys' soccer club, 1989-90; participant Supt.'s Ann. Planning Conf. Broward County Schs., 1989-90. Named Young Outstanding Educator, Milford Jaycees and Milford Bd. Edn., 1976, Cross Creek Tchr. of Yr., Broward County Schs., 1991; recipient award for Project H.E.L.P., Broward County Bd. Edn., 1989, 91, 96-97. Mem. Broward Tchrs. Union (faculty coun. rep. at Cross Creek), So. Assn. Colls. and Schs. (chair 1990-91), Ramblewood Club Assn. (bd. dirs. 1998—, sec.), Kappa Delta Pi, Kappa Delta Epsilon. Republican. Methodist. Avocations: reading, writing, soccer, horseback riding.

SALGADO, SUSANA, Musicologist, researcher, consultant; b. Montevideo, Uruguay, June 14, 1927; d. Juan Andres Salgado, Amelia Gomez-Eirin; m. Roberto O. Morassi. Musicologist, School of Humanities (Dept. of Musicology), Montevideo, Uruguay, 1954—65. Chair of Uruguayan Music Research School of Humanities (Dept of Musicology), Montevideo, Uruguay, 1965—71; Consultant to the Music Division Library of Congres, Washington, 1994—. Mem. bd. advisors Garland Publishing for Opera performances, New York, 1992—; lectr. in field. Author: (Scholarly Book) The Teatro Solis, 150 Years of Opera, Concert and Ballet in Montevideo, 2002, Breve Historia de la Musica Culta en el Uruguay, Montevideo, 1971, 1980; contbr. 5 Grove Dictionaries. N/A. N/A. Mem.: Women National Book Association. Avocation: Traveling, swimming, walking. Office: N/A Home Fax: 703-412-1481. Personal E-mail: saisalgado@aol.com.

SALGO, MICHAEL NICHOLAS, civil engineer, consultant; b. Oradea Mare, Romania, Jan. 17, 1914; came to U.S., 1914; s. Louis and Celia (Kain) S.; m. Ruth Farkas, Aug. 20, 1944; children: Peter Lloyd, Jeffrey Boyd. BS in Engring., Northwestern U., 1938; MS in Civil Engring., Va. Poly. Inst., 1938. Registered profl. engr., S.C., N.Y., N.J., others. Rsch. fellow Va. Poly. Inst., Blacksburg, 1937-38; teaching asst., instr. Ill. Inst. Tech., Chgo., 1938-39; subway rodman City of Chgo., 1939-40; naval architect, structural engr. U.S. Navy-Charleston (S.C.) Navy Yard, 1940-43; structural engr. U.S. Navy-Bur. Yards and Docks, Washington, 1943-46; prin. maintenance engr. U.S. Navy Superintending Civil Engring., N.Y.C., 1946-48; staff civil engr. U.S. Navy-Third Naval Dist., 1948-57; dir. facilities engring. CBS Inc., 1957-74; mgr. transp., sr. assoc., dir. engring. various cos., 1974-90. Author materials in field. Mem. Soc. Profl. Engrs., (life), ASCE (pres. met. sect. 1959-60, dir., v.p. 1963-66, 70-71, treas. 1976-88; elected to hon. membership 1994). Republican. Achievements include working as project director for CBS East Coast Broadcast Center and many other national and international facilities projects. Home: 137-32 76th Ave Flushing NY 11367-2818

SALGO, PETER LLOYD, internist, anesthesiologist, broadcaster, journalist, lecturer, consultant, pathologist, pilot; b. N.Y.C., Nov. 9, 1949; s. Michael Nicholas and Ruth F. Salgo. BA, Columbia U., 1971, MD, 1975. Diplomate Am. Bd. Internal Meidicne, Am. Bd. Anesthesiology; lic. physician, N.Y., Calif., Mass.; instrument rated comml. pilot. Internal medicine intern Columbia Presbyn. Med. Ctr., N.Y.C., 1975-76, resident in internal medicine, 1976-78; vis. faculty fellow intensive care medicine and anesthesiology, dept. anesthesiology Columbia U., 1979-81; lectr. Harvard Med. Sch., Boston; clin. prof. medicine and anesthesiology Columbia P&S; mem. staff in anesthesia and medicine Mass. Gen. Hosp., Boston; attending in anesthesia and internal medicine Presbyn. Hosp., N.Y.C., assoc. vice chmn. dept. anesthesiology, chmn. inter-I.C.U. com., assoc. dir. surg. ICU. Host syndicated TV broadcast Healthcare 2000; aviation med. examiner FAA; comml. pilot. instrument Rated; host nat. radio med. program Sta. PRN, 1979—81; writer, producer, host med. info. broadcast Sta. WCBS-TV, N.Y.C., 1980—; med. corr. Sta. WCBS News, 1981—; corr. CBS Network Radio News, 1982—92; host. Healthtalk, 1982—88; med. corr. Sta. CNBC, 1989—, CNBC TV Network, 1989—93; host The Doctor Is In, Eyada.com, 2000—01; cons. to networks on med. content of TV programs; corr. Patient Info. Network, 1989—; anchor Americas Vital Signs, CNBC TV Network, Med. Crossfire , 2001—; lectr. in field.; expert guest on John F. Kennedy, Jr., crash NTSB Report Discovery Network, 2002; expert guest, med. cons. Fox News, 2001—02. Recipient Leonard Pullman award Columbia U., 1971, Blakesley award Am. Heart Assn., Journalism award Medic-alert Found., Honorable Mention in Journalism, UPI, Alumni Assn. medal Columbia U. P&S, 1975, Emmy award for excellence in broadcast journalism, Journalism award Lions Eye Found. Fellow ACP; mem. AAAS, AMA, AFTRA, N.Y. State Med. Soc., N.Y. County Med. Soc., Am. Soc. Anesthesiologists. Home: Apt 33A 200 W 60th St New York NY 10023-8511 Office: Presbyn Hosp Dept Anesthesiology New York NY 10032 E-mail: pls1@columbia.edu.

SALIBA, GEORGE, Maltese government official; Rep. to UN Govt. of Malta, 1997-99; amb. of Malta to U.S., 1999—; high commr. for Malta to Can., 2000—; amb. of Malta to Mex., 2000—. Office: Embassy of Malta 2017 Connecticut Ave NW Washington DC 20008-6195 E-mail: george.b.saliba@magnet.mt.

SALIBA, JACOB, manufacturing executive; b. East Broughton, Que., Can., June 10, 1913; s. Said and Nazira (David) S.; m. Adla Mudarri, May 31, 1942; children: John, Thomas, Barbara. BS, Boston U., 1941. Sr. supervising engr. Thompson and Lichtner Co., Boston, 1944-49; pres. Kingston Dress Co., 1949-51, Indsl. & Mgmt. Assocs., Inc., Boston, 1951-54, Maine Dress Co., Cornish, 1948-61; exec. v.p., mem. exec. com. Cortland Corp., Inc. (formerly Brockway Motor Co., Inc.), N.Y.C., 1954-59; exec. v.p. Sawyer-Tower, Inc., Boston, 1955-56, pres., 1956-59; v.p. Farrington Mfg. Co.; exec. v.p. Farrington Packaging Corp., 1959-61, Farrington Instruments Corp.; pres. N.E. Industries, Inc., from 1961, also bd. dirs.; pres. Fanny Farmer Candy Shops, Inc., 1963-66, W.F. Schrafft & Sons Corp., 1967-68; pres. frozen foods div. W.R. Grace & Co., 1966-68; pres. Katy Industries, Inc., Elgin, Ill., 1969-88, chmn., CEO, 1988-94. Chmn. bd. dirs. Schon & Cie; bd. dirs. Dresdner RCM Europe Fund NYSE, Katy Industries, NYSE; spl. cons. Air Material Command, USAF, Dayton, Ohio, 1942-43; cons. to chief air staff USAF, 1952-54; co-chmn. Air Force Spare Study Group, 1953. Mem. corp. Mass. Gen. Hosp., Mus. Sci. Mem. Union League Club, Bridgton Club, Highlands Country Club, Palm Beach Yacht Club. Methodist. E-mail: salibagido@aol.com.

SALIBA, PHILIP E. archbishop; b. Abou-Mizan, Lebanon, 1931; came to U.S., 1956, naturalized, 1961; s. Elias Abdallah and Salema (Saliba) S. BA, Wayne State U., 1959; MDiv, DD, St. Vladimir's Sem., N.Y., 1964; DHL, Wayne State U., 1986. Became sub-deacon, deacon Antiochian Orthodox Christian Ch., 1945-49, ordained deacon, 1949-59, priest, 1959-66, consecrated archbishop, 1966, now met. and primate. Chmn. Standing Conf. Am.-Middle Eastern Christian and Moslem Leaders; chmn. Orthodox Christian Edn. Commn.; vice chmn. Standing Conf. Canonical Orthodox Bishops in Ams. Vice-chmn. St. Vladimir's Orthodox Theol. Sem. Address: 358 Mountain Rd Englewood NJ 07631-3727 E-mail: archdiocese@antiochian.org.

SALIBI, SLEIMAN SAMI, neurologist, flight surgeon; b. Bhamdoun, Lebanon, Nov. 14, 1961; came to U.S., 1980; s. Sami Sleiman and Wadad Khairallah Salibi. BS, Syracuse U., 1983; MD, Am. U., Beirut, 1987. Intern in gen. surgery New Eng. Med. Ctr., Boston, 1990-91, resident in neurology, 1991-93, La. State U. Med. Ctr., New Orleans, 1994-95, resident in internal medicine, 1995-96; fellow in clin. neurophysiology St. Louis U. Hosp., 1996-97; pvt. practice in neurology Lake Charles, La., 1997—. Maj. La.-ANG, 1994—. Mem. Am. Acad. of Neurology (jr. mem.). Presbyterian. Avocation: private pilot. Office: 707 S Ryan St Lake Charles LA 70601-5815 E-mail: ssalibi@pol.net.

SALIGMAN, HARVEY, retired consumer products and services company executive; b. Phila., July 18, 1938; s. Martin and Lillian (Zitin) S.; m. Linda Powell, Nov. 25, 1979; children: Martin, Lilli Ann, Todd Michael, Adam Andrew, Brian Matthew BS, Phila. Coll. Textiles and Sci., 1960. With Queen Casuals, Inc., Phila., 1960-88, v.p., 1966-68, pres., chief exec. officer, 1968-81, chmn., 1981-88; pres., chief operating officer Interco Inc., St. Louis, 1981-83, chief exec. officer, 1983-85, 1985-89, chmn., 1989-90; ret. Bd. dirs. Ameren Corp. (formerly Union Electric). Trustee Washington U., St. Louis, John Burroughs Sch., St. Louis Mem. St. Louis Club, Masons.

SALINAS, BARUJ, artist, architect; b. Havana, Cuba, July 6, 1935; came to U.S., 1959; s. Moises and Regina (Algazi) S.; 1 child, Shari Regina. BArch, Kent State U., 1958. Chief draftsman Calif. Exploration Co., Coral Gables, Fla., 1961-64; draftsman Stresscon, Miami, 1964-66; chief draftsman Pillsbury Co., 1966-70; artist Miami and Barcelona, Spain, 1970—. Instr. Winchester Sch. Art, Barcelona, 1992, 93, N.Y. Sch. Visual Arts, Barcelona, 1993; instr. art. Miami Dade Cmty. Coll. interam. campus, 1998-. Vol. Amnesty Internat., Paris, 1989-90; art coord. Internat. Com. for Human Rights, Miami, 1993-94, 95-96, 97, 98. Recipient fellowship Cintas Found., 1969, 70, 1st prize Ft. Lauderdale Mus. Art, 1969, 1st prize Cultura P.R., 1983. Democrat. Jewish. Avocations: travel, reading, music, sports. Home: 2740 SW 92nd Ave Miami FL 33165-3119

SALINAS, CARLOS FRANCISCO, dentist, educator; b. Iquique, Chile, Apr. 9, 1941; came to U.S., 1972; s. Carlos F. and Victoria (Cerda) S.; m. Maria Asunción Córdova, 1963; children: Carlos Miguel, Claudio Andres, Maria Asunción. BS, U. Chile, Santiago, 1958; DDS, U. Chile, 1963; DMD, Med. U. S.C., 1985. Cert. Fla., 1982, Tenn., 1982, S.C., 1985. Dentist Nat. Health Svc., Viña del Mar, Chile, 1963-65; pvt. practice, 1963-72; fellow in medicine/genetics Johns Hopkins U., Balt., 1972-74; faculty mem. Med. Univ. S.C., Charleston, 1974-88, assoc. prof., 1988-94, prof., 1994—, dir. divsn. craniofacial genetics, 1981—; dir. craniofacial anomalies and cleft lip palate ctr. Med. U. S.C., 1995—. Faculty mem. U. Chile, Valparaiso, 1965-74; dentist Dental Ctrl. Clinic for Chilean Navy, Valparaiso, 1964-66; vis. scientist U. Montreal, 1974; internat. cons. Interamerican Coll. Physicians and Surgeons, Ptnrs. of Ams., WHO/Pan Am. Health Orgn. Editor: Genetica Craniofacial, 1979, Craniofacial Anomalies: New Perspectives, 1982, (with R.J. Jorgenson) Dentistry in the Interdisciplinary Treatment of Genetic Diseases, 1980, (with K.S. Brown) Craniofacial Mesenchyme In Morphogensis and Malformations, 1984, (with J.M. Opitz) Recent Advances in Ectodermal Dysplasias, 1988; contbr. articles to profl. jours. Bd. dirs. Ptnrs. Am. (award 1992), East Cooper Cmty. Outreach, S.C. World Trade Ctr., Charleston; chmn. bd. S.C. Hispanic Coalition, 1994; founder Circulo Hispanoamericano de Charleston, pres. 1978-2000; hon. consul of Chile, 1978—; dental dir. Spl. Olympics S.C., 2001—. Fogarty Internat. Rsch. fellow; grantee NIH, 1972-74, HEW, 1979-80, 80-81, 81-82, 82-83, 83-84, Dept. Health and Human Svcs., 1983-84, 84-85, March of Dimes Birth Defects Found., 1984-85, S.C. State Health and Human Svcs. Fin. Commn., 1989, Healthy South Carolina Initiative, 1997-2001, S.C. Developmental Disabilities Coun., 2000-02; NIH-NIDCR, 2001, Duke Endowment, 2002. Mem. AAAS, Soc. Craniofacial Genetics (pres. 1985, 92, chmn. membership com. 1993-94), Iberoam. Soc. Human Genetics of N.Am. (v.p. 1992-94, pres. 1994-96, v.p. 2000-01), Hispanic Dental Assn.

(sci. program co-chair 2001), Hispano Am. Biomed. Assn. (v.p. 1997—), Am. Assn. Dental Schs., Am. Soc. Human Genetics, Am. Cleft Palate and Craniofacial Anomalies Assn., Internat. Assn. for Dental Rsch., Am. Assn. for Dental Rsch., Interam. Coll. Physicians and Surgeons (bd. dirs. chpt. faculty and rschrs. 1994—), Incontinentia Pigmenti Found. (sci. adv. coun. 1995—), Med. Assn. P.R. (hon.), Peruvian Soc. Human Genetics (hon.), Med. Soc. Western Dist. P.R. (hon.). Home: 948 Equestrian Dr Mount Pleasant SC 29464-3608 Office: Med Univ SC 171 Ashley Ave Charleston SC 29425-0001 E-mail: salinas@musc.edu.

SALINAS, MARTHA F. manufacturing executive; b. Santa Maria, Calif., Aug. 6, 1972; d. Panfilo and Faustina Salinas. BA in Bus. Adminstrn., U. Tex., Austin, 1994, MBA, 1996. Fin. mgr., mktg. mgr. Chase Manhattan Bank, Houston, 1996—99; database mktg. mgr. Compaq Computer Co. , 2000—. Mem.: Nat. Soc. Hispanic MBAs (exec. v.p. Houston 1998—99, pres. 1999—, Nat. Edn. Chair 2002—). Avocations: reading, community svc.. Mailing: 10801 Legacy Park Dr #415 Houston TX 77064*

SALINE, CAROL SUE, journalist; b. Phila., May 19, 1939; d. Carl and Gertrude (Feld) Auerbach; m. Jack Saline, June 3, 1962 (div. Sept. 1996); children: Sharon, Matthew. BA magna cum laude, Syracuse U., 1961. Sr. writer Phila. Mag., 1974—. Talk radio host WDVT-AM, Phila., 1986—89; freelance writer, 1970—; pub. affairs panelist WPVI-TV, Phila., 1986—98; host The Fretz Kitchen Comcast Cable Network, 2000—; nat. pub. spkr., lectr. Fischer-Ross Bur., N.Y.C., 1996—. Author: Straight Talk, 1981, Dr. Snow, 1988, Guide to Good Health, 1994-96; co-author: Sisters, 1994 (N.Y. Times Bestseller), Mothers and Daughters, 1997 (N.Y. Times Bestseller), Best Friends, 1998 (N.Y. Times Bestseller). Bd. dirs. Mayor's Commn. on Literacy, Phila., Ctr. for Literacy, Phila., Phila. Theater Co., Phila. CASA. Recipient Nat. Mag. award, Clarion award Women in Comm., Charles Stuart Mott award, Internat. Reading Assn. award, Health Journalism award Am. Soc. Chiropractors, Sarah award Women in Comms., Melitta Benz Woman of Achievement award 1995, Myrtle Wreath award Camden County Hadassah, 1990, Woman of Achievement award Women in Transition, 1987; named Woman of Yr. Delaware County Domestic Abuse Project, 1984. Mem. Phi Beta Kappa. Avocations: reading, fitness, theater, travel. Office: Philadelphia Mag 1818 Market St Fl 36 Philadelphia PA 19103-3683 E-mail: csaline@phillymag.com.

SALINGER, ANTHONY WILSHIRE, educator, organization consultant; b. N.Y.C., Dec. 4, 1938; s. Alan Bijur Salinger and Frances (Wilshire) Riordan; m. Nina Lois Popick, Feb. 20, 1965 (div. 1981); children: Kerri Rae, Beth Kendra; m. Joan Marie Kelleher, Jan. 15, 1983; 1 child, Victoria Lucy. AB, U. N.C., 1965; MBA, Colo. State U., 1995. Staff mgr. AT&T Long Lines, N.Y.C., 1970-72, planning engr., 1972-74, dist. engr. White Plains, N.Y., 1974-76, staff supr. Bedminster, N.J., 1976-82, AT&T Planning and Design, Bedminster, 1982-83; venture mgr. AT&T Mktg. Devel., Basking Ridge, 1983-87; staff mgr. AT&T Mktg. Info. Systems, 1987-88; sr. tng. cons. AT&T Corp. Edn. Ctr., 1988-89, product mgr., 1989-91, sales ops. mgr., 1991-92, orgn. devel. mgr., 1993-94; quality dir. AT&T Phone Ctr., Parsippany, N.J., 1992-94; quality mgr. fin. dept. AT&T Consumer Products, 1994-96; mgr. strategic planning Lucent Technologies Consumer Products, 1996-97; skills devel. mgr. Lucent Technologies Human Resources, 1997; mng. ptnr. Alexis Gill, Inc., 1998-99; cons. M.F. Smith & Assocs., Inc., 1988—. Adj. prof. NYU Stern Sch. Bus., 1988-2001; mem. faculty U. Phoenix Online Campus, 1996-2001, George Rothman Inst. Enterpreneurial Studies, Fairleigh Dickinson U., 1997-2000, Keller Graduate Sch. Mgmt., 2001; examiner N.J. Quality Achievement award, 1994, 98. Author: Enhancing Communications Between Users and DP Staff, 1983, (with others) American Management Association Handbook, 4th edit., 1994, Strategy, Quality and Information Technology, 1997, (with others) Handbook of Business Strategy. Mem. faculty Quality Assurance Inst., Orlando, Fla., 1982-85; mem. Pingel Design Group, 1995; mem. adv. bd. Jointure for Cmty. Adult Edn., 1987-90; mem. Strategic Leadership Forum, 1996. Served with U.S. Army, 1961-64. Recipient Oliver Innovation award AT&T Long Lines, 1973, Capitol award Nat. Leadership Coun., 1991. Mem. IEEE, Soc. for Info. Systems Quality (pres. 1987), Data Processing Mgmt. Assn. (pres. 1982-85, Individual Performance award 1985), Nat. Spkrs. Assn., Internat. Platform Assn., Internat. Biog. Assn., ASTD, Am. Soc. Quality (sr. mem., chair annual svc. quality conf. 1994, 95), Assn. Systems Mgmt., Assn. for Quality and Participation, Toastmasters (award 1983). Republican. Episcopalian. Home and Office: 32 Oak Ridge Rd Bernardsville NJ 07924-1878 E-mail: salinger@worldnet.att.net.

SALINGER, FRANK MAX, lawyer; b. Landau, Isar, Germany, Dec. 4, 1951; s. Karl and Ingeborg F. (Herold) S.; m. Susan Ann Wagner, May 20, 1978. Student, Columbia Union Coll., Takoma Park, Md., 1969-72; JD, U. Balt., 1975. Bar: Md. 1975, U.S. Dist. Ct. Md. 1975, U.S. Ct. Appeals (4h cir.) 1978, U.S. Tax Ct. 1978, U.S. Ct. Mil. Appeals 1978, U.S. Ct. Appeals (5th cir.) 1982, U.S. Supreme Ct. 1983, U.S. Ct. Appeals (11th cir.) 1984, U.S. Ct. Appeals (9th cir.) 1986, D.C. 1986, U.S. Ct. Appeals (3d cir.) 1989. Pvt. practice, Balt., 1975-77; counsel Md. State Senate, Annapolis, 1975-76; assoc. counsel Am. Fin. Corp., Silver Spring, Md., 1977-78; govt. rels. counsel Truck Trailer Mfrs. Assn., Washington, 1978-80; v.p., gen. counsel, dir. govt. affairs Am. Fin. Svcs. Assocs., 1980-92; v.p. govt. rels. Advanta Corp., Wilmington, Del., 1992—. Co-author: (with Alvin O. Wiese and Robert E. McKew) A Guide to the Consumer Bankruptcy Code, 1989; (with Robert W. Green) State Regulations and Statutes on Consumer Credit, 1989, Federal Consumer Credit Regulations and Statutes, 1989. City councilman, Laurel, Md., 1976-78, zoning commr., 1976-78; chmn. Md. State Young Reps., 1977-78; bd. dirs. Am. Bankruptcy Inst., Washington, 1986-88. Mem. ABA (mem. com. on consumer fin. svcs., subcoms. on interest rate regulation and state regulation), Am. League Lobbyists (chair fin. svcs. sect. 1995-97), Federalist Soc. Law and Pub. Policy, Woodmore Country Club, Capitol Hill Club, Ford's Theatre Soc. Republican. Lutheran. Office: Advanta Corp One Righter Pkwy Wilmington DE 19803

SALINGER, J(EROME) D(AVID), author; b. N.Y.C., Jan. 1, 1919; s. Sol and Miriam (Jillich) S.; m. Claire Douglas, 1953 (div. 1967); children: Margaret Ann, Matthew. Student, Valley Forge Mil. Acad., Columbia U. Author: Catcher in the Rye, 1951, Nine Stories, 1953, Franny and Zooey, 1961, Raise High the Roof Beam, Carpenters; and Seymour: An Introduction, 1963; contbr. stories to New Yorker mag. Sgt. AUS, 1942-46. Address: care Harold Ober Assocs 425 Madison Ave New York NY 10017-1110*

SALINGER, MICHAEL ALVIN, economist, educator; b. Cin., Aug. 24, 1956; s. James Alvin and Joyce (Joslin) S.; m. Julie Landsman, July 6, 1985; children: Philip Landsman, David Herbert, Nicholas Andrew. BA, Yale U., 1978; PhD, MIT, 1982. Asst. prof. Grad. Sch. Bus. Columbia U., N.Y.C., 1982-87, assoc. prof., 1987-90, Boston U., 1990—, faculty dir. undergrad. program, 1999-2000, chmn. dept. fin. and econ., 2000—, prof., 2001—. Economist FTC, Washington, 1985—86; acad. advisor Princeton Econs. Group, 1989—94; spl. cons. Nat. Econ. Rsch. Assocs., 1994—; vis. assoc. prof. MIT, 1997—98. Contbr. articles to profl. publs.; assoc. editor: Jour. Indsl. Econs., 1996—. Vol. The Alumni Fund, New Haven, 1978—. NSF fellow, 1979-82. Mem. Am. Econ. Assn. Jewish. Avocations: tennis, skiing. Office: Boston U Sch Mgmt 595 Commonwealth Ave Boston MA 02215-1704 E-mail: salinger@bu.edu.

SALINGER, PIERRE EMIL GEORGE, journalist; b. San Francisco, June 14, 1925; s. Herbert and Jehanne (Bietry) S.; m. Renee Laboure, Jan. 1, 1947; children: Marc (dec.), Suzanne (dec.), Stephen; m. Nancy Brook Joy, June 28, 1957; m. Nicole Helene Gillmann, June 18, 1965 (div. June 1988); 1 son, Gregory; m. Nicole Beauvillain de Menthon, June 17, 1989. BS, U. San Francisco, 1947. Reporter, night city editor San Francisco Chronicle, 1946-55; guest lectr. journalism Mills Coll., 1950-55; West Coast editor, contbg. editor Collier's mag., 1955-56; investigator select com. to investigate improper activities in labor or mgmt. field U.S. Senate, 1957-59; press sec. U.S. Senator Kennedy, 1959-60, Pres. Kennedy, 1961-63, Pres. Johnson, 1963-64; U.S. Senator from Calif., 1964; v.p. Nat. Gen. Corp., 1965; v.p. internat. affairs Continental Airlines, Inc. and Continental Air Services, Inc. (subsidiary), 1965-68; pres. Gramco Devel. Corp., 1968—; dep. chmn. Gramco (U.K.) Ltd., 1970-71; sr. v.p. AMROP Inc., 1969; L'Express, Paris, 1973-78; contbg. corr. ABC for Europe, 1977—, Paris bur. chief, 1979-87, sr. editor, 1988-90, ABC News, 1988-93; vice chmn. Burson Marsteller, Washington, 1993-96. Ind. pub. rels. profl., 1996—. Author: With Kennedy, 1966, On Instructions of My Government; editor A Tribute to John F. Kennedy, 1964, A Tribute to Robert F. Kennedy, 1968, Je Suis un Americain, 1975, La France et le Nouveau Monde, 1976, America Held Hostage-The Secret Negotiations, 1981, The Dossier, 1984, Mortal Games, 1988, Secret Dossier--The Hidden Agenda Behind the Gulf Crisis, 1991, PS-A Memoir, 1995, John F. Kennedy Commander in Chief, 1997. Press officer Calif. Stevenson for Pres. Campaign, 1952, Richard Graves for Gov. Calif. Campaign, 1954; trustee Robert F. Kennedy Meml. Found.; chmn. bd. trustees Am. U. in Paris, 1978-88, hon. chmn., 1988—. With USNR, World War II. Decorated officer Legion of Honor (France); recipient Ellis Island Medal of Honor, 1992. Mem. Nat. Press Club.

SALINGER, RUTH ANGIER, international trade company executive, environmental administrator; b. Newton, Mass., July 21, 1931; d. Ralph Loveland and Elizabeth Angier; children: Peter Dennison, Jennifer Angier. BS in Edn., Wheelock Coll., Boston, 1953. Cert. in elem. edn. Tchr. Claflin Sch., Newton, 1953-54; dir. religious edn. Eliot Ch. of Newton, 1955-60; dist. case worker Mass. Senate Ways and Means Com., Boston, 1983-85; dir. constituent svcs. Congressman Chester G. Atkins, Lowell, Mass., 1985; pres., founder Greeley Found., Concord, 1986-90; pres., co-founder The Salinger Group, Gloucester, 1990—; chief exec. officer, co-founder Global Initiatives, Inc., 1990—. Co-founder Just-A-Start, Boston and Cambridge, 1964-67; founder, pres. Concord-Carlisle Human Rights Council, 1979-83, Mass. Women Sch. Com. Mems., Boston, 1974-79. Co-editor: Forward Through the Ages, 1986. Chmn. Concord Sch. Com., 1972-79; trustee METCO, 1979-83; co-chmn. U.S./USSR Citizen Summit, Moscow, 1990; mem., adviser Women for Mut. Security, 1986—. Recipient Peace Day award Nat. Peace Day Com., 1986. Mem. Wheelock Coll. Alumnae Assn. (trustee 1979-83, chmn./pres. social action com. 1979-83, Centennial Alumnae award 1989). Democrat.

SALINGER, WARREN, writer; b. Berlin, Apr. 5, 1932; s. Curt and Bella Salinger(Stepmother); m. Martha Betty Herpich, Jan. 27, 1955; children: Lynn, Barbara Sienkiewicz, Kenneth, Lisa Lemieux. BA, Goddard Coll., 1973. Dir. devel. Unitarian Universalist Svc. Com., Boston, 1968—85; exec. dir. Greeley Found., Concord, 1987—90; owner Century-21 Cape Ann, Gloucester, 1990—97. Author: Close to the Wind, 1998, Counterclockwise, Phoenix and the Valley of the Sun. Mem. Marlboro Sch. Com., 0973—1977; chmn. Greater Wshington Assn. Unitarian Universalist Chs., 1966—68; chmn. bd. dirs. Paint Br. Unitarian Ch., Silver Spring, Md., 1964—67. Staff sgt. USAF, 1951—55, Germany. Democrat. Avocations: tennis, trivia, writing. Home: 15R Pleasant St Rockport MA 01966 Personal E-mail: wasal@igc.org.

SALINS, PETER D. academic administrator; b. Berlin, June 15, 1938; came to U.S., 1939; s. Irwin and Ilse Daisy (Lessler) S.; m. Rochelle Chensky, Apr. 4, 1971; children: Jessica Elizabeth, Jonathan Andrew. BArch, Syracuse U., 1961, M of Regional Planning, 1968, PhD, 1969. Registered architect, Mass. Chmn. dept. urban affairs and planning Hunter Coll., CUNY, N.Y.C., 1973-93, 96-97, prof. dept. urban affairs and planning, 1980-97, dir. grad. program in urban planning, 1993-95, dir. urban rsch. ctr., 1995-97; provost, vice chancellor acad. affairs SUNY Adminstrn., Albany, 1997—; prof. dept. polit. sci. U. Stony Brook, 1998. Dir. SUNY Rsch. Found., 1997—; sr. fellow Manhattan Inst. for Policy Rsch., N.Y.C., 1985—; mem. Planning Accreditation Bd., Chgo., 1990—; Catherine Bauer Wurster lectr. U. Calif., Berkeley, 1993. Author: The Ecology of Housing Destruction, 1980, Assimilation, American Style, 1997; co-author: Scarcity by Design, 1992; editor: Housing America's Poor, 1987, New York Unbound, 1988; co-editor Jour. of Am. Planning Assn., 1988-93 (Excellence award 1992, Journalism award 1994). Mem. planning com. Am. Acad. Sci., Washington, 1971-72; mem. adv. panel White House Domestic Policy Unit, Washington, 1977; dir. Citizens Housing and Planning Coun., N.Y.C., 1988—; trustee Lavanburg Found., N.Y.C., 1987—, Village of Baxter Estates, Nassau County, N.Y., 1992-99; mem. mayor's adv. commn. N.Y.C. Health and Hosps. Corp., 1995-96. Fellow: Am. Inst. Cert. Planners; mem.: ASPA (v.p. 1982—84, Luther Gulick award for outstanding acad. 1994), Am. Planning Assn. (v.p. 1986—88, policy bd. mem. 1986—, N.Y. Metropolitan chpt.), Lambda Alpha. Avocations: golf, reading, hiking. Office: SUNY Suny Plz Albany NY 12246-0001 E-mail: salinspd@syadm.suny.edu.

SALIOLA, FRANCES, retired corporate administrator; b. Westfield, N.J., Oct. 27, 1921; d. Antonio and Maria (Chironna) Ponturo; m. Peter Saliola, Aug. 25, 1945; 1 child, George. Grad. high sch., Westfield, N.J., 1939. Sec., bookkeeper Pearsall & Frankenbach, Inc., Westfield, 1939-45; legal sec. Dughi & Johnstone, 1945-51; exec. sec. Arthur Venneri Co., 1951-65; office mgr. Torcon, Inc., 1965-77, dir. mgmt. risk and finance, 1977-86, dir. adminstrv. mgmt., 1983-86, corp. sec., dir., 1965-90. Sec. Sodality of the Blessed Virgin, Westfield, 1938, Civic Club Westfield, 1944; mem. Union County Boys' Town of Italy, 1951-63; membership chair Rosary Soc., 1993—. Mem. Holy Trinity Srs. Social Club (sec. 1996—). Roman Catholic. Avocations: reading, knitting, crocheting, travelling.

SALISBURY, ALAN BLANCHARD, information systems executive; b. Newark, Jan. 21, 1937; s. Lloyd Wade and Elizabeth Barry (Blanchard) S.; m. Florence Dorothy Conrad, May 21, 1971; children: Katherine Anne, Barbara Lynn. BS with distinction, U.S. Mil. Acad., 1958; MSEE, Stanford U., 1964, PhD, 1973; postgrad., Indsl. Coll. of Armed Forces, Washington, 1978. Commd. 2d lt. Signal Corps U.S. Army, 1958, advanced through grades to Maj. Gen., ret., 1987; asst. prof. U.S. Mil. Acad., West Point, N.Y., 1964-67; chief of data communications lst Signal Brigade, Republic of Vietnam, 1968-69; tech. adv. Directorate of Mgmt. Info., Washington, 1970-71; dir. U.S. Army Ctr. for Tactical Computer Sci., Ft. Monmouth, N.J., 1975-77; project mgr. Operations Tactical Data Systems, 1978-82; program mgr. Joint Tactical Fusion Program, Washington, 1982-84; comdr. U.S. Army Info. Systems Engring., Ft. Belvoir, Va., 1984-87; pres. Contel Technology Ctr., Fairfax, 1987-91; exec. v.p. Microelectronics & Computer Tech. Corp., Austin, Tex., 1991-93; pres. Learning Tree Internat. USA, Inc., Reston, Va., 1993-99; ind. cons., 1999—. Bd. dirs. Sybase, Emeryville, Calif., Challenger Ctr. for Space Sci. Edn., Alexandria, Va.; trustee Mitretek Systems, Inc., McLean, Va.; bd. visitors Software Engring. Inst. Carnegie Mellon U., Coll. of Engring. U. Md. Author: Microprogrammable Computer Architectures 1976, numerous articles in profl. jours.; founding editor Journal of Systems & Software, 1979-85. Decorated Bronze Star (2), 1969, D.S.M., 1987. Mem. Inst. for Elec. & Electronic Engrs. (sr.), Assn. for Computing Machinery, Armed Forces Communications & Electronics Assn. (chpt. pres. 1981-82), Phi Kappa Phi, Soc. of the Sigma Xi. Office: PO Box 2910 Reston VA 20195-0910 E-mail: abslsbry@aol.com.

SALISBURY, DALLAS L. research institute executive; BA, U. Wash., 1970; MBA in Pub. Policy and Adminstrn., Syracuse U., 1973. With Pension and Welfare Benefits Adminstrn. of U.S. Dept. Labor, 1975-76, Pension Benefit Guaranty Corp., 1977-78, U.S. Dept. Justice, 1974, Wash. State Legislature, 1971-72, Employee Benefit Rsch. Inst., Washington, 1978—, pres., CEO, mem. bd. trustees; chmn., CEO Am. Savs. Edn. Coun. Bd. dirs. The Health Project; mem. adv. bd. Nat. Acad. on Aging; lectr. in field; cons. in field. Mem. editl. adv. bd. Employee Benefit News, Benefits Quar., Employee Benefits Jour., Healthplan; contbr. articles to profl. jours. Mem. ERISA adv. coun. Sec. of Labor; pres.'s adv. coun. PBGC. Fellow Nat. Acad. Human Resources. Office: Employee Benefit Research Inst 2121 K St NW Ste 600 Washington DC 20037-1800

SALISBURY, EUGENE W. lawyer, justice; b. Blasdell, N.Y., Mar. 20, 1933; s. W. Dean and Mary I. (Burns) S.; m. Joanne M. Salisbury, July 14, 1950; children: Mark, Ellen, Susan, David, Scott. BA in History and Govt. cum laude, U. Buffalo, 1959, JD cum laude, 1968. Bar: N.Y. 1960, D.C. 1973, U.S. Dist. Ct. (we. and no. dists.) 1961, U.S. Ct. Appeals (2d cir.) 1970, U.S. Ct. Appeals (D.C. cir.) 1973, U.S. Supreme Ct. 1973. Ptnr. Lipsitz, Green, Fahringer, Roll, Salisbury and Cambria, Buffalo, 1960—. Justice Village of Blasdell, 1961-2001; lectr. N.Y. Office Ct. Adminstrn., N.Y.C., 1961—; mem. N.Y. State Commn. on Jud. Conduct, 1989-2001, chmn., 2000-2001. Author: Manual for N.Y. Courts, 1973, Forms for N.Y. Courts, 1977. Capt. U.S. Army, 1949-54, Korea. Decorated Bronze Star, Purple Heart; recipient Citizen of Yr. award Indsl. Rels. Rsch. Assn., 2000; named Jurist of Yr., Erie County Judges and Police Conf., 2001, Magistrate of Yr., Erie County Magistrates Assn., 2001. Mem. ABA (del. spl. ct. sect. 1988-2001), D.C. Bar Assn., Erie County Bar Assn., N.Y. State Bar Assn., World Judges Assn., N.Y. State Magistrates Assn. (pres. 1973, Man of Yr. 1974), N.Y. State Jud. Conf., Upstate N.Y. Labor Adv. Coun., 1995—. Office: Lipsitz Green Fahringer Roll Salisbury and Cambria 42 Delaware Ave Ste 300 Buffalo NY 14202-3857 E-mail: esalisbury@lipsitzgreen.

SALISBURY, HELEN HOLLAND, education educator; b. Bedford, Ind., Dec. 15, 1923; d. Deward Julius and Zella (Kinser) Holland; B.S. in Home Econs., Ind. U., 1957; M.Ed., U. Va., 1967; Ed.D., Temple U., 1979; m. Charles Jackson Salisbury, Jan. 10, 1942; children: Creggie Helen Salisbury Henderson, Andrew Jackson II. Plating chemist Curtiss-Wright, Indpls., 1943; supr. sch. lunch program Charlottesville (Va.) Pub. Schs., 1963-65; dir. Harcum Jr. Coll. Lab. Sch., Bryn Mawr, Pa., 1966-68; prof. edn. Harcum Jr. Coll., Bryn Mawr, 1965-73; teaching assoc. Temple U., Phila., 1974; early childhood cons., 1979—; prof. edn. Harcum Jr. Coll., Bryn Mawr, 1982-94, dir. infant devel. practice, 1982-94; early childhood cons. Head Start, 1965; instr. Child Care Tng. Project, Pa., 1992-94. Mem. ASCD, DAR, Nat. Assn. Edn. Young Children, Delaware Valley Assn. Edn. Young Children, Orgn. Mondiale pour L'Education Prescolaire, Kappa Alpha Theta. Episcopalian. Co-author: Diagnosing Individual Needs for Early Childhood Education, 1975. Home: 3915 Nimit Dr Bloomington IN 47401-8964 Office: Harcum Jr Coll Montgomery Ave Bryn Mawr PA 19010

SALISBURY, RALPH JAMES, poet; b. Arlington, Iowa, Jan. 24, 1926; s. Charles Salisberry, Olive Ione McAllister; m. Joyce Eleanor Hurlbert (div. Mar. 1969); children: Jeff, Brian; m. Ingrid Wendt Salisbury, Sept. 19, 1944; 1 child Martina. BA, U. Iowa, MFA, 1951. Prof. Tex. A&M U., College Station, Tex., 1951—57, Drake U., Des Moines, 1957—60, U. Oreg., Eugene, 1960—. Author: Rainbows, 2000, The Last Rattlesnake, 1988. Sgt. USAF, 1944—46. Named Fulbright prof., Fulbright Found.; fellow Rockefeller Found. fellow. Home: 2377 Charnelton St Eugene OR 97405-2859

SALISBURY, ROBERT HOLT, political science educator; b. Elmhurst, Ill., Apr. 29, 1930; s. Robert Holt and Beulah (Hammer) S.; m. Rose Marie Cipriani, June 19, 1953; children: Susan Marie, Robert Holt, Matthew Gary. AB, Washington and Lee U., 1951; MA, U. Ill., 1952, PhD, 1955. Mem. faculty Washington U., St. Louis, 1955-65, prof., 1965-97, prof. emeritus, 1997—, chmn. dept. polit. sci., 1966-73, 86-92, dir. Center for Study Pub. Affairs, 1974-77, Sidney W. Souers prof. govt., 1982-97. Vis. prof. SUNY, Buffalo, 1965, So. Ill. U., Edwardsville, 1975; affiliated scholar Am. Bar Found., 1981-95; cons. U.S. Conf. Mayors, 1965, Hartford (Conn.) C. of C., 1964, NSF, 1973. Author: Interest Groups Politics in America, 1970, Governing America, 1973, Citizen Participation in the Public Schools, 1980, Interests and Institutions, 1992, The Hollow Core, 1993; contbr. articles to profl. jours. Mem. St. Louis County Charter Commn., 1967, Gov.'s Commn. on Local Govt., 1968-69. Guggenheim fellow, 1990; Rockefeller Ctr. scholar, 1990. Mem. Mo. Polit. Sci. Assn. (pres. 1964-65), Am. Polit. Sci. Assn. (exec. council 1969-71, v.p. 1980-81), Midwest Polit. Sci. Assn. (pres. 1977-78), Pi Sigma Alpha. Democrat. Methodist. Home: 709 S Skinker Blvd Saint Louis MO 63105-3225 Office: Washington U Dept Polit Sci Saint Louis MO 63130 E-mail: rhsalisb@artsci.wustl.edu.

SALISBURY, TAMARA PAULA, foundation executive; b. N.Y.C., Dec. 14, 1927; d. Paul Terrance and Nadine (Korolkova) Voloshin; m. Franklin Cary Salisbury, Jan. 22, 1955; children: Franklin Jr., John, Elizabeth, Elaine, Claire. BA, Coll. Notre Dame, 1948; postgrad., Am. U., George Washington U. Chemist depts. pathology and chemotherapy NIH Cancer Inst., Bethesda, Md., 1946-52; asst. to chief of Chemistry Br. Office of Naval Rsch., 1953-55; v.p., COO Nat. Found. Cancer Rsch., 1973—. Mem. Assn. Internat. Cancer Rsch., 1995. Decorated d'Officier De L'Ordre De Leopold II; outstanding contbns. award Internat. Soc. Quantum Biology, 1983, award of appreciation Beth Israel Hosp., Harvard Med. Sch., Brigham & Women's Hosp., 1993. Mem. AAAS, Am. Chem. Soc., N.Y. Acad. Scis., Inst. Phys. and Chem. Biology (fgn.), Krebforschung Internat., Nat. Liberal Club. Home: 10811 Alloway Dr Potomac MD 20854-1504 Office: Nat Found Cancer Rsch 4600 E West Hwy Ste 525 Bethesda MD 20814-6900

SALITERMAN, RICHARD ARLEN, lawyer; b. Aug. 3, 1946; s. Leonard Slitz and Dorothy (Sloan) S.; m. Laura Shrager, June 15, 1975; 1 child, Robert Warren. BA summa cum laude, U. Minn., 1968; JD, Columbia U., 1971; LLM, NYU, 1974. Bar: Minn. 1972, D.C. 1974. Mem. legal staff subcom. on antitrust and monopoly U.S. Senate, Washington, 1971-72; acting dir., dep. dir. compliance and enforcement divsn. Fed. Energy Office, N.Y.C., 1974; mil. atty. Presdl. Clemency Bd., White House, Washington, 1975; sr. ptnr. Saliterman & Saliterman, Mpls., 1975—. Adj. prof. law Hamline U., 1976-81. Author: Advising Minnesota Corporations and Other Business Organizations, 4 vols., 1975; chmn. Hennepin County Bar Jour., 1985-87. Trustee, sec. Hopkins Edn. Found.; trustee W. Harry Davis Found., 1990-96; pres. Twin Cities Coun.; mem. nat. bd. dirs. Navy League U.S., Washington, 1997—, nat. judge adv., 2001—.

SALIU, ION, software developer, computer programmer; b. Gemeni, Mehedinti, Romania, Mar. 9, 1950; came to U.S., 1985; s. Marin and Elena (Chiser) S.; m. Ofelia Foltean, June 30, 1979 (div. 1989); 1 child, Amy Ofelia. Diploma in Econs., Acad. Econ. Studies, Bucharest, Romania, 1976. Economist Silk Co., Deva, Romania, 1978-84; technician Inacomp Computer Ctr., Troy, Mich., 1987; worker Boyer Nursery, Biglerville, Pa., 1985; software developer Lotwon, 1989—. Author (software) on probability applied to lottery and computer programming, 1989-92; contbr. articles to profl. jours. Mem. N.Y. Acad. Scis. Achievements include discovery of repeat cycles in probabilistic events, incorporated in a computer software algorithm. Home and Office: Lotwon PO Box 400 Cashtown PA 17310-0400 Fax: (815) 550-4389. E-mail: ion@saliu.com.

SALJINSKA-MARKOVIC, OLIVERA T. oncology researcher, educator; b. Skopje, Macedonia; d. Trajko and Radmila; m. Nenad Markovic, July 9, 1961; 2 children. MD, Med. Faculty, Skopje, 1962; PhD, Med. Faculty, Belgrade, 1977; Specialist Med. Biochemistry, U. Kiril and Metodij, Skopje, 1969. Asst. prof. Med. Faculty, Skopje, 1964-79, assoc. prof., 1979-84; dir. clin. lab. U. Children's Hosp., 1974-84; sr. rsch. assoc. Pa. State U., State College, 1984-85; sr. fellow U. Pa., Phila., 1985-88; prof. U. Belgrade, 1988-93. Adj. prof. Med. Coll. of Pa., 1993-95; vis. scientist NIAMDD, NIH, Bethesda, 1976-77; vis. scientist Am. Type Culture Collection, Rockville, Md., 1995-96; dir. BioSciCon, Md., 1996—; primarius Univ. Children's Hosp., Skopje, 1983-86; head lab. for rsch. and devel., Clin. Ctr., Belgrade, 1990-93; mem. exam. com., State of Macedonia, 1980-90; adj. prof. U. Md. U. Coll., 1998, Am. U., Washington, 1999—; vis. prof. Georgetown U., Washington, 2000. Author: Quantitative Cytoch of Enzymes, 1986; contbr. articles to profl. jours., publs. Postdoctoral intern rsch. fellowship Fogarty Internat. Ctr., NIH, Bethesda, 1971-73; recipient several rsch. grants NIH, Pharm. Co., 1984-95. Mem. Histochem. Soc., Am. Assn. Clin. Chem., N.Y. Acad. Scis., Am. Assn. Cell Biology. Achievements include development of new concepts and methods in cancer diagnosis and treatment; patents for CAP-PAP test for cervical cancer screening, and Inosinic Acid Dehydrogenase Assay. Office: BioSciCon Inc Rockville MD 20852

SALKEVER, STEPHEN GREGORY, political science educator; b. Phila., Mar. 26, 1943; s. Louis R. and Edna T. Salkever; m. E. Jane Hedley; 1 child Emily Scott. BA, Amherst (Mass.) Coll., 1963; PhD in Polit. Sci., U. Chgo., 1972. Asst. prof. to prof. polit. sci. Bryn Mawr (Pa.) Coll., 1969—. Author: Finding the Mean: Theory & Practice in Aristotelian Political Philosophy, 1990. Avocation: choral singing. Office: Polit Sci Dept Bryn Mawr Coll 101 N Merion Ave Bryn Mawr PA 19010 E-mail: ssalkeve@brynmawr.edu.

SALKIND, MICHAEL JAY, technology administrator; b. N.Y.C, Oct. 1, 1938; s. Milton and Esther (Jaffe) S.; m. Miriam E. Schwartz, Aug. 16, 1959 (div. 1979); children: Michael Jay, Elizabeth Jane, Jonathan Hillson, Joshua Isaac; m. Carol T. Gill, Dec. 23, 1990. B in Metall. Engring., Rensselaer Polytech. Inst., 1959, PhD, 1962. Chief advanced metallurgy United Techs. Rsch. Labs., East Hartford, 1964-68; chief structures and materials Sikorsky Aircraft div. United Techs. Corp., 1968-75; dir. product devel. Avco Systems div., 1975-76; mgr. structures NASA, 1976-80; dir. aerospace scis. Air Force Office of Sci. Rsch., 1980-89; pres. Ohio Aerospace Inst., 1990—. Adj. faculty metallurgy Trinity Coll., Hartford; adj. faculty aerospace U. Md., 1982-85; adj. faculty materials Johns Hopkins U., 1985-89; chair Ohio Math. and Sci. Coalition. Cons. editor Internat. Jour. Fibre Sci. and Tech.; editor Applications

Composite Materials, 1973; contbr. to profl. jours. and textbooks. Evaluator Accreditation Bd. Engring. and Tech., 1989—; mem. Daniel Guggenheim Medal Bd. Awards, 1984-90; mem. Spirit of St. Louis Medal Bd., 1984-89; mem. bd. Citizens' Acad. Charter Sch.; mem. bd. NCCJ. Capt. U.S. Army, 1962-64. Recipient Disting. Leadership award, Cleve. Tech. Socs. Coun., 2002. Fellow AAAS, AIAA (assoc.), ASM Internat.; mem. ASME (Disting. lectr. 1989-93), ASTM (chmn. com. D-30 on high modulous fibers and their composites 1968-74), Am. Helicopter Soc., AIME, Brit. Inst. Metals, Rsch. Soc. Am., Plansee Soc., Cosmos Club, Union Club, 50 Club, Leadership Cleve., Sigma Xi, Alpha Sigma Mu. E-mail: michaelsalkind@oai.org.

SALL, JOHN, information technology executive; married; 4 children. BS, Beloit Coll.; MS, No. Ill. U. Co-founder, exec. v.p. SAS Inst., Cary, NC. Office: SAS Inst 100 SAS Campus Dr Cary NC 27513-2414

SALLAH, MAJEED (JIM SALLAH), real estate developer; b. Boston, Aug. 5, 1920; s. Herbert K. and Rose (Karem) S. Student, Gloucester (Mass.) pub. schs.; m. Aline C. Powers, Apr. 10, 1970; children: Christopher M., Melissa Rose. Pres., dir. Glo-Bit Fish Co., Gloucester, 1947-48, Live-Pak of Ohio, Inc., 1947-51, Cape Ann Glass Co., Inc., Gloucester, 1950-72, Cape Ann Realty Corp., Gloucester, 1961—, Marias Restaurant, Gloucester, 1960—; pres., treas., dir. Gloucester Hot-Top Constrn. Co., Gloucester, 1967-75; pres., bd. dirs. SGF Corp., Gloucester, 1983-85, SALFAD, Inc. Rossford, Ohio; pres., treas. Points East, Inc.; trustee Christopher Investment Trust; bd. dirs. Lutsal, Inc.; bd. dirs., ptnr. Barsal, Inc., Toledo, Ohio, Hamsal, Inc., Toledo. Pres. Lebanese-Am. Bus. Men's Club; treas. Lebanese-Maronite Soc. With U.S. Army, 1942-45. Decorated Bronze Star. Mem. Gloucester Assocs., Cape Ann Investment Corp., Am. Legion, Amvets, Gloucester Fraternity Assn., Order Ky. Cols. (hon.), Lions, Elks, Moose. Roman Catholic. Home and Office: PO Box 78 56 Hilltop Rd Gloucester MA 01931-0078

SALLEN, DAVID URBAN, lawyer; b. Ft. Madison, Iowa, June 23, 1952; s. Urban Frank and Lillian Virginia (Ashby) S.; m. Sheila Marie Strang, Jan. 5, 1985; children: Josef David, William James. BA in Sociology and Philosophy, St. Ambrose Coll., 1974; JD, U. Iowa, 1977. Bar: Iowa 1977, U.S. Dist. Ct. (no. and so. dists.) Iowa 1977, U.S. Ct. Appeals (8th cir.) 1978, U.S. Supreme Ct. 1980. Assoc. Morr & Shelton, Chariton, Iowa, 1977-79; asst. county atty. Lucas County, 1977-79; pub. defender Lee County, Ft. Madison, 1979—; sole practice, 1982-95. Chairperson Ft. Madison Human Rights Commn., 1980-86, Lee County Cmty. Action Agy., 1982-88; mem. jud. coordinating com. Iowa Supreme Ct., Des Moines, 1981-89, mem. commn. indigent def. transition com., 1985-90; coun. mem. St. Marys Paris, Ft. Madison, 1982-84; elected councilman 1st ward Ft. Madison City Coun., 1988—; mayor pro-tem Ft. Madison, 1994-96; pres. Iowa Pub. Defenders Assn., 1982-83; sec. Cmty. Svcs. Coun., 1983-88; mem. com. drinking drivers Iowa State Legis., Des Moines, 1984-85. Recipient Cert. of Appreciation, S.E. Iowa Cmty. Action Agy., 1984, Friends Reach Out, Inc., 1982. Mem. ABA, Nat. Assn. Criminal Def. Lawyers, Nat. Legal Aid and Defender Assn., Iowa State Bar Assn., Lucas County Bar Assn. (pres. 1978-79), Am. Judicature Soc., Lee County Bar Assn., Dominic Club, K.C. Home: 309 6th St Fort Madison IA 52627-4810 Office: 821 Avenue G Fort Madison IA 52627-4501

SALLEN, MARVIN SEYMOUR, investment company executive; b. Detroit, Oct. 15, 1930; s. Jack Samuel and Sara S.; m. Nancy Susan Berke; 1 child, Jack Samuel II. AB in Econs., U. Mich., 1952. V.p. Sonnenblick-Goldman Corp., Detroit, 1967-83; sr. v.p. Comerica Bank, 1983-87; pres. Comerica Mortgage Corp., 1983-87; mng. ptnr. Brick Ltd., Birmingham, Mich., 1988-90; mng. dir. Redcliffe Corp., 1990—.

SALLER, RICHARD PAUL, classics educator; b. Ft. Bragg, N.C., Oct. 18, 1952; s. George E. and Arthea E. (North) S.; m. Carol Joann Fisher, Jan. 12, 1974; children: John E., Benjamin T. BA in Greek and History, U. Ill., 1974; PHD in Classics, U. Cambridge, Eng., 1978. Asst. prof. Swarthmore (Pa.) Coll., 1979-84; assoc. prof. U. Chgo., 1984-89, prof., 1990—, dean of social scis., 1994—2001, provost, 2002—. Author: Personal Patronage, 1982, Patriarchy, Property and Death in the Roman Family, 1994; co-editor: Economy and Society in Ancient Greece, 1981; co-author: Roman Empire, 1987; editor Classical Philology, 1991-93. Rsch. fellow Jesus Coll., U. Cambridge, 1978-79; Ctr. for Adv. Study fellow, Stanford U., 1986-87; Trinity Coll., U. Cambridge fellow commoner, 1991. Mem. Am. Philol. Assn., Am. Hist. Assn. Office: U Chgo Dept History 1126 E 59th St Chicago IL 60637-1580

SALLES, FERNANDO JAVIER, molecular biologist, biotechnologist; b. Miami, Oct. 1, 1964; s. Jaime Carlos and Marta Diaz Salles. BS, U. Tampa, 1985; PhD, SUNY, Stony Brook, 1991. Postdoctoral rsch. assoc. SUNY, Stony Brook, 1992-94; staff investigator Picower Inst. Med. Rsch., Manhasset, N.Y., 1994-95; rsch. scientist SUNY, Stony Brook, 1996-98, instr., 1998-99, rsch. asst. prof., 1999-2000; STET Cogent Neurosci., Inc., Durham, N.C., 2000, dir., bus. and strategic devel., 2001—. Co-founder Two Entertaining, N.Y.C., 1995—. Choreographer (theater) And the World Goes 'Round, 1999. Rsch. grantee Alzheimer's Assn., 1994-95. Mem. Soc. Neurosci. Avocations: dancing, theater, travel. Office: Cogent Neurosci Inc # 200 4321 Medical Park Dr Durham NC 27704-2175 Fax: (919) 688-7156. E-mail: Fern@cogentneuroscience.com., Fsalles@nc.rr.com.

SALLESE, PAULA MARIE, critical care, resuscitation nurse; b. Balt., Apr. 27, 1959; d. Frank P. and Dorothy H. (Plichta) S. Diploma, Md. Gen. Hosp. Sch. Nursing, 1980. RN, Md.; cert. ACLS, advanced trauma life support. Staff nurse Md. Gen. Hosp., Balt., 1980-82; nurse critical care recovery unit Md. Inst. Emergency Med. Svcs. Systems, 1982-87; full ptnr. trauma resuscitation unit R. Adams Cowley Shock Trauma Ctr., 1987-98, clin. info. systems analyst, 1998—. Mem. AACCN, Soc. Trauma Nurses, Am. Trauma Soc. (program coord. nursing during the golden hour). Home: 8809 Richmond Ave Baltimore MD 21234-2929 E-mail: psallese@umm.edu.

SALLETTE, MARK KEVIN, utilities executive, sales executive; b. Mobile, Ala., Feb. 8, 1963; s. Edward LaCounte and Carol Dianne Sallette; m. Caroline Hammond Crumley; children: Joseph. BSBA, Brenau U., 1993, MBA, 1997. Cert. energy mgr., demand-side mgmt. profl. Residential mktg. rep. Ga. Power Co., Hartwell, 1994—98, sr. power mktg. rep. Athens, 1998—2000, field sales team leader Rome, 2000—. Program com. chair Leadership Athens, 1999—2000; local bus. coun. co-chair Athens Area C. of C., 1999—2000; mem. local adv. bd., vol. tchr. Jr. Achievement, 1998—2000; bd. dirs. Summer Opportunities, 1998—2000, Foothills United Way, Anderson, SC, 1995—96; venue site vol. Atlanta Com. for the Olympic Games, Athens, 1996; corp. sch. ptnr. coord. Barrow Elem. Sch., 1996—2000; pres. N.E. Ga. Power Credit Union, 1998—2000. Mem.: Assn. Energy Engineers (none). Methodist. Avocations: golf, children's sports, writing. Home: 51 Carrington Dr Cartersville GA 30120-6473 Office: Ga Power Co 800 Broad St Rome GA 30161 Home Fax: 678-721-9157; Office Fax: 706-236-1329. Personal E-mail: mksallet@bellsouth.net. E-mail: mksallet@southernco.com.

SALLEY, JOHN JONES, university administrator, oral pathologist; b. Richmond, Va., Oct. 29, 1926; s. Thomas Raysor and Kathryn (Josey) S.; m. Jean Gordon Cunningham, Dec. 21, 1950; children: Katharine Gordon, John Jones, Martha Cunningham. DDS, Med. Coll. Va., 1951; PhD, U. Rochester, 1954; DSc, Boston U., 1975. Research fellow U. Rochester, 1951-54; from instr. to prof., chmn. dept. oral pathology Med. Coll. Va., 1954-63, prof. emeritus, 1991—; prof. pathology, dean Sch. Dentistry U. Md., 1963-74, dean emeritus Sch. Dentistry, 1977—, ret., 1991; v.p. research and grad. affairs Va. Commonwealth U., Richmond, 1974-85; acting pres. Va. Ctr. for Innovative Tech., 1985, v.p., 1985-87. Cons. div. research grants NIH, 1962-66; cons. U.S. Naval Dental Sch., Bethesda, Md., 1966-75; spl. cons. Nat. Inst. Dental Research, NIH, 1957-64; cons. USPHS Hosp., Balt., 1963-74, U.S. Naval Hosp., Portsmouth, Va., VA Hosp., Balt., 1964-74; dental health div. USPHS; mem. Md. Adv. Council Comprehensive Health Planning, 1968-74, Nat. Health Council, 1970-71; pres. Am. Assn. Dental Schs., 1971-72, Conf. So. Grad. Schs., 1983-84; sr. program cons. Robert Wood Johnson Found., 1978-84; mem. career devel. rev. com. VA, 1974-78; mem. com. health care resources in VA, NRC, 1974-77; cons. WHO, 1969-75; mem. Va. Gov.'s Task Force Sci. and Tech., 1982-83, sci. advisor to Gov. of Va., 1984-86; mem. research com. Va. State Council Higher Edn., 1974-84; chmn. task force Council Grad. Schs. in U.S., 1979-82. Conbtr. articles in field; editorial rev. bd.: Jour. Dental Edn, 1974-78. Bd. dirs. Md. divsn. Am. Cancer Soc., 1963-70, Am. Fund Dental Health, Rappahannock C.C. Found., 1999—; bd. dirs. Nat. Found. Dentistry for the Handicapped, 1986, pres., 1992-94; mem. adv. bd. Va. Inst. for Devel. Disabilities, 1987-91; bd. trustees Middlesex County Pub. Libr., 1994-98, pres., 1995-97. With USAAF, 1944-46. Recipient Outstanding Civilian Service medal Dept. Army, 1961, Disting. Citizenship award State Md., 1974. Fellow AAAS, Am. Coll. Dentists; mem. ADA, Nat. Conf. Univ. Research Adminstrs., Am. Acad. Oral Pathology, Internat. Assn. Dental Research (Novice award 1953), Internat. Med. Informatics Assn. (chmn. working group 1989-92), Sigma Xi, Sigma Zeta, Omicron Kappa Upsilon. Episcopalian (vestryman). Home and Office: PO Box 838 Urbanna VA 23175-0838 E-mail: salleyj@oonl.com.

SALLIS, JAMES, writer; b. Helena, Ark., Dec. 21, 1944; s. Chappelle Horace and Mildred Clodine (Liming) S. Student, Tulane U., 1961-63, U. Tex., 1985-87. Tchr. intensive writing workshops Clarion (Pa.) Coll., U. Wash., Tulane U., Loyola U.; guest lectr. modern poetry, European lit., art; writer short stories, essays, poetry and trans. Editor New Worlds 1966-68; editor: (anthologies) The War Book, 1972, The Shores Beneath, 1973; features writer, reviewer, columnist Tex. Jazz, 1980-83, lead book reviewer Dallas Morning News, 1981-83; book reviewer Washington Post Book World, L.A. Times, 1993—; author: A Few Last Words, 1972, The Guitar Players, 1982, 94, Jazz Guitars, 1984, The Long-Legged Fly, 1992, Saint Glinglin (translator), 1993, Difficult Lives, 1993, Moth, 1993, Black Hornet, 1994, Limits of the Sensible World, 1994, Renderings, 1995, The Guitar in Jazz, 1996, Ash of Stars: On the Writings of Samuel R. Delany, 1996, Death Will Have Your Eyes, 1997, Eye of the Cricket, 1997, Bluebottle, 1999, Gently into the Land of the Meateaters, 2000, Chester Himes: A Life, 2000, Time's Hammers, 2000, Sorrow's Kitchen, 2000, Ghost of a Flea, 2001.

SALLOWAY, JOSEPHINE PLOVNICK, psychologist, marriage and family therapist, mental health counselor, psychology educator, college counselor; b. Brookline, Mass., July 30, 1944; d. Isadore B. and Gladys J. (Press) Plovnick; m. Richard B. Salloway, July 4, 1967; 1 child, Matthew. AB in History, Boston U., 1965, EdM in Counseling, 1966; cert. in human resource mgmt., Bentley Coll., 1980. Cert. sch. psychologist, sch. adjustment counselor, History Soc. Studies tchr.; clinically cert. forensic counselor, domestic violence counselor; lic. mental health counselor, lic. marriage and family therapist; nat. cert. psychologist. Counselor Boston Pub. Schs., 1966-78; counselor, psychologist ednl. enrichment program Milton (Mass.) Acad., 1970-71; psychologist Braintree (Mass.) Pub. Schs., 1983-89; psychologist, adjustment counselor Norwood Pub. Schs., 1990-92; sch. adjustment counselor Stoughton, Mass., 1993-94; cons. psychologist Waltham (Mass.) Schs., 1997—; pvt. practice Braintree, 1997—. Faculty psychology and child devel. Quincy (Mass.) Coll., 1997—, head counselor student support advisor, 1997—; mem. faculty psychology and early childhood edn. and devel., faculty advisor Massasoit C.C., 1999—; mem. faculty Program for Advancement of Learning (PAL) Curry Coll., 1999, mem. faculty psychology, 2000—, diagnostic tchr. Edn. and Diagnostic Ctr., 1999-00; field supr. dept. counselor edn. Harvard U., Cambridge, Mass., Northeastern U., Boston; lectr., presenter workshops on stress mgmt., parenting, child devel. spl. needs, time mgmt., test taking strategies and techniques and other subjects; del. Coastline Coun. for Children, Mass., 1985—; psychometrist Mass. Gen. Hosp., Boston; asst. coord. Boston U. Counseling Clinic; diagnostic tchr. Braintree, Mass., 1999—, Mass. Edn. Reform, Tutor, Canton Pub. Schs., 2000; mem. edn. reform Mass. Comprehensive Assessment Sys., 2000; commn. on child advocacy and domestic violence Dist. Atty.'s Office, 2000—; lectr. in field; presenter in field. Pub. dir. Curtain Call Theatre, 1997; contbg. editor Gazette newsletter, 1996—. Class agt. Boston U. Alumni Assn., 1996—; ednl. dir. House of Worship, Braintree, 1994—; del. Braintree Fair Housing Commn., 1994-2000, Braintree Multicultural Com., 1994-2000; pres., bd. chmn. Cmty. Friends for Human Svcs., Inc., Boston, 1995—, chmn. edn. bd.; vol. Genesis Fund Telethon. Recipient Presdl. award Cmty. Friends for Human Svcs., Inc., 1996-97, 2001, Svc. award, 1998, 99, 2001, Senatorial award, 1998; award for contbn. to svcs. for children Mass. Soc. for Prevention Cruelty to Children, 1998, 99, Senatorial award for outstanding contbn. to mental health Mass. Senate, 1998. Mem. ACA (clin.), NASP, Am. Assn. Marriage and Family Therapists (clin.), NAMP, Mass. Sch. Counselors Assn., Mass. Assn. Sch. Adjustment Counselors, Mass. Assn. Marriage and Family Therapists, Mass. Assn. Mental Health Counselors, Pi Lambda Theta. Avocations: antique collecting, reading, travel, volunteer work, theater . Home: 57 Cochato Rd Braintree MA 02184-4628 E-mail: jsalloway@aol.com.

SALLQUIST, GARY ARDIN, minister, non-profit executive; b. Sioux City, Iowa, July 7, 1938; s. Hal Thurston and Rosemary (Daggett) S.; m. Joyce Darleen Casey, June 10, 1960; children: Susan L. Rail, Steven P. BA, U. Nebr., Omaha, 1960; MDiv, Princeton Theol. Sem., 1993; D of Ministry, La. Bapt. U., 1997. ChFC, CLU. Ptnr. Sallquist-Wilkinson Inc., Omaha; pres. Planned Giving Sys., Cin., 1987-90; min. adult edn. Coll. Hill Presbyn. Ch., 1993-95; dir. planned giving Promise Keepers, Denver, 1995-98; v.p., divsn. higher edn. PhilanthroCorp, Woodland Park, 1998—2000; headmaster Miami Valley Christian Acad., Cin., 2002—. Author: A Seminary Journey, 1995, The Counsel of Many, 1999. Pres. Omaha Jaycees, 1966-67, Ednl. Found., Memphis, 1976; dirs. Creighton-St. Joseph Hosp., Omaha, 1975-81, Cin. Assn. CLUs, Leadership Cin. Alumni Assn., 1987-89. Recipient Golden Key award Nebr. Jaycees, 1975, Friar's Club award, N.Y.C., 1993. Mem. U. Nebr. Omaha Alumni Assn. (pres. 1968-70, Outstanding Alumnus award 1977), Pi Kappa Alpha (nat. pres. 1970-72). Avocations: basketball, running, tennis, reading, public speaking. Home: 5300 Barony Pl Cincinnati OH 45241 Office: Miami Valley Christian Acad 6830 School Rd Cincinnati OH 45244 E-mail: mvcaheadmaster@hotmail.com.

SALLS, JEAN R. nonprofit executive; b. Eugene, Oreg., July 13, 1940; d. Howard Peebles and Marguerite (Holding) S.; m. D.B. Hopps, July 15, 1961 (div. Apr. 1987); children: D. Brad, H. Robert, Kirsten M.; m. Paul Trescott Jackson, Oct. 17, 1998. BA, Western Wash. U., 1976. Bookkeeper Nelson Med. Group, Seattle, 1961-69; info. and referral program coord. Sr. Svcs. Snohomish County, Everett, Wash., 1976-77; instr. Milw. Area Tech. Coll., 1979-80; project coord. Cedar Valley C.C., Dallas, 1980-81; caseworker The Salvation Army, Seattle, 1983-86; program dir. YWCA of Seattle-King County, 1986-92; exec. dir. United Way of Island County, Oak Harbor, Wash., 1992—. Mem., bd. dirs. Concerts on the Cove Found., Coupeville, Wash., 1994—; v.p. Whidley Animal Improvement Found., Coupeville, 1996—; precinct com. King County Dems., Seattle, 1975; bd. dirs. Healthcare for the Homeless, Seattle, 1991, Montlake Cmty. Club, Seattle, 1975; pres. Montlake Coop. Presch., Seattle, 1973. Mem. United Ways of Wash. (treas. 1999—), Soroptimist Internat. Avocations: reading, music, hiking. Office: United Way of Island County 830 SE Bayshore Dr Oak Harbor WA 98277-5792

SALLS, JENNIFER JO, secondary school educator, consultant; b. Reno, May 8, 1952; d. Edmund Allenby and Georgia Theresa (Mullison) Naphan; m. Mitchell Aaron Marshall, Dec. 18, 1971; children: Kevin Alexander, Christopher Allen, Brian Andrew. BS, U. Nev., 1974, MEd, 1985. Cert. math., lang. and computer tchr., Nev. Tchr. Reno High sch., 1977-82; chair math. dept., tchr. McQueen High Sch., Reno, 1982-90; edn. cons. Nev. Dept. of Edn., Carson City, 1990-91; secondary math./computer coord. Washoe County Sch. Dist., Reno, 1991-94, K-12 math. coord., 1994-2000; tchr. Sparks (Nev.) H.S., 2000—. In-svc. instr. Washoe County Sch. Dist., Reno, 1980—; cons. U. Nev., Reno, 1986-87; referee Math. Tchr., Reston, Va., 1988—, mem. editl. bd., 1990-94. Co-author: Turtle Geometry, 1986; contbr.: (video course) Teaching Mathematics with Manipulatives Grades 7-12, 1995. NSF grantee, 1984. Mem. Nat. Coun. Tchrs. Math. (program com. annual meeting 1999, meeting the needs of beginning tchrs. com. 2000—, local arrangements com. ann. meeting 2002), Nat. Coun. Suprs. Math., Assn. State Suprs. Math., Calif. Math. Coun., Oreg. Coun. Tchrs. Math., No. Nev. Math. Coun. (pres. 1984-85, 87-88, treas. 2000-01), Nat. State Tchrs. Yr., Coun. Presdl. Awardees of Math. Democrat. Mem. Lds Ch. Avocations: needlework, tennis. Office: Sparks HS 820 15th St Sparks NV 89431 E-mail: jsalls@washoe.k12.nv.us.

SALMAGGI, GUIDO GODFREY, former diplomat, opera agent; b. Bklyn., July 22, 1916; s. Alfredo and Elvira (Canzano) S.; m. Nancy Stair, Feb. 11, 1944 (div. Oct. 1974); child: Linda; m. Maria Gargenti. Grad. h.s., Bklyn.; student, Bklyn. Conservatory of Music, Sch. of Drama & Arts, L.A. Artistic dir. N.Y. Opera Festival, Inc., Washington, 1956-64; artistic advisor Honolulu Symphony Opera, 1960-62; genl. dir. Bklyn. Opera Co., 1960-70; dir. of auditoriums City and County of Honolulu, 1969-71; with pub. rels. Hyatt Regency Waikiki Hotel, Honolulu, 1976-88; vice consul of Italy State of Hawaii, San Francisco, 1967-88. Opera debut in Verdi's La Traviata, N.Y. Hippodrome Theatre, 1938; sang national anthem for all U.S. Presidents from Franklin D. Roosevelt to George Bush; columnist Kahala Press Newspaper, 1972-78. Venerable Sons of Italy, Honolulu, 1969-71; dean Consular Corps. of Hawaii, 1973-75. Sgt. U.S. Army Spec. Svcs., PTO, 1941-45. Decorated commendatore Italian Govt., 1988; recipient Medal of Mil. Merit, U.S. Army, Honolulu, 1945. Mem. Sons of Italy (pres. 1971-73), Am. Soc. of the Italian Legions of Merit in N.Y.C. (hon.). Roman Catholic. Avocations: tennis, swimming, gardening.

SALMAN, ROBERT RONALD, lawyer; b. N.Y., Dec. 26, 1939; s. Samuel L. and Lillian Gertrude (Sincoff) S.; m. Reva Carol Rappaport, June 16, 1963; children: Elyse D. Spiewak, Suzanne A. BA magna cum laude, Columbia Coll., 1961, LLB cum laude, 1964. Bar: N.Y. 1965, U.S. Supreme Ct. 1974, U.S. Ct. Appeals (2nd cir.) 1967, U.S. Ct. Appeals (3rd cir.) 1993, U.S. Ct. Appeals (11th cir.) 1985, U.S. Ct. Appeals (9th cir.) 1979, U.S. Dist. Ct. so. dist., ea. dist.) N.Y. 1969. Assoc. Proskauer, Rose, Goetz & Mendelsohn, N.Y.C., 1964-67; asst. corp. counsel Law Dept. N.Y., 1967-69; assoc. Phillips, Nizer, 1969-73; ptnr. Phillips, Nizer, Benjamin, Krim & Ballon, 1973-87, Reavis & McGrath, N.Y.C., 1987-88, Carter, Ledyard & Milburn, N.Y.C., 1988-94, Phillips & Salman, N.Y.C., 1994-97, Phillips Salman & Stein, N.Y.C., 1997-2000, Duane Morris & Heckscher LLP, N.Y.C., 2001—. Adj. prof. Seton Hall Law Sch., Newark, N.J., 1995-98. Contbr. articles to profl. jours. Pres., founder The Assn. for A Better N.J. Inc., 1991—; pres. Marlboro Jewish Ctr., 1982-84. Recipient NEGEV Builder award Israel Bonds, 1980, Award of Honor UJA Fedn., 1981. Mem. N.Y. State Bar Assn., ABA, Assn. Bar City of N.Y. Avocations: charitable and communal work, baseball, reading, writing. Office: 111 Broadway New York NY 10006-1901 E-mail: RRSalman@aol.com., RRSalman@DuaneMorris.com.

SALMASSI, SADEGH, family practice physician; b. Baghdad, Iraq, Aug. 14, 1946; s. Jafar and Kobra (Alavi) S.; m. Tahereh Ali Nazari, Jan. 17, 1970; children: Ali (dec.), Nahal. BS, Pahlavi U., 1966, MD, 1973. Diplomate Am. Bd. Pathology, Am. Bd. Gen. Practice in Medicine and Surgery. Instr. pathology U. Ill. Sch. Medicine, Chgo., 1975-80; asst. prof. pathology, assoc. chmn. dept., dir. blood bank U. Mo., Kansas City, 1980-84; chmn. family practice Delano (Calif.) Regional Med. Ctr., 1984-86; pres. Delano Regional Med. Group, 1989-96. Chief of staff Delano Regional Med. Ctr., 1989. Fellow Am. Coll. Internat. Physicians, Coll. Am. Pathologists, Am. Acad. Family Physicians; mem. AMA, Am. Acad. Gen. Physicians, Calif. Med. Assn. E-mial. Office: Sadegh Salmassi MD & Assocs Urgent Care Ctr 719 Main St Delano CA 93215-2935 also: Salmassi Cosmetic and Med Inst 719 Main St Delano CA 93215 E-mail: mdfcap@aol.com.

SALMELA, DAVID DANIEL, architect; b. Wadena, Minn., Mar. 28, 1945; s. Laurie Fredrick and Lempi Christine (Matti) S.; m. Gladys Elaine Hanka, June 23, 1967; children: Cory, Chad, Tia, Kai, Brit. Grad. high sch., Sebeka, Minn. Registered profl. architect, Minn., Wis. Draftsman McKenzie Hague & Gilles, Mpls., 1965-66, A.G. McKee, Hibbing, Minn., 1966, ABI Contracting, Virginia, 1966-69, Archtl. Resources, Hibbing, 1969-70; designer, arch. Damberg Scott Peck & Booker, Virginia, 1970-89; arch. Mulfinger Susanka, Duluth, Minn., 1989-90; prin. Salmela Fospick Ltd., 1990-94, Salmela, Arch., Duluth, 1994—. Recipient Minn. Masonry Inst. award, 1987, citation Am. Wood Coun., 1994. Fellow: AIA (honor award for architecture 1998, Wood Design award 1994, Merit award 1997, Record House award 1998, AIA/PIA award 2000, Minn. Honor award 1985, 1987, 1990, 1992—2000). Office: Architect 852 Grandview Ave Duluth MN 55812-1170 E-mail: ddsalmela@aol.com.

SALMOIRAGHI, GIAN CARLO, physiologist, educator; b. Gorla Minore, Italy, Sept. 19, 1924; came to U.S., 1952, naturalized, 1958; s. Giuseppe Carlo and Dina (Rinetti) S.; m. Eva Tchoukourlieva, Dec. 5, 1970; 1 child, George Charles MD, U. Rome, 1948; PhD, McGill U., 1959; DSc (hon.), Hahnemann U., 1995. Sr. med. officer Internat. Refugee Orgn., Naples, Italy, 1949-52; research fellow Cleve. Clinic Found., 1952-55; lectr. dept. physiology McGill U., Montreal, Que., Can., 1956-58; from neurophysiologist to dir., div. spl. mental health research NIMH, Washington, 1959-73; assoc. commr. research N.Y. State Dept. Mental Hygiene, Albany, 1973-77; assoc. dir. for research Nat. Inst. Alcohol Abuse, HHS, Bethesda, Md., 1977-84; prof. neurology and physiology Hahnemann U., Phila., 1984-85, vice provost for research affairs, 1984-85, chmn. dept. physiology, asst. v.p sci. affairs, 1986-94; clin. prof. psychiatry George Washington U., 1966-73. Contbr. articles to profl. jours. Recipient Superior Service award HEW, 1970 Fellow Am. Coll. Neuropsychopharmacology; mem. AAAS, Am. Physiol. Soc., Am. Soc. Pharmacology and Exptl. Therapeutics, Internat. Brain Research Orgn., Internat. Soc. Psychoneuroendocrinology, Am. Psychiat. Assn., Soc. Neurosci., Royal Soc. Medicine, Soc. Biol. Psychiat., Assn. Research Neurol. and Mental Disease, Research Soc. Alcoholism, Assn. Chmn. Dept. Physiology, Sci. Research Soc., Sigma Xi. Clubs: Cosmos (Washington). Home: 8216 Hamilton Spring Ct Bethesda MD 20817-2714

SALMON, EDWARD LLOYD, JR. bishop; b. Jan. 30, 1934; s. Edward Lloyd Sr. and Helen Bernice (Burley) S.; m. Louise Hack, 1972; children: Catherine, Edward III. BA, U. of the South, 1956; BD, Va. Theol. Seminary, 1960. Ordained to deaconate Episc. Ch., 1960, to priesthood, 1961. Vicar St. Andrew's Ch., Rogers, Ark., rector, 1963-68; vicar St. James Ch., Eureka Springs, Ark., St. Thomas Ch., Springdale, Grace Ch., Siloam Springs; assoc. St. Paul's Ch., Fayetteville, 1968, rector, 1968-78, Ch. St. Michael and St. George, St. Louis, 1978-90; elected bishop Diocese S.C., 1990—. Pres. province IV Episcopal Ch.; chmn. bd. dirs. Speak, Inc., The Anglican Digest, Voorhees Coll., Denmark, S.C.; trustee, regent Univ. of South; pres. Nashotah House Seminary; pres. Kanuga Confs., Inc.; chmn. Anglican Inst. Chmn. bd. trustees Voorhees Coll. Office: PO Box 20127 Charleston SC 29413-0127 E-mail: elsalmon@dioceseofsc.org.

SALMON, JOHN HEARSEY MCMILLAN, historian, educator; b. Thames, New Zealand, Dec. 2, 1925; came to U.S., 1969; s. John Hearsey and Elizabeth (McMillan) S. MA, U. New Zealand, 1951; M.Litt., Cambridge (Eng.) U., 1957; Litt.D., Victoria U., 1970. Prof. history U. New S. Wales, Sydney, Australia, 1960-65; prof. history, dean humanities U. Waikato, New Zealand, 1965-69; Marjorie Walter Goodhart prof. history Bryn Mawr Coll., 1969-91, prof. emeritus, 1991—. Author: The French Religious Wars in English Political Thought, 1959, A History of Goldmining in New Zealand, 1963, Cardinal de Retz, 1969, Society in Crisis - France in The 16th Century, 1975, Renaissance and Revolt: Essays in the Intellectual and Social History of Early Modern France, 1987, Ideas and Contexts in France and England from the Renaissance to the Romantics, 2000; editor: The French Wars of Religion, 1967; co-editor: Francogallia by François Hotman, 1972, Historians and Ideologues, 2001; translator: The Muskets of Gascony by Armand Daudeyos, 2000; contbr. to hist. jours. Fellow Royal Hist. Soc. Home: 1853 County Line Rd Villanova PA 19085-1729 E-mail: jsalmon@brynmawr.edu.

SALMON, JOSEPH THADDEUS, lawyer; b. Auburn, Ala., Nov. 13, 1927; s. William Davis and Helen (Bowman) S.; m. Mabel Marie Groves, July 7, 1951; children: Joseph Thaddeus Jr., Bruce Groves. BS, Auburn U., 1949; JD, U. Ala., 1951. Bar: Ala. 1951. Practice in, Montgomery, 1953-93; sec., gen. counsel Alfa Mut. Ins. Co., Alfa Mut. Fire Ins. Co., Alfa Mut. Gen. Ins. Co., Alfa Corp., Alfa Ins. Corp., Alfa Gen. Ins. Corp., Alfa Life Ins. Co.; ret., 1993. Served with USNR, 1946-47; to 1st lt. USAF, 1951-53. Mem. Internat. Assn. Def. Counsel, Ala. Def. Lawyers Assn., Montgomery County Bar Assn., Phi Alpha Delta, Kappa Sigma. Episcopalian. Home: 2731 Lansdowne Dr Montgomery AL 36111-1741

SALMON, MARGARET BELAIS, nutritionist, dietitian; b. N.Y.C. m. Douglas A. Salmon; children: Robert, Betty Lynn, Donald. BS in Food Chemistry, Dietetics and Nutrition, U. Calif., Berkeley, 1941; MS in Human Nutrition, Columbia U., 1964, MS in Sci. Nutrition, 1982. cert. Hosp. Dietetics, Duke U. Hosp., 1943; specialist Nutrition Edn., Columbia U., 1967. Clin. dietitian Columbia-Presbyn. Med. Ctr., N.Y.C., 1943-44, research dietitian, 1956-66; teaching and therapeutic dietitian Englewood (N.J.) Hosp., Hackensack (N.J.) Hosp. and Holy Name Hosp., 1954-57; adminstrv. and therapeutic dietitian St. Luke's Hosp. Ctr., N.Y.C., 1966-70; chief dietitian, dir. dietetic traineeship program St. Joseph's Hosp. and Med. Ctr., Paterson, N.J.,

1971-82; pres. Salmon Cons., Harrington Park, 1970—. Assoc. dir. dietary dept. Bronx (N.Y.)-Lebanon Hosp. Ctr., 1970-71; lectr. in field. Author: Soy Discoveries: Over 700 Quick Soy Recipes, 2001, Diabetic Diet Handbook, 1998, Food Facts for Teenagers, 1965, (with A. Colby) Physician's Diet Handbook, 1975, rev., 1978, The Joy of Breastfeeding, 1977, 2d rev. edit., 1979, Diabetic Diet Handbook, 1977, Dieta Diabetica Para Buena Salud, 1979, Diabetic Diet Handbook for Low Sodium Diets, 1980, Breast Milk: Nature's Perfect Formula, 1994, Soy Expressions: Common Sense Way to Small Food Bills, 1999, Soy Discoveries: Over 700 Quick Soy Recipes, 2001; editor: Enjoying Your Restricted Diet, 1972, St. Joseph's Hosp. & Med. Ctr. Diet Man., 1977, rev., 1981; contbr. Career Guidance for Young Women, 1974, Easy and Delicious Rice Flour Recipes, 1974, A Professional Dietitian's Natural Fiber Diet, 1987, La Alegria De Alimentacion A Pecho (Joy of Breastfeeding, in spanish), 1987; contbr. articles profl. books and jours.; numerous TV appearances. Mary Swarz Rose scholar, 1961. Mem. Am. Dietetic Assn., Pi Lambda Theta, Omicron Nu, Kappa Delta Pi. Home: 435 Lynn St Harrington Park NJ 07640-1131 Office: Salmon Cons 435 Lynn St Harrington Park NJ 07640-1131 E-mail: salmonhp@yahoo.com.

SALMON, MARLA E. nursing educator, dean; b. Vermillion, S.D., May 2, 1949; d. Everett Lloyd and Marceline Louise (Adamson) S.; m. Jerry Steven Anderson, Aug. 1, 1984; children: Jessica Louise White, Matthew Lawrence White. BA cum laude, U. Portland, 1971, BSN cum laude, 1972; MSN, 1999; ScD, Johns Hopkins U., 1977. Dir. patient advocacy program Johns Hopkins U., Balt., 1974-75, instr., 1975-78; asst. prof. U. Minn., Mpls., 1978-82, asst. dir. PRONA, 1978-79, acting dir. PRONA, 1978-80, dir. pub. health nursing programs, 1980-85, assoc. prof., 1982-86; prof. pub. health nursing, chmn. dept. U. N.C., Chapel Hill, 1986-92; dir. nursing div., Bureau Health Professions HHS, Rockville, 1991-97; prof., dean Grad. Sch. Nursing U. Pa., Phila., 1997-99, dir. grad. studies; dean, prof. Nell Hodgson Woodruff Sch. Nursing Emory U., 1999—. Mem. Presdl. Task Force Health Care Reform, Washington, 1993; U.S. del. World Health Orgn., Geneva, 1995; cons. in field. Co-editor News Outlook, 1989-91; contbr. articles to profl. jours. Fulbright scholar, 1972-73; W.K. Kellogg fellow, 1984-87, Reflective Leadership fellow, 1985-86; Rsch. grantee, 1975-78; recipient Recognition award Assn. State Territorial Dirs. of Nursing, 1993, Achievement award Nat. Black Nurses Found., 1994, Presdl. award for meritorious exec. The White House, 1995. Mem. ANA (v.p. coun. community health nursing, 1988—, task force credentialing 1989), Am. Acad. Nursing, Am. Pub. Health Assn., Am. Tae Kwon Do Assn., Nat. League Nursing, N.C. League Nursing, N.C. Pub. Health Assn., N.C. Nurses Assn., Assn. Community Health Nurses Educators, Women's Health Leadership Trust, Sigma Theta Tau, Sigma Xi, Delta Omega. Avocations: athletics, gardening. Office: Emory U Nell Hodgson Woodruff Sch 1520 Clifton Rd Ste 402 Atlanta GA 30322-4207

SALMON, MATT, former congressman, communications company executive; b. Salt Lake City, Jan. 21, 1958; s. Robert James and Gloria (Aagard) S.; m. Nancy Huish, June, 1979; children: Lara, Jacob, Katie, Matthew. BA in English Lit., Ariz. State U., 1981; MA in Pub. Adminstrn., Brigham Young U., 1986. Mgr. pub. affairs U.S. West, Phoenix, 1988-94; mem. Ariz. State Senate, Mesa, 1990-94, U.S. Congress from 1st Ariz. dist., Washington, 1995-2001; mem. internat. rels. and sci. coms., asst. major whip; exec. v.p. APCO Worldwide, Scottsdale, Ariz., 2001—. Bd. dirs. Mesa United Way, 1990—, Ariz. Sci. Mus., 1992—. Recipient Outstanding Svc. award Ariz. Citizens with Disabilities, 1991, Excellence in Govt. award Tempe Ctr. for Handicapped, 1992; named Outstanding Young Phoenician, Phelps Dodge/Phoenix Jaycees, 1990, Outstanding Legislator, Mesa United Way, 1991. Republican. Mem. Lds Ch. Avocations: tennis, racquetball, cycling. Office: APCO Worldwide 6991 E Camelback Rd Ste D216 Scottsdale AZ 85251*

SALMON, MERLYN LEIGH, laboratory executive; b. Macksville, Kans., June 24, 1924; s. Kenneth Elbert and Inez Melba (Prose) S.; m. Flora Charlotte Sievers, Mar. 20, 1948; children: Charla Lee, Merlyn Leigh. BS, U. Denver, 1951, MS, U. Denver, 1952. Rsch. engr. Denver Rsch. Inst., U. Denver, 1951-56; owner-operator Fluo-X-Spec Lab., Denver, 1956-92; ret., 1992. Cons. in field. Contbr. articles to profl. jours. With AUS, 1943-45, 45-47. Mem. Am. Chem. Soc., Am. Soc. Metals, Sigma Xi, Tau Beta Pi, Phi Lambda Upsilon, Omicron Delta Kappa. Democrat. Address: 718 Sherman St Denver CO 80203-3511 E-mail: salmonm@webtv.net.

SALMON, RAPHAEL JACK, urban studies and public policy educator; b. Jerusalem, Jan. 29, 1931; came to U.S., 1949; s. Israel and Malka (deToledo) S.; divorced; children: Ron, Daniel, Tamar. BSc, Utah State Coll., 1953; MSPH, U. N.C., 1955; PhD in Health Edn., U. Md., 1970. prof. of Health Adminstrn. Ben-Gurion U., Ber-Sheba, Israel, 1972—. Civil engr. Metro. Engrng. Co., Salt Lake City, 1952-54; pub. health engr., economist Dept. Agrl., Israel, 1954-56, U.S. Dept. Health Edn. Welfare, Washington, 1958-60; exec. dir. Seaboard Z.Y. Commn., 1959-62; studies for Pres. Kennedy Nat. Acad. Sci., Washington, D.C., 1962-63; head dept. rsch., health and cmty. devel. No. Mich. U., Marquette, 1962-64; sr. rsch. analyst, economist Rsch. Triangle Inst., Durham, N.C., 1964-66; sr. economist, engr. Battelle Meml. Inst., Columbus, Ohio, 1966-68; dir. health and rehab. svcs., policy analysis and planning Health Edn. and Welfare, Washington, 1968-72; dir. planning and evaluation Nat. Acad. Scis., Brd. of Medicine, Washington, D.C., 1970-72; prof. urban studies and pub. policy Rutgers State U. of N.J., Moorestown, 1970—. Dir. planning and evalution Nat. Acad. Sch., Bd. Medicine, Washington, 1970-72. Contbr. 87 articles to profl. jours., author "Water; Social and Economic Aspects of Natural Resources," Fellow APHA (life), AAAS (life); mem. NEA, AAUP, IEEE (sr. mem.), Ops. Rsch. Soc. Am. (sr. mem.), Internat. Health Econ. and Mgmt. Inst., N.Y. Acad. Scis., Am. Econ. Assn., Am. Chem. Soc., Am. Water Works Assn., Nat. Cmty. Devel. Assn., Adult Edn. Assn. Home: 1919 Chestnut St Apt 2314 Philadelphia PA 19103-3441

SALMON, THOMAS PAUL, lawyer, academic administrator; b. Cleve. , Aug. 19, 1932; s. Thomas Aloysius and Lucy Moylan (Conlon) S.; m. Madeleine Salmon, Aug. 16, 1958 (div. 1983); children: Marguerite M., Anne Marie, Thomas M., Caroline M.; m. Susan J. Bisson, 1984. AB in History and Govt., Boston Coll., 1954, JD, 1957, hon. degree, 1975; LLM in Taxation, NYU, 1958; hon. degree, U. Vt., Burlington, 1980. Bar: Vt. Clk. Ryan, Smith and Carbine, Rutland, Vt., 1958-59; assoc. Robert J. Crotty, Bellows Falls, 1959; pvt. practice, 1960-72; gov. State of Vt., Montpelier, 1973-77; sr. ptnr. Salmon & Nostrand, Bellows Falls, 1977-91; interim pres. U. Vt., Burlington, 1991-93, pres., 1993—. Judge Mcpl. Ct., Bellows Falls, 1963-65; chmn. bd. dirs. Green Mountain Power Corp., Burlington; bd. dirs. Vt. Electric Co., Rutland, Banknorth Group, Burlington, Union Mut. Life Ins. Co., Montpelier, Ctrl. Vt. Railroad, St. Albans; chmn. Jud. Conduct Bd., Montpelier, 1984-88. Mem. Vt. Ho. of Reps., 1965-70, minority leader, 1969-71. Mem. AMA, Vt. Bar Assn., Windham County Bar Assn. Office: Green Mountain Power 163 Acorn Ln Colchester VT 05446

SALMON, WILLIAM COOPER, mechanical engineer, engineering academy executive; b. N.Y.C., Sept. 3, 1935; s. Chenery and Mary (Cooper) S.; m. Josephine Stone, Sept. 16, 1967; children: William Cooper, Mary Bradford, Pauline Alexandra. SB in Mech. Engring., MIT, 1957, SM in Mech. Engring., 1958, Mech. Engr., 1959, SM in Mgmt. Sci., 1969. Registered profl. engr., Mass. Research and teaching asst. MIT, Cambridge, 1957-59; sr. engr. Microtech, 1959-60; 1st lt. U.S. Army Ord. C., Aberdeen, Md., 1960; asst. sci. advisor U.S. Dept. State, Washington, 1961-74, sr. advisor for sci. and tech., 1978-86; counselor for sci. and tech. Am. embassy, Paris, 1974-78; exec. officer Nat. Acad. Engring., Washington, 1986-99, exec. officer emeritus, advisor to pres., 1999—2001; sec., treas. Internat. Coun. Acad. Engring. and Technol. Scis., Inc., 2000—. Recipient Superior Honor award Dept. State, 1984, Meritorious Svc. award Pres. U.S., 1968, Kenneth A. Roe award Am. Assn. Engring. Socs., 1996; Sloan fellow MIT, 1969. Fellow: ASME; mem.: NSPE, Am. Soc. Engring. Edn., Jr. Engring. Tech. Soc. (pres. 1998—2001), Soc. Colonial Wars, Cosmos Club, Masons. Episcopalian. Home and Office: 3601 N Peary St Arlington VA 22207-5345 E-mail: wsalmon@nae.edu., caets@nae.edu.

SALMONSON, MARTY LEE, stockbroker, consulting engineer; b. Wellsville, N.Y., Sept. 23, 1946; s. John William and Alice May (Olson) S.; Gail White, Sept. 17, 1971; children: René, Marci. AS in Engring. Sci., SUNY, Alfred, 1970; postgrad., SUNY, Buffalo, 1971; BS in Sci. and Bus. Mgmt., Empire State Coll., 1979. Engr. Dresser-Rand, Olean, N.Y., 1974-90, Petro-Marine, Gretna, La., 1990-91; stockbroker Franklin Lord, Scottsdale, Ariz., 1992, Charles Schwab, Phoenix, 1993—. Cons. engr., Phoenix, 1994—. With U.S. Army, 1967-69, Vietnam. Mem. NSPE, ASME, VFW, Moose, Elks. Episcopalian. Achievements include development of state of the art programs for centrifugal compressors. Home: PO Box 26601 Phoenix AZ 85068-6601

SALNY, ABBIE FEINSTEIN, psychologist; b. N.Y.C., July 3, 1926; d. Carl and Edith (Cooperman) Feinstein; m. Jerome E. Salny, July 12, 1973. BA, NYU, 1949; MA, Montclair State U., 1953; EdD, Rutgers U., 1966. Lic. psychologist, N.J.; diplomate Am. bd. Profl. Psychology. Sch. psychologist Bd. of Edn., Parsippany, N.J., 1959-66; prof., dep. chair, acting chair psychology dept. Montclair State U., 1966-79; supervisory psychologist Am. and Internat. Mensa, 1979—; trustee Mensa Edn. and Rsch. Found., 1971-96. Chmn. scholarship com. Mensa Edn. and Rsch. Found., 1973-82, dir. sci. and edn. Am. Mensa com., 1983-87, dir. rsch. rev. com., 1984-88. Co-author: Mensa Genius Quiz Book, 1981, Mensa Genius Quiz Book II, 1983, Mensa Think Smart Book, 1985; author: Quiz-A-Day Book, 1986, Book of Literary Quizzes, 1988, Page-A-Day Puzzle Calendar, 1995—, others; contbr. articles to profl. jours. Fellow Am. Acad. of Sch. Psychologists; mem. Am. Psychol. Assn., N.J. Psychol. Assn., British Psychol. Soc., Am. Soc. of Journalists and Authors, Am. Mensa Ltd. Avocation: travel, cooking. Home and Office: 407 Breckenridge Wayne NJ 07470-4072

SALO, ANN SEXTON DISTLER, lawyer; b. Indpls., Sept. 2, 1947; d. Harry W. and Ann (Malloy) Distler; m. Donald R. Salo, June 3, 1972 (div. Feb. 1983); 1 child, Eric V. Salo; m. Phillip G. Clark, May 5, 1990; children: Ann Potter Clark, Philip Gray Clark. BA, Purdue U., 1969; JD, George Washington U., 1972; LLM in Taxation, Emory U., 1976. Bar: Ga. 1973, U.S. Dist. Ct. (no. dist.) Ga. 1974. Assoc. Hansell & Post, Atlanta, 1972-78, mng. ptnr., 1978-89; ptnr. Grenwald and Salo, 1989-92, Long, Aldridge & Norman, Atlanta, 1992-95, Salo & Walker, Atlanta, 1995—. Adj. prof. law Emory U., 1983-86; mem. fin. planning adv. bd. Warren Gorham & Lamont, 1988-2000. Author: Estate Planning, 1988. Bd. dirs. Auditory Edn. Ctr., Atlanta, 1987-93, 98-2001; pres. Planned Parenthood of Atlanta, 1984-86; pres. Atlanta Humane Soc., 1990-93. Fellow Am. Coll. Trust and Estate Counsel (state chair 2001—); mem. Atlanta Estate Planning Coun., Atlanta Tax Forum. Office: Salo & Walker 2968 Lookout Pl NE Atlanta GA 30305-3272 E-mail: adsalo@bellsouth.net.

SALO, HARRY A. health care executive; b. Rahway, N.J., Jan. 27, 1944; s. E. Arthur and Nina (Hill) S.; m. Karen Waugh, Sept. 7, 1964 (div. 1972); 1 child, Jannine; m. Carol Ann Vath, Mar. 17, 1973; children: Jessica, Adam. BA, Cornell U., 1967; MA, Barry U., 1969, MA, 1974; postgrad., Columbia U., 1974, NYU, 1974-75. Tchr. Miami (Fla.) Country Day Sch., 1967-69, Fairfield (Conn.) Country Day Sch., 1968-74; MA Barry U., 1969; dir. admissions Fairfield (Conn.) Country Day Sch., 1972-74; adminstr. Med. Pers. Pool, Cin., 1975-77; v.p. Salo Inc., 1977-79; v.p., founder T.S.O. Mgmt. Corp., Media, Pa., 1979-84, pres., 1984-90, chmn., 1990—. Chmn. bd. dirs. Ind. Franchise Assn., San Francisco; mem. Owners Adv. Coun., Ft. Lauderdale, Fla., 1981-82, chmn., 1993-95. Bd. dirs. Women Against Rape, Delaware County, Pa., 1985-88; mem. leadership group, exec. dir.'s adv. coun. Amnesty Internat., N.Y.C., 1989—; leadership group Oxfam Am., N.Y.C., 1991—, internat. rescue com., 1992—, so. policy law ctr., 1993—. Home: PO Box 1324 East Dennis MA 02641-1324

SALOM, ROBERTO, financial executive; b. Bogota, Colombia, July 12, 1944; came to U.S., 1966; m. Estell Kathleen Millard; children: David Andres, Robert W.A. Student, U. Andes, Bogota, 1965; BS, San Francisco State U., 1969, MBA, 1972; postgrad., U. Calif., Berkeley, 1973; PhD in Econs., NYU, 1977. Rsch. assoc. Fed. Res. Bank San Francisco, 1968-70, fin. analyst, 1970-73; mem. staff UN Devel. Program/Fund for Population Activities, N.Y.C., 1973-82, dep. chief program planning, 1982-83, dep. chief fin. br., 1983-87, chief fin. br., 1987-94; sr. officer UN Adv. Com. on Adminstrv. and Budgetary Questions, 1995—. Presenter seminars in field. Home: 5 Elmwood Ave Rye NY 10580-3401 Office: United Nations UN Plaza New York NY 10017 E-mail: salom@un.org.

SALOMETO, PETER JAMES MORGAN, marketing consultant, lawyer; b. Garden City, N.Y., May 11, 1944; s. Peter James and Ann Rita (Skelly) S. AB, U. Pa., 1965; JD, St. Louis U., 1972. Bar: Mo. 1973, N.Y. 1982. Asst. gen. counsel Mass. Indemnity & Life, Clayton, Mo., 1973-77; sr. atty. Allstate Life Ins. Co., Northbrook, Ill., 1977; asst. gen. counsel MONY, N.Y.C., 1977-81; mktg. mgr. PW Comm., Secaucus, N.J., 1983-85, Avon Books, Hearst Corp., N.Y.C., 1985-86; v.p. mktg. McGraw-Hill, Inc., 1986-93; mng. ptnr. Peter J. Salometo & Assocs., N.Y.C., Phila., 1994—. Campaign dir. Funsch for Congress, St. Louis, 1972; chmn. Clayton Twp. Citizens for Reagan, Mo., 1976; alt. del. Rep. Nat. Convention, Kansas City, Mo., 1976; bd. dirs. Clayton Twp. Rep. Club, 1977; campaign mgr. Chase for Congress, St. Louis County, 1978; vol. Green for Congress, N.Y.C., 1978-92, Millard for City Coun., N.Y.C., 1991-93; Rep. committeman 8th ward City of Phila., 1998—. With U.S. Army, 1965-67, Vietnam. Recipient award of Appreciation, Leukemia Soc. Am., N.Y.C., 1990, Excellence in Leadership award Liberty Edn. Fund, 2000. Mem. Log Cabin Rep. Club Phila. (bd. dirs. 1997-2000, v.p. 1998-2000). Presbyterian. Avocations: travel, music, film, theater. Home: 1900 Rittenhouse Sq Philadelphia PA 19103-5767

SALOMON, DARRELL JOSEPH, lawyer; b. Feb. 16, 1939; s. Joseph and Rosalie Rita (Pool) S.; m. Christine Mariscal, Apr. 25, 1992; 1 child, Camilla Lind. Student, Georgetown U., 1957-59; BS, U. San Francisco, 1964, JD, 1966. Bar: Calif. 1970, U.S. Dist. Ct. (cen. and no. dists.) Calif. 1970, U.S. Supreme Ct. 1971. Assoc. Offices of Joseph L. Alioto, San Francisco, 1970, 72, 73; dep. city atty. City of San Francisco, 1972; pvt. prac., 1973—84; ptnr. Hill, Farrer & Burrill, L.A., 1984-87, Arter & Hadden, L.A., 1987-94; dir. of litigation Keck, Mahin & Cate, San Francisco, 1994-96; chmn. Commerce Law Group A Profl. Corp., 1996-99; chief asst. dist. atty. City of San Francisco, 2000; gen. counsel San Francisco Examiner, 2000—. Lectr. law Santa Clara U. Mem. Human Rights Commn. City and County of San Francisco, 1975; mem., past pres. Civil Svc. Commn., San Francisco, 1976-84; trustee San Francisco War Meml. and Performing Arts Ctr., 1984-88; bd. dirs. L.A. Symphony Master Chorale, 1985-87, Marin Symphony Assn., 1995-97. Recipient Disting. Svc. citation United Negro Coll. Fund, 1975; D'alton-Power scholar Georgetown U., 1957. Mem. ABA, Consumer Attys. of Calif. (bd. govs. 1977), Soc. Calif. Pioneers, Chit Chat Club, San Francisco Lawyers Club. Office: 988 Market St San Francisco CA 94102-4002 E-mail: dsalomon@s.f.examiner.com.

SALOMON, ELIZABETH LOWENSTEIN, social worker; b. Atlanta, Aug. 8, 1924; d. Max M. Lowenstein and Elizabeth (Wolf) Burak; m. Roger B. Salomon, June 14, 1950; children: Pamela Zuban, Wendy Salomon. BS, Northwestern U., 1945; postgrad., Simmons Sch. of S.W., 1949-50; MSW, U. Calif., Berkeley, 1951; cert. in child therapy, Smith Coll. Sch. Social Work, 1982. Lic. ind. social worker. Caseworker Jewish Family Svc. Assn., Cleve., 1967-72; cons. Community United Headstart, 1970-72; caseworker Child Study Ctr., Cleve. Met. Gen. Hosp., Cleve., 1974-78; chief social worker Dept. Ob-gyn., Univ. Hosps., 1979-81; caseworker, child therapist Parkview Therapeutic Pre-Sch., 1981-83; child therapist, adoption worker Bellfaire, Jewish Children's Bur., 1981-83, 84-87; cons. Bellflower Ctr. for Prevention of Child Abuse, 1987-89, Murtis Taylor Multi-Purpose Ctr., Cleve., 1989-2001; child therapist Cath. Social Svcs. of Cleve., 1991—2001; cons. Early Learning Ctr. Westside Ecumenical Ministry, Cleve., 2001—. Adj. instr. Mandel Sch. for Applied Social Scis., Cleve., 1988, 89; adj. instr. adult degree program Capital U., 1991-92, instr. master cert. program Mondel Sch. for Applied Social Sci., 1990; visitor Hampstead Child Therapy Clinic, London, 1972-78; invitational visit to People's Republic of China, 1988. Contbr. articles to profl. jours. Field supr. ACLU, Cleve., 1991; bd. trustees Groundworks Dance Theatre, 1998—. Mem. Ohio Soc. for Clin. Social Work (program chair 1982-83, v.p. 1983-84, chair symposium com. 1984-85, newsletter editor 1988-89, co-chair seminar com. 1991-92, 95-96), Cleve. Clin. Social Work Soc. (bd. dirs. 1982—). Democrat. Home: 2830 Coventry Rd Shaker Heights OH 44120-2231

SALOMON, FRANK ERNEST, classical music administrator; b. N.Y.C., Apr. 2, 1936; s. Albert and Anna Theresa (Lobbenberg) S.; m. Martha Laredo, June 1, 1961; children: Lisa Ana, Yana Elena. Student, NYU, N.Y.C., 1953-58. Asst. mgr. Symphony of the Air, N.Y.C., 1959-61; adminstrv. dir. New Sch. Concerts, 1959—; founder N.Y. String Orch. Seminar, 1969—; co-adminstr. Marlboro (Vt.) Music Sch. Festival, 1960—; mgr. Peoples' Symphony Concerts, N.Y.C., 1972—; pres. Frank Salomon Assocs., 1968—, Internat. Arts Found., N.Y.C., 1990—. Cons. Tokyo Opera City, 1995-98, Pablo Casals Hall, Tokyo, 1986-87; co-chair music panel, profl. tng. Nat. Endowment for Arts, Washington, 1970's-80's. Mgr. 1st U.S. tours Sir Simon Rattle City of Birmingham (Eng.) Symphony Orch., 1988, Sergiu Celibidache Munich Philharmonic, 1989, John Adams Ensemble Modern, Frankfurt, Germany, 1996, 1st inter-disciplinary project in conjunction with Orch. Tour Sir Simon Rattle CBSO, 1992. With N.Y. Nat. Guard, 1955-59. Mem. Assn. Performing Arts Profls., Internat. Soc. Performing Arts (Patrick Hayes award 2000), Nat. Assn. Performing Arts Profls. Office: 201 W 54th St Apt 1C New York NY 10019-5520 E-mail: salomonf@aol.com., frank@franksalomon.com.

SALOMON, LUCY, psychiatrist, educator; b. Zagreb, Yugoslavia, Jan. 25, 1925; came to U.S., 1950; d. Kornel and Jolanda (Schlesinger) Tarjan; m. Salomon M. Salomon, Feb. 4, 1950; children: Ronald M., Gary D., Melinda S. BS, Beloit Coll., 1962; MD, U. Wis., 1968. Diplomate Am. Bd. Psychiatry and Neurology, 1978. Rsch. assoc. in hematology and blood coagulation Tufts U.-New Eng. Med. Ctr., Boston, 1950-54; intern Madison (Wis.) Hosp., 1968-69; resident in psychiatry McLean Hosp., Belmont, Mass., 1969-71, fellow in psychiatry, 1969-72, assoc. attending psychiatrist, 1972-88, attending psychiatrist, 1989-96; resident in psychiatry Beth Israel Hosp., Boston, 1971-72; pvt. practice Brookline, Mass., 1972-95, Nantucket, 1992—. Clin. instr. psychiatry Harvard U. Med. Sch., Boston, 1972-96. Contbr. numerous articles on hematology and psychiatry to med. jours. Mem. Am. Psychiat. Assn., AMA. Address: PO Box 3368 Nantucket MA 02584-3368

SALOMON, MARILYN, batik artist; b. Ann Arbor, Mich., Jan. 30, 1943; d. William Iane and Sarah Sheon; m. Charles Sam. Salomon, Dec. 22, 1962; children: Teri(dec.) , Alicia, Cliff. BA, UCLA, 1965; postgrad., Calif. State U., Northridge, 1969-70, 88, Miriam Ariav, Israel, 1970. Elem. edn. tchr., Simi Valley, Calif., 1966-69; artist, 1970—. Guest lectr. on double layer techniques Internat. Batik Conf., Ghent, Belgium, 1999; asst. art curator mus. show, Lancaster, Calif., 1993; leader workshop Surface Designer Nat. Conf., Calif. State U., Northridge, 1988; represented by Horizon Fine Arts, Jackson, Wyo., Full Moon-Morro Bay, Calif., Feats of Clay, Idyllwild, Calif.; invited participant Internat. Batik Exhibit, Cologne, Germany, 2002, Ryman Found. show, 2000-02; lectr. in field; subject of TV interview Process of Batik, 2001. One-woman shows include Ranch House, Ojai, Calif., 1975-78, Gallerie 507, Carlsbad, Calif., 1984, Sun West Gallery, Prescott, Ariz., 1986, Art Beat Gallery, Agoura, Calif., 1987, Jewish Cmty. Ctr., Long Beach, Calif., 1985; exhibited in group shows at Cygnet Gallery, Santa Rosa, Calif., 1981, Jewish Fedn. Bldg., Olympic Exhbn., L.A., 1984, La Quinta Arts Found., 1985-91, Thousand Oaks Mus. Juried Show, 1988, 89 (1st pl. award 1988, purchase award 1989), Calif. Luth. U., 1989, Nat. Mus. History, Santa Barbara, Calif., 1990, City of La Quinta, 1991 (purchase award), Lancaster Mus., 1992, 93, 98, Conejo Valley Mus., 1992 (2d pl. award), Riverside Mus. Art, 1998, Walt Disney Ryman Found., Burbank, Calif., featured artist, 1997, 98, 99, Horizen Fine Arts, Jackson, 2002; represented in permanent collections City of Tempe, City of Thousand Oaks, City of La Quinta, Taft Entertainment, 1983, Cancer Inst. Ariz., 1983; featured in TV interview KTVK, Ariz., 2000; works appear in Batik for Artists & Quliters, 2000. Workshop leader Surface Designer's Nat. Conf., Calif. State U., Northridge, 1988; studio home tour Westlake Art Guild, Calif., 1989, Pan Hellenic Home Tour Riverside featured Salomon's Art, 1986. Recipient purchase award City of Tempe, Ariz., 1983, City of Thousand Oaks, Calif., 1989, City of La Quinta, 1991. Mem. (elected charter mem.) Women's Nat. Mus., Phoenix Art Mus. Avocations: hiking, yoga, reading, music. Home: HC 2 Box 261D Payson AZ 85541-9418

SALOMON, ROGER BLAINE, English language educator; b. Providence, Feb. 26, 1928; s. Henry and Lucia Angell (Capewell) S.; m. Elizabeth Helen Lowenstein, June 14, 1950; children— Pamela, Wendy. BA, Harvard, 1950; MA, U. Calif. at Berkeley, 1951, PhD, 1957. Instr. Mills Coll., Oakland, Calif., 1955-57; instr., then asst. prof. Yale U., New Haven, 1957-66; mem. faculty Case Western Res. U., Cleve., 1966—, prof. English, 1969—, Oviatt prof. English, 1990, chmn. dept., 1974-80, part-time prof. English, 1994-99; Oviatt prof. English emeritus, 1999—. Mem. adv. screening com. Am. lit. Sr. Fulbright-Hayes Program, 1973-76, chmn., 1975; mem. grants-in-aid selection com. Am. Council Learned Socs., 1976-78 Author: Twain and the Image of History, 1961, Desperate Storytelling: Post-Romantic Elaborations of the Mock-Heroic Mode, 1987, Images of the Serpent: An Anatomy of Horror Narrative, 2002. Served to 1st lt. USAF, 1952-53. Morse fellow, 1960-61; Guggenheim fellow, 1972-73 Mem. AAUP, MLA. Home: 2830 Coventry Rd Cleveland OH 44120-2231 Office: Case Western Reserve U Dept English Cleveland OH 44106

SALOMONE, JEFFREY PAUL, surgeon, educator; b. Reno, Dec. 6, 1961; s. Joseph Anthony and Peggy Ruth (Crompton) S. BS, U. Nev., 1983, MD, 1990. Diplomate Am. Bd. Surgery; cert. surg. critical care. Resident Tulane U. Med. Ctr., New Orleans, 1990-95, fellow in critical care, 1995-96; asst. prof. Emory U., Atlanta, 1996—2001, assoc. prof., 2001—. Cons. Nat. Registry of EMTs, Columbus, Ohio, 1996—. Fellow ACS; mem. AMA, Nat. Assn. Emergency Med. Svcs. Physicians, Am. Assn. for the History of Medicine, Soc. for Critical Care Medicine, Phi Kappa Phi. Avocations: gourmet cooking, photography, theater. Office: Emory U Dept Surgery TK Glenn Bldg Rm 312A 69 Butler St SE Atlanta GA 30303-3033

SALONER, GARTH, management educator; b. Johannesburg, South Africa, Jan. 18, 1955; came to U.S. 1978; s. Max and Rachel (Aronovitz) S.; m. Marlene Shoolman, Dec. 26, 1978; children: Amber, Romy, Kim. BCom, U. Witwatersrand, S. Africa, 1976; MBA, U. Witwatersrand, 1977; MS in Statistics, Stanford U., 1981, MA in Econs., PhD, 1982. Asst. lectr. U. Witwatersrand, 1977-78; asst. prof. econs. MIT, Cambridge, 1982-86, assoc. prof. econs. and mgmt., 1986-89, prof., 1990; vis. assoc. prof. bus. adminstrn. Harvard Bus. Sch., Boston, 1989-90; vis. assoc. prof. Stanford (Calif.) U., 1986-87, prof. strategic mgmt. and econs. Grad. Sch. Bus., 1990—, Robert A Magowan prof., 1993-99, dir. rsch. and curriculum devel., 1993-96, assoc. dean for acad. affairs, 1994-96, co-dir. Ctr. Elec. Bus. & Commerce, 1999—, Jeffrey S. Skoll prof., 2000—. Bd. dirs. Brilliant Digital Entertainment, Next Stage Entertainment, Quick Response Svcs., Inc., Synthean, Aplia, Covisint; rsch. assoc. Nat. Bur. Econ. Rsch., 1991—; mem. adv. bd. Voxeo, Talkie, eOneGlobal. Author: Strategic Management, 2001; assoc. editor Rand Jour. Econs., 1986-88, co-editor, 1988-95; assoc. editor Internat. Jour. Indsl. Orgn., 1988-95, Econs. of Innovation and New Tech., 1988-95, Strategic Mgmt. Jour., 1991-94; contbr. articles to profl. jours. Nat. fellow, Hoover Inst., 1986-87, Sloan fellow, 1987-89; grantee, NSF, 1982, 85, 88. Mem. Am. Econ. Assn., Acad. Mgmt. Jewish. Avocations: bicycling, photography. Home: 4151 Amaranta Ave Palo Alto CA 94306-3903 Office: Stanford U Grad Sch Bus Stanford CA 94305

SALOOM, JOSEPH A., III, diplomat; b. Urbana, Ill., Apr. 8, 1948; s. Joseph A. and Barbara (Bombard) S.; m. Anne Elizabeth Mayer, Jan. 22, 1972; children: Elizabeth, Shahin, Ilyas. BA in Econs., Georgetown U., 1970; MS, MIT, 1973. Joined Fgn. Svc.; comml. officer AM. Consulate Gen., Dusseldorf, Germany, 1974-76; econ. officer Am. Embassy, Rabat, Morocco, 1976-78, fin. economist Jidda, Saudi Arabia, 1978-80, econ. counselor Kinshasa, Zaire, 1983-87, dep. chief mission Niamey, Niger, 1987-90, U.S. amb. to Guinea Conakry, Guinea, 1993-96; transp. economist Dept. State, Washington, 1980-83, dir. office monetary affairs, 1990-91, dep. asst. sec., 1991-93, dir. econ. policy African-Affairs bureau, 1996-97; min.-counselor for econ. affairs Am. Embassy, Berlin, 1997—2001; sr. examiner Bd. of Examiners, Alexandria, Va., 2001—. Home: 6104 Fort Hunt Rd Alexandria VA 22307 E-mail: saloomja@state.gov.

SALOOM, KALISTE JOSEPH, JR. lawyer, retired judge; b. Lafayette, La., May 15, 1918; s. Kaliste and Asma Ann (Boustany) S.; m. Yvonne Adelle Nassar, Oct. 19, 1958; children: Kaliste III, Douglas James, Leanne Isabelle, Gregory John. BA with high distinction, U. La., 1939; JD, Tulane U., 1942. Bar: La. 1942. Atty. City of Lafayette, 1948—52; judge City and Juvenile Ct., Lafayette, 1952—93; ret., 1993; of counsel Saloom & Saloom, Lafayette, 1993—; Eniment Scholar endowed chair in polit. sci. U. La., 2001. Mem. jud. coun. La. Supreme Ct., 1960-64; bd. dirs. Nat. Ctr. for State Cts., Williamsburg, Va., 1978-84, adv. coun., 1984—, mem. assocs. com., 1986—; judge pro tempore La. Ct. Appeal 3d Cir., 1992; tech. adviser Jud. Adminstrn. of Traffic Cts. mem. adv. com. Nat. Hwy. Traffic Safety Adminstrn., U.S. Dept. Transp., 1977-80, Nat. Com. on Uniform Traffic Laws, 1986; mem. expert panel Drunk Driving Protection Act U.S. Congress, 1989-91. Mem. editl. bd. Tulane Law Rev., 1941; contbr. articles to profl. jours. Active Boy Scouts Am., Evangeline Area coun. With U.S. Army, 1942-45. Recipient Civic Cup, City of Lafayette, 1965, Pub. Svc. award U.S. Dept. Transp., 1980, Disting. Jurist award Miss. State U. Pre-Law Soc., 1987, Disting. Svc. award Nat. Ctr. State Cts., 1988, Disting. La. Jurist award La. State Bar Found., 1992, U.S. Supreme Ct. Chief Justice Warren E. Burger Soc. award, 1999. Mem. ABA (Benjamin Flaschner award 1981, vice chair JAD com. on traffic ct. program 1989-2002), Am. Judges Assn. (William H. Burnett award 1982), Nat. Coun. Juvenile Ct. Judges, La. City Judges Assn. (past pres., panel drafting La. children's code 1989-91), La. Juvenile Ct. Judges Assn. (past pres.), Order of Coif, Equestrian Order of Holy Sepulchre (knight comdr.), Oakbourne Country Club, Rotary (Paul Harris fellow), KC. Democrat. Roman Catholic. Home: 502 Marguerite Blvd Lafayette LA 70503-3138 Office: 211 W Main St Lafayette LA 70501-6843

SALOSCHIN, ROBERT L. lawyer; b. N.Y.C., Jan. 15, 1920; s. Bruno Benedix and Edna Saloschin; m. Neita L. Saloschin, Dec. 10, 1949; children: Mary Ann, Joan Janelle. BA, Columbia Coll., 1940; JD, Columbia Law Sch., 1947. Bar: N.Y. 1947, D.C. 1960, Md. 1980, U.S. Supreme Ct. 1956. Pers. adminstr. USN, Washington, 1941-43; atty. Cahill, Gordon, Reindel, N.Y.C., 1947-49, Housing & Home Fin. Agy., Washington, 1950-52, Civil Aeronautics Bd., Washington, 1952-58; atty. Office of Legal Counsel, dir. Office Info. Law U.S. Dept. Justice, 1958-81; of counsel Lerch Early & Brewer, Bethesda, Md., 1981—. Cons. standing com. on law and nat. security ABA, Washington, 1981-91; developed legal strategy for ending racial segregation in interstate bus transp., ICC; mediator for Am. athletics orgns. Olympic Games. Patentee air navigation device; editor: A Short Guide to the Freedom of Information Act, annually, 1974—; editor law rev. Columbia Law Sch., 1947. Organizer, pres. Citizens for Quality Civilization, Inc., Bethesda, 1990—; pres. West Fernwood Citizens Assn., Bethesda, 1962-65; officer North Bethesda Congress of Citizens Assocs., Bethesda, 1965-75. Lt. comdr. USN, WWII. Decorated Air medal with oak leaf cluster. Mem. Ret. Officers Assn., Herring Bay Yacht Club, Phi Beta Kappa. Avocations: coastal cruising, flying, reading, bridge, lecturing in schools. Home: 6603 Lone Oak Dr Bethesda MD 20817-1649

SALOVEY, PETER, psychology educator; b. Cambridge, Mass., Feb. 21, 1958; s. Ronald and Elaine Y. (Gross) S.; m. Marta Elisa Moret, June 15, 1986. BA in Psychology, MA in Sociology, Stanford U., 1980; PhD in Psychology, Yale U., 1986, MS in Psychology, 1983, MPhil in Psychology, 1984. Lic. psychologist, Conn. Asst. prof. Yale U., New Haven, 1986-90, assoc. prof., 1990-95, prof. psychology, epidemiology and pub. health, 1995—, chmn. dept. psychology, 2000—, Chris Argyris prof. psychology, 2001—. Cons. psychologist West Haven (Conn.) VA Med. Ctr., 1986—; dep. dir. Ctr. for Interdisciplinary Rsch. on AIDS, 1997—; mem. NSF Social Psychology Adv. Com., 1994-97; mem. NIMH Nat. Adv. Mental Health Coun. Behavioral Sci. Task Force, 2000. Author: Peer Counseling, 1983, The Remembered Self, 1993, Psychology, 1993; editor: Judgement and Inference in Clin. Psychology, 1988, The Psychology of Jealousy and Envy, 1991, Emotional Development and Emotional Intelligence, 1997, At Play in the Fields of Consciousness, 1999, The Wisdom in Feeling: Psychological Processes in Emotional Intelligence, 2002; editor: Rev. of Gen. Psychology, 1996-2002; assoc. editor Psychol. Bull., 1991-96, Emotion, 2000-2002; contbr. articles to profl. jours. Named Presidential Young Investigator, NSF, Washington, 1990. Fellow APA, Am. Psychol. Soc., Internat. Soc. for Rsch. on Emotion (treas. 1992-96, pres.-elect 2003), Soc. for Gen. Psychology, Phi Beta Kappa, Sigma Xi. Democrat. Jewish. Achievements include rsch. on psychological consequences of the arousal of mood and emotion, emotional intelligence, and motivators of health-protective behaviors, especially those relevant to the prevention of cancer and HIV/AIDS. Office: Yale U Dept Psychology 2 Hillhouse Ave New Haven CT 06511-6814 E-mail: peter.salovey@yale.edu.

SALOW, CYNTHIA LOUISE, legal assistant, paralegal, poet; b. Manchester, Iowa, Jan. 2, 1955; d. Clarence John Salow and Iris Marcheta (Grigg) McElmeel; children: Lea Ament, Jason Halfhill, Jessie Sage, Annie Sage. Legal sec. diploma, Kirkwood C.C., Cedar Rapids, Iowa, 1982. Paralegal, legal asst. Tom Riley Law Firm, LLC, Cedar Rapids, 1982-97; litigation sec. Lombardo & Gilles, Salinas, Calif., 1997-98; legal asst. Horan Lloyd Law Offices, Monterey, 1998—. Chmn. adv. bd. Kirkwood C.C., 1987-91. Author: Angel Poetry, 1995, Love and War in the American Home, 1997; contbr. poetry to lit. publs. Co-suptr. Sunday sch. Immanuel Luth. Ch., Earlville, Iowa, 1990-92, 94-97; supt. ch. sch. St. Timothy Luth. Ch., Monterey, Calif., 1997-99. Mem. Legal Secs. Assn. Monterey County. Avocations: study of angels, photography, writing poetry, snow skiing, hiking. Office: Horan Lloyd Law Offices 499 Van Buren St Monterey CA 93940-2623 E-mail: salow@horanlegal.com.

SALPETER, EDWIN ERNEST, physical sciences educator; b. Vienna, Austria, Dec. 3, 1924; came to U.S., 1949, naturalized, 1953; s. Jakob L. and Frieder (Horn) S.; m. Miriam Mark, June 11, 1950; children: Judy Gail, Shelley Ruth. MS, Sydney U., 1946; PhD, Birmingham (Eng.) U., 1948; DSc, U. Chgo., 1969, Case-Western Reserve U., 1970, U. Sydney, 1994, U. New South Wales, Sydney, 1996. Research fellow Birmingham U., 1948-49; faculty Cornell U., Ithaca, N.Y., 1949-97, now J.G. White prof. phys. scis. emeritus NY. Mem. U.S. Nat. Sci. Bd., 1979-85 Author: Quantum Mechanics, 1957, 77; mem. editorial bd. Astrophys. Jour, 1966-69; assoc. editor Rev. Modern Physics, 1971-92; contbr. articles to profl. jours. Mem. AURA bd., 1970-72. Recipient Gold medal Royal Astron. Soc., 1973, J.R. Oppenheimer Meml. prize U. Miami, 1974, C. Bruce medal Astron. Soc. Pacific, 1987, A. Devaucouleurs medal, 1992, Dirac Meml. medal U. New South Wales, 1996, Crafoord laureate Royal Swedish Acad. Scis., 1997, H. A. Bethe Prize, Am. Phys. Soc., 1999. Mem. NAS, Am. Astron. Soc. (v.p. 1971-73), Am. Philos. Soc., Am. Acad. Arts and Scis., The Royal Soc. (fgn.), Australian Acad. Sci., Deutsche Akademie Leopoldina. Home: 116 Westbourne Ln Ithaca NY 14850-2414 Office: Cornell U 612 Space Science Bldg Ithaca NY 14853-6801

SALSBERG, ARTHUR PHILIP, publishing company executive; b. Bklyn., Aug. 28, 1929; s. Solomon William and Rae (Miller) S.; m. Rhoda Gelb, Sept. 11, 1960; children: Charles Martin, Solomon William. BBA, CCNY, 1951. Mng. editor Ojibway Press, N.Y.C., 1957-64; advt. and promotion mgr. RCA Corp., Harrison, N.J., 1965-67; editor N.Am. Pub. Co., Phila., 1967-70; v.p., gen. mgr. Lawyers World, Inc., 1970-72; editorial dir. Ziff-Davis Pub. Co., N.Y.C., 1973-83; editor, assoc. pub. CQ Communications, Inc., Hicksville, N.Y., 1984—. Mag. and newspaper pub. cons.; electronics instr.; local campaign publicist, speech writer for town mayor, town coun., libr. bd., sch. bd. Author: Complete Book of Video Games, 1977, Collier's Ency. Yearbook, 1977, 78, 79, 80, 81, 82, First Book of Modern Electronics Fun Projects, 1986, Second Book of Modern Electronics Fun Projects, 1986; editor: Audio Mag, 1967-70, Lawyers World, 1970-72, Popular Electronics, 1973-83, Comm. Handbook, 1973-83, Stereo Directory, 1973-83, Tape Recorder Directory, 1973-83, Citizens Band Handbook, 1976-83, Invitation to Electronics, 1972-83, Modern Electronics, 1984-91, Computer Craft, 1992-93, MicroComputer Jour., 1994-96; assoc. pub.: Amateur Radio Equipment Buyers Guide, 1988, 89, 90, 91, 92, Amateur Radio Antenna Buyers Guide, 1989, 90, 91-92. Publicity chmn. Nassau coun. Boy Scouts Am., 1975; mem. adv. com. Bramson OR Tech. Inst., 1975. With AUS, 1951-53, Korea. Recipient Indsl. Mktg. Mag. award, 1959 Home: 7844 Lexington Club Blvd Apt A Delray Beach FL 33446-3426

SALSIG, DOYEN, photographer, photography studio owner; b. San Diego, Jan. 17, 1923; d. Felix and Fay (Doyen) Johnson; m. Budd Salsig, June 11, 1943; children: Winter, Kristin, Fay, Ben. AA, San Diego City Coll., 1965; BA in Biology, U. Calif., San Diego, 1970. Owner West Wind Studio, Flagstaff, Ariz., 1972-97. Photo workshop leader Mus. of No. Ariz., Flagstaff, 1978-93. Author: Parole: Quebec; Counter-sign: Ticonderoga, 1980 (grand prize Coconino County Women of the Arts 1985); contbr., photos and photographic essays to profl. jours. Bd. dirs., v.p. Grand Canyon (Ariz.) Natural History Assn., 1988-96; vice-chmn. Coconino County Rep. Com., Flagstaff, 1988-97; pres. Rep. Women's Club, Flagstaff, 1989-91; docent Mus. No. Ariz., Flagstaff, 1975-82; mem. Ariz. Humanities Coun., 1991-94; del. Rep. Nat. Conv., 1992, 96. Avocations: hiking, aerobics, swimming, camping, photography. Home and Office: 457 D Ave Coronado CA 92118-1759 E-mail: doyens1@msn.com.

SALSMAN, IAN, graphics designer; s. Stan and Ann Salsman; m. Carol Cavin. BS in Civil Engring., Carleton U., Ottawa, Ont., 1981—85. Customer svc. rep. Alphagraphics, Phoenix, 1997—99; graphic designer, digital pre press D&L Press, Inc., 1999—. Personal E-mail: AZSalsman@worldnet.att.net.

SALT, ALEC NICHOLAS, otolaryngology educator; b. Dewsbury, Yorkshire, Eng., May 4, 1952; arrived in U.S., 1984; s. Harold and Jean Salt; m. Devina Margaret Swan, Aug. 4, 1973; children: Lisa, Anthony. BSc, U. East Anglia, Norwich, Eng., 1973; MSc, U. Birmingham, Eng., 1974, PhD, 1977. Clin. physiologist Inst. for Sound and Vibration Rsch., Southampton, Eng., 1983; rsch. asst. prof. Washington U., St. Louis, 1984-87, asst. prof., 1987-93, assoc. prof. cochlear physiology, 1993—. Contbr. articles to profl. jours. Recipient Guyot prize for otolaryngology U. Groningen, The Netherlands, 1999; rsch. grantee NIH, Nat. Inst. Deafness and other Cumm. Disorders, Washington U., 1992—. Mem. Assn. for Rsch. in Otolaryngology, Acoustical Soc. Am. Avocation: radio controlled flying. Office: Washington Univ Med Sch Box 8115 660 S Euclid Ave Saint Louis MO 63110-1010 Fax: 314-362-7522. E-mail: salta@msnotes.wustl.edu.

SALT, ALFRED LEWIS, priest; b. Hackensack, N.J., Apr. 30, 1927; s. Alfred John and Lily (Tittle) S.; m. Elizabeth May Loveland, June 18, 1949; children: Richard John, Michael Rob, Christopher William, Katharine Anne. BA with honors, Bishop's U., Lennoxville, Can., 1949, MA in History, 1951, BD, 1960; grad. advanced mgmt. program, Harvard U., 1970; D Ministry, Grad. Theol. Found., 1988. Ordained to ministry Episcopal Ch. as deacon, 1951, as priest, 1952. Incumbent St. Philip's, Sawyerville, Que., Can., 1951-52, St. John the Evangelist, Porteuf, 1952-54; rector Christ Ch., Stanstead, 1954-62, St. Michael's Ch., Sillery, 1962-72, All Sts.' Ch., Millington, N.J., 1972-93. Bishop's chaplain Diocese of Que., 1962, hon. canon, 1970; pres. Morris Convocation. Morris County, N.J., 1974-78, retreat condr., 1979—; with Victorious Ministry Through Christ, Orlando, Fla., 1981-92, dir., 1986-92, v.p., 1989-92; dir. VMTC Can., 1995—; hon. asst. Grace Ch., Port Huron, Mich., 1993-98, Trinity Ch., Lexington, Mich., 1998-2001, St. Monica's Ch., Fla., 2002--. Author: Compass Book on Healing, 1996; contbr. articles to religious jour. Mem. Superior Coun. Edn., Que., 1964-70; commr. Que. Protestant Sch. Bd., 1970-72; trustee Heath Village, Hackettstown, N.J., 1974-76; mem. Passaic Twp. Welfare Bd., Millington, 1977-78, 82. With U.S. Army Air Corps Res., 1944-45; with USN, 1945-46. Mem. Blue Water Convocation, Order St. Luke (chaplain). Home: 4822 Martinique Way Naples FL 34119 also: North Hatley 190 Chemin du Lac Quebec QC Canada J0B 2C0 E-mail: alemsalt@aol.com. *The more I come to know Jesus, the more I come to know myself. The more I submit myself to Him, the less I depend upon myself.*

SALT, WILLIAM BRADLEY, II, physician; b. Cin., June 17, 1947; s. William Bradley and Shirley Jane (Betz) S.; m. Susan Sherron, July 30, 1948; children: Bradley, Shelley, Casey. BA, Ohio State U., 1969, MD, 1972. Diplomate Am. Bd. Internal Medicine. Intern medicine Vanderbilt U. Hosp., Nashville, 1972-73, resident medicine, 1973-74, fellow gastroenterology, 1974-76, chief resident medicine, 1976-77; pvt. practice Gastroenterology Inc., Columbus, Ohio, 1977-96, Ohio Gastroenterology Group, Columbus, 1996—. Clin. assoc., prof. medicine Ohio State U., Columbus, 1977—; chmn. continuing med. edn. com. Mt. Carmel Health, Columbus, 1987—. Author: Irritable Bowel Syndrome and the Mind-Body/Brain-Gut Connection, 1997, Fibromyalgia and the MindBodySpirit Connection, 2000, Irritable Bowel Syndrome and the MindBodySpirit Connection, 2002; contbr. articles to profl. jours. Mem. Am. Soc. Gastroent. Endoscopy. Republican. Luth. Home: 281 S Parkview Ave Columbus OH 43209-1649 Office: Ohio Gastroenterology Group 777 W State St Columbus OH 43222-1536 E-mail: drsalt@parkviewpub.com.

SALTEN, DAVID GEORGE, county agency administrator, academic administrator; b. N.Y.C., Aug. 23, 1913; s. Max Elias and Gertrude (Brauer) S.; m. Frances Claire Brown (div. 1983); children: Phoebe, Cynthia, Melissa; m. Adrienne O'Brien, 1989. ScB, Washington Sq. Coll., N.Y.C., 1933; AM, Columbia U., 1939; PhD, NYU, 1944; LLD (hon.), Lynn U., 1976; L.H.D., Nova U., Ft. Lauderdale, Fla., 1983; Sc.D. (hon.), N.Y. Inst. Tech., 1984; LHD (hon.), Hofstra U., 1996. Registered psychologist, N.Y. Chemist Almay Cosmetics, 1934-35, City of New York, 1938-40; tchr., chmn. dept., high sch. prin. N.Y.C. Bd. Edn., 1940-50; assoc. prof. Hunter Coll. Grad. Program, 1947-63; supt. of schs. City of Long Beach, N.Y., 1950-62, City of New Rochelle, 1962-65; exec. v.p. Fedn. of Jewish Philanthropies, N.Y.C., 1965-69; exec. v.p., provost N.Y. Inst. Tech., Old Westbury, 1969-90; chmn. Nassau County Indsl. Devel. Agy., Mineola, N.Y., 1985—; exec. dir. Nassau County Tax Relief Commn., 1990-93. Mem. White House Conf. on Edn., 1955, White House Conf. on Youth, 1960; U.S. resource person on edn. World Mental Health Congress, Paris, 1961; mem. Bd. Edn., Hawthorne, Cedar Knolls, N.Y., 1963-65; mem. adv. council Columbia U. Sch. of Social Work, 1967-69; chmn. adv. council NYU Sch. Edn., 1963-65; chmn. adv. council to Select Com. on Higher Edn. N.Y. Legislature, 1971-73. Author: Mathematics: A Basic Course, 1957. Editor instructional software. Contbr. articles on edn. and ednl. adminstrn. to profl. publs. Vice chmn. N.Y. State Mental Health Council, Albany, 1965-72; pres. N.Y. State Citizens Council, 1957, Nat. Council on Aging, Washington, 1975-77; chmn. Nassau County Local Devel. Agy., 1982—, Nassau County Local Devel. Corp., N.Y., 1982—, pres., 1992—; chmn. Nassau County Cultural Devel. Bd., 1980—; bd. dirs. NAACP Legal Def. Fund, 1964-74; chmn. bd. trustees The Hewlett Sch., 1991—. Recipient citation U.S. Navy, 1947, Mental Health Assn., Nassau County, N.Y., 1955, Long Beach Edn. Assn., N.Y., 1962, Council of City of New Rochelle, N.Y., 1965, Council of Town of Islip, N.Y., 1982. Fellow AAAS, Am. Orthopsychiat. Assn.; mem. Princeton Club (N.Y.C.). Avocations: opera, ballet, international travel, photography. Office: Nassau County Indsl Devel Agy 400 County Seat Dr Mineola NY 11501-4839

SALTER, CHRISTOPHER LORD, geography educator; BA, Oberlin Coll., 1961; MA, U. Calif. Berkeley, 1968, PhD, 1970. Prof. geography U. Mo., Columbia. Recipient George J. Miller award Nat. Coun. for Geog. Edn., 1992, Disting. Geography Educator award Nat. Geog. Soc., 1990, Disting. Tchg. Achievement award Nat. Coun. for Geog. Edn., 1999, Disting. Faculty award U. Mo. Alumni Assn., 1999. Office: Univ Mo Dept Geography Dept Geography 3 Stewart Hall Columbia MO 65211-6170

SALTER, DAVID WYATT, secondary school educator; b. Augusta, Ga., Aug. 10, 1950; s. Wyatt Jackson and Annie Lee (Coleman) S.; m. Dorothy Mikell Fishburne, Aug. 11, 1973; 1 child, Caroline Elizabeth. BS, U. S.C., 1973, MEd, 1977, postgrad., 1982-92, Clemson U., 1985. Cert. tchr., S.C. Tchr. biology Aiken (S.C.) High Sch., 1973—, chair dept. biology, 1985—. Curriculum assoc. for h.s. sci., Sch. Dist. of Aiken County, 1994—, adult edn. tchr., 1976-85, mem. h.s. sci. curriculum revision com., 1997; bd. dirs. S.C. Jr. Acad. Sci., 1984-97; mem. adult edn. curriculum com. S.C. Dept. Edn., 1984; mem. state textbook com., 1989, 92, 2002. Organist Warrenville (S.C.) United Meth. Ch., 1963-91, 93—, St. John United Meth. Ch., Graniteville, S.C., 1998—; dir. men's choir St. John's United Meth. Ch., Aiken, S.C., 1997—; spkr. Prayer Breakfast for H.S. Srs. St. John's United Meth. Ch., Aiken, 1984; mem. commn. on worship S.C. Ann. Conf. United Meth. Ch.; mem. edn1. adv. com. Aiken County Human Rels. Commn., 1993-95. Recipient Svc. award to S.C. Jr. Acad. Sci., 1994; named Outstanding Tchr. in Math. and Sci., Am. Nuclear Soc. Savannah River Sect., 1991-92, Midlands Sci. Tchr. of Yr., U. S.C. chpt. Sigma Xi, 1994, Sci. Tchr. of Yr., 1998, S.C. Acad. Sci. award Excellence in Sci. or Math. Teaching, 1995. Mem. NEA, Nat. Biology Tchrs. Assn., S.C. Edn. Assn., Aiken County Edn. Assn., S.C. Acad. Sci., S.C. Assn. Biology Tchrs. (2d v.p. 1993-94, 1st v.p. 1994-95, pres. 1996-97), S.C. Suprs. Assn., S.C. Sci. Coun., Nat. Sci. Tchrs. Assn., Am. Guild Organists (sub-dean Augusta chpt. 1993-94, dean 1994-96, treas. 2001--), Phi Delta Kappa. Methodist. Avocations: piano and organ music, fishing, travel. Home: PO Box 904 52 Sunnyside Ln Aiken SC 29803-9420 Office: Aiken High Sch 449 Rutland Dr NE Aiken SC 29801-4098 E-mail: dsalter@aiken.k12.sc.us., salterdav@aol.com.

SALTER, EDWIN CARROLL, retired physician; b. Oklahoma City, Jan. 19, 1927; s. Leslie Ernest and Maud (Carroll) S.; m. Ellen Gertrude Malone, June 30, 1962; children— Mary Susanna, David Patrick BA, DePauw U., 1947; MD, Northwestern U., 1951. Intern Cook County Hosp., Chgo., 1951-53; resident in pediatrics Children's Meml. Hosp., 1956-58, Cook County Hosp., Chgo., 1956-58; practice medicine specializing in pediatrics Lake Forest, Ill., 1958-97; attending physician Lake Forest Hosp., 1958—, pres. med. staff, 1981-82. Attending physician Children's Meml. Hosp., Chgo.; clin. faculty mem. dept. pediatrics Northwestern U. Med. Sch. Served to capt. M.C., U.S. Army, 1954-56 Mem. AMA, Ill. State Med. Soc., Lake County Med. Soc. (pres. 1984), Phi Beta Kappa Republican. Methodist. Home: 19 N Maywood Rd Lake Forest IL 60045-3233

SALTER, KEVIN THORNTON, lawyer; b. N.Y.C., Oct. 21, 1947; s. Hershel Fletcher and Elizabeth (Thornton) S.; m. Eleanor Raftery, Aug. 28, 1982. BA, Iona Coll., 1973; JD, St. John's U., 1977. Bar: N.Y. 1978, U.S. Dist. Ct. (so. and ea. dists.) N.Y., 1978. Atty. Nat. Coun. on Compensation Ins., N.Y.C., 1978-80; coun. James G. Barron, 1980-81; assoc. St. Regis Paper Co./Champion Internat., N.Y.C. and Stamford, Conn., 1981-88; sr. ptnr. Kroll & Tract, N.Y.C., 1988-94; ptnr. Peterson & Ross, 1994-98, Querrey & Harrow, 1998—. Bd. dirs. Realm Nat. Ins. Co., N.Y.C. With U.S. Army, 1967-69. Mem. N.Y. State Bar Assn., Brit. Ins. Law Assn. Office: Querrey & Harrow 120 Broadway Ste 3660 New York NY 10271-3699

SALTER, LESTER HERBERT, lawyer; b. Waterbury, Conn., Apr. 26, 1918; s. Nathan M. and Eva G. (Levy) S.; m. Nina P. Scheftel, Sept. 15, 1951; 1 child, Ellen Lee. BS in Econs, U. Pa., 1940, LLB, 1948. Bar: R.I. 1948. Trial atty. Office of Chief Counsel, IRS, Newark and Boston, 1949-53; pvt. practice Providence, 1953-57; partner Salter & McGowan, 1957-70, Salter, McGowan, Arcaro & Swartz, Providence, 1970-74; pres. Salter, McGowan, Swartz & Holden, Inc., 1974-95, Salter, McGowan & Swartz, Inc., Providence, 1995-97, Salter, McGowan, Swartz & Sylvia, Inc., Providence, 1997-99, Salter, McGowan, Sylvia & Leonard, Inc., Providence, 2000—. Lectr. Northeastern U., 1955-56; chmn. U. R.I. Fed. Tax Inst., 1972-77; chmn. disciplinary bd. Supreme Ct., R.I., 1975-81; mem. R.I. Adv. Commn. Jud. Appts., 1978-82, ethics adv. panel Supreme Ct., R.I., 1987-92. Assoc. editor: R.I. Bar Jour, 1961-68. Served with F.A. AUS, 1941-46. Decorated Bronze Star. Fellow: ABA, Am. Bar Found; mem.: Am. Law Inst., Am. Judicature Soc., New Eng. Bar Assn. (pres. 1996—97), R.I. Bar Assn. (pres. 1986—87), ABA (ho. of dels. 1987—2000, bd. govs. 1999—2000). Home: 75 Blackstone Blvd Providence RI 02906-5413 Office: 321 S Main St Providence RI 02903-7108

SALTER, LINDA LEE, security officer; b. Garden City, Mich., Oct. 10, 1953; d. Bertram Edward Salter and Gertrude Theresa (Barnes) Honeycutt; children: Korina Reshell Irene Miller, Terry Wayne Tomlin II. Grad., Henry Ford C.C., 1998; student, U. Detroit, 1999. Security supr. Guardsmark, Memphis, 1979-86, security officer, 1986-96, Detroit, 1998—, Detroit Newspapers, 1986-96, advt. officer, 1996—. Emergency first aid specialist ARC, Dearborn, Mich., 1993—. Pres. Downriver/Monroe County Women Involved in Wings, South Rockwood, Mich., 1991—; mem. Mich. Lupus Found., 1995—, Monroe County Humane Soc., 1993—, Ladies Aux., 9363, 1971—; reunion class tchr. Carlson H.S., Gibraltar, Mich., 1971; mem. Our Lady of the Woods Cath. Ch. Mem. C. of C. of Huron Twp. Roman Catholic. Avocations: reading, travel, horses, sports, gardening. Home: 22033 Verdun St Romulus MI 48174-9533 Office: Detroit Newspapers 615 W Lafayette Blvd Detroit MI 48226-3197 E-mail: llsalt@prodigy.net.

SALTER, MARY JO, poet; b. Grand Rapids, Aug. 15, 1954; d. Albert Gregory and Lormina (Paradise) S.; m. Brad Leithauser, 1980; children: Emily Salter, Hilary Garner. BA cum laude, Harvard U., 1976; MA, Cambridge U., 1978. Instr. Harvard U., 1978-79; instr. English conversation Japan, 1980-83; lectr. English Mt. Holyoke Coll., South Hadley, Mass., 1984—, Emily Dickinson lectr. in humanities, 1995—. Staff editor Atlantic Monthly, 1978-80; poet-in-residence Robert Frost Place, 1981; poetry editor The New Republic, 1992-95. Author: Henry Purcell in Japan, 1985, Unfinished Painting, 1989 (Lamont prize in poetry 1988), The Moon Comes Home, 1989, Sunday Skaters: Poems, 1994 (Nat. Book Critics Circle award nomination 1994), A Kiss in Space: Poems, 1999; co-editor: Norton Anthology of Poetry, 4th edit., 1996; contbr. to periodicals including New Yorker, New Republic, Kenyon Rev. Amy Lowell scholar, 1995; recipient Discovery prize Nation, 1983; Nat. Endowment for Arts fellow, 1983-84, Guggenheim fellow, 1993. Mem. Internat. P.E.N. Office: care Alfred A Knopf Inc 299 Park Ave New York NY 10171

SALTERS, RICHARD STEWART, engineering company executive; b. St. Johns, Mich., Apr. 4, 1951; s. Stewart Arthur and Mary Ann (Eiseler) S.; m. Patricia Lynn Shumsky, Oct. 23, 1971 (div. Mar. 1982); children: Tiffani, Destiny; m. Marilyn L. DeVille, Sept. 5, 1998; 1 child, Wyatt Richard. BS in Engring., Purdue U., 1974. Field engr. Henkels & McCoy, Inc., Blue Bell, Pa., 1972-77; area mgr. engring. dept. Harris McBurney Co., Inc., Jackson, Mich., 1977-81; project engr. Lambic Telcom, Inc., Ridgewood, N.J., 1981-82; pres. S & H Assocs., Inc., Lafayette, La., 1982—. Mem. Engring. Soc. of Detroit, City Club of Lafayette. Roman Catholic. Avocations: raising, racing thoroughbred horses, skiing, golf, tennis. Office: S & H Assocs Inc PO Box 52721 Lafayette LA 70505-2721 also: Seattle WA

SALTHE, STANLEY NORMAN, retired theoretical biology educator; b. N.Y.C., Oct. 16, 1930; s. Christian and Ruth (Idland) S.; m. Barbara May Salthe, May 23, 1959; children: Eric Peter, Rebecca May. BS, Columbia U., 1959, MA, 1960, PhD, 1963. Asst. prof. Bklyn. Coll. CUNY, 1965, assoc. prof. biology, 1971, prof., 1973—; prof. emeritus Bklyn. Coll., CUNY, 1991—; vis. scientist in biol. scis. Binghamton (N.Y.) U., 1992—. Author: Evolutionary Biology, 1972, Evolving Hierarchical Systems, 1985, Development and Evolution, 1993. With USAF, 1950-54 Woodrow Wilson fellow, 1959; rsch. grantee NSF, 1966-70, CUNY, 1970-73. Mem. Gen. Evolutionary Rsch. Group, Washington Evolutionary Systems Soc., Internat. Soc. for History, Philosophy and Social Studies Biology, Am. Soc. Naturalists, Phi Beta Kappa. E-mail: ssalthe@binghamton.edu.

SALTIEL, DAVID MICHAEL, lawyer; b. Boston; s. Abraham M. and Anna L. S.; m. Rhoda B., Sept. 3, 1961; 1 child, Marjorie Weinberger. BA, U. Mass., 1959; JD, Harvard U., 1962. Bar: Mass., U.S. Dist. Ct. Mass., U.S. Supreme Ct. Atty. Nutter, McClennen & Fish, Boston, 1962-89, Posternak, Blankstein & Lund, Boston, 1989—. Home: 95 Cynthia Rd Newton MA 02459-2836 Office: Posternak Blankstein & Lund 100 Charles River Plz Fl 9 Boston MA 02114-2794

SALTIEL, NATALIE, accountant; b. Chgo., Mar. 19, 1927; d. Henry Carl and Dorothy (Maremont) S.; m. Sidney D. Levin, Oct. 13, 1963; 1 chld, Erica Saltiel Levin. BBA with highest distinction, Northwestern U., 1948. CPA, Ill. Mem. staff acctg. firm, Chgo., 1948-52; pvt. practice acctg., 1952—. Bd. dirs., mem. exec. com., chmn. com. United Way Chgo., 1979-85, United Way/Crusade of Mercy, 1980-88; mem. adv. coun., chmn. com. Sta. WBEZ Chicagoland Pub. Radio, 1981-91; bd. dirs. Chgo. Fin. Exch., 1989-90; bd. dirs., treas., v.p., Jewish Coun. Urban Affairs, 1992-98. Mem. AICPA, Ill. CPA Soc., Am. Women's Soc. CPAs, Beta Gamma Sigma. Office: 105 W Madison St Ste 401 Chicago IL 60602-4603

SALTS, NANCY LEE, critical care, emergency nurse; b. Deer Run, W.Va., Nov. 19, 1945; d. Ralph A. and Neva A. (Mitchell) Rexrode; m. R.J. Salts, Apr. 20, 1973; children: Jason L., Angela S. AS, Fla. Keys Community Coll., Key West, 1980. RN, Iowa, Nebr., La.; cert. in advanced cardiac life support. ICU and med.-surg. nurse Community Meml. Hosp., Missouri Valley, Iowa; telemetry nurse Bergen Mercy Hosp., Omaha; emergency room and telemetry nurse Immanuel Med. Ctr.; emergency room pool nurse Pendleton Meml. Meth. Hosp., New Orleans, asst. head nurse emergency dept., 1993-96; owner Pooch Pit, Picayune, Miss., 1996—; clin. triage nurse Ochsner Clinic, 2000—; office nurse Dr. D.L. Bolton Family Practice, Picayune, Miss., 1001—. Developer pet grooming restraint. Vol. co-facilitator for systematic tng. for effective parenting; facilitator Navy Alcohol and Drug Safety Action Program.

SALTSMAN, JOHN B. former political party executive, commissioner; BS, MBA, Christian Bros. U. V.p. strategic planning McKenzie Mgmt. Co., Cleveland, Tenn.; West Tenn. field rep. Pres. Bush Re-election Campaign, 1992; with Office of Congressman Don Sundquist; campaign field dir. Don

Sundquist Gubernatorial Campaign, 1994; adminstrv. asst. Office of Gov. Sundquist; exec. dir. Tenn. Rep. Caucus, 1996; chmn. Tenn. Rep. Party, Nashville; commr. transp. State of Tenn., 1995—. Mem. state fin. com. Gov. Sundquist's Re-election Campaign, 1998. Office: James K Polk Bldg 505 Deaderick St Nashville TN 37243 Fax: 615-292-9619.*

SALTYKOV, BORIS GEORGIEVICH, economist, politician; b. Moscow, Dec. 27, 1940; s. Gregory N. and Evdokia M. (Pukaleva) S.; m. Lubov N. Clochkova; 2 children. Student, Moscow Inst. Physics & Tech. Rschr., chief engr. Ctrl. Econ. Math. Inst. USSR Acad. Scis., Moscow, 1967—73, sr. rschr., 1973—86, head dept. Inst. Econ. Forecasting, 1986—91, vice dir. Analytical Rsch. Ctr. on Problems Social, Econ. and Sci. Tech. Devel., 1991—96; min. for sci. and tech. policy, pub. affairs chmn. commn. to UNESCO, vice premier of Russian govt. Russian Fedn., 1992—93; mem. Russian Parliament, 1993—95. Pres. Russian House for Internat. S & T Coop., 1996—. Contbr. over 70 articles to profl. jours. Mem.: Am. Acad. Arts and Scis. (fgn.). Avocation: yachting. Office: Russian House for Interna S&T Coop Brusov per 11 103009 Moscow Russia E-mail: bsaltykov@osi.ru.

SALTZ, HOWARD JOEL, newspaper editor; b. Bronx, N.Y., Apr. 11, 1960; s. Fred Raymond and Sheila Lois (Goldberg) S. BA in Liberal Arts, SUNY, Stony Brook, 1983. Reporter Greenwich Time, So. Conn. Newspapers divsn. Times Mirror, 1983-85; with MediaNews Group, 1985—, N.J. Advance, Dover, 1985-87, editor, 1987-88, Hamilton (Ohio) Jour.-News, 1988-89, Fremont (Calif.) Argus, 1989-91; editor Johnstown Tribune-Democrat, 1991; dep. bus. editor Denver Post, 1996-98, dep. mng. editor features, 1998-2000, multimedia editor, 2000—02, assoc. editor/new media & strategic devel., 2002—. Adv. com. dept. journalism Ohlone Coll., Fremont, Calif., 1990-91. Bd. dirs. YMCA, Fremont-Newark, Calif., 1990-91, Johnstown Area Heritage Assn., 1991-93. Mem. Greater Johnstown C. of C. (bd. dirs. 1991-96), Soc. Profl. Journalists (bd. dirs. Northern Calif. chpt. 1990-91). Avocations: skiing, travel, scuba. Address: 535 Garfield St Denver CO 80206-4513 Office: Denver Post 1560 Broadway Denver CO 80202-5177 E-mail: hsaltz@denverpost.com.

SALTZBERG, JOANNE MARIA, company executive; b. Yonkers, N.Y., July 24, 1945; d. John Salvatore and Josephine Pauline (Aiello) Vasile; m. Jerald Stanley Saltzberg, Dec., 1971 (div. Mar. 1981). BS, Univ. Coll. Md., 1997. CLU; ChFC. Adminstr. Security Brokerage, Balt., 1970-79; adminstrv. mgr. The Phoenix Cos., Bethesda, Md., 1979-85, fin. planner, 1985-92; exec. dir. Md. Commn. for Women, Balt., 1992-99; COO Women Entrepreneurs of Balt., 1999—. Editor: Gender Composition of Maryland Boards and Commissions, 1965-93, 1994. Bd. dirs. Women's Alliance of Md., Balt., 1995—, Girl Scouts U.S., Ctrl. Md. Coun., Balt., 1996—; mem. Child Care Adv. Bd., Balt., 1994—, Equal Opportunity Coun., Balt., 1996—, Family Violence Coun., Annapolis, 1997, YWCA of Greater Balt., 1998—. Named Legis. Leader, Md. Network Against Domestic violence, 1995, Md.'s Top 100 Women, 1997, 99. Mem. NOW (sec. 1990-91). Democrat. Office: Women Entrepreneurs of Baltimore 1118 Light St Ste 202 Baltimore MD 21230-4135

SALTZBURG, STEPHEN ALLAN, law educator, consultant; b. Phila., Sept. 10, 1945; s. Jack Leonard and Mildred (Osgood) Adelman; m. Susan Lee, March 10, 1990; children: Mark Winston, Lisa Marie, Diane Elizabeth, David Lee Mussehl. AB, Dickinson Coll., 1967; JD, U. Pa., 1970. Bar: Calif. 1971, D.C. 1972, Va. 1976. Law clk. U.S. Dist. Ct. (no. dist.) Calif., San Francisco, 1970-71, U.S. Supreme Ct., 1971-72; asst. prof. law sch. U. Va., Charlottesville, 1972-74, assoc. prof., 1974-77, prof., 1977-87, Class of 1962 prof., 1987-90; Howrey prof. trial advocacy, litigation and profl. responsibility George Washington U. Sch. Law, Washington, 1990—. Reporter Alaska Rules of Evidence, 1976-77, Alaska Civil Jury Instrns., 1979-81, Adv. Com. on Rules of Criminal Procedure, 1984-89, Va. Rules on Evidence, 1984-85, Civil Justice Act Adv. Group, U.S. Dist. Ct. D.C., 1992-93, chmn., 1994-99; dep. asst. atty. gen. criminal divsn. U.S. Dept. Justice, 1988-89; mem. adv. com. on Fed. Rules of Criminal Procedure, 1989-95, on Fed. Rules of Evidence, 1992-95; mediator dispute resolution program U.S. Ct. Appeals, 1993—. Author: Evidence in America, 1987, American Criminal Procedure, 6th edit., 2000, Criminal Law: Cases and Materials, 1994, 2d edit., 2000, Evidence: The Objection Method, 1997, Federal Rules of Evidence Manual, 8th edit., 2002, Federal Rules of Evidence Trial Book, 1998, A Modern Approach to Evidence, 2d edit., 1982, Military Rules of Evidence Manual, 4th edit., 1997, Basic Criminal Procedure, 1994, 2d edit., 1997, Military Evidentiary Foundations, 1994, 2d edit., 2000, Trying Cases to Win: Anatomy of a Trial, 1999, Trying Cases to Win: Evidence: Weapons for Winning, 2000, California Federal Evidence Trial Book, 1999, Ohio Rules of Evidence Trial Book, 1999, Washington Evidence Trial Book, 1999. Mem.: ABA (chmn. com. on trial advocacy criminal justice sect. 1992—96, co-chmn. task force on civil trial stds. litig. sect. 1996—97, task force on Ind. Counsel Act litig. sect. 1997—99, mem. criminal justice sect. coun. 2000—, litigation sect. coun. 2001—, task force on terrorism and the law 2001—02, task force on gatekeeper regulation and the profession 2002—), Am. Law Inst. Office: George Washington U Law Sch 2000 H St NW Washington DC 20052

SALTZER, JEROME HOWARD, computer science educator; b. Nampa, Idaho, Oct. 9, 1939; s. Joseph and Helene (Scheuermann) S.; m. Marlys Anne Hughes, June 16, 1961; children— Rebecca, Sarah, Mark. BS, MIT, 1961, MS, 1963, Sc.D., 1966. Faculty dept. elec. engring. and computer sci. MIT, Cambridge, Mass., 1966—, now prof. emeritus and sr. lectr.; tech. dir. Project Athena, 1984-88. Cons. Chem. Abstracts Svc., 1968-88, IBM Corp., 1970-84. Mem. Mayor's Telecomms. Adv. Bd., Newton, Mass., 1984—. Fellow AAAS, IEEE; mem. NRC (computer sci. and telecom. bd. 1991-93), NAE, Assn. for Computing Machinery (mem. com. on computers and pub. policy 1984—), Eta Kappa Nu, Tau Beta Pi. Home: 54 Gammons Rd Waban MA 02468-1216 Office: MIT Lab Computer Sci 545 Technology Sq Cambridge MA 02139-3539 E-mail: saltzer@mit.edu.

SALTZMAN, BARRY, actor; b. Chgo., Nov. 1, 1961; s. Bernard William and Cynthia Iris (Gordon) S. BA in Theatre and Drama, Ind. U., 1983. Appeared in theatrical prodns. Rosencrantz and Guilderstern Are Dead, Stage Left Theatre, Chgo., 1984, On the Verge, Body Politic Theatre, Chgo., 1986, The Skin of Our Teeth, Baliwick Repertory, 1987, The Magic Barrel and Other Stories, Nat. Jewish Theatre, Skokie, Ill., 1988, Vampire Lesbians of Sodom, Royal George Theatre, Chgo., 1990, The Little Prince, Children's Classical Theatre Co., Chgo., 1990, Broadway Bound, Briar Street Theatre, Chgo., 1991, The Merry Widow, DuPage Opera Theatre, Glen Ellyn, Ill., 1991, The Miser, The Liar, Green Stockings, Festival Theatre, Wis., 1992, Julius Caesar, Next Theatre, Evanston, Ill., 1992, The Real Live Brady Bunch (nat. tour), 1993, Beachwood Palace Jubilee, L.A., 1994-95, Theft, Hudson Theatre, L.A., 1994, The Smell of Ennui, Theater/Theatre, L.A., 1995, The Big Time Jubilee, Acme Theatre, L.A., 1995-96, numerous others; on camera performances include Bradymania, ABC, 1993, others. Adminstr., fundraiser The Hunger Project, 1986-88; fundraiser Youth at Risk, 1988, AIDS Walk Chgo., 1990; group discussion leader, fundraiser Stop AIDS Chgo., 1987-90; various adminstrv. and enrollment roles Werner Erhard and Assocs., Chgo., 1986-90; mem. Human Rights Campaign Fund, 1990-94; adminstrv. vol. Gore-Lieberman, 2000; entertainment legal MGM Studios, 2001—. Recipient Medallion for Acting Excellence, Amoco Cos./Am. Coll. Theatre Festival, Kennedy Ctr., Washington, 1982. Mem. AFTRA. Home: 319 S Cloverdale Ave Los Angeles CA 90036-3433 E-mail: bjsaltzman@yahoo.com.

SALTZMAN, CHARLES MCKINLEY, educational consultant; b. N.Y.C., Apr. 6, 1937; s. Charles Eskridge Saltzman and Gertrude (Lamont) Saltzman Rockwood; m. Cornelia Metz Biddle, Sept. 3, 1965; children: Cornelia Biddle Saltzman Tierney, Charles Eskridge. AB, Harvard Coll., 1959, MA in Teaching, 1962. Cert. prin. and supr., La. Tchr., coach, dorm head St. Albans Sch., Washington, 1962-66, 67-73; tchr., coach Athenian Sch., Danville, Calif., 1966-67; headmaster Hannah More Acad., Reisterstown, Md., 1973-74, Metairie (La.) Park Country Day Sch., 1974-81, Madeira Sch., McLean, Va., 1981-88; cons. Ind. Ednl. Svcs., Princeton, N.J., 1988-95. Adj. instr. Gettysburg (Pa.) Coll., 1988—; dir. Upper Adams Sch. Dist., Biglerville, Pa., 1991-95, 96-97; cons. Search Assocs., 1996—. Capt. U.S. Army, 1959-61. Mem. Country Day Sch. Headmasters Assn. Episcopalian. Avocations: farming, gardening, tennis. Home and Office: 622 Chestnut Hill Rd Aspers PA 17304-9425 E-mail: csaltzman@supernet.com.

SALTZMAN, IRENE CAMERON, consumer products company executive; b. Cocoa, Fla., Mar. 23, 1927; d. Argyle Bruce and Marie T. (Neel) Cameron; m. Herman Saltzman, Mar. 23, 1946 (dec. May 1986); children: Martin Howard (dec.), Arlene Norma Hanly. Owner Irene Perfume and Cosmetics Lab., Jacksonville, Fla., 1972—. Mem. Cummer Mus. Art, Jacksonville, 1972-. Mem. Ret. Judge Advocates Assn. of USAF (hon.), First Coast Women in Internat. Trade, Cosmetic, Toiletry and Fragrance Assn., Ret. Officers Assn., Ponte Vedra Club, Jacksonville Naval Flying Club. Democrat. Episcopalian. Avocations: aviation, painting, travel, swimming, golf. Home: 2701 Ocean Dr S Jacksonville Beach FL 32250 E-mail: irene@ireneparfums.com.

SALTZMAN, JOSEPH, journalist, producer, educator; b. L.A., Oct. 28, 1939; s. Morris and Ruth (Weiss) S.; m. Barbara Dale Epstein, July 1, 1962; children: Michael Stephen Ulysses, David Charles Laertes. BA, U. So. Calif., 1961; MS, Columbia U., 1962. Freelance writer, reporter, prodr., 1960—; reporter Valley Times Today, L.A., 1962-64; editor Pacific Palisades Palisadian Post, 1964; sr. writer-prodr. CBS-KNXT TV, L.A., 1964-74; freelance broadcast cons., 1974—; prof. journalism U. So. Calif., 1974—; assoc. dir. Sch. Journalism U. So. Calif. Annenberg, 1996-99; assoc. dean Annenberg Sch. for Comm., 1999—; sr. prodr. investigative unit Entertainment Tonight, 1983; dir. Image of the Journalist in Popular Culture project Norman Lear Ctr., Annenberg Sch. Comm., U. So. Calif., 2001—. CFO The Jester & Pharley Phund. Author: Frank Capra and the Image of the Journalist in American Film, 2002; prodr.(writer): (documentaries) Black on Black, 1968, The Unhappy Hunting Ground, 1971, The Junior High School, 1971, The Very Personal: Death of Elizabeth Schell-Holt-Hartford, 1972, Rape, 1972, Why Me?, 1974, Entertainment Tonight, 1983, (films, video, audio) , 1984—93; editor (columnist): USA Today, 1983—; columnist: King Features Syndicate, 1983—92; contbg. editor: Emmy Mag., 1986—90, Roberts Reviewing Svc., 1964—95, others. Recipient AP certificates of excellence and merit, 1968, 72, 73, 74, 75, Edward R. Murrow awards for distinguished achievements in broadcast journalism, 1969, 72, Alfred I. duPont-Columbia U. award in broadcast journalism, 1973-74, Silver Gavel award Am. Bar Assn., 1973, Ohio State award Am. Exhbn. Ednl. Radio-Television Programs and Inst. for Edn. by Radio-TV Telecom. Ctr., 1974, Broadcast Media awards San Francisco State U., 1974, 75, Media award for excellence in comm. Am. Cancer Soc., 1976, Disting. Alumni award U. So. Calif., 1992; Seymour Berkson fellow, 1961; Robert E. Sherwood fellow, 1962; alt. Pulitzer traveling fellow, 1962-63. Mem. NATAS (regional Emmy awards 1965, 68, 74, 75), Radio-TV News Assn. (Golden Mike awards 1969, 71, 73, 75), Writers Guild Am., Greater Los Angeles Press Club (awards 1968, 74, 75), Columbia U., U. So. Calif. alumni assns., Skull and Dagger, Blue Key, Phi Beta Kappa, Sigma Delta Chi, Pi Sigma Alpha, Alpha Epsilon Rho. Home: 2116 Via Estudillo Palos Verdes Peninsula CA 90274-1931 Office: U So Calif Annenberg Sch Journalism Univ Park Los Angeles CA 90089-0001 E-mail: saltzman@usc.edu.

SALTZMAN, PHILIP, television writer, producer; b. Sonora, Mexico, Sept. 19, 1928; came to U.S., 1929, naturalized, 1948; s. Louis and Vanya (Liberman) S.; m. Caroline Veiller, Jan. 24, 1960; children: Jennifer, Daniel, Anthony. BA, UCLA, 1951, MA, 1953. Free lance writer, 1958-68. Pres. Woodruff Prodns., Inc. Writer: TV shows Alcoa Goodyear Theater, 1959, Richard Diamond, 1959, Rifleman, 1961, Perry Mason, 1964, Dr. Kildare, 1964, Fugitive, 1964, Twelve O'Clock High, 1966; producer, writer: TV shows Felony Squad, 1966-69, F.B.I, 1969-73, Barnaby Jones, 1973-77; producer, writer, creator Intertect, 1973; producer: TV movie The FBI vs. Alvin Karpis, 1974, Attack on Terror: The FBI vs. the KKK in Mississippi, 1975, Brinks: The Great Robbery, 1976; co-writer: feature film The Swiss Conspiracy, 1975; creator-writer-producer TV movie Crossfire, 1975; exec. producer: TV shows Barnaby Jones, 1978-80, Escapade, 1978, Colorado C-I, 1978, A Man Called Sloane, 1979, The Aliens Are Coming, 1979, Freebie and the Bean, 1980; producer: TV shows Bare Essence, 1982; supervising producer-writer Partners in Crime, 1984; producer-writer Crazy Like a Fox, 1985; producer, co-writer TV movie That Secret Sunday, 1986; exec. supervising producer The New Perry Mason movies, 1987-88; exec. supervising producer, writer Jake and The Fatman, 1987-88; supervising producer Columbo, 1989-90; creator-writer The Caller, 1991. Mem. dean's coun. Coll. Letters and Sci., UCLA, Friends of English, UCLA. Mem. Writers Guild Am., West, Caucus for Writers, Producers, Dirs., Acad. TV Arts and Scis., PEN Ctr. USA West. E-mail: cpsaltzman@aol.com.

SALVAN, SHERWOOD ALLEN, lawyer; b. N.Y.C., Dec. 2, 1942; s. Harry and Marie Ann (Deramo) S. BBA, St. Francis Coll., N.Y.C.; MBA, Pace U.; JD, postgrad., NYU. Bar: N.Y. 1969, U.S. Ct. Appeals (2d dist.) 1971, U.S. Dist. Cts. (so. and ea. dist.) N.Y. 1971, U.S. Cir. Ct. (2d cir.) 1972, U.S. Supreme Ct. 1980, D.C. 1981. Tax specialist Haskins & Sells, N.Y.C., 1969-71; sole practice, 1972—. Mem. cen. screening com. first dept. N.Y. Appellate Div., 1977-82; spl. master N.Y. County Supreme Ct., 1977-85; arbitrator Am. Arbitration Assn., 1976-89, N.Y. County and Bronx County Civil Cts., 1976-89; adminstrv. law judge Environ. Control Bd. City of N.Y., 1975-77. Contbr. articles to profl. jours. V.p. N.Y. County Dem. Club, 1980—; jud. del. N.Y. County dems., 1983—. Mem. N.Y. County Lawyers Assn. (chairperson com. word processing 1978-86), Am. Judge Assn., NY Law Sch. Alumni Assn. (bd. dirs. 1984—). Home: 526 E 83rd St New York NY 10028-7249 E-mail: woodmanlaw@aol.com.

SALVANESCHI, LUIGI, real estate and development executive, business educator; b. Casale, Italy, 1929; came to U.S., 1959; s. Ernesto and Carolina (Bassignana) S.; m. Lenore M. Rickels, Aug. 20, 1958; 1 child, Margherita Lina. Classical Maturity, Valsalice, Torino, Italy, 1950; PhD, Vatican U., Rome, 1958; cert. in real estate, UCLA, 1965. Restaurant mgr. McDonalds Co., Chgo., 1959-61, restaurant mgr. and supr. Los Angeles, 1961-63, real estate mgr., 1964-68, v.p. real estate Oakbrook, Ill., 1969-83; sr. v.p. real estate and constrn. Kentucky Fried Chicken, Louisville, 1983-88; pres., COO, dir. Blockbuster Entertainment, Ft. Lauderdale, Fla., 1988-91; disting. adj. prof. Barry Univ., 1991—. Adj. prof. Sch. Bus. U. Louisville, 1987; dir. Fla. Fun-Train subs. First Am. Rwys., Hollywood, Fla. Author: Location, Location, Location, 1997, Renaissance 2000: Liberal Arts Essentials for Tomorrow's Leaders, 1998. Dir. Ft. Lauderdale Internat. Movie Festival. Served as 2d lt. in Italian Infantry, 1945-46. Recipient Outstanding Italo-Am. award Italian Am. Fedn., 1991; named Colonel of the Commonwealth of Ky., 1984. Mem. Nat. Assn. Real Estate Execs. (co-founder, bd. dirs.). Roman Catholic. Avocations: reading classics in Latin and Greek, mountain hiking. Office: Barry Univ Sch of Bus 11300 NE 2nd Ave Miami FL 33161-6695

SALVATIERRA, OSCAR, JR. transplant surgeon, urologist, educator; b. Phoenix, Apr. 15, 1935; s. Oscar and Josefine S.; m. Pamela Moss; children: Mark, Lisa Marie. BS, Georgetown U., 1957; MD, U. So. Calif., 1961. Intern, resident in surgery and urology U. So. Calif.-Los Angeles County Med. Center, 1961-66; practice medicine Pomona, Calif., 1968-72; chief staff Casa Colina Hosp., 1972; post doctoral fellow in transplantation U. Calif.-San Francisco, 1972-73, asst. prof. surgery and urology, 1973-75, assoc. prof., 1975-81, prof., 1981-91, chmn. transplant service, 1974-91; attending surgeon and urologist Moffitt Hosp., 1973—; exec. dir. Pacific Transplant Inst., 1991-94; prof. surgery/pediatrics, dir. pediat. renal transplantation Stanford U. Med. Ctr., 1994—, attending surgeon, urologist and pediat. Mem. study sect. NIH, 1981-85, nat. adv. bd., 1986-92, chmn. nat. adv. bd. 1990-92, chmn. spl. study sect., 1997, 99. Contbr. over 250 articles and chpts. to med. lit.; mem. editorial bd. Transplantation and Immunology, 1984—, Transplantation, 1987—, Transplantation Procs., 1990—, Pediat. Transplantation, 1998—; assoc. editor Am. Jour. Kidney Diseases, 1987-89. Mem. nat. bd. advisors Agent Orange Class Assistance Program, 1988-96. Served with M.C., U.S. Army, Vietnam, 1966-68. Decorated Army Commendation medal; recipient Chancellor's award for pub. svc., U. Calif., 1986, Commendation resolution, Calif. State Legislature, 1990, Presdl. medal and Diploma of Honor, Argentina, 1999, Rambar-Mark award for excellence in patient care, Stanford U., 1999, Grand Ufficiale of Italian Rep. with title His Excellency award, Pres. of Italian Rep., 2000, ann. meeting Oscar Salvatierra Transplantation Fellows Symposium, named in his honor, 2001; grantee, NIH, 1974—76, 1980—83, 1988—90, USPHS, 1986—89. Fellow ACS (bd. govs. 1986-92); mem. Am. Surg. Assn., Am. Soc. Transplant Surgeons (bd. dirs. 1977-85, pres. 1983-84, chmn. adv. com. on issues 1984-87), Soc. Univ. Surgeons, Soc. Univ. Urologists, N.Y. Acad. Scis., Am. Soc. Nephrology, Internat. Transplantation Soc. (bd. dirs. 1984—, pres.-elect 1996-98, pres., 1998-2000), Soc. Pediatric Urology, Am. Urol. Assn., Nat. Kidney Found., Renal Physicians Assn. (bd. dirs. 1984-87), Pacific Coast Surg. Assn., San Francisco Surg. Soc., United Network Organ Sharing (bd. dirs. 1984-88, pres. 1985-86), Internat. Soc. for Organ Sharing (bd. dirs. 1991—, pres. 1993-95), Am. Soc. for Minority Health and Transplant Profls. (pres. 1992-94), Nafziger Surg. Soc. Achievements include being the principle lay figure in passage and enactment of National Organ Transplant Act, 1984; introduction of Pope John Paul II to the 18th International Transplantation Congress for Encyclical on Organ Transplantation, 2000. Office: Stanford U Med Ctr 703 Welch Rd Ste H2 Palo Alto CA 94304-1708 E-mail: oscar.salvatierra@medcenter.stanford.edu.

SALVATOR, JOSEPH C. law enrovcement, intelligence and security administrator, educator; b. Rockville Centre, N.Y., Aug. 16, 1974; s. Charles J. and Marilyn Salvator; m. Kathryn Levesque, July 23, 1999. BA in Criminal Justice (hon.), Norwich U., 1996; MS in Criminal Justice Adminstrn., Chaminade U. Honolulu, 1999. Adj. faculty Chaminade U., Honolulu, 1999-2000; security/intelligence ops. specialist Transp. Security Adminstrn., 2001—. Capt. USMC, 1996-2000. Mem. Internat. Assn. Chiefs of Police, Am. Soc. Indsl. Security. Roman Catholic.

SALVATORE, RICHARD JOHN, cinematographer, company executive; b. Bklyn., May 25, 1950; s. Peter Louis and Julia (Stampano) S. AA, Los Angeles Valley Coll., 1972. Artist George Whiteman & Assocs., Hollywood, Calif., 1968-72; ind. cinematographer, 1976—; founder RJS Motion Picture and TV, Northridge, 1991—; co-founder RJS Promotions, 1993—. Tchr. Prodrs. Assn., Hollywood, 1975—, Am. Film Inst., Beverly Hills, Calif., 1984—; CEO Omnicom Sys., Canoga Park, Calif., 1981—; co-owner Norman Borines World Bruce Lee Mus., Northridge, 1992—; founder RJS Comms., 1995—; bd. dirs., cinematographer Davidson Design Prodns., San Diego; cons. entertainment mktg. and advt. spl. projects (tie-ins and global exposure), 1991—; creative cons. for programming JM Entertainment, Hollywood, Calif., 1997—. Photographer: Solace, 1968 (Memorable mention Los Angeles County Fair 1968), Night Wind Dragon, 1972. Pres. Robert F. Kennedy campaign com., L.A., 1967, Gun Control Act of 1968, L.A.; dist. leader/area leader Muscular Dystrophy Assn., Los Angeles County, 1966-70. Recipient fin. grant U. Calif., 1972. Mem. Soc. Operating Cameramen (assoc.), Acad. TV Arts and Scis. (assoc.). Avocations: kung fu, collecting old movies. E-mail: richard@martial.com.

SALVATORELLI, JOSEPH J. engineer, consultant; b. Oct. 22, 1924; s. Luigi and Agnes (D'Amario) S.; m. Dolores A. Biello, Aug. 11, 1946; 1 child, Joel Girard. Diploma in civil engring., Drexel U., 1954, BSCE, 1956. Registered profl. engr., N.J., Pa., Md., Va., Del., N.Y., Nebr.; lic. sewage/water treatment plant operator; registered land surveyor. With Albright & Friel, Inc., Phila., 1946-59, ptnr., 1959-62, v.p., dir., 1962-71; sr. assoc. Taylor Wiseman Taylor, Mt. Laurel, N.J., 1971-75, v.p., ptnr., 1975-85; ret., 1985. Cons. in field, 1986—; mem. rsch. adv. coun. P.S.E.G. Rsch. Corp., 1986-89. Contbr. articles to profl. publs. Pres. Island House Unit Owners, 1974-76, 79-84; pres. Island House Condominium Assn., Margate, N.J., 1976-77. Sgt. U.S. Army, 1943-46, PTO. Recipient Alumni Achievement award Drexel U., 1959, named Alumnus of Yr., 1976. Mem. NSPE (life), ASCE (life, dir. Phila. sect., chmn. san. engring. divsn. 1968-69), Am. Acad. Environ. Engrs. (diplomate, life), Am. Water Works Assn. (life), N.J. Water Environment Assn. (life), Pa. Mcpl. Authorities Assn., N.J. Assn. Environ. Authorities (dir. 1972-74, hon. life), Environ. Assessment Assn. (cert. environ. inspector), Franklin Inst., Pa. Water Environ. Assn. (life, pres. 1971-72, High Hat award 1975, Hazeltine award 1980), Water Environ. Fedn. (life, dir. 1973-76, Arthur Sidney Bedell award 1973, Svc. award 1976), Ea. Pa. Water Pollution Control Operators Assn. (life, Svc. award 1973, Bolenius-Wiest Clean Streams award 1983), Alpha Sigma Lambda (ETA chpt.), Yeadon, Pa. Kiwanis (sec. 1968-70, pres. 1972, dir.). Roman Catholic.

SALVATY, BENJAMIN BENEDICT, lawyer; b. Chgo., Dec. 22, 1940; s. Benjamin Benedict and Marion Therese (Ryan) S.; m. Patricia Louise Recor, Aug. 29, 1964; children: Paul Benedict, Kathleen Anne. BBA, U. Notre Dame, 1962; JD, U. So. Calif., 1965. Bar: Calif. 1966, U.S. Dist. Ct. (no., cen., ea. and so. dists.) Calif., U.S. Ct. Appeals (9th cir.), U.S. Tax Ct., U.S. Supreme Ct. Sr. trial atty. Calif. Dept. Transp., 1966-79; gen. atty. The Atchison, Topeka and Santa Fe Railway Co., 1980-89; sr. ptnr. Hill, Farrer & Burrill, Los Angeles, 1990—. Mem. ABA (litigation sect. urban, state and local govt. law com. on condemnation, zoning and planning com.), Am. Bd. Trial Advs., Am. Judicature Soc., Internat. Right Way Assn., Irish Am. Bar Assn. (bd. dirs. 1985—, treas. 1991, sec. 1992, v.p. 1992-93, pres. 1993-94), Italian Am. Lawyers Assn., State Trial Attys. Assn. (pres. 1975-79), Calif. State Bar (chmn. condemnation com. 1987-88, vice chmn. 1986-87), Pasadena Bar Assn., L.A. County Bar Assn. (condemnation and land valuation com.). Office: Hill Farrer & Burrill LLP One California Plz 37th Fl 300 S Grand Ave Los Angeles CA 90071-3109 Fax: 213-624-4840.

SALVENDY, GAVRIEL, industrial engineer, educator; b. Budapest, Hungary, Sept. 30, 1938; came to U.S., 1968; s. Paul and Katarina (Brown) S.; m. Catherine Vivien Dees, Apr. 1, 1966; children: Laura Dorit, Kevin David. MSc in Engring. Prodn, U. Birmingham, Eng., 1966, PhD, 1968; Doctorate (hon.), Academia Sinica, 1995, Chinese Acad. Scis., 1995. Asst. prof. indsl. engring. SUNY, Buffalo, 1968-71; mem. faculty Purdue U., 1971—, prof. indsl. engring., chmn. human factors program, 1977, Fulbright distinguished prof., 1979-80, 81-82, NEC prof. indsl. engring., 1984-99; chmn. prof., head dept. indsl. engring. Tsinghua U., China, 2001—. Chmn. Internat. Commn. on Human Aspects in Computing, Switzerland, 1986-91. Co-author: Prediction and Development of Industrial Work Performance, 1973, Human Aspects of Computer Aided Design, 1987; sr. editor: Machine-Pacing and Occupational Stress, 1981, Social, Ergonomic and Stress Aspects of Work with Computers, 1987, Designing and Using Human-Computer Interfaces and Knowledge Based Systems, 1989; editor: Handbook of Industrial Engineering, 1982, 2d edit., 1992, Human Computer Interaction, 1984, Handbook of Human Factors, 1987, Cognitive Engineering in the Design of Human Computer Interaction and Expert Systems, 1987; founding editor: Internat. Jour. on Human-Computer Interaction, Internat. Jour. Human Factors in Mfg., Internat. Jour. of Cognitive Ergonomics; co-editor: Work with Computers: Organizational Management, Stress and Health Aspects, 1989, Human Computer Interaction: Software and Hardware Interfaces, 1993, Human-Computer Interaction: Applications and Case Studies, 1993, Design of Work and Development of Personnel in Advanced Manufacturing, 1994, Organization and Management of Advanced Manufacturing, 1994, Advanceds in Applied Ergonomics, 1996, Handbook of Human Factors and Ergonomics, 2d edit., 1997, Design of Computing Systems (2 vols.), 1997, Ergonomics in Manufacturing, 1998; contbr. articles to profl. jours., chpts. to books. Pres. Lafayette Jewish Sunday Sch., 1980-81. Recipient Mikhail Vasilievich Lomonosov medal USSR Acad. Sci., 1991. Fellow APA, Inst. Indsl. Engrs. (sr., Phil Carroll award 1973), Human Factors and Ergonomics Soc. (past officer), Ergonomics Soc. (hon., life mem.); mem. NAE. Office: Purdue U Sch Indsl Engring West Lafayette IN 47907

SALVESEN, B. FORBES, artist; b. Elgin, Ill., Nov. 6, 1944; d. Donald Behan and Helen Elaine (Krajacik) Forbes; m. Bruce Michael Salvesen, Sept. 3, 1966. Studied with Elvira Spivey, Barrington, Ill., 1972-74; studied with Peter Schoelch, Cary, Ill., 1975-82; student, Am. Acad. Art, 1976, Sch. Art Inst. Chgo., 1980-82, Kulick-Startk Byzantine Jewelry Sch., 1983. Asst. to purchasing agt. Harnischfeger, Crystal Lake, Ill., 1962-64; rec. sec. Electric Mfrs. Credit Bur., Cary, 1964-66; student and practicing artist, 1968—. Illustrator: (book) There were Reasons, 1983. Recipient Award of Excellence, Ill.-Arlington Heights Fine Arts Festival, 1995, Best of Show award 20th Ann. Cambridge Art Fair, 1995, 19th Ann. Fine Arts Festival, Downers Grove, Ill., 1995. Democratic. Roman Catholic. Avocations: writing, poetry, jewelry crafting, cross-country skiing, hiking. Home: 1312 Whippoorwill Dr Crystal Lake IL 60014-2614

SALVESEN, MAGDA ABERCROMBY, art historian, garden historian; b. Edinburgh, Scotland, June 20, 1944; came to US, 1976; d. Harold Keith and Marion Eleanora (Cameron) S.; m. Jon R. Schueler, July 29, 1976 (dec. Aug. 1992). MA, U. St. Andrews (Scotland), 1966, U. London, 1968; Cert. in Secondary Edn., Moray House Coll. Edn., Edinburgh, 1976. Asst. Richard Demarco Gallery, Edinburgh, 1968; exhibn. officer Scottish Arts Coun., 1969-71; tchr. middle sch. The Day Sch., N.Y.C., 1976-81; ESL tchr. Berlitz Sch. Langs., 1983-85; exec. adminstr. Archs./Designers/Planners for Social

Responsibility, 1985-88; lectr. art history New Sch. U., 1988—; lectr. garden history and theory N.Y. Botanical Garden, Bronx, 1990—. Lectr. in field. Editor: (manuscript by Jon Schueler) The Sound of Sleat: A Painter's Life, 1999; (dir., exec. prodr.): (video) Jon Schueler: A Life in Painting, 1999; contbr. Democrat. Avocations: museuming, reading, traveling, gardening. Address: 40 W 22nd St New York NY 10010 E-mail: msalvesen@juno.com.

SALWEN, MARIE (MANYA SALWEN), social worker, psychotherapist; b. N.Y.C., Aug. 16, 1931; d. Benjamin Kopman and Feiga Blumberg; m. Harold Salwen, June 11, 1950; children: Julie, Sharon, Cynthia, Nathan, Deborah, Fay. BA, Barnard Coll., 1952; MS in Social Work, Columbia U., 1979. Lic. social worker, N.Y., N.J. Psychiat. social worker Mt. Carmel Guild Community Mental Health Ctr., Newark, 1979-91, clin. supr., 1991-92, coord. outpatient dept., 1992-94; psychotherapist outpatient dept. Mountainside Hosp., Montclair, 1994—; pvt. practice N.Y.C., 1983—. Pvt. practice, N.Y.C., 1983—; field instr. Rutgers U. Sch. Social Work, New Brunswick, N.J., 1982-89, NYU Sch. Social Work, 1984; field instr. counseling program Seton Hall U., Newark, 1990-91. Mem. Teaneck (N.J.) Dem. Mcpl. Com., 1969-77, chmn., 1974-75; membership chmn. Teaneck Fair Housing Commn., 1964-70. Fellow Am. Inst. Psychotherapy and Psychoanalysis (cert. 1987); mem. NASW. Office: 27 W 72nd St New York NY 10023-3401

SALWEN, MARTIN J. pathologist, educator; b. Bklyn., Sept. 21, 1931; s. David Simon and Rose (Hittner) S.; m. Jane Stafford, July 21, 1979; children: Jennifer Artis, Zachary David; children by previous marriage: John Duncan, Jonathan M. BS, CCNY, 1953; MD, SUNY, Bklyn., 1957. Intern Hosp. of St. Raphael, New Haven, 1957-58; resident Yale-New Haven Hosp., 1958-59; fellow Yale U. Sch. Medicine, New Haven, 1959-61; attending pathologist Yale-New Haven Hosp., 1961-67; asst. prof. pathology Yale U., New Haven, 1965-71; prof. pathology Hahneman Med. Coll., Phila., 1971-79; clin. prof. pathology SUNY Health Sci. Ctr., Bklyn., 1979-93, disting. svc. prof., 1993—; dir. labs. U. Hosp. of Bklyn., 1986—97. Dir. pathology Kings County Hosp. Ctr., Bklyn., 1979-97, co-dir. residency tng. program, 1982-97, dir. labs. Monmouth Med. Ctr., Long Branch, N.J., 1967-78; chief Med. Lab. Ctr., USAF Hosp., Tachikawa, Japan, 1964-66; Jean Redman Oliver master tchr., 1992. Pres. Prospect Park South Assn., Bklyn., 2001—. Capt. USAF, 1964-66, Japan. Fellow Coll. Am. Pathologists, Am. Soc. Clin. Pathologists, Assn. Clin. Scientists, N.Y. Acad. Medicine, SUNY Alumni Assn. (chmn. bd. trustees 2000—, Disting. Svc. award 2002), Alpha Omega Alpha. Home: 934 Albemarle Rd Brooklyn NY 11218-2708 Office: SUNY Health Sci Ctr Bklyn 450 Clarkson Ave Brooklyn NY 11203-2056

SALWIN, ARTHUR ELLIOTT, software engineer; b. Chgo., Feb. 18, 1948; s. Harold and Shirley Salwin; m. Nancy Kessler, July 31, 1977; children: Edward, Rebecca. BS, U. Md., 1970; MA, Princeton U., 1972, PhD, 1975. Tech. staff Applied Physics Lab., Laurel, Md., 1976-78; rsch. staff Riverside Rsch. Inst., Arlington, Va., 1978-80; system engr. MITRE Corp./Mitretek Sys., McLean, 1980—, group leader, lead engr., 1983-95, prin. engr., 1996—98, sr. prin. software engr., 1998—. Instr. Fairfax County Adult Edn., McLean, 1982—; lectr. Georgetown U., Washington, 1980, 82. Fellow NSF, 1970, Noxell Found., 1969, Woodrow Wilson fellow, 1969. Mem. Reviewer Computing Revs., Phi Beta Kappa, Phi Kappa Phi, Phi Eta Sigma.

SALYER, STEPHEN LEE, media executive; b. Lexington, Ky., July 20, 1950; s. Ralph Conley Salyer and Margaret (Greenlee) Miles; m. Martha Ingels Ruddy, Apr. 21, 1985; children: Samuel Wilmot, Duncan Davis, Clara Josephine. BA, Davidson Coll., 1972; MPA, Harvard U., 1975. Pres. Citizens' Com. on Population and the Am. Future, Washington, 1972-73; cons. Rockefeller Family Assocs., N.Y.C., 1973-75; assoc. pub. issues program Population Coun., 1977-79; asst. to the pres. Ednl. Broadcasting Corp., Sta. WNET TV, 1975-76, v.p. corp. affairs, 1979-80, v.p. program devel. and mktg., 1981-82, sr. v.p. edn. divsn., 1982-86, sr. v.p. mktg. and comm., 1986-88; pres., CEO Pub. Radio Internat., Mpls., 1988—, also bd. dirs. Chmn. bd. dirs. Pub. Interactive, Inc., 1999—; bd. dirs. Minn. Meeting, McPhail Ctr. for the Arts, Philanthropic Rsch., Inc., 2001—; mem. nat. adv. com. Nat. Peace Found., 1991—. Co-author: (with James J. Bausch) Toward Safe, Convenient and Effective Contraceptives, 1978. Fellow Japan Soc. U.S.-Japan Leadership, 1996; mem. Nat. Commn. on Population Growth and the Am. Future, Washington, 1970-72. Root-Tilden scholar NYU Sch. Law, 1976-79. Mem. Harvard Club (N.Y.C.), Mpls. Club. Home: 1801 Irving Ave S Minneapolis MN 55403-2822 Office: Pub Radio Internat 100 N 6th St Ste 900 A Minneapolis MN 55403-1516

SALZBERG, BRIAN MATTHEW, neuroscience and physiology educator; b. N.Y.C., Sept. 4, 1942; s. Saul and Betty Bernice (Jacobs) S. BS, Yale U., 1963; PhD, Harvard U., 1971. Woodrow Wilson fellow in physics Harvard U., Cambridge, Mass., 1963-64, rsch. asst. in high energy physics, 1964-71; rsch. assoc. physiology Yale Med. Sch., New Haven, 1971-75; asst. prof. physiology U. Pa. Sch. Dental Medicine, Phila., 1975-80; assoc. prof. physiology U. Pa., 1980-82; prof. physiology U. Pa. Sch. Medicine, 1982-92, prof. neurosci. and physiology, 1992—. Arturo Rosenblueth vis. prof. CINVESTAV, Mexico City, 1987. Author more than 150 sci. articles on neurophysiology and biophysics. Trustee Marine Biol. Lab., Woods Hole, Mass., 1980-84, 87-95. Guest fellow Royal Soc., Cambridge U., 1991, fellow Japan Soc. for Promotion of Sci., Tokyo, 1989, STEPS fellow Marine Biol. Lab., 1977, 78; recipient Marine Biol. Lab. award, 1981. Fellow: AAAS, Am. Phys. Assn.; mem.: Soc. for Neurosci., Soc. Gen. Physiologists (coun. 1986—88), Biophys. Soc. (exec. bd. 1987—90, 1999—2001, coun. 1987—90, 1997—99), Sigma Xi, Phi Beta Kappa. Achievements include co-discovery of voltage-sensitive merocyanine, styryl, oxonol and cyanine dyes, dynamic optical properties of nerve terminals; application of optical methods to cell physiology and neuroscience. Avocation: marathon runner. Home: 4632 Spruce St Philadelphia PA 19139-4540 Office: U Pa Physiology Dept 234 Stemmler Hall Philadelphia PA 19104-6074

SALZER, LINDA PARSONS, clinical social worker; b. Middletown, Conn., June 13, 1951; d. Robert Nelson and Jean (Blanchard) Parsons; m. Richard Louis Salzer Jr., June 21, 1980; children: Eric, Scott. BA, Duke U.; MSS, Bryn Mawr Coll., 1975. Diplomate ACSW; lic. marriage counselor, N.J. Clin. social worker Life Guidance Svcs., Broomall, Pa., 1975-77, Albert Einstein Mental Health Ctr., Phila., 1977-78, Hackensack (N.J.) Hosp. Inst. for Child Devel., 1978-80, Community Mental Health Orgn., Englewood, N.J., 1980-83; pvt. practice clin. social work, 1982—. Author: Infertility: How Couples Can Cope, 1986, Surviving Infertility, 1991. Mem. Nat. Assn. Social Workers, Resolve, Inc. (pres. No. N.J. chpt. 1986-89), Phi Beta Kappa. Avocations: running, gardening, travel, piano. Office: 174 Grand Ave Englewood NJ 07631-3547

SALZMAN, ARTHUR GEORGE, architect; b. Chgo., June 20, 1929; s. Russell Harvey Salzman and Mildred Olive (Olsen) Erickson; m. Joan Marie Larson, Aug. 16, 1952; children: Lisa Jo Salzman Braucher, David Ralph. BS in Archtl. Engring., U. Ill., 1952; MArch, Ill. Inst. Tech., 1960. Registered architect, Ill., Mich., Nat. Coun. Archtl. Registration Bds. Architect Skidmore, Owings & Merrill, Chgo., 1960, Mies van der Rohe, Arch., Chgo., 1960-69; assoc. The Office of Mies Van Der Rohe, 1969-81; v.p. FCL Assocs., 1981-86; exec. v.p. Lohan Assocs., 1986-91; pvt. practice Evanston, Ill., 1992—. Bldg. code restructuring com. City of Chgo., 1994-96, bldg. code electronic version com., 1997, bldg. code rev. com., 1998—. V.p. Chgo. area Unitarian-Universalist Coun., Chgo., 1974—76; bd. dirs. Savoy-aires, Evanston, 1985—88, 1990—93, pres., 1992—93; active Chgo. Com. on High Rise Bldgs. Cpl. U.S. Army, 1952—54. Mem. AIA (bd. dirs. Chgo. chpt. 1992-96, sec. 1994-96), Constrn. Specifications Inst., Bldg. Ofcls. and Code Adminstrs. Internat. (profl.), Coun. on Tall Bldgs. and Urban Habitat, Am. Assn. for Wind Engring., Precast-Prestressed Concrete Inst., Cliff Dwellers Club, North Shore Musicians Club. Avocations: community theater, choral singing, sailing. Home: 1018 Greenwood St Evanston IL 60201-4212 Office: 1603 Orrington Ave Ste 1060 Evanston IL 60201-5041 E-mail: salzmanagev@att.net.

SALZMAN, BARNETT SEYMOUR, psychiatrist; b. N.Y.C., Feb. 15, 1939; s. George and Fanny (Pugach) S.; m. Sandra Christian, 1974 (div. 1978); m. Diana Toney, 1980 (div. 1989); m. Stacey Jean Severin, Jan. 7, 1992; children: Rachel Star, Sunshine Star, Priscilla Magdalene Star Barnett. BA, Hunter Coll., 1960; MD, SUNY, Buffalo, 1965. Diplomate SPEX, Am. Bd. Forensic Medicine, Am. Bd. Psychiatry and Neurology, Am. Bd. Forensic Examiners, Nat. Bd. Med. Examiners. Rsch. fellow in biochemistry Northeastern U., Boston, 1960, 61; intern Good Samaritan Hosp., L.A., 1965-66; chief resident in psychiatry Cedars-Sinai Med. Ctr., 1966-69; psychiatrist inpatient svcs. Fresno County HHS, 1997—2002. Pvt. practice gen. and forensic psychiatry, Calif., Hawaii, Fla., Ariz., Tex., Utah, Ohio; legal expert psychiatry U.S. Superior Cts., Fresno County Cts.; pres. New World Acad. Holopsychiatry, Holy Virgin Beauty Prodns., Inc.; video psychiatrist, holistic physician. Prodr., dir. (TV psychiatry series) Mind and Soul, 1973-96. Founder, dir. Laguna Beach (Calif.) Free Clinic, 1970. With USNR, 1962-73. Served to lt. comdr. USNR, 1962—73. Fellow Royal Soc. Health U.K., Am. Assn. Social Psychiatry, World Assn. Social Psychiatry, Am. Coll. Forensic Examiners, Am. Coll. Forensic Medicine; mem. Am. Chem. Soc., Nat. Forensic Ctr. Disting. Experts, N.Y. Acad. Sci. Office: 3222 W Menlo Ave Fresno CA 93711

SALZMAN, BEVERLY E. behavioral and social sciences educator, consultant; b. N.Y.C., July 25, 1960; d. Norman Erwin and Ruby Valerie (Freeman) S. BS in Psychology, BS in Phys. Edn., U. Bridgeport, 1982; MBA, Sacred Heart U., 1986; sr. profl. cert. application of psychol., U. New Haven, 1990. Sr. program dir. Lakewood-Trumbull divsn. YMCA Greater Bridgeport, Monroe, Conn., 1983-88; youth svc. bur. dir. City of Shelton, 1988-91; exec. dir. Big Bros. Big Sisters of Fairfield County, Inc., Bridgeport, 1991-92; instr. Housatonic Comty. Tech. Coll., 1992—; exec. dir. Alpha Home, Inc., 1992-96; instr. U. Bridgeport, 1996-98; asst. dir. of devel. Bridgeport Hosp. Found., 1996-97; instr. Albertus Magnus, New Haven, 1997. Mem. Housatonic Regional Adv. Coun., Bridgeport, 1990—2002; instr. Teikyo Post U., 1998—2000; nonprofit cons., 1992—. Exec. dir. Sexual Assault Crisis Ctr., Stamford, Conn., 1999—2000. Named Woman of Substance, Conn. Post, 1996. Avocations: travel, fitness, theater, reading. Home: 3275 Main St Bridgeport CT 06606-4240 E-mail: bsalzman@snet.net.

SALZMAN, DAVID ELLIOT, entertainment industry executive; b. Bklyn., Dec. 1, 1943; s. Benjamin and Rose Harriet (Touby) S.; m. Sonia Camelia Gonsalves, Oct. 19, 1968; children: Daniel Mark, Andrea Jessica, Adam Gabriel. BA, Bklyn. Coll., 1965; MA, Wayne State U., 1967. Dir. TV ops. Wayne State U., 1966-67; producer Lou Gordon Program, 1967-70; program mgr. Sta. WKBD-TV, Detroit, 1970-71, Sta. KDKA-TV, Pitts., 1971-72, gen. mgr., 1973-75; program mgr. Sta. KYW-TV, Phila., 1972-73; chmn. bd. Group W Prodns., N.Y.C and Los Angeles, 1975—; founder, pres. United Software Assocs., 1980-81; creator News Info. Weekly Service, 1981; exec. v.p. Telepictures Corp., 1980-84, vice chmn., 1984; pres. Lorimar Telepictures Corp. (merger Telepictures and Lorimar, Inc.), 1985-90, Lorimar TV, 1986-90; creator Newscope: Nat. TV News Cooperative, 1983; pres., CEO David Salzman Entertainment, Burbank, Calif., 1990-93; co-CEO Quincy Jones-David Salzman Entertainment (QDE), 1993—; exec. prodr. Jenny Jones Show, 1991—. Exec. prodr. Mad-TV, In the House, 68th Ann. Acad. awards, Concert of the Americas, 1995, Vibe-TV, 1997-98, Steel, 1997; CEO David Salzman Enterprises, 1998—; co-owner Vibe Mag., 1995—, Spin Mag., 1995—, Sta. WNOL-TV, 1995—, Sta. WATL-TV, 1995—, Sta. KCWE-TV, 1995, Sta. WGRB-TV, 1998; bd. dirs. 411.com, Broadwave USA, In Radio, Rimer Drive Networks; guest lectr. at schs.; bd. govs. Films of Coll. and Univ. Students; co-prodr. (Broadway shows) Urinetown, The Dinner Party, 2001, Into the Woods, 2002. Contbr. articles to Variety and numerous comms. trade pubs. Bd. dirs. Pitts. Civic Light Opera, Am. Blood Bank, Pitts., Hebrew Inst., Jewish Community Ctr., Harrison, N.Y., Temple Etz Chaim, USC Sch. Cinema-TV, Emory U. Ctr. for Leadership, Emory Bus. Sch., Bklyn. Coll. Found., HELP group. Recipient award Detroit chpt. Am. Women in Radio and TV, 1969, award Golden Quill, 1971, award Golden Gavel, 1971, local Emmy award, 1972, award AP, 1974, Gold medal Broadcast Promotion Assn., 1983, Lifetime Achievement award Bklyn. Coll., 1990, Disting. Alumnus award, Golden Plate award Am. Acad. Achievement, 1995; BPME Gold medal San Francisco Film Festival, 1984, N.Y., 1985, Chgo., 1986, Tree of Life award Jewish Nat. Fund, 1988. Mem. Acad. TV Arts and Scis., Nat. Assn. TV Program Execs., Radio-TV News Dirs. Assn., Am. Mgmt. Assn., Am. Film Inst., Brooklyn Coll. Found. Office: Mad TV Hollywood Ctr Studios 2d Fl 1040 N Las Palmas Bldg 2 Hollywood CA 90038 E-mail: Davids@madtv.com. *"We know what we are but not what we may be."*.

SALZMAN, ERIC, composer, writer; b. N.Y.C., Sept. 8, 1933; s. Samuel and Frances (Klenett) S.; m. Lorna Jackson, Dec. 24, 1955; children: Eva, Stephanie. BA in Music with honors, Columbia U., 1954; MFA, Princeton U., 1956. Music critic N.Y. Times, N.Y.C., 1958-62; dir. music Sta. WBAI-FM, 1962—63, 1968—72; music critic N.Y. Herald Tribune, 1963-66; asst. prof. Queens Coll. CUNY, Queens, 1966-68; artistic dir. Quog Music Theater, N.Y.C., 1970-80; co-founder, artistic dir. Am. Music Theater Festival, Phila., 1982-94; founder, artistic dir. MusicTheater/N.Y., 1994—. Mem. guest faculty NYU, Yale U., Banff Ctr. for Arts, Can., Conservatoire Nationale, Lyon, France; assoc. artistic dir. Ctr. Contemporary Opera, 2000—; founder, artistic dir. Electric Ear, Electric Circus, N.Y.C., 1967-68, New Image of Sound, Hunter Coll., N.Y.C., 1968-71, Free Music Store, N.Y.C., 1968-72. Prin. works include (compositions) String Quartet, 1955, Sonata for Flute and Piano, 1956, Night Dance for Orch., 1957; prin. works include (compositions) Whitman Songs for Voice and Piano, 1955—57; prin. works include (compositions) Partita for Violin, 1958, Cummings Set for Voice and Piano, 1958, Inventions for Orch., 1957, In Praise of the Owl and the Cuckoo for Soprano, Guitar, Violin, and Viola, 1963, Foxes and Hedgehogs, Verses and Cantos for 4 Voices, two Instrumental Groups with Sound Sys., 1964, Queens Collage, An Acad. Festival Overture for Tape, 1966, Larynx Music, Verses for Soprano, Guitar, and 4 track Tape, 1966, Helix, 1971, Fantasy on Lazarus, 1974, Accord, 1975, Variations on Sacred Harp Tunes, 1982, and numerous others, (radio opera) Voices, 1971, (mime-dance prodn.) The Peloponnesian War, 1967, (multimedia participatory work) Feedback, 1968, The Nude Paper Sermon, 1969, (multimedia environ. work) Can Man Survive?, 1969—71, (media poem) Ecolog, 1972, (musical theater prodn.) Saying Something, 1972, Biograffiti, 1972, Lazarus, 1973, (with Michael Sahl) The Conjurer, 1974, Stauf, 1974, Noah, 1978, The Passion of Simple Simon, 1979, Boxes, 1982 (Seagram Prodn. award), (opera buffa) Civilization and its Discontents, 1980 (Prix Italia award Assn European Broadcasters), (with Ned Jackson) Big Jim and the Small-time Investors, 1986, (with Valeria Vasilevski) The True Last Words of Dutch Schultz , 1996, (with Michel Rostain) La Prière du Loup (Wolfman Prayer), 1997, (media and live performance piece) Toward a New American Opera, 1985, (adaptations) Strike Up the Band, 1984, Love Life, 1990, The Silent Twins, 1992, prodr., dir (with Teresa Strata) The Unknown Kurt Weill, (with Joel Grey and N.Y.C. Opera) Silverlake, Civilization and its Discontents, The Tango Project (Record of Yr. award Stereo Rev.), Two to Tango, The Palm Court, The Waltz Project, Moore's Irish Melodies, A Portrait Album, Notebooks of Anna Magdalena Bach, An Old-Fashioned Christmas, Revelation in the Courthouse Park, Casino Paradise, recs. include Civilization and its Discontents, Wiretap, The Nude Paper Sermon, Noah, Accord; author: 20th Century Music: An Introduction, 1967, (4th edit.) , 2001, (translated into Spanish, Portuguese, Hungarian, and Japanese) ; editor: Musical Quar., 1984—91; contbg. editor, critic Stereo Rev., N.Y.C., 1970—99; contbr. N.Y. Times, New York Herald-Tribune, N.Y. Mag., others; composer: (commns., premiers) Can., 1995, France, 1997, The Netherlands, 1997; composer: (with premiers) Abel Gance à New York, 1999—; with Eva Salzman Francois Godin) Abel Gance à New York, 1999—; premiers Strike Up the Band, Cassandra; arranger French version: commns., premiers Strike Up the Band, 2000. Fulbright scholar St. Cecilia Acad., 1956-58, Darmstadt Ferienkurse, 1957; recipient Armstrong, Prix Italia radio awards, Sang prize for criticism. Mem. South Fork Nat. History Soc. (mem. coun.). Avocations: natural history, ornithology. Home: 29 Middagh St Brooklyn NY 11201-1339 E-mail: esalzman@aba.org.

SALZMAN, GARY SCOTT, lawyer; b. Portchester, N.Y., May 26, 1963; s. David Stuart and Francine (Selenow) S.; m. Suzanne Sansone, Apr. 2, 1990. BBA, U. Miami, 1985, JD, 1988. Bar: Fla. 1988, U.S. Dist. Ct. (so. dist.) 1989, Colo. 1991, U.S. Dist. Ct. (mid. dist.) Fla. 1992, U.S. Ct. Appeals (11th cir.) 1992, U.S. Supreme Ct. 1992; cert. arbitrator and mediator; cert. in bus. litigation, Fla. Assoc. Robinson & Greenberg, PA, Coral Gables, Fla., 1988-89, Buchbinder & Elegant, PA, Miami, 1989, Mishan, Sloto, Hoffman and Greenberg, PA, Miami, 1989-91, Dempsey & Assocs., Winter Park, Fla., 1991-92; pvt. practice, Orlando and Winter Park, 1992-95; ptnr. Marlowe, Appleton, Weatherford & Salzman, Winter Park, 1996-98, Brown, Ward, Salzman & Weiss, P.A., Orlando, 1998—. Comml.,employment and fin. arbitration panelist Am. Arbitration Assn. Mem. ABA, Fla. Bar Assn. (Fla. Bar BLSE, bus. litig. cert. com. 1995—), Bus. Exec. Network, Orange County Bar Assn. Office: 225 E Robinson St Ste 660 Orlando FL 32801 Fax: 407-425-9596. E-mail: gssalzman@orlandolaw.net.

SALZMAN, ROBERT JAY, accountant; b. Bklyn., Dec. 7, 1941; s. Irving and Sydelle (Feingold) S.; m. Constance A. Freeman, Sept. 16, 1990. BA, Allegheny Coll., Meadville, Pa., 1962; MBA, U. Pa., 1965; JD, N.Y. Law Sch., 1972. Bar: N.Y. 1973; CPA, N.Y. Acct., N.Y.C., 1965—; pvt. practice Robert J. Salzman, CPA, P.C., 1970—. Home: 10 E End Ave New York NY 10021-1106 also: 82 Sycamore Dr East Hampton NY 11937-1482 also: 2801 NE 183rd St Miami FL 33160-2100 E-mail: rsalzman@rjspc.com.

SALZMAN, STANLEY P. lawyer; b. N.Y.C., Jan. 30, 1931; s. George D. and Fanny M. (Pugach) S.; m. Leona Schames, June 18, 1958 (dec. Nov. 1967); m. Marilyn J. Bzura, Feb. 3, 1974; children: Ira J., Mark B., Debra G., Jeffrey M. David, Steven B. David. BA, Bklyn. Coll., 1952; JD, Bklyn. Law Sch., 1955. Bar: N.Y. 1956, U.S. Dist. Ct. (so. and ea. dists.) N.Y. 1960, U.S. Supreme Ct. 1964, U.S. Ct. Appeals (2d cir.) 1966. Assoc. Otterbourg, Steindler, Houston & Rosen, N.Y.C., 1957; ptnr. Venitt, Adler & Salzman, 1958-66, Friesner & Salzman, LLP, Great Neck, N.Y., 1966—. Bd. dirs. Colora Printing Inks Inc., Linden, N.J. Office: PO Box 220700 11 Grace Ave Great Neck NY 11021-2417 E-mail: legalsps@aol.com.

SALZMANN, GEORGE STEPHEN, biochemist, priest; b. Phila., June 19, 1948; s. George Edward and Jean Elizabeth (Bigley) S. BS in Math. and Physics, Allentown U., 1971; MS in Molecular Biophysics, Yale U., 1973; STL in Moral Theology and Bioethics, The Gregorian U., Rome, 1978; PhD in Biol. Chemistry, Harvard U., 1987. Ordained priest Roma Cath. Ch., 1977. Fellow dept. molecular biology, lectr. dept. religion Princeton (N.J.) U., 1987-91; chaplain grad. and profl. schs. Harvard U., Cambridge, Mass., 1992—, pres. Harvard Chaplains, 1995-97; assoc. pastor St. Paul's Ch., Harvard Sq., 1992—. Assoc. pastor St. Catherine Ch., Norwood, Mass., 1978-85, Holy Cross Ch., Wayne, N.J., 1986-87, St. Paul's Ch., Princeton, 1987-90, St. Anthony's Ch., Princeton, 1988-92. Founder A.W.N. Pugin Soc. N.Am.; trustee ADe Sales U, Center Valley, Pa., 1991—; pres. United Ministry, Harvard U., 1995—, pres. chaplains, 1995-97. Nat. Merit scholar, 1966; NSF fellow, 1971-73, Adams House/Harvard Coll. fellow, NIH fellow, 1978-85, Roche Inst. Molecular Biology fellow, 1985-87. Home: St Paul's Rectory 29 Mount Auburn St Cambridge MA 02138-6031 Office: Harvard-Radcliffe Cath Student Ctr 20 Arrow St Cambridge MA 02138-5102 E-mail: gsalzmann@fas.harvard.edu.

SALZMANN, ZDENEK, anthropology educator; b. Prague, Czechoslovakia, Oct. 18, 1925; came to U.S., 1947; s. Zdenko and Ludmila (Chrzova) S.; m. Joy Anne McCollum, Aug. 18, 1949; children: Anne Mitchell, Linda Joy, Erica Jane. Abitur, Realgymnasium, Prague, Czechoslovakia, 1944; Absolutorium, Charles U., Prague, Czechoslovakia, 1948; MA, Indiana U., 1949, PhD, 1963. Headmaster Verde Valley Sch., Sedona, Ariz., 1963-66; Instr. Phillips Exeter (N.H.) Acad., 1966-68; prof. Dept. of Anthropology U. Mass., Amherst, 1968—. Adj. prof. dept. Slavic langs. and lit. U. Mass., Amherst, 1975—; vis. prof. Albert-Ludwigs U., Freiburg, Fed. Republic Germany, 1970; lang. and culture cons. Arapaho Indians, Wyoming, 1949—; vis. lectr. Semester at Sea, U. Pitts., 1982; vis. prof. Yale U., New Haven, 1983. Author: Anthropology, 1969, 1973, 1977 (Spanish edition), The Arapaho Indians: a Research Guide and Bibliography, 1988; co-author Komarov: a Czech Farming Village, 1974, 1986, Humanity and Culture; an Introduction to Anthropology, 1978; compiler: Dictionary of Contemporary Arapaho Usage, 1983; contbr. numerous articles on Arapaho and Czech language and culture. Ceremonially named Arapaho Chief, 1985; grantee Am. Coun. of Learned Socs., Internat. Rsch. and Exchanges Bd., Fulbright-Hays, NIMH, NEH, Am. Philos. Soc. Fellow Am. Anthrop. Assn.; mem. Linguistic Soc. Am. (life), Am. Assn. Advancement Slavic Studies, Czechoslovak Soc. Arts and Scis. Avocation: travel, philately, carpentry. Office: U Mass Amherst MA 01003

SALZSTEIN, RICHARD ALAN, pharmaceutical sales administrator, biomedical engineer; s. Eli and Lorraine Salzstein; m. Sharon Lazar; 2 children. BS in Engring., U. Pa., 1981, MS in Engring., 1982, PhD in Bioengring., 1985. Rsch. fellow U. Pa., Phila., 1981-85; rsch. scientist Hercules, Inc., Wilmington, Del., 1986-2000, mkt. mgr., pharms., 2000—01, pharm. sales mgr., 2001—. Mem. Am. Assn. Pharm. Scientists., Tau Beta Pi. Recipient Kappa Delta award Bioelectrical Repair & Growth Soc., 1985; NSF fellow, 1981-85. Avocations: racquetball, skiing. Office: Hercules Inc Aqualon Divsn 1313 N Market St Wilmington DE 19894-0001

SAM, DAVID, federal judge; b. Hobart, Ind., Aug. 12, 1933; s. Andrew and Flora (Toma) S.; m. Betty Jean Brennan, Feb. 1, 1957; children: Betty Jean, David Dwight, Daniel Scott, Tamara Lynn, Pamela Rae, Daryl Paul, Angie, Sheyla. BS, Brigham Young U., 1957; JD, Utah U., 1960. Bar: Utah 1960, U.S. Dist. Ct. Utah 1966. Sole practice and ptnr., Duchesne, Utah, 1963-76; dist. judge State of Utah, 1976-85; judge U.S. Dist. Ct. Utah, Salt Lake City, 1985-97; chief judge U.S. Dist. Ct., 1997—99, sr. judge, 1999—. Atty. City of Duchesne, 1963-72; Duchesne County atty., 1966-72; commr. Duchesne, 1972-74; mem. adv. com. Codes of Conduct of Jud. Conf. U.S., 1987-91, Jud. Coun. of 10th Cir., 1991-93; mem. U.S. Del. to Romania, Aug. 1991. Chmn. Jud. Nomination Com. for Cir. Ct. Judge, Provo, Utah, 1983; bd. dirs. Water Resources, Salt Lake City, 1973-76. Served to capt. JAGC, USAF, 1961-63. Named Judge of Yr., Utah State Bar, 1999. Mem. Utah Bar Assn., Supreme Ct. Hist. Soc., Am. Inns of Ct. VII (counselor 1986-89), A. Sherman Christensen Am. Inn of Ct. I (counselor 1989-98), Utah Jud. Conf. (chmn. 1982), Utah Dist. Judges Assn. (pres. 1982-83), Order of Coif (hon. Brigham Young U. chpt.). Mem. Lds Ch. Avocations: beekeeping, reading, sports. Office: US Dist Ct 148 US Courthouse 350 S Main St Ste 441 Salt Lake City UT 84101-2180 E-mail: davidsam@utd.uscourts.gov.

SAMAD, NIDAL ABDUL, research scientist; b. Mazraa, Beirut, Lebanon, June 9, 1961; came to U.S., 1985; s. Nadim N. and Dalal N. Samad; m. Soha A., Sept. 9, 1988. BS in Chemistry, Lebanese U., Beirut, 1984; BSChemE with honors, Fla. Inst. Tech., 1987, MSChemE, 1989, MS in Environ. Sci., 1994. Plant operator, Cocoa, Fla., 1989-90; grad. rsch. asst. Fla. Inst. Tech., Melbourne, 1990-92, rsch. cons., 1991-92, rsch. scientist, 1991-93, Mainstream Engring., Rockledge, 1993—. Rsch. scientist, cons. Fla. Inst. Tech., Melbourne, 1991-93; rsch. scientist Mainstream Engring. Corp., Rockledge, 1993—. Mem. edn. com. UN, Brevard chpt., 1994. Recipient Rsch. assistantship Fla. Inst. Tech., 1997-89, teaching assistantship, 1991. Mem. AIChE, Sigma Xi (assoc.). Achievements include four patents pending, two in the area of water and waste water treatment and two in the area of air conditioning. Home: Apt 108 1050 Diamond Head Dr Merritt Island FL 32953-3247

SAMANIEGO, PAMELA SUSAN, organization administrator; b. San Mateo, Calif., Nov. 29, 1952; d. Armando C. and Harriott Susan (Croot) S. Student, UCLA, 1972, Los Angeles Valley Coll., 1970-72. Asst. new accts. supr. Beverly Hills Fed. Savings, 1970-72; asst. controller Bio-Science Enterprises, Van Nuys, Calif., 1972-74; adminstr. asst. Avery/Tirce Prodns., Hollywood, 1974-78; sr. estimator N. Lee Lacy and Assocs., 1978-81; head of prodn. Film Consortium, 1981-82; exec. producer EUE/Screen Gems Ltd., Burbank, Calif., 1982-88; advt. agency dir. Barrett & Assocs., Las Vegas, Nev., 1988-90; exec. producer Laguna/Take One, 1990-93; dir. Sta. KXLY-4 ABC, Spokane, Wash., 1993-94; dir. advt. and mktg. Appaloosa Horse Club, Moscow, 1994—2001; sr. mgr. mktg. Am. Quarter Horse Assn., Amarillo, Tex., 2001—. Author: Millimeter & Backstage, 1982-88. Emergency room vol. San Mateo (Calif.) County Hosp., 1968-70; Sunday sch. tchr. Hillsdale Meth. Ch., San Mateo, 1968-70; vol. worker Hillsdale Meth. Ch. Outreach, San Francisco, 1967-70. Recipient CLIO award CLIO Awards, Inc., 1985, ADDY award Las Vegas Advt. Fedn., 1988. Mem. Dirs. Guild Am. (2nd asst. dir. 1987-88), Assn. Ind. Comml. Producers, Am. Horse Show Assn., Internat. Arabian Horse Assn., AHASFV (sec. 1978-79), AHASC (sec. 1978-88). Democrat. Methodist. Avocations: breed and show Arabian horses. Home: 3630 Brennan Blvd 20F Amarillo TX 79121 Office: Am Quarter Horse Assn 1600 Quarter Horse Ln Amarillo TX 79104 E-mail: PamelaS@aqha.org.

SAMARTINI, JAMES ROGERS, retired appliance company executive; b. Cleve., Apr. 13, 1935; s. Leonard Henry and Grace Rogers (Tully) S.; m. Irene Ann Kurnava, Sept. 16, 1961 (dec. June 1994); m. Julia S. Rubin, Sept. 8, 1996; children: David L., James F., Patrick R. AB, Dartmouth Coll., 1957; MBA, Harvard U., 1961. Fin. supr. Ford Motor Co., Dearborn, Mich.,

1966-72; v.p. fin. and adminstrn. Thonet Industries Inc., York, Pa., 1972-74; from asst. controller to v.p., CFO Mead Corp., Dayton, 1974-86; CFO Whirlpool Corp., 1986-91, exec. v.p., chief adminstrv. officer Mich., 1991-95; ret., 1995. Bd. dirs. Peoples State Bank, St. Joseph, Mich., 1987-95. Mem. adv. bd. Salvation Army; chmn. bd. trustees Whirlpool Found., 1993—95; trustee Dayton Opera Assn., 1977—86, pres., 1985—86; bd. dirs. Epilepsy Assn. We. Ohio, 1986, S.W. Mich. Symphony Orch., 1991—93; bd. fin. Town of Kent (Conn.), 1999—2001, mem. zoning bd.appeals, 2001—02. Mem.: Fin. Execs. Inst. (dir. 1983—86). Home: PO Box 129 South Kent CT 06785-0129

SAMBALUK, NICHOLAS WAYNE, auditor, educator; b. Winnipeg, Can., Nov. 5, 1955; s. Nicoli and Mary (Homeniuk) S.; m. Rosalyn Eisterhold, Apr. 5, 1981; children: Nicholas Michael, Eric Preston. BS, Ariz. State U., 1977; MS in Adminstrn., Ctrl. Mich. U., 1999. CPA, Va.; cert. mgmt. acct.; cert. internal auditor. Auditor Office of Inspector Gen. for Health and Human Services, Jefferson City, Mo., 1978-82, Def. Contract Audit Agy., Ft. Worth, 1982-87; auditing instr. Def. Contract Audit Inst., Memphis, 1987-90; audit supr. Def. Contract Audit Agy., Dallas, 1990-91, program mgr. Hdqrs. Ft. Belvoir, Va., 1991-96, br. mgr. Arlington, Tex., 1996-99; regional resources mgr. ctrl. region Defense Contract Audit Agy., 1999—. Mem. AICPA, Nat. Assn. Accts. Democrat. Home: 721 Loggins Trail Poolville TX 76487-5617 Office: Def Contract Audit Agy Central Region 6321 Campus Circle Dr E Irving TX 75063-2712

SAMBASIVAM, SAMUEL E. computer science and mathematics educator; b. Edaiyur, Tamil Nadu, India, Apr. 7, 1956; came to U.S., 1987, naturalized, 1999; s. Sambasivam Kuppusamy and Valliyammal (Loganathan) S.; m. Vijayalakshmi Ramachandran, July 9, 1989; children: Richard Cecil, Joshua David. BS, Madras (India) U., 1976; MS, Mysore (India) U., 1978; MPhil, Indian Inst. Tech., 1981; PhD, Moscow State U., 1986; MS, We. Mich. U., 1990. Rsch. asst. Indian Inst. Tech., Delhi, 1979-81, instr. Bombay, 1981-82; rschr. Moscow State U., 1983-87; instr. Western Mich. U., Kalamazoo, 1987-88, grad. asst., 1988-90; assoc. prof. computer sci. and math. Mo. Western State Coll., St. Joseph, 1990-95, coord. computer sci., 1991-95; prof. computer sci. Azusa (Calif.) Pacific U., 1996—, acting chmn. computer sci., 1996-97, chmn. computer sci., 1997—. Contbr. articles to profl. jours. Merit scholar Nat. Coun. India, 1976-78, rsch. fellow, 1978-81; fellow Govt. of India, 1982-86; scholar Western Mich. U., 1989, Coun. of Chairpersons award, 1992. Mem. Assn. Computing Machinery (dir. Scholastic programming contest 1990—), Upsilon Pi Epsilon, Kappa Mu Epsilon. Avocations: travel, swimming, tennis, chess, racquetball. Home: 1350 E Comstock Ave Glendora CA 91741-2915 Office: Azusa Pacific U Computer Sci Dept Rte 66 Azusa CA 91702-2769 E-mail: ssambasi@apu.edu.

SAMBASIVAN, MAHADEVA IYER, neurosurgeon, consultant; b. Trivandrum, India, May 1, 1936; s. Iyer Mahadeva and Ammal Avudai; m. Gomathy Sambasivan, May 8, 1963; children: Mahesh, Kumar, Srividya. MBBS, Trivandrum Med. Coll., India, 1955; MS in Neurosurgery, Vellore Christian Med. Coll., Trivandrum, 1960; MS in Gen. Surgery, Trivandrum Med. Coll., India, 1966. From asst. prof. to assoc. prof. Med. Coll., Trivandrum, 1966-75, prof., 1975-82, dir., 1982-91, vice prin., 1989-91; cons. neurosurgeon Cosmopolitan Hosp., 1991—. Sci. program dir. World Fedn. N.S. Socs., 1985-89, v.p. 1997—; dep. chmn. Neurotrauma Com. WFIVS, 1990—. Contbr. articles to med. jours. Chmn. Sankara Free Med. Ctr., Trivandrum, 1993—; v.p. Swati Tirunal Sangeetha Sabha, Trivandrum, 1994—; patron Ctr. for Human Rights Legal Aid Rsch., Trivandrum, 1994. Fellow Royal Coll. Surgeons, Acad. Med. Scis.; mem. Neurological Soc. (sec. 1981-89, pres. 1995—), World Fedn. Neurosurg. Socs. (v.p. 1997—). Avocations: Sanskrit studies, Vedie literature, nature. Home: Sivapriya Tagore Gardens 695011 Trivandrum India Office: Cosmopolitan Hosp Pattom 695004 Trivandrum Kerala India E-mail: sambshiv@mol4vsml.net.in.

SAMBUR, MARVIN, federal agency administrator; B in Elec. Engring., CCNY, 1968; M in Elec. Engring., MIT, 1969, PhD in Elec. Engring., 1972. Tech. staff mem. Bell Labs., Murray Hill, NJ, 1968—77; sr. v.p. ITT Def. Comms., Nutley, 1977—88; pres., gen. mgr. electron tech. divsn. ITT, Easton, Pa., 1988—91, pres., gen. mgr. aerospace/comms. divsn. Ft. Wayne, Ind., 1991—98; pres., CEO ITT Def., McLean, Va., 1998—2001; asst. sec. for acquisition/svc. acquisition exec. Dept. Def., USAF, Washington, 2001—. Recipient Golden Apple award, 1999, Outstanding Leadership award, Inst. Environ. Mgmt. and Assessment, 1994. Mem.: IEEE (Centennial award), Acoustical Soc. Am., Eta Kappa Nu, Tau Beta Pi. Office: Dept Def Asst Sec for Acquisition/AF Acquisition 1060 Air Force Pentagon Washington DC 20330-1060

SAMBURG, A. GENE, security company executive; b. Indpls., Apr. 25, 1941; s. A. George and Hermine (Wittgenstein) S.; m. Lorrie Silverman, June 26, 1966; children: Kimberly Jill, Thomas Blair. BEE, Cornell U., 1964; OPM, Harvard U., 1985. Engr. Westinghouse Corp., 1964-72; founder, pres. and CEO Kastle Systems, Inc., 1972—. Adv. on bus. programs Cornell U.; spl. lectr. for numerous profl. and ednl. courses in field. Patentee in field. Named E&Y Master Entrepreneur of Yr., Washington, 1999. Mem. IEEE, ASME, CPP, Am. Soc. Indsl. Security, Woodmont Country Club, City Club (Washington), Tower Club (McLean, Va.). Home: 1206 Stable Gate Ct Mc Lean VA 22102-2516 Office: Kastle Systems Inc 1501 Wilson Blvd Arlington VA 22209-2403 E-mail: gene@kastle.com.

SAMEK, EDWARD LASKER, service company executive; b. N.Y.C., Oct. 26, 1936; s. Richard E. and Jane L. Samek; m. Marthann Lauver, June 26, 1960; children: Anne, Margaret, Elizabeth. BS in Commerce and Fin., Bucknell U., 1958; MBA, Columbia U., 1960. Brand mgr. Procter & Gamble Co., Cin., 1960-62; dir. new products Johnson & Johnson, New Brunswick, N.J., 1962-67; v.p., gen. mgr. Avon Products Inc., N.Y.C., 1967-75; pres., CEO Childcraft Edn. Corp., Edison, N.J., 1975-78, also dir.; pres. Hudson Pharm. Corp., W. Caldwell, 1978-82; CEO, chmn. bd., pres. Secrephone Ltd., Ft. Washington, Pa., various locations, 1982-94, exec. v.p. various locations, 1994-95; chmn., pres., CEO Medifax SecrePhone, Atlanta, 1995-96; chmn., CEO The MRC Group, Cleve., 1996-98; vice chmn. Medquist Inc., Marlton, N.J., 1998—. Bd. dirs. A. Gary Shilling & Co., MedPlus, Inc., Cin., VeriText LLC, Alliance Imaging, Inc., Anaheim, Calif., Third Millenniam Healthcare, Atlanta, N.Am. Mgmt. Corp., Boston. Pres. bd. trustees Hartridge Sch., Plainfield, N.J., 1969-76; v.p. bd. trustees Wardlaw-Hartridge Sch., Plainfield and Edison, 1975—; trustee, v.p. bd. Plainfield Symphony, 1976-86. Served with Ordinance Corps., U.S. Army, 1958-59. Mem. Young Pres. Orgn., Princeton Club, World Pres. Orgn. Home: 1717 Woodland Ave Edison NJ 08820-1039 Office: Ste 311 Five Greentree Ctr Marlton NJ 08053

SAMER, BILL FRED CARL, poet, publisher, writer; b. Elizabeth, N.J., Sept. 2, 1953; s. Fred Carl and Myrtle Edith (Levey) S. AA, Union Coll., Cranford, N.J., 1975; MA, Kean U. N.J., Union, 1980; BA, Concordia Coll., Bronxville, N.Y., 1994. Editor Top of the Stairs, Union, NJ, 1971—2002; founder Gracevine, 1975; cons. SIS, Pine Brook, NJ, 1978—. Reporter, columnist Live in New York. Author: Father and Daughter, Parson Larson, Addison's Rise. Walker CROP, Clifton, NJ, 1978; vol. I Found It TV campaign, NY, 1976; active Am. Cancer Soc., 2002; mem. Garden Club charter, William Samer Activist Orgn., 1987; del. to conv. Luth. Ch.-Mo. Synod, Ridgewood, NJ, 1976; mem. choir Grace Lutheran Ch., UnionClifton, 1983—85. Avocations: jogging, volleyball. Home and Office: Gracevine/WHAT 936 Louisa St Union NJ 07083-6725

SAMEROFF, ARNOLD JOSHUA, developmental psychologist, educator, research scientist; b. N.Y.C., Apr. 20, 1937; s. Stanley and Zeena (Shapiro) S.; m. Susan C. McDonough, Jan. 2, 1982; children: Shira, Rebecca, Crista, Andrew. BS, U. Mich., 1961; PhD, Yale U., 1965; MA (hon.), Brown U., 1987. Asst. prof. psychology, pediatrics and psychiatry U. Rochester, 1967-70, assoc. prof., 1970-73, prof., 1973-78, dir. developmental psychology tng. program, 1975-78; prof. psychology U. Ill., Chgo., 1978-86, assoc. dir. Inst. for Study Developmental Disabilities, 1978-86; assoc. dir., dir. rsch. Ill. Inst. for Developmental Disabilities, Ill. Dept. Mental Health and Developmental Disabilities, 1978-86; prof. psychiatry and human behavior Brown U., Providence, 1986-92; dir. Developmental Psychopathology Rsch. Ctr., Bradley Hosp., East Providence, 1986-92; prof. psychology, sr. rsch. scientist Ctr. for Human Growth and Devel. U. Mich., Ann Arbor, 1992—, dir. devel. and mental health Rsch. Ctr., 2000-01. Vis. prof. psychology Birkbeck Coll., U. London, 1974-75; vis. scientist Ctr. for Interdisciplinary Rsch., U. Bielefeld, Fed. Republic Germany, 1977-78; W.T. Grant Found. lectr. Soc. for Behavioral Pediatrics, 1984; dir. Summer Inst. on Human Devel. and Psychopathology, Ctr. for Advanced Study in Behavioral Scis., Stanford, Calif., 1989; mem. small grants adv. com. NIH, 1977-81, behavioral scis. assessment panel, 1987-88; mem. organizational planning com. Internat. Conf. for Infant Studies, 1980-84. Editor: (with R.N. Emde) Relationship Disturbances in Early Childhood: A Developmental Approach, 1989, (with F. Kessel and M. Bornstein) Contemporary Constructions of the Child: Essays in Honor of William Kessen, 1991, (with M. Haith) The Five to Seven Year Shift, 1996 (with F.F. Furstenberg et. al.) Managing to Make It: Urban Families and Adolescent Success, 1999, (with S. Miller) Handbook of Developmental Psychopathology, 2000; also monographs; mem. editl. bds. Devel. and Psychopathology, 1988-94, Jour. Devel. and Behavioral Pediatrics, 1989-93, Jour. Family Psychology, 1990-91, Parenting: Science and Practice, 2001, others. Mem. social and behavioral scis. rsch. adv. com. March of Dimes Birth Defects Found., 1977-94, rsch. adv. com. Little City Found., 1986-88; bd. dirs. Zero to Three: Nat. Ctr. for Infants Toddlers and Families, 1986—, exec. com., 1998—; mem. program on successful adolescent devel. among youth in high-risk settings John D. and Catherine T. MacArthur Found., 1986-95, network on early childhood transitions, 1989-92; mem. gov. coun. Soc. Rsch. in Child Devel., 1998—. Recipient rsch. scientist award NIMH, 1994-99; GE fellow Yale U., 1961; NIMH predoctoral rsch. fellow Yale U., 1962, NIMH postdoctoral rsch. fellow, 1965-67, Ctr. for Advanced Study in Behavioral Scis. fellow Stanford U., 1984-85. Fellow AAAS, Am. Acad. Mental Retardation, Am. Psychol. Soc., APA (mem. program com. devel. psychology divsn. 1978-90, chair 1979, mem. coun. 1980-83, mem.-at-large exec. com. 1985-88, pres. devel. psychology divsn. 1995-96, G. Stanley Hall rsch. award); mem. AAUP, Soc. for Rsch. in Child Devel. (governing coun. 1999—), World Assn. Infant Mental Health, Internat. Soc. for Infant Studies (pres. 2002—), Soc. for Rsch. on Adolescence, Zero-to-Three (bd. dirs. 1986—, exec. com. 1999—). E-mail: sameroff@umich.edu.

SAMET, DEAN HENRY, safety engineer; b. Elgin, Ill., Mar. 22, 1947; s. Henry Ralph and Ardella Mary (Schiebel) S.; m. Karen Rae Meyer, Feb. 11, 1979; children: Chris, Lisa, Sean. AAS, Elgin C.C., 1972; BS in Engring. Tech., So. Ill. U., 1974. Cert. healthcare safety profl. Internat. Healthcare Safety Profl. Cert. Bd. Project engr. McBro Planning & Devel. Co., Grand Island, Nebr., 1974-78; field constrn. engr. Arabian Am. Oil Co., Dhahran, Saudi Arabia, 1978-79; project engr. McCarthy Co., Jeddah, Saudi Arabia, 1979-81; sr. project engr. Univ. Mech., Riyadh, Saudi Arabia, 1981-82; staff engr. Joint Commn., Chgo., 1983-85; chief mech. cons. engr. Architects Collaborative, Baghdad, Iraq, 1985; codes and stds. engr. King Faisal Specialist Hosp., Riyadh, 1985-89; assoc. dir. Joint Commn., Oakbrook Terrace, Ill., 1989—. Architecture for health com. AIA, Washington, 1983-85. Co-author: The Environment of Care Handbook, 1998, Environment of Care Essentials, 2002. Staff sgt. USAF, 1966-69. Mem. Am. Soc. Hosp. Engring., Nat. Fire Protection Assn., Tenn. Squires Assn. Avocation: playing guitar. Office: Joint Comm 1 Renaissance Blvd Oakbrook Terrace IL 60181 E-mail: dsamet@jcaho.org.

SAMET, JACK I. lawyer; b. N.Y.C., Aug. 6, 1940; s. William and Tillie (Katz) S.; m. Helen Ray, Feb. 12, 1967; 1 son, Peter Lawrence. BA, Columbia U., 1961; JD, Harvard U., 1964. Bar: N.Y. 1964, Calif. 1973. Assoc. Whitman & Ransom, N.Y.C., 1966-69, Hall, Casey, Dickler & Howley, N.Y.C., 1969-73; ptnr. Ball, Hunt, Hart, Brown & Baerwitz, L.A., 1973-81, Buchalter, Nemer, Fields & Younger, L.A., 1981-94, Baker & Hostetler, L.A., 1994—, mem. policy com., 1997-98; ptnr.-in-charge, 1997-98. Arbitrator Nat. Assn. Securities Dealers, L.A., 1976—; speaker, panelist Calif. Continuing Edn. of Bar, 1988. Mem. ABA, Sports Club/L.A., Million Dollar Advocates Forum, Am. Bd. Trial Advocates, City Club L.A., City Club of Bunker Hill. Avocations: exercise, reading. Home: 2741 Aqua Verde Cir Los Angeles CA 90077-1502 Office: 333 S Grand Ave Los Angeles CA 90071-1504 E-mail: jsamet@bakerlaw.com.

SAMET, JONATHAN MICHAEL, epidemiologist, educator; b. Va., Mar. 26, 1946; AB in Chemistry and Physics, Harvard Coll., 1966; MD, U. Rochester, 1970; MS in Epidemiology, Harvard Sch. Pub Health, 1977. Diplomate Am. Bd. of Internal Medicine, Nat. Bd. Med. Examiners. Intern in medicine U. Ky. Med. Ctr., Lexington, 1970-71; asst. resident in medicine U. N.Mex. Affiliated Hosps., Albuquerque, 1973-74, sr. resident, 1974-75; rsch. fellow in clin. epidemiology Channing lab. Harvard Med. Sch., Boston, 1975-78, rsch. assoc. in medicine, 1978-83; epidemiologist Cancer Rsch. and Treatment Ctr. U. N.Mex., Albuquerque, 1980-87, asst. prof. medicine, 1978-82, assoc. prof. medicine, 1982-88, assoc. prof. family, cmty., and emergency medicine, 1985-88, prof. family, cmty., and emergency medicine, 1986-94, prof. medicine, 1988-94, clin. prof. medicine, 1994—; prof., chmn. dept. epidemiology The Johns Hopkins U., Balt., 1994—, co-dir. risk scis. and pub. policy inst., 1995—. Chief pulmonary divsn. U. N.Mex. Hosp., Albuquerque, 1985-94, chief pulmonary and critical care divsn. dept. medicine, 1986-94; mem. indoor air quality and total human exposure com., sci. adv. bd. U.S. EPA, 1987-95; chmn. biol. effects of ionizing radiation VI com. Nat. Rsch. Coun., 1994-98; Inst. Medicine, 1997; chmn. com. on rsch. priorities for airborne particulate matter, NRC, 1998—. Editor pro tem Am. Jour. of Epidemiology, 1991—92; editor: Am. Jour. of Epidemiology, 1992—98; assoc. editor Tobacco Control: An Internat. Jour., 1991—; editor: Epidemiologic Revs., 1994—, Epidemiology, 2002—. With U.S. Army, 1971-73. Recipient Clinton P. Anderson award Am. Lung Assn. N.Mex., 1988, Surgeon Gen.'s medallion, 1990, Award for Excellence in Environ. Health Rsch. The Lovelace Inst., 1996, Inst. of Medicine, Nat. Acad. Scis., 1997. Fellow: AAAS, Am. Coll. Epidemiology (pres. 2000—01); mem.: Md. Thoracic Soc., Internat. Soc. of Indoor Air Quality and Climate, Internat. Epidemiol. Assn., N.Mex. Thoracic Soc. (sec.-treas. 1982—83, v.p. 1983—84, pres. 1984—85), Am. Thoracic Soc. (long range planning com. environ. and occupational health assembly 1992—, program com. behavioral scis. sect. 1994—95), Soc. for Epidemiol. Rsch. (pres.-elect 1988—89, pres. 1989—90, exec. com. 1988—91), Delta Omega Alpha, Alpha Omega Alpha. Office: Dept Epidemiology The Johns Hopkins U 615 N Wolfe St Ste 6041 Baltimore MD 21205-2103 E-mail: jsamet@jhsph.edu.

SAMFORD, KAREN ELAINE, small business owner, consultant; b. Houston, Aug. 14, 1941; d. George C. and Agnes M. (Phillips) Sanford; m. Jeff E. Samford, Aug. 18, 1938; children: Jeffrey Barton, Keri Lynn. BA in English, History, Tex. Christian U., 1964. Cert. secondary tchr., Tex. Tchr. secondary schs., Tex., La., Mo., 1964-74; saleswoman, 1974-83; corp. trainer, 1983-86; owner Karen E. Samford Tng. Cons., Plano, 1986—. Republican. Home and Office: 3409 Haversham Dr Plano TX 75023-6109

SAMFORD, THOMAS DRAKE, III, lawyer; b. Opelika, Ala., Mar. 4, 1934; s. Thomas Drake and Aileen (Maxwell) S., Jr.; m. Jacqueline Screws, June 7, 1955; children: Thomas Drake IV, Jacquelyn, Robert Maxwell, Richard Drake. AB magna cum laude, Princeton U., 1955; JD, U. Ala., 1961. Bar: Ala. 1961. Owner firm Samford & Samford, 1961-88; judge Mcpl. Ct., Opelika, 1961-88; mem. Ala. Permanent Jud. Commn., 1979-83; gen. counsel Auburn U., 1965-95, gen. counsel emeritus, 1995—. Lectr. Ala. Law Inst., 1969, Am. Judicature Soc., 1969—. Editor-in-chief: Ala. Law Rev, 1960-61. Dir., bd. trustees Opelika Comty. Chest, 1965-68, pres., 1966-67; bd. dirs. U. Ala. Law Sch. Found., Jr. Achievement Chattahoochee-Lee; elder Presbyn. ch., 1974-94, Meth. ch., 1994—. Recipient John G. Buchanan prize politics, 1955, Jaycee Disting. Svc. award, 1996; Farrah, Order Jurisprudence U. Ala., 1956; named one of four Outstanding Young Men in Ala. Jr. C. of C., 1967. Mem. ABA, Lee County Bar Assn. (pres. 1965, Wright Jurisprudential award), Ala. State Bar, U. Ala. Nat. Alumni Assn. (pres. 1966-67), Opelika C. of C. (dir. 1967, pres. 1968), Phi Beta Kappa, Alpha Tau Omega, Phi Delta Phi, Omicron Delta Kappa. Lodges: Kiwanis (bd. dirs. 1966-67, pres. 1969-70). Home: PO Box 550 Opelika AL 36803-0550 Office: Auburn U Office Gen Counsel 101 Samford Hall Auburn AL 36849-5163

SAMFORD, YETTA GLENN, JR. lawyer, director; b. Opelika, Ala., June 8, 1923; s. Yetta Glenn and Mary Elizabeth (Denson) S.; m. Mary Austill, Sept. 6, 1949; children: Mary Austill Lott, Katherine Park Alford, Yetta Glenn III (dec.). BS, Ala. Poly. Inst., 1947; LLB, U. Ala., 1949, LLD (hon.), 1995; DHL (hon.), U. Mobile, 2001. Bar: Ala. 1949, U.S. Dist. Ct. (mid. dist.) Ala. 1950, U.S. Ct. Appeals (5th cir.) 1961, U.S. Ct. Appeals (11th cir.) 1981. Since practiced in, Opelika; ptnr. Samford, Denson, Horsley, Pettey & Bridges (& predecessors), 1949—. Mem. Ala. Senate from Lee and Russell counties, 1958-62; mem. State of Ala. Bd. of Corrections, 1969-75; mem. adv. bd. State Docks, 1987-2000. Trustee U. Mobile, 1963-92, life trustee, 1992—, trustee U. Ala., 1972-93, trustee emeritus, 1993—. Mem. Ala. Law Inst. Council (exec. com.), Ala. Acad. of Honor, Phi Delta Phi, Omicron Delta Kappa, Alpha Tau Omega. Lodges: Masons. Republican. Baptist. Home: 615 Terracewood Dr Opelika AL 36801-3850 Office: Samford Denson Horsley Pettey & Bridges PO Box 2345 Opelika AL 36803-2345 E-mail: pettey.sdhpb@mindspring.com.

SAMI, SEDAT, civil engineering, educator; b. Istanbul, Turkey, Oct. 23, 1928; came to U.S., 1956; s. Huseyin and Neyire S.; m. Dagmar Elisabeth Ellwanger, June 9, 1968; children: Iskender, Elisabeth. Diplom Ingenieur, Tech. U. Istanbul, Turkey, 1951; MS in Mech. and Hydraulics, U. Iowa, 1957, PhD in Fluid Mechanics, 1966. Registered profl. engr., Ill. Design engr. Chas. T. Main, Inc., Turkey, 1951-52, asst. chief engr. Turkey, 1952-55; chief desing engr. Eti Yapi Constrn. Co., Ltd., Ankara, Turkey, 1958-60, v.p. engring. Turkey, 1960-61; asst. prof. civil engring. Mid. East Tech. U., Turkey, 1961-63; asst. prof. engring. So. Ill. U., Carbondale, 1966-69, assoc. prof. engring. mechancis, 1969-72, prof. engring. mechanics, 1972—, chmn. dept. civil engring. and mechanics, 1992—. Co-author: Engineering Mechanics: Statics, 1994, Engineering MEchancis: Dynamics, 1994; contbr. over 40 articles to Jour. Fluid Mechancis, Jour. Hydraulic Engring., others. Advisor Ill. Gov.'s Sci. Adv. Com., Chgo., 1990—. Lt. C.E., Turkish Army, 1955-56. Fellow ASCE.

SAMIIAN, BARAZANDEH, business owner, educator; b. Tehran, May 13, 1939; came to U.S., 1958. B.A., Woodbury U., Los Angeles, 1961; B.A., Immaculate Heart Coll., Los Angeles, 1980; M.A., Webster U., Geneva, 1981; EdD U. North Fla., 1994. 1 child, Mina P. Cullimore. Cons., Design & Architecture, Tehran, 1965-72; bus. cons. multinat. corps., Calif., 1970-77; co-owner Samiian and Solomon Assocs., Geneva, 1978-86; owner, B. Samiian Assocs., Jacksonville, Fla., 1987—; adj. prof. Webster U., Geneva and North Fla. campuses, 1981—, U. North Fla., 1990-95; cons. and lectr. human resources and leadership devel.; regional acad. dir. North Fla. Campuses Webster U., 1995—. Mem. editl. bd. and pubs. com. Multicultural Edn., 1994—. Named Woman of Yr., 1983; recipient Gov's. citation State of Md., 1983. Mem. Nat. Assn. for Multicultural edn. (nat. bd. dirs. 1993—), Internat. Alliance Exec. Women (bd. dirs. 1988-92), Internat. Assn. of Human Resources Info. Mgmt. (bd. dirs. North Fla. 1995—), Phi Kappa Phi, Phi Delta Kappa. Office: Webster Univ Jacksonville Met Campus 6104 Gazebo Park Pl S Jacksonville FL 32257-1037

SAMIZAY, MOHAMMAD RAFI, architect, educator; b. Kabul, Afghanistan, May 12, 1946; s. Abdul Sami and Saleha Samizay; m. Sultana Nassery, Mar. 4, 1972; children: Wazhma, Gazelle. BArch, Ill. Inst. Tech., 1969; MArch in Advanced Studies, MIT, 1974. Registered arch., D.C. Head dept. arch. Kabul U., 1970-72; arch. Marcel Breuer & Assocs., N.Y.C., 1974-75; prin. Samizay-Seraj Archs., Kabul, 1975-81; liaison officer UNESCO, Paris, 1981-83; dir. Sch. of Arch. Wash. State U., Pullman, 1989-98, prof. of arch., 1998—. Author: Islamic Architecture in Herat, 1981; co-author: Traditional Architecture of Afghanistan, 1980. Mem. AIA, Assn. Collegiate Schs. Arch. Avocations: travel, photography. Address: 160 SE Water St Pullman WA 99163-2354 E-mail: samizay@arch.wsu.edu.

SAMMARCO, PAUL WILLIAM, ecologist, researcher; b. Hackensack, N.J., Oct. 18, 1948; s. Giacomo and Esther (Galanti) S.; m. Jean Sogioka, May 29, 1971 (div. 1996); children: Mimi Cecile, Dustin Paul, Jack Isao; m. Donna M. Melancon, Aug. 12, 1998; stepchildren: Lindsay Claire, Ben Charles. BA, Syracuse U., 1970, postgrad., 1970-71; cert., Marine Biology Lab., Woods Hole, Mass., 1971; cert. Fairleigh Dickinson U., W.I. Lab., U.S. V.I., 1972; PhD, SUNY, Stony Brook, 1977. Teaching asst. Syracuse (N.Y.) U., 1970-71; teaching asst. Discovery Bay Marine Lab. SUNY-Stony Brook Overseas Acad. Program, Jamaica, 1974; teaching asst. SUNY, Stony Brook, 1971-77; asst. prof. Clarkson U., Potsdam, N.Y., 1977-79; vis. asst. prof. tropical ecology in St. Croix, V.I., SUNY-Potsdam, 1979; sr. rsch. scientist Australian Inst. Marine Sci., Townsville, Queensland, 1979-89; coord. Shelf Seas Rsch. Program, 1985-86; dir. environ. rsch. of Resource Assessment Commn. Prime Minister's commn. on natural resources, Canberra, Australia, 1989-91; exec. dir. La. Univs. Marine Consortium, Chauvin, 1991-95, prof., 1995—. Dir. inter-univ. seminar program Assn. Colls. St. Lawrence Valley, Potsdam, 1977-79; adj. prof. La. State U., U. La. at Lafayette, U. New Orleans, Nicholls State U., U. Campinas-Brazil, Ctrl. Queensland U., Australia; pres. Endless Shores Music Pubs.; pres. P&J Records, LLC. Composer, arranger, prodr. popular and sacred music; former mem. Australian Chamber Choir, Wesley Choir, Canberra; editor (with M.L. Heron) The Bio-Physics of Marine Larval Dispersal, 1994, Marine Biology (Berlin), 2000—; contbr. numerous articles to profl. jours.; editl. advisor Marine Ecology Progress Series, 1985-93; co-editor Proceedings 6th Internat. Coral Reef Symposium, 1988, Procs. 8th Internat. Coral Reef Symposium. Mem. chancel choir First United Meth. Ch., Houma, La. Recipient Internat. Sci. Exch. award, 1988-89. Mem. ASCAP, Australian Marine Scis. Assn. (keynote speaker 1981, counselor 1984-89, chmn., organizer nat. conf. 1987, chmn. Australia Acad. Sci. Boden Conf. 1990), Internat. Soc. Reef Studies (counselor 1997-2000), Australian Coral Reef Soc., Australasian Performing Rights Assn., Sigma Xi. Democrat. Home: 200 Greenwood St Houma LA 70364-4542 Office: La Univs Marine Consortium 8124 Highway 56 Chauvin LA 70344-2110

SAMMET, JEAN E. computer scientist; b. N.Y.C. d. Harry and Ruth S. BA, Mt. Holyoke Coll., Sc.D. (hon.), 1978; MA, U. Ill. Group leader programing Sperry Gyroscope, Great Neck, N.Y., 1955-58; sect. head, staff cons. programming Sylvania Electric Products, Needham, Mass., 1958-61; with IBM, 1961-88; adv. program mgr. Boston, 1961-65; program lang. tech. mgr. IBM, 1965-68; programming tech. planning mgr. Fed. Systems div., 1968-74, programming lang. tech. mgr., 1974-79, software tech. mgr., 1979-81, div. software tech. mgr., 1981-82, programming lang. tech. mgr., 1983-88; programming lang. cons. Bethesda, Md., 1989—. Chmn. history of computing com. Am. Fedn. Info. Processing Socs., 1977-79; mem. exec. com. Software Patent Inst., 1991—, edn. com., 1992—, chair edn. com., 1992-93; bd. dirs. Computer Mus., 1983-93. Author: Programming Languages: History and Fundamentals, 1969; editor-in-chief: Assn. Computing Machinery Computing Revs, 1979-87; contbr. articles to profl. jours. Fellow Assn. for Computing Machinery, 1994, (charter, pres. 1974-76, Disting. Svc. award 1985), Computer History Mus.; mem. NAE, Upsilon Pi Epsilon. Home and Office: 3124 Gracefield Rd Apt 311 Silver Spring MD 20904-5818

SAMMIS, ANNE MIMI, sculptor, artist; b. Pitts., July 9, 1940; d. Jesse Fleet and Anne Candler (Baker) S.; m. Lee W. Patterson, Feb. 14, 1960 (div. 1969); m. Avery Rockefeller, Jr., Mar. 3, 1971 (dec. Dec. 1979). Grad. high sch., Middlebury, Conn. One-woman shows include Wally Findlay Gallery, N.Y.C., 1980, UN, N.Y.C., 1998, 2001, Capitol Bldg., Madison, Wis., 1999, Newport (R.I.) Art Mus., 2002; exhibited in group shows, including The Hague, The Netherlands, 1998Nat. Sculpture Soc., N.Y.C., 2002; represented in over 400 pub. and pvt. permanent collections in Am. and Europe, including Aspen (Colo.) Chapel, Rio Grand Trail, Aspen, Brockton (Mass.) Hosp., Unity Sch. Christianity, Unity Village, Mo., Women and Infants Hosp., Providence, Dance Aspen, Children's Mus., Providence, Town of Narragansett, R.I., Archbishop Canterbury Lambeth Palace, Eng.; prin. works in bronze range from 1 to 22 feet, incorporating fountains and moveable figures, including R.I. Women Vets. Meml., Exeter, Embrace of Life II, Rainbow of Souls, Three Dancing Children, Dancing on the World, Visitation, Dance of Peace. Recipient Artist of Merit award Courthouse Ctr. for Arts, Kingston, R.I., 2000. Studio: PO Box 335 Narragansett RI 02882 E-mail: mimisammis@yahoo.com.

SAMO, AMANDO, bishop; b. Moch Island, Federated States of Micronesia, Aug. 16, 1948; s. Benito and Esiper Samo. BA in Psychology, Chaminade U., 1973; diploma in religious edn., EAPI, Manila, Philippines, 1982. Ordained priest Roman Cath. Ch. Parish priest Cath. Ch., Truk, Federated States of Micronesia, 1977-87; bishop Diocese of the Carolines and Marshalls, 1987—. Founder, bd. dirs. Marriage Encounter-Carolines-Marshalls, Truk, 1982-88; dir. ch. leadership tng. programs, Truk, 1986—; mem. Bishop's Conf.

Oceania, 1988, pontificial commn. Cor Unum, Rome, 1995. Chmn. Bishop's commn. justice and devel., 1995. Home: PO Box 939 Chuuk FM 96942-0939 Office: Diocese Caroline Is PO Box 250 Chuuk FM 96942-0250

SAMO, TOBIAS CHARLES, physician; b. N.Y.C., May 20, 1952; s. Harvey W. and Eva Samo; m. Genie Landon, Aug. 15, 1982; children: Julia, Jordan. BA, Rutger Coll., 1974; MD, Chgo. Med. Sch., 1978. Bd. cert. internal medicine and infectious diseases. Intern, resident, fellow Baylor Coll. Medicine, Houston; pres. Infectious Diseases Assn., 1984—. Pres. Houston Med. Group, 1995—. Fellow: ACP, Infectious Diseases Soc. Am.; mem.: Am. Soc. Microbiology. Avocations: skiing, exercise. Office: Infectious Diseases Assoc Houston 6560 Fannin St Ste 1540 Houston TX 77030-2783 E-mail: tsamo@tmh.tmc.edu.

SAMODELOV, LEONID FEODOR, anesthesiologist; b. Villach, Austria, Mar. 3, 1948; s. Feodor Alexander and Valentina (Ropadin) S.; m. Gabriele Sauerland; children: Valentina, Sophia, Alexander. MS in Biology, Northeastern U., 1975; MD, U. Düsseldorf, Germany, 1984; BS in Biology, Boston Coll., 1970. Surg. orderly Mass. Gen. Hosp., Boston, 1964-70, rsch. technician respiratory ICU, 1970-75; rsch. assoc. sect. exptl. anesthesia U. Düsseldorf, 1975-83, software developer/programmer dept. anesthesiology, 1983-85, anesthesia resident, 1985-88; med. intern Mercy Cath. Med. Ctr., Upper Darby, Pa., 1988-89; anesthesia resident Albert Einstein Med. Ctr., Phila., 1989-91, Meridia-Huron Hosp., Cleve., 1991-94. Contbr. numerous articles to profl. publs. Avocations: electronic design and construction, software development, scuba diving, photography, flying. E-mial. Home: 20900 Fairlane Cir Fairview Park OH 44126-2007 Office: Meridia-Huron Hosp 13951 Terrace Rd Cleveland OH 44112-4399 E-mail: lsamodelov@aol.com.

SAMOJLA, SCOTT ANTHONY, accountant; b. Chgo., Dec. 29, 1955; s. Richard John and Jane Louise (Novosel) S. BS in Acctg., So. Ill. U., 1978; MBA, U. So. Calif., 1990. Staff acct. Price Waterhouse & Co., Chgo., 1979-81; sr. ops. acct. McGraw-Edison Co., Rolling Meadows, Ill., 1982-83, sr. internal auditor, 1983-85; asst. controller Dresser Industries Masoneilan N.Am. ops., Montebello, Calif., 1985, controller, 1985-90; contr. Masoneilan N.A./Far East Ops., Canton, Mass., 1990-93; divsn. contr. Waters Corp., Milford, 1993-94, group contr./dir. worldwide bus. ops., 1995—. Mem. Am. Inst. CPAs, Ill. Soc. CPAs (younger mem. com. 1982-83), Fin. Execs. Inst. Republican. Office: Waters Corp 34 Maple St Milford MA 01757-3696

SAMOJLIK, EUGENIUSZ, medical educator, clinical researcher; b. Kuchmy-Bialystok, Poland, Aug. 20, 1933; s. Michael and Anastazia S.; m. Anna Morozewicz, Apr. 10, 1965; children: Dorothy, Michael. BS in Biomedicine, U. Warsaw, 1958, PhD in Reproductive Endocrinology, 1964. Rsch. asst. Maternity Inst. Dept. Pharmacology, Warsaw, 1958-62, sr. asst., 1962-66; asst. prof., chief reproductive pharmacology & toxicology Inst. Pharmacy Dept. Pharmacology, 1966-70; assoc. prof., chief hormone rsch. lab. Med. Acad. Dept. Clin. Endocrinology, 1970-73; staff rschr. II Syntex, Inc. Rsch. Divsn., Palo Alto, Calif., 1974-75; asst. prof. physiology, dir. radioimmunoassay lab. Milton S. Hershey (Pa.) Med. Ctr., Divsn. Endocrinology, 1975-80; staff endocrinologist VA Med. Ctr. Dept. Medicine, Sect. Endocrinology, East Orange, N.J., 1980-82; dir. endocrine lab. Newark Beth Israel Med. Ctr., Dept. Medicine, 1982-92; assoc. prof. medicine divsn. endocrinology U. Medicine & Dentistry-N.J. Med. Sch., Newark, 1982—; chief endocrine lab. dept. Labs. NBIMC, 1994-96. Vis. researcher UCLA Sch. Medicine, Torrance, Calif., 1973; vis. scientist Nat. Inst. Child Health Human Devel., Reproductive Br., Bethesda, Md., 1973-74; lectr. in field. Mem. internat. adv. bd. Jour. Assisted Reproductive Tech. and Andrology, mem. editorial bd., 1996; contbr. articles to profl. jours. Grantee WHO, 1973-74, Ciba-Geigy, 1982-83, Nat. Cancer Inst., 1983-86, 85-88; tng. program fellow Worcester Found. Experimental Biology, Shrewsbury, Mass., 1967-69. Mem. AAAS, Am. Soc. Andrology, Am. Assn. Clin. Chemistry, Nat. Acad. Clin. Biochemistry, Acad. Medicine N.J., Endorcine Soc. Home: 73 Sykes Ave Livingston NJ 07039-1318 Fax: 973-972-5185. E-mail: samojleu@umdnj.edu.

SAMOREK, ALEXANDER HENRY, electrical engineer, mathematics and technology educator; b. Detroit, Feb. 14, 1922; s. Walter and Gladys (Kurys) S.; m. Deloris Gehrig 1944 (dec. Mar. 1948); 1 child, David A.; m. Matilda Louise Dusincki, May 10, 1952 (dec. Dec. 1998). Student, U. Detroit, 1946-49; BSEE, Detroit Inst. Tech., 1961. Electronics instr. Radio Electronic and TV Sch., Detroit, 1946-49; electronics inspector USAF Procurement Office, 1950-53; chief technician Wayne Engring. and Rsch. Inst., Wayne State U., 1954-57; elec. engr. Control Engring. Co., 1957-60; chief engr., engring. mgr. Weltronic Co. subs. Ransburg Corp., Clare, Mich., 1960-84; electronic instr. Redford High Sch., Redford Twp., 1966; instr. math. and elec./electronics Mid. Mich. Community Coll., Clare, 1984-95. With USAAF, 1942-46. Mem. (life) IEEE, Soc. Automotive Engrs. E-mail: samorek@quik.com.

SAMORS, NEAL, marketing executive; b. Chgo., July 10, 1943; s. Joseph and Bernette (Schulman) S.; m. Frieda Anschel, May 25, 1969; 1 child, Jennifer Laura. BS, U. Wis., 1965; MA, No. Ill. U., 1967; PhD, Northwestern U., 1979, MA, 2000. Lectr. polit. sci. Loyola U., Chgo., 1967-69; instr. polit. sci. Barat Coll., Lake Forest, Ill., 1969-74; profl. assoc. Ednl. Testing Svc., Evanston, 1974-80, asst. dir., 1980-84, sr. field mktg. rep., 1984-88, asst. dir. field mktg., 1989-93, exec. dir. field mktg., 1993-95, exec. dir. market devel., 1995-97, exec. dir. client acquisition and retention, 1997-99; pres. Samors & Assocs., Inc., Buffalo Grove, Ill., 1999—. Cons. and evaluator Alverno Coll., Milw., 1978-81, Madonna Coll., Livonia, Mich., 1978-81, Coll. St. Scholastica, Duluth, Minn., 1980-81; cons. Ednl. Testing Svc., Chauncey Group Internat., 1999—. Co-author: Chicago's Far North Side: Illustrated History of Rogers Park and West Ridge, 2000, Neighborhoods Within Neighborhoods: Twentieth Century Life on Chicago's Far North Side, 2002. Rschr. Stevenson for Senator, Chgo., 1970; dir. resource devel. Rogers Park/West Ridge Hist. Soc. Ford Found. fellow, 1967. Mem. Am. Assn. Higher Edn., Am. Hist. Assn., Orgn. Am. Historians, Chgo. Hist. Soc., Phi Delta Kappa (rsch. v.p. Northwestern chpt. 1980). Avocations: photography, sketching portraits, American history. Home: 282 Stanton Dr Buffalo Grove IL 60089-6841 Office: Samors & Assocs Inc 282 Stanton Dr Buffalo Grove IL 60089-6841 E-mail: nsamors@aol.com.

SAMOTIN, NANCY, lawyer, singer; b. N.Y.C., May 19, 1960; d. Julius and Mildred (Moser) S. BA, Binghamton U., 1981; JD, Hofstra Law Sch., 1984. Bar: N.Y. 1985, N.J. 1985. Ct. atty. OCA State of N.Y., N.Y.C., 1988-91, jud. hearing examiner Family Ct., 1991—. Mem. ABA, N.Y. County Lawyers Assn.

SAMOUILIDIS, LEONIDAS, psychoanalyst; b. Zagazig, Egypt, Dec. 15, 1930; came to U.S., 1957; s. Telemachus and Antigone (Calogeropoulou) S.; m. Alexandra Mantzorou, Nov. 12, 1967; children: Leo, Paul. MD, Athens U., 1956. Cert. psychoanalyst; cert. sex therapist. Gen. intern Deaconess Hosp., Cleve., 1957-58; resident in psychiatry St. Lawrence State Hosp., Ogdensburg, N.Y., 1958-59, Buffalo State Hosp., 1959-61, Pilgrim State Hosp., West Brentwood, N.Y., 1961-63; therapist Lincoln Inst. for Psychotherapy, N.Y.C., 1963-70, Karen Horney Clinic, N.Y.C., 1967-70, clin. asst. physician in-charge, 1965-72; med. dir. N.J. Mental Health Ctr., Passaic, 1970-76, Ctr. for Creative Living, Allendale, N.J., 1976—; pvt. practice Glen Roch, River Edge, 1970-85. Attending psysician St. Joseph's Hosp., Paterson, N.J., 1970-75, Lincoln Park (N.J.) Nursing Home, 1972-74. Contbr. articles to profl. jours. Mem. Masons. Avocations: collecting art, records, pipes. Home: 4 Lookout Dr Saddle River NJ 07458-3314

SAMPAS, DOROTHY MYERS, retired government official; b. Washington, Aug. 24, 1933; d. Lawrence and Anna Cornelia (Henkel) Myers; m. James George Sampas, Dec. 8, 1962; children: George, Lawrence James. AB, U. Mich., 1955; postgrad., U. Paris, 1955-56; PhD, Georgetown U., 1970; cert., Nat. War Coll., Washington, 1987, Naval Post Grad. Sch., 1993. With Bur. Pub. Affairs Dept. State, Washington, 1958-60, analyst Bur. of Adminstrn., 1973-75, div. chief, dep. chief Office of Position and Pay Mgmt., 1979-83, div. chief Office of Mgmt., 1983-84, dir. Office of Mgmt., 1984-86; vice consul Am. Consulate Gen., Hamburg, Fed. Republic Germany, 1960-62; cons. Trans Century Corp., Washington, 1972; gen. svcs. officer Am. Embassy, Brussels, 1975-79, embassy minister-counselor Beijing, 1987-90; minister-counselor U.S. Mission to UN, N.Y.C., 1991-94; Am. ambassador to Islamic Republic of Mauritania, 1994-97; ret., 1998. Presbyterian. Home: 4715 Trent Ct Chevy Chase MD 20815-5516

SAMPATH, SANJAY, science educator; b. Madras, Tamil Nadu, India, Sept. 22, 1962; s. Srirangam Rajagopalan and Sushila Sampath; m. Radha Raman; children: Aneesh, Adity. PhD, SUNY, Stony Brook, 1989. Advanced rsch. engr. Osram Sylvania, Towanda, Pa., 1989—93; prof. SUNY, Stony Brook, 1993—. Dir. Ctr. for Thermal Spray Rsch., Stony Brook, 2002—. Editor: (procs.) Functionally Graded Materials, 2001. Recipient Best Paper award, Jour. of Thermal Spray Tech., 1992. Mem.: ASM Internat. (com. mem. 1990—92). Office: SUNY Dept Materials Sci and Engring Stony Brook NY 11794 Office Fax: 631-632-7878. Business E-Mail: sanjay.sampath@sunysb.edu.

SAMPINO, ANTHONY F. physician, obstetrician and gynecologist; b. Bklyn., Jan. 13, 1965; s. Frank Paul-Joseph and Lillian Katherine (Cucinotta) S. D Osteopathic Medicine, N.Y. Coll. Osteopathic Medicine, 1991. Diplomate Am. Bd. Ob-Gyn, Am. Coll. Osteo. Bd. Ob-Gyn. Rotating intern St. Barnabas Hosp., Bronx, N.Y., 1991-92; resident ob-gyn. St. Vincents Med. Ctr. of Richmond, Staten Island, 1992-96; with dept. ob-gyn. Good Samaritan Hosp., West Islip, 1996—; pvt. practice Comprehensive Ob-Gyn of L.I., 2000—; dir. osteo. internship program Good Samaritan Hosp., 1998—. Clin. asst. prof. N.Y. Coll. Osteo. Medicine, 1996—. Fellow ACOG (jr., sect. chmn. 1992-94, bd. cert.); mem. AMA, Am. Osteo. Assn., Am. Coll. Osteo. Ob-gyn., Am. Osteo. Dirs. Med. Edn., Am. Soc. Colposcopy and Cervical Pathology, Am. Assn. Gynecologic Laparoscopists (Outstanding Resident in Gyn. Endoscopy 1996), Med. Soc. State of N.Y., L.I. Soc. Osteo. Physicians & Surgeons, Suffolk County Med. Soc. Home: 60 West Ln Bay Shore NY 11706-8616

SAMPINO, MICHELE, physician assistant; b. Bklyn., Feb. 24, 1971; d. Javier Hernan Rodriguez and Geraldine Palmer Arghiere. BS in Biology, Coll. S.I., 1996. Cert. physician asst. Physician asst. St. Vincents Hosp., S.I., 1998—2001, S.I. U. Hosp., 1999—2000. Recipient Cert. of Recognition Wellness Expo., 1999. Mem. Am. Acad. Physician Assts. Avocation: scuba diving. Home: 60 W Lane Bay Shore NY 11706

SAMPLE, FREDERICK PALMER, former college president; b. Columbia, Pa., May 22, 1930; s. William Walter and Erna Rebecca (Roye) S.; m. Mary Jane Drager, Aug. 19, 1951; children: Jeffrey Lynn, Roger Lee. AB, Lebanon Valley Coll., 1952; MEd, Western Md. Coll., 1956; DEd, Pa. State U., 1968; D in Pedagogy, Albright Coll., 1968. Tchr. Annville (Pa.) High Sch., 1952-53; tchr. Red Lion Area (Pa.) High Sch., 1953-57, prin., 1957-59, supervising prin., 1959-64; supt. Manheim Twp. Sch. Dist., Neffsville, Pa., 1964-68; pres. Lebanon Valley Coll., Annville, 1968-83; supt. Bellefonte (Pa.) Area Sch. Dist., 1987-92. Ednl. cons.; adminstr. Bucknell U., 1985-87. Mem. Phi Delta Kappa. Republican. Home: PO Box 92 Eagles Mere PA 17731-0092 E-mail: fpso522@epix.net. *Despite failures, difficulties, and disappointments I have tried to find the honorable, responsible, productive, true, and humane solutions to problems and make decisions for progress.*

SAMPLE, HERBERT ALLAN, reporter; b. L.A., Mar. 19, 1961; s. Herbert Warner and Ramona Winifred Sample. BA, Calif. State U., Sacramento, 1983. Reporter L.A. Times, 1983-85, Sacramento Bee, 1986-91, 92-93; bur. chief Dallas Times Hearald, Austin, 1991; reporter McClatchy Newspapers, Washington, 1993-2000, Sacramento Bee San Francisco Bur., 2001—. Mem. Nat. Assn. Black Journalists, Washington Assn. Black Journalists (v.p. 1998-99, pres. 1999). Avocations: biking, cooking, internet. Office: 360 Grand Ave #309 Oakland CA 94610 E-mail: hsample@sacbee.com.

SAMPLE, JOSEPH SCANLON, foundation executive; b. Chgo., Mar. 15, 1923; s. John Glen and Helen (Scanlon) S.; m. Patricia M. Law, Dec. 22, 1942 (div.); children: Michael Scanlon, David Forrest, Patrick Glen; m. Miriam Tyler Willing, Nov. 19, 1965. BA, Yale U., 1947. Trainee, media analyst, media dir. Dancer-Fitzgerald-Sample, Inc., advt. agy., Chgo., 1947-50, v.p., media dir., 1952-53; pres. Mont. Television Network KTVQ, Billings, KXLF-AM-TV, Butte, Mont., KRTV, Great Falls, KPAX-TV, Missoula, 1955-84; dir., prodr. Yellowstone Pub. Radio KEMC, Billings, 1993—. Pres. Greater Mont. Found., 1986—; chmn. Wheeler Ctr. Mont State U., 1988—. Served with AUS, 1943-46. With U.S. Army, 1950-52. Mem. Rotary, Yellowstone Country Club, Port Royal Club, Hole in The Wall Golf Club, Hilands Golf Club, Naples Yacht Club. Home: 606 Highland Park Dr Billings MT 59102-1909 Office: 14 N 24th St Billings MT 59101-2422 E-mail: scatman01@msn.com.

SAMPLE, STEVEN BROWNING, university executive; b. St. Louis, Nov. 29, 1940; s. Howard and Dorothy (Cunningham) Sample; m. Kathryn Brunkow, Jan. 28, 1961; children: Michelle Sample Smith, Elizabeth Ann Smith. BS, U. Ill., 1962, MS, 1963, PhD, 1965; DHULL (hon.) , Canisius Coll., 1989; LLD (hon.) , U. Sheffield, Eng., 1991; EdD (hon.) , Purdue U., 1994; DHL (hon.) , Hebrew Union Coll., 1994; DL (hon.) , U. Nebr., 1995. Sr. scientist Melpar Inc., Falls Church, Va., 1965—66; assoc. prof. elec. engring. Purdue U., Lafayette, Ind., 1966—73; dep. dir. Ill. Bd. Higher Edn., Springfield, 1971—74; exec. v.p. acad. affairs, dean Grad. Coll., prof. elec. engring. U. Nebr., Lincoln, 1974—82; prof. elec. and computer engring. SUNY, Buffalo, 1982—91; pres. U. So. Calif., L.A., 1991—, prof. elec. engring., 1991—, Robert C. Packard pres.'s chair, 1995—. Bd. dirs. Santa Catalina Island Co., UNOVA, William Wrigley Jr. Co., Advanced Bionics, AMCAP/AMF, U. So. Calif., Keck Sch. Medicine; vice-chmn. Western N.Y. Tech. Devel. Ctr., Buffalo, 1982—91; chmn. bd. dirs. Calspan-UB Rsch. Ctr., Inc., Buffalo, 1983—91; mem. Calif. Coun. Sci. and Tech., Irvine, Calif., L.A. Bus. Advisors, Nat. Acad. of Engring., 1998—; cons. in field; chmn. Pacific-10 Conf. , 1997—; bd. dirs. Galaxy Inst. Edn., 1991—94. Author: Contrarian's Guide to Leadership, 2001; contbr. articles to profl. jours. Timpanist St. Louis Philharm. Orch., 1955—58; chmn. Western N.Y. Regional Econ. Devel. Coun., 1984—91; trustee U. at Buffalo Found., 1982—91, Studio Arena Theatre, Buffalo, 1983—91, Western N.Y. Pub. Broadcasting Assn., 1985—91; chmn. Gov.'s Conf. on Sci. and Engring. Edn., Rsch. and Devel, 1989—91; sr. warden Ch. of Our Savior, 1996—98; mem. Calif. Bus.-Higher Edn. Forum (CBHEF), 1995—97; trustee LEARN, 1991—; mem. bd. dirs. 1st Interstate Bancorp, 1991—96; mem. bd. dirs. Galaxy Inst. Edn. , 1991—94, Niagara Mohawk Power Corp. , 1988—91; vestry Ch. of Our Savior, 1996—2001; mem. bd. govs. L.A. Annenberg Met. Project (LAAMP), 1994—2000; mem. bd. dirs. Western Atlas, Inc., 1994—97; mem. bd. dirs. The Presley Cos. , 1991—; bd. dirs. Buffalo Philharm. Orch., 1982—91, Regenstrief Med. Found., Indpls., 1982—, Rsch. Found. SUNY, 1987—91; bd. dirs. L.A. chpt. World Affairs Coun., Hughes Galaxy Inst. Edn., 1991—94; bd. dirs. Rebuild L.A. Com., L.A. Annenberg Metro Project, Coalition of 100 Club , L.A.; mem. bd. dirs. Dunlop Tire Corp., 1987—91, Greater Buffalo C. of C., 1985—91, United Way Buffalo and Erie County, 1985—91. Named Engr. of Yr., N.Y. State Soc. Profl. Engrs., 1985; recipient Disting. Alumnus award, U. Ill., 1980, Alumni Honor award, U. Ill. Coll. Engring., 1985, citation award, Buffalo Coun. on World Affairs, 1986, Outstanding Elec. Engr. award, Purdue U., 1993, Humanitarian award, Nat. Conf. Christians and Jews, 1994, Hollzer Meml. award, Jewish Fedn. Coun. Greater L.A, 1994, Eddy award, L.A. County Econ. Devel. Corp., 2000; fellow, Sloan Found., 1962—63, Grad. fellow, NSF, 1963—65, Am. Coun. Edn. fellow, Purdue U., 1970—71. Mem.: NAE, IEEE (Outstanding Paper award 1976), Assn. Am. Univs., Assn. Pacific Rim Univs. (chmn., co-founder 1997—), Coun. on Fgn. Rels., Nat. Assn. State Univs. and Land-Grant Colls. (ednl. telecommunications com. 1982—83, chmn. coun. of pres. 1985—86, edn. and tech. com. 1986—87, exec. com. 1987—89), Assn. Am. Univs. (chmn. 1998—99, exec. com. 1995—, vice-chmn. 1997—98, tenure com. 1997—, assessing quality of univ. edn. and rsch. com. 2000—, co-chair task force on rsch. accountability 2001—). Episcopalian. Achievements include patents for in field. Office: U So Calif Office of Pres University Park Adm 110 Los Angeles CA 90089-0012

SAMPLES, JERRY WAYNE, Registered profl. engr., Va. Lab. asst. Columbia Ribbon & Carbon, Glen Cove, N.Y., 1969-70; commd. 2d lt. U.S. Army, 1969, advanced through grades to col., 1991; asst. prof. mech. engring. U.S. Mil. Acad., West Point, N.Y., 1979-82; with Air Command and Staff Coll., Maxwell AFB, Ala., 1983; exec. officer 10th Engr. Bn., 1983-85, bn. comdr. 10th engr. bn. 3d inf. div., Fed. Republic Germany, 1987-89; assoc. prof. mech. engring. U.S. Mil. Acad., West Point, 1985-87, assoc. prof. dept. civil and mech. engr., 1989-96; prof. engring., dir. engring. tech. U. Pitts., Johnstown, Pa., 1996—. Home: 108 Laurlis Ln Johnstown PA 15904-1742 Office: U Pitts at Johnstown Dept Engring Tech Johnstown PA 15904 E-mail: samps2@twd.net.

SAMPLINER, LINDA HODES, psychologist, consultant; b. Cleve., Sept. 25, 1945; d. Walter J. and Caroline Jean (Klein) Hodes; m. Richard Evan Sampliner, July 31, 1966; children: Robert David, Steven Jay. BS, Western Res. U., Cleve., 1967; EdM, Boston U., 1972, EdD, 1975. Lic. psychologist, Ariz; cert. grief therapist, cons. in clin. hypnosis. Counselor The Family Life Ctr., Columbia, Md., 1976-80; psychologist Psychology & Rehab. Assocs., Tucson, 1981-85; pvt. practice, 1985—; cons., psychologist div. econ. security Child and Family Svcs., 1985—; psychologist Sonora Behavioral Health Assocs., 1994-99; pvt. practice, 2000—. Cons. SHARE, Tucson, 1985-98; trainer comm. skills for police Balt. County Dept. Mental Health, 1975-80, drub abuse adminstrn. trainer for counselors, 1975-80. Bd. dirs. Adapt Inc., Tucson, 1985-93, pres., 1990-91; bd. dirs. Mental Health Resources, 1993-95, 2000—; bd. dirs. Tucson Symphony Soc., 1984-89, v.p., 1987-89; pres. bd. dirs. Tucson Mus. of Art League, 1985-86; mem. adv. bd. dept. art U. Ariz., 1993-99. Mem. APA, Assn. Death Edn. and Counseling, Ariz. Psychol. Assn., So. Ariz. Psychol. Assn. Avocations: hiking, entertaining. Office: Pusch Ridge Assocs LLC 7440 N Oracle Rd # Casita 2B Tucson AZ 85704-6385 Fax: (520) 877-3339.

SAMPLINER, RICHARD EVAN, physician; b. Cleve., Apr. 14, 1941; m. Linda Sampliner. BA, Yale U., 1963; MD, Case Western Res. U., 1967. Diplomate Am. Bd. Internal Medicine, Am. Bd. Gastroenterology. Intern Univ. Hosps., Cleve., 1967-68; resident New England Med. Ctr., Boston, 1970-71; sr. resident Boston City Hosp., 1971-72; chief of gastroenterology VA Med. Ctr., Tucson, 1980—; prof. medicine U. Ariz., 1990—. Contbr. articles to profl. jours. With USPHS, 1968-70. Mem. Am. Coll. Gastroenterology. Office: VA Med Ctr 111G1 3601 S 6th Ave Tucson AZ 85723-0001 E-mail: samplinr@u.arizona.edu.

SAMPRAS, PETE, professional tennis player; b. Washington, Aug. 12, 1971; s. Sam and Georgia Sampras. Mem. U.S. Davis Cup team., named to Olympic Team Atlanta, 1996 Chairman ATP Tour Charities program, 1992. Winner tournaments including Phila., 1990, Manchester, 1990, U.S. Open, 1990, 1993, Grand Slam Cup, 1990, L.A., 1991, Indpls., 1991, Lyon, 1991, IBM/ATP Tour World Championship-Frankfurt, 1991, 94, U.S. Pro Indoor, 1992, Lipton Internat., 1993, Wimbledon, 1993, 94, 95, 97, 98, 99, 2000; Australian Open, 1994, 97, Italian Open, 1994, U.S. Open, 1990, 93, 95, 96, 2002, San Jose Open, 1996, Memphis Open, 1996, ATP Tour World Championship/Hannover, Germany, 1996, Australian Open Wimbledon, 1997, Advanta Championships, 1998; ranked # 1 during 1993, 94 season, finalist Australian Open, 1995. Achievements include 1st male to win the U.S Open, Wimbledon, and the Australian Open in succession, mem. U.S. Davis Cup Team, 1991, became only the fourth player to finish as No. 1three (or more) consecutive years, 1st player to surpass $5 million in a season,all-time leader in career earnings, named ATP Tour Player of the Year, 1993-94, Jim Thorpe Tennis Player, 1993. Office: ATP Tour 420 W 45th St New York NY 10036-3503*

SAMPSON, CINDY KATHLEEN STEWART, school social worker, educator; b. Scottsburg, Ind., June 23, 1958; d. Gordon Lee and Velva Kathleen (Henry) Stewart; m. Bradford Sampson, Jan. 15, 1998; 1 child Lois Kathleen. BS in Social Work, Ball State U., 1980; MS in Social Work, U. Louisville, 1981; PhD in Human Svcs., Walden U., 1992. Cert. social worker, Ky., clin. social worker, Ind.; lic. clin. social worker, Fla.; lic. sch. social worker, Ky., Ga., Fla.; diplomate Am. Bd. Examiners in Clin. Social Work. Therapist Washington County Guidance Ctr., Salem, Ind., 1981—83; psychiat. social worker Madison (Ind.) State Hosp., 1983—85; sch. social worker Bullitt County day treatment program Bullitt County Pub. Schs., Shepherdsville, Ky., 1985—92; sch. social worker Hillsborough County Schs., Tampa, Fla., 1992—; therapist Mental Health Care, Inc., 1998—2001; part-time social worker Access Home Health Care, 2000—. Prof. social work Lindsey Wilson Coll., Shepherdsville, Ky., 1991, U. Ky., Louisville, 1988-92; psychiat. social work cons. Ind. Rehab. Svcs., Indpls., 1984-85; ; instr. adult edn. Jefferson County Pub. Schs., Louisville, 1989-92; pvt. practice Price Counseling Assocs., New Albany, Ind., 1990; workshop facilitator dropout prevention Ashland Oil Co., 1989—; mem. foster care rev. bd. Jefferson County, 1988-92 Student sponsor ARC, Shepherdsville, 1989-92. Mem. NASW, Phi Delta Kappa, Alpha Kappa Delta. Baptist. Avocations: modeling, ceramics, acting, baking, travel.

SAMPSON, DAVID ALLAN, federal agency administrator; b. Washington, July 2, 1957; s. Beryl Harrel and Laura Evelyn (King) S.; m. Karen Ann Nichols, Dec. 10, 1978. BA, David Lipscomb Coll., Nashville, 1978; MDiv, New Orleans Bapt. Theol. Sem., 1982. Minister Westchurch Ch. of Christ, Hammond, Ind., 1978-82; sr. minister Park Row Ch. of Christ, Arlington, Tex., 1982—; pres., CEO Arlington (Tex.) C. of C.; chmn. Tex. Coun. on Workforce and Econ. Competitiveness; asst. sec. for econ. devel. Dept. Commerce, Washington, 2001—. Bd. dirs. emergency chaplain program Arlington Community Hosp., 1985—; adv. bd. Arlington Meml. Hosp., 1985—; bd. dirs. Neo-natal Bioethics Review Bd., 1986—. Contbr. articles to profl. jours. Mem. United Way; bd. dirs. Arlington Ind. Sch. Dists, Communications Bd., 1985—. Named Arlington's Minister of Yr., Kiwanis, 1985. Mem. Arlington C. of C. (bd. dirs. 1985—, chmn. emergency preparedness com. 1985—), Arlington Ministerial Assn. (pres. 1985-86), Soc. Biblical Lit., Internat. Ch. Soc. (chmn. North Tex. chpt.), Phi Alpha Theta. Lodges: Rotary. Republican. Avocations: travelling, tennis. Office: Dept Commerce Econ Devel Adminstrn 14th & Constitution Ave NW Washington DC 20230*

SAMPSON, DAVID SYNNOTT, lawyer; b. Troy, N.Y., Oct. 2, 1942; s. Stephen Hastings and Ruth (Hall) S.; m. Arlene Mernit, July 1, 1967; children: Christopher Hastings, Jamie Everett. BA, St. Lawrence U., 1965; JD, Albany Law Sch., 1973. Bar: N.Y. 1975, D.C. 1977, U.S. Ct. Appeals (D.C. cir.) 1977. Reporter Troy Record, 1965-67; newsman AP, 1967-70; spl. asst. N.Y. State Dept. Environ. Cons., Albany, 1972-74; panel dir. Com. on Critical Choices for Ams., N.Y.C., 1974-75; chief legis. asst. U.S. Rep. H.J. Heinz, Washington, 1975-77; assoc. Boasberg, Hewes, Finkelstein & Klores, 1977-79; exec. dir. Am. Land Forum, 1978-79; ptnr. Pattison, Sampson, Ginsberg & Griffin, Troy, N.Y., 1979-87; exec. dir. Hudson River Valley Assn., Troy and Cold Spring, 1987-89, Hudson River Valley Greenway Coun., Albany, 1989-2000; of counsel Martin, Shudt, Wallace, DiLorenzo & Johnson, Troy, 2001—; postgrad. in geology and planning U. Albany , 2001—. Adj. prof. Columbia U. Grad. Sch. Arch., Planning and Preservation, 2000—. Contbr. book revs., articles to profl. jours. Pres. Samaritan Hosp. Found., 1985-87; bd. dirs. Samaritan Hosp., Troy, 1985-88, St. Gregorys Sch., Loudonville, N.Y., 1982-87, Troy Pub. Libr. Found., 1991—, Scenic Hudson, Poughkeepsie, N.Y., 1982-92, 93-99; mem. Scenic Hudson Land Trust, 1996-01, Husdon River Found., 1999—, Hudsonia, 2001—; mem. adv. bd. Preservation League N.Y., Albany, 1989; mem. N.Y. State Freshwater Wetlands Appeals Bd., 1980-94, chmn., 1984-94; active U.S./UK Countryside Stewardship Exch., Eng., 1989; founder Czech-Hudson Greenway Project, 1992; bd. dirs. Hudson River Found., 1997—. Recipient Greenway award DuPont Corp., 1994, Environ. Alumni award Albany Law Sch., 1997. Mem. Am. Conservation Assn. (bd. dirs. 1987—), N.Y. Pks. and Conservation Assn. (founding dir. 1986-94), N.Y. State Bar Assn. (chmn. hist. preservation com. 1980-85, exec. com. 1985—, chmn. environ. law sect. 1990-91, Bar Assn. City of N.Y. Avocation: bicycling. E-mail: dvsampson@aol.com.

SAMPSON, EARLDINE ROBISON, education educator; b. Russell, Iowa, June 18, 1923; d. Lawrence Earl and Mildred Mona (Judy) Robison; m. Wesley Claude Sampson, Nov. 25, 1953; children: Ann Elizabeth, Lisa Ellen. Diploma, Iowa State Tchrs. Coll., 1943, BA, 1950; MS in Edn., Drake U., 1954; postgrad., No. Ill. U., Iowa State U., 1965-66, 74. Cert. tchr., guidance counselor, Iowa. Tchr. elem. sch. various pub. sch. sys., 1943-48; cons. speech and hearing Iowa Dept. Pub. Instrn., Des Moines, 1950-52; speech therapist Des Moines Pub. Schs., 1952-54, 55; lectr. spl. edn. No. Ill. U., DeKalb, 1964-65; tchr. of homebound Cedar Falls (Iowa) Pub. Schs., 1967-68; asst. prof. edn. U. No. Iowa, Cedar Falls, 1968; asst. prof., counselor Wartburg Coll., Waverly, Iowa, 1968-70; instr. elem. edn., then head of advising elem. edn. Iowa State U., Ames, 1972-82; field supr. elem. edn. U. Toledo, 1988, 89;

ind. cons. Sylvania, Ohio, 1989—. Cons. Des Moines Speech and Hearing Ctr., 1958-59, bd. dirs., 1962, 63; cons. Sartori Hosp., Cedar Falls, 1967-69; bd. dirs. Story County Mental Health Ctr., Ames, 1972-74. NDEA fellow, 1965. Methodist. Avocations: public speaking on preservation of prose and poetry, reading, music, photography. Home: 4047 Newcastle Dr Sylvania OH 43560-3450 *My creed is based on the words of Edwin Markham: "There is a destiny that makes us brothers; none goes his way alone. All that we send into the lives of others comes back into our own." Just reward came from a former student who stated "I have never known you to compromise your principles".*

SAMPSON, EDWARD COOLIDGE, humanities educator; b. Ithaca, N.Y., Dec. 20, 1920; s. Martin W. and Julia (Pattison) S.; m. Frances P. Hanford, Oct. 26, 1946 (div. 1968); children: Susan S. Wilt, Edward H.; m. Cynthia R. Clark, 1968. BA, Cornell U., 1942, PhD, 1957; MA, Columbia U., 1949. Instr. Hofstra Coll., Hempstead, N.Y., 1946-49; teaching fellow Cornell U., Ithaca, 1949-52; with faculty Clarkson Coll. Tech., Potsdam, N.Y., 1952-69, assoc. prof. humanities, 1957-61, prof., 1961-69, SUNY, Oneonta, 1969-82, ret., 1982. Author: Hemingway's The Killers, 1952, E.B. White, 1974, Afterword, The House of the Seven Gables, 1961, E.B. White: Dictionary of Literary Biography, 1982, Thomas Hardy, Justice of Peace, 1977. Capt. USAAF, 1942-46. Decorated Bronze Star medal; Fulbright prof. U. Panjab, 1959-60. Fellow Am. Coun. Learned Socs.; mem. MLA. Home: 89 Hemlock Dr Killingworth CT 06419-2225 E-mail: ecsampson@snet.net.

SAMPSON, HERSCHEL WAYNE, anatomy educator; b. Greenville, Tex., June 28, 1944; s. Clyde Edwin and Wanda Ruth (Brandon) S.; m. Joyce Ann Blissitte, Feb. 22, 2002; children: Nathan Paul, Susan Diane. BS, Arlington State Coll., 1967; PhD, Baylor U., 1970. Asst. prof. of anatomy Creighton U. Sch. Medicine, Omaha, 1970-72; asst to assoc. prof. of Anatomy Baylor Coll. Dentistry, Dallas, 1972-77; assoc. prof. Oral Roberts U. Sch. Dentistry, 1977-78; prof. Tex. A&M U. Coll. Medicine, College Station, Tex., 1979—. Adjunct prof. Dallas Bible Coll., 1972-79; exec. sec. Anatomical Bd., State of Tex., Dallas, 1974-77; coord. Med. Electron Microscope Facility Coll. Station, Tex., 1982-95; nutrition faculty Tex. A&M U., Coll. Station, 1989—. Co-author: Atlas of the Human Skull, 1991; contbr. articles to profl. jours. Bd. dirs. Greenville (Tex.) Christian Sch., 1976-77, Brazos Valley Rehab. Ctr., Bryan, Tex., 1979-85, Dallas Bible Coll., 1979-83; deacon Cen. Bapt. Ch., Bryan, 1984—. Mem. Am. Assn. Anatomy, Am. Soc. for Bone and Mineral Rsch., Internat. Conf. on Calcium Regulating Hormones, Tex. Soc. for Electron Microscopy (pres. 1984-90), Tex. Mineralized Tissue Soc., Rsch. Soc. Alcoholism, Tex. Soc. on Alcoholism, Endocrine Soc. Office: Coll of Medicine Tex A&m U College Station TX 77843-0001 E-mail: sampson@medicine.tamu.edu.

SAMPSON, JOHN DAVID, lawyer; b. Lackawanna, N.Y., Feb. 20, 1955; s. Hugh Albert and May (Davidson) Henderson S.; m. Carol Jasen, July 29, 1978; children: Rachel Henderson, Matthew David. BA, Canisius Coll., Buffalo, 1977; JD, Union U., Albany, N.Y., 1982. Bar: N.Y. (Bar) 1983, Pa. 1998, U.S. State Supreme Ct. 2001. Assoc. Damon & Morey, Buffalo, 1982-87, Lippes Silverstein Mathias & Wexler, Buffalo, 1987-88; ptnr. Walsh & Sampson, PC, 1988-93, Jasen, Jasen & Sampson PC, Buffalo, 1993-99, Underberg & Kessler LLP, Buffalo, 1999—. Paul Harris fellow, 1997. Mem. N.Y. State Bar Assn., Erie County Bar Assn., Def. Rsch. Inst., Rotary Club of Buffalo, Rotary Club of East Aurora (dir. 1993—, pres. 1995-96). Wesleyan Methodist. Avocations: golf, running, skiing. Home: 44 Elmwood Ave East Aurora NY 14052-2610 Office: Underberg & Kessler LLP 1900 Main Place Tower # 620 Buffalo NY 14202-3711 E-mail: dsampson@underberg-kessler.com.

SAMPSON, JOHN EUGENE, consulting company executive; b. Feb. 25, 1941; s. Delbert John and Mary Etta (Dodrill) S.; m. Mary Margaret Treanor, Aug. 14, 1965; children: J. Mark, Sharon. AB with distinction, Nebr. Wesleyan U., 1963; MBA, Ind. U., 1964. Mgmt. asst., exec. trainee Office Sec. Def., Washington, 1963—64; mem. staff Com. Econ. Devel., 1964—69; coord. environ. planning Gen. Mills Inc., Mpls., 1969—72, mgr. devel. planning, 1972—74; dir. corp. planning Cen. Soya Co. Inc., Ft. Wayne, Ind., 1974—76, v.p. corp. planning, 1976—80, v.p. corp. planning and devel., 1980—82, v.p. corp. devel., corp. sec., 1982—84; v.p. corp. planning and devel. Internat. Multifoods, Inc., 1984—96; pres. Sampson Assocs., Edina, Minn., 1996—. Mem. bd. govs. Nebr. Wesleyan U., 1974-80; chmn. bd. trustees St. Joseph United Meth. Ch., Ft. Wayne, 1984; bd. dirs., treas. North Ind. United Meth. Found., 1981-84; lay mem. North Ind. Ann. Conf. United Meth. Ch., 1980-84; bd. dirs. Anthony Wayne coun. Boy Scouts Am., 1984; lay mem. Minn. Ann. Conf. United Meth. Ch., 1985-91, 97-00; chmn. conf. bd. devel. Minn. United Meth. Conf., 1986-91; chmn. bd. trustees Hennepin Ave. United Meth. Ch., Mpls., 1990-92, chair adminstrv. coun., 1993-95, lay leader, 1995-98; chair exec. com. North Naples (Fla.) United Meth. Ch., 2002—. Mem. Ind. U. Sch. Bus. Alumni Assn. (pres. 1984-85), Interlachen Country Club, Country Club of Naples. Home: 6612 Gleason Ter Edina MN 55439-1131 also: Unit 1701 4451 Gulf Shore Blvd N Naples FL 34103 Office: Sampson Assocs 5200 Willson Rd Ste 404 Edina MN 55424-1345

SAMPSON, JOHN LAURENCE, physicist; b. Lynn, Mass., Dec. 14, 1929; s. Laurence Gordon and Ida Bray (Walkey) S.; m. Georgette Charlton McMurray, July 26, 1952; children— Thomas L., Gail P., Elizabeth L. B.S., MIT, 1951; M.S., Tufts U., 1954, Ph.D., 1962. Physicist U.S. Air Force, Cambridge, Mass., 1951; instr. dept. physics Tufts U., Medford, Mass., 1954-55; physicist Air Force Cambridge Research, Bedford, Mass., 1955-58; staff physicist Arthur D. Little Inc., Cambridge, 1961-62; research physicist U.S. Air Force/Rome Air Devel. Ctr., Bedford, 1962— . Contbr. articles to profl. jours. Patentee in field. Judge sci. fair Mass. State Sci. Fair, MIT, 1976-85. Recipient Sustained Superior Performance award U.S. Air Force, 1984. Mem. Am. Phys. Soc. Democrat. Unitarian. Avocation: choral singing. Office: US Air Force/ Rome Air Devel Ctr Hanscom AFB Bedford MA 01731

SAMPSON, ROBERT CARL, JR. psychiatrist; b. Concord, N.H., June 6, 1948; s. Robert Carl Sr. and Alice May (Bedor) S. BA magna cum laude, Yale U., 1970; MD, U. Pa., 1974; CAc, New Eng. Sch. Acupuncture, Watertown, Mass., 1984. Diplomate Nat. Bd. Med. Examiners, Am. Bd. Psychiatry and Neurology, Child Psychiatry. Intern Bryn Mawr (Pa.) Hosp., 1974-75; resident in psychiatry U. Mich., Ann Arbor, 1975-77; resident in child psychiatry New Eng. Med. Ctr., Boston, 1977-79; staff psychiatrist Beaverbrook Guidance Ctr., Waltham, Mass., 1979-89, med. dir., 1989-92, Sino-U.S. Qi Gong Health Scis. Devel. Ctr., Cambridge, 1985-87; psychiatrist Ctr. for Health, Newton Centre, 1986-89; pvt. practice Newton, 1992-95, Andover, 1996-2000, Billerica, 2000—. Instr. psychiatry Harvard U. Med. Sch., Boston, 1987-90; assoc. med. dir. Family Counseling and Guidance Ctrs., Inc., Marshfield, Mass., 1987-89; rsch. cons. Cambridge Hosp.-Psychiatry Dept., 1987-90; founder, cons. Stress Transformation Systems, Newton, Mass. and Londonderry, N.H., 1987-96, Beyond That Which Has Been Healing Ctr., 1996-99, Life Gate Ctr. for Health and Regeneration, 1999—. Co-author: Breaking Out of Environmental Illness: Essential Reading for People with Chronic Fatigue Syndrome, Allergies and Chemical Sensitivities, 1997; contbr. articles to profl. jours. Fellow: Am. Acad. Child and Adolescent Psychiatry; mem.: Phi Beta Kappa. Avocations: travel, meditation, hiking, ashtanga yoga, qigong. Home: PO Box 940 Londonderry NH 03053-0940 Office: 25 Bridge St Ste 7 Billerica MA 01821-1023

SAMPSON, ROBERT NEIL, natural resources consultant; b. Spokane, Wash., Nov. 29, 1938; s. Robert Jay and Juanita Cleone (Hickman) S.; m. Jeanne Louise Stokes, June 7, 1960; children— Robert W., Eric S., Christopher B., Heidi L. BS in Agr, U. Idaho, 1960; M.Public Adminstrn., Harvard U., 1974. Soil conservationist Soil Conservation Service, Burley, Idaho, 1960-61, work unit conservationist Orofino, 1962-65, agronomist Idaho Falls, 1967-68, info. specialist Boise, 1968-70, area conservationist, 1970-72, land use specialist Washington, 1974-77, dir. environ. services div., 1977; land use program mgr. Idaho Planning and Community Affairs Agy., Boise, 1972-73; exec. v.p. Nat. Assn. Conservation Dists., Washington, 1978-84, Am. Forestry Assn., Washington, 1984-95; sr. fellow Am. Forests, 1995-2000; affiliate prof. Dept. Forest Resources U. Idaho, 1997—. Instr. soils and land use Boise State U., 1972; F.K. Weyerhaeuser vis. fellow in comml. forestry Yale Sch. Forestry and Environ. Studies, 2001; pres., The Sampson Group, Inc., 1996—, Vision Forestry LLC, 2000—; rsch. scientist, Yale Sch. Forestry and Environ. Studies, 2001—. Author: Farmland or Wasteland: A Time To Choose, 1981, For Love of the Land, 1985; contbr. articles to profl. and popular publs. Pres. Orofino Golf Assn., 1966, Clearwater County Search and Rescue Unit, 1966-67; chmn. Nat. Commn. on Wildfire Disasters, 1992-94. Recipient President's citation Soil Conservation Soc. Am., 1978; named Boise Fed. Civil Servant of Year Boise Fed. Bus. Assn., 1972 Fellow Soil and Water Conservation Soc. (Hugh Hammond Bennett award 1992); mem. Soc. Am. Foresters. Presbyterian. E-mail: rneilsampson@cs.com.

SAMPSON, RUTH LOUISE, endocrinologist; b. Providence, Oct. 1, 1947; d. Albert Palmer and Winifred Silk (Lilly) S. AB in Biology, Brown U., 1969; MD, Tufts U., 1973. Diplomate Am. Bd. Internal Medicine, Am. Bd. Endocrinology. Resident NE Deaconess Hosp., Boston, 1973-76; fellow in endocrinology Baystate Med. Ctr., Springfield, Mass., 1976-78; practice medicine specializing in endocrinology Missoula, Mont., 1978—. Affiliate Missoula Community Hosp., St. Patrick Hosp., Missoula, 1978—. Treas. Mont. Libertarians, Missoula, 1980-82, 85-87, 90—, vice chairperson, 1983. Mem. Am. Diabetes Assn., Endocrine Soc., Am. Thyroid Assn., Phi Beta Kappa, Sigma Xi. Office: 516 S Orange St # A Missoula MT 59801-2510

SAMPSON, SAMUEL FRANKLIN, sociology educator; b. Malden, Mass., Sept. 22, 1934; s. Samuel Daniel and Margaret Louise (Grimes) S.; m. Patricia Katherine Driscoll, Apr. 8, 1972. BA, U. Okla., 1960, MA, 1961; PhD, Cornell U., 1968. Asst. prof. dept. sociology SUNY, Binghamton, 1965-66; research assoc. dept. sociology Cornell U., Ithaca, N.Y., 1966-67; lectr., chmn. bd. tutors and advs. Harvard U., Cambridge, Mass., 1967-72; assoc. prof. dept. urban studies and planning MIT, 1971-72; prof. sociology U. Vt., Burlington, 1972-2000, chmn. dept. sociology, 1972-76, 90-96, prof. emeritus, 2000—. Research and policy cons. Public & Community Agys. and Orgns., 1969— Gen. editor: Bobbs-Merrill Studies in Sociology, 1970-77; contbr. articles to profl. jours. Served with USAF, 1954-58. Mem. AAUP, AAAS, Internat. Sociol. Assn., Am. Sociol. Assn., Am. Acad. Arts and Scis., Ea. Sociol. Soc., Soc. Study Social Problems, New Eng. Sociol. Assn., Soc. Sci. Study Religion, Internat. Sociol. Assn. Home: 215 S Cove Rd Burlington VT 05401-5445 Office: Univ Vt Dept Sociology 31 S Prospect St Burlington VT 05405-1704 E-mail: lhcarew@zoo.uvm.edu.

SAMPSON, VALERIE K. MORMAN, music educator; b. Renton, Wash., Sept. 12, 1968; d. James Francis and Agnes Mary Morman; m. Owen Russell Sampson, July 20, 1996; children: Lauren Anne, Ethan Clark. BS in Edn. in Composite Music Edn., Valley City State U., 1990. Music tchr. grades K-12 Wishek (N.D.) Pub. Schs., 1990—94; music tchr. grades 4-6, choral tchr. grades 7-12 Grafton (N.D.) Pub. Schs., 1994—96; pvt. music instr. Devils Lake, 1997—2001; band instr. grades 5-6 St. Joseph Cath. Sch., 1999—2000; music instr. grades K-8 St. Alphonsus Sch., Langdon, ND, 2002—. Mem. NEA, 1990-96, Grafton Edn. Assn., 1994-96; sec. Wishek Area Dollars for Scholars, 1993-94; v.p. Wishek Edn. Assn., 1993-94. Mem.: Music Tchrs. Nat. Assn., N.D. Music Tchrs. Assn. (state sec. 1998—2001), Lake Region Curling Assn. (pres. 1998, media coord. 1999, chmn. USA curling nat. mixed championship 1999), Devils Lake Federated Music Club. Roman Catholic. Avocations: musical theatre, curling, tap dancing, gardening, home interior decorating. Home: 607 N Main St Edmore ND 58330

SAMPSON, WILLIAM ROTH, lawyer; b. Teaneck, N.J., Dec. 11, 1946; s. James and Amelia (Roth) S.; 1 child, Lara; m. Drucilla Jean Mort, Apr. 23, 1988; stepchildren: Andy, Seth. BA in History with honors, U. Kans., 1968, JD, 1971. Bar: Kans. 1971, U.S. Dist. Ct. Kans. 1971, U.S. Ct. Appeals (10th cir.) 1982, U.S. Ct. Claims 1985, U.S. Ct. Appeals (8th cir.) 1992. Assoc. Turner & Balloun, Gt. Bend, Kans., 1971; ptnr. Foulston & Siefkin, Wichita, 1975-86, Shook, Hardy & Bacon, Overland Park, 1987—. Adj. prof. advanced litig. U. Kans., 1994; mem. faculty trial tactics inst. Emory U. Sch. Law, 1994-97; mem. merit selection panel U.S. Dist. Ct. Kans., 1999; lectr., presenter in field. Author: Kansas Trial Handbook, 1997; mem. Kans. Law Rev., 1969-71, editor, 1970-71; contbr. articles to profl. jours. Chmn. stewardship com. Univ. Friends Ch., Wichita, 1984-86; bd. dirs. Friends U. Retirement Corp., Wichita, 1985-87; chmn. capital fund drives Trinity Luth. Ch., Lawrence, Kans., 1990-93, mem. ch. coun., 1990-92; bd. dirs. Lied Ctr. of Kans., 1994-97. Lt. USNR, 1971-75. Named among Best Lawyers in Am. Fellow: Kans. Bar Found., Am. Bar Found.; mem.: ABA, Order of the Coif, Am. Inn Ct. (Judge Hugh Means chpt. Master of Bench), Kans. U. Law Soc. (bd. govs. 1993—96), Kans. Assn. Def. Counsel (pres. 1989—90, legis. coun. 1991, 1993), Def. Rsch. Inst. (pres. elect 2002, nat. bd. dirs. 1998—2000, Kans. state rep. 1990—98, Exceptional Performance citation 1990, William H. Kahrs Disting. Achievement award 1994), Internat. Assn. Def. Coun. (faculty mem. trial acad. 1994), Am. Bd. Trial Advs. (pres. Kans. chpt. 1990—91, nat. bd. dirs. 1990—91), Wichita Bar Assn. (bd. dirs. 1985—86), Johnson County Bar Assn. (bench-bar com. 1989—99, Boss of Yr. award 1990), Douglas County Bar Assn., Kans. Bar Assn. (chmn. Kans. coll. advocacy 1986, long-range planning, CLE com. 1987—88), Assn. Def. Trial Attys., Lawrence Country Club, Omicron Delta Kappa, Phi Alpha Theta, Delta Sigma Rho. Republican. Episcopalian. Avocations: jogging, golf, snow skiing, travel, reading. Office: Shook Hardy & Bacon 10801 Mastin Ste 1000 Overland Park KS 66210-1669 E-mail: wsampson@shb.com.

SAMRA, SAID ABOU, plastic surgeon; b. Apr. 10, 1949; MD, U. Damascus, Syria. Pvt. practice, Middlesex and Monmouth, N.J., 1982—. Office: 733 N Beers St Ste U1 Holmdel NJ 07733-1528 also: 200 Perrine Rd Ste 228 Old Bridge NJ 08857-2871 E-mail: ssamramd@aol.com.

SAMS, JAMES FARID, real estate development company executive; b. Bay City, Mich., Apr. 21, 1932; s. James and Adele Sams; m. Betty Suham Hamady, Aug. 17, 1957; children: James Karl, Alicia Diane, Victoria Saab. BA, Northwestern U., 1954; JD, U. Mich., 1957; LLM, Harvard U., 1959. Com. counsel ABA spl. com. World Peace/Law, Washington, 1960-63; ptnr. Reeves, Harrison, Sams & Revercomb, 1964-69, Brown & Sams, Washington, 1969-71, Kirkwood, Kaplan, Russin, Veechi & Sams, Beirut, 1971-74; owner, prin. Am. Devel. Services Corp., Washington, 1978—. Rep. U.S. State Dept. Ams. Abroad, Washington, 1965; del. UN Com. on Internat. Trade Law, N.Y.C., 1970; adv. bd Ctr. for Internat. and Comparative Law, U. Mich. Law Sch.. Contbr. articles to profl. jours. Co-founder, dir. Am. Near East Refugee Aid, Washington, 1968-92; mem. adv. bd. Georgetown U. Ctr. for Arab Studies; mem. visitors com. U. Mich. Law Sch.; mem. adv. bd. Ctr. Internat. and Comparative Law; former chmn., dir. Grameen Found. USA, Washington. Served to lt. U.S. Army, 1957-58. Mem. ABA, Bar Assn. of Washington, Am. Soc. Internat. Law, Nat. Assn. Arab Ams. (pres. 1981, chmn. 1983), Cosmos Club. Avocations: skiing, sports. Home: 8907 Fernwood Rd Bethesda MD 20817-3015 Office: Am Devel Svcs Corp 5454 Wisconsin Ave Ste 1260 Bethesda MD 20815-6921 E-mail: adsc@erols.com.

SAMS, ROBIN DAHL, artist; b. Perth Amboy, N.J., Mar. 2, 1950; d. George Martin and Lillian Dorothy (Farr) Dahl; m. John Lawrence Sams, Aug. 3, 1973. BFA, R.I. Sch. Design, Providence, 1972. Illustrator U.S. Army, Vaihingen, West Germany, 1985-88; sole proprietor Peace & Plenty Studio, Tyner, N.C., 1993—; owner Edenton (N.C.) Art Gallery, 1998—. Exhbns. include Pasquotanic Arts Coun., 1995, Beaufort County Arts Coun., 1997, Chowan Arts Coun., 1998. Head conservation Gen. Fedn. Women's Clubs, 1998; rep. candidate Chowan County Commr., 1998; bd. dirs. Chowan Arts Coun. Grantee N.C. State Arts Coun., 1997, 99. Mem. Watercolor Soc. N.C., Psquotank County Arts Coun., Dare County Arts Coun., Edenton Womans Club (pres. 1997-99). Home and Office: 848 Dillards Mill Rd Tyner NC 27980-9616

SAMSEL, MAEBELL SCROGGINS (MIDGE SAMSEL), paralegal; b. Yazoo City, Miss., Aug. 15, 1940; d. Robert and Lela Estelle (Hammons) Scroggins; m. John Sanders Swain, Dec. 30, 1960 (div. Oct. 1968); 1 child, Stacy Melissa Swain Ramsey; m. Howard Swinehart Samsel, Oct. 8, 1981. BA, Miss. Coll., 1963. Sec. Standard Life Ins. Co., Jackson, Miss., 1963-64; legal sec. Gray & Montague Law Firm, Hattiesburg, 1964-65; personnel sec. Adj. Gen.'s Office, State of Miss., Jackson, 1965-70; paralegal State of Miss., Atty. Gen.'s Office, 1970-79, 84-86; sales agt. Prudential Ins. Co. Am., 1979-84. Chmn. acquisitions Miss. Mus. Art, Jackson, 1983, acquisitions vol., 1982, 89, chmn. Vols. at the Palette Restaurant, 1990-99, music chair Miss. Mus. Art Palette Restaurant, 1996, pres. aux., 1991-92, trustee, 1991-92, treas. Gallery Guild, 1998; mem. Jackson Symphony League, 1988—, Miss. Opera Guild, Jackson, 1991—; bd. dirs. Friends of the Internat. Ballet Competition, historian, 1996-97, pres.-elect, 1997, pres. 1998-99. Named Vol. of the Week, Miss. Mus. Art Palette Restaurant, 1989, Vol. of Yr., Miss. Mus. of Art, 1991-92. Mem. AAUW, Jackson Assn. Legal Secs. (pres. 1975-76, 77-78, del. to nat. convs. 1975-77, Outstanding Legal Sec. of Yr. 1975-76), Miss. Assn. Legal Secs., Nat. Assn. Legal Secs. (chmn. nat. spring bd. mtg. 1980), Miss. Coll. Alumni Assn., Petroleum Aux. (v.p. 1986-87, pres. 1988-89, treas. 1989-90, pres. 1994-96), Serendipity Bridge Club (treas. 1989-93, v.p. 1991-92, pres. 1992-93). Republican. Baptist. Avocations: fishing, piano, travel. Home: 1206 Bay Vis Brandon MS 39047-8650

SAMSELL, LEWIS PATRICK, municipal finance executive; b. Morgantown, Va., Feb. 20, 1943; s. Lewis Hildreth and Harriet Elizabeth (Gidley) S.; m. Linda Joyce Hewitt, July19, 1967. BSBA in Acctg., W.Va. U., 1970; MBA in Acctg., George Washington U., 1975. CPA, V.I.; cert. mgmt. acct.; cert. in govt. fin. mgmt.; cert. fin. mgmt. acct. Auditor GAO, Washington, 1971-79, Office of the U.S. Govt. Controller, St. Thomas, V.I., 1979-82; fin. officer City of Merced, Calif., 1982-86; dir. fin. City of Stockton, 1986—. Bd. dirs. Stockton Coun. U.S. Navy League, 1993—; mem. state controllers task force on single audit, Calif. CAP Composite Squadron 147 Sr. Programs Officer, Merced, 1985; resource allocation team leader United Way of San Joaquin County, treas., 1994—. With USN, 1964-67. Recipient Cert. of Achievement Service Corps of Retired Execs., St. Thomas, 1982. Mem. AICPA, Treas. Mgmt. Assn., Assn. Govt. Accts., Calif. Soc. Mcpl. Fin. Officers (profl. and tech. stds. com. 1983-93), Govt. Fin. Officers Assn., Nat. Assn. Accts. (pres. MPG chpt. 1979, nat. bd. dirs. 1989-91), Calif. Mcpl. Treas. Assn., The Inst. of Mgmt. Acctg. (pres. Golden West coun. 1994-95, mem. nat. ethics com.), Am. Mgmt. Assn., Kiwanis, Rotary, Elks. Avocations: fishing, camping. Home: 7034 Bridgeport Cir Stockton CA 95207-2359 Office: City of Stockton 425 N El Dorado St Stockton CA 95202-1997

SAMSON, ALLEN LAWRENCE, bank executive; b. Milw., Nov. 16, 1939; s. Harry E. and Rose (Landau) S.; m. Vicki Faye Boxer, July 3, 1977; children: Daniel, Rachel; children from previous marriage: Nancy, David. BS, U. Wis., 1962, LLB, 1965. Bar: Wis. 1965. Asst. dist. atty. Milw. County Dist. Attys. Office, 1965-67, dep. dist. atty., 1968-70; assoc. Samson & Nash, Milw., 1967-68; ptnr. Samson, Friebert, Sutton and Finerty, 1970-73; v.p., sec. Am. Med. Svcs., Inc., 1973-83, exec. v.p., chief exec. officer, 1983-86, chmn., chief exec. officer, 1986-90; cons. nursing homes Samson Med. Mgmt. Co., 1990-93; pres. Liberty Bank, 1994—2001; vice chmn. State Fin. Bank, 2001—. Pub. mem. nursing home study Wis. Legis. Bur., 1988-89; mem. bd. visitors U. Wis. Law Sch., 1992—; mem. health policy adv. coun. Med. Coll. Wis., 1992-96. Bd. dirs. Nat. Found. Jewish Culture, 1996—98; trustee Milw. Ballet, 1982—89, Milw. Art Mus., 2001—, pres. bd. trustees, 1992—95; bd. dirs. Milw. Symphony Orch., 1995—2002, treas., 1996—2000; bd. dirs. Wis. Womens Bus. Initiative, War Meml. Corp., 1993—95, Jewish Fedn., 1985—, pres., 2000—02; bd. dirs. Milw. Jewish Home, 1992—96, Jewish Cmty. Ctr., 1985—96; pres. Milw. Parks Found., 1998—; gen. chmn. Wis. Israel Bond Campaign, 1993—94, chmn., 1996—98, bd. dirs., exec. com., 1986—; gen. chmn. ann. camp Milw. Jewish Fedn., 1990—91; pres. Jewish Vocat. Svc., 1976—78; Alexis de Tocqueville's leadership chmn. United Way campaign, 1995. Recipient Kaplan prize for econ. devel. Govt. of Israel, 1986, United Way Fleur de Lys award, 1996, Israel Bonds Star of David award, 1999. Avocations: tennis, skiing, golf. Office: State Fin Bank 815 N Water St Milwaukee WI 53202-3529

SAMSON, ALVIN, former distributing company executive, consultant; b. N.Y.C., May 2, 1917; s. Morris and Jennie (Buitekant) S.; m. Ann Carol Furmansky, Aug. 15, 1942; children: Leslie Joan, Marla Adriane. Br. mgr. U.S. Hardware and Paper Co., 1947-51; mdse. mgr. U.S. Servateria, 1951-57; dir. purchasing U.S. Consumer Products, Los Angeles, 1959-64, v.p. ops., 1964-66, pres., 1966-72, San Diego, Bakersfield, Las Vegas, Phoenix, 1966-72, Zelman Co., Los Angeles, San Francisco and Las Vegas, 1968-72, Triple A Corp., Los Angeles, 1966-72, U.S. Consumer Products-Wesco Mdse., Los Angeles, 1972-74; v.p. APL Corp., N.Y.C., 1967-74; pres. USCP-WESCO, 1974-85; cons. A. Samson Cons., Beverly Hills, 1985-92; retired, 1992. Active USCG Aux., 1981—, divsn. capt., 1992—. With USAAF, 1942-45. Named Man of Year Housewares Club So. Calif., 1965 Mem. Nat. Assn. Service Merchandisers (dir. 1982-85)

SAMSON, CHARLES HAROLD, JR. (CAR SAMSON), retired engineering educator, consultant; b. Portsmouth, Ohio, July 12, 1924; s. Charles Harold and Gertrude (Morris) S.; m. Ruth Aileen Baumbach, Sept. 12, 1947; children: Peggy Aileen, Charles Harold III. BS, U. Notre Dame, 1947, MS, 1948; PhD, U. Mo., 1953. Registered profl. engr., Tex., Ind. Asst. field rep. Loebl, Schlossman and Bennett (architects and engrs.), Chgo., 1948-49; structures engr. Convair Aircraft, Fort Worth, 1951-52, sr. structures engr., 1952-53, project aerodynamics engr., 1956-58, project structures engr., 1958-60; asst. prof. civil engring. U. Notre Dame, 1953-56; office engr. Wilbur H. Gartner & Assocs., South Bend, Ind., 1954; grad. lectr. civil engring. So. Meth. U., Dallas, 1952-53, 56-60; prof. structural engring. and mechanics, depts. aerospace and civil engring. Tex. A&M U., College Station, 1960-64, prof. civil engring., 1964-94; prof. emeritus Tex. A&M, 1994—; head dept. Tex. A&M U., 1964-79, assoc. head dept., 1989-92, construction area engring. leader, dir. ctr. construction edn., 1992-93; rsch. engr. Tex. Transp. Inst., Tex. A&M U., 1960-62, head structural research dept., 1962-65, acting pres., 1980-81, v.p. planning, 1981-82. Pres. S.W. Athletic Conf., 1979-81; v.p. Nat. Collegiate Athletic Assn., 1981-83, mem. council, 1983-85; cons. systems engring. and quality mgmt.; Tex. Quality Award examiner, 1998-99, sr. examiner, 2000. Contbr. articles to profl. jours. Served to ensign USNR, 1943-46. Recipient Gen. Dynamics-Ft. Worth Excellence in Tchg. award, 1962, Engring. hon. award U. Notre Dame, 1982. Fellow ASCE (life), Nat. Inst. Engring. Mgmt. and Systems (pres. 1989-90), Nat. Soc. Profl. Engrs. (past v.p., chmn. profl. engrs. in edn., pres. 1987-88, award 2000); mem. Am. Soc. Engring. Mgmt., Am. Soc. Engring. Edn., Tex. Soc. Prof. Engrs. (past nat. dir., pres. 1973-74, Tex. Engring. Dream Team 2000), Nat. Assn. Parliamentarians, Internat. Soc. Systems Sci., Order of the Engr. (chmn., bd. govs. 1989-91), Am. Soc. for Quality, Internat. Coun. on Systems Engring., Nat. Inst. Engring. Ethics, Sigma Xi, Sigma Gamma Tau, Tau Beta Pi, Phi Kappa Phi, Chi Epsilon. Home: 810 Dogwood Ln Bryan TX 77802-1144 E-mail: samson@cox-internet.com.

SAMSON, DAVID, state attorney general; Law degree, Univ. Pa. Law Sch., 1965; BA, Rutgers Univ., 1961. Atty. gen. State of N.J., 2002—; founding prin. Wolff & Samson, former sr. ptnr. Mem. Gov. Commn., 1990—91; chmn. Gov. Task Force, 1987—89; gen. counsel N.J. Turnpike Authority, 1982—90; legal cons. Ethics Com., 1981—85, N.J. Supreme Court Com., 1973—77, Atty. Gen. Governmental Immunity, 1967—68. Mem.: U.S. Supreme Court, N.Y. Bar Assn., Am. Bar Found., Am. Bar Assn., N.J. State Bar Assn., Essex County Bar Assn. Office: Richard J Hughes Justice Complex 25 Market St CN 080 Trenton NJ 08625*

SAMSON, DUKE STAPLES, neurosurgeon; b. Odessa, Tex., Jan. 16, 1943; s. Horace Stanford and Ruby Sue (Nicholson) S.; m. Patricia Celine Bergen, July 15, 1989; children: Lorne Daniel, Gabriel Stanford. BA, Stanford U., 1965; MD, Washington U., St. Louis, 1969. Diplmate Am. Bd. Surgery, Am. Bd. Neurosurgery. Intern Duke U. Med. Ctr., Durham, N.C., 1969-70; neurosurg. resident U. Tex. S.W. Med. Sch., Dallas, 1970-75; fellow Ctr. Medico U. Hosp., Paris, France, 1972-73; vis. fellow dept. neurosurgery Katonspital U. Zurich, Switzerland, 1973; asst. prof. dept. surgery U. Tex. Health Sci. Ctr., Dallas, 1975-80, assoc. prof. dept. surgery, 1981-84, prof., chmn. divsn. neurosurgery, 1984-86, Clark prof. and chmn. divsn. neurosurgery, 1985-95, Lois C.A. and Darwin E. Smith disting. chair neurol. surgery, 1983—. Hosp. appts. VA Med. Ctr., Parkland Meml. Hosp., Children's Med. Ctr., Dallas, 1977—, Zale Lipshy U. Hosp., St. Paul Med. Ctr., Dallas, 1989—; cons. neurosurgery svc. Walter Reed Med. Hosp., Washington, 1982—; neurosurgery cons. Surgeon Gen. U.S. Army, 1983—; mem. editl. bd. Surg. Neurology; ad hoc reviewer Neurosurgery. Contbr. over 110 articles and abstracts to profl. jours., over 36 chpts. to books; author: (for symposium) Neurological Conflicts and Concerns, 1977. Honored visitor Royal Australasian Coll. of Surgeons, Disting. Vis. Prof. U. Buenos Aires, Argentina, 1996; grantee: Miles Labs., 1984-85, NIH, 1986-89, 89. Mem. Am. Assn. Neurol. Surgeons (Donaghy Lectureship 1997), Congress of Neurol. Surgeons (Honored Guest 1999), Soc. Neurol. Surgeons, Acad. Neurol. Surgery, Kason Rsch.

Soc., Neurosurg. Rsch. Soc. Avocations: creative writing, handgun shooting, horses. Office: U Tex SW Med Ctr Dept Neurol Surgery 5323 Harry Hines Blvd Dallas TX 75390-7208 E-mail: samson@utsw.swmed.edu.

SAMSON, FREDERICK EUGENE, JR. neuroscientist, educator; b. Medford, Mass., Aug. 16, 1918; s. Frederick Eugene and Annie Bell (Pratt) S.; m. Camila Albert; children Cecile Samson Folkerts, Julie Samson Thompson, Renée. DO, Mass. Coll. Osteopathy, 1940; PhD, U. Chgo., 1952. Asst. prof. U. Kans., Lawrence, 1952-57, prof. physiology, 1962-73, chmn., prof. dept. physiology and cell biology, 1968-73; prof. physiology U. Kans. Med. Ctr., Kansas City, 1973-89, prof. emeritus, 1989—; dir. Ralph L. Smith Rsch. Ctr. U. Kans., 1973-89. Staff scientist neurosci. rsch. program MIT, Cambridge, Mass., 1968-82, cons., 1982-91; vis. prof. neurobiology U. Catolica de Chile, Santiago, 1972; prof. Inst. de Investigaciones Citologicas, Valenica, Spain, 1981-89; hon. lectr. Mid-Am. State Univs. Assn., 1987. Editor: (with George Adelman) The Neurosciences: Paths of Discovery, II, 1992, (with Merrill Tarr) Oxygen Free Radicals in Tissue Damage, 1993; contbr. articles to profl. publs. Scientist, U.S.A., Spain Friendship Treaty, Madrid and Valencia, 1981. Staff sgt. U.S. Army, 1941-45, PTO. Recipient Rsch. Recognition award U. Kans. Med. Ctr., Kansas City, 1984; Van Liere fellow U. Chgo., 1948; Rawson fellow U. Chgo., 1949-51; USPHS fellow MIT, 1965 Fellow AAAS; mem. Am. Soc. Neurochemistry (chmn. program com. 1980), Am. Soc. Cell Biology (local host com. 1984), Am. Physiol. Soc. (emeritus 1990), Soc. Neurosci. (program com. 1972-73), The Oxygen Soc., N.Y. Acad. Sci., U. Chgo. Kansas City Club (chmn. alumni fund bd. 1975-82, pres. 1979-81), Sigma Xi (regional lectr. 1974-75, pres. Kansas City chpt. 1977-78, pres. neurosci. chpt. 1978). Avocations: writing, hand balancing. Home: 171 Lakeshore Dr S Lake Quivira KS 66217-8516 Office: U Kans Med Ctr Ralph L Smith Rsch Ctr Bldg 37 Kansas City KS 66160-0001

SAMSON, JEROME, communications executive, software engineer; b. Bagneres de Bigorre, Pyrenees, France, Mar. 20, 1967; came to U.S., 1990; s. Jean Claude and Denise S.; m. Martine Abadie; 2 children: Margot, Charlotte. BS in Sci. Studies, Pierre de Fermat, Toulouse, France, 1987; MS in Computer Sci., Grad. Sch. Software Engring., Paris, 1989; MBA, Carnegie Mellon U., 1991. From re-engring. mgr. to sr. prog. mgr. Nielsen Media Rsch., Tampa, Fla., 1992-96; dir., tech. & bus. strategy Nielsen Interactive Svcs., 1996—; credit ratings project mgr. Dun & Bradstreet, Paris, 1993; R & D mgr. Sales Technologies, Atlanta, 1993-94; bus. devel. mgr. IMS Am., Phila., 1994. Rsch. fellow CommerceNet consortium. Mem. Interactive TV Assn., Assn. for Interactive Media, Internat. Data Warehouse Assn., Internat. Soc. for Optical Engring., CommerceNet Consortium (rsch. fellow). Office: Nielsen Interactive Svcs 375 Patricia Ave Dunedin FL 34698-8190 E-mail: samson_jerome@yahoo.com.

SAMSON, RICHARD MAX, theatre director, investment/real estate executive; b. Milw., June 13, 1946; s. Harry E. and Rose (Landau) S.; m. Nancy K. Pinter; children: Gina Shoshana, Alayna Tamar; (stepson) Christopher P. BA, U. Wis., 1968. Dir., owner The Puppet Co., Jerusalem, 1972-73; pres. Century Hall, Inc., Milw., 1974-75; dir. purchasing Am. Med. Svcs., Inc., 1973-74, v.p., 1974-82, exec. v.p., 1982-86, pres., 1986-90, Samson Investments, Milw., 1990—. Bd. dirs. Liberty Bank, Milw.; sec. Super Sitters, Mequon, Wis., 1987—. Co-prodr./dir. Loss of Breath: The Unfinished Life and Death of Edgar Allan Poe, 1999; co-creator/dir. Einstein: Hero of the Mind, 2002. Pres. bd. Theatre X, Milw., 1982, Holton Youth Ctr., Milw., 1994, Children's Outing Assn., 1996, Jewish Found. for Econ. Opportunity, 1996—; v.p. bd. ArtReach, Milw., 1987; bd. dirs. Bnai Or Religious Fellowship, 1988-93, Milw. Jewish Coun., 1992-94; mem. funding bd. Wis. Cmty. Fund, 1989-93; dir. Mask and Puppet Co. Milw., 1992—; treas. nat. bd. Am. for Peace Now, 2002. Recipient Humanitarian Peace award Ecumenical Refugee Coun., 1989, Social Justice award Wis. Cmty. Fund, 1997, Human Rels. award Wis. region NCCJ, 1998, Cmty. Svc. Human Rels. award, Wis. chpt. Am. Jewish Com., 2000. Mem. Ams. for Peace Now (bd. dirs. 1990—). Avocations: chess, comic collecting, puppetry. Office: Samson Investments 100A E Pleasant St Milwaukee WI 53212-3975

SAMSONOVICH, ALEXEI VLADIMIR, neuroscientist, educator; b. Kiev, Ukraine, Nov. 18, 1956; arrived in U.S.A., 1991; s. Vladimir Alexei and Zinaida Vasiljevna Samsonovich. MSc, Moscow Phys. Tech. Inst., 1980; PhD, U. Ariz., 1997. Rsch. assoc. Ariz. Rsch. Labs. U. Ariz., Tucson, 1997—98; rsch. asst. psychology dept. U. Ariz., 1998—. Co-author: Computational Neuroanatomy, 2002. Recipient Golden medal, Phys. Math. Sch., 1974. Mem.: Internat. Soc. Molecular Elec. & Biocomputing, Assn. Scientific Study Consciousness (grant 1999—2000), Soc. Philos. & Psychology, Soc. for Neurosci. Home: 4450 Rivanna Lane 3717 Fairfax VA 22030 Office: Krasnow Inst at George Mason Univ 4400 University Dr MS 2A1 Fairfax VA 22030 E-mail: asamsono@gmu.edu.

SAMSOT, ROBERT LOUIS, newspaper editor, consultant; b. New Orleans, July 20, 1943; s. Robert Desposito and Mary Helen (Dohan) S.; m. A. Michael Newton, June 9, 1965; children: Kathleen Anderson Samsot English, Robert Dohan Samsot. BA in Journalism, U. N.C., Chapel Hill, 1965; cert. in Bus. Adminstrn., Rockhurst Coll., 1982. Reporter Rocky Mountain News, Denver, 1965-67, The Comml. Appeal, Memphis, 1967-72; reporter, editor Newsday, L.I., N.Y., 1972-80; Gannett prof.-in-residence U. Kans., Lawrence, 1980-81; met. editor The Kansas City (Mo.) Times, 1981-84; city editor The Plain Dealer, Cleve., 1984-87; lifestyle editor, dep. editor N.J., dep. editor nat. The Phila. Inquirer, 1987-97; regional editor Balt. Sun, 1997-98; sr. nat. editor USA Today, 1998-2000; asst. city editor The Washington Post, 2000—. Cons. W.K. Kellogg Nat. Fellowship, Battle Creek, Mich., 1984-93; freelance writer, 1965—. Youth soccer coach Northport, N.Y., 1976-80, dir., 1979-80, Shaker Heights, Ohio, 1984-87, Swarthmore (Pa.) Recreation Assn., 1987-88; coach Johnson County (Kans.) Soccer League, 1983-84, U. Kans. Women's Soccer Club, 1980-81; bd. dirs. Suffolk County Heart Assn., L.I., 1974-75. Mem. Nat. Assn. Hispanic Journalists, Investigative Reporters and Editors. Democrat. Roman Catholic. Avocations: travel, fishing, outdoor sports. Home: 10413 Breckinridge Ln Fairfax VA 22030-3417 Office: The Washington Post 1150 15th St NW Washington DC 20071-0002

SAMUEL, HOWARD DAVID, union official; b. N.Y.C., Nov. 16, 1924; s. Ralph E. and Florence (Weingarten) S.; m. Ruth H. Zamkin, Apr. 15, 1948; children: Robert H., Donald F., William H. BA, Dartmouth Coll., 1948. Various positions Amalgamated Clothing and Textile Workers (formerly Amalgamated Clothing Workers Am.), N.Y.C., 1949-60, asst. pres., 1960-64, v.p., 1966-77; dep. under sec. Bur. Internat. Labor Affairs Dept. Labor, Washington, 1977-79; pres. Indsl. Union Dept. AFL-CIO, 1979-92; v.p. New Sch. for Social Rsch., N.Y.C., 1964-65, Econ. Strategy Inst., 1992-98. Vice chmn. N.Y. Urban Coalition, 1968-74; mem. governing bd. Common Cause, 1971-77; sec. Nat. Com. Full Employment, 1975-77, sec.-treas., 1977-89; mem. Pres.'s Commn. on Indsl. Competitiveness, 1983-85; sr. fellow Coun. on Competitiveness, 1993-97, vice chmn., 1986-92; mem. U.S. Dept. Labor Task Force on Econ. Adjustment, and Worker Dislocation, 1985-87; mem. vis. com. advanced tech. Nat. Inst. Stds. and Tech., 1995-2000; mem. adv. com. Export-Import Bank. Author: (with Stephen K. Bailey) Congress at Work, 1952; Government in America, 1957; editor: Toward a Better America, 1968; author numerous mag. articles. Mem. Nat. Manpower Adv. Com., 1969-74; mem. Commn. Population Growth and the Am. Future, 1970-72; mem. Def. Mfg. Bd., 1988-89, Def. Sci. Bd., 1989-92; chmn. White Plains Dem. Com., 1960-64; vice-chmn. Westchester County com., 1957-70, alt. del. nat. conv., 1964; mem. Nat. Dem. Charter Revision Com., 1972-73; exec. dir. Nat. Labor Com. McGovern-Shriver, 1972; del. Dem. Conv. on Party Orgn. and Policy, Kansas City, 1974, Nat. Dem. Conv., 1976; trustee Carnegie Corp., 1971-77, Joint Coun. Econ. Edn., 1971-77; bd. dirs. ACLU, 1966-68; trustee Brookings Instn.; overseer RAND Inst. for Civil Justice, 1987-93. With AUS, 1943-46. Mem. Coun. on Fgn. Rels., Phi Beta Kappa. E-mail: HHDSamuel@aol.com.

SAMUEL, PAUL, cardiologist, educator; b. Janoshaza, Hungary, Jan. 17, 1927; came to U.S., 1954, naturalized, 1960; s. Adolf and Magda (Zollner) S.; m. Gabriella R. Zeichner, Mar. 27, 1954; children: Robert Mark, Adrienne Jill. Baccalaureat, Kemeny Zsigmond Gymnasium, Budapest, Hungary, 1945; MD, U. Paris, 1953. Intern Queens Hosp. Ctr., N.Y.C., 1954-55; resident L.I. Jewish Med. Ctr., New Hyde Park, N.Y., 1959-61; adj. prof. Rockefeller U., N.Y.C., 1971-81; adj. prof. medicine Cornell U., 1979—; pvt. practice, Forest Hills, N.Y., 1961—. Clin. prof. medicine Albert Einstein Coll. Medicine, Bronx, N.Y., 1981—; dir. Arteriosclerosis Rsch. Lab., L.I. Jewish-Hillside Med. Ctr., New Hyde Park, 1962—; chmn. N.Y. Lipid Rsch. Club, Rockefeller U., 1977-78. Contbr. articles to med. jours. Fellow Am. Coll. Cardiology; mem. ACP, Am. Heart Assn. (fellow coun. on arteriosclerosis, Disting. Achievement award), Am. Fedn. Clin. Rsch., Harvey Soc. Home: 25 Nassau Dr Great Neck NY 11021-2163 Office: 11020 71st Rd Forest Hills NY 11375-4945

SAMUEL, RALPH DAVID, lawyer; b. Augusta, Ga., May 8, 1945; s. Ralph and Louise Elizabeth (Wurreschke) S.; m. Lynn Christel Malmgren, June 12, 1971; children: Lynn Britt, Ralph Erik. AB, Dartmouth Coll., 1967; JD, Dickinson Sch. of Law, 1972. Bar: Pa. 1972, U.S. Dist. Ct. (ea. dist.) Pa. 1972, U.S. Ct. Appeals (3d cir.) 1973, U.S. Supreme Ct. 1976. Law clk. to hon. judge John P. Fullam U.S. Dist. Ct. (ea. dist.) Pa., Phila., 1972-74; assoc. MacCoy, Evans & Lewis., 1974-76; ptnr. Samuel and Ballard, P.C., 1976-98; pres., CEO Ralph D. Samuel & Co., P.C., 1998—. Established Samuel Poetry Fellow Dartmouth Coll., Hanover, N.H., 1994. *For over 25 years Ralph Samuel has fought for the rights of individual Americans to enjoy their civil rights, live and work free from discrination, and to be farily and adequately compensated for physical and economic injury. In 1977 he represented the appellants in taking on the nation's chieg prosecutor, Hon. Richard Thornburgh, in argument to the U.S. Supreme Court in the landmark Fith Amendment case by which Ralph Samuel secured the right of an immediate appeal when threatened with double jeopardy. Abeny, et al. v. United States, 431 U.S. 651, unanimous opinion by Chief Justice Burger. Additionally, Ralph Samuel has succesfully represented clients at all levels of the Pennsylvania state and federal courts. The law office of Ralph D. Samuel & Co., P.C. currently provides consultaions and accepts selected representation of 11 individuals, at all levels of compensation, to achieve their results in employment conflicts, injury and other civil cases.* Contbr. articles to profl. jours., poetry to publs. Trustee The George Sch., Newtown, Pa., 1983-90; chmn. bd. dirs. Stapeley in Germantown, 1985-90; mem. Chase Fund Com., 2000; chmn. budget com. Phila. Yearly Meeting of Friends, 1991-93; bd. dirs., mem. fin. com. Phila. Ranger Corps., 1992-94; pres. Cedar Park Neighbors, Phila., 1975-78, West Mt. Airy Neighbors, Phila., 1981-82. Mem. Pa. Soc., Athenaeum of Phila., Sunday Breakfast Club. Mem. Soc. Of Friends. Avocations: music, writing, squash, tennis. Office: PO Box 35185 Philadelphia PA 19128-0185 Fax: (215) 849-6859. E-mail: RalphSamuel@RalphSamuel.com.

SAMUEL, ROBERT THOMPSON, optometrist; b. Kansas City, Mo., June 27, 1944; s. Manlius Thompson and Helen Evelyn (Syverson) S. BA, William Jewell Coll., 1966; postgrad., U. Mo., Kansas City, 1967; MS, U. Mo., 1968; DOptometry, U. Tenn., Memphis, 1971; postgrad., U. Mo., St. Louis, 1995, Northeastern State U., 1998. Cert. optometrist, Mo. Buyer Recco, Inc., Kansas City, Mo., 1963-67; histology lab. instr. William Jewell Coll., Liberty, 1965-66; pvt. practice optometry Gladstone, 1972—; staff doctor O.H. Gerry Optical Clinics, 1996—. Panel doctor Ford Motor Co., Claycomo, Mo., 1985—, Union Pacific R.R., Kansas City, 1985—, TWA Airlines, 1990, Union Carbide, 1990. Publicity coord. Rep. Party, Kansas City, Mo., 1975-76; chmn. Save Your Vision Week, Kansas City, 1977; mem. Theatre League of Kansas City, 1976—, Kansas City Mus., 1986—, Friends of Art, 1985, Friends of Mo. Town 1955, 1980—. Recipient Outstanding Young Men of Am. award Jaycees, 1978, Good Citizens award DAR, 1962. Mem. Am. Optometric Assn., Mo. Optometric Assn., Optometric Soc. Greater Kansas City, Heart of Am. Contact Lens Congress, Am. Acad. Sports Vision, Vol. Optometric Svcs. for Humanity, Smithsonian Assocs., Lions (exec. bd. dir. Lions Eye Clinic 1974-84, bd. dirs. 1982—, Outstanding Svc. award 1973, 74, editor Lions Optometric Ctr. Quar. 1974-84), Kappa Alpha Order (treas. 1966). Republican. Lutheran. Avocations: photography, music, piano, swimming, travel. Home: 6325 N Monroe Ave Kansas City MO 64119-1923 Office: 1170 W 152 Hwy Liberty MO 64068-2035 also: 5601 NE Antioch Rd Kansas City MO 64119-2302

SAMUELI, HENRY, electrical engineering educator, entrepreneur; b. Buffalo, Sept. 20, 1954; s. Aron and Sala (Traubman) S.; m. Susan Faye Eisenberg, Aug. 22, 1982; children: Leslie Pamela, Jillian Meryl, Erin Sydney. BS, UCLA, 1975, MS, 1976, PhD, 1980. Staff engr. TRW Inc., Redondo Beach, Calif., 1980-83, section mgr., 1983-85; asst. prof. UCLA, 1985-90, assoc. prof., 1990-94, prof., 1994—. Cons. TRW, Inc., Redondo Beach, 1985-89; co-founder, chief scientist PairGain Techs., Inc., Tustin, Calif., 1989-94; co-founder, chief tech. officer Broadcom Corp., Irvine, Calif., 1991—. Named one of Top 20 Entrepreneurs of 1997, The Red Herring Mag., 1997, one of Top 50 Cyber Elite, Time Digital Mag., 1997. Mem. IEEE, Sigma Xi, Tau Beta Pi. Republican. Jewish. Avocations: skiing, basketball. Office: Broadcom Corp PO Box 57013 Irvine CA 92619-7013

SAMUELS, ABRAM, stage equipment manufacturing company executive; b. Allentown, Pa., Sept. 15, 1920; s. Irving and Ann (Friedman) S.; m. Harriet Ann Goodman, Sept. 1, 1945; children: Margaret A. Samuels Berger, Katherine E., Sally R. Samuels Slifkin, John A., Dorothy M. Samuels Lampl, Caroline J. Samuels Bagli. BS, Lehigh U., 1942; auditor philosophy, Princeton U., 1962-65. Pres. Automatic Devices Co., Allentown, 1946-75, chmn. exec. com., 1987-92, chmn. bd., 1975-87, 93—, Mchts. Bank, 1981-85, chmn. exec. com., 1985-91. Past guest lectr. Cedar Crest Coll., 1969-71, 84, Muhlenberg Coll., 1977-82, 92. Author: Where the Colleges Rank, 1973. Pres. Samuels Family Found., 1959—; past pres. Pa. Soc. for Crippled Children and Adults, 1957-58; past pres., hon. bd. dirs. Lehigh County Crippled Children's Soc., 1949-51; past pres. Lehigh County Humane Soc., 1960-64, Cedar Crest Coll. Assocs., 1968-70; bd. dirs. Allentown Hosp., 1977-88, chmn. bd., 1987; vice chmn. Allentown Hosp.-Lehigh Valley Hosp. Ctr., 1988; pres. Lehigh County Hist. Soc., 1976-78; past bd. dirs. Nat. Soc. for Crippled Children and Adults, Pa. Mental Health Assn., Merchants Bank, 1965-91, Lehigh County Indsl. Devel. Corp., Pa. Stage Co., 1983-84, Health East, Inc., 1985-91, Nightingale Awards of Pa., 1989-91; trustee St. Augustine's Coll., 1970-77, 92-95, Allentown YWCA, 1977-83, Cedar Crest Coll., 1996—; bd. dirs. Fund to Benefit Children and Youth of Lehigh Valley Inc., 1992—, Lehigh County Hist. Soc., 1999—. With AUS, 1942-46. Recipient Benjamin Rush award Lehigh County Med. Soc., 1954, Allentown Human Relations award, 1979; named Outstanding Young Man of Year Jr. C. of C., 1954. Mem. Hon. First Defenders, C. of C. (past v.p. 1960), Pa. German Soc., Am. Soc. Psychical Rsch. (trustee 1985-91, treas. 1990), Princeton Club (N.Y.C.), Rotary (pres. Allentown club 1955-56, dist. gov. 1964-65), Skytop Club. Republican. Office: 2121 S 12th St Allentown PA 18103-4751

SAMUELS, BARRY IVAN, radiologist, medical educator; b. Detroit, Oct. 31, 1940; s. Alex and Ida Samuels; m. Carole Paulette Samuels, June 20, 1964; children: Marc, Craig. BA, Wayne State U., 1961; MD, U. Mich., 1965. Lic. physician, Tex., Mich., Calif., La., Ariz. Assoc. prof. radiology U. Tex. M.D. Anderson Cancer Ctr., Houston, 1989—2002, prof. radiology, 2002—. Sr. asst. surgeon USPHS, 1966-68. Mem. Am. Coll. Radiology, Am. Inst. Ultrasound, Tex. Radiol. Soc., Tex. Med. Assn., Houston Radiol. Soc. Avocations: walking, reading, music, art, travel.

SAMUELS, BRIAN LOUIS, oncologist, researcher; b. Harare, Zimbabwe, May 6, 1954; m. Lesley Margaret Samuels, Jan. 5, 1979; children: David, Mark, Emma. MBChB, U. Rhodesia, 1976. Asst. prof. U. Chgo., 1988—95; assoc. prof. U. Ill. at Chgo., 1996—; dir. oncology rsch. Luth. Gen. Hosp., Park Ridge, Ill., 1991—. Office: Oncology Specialists SC 1700 Luther Ln Park Ridge IL 60068

SAMUELS, FERN JACQUELINE, artist, educator; b. Chgo., Feb. 16, 1931; d. Noah S. and Ann (Zager) Andrews; m. Howard Stanley Samuels, Sept. 17, 1950; children: Mitchell, Paul, David. BFA, Loyola U., 1973; MFA, Sch. Art Inst. Chgo., 1983. Instr.-coord. Mundelein Coll., Chgo., 1976-83; faculty Columbia Coll., 1978-2000. Instr. workshops Field Mus., Chgo., 1976, Lake Forest Coll., Chgo., 1976, Lincoln Park Cultural Ctr., Chgo., 1973, Ill. Inst. Tech., Chgo., 1980—, Latin Sch., Chgo., 1976; juror St. Louis Arts Guild, 1998. One-women shows include Northwestern U., 1988, Ea. Ill. U., Chgo., 1989, Countryside Gallery, 1988, Upstart Gallery, 1990, Soho 20, N.Y.C., 1993, Loyola U., 1995, Morraine Valley Coll., 1995, McDonough Mus. Art, 1997; exhibited in group shows including Smithsonian Air and Space Mus., 1983, Freeport Mus., 1995, Rockford Mus., 1996, Butler Inst. Am. Art, 1998, Lafayette Mus., 1999, Columbus Mus. Art, 2000, So. Ohio Mus., 2000, South Bend Regional Mus., 2000, Univ. Mus. S.D., 2001. Mem. LWV, Chgo., 1969—; founding mem. Alternative Fibers, Chgo., 1982; chairperson, coord. Seven Ethnic Museums, Chgo., 1986; membership chmn. ARC Gallery, Chgo., 1983-86, pres. 1988-90; bd. dirs. Artist Book Works, Chgo., 1992-93. Recipient Best of Show award Women in the Visual Arts, Boca Raton, Fla., 2001, Judges Recognition award, Boca Raton, 2001, 2nd prize Boca Mus. Artists Guild, 2001, 1st prize, 2002, 1st prize Women in Visual Arts, Del Ray, Fla., 2002, Mus. Exhibits, 2002, Jewish Mus., Miami, Norton Mus., West Palm Beach, Fla., 2002, Cornell Mus. of Art and Sci., Del Ray, 2002; grantee Columbia Coll., 1981; Fern Samuels Scholarship Fund est. Columbia Coll., Chgo. Mem. Arts Club Chgo., Chgo. Soc. Arts, Am. ORT, City of Hope (Bobby Blechman chpt. founding mem.), Sch. Art Inst. Chgo. Alumni (2d prize 2002). Democrat. Avocations: reading, music, theater, exercise. Home: 84 Saint James Ct Palm Beach Gardens FL 33418 E-mail: ucars1@aol.com.

SAMUELS, HANNA, artist; b. Buffalo, Apr. 26, 1908; d. Emil and Rachel (Span) S. Student, Art Inst. Buffalo, 1937-54. Sr. clk. in charge of catalog Buffalo State Coll., 1966-73, vol. cons. on art. Represented in permanent collections at Erie County Hist. Soc., Vincent Price Collection, Judaic Mus., Temple Beth Zion, Buffalo, Butler Libr., Buffalo State Coll., Cox Conv. Hall, Pentecostal Temple Ch., Buffalo, Burchfield-Penney Art Ctr., Buffalo; exhibited in group shows Smithsonian Instn., Kenan Ctr., Lockport, N.Y.; exhbns. of sculpture include Burchfield-Penney Art Ctr., Buffalo, Albright-Knox Art Gallery, Memphis, Jr. League, Smithsonian Instn., Washington, Castellani Art Mus., Smithsonian Assocs. Nat. Mem. The Libr. of Congress. Vol. USO, Buffalo, 1942-45. Mem. Patteran Artists (rec. sec.), Castellani Art Mus. Niagara U., Libr. Congress (nat.), Smithsonian Inst. (assoc.). Democrat. Avocations: painting, music. Address: 1190 Amherst St Buffalo NY 14216-3624

SAMUELS, JANET LEE, lawyer; b. Pitts., July 18, 1953; d. Emerson and Jeanne (Kalish) S.; m. David Arthur Kalow, June 18, 1978; children; Margaret Emily Samuels-Kalow, Jacob Richard Samuels-Kalow, Benjamin Charles Samuels-Kalow. BA with honors, Beloit Coll., 1974; JD, NYU, 1977. Bar: N.Y. 1978, D.C. 1980. Staff atty. SCM Corp., N.Y.C., 1977-80, corp. atty., 1980-83, sr. corp. atty., 1983-85, assoc. gen. counsel Allied Paper div., 1983-86, corp. counsel, 1986, Holtzmann, Wise & Shepard, 1986-88. Mem. N.Y. State Bar Assn., Mortar Board, Phi Beta Kappa. E-mail: jlsamuels@hotmail.com.

SAMUELS, JOHN STOCKWELL, III, mining company executive, financier; b. Galveston, Tex., Sept. 15, 1933; s. John Stockwell and Helen Yvonne (Poole) S.; children: Evelyn Kathleen, John Stockwell, Ainlay Leontine, Peter Ashton Hayes. AB, SM, Tex. A&M U., 1954; JD, Harvard U., 1960. Bar: N.Y. 1961. Assoc. Chadbourne, Parke, Whiteside & Wolff, N.Y.C., 1960-73; pres. Internat. Carbon & Minerals, 1973-78, Carbomin Group, Inc., N.Y.C., 1978—, U.S. Reduction Inc., 1996—. Chmn. bd. J.S. Samuels & Co. Bd. dirs. City Center Music and Drama, Inc., N.Y.C.; chmn. bd. dirs. N.Y.C. Ballet, N.Y.C. Opera, 1976-81, Lincoln Ctr. Theatre, N.Y.C., 1979-81, Lincoln Ctr., N.Y.C. With U.S. Army, 1954-57. Mem. Inst. Petroleum, Century Assn. Democrat. Episcopalian. E-mail: jss@usr-inc.com.

SAMUELS, LESLIE B. lawyer; b. St. Louis, Nov. 10, 1942; s. Joseph E. and Dorothy J. (Bernstein) S.; m. Judith B. Thorn, June 19, 1966 (div. Aug. 1976); children: Colin T., Polly B.; m. Augusta H. Gross, Nov. 8, 1980. BS in Econs., U. Pa., 1963; LLB magna cum laude, Harvard U., 1966; postgrad., London Sch. Econs., 1966-67. Bar: N.Y., 1969, U.S. Dist. Ct. (so. dist.) N.Y. 1973, U.S. Tax Ct., 1980, U.S. Supreme Ct. 1994; CPA. Tax analyst Gulf Oil Co., London, 1967-68; assoc. Cleary, Gottlieb, Steen & Hamilton, N.Y.C., 1968-75, ptnr., 1975-93, 96—; asst. sec. for tax policy U.S. Dept. Treasury, Washington, 1993-96; vice-chair com. fiscal affairs OECD, 1994-96. Mem. Pres.'s Com. on the Arts and the Humanities, Washington, 1994-96. Editor Law Rev.; contbr. articles to profl. jours. Dir. Lower Manhattan Cultural Coun., N.Y.C., 1981-93, Roy Lichtenstein Found., N.Y.C., 1999—; active Carter-Mondale Transition Planning Group, Washington, 1976-77. Fulbright fellow London Sch. Econs., 1966-67. Mem. N.Y. State Bar Assn., Assn. of Bar of City of N.Y., Harvard Club (N.Y.C.). Democrat. Office: Cleary Gottlieb Steen & Hamilton One Liberty Plaza New York NY 10006 E-mail: lsamuels@cgsh.com.

SAMUELS, LESLIE EUGENE, marketing and management consultant; b. St. Croix, V.I., Nov. 12, 1929; s. Henry Francis and Annamartha Venetia (Ford) S.; m. Reather James, Oct. 24, 1959; children: Leslie Jr., Venetia, Yvette, Philip. MusB, NYU, 1956; JD, Blackstone Sch. Law, 1975; MBA, Columbia Pacific U., 1984, PhD, 1985. Concert soloist Van Dyke Studios, N.Y.C., 1956-65; dir. Housing, Preservation and Devel., 1966—; bandmaster N.Y. State Dept. Rehab. and Recreation, 1967-76; pres., CEO Samuels and Co., Inc., 1986—, Coll. Philosophy and Edn., 1998—; exec. dir., CEO Samuels Inst. Hist. Rsch. of Christian Prins., 1991—. Cons. in field., 1984—; mem. N.Y., N.J. Minority Bus. Purchasing Coun., Inc., Nat. Minority Bus. Coun., Inc., Internat. Trade divsn.; evangelist, lectr. Principles of the Christian Faith; adj. prof. St. Martin's Coll. and Sem., 1995; dir. pvt. sch. state edn. dept., 1996. Author: Redemption, 2000. Mem. Bronx County Com., 1969; dist. leader Bronx 86th Assembly Dist., 1969; advisor Astor Home for Children, Bronx, 1973, Bronxville C. of C., Bklyn., 1975; charter mem. Rep. Presdl. Task Force, 1989; exec. dir. Samuels Inst. Hist. Rsch. Christian Principles, 1991—; mem. Nat. Rep. Senatorial Com., 1992. With U.S. Army, 1951-53. Mem. Maison Internationale des Intellectuels, Am. Mgmt. Assn., Nat. Black MBA Assn., Harvard Bus. Rev., Sloan Mgmt. Rev., Calif. Mgmt. Rev., Columbia Pacific U. Alumni Assn., Internat. Platform Assn., Smithsonian Assocs., Ind. Citizen's Club (pres. Bronx 1967-77). Republican. Avocation: sports. Home: 2814 Bruner Ave Bronx NY 10469-3403 E-mail: samuelsinstitut@webtv.net.

SAMUELS, LINDA S. science administrator; b. Mansfield, Ohio, Feb. 15, 1947; d. Robert Lloyd and Esther Sophia (Schwob) Garber; children: Marilyn L., Charles L. AB in Biology-Zoology, U. Cin., 1969, MS in Population Biology, 1971; MBA, Suffolk U., 2002. Anatomy and physiology instr. U. Cin., 1969—70; biology, chemistry, physics, algebra instr. Cambridge (Mass.) Acad., 1971—72; instr. biology Simmons Coll., Boston, 1972—73; instr. advanced biology, life sci., dance sci. Dana Hall Sch., Wellesley, 1972—2002; CEO Sci. of Learning Ctr., Boston, 2002—. Rap Around: Discussion Dissection in the Classroom, WBZ-TV, Boston, 1996-97; liaison com. to head of sch. Dana Hall Sch., Wellesley, Mass., 1995-98, developer dance sci. curriculum, 1998—; cons. NSF summer project Girls in Engring. engring. adv. com. Tufts U., 1997; mem. com. to study physiology of learning Harvard Med. Sch , 1998—; mem. neurosci. com. minority faculty devel. program, 1995 Author: Girls Can Succeed in Science, 1999; contbr. articles to sci. jours. Mem. Bar/Bat Mitzah Com. Temple Israel, Boston, 1995, adult choir, 1997; parent rep., Buckingham, Browne and Nichols Sch., Cambridge, 1995-98; mem. parking com. Back Bay Assn. Recipient Sci. Tchr. of Yr. award Norfolk County, 1994, sabbatical grant Dana Hall Sch., 1995, Disting. Alumni award U. Cin., McMicken Coll. Arts and Scis., 1996, H. Dudley Wright Fellowship for Innovative Sci. Edn. Tufts U., Medford, Mass., 1996-97; dedication of Linda S. Samuels Animal Behavior Lab. at Dana Hall; inductee Mass. Hall of Fame Educators, Boston, 1999. Mem. Nat. Assn. Biology Tchrs. (presenter 1986—, award for excellence in encouraging equity sect. on women 1997-98, Outstanding Biology Tchr. Mass. 1994), Nat. Sci. Tchrs. Assn. (presenter 1986—, Tchr. of Yr. award 1994), New Eng. Sci. Tchrs., Mass. Assn. Biology Tchrs. (v.p. 1997, pres. 1998), Mass. Assn. Sci. Tchrs. (presenter 1986-95, 99, Presdl. award state finalist Sec. Sch. Sci., Mass). Avocations: science business consulting, exercise. Office: 1148 Boylston St Chestnut Hill MA 02467-2324

SAMUELS, MARC, health care consultant; b. Bethesda, Md., Feb. 8, 1968; s. Monica (Leiter) Samuels; 1 child, Jeb. BA cum laude, U. Mich., 1989; MPH in Policy and Adminstrn., Yale U., 1992; JD, U. Tex., 1996. Staff asst. McManis Assocs., Health Care Consultants, Washington, Law Offices of Deborah L. Steelman, Washington, Office of Policy Devel., The White House, Washington, V.P.'s Domestic Policy Office, Washington; health care cons., legis. asst., health law sect. Jenkens & Gilchrist PC, Austin, Tex.; asst. to Gov. for Health Policy, Office of Gov. George W. Bush; personal asst. to commr. Tex. Health and Human Svcs. Commn.; prin. Samuels Health Strategies. Mem. adv. bd. U. Houston Health Law and Policy Inst.; advisor Tex. Lifescience Found., Austin. Co-author: The Managed Care Answer Book, 1996, 4th edit., 1999, Risk Contracting and Capitation Answer Book, 1998, 2d edit., 1999; contbr. articles to profl. jours. Dep. rsch. dir. Kay Bailey Hutchison for U.S. Senate, 1993; health care policy advisor George W. Bush for Gov., 1994, Jeb Bush for Gov., 1998, Bush for Pres. Campaign Exploratory Com., 1999; chmn. A Policy Forum for Young Am., 1996. Spencer Scholar Risk & Ins. Mgmt. Soc., 1996; recipient Baker and Botts prize, 1996. Fax: 512-480-8964. E-mail: samuelshs@mindspring.com.

SAMUELS, WILLIAM MASON, physiology association executive; b. Dover, Ohio, Jan. 17, 1929; s. William Mason and Anne Frieda (Fankhauser) S.; m. Joanne Gorenflo, Oct. 2, 1971; children: Robert Lee, Ann Frances. AB, U. Ky., 1951; postgrad., Georgetown U., 1952. Mng. editor for Ind., Courier-Jour. & Times, Louisville, 1955-65; dir. office of v.p. U. Ky. Med. Center, Lexington, 1965-70; exec. dir. Am. Soc. Allied Health Professions, Washington, 1973—78; assoc. Schs. Allied Health Professions, 1970—73; exec. dir. Am. Assn. Blood Banks, Washington, 1978-80, Nat. Soc. Med. Research Washington, 1980-84, Am. Physiol. Soc., Bethesda, Md., 1984-92; retired, 1992—. Contbr. articles to profl. jours. Mem. secretarist Nat. Commn. Health Certifying Agys.; v.p. Coalition Health Funding; cons. to fed. agys.; vol. Habitat for Humanity, Boca Raton. With USAF, 1951-53, USAFR, 1954-76, lt. col. ret. Named Ky. Man of Yr. Sigma Phi Epsilon, 1968 Mem.: AMA (mem. coun. on allied health edn. accreditation), Washington Soc. Assn. Execs., Health Staff Soc., Am. Hosp. Assn. (coun. on edn.), Am. Optometric Assn. (mem. coun. on edn., coun. on optimetric clin. care, nat. commn. on parraoptometric cert.), Am. Soc. Assn. Execs., Pinehurst (NC) Country Club, Lions. Presbyterian. Home: 6055 S Verde Trail H-120 Boca Raton FL 33433-4406

SAMUELSON, BILLIE MARGARET, artist; b. Long Beach, Calif., Apr. 11, 1927; d. William Christian and Gladys Margaret (Caffrey) Newendorp; m. Fritz Eric Samuelson, Aug. 12, 1950 (div. 1985); children: Craig Eric, Clark Alan, Dana Scott. Student, Long Beach City Coll., 1945—46. Pvt. art tchr., Wycokoff/Allendale, NJ, 1985. Workshop instr. Jane Law Studio, Long Beach Island, N.J., 1990—. Exhibited in solo show at Ridgewood (N.J.) Art Inst., 1985, West Wing Gallery, 1991, Chas. Austin Gallery, Saddle River, N.J., 1997; group shows include Craig Gallery, Ridgewood, 1979, Charisma Gallery, Englewood, N.J., 1981-83, Custom Gallery, Waldwick, N.J., 1985, Wyckoff (N.J.) Gallery, 1987-90, West Wing Gallery, Ringwood State Park, N.J., 1991, Union Camp Corp., 1992, Eisenhauer Gallery, Block Island, R.I., 1996—; featured in Am. Artists Mag., 2001. Recipient 1st in State N.J. Womens Clubs, 1978-80, Watercolor award N.J. Painters and Sculptors, 1981. Mem. DAR, Community Arts Assn. (pres. 1978-79), Am. Artists Profl. League (bd. dirs. 1985-87, watercolor prize 1992), Ringwood Manor Arts Assn. (sr. profl.), Catherine Lorillard Wolfe Art Club (cash award 1993), Salute to Women in the Arts, Art Ctr. Watercolor Affiliates, Nat. Mus. of Women in the Arts. Avocations: bridge, travel, museums, theatre, reading. Home: 1-3 Chestnut Pl Waldwick NJ 07463-1113

SAMUELSON, CYNTHIA, information technology executive; b. N.C. m. Lawrence Samuelson. BA in Math., Hampton U.; MS in Computer Sci., Fairleigh Dickinson U.; postgrad., U. So. Calif. Mathematician Westinghouse R&D Ctr., Pitts.; with FTC, Washington, U.S. Dept. Commerce, Washington, Nat. Edowment for the Arts; info. resource mgmt. dir. Dept. of Transp.; prin. dir. info. mgmt. Office of the Asst. Sec. of Def. for Command, Control, Comm. and Intelligence, Washington; bus. devel. dir. Lucent Technologies Govt. Solutions (now Avaya), Basking Ridge, NJ, v.p. mktg., telesales and svcs. Mem. Aero. and Space Engrng. Bd., NAS. Bd. dirs. Sch. Engring., Hampton U.; mentor Boy Scouts Am.; mentor various pub. and pvt. sector orgns. Named one of Fed. Computer Week's Top 100 Fed. Info. Tech. Execs.; recipient Bronze medal, Dept. Transp., Medal for Meritorious Civilian Svc., Dept. of Def., Exceptional Civilian Svc. award, Tech. award, Black Engr.'s Women of Color. Mem.: Armed Forces Comm. and Electronics Assn. (bd. dirs.). Office: Avaya 211 Mount Airy Rd Basking Ridge NJ 07920*

SAMUELSON, DENNIS RAY, retired pathologist; b. Burlington, Iowa, Jan. 4, 1940; s. Norman Russell and Josephine Katherine (McQueen) S.; m. Virginia Lea Matthews; children: Erik Sven, Heidi Jo, Alek Justin. BA, U. Iowa, 1958-62, MD, 1961-65. Diplomate Am. Bd. Pathology, 1970, Am. Bd. Nuclear Medicine, 1975, Am. Bd. Family Practice, 1979. Pathologist and physician McDonough Dist. Hosp., Macomb, Ill., 1972-98, pres. NuPath P.C., 1980-98; nuclear medicine physician Meml. Hosp., Carthage, Ill., 1973-98, Sarah D. Culbertson Hosp., Rushville, 1987-98; staff physician Beu Health Ctr., Western Ill. U., Macomb, 1998—2001; ret. Dir. lab., blood bank, nuclear medicine McDonough Dist. Hosp., 1976-97; asst. prof. pathology U. (Peoria) Ill., 1982—; instr. Western Ill. U., 1987—. Contbr. articles to profl. jours. Prof., chmn. McDonough County Unit Am. Cancer Soc., Macomb, Ill., 1982—. Fellow Coll. Am. Pathologist, Am. Soc. Clin. Pathologists, Am. Coll. Nuclear Medicine, Soc. Nuclear Medicine,Am. Acad. Family Physicians, AMA, Macomb Country Club; mem. Omicron Delta Leadership Soc., Alpha Omega Alpha, Macomb Bus. Boosters Breakfast Club (pres.). Methodist. Avocations: tennis, gardening, beer mktg.

SAMUELSON, DERRICK WILLIAM, lawyer; b. Mpls., July 24, 1929; s. Oscar W. and Ruth (Hill) S.; m. Diana L. Webster, Aug. 10, 1957; children: David W., Deirdre S. Columbia. BS, U.S. Mil. Acad., 1951; LL.B., Harvard U., 1957. Bar: N.Y. 1958. Assoc. firm Lowenstein, Pitcher, Hotchkiss, Amann & Parr, N.Y.C., 1957-60; staff atty. internat. div. Warner-Lambert Pharm. Co., Morris Plains, N.J., 1960-63; counsel internat. div. Olin Mathieson Chem. Corp., N.Y.C., 1964-65; v.p., gen. counsel ITT World Communications Inc., 1965-70, ITT Asia Pacific, Inc., N.Y.C., 1970-81; sr. counsel ITT Corp., 1981-87, asst. gen. counsel, asst. sec., 1987-92; of counsel Mulvaney, Kahan & Barry, San Diego, 1993—. Mem. panel neutrals and internat. panel Am. Arbitration Assn., 1995—; mem. bd. arbitrators Nat. Assn. Securities Dealers, Inc., 1996—. Pres. Am-Indonesian C. of C., 1976-79, Smoke Rise Club, 1976-77, 88-89; chmn. Am. ASEAN Trade Coun., Inc., 1978-92. With U.S. Army, 1951-54. Home: 2940 Via Asoleado Alpine CA 91901-3182 Office: First Nat Bank Bldg 401 W A St San Diego CA 92101-7901 E-mail: dsamuelson@prodigy.net.

SAMUELSON, DONALD B. state legislator; b. Brainerd, Minn., Aug. 23, 1932; s. Walter H. and Ellen (Gallagher) S.; m. Nancy O'Brien, 1952; children: Stephen, Laura, Paula, Christine. Chmn. 6th Dist. Com. on Polit. Edn. State of Minn., 1960-66; mem. Minn. Ho. of Reps., St. Paul, 1969-76, 1981-82, Minn. Senate from 12th dist., St. Paul, 1982—; pres. Minn. Senate, 2001—. Chmn. Health & Human Svc. Fin. Div. Com., mem. Commerce and Consumer Protection, mem. Family Svc. Com., mem. Fin. and Health Care Com.; former foreman Bor-Son Construct Co.; union bus. mgr. Chmn. 6th Dist. Com. on Polit. Edn., Minn., 1960-66; mem. State Ctrl. Com. Dem-Farmer-Labor Party, 1964-66, former chmn. Crow Wing County. Mem. Housing and Redevel. Authority, Minn. AFL-CIO, Bricklayers Union, Elks, Eagles, Moose. Democrat. Home: 1018 Portland Ave Brainerd MN 56401-4133 also: 121 Capitol 75 Constitution Ave Saint Paul MN 55155-1606*

SAMUELSON, DOUGLAS ALAN, information systems company executive; b. Reno, July 27, 1948; s. Norman Harold and Shirley (Leder) S.; m. Francine Ruth Kimel, Jan. 7, 1979; children: Andrew, Diane. BA, U. Calif., Berkeley, 1969; MS, George Washington U., 1981, DSc, 1990. Computer systems analyst Bank of Am., San Francisco, 1972-73; cons. San Rafael, 1973-75; ops. rsch. analyst U.S. Govt., Washington, 1975-82; analyst, v.p. Micro-Zeit/Internat. Telesystems Corp., Reston, Va., 1983-88; asst. prof. Memphis State U., 1990-92; pres. InfoLogix, Inc., Annandale, Va., 1988—; prin. scientist Puma Sys., Inc., Falls Church, 1997-98; chief statistician FMAS Dyncorp., Columbia, Md., 2000; sci. advisor ITT Rsch. Inst., 2001. Vis. rsch. scholar George Washington U., 1993—95, mem. nat. adv. coun. Sch. Engring. and Applied Sci., 1996—2000, adj. prof. lectr., 1997—; adj. assoc. prof. George Mason U., Fairfax, Va., 1994—96, external rsch. prof. Krasnow Inst. for Advanced Study, 2001—; adj. assoc. prof. U. Pa., Phila., 2001—. Co-editor, author (with others): Human Rights and Statistics: Getting the Record Straight, 1992, Health Information and Ethics: Protecting Fundamental Human Rights, 1997; author (column) The ORacle, 1986—; contbr. articles to profl. jours. Bd. dirs. George Washington U. Engr. Alumni Assn., 1994—, v.p., 1996-98, pres., 1998-2000. Mem. AAAS, Washington OR/MS Coun. (pres. 1989-90, 96-97), Am. Statis. Assn. (chair com. on scientific freedom and human rights 1985-88), Inst. for Ops. Rsch. and Mgmt. Sci. (bd. dirs. 1998-2000). Democrat. Jewish. Achievements include patent for systems for regulating arrivals of customers to servers. Office: InfoLogix Inc 8711 Chippendale Ct Annandale VA 22003-3807 E-mail: samuelsondoug@netscape.net.

SAMUELSON, KENNETH LEE, lawyer; b. Natrona Heights, Pa., Aug. 22, 1946; s. Sam and Frances Bernice (Robbins) S.; m. Marlene Ina Rabinowitz, Jan. 1, 1980; children: Heather, Cheryl. BA magna cum laude, U. Pitts., 1968; JD, U. Mich., 1971. Bar: Md. 1972, D.C. 1980, U.S. Dist. Ct. (trial bar) Md. 1984. Assoc. Weinberg & Green, Balt., 1971-73, Dickerson, Nice, Sokol & Horn, Balt., 1973; asst. atty. gen. State of Md., 1973-77; pvt. practice Balt., 1978; ptnr. Linowes and Blocher, Silver Spring (Md.), Washington, 1979-93, Semmes, Bowen & Semmes, Washington, D.C., and Balt., 1993-95, Wilkes Artis, Chartered, Washington, 1995-2001, Deckelbaum Ogens & Raftery, Washington and Md., 2001—. Spkr. in field of telecomms., fin. and real estate. Bd. govs. Wash. Bldg. Congress, 1998—2001; bd. dirs. D.C. Assn. Retarded Citizens, Inc., 1986—2001. Mem. ABA (coun. mem. sect. real property, probate and trust law 2000—, moderator various programs), Am. Coll. Real Estate Lawyers (moderator various programs), D.C. Bar (comml. real estate com., chmn. legal opinions project), Md. Bar Assn. (real property, planning and zoning sect., chmn. environ. subcom. legal opinions project 1987-89, litigation sect. 1982-84, chmn. comml. trans. com.), Md. Inst. Continuing Profl. Edn. Lawyers, Am. Arbitration Assn. (arbitrator and mediator), D.C. Bldg. Industry Assn., Washington Assn Realtors, Inc., Nat. Assn. of Corp. Real Estate Execs., Civil Code Drafting Com. of the Russian Legis., Apt. and Office Bldg. Assn. Met. Washington, East Coast Builders Conf., Internat. Coun. Shopping Ctrs. (organized, co-faculty program "univ." 1988, NAFTA 1992, condemnations 1994, leasing 1997, high tech. effects 1998, com. chmn. 1998-99, pub./pvt. partnerships 1999), Montgomery County Bar Assn. (jud. selections com. 1988-90), Phi Beta Kappa, Lambda Alpha. Office: Deckelbaum Ogens & Raftery Chartered # 165 2020 Pennsylvania Ave NW Washington DC 20006 E-mail: ksamuelson@bigfoot.com.

SAMUELSON, M. KRISTIN, music educator; b. Milw., May 11, 1951; d. Albert C. and Jeanlyn C. (Gunderson) S.; m. Edward Allen Joffe, May 22, 1982 (div. Oct. 1996); 1 child, Janine Kirsten Joffe. BA, Denison U., 1973; MMus, New Eng. Conservatory Music, 1976; EdD, Columbia U., 1999. Acad. advisor Dean's Office New Eng. Conservatory, Boston, 1976-79; singer/soloist Nat. Opera Co., Raleigh, N.C., 1980, Enchanted Circle Concerts, Boston, 1979, 84; singer/voice tchr. Monanea Festival, Leukerbad, Switzerland, 1989-90; singer/soloist Sixth Internat. Congress of Women in Music, N.Y.C., 1990; instr. Columbia U., 1994-98, N.Y.U./Lee Strasberg Theatrical Inst., N.Y.C., 1997—. Adj. asst. prof. Franklin & Marshall Coll., Lancaster, Pa., 1985—; soloist Boston Symphony Orchestra, 1976, Banff Festival, Alberta, Can., 1978, 79; lectr. in field; workshop leader Symposium for Care of Profl. Voice, 1999. Contbr. articles to profl. jours. Recipient Frances Yeend's Instr. scholarship Chautauqua Inst., N.Y., 1973, Florence C. Rowe Meml. scholarship New Eng. Conservatory, Boston, 1975-76. Mem.: Nat. Assn. Tchrs. of Singing (bd. dirs. N.Y.C. chpt.), N.Y. Singing Tchrs. Assn. (bd. dirs.). Avocations: bicycling, travel, langs., playing piano. E-mail: kristins@prodigy.net.

SAMUELSON, NORMA GRACIELA, architectural illustrator, artist; b. Mar del Plata, Argentina, May 29, 1957; came to U.S., 1979; d. Jose and Elsa Florinda (Camaras) Nunez; m. Jeffrey Thomas Samuelson, Oct. 9, 1982; 1 child, Taylor Sebastian. Student, Conservatory Mendelssohn, Mar del Plata, 1970-76; MFA, Superior Sch. Visual Arts, Mar del Plata, 1976. Tchr. art Domingo F. Sarmiento, Mar del Plata, 1976; graphic artist Atelier Marzoratti Munoz, 1976-79; archtl. illustrator Szabo Inc., Irvine, Calif., 1981-84; owner, archtl. illustrator Norma Samuelson Illustrations, Mission Viejo, 1985—. Represented by Artreps Calif., Studio Gallery, Calif. Illustrator: Centennial of Immigration Law, 1975 (2d nat. award), Historical Buildings in Los Angeles, 1995 (ltd. edits.); art work published in Best of Colored Pencil III and Architecture in Perspective 13, 14, 15, 16. Bd. dirs. Mus. Architecture, Capistrano, Calif. Mem. Color Pencil Soc. Am., Am. Soc. Archtl. Perspective. Avocations: playing piano, painting and drawing, foreign travel, French art and language. Home: 26862 Via Corta San Juan Capistrano CA 92675-5039 Office: 27001 La Paz Rd Ste 406B Mission Viejo CA 92691-5523

SAMUELSON, PAUL ANTHONY, economist, educator; b. Gary, Ind., May 15, 1915; s. Frank and Ella (Lipton) Samuelson; m. Marion E. Crawford, July 2, 1938 (dec.); children: Jane Kendall, Margaret Wray, William Frank, Robert James, John Crawford, Paul Reid; m. Risha Eckaus, 1981; 1 stepchild Susan Miller. BA, U. Chgo., 1935; MA, Harvard U., 1936, PhD (David A. Wells prize 1941), 1941; LLD (hon.) , U. Chgo., Oberlin Coll., 1961, Boston Coll., 1964, Ind. U., 1966, U. Mich., 1967, Claremont Grad. Sch., 1967; LLD (hon.) , Seton Hall U., 1971, U. N.H., 1971; LLD (hon.) , Keio U., 1971, Widener Coll., 1982; LLD (hon.) , Cath. U. at Riva Aguero U., Lima, Peru, 1980, Harvard, 1972; LLD (hon.) , Gustavus Adolphus Coll., 1974, U. So. Calif., 1975; LLD (hon.) , U. Pa., 1976; LLD (hon.) , U. Rochester, 1976, Emmanuel Coll., 1977, Stonehill Coll., 1978; LLD (hon.) , Indiana U. of Pa., 1993; DLitt (hon.) , Ripon Coll., 1962; DLitt (hon.) , No. Mich. U., 1973; DLitt (hon.) , Valparaiso U., 1987, Columbia U, 1988; LHD (hon.) , Williams Coll., 1971; DSc (hon.) , U. Mass., 1972; DSc (hon.) , U. R.I., 1972, Tufts U., 1988, East Anglia U., Norwich, Eng., 1966; DSc (hon.) , Rensselaer Poly. Inst., 1998; D (hon.) , U. Catholique de Louvain, Belgium, 1976, City U., London, 1980, New U. Lisbon, 1985, Univ. Nat. de Educacion a Distancia, Madrid, 1989, Univ. Politecnica de Valencia, Spain, 1991. Prof. econs. MIT, 1940—65, inst. prof., 1966, prof. emeritus, 1986; mem. staff Radiation Lab., 1944—45; prof. internat. econ. relations Fletcher Sch. Law and Diplomacy, 1945; cons. Nat. Resources Planning Bd., 1941—43, WPB, 1945, U.S. Treasury, 1945—52, 1961—74, Bur. Budget, 1952, RAND Corp., 1948—75, Fed. Res. Bd., 1965—; council Econ. Advisers, 1960—68; econ. adviser to Pres. Kennedy; sr. adviser Brookings Panel on Econ. Activity; mem. spl. commn. on social scis. NSF, 1967—68; cons. Congl. Budget Office, Federal Reserve Bd., 1965—; Gordon Y Billard Fellow MIT, Boston, 1986—; vis. prof of polit. econ. Ctr. Japan-U.S. Bus. and Econ. Studies, NYU, 1987—. Stamp Meml. lectr., London, 1961; Wicksell lectr., Stockholm, 62; Franklin lectr., Detroit, 62; Carnegie Found. reflective year, 1965—66; John von Neumann lectr. U. Wis., 1971; Gerhard Colm Meml. lectr. New Sch. for Social Rsch., N.Y.C., 1971; Sulzbacher Meml. lectr. Columbia Law Sch., N.Y.C., 1974; J. Willard Gibbs lectr. Am. Math. Soc., San Francisco, 1974; John Diebold lectr. Harvard, 1976; Alice E. Blumeuf lectr. Boston Coll., 1981; Horowitz lectr. Jerusalem and Tel Aviv, 1984; Marschak Meml. lectr. UCLA, 1984; Tennenbaum lectr. Ga. Inst. Tech., 1985; Julis Steinberg Meml. lectr. Wharton Sch., 1986; Godkin lectr. Harvard, 1986; Woodward lectr. U. B.C., 1987; lectr. Harvard 350 Symposium Harvard U., 1986; Olin lectr. U. Va., 1989; Commemorative lectr. Stonehill Coll., 1990; Lionel Robbins Meml. lectr. Claremont Coll., 1991; mem. nat. adv. com. Inst. for Rsch. on Poverty. Author: Foundations of Economic Analysis, 1947, Foundations of Economic Analysis, enlarged edit., 1983, Economics, 1948—95, Readings in Economics, 1955—73; author: (with R. Dorfman and R.M. Solow) Linear Programming and Economic Analysis, 1958; author: Collected Scientific Papers, 5 vols., 1966, 1972, 1978, 1986; co-author: numerous other books; columnist: Newsweek, 1966—81, assoc. editor: Jour. Pub. Econs., Jour. Internat. Econs., Jour. Fin. Econs., Jour. Nonlinear Analysis, adv. bd.: Challenge Mag., mem. editl. bd.: Proces NAS; contbr. articles to profl. jours. Chmn. Pres.'s Task Force Maintaining Am. Prosperity, 1964; mem. Nat. Task Force on Econ. Edn., 1960—61; econ. adviser to Pres. John F. Kennedy, 1959—63; mem. adv. bd. Nat. Commn. Money and Credit, 1958—60. Recipient David A. Wells prize, Harvard U., 1941, John Bates Clark medal, Am. Econ. Assn., 1947, Alfred Nobel Meml. prize, 1970, medal of Honor, U. Evansville, Ill., 1970, Albert Einstein Commemorative award, 1971, Alumni medal, U. Chgo., 1983, Britannica award, 1989, Gold Scanno prize, Naples, Italy, 1990, Paul A. Samuelson Professorship established in his name, MIT, 1991, Nat. Medal of Sci., Washington, 1996; fellow hon. fellow, London Sch. Econs. and Polit. Sci., Guggenheim, 1948—49, rsch. fellow, Ford Found., 1958—59. Fellow: Econometric Soc. (v.p. 1950, pres. 1951), Am. Philos. Soc., Am. Econ. Assn. (hon.; pres. 1961), Brit. Acad. (corr.); mem.: NAS, AAAS, Nat. Assn. Investment Clubs (Disting. Svc. award in Investment Edn. 1974), Leibniz-Akademie der Wissenschaften und der Literatur (corr.), Internat. Econ. Assn. (pres. 1966—68, hon. pres.), Com. Econ. Devel. (commn. on nat. goals, rsch. adv. bd. 1959—60), Club of Econ. and Mgmt. (medal, hon. Valencia, Spain 1990), Omicron Delta Epsilon (trustee), Phi Beta Kappa. Home: 94 Somerset St Belmont MA 02478-2010 Office: MIT E52 # 383C Dept Econs Cambridge MA 02139

SAMUELSON, RITA MICHELLE, speech language pathologist; b. Chgo., July 15, 1954; d. Mike Dabetic and Rita Lorraine (Stasny) Dabertin; m. K. Alan Samuelson, May 7, 1977; children: Amber Michelle, April Claire. BS, Ind. U., 1976, MA in Teaching, 1977. Speech lang. therapist East Maine Dist. 63, Des Plaines, Ill., 1977-80, Cmty. Cons. Dist. 59, Elk Grove, 1980-83, Fenton High Sch. Dist. 100, Bensenville, 1988-93, Addison (Ill.) Dist. 4, 1993-94, Elgin (Ill.) Dist. U-46, 1994—. Author: Sound Strategist, 1989, The Birthday Party Adventure, 1991, The Lizard Princess Adventure, 1991; contbr. chpt.: Yuletide Reverie, 1993. Mem. Am. Speech Lang. Hearing Assn., DuPage County Speech Hearing Lang. Assn. (v.p. bd. dirs. 1995—), Ill. Speech Lang. Hearing Assn., Villagers Club Bloomingdale, Writer's Workshop of Bloomingdale (steering com. rep.). Roman Catholic. Avocations: singing in church choir, lectr. in children and humor, doll collecting, antiquing. Home: 156 Longridge Dr Bloomingdale IL 60108-1416 Office: Oakhill Elementary Sch 502 S Oltendorf Rd Streamwood IL 60107-1575

SAMUELSON, WILLIAM ALLEN, music educator; b. Schenectady, N.Y., Sept. 17, 1957; s. Leonard Philip and Kathryn Allen Samuelson; m. Karen Joy Loughman, Aug. 20, 1983; children: Salem, Gifford, Guy, Evan, Zena, Laurel, Claire, Natalie, Camille. MusB in Edn., Oral Roberts U., 1979; MA in Pub. Policy, Regent U., 1987. Cert. Tchr. Calif., 2002. Libr. circulation supr. Regent U., Va. Beach, Va., 1984—87; tchr. Monte Vista Christian Sch., Watsonville, Calif., 1987—2000; instrumental music dir. Yosemite Union H.S. Dist., Oakhurst, 2000—02; music dir. Chawanakee Sch. Dist., North Fork, 2002—. Music team leader Sierra Pines Ch., Oakhurst, Calif., 2002—; mem. Oakhurst Cmty. Band, Oakhurst, Calif., 2001—. Inky's Basement Band, Mariposa, Calif., 2002—; guitarist Phil Miller Band, Coarsegold, Calif., 1995—; mem. Andy Lewis Band, Santa Cruz, Calif., 1996—. Composer: (soundtrack segments) Waves of Adventure, 1992, Bird in a Cage, 1987 (Student Acad. award, 1987), (jingle) Big Head Coffee Cola, 1996; musician: (albums) The Fairburns: OH!, 1997, Deliverance: Twin Lakes Saturday Worship, 1999, Deliverance: Refuel!, 2000, Phillip Hardy Miller: You Can Lean on Him, 2000. Recipient Citation of Excellence, Nat. Band Assn., 2001, 2002. Mem.: Calif. Band Dir. Assn., Fresno Madera Calif. Music Educator's Assn., Calif. Music Educator's Assn., Music Educators Nat. Conf. Republican. Avocations: surfing, reading, hiking, weightlifting. Home: 31490 Apache Road Coarsegold CA 93614 Personal E-mail: bsamuelson@sierratel.com.

SAMWAY, PATRICK H. secondary education educator; b. N.Y.C., May 12, 1939; s. Henry Lewis and Mary (Mahan) S. BA, Fordham U., 1962, MA, 1963, Licentiate in Philosophy, 1964; MDiv, 1969; PhD, U N.C., 1974. Joined Soc. of Jesus, 1957. Assoc. prof. English LeMoyne Coll., Syracuse, N.Y., 1974-84; lit. editor AMERICA (mag.), N.Y.C., 1984-99; Will and Ariel Durant Prof. of Humanities St. Peter's Coll., Jersey City, 1999-2001; MacLean prof. English. St. Joseph's U., Phila., 2001—. Various vis. univ. professorships, 1984—. Author: Walker Percy: A Life, 1997; editor: Signposts in a Strange Land, 1991, Letters of Walker Percy, 1994, others. Office: St Joseph's U 5600 City Ave Philadelphia PA 19131-1395 E-mail: psamwaysj@aol.com.

SANABRIA, SHERRY ZVARES, artist; b. Washington; d. Simon and Belle (Herzfeld) Zvares; m. Phillip Kasten, Aug. 31, 1958 (div. Dec. 1985); childrn: Jessica L., Alex S.; m. Robert Sanabria, Jan. 24, 1986. BA, George Washington U., 1959; MFA, Am. U., 1974. Freelance lectr. on her painting. One-woman shows include Touchstone Gallery, Washington, 1977, Phillips Collection, Washington, 1980, Baumgartner Galleries, Washington, 1981, 83, 86, 88, Genest Gallery, Lambertville, N.J., 1987, KPMG Peat Marwick, Washington, 1989, David Adamson Gallery, Washington, 1989, 91, 93, 95, Ellis Island Immigration Mus., N.Y.C., 1991-92, Marymount U., McLean, Va., 1992, Dorothy McRae Gallery, Atlanta, 1994, George Washington U., Ashton, Va., 1997, Washington Hebrew Congregation, 1998, Am. Inst. of Architects, Washington, 2002; exhibited in group shows, including Washington Women's Arts Ctr., 1977, So. Alleghenies Mus., Loretto, Pa., 1978, Arts Gallery, Balt., 1980, 81, Corcoran Gallery Art, Washington, 1980, Frostburg (Md.) State Coll., 1981, Art Barn, Washington, 1982, Am. Acad. Arts and Letters, N.Y.C., 1983, Williams Coll. Mus. Art, Williamstown, Mass., 1984, Cornell U., Ithaca, N.Y., 1985, Fed. Reserve System, Washington, 1985, 89, Washington County Mus. Fine Arts, Hagerstown, Md., 1986, Vanderbilt U., 1989, Gallery 10 ltd., Washington, 1991, Watkins Gallery, Am. U., Washington, 1992, U. Richmond, Va., 1992, Emerson Gallery, McLean, Va., 1993, U. Del., 1994, B'nai B'rith Kluznick Mus., Washington, 1996, Gallery Henoch, N.Y.C., 1999, Md. Art Place, Balt., 2000; represented in permanent collections Phillips Collection, Philip Morris USA, Associated Gen. Contractors Am., Artery Orgn., First Nat. Bank Boston, Owens and Minor Inc., Charles E. Smith Co., Ernst and Whinney, Northern Telecom., Inc., Loudoun Med. Ctr., Astrolink, McGraw Hill Pubs., Benchmark Capitol, Paul Hastings Law Firm, Carter Braxton Devel. Co., Am. Univ., others. Mem. Women's Caucus for Arts, Loudoun Arts Coun. E-mail: szspaint@aol.com.

SAN AGUSTIN, MUTYA, pediatrician; b. Manila, Nov. 25, 1934; d. Dionisio and Trinidad (Tolentino) San A.; m. Barry Shaw, July 27, 1969; children: Noel, Ariel, Angela, Joanna. MD, U. Philippines, 1957. Diplomate Am. Bd. Pediats. Intern, resident Sinai Hosp., Balt., 1960, chief resident in pediats., 1961; chief phys. devel. rsch. divsn. Nat. Coordinating Rsch. Ctr., Philippines, 1962-64; dir. Montefiore-Morrisania Comprehensive Health Care Ctr., Bronx, N.Y., 1968-76; dir. ambulatory care medicine North Ctrl. Bronx Hosp.- Montefiore Med. Ctr., 1976-97; dir. dept. primary care medicine Montefiore Med. Ctr., 1997—. Cons. internat. ednl. br. HEW, 1969-74; cons. health com. U.S. China People's Friendship Assn., 1975-81; cons. to pres. N.Y.C. Health and Hosps. Corp., 1979-89;dir. primary care residency in pediats. and internal medicine Albert Einstein Coll. Medicine, 1979-92, prof. pediat.- clin. epidemiology and social medicine, 1993; vis. prof. UCLA, 1985, Ben-Gurion U., Beer-Sheva, Israel; mem. N.Y. State Coun. Grad. Med. Edn., 1988-90, N.Y. State Hosp. Rev. and Planning Coun., 1990-95, N.Y. State Gov.'s Health Adv. Bd., 1991-95; mem. residency tng. rev. com. divsn. medicine Bur. Health Profls., HHS, 1990-94; project dir. internat. pediat. fellowship program Montefiore Med. Ctr., Albert Einstein Coll. Medicine, 1989—; lectr. in field. Pediats. fellow John Hopkins U., 1960-61; Grantee NIH, 1967, NIMH, 1990-92; Atram Found. scholar, 1980; recipient Hon. Fellow award Philippine Pediat. Soc., Inc., 1996. Mem. APHA, Am. Acad. Pediat., Am. Pediat. Soc., Royal Soc. Medicine, Soc. Gen. Internal Medicine, Ambulatory Pediat. Assn., N.Y. Acad. Medicine, Philippine Ambulatory Pediat. Assn. (founding pres. 1995). Office: Montefiore Med Ctr 111 E 210th St Bronx NY 10467-2401

SANAN, ABHAY, physician; b. Chandigarh, India, Dec. 12, 1967; came to U.S., 1970; s. Bal Krishan and Vinod Sanan; m. Priya Sanan, Sept. 4, 1994; children: Akash, Avi. BA, Boston U., 1987, MD, 1991. Resident U. Minn., Mpls., 1991-97; chief resident Mayo Clinic, Rochester, Minn., 1997-98; fellow U. Cin., 1998-99. Avocations: reading, hiking, travel, photography, computers. Office: Neurol Assocs Tucson 5300 E Erickson Dr Ste 116 Tucson AZ 85712-2809

SANAN, PUNEET, investment banker; s. Inder Kumar and Sneh Prabha Sanan; m. Shivani Khurana, July 22, 2000. BChemE, Panjab U., Chandigarh, 1994; MBA in Fin., U. Tex., 1998. Registered profl. engr.; NYSE/NASD broker. Project engr. Pfizer, Chandigarh, 1993; project/valuation engr. DSM, 1994—96; assoc. Royal Dutch/Shell, Houston, 1997; cons. Perform Cons. LLC, N.Y.C., 1998—99; hedge fund analyst Legg Mason, 1999—2000; assoc. dir. UBS Warburg/PaineWebber Inc., 2000—01; v.p. investment banking Fano Securities LLC, Purchase, 2001—. Author: (book) Research on Alternative Energy/Fuel Cells, 2002 (Commendations by DOE, CEOs, CFOs, 2002), North American Railcar Manufacturing, 2000, Specialty Chemicals, 2001, Undervalued Industrial Companies, 2000. Recipient Cert. award for design of common effluent treatment plan, HSIDC Ministry of Environment, India, 2002; scholar Fitzgerald Presdl. scholar, U. Tex. at Austin, 1996—98. Mem.: AIChE, Conn. Venture Group, Internat. Bus. Brokers Assn., NY Acad. Scis. Hindu. Avocation: travel. Personal E-mail: puneetsanan@yahoo.com.

SANANMAN, MICHAEL LAWRENCE, neurologist; b. Bklyn., Oct. 11, 1939; s. Jack and Sarey (Bykofsky) S.; m. Elisa Joan Freeman, Apr. 12, 1964; children: Amy, Peter. AB, Swarthmore Coll., 1960; MD, Columbia U., 1964. Diplomate Am. Bd. Psychiatry and Neurology. Intern U. Hosp., San Francisco, 1964-65; resident in neurology N.Y. Neurol. Inst., N.Y.C., 1966-69; practice medicine specializing in neurology Elizabeth, N.J., 1972—. Cons. neurologist Rahway (N.J.) Hosp., Trinitas Hosp., N.J., Union Hosp., N.J.; instr. neurology Columbia U., N.Y.C., 1971-75; assoc. clin. prof. neurology U. Medicine and Dentistry N.J., Newark, 1975—. Lt. comdr. M.C., USNR, 1969-71. Mem. AMA, Am. Acad. Neurology, Am. Epilepsy Soc., N.J. Acad. Medicine (chmn. neurology sect.), Am. Eastern EEG Socs., Am. Assn. EMG and Electrodiagnosis. Office: 700 N Broad St Elizabeth NJ 07208-2310 E-mail: Mikesan24@hotmail.com.

SANAYEI, MASOUD, civil engineering educator; b. Isfahan, Iran, June 9, 1954; came to U.S., 1978; m. Mojgan Montazeri. BSCE, Tehran, Iran, 1978; MS, UCLA, 1980, Engr., 1983, PhD, 1986. Prof. civil engring. Tufts U., Medford, Mass., 1986—. Office: Tufts U Dept Civil Engring Medford MA 02155 E-mail: masoud.sanayei@tufts.edu.

SANBORN, ANNA LUCILLE, pension and insurance consultant; b. Bklyn., Mar. 29, 1924; d. Peter Francis and Matilda M. (Stumpp) Galligen; 1 son, Dean Sanborn. BA, Bklyn. Coll., 1945. Head dept. benefit and estate planning Union Ctrl. Life Ins. Co., N.Y.C., 1949-51; adminstr. employee benefits Seaboard Oil Co., 1952-56; with Frank J. Walters Assocs., Inc., 1957—, pres., 1970—. Bd. dirs. Archdiocesan Svc. Corp. Mem. Am. Acad. Actuaries. Republican. Roman Catholic. Home: 58-11 Seabury St Elmhurst NY 11373-4825 Office: Frank J Walters Assocs 58-13 Seabury St Flushing NY 11373-4825 E-mail: fjwainc@aol.com.

SANBORN, GEORGE FREEMAN, JR. genealogist; b. Laconia, N.H., Jan. 18, 1944; s. George Freeman and Charlotte (Dearborn) S.; m. Melinde Laura Lutz, Mar. 30, 1984 (div.); children: Ruth Alice, Lowell Freeman. AB, Boston U., 1967; AM, U. Ill., 1968; MEd, U. N.H., 1981. French tchr. Souris (P.E.I., Can.) Regional H.S., 1968-69; French and occupational studies tchr. Massey-Vanier H.S., Cowansville, Que., Can., 1969-70; French and English tchr. Kings Coll. Sch., Windsor, N.S., Can., 1970-71; translator, revisor Province of N.B., Fredericton, 1971-73; sr. govt. revisor Province of Ont., Toronto, 1973-75; French and Spanish tchr. Tilton (N.H.) Sch., 1978-80; living unit coord. Laconia (N.H.) State Sch., 1982-83; ref. libr. New Eng. Hist. Geneal. Soc., Boston, 1983-85, acquisitions libr., dir. libr. ops., 1985-95, publs. asst., 1996-2000, ref. libr., 2000—. Editor The N.H. Geneal. Record, 1990-93; compiler Vital Records of Hampton, N.H., 1992, 98; contbr. articles to profl. jours. Fellow Am. Soc. Genealogists, Soc. Antiquaries Scotland; mem. Soc. of the Cin. in the State of N.H., Soc. of Mayflower Descendants in the State of N.H., New Eng. Hist. Geneal. Soc., P.E.I. Geneal. Soc., N.H. Soc. Genealogists (pres. 1988-95), Geneal. Soc. Vt. (chair publs. com. 1992-96). Democrat. Presbyterian. Avocations: gardening, bantam raising, Scottish Gaelic language, P.E.I. history, antique glass and china. Home: 24 Thornton St Derry NH 03038-1628 Office: New Eng Hist Geneal Soc Libr 99 Newbury St Boston MA 02116-3007

SANBORN, KATHY, career planning administrator, consultant; m. Wayne Ricci; children: Cherie, Meilani. Bachelor's, Calif. State U., Sacramento. Owner Life and Career Coaching, Sacramento. Author: (book) Grow Your Own Love, 2001; singer (composer): (CD) Critical Mass, 1996; contbr. articles to profl. jours.; columnist: various web sites. Mem.: Golden Key Honor Soc. (life). Office: Life and Career Coaching PO Box 215664 Sacramento CA 95821 Business E-Mail: kathy@lifeandcareercoaching.com.

SANBORN, MARCIA GAIL, legal assistant, writer; d. John Robert and Ellen Loretta Reese; children: Heather Mount, Joshua. Diploma, Jackson Career Ctr. Legal sec. Scott, Scriven & Wahoff LLP, Columbus, Ohio; adminstrv. asst. Bank One; adminstrv. asst./legal sec. Baker & Hostetler LLP; adminstrv. asst./exec. sec. Cambridge (Ohio) Savs. & Loan Assn. Gov. Legal Secretaries Assn., Cambridge. Author: (poetry) The First Snow, 1997 (1998 President's Award for Lit. Excellence, 1998); (prodr., performer): (concert for charity) Focus on Love, 1996; prodr.: (variety show for Operation Feed) , 1997; singer: (concert for arthritis benefit) Moulin Rouge Night, 1984; recording artist: 10 original songs You Gave Me My Song, 1984, recording artist: single I Was There, 1995, recording artist: home recording Holiday Hugs, 2001. Former vol. ARC, Cambridge, Ohio, 1973—74. Mem.: ASCAP. Avocations: ballroom dancing, reading, writing.

SANBORN, MELINDE LUTZ, genealogist, writer; b. Cleve., Jan. 30, 1956; d. Gilbert Francis and Helen Laura (Mann) Lutz; m. L. Tucker Hatfield, Mar. 31, 1976 (div. Oct., 1983); m. George Freeman Sanborn Jr., Mar. 30, 1984 (div. May 2001); children: Ruth, Lowell. BA, Miami U., Oxford, Ohio, 1978; postgrad., U. Oreg., 1978-80, Simmons Coll., 1989—. Genealogist, author, Derry, N.H., 1976—. Database author with ancestry.com. Editor: (book) Ancestry of Emily Jane Angell, 1992 (Jacobus award 1993), Ancestry of Samuel Blanchard Ordway, 1990, Ancestry of Eva Belle Kempton, 1995, 2001, Essex Probate Index, 1987; editor Oreg. Geneal. Soc., 1980-82, Mass. Geneal. Coun., 1986-87; co-author: The Great Migration, 1999. Vol. Sonshine Soup Kitchen, Derry, 1995—; sec. New England Reg. Genealogical Coun., 1999—, v.p., 2001—. Fellow Am. Soc. Genealogists; mem. N.H. Soc. Genealogists (publs. chair 1991—, program chair 1993, pres. 1999-01, editor 2001—). Avocation: photography. E-mail: melinde@attbi.com.

SANBORNE, LEWIS W. director, English educator; b. Syracuse, N.Y., Mar. 7, 1961; s. Sandy D. and Harriet C. Sanborne; m. Deborah A. Sanborne, Mar. 12, 1983; children: David, Thomas. BA in English, Idaho State U., 1983, MA in English, 1989; PhD in Higher Edn., Ill. State U., 2001. Writing coord. Acad. Support Ctr. St. Ambrose U., Davenport, Iowa, 1990-98, asst. prof., 1990—, coord. student success programs, 1998—. Mem. Nat. Acad. Advising Assn., Nat. Orientation Dir.'s Assn. Home: 2212 E 45th St Davenport IA 52807 Office: Saint Ambrose U 518 W Locust St Davenport IA 52803 E-mail: lsanbore@sau.edu.

SANCAKTAR, EROL, engineering educator; b. Ankara, Turkey, July 13, 1952; came to U.S., 1974; s. Mehmet Ali and Ulker Mualla (Elveren) S.; m. Teresa Sue Sancaktar, Feb. 16, 1979; children: Orhan Ali, Errol Alan. BS in Mech. Engring., Robert Coll., Istanbul, Turkey, 1974; MS in Mech. Engring., Va. Poly. Inst. and State U., 1975, PhD, 1979. Tchg. asst. Robert Coll., Istanbul, 1972-74; instr. Va. Poly. Inst. and State U., Blacksburg, Va., 1977-78; vis. scholar Kendall Co., Boston, 1985-86; assoc. prof. Clarkson U., Potsdam, N.Y., 1984-95; prof. U. Akron (Ohio), 1996—. Cons. to the UN Devel. Programme, 1987, ALCOA, 1990-91, U.S. Army Benet Labs., 1991. Mem. editl. adv. bd. Jour. Adhesion Sci. Tech., 1993—; assoc. tech. editor Transactions of the ASME, Jour. of Mech. Design, 1995—; contbr. articles to profl. jours.; patentee in field. Recipient various rsch. grants awarded by NSF, NASA, U.S. Army, N.Y., Grumman Corp., Kendall Co., GE, IBM. Fellow ASME (assoc. tech. editor transactions of ASME Jour. of Mech. Design 1995—, editor Reliability, Stress Analysis and Failure Prevention: Aspects of Composite and Active Materials, Issues in Fastening & Joining, Composite & Smart Structures, Numerical & FEA Methods, Risk Minimization, elected chair RSAFP tech. steering com.). Home: 465 Evergreen Dr Tallmadge OH 44278-1356 Office: Univ Akron Dept Polymer Engring Akron OH 44325-0001

SANCHELLI, CHARLES RAYMOND (CHUCK SANCHELLI), tennis company executive; b. Decatur, Ill., June 30, 1951; s. Charles R. and Mary E. (Metzger) S.; m. Delinda A. Martinez, July 7, 1990. BS in Bus., Purdue U., 1973. Tennis dir. French Lick (Ind.) Sheraton Resort, 1973-74; with U.S. Pro Tennis Tour, 1974-75; club mgr. Newk Plus Two, Inc., New Braunfels, Tex., 1975-77, Quail Valley Tennis Club, Missouri City, 1977-79; mgr., dir. Meadow Creek Racquet Club, 1979-84; pres., chief exec. officer Ft. Bend Tennis Svcs., Inc., Sugarland, 1984—. Engring. technician Sonat Exploration, Inc., Houston, 1984-89; computer specialist Sonat Svcs., Inc., Houston, 1989-90; v.p., chief fin. officer Day Camp Svcs., Inc., Sugar Land, 1990—. Chmn. Greater Houston Tennis Coun., 1991—. Mem. U.S. Pro Tennis Assn. (cert. pro level I), U.S. Tennis Assn. (nat. com. 1991-2000, Nat. Cmty. Svc. award 1994), Tex. Profl. Tennis Assn. (chmn. 1990-2001, state com., Svc. award 1989, 2000), Tex. Tennis Assn. (chmn. 1989-94, 2001—, state com. officer 1995-2000), Houston Tennis Assn. (pres. 1988-91, Svc. award 1988, bd. of dir. 2000—), Houston Profl. Tennis Assn. (founder, treas. 1988-94, 2001-02), Fort Bend C. of C., 1st Colony Assn. (recreation com. 1990—). Roman Catholic. Avocations: reading, tennis, music. Office: Ft Bend Tennis Svcs Inc 435 B-1 FM 1092 Stafford TX 77477 E-mail: fbts@pdq.net.

SANCHEZ, CHERYL PIMENTEL, pediatrician, educator; b. Manila, Mar. 12, 1961; came to U.S., 1983; d. Mariano Gayla Jr. and Consolacion Sanchez; m. Waseemuddin Kazi, Oct. 5, 1991; children: Amber Jasmine Kazi, Mikhail Amir Kazi. BS in Psychology cum laude, U. of The Philippines, Quezon City, 1982; MD, U. of The Philippines, Manila, 1986. Intern, then resident in pediat. Rush Presbyn.-St. Lukes Med. Ctr., Chgo., 1988-91; fellow in pediat. nephrology UCLA Med. Ctr., 1991-94, clin. instr. pediat., 1994-96, asst. prof. pediat., 1996-99; pediatrician, mem. adv. com. Women's Health U. Wis., Madison, 1999—. Mem. adv. com. Clin. Rsch. Ctr., L.A., 1996—. Contbr. chpts. to books, articles to med. jours. Recipient Clin. Assoc. Physician award Clin. Rsch. Ctr., NIH, 1995-98. Fellow Am. Acad. Pediat.; mem. Am. Soc. Nephrology, Am. Soc. Bone and Mineral Rsch., Am. Soc. Pediat. Nephrology, Nat. Kidney Found. (fellow 1993-94), Internat. Soc. Pediat. Nephrology, Phi Kappa Phi. Roman Catholic. Avocation: travel. Office: U Wis Med Sch 3590 MSC/Pediats 1300 University Ave Madison WI 53706-1510 E-mail: cpsanchez@facstaff.wics.edu.

SANCHEZ, FAUSTO H. advertising agency executive; b. Camaguey, Cuba, Oct. 21, 1953; came to U.S., 1966; s. Fausto Rene and Eloisa (Aparicio) S. AA, Miami (Fla.) Dade Community Coll., 1976; BA, U. Miami, 1979; postgrad., UCLA, 1980-82. Dir., newswriter, anchor Sta. KMEX-TV, Hollywood, Calif., 1980-82; producer, dir. Brighton Communications, 1982-84; dir. mktg. Edward J. DeBartolo Corp., Miami, 1984-86; chmn., pres., creative dir. Sanchez & Levitan Advt., 1986—. Author: Hispanic Market, 1982. Mgr. advt. Aida Levitan for Commr. Campaign, Miami, 1988. Recipient Media award Calif. N.G., 1983, award of excellence Nat. Addy, 1989, Best of Show, 1988, 2 1st place Gold Addy awards, 1987, Am. Advt. Fedn., 4th Dist., 1st place radio Se Habla Espanol Awards, 1988, Addy award, 1988. Mem. Advt. Fedn. of Greater Miami. Democrat. Avocations: films, tennis, sailing. Office: Sanchez & Levitan Advt Inc 3191 Coral Way Ste 510 Miami FL 33145-3220*

SANCHEZ, ISAAC CORNELIUS, chemical engineer, educator; b. San Antonio, Aug. 11, 1941; s. Isaac Jr. and Marce (Aguilar) S.; children: Matthew, Timothy. BS with honors, St. Mary's U., 1963; PhD, U. Del., 1969. Postdoctoral Nat. Bureau Standards, Gaithersburg, Md., 1969-71; assoc. scientist Xerox Corp., Webster, N.Y., 1971-72; asst. prof. U. Mass., Amherst, 1972-77; rsch. chemist Nat. Bureau Standards, Gaithersburg, 1977-86; fellow Alcoa, Pitts., 1986-88; prof. U. Tex., Austin, 1988—. H.A. disting vis. prof. U. Akron (Ohio), 1995. Mem. editorial bd. Jour. Polymer Sci., 1986-92, Polymer, 1987—; contbr. over 100 articles to profl. jours. Lt. USN, 1963-67. Recipient William J. Murray Endowed Chair in engring U. Tex., 1997, Bronze medal U.S. Dept. Commerce, 1980, Silver medal, 1983, E.U. Condon award Nat. Bur. Standards, 1983. Fellow Am. Phys. Soc.; mem. AAAS, AIChE, Am. Chem. Soc., Nat. Acad. Engring., Materials Rsch. Soc., Soc. Plastics Engrs. (Internat. Rsch. award 1996) Avocations: golf, lay ministry. Office: Univ Tex Chem Engring Dept Austin TX 78712

SANCHEZ, JAVIER ALBERTO, industrial engineer; b. San Cristobal, Tachira, Venezuela, Apr. 13, 1960; came to U.S., 1977; s. Leonidas and Ana Mireya (Albornoz) S. AA, Butler County C.C., El Dorado, Kans., 1979; BS in Indls. Engring., Wichita State U., 1982, MS in Engring. Mgmt., 1985. Indsl. cons. Ferronikel, C.A., Caracas, Venezuela, 1977-83; project mgr. Trabajos Viales, C.A., Venezuela, 1980; applications engr. Major, Inc., Wichita, Kans., 1983; mfg. engr. L.S. Industries, Inc., 1983-86; plant mgr. World Wide Mfg., Inc., Miami, Fla., 1986-88; prodn. mgr. Capitol Hardware Mfg. Co., Chgo., 1988-91; product mgr. Ready Metal Mfg.Co., 1991-92; engring. tech. resources and materials mgr. Taurus Internat. Mfg. Inc., Miami, 1992-95; materials mgr. Marino Tech., Inc., 1996; bus. cons. South Fla. Mfg. Tech. Ctr., 1996-2000; pres. Intesco, 2000—. Sr. cons. Ferronikel, C.A., Caracas, 1983—, mgr. internat. ops., 1988—. Recipient scholarship award Venezuelan Govt., 1977, Mariscal Ayacucho award, 1980, Recognition of Excellence award So. Fla. Mfg. Assn., 1998. Mem. Soc. Mfg. Engrs., Inst. Indsl. Engrs. (sr., pres. Greater Miami chpt. 2000—), Am. Soc. Safety Engrs., Nat. Safety Coun., Am. Prodn. and Inventory Control Soc., Soc. Plastic Engrs., Nat. Assn. Purchasing Mgmt, Assn. Facility Engrs. Roman Catholic. Achievements include development of applications of world class manufacturing techniques in tube fabricating, sheet metal operations and firearms production; cost estimating techniques for metal fabricators; design and manufacturing of retail store fixtures and racks; worldwide engineering and technical resources for firearms manufacturing and for international businesses; materials management techniques, procurement and negotiating, fabrication methods for bulk packaging manufacturing, outsourcing business, networking, outreach programs, operational assessments, performance benchmarking, safety and health programs, drug free programs, environmental engineering, ISO-9000, and QS-9000 implementation, continuous flow, lean manufacturing process mapping, cellular manufacturing. Home: 8357 W Flagler St PMB 308 Miami FL 33144-2072 Office: Intesco 8357 W Flagler St PMB 308 Miami FL 33144 E-mail: intecorp@gate.net.

SANCHEZ, JOSE, fine arts educator, producer, director, media consultant; b. Cochabamba, Bolivia, June 28, 1951; s. Victor Sanchez and Margarita Hermoso. MA, U. Mich., 1977, PhD, 1983. Camera operator NBC, WDIV/TV 4, Detroit, 1980-81; assoc. prof. Univ. del Sagrado Corazon, P.R., 1984-88; prof. Calif. State U., Long Beach, 1988—. Actor Ninon Davalos Co., Cochabamba, 1969, Dept. of Fine Arts, Guadalajara, Mexico, 1970—72; rsch. cons. U. Mich., Ann Arbor, 1984, media engr., 1982—83; photographer Mus. of Contemporary Art, L.A., 1989—; cons. Dept. of State. Cinematographer (film) Chautauqua: Famous American Voices of 1914, 1984; still photography (film) Secret Honor, 1984; dir. (video) Pope John Paul II, 1984; producer/dir. (videos) The Carillon Concert, 1979, Yo No Entiendo a la Gente Grande, 1986, Platinotipo, 1988, Artificial Intelligence, 1989, Partners for Success, 1990, The L.A. Mexican Dance Co., 1990, Rudolf Arnheim: A Life in Art, 1994, Ca/Rep 1995, Themes in Bicultural Education, 1991, Fue Cosa de Un Dia, 1992, (films) You and I, 1976, Who Cares About the Time?, 1977, Inside Cuba: The Next Generation, 1990; writer, producer, dir. (film) La Paz, 1994; dir. (film) The Delirium, 2001; writer (plays) La Paz, 1989, The Road to the Coast, 1999, News for Manuela on the Death of Bolivar, 2000; author: (book) The Art and Politics of Bolivian Cinema, 1999. Mem. The Long Beach Mus. of Art, Hispanic Acad. of Arts, 1987-89. Recipient Exceptional Achievement award Coun. Advancement and Support of Edn., 1982, Rackham Dissertation award U. Mich., 1982, Rackham scholarship, 1980-83. Mem. NEA, Latin Am. Found., Am. Film Inst., Profl. Photographers, Ptnrs. of the Ams., Ind. Feature Project/West. Avocations: travel, painting, music, movies, dancing. Office: Calif State U Film & Elec Arts Dept 1250 N Bellflower Blvd Long Beach CA 90840-0001 E-mail: sanchezh@csulb.edu.

SANCHEZ, LEONEDES MONARRIZE WORTHINGTON (HIS ROYAL HIGHNESS DUKE DE LEONEDES OF SPAIN SICILY GREECE), fashion designer; b. Flagstaff, Ariz., Mar. 15, 1951; s. Rafael Leonedes and Margaret (Monarrize) S. BS, No. Ariz. U., 1974; studied, Fashion Inst. Tech., N.Y.C., 1974-75; AA, Fashion Inst. D&M, L.A., 1975; lic., La Ecole de la Chambre Syndical de la Couture Parisian, Paris, 1976-78; certificate, La Mason de Couture, Paris, 2000. Lic. in designing. Contract designer/asst. to head designer House of Bonnet, Paris, 1976—; dress designer-in-residence Flagstaff, 1978—; mem. faculty No. Ariz. U., 1978-80; designer Ambiance, Inc., L.A., 1985—; designer Interiors by Leonedes subs. Studio of Leonedes Couturier, Ariz., 1977, Calif., 1978, London, Paris, 1978, Rome, 1987, Milan, Spain, 1989, Palazzo de Leonedes, 1998, designer Liturgical Vesture subs.; CEO Leonedes Internat., Design Consortium, Leonedes Internat. Ltd., 1999—; designer El Casillo de Nuevo Espana, Santa Fe, La Maison de Couture, Paris, 2000, La Maison de Couture de Leonedes Internat., Paris, 2001. Owner, CEO, designer Leonedes Internat., Ltd., London, Milan, Paris, Spain, Ambian Ariz, Calif., Appolonian Costuming, Ariz., London, Milan, Paris, El Castillo de Leonedes, Sevilla, Spain, Villa Apollonian de Leonedes, Mykonos, Greece, Palazzo de Leonedes Internat., Sicily; cons. House of Bonnet, Paris, 1976—, Bob Mackie, Studio City, Calif., 1974-75; CEO, designer artistical dir., Leonedes internat.; appointee commn. on religious antiquities Congregation on the Arts, The Vatican, Italy, 1998. Bd. dirs. Roman Cath. Social Svcs., 1985-86, Northland Crisis Nursery, 1985—; bd. dirs., chmn. Pine Country Transit, 1986-88; pres. Chicanos for Edn.; active master's swim program ARC, Ariz., 1979—; eucharistic min., mem. art and environ. com., designer liturgical vesture St. Pius X Cath. Ch.; vol. art tchr., instr. St. Mary's Regional Sch., Flagstaff, 1987-90, vol. art dir.; mem. Flagstaff Parks and Recreation Commn., 1994-96, citizens' adv. com. master plan, 1994-96; mem. cmty. bd. adv. com. Flagstaff Unified Sch. Dist., 1995; active Duke de Leonedes Found. de Nuevo Espana, Santa Fe, Duke de Leonedes Found. de Nuevo Espana, Santa Fe; prin. chair Duke de Leonedes Found., The Netherlands, 1995; de nuevo espana Duke de Leuedes Found., Santa Fe, N.Mex., 1996. Decorated Duke de Leonedes (Spain), 1994, His Royal Highness (Spain, Greece, Sicily), 1998; recipient Camellian Design award 1988, Atlanta. Mem. AAU (life, chairperson swimming Ariz. 1995, vice chairperson physique, mem. citizen adv. bd. parks and recreation, chairperson state of Ariz. physique, swimming, adv. to Olympic inquiry com., advisor to internat. Olympic com. on physique), Am. Film Inst., Am. Assn. Hist. Preservation, Costume Soc., Am. Nat. Physique Com., Internat. Consortium Fashion Designers, Nat. Cath. Ednl. Assn., La Legion de Honour de la Mode Parisienne, Social Register Assn., Phi Alpha Theta (historian 1972-73, pres. 1973-74), Pi Kappa Delta (pres. 1972-73, historian 1973-74). Republican. Avocations: body building, swimming. Office: El Castillo de Leonedes Seville Spain also: El Castillo de Nuevo Espana Santa Fe NM 87501 also: Villa de Apollonian de Leonedes Mykonos Greece

SANCHEZ, LORETTA, congresswoman; b. Anaheim, Calif., Jan. 7, 1960; BA, Chapman U., 1982; MBA, Am. U., 1984. With Orange County Transp. Authority, 1984-87, Fieldman Rolapp & Assocs., 1987-90; strategic mgmt. cons. Booz Allen & Hamilton; owner, operator AMIGA Advisors Inc.; mem. U.S. Congress from 46th Calif. dist., 1997—; mem. edn. and the workforce com., mem. armed svcs. com. Mem. Anaheim Rotary Club. Democrat. Office: US Ho of Reps 1230 Longworth Ho Office Bldg Washington DC 20515-0001*

SANCHEZ, LUIS ARTURO, forensic pathologist; b. P.R., Jan. 3, 1963; s. Luis Arturo and Emma (Maldonado) S. MD, U. Mass., 1988; postgrad., Columbia U., 1992, U. Miami, 1993. Diplomate in anat. and forensic pathology Am. Bd. Pathology. Forensic pathologist Office of the Chief Med. Examiner, Washington, 1993—2000, acting chief med. examiner, 1998, sr. dep. chief Houston, 2001—; asst. clin. prof. George Washington U., Washington, 1993—. Forensic expert advisor U.S. Dept. of Justice, Office of the Dep. Atty. Gen., Washington, 1994—; forensic pathology prof., Internat. Criminal Investigative Tng. Asst. Program, Ctrl. and S.Am. and Ctrl. Asia, 1995—; lectr. in homicide sch., Washington Police Dept., 1993-94. Contbr. articles to profl. jours. Mem. Am. Acad. Forensic Scis., Nat. Assn. Med. Examiners. Avocations: foreign languages, travel. Office: Office Chief Med Examiner 1885 Old Spanish Trail Houston TX 77054

SANCHEZ, MARLA RENA, controller; d. Tomas Guillermo and Rose Sanchez; m. Bradley D. Gaiser. BS, MS, Stanford U., 1979; MBA, Santa Clara U., 1983. Rsch. biologist Syntex, Palo Alto, Calif., 1980-81; fin. analyst Advanced Micro Devices, Sunnyvale, 1983-85; fin. mgr. ultrasound divsn. Diasonics, Inc., Milpitas, 1985-86, contr. therapeutic products divsn., 1989-93, contr. internat. divsn., 1992-93; contr. Ridge Computers, Santa Clara, 1986-88; dir. fin. VLSI Tech., Inc., San Jose, 1993-98; corp. contr. SDL, Inc., 1999-2001. Avocations: dancing, backpacking, rock climbing. Home: 1234 Russell Ave Los Altos CA 94024-5541

SANCHEZ, MARY ANNE, retired secondary school educator; b. Galesburg, Ill., Aug. 4, 1939; d. Stephen Mingare and M. Margaret Kennedy; m. J. Manuel Sanchez, Dec. 26, 1980. BS in Edn., Western Ill. U., 1961; MA, Ill. State U., 1970. Tchr., Stanford, Ill., 1962-64, Titusville, Fla., 1964-66, Montgomery County Bd. Edn., Chevy Chase, Md., 1969-72, Hillsborough County Bd. Edn., Tampa, Fla., 1972-96; ret., 1996. Mary Anne Sanchez Young Woman scholarship named in her honor by Social Studies Dept. Leto Comprehensive H.S., 1999. Mem. Nat. Coun. for Social Studies, Fla. Coun. for Social Studies, Adult Edn. Assn. Home: 2715 W Ivy St Tampa FL 33607-1922

SANCHEZ, MIGUEL RAMON, dermatologist, educator; b. Havana, Cuba, May 5, 1950; came to the U.S., 1962; s. Rodolfo and Maria Sanchez. BS, CCNY, 1971; MD, Albert Einstein Coll. Medicine, 1974. Instr. Montefiore Dept. Family Medicine, Bronx, N.Y., 1978-79; sr. med. specialist Kingsborough Psychiat. Ctr., Bklyn., 1979-80; med. dir. Ten Communities Health Ctr., Tulare, Calif., 1980-82; assoc. prof. clin. dermatology NYU, N.Y.C., 1982-83; assoc. dir. Dept. Dermatology Bellevue Hosp. Ctr, 1983—. Mem. Tulare County Mental Health Bd., 1980-81; mem. med. bd. Bellevue Hosp., 1990—. Contbr. articles to profl. jours. and chpts. to books; editor: (software) Derm-Rx, 1986-90, (book) Dermatology Educational Review Manual, 1993. Bd. dirs. Community Health Project, N.Y.C., 1993; mem. patient care com. community bd. Bellevue Hosp., 1990-93; co-founder, pres. Assn. Latino Faculty and Students. Recipient Testimonial of Appreciation So. Tulare County, 1981, 1st Place award Scientific Forum N.Y. Acad. Dermatology, 1985. Mem. Am. Acad. Dermatology, Acad. for Advancement Sci., Dermatologic Found. Democrat. Roman Catholic. Achievements include development of clinics for tropical dermatology, HIV skin disease, disorders of keratinization, connective tissue disease, and phototherapy; research in infectious diseases, dermatopharmacology and cutaneous manifestation of HIV infection. Office: NYU Dept Dermatology 562 1st Ave New York NY 10016-6402

SANCHEZ, RAFAEL CAMILO, physician, educator; b. Tampa, Fla., July 18, 1919; s. Francisco and Catalina (Mateo) S.; children: Stephen Francis, John Thomas, David Lear. BS, Loyola U., New Orleans, 1940; MD, La. State U., 1950. Diplomate: Am. Bd. Family Practice (bd. dirs. 1976-79, assoc. exec. dir. 1979-84). Intern U.S. Marine Hosp., New Orleans, 1950-51; gen. practice medicine, 1951-72; med. educator, dir. continuing med. edn. La. State U., 1963-77. prof. family medicine, 1979-84, East Carolina U. Sch. Medicine, Greenville, 1984-90, prof. emeritus, 1990—; dir. family practice residency program Charity Hosp. of Bogalusa, La., 1977-79. Dir. Continuing Med. Edn.; med. dir. Nat. Med. Info. Network, pres. RCS-CME Svcs. Mem. bd. curators Archives for Family Practice, 1993-99. Served with AUS, 1940-46. Recipient Recognition award Soc. Tchrs. Family Medicine, 1987, Willard M. Duff award Accreditation Coun. for Continuing Med. Edn. Fellow AMA, Am. Acad. Family Physicians (Thomas W. Johnson award 1978, Presdl. award 1983, Pres.'s award 1989); mem. Network for Continuing Med. Edn. (med. dir., chair archives com. alliance), Nat. Med. Info. Network of Lippincott-Raven Healthcare (sr. med. adv.), Alpha Omega Alpha. Democrat. Roman Catholic.

SANCHEZ, RAYMOND G. former state legislator; b. Albuquerque, Sept. 22, 1941; s. Gillie and Priscilla S.; 1 child, Raymond Michael. BA, U. N.Mex., 1964, JD, 1967. Bar: N. Mex. 1967. Practice law, Albuquerque; mem. N.Mex. Ho. of Reps., 1970—; speaker N. Mex. Ho. of Reps., 1983—84, 1987—88, 1992—2000; mem. judiciary com., rules and order of bus. com., voters and elections com.; interim mem. workers compensation, legis. reform study coms., legis. coun.; pres. Naleo Educational Fund, Albuquerque, 2001. Bd. dirs. New Mex. Amigos, N.Mex. Diamond Jubilee/U.S. Constl. Bicentennial Commn., New Mex. First, Albuquerque Com. Fgn. Rels., N. Valley Neighborhood Assn. Mem. Nat. Assn. Latino Elected and Apptd. Ofcls. (bd. dirs.), Alameda Optimist Club (bd. dirs., charter mem.), U. N.Mex. Sch. Law Alumni Assn. (bd. dirs.), Elks Club, Sigma Xi. Democrat. Avocations: handball, scuba diving, swimming, spectator sports. also: PO Box 1966 Albuquerque NM 87103-1966*

SANCHEZ, ROBERT FRANCIS, journalist; b. Bradenton, Fla., Jan. 1, 1938; s. Robert and Frances Alice (Thompson) S. BS in English Edn., Fla. State U., 1959, MS, 1962, postgrad., 1971-74. Mem. faculty Fla. State U., Tallahassee, 1962-67; mem. faculty Fla. A&M U., 1968-71; writer, editor Tallahassee Democrat, 1965-74; editl. writer Miami Herald, 1974-2000. Co-recipient Pulitzer Prize, 1983 Mem. Phi Delta Kappa, Sigma Delta Chi Republican. Methodist. Home: 2324 Williams Rd Tallahassee FL 32311 Office: Fla Dept Hwy Safety & Motor Vehicles 2900 Apalachee Pkwy Tallahassee FL 32399-0509

SANCHEZ, ROMULO MANALO, physician; b. Lipa, The Philippines, Apr. 6, 1936; came to U.S., 1970. s. Benito Laygo and Clara(Manalo) S.; m. Aurora Fernandez, April 3, 1967; children: Claire, Royce. BS in Chemistry, Manila Ctrl. U., 1960, MD, 1964. Diplomate Am. Bd. Family Medicine. Dir. respiratory dept. St. Joseph Hosp., Chippewa Falls, Wis., 1978—2002, chmn.

ICU, 1986-96; mem. staff Marshfield Clinic, 1994—, active staff Cadott Ctr. Cons. Cadott (Wis.) Sch., 1984-97. Fellow Am. Acad. Family Practice, Philippine-Am. Acad. Family Practice; mem. Am.Thoracic Assn., Wis. Lung Assn., Cadott C. of C. Avocations: fishing, reading, gardening. Office: 305 S Highway 27 Cadott WI 54727-9561

SANCHEZ, VICTOR DAVID, computer scientist; b. Lima, Peru, June 26, 1959; arrived in U.S., 1995; MS in Comm. Engring., U. Applied Sci., Karlsruhe, Germany, 1985; MSEE, U. Karlsruhe, Germany, 1986; PhD in Computer Sci., Nova Southeastern U., Ft. Lauderdale, Fla. Adj. assoc. prof. U. Miami, Coral Gables, Fla., 1995; chief tech. officer Thuris Corp., Newport Beach, Calif., 2000; owner ACIS, Pasadena, 1999—. Editor-in-chief Neurocomputing, 1989—. Recipient Nat. award, NASA, 1999. Fellow: IEEE; mem.: AAAS, IEEE Edn. Soc., IEEE Computer Soc. Home: PO Box 1424 La Canada CA 91012

SANCHEZ, WALTER MARSHALL, lawyer; b. Lake Charles, La., July 3, 1959; s. John Augustine Sanchez and Louise Page Dugas Meyer; m. Frances E. Morgan, Oct. 18, 1986; children: Clare, Madeline, Kate, John. BS, La. State U., Baton Rouge, 1981, JD, 1984. Bar: La. 1984, U.S. Supreme Ct. 1984; bd. cert. family law specialist, La. Bd. of Legal Specialization. Assoc. Godwin, Painter, Roddy, Lorenzi & Watson, Lake Charles, 1985-86; ptnr. Godwin, Roddy, Lorenzi Watson & Sanchez, 1986-90, Lorenzi, Sanchez & Palay, LLP, Lake Charles, 1990—. Vice chmn. La. Indigent Defender Bd., New Orleans, 1994-96; chmn. 14th Jud. Dist. Indigent Defender Bd., Lake Charles, 1987-96; mem. faculty trial advocacy tng. program La. State U. Law Ctr., 1993—; mem. Joint Legis. Com. for Study Indigent Def. Sys., 1996-97; mem. spl. com. to study reinstatement of fault in divorce La. State Law Inst., 1998-2001; apptd. judge pro tempore City Ct. of Sulphur, 1999—. Mem. La. Assn. Criminal Def. Attys. (bd. dirs. 1990—, pres. 1997-98), Am. Mensa, Order of St. Charles. Democrat. Roman Catholic. Office: Lorenzi Sanchez & Palay LLP PO Box 3305 Lake Charles LA 70602-3305

SANCHEZ ALVARADO, ALEJANDRO, embryologist, molecular biologist; b. Caracas, Venezuela, Feb. 24, 1964; came to U.S., 1982; s. Delfin Orestes and Vera Antonieta (Alvarado) S. BS, Vanderbilt U., 1986; PhD, U. Cin., 1992. Rsch. asst. U. Cin. Coll. Medicine, 1987-88, grad. student, 1988-92, rsch. assoc., 1992-93; postdoctoral fellow Carnegie Inst., Balt., 1994-96, staff assoc., 1996—2001; assoc. prof. U. Utah Sch. of Medicine, 2002—. Sci. corr. El Nacional, Caracas, 1996; UNESCO lectr., Venezuela, 1997, 99. Editor: Regenerative Medicine; contbr. articles to Jour. Biol. Chemistry, Devel. Dynamics, Devel. Biology, Proceedings of the NAS. Recipient Marine Biol. Labs. Embryology rsch. award, 1995, Marcus Singer rsch. regeneration award, 1999. Mem. AAAS, Am. Soc. Cell Biology, Soc. Devel. Biology, Singer Soc. for Regeneration, N.Y. Acad. Scis. Achievements include research in characterizing in vitro model for vertebrate cardiogenesis; development of an invertebrate model for the molecular study of regeneration. Office: U Utah Sch Medicine Dept Neurobiology and Anatomy 50 North Med Dr Salt Lake City UT 84132 E-mail: sanchez@neuro.utah.edu .

SANCHEZ DE LEON, ROBERTO J. physician, educator, writer; b. Caracas, Venezuela, Sept. 21, 1949; s. Pablo and Alicia (Santander) Sanchez de L.; m. Imperia Brajkovich, Feb. 14, 1975 (div.); m. Morella H. Ferrero; children: Vanessa, Michelle, Lorena, Geraldine, Giselle. MD, U. Caracas, Venezuela, 1972. Intern, resident in internal medicine Maternity Hosp., Caracas, Venezuela, 1972-78; resident in intensive care U. Hosp., 1978-80; asst. prof. U. Caracas, 1981-85; resident pulmonology and chest clinic Hammersmith Hosp. London U., 1982-84; resident in intensive care Manheim Hosp. Heidelberg U., Germany, 1984-85; assoc. prof. U. Caracas, 1985-90, prof., 1990—, head dept., 1999—. Author: (children's lit.) Papa's Stories, 1999, (poetry) Yo En Ti, 1997, Basics in Pulmonary Physiology. Fellow Royal Coll. Chest Physicians; mem. Am. Coll. Chest Physicians, Am. Thoracic Soc. (associated, regular prof.), L.Am. Thoracic Soc. Avocations: swimming, diving, art. Office: PO Box International 281 Miami FL 33102 E-mail: rsanchez@ven.net.

SANCHEZ-RAMOS, JUAN RAMON, physician, medical educator; b. Cabimas, Zulia, Venezuela, July 16, 1945; came to the U.S., 1950; s. Juan Ramon Sanchez y Sanchez and Carmen F. Ramos de Sanchez; m. Catherine O'Neill, Aug. 19, 1984; children: Zachary, Zoe Allegra, Sofia Isabel. BS, U. Chgo., PhD, 1976; MD, U. Ill., Chgo., 1981. Rsch. assoc. dept. pharmacology U. Chgo., 1976-78; med. intern Michael Reese Hosp., Chgo., 1981-82; resident in neurology U. Chgo., 1982-86; asst. prof. dept. neurology U. Miami, Fla., 1987-92, assoc. prof. dept. neurology, 1992-96; prof. U. South Fla., Tampa, 1996—, Helen E. Ellis endowed chair, 1996. Mng. editor Parkinson's Disease Update, 1994—; contbr. chpts. to books and articles to profl. jours. Recipient Clin. Investigator award NIH, Washington, 1988, Vets. Affairs Merit Rev., Washington, 1994, 98. Mem. AAAS, Am. Acad. Neurology, Am. Neurol. Assn., Movement Disorders Soc., Parkinsons Study Group, Oxygen Radical Soc. Avocations: drawing, painting. Office: Univ South Fla MDC55 12901 Bruce Downs Blvd Tampa FL 33620 E-mail: jsramos@hsc.usf.edu.

SAND, JOHN HALVDAN, obstetrician, gynecologist; b. San Diego, May 7, 1951; MD, U. Calif., Davis, 1976. Diplomate Am. Bd. Ob-Gyn. Intern USPHS, San Francisco, 1976-77; resident in internal medicine Mercy Hosp. Med. Ctr., San Diego, 1978-79; resident in ob-gyn. U. N.Mex., Albuquerque, 1979-81, Gallup Indian Med. ctr., Ellensburg, Wash., 1981-83; mem. staff Tucson Med. Ctr., 1986-89, Univ. Med. Ctr., Tucson, 1989-92, St. Joseph's Hosp., Tucson, 1989-92; pvt. practice, Ellensburg, 1992—. Mem. staff Kittitas Valley Cmty. Hosp., Ellensburg, 1983-86, chief OBG, 1992—. Fellow ACOG; mem. AMA, Am. Assn. Gynecol. Laparoscopists, Am. Inst. for Ultrasound in Medicine. Office: 611 S Chestnut St Ste B Ellensburg WA 98926-4815

SAND, MICHAEL, museum planner, interactive media designer; b. Bklyn., Aug. 9, 1940; s. Joseph H. and Ethel (Lichtenstein) S.; m. Margaret Emma Schmidt, Aug. 8, 1969; children: Zoe, Jessica. BFA in Indsl. Design, R.I. Sch. Design, 1963. Design dir. Boston Children's Mus., 1963-64; pres. Michael Sand, Inc., Brookline, 1964—. Acting dir. Richmond (Va.) Children's Mus., 1980-81, Muncie (Ind.) Children's Mus., 1977-78; vis. critic R.I. Sch. Design, Providence, 1967—; vis. instr. Ball State U., Muncie, 1977-78, Harvard U. Grad. Sch. Design, Cambridge, Mass., 1981-83; design dir. Edn. Devel. Ctr., Cambridge, 1969-77, Boston Zool. Soc., 1970-76; planner Nat. Mus. Boy Scouts Am., Murray, Ky., 1986-88. Active Brookline Arts Coun., 1986; founder, dir. Brookline Found., 1986; bd. dirs. Coolidge Corner Theatre Found., 1993-98. Mem. Am. Assn. Mus., Boston Computer Soc. (bd. dirs. 1992-96), Am. Assn. Youth Mus., Internat. Coun. Mus. Achievements include design of Lowell (Mass.) Nat. Park, 1996; The Wave, Boston, 1977; Mus. of Sci. Big Dig Exhibit, Boston, 1992; Boston Bicentennial Exhibit. Home and Office: Rare Media Well Done Inc 1110 Washington St Boston MA 02124-5522 E-mail: msand@aol.com.

SAND, STEPHANIE JO, accountant, consultant; b. Toledo, Oct. 19, 1969; d. James M. Bishop and Shirley J. Keiser; m. Howard L. Sand, Apr. 19, 1998; children: Zachery, Courtney. BSBA in Acctg., U. Nev., Las Vegas, 1993. CPA, Nev. Bus. cons. Stewart, Archibald & Barney, LLP, Las Vegas, 1993—2002, ptnr., 2002—. Mem. AICPA, Nev. Soc. CPAs. Avocations: camping, hiking, reading. Office: Ste 250 7881 W Charleston Blvd Las Vegas NV 89117

SAND, THOMAS CHARLES, lawyer; b. Portland, Oreg., June 4, 1952; s. Harold Eugene and Marian Anette (Thomas) S.; m. Rhonda Diane Laycoe, June 15, 1974; children: Kendall, Taylor, Justin. Student, Centro des Artes y Lenguas, Cuernavaca, Mex., 1972; BA in English, U. Oreg., 1974; JD, Lewis and Clark Coll., 1977. Bar: Oreg. 1977, U.S. Dist. Ct. Oreg. 1977, U.S. Ct. Appeals (9th cir.) 1984. Assoc. Miller, Nash, LLP, Portland, 1977-84, ptnr., 1984—, mng. ptnr., 1999—. Mem. Oreg. State Bar Com. on Professionalism, 1989, chmn., 1990; dir. young lawyers divsn. Multnomah County Bar Assn., 1980; spl. asst. atty. gen. Wasco County 1983 Gen. Election; speaker in field. Contbr. articles to legal jours. Mem. U.S. Dist. Ct. of Oreg. Hist. Soc., 1990—; bd. dirs. Portland Area coun. Camp Fire, Inc., 1978-90,pres., 1984-86; bd. dirs. Oreg. Indoor Invitational Track Meet, Inc., 1982-84. Recipient Boss of the Yr. award Portland Legal Secs. Assn., 1989. Mem. ABA (securities litigation com., subcom. on broker-dealer litigation), Oreg. Bar Assn., Multnomah Bar Assn. (bd. dirs. task force on structure and orgn. 1989, chmn. com. on professionalism 1988, nominating com. 1986, participating atty. in N.E. legal clin. Vol Lawyers project, award of merit for svc. to profession 1988), Securities Industry Assn. (compliance and legal divsn.), Northwestern Sch. of Law, Lewis and Clark Coll. Alumni Assn. (bd. dirs. 1992, pres. 1997), Valley Comm. Presbyterian Ch., Multnomah Athletic Club, Portland Golf Club. Avocations: golf, guitar, camping, river rafting, children's sports. Office: Miller Nash LLP 111 SW 5th Ave Ste 3500 Portland OR 97204-3699

SANDAHL, BONNIE BEARDSLEY, health services executive, educator; b. Washington, Jan. 17, 1939; d. Erwin Leonard and Carol Myrtle (Collis) B.; m. Glen Emil Sandahl, Aug. 17, 1963; children: Cara Lynne, Cory Glen. BSN, U. Wash., 1962, MN, 1974; cert. pediat. nurse practitioner, 1972. Dir. Wash. State Joint Practice Commn., Seattle, 1974-76; instr. pediatric nurse practitioner program U. Wash., 1976, course coord. quality assurance, 1977-78; pediatric nurse practitioner/health coord. Snohomish County Head Start, Everett, 1975-77; clin. nurse educator (specialist), nurse mgr. Harborview Med. Ctr., Seattle, 1978-97, dir. child abuse prevention project, 1986-97; mgr. Children's Ctr., Providence Health Sys. Northwest, 1997-2000; v.p. clin. svcs. and ops., COO Seattle Children's Home, 2000—. Spkr. legis. focus on children, 1987; clin. assoc. dept. pediatrics U. Wash. Sch. Medicine, 1987—; clin. faculty U. Wash. Sch. Nursing, 1987—97; nurse mgr. Providence Gen. Children's Ctr., Everett, 1997—2000; gov. appointee State Interagy. Coord. Coun., 1998—. Mem. Task Force on Pharmacotherapeutic Courses, Wash. State Bd. Nursing, 1985-86; Puget Sound Health Sys. Agy., 1975-88, pres., 1980-82; mem. child devel. project adv. bd. Mukilteo Sch. Dist., 1984-85; mem. parenting adv. com. Edmonds Sch. Dist.; chmn. hospice-home health task force Snohomish County Hospice Program, Everett, 1984-85, bd. dirs. hospice, 1985-87, adv. com. 1986-88; mem. Wash. State Health Coordinating Coun., 1977-82, chmn. nursing home bed projection methodology task force, 1986-87; mem. interim chair Nat. Coun. Health Planning and Devel., HHS, 1980-87; mem. adv. com. on uncompensated care Wash. State Legislature, 1983-84; mem. Joint Select Com., Tech. Adv. Com. on Managed Health Care Sys., 1984-85; pres., Alderwood Manor Cmty. Coun., 1983-85; treas. Wash. St. Women's Polit. Caucus, 1983-84; mem. com. to examine changes in Wash. State Criminal Sex Law, 1987; appointee county needs assessment com. Snohomish County Govt. United Way, 1989, 94; chair human svcs. adv. coun. Snohomish County Human Svcs. Dept., chair adv. com., 1998-; gubernatorial appointee State Interagency Coordinating coun. Health Svcs. Adv. Com. for Wash. State, 1995-97; apptd. Snohomish County Children's Commn., 1997—; apptd. by gov. State Interagy. Coordinating Coun., 1998—. Recipient Golden Acorn award Seattle-King County PTA, 1973, Katherine Rickey Vol. Participation award, 1987. Mem. ANA (chmn. pediatric nurse practitioner subcom. Com. Examiners Maternal-Child Nursing Practice, 1986-92, chair Com. Examiners Maternal-Child Nursing Practice 1988-90), Wash. State Nurses Assn. (hon. leadership award 1981, chair healthcare reform task force 1992-96), King County Nurses Assn. (Nurse of Yr. 1985, 1st v.p. 1992-96, pres. 1996-97), Sigma Theta Tau. Home: 1814 201st Pl SW Lynnwood WA 98036-7060 Office: Seattle Childrens Home Seattle WA 98119-2899

SANDALOW, TERRANCE, law educator; b. Chgo., Sept. 8, 1934; s. Nathan and Evelyn (Hoffing) Sandalow; m. Ina Davis, Sept. 4, 1955; children: David Blake, Marc Alan, Judith Ann. AB, U. Chgo., 1954, JD, 1957. Bar: Ill. 1958, Mich. 1978. Law clk. to judge Sterry R. Waterman U.S. Ct. Appeals (2d cir.), 1957-58; law clk. to justice Potter Stewart U.S. Supreme Ct., Washington, 1958-59; assoc. Ross, McGowan & O'Keefe, Chgo., 1959-61; assoc. prof. law U. Minn., Mpls., 1961-64, prof., 1964-66; prof. law U. Mich., Ann Arbor, 1966-2000, dean Law Sch., 1978-87, Edson R. Sunderland prof. law, 1987-2000, dean emeritus and Edson R. Sunderland prof. law emeritus, 2000—. Author (with F. I. Michelman): (book) Government in Urban Areas, 1970; author: (with E. Stein) Courts and Free Markets, 1982; contbr. articles to legal jours. and periodicals. Mem. Mpls. Commn. Human Rels., 1965—66. Recipient Profl. Achievement award, U. Chgo. Alumni; fellow, Ctr. Advanced Study in Behavioral Scis., 1972—73. Fellow: Am. Acad. Arts Scis.; mem.: Order of Coif (nat. pres. 2001—), Phi Beta Kappa (hon.). Office: U Mich Law Sch Hutchins Hall Ann Arbor MI 48109-1215 E-mail: sandalow@umich.edu.

SANDARS, LEIBERT JOVANOVICH, radiologist; b. Balt., Apr. 17, 1914; s. Michael and Katherine (Jovanovich) Skandarski; m. Annel Branch, 1947; children: Jill Bonifield, Judy Klaich. MD, U. Chgo., 1941. Diplomate Am. Bd. Radiology. Intern St. Lukes Hosp., San Francisco, 1941-42; resident in radiology U. Calif., 1949-52; dir., founder Dept. Radiology, Washoe Med. Ctr., Reno, 1952-88; dir., cons. radiologist VA Hosp., 1954-68; chmn. Reno Radiol. Assocs., 1958-88. Artist in watercolor and oils. Lt. (j.g.) USNR, 1941-43. Fellow Am. Coll. Radiology (Nev. councilor 1954-68); mem. No. Calif. Radiol. Soc. (pres. 1964), Washoe County Med. Soc. (pres. 1964), Prospectors Club. Republican. Avocation: art, golf. Home: 3340 Piazzo Cir Reno NV 89502-9597

SANDBACH, CHARLIE BERNARD, accountant; b. Litchfield, Ill., July 19, 1933; s. Samuel Bernard and Eva Benoid (Weck) S.; m. Janet Lee Koch, Aug. 12, 1955; children: Debra Lee, Cynthia Joan, Charlie Bernard Jr. BA, Greenville (Ill.) Coll., 1955; postgrad., Washington U., St. Louis, 1961, St. Louis U., 1961. CPA, Mo. Acct. CPA firm, 1958-67; pres. Charlie B. Sandbach CPA, Inc., St. Louis, 1967-95. With U.S. Army, 1955-57. Mem. AICPA, Mo. Soc. CPA's, Ill. Soc. CPA's, Mo. Assn. Tax Practitioners (bd. dirs. 1965-89, pres. 1972-73). Mem. Nazarene Ch. Avocation: golf. Office: 319 N 4th St Saint Louis MO 63102-1906

SANDBACK, WILLIAM ARTHUR, lawyer; b. N.Y.C., Aug. 2, 1945; s. William A. and Gertrude E. (Ryan) S.; married; children: Lauren, Adam. BA, Villanova U., 1967; postgrad. in English, L.I. U., 1968; JD, N.Y. Law Sch., 1971; LLM in Labor Law, NYU, 1974. Bar: N.Y. 1972, Fla. 1973, U.S. Dist. Ct. (ea. and so. dists.) N.Y. 1973. Fin. planner Aims Group, N.Y.C., 1971-72; asst. dist. atty. Nassau County, N.Y., 1972-73; law sec. to presiding justice Nassau County Ct., 1973-77; ptnr. Sandback, Birnbaum & Michelen, Mineola, N.Y., 1977—. Committeeman Nassau County Rep. Com., 1979-86. Mem. ABA, Nassau County Bar Assn. (com. mem.), Lions (pres. 1983-84). Roman Catholic. Avocation: golf. Office: Sandback Birnbaum Michelen 200 Old Country Rd Mineola NY 11501-4235 also: 2 Penn Plz Rm 1996 New York NY 10121-1999

SANDBANK, HENRY, photographer, film director; b. Burg, Germany, Mar. 20, 1932; came to U.S., 1939, naturalized, 1950; s. Sylvan and Bella (Spatz) S.; m. Judith Lebow, July 4, 1952; children: Kenneth, Laura, Lisa, David. Ed. pub. schs. Ptnr. Beach & Sandbank, Syracuse, N.Y., 1960-63; sr. ptnr. Sandbank & Ptnrs., N.Y.C., 1963-88; pres., film dir. Sandbank Films Co., Inc., 1972—; dir. Vantage Films, 1979—; sr. ptnr. Sandbank Kamen & Ptnrs., 1992-94; dir. AEGIS Prodns., N.Y.C. and Hollywood, Calif. Lectr. Syracuse U., 1972, lectr. Coll. Visual and Performing Arts, 2002; lectr. Mus. Modern Art, 1994, for Eastman Kodak, Tokyo, 1994; cons. Fashion Inst. Tech., 1974—80. Recipient Gold medal Art Dirs. and Copywriters Show, Gold medal Film Festival of the Americas, several Clio and Andy awards, Cannes Festival award, Gold medal for film documentary Houston Internat. Film Festival 1980. Served to sgt. AUS, 1952-54, Korea. Mem. Am. Soc. Mag. Photographers (chmn. exec. com. 1978-79, Outstanding Achievement award 1981), Soc. Photographers in Communications (trustee 1974-81, 2d v.p. 1975-76, 1st v.p. 1977, chmn. exec. com. 1979) Home and Office: 24 Nutmeg Dr Greenwich CT 06831-3211 E-mail: hankjudy@optonline.net.

SANDBERG, IRWIN WALTER, electrical and computer engineering educator; b. N.Y.C., Jan. 23, 1934; s. Ben and Estelle (Hornick) S.; m. Barbara A. Zimmerman, June 15, 1958; 1 dau. Heidi L. Ed., CCNY, 1951-53; B.E.E., Poly. Inst. Bklyn., 1955, M.E.E., 1956, D.E.E., 1958. Tech. aid Bell Telephone Labs., Inc., Murray Hill, N.J., summer 1954, mem. tech. staff, 1958-67, head systems theory research dept., 1967-72, mem. math. and statis. research ctr., 1972-86; prof. elec. and computer engring. U. Tex., Austin, 1986—, now holder Cockrell Family Regents Chair in Engring.; engr. Wheeler Labs., Great Neck, N.Y., summer 1955. Vis. prof. U. Calif.-Berkeley, 1965; U.S. del. Union Radio Scientifique Internationale, Munich, Germany, 1966; U.S. nat. inst. rep. Advanced Study Inst. on Network and Signal Theory, NATO, Bournemouth, Eng., 1972; lectr. study inst. NATO (Knokke), Belgium, 1966, Copenhagen, 1970; disting. invited spkr. Asilomar Conf., 1973-74; main lectr. European Conf. on Circuit Theory and Design, The Hague, 1981; advisor Inst. Electronics, Info. and Comm. Engrs., Tokyo; advisor Am. Men and Women of Sci., 1993. Patentee (in field). Recipient Best Paper award Asilomar Conf., 1970, Achievement award IEEE Circuits and Systems Soc., 1986, Classic Paper citation ISI press, 1984, Outstanding Alumnus award Poly. U., 1993. Fellow IEEE (life, adminstrv. com. group circuit theory 1969-70, vice chmn. group circuit theory 1971-72, Centennial medal, Millennial medal, Cirs. and Sys. Soc. Golden Jubilee medal, Cirs. and Sys. Soc. disting. lectr.), AAAS; mem. NAE, Soc. for Indsl. and Applied Math., Eta Kappa Nu, Sigma Xi, Tau Beta Pi Home: 8505 Hickory Creek Dr Austin TX 78735-1527 Office: Univ Tex Dept Elec Comp Engr Austin TX 78712 E-mail: sandberg@ece.utexas.edu.

SANDBERG, KAREN ELIZABETH, nurse, writer; b. Mpls., June 29, 1942; d. Vernon E. and Marcia F. Sandberg; children: Eric, Ben; m. Thomas Harry Bliss, Apr. 18, 1992; stepchildren: Petr, Brigid. Student, U. Minn., 1960-63; AS, Rochester Cmty. Coll., 1977. RN Minn. Obstet. nurse Mayo Clinic, Rochester, Minn., 1977—. Author poetry. Unitarian Universalist. Home: 11128 Cedar Beach Dr NW Oronoco MN 55960 E-mail: ironpoint@hotmail.com.

SANDBERG-MORGAN, BARBARA, retired communication and women's studies educator; b. McAllen, Tex., Dec. 19, 1934; d. Dean M. and Katherine (Hurlbert) Baer; m. Robert Morgan, July 31, 1976 (dec. Nov. 1994); 1 chld, Allison Morgan. BS, Ind. U., 1959; MA, Columbia U., 1963, EdD, 1974. Registered drama therapist. Prof. William Paterson U., Wayne, N.J., 1963-2000, prof. emerita NJ, 2000—. Instr. Tchrs. Coll./Columbia U., N.Y.C., 1971-77; drama therapist, 1979—; mem. adv. bd., drama cons. Jersey Shore Arts Ctr., Ocean Grove, N.J., 1996—; dir. edn. Inner City Ensemble, Paterson, N.J., 1984-89; dir. Washington St. Gallery, Paterson, 1989-93. Dir. Paterson Bicentennial Pageant, Hist. Commn., 1992; dir. Washington St. Cultural Activities Assn., Paterson, 1990-93. Recipient Heritage Citizen award Paterson, 1993, citation for tchg. excellence William Paterson U., 1994; named Woman of Yr., World of the Arts-Girl Scout Coun., 1995. Mem. Nat. Assn. for Drama Therapy (founding; bd. dirs.). Avocations: acting, directing, gardening. E-mail: millik@sedona.net.

SANDBORN, VIRGIL ALVIN, civil engineer, educator; b. Conway Springs, Kans., Apr. 30, 1928; s. Kenneth Arthur and Mamie Una (Durham) S.; m. Virginia Ruth Cerny, June 12, 1955; children: Peter Alan, Paticia Marie. B in Aero. Engring., U. Kans., 1950; M in Aero. Engring., U. Mich., 1953. Aero. research scientist NACA-NASA, Cleve., 1951-62; cons. scientist AVCO R&AD, Wilmington, Mass., 1962-63; prof. Colo. State U., Ft. Collins., 1963—. Vis. scientist NASA-Ames Research Ctr., Moffett Field, Calif., 1972-73, Navy Underwater Ctr., Newport, R.I., 1984-85. Author: Resistance Temperature Transducers, 1972, Classnotes for Experimental Methods in Fluid Mechanics, 1981. Mem. AIAA, Sigma Xi. Home: 917 Cheyenne Dr Fort Collins CO 80525-1559

SANDBOWER, NANCY NORMINE, potter, educator; b. Balt., Oct. 13, 1935; d. Fitzhugh Lee and Alice Mildred (Hine) N.; children: Beth Allison, John Cary, Katie McLean. Student, Peabody Sch. Music, Balt., 1941-53; BS, Towson (Md.) U., 1957; MFA, Antioch U., Columbia, Md., 1980. Tchr. Halethorpe Elem. Sch., Balt., 1957-59, Samuel Ready Sch., Balt., 1970-71, Potter's Guild Balt., 1981-82, Dundalk (Md.) C.C., 1982-83, Howard C.C., Columbia, Md., 1985, 86, Towson U., 1986, 87-88; potter Oak Forest Pottery, Catonsville, Md., 1982, 84, 89, 91-96. Pres. PTA Hillcrest Elem. Sch., Balt., 1972, Thomas Jefferson Sch., Balt., 1969. Dir. 16mm movia A. Hospital Adventure, 1972; curator art and lit. show Poetry and Pots, 1986; artistic dir., project coord. clay mural "The Children's Mural" for the Catonsville Libr., 1995-96; installer 2 shows Balt. Clayworks and Jewish Cmty. Ctr., 1995; exhibited in group shows at Balt. Sch. for the Arts, 1981, Gallery 1734, Washington, 1982, Tomlinson Craft Collection, Balt., 1983, Slayton House Gallery, Columbia, Md., 1983, Village of Wildelake, Columbia, 1984, Foundry St. Studio, Savage, Md., 1984, Rockland Art Ctr., Ellicott City, 1984, New Art Ctr., Washington, 1987, Life of Md. Gallery, Balt., 1987, Walter's Art Gallery, 1994, Clayworks, 1995, Dundalk Cmty. Coll. Gallery, 1997, Balt. Clayworks, 1997, 98; designer, builder displays Nat. Mus. Ceramic Arts Booth, Am. Crafts Coun., Balt. Conv. Ctr., 1988-91, Clayworks Booth, 1994, 95; creator, prodr., dir. Three Penny Puppets, Balt., 1971-74. Docent Balt. Zoo, 1972-75; mus. shop dir., buyer Nat. Mus. Ceramic Art, Balt., 1988-91; bd. mem. Nat. Mus. Ceramic Art, Balt., 1988-93. Mem. Balt. Clayworks (pres. 1992-95, bd. dirs. 1991—), Potters Guild Balt., Garden Club Am. (Catonsville). Avocations: hiking, cooking, travel, wine collecting. Home: 505 Patleigh Rd Baltimore MD 21228-5634

SANDBROOK, DAVID LEE, forest service specialist, database administrator; b. Corona, Calif., Apr. 26, 1954; s. John Henry and Frances Virginia Sandbrook; m. Patricia Lynn Osborn, Jan. 25, 1975; 1 child, Amanda. AS, Coll. of Canyons, Valencia, Calif., 1979. Helitack cpt. USDA Forest Svc., Chester, Calif., 1979-97, database mgr./geographic info. system specialist, 1997—. Author short stories. Mem. bd. dirs. Peoples Ch., Westwood, Calif., 1995—. Mem. Soc. Am. Foresters. Avocations: mountain bike riding, hiking, history. Office: USDA Forest Svc PO Box 767 Chester CA 96020 E-mail: dsandbrook@fs.fed.us.

SANDBURG, HELGA, author; b. Maywood, Ill., Nov. 24, 1918; d. Carl and Lilian (Steichen) S.; m. George Crile, Jr., Nov. 9, 1963; children by previous marriage: John Carl Steichen, Paula Steichen Polega. Student, Mich. State Coll., 1939-40, U. Chgo., 1940. Dairy goat breeder, also personal sec. to father, 1944-51; sec. manuscripts div., also for keeper of collections Library of Congress, 1952-56; adminstrv. asst. for papers of Woodrow Wilson, 1958-59; writer, lectr., 1957—. Author: (novels) The Wheel of Earth, 1958, Measure My Love, 1959, The Owl's Roost, 1962, The Wizard's Child, 1967; (non-fiction) Sweet Music, A Book of Family Reminiscence and Song, 1963; (with George Crile, Jr.) Above and Below, 1969; (poetry) The Unicorns, 1965; To A New Husband, 1970, The Age of the Flower, 1994; (young adult novels) Blueberry, 1963; Gingerbread, 1964; (juveniles) Joel and the Wild Goose, 1963; Bo and the Old Donkey, 1965, Anna and the Baby Buzzard, 1970, Children and Lovers: 15 Stories by Helga Sandburg, 1976; (biography) A Great and Glorious Romance: The Story of Carl Sandburg and Lilian Steichen, 1978; "...Where Love Begins", 1989, (recorded poems) From in the Dream: Helga Sandburg Reads her Poems, 2001; also numerous short stories; rep. in collections.; contbr.short stories, poems, articles to popular mags. including Seventeen. Recipient Va. Quar. Rev. prize for best short story, 1959, Borestone Mountain poetry award, 1962, Poetry award Chgo. Tribune, 1970; 2d prize 7th Ann. Kans. Poetry Contest, Florence Roberts Head Ohioana Book award, 1990; grantee Finnish Am. Soc. and Svenska Inst., 1961 Mem. Authors Guild, Poetry Soc., Am. Milk Goat Record Assn., Am.-Scandinavian Found., Nat. Nubian Club, Coun. Save the Dunes, Am. Luxembourg Soc., Acad. Am. Poets. Address: 2060 Kent Rd Cleveland Heights OH 44106-3339 E-mail: helgacrile@aol.com.

SANDDAL, NELS DODGE, foundation executive, consultant; b. Salt Lake City, Feb. 17, 1949; s. James Wesley and Charlotte Jean (Ewer) S.; m. Brenda Kay Lille Griffin, Sept. 27, 1970 (div. June 1990); m. Theresa Louise Knipe, Oct. 10, 1992; 1 child, Jami. BA in English, Carroll Coll., 1966-70; MS in Psychology, Mont. State U., 1996. In-svc. trainer Boulder (Mont.) River Sch. and Hosp., 1974-75; group home mgr. REACH, Inc., Bozeman, Mont., 1975-76; community home trainer Devel. Disabilities Tng. Inst., Helena, 1976-77; tng. coord. emergency med. svcs. bureau State Dept. Health and Environ. Scis., 1977-82; cons., lead staff Nat. Coun. State Emergency Med. Svcs. Tng. Coords., Inc., Lexington, Ky., 1981-86; account exec., lead staff Nat. Assn. Emergency Med. Techs., Clinton, Miss., 1986-87; pres., CEO Assn. Mgmt. and Cons., Inc., Boulder, 1983-89; writer, prodr., dir. North Country Media Group, Great Falls, Mont., 1990-91; chief conf. planner S.O.S. Conf. Planning Consortium, 1991-92; exec. dir. Critical Illness & Trauma Found., Bozeman, Mont., 1986-91, pres., CEO, 1991—. Season course leader Nat. Outdoor Leadership Sch., Lander, Wyo., 1966—74; mem. exec. com. Nat. Coun. State EMS Tng. Coords., 1977—82, chmn., Ky., 1979—81; mem. adv. com. pediatric emergency med. svcs. tng. project Children's Hosp. Nat. Med. Ctr., Wash., 1985—88, pediatrics emergency instr., 1986—90; mem. grant peer rev. com. divsn. injury epidemiology Ctrs. for Disease Control, Atlanta, 1986—87; cons. Emergency Med. Svcs. Bureau , Helena, 1977, Devel. Disabilities Tng. Inst., Helena, 1977—78; mem. injury prevention profls. New Eng. Network to Prevent Childhood Injuries, Newton, Mass., 1988—95; mem. core faculty devel. trauma sys. tng. program U.S. Dept. Transp., Wash., 1989—; tech. assistance team mem. EMS, 1991—93; EMS instr. and program coord. Great Falls Vocat. Tng. Ctr., 1991—93; rsch. asst. inst. for cmty. studies U. Mo., Kansas city, 1983—95; assoc. rsch. prof. psychology Mont. State U., 1999—; asst. clin. prof. surgery U. Nev. Sch. Medicine, 1999—; exec. com. Intermountain Regional EMS Children Coord. Coun., Bozeman, Mont., 1994—2002; site reviewer Commn. for Accreditation of Ambulance Svcs., Glenview, Ill., 1997—; firefighter/EMS trainer Gallatin Gateway Vol. Fire Dept., Gallatin Gateway, Mont., 1998—2001; asst. chief Gallatin Gateway Fire Dept. , 2001—; bd. dirs. Five Rivers chpt. ARC, Bozeman, Mont., 1998—2001; med. officer Gallatin River Ranch, 2001—. Editor and tech. cons.: Workbook for Prehospital Care and Crisis Intervention, 4th edit., 1992, 5th edit., 1993, Instructor Resource Manual for Prehospital Care and Crisis Intervention, 4th edit., 1992, Workbook for First Responder, 1990; contbg. editor Jour. of Prehospital Care, 1984-85, The EMT Jour., 1980-81; editl. cons. Am. Acad. Orthopaedic Surgeons, 1980-81; contbr. numerous articles to profl. jours.; video prodr. and presenter in field. Mem. Park County DUI Task Force, Livingson, 1993-96; inaugural coord. Mont. Safe Kids Coalition, Big Timber, 1988-90; adv. com. Nat. Significance Project for Respite Care, 1977-78; mem. basic life support com. of Mont., Mont. Heart Assn., 1977-82. Recipient Golden award for humanity ARC, 1976, 500 Hour award, 1976, Outstanding Svc. award Nat. Coun. State EMS Tng. Coords., 1979, Leadership award, 1981, Charter Membership award, 1984, J.D. Farrington award for excellence Nat. Assn. Emergency Med. Technicians, 1981, Jeffrey S. Harris award, 1985, Outstanding Svc. award Am. Heart Assn., 1982, Appreciation cert. for paramedic emergency care U.S. Dept. Transp., 1984, appreciation awards Colo. Trauma Inst., 1993, Healthy Mothers/Healthy Babies, Helena, Mont., 1997, Kans. Bd. of EMS, Topeka, 1996, 98, Intermountain Regional EMS for Children Coordinating Coun., Inc., 1998. Mem. Nat. Registry EMTs (20 yr. recognition), Mont. Bd. Med. Examiners. Democrat. Avocations: mountaineering, hiking, sailing, golf, skiing. Home: 115 Lay Pass Manhattan MT 59741 Office: 115 Lay Pass Rd Manhattan MT 59741-8032 E-mail: nsanddal@citmt.org.

SANDE, THEODORE ANTON, architect, educator, foundation executive; b. New London, Conn., Nov. 21, 1933; s. Lars Anton and Viola (Edgcomb) S.; m. Solveig Inga-Maj Imselius, Aug. 6, 1960; children: Susanne Ingrid, Lars Michael. BSc in Architecture, R.I. Sch. Design, 1956; MArch, Yale U., 1961; PhD, U. Pa., 1972; grad. Cultural Instns. Mgmt. Program, Mus. Collaborative, 1983; postgrad., Attingham (Eng.) Summer Sch., 1980. Vis. prof. history of architecture Rensselaer Poly. Inst., fall 1973-74, U. Pa., 1976-77; adj. prof. Am. studies and history Case-Western Res. U., 1981—. Vis. lectr. in historic preservation Cleve. State U., summer 1994, spring 1998; lectr. art Williams Coll., 1972-75; attended teleconfs. non-profit orgn. mgmt. Drucker Found., 1992. Designer, Arkitekt, Hakon Ahlberg, SAR, Arkitekt, Stockholm, 1960, designer, Washburn, Luther & Rowley, Architects, Attleboro, Mass., 1961-62, Barker & Turoff, Architects, Providence, 1962-63, jr. partner, Turoff Assocs., Architects, 1964-67, partner, Turoff & Sande, Architects, Providence, 1968-70, prin., Ted Sande, Architect, Cranston, R.I., 1970, Cleve., 1993—; author: Industrial Archaeology: A New Look at the American Heritage, 2d edit, 1978; contbg. author: Guidebook to Philadelphia Architecture, 1974; editor: New England Textile Mill Survey, 1971; co-editor: Historic Preservation of Engineering Works, 1981; contbr. articles to profl. jours.; two-man show drawings, Providence Art Club, 1970. Dir. profl. svcs. office hist. properties Nat. Trust Hist. Preservation, Washington, 1975-77, dir. planning and devel., 1977-78, acting v.p. office hist. properties, 1978-79, v.p., 1979-80; mem. Old Georgetown Bd. Nat. Commn. Fine Arts, 1979-81; exec. dir. Western Res. Hist. Soc., Cleve., 1981-93, exec. dir. emeritus, 1993—; cons. architecture Mus. and Hist. Soc. Mgmt., Historic Preservation and Archtl. Hist., 1993—; co-chmn. Conf. Indsl. Archeology, Smithsonian Instn., 1971; active Shaker Heights Landmark Commn., 1982-84, Cleve. Landmarks Commn., 1985—, Archtl. Bd. of Review, Village of Hunting Valley, Ohio, 2000—, Leadership Cleve. Class 86/87, Ohio Gov.'s Commn. on the Bicentennials the NW Ordinance and U.S. Const., 1986-89, Cleve. Bicentennial Commn., 1992-94; trustee Univ. Circl Inc., 1981-93, Lakeview Cemetery Found., 1985—, Nat. Rock and Roll Mus. and Hall Fame, mem. exec. bldg. com., 1993-95, instnl. rep. Cleve. Arts Consortium, 1987-93; pres. Cleve. Restoration Soc., 1994-97; mem. historic properties and collections com. Stan Hywet Hall and Gardens, Akron, Ohio, 1996—; trustee Stan Hywet Hall & Gardens, 1997—; cjaor Schweinfurth Trust, 1999—. Mem.: SAR, AIA (com. hist. resources 1972—74), Ohio Mus. Assn. (trustee 1982—87), Am. Assn. Mus., Internat. Com. for Conservation of Indsl. Heritage (chmn. bd. dirs. 1978—81), Soc. Archtl. Historians (preservation com. 1972—74), Soc. Indsl. Archeology (co-founder, 1st pres. 1971—72, dir. 1973—76, project supr. handbook on adaptive use of indsl. bldgs., gen. chmn. 15th ann. conf.), Philos. Club Cleve. (past pres.), Rowfant Club (coun. of fellows, pres. 2002—). Episcopalian. Home: 13415 Shaker Blvd Cleveland OH 44120-1586

SANDEFER, G(EORGE) LARRY, lawyer; b. Washington, Mar. 2, 1950; s. George Hall and Mary Gray (Babers) S. BS, Auburn U., 1972; JD, U. Fla., 1978. Bar: Fla. 1978, U.S. Dist. Ct. (mid. dist.) Fla. 1978, U.S. Ct. Appeals (5th and 11th cirs.) 1981, U.S. Supreme Ct. 1982; cert. in criminal trial law Fla. Bar. Asst. state atty., criminal divsn., lead trial atty. State of Fla., Clearwater, 1977-86; sole practice, 1986-88; assoc. Kimpton, Burke and White, P.A., 1988-90; pvt. practice, 1991—. Mem. Indian Rocks Civic Assn., 1994-2000, Leadership Pinellas; city commr. Indian Rocks Beach, 1994-00. 1st lt. USAF, 1973-75. Mem. ATLA, Pinellas County Trial Lawyers Assn., Fla. Assn. Criminal Def. Attys., Colo. Bar Assn., Fla. Bar Assn., Clearwater Bar Assn., St. Petersburg Bar Assn., Kiwanis. Avocations: tennis, skiing, boating. Address: 111 N Belcher Rd Ste 202 Clearwater FL 33765-3259

SANDEFUR, JAMES TANDY, mathematics educator; b. Madison, Ind., Apr. 25, 1947; s. James Tandy and Evelyn (Gayle) S.; m. Mary Elizabeth Epes, Sept. 6, 1969 (div. 1982); m. Helen Moriarty, Apr. 14, 1984; 1 child, Scott David. BA, Vanderbilt U., 1969; MA, U. Denver, 1971; PhD, Tulane U., 1974. Prof. math. Georgetown U., Washington, 1974—, chair honor coun.; faculty chair Georgetown Honor Coun., 2000—. Vis. assoc. prof. Ctr. for Applied Math., Cornell U., Ithaca, N.Y., 1981-82; vis. prof. U. Iowa, Iowa City, 1988-89; math. cons. It's Academic TV show, Altman Prodns., Washington, 1985—; prin. investigator, dir. math. modelling workshop NSF, Washington, 1988-91; visitor Freudenthal Inst., Utrecht, The Netherlands, 1996; writing team Principles and Stds. for Sch. Math., 2000; mem. adv. bd. Exploratorium's Math Explorer Project; cons. Cerebellum Corp. Author: Discrete Dynamical Systems: Theory and Applications, 1990, Discrete Dynamical Modeling, 1993; adv. bd. to Annenberg/CPB math. and sci. project's Guide to Math and Science Reform; contbr. articles to math. jours. Program dir. in Instrl. Materials Devel. for Div. of Materials, Devel., Rsch. and Informal Sci. Edn.; directorate for Edn. and Human Resources NSF. NSF grantee, prin. investigator Tchr. Leadership Inst., 1993—. Mem.: Nat. Coun. Teachers Math. (adv. panel Yearbook Discrete Math., mem. writing team for standards 2000, ed. panel Math. Teacher), Nat. Faculty, Math. Assn. Am. (former chmn. minicourse com.), Am. Contract Bridge League (chap. bd. dir. 1983-85) (life). Democrat. Avocations: bridge, tennis, skiing. Office: Georgetown U Dept Math Washington DC 20057-0001

SANDEL, RANDYE NOREEN, artist; b. L.A., June 2, 1942; d. Alexander and Sara Lisa (Cohen) Newman. BA in Latin, UCLA, 1965, MFA in Painting and Print Making, 1969. Art instr. L.A. Valley Coll., Van Nuys, 1970-87, L.A. Harbor Coll., Wilmington, 1969-82. One-woman shows include Stanislaus State Coll., Turlock, Calif., 1971, L.A. Mcpl. Art Gallery, 1979, Calif. State Art Gallery, Northridge, 1988, Sherry Frumkin Gallery, Santa Monica, Calif., 1990, 1992, 1994, 1996, 1998, 2001, Riverside (Calif.) Art Mus., 1989, Stella Polaris Gallery, Beverly Hills, Calif., 1985, Space Gallery, L.A., 1977, 1983, others, exhibited in group shows at Orange County Contemporary Arts, 2001, Occidental Coll., L.A., 1996, Danville Fine Arts Ctr., Calif., 1996, Irvine (Calif.) Med. Ctr., 1991, Mt. Saint Mary's Coll., Brentwood, Calif., 1989, L.A. Inst. Contemporary Art, 1976—78, Laguna Beach (Calif.) Art Mus., 1975, Market St. Project, 1973, others, Represented in permanent collections BankAmerica: Corporate Art Collection, Devon Industries, River Forest (Ill.) State Bank. Home: 12240 Hartsook St Valley Village CA 91607

SANDELANDS, ERIC ALAN, publisher, educator, editor; b. Workington, Cumbria, Eng., June 27, 1963; s. Alan and Elizabeth Russel (Wilson) S.; m. Claire Huntley, Aug. 20, 1988; children: Luke, Chloe. DPhil, Internat. Mgmt. Ctrs.; MBA, U. Teesside, Eng., 1993; postgrad., Internat. Mgmt. Ctr., Buckingham, Eng., 1993-98. Ops. mgr. TSC, Middlesbrough, Eng., 1985-92; editor-in-chief MCB Univ. Press, Bradford, Eng., 1992-94, dir. pub. Eng., 1994-95; COO Anbar Electronic Intelligence, 1995, CEO, 1995-96, sr. advisor, 1996-99; prin. Eric Sandelands Assocs., Middlesbrough, 1996-98. Cons. Info. for Success, Bedford, Eng., 1996-98; proprietor Virtual Univ. Jour., 1996-98; dean Canadian Sch. Mgmt., 1999—, Americas Internat. Mgmt. Ctrs., 1999—. Editor Mgmt. Express, 1996-98; editor-in-chief Strategic Direction, 1992-95, Anbar Mgmt. Intelligence (info. database), 1992-95. David Sutton fellow Internat. Mgmt. Ctr., 1996, Internat. Bus. fellow U. Surrey/IMC, 1994. Mem. Inst. of Mgmt. Avocations: hiking, cinema, literature, playing squash. Home: RR # 1 553291 Grey Rd 23 Priceville Ontario ON Canada N0C 1K0 Office: Canadian Sch Mgmt Ste 1120 335 Bay St Toronto ON Canada M5H 2R3 E-mail: esandelands@c.s.m.org.

SANDENAW, THOMAS ARTHUR, JR. lawyer; b. Harlowton, Mont., Mar. 17, 1936; s. Thomas A. Sr. S.; m. Colleen A. Andrews, June 3, 1956 (div. May 1981); children: Cheryl Lea, Kevin K., Dana Scott; m. Deborah Rose Hammel, Sept. 26, 1981. BS, Mont. State U., 1958; JD, U. N.Mex., 1967. Bar: N.Mex. 1967, U.S. Dist. Ct. N.Mex. 1968, U.S. Ct. Appeals (10th cir.) 1968. Atty. Wilkinson, Durrett & Conway, Alamogordo, N.Mex., 1968-69, Spence & Sandenaw, Alamogordo, 1969-71, Shipley, Durrett, Conway & Sandenaw, Alamogordo, 1971-77; judge 12th jud. dist. Lincoln and Otero Counties, 1978-79; atty. Overstreet & Sandenaw, 1979-82; ptnr. Weinbrenner, Richards, Paulowsky, Sandenaw & Ramirez, Las Cruces, 1982-92; pvt. practice, 1992—. Dir. St. Lukes Health Care, Las Cruces, 1992—, Mesilla Valley Hospice, Las Cruces, 1992-95. Mem. Am. Bd. Trial Advocates, Am. Bd. Profl. Liability Attys. (diplomat 1993—), Nat. Bd. Trial Advocacy (cert. civil trial practice 1989), State Bar N.Mex. (chmn. pub. rels. com. 1967-68, bd. mem. family law sect. 1983-86, chmn. trial practice sect. 1987-88, bd. dirs. 1990-94), N.Mex. Def. Lawyers Assn. (sec. 1984-85, v.p. 1985-86, pres. 1987-88, bd. dirs. 1983—, chmn. Amicus Curie com. 1991-96), N.Mex. Bench and Bar Com., Dona Ana County Bar Assn., Assn. Def. Trial Attorneys (exec. coun. 1996-99), Rotary (past pres. Rio Grande chpt.), Am. Inn of Courts. Republican. Lutheran. Avocations: skiing, sailing, woodworking. Office: Sandenaw Carrillo & Piazza PC 2951 N Roadrunner Pkwy # A Las Cruces NM 88011-0814 E-mail: lgltas@zianet.com.

SANDER, DONALD HENRY, soil scientist, researcher; b. Creston, Nebr., Apr. 21, 1933; s. Paul L. and Mable O. (Wendt) S.; m. Harriet Ora Palmateer, Dec. 27, 1953; children: Ben, Joan. BS, U. Nebr., 1954, MS in Agronomy, 1958, PhD in Agronomy, 1967. Soil scientist, researcher USDA Forest Svc., Lincoln, Nebr., 1958-64; asst. prof. agronomy, soil fertility specialist Kans. State U., Manhattan, 1964-67; prof. agronomy U. Nebr., Lincoln, 1967-98; ret., 1998. Contbr. numerous rsch. articles to jours. including Soil Sci. Soc. Am. Jour. 1st lt. U.S. Army, 1954-56, Korea. Recipient Agronomic Achievement award, 1985, USDA Superior Svc. award, 1987, Soil Sci. Applied Rsch. award, 1989, Great Plains Leadership award, Denver, 1990. Fellow Am. Soc. Agronomy, Soil Sci. Soc. Am.; mem. Gama Sigma Delta, Sigma Xi. Republican. Presbyterian. Avocation: woodworking. Home: 6548 Darlington Ct Lincoln NE 68510-2362 Office: Univ Nebr Dept Agronomy Lincoln NE 68583

SANDER, DOROTHY E. manufacturing executive; V.p. adminstrn. and benefits Hanson Industries, 1984-95; assoc. dir. Hanson PLC, 1993-95; v.p. adminstrn. U.S. Industries, Inc., Iselin, NJ, 1995—98, sr. v.p. adminstrn., 1998—, West Palm Beach, Fla., 2000—. Mem. adv. bd. Bank of N.Y. Bd. editors HR-Law and Practice mag., Feminist Press. Office: US Industries Inc 777 S Flagler Dr Ste 1112 West Palm Beach FL 33401

SANDER, FRANK ERNEST ARNOLD, law educator; b. Stuttgart, Germany, July 22, 1927; came to U.S., 1940, naturalized, 1946; s. Rudolf and Alice (Epstein) S.; m. Emily Bishop Jones, Apr. 26, 1958; children: Alison Bishop, Thomas Harvey, Ernest Ridgway Sander. AB in Math. magna cum laude, Harvard U., 1949, LLB magna cum laude, 1952. Bar: Mass. 1952, U.S. Supreme Ct 1952. Law clk. to Chief Judge Magruder U.S. Ct. Appeals, 1st Cir., 1952-53; law clk. to Justice Frankfurter, U.S. Supreme Ct., 1953-54; atty. tax divsn. Dept. Justice, 1954-56; with firm Hill & Barlow, Boston, 1956-59; mem. faculty Harvard Law Sch., 1959—, prof. law, 1962—, Bussey prof., 1981—, assoc. dean, 1987-2000. Spl. fields fed. taxation, family law, welfare law, dispute resolution; chmn. Coun. on Role of Cts.; mem. panels Am. Arbitration Assn., Fed. Mediation and Conciliation Svc.; chmn. Coun. on Legal Edn. Opportunity, 1968—70; cons. Dept. Treasury, 1968; treas. Harvard Law Rev., 1951—52; vice chair dispute resolution standing com. Mass. Supreme Jud. Ct., 1994—; drafting com. Uniform Mediation Act, 1998—2001. Author: (with Westfall and McIntyre) Readings in Federal Taxation, 2d edit., 1983, (with Foote and Levy) Cases and Materials on Family Law, 3d edit., 1985, (with Gutman) Tax Aspects of Divorce and Separation, 4th edit., 1985, (with Goldberg and Rogers) Dispute Resolution, 3d edit., 1999. Mem. tax mission Internat. Program Taxation to Republic of Colombia, 1959; mem. com. on civil and polit. rights President's Commn. on Status of Women, 1962-63; trustee Buckingham Browne and Nichols Sch., 1969-75; chmn. Mass. Welfare Adv. Bd., 1975-79. With AUS, 1945-46. Recipient Whitney North Seymour medal Am. Arbitration Assn., 1988, spl. award for disting. svc. to dispute resolution Ctr. for Pub. Resources Inst. for Dispute Resolution, 1990. Mem. ABA (chmn. standing com. dispute resolution 1986-89, Kutak medal 1993, D'Alemberte-Raven award 1999), Boston Bar Assn., Phi Beta Kappa. Home: 74 Buckingham St Cambridge MA 02138-2229 Office: Harvard U Sch of Law Cambridge MA 02138

SANDER, SUSAN BERRY, environmental planning engineering corporation executive; b. Walla Walla, Wash., Aug. 26, 1953; d. Alan Robert and Elizabeth Ann (Davenport) Berry. BS in Biology with honors, Western Wash. U., 1975; MBA with honors, U. Puget Sound, 1984. Biologist, graphic artist Shapiro & Assocs., Inc., Seattle, 1975-77, office mgr., 1977-79, v.p., 1979-84, pres., owner, 1984—; also bd. dirs. Shapiro & Assocs., Inc., NHS Scholarship Found. Adv. bd. mem. A-Pro, Inc.; bd. dirs. Index, Inc. Co-pres. Tyree Middle Sch. PTSA. Named Employer of Yr., Soc. Mktg. Profl. Svcs., 1988, Small Bus. of Yr., City of Seattle, Environ. Cons. of Yr., King County; recipient Identity award, PEMA Corp., 1996, Mktg. award, Soc. Mktg. Svc. Profls., 2000, 2001, merit scholar, Overlake Svc. League, Bellevue, Wash., 1971, scholar, Wester Wash. U. Bellingham, 1974—75, U. Puget Sound, 1984. Mem.: WTS, Am. Coun. Engring. Cos., Student Conservation Assn. (bd. dirs.), Portland C. of C., Seattle C. of C. Avocation: swimming, hiking, travel, painting. Office: 101 Yesler Way Ste 400 Seattle WA 98104-3425 E-mail: ssander@shap.com.

SANDER, THERESA MARIE, nurse practitioner; b. Renovo, Pa., Jan. 12, 1952; d. Francis Michael and Anita Marie (Perri) Pompili; m. Steven John Sander, Oct. 28, 1978; children: Christina Michele, Jonathan Francis, Andrea Lynn. Diploma, Williamsport Hosp Sch. Nursing, 1974; AD in Gen. Studies, Pa. Coll. Tech., Williamsport, 1991; BSN cum laude, Coll. Misericordia, Dallas, Pa., 1993, MSN, 1996. RN, Pa.; cert. family nurse practitioner. Staff med. surg. nurse Williamsport Hosp., 1974-84; vis. nurse Vis. Nurse Assn., Williamsport, 1984-86; emergency rm. nurse Divine Providence Hosp., 1986-89; ICU nurse Muncy (Pa.) Valley Hosp., 1989-90; nurse Stat Nurse, Inc., Montoursville, Pa., 1990-96; nurse practitioner Susquehanna Health Sys., Williamsport, 1996-99; pvt. practice, 1999—. Office nurse, Williamsport, 1987-89; clin. instr. Pa. Coll. Tech., Williamsport, 1994-96. Contbr. articles to profl. jours. Mem. Am. Acad. Nurse Practitioners (cert.). Avocations: biking, swimming, traveling, Italian cuisine. Home: 208 Ridge Rd Cogan Station PA 17728-9734 E-mail: treefnp@pcspower.net.

SANDERCOX, ROBERT ALLEN, college official, clergyman; b. Akron, Ohio, May 20, 1932; s. Monroe J. and Elverda (Arnold) S.; m. Nancy Lee Wertz, Sept. 13, 1958; children— Alison Grace, Megan Louise, Robert Philip BA, Bethany Coll., W. Va., 1954; M.Div., Yale U., 1957; postgrad., U. Buffalo, W.Va. U.; LittD, Bethany Coll., 1989. Ordained to ministry Christian Ch. (Disciples of Christ). Asst. minister Park Ave Christian Ch., N.Y.C., 1954-57; asst. provost Bethany Coll., 1957-60, v.p., dean students, 1960-75, v.p., dir. devel., 1975-79, interim pres., 1979-80, v.p., provost for coll. advancement, 1980-89, sr. v.p., 1989-95, cons. to the pres., 1995-97, sr. v.p. emeritus, 1997—. Trustee Christian Ch. Disciples of Christ in W.Va., Parkersburg, 1984-88; chmn. Brooke County Landmarks Commn., 1988-98, Brooke County Mus. Bd., 1995-98. Recipient Alumni Disting. Service award Bethany Coll., 1982 Mem. Coun. for Advancement and Support Edn., Duquesne Club (Pitts.), Order of Symposiarch, Rotary, Kiwanis (pres. 1967), Alpha Sigma Phi (nat. treas. 1982-84, v.p. 1984-86, grad. sr. pres. 1986-88, bd. dirs., trustee Ednl. Found. 1982-95, chmn. Ednl. Found. 1994-95, Delta Beta Xi svc. award 1960). Republican. Home: 4557 Middleton Park Cir E Jacksonville FL 32224-6609 Address: 715 Buckwood Ln Lititz PA 17543 E-mail: r.sandercox@prodigy.net.

SANDERLIN, TERRY KEITH, counselor; b. Ashland, Oreg., Aug. 5, 1950; s. Calvin Carney and Myrtle Estell (Cope) S.; m. Theresa Emma Garcia, Jan. 19, 1969 (div. Feb. 1976); 1 child, Sean Eric; m. Margaret Lillian Lutz, Dec. 26, 1987. B in Bus., U. N.Mex., 1982, M in Counseling, 1983, EdD, 1993. Diplomate Am. Psychotherapy Assn.; lic. clin. mental health, N.Mex., sch. counselor, N.Mex.; cert. hypnotherapist Internat. Assn. Counselors and Therapists; pvt. pilots lic.; glider lic.; keelboat cert. Unit supr. Bernalillo County Juvenile Detention Ctr., Albuquerque, 1978-80; counselor Independence Halfway House, 1980-81; mental health worker Bernalillo County Mental Health Ctr., 1981-82; probation parole officer N.Mex. Probation/Parole, 1982-87, dist. supr. Gallup, 1987-88; vocat. counselor Internat. Rehab. Assn., Albuquerque, 1989-91; counseling psychologist VA, 1991-98; owner, dir. Counseling and Tng. Specialist, 1988—. Counselor Albuquerque (N.Mex.) Counseling Specialist, 1983-86; guest lectr. sociology dept. U. N.Mex., Albuquerque, 1992; presenter 5th Annual S.W. Substance Abuse Conf., Albuquerque, 1992; presenter N.Mex. Corrections Dept., Santa Fe, 1993. Author: (video tapes) Breathing Free & Good, 1991, Understanding Adolescent Satanism, 1991, (manual) Social Skills and Anger Management, 1993, Anger Management Intervention with Offender Populations, 1998, The Impulsivity Factor in Offender Behavior, 1999; contbr. articles to profl. jours. Vol. counselor Adult Misdemeanor Probation, Albuquerque, 1974-76; panel mem. Cmty. Corrections Selection Panel, Albuquerque, 1987-90. With U.S. Army, 1969-72, Vietnam. Recipient Outstanding Citizenship, Albuquerque Police Dept., 1974; N.Mex. Dept. Pub. Safety rsch. grantee, 1995. Mem.: Am. Psychotherapy Assn., Am. Counseling Assn. Democrat. Avocations: scuba diving, martial arts, canoeing, flying, sailing. Office: Counseling & Tng Specialist 127 Bryn Mawr Dr SE Ste E Albuquerque NM 87106-2209 E-mail: TSanderlin@juno.com.

SANDERS, AARON PERRY, radiation biophysics educator; b. Phoenix, Jan. 12, 1924; s. DeWitt and Ruth (Perry) S.; m. Betty Mae Gelein, Aug. 11, 1944 (div.); children: Merle Sanders Ireland, Julie Sanders Carpenter, James DeWitt; m. Georgia Anne Bullock, Nov. 26, 1972 (div.); 1 child, Kai Marie; m. Vallie E. Flint. BS, U. Tex., El Paso, 1950; MS (AEC fellow), U. Rochester, 1952; PhD, U. N.C., 1964. Diplomate: Am. Bd. Health Physics. Baggage clk., ticket agt. Greyhound Bus Lines, Phoenix, 1942, dispatcher, ticket agt. El Paso, Tex., 1946-50; asso. health physicist Brookhaven Nat. Lab., Upton, N.Y., 1951-53; instr. physics, radiol. safety officer N.C. State Coll., 1953; instr. radiology Duke Med. Center, Durham, N.C., 1953-56, dir. radiosotope lab., 1953-65; asso. in radiology Duke Med. Ctr., 1956-57, asst. prof., 1957-64, assoc. prof., 1964-65, assoc. prof., dir. div. radiobiology, 1965-70, prof., dir. div. radiobiology, 1970-83, prof. emeritus, 1983—; chmn. Biomed. Physics Dept. King Faisal Specialist Hosp., Riyadh, Saudi Arabia, 1984-86. Fulbright sr. lectr. radiol. physics, Argentina, 1958-59; cons. N.C. Bd. Health, 1961-76; mem. N.C. Radiation Protection Commn., 1976-83, chmn., 1978-79 Contbr. articles to profl. jours. Served with USNR, 1942-45. Mem. AAAS, Am. Assn. Physicists in Medicine, AAUP, Soc. Exptl. Biology and Medicine, Health Physics Soc., Soc. Nuclear Medicine, Biophys. Soc., Radiation Research Soc., Undersea Med Soc., Sigma Xi, Sigma Pi Sigma. Home and Office: 6945 E Main St Apt 3159 Mesa AZ 85207-8220 *Each individual has an obligation to himself and society to pursue an education to his maximum capability. This capability should then be used in his career in an effort to contribute to society as much, or more, than he receives. In work and personal relations you must never deny a man the dignity of his work by ridicule or denigration, and you must never use people.*

SANDERS, ADELLE (CATHERINE SANDERS), social worker, educator; b. Huntsville, Ala., Dec. 22, 1946; d. Willie Marion and Harriet Catherine (Worley) S.; 1 child, Eric Daniel Jones. Student, Monterey Peninsula Coll., 1973-75; BS in Human Devel., U. Calif., Davis, 1977; MSW, Calif. State U., Sacramento, 1980; postgrad., U. So. Calif., 1992—. Social svcs. planner Placer County Human Rels. Commn., Auburn, Calif., 1980-81; Indian desk coord. Calif. Office Econ. Opportunity, Sacramento, 1981-82; cons. Robinson Rancheria, Clear Lake, Calif., 1980-87; community devel. coord. Sacramento Housing and Redevel. Agy., 1984-88; cons. Grey Eagle & Assocs., West Sacramento, Calif., 1989-90, Sacramento Regional Purchasing Coun., 1990-91, Solano-Napa Agy. on Aging, Vallejo, Calif., 1992; cons., owner Sanders & Assocs., Sacramento, 1980—; prof. social work Calif. State U., 1986—. Commr., vice chair Sacramento Human Rights/Fair Housing Commn., 1991—; commr. Sacramento History and Sci. Commn., 1992—; mem. Sacramento Cultural Competency and Sensitivity Task Force, 1992—, Sacramento Human Svcs. Cabinet, 1992—. Recipient Doctoral Incentive award Calif. State U., 1990. Home: 2345 Mossy Bank Dr Apt 1 Sacramento CA 95833-2387 Office: Calif State U Dept Social Work 6000 J St Dept Social Sacramento CA 95819

SANDERS, ADRIAN LIONEL, educational consultant; b. Paragould, Ark., Aug. 3, 1938; s. Herbert Charles and Florence Theresa (Becherer) S.; m. Molly Jean Zecher, Dec. 20, 1961. AA, Bakersfield Coll., 1959; BA, San Francisco State U., 1961; MA, San Jose State U., 1967. 7th grade tchr. Sharp Park Sch., Pacifica, Calif., 1961-62; 5th grade tchr. Mowry Sch., Fremont, 1962-64; sci. tchr. Blacow Sch., 1964-76; 5th grade tchr. Warm Springs Sch., 1977-87, 5th grade gifted and talented edn. tchr., 1987-94; edn. cons., 1994—. Mem. San Diego Hist. Soc., 1999, Nat. Geog. Soc., Washington, 1976—, Alzheimer's Family Relief Program, Rockville, Md., 1986; vol. 7 km. Race for Alzheimer's Disease Willow Glen Founders Day, San Jose, 1988-92. Named Outstanding Young Educator, Jr. C. of C., Fremont, Calif., 1965. Mem. Zoolog. Soc. San Diego, Calif. Ctr. for the Arts (Escondido). Avocations: photography, traveling, visiting presidents' birthplaces, collecting license plates, collecting matchbooks worldwide. Home and Office: 1437 Stoneridge Cir Escondido CA 92029-5514

SANDERS, ARTHUR, political scientist, educator; b. Ardmore, Okla., Nov. 15, 1955; s. Saul and Elinor Sanders; m. Deborah Pappenheimer, June 27, 1982; 1 child Benjamin Pappenheimer. AB, Franklin & Marshall U., 1978; PhD, Harvard U., 1982. Asst. prof. polit. sci. Hamilton Coll., Clinton, NY, 1982—90, Drake U., Des Moines, 1990—93, assoc. prof. polit. sci., 1993—2002, prof., 2002—. Author: Making Sense of Politics, 1990, Victory, 1992, Prime Time Politics, 2002. Jewish. Avocations: gourmet cooking, pickup basketball. Home: 3802 Forest Ave Des Moines IA 50311 Office: Drake U Dept Politics Des Moines IA 50311

SANDERS, BERNARD (BERNIE SANDERS), congressman; b. Sept. 8, 1941; s. Eli and Dorothy (Glassberg) S.; m. Jane O'Meara, 1988; children: Levi, Heather, Carina, David. BA, U. Chgo., 1964. Freelance writer, carpenter, youth counselor, 1964-76; with Govt. Vt., 1965-66; dir. Am. People's Hist. Soc., Burlington, Vt., 1976-81; mayor of Burlington, 1981-89; mem. U.S. Congress from Vt., 1991—. Mem. progressive caucus, mem. com. fin. svcs., com. on govt. reform. Author filmstrips and articles on social, hist. and polit. subjects. Chmn. Vt. Liberty Union Party, 1975-76, candidate for gov., 1972, 76, 86, U.S. Senate, 1971, 74. Jewish. Office: US Ho of Reps 2135 Rayburn Ho Office Bldg Washington DC 20515-0001*

SANDERS, BOBBY LEE, lawyer; b. Ben Wheeler, Tex., Jan. 12, 1935; s. Levi Franklin and Veta Lee (Bigony) S.; m. Elsie Jean Beard, May 29, 1954; children: Samuel Franklin, Cynthia Lee. BS, East Tex. State U., 1956; MS, Fla. State U., 1958, PhD, 1962; JD, So. Methodist U., 1977. Bar: Tex. 1976. From asst. prof. to prof. Tex. Christian U., Ft. Worth, 1962-77; ptnr. Sanders & Sanders, Canton, Tex., 1977-86; pvt. practice, 1977—. Bd. dirs. Mental Health/Mental Retardation Regional Ctr. East Tex., Tyler, 1978-94; mem. Van Zandt County Libr. Adv. Bd., Canton, 1987-91; pres. Van Zandt County Assn. Retarded Citizens, Canton, 1979-81. Mem. Tex. State Bar Assn., Van Zandt County Bar Assn. (pres. 1987-89). Democrat. Methodist. Avocations: golf, computers. Home and Office: PO Box 416 Canton TX 75103-0416 E-mail: ssanders@vzinet.com.

SANDERS, CHARLES F. dean; DDS Dental-Orthodontics, Howard U., 1968. Dentist. Office: 600 W St NW Washington DC 20059*

SANDERS, CHARLES FRANKLIN, management and engineering consultant; b. Louisville, Dec. 22, 1931; s. Charles Franklin and Maragret Rhea (Timmons) S.; m. Marie Audrey Galuppo, Dec. 29, 1956; children: Karen Lynn, Craig Joseph, Keith Franklin. B.Chem. Engring., U. Louisville, 1954, M.Chem. Engring., 1958; PhD, U. So. Calif., 1970. Research engr. Exxon Research and Engring. Co., Linden, N.J., 1955-62; asst. prof. engring. Calif. State U., Northridge, 1962-68, assoc. prof., 1968-71, prof., 1971-82, chmn. dept., 1969-72, dean Sch. Engring. and Computer Sci., 1972-81; pres., chief exec. officer, dir. Rusco Industries, Los Angeles, 1981-82; exec. v.p. Energy Systems Assocs., Tustin, Calif, 1982-89, Energeo, San Francisco, 1989-95, also bd. dirs.; v.p. tech. Smith-Bellingham Capital, 1989-91. Bd. dirs. Clean-Air Tech., Inc., L.A., 1997-99, Applied Tech. Solutions, Inc., Costa Mesa, 1999-2002. Bd. dirs. San Fernando Valley Child Guidance Clinic, 1979-81. Served to 1st lt. U.S. Army, 1956-57. NSF fellow, 1965-67 Mem. AIChE, NSPE, Calif. Soc. Profl. Engrs., Am. Soc. for Engring. Edn. Republican. E-mail: cfs@cox.net.

SANDERS, DALE R. lawyer; b. N.Y.C., Feb. 1, 1946; m. Jo-Ann Sanders, Dec. 25, 1967; 1 child. Bar: Fla. 1970, Wyo. 1991, U.S. Dist. Ct. (so. dist.) Fla. 1971, U.S. Tax Ct. 1972. Atty. Kirsch & Druck, P.A., Ft. Lauderdale, Fla., 1970-71, Kirsch, Digiulian, Druck et al, Ft. Lauderdale, 1971-72, Digiulian, Spellacy, Lyons, Ft. Lauderdale, 1972-77, Lyons & Sanders, Chartered, Ft. Lauderdale, 1977—. With USAR, 1969-75. Mem.: Broward City Trial Lawyers, Broward City Bar (pres. 1990), Fla. Bar Assn. (bd. govs. 1991—95, mem. 17th cir. jud. nominating commn. 1992—96, mem. State of Fla. jud. qualifications commn., vice chair 1996—). Office: Lyons and Sanders Chartered 600 NE 3rd Ave Fort Lauderdale FL 33304-2618

SANDERS, DAVID, university press administrator; BFA in Creative Writing, Bowling Green State U., 1977; MFA, U. Ark., 1983, postgrad., 1986-88. Owner, propr. Hays & Sanders Bookshop, Fayetteville, Ark., 1983-86; vis. asst. prof. dept. English U. Ark., 1984-88; asst. dir. U. Ark. Press, 1988-89, assoc. dir., 1989-90, assoc. dir., editor-in-chief, 1991-92; dir. Purdue U. Press, West Lafayette, Ind., 1992-95, Ohio U. Press/Swallow Press, Athens, 1996—. Author: Time in Transit, 1995, Nearer to Town, 1998; contbr. translations: Poetry Miscellany; Sparrow. Literature of the Western World, Vol. One, 1988; contbr. poetry to New Orleans Rev., Poetry East, Christian Sci. Monitor, S.I. Rev., Mankato Rev., Kans. Quar., Stand Mag., Yarrow, Caesura, Epigrammatist, Zone 3, Hiram Poetry Rev., others. Recipient Christopher McKean award for poetry, 1982, Kenneth Patchen Poetry award, 1982, Dudley Fitts Translation award, 1986, 87, Lily Peter Found. award, 1987. Office: Ohio Univ Press Scott Quadrangle Athens OH 45701

SANDERS, DAVID H. civil engineering educator; BS with honor and distinction, Iowa State U., 1984; MS, U. Tex., Austin, 1986, PhD, 1990. Asst. structural engr. Chgo. Bridge & Iron, Oak Brook, Ill., 1982; rsch. asst. Ferguson Structural Engring. Lab., Austin, Tex., 1984-89; asst. prof. dept. civil engring. U. Nev., Reno, 1990-96, assoc. prof., 1996—. Vis. prof. Nat. Ctr. for Earthquake Engring. Rsch., Buffalo, 1996. Contbr. articles to profl. jours.; author reports and conf. procs.; presenter in field. Soccer coach High Sierra Soccer, Reno, 1997-99; baseball coach Reno Continental, 1998, 99, 2002; vol. Jr. Ski Program, Reno, 1997—; scoutmaster Boy Scouts Am., Austin, 1986-89. Named Iowa State U. Outstanding Young Alumnus, 2000. Fellow Am. Concrete Inst. (chair earthquake resistant concrete bridge com. 1998—); mem. ASCE (treas. 1993-94, v.p. 1995-96, pres. 1996-97), Transp. Rsch. Bd., Earthquake Engring. Rsch. Inst. Avocations: skiing, golf, camping, hiking. Office: U Nev Reno Dept Civil Engring 258 Reno NV 89557-0001 E-mail: sanders@unr.edu.

SANDERS, DEION LUWYNN, professional football player; b. Ft. Myers, Fla., Aug. 9, 1967; Student, Fla. State U. Baseball player N.Y. Yankees, 1988-90, Atlanta Braves, 1991-94, Cin. Reds, 1994, 97; football player Atlanta Falcons, 1989-94, San Francisco 49ers, 1994, Dallas Cowboys, 1995—. Named to Sporting News Coll. All-Am. football team, 1986-88, Sporting News NFL All-Pro Football Team, 1991, 92, 94, Pro Bowl team, 1991-94; recipient Jim Thorpe award, 1988. NFL kickoff return leader, 1992, Nat. League Triples Leader, 1992; mem. Championship team Super Bowl XXIX, 1994, Super Bowl XXX, 1995. Office: Dallas Cowboys 1 Cowboys Pkwy Irving TX 75063-4999

SANDERS, DOUGLAS WARNER, JR. lawyer, municipal judge; b. Oklahoma City, Jan. 13, 1958; s. Douglas Warner Sr. and Jane (Livermore) S.; m. Brenda Gail Cox, Apr. 20, 1990; children: Douglas Warner III, Noel Layne, Jonathan Scott, Stephanie Marie. BS, Okla. State U., 1980; JD, Oklahoma City U., 1983. Bar: Okla., U.S. Dist. Ct. (ea., no. and we. dists.) Okla., U.S. Dist. Ct. (we. dist.) Ark. Assoc. Stipe Law Firm, Oklahoma City, 1983-85; ptnr. Sanders, Sanders & Sullivan, Poteau, Okla., 1985—. Mcpl. judge City of Poteau, 1994—, City of Spiro, Okla., 1994—, Town of Shady Point, Okla., 1994—; mem. Okla. Bd. Bar Examiners, 2000—. Recipient Outstanding Alumnus award Oklahoma City U. Law Sch., 1999. Fellow ABA; mem. Okla. Bar Assn. (bd. govs. 1992-94, v.p. 1997, pres. 1999, Pres.'s award 1997, Disting. Svc. award 1999), LeFlore County Bar Assn. (Pres.'s award 1997). Democrat. Presbyterian. Avocation: golf. Home: 900 N Witte St Poteau OK 74953-3636 Office: Sanders Sanders & Sullivan 104 S Church St Poteau OK 74953-3344 E-mail: dougal@clnk.com.

SANDERS, EDWIN PERRY BARTLEY, judge; b. Madisonville, Ky., July 12, 1940; s. Virgil Perry and Eunice Jane (Denton) S.; m. Kathryn Walker, Jan. 28, 1967; children: Christopher Charles, Carroll Denton. BS in Bus., Stetson U., 1965, JD, 1968. Bar: Fla. 1968. Ptnr. Ford, Wren and Sanders, 1968-69; mem. Landis, Graham, French, Husfeld and Ford, PA, DeLand, Fla., 1970-83; prof. real estate Stetson U. Sch. Bus. Adminstrn., 1980-83; judge 7th Jud. Cir. Ct. Volusia County, DeLand, Fla., 1983—. With U.S. Army. Mem. Fla. Bar Assn., Volusia County Bar Assn., Lake Beresford Yacht Club, Rotary. Democrat. Episcopalian. Home: 340 Washington Oaks Dr Deland FL 32720-2760 Office: Volusia County Jail Bldg 130 W New York Ave Rm 104 Deland FL 32720-5416 also: PO Box 611 Deland FL 32721-0611

SANDERS, ELIZABETH ANNE WEAVER (BETSY SANDERS), management consultant; b. Gettysburg, Pa., July 25, 1945; Student, Gettysburg (Pa.) Coll., 1963-65; BA in German Lang. and Linguistics, Wayne State U., 1967; MEd, Boston U., 1970; postgrad., U. Wash., 1976-78. Prin. The Sanders Partnership, Sutter Creek, Calif., 1971-90; founder, dir. Nat. Bank So. Calif., 1971-90; v.p., gen. mgr. Nordstrom Inc.; prin. The Sanders Partnership, Sutter Creek, Calif. Bd. dirs. Wal Mart Stores, Inc., Washington Mut., Wellpoint Health Sys., Inc., Wolverine Worldwide, Inc., Advantica Restaurant Group, H.F. Ahmanson Co., Carl Karcher Enterprises, Sport Chalet, St. Joseph Health Sys. Trustee Gettysburg Coll. Recipient Woman of Achievement in Bus. award YWCA South Orange County, Director's Choice award, 1997; named Woman of Yr. Bus. and Industry YWCA North Orange County, Humanitarian of Yr. NCCJ, Author of Yr., 1996. Mem. Internat. Women's Forum. Office: The Sanders Partnership PO Box 14 Sutter Creek CA 95685-0014

SANDERS, FRANKLIN D. insurance and reinsurance consultant; b. Newton, Mass., Apr. 24, 1935; s. Franklin and Ethel Shriner (Dulaney) S.; m. Jane Gray Collier, June 18, 1960; children— Cynthia, Franklin D., Nancy, Carolyn AB, Amherst Coll., 1957; MBA, Harvard U., 1959. With 1st Boston Corp., N.Y.C., 1960-86, mng. dir., 1976-86; pres. Aegis Ins. Services Inc., Jersey City. Treas., bd. dirs. Assoc. Electric & Gas Ins. Services, Ltd., Hamilton, Bermuda, 1986-97. Chmn. Republican Exec. Com., Bernardsville, N.J., 1965-72, Bernardsville Zoning Bd. of Adjustment, 1966-99. Mem. Harvard Club (N.Y.C.). Episcopalian. Avocations: sailing, skiing, golf.

SANDERS, GARY GLENN, electronics engineer, consultant; b. Gettysburg, Pa., Dec. 21, 1944; s. James Glenn Sanders and Martha Maybelle (Fleming) Ehlert; m. Elizabeth Marie Rega, Sept. 9, 1977 (div. Sept. 1981). Cert. med. technologist, Chgo. Inst. Tech., 1970; AA, Mayfair Coll., 1972; BS in Electronic Engring., Cooks Inst., Jackson, Miss., 1982. Registered Internat. Med. Techs. Cons. engr. Electronics Design Services, Chgo., 1977-79; applications engr. Nationwide Electronics Systems, Streamwood, Ill., 1979-80; mng. engr. Electronics Design Ctr. Case Western Res. U., Cleve., 1980-82; sr. project mgr. Scott Fetzer Co., 1982-89; v.p. engring. Penberthy, Inc., 1990—. Comml. pilot; electronic transduction cons. Teltech Inc., Mpls., 1989—; mem. adv. bd. Electronics Search Group, Indpls., 1991—. Contbr. articles on electronics in medicine and biology to profl. confs. and publs.; patentee in biomed. electronics and indsl. instrumentation, inventor, 1985—. Served with U.S. Army, 1962-68, Vietnam. Decorated DFC, Bronze Star, Air medal, Purple Heart. Fellow Internat. Coll. Med. Technologists; mem. IEEE, AAAS, NRA, DAV, VFW, Instrument Soc. Am. (sr. mem.), Internat. Microelectronics and Packaging Soc., N.Y. Acad. Scis., Ohio Acad. Sci., Nat. Fire Protection Assn., Am. Legion, Am. Soc. Materials Internat., Boy Scouts Am. Alumni, Nat. Eagle Scout Assn. Republican. Avocations: marquetry, archery. Home: 3104 Prophetstown Rd Rock Falls IL 61071-2556 Office: Penberthy Inc 320 Locust St Prophetstown IL 61277-1147

SANDERS, GARY HILTON, physicist; b. N.Y.C., Aug. 27, 1946; s. Sidney Simon and rose (Kershner) S.; m. Marjorie Clark King, June 9, 1973; children: David Ethan, Laurie Kate. AB, Columbia U., 1967; PhD, MIT, 1971. Rsch. asst. MIT, Cambridge, 1967-71; rsch. assoc. Princeton U., 1971—78, asst. prof., 1971—78; mem. staff Los Alamos (N.Mex.) Nat. Lab., 1978-94; project mgr., dep. dir. laser interferometer gravitational wave obs. Calif. Inst. Tech., Pasadena, 1994—. Guest physicist DESY, Hamburg, Germany, 1968-71; guest scientist Brookhaven Nat. Lab., Upton, N.Y., 1971-75, 84-89; vis. scientist Fermi Nat. Accelerator Lab., Batavia, Ill., 1977-79. Contbr. articles to profl. jours. Chmn. N.Mex. Conservation Voters Alliance, 1983-90, Govs. Task Force on Water Resources, N.Mex., 1984-85; bd. dirs. N.Mex. Citizens for Clear Air and Water, 1979-94. Mem. Am. Phys. Soc. Democrat. Home: 572 Alta Vista Way Laguna Beach CA 92651-4039 Office: Calif Inst Tech Mail Code 18 34 Pasadena CA 91125-0001 E-mail: sanders@ligo.caltech.edu.

SANDERS, GEORGE BENTON, surgeon; b. Kingston, Jamaica, Dec. 28, 1910; s. George Crittenden and Eleanora Jane (Georges) S.; m. Elizabeth Shwab, Apr. 30, 1960; children by previous marriage— Ann Sanders Houston, George Benton. AB, Cornell U., 1932, MD, 1935. Resident in surgery Barnes Hosp., St. Louis, 1935-39; research fellow in surgery U. Pa., Phila., 1939-42; practice medicine, specializing in surgery Louisville, 1946—. Mem. faculty U. Louisville, 1947— , asst. prof. surgery, 1948-58, clin. prof., 1958— ; pres. med. staff Norton Meml. Infirmary, 1954-55 Contbr. articles to profl. jours. Bd. dirs. Ky. div. Am. Cancer Soc., 1962— , pres., 1977, recipient Annual award, 1977. Served to lt. col. M.C. AUS, 1942-46, Middle East. Fellow A.C.S.; mem. Ky. Med. Assn. (Aesculapius award 1966), AMA, So. Surg. Assn., Central Surg. Assn., Southeastern Surg. Congress, So. Surgeons Club, Societe Internationale de Chirurgie, Societe Internationale de Chirurgia Gastroenterologica, Soc. Surgery Alimentary Tract, N.Y. Acad. Scis., Ky. Surg. Soc., Louisville Surg. Soc., Innominate Soc., Jefferson County Med. Soc. Clubs: River Valley, Louisville Country, Wynn-Stay; Hillsboro (Pompano Beach); So. Surgeons. Republican. Episcopalian. Research on gastrointestinal surgery, breast cancer surgery. Office: 558 Medical Towers S Louisville KY 40202-1966

SANDERS, GEORGIA ELIZABETH, secondary school educator; b. Holmwood, La., July 14, 1933; d. Frederick Rudolph and Susie W. (Hackett) S. Student, La. Coll., 1951-53, La. State U., 1959-60; BS, then MS in Microbiology, U. Southwestern La., 1970; MS in Math., U. So. Miss., 1983. Instr. dept. biology U. New Orleans, 1976-79, instr. dept. math., 1983-86; tchr. East Baton Rouge Parish Schs., 1988-89; tchr. math. St. Tammany Parish, La., 1990—. Mem. NEA, Am. Math. Soc., Math. Assn. Am., Nat. Coun. Tchrs. Math. Home: PO Box 968 Slidell LA 70459-0968 E-mail: gsan863722@aol.com.

SANDERS, GERALD HOLLIE, communications educator, educator; b. Mt. Vernon, Tex., Dec. 10, 1924; s. Elmer Hugh and Velma Mae (Hollowell) S.; m. Mary Dean Crew, July 18, 1947; children: Michael Dwaine, Rose Ann, Susan Kathleen, Randall Wayne. BA, Southeastern Okla. U., 1947; MA, Tex. Tech U., 1969; PhD, U. Minn., 1974. Program dir. Sta. WEWO, Laurenburg, N.C., 1947-49; sports dir. Sta. KFYO, Lubbock, Tex., 1949-50; gen. mgr. Sta. KLVT, Levelland, 1950-51, 53-54; sports dir. Sta. KCUL, Ft. Worth, 1954-55; asst. mgr. Sta. KDAV, Lubbock, 1955-57; mgr. Sta. KCBD, 1957-58; owner Sta. KSEL, 1958-67, Sta. KBUY, Amarillo, Tex., Sta. KERB, Kermit, Sta. KBEK, Elk City, Okla., Sta. KZZN, Littlefield, Tex.; lectr. communications The Coll. of Wooster, Ohio, 1967-68, asst. prof., 1968-75, assoc. prof., 1975-81, chmn. dept. communication, 1974-81, Miami U., Oxford, 1981-92, prof. emeritus comm., 1992—. Disting. lectr. Jinan U., Zhong Shan U., Fudan U., Nanjing U., Beijing U., China, 1989; cons. in field, Oxford, 1982—; polit. and trial cons., 1996—. Author: Introduction to Comtemporary Academic Debate, 1983; also articles. Active Political Campaigns. Served to col. USMC, 1943-46, PTO, 1951-53, Korea. Recipient Disting. Svc. award Delta Sigma Rho-Tau Kappa Alpha, 1991, Am. Forensic Assn., 1991. Mem. Am. Forensic Assn. (pres. 1978-82), Speech Communication Assn., Speech Communication Assn. of Ohio (pres. 1976-77), Disting. Svc. award 1978), Am. Inst. Parliamentarians, Soc. Trial Cons. Presbyterian. Avocations: sports, political campaigns. Home: 200 Country Club Dr Oxford OH 45056-9050 Office: Advocacy Unltd PO Box 457 Oxford OH 45056-0457 E-mail: gsanders@one.net.

SANDERS, HAROLD BAREFOOT, JR. federal judge; b. Dallas, Feb. 5, 1925; s. Harold Barefoot and May Elizabeth (Forrester) S.; m. Jan Scurlock, June 6, 1952; children— Janet Lea, Martha Kay, Mary Frances, Harold Barefoot III. BA, U. Tex., 1949, LLB, 1950. Bar: Tex. bar 1950. U.S. atty. No. Dist. Tex., 1961-65; asst. dep. atty. gen. U.S., 1965-66; asst. atty. gen., 1966-67; legis. counsel to President U.S., 1967-69; partner firm Clark, West, Keller, Sanders & Butler, Dallas, 1969-79; U.S. dist. judge for No. Dist. Tex., 1979—, chief judge, 1989-95. Mem. Tex. Ho. of Reps., 1952-58; Dem. nominee U.S. Senate, 1972. Lt. (j.g.) USNR, World War II. Mem. ABA (chmn. nat. conf. fed. trial judges 1988-89), Fed. Bar Assn. (Disting. Svc. award Dallas 1964), Dallas Bar Assn., State Bar Tex. (jud. conf. U.S. 1989-92, jud. panel on multidistrict litigation 1992-2000), Blue Key, Phi Delta Phi, Phi Delta Theta. Methodist. Office: US Courthouse 1100 Commerce St Ste 15 Dallas TX 75242-1016

SANDERS, IRWIN TAYLOR, sociology educator; b. Millersburg, Ky., Jan. 17, 1909; s. Robert Stuart and Lucy (Taylor) S.; m. Margaret Rydberg, June 23, 1934 (dec. Feb. 1997); children: Gerda S. (Groff), Robert Stuart (dec. Sept. 1998); m. Mary Ann Hawkes, Nov. 1, 1997. Student, Tenn. Mil. Inst., 1920-25; AB, Washington and Lee U., 1929; student, Theol. Sem., Princeton, 1932-33; PhD, Cornell U., 1938; D.Pedagogy (hon.), R.I. Coll., 1981; Litt.D. (hon.), Washington and Lee U., 1981. Instr. American Coll., Sofia, Bulgaria, 1929-32, dean, 1934-37; asst. prof. sociology Ala. Coll., 1938-40; successively asst. prof., asso. prof., prof., head dept. sociology, distinguished univ. prof. U. Ky., 1940-56; lectr. sociology Harvard Sch. Pub. Health, 1958-62; chmn. dept. sociology and anthropology Boston U., 1960-63, 69-72, prof. sociology, 1972-77, Univ. lectr., 1973-74, also co-dir. community sociology tng. program. Research dir. Assos. Internat. Research, Inc., Cambridge, Mass., 1956-60; asso. dir. Internat. Tng. and Research Program, Ford Found., 1962-66; v.p. Edn. and World Affairs, 1967-69; social science analyst Bur. Agrl. Econ., U.S. Dept. Agr., summer 1943; sr. social scientist Bur. Agrl. Econ., U.S. Dept. Agr. (Office Fgn. Agrl. Relations), 1943; social sci. Bur. Agrl. Econ., U.S. Dept. Agr. (Extension Service), summer 1944; agrl. attaché Am. Embassy, Belgrade, Yugoslavia, 1945-46; research assoc. Harvard, 1952-53; cons. rural welfare division FAO Author: Balkan Village, 1949, The Community, 1958, 3d rev. edit., 1975, Rainbow in the Rock, People of Rural Greece, 1962, Rural Society, 1977; co-author: Alabama Rural Communities, 1940, Sociological Foundations of Education, 1942, Kentucky: Designs for Her Future, 1944, Farmers of the World, 1945, Making Good Communities Better, 1950, Bridges to Understanding: International Programs at U.S. Colleges and Universities, 1970; Editor: Societies Around the World, 1953, Collectivization of Agriculture in Eastern Europe, 1958, The Professional School and World Affairs, 1968; series editor: Social Movements: Past and Present, 1980-95. Bd. dirs. Am. Farm Sch., Thessaloniki, Greece, Sofia Am. Schs., Inc., Assn. for Study Southeastern Europe, Bucharest, Rumania; mem. corp. bd. Mass. Half-Way Houses, Inc., 1988—. Decorated Royal Order of Phoenix Greece). Mem. Am. Sociol. Soc. (disting. cmty. sect. award 1983), Eastern Sociol. Soc., So. Sociol. Soc. (pres. 1955-56), Rural Sociol. Soc. (pres. 1956-57, Disting. Rural Sociologist 1993), New Eng. Sociological Assn. (Apple award 1993), Am. Assn. Advancement Slavic Studies, Bulgarian-Am. Studies Assn. (hon. pres.), Modern Greek Studies Assn. (council), Am. Assn. for S.E. European Studies (pres. 1980), Société European de Culture (Venice), Rumanian Studies Soc. (council), Bulgarian Acad. Scis. (fgn. mem.), Am. Assn. for Promotion Bulgarian Culture (hon. pres.), Cornell Club (N.Y.), Phi Beta Kappa, Omicron Delta Kappa, Kappa Phi Kappa, Delta Sigma Rho, Delta Upsilon. Democrat. Presbyterian. Home: 99 Norumbega Rd #141 Weston MA 02493-2495 Office: 96 Cummington St Boston MA 02215-2407 E-mail: maits@mediaone.net.

SANDERS, JACK FORD, physician; b. St. Louis, July 16, 1918; s. Ford and Viva (Marvin) S.; m. Gretchen A. Jellema, Feb. 2, 1945; children: Karen Jean, Vicki Leigh, Mary Beth, Donald Curtis, Wendy Lynn BS summa cum laude, Alma Coll., Mich., 1939; MD, U. Mich., 1945; LL.D., Northwood U. Diplomate Am. Bd. Internal Medicine; cert. flight instr. aircraft and instruments, airplane single and multi-engine land and sea; flight safety counselor FAA; CAP check pilot; sr. aviation med. examiner. Intern Henry Ford Hosp., 1945-46, resident in internal medicine, 1947-50; practice medicine specializing in internal medicine Alma, Mich.; sr. attending physician internal medicine Butterworth Hosp., Blodgett Hosp., Grand Rapids; cons. St. Mary's Hosp., Ferguson-Droste-Ferguson Hosp.; med. dir. Mich. Masonic Hosp., Alma, 1960-77; med. dir. rehab. div., chmn. dept. medicine, chief staff Gratiot Community Hosp.; chmn. dept. medicine Tri-County Hosp., Edmore, Mich.; clin. assoc. prof. medicine Coll. Human Medicine, Mich. State U. Mem. Com. on Aging, Gov's Adv. Coun. on Heart Disease, Cancer and Stroke; del White Ho. Conf. on Aging; bd. dirs. Mich. Masonic Home and Hosp.; chmn. bd. Cen. Mich. Wendy's, Inc.; sec., treas. Gratiot Aviation, Inc. Contbr. articles to profl. jours. Chmn. bd. govs. Mich.; bd. dirs. Northwood U., Gratiot Cmty. Airport Bd. Instr. ACTS, U.S. Air Corps and lt. (j.g.) M.C., USNR, WWII. Fellow ACP, Am. Geriatrics Soc.; mem. AMA, Mich. State Med. Soc., Gratiot Med. Soc., Kent Med. Soc., Gratiot-Isabella-Clare County Med. Soc. (pres. 1965), Am. Diabetes Assn., Am. Heart Assn., Am. Multiple Sclerosis Soc., Mich. Crippled Children and Adults Soc., East Ctrl. Mich. Health Svc. Assn., Mason (33d degree), Rotary, Phi Sigma Pi (hon.). Home: 250 Purdy Dr Alma MI 48801-2174 Office: Mich Masonic Pathways Alma MI 48801-2174

SANDERS, JACK THOMAS, religious studies educator; b. Grand Prairie, Tex., Feb. 28, 1935; s. Eula Thomas and Mildred Madge (Parish) S.; m. M. Patricia Chism, Aug. 9, 1959 (dec. Oct. 1973); 1 son, Collin Thomas; m. Susan Elizabeth Plass, Mar. 3, 1979. BA, Tex. Wesleyan Coll., 1956; M.Div., Emory U., 1960; PhD, Claremont Grad. Sch., 1963; postgrad., Eberhard-Karls U., Tuebingen, Germany, 1963-64. Asst. prof. Emory U., Atlanta, 1964-67, Garrett Theol Sem., Evanston, Ill., 1967-68, McCormick Theol. Sem., Chgo., 1968-69; assoc. prof. U. Oreg., Eugene, 1969-75, prof., 1975-97, head dept. religious studies, 1973-80, 85-90, prof. emeritus, 1997—. Author: The New Testament Christological Hymns, 1971, Ethics in the New Testament, 1975, 2d edit., 1986, Ben Sira and Demotic Wisdom, 1983, The Jews in Luke-Acts, 1987, Schismatics, Sectarians, Dissidents, Deviants: The First One Hundred Years of Jewish-Christian Relations, 1993, Charisma, Converts, Competitors: Societal and Sociological Factors in the Success of Early Christianity, 2000; editor: Gospel Origins and Christian Beginnings, 1990, Gnosticism and the Early Christian World, 1990; mem. edit. bd. Jour. Bibl. Lit., 1977-83. Mem. policy bd. Dept. Higher Edn. Nat. Council Chs., N.Y.C., 1971-73. NDEA grad. study fellow, 1960-63; Fulbright Commn. fellow, 1963-64; Am. Council Learned Socs. travel grantee, 1981; NEH fellow, 1983-84 Mem. AAUP (chpt. pres. 1981-82), Studiorum Novi Testamenti Soc., World Union Jewish Studies, Assn. for Jewish Studies, Soc. Bibl. Lit. (regional sec. 1969-76, sabbatical rsch. award 1976-77), Archeol. Inst. Am. (chpt. pres. 1988-89), Soc. for Sci. Study of Religion, Assn. for Sociology Religion. Democrat. Home: 2555 Birch Ln Eugene OR 97403-2191 Office: U Oregon Dept Religious Studies Eugene OR 97403 E-mail: jsanders@oregon.uoregon.edu.

SANDERS, JACQUELYN SEEVAK, psychologist, educator; b. Boston, Apr. 26, 1931; d. Edward Ezral and Dora (Zoken) Seevak; 1 son, Seth. BA, Radcliffe Coll., 1952; MA, U. Chgo., 1964; PhD, UCLA, 1972. Counselor, asst. prin. Orthogenic Sch., Chgo., 1952-65; research assoc. UCLA, 1965-68; cons. Osawatomie State Hosp. (Kans.), 1965-68; asst. prof. Ctr. for Early Edn., L.A., 1969-72; assoc. dir. Sonia Shankman Orthogenic Sch., U. Chgo., 1972-73, dir., 1973-93, dir. emeritus, 1993—; curriculum cons. day care ctrs. L.A. Dept. Social Welfare, 1970-72; instr. Calif. State Coll., L.A., 1972; lectr. dept. edn. U. Chgo., 1972-80, sr. lectr., 1980-93, clin. assoc. prof. dept. psychiatry, 1990-93, emeritus, 1993—; instr. edn. program Inst. Psychoanalysis, Chgo., 1979-82; reading cons. Foreman High Sch., Chgo. Author: Greenhouse for the Mind, 1989; editor: (with Barry L. Childress) Psychoanalytic Approaches to the Very Troubled Child: Therapeutic Practice Innovations in Residential & Educational Settings, 1989, Severly Disturbed Children and the Parental Alliance, 1992, (with Jerome M. Goldsmith) Milieu Therapy: Significant Issues and Innovative Applications, 1993, The Seevak Family, The Zoken Family; contbr. articles to profl. jours. Mem. vis. com. univ. sch. rels. U. Chgo.; bd. dirs. KAM Isaiah Israel Congregation, 1997-2001. UCLA Univ. fellow, 1966-68; Radcliffe Coll. Scholar, 1948-52; recipient Alumna award Girls' Latin Sch., Boston, Bettelheim award Am. Assn. Children's Residential Ctrs., Dist. Svc. award Radcliffe Assn. Mem. Assn. Children's Residential Ctrs. (past pres.), Quadrangle Club, Radcliffe Club (Chgo., sec/treas. 1986-87, pres. 1987-89), Harvard Club (Chgo., bd. dirs. 1986-2001). Home: 5842 S Stony Island Ave Apt 2G Chicago IL 60637-2033

SANDERS, JAMES ALVIN, minister, religious studies educator; b. Memphis, Nov. 28, 1927; s. Robert E. and Sue (Black) S.; m. Dora Cargille, June 30, 1951; 1 son, Robin David. BA magna cum laude, Vanderbilt U., 1948, BD with honors, 1951; student, U. Paris, 1950-51; PhD, Hebrew Union Coll., 1955; DLitt, Acadia U., 1973; STD, U. Glasgow, 1975; DHL, Coe Coll., 1988, Hebrew Union Coll., 1988, Hastings Coll., 1996, Calif. Luth. U., 2000. Ordained teacher Presbyn. Ch., 1955; instr. French Vanderbilt U., 1948-49; faculty Colgate Rochester Div. Sch., 1954-65, assoc. prof., 1957-60, Joseph B. Hoyt prof. O.T. interpretation, 1960-65; prof. O.T. Union Theol. Sem., N.Y.C., 1965-70, Auburn prof. Bibl. studies, 1970-77; adj. prof. Columbia, 1966-77; prof. Bibl. studies Sch. Theology and Grad. Sch., Claremont, Calif., 1977-97; vis. prof. Union Theol. Seminary and Columbia U., 1997-98, Yale Divinity Sch., 1998, Jewish Theol. Seminary, 2001. Ann. prof. Jerusalem Sch. of Am. Schs. Oriental Rsch., 1961-62; fellow Ecumenical Isnt., Jerusalem, 1972-73, 85; Ayer lectr., 1971, 79, Shaffer lectr., 1972, Fondren lectr., 1975, Currie lectr., 1976, McFadin lectr., 1979, Colwell lectr., 1979; guest lectr. U. Fribourg, Switzerland, 1981, 90, Hebrew Union Coll., 1982, 88, Oral Roberts U., 1982, Tulsa U., 1982, Ind. U., 1982, Coe Coll., 1983, Garrett Sem., 1984, Pepperdine U., 1985, Western Sem., 1985, Bethany Sem., 1986; lectr. Union Sem. Sesquicentennial, 1987, U. Wis., 1987, U. Chgo., 1987; Gray lectr. Duke U., 1988; guest lectr. Notre Dame U., Georgetown U., Tex. Christian U., 1989, Alexander Robertson lectr. U. Glasgow, 1990-91, Gustavson lectr. United Theol. sem., 1991; assoc. program lectr. Smithsonian, 1990, Am. Bible Soc. Sesquicentennial, 1991, U. N.Mex., 1992, 94, 97, Am. Interfaith Inst., 1992, Georgetown U., 1992; Lily Rosmen lectr. Skirball Mus., 1992; vis. prof. U. N.Mex., 1992, Southwestern U., 1992, Calif. Luth. U., 1992, 94, Willamette U., 1993, Peter Craigie lectr. U. Calgary, 1993, U. So. Ariz., 1993; Samuel Iwry lectr. John Hopkins U., 1993; lectr. San Diego State U., 1994, Creighton U., 1995, The Mercantile Libr., N.Y.C., 1995, U. Heidelberg, Germany, 1995, U. Mich., 1995; session chair, Internat. Congress for Fiftieth Anniversary of Dead Sea Scrolls, Jerusalem, 1997; Womack lectr. The Methodist Coll., 1996; Purcell lectr. Barton Coll., 1997, Vatican Symposium, 1999, Temple Emanu-El, 1999, Hebrew Union Coll., 2001; mem. internat. O.T. text critical com. United Bible Socs., 1969—; mem. nat. adv. acad. bd. Hebrew Union Coll., 1997—; bd. dirs. Mobilization for the Human Family, 1998—; exec. officer Ancient Bibl. Manuscript Ctr. for Preservation and Rsch., 1977-80, pres., 1980—, VIS. PROF., Jewish Theological Seminary, 2001—. Author: Suffering as Divine Discipline in the Old Testament and Post-Biblical Judaism, 1955, The Old Testament in the Cross, 1961, The Psalms Scroll of Qumran Cave 11, 1965, The Dead Sea Psalms Scroll, 1967, Near Eastern Archaeology in the Twentieth Century, 1970, Torah and Canon, 1972, 74, Identité de la Bible, 1975, God Has a Story Too, 1979, Canon and Community, 1984, From Sacred Story to Sacred Text, 1987, Luke and Scripture, 1993; editor: Paul and the Scriptures of Israel, 1993, Early Christian Interpretation of the Scriptures of Israel, 1997, The Function of Scripture in Early Jewish and Christian Tradition, 1998, The Canon Debate, 2002; contbr. over 250 articles to profl. jours.; mem. editorial bd. Jour. Bibl. Lit., 1970-76, Jour. for Study Judaism, Bibl. Theology Bull., Interpretation, 1973-78, New Rev. Standard Version Bible Com.; 2 vols. of essays: A Gift of God in Due Season, 1996, The Quest for Context and Meaning, 1997 pub. in honor of Sanders' retirement. Trustee Am. Schs. Oriental Research. Fulbright grantee, 1950-51, Lilly Endowment grantee, 1981, NEH grantee, 1980, 91-92; Lefkowitz and Rabinowitz interfaith fellow, 1951-53, Rockefeller fellow, 1953-54, 85, Guggenheim fellow, 1961-62, 72-73, Human Scis. Rsch. fellow, 1989. Mem. Soc. Bibl. Lit. and Exegesis (pres. 1977-78), Phi Beta Kappa, Phi Sigma Iota, Theta Chi Beta. Home: PO Box 593 Claremont CA 91711-0593 Office: Ancient Bibl Manuscript Ctr 1325 N College Ave Claremont CA 91711-3154 E-mail: SandersJA@aol.com.

SANDERS, JAMES GRADY, biogeochemist; b. Norfolk, Va., June 10, 1951; s. Allen Buford and Maple Seretha (Myers) S.; m. Dorothea L. Palmer, 2001. BS in Zoology, Duke U., 1973; MS in Marine Scis., U. N.C., 1975, PhD in Marine Scis., 1978. Postdoctoral investigator Woods Hole (Mass.) Oceanographic Instn., 1978-80; vis. scientist Chesapeake Biol. Lab. U. Md., Solomons, 1980-81; asst. curator Benedict (Md.) Estuarine Rsch. Ctr., Acad. Natural Scis., 1981-85, assoc. curator, 1985-89, curator, 1989-99, dir., 1983-99, v.p., 1999; chair dept. ocean, earth and atmospheric scis. Old Dominion U., Norfolk, Va., 1999-2001; dir. Skidaway Inst. Oceanography, Savannah, Ga., 2001—. Cons. EPA Sweden, Stockholm, 1985-90; mem. Md. Sea Grant Adv. Com., College Park, 1983-90, Environ. Commn., Calvert County, Md., 1981-88; mem. environ. biology panel Office R & D EPA, Washington, 1986-95; regional rep. Coastal Resources Adv. Commn., Md., 1983-86; bd. dirs. Am. Chestnut Land Trust. Assoc. editor Estuaries, 1996-99; mem. editl. bd. Environ. Toxicology and Chemistry, 2000—; contbr. more than 70 articles to sci. jours. Grantee NOAA, 1981—, EPA, 1983—. Mem. AAAS, Am. Geophys. Union, Am. Soc. Limnology and Oceanography, Soc. for Environ. Toxicology and Chemistry, Estuarine Rsch. Fedn. (treas. 1993-97), So. Assn. Marine Labs. (pres.-elect 2001—). Achievements include first identification of relationships between algal growth and chemical transformations of arsenic in aquatic systems. Office: Skidaway Inst Oceanography 10 Ocean Science Cir Savannah GA 31411 Home: 11 Wesley Crossing Savannah GA 31411 E-mail: sanders@skio.peachnet.edu.

SANDERS, JIMMY DEVON, public administration and health services educator; b. Montgomery, Ala., Nov. 6, 1945; s. Harold Wright Sanders and Elsie M. (Huett) Harris; m. Linda Ruth Sweatt, Mar. 25, 1966; children: Richard Devon, Robert Pearson. B Gen. Studies, U. Nebr., Omaha, 1968; MPA, U. Okla., 1973, U. So. Calif., 1988, D Pub. Adminstrn., 1989. Commd. officer USAF, 1964, advanced through grades to lt. col., 1985, various health svc. adminstrv. positions, 1964-83, dir. base med. svcs. Italy, 1980-83; sr. health policy analyst Dept. Def., Washington, 1983-88; ret., 1988; assoc. prof. mgmt. and healthcare mgmt. Marymount U., Arlington, Va., 1988-91; dir. Atlantic region Troy State U., Norfolk, 1991-94; dir. Fla. region Troy State U., Ft. Walton Beach, 1995-96, assoc. prof. pub. adminstrn., 1996—. Health care cons. various hosps. and cities, 1987—, Ret. Officers Assn., Arlington, 1988-90. Fellow Am. Coll. Health Care Execs.; mem. Assn. Mgmt./Internat. Assn. Mgmt. (pres. 1996-97), Internat. Soc. Rsch. in Healthcare Fin. Mgmt., 2000—. Republican. Lutheran. Avocations: walking, reading, golf. Home: 10850 US Highway 331 Montgomery AL 36105-6105 Office: Troy State U PO Box 2829 Fort Walton Beach FL 32549-2829

SANDERS, JOAN MARY, artist, educator; b. N.Y.C., July 27, 1931; d. Charles Leonard and Clementine Strack; m. Robert William Sanders, June 12, 1954; children: Robert, Dean, Alicia. Student, Fordham U. Illustrator Mercantile Stores, N.Y.C., 1949—63. V.p. Art League Nassau County, N.Y.C., 1988—97; pres. Waterway Artists, Calabash, NC, 2000. Mem.: Waterway Art League (9 awards), Waccamaw Art League (3 awards), Wilmington Art League (7 awards). Republican. Roman Catholic. Avocations: birdwatching, gardening, cooking, travel. Home: 8 Calabash Ct Calabash NC 28467

SANDERS, JOE MAXWELL, JR. pediatrician, association administrator; b. Hartsville, S.C., July 5, 1940; m. Dorothy Garvin, June 6, 1963; children Joe M. III, Eric T. BS, The Citadel, 1962; MD, Med. U. S.C., 1967. Diplomate Am. Bd. Pediatrics. Rotating intern, resident in pediatrics Letterman Army Med. Ctr., San Francisco, 1967-70; fellow in adolescent medicine San Francisco Children's Hosp., 1970-71; chief adolescent medicine svc. Fitzsimmons Army Med. Ctr., 1971-86; dir. adolescent medicine svc. Med. Coll. Ga., 1986-88; assoc. exec. dir. Am. Acad. Pediatrics, Elk Grove Village, Ill., 1988-93, exec. dir., 1993—. Asst. clin. prof. pediatrics U. Colo. Health Scis. Ctr., 1971-76, assoc. clin. prof., 1976-83, clin. prof. 1983-86; assoc. prof. pediatrics Med. Coll. Ga., 1986-88; clin. prof. pediatrics, U. Chgo., 1991—; cons. for adolescent medicine Surgeon Gen. Army, 1976-86; mem. med. com. Rocky Mt. Planned Parenthood, 1981-86; vis. prof. dept. pediatrics U. Kansas (Wichita), 1984, 87, dept. pediatrics and family practice, E. Tenn. State U., Johnson City, 1985, U. Fla., Gainesville, 1987, Fitzsimmons Army Med. Ctr., Denver, 1989, U. Chgo., 1991, Baylor Coll., Houston, 1994, others. Contbr. numerous articles and abstracts to profl. jours., chpts. to books; mem. editl. bd. Jour. Current Adolescent Medicine, 1979-81, Substance Abuse: A Guide for Profls., 1985-88; reviewer Pediatrics, 1984—, Jour. Pediatrics, 1986—, Jour. Adolescent Health, 1986—, Am. Jour. Diseases of Children, 1987—, Jour. Am. Med. Assn., 1987—; guest lectr., speaker at many sci. confs. and med. soc. meetings. Mem. teenage coord. coun. Richmond County Health Dept., 1986-88, head start health adv. com. CSRA Econ. Opportunity Authority, Inc., 1986-88; med. cons. Alexian Bros. Med. Rels. Com. Decorated Legion of Merit, U.S. Army, 1987; recipient Adele Hoffman award, Sect. on Adolescent Health, 1988. Fellow Am. Acad. Pediatrics (com. on adolescence 1980-87, chmn. 1983-87, chmn. uniformed svcs chpt. 1981, 84, mem. exec. com. mil. pediatrics sect. 1976-79, sec.-treas. 1976-77, chmn. 1977-79, mem. steering com. to establish non-geographic mil. dist. chpt., mem sect. on adolescent health 1979—, program com. 1981-83, task force on substance abuse, chmn. 1984-85, cons. 85-87, task force on sch. based clinics, 1987—), Soc. Adolescent Medicine (edn. com., ambulatory care com., 1975-80, chmn. nominating com. 1978, exec. coun. 1980-83, chmn. awards com. 1990-93, pres. 1987-88, past pres's. coun. 1988—, Outstanding Achievement award 1994); mem. AMA (mem. planning com. nat. coalition on adolescent health, rep. Am. Acad. Pediatrics, Soc. Adolescent Medicine to Coalition 1987—, chmn. working group on rsch. agenda 1987-88, adv. com. on unintentional injuries 1987), Ambulatory Pediatric Assn., So. Soc. for Pediatric Rsch., Soc. Med. Cons. to Armed Forces, Order Mil. Med. Merit, Sigma Xi. Home: 449 W Rosiland Rd Palatine IL 60074-1098 Office: Am Acad Pediatrics 141 Nortwest Point Blvd Elk Grove Village IL 60007

SANDERS, JOHN KENNETH, marketing communications executive; b. Tucson, Nov. 1, 1939; s. Autie Alfred and Ina Fae (Davis) S.; m. Diane Evelyn Nasby, Sept. 16, 1958 (div. 1981); children: John Kenneth Jr., Jeffrey Neil; m. Cathleen Victoria Watson, May 24, 1981; children: Brian Charles, Riley Scott, Julia Fae. BA, Art Ctr. Coll. of Design, 1963; MA, Syracuse U., 1994. Corp. art dir., asst. advt. mgr. Southern Pacific Co., San Francisco, 1963-66; head art dir., asst. creative dir. Botsford, DeGarmo & Day, London, 1966-67; sr. art dir. Milici Advt. Inc., Honolulu, 1968-69, Lennon & Newell Pacific, Honolulu, 1970-71; pres., creative dir. Sanders & Gamlin, 1971-75, Sanders & Printup Inc., Honolulu, 1975-82; dir. creative & mktg. svcs. Home Vue Hawaii, 1984; pres., creative dir. Sanders Mktg., 1984-88, 1994—; dir. mktg., pub. rels., & fin. devel. Am. Red Cross, Hi State Chpt., 1988-92. Adv. bd. bus. banking coun. Bank Am., Honolulu, 1996-2000; co-founder, pres., creative dir. Hawaii-Aloha.com., 1999—; bd. dirs., mktg. officer Ocean News Network Internat. Contbr. articles to profl. mags.; designer of numerous advt. campaigns. Bd. dirs. Kailua Urban Design Task Force, Honolulu, 1995-96, past chmn.; bd. dirs. Am. Red Cross, Honolulu, 1977-88, chmn. mktg. 1979-85; adv. Boy Scouts Am., 1977-78, vol. 1996-97; bd. dirs. Lanikai Cmty. Assn., 1988-91, chmn. playground com., 1988-91; adv. com. Mental Health Assn., 1978-79, designer 1978-79; adv. com. March of Dimes Assn., 1977-78; bd. dirs. Cmty. Scholarship Assn., 1976-78. With USAR, 1957-65. Grantee State Found. Culture & Arts, 1982; recipient Pres.'s award Am. Red Cross Hawaii State chpt. 1979; first recipient of the Hon. Lifetime Membership Award (nationally and in Hawaii). First chmn. of Ad II Divsn. of Am. Advt. Fedn., 1968-69; mem. Honolulu Advt. Fedn. (pres. 1971-72, lt. gov. 1972-76, gov. 1976-78, Ad Man Yr. award 1972-73), Am. Advt. Fedn. (Printer's Ink silver medal 1966), Kailua C. of C., Hawaii Alliance Arts Edn. (pub. rels. com. 1995-97, bd. dirs.), Honolulu Symphony Soc., 1978-83. (chmn. fundraising/Night of Stars, 1981-83), chmn. mktg. and pub. rels. com. 1995-99, bd. dirs.), Rotary (chairman programs 1996-97). Avocations: cmty. svc., architecture, building, aerobics, sports. E-mail: Ken@hawaii-aloha.com.

SANDERS, JUDITH BROWN, clinical nurse specialist; b. York, Pa., Sept. 27, 1940; d. Robert Lawrence and Melvine Louise (Schroeder) Brown; children: Jonathan, Robert. Diploma, Del. Hosp. Sch. Nursing, Wilmington, 1964; BS, U. Del., 1964; MS in Nursing, U. Md., 1967; Basic Cert. in Gerontology, U. Vt., 1990. Psychiat.-mental health nursing cons. Dept. Mental Health State of Mo., Jefferson City, 1978-80; asst. prof. U. Mo. Sch. Nursing, Columbia, 1976-83; dir. dept. nursing Fulton (Mo.) State Hosp., 1980-83; nurse exec. The Brattleboro (Vt.) Retreat, 1983-95; psychiat. clin. nurse specialist Christiana Care Health Sys., Wilmington, Del., 1996—. Contbr. articles to profl. jours. Mem. AAUW, Am. Nurses Assn., Del. Nurses Assn., Am. Orgn. Nurse Execs., Am. Coll. Mental Health Adminstrn., Am. Coll. Health Care Execs., Sigma Theta Tau. E-mail: jsanders@christianacare.org.

SANDERS, KEITH PAGE, journalism educator; b. Ashland, Ohio, Sept. 25, 1938; s. Merwin Morse and Phyllis Pearl (Snyder) S.; m. Jane Carmel Adams, June 11, 1966; children: Paige Ann, Kevin Scott. BS in Journalism, Bowling Green State U., 1960; MS in Journalism, Ohio U., 1964; PhD in Mass. Comm., U. Iowa, 1967. Sports editor Ashland (Ohio) Times Gazette, 1960-61, Dover (Ohio) Daily Reporter, 1961-62; instr. journalism Bowling Green (Ohio) State U., 1963-64, U. Iowa, Iowa City, 1965-67; prof. journalism U. Mo., Columbia, 1967—2001, assoc. dean grad. studies Sch. Journalism, 1986-87, 90-91, O.O. McIntyre disting. prof., 1993, prof. emeritus, 2002—. Cons. in field. Contbr. articles to profl. jours. including Journalism Quar., Mass Media Rev., Jour. Broadcasting, Electronic Jour. of Comm.; assoc. editor Mass Comm. Rev., 1981-92, mem. editl. bd., 1972-98; mem. editl. bd. Journalism Monographs, 1973-80, Mass Comm. and Soc., 1998—. Recipient Award for Outstanding Achievement U. Mo. Alumni Assn., 1986; Joyce Swan Disting. Faculty award U. Mo., 1973; inducted into Columbia Bowling Hall of Fame, 1999. Mem. Internat. Soc. for Sci. Study of Subjectivity (treas. 1990-95), Assn. for Edn. in Journalism/Mass. Comm. (Trayes Prof. of Yr. 1987), Soc. Profl. Journalists, Mo. State Bowling Assn. (bd. dirs. 2000—), Kappa Tau Alpha (exec. dir. 1991—), Omicron Delta Kappa. Avocations: bowling, golf, fishing. Home: 6551 N Creasy Springs Rd Columbia MO 65202-8093 Office: Univ of Missouri Sch Journalism Columbia MO 65211-1200 E-mail: sandersk@missouri.edu.

SANDERS, MANUEL JACKSON, III (BUD SANDERS), mathematician; b. Denver, Oct. 20, 1964; s. Manuel Jackson Jr. and Regina Marie Sanders; m. Helen Anne Buchholz, Oct. 21, 1989; children: Gretchen Elise, Manuel Jackson IV. PhD, U Tenn., Knoxville, 1999. Asst. prof. of math. Clarke Coll., Dubuque, Iowa, 1999—2000, McMurry U., Abilene, Tex., 2000—02, Armstrong Atlantic State U., Savannah, Ga., 2002—. Mem.: Am. Math. Soc. Home: 2101 River Oaks Cir Abilene TX 79605 Office: McMurry Univ S 14th & Sayles Ave Abilene TX 79697 E-mail: msanders@cs1.mcm.edu.

SANDERS, MARC ANDREW, computer technical consultant; b. Chgo., Apr. 21, 1947; s. Edward and Elizabeth Sanders. BA, Roosevelt U., 1973; MAS, Fla. Atlantic U., 1987. Computer programmer Market Facts, Inc., Chgo., 1973-76, N.E. Ill. Planning Commn., Chgo., 1977; salesman Radio Shack, Tamarac, Fla., 1982-83; sr. analyst/tech. cons. Birch/Scarborough Rsch., Coral Springs, 1984-91; programmer/analyst Datateam, Inc., Margate, 1992-93, SIRS, Inc., Boca Raton, 1994-99, Bristol West Ins. Group, 2000—. Mem. ACM, IEEE Computer Soc., Phi Kappa Phi, Beta Gamma Sigma, Upsilon Pi Epsilon. Democrat. Jewish. Avocations: golf, working-out, walking, writing, science fiction. Office: SIRS PO Box 9742 Coral Springs FL 33075-9742

SANDERS, MARGUERITE DEES, retired educational administrator; b. Many, La., Sept. 1, 1914; d. W.E. and Mary J. (White) Dees; BA in Edn., Math. and Physics, La. State Normal Coll., Natchitoches, La., 1934; MEd in Secondary Edn., Stephen F. Austin U., Nacogdoches, Tex., 1955; postgrad. U. Colo., Stephen F. Austin U., Baylor U., Northwestern U., 1959-69; m. Horace I. Sanders (dec.); 1 dau., Dorothy Sanders Tidwell. Math. coord. N. La. Supplemental Edn. Ctr., Natchitoches, La., 1967-69; curriculum coord. Title 1, Sabine Parish Sch. Bd., Many, La., 1970-73, dir. Title I, 1973-74, dir. federal programs, 1974-76, asst. supt. Sabine Parish Schs., 1976-80, ret., 1980. Mem. NEA, La. Tchrs. Assn., La. Assn. Sch. Adminstrs. (federally assisted programs), La. Unit Assn. Sch. Curriculum Developers, La. Suprs. Assn., La. Sci. Tchrs. Assn. (pres., sec.), La. Math. Tchrs. Assn., Nat. Ret. Tchrs. Assn., Sa. Ret. Tchrs. Assn., La. Ret. Tchrs. Assn., Delta Kappa Gamma (Outstanding educator award 1988, chpt. treas. 1990-94), Kappa Delta Pi. Recipient La. Sci. Tchrs. Honor Award, 1963, tchr. Sunday Sch. 1st Baptist Ch., hostess com. 1989-95. Author revision of sch. bd. policy manual Sabine Parish Sch. Bd. Home and Office: 2548 Texas Hwy Many LA 71449-3953

SANDERS, MARION YVONNE, geriatrics nurse; b. St. Petersburg, Fla., Dec. 4, 1936; d. Ira Laurey and Maude Mae Cherry Sanders; children: Dwayne Irwin, Princess Charrie. BS, Fla. A&M U., 1959; MS, Nova U., Ft. Lauderdale, Fla., 1992. RN, Fla. Staff nurse Lantana (Fla.) TB Hosp., 1960-61, Mercy Hosp., St. Petersburg, 1961; gen. duty nurse VA, Tuskegee, Ala., 1961-62; staff nurse John Andrews Hosp., 1962-63; gen. duty staff nurse Brewster Meth. Hosp., Jacksonville, Fla., 1963-65, Duval Med. Ctr., Jacksonville, 1965-66; pvt. duty nurse Dist. 2 Registry, 1966-70; supr. Eartha White Nursing Home, 1970; staff nurse Bapt. Hosp., 1971-73, City-County Methadone Clinic, Jacksonville, 1976-78; pvt. duty nurse Home Nursing, 1982-86, pvt. duty geriatric nursing and gerontology specialist, 1995—, Sr. Companion Svc. Corp., 1997-98. Respite and relief sr. companion vol. Urban Jacksonville Cathedral Found., 1996-98. Mem. Ideas for Am.'s Future, 1997, 1998, NAACP, 1997—98; vol. shelter mgr. ARC, Miami, Fla., 1992—94; vol. cmty. activist, 1994; vol. Jacksonville Cmty. Rels. Bd., 1996, Jacksonville Inc. Cathedral Found., 1997—; sr. companion Svc. Corp., 1997—98, 1999; mem. Brewseter's and Cmty. Nurses Alumni, 1998—2000, 2001—02; vol. Rep. Senatorial Com., 1999; vol. cmty. svcs., elem. grades tutor, polit. campaigns, tchr. health edn.; vol. Rep. Nat. Com., 1997—2000, 2001—02, Rep. Com. Fla., 1997—98, Northside Rep. Club, 1997, 1998, 1999; active St. Stephen AME Ch., Jacksonville, tch. Bible studies for youth, advocate for poor, homeless and prisoners. Recipient Cert. of Recognition, Rep. Party, Fla. and Wash., 1990, Rep. Congl. Orgn., 1988, 90, 91. Mem. ANA (mem. polit. action coms.), Fla. Nurses Assn., Women's Missionary Soc. (life). Republican. Methodist. Avocations: reading the Holy Bible, teaching Sunday school, volunteer work. Home: 4832 N Main St Apt 14 Jacksonville FL 32206-1458

SANDERS, MARLENE, anchor, journalism educator; b. Cleve., Jan. 10, 1931; d. Mac and Evelyn (Menitoff) Sanders; m. Jerome Toobin, May 27, 1958 (dec. Jan. 1984); children: Jeff, Mark. Student, Ohio State U., 1948-49. Writer, prodr. Sta. WNEW-TV, N.Y.C., 1955-60, P.M. program Westinghouse Broadcasting Co., N.Y.C., 1961-62; asst. dir. news and public affairs Sta. WNEW, 1962-64; anchor, news program ABC News, 1964-68, corr., 1968-72, documentary prodr., writer, anchor, 1972-76, v.p., dir. TV documentaries, 1976-78; corr. CBS News, 1978-87; host Currents Sta. WNET-TV, 1987-88; host Met. Week in Review, 1988-90; host Thirteen Live Sta. WNET-TV, 1990-91; prof. dept. journalism NYU, N.Y.C., 1991-93; adj. prof. journalism, adminstr. Columbia U. Grad. Sch. Journalism, 1994-95; adj. prof. journalism NYU, 1996—. Profl.-in-residence Freedom Forum Media Studies Ctr., 1997-2000; freelance broadcaster, narrator. Co-author: Waiting for Prime Time: The Women of Television News, 1988. Recipient award N.Y. State Broadcasters Assn., 1976, award Nat. Press Club, 1976, Emmy awards, 1980, 81, others. Mem. Am. Women in Radio and TV (Woman of Yr. award 1975, Silver Satellite award 1977), Women in Comm. (past pres.), Soc. Profl. Journalists (mem. coun. on fgn. rels.). E-mail: msanders110@aol.com.

SANDERS, MARY ELIZABETH, author, historian; b. Baton Rouge, May 25, 1923; d. Jared Young and Mary (Briggs) S. BA, La. State U., 1944, MA, 1955. Adminstrv. asst. Congressman J.Y. Sanders, Washington, 1942-43, Sanders, Miller, Downing, Rubin & Kean, Baton Rouge, 1946-48; librarian, archivist New Orleans Pub. Libr., 1955-57. Appeared on Restore Am.-La. program Home & Garden TV, 1999. Author: Avoca Plantation Receipts and Other Family Favorites, 1995; editor: Letters of a Southern Family, 1816-1941, 2001, Diary in Gray: Civil War Journal of J. Y. Sanders, 1994; compiler Records of Attakapas District, La., 1739-1811, 1962, Records of Attakapas District, La., Vol II: St. Mary Parish, 1811-1860, 1963, Records of Attakapas District, La., Vol. III: St. Martin Parish, 1808-1860, 1974, St. Mary Parish, Louisana, Heirship Series: Vol. I—Annotated Abstracts of the Successions, 1811-1834, 1972, Vol. II—Selected Annotated Abstracts of Marriage Book 1, 1811-1829, 1973, Vol. III—Selected Annotated Abstracts of Court Records, 1811-1839, 1978. Mem. La. Hist. Records Adv. Commn., Baton Rouge, 1981-85; charter mem., pres. La. Genealogy and Hist. Soc., 1954-56, editor, 1957-58; hon. mem. Morgan City (La.) Arch. Commn., 1985—; co-trustee J. Y. Sanders Found., Baton Rouge, 1988—; pres. La. Archives Found., Baton Rouge, 1988-96, Young-Sanders Ctr. Found., Morgan City, 1998—; mem. La. State U. Found., Baton Rouge, 1988-92; mem. nat. bd. Coun. Conservative Citizens, St. Louis, 1997—; hon. chmn. La. Sovereignty Party, Baton Rouge, 1999. Named Hon. Citizen Morgan City, La., 1985; recipient award of commendation La. State Dept. Archives, Records Mgmt. and History, 1988, cert. of appreciation Coun. Conservative Citizens, 1996, cert. of honor Jud. Watch, 1999. Mem. DAR (registrar La. soc. 1983-86, nat. vice chmn. flag com. 1986-89, corr. sec. 1992-95), United Daus. of the Confederacy (divsn. corr. sec. 1989-91, divsn. pres. 2000-2002, Jefferson Davis medal 1989, cert. of merit 1998), Huguenot soc. of Founders of Mamakin in Colony of Va. (nat. registrar 1979-85), Colonial Dames Am. Republican. Christian Scientist. Avocations: genealogy, preservationist, cooking. Home: 2332 Wisteria St Baton Rouge LA 70806-5352

SANDERS, MICHAEL, social services organization executive; b. Phelps, Ky., Apr. 8, 1950; s. John Bennett and Patsy Marie (Tabor) S.; m. Jacquline Marie Taylor, June 26, 1971; children: Melissa Rene Sanders, Michael Bennett, Kelli Ann. Student, U. Ky., Baldwin Wallace Coll. Pres. Christian Appalachian Project, Lancaster, Ky. Vol. Habitat for Humanity. With U.S. Army, Vietnam. Mem. Garrard County (Ky.) C. of C. (bd. dirs.), Rotary Club. Roman Catholic. Avocations: boating, fishing, restoring old automobiles, horsemanship. Home: 101 Long Branch Dr Lancaster KY 40444-9569 Office: Christian Appalachian Project 322 Crab Orchard Rd Lancaster KY 40444-9777

SANDERS, PAUL DAVID, music educator; b. Poplar Bluff, Mo., Sept. 30, 1956; s. Kenneth Randolph and Bitha Ovena Sanders; m. Edie Loraine Norlin, Oct. 8, 1962; children: Peter, Jacob. BA, Sch. of the Ozarks, Point Lookout, Mo., 1979; MusM, U. Okla., 1981, PhD, 1991. Music instr. Silver Lake Coll., Manitowoc, Wis., 1988—92; asst. prof. music edn. Ohio State U. , Newark, 1992—98, assoc. prof. music edn., 1998—. Dir. music edn. Silver Lake Coll., 1990—92; asst. acad. dean Ohio State U., Newark, 1999—2001. Editor and compiler 53 Rounds for All Ages, 2001, 53 More Rounds for All Ages, 2002; contbr. articles to profl. jours. Mem.: Midwest Kodály Music Educators (jour. editor and bd. mem. 1996—98), Orgn. Am. Kodály Educators (jour. editor and bd. mem. 1998—2001), Ohio Choral Dirs. Assn. (bd. mem. 1999—2002). Office: Ohio State U at Newark 1179 University Dr Newark OH 43055 Office Fax: 740-366-5047. E-mail: sanders.102@osu.edu.

SANDERS, PHILIP F., JR. artist, computer art educator; b. Phila., Feb. 5, 1950; s. Philip F. and Doris Sanders; m. Joanna M. Dawe, Dec. 23, 1979; 1 child, Amelia. Diploma in painting, Pa. Acad. Fine Arts, Phila., 1976; BFA in Computer Art, Guilford Coll., 1979; MA in Computer Art, NYU, 1991. Graphic artist Village Voice, N.Y.C., 1981-85; computer graphics specialist Fashion Inst. Tech., 1986-89; faculty Seton Hall U., West Orange, N.J., 1987-88, Sch. Visual Arts, N.Y.C., 1987-90; rsch. scientist NYU Interactive Telecomm. Program, 1990-94; faculty NYU Interactive Telecomm. Program/Gallatin Sch., 1992—, Coll. of N.J., Ewing, 1994—. Lead artist, organizer Internat. Painting Interactive, L.A., 1992; juror Marche Internat. Multimedia, Montreal, Que., Can., 1996; presenter, Multimedia Creators Exch., Images du Futur, Montreal, 1996. Computer art works featured Internat. Symposium Electronic Art, 1988, 95-97, SIGGRAPH Art Gallery, 2000, SIGGRAPH Studio, 2001, others. Co-founder, dir. RYO Art & Tech. Gallery, 1984—. Recipient Truvision prize Calif. Mus. Sci., L.A., 1987. Mem. Coll. Art Assn. (panel chair 1997), Assn. Computing Machinery/SIGGRAPH (internet artist, L.A., 1995, Educators grant 1996, SIGGRAPH Sketches and Applications award 1999, SIGGRAPH Creative Applications Lab award 2000), N.Y. Alias Users Group (founder, pres. 1993—), N.J. Alias Wavefront Global users Assn. (founder, chair 2001). Office: College of NJ 2000 Pennington Rd Ewing NJ 08618-1104 Fax: 609-637-5193. E-mail: sanders@tcnj.edu.

SANDERS, RICHARD BROWNING, state supreme court justice; b. Tacoma; 1 child: Laura. BA, U. Wash., 1966, JD, 1969. Assoc. Murray, Scott, McGavick & Graves, Tacoma, 1969, Caplinger & Munn, Seattle, 1971; hearing examiner State Wash., Olympia, 1970; pvt. practice Wash., 1971-95; justice Wash. Supreme Ct., Olympia, 1995—. Adj. prof. U. Wash. Sch. Law; lectr. in field. Contbr. articles to profl. jours. Office: Supreme Court of Washington Temple of Justice PO Box 40929 Olympia WA 98504-0929 Fax: (360) 357-2092. E-mail: j_r.sanders@courts.wa.gov.

SANDERS, RICHARD HENRY, lawyer; b. Chgo., Apr. 10, 1944; s. Walter J. and Marian (Snyder) Sikorski; m. Sharon A. Marciniak, July 8, 1967 (div. Oct. 1979); 1 child, Douglas Bennett. BS, Loyola U., Chgo., 1967; JD, Northwestern U., 1969. Bar: Ill. 1969, Ind. 1990, D.C. 1990, U.S. Dist. Ct. (no. dist.) Ill. 1970, U.S. Dist. Ct. (no. and so. dists.) Ind. 1990, U.S. Ct. Appeals (7th cir.) 1990, U.S. Supreme Ct. 1990. Assoc. Vedder, Price, Kaufman & Kammholz, Chgo., 1969-76, ptnr., 1976—, mem. exec. com., 1991-93, health law area leader, 1989-91, 93-95, 2001—. Adj. prof. Sch. of Law Northwestern U., 1994—; mem. svc. dispute resolver panel Am. Health Lawyers Assn. Alt. Dispute Resolution, 2000—. Mem. ABA, Ill. Bar Assn. (chmn. health sect. 1989-90), Chgo. Bar Assn., Ind. Bar Assn., D.C. Bar Assn., Am. Health Lawyers Assn., Ill. Assn. Health Attys., Univ. Club, Evanston Golf Club (Skokie). Avocations: skiing, diving, photography, golf. Office: Vedder Price Kaufman & Kammholz 222 N La Salle St Ste 2600 Chicago IL 60601-1100 E-mail: rsanders@vedderprice.com.

SANDERS, RICHARD KINARD, actor; b. Harrisburg, Pa., Aug. 23, 1940; s. Henry Irvine and Thelma S. BFA, Carnegie Inst. Tech., 1962; postgrad. (Fulbright scholar), London Acad. Music and Dramatic Art, 1962-63. Pres. Blood Star, Inc. Mem. various acting cos., Front St., Memphis, Champlain Shakespeare Festival, Vt., Center Stage, Balt., N.Y. Shakespeare Festival, N.Y.C., Chelsea Theater Center, N.Y.C., Mark Taper Forum, Los Angeles, Arena Stage, Washington; appeared on: (Broadway) Raisin; (TV series) Les Nessman on WKRP in Cincinnati and The New WKRP in Cincinnati, Paul Sycamore in You Can't Take It With You, Mr. Beanley in Spenser; writer of many episodes of WKRP and other situation comedies; writer NBC movie Max and Sam; numerous TV and film appearances. Vol. Peace Corps, Northeastern Brazil, 1966-69. Recipient Buckeye Newshawk award, 1974-79, Silver Sow award, 1979 Mem. Writers Guild Am., Screen Actors Guild, AFTRA, Actors Equity Assn. Office: PO Box 1644 Woodinville WA 98072-1644

SANDERS, RICHARD LOUIS, executive editor; b. Rockville Centre, N.Y., July 14, 1949; s. Louis Chadrone and Grace Marie (Clarke) S.; m. Laurie Anne Miroff, July 24, 1970. BFA in Film, NYU, 1976. Sr. editor Us mag., N.Y.C., 1978-83, exec. editor, 1983-85; sr. editor People mag., 1985-91; gen. editor Entertainment Weekly, 1991-92, assistant mng. editor, 1993-95, exec. editor, 1995—. Office: Entertainment Weekly 1675 Broadway New York NY 10019-5820

SANDERS, RUSSELL EDWARD, protective services official; b. Louisville, Oct. 6, 1949; s. Robert George Sr. and Jean Francis (Stevens) S.; m. Mary Ann Miller, Feb. 12, 1972; children: Scott, Jason. BA in Psychology, U. Louisville, 1976, MEd in Pers. Svcs., 1980, MS in Community Devel., 1987. Firefighter Louisville Fire Dept., 1967-74, sgt., 1974-77, capt., 1977-81, dist. chief, 1981-86, chief, 1986-95; regional mgr. Nat. Fire Protection Assn., Louisville, 1995—. Adj. instr. Nat. Fire Acad., Emmitsburg, Md., 1985-86; instr. Western Oreg. State Coll., Monmouth, 1984; cons. numerous locations; tchr. Jefferson County Pub./Cath. Sch. Systems, Louisville, 1976-80; bd. dirs. Gov's. Commn. on Pers. Standards, Frankfort, Ky. Contbr. numerous articles to profl. publs. Tennis coach St. Barnabas Cath. Sch., Louisville, 1985-86; baseball coach Hikes Point Optimist, Louisville, 1988; bd. dirs. Stage One Childrens Theater, 1992-95. Sgt. U.S. Army, 1969-71. Recipient People to watch award Louisville mag., 1988, Dean's Citation/Outstanding Svc. award U. Louisville, 1988; Fed. Emergency Mgr. Agy. fellow Harvard U., 1987. Mem. Nat. Inst. Bldg. Scis. (bd. dirs.), Metro Fire Chiefs Assn. (sec. 1988-89, chmn. 1990-91), Comité Technique Internationale de Prévention d'Extinction de Feu (v.p. 1998—), Soc. Exec. Fire Officers, Internat. Soc. Fire Svc. Instrs., U. Louisville Alumni Assn. (pres. 1996-97,

Outstanding Alumni award 1987). Democrat. Roman Catholic. Avocations: bicycling, skiing. Home and Office: Nat Fire Protection Assn 3257 Beals Branch Rd Louisville KY 40206-3060 E-mail: rsanders@nfpa.org.

SANDERS, SCOTT REED, healthcare company administrator; b. Sterling, Ill., Mar. 27, 1956; s. Jack Reed and Charlene Deanne Sanders; m. Bobbi Jo Barker, May 24, 1980; children: Amy Lynn, Sara Nicole. BA, U. Denver, 1978. Owner Metro County Decorations, Englewood, Colo., 1975-80; mgr. product mktg. Electromedics, 1980-85; product mgr. Pfizer Valleylab, Boulder, Colo., 1985-88, dir. mktg., 1990—97, dir. corp. sales, 1997—99; mktg. mgr. Aegis Med., Denver, 1988-90; v.p. sales, mktg. Panoramic Care Sys., Wheat Ridge, 1999; sr. v.p. Strategic Med. Comms., Denver, 1999—2001; v.p. mktg. Gyrus Med. Inc., Maple Grove, Minn., 2001—. Mem. Med. Mgmt. Assn. Republican. Avocations: golf, ski, mountain bike, tennis, roller hockey. Office: Gyrus Med Inc 6655 Wdegwood Rd Maple Grove MN 55311 Business E-Mail: ScottS@gyrusmed.com. E-mail: ScottRSand@aol.com.

SANDERS, TENCE LEE WALKER, elementary education educator; b. Ridgeville, S.C., June 15, 1937; d. Joseph Thomas and Rosalee (Simmons) Walker; divorced; children: Carsandra, Torin Travis. BS, Allen U., 1960; postgrad., S.C. State Coll., 1960-61, CCNY, 1969-70; MA, Antioch Coll., 1974. Lic. tchr., N.Y., N.J. Tchr. Mary Ford Sch., Charleston, S.C., 1960-61, St. Thomas Apostle Sch., N.Y.C., 1966-72, New Rochelle Sch. System, N.Y.C., 1972-94, ret., 1994. Reading coord. YWCA, N.Y.C., 1966; tchr. Project Head Start, N.Y.C., 1967, 69. Chairperson award com. Allen U., 1985-88; active St. Peters A.M.E. Ch., 1989. Recipient cert. of merit Delta Sigma Theta, 1955, S.C. Hwy. Dept., 1956, Williams Alanson White Inst. Psychology, Psychiatry and Psychoanalysis, 1971, Outstanding Svc. in Field of Edn. award Allen U., 1989. Mem. Am. Fedn. Tchrs., N.Y. State United Tchrs., New Rochelle Fedn. United Sch. Employees, Gen. Alumni Assn. Allen U. (pres. Met. N.Y.C. chpt. 1983-93, Outstanding Svc. Beyond Call Duty met. alumni chpt. 1989, Outstanding Leadership and Dedicated Svc. award 1992, Outstanding Leadership, Unwavering Loyalty and Selfless Devotion award 1996), Alpha Kappa Alpha (Tau Nu Omega chpt.). Democrat. Methodist. Avocations: traveling, theatre, dancing, photography. Home: PO Box 5196 Charleston SC 29405-1002 E-mail: SandersT1061@aol.com.

SANDERS, THERESA LYNN, writer, systems analyst, consultant; b. Springfield, Mo., July 26, 1957; d. William Lee and Mary Catherine (Berg) Lambeth; m. Jeffery Gale Sanders, June 5, 1976; children: David, Christopher, Holly, Wendy. BS in Psychology, BS in Tech. Mgmt., U. Md., 1985. Programmer Am. Nat. Ins., Springfield, Mo., 1977-81, Potomac Electric Power, Washington, 1981-82; lead programmer Chevy Chase (Md.) Savs. & Loan, 1982-83; programmer analyst GTE, Reston, Va., 1983-84; supr. documentation/tng. Calvert Group, Bethesda, Md., 1985-87; freelance writer St. Peters, Mo., 1987—. Sys. cons. Washington Area Transit Authority, 1985; tech. writing cons. Edn. Employment Credit Union, Bridgeton, Mo., 1992. Author: (manual) Documentation Guidelines, 1986. Mem. NAFE, Soc. Tech. Comms. (contbg. editor 1986-87), Romance Writers Am. (Mo. pres. 1990-91). Avocations: reading, aerobics.

SANDERS, W. J., III, information technology executive; BSEE, U. Ill., 1958. Chmn. bd., founder Advanced Micro Devices, Sunnydale, Calif., 1969—; various positions with engrng. dept Douglas Aircraft Co.; sales and mktg. positions Motorola Semicondr.; various positions with semicondr. divsn., including sales mgr., area sales mgr., dept. head, dir. mktg., group dir. mktg. worldwide Fairchild Camera and Instrument Corp., 1967—69. Co-founder Semicondr. Industry Assn., Santa Clara Mfg. Group, Semicondr. Rsch. Corp., Microelectronics and Computer Tech. Corp. Recipient Robert N. Noyce award, Semicondr. Industry Assn., 1998, Medal of Achievement, AeA, 2001. Office: AMD 1 AMD Pl Sunnyvale CA 94086

SANDERS, WALLACE WOLFRED, JR. civil engineer; b. Louisville, June 24, 1933; s. Wallace Wolfred and Mary Jane (Brownfield) S.; m. Julia B. Howard, June 9, 1956; children— Linda, David. B.C.E., U. Louisville, 1955; MS, U. Ill., Urbana, 1957, PhD, 1960; M.Engring., U. Louisville, 1973. Research asst., then research assoc. U. Ill., 1955-60, asst. prof., 1960-64; mem. faculty Iowa State U., Ames, 1964-98, prof. civil engring., 1970-98, assoc. dir. engrng. research, 1980-91, assoc. dean research, 1988-91, interim asst. vice provost for research and advanced studies, 1991-92. Cons. to govt. and industry. Contbr. numerous papers to profl. jours. Bd. dirs. Northcrest Retirement Cmty., Ames, 1976-82, 92-98, pres., 1987-91, 96—; bd. dirs. Am. Bapt. Homes of the Midwest, Mpls., 1998—. Mem. ASCE (R.C. Reese research prize 1978), Am. Welding Soc. (Adams Meml. membership award 1971), Am. Ry. Engring. Assn., Am. Soc. Engring. Edn. Baptist. Home and Office: Iowa State U 1924 Northcrest Cir Ames IA 50010-5113 E-mail: wsanders@iastate.edu.

SANDERS, WAYNE R. paper products manufacturing executive; b. Chgo., July 6, 1947; s. Ralph G. and Bernice F. (Swanson) S.; m. Kathleen E. Lessard, Aug. 22, 1970; children: Tracy, Amy, Megan. BCE, Ill. Inst. Tech., 1969; MBA, Marquette U., 1972. Fin. analyst Ford Motor Co., Dearborn, Mich., 1972-75; sr. fin. analyst Kimberly-Clark Corp., Neenah, Wis., 1975, dir. bus. planning internat., 1976-80, dir. bus. planning U.S. consumer bus., 1980-81; v.p. strategic planning Kimberly-Clark of Can., Toronto, Ont., 1981-82, pres., 1982-85; sr. v.p. Kimberly-Clark Corp., Dallas, 1986, pres. infant care sector Neenah, Wis., from 1987, former pres. personal care div., pres., chief oper. officer world consumer, nonwovens and svc. and indsl. ops., 1990—, pres., CEO, 1990-91, chmn., CEO, 1992—. Elected mem. Neenah Sch. Bd., 1980-81; nat. trustee Boys and Girls Clubs Am., 1994; trustee Marquette U., Milw. Roman Catholic.*

SANDERS, W(ILLIAM) EUGENE, JR. physician, educator; b. Frederick, Md., June 25, 1934; s. W(illiam) Eugene and E. Gertrude (Wilburn) S.; m. Christine Culp, Feb. 22, 1974. AB, Cornell U., 1956, MD, 1960. Diplomate: Am. Bd. Internal Medicine. Intern Johns Hopkins Hosp., Balt., 1960-61, resident, 1961-62; instr. medicine Emory U. Sch. Medicine, Atlanta, 1962-64; chief med. resident, instr. U. Fla. Coll. Medicine, Gainesville, 1964-65, asst. prof. medicine and microbiology, 1965-69, asso. prof., 1969-72; prof., chmn. dept. med. microbiology, prof. medicine Creighton U. Sch. Medicine, Omaha, 1972-95, prof. emeritus, 1995—. Cons.-in-research Fla. Dept. Health and Rehab. Services, 1966— *Recipient of 11 awards for teaching excellence and 7 awards for research achievements. Honored by lectureships at the Pasteur Institute in Paris and the Jules Bordet Institute in Brussels. Co-recipient of 9 patents for anti-infective substances and antibiotics. Authored or co-authored 203 scientific articles and acted as editor or co-editor of 5 scientific books and monographs. Also co-authored book outside the scientific arena entitled "Pocket MatchSafes: Reflections of Life and Art, 1840-1920." Recognized by Creighton University as Distinguished Professor and recipient of Distinguished Faculty Service Award.* Editor: Am. Jour. Epidemiology, 1974-95; contbr. sci. articles to profl. jours. Served as med. officer USPHS, 1962-64. Recipient NIH Research Career Devel. award, 1968-72; John and Mary R. Markle scholar in acad. medicine, 1968-73 Mem. Am. Soc. for Microbiology, Infectious Diseases Soc. Am., Soc. for Epidemiol. Research, Am. Lung Assn., Thoracic Soc., N.Y. Acad. Scis., Phi Beta Kappa, Sigma Xi, Phi Kappa Phi. Achievements include patent on enocin antibiotic and RBE limonene and perrilyl alcohol. Home: 1901 Pennsylvania Ave Englewood FL 34224 E-mail: ecsanders@gls3c.com. *Each day provides more challenges and more opportunities than the preceding. No individual can possibly cope with each of these in any given day. Success depends upon establishing priorities and maintaining them. Fight only those battles and pursue with fervor only those opportunities that improve both one's self and one's fellow man.*

SANDERS, WILLIAM EUGENE, marketing executive; b. Asheboro, N.C., Nov. 16, 1933; s. Arthur Ira and Picola (Loftin) S.; m. Velna Elizabeth Sumner, June 8, 1957; children: William Eugene Jr., George Herbert Sumner. AB in Polit. Sci., U. N.C., 1956, postgrad. in Law, 1956-57. Marketing rep. Encyclopaedia Britannica, Greensboro, N.C., 1957-60, Am. Pubs., Chgo., 1960-66; pres. S&W Distbrs., Inc., Greensboro, 1966—. Little league coach Civitans, Greensboro, 1967-68. With U.S. Army Res., 1957-63. Named Hon. Amb. Dept. of Labor, Ky., 1976, Ky. Col., 1976, Hon. Mem. La. Lt. Gov. Staff, 1984; recipient Cert. Appreciation Jefferson Davis Parish Libr., Jennings, La., 1986, Top Sales award Am. Media. Corp., 1996, Marshall Cavendish Top Prodn. award, 1990-91, Mktg. award Am. Media, 1995, Gold Cir. award Penworthy Books, 1999, 2000, 01, Marshall Cavendish quota Prodn. award, 1999, 2000. Mem.: Gen. Alumni Assn. (co-chmn. Greensboro chpt. 1979—80, Rosen Prodn. award 2001—02), State Libr. Assn. S.C., State Libr. Assn. N.C., State Libr. Assn. La., State Libr. Assn. W.Va., State Libr. Assn. Va. Democrat. Methodist. Office: S&W Distbrs Inc 1600 E Wendover Ave # H Greensboro NC 27405-6854

SANDERS, WILLIAM H, music educator; b. New Castle, Pa., July 12, 1948; s. Harry A. and Jeanne B. Sanders; m. Gail C. Hughes, Sept. 11, 1971; children: William D., Mark. BS - Music Edn., Geneva Coll., Beaver Falls, PA, 1970; MED, Westminster Coll., New Wilmington, PA, 1974. Music tchr. New Castle Area Schools, New Castle, Pa., 1971—. Mem.: PA Music Educators Assn., New Castle Fedn. of Teachers. Avocations: stock car racing, stock car racing. Home: 10 Coates Avenue New Castle PA 16101

SANDERS, WILLIAM JOHN, research scientist; b. Detroit, July 10, 1940; s. John William and Charlotte Barbara (Linsday) Steele; m. Gary Roberts, Sept. 12, 1961; children: Scott David, Susan Deborah. BS, U. Mich., 1962; MSEE, U. Calif., Berkeley, 1964. Sr. rsch. scientist Stanford (Calif.) U., 1967-97; pres. Sanders Data Systems, 1991—. Pres. Computers in Cardiology, 1990-93, dir., 2000—, dir. info. svcs., 2001—. Inventor cardiac probe; contbr. articles to profl. jours. Mem. IEEE Computer Soc., Assn. Computing Machinery. Avocations: bicycling, wind surfing. Office: Sanders Data Sys 3980 Bibbits Dr Palo Alto CA 94303-4531 E-mail: bill@sandersdata.com.

SANDERS-COCHRAN, RACHEL DEANNA, lawyer; b. Heflin, Ala., Aug. 4, 1962; m. Gregory D. Cochran, Nov. 4, 1994; children: William G., S. Sanders. BS magna cum laude, Auburn U., 1988; JD cum laude, Samford U., 1991. Bar: Ala. 1991, U.S. Dist. Ct. (mid. dist.) Ala. 1991, U.S. Dist. Ct. (no. and so. dist.) Ala. 1994, U.S. Ct. Appeals (11th cir.) 1994. Atty. Capell, Howard, Knabe & Cobbs, Montgomery, Ala., 1991-94, Pierce, Carr, Alford, Mobile, 1994-96, Carr, Alford, Clausen, Mobile, 1996, Rushton, Stakely, Johnston & Garrett, Montgomery, 1997—. Mem. ABA, Def. Rsch. Inst., Ala. Bar Assn. (mem. exec. com. young lawyers divsn.), Ala. Def. Lawyers Assn. Office: Rushton Stakely Johnston & Garrett 184 Commerce St Montgomery AL 36104-2538

SANDERSON, ARTHUR CLARK, engineering educator; b. Providence, Oct. 23, 1946; s. Robert Leroy and Julia Ayer (Oldham) S.; m. Susan Rita Walsh, Aug. 14, 1971; children: Angeline Mirada, Andrew McWain. BS, Brown U., 1968; MS, Carnegie-Mellon U., 1970, PhD, 1972. Rsch. engr. Westinghouse Electric Corp., Pitts., 1968-70; vis. rsch. scientist Delft (The Netherlands) U. Tech., 1972-73; prof. Carnegie-Mellon U., Pitts., 1973-87, co-dir. robotics inst., 1981-87; rsch. dir. Philips Rsch. Labs., Briarcliff Manor, N.Y., 1985-87; prof., dept. chmn. Rensselaer Poly. Inst., Troy, 1987—; divsn. dir. elec. & comm. systems NSF, Arlington, Va., 1998-2000; v.p. rsch. Rensselaer Poly. Inst., 2000—. Vis. prof. Univ. Iberoamericana, Mexico City, 1975-77, Inst. Info. Sci. & Elecs., U. Tsukuba, Japan, 1996-97. Contbr. 3 books, over 250 articles to profl. jours. Fellow AAAS, IEEE (pres. robotics and automation soc. 1989, 90); mem. AIAA (mem. space automation and robotics tech. com.), Am. Assn. Artificial Intelligence, Soc. Mfg. Engrs. Home: 26 Riverwalk Way Cohoes NY 12047-3335 Office: Rensselaer Poly Inst 110 8th St Troy NY 12180-3522 E-mail: sandea@rpi.edu.

SANDERSON, DAVID R. physician; b. South Bend, Ind., Dec. 26, 1933; s. Robert Burns and Alpha (Rodenberger) S.; divorced, 1978; children: David, Kathryn, Robert, Lisa; m. Evelyn Louise Klunder, Sept. 20, 1980. BA, Northwestern U., 1955, MD, 1958. Cons. in medicine Mayo Clinic, Rochester, Minn., 1965-87, chmn. dept. thoracic disease, 1977-87, cons. in medicine Scottsdale, Ariz., 1987—2000, chmn. dept. internal medicine, 1988-96, vice chmn. bd. govs., 1987-94. Assoc. dir. Mayo Lung Project, Nat. Cancer Inst., Rochester. Contbr. articles to profl. jours. Recipient Noble award Mayo Found., Rochester, Chevalier Jackson award Am. Bronchoesophagologic Assn., 1990. Fellow ACP, Am. Coll. Chest Physicians (gov. for Minn. 1981-87); mem. Am. Bronchoesophagologic Assn., World Assn. for Bronchology, Internat. Bronchoesophagologic Assn., Internat. Assn. Study of Lung Cancer, AMA, Sigma Xi, Sigma Chi (Significant Sig award 1989). Presbyterian. Home: 10676 E Bella Vista Dr Scottsdale AZ 85258-6086 Office: Mayo Clinic Scottsdale 13400 E Shea Blvd Scottsdale AZ 85259-5499 E-mail: dsanderson958@md.northwestern.edu.

SANDERSON, DOUGLAS JAY, lawyer; b. Boston, Apr. 21, 1953; s. Warren and Edith S. Sanderson; m. Audrey S. Goldstein, June 6, 1982; children: Scott M.G., Phoebe H.G. BA, Trinity Coll., Hartford, Conn., 1974; JD, George Washington U., 1977. Bar: Va. 1977, D.C. 1978, U.S. Dist. Ct. (ea. dist.) Va. 1978, U.S. Ct. Appeals (4th cir.) 1978. Assoc. Bettius, Rosenberger & Carter, P.C., Fairfax, Va., 1977-82; ptnr. Bettius & Sanderson, P.C. and predecessor firms, 1982-86; prin. Miles & Stockbridge P.C., 1986-95; br. head Miles & Stockbridge, 1989-91; co-owner McCandlish & Lillard, P.C., 1995—. Trustee Cambridge Ctr. Behavioral Studies, Cambridge, 1981-90. Editor: Consumer Protection Reporting Svc., 1976-77. Bd. dirs. Legal Svcs. No. Va., Inc., 1991-97, pres., 1993-95; vol. counsel Arts Coun. of Fairfax County, Inc., 1991--. Mem. ABA, Va. Bar Assn., Fairfax Bar Assn., Ctrl. Fairfax C. of C. (bd. dirs. 1988-93). Avocations: sports, reading. Office: McCandlish & Lillard 11350 Random Hills Rd Ste 500 Fairfax VA 22030-6044

SANDERSON, EDWARD J., JR. information technology executive; B, U.S. Naval Acad.; MBA, George Washington U. Ptnr. Arthur Andersen (now Andersen Cons.); also bd. dirs.; ptnr. McKinsey & Co.; pres. worldwide info. svcs. Unisys; exec. v.p. Oracle Corp., Redwood City, Calif. Office: Oracle Corp 500 Oracle Pkwy Redwood City CA 94085*

SANDERSON, GEOFF, professional hockey player; b. Hay River, N.W.T., Can., Feb. 1, 1972; Hockey player Hartford, 1990-97, Carolina Hurricanes, 1997-98, Vancouver Canucks, 1998, Buffalo Sabres, 1998-2000, Columbus Blue Jackets, 2000—. Office: Columbus Blue Jackets 150 E Wilson Bridge Rd Columbus OH 43085-2328

SANDERSON, GLEN CHARLES, science director; b. Wayne County, Mo., Jan. 21, 1923; married; 2 children. BS, U. Mo., 1947, MA, 1949; PhD, U. Ill., 1961. Game biologist Iowa State Conservation Commn., 1949-55, Ill. Dept. Conservation, 1955-60; from game biologist to prin. scientist emeritus, dir. Ill. Nat. History Survey, Champaign, 1955—90, prin. scientist emeritus, dir., 1990—; prof. U. Ill., 1965—92. Adj. rsch. prof. So. Ill. U., 1964, adj. prof. 1964-84. Editor Jour. Wildlife Mgmt., 1971-72. Recipient Oak Leaf award Nature Conservancy, 1975. Mem. AAAS, Am. Soc. Mammal, Am. Inst. Biol. Sci., Wildlife Soc. (Aldo Leopold Meml. award 1992). Achievements include research in population dynamics of wild animals, especially furbearers, physiological factors of reproductive and survival rates, and lead poisoning in waterfowl. Office: Ill Natural History Survey Ctr Wildlife Ecology 711 S State St Champaign IL 61820-5114

SANDERSON, HOLLADAY WORTH, priest; b. Raleigh, N.C., May 17, 1950; d. Hal Venable Jr. and Mary Simmons (Andrews) W.; m. Glen Wessel Potter, Apr. 15, 1978 (div. Sept. 1980); m. Stanley McNaughton Sanderson, July 2, 1984. AB in Music and French, U. N.C., 1972; MMEd, East Carolina U., 1975; cert. advanced acctg./data processing, Kinman Bus. U., 1985; MDiv, Va. Theol. Sem., 2001. Ordained priest Episcopal Ch., 2001, ordained deacon 2001. Orch. tchr. New Hanover County Schs., Wilmington, N.C., 1972-74, 75-78, Fairfax (Va.) County Schs., 1978-80, 86-89, Missoula (Mont.) Elem. Sch. Dist., 1983-84; musician, music tchr. Coeur d'Alene, Idaho, 1980-83, 84-86, 1989-91; adj. music faculty, violin, viola, chamber music North Idaho Coll., 1980-83, 84-86; organist, choir dir. St. Luke's Episcopal ch., 1980-83, 84-86, St. Luke's Episcopal Ch., Coeur d'Alene, 1989-95; gen. mgr., artistic dir. Coeur d'Alene Summer Theatre, 1991-92; bookkeeper, adminstrv. asst. Women's Ctr., 1993-95, exec. dir., 1995-98; rector St. Martin's Episcopal Ch., Moses Lake, Wash., 2001—. Sec. Idaho Coalition Against Sexual and Domestic Violence, 1995-98; sec.-treas. North Idaho Coalition on Domestic Violence, 1995-98; bd. dirs. Idaho Women's Network, 1997-98; mem. vestry St. Luke's Episcopal Ch., 1995-97, chair audit com., 1992-95, lay reader, chalice bearer, 1992-98, parliamentarian, 1996, sr. warden, 1997; orch. dir. Pend Oreille Chamber Orch., Sandpoint, Idaho, 1994-95, North Idaho Symphony, 1991, Coeur d'Alene Summer Theatre, 1982-85; cert. QPR suicide prevention gatekeeper instr. Greentree Behavioral Ctr., Spokane, 1996—; mem. Nat. Coalition Against Domestic Violence, Washington State Coalition Against Domestic Violence; bd. dirs. Idaho Woman's Network, 1997-98. Democrat. Avocations: reading, cross-stitch, feminist theology. Home: 3805 Sherwood Dr Coeur D Alene ID 83815-7834 Address: 415 E State St Moses Lake WA 98837 Office: St Martins Episcopal Ch 416 E Nelson Rd Moses Lake WA 98837

SANDERSON, JAMES RICHARD, naval officer, planning and investment company consultant; b. Selma, Calif., Dec. 27, 1925; s. Charles Maxwell and Edith (Wente) S.; m. Betty Lee Bradley, Sept. 19, 1947. Student, U. Calif.-Berkeley, 1943-44, U. Wash., 1944, U. Willamette, 1944-45; grad., USNR Midshipman Sch. at Columbia U., 1945, Nat. War Coll., 1966; student, Gen. Line Sch., Monterey, Calif., 1953, Sr. Officers Ship Material Mgmt. Course, Idaho Falls, Idaho, 1979; BA in Internat. Affairs, George Washington U., 1968. Served as enlisted man U.S. Naval Res., 1943-45; commd. ensign USN, 1946, advanced through grades to vice adm., 1980; gunnery officer U.S.S. Mansfield, 1946-47, U.S.S. Bausell, 1947-48; flight trainee Naval Air Sta., Pensacola, Fla., 1949, Corpus Christi, Tex., 1950; served in Attack Squadron 195, Alameda, Calif., 1950-52; flight instr. Naval Air Sta., Pensacola, 1953-55; served in Attack Squadron 16, 1955-57; air ops. officer on staff Comdr. Carrier Div. Four, U.S.S. Forrestal, 1957-60; ops. officer Attack Squadron 43, Naval Air Sta., Oceana, Va., 1960-62; comdg. officer Attack Squadron 76, 1962-63; comdr. Attack Carrier Air Wing Three in U.S.S. Saratoga, 1963-65; spl. support plans officer, Pacific Area Strategic Plans and Policy Div., Office of Chief of Naval Ops., Washington, 1966-67; exec. asst. and sr. aide to dep. chief. naval ops., 1967-69; comdg. officer U.S.S. Ranier, 1969-70; dep. chief of staff for ops. and plans U.S. Sixth Fleet, 1970-71; comdg. officer U.S.S. Saratoga, 1971-73; dep. comdr. Naval Striking and Support Forces, So. Europe, Naples, Italy, 1973-76; vice dir. ops. Joint Chiefs of Staff, Washington, 1976-77; asst. dep. chief naval ops. for plans, policy and ops., 1977-79; comdr. Task Force Sixty, U.S. 6th Fleet, 1979-80, Carrier Group Two, 1979-80, Battle Force Sixth Fleet, 1979-80, Carrier Striking Force So. Region, 1979-80; dep. and chief staff, comdr. in chief Atlantic/U.S. Atlantic Fleet, Norfolk, Va., 1980-83; ret., 1983; exec. cons. Exec. Planning & Investment Co., Inc., Virginia Beach, Va., 1983-85; sr. v.p. for corp. ops. Computer Dynamics, Inc., 1984-86; asst. to pres. Eastern Computers, Inc., 1986—; cons., prin. Exec. Planning and Investment Co., Inc., 1986-94; sr. fellow joint and combined warfare course Armed Forces Staff Coll., 1994—. Decorated 21 campaign medals, including D.S.M., Legion of Merit with 3 gold stars, D.F.C., Meritorious Service medal, Air medal with 4 gold stars, Navy Commendation medal with combat distinguishing device. Mem. NRA, KT, U. Calif. Alumni Assn., George Washington U. Alumni Assn., Nat. War Coll. Alumni Assn., Naval Acad. Athletic Assn., Assn. Naval Aviation, Tailhook Assn., Smithsonian Assn., Nat. Eagle Scout Assn. (regent, Disting. Eagle Scout award 1994), Nat. Skeet Shooting Assn., KT Eye Found., Nat. Assn. Individual Investors, Nat. Wildlife Assn., Order of Daedalians, Army Navy Country Club (Arlington, Va.), Masons (33d degree), Shriners, Sojourners, Royal Order of Scotland. Clubs: Army Navy Country (Arlington, Va.). Lodges: Masons (33 degree), Shriners, Knight Templer, Sojourners.

SANDERSON, JEROME ALAN, survey statistician, accountant; b. Nashville, Nov. 18, 1945; s. Bernard and Anna Sanderson; m. Rhona J. Flehinger, Oct. 5, 1990. BSBA, U. Tenn., 1968; MS in Tech. of Mgmt., Am. U., 1974. CPA, Md. Survey statistician Bur. of Census, Washington, 1968-80, U.S. Dept. Energy-Energy Info. Adminstrn., Washington, 1980—. Chief minerals & metals sect. Bur. of Census Fgn. Trade Divsn., Washington, 1977-80. Mem. Hexagon, Inc., Washington, 1984—, Camelot Community Neighborhood Watch, Annandale, Va., 1993—. Mem. Greater Washington Soc. of CPAs, Md. Assn. CPAs, Alpha Epsilon Pi. Avocations: amateur radio, philately. Home: 3806 King Arthur Rd Annandale VA 22003-1323 Office: US Dept Energy 950 Lenfant Plz SW Washington DC 20024-2123

SANDERSON, MARY LOUISE, medical association administrator; b. Fairmont, W. Va., Oct. 29, 1942; d. Lawrence Oliver and Frances Evelyn (Shuttleworth) Shingleton; m. William W. Olmstead III, Dec. 1966 (div. June 1974); children: William W. IV, Happy; m. Lester F. Davis, III, Oct. 1979 (div. Dec. 1986); m. David S. Sanderson, Sept. 1992. Student, Vassar Coll., 1960-62, Carnegie Mellon, 1962-63. Real estate broker, N.C. Exec. sec. Creative Dining, Raleigh, N.C., 1980-83, Sea Pines Plantation Co., Hilton Head, S.C., 1973-79; adminstr. Am. Bd. Neurological Surgery, Houston, 1983—. Vol. Interact, Raleigh, 1984-86, M.D. Anderson Cancer Ctr./Camp Star Trails, 1994—; docent Mordicai House Hist. Preservation, Raleigh, 1981-83; mem. Reach to Recovery, 1995—. Recipient Vol. award N.C. State Gov., 1986. Mem. Am. Soc. Assn. Execs. Democrat. Episcopalian. Office: Am Bd Neurol Surgery 6550 Fannin St Ste 2139 Houston TX 77030-2718*

SANDESON, WILLIAM SEYMOUR, cartoonist; b. Mound City, Ill., Dec. 16, 1913; s. William Stephen and Jessie Mae (Mertz) S.; m. Ione Wear, June 4, 1938 (dec. 1975); 1 son, William Scott; m. Ruth Cress, Dec. 31, 1978. Student, Chgo. Acad. Fine Arts, 1931-32. Free-lance cartoonist for nat. mags., 1932-37; editorial cartoonist New Orleans Item-Tribune, 1937-41; cartoonist, picture editor and art dir. St. Louis Star-Times, 1941-51; editorial cartoonist Ft. Wayne (Ind.) News-Sentinel, 1951-82; ret., 1982. Drew daily cartoon feature for, Star-Times, Sketching Up With the News. Recipient Honor medal Freedoms Found., 1952, 53, 56, George Washington Honor medal, 1954, 55, 57, 58, 59, 60, Disting. Service award, 1961-72, cartoon award, 1982;, Ind. Sch. Bell award, 1967, Disting. Service awards, 1971-76, prin. cartoon award, 1977, cartoon award, 1978; co-recipient Pulitzer prize for gen. local reporting, 1982 Mem. Nat. Cartoonist Soc., Assn. Am. Editorial Cartoonists. Clubs: Fort Wayne Press (pres. 1965). Congregationalist. Home: 119 W Sherwood Ter Fort Wayne IN 46807-2846 *Until I'm listed in WHO WAS WHO, I intend to dip my brush in a mixture of self-improvement, stubbornness, and sincere thoughtfulness of my fellow American.*

SANDFORD, JUANITA DADISMAN, sociologist, educator, writer; b. Wichita, Kans., June 20, 1926; d. Carl Orville and Mabel Bernice (Stearman) Dadisman; m. Herman Prestridge Sandford, Dec. 22, 1946; children: Susan Jane, Linda Ann, Mary Kaye. BA, Baylor U., 1947, MA, 1948; LLD (hon.), Hendrix Coll., 1991. Instr. sociology Wayland Bapt. Coll., Plainview, Tex., 1948-49, Ft. Smith (Ark.) Jr. coll., 1959, Ouachita Bapt. U., Arkadelphia, Ark., 1960-68, adj. prof., 1996—; asst. prof. sociology Henderson State U., 1968-89, coord. women's studies, 1975-89; ret., 1989; adj. tchr. Ouachita Bapt. U., 1996—. Chmn. bd. Coll. Cmty. Action, Inc., 1974-78; cons. human rels. Ark. Tech. Assistance & Consultative Ctr., 1964-78; mem. Gov. Ark. Commn. on Status of Women, 1975-80, Atty. Gen. Consumer Adv. Bd., 1977-79. Author: I Didn't Get a Lot Done Today, 1974, Poverty in the Land of Opportunity, 1978, Sunbonnet Sue: The Crone, 1996; contbg. author Women & Religion: Images of Women in the Bible, 1977, Arkansas: State in Transition, 1981, Arkadelphia: 2000 AD, 1982. Bd. dirs. Ctrl. Ark. Devel. Coun., 1975-80, Ark. Hunger Project, 1983-86, Ark. Advs. for Children and Families, 1986-89. Recipient Ark. Woman of Achievement award Ark. Womens Polit. Caucus, 1975. Mem. NOW, Ark. Sociolog. & Anthropolog. Assn. (pres. 1991-92), Inst. Noetic Sci. Avocations: quilting, flower gardening. Home: 959 N 8th St Arkadelphia AR 71923-3201 E-mail: sandford@ezclick.net.

SANDFORD, VIRGINIA ADELE, motivational speaker, writer; b. Tacoma, Nov. 29, 1926; d. Fred John and Lucille Lillian (Skok) Wepfer; m. Calvert H. Sandford, Sept. 16, 1949 (div. 1970); children: Susan L., Kaye E., James C. Student, U. Wash., 1946-49. Tchr. stringed instruments dept. music Puyallup (Wash.) Sch. Dist., 1944-46; sec. Fife (Wash.) Sch. Dist., 1969-72; exec. sec. Tacoma (Wash.) Sch. Dist., 1972-75; tchr. ednl. sec. program Clover Park Vocat. Tech. Inst., Tacoma, 1975-82; profl. spkr., seminar prodr. Virginia Sandford & Assocs., 1982—. Author: You Can't Smell the Roses When You're Pushing Up Daisies, 2001. Violinist, Tacoma Symphony, 1972-75. Mem. Am. Vocat. Assn., Wash. Vocat. Assn., Ednl. Office Personnel, Nat. Spkrs. Assn., Pacific N.W. Spkrs. Assn., Alpha Chi Omega. E-mail: vsandford@nventure.com.

SANDHU, HARVINDER SINGH, spinal surgeon, educator; b. Jalandhar, Punjab, India, Mar. 18, 1962; s. Jagtar singh and Shivtej Kaur Sandhu; m. Sonia Kaur Chattha, May 25, 1997; 1 child, alexi. BS, Northwestern U., 1982, MD, 1987; MBA, Columbia U., 2001. Diplomate Am. Bd. Orthopedic Surgery, Nat. Bd. Med. Examiners. Attending spine surgeon UCLA, 1994-97, Hosp. for Spl. Surgery, N.Y.C., 1997—. Pres. Sandhu Cons., Scarsdale, N.Y., 1999—. Recipient Outstanding Sci. Exhibit award Internat. Soc. for Study of the Lumbar spine, 1999, Volvo award for Lumbar Spine Rsch., 2002. Mem. Am. Acad. Orthopedic Surgery (biologic implants com. 2000—), Orthopedic Rsch. Soc., N.Am. Spine Soc. (Outstanding Sci. Exhibit award 1996), Scoliosis Rsch. Soc., Beta Gamma Sigma. Office: Hosp for Spl Surgery 535 E 70th St New York NY 10021 Fax: (212) 774-2600. E-mail: sandhuh@hss.edu.

SANDIDGE, JUNE CAROL, retired physical education educator; b. Lynchburg, Va., Mar. 16, 1936; d. Fred Brown and Sarah Elizabeth (Cocks) S. BS, Longwood Coll., Farmville, Va., 1959; MEd, U. Va., 1967; cert. advanced grad. studies, Va. Tech. Inst., 1981. Tchr. Roanoke (Va.) City Schs., 1959-65; prof. phys. edn. and recreation Ferrum (Va.) Coll., 1965-2001; ret. Asst. dir. YWCA Camp-on-Craig, Roanoke, 1965-83, dir., 1984-85; interim dir. Henry Forks Svc. Ctr., United Meth. Ch., Rocky Mount, Va., 1986-87, chair bd., 1989-91, cons. ARC, Roanoke, 1986-90, chair S.W. Va. territory, 1988-91, chair Va./D.C. field svc., 1992-95. Recipient Disting. Service Alumni award Longwood Coll., 1984, Honor award for vol. svc. ARC, 1982. Mem. AAUW, AAHPERD, Va. Assn. Health, Phys. Edn., Recreation and Dance (rep. aquatic coun. so. dist. 1991-93), Coun. Nat. Coop. Aquatics, Phi Delta Kappa. Baptist. Home and Office: 437 Hedgelawn Ave Roanoke VA 24019

SANDIDGE, KANITA DURICE, consultant, retired communications executive; b. Cleve., Dec. 2, 1947; d. John Robert Jr. and Virginia Louise (Caldwell) S. AB, Cornell U., 1970; MBA, Case Western Res. U., 1979. Supr. assignments service ctrs. and installation AT&T, Cleve., 1970-78, chief dept. data processing and acctg., 1979-80, adminstrn. mgr. exec. v.p. staff N.Y.C., 1980-83, sales forecasting and analysis mgr. resources planning Newark, 1983-86; planning and devel. mgr. material planning and mgmt. AT&T Network Systems, Morristown, N.J., 1986-87, dir. adminstrv. services Lisle, Ill., 1987-89, dir. divsn. staff customer support and ops. Morristown, 1990-94; dir. global procurement minority and women bus. enterprises AT&T, Basking Ridge, N.J., 1994-98; prin. Sandidge Cons. Group, Randolph, 1999—. Mem black exchange program Nat. Urban League, N.Y.C., 1986-98. Named Black Achiever in Industry, Harlem YMCA, 1981; recipient Tribute to Women and Industry Achievement award YWCA, 1985; one of Minority Bus. News USA's Women Who Mean Business; named Nat. Minority Supplier Devel. Coun. MBE Coord. of the Yr., 1996; recipient Nat. Fedn. of Black Women Bus. Owners Black Women of Courage Woman Owned Bus. Advocate award, 1997. Mem. Nat. Black MBA's, Alliance Black AT&T Mgrs., Am. Mgmt. Assn., Nat. Assn. for Female Execs., NAACP, Beta Alpha Psi. Mem. African Meth. Episcopal Ch. Home and Office: 10 Trade Winds Dr Randolph NJ 07869-1238 E-mail: kdsandidge@att.net.

SANDIFER, KEVIN WAYNE, archival services executive; b. Shreveport, La., Sept. 5, 1956; s. Glenn Eugene and Beverly Sue (Mauritzen) S. BS in Libr. Sci., La. State U., Shreveport, 1985, BA in History, 1987; M in Spl. Libr. Instrn., U. Arlington, 1989. Pub. Red River Press, Blanchard, La., 1985-87; pres., CEO Archival Svcs., Inc., 1988—. Author: Layman's Look at Starting a Religious Archive, 1982 (Disting. Writing award 1983), Complete Document Restoration Manual, 1986, Introduction to Religious Archival Science, 1988. 2d edit., 1998, Public Relations are an Asset for the Museum and Archives, 1986, 2d edit., 1998, Photography Simplified for the Archivist, 1990, 2d edit., 1995, Christianityn and the Ark of the Covenant, 1998, others; editor: (textbook) Oral History, 1985. Archivist Grandstone Bluff Mus., 1985-90. Named Outstanding Historian Northwest La., Shreveport Jour., 1982, Expert Archivist Shreveport Times, 1983. Fellow Soc. Am. Archivists; mem. Am. Assn. State and Local History, La. Hist. Soc., North La. Hist. Assn. Southern Baptist. Avocations: reading, writing, running track. Home and Office: 3900 Roy Rd Apt 37 Shreveport LA 71107-9631

SANDITEN, EDGAR RICHARD, investment company executive; b. Okmulgee, Okla., Feb. 1, 1920; s. Herman and Anna (Sanditen) S.; m. Isabel Raffkind, Jan. 26, 1945; children: Linda Caryl, Judith Marie, Ellen Jane, Michael Jay. Student, Western Mil. Acad., 1934-37; BS in Bus., Okla. U., 1941. With Otasco, Inc., Tulsa, 1941-87, v.p., 1970, pres., 1974-77, chmn., chief exec. officer, 1977-83, chmn. employees retirement trust, 1983-87; prin., chmn. Sanditen Investments, Ltd., 1987—. Fin. advisor Bank of Okla., 1978-84. Chmn. Tulsa Charity Horse Show, 1969-71, 80-84; bd. dirs. Tulsa Opera, 1979—, chmn., 1979-81, 83-85, v.p., 1989 (Champion Fundraiser, 1989-96); bd. dirs. Tulsa Ballet Theatre (Dimedici award 1989), Tulsa Philharm. 1990—, Tulsa Hist. Soc., 1995-99, Fenster Mus., 1983-85, Ret. Sr. Vols., 1997—; mem. B'nai Emunah Synagogue; pres. Temple Israel, 1968-70; chmn., pres. Children's Med. Ctr., 1979-81; bd. dirs. NCCJ, 1983—, pres., 1985-87; mem. adv. bd. dirs. U. Okla. Coll. Bus. Adminstrn., 1986—; hon. chmn. Ronald McDonald House, 1991; bd. dirs. St. John Med. Ctr., 1978-87, chmn., 1978-81. With USAAF, 1943-46. Recipient Nat. Humanitarian award Nat. Jewish Hosp., 1987, Brotherhood award NCCJ, 1991, Alfred Aaronson Cmty. Rels. award, 1993; named Boss of Yr., Am. Bus. Women's Assn., 1976; named to Tulsa Hall of Fame, 1996. Mem. Tulsa Jr. C. of C. (honor award 1943), Tulsa C. of C. (v.p. 1978-79), Quarter Century Club Automotive Industry, So. Hills Country Club (bd. dirs. 1990-96, fin. chmn., exec. com., v.p. 1992, pres. 1995). Office: Sanditen Investments Ltd 3314 E 51st St Ste 207K Tulsa OK 74135-3527

SAND LEE, INGER, artist; b. Sauda, Norway, Apr. 8, 1938; came to U.S., 1960; d. Inge Sigvald and Johanne Elise (Hamre) Sand; m. Charles Allen Lee, Aug. 28, 1981. Cert. in decorative art, N.Y. Sch. Interior Design, 1968; BFA, Marymount Manhattan Coll./N.Y. Sch. Interior Design, 1980; cert. completion, Art Students League, 1993; postgrad., Nat. Acad. Design, 1993-94. Auction benefit ASID 85th Anniversary, 2001; juror small works Wash. Sq. East Galleries Dept. or N.Y.U., 2002. One-woman shows include Art 54, N.Y.C., 1988, Pyramid Gallery, N.Y.C., 1990, Exhbn. Space, N.Y.C., 1991, Denise Bibro Fine Art, N.Y.C., 1993, 95, 97, 98, 99, 2000, 01, DYN-CORP, Oak Ridge, Tenn., 1998, En Vogue Gallery, Knoxville, 1999; selected exhbns. include Lincoln Ctr., N.Y.C., 1988, Avery Fisher Hall, N.Y.C., 1988, Mus. Atheism and Realism, Lviv, USSR, 1990, Lever House, N.Y.C., 1991, Nat. Acad. Mus., N.Y.C., 1994, Albright-Knox Mus., Buffalo, N.Y., 2000; group exhbns. include Pyramid Gallery, N.Y.C., 1989, 90, 91, Ariel Gallery, N.Y.C., 1991, Broome Street Gallery, N.Y.C., 1992, 93, Ward-Nasse Gallery, N.Y.C., 1992, Hudson Guild Art Gallery, N.Y.C., 1992, Denise Bibro Fine Art, N.Y.C., 1992, 94, 95, 97, 99, 2000, Frank Bustamante Gallery, N.Y.C., 1993, Southern Alleghenies Mus. Art, Loretto, Pa., 1994, Edward William Gallery, 1996, Knoxville (Tenn.) Opera Guild, 1996, Fairleigh Dickinson U., 1996, N.Y. Internat. Film and Video Festival, 1998, Gramercy Park Armory, N.Y.C., 1998, Jacob K. Javits Conv. Ctr., N.Y.C., 1998, DYN Corp., Oak Ridge, Tenn., 1998, Denise Bibro Fine Art, N.Y., 1999, 2001, Cambridge Fin., Knoxville, 2000; group shows include En Vogue Gallery, Knoxville, Tenn., 1999, Art at the Mill, Millwood, Va., 1999, Adventures in Art The Women's Nat. Republican Club, 2001. Mem. presdl. victory team Republican Nat. Com., 2001. Grantee Cork Gallery, Lincoln Ctr., N.Y.C.; recipient Alumni award N.Y. Sch. Interior Design, 1979; merit scholar Art Student's League, 1991. Mem. Archtl. League N.Y., Friends N.Y. Libr., Ams. Soc. (N.Y.), Nat. Geog. Soc., Nat. Mus. Women in the Arts, Pres.'s Cir. Smithsonian Nat. Mus. Am. History (charter, name inscribed on wall of Am. history patrons), Frick Mus., Guggenheim Mus, The Women's Nat. Republican Club. Address: PO Box 2036 New York NY 10021-0051

SANDLER, GERALD HOWARD, computer science educator, company executive; b. N.Y.C., Sept. 17, 1934; s. Irving and Sally S.; m. Ann Sandler; children: Eric, Steven. BS, CUNY, 1956, MS, 1957. With Grumman Aerospace, 1963-83; past pres. Grumman Data Systems & Svcs., Bethpage, N.Y., 1983-95; pres. GHS Enterprises, 1995—; prof. computer sci. Poly. U., Farmingdale, N.Y., 1995—. Author: System Engineering, 1963. Home: 46 Bonnie Dr Westbury NY 11590-2804

SANDLER, IRVING HARRY, art critic, art historian; b. N.Y.C., July 22, 1925; s. Harry and Anna (Robin) S.; m. Lucy Freeman, Sept. 4, 1958; 1 child, Catherine Harriet. BA, Temple U., 1948; MA, U. Pa., 1950; PhD, NYU, 1976. Instr. in art history NYU, 1960-71; prof. art history SUNY, Purchase, 1971—; art critic N.Y. Post, N.Y.C., 1960-65. Author: The Triumph of American Painting: A History of Abstract Expressionism, 1970, The New York School: Painters and Sculptors of the Fifties, 1978, Alex Katz, 1979, Al Held, 1984, American Art of the 1960s, 1988; editor (with Amy Newman) Defining Modern Art: Selected Writings of Alfred H. Barr Jr., 1986, Mark di Suvero at Storm King Art Ctr., 1996, Art of Postmodern Era: From Late 1960s to Early 1990s, 1996, Natvar Bhavsar, 1998, Stephen Antonakos, 1999. John Simon Guggenheim fellow, 1965; Nat. Endowment for Arts fellow, 1977. Mem. Coll. Art Assn., Internat. Assn. Art Critics. Home: 100 Bleecker St New York NY 10012-2202 Office: SUNY at Purchase Dept Visual Arts 735 Anderson Hill Rd Dept Visual Purchase NY 10577-1400

SANDLER, LUCY FREEMAN, art history educator; b. N.Y.C., June 7, 1930; d. Otto and Frances (Glass) Freeman; m. Irving Sandler, Sept. 4, 1958; 1 child, Catherine Harriet. BA, Queens Coll., 1951; MA, Columbia U., 1957; PhD, NYU, 1964. Asst. prof. NYU, 1964-70, assoc. prof., 1970-75, prof. fine arts, 1975-86, Helen Gould Sheppard prof. art history, 1986—, chmn. dept., 1975-89; editorial cons. Viator, UCLA, 1983-97. Author: The Peterborough Psalter in Brussels, 1974, The Psalter of Robert De Lisle in the British Library, 1983, new edit., 1999, Gothic Manuscripts 1285-1385, 1986, 'Omne Bonum': A Fourteenth-Century Encyclopedia of Universal Knowledge, 1996, The Ramsey Psalter, 1999; editor: Essays in Memory of Karl Lehmann, 1964, Art the Ape of Nature: Studies in Honor of H.W. Janson, 1981, Coll. Art Assn. Monograph Series, 1970-75, 86-89, Gesta, 1991-94; asst. editor Art Bull., 1964-67, mem. editl. bd., 1994; mem. editl. bd. Jour. Jewish Art, 1978, Speculum, 1994. Trustee Godwin-Ternbach Mus., Queens Coll., 1982-94; chair dels. exec. com. Am. Coun. Learned Socs., 2002--. NEH fellow, 1967-68, 77; fellow Pierpont Morgan Library; Guggenheim fellow, 1988-89. Fellow Medieval Acad. Am. (councillor 2002), Soc. Antiquaries (London); mem. AAUP, Coll. Art Assn. (pres. 1981-84), Internat. Ctr. Medieval Art (adv. bd., bd. dirs. 1976-80, 84-87, 89-92, 1995-2001). Home: 100 Bleecker St Apt 30A New York NY 10012-2207 Office: NYU Dept Fine Arts New York NY 10003

SANDLER, ROBERT MICHAEL, insurance company executive, actuary; b. N.Y.C., Apr. 20, 1942; s. Albert and Ruth (Marcus) S.; m. Annette L. Marchese, Aug. 18, 1963; children— David, Glenn BA in Math., Hofstra U., 1963. Various actuarial positions Met. Life, N.Y.C., 1963-68; various actuarial positions Am. Internat., 1968-80; v.p., casualty actuary American Internat. Group, Inc., 1980-84, sr. v.p., sr. actuary, sr. claims officer, 1984-95, exec. v.p., 1995—, dir. various subs. Mem. Casualty Acturial Soc. (assoc.), Am. Acad. Actuaries, Internat. Actuarial Assn., Am. Internat. Underwriters (chmn. 1994—). Republican. Home: 3 Crestwood Dr Bridgewater NJ 08807-2209 Office: Am Internat Group 70 Pine St New York NY 10270-0002

SANDLER, ROSS, law educator; b. Milw., Jan. 31, 1939; s. Theodore T. and Laurette (Simons) S.; m. Alice R. Mintzer, Sept. 15, 1968; children: Josephine, Jenny, Dorothy. AB, Dartmouth Coll., 1961; LLB, NYU, 1965. Bar: N.Y. 1965, Fla. 1965. Assoc. atty. Cahill Gordon Reindel & Ohl, N.Y.C., 1965-68; asst. U.S. atty. So. Dist. N.Y., 1968-72; assoc. atty. Trubin Sillcocks Edelman & Knapp, N.Y.C., 1972-75; sr. staff atty. Natural Resources Def. Coun., 1975-81, 83-86; spl. advisor to mayor City of N.Y., 1981-82; exec. dir. Hudson River Found., N.Y.C., 1983-86; commr. N.Y.C. Dept. Transp., 1986-90; ptnr. Jones Day Reavis & Pogue, N.Y.C., 1991-93; law prof. N.Y. Law Sch., 1993—, dir. Ctr. for N.Y.C. law, 1993—; pres. N.Y. Legis. Svc., 1998—. Mem. N.Y.C. Procurement Policy Bd., 1994—; vis. lectr. Yale Law Sch., New Haven, 1977; adj. prof. law NYU Law Sch., 1976-94; chair, mem. N.Y.C. Taxi and Limousine Commn., 1980-90. Co-author: A New Direction in Transit, 1978; columnist Environ. Mag., 1976-80; editor: (jour.) City Law; contbr. book chpt., op-ed columns, articles to profl. jours.; lectr. environ. law, spkr. confs. Trustee Woods Hole (Mass.) Rsch. Ctr., 1983—; mem. exec. com. Hudson River Found., 1986-96; mem. adv. coun. Ctr. Biodiversity and Conservation Am. Mus. Nat. History, 1996—. Recipient Pub. Interest award NYU Law Alumni, 1987, Louis J. Lefkowitz award Fordham Law Sch. Urban Law Jour., 1989, Lifetime Achievement award N.Y. State Bar Assn., 1998. Mem. City Club of N.Y. (chair 1992-93, trustee). Office: NY Law Sch 57 Worth St New York NY 10013-2959

SANDLER, STANLEY IRVING, chemical engineering educator; b. N.Y.C., June 10, 1940; s. Murray C. and Celia M. (Kamenetsky) S.; m. Judith Katherine Ungar, June 17, 1962; children: Catherine Julietta, Joel Abraham, Michael Howard. BChemE, CCNY, 1962; PhD, U. Minn., 1966. NSF postdoctoral fellow Inst. Molecular Physics, U. Md., College Park, 1966-67; successively asst. prof., assoc. prof., prof. dept. chem. engring. U. Del., Newark, 1967-82, H.B. du Pont prof., 1982-2000, chmn. dept., 1982-86, dir. Ctr. for Molecular and Engring. Thermodynamics, 1992—, interim dean Coll. of Engring., 1992, H.B. duPont chair, 2000—. Vis. prof. Imperial Coll., London, 1973-74, U. Nat. del Sur, Bahia Blanca, Argentina, 1985, Tech. U., Berlin, 1981, 88-89, U. Queensland, Brisbane, Australia, 1989, 96, U. Calif., Berkeley, 1995; cons. maj. oil and chem. cos. Author: Chemical and Engineering Thermodynamics, 1977, 3d rev. edit., 1998, Modeling Vapor-Liquid Equilibrium, 1998; editor: Fluid Properties and Phase Equilibria, 1977, Chemical Engineering Education in a Changing Environment, 1989, Kinetic and Thermodynamic Lumping of Multicomponent Mixtures, 1991, Models for Thermodynamic and Phase Equilibria Calculations, 1993, AI Chem E. Jour., 2000—; mem. adv. bd. Jour. Chem. Engring. Data, Chem. Engring. Edn., Indsl. Engring. Chem. Rsch., Indian Chem. Engr., Engring. Sci. and Tech. (Malaysia); also numerous articles. Mem. adv. bd. chem. engring. La. State U., Carnegie-Mellon U., Princeton U. Recipient U.S. sr. Scientist award Alexander von Humboldt Found., 1988, Francis Alison award U. Del., 1993, Ashton Cary award Ga. Tech. U., 1994, Phillips Lecture award Okla. State U., 1993, Rossini Lectureship award Internat. Union Pure Applied Chemistry, 1998. Mem. AIChE (jour. adv. bd., editor 2000—, Profl. Progress award 1984, Warren K. Lewis award 1996, Del. Soc. award 1998), U.S. Nat. Acad. Engring., Am. Chem. Soc. (award Del. sect. 1989, E.V. Murphree award 1997), Am. Soc. Engring. Edn. (lectr. chem. engring. div. 1988), Cosmos Club (Washington). Jewish. Avocations: jogging, philately. Home: 202 Sypherd Dr Newark DE 19711-3627 Office: U Del Dept Chem Engring Newark DE 19716 E-mail: sandler@udel.edu.

SANDLER, SUMNER GERALD, medical educator; b. Lawrence, Mass., Jan. 13, 1935; s. Maurice Lewis and Dorothy Gretchen (Alman) S.; m. Katherine Cushing Rosenberg, May 9, 1969; children: Lisah, David, Jonathan, Joel. AB, Princeton U., 1957; MD, NYU, 1962. Diplomate Am. Bd. Internal Medicine, Am. Bd. Pathology (blood banking). Intern NYU-Bellevue Hosp. Ctr., N.Y.C., 1962-63, assoc. med. resident, 1963-64; clin. assoc. NCI, NIH, 1964-66; hematology fellow NYU-Bellevue Hosp. Ctr., N.Y.C., 1966-68; clin. assoc. NIH, 1964-66; teaching asst. NYU Sch. Medicine, N.Y.C., 1966-67; instr. medicine Georgetown U., Washington, 1968-72, asst. prof. medicine, 1970-72, prof. medicine and pathology, 1991—; sr. lectr. Hebrew U.-Hadassah Med. Ctr., Jerusalem, 1972-78, assoc. prof. medicine, 1977-78; assoc. dir. blood svcs. nat. hdqs. ARC, Washington, 1978-84, assoc. v.p., 1984-90, med. dir., 1989-90, chief med. officer, 1990-91. Med. dir. Nat. Reference Lab., ARC, Rockville, Md., 1978-95; sr. lectr. Hebrew U. Sch. Medicine Hebrew U. Hadassah Sch. Medicine, Jerusalem, 1977-78; head blood bank, Hadassah U. Hosp., Jerusalem, 1972-78; profl. lectr. dept. medicine, George Washington U. Sch. Medicine, Washington, 1988-91, others. Editor: Immunobiology of the Erythrocyte, 1980, Autologous Transfusion, 1983, Advances in Immunobiology, 1984; mem. editl. bd. Haematologia, 1990—, Immunohematology, 1995—, Transfusion, 1982—, assoc. editor, 1996—. Lt. Comdr. USPHS, 1964-66; capt. med. corps. reserve, Israel Def. Forces, 1976-81; bd. mgrs. Adas Israel Congregation, Washington, 1986-92. Recipient FDA Commrs. Spl. Citation, 1988, Vicenniel medal Georgetown U., Washington, 1989, Charles E. Walter Meml. award Mid-Atlantic Assn. Blood Banks, 1996. Fellow Am. Coll. Physicians, Coll. Am. Pathologists; mem. Internat. Soc. Blood Transfusion (hon., counsellor 1986-91, v.p. 1991-94, Svc. award 1990), Am. Assn. Blood Banks, Leukemia Soc. Am. (med. adv. bd. 1970-72, D.C. chpt. chmn. 1971-72, bd. dirs. 1970-72), Israel Soc. Hematology and Blood Transfusion (exec. com. 1976), Am. Soc. Hematology, others. Jewish. Avocation: Torah Bible study. Home: 5808 Ogden Ct Bethesda MD 20816-1263 Office: Georgetown U Med Ctr 3800 Reservoir Rd NW Washington DC 20007-2113 E-mail: sandlerg@gunet.georgetown.edu.

SANDLER, THOMAS R. accountant; b. Mt. Kisco, N.Y., Dec. 16, 1946; s. Louis and Susan (Rosen) S.; m. Alison G. Corneau, Aug. 26, 1972; children—Justin C., Shawn A. BS summa cum laude, Ithaca Coll., 1968; MS, SUNY-Binghamton, 1972. C.P.A., N.Y., Colo. 1982. Asst. acct. KPMG Peat Marwick, White Plains, N.Y., 1972, mgr. Phoenix, 1975, sr. mgr. N.Y.C., 1978, ptnr. Denver, 1981-92, ptnr. in-charge corp. recovery svcs. N.Y.C., 1993-94; mng. ptnr. BDO Seidman, Denver, 1994-95; CFO, treas., sec. Samsonite Corp., 1995-98; pres. Samsonite Am., 1998—. Contbr. articles to profl. jours. Past trustee, past pres. Colo. Children's Chorale; treas., past pres., gov., mem. exec. com., committeeman Colo. Golf Assn.; committeeman U.S. Golf Assn. bd. dirs. Pacific Coast GOlf Assn.; chair-elect Travel Goods Assn. Mem. AICPA, Colo. Soc. CPAs (chmn. real estate and govt. acctg. com.), Bear Creek Golf Club, Country Club at Castle Pines. E-mail: Tom. Home: 896 Anaconda Ct Castle Rock CO 80108-9044 Office: Samsonite Corp Corp Bldg 11200 E 45th Ave Denver CO 80239-3000 E-mail: tom_sandler@Samsonite.com.

SANDLER, TODD MICHAEL, economist, educator, political scientist, educator; b. Mt. Kisco, N.Y., Dec. 16, 1946; s. Louis and Susie Sandler; m. Jean Marie Murdock, June 28, 1985; 1 child Tristan Jon. BA, SUNY, Binghamton, 1968, MA, 1969, PhD, 1971. Asst. prof. Ariz. State U., Tempe, 1971-76; assoc. prof. U. Wyo., Laramie, 1976-79, prof., 1979-85, U. S.C., Columbia, 1985-86; prof. econs. and polit. sci. Iowa State U., Ames, 1986-2000, Disting. prof., 1995—2001; Dockson prof. U. So. Calif., L.A., 2000—. Author: (book) Collective Action: Theory and Applications, 1992, The Economics of Defense, 1995, Global Challenges, 1997, Economic Concepts for the Social Sciences, 2001; co-author: The Theory of Externalities, Public Goods and Club Goods, 1986, The Theory of Externalities, Public Goods and Club Goods, 2d edit., 1996, International Terrorism in 1980s, 1989, Handbook of Defense Economics, 1995, The Political Economy of NATO, 1999; co-editor: Defense Economics, 1989—94; assoc. editor: Jour. Environ. Econs. and Mgmt., 1988—89, assoc. editor: Jour. Pub. Econ. Theory, 1999—, mem. editl. bd.: Social Sci. Quar., mem. editl. bd.: Pub. Fin. Rev., mem. editl. bd.: Fiscal Studies, mem. editl. bd.: , mem. editl. bd.: Def. and Peace Econs., mem. editl. bd.: Bull. Econ. Rsch., mem. editl. bd.: Internat. Studies Quar. Fellow NATO postdoctoral, 1977, 1998—2000, Australian Nat. U., 1981, 1994, Sr., Inst. Policy Reform, 1990—91, 1992—94, Hon., U. Wis.-Madison, 1990; grantee NSF, 1989, 1993. Mem.: Pub. Choice Soc., So. Econ. Assn., Assn. Environ. and Resource Econs. (editl. bd.), Royal Econ. Soc., Am. Econ. Assn., Internat. Def. Econs. Assn. (exec. bd.). Home: 307 Alta Vista Ave South Pasadena CA 91030-3501 Office: U So Calif Sch Internat Rels Los Angeles CA 90089 E-mail: tsandler@usc.edu.

SANDLIN, ANATHALEE GRAY, writer, music company owner; b. Hastings, Nebr., Nov. 12, 1945; d. Lloyd Vern and Elizabeth Powers Gray; m. John Everett Sandlin, Jr.; children: Leigh Ellen Cauthen, Kristin Ann Spain, Heidi Anathalee Wilson. Columnist Nat. Skeet Shooters Review, 1982-83; bus. mgr. Ducktape Music Prodns., Decatur, Ala., 1984—; prin., owner Rockin Rabbit Music Other Ducks Music, 1986—, AGS Publishing, Decatur, 1997—. Artist-media liason various tv award shows and benefit concerts, Southeast, U.S., 1986-96; bd. dirs. Tenn. Valley Homeless Shelter, Ala.; lectr. in field. Author: When Grandma Was Really Cooking, 1989, The Decatur Daily Cookbook, 1993, The Rosary-A Treasure of Graces, 1997. Mem. ASCAP, BMI, North Ala. Songwriters Assn. (bd. dirs., chmn. 1984-86). Avocations: painting, cooking, full time grandmother. Office: PO Box 2854 Decatur AL 35602-2854

SANDLIN, DEBBIE CROWE, critical care nurse; b. Columbia, Tenn., Oct. 1, 1953; d. William Taylor and Jean (Burns) Crowe; divorced; 1 child, Ashley Taylor. AS cum laude, Columbia State Coll., 1973; student, U. Tenn., Nashville, 1974-76. RN, Tenn.; cert. post anesthesia nurse; cert. ACLS, BCLS, U. Tenn. critical care curriculum. Charge nurse surg. unit Maury Regional Med. Ctr., Columbia, 1973-74; charge nurse surg. ICU HCA Pk. View Med. Ctr., Nashville, 1974-76; staff nurse post anesthesia care unit HCA Westside Hosp., 1976-79; head nurse Columbia Centennial Surgery Ctr., 1979-85; nurse mgr. Columbia So. Hills Med. Ctr., 1985—, post anesthesia care unit nurse, 1985—; cert. post anesthesia nurse, 2000—. Mem. Am. Bd. Peri-Anesthesia Nursing Certification Appeals Bd. Surg. missionary Chocola, Guatemala, 1998. Recipient Excellence Critical Care Nursing award U. Tenn.; Maury Regional Med. Ctr. Aux. scholar, 1971; Dr. Frist Humanitarian award nominee, 1989, 95, 96, 97. Mem. Am. Bd. Peri Anesthesia Nursing (cert. rev. task force 1998-99), Mid. Tenn. Soc. Post Anesthesia Nurses (founder, pres. 1986, bd. dirs. 1986-88, Outstanding Svc. award 1986-87, pub. newsletter, editor 1986-87, various coms.), Tenn. Soc. Post Anesthesia Nurses (v.p. 1986-87, pres. 1987-88, bd. dirs. 1986-93, state seminar com. chairperson 1993-94, congl. rep. Point Sys. Winner 1987, 88, chair edn. com. 1994-98, chair TSPAN mid-yr. seminar 1996, various coms.), Am. Soc. Post Anesthesia Nurses (Tenn. dir. 1990-93, membership com. 1993-95, ethics com. 1993-94, new products com., exec. com. 1992-93, chair bylaws com. 1992-93, nat. conf. com. 1991-92, amb. to Nat. Assn. Orthopaedic Nurses 1994, Pres. Appreciation award 1992, 93, 94, Amb. award 1995, 96, product evaluation com. 1995-96, edn. approver com. 1997-98, liasion to emergency nurses assn. nat. conf. 1995, scholar 1997, standards guidelines com. 1998-99, 99-00, mktg. com. 1998-99, 2000-02, computer tech. com., computer tech. com. 1998-99, 2000-01), Am. Assn. Oper. Rm. Nurses, publ. com. 2001-02, mem. mktg. com. 2001-02, editl. bd. of jour. of peri-anesthesia nursing 2000-03, resource guide columnist jour. & peri-anesthesia nursing 2000-03. Home: 508 Michele Dr Antioch TN 37013-4109

SANDLIN, DOROTHY, artist; b. Chgo., Feb. 20, 1930; d. Clarence L. and Mary E. Sehnert; m. Henry L. Sandlin, July 18, 1953 (div. Mar. 1973); children: Lee Henry, Neil Bryan; m. Michael C. Lazich, Jan. 18, 1985. AA, North Park Coll., 1949; student, Ariz. State U., 1950, 52, Art Inst. Chgo., 1955-65, Am. Acad. Art, 1994-96. Legal sec. Sidley & Austin, Chgo., 1975-94. Represented by Weatherburn Gallery, Naples, Fla., 2000—. One woman shows include Elmhurst (Ill.) Art Mus., 1996, Strawn Gallery, Jacksonville, Ill., 1998, 2001, Tall Grass Gallery, Park Forest, Ill., 1997, 2000, Deer Path Gallery, Lake Forest, Ill., 2000; featured in Best of Pastel, 1996, Landscape Inspirations, 1997. Recipient 1st place in various art festivals, Springfield, Ill., Wilmette, Ill.,Woodstock, Ill., Glenview, Ill., Top 200 award Arts for the Parks nat. competition, Jackson Hole, Wyo, 1998. Mem. Pastel Soc. Am. (signature mem.), Midwest Pastel Soc. (signature mem., Hon. Mention 1994), Oil Painters Am., Chgo. Artists Coalition, Art Inst. Chgo. Alumni Assn. Home: 3239 W 205th St Olympia Fields IL 60461 Studio: 218 Forest Blvd Park Forest IL 60466

SANDLIN, JAMES DELACY, III, investment broker; b. Kinston, N.C., Nov. 7, 1949; s. James Delacy, Jr. and Dorothy Southerland (Johnson) S.; m. Luanne Robinson, Dec. 16, 1950; children: Michael J., Ryan D. BA, E. Carolina U., 1972. Ins. agent Pilot Life, Raleigh, N.C., 1975-83; investment broker, planner FSC Securities, 1985—91; investment broker Sandlin Fin. Svcs. and Investacorp, Inc., 1991—. Investment broker Marion Bass Securities, Raleigh, 1983-85, FSC Securities, Raleigh, 1983-85. Asst. scoutmaster Boy Scouts Am., Raleigh, 1992—; active St. Paul's Episcopal Ch., Cary, N.C. Master sgt. USAR, 1972-95, ret. Presbyterian. Avocations: woodworking, fishing, golfing. Home: 8404 Southbriar Dr Raleigh NC 27606-9617 Office: 3301 Womans Club Dr Ste 112 Raleigh NC 27612-4841 E-mail: jsandlin1@mindspring.com.

SANDLIN, MAX ALLEN, JR. congressman; b. Texarkana, Ark., Sept. 29, 1952; s. Max Allen and Margie Beth (Barnett) S.; children: Hillary, Max III, Emily, Christian. BA, Baylor U., 1975, JD, 1978. Bar: Tex. Assoc. Huffman & Palmer, Inc., Marshall, Tex., 1978-82; ptnr. Sandlin & Buckner, 1982-96; judge County of Harrison, 1986-89, county ct. judge, 1989-96; v.p., gen. counsel Howell & Sandlin, Inc., 1990-96; mem. Congress from 1st Tex dist., 1997—. Mem. exec. com. Tex. Supreme Ct. Jud. Edn. Com., Austin, 1987—; bd. dirs. Security State Bank, Elysian Fields, Tex., East Tex. Legal Svcs., Nacogdoches; bd. dirs., treas. East Tex. Housing & Fin. Corp., Marshall, 1990—. Chairman Harrison County Dem. Party, Marshall, 1982-88; mem. exec. com. Marshall-Harrison County Industries, Marshall, 1986-89; founder, sponsor, mem. Michelson-Reves Mus. Art; post supr. Boy Scouts Am., 1982-86; mgr. Marshall Youth Baseball, 1980. Recipient Appreciation award Tex. Dept. Human Resources, 1985. Mem. Harrison County Bar Assn. (pres. 1982-84), Baylor U. Alumni Assn. (bd. dirs.), Marshall Symphony Soc. (bd. dirs. 1988-90), Marshall Rotary. Baptist. Avocations: politics, hunting, fishing, baseball, classical cars. Office: 324 Cannon Washington DC 20515-0001*

SANDLOW, LESLIE JORDAN, physician, educator; b. Chgo., Jan. 7, 1934; s. Harry H. and Rose (Ehrlich) S.; m. Joanne J. Fleischer, June 16, 1957; children: Jay, Bruce, Lisa. BS, U. Ill., 1956; MD, Chgo. Med. Sch., 1960. Intern Michael Reese Hosp. and Med. Ctr., Chgo., 1961, med. resident, rsch. fellow gastrointestinal rsch., 1961-64, physician-in-charge clin. gastroenterology lab., 1963-74, asst. attending physician, 1964-67, assoc. attending physician, 1967-72, vice chmn. divsn. gastroenterology, dir. ambulatory medicine, 1968, dir. ambulatory care, 1969-76, attending physician, 1972—, assoc. med. dir., 1972-73; clin. asst. Chgo. Med. Sch., 1963-68, clin. instr., 1966; asst. prof. dept. medicine Pritzker Sch. Medicine, U. Chgo., 1973-76, assoc. prof., 1976-85, prof., 1985-90; prof. clin. medicine and med. edn. U. Ill. Coll. Medicine, Chgo., 1990-91, prof. medicine and med. edn., 1992—, sr. assoc. dean for grad. and continuing med. edn., 1993—, head dept. med. edn., 1993—, sr. assoc. dean for med. edn. affairs, 1994—. Dep. v.p. profl. affairs Michael Reese Hosp. and Med. Ctr., 1973-78, dir. Office Ednl. Affairs, 1976-81, assoc. v.p. acad. affairs, 1978-82, dir. quality assurance program, 1981-91, v.p. planning, 1982-83, v.p. profl. affairs and planning, 1983-88, dir. divsn. internal medicine, 1986-93, v.p. profl. and acad. affairs, 1988-91, med. dirs. acad. and med. affairs, 1992-94; med. dir. Michael Reese Health Plan, Inc., 1972-74, interim exec. dir., 1976-77; cons. gastroenterologist Ill. Ctrl. Hosp., 1978-80; vis. prof. Pontifica U. Catolica Rio Grande do Sul, Brazil, 1978, U. Fed. Espirito Santo, Brazil, 1978, Nordic Fedn. for Med. Understanding, Akureyri, Iceland, 1978, Seoul Nat. U. Sch. Medicine, 1981, Coll. Physicians and Surgsons, Kharachi, Pakistan, 1994, U. Tex., Ft. Worth, 1977, U. Ariz., Tucson, 1977, Loyola U. Med. Sch., Maywood, Ill., 1979; cons. in field; coord. Health Scis. Librs. in Ill.; mem. Midwest Med. Libr. Network; mem. subcom. on delivery of ambulatory med. care Inst. Medicine Chgo.; mem. cmty. resources task force Interinstnl. Cardiovascular Ctr.; chmn. steering group Ill. Regional Med. Program; past co-chmn. curriculum com. U. Chgo. Reviewer Rsch. in Med. Edn./Assn. Am. Med. Colls., 1985—, Acad. Medicine/Assn. Am. Med. Colls., 1989; contbr. numerous articles to profl. publs. Mem. Skokie (Ill.) Bd. Health, 1973-85, chmn., 1976-85; bd. dirs. Group Health Assn. Am., 1976-78, Portes Ctr., 1980—; bd. dirs. Good Health Program Skokie Valley Hosp., 1978-80; bd. dirs., exec. com. Rsch. and Edn. Found. of Michael Reese Hosp. Med. Staff, 1992—. Recipient numerous grants, including NIH, 1988, Michael Reese Hosp. Found., 1994-95, Chgo. Cmty. Trust, 1994-95. Fellow Am. Coll. Gastroenterology; mem. N.Y. Acad. Scis., Inst. Medicine, Assn. Am. Med. Colls., Am. Coll. Physician Execs. (co-chair resource mgmt. com. of quality assurance forum), Soc. Dirs. Med. Coll. Continuing Med. Edn., Soc. Dir. Rsch. in Med. Edn. Home: 2314 N Lincoln Park W Chicago IL 60614-3455 Office: U Ill Coll Medicine Med Edn MC 784 1819 W Polk St Chicago IL 60612-7331

SANDMAN, IRVIN W(ILLIS), lawyer; b. Seattle, Mar. 19, 1954; BA summa cum laude, U. Wash., 1976; JD, UCLA, 1980. Bar: U.S. Dist. Ct. (we. and ea. dists.) Wash. 1980. Prin. Graham & Dunn, Seattle, 1980—. Staff mem. UCLA Law Review. Mem. ABA (co-chair resort and tourism com. 1996-2001, co-chair 2001—), Acad. Hospitality Attys. (charter), Wash. State Bar Assn. (chmn. creditor/debtor sect. 1988-90, editor newsletter 1984—, speaker continuing legal edn.). Office: Graham & Dunn 1420 5th Ave Fl 33 Seattle WA 98101-4087

SANDMAN, PETER M. risk communication consultant, speaker; b. N.Y.C., Apr. 18, 1945; s. Howard Edwin and Gertrude Leah (Orgel) S.; m. Susan Marie Goertzel, June 18, 1967 (div. 1975); m. Jody Sue Lanard, June 10, 1990; children: Alison, Jennifer; 1 stepchild, James Sachs. BA in Psychology, Princeton U., 1967; MA in Comm., Stanford U., 1968, PhD, 1971. Reporter Toronto (Ont.) Star, Can., 1966; stringer Time, 1966-67; instr. comm. Stanford (Calif.) U., 1968-70; instr. journalism Calif. State Coll., Hayward, 1970; sr. editor The Magazine, 1970; asst. prof. Ohio State U., Columbus, 1971-72; asst. prof. natural resources, journalism U. Mich., Ann Arbor, 1972-75, assoc. prof. natural resources, 1975-77; assoc. prof. comm., coord. Cook Coll. comm. program Rutgers U., New Brunswick, N.J., 1977-83, prof. journalism, 1983-94, prof. dept. human ecology, 1992-94; adj. prof., 1994—. Adj. prof. TV, radio Ithaca (N.Y.) Coll., 1976, grad. program in pub. health Rutgers U., 1986—, dept. environ. and cmty. medicine Robert Wood Johnson Med. Sch., Rutgers U., 1987—; adv. com. environ./occupl. health info. program 1984-89; founder, dir. environ. comm. rsch. program N.J. Agrl. Exptl. Sta., Rutgers U., 1986-92; vis. scholar urban and environ. policy Tufts U., Medford, Mass., 1990-91; rsch. prof. George Perkins Marsh Inst., Clark U.; comm. coun. Environ. Def. Fund, 1985—; bd. advisors grad. program in tech. and sci. comm. Drexel U., Phila., 1988—; cons. on comm. ACP, 1976-79, The Cousteau Soc., 1977-79, Pres. Com. on the Accident at Three Mile Island; specialist in comm. coop. ext. svc. U.S. Dept. Agr., 1977-86; cons. risk commn. office policy analysis EPA, 1986-88; exec. com. Sci. Writing Educators Group, 1978-81; cons. ARCO Chem., Boise Cascade, Chevron, Ciba-Geigy, Consumers Power, Dow, Du Pont, Johnson and Johnson, Johnson Wax, Procter and Gamble, Union Carbide, others. Cons. editor Random House, 1982-89, McGraw-Hill, 1989-94, Holt, Rinehart and Winston, 1978-81; contbg. editor Apt. Life, 1971-75; freelance writer, 1966—; editl. bd. Pub. Rels. Rsch. Ann., 1981-91, Jour. Pub. Rels. Rsch., 1991-94; editl. adv. bd. Environ. and Behavior, 1976-86; contbr. articles to profl. jours. Bd. dirs. N.J. Environ. Lobby, 1984-90, Nuclear Dialogue Project, 1985-90, pres. 1986-90; pub. info. com. N.J. chpt., Am. Cancer Soc., 1981-86, vice-chmn., 1983-86; comm. coord. N.J. Campaign for a Nuclear Weapons Freeze, 1982-85; socioeconomic subcom., com. on biotechnology agr. divsn. Nat. Assn. State Univs. and Land Grant Colls., 1988-90; bd. advisors Environ. Scientists for Global Survival, 1988-91; sci. review panel, radium/radon adv. bd. N.J. Dept. Environ. Protection, 1987-88; com. to survey the health effects mustard gas and lewisite Inst. Medicine, NAS, 1992. Mem. AAUP, ACLU (bd. dirs. N.J. chpt. 1984-87), Environ. Def. Fund, Nat. Assn. Profl. Environ. Communicators, Sci. Writing Educators Group, Soc. for Risk Analysis, Soc. Environ. Journalists, Internat. Assn. Pub. Participation Practitioners, Sigma Delta Chi. Home: 59 Ridgeview Rd Princeton NJ 08540-7601 Fax: 609 683-0566. E-mail: peter@psandman.com.

SANDMEYER, E. E. toxicologist, consultant; b. Winterthur, Zurich, Switzerland, Aug. 9, 1929; came to U.S., 1955; BSChemE, Technikum, Winterthur, 1951; MS in Organic Chemistry, Ohio State U., 1960, PhD in Biochemistry, 1965. Cert. civil svc. chemist II, Nev., biochemist II, Pa., clin. lab. dir. Ctrs. for Disease Control. Asst. prof. sci., gen. chemistry, organic chemistry Friends U., Wichita, 1965-66; asst. prof. biochemistry, labs., and rsch. U. Nev., Reno, 1966-71; head corp. toxicology Gulf Oil Corp., Pitts., 1971-76; divsn. head organic analysis Barringer Labs., Denver, 1987-88; pres., toxicologist, owner Transcontec, Inc., Kelseyville, Calif., 1976—. Div. head organic analysis Barringer Labs., Denver, 1986-88. Contbg. author: Patty's Industrial Hygiene and Toxicology, 1981, A Guide to General Toxicology, 1983. Mem. AAAS, Am. Chem. Soc., Soc. Environ. Health, Sigma Xi, Sigma Delta Epsilon. Office: Transcontec 7305 Live Oak Dr Kelseyville CA 95451-7862

SANDMORE, DONALD ROBERT, research and development engineer; b. Chgo., Nov. 27, 1960; s. Donald Kenneth and Marilynn Joyce (Warner) S.; m. Anne Pepperdine. BS, U. Ill., Chgo., 1982, BS, 1985; cert., Coll. of DuPage, 1990. R & D engr. C. R. Bard, Davol Div., Lombard, Ill., 1986-91; sr. mech. engr. Physio-Control Corp., Redmond, Wash., 1991-95; prin. project engr. Medtronic, Inc., Grand Rapids, Mich., 1995—. Grand Rapids chpt. chmn. Medtronic Tech. Forum. Patentee in field. Mem. Am. Soc. Mech. Engrs., Soc. Plastics Engrs. Avocations: football, photography. Office: Medtronic 620 Watson St SW Grand Rapids MI 49504 E-mail: Sandmd1@medtronic.com.

SANDOR, GYORGY, pianist; b. Budapest, Hungary; came to U.S., 1938, naturalized, 1943; s. Ignac and Zsenka (Czipszer) S.; 1 child, Michael. Student, Liszt Ferenc Acad., Budapest, 1927-33; studied piano with, Bela Bartok; composition with, Zoltan Kodaly. Mem. piano faculty Juilliard Sch., 1982—. Made concert debut, Budapest, 1931; toured, Europe, 1931-38, Am. debut Carnegie Hall, N.Y.C., 1939, touring throughout U.S., Mexico, Can., W.I., North Africa, C.Am., S.Am., Europe, Australia, Far East; rec. with N.Y. Philharm. and Phila. orchs., also solo rec. (Grand Prix du Disque for rec. entire piano repertory of Bela Bartok's works 1964); rec. entire solo piano repertory of Prokofiev, 1967, Kodály, 1973; author: On Piano Playing, 1981; world premieres include Bartok's 3d Piano Concerto, Ormandy and Phila. Orch., 1946, Dance Suite, Carnegie Hall, 1945, Concerto for Orch., piano version by Bartok, 1990, Sony Classical, Vox Candide Turnabout, Columbia Records, Trio, Phillips Records, Brahms 2d Piano Concerto, Chopin 1st Concerto, De FaMia Nights in the Gardens of Spain.

SANDOVAL, AMADA, director; Interim dir. women's ctr. Princeton U., NJ. Mem.: Modern Lang. Assn. Am. (exec. coun. 2002—). Office: Princeton Univ 243 Frist Campus Ctr. Princeton NJ 08544-2142 Office Fax: 609-258-2142. E-mail: sandoval@princeton.edu.*

SANDOVAL, ARTURO ALONZO, art educator, artist; b. Espanola/Cordova, N.Mex., Feb. 1, 1942; s. Lorenzo Sandoval and Cecilia Eulalia (Archuleta) Harrison; (div. Sept. 1982); 1 child, Avalon Valentine Galaglorial. Student, U. Portland, 1959; BA, Calif. State Coll., L.A., 1964, MA, 1969; MFA, Cranbrook Acad. Art, Bloomfield Hills, Mich., 1971. Designer, illustrator Western Lighting Corp., L.A., 1964-66; advt. designer, adult edn. instr. spl. svcs. USN, Yokosuka, Japan, 1966; interior design asst. Walter B. Broderick & Assocs., La Mesa, Calif., 1967; asst. prof. art dept. U. Ky., Lexington, 1974-76, assoc. prof., 1976-86, full prof., 1986—, dir. art dept. Barnhart Gallery, 1976—, curator, 1979—. Teaching asst. Calif. State Coll., L.A., 1969, Cranbrook Acad. Art, Bloomfield Hills, 1969-71; fiber art demonstrator Mus. Art, Grand Rapids, Mich., 1970; batik and tie-dye demonstrator Gwynn's Fabric Shop, Birmingham, Mich., 1970; instr. Calif. State Coll., L.A., 1970, So. Ill. U., Carbondale, 1971, Edwardsville, 1971, 72, 73, asst. prof., 1971-73; presenter various lectures and workshops throughout the U.S., 1973—; juror Mo. Women Festival Arts, St. Louis, So. Ill. U., East St. Louis, 1974, Paramount Arts Assn., Ashland, Ky., 1975, Ind. Weavers Guild, Indpls., 1979, Fed. Corrections Inst., Lexington, 1979, Hawaii Craftsman Hui and Art Dept. U. Hawaii, Manoa, Honolulu, 1982, art dept. Va. Intermont Coll., Bristol, 1982, Arrowmont Sch. Arts and Crafts, Gatlinburg, Tenn., 1984, Ctr. Contemporary Art, U. Ky., Lexington, 1984, Guild Greater Cin.,Carnegie Art Ctr., Covington, Ky., 1989, S.C. Arts Commn., Charleston, 1990, Adams Art Gallery, Dunkirk, N.Y., 1994; visual arts cons. Ky. Arts Commn., Frankfort, 1977; curator Visual Arts Ctr. Alaska, Anchorage, 1982, Ky. Art and Crafts Found., Inc., Louisville, 1985; mem. artist adv. panel Ky. Art and Crafts Found., Louisville, 1986, 87, 92-2000; visual arts cons. Arts Midwest, 1987; artistic advisor Ky. Guild Mktg. Bd., Berea, 1988, 91, 92, 93; bd. trustees Ky. Guild 1995-98, Am. Craft Coun., N.Y.C., 1996—; vis. artist/critic Allen R. Hite Inst., U. Louisville, 1992; vis. artist Coll. Human Environ. Scis., U. Ky., Lexington, 1993; vis. artist/ lectr. fiber dept. Cranbrook Acad. Art, Bloomfield Hills, Mich., 1994, Art. Dept. St. Louis Comm. Coll.-Florissnat Valley, 2001, U. Arizona, 2001; curator, Art Wuilts 2001, River Oaks Square Art Ctr., Louisiana, 2001. Exhibited in group shows at Yeiser Art Ctr., Paducah/Paramount Arts Ctr., Ashland/S.E. Cmty. Coll., Cumberland, 1994, Textile Arts Centre, Chgo., 1994, Winnipeg (Man., Can.) Art Gallery, 1994, Riffe Gallery, Ohio Arts Coun., Columbus, 1994, Royal Hiberian Acad., Gallagher Gallery, Dublin, Ireland, Cooper Gallery, Barnsley, South Yorks, Gt. Britain, Shipley Art Gallery, Gateshead, Gt. Britain, 1994, Grand Rapids (Mich.) Art Mus., 1994, Whatcom Mus. History and Art, Bellingham, Wash., The Rockwell Mus., Corning, N.Y., Mus. Art, Washington State U., Pullman, The Hyde Collection, Glen Falls, N.Y., 1994, U. Art Galleries, U. S.D., Vermillion, 1994, Barnhart Gallery, U. Ky., Lexington, 1994, Sawtooth Ctr. Visual Art, 1994, Santa Fe Gallery, Santa Fe Cmty. Coll., Gainesville, Fla., 1994, Liberty Gallery, Louisville, 1994, Asahi Shimbun Gallery, Tokyo, Takashimaya Gallery, Osaka, 1994, Minn. Mus. Art, Landmark Ctr., St. Paul, 1994, S.C. State Mus., Columbia, 1994, Galbreath Gallery, Lexington, 1994, U.K. Art Mus., 1998; represented in permanent collections at Wabash Coll., Crawfordsville, Ind., Greenville County Mus. Art, Greenville, S.C., Mus. Modern Art, N.Y.C., St. Mary's Coll., Notre Dame, Ind., Coll. St. Rose, Albany, N.Y., Bowling Green (Ohio) StateU., U. Notre Dame, Transylvania U., Lexington, U. Ky. Mus. Art, Lexington, Mid-Am. Rare Coin Auction Galleries, Lexington, Henry Luce Found., N.Y.C., Lexington Ctrl. Libr., UK Art Mus., 1998, Nat. Mus. Am. Art, Renwick Gallery, 1999, J.B. Speed Art Mus., Louisville, 2000; Linda Schwartz Gallery, 2000, Tuska Gallery, 2000, President's Room, KY, 2000, Shands Gallery, 2001, Friedman Gallery, 2001, KGAG Offices, 2001, Actor;s Theater, 2001, Ronald Barr Gallery, 2001, Opera House Gallery, 2001. Recipient Alexandra Korsakoff Galston Meml. prize St. Louis Artist's Guild, 1971, Mus. Merit award Mus. Arts and Scis., Evansville, 1972, Creative Rsch. Grant So. Ill. U.-Edwardsville Rsch. Found., 1972, Craftsman fellowship Nat. Endowment for Arts, Washington, 1973, Friend of Mus. award Mus. Arts and Scis., Evansville, 1973, Clay Eugene Jordan ann. bequest prize for crafts St. Louis Artist's Guild, 1973, Teaching Improvement grant U. Ky. Rsch. Found., 1974, Travel grant U. Ky. Rsch. Found., 1977, Judges Choice award Berea (Ky.) Coll., 1978, Handweaver's Guild Am. award, 1978, Fiber award LeMoyne Art Found., Tallahassee, 1981, Elise Strout Merit award Mus. Arts and Scis., Evansville, 1981, Handweavers Guild Am. award, 1983, Martha Ryan Merit award Mus. Arts and Scis., Evansville, 1984, Best of Show award Gayle Willson Galleries, Southampton, 1984, Juror's merit award Brenau Coll., Gainesville, Ga., 1985, Installation Grant Ind. Arts Commn., Ft. Wayne, 1985, All Smith fellowship Ky. Arts Coun., Frankfort, 1987, Merit award Spotlight '88 Am. Craft Coun. Southeast Conf., Tuscaloosa, Ala., 1988, Merit award Mus. Arts and Scis., Evansville, 1989, Design Grant, Arts and Cultural Coun. for O.A. Singletary Ctr. for Arts, Lexington, 1990, Visual Arts fellowship Nat. Endowment for Arts, Washington, 1992, Hon. award Ky. Crafts Mktg. Bd., Frankfort, 1994, Rude Osolnik Craftsman award Ky. Crafts Mktg. & KAC Fund, 1998, 1st pl. Lexington Art League, Reverse Raffle, Lexington, 1999; NEA vis. artist grantee Pyramid Atlantic Press, Riverdale, Md., 1996. Mem. Lexington Fiber Guild Inc., Louisville Visual Arts Assn., Ky. Art and Craft Found., Inc., Ky. Guild Artists and Crafstmen, Am. Craft Coun., Friends of U. Ky. Mus. Art, Friends of Fiber Art, Surface Design Assn. Home: PO Box 25153 Lexington KY 40524-5153 Office: U Ky Dept Art 207 Fine Arts Bldg Lexington KY 40506-0022 E-mail: arturo6@prodigy.net.

SANDOVAL, ISABELLE MEDINA, education educator; b. Laramie, Wyo., Sept. 30, 1948; d. John Ben and Ida Medina Sandoval; 1 child, Tomas Andres Duran. BA, U. N.Mex., 1970; MA, U. Mo., 1976; EdD, U. Wyo., 1982. Cert. Spanish, reading, English, adminstrn. Tchr. Spanish and English Menaul Sch., Albuquerque, 1971-73; tchr. bilingual edn. and reading Kansas City, Mo., 1973-78; tchr. title I Sch. Dist. #60, Pueblo, Colo., 1978-83, adminstr., 1983-88, Acad. Dist. 20, Colorado Springs, Colo., 1988-95; human resources coord. Harrison Dist. 2, 1995-98; prof. education Coll. of Santa Fe, N.Mex. V.p. Hispano Crypto Jewish Resource Ctr., Denver. Author of poetry. Mem. Geneal. Soc. Hispanic Am., Hispanic Geneal. Rsch. Ctr. N.Mex., Mana del Norte, Olibama Lopez Tushar Hispanic Legacy Rsch. Ctr., N.M. Jewish Hist. Soc., Soc. for Crypto Judaic Studies, Nat. Assn. Sephardic Artists, Writers and Intellectuals, Hispano Luncheon Club, Phi Kappa Phi, Kappa Delta Phi, Phi Delta Kappa. Jewish. Avocations: writing poetry, researching family history and Hispano Jewish materials. Home: 4358 Lost Feather Santa Fe NM 87507-2580 Office: Coll of Santa Fe 1600 Saint Michaels Dr Santa Fe NM 87505-7615

SANDOVAL, LISA ANN, occupational therapist; b. Joliet, Ill., May 18, 1972; d. Manfred W. and Jo-Ann P. (Benko) K.; m. Melvin Sandoval; children: Cherie, Isaiah, Cedrick. BS, N.Y.U., 1995. Occupl. therapist IHS, Aurora, 1998—, Therapy Cons. Innovations, Denver, 1999—, Specialty Select Med. Hosp., Denver, 2001—. Writer N.Y.U. Occupl. Therapist Alumni, 1996. Mem. Hadassah, Nat. Indian Relief Coun. Democrat. Jewish. Avocations: walking, swimming, study of Native American culture. Home: 10293 Bentwood Ln Highlands Ranch CO 80126

SANDOVAL, RIK (CHARLES SANDOVAL), broadcasting executive; b. Chgo., May 20, 1952; s. Placido Jr. and Ophelia (Lugo) S. BA in Communications, Columbia Coll., 1974. With prodn. dept. Sta. WSNS-TV, Chgo., 1971-72; dir., producer Sta. WCAE-TV, St. John, Ind., 1972-73; producer Sta. WBBM-FM, Chgo., 1973-74; prodn. mgr. Sta. WLS-TV, 1972-76, on-air mgr., 1976-77; sr. publicist, producer Sta. KABC-TV, Hollywood, Calif., 1977-79; dir. creative svcs. Sullivan & Assocs, L.A., 1979-81; producer ABC, Hollywood, 1981-82; pres. Sandoval Prodns., Studio City, Calif., 1982-87; sr. v.p. The Agy., 1987-88; pres. Tri-Mark Group, Inc., 1988-92; dir. world wide ops. publicity MGM Studios, Culver City, Calif., 1992; mgr. interactive video prodn. Entergamement, Inc., L.A., 1993-94; dir. ops. GTE Interactive Media, Carlsbad, Calif., 1994-97, dir. corp. comm., 1994-97; v.p. pub. rels. and mktg. comm. Neale-May & Ptnrs., Palo Alto, 1998—; v.p. tech., sr. exec. on iMac launch Edelman Pub. Rels. World Wide, Mountain View, 1998—; v.p. publ. rels. Access Comms. Sega Dreamcast Launch and .com Strategic Svcs., 1999—; sr. dir. corp. comm. Silicon Motion, Inc., San Jose, Calif., 2000—. Judge The Clio Awards; prodr., writer Miss Hawaiian Tropic Beauty Pageant, 1992; head writer Mad Scientist Toon Club, 1993; exec. dir. Computer Game Developers Assocs., Los Altos, Calif., 1997. Producer, writer: (broadcast promotions) A.K.A. Pablo, 1984 (Silver award), Entertainment Tonight, 1984 (Silver award), Hunter, 1985, People, 1985 (Telly award, 1985, Gold Statuette award); head writer Mad Scientist Toon Club, 1993. Mem. NOSOTROS, L.A., 1987. Recipient 8 Clio nominations, 1977, 79-81, 2 Gold medals Internat. Radio Festival N.Y., 1985, 4 Bronze Telly awards, 1983-88, Silver Telly award, 1988, 2 ITVA awards, 1988, 3 Silver Telly awards, 1991, 4 Silver Telly awards, 1992, 2 Bronze Telly awards, 1992. Mem. Broadcast Promotion Mktg. Execs. (Gold medal, Silver medal 1985, 2 Bronze Telly award statuettes 1989, Silver Telly award statuette 1989. ITVA award), Nat. Assn. Broadcasters (cert. merit 1974), The Publicist Guild, Acad. TV Arts and Scis., Pub. Rels. Soc. Am. Roman Catholic. Avocations: Art Deco antiques, fine wine collector, karate, pre-Columbian artifacts, modern art collector. Home: PO Box 712 Belmont CA 94002-0712

SANDOWSKI, NORMA J. safety engineer; b. Tulsa, Dec. 30, 1940; d. Norman Jesse Sandusky and Gulia Ida (Poynor) Foster; divorced; children: Sheila Jewell Lester, Sheryl Lee Sanders, Michael Lance Sandowski. AS in Welding Tech., Tulsa Jr. Coll., 1970; BS in Indsl. Safety, Cen. State U., 1983; MS in Environ. Sci., Nova U., 1987; cert. in hazardous materials mgmt., U. Calif., Davis, 1988. Cert. assoc. risk mgmt.; cert. assoc. loss control mgmt. Safety and personnel dir. Utility Contractors, Tulsa, 1976-77; safety officer City of Tulsa Water and Sewer Dept., 1977-78; risk control rep. Comml. Union Ins., Dallas, Oklahoma City, 1978-81; cons. Parallel Resources, Oklahoma City, San Francisco, 1981-86; mgr. environ. and occupational health Linde div. Union Carbide, Santa Rosa, Calif., 1987; mgr. tech. svcs., asst. v.p. risk engrng. dept. Zurich-Am. Ins., Schaumburg, Ill., 1987—; mgr. safety & indsl. hygiene JLM Chems. Inc., Blue Island. Author: Right to Know in Educational Institutions, 1986, Environmental Auditing and Recordkeeping, 1987, Chemical Industry and its Accidents, 1991, Future of Ammonia, 1992. Mem. Adult Literacy Coun., Make Today Count-Am. Cancer Soc.; vol. Take-A-Hike. Pres.' scholar Tulsa Jr. Coll., 1969, Flint Steel scholar, Tulsa, 1970; recipient Danforth award Cities Svc. Oil, Bartlesville, Okla., 1958, Silver Trefoil Woman of Achievement award Ill. Crossroads coun. Girl Scouts U.S.A., 1994. Mem. Am. Soc. Safety Engrs. (profl.). Jewish. Otoe Indian. Avocations: bicycling, running. Office: 3350 131st St Blue Island IL 60406-2365

SANDQUIST, DIANE L. foundation administrator; b. Pottstown, Pa., Apr. 4, 1939; d. Bernard O. and Kathryn M. (Masleh) Sandquist; m. Walter K. Swartzkopf, Aug. 19, 1961 (div. 1985); children: Erika Jansson, Walter Kalt. III. AB, Wilson Coll., Chambersburg, Pa., 1961. Pub. info. officer Harrisburg (Pa.) Redevel. Authority, 1980-83; pres. The Greater Harrisburg Found., 1980-94, Cmty. Found. of Ctrl. Fla., Orlando, 1994—. Corp. sec. Delta Dental of Pa., Mechanicsburg, 1982-94; dir. Commonwealth Cmty. Founds., Harrisburg, 1989-94. Bd. dirs. Planned Giving Coun., 1996-97; mem. Jr. League of Greater Orlando, 1994-97. Recipient Cmty. Svc. award Rotary of Harrisburg, 1991, Liberty Bell award Dauphin County Bar Assn., 1988, Partnership award City of Harrisburg, 1990; honored at Diane Sandquist Day, City of Harrisburg, 1994, Dauphin County, 1994. Mem. Rotary Club of Orlando. Avocations: travel, gardening, international cooking. Home: 1390 Augusta National Blvd Winter Springs FL 32708-4230 Office: Community Found Ctrl Fla PO Box 2071 Orlando FL 32802-2071

SANDQUIST, GARY MARLIN, engineering educator, researcher, consultant, writer; b. Salt Lake City, Apr. 19, 1936; s. Donald August Sandquist and Lillian (Evaline) Dunn; m. Kristine Powell, Jan. 17, 1992; children from previous marriage: Titia, Julia, Taunia, Cynthia, Carl; stepchildren: David, Michael, Scott, Diane, Jeff. BSME, U. Utah, 1960; MS in Engrng. Sci., U. Calif., Berkeley, 1961; PhD in Mech. Engrng., U. Utah, 1964, MBA, MBA, U. Utah, 1995. Registered profl. engr., Utah, N.Y., Minn., Calif.; cert health physicist, quality auditor; diplomate in environ. engrng. Staff mem. Los Alamos (N.Mex.) Sci. Lab., 1966; postdoctoral fellow MIT, 1969-70; rsch. prof. surgery Med. Sch., U. Utah, Salt Lake City, 1974—, prof., dir. nuc. engrng. dept. mech. engrng., 1975—, acting chmn. dept., 1984-85; expert in nuc. sci. Internat. Atomic Energy Agy., UN, 1980—; chief scientist Rogers and Assocs. Engrng. Corp., Salt Lake City, 1980—; mgr., owner Applied Sci. Profls., LLC, 1999—. Vis. scientist MIT, Cambridge, Mass., 1969-70; vis. prof. Ben Gurion U., Israel; advisor rocket design Hercules, Inc., Bachus, Utah, 1962; sr. nuc. engr. Idaho Nat. Engring. Lab., Idaho Falls, 1963-65; cons. nuc. sci. State of Utah, 1982—; vis. prof. Ben Gurion U., Beer Sheva, Israel, 1985; cons. various cos.; spkr. Nuc. Energy Inst., 1990—. Author: Geothermal Energy, 1973, Introduction to System Science, 1985. Comdr. USNR, 1954-56, Korea; ret. Recipient Glen Murphy award in nuc. engrng. Am. Soc. Engrng. Edn., 1984. Fellow ASME, Am. Nuc. Soc.; mem. Am. Soc. Quality (sr.), Am. Health Physics Soc., Alpha Nu Sigma, Sigma Xi, Tau Beta Pi, Pi Tau Sigma. Republican. Mem. Lds Ch. Home: 2564 Neffs Cir Salt Lake City UT 84109-4055 Office: U Utah 2116 Merrill Engrng Bldg Salt Lake City UT 84112 E-mail: gms@asp-llc.com.

SANDRICH, JAY H. television director; b. L.A., Feb. 24, 1932; s. Mark R. and Freda (Wirtschafter) S.; m. Nina Kramer, Feb. 11, 1952 (div.); children: Eric, Tony, Wendy; m. Linda Green Silverstein, Oct. 4, 1984. BA, UCLA, 1953. Producer (TV show) Get Smart, 1965; dir. (TV shows) He and She, 1967, Mary Tyler Moore Show, 1970-88, Soap, 1977-79, Cosby Show, 1984-92; dir. (films) Seems Like Old Times, 1980, For Richer, For Poorer (HBO), 1992, Neil Simon's London Suite (NBC), 1996. Served to 1st lt. Signal Corps U.S. Army, 1952-55. Mem. Dirs. Guild Am. (award 1975, 85, 86), TV Acad. Arts and Scis. (Emmy award 1971, 73, 85, 86).

SANDRIDGE, WILLIAM PENDLETON, JR. lawyer; b. Winston-Salem, N.C., Jan. 27, 1934; m. Jane Carolyn Yeager, Dec. 10, 1966; children: Jane, William. AB, U. N.C., 1956; LLB, U. Va., 1961. Bar: N.C. 1961. Mem.. Womble Carlyle Sandridge & Rice, PLLC, Winston-Salem, 1962—. Chmn., bd. dirs. Horizons Residential Care Ctr., 1980, Food Bank N.W. N.C., Inc., 1988-89, Data Max Corp., 1996. Mem.: ABA. Office: Womble Carlyle Et Al PO Drawer 84 1600 BB&T Plz Winston Salem NC 27102

SANDRIN, COLLEEN LOUISE, social welfare administrator; b. Litchfield, Ill., Oct. 28, 1953; d. Elmer Sandrin and Bernadine Mary (Kline) Buffington. Student, U. Colo., 1971-74; BA, U. No. Colo., 1977. Staff asst. judiciary Sen. Floyd K. Haskell, Washington, 1974-75; title IX coord. U. No. Colo., Greeley, 1976; pub. rels. dir. Pikes Peak United Way, Colorado Springs, Colo., 1978-79, assoc. campaign dir., 1979-81; dir. resource and fund devel. Sacramento Area United Way, 1981-83; exec. dir. Am. Cancer Soc., Sacramento, 1983-87; exec. v.p. Woodland (Calif.) Meml. Health Found., 1987—97; devel. dir. U. Calif., Irvine, 1998—2000; sr. v.p. resource devel. and mktg. Orange County United Way, 2000—. Named Big Sister of Month, Big Bros./Big Sisters Program, 1985; recipient Innovative Program of Yr. award Calif. Assn. Pub. Hosps., 1989; 1st place award (grantsmanship category) Assn. Healthcare Philanthropy Showcase, 1990; The Healthcare Forum outreach and edn. grantee, 1991. Mem. Assn. Fundraising Profls., Nat. Com. Planned Giving, Planned Giving Roundtable, Woodland Rotary Club. Democrat. Episcopalian. Avocations: travel, gardening, photography, wooden barns and animals. Office: Orange County United Way 18012 Mitchell Ave S Irvine CA 92614

SANDROK, RICHARD WILLIAM, lawyer; b. Evergreen Park, Ill., July 8, 1943; s. Edward George and Gertrude Jeanette (Van Stright) Sandrok; m. Rebecca Fittz, June 19, 1973; children: Richard William, Jr., Alexander Edward, Philip Robert, Erika Joy. BA, Wheaton (Ill.) Coll., 1965; JD, U. Ill., 1968. Bar: Ill. 1968, U.S. Dist. Ct. (no. dist.) Ill. 1971. Assoc. Hinshaw Culbertson Moelmann Hoban & Fuller, Chgo. and Wheaton, 1971-75, ptnr. Wheaton, 1976-89, Lisle, 1989—. Reviewer: Legal Checklists. Capt. U.S. Army, 1969—71. Mem.: ABA, Def. Rsch. Inst., Assn. Def. Trial Attys., DuPage County Bar Assn. (chmn. med./legal com. 1978—79), Am. Arbitration Assn. (arbitrator), Chgo. Bar Assn., Ill. Bar Assn. Home: 818 Revere Rd Glen Ellyn IL 60137-5537 E-mail: RWS283@aol.com.

SANDS, CHRISTINE LOUISE, English educator; b. Johnstown, Pa., Oct. 13, 1947; d. Joseph and Margaret (Kocsis) Migut; m. Angelo Joseph Sands, Dec. 28, 1968 (div. Nov. 1989); children: Vincent, Linda. BS in German, Indiana U. Pa., 1969, BS in English, 1975; postgrad., Slippery Rock U., 1971-76. Tchg. cert. Pa. Educator New Castle (Pa.) Schs., 1969—. Student advisor, judge Forensics, New Castle, 1981-96, Youngstown (Ohio) Reading Festival, 1981-95. Pres. New Castle City Coun., 1996; parish coun. St. Vitus

Ch., New Castle, 1986-92; basketball referee PIAA, Mechanicsburg, Pa., 1972-91; coach New Castle H.S. Bowling, 1986-97. Democrat. Roman Catholic. Avocations: reading, traveling, sports, cooking, politics. Home: 819 E Hillcrest Ave New Castle PA 16105-2256 Office: New Castle HS 230 N Jefferson St New Castle PA 16101-2274

SANDS, DARRY GENE, lawyer; b. Charleston, Ark., Jan. 4, 1947; s. Anthony Wayne and Marjorie (Elkins) S.; m. Charlotte Moore, Dec. 28, 1968; 1 child, Spencer Justin. BS, U. Ark., 1969; JD, U. Kans., 1974. Bar: Mo. 1974, U.S. Dist. Ct. (we. dist.) Mo. 1974. Dir. Dicus, Davis, Sands & Collins, P.C., Kansas City, Mo., 1991—. Spkr. in field. Contbr. articles to profl. jours. Bd. dirs. Hope House. Mem. ABA, Nat. Assn. Coll. and Univ. Attys., Mo. Bar, Kansas City Met. Bar Assn. (chmn., past chair coll. and univ. law com., local govt. com.), Order of Coif, Lake Quivira Country Club. Democrat. Home: 5341 Canterbury Rd Shawnee Mission KS 66205-2612 Office: Dicus Davis Sands & Collins PC 1930 City Center Sq 1100 Main St Kansas City MO 64105-2105 E-mail: dsands@ddsc-law.com.

SANDS, FRANK MELVILLE, investment manager; b. Kansas City, Mo., Sept. 5, 1938; s. Melville Reynolds Sands and Louise (Evison) Olmstead; m. Marjorie Kay Root, July 20, 1963; children: Frank M. Jr., Katharine I., Laura E. BA, Dickinson Coll., 1960; MBA, U. Va., 1963. CFA. Security analyst Loomis Sayles & Co., Boston, 1969-72; sr. v.p., dir. David L. Babson & Co., Inc., 1972-83, Eppler, Guerin & Turner, Inc., Dallas, 1983-86; chief investment officer Folger Nolan Fleming Douglas, Inc., Washington, 1986-92; pres. Sands Capital Mgmt., Arlington, Va., 1992—. Treas., bd. dirs. Arlington Hosp. Found., 1987-93; trustee Arlington Cmty. Found., 1994-2000; bd. dirs. Arlington Free Clin., 2000—. 1st lt. U.S. Army, 1960-61. Mem. Washington Soc. Investment Analysts, Inc. Office: Sands Capital Mgmt Inc 1001 N 19th St Ste 1250 Arlington VA 22209

SANDS, HAROLD WINTHROP, banker, financial adviser; b. N.Y.C., Aug. 25, 1926; s. Harold Aymar and Muriel Winthrop Sands; m. Joan Hodges Baker, Sept. 6, 1961; children: Harold, Serena. Student, EBS-NBS Tellers' Acad., 1950-52, Am. Inst. Banking, 1967-69; postgrad., Miami Dade U., 1968-71. V.p., devel. officer, regional mgr. S.E. Banks, Miami, London, Europe, Caribbean, 1967-79; v.p. Marine Midland Bank N.V., London, 1979-85; sr. cons., fin. adviser Sun Life Assurance Soc., 1985-87; U.K. rep. Wright Investment Svc., 1987-92; v.p. Kreditbank Global Mgmt., Miami, 1993-94; dir., trustee Kapok Bermuda Ltd., London, 1994-96; gen. ptnr. The Winthrop Group L.P., Newport, R.I., 1996-2001; mgr. Pre-paid Legal Svcs., Inc., RI, 2001—. Founder Lorimex Internat., N.Y.C., 1952-60; CEO Account Solomon Paramount Pictures Corp., N.Y.C., 1950-52; founder, CEO Distbrs. for Mexico Rex Chain Belt, Ampudia A.S. Mex., 1960-67. Chairperson N.Am. com. London C. of C., 1985-88, chmn. Caribbean com.; hon. treas. European Atlantic Group, 1980—; mem. Rep. Com.; mem. Woolnoth Soc. Coun., City of London, 1980-93; trustee La Farge Restoration Fund of Newport, 1996—; trustee Preservation Soc. Newport, mem. fin. and edn. coms., 1994—; com. mem. Tall Ships Salute, 1995. Master sgt. U.S. Army, 101st Armed Calvery, 1949-54. Decorated Imperial House of David, 1995, Comdr. of Most Revered Order of the Star of Ethiopia. Mem.: SAR (Newport chpt.), Monday Lunch Club London, The Guild of Internat. Bankers London, Order of 1st Families of R.I., Soc. Colonial Wars (Providence and Boston chpts.), Ida Lewis Club (Newport, R.I.), Clambake Club, Reading Rm. Club, Ends of the Earth Club London, Broad St. Ward Club London, Bankers Club of London, Rotary Internat., Pilgrim's London, Masons (Holland lodge #8, United Lodge of Prudence London). Avocations: sailing, tennis, skiing, boating, chess. Home: 10 Cherry Creek Rd Newport RI 02840 E-mail: hss6518@aol.com.

SANDS, HARRY, psychologist, health administrator, researcher; b. N.Y.C., Jan. 6, 1917; s. Morris and Lena Sandrowitz; m. Helene Purl, June 24, 1945; children: Jeffrey, Richard. AB, NYU, 1941, PhD in Psychology, 1952. Diplomate Am. Bd. Profl. Psychology; lic. psychologist, N.Y. Rsch. fellow dept neurology Neurol. Inst./Columbia U. Phys. and Surg., N.Y.C., 1941-42, rsch. chief psychophysiologist Head Injury Project, 1942-44; assoc. dir., chief psychologist Baird Found. Clinic for Children with Epilepsy/Beth David Hosp., 1944-46; instr. Washington Sq. Coll./NYU, 1947-50, Bklyn. Coll., 1950-52; exec. dir. Com. Pub. Understanding of Epilepsy, N.Y.C., 1952-53, United Epilepsy Assn. Am., N.Y.C., 1953-56; dir. and clin. psychologist Psychol. Lab., Inc., 1955-61; dir. Epilesy Assn. N.Y., Epilepsy Found. Am., 1956-68; dir. program planning and evaluation Epilepsy Found. Am., Washington, 1972-74; assoc. staff adult therapy clinic Postgrad. Ctr. for Mental Health, N.Y.C., 1962-66, assoc. staff supervision therapeutic process, 1971-73, assoc. supr., sr. supr. psychoanalysis, psychotherapy, 1974—85, tng. analyst, pyschoanalysis, psychotherapy, 1993-98, exec. v.p., CEO, 1979—87, exec. dir., CEO, 1987—88. Pvt. practice pyschoanalysis and psychotherapy, N.Y.C., 1952-98; cons. divsn. resource devel. Nat. Inst. on Drug Abuse, Rockville, Md., 1978-79, Commn. for Control of Epilepsy and its Consequences, HEW, Washington, 1977, legal and protective svcs. project, Harvard U. Sch. of Pub. Health, Boston, 1974, cons. classification exceptional children, adequacy of classification for physically and sensorially handicapped, Vanderbilt U., Knoxville, 1974, bd. trustees, exec. com., 1988—; bd. dirs. Postgrad. Ctr. Residences, I, II, and III, N.Y.C., 1991-96, sec., 1991-2000, 2002—, pres. Editor: (book) Epilepsy: A Handbook for the Mental Health Professional, 1982 (Book of Yr. award ANA, 1982); co-author: (books) Epilepsy Fact Book, 1979, Education and Training Beyond the Doctoral Degree, 1995, Impact of Managed Care on Psychodynamic Treatment, 1996, The Guide to Pastoral Counseling and Care, 2000; contbr. chpts. in books, articles to profl. jours. Mem. tech. adv. com. on epilepsy N.Y. Dept Health, N.Y.C., 1945, planning com. advisory com on epilepsy, N.Y. State Dept. Mental Hygiene, Albany, 1952, joint legis. com. of State of N.Y. on program of pub. health, medicaid and compulsory health and hosp. ins., Albany, 1953; mem com. on Neurol. Disorders in Industry and com. on Emergency Med. Identification, AMA, Chgo., 1953, com. of info. svcs. and employment com., handicapped sect., Comty. Coun. of Greater N.Y., N.Y.C., 1954, joint legis. com. on mental retardation and physical handicaps, State of N.Y., Albany, 1956. Recipient fellowship Internat. Rehab. Rsch. Program of Social and Rehab. Svcs., HEW, Washington, 1972, Gold medal award for lifetime achievement in practice of psychology, Am. Psychol. Found., Washington, 1995; grantee Social Rehab. Svcs, HEW, Washington, 1968, 78. Fellow APA (bd. govs. coll. profl. practice 1994-99, co-chair nat. conf. on postdoctoral edn. and tng., Washington, 1992-94, bd. govs. coll. profl. practice, 1994-99, coun. reps. 1988-91, 1994, treas. com. for advancement profl. practice, practice directorate, 1992-94, cons. 1995, Karl F. Heiser Presdl. award 1993, Disting. Psychologist award Divsn. Psychotherapy 1995); mem. Am. Acad. Psychology, N.Y. State Psychol. Assn. (pres. 1978-79, 1985-86, coun. of reps. 1957-60, 1986-91, Allen J. Williams Jr. Meml. award 1993), Postgrad. Psychoanalytic Soc., Nat. Acad. of Practices (Disting. Practitioner in Psychology 1995), Psi Chi, Sigma Xi. Democrat. Jewish. Avocations; travel, theatre, music, ballet. Home and Office: 219 E 69th St Apt 7 D New York NY 10021-5455 E-mail: hasands@aol.com.

SANDS, MARTHA MERCER (NICHOLE RENÉ), artist, musician, poet, entertainer; b. Flemington, N.J., Sept. 19, 1954; d. William Franklin and Sarah Marshall (Darlington) Sands. Theatrical apprentice in theater technology, Garrick Players, Washington, 1968-69; theatrical apprentice, Wash. Theatre Club, Wash., D.C., 1970-72; acting student, Owen Jordan, Cuernavaca, Mex., 1974; student of fine arts, Instituto Allende, San Miguel Allende, Mexico, 1974; AS, SUNY, Stoneridge, 1990; student, Quincy U., 1991. Soundman various bands, Washington, 1977—; mgr. Skyline Inn, 1981-82; chef The Bear Café, Bearsville, N.Y., 1982-83; ops. mgr. Dreamland Studio, West Hurley, 1984-85; post prodn. ops. Silverhawk Films, Woodstock, NY, 1986-87; publicity dir. Arthritis Found., Quincy, Ill., 1991; owner Blue Rose Prodns., Woodstock, 1992—. Asst. to dir. Garrick Players, Washington, 1969—70; bd. mem. Mid-Hudson Legal Aid, Poughkeepsie, NY, 1987—89; tech. cons. Folger Theater, Washington, 1980—82; sound cons. Blues Alley; mgmt. cons. Tinker St. Café, Woodstock, 1989—90; prodr. Pub. Access TV, Woodstock, 1989—. Author: Images/Collected Works, 1968—70. Com. mem. Christmas Com., Woodstock; organizer benefit concerts; vol. daily bread/soup kitchen; child advocate. Named Child of Mary, Order of Sacred Heart, Phila., 1969; recipient Golden Spoon award, Hudson Valley Mag., 1983. Mem.: Assn. Women Geoscientists, Phi Theta Kappa (scholar 1990). Avocations: gardening, computers, herbal medicine. Home and Office: PO Box 374 Bearsville NY 12409-0374

SANDS, MATTHEW LINZEE, physicist, educator; b. Oxford, Mass., Oct. 20, 1919; m. Freya Kidner, 1978; children: Michael, Richard, Michelle. BA, Clark U., 1940; MA, Rice U., 1941; PhD, MIT, 1948. Physicist U.S. Naval Ordnance Lab., 1941-43, Los Alamos Sci. Lab., 1943-46; research asso., then asst. prof. physics Mass. Inst. Tech., 1946-50; sr. research fellow, asso. prof., prof. physics Calif. Inst. Tech., 1950-63; prof., dep. dir. Linear Accelerator Center, Stanford, 1963-69; prof. physics U. Calif.-Santa Cruz, 1969-85, prof. emeritus, 1985—, fellow Kresge Coll.; vice chancellor for sci., 1969-72; pres. Sands-Kidner Assocs., Inc., 1986-90. Vis. prof. U. Paris-Sud, spring 1976; mem. Commn. Coll. Physics, 1960-66, chmn., 1964-66; cons. Office Sci. and Tech., ACDA, Inst. Def. Analyses, 1962-67; mem. Pugwash Conf. Sci. and World Affairs, 1960-63; cons. on accelerator physics, 1975-93. Author: (with W.C. Elmore) Electronics-Experimental Techniques, 1948, (with R.P. Feynman and R.B. Leighton) The Feynman Lectures on Physics, 3 vols, 1965, (with others) Physical Science Today, 1973; also articles.; Mem. editorial bd.: Il Nuovo Cimento, 1972-85. Fulbright scholar Italy, 1952-53 Fellow Am. Phys. Soc. (Robert R. Wilson prize 1998); mem. Am. Assn. Physics Tchrs. (Disting. Service award 1972), Fedn. Am. Scientists, AAAS. Achievements include special research electronic instrumentation for nuclear physics, cosmic rays, accelerators, high-energy physics, science education, science and public affairs, electron storage rings. Home: 160 Michael Ln Santa Cruz CA 95060-1704 E-mail: sands@scipp.ucsc.edu.

SANDS, NORMAN EARL, elementary school educator, composer; b. Meshoppen, Pa. s. Gifford Leroy and Ruby Venorma (Carpenter) S. BS in Music Edn., Pa. State U., 1985. Cert. all-level music tchr., Tex., Pa. Tchr. elem. music Bellefonte (Pa.) Area Sch. Dist., 1985-93, tchr. grade 6, 1993-95; tchr. elem. music Donna (Tex.) Ind. Sch. Dist., 1995-96, Sharyland Ind. Sch. Dist., Mission, Tex., 1996-98; owner The Write Stuff, McAllen, 1998—; product mgr. Schoolmusic.com, Amherst, NH, 2000—01; tchr. elem. music La Joya Ind. Sch. Dist., 2001—. Music editor, composer, pub. SandSounds, McAllen, Tex., 1992-97; cons. Shawnee Press, Delaware Water Gap, Pa., 1990—; reviewer, composer Plank Rd. Pub., Wauwatosa, Wis., 1991-95. Author: Blowin' With the Beat, 1991, Les't Play—Right Away!, 1992, Who Pushed Humpty?, 1993, Songs for Singin' and Playin,' 1994. Mem. Music Educators Nat. Conf., Tex. Music Educators Assn. Democrat. Avocations: health, fitness. Home: 4149 Carnation Ave Mcallen TX 78501-3405

SANDS, ROBERTA ALYSE, real estate investor; b. N.Y.C., Oct. 7, 1937; d. Harry and Irene (Mytelka) S. BEd, U. Miami, 1960; postgrad., U. Oslo, 1960. Cert. secondary educator biology, Mass. Phys. edn. instr. Key Biscayne and Ludlam Elem. Sch., Miami, 1961-63; sci. tchr. Plantation (Fla.) Mid. Sch., 1969-71, Rickards Middle Sch., Ft. Lauderdale, Fla., 1972-76. Founder U. Miami Diabetes Rsch. Inst., 1989. Author: Biology on the Secondary Level, 1970. Vol. Douglas Garden Retirement Home, Miami, 1988-92, Mus. of Art, Ft. Lauderdale, 1988-92, Imperial Point Hosp., Ft. Lauderdale, 1981-83. Mem. AAUW (rec. sec. 1988-92, cultural chair 1993-94, legis. chair Ft. Lauderdale br. 1994-95, women's issue chair Ft. Lauderdale 1994—, edn. chair Pompano Beach br. 1994-96, Recognition of Significant Svc. award 1983). Avocations: oil painting, golf, embroidery, travel. Home: 4250 Galt Ocean Dr Apt 8S Fort Lauderdale FL 33308-6113

SANDS, ROBERTA G. social work educator; b. Bklyn., Oct. 28, 1941; d. Alan Nathan and Alice Louise Goldsamt; m. Morris M. Wilhelm, Mar. 13, 1966 (div. Nov. 1972); children: Philip Wilhelm, Bonnie Wilhelm Moskoff; m. Samuel Z. Klausner, Nov. 26, 1992. BA, Bryn Mawr Coll., 1963; MSW, Hunter Coll., 1965; PhD, U. Louisville, 1979. Psychiat. social worker River Region Mental Health, Louisville, 1972-75; psychiat. social worker/rschr. U. Louisville, 1975-78; instr. Spalding Coll., Louisville, 1978-79; lectr. Cornell U., Ithaca, N.Y., 1979-80; psychiat. social worker Willard (N.Y.) Psychiat. Ctr., 1980-81; asst. prof. Ohio State U., Columbus, 1981-87, assoc. prof., 1987-90, U. Pa., Phila., 1990—. Author: Clinical Social Work Practice in Community Mental Health, 1991, Clinical Social Work Practice in Behavioral Mental Health, 2d edit., 2001; author: (with M. McClelland) Interprofessional and Family Discourses, 2002; contbr. over 60 articles and book revs. to profl. jours., chapters to books. Rsch. grantee AARP Andrus Found., Washington, 1995-96. Mem. NASW (bd. dirs. Ohio chpt. 1985-87), Coun. on Social Work Edn. Jewish. Avocation: writing. Office: U Pa Sch Social Work 3701 Locust Walk Philadelphia PA 19104-6214 E-mail: rgsands@ssw.upenn.edu.

SANDS, SHARON LOUISE, graphic design executive, art publisher, artist; b. Jacksonville, Fla., July 4, 1944; d. Clifford Harding Sands and Ruby May (Ray) MacDonald; m. Jonathan Michael Langford, Feb. 14, 1988. BFA, Cen. Washington U., 1968; postgrad, UCLA, 1968. Art dir. East West Network, Inc., L.A., 1973-78, Daisy Pub., L.A., 1978; prodn. dir. L.A. mag., 1979-80; owner, creative dir. Carmel Graphic Design, Carmel Valley, Calif., 1981-85; creative dir., v.p. The Video Sch. House, Monterey, 1985-88; graphic designer ConAgra, Omaha, 1988; owner, creative dir. Esprit de Fleurs, Ltd., Carmel, Calif., 1988-99; owner, dir. Sands Studios, 1999—; owner Sweden by the Sea, Carmel, Calif., 1999—2001. Lectr. Pub. Expo, L.A., 1979, panelist Women in Mgmt., L.A., 1979; redesign of local newspaper, Carmel, Calif., 1982. Contbr. articles to profl. mags. Designer corp. ID for Carmel Valley C. of C., 1981, 90. Recipient 7 design awards Soc. Pub. Designers, 1977, 78, Maggie award, L.A., 1977, 5 design awards The Ad Club of Monterey Peninsula, 1983, 85, 87, Design awards Print Mag. N.Y., 1986, Desi awards, N.Y., 1986, 88, Oil Painting awards Jazz Festival, 1999. Mem. NAFE, Soc. for Prevention of Cruelty to Animals, Greenpeace. Democrat. Avocations: oil painting, interior decorating. Home and Office: 175 Ford Rd Carmel Valley CA 93924-9621

SANDS, VELMA AHDA, lawyer; d. John T. and Thelma Jane (Davis) Carlisle. BS, Calif. State U., Dominguez Hills, 1976; JD, Southwestern U., 1985. CPA. Cons. Peat Marwick Main, L.A., 1980-81; v.p. Security Pacific Bank, 1981-86; contr. L.A. Investors, 1986; mgr. IRC div. FN Realty Svcs., Pasadena, Calif., 1986-88; mgr. fin. reporting Luz Internat. Ltd., L.A., 1988-89; pvt. practice law, 1990—; temporary judge L.A. Mcpl. Ct., 1996—. Instr. Fame Entrepreneurial Tng. Program; co-pres. Multicultural Bar Alliance, 2001-02. Participant career day programs for local high schs.; mem. United We Stand. Nat. Assn. Black Women Lawyers scholar, 1982. Mem. ABA, NAFE, Bd. Black Women Lawyers (bd. dirs.), Nat. Assn. Bank Women (chair ways and means com. of scholarship fund 1986, scholar 1984), So. Calif. Chinese Lawyers Assn., Am. Bridge Assn., L.A. County Bar Assn., Langston Bar Assn. (pres. 2000), L.A. Bench and Bar Affiliates (scholarship com., meeting host, scholar 1983), Phi Alpha Delta. Home and Office: 3435 Wilshire Blvd Ste 2700 Los Angeles CA 90010-2013 Address: 14122 Friar St Van Nuys CA 91401-2105

SANDSTEAD, HAROLD HILTON, medical educator; b. Omaha, May 25, 1932; s. Harold Russel and Lula Florence (Hilton) S.; m. Kathryn Gordon Brownlee, June 6, 1959 (dec. May 13, 1989); m. Victoria Regan Liddle, Feb. 14, 1990 (div. Oct. 1993); children: Eleanor McDonald, James Brownlee, William Harold. BA, Ohio Wesleyan U., 1954; MD, Vanderbilt U., 1958. Diplomate Am. Bd. Internal Medicine, Am. Bd. Nutrition. Intern, asst. resident in internal medicine Barnes Hosp. Washington U., St. Louis, 1958-60; asst. resident in pathology Vanderbilt Hosp., Nashville, 1960-61; asst. surgeon USPHS U.S. NAMRU 3, Cairo, Egypt, 1961-63; asst. resident in internal medicine Thayer VA Hosp. Vanderbilt, Nashville, 1963-64; chief resident in internal medicine Vanderbilt Hosp., 1964-65; instr. internal medicine, asst. prof. biochemistry Med. Sch. Vanderbilt U., 1965-70, asst. prof. internal medicine, assoc. prof. nutrition, 1970-71; dir. USDA-ARS Human Nutrition Rsch. Ctr., Grand Forks, N.D., 1971-84; adj. prof. biochemistry and internal medicine Sch. Medicine U. N.D., 1971-84; dir. USDA-ARS Human Nutrition Rsch. Ctr. on Aging, Boston, 1984-85; prof. nutrition Tufts U., Medford, Mass., 1984-85; prof. preventive medicine and community health U. Tex. Med. Br., Galveston, 1985—; chmn. preventive medicine and community health Med. Br. U. Tex., 1985-90, prof. internal medicine, human biol. chemistry & genetics, 1986—. Cons. NAS, NRC, NIH, WHO, USDA; Joseph Goldberger vis. prof. AMA, 1976, Ellen Swallow Richards Meml. lectr., 1984; W.O. Atwater lectr. USDA, 1984; Sam E. and Mary F. Roberts lectr., 1985, Raymond Ewell Meml. lectr., 1985; Welcome prof. in basic sci. Fedn. Am. Socs. Exptl. Biology, 1988. Contbr. articles to profl. jours. Recipient Future Leader award Nutrition Found., 1968-70, Hull Gold medal AMA, 1970. Fellow ACP, Am. Soc. Nutrition Scis. (Mead Johson award 1972); mem. Am. Soc. Clin. Nutrition (various office including pres.), Sigma Xi, Alpha Omega Alpha. Avocations: gardening, fishing, reading. Office: U Tex Med Br Ewing Bldg Galveston TX 77555-0001 E-mail: hsandste@utmb.edu.

SANDSTROM, ALICE WILHELMINA, accountant; b. Seattle, Jan. 6, 1914; d. Andrew William and Agatha Mathilda (Sundius) S. BA, U. Wash., 1934. CPA, Wash. Mgr. office Star Machinery Co., Seattle, 1935-43, Howe & Co., Seattle, 1943-46; pvt. practice acctg., 1945-85. Controller Children's Orthopedic Hosp. and Med. Ctr., Seattle, 1948-75, assoc. adminstr. fin., 1975-81; lectr. U. Wash., Seattle, 1957-72. Mem. Wash. state Title XIX Adv. Com., 1975-82, Wash. State Vendors Rate Adv. Com., 1980-87, Mayor's Task Force for Small Bus., 1981-83; bd. dirs. Seattle YWCA, 1981—, pres., 1986-88; bd. dirs. Sr. Svcs. Seattle King Co., 1989-95, bd. dirs. Sr. Svcs. Seattle/King County, 1985, treas., 1986, pres., 1988-90; bd. dirs. Children's Orthopedic Hosp. Found., 1982-90; mem. LWV, 1997. Recipient Jefferson award for vol. svcs., 1997, Alumnus award, U. Wash. Bus. Sch., 2002. Fellow Hosp. Fin. Mgmt. Assn. (charter, state pres. 1956-57, nat. treas. 1963-65, Robert H. Reeves merit award 1970, Frederick T. Muncie award 1985; mem. Wash. State Hosp. Assn. (treas. 1956-70), Am. Soc. Women Accts. (pres. Seattle chpt. 1946-48), Am. Soc. Women CPAs, Wash. Soc. CPAs, Seattle Women's Voters League, Women's Univ. Club (Seattle), City Club (Seattle, charter mem.), Beta Alpha Psi (Outstanding Alumnus award 2001). Home and Office: 5725 NE 77th St Seattle WA 98115-6345 E-mail: sandstromaw@hotmail.com.

SANDSTROM, DALE VERNON, state supreme court judge; b. Grand Forks, N.D., Mar. 9, 1950; s. Ellis Vernon and Hilde Geneva (Williams) S.; m. Gail Hagerty, Mar. 27, 1993; children: Jack, Carrie, Anne. BA, N.D. State U., 1972; JD, U. N.D., 1975. Bar: N.D. 1975, U.S. Dist. Ct. N.D. 1975, U.S. Ct. Appeals (8th cir.) 1976. Asst. atty. gen., chief consumer fraud and antitrust div. State of N.D., Bismarck, 1975-81, securities commr., 1981-83, pub. svc. commr., 1983-92, pres. commn., 1987-91, justice Supreme Ct., 1992—. Chair N.D. Commn. on Cameras in the Courtroom, 1993—, Joint Procedure Com., 1996—; mem. exec. com. N.D. Jud. Conf., 1995—, chair-elect, 1997-99, chair, 1999-2001; mem. Gov.'s Com. on Security and Privacy, Bismarck, 1975-76, Gov.'s Com. on Refugees, Bismarck, 1976; chmn. Gov's Com. on Comml. Air Transp., Bismarck, 1983-84. Mem. platform com. N.D. Reps., 1972, 76, exec. com., 1972-73, 85-88, dist. chmn., 1981-82; former chmn. bd. deacons Luth. Ch.; mem. ch. coun., exec. com., chmn. legal and constl. rev. com. Evang. Luth Ch. Am., 1993—; mem. exec. bd. dirs., No. Lights Coun., dist. chair Boy Scouts Am., 1998-2000. Named Disting. Eagle Scout, Boy Scouts Am., 1997. Mem. ABA, N.D. Bar Assn., Big Muddy Bar Assn., Nat. Assn. Regulatory Utility Commrs. (electricity com.), N.A. Assn. Securities Adminstrs., Order of De Molay (grand master 1994-95, mem. Internat. Supreme coun., Legion of Honor award), Nat. Eagle Scouts Assn. (regent for life), Shriners, Elks, Eagles, Masons (33d degree, chmn. grand youth com. 1979-87, Youth Leadership award 1986), Bruce M. VanSickle Am. Inn of Court (pres. 1999-2001). Office: State ND Supreme Court Bismarck ND 58505*

SANDSTROM, DIRK WILLIAM, air force officer, hospital administrator; b. Ogden, Utah, Oct. 27, 1963; s. William Arthur and Jeanene Melva (Curtis) S.; m. Lisa Marie Nelson, Dec. 29, 1992; children: Elisabeth Annette, Matthew Daren, Sarah Janene. BS cum laude, U. Utah, 1990, MPH, 1994. Rsch. asst. U. Iowa, Iowa City, 1990-92; freelance writer Blackwell Cons., Inc., Salt Lake City, 1993-94; commd. capt. USAF, 1994; asst. adminstr. 7th Med. Group, Dyess AFB, Tex., 1995-96; mem. adv. coun. health care consumer adv. coun. 7th and 15th Med. Group, 1995-96, 98-99; chief info. officer 7th Med. Group, 1996-98; ops. officer 15th Med. Group, Hickam AFB, Hawaii, 1998-99; flight comdr. Med. Logistics, 1999-2001; adminstr. 71st Med. Group, Vance AFB, Okla., 2001—. Lectr. U. Utah, Salt Lake City, 1993-94, Salt Lake C.C., Salt Lake City, 1993-94; mem. adv. bd. Salt Lake City-County Health Dept., 1993-94; instr. Embry-Riddle Aero. U., 1998—; instr. Hawaii Pacific U., 2000—. Author: How To Own a Home Business, 1994; editor Utah Pub. Health Assn. Newsletter, 1993-94. Scout Master Boy Scouts Am., Salt Lake City, 1993-94; loaned exec. United Way Abilene, Tex., 1996; dir. combined fed. campaign Dyess AFB, 1996, Hickam AFB, 1998, 2000. Mem. Am. Coll. Healthcare Execs., Air Force Assn., Co. Grade Officers Assn., Golden Key, Phi Beta Kappa, Phi Kappa Phi, Beta Sigma. Republican. Mem. Lds Ch. Avocations: sports, cooking, travel, reading, fine arts. Office: 15th Med Group/71 MDSS/SGA 755 Scott Cir Hickam AFB HI 96853-5399 Home: 1296 Hurst Dr Enid OK 73703-8540

SANDSTROM, ROBERT EDWARD, pathologist; b. Hull, Yorkshire, Eng., Apr. 4, 1946; came to U.S., 1946; s. Edward Joseph and Ena Joyce (Rilatt) S.; m. Regina Lois Charlebois (dec. May 1987); children: Karin, Ingrid, Erica. BSc, McGill U., Montreal, 1968; MD, U. Wash., 1971; MBA, U. Calif., Irvine, 1999. Diplomate Am. Bd. Pathology, Am. Bd. Dermatopathology. Internship Toronto (Can.) Gen. Hosp., 1971-72; resident pathologist Mass. Gen. Hosp., Boston, 1974-78; clin. fellow Harvard U. Med. Sch., 1976-78; cons. King Faisel Hosp., Riyadh, Saudi Arabia, 1978; pathologist St. John's Med. Ctr., Longview, Wash., 1996-2001; v.p. Intersect Systems Inc., 1990—; pres. Lower Columbia Pathologists, 2001—. Chmn. bd. Cowlitz Med. Svc., Longview, 1988; participant congl. sponsored seminar on AIDS, Wash., 1987; vis. mem. Darwin Coll., Cambridge U., 2001-02. Script writer movie Blood Donation in Saudi Arabia, 1978; contbr. articles to profl. jours. Surgeon USPHS, 1972-74. Fellow Coll. Am. Pathologists, Royal Coll. Physicians; mem. Cowlitz-Wahkiakum County Med. Soc. (past pres.). Roman Catholic. Avocations: sport fishing, mountain climbing, philately. Home: 49 View Ridge Ln Longview WA 98632-5556 Office: Lower Columbia Pathologists 1606 E Kessler Blvd Ste 100 Longview WA 98632-1841

SANDSTRUM, STEVE D. engineering executive; b. Ulysses, Kans., Dec. 8, 1953; s. Don Eugene and Alleene (Lawrence) Sandstrum; m. Nancy Heinzer, Aug. 28, 1976; 1 child Andrew. BS in Zoology, Okla. State U., 1976, MS in Engring., 1980. Registered engr. in tng. Devel. engr. Phillips Driscopipe, Richardson, Tex., 1984-85, sr. tech. engr., 1985-86, quality assurance specialist, 1986-88; sr. polymer engr. Solvay Polymers, Houston, 1988; tech. svc. mgr. Poly Pipe Industry, Gainesville, 1988; group leader Solvay Polymers, Houston, 1988-91, mktg. mgr. profl. engr., 1991-92, industry mgr., 1992-96, product devel. mgr., 1997—. Exec. bd. Plastics Pipe Inst., Wayne, NJ, 1989—91, adv. bd., 1991—94, hydrostatic bd., 1991—; tchr. Okla. State U., Stillwater, 1979—80; pres. Plastics Pipe Inst., Washington, 1995—97. Co-author: Pipeline Rehabilitation, 1987, Above Ground Applications, 1989; author: Pellets to Pipe, 1995, What is PE100?, 1999, PE3408 vs. PE100, 1999, PE100: Performance Plus, 1999, ISO 9080 and the U.S. Gas Distribution Industry, 2000; editor: Handbook of Polyethylene Pipe, 1991. Pres. Sea Lion Swim team, Kingwood, Tex., 1995. Recipient Rsch. award, GM, 1981. Mem.: ASTM, NSPE, Tex. Soc. Profl. Engrs., Am. Pub. Works Assn., Plastics Pipe and Fittings Assn., Am. Water Works Assn., Soc. Plastic Engrs., Alpha Phi Mu. Republican. Presbyterian. Achievements include patents for. Office: Solvay Polymers 1230 Battleground Rd Deer Park TX 77536-1000

SANDT, JOHN JOSEPH, psychiatrist, educator; b. N.Y.C., June 29, 1925; s. John Jacob and Victoria Theodora Sandt; m. Mary Cummings Evans, Sept. 14, 1946; children: Christine, Karen, John K., Kurt, Colin, Carol; m. Mary W. Griswold, July 10, 1992 (dec. Dec. 1998). BA, Vanderbilt U., 1948; MA, Yale U., 1951; MD, Vanderbilt U., 1957. Instr. English Vanderbilt U., Nashville, 1951-52, Syracuse (N.Y.) U. Coll., 1960-61; intern SUNY Upstate Med. Ctr., Syracuse, 1957-58, resident, 1958-61; instr. psychiatry Southwestern Med. Sch., Dallas, 1961-63; chief psychiatry VA Med. Ctr., 1961-63; chief outpatient clinic Dept. Mental Health, Springfield, Mass., 1963-66; asst. prof. psychiatry U. Rochester (N.Y.) Med. Sch., 1966-75, clin. assoc. prof. psychiatry, 1975-98; chief psychiatry Clifton Springs (N.Y.) Hosp., 1985-88, VA Med. Ctr., Bath, N.Y., 1988-96; pvt. practice Hammondsport, 1996—. Cons. psychiatry VA Med. Ctr., Northampton, Mass., 1965-66, Springfield Coll., 1964-66, Brockport (N.Y.) State Coll., 1966-75, Fairport (N.Y.) Bapt. Home, 1966-88; asst. dir. ind. study program U. Rochester Med. Sch., 1971-75. Author: Clinical Supervision of Psychiatric Resident, 1972; contbr. articles to profl. jours. Vestryman All Saints Episcopal Ch., South Hadley, Mass., 1963-66. With USNR 1944-46, PTO. Nathaniel Currier fellow Yale Grad. Sch., 1948-49. Mem. AAAS, Am. Psychiat. Assn.

SANDU, ADRIAN, mathematician, computer scientist, educator; b. Bucharest, Romania, Nov. 28, 1965; came to U.S., 1992; s. Gheorghe and Marioara Sandu; m. Corina S., June 20, 1992; children: Andreea, Monica. BS, MS, Tech. U. Bucharest, 1990; MS, PhD, U. Iowa, 1997. Instr. Tech. U. Bucharest, 1990-92; rsch. assoc. Courant Inst. Math. Scis., N.Y.C., 1997-98; asst. prof. computer sci. Mich. Technol. U., Houghton, 1998—. Contbr. articles to profl. jours. Mem. Am. Math. Soc., Soc. Indsl. and Applied Math. Avocations: skiing, rollerskating, camping. Home: 511 Jacker Ave Houghton MI 49931 Office: Mich Technol U Dept Computer Sci 1400 Townsend Dr Houghton MI 49931-1200 E-mail: asandu@mtu.edu.

SANDU, CONSTANTINE, process development engineer; b. Costesti, Arges, Romania, Nov. 9, 1943; came to U.S. 1979, naturalized 1984; s. Dumitru and Maria (Calinoiu) S. Eng., U. Galatz, Romania, 1966; PhD, U. Wis., 1989. Plant engr. Fruit and Vegetables Co., Riureni, Romania, 1967-68; prof.'s asst. U. Galatz, Romania, 1968-75; vis. scientist Fed. Rsch. Ctr. Nutrition, Karlsruhe, Ger., 1975-77; R & D engr. Soc. for Ind. Heating & Engring., Krefeld, Ger., 1978-79; rsch. asst. U. Wis., Madison, 1979-86; sr. devel. engr. The Quaker Oats Co., Barrington, Ill., 1986-95; process devel. mgr. ConAgra Grocery Products Co., Irvine, Calif., 1995—. Adj. prof. Purdue U., W. Lafayette, Ind. 1989-95. Author: Physicomathematical Model for Milk Fouling in a Plate Heat Exchanger, 1991; editor: Fouling and Cleaning in Food Processing, 1985; contbr. articles to profl. jours. Mem. Inst. Food Technologists, Math. Assn. Am., Sigma Xi, Phi Tau Sigma. Avocations: philosophy, history, foreign languages, body building, tennis. Home: 2889 Player Ln Tustin CA 92782-1534 Office: ConAgra Grocery Products 3353 Michelson Dr Irvine CA 92612-0650 E-mail: csandu@cagpc.com.

SANDUM, HOWARD E. literary agent; b. Devils Lake, N.D., July 7, 1929; s. Howard E. Sandum and Gladys I. Lien; m. Evangeline M. Olson, May 12, 1955 (dec. Feb. 1972); children: Kyrie L. (dec.), Beret S. Canakes, Rachel S. Tune, Joseph H., Marn S. Turley; m. Marta R. Enebuske, July 28, 1975. BA, St. Olaf Coll., Northfield, Minn., 1951; postgrad., U. Minn., 1954-56, 60-62. Editor trade religion The Macmillan Co., N.Y.C., 1962-63, editor-in-chief Collier Books divsn., 1963-71; editor-in-chief Adult Trade divsn. The World Pub. Co., 1971-73; dir. office for comm. Luth. Ch. in Am., 1973-76; editl. dir. The Saunders Press (W.B. Saunders Co.), Phila., 1979-81; editl. dir. Harvest Books Harcourt Brace Jovanovich, N.Y.C. and San Diego, 1982-83; mng. dir. Sandum & Assocs. Lit. Agy., N.Y.C., 1987—. Founder, dir. The Pub. Inst., U. Pa., Phila., 1980-82; dir. pub. info. The Am. Luth. Ch., Mpls., 1960-62; night editor AP, Boise, Idaho, 1956-60. Editor Scandinavian Rev., 1976-78. Lay reader, usher Ch. of Holy Trinity, N.Y.C., 1990—; planning chmn. New St. Peters Lutheran Ch. at Citicorp Ctr., N.Y.C., 1970-78. Capt. USMC, 1952-54, res. Recipient Disting. Alumnus award St. Olaf Coll., 2000. Mem. Met. Mus. Art (sustaining), N.Y. Soc. Libr. Episcopalian. Avocations: cooking, museums, urban walking. Home and Office: Sandum & Assocs a Lit Agy 144 E 84th St New York NY 10028-2004

SANDUSKY, CHRISTINE ANN, English language educator; b. Flushing, N.Y., June 28, 1952; d. Charles Stanley and Lorna Joyce (Kunz) Downey; m. Michael James Sandusky, Aug. 24, 1974; children: Carl, Sarah. BA in English, Western Ill. U., 1974, MS in Edn.-Reading, 1976. Cert. tchr., Minn. Tchr. lang. arts 7th grade Edison Jr. H.S., Macomb, Ill., 1976-83; tchr. English, English as Second Lang. Elk River (Minn.) Sch. Dist., 1984-95; tchr. English, Reading Elk River Area Sr. H.S., 1995—. Mem. Elk River Edn. Assn., Delta Kappa Gamma. Office: Elk River Area Sr H S 900 School St Elk River MN 55330-1336 E-mail: csandusky@elkriver.k12.mn.us.

SANDWEISS, MARTHA A. author, American studies and history educator; b. St. Louis, Mar. 29, 1954; d. Jerome Wesley and Marilyn Joy (Gilk) S. BA magna cum laude, Radcliffe Coll., 1975; MA in History, Yale U., 1977, MPhil in History, 1981, PhD, 1985. Smithsonian-Nat. Endowment Humanities fellow Nat. Portrait Gallery, Washington, 1975-76; curator photographs Amon Carter Mus., Ft. Worth, 1979-86; adj. curator photographs, 1987-89; dir. Mead Art Mus. Amherst Coll., 1989-97, adj. assoc. prof. of fine arts and Am. studies, 1989-94, assoc. prof. Am. studies, 1994-97, assoc. prof. Am. studies and history, 1997-2000, prof. Am. studies and history, 2000—. Author, American studies and history educator; b. St. Louis, Mar. 29, 1954; d. Jerome Wesley and Marilyn Joy (Glik) S. BA magna cum laude, Radcliffe Coll., 1975; MA in History, Yale U., 1977, MPhil in History, 1981, PhD, 1985. Smithsonian-Nat. Endowment Humanities fellow, Nat. Portrait Gallery, Washington, 1975-76; curator photographs Amon Carter Mus., Ft. Worth, 1979-86, adj. curator photographs, 1987-89; dir. Mead Art Mus. Amherst Coll., 1989-97, adj. assoc. prof. of fine arts and Am. studies, 1989-94, assoc. prof. Am. studies, 1994-97, assoc. prof. Am. studies and history, 1997-2000; prof. Am. studies and history, 2000—. Author: Carlotta Corpron: Designer with Light, 1980, Masterworks of American Photography, 1982, Laura Gilpin: An Enduring Grace, 1986, (catalogue) Pictures from an Expedition: Early Views of the American West, 1979; co-author: Eyewitness to War: Prints and Daguerreotypes of the Mexican War, 1989; editor: Historic Texas: A Photographic Portrait, 1986, Contemporary Texas: A Photographic Portrait, 1986, Denizens of the Desert, 1988, Photography in Nineteenth Century America, 1991; co-editor: Oxford History of the American West, 1994. Fellow Ctr. for Am. Art and Material Culture, Yale U., 1977-79, NEH, 1988, Am. Coun. Learned Socs., 1996-97, Weatherhead Fellowship, 2000—. Author: Carlotta Corpron: Designer with Light, 1980, Masterworks of American Photography, 1982, Laura Gilpin: An Enduring Grace, 1986, (catalogue) Pictures from an Expedition: Early Views of the American West, 1979; co-author: Eyewitness to War: Prints and Daguerreotypes of the Mexican War, 1989; editor: Historic Texas: A Photographic Portrait, 1986, Contemporary Texas: A Photographic Portrait, 1986, Denizens of the Desert, 1988, Photography in Nineteenth Century America, 1991, Print the Legend: Photography and the American West, 2002; co-editor: Oxford History of the American West, 1994. Fellow Ctr. for Am. Art and Material Cultures, Yale U., 1977-79, NEH, 1988, Am. Coun. Learned Socs., 1996-97, Weatherhead, 2000-2001. Office: Amherst Coll Am Studies Dept PO Box 2225 Amherst MA 01004-2225

SANDWELL, KRISTIN ANN, special education educator; b. Topeka, Jan. 13, 1955; d. Edwin C. and E. Maxine (Nelson) Henry; m. Steve Sandwell, Dec. 27, 1997; children: Dustin Grimm, Chris Creek, Brandon Grimm, Sarah Sandwell, Paul Sandwell. AA, Hutchinson (Kans.) C.C., 1986; BS, McPherson (Kans.) Coll., 1989; MEd, Wichita State U., 1992. Cert. tchr. elem., gifted. Math/parenting tchr. Flint Hills Job Corps Ctr., Manhattan, Kans., 1992; gifted facilitator Unified Sch. Dist. 353, Wellington, 1993-94, Unified Sch. Dist. 260, Derby, 1995-97; tchr. City of Wichita Summer Youth Employment Program-Edn., 1997—; gifted facilitator Unified Sch. Dist. 259, 1998—. Head injury counselor, life skills trainer Three Rivers Ind. Living Ctr., Wamego, Kans., 1992; facilitator Summer Youth Employment Edn. Program, 1997-98. Epiphany Festival prodr. Trinity Luth. Ch., McPherson, 1991, 93; CASA organizer McPherson Coll., 1988-89; vol. Coun. on Violence Against Persons, McPherson, 1990-92. Mem. ASCD. Avocations: reading, travel, working with disability issues. E-mail: ksandwell@yahoo.com., ksandwell@usd259.net.

SANDY, JOHN A. state legislator; b. Twin Falls, Idaho, June 8, 1948; m. Robin Sandy; 1 child, Alex McConnell. BS in Agr., U. Idaho. Farmer; apptd. senator, dist. 22 Idaho Senate, Boise, 1995-98, elected senator, dist. 22, 1998—. Mem. agrl. affairs, state affairs, edn., and transp. coms. Idaho state Rep. 1st vice chair, 1992-98; chmn. Idaho Republican Party, 2002-. Republican. Methodist. Office: State Capitol PO Box 83720 Boise ID 83720-3720*

SANDY, LEWIS GORDON, physician, foundation executive; b. Detroit, July 18, 1958; s. William Haskell and Marjorie Mindel (Mazor) S.; m. Kathleen Anne Morgan, June 17, 1984; children: Matthew, Natalie, Jonah. BS, U. Mich., 1979, MD, 1982; MBA, Stanford U., 1988. Diplomate Am. Bd. Internal Medicine, Nat. Bd. Med. Examiners. Intern Beth Israel Hosp., Boston, 1982-83, resident, 1983-85; Robert Wood Johnson clin. scholar U. Calif., San Francisco, 1985-86, clin. fellow in medicine, 1986-88; instr. Harvard Med. Sch., 1988-91; assoc. chief internal medicine Harvard Community Health Plan, Boston, 1988-89, dir. Health Ctr., 1989-91; v.p. Robert Wood Johnson Found., Princeton, N.J., 1991-96, exec. v.p., 1997—; clin. assoc. prof. medicine U. Medicine and Dentistry N.J./Robert Wood Johnson Med. Sch., 1991—. Cons. Kaiser Found. Health Plan, Oakland, Calif., 1987-88. Fellow ACP; mem. APHA, AMA, Am. Coll. Physician Execs., N.J. Med. Soc., Middlesex County Med. Soc., N.J. Acad. Medicine, Soc. Gen. Internal Medicine, Alpha Omega Alpha. Office: Robert Wood Johnson Found PO Box 2316 Princeton NJ 08543-2316

SANDY, STEPHEN, writer, educator; b. Aug. 2, 1934; s. Alan Francis and Evelyn Brown (Martin) S.; m. Virginia Scoville, 1969; children: Nathaniel Merrill, Clare Scoville. AB, Yale U., 1955; AM, Harvard U., 1958, PhD, 1963. Instr. Harvard U., 1963-67; vis. prof. U. Tokyo, 1967-68; asst. prof. Brown U., Providence, 1968-69; mem. faculty Bennington (Vt.) Coll., 1969—2002; McGee prof. writing Davidson (N.C.) Coll., 1994. Lectr. U. R.I., 1969; prof. Summer Sch. Harvard U., 1986, 87, 88; poetry workshop dir. Chautauqua Instn., 1975, 77, Johnson (Vt.) State Coll., 1976, 77, Bennington Coll., 1978-80, 89, Bennington Writing Seminars Program, 1994-96, Wesleyan Writers Conf., 1981. Author: Stresses in the Peaceable Kingdom, 1967, Roofs, 1971, End of the Picaro, 1977, The Hawthorne Effect, 1980, The Raveling of the Novel: Studies in Romantic Fiction from Walpole to Scott, 1980, Riding to Greylock, 1983, To a Mantis, 1987, Man in the Open Air, 1988, The Epoch, 1990, Thanksgiving Over the Water, 1992; translator: Seneca's Hercules Oetaeus, 1995, Vale of Academe A Prose Poem for Bernard Malamud, 1996, Marrow Spoon, 1997, Aeschylus's Against Thebes, 1998, The Thread, New and Selected Poems, 1998, Black Box, 1999, Surface Impressions:A Poem, 2002. Councillor English Harvard Grad. Soc. Coun., 1969-74. With U.S. Army, 1955-57. Recipient Fulbright postdoctoral award, 1967-68; Dexter fellow, 1961, Yaddo fellow, 1963-68, 76, 93, 97, 98, 00, 02, Invited Poetry fellow Breadloaf Writers Conf., 1968, Ingram Merrill Found. fellow, 1985, MacDowell Colony fellow, 1986, 93, Blue Mt. Ctr. fellow, 1985, 88, Creative Writing fellow Nat. Endowment Arts, 1988, Vt. Coun. Arts fellow, 1988—, Sr. fellow Provincetown Fine Arts Work Ctr., 1998, Rockefeller Found. residency Bellagio Study and conf. ctr., 2001, Huber Found. grantee, 1973, Vt. Coun. Arts grantee, 1974; nominee for Pulitzer Prize, 1971. Mem. Signet Soc., Elizabethan Club.

SANDY, WILLIAM HASKELL, training and communication systems executive; b. N.Y.C., Apr. 28, 1929; s. Fred and Rose S.; m. Marjorie Mazor, June 15, 1952; children: Alan, Lewis, Barbara. AB, U. Md., 1950, JD, 1953; postgrad. Advanced Mgmt. program, Harvard Bus. Sch., 1970-71. Bar: Md. 1953. From planner-writer to acct. supr. Jam-Handy Orgn., Detroit, 1953-64, v.p., 1964-69, sr. v.p., 1969-71; pres. Sandy Corp., Troy, Mich., 1971-88, chmn., 1988-96; pres. Rudgate Corp., Bloomfield Hills, Mich., 1996—. Author: Forging the Productivity Partnership, 1990. Bd. govs. Northwood Inst., 1976-80; bd. dirs. Cranbrook Sci. Inst., Met. Ctr. High Tech., 1993, Birmingham (Mich.) Cmty. House, 1997-2002, Mich. Opera Theatre; pres. Graphic Arts Coun., 1992-93; trustee Detroit Inst. Arts, 1992-93; v.p. nat. exec. coun. Harvard Bus. Sch., 1985-89; mem. Bloomfield Hills Zoning Bd., Walsh Coll. Leader in Residence, Pres.'s Adv. Coun.; mayor City of Bloomfield Hills, 1996-97; mem. Troy Downtown Devel. Authority, 1996-99; Inst. for Humanities trustee U. Mich. Mem. ASTD, Am. Mktg. Assn. (pres. Detroit chpt. 1975), Nat. Found. Am. Mktg. Assn (bd. dirs.), S.E. Mich. BBB (bd. dirs.), Adcraft Club, Nat. Assn. Ednl. Broadcasters, Harvard Bus. Sch. Club (pres. Detroit chpt. 1983-85), The Hundred Club. Home: 596 Rudgate Rd Bloomfield Hills MI 48304-3355 Home (Winter): 535 Sanctuary Dr Longboat Key FL 34228-3852

SANERA, MARGE See KRASCHNESKE, MARGARETHE REGINA

SANES, KEN ROSS, critic; b. Bklyn., Mar. 4, 1953; s. William and Frances Sanes. BA magna cum laude, Tufts U., 1975. Columnist, editor, mem. editl. bd. Palm Beach Post, West Palm Beach, Fla., 1980—89; writer, media critic, 1989—. Writer, designer Transparency website, 1997— (Britannica Internet Guide award, Internet Bros. Elite Site award and Helpware award, NetMagick Master of Content award, Ednl. Site award of excellence, Innovative Tchg. Concepts, Channel One Network resource, resource of numerous univs., schs., and media orgns.). E-mail: editor@transparencynow.com.

SANETO, RUSSELL PATRICK, pediatric neurologist, epileptologist, neurobiologist; b. Burbank, Calif., Oct. 10, 1950; s. Arthur and Mitzi (Seddon) S.; m. Kathleen D. Saneto. BS with honors, San Diego State U., 1972, MS, 1975; PhD, U. Tex. Med. Br., 1981; DO, U. Osteo. Medicine and Surgery, 1994. Tchg. asst. San Diego State U., 1969-75; substitute tchr. Salt Lake City Sch. Dist., 1975; tchg. and rsch. asst. U. Tex. Med. Br., 1976-77, NIH predoctoral fellow, 1977-81, postdoctoral fellow, 1981; Jeanne B. Kempner postdoctoral fellow UCLA, 1981-82, NIH postdoctoral fellow, 1982-87; asst. prof. divsn. neurosci. Oreg. Regional Primate Rsch. Ctr., Beaverton, 1987-89; asst. prof. dept. cell biology and anatomy Oreg. Health Scis. U., Portland, 1988-90, U. Osteo. Medicine and Surgery, 1991-94, Cleve. Clinic, 1994-2001; asst. prof. divsn. pediat. neurology and pediatrics U. Wash. Children's Hosp. and Regional Med. Ctr., Seattle, 2001—. Lectr. rsch. methods Grad. Sch., 1982; vis. scholar in ethics So. Baptist Theol. Sem., Louisville, 1981. Contbr. articles to profl. jours. Recipient Merit award Nat. March of Dimes, 1978; named one of Outstanding Young Men in Am., 1979, 81, one of Men of Significance, 1985. Mem. AAAS, Am. Acad. Pediats., Am. Acad. Neurology, Am. Epilepsy Soc., Bread for World, Winter Confs. Brain Rsch., Neuroscis. Study Program, N.Y. Acad. Scis., Am. Soc. Neurochemistry, Soc. Neurosci., Sigma Sigma Phi. Democrat. Mem. Evangelical Free Ch. Office: Childrens Hosp and Regional Med Ctr 4800 Sand Point Way NE CH- 9 Seattle WA 98105 E-mail: rsanet@chmc.org.

SANETTI, STEPHEN LOUIS, lawyer; b. Flushing, N.Y., June 25, 1949; s. Alfred Julius Sanetti and Yolanda Marie (DiGioia) Boyes; m. Carole Leighton Koller, Sept. 21, 1974; children: Christopher Edward, Dana Harrison. BA in History with honors, Va. Mil. Inst., 1971; JD, Washington and Lee U., 1974. Bar: Conn. 1975, U.S. Ct. Mil. Appeals 1975, U.S. Dist. Ct. Conn. 1978, U.S. Ct. Appeals (2d cir.) 1979, U. S. Supreme Ct. 1980. Litigation atty. Marsh, Day & Calhoun, Bridgeport, Conn., 1978-80; gen. counsel Sturm, Ruger & Co., Southport, 1980—, v.p., 1993-2000, also bd. dirs., 1998-2000, vice chmn., sr. exec. v.p., 2000—. Dir. Product Liability Adv. Coun. Tech. advisor Assn. Firearm and Toolmark Examiners; chmn. legis. & legal affairs com. Sporting Arms & Ammunition Mfrs. Inst., 1993-2001; bd. govs. Nat. Shooting Sports Found., 2002-. Served to capt., chief criminal law 1st Cavalry Div. Staff Judge Advocate, U.S. Army, 1975-78. Mem. Am. Acad. Forensic Sci., Def. Rsch. Inst. Republican. Roman Catholic. Office: Sturm Ruger & Co Inc 1 Lacey Pl Southport CT 06490-1241

SANFELICI, ARTHUR H(UGO), editor, writer; b. Haledon, N.J., May 23, 1934; s. Hugo and Anna (Schilder) S.; m. Betty Louise Van Riper, Aug. 10, 1957; children: Brian Arthur, Amy Elizabeth, Gary Hugh, Bruce Richard. Attended, Lehigh U., 1952-55. Assoc. editor Flying Mag., N.Y.C., 1961-64; mng. editor Am. Aviation Mag., Washington, 1964-68; dist. sales mgr. Gates Learjet Co., N.Y.C., 1969-71; exec. editor Airport World Mag., Westport, Conn., 1971-74; spl. project editor Aircraft Owners & Pilots Assn., Washington, 1974-75, mng. editor Pilot mag., 1975-79, editor AOPA Newsletter, AOPAirport Report, Gen. Aviation Nat. Report, 1979-88; pub. cons., 1989-90; sr. editor Flight Safety Found., Washington, 1989-92; editor S-Cubed divsn. Maxwell Labs., Alexandria, Va., 1992-95; comms. dir. Helicopter Assn. Internat., 1996-97; editor Shooting Sports USA, 1997-98. Editor, compiler: Yesterday's Wings; Editor Aviation History Mag., Leesburg, Va., 1990—. Served with USAF, 1955-60. Mem. Nat. Aeronautic Assn., Aero Club of Washington, Soc. Aerospace Comms. Home: 5 Oak Shade Rd Sterling VA 20164-1163

SANFILIPPO, ALFRED PAUL, pathologist, educator; b. Racine, Wis., Aug. 30, 1949; s. Paul Joseph and Therese (Rhode) S.; m. Janet Lee Thompson, 1973; children: Lisa, Joseph. Student, Max Planck Inst. Exptl. Med., Gottingen, Germany, 1966-68, U. Pa., 1969-70, BA and MS in Physics, 1970; postgrad., Duke U., 1972-75, PhD in Immunology, 1975, MD, 1976. Diplomate Am. Bd. Pathology; lic. physician N.C., Md. Postdoctoral rschr. divsn. tumor virology dept. surgery, 1976-79; intern in anatomic pathology Duke U. Hosp., 1976-77, resident in anatomic and clin. pathology, 1977-79; asst. prof. pathology and exptl. surgery, lectr. immunology Duke U., Durham, 1979-84, from assoc. prof. to prof. pathology, 1984-93, from assoc. prof. to prof. exptl. surgery, 1985-93, prof. immunology, 1990-93; attending pathologist Duke U. and Durham VA Hosps., 1979-93; staff mem. Duke Surg. Pvt. Diagnostic Clinic, 1979-93; dir. Transplantation Lab. Durham VA Hosp., 1979-93; dir. immunopathology Duke U. Med. Ctr., 1982-93, exec. com. dept. pathology, 1989-91; pathologist-in-chief Johns Hopkins Hosp., Balt., 1993-2000; Baxley prof., dir. dept. pathology Johns Hopkins U., 1993-2000; sr. v.p. health scis., dean Coll. Medicine & Pub. Health Ohio State U., Columbus, 2000—. Adj. prof. pathology and immunology Duke U., 1993-95, clin. rsch. unit sci. adv. com., 1988-91, at-large rep. basic sci. faculty steering com., 1989-91, dir. interdisciplinary program in transplantation, 1991-93; mem. Duke Comprehensive Cancer Ctr., 1979-93; chmn. comprehensive transplant ctr. planning com. Johns Hopkins Med. Instns., 1993-96, mem. physician coun. for Atlantic Alliance, 1994-95; med. bd. Johns Hopkins Hosp., 1993—, strategic planning work group, 1993-95, quality assessment and improvement com., 1994-97, re-engring. steering com., 1994-97; Osler prof., dir. medicine search com. Johns Hopkins U. Sch. Medicine, 1994-95, DeVelbiss fund com., 1994—, Clayton fund com., 1993—, Shelley vis. prof. com., 1993—, faculty compensation com., 1993-97, bd. dirs. clin. practice assn., 1993—, chair profl. promotions, 1997—, internat. affairs adv. com., 1997—, dir. Rsch. Comp. Transplant Ctr., 1996—, mem. scientific adv. coun., 1998—; mem. orgn. student reps. Assn. Am. Med. Colls., 1973-75; sec. Carolina Organ Procurement Agy., 1987-89, exec. com., 1987-93, v.p., 1989-91, pres., 1991-93; com. med. student affairs N.C. Med. Soc., 1972-76, del. Durham County, 1974; cons. Battelle Human Affairs Rsch. Ctrs., Seattle, 1985-93, NSF of Switzerland, 1992-93, also numerous U.S. govt. adv. coms.; speaker and presenter in field. Guest editor: Human Immunology, Vol. 14, 1987; mem. editl. bd. Transplantation, 1985—, Pathobiology, 1989—, Transplantation Now (Japan) 1989—, Pathology, Rsch. and Practice, 1990—, Human Immunology, 1992—, Lab. Investigation, 1993—, Xeno, 1994—, Vircholos Archiv, 1998—, Transplant Immunology; reviewer Am. Jour. Kidney Diseases, Am. Jour. Ophthalmology, Am. Jour. Pathology, New Eng. Jour. Medicine, Blood, Jour. of AMA, Jour. Am. Soc. Nephrology, Jour. Clin. Investigation, Jour. Leukocyte Biology, Kidney Internat., others; contbr. numerous articles to profl. jours. Recipient Kermit G. Osserman award Myasthenia Gravis Found., 1976, Wiley D. Forbus award N.C. Soc. Pathologists, 1979, Reach for Sight Physician Investigator award, 1990; NIH predoctoral fellow Duke U., 1970-76, fellow in exptl. pathology Duke U., 1978-79; numerous rsch. grants. Fellow Coll. Am. Pathologists (mem. coun. govt. profl. affairs 1995-97), Am. Soc. Clin. Pathologists (coun. on edn. and rsch. 1994-96); mem. AMA (Physician Recognition award 1979-84), Am. Assn. Immunologists, Am. Soc. Investigative Pathology (councillor 1996—), Am. Assn. Med. Colls. (mem. coun. Acad. Soc. 1998—, adminstrv. bd. 1999—), U.S.-Can. Acad. Pathology (mem. exec. coun. 1997—), Nat. Coun. Basic Biomed. Chairs, Southeastern Organ Procurement Found. (sci. projects and publs. com. 1980-97, organ preservation com. 1981-83, exec. com. 1992-97, sec. 1992-93, treas. 1993-94, v.p. 1994-95, pres. 1995-96 bd. dirs. med. svcs. 1992-96, pres. med. svcs. 1994-95), Transplantation Soc., Am. Soc. Histocompatibility and Immunogenetics (chmn. clin. affairs com. 1987-90, chmn. cornea transplant standards subcom. 1985-86), Assn. for Rsch. in Vision and Ophthalmology, Am. Soc. Transplant Physicians (pres.-elect 1984-85, pres. 1985-86, chmn. sci. studies com. 1991-92), Am. Soc. Nephrology, N.C. Kidney Coun. (rep. histocompatibility 1981-92), Md. Soc. Pathologists, Assn. Pathology Chmn. (rep. 1993—, pres.-elect 1999—), Transplant Resource Ctr. (bd. dirs. 1993—), Univ. Assn. Edn. in Pathology (bd. dirs. 1994—, pres. 1998—), Intersoc. Pathology Coun. (chair 1998—), Alpha Omega Alpha. Office: 200 A Meiling Hall 370 W 9th Avey 415 Columbus OH 43210 E-mail: sanfilippo.5@osu.edu.

SANFILIPPO, HELENA MARY, development director, educator; b. Buffalo; BA in History, San Francisco Coll. Women, 1957; MA in History, U. San Francisco, 1967; PhD in History, U. Notre Dame, 1972. Cert. tchr. Calif. Tchr. various elem. and h.s., Calif., 1950-66; governing coun. Sisters of Mercy, Burlingame, 1972-74, archivist, 1977-87; acad. dean Russell Coll., 1974-82; educator King Coll., Bristol, Tenn., 1988-90, Va. Intermont Coll., 1989-90; founder, exec. dir. Tri-County (Free) Health Clinic, Richlands, Va., 1989-95; educator Chabot/Los Positas C.C. Dist., Hayward/Livermore, Calif., 1996—; devel. dir. Mercy Retirement and Care Ctr., Oakland, 1997—. Author: Inward Wealth and Outward Splendor: New England Transcendentalists View the Roman Catholic Church, 1987. Bd. govs. Cath. Healthcare West-S.W., 1995—, Tri-County Health Clinic, Richlands, Va., 1991-95, Assn. Free Clinics, Va., 1993-95, Mercy Hosp. and Med. Ctr., San Diego, 1982-88, St. Rose Hosp., Hayward, Calif., 1981-87, Soc. Calif. Archivists, 1981-85, Mercy H.S., Burlingame, Calif., 1980-84, St. Mary's Hosp. and Med. Ctr., San Francisco, 1974-77, Mercy Retirement & Care Ctr., Oakland, Calif., 1974-77; bd. dirs. United Way of S.W. Va., Lebanon, 1993-95; cmty. outreach vol. SHARE, HelpLine, Mercy Project, Food Bank, Meals on Wheels, Water Project of Clinch Valley, Va., 1987-95. Recipient Outstanding Vol. Svc. award, Appalachian Agy. Sr. Citizens, 1995, Disting. Citizen of Yr. award, Richlands Area C. of C., 1994, Outstanding Citizen award, Woodmen of the World, 1994, Cmty. Builder's awards, Masons, 1992, 93, Gov.'s Gold award for volunteering excellence, Commonwealth of Va., 1992. Mem. Orgn. of Am. Historians, Am. Hist. Assn., Am. Cath. Hist. Soc. Roman Catholic. Avocations: volunteering, travel, crossword puzzles, reading, choral singing. Fax: 415-333-5238. E-mail: helenarsn@yahoo.com., hsanfilippo@eldercarealliance.org.

SANFILIPPO, JON WALTER, lawyer; b. Milw., Nov. 10, 1950; s. Joseph Salvator and Jeanne Catherine (Lisinski) S.; m. Pamela Joy Jaeger, July 8, 1972; children: Kerri, Jessica, Jennifer. AS, U. Wis., West Bend, 1972; BS, U. Wis., Milw., 1974, MS, 1978; JD, Marquette U., 1988; postgrad., Nat. Jud. Coll., 1996. Bar: Wis. 1988, U.S. Dist. Ct. (ea. dist.) Wis. 1988, U.S. Ct. Appeals (7th cir.) 1988, U.S. Dist. Ct. (we. dist.) Wis 1989, U.S. Supreme Ct. 1994; cert. elem. tchr., ednl. adminstr., Wis. Collection agt. West Bend Co., 1970-72; educator, athletic dir., coach St. Francis Cabrini, West Bend, 1974-77; clk. of cir. ct. Washington County, 1976-89; ptnr. Schowalter, Edwards & Sanfilippo, S.C., 1989-94; sch. prin.K-8 Campbellsport (Wis.) Sch. Dist., 1994-95; chief dep. clk. Cir. Ct. Milw. County, Milw., 1995—, acting clk., 1997-98; jud. ct. commr. Milw. County, 1997—. Judo tchr. City of West Bend, 1967—; phys. edn. instr., judo coach U. Wis., West Bend, 1992—; fellow ct. exec. devel. program Inst. Ct. Mgmt. Nat. Ctr. State Cts., 1999. Author: Judo for the Physical Educator, 1981, Proper Falling for Education Classes, 1981. Mem. sch. bd. West Bend Sch. Dist., 1979-80; dist. chmn. Wis. Clk. of Cts. Assn., 1976-79, mem. exec. com., 1976-82, 97-98, mem. legis. com., 1982-84, 97-98. Recipient cert. study internat. and Chinese law East Chinese Inst. Politics and Law, Willamette U. Law Sch., Shanghai, People's Republic China, 1988. Mem. ABA, Nat. Jud. Coll., Nat. Assn. for Ct. Adminstrn., Wis. Bar Assn. (bench/bar com. 1986-88, 97—), Milw. Bar Assn. (cts. com. 1995—, criminal bench/bar com. 1997—, family bench/bar coun. 1997—), Washington County Bar Assn., U. Wis.-Washington County Found. Inc. (bd. dirs. 1993-94), Assn. Wis. Sch. Adminstrs., Justinian Soc., Universal Tae Kwon Do Assn. (3d degree Black Belt 1988), U.S. Judo Assn. (6th degree Black Belt 1995), U.S. Martial Arts Assn. (7th degree Black Belt Judo 2000, inductee Martial Arts Hall of Fame 2002), Rotary (bd. dirs. West Bend Sunrise Club 1990-91, Paul Harris fellow). Roman Catholic. Avocations: Tae Kwon Do, Tai Chi, Judo, photography, model railroading. Office: Milw County Ct House Rm 104 901 N 9th St Milwaukee WI 53233-1425 E-mail: jon.sanfilippo@milwaukee.courts.state.wi.us.

SANFILIPPO, JOSEPH SALVATORE, physician, reproductive endocrinologist, educator; b. Bklyn., Feb. 28, 1948; s. Joseph Philip and Elena Teresa (Canepa) S.; m. Patricia M. Cantwell, June 21, 1974; children: Angela, Andrea, Luke. BS, St. John's U., N.Y.C., 1969; MD, Chgo. Med. Sch., 1973. Diplomate Am. Bd. Ob-Gyn., spl. qualification in reproductive endocrinology. Intern Milwaukee County Gen. Hosp.; resident in ob-gyn. SUNY Upstate Med. Ctr., Syracuse; instr. dept. ob-gyn. U. Louisville Sch. Medicine, 1977—79, asst. prof., 1979—83, assoc. prof., 1983—89, prof., 1989—98, dir. div. reproductive endocrinology, 1993—98; prof. ob-gyn. and reproductive scis. U. Pitts., Sch. Medicine, 1998—2001; vice chmn. reproductive scis. Magee-Women's Hosp., Pitts., 1998—; chmn. ob-gyn. Alleghney General Hosp., 1998—2001. Pres. med. staff Alliant Health System/Norton Hosp. and Alliant Med. Pavilion, Louisville, 1994—; dir. gynecology Kosair-Children's Hosp., Louisville, 1979—. Editor: Risk Management for Healthcare Professionals, 2001, MBA Handbook for Healthcare Professionals, 2002; editor-in-chief: Jour. Pediat. Adolescent Gynecology, 1989—. Named Disting. Alumnus, Chgo. Med. Sch., 1990. Fellow: N.Am. Soc. for Pediat. Adolescent Gynecology (pres. 2000), Am. Soc. for Reproductive Medicine (bd. dirs.); mem.: ACOG (chair gen. prologus fifth ed.). Avocations: jogging, boating, fishing, ham radio. Office: Magee-Womens Hosp 300 Halket St Rm 2232 Pittsburgh PA 15213-3180

SANFILIPPO, STEPHEN NICHOLAS, educator; b. Bklyn., Sept. 27, 1948; s. Niccolo Sanfilippo and Ottilie Fredericka Nalbach; m. Susan Margaretha Joyce, June 20, 1970. BS in Edn. and History, Northeast Mo. State U., 1970; postgrad., Old Dominion U., 1971-74; MA in Liberal Studies, SUNY, Stony Brook, 1997, postgrad., 1997—. Tchr. history Longwood Sr. H.S., Mid. Island, N.Y., 1974—. Advisor Colonial-Am. Music, East Hampton (N.Y.) Hist. Soc., 1996—; interpreter music of the Whitman era, Walt Whitman Birth Place Assn., Huntington, N.Y., 1988—. Host Sta. WUSB-FM, Stony Brook, N.Y., 1980—. With USN, 1970-74. Mem. L.I. Coun. Social Studies, L.I. Traditional Music Assn. (pres. 1981-83), Suffolk County Hist. Soc., SUNY Italian Cultural Studies Ctr. Democrat. Roman Catholic. Avocations: bird watching, camping, canoeing, folk music and folk musical instruments, hand puppeteer. Home: 113 Woodlot Rd Ridge NY 11961-1938 Office: Longwood Sr HS 100 Longwood Rd Middle Island NY 11953 E-mail: ssanfili@longwoodcsd.com.

SANFORD, BRUCE WILLIAM, lawyer; b. Massena, N.Y., Aug. 5, 1945; s. Doris (Suhrland) Sanford; m. Marilou Green, May 17, 1980; children: Ashley Anne, Barrett William. BA, Hamilton Coll., 1967; JD, NYU, 1970. Bar: N.Y. 1970, Ohio 1971, D.C. 1981, Md. 1985. Staff reporter Wall St. Jour., 1966-67; assoc. Baker and Hostetler, Washington, 1971-79, ptnr., 1979—. Author: Sanford's Synopsis Law of Libel and Privacy, rev. edit., 1991, Libel and Privacy, 2nd edit., 1991, Don't Shoot the Messenger: How Our Growing Hatred of the Media Threatens Free Speech for All of Us, 1999. Trustee Nat. Symphony Orch. Assn.; bd. dirs. Thomas Jefferson 1st Amendment Ctr., U. Va., Charlottesville; pres. Washington Nat. Cathedral Assn., 2002--. Mem. ABA (governing bd., forum com. on communication law, chmn. defamation torts com. 1985-86). Office: Baker & Hostetler LLP 1050 Connecticut Ave NW Washington DC 20036-5304

SANFORD, DARRYL WARREN, real estate and investment consultant, real estate developer, corporate executive; b. Syracuse, N.Y., July 13, 1945; m. Linda J. Rice; children— Darryl W. II, Shanna L.. Cert. real estate appraiser. Field engr. RCA Corp., Cherry Hill, N.J., 1967-72, Data Gen. Corp., Westboro, Mass., 1973-77; founder, pres., chief exec. officer Cen. Computer Services Corp., Syracuse, 1977-83, chmn., dir., 1983-86; dir. Delta Computec Inc., Rochester, N.Y.; pres., dir. Salt City Devel. Corp., Syracuse, 1983—, Microwave North, Inc., Pulaski, N.Y., 1983—; v.p., dir. No. Devel. Corp., Pulaski, 1983—; pres., dir. Golden Fin. Network, Inc., Ft. Meyers, Fla., 1986—; comml. and exchange assoc. ReMax Realty Group II, Lee County, Fla., 1988—; field engr. in computer electronics; engring. cons. in home constrn. and real estate mgmt.; pvt. investor; lic. real estate sales assoc., Fla.; lic. pvt. pilot. Mem. Am. Congress Real Estate, Nat. Assn. Real Estate Appraisers, Aircraft Owners and Pilots Assn., Acad. Model Aeronautics.

SANFORD, DAVID BOYER, writer, editor; b. Denver, Mar. 4, 1943; s. Filmore Bowyer and Alice Irene (Peterson) S. BA with honors, U. Denver, 1964; MS in Journalism with honors, Columbia U., 1965. With New Republic mag., Washington, 1965-76, mng. editor, 1970-76, Politics Today (formerly Skeptic), Santa Barbara, Calif., 1976-78, contbg. editor, 1978-79; editorial writer Los Angeles Herald Examiner, 1978-79; mng. editor Harper's mag., N.Y.C., 1979-80; editor Wall St. Jour. mag., 1980-81; sr. spl. writer Wall Street Jour., 1981—. Syndicated columnist, 1970-71; commentator Can. Broadcasting Corp., 1967-76; judge Heywood Broun award Newspaper Guild, 1971; mem. print screening com. Champion-Tuck awards, 1985, 86, Judge Wuxtry award, 1990. Author: Who Put the Con in Consumer?, 1972, Me and Ralph, 1976; editor, co-author: Hot War on the Consumer, 1970. Recipient Sackett Law prize Columbia, 1965, Eckenberg prize, 1965, Gold award N.Y. Art Dirs. Club, 1977, Wuxtry award for disting. achievement in headline writing Internat. Soc. for Gen. Semantics, 1989, Pulitzer prize, 1997; Centennial scholar, 1960-64; N.Y. Newspaper Guild fellow, 1964-65. Mem. Phi Beta Kappa, Omicron Delta Kappa. Democrat. Home: 118 Prospect Park W Brooklyn NY 11215-4270

SANFORD, DAVID HAWLEY, philosophy educator; b. Detroit, Dec. 13, 1937; s. Hawley Seager and Alice Katherine (Brown) S.; m. Anne Irene Zeleney, July 10, 1965; children: Daria Margaret, Katherine Eugenia. Student, Oberlin Coll., 1955-57; BA, Wayne State U., 1960; PhD, Cornell U., 1966. Instr., asst. prof. philosophy Dartmouth Coll., Hanover, N.H., 1963-70; assoc. prof. Duke U., Durham, N.C., 1970-78, prof., 1978—, chmn. dept., 1986-89. Vis. faculty U. Oreg., U. Mich., Dalhousie U. Author: If P, then Q: Conditionals and the Foundations of Reasoning, 1989, paperback edit., 1992; contbr. articles to profl. jours. Samuel S. Fells fellow, 1962-63, NEH fellow, 1974-75, 82-83, 89-90, Nat. Humanities Ctr. fellow, 1989-90 Mem. Am. Philos. Assn. (exec. com. Eastern div. 1979-81), N.C. Philos. Soc. (pres. 1983-85), Soc. for Philosophy and Psychology, Phi Beta Kappa. Home: 2227 Cranford Rd Durham NC 27705-1007 Office: Duke Univ Dept Philosophy PO Box 90743 Durham NC 27708-0743 E-mail: dhs@duke.edu.

SANFORD, DAVID ROY, journalist, educator; b. Seattle, Apr. 6, 1959; s. Roy Arnold and Venetta Maxine Sanford; m. Renée Shawn Hord, Sept. 11, 1982; children: Elizabeth, Shawna, Jonathan, Benjamin. BS in Religious Edn. with hons., Multnomah Bible Coll., Portland, Oreg., 1982. V.p. pub. & internet ministries Luis Palau Evangelistic Assn., Portland, 1983—. Adj. prof. Western Bapt. Coll., Salem, Oreg., 1995-98, 2001—; lectr. in field, literary agent. Author: Living Faith Bible, 2000; co-author: Calling America & the Nations to Christ, 1994, 2000, God Is Relevant, 1997; contbg. author: More Than Conquerors, 1992 (Gold Medallion 1993), God's Abundance, 1997, 2002, Lists to Live By, 3 vols., 1999, 2000, 02, An Expressive Heart, 2001; exec. editor: Starting Point Study Bible, 2 vols., 2002; editor more than 30 books; contbr. articles to profl. jours.; editl. cons., 1990—; freelance writer, editor, 1982— . Lay pastor Spring Mountain Bible Ch., 1991—; dir., v.p. alumni bd. Multnomah Bible Coll, 1993-98. Mem. Evang. Press Assn. (Merit award 1991, 92, 98, Excellence award 1996), Christian Booksellers Assn. (Gold Medallion award second round judge 1999—), Delta Epsilon Chi. Avocations: travel. Home: 6406 NE Pacific St Portland OR 97213-4930 Office: Luis Palau Evang Assn 1500 NW 167th Pl Beaverton OR 97006-7342

SANFORD, ERIC, lawyer; b. Potsdam, N.Y., July 11, 1951; s. Gerald Ernest Sanford and Annabelle Esther Slater; m. Janis Desmond, Oct. 9, 1977 (div. Feb. 1984); 1 child, Janine. BS in Econ., Ariz. State U., 1993; JD, Stanford U., 1996. Bar: N.Y. 1997. Co-owner Redwood Constrn. Inc., Phoenix, 1986-88; legal asst. Charles P. Franklin, P.C., Tempe, Ariz., 1990-91; rsch. asst. Econ. Analysis Corp., 1992-93; summer assoc. Comptroller of Currency, Washington, 1994; assoc. Cadwalader, Wickersham & Taft, N.Y.C., 1996-99, Milbank, Tweed, Hadley & McCloy LLP, N.Y.C., 1999—. Exec. editor Stanford Law Rev., 1995-96. Student Found. Leadership scholar Ariz. State U. Student Found., 1992; Turken Found. scholar Sam and Ida Turken Found., 1992. Mem. ABA, Phi Beta Kappa. Avocations: bicycling, travel, computers, skiing, reading. Office: 1 Chase Manhattan Plz New York NY 10005-1401

SANFORD, GERALDINE AGNES, retired editor, retired English language educator; b. Sioux Falls, S.D. d. Francis Meredith and Opal Mae (Weimer) Jones; m. Dayton Marshall Sanford, Aug. 28, 1948 (div. July 1972); children: Scott Elliot, Melissa Drue, Corey Todd, Craig Marshall, Reed Meredith. BA, Augustana Coll., Sioux Falls, 1971; MA, U. S.D., 1977. Instr., lectr. U. S.D., Vermillion, 1978-79; instr. English, U. Minn., Morris, S.D., 1979-82; part-time editor S.D. Rev., Vermillion, 1983-99. Presenter Coun. English Tchrs., Yankton, S.D., 1977; panelist Poetry Socs. Conf., Sioux Falls, 1978, Composition Conf., Morris, 1991. Author: Unverified Sightings, 1996; contbr. essays to jours. Grantee S.D. Arts Coun., 1995-96. Democrat. Methodist. Avocations: reading, research, writing, nurturing progeny and plants.

SANFORD, GLENDA LEVONNE, educational administrator; b. Mpls., Apr. 3, 1935; d. Robert Emmanuel and Stella Glendora (Larson) Carlson; m. Reed Ellis Sanford, June 17, 1955 (div. June 1979); children: Kenneth, Paul, Sheryl Sanford Vanscoy; m. Vernon Edward Almlie, Aug. 12, 1995; stepchildren: Jurgan, William, Ann Almlie Iglehart. AA, U. Minn., 1955; BA, Moorhead (Minn.) State U., 1979; MS, N.D. State U., 1986. Bus. office mgr. U. Minn. Health Svc., Mpls., 1955-58; office mgr. Reed E. Sanford Inc., Fargo, 1958-77; exec. dir. YWCA of Fargo-Moorhead, 1979-85; owner, mgr. farm and rental properties, Fargo, 1981-89; pres. Sanford Money Mgmt. Inc., 1987—; program coord. Early Childhood Tracking Sys. State of N.D., Bismarck, 1989-98; spl. pub. adminstr. Cass County, Fargo, 1988-89; tax preparer H&R Block, 1999—. Spkr. Women in Leadership N.D. State U. and KFME, Fargo, 1975-76; advisor N.D. Office Vol. Svcs., Bismarck, 1984-86. Mem. bds. YWCA, LWV, AAUW, Fargo, 1989-92; pres., treas. Jr. League Fargo-Moorhead, 1971-75; pres., bd. mem. Hot Line, Inc., Fargo, 1970-76, United Way of Cass County, Fargo, 1983, N.D. Dental Aux., Fargo, 1975-77; del. White House Conf. on Family, L.A., 1981. Recipient Women Helping Women award Soroptomist Internat., Moorhead, 1984. Mem. AAUW, LWV (treas. 1990-92), Women's Polit. Caucus (fundraising chair 1989-94), N.D. Mental Health Assn. Republican. Lutheran. Avocation: reading. Home and Office: 2101 10th St S Fargo ND 58103-5307

SANFORD, JAMES KENNETH, public relations executive; b. Clyde, N.C., Jan. 23, 1932; s. James Edward S. and Bernice (Crawford) Peebles; m. Judith Bullard Lonashore, 2001; children: Timothy, Scott, Jeannette. AA, Mars Hill (N.C.) Coll., 1952; AB, U. N.C., 1954, MA, 1958. Pub. rels. officer Asheville (N.C.) United Appeal, 1954; reporter, copy editor Winston-Salem (N.C.) Jour., 1957-59, asst. state editor, 1959-61, news editor, 1961-63, editorial writer, 1963-64; dir. pub. info. and publs. U. N.C., Charlotte, 1964-94; pub. rels. cons. N.C., 1994—. Cons. Commn. on Future of Mars Hill Coll., 1990-91, City of Charlotte, 1991. Author: Charlotte and UNC Charlotte: Growing Up Together, 1996, Building Future From the Past: The History of Gaston College 1964-99, 1999; co-author: Fifty Favored Years, 1972; contbr. numerous articles to mag. and newspapers. Mem. attractions com. Charlotte Conv. and Visitors Bur., 1994; pres. elect Internat. House, 2001—, adv. com. Sta. WTVI Pub. TV, Charlotte, 1986-94; chmn. bd. deacons local ch., 1994-95; mem. gen. bd. Bapt. State Conv. of N.C., 2000; mem. Coun. on Christian Higher Edn., 2000—; v.p. Mars Hill Coll. Nat. Alumni Assn., 2001. With U.S. Army, 1954-56. Elected to N.C. Pub. Rels. Hall of Fame, 1995; recipient Alumnus by Choice award U. N.C. at Charlotte, 1996. Fellow Pub. Rels. Soc. Am. (chmn. S.E. dist. 1991); mem. Coll. News Assn. Carolinas (Lewis Gaston award 1982), Charlotte Pub. Rels. Soc. (pres. 1974, Infinity award 1986), Coun. for Advancement and Support Edn. (asst. dist. chmn. 1975-76), Phi Kappa Phi. Baptist. Avocations: writing, hiking, photography. Home and Office: 4 Lake Ridge Rd Lake Wylie SC 29710

SANFORD, LINDA S. information technology executive; b. Jan. 21, 1953; d. William J. and Catherine A. Sanford; 2 children. BA, St. John's U.; MS in Ops. Rsch., Rensselaer Poly. Inst. With IBM, Westchester, NY, 1975—, mgr. hardware and software prodn., 1979, exec. asst. to chmn., 1985—87, product mgr. distributed program exec., 1987—89, dir. networking sys., 1989—92, lab. dir. enterprise systems, 1992—93, gen. mgr. Syst/390 Sys., 1993—95, gen. mgr. Syst/390 divsn./global industries, 1995—99, gen. mgr. storage subsys. divsn. Somers, 1999—2000, sr. v.p., group exec. storage sys. group, 2000—. Bd. dirs. ITT Industries. Bd. dirs. St. John's U., Rensselaer Poly. Inst. Named one of 50 Most Influential Women in Bus., Fortune Mag., Top 10 Innovators in Tech. Industry, Info. Week Mag., 10 Most Influential Women in Tech., Working Woman Mag.; named to Women in Tech. Internat. Hall of Fame. Mem.: NAE. Office: IBM Corp Rte 100 Somers NY 10589

SANFORD, MARSHALL (MARK SANFORD), former congressman; b. Ft. Lauderdale, Fla., May 28, 1960; m. Jenny Sullivan; 3 children. BA, Furman U., 1983; MBA, U. Va., 1988. With Goldman Sachs, 1988, CRC Realty, 1988-89; prin. Southeastern Ptnrs., 1989—, Norton & Sanford, 1993-95, 2001—; mem. U.S. Congress from 1st Dist. S.C., 1995-2001; mem. govt. reform and oversight com., internat. rels. com., sci. com., joint econ. com. Republican. Office: Norton & Sanford 171 Church St Ste 215 Charleston SC 29401*

SANFORD, RHONDA LEMKE, English educator; b. Osmond, Nebr., July 11, 1952; d. Darrell Dean and Frieda Marie (Huttmann) Lemke; m. Stephen Lee Sanford. BA in English, U. Colo., 1975, MBA, 1989, MA in English Lit., 1993; PhD in English Lit., U. Colo., Boulder, 1998. Asst. prof. English Fairmont (W.Va.) State Coll., 1999—. Author: Maps and Memory in Early Modern England: A Sense of Place , 2002. Mem. MLA, Renaissance Soc. Am., Shakespeare Assn. Am., 16th Century Studies Conf., W.Va. Assn. Coll. English Tchrs., W.Va. Shakespeare and Renaissance Assn., Rocky Mountain Medieval and Renaissance Assn. Home: 12 Sunset Dr Fairmont WV 26554 Office: Fairmont State Coll 1201 Locust Ave Fairmont WV 26554 E-mail: rsanford@mail.fscwv.edu.

SANFORD, SUSAN HASPEL, not-for-profit executive; b. Memphis, Nov. 14, 1944; d. Sam M. and Geraldine F. Haspel; m. Jeffry B. Sanford, Feb. 12, 1966 (div. 1990); children: Julie Ann, Jill Suzanne. BS, U. Wis., Madison, 1967. Sr. rsch. assoc. WHBQ-TV, Memphis, 1982-83; dir. devel. Memphis Brooks Mus. Art, 1983-87; v.p. Memphis Arts Coun., 1987-91; exec. dir. Memphis Food Bank, 1991—. Pres. Memphis sect. Nat. Coun. Jewish Women, 1978-80; trustee Day Found., Memphis, 1981-85; sec.-treas. Leadership Memphis, 1982-83; chair United Way Greater Memphis, 1988-89; bd. dirs. Am. Second Harvest, 1998-, vice-chair 2000-02. Named Vol. of Yr., Vol. Ctr. Memphis, 1980, Comml. Appeal Thousand Points of Light award, 1989. Mem.: Rotary (chair tchr. initiative grant com. 1994, chair program com. 1999, project study com. 1998, pres. 2001—02). Democrat. Office: Memphis Food Bank 239 S Dudley St Memphis TN 38104-3244 E-mail: ssanford@secondharvest.org.

SANFORD-FALL, LINDA BARROWS, trauma technician; b. Irvington, N.J., Jan. 6, 1959; d. Joyanna Paul; children: Shawn David Sanford, Brittany Renee Sanford; m. Dennis James Fall, May 13, 1994. Cert. EMT, Midland Coll., 1988. Cert. BLS instr., BCLS instr. Unit coord. EMT, Midland (Tex.) Meml. Hosp., 1980; EMT, Lifecare Ambulance Svc., Odessa, Tex., 1988. Mem. Nat. Assn. EMT's, Tex. Assn. EMT's. Office: Meml Hosp and Med Ctr 2200 W Illinois Ave Midland TX 79701-6407

SANFORD-HUGUS, BARBARA, geneticist, consultant; b. Brockton, Mass., Oct. 7, 1927; d. Arthur A. and Grace Brennan Hendrick; m. George R. Sanford, Nov. 25, 1950 (div. Jan. 15, 1971); children: Arthur, Jane, Brian, Paul; m. J. Edward Hugus, Apr. 14, 1992. BS, BA, Boston U., 1949; MA, Brown U., 1960, PhD, 1963; DSc (hon.) , Bates Coll., 1986. Assoc. biologist Mass. Gen. Hosp., Boston, 1963—73; br. chief biology br. Nat. Cancer Inst., Bethesda, Md., 1973—78; assoc. prof. pathology Harvard Med. Sch., Boston, 1978—81; rsch. dir. Dana Farber Cancer Ctr., 1978—81; dir. Jackson Lab., Bar Harbor, Maine, 1981—88. Trustee U. Maine, Bangor, 1983—88, Jackson Lab., Bar Harbor, 1988—, Dana Farber Cancer Inst., Boston, 1981—. Contbr. Grantee, NIH, 1963—88. Mem.: Am. Assn. for Cancer Rsch. Home: 1090 Mission Rd Pebble Beach CA 93953 E-mail: bhhugus@msn.com.

SANFTLEBEN, KURT ALLEN, career officer; b. St. Louis, Oct. 28, 1952; s. George P. and Betty J. (Zimmer) S.; m. Gail Elizabeth Miller, Dec. 13, 1980; 1 child, Amy Elizabeth. BA, Mich. State U., 1974; MA, Calif. State U., 1989; EdD, Coll. of William and Mary, 1993. Cert. postgrad. tchr., phys. distbn. mgmt. profl. Commd. med. svc. corps U.S. Army, 1974, advanced through ranks to lt. col., 1992, platoon leader 7th inf. divsn. Calif., 1974-76; logistics officer U.S. Army Hosp., Fort Stewart, Ga., 1976-80; company comdr. 3rd Inf. Divsn., Aschaffenburg, Germany, 1981-83; logistics officer Walter Reed Army Med. Ctr., Washington, 1983-86; bat. exec. officer 2d Armored Divsn., Fort Hood, Tex., 1986-88; logistics officer U.S. Army III Corps Surgeon's Office, 1988-90; chief med. plans and ops. U.S. Atlantic Command, Norfolk, Va., 1990-93; prof. mil. medicine Uniformed Svcs. Univ. of the Health Scis., Bethesda, Md., 1993-94, ret., 1994; dep. dir. Va. Commonwealth Challenge, 1994-97. Dir. USMC Rsch. Ctr., 1998—; mem. Sch. Edn. Deans Coun., Coll. William and Mary, mem. sch. edn. devel. bd., mem. bd. dirs. The Assoc. of 1775. Author: Meeting the Challenge: A Successful Dropout Recovery Program, 1997, The Unofficial Joint Medical Officer's Guide, 1995; contbg. author: Planning for Health Service Support, 1993, Postal History of the American Expeditionary Force, 1917-1921, 1990. Decorated Legion of Merit, Def. Meritorious Svc. medal, Expert Field Med. badge; recipient Pres.'s award Mich. State U., 1974. Mem. ASCD, ALA, ASTD, Am. Assn. Higher Edn., Assn. Mil. Surgeons of U.S., Nat. Eagle Scout Assn., Kappa Delta Pi. Libertarian. Unitarian Universalist. Home: 4928 Breeze Way Dumfries VA 22026-1253 Office: Marine Corps Rsch Ctr MCCDC 2040 Broadway St Quantico VA 22134-5139 E-mail: sanftlebenka@tecom.usmc.mil., kurt@sanftleben.com.

SANG, GREG, property development manager; b. Auckland, New Zealand, Nov. 16, 1965; s. Len and Joanna S.; m. Linda Spaeth, Dec. 18, 1993; children: Zachary, Erin, Jessica. BEngring., U. Auckland, 1989. Cert. engr. New Zealand. Sr. project mgr. Cen. Waterfront Property Project Mgmt. Co., Ltd., Hong Kong, 1997—. Office: Cen Waterfront Property Rm 1123 Sun Hung Kai Ctr Wanchai Hong Kong

SANGER, EILEEN, artist; b. Far Rockaway, N.Y., Mar. 24, 1952; d. Edward Herbert and Gladys Minerva Sanger; m. Freddy Profit, May 28, 1989; 1 child, Kristen. Student, Roslyn Sch. Painting, 1975—77. Accounts receivable supr. Kwik Kopy Printers, Inc., N.Y.C., 1978-82; acctg. supr. Insul-lite Window Mfg., Inc., Garden City, N.Y., 1984-89; ptnr., owner Sweet'ms, Rocky Point, 1991-93, Bellport (N.Y.) Lane Art Gallery, 1994-98. Exhibited in group shows at Mills Pond House Gallery, St. James, N.Y., 1993—94, Vanderbilt Mus., Northport, N.Y., 1993—94, Guild Hall, East Hampton, N.Y., 1993—95, 1997, Gallery North, Setauket, N.Y., 1993—95, 1997, 1998, 1999, B.J. Spoke Gallery, Huntington, N.Y., 1994, Stony Brook (N.Y.) Mus., 1999, Represented in permanent collections Neo-Futurarium Hall of Pres., Chgo., Port Jefferson (N.Y.) Free Libr., represented by. N.Y. Found. for Arts spl. opportunity grant, 1994, 96; Stu-Art Oils award Suburban Art League, 1993, Grumbacher Oils award Wet Paint Studio Group, 1994-97. Mem. Nat. League Am. PEN Women, Smithtown Twp. Arts Coun., Southbay Arts Assn. (1st pl. 1995, 2d pl. 1996), East Ends Arts Coun., Brookhaven Arts Coun., Long Island Plein Air Painters Soc. (founding mem.). Avocation: gourmet cooking. Home: 49 Rolling Rd Miller Place NY 11764-2223

SANGER, FREDERICK, retired molecular biologist; b. Rendcomb, Gloucestershire, Eng., Aug. 13, 1918; s. Frederick and Cicely Sanger; m. Joan Howe, 1940; children: Robin, Peter Frederick, Sally Joan. BA, St. John's Coll., Cambridge U., 1940, PhD, 1943; D.Sc. (hon.), Leicester U., 1968, Oxford U., 1970, Strasbourg U., 1970, Cambridge U. Beit Meml. Med. Research fellow U. Cambridge, 1944-51, research scientist dept. biochemistry, 1944-61, research scientist, div. head Med. Research Council Lab. of Molecular Biology, 1962-83. Contbr. articles in field to sci. jours. Recipient Nobel prize for chemistry, 1958, 80; Gairdner Found. ann. award, 1971, 79, William Bate Hardy prize Cambridge Philos. Soc., 1976, Copley medal Royal Soc., 1977; fellow King's Coll., Cambridge U., 1954. Mem. Am. Acad. Arts and Scis. (hon. fgn. mem.), Am. Soc. Biol. Chemists (hon.), Fgn. Assn., NAS. Home: Far Leys Fen Ln Swaffham Bulbeck Cambridge CB5 ONJ England

SANGER, JOSEPH WILLIAM, cell biologist; b. N.Y.C., Feb. 25, 1941; s. Joseph James and Mary Jackson S.; m. Jean McGilvray, Sept. 12, 1964; children: John McGilvray, Matthew Kernan. BS, Manhattan Coll., 1962; PhD, Dartmouth Coll., 1968; MA (hon.), U. Pa., 1976. Assoc. in anatomy U. Pa. Sch. Medicine, Phila., 1971-72, asst. prof., 1972-76, assoc. prof., 1976-85, prof., 1985—; chair, cell biology grad. program U. Pa., 1990-95. Exec. trustee Marine Biol. Lab., Woods Hole, Mass., 1991-93, trustee, 1990-93, Bermuda biol. St., Saint George's Bermuda, 1977-82. Editl. bd. cell motility and cytoskeleton Wily-Liss, N.Y.C., 1986—. Editor (video) Cell Notility, 1991-98; contbr. articles to profl. jours. Humboldt fellow Humboldt Found., 1979-80. Fellow AAAS (nominating com. 2000—). Office: U Pa 421 Curie Blvd Philadelphia PA 19104-6058 E-mail: sangerj@mail.med.upenn.edu.

SANGER, STEPHEN W. consumer products company executive; b. 1945; With Gen. Mills, Inc., Mpls., 1974—, v.p., gen. mgr. Northstar Divsn., 1983, v.p., gen. mgr. new bus. devel., 1986, pres. Yoplait USA, 1986, pres. Big G Divsn., 1988, sr. v.p., 1989, vice chmn. bd., 1992-96, pres., 1993-95, CEO, chmn. bd., 1995—. Bd. dirs. Donaldson Co., Inc., Mpls. Treas. Guthrie Theatre Found., Mpls. Office: Gen Mills Inc One General Mills Blvd Minneapolis MN 55426*

SANGERMAN, JAY J. lawyer, rabbi; b. Chgo., Mar. 7, 1944; s. Alfred and Helen (Eisenberg) S.; m. Barbara Lee Weiss, July 12, 1981. BA in Philosophy, U. Ill., 1968; BHL, MHL, Hebrew Union Coll., Cin., 1971; JD cum laude, Yeshiva U., N.Y.C., 1987. Bar: N.Y. 1988, N.J. 1990, Fla. 1990. Rabbi Etz Chaim Congregation, Lombard, Ill., 1968-73, Temple Sholom, New Milford, Conn., 1973-74, Beth Sholom, Bklyn., 1975-81, Union Temple, Bklyn., 1981-83; assoc. Fried, Frank, Harris, Shriver & Jacobson, N.Y.C., 1987-90; prin. Jay J. Sangerman & Assocs., 1990—. Asst. adjunct prof. in estate planning for the elder protection N.Y. Univ. Sch. Profl. Studies., 1997—. Trustee Jewish Bd. Family and Children's Svcs. Alexander fellow Cardozo Sch. Law, 1986. Mem. N.Y. State Bar Assn. (past chair elder law practice and ethics com. of elder law sect. 1991-97), Assn. of the Bar of the City of N.Y. (legal problems of aging com.), Nat. Acad. of Elder Law Attys. Home: 171 E 84th St New York NY 10028-2000 Office: 60 E 42nd St Rm 650 New York NY 10165-0699 E-mail: law@sangerman.com.

SANGHOEE, SANJAY, investment banker; b. Bombay, India, Aug. 15, 1972; arrived in U.S., 1991; s. Subhash Sanghoee, Saroj Sanghoee. BS in Computer Engring., Columbia U., 1995, MBA, 2000. Investigator Strategic Intelligence Network, N.Y.C., 1993—95; fin. analyst PaineWebber, 1995—96, Lazard Freres & Co. LLC, N.Y.C., 1996—98; CEO, pres. Destiny New Media Inc., 1999—2001; assoc. Dresdner Kleinwort Wasserstein, 2001—02. Author: (novels) Merger, 2002. Scholar Ethics in Bus. scholar, Columbia Bus. Sch., 1999. Mem.: Motion Picture Financing Club (founder, pres. 1998—2000). Personal E-mail: sanjay9000@yahoo.com.

SANGIULIANO, BARBARA ANNA, tax consultant; b. Bronx, N.Y., Dec. 28, 1959; d. Patrick John and Mildred (Soell) Gallo; m. John Warren Sangiuliano, Aug. 28, 1982. BA, Muhlenberg Coll., 1982; MST, Seton Hall U., 1989, JD, 1997. Bar: N.J. 1997; CPA, N.J.; 1987; CMA. Sr. tax mgr. KPMG Peat Marwick, Short Hills, N.J., 1988-92; sr. tax analyst Allied Signal, Morristown, 1992-93; tax mgr. AT&T, 1993-96, Lucent Techs., Morristown, 1996-97; tax atty. Witman, Stadtmauer & Michaels, Florham Park, 1997-98; tax cons. Ernst & Young LLP, Iselin, 1998—. Mem. AICPA, ABA, N.J. Soc. CPAs (v.p. Union County chpt.), N.J. Bar Assn., Inst. Mgmt. Accts., Mensa, Omicron Delta Epsilon, Phi Sigma Iota. Republican. Roman Catholic. Avocations: reading, bicycling, fencing. Home: 340 William St Scotch Plains NJ 07076-1430 Office: Ernst & Young LLP Metropark 99 Wood Ave S Ste 702 Iselin NJ 08830-2729 E-mail: pudd__bear@msn.com., barbara.sangiuliano@ey.com.

SANGMEISTER, GEORGE EDWARD, lawyer, consultant, former congressman; b. Joliet, Ill., Feb. 16, 1931; s. George Conrad and Rose Engaborg (Johnson) S.; m. Doris Marie Hinspeter, Dec. 1, 1951; children: George Kurt, Kimberley Ann. BA, Elmhurst Coll., 1957; LLB, John Marshall Law Sch., 1960, JD, 1970. Bar: Ill. 1960. Ptnr. McKeown, Fitzgerald, Zollner, Buck, Sangmeister & Hutchison, 1969-89; justice of peace, 1961-63; states atty. Will County, 1964-68; mem. Ill. Ho. of Reps., 1972-76, Ill. Senate, 1977-87, 101st-103rd Congresses from 4th (now 11th) Dist. Ill., 1989-95; ret., 1995; cons. McKeown, Fitzgerald, Zollner, Buck, Hutchison, Ruttle and Assocs., 1990—. Chmn. Frankfort Twp. unit Am. Cancer Soc., Will County Emergency Housing Devel. Corp.; past trustee Will County Family Svc. Agy.; past bd. dirs. Joliet Jr. Coll. Found., Joliet Will County Ctr. for Econ. Devel., Silver Cross Found., Silver Cross Hosp. With inf. AUS, 1951-53. Mem. ABA, Ill. Bar Assn., Assn. Trial Lawyers Am., Am. Legion, Frankfort (past pres.), Mokena C. of C., Old Timers Baseball Assn., Lions. Home: 20735 Wolf Rd Mokena IL 60448-8927

SANGREE, WALTER HINCHMAN, social anthropologist, educator; b. N.Y.C., June 15, 1926; s. Carl Michael and Constance (LaBoiteaux) S.; m. Mary Lucinda Shaw, June 14, 1952 (div. Jan. 1986); children: Margaretta Elizabeth, Mary Cora; m. Ilse Michaelis, Dec. 31, 1988. AB, Haverford Coll., 1950; MA, Wesleyan U., 1952; PhD, U. Chgo., 1959. Asst. prof. anthropology U. Rochester, N.Y., 1957-64, assoc. prof., 1964-73, prof., 1973-95, prof. emeritus, 1995—, chmn. dept. anthropology, 1974-77, acting chmn. dept., 1990; vis. scholar dept. anthropology Harvard U., 1979-80. Vis. scholar Ctr. for Population Studies, Harvard U., 1986-87; rsch. fellow Ctr. for African Studies, Boston U., 1998—. Author: Age, Prayer & Politics in Tiriki, Kenya, 1966; contbr. articles to profl. jours. Co-clk. Rochester Friends Meeting, 1977-79. Fulbright scholar U.K. and Kenya, 1954-56; NSF research fellow Nigeria, 1963-65 Mem. Am. Anthrop. Assn., African Studies Assn., Sigma Xi. Democrat. Mem. Soc. Of Friends. Home and Office: PO Box 1290 65 Meadow View Dr Nantucket MA 02554-2717 E-mail: sangree@attbi.com.

SANI, ROBERT LEROY, chemical engineering educator; b. Antioch, Calif., Apr. 20, 1935; m. Martha Jo Marr, May 28, 1966; children: Cynthia Kay, Elizabeth Ann, Jeffrey Paul. BS, U. Calif.-Berkeley, 1958, MS, 1960; PhD, U. Minn., 1963. Postdoctoral researcher dept. math Rensselaer Poly. Inst., Troy, N.Y., 1963-64; asst. prof. U. Ill., Urbana, 1964-70, assoc. prof., 1970-76; prof. chem. engring. U. Colo., Boulder, 1976—; co-dir. Ctr. for Low-g Fluid Mechanics and Transport Phenomena, U. Colo., 1986-89, dir., 1989—. Assoc. prof. French Ministry Edn., 1982, 84, 86, 92, 94, 95, 96, 97; cons. Lawrence Livermore Nat. Lab., Calif., 1974-84. Contbr. numerous chpts. to profl. publs.; co-author three books; mem. editorial bd. Internat. Jour. Numerical Methods in Fluids, 1981—, Revue Européenne des Éléments Finis, 1990—, Internat. Jour. Computational Engring. Sci., 1998—, Internat. Jour. Computational & Numerical Analysis & Applications, 2000-. Guggenheim fellow, 1970 Mem. AICE, Soc. for Applied and Indsl. Math., World User Assn. in Applied Computational Fluid Dynamics (bd. dirs.). Democrat. Office: U Colo Dept Chem Engring PO Box 424 Boulder CO 80309-0424 E-mail: sani@pastis.colorado.edu.

SANIAL, EMILY ANNE, research scientist; b. Groton, Conn., Aug. 11, 1977; d. Patricia Beach Sanial and James Andrews Sanial Jr. BS in Biology, Villanova U., 1998. Med. indexer BIOSIS, Phila., 1998—2000; clin. rsch. assoc. Merck and Co., Inc, Blue Bell, 2000—. Mem.: Am. Med. Writers Assn. (Core Curriculum cert. 2002).

SANIGA, ERWIN MARTIN, educator; b. Charleroi, Pa., June 16, 1946; s. Erwin and Gloria Lee Saniga; m. Karen Lee Geary, May 15, 1971 BS, Pa. State U., 1969, MBA, 1970, PhD, 1975. Asst. prof. U. Del., Newark, 1977-79, assoc. prof., 1979-82, prof., 1982—, Dana Johnson prof., 2000. Cons. Campbells Soup Co., Camden, N.J., 1985-87, Quantum Devel. Corp., Wilmington, Del., 1989—. Contbr. articles to profl. jours. Supr. Little Britain Twp., Nottingham, Pa., 1996—. Capt. U.S. Army, 1971-72. Mem. Am. Soc. Quality, Phi Kappa Phi, Beta Gamma Sigma, Alpha Pi Mu. E-mail: sanigae@be.udel.edu.

SANISLO, PAUL STEVE, lawyer; b. Cleve., Feb. 8, 1927; s. Paul and Bertha (Kasa) S.; m. Mary Ellen P. Conroy, May 7, 1949; 1 child, Susan J. BA, Baldwin-Wallace Coll., 1948; JD, Cleve. State U., 1961. Bar: Ohio 1961, U.S. Dist. Ct. (no. dist.) Ohio 1964. Order clk. Am. Agrl. Chem. Co., Cleve., 1948-52; safety engr. Park Drop Forge Co., 1952-62, personnel mgr., 1954-62; assoc. then ptnr. Spohn & Sanislo, L.P.A., 1962-81; pres., 1981-86; ptnr., pres. Sanislo, Bacevice & Assocs. LPA, Cleve., 1987-98; pres. Sanislo & Assocs. Co. LPA, 1998-2000; of counsel Stewart & Dechant, Cleve., 2000—. Spl. counsel Atty. Gen. Ohio, 1971; arbitrator Am. Arbitration Assn., 1972-78. Mem. Cleve. City Coun., 1964-67; trustee Cleve.-Marshall Law Sch., 1962-63; trustee Cleve.-Marshall Ednl. Found., 1963-68, pres., 1980-83; mem. Solon city Bd. Edn., Ohio, 1972-83, pres., 1974-83; chmn. Solon Charter Rev. Commn., 1971, mem., 2000—; past mem., organizer, legal adv. Solon Drug Abuse Ctr.; mem. Cuyahoga County Dem. Exec. Com.; ward leader 29th Ward Dem. Club, 1965-71, also past pres.; trustee Solon Dem. Ward Club, 1972-75. Recipient Disting. Svc. award City of Solon, 1984, Solon Bd. Edn., 1984, Solon Edn. Assn., 1984. Mem. Bar Assn. Greater Cleve. (Merit Svc. award 1978-79, chmn. workers compensation sect. 1975-96), Ohio Bar Assn., Cuyahoga County Bar Assn., Assn. Trial Lawyers Am., Cleve.-Marshall Law Sch. Alumni Assn. (pres. 1967-68), Hungarian Bus. and Tradesmen's Club (pres. 1967-68), Cleve. Assn. Compensation Attys. (pres. 1973-86). Democrat. Roman Catholic. Avocations: golf, travel. Office: Stewart & DeChant 1440 Standard Bldg Cleveland OH 44113 E-mail: psanislo@stewartdechant.com.

SAN JOSE, ANGEL MOLINA, surgeon; b. Manila, Dec. 9, 1939; came to U.S., 1966; MD, Far Ea. U., Manila, 1965. Diplomate Am. Bd. Surgery. Intern to resident in gen. surgery Mt. Sinai Hosp., Cleve., 1966-67, 67-71; ptnr. Dixie Med & Surg. Assocs., Homewood, Ill., 1973—; pvt. med. practice, 1973—. Attending physician Ingalls Meml. Hosp., Harvey, Ill., South Suburban Hosp., Hazel Crest, Ill. Fellow ACS; mem. AMA, Ill. State Med. Soc., Ill. Surg. Soc., Chgo. Med. Soc., Am. Soc. Gen. Surgeons. Office: Dixie Med & Surg Assocs 17901 Governors Hwy 103 Homewood IL 60430-1144

SANKAR, SUBRAMANIAN VAIDYA, aerospace engineer; b. New Delhi, India, June 22, 1959; came to U.S. 1982; s. V.S.S. and Bala (Sankar) Narayanan; m. Asha Govindarajan, July 31, 1988; children: Sitara, Ankita. B.Tech., Indian Inst. Tech., Madras, 1982; MSAE, Ga. Inst. Tech., Atlanta, 1983; PhD, Ga. Inst. Tech., 1987. R & D dir. Aerometrics, Inc., Sunnyvale, Calif., 1987-97; engring. mgr. Schlumberger ATE, San Jose, 1998-2000; sr. tech. program mgr. KLA-Tencor, Milpitas, 2000-01, dir. engring. San Jose, 2001—. Contbr. articles to profl. jours. J.N. Tata scholar, India. Mem. AIAA, AAAS, Nat. Geog. Soc., Inst. Liquid Atomization and Spray Sys. Home: 34211 Petard Ter Fremont CA 94555-2611 Office: KLA-Tencor 160 Rio Robles San Jose CA 95134-1809 E-mail: ionbeam@attbi.com., subra.sankar@kla-tencor.com.

SANKARANARAYANAN, VENKATA SUBRAMANIAN, researcher, educator; b. Vadodara, Gujarat, India, June 10, 1969; s. Indira Sankaranarayanan and Sankaranarayanan Venkateswara Iyer; m. Nithya Subramanian. BA with hons., U. Delhi, India, 1989; MA, U.Delhi, India, 1991, MPhil, 1993; PhD, U.Portsmouth, Eng., 1999. Scholar Pedagogical Inst., Graz, Austria, 1998—; instr., fellow Harvard Sch. of Pub. Health, Boston, 1999—2002, asst. prof., 2002—. Cons. Nat. Inst. of Pub. Health, Quebec, Canada, 2000—; cons. Nat. Inst. Pub. Health Svc. Mgmt., Tokyo, 2001; advisor U. of Bristol (DFID project), Bristol, 2001—; referee Am. Jour. of Epidemiology, 2000—, Health and Place, Internat. Jour. Epidemiology, Social Sci. and Medicine, Wellcome Trust; vis. prof. Cath. U., Santiago, Chile, 2001—02; vis. faculty Cath. U. , Brussels, 2000—02, Deakin U., Melbourne, Australia, 2000—, Children's Hosp. U. Zurich, Switzerland, 2002—. Editor: (book) Epidemiology: an introduction, 2000; author: (book chapter) Multilevel models: a unified methodological framework for public health research, 2002; contbr. articles (numerous) to profl. jours., also monographs. Recipient Overseas Rsch. Student award, Com. of Vice Chancellors and Principals of the Universities of UK, 1996-1999; grantee U. Grants Commn. Cert. on Nat. Eligibility for Fellowship and Lectureships, Govt. of India, 1994, Rsch. Bursary, U. of Portsmouth, 1995-1999, Bursary, UK Econ. and Social Rsch. Coun., 1997, David E. Bell Fellowship, Harvard U., MacArthur Leadership Program, 1999-2000. Office: Harvard Sch Pub Health 677 Huntington Ave 7th Floor Boston MA 02115-6096

SANKEY, MIKIO, nutritionist, writer, acupuncturist; b. Tokyo, Japan, Aug. 9, 1948; s. George Kiyoshi and Anita Mitsuko Sankey. PhD, Honolulu U., 1992; MSc in Oriental Medicine, Samra U., L.A., 1993. Author: Esoteric Acupuncture Vol. I, 1999, Discern The Whisper, Esoteric Acupuncture Vol. II. Recipient Cert. of Tribute, City of L.A., 1988, Cert. of Recognition, Sen. Herschel Rosenthal, 1988, Award of Honor, County of L.A., 1989.

SANKOVICH, JOSEPH BERNARD, cemetery management consultant; b. Johnstown, Pa., Feb. 6, 1944; s. Joseph George and Helen Mary (Kasprzyk) S. Student, St. Francis Sem., 1964-68; BA, St. Francis Coll., 1966; postgrad., St. John Provincial Sem., 1968-69; MA, U. Detroit, 1973. Cert. cemetery exec., cath. cemetery exec., profl. cons. Assoc. pastor St. Mary's Ch., Nanty Glo, Pa., 1970-71, Sacred Heart Ch., Dearborn, Mich., 1971-74; dir. Mt. Kelly Cemetery, 1972-84; admissions counselor U. Detroit, 1974-81; dir. religious edn. St. James Ch., Ferndale, Mich., 1981-84; exec. Diocesan Cemetery Cons., Wyoming, Pa., 1984-86; dir. cemeteries Archdiocese of Seattle, 1986-91; mgmt. cons., owner Joseph B. Sankovich & Assocs., Edmonds, Wash., 1991—, Tucson, 1997—. Cons. Archdiocese St. Paul and Mpls., 1990—, Diocese San Diego, 1991—, Archdiocese Santa Fe, 1991—, Diocese Tucson, 1991—, Diocese Toledo, 1992—, Diocese Saginaw, 1992—, Archdiocese Edmonton, Alta., Can., 1993—, Diocese Monterrey, 1993—, Diocese Fresno, Calif., 1994—, Archdiocese Anchorage, 1995, Diocese Gaylord, Mich., 1996, Trustees of St. Patrick's Cathedral, 1997, Diocese of Nashville, 1997; Diocese of London, Ont., Can., 1998, Diocese of Springfield, Mass., 1998, Archdiocese of Detroit, 1999, Archdiocese of Boston, 2000, Archdiocese of Newark, 2001, Diocese of Providence, 2001, Diocese of Wilmington, 2001, Diocese of Wheeling-Charleston, 2001, Minn. Cath. Conf., 2001; mem. Task Force on Cremation of Bishops Com. on Liturgy Nat. Conf. Cath. Bishops, 1990-92; instr. A. Cemetery Assn. Univ. Ops./Maintenance, 1994; interim dir. cemeteries Diocese of Tucson, 1992-93, Diocese of Saginaw, 1995-96, Diocese of Springfield, Mass., 1998-2000. Author, editor: Directory of Western Catholic Cemeteries, 1992, 94; author mgmt. assessments, sales programs, market analyses, 1986—; contbr. articles to profl. jours. Mem. Internat. Cemetery and Funeral Assn., Nat. Cath. Cemetery Conf., Wash. Interment Assn. (bd. dirs. 1990-91), Cath. Cemeteries of the West (founder 1987, governancy com. 1987-90). Avocations: travel, reading. Address: Joseph B Sankovich & Assocs 7273 E Shoreward Loop Tucson AZ 85715-3455

SANKOVITZ, JAMES LEO, retired development director, lobbyist; b. St. Paul, July 3, 1934; s. John L. and Mabel A. (Hanrahan) S.; m. Margaret E. Mathews, Aug. 3, 1957; children: Richard, Therese, Patrick, Margaret, Katherine. BS in Journalism, Marquette U., 1956; MA in Speech, U. Denver, 1963. Dir. pub. rels. Coll. of St. Mary of the Wasatch, Salt Lake City, 1956-57; dir. pub. info. Colo. Sch. of Mines, Golden, 1957-63; assoc. dir. devel. Marquette U., Milw., 1963-66, dir. alumni fund, 1966-67, dir. alumni rels., 1967-69, asst. v.p. univ. rels., 1969-70, v.p. univ. rels., 1970-78, v.p. govtl. rels., 1978-86, v.p. govtl. and community affairs, 1986-97; ret., 1997. Contbr. articles to profl. jours. Founding dir. Univ. Nat. Bank, Milw., 1971-74; bd. dirs. St. Coletta Sch., Jefferson, Wis., 1970-76, 86-93, chair, 1974-76. Mem. Nat. Assn. for Ind. Colls. and Univs. (bd. dirs. Washington 1986-90), Disting. Svc. award 1986), Assn. Jesuit Colls. and Univs. (fed. affairs cons. Washington 1974-90), Assn. Cath. Colls. and Univs. (fed. affairs cons. Washington 1974-85, Blue Key, Alpha Sigma Nu. Roman Catholic. Avocations: woodworking, reading. Home: 4057 N Prospect Ave Milwaukee WI 53211-2121 E-mail: ztiv@aol.com.

SANKS, ROBERT LELAND, environmental engineer, emeritus educator; b. Pomona, Calif., Feb. 19, 1916; s. John B. and Nellie G. (Church) S.; m. Mary Louise Clement, May 16, 1946 (dec. Oct. 1994); children: Margaret Nadine, John Clement; m. Edith Millen Harrington, Dec. 2, 1999. Registered profl. engr., Mont. Draftsman City of La Habra Calif., 1940; asst. engr. Alex Morrison cons. engr., Fullerton, Calif., 1941; jr. engr. U.S. Army Engrs., Los Angeles, 1941-42; asst. research engr. dept. civil engring. U. Calif.-Berkeley, 1942-45; structural engr. The Austin Co., Oakland, Calif., 1945-46; instr. dept. civil engring. U. Utah, Salt Lake city, 1946-49, asst. prof. Salt Lake City, 1949-55, assoc. prof., 1955-58; structural engr. The Lang Co., 1950; instrument man Patti McDonald Co., Anchorage, 1951; checker Western Steel Co., Salt Lake City, 1952; structural engr. Moran, Proctor, Meuser and Rutledge, N.Y.C., 1953, F.C. Torkelson Co., Salt Lake City, 1955; soils engr. R.L. Sloane & Assocs., 1956; prof., chmn. dept. civil engring. Gonzaga U., Spokane, Wash., 1958-61; prof. dept. civil engring.-engring. mechanics Mont. State U., Bozeman, 1966-82, prof. emeritus, 1982—; vis. prof. U. Tex.-Austin, 1974-75; part-time sr. engr. Christian, Spring, Sielbach & Assoc., Billings, Mont., 1974-82. Cons. engr., 1945—; lectr. at pumping sta. design workshops, 1988—; assoc. specialist San. Engring. Research Lab., 1963-65, research engr., 1966. Author: Statically Indeterminate Structural Analysis, 1961; co-author: (with Takashi Assano) Land Treatment and Disposal of Municipal and Industrial Wastewaters, 1976, Water Treatment Plant Design for the Practicing Engineer, 1978; editor-in-chief: Pumping Station Design, 1989 (award Excellence profl. & scholarly pub. div. Assn. Am. Pubs. 1989), 2d edit., 1998; contbr. articles on civil engring. to profl. publs. Mem. Wall of Fame, Fullerton High Sch., 1987; NSF fellow, 1961-63 Mem. ASCE (life, chmn. local qualifications com. intermountain sect. 1950-56, pres. intermountain sect. 1957-58), Am. Water Works Assn. (pres. Mont. sect. 1981-82, George Warren Fuller award), Mont. Water Environ. Fedn., Assn. Environ. Engring. Profs., Rotary, Sigma Xi, Chi Epsilon. Home: 411 W Dickerson St Bozeman MT 59715-4538 E-mail: sanks@mcn.net.

SAN MIGUEL, LOLITA, artistic director; Student, Sch. Am. Ballet. Performer Robert Joffrey Co., Benjamin Harkarvy Co., Slavenska-Franklin Ballet; soloist Met. Opera Ballet; founder Puerto Rican Dance Theatre, N.Y., 1970; artistic dir., founder Ballet Concierto de P.R., Santurce, 1978—. Tchr., ballet mistress Ballet Hispánico, N.Y.; tchr. Dance Theatre Harlem, Performing Arts H.S., Adelphi Coll., Hofstra U., L.I. U., Clark Ctr., Met. Opera. Office: Ballet Concierto de PR PO Box 13245 San Juan PR 00908-3245*

SAN MIGUEL, MANUEL, painter, historian, composer, poet, art collector; b. Guayama, P.R., Sept. 29, 1930; s. Manuel and Luisa (Griffo) San M.; m. Sandra Bonilla, July 12, 1969; children: Manuel, Ana. Student, U. P.R., 1947-51, U. Pa., 1966-68, Arts Students League, N.Y.C., 1968-69. Historian San Juan Nat. Historic Site, Nat. Park Svc., 1953-63; exec. sec. Acad. Arts and Scis., San Juan, 1963-64. Founder of mus. and study collection El Morro Castle San Juan Nat. Hist. Site; painter, writer, musician, 1964—; cons. in field. Exhibited in U. P.R., 1958, 62, Ateneo de P.R., 1962, Pan-Am. Union, Washington, 1963, Bienal Mex., 1972, Bienal Rio de Janeiro, 1976, Orange County Schs. Mus. Art, Orlando, Fla., 1992, Mus. Modern Art, Paris, 1994, Expo of the Americas, Orlando, 1996, 98, Galeriá Santiago, San Juan, P.R., 2000, Galeria Campeche, San Juan, P.R., 2001, Simon Bolivar Gallery, Caracas, 2001, and numerous other nat. and internat. exhbns.; contbr. monographs on historical work in San Juan Nat. Historic Site to U.S. Nat. Archives, Washington; contbr. poetry to anthologies including Anthology of Latin American Poets, vol. III, 1987; rec. artist popular music of P.R.; soloist U. P.R. choir, Carnegie Hall, N.Y.C., 1949. Capt. U.S. Army, 1951-53, Korea. Decorated Bronze Star with valor clasp and oak leaf cluster, Purple Heart, Combat Infantryman Badge, others; named One of Ten Outstanding Hispanic Men, Orlando, Fla., 1991; recipient Recognition award for contbns. to Hispanic Am. Culture, Govt. P.R., 1996, Hispanic Heritage Found., medal Painters & Designers 20th Century, Cambridge, Eng., 2000; Coqui de Oro award for contbns. to Puerto Rican arts Casa de P.R., Inc., 1999. Mem. AAAS, VFW (life), Disabled Am. Vets. (life), Am. Legion, Ateneo de P.R. (bd. govs. 1959-60), Am. Biog. Inst. (bd. advisors, life mem. bd. govs.), Am. Philatelic Soc. (postal commemorative soc.), Inst. P.R. Culture (cons.), P.R. Philatelic Assn. (charter), Internat. Platform Assn., Lions (Lion of Yr. 1962-63). Achievements include documentary research in the restoration of Castillo San Marcos, St. Augustine, Fla., Castillo San Felipe de Barajas, Colombia, South Am., and restoration of San Juan fortifications and city walls. Home: 1214 Howell Creek Dr Winter Springs FL 32708

SAN MIGUEL, SANDRA BONILLA, social worker; b. Santurce, P.R., May 23, 1944; d. Isidoro and Flora (Carrero) Bonilla; m. Manuel San Miguel, July 12, 1969. BA, St. Joseph's Coll., 1966; MS in Social Work, Columbia U., 1970. Cert. social work mgr., sch. social work specialist. Case worker Dept. Labor, Migration Divsn., N.Y.C., 1966-68; clin. social worker N.Y.C. Housing Authority, 1968-69, Children's Aid Soc., N.Y.C., 1969-71; sr. social worker Traveler's Aid Soc., San Juan, P.R., 1971-74; coord., supr. Dept. Addiction Control Svcs., 1974-77; substance abuse div. dir. Seminole County Mental Health Ctr., Altamonte Springs, Fla., 1978-81; cons. pvt. practice Hispanic Cons. Svcs., Winter Springs, 1982—; adj. prof. Seminole C.C., Lake Mary, 1986-90; sch. social worker Seminole County Pub. Schs., Sanford, 1986-91, lead sch. social worker, 1991—. Pres.'s minority adv. coun. U. Ctrl. Fla., 1982—, vice-chair, 1982-86, chair, 1986-90; bd. regents EEO adv. com. State U. Sys. Fla., 1985-89; bd. dirs. Seminole Cmty. Mental Health Ctr., 1986-94, 95-2001, v.p., 1988-90, pres., 1990-91; adv. bd. Nat. Devereux Found. Ctrl. Fla., 1993-98, women's adv. bd. South Seminole Hosp., Fla., 1994-96; mem. multicultural cmty. adv. com. Seminole County Pub. Schs., 1993—; mem. Fla. Consortium on Tchr. Edn. for Am. Minorities, 1990-96; mem. local com. Hispanic Info. and Telecomms. Network, 1990; mem. Seminole County (Fla.) Juvenile Justice Coun., 1993—; mem. statewide student svcs. adv. com. Dept. Edn. Fla., 1993-96, student svcs. adv. group, 1996-97. Named Ednl. Support Ctr. Tchr. of Yr., Seminole County Pub. Schs., 2000; recipient Pres.'s Oustanding Svc. award, UCF, 1991, Ponce de Leon Hispanic Cmty. award, 1992, Bd. Svc. Recognition Plaque, Seminole Cmty. Mental Health Ctr., 1991, Outstanding Contribution to Student Svcs. cert., Fla. Dept. Edn., 1995, Manuel Martinez award for Outsanding Contbns. to Puerto Rican Cmty. in Ctrl. Fla., La Casa de Puerto Rico, 1999. Mem.: NASW (appt. nat. sch. social work credential com. 1996—99), Nat. Network Social Work Mgrs., Collegiate Social Workers P.R., Fla. Assn. Student Svcs. Adminstrs., Sch. Social Work Assn. Am. (founding mem.), Fla. Assn. Sch. Social Workers (co-founder minority caucus 1988, columnist quar. newsletter article Minority Corner 1988—92, bd. dirs. 1989—, website article From the Gallery 2001—, sec. 1990—92, v.p. 1992—93, pres. 1993—94, Leadership Plaque 1994, Adminstr. of Yr. 1999), Nat. Network Social Work Mgrs., St. Joseph's Coll. Alumni Assn., Columbia U. Alumni Assn. (nat. bd. dirs. 1997—). Office: PO Box 195933 Winter Springs FL 32719-5933 E-mail: sanmiguel1969@earthlink.net.

SANNA, CATHERINE LEE, special education educator; b. Anchorage, Dec. 11, 1951; d. Julius Anthony and Willa Lee Sanna. BA in Elem. Edn., SUNY, Stony Brook, 1974; MS in Edn. and Spl. Edn., Hofstra U., 1978. Remedial math tchr. South Huntington (N.Y.) Pub. Schs.; resource rm. tchr. Lindenhurst (N.Y.) Pub. Schs.; health conservation tchr. Flushing Queens N.Y.C. Pub. Schs. Host Spl. People show Radio Sta. WNYG, Babylon, NY, 1980—83. Author: A Forest Christmas: Campfire Girls, 1963 (award, 1965). Founder Police Survivors; active WWII Vet. Meml., British Am. & Am. Air Mus. Mem.: DAV, Am. Legion. Republican. Roman Catholic. Home: 161 S 6th St Lindenhurst NY 11757 Home Fax: 631-715-1436 .

SANNER, GEORGE BRADLEY, bank executive; b. Balt., Sept. 20, 1953; s. George E. and Marjorie (Hohman) S.; m. Ann Margaret Tehan, Aug. 31, 1991 (div.); children: Anne, Meredith, Kimberly. BA, U. Va., 1974; MBA, Loyola Coll., Balt., 1978. Asst. v.p. Union Trust Co., Balt., 1974-82; v.p. Am. Security Bank, Washington, 1982-86; sr. v.p. Bank of Md., Towson, 1986-87; mng. dir. Provident Bank of Md., Balt., 1987-94; sr. v.p. FCNB Bank, Frederick, Md., 1994-95; pres./CEO Regal Bancorp, Owings Mills, 1995—; also bd. dirs. Bd. dirs. Md. Bank Svcs., Inc., Chesapeake Bus. Fin. Corp.; pres., CEO Regal Bank and Trust, 1995—. Airman USAF, 1973-75. Mem. Md. Bankers Assn. (bd. dirs. 2001—), Alpha Sigma Nu. Republican. Methodist. Avocations: golf, tennis, amateur radio. Office: Regal Bancorp 10123 Reisterstown Rd Owings Mills MD 21117-3814 E-mail: bsanner@regalbankandtrust.com.

SANNER, GEORGE ELWOOD, electrical engineer; b. Rockwood, Pa., Aug. 30, 1929; s. Dennis Charles and Alverda (Growall) S.; m. Marjorie Mary Hohman, July 1, 1951; children: George Bradley, Marjorie Rosalie, Cathy Ann. BS, U. Pitts., 1951; postgrad., Johns Hopkins U., 1957-59; cert. network engr., Mercer U., 1999. Registered profl. engr., Md.; cert. cost acctg. mgmt.; Microsoft profl. network cert. MCP, MCP+I, MCSE. Supervisory engr. Westinghouse Electric Corp., Balt., 1952-58, chief scientist, cons. def. and space ctr., 1964-72; chief engr., program mgr. radio div. Bendix Corp., 1958-64, engring. mgr. jet propulsion labs. Pasadena, Calif., 1980-81; pres., gen. mgr. Santron Corp., Balt., 1972-79; v.p. engring. M-Tron Industries div. Curtiss Wright Corp., Yankton, S.D., 1979-80; sr. engring. specialist engring. ctr. Litton Data Systems, New Orleans, 1981-83; cons. engring. mgmt. AIL div. Eaton Corp., Deer Park, N.Y., 1983-87; sr. prin. engr. Am. Electronics Labs, Inc., Lansdale, Pa., 1987-92; cons. Atlanta, 1992—. Rep. People to People Tour, various countries, 1978. Patentee in field. Vestryman Immanuel Ch., Sparks-Glencoe, Md., 1969-70; trustee St. Paul's Sch. for Boys, Balt., 1965-67; mem. bishop's secretariat Diocese of L.I., Garden City, N.Y., 1985-87; mem. exec. com. Scriptural Coalition, Diocese of Phila., 1990-92; mem. Rep. Nat. Com., Rep. Presdl. Trust, Nat. Rep. Senatorial Com. A.K. Mellon Found. scholar, 1947-50, Carnegie Inst. Tech. scholar, 1947-51. Mem. IEEE (life), Quarter Century Wireless Assn. Lutheran. Address: 2501 Hidden Hills Dr Marietta GA 30066-5241 E-mail: geste@msn.com.

SANNER, JOHN HARPER, retired pharmacologist; b. Anamosa, Iowa, Apr. 29, 1931; s. Lee Michael and Helen (Grace) S.; m. Marilyn Joan Eichorst, Dec. 28, 1958; children: Linda Leigh, Steven Bradley. BS, U. Iowa, 1954, MS, 1961, PhD, 1964. Rsch. investigator G.D. Searle & Co., Skokie, Ill., 1963-69, sr. rsch. investigator, 1969-75, rsch. fellow, 1975-86, ret., 1986—. Conducted pioneering rsch. in prostaglandin antagonists; contbr. articles to profl. jours. Mem. Deerfield (Ill.) Cable and Telecomm. Commn. 1st lt. USAFR, 1955-57. Mem. Am. Soc. for Pharmacology and Exptl. Therapeutics (ret.), Ill. Videomakers Assn., Wedding and Event Videographers Assn. Internat., Deerfield C. of C. Republican. Avocations: video photography and production. Office: Sanner Video Svc PO Box 199 Deerfield IL 60015-0199 E-mail: johnsanner@aol.com.

SANNER, KENNETH LEROY, inspection systems specialist; b. Smithton, Pa., Apr. 26, 1952; s. Kenneth James and Esther (Lebe) S.; m. Debbie R. Aguillard, Apr. 10, 2000. A of Engring. Tech., Grantham Coll., 1988. NDT tech. Bucyrus Engring., Glassport, Pa., 1971-73, metallurgy lab. tech., 1973-75, metallurgy lab. supr., 1975-81; supr. NDT Timken Latrobe (Pa.) Steel Co., 1981-83, NDT specialist, 1983-86, supr. NDT, 1986-87, supr. NDT, Lims, 1987-90, inspection systems analyst, 1990-96; mgr. Quality Systems, 1996-2000; specialist NDT & Inspection Systems, 2000—. Mem. Am. Soc. Nondestructive Testing, Am. Soc. Quality Control, Am. Soc. Testing & Materials, NRA, Masons. Avocations: aviation, ham radio, computers, hunting, shooting. Office: PO Box 31 Latrobe PA 15650-0031 E-mail: sannerk@timken.com.

SANNER, ROYCE NORMAN, lawyer; b. Lancaster, Minn., Mar. 9, 1931; s. Oscar N. and Clara Sanner; m. Janice L. Sterne, Dec. 27, 1972; children—Michelle Joy, Craig Allen. BS, Minn. State U., Moorhead, 1953; LLB cum laude, U. Minn., 1961. Bar: Minn. 1961, U.S. Dist. Ct. Minn. 1961, U.S. Supreme Ct. 1981. Tchr. English Karlstad (Minn.) High Sch., 1955-57; counsel IDS Life Ins. Co., Mpls., 1961-68, v.p., gen. counsel, 1969-72, exec. v.p., gen. counsel, 1972-77; dir. corp. devel. Am. Express Fin. Advisors, Mpls., 1968-69, v.p., gen. counsel, 1975-78, v.p., 1978-80, v.p., gen. counsel, 1980-82; v.p. law Northwestern Nat. Life Ins. Co., 1982-83, sr. v.p., gen. counsel, sec., 1983-96, ReliaStar Fin. Corp. (formerly known as NWNL Cos., Inc.), Mpls., 1988-96; of counsel Maslon Edelman Borman & Brand, 1996—. Bd. dirs. Fairview Univ. Med. Ctr., Friendship Found., Inc., Fraser Cmty. Svcs., Fairview Health Svcs. Served with U.S. Army, 1953-55. Mem. ABA, Minn. Bar Assn., Hennepin County Bar Assn., Fed. Bar Assn., Assn. of Life Ins. Counsel, Minn. Corp. Counsel Assn., Rotary. Home: 734 Widsten Cir Wayzata MN 55391-1784 Office: Maslon Edelman Borman & Brand 3300 Wells Fargo Ctr 90 S 7th St Ste 3300 Minneapolis MN 55402-4140 E-mail: rsampls@aol.com.

SANO, EMILY JOY, museum director; b. Santa Ana, Calif., Feb. 17, 1942; d. Masao and Lois Kikue (Inokuchi) S. BA, Ind. U., 1967; MA, Columbia U., 1970, MPhil, 1976, PhD, 1983. Lectr. Oriental Art Vassar Coll., Poughkeepsie, N.Y., 1974-79; curator Asian Art, asst. dir. programs Kimbell Art Mus., Ft. Worth, 1979-89; dep. dir. collections and exhbns. Dallas Mus. Art, 1989-92; dep. dir., chief curator Asian Art Mus., San Francisco, 1993-95, dir., 1995—. Author: Great Age of Japanese Buddhist Sculpture, 1982; editor: The Blood of Kings, 1986, Weavers, Merchants and Kings, 1984, Painters of the Great Ming, 1993. Active Assn. Art Mus. Dirs.; vis. com. Harvard U. Art Mus. Woodrow Wilson Fellow, 1966-67; grantee Carnegie, 1963-64, Fulbright-Hays, 1977-78. Office: Asian Art Mus Golden Gate Park San Francisco CA 94118 E-mail: esano@asianart.org.

SANO, KEIJI, neurosurgeon, educator; b. Shizuoka Prefecture, Japan, June 30, 1920; s. Takeo and Haru (Sase) S.; m. Yaeko Sano. MD, U. Tokyo, 1945, PhD, 1951. Asst. U. Tokyo, 1945-56, lectr., chief out patient clinic, 1956-57, assoc. prof. neurosurgery, 1957-62, prof. neurosurgery, 1962-81, emeritus prof., 1981—; prof. neurosurgery Teikyo U., 1981-96; dir. Fuji Brain Inst., 1986—. Pres. 5th Internat. Congress Neurol. Surgery, 1973; pres. Internat. Conf. on Cerebral Vasospasm, 1990; chmn., dir Nat. Com. for Brain Rsch., Sci. Coun. of Japan, 1987-91. Mem. Japan Neurosurg. Soc. (pres. 1965), Japanese Assn. Rsch. in Stereo-ancephalotomy (pres. 1966), Asian and Australasian Soc. Neurol. Surgeons (pres. 1967-71, hon. life pres. 1971—), World Fedn. Neurosurg. Socs. (pres. 1969-73, hon. life pres. 1973—), Japanese Soc. CNS CT (pres. 1978—), Am. Assn. Neurol. Surgeons (hon.), Deutsche Gesellschaft für Neurochirurgie (hon.), Academia Eurasiana Neurochirurgie (hon.), Academia Eurasiana Neurochirurgica (pres. 1986), Soc. Neurol. Surgeons (hon.), Am. Acad. Neurol. Surgery (hon.), Congress Neurol. Surgeons (hon.), Scandinavian Neurosurg. Soc. (corr.), Am. Surg. Assn. (sr.), Am. Neurol. Assn. (corr.), ACS (hon.). Achievements include research on treatment of brain tumors, aneurisms, stereo-encephalotomy, vascular lesions. Home: 4-22-6 Den-en-chofu Ota-ku Tokyo 145 0071 Japan

SANOFF, ALVIN PAUL, education consultant, writer; b. N.Y.C., July 1, 1941; s. Harry and Sema (Kravitz); m. Jane O. Blakely, Aug. 25, 1968; children: Geoffrey L., Scott L., Michael B. AB cum laude in Sociology, Harvard Coll., 1963; MS in Journalism, Columbia U., 1964. Reporter Washington Star, 1965; editor Newhouse Newspapers Washington Bur., 1965-66; pub. info. officer Sm. Bus. Adminstrn., Washington, 1966-67; reporter Balt. Sun, 1967-71; editoral page editor Dayton (Ohio) Jour. Herald, 1971-77; from assoc. editor to asst. mng. editor U.S. News & World Report Mag., Washington, 1977-98, mng. editor Guides to Am.'s Best Colls. and Grad

Schs., 1992-98. Sr. v.p. Maguire Assocs., Bedford, Mass., 1998-2000; dir. Schs. Edn. Rsch. Project, Tchrs. Coll., Columbia U., 2000—. Creator, series editor: Authors' America TV Series, 1992-95; contbg. editor Prism Mag., 2000—. Recipient Best Editl. Writing award Ohio AP, 1974; NEH Fellow, 1974-75. Jewish. Avocations: reading, music, walking, traveling. Office: 5510 Johnson Ave Bethesda MD 20817-3518 E-mail: apsanoff@erols.com.

SAN PEDRO, OFELIA, transportation services executive, energy planner; b. Havana, Cuba, Apr. 11, 1953; d. Carlos and Ofelia (Uset) Martinez; m. Pablo Alvarado, June 24, 1976 (div. May 1981); m. Miguel San Pedro, Apr. 26, 1986; children: Victoria, Miguel. B in Indsl. Engring., U. Miami, 1975, MBA, 1979. Mgmt. engr. Mercy Hosp., Miami, Fla., 1973-75; cons. Arthur Andersen & Co., 1975-76; project mgr. Ea. Airlines, 1976-79; sr. EDP auditor Ryder System Inc., 1979-80; mgr. energy planning Ryder Truck Rental, 1980-81; mgr. planning & control Ryder System Inc., 1981-84, dir. planning & control, 1984-91; v.p., contr. Ryder Energy Distbn. Corp., 1991-96; pres. Ryder Energy Distbn., 1996-97; v.p. Global Procurement Ryder Sys., 1997—. Adj. prof. U. Miami, 1979-90; bd. dirs. Miami Mus. Sci., Columbia-Deering Hosp. Bd. dirs. U. Miami Engring. Alumni Assn., 1990. Mem. NASE, Nat. Soc. Hispanic MBAs, Ryder Women's Mgmt. Assn. Home: 200 NW 136th Ave Miami FL 33182-1955 Office: Ryder System Inc 3600 NW 82nd Ave Miami FL 33166-6623

SANSALONE, WILLIAM ROBERT, biochemistry educator, researcher; b. Vineland, N.J., Feb. 16, 1931; s. Fortunato and Rosa (Pelle) S.; m. Alice E. Koury, June 25, 1960; 1 child, Catherine. *William Sansalone's parents left Gerace, a historic cathedral town in Calabria, Italy, in 1913, for Philadelphia. In 1916, they purchased a parcel of woodland and settled in Malaga, a farming community in southern New Jersey. All of their 44 descendants were born in the United States.* BS, Rutgers U., 1953, PhD, 1961; MS, U. N.H., 1955. Biochemistry rsch. asst. U. Conn., Storrs, 1955-56; instr. biochemistry SUNY Downstate Med. Ctr., Bklyn., 1961-64, asst. prof. biochemistry, 1964-70, assoc. prof., 1970-71; project scientist NIH, Bethesda, Md., 1971-72, sr. project scientist, 1972-73, exec. sec. biochemistry study sect., 1973-74, program dir. rev., 1974-83, assoc. dir. sci. program ops., 1983-87, dir. office of program planning and evaluation, 1987-96; sr. fellow Georgetown U., Washington, 1999—. Vis. assoc. prof. physiology and biophysics Med. Coll. Pa., Phila., 1970. *After retiring from the National Institutes of Health in 1996, William Sansalone launched a writing career, having completed the Certificate Program in Editing and Publications at Georgetown University, Washington, DC, in 1997. His publications from 1997-98 include a history of St. Mary's Church in Malaga, New Jersey, founded in 1922, and a biography of distinguished Cornell University biochemist Harold H. Williams (1907-91). In 1999, Dr. Sansalone was appointed adjunct fellow at the Georgetown University Center for Food and Nutrition Policy, where he was a writer-editor. In 2001, he transferred to Georgetown University Medical Center as a senior fellow.* Contbr. articles to profl. jours. Served to 1st lt. USAF, 1956-58. Mem. AAAS, Harvey Soc., Biophys. Soc., Am. Soc. Nutritional Scis., Soc. Exptl. Biology and Medicine, Sigma Xi, Alpha Gamma Rho (chpt. treas. 1968-70). Roman Catholic. Home: 6835 Old Stage Rd Rockville MD 20852-4359 E-mail: ws31@prodigy.net., ws23@georgetown.edu.

SANSBURY, BARBARA ANN PETTIGREW, nursing administrator; b. Florence County, Aug. 6, 1951; d. Simon and Mary Magaline (Quillen) Pettigrew; 1 child, Terrence Urice. LPN, Southside Area Vocat. Ctr., 1970; AD, Florence (S.C.) Darlington Tech. Sch., 1978; BSN, Med. U. of S.C., 1987, MSN, 1991. RN, S.C. Staff and charge nurse McLeod Regional Med. Ctr., 1970-91; staff nurse Faith Health Care Facility, Florence, 1983-84; sch. nurse Timmonsville (S.C.) High Sch., 1983-84; clin. instr. Florence Darlington Tech., 1989-90; sr. staff nurse Med. U. S.C., 1991-92; nurse mgr. VA Med. Ctr., Augusta, Ga., 1992-97, 2000—, nurse case mgr., 1997-2000, nurse mgr., 2000—. Mem. USAR, ANA (cert. psychiat. nurse), Ga. Nurses Assn. (chair psychiat. and mental health coun., chair of cabinet on nursing practice 1999), Chi Eta Phi Sorority Inc., Sigma Theta Tau Internat. Home: 3545 Crawfordville Dr Augusta GA 30909-9437

SANSBURY, MICHAEL TODD, lawyer; b. Atlanta, Apr. 27, 1976; s. Roy Kenneth and Ann (Walker) S.; m. Tamara Nichole Vansant, Dec. 30, 1997; children: Michael Todd Jr., Mabry. BA, U. of South, 1998; JD, Yale U., 2001. Bar: Ga. 2001. Law clk. to Hon. Emmett Ripley Co. U.S. Ct. Appeals for 11th Circuit, Mobile, Ala., 2001—. Mem. exec. com. Yale Law Sch., New Haven, 2001—. Bd. dirs. St. Thomas' Day Sch., New Haven, 2000-01. John M. Olin fellow Yale U. Law Sch., 1998-2001. Mem.: ABA, Internat. Soc. for Philos. Inquiry (assoc.), Am. Mensa, Hon. Order Ky. Cols., Phi Beta Kappa, Chi Psi (life). Episcopalian. Home: 901 Gayfer Ave Apt 1012 Fairhope AL 36532-3905 Office: 113 St Joseph St Rm 433 Mobile AL 36602 Fax: 801-640-0616. E-mail: michael.sansbury@mindspring.com.

SANSBURY, OLIN BENNETT, JR. retired university/orchestra administrator; b. Florence, S.C., Dec. 10, 1937; s. Olin Bennett and Gladys Ruth (Snipes) S.; m. Helen Cecile Hyman, Aug. 24, 1963; 1 child, Olin Bennett, III. BA in History, Wofford Coll., 1959; PhD in Internat. Studies, U. S.C., 1972. Reporter, editorial writer WBTW-TV, Florence, 1963-64, 1966-67; asst. dir. student affairs U. S.C., 1969-70, dean students, Francis Marion Coll. Columbia, 1970-71, asst. vice provost, asst. prof. govt. and internat. studies, 1971-73, chancellor, assoc. prof. govt. and internat. studies Spartanburg, 1973-93, chancellor emeritus, 1993—; exec. dir. Greenville Symphony Assn., 1994-99; ret. Bd. dirs. S.C. Coun. Econ. Edn., 1977-94, S.C. Coun. for the Humanities, 1986-96, Am. Coun. Edn. Commn. Govtl. Rels., 1991-93, S.C. Arts Alliance, 1996-99; rep. Pres.' Commn. Divsn. II NCAA, 1991-93; founding com. bd. regents Leadership, Spartanburg, 1980-85. With U.S. Army, 1960-63. H.B. Earhart fellow, 1965-66, 69 Mem. Am. Assn. State Colls. and Univs. (bd. dirs. 1989-92).

SANSEIGNE, MARY JOSEPHINE, nurse anesthetist; b. Kearny, N.J., Aug. 29, 1931; d. Joseph A. and Catherine E. (Ward) Mac Neill; m. Alain Sanseigne, Nov. 1, 1952 (div. 1958); 1 child, Katherine; m. James C. Candy, June 18, 1983. Student, Jersey State Coll., 1950-53; RN, Jersey City Med. Ctr., 1953; cert. RN anesthetist, Jersey Shore Med. Ctr., Neptune, N.J., 1966, Jersey State Coll., Monmouth Coll., 1977-78. RN Army Hosp., Ft. Monmouth, N.J., 1957-64; chief cert. RN anesthetist Plainfield, 1968-82; staff cert. RN anesthetist Univ. Hosp., Newark, 1984-88; chief cert. RN anesthetist Centra State Med. Ctr., Freehold, N.J., 1988-92. Mem. Property Owner's Assn., Neptune, 1990-91. Mem. N.J. Assn. Nurse Anesthetists (bd. trustees 1972-74, pub. rels. 1970-72, legal adv. 1971-72), Am. Assn. Nurse Anesthetists (McGaw award 1968), N.J. Hosp. Assn. Republican. Roman Catholic. Avocations: dancing, reading, travel. Home: 69 Blue Ridge Dr Brick NJ 08724-2023

SANSEVERINO, RAYMOND ANTHONY, lawyer; b. Bklyn., Feb. 16, 1947; s. Raphael and Alice Ann (Camerano) S.; m. Karen Marie Mooney, Aug. 24, 1968 (dec. 1980); children: Deirdre Ann, Stacy Lee; m. Victoria Vent, June 6, 1982 (div. 1995); m. Kimberley Frank, May 11, 2002. AB in English Lit., Franklin & Marshall Coll., 1968; JD cum laude, Fordham U., 1972. Bar: N.Y. 1973, U.S. Dist. Ct. (so. and ea. dists.) N.Y. 1973, U.S. Ct. Appeals (2d cir.) 1974, U.S. Supreme Ct. 1986. Assoc. Rogers & Wells, N.Y.C., 1972-75, Corbin & Gordon, N.Y.C., 1975-77; ptnr. Corbin Silverman & Sanseverino LLP, 1978—2001, mng. ptnr., 1985—2001; ptnr. Brown Raysman Millstein Felder & Steiner LLP, 2001—, head comml. real estate leasing group, 2001—. Contbr. articles to profl. jours.; articles editor Fordham Law Rev., 1971-72. Recipient West Pub. Co. prize, 1972. Mem. ABA, Assn. Bar City of N.Y., N.Y. State Bar Assn., Twin Oaks Swim and Tennis Club (bd. dirs. 1981—, pres. 1993-2001), Alumni Assn. Franklin and Marshall Coll. (bd. dirs. 2001—) Republican. Roman Catholic. Office: Brown Raysman et al 900 3d Ave New York NY 10022 E-mail: rsanseverino@brownraysman.com.

SANSONE, ROSEMARY MARGARET, gifted and talented education educator; b. Medina, N.Y., Sept. 19, 1947; d. Leonard Joseph and Mary Elizabeth (Slattery) Matusak; m. James Joseph, Nov. 29, 1969; 1 child, Samantha Ellen. BS in Elem. Edn., SUNY, Brockport, 1969; MS in Elem. Edn., SUNY Coll. at Buffalo, Buffalo, 1973, cert. creative studies, 1987; PhD in Elem. Edn., SUNY, Buffalo, 1994. Elem. tchr. Lockport (N.Y.) Sch. Dist., 1969-81, enrichment tchr., 1987; rsch. asst. early childhood rsch. dept. SUNY, Buffalo, 1987-88; tchr. gifted/talented Lockport (N.Y.) Sch. Dist., 1988—. Facilitator lang. arts curriculum devel. Nat. Javits Found., 1991. Contbr. articles on gifted edn. and emerging literacy to profl. jours. Mem. Lockport Cath. Sch. Bd., 1987, Krull Olcott Devel. Com., 2000—. Tchr. fellow N.Y. State PTA, 1992-93; Internation Women's Decade II honoree, 1995, N.Y. State Senate's Women of Distinction Nominee, 1998. Mem.: Olcott Beach Carousel Pk. Assn. (chmn. 2002—), Advocacy for Gifted and Talented Edn., Elem. Tchrs., Assn. Gifted, Coun. Exceptional Children, Nat. Assn. Gifted Children, Olcott Beach Cmty. Assn. (co-sec. 2001—). Roman Catholic. Avocations: writing, aerobics, boating, reading, researching local history. Home: PO Box 308 5853 Ontario St Olcott NY 14126 Office: Charles Upson Elem 28 Harding Ave Lockport NY 14094-6021

SANSONETTI, THOMAS L. federal agency administrator; Grad., MBA, U. Va.; JD, Washington and Lee U. Chief of staff, legis. dir. Congressman Craig Thomas; assoc. solicitor on energy and natural resources Dept. Interior, solicitor, 1990; ptnr. Holland and Hart, Cheyenne, Wyo., 1993—2001; asst. atty. gen. Environment and Natural Resources Divsn. U.S. Dept. Justice, Washington, 2001—. Chmn. rules com. Rep. Nat. Com., 1996—2000; mem. Wyo. Rep. State Com. Office: US Dept Justice Environment and Natural Resources Divsn 950 Pennsylvania Ave NW Washington DC 20530-0001*

SANSTEAD, WAYNE GODFREY, state superintendent, former lieutenant governor; b. Hot Springs, Ark., Apr. 16, 1935; s. Godfrey A. and Clara (Buen) S.; m. Mary Jane Bober, June 16, 1957; children: Timothy, Jonathan. BA in Speech and Polit. Sci, St. Olaf Coll., 1957; MA in Pub. Address, Northwestern U., 1966; Ed.D., U. N.D., 1974. Tchr., Luverne, Minn., 1959-60; dir. forensics Minot (N.D.) High Sch., 1960-71, tchr. social sci., 1960-78; mem. N.D. Ho. of Reps., 1965-70, 83-85, N.D. Senate, 1971-73; lt. gov. N.D. Bismarck, 1973-81; supt. pub. instrn. N.D., 1985—. Served with AUS, 1957-59. Recipient Disting. Alumnus award St. Olaf Coll., 1991; named Outstanding Freshman Senator A.P., 1971, Outstanding Young Educator, N.D. Jr. C. of C., 1967, Outstanding Young Man, Minot Jr. C. of C., 1964; Coe Family Found. scholar, 1963, Eagleton scholar Rutgers U., 1969. Mem. N.D. Edn. Assn., NEA (legis. com. 1969—), Central States Speech Assn., Am. Forensic Assn., Jr. C. of C., Sons of Norway. Democrat. Lutheran (chmn. Western N.D. research and social action com. 1962-68). Clubs: Elk, Toastmaster. Home: 1120 Columbia Dr Bismarck ND 58504-6514 Office: Dept Pub Instrn 600 E Boulevard Ave Bismarck ND 58505-0660

SANSWEET, STEPHEN JAY, journalist, author, marketing executive; b. Phila., June 14, 1945; s. Jack Morris and Fannie (Axelrod) S. BS, Temple U., 1966. Reporter Phila. Inquirer, 1966-69; reporter Wall Street Jour., Phila., 1969-71, Montreal, Que, Can., 1971-73, L.A., 1973-84, dep. bur. chief, 1984-87, bur. chief, 1987-96; dir. speciality mktg. Lucasfilm Ltd., San Rafael, Calif., 1996-97, dir. content mgmt. and fan rels., 1997—; sr. editor Star Wars Galaxy Mag., 1996-2000; columnist Star Wars Insider, 1994—. Lectr. bus. journalism U. So. Calif., L.A., 1984-87. Author: The Punishment Cure, 1976, Science Fiction Toys and Models, 1981, Star Wars: From Concept to Screen to Collectible, 1992, Tomart's Price Guide to Worldwide Star Wars Collectibles, 1994, 2d edit., 1997, The Quotable Star Wars, 1996, Star Wars Scrapbook: The Essential Collection, 1998, Star Wars Encyclopedia, 1998, Star Wars Collectibles: A Pocket Manual, 1998, Anakin Skywalker: The Story of Darth Vader, 1998, Star Wars: The Action Figure Archive, 1999; cons. editor: Star Wars Galaxy card sets, 1993, 2d series, 1994, 3d series, 1995; editor: Star Wars Trilogy Spl. Edn. card sets, 1997. Recipient award for best fire story Phila. Fire Dept., 1968, Pub. Svc.-Team Mem. award Sigma Delta Chi, 1977; finalist Loeb award, 1990. Mem. Soc. Profl. Journalists. Avocation: collecting toys and movie memorabilia. Office: Lucasfilm Ltd PO Box 2009 San Rafael CA 94912-2009

SANT, JOHN TALBOT, lawyer; b. Oct. 7, 1932; s. John Francis and Josephine (Williams) S.; m. Almira Steedman Baldwin, Jan. 31, 1959; children: John Talbot Jr., Richard Baldwin, Frank Williams. AB, Princeton U., 1954; LLB, Harvard U., 1957. Bar: Mo. 1957. Assoc. Thompson, Mitchell, Douglas & Neill, St. Louis, 1958-60; atty. McDonnell Aircraft Co., 1960-61; asst. sec., 1961-62; sec., 1962-67, McDonnell Douglas Corp., St. Louis, 1967-76; asst. gen. counsel, 1969-74; corp. v.p. legal, 1974-75; corp. v.p., gen. counsel, 1975-88; bd. dirs., 1978-82; sr. v.p., gen. counsel, 1988-91; ptnr. Bryan Cave, 1991-96; of counsel, 1997. Vestry of St. Michael and St. George, St. Louis, 1979-82, 87-90, 93-95; bd. dirs. Grace Hill Neighborhood Svcs., Inc., St. Louis, 1987-93; pres. Grace Hill Settlement House, 1996-97; mem. transition task force Supt. Elect. of St. Louis Pub. Schs., 1996, found. dir. St. Louis Pub. Schs. Found., chair Partnership For Youth, Inc., 2001—. Mem. ABA (pub. contracts sec., coun. 1987-91), Mo. Bar Assn., St. Louis Bar Assn. Home: 9 Ridgewood St Saint Louis MO 63124-1849 Office: Bryan Cave 1 Metropolitan Sq Ste 3600 Saint Louis MO 63102-2750

SANTA-COLOMA, BERNARDO, secondary school educator, counselor; b. N.Y.C., May 31, 1934; s. Bernardo Santa-Coloma Sr. and Belma Remotti; m. Sofia A. Santa-Coloma, Dec. 22, 1981; childen: Ananda, Anita. BA in Humanistic Psychology, U. Calif., Santa Cruz, 1973; MA in Integral Counseling Psychology, Calif. Inst. Integral Studies, San Francisco, 1976; MEd in Secondary Edn., U. Nev., Las Vegas, 1979; 3 level cert., Feuerstein's Instrumental, Enrichment Program; postgrad., U. Sarasota and U. Houston. Cert. secondary edn. tchr. ESL, history, English Tex., guidance counselor Tex. Edn. Assn., lic. marriage and family therapist Tex., cert. nat. cert. counselor, lic. profl. counselor Tex., cert. supr. LPC/LMFT interns/Medicaid providers. Mem. tchr. corps., vol. VISTA, Las Vegas, Nev., 1976-79; family counselor, English tutor Diocese of Matamoros and Valle Hermoso Tamps, Mexico, Cath. Family Svcs. and Vol. Ednl. and Social Svcs., Amarillo, Tex., 1980-82; grad. asst. Pan Am. U., Brownsville, 1983-84; at-risk program, low-level reading instr. Brownsville Ind. Sch. Dist., 1984-94; basic skills instr. James Pace High Sch., Brownsville; pres. Alternative Edn. Ctr./Brownsville Ind. Sch. Dist., 1994—. Counselor and psychotherapist Family Effectiveness and Devel. Program, Kids in Crisis Teenage Crisis Hotline, La Casa Esperanza Home for Boys; basic adult reading instr. Southmost Coll.; ESL, lang. arts tchr. Alternative Ctr.; at-risk tchr., pvt. practice counselor, Brownsville Ind. Sch. Dist. Family Ctrs., 1994—; part-time counselor Holistic Mind and Health Inst., Brownsville, 1998; cons., contract worker, counselor supr. chem. dependeny counselor Recovery Ctr., Cameron County Housing Authority, 1999-2001, Citadel Group, 2000—; medicaid provider, individual approved supr. LPC interns, LMFT assocs.; instr., supr. Weslaco. Contbr. articles to profl. jours. in U.S. and Mex. including Integracion Integral, Journey in Matamoros. Vol. VISTA, 1976-79, VISTA Tchr. Corps, Las Vegas, Peace Corps, Thailand, 1979, Vol. Edn./Soc. Svc., Tex., Mex., 1980-82. With USN, 1952-56, medic neuropsychiatric wards San Diego and Guam. Recipient scholarship U. Calif.-Santa Cruz, 1971-73, U. Nev. tchr. corps, 1977-79; named grad. asst. Calif. Inst. Integral Studies, 1974-76. Home: PO Box 3941 Brownsville TX 78523-3941 also: Country Club 2009 Madero Dr Brownsville TX 78526-1734 Fax: 956-982-2868. E-mail: bstacoloma@aol.com. *Waking up is really the seed of perfection, of personal and transpersonal realization - involution precedes evolution! To be is to do and to do IS. In the final analysis, final judgment, what shall we - yes, you and I contribute to our fellowman, to posterity? - we often die before giving birth to ourselves - truly to be reborn is not easy; we create, instead, an intense paradox, toward life, toward our destiny (i.e., a paradoxical process of self denial instead of one of genuine self interest, self-realization,-actualization, ad infinitum, in tune with spirit, the cosmos...'Like trees", we begin with a seed. Some do not develop at all. Some die young. And some grow into towering heights with many flourishing branches).*

SANTAELLA, JUAN, banker, investment advisor; b. Caracas, Venezuela, Jan. 2, 1945; came to U.S., 1993; s. Hector Santaella and Margarita Telleria; m. Alicia Zamora de Santaella, Sept. 16, 1967; children: Hector, Juan B., Maria Antonia. Degree in econs., Cath. U. Andres Bello, Caracas, 1967. Gen. mgr. Metalanca, Caracas, 1968-83; v.p. S.F. Atlantica, 1977-80; pres., CEO Corpofin, 1983-94, Bancor, Caracas, 1985-94; pres. Valcorp Securities, Miami, 1995—; chmn. bd. Ea. Nat. Bank, 1983-99. Dir. Fedecamaras, Caracas, 1989-93, Venezuelan Banking Coun., Caracas, 1990-92; chmn. bd. dirs. Haverfield Corp., Gettysburg, Pa., 1998—; pres. Intercapital Holdings, Miami, 1999—; chmn. Emida Techs., Miami. Treas. Mus. Am. Found., Washington, 1999-2002; mem. Hispanic Coun. on Internat. Rels., Washington. Mem. Venezuelan Banking Assn. (v.p. 1992-94), Key Biscayne (Fla.) Yacht Club, Riviera Country Club. Roman Catholic. Avocations: jogging, golf, skiing. Office: Valcorp Securities 2200 S Dixie Hwy Ste 603 Miami FL 33131-

SANTAMARIA, BARBARA MATHENY, retired nurse practitioner; b. Parkersburg, W.Va., Dec. 25, 1930; d. Richard H. and Vivian L. (Effinger) Matheny; children: Angelo Jr., Mark E., Annette B. Diploma in nursing, Union Meml. Hosp., 1953, adult nurse practitioner cert., 1975; BS, Johns Hopkins U., 1977, MPH, 1978. RN Md.; cert. nurse practitioner, Md. Adminstrv. supr. Balt. County Dept. Health, Towson, Md., 1976—83; cons. with Respiratory Disease Program Md. State Dept. Health and Mental Hygiene, Balt., 1983—85; asst. dir. profl. health svcs. HomeCall, Inc., Frederick, 1985—86, dir. profl. health svcs., 1986—88; nurse practitioner, home-based primary care VA Med. Ctr., Balt., 1988—2001; ret., 2001; pt. time nurse practitioner clin. pharmaceutical rsch. Balt. Rsch. Edn. Found., Balt., 2002—. Congl. dist. coord., 1985-94. Contbr. chpts. to books. Recipient scholarship and grant Dept. Health, Edn. and Welfare, 1978-79. Mem. Am. Nurses Assn. (cert. family nurse practitioner), Coun. Primary Health Care Nurse Practitioners, Md. Nurses' Assn. (pres. 1982-85, pres. coun. nurse practitioners 1992-93), Md. League Nursing, Am. Lung Assn. Md. (bd. dirs. 1986-90), Am. Red Cross Assn. (nursing and edn. com. 1985-92, chair nursing and health com. 1988-92, named Outstanding Vol. 1990), Nat. Heart, Lung and Blood Inst. (coord. com. nat. asthma edn. program, 1988-2000), Balt. County LWV (bd. dirs. 1986-87), Md. Bd. Nursing (mem. home health credentialing standards com. 1988-92), Sigma Theta Tau. Home: 74 Open Gate Ct Baltimore MD 21236-1681

SANTANA, ROBERT RAFAEL, lawyer; b. Bklyn., Apr. 22, 1961; s. Carlos Roberto and Hilda Eva (Cabrera) S.; children: Robert Jr., Alexis. BBA, Fordham U., 1985; JD, NYU, 1990. Bar: N.Y. 1992, U.S. Dist. Ct. (ea. dist.) 1992, U.S. Dist. Ct. (so. dist.) 1993. Police officer N.Y.C. Police Dept., 1981-93, sgt., 1993-94. Assoc. Morales & Silva, P.C., N.Y.C., 1992-94, ptnr., 1995-96; ptnr. Morales & Assocs., 1996-97, pvt. practice, 1997—. Mem. ABA, N.Y. State Bar Assn., N.Y. County Lawyers Assn., Puerto Rican Bar Assn., Hispanic Nat. Bar Assn. Democrat. Roman Catholic. Avocations: basketball, football, baseball, travel, reading. Office: 11 Park Pl Rm 617 New York NY 10007-2801

SANTANGELO, MARIO VINCENT, dentist; b. Youngstown, Ohio, Oct. 5, 1931; s. Anthony and Maria (Zarlenga) S. Student, U. Pitts., 1949-51; DDS, Loyola U., Chgo., 1955, MS, 1960. Instr. Loyola U., 1957-60, asst. prof., 1960-66, assoc. prof., 1966-70, chmn. dept. radiology, 1962-70, dir. dental aux. utilization program, 1963-70, chmn. dept. oral diagnosis, 1967-70, asst. dean, 1969-70; pvt. practice, Chgo., 1960-70. Cons. Cert. Bd. Am. Dental Assts. Assn., 1967-75, VA Rsch. Hosp., 1969-75, Chgo. CSC, 1967-75; counselor Chgo. Dental Assts. Assn., 1966-69; mem. dental student tng. adv. com. divsn. dental health USPHS, HEW, 1969-71; cons. dental edn. rev. com. NIH, 1971-72; cons. region IV, USPHS, HEW, Atlanta, 1973-76, region V, Chgo., 1973-77; mem. Commn. on Dental Edn. and Practice, Fedn.Dentaire Internat., 1984-92; mem. bd. visitors Washington U. Sch. Dental Medicine, St. Louis, 1974-76 Contbr. articles to dental jours. Capt. USAF, 1955-57. Recipient Dr. Harry Strusser Meml. award NYU Coll. Dentistry, 1985. Fellow Am. Coll. Dentists (life); mem. ADA (life, asst. sec. coun. dental edn. 1971-81, acting sec. 1981-82, sec. 1982-90, dir. 1990-92, asst. sec. commn. on dental accreditation 1975-81, acting sec. commn. on continuing dental edn. 1981-82, sec. 1982-85), Ill. State Dental Assn. (life), Chgo. Dental Assn. (life), AMA (edn. work group 1982-86), Assembly Specialized Accrediting Bodies (coun. on postsecondary accreditation 1981-92, award of merit 1992), Am. Assn. Dental Schs., Odontographic Soc. Chgo. (life), Am. Acad. Oral Pathology, Am. Acad. Dental Radiology, Can. Dental Assn. (commn. on dental accrediation award of merit 1992), Am. Acad. Oral Medicine, Am. Assn. Dental Examiners (hon.), Blue Key, Omicron Kappa Upsilon, Xi Psi Phi. Home: 1440 N Lake Shore Dr Chicago IL 60610-1626

SANTANGELO, STEPHEN, portfolio manager; b. Bklyn., Apr. 30, 1960; s. Joseph P. and Theresa (Carfizzi) S. SBA in Finance and Investments, Bernard Baruch Coll., N.Y., 1982. CFA. Officers asst. Chemical Bank, N.Y., 1982-85; mng. dir., fixed income portfolio mgr. Trust Co. of the West, 1985-99; mng. dir. R.W. Pressprich & Co., 2000—. Mem. N.Y. Soc. of Security Analysts, Assn. for Investment Mgmt. Rsch.

SANTANIELLO, ANGELO GARY, retired state supreme court justice; b. New London, Conn., May 28, 1924; s. Samuel C. and Katie Santaniello; m. Catherine A. Driscoll, June 1948 (dec.); children: Samuel Gary, Lisa Mary; m. Catherine M. Cooper, Sept. 27, 1968; 1 child, Maria Roberta. BA, Coll. Holy Cross, 1945; JD, Georgetown U., 1950. Bar: Conn. 1950, U.S. Dist. Ct. Conn. Sole practice, New London, 1950-53; sr. ptnr. Santaniello & Satti, 1953-61, Santaniello Satti Wilensky & Schwartz, 1962-65; judge Conn. Cir. Ct., 1966-71, Conn. Ct. Common Pleas, 1971-73, Conn. Superior Ct., 1973-85, adminstrv.judge, 1978-85, chief adminstrv. judge, civil divsn., 1979-85; assoc. justice Conn. Supreme Ct., Hartford, 1985-87, sr. assoc. justice, 1987-94; chief mediator State-Fed. ADR, Inc., 1993-95; mediator Conn. Superior Ct. Annexec Mediation Program, 1996—. Asst. pros. atty. New London Police Ct., 1951-55; bd. dirs. New London Fed. Savs. and Loan. Trustee New London Pub. Libr., Lawrence and Meml. Hosp.; bd. dirs. Am. Cancer Soc.; chmn. New London Rep. Party, 1956-65; nat. committeeman Conn. State Young Reps., 1959-61; legal counsel Conn. State Senate Rep. Minority, 1961-65; campaign mgr. for gubernatorial candidate, 1962; mem. athletic coun. Holy Cross Coll., 1971-77, chmn., 1972-73; trustee Mitchell Coll., 1976-89, chmn., 1988-91. Served to lt. (j.g.) USNR, 1942-46. Recipient Columbus award Italian-Am. Civic Assn., 1964, In Hoc Signo award Holy Cross Coll., 1976, 1st Humanitarian award Eastern Conn. chpt. March of Dimes, 1983, Conn. Supreme Ct. Law Day award, 1999. Mem. Conn Bar Assn. (Henry J. Naruk award 1999), New London Bar Assn., Am. Justinian Soc., Holy Cross Alumni Assn. (bd. dirs., pres. 1981-82), Conn. Trial Lawyers Assn. (Jud. award). Roman Catholic. Home: 25 Shirley Ln New London CT 06320-2929 Office: 70 Huntington St New London CT 06320-6113

SANTAVICCA, EDMUND FRANK, information scientist; b. Detroit, Jan. 4, 1947; BA in Comparative Lit., French, Wayne State U., 1968, MA in French, 1972; AMLS, U. Mich., 1971, PhD of Libr. and Info. Sci., 1977. Cert. hypnotherapist, Atwood Inst., 1996. Bibliographer U. Va., Charlottesville, 1971-74; asst. prof. libr. sci. Vanderbilt U., Nashville, 1979-81; bibliographer, head collection mgmt. svcs. Cleve. State U., 1983-89; head reference svcs. Ariz. State U., Tempe, 1990-94; faculty info. access Estrella Mountain C.C., Avondale, Ariz., 1994-95, dir. info. resources, 1995-2000; libr. Phoenix Coll., 2000—02; free-lance writer, 2002—. Author: Reference Work in the Humanities, 1980, Four French Dramatists, 1974, (play) Maximum Tumescence, 1989, Faux Sexe, 1992, Pathetic Fallacies, 2000. Concours de poesie French Govt., 1969; recipient Pres.'s Program award Libr. Adminstn. and Mgmt. Assn., 1986; named Writer-in-Residence Found. Karolyi, 1989. Mem. ALA. E-mail: ed.santa@yahoo.com.

SANTEE, DALE WILLIAM, lawyer, air force officer; b. Washington, Mar. 28, 1953; s. Robert Erwin and Elsbeth Emma (Bantleon) S.; married; 1 child, Enri De'Von; m. Junko Mori, June 2, 1992. BA, Washington & Jefferson Coll., 1975; MA, U. No. Ariz., 1982; JD, U. Pitts., 1978. Bar: Pa. 1978, U.S. Ct. Mil. Appeals 1979, Calif. 1989. Floor mgr., commn. salesman J.C. Penney Co., Washington, 1971-76; asst. mgr. Rach Enterprises, Charleroi, 1977-78; legal intern Washington County Pub. Defender; commd. 2d lt. USAF, 1979, advanced through grades to col., 2001; from asst. staff judge advocate to area def. counsel Luke Air Force Base, Ariz., 1979-81; claims officer 343 Combat Support Group/Judge Advocate, Eielson AFB, Alaska, 1981-83; sr. staff legal adviser Dept. Vet. Affairs, Washington, 1983-89; asst. staff judge advocate Mil. Justice div. Air Force Judge Advocate Gen.'s Office, 1986-89, 63CSG/Judge Advocate, Norton Air Force Base, Calif., 1989-91; dep. pub. defender Juvenile div. San Diego County, 1990-93, dep. alt. pub. defender, 1993-98; asst. staff judge advocate 452 AMW, March Air Res. Base, Calif., 1991-99, staff judge advocate, 1999-2001; supervising dep., alt. pub. defender Conflict Parent-Child Office, 1998-2001, dep. alt. pub. defender, 2001—; sr. IMA 21 AF/JA, Mc Guire AFB, NJ, 2001—. V.p. Neuer Enterprises, Nanjemoy, Md., 1983-89; participant MgmT. Devel. Seminar, 1988. Mem. San Diego County Rep. Party; pres., co-chmn. legis. com. PTA Zamorano Elem. Sch., San Diego, chmn. SITE com.; mem. San Diego County Child Abuse Coord. Coun., San Diego County Commn. on Children and Youth, San Diego County Juvenile Ct. Mental Health Task Force, San Diego County Unified Sch. Dist. Parent Adv. Coun.; bd. dirs. San Diego County Youth Ct. Program, Pub. Defenders Assn., Train Ct. Apptd. Spl. Advocates for Voices for Children, McGill Ctr. Creative Problem Solving Youth Curriculum Com. Decorated Air

Force Commendation medal, 1981, 89, Air Force Meritorious Svc. medal, 1991, 96, 99, Air Force Achievement medal, 2000; named Outstanding Young Man of Am., U.S. Jaycees, Montgomery, Ala., 1981; acad. scholar Washington & Jefferson Coll., 1971-75, Beta scholar Washington & Jefferson Coll., 1974, Pa. Senatorial scholar Pa. Senate, 1975-78; named Juvenile Justice Commn. Atty of Yr., 1997; recipient Clara Shortridge Foltz award ABA/Nat. Legal Aid and Defender Assn., 1999, Judge Advocates Assn. Outstanding Career Armed Svcs. Atty. award, 2000. Mem. Pa. Bar Assn., Calif. Bar Assn., San Diego County Bar Assn., San Diego County Psych-Law Soc. Avocations: swimming, softball, stamp and coin collecting, foreign travel. Office: 765 3d Ave STe 305 Chula Vista CA 91910 E-mail: Dale.Santee@sdcounty.ca.gov.

SANTHANAM, BALU, engineering educator; b. Chrompet, India, Jan. 21, 1971; s. Thalanayar S. and Kamakshi Santhanam; m. Deepa D. Santhanam, July 15, 1998. BSEE, St. Louis U., 1992; MSEE, Ga. Inst. Tech., 1994, PhD in Elec. Engring., 1998. Grad. rsch. asst. Ga. Inst. Tech., Atlanta, 1994-98; postdoctoral rsch. fellow U. Calif., Davis, 1998-99; asst. prof. dept. elec. and computer engring. U. N.Mex., Albuquerque, 1999—. Reviewer IEEE Transactions on Signal Processing, IEEE Transactions on Comm., IEEE Signal Processing Letters, IEEE Transactions on Circuits and Systems. Mem. IEEE, IEEE Signal Processing Soc., IEEE Comm. Soc. Avocations: Indian percussion (Mirdangam), philosophy, theology, cricket. Office: Univ of New Mexico Dept Elec Eng/Computer Eng Albuquerque NM 87131 E-mail: bsanthan@eece.unm.edu.

SANTIAGO, GWENDOLYN SELBY, educational association administrator; b. Taylor, Tex., Mar. 10, 1940; d. Rudolph Gust and Doris Gwendolyn (Anderson) Wallin; m. Ted Shearer Selby, Oct. 4, 1958 (dec. May 1992); children: Mark Wayne, Shana Lynn Selby Muske; m. Joseph Albert Santiago, May 23, 1998. BLS, St. Edward's U., 1978, MBA, 1988. Cert. sch. bus. adminstr., Tex. CFO Round Rock (Tex.) Ind. Sch. Dist., 1967-90, N.E. Ind. Sch. Dist., San Antonio, 1990-97; CEO Tex. Assn. Sch. Bus. Ofcls., Austin, 1997—. Mem. Tex. Assn. Sch. Bus. Ofcls. (bpres. 1986-87, bd. dirs. 1993-95, Bus. Ofcl. of Yr. 1994, chmn. legis. com. 1988-97), Tex. Sch. Alliance (chmn. 1996-97), Assn. Sch. Bus. Ofcls. (vice chmn. legis. com. 1997—), Tex. Coun. Women Sch. Execs. Lutheran. Avocations: music, art, exercise. Office: Tex Assn Sch Bus Ofcls 2538 S Congress Austin TX 78704 E-mail: gwen@tasbo.org.

SANTIAGO, SAM, business owner, computer consultant; b. N.Y.C., Jan. 6, 1976; s. Samuel and Aurora Iris (Gonzales) S.; m. Christina. Student, Cittone Inst., Edison, N.J., 1994; cert. Novell adminstr., Middlesex County Coll., Edison, 1995. Cert. Cisco network assoc. INT Solutions. Exec. PC support cons. AT&T, Basking Ride, N.J., 1995-96, info. tech. mgr. Basking Ridge, 1997-98, Prudential, Newark, 1996-97; CEO, Exec. PC-Support Svcs., Inc., Morris Plains, N.J., 1999—; desktop support specialist Century 21 Dept. Store, N.Y.C., 1994-95. Pres. AHA! Incentives, NJ. Republican. Roman Catholic. Avocations: video games, watching World Wrestling Federation, listening to tapes by motivational speakers, going to batting cages. Office: Exec PC-Support Svcs Inc 2647 Rte 10 Bldg 45-7A Morris Plains NJ 07950-1202 E-mail: samsantiago@ahaincentives.com.

SANTIAMO, JOSEPH PATRICK, geriatrician; b. S.I., N.Y., Aug. 4, 1955; s. Pat Santiamo and Josephine Lucy (Iannacone) Jastremski; m. Andrea Marie Barbini, Apr. 23, 1988; children: Joseph Edward, Marisa Ann. BS in Biology, St. Peter's Coll., Jersey City, 1977; MD, Autonomous U. Guadalajara, Mexico, 1981. Diplomate Am. Bd. Internal Medicine. Intern/resident L.I. Coll. Hosp., Bklyn., 1983-86; fellow in geriatrics L.I. Jewish-Hillside Med. Ctr., New Hyde Park, N.Y., 1986-88; house attending physician Bayley-Seton Hosp., S.I., 1988-89; pvt. practice, 1989—. Bd. dirs. Alzheimer's Assn. S.I., 1st v.p., 1997-99; assoc. clin. prof. N.Y. Med. Coll., Valhalla, 1991—; dir. geriatrics St. Vincent Med. Ctr. Named one of Top Drs. in N.Y. New York mag., 1996, 99. Mem. Am. Geriatrics Soc., Richmond County Med. Soc. Avocation: gardening. Office: 4268 Richmond Ave Staten Island NY 10312-6239

SANTILLAN, ANTONIO, financial company executive; b. Buenos Aires, May 8, 1936; naturalized, 1966; s. Guillermo Spika and Raphaella C. (Abaladejo) S.; children: Andrea, Miguel, Marcos. Grad., Morgan Park Mil. Acad., Chgo., 1954; BS in Psychology, Coll. of William and Mary, 1958. Cert. real estate broker. Asst. in charge of prodn. Wilding Studios, Chgo., 1964; pres. Adams Fin. Services, Los Angeles, 1965—. Writer, producer, dir. (motion pictures) The Glass Cage, co-writer Dirty Mary/Crazy Harry, Viva Knievel; contbg. writer Once Upon a Time in America; TV panelist Window on Wall Street; contbr. articles to profl. fin. and real estate jours. Served with USNR, 1959. Recipient Am. Rep. award San Francisco Film Festival, Cork Ireland Film Fest, 1961. Mem. Writer's Guild Am., L.A. Bd. Realtors, Beverly Hills Bd. Realtors (income/investment divsn. steering com.), Westside Realty Bd. (bd. dirs.), L.A. Ventures Assn. (bd. dirs.), Jonathan Club (L.A.), Rotary, Roundtable, Toastmasters Internat. Avocations: golf, tennis, skiing. Office: Adams Fin Svcs Inc 425 N Alfred St West Hollywood CA 90048-2504

SANTILLO, HUMBART DOMINIC, JR. naturopathic physician, writer; b. Lockport, N.Y., June 6, 1948; s. Humbart and Amelia Santillo; m. Dawn Valerie Santillo, May 9, 1986; children: Nicholas, Jessica. Degree in elem. edn., Edinboro U., 1970; degree in naturopathic medicine, Am. Naturopathic Med. Assn., 1993. Tchr. 6th grade, Lockport; jazz saxophonist; naturopathic physician Ariz./N.Y. Cons. Nat. Enzyme Co., Forsyth, Mo., Natural Alts. Internat., San Marcos, Calif., Nat. Safety Assn., Memphis. Author: Natural Healing with Herbs: The Complete Reference Book for the Use of Herbs, 1984, Food Enzymes: The Missing Link to Radiant Health, Intuitive Eating: Everybody's Natural Guide to Total Health & Lifelong Vitality thru Food, (audiocassettes) Dead Dogs Don't Lie, Natural Health from Within, Weight-Loss Seminar, Herbs, Nutrition & Healing, Food Enzymes: Live Educational Seminar, Fruits & Vegetables: The Basis of Health, Energetics of Juicing: The Key to Longevity; inventor predigested foods, juice powders, Juice Plus, other health products.

SANTINA, DALIA, nutritionist, writer; b. Amman, Jordan, Sept. 24, 1954; d. Mahmoud Daoud Abbasi, Widad Abbasi; m. Mohammed Shafiq Santina. BA in English Lit., U. Riyadh, Saudi Arabia, 1977; diploma in computer programming, Western Bus. Coll., 1980; diploma in Skin Aesthetics, Career Acad. Beauty, 1989; PhD in Holistic Nutrition, Am. Holistic Coll. Nutrition, 1994. Cert. paramedical acne 1990, glycolic acid services 1991, mgmt. aging and sun-damaged skin 1992, natural pharmacology 1992, aesthetic peeling 1992, oxygenation of the skin 1993, lymphatic drainage massage techniques 1994, homeopathic esthetiocology 1994, iridology diploma 1995, cert. chem. peels 1996, hydrotherapy 1997, glycolic treatments 1998. Exec. asst. to v.p. Am. Health Ctr., Newport Beach, Calif., 1988—89; skin care co. Skinclub, Huntington Beach, 1991—96; lectr. holistic nutrition/skin health issues, 1999—. Translator computer sys. tng. manuals, Dallas, 1983—84; tech. translator England and No. Ireland, 1984. Author: Holistic Skin Is...In, 2001, Smart Nutrition for Skin, Body & Mind, 2001; contbr. articles. Recipient Gold medal in Table Tennis, Sports Bd., Kuwait, 1972. Avocations: horseback riding, reading, antiques. Personal E-mail: Dalia4skin@msn.com. Business E-Mail: Dalia4skin@msn.com.

SANTINI, GINO, marketing professional; Pres. SERM and skeletal products; pharm. dir. Lilly affiliate, Belgium, 1990, gen .mgr. Mexico, 1991, area dir. to v.p. corp. strategy and bus. devel., 1994—95; pres. Am. ops. and global mktg. Eli Lilly and Co., 1999—. Office: Eli Lilly and Co Lily Corp Ctr Indianapolis IN 46285*

SANTINI, ROSEMARIE, writer; Lectr. in field. Author: (fiction) The Dienchanted Diva, A Swell Style of Murder, Ask Me What I Want, Beansprouts, (non-fiction) The Secret Fire, (novelization) All My Children; contbr. articles to numerous mags., anthologies; poetry performances include ATA Theater, Westbeth Cabaret, Greenwich Music Sch., St. Peter's Ch., Greenwich Ho. Recipient Macavity award, Blaggart award. Mem.: NATAS, PEN, Sisters in Crime, Internat. Assn. Crime Writers, Dramatists Guild, Soc. Am. Journalists and Authors, Poetry Soc. of Am., Poets & Writers, Authors Guild, Mystery Writers of Am. (N.Y. bd.). Address: c/o Donald Maass Lit Agy 160 W 95th St Apt 1B New York NY 10025

SANTMAN, LEON DUANE, lawyer, former federal government executive; b. Phila., July 29, 1930; s. Elmer William and Anna Mary (Moffitt) S.; m. Juliet Gloria Peacock, June 16, 1952; 1 dau., Lorri Leigh Santman Myers. BS, U. S., COAST Guard Acad., 1952; LLB, U. Houston, 1953; LLM, George Washington U., 1968. Bar: Tex. 1963, Md. 1974. Commd. ensign U.S. Coast Guard, 1952, advanced through grades to comdr., 1967, ret., 1972; assoc. gen. counsel Cost of Living Council, Washington, 1972-74; asst. gen. counsel U.S. Dept. Transp., 1974-77, dir. Materials Transp. Bur., 1977-85; dir. ship ops. Maritime Adminstrn., 1985-88. Episcopalian.

SANTOLA, DANIEL RALPH, lawyer; b. Syracuse, N.Y., Oct. 25, 1949; s. Dan D. and Sophie Irene (Podszebka) S.; m. Kathleen Elaine Beach, Aug. 21, 1971; children: Daniel, Jonathan. BA, SUNY, Buffalo, 1971; JD, Union U., Albany, N.Y., 1974. Bar: N.Y. 1975, U.S. Dist. Ct. (no. dist.) N.Y. 1975, U.S. Dist. Ct. Vt. 1986, U.S. Dist. Ct. (we. dist.) N.Y. 1992, U.S. Dist. Ct. (so., ea. dist.) N.Y., 1993. Assoc. Martin Brickman, Esq., Albany, N.Y., 1974-75; assoc. prof. Rensselaer Poly. Inst., Troy, 1976-77, dir. law mgmt. program, 1976-77; assoc. Morris J. Bloomberg, Esq., Albany, 1978-81; ptnr. Bloomberg & Santola, Esq., 1982-87, Powers and Santola, LLP, Albany, 1987—. Asst. town atty. Town of Bethlehem, Delmar, N.Y., 1978—. Author: (with others) Products Liability Practice Guide, Medical Equipment, 1988, N.Y. Negligence Guide, Construction Accidents, 1989, Compensating the Catastrophically Injured, 1990, Using SPECT Scans to Show Head Injuries. Mem. N.Y. State Bar Assn. (ho. of dels. 1995—), N.Y. State Trial Lawyers Assn. (past pres. capitol dist. affiliate, bd. dirs. 1988—), Albany County Bar Assn. (pres. 1997), Am. Bd. Trial Advs., N.Y. State Trial Lawyers Inst. (dir. decisions seminar 1984—), Capital Dist. Trial Lawyers Assn. (pres. 1985), Am. Bd. Trial Adv. (Albany chpt., pres. 2000). Republican. Roman Catholic. Avocations: golf, snowboarding, scuba diving. Office: Powers and Santola Esq 39 N Pearl St Ste 6 Albany NY 12207-2785 E-mail: DSantola@Powers-Santola.com.

SANTOLAYA-FORGAS, JOAQUIN, gynecologist, educator; b. Madrid, Feb. 15, 1956; s. Joaquin Santolaya and Montserrat Forgas; m. Carmen Arroyo; 1 child Jacobo Leopoldo Santolaya-Arroyo. MD, Autonoma U., Madrid, 1980; PhD, U. London, 1989. Cert. ob-gyn., clin. genetics, clin. molecular genetics. Resident in ob-gyn. Fundacion Jimenez Diaz. , Madrid, 1981—85; fellow divsn. maternal fetal medicine Ea. Va. Mid. Sch., Norfolk, Va., 1999—2000; fellow clin. genetics U. Ill., Chgo., 1992—94, asst. prof. ob-gyn., 1994—97, assoc. prof. ob-gyn., 1997—2000; fellow clin. molecular genetics Yale U., New Haven, 1998—99; prof. ob-gyn. Texas Tech. U., Amarillo, Tex. Dir. reproductive genetics U. Ill., Chgo., 1994—98; dir. reproductive genetics fetal medicine and ultrasound Texas Tech. U., Amarillo, 2000—; dir. Women's Rsch. Inst., Amarillo, 2002—. Author: (book) Interventional Ultrasound in Obstetrics, Gynecology and the Breast., 1998 (Outstanding Sci.Paper of the Chairs of Ob-Gyn. of Med. Schs. in Chgo., 1997); contbr. numerous articles to profl. jours. Master: Internat. Fetal Medicine and Surg. Soc.; fellow: Am. Soc. Reproductive Medicine, Am. Coll. Human Genetics; mem.: Fetal Medicine Found., Am. Inst. Ultrasound in Medicine. Office Fax: 806-354-5516. Business E-Mail: jsf@ama.ttuhsc.edu.

SANTOLERI, NICHOLAS PETER, artist, art publishing company executive; b. Bryn Mawr, Pa., Jan. 14, 1957; s. Nicholas C. and Lynette J. (Martinelli) S.; m. Frances Louise Scholl, Aug. 28, 1976; children: Tracy, Christine, Katie, Frances, Laura. Masonry contractor N.P. Santoleri, Ardmore, Pa., 1978-88; real estate broker Carr Real Estate, Drexel Hill, 1985-88; pres. Pine Ridge Prodns., Inc., Havertown, 1997—. Represented in permanent collections AT&T, Arco Chem. Co., DuPont Corp., Thomas Jefferson Med. Coll., The Rittenhouse, Free Libr. Phila.; creator ltd. edition prints. Pres. Katie Santoleri Meml. Fund, Havertown, Pa., 1992; vol. disaster svcs. ARC, 1993—; active Walden Woods Project. Mem. Am. Watercolor Soc. (assoc.), Nat. Watercolor Soc. (assoc.), Pa. Watercolor Soc., Phila. Sketch Club, Thoreau Soc. Home: 221 Pine Ridge Rd Havertown PA 19083-4734

SANTOMERO, ANTHONY M. bank executive, public policymaker; b. N.Y.C., Sept. 29, 1946; s. Camillo and Jean (Oddo) S.; m. Marlena Belviso, Aug. 21, 1971; children: Jill Renee, Marc Anthony. AB, Fordham U., 1968; PhD, Brown U., 1971; EDhe (hon.), Stockholm Sch. Econs., 1992. Successively asst. prof., assoc. prof., prof. fin. Wharton Sch., U. Pa., Phila., 1972-84, R.K. Mellon prof. fin., 1984—2002, R.K. Mellon prof. emeritus of fin., 2002—, vice dean, dir. grad. div., 1984-87, dep. dean, 1990-94; dir. Wharton Fin. Instns. Ctr., 1995-2000; pres. Fed. Reserve Bank, Phila., 2000—. Asst. prof. econs. Baruch Coll., CUNY, 1971-72; vis. prof. European Inst. Advanced Studies in Mgmt., Brussels, 1977-78, Stockholm Sch. Econs., 1989-90, U. Rome, Tor Vergata, 1994-97, Ecole Superieure des Sciences Economiques and Commerciales, France, 1977-78. Author: Financial Markets, Instruments and Institutions, 1997, 2001, Challenges for Modern Central Banking, 2001; assoc. editor: Jour. Banking and Fin., 1978—, assoc. editor: Jour. Money, Credit and Banking, 1980—, assoc. editor: Jour. Econs. and Bus., 1979—, assoc. editor: Jour. Fin. Svc. Rsch., 1992—, assoc. editor: Euro Fin. Rev., 1995—, bd. editors: Advances in Internat. Banking and Fin., 1993—; co-editor: Brookings-Wharton Papers on Finalcial Policy, 1997—2000; adv. bd. : European Banking Report, 1994—, adv. bd. : Jour. Internat. Econ. Law, 1997—; contbr. articles to profl. jours. Mem. European Fin. Assn. (exec. com. 1984-87), Am. Fin. Assn., Am. Econs. Assn. Roman Catholic. Home: 310 Keithwood Rd Wynnewood PA 19096-1224 Office: Fed Reserve Bank Phila 10 Independence Mall Philadelphia PA 19106-1574 E-mail: santomero@phil.frb.org.

SANTONI, RONALD ERNEST, philosophy educator; b. Arvida, Que., Can., Dec. 19, 1931; s. Fred Albert and Phyllis (Tremaine) S.; m. Marguerite Ada Kiene, June 25, 1955; children: Christina, Marcia, Andrea, Juanita, Jonathan, Sondra. BA, Bishop's U., Lennoxville, Que., 1952; MA, Brown U., 1954; PhD, Boston U., 1961; postgrad., U. Paris-Sorbonne, 1956-57. Asst. prof. philosophy U. Pacific, Stockton, Calif., 1958-61; postdoctoral rsch. fellow Yale U., New Haven, 1961-62; asst. prof. philosophy Wabash Coll., Crawfordsville, Ind., 1962-64; mem. faculty Denison U., Granville, Ohio, 1964—, prof. philosophy, 1968—, chmn. dept., 1971-73, 82-84, 92, Maria Theresa Barney chair in philosophy, 1978—. Peace lectr. Bethel Coll., 1985; vis. scholar in philosophy Cambridge U., Eng., 1986, 90, 94, 97, 99, 2001, also vis. lectr. in philosophy, 1990; vis. fellow Clare Hall, Cambridge U., 1986; vis. fellow in philosophy Yale U., 1975, 81, 93-94, 97; keynote speaker 2d Internat. Conf. on Nuclear Free Zones, Cordoba, Spain, 1985; Internat. Studies Assn., London, 1989, speaker and U.S.A. co-chair Internat. conf. Internat. Philosophers for Prevention of Nuclear Omnicide, Moscow, 1990; speaker World Congress Universalism, Warsaw, Poland, 1993; del. and raporteur UN meeting of Peace Messenger Orgns., Dagomys, Sochi, USSR, 1991; invited plenary speaker 2d Internat. Cong. Violence and Co-existence, Montreal, Can., 1992; invited participant Colloquium on Technological Risks to Environment, Montreal, 1993; participant, spkr. numerous nat. and internat.profl. confs. Contbg. author: Current Philosophical Issues: Essays in Honor of C.J. Ducasse, 1966, Towards an Understanding and Prevention of Genocide, 1984, Nuclear War: Philosophical Perspectives, 1985, Genocide: A Critical Bibliographic Review, 1988, Just War, Nonviolence and Nuclear Deterrence: Philosophers on War and Peace, 1992, The Institution of War, 1991, Violence and Human Co-Existence, 1994, Hiroshima's Shadows, 1998, The Encyclopedia of Genocide, 1999, Human Coexistence and Sustainable Development, 2001, Das Sein und das Nichts, 2002; author: Bad Faith, Good Faith and Authenticity in Sartre's Early Philosophy, 1995; editor, contbr. Religious Language and the Problem of Religious Knowledge, 1968; co-editor Social and Political Philosophy, 1963; contbg. editor Internet on the Holocaust and Genocide; contbr. over 130 articl and revs. to profl. jours., also to The Progressive, The Human Quest, Churchman; bd. editors Jour. Peace and Justice Studies. V.p. NAACP, Licking County, 1967; co-organizer Crawfordsville Human Rels. Coun., 1962-64; mem. nat. exec. com. Episcopal Peace Fellowship, 1968-78; mem. internat. coun. Internat. Inst. on the Holocaust and Genocide, 1985—; mem. nat. coun. Fellowship of Reconciliation, 1988-89; trustee Margaret Hall Sch., Versailles, Ky., 1972-74; nat. bd. dirs. Promoting Enduring Peace, 1982—. Canadian Govt. Overseas fellow Royal Soc. Can., 1956-57; Church Soc. for Coll. Work faculty fellow, 1961-62; Yale postdoctoral rsch. fellow, 1961-62; Danforth assoc., 1963-64; Soc. for Religion in Higher Edn. postdoctoral fellow, 1972—; Yale rsch. fellow, 1975; guest fellow Berkeley Coll., Yale U., 1975, 81, 93-94, 97, elected assoc. fellow, 1994—; vis. fellow in philosophy Yale U., 1981, 93-94, 97; Robert C. Good faculty fellow Denison U., 1985-86, 2000-01—, Robert C. Good Faculty Rsch. fellow, 1993-94 elected life mem. Clare Hall, Cambridge (Eng.) U., 1986; elected mem. High Table, King's Coll., Cambridge U., 1999; recipient Mellon award for disting. faculty Denison U., 1972, Crossed Keys Faculty of Yr. award Denison U., 1986-87. Mem. Am. Philos. Assn., Ch. Soc. for Coll. Work, Soc. for Phenomenology and Existential Philosophy, Internat. Philosophers for Prevention of Nuclear Omnicide (v.p. 1983-85, v.p. cen. div. 1990-91, internat. pres. 1991-96, internat. exec. com. 1996—), Sartre Soc. of N.Am. (exec. com. 1994—), Sartre Circle (coord. 1997—), le groupe d'Etudes Sartriennes, Gandhi-King Soc., Union of Bi-Nat. Profls. Against Omnicide (v.p. 1978—), Concerned Philosophers for Peace (founding 1980—, pres. 1996-97), Fellowship of Reconciliation. Episcopalian. Home: 500 Burg St Granville OH 43023-1005 E-mail: santoni@denison.edu. *Gratitude for what one has been given, commitment to personal growth and integrity, some "gracious gall", listening to the world's humiliated, and a recognition that genuine success is a gift of grace, never fully deserved.*

SANTOPIETRO, ALBERT ROBERT, lawyer; b. Providence, R.I., Oct. 18, 1948; s. Alfred and Marie (Epifanio) S.; m. Linda Stuart, 1994; children: Hope, Spencer, Anna. BA, Brown U., 1969; JD, U. Va., 1972. Bar: R.I. 1973, Mass. 1997, U.S. Dist. Ct. R.I. 1973, Ill. 1974, Conn. 1983, Mass. 1997. Atty. Met. Life Ins. Co., Oak Brook, Ill., 1974-75, Seligman Group, N.Y.C., 1975-76; atty. Mut. Benefit Life Ins. Co., Newark, 1976-78, asst. counsel, 1978-81; atty. Aetna Life and Casualty, Hartford, Conn., 1981-82, counsel, 1982—; assoc. counsel Conn. Mut. Life Ins. Co., Hartford, 1991-95, counsel, 1995—; 2d v.p. & assoc. gen. coun. Mass Mutual. Home: 142 Pond Brook Rd Huntington MA 01050-9620 Office: 1500 Main St Ste 2800 Springfield MA 01115 Office Fax: 413-226-2068. E-mail: asantopietro@massmutual.com.

SANTORA, CAROL ANNE, artist, educator; b. Leominster, Mass., Aug. 5, 1954; d. Albert Rainier Cristofono and Irene Anne Caiazzi; m. David Henry Santora, May 14, 1983; 1 child, Albert Anthony. ASN, Mount Wachusett C.C., Gardner, Mass., 1980, AA, 1985; BFA, Framingham State Coll., 1995. RN, Mass. Pvt. practice artist, tchr., Westminster, Mass., 1996—. Art therapist Art With Elders Program, various nursing homes and sr. ctrs., Lunenburg, Westminster, Worcester, Clinton, Athol, Fitchburg, Lancaster, Baldwinville, Ayer, Mass., 1993—; continuing edn. instr. Montachusett Regional Vocat. Tech. Sch., Fitchburg, 1996—; art instr. Fitchburg (Mass.) Art Mus., 1997—; juried mem. Art Guild of Kennebunks; bd. dirs., newsletter editor Ctrl. Mass. Women's Caucus for Art, 2002-. Bd. dirs. Ctrl. Mass. Women's Caucus for Art, 2002—. Recipient Cheap Joe's award for watercolor, 2000, 2001, Best of Show, Gardner Art Assn., 2002, Best of Category in Watercolor, Mixed Media, Downcast Regional Wildlife Show, 2001, over 45 regional awards. Mem. Maine Women in the Arts, York Art Assn., Artsworcester, Gardner Artists Assn. (bd. dirs. 2002-), Art Guild of the Kennebunks (juried mem.). Avocation: travel. Home and Office: Brush N Palette Etc 5 Kurikka Pl Westminster MA 01473-1310 Studio: PO Box 578 Alfred ME 04002 also: 2304 Alfred Rd Box 578 Alfred ME 04002 E-mail: casantora@yahoo.com.

SANTORA, NORMAN J. chemical information specialist, webmaster; b. Camden, Nj, Sept. 17, 1935; s. Rocco Nunzio Santora and Mae Catherine Crullo; m. Mary Bernadette Pascarella, Feb. 8, 1940; children: David Norman, Stephen Norman, Paul Norman. BA, Temple U., Philadelphia, PA, 1957, MA, 1960, PhD, 1965. Med. chemist William H Rever, Fort Washington, Pa., 1968—83; chem. info. specialist Smithkline Beach, King of Prussia, 1983—90, Johnson & Johnson Co., Spring House, 1991—98, Roshyo, 1998—. Webmaster Chem. Consultants Network, Bala Lynand, Pa., 2002—02. Author: (textbook) Math Fun. Fellow: Sigma Xi; mem.: Am. Chem. Soc. Home: 1323 Partridge Road Roslyn PA 19001-2807 Home Fax: 215-659-6124. Personal E-mail: n55mbs@msn.com.

SANTORA, OLGA MARIE, retired education educator; b. Paterson, N.J., Dec. 17, 1915; d. Joseph and Mary (Mondon) S. Tchg. cert., SUNY, Oneonta, 1935; BS in Elem. Edn., Columbia U., 1942; MS in Elem. Edn., Harvard U., 1952; EdD in Elem. Edn., SUNY, Albany, 1972. 1-8 grade tchr. one rm. sch., East Peacham, Vt., 1937-40, 1-6 grade tchr. Carlisle, N.Y., 1942-43; 1-4 grade tchr. Barnet (Vt.) Schs., 1940-42; 4th grade tchr. Waterville (N.Y.) Schs., 1943-47; 2d grade tchr. Schenectady (N.Y.) Schs., 1947-53; prin. K-6 sch. Coxsackie (N.Y.) Schs., 1953-60; prin. 1-6 sch. U.S. Dependent Schs., Wiesbaden, Germany, 1960-63; prof. directed grad. reading SUNY, New Paltz, 1963-85, prof. intensive tchr. tng., summers 1957-60; ret., 1985. Spkr., presenter workshops in field; organizer Children's Lit. Festival SUNY, New Paltz, organizer, dir. master's reading program and reading clinic. Mem. planning com. Columbia Greene C.C., Hudson; mem., sec. Mid Hudson Libr. Svc., Poughkeepsie, N.Y.; v.p. Greene County Hist. Soc., Coxsackie. Honored by Columbia Greene C.C. 25th Yr. Reception; recipient Ann. Svc. award VFW, 1997. Mem. Columbia-Greene Reading Coun. (pres., charter mem.), Bus. and Profl. Women (pres., Woman of Yr.), Ulster County Reading Coun. (founder, advisor, Literacy award, found. rep.), Phi Delta Kappa (advisor), Kappa Delta Pi (counselor). Home: 69 Ely St Coxsackie NY 12051-1415

SANTORO, ANTHONY RICHARD, history educator; b. Feb. 2, 1939; m. Carol Lynne; 1 child, Melissa. AB, Coll. of the Holy Cross, 1960; MA, U. Calif., 1962; PhD, Rutgers U., 1978. Instr. history Monmouth Coll., West Long Branch, N.J., 1963-67; v.p. for adminstrn., chair depts history and philosophy, registrar Briarcliff Coll., Briarcliff Manor, N.Y., 1967-77; v.p. Devel. and Coll. Rels. Ladycliff Coll., Highland Falls, 1977-88; pres. St. Joseph's Coll., Standish, Maine, 1979-87, Christopher Newport U., Newport News, Va., 1987-96, pres. emeritus, disting. prof. history, 1996—. Author: Theophanes Chronographia: A Chronicle of 8th Century Byzantium, 1982; co-author: An Eyewitness to History: The Short History of Nikephoros the Patriarch of Constantinople, 1991, (4-track DVD) Triumph of the Will (Leni Riefenstahl), 2001. Office: Christopher Newport U Smith Hall 164 1 University Pl Newport News VA 23606-2998 Fax: 757-594-7718. E-mail: santoro@cnu.edu.

SANTORO, CHARLES WILLIAM, investment banker; b. N.Y.C., Apr. 20, 1959; s. Dino and Dorice (Gillick) S.; m. Vanessa Lee Bishop; 1 child, Olivia Charlotte. BA in Econs., Columbia U., 1982; MBA, Harvard U., 1984. With Morgan Stanley & Co., N.Y.C., 1984-88; sr. v.p., coord. officer European mergers and acquisitions Morgan Stanley Internat., London, 1989-90; mng. dir., head internat. investment banking, bd. dirs. Smith Barney, Inc., N.Y.C., 1991-93, head investment banking new bus. group, 1993-95; mng. dir., head. indsl. corp. finance Paine Webber Inc., 1995-96, vice chmn. investment banking, 1996-2000; co-founder, mng. gen. ptnr. Sterling Investment Ptnrs. LP, Westport, Conn., 1999; co-founder, mng. ptnr. Sterling Investment Advisors LLC, 1999—, Sterling Investment Ptnrs. Mgmt. LLC, 1999—. Bd. dirs. Interline Brands, Inc. (formerly Wilmar Industries, Inc.). Recipient fellowship Harvard Bus. Sch., 1983. Mem. Harvard Club of N.Y., N.Y. Athletic Club, Columbia Coll. Alumni Assn. (co-chmn. class of '82 com. 1982—), Kings Crown Rowing Assn. of Columbia U. (trustee). Republican. Roman Catholic. Home: 3 Alden Ter Greenwich CT 06831-4422 Office: 276 Post Rd W Westport CT 06880-4703 E-mail: santoro@sterlinglp.com.

SANTORO, THOMAS MEAD, lawyer; b. Glens Falls, N.Y., Feb. 16, 1946; m. Corinne Collins, Mar. 27, 1981. AB, Colgate U., 1967; JD, Union U., Albany, N.Y., 1972. Bar: N.Y., Fla., U.S. Dist. Ct. (no., so., ea. and we. dists.) N.Y., U.S. Dist. Ct. (so. dist.) Fla., U.S. Ct. Appeals (2d and 11th cirs.), U.S. Supreme Ct. Atty. Legal Aid, N.Y.C., 1972-73, Cmty. Legal Rights Found., Inc., Albany, N.Y., 1973-74; asst. atty. gen. N.Y. State Dept. Law, 1974-76; asst. counsel SUNY, 1976-79; assoc. Bouck, Holloway & Kiernan, 1979-81; dep. univ. counsel Cornell U., Ithaca, N.Y., 1981-97; gen. counsel Fla. Internat. U., Miami, 1997—. Contbr. chpt. to book. Trustee Albany Law Sch. of Union U., 1992—. Mem. N.Y. State Bar Assn., Fla. Bar Assn., Dade County Bar Assn., Nat. Assn. Coll. and Univ. Attys. Avocations: boating, skiing, bicycling. Home: 4161 Malaga Ave Coconut Grove FL 33133-6324 Office: 11200 SW 8th St Miami FL 33199-0001 E-mail: santoro@fiu.edu.

SANTORUM, RICK, senator; b. Winchester, Va., May 10, 1958; s. Aldo and Catherine (Dughi) S.; m. Karen Garver, June 2, 1990; children: Elizabeth Anne, Richard John Jr., Daniel James, Sarah Maria, Peter Kenneth. BA in Polit. Sci., Pa. State U., State College, 1980; MBA, U. Pitts., 1981; JD, Dickinson Sch. Law, 1986. Bar: Pa. 1986. Adminstrv. asst. State Sen. Doyle Corman, Harrisburg, Pa., 1981-86; exec. dir. local govt. com. Pa. State Senate, 1981-84, exec. dir. transp. com., 1984-86; assoc. atty. Kirkpatrick and Lockhart, Pitts., 1986-90; mem. 102nd-103rd Congresses from 18th Pa. dist.,

Washington, 1991-95; U.S. Senator from Pa., 1995—. Mem. Agr. Com., Armed Svcs. Com., Rules and Adminstrn. Com., Spl. Com. on Aging, Com. on Banking. Bd. dirs. Mt. Lebanon Extended Day Program, 1987-91; mem. Child Advocacy Project, 1987-91. Mem. KC, Italian Sons and Daus. Assn. Republican. Roman Catholic. Avocations: golf, racquet sports. Office: US Senate 120 Russell Senate Office Bldg Washington DC 20510-0001 also: Widener Bldg One South Penn Sq Ste 960 Philadelphia PA 19107*

SANTOS, ANDREW J., III, priest; b. Evergreen Park, Ill., May 31, 1971; s. Andrew J. and Mary M. Santos. BA in Liberal Arts, Loyola U., Chgo., 1993; MDiv, U. St. Mary of the Lake, Mundelein, Ill., 1997. Assoc. pastor St. Lawrence O'Toole Ch., Matteson, Ill., 1997—2000, Infant Jesus Prague Cath. Ch., Flossmoor, 2000—. Admin. asst. Bishop Thaddeus Jarubowski, Chgo., 1995—; regional state chaplain Alhambra, 1998—; liturgical cons. St. Stephen Cath. Ch., Tinley Park, Ill., 2000—. Cons., activist Ill. Rep. Party, 1998. Recipient Pres. medal, Niles Coll. Seminary, 1993. Republican. Roman Catholic. Home and Office: 1131 Douglas Ave Flossmoor IL 60433 Office Fax: 708-799-5462. Business E-Mail: andrewJ.SantosIII@prodigy.net.

SANTOS, GILBERT ANTONIO (GIL SANTOS), radio and television sportscaster; b. Achusnet, Mass., Apr. 19, 1938; s. Arthur Nunes and Herminia Rego (Torres) S.; m. Roberta Marie Reul, Apr. 19, 1961; children: Mark Joseph, Kathleen Marie. Student, Southeastern Mass. U., New Bedford, 1956-58; grad., New Eng. Broadcast Sch., Boston, 1959. Sportscaster WBSM Radio, New Bedford, 1958-64, WNBH Radio, New Bedford, 1964-70, WBZ Radio/TV, Boston, 1971—. Vol. Easter Seal Soc. Southeastern Mass., 1974-82, Multiple Sclerosis Soc., Mass. chpt., 1995—. Staff sgt. U.S. Army, 1961-62; staff sgt. Mass. Army N.G., 1963-67. Named Mass. Sportscaster of Yr., Nat. Sportscasters Assn., 1980, 84, 86, New Eng. Emmy TV Play-By-Play, 1980, 21 AP Best Sportscaster award, 1976-98, Play-By-Play Mass., 1976-96, 2 UPI Best in Nation Sportscaster awards, 1988, 90. Roman Catholic. Avocations: reading, gardening, cooking, bicycling, history. Home: 499 King St Raynham MA 02767-1384 Office: WBZ Radio/TV 1170 Soldiers Field Rd Boston MA 02134-1004

SANTOS, HERBERT JOSEPH, JR. lawyer; b. Reno, Feb. 17, 1963; s. Herbert Joseph Sr. and Jeanette Dorothy (Olivera) S.; m. Kimberly Ellen Saylors, Mar. 8, 1986; children: Herbert Joseph III, Jarred Adam, Hannah McKenzie. BA in Sociology, U. Nev., Las Vegas, 1985; JD, U. of the Pacific, 1991. Bar: Nev. 1991, Calif. 1992, U.S. Dist. Ct. Nev. 1992, U.S. Supreme Ct. 1999. Head social worker Cmty. Welfare, Inc., Reno, 1986-87; inspector Nev. Athletic Commn., 1986-87; sr. legal rsch. asst. County Sacramento, Calif., 1987-91; assoc. Law Offices of Terry A. Friedman, Ltd., Reno, 1991-98; owner The Law Firm of Herb Santos Jr., 1999—. Mem. State Bar Law Office Mgmt. and Procedures Com., 1996-98; chair election canvassing com. Nev. Bd. Govs, access to justice com., 1998, temp. apptd. jud. selection com. Author (instrn. manual) ORR, County of Sacramento Bankruptcy Forms and Procedures Manual with Practice Pointers, 1990; editor: The Writ, 1997-98; appeared in: (films) Kingpin, Father's Day, (TV miniseries) The Last Don, The Cheater's Partner in Mafia!, Body and Soul, Diamonds. Mem. Cmty. Coalition, Reno, 1986-87; mentor U. Nev., Reno, 1993—. Recipient Am. Jurisprudence award, 1991, Mem. ABA (young lawyers divsn., del. for State of Nev. 1996, 97, 98, 99), ATLA, Nev. Trial Lawyers Assn., State Bar Nev. (exec. coun. mem. young lawyers sect. 1993—, pres. young lawyers sect. 1996-97, com. chair Ask-a-Lawyer young lawyers sect. 1994—. chair pub. com. 1996-97, Pro-Bono award 1997, apptd. alternate dispute resolution sect.-long range planning 1998), Washoe County Bar Assn. (exec. coun., sgt.-at-arms 1997-98, treas. 1998-99, sec. 1999—, Bar Leader award 1998), Am. Inns of Ct. (Hon. Bruce Thompson chpt. 1995-97). Republican. Roman Catholic. Avocations: family, boxing, basketball, golf. Office: The Law Firm of Herb Santos Jr Liberty Ctr 350 S Center St Ste 350 Reno NV 89501-2113

SANTOS, LEONARD ERNEST, lawyer; b. Caracas, Venezuela, Aug. 5, 1946; s. Paul Joseph and Frieda (Epstein) S.; m. Jeannie Bernadette Niedermeyer, Oct. 28, 1978; children: Jonathan, Matthew, Andrew. BA cum laude, Tufts U., 1967; JD, NYU, 1971. Bar: Ariz. 1972, D.C. 1972, U.S. Dist. Ct. D.C. 1972, U.S. Ct. Appeals (9th and 5th cirs.) 1972, U.S. Supreme Ct. 1972. Law clk. to cir. judge U.S. Ct. Appeals (9th cir.), San Francisco, 1971-72; assoc. Hogan & Hartson, Washington, 1972-76; sr. atty. internat. affairs U.S. Dept. Treasury, 1976-83; internat. trade counsel U.S. Senate Fin. Com., 1983-87; ptnr. Verner, Liipfert, Bernhard, McPherson & Hand, 1987-89, Perkins Coie, Washington, 1989-98, World Mae, Washington, 1998-99, Santos Family Found., Washington, 2000—; pres. Martin Santos Properties, LLC, 2001—. Note and comment editor NYU Law Jour., 1970; contbr. legal publs.; editor ABA Compendium of Foreign Trade Remedy Laws, 1998. Exec. dir. Dole for Pres. campaign, Washington, 1988, 96. Mem. NAFTA (chpt. 19 dispute settlement panels) Republican. Roman Catholic. Avocations: architecture, economics. Office: Santos Family Found Ste 400 1775 Pennsylvania Ave NW Washington DC 20006 E-mail: santlen@aol.com.

SANTOS, LISA WELLS, critical care nurse; b. Richardson, Tex., Oct. 25, 1963; d. Malcolm R.N. and Maitland Anne (MacIntyre) Wells; m. Ignacio Santos, Jr., Dec. 17, 1988. Cert. med. asst., x-ray-lab. technician, Tex. Coll. Osteopathy, 1983; ASN, El Centro Coll., 1988; postgrad., U. North Tex.; BS in Bus. Mgmt., Le Tourneau U., 1993; postgrad., U. Phoenix, 1995—. RN, Tex.; cert. in CPR; cert. case mgr., cert. profl. health care quality, advanced competency certification in continuity of care Nat. Bd. Competency in Continuity of Care; assoc. cert. mgr. Inst. Cert. Profl. Mgrs.; cert. disability analyst, fellow Am. Bd. Disability Analysts. Med. technologist Family Med. Ctr., Dallas, 1984-85, Beltline Med. Clinic, Dallas, 1985-86; nurse, lab. technician Primacare, Dallas, Plano, Richardson, 1986-88; charge nurse telemetry unit NME Hosp.-RHD Meml. Hosp., Denton, 1988-89; nurse ICU Denton (Tex.) Regional Med. Ctr.; nurse Angel Touch, Dallas, 1989; nurse cons. Travelers Ins., Richardson, 1990-91; med. rev. specialist Nat. Group Life, Las Colinas, 1991-94, mgr. coordinated care, 1994-95; pres. San Cal Health Care Options, Lewisville, Tex., 1994-95; clin. dir. PRN Associated Care/ Am. Care Source, Dallas, 1995-97; quality health mgr., utilization review mgr. Mutual of Omaha, 1997; with Cigna Integrated Care, 1998—2002; owner Monitos, 1997—, case mgr., 2002—; realtor New Castle Properties, 2002—. Contbr. articles to profl. jour. Mem. AACN, NAFE, Nat. Assn. Health Care Quality (cert.), Nat. Assn. Quality Assurance Profls., Assn. Nurses in AIDS Care, Case Mgmt. Soc. Am., Am. Assn. Law Ethics and Medicine, Am. Assn. Continuity of Care, Alpha Epsilon Delta, Alpha Beta Kappa, Gamma Beta Phi.

SANTOS, ORLANDO, aerospace scientist, researcher; b. Havana, Cuba, July 31, 1957; s. Mario Orlando and Celia Garcia Santos, Celia Garcia Santos. BS, U. Fla., Gainesville, 1975—80; MS, U. Miami, Coral Gables, 1981—83; PhD, U. Miami, 1984—89. Sr. rsch. scientist Hybritech, Inc., San Diego, 1991—94; sr. scientist Agouron Pharmaceuticals, Inc., 1994—96; sr. rsch. scientist Amur Pharmaceuticals, Inc., Belmont, 1997—97, Shaman Pharmaceuticals, Inc., South San Francisco, 1998—99; scientist VI Lockheed Martin Engring. & Scis. Co., Moffett Field, 1999—2000; SSBRP science lead NASA/Ames Rsch. Ctr., 2000—. Cons. The John E. Fetzer Inst., Kalamazoo, 1991; mem sci. adv. bd. Kerix, LLC, Mountain View, Calif., 2000—. Contbr. articles. Mem.: Am. Inst. of Aeronautics and Astronautics, Am. Soc. for Gravitational and Space Biology, Radiation Rsch. Soc., Am. Assn. for Cancer Rsch. Avocations: swimming, scuba diving. Office: NASA/Ames Rsch Ctr Mail Stop 244 19 Mountain View CA 94035 Office Fax: 650-604-0673. Business E-Mail: osantos@mail.arc.nasa.gov.

SANTOS, RICHARD J. associate administrator; m. Linda Lee Perry; children: Betsy Lee, Lee, Steffen. Ins. claim rep.; nat. comdr. Am. Legion, Indpls., 2001—. Commr. Md. Vets. Commn., Md. Mil. Monuments Commn. With USNR. Mem.: Am. Legion (life; mem. vets. affairs and rehab. commn., citizens flag alliance, policy coordination and action group, vets. planning and coord. com., legis. commn., NEC liaison to VA&R commn., chmn. pub. rels. commn.). Office: American Legion PO Box 1055 700 N Pennsylvania St Indianapolis IN 46206*

SANTOS, SHARON LEE, parochial school educator; b. Perth Amboy, N.J., June 23, 1955; d. John Anthony Santos and Dolores Estelle Barrett. BA in History, Kean U., 1978, MA in Guidance and Counseling, 1985; MA in Systematic Theology, Seton Hall U., 1998. Religious sr. Franciscan of Our Lady of Guadalupe; cert. tchr. K-12, guidance counelor N.J., religion tchr. Diocese of Metuchen, N.J. Tchr. Archdiocese of Newark, Diocese of Metuchen, Perth Amboy, Fords, Woodbridge; dir. religious edn. Vicariate of Perth Amboy, St. Mary Parish, New Monmouth. Guest spkr. on biblical and doctrinal topics various cities in N.J., 1993—; adv. bd. on evangelization Diocese of Meetuchen, 1999. Mem.: Fellowship of Cath. Scholars, St. Edith Stein Guild (life), Kappa Delta Phi. Avocations: astronomy, gardening. Home: 44 Thomas St South River NJ 08882 Office: St Mary Cath Ch 26 Leonardville Rd New Monmouth NJ 07748

SANTOS, WILMA, missionary; b. Cayey, P.R., Apr. 15, 1945; d. Faustino Escalera, Isabel Ortiz; m. Eugenio Santos, Nov. 22, 1964; children: Carlos Eugenio, Joann Lisa, Luis Ricardo, Hector. Missionary, Theol. Inst. Assemby of Christian Chs. Inc., Rochester, N.Y., 1975; BA, SUNY, Brockport, 1982. Cert. tchr. N.Y. Consumer educator Rochester City Sch. Dist., NY, 1968—77, coord. CommUniv. program, 1977—78, elem. tchr., 1982—84, translator, 1985—86, lang. assessor, placement ctr., 1985—90; Spanish tchr. Cath. Diocese of Rochester, 1988—90, Charles Finney H.S., 1996—98; tutor Integrated Learning Ctr. Monroe C.C., 1995—. Tchr. God's Work Pentecostal Ch., Rochester, 1975—; missionary to Mex.; tchr. Bible studies; prodr. tchg. tapes; facilitator confs. various locations. Author: (book of poetry) Rayitos de Inspiración; contbr. Founder Spanish Christian Svc. Monroe County Jail; vol. Albion Correctional Facilities. Pentecostal Ch. Office: To God be the Glory Ministry PO Box 13225 Rochester NY 14613

SANTOSO, IRENE, art director, graphics designer; b. Surabaya, Indonesia, Mar. 13, 1974; d. Bing Santoso and Soezana Djohan-Lie. AAS, Fashion Inst. Tech., 1994; BFA, Parsons Sch. Design, 1996. Sr. art dir. Tribal DDB, N.Y.C., 2001—02; creative dir. Hooloo.com, 2001, USWeb/CKS Cornerstone, N.Y.C., 1997—2000; graphic artist Polo Ralph Lauren, 1996—97. Design book (IMS SRC 100); author: (poetry) Am. Poetry Soc., 1999; website (Outstanding Female Designer, 2001), mag. Graphic Design: USA (Am. Graphic Design awards, 2000), (Student award, 1996). Avocation: fluent in spoken and written Mandarin, Cantonese, Japanese, Bahasa Indonesia. Personal E-mail: irene@irenesantoso.com.

SANTOS-PÉREZ, EILEEN, management consultant; b. Morristown, N.J., Feb. 27, 1965; d. Angel Jesus and Arsenia (Quiles) S.; m. Reinaldo Pérez, July 12, 1997. BS in Engring., Rutgers U., Piscataway, N.J., 1987; MBA, Columbia U., 1992. Assoc. engr. Westinghouse Elec. Corp., Balt., 1987-89; asst. mgr. N.J. Bell, Newark, 1989-90; ops. specialist Philp Morris Mgmt. Corp., N.Y.C., 1992-94; sr. bus. cons. Am. Mgmt. Systems, Inc., Roseland, N.J., 1994-97; mgr. change mgmt. Andersen Cons., N.Y.C., 1997—. Chair profl. com., Soc. Hispanic Profl. Engrs., Washington, 1988, client svc. team Vols. for Med. Engring, 1988; chair pub. rels. com., mem. exec. bd. Coun. of Action for Minority Profls., Newark, 1989; v.p. Hispanic Bus. Assn., 1991. Recipient Cora and Rose Morgan fellowship Columbia U., 1991. Mem. NAFE, Nat. Soc. Hispanic MBAs. Democrat. Roman Catholic. Avocation: folk art collector. Office: Andersen Cons 1345 Avenue Of Americas New York NY 10105-0302

SANTRY, BARBARA LEA, venture capitalist; b. Key West, Fla., Jan. 20, 1948; d. Jere Joseph and Frances Victoria (Appel) S. BS in Nursing, Georgetown U., 1969; MBA, Stanford U., 1978. Program analyst, br. chief U.S. Dept. HEW, Washington, 1973-76; mgr. cons. div. Arthur Andersen and Co., San Francisco, 1978-80; asst. v.p. Am. Med. Internat., Washington, 1980-83; v.p. Alex Brown and Sons, Inc., Balt., 1983-86; ptnr. Wessels, Arnold and Henderson, Mpls., 1986-88; v.p. Dain Bosworth Inc., 1988-90, sr. v.p., 1990-91; ptnr. Pathfinder Venture Capital Funds, Menlo Park, Calif., 1991—, Capstone Ventures, Menlo Park, 1996—. Trustee Stanford Bus. Sch. Trust, 1996—. Served to lt. USNR, 1967-72. Office: Bldg 1 3000 Sand Hill Rd Ste 290 Menlo Park CA 94025-7113

SANTSCHI, PETER HANS, marine sciences educator; b. Bern, Switzerland, Jan. 3, 1943; came to U.S., 1976; s. Hans and Gertrud (Joss) S.; m. Chana Hoida, Mar. 28, 1972; children: Rama Aviva, Ariel Tal. BS, Gymnasium, Bern, 1963; MS, U. Bern, 1971, PhD summa cum laude, 1975; Privatdozent, Swiss Fed. Inst. Tech., Zurich, Switzerland, 1984. Lectr. chemistry Humboltianum Gymnasium, Bern, 1968-70; teaching rsch. asst. U. Bern, 1970-75; rsch. scientist Lamont-Doherty Geol. Obs., Columbia U., Palisades, N.Y., 1976-77; rsch. assoc. Lamont-Doherty Geol. Obs. Columbia U., 1977-81; sr. rsch. scientist Lamont-Doherty Geol. Obs., Columbia U., 1981-82, Swiss Inst. Pollution Control, Zurich-Duebendorf, Switzerland, 1982-88; prof. oceanography Tex. A&M U., College Station, 1988—, prof. marine scis. Galveston, Tex., 1988—, sect. head chem. oceanography dept. oceanography College Station, 1990—. Head isotope geochemistry and radiology sect. Swiss Inst. Water Resources and Water Pollution Control, Zurich, 1983-88; mem. rev. panel on chem. oceanography NSF, 1990-91. Contbr. articles to profl. jours. Cpl. Swiss Army, 1964-65. Mem. AAAS, Am. Chem. Soc., Am. Geophys. Union, Oceanography Soc., Am. Soc. Limnology and Oceanography. Avocation: swimming. Office: Tex A&M U Oceanography Dept Galveston TX 77553-1675 E-mail: santschi@tamug.tamu.edu.

SANWICK, JAMES ARTHUR, international executive recruiter, management consultant; b. Balt., Feb. 15, 1951; s. Alfred George and Catherine Anne (von Sas) S.; m. Brenda Julia Tietz, Sept. 20, 1980; children: Luke Graham, Sierra Catherine. AS, Catonsville (Md.) C.C., 1975; BS, U. No. Colo., 1976; M in Pub. Administn., U. Alaska S.E., 1985. Lic. tchr. Dr. Edward deBono Thinking Skills Courses; cert. sr. profl. in human resources. Recreation therapist Md. Sch. for the Blind, Balt., 1974; dir. camp New Horizon United Cerebral Palsy Md., 1975; sub-dist. mgr. Nat. Park Svc., various, 1976-82; freelance mgmt. cons. Juneau, Alaska, 1982-84; regional mgr. div. labor standards Alaska Dept. Labor, 1983-88; adj. faculty sch. bus. and pub. administrn. U. Alaska S.E., 1985-93; mgr. Alaska Productivity Improvement Ctr., 1989-93; mgr. human resources and pub. affairs Greens Creek Mining Co., 1989-93; mgr. human resources, security and pub. affairs Rawhide Mining Co., Fallon, Nev., 1993-98; founder Ctr. for Innovation and Comm., Truckee, Calif., 1997—; v.p. Mgmt. Resources Cons., 1998—. Owner Sierra Bldg. Alternatives, 1995—; bd. dirs. Gov.'s Com. on Employment Disabled Persons, Alaska Acad. Decathalon Inc.; chmn. Job Svc. Employer Com., Alaska, 1989-93; bd. advisors Inst. Mine Tng. U. Alaska S.E., 1989-93; bd. dirs. Sierra High Tech. Group, v.p. strategic devel. Co-author: (info. pamphlet) Blue Water Paddling in Alaska, 1980; editor: (film) Green's Creek Project, 1990; photographic editor: Inside Passage Mag., 1982, 83; photographer: (book) Death Valley, 1977. Patrolman Nat. Ski Patrol System, Juneau, 1978—83; instr., trainer ARC, Alaska, 1979—82, Utah, 1979—82, Ariz., 1979—82; v.p. bd. dirs. Alaska Acad. Decathlon; mem. Reno Exec. Roundtable, 1995—; v.p. strategic devel. Sierra High Tech. Group, 2000—. Recipient Nat. New Svc. award United Cerebral Palsey, 1975; named Candidate of Yr. Nat. Ski Patrol System, 1979. Mem. ASTD, Am. Creativity Assn., Nev. Mining Assn. (human resources com. 1993—), Soc. Human Resources Mgmt., Juneau Ski Club. Avocations: skiing, hiking, scuba diving, guitar, tennis. Office: PO Box 1793 Truckee CA 96160-1793 E-mail: Innovate@ltol.com.

SANYOUR, MICHAEL LOUIS, JR. financial services company executive; b. Richmond, Va., Aug. 24, 1930; s. Michael Louis, Sr. and Betty (Toobert) S.; m. Therese Marie McCarthy, June 1, 1951; children: Jeffrey, Mark, Jennifer, Florence, Norman, Ned. AA, Union Coll., 1952; S.B., Rutgers U., 1954, postgrad., 1978-82; MBA, Harvard U., 1956; postgrad., Am. Coll., 1987-92. CLU, ChFC. Vice pres. Harbridge House, Inc., Boston, 1956-63; also dir; corp. v.p. mktg. Volkswagen of Am., Inc., Englewood Cliffs, N.J., 1963-70; pres., chief exec. officer Subaru of Am., Pennsauken, 1970-75, also dir.; exec. v.p., dir. Sci. Mgmt. Corp., 1975-82; pres., chief exec. officer Wofac Co., Bridgewater, N.J., 1975-82; pres., chief exec. officer, dir. Metrologic Instruments Inc., Blackwood, 1982-85; pres., chief operating officer, dir. Avant-Garde Computing, Inc., Mt. Laurel, 1985-86; principal, dir. CMS Cos., Phila., 1986—. Bd. dirs. CSS Industries Inc. Contbr. to: Chief Executive's Handbook, 1975, Am. Mgmt. Assn.'s Publs., 1990. Trustee West Jersey Chamber Music Soc., 1983—, pres., 1987-88; councilman Moorestown, N.J., 1988—, dep. mayor, 1999—; bd. dirs. Union League of Phila., 1993-97, Meml. Health Alliance, 1992-97, ARC of Burlington County, 1989-94, Coriell Inst. for Med. Rsch., 1992—, World Affairs Coun. Phila., 1992-98; bd. dirs. Phila. Pres.'s Orgn., 1994-97, vice chmn., 1992-93, chmn., 1993-94; class sec. HBS Class of '56, 1986-96. With USNG, 1948-56. Recipient Alumni award Rutgers U., 1954, awards Am. Cancer Soc., 1978, 79 Mem. World Pres.'s Orgn., Legatus, Am. Mensa Ltd., Automotive Orgn. Team, World Affairs Coun. Phila., South Jersey C. of C. (v.p., dir.), Rotary (pres. Moorestown 1987-88, bd. dirs.), Beta Gamma Sigma, Delta Sigma Pi. Clubs: Harvard (N.Y.C.); Union League (Phila.), Harvard Bus. Sch. (Phila.) (pres. 1980-81, chmn. 1983-84, dir. 1984—). Home: 201 E Maple Ave Moorestown NJ 08057-2011 Office: 1926 Arch St Philadelphia PA 19103-1444 E-mail: mlsanyour@aol.com., mls@cmsco.com.

SANZONE, DONNA S. publishing executive; b. Bklyn., Apr. 4, 1949; d. Joseph J. Seitz and Faye (Brooks) Rossman; m. Charles F. Sanzone, Jan. 2, 1972; children: Danielle, Gregory. BA magna cum laude, Boston U., 1970; MA, Northeastern U., 1979. Grad. placement specialist Inst. Internat. Edn., N.Y.C., 1970-72; adminstr. AFS Internat. Scholarships, Brussels, 1972-74; editor Internat. Ency. Higher Edn., Boston, 1974-76, G.K. Hall & Co., Pubs., Boston, 1977-81, exec. editor, 1981-91, editor-in-chief, 1991-96; v.p. Oryx Press, 1996-2000; editor-in-chief Grolier Acad. Reference, Danbury, Conn., 2000—. Contbg. author: Access to Power, 1981. Mem.: ALA, Libr. and Info. Tech. Assn., Assn. Coll. and Rsch. Librs., Soc. for Scholarly and Profl. Pub., Assn. Am. Pubs. Office: Grolier Acad Ref 18 Pine St Weston MA 02493-1116

SAON, GEORGE A. computer scientist, researcher; b. Brasov, Romania, Oct. 6, 1970; s. Elena Florina Tripsa and Stelian Saon. PhD in Computer Sci., Henri Poincare U., Nancy, France, 1997. Asst. lectr. Academie de Nancy-Metz, Nancy, 1997—98; rschr. IBM, Yorktown Heights, NY, 1998—. Contbr. articles. Recipient 1st prize at regional final Alsace-Lorraine, Internat. French Math Problem Solving Championship, 1998. Mem.: AAAS. Avocations: reading, skiing. Home: 10 Brookside Dr Apt LD Greenwich CT 06830 Office: IBM TJ Watson Rsch Ctr Rt 134 Yorktown Heights NY 10598 Business E-Mail: saon@watson.ibm.com.

SAPER, CLIFFORD BAIRD, neurobiology and neurology educator; b. Chgo., Feb. 20, 1952; s. Julian and Susan Menkin S.; m. Barbara Susan Farby, Aug. 26, 1973; children: Rebecca Michelle, Leah Danielle, Sean Zachary. BS, MS, U. Ill., 1972; MD, PhD, Washington U., 1977. Diplomate Am. Bd. Psychiatry and Neurology. Intern Jewish Hosp., St. Louis, 1977-78; resident New York Hosp., N.Y.C., 1978-81; asst. prof. Washington U., St. Louis, 1981-84, assoc. prof., 1984-85, U. Chgo., 1985-88, prof., 1988-92, chmn. com. on neurobiology, 1987-92; James Jackson Putnam prof. neurology and neurosci. Harvard Med. Sch., 1992—; chmn. dept. neurology Beth Israel Deaconess Med. Ctr., Boston, 1992—. Editor-in-chief Jour. of Comparative Neurology, 1994—; contbr. articles to profl. jours. Mem. Am. Neurol. Assn., Am. Acad. Neurology, Am. Physiol. Soc., Soc. for Neurosci. Office: 330 Brookline Ave Boston MA 02215-5400

SAPERS, CARL MARTIN, lawyer, educator; b. Boston, July 16, 1932; s. Abraham E. and Anne (Herwitz) S.; m. Judith H. Thompson, Nov. 29, 1959; children: Jonathan Simonds, Rachel Elizabeth, Benjamin Lovell. AB, Harvard U., 1953, JD, 1958. Bar: Mass. 1958. Assoc. Hill, Barlow, Goodale & Adams, Boston, 1958—65; ptnr. Hill & Barlow, 1965—96, of counsel, 1997—2002. Spl. asst. atty. gen. criminal divsn. Commonwealth of Mass., 1963-65; adj. prof. Harvard Grad. Sch. Design, 1983—; spl. cons. Mass. Ethics Commn., 1978-79; mem. Mass. Bd. Registration in Medicine, 1995-98, vice chair, 1997-98. Moderator Town of Brookline, 1982-91. With U.S. Army, 1953-55. Mem.: AIA (hon. Allied Professions medal 1975), Am. Coll. Constrn. Lawyers (bd. dirs. 1989—, pres. 1993), Am. Arbitration Assn. (bd. dirs. 1987—2000, Whitney North Seymour medal 1991), Boston Bar Assn. (coun. 1970—73, 1991—94). Home: 26 Chesham Rd Brookline MA 02445-5811 Office: Hill & Barlow One International Pl Boston MA 02110

SAPERSTEIN, DAVID, novelist, screenwriter, film director; b. Bklyn. s. Louis and Celia S.; m. Ellen Mae Bernard; children: Ivan, Ilena. Student, CCNY Film Inst., CCNY. With CBS-TV Ed Murrow Show-Person To Person; writer, prodr., dir. Skyline Films, Inc., 1963-83. Asst. prof. film NYU Grad. Sch., Tisch Sch. Arts, 1992-93; instr. screenwriting Manhattan Marymount Coll., 1996-99, N.Y. Film Acad., 1997. Lyricist 70 pub. songs; theatrical prodns. include musicals Blue Planet Blue, Clowntown; author: Cocoon, 1985 (bestseller), Fatal Reunion, 1987 (Book of the Month selection), Metamorphosis, 1988, Red Devil, 1989, Funerama, 1994, Dark Again, 1999; movies include Cocoon (Best Original Story for Screen 1985, 2 Acad. awards); writer, dir. My Sister's Keeper, Personal Choice (Beyond the Stars), Hearts & Diamonds; writer Torch, Sara Deri, Queen of America, Italian Ices, Joshua's Golden Band, Roamers, Vets, Do Not Disturb, Snatched, Jack in the Box, SchoolHouse, Point of Honor, Roberto!, The John Gill Story: In Defense of Ivan the Terrible, Joshua's Golden Band, Fighting Back, Babs' Labs, Silyan, A Christmas Visitor; writer, dir. music videos Dr. Bill, Teenage Mutant Ninja Turtles, Fallow Angel, Wowii; segment prodr. for Northstar Ent./PBS Reppies; dir. over 300 TV commls.; writer dir. over 200 documentaries, corp. and indsl. films, videos including Dance of the Athletes (Emmy nomination), Explorers in Aqua-Space, Rodeo: A Matter of Style; creator first interactive internet publishing at www.darkagain.com. Recipient Cine Golden Eagle award, N.Y. Film Festival award, San Francisco Film Festival award, Venice Film Festival award, Melbourne Film Festival award, N.Y. Art Dirs. award, Chgo. Film Festival award, Townsend Harris medal CCNY, 1998. Mem. Writer Guild of Am., Dir. Guild of Am., BMI Nat. Honor Soc. Office: Ebbets Field Prodns Ltd Wykagyl Station PO Box 42 New Rochelle NY 10804-0042 E-mail: zap@topnet.net.

SAPERSTEIN, HARRY W. physician, dermatologist; b. L.A., Feb. 6, 1952; s. Jerome and Rose B. Saperstein; m. Joan W. Saperstein, June 10, 1973; children: Jacob, Ruth. BA, Pomona Coll., Claremont, Calif., 1973; MD, U. So. Calif., 1977. Diplomate Am. Bd. Dermatology. Attending physician UCLA Med. Ctr., 1981—; assoc. clin. prof. UCLA, 1994—; chmn. pediatric dermatology Cedars-Sinai Med. Ctr., L.A., 1985—, chief divsn. dermatology, 1997—. Mem. adv. bd. So. Calif. Lupus Found., L.A., 1985—. Co-editor Dermatology USA; contbr. articles to profl. jours. Named Clin. Tchr. of Yr., UCLA, 1986; Merck schoalr, 1977. Mem. Phi Beta Kappa, Alpha Omega Alpha. Office: 8920 Wilshire Blvd Ste 545 Beverly Hills CA 90211-2009

SAPERSTEIN, LEE WALDO, mining engineering educator; b. N.Y.C., July 14, 1943; s. Charles Levy and Freda Phyllis (Dornbush) S.; m. Priscilla Frances Hickson, Sept. 16, 1967; children: Adam Geoffrey, Clare Freda. BS in Mining Engring., Mont. Sch. Mines, 1964; DPhil in Engring. Sci., Oxford U., 1967. Registered profl. engr., Ky., Mo., Pa. Laborer, miner, engr. The Anaconda Co., Butte, Mont., and N.Y.C., 1963-64; asst. prof. mining engring. Pa. State U., University Park, 1967-71, assoc. prof., 1971-78, prof., 1978-87, sect. chmn., 1974-87; prof., chmn. dept. mine engring. U. Ky., Lexington, 1987-93; dean, prof. mining engring. Sch. Mines and Metallurgy U. Mo., Rolla, 1993—. Chmn. engring. accreditation commn., 1989-90, bd. dirs. Accreditation Bd. for Engring. and Tech., 1992-2001, sec. of bd., 1995-98, pres.-elect, 1998-99, pres. 1999-2000, ABET fellow. Contbr. articles to refereed jours. Rhodes scholar Oxford U., 1964-67. Mem. NSPE, ASEE, Soc. Mining, metallurgy and Exploration, Inc. (disting. mem. AIME-Soc. Mining Engrs.), Am. Assn. Rhodes Scholars. Home: 801 Laurel Dr Rolla MO 65401-3841 Office: U Mo 305 V H Mc Nutt Hl Rolla MO 65409-0810 E-mail: saperste@umr.edu., saperste@rollanet.org.

SAPERSTEIN, MARC ELI, religious history educator, rabbi; b. N.Y.C., Sept. 5, 1944; s. Harold Irving and Marcia Belle (Rosenblum) S.; m. Roberta Shapiro, June 17, 1970; children: Sara Michal, Adina Ruth. AB, Harvard U., 1966, PhD, 1977; student, Pembroke Coll., U. Cambridge, Eng., 1966-67; MA, Hebrew U., Jerusalem, 1971, Hebrew Union Coll., N.Y.C., 1972. Ordained rabbi, 1972. Lectr. in Hebrew lit. Harvard U., Cambridge, Mass., 1977-79; lectr. in Jewish studies Harvard U. Divinity Sch., 1979-81, asst. prof. Jewish studies, 1981-83, assoc. prof., 1983-86; Gloria M. Goldstein prof. Jewish history and thought Washington U., St. Louis, 1986-97, chmn. program Jewish and Near Eastern Studies, 1989-97; rabbi Temple Beth David, Canton, Mass., 1973-86; Charles E. Smith prof. of Jewish history George Washington U., Washington, 1997—, dir. Judaic studies, 1997—. Mem. exec. bd. Cen. Conf. Am. Rabbis, 1985-87. Author: Decoding the Rabbis, 1980, Jewish Preaching, 1200-1800, 1989, Moments of Crisis in Jewish-Christian Relations, 1989, Your Voice Like a Ram's Horn, 1996, also articles; editor: Essential Papers on Messianic Movements and Personalities in Jewish History, 1992, Witness from the Pulpit, 2000. Fellow Charles and Julia Henry Fund, 1966-67, Am. Coun. Learned Socs., 1983-84, Inst. Advanced Studies Hebrew U., Jerusalem, 1989, Am. Acad. for Jewish Rsch., 1994—, Ctr. for Judaic Studies, U. Pa., 1995-96; Danforth Found. Kent fellow, 1973-77. Mem. Assn. Jewish

Studies (bd. dirs. 1983-99, book rev. editor 1997—), Am. Acad. Jewish Rsch. (exec. bd. 2000—), Phi Beta Kappa. Office: George Washington U Dept History 2142 G St NW Washington DC 20037-2721 E-mail: msaper@gwu.edu.

SAPHIR, RICHARD LOUIS, pediatrician; b. N.Y.C., May 1, 1933; s. Samuel and Grace (Greenberg) Saphir; m. Judith Schwartz, Dec. 6, 1958; 1 child Steven. BA, NYU, 1954; MD, SUNY, NYC, 1958. Diplomate Nat. Bd. Med. Examiners, Am. Bd. Pediat. Asst. attending physician Mt. Sinai Hosp., NYC, 1965—71, asst dir., pediat. acute care clinic, 1970—78, 1971—82, assoc. clin. prof. pediat., 1982—88, attending pediatrician, 1982—; chief, pediatric svcs. U.S. Naval Hosp., Newport, RI, 1967—69; clin. prof. pediat. Mt. Sinai Sch. Medicine, NYC, 1988—. Bd. dirs. Mt. Sinai Children's Ctr. Found., N.Y.C., 1987—. Contbr. articles to profl. jours. Chmn. cmty. and adv. com. N.Y.C. Info. and Counseling Program for Sudden Infant Death Syndrome, 1979—81; med. bd. YMHA, N.Y.C., 1982—86. Comdr. USNR, 1967—69. Fellow: N.Y. County Med. Soc. (vice chmn. com. child welfare 1974—85), N.Y. Pediat. Soc. (pres. 1978—79), Am. Acad. Pediats. (com. sci. meetings 1985—97, chmn. prep course 1991—96, editl. adv. bd. Continuing Med. Edn. audiotapes 1991—2001, ednl. program rep. ambulatory care quality improvement program 1992—2002, ednl. advisor proficiency testing program 1996—99, editl. bd. Pediat. in Rev. 1997—, ednl. adv. Uniformed Svcs. pediat. seminar 1997—, mem. super cont. med. edn. planning com. 2000—, chmn. super cont. med. edn. planning com. 2002—), N.Y. Acad. Medicine (treas. 1987—89). Office: BSM Pediatrics PC 55 E 87th St New York NY 10128-1043 E-mail: richard.saphir@verizon.net.

SAPIN, BURTON MALCOLM, political science educator, foreign policy analyst; b. N.Y.C., Dec. 14, 1926; s. Julius Sidney and Selma (Greifer) S.; m. Barbara Miller Piane, Dec. 11, 1960 (div. Aug. 1984); children: Julia Elizabeth, David Ralph; m. Judith Leitner, Sept. 12, 2001. AB, Columbia U., 1945, AM, 1947; PhD, Princeton U., 1953. Rschr. Brookings Instn., Washington, 1958-60; asst. prof. MIT, Cambridge, Mass., 1960-61; policy ofcl. U.S. Dept. State, Washington, 1961-65; prof. polit. sci. U. Minn., Mpls., 1965-69; dean Sch. Internat. Affairs George Washington U., Washington, 1969-83, prof. polit. sci. and internat. affairs, 1969-94, prof. emeritus, 1994—. Cons. Rand, Washington, 1994-97; vis. prof. Kansai U., Osaka, Japan, summer, 1991, Internat. U. Japan, Niigata, Japan, 1985, Hopkins-Nanjing Program, Nanjing, China, 1987-88. Author: Decision Making, 1954, Making of U.S. Foreign Policy, 1966; contbr. articles to profl. jours. With USN, 1945-46. Democrat. Jewish. Home: 5500 Friendship Blvd Apt 1816N Chevy Chase MD 20815-7267

SAPINSKY, JOSEPH CHARLES, magazine executive, photographer; b. N.Y.C., Dec. 13, 1923; s. Simon Moses and Janet (Charles) S.; m. Jane Tomney, Oct. 21, 1970; children— Michael Joseph, Jane Anne, Laura Alexandra. Certificate illustration, Pratt Inst., 1943; certificate advt. design, 1947; postgrad., Colgate U., 1943, Cornell U., N.C. U. Art dir. Today's Living, N.Y. Herald Tribune, N.Y.C., 1960-63; art dir. N.Y. Mag., 1963-65; asso. art dir., dir. photography Sat. Evening Post, 1965-67; dir. publs. I.O.S., Geneva, 1967-69; art dir. This Week, N.Y.C., 1969, Jock N.Y. mag., N.Y.C., 1970; dir. publs. I.I.G., London, 1970; art dir. Woman's Day mag., N.Y.C., 1971-83; exec. art dir. Woman's Day Spls., 1983-92; comml. photographer, 1992—. Cons. art dir. Infinity mag., N.Y.C., 1971-73; instr. dept. photography Sch. Visual Arts, N.Y.C., New Sch., N.Y.C. Served with USNR, 1943-46; capt. Res. ret. Recipient numerous art dir. awards. Mem. Am. Soc. Mag. Photographers, Soc. Illustrators, Am. Soc. Mag. Editors, Am. Inst. Graphic Arts, Soc. Publ. Designers, Res. Officers Assn. E-mial. Home: 242 Campbell Rd Box 207 Cherry Valley NY 13320-0207 E-mail: snipas@telenet.net.

SAPIRO, GUILLERMO, engineering educator, consultant; b. Montevideo, Uruguay; s. Jacob Sapiro and Miriam Schwartz; m. Daila Gheiler, Dec. 17, 1994; children: Eitan, Nahdav. PhD, Technion U., Israel, 1993. Postdoctoral assoc. MIT, Cambridge, Mass., 1993-94; mem. tech. staff HP Labs., Palo Alto, Calif., 1994-97; assoc. prof. U. Minn., Mpls., 1997—. Cons. HP, Motorola, Summus, Optibase. Author: Goemetric PDE's and Image Analysis, 2001. Recipient award PECASE White House, Young Investigator award ONR, Career award NSF. Office: U Minn 200 Union St SE Minneapolis MN 55455 Fax: 625-625-4583. E-mail: guille@ece.umn.edu.

SAPIRO, LELAND, mathematician, educator, editor; b. Chgo., Apr. 14, 1924; s. Aaron and Janet (Arndt) S. BA in French, U. Fla., 1978; MA in Math., UCLA, 1953; PhD in Math., U. Tex., Dallas, 1987. Teaching asst. U. Saskatchewan (Can.), Saskatoon, 1965-67; lectr. U. Regina, Saskatchewan, Can., 1967-73; instr. U. Wis., Sheboygan, 1980-81; asst. prof. Coker Coll., Hartsville, S.C., 1981-83; teaching asst. U. Tex., Dallas, 1983-87; prof. Paul Quinn Coll., Waco, Tex., 1987-89; asst. prof. math. McNeese State U., Lake Charles, La., 1989-92; assoc. prof. math. Jarvis Christian Coll., Hawkins, Tex., 1992—; instr. Willie Velasquez Learning Ctr., 1995-97; prof. Cen. Tex. Coll., 1997-98, Marion Mil. Inst., Marion, Ala., 1998—. Editor Riverside Quar., 1965—. V.p. Wascana Student Housing Coop., Regina, Can., 1971; pres. Reid Student Housing Coop., Gainesville, Fla., 1976. Mem. Am. Math. Soc., Math. Assn. Am., Sci. Fiction Rsch. Assn., Modern Lang. Assn. Democrat. Jewish. Home: 1005 Fikes Ferry Rd Apt 201 Marion AL 36756-3527 Office: Marion Military Inst 1101 Washington St Marion AL 36756-3207

SAPOFF, MEYER, electronics component manufacturer; b. N.Y.C., June 2, 1927; s. Benjamin and Mary (Charney) S. Student, Mohawk Coll., 1946-48, Poly. Inst. Bklyn., 1948-50, 52-53, BS in Elec. Engring. magna cum laude, 1950, postgrad., 1952-53, MIT, 1951, U. Pa., 1951-52; MS in Elec. Engring., Drexel Inst. Tech., 1952. Rsch. engr. Franklin Inst. Labs., Phila., 1950-52; rsch. fellow sr. grade Poly. Inst. Bklyn., 1952-53; dir. rsch. Victory Engring. Corp., Springfield, N.J., 1953-57, dir. engring., 1957-63, v.p., 1963-69; cons., sr. staff scientist Keystone Carbon Co., St. Mary's, Pa., 1969-70; pres. Thermometrics, Inc., Edison, N.J., 1970-86, chmn. bd. dirs., 1986-93, sr. staff cons., 1993-96; pres. MS Cons., Princeton, 1993—. Cons. in field, chmn. E20 Temperature com., session on thermistors 6th Symposium on Temperature, Measurement and Control in Sci. and Industry; U.S. del. to tech. com. 65 Internat. Electrotech. Commn. Contbr. articles to profl. jours.; patentee in field. Active Citizens League West Orange, 1962-75, West Orange PTA, 1960-76; trustee George St. Playhouse, New Brunswick, N.J., 1993-2001; bd. dirs. The Jewish Ctr., Princeton, N.J., 1995-98, fin. chmn., 1995-96, v.p. fin., 1995-98; bd. dirs. United Jewish Fedn. Princeton Mercer Bucks, 1998—, treas., 2001—. With USN, 1945-46. Recipient Indsl. Rsch. IR-100 award, 1974; State of NYU scholar, 1948-50; Poly. Inst. Bklyn. fellow, 1953. Mem. IEEE, ASTM (chmn.. E20.08 med. thermometry subcom. 1976—, 1st vice-chmn. E20 com. on temperature measurement 2000—, award of merit 1998), AAAS, Poly. Inst. Bklyn. Alumni Assn., Am. Ceramic Soc., Eta Kappa Nu, Tau Beta Pi. Home: 1137 Stuart Rd Princeton NJ 08540-1216

SAPOLSKY, HARVEY MORTON, political scientist, educator; b. Haverhill, Mass., Feb. 21, 1939; s. Abraham and Anne Betty (Selig) S.; m. Karen P. Stenbo, Aug. 27, 1966. BA, Boston U., 1961; MPA, Harvard U., 1963, PhD, 1967. Mem. faculty MIT, 1966—, prof. polit. sci., 1977—, dir. comm. forum, 1987-95, dir. security studies program, 1989—; dep. dir. Univ. Health Policy Consortium, 1978-83, assoc. chmn. faculty, 1981-83. Vis. prof. U. Mich., 1971-72; cons. Artificial Heart Assessment Panel Nat. Heart and Lung Inst., Washington, 1972-73; mem. Ethics and Health Policy Panel Hastings (N.Y.) Ctr., 1979-80; mem. com. on Fed. Rsch. on Effect of Ionizing Radiation NRC, Washington, 1980-81; mem. com. on Risk Perception and Comm. NRC, 1987-88, mem. com. on tech. alternatives to anti-pers. mines, 1999-2001; mem. Sec. of Energy's Task Force on Alternative Futures for Dept. of Energy Labs., 1994-95. Author: The Polaris System Development, 1972, (with D. Altman and Richard Greene) Health Planning and Regulation, 1981, (with A. Drake, S. Finkelstein) The American Blood Supply, 1982, Science and the Navy, 1990; editor: Consuming Fears: The Politics of Product Risks, 1986; co-editor: Federal Health Programs, 1981, (with S. Altman), 1981, (with R. Crane, W.R. Newman and E. Noam) The Telecommunications Revolution, 1992; also articles. Mem. AAAS (sec. sect. social and econ. scis. 1968-73), Am. Polit. Sci. Assn., Nat. Acad. Social Ins., Coun. on Fgn. Rels. Home: 37 Edgemoor Rd Belmont MA 02478-3916 Office: MIT Security Studies Program E38-600 Cambridge MA 02139

SAPORTA, JACK, psychologist, educator; b. N.Y.C., Oct. 21, 1927; s. David and Victoria (Fils) S.; m. Judith Hammond, May 28, 1967 (div. 1979); children: David, Victoria. AB cum laude, Adelphi U., 1951; PhD, U. Chgo., 1962. Diplomate Am. Bd. Profl. Psychology; lic. clin. psychologist. Pvt. practice, 1962-99; supt. Tinley Park (Ill.) Mental Health Ctr., 1975-78; chief manpower tng. and devel. Ill. Dept. Mental Health, Chgo., 1978-82; dean, prof. Forest Inst. Profl. Psychology, Des Plaines, Ill., 1982-85; coord. studies Fielding Inst., Santa Barbara, Calif., 1984—; prof. Ill. Sch. Profl. Psychology, Chgo., 1985-97. Mem. adj. faculty psychology Lake Forest Grad. Sch. Mgmt., 1987-97; mem. Ill. State Clin. Psychology Lic. and Disciplinary Com., Springfield, 1984-93; profl. staff Forest Hosp., Des Plaines, 1977-96; mem. attending doctoral profl. staff Luth. Gen. Hosp., Park Ridge, Ill., 1986-2000, emeritus, 2000—. Served with U.S. Army, 1946-47, Germany. Named Educator of Yr., Forest Inst., 1982, Outstanding Faculty Mem. Lake Forest Grad. Sch. Mgmt. Fellow Acad. Clin. Psychology, NTL-Inst. (faculty); mem. APA (accreditation site vis. team), Ill. Psychol. Assn., Chgo. Psychol. Assn. (cert. recognition 1999, mem. exec. bd.). Avocations: tennis, computers, do-it-yourself home projects. Home: 13077 Stone Creek Court Huntley IL 60142

SAPP, DONALD GENE, retired minister; b. Phoenix, Feb. 27, 1927; s. Guerry Byron and Lydia Elmeda (Snyder) S.; m. Anna Maydean Nevitt, July 10, 1952 (dec.); m. Joann Herrin Mountz, May 1, 1976; children: Gregory, Paula, Jeffrey, Mark, Melody, Cristine. AB in Edn., Ariz. State U., 1949; MDiv, Boston U., 1952, STM, 1960; D Ministry, Calif. Grad. Sch. Theology, 1975. Ordained to ministry Meth. Ch., 1950. Dir. youth activities Hyde Park (Mass.) Meth. Ch., 1950-52; minister 1st Meth. Ch., Peabody, Mass., 1952-54, Balboa Island (Calif.) Cmty. Meth. Ch., 1954-57, Ch. of the Foothills Meth., Duarte, Calif., 1957-63; sr. minister Aldersgate United Meth. Ch., Tustin, 1963-70, Paradise Valley (Ariz.) United Meth. Ch., 1970-83; dist. supt. Cen. West Dist. of Desert S.W. Conf. United Meth. Ctr., Phoenix, 1983-89. Editor Wide Horizons, 1983-89; contbr. articles to profl. jours. Chaplain City of Hope Med. Ctr., Duarte, 1957-63; trustee Plaza Community Ctr., L.A., 1967-70; corp. mem. Sch. Theology at Claremont, Calif., 1972-80; pres. Met. Phoenix Commn., 1983-85; del. Western Jurisdictional Conf. United Meth. Ch., 1984, 88; bd. dirs. Coun. Chs., L.A., 1963-67, Orange County (Calif.) Human Rels. Coun., 1967-70, Interfaith Counseling Svc. Found., 1982-89, Wesley Cmty. Ctr., Phoenix, 1983-89; gen. conf. United Meth. Ch., 1988. With USN, 1945-46. Mem. Ariz. Ecumenical Coun., Bishops and Exec. Roundtable, Rotary (pres.), Kappa Delta Pi, Tau Kappa Epsilon. Democrat. Avocation: overseas travel. Home: 7316 E Krall St Scottsdale AZ 85250-4518

SAPP, JOHN RAYMOND, lawyer; b. Lawrence, Kans., June 18, 1944; s. Raymond Olen and Amy (Kerr) S.; m. Linda Lee Tebbe, July 3, 1965; children: Jeffrey, Jennifer, John. BA, U. Kans., 1966; JD, Duke U., 1969. Bar: Wis. 1969, U.S. Dist. Ct. (ea. dist.) Wis. 1969, U.S. Ct. Appeals (7th cir.) 1974, U.S. Ct. Appeals (4th cir.) 1984, U.S. Supreme Ct. 1974. Assoc. Michael, Best & Friedrich, Milw., 1969-76, ptnr., 1976-90, mng. ptnr., 1990—. Dir. Roadrunner Freight Systems, Milw., 1992—. Bd. dirs. Milw. Symphony, 1981-95, mem. exec. com., 1993-95; bd. dirs. Boy Scouts Am., Milw., 1986—, pres. 1990-92; mem. Milw. Arts Bd., 1990, Greater Milw. Com.; bd. dirs. Zool. Soc., 1995—, v.p., 2000—; bd. dirs. Lex Mundi, 1997-2000, mem. exec. com., 1997-2001; bd. dirs. Jr. Achievement Greater Milw., 2001—. Avocations: golf, curling, print collecting. E-mail: jrsapp@mbf-law.com.

SAPP, LAUREN B. librarian, educator; b. Smithfield, N.C., Aug. 22; d. Lee and Senoria Burnette Sapp; m. Chester L. Williams, June 22, 1968 (div. Aug. 1990); children: Corey T., Christopher J., Cheston L. Williams. BA, N.C. Ctrl. U., 1967; MLS, U. Mich., 1971; advanced masters, Fla. State U., 1979, PhD, 1984. Instr. libr. Voorhees Coll., Denmark, S.C., 1971-74; libr. Fla. State U., Tallahassee, 1974-84, Duke U., Durham, N.C., 1984-96; libr. dir. Fla. A&M U., Tallahassee, 1996—. Vis. lectr. U. N.C. Sch. Libr. and Info. Sci.; adj. assoc. prof. N.C. Ctrl. Univ. Sch. Libr. and Info. Sci., 1995-96. Bd. dirs. Durham Vol. Ctr., 1995-96; chair Lit. Program Long Range Planning, Leon County Pub. Libr., Tallahassee, 1999. Fellow U. Mich., 1970-71, Bd. Regents-Fla., 1978-79, 82. Mem. ALA, Assn. Coll. and Rsch. Libr. (mem. internat. rels. com. 1994-99), Libr. Adminstrn. and Mgmt. (mem. cultural diversity com. 1997—), Black Caucus-ALA, 1890 Libr. Dirs. Assn. (treas. 1997—), Beta Phi Mu. Democrat. Episcopalian. Home: PO Box 6326 Tallahassee FL 32314-6326 Office: Fla A&M U Coleman Libr 1500 S Martin Luther King Tallahassee FL 32307 E-mail: lauren.sapp@famu.edu.

SAPP, NANCY L. educational administrator; b. Joplin, Mo., July 22, 1951; d. Jim L. and Leah (Smith) Hayes; children: Michael A., Julie D. B in Music Edn., Pittsburg (Kans.) State U., 1973; MEd in Psychology, Wichita State U.; cert. in elem./secondary sch. adminstrn., Emporia State U., 1994. Cert. elem./secondary vocal/instrumental music tchr., learning disabled tchr., behavior disorder tchr., adminstr., dist. level adminstrn. dir. spl. edn. Vocal and instrumental music instr., Cherokee, Kans., 1973-75, Holy Cross Grade Sch., Hutchinson, 1980-85, Trinity H.S., Hutchinson, 1980-82; learning disabilities tchr. Unified Sch. Dist. # 308, 1987-89, behavior disorder tchr., 1989-95, behavior cons., 1990-95; asst. sch. prin. Unified Sch. Dist. 308, 1995-97; prin., coord. student svcs. Unified Sch. Dist. 443, Dodge City, Kans., 1997-99; asst. dir. spl. edn. Southwest Kans. Area Coop. Dist., 1999—. Prin. second violin Hutchinson Symphony, 1991-97; pres. exec. bd. Hutchinson Regional Youth Symphony, 1994-95; bd. dirs. Reno Choral Soc., Kans. Youth Soc. Grantee Southwestern Bell Tel., Hutchinson, 1992. Mem. Internat. Reading Assn., NEA, Kans. NEA, Kans. Reading Assn., Hutchinson NEA (bldg. rep. 1992-94), Ark Valley Reading Assn. (pres. 1994-95), Phi Delta Kappa. Republican. Methodist. Avocations: theater, music, cross stitch, quilting. Home: 108 La Vista Blvd Dodge City KS 67801-2848

SAPP, WALTER WILLIAM, lawyer, energy company executive; b. Linton, Ind., Apr. 21, 1930; s. Walter J. and Nona (Stalcup) S.; m. Eva Kaschner, July 10, 1957 (dec.); children: Karen Elisabeth, Christoph Walter. AB magna cum laude, Harvard, 1951; JD summa cum laude, Ind. U., 1957. Bar: Ind. 1957, N.Y. 1959, Colo. 1966, U.S. Supreme Ct. 1972, Tex. 1977. Pvt. practice, N.Y.C., 1957-60, 63-66; practice in Paris, France, 1960-63, Colorado Springs, 1966-76; assoc. atty. Cahill, Gordon, Reindel & Ohl, Paris, 1960-63, N.Y.C., 1957-60, 63-65, partner, 1966; gen. counsel Colo. Interstate Corp., 1966-76, v.p., 1968-76, sec., 1971-76, sr. v.p., dir., exec. com., 1973-75, exec. v.p., 1975-76; v.p. Coastal States Gas Corp., 1973-76; sr. v.p., gen. counsel Tenneco, Inc., Houston, 1976-92, sec., 1984-86; pvt. practice, 1992—. Editor-in-chief Ind. U. Law Jour., 1956-57. Trustee Houston Ballet, 1982-85, Awty Internat. Sch., 1989-98, 99—, vice-chmn., 1994-97, pres. 1997-98, chmn., 1999-2002, pres., 2002—; bd. dirs. Harris County Met. Transit Authority, 1982-84, Houston Internat. Protocol Alliance, 1992-94, Houston Symphony, 1989—, v.p., 1991-94, 2001-; adv. bd. Inst. for Internat. Edn. S.W. region, 1987—, chmn., 1992-94, Internat. and Comparative Law Ctr. Southwestern Legal Found., 1976-92. Lt. USNR, 1951-54. Recipient Chevalier, Ordre Nat. du Mérit, France. Mem. ABA, N.Y. State Bar Assn., Tex. Bar Assn., Assn. of Bar of City of N.Y., Houston Bar Assn., Order of Coif, French-Am. C. of C. (bd. dirs. 1987-92), Alliance Française Houston (bd. dirs. 1989—, v.p. 1991-94, 98—). Mem. United Ch. of Christ. Office: 1111 Hermann Dr Unit 8B Houston TX 77004-6928

SAPP, WARREN CARLOS, football player; b. Orlando, Fla., Dec. 19, 1972; m. Jamiko, 1998; 1 child, Mercedes. Student, U. Miami. Defensive tackle Tampa Bay Buccaneers. Avocation: swimming. Office: Tampa Bay Buccaneers 1 W Buccaneer Pl Tampa FL 33607-5797*

SAPPENFIELD, CHARLES MADISON, architect, educator; b. Columbia, S.C., Mar. 17, 1930; s. Charles Madison and Elizabeth Olive (Moss) S.; m. Mary Frances McGowan Dec. 14, 1963 (div. June 1990); children— Charles Ross, Sarah Kathleen B.Arch., N.C. State U., 1956; Cert., Denmark's Royal Acad., Copenhagen, 1961. Registered architect, Ind., N.C. Asst. prof. N.C. State U., Raleigh, 1956-57, asst. prof., 1961-63; head archtl. firm C.M. Sappenfield, Asheville, N.C. and Muncie, Ind., 1961—; assoc. prof. Clemson U., S.C., 1963-65; prof. architecture Ball State U., Muncie, Ind., 1965-94, prof. emeritus, 1994—, dean, 1965-81, dean emeritus, 1994—, dir. Design Indiana, 1983-88. Awards juror Interfaith Forum on Religious Art and Architecture, 1981, Am. Cons. Engrs. Council, 1982; mem. accreditation teams Nat. Archtl. Accrediting Bd., 1967-82. Archtl. works include: Dormitories, U. N.C., Gumpert residence, Dave residence Pres. Asheville Art Mus., N.C., 1964-65; chmn. Ind. Commn. on Aging, Indpls., 1983-85; pres. Alpha Day Care Ctr. for Elderly, Muncie, 1985; mem. State Planning Adv. Commn., Indpls., 1974-82. Served with U.S. Army Recipient Gold medal for service Ball State U., 1983; named Sagamore of the Wabash, Gov. of Ind., 1982 Fellow AIA (dir. nat. bd. dirs. 1989-92); mem. Ind. Soc. Architects (pres. 1976), Ind. Archtl. Found. (chmn. 1975), Am. Soc. Landscape Architects (awards juror 1983), Danish Fedn. Architects (hon., Aeresmedallion 1987), Fulbright Alumni Assn., Alpha Rho Chi. Lodges: Rotary, Civitan. Republican. Episcopalian. Avocations: bicycling, boating, photography. Home and Office: E-31 1250 Tennis Place Ct # 31 Sanibel FL 33957-3700

SAPPENFIELD, DIANE HASTINGS, real estate executive, civic worker; b. Marion, Ohio, Apr. 22, 1940; d. Edgar Dean and Marguerite Elizabeth (Alexander) Hastings; B.A. in Sociology and Econs., Mills Coll., 1962; tchr.'s cert. Calif. State U., Los Angeles, 1963; M.S. in Fin. and Real Estate, Am. U., 1986; m. Ronald Eugene Sappenfield, July 6, 1962; children: Derek Ronald, Ann Elizabeth. Tchr. elem. sch., El Segundo, Calif., 1963-66; asst. dir. admissions Mills Coll., 1972-74; v.p., dir. DDA Assocs., Inc., McLean, Va., 1978—; real estate investment cons., Shannon and Luchs, Washington, 1987-92, Long and Foster Commercial Real Estate, Washington, 1992—; asst. to chmn. bd. Watergate Complex, Washington, 1979-81; dir. corp. mktg. Watergate Devel. Inc., McLean, 1981-82; pres. Am. U. Real Estate Alumni Chpt.; Vol. tchr. Saugatuck Elem. Sch., Westport, Conn., 1976-79; active benefits for Corcoran Sch. Art, Nat. Symphony Orch., Women's Bd. Am. Heart Assn., Hope Ball, Meridian House, Washington; chmn. Meridian House Ball, 1990, Am. Heart Assn. Ann. Luncheon, 1993; bd. dirs. Westport-Weston Arts Council, 1973-79, Young Concert Artists, 1984—; mem. Levitt Pavilion Governing Com., 1974-79; pres. Friends of Levitt Pavilion, 1977; trustee Stauffer-Westport Fund, 1976-79; mem. Westport Young Woman's League, 1969-79, pres., 1975-76, Jr. League of Washington D.C., 1980—; bd. dirs. Stamford-Norwalk br. Jr. League, 1977-78. Mem. Washington D.C. Bd. Realtors, No. Va. Bd. Realtors, Mills Coll. Club N.Y., Washington Jr. League (sustainer). Home: 7612 Georgetown Pike Mc Lean VA 22102-1412

SAPPENFIELD, MAEDEANE L. piano and organ teacher; b. Belmond, Iowa, Nov. 1, 1927; d. Henry Gerhard and Lucille Bernice (Legge) Mennenga; m. David Reddick Sappenfield, May 14, 1948 (dec. Apr. 1997); children: Valoris Jane, Linda Jo-Anne, David Clark. Lic. pvt. pilot. Sec. at airport Bram Air Svc., Clarion, Iowa, 1947-48; sec. to sec. C. of C., 1948-49; sales, demonstrator, tchr. Jones Piano and Organs, Mason City, Iowa, 1970-85. Tchr. piano and organ. Composer organ solo (state winner Adult Composer, Fed. Music Club 1987). Leaders chair Campfire Girls Am., Belmond, 1959-61; pres. Women's Missionary Fedn., Belmond, 1963-64; pres. Luth. Ch. Women, Osage, Iowa, 1967-69, sec. Mason City conf., 1970-75; organist various chs., presently at Ch. of Christ Scientist, Clear Lake, Iowa. Mem. Music Tchrs. Nat. Assn., North Iowa Music Tchrs., Matinee Musicale Club (pres. 1989-90), Am. Guild Organists (dean 1975-78). Avocations: creative design/sewing, composing, photography, gourmet cooking. Home: One S Taylor Mason City IA 50401

SAPPINGTON, LYNDA LOUISA BURTON, artist; b. Alexandria, Va., Jan. 31, 1950; d. Raymond David and Helen Geraldine (Lamphiear) Burton; m. John Oliver Sappington, July 17, 1971; children: Jennifer Louisa, David John. MusB, Furman U., 1971; student Gwen Reardon Workshop, Am. Acad. Equine Art, 1997, student Kathleen Friedenberg Workshop, 1998. Artist advt. and pub. rels. Rocking Horse Studio, Lewisburg, Ohio, 1992-96; artist brochures and pub. rels. The Country Artist, 1993-96; artist, sculptor, owner Whimsy Hill Studio, West Alexandria, Ohio, 1996—. Cons. Collins Entertainment Concepts, Kettering, 1996; juror Equine Art Guild Internat. Show, 2001. Contbr. articles to profl. publs. Recipient Best of Show award Greenville Art Assn./Gt. Darke Co. Fair, 1998, Joel Meisner Co. Foundry award Am. Acad. Equine Art Fall Showcase, 1998, Best in Show 3-D award Black Stallion Show, Ocala, Fla., 2002. Mem.: Art Faces/Art Places (bd. dirs., v.p., editor-in-chief Art Voices Mag. 1998—2001), Nature Art Network, Equine Art Guild (contbr. to The Palette 1997—). Republican. Southern Baptist. Southern Baptist. Avocations: horses, singing, writing, reading, Web design. Office: Whimsy Hill Studio 15401 Eaton Pike West Alexandria OH 45381-9610 E-mail: lynda@thesculptedhorse.com., info@thesculptedhorse.com.

SAPRA, SUNIL K. economics educator; b. New Delhi, July 15, 1953; came to the U.S., 1979; s. Chaman and Usha Sapra; m. Santosh Baghat, Jan. 16, 1986. MA in Econs., Delhi Sch. Econs., 1976; PhD in Econs., Columbia U., 1983. Asst. prof. dept. econs. SUNY, Buffalo, 1983-91; assoc. prof. dept. econs. and stats. Calif. State U., L.A., 1991-94, prof. dept. econs. and stats., 1994—. Cons. Argonne Nat. Labs., 1984-87; statis. cons. Barksdale, Inc., L.A., 1994; presenter in field. Referee Econometrica, Econometric Revs., Jour. Econometrics, Jour. Applied Econometrics, Jour. Royal Statis. Soc., Explorations in Econ. History, Jour. Quantitative Econs., Jour. Bus. and Econ. Stats., Bull. Econ. Rsch., Rev. Internat. Econs., Procs. Far Ea. Econometric Soc., NSF, Acad. Internat. Bus.; contbr. articles to profl. jours.; mem. editl. bd. InterStat, Bus. Functions and Applications. Grantee NSF, 1989-90. Mem. Am. Statis. Assn., Indian Econometric Soc., Western Econ. Assn. (instnl. rep.). Avocations: solving mathematical and statistical puzzles, playing cricket. Office: Calif State Univ Dept Econs 5151 State University Dr Los Angeles CA 90032-4226 E-mail: ssapra@calstatela.edu.

SAPSOWITZ, SIDNEY H. entertainment and media company executive; b. N.Y.C., June 29, 1936; s. Max and Annette (Rothstein) Sapsowitz; m. Phyllis Skopp, Nov. 27, 1957; children: Donna Dawn Chazen, Gloria Lynn Aaron, Marsha Helene Gleit. BBA summa cum laude, Paterson State U. (N.J.), 1980. Various fin. and oper. systems positions Metro Goldwyn Mayer, Inc., N.Y.C., 1957-68; exec. v.p., dir. Penta Computer Assoc. Inc., 1968-70, Cons. Actuaries Inc., Clifton, N.J., 1970-73; exec. v.p., CFO Am. Film. Theatre, N.Y.C., 1973-76, Cinema Shares Internat Distrb. Corp., N.Y.C., 1976-79; sr. cons. Solomon, Finger & Newman, 1979-80; exec. v.p., CFO Met. Goldwyn Mayer, L.A., 1980-82; various positions leading to exec. v.p. fin. and adminstrn., CFO MGM/UA Entertainment Co., Culver City, Calif., 1982-86, also bd. dirs. L.A.; fin. v.p.; chief bus. and ops. officer, Office of Pres., dir. United Artists Corp., Beverly Hills, Calif., 1986-87; chmn. bd., CEO MGA/UA Telecommunications Corp., 1986-89; sr. exec. v.p., dir., mem. exec. com. MGA/UA Communications Co., 1986-89; chmn., CEO Sid Sapsowitz & Assocs., Inc., 1989—. Pres., Wayne Conservative Congregation, N.J., 1970-77. Mem. Am. Mgmt. Assn., Am. Film Inst., Acad. Motion Picture Arts and Scis., Fin. Exec. Inst., TV Acad. Arts and Scis., KP (chancellor comdr.).

SARACEVIC, TEFKO, information science educator; married; 2 children. MS in Libr. Sci., Case Western Reserve U., 1962, PhD in Info. Sci., 1970. Prof. comm., info. and libr. studies Rutgers U., New Brunswick, NJ. Editor-in-chief: Info. Processing and Mgmt., 1985—. Avocations: reading, skiing. Office: Rutgers U Sch Comm Info & Libr Studies 4 Huntington St New Brunswick NJ 08901-1071 E-mail: tefko@scils.rutgers.edu.

SARACHIK, MYRIAM PAULA MORGENSTEIN, physics educator; b. Antwerp, Belgium, Aug. 8, 1933; came to U.S., 1947; d. Solomon and Sarah (Segal) Morgenstein; m. Philip E. Sarachik, Sept. 6, 1954; 1 child, Karen Beth. AB, Barnard Coll., 1954; MS, Columbia U., 1957, PhD, 1960. Rsch. assoc. IBM Watson Labs., Columbia U., N.Y.C., 1960-61; mem. tech. staff Bell Telephone Labs., Murray Hill, N.J., 1962-64; asst. prof. physics CCNY, 1964-67, assoc. prof., 1967-70, prof., 1971—, Disting. prof., 1995—. Advisor NSF, NRC. Contbr. articles to profl. jours. Recipient N.Y.C. Mayor's award for excellence in sci. and technology, 1995. Fellow AAAS, Am. Phys. Soc. (v.p. 2001, pres.-elect 2002), N.Y. Acad. Scis.; mem. NAS, Am. Acad. Arts and Scis. Office: CCNY Physics Dept Convent Ave and 138 St New York NY 10031 E-mail: sarachik@sci.ccny.cuny.edu.

SARAF, DILIP GOVIND, management consultant; b. Begaum, India, Nov. 10, 1942; s. Govind Vithal and Indira Lazman (Divekar) S.; m. Mary Lou Arnold, July 25, 1970; 1 child, Rajesh Dilip. BTech with honors, Indian Inst. Tech., Bombay, 1965; MSEE, Stanford U., 1969. Sr. mgmt. trainee Delhi Cloth and Gen. Mills Co. (India), 1965-68; sr. rsch. engr. SRI Internat., Menlo Park, Calif., 1969-78; project dir. Kaiser Electronics, San Jose, 1978-87; sr. engring. mgr. Varian Assocs., Santa Clara, 1987-90; pres. TOTAL QUALITY, 1990-94; sr. cons. QI Internat., St. Paul, 1994-98; dir. Louis Allen Assocs., San Jose, 1998-99; sr. cons. Pers. Decisions Internat., San Francisco, 1999—2001; pvt. practice mgmt. and orgnl. cons., exec. coach, 2001—. Cons. tchg. U.

Santa Clara, 1972, 73. Contbr. articles to profl. jours.; patentee in field. Bd. dirs. Peninsula Children's Ctr., Palo Alto, Calif. Mem. IEEE, Am. Inventors, Am. Soc. Quality Control, Speakers' Bur. Home: 33106 Lake Champlain St Fremont CA 94555-1217

SARANAM, SANKARA, b. Miami Beach, Fla., Feb. 15, 1968; s. Alon Ben-Meir and Dina Dabby; life ptnr. Wendy Saranam. Bachelors, Columbia U., 1998; Masters, St. John's Coll., 2000. Monk Self-Realization Fellowship, L.A., 1991—94; pres. Pranayama Inst., Inc., Santa Fe, 1998—. Self-employed author, Arad, Israel, 1994—96. Author: Yoga and Judaism, 1997, Pranayama in Theory and Practice, 1998, The Cup of Eternity: Spiritual Commentary on the Rubaiyat of Hafiz, 1999, (booklet) How to Get Straight A's as an Undergraduate, 1998; composer: (assorted msic) Absolute, 1998; columnist A Message from Sankara Saranam, 1999. Socialist. Avocations: travel, camping, yoga. Home: PO Box 1103 Peralta NM 87042-1103 Office: Pranayama Inst 17 Mangham Ct Peralta NM 87042 E-mail: SSaranam@pranayama.org.

SARANDON, SUSAN ABIGAIL, actress; b. N.Y.C., Oct. 4, 1946; d. Phillip Leslie and Lenora Marie (Criscione) Tomalin; m. Chris Sarandon, Sept. 16, 1967 (div. 1979); children: Eva Maria Livia Amurri, Jack Henry Robbins, Miles Guthrie Robbins. BA in Drama and English, Cath. U. Am., 1968. Actress: (plays) include An Evening with Richard Nixon, 1972, A Coupla White Chicks Sittin' Around Talkin', 1980-81, A Stroll in the Air, Albert's Bridge, Private Ear, Public Eye, Extremities, 1982, (films) Joe, 1970, Lady Liberty, 1972, The Rocky Horror Picture Show, 1975, Lovin' Molly, 1974, The Front Page, 1974, The Great Waldo Pepper, 1975, Dragon Fly, 1976, Crash, 1976, The Other Side of Midnight, 1977, The Last of the Cowboys, 1978, Checkered Flag or Crash, 1978, Pretty Baby, 1978, King of the Gypsies, 1978, Something Short of Paradise, 1979, Loving Couples, 1980, Atlantic City, 1980 (Prix Genie Best Fgn. Actress award 1981, Acad. award nominee 1981), Tempest, 1982 (Best Actress award Venice Film Festival 1982), The Hunger, 1983, Buddy System, 1984, Compromising Positions, 1985, The Witches of Eastwick, 1987, Bull Durham, 1988, Sweet Hearts Dance, 1988, A Dry White Season, 1989, The January Man, 1989, White Palace, 1990, Thelma and Louise, 1991 (Acad. award nominee for best actress 1992, Golden Globe award nominee 1992), The Player, 1992, Light Sleeper, 1992, Bob Roberts, 1992, Lorenzo's Oil, 1992 (Acad. award nominee 1993), The Client, 1994 (Acad. award nominee for best actress), Little Women, 1994, Safe Passage, 1994, Dead Man Walking, 1995 (Golden Globe award nominee for best actress 1996, Acad. award for best actress 1996), James and the Giant Peach (voice), 1996, 187 (voice), 1997, Illuminata, 1998, Twilight, 1998, Stepmom (also producer), 1998, Joe Gould's Secret, 1999, Baby's in Black, 1999, Cradle Will Rock, 1999, Anywhere But Here, 1999; TV appearances The Haunting of Rosalind, 1973, F. Scott Fitzgerald and The Last of the Belles, 1974, Who Am I This Time, 1982, A.D., 1985. Mussolini: The Decline and Fall of Il Duce, 1985, Earthly Possessions, 1999, (TV series) A World Apart, 1970-71, Search for Tomorrow, 1972-73. Mem. AFTRA, Screen Actors Guild, Actors Equity, Acad. Motion Picture Arts and Scis., NOW, MADRE, Amnesty Internat., ACLU Office: Internat Creative Mgmt care Samuel Cohen 40 W 57th St New York NY 10019-4001

SARANGAPANI, JAGANNATHAN, embedded systems and networking engineer, educator; b. Madurai, India, June 14, 1965; s. Jagannathan and Janaki (Ramaswamy) S.; m. Sandhya (Srinivasan), June 16, 1997; 1 child, Sadhika. BS, Anna U., Madras, 1987; MS, U. Sask., Can., 1989; PhD, U. Tex., Arlington, 1994. Engr. Engr. India Ltd., New Delhi, 1986-87; rsch. asst. U. Sask., Saskatoon, 1987-89; rsch. assoc. U. Man., Winnipeg, Can., 1990-91; rsch. asst. Automation and Robotics Rsch. Inst., Ft. Worth, 1992-94; cons., rsch. Caterpillar, Inc., Peoria, Ill., 1994-98; asst. prof. elec. engring. and computer engring., dir. embedded sys. and networking lab. U. Tex., San Antonio, 1998—2001; assoc. prof. elect. and computer engring. U. Mo., Rolla, 2001—. Cons., collaborator Adv. Sensors and Controls Group, Ft. Worth, 1994-98; cons. Caterpillar Inc., 1994-98. Co-author: Neural Network Control of Robot and Nonlinear systems, 1999; contbr. chpts. to books, over 90 articles to profl. jours. Recipient Presdl. award for Rsch. Excellence, 2001, also several gold medals and scholarships; U. Tex. fellow, 1992-94; Sigma Xi doctoral rsch. awardee, 1994; NSF career awardee, 2000. Mem. IEEE (sr.; program chmn. Illinois Valley sect. 1994, program com. symposium on int. control, fin. chair symposium on intelligent control, conf. on recisions finance chair in control, 2004), Sigma Xi, Tau Beta Pi, Eta Kappa Nu. Achievements include 15 patents and 9 patents pending; development of novel neural network methods for control and relaxation of certainty equivalence assumption, linearity in the parameters, and persistence of excitation; novel prognostic algorithms. Avocations: tennis, jogging, walking, chess, biking. Office: Dept Elec and Computer Engring 133 Emerson Electric Hall Rolla MO 65409 E-mail: sarangap@umr.edu.

SARANTOS, ATHENA APANOMITH, interior designer; b. Elizabeth, N.J., Oct. 27, 1930; d. James and Mary (Ayianis) Apanomith; m. S. Randy Sarantos, June 18, 1955; children: Valerie Sarantos Cruice, Jean. BA, U. Rochester, 1952; MA, Columbia U., 1954; cert., N.Y. Sch. Interior Design, 1968. Music tchr. Elizabeth (N.J.) Pub. Sch. System, 1952-54, San Diego State Tchr.'s Coll., 1955-56; pvt. practice piano instrn. Elizabeth, 1956-68; pvt. practice interior designer Bernardsville, N.J., 1968—. Recipient Citizenship medal DAR, 1945.

SARASTE, JUKKA-PEKKA, conductor; b. Heinola, Finland, 1956; Doctorate(hon.) , York U., Toronto, Ont., 1995. With Finnish Radio Symphony Orch., 1978—, prin. condr., 1987—, Scottish Chamber Orch., 1987-91; music dir. The Toronto Symphony Orch., 1994—2001. Guest condr. Helsinki Philharm., Beijing Cen. Opera Orch., Symphonic Orch. Chengdu, Rotterdam Philharm. Orch., Chamber Orch. Europe, Bavarian Radio Symphony Orch., Junge Deutsche Philharm., Detroit Orch., Minn. Orch., Vienna Symphony Orch., Rome's Santa Cecilia Orch., Cleve. Orch., Boston Symphony Orch., L.A. Philharm. Orch., others; co-founder Avanti Chamber orch.; condr. more than 39 recs. with Finnish Radio Symphony Orch. and Scottish Chamber Orch. Recipient 1st prize, Scandinavian Conducting Competition, 1981. Office: Radio Symphony Orch Yleisradio Ja 14 SF-00240 Helsinki 24 Finland

SARATH, CAROL ANN, library/media coordinator; b. Ossining, N.Y., Apr. 2, 1952; d. Edward Noah and Florence Louise (Cafarelli) S.; m. Karl Burton Lohmann, July 9, 1986; children: Maria Estella, Patrick Noah. BS in Early Childhood Edn., So. Conn. State U., 1974; MLS, U. Ariz., 1980. Tchr. Gallup (N.Mex.) McKinley County Schs., 1975-79, libr./media coord., 1982—; rschr. Fenn Galleries, Santa Fe, 1980-82. Chair libr. br. Octavia Fellin Pub. Libr., Gallup, 1990—; libr. adv. coun. State of N.Mex., Santa Fe, 1992-2000. Contbr.: Exploring the Southwest Through Childrens Literature, 1994. Bd. mem. Red Rock Balloon Rally Assocs., Gallup, 1983—. Mem. ALA, AECT, N.Mex. Libr. Assn., Assn. Ednl. Comm. and Tech. Avocations: hot air ballooning, gardening. Office: Gallup McKinley County Schs PO Box 1318 Gallup NM 87305 E-mail: csarath@gmcs.k12.nm.us.

SARAVAY, STEPHEN MARTIN, psychiatrist; b. Bklyn., Apr. 26, 1938; s. George and Bess (Levine) S.; m. Jill; children: Adam, Nancy, Leslie. BS, Bklyn. Coll., 1958; MD, SUNY, Bklyn., 1962. Intern Maimonides Hosp., Bklyn., 1962-63; resident in psychiatry Kings County Hosp., 1963-66; asst. chief gen. psychiat. svc. NIMH Clin. Rsch. Ctr., Ft. Worth, 1966-68; unit chief Hillside Hosp., Glen Oaks, N.Y., 1968-72; physician in charge clin. svcs. L.I. Jewish Hosp., New Hyde Park, 1972-81, chief psychiatric consultation liason, 1981—; clin. assoc. prof. Albert Einstein Coll. Medicine, 1991-97, clin. prof., 1997—. Cons. Nassau County Dept. Mental Health, 1978-92. Contbr. chpt. in book, articles to profl. jours. With USPHS 1966-68. NIMH grantee, Squibb Pharm. grantee. Fellow: Acad. Psychosomatic Medicine (chair task force outcome studies 1991—95, mem. coun. 1997—2001, chair rsch. com. 1996—2001, sec. 2001), Am. Psychiat. Assn. (local arrangements com. 1989—90); mem.: Am. Psychosomatic Soc. Home and Office: 7 Dogleg Ln Roslyn Heights NY 11577-2701

SARAVOLATZ, LOUIS DONALD, epidemiologist, physician educator; b. Detroit, Feb. 15, 1950; s. Samuel and Saya Betty (Chonich) S.; m. Yvette Susanne Braymer, Oct. 6, 1990; children: Samuel Francis, Louis Donald II, Stephanie Nicole. BS, U. Mich., 1972, MD, 1974. Fellow Am. Coll. Epidemiology. Intern Henry Ford Hosp., Detroit, 1974-75, 1975-77, fellow, 1977-79, dir. hosp. epidemiology, 1979-82, divsn. head infectious diseases, 1982-96, dir. infectious diseases rsch. lab., 1982-96; prof. medicine Case-Western Res. U., 1993-96, Wayne State U. Sch. Medicine, Detroit, 1996—. Clin. prof. medicine U. Mich. Med. Sch., Ann Arbor, 1986-96; mem. AIDS clin. drug devel. com. NIH, 1990-95; chmn. dept. internal medicine St. John Hosp. and Med. Ctr., 1996—. Contbr. over 100 articles to profl. publs. Active Blue Ribbon Com. on AIDS State of Mich., Detroit, 1990; chmn. physician com. on AIDS Greater Detroit Health Coun., 1989. Fellow ACP, Infectious Diseases Soc. Am. (chmn. antimicrobial use and clin. trials com.), Royal Soc. Medicine (London).

SARAZIN, CRAIG LEIGH, astronomer, educator; b. Milw., Aug. 11, 1950; s. Valley V. and Martha V. (Gustafson) S.; m. Jane Curry, June 12, 1971; children: Stephen N., Andrew T. BS in Physics, Calif. Inst. Tech., 1972; MA in Physics, Princeton U., 1973, PhD in Physics, 1975. Millikan fellow Calif. Inst. Tech., Pasadena, 1975; mem. Inst. Advanced Study, Princeton, N.J., 1975-77; asst. prof. U. Va., Charlottesville, 1977-79, assoc. prof. dept. astronomy, 1979-86, prof., 1986-96, W.H. Vanderbilt prof. astronomy, 1996—, chmn. dept., 1992-95. Vis. asst. prof. U. Calif., Berkeley, 1979; vis. scientist Nat. Radio Astronomy Obs., Charlottesville, 1977-82; vis. prof. physics Inst. Advanced Study, 1981-82, Joint Inst. Lab. Astrophysics vis. fellow U. Colo., Boulder, 1985-86; mem. com. on Space Astronomy Astrophysics, Washington, 1984-86, mem. x-ray astronomy working group, 1989-99, mem. Heineman prize com., 1995-98; chmn. Chandra users com., 1993-01, Advanced Satellite for Cosmology and Astrophysics users com., 1995-2000; mem. High Energy Astrophysics from Space Panel, 1999-2000, USRA Sci. Coun., 2000—. Author: X-ray Emission from Clusters of Galaxies; contbr. numerous articles to profl. jours. NSF grantee, 1981-86, NASA grantee, 1979-82, 86—; recipient Haren Fischer Physics prize Calif. Inst. Tech., 1971. Mem. Am. Astron. Soc., Internat. Astron. Union. Home: 2574 Kimbrough Cir Charlottesville VA 22901-9516 Office: Leander J McCormick Obs Dept of Astronomy U of Va PO Box 3818 Charlottesville VA 22903-0818 E-mail: sarazin@virginia.edu.

SARBANES, PAUL SPYROS, senator; b. Salisbury, Md., Feb. 3, 1933; s. Spyros P. and Matina (Tsigounis) S.; m. Christine Dunbar, June 11, 1960; children— John Peter, Michael Anthony, Janet Matina. AB, Princeton, 1954; BA (Rhodes scholar), Oxford (Eng.) U., 1957; LL.B., Harvard, 1960. Bar: Md. bar 1960. Law clk. to judge Morris Soper U.S. Ct. Appeals (4th cir.), 1960-61; asso. Piper & Marbury, Balt., 1961-62; adminstrv. asst. Walter W. Heller; chmn. Council Econ. Advisers, 1962-63; exec. dir. Charter Revision Commn., Balt., 1963-64; asso. Venable, Baetjer & Howard, 1965-70; mem. Md. Ho. of Dels., 1967-71, 92d Congress from 4th Dist. Md., 93d-94th congresses from 3d Dist. Md.; U.S. senator from Md., 1977—; chmn. banking, housing & urban affairs com.; fgn. rels. com., joint econ. com., senate Dem. polich com.; budget com. Democrat. Greek Orthodox. Office: US Senate 309 Hart Senate Bldg Washington DC 20510-0001 also: Tower 1 Ste 1710 100 S Charles St Baltimore MD 21201-2725*

SARBIN, HERSHEL BENJAMIN, management consultant, business publisher, lawyer; b. Massillon, Ohio, Dec. 30, 1924; s. Joseph I. and Sarah Charlotte (Reich) S.; m. Susan Challman, July 24, 1973; children by previous marriage: Penelope Sarbin Burke, Richard, Barbara; 1 stepdau., Caroline Cooley. AB, Western Res. U., 1946; JD, Harvard U., 1950. Bar: Ill. 1950, N.Y. 1953. Assoc. firm Lewis and MacDonald, N.Y.C., 1953-58; with Ziff-Davis Pub. Co., 1950-81; pub. Popular Photography mag., 1965-66, sr. v.p. co., 1967-74; assoc. pub. Travel Weekly, 1967-68, pub., 1969-74, pres., pub. dir., chief exec. officer photog. div., 1968-69, pres. Pub. Transp. and Travel div., 1970-74; pres. Ziff-Davis Pub. Co., 1974-78; exec. v.p. Ziff Corp., 1978-81, also dir.; chmn., pres. Hershel Sarbin Assocs., Inc., 1981—. Vis. assoc. prof. Fla. Internat. U., 1980; mem. exec. com., nat. photography coordinator Pres.'s Council Youth Opportunity, 1968; fed. commr. Nat. Commn. on New Technol. Uses of Copyrighted Works, 1975-78; mem. policy rev. bd. Public Agenda Found.; pres., CEO Cowles Bus. Media, Inc., 1991-95; Sr. Advisor Cowles Media, 1995; sr. dir. Peppers & Rogers Group, Stamford, Ct., 1998-2001. Author (with George Chernoff): Photography and the Law, 1958, rev. edit., 1977; author: A Different Game: Golf After 50, 2001. Mem. exec. com. Westchester County (N.Y.) Sch. Bd., 1964-66; mem. ethical practices com. N.Y. Sch. Bd. Assn., 1965-68; pres. Hastings-on-Hudson Bd. Edn., 1966-67. Served with AUS, 1946-47. Mem. Harvard Club, Bedford (N.Y.) Golf and Tennis Club, Phi Beta Kappa. Home: 756 Guard Hill Rd Bedford NY 10506-1042 Office: PO Box 196 Bedford NY 10506

SARD, SUSANNAH ELLEN, non-profit executive; b. Boston, May 10, 1944; d. Russell Ellis and Miriam Clark Sard. AB, Bryn Mawr Coll., 1966. Devel. adminstr. Ky. Ednl. TV, Lexington, 1978-88; dir. found. and corp. rels. Sarah Lawrence Coll., Bronxville, N.Y., 1991-96; dir. devel. The Town Hall, N.Y.C., 1998—. Mem. Women in Devel. Office: The Town Hall 123 W 43d St New York NY 10036 Office Fax: 212 997-1929. E-mail: sard@optonline.net., ssard@the-townhall-nyc.org.

SARDELLA, EDWARD JOSEPH, television news anchor; b. Buffalo, June 2, 1940; s. Joseph Edward and Josephine Jenny (D'Amico) S.; m. Sandra K. Lorenzen, Jan. 17, 1975. BA in Speech Arts, Occidental Coll., L.A., 1962. Radio disc jockey, newsman KWIN/KTIL/KERG, Ashland/Tillamook/Eugene, Oreg., 1966-69; reporter KVAL-TV, Eugene, 1969-70; reporter/anchor KOIN-TV, Portland, Oreg., 1970-72, KMGH-TV, Denver, 1972-74; news anchor/sr. editor KUSA-TV, 1974—. Adj. instr. journalism U. Colo., Boulder, 1984-92. Author: Write Like You Talk, 1984; co-author: The Producing Strategy, 1995. Olympic torchbearer, 1996. Capt. USMC, 1962-66. Recipient Emmy award Nat. Assn. TV Arts and Scis., 1992, 93, 94, 95, 96, also Silver Circle Career Achievement award, 1999; named Colo. Broadcaster of Yr., 1997, Journalist of Yr. Colo. chpt. Soc. Profl. Journalists, 2000; inducted into Denver Press Club Hall of Fame, 2002. Office: KUSA TV 500 E Speer Blvd Denver CO 80203-4187

SARDESON, LYNDA SCHULTZ, nurse, parish nurse, diabetes educator; b. LaPorte, Ind., Nov. 5, 1946; d. Wilbur W. and Helen (Winkfein) Schultz; children: Brian Michael, Eric Matthew. BS, Purdue U., Westville, Ind., 1976; MSA, U. Notre Dame, 2000. Cert. diabetes educator. Emergency room nurse LaPorte Hosp., 1971-88, sr. clin. instr., 1988—94, diabetes edn. program coord., 1993—2000; med. missionary to Roatan, Honduras, 1998; nurse specialist to Prince and Princess of Kingdom of Saudi Arabia, 2000—01; parish nurse Bethany Luth. Ch., LaPorte, Ind., 2000—. Adj. prof. Commonwealth Bus. Coll., Michigan City, Ind., 2002; guest presenter 1st Ann. Med. Congress, Izhevsk, Russia, 1996; med. missionary Russia, 1996, 97. Past pres. People to People Internat., Vietnam Women's Meml.; chmn. wellness ministry Bethany Luth. Ch., 1994—. With U.S. Army, 1967-70. Mem. ADA, Am. Assn. Diabetes Educators, No. Ind. Assn. Diabetes Educators (pres.-elect, Diabetes Educator of Yr. 1997-98), Am. Legion.

SARDI, ELAINE MARIE, special education educator; b. Shippenville, Pa., Dec. 2, 1952; d. Willis Henry and Genevieve Evelyn (Hanby) Etzel; m. Michael James Sardi, Dec. 28, 1974; children: Jason Michael, Justin James. BS in Spl. Edn., Clarion State Coll., 1974; MEd in Reading, Clarion U., 1991. Tchr. spl. edn. North Clarion Sch. Dist., Leeper, Pa., 1974-75, Riverview Intermediate Unit, Shippenville, 1986-92; tchr. learning support Keystone H.S., Knox, Pa., 1992-97; lead tchr. Riverview Intermediate Unit, Shippenville, 1991-92; cross-categorical tchr. Louisburg (N.C.) H.S. Franklin County Sch. Sys., 1998; learning disabilities specialist Wake Tech. C.C., Raleigh, N.C., 1998—. Clin. field supr. Clarion (Pa.) U., 1988-97; Lamaze instr. Clarion Orgn. Parent Edn., 1976-83; mentor tchr. Keystone Sch. Dist., 1993-94. Sunday sch. tchr. 1st United Meth. Ch., Clarion, 1977-86; treas. Clarion County Spl. Olympics, 1986-93. Mem. DAR, Nat. Coun. Tchrs. English, Coun. Exceptional Children, Internat. Reading Assn., Learning Disabilities Assn. Wake County, Daus. Union Vets., Kappa Delta Pi, Delta Kappa Gamma. Republican. Avocations: reading, cooking, travel. Home: 8812 Valley Springs Pl Raleigh NC 27615-8120 E-mail: emsardi@mindspring.com.

SARDO, SANFORD, music educator; b. New York, NY, Aug. 29, 1969; s. Joan Marie and Joseph James Smith(Stepfather); m. Jennifer Lynn McKenna, July 3, 1999. BA, SUNY, Stony Brook, NY, 1992; MSc in Edn., CUNY-Queens Coll., , 1998. Cert. Tchr. N.Y., 1993, Music Edn. Orff-Shulwerk, 1995. Tech. dir. Broadhollow Theaters, Lindenhurst, NY, 1989—93; dir. choral activities Calhoun High School Choral Pgm., 1993—. Music counselor MapleWood Sch. Day Camp, Wantagh, NY, 1991—94. Singer: (performance) Back-up Choir @ Kenny Rogers Christmas Show, 1998; dir., dir.: Choir Performance @ Disney's Magic Music Days, 1998. Recipient Choral Soc. Award in Music Edn., CUNY- Queens Coll., 1993, Music Educator of the Yr., Long Island Musicians Assn., 1995, Tchr. Recognition Award, Kiwanis Club of Merrick, 1998, Legis. Citation, Nassau County Legis., 1998, Cert. of Recognition, Merrick C. of C., 2002, Nassau County Legis., 2002. Mem.: Nassau Music Educators Assn., NY State Sch. Music Assn., Music Educators Nat. Conf., Am. Fedn. Tchrs., NY Congress of PTAs (life). R-Consevative. Roman Catholic. Home: 89 Charles St Lindenhurst NY 11757 Office: Calhoun HS Choral Program 1786 State St Merrick NY 11566 Personal E-mail: sardomus@aol.com. E-mail: chschoir@aol.com.

SAREMBOCK, IAN JOSEPH, internist; b. Cape Town, Republic of South Africa, June 9, 1951; m. Ghita Marueen Sarembock; children: Craig Murray, Kerri Lauren. MD, U. Cape Town, 1975, PhD, 1988. Diplomate Am. Bd. Internal Medicine, Am. Bd. Cardiovascular Medicine, Am. Bd. Interventional Cardiology. Sr. house officer dept. internal medicine U. Cape Town and Groote Schuur Hosp., Cape Town, 1979-80, resident in internal medicine, 1980-83, sr. registrar Cardiac Clinic, 1985-86; Velva Schrire meml. rsch. fellow Cardiac Clinic Groote Schur Hosp., 1983-85; postdoctoral rsch. assoc. divsn. cardiology Yale U., New Haven, 1986-88; attending cardiologist divsn. cardiology VA Ctr., West Haven, Conn., 1987-88; asst. prof. internal medicine cardiovascular divsn. U. Va. Health Scis. Ctr., Charlottesville, 1988-93, assoc. prof. internal medicine cardiovascular divsn., 1993-99, dir. coronary care unit, 1988—, prof. internal medicine cardiovasc. divsn., 1999—; interventional cardiologist, 1988—; cardiology cons. Salem (Va.) VA Med. Ctr., 1988—. Lectr., presenter in field; invited prof. Heart-Lung Inst., Utrecht, The Netherlands, 1992; mem. faculty restenosis summits, Cleve. Clinic, 1992, 93, 97 Contbr. articles to profl. publs. Mem. policy working com., house staff supervision Commonwealth of Va., 1990—. Grantee U. Va. Sch. Medicine, 1989, Beecham Labs., 1989-90, Am. Heart Assn., 1989-91, 91-92, 95-98, NIH, 1991-94, 2000—. Fellow ACP, Coll. Physicians South Africa, Am. Coll. Cardiology (allied health profls. com. 1993—), Coun. Thrombosis Atherosclerosis and Vascular Biology; mem. AAAS, Am. Heart Assn. (bd. dirs. Charlottesville/Albermarle divsn. 1991—, mem. Va. affiliate rsch. peer rev. subcom. 1992—, thrombosis coun. 1987, fellow coun. on clin. cardiology 1989), South African Med. and Dental Coun. Office: U Va Dept Cardiology PO Box 158 Charlottesville VA 22908-0001 Fax: 434-982-0901.

SARFATY, SUZANNE, internist and educator; b. Irvington, N.Y., Apr. 11, 1962; d. Sam and Pat (Petrovich) S. BS, Boston U., 1984, MD, 1988, MPH, 1994. Diplomate Am. Bd. Internal Medicine. Intern and resident Boston City Hosp., 1988-91; asst. prof. medicine Boston U., 1991-93, asst. prof. medicine and pub. health, 1995—, asst. dean of student affairs, 1995—. Mem. prof. com. Am. Cancer Soc., Boston, 1991—; mentor Boston Ptnrs. for Edn., 1991—. Recipient Cmty. Svc. award CIBA Geigy, 1986; Dana Farber cancer prevention fellow, 1993-94. Fellow ACP. Avocations: cooking, travel, reading, Spanish language. Home: 11 Verndale St Brookline MA 02446-2415

SARFATY, WAYNE ALLEN, insurance agent, financial planner; b. Rochester, N.Y., Apr. 18, 1951; s. Benjamin and Grace (Rowan) S.; m. Karen Nugent, July 12, 1957, Apr. 18, 1951; children: Melissa A., Gabrielle M. Student, Parsons Coll., 1971-74. Cert. ins. agt. Sales rep. Met. Life, Rochester, N.Y., 1979-81; register rep. Prudential Fin. Svcs., 1981-92; owner, broker Wayne A. Sarfaty & Assocs., 1992—. Dir. tng. films. Mem. Eagle Club. Recipient Nat. Quality award Nat. Assn. Life Underwriters, 1982-90; named to Million Dollar Round Table, NALU, 1987. Mem Eagle Club, Am. Legion. Avocations: camping, auto racing, darts. Home: PO Box 182 Cohocton NY 14826-0182

SARGEANT, ERNEST JAMES, lawyer, educator; b. Spokane, Wash., Sept. 26, 1918; s. Ernest Edward and Louise (McWhinnie) S.; m. Helene Sophie Kazanjian, Jan. 29, 1944 BA cum laude, Harvard U., 1940, LL.B. magna cum laude, 1947. Bar: Mass. 1947. Assoc. Ropes & Gray, Boston, 1947, 52-56, ptnr., 1956-90, of counsel, 1991—. Lectr. law Harvard U. Law Sch., Cambridge, Mass., 1961-62, 65-92; adj. prof. Boston Coll. Law Sch., 1990-98. Grad. treas. Harvard Law Rev., Cambridge, 1971-98. Capt. U.S. Army, 1942-46, 51-52. Mem. Am. Law Inst. (council), ABA, Boston Bar Assn. Clubs: Union (Boston); Country (Brookline, Mass.). Home: 24 Highgate Wellesley Hills MA 02481-1420 Office: Ropes & Gray 1 International Pl Boston MA 02110-2624

SARGEANT, STEPHEN T. military officer; b. Defiance, Ohio, June 29, 1956; s. Robert P. Sargeant and Mary K. Lero; m. Vivienne L. Condon, Oct. 18, 1980; children: Patrick T., Michelle F., Rosemary L.(dec.) 1 stepchild Holly M. BS Polit. Sci. Nat. Security, USAF Acad., Colorado Springs, 1978; grad. disting., Squadron Officer Sch., Maxwell AFB, Ala., 1983, USAF Fighter Weapons Sch., Nellis AFB, Nev., 1983; MS Aeronautical Sci., Embry Riddle U., 1984, MS Bus. Adminstrn. Aviation, 1987; grad., Air Command and Staff Coll., 1986. Commd. 2nd lt. USAF, 1978, advanced through grades to brig. gen., 2001; exec. officer 3371st Student Tng. Squadron, Chanute AFB, Ill., 1978; chief weapons and tactics 509th Tactical Fighter Squadron, Royal Air Force Base Bentwaters, England, 1983—84; chief tactics and tng. weapons divsn. 81st Tactical Fighter Wing, England, 1984; air staff tng. program action officer Sec. of the air force personnel coun. Hdqrs. USAF, Washington, 1984, air staff tng. program exec. officer Office asst. sec. of air force for manpower, installations and reserve affairs, 1984—85; F-16 pilot, instr. pilot, chief scheduling and programming 306th Tactical Fighter Squadron, Homestead AFB, Fla., 1985—90, chief weapons and tactics, flight comdr., 1985—90; chief standardization and evaluation 31st Tactical Fighter Squadron, 1985—90; chief safety wing 8th Tactical Fighter Wing, Kunsan AB, Republic of Korea, 1990; ops. officer 35th Tactical Fighter Squadron, Republic of Korea, 1990—91; mem. air force chief of staff ops. group Hdqrs. USAF, Washington, 1991—92; mil. asst. to exec. sec. of Dept. Def., 1992—93; mil. asst. to deputy Sec. of Def., 1993—94; mil. asst. to Sec. of Def. Office of Sec. of Def., 1994; nat. def. fellow Brookings Instrn., 1994—95; dep. comdr. 23rd Ops. Group, Pope AFB, NC, 1995—96; commandant USAF Weapons Sch., Nellis AFB, Nev., 1996—98; comdr. 8th Fighter Wing, Kunsan AB, Republic of Korea, 1998—99; dep. exec. sec. Nat. Security Coun. The White House, Washington, 1999—2000; comdr. 56th Figher Wing, Luke AFB, Ariz., 2000—02; dir. Hdqrs. AETC, plans and programs Randolph AFB, Tex., 2002—. Mem. Coun. on Fgn. Rels., N.Y.C., 1994—. Contbr. columns in newspapers quar. column. Active Jaycees, Vienna, 1984—85. Decorated Def. Superior Svc. medal, Legion of merit with 2 oak leaf clusters, Meritorious Svc. medal with 2 old leaf clusters, Aerial Achievement medal with oak leaf cluster, Commendation medal, Achievement medal, Outstanding Unit award with three oak leaf clusters, Orgnl. Excellence award with oak leaf cluster, Combat Readiness medal with two oak leaf clusters, Nat. Def. Svc. medal with svc. star, Longevity Svc. award ribbon with six oak leaf clusters, others. Mem.: Daedalians (flight capt.), Air Force Assn. Alumni Assn., Air Force Assn. Roman Catholic. Avocations: running, fitness, golf, hunting, fishing. Home: 11 E Park Universal City TX 78148 Personal E-mail: burner0140@aol.com. Business E-Mail: steve.sargeant@randolph.af.mil.

SARGENT, ANGELA DENISE, geneticist, writer; b. Denver, Jan. 12, 1976; d. Joshua and Virgie Ann Sargent; 1 child. BA in Biology, George Mason U., 2000. Lead tchr. Children's World, Woodbridge, Va., 1999—2000; referral technician Am. Med. Lab., Chantilly, 2000—01; cytogeneticist Genetics & IVF Inst., Fairfax, 2001—. Recipient Black Achievement award, NAACP, 2000. Mem.: NOW. Democrat. Avocations: hiking, writing, theater . Office: Genetics & IVF Inst 3020 Javier Road Fairfax VA 22031

SARGENT, CHARLES LEE, manufacturing company executive; b. Flint, Mich., Mar. 22, 1937; s. Frank T. and Evelyn M. (Martinson) S.; m. Nancy Cook, June 9, 1962; children: Wendy L., Joy A., Candace L. B ME, GM Inst., 1960; MBA, Harvard U., 1962. Reliability engr. AC Spark Plug div. GM, Flint, 1962-63; with Thetford Corp., Ann Arbor, Mich., 1962-95, pres., chmn. bd. dirs., 1974-95, Thermassan Corp., 1969-72; pres., owner Quality Boat Lifts, Inc., Fort Myers, Fla., 1996—. Trustee Lincoln Cons. Schs., 1973-77, Ketterine U., 1989, chmn. 1995-97. Patentee in field. Elder Presbyn. Ch. Recipient Entrepreneurial Achievement award GMI, 1989; named Entrepreneur of the Yr., Harvard Bus. Sch. Club of Detroit, 1981, Engring. Achievement award Kettering U., 1999. Mem. Barton Hills Country Club (bd. dirs. 1985-87, pres. 1987), Harvard Bus. Sch. Club of Detroit (bd. dirs. 1983-93). Avocations: traveling, golf. Home: 27701 Marina Point Dr Bonita Springs FL 34134-0762

SARGENT, DOUGLAS ROBERT, air force officer, engineer; b. Manchester, N.H., Jan. 15, 1953; s. Robert Charles and Hazel Marie (Dearborn) S.; m. Pauline Elizabeth Conn, June 7, 1975; 1 child, Amber Marie. BS, Worcester Polytech. Inst., 1975; postgrad. Squadron Officers Sch., Air U., Maxwell AFB, Ala., 1982, postgrad Air Command and Staff Coll., 1992. Logistics officer 1st BN 3d Field Artillery, Ft. Hood, Tex., 1975-78; programs dir. Armed Forces Examining & Entrance Sta., Portland, Maine, 1978-81; chief contract mgmt. Shaw (S.C.) AFB, 1981-83; programs & engring. dir. Thule AFB, Greenland, 1983-84; chief contracting br. USAF, Ramstein AFB, Germany, 1984-87; chief engr. & environ. planning Aviano AFB, Italy, 1988-90; asst. dir. plans & environ. engr. USAF Electronic Systems Div., Hanscom AFB, Mass., 1991-95; project mgr. A.B. Lloyd Constrn., Inc., Manchester, N.H., 1996-97; pres. Sargent Enterprises, Northwood, 1995—; asst. dir. pub. works Town of Wolfeboro, 1997-99, dir. engring. and tech. svcs., 1997-99; project mgr. C&L Constrn., Greenland, N.H., 1999-2000; dir. pub. works Town of Ossipee, 2000—. Moderator Environ. Protection Com., Aviano, 1988-90, Space Planning Com., Aviano, 1988-90; advisor Mgmt. Assistance Team, Europe, 1985-87; lectr. 1986-88. Chmn. Protestant Parish Fund Coun., Aviano, 1989-90, mem. Ramstein, 1985-87, co-chair, Thule, 1984; bd. dirs. Pleasant Lake Assn., 1993-96. Mem. ASCE (tech. com. N.H. sect. 1993-94), Soc. Am. Mil. Engrs., Constrn. Specifications Inst. (sec. N.H. chpt. 1993-96, v.p. 1996-98, pres. 1998-2000, dir. 2000—), Mt. Washington Obs. Office: PO Box 67 Ossipee NH 03864-0067 E-mail: ossdpw@worldpath.net.

SARGENT, HERB, writer, television producer; b. Phila., July 15, 1923; m. LeGrand Council Mellon. Student, Pa. State U., 1941—43, U. Calif., L.A., 1946—48. Writer (TV series) Broadway Open House-NBC, 1950-51, Colgate Comedy Hour (Fred Allen)-NBC, 1951-52, Victor Borge Show-NBC, 1953, Tonight Show (Steve Allen)-NBC, 1954-58, Steve Allen Sunday Show-NBC, 1958-61, Tonight Show (Johnny Carson)-NBC, 1962-63, The Perry Como Show-NBC, 1963-64, That Was the Week That Was-NBC, 1964-65, The Corner Bar-ABC, 1972-73, Ivan the Terrible-CBS, 1976, The News is the News-NBC, 1983, (TV spls.) The Steve Allen Show with Peter Ustinov, Louis Armstrong and Van Cliburn-NBC, 1959, Music from Shubert Alley-NBC, 1959, Bing Crosby Special-ABC, 1961, Milton Berle Special-NBC, 1962, 9 Perry Como Spls.-NBC, 1963-64, Annie: The Women in the Life of a Man-CBS, 1970, 3 Burt Bachrach Spls., 1970-71, (Sammy Davis Spl.) Sammy, 1972, (Paul McCartney spl.) James Paul McCartney, 1973, Lily-CBS, 1973, The Best of Saturday Night Live-NBC, 1979, The 40th Annual Emmy Awards-Fox, 1988, Diet America Challenge-CBS, 1989, Time Warner Presents: The Earth Day Special-ABC, 1990, The 43rd Annual Primetime Emmy Awards Presentation-Fox, 1991, Saturday Night Live: All the Best of the Mother's Day-NBC, 1992, The 2nd Annual Saturday Night Live Mother's Day Special-NBC, 1993; writer, script cons. Saturday Night Live-NBC, 1975-95, NBC 75th Anniversary, 2002; prodr. (TV series) That Was the Week That Was-NBC, 1964-65, The News is the News, 1983, (TV spls.) The Wonderful World of Aggravation, 1972, Alan King Looks Back in Anger-A Review of 1972, 73, Lily-CBS, 1973, The George Segal Show, 1974, Happy Endings, 1975, Love, Life, Liberty, and Lunch, 1976, (radio) NPR's Backfire!, 1992—, (screenplay) Bye Bye Braverman, 1968; co-creator (TV series) The Corner Bar-ABC, 1972-73, Ivan the Terrible-CBS, 1976, others. Writer People for the Am. Way, 1970—. Sgt. U.S. Army Air Corps, 1943-46. Recipient 6 Emmy awards, 6 Writers Guild awards. Mem. NATAS (bd. govs.), Writers Guild Am. East (coun. mem. 1985-91, pres. 1991—), Dramatists Guild, Songwriters Guild Am. Office: Writers Guild Am East 555 W 57th St New York NY 10019-2925

SARGENT, JOANNE ELAINE, lawyer; b. Miami, Fla., Aug. 6, 1947; BE cum laude, Fla. State U., 1969; ME summa cum laude, Fla. Atlantic U., 1973; JD, Vt. Law Sch., 1985. Bar: Fla. 1986, Vt. 1986, U.S. Dist. Ct. (so. dist.) Fla. 1986, U.S. Ct. Internat. Trade 1986, U.S. Dist. Ct. D.C. 1988, U.S. Ct. Appeals (11th cir.) 1988, U.S. Claims Ct. 1988, U.S. Ct. Appeals (D.C. cir.) 1989, U.S. Dist. Ct. (mid. dist.) Fla. 1989. Law clerk atty. gen.'s office State Dept. Edn., Montpelier, Vt., 1983, 84; law clerk DuFresne and Bradley, P.A., Coconut Grove, Fla., 1985-86; assoc. Sandler, Travis & Rosenberg, P.A., Miami, 1986-88; pvt. practice Coral Gables, 1989-90; career atty. Fla. Ct. Appeal (3d dist.), Miami, 1990—. Tchr. math., sci. Mt. Greylock Regional H.S., Williamstown, Mass., 1969—76, dir. student svcs., Mass., 1976—81; family alcoholism counselor Detoxification Ctr. Hillcrest Hosp., Pittsfield, Mass., 1974—75; sch. adminstr. Drury Mid. Sch., North Adams, Mass., 1975—76; presenter ednl. conf. for hearing officers Supreme Ct. Va., 1985, 86; cons. U. Mass. Bus. adv. counsel Fellowship Ho., Miami, 1994; bd. dirs. Hope Ctr., Children Have All Rights - Legal, Ednl., Emotional Homes for Children. Mem.: Dade County Bar Assn., Coral Gables Bar Assn. (pres. 1999), Fla. Bar Assn., Peter T. Faye Inn of Ct. Office: Fla Ct Appeal 3d Dist 2001 SW 117th Ave Miami FL 33175-1716

SARGENT, JOSEPH DENNY, insurance executive; b. West Hartford, Conn., Sept. 11, 1929; s. Thomas Denny and Elizabeth (Owen) S.; m. Mary A. Tennant, June 25, 1955; children: Robert Tennant, Thomas Denny II, Mary Diane, Suzanne Davis. BA, Yale U., 1952. Ptnr. Conning & Co., Inc., Hartford, Conn., 1957-86, mng. ptnr., 1986-92; chmn., CEO Conning & Co., 1986-91, chmn., 1992, vice-chmn., 1993-95; chmn. Conning Internat., London, 1986-92; vice chmn. Conning & Co., 1993-95; chmn. Bradley, Foster & Sargent, 1995—. Bd. dirs. Beekley Corp., Bristol, Conn., Tenwick Reins., Stamford, Conn.; past trustee MMI Co., Chgo., Mut. Risk, Bermuda, Policy Mgmt. Sys., Columbia, S.C.; chmn. Conn. Surety Corp., Hartford, 1993-97, Bradley, Foster & Sargent, Hartford, Beazley Furlonge Holdings, Ltd., London; trustee McLean Fund; chmn., treas. SKI Ltd, 1956-96. Past trustee Wadsworth Atheneum, Children's Svcs. of Conn.; trustee Hartford Hosp. Mem. Yale Club (Hartford), Hartford Club, Hartford Golf Club. Home: 25 Colony Rd West Hartford CT 06117-2215 Office: City Place II 185 Asylum St Hartford CT 06103-3408

SARGENT, JOSEPH DUDLEY, insurance executive; b. Phila., Apr. 16, 1937; s. Gerald Thomas and Nora (Oliver) S.; m. Sheila Reidy, Apr. 27, 1963; children: Moira, Colleen, Joseph, Sean, Liam, Bridget. AB, Fairfield U., 1959. CLU. Agy. sec. The Guardian Life Ins. Co. Am., N.Y.C., 1959-70, v.p., 1970-79, sr. v.p. health ins., 1980-83, sr. v.p. life ins., 1984-88, exec. v.p., 1989-92, pres., 1993—, pres., CEO, 1996, also bd. dirs.; pres.-guardian Ins. and Annuity Co., 1993; chmn., CEO, bd. dirs. Berkshire Life Ins. Co., 2002—. Mem. bus. adv. coun. Sch. Bus., Baruch Coll., N.Y.C.; bd. dirs. Life Ins. Mktg. and Rsch. Inst., Life Office Mgmt. Assn., The Discovery Mus. Bridgeport, Life Ins. Coun. of N.Y.; treas., United Way of N.Y.C. With U.S. Army, 1960-64. Recipient Ellis Island Medal of Honor Profl. Achievement award Fairfield U.; named to Irish Am. Mag. Bus. 100, 1999, 2000, 01. Mem. Nat. Assn. Life Underwriters, Am. Coun. Life Insurers (bd. dirs.). Republican. Roman Catholic. Avocations: boating, fishing. Office: Guardian Life Ins Co of Am 7 Hanover Sq New York NY 10004-2616 E-mail: joseph_sargent@glic.com.

SARGENT, LIZ ELAINE (ELIZABETH SARGENT), safety consulting executive; b. Meadville, Pa., Apr. 17, 1942; d. Melvin Ellsworth and Roberta Jean (Beach) Taylor; m. Lawrence Sargent, Sept. 6, 1969; 1 child, Kathy-Dawn. AA cum laude, Cuyahoga C.C., Cleve., 1987, Assoc. in Transp. cum laude, 1989. Car distbr. Norfolk and Western R.R., Cleve., 1963-69; account mgr. Ill. Cen. R.R., 1970-73; traffic coord. Carlon Pipe, Mantua, Ohio, 1973-75; chief dispatcher X.L. Trucking, Coshocton, 1975-77; corp. log auditor Anchor Motor Freight, Beachwood, 1977-78; cons. Saf-T, Parma, 1978-84, v.p. safety Shaker Heights, 1987-91; dir. safety Sherwin Williams, Cleve., 1984-87; pres. Safety Advisors for Transp., Inc., Beachwood, Ohio, 1991—; founder Love Keepers, 1996. Spkr. Coshocton (Ohio) Traffic Club, 1984, Am. Indsl. Hygiene, Cleve., 1985, All-Ohio Safety and Health Congress, 1996. Author: Hall Chemical-Safety Procedures, 1983-84, Progressive Insurance, 1987, RL Lipton Co. manual, 1995; contbr. articles to profl. jours. Chairperson intergenerational com. Ch. in Aurora, Ohio, 1984-86, Valley View Village Ch. libr. chairperson, mem. choir; bd. dirs. Shaker Heights Teen Recreational Com., 1984-87. Delta Nu Alpha scholar, 1977. Mem. Ohio Trucking Assn. (nat. safety coun.), Cleve. Bd. Realtors, Motor Fleet Safety Suprs. (nat. com.), Fleet Maintenance Coun., Phi Theta Kappa. Republican. Avocations: interior design, painting, writing poetry and short stories, dried floral arrangements, hiking. Office: Saf-T 14716 Rockside Rd Maple Heights OH 44137-4016 E-mail: sargeantee@yahoo.com.

SARGENT, PAMELA, writer; b. Ithaca, N.Y., Mar. 20, 1948; BA, SUNY, Binghamton, N.Y., 1968, MA, 1970. Mng. editor, Binghamton, N.Y., 1970-73; asst. editor, 1973-75; Am. editor Bull. Sci. Fiction Writers Am., Johnson City, 1983-91. Author: Cloned Lives, 1976, Starshadows, 1977, The Sudden Star, 1979, Watchstar, 1980, The Golden Space, 1982, The Alien Upstairs, 1983, Earthseed, 1983, Eye of the Comet, 1984, Homesmind, 1984, Venus of Dreams, 1986, The Shore of Women, 1986, The Best of Pamela Sargent, 1987, Alien Child, 1988, Venus of Shadows, 1988, Ruler of the Sky, 1993 (Nebula best novelette award 1992, Locus best novelette award 1993, Electric Sci. Fiction award 1993), Climb the Wind: A Novel of Another America, 1999, (with Ron Miller) Firebrands: The Heroines of Science Fiction and Fantasy, 1998, Child of Venus, 2001, Behind the Eyes of Dreamers and Other Short Novels, 2002, The Mountain Cage and Other Stories, 2002; editor: (anthology) Women of Wonder, 1975, Bio-Futures, 1976, More Women of Wonder, 1976, The New Women of Wonder, 1978, (with Ian Watson) Afterlives, 1986, Women of Wonder, The Classic Years, 1996, Women of Wonder, The Contemporary Years, 1995, Nebula Awards 29, 1995, Nebula Awards 30, 1996, Nebula Awards 31, 1997. Office: care Richard Curtis Assocs Inc 171 E 74th St New York NY 10021-3221

SARGENT, ROBERT GEORGE, engineering educator; b. Port Huron, Mich., June 14, 1937; s. George O. and Marie L. (Roome) S.; m. Dorothy Baum, 1970; 1 dau., Tiffany. BSE, U. Mich., 1959, MS, 1963, PhD, 1966. Elec. engr. Hughes Aircraft Co., Culver City, Calif., 1959-61; faculty mem. Syracuse U., 1966—, asst. prof., 1966-70, assoc. prof., 1970-81, prof. indsl. engring. and ops. research, 1982-96, chmn. dept., 1982-85, prof. elec. and computer engring., 1994-96, prof. elec. engring. and computer sci., 1996—. Vis. faculty Cornell U., 1981-82, Ctr. Econ. Rsch. Tilburg U., 1996; bd. dirs. Winter Simulation Conf., 1974-84, chmn. bd., 1979-81, gen. chmn., 1977; chmn. TIMS Coll. on Simulation and Gaming, 1978-80. Dept. editor: Communications of Assn. Computing Machinery, 1980-85; editorial adv. bd. ACM Transactions on Modeling and Simulations, 1989-98; contbr. articles to profl. jours. Recipient Service award Winter Simulation Conf., 1984. Mem. Assn. Computing Machinery (nat. lectr. 1985-89, Svc. award 1985), Inst. for Ops. Rsch. and the Mgmt. Scis. (Disting. Svc. award for Simulation 1985), Inst. Indsl. Engrs. (Svc. award 1985), Soc. Computer Simulation (bd. dirs. 1984-87), Computer Soc. of IEEE (mem. exec. com. simulation 1985-99). Office: Syracuse U Dept Elec Engring & Computer Sci 253 Link Hall Syracuse NY 13244-0001

SARGENT, RONALD L. retail office and business products executive; BS, MBA, Harvard U. Various mgmt. and planning positions with Kroger Co., 1974-89; regional v.p. ops. Staples Inc., 1989, pres. N.Am. ops., 1998—2002, pres., COO, 2002—. Office: Staples Inc PO Box 9265 Framingham MA 01701-9265

SARGENT, THOMAS ANDREW, retired political science educator; b. Indpls., Apr. 24, 1933; s. Thomas Edward and Inez (Secrest) S.; m. Cecily Constance Fox-Williams, 1965 (dec.); children: Sarah Beatrice, Andrew Fox; m. 2d Frances Petty, 1987. BA, DePauw U., Greencastle, Ind., 1955; MA, Fletcher Sch. Law and Diplomacy, Tufts U., 1959, MA in Law and Diplomacy, 1968, PhD, 1969. With First Nat. City Bank, N.Y.C., 1959-64, asst. accountant, 1963-64; asst. sec. Irving Trust Co., 1964-66; mem. faculty Ball State U., Muncie, Ind., 1969-89, dir. London Ctr., 1973-74, chmn. polit. sci. dept., 1977-80, prof. polit. sci., 1979-89, prof. emeritus, 1989—, acting asst. to dean Coll. Scis. and Humanities, 1981-82, assoc. dean Coll. Scis. and Humanities, 1982-85, dir. spl. programs Minnetrista Ctr., 1985-87; dir. E.B. Ball Ctr., 1987-89, dir. emeritus, 1989—. Contbg. editor Ripon Forum, 1973-78. Bd. dirs., exec. v.p. Ea. Ind. Cmty. TV, Muncie, 1974-76, pres., 1976-77; mem. nat. bd. govs. Ripon Soc., Washington, 1976-84; mem. Indpls. Com. Fgn. Rels., 1977—; bd. dirs. Hist. Muncie, Inc., 1979-85, pres., 1980; bd. dirs. Muncie Civic Theatre Assn., 1978-81, 90-96, 1st v.p., 1992-96; exec. dir. Ind. Consortium for Internat. Programs, 1982-88; mem. Ind. Real Estate Commn., 1983-91; trustee DePauw U., 1983—; bd. dirs. Muncie Symphony Orch., 1985-95, pres., 1991-93; mem. bd. govs. Minnetrista Cultural Ctr., Muncie, 1989-94, chmn., 1992-94; trustee Malpas Trust, 1990—, pres., 1997—; bd. dirs. Arts Ind., Inc., 1992-99. Muncie Children's Mus., 1994-2000, v.p., 1996-97, pres. 1997; trustee Ind. Colls. Ind., 1996—, United Meth. Meml. Home, Warren, Ind., 1997—. 1st lt. USAF, 1955-58. Named Sagamore of Wabash, 1988. Mem. Am. Polit. Sci. Assn., Delaware County Hist. Alliance (bd. dirs. 1980-86, 87-95, pres., 1987-91), Soc. Profl. Journalists, Delaware Country Club, Columbia Club (Indpls.), Maxinkuckee Yacht Club (Culver, Ind.), Rotary, Phi Delta Theta. Republican. Methodist. E-mail: tsarg123@aol.com.

SARGENT, WALLACE LESLIE WILLIAM, astronomer, educator; b. Elsham, Eng., Feb. 15, 1935; s. Leslie William and Eleanor (Denniss) S.; m. Anneila Isabel Cassells, Aug. 5, 1964; children: Lindsay Eleanor, Alison Clare. B.Sc., Manchester U., 1956, M.Sc., 1957, PhD, 1959. Research fellow Calif. Inst. Tech., Pasadena, 1959-62; sr. research fellow Royal Greenwich Obs., 1962-64; asst. prof. physics U. Calif., San Diego, 1964-66; mem. faculty dept. astronomy Calif. Inst. Tech., 1966—, prof., 1971-81, Ira S. Bowen prof. astronomy, 1981—, dir. Palomar Obs., 1997-2000. Miller prof. U. Calif., Berkeley, 1993; Thomas Gold lectr. Cornell U., Ithaca, NY, 1994—95; Sackler lectr. Harvard U., Cambridge, Mass., 1995, U. Calif., Berkeley, 1996; Icko Iben lectr. U. Ill., 2002. Contbr. articles to profl. jours. Alfred P. Sloan fellow, 1968-70. Fellow Am. Acad. Arts and Scis., Royal Soc. (London); mem Am. Astron. Soc. (Helen B. Warner prize 1969, Dannie Heineman prize 1991, Henry Norris Russell lectr. 2001), Royal Astron. Soc. (George Darwin lectr. 1987, assoc. 1998), Astron. Soc. Pacific (Bruce Gold medal 1994), Internat. Astron. Union. Clubs: Athenaeum (Pasadena). Home: 400 S Berkeley Ave Pasadena CA 91107-5062 Office: Calif Inst Tech Astronomy Dept 105-24 Pasadena CA 91125-0001

SARGENT, WESLEY EVERETTE, civil engineer, consultant; b. Putham, Conn., June 28, 1933; s. William H. and Mildred T. Sargent; m. Patricia R. Collins, July 2, 1960; children: Robert, Gary. BS, U. Conn., 1956. Registered profl. engr., Conn. Div. engr. Met. Dist., Hartford, Conn., 1959-81; project engr. Close, Jensen & Miller, Wethersfield, 1991—. Mem. Planning and Zoning Commn., Wethersfield, 1969-73; chmn. Inland Wetlands, Wethersfield, 1971-82. With U.S. Army, 1956-58. Mem. ASCE. Home: 39 Randy Ln Wethersfield CT 06109-3763 Office: Close Jensen & Miller 1137 Silas Deane Hwy Wethersfield CT 06109-4296

SARGENT, WILLIAM WINSTON, retired anesthesiologist; b. Oshkosh, Wis., Feb. 28, 1933; s. Sprague Spencer and Lila Jane (Gjermundson) S. BS in Medicine, U. Ill., Chicago, 1955, MD, 1957; MS in Anesthesiology, U. Minn., 1967. Diplomate Am. Bd. Anesthesiology. Staff anesthesiologist St. Anthony Hosp., Rockford, Ill., 1960-61, Swedish Am. Hosp., Rockford, 1960-61; instr. anesthesiology U. Minn., Mpls., 1967-74, asst. prof. anesthesiology, 1974-80; staff anesthesiologist St. Luke's Hosp., Duluth, Minn., 1980-95, ret., 1995. Contbr. articles to profl. jours. Capt. USAF, 1961-64, France. Fellow Am. Coll. Anesthesiologists; mem. AMA, Am. Soc. Anesthesiologists, Minn. Soc. Anesthesiologists, Minn. State Med. Assn., St. Louis County Med. Soc. Presbyterian.

SARGUS, EDMUND A., JR. judge; b. Wheeling, W.Va., July 2, 1953; s. Edmund A. Sr. and Ann Elizabeth (Kearney) S.; m. Jennifer L. Smart, Jan. 7, 1978; 2 children. AB with honors, Brown U., 1975; JD, Case Western Res. U., 1978. Bar: Ohio 1978, U.S. Dist. Ct. (so. dist.) Ohio 1979, U.S. Dist. Ct. (no. dist.) Ohio 1981, U.S. Ct. Appeals (6th cir.) 1985, U.S. Dist. Ct. (no. dist.) W.Va. 1988, U.S. Ct. Appeals (4th cir.) 1988. Assoc. Cinque, Banker, Linch & White, Bellaire, Ohio, 1978-79, Stanley C. Burech, St. Clairsville, 1980-82; ptnr. Burech & Sargus, 1983-93; U.S. Atty. Dept. of Justice, Columbus, Ohio, 1993-96; dist. judge U.S. Dist. Ct. (so. dist.) Ohio, 1996—. Spl. counsel Ohio Atty. Gen., Columbus, 1979-93; treas. Coalition for Dem. Values, Washington, 1990-93. Solicitor Village of Powhattan Point, Ohio, 1979-93; councilman City of St. Clairsville, 1987-91. Mem. ABA, Ohio Bar Assn. Office: US Dist Ct 85 Marconi Blvd Columbus OH 43215-2823

SARHAN, MANSOOR MOHAMED, library director; b. Nuwidrat, Bahrain, Jan. 1, 1945; s. Mohamned Abdulla and Sukainah Ahmed (Ismail) S.; m. Zahra Abul Kassim Dashti, Aug. 22, 1971; children: Nazha, May, Mohamed. BA in History, Beirut (Lebanon) Arab U., 1972; B in Libr. Sci., U. Bombay, India, 1980; MA in Librarianship, Leeds (Eng.) Poly., 1985; diploma exec. mgmt., U. Bahrain, Isa Town, 1990. Tchr. for English lab. Ministry of Edn., Manama, Bahrain, 1963-73, libr. Manama (Bahrain) Pub. Libr., 1973-82, head pub. librs., 1982-88, dir. pub. librs., 1989—. Gen. organizer Bahrain Internat. Book Fair, Manama. Author: The Book and the Libraries, 1983, Cultural Movement in Bahrain 1940-1990, 1993, Bahrain National Bibliography, 1995, Libraries in Islamic Dynasties, 1997, Survey of Cultural Movement in Bahrain during Twentieth Century, 2000, Pioneers of Bookshops in Bahrain, 2000, Libraries in Bahrain, 2001. Lectr. schs., clubs and assns., Bahrain, 1975—; gen. organzer yearly piano concert Ministry of Edn., Bahrain, 1988—. Mem. Bahrain Libr. Assn. (pres. 1994—), Arab Fedn. for Librs. and Info., Nuwidrat Club (pres. 1966—). Avocations: reading, music, tennis, chess. Home: House 46 Rd 4301 Nuwidrat 643 Bahrain Office: Ministry of Edn PO Box 43 Manama Bahrain

SARICKS, JOYCE GOERING, librarian; b. Nov. 8, 1948; d. Joe W. and Lovella Goering; m. Christopher L. Saricks, Aug. 21, 1971; children: Brendan James, Margaret Katherine. BA with highest distinction in Eng.& Ger, U. Kans., 1970; MA in Comparative Lit., U. Wis., 1971; MA/MAT in Library Sci., U. Chgo., 1977. Reference librarian Downers Grove (Ill.) Pub. Library, 1977-80, head tech. svcs., 1980-83, coord. lit. and audio svcs., 1983—. Presenter workshops in field. Author: (with Nancy Brown) Readers' Advisory Service in the Public Library, 1989, revised edit., 1997, The Readers' Advisory Guide to Genre Fiction, 2001. Mem. Read Ill. adv. com., 1990-91. Woodrow Wilson fellow, 1970; recipient Allie Beth Martin award Pub. Library Assn., 1989, No. Ill. Libr. of Yr. award Windy City Romance Writers, 1995, Libr. of the Yr. award Romance Writers of Am., 2000. Mem. ALA, Ill. Library Assn., Adult Reading Round Table (founder), Phi Beta Kappa, Delta Phi Alpha, Pi Lambda Theta, Beta Phi Mu. Home: 1116 61st St Downers Grove IL 60516-1819 Office: Downers Grove Pub Library 1050 Curtiss St Downers Grove IL 60515-4606 E-mail: saricksj@juno.com.

SARIDAKIS, ANDREW PETER, international trader and business consultant; b. Smithtown, N.Y., Mar. 14, 1965; s. Andrew and Dorothy Elizabeth (Kritikos) S. BS, SUNY, Buffalo, 1987, postgrad. Lic. pvt. pilot. Internat. textile trader Nichimen Am. Inc., N.Y.C., 1987-88; internat. account exec. Belding Hausman Inc., 1988-89; internat. credit analyst Belding Heminway Inc., 1989-90; v.p. Internat. Trading Group, Long Island City, N.Y., 1990-95; corp. sales mgr. M.O. Air Internat., Roslyn Heights, 1995—; instr. World Trade Inst. Pace U., N.Y.C., 1998—. Mem. Ednl. Soc. for Resource Mgmt., Am. Prodn. and Inventory Control Soc. Republican. Avocations: golf, flying, Greek anthropology. Office: M O Air Internat Inc 4 Expressway Plz Ste 120 Roslyn Heights NY 11577-2034

SARIDIS, GEORGE NICHOLAS, electrical, computers and system engineering educator, robotics and automation researcher; b. Athens, Greece, Nov. 17, 1931; arrived in U.S., 1961, naturalized, 1971; s. Nicholas and Anna (Tsofa) S.; m. Panayota Dimarogona, Apr. 10, 1985. Diploma in Mech. and Elec. Engring., Nat. Tech. U., Athens, 1955; MSEE, Purdue U., 1962, PhD, 1965. Instr. Nat. Tech. U., 1955-63, Purdue U., West Lafayette, Ind., 1963-65, asst. prof., 1965-70, assoc. prof., 1970-75, prof., 1975-81; prof. elec., computer and sys. engring. Rensselaer Poly. Inst., Troy, N.Y., 1981-96, dir. Robotics and Automation Lab., 1982-96, prof. emeritus, 1997—. Dir. NASA Ctr. for Intelligent Robotic Systems for Space Exploration, 1988-92; engring. program dir. NSF, Washington, 1973; hon. prof. Huazhong U., Wuhan, China. Author: Self-Organizing Control of Stochastic Systems, 1977, Stochastic Processes Estimation and Control, 1995, Entropy in Control Engineering, 2001, Hierachically Intelligent Machines, 2002; co-author: Intelligent Robotic Systems: Theory and Applications, 1992, Reliable Plan Selection by Intelligent Machines, 1996, Design of Intelligent Control System Based on Hierarchical Stochastic Automata, 1996; contbr. articles to profl. publs.; co-author: Intelligent Robotic Sys.; co-editor, contbg. author: Fuzzy Automata, 1977, editor, contbg. author: Advances in Automation and Robotics, Vol. 1, 1985, editor, contbg. author: Advances in Automation and Robotics, Vol. 2, 1990. Fellow IEEE (founding pres. robotics and automation coun. 1981-84, Centennial medal 1984, Third Millennium medal 2000, Disting. Mem. award Control Sys. Soc. 1989); mem. ASME, Soc. Mfg. Engrs./Robotics Internat.-Machine Vision Assn. (sr.), Am. Soc. Engring. Edn., N.Y. Acad. Scis., Acad. Athens (Greece). Home: 38 Loudonwood E Loudonville NY 12211-1465 Office: Rensselaer Poly Inst Dept Electrical Computer & Sys Engring Sch of Engring Troy NY 12180-3590

SARIDIS, PANAYOTA DIMAROGONA, civil engineer; b. Pireaus, Greece, June 28, 1953; d. Dimos Andrew and Maria (Bekakos) Dimarogonas; m. George Nicholas Saridis, Apr. 10, 1985. Diploma in Civil Engring., U. Patras, Greece, 1977; MS in Computer Sci., Renselaer Poly. Inst., 1987. Registered profl. engr. Instr. U. Patras, 1978-85, Purdue U., West Lafayette, Ind., 1980-81, Siena Coll., Albany, N.Y., 1987-88; civil engr. Dept. Transp. State N.Y., 1988—. Cons. engr. Dimarogonas Bros. Co., Athens, Greece, 1977-85; pres. Engring. Software, Albany, 1989—. Contbr. articles to profl. jours. Mem. IEEE, ASCE, NSPE, LWV, Profl. Engrs. in Govt. Home: 38 Loudonwood E Albany NY 12211-1465 E-mail: saridis@aol.com.

SARINO, EDGARDO FORMANTES, radiologist, physician; b. Laoag City, Ilocos Norte, Philippines, Nov. 6, 1940; came to U.S., 1965, naturized, 1983; s. Epafrodito Cruze and Esperanza Raval Formantes S.; m. Milagros Felix Ona, Dec. 6, 1965; chldren: Edith Melanie, Edgar Michael, Edenn Michele. MD, U. of the East, 1964; MBA in Healthcare Svcs. Mgmt. Emphasis, W.Va. U., 1999, . Diplomate Am. Bd. Radiology. Rotating intern St. Clare's Hosp., N.Y.C., 1965-66; resident in anatomical pathology Coney Island Hosp, 1966; resident in gen. surgery Manhattan VA Hosp., 1966-67, U. Bellevue Med. Ctr., N.Y.C., 1967-68; resident in radiology Manhattan VA Hosp., 1968-71; fellow in diagnostic radiology, 1968-71; staff radiologist Mercer Med. Ctr., Trenton, N.J., 1973-83; chief nuclear medicine svc. Louis Johnson VA Med. Ctr., Clarksburg, W. Va., 1983-93, acting chief radiology svc., 1988-92, chief imaging svc., 1993—, assoc. chief staff imaging, 1998—; clin. assoc. prof. radiology U. W.Va. Sch. Med., 1989—; teaching asst. gen. surgery N.Y.U.-Bellevue Med. Ctr., N.Y.C., 1967-68. Contbr. articles to med. jours. Recipient Cert. of Merit Mallinkrodt Pharm., 1969. Mem. Am. Coll. Physician Execs., Soc. Nuclear Med., Am. Coll. Radiology, Radiol. Soc. N.Am., Harrison County Med. Soc., W. Va. Radiol. Soc., Assn. Phillipine Practicing Physicians in Am. Philippine Radiol. Soc. Am. Home: 96 Garden Cir Bridgeport WV 26330-1367 Office: Louis Johnson VA Med Ctr Clarksburg WV 26301 E-mail: efsarino@msn.com.

SARIPALLI, PRASAD KANAKA, research scientist; s. Sriramamurty and Kanaka Mahalakshmi Saripalli; m. Ratna V. Saripalli, Sept. 23, 1994; 1 child Arvind. PhD, U. of Fla., 1996. Cert. P. E. 1998. Sr. rsch. scientist Pacific Northwest Nat. Lab., Richland, Wash., 1999—. Mem.: Am. Geophys. Union. Office: Pacific Northwest Nat Lab Battelle Blvd Richland WA 99352

SARIS, PATTI BARBARA, federal judge; b. 1951; BA magna cum laude, Radcliffe Coll., 1973; JD cum laude, Harvard U., 1976. Law clerk to Hon. Robert Braucher Mass. Supreme Judicial Ct., 1976-77; atty. Foley Hoag & Eliot, Boston, 1977-79; staff counsel U.S. Senate Judiciary Com., 1979-81; atty. Berman Dittmar & Engel, Boston, 1981-82; chief civil divsn. U.S. Atty.'s Office, 1984-86; U.S. magistrate judge U.S. Dist. Ct. Mass., 1986-89; assoc. justice Mass. Superior Ct., 1989-94; dist. judge U.S. Dist. Ct. Mass., 1994—. Bd. overseers, chair com. on defender svcs. judicial conf. Harvard. Bd. trustees Beth Israel Hosp.; active Wexner Heritage Found. Recipient award Haskell J. Cohn Disting. Jud. Svc. award Boston Bar Assn.; Nat. Merit scholar, 1969. Mem.: Phi Beta Kappa. Office: US Courthouse Courthouse Way Ste 6130 Boston MA 02210

SARJEANT, PETER THOMSON, retired research director; b. Orillia, Ont., Can., June 24, 1929; came to U.S., 1957; s. Stanley Robert and Barbara Isobel (Thomson) S.; m. Marjorie Jean Gilbert, Nov. 3, 1956; children: Evelyn Joan, Sandra Gayle. BSc, Queen's U., Kingston, Ont., 1953, MSc, 1956; PhD, Pa. State U., 1967. Pharm. prodn. supr. Merck Sharpe & Dohme, Montreal, 1954-57; rsch. engr. Westvaco Corp., Charleston, S.C., 1957-60, product devel. supr. (lignin products), 1960-63, rsch. group leader printed products Columbia, Md., 1967-70, rsch. dir. papermaking Covington, Va., 1970-79, rsch. group mgr. lignin/ink resins Charleston, 1979-91; ret. Author: Hand Papermaking, 1973; contbr. articles to profl. jours. Mem. TAPPI, Am. Chem.

Soc. Republican. Presbyterian. Achievements include 5 patents on lignin in binders, purification of active carbon-1. Avocations: gardening, swimming, bridge, bagpiping. Home: PO Box 212 Highlands NC 28741-0212

SARJEANT, WALTER JAMES, electrical and computer engineering educator; b. Strathroy, Can., Apr. 7, 1944; s. Walter Burns and Margaret (Laurie) S.; m. Ann Richards, June 30, 1972; children: Eric, Cheryl. BSc in Math, Physics, U. Western Ont., Can., 1966, MSc in Physics, 1967, PhD in Physics, 1971. Asst. dir. R&D Gen-Tec Inc., Quebec City, Que., Can., 1971-73; program mgr. Lumonics Rsch. Ltd., Ottawa, Ont., Can., 1973-75; staff scientist Nat. Rsch. Coun., Can., 1975-78; project leader Los Alamos (N.Mex.) Nat. Lab., 1978-81; James Clerk Maxwell prof. elec. engring. SUNY, Buffalo, 1981—. Dir. High Power Electronics Inst. Author: High Power Electronics, 1989. Fellow IEEE; mem. Electromagnetics Acad., Electrostatics Soc., N.Y. Acad. Scis., Rotary, Eta Kappa Nu. Office: SUNY Elec Engring Dept PO Box 601900 312 Bonner Hall Buffalo NY 14260-1900

SARKAR, ARINDAM, information technology executive; b. Guwahati, Assam, India, Sept. 30, 1970; s. Amit and Reba Sarkar; m. Monica Mallick, Sept. 10, 1970; 1 child Amisha. BA with honors, Delhi U., 1991; MBA, Modern Inst. Mgmt., New Delhi, 1994. Pres. Interactive Group, Fremont, Calif., 1995—99; chmn., CEO YBE Info Sys., Inc., Foster City, 1999—2001; CEO, pres. IG2000 Info Sys., Inc., Fremont, 2001—. Mem.: Fedn. Indo-Am. Assns. of No. Calif. (sr. v.p. 2001—02). Hindu. Avocations: travel, sports, photography, outdoors. Office: IG2000 Info Sys Inc 47550 Kato Rd San Mateo CA 94404 Office Fax: 510-490-9212. Personal E-mail: ary@ig2000systems.com. Business E-Mail: ary@ig2000systems.com.

SARKAR, INDRA NEIL, medical informatician; b. Framingham, Mass., June 23, 1977; s. Basu Deb and Mahamaya S. BS, Mich. State U., 1999; MPhil, Columbia U., 2002. Tchg. asst., rsch. asst. Mich. State U., East Lansing, 1995-99; rsch. asst. Am. Mus. Natural History, N.Y.C., 2000—; tchg. asst. Columbia U., 2001—02. Dir. Mosaic Data Sys., Bedford, Mass., 1995—. Mem. Am. Med. Informatics Assn., AAAS, N.Y. Acad. Scis., Union Concerned Scientists., Am. Inst. Biol. Scis. Avocations: reading, cooking, soccer, programming, writing. Office: Columbia Presbyn Med Ctr Vanderbilt Clin 5 622 W 168th St New York NY 10032

SARKAR, SIDDHARTHA, pathologist; b. Khargpur, India, Aug. 9, 1936; s. Sailabala and Manmatha Nath S.; m. Patricia French, Apr. 6, 1963; children: Jayashri. BS, Calcutta U., 1956; MS, Cornell U., 1957; GVS, Vet. Coll., Calcutta, 1956; PhD, MIT, 1963. Mem. WHO, Geneva, 1975-77; clin. prof. SUNY Upstate Med. U., Syracuse, N.Y., 1999—. Dir. SUNY Ob/Gyn Andrology Svc., Syracuse, 1989—. Patentee in field. Durnham fellow oncology, Am. Cancer Soc., 1966-71. Office: SUNY Upstate Med Univ 750 E Adams St Syracuse NY 13210-2399

SARKIS, J. ZIAD, management consultant; b. Beirut, Lebanon, July 8, 1968; arrived in France, 1975; s. Nicolas Ata and Claude (Moussalli) Sarkis; m. Elisabeth Kalman, June 21, 1997; 2 children. BAS in Anthropology, Econs. and Math. with distinction and honors, MS in Engring. and Mgmt., Stanford U., 1990; DPhil in Econs., Oxford U., Eng., 1998. Cons. McKinsey & Co., San Francisco, 1990, N.Y.C., 1991—92, Paris, 1992; co-founder, sr. ptnr., bd. dirs. Mitchell Madison Group (formerly AT Kearney FI/SP), N.Y.C., 1992—2000; ptnr. Paribas Capital, London, 2001—. Gen. sec. Phoenixia-X, Paris, 1993—. Greek Catholic. Office: Paribas Capital 28 Old Brompton Rd #320 London SW7 3SS England

SARKISIAN, EDWARD GREGORY, dentist; b. Detroit, Oct. 6, 1952; s. Albert Nicholas and Nina (Doctorian) S.; m. Anna Svirid, July 12, 1975; children: Sara, Aram. BS, cert. in med. tech., U. Mich., 1974; DDS, U. Detroit, 1978. Lic. Bd. Dentistry, Mich. Gen. practice dentistry, Dearborn, Mich., 1978—. Mem. staff Harper Grace Hosp., Detroit, 1978-88; clin. instr. dept. otolaryngology Wayne State U. Sch. Medicine, Detroit, 1982-90. Fellow Am. Coll. Dentists, Pierre Fauchard Acad. (treas. Mich. sect.); mem. ADA, Mich. Dental Assn. (ho. of dels. 1999-2001), Detroit Dist. Dental Soc. (strategic planning com. 1996—, del. 1999-2001), Armenian Gen. Benevolent Union Am., Francis Vedder Soc. Crown and Bridge Prosthodontics, Nat. Eagle Scout Assn. Armenian Orthodox. Clubs: U. Mich. Pres.'s, U. Mich. Victors. Lodge: Knights of Vartan (Nareg chpt. comdr. 1984-85, midwest rep. 1986-87). Office: 22190 Garrison Suite 201 Dearborn MI 48124

SARKISIAN, PAMELA OUTLAW, artist; b. Spokane, Sept. 26, 1941; d. Willard Clinton and Frances (Montieth) Outlaw; m. Ronald Edward Sarkisian, Nov. 11, 1960; children: Ronald Abraham, Michelle Suzanne. Grad. high sch., Stockton, Calif. Art student, Oceanside, Calif., 1972-80; founder Palette 'N Easel Studio, 1980—, operator, mgr., 1980—, art tchr. in residence, 1985—. Publisher greeting cards Polytint, Ltd., England, 1995, 96; fine art prints pub. by Bentley House, Ltd., Walnut Creek, Calif., 1994-97. Designer floral collector plate series Danbury Mint/MBI, Inc., gift items Enesco Internat. Gift Co.; represented by Casay Gallery, Kailau, Kona, Hawaii, 1991, Galeria Jean Lammelin, Paris, 1991, 2d St. Gallery, Encinitas, Calif., 1991, Blondes Gallery, San Diego, 1992, Valentine-Owens Gallery, Santa Monica, Calif., 1992, Sodarco Gallery, Montreal, 1993, Surtex, 1993, Jacob G. Javity Conv. Ctr., N.Y.C., 1993, Laura Larkin Gallery, Del Mar, Calif., 1993-94, Charles Hecht Galleries, Tarzana and Palm Desert, Calif., 1993-94, 95-96, Lou Martin Gallery, Laguna Beach, Calif., 1994, Charles Hecht Gallery, La Jolla, Calif., 1995-96, Calif. Art Gallery, Laguna Beach, 1996, Hunter Gallery, Tucson, 1996, Cottage Gallery at Carmel, Calif., 1996, Dy'ans-Branham Gallery, Laguna Beach, 1997-98, 99, Aka'mai Gallery, Del Mar, 1998, 99, Gallery Adrienne, La Jolla, 1998, Cosmopolitan Gallery, La Jolla, Calif., 1998-99, The Lillian Berkley Collection, Escondido, Calif., 1999—; one-woman shows include AKA Mai Gallery, 1999, Lillian Berkeley Collection, 2001, Four Seasons-Aviara, La Costa, Calif., 2001. Pres. Zonta Internat., Oceanside, 1980-81; mem. Emblem Club #177, Oceanside, 1971-98; princess Daughters of the Nile, San Diego, 1974; bd. dirs. Oceanside Girls Club, 1980. Recipient 1st Pl. award San Dieguito Art Guild, 1978, 85, 2nd Pl. award, 1983, 89, 3rd Pl. award, 1983, 1990; winner People's Choice award Internat. Show of Women Artists of the West, Las Vegas, 1992. Mem. North County Art Assn. (founder), Carlsbad Oceanside Art League, 1978, San Dieguito Art Guild, Fallbrook Art Assn., San Diego Art Inst., Assn. pour Promotion Artiste Français, ARTISPHERE. Avocations: ceramics, sculpture, swimming. Office: Palette 'N Easel Studio 1021 S Coast Hwy Oceanside CA 92054-5004 E-mail: Pammie.wiggle@worldnet.att.net.

SARKISSIAN, NAVER AGOP, pathologist; d. Yuhaper Garabed and Agop Sarkis Hazarosyan; m. Assen Petrov Bogdanov, Sept. 21, 1995; children: Mark Alan Bogdanoff, Marie Juliette Bogdanoff. BS, Med. Coll., Varna, Bulgaria, 1980; MD, Med. Sch., Varna, Bulgaria, 1987; PhD, Med. Acad., Moscow, 1993. Lab. technologist dept. microbiology, virology and immunology Sch. of Medicine, Varna, 1980—81; clin. pathologist divsn. med. microbiology and virology Inst. of Epidemiology, 1987—89; post-doctoral rsch. assoc. St. Jude Children's Rsch. Hosp., Memphis, 1994—96; rsch. scientist Columbia U. Coll. of Physicians and Surgeons, N.Y.C., 1996—98, Cornell U. Med. Coll., N.Y.C., 1998—99. Recipient fellowship in med. virology, Bulgarian Ministry of Edn., 1989—93. Mem.: Union of Bulgarian Physicians, Internat. Med. Assn., Bulgaria, Am. Soc. for Virology. Avocations: travel, music, crafts, reading, cooking. Home: 31-11 Crescent St Apt C-5 Astoria NY 11106 Home Fax: 718-726-1517. Personal E-mail: n_sarkissian@hotmail.com.

SARLAT, GLADYS, public relations consultant; b. Elizabeth, N.J., July 22, 1923; d. Max and Dora (Levin) S. BS, U. Wash., 1946. Asst. Kay Sullivan Assocs., N.Y.C., 1949-50; fashion dir. Warsaw & Co., 1950-54; asst. fashion coord. Emporium Dept. Store, San Francisco, 1955-56; prodn. mgr. Cunningham & Walsh Advt., 1957-58; v.p., pub. rels. dir. Harwood Advt. Inc., Tucson and Phoenix, 1959-68; v.p., dir. Waller & Sarlat Advt. Inc., Tucson, 1968-69; pres. Godwin & Sarlat Pub. Rels., Inc., 1970-87, cons., 1988—; of counsel Liess Peck & Godwin, LP&G, 1993—. Cons. in field. Mem. adv. com. Downtown Devel. Corp., 1979-85, Festival in the Sun; bd. dirs. Tucson Conv. and Vis. Bur., 1993-95, Greater Tucson Devel. Com., 1999—. Named Woman of Yr. for Bus., Ariz. Daily Star, 1963; recipient Lulu award L.A. Woman in Advt., 1962. Mem. Pub. Rels. Soc. Am. (past bd. dirs., counselors acad.), Fashion Group, Tucson Met. C. of C. (v.p., dir. 1976-85, chmn. bd. 1986-87, Tucson Woman of Yr. 1990). Republican. Jewish. Home: 5530 N Camino Arenosa Tucson AZ 85718-5417 Office: 177 N Church Ave Ste 315 Tucson AZ 85701-1154 E-mail: gspr@mindspring.com.

SARLE, CHARLES RICHARD, health facility executive; b. Saratoga Springs, N.Y., Sept. 21, 1944; s. John Robert and Marjorie Elizabeth (Swick) S.; m. Marion D. Wallace, June 21, 1968; children: Richard Charles, Robert Edmond. BBA cum laude, Northea. U., 1968; MBA, Babson Coll., 1973. CPA, Mass., Vt. Staff acct. Price Waterhouse & Co., Boston, 1968-70, George Kanavich, CPA, Wellesley, Mass., 1970-72; controller Human Resource Inst., Boston, 1972-73, adminstr., 1973-77; controller Brattleboro (Vt.) Retreat, 1977-78, dir. adminstrn., 1978-85, v.p., 1985-88, chief exec. officer, 1988-97; pres., CEO Carrier Found., Belle Mead, N.J., 1997—. Speaker in field. Mem. commn. Vt. Health Bldg. Fin. Agy., 1978-90; trustee Austine Sch. for Deaf and Hard of Hearing, 1990-97, pres., 1994-97; trustee Winston Prouty Ctr. for Child Devel., 1982-97, treas., 1983-90, sec., 1991-97; trustee Health Rsch. and Edn. Trust N.J., 1998-99, N.J. Hosp. Assn., policy devel. com., 1998-01, fin. com., 2000-01; bd. govs. Nat. Conf. Christians and Jews, 1998—, exec. com., 1999—. Recipient recognition award Brattleboro C. of C., 1985. Fellow AICPA, Mass. Soc. CPAs, Am. Coll. Healthcare Execs. (regent Va. br. 1991-95); mem. Am. Hosp. Assn. (del.-at-large 1988-92, del.-at-large to regional policy bd.), Nat. Assn. Pvt. Psychiat. Hosps. (bd. dirs. polit. action com. 1983-93, trustee 1998-2000), Nat. Psychiat. Alliance (trustee 1989-96, pres. 1994-96), Vt. Soc. CPAs (Comty. Svc. award 1984), Hosp. Fin. Mgmt. Assn. (mem. hosp. cost com. 1985-96), Rescue, Inc. (trustee 1982-83), New Eng. Healthcare Assembly (trustee 1995-97). Republican. Avocations: skiing, fishing, tennis, photography. Home: PO Box 840 Belle Mead NJ 08502-0840 Office: Carrier Foundation Rt 601 Belle Mead NJ 08502 E-mail: rsarle@carrierclinic.com.

SARLES, HARVEY B. humanities educator; b. Buffalo, July 12, 1933; s. Leonard and Hattie (Rosen) S.; m. Janis Marie Hardy, Nov. 18, 1956; children: Amy Sarles Oakes, Stefan Hardy. BA, SUNY, Buffalo, 1954, MA, 1959; PhD, U. Chgo., 1966. Mathematician Cornell Aero. Lab., Buffalo, 1955-57; asst. prof. anthropology U. Pitts., 1962-66; from assoc. prof. to prof. anthropology U. Minn., Mpls., 1966-86, prof. cultural studies, comparative lit., 1986—. Adj. faculty Humanist Inst., N.Y.C., 1986—; dir. Ctr. Comparative Thought, Mpls., 1980-86. Author: Language and Human Nature, 1985, Teaching As Dialogue, 1993, Nietzsche's Prophecy, 2001. Mem. MLA. Avocation: playing violin. Home: 1225 Lasalle Ave Minneapolis MN 55403-2361 Office: Univ Minn CSCL-350 Folwell Minneapolis MN 55455 E-mail: sarle001@umn.edu.

SARLES, RICHARD M. medical educator; b. May 29, 1935; BS, Georgetown U., 1957; MD, U. Md., Balt., 1961. Dir. child and adolescent psychiatry Sheppard Pratt Hosp., 1983-92, U. Md., 1992-99. Contbr. over 75 articles to profl. jours. and books. Office: U Md Sch Medicine 701 W Pratt St Baltimore MD 21201-1549

SARMA, P. S. BALASUBRAMANIA, medical educator; b. India, Aug. 8, 1941; came to U.S., 1964; m. Diana Sarma; 3 children. MB BS, U. Madras, India, 1964. Bd. cert. in psychiatry and child and adolescent psychiatry. Assoc. prof. dept. psychiatry Finch U. Health Sci. Chgo. Med. Sch., North Chicago, Ill., 1980—. Mem. Ill. Med. Disciplinary Bd., Chgo., 1992-98, chmn., 1998-2000. Office: Chgo Med Sch Finch U Health Sci 3333 Greenbay Rd North Chicago IL 60064

SARNA, HELEN HOROWITZ, retired librarian, educator; b. London, Aug. 3, 1923; came to U.S., 1951; d. Elisha and Rachel Leah (Landau) Horowitz; m. Nahum M. Sarha; children: David E.Y., Jonathan D. BS, Columbia U.; B in Hebrew Lit., Jewish Theol. Sem.; M in Hebrew Lit., Hebrews Coll.; MLS, Simmons Coll. Libr. Asst. dir. Hebrew Coll., Brookline, Mass., 1965-90; libr. dir. Hist. Soc., Waltham, Am. Jewish Hist. Soc., Boston, 1992-95, Fla. Atlantic U., Boca Raton, Fla., 1995-96; ret., 1996. Mem. Assn. Jewish Librs. Democrat. Jewish. Avocations: reading, studying. Home: 7886 Chula Vista Cres Boca Raton FL 33433-4101 Fax: (561) 395-7289. E-mail: nmsarna@juno.com., nsarna@fau.edu.

SARNA, JONATHAN DANIEL, history educator; b. Phila., Jan. 10, 1955; m. Ruth Langer; children: Aaron Yehuda, Leah Livia. B of Hebrew Lit. with honors, Hebrew Coll., 1974; BA in Judaic Studies and History summa cum laude with highest honors, Brandeis U., 1975; MA in History, Yale U., 1976, MPhil in History, 1978, PhD in History, 1979. Vis. lectr. Hebrew Union Coll.-Jewish Inst. Religion, 1979-80, from asst. prof. to assoc. prof. to prof. Am. Jewish History, 1980-90; Joseph H. & Belle R. Braun prof. Am. Jewish History Brandeis U., Waltham, Mass., 1990—, chmn. dept., 1992-95, 98-01. Cons. Am.-Holy Land Project, 1978—, rschr., 1975-77; abstractor, cons. ABC-CLIO, 1981—; core constituency mem. Conf. on Religion and Life of Nation, Indpls., 1983-85; adv. bd. Maurice Amado Found., 1990-95; mem. grad. fellowship com. Wexner Found., 1989-93; adj. com. Ctr. for Study of N.Am. Jewry, Ben-Gurion U., Israel, 1991—, Ctr. for Am. Jewish History, Temple U., 1991—; dir. Am. Jewish Experience Curriculum Project, 1982—, Boston Jewish History Project, 1992-95, Ctr. for Study Am. Jewish Experience, 1986-90, acad. advisor, 1981-84, acad. directory, 1984-86; asst. in Am. history Yale U., 1978; vis. assoc. prof. Hebrew U., Jerusalem, 1986-87; vis. asst. prof. Judaic studies U. Cin., 1983-84; chmn. bd. Hebrew-Judaic Online Network in Jewish Studies; chair acad. adv. and editl. bd. Jacob-Rader Marcus Ctr. of Am. Jewish Archives; dir. Gralla Fellowship Program for Journalists in the Jewish Press, Bernard and Rhoda Sarnat Ctr. for the Study of Anti-Jewishness.lectr. in field. Author: Jacksonian Jew: The Two Worlds of Mordecai Noah, 1981, The American Jewish Experience: A Reader, 1986, rev. edit., 1997, JPS: The Americanization of Jewish Culture (A History of the Jewish Publication Soc. 1888-1988), 1989, (with Alexandra S. Korros) American Synagogue History: A Bibliography and State-of-the-Field Survey, 1988, (with Janet Liss) Yahadut Amerika: American Jewry: An Annotated Bibliography of Publications in Hebrew, 1991, (with Nancy H. Klein) The Jews of Cincinnati, 1989, (with Ellen Smith) The Jews of Boston, 1995, (with David G. Dalin) Religion and State in the American Jewish Experience, 1997 (Choice Outstanding Acad. Book of 1998); editor, translator People Walk on Their Heads: Moses Weinberger's Jews and Judaism in New York, 1982; co-editor: Jews and the Founding of the Republic, 1985; editor: (with Daniel J. Elazar and Rela Geffen Monson) A Double Bond: The Constitutional Documents of American Jewry, 1992, (with Henry D. Shapiro) Ethnic Diversity and Civic Identity: Patterns of Conflict and Cohesion in Cincinnati Since 1820, 1992, (with Lloyd Gartner) Yehude Artsot Ha-Berit, 1992, (with Mark A. Raider and Ronald W. Zweig) Abba Hillel Silver and American Zionism, 1997, (with Pamela S. Nadell) Women and American Judaism: Historical Perspectives, 2001; editor: Observing America's Jews (Marshall Sklare), 1993, Minority Faiths and the American Protestant Mainstream, 1997. Acting asst. libr. Am. Jewish Hist. Soc., 1973-75, chmn. acad. coun., 1992-95; v.p. Cin. chpt. Am. Jewish Com., 1985-88, bd. dirs., 1982-84, 88-90; dir. Cin. Coun. for Soviet Jews, 1986—, chmn. adv. bd., 1987-90; leadership coun. Cin. Jewish Fedn., 1981-88, edn. planning and budgeting com., 1982-84, strategic planning com., 1985-86; bd. dirs. Congregation B'nai Tzedek, chmn. adult Jewish edn., 1981-86; bd. dirs. U. Cin. Hillel Found., 1981-86, New Jewish H.S.; active Am. Hist. Assn., Can. Jewish Hist. Soc. Recipient Benjamin J. Shevach Meml. prize for disting. leadership in Jewish edn., 2000; Hebrew Free Loan Assn. fellow Am. Jewish Hist. Soc., 1974-75, Charles Andrew fellow Yale U., 1976-77, Howard F. Brinton fellow Yale U., 1977-78, Loewenstein-Wiener fellow Am. Jewish Archives, 1977, fellow Nat. Found. for Jewish Culture, 1977-79, Meml. Found. for Jewish Culture, 1977-79, 82, 83, Lady Davis Endowment, 1986-87, 2001, Bernard and Audre Rapoport fellow Am. Jewish Archives, 1979-80; PEW endowment grantee, 1991-94, Lilly Endowment grantee, 1984-93. Mem. Am. Acad. Religion, Assn. for Jewish Studies, Orgn. Am. Historians, Am. Hist. Assn., Am. Jewish Hist. Soc., Phi Beta Kappa. Office: Brandeis UDept Near Eastern & Judaic Studies MS 054 Waltham MA 02454 Fax: (781) 736-2070. E-mail: sarna@brandeis.edu.

SARNAT, BERNARD GEORGE, plastic surgeon, educator, researcher; b. Chgo., Sept. 1, 1912; s. Isadore M. and Fanny (Silverman) S.; m. Rhoda Elaine Gerard, Dec. 25, 1941; children: Gerard, Joan. SB, U. Chgo., 1933, MD, 1937; MS, DDS, U. Ill., 1940. Diplomate Am. Bd. Plastic Surgery. Intern Los Angeles County Gen. Hosp., 1936-37; resident oral and plastic surgery Cook County Hosp., Chgo., 1940-41; asst. to Dr. Marshall Davison (gen. surgery) Univ. Hosp., 1942-43; asst. to Drs. Vilray P. Blair and Louis T. Byars (plastic and reconstructive surgery), St. Louis, 1943-46; practice medicine specializing in plastic surgery Chgo., 1946-56, Beverly Hills, Calif., 1956-91; asst. histology U. Ill. Coll. Dentistry, 1937-40, prof., head dept. oral and maxillofacial surgery, 1946-56; asst. dept. surgery, divsn. plastic surgery Washington U. Sch. Medicine, St. Louis, 1944-46; prof., dir. dept. oral and plastic surgery St. Louis U. Coll. Dentistry, 1945-46; clin. asst. prof. surgery (plastic surgery) U. Ill. Coll. Medicine, 1949-56; adj. prof. oral biology Sch Dentistry UCLA, 1969—, mem. Dental Rsch. Inst., 1974-95, adj. prof. plastic surgery Sch. Medicine, 1974—; attending staff Cedars-Sinai Med. Ctr., L.A., 1956-91, emeritus, 1991—, mem. staff, sr. rsch. scientist, chief plastic surgery, 1961-81. Cons. in gen., plastic and maxillofacial surgery VA Regional Office, Chgo., until 1956; lectr. in field. Sr. author: (with Dr. Isaac Schour) Oral and Facial Cancer, 2nd edit., 1957, (with Dr. Daniel Laskin) Surgery of the Temporomandibular Joint, 1964; editor: (with Daniel Laskin) The Temporomandibular Joint A Biological Basis for Clinical Practice, 4th edit., 1991, (with Andrew D. Dixon) Factors and Mechanisms Affecting Growth of Bone, 1982, Normal and Abnormal Bone Growth: Basic and Clinical Research, 1985, Fundamentals of Bone Growth: Methodology and Applications, 1991; contbr. chpts. to textbooks, articles to surg. and sci. jours., other pubs. Co-winner Joseph A. Capps prize for med. rsch. Inst. Medicine, Chgo., 1940, Frederick B. Noyes prize, 1940; recipient Kerbs award for rsch. plastic and reconstructive surgery, 1950, 1st prize, sr. award Found. Am. Soc. Plastic and Reconstructive surgeons, 1957, Beverly Hills Acad. of Medicine award, 1959, Nat. Achievement award medicine Phi Epsilon Pi, 1964, 1st prize Am. Rhinologic Soc., 1980, medal Hebrew U., Jerusalem, 1985, medal Tel Aviv U., 1985, Disting. Svc. Alumni award U. Chgo. Pritzker Sch. Medicine, 1987, hon. award Am. Soc. Maxillofacial Surgeons, 1990, Dallas B. Phemister Profl. Achievement award Dept. Surgery U. Chgo., 1993, Disting. Alumnus award U. Ill. Coll. Dentistry, 1994, Craniofacial Biology Rsch. award Internat. Assn. for Dental Rsch., 1995, Disting. Scientist award, Pioneer in Medicine award Cedars-Sinai Med. Soc., L.A., 1999. Fellow ACS, AAAS, Am. Assn. Plastic Surgeons (hon. award 2000); mem. Calif. Med. Soc., L.A. Med. Soc., Am. Soc. Plastic and Reconstructive Surgeons, Plastic Surgery Rsch. Coun. (founding mem. 1955, chmn. 1957), Calif. Soc. Plastic Surgeons, Beverly Hills Acad. Medicine (pres. 1962-63), Internat. Assn. Craniofacial Biology, Am. Assn. Pediat. Plastic Surgeons (hon.), Am. Assn. Phys. Anthropologists, Internat. Assn. Study Dento-Facial Abnormalities (hon.), Sigma Xi, Omicron Kappa Upsilon, Zeta Beta Tau, Phi Delta Epsilon, Alpha Omega (Internat. Achievement medal 1988). Home: 1875 Kelton Ave Apt 301 Los Angeles CA 90025-8505 E-mail: bsarnat@earthlink.net.

SARNELLE, JOSEPH R. electronic publishing specialist, magazine and newspaper editor; b. Bklyn., Aug. 24, 1951; s. Alphonse Louis and Julie Lena (Mingarelli) S.; m. Ruth Patricia Cullen, Aug. 5, 1982; children: Cullen Joseph, D'Arcy Emilie. BA, Cornell U., 1973; postgrad., Sch. Visual Arts, N.Y.C., 1976-77, The New Sch., 1979-80. Graphic artist Lewahl KC Graphics, N.Y.C., 1974-76; editor United Bus. Publs., 1976-79; mng. editor Lebhar-Friedman Inc., 1979-88; assoc. mng. editor HomeOwner Mag., 1988-90; mgr. online sys. devel. Info. Builders Inc., 1990—. Cons. video Markham-Novelle Pub. Rels., N.Y.C., 1988-89; cons. Best info. Family Media, N.Y.C., 1990-91. Author, dir. (videos) J. Roland Pepe's Guide to New York City, 1980, Underground Roundup, 1981. Recipient McMullen scholar, Cornell U., Regents scholar, State of N.Y., 1969; Best Headline of Year award Lebhar-Friedman Inc., 1982. Office: Info Builders Inc 2 Penn Plz New York NY 10121

SARNER, RICHARD ALAN, lawyer; b. Stamford, Conn., Aug. 6, 1955; s. George and Patricia (Sloman) S.; m. Sharyn Frank, Apr. 5, 1986; children: Bryan, Lauren. BA, Dartmouth Coll., 1977; JD, Hofstra U., 1980. Bar: N.Y. 1982, U.S. Dist. Ct. (so. and ea. dists.) N.Y. 1982, U.S. Ct. Appeals (2d cir.) 1985, U.S. Dist. Ct. (no. dist.) N.Y. 1989, Conn. 1990, U.S. Dist. Ct. Conn. 1991, U.S. Supreme Ct. 1991. Assoc. Shea & Gould, N.Y.C., 1980-82, D'Amato & Lynch, N.Y.C., 1982-84, Lowenthal, Landau, Fischer & Ziegler, P.C., N.Y.C., 1984-90; sole practice Stamford, Conn., N.Y.C., Conn., 1990—. Bd. dirs. The Stamford Mus. and Nature Ctr., 1993-99; trustee King & Low-Heywood Thomas Sch., 1994—. Mem. ABA, N.Y. State Bar Assn., Conn. Bar Assn., Stamford/Norwalk Regional Bar Assn., Nat. Network Estate Planning Attys. Democrat. Home: 122 Frost Pond Rd Stamford CT 06903-3031 Office: 184 Atlantic St Stamford CT 06901-3518 also: 465 Park Ave Ste 10C New York NY 10022 E-mail: rsarner@sarnerlaw.com.

SARNEY, SAUL RICHARD, lawyer; b. Bklyn., Dec. 6, 1948; s. Albert Abraham and Edna (Goldstein) S. BA, Binghamton U., 1970; JD, U. Denver, 1973. Founding ptnr./shareholder Sarney, Trattler & Waitkus, PC, Denver, 1974—93; ptnr. Pelz & Sarney P.C., 1993—96; ptnr., shareholder Sarney & Pierson, PC, 1996—2001; pvt. practice Law Firm of Saul R. Sarney, P.C., 2001—. Guest lectr. Aurora (Co.) C.C., 1992—; seminar spkr. Profl. Edn. Syss., Inc., various seminars, programs & classes, 1976—. Past pres., bd. dirs. Diana Price Fish Found., Denver, 1993—; cornerstone ptnr. Colo. AIDS Project, Denver, 1993—. Mem. ATLA (ins., motor vehicle, profl. negligence and r.r. law sects.), Colo. Bar Assn. (chmn. interprofl. com., legal fee arbitration com.), Colo. Trial Lawyers Assn., Nebr. Trial Lawyers Assn., Denver Bar Assn. Avocations: film, cycling, scuba diving, wine, travel. Office: Law firm of Saul R Sarney 3900 E Mexico Ave Ste 330 Denver CO 80210-3942

SARNO, MARIA ERLINDA, lawyer, scientist; b. Manila, Philippines, July 26, 1944; BS in Chemistry magna cum laude, U. Santo Tomas, Philippines, 1967; MS in Chemistry summa cum laude, Calif. State U., Long Beach, 1975; JD cum laude, Western State U., 1993. Bar: Calif. 1994, U.S. Patent Office, 1993. Instr. U. Santo Tomas, Philippines, 1967-68; sr. chemist, analytical rsch. and quality assurance Rachelle Labs., Long Beach, Calif., 1969-74; teaching/rsch. asst. Calif. State U., Long beach, 1971-73; mgr. in charge of radioisotope section Curtis Nuclear Lab., L.A., 1974; assoc. chemist, asst. to dir. quality control Nichols Inst., San Pedro, Calif., 1974-75; mgr. rsch. and devel. Baxter Healthcare, Hyland, 1975-91; legal coord. sci. affairs Immunotherapy div. Baxter Biotech, Irvine, 1991-93, mgr. regulatory affairs, 1994-95; pvt. law practice, 1994—; bd. dirs. Small Bus. Fin. Devel. Corp. Editorial bd: (tech. editor) Western State U. Law Review; Contbr. articles to profl. jours.; patentee in field. Pres. Asian Bus. Assn. Orange County, 2001. Mem. ABA, Los Angeles County Bar Assn., Am. Chem. Soc., Am. Intellectual Property Law Assn., Filipino Am. C. of C. Orange County (asst. treas.). Home: 12541 Kenobi Ct Cerritos CA 90703-7756 E-mail: lindasarno@aol.com.

SARNO, MARTHA TAYLOR, speech and language pathologist, educator; b. N.Y.C., Nov. 25, 1927; d. Edward and Milagros Abril-Lamarque; m. John Ernest Sarno, Jan. 8, 1967; 1 child, Christina. BA, Mich. State U., 1949; MA, NYU, 1954; D in medicine honoris causa, U. Goteborg, Sweden, 1982. Cert. Am. Bd. Neurogenic Comm. Disorders in Adults and Chilren. Speech-lang. pathologist Goldwater Meml. Hosp., N.Y.C., 1949-50; dir. speech-lang. pathology dept. Rusk Inst. Rehab. Medicine, 1950—; instr. prof. dept. rehab. medicine NYU Sch. Medicine, 1957-65, asst. prof. dept. rehab. medicine, 1965-78, assoc. prof., 1978-90, prof., 1990—; asst. prof. dept. speech-lang. pathology NYU Sch. Edn., 1964-73. Faculty Kurt Goldstein Inst. Neuropsychology, Straubing, Germany, 1995—; chmn. tech. adv. speech and lang. disorder Dept. Health, N.Y.C., 1967-77; mem. task force to study ethics in rehab. medicine Hastings Ctr., Briarcliff Manor, N.Y., 1985-88; cons. editor jour. Comm. Disorders, 1967-91. Co-author: Stroke: The Condition and The Patient, 1979; editor: Acquired Aphasia, 1981, 3rd edit., 1999; editor: Topics in Stroke Rehabilitation, 1995. Founder, pres. Nat. Aphasia Assn., 1987—; charter mem. Acad. Aphasia, 1962—, bd. govs., 1979-83, 90-96. Recipient Outstanding Alumni award Mich. State U., 1976, Rusk award Howard A. Rusk Inst. Rehab. Medicine, 1985, Frank Kleffner Lifetime Career Achievement award Speech Found. Am., 1998. Fellow Am. Speech-Lang.-Hearing Assn. (Honors of the Assn. award 1999); mem. Am. Congress Rehab. Medicine (Gold Key award 1974), Acad. Aphasia (chmn. sci. program com. 1969-72), Acad. Neurologic Comm. Disorders and Scis. (bd. cert.), Daily Points of Light award 2001). Office: New York Univ Sch Medicine Dept Rehab Medicine 400 E 34th St New York NY 10016-4901

SARNOFF, IRVING, retired psychology educator, author; b. Bklyn., May 5, 1922; s. Nathan and Rose (Gelfand) S.; m. Suzanne Fischbach, Nov. 28, 1946; children: David, Sara Sarnoff Palmer. BA, CUNY, 1946; MA, U. Mich., 1949, PhD, 1951. Mental hygienist, sr. psychologist Student Health Svc., U. Mich., Ann Arbor, 1951-54; asst. prof. psychology Yale U., New Haven, 1955-60;

prof. psychology and social work Western Res. U., Cleve., 1960-62; prof. psychology NYU, N.Y.C., 1962-92, prof. emeritus, 1992—. Editl. advisor Ency. Brit., Chgo., 1968-98. Author: Personality Dynamics and Development, 1962, Society with Tears, 1966; co-editor (with Suzanne Sarnoff): Testing Freudian Concepts, 1971; author: Sexual Excitement/Sexual Peace, 1979, Love-Centered Marriage in a Self-Centered World, 1989, Intimate Creativity, 2002. With U.S. Army, 1943-46, PTO. Fulbright advanced rsch. scholar Univ. Coll., London, 1954-55; NIMH sr. grantee Tavistock Ctr., London, 1968-69. Mem. APA... Avocation: art. Home: 1 Washington Square Vlg Apt 14V New York NY 10012-1610

SARNOFF, JOSEPH C. academic administrator; b. Bronx, N.Y., Apr. 3, 1946; s. Philip and Jeannette (Seiden) S.; divorced; children: Allison, Philip, Julie. BA, Northland Coll., 1968; MS, U. Wis., Milw., 1969, Clarkson U., 1978. Lectr. biology Bronx Cmty. Coll., 1970; from assoc. dir. student union to dir. student union, activities and volunteerism SUNY, Potsdam, 1970—. Acting village justice Village of Potsdam, 1986, 89—, chair zoning bd., 1988-90, co-chair com. to rewrite zoning codes, 1989. Recipient Pres. award for excellence in pub. svc. SUNY, Potsdam, 1992, Point of Excellence award Kappa Delta Pi, 1995. Mem. Assn. Colls. & Univs. Internat., Nat. Assn. Coll. Activities, N.Y. State Magistrates Assn., SUNY Coll. Union Profls., Points of Light Found. Avocations: long distance running, biking, refinishing antique furniture. Office: SUNY Potsdam 44 Pierrepont Ave Potsdam NY 13676-2294

SARNOFF, LILI-CHARLOTTE (LOLO SARNOFF), artist, executive; b. Frankfurt, Germany (as Swiss citizen), Jan. 9, 1916; arrived in U.S., 1940; d. Willy and Martha (Koch von Hirsch) Dreyfus; m. Stanley Jay Sarnoff, 1948; children: Daniela Martha Bargezi, Robert L. Grad., Reimann Art Sch., Germany, 1936, U. Berlin, 1936-38; student, U. Florence, Italy, 1948-54. Rsch. asst. Harvard Sch. Pub. Health, 1950-54; rsch. assoc. cardiac physiology Nat. Heart Inst., Bethesda, Md., 1954-59; pres. Rodana Rsch. Corp., 1959—61; v.p. Catrix Corp., 1959—61. Inventor Flolite light scupltures under name Lolo Sarnoff, 1968—; one-woman shows include: Agra Gallery, Washington, 1969, Corning (N.Y.) Glass Ctr. Mus., 1970, Gallery Two, Woodstock, Vt., 1970, Gallery Marc, Washington, 1971, 72, Franz Bader Gallery, Washington, 1976, Gallery K, Washington, 1978, 81, 85, 87, 91, Restrospective Show 1995, Alwin Gallery, London, 1981, Galerie von Bartha, Basel, Switzerland, 1982, La Galerie L'Hotel de Ville, Geneva, 1982, Pfalzgalerie, Kaiserslautern, Fed. Republic Germany, 1985, Galerie Les Hirondelles, Geneva, 1988, Rockville (Md.) Civic Ctr., 1988, Washington Square Sculpture group, 1989, Internat. Sculpture Congress, Washington, 1990, Sculpture on the Grounds, Rockville, 1996; represented in collections: Brookings Inst., Washington, Corning Glass Ctr. Mus., Nat. Air and Space Mus., Washington, Kennedy Ctr., Washington, Nat. Acad. Sci., Washington, Chase Manhattan Bank, N.Y.C., Israel Mus., Jerusalem, Nat. Mus. Women in Arts, Washington, Corcoran Gallery of Art, Washington, others; transcriber: Dara Autobiography of a Chesapeake Bay Retriever, 1999. Founder, pres. Arts for the Aging, Inc., Bethesda, 1988—; active Washington Opera Soc., Washington Ballet Soc., bd. overseers Corcoran Gallery Art, 1991--; pres. Dara's Canine Found., Inc., 1999—. Recipient Golda Meir award, 1995; recipient Life Commitment to the Arts award Swiss Am. Cultural Exch., 1999, Path of Achievement award for Arts and Humanities, Montgomery County, Md., 2000, Outstanding Citizen award Iona Sr. Citizen Svcs., Washington, 2002. Home: 7507 Hampden Ln Bethesda MD 20814-1331 E-mail: lolos@erols.com.

SARNOFF, THOMAS WARREN, television executive; b. N.Y.C., Feb. 23, 1927; s. David and Lizette (Hermant) S.; m. Janyce Lundon, May 21, 1955; children: Daniel, Timothy, Cynthia. Grad., Phillips Acad., 1939-43; student, Princeton, 1943-45; BS in Elec. Engring., Stanford U., 1948, postgrad. Sch. Bus. Adminstrn., 1948-49; D.H.L., Columbia Coll. Engaged in prodn. and sales with ABC, Inc., 1949-51; prodn. Metro-Goldwyn-Mayer, 1951-52; with NBC, 1952-77; v.p. prodn. and bus. affairs NBC (Pacific div.), 1956-60, v.p. adminstrn. West Coast, 1960-62, v.p. charge West Coast, 1962-65, staff exec. v.p. West Coast, 1965-77; pres. NBC Entertainment Corp., 1972-77, Sarnoff Internat. Enterprises, 1977-81, Sarnoff Entertainment Corp., 1981—; exec. v.p. Venturetainment Corp., 1981-87, pres., 1987—. Bd. dirs. Multimedia Games, Inc., 1998—. Exec. producer Bonanza: The Next Generation, 1987, Bonanza: The Return, 1993, Back to Bonanza Retrospective, 1993, Bonanza: Under Attack, 1995. Mem. Calif. Commn. for Reform Intermediate and Secondary Edn. Pres., Research Found., St. Joseph Hosp., Burbank, 1965-73, Permanant Charities Com. of Entertainment Industries, 1971-72; nat. trustee Nat. Conf. Christians and Jews. Served with Signal Corps AUS, World War II. Mem. Acad. TV Arts and Scis. (chmn. bd. trustees 1972-74, chmn. past pres.'s coun. 1989-92), Acad. TV Arts and Scis. Found. (pres. 1990-99, chmn., CEO 1999—), The Caucus for Prodrs., Writers and Dirs. Office: 2451 Century Hl Los Angeles CA 90067-3510

SAROCCO, PHIL(LIP) W(ILLIAM), health economist, researcher, pharmacist; b. Pittsfield, Mass., Dec. 15, 1960; s. Philip Victor and Rosemary Josephine Sarocco; m. Mary Jane Sarocco, June 6, 1992; children: Adriana, Julia, Erin. MSc, Harvard U., 1993; RPh, Mass. Coll. Pharmacy, 1988. Registered clin. pharmacist. Home health care/hosp. clin., Boston and Chgo., 1989-93; clin. pharmacist Children's Meml. Hosp., Chgo., 1990-91; project mgmt. officer environ. health and devel. UN Office Project Svcs., N.Y.C., 1993-94; rsch. analyst UN Population Fund, 1994; health outcomes rsch. cons. Pfizer Internat. Pharms., 1994-95; mgr. outcomes rsch. Abbott Labs., Chgo., 1995-97; dir. health care econs. Parke-Davis, Morris Plains, N.J., 1997—. Mem. nat. com. on quality Nat. Pharm. Coun., Washington, 1997—; co-chmn. Harvard U. Sch. Pub. Health Student Govt., 1992-93. Co-author: International Perspectives on Environment, Health Development, 1996; contbr. articles to profl. jours. Ensign USPHS, 1992. Recipient scholarship Harvard U., 1992-93. Fellow Am. Diabetes Assn.; mem. Drug Info. Assn. (advisor 1996-98). Avocations: cycling, guitar, skiing, photography. Home: 5 Hilltop Cir Morristown NJ 07960-6312 Office: Aventis US Pharma 300 Somerset Corp Blvd Bridgewater NJ 08807

SARODE, SATYESWARA KRISHNAPPA, physician; b. Bangalore, Karnataka, India, Apr. 17, 1955; came to U.S., 1985; s. Krishnappa P. Sarode and Gangamma Jinde; m. Shashikala Sarode, May 6, 1984 (dec. Apr. 2002); children: Shubha, Sudha, Shilpa. MB BS, Bangalore Med. Coll., 1978. Intern joint diseases North Gen. Hosp., NY; resident Sinai Hosp. Detroit, St. Barnabas Hosp., LaGuardia Hosp. (now North Shore U. Hosp.); house staff St. Claires Hosp.; med. dir. Damon House, New Brunswick, NJ. Mem. ACP, Am. Soc. Internal Medicine. Avocations: working, reading, discussion, gardening. Office: 1445 Us Highway 130 New Brunswick NJ 08902-3100

SARPEL, SULEYMAN CELALETTIN, oncologist; b. Konya, Turkey, June 29, 1943; came to U.S., 1973; s. Namik and Zisan (Arcasoy) S.; m. Gunseli Rasa, Jan. 10, 1970; children: Umut, Dost. MD, Hacettepe U., Ankara, Turkey, 1969. Diplomate in internal medicine and oncology Am. Bd. Internal Medicine. Resident, then fellow in hematology and oncology U. Ill. Hosps., Chgo., 1973-78; instr., then asst. prof. medicine U. Ill., 1978-81; assoc. prof. medicine, chief med. oncology Cukurova U., Adana, Turkey, 1981-83; asst. prof., assoc. prof. medicine U. Health Scis./Chgo. Med. Sch., North Chicago, Ill., 1983-90; pvt. practice oncology Niagara Falls, N.Y., 1990—. Mem. attending staff North Chicago VA Med. Ctr.; vis. prof. Tokten Program, UN, 1990. Contbr. articles to profl. publs. Mem. ACP, Internat. Soc. Exptl. Hematology, Am. Soc. Clin. Oncology, Am. Assn. Cancer Rsch., Turkish Soc. Hematology. Avocations: photography, computers. Office: 6932 Williams Rd Niagara Falls NY 14304-3071

SARRAF, ROBERTA JEAN, planning consultant; b. Pitts., Nov. 9, 1945; d. Walter H. and Margaret E. (Ondof) S. BA, U. Pitts., 1967, M in Urban and Regional Planning, 1969. Intern Rep. James G. Fulton, Washington, 1965; planner Pa. Dept. Community Affairs, Pitts., 1970-76; dir. community devel. Twp. of Upper St. Clair, 1976-82; cons. planning, 1982—. Instr. Pa. Dept. Cmty. Affairs, 1976-95; del. Environ. Planning to People's Republic of China, 1983. Creator and performer (musical program), History of Am. Popular Music. Sec., bd. dirs. Chartiers Mental Health Ctr., Bridgeville, Pa., 1986-90; vol. U. Pitts. Ann. Giving Fund, 1973-90; dem. committeewomen, Mt. Lebanon, Pa., 1965-68, 82-88; mem. long range planning com. and choir Bower Hill Cmty. Ch., elder, 1990-92, sec. meml. gifts com., 1995-96, mem. adminstrn. and pers. com., 1996-98; mem. devel. com. South Hills Family Hospice, 1990-95, Mt. Lebanon Pub. Safety Bldg. Capital Campaign Com., 1998-99. Mem. Am. Planning Assn. (pres. Pitts. chpt. 1982-83), Nat. Assn. Housing and Redevel. Ofcls. (v.p. Pitts. chpt. 1980-81), Pa. Planning Assn. (bd. dirs. 1975-76, state conf. chmn. 1981), Women in Community Devel. (charter), Am. Fedn. Musicians, Grad. Sch. Alumni Assn. (chmn. com. 1987-88), Am. Inst. Cert. Planners, Three Rivers Corvette Club (activities com. 1987), Lions Club (pres. 1990-91, zone chmn. 1991-92, region chmn. 1992-93). Democrat. Presbyterian. Avocations: music, sports, photography, needlework, travel. Home and Office: 1316 Bower Hill Rd Pittsburgh PA 15243-1308

SARREALS, SONIA, data processing consultant; b. N.Y.C., Sept. 17, 1938; d. Espriela and Sadie Beatrice (Scales) Sarreals; m. Waldro Lynch, Sept. 18, 1981 (div. Oct. 1983). BA in Langs. summa cum laude, CCNY, 1960; cert. in French, Sorbonne, Paris, 1961. Systems engr. IBM, N.Y.C., 1963-69; cons. Babbage Systems, 1969-70; project leader Touche Ross, 1970-73; sr. programmer McGraw-Hill, Inc., Hightstown, N.J., 1973-78; staff data processing cons. Cin. Bell Info. Systems, 1978-89; sr. analyst AT&T, 1989-92; lead tech. analyst Automated Concepts Inc., Arlington, Va., 1992-96; tech. cons. Teksystems, Reston, 1996—. Elder St. Andrew Luth. Ch., Silver Spring, 1992-96. Downer scholar CUNY, 1960; Dickman Inst. fellow Columbia U., 1960-61. Mem. Assn. for Computing Machinery, Phi Beta Kappa. Democrat. Avocations: needlework, sewing. Home: 13705 Beret Pl Silver Spring MD 20906-3030 Office: Teksystems 12343 Sunrise Valley Dr Reston VA 20191 E-mail: ssarreals@teksystems.com.

SARRINGAR, MICHAEL RAY, manufacturing executive; b. Fairfax, Mo., Oct. 30, 1959; s. Donald Ray and Marjorie Ann Sarringar; m. Mary Ruth Jordan; children: Stephanie, Jennifer. BSBA, U. Cin., 1981. Operator NOWSCO Svcs., Houston, 1981—83; chem. salesman Uni Lab, 1983—84; tech. mgr. The Goodyear Tire & Rubber Co., Yuba City, Calif., 1984—. Conservative. Presbyterian. Home: 532 Windsor Dr Yuba City CA 95991 Office: Goodyear Tire & Rubber Co 532 Windsor Dr Yuba City CA 95991 Home Fax: 530-751-2445; Office Fax: 530-751-1175. Personal E-mail: Msarringar@aol.com. Business E-Mail: mike_sarringar@goodyear.com.

SARRIS, ANDREW GEORGE, film critic; b. Bklyn., Oct. 31, 1928; s. George Andrew and Themis (Katavolos) S.; m. Molly Clark Haskell, May 31, 1969. AB, Columbia, 1951. Film critic Village Voice, N.Y.C., 1960-89, N.Y. Observer, 1989—. Editor-in-chief Cahiers du Cinema in English; instr. Sch. Visual Arts, 1965-67; asst. prof. N.Y. U., 1967-69; assoc. prof. films Columbia Sch. Arts, N.Y.C., 1969-81, prof., 1981— Author: The Films of Josef Von Sternberg, 1966, Interviews with Film Directors, 1967, The Film, 1968 The American Cinema, 1968, Confessions of a Cultist, 1970, The Primal Screen, 1973, The John Ford Movie Mystery, 1976, Politics and Cinema, 1978. Served with Signal Corps AUS, 1952-54. Guggenheim fellow, 1969 Mem. Am. Film Inst. (dir.), Soc. Cinema Studies, Nat. Soc. Film Critics, N.Y. Film Critics. *I keep on working toward that last deadline.*

SARRO, MICHAEL THOMAS, network administrator; b. Miami Beach, Fla., Dec. 12, 1962; s. Leonard and Annette Frances (Helms) S. BA, Iona Coll., 1985. Libr. Iona Coll., New Rochelle, N.Y., 1989-94; database mgr. Mercy Coll., Dobbs Ferry, 2000—. Author (computer software) Computers and Librs., 1993. Inspector Bd. of Elections, White Plains, N.Y., 1994—; mem. county com. Working Families Party; co-chair Westchester Tenants Coalition. Mem. Assn. of Info. Tech. Profls., N.Y. Jewish Geneal. Soc.. Socialist. Episcopalian. Avocations: computer science, writing and religious research. Home: 5 Prospect St Apt 4S New Rochelle NY 10805-2837 Office: Mercy Coll 555 Broadway Dobbs Ferry NY 10522 E-mail: msarro@mercynet.edu.

SARROCCO, CLARA ANNA, editor, educator; b. Queens, Ny, Mar. 26, 1938; d. Galileo Hugo Sarrocco and Ada Catherine Troiano Sarrocco. BS, Fordham U., New York, NY, 1960; MA, Hunter Coll., New York, NY, 1964; PhD, St. John's U., Queens, NY, 1974, DA, 2000. English educator All Saints H.S., Brooklyn, NY, 1960—73, The Albert Shanker, Long Island City, 1973—2001; exec. assistatn Coun. on Sch. and Nat. Literatures, Queens, 2001—; editor Coun. on Nat. Literatures, 2001—. Contbr. articles to profl. jours. Treas. Glendale Property Owners Inc., Glendale, NY, 1998—2002. Mem.: The NY C.S. Lewis Soc. (sec., treas. 1989—2002). Roman Catholic. Home: 84-23 77 Avenue Glendale NY 11385 Office: Council on National Literatures 68-02 Metropolitan Avenue Middle Village NY 11379

SARROS, P. PETER, diplomat, consultant; b. Greece, Aug. 20, 1935; (parents Am. citizens); s. Basil and Helen Sarros. BA summa cum laude, Hobart Coll., 1957; M Pub. and Internat. Affairs, Princeton U., 1959, PhD, 1964. U.S. fgn. svc. officer Dept. of State, Washington, 1960-92, sr. fgn. affairs cons., 1992—2002. Spl. amb. to the Vatican, 1978; charge US Mission to the Vatican, 1975-80; acting dep. asst. sec. for Human Rights, 1980-82; dir. Regional Polit. Affairs for Latin Am., 1985-92; adj. prof. diplomacy, George Mason U., 1992-93; dipomatic assignments in Venezuela, the Dominican Republic, and Iceland, 1961-67; diplomat in residence Johns Hopkins Sch. Advanced Internat. Studies, 1972-73. W. Wilson fellow Princeton U., 1957-60. Mem. Am. Fgn. Svc. Assn., Ft. Myer Officers Club, Phi Beta Kappa. Avocations: bibliophile. Home: 1200 N Nash St Arlington VA 22209-3616 Office: Dept of State IRM/OPS Washington DC 20520 E-mail: sarrospp@state.gov.

SARRY, CHRISTINE, ballerina; b. Long Beach, Calif., May 25, 1946; d. John and Beatrice (Thomas) S.; 1 child, Maximilian Sarry Varriale. With Joffrey Ballet, 1963-64, Am. Ballet Theatre, 1964-68, prin. dancer, 1971-74; leading dancer Am. Ballet Co., 1969-71; ballerina Eliot Feld Ballet, 1974-81. Mem. faculty Ballet Tech., N.Y.C., also freelance guest tchr. Performed ballets for Agnes DeMille, Antony Tudor, Jerome Robbins, Eliot Feld; appeared at White House, 1963, 67; U.S. Dept. State tours include, Russia, 1963, 66, S.Am., 1964, 76, various tours of N.Am., Orient, Europe, various appearances U.S. nat. TV; partnered by Mikhail Baryshnikov.

SARTAIN, JAMES EDWARD, lawyer; b. Ft. Worth, Feb. 9, 1941; s. James F. and May Belle (Boaz) S.; m. Barbara Hardy, Aug. 17, 1962; 1 child, Bethany Sartain Hughes. BA, Tex. A&M U., 1963; LLB, Baylor U., 1966. Bar: Tex. 1966, U.S. Ct. Mil. Appeals, 1971, U.S. Dist. Ct. (no. dist.) Tex. 1974. Staff atty. Dept. Justice, Washington, 1970-72; staff atty. to U.S. Sen. William L. Scott Fairfax, Va., 1972; pvt. practice Ft. Worth, 1973—; sec. Esprit Comm. Corp., Austin, Tex. Bd. dirs. Ft. Worth Boys Club, 1980-89, Oakwood Cemetery, Ft. Worth, 1979-84; adv. dir. Grady McWhinney Rsch. Found., Abilene, Tex., CAP Initiatives, LLC, Austin, Tex. Capt. arty. U.S. Army, Vietnam. Fellow Coll. State Bar Tex.; mem. ABA, NRA, VFW, Abilene Bar Assn., Baylor Law Alumni Assn., Masons, Phi Delta Phi. Republican. Presbyterian. Home: PO Box 450 Abilene TX 79604-0450

SARTOR, DANIEL RYAN, JR. lawyer; b. Vicksburg, Miss., June 2, 1932; s. Daniel Ryan and Lucy Leigh (Hubbs) S.; m. Olive Guthrie Moss, Oct. 12, 1957; children— Clara M., Daniel Ryan, Walter M. BA, Tulane U., 1952, LL.B., 1955. Bar: La. 1955. Instr. Tulane U., New Orleans, 1955-56, asst. prof., 1956-57; ptnr. Snellings, Breard, Sartor, Inabnett & Trascher, Monroe, La., 1957—. Contbr. articles to profl. jours. Fellow Am. Coll. Trust and Estate Counsel, Am. Coll. Mortgage Attys., Am. Bar Found., La. Bar Found.; mem. La. State Law Inst. (mem. council 1969— , sec. civil law sect. 1969-97, sr. officer 1997—), La. State Bar Assn. (chmn. sect. on trust estate, probate and immovable property 1973-74, bd. govs. 1974-75), Lotus Club, Bayou DeSaird Country Club. Democrat. Methodist. Home: 2405 Pargoud Blvd Monroe LA 71201-2326 Office: Snellings Breard Sartor 1503 N 19th St Monroe LA 71201-4960

SARTORE, J. CHRISTOPHER, family practice physician; b. Ft. Irwin, Kans., July 12, 1962; s. James Ray and Darlene Vivian (Hedrick) S.; m. Rosetta H. Auffart, Oct. 18, 1987; children: Rosanna M., Breanna C., Sara N. AS, Vincennes U., 1982; BS, U. So. Ind., 1984; MD, Ind. U., 1988. Diplomate Am. Bd. Family Practice. Resident in family practice Deaconess Hosp., Evansville, Ind., 1988-89, 93-95; gen. med. officer U.S. Army, Mainz, Germany, 1989-93; family practice physician Welborn Clinic, Evansville, 1995—. Clin. asst. prof. family medicine Ind. U. Sch. Medicine. Mem.: AMA, Vanderburgh County Med. Soc., Ind. Acad. Family Physicians, Am. Acad. Family Practice, KC. Roman Catholic. Avocations: gardening, landscaping, photography, science fiction, golfing. Office: Welborn Clinic Highland 1137 W Mill Rd Evansville IN 47710-3845

SARTORELLI, ALAN CLAYTON, pharmacologist, educator; b. Chelsea, Mass., Dec. 18, 1931; m. Alice C. Anderson, July 7, 1969. BS, New Eng. Coll. Pharmacy Northeastern U., 1953; MS, Middlebury (Vt.) Coll., 1955; PhD, U. Wis., 1958; MA (hon.) , Yale U., 1967. Rsch. chemist Samuel Roberts Noble Found., Ardmore, Okla., 1958—60, sr. rsch. chemist, 1960—61; mem. faculty dept. pharmacology Yale Sch. Medicine, New Haven, 1961—, prof., 1967—, head devel. therapeutics program Comprehensive Cancer Center, 1974—90, chmn. dept. pharmacology, 1977—84, 1998—2000, dep. dir. Comprehensive Cancer Ctr., 1982—84, dir. Comprehensive Cancer Ctr., 1984—93, Alfred Gilman prof. pharmacology, 1987—, prof. epidemiology, 1991—97. Charles B. Smith vis. rsch. prof. Meml. Sloan-Kettering Ctr., 1979; William N. Creasy vis. prof. clin. pharmacology Wayne State U., 1983; Mayo Found. vis. prof. oncology Mayo Clinic, 1983; Walter Hubert lectr. Brit. Assn. Cancer Rsch., 1985; Pfizer lectr. in clin. pharmacology U. Conn. Health Ctr., 1985; William N. Creasy vis. prof. clin. pharmacology Bowman Gray Sch. Medicine, 1987; Wellcome vis. prof. basic sci. U. Pitts. Sch. Medicine, 1990; mem. sci. adv. bd. ImmunoGen, Inc., 1981—90, U. Ind. Cancer Ctr., 1992, Cancer Inst. N.J., 1993—, Cell Pathways, Inc., 1993—; chmn. cancer sci. adv. bd. ViraChem., Inc., 1986—93, The Liposome Co., 1986—2001, Vion Pharms., 1993—, bd. dirs., chmn. sci. adv. bd., 1993—; chmn. vis. sci. adv. com. Columbia U. Comprehensive Cancer Ctr., 1986—99; chmn. pres.'s cancer adv. bd. Fox Chase Cancer Ctr., 1992—; mem. cancer clin. investigation rev. com. Nat. Cancer Inst., 1968—72, mgmt. cons. to dir. divsn. cancer treatment, 1975—77, bd. sci. counselors, divsn. cancer treatment, 1978—81, chmn. com. to establish nat. coop. drug discovery groups, 1982—83, chmn. spl. rev. com. Outstanding Investigator grant applications, 1992, chmn. ad hoc contracts tech. rev. group, 93; mem. instnl. rsch. grants com. Am. Cancer Soc., 1971—76, coun. analysis and projection, 1978—79; cons. in biochemistry U. Tex. M.D. Anderson Hosp. and Tumor Clinic, Houston, 1970—76; cons. Sandoz Forschungs-Institut, Vienna, 1977—80; mem. exptl. therapeutics study sect. NIH, 1973—77, working cadre nat. large bowel cancer project, 1973—76; mem. adv. com. Cancer Rsch. Ctr., Washington U. Sch. Medicine, 1971—75, SLSB Ptnrs., L.P., 1992—96; mem. sci. adv. com. U. Iowa Cancer Ctr., 1979—83; mem. external adv. com. Wis. Clin. Cancer Ctr., 1978—79, Duke Comprehensive Cancer Ctr., 1983—94; mem. external adv. bd. U. Ariz. Cancer Ctr., 1982—92, U. So. Calif. Cancer Ctr., 1983—93, Clin. Cancer Rsch. Ctr., Brown U., 1980—86; mem. nat. program com. 13th Internat. Cancer Congress, 1979—81; cons. Bristol-Myers Co., 1982—93, mem. selection com. prize in cancer rsch., 1977—85, chmn., 1979—81, chmn. selection com. award for disting. achievement in cancer rsch. , 1989—92; bd. advisors Drug and Vaccine Devel. Corp. (Ctr. for Pub. Resources), 1980—81, Specialized Cancer Ctr., Mt. Sinai Med. Ctr., 1981—90, Grace Cancer Drug Ctr., Roswell Park Meml. Inst., 1986—89; mem. med. and sci. adv. com. grants rev. subcom. Leukemia Soc. Am., 1983—88; vs. dirs. Metastasis Rsch. Soc., 1984—90; mem. program planning com. Mary Lasker-Am. Cancer Soc. Conf., 1986; mem. external sci. rev. com. Massey Cancer Ctr., 1989—94; bd. visitors Moffit Cancer Ctr. U. South Fla., 1989—92; dep. dir. Cancer Prevention Rsch. Unit for Conn., 1989—93, acting dir., 1991—93; mem. nat. bd. Cosmetic Toiletry and Fragrance Assn.'s Look Good...Feel Better Program, 1989—91; mem. organizing com. Conf. on Bioreductive Drug Activation, 1993—94; chmn. bd. spl. cons. Inst. for Cancer Therapeutics, 1993—; scientific adv. bd. U. Ill. Cancer Ctr., 2001—. Regional editor Am. Continent Biochem. Pharmacology, 1968—, exec. editor, 1993—, editor-in-chief Cancer Comm., 1969—91, Oncology Rsch., 1993—; editor: Handbuch der experimentellen Pharmakologie vols. on antineoplastic and immunosuppressive agts., series on cancer chemotherapy Am. Chem. Soc. Symposium, 1976, 1976; exec. editor Pharmacology and Therapeutics, 1975—, editl. bd. Internat. Ency. Pharmacology and Therapeutics, 1972—94, Seminars in Oncology, 1973—83, Chemico-Biol. Interactions, 1975—78, Jour. Medicinal Chemistry, 1977—82, Cancer Drug Delivery, 1982—85, Jour. Enzyme Inhibition, 1984—, Jour. Liposome Rsch., 1986—92, In Vivo, 1990, Cancer Biotherapy, 1992—, Cancer Rsch., Therapy and Control, 1993—97, Oncology Reports, 1995—, Molecular and Cellular Differentiation, 1995—, mem. adv. bd. Advances in Chemistry Series, ACS Symposium Series, 1977—80, editl. adv. bd. Cancer Rsch., 1970—71, assoc. editor, 1971—78, Current Awareness in Biol. Scis., Current Advances in Pharmacology and Toxicology, 1983—, Cancer Cells, 1989—91, Jour. Exptl. Therapeutics and Oncology, 1995—, mem. exec. adv. bd. Ency. of Human Bioloty, 1987—90, Dictionary of Sci. and Tech., 1989—91, editl. cons. Biol. Abstracts, 1984—; contbr. articles to profl. jours. Bd. dirs. Schubert Performing Arts Ctr., 1992—2001, Schubert Opera Bd., 1991—2000, chmn., 1993—. Recipient Outstanding Alumni award, Northeastern U., 1987, Mike Hogg award, M.D. Anderson Cancer Ctr., U. Tex., 1989, Alumni Achievement award, Middlebury Coll., 1990, AACR-Bruce F. Cain Meml. award, 2001. Fellow: AAAS, N.Y. Acad. Scis.; mem.: Coun. Biology Editors, Conn. Acad. Sci. and Engring., Inst. Medicine NAS (com. on govt. industry collaboration in biomed. rsch. and edn. 1989, mem. Forum on Drug Devel. and Regulation 1989—93), Assn. Am. Cancer Insts. (v.p. 1986, liaison rep. to Nat. Cancer Inst. 1986, bd. dirs. 1986—89, pres. 1987—88, chmn. bd. dirs. 1989), Am. Soc. Pharmacology and Exptl. Therapeutics (award com. 1988, chmn. 1992, award in exptl. therapeutics 1986, Otto Krayer award 2002), Am. Soc. Cell Biology, Am. Soc. Biochemistry and Molecular Biology, Am. Soc. Microbiology, Am. Chem. Soc., Am. Assn. Cancer Rsch. (dir. 1975—78, chmn. publs. com. 1981—88, dir. 1984—87, v.p. 1985—86, fin. com. 1985—88, exec. com. 1985—89, pres. 1986—87, chmn. exec. com. 1987, chmn. awards com. 1987, chmn. nominating com. 1993—95, mem. devel. com. 1995—97). Home: 4 Perkins Rd Woodbridge CT 06525-1616 Office: Yale U Dept Pharmacology 333 Cedar St New Haven CT 06510-3289

SARTORI, BRIDGET ANN, home health care nurse; b. Plattsburg, N.Y., July 17, 1957; d. Francis McCarthy and Phyllis (Harvey) McCarthy/Haegler; m. Robert S. Sartori, May 20, 1978; children: Robert F., Ryan R. BSN, Mt. St. Mary's Coll., Newburgh, N.Y., 1990. RN, N.Y. Staff nurse CCU White Plains (N.Y.) Hosp., 1990-91; nurse in home care divsn. Putnam Hosp. Ctr., Carmel, N.Y., 1991—, acting long term home health cert. program coord. home care divsn., 1995-97; supr. clin. svcs. Homecare, Inc., Brookfield, Conn., 1997-98; intravenous therapy nurse Anytime Home Care, Poughkeepsie, N.Y., 1992-93; substitute tchr., nurse Dover Union Free Sch. Dist., 1994—. Children's adv. Astor Head Start, Dover Plains, N.Y., 1989-92; pres. J.H. Ketcham Hose Co., 1998. Rescue squad J.H. Ketcham Hose Co., Dover Plains, 1978—, mem. ladies aux., 1978—, fire prevention officer, 1994-95, corp. sec., 1996-97; 1st v.p. J.H. Ketcham Hose Co. Fire Police, 1994—, pres., 1998; coach Dover Little League, 1994, 95; pres. J.H. Ketcham Hose Co., 1998, 2000, 2001; 1st v.p. Dutchess County Assn. Fire Dist., 2000, 2001; mem. Dutchess County Fire Adv. Bd., 1998—. Recipient Army Nurse Perseverance award U.S. Army, 1990. Republican. Roman Catholic. Avocations: reading, biking. Office: Putnam Hosp Homecare Clocktower Commons Bldg Rt 22 Brewster NY 10509 E-mail: bsartori@aol.com.

SARTORI, GIOVANNI, political scientist, educator; b. Florence, Italy, May 13, 1924; s. Dante and Emilia (Quentin) S.; 1 child, Ilaria. PhD, U. Florence, 1956; Doctor honoris causa, U. Genoa, 1992, Georgetown U., 1994, U. Guadalajara, 1996, U. Buenos Aires, 1998, U. Madrid, 2001, U. Bucharest, 2001. Assoc. prof. U. Florence, 1956-62, prof., 1962-76, dean faculty of polit. scis., 1968-71; prof. polit. sci. Stanford U., 1976-79; Albert Schweitzer prof. in the humanities Columbia U., N.Y.C., 1979—. Fellow Ctr. Advanced Study Behavioral Scis., 1971-72; sr. fellow Hoover Instn., 1976-79. Author: Democratic Theory, 1962, Parties and Party Systems: A Framework for Analysis, 1976, La Politica, 1979, The Theory of Democracy Revisited, 1987, Elementi di Teoria Politica, 1990, Democrazia, 1993, Comparative Constitutional Engineering, 1994, Homo Videns, 1998, La Sociedad Multietnica, 2001. Guggenheim fellow, 1979, Russell Sage Found. fellow, 1988-89. Mem. Am. Acad. Arts and Scis, Accademia dei Lincei. Home: 25 Central Park W Apt 270 New York NY 10023-7253

SARTORIS, GEORGIA PORTER, artist; b. Denver, Sept. 8, 1943; d. Glen Porter and Marguerite C. (Downey) Arnold; m. James J. Sartoris, Apr. 30, 1966; 1 child, Aspen Claire. BA, Colo. State U., 1965. One-woman shows include Volcano Art Ctr., Hawaii, 1994, Emmanuel Gallery U. Colo. Auraria

Ctr., Denver, 1989, Robischon Gallery, Denver, 1984, 86, 87, Cohen Gallery, Denver, 1982, Colo. Mountain Coll., Breckenridge, 1981, Ohio State U., Newark, 1979; exhibited in group shows Artists of Hawaii, Honolulu Acad. Art, 1996, Hawaii Craftsmen Ann. Exbhn., Honolulu, 1994, 96-99, Denver Art Mus., 1983, 84, 86, San Angelo (Tex.) Mus. Fine Arts, 1989, Craft Nat., Buffalo, 1985, Colo. Springs (Colo.) Fine Arts Ctr., 1985, 8th Ann. Biennial of Ceramic Art, Vaullaris, France, 1982, Marietta (Ohio) Coll. Craft Nat., 1981, Aspen (Colo.) Found. for Arts, 1978, Tweed Mus., Duluth, Minn., 1975, 77; represented in permanent collections at Colo. U., Boulder, Colo. Springs Fine Arts Ctr., Forum Hotel, Chgo., Paine Weber, Tucson, Mountain Bell, Denver, Pa. Bell, Phila., Kimball Internat. Design, L.A., Hughes Aircraft PNL, L.A. Bd. dirs. Hamakua Incubator Kitchen and Craft, Inc., Honokaa, Hawaii, 1993-99. Recipient Best of Show award Foothills Art Ctr., Golden, Colo., 1975, Excellence in Ceramics award Colo. Artist Craftsman, Denver, 1979, 80, 81, Cash award Craft Design Ctr., 1988. Mem. Hawaii Artist/Craftsmen. Avocations: swimming, surfing, horseback riding, golf, hiking. Home: PO Box 392 Paauilo HI 96776-0392

SARU, GEORGE, artist; b. Checea, Timis, Romania, Mar. 1, 1920; s. George and Zorca (Pavlov) S.; m. Semizaliana Brinzan, Aug. 31, 1945; children: Dorian, Horia. BFA, Acad. Fine Arts, Jassy, Romania, 1944; MFA, Acad. Fine Arts, Bucharest, Romania, 1948; Diplomate, Acad. Di Belle Arti, Perugia, Italy, 1963. Editor-in-chief Arta Mag., Bucharest, 1950-64; dep. chancellor Inst. Fine Arts, Bucharest, 1966-67, prof., 1948-82. Exhibited in group shows at Biennale di Venezia, 1954, 56, Mus. of Modern Art, Sczecin, Poland, 1965, 75, Vienna, Austria, 1956, Moscow, 1958, Geneva, 1961, Berlin, 1963, Paris, 1968, Leningrad, 1972, Orly, France, 1972, San Sebastian, Spain, 1973, Washington, 1973, Cairo, Egypt, 1974, Quebec, 1975, Prague, Czechoslovakia, 1979; one-man shows include Dalles Art Gallery, Bucharest, 1956, 70, 77, 81, Pushkin Mus., Moscow, 1960, LeMire Gallery, New Orleans, 1983, Alex Gallery, Washington, 1987, Morin Miller Gallery, N.Y.C., 1988, 89, 90, Dome Gallery, N.Y.C., 1991, The York Sq. Gallery, New Haven, 1995, Romanian Cultural Ctr., 1997, N.Y. Gallery @49, N.Y., 1999; represented in permanet collections The Weisman Mus. Art, Mpls., Nat. Mus. Art Romania. Recipient Nat. award for Painting, Bucharest, 1950, Laureat of the State prize Bucharest, 1951, Internat. award for Painting, 1953, Gold medal Laureat or Triennial, Sofia, Bulgaria, 1976, Aachen, Germany, 1996; named Internat. Man of Yr. Internat. Biog. Ctr. Cambridge, Eng., 1995-96. Mem. UNESCO, Fine Arts Guild of Romania, Internat. Assn. Fine Arts, Assn. Internat. Arts Plastiques. Avocations: music, sculpture, etching, travel. Home and Office: 560 Main St Apt 446 New York NY 10044-0014 E-mail: compur@aol.com.

SARUBBI, JUDITH ALICE CLEARWATER, guidance counselor; b. Engelwood, N.J., Oct. 5, 1956; d. Jasper and Mary (Fadden) Clearwater; m. Edward J. Sarubbi, July 7, 1979; children: Brian, Alyssa, Christopher. BA, William Paterson Coll., 1978; MA, Kean Coll. N.J., 1983. Cert. tchr., spl. edn. tchr., reading specialist, guidance and counseling, N.J. Tchr. Bergen County Bd. Spl. Svcs., Paramus, N.J., 1978-82; asst. dir. Day Camp Oratam, Harriman State Park, N.Y., 1980-82; co-dir. Skyland Learning and Guidance Assocs., Ringwood, N.J., 1985--89; guidance counselor Wharton (N.J.) Borough Pub. Schs., 1992—. Cons. Embossography, Paramus, 1979-81. Steering com. Alliance of Wanaque (N.J.) and Ringwood for Edn. and Substance Abuse Prevention, 1989-92. Mem. ASCD, ACA, Pi Lambda Theta. Roman Catholic. Avocations: reading, collecting farm antiques, skiing, crafts, computers. Office: Alfred C MacKinnon Mid Sch 137 E Central Ave Wharton NJ 07885-2431

SARUTTO, ANNE MARIE RITA, research scientist; b. Bklyn., Feb. 13, 1950; d. Michael Robert and Margaret Lorraine Sarutto. BA in Meteorology, U. St. Thomas, 1994. Interviewer Pa. State U., Phila., 1973—74; biol. aid U.S. Wildlife Fisheries, NOAA, Galveston, 1974—75; cen. supply technician Pub. Health Hosp., Tex., 1975—76, phys. therapy aid, 1976—81; med. asst. Army Reentry Examining Unit, Houston, 1981—82; rsch. asst. NSF, N.Y.C., 1995—97; weather technician CCNY, 1995—96. Peer mentoring program CCNY, N.Y.C., 2002—, student sen., 1995—96. Contbr. poetry to anthologies. Grantee minority rsch. grantee, Geol. Soc. Am., 1993—94. Mem.: Math. Soc. Am., Am. Geophys. Soc., Am. Meteorol. Soc., Alpha Phi Delta. Avocations: walking, weather observing, astronomy, creative and poetry writing. Home: 202 Bay 17th St Brooklyn NY 11214 Personal E-mail: AMSARUTTO@AOL.COM.

SARVIS, ELAINE MAGANN, assistant principal; b. Conway, S.C., May 11, 1947; d. John Thomas and Gloria (Winkler) Duckett; m. John Wesley Magann, Aug. 2, 1969 (dec. Nov. 1975); children: Christiane, James Wesley; m. Francis Mack Sarvis, Dec. 18, 1982. BA in Elem. Edn., U. S.C., 1969, MEd in Early Childhood, 1976, postgrad., 1990. Cert. elem. adminstrn. tchr., S.C. Tchr. Southside Elem. Sch., Augusta, Ga., 1969-70, Homewood Elem. Sch., Conway, 1970-71, Timmerman Sch., Columbia, S.C., 1972-73, South Conway Elem. Sch., Conway, 1973-74, 1975-76, instructional specialist, 1976-80, tchr., 1980-90, Horry County Gifted and Talented Program, Conway, 1990-91. Mem. com. Horry County Tchr. Incentive Program, Conway, 1989-91; bd. dirs. Horry County Sick Leave Bank Program, 1990-92. Mem. First Bapt. Ch., Conway, 1958-99, Ocean Dr. Presbyn. Ch., 1999—, North Myrtle Beach High Parent Tchr. Orgn., 1990; neighborhood chmn. Am. Heart Assn., Conway, 1978. Named Tchr. of Yr. County of Horry, 1990. Republican. Baptist. Avocations: reading, walking, movies, classical music, travel. Office: South Conway Elem Sch 3001 4th Ave Conway SC 29527-5914 E-mail: esarvis@sce.sccoast.net.

SARWER-FONER, GERALD JACOB, physician, educator; b. Volkovsk, Grodno, Poland, Dec. 6, 1924; arrived in Can., 1932, naturalized, 1935; s. Michael and Ronia (Caplan) Sarwer-F.; m. Ethel Sheinfeld, May 28, 1950; children: Michael, Gladys, Janice, Henry, Brian. BA, Loyola Coll. U., Montreal, 1945, MD magna cum laude, 1951; DPsychiatry, McGill U., 1955. Diplomate: Am. Bd. Psychiatry and Neurology. Intern. Univ. Hosps. U. Montreal Sch. Medicine, 1950-51; resident Butler Hosp., Providence, 1951-52, Hosps. Western Res. U., Cleve., 1952-53, Queen Mary Vets. Hosp., Montreal, 1953-55; cons. psychiatry, dir. psychiatric rsch., 1955-61; lectr. psychiatry U. Montreal, 1953-55; lectr., assoc. prof. McGill U., 1955-70; dir. dept psychiatry Queen Elizabeth's Hosp, Montreal, 1964-71; prof. psychiatry U. Ottawa, Ont., 1971-89, prof., chmn. psychiatry, 1974-86, prof., 1989—; dir. dept. psychiatry Ottawa Gen. Hosp., 1971-87; dir. Lafayette Clinic, Detroit, 1989-92; prof. psychiatry and behavioral Neurosciences Wayne State U., 1989—. Cons. in psychiatry Ottawa Gen. Hosp., Royal Ottawa Hosp., Children's Hosp. of Eastern Ont., Ottawa, Windsor (Ont.) Western Hosp. Ctr., Ottawa Sch. Bd.; Z. Lebensohn lectr. Silbey Meml. Hosp. Cosmos Club, Washington, 1991; disting. lectr. XI World Congress Psychiatry, Hamburg, 1999, XII World Congress Psychiatry, Yokohama, Japan, 2002; mem. test com. Nat. Bd. Med. Examiners, 1975-81; pres. Que. Psychiat. Assn., 1966-68; mem. adv. panel on psychiatry Def. Rsch. Bd. Can., Dept. Nat. Def., 1958-62. Editor: Dynamics of Psychiatric Drug Therapy, 1960, Research Conference on the Depressive Group of Illnesses, 1966, Psychiatric Crossroads-the Seventies, Research Aspects, 1972, Social Psychiatry in the Late 20th Century, 1993; editor in chief Psychiat. Jour. U. Ottawa, 1976-90, emeritus editor in chief, 1990—; mem. editorial bds. of numerous internat. and nat. profl. jours.; editor numerous audio-video tapes; contbr. to more than 200 articles to profl. jours. Bd. govs. Queen Elizabeth Hosp., Montreal, 1966-71; life gov. Queen Elizabeth Hosp. Found.; cons. Protestant Sch. Bd., Westmount, Que., 1966-71; advisor Com. on Health, City of Westmount, 1969-71. Served to lt. col. Royal Can. A Med. Corps, 1949-62. Fulbright fellow, 1951-53; recipient Sigmund Freud award Am. assn. Psychoanalytic Physicians, 1982, William V. Silverberg Meml. award Am. Acad. Psychoanalysis, 1990, Poca award Assn. Psychiat. Out Patient Ctrs. Am., 1990; Simon Bolivar lectr. Am. Psychiat. Assn., New Orleans, 1981; Can. Decoration, Knight of Malta. Fellow: AAAS, Am. Assn. Social Psychiatry (v.p. 1987—89, pres.-elect 1990, pres. 1992—94), World Psychiat. Assn. (chair Sci. program VI World congress 1974—77, v.p. sect. on edn. 1989—, mem. internat. adv. com. 9th World Congress Rio de Janeiro 1993, disting. lectr. 1996, XI World Congress Hamburg 1999, organizing com. sci. com. X World Congress in Madrid, mem. nominating com.), Benjamin Rush Soc. (bounding mem., councillor), Am. Coll. Psychiatrists (bd. regents 1978—80, pres. com. long range planning and policy 1986—89, emeritus), Am. Psychopath. Assn., Collegium Internat. Neuropsychopharmacology, Am. Coll. Psychoanalysts (VI World Congress of Psychiatry Honolulu 1974—77, pres.-elect 1983, pres. 1984—85, chair by-laws and constn. com. 1994—2001, Henry Laughlin award 1986), Internat. Coll. Psychosomatic Medicine (sec.-gen. 1979—83), Royal Coll. Physicians and Surgeons (exec. sec. test psychiat. com. 1987—89), Am. Acad. Psychiatry and the Law (sr.; pres. 1977, Silver Apple award), Am. Coll. Neuropsychopharmacology (life; charter fellow), Can. Coll. Neuropsychopharmacology (life; hon. found. 1958—), Am. Psychiat Assn. (life; chair com. psychiatry, law 1975—77, chair task force model commitment code 1976—80, chair sci. program com.), Am. Coll. Mental Health Adminstrn. (life), Can. Psychiat. Assn. (life; bd. dirs. 1958—62, founder, chair com., sect. psychotherapy 1962—64), Royal Coll. Psychiatry (Found. fellow), Internat. Psychoanalytical Assn. (mem. program com. 31st congress NY 1979); mem.: Am. Psychoanalytic Assn. (mem. program com. 1972—76), Alliance for Mental Health Svcs. (pres. 1999—2000), Mich. Psychoanalytic Soc., Soc. Biol. Psychiatry (sr.; pres. 1983—84, H. Azina Meml. lectr. 1963, George M. Thompson award 1997), Can. Assn. Profs. Psychiatry (pres. 1976—77, 1982—86), Can. Psychoanalytic Soc. (pres. 1979—81), Royal Can. Mil. Inst. Club, Cosmos Club. Home and Office: 3220 Bloomfield Shr West Bloomfield MI 48323-3300 Fax: 248 855-8321. E-mail: sarwfon@aol.com.

SASAHARA, ARTHUR ASAO, cardiologist, educator, researcher; b. Del Rey, Calif., May 11, 1927; s. Harold Hango and Blanche (Takayama) S.; m. Alice Ann Guenther, Apr. 2, 1955; children: Ann Mariko, Claire Michiko, Ellen Reiko, Karen Hideko, Mark Tadao. AB, Oberlin Coll., 1951; MD, Case Western Res. U., 1955; AM (hon.), Harvard U., 1987. Diplomate Am. Bd. Internal Medicine. Intern Boston City Hosp., 1955-56; jr. asst. med. resident Mass. Gen. Hosp., Boston, 1956-57; fellow in cardiology West Roxbury VA Med. Ctr., Mass., 1957-58, Children's Hosp. Med. Ctr., Boston, 1958-59; sr. resident in medicine Yale-New Haven Med. Ctr., 1959-60; asst. chief med. svc., dir. cardiopulmonary lab., dep. chmn. rsch. and edn. com. VA Hosp. West Roxbury, 1960-70, chief cardiopulmonary sect., 1971-74, assoc. chief staff for rsch. and edn., 1970-76, chief med. svc., 1974-82, West Roxbury-Brockton VA Hosp., 1982-87; prof. medicine Harvard Med. Sch., Boston, 1974-93, prof. emeritus, 1993—; cons. cardiovascular-pulmonary diseases Boston, 1965-87; cons. pediatric cardiology Children's Hosp. Med. Ctr., 1976-86; physician Brigham and Women's Hosp., 1979-82, sr. physician, 1982—. Dir. thrombolytics rsch. pharm. products divsn. Abbott Labs., Abbott Park, Ill., 1987—95, sr. med. dir., 1995—97; sr. physician cardiovascular divsn. Brigham and Women's Hosp., 1998—. Author-editor: Pulmonary Embolic Disease, 1965, Pulmonary Emboli, 1975, New Therapeutic Agents in Thrombosis and Thrombolysis, 1997, 2d edit., 2002; contbr. articles to profl. jours.; designer constant infusion med. pump, Harvard Apparatus Co., 1973; editorial bd. Jour. Nuclear Medicine, 1981-83, Am. Jour. Medicine, 1971-72, Circulation, 1973-78, VASA, 1978-85, Jour. Cardiovascular Medicine, 1980-86, Primary Cardiology, 1986-89. With U.S. Army, 1945-47. NIH grantee, 1963-82; VA grantee, 1961-87. Fellow ACP, Am. Coll. Chest Physicians, Am. Coll. Cardiology; mem. AAAS, Internat. Soc. Fibrinolysis and Thrombolysis, Am. Fedn. Clin. Rsch., Internat. Soc. Thrombosis and Hemostasis, Am. Heart Assn., Alpha Omega Alpha. Democrat. Episcopalian. Home: 1115 Beacon St # 12 Newton MA 02461-1154

SASAKI, CLARENCE TAKASHI, surgeon, medical educator; b. Honolulu, Jan. 24, 1941; s. Tsutomu and Carla Harumi (Mirikitani) S.; m. Carolyn Elizabeth Lindahl, June 26, 1967; children: Peter Gordon, John Eric. BA, Pomona Coll., 1962; MD, Yale U., 1966. Diplomate: Am. Bd. Otolaryngology. Intern San Francisco Hosp., U. Calif., 1966-67; resident in surgery Dartmouth Med. Sch., 1967-68; resident in otolaryngology Yale U. Med. Sch. Hosps., New Haven, 1970-73, faculty mem., 1973—, assoc. prof., 1977-82, prof. surgery, 1982—, chief sect. otolaryngology, 1981—, Charles Ohse prof. surgery, 1988—, vice chmn. dept. surgery, 1996. Author: Surgery of the Skull Base, Head and Neck Surgery, Vol. 1 Atlas Otolarynogology, Vocal Fold Physiology, Laryngeal Function in Phonation and Respiration, Neurological Diseases of the Larynx; mem. editorial bd. profl. jours. Served to maj. M.C. U.S. Army, 1968-70. Recipient award Fowler Triological Soc., 1979 Mem. Am. Acad. Otolaryngology (1st prize clin. rsch.), Am. Soc. Head and Neck Surgery (coun.), Assn. Rsch. Otolaryngology, Am. Laryngol. Rhinol. and Otol. Soc. (coun., sec. ea. sect. 1990, v.p. 1998), New Eng. Otolaryngology Soc. (pres. 1987, coun.), Assn. Acad. Depts. Otolaryngology (coun.), Am. Laryngol. Assn. (Casselberry award 1999), Pan Pacific Surg. Assn., Soc. for Neurosci., Soc. Neurovascular Surgery, Soc. for Head and Neck Surgeons, Am. Neurotolog. Soc., Pan Am. Assn. Oto-rhino-laryngology and Bronchoesophagology, Conn. Med. Soc., N.Y. Acad. Scis., Soc. Univ. Otolaryngologists, Collegium ORLAS, Cartesian Soc., Am. Bronchoesophagological Assn.(mem. coun.), N.Am. Skull Base Soc., Laryngeal. Cancer Assn. (Padua), Am. Otol. Soc., Dysphagia Rsch. Soc. (treas., pres.), Lawn Club, Mory's Assoc., Yale Club, Phi Beta Kappa, Sigma Xi. Office: Yale U Med Sch Dept Surgery PO Box 208041 333 Cedar St New Haven CT 06520-8041

SASAKI, JOHN ERIC, art company executive, artist; b. New Haven; s. Clarence and Carolyn S. BFA, Pepperdine U., 1994. Supr. Cinesite Digital Studios, Hollywood, Calif., 1994-95, composite supr., 1995-96; compositor Digital Domain, Venice, 2000—02; composite supr. Manex Visual Effects, Alameda, L.A., 1998-2000; compositor Sony Pictures Imageworks, 2001—02. CEO John E Sasaki Inc., Pacific Palisades, Calif., 1998—. Visual effects credits include (films) Titanic, The Matrix, The Fifth Element, Armageddon, Sphere, Space Jam, Waterworld, Deep Blue Sea, Almost Famous, Crouching Tiger, Hidden Dragon, How the Grinch Stole Christmas. Vol. Rep. Party, L.A., 1990—. Mem. Pepperdine Alumni. Salisbury Sch. Alumni (class agt.). Home and Office: 16100 W Sunset Blvd Pacific Palisades CA 90272-3454 E-mail: johnesasaki@hotmail.com.

SASAKI, JOSEPH DONALD, optometrist; b. Fresno, Calif., Jan. 7, 1912; m. Wakako M. Morimoto (dec. Jan. 1982); 1 child Edwin F. ; m. Pamela Jane Curtis. BA, OD, U. Calif., Berkeley, 1938. Cert. sch. optometrist Calif. Bd. Edn., 1940. Asst. placement officer Jerome Relocation, Denson, Ark., 1943-44; instr. U. Mich., 1944-45; pvt. practice Fresno, 1938-42, Ann Arbor, Mich., 1945-78; ret., 1978. Syn-holistic clin. investigator in field of optometry and gerontology, 1947—. Author: Japanese Picture Dictionary, 1945; contbr. (Beta Sigma Kappa award, 1950). Active Japanese Am. Citizens League, 1938—, Boy Scouts Am., 1924—80; mem. county bd. supts. City of Ann Arbor, 1955—58; vol. instr. arts Ann Arbor Pub. Sch. Dist., 1984. Named Joseph D. Sasaki scholarship to 3d yr. student Mich. Sch. Optometry, Ferris State U.; recipient Emil Arnold Sci. award, Mich. Optometric Assn., 1950, Award of Honor, Wisdom Soc., 1971, Appreciation award, S.E. Mich. Optometric Study Group, 1975, Honor Dist. and Internat. Pres. Prospector award, 1968, Physianthropist award, Am. Holistic Sci. Assn., 1985. Fellow: Soc. Nutrition and Preventive Medicine, Internat. Acad. Med. Preventics, Am. Nutritional Med. Assn. (hon. doctorate Nutritional Medicine), Acad. Psychosomatic Medicine (assoc.), Royal Soc. Health; mem.: APHA, AAAS, Mich. Pub. Health Assn., Ophthal. Allied Sci. (life), N.Y. Acad. Scis., Mich. Optometric Assn. (life; life, Emil Arnold Sci. award), Washington Inst. Medicine, Ophthalmology and Allied Sci. (life), Mich. Acad. Sci., Arts, and Letters (life; life), Assn. Holistic Health (founder), Soc. Health Human Value (hon.), Am. Acad. Religion, Am. Sch. Health Assn., Gerontol. Soc. Am., Am. Optometric Assn. (life), U. Calif. Optometric Alumni Assn. (life), Optimist Club (past disting. gov. Mich. dist., past pres. Ann Arbor club), Mason (life), Beta Sigma Kappa (doctorate of Ocular Sci.). Achievements include development of test technique "neuroophthalmomyometry" to determine state of systemically existing Chronic hypoxic-hypothiaminic tissue acidosis leading to lowering pH to affect the various parts of the body protein; tissues and enzymes towards aging process attributed to oxygen insufficiency and thiamine insufficiency combined; discovery of photo sensitivity of the retina of the eyes that is known to release thyrotrlpin releasing hormone (TRH) and at the same time transduct signal through known existence of retino-hypothalamic tract; to the superchiasmic nucleus of hypothalamus to act upon the anterior pituitary to release thyrotropin to act upon the thyroid to release thyroxin and tri-iodothyronine where they enhance the oxygen; uptake and suppress the development of cholesterol with this thyroid hormone enhances the release of thiamine from the liver into the circulating blood, which means retina helps to maintain the need; of thiamine to the retina, brain, heart, and optic nerve. Thus the retina serves as thiamine maintenance (homeostasis); discovery of retina must have continuing supply of thiamine including optic nerve and brain as well to form acetylcholine, neurotransmitter that the brain needs. Home: 4320 Fresno Lane Ann Arbor MI 48108-1246 E-mail: psasaki@ic.net.

SASAKI, RAY K. music educator; b. Fresno, Calif., Oct. 22, 1948; s. Masaru and Hinako Sasaki; m. Jeanne Dayton Sasaki, Nov. 1, 1986; children: Sara, Miki. BA, Calif. State U. Fresno, Fresno, CA, 1968—72; MM, U. of North Tex., Denton, TX, 1972—75. Music educator U. of Ill., Urbana, Ill., 1975—2001; educator U. of Tex. at Austin, Austin, Tex., 2001—. Mem. Tone Rd. Ramblers Band, New York, NY, 1979, St. Louis Brass Quintet, St. Louis, 1990—. Recipient Outstanding Faculty, U. of Ill., 1996. Mem.: Internat. Trumpet Guild (dir. 1994—96). Home: 5806 Tributary Ridge Drive Austin TX 78759 Office: The University of Texas at Austin School of Music Austin TX 78712 Home Fax: 512-343-6263. Personal E-mail: sasaki@mail.utexas.edu.

SASAKI, TSUTOMU (TOM SASAKI), real estate company executive, international trading company executive, consultant; b. Tokyo, July 28, 1945; came to U.S., 1979; s. Tsuneshiro and Kimiko (Fujiwara) S.; m. Yoko Katsura, Feb. 21, 1971; children: Mari, Tomoko. BA, Sophia U., Tokyo, 1969. Plant export adminstrn. Ataka & Co., Ltd., Osaka, Japan, 1969-76; officer Seattle-First Nat. Bank, Tokyo, 1976-79, AVP bus. mgr., 1982-84, AVP Japan mgr. Seattle, 1979-82, v.p. Japan mgr., 1984-90; owner, pres. BBS Internat., Inc., 1990—. Bd. dirs. Wired, Inc., Seattle, InterPac Devel. Inc., InterPac Mgmt., Inc., Riverplace Mgmt., Inc., BBS Bus. Svc., Inc., N.W. Club Mgmt., Inc. Bd. dirs. Adopt-a-Stream Found., Everett, Wash., 1987X; bd. trustees N.W. Sch., Seattle. Am. Field Svc. scholar, 1963-64. Mem. Japan Am. Soc. Wash. (chmn. membership com. 1988, bd. dirs. 1997X), British Am. Bus. Coun., Fairwood Golf & Country Club, Wash. Athletic Club. Avocations: golf, gardening, music, photography. Home: 4625 136th Ave SE Bellevue WA 98006-3007 Office: BBS Internat Inc 720 Olive Way Ste 1025 Seattle WA 98101-1880

SASAKI, Y(ASUNAGA) TITO, engineering executive; b. Tokyo, Feb. 6, 1938; came to U.S., 1967; s. Yoshinaga and Chiyoko S.; m. Janet L. Cline; 1 child, Heather N. Diploma in Indsl. Design, Royal Coll. Art, London, 1962; MS in Ekistics, Athens (Greece) Tech. Inst., 1965. Cert. planner Am. Inst. Cert. Planners. Tech. officer London County Coun., 1962-63; sr. rschr. Inst. Battelle, Geneva, Switzerland, 1965-67; planning dir. Golden Gate Bridge, San Francisco, 1970-74; pres. Visio Internat., Inc., 1974-85, Quantum Mechanics Corp., Sonoma, Calif., 1981—. Mem. ASME, AIAA, Am. Vacuum Soc., Am. Welding Soc. Achievements: co-developer of the world's most sensitive helium leak detector and the world's lowest out-gasing stainless steel. Home: PO Box 200 Vineburg CA 95487-0200 Office: Quantum Mechanics Corp 21885 8th St E Sonoma CA 95476-9797 E-mail: TitoSasaki@attglobal.net.

SASEEN, SHARON LOUISE, artist, painter, educator; b. Savannah, Ga., Jan. 23, 1949; d. Edward James and Lois Saseen; m. Joseph A. Dillon (div. 1978; 1 child, Edward Saseen Dillon. BFA, U. Ga., 1970, MAE, 1972; MFA in Illustration, Syracuse U., 1988; postgrad., Savannah Coll. Art & Design, 1982-84. Art tchr. James Island Middle Sch., Charleston, S.C., 1973, Savannah/Chatham County Bd. Edn., 1973-79, 1978-79; lower sch. art tchr. Savannah Country Day Sch., 1979-84; artist-in-residence Savannah Art Assn., 1976-79; ptnr. Signature Gallery in City Market, Savannah, 1992—. Ptnr. Gallery 209, Savannah, 1978—, pres., 2000; pres. Gallery 2000. One woman shows include Savannah Coll. Art and Design, Exhibit A Gallery, 1983, Historic Savannah Found., An Exhbn. Daufsuike S.C. Impressions, 1986, Atlanta Fin. Ctr., 1990, Internat. Oasis Gallery, 1991; exhibited in group shows Hilton Head Island/Pink Island Gallery, 1986, Lord and Taylor of Fifth Ave., 1987; illustrator Where Did My Feather Pillow Come From?, 1982, 2d edit.; cover designer Southern Bell Telephone Book, 1991, 92. Recipient Savannah Art Assn. Mem. Show award, 1976; first prize in show award Savannah Arts Festival, 1978, Friedman's award, 1979; named Best Local Artist, Creative Loafing, 2001. Mem. Nat. League Am. Pen Women, Inc. Avocations: reading, gardening, writing and illustrating childrens books.

SASEK, GLORIA BURNS, English language and literature educator; b. Springfield, Mass., Jan. 20, 1926; d. Frederick Charles and Minnie Delia (White) Burns; m. Lawrence Anton Sasek, Sept. 5, 1960. BA, Washington Coll. of the U. Va., 1947; postgrad., U. Paris, 1953; Postgrad., U. Stranieri, Perugia, Italy, 1955; MA, Radcliffe Coll., 1954; EdM, Springfield Coll., 1955. Tchr., head dept. jr. and sr. high sch. English, publ schs., Somers, Conn., 1947-59; tchr. English, Winchester (Mass.) Pub. Schs., 1959-60; mem. faculty La. State U., Baton Rouge, 1961—, asst. prof. English, 1971-96, chmn. freshman English, 1969-70. Named Gumbo Favorite Prof., 1978; recipient Disting. Undergrad. Tchg. award Amoco Found., 1994, commendation La. Ho. of Reps., 1996. Named La. State U. Yearbook Favorite Prof., 1978; recipient George H. Deer Disting. Tchg. award, La. State U., 1977, Disting. Undergrad. Tchg. award, Amoco Found., 1994, commendation, La. Ho. of Reps., 1996. Mem. MLA, AAUP (chpt. v.p. 1981-84), South Ctrl. MLA, South Ctrl. Renaissance Soc., South Ctrl. Conf. on Christianity and Lit. Address: 1458 Kenilworth Pky Baton Rouge LA 70808-5737 E-mail: glsasek@worldnet.att.net.

SASENICK, JOSEPH ANTHONY, animal health and food safety company executive; b. Chgo., May 18, 1940; s. Anthony E. and Caroline E. (Smicklas) S.; m. Barbara Ellen Barr, Aug. 18, 1962; children: Richard Allen, Susan Marie, Michael Joseph. BA, DePaul U., 1962; MA, U. Okla., 1966. With Miles Labs., Inc., Elkhart, Ind., 1963-70; product mgr. Alka-Seltzer, 1966-68, dir. mktg. grocery products divsn., 1968-70; with Gillette Corp., Boston, 1970-79, dir. new products/new ventures, personal care divsn., 1977; v.p. diversified cos. and pres. Jafra Cosmetics Worldwide, 1977-79; mktg. dir. Braun AG, Kronberg, W. Ger., 1970-73; chmn. mng. dir. Braun U.K. Ltd., 1973-77; with Abbott Labs., North Chicago, 1979-84, corp. v.p., pres. consumer products divsn., 1979-84; pres., CEO, Moxie Industries, 1984-87; pres., CEO Personal Monitoring Technologies, Rochester, N.Y., 1987; pres. Bioline Labs., Ft. Lauderdale, Fla., 1988; mng. dir., ptnr. Vista Resource Group, Newport Beach, Calif., 1988-90; pres., CEO, Alcide Corp., Redmond, Wash., 1991-92, chmn., CEO, 1992—, 2001—. Mem. Columbia Tower Club, El Niguel Club, Wash. Athletic Club, Tech. Alliance, Rainier Club. Home: 1301 Spring St Apt 24J Seattle WA 98104-1353 Office: Alcide Corp PO Box 89 Redmond WA 98073-0089

SASHIN, DONALD, pet physicist, radiological physicist, educator; b. N.Y.C., Dec. 11, 1937; s. David and Pearl (Taub) S.; m. Kathleen Flaherty, July 24, 1967; children: Deirdre Moira, Courtenay Aileen. BS in Physics, MIT, 1960; MS in Physics, Carnegie Inst. Tech., 1962; PhD in Physics, Carnegie Mellon U., 1968. Instr. radiology and radiation health U. Pitts., 1967-70, asst. prof. radiology, 1970-74, asst. prof. indsl and environ. health, 1970-77; asst. prof. radiation health, 1977-87; assoc. prof. radiology U. Pitts., 1974—, assoc. prof. radiation health, 1987-89, assoc. prof. environ. and occupl. health, 1989-2000. Contbr. articles to profl. jours., patentee in field. Recipient Cum Laude award sci. exhibit Radiol. Soc. N.Am., 1977, cert. of merit sci. exhibit, 1979. Mem. IEEE, AAAS, Am. Phys. Soc., Am. Assn. Physicists in Medicine, Soc. Nuclear Medicine, Health Physics Soc., Sigma Xi. Democrat. Roman Catholic. Avocations: golf, fishing, swimming, sailing. Home: 4360 Centre Ave Pittsburgh PA 15213-1403 Office: PET Facility B938 PUH/UPMC 200 Lothrop St Pittsburgh PA 15213-2546

SASMOR, JAMES CECIL, publishing representative, educator; b. N.Y.C., July 29, 1920; s. Louis and Cecilia (Mockler) S.; 1 child from previous marriage, Elizabeth Lynn; m. Jeannette L. Fuchs, May 30, 1965. BS, Columbia U., 1942; MBA, Calif. Western U., 1977, PhD, 1979. Fellow, Diplomate Am. Bd. Med. Psychotherapists, Am. Assn. Sex Educators, Counselors and Therapists; lic. healthcare risk mgr., Am. Inst. Med. Law; diplomate Am. Bd. Sexology, Am. Bd. Disability Analysts (sr. analyst); cert. tchr. health scis.. Registered rep. Nat. Assn. Security Dealers, 1956-57; founder, owner J.C. Sasmor Assocs., Pub.'s Reps., N.Y.C., 1959-89; co-founder, pres., dir. adminstrn. Continuing Edn. Cons., Inc., 1976—. Pub. cons., 1959—; clin. assoc. U. So. Fla. Coll. Medicine, 1987-89, mem. adj. faculty Coll. Nursing, 1980-89; dir. Ednl. Counseling Comprehensive Breast Cancer Ctr., U. So. Fla. Med. Ctr., 1984-89, client librn. mental health inst., 1979-89; lectr. divsn. allied health nursing and pub. svc. Yavapai Coll. Author: Economics of Structured Continuing Education in Selected Professional Journals, Perception May Be Reality; contbr. chpts. to Childbirth Education: A Nursing Perspective; contbr. articles to profl. jours. Team tchr. childbirth edn. Am. Soc. Childbirth Educators; bd. dirs. Tampa chpt. ARC; pres. Sedona (Ariz.) unit Am. Cancer Soc., 1995—, co-chmn. adult edn. com., founder Am. Cancer Soc. edn. dept. Sedona Med. Ctr.; bd. dirs. Ariz. divsn., mem. pub. edn.

com.; county nursing ednl. cons. ARC, chmn. instrnl. com. on nursing and health, 1979-85; founding mem. coun. trustees Ariz. Nurses Found., 1998. With USN, 1942-58, PTO; lt. USNR ret. Recipient cert. of appreciation ARC, 1979, Am. Fgn. Svc. Assn., 1988, Dept. Health and Rehab. Svcs. award for Fla. Mental Health Inst. Svc., 1980; Internat. Coun. Sex Edn. and Parenthood fellow Am. U., 1981. Mem. NAACOG (bd. dirs. Tampa chpt.), Nat. Assn. Pubs. Reps. (pres. 1965-66), Am. Soc. Psychoprophylaxis in Obstetrics (dir. 1970-71), Am. Soc. Childbirth Educators (co-founder, dir. 1972—), Internat. Coun. Women's Health Issues (chmn. resources com.), Health Edn. Media Assn., Nursing Educators Assn. Tampa, Lions (bd. dirs. Found. Ariz. 1991-2000, past pres. Sedona club, chair sight, hearing, and scholarship coms.), Phi Theta Kappa (hon., advisor Beta Gamma Pi chpt.). Home: 235 Arrowhead Dr Sedona AZ 86351-8900 Office: PO Box 2282 Sedona AZ 86339-2282 E-mail: jsasmor@sedona.net.

SASMOR, JEANNETTE LOUISE, educational consulting company executive; b. N.Y.C., May 17, 1943; d. Sol and Willmyra J. (Reilly) Fuchs; m. James C. Sasmor, May 30, 1965. BS, Columbia U., 1966, MEd, 1968, EdD, 1974; adult primary care nurse practitioner, U. Md., Balt., 1982; MBA, U. South Fla., 1990. Cert. women's health nurse practitioner Assn. Women's Health, Obstetrical and Neonatal Nurses; lic. health care risk mgr., Fla. Agy. for Healthcare Adminstrn. Coord. ANA Divsn. Maternal Child Health, N.Y.C., 1972-73; maternal child health cons. test constrn. divsn. Nat. League for Nursing, 1973; prof., dir. continuing nursing edn. U. South Fla., Tampa, 1973-89; v.p. and dir. edn. Continuing Edn. Cons. Inc., Fla., 1976-89, Sedona, Ariz., 1989—; coord. maternal child health, dir. H.E.A.L.T.H. Yavapai Coll., Prescott, 1994—. Dir. internat. study tours USSR, 1986, New Zealand/Australia, 1990, Scandinavia, 1992, China, 1996, Spain, 1999; mem. scope practice com. Ariz. Bd. Nursing, 1994-99. Author: What Every Husband Should Know About Having a Baby, 1972, Father's Labor Coaching Log and Review Book, 1972, 82, Childbirth Education: A Nursing Perspective, 1979. Del. White House Conf. on Children and Youth, 1970, White House Conf. on Families, 1980; bd. dirs. Ariz. divsn. Am. Cancer Soc., 1992-97. Am. Acad. Nursing fellow, 1977, Robert Wood Johnson Nurse faculty fellow in primary care, 1981-82; recipient NEAA Nursing Practice award Tchrs.'s Coll. Columbia U., 1992, Vol. of Yr. award Sedona-Oak Creek unit Am. Cancer. Soc., 1992; inductee Nursing Hall of Fame, Tchr.'s Coll., Columbia U., 1999. Mem. Am. Soc. Childbirth Educators (pres. 1972-78), Fla. Nurses Assn. (pres. dist. 4 1976-77), Ariz. Nurses Assn. (continuing edn. review com. 1990—), Ariz. Bd. Nursing (scope of practice com. 1994-99), Lions (treas. Sedona-Oak Creek Canyon Club 1990-99, Melvin Jones fellow 1996), Ariz. Nurses Assn. (dir. fundraising 1999—), One Good Turn Inc. (pres. 1992-95), Phi Theta Kappa (founding pres. Lambda Nu chpt. 1962, faculty advisor Beta Gamma Pi chpt. 1996—, Horizon award 1999), Pi Lambda Theta, Sigma Theta Tau (chpt. treas. 1992-96, newsletter editor 1991-94, Outstanding Cmty. Leader award Lambda Omicron chpt. 1994), Kappa Delta Pi. Avocations: traveling, writing. Office: Yavapai Coll 1100 E Sheldon St Prescott AZ 86301-3220 E-mail: jsasmor@sedona.net.

SASS, ARTHUR HAROLD, educational executive; b. N.Y.C., Nov. 22, 1928; s. Maxwell Sigmund and Alice May (McGillick) S.; m. Eleanore G. Schmidt, Dec. 31, 1949; children: Nancy, Arlene, Susan, Eric. BS, Oswego (N.Y.) State Coll., 1949; EdM, Rutgers U., 1959, postgrad., 1960-68. Cert. chief sch. adminstr. Tchr. Millsboro (Del.) Pub. Sch. System, 1949-51, Eatontown (N.J.) Pub. Sch. System, 1955-66; coord. coop. indsl. edn. Monmouth Regional High Sch., Tinton Falls, N.J., 1966-68; prin. Mt. Holly (N.J.) Pub. Sch. System, 1968-71; supt. schs. Lumberton Twp. (N.J.) Pub. Sch. System, 1971-72, Lacey Twp. (N.J.) Pub. Sch. System, 1972-74; analyst mil. pers. Naval Sea Systems Command, Washington, 1975-79; head employee devel. Naval Rsch. Lab., 1979-83, 85-90; acad. dir. Naval Res. Engring. Duty Officer Sch., Leesburg, Va., 1983-85. Pres. DEVPRO, Inc., Warrenton, Va., 1985—; prin. founder Dept. Def. Sci. and Engring. Apprentice Program; established nation's first fed. svc. high sch. coop. indsl. edn. program, 1967. Author: Guide to the Naval Ammunition Depot, 1967; editor: (brochure) Commodore John Barry-Father of the U.S. Navy, 1976. Chmn. Shade Tree Commn., Little Silver, N.J., 1968-75, Rapidan/Rappahannock (Va.) Cmty. Mental Health Ctrs., 1980-81; deacon Warrenton Ch. of Christ, 1985, elder, 1995-99; mem. Va. Gov.'s Adv. Bd. for Emergency Med. Svcs., 1994-96, Shade Tree Commn., Monmouth Coutny, N.J., 1969-75. With USN, 1952-55; capt. USNR, 1952-88. Recipient Tng. Officers' Conf. Disting. Svc. award, 1988, Outstanding Contbn. to Engring. Edn. and Rsch award George Washington U., 1991. Mem. Am. Soc. Tng. and Devel., Res. Officers Assn. (v.p. Va. chpt. 1982-83), Naval Res. Assn. (Plimsoll Mark award 1975), Am. Soc. Naval Engrs., Navy League, Wash. Acad. Scis., Tng. Dirs. Forum. Republican. Avocation: outdoor activities. Home and Office: 604 Dam Lake Ct Williamsburg VA 23185-2796

SASS, LOUIS ARNORSSON, psychology educator; b. N.Y.C., Jan. 10, 1949; s. Louis DeWald and Hrafnhildur (Einarsdottir) S. BA, Harvard U., 1970; MA in Psychology, U. Calif., Berkeley, 1972, PhD in Psychology, 1979. Lic. psychologist, N.Y., N.J. Teaching asst. psychology dept. U. Calif., Berkeley, 1970-72; mental health coord. Charles Drew Family Life Ctr., Dorchester, Mass., 1972-73; vis. lectr. in psychology Assumption Coll., Worcester, 1973-76; instr. psychology Holy Cross Coll., 1977-79, asst. prof. psychology, 1979-83; mem. Inst. for Advanced Study, Sch. Social Sci., Princeton, N.J., 1982-83; asst. prof. clin. psychology Rutgers U., New Brunswick, 1983-88, assoc. prof. clin. psychology, 1988-94, prof., 1994—; vis. assoc. prof. theoretical and exptl. psychology Leiden U., The Netherlands, 1991; chair dept. Clin. Psychology, regent Rutgers U., 2001—03. Vis. prof. psychology (human devel.) and social sci. U. Chgo., 1995; intern in clin. psychology Westchester divsn. N.Y. Hosp., Cornell U. Med. Coll., 1980-81; rsch. and writing project on madness and modernism Inst. Advanced Study Sch. Social Sci., 1982-83; prin. investigator family rsch. project McLean Hosp., 1977-80; asst. attending psychologist, 1979-86, rsch. affiliate in psychology, Labs. for Psychiat. Rsch., 1987-89; instr. psychology Harvard Med. Sch., 1979-86, lectr. 1987-89; presenter in field. Author: (Book) Madness and Modernism, 1992, The Paradoxes of Delusion, 1994; co-editor: Hermeneutics and Psychological Theory, 1988; mem. editl. bd. Cultural Anthropology, 1992—95; mem. editl. bd.: Jour. Theory and Psychology, 2000—03, mem. editl. bd.: Jour. Phenomenenology and the Cognitive Scis., 2002—; contbr. articles to N.Y. Times Mag., Harper Mag and profl. jours. Fellow NEH, 1982-83, Henry Rutgers Found., 1985-87, Deutscher-Akademischer Austawschedienst, 1993; grantee N.J. Dept. Higher Edn., 1985. Fellow: N.Y. Inst. Humanities; mem.: APA, AAAS, Assn. Advancement Philosophy and Psychology (exec. bd.), Inernat. Soc. Theoretical Psychology (exec. bd.), World Fedn. for Mental health. Avocations: swimming, tennis. Office: Rutgers U Busch Campus GSAPP 152 Frelingheysen Rd Piscataway NJ 08854-0819

SASS, NEIL LESLIE, toxicologist; b. Balt., Oct. 24, 1944; s. Samuel and Blanche (Radoon) S.; m. Anita Paige Hoswell, June 29, 1984. BS, Wake Forest Coll., 1966; MS, W.Va. U., 1969, PhD, 1971; MS, Johns Hopkins U., 1984. Commd. officer USPHS, 1966, advanced through grades to capt., 1988, comdr. Preventive Medicine unit, 1989; served as rsch. toxicologist med. labs. U.S. Army, Edgewood Arsenal, Md., 1971-74; chief clin. investigations William Beaumont Med. Ctr., El Paso, Tex., 1974-77; toxicologist Bur. of Foods FDA, Washington, 1977-82; spl. asst. to dir. Ctr. for Food Safety and Applied Nutrition, 1982-99, dir. divsn. toxicol. rsch., 1996-99; chief toxicologist, state counterterrorism coord. Ala. Dept. Pub. Health, Montgomery, 1999—. Jewish. Home: 379 Westcott Dr Wetumpka AL 36093-1444 Office: Ala Dept Pub Health The RSA Tower 201 Monroe St Ste 1450 Montgomery AL 36104-3735 E-mail: nsass@adph.state.al.us.

SASS, RONALD LEWIS, biology and chemistry educator; b. Davenport, Iowa, May 26, 1932; s. Erwin Leese and Flora Alice (Puck) S.; m. Joyce R. Moorhead, 1951 (div. 1968); children: Dennise, Andria; m. Margaret Lee Macy, Apr. 4, 1969; children: Hartley, Dennis. BA, Augustana Coll., Rock Island, Ill., 1954; PhD, U. So. Calif., L.A., 1957. Chemist U.S. Army, Rock Island (Ill.) Arsenal, 1951-54; asst. prof. Rice U., Houston, 1958-62, assoc. prof., 1962-66, prof., 1966—, chmn. biology, 1981-87. Co-dir. Rice Ctr. for Edn., Houston, 1988—; chair Rice Earth Sys. Inst., Houston, 1990—, Ecology and Evolutionary Biology, 1995—; cons. EPA, Washington, 1990—, Coll. Bd., N.Y.C., 1988-96. Contbr. articles on chemistry, biology and biochemistry to profl. jours. NSF predoctoral fellow U. So. Calif., 1954-57, fellow AEC, 1957-58, Guggenheim fellow, 1965, sr. rsch. fellow NRC, 1988. Mem. Internat. Geospher-Biosphere Program (com. chair 1990—). Avocations: tennis, fishing. Office: Rice U Ecology & Evolutionary Biology Mail Stop 170 Houston TX 77251 E-mail: sass@rice.edu.

SASS, STEPHEN LOUIS, education educator; b. N.Y.C., Mar. 11, 1940; s. Abraham Silver and Betty (Gelb) S.; m. Karen Rae Sande Sass, Feb. 19, 1966; children: Adam Joshua Sass, Erik Nathaniel Sass. BChe, CCNY, 1961; PhD, Northwestern U., Evanston, Ill., 1966. Asst. prof. Cornell U., Ithaca, N.Y., 1967-73, assoc. prof., 1973-79, prof., 1979—. External review com. U. Ill., Champaign, Ill., 1995—; review com. Energy Technologies, Argonne, Ill., 1997—. Author: The Substance of Civilization, 1998; contbr. more than 170 papers in field. Fellow Am Phys. Soc., ASM. Named Stephen H. Weiss Presdl. fellow, Cornell U.; recipient Outstanding Paper award, Scripta Metallurgica, 1984, Acta Metallurgica, 1996. Fellow: Am. Phys. Soc.; mem.: Am. Soc. Materials. Home: 1025 Highland Rd Ithaca NY 14850-1447 Office: Bard Hall Dept Materials Sci/Engring Cornell U Ithaca NY 14853 E-mail: sls7@cornell.edu.

SASSER, CHARLES WAYNE, journalist, educator, writer; b. Sallisaw, Okla., Jan. 3, 1942; s. Ben Garland and Mary Louise Sasser; m. Dianne Carol Reilly, Oct. 8, 1965 (div. 1978); children: David, Michael; m. Katherine Renee, Feb. 2, 1979 (div. Oct. 1986); 1 adopted child, Joshua Dale; m. Donna Sue Baker, Oct. 7, 1995; stepchildren: DeAnn, Darren, Michael. AA, Miami (Fla.)-Dade Jr. Coll., 1968; BA, Fla. State U., 1969; postgrad., Okla. State U., 1977-78. Police officer Miami Police Dept., 1965-68; detective Tulsa Police Dept., 1970-79; coll. instr. Tulsa Jr. Coll., 1976—; freelance journalist, 1979—. Horse rancher, trainer, Mannford, Okla., 1971-78, Chouteau, Okla., 1996—; dir. criminal justice program Am. Christian Coll. Tulsa, 1974-78; profl. rodeo clown Profl. Rodeo Cowboy Assn., Okla., 1984-86; pres., CEO Fly High Inc., 2000—. Author: No Gentle Streets, 1984, The Girl Scout Murders, 1989, The Walking Dead, 1989, One Shot-One Kill, 1990, Homicide!, 1990, The 100th Kill, 1992, Always a Warrior, 1994, Shoot to Kill, 1994, Last American Heroes, 1994, In Cold Blood: Oklahoma's Most Notorious Murders, 1994, Smoke Jumpers, 1996, First Seal, 1997, Doc: Platoon Medic, 1998, Fire Cops, 1998, At Large, 1998, Arctic Homestead, 2000, Liberty City, 2000, Operation No Man's Land, 2000, Taking Fire, 2001, The War Chaser, 2001, The Return, 2001, Delta Detachment: Operation Punitive Strike, 2002, The Raider, 2002, The Encyclopedia of Navy Seals, 2002; editor Keystone Sportsman Mag., 1975-78; contbr. articles to periodicals; actor Wagoner (Okla.) Playhouse Dinner Theater, 1997—. Pres. Keystone Crossroads Hist. Assn., Mannford, 1977; del. Creek County Reps., Sapulpa, Okla., 1977-78, Sequoyah County Reps., Sallisaw, Okla., 1984-85. With U.S. Army Spl. Forces, 1966-67, 72-83; 1st sgt. USAR, 1991-97, ret.; with USN, 1960-64. Recipient Tulsa Author's award, City of Tulsa, 1992. Mem. Okla. Writers Fedn., Tulsa Nightwriters (Nightwriter of the Yr. 1990, 96). Avocations: martial arts, steer roping, scuba diving, parachuting, horses. Home and Office: RR 1 Box 288 Chouteau OK 74337-9617

SASSER, JONATHAN DREW, lawyer; b. Monroe, N.C., Mar. 1, 1956; s. Herman Wallace and Faith Belzora (Harrington) S.; m. Debra A. Smith, Feb. 22, 1994. BA with honors, U. N.C., 1978, JD with honors, 1981. Bar: N.C. 1981, N.Y. 1983, U.S. Dist. Ct. (so. and ea. dists.) N.Y. 1983, U.S. Dist. Ct. (no. dist.) Tex. 1983, U.S. Dist. Ct. (ea. dist.) N.C. 1986, U.S. Ct. Appeals (4th cir.) 1987, U.S. Dist. Ct. (mid. dist.) N.C. 1987, U.S. Supreme Ct. 1988. Law clk. to assoc. justice N.C. Supreme Ct., Raleigh, NC, 1981—82; assoc. Paul, Weiss, Rifkind, Wharton & Garrison, N.Y.C., 1982—86, Moore & Van Allen and predecessor firm Powe, Porter & Alphin P.A., Durham, NC, 1986—89; ptnr. Moore & Van Allen PLLC, Raleigh, 1990—. Editor: Cellar Door, 1977-78. Dem. precinct chmn., Chapel Hill, N.C., 1976-82. John Motley Morehead Found. fellow, Chapel Hill, 1978; John Motley Morehead Found. scholar, Chapel Hill, 1974. Mem. ABA, N.C. State Bar Assn., N.C. Bar Assn., N.Y. State Bar Assn. Methodist. Avocations: running, triathlons, mountain climbing. Home: 311 Calvin Rd Raleigh NC 27605-1707 Office: Moore & Van Allen 1 Hannover Sq Ste 1700 Raleigh NC 27601-1794

SASSER, WILLIAM JACK, retired federal agency administrator, consultant; b. Arcadia, Okla., Aug. 12, 1934; children: Sam, Steve, Susan, Sandra. BS in Sociology and Psychology, Okla. Bapt. U., 1956; postgrad., S.W. Bapt. Sem., 1957-60, George Washington U., 1966. Lic. comml. pilot with instrument rating. Air traffic control specialist S.W. region FAA Air Route Traffic Control Ctr., Ft. Worth, 1963-65, pers. officer, 1970-71; tech. intern FAA, Washington, 1965-66, employee devel. officer S.W. region Houston and Ft. Worth, 1966-70, chief tng. br. pers. div. Gt. Lakes region Des Plaines, Ill., 1971-73, with exec. devel. program Gt. Lakes and ctrl. regions Des Plaines, Kansas City, Mo., 1973-75, asst. chief airports div. ctrl. region Kansas City, 1975-76, mgr., 1977-87, mgr. airports div. S.W. region Ft. Worth, 1987-89, dep. regional adminstr. S.W. region, 1989-95; ret. S.W. region, 1995; pvt. cons., 1995—. Home: PO Box 162595 Fort Worth TX 76161-2595

SASSIN, JAMES MICHAEL, civil engineer, researcher; b. Weimar, Tex., Nov. 8, 1958; s. John Vaclav and Viola Dorothy (Holub) S. BCE, Tex. A&M U., 1981, M of Pub. Affairs, 1995. Registered profl. engr., Tex. Engr. asst. Tex. State Dept. Hwys., Austin, 1982-87, pavement engr., 1988-89, sr. pavement engr., 1989-91; rsch. engr. Nat. Rsch. Coun., Washington, 1987-88, Transp. Rsch. Inst., Brno, Czechoslovakia, 1991-92; U.S. fgn. svc. intern Am. Embassy, Prague, 1994; project mgr. surface transp. N.Mex., Tex., and Minn. Presenter papers in U.S. and Europe. Co-author: (textbook) Pavement Design, 1990; editor: (newsletter) Shrp'er Focus, 1990; contbr. articles to profl. publs. Lay min. Roman Cath. Ch., 1980-91, College Station and Austin; neighborhood vol. Arthritis Found., Austin, 1990; overseas vol. Coun. for Internat. Edn. Exch., Czechoslovakia, 1989; vol. Nat. Wildflower Rsch. Ctr., Austin, 1994—; mem. Transp. Rsch. Bd., 1995—; mem. Transp. Rsch. Forum, 1996—, mem. com. A5006 internat. trade and transp.; vol. Citizens Democracy Corps, 1991—, Edn. for Democracy, 1991-92. Mem. Nat. Soc. Profl. Engr. (mathcounts 1987-91, minuteman, Austin 1989-91). Democrat. Avocations: running, cycling, sailing. Home: 2205 Tower Dr Austin TX 78703-2319 Office: EP Hamilton & Assoc Inc 1406 Three Points Rd Ste B9 Pflugerville TX 78660-3139

SASSO, CLAUDE, historian, educator; b. Chgo., Jan. 4, 1944; s. Henry Erwin Sasso and Jean Francis Puglise; m. Patricia Ann Connor; children: Gena Lynn Sasso Perry, Michele Marie Sasso Visser, John Claude. BA in History, Loyola U., Chgo., 1966, MA in Am. History, 1968, PhD in European History, 1980; BA in Slavic Lang. and Lit., U. Kans., 1989. Commd. officer U.S. Army, 1966, advanced through grades to maj., ret., 1987; adj. asst. prof. history William Jewell Coll., Liberty, Mo., 1987—, Maple Woods C.C., Kansas City, 1987—; dir. L&C Software, Inc., 1998—, pres., 2002—. Author: Soviet Night Operations in WWII, 1980; contbr. articles to profl. jours. V.p. St. Vincent De Paul Soc., Kansas City, 1994—98. Mem.: Ret. Officers Assn., Slavic Studies Assn., Am. Hist. Assn. Roman Catholic. Avocations: Bible study, golf, tennis, history. Office: 5201 NW 58th Terr Kansas City MO 64151

SASSON, ARLEY ALBERTO, investment company executive; b. Mexico City; came to U.S., 1992; BS in Econs., U. Pa., 1996. Analyst emerging debt markets Goldman, Sachs & Co., N.Y.C., 1996-99, assoc. equity derivatives, 1999-2000; v.p. Donaldson, Lufkin & Jenrette, 2000—01, Deutsche Bank, N.Y.C., 2002—. Office: Deutsche Bank 31 W 52nd St 2d Fl New York NY 10019

SASSONE, MARCO MASSIMO, artist; b. Florence, Italy, July 27, 1942; came to U.S., 1967; s. Nicola and Anna Maria (Freschi) S.; m. Diane Nelson, Jan. 25, 1972 (div. 1983); 1 child, Nicola. Student, Inst. Galileo Galilei, Florence, 1959-62, Fine Arts Acad., 1963. One-man shows include Galleria Arte Internat., Florence, 1973, Laguna Art Mus., Laguna Beach, Calif., 1979, L.A. Mcpl. Art Gallery, 1988, Mus. Italo Am., San Francisco, 1994, Italian Cultural Inst., L.A., 1996, Cloisters of Santa Croce, Florence, 1997, Odon Wagner Gallery, Toronto, Can., 2000, MB Modern, N.Y., 2000; exhibited in group shows Nat. Acad. Design, N.Y.C., 1977, Orange Coast Coll., Costa Mesa, Calif., 1978, Univ. Calif., San Francisco, 1987, L.A. Contemporary Exhibitions, 1992, Mus. Italian Am., San Francisco, 1994; subject of film, book, video documentary; TV guest. Recipient Gold medal Italian Acad., 1978, Mayor's commendation, L.A., 1987, Marco Sassone Day declared in his honor, San Francisco, 1994; knighted by Sandro Pertini, Pres. of Italy, 1982. Avocations: culinary arts, tennis, boxing. Studio: Marco Sassone Studio 2140 Bush St Apt 8 San Francisco CA 94115-3166 E-mail: marco@marcosassone.com.

SASSOON, ANDRE GABRIEL, lawyer; b. Cairo, Apr. 13, 1936; came to U.S., 1959; s. Gabriel and Sarine (Tawil) S.; m. Barbara Dee Freedman, Aug. 15, 1965 (div. 2001); children: Daniel, Gabriel, Sarina. GCE, Oxford & Cambridge, England, 1953; JD, Villanova U., 1969; LLM, Harvard U., 1970. Bar: Pa. 1969, N.Y. 1970. Product mgr. Rohm & Haas Co., Phila., 1960-66; law clk. Dist. Atty.'s Office, 1968; assoc. Weil, Gotshal & Manges, N.Y.C., 1970-73; pvt. practice, 1973—; pres., CEO Sterimed Internat., Inc., 1999—. Dir. elem. Youth in Distress, N.Y.C., 1982—; v.p., dir. internat. Anti-Drug Abuse Found., N.Y.C., 1987—; v.p., dir., mem. exec. com. Hebrew Immigrant Aid Soc., N.Y.C., 1977—; internat. sec., gov. bd. internat. govs. World Sephardi Fedn., N.Y.C., 1988—; co-pres., chmn., U.S. com., dir. internat. Jewish Com. for Sephardi '92, N.Y.C., 1989—; mem. N.Y. State Christopher Columbus Quincetenary Comm., Statewide Outreach Com., 1991—; pres., CEO Sterimed Internat., Inc., 1999—. Editor Villanova Law Rev.; contbr. articles to profl. jours. Chmn. bd. Sloan's Auctioneers & Appraisers, 2001, chmn., 1953—. With USAR, 1960—66. Recipient Israel Trade award Govt. of Israel, 1985. Mem. ABA, Am. Arbitration Assn. (panel mem. 1971—), Am. Soc. Internat. Law, Order of the Coif, 0840 Internat. Pvt., 0860 Internat. Pub., SteriMed Internat. (pres. 1999). Home: 641 Fifth Ave Apt 30H New York NY 10022 Office: 600 Madison Ave New York NY 10022-1615 E-mail: AndreSassoon@aol.com.

SASSOUNI, CHRIS GARO, healthcare company executive; b. Phila., Dec. 1, 1957; s. Viken and Henriette (Bergè) Sassouni; m. Carol Ann Procoffie, Dec. 27, 1980; children: Michelle Christine, Christopher Carl-Viken. BA, U. Pitts., 1979, DMD, 1985; MBA, U. N.C., 1989. Intern Isotechnologies Inc., Hillsborough, N.C., 1988-89; pharm. rep. Merck & Co., Cin., 1989-90; v.p. Raymond James, St. Petersburg, Fla., 1990-96; sr. v.p. NatWest Securities, Clearwater, 1996-97; mng. dir. HSBC Securities Inc., 1997-98; CEO HealthCare Capital Advisors, Inc., 1999—. Mem.: World Future Soc., Phi Beta Kappa. Avocation: Avocations: bodybuilding, reading, acoustic guitar. Home: 2259 St Charles Dr Clearwater FL 33764-4941 Office: HealthCare Capital Advisors Inc 2259 St Charles Dr Clearwater FL 33764-4941 E-mail: csassouni@healthcarecapital.net.

SASTROWARDOYO, TERESITA MANEJAR, nurse; b. Iloilo, Philippines; came to U.S., 1960; d. Timoteo and Monica (Casianan) Manejar; m. Sumarsongko H. Sastrowardoyo, June 8, 1962; children: Timoteo, Daniel (dec.), Benjamin. BSN, Ctrl. Philippine U., Iloilo, 1957; cert. operating rm. and surgical nursing, St. Luke's Hosp Ctr., N.Y.C., 1960-61. Head nurse med. unit Emmanuel Hosp., Roxas City, Philippines, 1957-58; supr. oper. rm. Brent Hosp., Zamboanga City, Philippines, 1958-60; staff nurse oper. rm. Jewish Meml. Hosp., N.Y.C., 1961-62; evening staff nurse oper. rm. Flower and Fifth Ave Hosp., 1963-65; staff nurse oper. rm., charge nurse night shift St. Lukes Hosp. Ctr., 1966-76; staff nurse oper. rm. South Side Hosp., Bayshore, N.Y., 1976—. Mem.: N.Y. State Nurses Assn., Ctrl. Philippine U. Alumni Assn. N.Y., N.J. and Conn. (bd. dirs. 1994—95, 1995—97). Baptist. Avocations: gardening, reading.

SASTRY, SRIN, scientist, researcher, educator; b. Eluru, India, Mar. 1, 1953; s. S.B.R. Murthy and Vasundhara Devi; m. Nora L. Linderoth, July 12, 1986; 1 child, Olivia. PhD, Madurai U., India, 1983; postgrad., U. Calif., Berkeley, 1983-93. Fellow Louis B. Mayer Found., N.Y.C., 1993-96; asst. prof. Rockefeller U., 1993—. Grantee Hewlett-packard Found., Cancer Rsch. Inst., 2000; recipient Postdoctoral Trainee award NIH, 1990-93; rsch. fellow Indian Coun. Agrl. Rsch., 1979-83; merit scholar Indian Coun. Agrl. Rsch., 1970-72. Mem. AAAS, Am. Chem. Soc., Am. Soc. Biochemistry and Molecular Biology, Am. Soc. Photobiology. Office: Rockefeller U Box 174 1230 York Ave New York NY 10021 E-mail: sastrys2000@yahoo.com.

SATAN, MIROSLAV, professional hockey player; b. Topolcany, Slovakia, Oct. 22, 1974; Left wing Edmonton Hockey Team, Buffalo Sabres, 1997—. Mem. Slovakian Nat. Team, 1996 World Championships. Office: Buffalo Sabres Marine Midland Arena One Seymour H Knox III Plz Buffalo NY 14203*

SATAVA, DAVID RICHARD, accountant, educator; b. San Francisco, May 1, 1951; s. Marvin Satava and Louise Gibbons; m. Susan E. Brown, Oct. 7, 1973; 1 child, Steven. BA, San Francisco State U., 1979, MBA, 1987; DBA, Miss. State U., 1994. CPA, Calif. Acct. Boydstun & Klingner, San Francisco, 1983-86; contr. Audubon Cellars, Berkeley, 1986-89; pvt. practice Oakland, 1985-96; asst. prof. acctg. Ga. So. U., Statesboro, 1994-95; assoc. prof. acctg. U. Houston, Victoria, Tex., 1995—. Contbr. articles to profl. jours. Advisor Gamma Beta Phi, Victoria, 1995—; pres. PTO, Victoria, 1996. Recipient Meritorious Svc. award Gamma Beta Phi, 1996; named Tchr. of Yr., U. Houston, Victoria, 1998. Mem. AICPA, Am. Acctg. Assn. Avocation: golf. Office: U Houston-Victoria 2506 E Red River St Victoria TX 77901-4450

SATCHER, CLEMENT MICHAEL, education educator; b. L.A., Aug. 21, 1939; s. Dexter Getzwiller and Vera Janette (Laney) S.; m. Brenda Susan McMonigle, Oct. 1972 (div. Dec. 1980); children: Monica, Catherine. AA, Santa Monica Coll., 1972; BA, Calif. State U., Northridge, 1975; cert., Calif. State U., San Bernardino, 1997. Cert. tchr. Illustrator, film and sound operator U.S. Army Engr. Sch., Fort Belvoir, Va., 1961-63; lighting design engr. Walt E. Disney Enterprises, Glendale, Calif., 1981-82, elec. designer Anaheim, 1987-88; lighting technician Theater Vision Inc., North Hollywood, 1984; elec. engr. Tippetts-Abbett-McCarty-Stratton, L.A., 1984-85; architect Azarak Corp., Westlake Village, Calif., 1985-87, Ward Investment Co., Costa Mesa, 1988; portrait photographer DeSpain Portrait Svc., Milford, Iowa, 1989-90; checker Looking Glass Enterprises, Yucca Valley, Calif., 1990-92; caretaker Dusty Rose Ranch, Desert Hot Springs, 1992-94; chem. dependency technician Betty Ford Ctr., Rancho Mirage, 1994. Sr. elec. draftsman Hughes Telecomm., El Segundo, Calif., 1969-73, elec. designer, 1973-76; architect Dept. Water Resources, State Calif., Santa Barbara, 1990; poet, painter, cartoonist. Author: Out of the Flock, 1965, 72; poetry included in anthologies; paintings represented in permanent collections ACLU Headquarters, L.A., Archbiship Office, L.A. With U.S. Army, 1961-63. Recipient Golden Poet award World of Poetry, 1989-90, Best Poets award Nat. Libr. Poetry, 1995-96. Mem. Internat. Soc. Poets, Beyond Baroque (Venice, Calif. chpt., mem. poet), 521 Studio Washington. Home: 34560 Judy Ln Cathedral City CA 92234-6309 E-mail: SikeMatcher@aol.com.

SATCHER, DAVID, public health service officer, federal official; b. Anniston, Ala., Mar. 2, 1941; s. Wilmer and Anna Satcher; m. Nola Satcher; children: Gretchen, David, Daraka, Daryl. BS, Morehouse Coll., 1963; MD, PhD, Case Western Reserve U., 1970. Faculty UCLA Sch. Medicine; faculty, chair dept. family medicine King-Drew Med. Ctr., interim dean, 1977—79; dir. King-Drew Sickle Cell Rsch. Ctr.; prof., chmn. dept. cmty. and family medicine Morehouse Sch. Medicine, Atlanta; pres. Meharry Med. Coll., Nashville, 1982—93; dir. Ctrs. for Disease Control and Prevention, Atlanta, 1993—98; adminstr. Agy. for Toxic Substances and Disease Registry, 1993—98; asst. sec., surgeon gen. HHS, Washington, 1998—2002; sr. vis. fellow Kaiser Family Found., 2002—. Apptd. mem. Coun. of Grad. Med. Edn., 1986, chmn. Named Nashvillian of Yr., 1992; recipient Watts Grassroots award for cmty. leadership, 1978, Nat. Conf. Christians and Jews awards, 1985, Black Achivement award, Ebony Mag., 1994, Brewslow award in pub. health, 1995, Dr. Nathan B. Davis award, AMA, 1996. Mem.: Inst. Medicine NAS, Alpha Omega Alpha, Phi Beta Kappa. Office: Kaiser Family Foundation Ste 250 1450 G St NW Washington DC 20005

SATERFIEL, THOMAS HORNE, education researcher, administrator; b. Hattiesburg, Miss., Dec. 14, 1950; s. Thomas Walton and Maybell (Horne) S.; m. Susan McKinley, June 1, 1974; children: Wayne Thomas, John Michael. BS, Miss. State U., 1972, MEd, 1973; PhD, Fla. State U., 1977; postgrad., Harvard U., 1985. Asst. prin. Tupelo (Miss.) Pub. Schs., 1972-73; tchr. math. Amory (Miss.) Pub. Schs., 1973-74; dir. devel. Blue Mountain (Miss.) Coll., 1974-75; asst. prof. ednl. psychology Miss. State U., Mississippi State, 1976-81, assoc. prof., 1981-85, dir. program. rsch. and evaluation for pub. schs., 1976-85; dep. state supt. Miss. Dept. Edn., Jackson, 1985-90; v.p. for rsch. Am. Coll. Testing (now ACT, Inc.), Iowa City, 1990-98, sr. v.p., 1998—.

Mem. outcomes accreditation panel Office Gov. of Miss., Jackson, 1981-83, study commn. Coun. of Chief State Sch. Officers, Washington, 1985-90; chair planning and evaluation Southeastern Ednl. Rsch. Lab., Raleigh, N.C., 1987-90; exec. com. Nat. Forum on Ednl. Stats., Washington, 1989-90. Contbr. articles to profl. jours. Sec.-treas. Optimist Club, Starkville, Miss., 1977-85, bd. dirs., Jackson, 1985-90; deacon 1st Bapt. Ch., Starkville, 1982-85. Recipient Outstanding Young Adminstr. award Phil Hardin Found., 1975; named one of Outstanding Young Men in Am., U.S. Jaycees, 1977; Kellogg Nat. fellow W.K. Kellogg Found., 1983-86. Mem. Nat. Coun. on Measurement in Edn., Am. Ednl. Rsch. Assn., Am. Mgmt. Assn., Phi Kappa Phi, Phi Delta Kappa (pres. Mississippi State chpt. 1983-84, Peer award, 1982, Outstanding Educator award 1984). Avocations: music, running. Home: 49 Samuel Dr Iowa City IA 52245-5652 Office: ACT Inc 2201 N Dodge St Iowa City IA 52243-0001

SATHER, EVERETT NORMAN, accountant; b. Story City, Iowa, July 20, 1935; s. George John and Laura Josephine (Bakka) S.; m. Patricia Ann Johnson, Apr. 24, 1955; children: Kimberly L., Kristine J., Kendall D. Student, Am. Inst. Bus., Des Moines, 1953-55. CPA, Iowa, Nebr., Ill. Office mgr. Story Polk Farm Svc., Nevada, Iowa, 1955-57; office mgr., bookeeper Capital City Electric Co., Des Moines, 1958-59; staff acct. Willard C. Randol, CPA, 1959-60, Ryun, Givens and Co., Des Moines, 1960-63; acct. Everett N. Sather, CPA, 1963-66; acct., ptnr. Denman and Co., 1966—. Officer, dir. Ditch Witch-Iowa, Inc., 1971—; pres., chmn. Ankeny (Iowa) Nat. Bank, 1972-82; pres. Triple K Ltd., Ankeny, 1983-2001, Boone (Iowa) Speedways, Inc., 1976-96, Sather Enterprises, Ltd., 1998—, JR Motorsports, Ltd., 1997—, Convenience Corp. No. Iowa Ltd., 1988-2001, E&P Enterprises, Ltd., 1995-2001; bd. dirs. Gateway Savs. Bank. Active Polk County Bd. Rev., Des Moines, 1970—; chmn. bd. Greater Des Moines Aviation Expo, 1989—; treas. Des Moines Grand Prix, 1988-94; bd. dirs. Care Initiatives, 1993-2000, 2001--. Mem. AICPA, Ill. Soc. CPAs, Iowa Soc. CPAs, Rotary (bd. dirs. 1990-93, pres. 1994-95), Zagszig Shrine, Scottish Rite, MAsons. Lutheran. Avocation: sports. Office: Denman and Co 1601 22nd St Ste 400 West Des Moines IA 50266-1453

SATHYAMOORTHY, MUTHUKRISHNAN, engineering researcher, educator; b. Sathanur, Tamil Nadu, India, Feb. 21, 1946; s. Kuppusamy and Visalakshi Muthukrishnan; m. Chitra Subbiah, May 26, 1971; children: Mohanakrishnan, Kumaran. B in Civil Engring., U. Madras, India, 1967; M in Engring. Mechanics, Indian Inst. of Tech., Madras, India, 1969, PhD in Aero. Engring., 1973. Lectr. Indian Inst. of Tech., Madras, India, 1969-74; rsch. fellow U. Birmingham, Eng., 1974-76; asst. prof. Clarkson U., Potsdam, NY, 1979-82, assoc. prof., 1982-92, assoc. prof., exec. officer, 1992-94, prof., exec. officer, 1994-97, prof., chair, 1997-2001; dean engring. W. Va. Univ. Inst. Tech., 2001—. Vis. rsch. faculty U. Calgary, Can., 1977-79. Contbn. author: Handbook of Civil Engineering Practice, 1988; editor: Material Nonlinearity in Vibrations, 1985; author: Nonlinear Analysis of Structures, 1998. Recipient Appreciation cert. U.S. Army, 1990, Outstanding Advisor award Clarkson U., 1993, Tau Beta Pi Faculty award, 1997, Disting. Tchg. award Clarkson Univ., 2001. Fellow ASME (mem. nat. student sect. com. 1992-94, mem. gen. awards com. 1994-99, Nat. Faculty Advisor award 1993, Dedicated Svc. award 1999); AIAA (assoc.), Aero. Soc. India. Avocations: overseas travel, camping, photography, fishing. Office: Office of Dean of Engring W Va Univ Inst Technology Montgomery WV 25136 Home: 321 2nd Ave Montgomery WV 25136-2403 E-mail: msathy@wvutech.edu.

SATHYAMOORTHY, VENUGOPAL, research biologist; b. Arcot, India, Jan. 20, 1954; s. Venugopal and Vanaroja (Natesan) V.; m. Neeraja, Nov. 27, 1981; children: Vinayak, Vidya. BS, U. Madras, 1974, MS, 1976, MPhil, 1977, PhD, 1981. Rsch. assoc. U. Wis., Madison, 1981-84, asst. scientist, 1984-87; rsch. biologist FDA, Washington, 1992—. Rsch. fellow U. Madras, India, 1976-81, Sr. Staff fellow NIH, Bethesda, Md., 1987-90, FDA, 1990-92. Mem. AAAS, Am. Soc. Microbiology. Home: 11401 Potomac Oak Dr Rockville MD 20850-3576 Office: FDA 200 C St SW # HFS-327 Washington DC 20204-0001 E-mail: VSathya@aol.com.

SATIN, CLAIRE JEANINE, sculptor, book artist; b. Bklyn., Jan. 9, 1942; BA, Sarah Lawrence Coll., 1956; MFA, Pratt Inst., 1968. Instr. art edn. dept. edn. Bklyn. Mus., 1958-59; instr. dept. edn. and dept. Fine Arts Broward Cmty. Coll., Ft. Lauderdale, Fla., 1971-83; dir. Broward Cmty. Coll. Gallery, 1975-76. Artist rep. Vorpal Gallery, Soho, N.Y.C., Jan van der Donk Gallery, Chelsea, N.Y.C. Collections include Victoria and Albert Mus., London, Getty Ctr. Hist. Art and Humanities, L.A., Mus. Modern Art, N.Y.C., Mus. Art, Ft. Lauderdale, King Stephen Mus., Szekesfehrdr, Hungary, Ruth and Marvin Sackner Archive of Concrete and Visual Poetry, others; commd. works include: Chapman Chronicles, State of Alaska, U. Alaska, Fairbanks, 1992, Alphawalk, New Tampa Regional Libr., Hillsborough County, Tampa, Fla., 1997 (catalog); Alphastory, Pembroke Pines Libr., Pembroke Pines, Fla., Broward County Art in Pub. Places Program (brochure), Am. Ctrs., New Delhi, Bombay, India. Bd. dirs. Broward County Cultural Affairs Coun., Ft. Lauderdale, 1975-83, hon. chair, 1981—. Recipient S. Fla. Cult Consortium award Miami Art Mus., Fla., 1997-98; So. Arts Fedn./NEA Regional Visual Arts fellow, 1996; Fla. State Individual Artist fellow Statewide Exhbn., 1978, 97-98; Cult Consortium fellow Miami Art Mus., 1997-98; Tiffany Found. grantee, 1968-69, Meml. Found. for Jewish Culture, 2001-02. Mem. Internat. Sculpture Ctr., Am. Craft. Coun., Ctr. Book Arts, Fonteneda Soc. (bd. dirs. 1997—). Office: care ARTWORKS/ARTSPACE 101 SW 1st St Dania FL 33004-3628

SATIN, JOSEPH, language professional, university administrator; b. Phila., Dec. 16, 1920; s. Reuben Philip and Harriet (Price) Satin; m. Selma Rosen (dec. 1978); children: Mark, Diane; m. Barbara Jeanne Dodson (dec. 1987); m. Terrye Sagan, 1992. BA, Temple U., 1946; AM, Columbia U., 1948, PhD, 1952. Instr. integrated studies W.Va. U., Morgantown, 1952-54; prof. English and Comparative Lit. Moorhead (Minn.) State U., 1954-63; chmn. dept. English and Journalism Midwestern U., Wichita Falls, Tex., 1963-73; dean Sch. Arts and Humanities Calif. State U., Fresno, 1973-89. Mgr concert series Moorhead State Univ, 1956—61; mem nat bd consult NEH, Washington, 1979—; dir London semester Calif State Univ, Fresno, 1982—92; dir Frank Lloyd Wright Auditorium Project. Author: (book) Ideas in Context, 1958, The 1950's: America's "Placid" Decade, 1960, Reading Non-Fiction Prose, 1964, Reading Prose Fiction, 1964, Shakespeare and His Sources, 1966, Reading Literature, 1968, The Humanities Handbook (2 vols), 1969, (poems) The Journey Upward, 1999, Poems on the Internet (www.Poetry.com), 2000; editor: (book) Frank Lloyd Wright-Letters to Apprentices, 1982, Letters to Architects, 1984, Letters to Clients, 1986, Treasures of Taliesin, 1985, The Guggenheim Correspondence, 1986, Frank Lloyd Wright: His Living Voice, 1987, Frank Lloyd Wright, The Crowning Decade, 1989; translator: Federico Fellini, Comments on Film, 1987; contbr. ; dir: Univ Press, Calif State Univ, 1982—92. With U.S. Army, 1943—46, ETO. Named Nat Grand Prize Winner, Nat Library Poetry N Am Ann Poetry Contest, 1998. Jewish. Avocations: creative writing, music, parcheesi. Home: 65 Maywood Dr San Francisco CA 94127-2007 E-mail: terryellen1965@hotmail.com.

SATIN, KAREN W. university publications director; b. Chgo., Apr. 12, 1938; d. Harry E. and Gertrude (Plotkin) Weiss; m. Lawrence Z. Satin, Sept. 11, 1960 (div. 1980); children: Wendy, Scott, Kimberly. BA in English and Sociology, U. Conn., 1958; MA in Journalism, U. Md., 1984. Prodn. editor Encyclopedia Britannica, Chgo., 1960-64; freelance editor Washington, 1977-81; program editor Nat. Sci. Tchrs. Assn., 1981-83; sr. tech. writer Computer Scis. Corp., Arlington, Va., 1983-84; publs. mgr. Sci. Applications Rsch., Lanham, Md., 1984-89; dir. publs., adj. faculty comm. studies U. Md. Univ. Coll., College Park, 1989—. Office: U Md Univ Coll University Blvd At Adelphi Rd College Park MD 20742-0001

SATIN, MARK, editor, lawyer; b. N.Y.C., Mar. 16, 1946; s. Joseph Henry and Selma (Rosen) S. BA, U. B.C., Vancouver, Can., 1972; JD, NYU, 1995. Bar: D.C. 1999. Exec. dir. Toronto Anti-Draft Programme, 1967—68; freelance writer Vancouver, 1972-78; exec. dir. New World Alliance, Washington, 1979—81; editor New Options Newsletter, 1983-92; gen. ptnr. Mark Satin Prodns., LP, N.Y.C. and Washington, 1996—2002; gen. counsel Ctr. Visionary Law, Denver and Washington, 1998—; editor Radical Middle Newsletter, Washington, 1998—; webmaster www.radicalmiddle.com, 2000—. Mem. adv. bd. The Other Econ. Summit, N.Y.C., 1987-92, Elmwood Inst., Berkeley, Calif., 1986-92. Author: Manual for Draft-Age Immigrants to Canada, 1968, Confessions of a Young Exile, 1976, New Age Politics, 1979, New Options for America, 1991; contbr. articles to jour. Activist U.S. Green Party, Washington, 1984-90; civil rights worker Student Non-Violent Coord. Com., Holly Springs, Miss., 1964-65. Recipient Alternative Press award for gen. excellence Utne Reader, 1989. Mem. D.C. Bar, World History Assn., World Future Soc. Avocations: jogging, vegetarian cooking, art appreciation, Karma yoga. Office: Radical Middle Newsletter PO Box 57100 Washington DC 20037-0100

SATINE, BARRY ROY, lawyer; b. N.Y.C., July 25, 1951; s. Norman S. and Fay (Mekles) S.; m. Janice Bea Halfond, Aug. 4, 1974; children: David, Leah. BA, CCNY, 1972; JD, George Washington U., 1975. Bar: N.Y. 1976, D.C. 1977, U.S. Dist. Ct. (so. dist.) N.Y. 1978, U.S. Supreme Ct. 1979, U.S. Dist. Ct. (ea. dist.) N.Y. 1982, U.S. Ct. Appeals (2d cir.) 1989. Trial atty. U.S. Civil Svc. Commn., Washington, 1975-78; atty. AT&T, N.Y.C., 1978-81, N.Y. Tel. Co., N.Y.C., 1981-82; mem. assoc. Surrey & Morse, 1982-84, ptnr., 1985, Jones, Day, Reavis & Pogue, 1986—. Mem.: Assn. of Bar of City of N.Y. Office: Jones Day Reavis & Pogue 222 East 41st Street New York NY 10017 E-mail: barryrsatine@jonesday.com.

SATINOVER, JEFFREY B. psychiatrist, writer, health facility administrator, physicist; b. Chgo., Sept. 4, 1947; s. Joseph and Sena (Rotman) S.; m. Julie Rachel Leff, June 10, 1982; Sarah Katherine, Anne-Rebecca, Jenny Leigh. BS, MIT, 1971; EdM, Harvard U., 1973; MD, U. Tex., 1982; Diplomate, C.G Jung Inst., Zurich, Switzerland, 1976; postgrad., Yale U., 1998—; postgrad. in physics, 2001—. Diplomate Am. Bd. Psychiatry and Neurology, Am. Bd. Geriat. Psychiatry. Fellow dept. psychiatry and child psychiatry Yale U., New Haven, 1982-86; founder, exec. dir. Sterling Inst., Stamford, Conn., 1985-92; med. dir. Temenos Inst., Westport, 1984—; pvt. practice, 1992—. Relativistic heavy ion group dept. physics, Yale U.; pres. C.G. Jung Found. N.Y., 1988-92; catchment area coun. S.W. Regional Mental Health Bd., 1988-92; William James lectr. psychology and religion Harvard U., 1975; mem. Lower Fairfield County Regional Action Coun. Against Substance Abuse, 1990-92. Author: Homosexuality and the Politics of Truth, 1994, The Empty Self: Gnostic Foundations of Modern Identity, 1994, Feathers of the Skylark, 1996, Cracking the Bible Code, 1997, The Quantum Brain, 2001; co-author: Jungian Psychotherapy, 1984, Science and the Fragile Self, 1990, Jungian Analysis, 1993; contbr. articles to profl. jours. Founder, exec. bd. com. Save Our Schs., 1994—; bd. dirs. Towrd Tradition; bd. advisors Family Inst. Conn., 1996—; active nat. physician's resource coun. Focus on Family, 1994-97; bd. dirs. Klingberg Family Ctrs., 1994-96. Capt. USAR N.G., 1989-94; maj. USAR, 1995—. Recipient Seymour Lustman Residency Rsch. 2d place award Yale U. psychiatry dept., 1983, 85. Mem. Am. Psychiat. Assn. (Burroughs-Wellcome fellow 1983-85), Internat. Assn. Analytical Psychology, Aspetuck Valley Country Club, Alpha Omega Alpha. Republican. Jewish. Avocations: tennis, harpsichord, jazz keyboard. also: Relativistic Heavy Ion Group PO Box 208124 272 Whitney Ave New Haven CT 06520-8124 Office: 22 Wilton Crst Wilton CT 06897-4050

SATINSKAS, HENRY ANTHONY, airline services company executive; b. Kaunas, Lithuania, Dec. 22, 1936; came to U.S., 1949; s. Henry Francis and Donna (Olechnavicius) S.; m. Lucia Aldona Sestakauskas, Dec. 7, 1963; children: Henry Arnold, Paul Steven (dec.), Laura Monica. Student, Drexel U., 1957-60; BS in Bus. Adminstrn., Temple U., 1963. Mgmt. trainee Pub. Service Coordinated Transp., Maplewood, N.J., 1964; asst. garage supr. Jersey City, 1965-66; charter service mgr. Suburban Transit Corp., New Brunswick, N.J., 1966-68; gen. mgr. Ave B and E Byway Transit Co., N.Y.C., 1968-71, St. John's (Newfoundland, Can.) Transp. Commn., 1971-73; asst. dir. transp. planning Montgomery County Govt., Rockville, Md., 1973-76; gen. mgr. Airway Limousine Service subs. Hudson Gen. Corp., Balt., 1976-78; dir. transp. services Airway Services subs. Hudson Gen. Corp., Jamaica, N.Y., 1978-81; v.p. Hudson Gen. Corp. (now Globe Ground N.Am. LLC), Great Neck, NY, 1981—; bd. mem., mem. reps., mng. dir. Airport Carts LLC, 1999—. Mem. adv. coun. on edn. Province of Newfoundland and Labrador, St. John's, 1972; bd. dirs. Greater Jamaica Devel. Corp., 1987-90. Republican. Roman Catholic. Avocations: reading, gardening, travel, biking. Home: 35 Woodvale Dr Syosset NY 11791-1213 Office: Hudson Gen Corp 111 Great Neck Rd Ste 600 Great Neck NY 11021-5401

SATINSKY, BARNETT, lawyer; b. Phila., June 17, 1947; s. Alex and Florence (Talsky) S.; m. Fredda Andrea Wagner, June 17, 1973; children: Meagen, Sara Beth, Jonathan. AB, Brown U., 1969; JD, Villanova U., 1972. Bar: Pa. 1972, U.S. Dist. Ct. (ea. dist) Pa. 1975, U.S. Dist. Ct. (mid. dist.) Pa. 1975, U.S. Ct. Appeals (3d cir.) 1981. Law clk. Phila. Ct. Common Pleas, 1972-73; dep. atty. gen. Pa. Dept. Justice, Harrisburg, 1973-75; 1st asst. counsel Pa. Pub. Utility Commn., 1975-77, chief counsel, 1977; assoc. Fox, Rothschild, O'Brien & Frankel, LLP, Phila., 1978-81; ptnr. Fox, Rothschild, O'Brien & Frankel, 1981—. Children Svcs. Rev. com., United Way Southeast Pa., 1984-86; bd. dirs. ACLU, Harrisburg, 1973-74, Voyage House, Inc., 1994-96. Mem. ABA (pub. utility, labor and employment law sects., employee benefits com. 1984—), Pa. Bar Assn. (labor rels., pub. utility law sects. 1980—, pub. utility law com., governing coun. 1991-93), Phila. Bar Assn. (labor law com. 1980—, chmn. pub. utility law com. 1988-91), Nat. Assn. Coll. and Univ. Attys., Nat. Assn. Regulatory Commrs. (staff subcom. law 1977), Soc. for Human Resource Mgmt., Tau Epsilon Law Soc. Democrat. Jewish. Office: Fox Rothschild O'Brien & Frankel LLP 2000 Market St Philadelphia PA 19103-3291 E-mail: bsatinsky@frof.com.

SATISH, MALINI, physician, educator; b. Madras, India, Dec. 23, 1950; m. 1 child. Cert., Madras U., 1967; MBBS with honors, Sree Venkateswara Med. Coll., 1973. Diplomate Am. Bd. of Pediats.; cert. infant massage, NIDCAP. Intern Sree Venkateswara Med. Coll., Tirupathi, India, 1973-74; resident in ob-gyn. Andhra Mahila Sabha Hosp., 1975; resident in pediat. Med. Coll. of Ohio, Toledo, 1978-79; neonatal fellow The Toledo Hosp., 1980-81; assoc. clin. dir. neonatal svcs. Children's Med. Ctr. for N.W. Ohio Toledo Children's Hosp., 1982—; founder SAPTA Newborn Individualized Devel. Care and Assessment Plan Tng. Ctr., 1995, med. dir., 1995-96. Dir. NICU follow-up program Children's Med. Ctr. of N.W. Ohio, 1987—; courtesy staff Flower Meml. Hosp., Sylvania, Ohio, 1985-89; provisional staff Flower Hosp., 1996—; courtesy staff Firelands Cmty. Hosp., Sandusky, Ohio, 1997—; clin. instr. dept. of pediat. Med. Coll. of Ohio, Toledo, 1981-84, clin. asst. prof. dept. of pediat., 1984-95, clin. assoc. prof. dept. of pediat., 1995—; mem. Nat. Neonatal Database Med. Adv. Bd., 1995—; com. mem. The Toledo Hosp. Blood Utilization, The Toledo Hosp. Critical Care com., Dr. G raven's com. on Effects of Sound, Light and Positioning on VLBW Infants in NICU, Am. Acad. Pediats. com. Contbr. articles to profl. jours. Cert. prin. investigator Supplemental Therapeutic Oxygen for Prevention of Retinopathy of Prematurity. Recipient numerous grants. Fellow AMA, Am. Acad. of Pediats. (com. on children with devel. disabilities), N.W. Ohio Pediat. Soc. Home: 2326 Plum Leaf Ln Toledo OH 43614-1141 Office: Toledo Childrens Hosp 2142 N Cove Blvd Toledo OH 43606-3895 E-mail: msatish@pol.net.

SATITPUNWAYCHA, PON, surgeon; b. Bangkok, 1936; MD, Chulalongkorn Hosp. U., Bangkok, 1962. Intern Passavant Meml. Hosp., Chgo., 1963; resident Northwestern U. Med. Sch., 1964-69; surgeon Cypress Fairbanks Med. Ctr. Hosp., Houston. Mem. ACS (life; Disting. Philanthropy award 2001), AMA (life), Soc. Am. Gastrointestinal Endoscopic Surgery, Soc. Laparascopic Surgery, Am. Soc. Colo-rectal Surgeons, S.W. Surg. Congress. Office: 11301 Fallbrook Dr Ste 101 Houston TX 77065-4269

SATO, EUNICE NODA, former mayor, consultant; b. Livingston, Calif., June 8, 1921; d. Bunsaku and Sawa (Maeda) Noda; m. Thomas Takashi Sato, Dec. 9, 1950; children— Charlotte Patricia, Daniel Ryuichi and Douglas Ryuji (twins). AA, Modesto Jr. Coll., 1941; BA, U. No. Colo., 1944; MA, Columbia U., 1948. Public sch. tchr. Mastodon Twp. Schs., Alpha, Mich., 1944-47; ednl. missionary Reformed Ch. Am., Yokohama, Japan, 1948-51; coun. mem. City of Long Beach, Calif., 1975-86; mayor, 1980-82. Sec. corp. bd. Los Angeles County Health Systems Agy., 1978-79 Monthly contbr. articles to 2 neighborhood papers, 1975-86. Bd. dirs. Long Beach chpt. ARC, 1975-2000, mem. exec. com., 1978-91, 93-99, past pres. and v.p., mem. Calif. state svc. coun., A.R.C., 1995-2001; bd. dirs. Goodwill Industries, 1978-82 ; trustee St. Mary's Bauer Med. Ctr., 1977—; pres. Industry Edn. Coun., Long Beach, 1984-86, mem. exec. bd., 1984—; bd. dirs. Industry Edn. Coun. of Calif.; treas. So. Calif. Consortium of I.E.C., 1984-86, pres., 1988-89; mem. State Adv. Group on Juvenile Justice and Delinquency Prevention, 1983-91, Calif. Coun. Criminal Justice, 1983-95, legis. com. Girl Scout coun. Calif., 1986-92, chair, 1991-92; bd. dirs. Long Beach council Girl Scouts U.S., 1986-92, Region III United Way, 1974-88; mem. Asian Pacific adv. com. Calif. Dept. Rehab., 1985-87, recreation commn. City of Long Beach, 1985-86, pub. safety policy com. League Calif. Cities, 1981-86, community econ. and housing devel. com. So. Calif. Assn. Govts., 1976-86, Calif. Task Force to Promote Self-Esteem and Personal and Social Responsibility, 1987-90; Long Beach chpt. pres. NCCJ, 1987-88; pres. Internat. Community Coun., 1986-87, bd. dir. 1986-2001, pres. Japanese Am. Reps., 1987, 88, exec. bd. mem. 1987-2001; presdl. appointee Nat. Adv. Coun. Ednl. Rsch. and Improvement, 1991-94; pres. Aux. to Sch. Theology, Claremont, 1990-91, exec. bd. 1989-91, nat. selective svc. sys. local bd. 138, 1990-2001, SCA Edison Co. Equal Opportunity adv. coun., 1990-94; chair selection com. Leadership Long Beach, 1990-91, sec. exec. bd., 1991-92; chair adv. bd. AIESEC, 1990-92; chmn. Long Beach Area Rep. Party, 1990-92; asst. sec. cen. com., L.A, 1990-92; sec.-gen. coun. on fin. and administrn. United Meth. Ch., 1992-2000; appointed by Gov. to commn. on teacher credentialing State Calif., 1994, L.A. coun. svc. coun. A.R.C., 1995-99; chair adminstrv. bd. Leisure World Cmty. Ch., 1996—; rep. to South Coast Ecumenical Coun., 1993—, chair pastor parish rels. com., 2000; chair Parents Day Festival com. greater L.A. county, 1996-2000, Blue Ribbon Com. for Effective Parenting in Long Beach, 1997-99. Recipient Outstanding Svc. award Long Beach Coord. Coun., 1969, Mother of Yr. award Silverado United Meth. Ch., 1973, Hon. Svc. award Calif. PTA, 1963, Continuing Svc. award, 1974, hon. life membership award Nat. PTA, 1974, Outstanding Laywoman of Yr. award Long Beach Area Coun. Chs., 1976, Woman of Yr. award State Women's Coun.-C. of C., 1979, Long Beach Iternat. Bus. and Profl. Women's Club, Nat. Merit award DAR, 1982, Citizen of Yr. award Los Altos YMCA, 1982, Calif. Cmty. Pool for Handicapped, 1982, Outstanding Citizen award Torch Club of Long Beach, 1983, W. Odie Wright award Industry Edn. Coun., 1990, Humanitarian award NCCJ, 1992, Vol. of Yr. award ARC, 1995, 1st Life Membership award Long Beach chpt. UN Assn., Kunsho award of Order of the Sacred Treasure, Gold Rays with rosette from Japanese Govt., 1996, Sr. Vol. of Yr. Long Beach C.C., 1999. Mem. Industry Edn. Coun. Long Beach (hon. life), Long Beach C. of C. (Dewey Smith cmty. svc. award), Lions (hon. life), Alpha Iota (hon.). Republican. Methodist. Home: Bixby Village 551 Pittsfield Ct Unit 101 Long Beach CA 90803-6355

SATO, GLENN KENJI, lawyer; b. Honolulu, Jan. 6, 1952; s. Nihei and Katherine (Miwa) S.; m. Donna Mae Shiroma, Apr. 4, 1980 (dec. Aug. 1985); m. Nan Sun Oh, Mar. 27, 1987 (dec. Nov. 1997); children: Gavan, Allison, Garrett; m. Sandra K. Kumagai, Nov. 21, 1999. BBA, U. Hawaii, 1975; JD, U. Calif., San Francisco, 1977. Bar: Hawaii 1978, U.S. Dist. Ct. Hawaii, 1978, U.S. Ct. Claims 1990. Assoc. Fujiyama, Duffy & Fujiyama, Honolulu, 1978-80, 83-87, ptnr., 1987-95; stockholder Law Offices of Glenn K. Sato, 1980-82; pres. ISL Svcs., Inc., 1983; ptnr. Sato & Thomas, 1995-98; pvt. practice, 1998—. Vice chmn. Pattern Jury Instrn. Com., State of Hawaii, Honolulu, 1993. Treas. Polit. Action Com., Honolulu, 1993. Mem. Platform Assn., Beta Gamma Sigma. Avocations: golf, hunting, target shooting, surfing. Office: Ste 1020 1001 Bishop St Honolulu HI 96813-3481

SATO, KAZUYOSHI, pathologist; b. Shibata, Niigata, Japan, Apr. 3, 1930; came to U.S., 1968; s. Katsueita and Kyo (Sakagawa) S.; m. Ann Marie Farrenkopf, July 5, 1964 (dec. Aug. 1983); children: P.T. Sachiko, P. Miyoko, Michael T., Phillip K. Student, Niigata U., Japan, 1954, MD, 1958. Diplomate Am. Bd. Pathology, Anatomic and Clin. Pathology. Intern USAF Hosp., Tachikawa, Japan, 1958-59, Ellis Hosp., Schenectady, N.Y., 1959-60, asst. resident in pathology, 1960-61; resident in pathology Free Hosp. for Women, Brookline, Mass., 1961-62, The Children's Hosp. Med. Ctr., Boston, 1962-63, resident in neuropathology, 1963-64; resident fellow in pathology Mayo Grad. Sch. Medicine, Rochester, Minn., 1968-70; dir. labs. Falmouth (Mass.) Hosp., 1972-96; dir. Falmouth Hosp. Service Lab., Sandwich, Mass., 1986-93. Pathologist and rsch. assoc. Atomic Bomb Casualty Commn., Nagasaki, Japan, 1964-68; pathologist, chief of pathology USPHS Hosp., Norfolk Va., 1970-72, Falmouth (Mass.) Hosp., 1972-97. Recipient Fulbright scholarship, 1959. Fellow Coll. Am. Pathologists, Am. Soc. Clin. Pathologists; mem. Assn. Mil. Surgeons U.S. Home: 88 Two Ponds Rd Falmouth MA 02540-2225

SATO, MOTOAKI, geologist, researcher; b. Tokyo, Japan, Oct. 11, 1929; came to U.S., 1955, 63. s. Iwazo and Kyoko (Ito) S.; m. Ellen B. Levinson, Feb. 11, 1961 (div. Sept. 1978); children: Emily Coates, Alice Isomé, Thomas Bartlett. BS in Geology, U. Tokyo, Japan, 1953, MS in Geology, 1955; PhD in Geology, U. Minn., 1959. Research asst. dept. geophysics Univ. Minn., Mpls., 1956-58; rsch. fellow in geophysics dept. geol. scis. Harvard Univ., Cambridge, Mass., 1958-61; assoc. prof. geology Inst. Thermal Springs Research, Misasa, Tottori, Japan, 1961-63; research geologist U.S. Geological Survey, Washington, 1963-65, geologist, project chief Washington/Reston, Va., 1965-95, scientist emeritus, 1995—. Prin. investigator Lunar Sample & Sci. Program, NASA, 1971-80. Contbg. author books and articles in profl. jours. Fulbright/Smith-Mundt fellow Inst. Internat. Edn., 1955-57, Gilbert fellow U.S. Geol. Survey, Reston, Va., 1982-83. Mem. Am. Geophysical Union, Geochemical Soc., Geological Soc. Washington (2d v.p. 1982-83), Geochemistry Div. Am. Chem. Soc. Achievements include patent pending on mitigation of acid mine drainage. Home: 11173 Lake Chapel Ln Reston VA 20191-4308 Office: US Geol Survey 956 National Ctr Reston VA 20192-0001 E-mail: msato@usgs.gov., motoaki@aol.com. *Remember that we did not design the way Nature works; Nature designed us, too. So let's listen ever so carefully, with an open mind, to what Nature is trying to tell us.*

SATORIUS, DANIEL MARK, lawyer, motion picture and television producer; b. Normal, Ill., July 13, 1951; s. Richard Ben and Erma Satorius; m. Tonda Lu Mattie, Aug. 10, 1974; children: Ashley Mattie, Taylor Mattie, Perry Mattie. BA, U. Iowa, 1973, MA, 1976; JD, So. Ill. U., 1978. Bar: Ill. 1978, Minn. 1979, U.S. Dist. Ct. Minn. 1979. Shareholder Satorius and Mattie P.A., St. Paul, 1981-89; of counsel Leonard, Street & Deinard, Mpls., 1989-94; shareholder, officer Abdo Abdo Broady & Satorius PA, 1994—. Adj. prof. law William Mitchell Law Sch., St. Paul, 1997—; adj. faculty, lectr. Mpls. Cmty. & Tech. Coll., Mpls., 1989—, Music Tech., Mpls., 1995-98; nat. spkr., writer on entertainment law topics. Editor, prin. author: The Practical Musician, 1993; filmmaker: (motion picture) Fear and Trembling, 1976 (Acad. award nomination student film award competition); assoc. editor Entertainment and Sport Lawyer. Officer, bd. dirs. Ind. Feature Project North, Mpls., 1987—; bd. dirs. Resources and Counseling for Arts, St. Paul, 1991-97; mem. adv. bd. Minn. Chorale, Mpls., 1994—; mem. Gov.'s Task Force on Music and Recording Arts, St. Paul, 1984. Mem. ABA (Entertainment and Sports Forum 1981—, assoc. editor., Entertainment and Sports Law Lawyer, 1999—), NARAS, Minn. State Bar Assn. (mem., past chair art and entertainment law sect. 1985—).

SATO-VIACRUCIS, KIYO, nurse, inventor, entrepreneur, consultant; b. Sacramento, May 8, 1923; d. John Shinji and Mary Tomomi (Watanabe) Sato; m. Gene Viacrucis, Aug. 9, 1958 (div. May 1976); adopted children: Cia, Jon, Paul, Tanya. BS, Hillsdale Coll., 1944; M in Nursing in Grad. Studies/Pub. Health Nursing, Western Res. U., 1951. Cert. health and devel. specialist, Calif., pub. health nurse, Calif., audiologist. Nursery sch. attendant Poston (Ariz.) II Concentration Camp, 1942; staff nurse U. Hosps., Cleve., 1948; pub. health nurse Sacramento County Health Dept., 1948-50, 52-53; sch. nurse U. Oslo, 1953, Sacramento County Schs., 1954-58; presch. nurse Sacramento City Unified Sch. Dist., 1973-85; pvt. practice cons. Blackbird Vision Screening System, Sacramento, 1985—. Cons., speaker Blackbird Vision Screening System, 1973—; cons. state task force Vision Screening Guidelines, 1981. Inventor Blackbird presch. vision screening method; cons. vision screening; contbr. articles to profl. jours. Served to capt. USAF, 1951-52. Recipient Excellence in Nursing award RN Mag. Found., 1983. Mem. Nat. Sch. Nurses Assn., Calif. Sch. Nurses Orgn., Japanese Am. Citizens League (pres. 1950), Am. Assn. Ret. Persons, VFW (pub. rels., post surgeon 1985—, cmty. activities 1986—, speaker's bur. Internment of Am. of Japanese Descent and the U.S. Constn.). Democrat. Avocations: writing, pottery, hula dancing, Tai Chi, grandchildren. Office: Blackbird Vision Screening PO Box 277424 Sacramento CA 95827-7424 E-mail: blackbird@softcom.net.

SATOVSKY, ABRAHAM, lawyer; b. Detroit, Oct. 15, 1907; s. Samuel and Stella (Benenson) S.; m. Toby Nayer, Sept. 4, 1938 (dec.); children: Sheldon Baer, James Bennett. BA, U. Mich., 1928, JD, 1930. Bar: Mich. 1930, U.S. Supreme Ct. 1930. Assoc. William Henry Gallagher, Detroit, 1930-65. Bldg. chmn. lawyers com. United Found. and Torch Dr. Co-chmn. profl. divsn. Allied Jewish Campaign; adv. coun. United Synagogue Am.; del. Jewish Cmty. Coun. Detroit; v.p. Mosies Chetim Orgn. Detroit; bd. dirs. Detroit Svc. Group, past chmn. fgn. mission; active fund raiser Greater Miami United Jewish Appeal; mem. fund dr. com. U. Mich. Law Sch.; trustee Clover Hill Park Cemetery, 1978-81, trustee emeritus, 1982—; bd. dirs. Congregation Shaarey Zedek, Southfield, Mich., past pres., 1959-62. Recipient Sem. award Jewish Theol. Sem. Am., 1952; citation of merit Jewish Welfare Fedn., Detroit; Jerusalem award State of Israel Bond Orgn.; numerous other awards. Mem. ABA, Mich. Bar Assn., Detroit Bar Assn., Oakland County Bar, Nat. Fedn. Jewish Men's Clubs (founder, past pres., hon. life pres., Gt. Lakes regional award 1977, Ma'Asim Tovim (Good Deeds) award 1989), Am. Arbitration Assn., Jewish Hist. Soc. Mich. (mem. adv. bd.), Am. Jewish Hist. Soc., Am. Judicature Soc., Men's Club Congregation Shaarey Zedek (past pres., hon. life pres.), Standard Club, B'nai B'rith (past pres. Detroit), Hadassah (life), Phi Beta Delta (merged with Pi Lambda Phi). Home and Office: 28455 Northwestern Hwy Southfield MI 48034-1823 *With a desire and willingness to improve my profession, my religious beliefs, and help the community, I have devoted a good portion of my time and efforts for those purposes. I, too, have been enriched by the association, have hopefully directed and encouraged others, and hope to continue to do so.*

SATTER, RAYMOND NATHAN, judge; b. Denver, Oct. 19, 1948; s. Charles Herbert and Muriel Vera (Tuller); m. Suzanne Elizabeth Ehlers, May 28, 1977. BA, U. Denver, 1970; JD, Cath. U., 1973. Bar: Colo. 1973, U.S. Dist. Ct. Colo. 1973, U.S. Ct. Appeals (10th cir.) 1973, U.S. Supreme Ct. 1976, U.S. Tax Ct. 1981. Assoc. Wallace, Armatas & Hahn, Denver, 1973-75; ptnr. Tallmadge, Wallace & Hahn, 1975-77; pvt. practice, 1978-87; Denver County judge, 1987—; presiding judge Denver County Ct., 2001—. Gen. counsel Satter Dist., Denver, 1977-78; assoc. mcpl. judge City of Englewood, Colo., 1985-86; mem. Colo. Supreme Ct. Com. on Civil Rules. Pres. Young Artists Orch. Denver, 1985-87; sec. Denver Symphony Assn., 1985-86. Mem. Colo. Bar Assn. (ethics com.), Denver Bar Assn. (bd. trustees 1998-2001, Jud. Excellence award 1992, 95). Avocations: sailing, opera, classical music, fishing, bridge. Office: Denver County Ct 108 City & County Bldg 1437 Bannock St Denver CO 80202-5337 E-mail: rsatter@ci.denver.co.us.

SATTERFIELD, CHARLES NELSON, chemical engineer, educator; b. Dexter, Mo., Sept. 5, 1921; s. Charles David and Hermine (Weber) S.; m. Anne Pettingell, July 6, 1946; children— Mark Edward, Joye. BS cum laude, Harvard U., 1942; MS, MIT, 1943, Sc.D., 1946. Registered profl. engr., Mass. Asst. prof. chem. engring. Mass. Inst. Tech., Cambridge, 1946-53, asso. prof., 1953-59, prof., 1959-92; emeritus prof., 1992—. Lectr. indsl. chemistry Harvard, 1948-57; cons.on rocket propellants Dept. Def., 1952-60; mem. com. chem. kinetics NRC, 1960-66; chmn. ad hoc panel on abatement nitrogen oxide emissions from stationary sources Nat. Acad. Engring., 1970-72; indsl. cons. to major cos. in petroleum and chem. industries. Co-author: Thermodynamic Charts for Combustion Processes, 1949, Hydrogen Peroxide, 1955 (translated into Russian 1957), Role of Diffusion in Catalysis, 1963; author: Mass Transfer in Heterogeneous Catalysis, 1970 (translated into Russian 1976), Heterogeneous Catalysis in Practice, 1980 (translated into Russian 1984), repub. as Heterogeneous Catalysis in Industrial Practice, 1991, also more than 140 tech. papers; mem. editl. adv. bd. Indsl. and Engring. Chemistry, 1966-68, Advances in Chemistry Series, 1971-73, 82-86, Energy and Fuels, 1990-95, Applied Cata lysis, 1995—; patentee in field. Fellow Am. Acad. Arts and Scis.; mem. Am. Chem. Soc., Am. Inst. Chem. Engrs. (Wilhelm award 1980), Sigma Xi, Tau Beta Pi. Home: 38 Tabor Hill Rd Lincoln MA 01773-2906 Office: Dept Chem Engring Mass Inst Tech Cambridge MA 02139

SATTERFIELD, JOHN ROBERTS, JR. retired college president and music educator; b. Danville, Va., Dec. 4, 1921; s. John Roberts and Sara Elise Council Satterfield; m. Carolyn Talley, Dec. 18, 1948; children: John Roberts III, Kenneth Scott, Keith Charles, Jean Council. BA, U. N.C., 1949, MusM, 1950, MA, 1955, PhD, 1962. Asst. prof. music Davidson (N.C.) Coll., 1953-60; assoc. prof. music Fla. Prebyn. Coll., St. Petersburg, 1960-63, prof. music, 1963-67, prof. humanities and music, 1967-68; v.p. acad. affairs, prof. humanities and music Elmira (N.Y.) Coll., 1968-70; asst. dir. N.C. Bd. Higher Edn., Raleigh, 1970-72; asst. v.p. acad. affairs U. N.C. Gen. Adminstrn., Chapel Hill, 1972, dir. Ctr. Continuing Renewal of Higher Edn., 1972; provost Kalamazoo (Mich.) Coll., 1972-75, exec. v.p., 1973-75; pres. Wagner Coll., Staten Island, N.Y., 1975-81; ret., 1981; part-time instr. music Durham (N.C.) Tech. C.C., 1997. Vis. prof. music U. Ky., Lexington, 1964, U. Tex., Austin, 1966; cons. Fla. State Dept. Edn., N.Y. State Depts. Edn. and Civil Svc., U.S. Office Edn., N.C. Bd. Higher Edn., Siena Coll., Coll. St. Benedict, U. Dayton, Davidson Coll., Ohio U. Editor: Christopher Tye: The Latin Ch. Music, Part I: The Masses, 1973, Part II: The Shorter Latin Works, 1973; translator: The Technique of My Musical Language (Olivier Messaien), 2 vols., 1956; chief author: Private Higher Education in North Carolina: Conditions and Prospects, 1971, (video) Myth and Symbol: An Occasional Lecture, 2000; contbr. numerous articles and revs. to profl. jours. and newspapers, short stories to quars., chpts. to books; composer music; keyboardist (movie) The Handmaid's Tale, 1990. Bd. mem., Empire State Found. Ind. Liberal Arts Colls., N.Y.C., 1975-81, United Meth. City Soc., N.Y.C., 1975-81. Capt., USAF, 1942-45. Decorated Bronze Star, Presdl. Citation with Cluster, Belgian Fourragère, Croix de Guerre; recipient Composers award N.C. Symphony Soc., 1951, Harbison award, the Danforth Found., 1965-66. Mem. The Melville Soc. Avocations: reading, travel, cooking. Home: 1401 Brigham Rd Chapel Hill NC 27517-3403

SATTERFIELD-HARRIS, RITA, workers compensation representative; b. Bklyn., Oct. 14, 1949; d. Wilton Anthony and Hattie Eva (Tunstall) Satterfield; m. Sidney Harris, Jan. 5, 1973; 1 child, Marcial A.H. BA in Psychology, Bernard Baruch Coll., N.Y.C., 1983; student, CCNY, 1971-74; Cert. in Paralegal Studies, L.I. U., Bklyn., 1982; cert. unemployment ins. benefits law, Cornell U., 1984. Lic. workers' compensation rep. N.Y.; registered agt. N.Y. State Unemployment Ins. Dir. social svcs. Lincoln Sq. Neighborhood Ctr., N.Y.C., 1979-88; pvt. practice, 1988—. Writer of proposals funded by N.Y.C. Dept. for Aging Inc., 1980-82, and N.Y.C. Cmty. Devel. Agy., 1984-88. Recipient Cert. of Appreciation for participation in vol. income tax assistance program Dept. Treasury, IRS, 1985, 86, Ptnrs. in Change award Nat. Displaced Homemakers Network, 1991. Mem. Workers' Def. League, Nat. Orgn. Social Security Claimant's Reps. Avocations: rollerskating, music, gourmet cooking. Office: 141 Livingston St Brooklyn NY 11201-5133

SATTERLEE, GEORGE LEONARD, JR. retired civil engineer, consultant; b. Kansas City, Mo., Dec. 31, 1930; s. George Leonard and Mary Anna (Goelz) S.; m. Lois Jean Johnson, Feb. 10, 1956; Jane Satterlee Neihart, George L. III. BSCE, U. Mo., Columbia, 1952. Registered profl. engr., Mo. Dist. surveys and plans engr. Mo. Hwy. and Transp. Dept., Kansas City, 1963-68, dist. ops. engr., 1968-70, dist. engr., 1970-86; dir. pub. works City of Kansas City, 1986-93; spl. projects engr. HNTB Corp., 1994-2000; ret., 2000. Mem., bd. dirs. St. Luke's Hosp. Kansas City, 1992-2001. 1st lt. U.S. Army Corps of Engrs., 1952-55. Recipient Faculty Alumni award U. Mo., 1996, Disting. Engr. Svc. award, 1993. Fellow ASCE (pres. Kansas City sect. 1970-71, Govt. Engr. of Yr. 1995); mem. MSPE (bd. dirs. 1975-78), APWA, Mo. Hwy. Engrs. Assn. (pres., bd. dirs. 1988-89), Mo. Transp. Coun. (v.p., bd. dirs. 1993-98), Native Sons Kansas City (past bd. dirs.). Episcopal. Avocation: fishing.

SATTERLEE, PETER HAMILTON, communications executive, military officer; b. Mt. Vernon, N.Y., Oct. 5, 1946; s. Arthur H. and Gladys M. (Clarke) S.; m. Barbara Ann Ralston (div. Nov. 1970); children: Wade Charles, Tara Ann; m. Lillian Gail Lordi, Dec., 1971. BA in Broadcasting, U. Miami, 1973; student, U. S.C., 1980; MS in Ednl. Psychology, U. Okla., 1981; student, Command and Gen. Staff Coll., 1983. Commd. 2d lt. U.S. Army, 1966; officer in charge Am. Forces Network TV, Ramstein, Fed. Republic Germany, 1973-75; comdr. So. European Network, Vicenza, Italy, 1975-76; chief Ednl. TV U.S. Army Tng. and Doctrine Command, Ft. Eustis, Va., 1976-79; comdr. So. Command Network, Republic of Panama, 1979-82, U.S. Army Combat Pictorial Detachment, Washington, 1982-84; advanced through grades to lt. col. U.S. Army, 1984; chief radio-TV prodn. office Armed Forces Radio and TV Service, Washington, 1984-90; ret. U.S. Army, 1990; gen. mgr. NASA-TV, Washington, 1992-95; prodn. mgr. ABC News "Nightline", 1996-98; pvt. practice media cons., future/equity trader, 1999—. Author: (with others) Educational Television Handbook for Training Developers, 1978; exec. producer over 3,000 radio and TV commls., 1985-89. Recipient Disting. Broadcast award Dept. of Def., 1981. Mem. Armed Forces Broadcasters Assn. Avocations: sailing, diving. Home: 354 Desoto Dr New Smyrna Beach FL 32169-5201 Office: S Cube 354 DeSoto Dr New Smyrna Beach FL 32169-5201 E-mail: pete@s-cube.com.

SATTERLEE, TERRY JEAN, lawyer; b. Kansas City, Mo., Aug. 28, 1948; d. Charles Woodbury and Francis Jean (Shriver) S.; m. William W. Rice, Jan. 9, 1982; children: Cassandra Jean Rice, Mary Shannon Rice. BA, Kans. U., 1970; JD, U. Mo., 1974. Bar: Mo. 1974. Lawyer Arthur Benson Assocs., Kansas City, Mo., 1974-77, Freilich & Leitner, Kansas City, 1977-78, U.S. Environ. Protection Agy., Kansas City, 1978-83; of counsel Lathrop & Norquist, 1985-87, ptnr., 1987—, mem. exec. com., 1997-2001. Contbr. articles to profl. jours. Chmn. Bd. Zoning Adjustment, Kansas City, 1983-87, Mo. State Parks Adv. Bd., 1997-2002; Kansas City Hazardous Materials com; steering com. COMPASS Met. Planning, Kansas City, 1990-93. Mem. Mo. Bar Assn. (chair environ. com. 1990-93), Kansas City Bar Assn. (environ. com. chmn. 1986-90, chair 2001), Mo. C. of C. (natural resource coun. 1990-2002, bd. dirs. 1999-2002, chair 1998-2002), Kansas City C. of C. (environ. com. chmn. 1992), Women's Pub. Svc. Network (named Top 25 US Women in Bus. 2000). Democrat. Episcopalian. Office: Lathrop & Gage 2345 Grand Blvd Kansas City MO 64108-2612

SATTERLEE, WARREN SANFORD, II, retail management professional; b. Harlingen, Tex., Dec. 8, 1946; s. Ralph Pickard and Diane (Royall-Mann) S.; m. Virginia Lou Schumacher, July 17, 1971; 1 child, Heather Irene. AA, Cayuga C.C., Auburn, N.Y., 1972; BA, St. Cloud State U., 1974; cert. in Theol. Studies, Tex. Christian U., 1991. Supr. and bakery support staff Schlotzsky's, Arlington, Tex., 1989-93, Schlotzsky's Deli Sandwich Shop, Arlington, 1993-96; retail mgmt. Eckerd Drug #3156, 1995-2000; mem. customer svc. staff Office Depot, 1998; mem. mgmt. tng. program retail mgmt. practices Eckerd Drug, 1999, mem. supervisory tng. program, 1999; retail mgmt. staff Ross Dress For Less, Ft. Worth, 2000—. Author: Meditation, 1997, Meditation III, 1997; contbr. monthly column Meditations to The Pillar and Post newsletter, 1999—; contbr. articles to religious publs.; author poetry. Mem. Rite I, Ch. of Sts. Peter and Paul Episcopal Ch. Choir, Arlington, Tex., 1999—. With USAF, 1966-70. Mem. Hereditary Register of the U.S.A. (contbr.), Internat. Order of St. Luke the Physician, Crowley Art Guild, Ft. Worth Geneal. Soc. Episcopalian. Avocations: creative writing, making church worship banners and visuals, music, crafts. Home: 4004 Bradley Ln Arlington TX 76017-4148

SATTERTHWAITE, CAMERON B. physics educator; b. Salem, Ohio, July 26, 1920; s. William David and Mabel (Cameron) S.; m. Helen Elizabeth Foster, Dec. 23, 1950 (div. July 31, 1979); children: Mark Cameron, Tod Foster, Tracy Lynn, Keith Alan, Craig Evan (dec.). BA, Coll. Wooster, 1942; postgrad., Ohio State U., 1942-44; PhD, U. Pitts., 1951. Chemist Manhattan dist. project Monsanto Chem. Co., Dayton, Ohio, 1944-47; research chemist DuPont, Wilmington, Del., 1950-53; researcher, adv. physicist Westinghouse, Pitts., 1953-61; asso. prof. physics U. Ill., Urbana, 1961-63, prof., 1963-79, prof. emeritus, 1979—; prof. physics Va. Commonwealth U., Richmond, 1979-85, prof. emeritus, 1985—, chmn. dept. physics, 1979-82. Program dir. NSF, 1975-76; field sec. Friends Com. on Nat. Legis., 1988-90. Contbr. articles to profl. jours.; patentee in field. Sch. dir., Monroeville, Pa., 1959-61; trustee, mem. fin. com. Southeastern Univs. Research Assn., 1980-85; Democratic nominee for U.S. Congress, 1966; del. to Dem. Nat. Conv., 1968, 72, 2000; sec. Urbana Free Libr. Found., 1998-2000. Fellow Am. Phys. Soc.; mem. Fedn. Am. Scientists (chmn. 1968). Home: 308 E Colorado Ave Unit 1 Urbana IL 61801-5918 E-mail: csattert@uiuc.edu.

SATTERTHWAITE, FRANKLIN BACHE, JR. management educator, executive coach; b. Mt. Holly, N.J., Apr. 30, 1943; s. Franklin Bache and Emily Vaux (Cresson) S.; m. Antonia Mitchell, Oct. 6, 1987 (div. Oct. 1992); m. Martha Werenfels, May 21, 1994; children: Peter Franklin, Thomas Peabody. AB, Princeton U., 1965; M in Urban Studies, Yale U., 1968, MPhil, 1972, PhD, 1975. Sci. faculty Escola Americiana, Rio Janeiro, Brazil, 1965-66; planner Nat. Inst. Mental Health, Chevy Chase, Md., 1968-70; cons. Battelle Meml. Inst., Columbus, Ohio, 1971-72; touring squash pro W.P.S.A., N.Am., 1976-84; sr. cons. Brown Cronson Assocs., N.Y.C., 1981-87; prin. Frank Satterthwaite, 1982—, R.I., 1995—; asst. prof. Johnson & Wales U., Providence, 1993-97, assoc. prof., 1997—; prin. Dimensional Leadership L.L.C., 1999—, dir. Grad. Ctr. for Bus., 1999—2000. Cons. Cost of Living Coun., Washington, 1972-73; dir. Grad. Ctr. for Global Enterprise Leadership, 2000-01, Johnson and Wales U., 1999—; prin. Career P.E.A.K.S., LLC, 2001—. Author: The Three-Wall Nick and Other Angles, 1979. Lt. USPHS, 1968-70. Mem. Acad. Mgmt. Avocations: squash (World Profl. Vets. Squash Champion 1984), tennis, golf, piano, travel. Home: 107 Shaw Ave Cranston RI 02905-3828 Office: Johnson and Wales U 8 Abbott Park Pl Providence RI 02903-3775

SATTERTHWAITE, GEORGE, II, security firm executive; b. San Jose, Costa Rica, Apr. 18, 1935; s. Livingston Lord andAdelaide (Bristol) S.; m. Helen Marie McCann, June 28, 1958 (div. July 1982); children: Patricia Ann, Livingston Lord, Frank Lord; m. Deanna Marie Kelliher, Apr. 30, 1983; 1 child, Kelley Elizabeth. BA in Internat. Rels., U. Pa., 1957; MA in History, Johns Hopkins U., 1965. Commd. 2d lt. U.S. Army, 1957, advanced through grades to col., 1979, retired, 1987; chief indsl. security Planning Rsch. Corp., McLean, Va., 1987-89; corp. dir. security PRC Inc., 1989-96; cons., 1996-98; cons., contracts officer SSI Inc., McLean, Va., 1998—2000, photography and security cons., 2000—. Mem.: Am. Soc. Indsl. Security. Republican. Roman Catholic. Avocations: photography, music, volks marching, travel. Home and Office: 513 Holly Rd Fort Washington MD 20744-6606 E-mail: GS2nd@aol.com.

SATTERTHWAITE, HELEN FOSTER, retired state legislator; b. Blawnox, Pa., July 8, 1928; d. Samuel J. and Lillian (Schreiber) Foster; m. Cameron B. Satterthwaite, Dec. 23, 1950 (div. July 1979); children: Mark Cameron, Tod Foster, Tracy Lynn, Keith Alan, Craig Evan (dec.). BS in Chemistry, Duquesne U., 1949. Biol. technician USDA, 1967-68; lab. technician U. Ill. Coll. Agr., 1968-70; rsch. asst. Iowa State U. Coll. Agr., 1971, Gulf R & D, Harmarville, Pa., 1950; rsch. chemist E.I. duPont de Nemours & Co., Wilmington, Del., 1951-53; technician Nat. Sci. Lab., fU. Ill. Coll. Vet. Medicine, 1971-74; rep. Ill. Ho. of Reps., Springfield, 1974-92, majority leader, 1991-92, mem. sch. fin. task force, 1990-92, chmn. com. on higher edn., 1983-91, vice chmn. elem. and secondary edn., 1983-91; ret., 1993. Mem. Commn. on Mental Health and Devel. Disabilities, 1975-85, mem. exec. com., 1977-85, vice chmn., 1979-85; mem. Commn. to Visit and Examine State Instns., 1977-85, Ill. Coun. Mental Health, 1992-95, Task Force on Global Climate Change, 1991-96; treas. LWV, 1995-98, sec., 1998-2001; treas. Bus. and Profl. Women's Club, 1993-94, sec., 1994-95; bd. dirs. East Ctrl. Ill. Health Sys. Agy., 1977-79, Champaign County Mental Health Ctr., 1993—, Univ. YWCA, U. Ill., 1987—, Girls Inc., 1992-96; bd. dirs. Champaign County United Way, 1970-74, mem. budget com., 1973-74, mem. joint rev. com. on funding Champaign County mental health programs, 1973; co-chmn. task force on mental retardation Champaign County Mental Health Bd., 1973; mem. Ill. Devel. Disability Advocacy Authority, 1977-85, vice chmn., 1979-80; chmn. Ill. House Dem. Study Group, 1979-81; mem. Edn. Commn. on States, 1985-92, Nat. Conf. State Legis. Commn. on Labor and Edn., 1985-92; bd. govs. U. YWCA, 1995-. Recipient Freshman Legislator of Yr. award Ill. Edn. Assn., 1975, commndation Ill. State's Attys. Assn., 1975, Best Legislator award Ind. Voters Ill., 1976, 78, 80, 82, 84, 86, 88, 90, cert. of honor Assn. Student Govts., 1977, Disting. Svc. cert. AMVETS, 1977, Environ. Legislator of Yr. award Ill. Environ. Coun., 1977, 79, 81, 83, Meritorious Svc. award Champaign County Coun. on Alcoholism, 1978, Ill. C.C. Trustees ASsn., 1986, Perfect Voting Record award Ill. Credit Union League, 1979, Ill. Wildlife Fedn., 1979, cert., of spl. recognition Ill. Women's Polit. Caucus, 1979, 80, Pub. Svc. award Izaak Walton League, 1980, Friend of Edn. award Ill. Bd. Edn., 1985, cert. of appreciation Champaign County Urban League, 1987, Resolution of Honor, Ill. Libr. Assn., 1987, 100 Percent award Ill. Coun. Sr. Citizens Orgns., 1989, Dare To Be Great award Ill. Women Adminstrs., 1989; named Person of Yr., Champaign County Mental Health Assn., 1981, Pub. Citizen of Yr., Illino Dist. and Ill. chpt. NASW, 1981, Legislator of Yr., Ill. Assn. Sch. Social Workers, 1989. Mem. Ill. Conf. Women Legislators (co-convenor 1981-83), Nat. Order Women Legislators (bd. dirs. region IV 1982, treas. 1983-84), Delta Kappa Gamma. Mem. Soc. Of Friends.

SATTERWHITE, HARRY VINCENT, lawyer, writer; b. Columbus, Miss., Jan. 15, 1963; s. Gordon Andrew and Rosalyn Kathleen (Moore) S.; m. Aline Jackson Martin, Dec. 12, 1987; children: Harry Vincent Jr., Jackson Martin, Samuel Wood Satterwhite. BA, U. Ala., Tuscaloosa, 1985, MA, 1991, JD, 1994. Bar: Ala. 1994, Fla. 1997, Miss. 1997, U.S. Dist. Ct. (so. and no. dists.) Ala. 1994, U.S. Dist. Ct. (no., mid. and so. dists.) Fla. 1997, U.S. Dist. Ct. (no. and so. dists.) Miss. 1997, U.S. Ct. Appeals (11th cir.) 1994, U.S. Ct. Appeals (5th cir.) 1997, U.S. Supreme Ct. 1998. Reporter, photographer Foley (Ala.) Onlooker, 1985-86, Tuscaloosa News, 1986-91; assoc. Gillion, Brooks and Hamby, P.C., Mobile, Ala., 1994-96, Brooks and Hamby, P.C., Mobile, 1996-98, Janecky Newell, P.C., Mobile, 1998—; ptnr. Janecky Newell P.C., 2000—01; founding mem. Satterwhite & Erwin, L.L.C., 2001—. Author: Alabama's Open Meetings Law, 1991. Mem. Kappa Tau Alpha. Roman Catholic. Avocations: coaching youth baseball, golf. Office: Satterwhite & Erwin LLC 1203 Dauphin St Mobile AL 36604

SATTERWHITE, ROBERT LEE, library director; b. Oil city, Pa., July 16, 1941; s. Robert Linwood and Mettie Elizabeth S.; m. Mary Willis Woodruff, Aug. 12, 1972; childre; Benjamin, Elizabeth. BA in English, Hiram Coll., 1965; MA in English, U. Mich., 1966; MLS, U. Pitts., 1973. Instr. English W.Va. Inst. Tech., Montgomery, 1966-71; supr. ref. dept. Northwest Regional Libr. System, Panama City, Fla., 1973-77; regional ref. libr. Florence (S.C.) County Libr., 1977-80; dir. Vienna (W.Va.) Pub. Libr., 1980-89, Hopkinsville (Ky.) - Christian County Pub. Libr., 1989—. Recipient Pub. Svc. award Hopkinsville Human Rels. Commn., 1998. Mem. Ky. Libr. Assn.(treas. pub. libr. sect. 1994-95, sec. pub. libr. sect. 1995-96, mem. legis. com. 1996-97), Hopkinsville Civitan Club (sec. 1998-99). Avocations: creative writing, reading, guitar. Office: Hopkinsville-Christian County Pub Libr 1101 Bethel St Hopkinsville KY 42240-2051

SATTIN, ALBERT, psychiatry and neuropharmacology educator; b. Cleve., Oct. 5, 1931; s. Sam and Edith Sattin; m. Renee Schnider, Dec. 16, 1962; children: Rebecca Lee, Michael M. BS, Western Res. U., 1953, MD, 1957. Diplomate Am. Bd. Psychiatry and Neurology. Intern Washington U., St. Louis, 1957-58; resident in psychiatry Case-Western Res. U., Cleve., 1958-62; fellow dept. biochemistry U. London., 1965-66; instr., sr. instr. Case-Western Res. U. Sch. Medicine, 1965-70, asst. prof. psychiatry and pharmacology, 1970-77; assoc. prof. psychiatry Ind. U. Sch. Medicine, Indpls., 1977-84; assoc. prof. psychiatry and neurobiology Ind. U. Grad. Sch., 1984-91; assoc. prof. psychiatry and biobehavioal scis. UCLA, 1991—. Chief Antidepressant Neuropharmacology Lab, West L.A. and Sepulved VA Med. Ctrs., 1991—; mem. Brain Rsch. Inst., UCLA, 1997—. Contbr. articles to profl. jours. Grantee NIMH, NSF, VA. Fellow Am. Psychiat. Assn. (life); mem. Soc. for Neurosci. Soc. Biol. Psychiatry, Internat. Soc. Neurochemistry. Office: West LA VA Med Ctr PO Box 84122 11301 Wilshire Blvd Los Angeles CA 90073-1003

SATTINGER, MICHAEL JACK, economics educator, researcher; b. Toledo, Aug. 23, 1943; s. Irvin J. and Barbara R. (Lowenthal) S.; m. Ulla M. Jensen, Oct. 25, 1969; children: Graham, Andrew, Nicholas. BS, U. Mich., 1965; MS, Carnegie-Mellon U., 1969, PhD, 1973. Asst. prof. economics SUNY, Stony Brook, N.Y., 1970-77; assoc. prof. Miami U., Oxford, Ohio, 1977-81; assoc. prof. econs. SUNY, Albany, 1981-91, prof. econs., 1991—. Adj. lectr. Aarhus U., Denmark, 1974-75, lectr., 1982-83. Author: Capital and the Distribution of Labor Earnings, 1980, Unemployment, Choice and Inequality, 1985; contbr. articles to profl. jours. Grantee N.Y. Dept. Social Svcs., 1989-90. Avocation: cycling. Home: 271 Mccormick Rd Slingerlands NY 12159-9320 Office: SUNY 1400 Washington Ave Albany NY 12222-1000

SATTLER, ROLF, retired plant morphologist, educator; b. Göppingen, Germany, Mar. 8, 1936; arrived in Can., 1962; s. Otto and Emma (Mayer) S.; m. Liv Hamann, May 1, 1963 (div. 1985). PhD, U. Munich, 1961; DSc (hon.), Colombo U. Asst. prof. McGill U., Montreal, Que., Can., 1964-69, assoc. prof. Can., 1969-77, prof. Can., 1977-97, emeritus prof. Can., 1997—. Author: Organogenesis of Flowers, 1973 (Lawson medal 1974), Biophilosophy, 1986; editor: Theoretical Plant Morphology, 1978, Axioms and Principles of Plant Construction, 1981; contbr. articles to profl. jours. NATO fellow, 1962-64. Fellow Royal Soc. Can., Linnean Soc. London; mem. Can. Bot. Assn., Sci. and Med. Network.

SATTLER, STEPHEN CHARLES, writer, editor, communications consultant; b. Cleve., Feb. 22, 1962; s. Leo Anthony and Gertrude Louise (Hoffman) S.; life ptnr. Cornelius O'Neil O'Farrell, Jr., June 3, 1987. AB in History, Georgetown U., 1985; MS in Mktg., Johns Hopkins U., 1998. Mng. editor Nat. Press, Washington, 1987-88; publs. and membership coord. Amideast, 1988-91; dir. mktg. and comm. Am. Coun. on Edn., 1992-99; dir. comm. Boston Soc. Architects, 1999-2000; mktg. dir., mem. editl. bd. Architecture Boston mag., 1999-2000; dir. mktg. and comm. Mass. Hort. Soc., Boston, 2000—01; dir. mktg. Forest City Comml. Group, 2001—. Ptnr. O'Farrell & Sattler, Washington, 1990—. Editor: The Golden Circle, 1987, On My Own: A Single Mother by Choice, 1987, Black Mondays: Worst Decisions of the Supreme Court, 1987, Katharine the Great: Katharine Graham and the Washington Post, 1987; editor: (ref. books) Introduction to the Arab World, 1989, National Guide to Educational Credit for Training Programs, 1992-93, 93-94, Guide to the Evaluation of Educational Experiences in the Armed Services, 1994, GED Candidates in Canada, 1994, The Literacy Proficiencies of GED Examinees, 1995, Guiding Principles for Distance Learning in a Learning Society, 1996, Distance Learning Evaluation Guide, 1996. Bd. dirs. Coalition of Lifelong Learning Orgns., 1998-99, Trees for Capitol Hill, Washington, 1993-98; vol. Whitman-Walker Food Bank, Washington, 1994-97; active mem. Ch. of Epiphany, Washington, 1993-99, Emmanuel Ch., Boston, 2000—. Recipient pub. excellence (APEX) awards Comm. Concepts, 1994-98, Bronze Apple award Nat. Ednl. Film and Video Festival, 1989. Mem. Am. Mktg. Assn. (v.p. Boston 2000-2001). Episcopalian. Home: 44 Newburg St Boston MA 02131-2807

SATULOFF, BARTH, accounting executive, dispute resolution professional, publisher; b. Buffalo, Dec. 13, 1945; s. Bernard and Annette (Lurie) S.; m. Gail Lois Seid Jaffe, Aug. 23, 1992. BBA in Acctg., U. Miami, 1967, MBA, 1969. CPA, Fla., N.Y., Ill., La.; registered securities arbitrator, NYSE, AMEX, NASD; cert. state ct. arbitrator, Fla.; Spl. Master, Fla. pvt. property and land use cases; cert. comml. arbitrator Am. Arbitration Assn.; appt. spl. arbitrator Prudential Ins. remediation cases, Fla. Staff acct. Price Waterhouse, Miami, Fla., 1969-71; tax specialist Laventhol & Horwath, 1973-74; mng. dir. Barth Satuloff, CPA, 1974-99. Pres., bd. dirs. Satuloff Bros., Inc., Buffalo, 1974-94, Miami, 1994-97. Satuloff Bros. Nev., Inc., Reno, 1997—; CEO, dir. Papillon Press, Inc., Miami, 1998—. Mem. Ctr. for the Arts, Vero Beach, Fla., Met. Mus. Art, N.Y.C.; mem. Fla. state com. Nat. Mus. Women in the Arts, Washington. With Fla. N.G., 1970—76. Mem.: AICPA (mem. small bus. taxation com. of tax divsn. 1993—96, mem. fed. tax forms com. of tax divsn. 1997—99), Am. Arbitration Assn. (nat. panel arbitrators and mediators), Fla. Inst. CPAs, Idaho Rivers United, Nature Conservancy, Miami Country Day Sch. Alumni Assn. (sec. 1987—93, bd. dirs. 1987—, treas. 1994—), Audubon Soc., Nat. Wild Turkey Fedn., Rocky Mountain Elk Found. (founder Indian River chpt.), Antique Automobile Club Am., Cadillac-LaSalle Club, Am. Rivers. Avocations: hunting, fishing, photography, antique automobiles. Home and Office: 910 11th Ct Vero Beach FL 32960

SATURNELLI, ANNETTE MIELE, school system administrator; b. Newburgh, N.Y., Dec. 1, 1937; d. William Vito and Anna (Marso) M.; m. Carlo F. Saturnelli, Oct. 15, 1960; children: Anne, Karen, Carla. BA, Vassar Coll., 1959; MS, SUNY, New Platz, 1978; EdD, NYU, N.Y.C., 1993. Rsch. chemist Lederle Labs/Am. Cyanamid, Pearl River, N.Y., 1959-64; sci. coord. Marlboro (N.Y.) Cen. Sch. Dist., 1974-84; state sci. supr. N.Y. State Dept. Edn., Albany, 1984-86; dir. sci. edn. Newburgh (N.Y.) City Sch. Dist., 1986-98, exec. dir. funded programs, 1998—2001; deputy supt. of schs. Newburgh City Sch. Dist., NY, 2001—. Project dir., proposal reviewer NSF, Washington, 1984—;

state coord. N.Y. State Sci. Olympiad, 1985-86; mem. Gov. Cuomo's Task Force on Improving Sci. Edn., Albany, N.Y., 1989—; mem. adv. bd. N.Y. State Systemic Initiative, 1993—, N.Y. State Tech. Edn. Network, 1993— Author: Focus on Physical Science, 1981, 87; editor: Transforming Testing in New York State--A Collection of Past, Present and Future Assessment Practices, 1994. Project dir. Goals 2000: Educate America Act, 1996, 97, 98, 99. Recipient Presdl. award Excellence in Sci. Tchg., Washington, 1983, Pillars of the Cmty. award, City of Newburgh Family Health Ctr., 2001, Orange County Women of Achievement award, 2002; NSF 3-yr. summer sci. camp grantee, 1995, 96, 97, N.Y. State Edn. Dept. Workforce Preparation grantee, 1993-94, N.Y. State Edn. Dept. Sch.-to-Work grantee, 1995-96, 96-97, NSF Comprehensive Partnership for Math. and Sci. Achievement grantee, 1996—, Goals 2000 Educate Am. Act grantee, 1996, 97, 98, 99, Obey-Porter Comprehensive Sch. Reform Demonstration Programs grantee, 1998-99, 99-2000, 21st Century Comty. Learning Ctrs. grantee, 1999—, U.S. Dept. Edn. Small Learning Cmtys. grantee, 2000—. Mem. ASCD, Nat. Sci. Tchrs. Assn. (Exemplary Sci. Tchrs. award 1982), N.Y. State Sci. Suprs. (bd. dirs., pres. 1991, Mid Hudson Sch. Study Coun. Excellence in Adminstrn. award 1993), Sci. Tchrs. Assn. N.Y. State (pres. 1993, Outstanding Sci. Tchrs. award 1983, N.Y. State Outstanding Sci. Supr. award 1988, Fellows award 1990), Phi Delta Kappa, Delta Kappa Gamma. Home: 3 Taft Pl Cornwall On Hudson NY 12520-1713 Office: Newburgh Enlarged City Sch Dist Bd Edn 124 Grand St Newburgh NY 12550-4615

SATZ, JEFFREY S. telecommunications industry executive, consultant; b. Jackson Heights, N.Y., Feb. 10, 1973; s. Robert L. and Linda J. Satz; m. Elizabeth Stacy Panzer, Dec. 27, 1997; 1 child Zachary C. BSME, Rensselaer Poly. Inst., 1995. EIT N.Y. Engr. Nortel Networks, Richardson, Tex., 1995—98, sr. engr., 1998—2000, mgr., 2000—. Mem.: IEEE, NY Acad. Scis., Mensa. Avocations: home repair, reading, walking. Home: 4456 Big Sky Dr Plano TX 75024

SATZ, LOUIS K. publishing executive; b. Chgo., Apr. 28, 1927; s. Harry Addison and Faye (Pollen) S.; m. Janet Maas, Jan. 2, 1952 children: Jay, Jonathan. BS in Mktg, U. Ill., 1949. Circulation dir. Pubs. Devel. Corp., Chgo., 1953, Guns mag., Jr. Arts and Activities, 1961; wholesaler sales mgr., then v.p., dir. sales Bantam Books, Inc., N.Y.C., 1962-80, sr. v.p., dir. diversified markets, 1980-84; pub. Passport Books, Lincolnwood, Ill., 1985-88; pres. Louis K. Satz Assocs., Pub. Cons., N.Y.C., 1988-91; ptnr. Scott/Satz Group, Pub. Cons., Walnut Creek, Calif., 1991—. Guest lectr. Sarah Lawrence Coll.Pub. Sch., Pace U.; faculty Hofstra U., Denver Pub. Inst.; cons. World Book Encyclopedia, 1995—; bd. dirs. N.Y. is Book Country, Brandeis U. Pub. Scholarship Fund, Oscar Dystel Fellowship NYU. Served with AUS, World War II, ETO. Mem. Am. Assn. Pubs. (chmn. small books mktg. div. 1975) Office: Scott Satz Group 558 Monarch Ridge Dr Walnut Creek CA 94596-2956

SATZ, RONALD WAYNE, systems engineer, consultant; b. Seattle, May 24, 1951; s. Martin Allen and Miriem Fay (Lerner) S. BS and M in Engring., Rensselaer Polytech. Inst., 1974; postgrad., MIT, 1974; PhD, Columbia Pacific U., 1991. Design engr. Internat. Harvester, Ft. Wayne, Ind., summer 1973; rsch. engr. Caterpillar Tractor Co., Peoria, Ill., 1975; chief engr. Transpower Corp., Mpls., 1976-77; advanced project engr. 3M Co., St. Paul, 1977-78; product rsch. engr. Budd Co., Ft. Washington, Pa., 1978-80; sr. systems engr. GE, Valley Forge, 1980-82; pres. Transpower Corp., Parkerford, 1982—. Author: The Unmysterious Universe, 1971, Theory and Design of the New Rational Combustion Engine, 1978, Optimal Manager Software Package, 1982, Expert Thinker Software Package, 1988, Optimal Engineer Software Package, 1991, Optimal Scientist Software Package, 1993; inventor rotary positive displacement hot gas regenerative engine. Mem. ASME, Internat. Soc. Unified Sci. (sec. 1971-90, pres. 1991-95), Soc. Automotive Engrs., Ops. Rsch. Soc. Am. Republican. Avocation: testing new machines. Home and Office: Transpower Corp 3444 Rose Ave Trevose PA 19053-4939

SATZIK, JULIE ANN, archivist; b. Chgo., May 12, 1965; d. Edward Max and Jeanette Kinga (Kulik) S. BA in History, Northeastern Ill. U., 1987, MA in History, 1994. Intern Mus. Broadcast Comm., Chgo., 1987; archival intern Archdiocese Chgo. Archives and Records Ctr., 1988-93, asst. rsch. archivist, 1993—. Scholar Ill. State Commn., 1983-84. Mem. Assn. Cath. Diocesan Archivists, Midwest Archives Conf., Phi Alpha Theta. Avocations: reading, old movies and TV, music, cross stitching, puzzles. Office: Archdiocese Chgo Archives and Records 711 W Monroe St Chicago IL 60661-3515 E-mail: jsatzik@chgocatholicarchives@org.

SAUCIER, GENE DUANE, retired state legislator; b. Dallas, Sept. 25, 1931; s. Albert L. and Myrtle Irene (West) S.; m. Marilyn Emmy Cox, Dec. 27, 1952 (dec. Sept. 1980); children: Alan, Steve, Renee; m. Giulia Riga LaCagnina, Nov. 28, 1981. BS in Agronomy Soils, Miss. State U., 1953; MS in Counseling, U. So. Miss., 1970, EdD in Adult Edn., 1978. Builder, developer Saucier Co., Hattiesburg, Miss., 1957-70; dir. admissions U. So. Miss., 1970-74, dean spl. acad. svcs., 1974-84, asst. v.p. bus. and fin., 1984-93; mem. Miss. Ho. of Reps., Jackson, 1993-99; ret., 1999. Scoutmaster Boy Scouts Am., 1960—70, chmn. campaing and activities Pine Burr area, 1970; bd. dirs. Forrest Hub Coun., 2000, Miss. Wild Turkey Fedn., Pine Burr chpt., 2000. 1st lt. USAF, 1953—56. Named Forrest County Tree Farmer of Yr., 1996, Miss. Tree Farmer Yr., 1996; recipient Forestry award Miss. Wildlife Fedn., 1997, Legislator of Yr. Coastal Conservation Assn., 1997. Mem. So. Assn. Collegiate Registrars and Admissions Officers (bd. dirs. 1981, local arrangements chmn. 1981, v.p. admissions and fin. aid 1982-83, pres. 1985-86), Miss. Assn. Collegiate Registrars and Admissions Officers, Miss. Forestry Assn. (exec. bd. dirs. 1992-94, bd. dirs. 1992-94), Miss. Nature Conservancy, Forrest/Lamar Forestry Assn. (pres. 1989-92), Sigma Chi, ODK, Phi Delta Kappa, Omicron Delta Kappa.

SAUCIER, GERARD, psychologist, educator; b. Bryan, Tex., Feb. 21, 1955; s. Walter J. Saucier and Helen A. Nobles. BA with honors, U. N.C., 1978; MA, John F. Kennedy U., 1984; PhD, U. Oreg., 1991. Lic. psychologist Ill. Therapist O.E. Youth Svc. Ctr., Portland, Oreg., 1984—86, Employee Assistance Profls., Portland, 1985—89, Ctr. for Cmty. Mental Health, Portland, 1988—90; psychology intern U. Maine, Orono, 1990—91; asst. prof. Ea. Ill. U., Charleston, 1991—93, Calif. State U., San Bernardino, 1993—97; from asst. to assoc. prof. U. Oreg., Eugene, 1997—. Assoc. editor: Jour. Rsch. in Personality, 2001—, consulting editor: Jour. Personality and Social Psychology, 1998—, consulting editor: Jour. Personality, 2001—. Mem.: Soc. for Personality and Social Psychology, Soc. Multivariate Exptl. Psychology (Cattell award 2000), Am. Psychol. Soc. Achievements include research in evaluation of neutral model of personality description, four-factor structure of isms (social attitudes) in natural languages. Office: U Oreg Dept Psychology 1227 University of Oregon Eugene OR 97403

SAUCIER, GUYLAINE, corporate director; b. Noranda, Que., Can., June 10, 1946; d. Gérard and Yvette (Thiffault) S. Chartered acct., École Hautes Etudes Commls., Montreal, Can., 1971. Chair Joint Com. on Corp. Governance. Bd. dirs. Petro-Can., Bank Montreal, Nortel Networks Corp.; mem. Commn. Inquiry Unemployment Ins. Fellow Inst. Chartered Accts.; mem. Order Can. Avocation: tennis. E-mail: gusauci@attglobal.net.

SAUCIER LUNDY, KAREN, nursing educator; b. Hattiesburg, Miss., Oct. 7, 1954; d. William Marshall and Ruth (Landers) S.; m. Joel Christopher Lundy, Dec. 27, 1986; 1 child, Marshall Parker. BSN, U. So. Miss., 1975; MS in Cmty. Health Nursing, U. Colo. Health Scis. Ctr., 1978; MA in Sociology, PhD in Sociology, U. Colo., Boulder, 1987. RN. Clin. nurse U. Miss. Med. Ctr., Jackson, 1976-77; clin. specialist HEW, USPHS, Atlanta, 1978-80; clin. instr. U. Miss. Med. Ctr. and Med. Sch., 1980-81; asst. prof. Loretto Heights Coll., Denver, 1983-85; instr. U. Colo., Boulder, 1982-85; prof., dean sch. nursing Delta State U., Cleveland, Miss., 1985-90; assoc. prof. U. So. Miss. Coll. Nursing, Hattiesburg, 1990-92, 1992-2001, prof., 2001—. Mem. Miss. Bd. Nursing, 1990-94. Author: Community Health, 1987, nursing text, 1991, Family and Community Health Nursing, 1991 (AJN Book of the Year 1991), Community Health Nursing, 2001 (AJN Book of the Yr. 2001). Vol. Spl. Olympics, Miss., Fla., 1979-80; mem. ARC, 1978—; cons. Sierra Club, Denver, 1977-78, Headstart, Tampa, Fla., 1978-79; bd. dirs. March of Dimes, Jackson, 1979-81, Am. Cancer Soc., 1985—. Am. Coll. Test Merit scholar 1972-75; USPHS fellow, 1977; named Educator Nurse of Year Miss. Nurses' Assn., 1989. Mem. ANA, APHA, Assn. Cmty. Health Nurse Educators, Am. Sociol. Assn., So. Sociol. Assn., Am. Assn. Colls. Nursing (accreditation site evaluator 2000--), Nat. League Nursing (accreditation site visitor 1988—), Kappa Delta. Democrat. Avocation: photography. Home: 89 James Switzer Rd Purvis MS 39475-3036 Office: U So Miss PO Box 5095 Hattiesburg MS 39406-5095 Fax: 601-794-9369. E-mail: karen.lundy@usm.edu, KSLundy@msn.com.

SAUDEK, CHRISTOPHER D. medical association administrator, medical educator; b. Bronxville, N.Y., Oct. 8, 1941; s. Robert and Elizabeth (Koch) S.; m. Susan Saudek; children: Mark S., Deborah M., Christina A., Anthony C. AB, Harvard U., 1963; MD, Cornell U., 1967. Resident in medicine Presbyn. St. Luke's Hosp., Chgo., 1967-69, Boston City Hosp., 1969-70; fellow in metabolism Thorndike Lab, Harvard U., Cambridge, Mass., 1970-72; asst prof. Cornell U., Ithaca, N.Y., 1973-80; assoc. prof. Johns Hopkins U., Balt., 1981-91, prof., 1991—; pres. American Diabetes Assoc., 2001—. Author: (book) Johns Hopkins Guide to Diabetes, 1997. Office: Johns Hopkins U Med Sch Osler 576 600 N Wolfe St Baltimore MD 21287-0005*

SAUDER, VIRGINIA LYNNE HEISEY, paralegal; b. Feb. 13, 1975; BA in History/Social Studies, Messiah Coll., Grantham, Pa., 1997. Cert.: Pa. (paralegal). Adminstrv. asst. Roxbury (Pa.) Holiness Camp, 1992-97; adminstrv. asst., alumni dir. Messiah Coll., 1997-98; paralegal Menges, Gent & McLaughlin, LLP, York, Pa., 1998-2000, firm adminstr., paralegal, 2000—. Asst. youth group leader Glenview Christian and Missionary Alliance Ch., 1999—. E-mail: mgm@yorklawoffice.com.

SAUDINO, KIMBERLY JANE, psychology educator; b. Calgary, Alta., Can., Nov. 5, 1959; d. Hugo Martin and Beverly Jeanne (McKay) S.; m. Jeffrey Alan Zapfe, Aug. 10, 1985 BSc, U. Toronto, 1980; MA, U. Man., 1989, PhD, 1992. Psychoednl. cons. York Region Bd. Edn., Aurora, Can., 1982-86; postdoctoral rsch. fellow Pa. State U., University Park, 1992-95; asst. prof. Boston U., 1995-2001, assoc. prof., 2001—. Reviewer various psychol. jours., 1995—. Author book chpts. and sci. articles. Grantee NIMH, 1999-2001, Social Scis. and Humanities Rsch. Coun., 1993-96, 92-94; Sigma Xi awardee. Mem. Am. Psychol. Soc., Soc. Rsch. in Child Devel., Behavior Genetics Assn. Avocation: curling. Office: Psychology Dept Boston U Boston MA 02215

SAUER, BRIAN, molecular geneticist, researcher; b. Columbus, Wis., Sept. 18, 1949; s. Alan and V.E. Sauer. BS, U. Wis., 1972; PhD, U. Calif., Berkeley, 1979. Staff scientist Frederick (Md.) Cancer Rsch. Facility, 1982—84; prin. investigator DuPont Co., Wilmington, Del., 1984—90; sr. rsch. scientist DuPont-Merck Co., 1991—93; expert NIH, Bethesda, Md., 1993—96, sr. staff fellow NIDDK, 1996—98; mem./head devel. biology, dir. Transgenic Core Facility Okla. Med. Rsch. Found., Okla. City, 1998—2001; dir. transgenic tech. Stowers Inst. for Med. Rsch., Kansas City, Mo., 2001—. Vis. asst. prof. Hood Coll., Frederick, 1983; adj. prof. cell biology U. Okla., 2000—. Mem. editorial bd. Analytical Biochemistry, 1994—, Nucleic Acids Rsch., 2001—; patentee in field. Damon Runyon-Walter Winchell Cancer Fund postdoctoral fellow Stanford U., 1979. Mem. AAAS, Am. Soc. for Microbiology, Genetics Soc. Am., Sierra Club. Office: Stowers Inst 1000 E 50th St Kansas City MO 64110

SAUER, DAVID ANDREW, librarian, technical writer; b. Urbana, Ill., Feb. 25, 1948; s. Elmer Louis and Frances (Hill) S. BA, Northwestern U., 1970; MS, Simmons Coll., 1975. Reference libr. Boston U., 1976-78, bibliographer, 1978-84, sr. bibliographer, 1984-88, founder and head libr. Stone Sci. Libr., 1988-94; v.p. info. svcs. CyberHelp, Inc., 1995-98; sr. tech. editor Qualcomm., Inc., 1997-2000; tech. pubs. supr. QCP Inc., 2000—01, staff tech. writer/libr., 2001—02. Co-author of 12 books including: Access for Windows 95: The Visual Learning Guide, 1995, Windows NT 4.0 Visual Desk Reference, 1997, Discover Netscape Communicator, 1997. Mem. S.W. Corridor Project, Boston. 1977-87, Forest Hills Neighborhood Improvement Assn., Boston, 1977-90, Forest Hills/Woodbourne Neighorhood Group, 1991-94. Mem. ALA, IEEE, Spl. Librs. Assn., Soc. Tech. Comm., Nat. Assn. of PhotoShop Profls., Hillside Colony Homeowners Assn. Democrat. Home: 1802 Mckee St Unit C4 San Diego CA 92110-1964

SAUER, GEOFFREY FRANCIS KENNEDY, engineering educator; b. Bloomington, Ind., Oct. 10, 1968; s. David Kennedy and Janice S. PhD, Carnegie Mellon U., 1998. Asst. prof. literary and cultural theory Carnegie Mellon U., Pitts., 1998-2000; prof. engring. U. Wash., Seattle, 1999—. Dir. EServer, Seattle, 1990—. Author: Negotiating Internet Culture, 2001. Internet dir. Greater Pitts. ACLU, 1993-2000. Fellow Acad. Voltaire (co-dir. 1994-2000, recognition of contbn. to study of 18th century philosophy 1994). Office: U Wash Box 352195 Seattle WA 98195-2195

SAUER, GORDON CHENOWETH, dermatologist, educator; b. Rutland, Ill., Aug. 14, 1921; s. Fred William and Gweneth (Chenoweth) S.; m. Mary Louise Steinhilber, Dec. 28, 1944; children: Elisabeth Ruth, Gordon Chenoweth, Margaret Louise, Amy Kieffer.; m. Marion Green, Oct. 23, 1982. Student, Northwestern U., 1939-42; BS, U. Ill., 1943, MD, 1945. Diplomate Am. Bd. Dermatology and Syphilology. Intern Cook County Hosp., Chgo., 1945-46; resident dermatology and syphilology N.Y.U.-Bellevue Med. Center, 1948-51; dermatologist Thompson-Brumm-Knepper Clinic, St. Joseph, Mo., 1951-54; pvt. practice Kansas City, 1954—; mem. staff St. Luke's, Research, Kansas City Gen. hosps.; assoc. instr. U. Kans., 1951-56, vice-chmn. sect. dermatology, 1956-58, assoc. clin. prof., 1960-64, clin. prof., 1964-93; clin. prof. emeritus, 1993—; head sect. dermatology U. Kans., 1958-70. Clin. assoc., acting head dermatology sect. U. Mo., 1955-59, cons. dermatology, 1959-67, clin. prof., 1967—; cons. Munson Army Hosp., Ft. Leavenworth, Kans., 1959-68; dermatology panel, drug efficacy panel Nat. Acad. Sci.-FDA, 1967-69. Author: Manual of Skin Diseases, 1959, 7th edit., 1995, Teen Skin, 1965, John Gould Bird Print Reproductions, 1977, John Gould's Prospectuses and Lists of Subscribers to His Work on Natural History: With an 1866 Facsimile, 1980, John Gould The Bird Man, 1982, John Gould The Bird Man: Associates and Subscribers, 1995, John Gould The Bird Man: Bibliography 2, 1996, John Gould The Bird Man: Correspondence, Vol. 1 through 1838, 1998, vol. 2 through 1841, 1998, vol. 3, 1842-45, 1999; editor Kansas City Med. Bull., 1967-69; contbr. articles to profl. jours. Bd. dirs. Kansas City Area coun. Camp Fire Girls Am., 1956-59, Kansas City Lyric Theatre, 1969-74, Kansas City Chamber Choir, 1969-74, Chouteau Soc., 1985-97, U. Mo.-Kansas City Friends of Libr., 1988-92; bd. dirs. Mo. br. The Nature Conservancy, 1984-91. Sr. asst. surgeon USPHS, 1946-48. Named Dermatology Found. Practitioner of Yr., 1992; recipient Soc. for History of Natural History Founders' award, London, 2001. Fellow Am. Acad. Dermatology and Syphilology (dir. 1975-79, v.p. 1980); mem. Mo., Jackson County med. socs., Mo. Dermatol. Soc. (pres. 1974-75), Dermatology Found. (trustee 1978-83), Am. Ornithol. Union, Wilson Ornithol. Soc., Royal Australasian Ornithologists Union, Soc. Bibliography Natural History, Am. Dermatol. Assn., Alpha Delta Phi, Nu Sigma Nu. Presbyterian. Office: 4550 Warmick Kansas City MO 64111

SAUER, HAROLD JOHN, physician, educator; b. Detroit, Dec. 1, 1953; s. Peter and Hildegard (Muehlmann) S.; m. Kathleen Ann Iorio, Sept. 4, 1982; children: Angela Karin Ferrante, Peter Rolf Jan Muehlmann, Josef Andrew John Iorio. BS, U. Mich., 1975; MD, Wayne State U., 1979. Diplomate Am. Bd. Ob-Gyn. Resident in ob-gyn William Beaumont Hosp., Royal Oak, Mich., 1979-83, fellow in reproductive endocrinology and infertility, 1983-85; asst. prof. dept. ob-gyn and reproductive biology Mich. State U., East Lansing, 1985-91, assoc. prof. ob.-gyn, 1991—, chmn. group practice clinicians coun., 1995—, interim chmn., 1996-98, 2002—, dept. vice chair, 1998—. Mem. staff St. Lawrence Hosp., Lansing, Mich., 1985—98, Sparrow Hosp., Lansing, 1985—; cons. Mich. Dept. Social Svcs., Lansing, 1985—; mem. Mich. Bd. Medicine, 1992—2000, chmn., 1994—97; bd. dirs. Fedn. State Med. Bds.; examer Am. Bd. Ob-gyn., 1998—. Fellow Am. Coll. Ob.-Gyn. (sec. Mich. sect. 1990-96, treas. 1996-99, vice-chmn. 1999—); mem. AMA, Ingham County Med. Soc., Lansing Ob-Gyn. Soc., Am. Soc. Reproductive Medicine, Am. Assn. Gynecol. Laparoscopists, Wayne State U. Med. Alumni Assn., Mich. Soc. Reproductive Endocrinology (sec.-treas. 1991-93). Roman Catholic. Avocations: classical piano, microcomputers, skiing. Home: 2601 Creekstone Trl Okemos MI 48864-2455 Office: Mich State U Dept Ob-Gyn Reproductive Biology 1200 E Michigan Ave Ste 730 Lansing MI 48912-1895 E-mail: sauerh@msu.edu.

SAUER, HARRY JOHN , JR. mechanical engineering educator, university administrator; b. St. Joseph, Mo., Jan. 27, 1935; s. Harry John and Marie Margaret (Witt) S.; m. Patricia Ann Zbierski, June 9, 1956; children: Harry John, Elizabeth Ann, Carl Andrew, Robert Mark, Katherine Anne, Deborah Elaine, Victoria Lynn, Valerie Joan, Joseph Gerard. BS, U. Mo., Rolla, 1956, MS, 1958; PhD, Kans. State U., 1963. Instr. mech. engring. Kans. State U., Manhattan, 1960-62; sr. engr., cons. Midwest Rsch. Inst., Kansas City, Mo., 1963-70; mem. faculty dept. mech. and aerospace engring. U. Mo., Rolla, 1957—, prof., 1966—, assoc. chmn., 1980-84, dean grad. study, 1984-92. Cons. in field; mem. Gov.'s Commn. on Energy Conservation, 1977; mem. Mo. Solar Energy Resource Panel, 1979-83; mem. Accreditation Bd. for Engring. and Tech. Co-author: Environmental Control Principles, 1975, 4th edit., 1985, Thermodynamics, 1981, Heat Pump Systems, 1983, Engineering Thermodynamics, 1985, Principles of Heating, Ventilating and Air Conditioning, 1991, 4th edit., 2001; contbr. articles to profl. jours. Pres. St. Patrick's Sch. Bd., 1970-72, St. Patrick's Parish Council, 1975-76. Recipient Ralph R. Teetor award Soc. Automotive Engrs., 1968; Hermann F. Spoehrer Meml. award St. Louis chpt. ASHRAE, 1979; also E. K. Campbell award of merit, 1983; Louise and Bill Holladay disting. fellow, 1999. Mem. ASME, ASHRAE (disting. svc. award 1981, exceptional svc. award 2001), NSPE, Soc. Automotive Engrs., Am. Soc. Engring. Edn., Mo. Soc. Profl. Engrs., Mo. Acad. Sci., Sigma Xi. Roman Catholic. Home: 10355 College Hills Dr Rolla MO 65401-7726 Office: Dept of Mech Engring U Mo Rolla MO 65401 E-mail: sauer@umr.edu.

SAUER, JAMES LESLIE, librarian, educator; b. Buffalo, Aug. 7, 1953; s. Edwin C. and Margaret M. (Denne) S.; m. Paula J. Westerling, Aug. 20, 1977; children: Jacob, Adam, Joseph, Ariel, Abigail, Isaac, Mary Denise, Martha. BA, SUNY, Buffalo, 1975, MLS, 1977; MA, Villanova U., 1985. Libr. Buffalo and Erie County Pub. Librs., 1977-78, Masten Park Rehab. Ctr., 1979; dir. libr. Eastern Coll., St. Davids, Pa., 1980—. Pres. Tri-State Coll. Libr. Coop., 1999—. Coun. Biblical Manhood and Womanhood, 1996—. Mem. ALA, Pa. Libr. Assn., Assn. Christian Librs., Evang. Theol. Soc., Timothy Bitterman Soc. Republican. Presbyterian. Avocations: homeschooling, parenting. Home: 1207 Stirling St Coatesville PA 19320-3526 Office: Eastern Univ Warner Libr 1300 Eagle Rd Saint Davids PA 19087-3617 E-mail: jsauer@eastern.edu.

SAUER, JAMES BENSON, philosopher, educator; b. Richmond, Va., Dec. 31, 1948; s. James Brandon and Anna Ruth (Adkins) S.; m. Susan Parrish Grigg, Aug. 16, 1968; children: James Joseph, Christopher Dietrich, Noel Nathan. BA in Philosophy and English, U. Richmond, 1970; MDiv, Union Theol. Sem., 1974, DMin., 1979; MA, St. Paul's U., Ottawa, Ont., Can., 1990, PhD, 1992. Ordained to ministry Presbyn. Ch., 1973. Prof. theology Inst. Superior Theol., Ndesha, Zaire, 1974-79; min. Presbyn. Ch. Can., Toronto and Ottawa, Ont., 1979-91; assoc. prof. philosophy St. Mary's U., San Antonio, 1993—2002, site dir. London semester, 1999-2000, profl., 2002—. Cons. ethics, 1988-97; writer, translator Novalis Press, Ottawa, 1992-97; pres. Mid-South Philosophy Conf., Memphis, 1996, 97. Author: Envisioning the Future for Leadership Development, 1979, Conscience and Deliberation, 1992, Faithful Ethics, 1997, Commentary on Lonergan's Method in Theology, 2002; editor Philosophy in the Contemporary World, 1999—; mng. editor Personalist Forum, 1997—; contbr. articles to profl. jours. Mem. Strategic Planning Task Force, San Antonio, 1994; mem. Personalist Forum Found., Oklahoma City, 1997. Grantee St. Mary's U., 1994—. Mem. Am. Philos. Assn., Soc. Philosophy Contemporary World (treas. 1995-99), N.Mex. Mid-West Tex. Philos. Soc., Can. Soc. Practical Ethics, Am. Cath. Philos. Soc., Soc. for Philosophy and Econs., Soc. for Philosophy of Religion, Lonengan Philos. Soc. Avocations: hiking, reading, technology. Home: 7115 Forest Brk San Antonio TX 78240-3204 Office: St Marys U Dept Philosophy One Camino Santa Maria San Antonio TX 78228 E-mail: philjim@stmarytx.edu.

SAUER, JANE GOTTLIEB, artist, educator; b. St. Louis, Sept. 16, 1937; d. Leo and Sally (Walpert) Gottlieb; m. Martin Rosen, June 6, 1959 (div. 1967); children: Julie, Leo, Rachel; m. Donald Carl Sauer, Oct. 31, 1972; children: Jeffrey, Diane. BFA, Washington U., St. Louis, 1960; pvt. study with Leslie Laskey, 1976-78. Artist in residence New City Sch., St. Louis, 1976-78; artist in schs. Mo. Arts Council, 1979; studio artist, 1979—. Tchr. Craft Alliance Art Ctr., St. Louis, 1979-82; cons. Harris Stowe Tchrs. Coll., St. Louis, 1980-84; lectr. and workshop leader various orgns. throughout country, 1979—. Represented in collections Wash. U., Joseph & Emily Rauh Pulitzer, St. Louis, Nordenfjeldske Kunstindustrimuseum, Tronndheim, Norway, Vera Mott U. Mo., Columbia, Prudential Ins. Co. Am., Dallas, Erie (Pa.) Art Mus., Mus. of Nanjing, Republic of China, Mus. of Suwa, Japan, Wadsworth Atheneum Mus., Hartford, Conn., Jack Lenor Larsen, N.Y.C., Am. Craft Mus., Ark.Art Mus., Detroit Inst. of Art, M. H. De Young Mus., San Francisco, Phila. Mus. of Art, Racine (Wis.) Mus. of Art, Smithsonian Mus. of Am. Art, others; one and two person exhibits Craft Alliance Gallery, St. Louis, 1981, The Hand and the Spirit Gallery, Scottsdale, Ariz., 1982, 85, Am. Craft Mus., N.Y.C., 1986, Miller Brown Gallery, San Francisco, 1987, Del. Ctr. for Contemporary Art, Johnson Mus. Art, Ithaca, N.Y., Chgo. Cultural Arts Ctr., Grand Rapids (Mich.) Art Mus., Ella Sharp Mus., Jackson, Mich., B.Z. Wagman Gallery, St. Louis, St. Louis Art Mus., 1988, Bellas Artes Gallery, Santa Fe, 1989, The Works Gallery, Phila., 1989, Folk & Craft Art Mus., San Francisco, 1989; numerous selected exhibitions, U. Nebr., 2001, Ark. Art Mus., 2000, Mint Mus. of Craft and Design, 2000, R. Duane Reco Gallery, 2000 and 2002; contbr. articles to profl. publs. Mem. Sch. of Fine Arts Nat. Coun., Washington U., St. Louis; trustee New Mex. Mus. Found., 2002. Recipient Critic's Choice award, Christmas Exhibit Craft Alliance Gallery, 1979—80, Vera Mott Purchase award, 1981, Disting. Alumni award, Washington U., St. Louis, 2000, Disting. Citizen award, Arts and Edn. Coun. St. Louis, 1999; grantee, Nat. Endowment for Visual Arts, 1984, 1990, Mo. Arts Coun., 1986. Fellow: Am. Craft Coun. (hon.; trustee); mem.: St. Louis Weavers Giuild, Area Coordinating Coun. (sec 1984—86, past bd. dirs.). Home: 1379 Cerro Gordo Rd Santa Fe NM 87501-6108 Office: 1379 Cerro Gordo Rd Santa Fe NM 87501-6108

SAUER, KATHY R. health information administrator; b. Milw., Mar. 10; m. Gordon T. Sauer; 1 child, Jennifer Lynn Wisneski. BS, U. Wis., 1984. Registered health info. adminstr. Dept. adminstr. U. Wis., Milw., 1970-84; dir. med. records Hartford (Wis.) Meml. Hosp., 1984-85; dir. med. records and clin. svcs. St. Francis Hosp. and Health Ctr., Blue Island, Ill., 1985-88; Midwest ops. mgr. Hosp. Corr. Copiers, Rosemont, 1988; dir. med. records Ingalls Meml. Hosp., Harvey, 1988-92; dir. health info. mgmt. Michael Reese and Grant Hosp., Chgo., 1992-99; sr. dir. Evanston Northwestern Healthcare, 1999—. Mem. adv. bd. Ill. State U. Med. Record Adminstrn. Program, Bloomington, Ill., 1989-91; bd. dirs. mentor program Oakton C.C. Bd. dirs. Stage Left Theatre, Chgo., 1998—. Mem. Am. Health Info. Mgmt. Assn., Ill. Med. Record Assn. (dir. 1985—, Ambassador to Edn. 1986—), Chgo. and Vicinity Med. Record Assn. (pres. 1985—). Avocations: golf, theater, walking, travel. Home: 1516 N State Pkwy Chicago IL 60610-1677 E-mail: ksauer@enh.org.

SAUER, PETER WILLIAM, electrical engineering educator; b. Winona, Minn., Sept. 20, 1946; s. Alfred von Rohr and Eleanor Francis (Sawyer) S.; m. Sylvia Louise Stenzel, Aug. 23, 1969; children: Katherine Dora, Daniel Alfred. BSEE, U. Mo., 1969; MSEE, Purdue U., 1974, PhD, 1977. Registered profl. engr., Va., Ill. Design engr. Langley AFB, Hampton, Va., 1969-73; asst. prof. elec. engring. U. Ill., Champaign-Urbana, 1977-82, assoc. prof., 1982-85, prof., 1985—, Grainger prof., 1998—. Elec. engr. Chanute AFB, Rantoul, Ill., 1983-89, res. dir. engring. ops., 1989-93; chief engring. programs, East HQ AMC, Scott AFB, Ill., 1993—. Author: Power System Dynamics and Stability; contbr. articles to IEEE Transactions on Power Apparatus, IEEE Transactions on Power Systems, IEEE Transactions on Cirs. & Systems. Pres. Trinity Luth. Ch., Urbana, 1990-93, treas., 1994—. Maj. USAF, 1989-96, lt. col., 1996. Named Outstanding Young Coll. Educator, Champaign-Urbana Jaycees, 1982. Fellow IEEE (chpt. chmn. Ctrl. Ill. sect. 1982-83, chmn. power engring. 1988—, outstanding power engr. 1997). Lutheran. Achievements include development of systematic dynamic model reduction techniques for electric machines and power systems, explaining the relationship between power system stability and steady-state solutions. Office: U Ill 1406 W Green St Urbana IL 61801-2918

SAUER, RICHARD JOHN, retired non-profit executive; b. Walker, Minn., Nov. 15, 1939; s. Herman and Katherine Elizabeth (Rieder) S.; m. Elizabeth Louise Hornstein, Aug. 18, 1962; children: Michele, Alison, Maria, Peter. BS in Biology, St. John's U., Collegeville, Minn., 1962; MS in Zoology, U. Mich., Ann Arbor, 1964; PhD in Entomology, N.D. State U., 1967. Asst. prof. biology St. Cloud (Minn.) State U., 1967-68; asst. prof., then assoc. prof. entomology Mich. State U., East Lansing, 1968-76, acting assoc. dir. Mich. Agrl. Expt. Sta., 1975-76; prin. entomologist Coop. State Rsch. Svc., USDA, Washington, 1974-75; prof., head dept. entomology Kans. State U., Manhattan, 1976-80; dir. Agrl. Expt. Sta. U. Minn., St. Paul, 1980-89, v.p. agriculture, forestry and home econs., 1983-89, interim pres. Mpls., 1988-89; pres., CEO Nat. 4-H Coun., Chevy Chase, Md., 1989-2000, retired, 2000. Roman Catholic. Home: 405 NE Tahoe Dr Blue Springs MO 64014-2053

SAUER, TIMOTHY DUWAYNE, mathematician, educator; b. Valley City, N.D., May 21, 1956; s. DuWayne Morris and Phyllis Jeannine (Jansen) S.; m. Kathleen Tongue Alligood, Oct. 21, 1987; 1 child, Katherine Anne. BS in Math., Mich. State U., 1977; PhD in Math., U. Calif., Berkeley, 1982. Lectr. Mich. State U., East Lansing, 1982-85; asst. prof. George Mason U., Fairfax, Va., 1985-90, assoc. prof., 1990-96, prof., 1996—, disting. prof. Coll. Arts and Scis., 1999—. Co-author: Chaos: An Introduction to Dynamical Systems, 1996; co-editor: Coping with Chaos, 1994. Mem. Am. Math. Soc., Soc. Indsl. and Applied Mathematicians. Office: Math Sci Dept George Mason Univ Fairfax VA 22030

SAUERBREY, ELLEN ELAINE RICHMOND, former radio talk show host; b. Balt., Sept. 9, 1937; d. Edgar Arthur and Ethel Frederika (Landgraf) Richmond; m. Wilmer John Emil Sauerbrey, June 27, 1959. AB summa cum laude in Biology and English, Western Md. Coll., 1959. Biology instr., chmn. sci. dept. Baltimore County Sch. System, 1959-64; dist. mgr. Baltimore County U.S. Census, 1970; Md. Ho. of Dels., Annapolis, 1978-94, minority leader, 1986-94; radio talk show host Sta. WBAL, Balt., 1996; U.S. rep. com. status women UN, 2002—. Rep. nominee for Gov., 1994; Rep. nominee for Gov., 1998; bd. dirs. BBB; U.S. del. to UN Commn. on Human Rights, 2001; U.S. rep. to UN Commn. on Status of Women, 2002-. Nat. chmn. Am. Legis. Exec. Coun., 1990—91; trustee Md. Coun. Econ. Edn., Franklin Sq. Hosp.; founder United Citizen's for Md.'s Future; bd. advisors Yorktown University; Rep. Nat. Com. Woman Md., 1996—; Rules com., 1996; del. Rep. Nat. Convs., 1968, 1976, 1984, 1988, 1992, 1996, 2000, platform com., chmn. subcom. on economy, 1977; nat. adv. bd. Nat. Conservative Campaign Fund; mem. credentials com. Rep. Nat. Convs., 1984; vice chmn. Rep. State Ctrl. Com. of Balt. County, 1966—71; state chmn. Md. chpt. George W. Bush for Pres., 1999—2000. Recipient Pvt. Property award Greater Balt. Bd. Realtors, 1984; named Legislator of Yr., Md. Assn. Builders and Contractors, 1982, Am. Legis. Exec. Coun., 1986, Western Md. Coll. Alum of Yr., 1988, Outstanding Legis. Leader, Am. Legis. Exec. Coun., 1992, Rep. Woman of Yr., Md. Rep. Party, 1995, NFIB (Natl. Federation of Independent Bus.), Guardian of Small Bus. award, 1989; named one of top 100 Md. women The Daily Record, 1998. Mem. DAR, Nat. Fedn. Rep. Women (Margaret Chase Smith award 1995), Md. Fedn. Rep. Women, Am. Legis. exch. Coun. (chmn. emeritus), Md. Farm Bur., Md. Conservative Union, Beta Beta, Beta, Phi Beta Kappa. Presbyterian. Avocations: gardening, travel.

SAUERBRUNN, GARY LEE, music educator; b. Anna, Ill., Aug. 29, 1942; s. Cleo George and Glenna Mae Sauerbrunn; m. Diane Louise Sauerbrunn, Mar. 21, 1986; children: Christopher, Nicki; m. Deanna Marie Sauerbrunn, Nov. 28, 1965 (dec. Jan. 28, 1985). MS Music, U. of Ill., Urbana, Illinois, 1970; BME, So. Ill. U., Carbondale, Illinois, 1965. Cert. Secondary Education Music State of Ill. Band dir. Mesa Schools, Kino, Mesa, Ariz., 1982—; music dir. Mesa Schools, Taft, 1980—82; band dir. Herscher Pub. Sch., Herscher, Ill., 1975—80. Hoopston, East Lynn Schools, Hoopston, 1967—75; music dir. Pub. Sch., Rankin, 1965—67. Condr./clinician Mesa Elem. Honor Band, Mesa, Ariz., 1983—2002, U. Music Camp, Ariz., 1994—96, Tempe Jr. High Honor Band, Tempe, Ariz., 1992. Contbr. articles in professional magazines. Recipient Outstanding Music Educator, Old Pueblo Music Festival, 2000. Mem.: NEA, Masonic Star Lodge 709 (organist 1973), Phi Beta Mu (v.p. 1974). Avocations: tennis, golf, fishing, reading. Home: 1857 East Barbarita Avenue Gilbert AZ 85203 Office: Kino Junior High School 848 North Horne Street Mesa AZ 85203 Personal E-mail: doubletroublex6@aol.com.

SAUERHAFT, STAN, public relations executive, consultant; b. N.Y.C. s. Al and Rae S.; m. Rosalie Cynthia Tolkin; children: Richard Craig, Douglas Clark, Robert James. BA, U. Mich., 1948, MA, 1949. Editor, scriptwriter Paramount News, 1950-51; scriptwriter Hearst Metrotone News, N.Y.C., 1951-52; editor Food Bus. Mag., 1952-53; acct. supr. Selvage, Lee & Chase, 1953-55; v.p., mem. creative plans bd. Communications Counselors, Inc. McCann-Erickson, 1955-59; pres. Chase and Sauerhaft Assocs., 1959-65; exec. v.p., dir., mem. mgmt. com. Hill & Knowlton, Inc., 1965-86; vice chmn. bd. , dir. Burson-Marsteller, U.S., 1987-88; vice chmn., dir. Burson-Marsteller Internat., 1988—. Instr., lectr. Columbia U. Grad. Sch., 1962-65, Wharton Grad. Sch., 1968, U. Mich. Bus. Sch., 1969, NYU Grad. Bus. Sch., 1984-87. Author: The Merger Game, 1971, Handbook of Strategic Public Relations and Integrated Communications, 1998, (chpt.) The Role of Public Relations in Mergers and Acquisitions; co-author: Image Wars, 1989; contbr. bus. articles and chpts. to anthologies. Chmn. West Point Civilian Pub. Affairs Adv. Com., 1986—; mem. exec. com. of bd. Inst. for Pub. Rels. Rsch. and Edn., 1984-87, LS&A Coll. of U. Mich., 1990-95. Staff sgt. AUS, 1945-46. Coll. of Fellows Pub. Rels. Soc. Am. (nat. accreditation bd. 1981-83), Pub. Rels. Soc. N.Y. (pres. 1983-85); mem. Soc. Profl. Journalists, Authors Guild Inc., Pub. Affairs Coun., Am. Platform Tennis Assn. (v.p.), U. Mich. Alumni Club, Union League Club N.Y. (chmn. pub. affairs com. 1980-84), Burning Tree Country Club (Greenwich, Conn.), Windmill Club (Armonk, N.Y.), Seabrook Island Club (S.C.), Sigma Delta Chi. Republican. Avocations: golf, platform tennis, bridge. Office: Burson-Marsteller 230 Park Ave S New York NY 10003-1513 Personal E-mail: rosauerh@aol.com. *A father's advice to his sons: If you can't outthink them, outwork them. But better yet, try to do both. Also, the best luck seems to befall the hardest workers.*

SAUERS, WILLIAM DALE, lawyer, playwright; b. Santa Cruz, Calif., June 18, 1926; s. Myrl Melvin and Helen (Fightmaster) S.; m. Barbara Gean Cole, May 9, 1945; children: Kathleen McCarty, Deborah Nelson, Susan Reeves. AB, Fresno State U., 1949; JD, Stanford U., 1952. Bar: Calif. 1953, U.S. Dist. Ct. (no. dist.) Calif. 1953, U.S. Ct. Appeals (9th cir.) 1953, U.S. Supreme Ct. 1964. Asst. sec. State Bar of Calif., San Francisco, 1952-55; dep. dist. atty. County of Santa Clara, San Jose, Calif., 1955-58; ptnr. Finch, Sauers et al., Palo Alto, 1958-88; pvt. practice law, 1988—. Playwright: A Rainbow on Mt. Olympus, 1993, Did Not I Dance with You?, 1994, A Fork in the Road, 1995, What'll We Do With Mama, 1996, Reluctant Strangers, 1997, Lynch Mob Hunt, 1998. Sec. Urban Coaliton of Palo Alto, 1969-72; chmn. ARC chpt. Palo Alto, Calif., 1973-76, Family Svc. Assn., 1973-76, Sr. Corp. Affiliates, Palo Alto, 1981-85; chmn. bd. trustees Menlo Coll., Atherton, Calif., 1984-88;, dir. Oreg. Shakespeare Festival, Ashland, 1989-95; pres. San Jose Repertory Theatre, 1989-91; chmn. San Francisco Shakespeare Festival, 1994-98. Mem. ABA, Calif. State Bar Assn., Phi Delta Phi. Republican. Episcopalian. Avocations: skiing, tennis, golf, fly fishing, back packing. Office: Mount & Stoelker Riverpark Tower Ste 1650 333 W San Carlos San Jose CA 95110-2711 E-mail: wsauers@mount.com.

SAUFER, ISAAC AARON, lawyer; b. Bronx, N.Y., June 16, 1953; s. Solomon and Beatrice (Kanofsky) S.; m. Debra Edith Goldberg, June 26, 1977; children: Suzanne, Nancy, Scott, Daniel, Jonathan. BA, Yeshiva U., N.Y.C., 1975; JD, Bklyn. Law Sch., 1978; LLM in Taxation, NYU, 1982. Bar: N.Y. 1979, N.J. 1986, Fla. 1986, Conn. 1987. Summer intern N.Y. County Dist. Attys. Office, N.Y.C., 1976; legal editor Prentice-Hall, Inc., Englewood Cliffs, N.Y., 1979-80; assoc. Kurzman Karelsen & Frank, LLP, N.Y.C., 1980-85, ptnr., 1986—. Adj. assoc. prof. NYU Sch. Continuing and Profl. Studies, N.Y.C., 1988—; lectr. seminars, 1991, 93, 95, 97, 98, 2000, 2001. Co-author: (N.Y. real property forms) Bergerman & Roth, 1986-87. Office: Kurzman Karelsen & Frank LLP 230 Park Ave Rm 2300 New York NY 10169-2399

SAUL, B. FRANCIS, II, bank executive, director; b. Washington, Apr. 15, 1932; s. Andrew Maguire and Ruth Clark (Sheehan) S.; m. Elizabeth Patricia English, Apr. 30, 1960; children: Sharon Elizabeth, B. Francis III, Elizabeth Willoughby, Andrew Maguire II, Patricia English. Grad., Georgetown Prep. Sch., 1950; BS, Villanova U., 1954, DCS (hon.) , 1989; LLB, U. Va., 1957; LLD (hon.) , Nat. U. Ireland, 1998. Bar: D.C. 1959. Chmn., pres. B.F. Saul Co., Chevy Chase, Md., 1957—; chmn., trustee B.F. Saul Real Estate Investment Trust Co., 1964—; with Chevy Chase Bank, F.S.B., 1969—, chmn., CEO, founder; chmn. Fin. Gen. Bankshares, Inc., 1978-82; chmn., CEO, trustee Saul Ctrs., Inc., 1993—. Chmn. bd. dirs. 1st Am. Bankshares, Inc., Washington, 1978-85; dir. Colonial Williamsburg Hotel Properties, Inc., 1983-96; Archdiocese fin. coun. for Archbishop of Washington, 1990—; honors com. John F. Kennedy Ctr. Performing Arts, 1995—; trustees coun. Nat. Gallery of Arts, 1995—, dir. bd. vis. and govs. Washington Coll., 1995—; bd. adv. CLW Life and Annuity Acquisition Corp., 1994-96. Trustee Fed. City Coun., Nat. Geog. Soc., 1985—, Suburban Hosp., 1972-76, Johns Hopkins Med. Bd., 2000-; bd. dirs. Wadsworth Preservation Trust, 1983-91; trustee Corcoran Gallery Art, Washington, 1972-90; vis. com. Sch. Arch. U. Va., greenway, Va., 1985-90, Portsmouth Abbey Sch., R.I., 1979-84, United World Coll. of Am. West, Montezuma, N.Mex., 1982-85, D.C. Fund for Creative Space, 1980-82, D.C. chpt. ARC, 1964-86, Cork U. Found., 1997—; pres. D.c. Soc. for Crippled Children, 1973-75; mem. Vice Pres.'s Residence Found., 1997—. Mem. Mortgage Bankers Assn. Met. Washington (pres. 1968), Nat. Assn. Real Estate Investment Truste (pres. 1973-74), Internat. Coll. Auditors Prefecture Econ. Affairs Holy See, Alfalfa Club, Alibi Club, Met. Club, Knights of Malta, Chevy Chase Club, Burning Tree Club, Friendly Sons of St. Patrick (pres. 1992), Wianno Club, The Brook Club, Bohemian Club, Md. Club. Roman Catholic. Home: 1 Quincy St Chevy Chase MD 20815-4226 Office: BF Saul Co 7501 Wisconsin Ave Bethesda MD 20814

SAUL, IRVING ISAAC, lawyer; b. July 9, 1929; s. Israel Jacob and Jennie (Green) S.; m. Lita Brown, Dec. 29, 1950; children: Joanne Ilene, Sandra Lynn. BA, Washington and Jefferson Coll., 1949; LLB, U. Pitts., 1952; postgrad., Georgetown U., 1949, Ohio State U., 1951. Bar: Ohio 1952, U.S. Dist. Ct. (so. dist.) Ohio 1954, U.S. Supreme Ct. 1961, U.S. Ct. Appeals (6th cir.) 1966, U.S. Dist. Ct. (no. dist.) Ohio 1967, U.S. Dist. Ct. (ea. dist.) Wis. 1973, U.S. Ct. Appeals (7th cir.) 1978, U.S. Ct. Appeals (4th cir.) 1978, U.S. Ct. Appeals (fed. cir.) 1991. Pvt. practice, Dayton, Ohio, 1952—. Cons. in antitrust litigation; bd. advs. Fed. Civil Practice Abstracts, 1986-88, Ohio Dist. Ct. Rev., 1988—; adj. prof. complex litigation Sch. of Law U. Dayton, 1996-98; lectr. in field. Contbr. articles to profl. jours. James Gillespie Blaine scholar, 1948. Mem. Ohio Bar Assn. (chmn. fed. cts. and practice com. 1977-79, chmn. pvt. enforcement com. 1979-92, bd. govs. antitrust sect. 1982-94), Dayton Bar Assn. (chmn. fed. ct. practice com. 1976-77, 78-80, chmn. com. on judiciary 1987-88), Am. Judicature Soc., Masons (Shriner), Phi Beta Kappa. Jewish. Office: 113 Bethpolamy Ct Dayton OH 45415-2512

SAUL, JOHN WOODRUFF, III, writer; b. Pasadena, Calif., Feb. 25, 1942; s. John Woodruff and Adeline Elizabeth (Lee) S. Student, Antioch Coll., 1959-60, Cerritos Coll., 1960-61, Mont. State U., Missoula, 1961-62, San Francisco State Coll., 1963-65. In various positions, primarily in L.A. and San Francisco, 1965-76. Author: Suffer The Children. 1977, Punish the Sinners, 1978, Cry for the Strangers, 1979, Comes the Blind Fury, 1980, When the Wind Blows, 1981, The God Project, 1982, Nathaniel, 1984, Brainchild, 1985, Hellfire, 1986, The Unwanted, 1987, The Unloved, 1988, Creature, 1989, Second Child, 1990, Sleep Walk, 1990, Darkness, 1991, Shadows, 1992, Guardian, 1993, The Homing, 1994, Black Lightning, 1995, The Blackstone Chronicles, 1997, The Presence, 1997, The Right Hand of Evil, 1999, Nightshade, 2000, The Manhattan Hunt Club, 2001, Midnight Voices, 2002; also other novels under pseudonyms; creator computer game "John Saul's Blackstone Chronicles," 1998. Bd. dirs. Seattle Theatre Arts, 1978-80; bd. govs. Tellurian Communities, Inc., Madison, Wis.; v.p. Chester Woodruff Found., N.Y.C. Mem. Authors Guild. Democrat. Swedenborgian. Office: care Jane Rotrosen 318 E 51st St New York NY 10022-7803 *For a writer, the education of experience is without doubt the best education.*

SAUL, MARK E. mathematics educator, consultant; b. N.Y.C., June 17, 1948; s. Sidney R. and Shura S.; m. Carol Portnoy, June 26, 1968; children: Susanna, Michael, Peter. BA, Columbia U., 1969; MS, Courant Inst. Math. Scis., NYU, 1975; PhD, NYU, 1987. Tchr. math. and computer sci. Bronx High Sch. Sci., N.Y., 1969-85; teaching fellow Adm. Hyman H. Rickover Found., 1985; computer cons./coord. Bronxville Schs., N.Y., 1985—; dir. Research Sci. Inst. Ctr. Excellence in Edn., McLean, Va., 1987, San Diego, 1990, Cambridge, Mass., 1992-99; cons. computer graphics 1984 Olympics ABC-TV, N.Y.C., 1983-84; pres. N.Y.C. Interscholastic Math. League, N.Y.C., 1979-89, Am. Regions Math. League, 1989-2000; dir. ARML-Soviet Student Exch., 1991-96; cons. Ednl. Testing Service, Princeton, N.J., 1980-82; panelist/cons. LaGuardia High Sch. Performing Arts, N.Y.C., 1977-86; tchr. trainer N.Y.C. Bd. Edn., 1981; tchr.-coord. computer sci. Hollingworth Ctr. for Gifted, Tchrs. Coll., Columbia U., 1984; instr. Lehman Coll., 1984-92, Johns Hopkins U. Ctr. Talented Youth, 1986, Sophie Davis Biomed. Ctr. CCNY, 1986-94, Sarah Lawrence Coll., 1987-94; mem. U.S. del. to Internat. Congress Math. Educators, Budapest, 1988, Quebec, 1992, Seville, 1996, Tokyo, 2000; cons. Ednl. Devel. Ctr., Newton, Mass., 1999-2000; mem. math. scis. edn. bd. NRC, 1997-2000, mem. exec. bd., 1998-2000, others. Co-author: Science/Mathematics Research Programs in the High School, 1982, The New York City Problem Book, 1986, Read the Question: A Thinking Student's Guide to the SAT's, 1992, (with I.M. Gelfand) Trigonometry, 2001; author: Enrichment Problems in Leadership Manual for High School Supervisors in Mathematics, 1982; assoc. editor edn. Notices of Am. Math. Soc., 1996—; contbr. Jour. N.Y. State Assn. Computers and Tech. in Edn. Judge Internat. Math. Olympiad, Washington, 1981, chief guide, 2001; author contest questions Mass. Math. League Ann. Contest, 1981; math. field editor Quantum, 1991-2001; mem. editorial bd. Mathematics and Informatics Jour., 1991—, Mathematical Horizons Jour., 1992—; mem. editl. panel MAA New Math. Libr., 1996—; mem. authors' com. Educating Teachers of Science, Mathematics, and Technology: New Practices for the New Millennium, 1998-2000. Tandy Tech. scholar, 1994, Gabriela and Paul Rosenbaum Found. fellow, 1995; recipient Presdl. award for Excellence in Teaching Math., NSF, 1984, Paul Erdos award World Fedn. Nat. Math. Competitions, 1998. Mem. Assn. Tchrs. Math. (exec. bd. mem. 1980-85), Math. Assn. Am. (mem. com. on high sch. contests 1981-92), Am. Math. Soc., Nat. Council Tchrs. Math. (bd. dirs. 2001—). Avocations: music, art. Home: 711 Amsterdam Ave Apt 27K New York NY 10025-6929

SAUL, NORMAN EUGENE, history educator; b. LaFontaine, Ind., Nov. 26, 1932; s. Ralph Odis and Jessie (Neff) S.; m. Mary Ann Culwell, June 27, 1959; children: Alyssa, Kevin, Julia. BA, Ind. U.- Bloomington, 1954; MA, Columbia U., 1959, PhD, 1965; postgrad., Leningrad State U. (USSR), 1960-61. Asst. prof. Brown U., 1965-68; vis. assoc. prof. Northwestern U., 1969-70; assoc. prof. U. Kans., Lawrence, 1970-75, prof. history, 1975—, chmn. dept. history, 1981-89. Inst. Advanced Study, Princeton U., 2000. Author: Russia and the Mediterranean 1797-1807, 1970, Sailors in Revolt, 1978, Distant Friends: The United States and Russia, 1763-1867, 1991, Concord and Conflict: The United States and Russia, 1867-1914, 1996, War and Revolution: The United States and Russia, 1914-1921, 2001; editor: Russian-American Dialogue on Cultural Relations, 1776-1914, 1997. Fulbright scholar, London, 1954-55, Helsinki, 1968-69, Soviet Am. Exch. scholar Internat. Rsch. and Exch. Bd., Moscow, 1973-74, 91-92; fellow Ford Found., 1957-59, Hall Ctr. for Humanities, 1989, 95; recipient Byron Caldwell Smith Book award for Distant Friends Hall Ctr. for Humanities, 1993, Robert H. Ferrell book award for concert and conflict Soc. Historians Am. Fgn. Rels., 1997, Pub. Scholar award Kans. Humanities Coun., 1997, Higuchi Rsch. award U. Kans., 1997, Steeples award for Svc. to Kans., 2000, Herbert Hoover Libr. Assn. award, 2001. Mem. Am. Assn. Advancement of Slavic Studies, Kans. State Hist. Soc. Home: 1002 Crestline Dr Lawrence KS 66049-2607 E-mail: nsaul@ku.edu.

SAUL, RALPH SOUTHEY, financial service executive; b. Bklyn., May 21, 1922; s. Walter Emerson and Helen Douglas (Coutts) S.; m. Bette Jane Bertschinger, June 16, 1956; children: Robert Southey, Jane Adams. BA, U. Chgo., 1947; LL.B., Yale U., 1951. Bar: D.C. 1951, N.Y. 1952. With Am. Embassy, Prague, Czechoslovakia, 1947-48; assoc. Lyeth & Voorhees, N.Y.C., 1951-52; asst. counsel to gov. State of N.Y., 1952-54; staff atty. RCA, 1954-58; with SEC, 1958-65, dir. div. trading and markets, 1963-65; v.p. corporate devel. Investors Diversified Services, Inc., Mpls., 1965-66; pres. Am. Stock Exch., N.Y.C., 1966-71; co-chief exec., chmn. mgmt. com. 1st Boston Corp., 1971-74; chmn., CEO. INA Corp., Phila., 1975-82, CIGNA Corp., Phila., 1982-84. Trustee Com. for Econ. Devel., Brookings Inst. With USNR, 1943-46, PTO. Mem. ABA, N.Y. Stock Exch. (regulatory adv. com.), Union League , Merion Golf Club, Links Club. Office: Cigna Corp One Logan Square PO Box 7716 18th and Cherry Sts Philadelphia PA 19192

SAUL, WILLIAM EDWARD, civil engineering educator; b. N.Y.C., May 15, 1934; s. George James and Fanny Ruth (Murokh) S.; m. J. Muriel Held Eagleburger, May 11, 1976. BSCE, Mich. Tech. U., 1955, MSCE, 1961; PhD in Civil Engring., Northwestern U., 1964. Registerd profl. engr., Wis., Idaho, Mich., profl. structural engr., Idaho. Mech. engr. Shell Oil Co., New Orleans, 1955-59; instr. engring. mechanics Mich. Tech. U., Houghton, 1960-62; asst. prof. civil engring. U. Wis., Madison, 1964-67, assoc. prof., 1967-72, prof., 1972-84; dean, prof. civil engring. U. Idaho Coll. Engring., Moscow, 1984-90; prof. civil engring. Mich. State U., East Lansing, 1990—2000, chmn. dept. civil and environ. engring., 1990-95, chmn. emeritus, prof. emeritus, 2000. Cons. engr., 1961—; vis. prof. U. Stuttgart, Germany, 1970-71. Co-editor Conf. of Methods of Structural Analysis, 1976. Bd. dirs. Idaho Rsch. Found., 1984-90. Fulbright fellow 1970-71; von Humboldt scholar, 1970-71. Fellow ASCE (pres. Wis. sect. 1983-84), Mich. Soc. Profl. Engrs.; mem. NSPE, Internat. Assn. Bridge and Structural Engrs., Am. Concrete Inst., Am. Soc. Engring. Edn., Sigma Xi, Phi Kappa Phi, Tau Beta Pi, Chi Epsilon. Avocations: hiking, reading, travel, gadgets. Home: 1971 Cimarron Dr Okemos MI 48864-3905 Office: Mich State U 3546 Engring Bldg E East Lansing MI 48824

SAULLE, NUNZIO, physiatrist; b. Bklyn., Feb. 23, 1964; MD, SUNY, Bklyn., 1990. Diplomate Am. Bd. Physical Medicine and Rehab. Intern Winthrop Univ. Hosp., Mineola, N.Y., 1990-91, resident, 1991-93, L.I. Jewish Med. Ctr., New Hyde Park, 1993-96, physiatrist, 1996—; pvt. practice Mineola, 1999—. Named Attending Physician of the Yr. L.I. Jewish Med. Ctr., 1996-97. Fellow Am. Acad. Phys. Medicine and Rehab. Office: Progressive Phys Med and Rehab 131 Jericho Tpke Mineola NY 11501-1800

SAULMON, SHARON ANN, college librarian; b. Blackwell, Okla., June 13, 1947; d. Ellis Gordon and Willa Mae Overman; 1 child, John Henry. AA, No. Okla. Coll., 1967; BA, Ctrl. State U., 1969, MBA, 1987; MLS, U. Okla., 1974; postgrad., Okla. State U., 1982. Children's libr. Met. Libr. Sys., Oklahoma City, 1969-74, coord. pub. svcs., 1974-77, asst. chief ext. svcs., 1977-80; reference/special projects libr. Rose State Coll., Midwest City, Okla., 1980-91, head libr., 1991—. Adj. faculty Rose State Coll., 1983—; program chair Global Okla. Multi-Cultural Festival, 1993; mem. Nat. Adv. Panel for Assessment of Sch. and Pub. Librs. in Support of Nat. Edn. Goals, 1995—96, project dir. internet tng., 1997, chair website com., 1996—98, v.p. profl./adminstrv. staff, 1998—99, pres., 1999—2000; vice chair Okla. Coun. Acad. Libr. Dirs., 2001—02; spkr. various civic and profl. orgns. Contbr. articles to profl. jours. Bd. dirs. Areawide Aging Agy., 1974-77; chair Met. Libr. Commn., 1990-98, disbursing agt., chair fin. com., 1986-88, long-range planning com., 1985-87; chair bd. dirs. Met. Librs. Network Ctrl. Okla., 1989-90, chair alternative funding com., 1990-98, newsletter editor, 1987-89, chair electronic media com., 1987-89, chair bd. dirs., 1997-98, Webmaster, 1997-2000. Recipient Outstanding Contbn. award Met. Libr. Sys., Friends of the Libr., 1990, Disting. Svc. award Okla. Libr. Assn., 1995, OLA/SIRS Intellectual Freedom award 1999. Mem. AAUW, ALA (mem. legis. com. 1996-98, adv. bd. 1996-98, Cited Trustee award 1999), Am. Libr. Trustee Assn. (bd. dirs. 1997-98, pres. 1994-95, 1st v.p., pres. elect 1993-94, newsletter editor 1989-93, 99—, chair publs. com. 1987-92, regional v.p. 1985-88, chair speakers bur. com. 1991-92, chair awards com. 1998-99), Assn. Coll. and Rsch. Librs. (Cmty. and Jr. Coll. sect.), Pub. Libr. Assn., Am. Mktg. Assn., Okla. Libr. Assn. (conf. preview editor 1990-91, chair trustees divsn. 1989-90, mem. coms., disting. svc. award 1995, chair divsn. univ. colls. 1996-97, chair program com. 1998-99, v.p. 1999-2000, pres. 2000-01, budget com. chair 2001-02, navigating info. chair 2002-03), Profl. and Adminstrv. Staff Assn. (v.p. 1998-99, pres. 1999-2000), Am. Guild Organists. Democrat. Methodist. Office: Rose State Coll Libr 6420 SE 15th St Midwest City OK 73110-2704 E-mail: ssaulmon@yahoo.com.

SAULNIERS, ALFRED HERVEY, economics educator; b. Acushnet, Mass., June 22, 1945; s. Hervey Raymond and Aline Cecile (Ledoux) S.; m. Suzanne M. Smith, June 17, 1970; 1 child, Catherine Regine. AB, Boston Coll., 1967; PhD, U. Wis., Madison, 1972. Research assoc. U. Mich., Ann Arbor, 1973-76, U. Tex., Austin, 1976-86; project assoc. Harvard Inst. Internat. Devel., Cambridge, Mass., 1986-91; sr. mgr. office govt. svcs. Price-Waterhouse Internat., Washington, 1991—. Cons. Internat. Labor Orgn., Arusha, Tanzania, 1983-84, World Bank, Lima, Peru, 1981, USDA, Kinshasa, Zaire, 1979, 82, USAID, Dakar, Senegal, 1988. Editor: Public Sector in Latin America, 1984, Economic and Political Roles of the State, 1985, Las Empresas Publicas en el Peru, 1985; Cuatro Mitos Sobre Empresas Publicas en America Latina, 1985; compiler book bibliography Public Enterprise, 1985, supplement, 1986, Public Enterprises in Peru, 1988. Fulbright lectr. Council for Internat. Exchange of Scholars, Lima, 1985. Mem. Am. Econ. Assn., Latin Am. Studies Assn., Econ. History Assn. Avocation: reading science fiction. Home: 41 Jean St Acushnet MA 02743-2703

SAULPAUGH, CHRISTOPHER FRANCIS, publishing executive; b. West Point, N.Y., Apr. 1, 1962; s. Richard R. and Susan T. S. BS in Bus. Adminstrn., Calif. State U., San Bernardino, 1992. Reg. software beta tester; cert. mil. instr. Sys. engr. Computer Connection, Victorville, Calif., 1990-93; MIS dir., cd-rom developer and software programmer, project mgr. software into fgn. langs. Roger Wagner Pub., El Cajon, 1993—. Owner Future Tech. Sys., Apple Valley, Calif., 1987-92, Santee, Calif., 1993—; workshop presenter in the field. Cons.: (book) HyperStudio in an Hour, 1993; graphics designer HyperStudio in an Hour for Windows; author Getting Started Manual for HyperStudio for Macintosh, HyperStudio for Windows, 1994-98, How to Burn a CD-Rom in Three Bazillion Easy Steps, 1998; software developer. Vol. Calif. Dept. Forestry, San Bernardino, 1988-93; mortar platoon sect. leader Calif. Nat Guard, San Bernardino, 1986-93. Sgt. U.S. Army, 1982-86. Mem. IEEE, NRA (life), Am. Legion, Apple Valley Gun Club (v.p. 1986-87), Microsoft Devel. Network (registerd). Avocations: camping, computers, travel. Office: Roger Wagner Pub Inc 19840 Pioneer Ave Torrance CA 90503-1660

SAULSON, SAUL S. chemical company executive; b. Detroit, Nov. 30, 1928; s. Morse R. and Fannie W. Saulson; m. Laela Miller, Nov. 25, 1964 (dec. Oct. 1967); children: Melinda, Eli; m. Marjorie S. Saulson, Jan. 11, 1970. BA in Bus. Adminstrn., Wayne State U., 1951. V.p., gen. mgr. Frank W. Kerr Chem. Co., Novi, Mich., 1955—. Inventor first ready-to-use charcoal antidote for use in hosp. emergency dept., cherry flavored charcoal antidote, magnetic device for vacuums. Avocations: photography, painting, woodworking, swimming, bicycling. Home: 26662 Scenic Hwy Franklin MI 48025-1321 Office: Frank W Kerr Chem Co 43155 W 9 Mile Rd Novi MI 48375-4117

SAUMIER, ANDRE, finance executive; b. Montreal, Que., Can., Aug. 26, 1933; s. Robert and Georgette (Sansoucy) S.; children: Sonia, Genevieve, Verushka BA, U. Montreal, 1950; LTh, Angelicum U., Rome, 1955; MA, U. Chgo., 1958; MBA, Harvard U., 1962. Rsch. assoc. Battelle Inst., Columbus, Ohio, 1962-63; dir. rsch. Urban Affairs Coun., Ottawa, Ont., Can., 1963-67; asst. dep. minister rural devel., regional devel., urban affairs Govt. of Can., 1967-75; dep. sec. gen. to cabinet, dep. minister of mines, water & energy Govt. of Que., Quebec City, 1975-79; sr. v.p. Richardson Greenshields Co., Montreal, 1979-85; pres., CEO Montreal Stock Exch., 1985-87; chmn. Saumier Morrisson & Davidson Inc., Investment Bankers, Montreal, 1987-89, Saumier Freres Conseil, Fin. Advisors, Montreal, 1989—. Bd. dirs., chmn. Societe Nat. de L'Amiante, Montreal; chmn. Sebentar Holdings Inc., Vista Info. Tech. Inc., Vancouver, Can. ASEAN Ctr., Singapore; advisor World Resources Inst., Washington, Ministry of Fin. of Indonesia, Jakarta, Ministry of Fin. of Gabon, Libreville, Ministry of Fin. of Kazakhstan, Almaty, Office of Prime Min., Govt. of Vietnam, Hanoi; bur. de consultation de Montreal, City of Montreal, Que. Contbg. author books on environment Bd. govs. Nouveau-Monde Theater, Montreal, 1983—, Que. Assn. MBA, Montreal Coun. Internat. Affairs. Decorated officer Nat. Order of Niger, 1972, Order of St.-Lazarus of Jerusalem, 1987; recipient Merit award Montreal C. of C., 1985, 88. Home and Office: 65 Saint Paul W Apt 403 Montreal QC Canada H2Y 3S5

SAUNDERS, ALEXANDER HALL, real estate executive; b. Tallahassee, Oct. 5, 1941; s. Irvin Jasper and Perry Francis (Watson) S.; m. Pamela Wightman, July 24, 1970; 1 child, Anne Marguerite. AA, Norman Coll., 1961; BA, Mercer U., 1966. Planning adminstr. Ga. Dept. Corrections, Atlanta, 1969-70; mgmt. analyst Ga. Dept. Transp., 1970-71, tng. adminstr., 1971-72, asst. to research and devel., 1972-73, adminstr., asst. to dir., 1974-82; pres. ERA Towne Square Realty, Inc., Stone Mountain, Ga., 1982—. Named one of Top Real Estate Execs. in Am., ERA, 1987. Mem. Nat. Assn. Realtors, Ga. Assn. Realtors, DeKalb Bd. Realtors, ERA North Ga. Brokers Coun. (trustee 1983-86, pres. 1988-89, v.p., dir. fin. 1989-)., Metro Listing Svc., U.S. C. of C., DeKalb C. of C., Better Bus. Bur., Mercer U. Alumni Assn. (bd. dirs. 1997—), Alpha Tau Omega, Delta Theta Phi. Avocations: tennis, racquet ball, golf.

SAUNDERS, BARRY COLLINS, civil engineering consultant; b. St. Louis, Dec. 17, 1931; s. William Flewellyn and Naomi Harriet (Kober) S.; m. Marjorie Ruth Nordholm, June 11, 1960; children: Kristin Ruth, Jennifer Ann Saunders Gerlach. BS, St. Louis U., 1953; MBA, U. Denver, 1961; MS, Utah State U., 1967. Registered prof. engr., Colo. Test engr. McDonnell Aircraft Corp., St. Louis, 1956-58; sr. engr. Stanley Aviation Corp., Denver, 1958-62, Thiokol Chem. Corp., Brigham City, Utah, 1962-66; assoc. dir. Utah State Divsn. Water Resources, Salt Lake City, 1967-95; natural resources cons., 1995—. With U.S. Army, 1954-56. Mem. ASCE. Lutheran.

SAUNDERS, BARRY WAYNE, state official; b. Roxboro, N.C., June 9, 1944; s. Charlie Clifton and Mary Louise (Mooney) S.; m. Brenda Kaye Bell, Oct. 18, 1987; children: Dara Louise Saunders Lockamy, Erin Elissa (dec.). BA, Campbell u., 1971; MEd, U. N.C., 1974; EdD, N.C. State U., 1990. Tchr. Granville County Sch. System, Oxford, N.C., 1966-69; mental health counselor Vocat. Rehab., Henderson, 1971-75; staff devel. specialist John Umstead Hosp., Butner, 1975-82; trainer, asst. mgr., mgr. tng. N.C. Dept. Transp., Raleigh, 1982—; mgr. tng. (on loan from N.C. Dept. Transp.) Gov.'s Office of Quality Improvement, 1995-96; mgr. tng. N.C. Dept. Transp., Raleigh, 1996-2000; ret., 2000. Pres. Omicron Cons., Mill Spring, NC, 1982—. Contbr. articles to profl. jours., poems to N.C. Poetry Soc., 1981. Sec. Dem. Party, Person County, N.C., 1980-84. Mem. Nat. Mgmt. Assn. (bd. dirs. state govt. chpt. 1992-95, v.p. 1997-98), Triangle Quality Coun. (bd. dirs. 1995-96), Nat. Transp. Tng. Dirs. Assn. (v.p. 1997-2000). Methodist. Home: 121 Canoe Dr Mill Spring NC 28756

SAUNDERS, BRIAN KEITH, consulting company executive; b. Columbus, Ohio, June 4, 1961; BSEE, Purdue U., 1983; MBA, Dartmouth U., 1988. Asst. mgr. engring. New Eng. Telephone, Boston, 1983-85, asst. product mgr., 1985-86; assoc. Booz Allen & Hamilton, N.Y.C., 1987-90; dir. strategy and planning Pacific Bell, San Ramon, Calif., 1991-92; gen. mgr. Compus Svcs. Corp., Pleasanton, 1993-94; prin. cons., designer BKS Design, San Ramon, 1994—; sr. prin. The McKenna Group, Palo Alto, 1995-97; chief synergist The BKS Group, San Ramon, 1997-99; client ptnr. Organic Online, 1999-2000; v.p. profl. svcs. Telephia, Inc., San Francisco, 2001—. Instr. U. Calif.-Berkeley Extension, 1999—; bd. dirs. Children's Media Lab., Berkeley, Calif., 1993-97, Family Stress Ctr., Concord, Calif., 1995-97; mem. industry coun. Mt. Diablo Coll., Pleasant Hill, Calif., 1993-95; mem. exec. coun. Tuck MBEP Alumni Assn. Dartmouth Coll., Hanover, N.H., 1994—. Mem. Computer Game Developers Assn., Bay Area Video Coalition, MDG.org., World Future Soc. Avocations: jazz, history, science fiction, martial arts.

SAUNDERS, BRYAN LESLIE, lawyer; b. Newport News, Va., Apr. 18, 1945; s. Raymond Hayes and Lois Mae (Pair) S.; divorced; children: Kelly Brooke, Justin Lee; m. Anne Mason Dunbar, July 15, 1995. BS, East Tenn. State U., 1967; JD, U. Tenn., 1973. Bar: Va. 1973, U.S. Dist. Ct. (ea. dist.) Va. 1973, U.S. Ct. Appeals (4th cir.) 1991. Lawyer Cogdill & Assocs., Newport News, Va., 1973—76; pvt. practice, 1976—; ptnr. Saunders & Lawrence, 2002—. Commr. in chancery Cir. Ct. of Newport News, 1990-97. Sgt. U.S. Army, 1968-71. Decorated Bronze star, 1971; recipient Outstanding Svc. to Law Enforcement Newport News and Police Dept., 1986. Mem. Va. Bar Assn., Nat. Assn. Criminal Def. Lawyers, Va. Coll. Criminal Def. Attys., Pi Kappa Phi, Pi Gamma Mu. Avocations: chess, bridge, bowling. Office: 728 Thimble Shoals Blvd Ste C Newport News VA 23606-4546 E-mail: bryansaund@aol.com.

SAUNDERS, CHARLES ALBERT, lawyer; b. Boulder, Colo., Jan. 18, 1922; s. Charles and Anna (Crouse) S.; m. Betti Friedel, Oct. 18, 1946; children— Melanie, Stephen, Cynthia, Shelley. BA, U. Houston, 1942; LLB, U. Tex., 1945. Bar: Tex. bar 1945. Since practiced in, Houston; partner firm Fulbright & Jaworski, L.L.P., 1959—. Editor: How To Live-and Die-With Texas Probate, 8 vols., 1968, Texas Estate Administration, 1975. Bd. dirs. Houston Symphony Soc., 1964— ; bd. dirs. Am. Lung Assn., San Jacinto, 1965— , pres., 1972-73; past mem. bd. govs. U. Houston. Recipient Leon Jaworski award for cmty. svc. Houston Bar Assn., 1997, U. Tex. Law Sch. Disting. Alumnus award in Cmty. Svc., 1999. Mem. ABA, State Bar Assn., Houston Bar Assn., Am. Coll. Trust and Estate Coun. (regent 1972-80, pres. 1978-79), Internat. Acad. of Estate and Trust Law, Assn. Cmty. TV (bd. dirs. 1970—). Republican. Presbyterian. Home: 19 Willowron Dr Houston TX 77024-7618 Office: Fulbright & Jaworski 1301 Mckinney St Ste 5100 Houston TX 77010-3031 E-mail: csaunders@fulbright.com.

SAUNDERS, CHARLES BASKERVILLE, JR. retired association executive; b. Boston, Dec. 26, 1928; s. Charles Baskerville and Lucy (Carmichael) S.; m. Margaret MacIntire Shafer, Sept. 9, 1950; children— Charles Baskerville III, George Carlton, Margaret Keyser, Lucy C., John R. Grad., St. Mark's Sch., 1946; AB, Princeton, 1950. News reporter, polit. columnist Ogdensburg (N.Y.) Jour., 1950-51; edn. reporter Hartford (Conn.) Times, 1951-53; asst. dir. pub. relations Trinity Coll., Hartford, 1953-55; asst. dir. pub. info. Princeton, 1955-57; legis. asst. Sen. H. Alexander Smith, 85th Congress, 1957-58; asst. to asst. sec. for legislation HEW, 1958-59; asst. to sec. Arthur S. Flemming, 1959-61, dep. asst. sec. for legislation, 1969-71; asst. to pres. Brookings Instn., 1961-69; dep. commr. of edn. for external affairs U.S. Office Edn., 1971-72; dep. asst. sec. for edn. HEW, 1973-74; dir. govt. relations Am. Council on Edn., 1975-78, v.p. for govt. relations, 1978-87, sr. v.p., 1987-92. Author: Brookings Institution: A Fifty-Year History, 1966, Upgrading the American Police, 1970, Four Centuries in America, 2000. Mem. Montgomery County Bd. Edn., 1966-70, Md. Higher Edn. Commn., 1989-2002 (chmn. 1994-95, vice chmn. 1995-2002); chmn. bd. dirs. Md. Higher Edn. Loan Corp., 1994-95. Mem. Jamestowne Soc. Democrat. Presbyterian. Home: 7622 Winterberry Pl Bethesda MD 20817-4848

SAUNDERS, CHARLES DAVID, state official; b. Evanston, Ill., May 17, 1962; s. Charles Albert and Carol Ann (Tarpey) S.; m. Kazuko Uchino, June 8, 1986; children: Elizabeth Moeko, Sarah Kanae. BA, Lawrence U., 1984; MBA, Columbia U., 1988. CFA. Mombusho Japan fellow Japanese Ministry Edn., Kumamoto, 1984-86; fin. analyst J. Henry Schroder Bank & Trust, N.Y.C., 1987-88; v.p. Indsl. Bank Japan, Tokyo, 1988-94; investment dir. Wis. Investment Bd., Madison, 1994—. Mem. Internat. Fin. Analysts Soc., Milw. Fin. Analysts Soc. Episcopalian. Home: 1107 Oak Way Madison WI 53705-1420 Office: Wis Investment Bd Box 7842 121 E Wilson St Madison WI 53707-7842 E-mail: chuck.saunders@swib.state.wi.us., chucksaunders@msn.com.

SAUNDERS, DONALD LESLIE, hotel owner, real estate investor; b. Brookline, Mass., Jan. 28, 1935; s. Irving M. Saunders and Shirley Brown; children: Lisa M., Pamela R. AB in Econs., Brown U., 1957; grad., Inst. Real Estate Mgmt., 1963; LLB (hon.), Pine Manor Coll., 1989. Real estate broker, R.I., Mass. Chmn., CEO Saunders Real Estate Corp., Boston, 1957—; CEO, gen. mgr. Saunders Real Estate, Hotels L.C.; co-owner Boston Pk. Plz. Hotel & Towers, 1976—; gen. ptnr. SaunStar Land Co., LLC. Bd. dirs. Park Sch. Corp., Brookline, Mass., Jerusalem Found., Inc., U.S.A.; pres. Farview Inc.; vice chmn. facilities and design com. Brown U., trustee emeritus, 1972—; mem. nat. adv. com. U.s. Com. for UNICEF; trustee Boston Ballet Co.; bd. dirs. Jerusalem Inst. Mgmt. Inc. at Harvard Bus. Sch.; bd. dirs. John Carter Libr. of Americana at Brown U. Recipient Nat. Jewish Hosp. and Research Ctr. Nat. Asthma Ctr. Humanitarian award, 1979, Back Bay Fedn. Community Devel. Ann. award, 1981, Historic Neighborhoods Found. award, 1986. Mem. Internat. Hotel Assn., Inst. Real Estate Mgmt. (key 2299), Nat. Assn. Realtors, Great Boston Real Estate Bd., Ocean Reef Club (Racquet Club), Brown U. Club, Lotos Club, The Players, Union League Club, Hope Club, Boston Tennis and Racquet Club, Ea. Point Yacht Club, Belmont Country Club, Bay Club, Downtown Club, Union Club Boston, Charles River Yacht Club. Office: Saunders Real Estate Corp Statler Bldg 700 20 Park Plz Boston MA 02116-4303

SAUNDERS, DONNA M. accountant; b. Washington, July 23, 1969; d. Ellridge Everette Carey and Joyce Bernice Ramey; m. Gary Roland Saunders, June 10, 2000. BS, U. Md., 1991. Market rschr. Nat. Rsch. Inc., New Carrollton, Md., 1986-87; clk.-typist USN, Washington, 1987; student asst. U. Md. College Park, 1987-91; sr. acct. Bert Smith & Co., 1992-94; staff acct. Arrow Gen., Alexandria, 1994; accts. payable supr. Franklin Acceptance, Greenbelt, Md., 1994-96; acctg. mgr. Rental Tools, Upper Marlboro, 1996-99; sr. acct. FTI Cons., Annapolis, 1999; acctg. mgr. Safeware, Inc., Largo, 1999—. Mem. AICPAs, Md. Assn. CPAs. Democrat. Baptist. Avocations: bowling, writing poetry, missionary youth work.

SAUNDERS, GEORGE LAWTON, JR. lawyer; b. Mulga, Ala., Nov. 8, 1931; s. George Lawton and Ethel Estell (York) S.; children: Kenneth, Ralph, Victoria; m. Terry M. Rose. BA, U. Ala., 1956; JD, U. Chgo., 1959. Bar: Ill. 1960. Law clk. to chief judge U.S. Ct. Appeals (5th cir.), Montgomery, Ala., 1959-60; law clk to Justice Hugo L. Black U.S. Supreme Ct., Washington, 1960-62; assoc. Sidley & Austin, Chgo., 1962-67, ptnr., 1967-90; founding ptnr. Saunders & Monroe, 1990—. With USAF, 1951-54. Fellow: ACLA; mem.: ABA, Law Club, Quadrangle Club, Chgo. Club, Point-O-Woods Club, Order of the Coif, Phi Beta Kappa. Democrat. Baptist. Home: 179 E Lake Shore Dr Chicago IL 60611-1306 Office: Saunders & Monroe Ste 1302 33 N Dearborn St Chicago IL 60602

SAUNDERS, GEORGE WENDELL, management consultant, retired government official; b. Hubbard, Ohio, Oct. 17, 1917; s. Phillip and Mary (Shafer) S.; m. Audrey Edna Bogue (dec. Nov. 1979); children: Wayne George, Wendy Jean; m. Virginia Hutson Baker, June 25, 1987; stepchildren: John Milton Jr., Kathee Eloise. B in Acctg., Rider Coll., 1937; postgrad, Harvard U., 1943; grad., Indsl. Coll. Armed Forces, 1955, Fgn. Service Inst., Naval War Coll.; student, Grad. Sch. Dept. Agr., Dept. Def. Computer Inst. Auditor, acct. U.S. Rubber Co., N.Y.C., 1937-39; acct., office mgr. S. King Fulton, Inc., Washington, 1939-40; with War Dept. and Civil Aero. Adminstrn., 1940-41; adminstrv. asst., sr. investigator Bur. Fed. Supply Treas. Dept., 1941-47; ops. planning analyst, orgn. and methods examiner, supply specialist Fed. Supply Services GSA, 1957-55, dep. dir. stores mgmt. div., 1955-61, dir. supply distbn. div., acting asst. dir. nat. buying div., 1956-61, dir. distbn. programs div., 1961-64, asst. commr. supply distbn., 1964-71, asst. commr. trans. and pub. utilities, 1971-73, dep. commr., 1973-75; v.p. Washington Mgmt. Group, Washington Mktg. Group, 1975-79; pvt. practice cons., 1979—. Mem. Fed. Safety Council, Fed. Fire Council and Nat. Def. Trans. Bd., 1970-75 Contbr. to govt. publs. Chmn. bd. dirs., past pres. North Chevy Chase Swimming Pool Assn., 1960; vestryman, treas. Episc. Ch., Silver Spring, Md., 1950. Served with USN World War II, PTO, ATO, comdr. Res. ret., 1975. Recipient Adminstrs. Exceptional Service award GSA, 1975. Mem. Ret. Officers Assn., Am. Legion (exec. bd. Thad Dulin chpt. 1986-87, adj. 1988, vice comdr. 1989-91, comdr. 1994-95), Leisure World Golf Club, Kenwood Country Club, Montgomery Village Golf Club, Lions (pres. Rossmoor Club Silver Spring, 1988-89), Fireside Forum (v.p., bd. dirs.), Leisure World. Republican. Avocations: golf, travel,aviation, swimming. Home and Office: 15107 Interlachen Dr Apt 812 Silver Spring MD 20906-5633

SAUNDERS, HAROLD HENRY, foundation administrator; b. Phila., Dec. 27, 1930; s. Harold Manuel Saunders and Marian Elizabeth Weihenmayer; m. Barbara Mc Garrigle, May 4, 1963 (dec. Oct. 1973); children: Catherine Elizabeth, Mark Harril; m. Carol Eleanor Jones Cruse, June 2, 1990. AB, Princeton U., 1952; PhD, Yale U., 1956; LittD, New England Coll., 1999. With CIA, Washington, 1959-61; sr. staff Nat. Security coun., 1961-74; dir. intelligence and rsch., asst. sec. Near East and South Asian affairs Dept. of State, 1974-81; fellow Am. Enterprise Inst. Brookings Inst., 1981-91; professorial lectr. Johns Hopkins U. SAIS, George Mason U., 1984—91; dir. internat. affairs Kettering Found., Washington, 1991—; pres. Internat. Inst. for Sustained Dialogue, 2002—. Prof. lectr. John Hopkins Univ., SAIS, George Mason Univ., 1984—91. Author: The Other Walls: Arab-Israeli Peace Process in Global Perspective, 1985, 91, A Public Peace Process: Sustained Dialogue to Transform Racial & Ethnic Conflicts, 1999. Trustee Princeton U., 1996—2000; ruling elder Lewinsville Presbyn. Ch., McLean, Va., 1971—; bd. dirs. East-West Inst., N.Y.C., 1981—89, Ptnrs. Dem. Change, San Francisco, 1995—, InterNews, Arcata, 1999—2001. Lt. USAF, 1957—59. Recipient Disting. Fed. Civilian Svc. award Pres. U.S., 1978, Disting. Honor award Dept. of State, 1981, First Disting. Achievement Award, Germantown Acad., Phila. Mem. Internat. Sc. Polit. Psychology (gov. coun. 1991-94), Coun. on Fgn. Rels., Princeton Club N.Y., Phi Beta Kappa. Avocation: writing. Home: 2101 Lorraine Ave Mc Lean VA 22101 Office: Kettering Found. 444 N Capitol St NW Washington DC 20001

SAUNDERS, JACQUELYN RAE, exterior designer; b. Youngstown, Ohio, Mar. 10, 1938; d. Thomas Gilbert Madden and Hazel Elizabeth (Ward) Anderson; divorced; 1 child, Heidi Lee Graber. Student, Kent State U., 1956-57. From sales person to mgmt. Index Pubs., Chgo., 1966-67, owner, 1975-80, Lockman Printing, Blue Island, Ill., 1973-80, Colortone, Inc., Blue Island, 1976-80, Sheldon Offset, Blue Island, 1978-80; mgr. classified advt. Houston Post, 1980-81; from mktg. mgmt. to gen. mgr., v.p. ops. Trim Home Design, Inc., Houston, 1983—. Illustrator, cons. Test Yourself Book, 1980. Mem. Ill. Presswomens Assn. Republican. Unitarian Universalist. Avocations: golf, oil and watercolor painting, reading, sailing.

SAUNDERS, JAMES C. neuroscientist, educator; b. Elizabeth, N.J., May 8, 1941; s. Charles Oliver and Elizabeth Veronica (Drake) S.; m. Elaine Priscilla Edwards, Oct. 14, 1967; children: Breton Morris, Drew Charles. BA, Ohio Wesleyan U., 1963; MA, Conn. Coll., 1965, U. Pa., 1979; PhD, Princeton U., 1968. Lectr. dept. psychology Monash U., Victoria, Australia, 1969-72; rsch. assoc. Cen. Inst. for Deaf, St. Louis, 1972-73; asst. prof., then prof. dept. otorhinolaryngology U. Pa., Phila., 1973-89, acting dir. Inst. Neurol. Scis., 1980-83. Guest scientist Karolinska Inst., Stockholm, 1984-85; exec. com. CHABA, Nat. Rsch. Coun., Washington, 1986-89; chmn. disorders rev. com. NIDCD, Bethesda, Md., 1987-89; mem. exec. coun., long range planning com., Assn. Rsch. Otolaryngology, Chgo., 1988-91; mem. com. on hearing and bioacoustics Nat. Inst. on Deafness and Other Communications Disorders; chair Med. Sch. Fac. Senate, U. Pa., 1998-99; chair faculty 2000 project U. Pa., 1999—. Contbr. chpts., rev. papers to books on biology of hearing; contbr. articles on auditory neurobiology to profl. jours; author abstracts of meeting presentations on hearing. Recipient Basic Sci. Rsch. award Am. Acad. Otolaryngology, 1978, 87, Pa. Acad. Otolaryngology, 1982, Basic Sci. Excellence award (Claude Pepper award) NIDCD, 1988. Mem. AAAS, Acoustical Soc. Am., Soc. Neurosci., N.Y. Acad. Sci., Sigma Xi (legal cons. effects of noise on hearing). Democrat. Office: U Pa 5 Ravdin ORL 3400 Spruce St Philadelphia PA 19104-4206 Home: 417 Bryn Mawr Ave Bala Cynwyd PA 19004-2619 E-mail: saundrej@mail.med.upenn.edu.

SAUNDERS, JAMES DALTON, lawyer; b. Sept. 6, 1969; s. James Cranford Saunders Jr. and Caroline Elizabeth Dalton Saunders. BA, BS, Case Western Res. U., 1990, MBA, 1991, JD, 1996, LLM, 1999; MSc, Imperial Coll., London, 1992. Bar: Ohio 1997, Fla. 1998, D.C. 1999, U.S. Tax Ct. 1999, U.S. Dist. Ct. N.D. 2001, U.S. Dist. Ct. Ohio 2001. Interest rate options analyst Security Pacific Hoare Govett Merchant Bank, London, 1988-90; comml. lending asst. Hong Kong and Shanghai Banking Corp., Hong Kong, London, 1991-93; atty. in pvt. practice Cleve., Boca Raton, Fla., 1997—. Treas. Cleve. Orch. Chorus, 1995-98. Republican. Episcopalian. Avocations: music, literature, architectural design, hiking. Home: 16210 Shaker Blvd Shaker Heights OH 44120-1664 Office: 23220 Chagrin Blvd Cleveland OH 44122

SAUNDERS, JAMES HARWOOD, accountant; b. Carlsbad, N.Mex., Apr. 2, 1948; s. Eugene C. and Ruth (Powelson)S.; m. Kathleen Sue Matson, Jan. 26, 1974 (div. Apr. 1982); m. Bette Kim McCutcheon, Sept. 4, 1982 (div. Oct. 1997); children: James C., Carl J., William K.; m. Tricia Eggleston, Feb. 20, 2002. AA in Adminstrn. Justice, Glendale Coll., Glendale, Ariz., 1975; BSBA, Ariz. State U., 1978. CPA, N.M., Ariz., Colo., Nev., Utah; lic. funeral dir. and embalmer; cert. fraud examiner; lic. pvt. investigator. Embalmer Denton Funeral Home, Carlsbad, 1964-69; clk., trainee Sears & Roebuck Co., Dallas and Albuquerque, 1969-71, Phoenix, 1971-73; police sgt. spl. ops. Phoenix Police Dept., 1973-80; staff acct. various CPA firms, Carlsbad, 1980-83; owner James H. Saunders Acctg., 1983-86; pvt. practice acctg. Eagar, Ariz., 1987—. Auditor, mgmt. advisor to several Ariz. municipalities, 1987—. Vol. fireman Carlsbad Fire Dept., 1965-68; reserve dep. Bermallio County Sheriff Dept., Albuquerque, 1969-70. Mem. AICPA, Ariz. Soc. CPAs, N.Mex. Soc. CPAs, N.Mex. Assn. Funeral Dirs., Lions (sec. Carlsbad chpt. 1985-87, pres. Springerville, Ariz. chpt. 1987-91). Avocations: coin collecting, hunting, fishing, old movies, reading. E-mail: jamesH49@aol.com.

SAUNDERS, JAMES ROBERT, English educator; b. Richmond, Va., Apr. 4, 1953; s. Marjorie Charlotte (Wilson) S.; m. Renae Nadine Shackelford, July 6, 1982; 1 child, Monica. BA, U. Va., 1975, MA, 1981; JD, Harvard U., 1978; PhD, U. Mich., 1986. Instr. U. Va., Charlottesville, 1973-74, 80-82; lectr. Mary Washington Coll., Fredericksburg, Va., 1981-82; instr. U. Toledo, 1985-86, asst. prof., 1986-90, assoc. prof., 1990-96, prof., 1996-97, Purdue U., West Lafayette, Ind., 1997—. Vis. scholar U. Mich., 1996-97. Author: The Wayward Preacher in the Literature of African American Women, 1995, Tightrope Walk: Identity, Survival and the Corporate World in African American Literature, 1997; co-author (with Renae Nadine Shackelford) Urban Renewal and the End of Black Culture in Charlottesville, Virginia: An Oral History of Vinegar Hill, 1998, (with Monica Renae Saunders) Black Winning Jockeys in the Kentucky Derby, 2002; reader Jour. Soc. for Study of Multi-Ethnic Lit. of U.S., 1996-99); editor: (with Renae Nadine Shackelford) The Dorothy West Martha's Vineyard: Stories, Essays and Reminiscences by Dorothy West Writing in the Vineyard Gazette, 2001; contbr. essays to Gloria Naylor, Readings on Native Son: Critical Perspectives Past and Present, The Critical Response to Gloria Naylor; mem. editl. bd. Modern Fiction Studies; contbr. articles to profl. jours. including So. Lit. Jour., Hollins Critic, Langston Hughes Rev., Lit. of U.S., Modern Fiction Studies, Obsidian II, Coll. Lit. Dir. Vinegar Hill Oral History Project, Charlottesville, 1980. Faculty rsch. fellow U. Toledo, 1988, 90, 95; recipient Cert. of Excellence Options, Inc., 1996, Somia Soul award 2001. Mem. Richard Wright Circle. Avocations: basketball, reading, hiking, pet collecting, attending plays. Office: Purdue U Dept English 1356 Heavilon Hall Dept English West Lafayette IN 47907-1356

SAUNDERS, JANET MCGEE, small business owner, healthcare administrator; b. Portsmouth, N.H., June 11, 1958; d. John P. and Louise (Flynn) McG.; m. Peter C. Saunders. AA in Recreation Leadership, Colby-Sawyer Coll., New London, N.H., 1979; AS in Natural Scis., Colby-Sawyer Coll., 1980, BS in Health Records Adminstrn., 1981; Cert. in Health Records Adminstn., US Pub. Health Svc. Hosp., Balt., 1981. Registered record adminstr., Am. Health Info. Mgmt. Assn.; lic. real estate agt., Ga. Med. record technician, supr. patient accounts U.S. Pub. Health Svc. Hosp., 1981-82; chief fin. counselor Champus HBA Wyman Pk. Health System Inc. (formerly USPHS), 1981-82; claims specialist Blue Cross/Blue Shield, Atlanta, 1982-83; health record adminstr., quality control mgr. Computer Health Corp., 1983-84; sales assoc. Ernst Resort Devel., 1984-86; owner Errands Etc., 1984-87; sales mgr. Am. Svc. Life Ins. Co., 1988-92; health benefits cons., 1988—; healthcare practice mgmt. cons. Ga., N.H., 1988—; prin. Saunders Auctioneers & Appraisers, N.H. and Mass., 1997—, Antiques, Arts & Books @ Sign of Mermaid, Kingston, N.H., 1999—; property mgr. Cons. health benefits mgmt. for small businesses and individuals, S.E., U.S., 1989—. Contbr. articles to prof. jours., manuals. Counselor to delinquent youths Youth Svcs., USA, 1975-76. Gov.'s. funded program Commn. on Crime and Delinquency, 1976-77; mem. Nat. Right to Life Com., 1985-90; chmn. Summerfest-MDA fundraiser, Atlanta, 1989; coord., fundraising and devel. N.H. Soc. Prevention of Cruelty to Animals, 1992-93; chair charity events MDA. Mem. U.S. Pub. Health Svc. Officers Club (Balt., sec.-treas. 1980-82), Am. Vet. Health Info. Mgmt. Assn., Nat. Auctioneers' Assn., Alpha Chi, Phi Theta Kappa. Roman Catholic. Avocations: books, lit., history and preservation, danicng, horseback riding. Home and Office: PO Box 360 187 Main St Kingston NH 03848 E-mail: jsaunders@jmacofnh.com.

SAUNDERS, JIMMY DALE, aerospace engineer, physicist, naval officer; b. Bronte, Tex., Dec. 16, 1948; s. James Howard and Wanda Lee (Lackey) S.; m. Judy Karon Falconer, Aug. 2, 1969; children: Jennifer Rebecca, Rachel Lee, Jason Allan. BS in Physics, U. Miss., 1976; MS in Physics, Naval Postgrad. Sch., Monterey, Calif., 1986. Enlisted USN, 1970, advanced through grades to comdr., 1991; ret., 1993; intelligence officer Comdr. Submarines Mediteranean, Naples, Italy, 1979-82; weapons officer USS George Bancroft, 1982-84; asst. for strategic weapons systems Strategic Systems Programs, Washington, 1987-88, asst. head missile ops., 1988, asst. head missile engring., 1988-90, asst. for advanced systems, 1990-91, head missile engring., 1991-93; asst. dir. Applied Rsch. Labs. U. Tex., Austin, 1994-98, dir. space & geophys. lab., 1998-2000; pres. J3S, Inc., 2000—. Staff assoc. Chief Naval Ops. for Spl. Studies, 1989-90, Def. Sci. Bd., 1990; tech. advisor Strategic Arms Reductions Treaty, Geneva, 1990-91. Contbr. article to Phys. Rev. Mem. County Sch. Adv. Coun., Goose Creek, S.C., 1982-84; commr. Springfield (Va.) Youth Football Program, 1990-93; bd. dirs. Springfield Youth Club, 1990-93. Mem. AAAS, Am. Phys. Soc., Am. Soc. Naval Engrs., Sigma Xi. Methodist. Home: 9601 State Highway 29 W Georgetown TX 78628-6801 Office: J3 Corp 9651 W Hwy 29 Georgetown TX 78628

SAUNDERS, JOSEPH ARTHUR, office products manufacturing company executive; b. Creston, Mont., July 9, 1926; s. Albert Henry and Edith Margaret (Rhodes) S.; m. Lois Evelyn White, June 19, 1948 (dec. Oct. 1986); children: Albert Henry II, Margaret Jean; m. Eva Homor, July 18, 1987; stepchildren: Rodney, Charmaine. Educated pub. schs., Youngstown, Ohio and Winthrop, Maine. With Saunders Mfg. Co. Inc., doing bus. as Saunders, Winthrop, 1947—, exec. v.p., 1967-77, pres., 1977-88, CEO, 1967-96, chmn. bd., 1988—. Chmn. Saunders Internat. B.V., Netherlands, Graphic Utilities, 1999—, RhinoSkin, Inc., 2000—; co-founder, sec., bd. dirs. Dirigo Bank and Trust Co., Augusta, Maine, 1969-86; co-founder, dir. Cushnoc Bank and Trust Co., Augusta, Maine, 1988-94. Chmn. jour. ADL Torch of Liberty Award, 1997. With U.S. Army, 1945-47. Recipient ADL Torch of Liberty award, 1998. Mem. Maine C. of C. and Industry (bd. dirs. 1976-81, chmn. mfg. coun. 1978-82), Maine Metal Products Assn. (bd. dirs. 1983-84), Soc. Mfg. Engrs. (cert. new product engr.), Internat. Bus. Forms Industries (chmn. assocs. 1976-77, co-chmn. exhibits com. 1978-82), Order of the Black Leaf, Document Mgmt. Industries Assn., Bus. Products Industry Assn., Office Products Mfrs. Assn. (bd. govs. 1988-94, v.p. 1990), Am. Legion, Masons, Shriners, others. Achievements include patentee in field. Home: PO Box 123 Readfield ME 04355-0123 Office: Saunders Mfg & Mktg PO Box 243 Winthrop ME 04364-0243

SAUNDERS, JOSEPH W. financial services company executive; Head credit card svcs. Household Credit Svcs.; chmn. & CEO Fleet Credit Card LLC, 1997—2001; chmn. bd, CEO & pres. Providian Fin. Corp., 2001—. Office: 201 Mission St San Francisco CA 94105*

SAUNDERS, KAREN ESTELLE, secondary school educator; b. San Carlos, Ariz., June 13, 1941; d. Walter Carl and Irma Marie (Gallmeyer) Sorgatz; m. John Richard Saunders, Dec. 27, 1962 (div. Nov. 1981). BA, Ariz. State U., 1964, MA, 1968, postgrad., 1982—. Tchr., chair art dept. McClintock H.S., Tempe, Ariz., 1964-77; tchr. Corona del Sol H.S., 1977-98, chair art dept., 1977-87, adminstv. counc., 1977-97, chair fine arts dept., 1987-97. Coord. artists-in-schs. program Tempe Union H.S. Dist., 1975-80, program adminstr. travel/study program, 1976-78, 80, Corona del Sol H.S., 1994-95; Arizona North Central Assn. Evaluation Vis. Teams, 1969-89, program chair Four Corners Art Educators Conf., Scottsdale, Ariz., 1982; co-chair S.W. Indian Art Collectibles Exhbn., Carefree, Ariz., 1982, also editor, designer catalogue; adv. editorial bd. Sch. Arts Mag., 1989-96; artist-in-schs. coord. Corona del Sol High Sch., 1994-95; strategic planning team Tempe Union H.S. Dist., 1993-96; mem. occupational edn. adv. com. Tempe Union H.S. Dist., 1995-98; East Valley Sch.-To-Work-Equity Team liason to Corona Del Sol H.S., 1996-98; editor Connections to Career Pathways newsletter Union H.S. Dist. Sch.-to-Work Liason Team, 1997-98 Editorial bd. Jour. Art Edn., 1982-85; dir. mural project Corona Del Sol H.S., 1994-95. Mem. State Art Guide Com., Tempe, 1975-77; mem. planning com. Sheldon Lab. Systems Facilities, 1980-83; chmn. Tempe Sculpture Competition, Fine Arts Ctr., 1983; mem. Ariz. Scholastic Art Adv. Bd., Phoenix, 1983-87; judge Mill Ave. Arts Festival, Tempe, 1989, 1991-94; bd. dirs. Hackett House, 1998—, Tempe Sister Cities, 1999—. Recipient Vincent Van Gogh award Colo. Alliance for Arts Edn., 1978, Ariz. Art Educator of Yr. award Ariz. Art Edn. Assn., 1979, Leadership award Four Corners Art Educators Conf., 1982, Lehrer Mel. award Ariz. State U. Sch. Art, 1986, Tempe Diablos Ednl. Excellence awards, 1991; Ariz. State U. fellow, 1967-68. Mem. NEA, Nat. Art Edn. Assn. (v.p., bd. dirs. 1980-82, chmn. leadership workshop 1979, Nat. Assn. Gender Diversity Tng. (mem. profl. counsel com. 1998), Pacific Secondary Art Educator of Yr. award 1985, co-chair Pres.' Day 1992-95 Conv.), Assn. Secondary Curriculum Devel., Ariz. Alliance for Arts Edn. (bd. dirs. 1976-81, co-chmn. western regional conf. 1978), Tempe Secondary Edn. Assn., Ariz. Art Edn. Assn. (pres. 1976-78), Tempe Sister Cities Orgn. (bd. mem., exch. tchr. Regensburg, Germany 1992, Tchr. Exchange Core Team, 1997-2002, chmn. young artist program 1997-2002, Hackett House bd.), Mortar Bd., Phi Delta Kappa, Alpha Phi. Avocations: art, photography, flying, travel. Home: 930 S Dobson Rd Unit 22 Mesa AZ 85202-2912

SAUNDERS, KATHRYN A. retired data processing administrator; b. Elgin, Minn., Apr. 12, 1920; d. William P. and Mathilda M. (Mielke) Hagner; m. James L. Saunders, June 14, 1952 (dec. 1992); children: Gary, Wade, Brian. BA, U. Calif., Berkeley, 1941; cert., Coll. of Marin, Kentfield, Calif., 1948. Mem. gen. staff Fed. Res. Bank, San Francisco; with civilian pers./payroll dept. USAF, Hamilton AFB, Calif.; coord. data processing Sir Francis Drake High Sch., San Anselmo. Sec. program resource United Meth. Women, 1988—, treas., 1994-99; mem. decorations guild Marin Art and Garden Ctr., 1996—. Mem. AAUW, Calif. Sch. Employees Assn., Calif. Scholarship Fedn. (life), Nat. Assn. Ret. Fed. Employees, Coll. of Environ. Design Alumni Assn. of U. Calif. Berkeley, Order of Golden Rose of Delta Zeta, Commonwealth Club of Calif. Avocations: sewing, knitting, art work, piano, volunteer work. Address: 118 Tamal Vista Dr San Rafael CA 94901-1646

SAUNDERS, KENNETH D. insurance company executive, consultant, arbitrator; b. Chgo., Jan. 4, 1927; s. Maurice and Mildred (Cochrane) S.; m. Jean S. Davies, Dec. 17, 1949; children: Karen Saunders Waugh, William Thomas. AB, Dartmouth Coll., 1949. With Continental Casualty Co., Chgo., 1949-59, asst. v.p., 1957-59; exec. asst. Standard Accident Ins. Co., Detroit, 1959-62; with Combined Ins. Co. Am., Chgo., 1962-86, v.p., 1969-74, sr. v.p., 1974-86; with Rollins, Burdick, Hunter, 1986-87. With USMC, 1945-46. Mem. Tavern Club (Chgo.), Exmoor Country (Ill.) Club, John's Island (Fla.) Club. Office: 1418 Woodhill Dr Northbrook IL 60062-4661

SAUNDERS, LONNA JEANNE, lawyer, newscaster, talk show host; b. Cleve. d. Jack Glenn and Lillian Frances (Newman) Slaby. Student, Dartmouth Coll.; AB in Polit. Sci. with hons., Vassar Coll.; JD, Northwestern U., 1981; cert. advanced study in Mass Media, Stanford U., 1992. Bar: Ill. 1981. News dir., morning news anchor Sta. WKBK-AM, Keene, N.H., 1974-75; reporter Sta. KDKA-AM, Pitts., 1975; pub. affairs dir., news anchor Sta. WJW-AM, Cleve., 1975-76; helicopter traffic reporter WERE-AM Radio, 1976-77; morning news anchor Sta. WBBG-AM, 1978; talk host, news anchor Sta. WIND-AM, Chgo., 1978-82; atty. Arvey, Hodes, Costello & Burman, 1981-82; host, "The Stock Market Observer", news anchor WCIU-TV, 1982-85; staff atty. Better Govt. Assn., 1983-84; news anchor, reporter Sta. WBMX-FM, 1984-86; pvt. practice, 1985—; news anchor Sta. WKQX-FM, 1987. Instr. Columbia Coll., Chgo., 1987-90; guest talk host Sta. WMCA, N.Y.C., 1983, Sta. WMAQ, Chgo., 1988, Sta. WLS, Chgo., 1989, Sta. WWWE, Cleve., 1989, Sta. KVI, Seattle, 1994, WCBM-AM, Balt., 1996, WRC-AM, Wash., D.C., 1997; host, prodr. The Lively Arts, Cablevision Chgo., 1986; talk show host The Lonna Saunders Show, Sta. KIRO-AM, Seattle, 1995-96; news anchor, WTOP-AM Radio, Washington, D.C., 1996-97; talk host, "Today and Tomorrow show", WMAL-AM radio, Washington, D.C., 1997, freelance reporter, CBS Radio Network, N.Y.C., 1995—; writer, General Media, N.Y.C., 1996—; atty. Lawyers for Creative Arts, Chgo., 1985-91; guest columnist Gainesville (Fla.) Sun Newspaper, 1998-99; freelance writer Indians Ink mag., 1998—. Columnist Chgo. Life mag., 1986—; editl. bd. Jour. Criminal Law and Criminology, 1979-81; contbr. articles to profl. jours.; creator pub. affairs program WBBM-AM, Chgo., 1985. Recipient Akron Press Club award for best pub. affairs presentation, 1978; grantee Scripps Howard Found., 1978-81; AFTRA George Heller Meml. scholar, 1980-81. Fellow Am. Bar Found.; mem. ABA (mem. exec. coms. Lawyers and the Arts, Law and Media 1986-92, chmn. exec. com. Law and Media 1990-91, 91-92, Young Lawyers divsn. liaison to Forum Com. on Communications Law 1991-93, Commn. for Partnership Programs 1993-94, regional divsn. chair Forum on Communications Law 1995-96). Roman Catholic. Avocations: theater, piano, baseball.

SAUNDERS, MARK A. lawyer; b. N.Y.C., July 9, 1946; s. Phillip George and Florence (Schell) S.; m. Paula Squillante, Sept. 2, 1972; children: David Prescott, Christina Joy. BA cum laude, Fordham U., 1968; JD, U. Va., 1972. Bar: N.Y. 1973, U.S. Dist. Ct. (so. dist.) N.Y.) 1973, U.S. Ct. Appeals (2d cir.) 1974, U.S. Ct. Appeals (D.C. cir.) 1987, U.S. Supreme Ct. 1987. Sr. ptnr. Holland & Knight, N.Y.C.; counsel to corp. fin. and mergers acquisitions depts. Morgan Stanley & Co. Inc., 1975-80; mem. faculty Internat. Law Inst., Washington, 1985—. Mem. comparative law delegation to govt. of People's Rep. of China, 1986; gen. counsel Softstrip Internat. Ltd. subs. Eastman Kodak Co., 1987; mem. adv. bd. Southwestern Legal Found. Author: Amrican Depositary Receipts: An Introduction to U.S. Capital Markets For Foreign Companies, 1993, Fordham Internat. Law Jour., 1993; mng. bd. editors Va. Jour. Internat. Law, 1971-72; cons. editor China Banking and Fin., 1988-92. Chmn. charity benefit Ann. Good Counsel Awards Celebration, 1999, 2000; apptd. fed. adv. bd. nat. polit. action com., 1999; mem. fed. adv. bd. Ann Arbor Polit. Action Com. Jervey fellow in fgn. and comparative law Columbia U. Parker Sch. Internat. Law, 1972. Fellow Am. Coll. Investment Counsel; mem. ABA (coms. fed. securities, regulation and internat. securities matters and fgn. investment in U.S.), Assn. Bar City N.Y., Internat. Bar Assn., Legatus (pres. N.Y.C. chpt. 1998-2000), Phi Beta Kappa. Roman Catholic. Home: 3 Nutmeg Dr Greenwich CT 06831-3211 Office: Holland & Knight 195 Broadway New York NY 10007-3100 E-mail: msaund@hklaw.com.

SAUNDERS, MICHAEL ALAN, science educator, researcher; b. Christchurch, Canterbury, New Zealand, Jan. 6, 1944; s. John Leo and Zita Ruahine Saunders; m. Prudence Louise Rowland, Dec. 8, 1947; children: Tania, Emily. BSc with honors, U. Canterbury, 1965; PhD, Stanford U., 1972. Sci. officer DSIR, Wellington, New Zealand, 1966—79; sr. rsch. assoc. Stanford U., 1979—87, prof. rsch., 1987—. Coauthor (computer software) MINOS, 1983 (Orchard-Hays prize Math. Programming Soc., 1985). Home: 2671 Ross Rd Palo Alto CA Office: Stanford Univ Dept Mgmt Sci & Engring Stanford CA 94305-4026 E-mail: saunders@stanford.edu.

SAUNDERS, NINA ALEXANDER, interior designer; b. Lemberg, Poland, Jan. 1, 1934; came to U.S., 1951, naturalized, 1955; d. Leopold and Ann (Erbsen) Alexander; m. Roger Alfred Saunders, Oct. 4, 1953; children— Gary L., Jeffrey G., Todd R., Tedd R. Student CCNY, 1951-52, NYU, 1952-53. Ptnr., J & N Interior Design, Brookline and Chestnut Hill, Mass., 1971-79; pres. Interior Design Assocs. Boston, 1979— ; Jr. League showhouse invitee, Newton, Milton and Brookline, 1975, 76, 77; dir. Hotels of Tradition, Boston, 1980— ; judge nat. lodging-hosp. design awards, 1983. Bd. dirs. women's div. Combined Jewish Philanthropies, Boston, 1985— , Friends of Pub. Garden, Boston, 1985— ; trustee New Eng. Aquarium, Boston, 1981— , Met. Opera Boston, 1982— ; mem. exec. bd. Mus. Fine Arts Ladies Com., Boston, 1982— . Honored by proclamation Nina A. Saunders Day, Mayor of Boston, 1981. Clubs: Longwood Cricket (Chestnut Hill); Belmont Country (Mass.); Algonquin, Badminton and Tennis (Boston). Avocations: tennis; skiing; painting; travel; entertaining. Home: Boston, Mass. Died Nov. 3, 1991.

SAUNDERS, NORMAN THOMAS, consultant; b. Amityville, N.Y., Oct. 19, 1942; s. Norman George and Marjory (Scott) S.; m. Christine Patricia Miller, Feb. 24, 1968; children: Thomas, Carré. BS, USCG Acad., 1964; MS, Naval Postgrad. Sch., Monterey, Calif., 1972; grad., Nat. War Coll., 1985. Commd. officer USCG, 1964, advanced through grades to Radm., 1991, br. chief edn. and tng. divsn., 1972-76; exec. officer USCGC COURAGEOUS, Port Canaveral, Fla., 1976-78; from spl. projects officer to br. chief personnel divsn. USCG, Washington, 1978-82; comdg. officer USCGC DEPENDABLE, Panama City, Fla., 1982-84; spl. projects officer R & D USCG, Key West, 1985-86; comdr. USCG Group, 1986-88; chief intelligence and law enforcement br. 7th CG Dist., Miami, Fla., 1988-90; chief ops. divsn. 7th USCG Dist., 1990-91; comdr. 2nd USCG Dist., St. Louis, 1991-93; mil. pers. command Washington, 1993-94; asst. commandant for ops., 1994-97; comdr. Seventh CG Dist., Miami, 1997-99; ret. Mem. Mil. Order World Wars, Naval Order U.S., Coast Guard Combat VA, Ret. Officers Assn., Sigma Xi. Republican. Methodist. Avocations: running, tennis, fishing, reading. Home: 13479 Pt Pleasant Dr Chantilly VA 20151-2446 E-mail: norm.saunders@tsanda.com.

SAUNDERS, PAMELA RUTH, lawyer, mediator; b. Portsmouth, Va., Sept. 22, 1955; d. Jerald Allen and Rose Ann (Russell) S.; m. Thomas F. Selleys, Jr., 1995. BA, U. Minn., 1977; JD cum laude, William Mitchell Coll. Law, 1981. Bar: Minn., 1981. Assoc. Dorsey and Whitney, Mpls., 1981-87; pvt. practice St. Paul, 1988-89, Mpls., 1989-90; atty. U.S. Dept. Vet. Affairs, 1990—. Bd. dirs. Rock Lake Mfg., Inc. Mem. Legal Advice Clinics, Ltd., Mpls., 1982-90; mediator Minn. Human Rights Dept. Project. Recipient Am. Jurisprudence awards, 1978, 80; named "Hot" Atty. of Yr., VA, 1995, Friend of Social Work, 1996; recipient Hammer award 1996, Partnership award 1997. Mem. ABA, Minn. State Bar Assn., Am. Health Lawyers Assn., Hennepin County Bar Assn. Democrat. Avocations: swimming, reading, computers. Office: US Dept Vet Affairs Va Med Ctr 1 Veterans Dr Minneapolis MN 55417

SAUNDERS, PATRICIA GENE, freelance writer, editor; b. Tulsa, Okla., Nov. 29, 1946; d. Eugene Merritt and Patricia May (Hough) Knight; m. Joseph Eugene Saunders, June 24, 1989. BA, Baylor U., 1969. Nat. advt. sec. KTVT-TV, Ft. Worth, 1969-71; tchr. Arlington (Tex.) Ind. Sch. Dist., 1971-77, Garland (Tex.) Ind. Sch. Dist., 1977-79; payroll, spl. projects assoc. Electronic Data Systems, Dallas, 1979-81; adminstrv. asst. Diversifield Innovators, 1981-82; system ops. mgr. Span Instruments, Plano, 1982-86; data processing mgr. Claire Mfg., Addison, Ill., 1986-87. Everpure, Inc., Westmont, 1987-88; software cons. Software Alternatives, Inc., Downers Grove, 1988-89; sys. ops. asst., cons. J&J Maintenance, Inc., Austin, Tex., 1989-90; pres., computer cons. Cardinal Software Solutions, Inc., 1990-93; editor Holt, Rinehart & Winston, 1993-99. Mem.: Writers' League of Tex., Soc. of Children's Book Writers and Illustrators, N.Y. Met. Mus. Fine Art, Smithsonian Instn., Nat. Mus. Women in the Arts, Nat. Arbor Day Found., Lady Bird Johnson Wildflower Ctr. Republican. Baptist. Avocations: gardening, travel, reading, movies, cats. Home: 410 Teal Ln Kyle TX 78640-8888 E-mail: pat.s@ix.netcom.com.

SAUNDERS, PAUL CHRISTOPHER, lawyer; b. N.Y.C., May 21, 1941; s. John Richard and Agnes Grace (Kelly) Saunders; m. Patricia Newman, Aug. 14, 1968; children: Paul Christopher, Michael Eagan. AB, Fordham Coll., 1963; JD, Georgetown U., 1966; Certificat d'Études Politiques, Institut d'Études Politiques, Paris, 1962. Bar: NY 1966, DC 1967, US Supreme Ct 1969. Assoc. Cravath, Swaine & Moore, N.Y.C., 1971-77, ptnr., 1977—. Bd dirs Office Appellate Defender. Mem ed bd: Georgetown Law Jour, 1965—66; editor (editor-in-chief): The Advocate, 1969—70. Trustee Fordham Univ, 1991—96; bd regents Georgetown Univ; chmn. bd. visitors Law Ctr. Georgetown Univ., 1996—97; trustee, vice-chmn Fordham Prep Sch, 1986—94; v.p., bd. dirs. Legal Aid Soc., 1983—88; bd dirs, trustee Lawyers Comt Civil Rights Under Law, 1985—, co-chair, 1995—97; v.p., trustee Vols. Legal Svc., Inc., 1999—; bd. dirs. Office of the Appellate Defender, 1999—; mem. N.Y. State Judicial Inst. on Professionalism in the Law, 2000—; mem Cardinal's Comt Laity, 1982—90; chmn bd dirs Const Project, 2000—. Capt JAGC U.S. Army, 1967—71. Decorated Meritorious Svc. medal; recipient John Carroll medal, Georgetown U., 1995, Whitney N. Seymour award, Lawyers Com. Civil Rights Under Law, 2000. Fellow: Am. Bar Found., Am. Coll. Trial Lawyers; mem.: ABA, London Ct. Internat. Arbitration, Assn. Bar City N.Y., N.Y. State Bar Assn., Westchester Country Club (Rye, N.Y.), Apawamis Club, Knights Malta, Phi Beta Kappa, Pi Sigma Alpha. Democrat. Roman Catholic. Home: 1220 Park Ave New York NY 10128-1733 also: 455 Polly Pk Rd Rye NY 10580-1960 Office: Cravath Swaine & Moore Worldwide Plz 825 8th Ave Fl 39 New York NY 10019-7475 E-mail: psaunders@cravath.com.

SAUNDERS, PETER PAUL, investor; b. Budapest, Hungary, July 21, 1928; emigrated to Can., 1941, naturalized, 1946; s. Peter Paul and Elizabeth (Halom) Szende; m. Nancy Louise McDonald, Feb. 11, 1956; children: Christine Elizabeth McBride, Paula Marie. Student, Vancouver Coll., 1941-44; B.Com., U. B.C., 1948. Acct. Canadian Pacific Rly. Co., 1948-50; founder, pres. Laurentide Fin. Corp., Ltd., 1950-66, vice chmn., 1966-67; chmn., pres. Coronation Credit Corp. Ltd., Vancouver, B.C., Can., 1968-78, Versatile Corp. (formerly Coronation Credit Corp. and Cornat Industries Ltd.), Vancouver, Can., 1978-87; prin., pres. Saunders Investment Ltd., 1987—. Bd. dirs. Computrol Security Sys. Ltd., Greene Valley Concessions.; chmn., dir. Harlan Fairbanks Co. Ltd. Past pres. Vancouver Symphony Soc., 1968-70, Can. Cancer Soc., B.C. and Yukon Rdgion, 1975-77, Vancouver Art Gallery Assn., 1981-83; chmn. Vancouver Opera Round Table, 1984-92. Mem. Vancouver Club, Shaughnessy Golf and Country Club, Royal Vancouver Yacht Club, Thunderbird Country Club (Rancho Mirage, Calif.). Avocations: golf, skiing, hunting, boating. Home: 3620 Alexandra St Vancouver BC Canada V6J 4B9 Office: Saunders Investment Ltd PO Box 49352 Bentall Ctr Vancouver BC Canada V7X 1L4

SAUNDERS, PHILIP D. professional basketball coach; b. Cleve., Feb. 23, 1955; m. Debbie Saunders; children: Ryan, Mindy, Rachel and Kimberly (twins). Student, U. Minn. Asst. coach U. Minn Golden Golphers, 1982-86, U. Tulsa, 1986-88; head coach Continental Basketball Assn. Rapid City (S.D.) Thrillers, 1988-89, La Crosse (Wis.) Catbirds, 1989-94, gen. mgr., 1991-93, team pres., 1991-94; head coach Continental Basketball Assn. Sioux Falls (S.D.) Skyforce; gen. mgr., head coach Minn. Timberwolves, 1995—. Named CBA Coach of the Yr., 1989, 92. Office: Minn Timberwolves 600 1st Ave N Minneapolis MN 55403-1416*

SAUNDERS, ROBERT M. lawyer; b. N.Y.C., July 31, 1959; s. Herbert L. and Loretta (Tymon) S.; m. Cheryl D. Lambek, Nov. 6, 1988; children: David, Dana. BA, SUNY, Buffalo, 1980; JD, U. Chgo., 1983. Bar: N.Y. 1984, U.S. Dist. Ct. (so. and ea. dist.) N.Y. 1988, Fla. 1995, U.S. Dist. Ct. (so. dist.) Fla. 1995. Assoc. LeBoeuf, Lamb, Leiby & MacRae, N.Y.C., 1983-86, Brown & Wood, N.Y.C., 1986-88, Willkie Farr & Gallagher, N.Y.C., 1988-92, spl. counsel, 1993-95; sole practice Weston, Fla., 1995—. Office: 4300 N University Dr Ste C203 Fort Lauderdale FL 33351-6244 Address: 96 Flintlock Ln Bell Canyon CA 91307-1129

SAUNDERS, ROBERT SAMUEL, venture capital executive; b. Akron, Ohio, Dec. 3, 1951; s. Samuel Robert and Rose Saunders; m. Heidi Ruth Fulkerson, Mar. 18, 1978. AB with distinction, Stanford U., 1973; MSc with distinction, London Sch. Econs., 1974; diploma, U. Stockholm, 1976; MA, Harvard U., 1978. Cons. World Bank, Washington, 1975-77; sr. cons. Boston Cons. Group, 1978-82; dir. competitive strategy analysis Bain and Co., Boston, 1982-86; sr. v.p., chief planning officer Krupp Cos., 1986-88. Chmn. Saunders Capital Group, Boston, 1988—94; mng. dir. Providian Capital Mgmt., Louisville, 1993—97; sr. mng. dir. Chrysalis Ventures, Louisville, 1997—; vice chmn. High Speed Access Corp., Louisville; chmn. Telemics, Inc., Louisville, Internat. Mktg. Concepts, Louisville; fin. com. chmn. Pub. Radio Partnership, Louisville, 1996—; chmn. Venture Club Louisville, 1995—; investment com. chmn. African Am. Venture Capital Fund, 1993—; chmn. adv. bd. dept. computer engring. and computer sci. U. Louisville; bd. dirs. Genscape Inc. , Louisville. Editor: Stanford Quar. Rev., 1973. Del. Mass. Dem. Nat. Conv., San Francisco, 1984; co-founder Weston Conservation Trust, Mass., 1988. Marshall scholar, 1973-75; NEH fellow, 1978; Swedish Govt. Fulbright grantee, 1975, U.S. Congress Profl. Devel. grantee, 1976. Mem. Am. Econ. Assn., Internat. Union for Sci. Study of Population. Unitarian Universalist. Home: PO Box 99252 Louisville KY 40269-0252 Office: Chrysalis Ventures Ste 1650 National City Tower, 5th St Louisville KY 40202

SAUNDERS, SALLY LOVE, poet, educator; b. Bryn Mawr, Pa., Jan. 15, 1940; d. Lawrence and Dorothy (Love) S. Student, Sophia U., Tokyo, Japan, 1963, U. Pa., Columbia; BS, George Williams Coll., 1965. Tchr. Shipley Sch., Bryn Mawr, 1962-65, Agnes Irwin Sch., Wynnewood, Pa., 1964-65, Montgomery County Day Sch., Wynnewood, 1962, Miquon (Pa.) Sch., Waldron Acad., Merion, Pa., 1965-66, Phelps Sch., Malvern, 1965-70, Frankford Friends Sch. Phila., 1965-66, Haverford (Pa.) Sch., 1965-66, Friends Sem. Sch., N.Y.C., 1966-68, Ballard Sch., N.Y.C., 1966-67, Lower Merion Sch., Ardmore, Pa., nights 1967-71, Univ. Settlement House, Phila., 1961-63, Navajo Indian Reservation, Fort Defiance, Ariz., 1963, Young Men's Jewish Youth Center, Chgo., 1964-65, Margaret Fuller Settlement House, Cambridge, Mass., 1958-61; poetry therapist Pa. Hosp. Inst., 1969-74, also drug rehab. house; poet in residence Tyrone Guthrie Ctr., Newbliss, Ireland, Aug. 1988; poetry workshop leader Pendle Hill Quaker Ctr., Wallingford, Pa., Apr. 1988; poetry week leader Ferry Beach, Saco, Maine, summer 1988. Pioneer in poetry therapy. Poet, 1946—; poems pub. in periodicals including others; author: Past the Near Meadows, 1961, Pauses, 1978, Fresh Bread, 1982, Random Thoughts, 1992, Patchwork Quilt, 1993, Quiet Thoughts and Gentle Feelings, 1996, Word Pictures, 1998; contbr. poems to newspapers. Mem. Acad. Am. Poets, Nat. Fedn. State Poetry Socs., Am. Poetry League, Nat. League Am. Pen Women, Poetry Therapy Assn. (v.p.), Avalon Orgn., Authors Guild, Nat. Writers Club, Pen and Brush Club, N.H., Pa. poetry socs., Cath. Poetry Soc. (asso.), Fla. State Poetry Soc. (asso.) Episcopalian. Home: 2030 Vallejo St Apt 501 San Francisco CA 94123-4854 Office: 609 Rose Hill Rd Broomall PA 19008-2254 *So often during my life I have found great comfort and strength in writing and reading poetry. With my poetry I want to help others to get in touch with their own powers. Poetry, to me, is a rare and beautiful freedom and this is what I want to share with others.*

SAUNDERS, SUSAN PRESLEY, real estate executive; b. South Bend, Ind., Feb. 27, 1956; d. William Presley Jr. and Anne Summers (Winburn) S. Student, Converse Coll., 1974-77, Sandhills Community Coll., Southern Pines, N.C., 1978-86. Lic. real estate broker, N.C.; ins. lic., N.C.; notary pub.; accredited Relo coord. With Gouger, O'Neal & Saunders, Southern Pines, 1973-74, 75, Ceralon Mfg., Aberdeen, N.C., 1976; bank teller The Carolina Bank, 1977-78; from clk. to v.p. fin. G.O.S., Inc., Southern Pines, 1978—. Mem. NAFE, Am. Soc. Profl. and Exec. Women, Am. Inst. Profl. Bookkeepers, Sandhills Area C. of C. (membership com. So. Pines chpt. 1989-94), Moore County Leadership Inst. Democrat. Presbyterian. Avocations: reading, snow skiing, swimming, traveling. Home: 130 Pebble Bch Southern Pines NC 28387-2345 Office: GOS Inc 177 W Pennsylvania Ave Southern Pines NC 28387-5428

SAUNDERS, TED ELLIOTT, accountant; b. Nashville, Feb. 19, 1952; s. Owen Felts and Dora Dean (Dorris) S.; m. Susan Sherrill, July 14, 1984; children: Scott Thomas, Shelley Eileen. BS, Mid. Tenn. State, 1973. Asst. mgr. Bill Crooks Foodtown, Nashville, 1974-75; bookkeeper Odom Sausage Co., Inc., Madison, Tenn., 1975-84; partnership acct. Transatlantic Exploration Ltd., Nashville, 1984-86; chief acct. B.A. Pargh Co., Inc., 1986-89; comptroller Built More Homes, Inc., Lavergne, Tenn., 1989-92; bus. mgr. St. Edward Ch. and Sch., Nashville, 1992—. Bd. dirs. Tenn. Pride Employees Credit Union, 1977-83; pres. Danbury Condominium Assn., Nashville, 1986-88. Mem. Nat. Assn. Accts. Democrat. Baptist. Avocations: jogging, reading, softball. Office: St Edward Ch and Sch 190 Thompson Ln Nashville TN 37211-2451 E-mail: tsaunders@stedward.org.

SAUNDERS, TERRY ROSE, lawyer; b. Phila., July 13, 1942; d. Morton M. and Esther (Hauptman) Rose; m. George Lawton Saunders Jr., Sept. 21, 1975. BA, Barnard Coll., 1964; JD, NYU, 1973. Bar: D.C. 1973, Ill. 1976, U.S. Dist. Ct. (no. dist.) Ill. 1976, U.S. Ct. Appeals (7th cir.) 1976, U.S. Supreme Ct. 1983. Assoc. Williams & Connolly, Washington, 1973-75, Jenner & Block, Chgo., 1975-80, ptnr., 1981-86, Susman, Saunders & Buehler, Chgo., 1987-94; pvt. practice Law Offices of Terry Rose Saunders, 1995—. Author: (with others) Securities Fraud: Litigating Under Rule 10b-5, 1989. Recipient Robert B. McKay award NYU Sch. Law. Mem. ABA (co-chair class actions and derivative suits com. sect. litig. 1992-95, task force on merit selection of judges, co-chair consumer and personal rights itig. com. sect. litig.), Ill. State Bar Assn., Chgo. Bar Assn., Order of Coif, Union League Club. Office: 30 N La Salle St Chicago IL 60602-2590 E-mail: trslawfirm@aol.com.

SAUNDERS, WARD BISHOP, JR. retired aluminum company executive; b. Gilroy, Calif., Nov. 26, 1919; s. Ward Bishop and Lamira (Doan) S.; m. Elaine McDermott, Oct. 11, 1942; children: Douglas L., Myra K., Leslie J. BS, U. Calif., Berkeley, 1942; JD, Stanford U., 1948. Bar: Calif. 1948, U.S. Dist. Ct. (no. dist.) Calif. 1948, U.S. Supreme Ct. 1956. Atty. Kaiser Aluminum & Chem. Corp., Oakland, Calif., 1951-65, div. v.p., 1965-71, v.p., 1971-84. Dir. Volta River Authority, Accra, Ghana, Aluminium Bahrain, Manama, Bahrain, Hindustan Aluminium Co., Bombay, India; mng. dir. Volta Aluminium Co. Ltd., Tema, Ghana, 1971-84. Served to lt. USNR, 1942-46. Mem. Kaiser Aluminum Salaried Retirees Assn. (bd. dirs. 1988-94, pres. 1992-93, v.p. 1995-98), Commonwealth Club of Calif. Republican. Unitarian Universalist. Home: 6123 Estates Dr Oakland CA 94611-3117

SAUNDERS, W(ARREN) PHILLIP, JR. economics educator, consultant, author; b. Morgantown, W.Va., Sept. 3, 1934; s. Warren Phillip and Thelma Marie (Dotson) S.; m. Nancy Lee Trainor, June 16, 1956; children: Kathleen M., Kevin W., Keith A., Kent T., Kristine A. BA, Pa. State U., 1956; MA, U. Ill., 1957; PhD, MIT, 1964. Instr. econs. Bowdoin Coll., Brunswick, Maine, 1961-62; rsch. assoc., from asst. to assoc. prof. econs. Carnegie-Mellon U., Pitts., 1962-70; prof. econs. Ind. U., Bloomington, 1970—; assoc. dean Coll. of Arts and Scis. Ind. U., 1974-78, chmn. dept. econs., 1988-92. Cons. Agy. for Instructional Tech., Bloomington, 1976-78, 81-84, 92-93. Author: (books) Political Dimension of Labor-Management Relations, 1986; author, editor: Framework for Teaching Basic Economic Concepts, 1995; (Workbooks) Introduction to Macroeconomics (18th edit.), 1998, Introduction to Microeconomics (18th edit.), 1998; contbr. articles to Am. Econ. Rev., 1964—. Chmn. staff-parish rels. com. First United Meth. Ch., Bloomington, 1982-94. Recipient Vilard award for disting. rsch., Nat. Assn. Econ. Educators, N.Y.C., 1986, Leavey award for edn. Freedoms Found., Valley Forge, Pa., 1986, Disting. Svc. award. Nat. Coun. Econ. Edn., 1995. Mem. Am. Econ. Assn., Midwest Econ. Assn. (1st v.p. 1988-89), Soc. Econs. Educators (pres. 1992-93). Home: 3725 E Brownridge Rd Bloomington IN 47401-4209 Office: Ind Univ Dept Econs Bloomington IN 47405 E-mail: saunders@indiana.edu.

SAUNDERS, WESLEY HUGH, librarian; b. Eureka, Calif., Feb. 19, 1966; s. John Dewey and Janet L. Fouch Saunders; m. Sheila L. Saunders, Aug. 11, 1987; children: Erin Rae, William John. B of Gen. Studies, La. State U., 1988, M of Libr. and Info. Sci., 1989. Reference libr. La. Coll., Pineville, 1989-90; cataloging libr. USL, Lafayette, La., 1990-91; reference coord. Rapides Parish Libr., Alexandria, 1991-97; dir. Evangeline Parish Libr., Ville Platte, 1997-99; main libr. adminstr. Rapides Parish Libr., 1999—. With U.S. Army Res., 1984-90. Mem. K.C. (3rd degree). Democrat. Roman Catholic. Home: 1165 Regile Ln Ville Platte LA 70586-8372 Office: Rapides Parish Libr 411 Washington St Alexandria LA 71301-8338 E-mail: whughs@hotmail.com.

SAUNDERS, WILLIAM ARTHUR, management consultant; b. Ottawa, Ont., Can., Oct. 13, 1930; BS with honors, McGill U., 1954; MBA in Econs. and Fin., U. Western Ont., 1956; M Commerce in Econs. and Mktg., U. Toronto, 1960. Econ. analyst Imperial Oil Ltd., Toronto, Ont., 1956-63; supr. distbrn. Polysar Ltd., Sarnia, 1963-69; venture mgr. Polysar Plastics, Inc., Westport, Conn., 1969-77; adv. strategy devel. Gulf Oil Chems. Co., Houston, 1977-82; mgmt. cons., 1982—; pres. William A. Saunders Co., 1987—. Mem. Assn. Corp. Growth. Methodist. Home and Office: 8585 Woodway Dr Apt 112 Houston TX 77063-2438

SAUNIER, BERNARD-MARIE, civil engineer; b. Cholet, France, July 6, 1948; s. Rene and Madeleine (Guerin) S.; m. Elisabeth Marie Raphaelle Levy, Sept. 8, 1973; children: Juliette, Xavier, Florence. Civil Engr., Enitrts (1), Strasbourg, France, 1971; San. engr., ENSP (2), Rennes, France, 1972; MS in Civil Engring., U. Calif., Berkeley, 1973; PhD, U. Calif., 1976. Assoc. prof. ENSP (2), Rennes, France, 1971-72; rsch. asst. Sanitary Engr. Rsch. Lab. U. Calif., Berkeley, 1974-76; pres., gen. mgr. Saunier Eau et Environment, St. Gregoire, France, 1976—, SAFEGE, Nanterre, France, 1986—, LYSA, Nanterre, France, 1990—. Lectr. in field.$det, France, July 6, 1948; s. Rene and Madeleine (Guerin) Contbr. articles to profl. jours; patentee in field. Recipient 1st prize Am. Water Works Assn. for PhD thesis, 1976. Mem. Am. Water Works Assn., Am. Soc. Limnology and Oceanography, ASCE, Water Pollution Control Fedn., Internat. Water Supply Assn., Association generale des Hygienistes et Techniciens Muncipaux. Home: 25 rue Victor Hugo 78420 Carriéres s/Seine France

SAURMAN, ANDREW (SKIP SAURMAN), state agency executive; b. Abington, Pa., Feb. 11, 1951; s. Andrew Charles and Doris (Margerum) S.; m. April Diane Young, Aug. 15, 1973 (div. June 1982); 1 child, Wendy Dawn; m. Susan Lynne MacMillan, July 30, 1988; children: Shelly Lloyd, Aaron Lloyd. BS in Vocat. Edn., So. Ill. U., 1993. Cert. master automotive technician. Automotive and truck technician various dealerships, Albuquerque and Belen, N.Mex., 1972-83; automotive instr. Santa Fe H.S. and Santa Fe C.C., 1984-95;

state supr. for trade, indsl. and tech. edn. N.Mex. State Dept. Edn., Santa Fe, 1995—; owner Automotive Svc. Cons. Tech. cons. N.Mex. Better Bus. Bur., Albuquerque, 1987—, Megatech Corp., Tewksbury, Mass., 1989—, N.Mex. Atty. Gen.'s Office, Santa Fe, 1994—; facilitator N.Mex. Automotive Adv. Com., Santa Fe, 1995—; contract instr. for snap-on tools; arbitrator Nat. Ctr. for Dispute Settlement. Served with U.S. Army, 1969-72, Vietnam. Decorated Bronze Star medal; recipient Gold Wrench award Snap-on Tools, 1990, Gt. Tchr. award Century Savs. and Loan, Santa Fe, 1993. Mem. N.Am. Coun. Automotive Tchrs., Skills USA-Vocat. Clubs Am., Assn. for Career and Tech. Edn., N.Mex. Assn. for Career and Tech. Edn., Svc. Technician Soc., Soc. Automotive Engrs., Nat. Automotive Technicians Edn. Found. (cert.). Avocations: backpacking, camping, boating, other outdoor activities. Home: 7 Manzano Ln Santa Fe NM 87508-8214 Office: NMex State Dept Edn 300 Don Gaspar Ave Santa Fe NM 87501-2752 E-mail: ssaurman@sde.state.nm.us., fixum4u@juno.com.

SAURMAN, GEORGE EDWIN, legislator, retired; b. Houston, Jan. 15, 1926; s. Benjamin F. Saurman and Marcelene B. Quay; m. Mary E. Saurman, June 7, 1950; children: Nancy L. Ruane, Richard B., George W., Robert A. BA, Ursinus Coll., 1950. Asst. mgr. Levenwood Dairies, Pottstown, Pa., 1950-58; dist. supr. Sun Life of Can., 1958-62; gen. mgr., v.p. Sellers Kirk & Co., Ambler, Pa., 1962-80; mem. Ho. Reps. 151st dist. Commonwealth of Pa., Harrisburg, 1980-94, ret., 1994. Chmn. task force Am. Legis. Exchange Coun., Washington, 1986-94. Mem. Ambler (Pa.) Borough, 1966-70, 95-99 (pres. 1997-99), mayor, 1970-81. Mem. Am. Cancer Soc. (bd. dirs.; hon. life mem.), Am. Trauma Soc., Ursinus Coll. Alumni Assn., Kiwanis Club (pres. 1958). Republican. Methodist. Avocations: sports, fishing, craft work, writing. Home: 1264 Ft Washington Ave S-10 Fort Washington PA 19034

SAURO, JOSEPH PIO, physics educator; b. New Rochelle, N.Y., Apr. 4, 1927; s. Francesco Giovanni and Lucia (Arrivebene) S.; m. Elizabeth Joann Schellman, May 2, 1948; children: Brian, Michael, Joseph. BS, Poly Inst. Bkyn., 1955, MS, 1958, PhD in Physics, 1966. Dir. coll. sci. improvement program U. Mass., North Dartmouth, 1969-71, dean grad. sch., 1969-71, interim dean Coll. of Engring., 1978-80, dean Coll. Arts and Scis., 1969-80, prof. physics, 1965-93, prof. emeritus, 1995—. Participant Symposium on Devel. of Physicist's Conception of Nature, Trieste, 1972. With USN, 1944-46. Sci. Faculty fellow NSF, 1964; State War Svc. scholar State of N.Y., 1953. Mem. Am Assn. Physics Tchr., Sigma Xi, Sigma Pi Sigma. Avocations: photography, travel, music. Home: 8 Captain Wing Rd East Sandwich MA 02537-1122 Office: U Mass North Dartmouth MA 02747

SAUSMAN, KAREN, zoological park administrator; b. Chgo., Nov. 26, 1945; d. William and Annabell (Lofaso) S. BS, Loyola U., 1966; student, Redlands U., 1968. Keeper Lincoln Park Zoo, Chgo., 1964-66; tchr. Palm Springs (Calif.) Unified Sch., 1968-70; ranger Nat. Park Svc., Joshua Tree, Calif., 1968-70; zoo dir. The Living Desert, Palm Desert, 1970—. Natural history study tour leader internat., 1974—; part-time instr. Coll. Desert Natural History Calif. Desert, 1975-78; field reviewer conservation grants Inst. Mus. Svcs., 1987—, MAP cons., 1987—, panelist, 1992—; internat. studbook keeper for Sand Cats, 1988-2001, for Cuvier's Gazelle, Mhorr Gazelle, 1990-2000; co-chair Arabian Oryx species survival plan propogation group, 1986-95; spkr. in field. Author Survival Captive Bighorn Sheep, 1982, Small Facilities- Opportunities and Obligations, 1983; wildlife illustrator books, mags, 1970—; editor Fox Paws newsletter Living Desert, 1970—, ann. reports, 1976—; natural sci. editor Desert Mag., 1979-82; compiler Conservation and Management Plan for Antelope, 1992; contbr. articles to profl. jours. Past bd. dirs., sec. Desert Protective Coun.; adv. coun. Desert Bighorn Rsch. Inst., 1981-85; bd. dirs. Palm Springs Desert Resorts Convention and Visitors Bur., 1988-94; bd. dirs., treas. Coachella Valley Mountain Trust, 1989-92. Named Woman Making a Difference Soroptomist Internat., 1989, 93, 97, Woman of Distinction, Riverside Bus. Press, 2000. Fellow Am. Assn. Zool. Parks and Aquariums (bd. dirs., accredation field reviewer, desert antelope taxon adv. group, caprid taxon adv. group, felid taxon adv. group, small population mgmt. adv. group, wildlife conservation and mgmt. com., chmn. ethics com. 1987, mem. com., internat. rels. com., ethics task force, pres'. award 1972-77, outstanding svc. award 1983, 88, editor newsletter, Zool. Parks and Aquarium Fundamentals 1982); mem. Internat. Species Inventory System (mgmt. com., policy adv. group 1980-96), Calif. Assn. Mus. (v.p. 1992-96), Calif. Assn. Zoos and Aquariums, World Assn. Zoos and Aquariums (coun. 2002--, governing coun. 2002--), Western Interpretive Assn. (so. Calif. chpt.), Am. Assn. Mus., Arboreta and Botanical Gardens So. Calif. (coun. dirs.), Soc. Conservation Biology, Nat. Audubon. Soc., Jersey Wildlife Preservation Trust Internat., Nature Conservancy, East African Wildlife Soc., African Wildlife Found., Kennel Club Palm Springs (past bd. dirs., treas. 1978-80), Scottish Deerhound Club Am. (editor Scottish Deerhounds in N.A., 1983, life mem. U.K. chpt.), Internat. Bengal Cat Soc. (pres. 1994-96). Avocations: pure bred dogs, cats, dressage, painting, photography. Office: The Living Desert 47 900 Portola Ave Palm Desert CA 92260 E-mail: kastld@aol.com.

SAUSSER, GAIL DIANNE, lawyer; b. Richland, Wash., May 8, 1952; d. Lenard Merl and Julia Esther (Saxerud) Oathes; m. Harvey Wilson Sausser III, 1979 (div. 1982). BA in Humanities, Heritage Coll., Spokane, Wash., 1974; MA in Psychology, Antioch West, Vancouver, B.C., Can., 1977; postgrad., Seattle U., 1996-97; JD magna cum laude, Am. U., 1999. Cert. asst. risk mgmt., Ins. Inst. Am. Counselor Chem. Dependency Program, Seattle, 1982-84; acctg. asst. Newdata Corp., 1986-87; adminstrv. ins. broker Johnson & Higgins, 1987-96, Ctr. Health Policy Rsch., George Washington U., 1998-99; assoc. Vinson & Elkins, Washington, 1999—2002. Counselor Cmty. Mental Health Inst., Spokane, Wash., 1972-75, Seattle Mental Health Inst., 1975-77; pres. Acupuncture Rsch. Treatment Assn., Seattle, 1992-96; mem. rsch. roundtable King County Natural Health Clinic, Seattle, 1993-95, adv. bd., 1996-97; mem., co-chmn. evaluation com., managed care com. King County HIV/AIDS Planning Coun., Seattle, 1996-97. Fellow, Ctrs. for Medicare and Medicaid Svcs., 1998. Mem.: Healthcare Fin. Mgmt. Assn. Avocations: writing. Home: Apt 732 4000 Massachusetts Ave NW Washington DC 20016-5125

SAUTE, ROBERT EMILE, drug and cosmetic consultant; b. West Warwick, R.I., Aug. 18, 1929; s. Camille T. and Lea E. (Goffinet) S.; m. Arda T. Darnell, May 18, 1957; children: Richard R., Steven N., Allen K. BS, R.I. Coll. Pharmacy, 1950; MS, Purdue U., 1952, PhD, 1953. Registered pharmacist. Tech. asst. to pres. Lafayette (Ind.) Pharmacal, 1955-56; sr. rsch. and devel. chemist H.K. Wampole Denver Chem. Co., Phila., 1956-57; supt. Murray Hill (N.J.) plant Strong Cobb Arner Inc., 1957-60; adminstrv. dir. rsch. and devel. Avon Products Inc., Suffern, N.Y., 1960-68; dir. rsch. and devel. toiletries div. Gillette Co., Boston, 1968-71; group v.p. Dart Industries, L.A., 1972-75; pres. Saute Cons., Inc., 1975—. Bd. dirs. Joico Labs., Inc., Cosmetics Enterprises, Ltd. Contbr. to books; patentee in field. With U.S. Army, 1953-55. Fellow Soc. Cosmetic Chemists (bd. dirs. 1987-89, 94-96, chmn. Calif. chpt. 1986); mem. AAAS, N.Y. Acad. Scis., Soc. Investigative Dermatology, Am. Assn. Pharm. Scientists, Sigma Xi, Rho Chi. Avocations: travel, art, music, cooking, wine.

SAUTER, GAIL LOUISE, speech pathologist; b. Williamsport, Pa., Mar. 14, 1951; d. Irvin Lamont and Mary Christine (Gephart) Guthrie; m. Gary Lee Sauter, Apr. 1974; children: Amberlynn Marie, Steven James. BS in Edn., Calif. State Coll., 1974; M of Communicative Disorders, Brigham Young U., 1985. Cert. clin. speech/lang. pathologist, resource tchr.; lic. speech pathologist. Asst. dir., dir. rehab. Summer Camp for Handicapped Children, Amherst, Ohio, 1976-77; speech/lang. pathologist Easter Seal Summer Clinic, Lorain, 1978, Vermilion (Ohio) Sch. System, 1975-80, Alpine Sch. Dist., Orem, Utah, 1980-86, spl. edn. tchr., 1986—. Mentor Alpine Sch. Dist.; ednl. cons. Accelerated Learning Ctr., also mem. adv. bd. Pres. No. Ohio Speech & Lang. Assn., 1978-79. Mem. Am. Speech/Lang. Hearing Assn., Utah Speech/Lang. Assn., Learning Disabilities Assn. Utah. Republican. Home: 920 N 840 E Orem UT 84097-3437 Office: Orchard Elem Sch 1035 N 800 E Orem UT 84097-3462

SAUTER, GAIL E. artist; b. San Antonio, July 16, 1949; d. Eugene Aaron and Phyllis Leone (Wolfe) Englert. BFA, U. Okla., 1970. Exhibited paintings in numerous shows including Shapiro Gallery N.H. Coll., 1993, Nature N.H. Statewide Traveling Exhbn., 1992, Faber Birren Color show, Stamford, Conn., 1992, 88, League of N.H. Craftsmen Gallery, 1992, Belknap Mills Soc. Visual Arts Coalition Statewide Exhbn., Laconia, N.H., 1991, Sharon (N.H.) Gallery, 1989, Newport (R.I.) Art Mus., 1987, others; paintings represented in numerous corp. collections including Salomon Bros. Investments, Chubb Life Am., Browning Ferris Industries. Art colony fellow Va. Ctr. for Creative Arts, 1991, 92, Vt. Studio Colony, 1991. Mem. Pastel Soc. Am. (master), Copley Soc. (Copley artist), League N.H. Craftsmen, Women's Caucus for Art, N.H. Art Assn. Home: 9 Government St Kittery ME 03904-1653

SAUTER, JOHNNY, race car driver; Race car driver Richard Childress Racing, Welcome, NC. Named 10 Time Champion, Am. Speed Assn., 2001, Pat Schauer Rookie of the Yr., Midwest Late Model Touring Series, 2001. Office: c/o Richard Childress Racing PO Box 1189 236 Industrial Dr Welcome NC 27347*

SAUTNER, BARRY ROBERT, artist; b. Phila., Jan. 20, 1952; s. Alfred Carl and Elva Mae (Ehly) S.; children: Heather Lynn, Jason Barry. First to use sandblasting to create cameo glass, 1979; devel. 3 dimensional undercut cameo glass, 1982, insculpture-diatreta paperweight, 1984; incorporated posts into diatreta design, 1985; creator double diatreta vase, 1987, postless double diatreta vase, 1988; carved vase on entire outside and inside, 1992; exhibited glass carvings in several shows including Bergstrom-Mahler Mus., Neenah, Wis., 1994, Am. Mus. Glass, Millville, N.J., 1993, Mus. Fine Arts, Houston, 1991, Corning (N.Y.) Mus. Glass, 1982, William Traver Gallery, Seattle, 1995, Habatat Gallery, Boca Raton, Fla., 1993, Judy Youens Gallery, Houston, 1993, Georgeo's Collection, Beverly Hills, Calif., 1993, Habatat Gallery, Aspen, Colo., 1993, Sandra Ainsley Gallery, Toronto, 1993, Habatat Gallery, Pontiac, Mich., 1993, Grohe Glass Gallery, Boston, 1993, Leo Kaplan Gallery, N.Y.C., 1995, others. Home: 1855 79th Ave Vero Beach FL 32966-1358

SAUTNER, ZENOBIA ZOE, office manager; b. Phillipsburg, N.J., June 2, 1972; d. Alfred Carl Sautner Jr.and Vanessa Amy (Fleming) Thatcher. AS in Chemistry, Raritan Valley C.C., 1998; student, Rutgers U., 1998—. Tax adminstr. Chapman, Bird & Grey, L.A., 1990-94; exec. asst. Yale Materials Handing Corp., Flemington, N.J., 1994-97; office manager Payback Tng. Systems, Morristown, 1997—. Mem. Phi Theta Kappa (v.p. fundraising), Alpha Epsilon Pi. Baptist. Avocations: hiking, biking, foreign films, theater, fine music. Home: 505 Spring Mills Rd Milford NJ 08848-1949

SAUTTER, CAROLYN HUBER, librarian; b. Chilton, Wis., Aug. 26, 1968; d. Carl Joseph and Carol Marie (Wolf) Huber; m. Richard Haines Sautter, 1996; 1 child, William. BA in History summa cum laude, U. Notre Dame, 1990; diploma, U. Oxford, Eng., 1992; MLS, Rutgers U., 1995. Cert. pub. libr., Pa. Libr. asst. Allentown (Pa.) Pub. Libr., 1984-89, reference libr., 1990—; resident asst. U. Notre Dame, London, 1990. Actress Muhlenberg Coll. Summer Musical Theatre, 1988-89, 91, 93; singer Lehigh U. Choral Union, 1992—; contbr. article to profl. jour. Catechist for children's masses St. Thomas More Parish, Allentown, 1995—. Mem. ALA, Pa. Libr. Assn., Pa. Shakespeare Festival (relief com. co-chair 1992-93), Notre Dame Club Lehigh Valley, Phi Beta Kappa, Phi Alpha Theta (Notre Dame chpt. sec. 1989-90). Avocations: travel, history, reading, theater, music. Office: Allentown Pub Libr 1210 W Hamilton St Allentown PA 18102-4371

SAUVÉ, CAROLYN OPAL, writer, journalist, poet; b. Columbus, N.C., Apr. 30, 1934; d. Anthony Floyd and Nina Morris Pittman; m. Joseph Ernest Sauvé, Mar. 31, 1953; children: Floyd, Kenneth, Timothy. Student, Spartanburg Meth. Coll., 1952-53; AAS, Isothermal C.C., 1976. Editor, author, photographer: History of Polk County, 1983; author, photograph APP Jour., 1999; author: Spirit of the Age, 1996. Trustee Isothermal C.C., Spindale, N.C., 1985-93; bd. dirs. Area Mental Health Bd., Spindale, 1985-91; v.p., sec., edn. chmn. Am. Cancer Soc., Polk County, N.C., 1975-79; bd. dirs. Juvenile Justice Bd., Rutherfordton, N.C., 1978-82; chmn. Polk County Commn., Columbus, 1978-82; chmn. Polk County Rep. Party, Columbus, 1984-86, 95-98; vice chmn., dist. chmn. N.C. Rep. Women's Club, Raleigh, 1975-79; chmn. World Missions Com., 1994-2000. Mem. Polk County Hist. Assn. (pres. 1984-86, v.p. 1996-2000). Presbyterian. Avocations: creative writing, boating, water-skiing, cake decorating, grandchildren. Home: 165 Landrum Rd Columbus NC 28722-9545

SAVAGE, BLAIR DEWILLIS, astronomer, educator; b. Mt. Vernon, N.Y., June 7, 1941; s. Rufus Llewellyn and Christine (Burney) S.; m. Linda Jean Wilber, June 25, 1966; children: Reid Hamilton, Keith Wesley. B.Engring. Physics, Cornell U., 1964; MS, Princeton U., 1966, PhD, 1967. Research assoc. Princeton U., 1967-68; asst. prof. U. Wis., Madison, 1968-73, assoc. prof., 1973-78, prof. astronomy, 1978—, chmn. dept., 1982-85, Karl Kansky prof. astronomy, 1999—. Vis. fellow Joint Inst. Lab. Astrophysics, Boulder, Colo., 1974-75; investigator space astronomy projects NASA, 1968—; bd. pres. Wis., Ind., Yale Nat. Optical Astronomy Obs. Telescope Consortium, 1990-96. Contbr. articles to profl. jours. Peyton fellow Princeton U., 1964-66; NASA fellow Princeton U., 1966-67; research grantee NASA, NSF, 1968—. Mem. Am. Astron. Soc. (councilor 1994-97), Internat. Astron. Union, Nat. Rsch. Coun. (space sci. bd. mem. 1985-88, chmn. com. for space astronomy and astrophysics 1985-88, astronomy and astrophysics survey com. 1989-90, com. for astronomy and astrophysics 1998-2001), Assn. for Univ. Rsch. in Astronomy (bd. dirs. 1989-92, space telescope Sci. Inst. coun. 1999-2002), Tau Beta Pi. Home: 4015 Hiawatha Dr Madison WI 53711-3037 Office: Dept Astronomy U Wis 475 N Charter St Madison WI 53706-1507

SAVAGE, CARLA LEE, insurance agent; b. Howell, Mich., Dec. 12, 1963; d. Evert and Gloria Jean (Andrews) Van Raden; m. Matthew Paul Savage, Apr. 9, 1994; 1 child, Trevor MacKenzie. AA, Yakima Valley C.C., Yakima, Wash., 1984; BA cum laude, Ctrl. Wash. U., 1986. Asst. mgr. Jay Jacobs, Yakima, Wash., 1983-85; probation counselor Kittitas Co. Probation Svc., Ellensburg, 1985-86; staff asst. N.W. Adminstr., Inc., Seattle, 1986-89; svc. rep., agent Sedgwick Noble Lowndes, Yakima, 1989-94; sales exec., agent Marsh Advantage America/Seabury & Smith, 1995—. Mem. adv. bd. health care reform Yakima Herald Republic, 1996. Vol. phone lines Crisis Line, Ellensburg, 1985, ARC, YMCA, Yakima Greenway, Pub. TV, Yakima C. of C., Kiwanis. Recipient Bus. Edn. award U.S. Achievement Acad., 1982. Avocations: boating, fishing, camping, sewing, furniture refinishing. Office: Marsh Advantage Amer/Seabury & Smith Lake Aspen Office Park 1430 N 16th Ave Yakima WA 98902-1381 E-mail: carla.l.savage@seabury.com.

SAVAGE, CHRISTINE DADEZ, women's health nurse, educator; b. Clinton, Iowa, Aug. 3, 1958; d. LeRoy D. and Carolyn A. Smith; children: Chelsea R. Dadez, Aleana R. Savage. AAS, Highland Cmty. Jr. Coll., Freeport, Ill., 1980; AS with honors, Rock Valley Jr. Coll., Rockford, Ill., 1986; BSN with honors, No. Ill. U., 1991; MSN, U. Wis., Milw., 1998. Cert. in childbirth edn., in-house obstetrics, women's health nurse practitioner. Staff nurse, labor and delivery Rockford Meml. Hosp., 1980-91; co-owner, instr. childbirth edn. Rockford Childbirth Edn., 1989—; staff nurse practitioner Rockford (Ill.) Meml. Hosp., 1991—. Women's health nurse practitioner U. Wis., Milw. Mem. No. Ill. Perinatal Regional Adv. Coun.; mem. Planned Parenthood of Wis., 1993. Mem. Internat. Childbirth Edn. Assn. (cert. childbirth educator), Am. Soc. for Psychoprophylaxis in Obstetrics, Nat. Assn. for Nurse Practitioners in Reproductive Health, Perinatal Assn. Ill., Golden Key, Sigma Theta Tau. Home: 1838 W Walters Rd Beloit WI 53511-8819

SAVAGE, CYNTHIA GAIL, business owner; b. Stuttgart, Germany, Feb. 15, 1958; d. Roscoe E. and Frances M. Savage. BS, San Jose State Univ., 1986; postgrad., Monterey Inst., 1993. Owner Honey Bears Deli Cafe, Pacific Grove, Calif., 1991-93, Imusination Music Pub., Pacific Grove, 1997—. Composer numerous songs. Mem. Eta Phi Beta, Beta Gamma (pres., 1978-81). Home: 3009 Eddy St Marina CA 93933-4004

SAVAGE, DONNA ROTHENBERG, association administrator; b. N.Y.C., May 4, 1952; d. Richard and Carol E. Rothenberg; m. Allan G. Savage, June 28, 1981. BA in Polit. Sci., Grinnell Coll., 1974; MEd in Adminstrn. and Counseling, Northeastern U., 1979; postgrad., Wellesley coll., 1986-87. Lic. social worker, Mass. Outreach counselor Quincy (Mass.) Jr. Coll., 1979-81; career counselor Grinnell (Iowa) Coll., 1981-83, asst. coord. pers. devel. program, 1983-84, residence hall dir., 1981-84; asst. dean of students Hamilton Coll., Clinton, N.Y., 1984-86, assoc. dean of students, 1986-88; dean of students Mount Vernon Coll., Washington, 1988-89; curriculum specialist, publs. mgr. Univ. Rsch. Corp., Bethesda, Md., 1990-92; projects coord. Sharon Sloane Enterprises, Inc., Rockville, 1991-93; mgr. Nat. Transit Resource Ctr. Community Transp. Assn. Am., Washington, 1993—. Mem. planning com. Nat. Conf. for Coll. Women Students Leaders, 1990-92; cons., workshop facilitator Myers-Briggs Type Indicator, 1985—. Editor: (newsletter) Montgomery County NOW, 1993—. Mem. Kensington Heights (Md.) Citizens Assn., 1992—; vol. Friendly Vis. Program Montgomery County, Md., 1990—; career counselor YMCA Counseling Ctr., Boston, 1980-81, Northeastern U., Boston, 1978-79, Acess Hotline, Cambridge, Mass., 1977-78; field organizer, county campaign mgr. Iowa Dem. Com., Des Moines, 1974. Mem. Nat. Assn. Women in Edn., Am. Coll. Pers. Assn., Assn. for Psychol. Type (cert. facilitator). Democrat. Jewish. Home: 10804 Mccomas Ct Kensington MD 20895-2210

SAVAGE, EDWARD BRUCE, surgeon; b. Brooklyn, N.Y., Nov. 7, 1959; BA, Columbia Coll., 1981; MD, Yale Med. Sch., 1985. Diplomate Am. Bd. Surgery, Am. Bd. Thoracic Surgery. Resident surgery Hosp. of U. Pa., Phila., 1985-92; resident in cardiothoracic surgery Brigham and Women's Hosp., Boston, 1992-94; asst. prof. surgery Hahnemann Sch. Medicine, Pittsburgh, 1994-98; cardiothoracic surgeon Allegheny Gen. Hosp., 1994-98; assoc. prof. cardiothoracic surgery Rush Med. Coll., Chgo., 1999—; chmn. divsn. cardiothoracic surgery Cook Co. Hosp., 1999—. Editor: (book) Essentials of Basic Science in Surgery, 1993. Mem. Soc. Thoracic Surgeons, Am. Coll. Surgeons, Internat. Soc. Heart and Lung Transplantation. Avocations: swimming, reading, fitness. Office: U Cardiovascular Surgeons 1725 W Harrison St Ste 1156 Chicago IL 60612-3835 Fax: 312-829-8680. E-mail: EBSavage@attbi.com.

SAVAGE, JAMES FRANCIS, editor; b. Boston, July 23, 1939; s. James and Hanora (Enright) S.; m. Sharon Kaye Base, May 29, 1965; 1 son, Sean. AA, Boston U., 1959, BS, 1961. Reporter Quincy (Mass.) Patriot Ledger, 1961-63; reporter Miami (Fla.) Herald, 1963-67, investigative reporter, 1967-78, investigations editor, 1978-84, assoc. editor investigations, 1984—. Investigative reporter Boston Herald Traveler, 1967 Served with AUS, 1962. Recipient Nat. Headliners award, 1969, Fla. Press Assn. award, 1972, George Polk Meml. award for investigative reporting, 1973, 80, Pub. Service award Nat. A.P. Mng. Editors, 1974, 80, award Fla. Soc. Newspaper Editors, 1974, 75, Nat. Disting. Service award Sigma Delta Chi, 1979, 87, Pulitzer Prize Staff award for Nat. Reporting, 1987, Outstanding Investigative Reporting award Investigative Reporters and Editors, 1988, Disting. Alumni award Boston U. Coll. Communications, 1990, Pulitzer Prize Staff Pub. Svc. award, 1993; Profl. Journalism fellow Stanford, 1974-75 Home: 1004 Orange Is Fort Lauderdale FL 33315-1651 Office: 1 Herald Plz Miami FL 33132-1609

SAVAGE, JOHN EDMUND, computer science educator, researcher; b. Lynn, Mass., Sept. 19, 1939; s. Edmund J. and Eldora A. (Guay) S.; m. Patricia Joan Landers, Jan. 29, 1966; children: Elizabeth, Kevin, Christopher, Timothy ScB, ScM, MIT, 1962, PhD, 1965. Mem. tech. staff Bell Telephone Labs., Holmdel, N.J., 1965-67; prof. computer sci. Brown U., Providence, 1967—, chmn. dept. computer sci., 1985-91. Vis. prof. U. Paris, 1980-81, Warwick U., Eng., 1991-92; mem. dept. vis. com. elec. engring. and computer sci. MIT, 1991—; cons. in field. Author: The Complexity of Computing, 1977; (with others) The Mystical Machine, 1986, Models of Computation: Exploring the Power of Computing, 1998; editor: (with Thomas Knight) Advanced Research in VLSI and Parallel Systems, 1992; chmn. editl. bd. Computing Rsch. News, 1990-96; mem. editl. bd. Jour. Computer and Sys. Scis., 1993—; patentee data scrambler, 1970, means and methods for generating permutation of a square, 1976. Mem. MIT Corp. visiting com. dept. elec. engring. and computer sci. Fulbright-Hays grantee, 1973; NSF fellow, 1961, Guggenheim fellow, 1973 Fellow AAAS, IEEE, Assn. Computing Machinery; mem. Computing Rsch. Assn. (bd. dirs. 1990-96), Sigma Xi, Tau Beta Pi. Avocations: reading, skiing, bicycling, walking. E-mail: john. Office: Brown U Dept Computer Sci 115 Waterman St Providence RI 02912-9016 E-mail: john_savage@brown.edu.

SAVAGE, JOHN WILLIAM, lawyer; b. Seattle, Oct. 11, 1951; s. Stanley and Jennie Sabina (Siggstedt) S.; m. Rebecca Lee Abraham, Oct. 1, 1983; children: Bennett William, James Oliver. Student, Lewis and Clark Coll., 1969-71, JD Northwestern Sch. Law, 1977; BA, U. Wash., 1973. Bar: Oreg. 1977, U.S. Dist. Ct. Oreg. 1977, U.S. Ct. Appeals (9th cir.) 1977, U.S. Supreme Ct. Pvt. practice law, Portland, Oreg., 1977-79; ptnr. Bailey, Olstad, Rieke, Geil & Savage, P.C., 1979-80; ptnr., shareholder Rieke, Geil & Savage, P.C., 1980-95; shareholder Rieke & Savage, P.C., 1995—. Mem. Oreg. Literacy Inc., Portland, 1979-85; mem. standing com. City Club, Portland, 1984-88, chmn. law and pub. safety standing com. 1986-87. Recipient award of merit Gerry Spence's Trial Lawyers Coll., 1999. Mem. ABA (chairperson young lawyers sect. Nat. Cmty. Law Week 1983-84, inmate grievance com. 1984-88), Assn. Trial Lawyers Am., Trial Lawyers for Pub. Justice, Oreg. Trial Lawyers Assn., Oreg. Bar Assn. (def. of indigent accused com. 1985-89), Oreg. Criminal Def. Lawyers Assn. (bd. dirs. 1984-86), Multnomah Bar Assn. (v.p. young lawyers sect. 1980, pres.-elect 1981, pres. 1982, Disting. Svc. award, bd. dirs. 1989-92, task force chair 1992-93, jud. selection com. 1998-99, Award of Merit 1994). Home: 397 Furnace St Lake Oswego OR 97034-3957 Office: Rieke & Savage PC 140 SW Yamhill St Portland OR 97204-3007 E-mail: jwsavage@rieke-savage.com.

SAVAGE, JOSEPH GEORGE, hospital administrator; b. Bklyn. s. Joseph George Jr. and Eileen (Schnell) S.; m. Lynn Ann Campbell; children: Kimberly, Patricia, Joseph IV. BA, Oswego Coll., 1977; postgrad., Seton Hall U., 1985. Pub. affairs dir. L.I. chpt. Nat. Multiple Sclerosis Soc., N.Y.C., 1977-79, exec. dir. Conn. chpt., 1979-80; dir. devel., mktg. Clara Mass Meml. Med. Ctr., Belleville, N.J., 1980-81; exec. dir. Found. of St. Joseph's Hosp. Med. Ctr., Paterson, 1981-89; sr. v.p. St. Francis Hosp. Heart Ctr., Roslyn, N.Y., 1989-92; v.p. St. Vincents Hosp. and Med. Ctr., N.Y.C., 1992-98, Cathedral Health Care Sys., Newark, 1998—. Commr. health City of Clifton, 1990-94; bd. dirs. N.Y. Heart Coun., 1989-93, Cath. Family and Cmty. Svcs., 1992—, Osweo Coll. Alumni, 1992—, St. Mary's Hosp., Passaic, N.J., 1993—, v.p., 1998—. Fellow Nat. Assn. Hosp. Devel. (communication chair 1982-85, edn. chair 1985-86, bd. dirs., regional dir. 1988-89), Friendly Sons of St. Patrick, Ancient Order of Hibernians, Rotary (past pres. Clifton Club, Paul Harris fellow, Walter Head fellow). Roman Catholic. Avocations: swimming, golf. Office: Cathedral Health Care Sys 219 Chestnut St Newark NJ 07105-1558 Home: 14 Limonite Rd Hackettstown NJ 07840-4821

SAVAGE, JOSEPH SCOTT, physician; b. Malden, Mass., Dec. 30, 1958; s. Jospeh Edward and Arlene Barbara S.; m. Gwendolyn Kieko Uezo, July 4, 1979 (div); m. Terri Armstrong, Apr. 2, 1998; 1 child, Colin Eric. BA, Wheaton Coll., 1983; DO, Osteopath, Medicine, Kirksville Coll., 1987. Diplomate Am. Bd. Osteopathic Med. Examiners, Am. Bd. Emergency Medicine. Coomd. maj. USAF, 1988; coord. EMS svcs. Wright Patterson AFB, Dayton, Ohio, coord. disater svcs.; attending physician USAF hosp., Lakenheath, Eng., 1988-91, asst. dir. emergency dept. Eng., 1990-91; dir. emergency tng. we. Europe divsn. USAF RAF, Eng., 1990-91; flight surgeon USAF Hosp. Holloman AFB, N. Mex., 1991-92; flight surgeon Space Shuttle contigency opers. USAF, Holloman AFB, 1991-92; resident physician Wright State U./USAF, Dayton, 1992-95; staff physician, instr. tactical medicine USAF Hosp., Wright Patterson AFB, 1995-97, EMS dir., 1996-97; clin. instr. emergency medicine Wright State U., 1996—; clin. tng. in mind-body medicine The Mind-Body Med. Inst., Deaconess-Beth Israel Hosp., Boston, 1997; staff physician New Century Physicians, Dayton, 1997—. Med. dir. Ohio Acad. Holistic Health, Dayton, 1998-99, Ohio Wellness Ctr., 1998-99; spl. asst. Dept. Health and Human Svcs., Rockville, Md., 1986; health policy fellow U.S. Senate, Wash., 1988; chief cons. Dayton, SWAT Team, 1994-96; keynote spkr. Ohio State EMS, Columbus, 1995; Ohio Holistic Health Expo, 1998; spl. lectr. mind-body medicine, Ohio Wellness Ctr.; keynote spkr. Ohio Holistic Health Expn., 1998; guest lectr. grand rounds Good Samaritian Hosp., 1998; Spl. lectr. Unitarian Universalist Ch., Oakwood, Ohio, 1993; guest lectr., Rotary Club, 1999. Contr. Chpt: (textbook) Emergency Medicine Reference Book, 1999. Decorated Commendation medal USAF, 1993, 97, Meritorious Svc. medal, 1991, recipient Dir's award USPHS U.S. Surgeon Gen., 1987; named to Internet Book of Honor, 1999. Fellow Internat. Biog. Assn. (life), mem. Am. Coll. Emergency Physicians. Avocations: fine arts, athletics. Home: 1211 W Main St Bldg 1205 Troy OH 45373-2564

SAVAGE, KARLEEN SUE, small business owner; b. San Diego, Oct. 16, 1963; d. Joseph Conrad Olayan and Terri Eileen Anderson; m. Donald Edward Savage, Nov. 11, 1988; children: Shendileen, Loraleen, Donald Jr., Anderson, Shaileen, Morgan. Cert. legal sec., Cascade Bus. Coll., 1985. Loan svc. rep.

Mellon Fin., Bellingham, Wash., 1985-86; office mgr. to Dr. Austin McGreal D.D.S. Upland, Calif., 1987-88; mgr. Expectation Party Sales, Riverside, 1991-92; owner Prime Affaire, 1992—. Lectr. in field. Tchr. relief soc. Latter Day Saints, Bloomington, Calif., 1991, primary counselor, 1993, nursery leader, Riverside, 1994; pres., v.p., mem. PTA, Bloomington. Pres.'s award PTA, Bloomington, 1989, 90. Republican. Avocations: reading, cooking, sewing, travel. Office: Prime Affaire 231 E Alessandro Blvd # A-338 Riverside CA 92508-6039

SAVAGE, LAURA L. ministry consultant, author, speaker; b. Houston, June 13, 1961; d. Edgar Lee Jr. and C. Joyce (Spelce) S. BS, Houston Bapt. U., 1983; MA in Comm., Southwestern Bapt. Theol. Sem., 1986. Tchr. Liestman Elem. Sch., Houston, 1983-84; dir. publs. Wedgwood Bapt. Ch., Ft. Worth, 1986-88; graphic designer Radio & TV Commn., 1987-88; comms. specialist ABB Impell Corp., 1989-90; v.p. pub. rels. H&S Comms. Group, 1990-91; dir. internal comms. Dallas Bapt. U., 1991-93; prodn. editor Woman's Missionary Union, Birmingham, Ala., 1993-95, ministry cons., 1995—. Prodn. editor mags. Contempo, 1993-95, Royal Service, 1993-95, Missions Mosaic, 1995; co-author: (cassette) Gifted By God: Leading, Loving, and Teaching with Your Life, 1997; co-author: In and Not of the World: Life Mission for a World Christian; writer Missions Mosaic. Mem. youth com. Bapt. World Alliance. Recipient 1st Pl. award for nat. student tchg. NEA, 1983. Mem. Christians for Biblical Equality. Avocations: travel, writing, interior decorating, musicals, Bible studies. Office: Woman's Missionary Union Hwy 280E 100 Missionary Ridge Dr Birmingham AL 35242-5235 E-mail: LSavage@wmu.org.

SAVAGE, MARK RANDALL, lawyer; b. Chicopee, Mass., Mar. 10, 1959; m. Lucia Clara Savage; children: David, Ryan. BA, U. Calif., Berkeley, 1982; JD, Stanford U., 1988. Bar: Calif. Jud. law clk. to Judge James Holden, North Bennington, Vt., 1988-89; mng. atty. Pub. Advocates, Inc., San Francisco, 1989—. Gen. counsel Cmty. Tech. Found. Calif., San Francisco, 1998—. Contbr. articles to profl. jours. Bd. dirs. Inst. for Civic Arts and Pub. Spaces, Inc., Albuquerque, 1996—2001. Recipient Drum Maj. award for contbns. to peace and justice So. Christian Leadership Conf., 1998, award Diversity, Innovation and Reform in Edn., 1995, El Fuego Nuevo award for work in edn. Assn. Mex. Am. Educators, 1999, Leadership Recognition award for work in health care for immigrant cmty. Calif. Primary Care Assn., 1999. Office: Pub Advocates Inc 1535 Mission St San Francisco CA 94103-2500 E-mail: MarkSavage@igc.org.

SAVAGE, MICHAEL PAUL, medicine educator, interventional cardiologist; b. Wilkes-Barre, Pa., Jan. 25, 1955; s. Peter J. and Olga J. (Sekerchak) S.; m. Kathleen A. Gallagher, June 1989; children: Katherine, Andrew. BA, Wesleyan U., Middletown, Conn., 1976; MD, Jefferson Med. Coll., 1980. Diplomate Am. Bd. Internal Medicine, Am. Bd. Cardiovascular Disease Interventional Cardiology, Nat. Bd. Med. Examiners. Intern, then resident New Eng. Deaconess Hosp.-Harvard U. Med. Sch., Boston, 1980-83; fellow Jefferson Med. Coll., Phila., 1983-86, asst. prof. medicine, 1986-91, assoc. prof., 1991—, dir. cardiac catheterization, 1990—, dir. interventional cardiology sect., 1996—. Cons. Johnson & Johnson Interventional Sys. Co., Warren, N.J., Scimed/Boston Scientific, Maple Grove, Minn., GlaxoSmithKline, Phila.; lectr. coronary angioplasty and cardiac catheterization. Contbr. articles to profl. jours. including New Eng. Jour. Medicine, Circulation, Am. Jour. Cardiology, Jour. Am. Coll. Cardiology, JAMA, Lancet, chpts. to books. Fellow Am. Coll. Cardiology, Soc. Cardiac Angiography and Interventions, Pa. Med. Soc., Am. Heart Assn., Am. Fedn. for Clin. Rsch. Roman Catholic. Achievements include rsch. in interventional cardiology concerning new techniques in treatment of coronary artery disease, culminating in international, prospective trials demonstrating superiority of implantable coronary stents over conventional balloon angioplasty. Office: Jefferson Med Coll 1025 Walnut St Ste 410 Philadelphia PA 19107-5001

SAVAGE, MICHAEL JOHN, agrometeorologist, researcher, educator; b. Germiston, Gauteng, South Africa, Jan. 7, 1953; s. Ronald Dennis and Blanche Mary (Williams) S.; m. Meryl Ann Venter, Dec. 24, 1977. BSc, U. Natal, Pietermaritzburg, South Africa, 1974, BSc with honors, 1975, PhD, 1983. Lectr. U. Natal, Pietermaritzburg, 1977-81, sr. lectr., 1982-83, assoc. prof., 1985-87, ad hominem prof., 1988-89, prof. (post level 7), 1994—, prof., head dept. agronomy, 1994-98, vice chmn. rsch. com. Durban, Pietermaritzburg, 1996-99, prof. Sch. Applied and Environ. Scis., 1999—. Vis. scientist Blackland Rsch. Lab., USDA, 1984, Mich. State U., East Lansing, 1984, Tex. A&M U., College Station, 1992, U. Ga., 2000; dir. Campbell Sci. South Africa, Stellenbosch, 1997. Co-editor and author: South African National Scientific Programs Report (monograph), 1989; contbr. numerous articles to profl. jours., chpts. to books. Preacher Christian Fellowship, Pietermaritzburg, 1994—; boardermaster St. Charles Coll., Pietermaritzburg, 1976-78. Lt. South African Army, 1976-93. Named one of Four Outstanding Young South Africans, Jr. C. of C., Johannesburg, 1990; recipient Comprehensive Rsch. award Found. for Rsch. Devel., 1985—, Cert. of Merit U. Natal, 1972, 77; Prin. Fulbright scholar Coun. for Internat. Exch. of Scholars, 1992, Satbel scholar, 1971-73; U. Natal fellow, 1996. Mem. Am. Meteorol. Soc., Agrl. Sci. Assn. Natal (pres. 1976-80, 85-86), Am. Soc. Agronomy, Internat. Soil Sci. Soc., South African Soc. Crop Prodn. (gold medal 1998). Pentecostal Ch. Avocations: photography, reading computer magazines. Office: U Natal Applied Environ Sci P Bag X01 Scottsville 3209 South Africa

SAVAGE, MICHAEL JOHN KIRKNESS, oil company and arts management executive; b. Birmingham, Eng., Oct. 28, 1934; came to U.S., 1962, naturalized, 1981; s. Leonard W. H. and Hilda C. (Fletcher) S.; m. Elisabeth Karl, June 21, 1965 (div.); m. Virginia Hooper, Aug. 31, 1978; 1 child, Matthew Nicholas. MA in Econs. and Law with honors, Cambridge U., 1958; postgrad., Manchester (Eng.) Bus. Sch., 1965; Diploma in Arabic, Middle E. Ctr. for Arab Studies, Shemlan, Lebanon, 1967. Various positions The British Petroleum Co. Ltd., England, Kuwait, Lebanon, Abu Dhabi, Alaska, Can., U.S., 1958-82; pres. BP Alaska Inc., San Francisco, 1977, Sohio Petroleum Co., San Francisco, 1978-82; internat. dir. The Brit. Petroleum Co. Ltd., London, 1982; founder/pres. Merlin Petroleum Co., San Francisco, 1983-88, Savage Petroleum Co., Sausalito, 1992—95; bd. dirs., mng. dir. San Francisco Opera, 1994-99; exec. dir., bd. dirs. Napa Valley Opera House, Napa, Calif., 2000—. Trustee Alaska Pacific U., 1982-86; trustee San Francisco Conservatory of Music, 1983—, chmn., 1990-94. Mem. Brit.-Am. Chamber (San Francisco), Belvedere (Calif.) Tennis Club (bd. dirs. 1994-96). Avocations: Music, tennis, skiing, mountain walking. Office: Napa Valley Opera House 1040 Main St Napa CA 94559

SAVAGE, PATRICIA WERNER, nonprofit health and human service agency executive; b. Reading, Pa., Nov. 17, 1949; d. Carl Clenroy and Margaret Evelyn (Harris) Werner; m. John William Savage, Jr., Aug. 16, 1975 (dec. Jan. 1997). BA, Alvernia Coll., 1971; MSW, Marywood U., Scranton, Pa., 1976; MS, U. Scranton, 1988; postgrad, Union Inst., Cin. Lic. social worker, nursing home adminstr., Pa. Dir. sr. companion program TELEPOND, Scranton, 1976-78; coord. spl. svcs. N.E. Tricounty Mental Health-Mental Retardation, Carbondale, Pa., 1978-85; dir. St. John Hospice, Luth. Welfare Svc., Hazleton, 1985-88, v.p. program ops., 1988-96; pres., CEO, Allegheny Luth. Social Ministries, Hollidaysburg, 1996—. Mem. coun. Evang. Luth. Coalition for Mission in Appalachia, Indiana, Pa., 1990—; mem. adv. com. Somerset County Aging Office, Somerset, Pa., 1996—; mem. adv. coun. for sr. citizens Office Senator Robert Jubelier, Altoona, Pa., 1996. Mem. Hollidaysburg Area Women's Club, Friends of Hollidaysburg Libr.; bd. dirs. divsn. for ministry ELCA, 2001--. Recipient Athena award Hazleton C. of C., 1991, P.E.A.R.L. award YWCA, Hazleton, 1991. Mem. Acad. Cert. Social Workers, Am. Coll. Healthcare Adminstrns., Rotary, Sigma Phi Omega. Lutheran. Avocations: reading, travel, cross-country skiing, golf. Office: Allegheny Luth Social Ministries 915 Hickory St Hollidaysburg PA 16648-2247 E-mail: patricia.savage@alsm.org., trish20146@aol.com.

SAVAGE, RANDALL ERNEST, journalist; b. Commerce, Ga., Mar. 3, 1939; s. Ernest Kyle and Sara Beatrice (Collins) S.; m. Joyce Carol Martin, Nov. 26, 1964 (div. May 1984); children: Kimberly Dawn, Bradley Kyle; m. Mary Elizabeth Hallmark, Aug. 4, 1984; children: Brock Morgan, Laura Marie, Shaw Hamilton. Student, U. Md.-European Div., RAF Bentwaters, Eng., 1967-69; BA in Journalism, U. Ga., 1972. Service sta. worker Collins Service Sta., Commerce, Ga., 1958; billing clk. Benton Rapid Express, Atlanta, 1958-61; truck driver So. Oil Co., High Point, NC, 1964-65; reporter Commerce News, Ga., 1972; sr. spl. projects reporter Macon Telegraph and News, 1972—, polit. and investing reporter. Served with U.S. Army, 1961-64; with USAF, 1966-69. Recipient 3rd place in news AP, Atlanta, 1976, 2nd place in news AP, Atlanta, 1976, 1st place in sports AP, Atlanta, 1984; 2d place in news Green Eyeshades award, 1976; Pulitzer prize, 1985, Outstanding Alumnus award Henry W. Grady Coll. of Journalism and Mass Communication, U. Ga., 1989. Baptist. Avocations: jogging, softball, fishing, free-lance writing. Home: 985 Chads Ford Ct Macon GA 31210-1572 Office: WMAZTV 1314 Gray Hwy 31211 Macon GA 31201

SAVAGE, RICHARD MARK, quality manager; b. Rockville Centre, N.Y., Feb. 8, 1950; s. Jack Earl and Margaret Ruth (Davis) S.; m. Jean Ann Hively, Sept. 19, 1970; children: Michael A., David A. Cert. in mid-mgmt. with honors, Wilbur Wright Jr. Coll., Chgo., 1974; AA in Sci., Community Coll. of USAF, 1979; assoc. tech. degree, GTE Corp., 1987, Assoc. Mgmt., 1991; BSBA, LeTourneau U., 1996. Enlisted USAF, 1969, advanced through grades to staff sgt., 1973, airman, student security service Tex., 1969-70, radio communications analyst Greece, 1970-72, Shepherd, Eng., 1972-77, instr. San Angelo, Tex., 1977-79, resigned, 1979; personnel and sales recruiter Interglobal Tech. Services, Austin, Tex., 1979-80; switching services maint. analyst GTE of the Southwest, Baytown, 1981-83, switching services budget analyst San Angelo, 1983-85, switching services systems analyst, 1985-87, adminstrn. results supr., 1987-89; sr. adminstr. GTE Telephone Ops., 1989-90; staff adminstr., 1990-94; industry sales, sys. mgr. GTE Supply, Irving, Tex., 1994-96; worldwide ops. mgr. GTEINS, 1996-98, tech. & planning mgr., 1998-1999; sr. sys. engr. TSI, 2000—. Cons. to local bus., Dallas Metroplex, 1985—; pres., owner Savage Innovations, Dallas, 1986—. Commr., cubmaster Boy Scouts Am., San Angelo, 1986-87; pres. McGill PTA, San Angelo, 1987-89; mem. adult coun. Sierra Vista Meth. Ch., San Angelo, 1987-88. Named one of Outstanding Young Men Am., 1985. Avocations: golf, computer programming, tole painting, auto mechanics, woodworking. Office: TSI HQXAAINS 1333 Corporate Dr Ste 300 Irving TX 75038-2535

SAVAGE, ROBERT HEATH, advertising executive; b. Chillicothe, Ohio, Nov. 24, 1929; s. Russell Heath and Frances (Hunt) S.; m. Lorna Dale, May 2, 1970. BA, Principia Coll., 1951; MBA, Harvard U., 1956. Brand mgr. Procter & Gamble, Cin., 1956-60; sr. v.p., mgmt. supr., dir. Ogilvy & Mather, Inc., N.Y.C., 1960-71; mktg. mgr. personal products div. Lever Bros., 1971; exec. v.p. Botsford Ketchum, Inc., San Francisco, 1972, pres., 1972-78, chmn., 1978-81; pres. KM&G Internat., Inc., 1978-81, Saatchi and Saatchi Compton, Inc., N.Y.C., 1981-83; mng. dir. Henson Assocs., 1983-86; ptnr. CMA Assocs., Southport, Conn., 1987—. Mngt. cons., sports and video mktg. cons., 1987—; chmn. Flying Rhinoceros, Inc., 1996—. With USMCR, 1951-54. Mem. Gipsy Trail Club, Colliers Reserve Country Club, Brooklawn Country Club. Home and Office: 273 Harbor Rd Southport CT 06490-1320 E-mail: rsavage881@aol.com.

SAVAGE, RUTH HUDSON, poet, writer, speaker; b. Childress, Tex., Apr. 29, 1932; d. John Floyd and Eula Jemima (Cornelius) Hudson; m. Robert Berkes, Nov. 6, 1950 (div. June 1963); children: Donna, Mike, Kelly, Rex; m. Martin Thomas Savage, Sept. 18, 1965. Pres. Poets of Tarrant County, 1992—94; founder, pres. New Millennium Poets, Arlington, Tex., 2000; judge local, nat. and state poetry contests; featured spkr., writer, Tex.; sponsor poetry contests. Author: (poetry) Voices in the Wind, 1982, (CD-ROM books of poetry) Savage Whispers, 1999, Texas Tuff, 2001, (plays) Tumbleweed Christmas, 1989, numerous poems ; contbr. to poetry jours. and anthologies; : Simply Savage, 1992. Judge various chpts. Poetry Soc. Tex. and Tex. Students, 1987—. Recipient numerous awards for poetry. Mem.: New Millennium Poets (founder), Poetry Soc. Tex. (judge various chpts. 1987—, councilor 2000—, sch. liaison 2000—, rec. sec. 2000—, sec. 2000—), Acad. Am. Poets, Nat. Fedn. State Poetry Socs. Avocations: art, speaking, writing. Home: 1700 Ocho Rios Ct Arlington TX 76012-2023 E-mail: ttsavage@arlington.net.

SAVAGE, SANDRA HOPE SKEEN, mathematics educator, curriculum writer; b. Charleston, W.Va., Apr. 4, 1938; d. Raymond and Freda (Burgess) Skeen; m. Steven William Savage, Aug. 17, 1963; 1 child, Samantha. BS in Secondary Edn. Math and English, Bob Jones U., 1960; MS in Math., Ill. Inst. Tech., 1966; EdD in Math. Edn., Columbia U., 1976. Cert. tchr., Calif., N.Y., Ill., Fla., W.Va., Minn. Math. tchr. S. Charleston Jr. High Sch., 1960-61, Citrus Grove Jr. High Sch., Miami, Fla., 1961-62, Skiles Jr. High Sch., Evanston, Ill., 1962-65, Evanston Twp. High Sch., 1965-67, White Plains (N.Y.) High Sch., 1967-68; chmn. math. dept. The Scarborough Sch., Scarborough-on-Hudson, N.Y., 1968-71; math. tchr. Alexander Ramsey High Sch., Roseville, Minn., 1971-72, Minnehaha Acad., Mnpls., 1971-72; lectr. math. Pace U., Westchester County, N.Y., 1972-73; team leader, math. tchr. Fox Lane Mid. Sch., Bedford, 1973-74; prof. math. Orange Coast Coll., Costa Mesa, Calif., 1977—. Lectr. math. edn. North Park Coll., Chgo., 1965; judge Odyssey of the Mind Competition, 1995; math. media cons. Annenberg Found., Washington, 1991; cons Business Link, Costa Mesa, 1990—. Designer/developer Mathematics Video Series, 1996-97, CD-ROM Design/Development, 1997. Speaker Expanding Your Horizons Women's Conf., Irvine, Calif., 1984-87; guild mem. Orange County Performing Arts Ctr., Costa Mesa, 1985-87; asst. troop leader Girl Scouts Am., Laguna Niguel, Calif., 1985-87; active Geneva Presbyn. Ch., Laguna Hills, Calif., 1983—. Recipient Cert. Merit, Nat. Merit Scholarship Corp., 1956, Tchr. of Yr. award Orange County Tchrs., 1994, Nat. Inst. for Staff and Orgn. Devel. awrd U. Tex., 1993, U.S.A. Today Teaching Excellence award, 1993; Dept. Edn. Nat. Workplace Literacy Program grantee, 1995. Fellow NSF (grantee 1983); mem. AAUW, Am. Math. Assn. Two Yr. Colls., Math. Assn. Am., Assn. for Women in Sci., Calif. Math. Coun., Orange County Math. Assn. (sec. 1982-83), Phi Delta Kappa (pres. Trabuco chpt. 1986-87, 95-96). Democrat. Avocations: music, computer graphics, multimedia/CD-ROM design, poetry. Office: Orange Coast Coll PO Box 5005 2701 Fairview Rd Costa Mesa CA 92626-5563 Home: Apt P 24832 Hidden Hills Rd Laguna Niguel CA 92677-8857

SAVAGE, STEPHEN MICHAEL, lawyer; b. Norwich, Conn., Apr. 23, 1946; s. Alfred and Iva (Allen) S.; m. Lois Palestine, July 4, 1968; children: Meredith, William, Sam. BA, U. Pa., 1968; JD, Harvard U., 1973. Bar: Ariz. 1973, U.S. Dist. Ct. Ariz. 1973. With Fennemore Craig, Phoenix, 1973—, chmn. mgmt. com., 1988—. Mem. Greater Phoenix Leadership; bd. dirs. Ariz. Diabetes Assn., Phoenix, 1983-87; chmn. bd. trustees Ariz. Sci. Ctr., Phoenix; chmn. bd. dirs. All Saints' Episcopal Day Sch., Phoenix, 1988; comdr., pres. Mounted Sheriff's Posse Maricopa County, Phoenix, 1992-93. Mem. ABA, State Bar Ariz. (chmn. sect. corp., banking and bus. law 1983-84), Maricopa County Bar Assn., Assn. Corp. Growth, Phoenix Country Club. Avocations: team roping, golf. Office: Fennemore Craig 3003 N Central Ave Ste 2600 Phoenix AZ 85012-2913

SAVAGE, SUSAN M. former mayor; b. Tulsa, Okla., 1936; married; 2 children. Student, U. Aix-Marseilles, Aix-en-Provence, France, 1969, City of London Poly., Eng., 1972; BA in Sociology with honors, Beaver Coll., 1974. Pre-trial rep. Phila. Ct. Common Pleas, 1974-75; criminal justice planner Montgomery County Criminal Justice Unit, 1975-77; exec. dir. Met. Tulsa Citizens Crime Com., 1977-87; vol. coord. Vote Yes For Tulsa, 1987; chief of staff to mayor City of Tulsa, 1988-92, mayor, 1992—2002. Active Lee Elementary Sch. PTA; bd. dirs., treas. Okla. Crime Prevention Assn.; bd. dirs. Youth Svcs. of Tulsa County, 1984-88, pres., 1986-87; co-chair Safe Streets/Enhanced 911 Steering Com., 1987; mem. C. of C. Task Force/Community Edn. Network, 1983. Mem. U.S. Conf. Mayors (chmn. com. energy and environment).*

SAVAGE, TERRY RICHARD, information systems executive; b. St. Louis, Oct. 21, 1930; s. Terry Barco and Ada Vanetta (Cochran) S.; m. Gretchen Susan Wood, Sept. 26, 1964; children: Terry Curtis, Christopher William, Richard Theodore. AB, Washington U., St. Louis, 1951, MA, 1952; PhD, U. Pa., 1954. Mgr. system software IBM Rsch., Yorktown Heights, N.Y., 1956-63; dir. data processing Documentation Inc., Bethesda, Md., 1963-64; mgr. info. systems Control Data Corp., Rockville, 1964-67; dir. rsch. Share Rsch. Corp., Santa Barbara, Calif., 1967-68; computer-aided acquisition and logistic support program mgr. TRW, Redondo Beach, 1968-92; ret., ind. cons. pvt. practice, 1992—. Expert witness for various coms. U.S. Congress, 1981, 84, 88, 89. Contbr. articles to profl. jours. Bd. dirs. ABC-Clio Press, Santa Barbara, 1970-75, Help the Homeless Help Themselves, Rancho Palos Verdes, Calif., 1988-94, ChorusLiners, Rancho Palos Verdes, 1983—, Savage Info. Svcs., Inc., Torrance, Calif., 1992—. Mem.: Cosmos Club. Home and Office: 30000 Cachan Pl Rancho Palos Verdes CA 90275-5412 E-mail: terrysavage@cox.net.

SAVAGE, THOMAS JOSEPH, executive development company executive, priest; b. Medford, Mass., Oct. 28, 1947; s. Frank James and Viola Augustine (Ballou) S. B.A. summa cum laude, Boston Coll., 1971; M. City Planning, U. Calif.-Berkeley, 1973; M. Pub. Policy, Harvard U., 1982, EdD, 1985. Assoc. Cheswick Ctr., Boston, 1973, dir., 1984—; assoc. Instl. Strategies Assocs., Cambridge, Mass., 1975-87; asst. acad. v.p. Fairfield (Conn.) Univ., 1986-88; pres. Rockhurst Coll., Kansas City, Mo., 1988-96, pres. Nat. Seminars Group., Shawnee Mission, Kans., 1991—; sr. cons. William M. Mercer, Inc., San Francisco, 1998—; adj. faculty Lesley Coll., Cambridge, 1982-85; cons. Lilly Endowment, Indpls., 1983-87; chmn. planning com. Jesuits New Eng. Province, Boston, 1985-88. Author: Seven Steps to a More Effective Board, 1994, The Goverance of Catholic Health Care Institutions, Catholic Health Assn., Spring, 1988; also articles. Del. Bridges for Peace, Soviet Union, 1985; Trustee Regis U., 1989-97, U. Detroit Mercy, 1995—, St. Louis U., 1991—, Loyola Marymount, 1994—; bd. dirs. Valentine-Radford Comm., 1992—, Preferred Health Profls., 1992-97, Kauffman Found., 1993—, Menning er Clinic, 1993—; co-chair FOCUS (Comprehensive Strategic Plan for Kansas City), 1992-97; founding chmn. Brush Creek Ptnrs., 1994-96. Mellon fellow, 1971-73. Mem. Am. Planning Assn., Nat. Policy Assn., AAAS, Assn. Jesuit Colls. and Univs. (bd. dirs. 1989-96), World Future Soc., Bostonian Soc., Phi Beta Kappa. Roman Catholic. Club: Harvard. Office: William M Mercer Inc Three Embarcadero Ctr San Francisco CA 94111

SAVAGE, THOMAS WARREN, engineering director; b. Morgantown, W.Va., Feb. 6, 1959; s. Thomas Louis Savage and Sandra Mabel (Ferguson) Crawford; m. Cydney Ellen Fry, May 8, 1981; children: Jessica Louise, Kristin Anne, Thomas Dylan. BS in Computer Engring., Santa Clara U., 1993; MBA, Pepperdine U., 1999. Electronic technician ITT North, Galion, Ohio, 1977-79; electronic test engr. Fairchild Test Systems, San Jose, Calif., 1979-82; design engr. Tandem Computers, Cupertino, 1982-94, engring. mgr., 1994-95; dir. Synopsys Inc., Mountain View, Calif., 1995—. Patentee in field. Mem. Order of the Engr. Avocations: archaeology, baseball, golf, skiing. Home: 1648 Capitancillos Pl San Jose CA 95120-5701 Office: Synopsys Inc PO Box 7670 Mountain View CA 94039-7670 E-mail: warren@savageplace.com.

SAVAGE, TIMOTHY JOSEPH, lawyer; b. Phila., Mar. 24, 1946; s. Norbert J. and Edna M. (Mawson) S.; m. Linda S. Siegle, June 22, 1968; children: Timothy J., Daniel J., Christian S. BA, Assumption Coll., 1968; JD, Temple U., 1971. Bar: Pa. 1971, U.S. Dist. Ct. (ea. dist.) Pa. 1971, U.S. Supreme Ct. 1980, U.S. Ct. Appeals (2d and 3d cirs.) 1981, U.S. Dist. Ct. N.J. 1985, N.J. 1985, U.S. Tax Ct. 1985. Assoc. MacCoy, Evans & Lewis, Phila., 1971-74; ptnr. Savage and Ciccione, 1976-77; atty. examiner Pa. Liquor Control Bd., Harrisburg, 1976—; pvt. practice Phila., 1977—. Vice chmn. Frankford Econ. Revitalization Com., 1976—80; mem. Phila. Dem. County Exec. Com., 1976—; leader 23d Ward Dem. Exec. Com., 1976—; chmn. bldg. and fin. com. St. Joachim Roman Cath. Ch.; bd. dirs. Met. lub Am.; sec., bd. dirs. N.E. Cmty. for Mental Health/Mental Retardation, 1974—81; pres. Frankford Spl. Svcs. Dist., 1995—99; counselor N.E. Boys and Girls Club. Mem. ABA, Assn. Trial Lawyers Am., Pa. Bar Assn., Pa. Trial Lawyers Assn., Phila. Trial Lawyers Assn. Avocations: boating, fishing. Office: 5030 Oxford Ave Philadelphia PA 19124-2520

SAVAGE, TOM, poet; b. N.Y.C., July 14, 1948; s. Thomas Upton and Anna Joyce Savage. BA, Bklyn. Coll., 1969; MLS, Columbia U., 1980. Cert. N.Y. state libr. Tchr. poetry workshops The Poetry Project, N.Y.C., 1983-85; tchr. poetry master class Juilliard Sch. Music, 1998; video libr., 1998—. Author: (books) Personalities, 1978, Filling Spaces, 1980, Slow Waltz on a Glass Harmonica, 1980, Housing, Preservation, & Development, 1988, Processed Words, 1990, Political Conditions/Physical States, 1993, Brain Surgery Poems, 1999; contbr. poetry to anthologies including A Day in the Life, 1990, Out of this World, 1991, Unbearables, 1995, Staring Back: The Disability Experience from the Inside Out, 1997, also to periodicals including N.Y. Times, New Am. Writing, Lungfull, Talisman; editor: (mag.) Gandhabba, 1983-88; founding and assoc. editor: ROOF, 1976-78; contbg. editor: The World, 1990-95. Vol. libr. Met. Mus. Art, N.Y.C. Grantee PEN, 1978, Fund for Poetry, 1989, 98. Buddhist. Home and Office: 622 E 11th St New York NY 10009-4127

SAVAGE, TOY DIXON, JR. lawyer; b. Norfolk, Va., Oct. 12, 1921; s. Toy Dixon and Hildreth Gatewood S.; m. Mary Hunter Hankins, Oct. 19, 1946; children: Tracy G., Toy D. III. BA in Econ., U. Va., 1943, LLB, 1948; LittD (hon.), Ea. Va. Med. Sch., 1995. Assoc., ptnr. Willcox & Savage PC, Norfolk, 1948—. Mem. ho. of dels. Gen. Assembly Va., 1954-63; bd. dirs. Sentara Health Sys., United Cmty. Fund, 1968-73; chmn. Norfolk Found. Distribution Com., Hampton Rds. Areawide Coop. Com., 1963-64, 76-78; trustee Chrysler Mus., Va. Found. for Ind. Coll., Camp Found., North Shore Found., Va. Hist. Soc., Ea. Va. Med. Sch. Found., Va. Mus. Fine Arts, 1975-85; trustee, deacon Freemason St. Bapt. Ch.; mem. Govs. Adv. Bd. on Indsl. Devel., 1983-92; chmn. task force on health care Govs. Commn. on Future of Va., 1984-85; pres. Old Dominion U. Ednl. Found., 1972-73, Med. Ctr. Hosps., 1966-68; vice-chmn. Ea. Va. Med. Authority, 1964-66. Home: 3100 Shore Dr Virginia Beach VA 23451

SAVAGE, WILLIAM EARL, savings and loan executive, religious educator; b. Wilmore, Ky., Feb. 5, 1918; s. Earl Wilson and Mary Nell (Jones) S.; m. Dorothy Jane Dorrycott, Dec. 28, 1939; children: Sue Ann, William Earl II, Carolyn. AB, Asbury Coll., Wilmore, Ky., 1939; LHD, Asbury-Theol. Sem., 1995. V.p. Pineland Coll., Deland, Fla., 1939-42; bus. mgr. Ky.-Wesleyan Coll., Owensboro, 1942-44; v.p. bus. adminstrn. Asbury Theol. Sem., 1946-76; pres. First Fed. Savs. and Loan, Lexington, Ky., 1982-85, vice chmn. bd. dirs., 1982—; ret. Mem. United Meth. Bd. Global Ministries, 1960-72; mem. adminstrv. bd. Park United Meth. Ch., Lexington, 1960—; mem. World Meth. Coun., 1961—, exec. com., 1975—; bd. dirs. Asbury Theol. Sem., Wilmore, 1945—; lay leader Ky. Conf. United Meth. Ch., 1964-68; treas. bd. dirs. Ky. Meth. Found., 1982-88. Trustee Cardinal Hill Children's Hosp., Lexington, 1954-60, Good Samaritan Hosp., Lexington, 1964-92; bd. dirs. Lexington Coun. Arts, 1980-86. Mem. Ky. Savs. Loan League, Nat. Assn. Cert. Revenue Appraisers, U.S. Savs. League, Ky. Crippled Children's Soc. Democrat. Home: 4111 Harrodsburg Rd Lexington KY 40513-1366

SAVAGE, WILLIAM WOODROW, JR. historian, consultant, educator; b. Richmond, Va., Oct. 13, 1943; s. William Woodrow and Margaret (Clarke) S.; m. Sheila Bobalik, July 30, 1983; 1 child, William Woodrow III. BA in Journalism, U. S.C., 1964, MA in History, 1966; PhD in History, U. Okla., 1972. Instr. Coll. Gen. Studies U. S.C., Columbia, 1966; vis. lectr. history Iowa State U., Ames, 1970; asst. editor U. Okla. Press, Norman, 1972-75; asst. prof. history U. Okla., 1974-80, assoc. prof. history, 1980-89, prof. history, 1989—. Tech. adviser Korine-Dunlap Prodns., Nashville, 1982-83; adviser Am. Frontier Project, N.Y.C., 1982-85; bd. cons. editors Popular Culture in Librs., Binghamton, N.Y., 1991-99; co-prodr., host Norman Cable TV, 1986-88. Author: The Cherokee Strip Live Stock, 1973, The Cowboy Hero, 1979, Singing Cowboys and All that Jazz, 1983, Comic Books and America 1945-54, 1990; editor: Indian Life, 1977, Cowboy Life, 1993; editor: Cowboy Life, 1975, Indian Life, 1977; co-editor: The Frontier, 1979; newsletter editor Comparative Frontier Studies, 1975-86, Norman and Cleveland County Hist. Mus., 1975-86; columnist Okla. Gazette, 1993-95. Recipient Spl. Recognition award Okla. Jazz Hall of Fame, 1993. Mem. Okla. Hist. Soc., So. Hist. Assn., Western History Assn., Sigma Delta Chi. Avocations: panelology, mixed media and collage. Home: 1021 Connelly Ln Norman OK 73072 Office: U Okla Dept History 455 W Lindsey Rm 424 Norman OK 73019

SAVAGEAU, MICHAEL ANTONIO, microbiology and immunology educator; b. Fargo, N.D., Dec. 3, 1940; s. Antonio Daniel and Jennie Ethelwin (Kaushagen) S.; m. Ann Elisa Birky, July 22, 1967; children— Mark Edward, Patrick Daniel, Elisa Marie BS, U. Minn., 1962; MS, U. Iowa, 1963; PhD, Stanford U., 1967, postgrad., 1968-70, UCLA, 1967-68. Research fellow UCLA, Los Angeles, 1967-68; lectr. Stanford U., Calif., 1968-69; from asst. to full prof. U. Mich., Ann Arbor, 1970—; sr. research fellow Max Planck Inst., Göttingen, Fed. Republic of Germany, 1976-77; fellow Australian Nat. U., Canberra, 1983-84; prof. microbiology and immunology U. Mich., Ann

Arbor, 1978—, chmn. dept., 1982-85, 92—, prof. chem. engring., dir. cellular biotech. labs., 1988-91, dir. NIH tng. program in cellular biotechnology, 1991-92, dir. bioinformatics program, 1998-2001, Nicolas Rashevsky disting. univ. prof., 2002—. Vis. prof. Institut des Hautes Etudes Scientifiques, Bures-Sur-Yvette, France, 2002; vis. prof. dept. biochemistry U. Ariz., Tucson, 1994; cons. Upjohn Co., Kalamazoo, 1979—81, NIH, Bethesda, Md., 1981—82, Bethesda, 1994—95, Bethesda, 1997—2000, Synergen, Boulder, Colo., 1985—87, NRC/Howard Hughes Med. Inst., 1997—, NSF, 1999—, Swedish Found. for Strategic Rsch., 2001—02, Stockholm, 2001—02, Cigene Ctr. for Integrated Genetics, Agrl. U. Norway, Aas, 2001—. Author: Biochemical Systems Analysis, 1976; mem. editl. bd. Math. Scis., 1976-95, editor, 1995—; mem. editl. bd. Jour. Theoretical Biology, 1989-96, mem. adv. bd., 1996—; mem. editl. bd. Nonlinear World, 1992—, Nonlinear Digest, 1992—, inSight, 1998—, BioComplexity, 2000—; co-editor Math. Ecology, 1986—. Guggenheim Found. fellow N.Y.C., 1976-77; Fulbright Found. sr. rsch. fellow, Washington, Fed. Republic of Germany, 1976-77; sr. fellow Mich. Soc. Fellows, 1990-94; grantee NIH, NSF, ONR, 1964—. Fellow AAAS; mem. Am. Chem. Soc., Am. Soc. Microbiology, IEEE (sr.), Soc. Indsl. and Applied Math., Biophys. Soc., Soc. Gen. Physiologists, Soc. Math. Biology (bd. dirs. 1987-90), Internat. Fedn. Nonlinear Analysts (bd. dirs. 1997—). Office: U Mich Dept Microbiology and Immunology 5641 Med Sci II Ann Arbor MI 48109-0620

SAVAGE-NEUMAN, MARY SUSAN, art dealer; b. Deerfield, Mass., Dec. 15, 1944; d. John George and Mary Margaret (Sabolinski) Savage; m. Robert Sterling Neuman, June 3, 1979; 1 child, Christina Mary Savage Neuman. Student, U. de Mediterranee, Nice, France, 1965; BA, Lake Erie Coll., 1966; postgrad., Western New Eng. Law Coll., 1967-68. Asst. to adminstr. Mayor's Office of Pub. Svc., Boston, 1968-70; dir. art rental gallery Inst. Contemporary Art, 1970-71; art cons. Cir. Art Gallery, 1971-75; dir., owner Sunne Savage Gallery, 1975-83, pvt. art dealer Winchester, Mass., 1983—. Fine arts project coord. Park Meadow, Denver, Belluschi Architects, Chgo.; curator of Herbert W. Plimpton Collection, 1976-80, Wingspread Gallery, Northeast Harbor, Maine, 1990—; conceptual advisor to Monumenta Exhibit, Newport, R.I., 1974; initiated various art shows including Rose Art Mus., Waltham, Mass., Oakland Mus. Art, Calif.; represents various 20th century Am. and European artists. Conservation chair Winchester (Mass.) Home & Garden, 1994-96, program chair, 1998—; active Fogg Mus., Harvard U., 1985—, Mus. Fine Arts Boston, 1985—, Gore Place, Waltham, Mass., 1990—, Historic Deerfield, Mass., 1990—; program com. St. Mark's Sch. Parents Assn., 1996-97; pres. coun. Wheaton Coll., 2000—; mem. Portland Mus. Art, 2000—, DeCordova Mus., Lincoln, Mass., 2000—, Worcester (Mass.) Art Mus., 2002, Colby Art Mus., Waterville, Maine, 2000—; patron Mus. Fine Arts, Boston, 2001—. Named Forbes fellow, Harvard U. Art Mus., 2001—02. Mem. Archives of Am. Art (co-chair state street benefit 1989, vice chair art fair 1990, co-chair art libr 1992), William Farnsworth Libr. and Art Mus. (Rockland, Maine), Mus. Modern Art (N.Y.C.), Met. Mus. Modern Art, Guggenheim Mus. Republican. Roman Catholic. Avocations: tennis, hiking, cooking, traveling to Europe. Home: 135 Cambridge St Winchester MA 01890-2411

SAVANNAH, MILDRED THORNHILL, public school educator; b. Lynchburg, Va., Aug. 10, 1951; d. Norman Nemrod and Ruby (Brown) Thornhill; m. Ronald L. Savannah, June 17, 2000. BS in Edn., Elizabeth City State U., 1973; postgrad., U. Va., 1974-82, U. Tex., 1986-87; M in Ednl. Adminstr., U. North Tex., 1994. Cert. tchr., Va., Tex. Tchr. Campbell County Pub. Sch., Rustburg, Va., 1973-84; leader recreation City Lynchburg, 1976-77; tchr. Dallas Ind. Sch. Dist., 1984—99, instrnl. specialist for mid. schs. math. dept., 1999—. Dir. Dealey After Sch. Tutoring Program. Officer NAACP, Campbell County, Va., 1980-84; sch. coord. March of Dimes; mem. Task Force Excellence in Edn., Richmond, 1982-84; charter mem. leadership edn. com. S.W. Edn. Devel. Labs., Austin, 1985-86; dir. youth dept. devel. programs Bethany Bapt. Ch., 1974-83; chaplain, tchr. Missionary Soc.-1st Bapt. Ch., Hamilton Park; v.p. mission 2 South Oak Cliff Bapt. Ch., deaconess; adult leader Campbell County 4-H Clubs, 1973-83; appointee Tex. Edn. Agy. Grant Reader Rev. Com. Named Outstanding Young Woman Am., 1981. Mem. NEA, Nat. Mid. Sch. Assn., Nat. Coun. Tchrs. Math., Nat. Coun. Supr. Math., Classroom Tchrs. Dallas (minority affairs chair, black caucus chair, instrnl. and profl. devel. chair, v.p. region 19 exec. bd.), Va. Edn. Assn., Campbell County Edn. Assn. (pres. 1982-83), Tex. State Tchrs. Assn. (cert. trainer for profl. staff devel. 1984—, campus coord. Project Early Options, chair, regional rep. to state instrnl. advocacy com., pres., bd. dirs. region 19 2000-), Elks, Zeta Phi Beta (chair, 3d v.p. Kappa Zeta chpt.), Phi Delta Kappa. Baptist. Home: 1207 Shady Ln Lancaster TX 75146 Office: PO Box 77 3700 Ross Ave Dallas TX 75204

SAVARD, CHRISTINE ELIZABETH, music educator; b. Boston, Apr. 25, 1940; d. Albert Eugene and Catherine Marie (Lusk) Lloyd; m. Emile Joseph Savard, June 27, 1964; children: Peter Joseph, Paul Eugene, Elizabeth Jane. BS, New Eng. Conservatory of Music, 1964; MM in Arts Edn., Spring Arbor U., 2002. Music tchr. Glen Cove (Maine) Christian Acad., 1962-63, The Pub. Schs., Malden, Mass., 1964-65, Vestal (N.Y.) Ctrl. Schs., 1965-68, Johnson City (N.Y.) Ctrl. Sch. Dist., 1969, Ctrl. Bapt. Christian Acad., Binghamton, 1975-78, Ross Corners Christian Acad., Vestal, 1978-82, Tamworth (N.H.) Sch. Dist., 1987-90, Rogers City (Mich.) Area Schs., 1991-96; elem. music supr., tchr. Onaway Area Cmty. Schs., 1996-97; music tchr. Cedar Lake Elem. Sch., Oscoda, Mich., 1999—2002, Richardson Elem. Sch., Oscoda, 2002—. Music tchr. Freedom & Madison (N.H.) Sch. Dists., 1988-89. Profl. entertainer, singing and playing 8 instruments at each performance. Competition judge N.Y. State Talents for Christ, 1977-85; choir dir. First Baptist Ch., N. Conway, N.H., 1970-74; organist Mich. Home Health Care Hospice, Indian River, Mich., 1993. Mem. No. Mich. Gen. Assn. Regular Baptist Chs. (pres., spkr. ladies group 1991-96). Home: 7768 E County Line Rd South Branch MI 48761-9645

SAVARI, SERAP AYSE, electrical engineer, researcher; b. Astoria, N.Y., Nov. 4, 1968; d. Aykut and Sirin Savari. MS, MIT, 1991, PhD, 1996. Mem. tech. staff Bell Labs., Lucent Techs., Murray Hill, N.J., 1996—. Mem. program com. Data Compression Conf. , 2000, 01, 02. Contbr. articles to profl. jours. Mem.: IEEE (program com. Internat. Symposium on Inf. Theory 2001—02), Toastmasters, Tau Beta Pi, Phi Beta Kappa. Home: 25 Hickory Pl Apt D22 Chatham NJ 07928-1481 Office: Bell Labs Lucent Techs 600 Mountain Ave Rm 2c-451 New Providence NJ 07974-2008 E-mail: savari@research.bell-labs.com.

SAVAS, EMANUEL S. public management and public policy educator; b. N.Y.C., June 8, 1931; s. John and Olga (Limbos) S.; m. Helen Andrew, Dec. 25, 1955; children: Jonathan, Stephen. BA, U. Chgo., 1951, BS, 1953; MA, Columbia U., 1956, PhD, 1960; PhD (hon.), U. Piraeus, Greece, 2000. Control systems cons. IBM, Yorktown Heights and White Plains, N.Y., 1959-65; urban systems mgr. N.Y.C., 1966-67; 1st dep. city adminstr. Office of Mayor of N.Y.C., 1967-72; chmn. Mayor's Urban Action Task Force, 1969-72; prof. pub. mgmt. Columbia U., N.Y.C., 1972-83, dir. Center for Govt. Studies, 1973-83, assoc. dir. Center for Policy Rsch., 1973-81; asst. sec. for policy devel. and rsch. HUD, Washington, 1981-83; prof. mgmt. Baruch Coll., CUNY, 1981-94, prof. public policy, 1994—, dir. public policy program, 1994-97, chm. dept. mgmt., 1986-93; dir. Privatization Rsch. Orgn., 1986—. Cons. NSF, HUD, Dept. Transp., Dept. Energy, World Bank, AID, U.S. Dept. State, Pres.'s Commn. on Privatization, UN, UN Devel. Program, ILO, UNIDO, USIA, also others; mem. voting bd. Blue Cross and Blue Shield Greater N.Y., 1976-79, bd. dirs., 1979-81; mem. Pres.-Elect's Urban Affairs Task Force, 1980, N.Y. State Senate Adv. Commn. on Privatization, 1990-95; mem. Gov. Pataki privatization coun., N.Y., 1995-2000; dir. U.S.-USSR Joint Project on Mgmt. of Large Cities, 1973-81; advisor on privatization Govt. Poland, 1990-92, Govt. Lesotho, 1992, Govt. Ukraine, 1993, N.Y.C. mayor, 1994-2000, Govt. South Africa, 1996, Govt. Botswana, 1996, Govt. Philippines, 1997, others. Author: Computer Control of Industrial Processes, 1965, Organization and Efficiency of Solid Waste Collection, 1977, Privatizing the Public Sector, 1982, Moscow's City Government, 1985, Privatization, 1987, Privatization and Public-Private Partnerships, 2000, 15 fgn. edits., others; editor: Alternatives for Delivering Public Services, 1977, Privatization for New York, 1992, The New Public Management, 2002; mem. editorial bd. Urban Affairs Quar., Privatization Report, Privatization Watch, State and Local Govt. Rev.; contbr. 110 articles to profl. jours. Mem. N.Y.C. Mayor-elect Giuliani transition team, 1993, N.Y. Gov.-elect Pataki transition team, 1994; mem. Tenafly (N.J.) Borough Coun., 1996. With U.S. Army, 1953-54, Korea. Recipient Systems Sci. and Cybernetics award IEEE, 1968, Louis Brownlow award Am. Soc. Public Adminstrn., 1970, Honor award Templeton Found., 1989, Leadership award Nat. Coun. Pub.-Private Partnerships, 1993, Outstanding Acad. award Am. Soc. Pub. Adminstrn., 1996. Mem. Sigma Xi, Psi Upsilon. Clubs: City of N.Y. (trustee 1974-77, Richard Childs award 1979). Greek Orthodox. Office: CUNY Baruch Coll Box C-207 17 Lexington Ave New York NY 10010-5518 E-mail: prisect@aol.com.

SAVEDGE, ANNE CREERY, artist, photographer; b. Richmond, Va., Jan. 29, 1947; d. Leslie Roy Jr. and Dorothy (Rakes) C.; m. Edwin Clement Savedge Jr., Aug. 11, 1967; 1 child, Ross Alan. BS, James Madison U., 1969; M in Art Edn., Va. Commonwealth U., 1977. Art instr. Colonial Heights (Va.) High Sch., 1969-78; instr. Va. Mus. Robinson House, Richmond, 1983-86; vis. artist Office of Youth and Community Svcs., Dinwiddie, Va., 1986-87; artist-in-residence Richmond Children's Mus., 1987-88; instr. Shenandoah Photographic Workshops, 1988. Adj. faculty U. Richmond, 1978-2000—; artist-in-residence Va. Mus. of Fine Arts, Richmond, 1984-86, Richmond Children's Mus., 1987-88; curator Bedford Gallery Photoshow Longwood Coll., Farmville, Va., 1985, Light Images Gallery Photoshow James Madison U., Harrisonburg, Va., 1985, 1708 East Main Gallery Photoshow, Richmond, 1987, 90, New Realities/Digital Transformations show, 1997; artist Fay Gold Gallery, Atlanta, 1985-87, Nat. Copier Art Show; artist-in-edn. gifted program Dinwiddie, Va., 1988; instr. Chesterfield Tech. Ctr., 1989—. One-woman shows include Marsh Gallery, U. Richmond, 1986, 1708 Gallery, 1994, Baton Rouge, 1991, "Pinholes & Pixels" 1912 Gallery, 2000, Cultural Arts Ctr. at Glen Allen, 2002; exhibited in group shows Pleiades Gallery, N.Y.C., 1989, Martin Gallery, Washington, 1989, Midwest Invitational, 1993-94, Mars Gallery, Ariz., 1994, Bloom Gallery, Milan, 1995, Longwood Ctr. for Visual Arts, 1997, Chrysler Mus., 1999, Art Mus. Western Va., 2002; represented in permanent collections Polaroid Internat. Collection, Fed. Res. Bank, Chrysler Mus., Valentine Mus., Longwood Ctr. for Visual Arts, Va., Art Mus. Western Va.; pub. in Magic Wand, 1st and 2nd edits., 1998. Adv. coun. Richmond Arts Coun.; evaluation com. Partners-in-Arts; master tchr. Va. State T&I Skills USA Nat. Conf.; chmn. 1708 Gallery Exhbns., 1995-96. Named Art Tchr. of Yr., Chesterfield County, 1997-98, Art Educator of Yr., Va. Art Edn. Assn., 1999, hon. mention Excellence in Photographic Tchg. award Santa Fe Ctr. for the Visual Arts; individual artist fellow Va. Commn. for Arts, 1999m, profl. fellow Va. Mus. Fine Arts. Mem. Nat. Art Edn. Assn. (presenter Chgo. chpt. Nat. Conf. 1998, Chgo. chpt. Washington Nat. Conf. 1999, Southeastern Art Educator of Yr. 2000), Richmond Artists Assn. (pres. 1978-80, cert. distinction 1980), Soc. for Photographic Edn., Va. Soc. for Photographic Arts (steering com. 1976—, fundraising chmn. 1978—, mem. chmn. 1980-86). Methodist. Home: 5318 Verlinda Dr Richmond VA 23237-3307 E-mail: asavedge@savedge.com.

SAVEDRA, JEANNINE EVANGELINE, art educator, artist; b. Montebello, Calif., Dec. 21, 1965; d. Robert Anthony Savedra and April Elizabeth (Sanchez) Baroth. Student, Pasadena C.C., Calif., 1985-87, Otis Art Inst./Parsons Sch., 1987-88; BA in Studio Art, Calif. State U., L.A., 1991; postgrad., 1992-93; MA in Art/Humanities, Calif. State U., Dominguez Hills, 1999; postgrad. IMMEX Inst., UCLA, 1999; postgrad., Getty Edn. Inst. for Arts. Cert. art tchr., Calif. Children's counselor Salvation Army, Pasadena, Calif., 1987-88; graphic artist Calif. State U., L.A., 1989; pvt. investigator Larry J. Larsen Investigations and Trial Preparations, 1990-93; art instr. Pasadena Unified Sch. Dist., 1994-95; studio art instr. Visual Arts and Design Acad., Pasadena, 1995—, coord./lead tchr., 1999-00. Supr. mural Pasadena Playhouse Improvement Assn., 1995-96; mentor Puente program U. Calif., Berkeley, 1995—; educator Nat. Conf. Human Rels., Temescal Canyon, Calif., 1996, Annenberg Inst. Sch. Reform, Brown U., 1998—; apptd. to ednl. adv. com. Jack Scott, mem. Assembly, Calif. State Legislature, 1997—; apptd. to Sierra Madre Arts Commn., 1999; artist exch. program Cultural Min., Havana, Cuba, 2000. Co-author interactive multi-media ednl. CD-ROM. Appt. to Sierra Madre Downtown Improvement Com., 2000; founding mem. Nat. Campaign for Tolerance, Montgomery, Ala. Calif. Partnership Acad. grantee, 1996—; recipient Excellence in Visual Arts award Calif. State U., 1990. Mem. Nat. Art Edn. Assn., L.A. County Mus. Art, Mus. Contemporary Art, Nat. Soc. Women Artists, Mus. Tolerance, Pasadena Armory Ctr. for Arts, Armand Hammer Art Mus. Office: Visual Arts and Design Acad 2925 E Sierra Madre Blvd Pasadena CA 91107-1846

SAVELKOUL, DONALD CHARLES, retired lawyer; b. Mpls., July 29, 1917; s. Theodore Charles and Edith (Lindgren) S.; m. Mary Joan Holland, May 17, 1941; children: Jeffrey Charles, Jean Marie, Edward Joseph. BA magna cum laude, U. Minn., 1939; JD cum laude, William Mitchell Coll. Law, 1951. Bar: Minn. 1951, U.S. Dist. Ct. Minn. 1952, U.S. Ct. Appeals (8th cir.) 1960, U.S. Supreme Ct. 1971. Adminstrv. work various U.S. govt. depts., including Commerce, War, Labor, Wage Stblzn. Bd., 1940-51; mcpl. judge Fridley, Minn., 1952-53; pvt. practice law Mpls., St. Paul, Fridley, 1951-96; ret., 1997. Chmn. bd. Fridley State Bank, 1962-95; pres. Banrein, Inc., 1962-95, Babbscha Co., 1962-95; mem. faculty William Mitchell Coll. Law, 1952-59, corp. mem., 1956-99; sec. Fridley Recreation and Svc. Co., 1955-97; mem. Minn. Legislature, 1967-69. Mem. Gov.'s Com. Workers Compensation, 1965-67, Gov.'s Adv. Coun. on Employment Security, 1957-60, 62-63; gen. counsel Minn. AFL-CIO Fedn. Labor, 1952-71. 1st lt. AUS, 1943-46. Decorated Bronze Star; recipient Disting. Alumni award Coll. Liberal Arts U. Minn., 1995, Outstanding Alumnus award William Mitchell Coll. Law Alumni/ae Assn., 1997. Mem. ABA, Minn. Bar Assn. (chmn. 1957-58, bd. dirs. 1958-62, 68-69, labor law sect.), Justice William Mitchell Soc., Am. Legion, U. Minn. Pres.'s Club, Phi Beta Kappa. Roman Catholic. Office: 916 Moore Lake Dr W Fridley MN 55432-5148

SAVELL, EDWARD LUPO, lawyer; b. Atlanta, Apr. 29, 1921; s. Leon M. and Lillian (Lupo) S.; m. Bettie Patterson Hoyt, Oct. 11, 1944; 1 dau., Mary Lillian Savell Clarke. BBA, Emory U., 1947, LL.B., 1949. Bar: Ga. 1948, U.S. Dist. Ct. (mid. and no. dist.) Ga.; registered mediator and arbitrator, Ga. Assoc. A.C. Latimer, Atlanta, 1948-53; ptnr. Carter, Latimer & Savell, 1953-56, Woodruff, Latimer & Savell (and successor firms), Atlanta, 1956-87; of counsel Savell & Williams, 1987—. Instr. John Marshall Law Sch., 1951-55; dir. Legal Aid Soc., 1955-58; arbitrator Am. Arbitration Assn. and Fulton Superior Ct. Contbr. articles to legal jours. With USAF, 1942-45, CBI. Fellow Internat. Acad. Trial Lawyers (pres. 1978-79, Dean of Acad. 1976); mem. Atlanta Bar Assn. (sec.-treas. 1953-54), ABA, State Bar Ga., Ga. Def. Lawyers Assn. (founder, v.p.), Internat. Assn. Ins. Counsel, Atlanta Claims Assn., Lawyers Club Atlanta, Chi Phi, Phi Delta Phi. Clubs: Cherokee Town and Country, Commerce, Univ. Yacht (past commodore). Presbyterian. Office: Savell and Williams 1500 Equitable Bldg 100 Peachtree Atlanta GA 30303

SAVELL, POLLY CAROLYN, lawyer; b. N.Y.C., Oct. 24, 1960; d. Joel Morton and Elise Rhea (Crane) S. BA, U. Md., 1982; diploma, Internat. Comp. Law Inst., Paris, 1983; JD, NYU, 1985. Bar: N.Y. 1986. Assoc. corp. and entertainment divsn. Battle Fowler, N.Y.C., 1986-87; atty. Columbia Pictures Entertainment Inc., 1987-89; counsel Turner Broadcasting Sys. Inc., Atlanta, 1989-91; sole practice, 1991-93; asst. gen. counsel WorldCom Inc., N.Y.C., 1993—2001; pvt. practice, 2001—. Bd. dirs. Eviction Intervention Svcs., Homeless Prevention, Inc. Mem. ABA, Fed. Comm. Bar Assn., Am. Corp. Counsel Assn., Assn. of Bar of City of N.Y. (telecom. law com.). Democrat. Methodist. Office: 410 Park Ave Ste 1530 New York NY 10022

SAVELSBERG, JOACHIM JOSEF, sociologist, educator; b. Ahlen, Germany, Mar. 29, 1951; came to U.S., 1989; s. Heinrich Paul and Gertrud Maria Savelsberg; m. Pamela L. Feldman-Savelsberg, June 26, 1958; children: Anna, Rebecca. D, U. Trier, Germany, 1982. Instr. U. Trier, 1978-82; rsch. scientist U. Bremen, Germany, 1983-86; assoc. dir. Criminological Rsch. Inst. Lower Saxony, Hannover, Germany, 1986-89; assoc. prof. U. Minn., Mpls., 1989—. Author: Constructing White Collar Crime , 1995 (Disting. Book award American Society of Criminology internat. divsn.). Recipient Rsch. award NSF, 1993-96; Jr. fellow Johns Hopkins U. and German Exch. Svc., 1982-83, John F. Kennedy Meml. fellow Harvard U., 1997-98. Mem. Am. Sociol. Assn. (sec., treas. law sect. 1993-94), Am. Soc. Criminology, Deutsche Gesellschaft Soziologie, Law and Soc. Assn. Home: 1745 Ashland Ave Saint Paul MN 55104 Office: U Minn Dept Sociology 909 Social Scis Tower Minneapolis MN 55455 Fax: 612-624-7020. E-mail: savelsbg@atlas.socsci.umn.edu.

SAVENOR, BETTY CARMELL, painter, printmaker; b. Boston, Sept. 2, 1927; d. Harry Hyman and Sally Carmell; m. Jack Savenor, June 1, 1948; children: Alan, Barry, Ronald. Student, Jackson Van Ladau Sch. Fashion, Brandeis U., DeCordova Mus.; BFA, Mass. Coll. Art, 1993. Represented by Art 3, Inc., Manchester, NH, Diane Levine, Boston, Gallery 333, Falmouth, Mass., So.Watercolor Soc. Exhibited in group shows at Guild of Boston Artists, Salmagundi Club, N.Y., Boston Printmakers, U. Mass., Harvard U., Okla. U., Brandeis U., Purdue U., Ind., Attleboro (Mass.) Mus., Western N.Mex. U., Montclair Art Mus., N.J., Duxbury Art Complex, Mass., Morris Mus. Arts & Scis., N.J., George Walker Vincent Smith Mus., Mass., Nat. Gallery, N.Y., Fairleigh Dickinson U., N.J., Fitchburg Art Mus., Mass., Boston C. of C., Fed. Res. Bank of Boston, Adelphi U., N.Y., Stonehill Coll., Cahoon Mus. Am. Art, Midwest Mus. Art, Ind., Allied Artists Am., N.Y., Bentley Coll., Mass.; represented in permanent collections Fairfield Med. Assn., Vackerville, Calif., Bank of Boston, Data Products, NEC Info. Sys., Inc., Skowhegan Bank, Maine, Sheraton Corp., Hollywood, Calif. and New Orleans, Meadows Country Club, Fla., U. Tampa, First Bank of Concord, N.H., Indian Head Bank, N.H., New Eng. Life Ins. Co., Conn. Mut. Ins. Co., Liberty Mut. Ins. Co., Velcro Mgmt., Jo-Ann Fabrics, Tampa Energy Corp., Fla., Weisner Assocs., Fla.; pubs. include Collograph Printmaking, Best of Watercolor, Painting Textures, Best of Watercolor, The Collected Best of Watercolor. 2002. Juror for numerous art shows, Mass.; demonstrator for many art socs. Recipient Nicholas Reale Meml. award for graphics Allied Artists Am., First Frontier Collage Soc., Guiller Gall. Awd., TX, 1999, Sarasota Visual Art Ctr., First Prize, 1999-00, FL, Art League of Manatee, FL, Printmaker Awd., 2000. Mem. Nat. League of Am. Pen Women (award of excellence 1998), New Eng. Watercolor Soc. (sec. 1983-93, Best Contemporary Watercolor prize 1990, Pelikan Disting. award 1997, Bronze medal 1998), Nat. Assn. Women Artists (prize 1982, 87, 89), Northwest Watercolor Soc. (signature mem.), Cape Cod Art Assn. (Jurors Merit award 1992-94, 1st prize in graphics 1993-95, 97), Nat. League Am. PEN Women (Best in State award 1983-95, 39th Nat. Exhbn. award of excellence 1998), Concord Art Assn. (Gold medal 1985, 1st prize 1991, Yarmouth Art award 1998), Falmouth Art Guild (best in show 1997). Democrat. Jewish. Avocations: tennis, swimming, decorating. Home: 4305 Highland Oaks Cir Sarasota FL 34235-5173

SAVERCOOL, JOHN G. professional society administrator; b. Endicott, N.Y., Apr. 1, 1959; s. George W. Savercool and Martha A. Rudiman; m. Mary K. Hathway, Feb. 12, 1988; children: Charlotte, Annie, Jack. BS, Frostburg State U., 1981. Staff asst. U.S. Rep. Mike Oxley, Washington, 1981; legis. asst. U.S. Rep. Phil Gramm, 1982-84, state projects dir., 1985-94, adminstrv. asst., 1994-99; chief staff U.S. Senator Kay Bailey Hutchison, 1994; v.p. fed. affairs Am. Ins. Assn., 1999-2000. Apptd. advisor Ea. Montgomery County Master Plan Assn., Silver Spring, Md., 1994-2000. Mem. Knights. Office: Am Ins Assn 1130 Connecticut Ave NW Washington DC 20036 E-mail: jsavercool@aiadc.org.

SAVERINO, CASSIO ANTHONY, secondary school educator; b. N.Y.C., Sept. 28, 1956; s. Salvatore Anthony Saverino and Bernice Bengford; m. Noel Christina Carpino, Aug. 27, 1978; children: Tara, Marc. BA, SUNY, Cortland, 1978; Master's degree, No. Ariz. U., 1985. Cert. secondary edn. Tchr. Willis Jr. H.S., Chandler, Ariz., 1979—80, Mountain View H.s., Mesa, 1980—81, Deer Valley Jr. H.S., Phoenix, 1981—82; tchr., dept. coord. Deer Valley H.S., Glendale, 1982—. Roman Catholic. Avocations: scuba diving, juggling, football official. Home: 7273 W Bloomfield Peoria AZ 85381 Office: Deer Valley H S Glendale AZ 85308

SAVEROT, PIERRE-MICHEL, nuclear waste management company executive; b. Charnay les Macon, France, Aug. 30, 1952; m. Francoise Solamito; children: Cyprien, Luc, Scott-Eugene. MS, Northwestern U., 1977. Formerly with SGN, Sybelpro, Cogema Inc., Numatec, West Valley Nuclear Svcs., NUSYS; sr. cons., asst. to pres. JAI Corp., Fairfax, Va., 1994—. Mem. Inst. Nuclear Waste Mgmt. (chmn. 1996—). Home: 3112 White Daisy Pl Fairfax VA 22031-1463 Office: JAI Corp 4103 Chain Bridge Rd Ste 200 Fairfax VA 22030-4107

SAVETH, EDWARD NORMAN, history educator; b. N.Y.C., Feb. 16, 1915; s. Isidor and Eva (Vasa) S.; m. Harriet Obstler, June 22, 1975; 1 child by previous marriage, Henry. BSS., CCNY, 1935; MA, Columbia U., 1937, PhD, 1946. Prof. history Grad. Faculty New Sch. for Social Research, N.Y.C., 1960-63; Fulbright prof. Kyoto U., Kyoto, Japan, 1964-65; prof. Dartmouth Coll., 1965-66; Disting. vis. prof. Tex. Lutheran Coll., Seguin, 1966-67; Disting. prof. SUNY-Fredonia, 1967-85; adj. prof. SUNY, Buffalo, 1987—; lectr. USIA, Nepal, 1965, Morocco, 1977; Fulbright prof. Hebrew U., Jerusalem, 1981. Vis. prof. U. Rochester, 1972; lectr. Beijing Tchrs. Coll., 1989. Author: American historians and European Immigrants, 1947; author, editor: Understanding the American Past, 1954, Henry Adams, 1963, American History and the Social Sciences, 1964; revisions editor: Ency. Americana, 1962; contbr. numerous articles to mags. Mem. Am. Hist. Assn., Orgn. Am. Historians Home: 11 High Ct Snyder NY 14226-3527 Office: SUNY-Buffalo Dept History Buffalo NY 14260-0001

SAVIA, ALFRED, conductor; b. Livingston, NJ; Asst. condr. Omaha Symphony, 1976-78, Fla. Symphony Orch., 1978-78, assoc. condr., 1979-86, prin. guest condr., 1986-87; asst. condr. Colo. Philharm., 1979-81; resident condr. New Orleans Symphony, 1986-88, assoc. condr., 1988-89; resident condr. Philharm. Orch. Fla. (now Fla. Philharm. Orch.), 1987-89; music dir. Evansville (Ind.) Philharm., 1989—; assoc. condr. Indpls. Symphony Orch., 1990-96, artistic dir., prin. condr. summer season, 1991-96. Guest condr. Indpls. Symphony, New Orleans Symphony, Kitchener-Waterloo Symphony, Can., Presdl. Symphony Ankara, Turkey, Aalborg Symphony, Denmark, Korea Philharm., San Antonio Symphony, Alabama Symphony, Hudson Valley Philharm., Fla. Symphony Orch., Colo. Philharm., Denver Chamber Orch., Lubbock Symphony, Nebr. Chamber Orch., Miami Ballet, Orlando Opera Co., St. Louis Symphony, R.I. Philharm., Nat. Repertory Orch., Ill. Symphony, Grant Park Symphony, Osnabruck Symphony Orch., others. Recipient High Fidelity Musical Am. Young Artist award, 1985. Office: Evansville Philharm Orch PO Box 84 Evansville IN 47701-0084 also: Parker Artists 382 Central Park W Apt 9G New York NY 10025-6032*

SAVILLE, KATHLEEN JO, instructional technologist; b. Clifton Forge, Va., Nov. 18, 1955; d. Leon Hunter and Elizabeth Pignato Saville. BS, James Madison U., 1978, MEd, 1982. Sch. libr. Clarksville (Va.) Primary Sch., 1979; sch. libr., media specialist Woodstock (Va.) Mid. Sch., 1979-82; instr. No. Mich. U., Marquette, 1982—. Mem. Assn. Ednl. Comm. and Tech. (sec., treas. 1999—). Office: No Mich U 1401 Presque Isle Ave Marquette MI 49855 Fax: 906-227-1333. E-mail: ksaville@nmu.edu.

SAVILLE, PAT, state senate official; b. Marysville, Kans., Sept. 10, 1943; Sec. Kans. Senate, Topeka, 1991—. Mem.: Am. Soc. Legis. Clks. and Secs. (past pres.). Office: Kans Senate State House 360 East Topeka KS 66612 E-mail: pats@senate.state.ks.us.

SAVILLE, THORNDIKE, JR. coastal engineer; b. Balt., 1925; s. Thorndike and Edith Saville; m. Janet Foster, Aug. 28, 1950; children: Sarah, Jennifer, Gordon. AB, Harvard U., 1947; MS, U. Calif., Berkeley, 1949. Rsch. asst. U. Calif., Berkeley, 1947-49; hydraulic engr. Beach Erosion Bd. and Coastal Engring. Rsch. Ctr., Ft. Belvoir, Va., 1949-81, chief rsch. divsn., 1964-71, tech. dir., 1971-81; cons., 1981—. Contbr. articles to engring. and sci. publs. With USAAF, 1943—46. Recipient Meritorious Civilian Svc. award, Dept. Army, 1981, Comdr.'s award, 1998. Fellow: ASCE (Huber award 1963, Moffatt-Nichol award 1979, Internat. Coastal Engring. award 1991), AAAS, Wash. Acad. Scis.; mem.: Am. Shore and Beach Preservation Assn. (bd. dirs. 1976—97, v.p. 1988—95, M. P. O'Brien award 1997), Permanent Internat. Assn., Navigation Congresses (hon.; U.S. commr. 1971—78, U.S. commr. emeritus 1987—, U.S. rep. PTC II 1991—98), Nat. Acad. Engring., Am. Geophys. Union, Cosmos Club (Washington). Home and Office: 5601 Albia Rd Bethesda MD 20816-3304

SAVINELL, ROBERT FRANCIS, engineering educator; b. Cleve., May 26, 1950; s. Robert D. and Lotte R. Savinell; m. Coletta A. Savinell, Aug. 23, 1974; children: Teresa, Robert, Mark. BSChemE, Cleve. State U., 1973; MS, U. Pitts., 1974, PhD, 1977. Registered profl. engr., Ohio. Rsch. engr. Diamond Shamrock Corp., Painesville, Ohio, 1977-79; assoc. prof. U. Akron, 1979-86; prof. Case Western Reserve U., Cleve., 1986—, dir. Ernest B. Yeager Ctr. for

Electrochem. Scis., 1991—, assoc. dean engring., 1998—, interim dean of engring., 2000, dean engring., 2001. Divsn. editor Jour. Electrochem. Soc., 1988-91; N.Am. editor Jour. Applied Electrochemistry, 1991-97; contbr. articles to profl. jours. Named Presdl. Young Investigator, NSF, Washington, 1984-89, Outstanding Engring. Alumnus, Cleve. State U., 1984. Fellow Electrochem. Soc.; mem. AIChE (program chmn. 1986-92), Electrochem. Soc. (divsn. officer 1992—), Internat. Soc. Electrochemistry (v.p. 1995-98). Avocations: sailing, skiing. Office: Case Western Reserve U AW Smith Bldg Dept Chem Eng 10900 Euclid Ave Cleveland OH 44106-4901 E-mail: Rfs2@PO.cwru.edu.

SAVINETTI, LOUIS GERARD, lawyer; b. Sea Cliff, N.Y., Sept. 5, 1955; s. Louis Philip and Alice Margaret (Stanco) S.; m. Holly Pinto, Apr. 30, 1983; 1 child, Scott Pinto. BA in Edn., L.I. U., Brookville, N.Y., 1979, MPA, 1987; JD, Touro Sch. Law, Huntington, N.Y., 1996. Asst. dir. Office of County Devel. County of Nassau, Roslyn Harbor, N.Y., 1981-88; asst. to commr. Town of Oyster Bay, 1988-92, dep. commr. planning and devel., 1992-96, councilman, 1994-98; atty., adminstr. Met. Transp. Authority, N.Y.C., 1997-98, gen. counsel L.I. Bus Garden City, 1998-99; exec. v.p., gen. coun. Nassau Health Care Corp., 1999—. Exec. leader Republican Party, Glen Head, Glenwood Landing and Old Brookville, N.Y., 1992-2001. Founder Geographic Info. Systems Commn., Cmty. Congress Citizens Adv. Bd.; bd. dirs. Syosset Hosp.; founder Fire Adv. Bd., Marine Adv. Bd., Environ. Coord. Coun.; fundraising chmn. Coalition to Save Hempstead Harbor, 2001—. Mem. Grenville Baker Boys and Girls Club Alumni (fundraising chmn. 2001), Glen Head/Glenwood Bus. Assn., L.I. U. Alumni Assn., Salve Soc. Vassar Coll. Episcopalian. Avocations: photography, music. Home: 43 Kissam Ln Glen Head NY 11545-1013

SAVING, THOMAS ROBERT, economics educator, consultant; b. Chgo., Dec. 27, 1933; s. Harold John and Frances Josephine (Fillipino) S.; m. Barbara Jean Sorby, Aug. 22, 1959; children: Jason Lee, Nicole Aline. B.A. in Econs., Mich. State U., 1957; M.A. in Econs., U. Chgo., 1958, Ph.D. in Econs., 1960. Asst. prof. U. Wash., Seattle, 1960-61; asst. prof. Mich. State U., East Lansing, 1961-63, assoc. prof., 1965-66, prof., 1966-68; head dept. econs. Tex. A&M U., College Station, 1985-91, dir. Pvt. Enterprise Rsch. Ctr., 1991—, prof. econs., 1968-89, disting. prof. econs., 1989—; pres. RRC, Inc., College Station, 1979-89, chmn. bd., 1989—. Author: Money, Wealth, Economic Theory, 1966. Mem. Am. Econ. Assn., So. Econ. Assn. (pres. 1981-82), Western Econs. Assn. (pres. 1971-72), Econometric Soc., Mont Pelerin Soc. Home: 1402 Post Oak Cir College Station TX 77840-2322 Office: Tex A&M U Pvt Enterprise Rsch Ctr College Station TX 77843-0001

SAVINO, MICHAEL ANTHONY, surgeon; b. Queens, N.Y., May 8, 1953; s. Daniel Joseph and Lucille Savino; m. Debra Graffeo, July 9, 1977; children: Arielle, Jared, Troy. BS, Richmond Coll., Staten Island, N.Y., 1975; MD, U. Guadalajara, Mex., 1979. Diplomate Am. Bd. Urology. Intern Coney Island Hosp., 1979-80; resident in surgery Maimonides Med. Ctr., 1980-82, resident in urology, 1982-85; surgeon in group practice Staten Island, 1985—. Fellow ACS; mem. Am. Assn. Clin. Urologists, Am. Urologic Assn. Avocations: karate, tennis, physical fitness. Office: Todt Hill Urologic Group PC 78 Todt Hill Rd Staten Island NY 10314-4528

SAVITS, BARRY SORREL, surgeon; b. Phila., Feb. 14, 1934; s. Frank and Sophia (Cohen) S.; children: George, Frank, Alexander. BA, Princeton U., 1955; MD, U. Pa., 1959; cert. surg. residency, Mt. Sinai Hosp., N.Y.C., 1965. Prof. surgery Project Hope, Ecuador, 1965-66; instr. surgery Albert Einstein Med. Coll., Bronx, N.Y., 1966-67; surgeon LaGuardia Med. Group, Queens, 1970-72; dir. surgery St. Mary's Hosp., Bklyn., 1973-91, Kingsbrook Jewish Med. Ctr., Bklyn., 1991-2000; attending N.Y. Meth. Hosp., 2000—, N.Y. Cmty. Hosp., 2001—. Vis. surgeon Hope-Ecuador, 1965-66, Care-Medico, Afghanistan, 1976. Comdr. USN, 1967-69. Fellow ACS (gov. 1991-97); mem. Soc. Am. Gastrointestinal Endoscopic Surgeons, Assn. Acad. Surgery, Assn. Surg. Program Dirs., Bklyn. Surg. Soc. (pres. 1992-93). Jewish. Avocations: reading, children. Office: 263 7th Ave Ste 4E Brooklyn NY 11215 Fax: (718) 369-8121. E-mail: bsavits@aol.com.

SAVITSKY, DANIEL, engineer, educator; b. N.Y.C., Sept. 26, 1921; s. Maxim and Anna (Oleksiw) S.; m. Mary Wysocki; children: Jean, James, Anne. BCE, CCNY, 1942; MSc, Stevens Inst. Tech., 1952; PhD, NYU, 1971. Registered profl. engr., N.Y. Structural engr. EDO Corp., College Point, N.Y., 1942-44; aero. rsch. scientist Nat. Adv. Com. for Aero., Langley Field, Va., 1944-47; prof. emeritus Stevens Inst. Tech., Hoboken, N.J., 1947—. Chmn. high speed vehicle com. Internat. Towing Tank Conf., 1978-88; cons. Naval Studies Bd., Nat. Rsch. Coun. Author: (with others) Yearbook of Science and Technology, 1987; patentee hydrofoil controls. Fellow Soc. Naval Architects and Marine Engrs. (Adm. Cochrane award 1967, Davidson medal 1996), Am. Soc. Naval Engrs., Niantic Bay Yacht Club (Conn.), Sigma Xi. Roman Catholic. Avocations: sailing, skiing, tennis. Home: 597 Delcina Dr Westwood NJ 07675-6111 Office: Davidson Lab 711 Hudson St Hoboken NJ 07030-5953 E-mail: dsavitsk@stevens-tech.edu.

SAVITSKY, MAUREEN ELIZABETH, pharmacist; b. Plainfield, N.J., Aug. 12, 1959; d. Jerome Joseph and Mary Elizabeth (Leonard) S. BS in Pharmacy, Mercer U., Atlanta, 1982, PharmD, 1983. Clin. pharmacy resident U. Nebr. Med. Ctr., Omaha, 1984-85; drug info. resident U. Mich. Med. Ctr., Ann Arbor, 1985-86; dir. drug info. svc. U. Chgo. Hosps., 1986-88; coord. clin. and drug info. svcs. Geisinger Med. Ctr., Danville, Pa., 1988-97; dir. formulary svcs. Pa. State Geisinger Health Sys., 1997-2000, Geisinger Health Sys., 2000—; clin. asst. prof., group facilitator for working profl. Doctor of Pharmacy program, U. Fla. Coll. Pharmacy, 2000—. Contbr. articles to profl. jours.; reviewer journal manuscripts for scientific publs.; mem. editorial bd. Jour. Pharmacy Practice, 1993-96. Mem. Am. Soc. Hosp. Pharmacists, Pa. Soc. Hosp. Pharmacists (pres. No. Ctrl. chpt. 1991-92, bd. dirs. 2000—), Drug Info. Assn., Acad. Managed Care Pharmacy, Kappa Epsilon, Phi Kappa Phi, Phi Lambda Sigma, Rho Chi. Office: Geisinger Med Ctr 100 N Academy Ave Danville PA 17822-4201 E-mail: msavitsky@geisinger.edu.

SAVITT, STEVEN LEE, computer scientist; b. Mpls., May 25, 1949; s. Leonard Robert and Claire (Hurwitz) S.; m. Gloria Lynn Kumagai; children: Mariko, Leilani, Joshua. BSEE, U. Minn., 1971, PhD in Computer Sci., 1992. Founder, CEO Compmark I Corp., Mpls., 1972-83; rsch. sect. head Honeywell, Inc., 1983-89; rsch. staff scientist Alliant Techsystems, Inc., 1989-96, engring. sect. head, 1996—. Co-chair database com. Automatic Target Recognizer Working Group, 1985-87. Mem. IEEE, Japanese-Am. Citizens League. Avocations: piano, classic car collecting, canoeing, tennis, swimming. Home: 332 Westwood Dr N Golden Valley MN 55422-5263

SAVITT, SUSAN SCHENKEL, lawyer; b. Bklyn., Aug. 21, 1943; d. Edward Charles and Sylvia (Dlugatch) S.; m. Harvey Savitt, July 2, 1969 (div. 1978); children: Andrew Todd, Daniel Cory. BA magna cum laude, Pa. State U., 1964; JD, Columbia U., 1968. Bar: N.Y. 1968, U.S. Dist. Ct. (so. and ea. dists.) N.Y. 1973, U.S. Tax Ct. 1973, U.S. Ct. Appeals (2d cir.) 1981, U.S. Supreme Ct. 1980, U.S. Dist. Ct. (we. dist.) N.Y. 1996. Atty. Nassau County Legal Svcs., Freeport, N.Y., 1973-74; asst. corp. counsel City of Yonkers, 1977-78; from assoc. to ptnr. Epstein, Becker & Green, P.C., N.Y.C., 1978-94; ptnr. Winston & Strawn, 1994—. Adj. prof. Elizabeth Seton Coll., Yonkers, 1982-83; mem. NYU exec. coun. Met. Ctr. for Ednl. Rsch. Devel. and Tng., 1987-90; mediator Vol. Mediation Panel, U.S. Dist. Ct. (so. dist.) N.Y., 1997—, U.S. Dist. Ct. (ea. dist.) N.Y., 1999—. Mem. Hastings-on-Hudson (N.Y.) Sch. Bd., 1984-93, v.p., 1986, 87-88, pres., 1989-90, 92-93; bd. dirs. Associated Blind, 1993-95, Nat. Child Labor Com., 2001—, Liberal Arts Alumni Coun., Pa. State U., 2001—; bd. dirs. Search for Change, 1996—, sec., 1998—; bd. dirs. Pa. State Profl. Women's Network of N.Y., 1996—, pres., 1998-2000. Mem. ABA (internat. law sect., litigation and labor law sect.), N.Y. State Bar Assn. (labor law sect., comml. litigation sect.), Women's Bar Assn., Fed. Bar Coun., Pa. State Alumni Club (v.p. Westchester County 1985-87), Phi Beta Kappa, Alpha Kappa Delta, Phi Gamma Mu, Pi Kappa Phi. Office: Winston & Strawn 200 Park Ave New York NY 10166-0005

SAVITZ, FRED, education educator; b. Phila., Sept. 2, 1946; m. Jill Lynn, Dec. 21, 1968; children: Ryan, Ian. BA, Ursinus Coll., 1968; EdM, Temple U., 1970, EdD, 1977. Asst. prof. St. Joseph's U., Phila., 1980-86; divsn. chairperson Neumann Coll., Aston, Pa., 1986-92, prof., 1992—. Motivational spkr. Chester (Pa.) Edn. Found. Author (curriculum): Odyssey of the Mind; contbr. articles to profl. jours. Mem. Pa. Assn. of Colls. and Tchr. Educators (bd. dirs. 2000—). Avocations: running, music. Home: 1532 Willowbrook Ln Villanova PA 19085 E-mail: fsavitz@home.com.

SAVITZ, MARTIN HAROLD, neurosurgeon; b. Boston, Jan. 20, 1942; s. Nathan and Bernice Beatrice (Segal) S.; m. Susan Rayna Gordon, June 23, 1968 (div. Sept. 1977); 1 child, Sean Isaac; m. Harmony Gwynne Keys, Oct. 28, 1979; 1 child, Ariel Austryn. AB, Harvard U., 1963; MD, Hahnemann U., 1969; MS in Psychology, Calif. Coast U., 1998. Diplomate Am. Bd. Neurol. Surgery, Am. Bd. Clin. Neurol. Surgery, Nat. Bd. Med. Examiners, Am. Bd. Forensic Medicine, Am. Bd. Minimally Invasive Spinal Surgery. Intern Boston City Hosp., 1969-70; resident in neurosurgery Mount Sinai Hosp., N.Y.C., 1970-74; clin. instr. dept. neurosurgery Mt. Sinai Sch. Medicine, 1974-82, asst. clin. prof., 1982-86, assoc. clin. prof., 1986-97. Vis. prof. neurosurgery Med. Coll. Pa.-Hahnemann Sch. Medicine, 1998-99, adj. prof. bioethics, 1998—; provost, dean acad. affairs, prof. med. rsch. Am. Internat. U., 1999—; adj. prof. pain mgmt. U. N.Mex. Sch. Medicine, 2002-; adj. prof. surgery, U. Health Services, Antigua; attending neurosurgeon Nyack (N.Y.) Hosp., 1974-99, Good Samaritan Hosp., Suffern, N.Y., 1974-99, Cmty. Hosp., Dobbs Ferry, N.Y., 1995-99, Westchester Med. Ctr., Valhalla, N.Y., 1998-99; mem. pres.'s coun. Harvard Coll., 1991-99, marshal of commencement, 1993—, admissions and fin. aid com., 1978—; mem. alumni bd. trustees Hahnemann U., 1991-94; head exam com. Am. Bd. Clin. Neurosurgery, 1995-99; lectr. in field. Contbg. editor Mt. Sinai Jour. Medicine, 1976-90, asst. editor, 1990—; mem. editl. bd. Jour. Orthopaedic Neurol. Medicine and Surgery, 1991-99; exec. editor Minimally Invasive Global Update, 1999—; editor-in-chief Jour. Mininally Invasive Spinal Technique, 2000—; asst. editor Jour. Royal Coll. Physicians and Surgeons, 2000—; contbr. chpts. to textbooks, numerous articles to profl. jours. Named Internat. Man of Yr., Internat. Biographical Ctr., 1994. Fellow: ACS, Am. Back Soc., Am. Acad. Minimally Invasive Spinal Medicine and Surgery (exec. dir. 1999—), Internat. Biog. Ctr. (dep. dir. gen. 2001—, Man of Yr. 1994), Murphy Ctr. for Codification of Human Orgnl. Law, Am. Acad. Neurol. Orthopaedic Surgeons (bd. dirs. 1994—99, Lifetime Achievement award 1998), N.Y. Acad. Medicine, Am. Biog. Inst. (Man of Yr. 1995), Royal Coll. Physicians and Surgeons (U.S., exec. dir. 2000—01, prof. minimally invasive spinal surgery, vice chancellor 2002—), Internat. Coll. Surgeons (chmn.-elect U.S. sect. neurosurgery 1992, chmn. 1993, exec. com. 1994, chmn.-elect 1995, chmn. 1996, bd. regents 1997—2002, v.p. 1998—2000), Phila. Coll. Physicians, Am. Forensic Examiners Coll. (ethics com. 1995—); mem.: AAAS, AMA, N.Y. Acad. Scis., Hastings Ctr., Internat. Soc. Minimal Intervention in Spinal Surgery, Internat. Fedn. of Surg. Colls., N.Y. State Neurosurg. Soc., Congress Neurol. Surgeons, N.Y. Soc. Neurosurgery, Am. Coun. Bd. Certification (exec. dir. 2001—), Am. Fedn. Med. Accreditation (vice-chmn. 1997, chmn. 1998—99), Am. Assn. Neurol. Surgeons, John Harvard Soc., Phi Delta Epsilon, Alpha Omega Alpha. Jewish. Avocations: travel to all 7 continents, photography of rare fauna and flora, archeology. Home: Hobbit Holw New City NY 10956 Office: 30 Old Phillips Hill Rd New City NY 10956-2108 Fax: 845 634-5075. E-mail: drbcasey@aol.com.

SAVITZ, MAXINE LAZARUS, aerospace company executive; b. Balt., Feb. 13, 1937; d. Samuel and Harriette (Miller) Lazarus; m. Sumner Alan Savitz, Jan. 1, 1961; children: Adam Jonathan, Alison Carrie. BA in Chemistry magna cum laude, Bryn Mawr Coll., 1958; PhD in Organic Chemistry, MIT, 1961. Instr. chemistry Hunter Coll., N.Y.C., 1962-63; sr. electrochemist Mobility Equipment Rsch. and Devel. Ctr., Ft. Belvoir, Va., 1963-68; prof. chemistry Federal City Coll., Washington, 1968-72; program mgr. NSF, 1972-74; dir. FEA Office Bldgs. Policy Rshc. U.S. Dept. Energy, 1974-75, dir. div. indsl. conservation, 1975-76, from dir. div. bldgs. and community systems to dep asst sec., 1975-83; pres. Lighting Rsch. Inst., 1983-85; asst. to v.p. engring. Ceramic Components div. The Garrett Corp., 1985-87; gen. mgr. ceramic components divsn. AlliedSignal Inc., Torrance, Calif., 1987-99; gen. mgr. tech. partnerships Honeywell, 1999—2001, ret., 2001. Bd. dirs. Am. Coun. for Energy Efficient Economy, EPRI; cons. State Mich. Dept. Commerce, 1983, N.C. Alternative Energy Corp., 1983, Garrett Corp., 1983, Energy Engring. Bd., Nat. Rsch. Bd., 1986—93, Office Tech. Assessment, U.S. Congress Energy Demand Panel, 1987—91; nat. materials adv. bd. NRC, 1989—94; bd. dirs. U.S. Advanced Ceramic Assn., 1989—98, chmn., 1992; adv. com. divsn. ceramics/materials ORNL, 1989—92, adv. com. dir., 1992—96; mem. lab. adv. com. Pacific N.W. Nat. Lab., 2000—; adv. bd. Sec. Energy, 1992—; mem. Def. Sci. Bd., 1993—96; vis. com. adv. tech. Nat. Inst. Stds. and Tech., 1993—98, Nat. Sci. Bd., 1999—. Editor Energy and Bldgs.; contbr. articles to profl. jours. Mem. policy com. NAE, 1994-98. NSF postdoctoral fellow, 1961, 62, NIH predoctoral fellow, 1960, 61. Mem. Nat. Acad. Engring. E-mail: maxinesavitz@aol.com.

SAVITZ, SAMUEL J. actuarial consulting firm executive; b. Phila., Dec. 23, 1936; s. Paul and Ann (Gechman) S.; m. Selma Goldberg, June 15, 1958; children: Jacqueline Beverly, Steven Leslie, Michelle Lynn. BS in Adminstrn., Temple U., 1958; postgrad., 1965, U. Pa., 1960-62. Pension analyst provident Mut. Life Ins. Co., Phila., 1958-61; v.p. The Wirkman Co., 1961-64; pres. Samuel J. Savitz & Assoc., Inc., 1964-86; sr. prin. Laventhol & Horwath, 1986-90; chmn. Savitz Orgn., Inc., 1990—. Vis. lectr. U. Pa., Phila., 1960, La. State U., 1972-74; faculty Villanova U., 1971-75; cons. in field. Contbr. articles to profl. jours. Mem. pension com. Fedn. JewishAgys., Phila., 1960; bd. dirs. Am. com. Weizmann Inst. Sci., 1984-85, Phila. All-Star Forum, 1987-95, Mann Music Ctr., 1992—; trustee Fgn. Policy Rsch. Inst., 1996—, Pa. Acad. Fine Arts, 1998—, Nat. Liberty Mus. and Edn. Ctr., 1999—, Am. Interfaith Inst., 1999—, Encore Series, Inc., 1999—; pres. Philly Pops, 1999—, Florentine Festivals USA, Inc., 2000—, Regional Performing Arts Ctr., 2002—, Kimmel Ctr. for the Performing Arts, 2002—, Nat. Mus. of Am. Jewish History, 2002—. With USAR, 1954-62. Mem. Am. soc. Pension Actuaries (dir. 1969-75), Union League Phila. Jewish. Home: 470 Conshohocken State Rd Bala Cynwyd PA 19004-2639 Office: 1845 Walnut St Philadelphia PA 19103-4708

SAVITZKY, EVELYN ROBBINS, information specialist, librarian; b. Yonkers, N.Y. d. Samuel and Tanya (Sanoff) Robbins; m. Abraham Savitzky, Nov. 2, 1942; children: Stephen, Alan. BA, SUNY, Albany, 1943; MLS, So. Conn. State U., 1966. Technician physics dept. Nat. Bur. Stds., Washington, 1942; lab. asst. organic chemistry Rockefeller Inst., Princeton, N.J., 1942-45; library asst. Westport (Conn.) Bd. Edn., 1960-66; librarian Perkin-Elmer Corp., Norwalk, Conn., 1966-84; library cons. ITT Corp., Stamford., 1979; lib. cons. NYNEX, White Plains, N.Y., 1984-91, Engring. Socs. Lib., N.Y.C., 1991-93; lib. and info. specialist, v.p. Silvermine Resources Inc., 1984-97; lib. and info. specialist various companies, 1993—. Mem. Conn. state adv. bd. State Lib., Hartford, 1989-91; mem. bd. Bibliomation lib. automation, Stratford, Conn., 1993-95. Author, actress: (film) How to Search Nat. Tech. Info. Svcs. Files, 1983; contbr. chpt. to Computer Online Database Literature Searching, 1985. V.p., mem. bd. Wilton (Conn.) Lib. Bd., 1982-95; chmn. Weir Preserve Stewardship com., Wilton, Conn., 1994-99; librarian Save the Sound, Stamford, Conn., 1992-98. Named Outstanding Lib. Trustee of Yr., Conn. Assn. Lib. Trustees, 1995. Mem. Spl. Libs. Assn., Assn. Ind. Info. Profls., We. Conn. Lib. Coun. Avocations: gardening, needlework, reading, travel, nonprofit catalog work. Home: 4236 Longshore Way S Naples FL 34119 E-mail: abesa@infi.net.

SAVOCCHIO, JOYCE A. former mayor; b. Erie, Pa. d. Daniel and Esther Savocchio BA in History, Mercyhurst Coll., 1965; MEd, U. Pitts., 1969; cert. secondary sch. adminstrn., Edinboro U., 1975; LLD (hon.), Gannon U., 1990. Tchr. social studies Erie Sch. Dist., 1965-85, asst. prin. Strong Vincent High Sch., 1985-89, tchr. coord. high sch. task force, 1971-75; pres. Erie Edn. Assn., 1975-76; mem. coun. City of Erie, 1981-90, pres. coun., 1983, mayor, 1990—2001. Mem., past pres. Pa. League League of Cities and Municipalities, Northwestern Pa. Mayors' Roundtable; mem. subcoms. on transp. and comms. U.S. Conf. of Mayors; mem., sec. Electoral Coll. for Commonwealth of Pa.; v.p. Christopher Columbus Found.; past pres., mem. Coun. of Govts. of the Greater Erie Area. Past pres. Erie Hist. Mus.; mem. Pa. Gov.'s Flagship Commn., Cmty. Task Force on Drug and Alcohol Abuse; treas., v.p., pres. Erie Area Job Partnership Tng., Inc. Named Woman of Yr., Dem. Women Erie, 1981, Italian Am. Women's Assn., 1987, Outstanding Citizen of Yr., MECA United Cerebral Palsy, 1991; recipient Disting. Alumna award Mercyhurst Coll., 1990, Disting. Citizen award French Creek coun. Boy Scouts Am., 1991, Tree of Life award Jewish Nat. Fund, 1995; named to Pa. Honor Roll of Women. Roman Catholic.*

SAVOIE, JAMES ANTHONY, university official; b. Hastings, Minn., Aug. 19, 1963; s. Paul Anthony and Arlene Marie Palmer Savoie; m. Jennifer Caroline Meisle, Oc. 22, 1965; 1 child, Caroline. BA, U. St. Thomas, Minn., 1985; MA, U. Maine, Orono, 1988; postgrad., NYU, 1989. Dir. acad. svcs. NYU-Tisch Sch. of the Arts, 1989-2000; asst. dean acad. affairs Phila. U., 2000—. Mng. dir. Richard Schechner's East Coast Artists, N.Y.C., 1996-98. Mem. Assn. Theatre in Higher Edn. Democrat. Avocations: travel, reading, research. Office: Phila U Henry Ave and School House Ln Philadelphia PA 19144 Fax: (215) 951-2569. E-mail: savoiej@philau.edu.

SAVOIE, LEONARD NORMAN, transportation company executive; b. Manchester, N.H., Aug. 8, 1928; s. Joseph Peter and Angelina (Desmarais) S.; m. Elsie Anne Berscht, June 9, 1951; children: Deborah Anne, Judith Lynn, Andrew Peter. BS, Queen's U., 1952; MBA, U. Detroit, 1955. Indsl. engr. Kelsey-Hayes Can. Ltd., Windsor, Ont., Can., 1952-60; mgmt. cons. P.S. Ross & Partners, Toronto, 1960-64; pres., gen. mgr. Kelsey-Hayes Can. Ltd., 1964-70; pres., chief exec. officer Algoma Central Ry., Sault Ste. Marie, Ont., 1970-93, vice-chmn., 1993-96. Bd. dirs. Can. Gen. Ins. Co., E-L Fin. Corp. Ltd., Empire Life Ins. Co., Newaygo Forest Products Ltd., Gt. Lakes Power Ltd. Bd. dirs. United Appeal. Mem. Profl. Engrs. Ont., Engring. Inst. Can., Canadian, Sault Ste. Marie chambers commerce. Clubs: Rotary, Toronto, Toronto Ry, Sault Ste. Marie Golf. Office: 517 Conservation Dr Brampton ON Canada L6T 3S1 E-mail: lens@sprint.ca.

SAVOIE, PAUL-ANDRÉ, information technology executive; BA in Commerce, Concordia U. Pres., tech. dir. R.A.N.K.I.N. Techs.; pres. Datacom Wireless Corp., Laval, Canada, 1999—. Gov. Le Portage; bd. dirs. Fondation Roméo Dallaire, Ambulance St.-Jean. Named one of Top 40 Under 40, 2002. Office: Datacom Wireless Corp 440 Armand-Frappier Blvd Ste 350 Laval QC Canada H7V 4B4

SAVOLT, LOUANN SUE, retailer; b. Ft. Wayne, Ind., Sept. 28, 1942; d. Harold Edwin and Norma Esther (Mertz) Hartman; m. Larry Gene Savolt, Sept. 6, 1980; children: Neil Reith, Sheila Reith. AD in Nursing, Garden City Community Coll., 1977. RN, Kans. Health nurse Garden City Community Coll., Kans., 1977-80; staff nurse St. Catherine Hosp., Garden City, 1983; owner, mgr. Personally Yours, Garden City, 1984—; ptnr. Big Sky Farms, Inc., 1986—. Vol. hot line Family Crisis Svcs., Finney County, Kans., 1982-84; pub. edn. chmn. Am. Cancer Soc., Finney County, 1978-84; co-chmn. Coalition for Prevention of Child Abuse and Neglect, Finney County, 1978-79, chmn., 1979-80. Recipient Svc. award Finney County Am. Cancer Soc., 1981, Family Crisis Svcs., 1984. Mem. NAFE, Women's C. of C. Avocations: reading, snowmobiling, travel. Home: RR 2 Box 51 Holcomb KS 67851-9803

SAVOY, DOUGLAS EUGENE, bishop, religious studies educator, explorer, writer; b. Bellingham, Wash., May 11, 1927; s. Lewis Dell and Maymie (Janett) S.; m. Elvira Clarke, Dec. 5, 1957 (div.); 1 son, Jamil Sean (dec.); m. Sylvia Ontaneda, July 7, 1971; children: Douglas Eugene, Christopher Sean, Sylvia Jamila. Student, U. Portland, 1947-8; DST, D Canon and Sacred Law, Jamilian U. of the Ordained, 1980. Ordained to ministry Internat. Community of Christ Ch., 1962, bishop, 1971. Head bishop Internat. Community of Christ Ch., 1971—; lectr. in ministerial tng. studies, 1972—; pastor Univ. Chapel, Reno, 1979—; founder Jamilian Parochial Sch., 1976; chancellor, founder Sacred Coll. of Jamilian Theology; pres., founder Jamilian U. of the Ordained, 1980; pres. Advs. for Religious Rights and Freedoms; chmn. World Coun. for Human Spiritual Rights, 1984—; head Jamilian Order of Patriarchs, 1990—; engaged in newspaper pub. West Coast, 1949-56; began explorations in jungles east of Andes in Peru to prove his theory that high civilizations of Peru may have had their origin in jungles, 1957; pres., founder Andean Explorers Found & Ocean Sailing Club, Reno. Expedition dir. Grand Ophir Sea Expedition; capt. Feathered Serpent III-Ophir, 1997-98. Author: Antisuyo, The Search for Lost Cities of the High Amazon, 1970, Vilcabamba, Last City of the Incas, 1970, The Cosolargy Papers, vol. 1, 1970, vol. 2-3, 1972, The Child Christ, 1973, Arabic edit., 1976, Japanese edit., 1981, The Decoded New Testament, 1974, Arabic edit., 1981, Millenium Edition, 1983, On The Trail of The Feathered Serpent, 1974, Code Book and Community Manual for Overseers, 1975, Prophecies of Jamil, First Prophecy to the Americas, vol. 1, 1976, Second Prophecy to the Americas, 1976, The Secret Sayings of Jamil, The Image and the Word, vol. 1, 1976, vol. 2, 1977, Project X— The Search For the Secrets of Immortality, 1977, Prophecy to the Races of Man, Vol. 2, 1977, Solar Cultures of The Americas, 1977, Dream Analysis, 1977, Vision Analysis, 1977, Christoanalysis, 1978, The Essaei Document: Secrets of an Eternal Race, 1978, Millennium edit., 1983, The Lost Gospel of Jesus: Hidden Teachings of Christ, 1978, Millennium edit., 1983, Secret Sayings of Jamil, vol. 3., 1978, vol. 4, 1979, Prophecy to The Christian Churches, vol. 3, 1978, The Sayings, vol. 4, 1979, Solar Cultures of Oceania, 1979, Prophecy of The End Times, vol. 4, 1980, Solar Cultures of Israel, vols. 1 and 2, 1980, Solar Cultures of China, 1980, Christotherapy, 1980, Christophysics, 1980, Christodynamics, 1980, Code Book of Prophecy, 1980, The Sayings, vol. 5, 1980, vol. 6, 1981, Solar Cultures of India, 1981, Prophecy on the Golden Age of Light and the Nation of Nations, Vol. 5, 1981, Solar Cultures of Israel, vol. 3, 1981, The Counsels, 1982, Prophecy of the Universal Theocracy, vol. 6, 1982, Prophecy of the New Covenant, vol. 7, 1982, The Book of God's Revelation, 1983, Miracle of the Second Advent, 1984, Clerical Studies in Theology, Book I, Book II, Book III, Book IV, Transformative Theology: The School of Revelation, Transformative Theology: The School of Prophecy, Liturgical Theology: Preparation for Advanced Degrees, 1993; over 400 audio tape rec. lectures, 1974—, numerous others.; dir. documentary film Adventure: Trail of the Feathered Serpent, 1970, Lost City of the Andes, 1987; wrote, dir. videos Royal Roads to Discovery, Mystery of the Essenes of Old Israel, Secrets From the High Andes of Peru, 1993, The Gran Vilaya Expeditions, 1996; contbr. articles on Peruvian cultures to mags., also articles on philosophy and religion; discoverer lost city of Incas at Vilcabamba Cuzco, numerous ancient cities in Amazonia including Gran Pajaten, Gran Vilaya, Monte Peruvia, Twelve Cities of the Condor, Gran Saposoa. Trustee in Trust Head Bishop Internat. Community of Christ. Served with AS USNR, 1944-46. Decorated Order of the Grand Cross Senate of Peru, 1989; recipient Participant's medallion Seawanhaka Yacht Club, 1977; Gold medal Ministry Industry and Tourism Peru, Silver Hummingbird, 1987; Silver medal and scroll City of Ica, Peru; honored with Gene Savoy Day by City of Reno, 1996, numerous exploring awards. Mem. Geog. Soc. Lima, Andean Explorers Found., Ocean Sailing Club (Explorer of the Century 1989, Flag awards), World Coun. for Human Spiritual Rights, Advs. for Religious Rights and Freedoms, Authors Guild, Explorers Club (N.Y.C., Flag awards), L.A. Yacht Club. Home: 2025 La Fond Dr Reno NV 89509-3025 Office: 643 Ralston St Reno NV 89503-4436 E-mail: gene@savoy.reno.nv.us. *One who makes dreams come true is that person who gets an idea, figures out how to make it work and then throws all of his energy into the project, stopping at nothing.*

SAVOY, SUZANNE MARIE, advanced practice nurse; b. N.Y.C., Oct. 18, 1946; d. William Joseph and Mary Patricia (Moclair) S. BS, Columbia U., 1970; M in Nursing, UCLA, 1978. RN, cert. clin. nurse specialist, cert. critical care nurse. Staff nurse MICU, transplant Json Meml. Hosp., Miami, 1970-72; staff nurse MICU Boston U. Hosp., 1972-74, VA Hosp., Long Beach, Calif., 1974-75; staff nurse MIRU Cedars-Sinai Med. Ctr., L.A., 1975-77; critical care clin. nurse specialist Anaheim (Calif.) Meml. Hosp., 1978-81; practitioner, instr. Rush-Presbyn.-St. Luke's Med. Ctr. Coll. Nursing, Chgo., 1982-88; rsch. assoc. dept. neurosurgery Rush U., 1984-88; clin. rsch. assoc. Medtronic, Inc. Drug Adminstrn. Sys., Mpls., 1988-91; staff nurse crit. care Harper Hosp., Detroit, 1992-93; clin. nurse specialist, surg./trauma crit. care Detroit Receiving Hosp., 1993-95; clin. instr. Wayne State U. Coll. of Nursing, Detroit, 1991-96, adj. faculty staff, 1996-98. Program coord. Crit. Care ACNP-CC MSN, Wayne State U., 1993-96; adult crit. care clin. nurse specialist Saginaw Gen. Hosp., 1996-98; card. clin. nurse specialist Covenant Healthcare Sys., Saginaw, 1998—; neurosci. clinician acute stroke unit Harper Hosp., Detroit, 1989; edn. cons. Crit. Care Svcs., Inc., Orange, Calif., 1979-81. Co-author articles for profl. jours. Mem. Am. Assn. Neurosci. Nurses (treas. Ill. chpt. 1983-85, pres. 1986-87, SE Mich. chpt. 1992-98, bd. dirs., treas., program chair), Am. Assn. Crit. Care Nurses (bd. dirs. Long Beach chpt. 1981-82, treas. NEMC chpt. 1999-2001), Assn. Healt Care Quality (treas. 2002—, Am. Assn. Spinal Cord Injury Nursing (mem. rsch. com. 1993-95), Lambda and Gamma Phi (bd. dirs. 1994-96), Sigma Theta Tau. Roman Catholic. E-mail: ssavoy@chs-mi.com.

SAVRIN, LOUIS, lawyer; b. Phila., Jan. 20, 1927; s. William Philip and Anna (Sass) S.; m. Barbara J. Schwimmer, Jan. 16, 1954; children: Jonathan Eric, Philip Wade, Daniel Scott. BS, N.Y. U., 1948; JD, U. Pa., 1951. Bar: N.Y. 1952. Atty. tax dept. Arthur Young & Co. (C.P.A.'s), N.Y.C., 1951-55; pvt. practice, 1955—. Gen. counsel, sec. Pickwick Internat., Inc., N.Y.C., 1965-77 Assoc. editor: U. Pa. Law Rev, 1949-51. Mem. sch. bd. Dist. 21, Bklyn., 1962-68. With AUS, 1945-46. Mem. N.Y. State Bar Assn., N.Y. County Lawyers Assn., Real Estate Tax Rev. Bar Assn.; mem. B'nai B'rith (pres. lodge 1957-59, named to lodge Hall of Fame 1967, Torch of Freedom award Anti-Defamation League 1982) Clubs: Mason. Home: 50 Park Ave Apt 17H New York NY 10016-3082 Office: 60 E 42nd St New York NY 10165-0006

SAVRUN, ENDER, engineering executive, researcher, engineer; b. Adana, Turkey, July 29, 1953; came to U.S., 1978; s. Yusuf and Nemide Savrun; m. Canan Erdamar, Oct. 23, 1979; children: Altay, Seray. BS, Istanbul (Turkey) Tech. U., 1976, MS, 1978; PhD, U. Wash., 1986. Rsch. engr. Charlton Industries, Redmond, Wash., 1984-85; rsch. scientist Flow Industries, Kent, 1985-87, Photon Scis., Bothell, 1987-88; mgr. rsch. Keramont Rsch. Corp., Tucson, 1988-89; v.p. R & D Keramont Corp., 1989-92; founder, pres. Sienna Techs., Inc., 1992—. Contbr. articles to profl. jours.; patentee in field. Turkish Govt. scholar, 1979. Mem. Materials Rsch. Soc., Am. Soc. for Metals, Am. Ceramic Soc. Avocations: cross-country skiing, camping, travel.

SAVUKINAS, ROBERT STEVEN, educator; b. Washington, June 2, 1971; s. John and Margaret Savukinas. BA in Spanish and Politics, Duquesne U., 1993; MA in Spanish Lit., Cath. U. Am., 1997; postgrad., George Washington U., 1998—. Staff asst. U.S. Ho. of Reps., Washington, 1993-94; instr. in Spanish Cath. U. Am., 1995-97; instr. Acad. of Holy Cross, Kensington, Md., 1997-99; grad. asst. George Washington U., Washington, 1999—2001; dir. info. mgmt. Health Resource Ctr., 2000—. Contbr. articles to profl. jours. Capt. USAR, 1993—. Army ROTC scholar Dept. Def., 1990. Mem. Am. Assn. Tchrs. Spanish and Portuguese, Am. Translators Assn., Am. Assn. CCs. Republican. Roman Catholic. Avocations: car racing, boating. Home: 1600 N Oak St Arlington VA 22209 Office: Health Resource Ctr 2121 K St NW Ste 220 Washington DC 20037 E-mail: rss@gwu.edu.

SAWABINI, WADI ISSA, retired dentist; b. Jaffa, Palestine, Jan. 14, 1917; s. Issa J. and Julia C. (Malak) S.; m. Harriet Colgate Abbe Lack, Aug. 6, 1949; children— Wadi' Issa, Frederick Lack, Stuart John, Julia Malak. Student, College des Ecoles Chrétiennes, 1924-32; D.D.S., Am. U. Beirut, 1940. Grad. study Forsyth Dental Infirmary, 1940-41; intern Med. Center Hosp. Vt. (formerly DeGoesbriand Meml. Hosp.), Burlington, 1941-42; attending staff; assoc. pvt. practice Dr. Charles I. Taggart, 1942-51; pvt. practice Burlington, 1951-88, ret.; instr. oral pathology U. Vt., 1951-58; dir. U. Vt. (Sch. Dental Hygiene), 1953-72; asst. prof. oral hygiene U. Vt. (Coll. Medicine), 1958-72; chief dental staff Mary Fletcher Hosp., 1958-68, assoc. prof. dept. allied health scis., 1969-72. Mem. adv. bd. Vt. Pub. Health Dept.; mem. Vt. Bd. Health, 1980-86; v.p. bd. dirs. Overlake Day Sch., 1962-63; mem. Ethan Allen Homestead Fundraising Com., 1990—. Paul Harris fellow Burlington Rotary. Fellow Internat. Coll. Dentists (mem. exec. council 1950-54), Am. Coll. Dentists; mem. Vt. Dental Soc. (pres. 1956-57, mem. bd. rev., Disting. Service award 1972), New Eng. Dental Soc., Champlain Valley Dental Soc., C. of C., ADA, Fedn. Dentaire Internat. Republican. Episcopalian (vestryman). Clubs: Mason (Shriner), Rotary (dir. 1955-56, pres. 1961-62), Ethan Allen (Burlington). Home: 512 Acorn Ln Gardenside Shelburne VT 05482-7316 E-mail: wsawabini@iopener.net. *I attribute my life's happiness to my alma mater, The American Univeristy of Beirut. It gave me technical expertise and love to seek knowledge, international understandings, and service to fellowman without regard to color nationality or religion.*

SAWCZUK, IHOR S. urologist; b. N.Y.C., Oct. 5, 1952; s. Stefan and Stefania (Mruczkewycz) S. BA, NYU, 1974; MD, Med. Coll. of Pa., 1979. Diplomate Am. Bd. Urology. Chief Allen Pavilion Urology Columbia-Presbyn. Med. Ctr., N.Y.C., 1988—99; prof. urology Columbia U., 1993—, vice chmn. Dept. of Urology, 1994—2001; chmn. urology Hackensack (NJ) U. Med. Ctr., 2001—, chief urologic oncology Cancer Ctr. Adv. bd. Nat. Kidney Cancer Assn., 1994—; dep. dir. Internat. Coop. Urological Edn. Project, 1994-96. Co-editor: (book) Urologic Clinics of North America, 1993. Counselor Boy Scouts of Am., N.J., 1970—; bd. dirs. Children of Chernobyl, Short Hills, N.J., 1992-98. Recipient Young Investigator award Nat. Kidney Found., 1987. Mem. ACS, Am. Urological Assn. (scholar 1986), N.Y. Acad. Scis., Soc. Internat. de Urologie, Soc. Urologic Oncology.

SAWDEY, SHERRY N. real estate broker; b. Boulder, Colo., July 21; d. William L. and Evelyn Fae Sheets; m. Robert I. Sawdey, Aug. 31, 1962; children: Richard, LeeRoy. Grad., Realtors Inst. Utah, 1991. Cert. residential specialist. Broker assoc. Wardley Better Home & Gardens Corp., Heber City, Utah, 1990—. Mem. Utah Assn. Realtors (conv. com.), Wasatch County Bd. Realtors (v.p. 1985, pres. 1986, sec.-treas. 1987-89, chmn. membership 1988-91). Home: 2777 S Mill Rd Heber City UT 84032-3518 Office: Wardley Better Homes & Gdns 76 E Center St Heber City UT 84032-1941

SAWERS, PETER RITCHIE, management consultant, educator, retired; b. Milw., Apr. 3, 1933; s. Arthur Ritchie and Bernardine (Chesley) S.; m. Mary Howell, Apr. 4, 1959; children: Gregory, Andrew, Emily. BA, Yale U., 1955; MBA, Harvard U., 1957. Cert. mgmt. cons., chartered fin. analyst. Rsch. analyst Dominick & Dominick, N.Y.C., 1957-59; v.p. Chesley & Co., Chgo., 1959-62; sr. cons. IIT Rsch. Inst., 1962-65; sr. lectr. Robert Gordon U., Aberdeen, Scotland, 1974-75; sr. v.p. Hayes/Hill Inc., Chgo., 1965-88; exec. dir. Towers Perrin, Sydney, Australia, 1988-90, ret. Australia, 1990. Bd. dirs. Exec. Svc. Corps., Chgo.; mem. Internat. Exec. Svc. Corps, Stamford, Conn., 1992—. Chmn. Civil Svc. Commn., Evanston, Ill., 1975-85; chmn., bd. dirs. Hadley Sch. for Blind, Winnetka, Ill., 1975-88; trustee Evanston Hist. Soc., 1982-86; mem. Com. for Econ. Devel. Australia, Sydney, 1990; trustee, bd. dirs. Inst. Mgmt. Cons., N.Y.C., 1986-88. Mem. Sheridan Shore Yacht Club (commodore 1992-94). Republican. Avocations: sailing, travel, reading, history. Home: 22 The Landmark Northfield IL 60093

SAWICK, KAREN ANN, real estate agent; b. Elizabeth, N.J., Apr. 6, 1947; d. Florian Albert and Janet Gloria (Anthony) Smiles; m. Richard Henry Sawick, July 6, 1996; children: Robert Richard, Jeffrey Christopher. Student, Fairleigh Dickinson U. Lic. real estate salesperson, N.J. Dental asst. Dr. Ferrec, Ramsey, N.J., 1965-67; office mgr. Dr. Walter Stocker, Basking Ridge, 1974-76; sec.-treas. N.E. Atlantic Airlines, Somers Ct., Westfield, Mass., 1971-76; real estate salesperson Schlott Realtors, Better Homes and Gardens, Chester, N.J., 1976-80. Poet/author: Diamonds and Pearls, 1997. Vol. Morristown Meml. Hosp., 1974; mem. Chaplain's Conf. Somerset County, 1974; active vol. Red Cross, 1976, C. of C., Marion/Ocala. Mem. Suncoast Better Bus. Fedn., Ocala/Marion C. of C., Bd. Realtors of Hunterdon County and Somerset County. Presbyterian. Avocations: writing, humane animal societies. Home: 8919 SW 204th Cir Dunnellon FL 34431-5726

SAWICKI, ZBIGNIEW PETER, lawyer; b. Hohenfels, Germany, Apr. 13, 1949; came to U.S., 1951; s. Witold and Marianna (Tukiendorf) S.; m. Katheryn Marie Loman, Aug. 19, 1972; children: James, Jeffrey, Jessica, Jason. BSChemE, Purdue U., 1972; MBA, Coll. St. Thomas, St. Paul, 1977; JD, Hamline U., 1980. Bar: Minn. 1980, U.S. Dist. Ct. Minn. 1981, U.S. Ct. Appeals (8th cir.) 1981, U.S. Patent and Trademark Office 1981, U.S. Ct. Appeals (fed. cir.) 1982, Can. Patent Office 1994, Can. Trademark Office 1995. Process engr. 3-M Co., St. Paul, 1973-75; process engring. supr. Conwed Corp., 1975-77; shareholder, bd. dirs. Kinney & Lange, Mpls., 1980—. Bd. dirs. Orono (Minn.) Hockey Boosters, 1992—. With USAF, 1970-72. Mem. ABA, Am. Intellectual Property Assn., Internat. Trademark Assn., Minn. Intellectual Property Assn. (past treas.), Am. Legion. Home: 4510 N Shore Dr Mound MN 55364-9602 Office: Kinney & Lange 312 S 3d St Minneapolis MN 55415-1624 E-mail: zpsawicki@kinney.com.

SAWIN, CLARK TIMOTHY, endocrinologist; b. Boston, May 23, 1934; s. W. Clark and E. Loretta (Keegan) S.; m. Leslie, Jan. 10, 1982; children: Jennifer, Philip, Kenneth. BA, Brandeis U., Waltham, Mass., 1954; MD, Tufts U., Boston, 1958. Diplomate Am. Bd. Internal Medicine, Endocrinology and Metabolism. Intern U. Ill. Rsch./Ednl. Hosp., 1958-59; fellow endocrinology Tufts-New Eng. Med. Ctr., 1962-63, 65-66, resident internal medicine, 1963-64, Boston VA Hosp., 1964-65; chief endocrine diabetes sect. Boston VA Med. Ctr., 1966—; prof. medicine Tufts U., Boston, 1981—, Boston U., 1994—. Contbr. over 100 articles to profl. jours. Capt. Med. Corps U.S. Army, 1959-62. Recipient Reynolds award, Am. Physiol. Soc., 1990, Disting. Career Tchg. award Tufts U., 1997. Achievements include definition of changes in thyroid function in older persons. Office: VA Hqrs 810 Vermont Ave NW Washington DC 20420-0001

SAWIRIS, MILAD YOUSSEF, statistician, educator; b. Cairo, Jan. 11, 1922; came to U.S., 1966, naturalized, 1972; s. Youssef Sawiris and Faika Botros Samaan. B.Sc., Cairo U., 1942, diploma in edn., 1944, diploma higher edn., 1959; MA, U. London, 1963, PhD, 1965; MS, Stanford U., 1975. Tchr. math. Egyptian Govt. schs., 1944-48, 57-61, Sudan Govt. schs., 1948-57; mem. faculty Calif. State U., Sacramento, 1966-86, prof. emeritus, 1986—. Author research papers. Mem. Am. Statis. Assn. Mem. Coptic Orthodox Ch. Home: 8308 Caribbean Way Sacramento CA 95826-1657

SAWKAR, LAXMIDAS ANANT, retired internist, oncologist; b. Chendia, India, July 5, 1936; came to U.S., 1967; s. Anant Raghunath and Gopika Anant (Kamat) S.; m. Bharati Krishna Gaitonde, Dec. 7, 1966; children: Vineeta, Ashish. MBBS, Baroda (India) U., 1963, MD, 1966. Diplomate Am. Bd. Internal Medicine, Am. Bd. Medical Oncology. Intern SSG Hosp., Baroda, 1961-62; resident in internal medicine Mt. Sinai Hosp. Svc., Elmhurst, N.Y., 1967, resident in hematology, 1968; fellow in cardiopulmonary Grassland Hosp., Valhalla, 1968-69; fellow in medical oncology U. Kans. Med. Ctr., Kansas City, 1973-74; private practice Shawnee Mission, 1974-2000; section chief hematology-oncology Bethany Med. Ctr., Kansas City, 1976-2000, chmn. dept. medicine, 1993-94, Shawnee-Mission (Kans.) Med. Ctr., 1979-80; dir. Mid Am. Hospice Care, Kansas City, 1991-92; asst. clin. prof. med. U. Kans., 1974-2000; ret., 2000. Pres. Wyandotte County Med. Soc., 1997; pres. med. and dental staff Bethany Med. Ctr., 1998. Contbr. articles to profl. jours. Mem. ACP (chmn. fin. com. Kans. chpt. 1989-91), Am. Coll. Chest Physicians, Am. Soc. Clin. Oncology, Am. Coll. Internat. Physicians. Hindu. Home: 10314 Catalina St Overland Park KS 66207-4010

SAWKO, FELICJAN, civil engineering educator; b. Wilczuki, Poland, May 17, 1937; s. Czeslaw and Franciszka (Nawrot) S.; m. Genowefa Stefania Bak, Apr. 18, 1960; children: Andrew, Barbara, Piotr, Ryszard, Paul. BSc, Leeds (Eng.) U., 1958, MSc, 1960, DSc, 1973. Chartered engr. Civil enr. Rendel, Palmer & Tritton, Eng., 1959-62; lectr. Leeds U., 1962-67; prof. Liverpool (Eng.) U., 1967-86; prof., head dept. civil engring. Sultan Qaboos U., Oman, 1986-95; ret., 1995. Cons. in civl engring., 1962-86. Editor: Developments in Prestressed Concrete, 1978, Computer Methods for Civil Engineers, 1984; contbr. articles to profl. jours. Fellow Instn. Civil Engrs. Roman Catholic. Avocations: bridge, photography, numismatics, travel. Home: 23 Floral Wood Liverpool L17 7HU England

SAWOROTNOW, PARFENY PAVLOVICH, mathematician, educator; b. Ust Medveditskaya, Russia, Feb. 20, 1924; came to U.S., 1949, naturalized, 1965; s. Pavel Ivanovich and Anna Davidovna (Soloview) S.; student U. Graz (Austria), 1946-49; MA (Peirce scholar), Harvard U., 1951, PhD (Shattuck fellow), 1955. Teaching fellow Harvard U., 1953-54; instr. math. Cath. U. Am., Washington, 1954-57, asst. prof., 1957-62, assoc. prof., 1962-67, prof., 1967-96, prof. math. emeritus, 1997—. NSF grantee, 1967, 70; with Georgetown U. and George Washington U., 1971-77. Mem. Am. Math. Soc., Math. Assn. Am., Calcutta Math. Soc., N.Y. Acad. Scis., Sigma Xi. Mem. Eastern Orthodox Ch. Contbr. articles to and referred papers for math. rsch. jours. Home: 6 Avon Pl Hyattsville MD 20782-3328 Office: Cath U Am Dept Math 4th And Michigan Ave NE Washington DC 20064-0001

SAWTELLE, CARL S. psychiatric social worker; b. Boston, July 14, 1927; s. Carl Salvador and Martha (Bellamacina) S.; BA, Suffolk U., Boston, 1951; MSW, Simmons Sch. Social Work, 1953; m. Thelma Florence Ramsay, Aug. 20, 1950; children: Tracy Lynn, Lisa June. Social worker Tewksburry (Mass.) State Hosp., 1952; psychiat. social worker, head psychiat. social worker, dir. clin. social work Taunton (Mass.) State Hosp., 1953-74; 1st dir. clin. social work, Plymouth, Mass., 1974-78; co-founder, v.p. 1st legally established War On Poverty program Triumph, Inc., Taunton; co-founder 1st Greater Taunton Coun. on Alcoholism, 1972. With USCG, 1944-46. 1st lic. social worker in Mass., 1980. Mem. Nat. Assn. Social Workers (co-founder Southeast Mass. chpt. 1957, pres. 1957, Spl. Mass. Chpt. award 1978), Acad. Cert. Social Workers (chmn. 1962-72), Am. Legion, Mass. Mental Health Social Workers Assn. (co-founder, pres. 1972-74, other offices). Created innovated programs, resources, opportunities, svcs. to state mental hosp. patients and their families; mentor to young social workers; contbr. advancement of knowledge, practice quality and standards of psychiat. social work; father of licensing and registration of Social Workers in Mass. Home: 9 Tracywood Rd Canton MA 02021-3501

SAWYER, ANA MARIA RAMIREZ, clinical psychologist; b. Tegucigalpa, Honduras, Mar. 21, 1954; came to U.S., 1965; d. Jaime Antonio Ramirez Quesada and Ofelia Ochoa de Ramirez; m. Richard S. Sawyer, Dec. 21, 1984 (div. June 1990); children: Briant Boru, Rory Conor, Brendan Patrick. Cert. stenographer, Soulé Bus. Coll., 1976; BS, U. South Ala., 1980, MS, 1982. Counselor Cuban Haitian concerns Mobile (Ala.) Mental Health Ctr., 1982; sec. I U.S. Agy. Internat. Devel. Procurement and Contracting, Tegucigalpa, Honduras, 1982; visa examiner Am. Consulate, Am. Embassy, 1982; habilitation supr. Albert P. Brewer Devel. Ctr., Mobile, 1983-85; temp. sec. Kelly Svcs. Inc., 1985-86; contract therapist Cath. Soc. Svcs. Counseling Program, 1985-88; coord. students with spl. needs U. South Ala., 1986-88; coord. day treatment program Searcy Hosp., Mt. Vernon, Ala., 1988-91; behavior mgmt. splst. Albert P. Brewer Devel. Ctr., Mobile, 1991—, habilitation treatment coord. II, 1992—99; adv. dept. mental health and mental retardation State of Ala., 1999—. Bd. mem. Ala. Orgn. Mental Health Technologists and Human Svc. Workers, 1988-89; designer/developer behavioral mgmt. programs; presenter, cons. workshops. Presentor/trainer Cath. Soc. Svcs., Mobile, 1987-88, Cath. Youth Ministries, 1988. Mem. APA (assoc.), Nat. Assn. M's in Psychology, Ala. Assn. M's in Psychology, Ala. Orgn. for Mental Health Technologists and Human Svc. Workers (bd. mem. 1988-89), Ala. Coun. on Learning Disabilities (Mobile County chpt. edn. chmn. 1987), Alpha Lambda Delta, Omicron Delta Kappa. Democrat. Roman Catholic. Avocations: aerobics, fgn. travel, reading, drawing, painting. Home: 2528 Woodland Rd Mobile AL 36693-3063

SAWYER, CHARLES HENRY, anatomist, educator; b. Ludlow, Vt., Jan. 24, 1915; s. John Guy and Edith Mabel (Morgan) S.; m. Ruth Eleanor Schaeffer, Aug. 23, 1941; 1 dau., Joan Eleanor. BA, Middlebury Coll., 1937, DSc honoris causa, 1975; student, Cambridge U., Eng., 1937-38; PhD, Yale, 1941. Instr. anatomy Stanford, 1941-44; assoc., asst. prof., assoc. prof., prof. anatomy Duke U., 1944-51; prof. anatomy UCLA, Los Angeles, 1951-85, prof. emeritus, 1985—, chmn. dept., 1955-63, acting chmn., 1968-69, faculty research lectr., 1966-67. Editorial bd.: Endocrinology, 1955-59, Proc. Soc. Exptl. Biology and Medicine, 1959-63, Am. Jour. Physiology, 1972-75; Author papers on neuroendocrinology. Mem. Internat. Brain Research Orgn. (council 1964-68), AAAS, Am. Assn. Anatomists (v.p. 1969-70, Henry Gray award 1984), Am. Physiol. Soc., Am. Zool. Soc., Neurosci. Soc., Endocrine Soc. (council 1968-70, Koch award 1973), Am. Acad. Arts and Scis., Nat. Acad. Scis., Soc. Exptl. Biology and Medicine, Soc. Study Reprodn. (dir. 1969-71, Hartman award 1977), Internat. Neuroendocrine Soc. (council 1972-76), Hungarian Soc. Endocrinology and Metabolism (hon.), Japan Endocrin Soc. (hon.), Phi Beta Kappa, Sigma Xi. Home: 466 Tuallitan Rd Los Angeles CA 90049-1941 Office: U Calif Sch Medicine Dept Neurobiology Los Angeles CA 90095-1764

SAWYER, CHARLES HENRY, art educator, art museum director emeritus; b. Andover, Mass., Oct. 20, 1906; s. James Cowan and Mary Pepperrell (Frost) S.; m. Katharine Clay, June 28, 1934. BA, Yale U., 1929, MA, 1947; student, Harvard Law Sch., 1929-30; student of Fine Arts, Harvard U. Grad. Sch., 1930-32; LHD, Amherst Coll., 1950; DFA, U. New Hampshire, 1951; LHD, Clark U., 1953. Dir. Addison Gallery of Am. Art, art instr. Phillips Acad., Andover, Mass., 1930-40; dir. Worcester (Mass.) Art Mus., 1940-46; dir. divsn. of the arts, prof. history of art Yale U., New Haven, 1947-56; master Timothy Dwight Coll. Yale U., 1947-53; dean Sch. of Architecture and Design, Yale U., 1947-56; dir. mus. of art U. Mich., Ann Arbor, 1957-72, prof. history of art, 1957-76, dir. emeritus mus. of art, 1973—, prof. emeritus history of art, 1977—. Mem. art adv. commn. Harvard U., 1940-58, Cambridge, , Amherst (Mass.) Coll., 1948-60, Smith Coll., Northampton, Mass. 1948-55, U. Notre Dame, Ind., 1973-82, Smithsonian Art Commn., Smithsonian Instn., Washington, 1953-80; trustee Corning (N.Y.) Mus. of Glass, 1950-75. Author: (book) Art in English Public Schools, 1936; author various articles, exhibition catalogues etc., 1931—. Mem. Art Commn. State of Mass., Boston, 1940-44, Historic Sites Commn., State of New Hampshire, Concord, 1948-58, Arts Coun., State of Mich., Lansing, 1964-72. Named Hon. Mem. NMAA Commn. Washington, 1985—. Fellow Am. Acad. Arts and Scis.; mem. Assn. Art Mus. Dirs. (hon. mem. 1973—), Century Assn. N.Y., Am. Antiquarian Soc. Episcopalian. Avocations: hist. rsch., gardening. Home: 801 W Middle St Apt #172 Chelsea MI 48118

SAWYER, CHARLES S. environmental engineer, engineering educator; b. Jan. 8, 1959; s. Joshua S. Sawyer, Regina S. George; m. Marvel A. Cole; children: Marvin. BSME, U. Sierra Leone, 1980; MS in Chem. Engring., Va. Poly. Inst. and State U., Blacksburg, 1987; PhD in Environ. Engring., U. Conn., 1992. Registered prof. engr., Conn.; cert. qualified environ. profl. Pres., prin. engr. Bryxx Engring. Inc., North Haven, Conn., 2001—; prof. U. Conn., Storrs, 1992—. Bd. dirs. Amistad Am. Inc, 2001—. Contbr. articles. Mem.: ASCE, Conn. Soc. Civil Engrs. (chmn. water resources com. 1995—2000, newsletter editor 2001—), Am. Soc. of Engring. Edn., Am. Geophys. Union. Home and Office: 15 Patten Rd North Haven CT 06473-2828 Home Fax: 203-239-7438; Office Fax: 203-239-7438. Personal E-mail: csswayer@aol.com. Business E-Mail: Bryxxinc@aol.com.

SAWYER, DAVID JONATHAN, educator; b. Fayetteville, N.C., Aug. 26, 1927; s. Noah Devon and Mary Woodie (Jackson) S.; m. Margaret T. Sawyer, June 16, 1950 (dec.); 1 child, Phyllis (dec.); m. Carolyn Gertrude Sawyer, June 29, 1975; children: Phyllis, Lois. Grad. H.S., Fayetteville. Prodn. operator Glidden Chem. Co., Balt.; paraprofl. Balt. City Sch. With U.S. ARmy, 1946. Mem. Homeless Children Balt. (bd. mem., transport rep. 1997—). Democrat. Baptist. Avocations: writing, playing pool, traveling. Home: 3524 Elmora Ave Baltimore MD 21213 Office: 1220 E 20th St Baltimore MD 21218-6314 E-mail: sawyerdj73@aol.com.

SAWYER, DEBORAH CHRISTINE, information services company executive; b. Ince-in-Makerfield, Eng., Jan. 28, 1953; d. Terence John and Joan Margaret (Hatcher) S. BA, Univ. Coll., Toronto, 1974; MLS, U. Toronto, 1976; cert., Brit. Inst. Homeopathy, 2000. Registered nutritional cons., Can. Sch. Natural Nutrition, 1998. Editor CEI/RCE Can. Edn. Assn., Toronto, 1976-79; pres. Info. Plus, 1979—, Buffalo, 1990—. Vis. lectr. SUNY Buffalo, 1994; speaker at confs. and seminars, U.S. and Can. Author: Sawyer's Survival Guide for Info Brokers, 1995, Getting It Right: Avoiding the High Cost, 1998, Sawyer's Success Tactics for Information Businesses, 1998, Smart Services: Competitive Information Strategies, Solutions and Success Stories for Service Businesses, 2002; editor: Tradecraft, vol. I, 1995, vol. II, 1999; columnist Info. Broker, 1987-98, CIR, 1995-2001. Vol. tutor Boys and Girls Club St. Alban's, Toronto, 1993, Frontier Coll./Reading Cir., Toronto, 1989-91; vol. adult literacy tutor, Toronto, 1986-87. Mem. Am. Soc. for Indsl. Security, World Future Soc. Avocations: painting, sewing, walking, swimming, reading. Office: Info Plus 575 Madison Ave 10th Fl New York NY 10022

SAWYER, DIANE (L. DIANE SAWYER), television journalist; b. Glasgow, Ky., Dec. 22, 1945; d. E.P. and Jean W. (Dunagan) S.; m. Mike Nichols, Apr. 29, 1988. BA, Wellesley Coll., 1967. Reporter Sta. WLKY-TV, Louisville, 1967-70; adminstr. press office White House, 1970-74; rschr. Richard Nixon's memoirs, 1974-78; gen. assignment reporter, then Dept. State corr. CBS News, 1978-81; co-anchor Morning News CBS, from 1981, co-anchor Early Morning News, 1982-84; corr., co-editor 60 Minutes CBS-TV, 1984-89; co-anchor Prime Time Live (now known as 20/20) ABC News, 1989—; co-anchor Day One, 1995, Turning Point, 1996, Good Morning Am. ABC News, N.Y.C., 1999—. Recipient 2 Peabody awards for Pub. Svc., 1988, Robert F. Kennedy award 10 Emmy awards, Spl. Dupont award, IRTS Lifetime Achievement award; named to TV Hall of Fame, 1997. Office: Good Morning America 147 Columbus Ave Fl 10 New York NY 10023-5900*

SAWYER, DIANNE M. obstetrician-gynecologist; b. Evanston, Ill., Sept. 11, 1953; d. Tom M. and Cynthia (Lewis) S.; m. David M. Lipkin, Feb. 19, 1983; children: Emily, Michael. BS in Medicine, MD, Northwestern U., 1977. Diplomate Am. Bd. Ob-Gyn. Intern Northwestern U. Med. Ctr., Chgo., 1977-78, resident in ob-gyn., 1978-81. Fellow ACOG.

SAWYER, DIANNE WADDELL, obstetrician-gynecologist; b. Amarillo, Tex., Dec. 24, 1956; d. Lowell Morton and Peggy E. Waddell; m. J. Clay Sawyer, May 11, 1979. BS, Tex. Woman's U., 1977; MD, U. Tex., Galveston, 1982. Diplomate Am. Coll. Ob-gyn. Intern St. Luke's Hosp., Cleve., 1982-83, ob-gyn. resident, 1983-86; pvt. practice ob-gyn. Waco, Tex., 1986—. Chief ob-gyn. Hillcrest Bapt. Med. Ctr., Waco, 1994-97; sec. med. staff Hillcrest Hosp., 1997—, pres.-elect med. staff, 1999, pres. med. staff, 2000; bd. dirs. Hillcrest Bd. Devel., Hillcrest Clins., Waco Family Practice Clin. Bd. dirsmem. Am. Cancer Soc., Waco, 1987-89, Ctr. for Acting Against Sexual Assau Waco, 1989-93, asst. creating sexual assault nurse examiners, 1992-94; sec. bd. dirs. Cameron Park Zoo, treas. 2002. Named United Way Vol. of the Yr., United Way, Waco, 1995, Brian Aynesworth Family Practice Clinic Tchr. of the Yr., Family Practice Clinic, Waco. Mem. Am. Med. Women's Assn., Jr. League Waco (treas. 1996-97, v.p. fin. 1997-98, pres.-elect. 2001-2002, pres. 2002-2003, Excellence in Volunteerism award 1999). Avocations: sailing, reading, gardening. Office: 3115 Pine Ave Ste 903 Waco TX 76708-3250

SAWYER, DOLORES, motel chain executive; b. Shreveport, La., Oct. 16, 1938; d. Orlan B. Greer and Doris Lucile (Sanders) Eckman; m. Raymond Lee Sawyer Jr., June 11, 1960; children: Lisa Kay, Linda Faye. BSN, Northwestern State Coll., 1960, MSN, Tex. Woman's U., 1975. Supr. obstetrics dept. Highland Hosp., Shreveport, La., 1962-64; head nurse (3-11 shift) Scott and White Meml. Hosp., Temple, Tex., 1966-71, dir. of nursing edn., 1975-76; sch. nurse Temple Ind. Sch. Dist., 1971-72; instr. Mary-Hardin Baylor Coll., Belton, Tex., 1972-74; asst. prof., clin. specialist U. Tex. Arlington, 1976-86; v.p. Budget Host Internat., Arlington, Tex., 1986-96, sr. v.p., 1996—. Recipient Amoco Outstanding Tchg. award, 1981. Mem. Sigma Theta Tau. Republican. Methodist. Avocations: reading, tole painting, gardening, crafts, piano. Office: Budget Host Internat Ste B 2307 Roosevelt Dr Arlington TX 76016-5865 E-mail: rsawyerl@airmail.net., mail@budgethost.com.

SAWYER, DONALD E. physician, urologist; b. Cambridge, Mass., Sept. 11, 1944; m. Anne Ross, June 30, 1968. BA, U. Vt., 1966; MD, N.Y. Med. Coll., 1970. Diplomate Am. Bd. Urology. Intern N.Y. Med. Coll., 1970-71, resident, 1971-72, Lahey Clinic, 1972-75; urologist in pvt. practice, Long Beach, Calif., 1979-99, Los Alamitos, 1979-99, Ocean Springs, Pascagoula, Miss., 1999—; asst. prof. urology U. Miss. Med. Ctr, Jackson, 2001—. Contbr. articles to profl. jours. Served as lt. comdr. USN, 1975-79. Mem. Rotary Internat. Avocations: travel, walking. Office: VA Med Ctr Surg Svc (112) 1500 E Woodrow Wilson Dr Jackson MS 39216

SAWYER, FRANK DENZIL, clergyman; b. Brantford, Ont., Can., Jan. 29, 1971; came to U.S., 1999; s. Denzil Brooks and Catherine Louise (Froud) S.; m. Ginnelle Margaret Elliott, Sept. 19, 1998. BA in Philosophy, U. Toronto, Can., 1993; MDiv, U. Toronto, 1997. Ordained deacon, 1997; ordained to ministry Anglican Ch., 1998. Lectr. in English Vyssi Obchodni Podnikatelska Škola, Prague, Czech Republic, 1994-95; curate St. Clement's Ch., Toronto, 1997-99; chaplain St. Clement's Sch., 1997-99, Cathedral Sch. for Boys, Grace Cath., San Francisco, 1999—. Mem. planning com. Anglican/Episcopal Stewardship and Fin. Devel. Confs., 1998, 99; mem. senate Trinity Coll. U. Toronto, 1995-97, mem. of corp., 1992-94; field edn. supr. Ch. Sch. of Pacific, Berkeley, 2000—; co-chair boys study com. Cathedral Sch., 2001—. Wellington scholarship Trinity Coll. U. Toronto, 1990. Mem. Nat. Assn. of Episcopal Schs. (chaplain), Internat. Coalition Boys Schs., Golden Gateway Club. Avocations: traveling, sailing, marathon running. Office: Cathedral Sch for Boys 1275 Sacramento St San Francisco CA 94108

SAWYER, HOWARD JEROME, physician; b. Detroit, Nov. 17, 1929; s. Howard C. and Dorothy M. (Risley) S.; m. Janet Carol Hausen, July 24, 1954; children: Daniel William, Teresa Louise BA in Philosophy, Wayne State U., 1952, MD, 1962, postdoctoral, 1969-72. Diplomate Am. Bd. Preventive Medicine in Occupational and Environ. Medicine. Intern William Beaumont Hosp., Royal Oak, Mich., 1962-63, resident in surgery, 1963-64; chief physician gen. parts div. Ford Motor Co., 1964-66; med. dir. metall. products dept. Gen. Electric Co., Detroit, 1966-73, chem. and metal div., 1972-73; staff physician Detroit Indsl. Clinic, Inc., 1973-74; pres., med. dir. OccuMed Assocs., Inc., Farmington Hills, Mich., 1974-84; dir. OccuMed div. Med. Service Corp. Am., Southfield, 1984-86; dir. occupational, environ. and preventive medicine Henry Ford Hosp., 1987-91; pres. Sawyer Med. Cons., P.C., 1991—. Adj. asst. prof. occupational and environ. health scis. Wayne State U., 1974— , lectr. occpl. and environ. medicine Sch. of Medicine, 1998—; lectr. Sch. Pub. Health, U. Mich., Ann Arbor, 1977-88 ; cons. med. dir. St. Joe Minerals Corp., 1976-87, Chesbrough Pond's Inc., 1979-83; cons. Anaconda, Bendix, Borg Warner Chems., Fed. Mogul, Gen. Electric, Gt. Lakes Chems., other corps. Contbr. articles to profl. jours., chpts. to textbooks. Fellow Am. Coll. Preventive Medicine, Am. Occupational and Environ. Med. Assn., Mich. Occupational and Environ. Med. Assn. (pres. 1986), Am. Acad. Occupational Medicine; mem. AMA, Detroit Occupational Physicians Assn. (pres. 1984), Mich. State Med. Soc., Oakland County Med. Soc., Am. Indsl. Hygiene Assn., Mich. Indsl. Hygiene Soc. E-mail: buzsaw@mediaone.net.

SAWYER, JOHN EDWARD, management educator; b. Florence, Ariz., July 26, 1954; s. Almus Wilmore and Betty (Mossman) S.; m. Dana Lee Strandberg, Aug. 5, 1989; children: Adrian John, Alexander Lyn, Jordan Estelle. BA in Psychology, Calif. State U., Long Beach, 1977; MA in Counseling Edn., Calif. State U., Fresno, 1979; AM in Indsl./Orgnl. Psychology, U. Ill., 1985, PhD of Indsl./Orgnl. Psychology, 1987. Project dir. Youth Svc. Bur., Modesto, Calif., 1979-81; counselor Horizons Youth Svc. Bur., Livermore, 1981-82; lectr., tchg. asst. U. Ill., Urbana, 1982-87; asst. prof. Tex. A&M U., College Station, 1987-91; asst. prof. mgmt. U. Del., Newark, 1991-95, assoc. prof., 1995—, mgmt. area head, 1998—2001, chair dept. bus. adminstrn., 2001—. Human resources rschr. Xerox Corp., Rochester, N.Y., 1985-86; orgnl. cons. Mercy Hosp., Urbana, 1983, Tex. Dept. Mental Health, San Antonio, 1989-90; trainer, cons. DuPont Merck Pharm. Co., Wilmington, 1994, Hercules, Wilmington, 1996. Mem. editl. bd. Jour. Mgmt.; contbr. chpt. in book and articles to profl. jours. Grantee Tex. Engring. Experiment Sta., 1989, Tex. Higher Edn. Coordinating Bd., 1990, Gen. Univ. Rsch. Program, 1993, Ctr. for Info. Sys. Mgmt. Edn. and Rsch., 1994. Mem. APA, Acad. Mgmt. (invited guest editl. bd.), Judgment and Decision Making Soc., Soc. Indsl. and Orgnl. Psychology. Home: 214 Cullen Way Newark DE 19711-6112 Office: Univ Delaware Dept Bus Adm Newark DE 19716 E-mail: sawyerj@be.udel.edu.

SAWYER, MARGO LUCY, artist, educator; b. Washington, May 6, 1958; d. Eugene Douglas and Joan Imogen (Alford) S. BA hons., Chelsea Sch. Art, London, 1980; MFA, Yale U., 1982. Assoc. prof. U. Tex., Austin, 1988—. Vis. artist Chelsea Sch. Art, London, 1982—. One-person shows include Brit. Coun., Bombay, India, 1983, Barbara Toll Fine Arts, N.Y.C., 1989, 91, Sagacho Exhibit Space, Tokyo, 1996, Gallery Gallery, Kyoto, Japan, 1996, Internat. House of Japan, Tokyo, 1996, Austin (Tex.) Mus. Art, 1998, Artplace, 2000, others; group shows include Whitechapel Gallery, London, 1979, ICA, London, 1979, 80, Leo Castelli Gallery, N.Y.C., 1986, Portland (Maine) Mus. Art, 1987, U. Md. Art Gallery, Balt., 1988, Meyers/Bloom Gallery, Santa Monica, Calif., 1989, Archer M. Huntington Art Gallery, Austin, Tex., 1990, 91, 92, 93, 94, Harn Mus. Art, Gainesville, Fla., 1992, Laguna Gloria Art Mus., Austin, 1994, Abilene (Tex.) Outdoor Sculpture exhbn., 1995-96, Artspace A Found. for Contemporary Art, 2000, Finesilver Gallery, San Antonio, 2002; permanent collections include Hyde Park, London, Cityarts Workshop, Portland Mus. Art, Samuel O. Harn Mus. Art, U. Fla., Prudential Ins., Chem. Bank, Champion Paper, and various pvt. collections. Recipient Louis Comfort Tiffany Found. award, 2001; Am. Acad. Rome fellow, 1986-87, Japan Found. visual arts fellow, 1996; Travel grantee Ford Found., 1981, Fulbright rsch. grantee, India, 1982-83, Japan, 1995-96, N.Y. State Coun. on Arts grantee, 1987, Travel grantee NEA, 1994. Office: U Tex Dept Art and Art History Austin TX 78712-1104

SAWYER, MARY CATHERINE, retired hospital administrator; b. Borger, Tex., Dec. 8, 1931; d. Andrew Rodgers and Mary Elizabeth (Slater) Hill; m. Edmond Eugene Sawyer, Aug. 26, 1963; children: Slater Shane, Anthony Barrett, Maronda Rae. BBA, Tex. Tech U., 1956; cert. in med. records, U. Tex. Med. Br., Galveston, 1957. Registered med. adminstr.; cert. coding specialist. Med. record adminstr. Taylor Hosp., Inc., Lubbock, Tex., 1957-63; pvt. practice cons. Paris, 1963-79; med. record adminstr., coding specialist St. Joseph's Hosp., 1979-98; ret., 1998. Mem. DAR (corr. sec. 1989-91, treas. 1991-93, 1st vice regent 1994-96, def. chmn. 1990-96), Gordon Country Club, Phi Gamma Nu. Methodist. Avocation: genealogy. Home: PO Box 128 Deport TX 75435-0128

SAWYER, MERLIN HOWARD, financial executive; b. Madison, S.D., July 15, 1955; s. Richard James Sawyer and Dorothy Elizabeth Cherrey; m. Leann Marie Lutmer, Apr. 25, 1987; children: Michelle, Samuel, Ethan. BSBA, U. S.D., 1977. CPA. Staff acct. to supervisory sr. acct. Eide Helmeke & Co., CPAs, Sioux Falls, S.D., 1977-84; staff mgr. Nat. Exch. Carrier Assn., Omaha, 1984-87; CFO Mo. River Energy Svcs., Sioux Falls, 1987—. Vice chair, chair acctg., fin. and audit com. Am. Pub. Power Assn., Washington, 1996-98, 2001-02; chmn. tech. working group Mid-West Electric Consumers Assn., Denver, 1993-97; chair audit com. Mo. Brain Power Project, 1991-92, 98-2002. Vice chair, chair allocations divsn. Sioux Empire United Way, 1992-96, bd. dirs., 1993-96; vice chair, chair parish coun. Risen Savior Cath. Ch., Brandon, S.D., 1991-92; chair fin. com. Risen Savior Cath. Ch., Brandon, 1990-92. Mem. AICPA, Sioux Falls Soccer Assn. (asst. coach, coach), Brandon Valley Youth Softball Assn. (coach), Brandon Baseball Assn. (coach). Republican. Roman Catholic. Avocations: hunting, golf, horseback riding, genealogy.

SAWYER, MICHAEL E. library director; b. Martinez, Calif., June 8, 1953; s. William and Shirley (Greenberg) S. BA, Columbia Coll., 1974; MLS, U. Pitts, 1976, cert. advanced study, 1978. Libr. So. Ohio Correctional Facility, Lucasville, 1977-84; adminstrv. asst. Findlay-Hancock County Pub. Libr., Findlay, Ohio, 1984-85; libr. Chillicothe (Ohio) Correctional Inst., 1985-89; dir. Auglaize County Pub. Dist. Libr., Wapakoneta, Ohio, 1989-92, Clinton (Iowa) Pub. Libr., 1993-98, Northwestern Regional Libr., Elkin, N.C., 1998—. Author: (book) A Bibliographical Index of Five English Mystics, 1978; co-editor Classics Jour., 1983-87; contbr. articles to profl. jours. Trustee U.S. Jaycees Found. Recipient Al Maresh award Correctional Ednl. Assn., Grand Rapids, Mich., 1988, ASCLA Exceptional Svc. award ALA, Dallas, 1989, Jaycees Bill Butler Meml. award, 1987, Nat. Achievement Citation award Pub. Libr. Assn., 1994; named One of Five Outstanding Ohioans, Ohio Jaycees, 1988, Outstanding Svc. Innovation award NCPLDA, 2001. Mem. ALA (Libr. of the Future award 2002), N.C. JCI Senate (historian 1997—), N.C. Libr. Assn., Rotary. Home: 143 Thornecliffe Dr State Road NC 28676-9240 Office: Northwestern Regional Libr 111 N Front St Elkin NC 28621-3342

SAWYER, MILDRED CLEMENTINA, retired real estate agent; b. Boston, Nov. 19, 1928; d. Joseph Felix and Assunta (Malone) Volpe; m. Frederick Myles Sawyer, June 15, 1957 (dec. Jan. 1995); children: Frederick G., Bernard G. Grad. h.s., Brockton, Mass. Clk. Prudential Ins. Co., Brockton, Mass., 1947-57, Clark Bros., Olean, N.Y., 1957-58; typist N.J., R.I., 1958-87; real estate sales rep. JLC & Home Realty, Chepachet, No. Scituate, 1984-97; ins. sales agt. Mass. Indemnity Life Ins. Co., Cranston, R.I., 1984-89; security sales rep. First Am. Nat. Securities, 1986-89; ret., 1995. Author: A Lifetime of Hints for Everyday Living, 1996, The Path Into Vietnam: An Historical Reflection, 2002; author numerous poems. Sec. Cold Springs Harbor Heights Civic Assn., Huntington, L.I., N.Y., 1961-63, Save All Foster's Environ., Foster, R.I., 1969-87, Students for a Dem. Soc., Warwick, 1970-72. Mem. Soc. of Children's Books, Writers and Illustrators, Soc. of Childrens Books Writers and Illustrators of New England, Noetic Sci. Avocations: reading, exercising, gardening, cooking, sewing. Home: 49A Mount Hygeia Rd Foster RI 02825-1923

SAWYER, MIRIAM, library director; b. Columbus, Ohio, Mar. 20, 1937; d. Nathan and Goldie (Kanter) Mayer; m. Richard J. Sawyer, Oct. 201 1957; children: Rachel, Louisa Sawyer Lindquist. AB, Ohio U., 1955; MLS, SUNY, Albany, 1970. Dir. William E. Dermody Libr., Carlstadt, N.J., 1978-81, Little Falls (N.J.) Libr., 1981-91, Rutherford (N.J.) Libr., 1991—. Reviewer Multicultural Rev., N.Y.C., 1996—. Author: African-American Aviators and Astronauts, 2001; editor N.J. Librs., 1994-96; contbr. numerous articles to profl. jours. Mem. ALA, N.J. Libr. Assn. (com. chmn. 1994-96, 1999-2000). Office: Rutherford Libr 150 Park Ave Rutherford NJ 07070-1959 E-mail: miriamms@juno.com.

SAWYER, NELSON BALDWIN, JR. credit union executive; b. Jacksonville, Fla., Nov. 11, 1948; s. Nelson Baldwin and Nancy (Watson) S.; m. Carla Lee Dowden, Aug. 9, 1986. BA, U. North Fla., 1974. Program cons. State of Fla., Jacksonville, 1974-81; product mgr. Qualified Plan Designs, Inc., 1981-83, Associated Gen. Contractors, Jacksonville, 1983-86; membership mgr. Calif. Credit Union League, Pomona, 1986-87, comm. mgr., 1987-90; sr. v.p., COO Calif. League Svcs. Corp., 1990-93; sr. v.p. Wescorp, San Dimas, Calif., 1994-97; v.p. Travis Fed. Credit Union, Vacaville, 1997-2000; pres., CEO Chevron Valley Credit Union, Bakersfield, 2000—. Chmn. bd. dirs. Calif. Ctr. Credit Union, 1996-97, Product Rsch. Orgn. for Credit Unions. Bd. dirs. Jacksonville C. of C., 1983-84, Taft Coll. Found., 2001—. Mem. U.S. Jaycees (pres. Jacksonville 1983-84, chmn. bd. '84-85, senator, U.S., 1984—, internat. senator 1984—, Outstanding Young Man Am. 1983), Fla. Yacht Club. Republican. Episcopalian. Office: Chevron Valley Credit Union 8200 Granite Falls Dr Bakersfield CA 93312-5592

SAWYER, PHILIP NICHOLAS, surgeon, educator, health science facility administrator; b. Bangor, Maine, Oct. 25, 1925; s. Frank S. and Linda (Makanna) S.; m. Grace Makla, June 13, 1953; children: Margaret Ann, Elizabeth Lynn, Susan Jean, Philip Michael. BS, Harvard U., 1947; MD, U. Pa., 1949. Diplomate Am. Bd. Surgery, Am. Bd. Thoracic Surgery. Intern Hosp. of U. Pa., Phila., 1949-50, resident in surgery, fellow, 1953-56; chief resident in surgery, fellow in pathology St. Luke's Hosp., N.Y.C., 1956-57; instr., asst. prof. surgery SUNY Downstate Med. Ctr., Bklyn., 1957-62, assoc. prof., 1962-66, prof., head vascular surgery svc., 1966-84, prof. emeritus, 1985—; pres. Interface Biomed. Labs. Corp.; prof. surgery N.Y. Med. Coll., 1991-96; vis. surgeon, head vascular surg. svcs. Kings County Hosp., Bklyn., 1972-85. Hon. cons. Meth. Hosp., Bklyn.; hon. assoc. attending, head vascular surg. svcs. St. John's Episcopal Hosp., Far Rockaway, N.Y.; hon. attending surgery VA Hosp., Bklyn.; hon. cons. cardiovascular and thoracic surgeon Norwalk (Conn.) Hosp.; hon. cons. vascular surgeon Caledonian Hosp., Bklyn.; prin. investigator Office Naval Rsch., NIH, Am. Heart Assn., 1953-84, NIH, 1957-86; disting. lectr. worldwide. Founding editor Jour. Investigative Surgery; assoc. editor: Am. Jour. Med. Electronics, Jour. Biomed. Rsch. Engring.; editor: Biophysical Mechanisms in Vascular Homeostasis & Intravascular Thrombosis, 1965, Vascular Grafts, 1976, Modern Vascular Grafts, 1987; co-editor: Surgical Resident's Manual, 1980, Vascular Diseases, Current Controversies, 1981; contbr. over 300 articles to med. jours.; numerous patents on heart valves, vascular grafts, hemostatic agts., vascular wall protective agts. Recipient Clemson award for basic biomaterials rsch. Soc. for Biomaterials, 1985; Markle scholar, 1959-64. Mem. Acad. Surg. Rsch. (Jacob Markowitz award 1986), AAAS, Am. Assn. for Thoracic Surgery, Am. Chem. Soc., Am. Coll. Cardiology, ACS, Am. Coll. Chest Physicians, AMA, Am. Heart Assn., Am. Nuclear Soc., Am. Soc. for Artificial Internal Organs, IEEE, Internat. Cardiovascular Soc., Soc. for Thoracic Surgeons, Soc. Univ. Surgeons, Soc. for Vascular Surgery, European Soc. for Microcirculation, Fedn. Am. Socs. for Exptl. Biology, Cardiovascular Soc. (pres.), Harvard Club (N.Y.C.), Sigma Xi, others. Avocation: collecting historical weapons. Office: 7324 Ridge Blvd Brooklyn NY 11209

SAWYER, RAYMOND TERRY, lawyer; b. Cleve., Oct. 1, 1943; s. R. Terry and Fanny Katherine (Young) S.; m. Katherine Margaret Schneider, Aug. 5, 1972; children: Margaret Young, John Terry. BA, Yale U., 1965; LLB, Harvard U., 1968. Bar: Ohio 1969, U.S. Dist. Ct. (no. dist.) Ohio 1970. Assoc. Thompson Hine LLP, Cleve., 1968-76, ptnr., 1976—83, 1986—2001, chmn. bus. transactions and org. dept., 1998—2001, of counsel, 2002—; exec. dir. Ohio Housing Fin. Agy., Columbus, 1983-84; counsel to gov. State of Ohio, 1984, chief of staff, 1985-86, chmn. Gov.'s commn. on housing, 1989-90. Bd. dirs. Premix, Inc., North Kingsville, Ohio. Vol. VISTA, East Palo Alto, Calif., 1968—69; mem. Tech. Leadership Coun., 1987—95, Leadership Cleve., 1986—87, Cleve. Found. Study Commn. on Med. Rsch. Edn., 1991—92; chmn. George W. Codrington Charitable Found.; mem. Ohio Bd. Regents, Columbus, 1987—96, chmn., 1992—93; trustee Cleve. Ballet, 1987—2000; trustee Cleve. Orch., 1993—; mem. exec. com. MetroHealth Sys., 1998—; mem. Julliard Coun. Julliard Sch.; mem. pres.'s adv. coun. Case Western Res. U. Named Man of Yr. Womanspace, 1982. Mem. ABA, Ohio State Bar Assn. (chair corp. law com. 1993-95), Clevel. Bar Assn., Yale U. Alumni Assn. (pres. Cleve. chpt. 1980-81), Assn. Yale Alumni (del. 1996-99). Democrat. Presbyterian. Office: Thompson Hine LLP 3900 Key Ctr Cleveland OH 44114-1216

SAWYER, ROBERT MCLARAN, history educator; b. St. Louis, Nov. 12, 1929; s. Lee McLaran and Harrie (Alcock) S.; m. Patricia Ann Covert, Nov. 23, 1955; children— Ann Marie, Lee McLaran, Gail Louise. BS, S.E. Mo. State Coll., 1952; MA, U. Ill., 1953; PhD, U. Mo., 1966. Tchr. Rolla (Mo.) Public Schs., 1955; asst. prof., then asso. prof. history U. Mo., Rolla., 1956-67; mem. faculty U. Nebr., Lincoln, 1967—, prof. history of edn., 1969—, chmn. dept. history and philosophy of edn., 1975-81; mem. council U. Nebr. (Coll. Arts and Scis.), 1979—. Vis. prof. Ark. State U., Jonesboro, summer 1966; proposal reviewer Nat. Endowment Humanities, 1979 Author: The History of the University of Nebraska, 1929-1969, 1973, The Many Faces of Teaching, 1987, The Art and Politics of College Teaching, 1992, The Black Student's Guide to College Success, 1993, The Handbook of College Teaching, 1994; also articles, revs. Served with AUS, 1953-55. Mem. Orgn. Am. Historians, History Edn. Soc., Am. Ednl. Studies Assn., Soc. Profs. Edn., Phi Alpha Theta, Phi Delta Kappa. Home: 2640 S 35th St Lincoln NE 68506-6623 Office: Univ Nebr 29 Henzlik Hall Lincoln NE 68588

SAWYER, THOMAS C. congressman; b. Akron, Ohio, Aug. 15, 1945; m. Joyce Handler, 1968; 1 child, Amanda. BA, U. Akron, 1968, MA, 1970. Pub. sch. tchr., Ohio; adminstr. state sch. for delinquent boys; legis. agt. Ohio Pub. Utilities Commn.; mem. Ohio House Reps., Columbus, 1977-83; mayor City of Akron, 1984-86; mem. U.S. Congress from 14th Ohio dist., Washington, 1987—; mem. energy and commerce com. Democrat. Office: US Ho of Reps 1414 Longworth Hob Washington DC 20515-3514 also: District Office 411 Wolf Ledges Parkway, Suite 105 Akron OH 44311*

SAWYER, THOMAS EDGAR, management consultant; b. Homer, La., July 7, 1932; s. Sidney Edgar and Ruth (Bickham) S.; m. Joyce Mezzanatto, Aug. 22, 1954; children: Jeffrey T., Scott A., Robert J., Julie Anne. BS, UCLA, 1959; MA, Occidental Coll., 1969; PhD, Walden U., 1990. Project engr. Garrett Corp., L.A., 1954-60; mgr. devel. ops. TRW Systems, Redondo Beach, Calif., 1960-66; spl. asst. to gov. State of Calif., Sacramento, 1967-69; prin., gen. mgr. Planning Rsch. Corp., McLean, Va., 1969-72; dep. dir. OEO, Washington, 1972-74; assoc. prof. bus. mgmt. Brigham Young U., 1974-78; pres., chmn. bd. Mesa Corp., Provo, Utah, 1978-82; pres. and dir. Sage Inst. Internat., Inc., 1982-88; chmn. bd., CEO Pvt. Telecom Networks, Inc. (name changed to Nat. Applied Computer Techs, Inc.), Orem, 1988-98; chief tech. officer GST Telecom. (formerly Greenstar Telecom., Inc.), San Francisco, 1993-98, also bd. dirs. Vancouver, Wash., 1995-98; chmn. bd. NeTrue Comm., Inc., Fullerton, Calif., 1998—2002. Dir. Intechna Corp., HighTech Corp., Indian Affiliates, Inc., Greenstar USA, Inc., San Francisco, 1994-98, GST Global Comm., Inc., Vancouver, Can., 1998-2002, Highpoint Telecom., Inc., Vancouver, Can., 1998-2002, World Wide Wireless Comm., Inc., Salt Lake City, 1998-2001, Columbia Hosp., Orem, Utah, 1998—. Author: Assimilation Versus Self-Identity: A Modern Native American Perspective, 1976, The Promise of Funding a New Educational Initiative Using the Microcomputer, 1988, Computer Assisted Instruction: An Inevitable Breakthrough, Current Challenges of Welfare: A Review of Public Assistance as Distributive Justice, 1989, New Software Models for Training and Education Delivery, 1989, New Organizations: How They Deviate from Classical Models, 1989, Increasing Productivity in Organizations: The Paradox, 1989, An Introduction and Assessment of Strategic Decision Making Paradigms in Complex Organizations, 1989, The Future of Technology in Education, 1989, Impact of Failure by Senior Executives to Receive Accurate Critical Feedback on Pervasive Change, 1990, The Influence of Critical Feedback and Organizational Climate on Managerial Decision Making, 1990. Chmn. Nat. Adv. Coun. Indian Affairs, Utah State Bd. Indian Affairs, So. Paiute Restoration Com.; bd. trustees Utah Valley State Coll., Orem, 2000—, Coll. Ea. Utah, Price, 2001—; mem. Utah Dist. Export Coun., Utah dist. SBA Coun.; mem. adv. coun. Nat. Bus. Assn.; mem. Utah Job Tng. Coordinating Coun. Served with USMC, 1950-53. Mem. ASPA, Am. Mgmt. Assn., Utah Coun. Small Bus. (dir.), Utah State Hist. Soc. (bd. dirs. 1993-99), Masons. Republican. Mem. Lds Ch. Home: 548 W 630 S Orem UT 84058-6154 Office: 1450 E 820 N Orem UT 84097-5481

SAWYER, THOMAS HARRISON, health, physical education and recreation educator; b. Norwich, N.Y., Apr. 5, 1946; s. Harrison Donald and M. Daughn (Geer) S.; m. Kathleen Ann Daly, July 5 1969; children: Shawn Thomas, Meghan Daly. BS, Springfield Coll., 1968, MPE, 1971; EdD, Va. PolyTech Inst., 1977. Instr. health, phys edn., recreation Va. Mil. Inst., Lexington, 1969-72, asst. prof., 1972-75, assoc. prof., 1975-79; dir. recreation ctr. U. Bridgeport, 1979-81; assoc. prof., head dept. Mont. Tech. Inst., Butte, 1981-84; prof., chmn. phys. edn. dept. Ind. State U., Terre Haute, 1984-89, prof., 1984—, coord. sport mgmt. programs, 1984—; cons. Mont. Fitness, Butte, 1981-84, ARC, Mont., 1981-83, Wellness-Pillsbury Co.; pres. Ind. Ctr. Sport Edn., Inc., 1995—. Mem. edit. bd. Jour. for Employee Health and Fitness, Mag. for Health Mgrs., 1984-89; contbr. articles to profl. jours. Bd. dirs. YMCA, Butte, 1981-84; mem. Sch. Bd. Dist. 1, Butte, 1982-84; mem. bd. dirs. Vocation Edn. Council Mont., 1983-84; chair Task Force for Encouragement of Quality, Daily Physical Edn. Programs for Ind. Pub. Schs., 1987-88, Physical Edn. Adv. Task Force, 1988-91; dir. The Ctr. for Coaching Edn., 1988-94; dir. Ind. PACE, 1994-99, Ind. LANCE, 1999—. NDEA scholar, 1968; recipient Founder's award Alcohol Services, Buena Vista, Va., 1979, Vol. Safety award ARC, Conn., 1981, Red Triangle, YMCA, Butte, 1982; N. Am. fellow Health, Phys. Edn., Recreation, Sport, and Dance, 2000. Mem. Am. Alliance for Health, Phys. Edn., Recreation and Dance (editl. bd. 1991-95, chair 1993-95, Honor award 1991), ARC (bd. dirs. Terre Haute 1985-87, 88—, svc. coun., 1993, chair 1994-97), Ind. Assn., Phys. Edn., Recreation and Dance (editor jour. and newsletter 1987—, conv. coord. 1992-2000), Nat. Assn. Sports Offcls., Assn. Fitness in Bus., Employee Svcs. Mgmt. Assn., Nat. Assn. Sport and Phys. Edn., North Am. Soc. Sport Mgmt., Am. Assn. Active Lifestyles and Fitness (pres.-elect 1996-97, pres. 1997-2000), Coun. Facilities and Equipment (chair 1995-97), Soc. Study of Legal Aspects of Sport and Phys. Activity (treas. 1994-96, exec. dir. 1997-2001, editor Jour. Legal Aspects of Sports, 1995-2000). Office: Ind State U Dept Rec Sport Mgmt Terre Haute IN 47809-0001

SAWYER, THOMAS WILLIAM, career officer; b. Turlock, Calif., Nov. 19, 1933; s. Everett Edward and Marie Georgine (Gunderson) S.; m. Faith Barry Martin, Feb. 16, 1957; children: William Everet, John Martin, Susan Quincy BS in Mil. Sci., U. Nebr., 1965; MS in Internat. Rels., George Washington U., 1974. Enlisted U.S. Air Force, 1952, commd. and advanced through grades to maj. gen., 1983; comdr. 57th Fighter Squadron, Keflavik, Iceland, 1971-73; chief internat. relations div. Hdqrs. U.S. Air Force, Washington, 1974-77; vice comdr. 20th Air Div., Fort Lee, Va., 1977-78; mil. asst. to Sec. Air Force, 1978-80; comdr. 26th Air Div., Luke AFB, Ariz., 1980-82; dep. ops. NORAD and Space Command, Colorado Springs, Colo., 1982-86; retired USAF, 1986; founder, pres. Aerospace Network Inc., 1986-98; pres. Pathfinder Tech., Inc., 1998—. Bd. dirs. Pikes Peak chpt. ARC, Colo./Wyo. chpt. Am. Def. Preparedness Assn. Decorated Disting. Service medal, Def. Disting. Service medal, Legion of Merit with 2 oak leaf clusters, Silver Star (2) Mem. Phoenix C. of C. (bd. dirs. 1980-82), Colorado Springs C. of C. Avocations: nat. security affairs, woodworking, automobile bldg. Office: Pathfinder Tech Inc 3730 Sinton Rd Ste 250 Colorado Springs CO 80907

SAWYER, WILLIAM C. lawyer; b. Bangor, Maine, Aug. 26, 1929; s. Frank S. and Linda M. (Makanna) S.; m. Mary A. Eaton (div.); m. Joan N. Gardner; children: William D., Constance, Faith. AB cum laude, Harvard Coll., 1951, JD, 1954. Bar: Mass., U.S. Dist. Ct. Mass., U.S. Ct. Mil. Appeals, U.S. Supreme Ct. Assoc. Palmer & Dodge, Boston, 1958-61; ptnr. Sawyer, Burlingham, Tucker & Salloway, 1961-85, Dicara, Selig, Sawyer & Holt, Boston, 1985-90, Clarkin, Sawyer & Phillips, P.C., Boston, 1990—. Bd. dirs. Jones & Vining, Inc., Ayer Sales, Inc., Applied Geographics, Inc., Applied Tech., Inc., others. Contbr. articles to profl. jours. Bd. trustees Mass. Conv. Ctr. Authority, 1991-97; pres., treas., chmn. Metro. Area Planning Coun., 1975-87; pres. Mass. Assn. Regional Planning Agys., 1980, 87; bd. dirs. Nat. Assn. Regional Couns., 1980-86; mem. Mass. Selectman's Assn., 1975—; bd. selectman Town of Action, 1967-75, chmn., 1969, 75; Rep. candidate Mass. Atty. Gen., 1990; pres. New Eng. Rep. Coun.; mem. Rep. State Com.; Rep. candidate Congress, 5th Congl. Dist., Mass., 1980. 1st lt. U.S. Army, 1955. Recipient Regional Leadership award Planning Commns. and Couns. New Eng., 1987, and others. Mem. ABA, Mass. Bar Assn., Boston Bar Assn. Avocations: tennis, painting, reading. Office: Clarkin Sawyer & Phillips PC 1 Center Plz Ste 240 Boston MA 02108-1801

SAWYER, WILLIAM CURTIS, pest control company executive; b. Lockport, N.Y., Jan. 25, 1933; s. Fletcher D. and Mildred R. (Schnurstein) S.; m. Noreen T. Doran, Aug. 8, 1959 (div. 1987); children: Curtis P., Todd T.; m. Gail P. Mangan, 1988. Student, Cornell U., 1950-52. Technician McLeod Indsl. Fumigators, Buffalo, 1949-50; v.p. Sawyer's Exterminating, Rochester, N.Y., 1958-76, pres., 1976—. Sgt. USMC, 1952-56. Mem. Nat. Pest Control Assn. (bd. dirs. 1981-88), Empire Pest Control Assn. (treas. 1981-85, bd. dirs. 1978-85), N.Y. State Pest Control Assn. (bd. dirs. 1981-85), Small Bus. Assn. Rochester (bd. dirs. 1981-85), Meml. Art Gallery, Rochester Area C. of C., Rochester Club, Masons, Shriners, Rochester Rotary. Republican. Avocations: flying, ballroom dancing, scuba diving. Home: 3126 Brockport Rd Spencerport NY 14559-2164 Office: Sawyers Exterminating Unit 3 1270 Creek St Webster NY 14580-2261

SAWYER, WILLIAM DALE, physician, educator, university dean, foundation administrator; b. Roodhouse, Ill., Dec. 28, 1929; s. Cloyd Howard and Eva Collier (Dale) S.; m. Jane Ann Stewart, Aug. 25, 1951; children— Dale Stewart, Carole Ann Student, U. Ill., 1947-50; MD cum laude, Washington U., St. Louis, 1954; ScD (hon.), Mahidol U., Bangkok, 1988; DPH (hon.), Chiang Mai U., Thailand, 1993, Chulalongkorn U., 1998. Intern Washington U.-Barnes Hosp., 1954-55, resident, 1957-58, fellow, 1958-60; asst. prof. microbiology Johns Hopkins U., Balt., 1964-67; prof., chmn. dept. microbiology Rockefeller Found.-Mahidol U., Bangkok, 1967-73, Ind. U. Sch. Medicine, Indpls., 1973-80; prof. depts. medicine, microbiology and immunology Wright State U., Dayton, Ohio, 1981-87, dean Sch. Medicine, 1981-87; pres. China Med. Bd. N.Y., Inc., 1987-97. Adj. prof. biology Ball State U., Muncie, Ind., 1978-80; hon. prof. microbiology Sun Yat Sen U. Med. Sci., 1987; hon. prof. Peking Union Med. Coll., 1989; hon. advisor Beijing Med. U.; cons. U.S. Army Med. R & D Command, WHO Immunology Ctr., Singapore, 1969-73; mem. bd. sci. advisers Armed Forces Inst. Pathology, 1975-80, chmn., 1979-80; adj. prof. medicine and microbiology and immunology N.Y. Med. Coll., Valhalla, 1990-96; hon. prof. China Med. U., 1995, West China U. Med. Sci., 1995, Zhejiang Med. U., 1995, Jiujang Med. Coll., 1995, Hunan Med. U., 1996, Xian Med. U., 1996, Shanghai Med. U., 1996. Contbr. numerous articles to profl. jours. Mem. Lobund adv. bd. U. Notre Dame; dir. Georgetown Area Cmty. Found., 1998-2002, pres. 1999. Served to maj. M.C., UAS, 1955-64. Recipient Gold medal of merit Airlangga U., Indonesia, 1992, Pub. Health Recognition award Asia-Pacific Acad. Consortium Pub. Health, 1993, China Health medal, 1996, White Magnolia award, 1996. Fellow ACP; mem. AAAS, Am. Soc. Microbiology (br. pres. 1976), Sci. Rsch. Soc. Am., Am. Fedn. Clin. Rsch., Ctrl. Soc. Clin. Rslch., Infectious Diseases Soc. Am., Soc. Exptl. Biology and Medicine, Am. Acad. Microbiology, Am. Assn. Pathologists, Assn. Am. Med. Colls. (coun. deans 1980-87), Phi Beta Kappa, Sigma Xi, Alpha Omega Alpha. Home: 124 Poppy Hills Cv S Georgetown TX 78628-1179 E-mail: wllmsawyer@aol.com.

SAWYER-MORSE, MARY KAYE, nutritionist, educator; b. Ft. Stockton, Tex. BA in psychology, Southwest Tex. State U., 1978; MS in nutrition, Incarnate Word Coll., 1987; PhD, U. Tex., 1997. Lic. dietitian. Nutrition svcs. con. Christian Sr. Svcs., 1985-87; nutrition svcs. cons. The Alternative Adult Day Care Ctr., 1989-90; pvt. con. dietitian, 1990—; exec. dir. Christian Sr. Svcs., 1987-90; community dietitian Health Enhancement Ctr. Humana Hosp. Met., 1990-91; dietetic program dir., assoc. prof. U. of the Incarnate Word, San Antonio, 1991—. Presenter Diabetic Homebound Svcs. Nat. Conf. of Meals-On-Wheels Am., 1989. Innovative Nutrition Svc. Model Southwest Tex. Gerontological Soc. Annual Meeting, 1988; spkr. in field. Contbr. articles to profl. jours. Recipient Disting. Rsch. award, 1977, 78, Acad. Excellence award, 1978, YWCA Women's Leadership award, 1988, Creative Tchg./Rsch. award, 1994, Carnation Corp. scholar, 1995; U.S. Dept. Edn. grantee,

1997-00. Mem. Am. Dietetic Assn. (sec. 1990-92, nominating com. 1993-94, dietetic educator's practice group), Tex. Dietetic Assn., San Antonio Dist. Dietetic Assn., Nat. Spkrs. Assn. (devel. dir. 2000-01). Office: U of the Incarnate Word 4301 Broadway St San Antonio TX 78209-6318 E-mail: morsemk@msn.com.

SAWYERS, CLAIRE ELYCE, arboretum administrator; b. Maryville, Mo., May 30, 1957; d. Scott Kirkir and Betty Jane (Alexander) S. BS with distinction, Purdue U., 1978, MAg., 1981; MS, U. Del., 1984. Dir. Scott Arboretum of Swarthmore (Pa.) Coll., Swarthmore, Pa., 1990—. Recipient Disting. Alumna award, U. Del., 2001, Purdue U. Dept. Horticulture, 1999. Office: Scott Arboretum 500 College Ave Swarthmore PA 19081-1306 E-mail: csawyer1@swarthmore.edu.

SAWYERS, ELIZABETH JOAN, librarian, administrator; b. San Diego, Dec. 2, 1936; d. William Henry and Elizabeth Georgiana (Price) S. AA, Glendale Jr. Coll., 1957; BA in Bacteriology, UCLA, 1959, M.L.S., 1961. Asst. head acquisition sect. Nat. Library Medicine, Bethesda, Md., 1962-63, head acquisition sect., 1963-66, spl. asst. to chief tech. services div., 1966-69, spl. asst. to assoc. dir. for library ops., 1969-73; asst. dir. libraries for tech. services SUNY-Stony Brook, 1973-75; dir. Health Scis. Library Ohio State U., Columbus, 1975-90, spl. asst. to dir. Univ. librs., 1990—. Mem. Assn. Acad. Health Scis. Library Dirs. (sec./treas. 1981-83, pres. 1983-84), Med. Library Assn., Am. Soc. for Info. Sci., Spl. Libraries Assn., ALA Office: Ohio State Univ Librs 1858 Neil Ave Columbus OH 43210-1225

SAX, BORIA, German studies educator, writer; b. N.Y.C., Mar. 31, 1949; s. Saville and Susan Sax; m. Linda Jean Wooh, Apr. 16, 1977. BA, U. Chgo., 1972; MA in German, SUNY, Buffalo, 1978, PhD in German and History, 1981. Adj. full prof. Pace U., White Plains, N.Y., 1982-91; adj. prof. Mercy Coll., Dobbs Ferry, 1986—; instr. N.Y. Bot. Garden, 1998—, Audrey Cohen Coll., N.Y., 2000-01; coord. online learning Mercy Coll., 2000—. Cons. Ammesty Internat., N.Y.C., 1988-89, Eastern Europe coord., 1981-90; pres. Nature in Legend and Story, White Plains, 1992—. Author: (nonfiction) The Frog King, 1990, The Parliament of Animals, 1992, The Serpent and the Swan, 1998, Animals in the Third Reich, 2000, The Mythological Zoo, 2001, (poetry) Rheinland Market, 1987. Grantee Modern German Studies, 1979, Pace U., 1985-90, N.Y. Coun. Humanities, 1993, 96, 98. Mem. Internat. Soc. for Anthrozoology. Avocations: jewelry making, miniature sculptures, hiking, history. Home: 25 Franklin Ave Apt 2F White Plains NY 10601-3819 Office: Mercy Coll 555 Broadway Dobbs Ferry NY 10522 E-mail: vogelgreif@aol.com.

SAX, DANIEL SAUL, neurologist, educator; b. Balt., Jan. 27, 1935; s. Benjamin J. and Miriam (Helfgott) S.; m. Joan Atherton Bond, Mar. 25, 1962; children: Karen Bond, John Derek, Diana Atherton. AB, Johns Hopkins U., 1955; MD, U. Md., 1959. Diplomate Am. Bd. Psychiatry and Neurology. Intern Boston City Hosp., 1959—60, resident in neurology and neuropathology neurologic unit, 1961—67; resident in neurology N.E. Med. Ctr., 1961; asst. prof. neurology Northwestern U., Chgo., 1966-67; assoc. prof. neurology Albert Einstein Med. Sch., N.Y.C., 1967-69, Boston U. Sch. Med., 1969-76, prof. neurology, 1976-2000, prof. emeritus neurology, 2000—. Chief neurology svcs. Boston VA Outpatient Clinic, 1974-90; EEG lab. dir., cons. Gifford Med. Ctr., Randolph, Vt., 1977—, neurologist, 1977—; cons. neurology Boston VA Med. Ctr., 1991-2000. Clin. adv. com. Vt. divsn. Nat. MS Soc., 2001, clin. adv. com. ctrl. N.E. chpt., 1977—. Lt. comdr. USNR, 1964-66. Fellow: Am. Acad. Neurology; mem.: AMA, Internat. Soc. Women in Health and Sexuality, Huntington's Study Group, Huntington's Dx Soc. (mem. adv. bd. Mass. chpt. 1980—2000, clin. adv. bd. 2001—), Multiple Sclerosis Soc. (clin. adv. bd. 1977—), Boston Soc. Neurology and Psychiatry (pres. 1982—83, exec. com. 1985—), Mass. Med. Soc., Am. Soc. Neuroimaging, Am. Assn. for Study of Headache, Am. Neurol. Assn. Avocations: tree farmer, oenology. Office: Gifford Med Ctr Neurology 44 S Main St Randolph VT 05060 also: 258 W Cummings Park Woburn MA 01801 E-mail: saxdj@bu.edu., dsax@adelphia.net.

SAX, JOSEPH LAWRENCE, lawyer, educator; b. Chgo., Feb. 3, 1936; s. Benjamin Harry and Mary (Silverman) S.; m. Eleanor Charlotte Gettes, June 17, 1958; children: Katherine Elaine Dennett, Valerie Beth, Amber Sax Rosen. AB, Harvard U., 1957; JD, U. Chgo., 1959; LLD (hon.), Ill. Inst. Tech., 1992. Bar: D.C. 1960, Mich., 1966, U.S. Supreme Ct. 1969. Atty. U.S. Dept. Justice, Washington, 1959-60; pvt. practice law, 1960-62; prof. U. Colo., 1962-65, U. Mich., Ann Arbor, 1966-86; dep. asst. sec. and counselor U.S. Sec. Interior, Washington, 1994-96; prof. U. Calif. Law Sch., Berkeley, 1986—. Fellow Ctr. Advanced Study in Behavioral Scis., 1977-78. Author: Waters and Water Rights, 1967, Water Law, Planning and Policy, 1968, Defending the Environment, 1971, Mountains Without Handrails, 1980, Legal Control of Water Resources, 3rd edit., 2001, Playing Darts with a Rembrandt, 1999. Fellow AAAS; mem. University Club (San Francisco). E-mail: saxj@law.berkeley.edu.

SAX, MARY RANDOLPH, speech pathologist; b. July 13, 1925; d. Bernard Angus and Ada Lucile (Thurman) TePoorten; m. William Martin Sax, Feb. 7, 1948. BA magna cum laude, Mich. State U., 1947; MA, U. Mich., 1949. Cert. clin. competence in speech and lang. pathology. Supr. speech correction dept. Waterford Twp. Schs., Pontiac, 1949-69; lectr. Marygrove Coll., Detroit, 1971-72; pvt. practice in speech and lang. pathology Wayne & Oakland Counties, Mich., 1973—. Co-investigator Support Pers. Profl. Practice of Speech-Lang. Pathology; mem. stroke com. Mich. Heart Assn., 1982—99; counselor to divsn. stroke liaisons Am. Heart Assn. Mich.; stroke advisor for Midwest affiliate Am. Heart Assn., 1999—, advocacy com. for Midwest affiliate of Ill., Ind. and Mich., 1999—; liaison between Am. Heart Assn. of Mich. and Am. Heart Assn., Dallas, 1996—98; adj. speech pathologist, Southfield, Mich.; lectr. on stroke Mich. Spkrs. Bur., Am. Heart Assn., 1990—; pub. spkg. coach, 1989—; mem. adj. faculty SS Cyril and Methodius Sem., Orchard Lake, Mich., 1989—90; adj. St. Mary's Prep. Sch., Orchard Lake, 1990—; mem. Met. Detroit Stroke Task Force of Am. Stroke Assn., 1999—; founder, mem. Stroke Project Task Force for Detroit, 1993—98; com. mem. Charette, study Arch. and Design for phys. restructuring Franklin, Mich., 1993; invited speech pathology del. nternat. Health Programs People to People Citizen Amb. Program, 1996; mem. sci. coun. on stroke Am. Heart Assn., 1980—. Contbr. articles to profl. jours. including Lang. and Lang. Behavior Abstracts, Lang. Speech & Hearing Svcs., Speech Lang. Hearing Jour. Active Franklinites for Responsible Govt. Recipient Svc. Recognition award Coll. Edn. Mich. State U.; grantee Inst. Articulation and Learning, 1969, others; Christian svc. commn. St. Owen, Birmingham co-chmn. blood dr. Red Cross, Franklin, Mich., 1991—. Mem.: Founders Soc. of Detroit Inst. Arts, Franklin Found. (mem. natural resources adv. coun. 1991—99, bd. dirs. 1994—98), Pvt. Practitioners Speech-Lang. Pathology (co-founder), Internat. Assn. Logopedics and Phoniatrics (Switzerland), Am. Heart Assn. Mich. (mem. stroke awareness seminars, continuing edn. for physicians and other profls., planning and operation edn.), Mich. Speech-Lang.-Hearing Assn. (pvt. practitioner liaison 1991—, com. comty. and hosp. svcs., mem. state award selection com., developer structural parameters for State Clin. Svc. award 1999—), Am. Speech-Lang.-Hearing Assn. (clin. competence cert.), Mich. Humane Soc., Gamma Phi Beta, Kappa Delta Pi, Phi Kappa Phi, Theta Alpha Phi. Achievements include research in language and speech acquisition in children in reference to the development of and prediction of biological speech change; research interests in developmental phonatory voice disorders, and in adult acquisition of language and speech relative to central and autonomic nervous systems. Office: 31320 Woodside Dr Franklin MI 48025-2027

SAX, ROBERT EDWARD, food service equipment company executive; b. Phila., Nov. 2, 1938; s. Sam and Jessie (Sirisky) S.; m. Rochelle E. Sax, Jan. 11, 1959; children: Nathan, Beverly. Student, U. Pa., 1960-66; diploma, Xerox Sys., Chgo., 1987. Pres. Robert E. Sax Assocs., Inc., Blackwood, N.J., 1965-79; sr. sales mgr. Household Internat., Inc., Veron Hills, Ill., 1979-90; v.p. nat. accounts True Food Svc. Equipment, O'Fallon, Mo., 1990—. Author: It's Yours Just Ask, 1975. Pres. Assn. Representing Children Handicaps, Berlin, N.J., 1971. Named Man of Yr. Sta. WPEN-AM, Camden, N.J., 1969. Mem. Nat. Hot Rod Assn., Rolls Rovce Owner's Club, Masons. Home: 305 Old Orchard Rd Cherry Hill NJ 08003-1216 Fax: 856-751-0035.

SAXBE, WILLIAM BART, lawyer, former government official; b. Mechanicsburg, Ohio, June 24, 1916; s. Bart Rockwell and Faye Henry (Carey) S.; m. Ardath Louise Kleinhans, Sept. 14, 1940; children: William Bart, Juliet Louise Saxbe Blackburn, Charles Rockwell. AB, Ohio State U., 1940; LL.B., 1948; hon. degrees, Central State U., Findlay Coll., Ohio Wesleyan U., Walsh Coll., Capital U., Wilmington Coll., Ohio State U., Bowling Green State U. Bar: Ohio 1948. Practiced in, Mechanicsburg, 1948-55; partner Saxbe, Boyd & Prine, 1955-58; mem. Ohio Gen. Assembly, 1947-48, 49-50; majority leader Ho. Reps., 1951-52, speaker, 1953-54; atty. gen. Ohio, 1957-58, 63-68; partner Dargusch, Saxbe & Dargusch, 1960-63; mem. U.S. Senate from, Ohio, 1969-74; atty. gen. U.S., 1974; ambassador to India, 1975-77; partner firm Chester, Saxbe, Hoffman & Wilcox, Columbus, Ohio, 1977-81; of counsel firm Jones, Day, Reavis & Pogue, Cleve., 1981-84, Pearson, Ball & Dowd (merger Pearson, Ball & Dowd and Reed, Smith & McClay), Washington, 1984-93; ind. spl. counsel Central States Teamsters Pension Fund, 1982—; of counsel Chester Willcox & Saxbe, Columbus, Ohio, 1994—. Served with 107th Cav. AUS, 1940-42; Served with 107th Cav. USAAF, 1942-45; col. Res. Mem. Am., Ohio bar assns., Am. Judicature Soc., Chi Phi, Phi Delta Phi. Clubs: Mason (33d degree) (Columbus), University (Columbus), Columbus Athletic (Columbus), Columbus (Columbus), Scioto Country (Columbus); Urbana (Ohio) Country; Burning Tree Country (Bethesda, Md.); Country of Fla. (Boynton Beach). Republican. Episcopalian. Home: 1171 N Ocean Blvd Gulf Stream FL 33483-7273 Office: 4600 N Ocean Blvd 2nd Fl Boynton Beach FL 33435-7365

SAXBERG, BORJE OSVALD, management educator; b. Helsinki, Finland, Jan. 25, 1928; came to U.S., 1950, naturalized, 1966; s. Oskar Valdemar and Martha (Granberg) S.; m. A. Margrete Haug; children: Bo Erland Haug, Bror Valdemar Haug. BA, Swedish Sch. Bus. and Econs., 1950; BS, Oreg. State U., 1952; MS, U. Ill., 1953, PhD, 1958. Teaching asst., instr. U. Ill., 1953-57; prof. dept. mgmt. and orgn. U. Wash., 1957—; asso. dean U. Wash. (Bus. Sch.), 1967-70, chmn. dept. mgmt. and orgn., 1972-76, chmn. faculty senate, 1980-81, chmn. dept. mgmt. and orgn., 1989-93; dir. program in entrepreneurship and innovation, 1989-95. Cons. in field. Author: (with R. Joseph Monsen) The Business World, 1967, (with H.P. Knowles) Personality and Leadership Behavior, 1971, (with R.A. Johnson) Management, Systems and Society, 1976, (with B. Mar) Managing High Technology, 1985. Ford Found. fellow, 1960-61 Mem. Am. Sociol. Assn., Rainier Club, Swedish Club (Seattle). Home: 7336 58th Ave NE Seattle WA 98115-6257 Office: Univ Wash Grad Sch Bus 353200 Seattle WA 98195-0001

SAXE, DEBORAH CRANDALL, lawyer; b. Lima, Ohio, July 23, 1949; d. Robert Gordon and Lois Barker (Taylor) Crandall; m. Robert Saxe, June 3, 1989; children: Elizabeth Sara, Emily Jane. BA, Pa. State U., 1971; MA, UCLA, 1973, JD, 1978. Bar: Calif. 1978, D.C. 1979, U.S. Dist. Ct. D.C. 1979, U.S. Dist. Ct. (ea. dist.) Calif. 1981, U.S. Dist. Ct. (ctrl. dist.) Calif. 1982, U.S. Dist. Ct. (no. and so. dists.) Calif. 1987, U.S. Ct. Appeals (4th and D.C. cirs.) 1979, U.S. Ct. Appeals (6th cir.) 1985, U.S. Ct. Appeals (8th and 9th cirs.) 1987, U.S. Ct. Appeals (2nd cir.) 1990, U.S. Supreme Ct. 1982, U.S. Dist. Ct. (no. dist.) Ill. 2001, U.S. Ct. Appeals (7th cir.) 2001. Assoc. Seyfarth, Shaw, Fairweather & Geraldson, Washington, 1978-83, Jones, Day, Reavis & Pogue, Washington, 1983-85, L.A., 1985-87, ptnr., 1988-97; shareholder Heller Ehrman White & McAuliffe LLP, 1997—. Judge pro tem, Small Claims Ct., L.A., 1985-88. Co-author: Advising California Employers, 1990, 2d edit., 1995; contbg. editor Employment Discrimination Law, 1989. Bd. dirs. Constitutional Rights Found., 1997—2002, Eisner Pediatric and Family Med. Ctr., L.A., 1990—, chair, 1996—98; bd. dirs. L.A. County Bar Found., 1997—99. Mem.: ABA (labor law sect. 1978—), L.A. County Bar Assn. (labor and employment law sect. 1985—, mem. exec. com. 1988—2002, vice chair 2001—02, chair 2002—, treas. 2000—01), Calif. Bar Assn. (labor law sect. 1985—), Phi Beta Kappa, Pi Lambda Theta. Office: Heller Ehrman White & McAuliffe 601 S Figueroa St Fl 40 Los Angeles CA 90017-5704 Fax: 213-614-1868. E-mail: dsaxe@hewm.com.

SAXE, IRVING HENRY, obstetrician-gynecologist; b. Passaic, N.J., Nov. 24, 1909; MD, Harvard Med. Sch., 1935. Intern Beth Israel Hosp., Boston, 1935-36; resident N.Y. Polyclinic Med. Sch., N.Y.C., 1936-38. Fellow Am. Coll. Ob.-Gyn., Internat. Coll. Surgeons; mem. Am. Fertility Soc., AMA. Home: 75 Central Park W New York NY 10023-6011

SAXE, THELMA RICHARDS, secondary school educator, consultant; b. Ogdensburg, N.J., Apr. 21, 1941; d. George Francis and Evelyn May (Howell) Richards; m. Kenneth Elwood Meeker, Jr., June 22, 1957 (div. 1965); children: Sylvia Lorraine Meeker Hill, Michelle Louise Meeker Aromando, David Sean (dec.); m. Frederick Ely Saxe, Feb. 18, 1983; stepchildren: Jonathan Kent, Holly Harding Schenker. BA, William Paterson Coll., Wayne, N.J., 1972, MEd, 1975, postgrad., 1983-84; Dyslexia cert., Fairleigh Dickinson U., 1994; voice student, Dr. Roberta Moger. Cert. paralegal. Tchr. handicapped Sussex (N.J.)-Wantage Regional Sch. Dist., 1972-75; resource rm. tchr. Sussex County Vo-Tech Sch., Sparta, N.J., 1975-77, learning cons., 1977-83; learning specialist Bennington-Rutland Supervisory Union, Manchester, Vt., 1986-87; learning cons. Stillwater (N.J.) Twp. Sch., 1987-88, Independence Twp. Cen. Sch., Great Meadows, N.J., 1989; learning cons., tutor in pvt. practice specializing dyslexia Sparta, 1986-97; asst. prin. Harmony Twp. Sch., Harmony, N.J., 1989-92; learning cons. Montague (N.J.) Elem. Sch., 1996-98; coord. gifted/talented Sussex Vo-Tech, 1980-83; coord. child study team Stillwater Twp. Sch., 1987-88, Montague Twp. Sch., 1996-98; ret., 1998; learning cons. Sandyston-Walpack Consolidated Sch., 1997-98. Soprano mem. Nature Coast Festival Singers, Spring Hill, Fla.; soprano Citrus Hills Chorus, Hernando, Fla. Mem.: Kappa Delta Pi. Democrat. Presbyterian. Avocations: music, singing, piano, autoharp, skiing, hiking, travel. Home: 3029 N Annapolis Ave Hernando FL 34442-4718

SAXENA, ARJUN NATH, physicist; b. Lucknow, India, Apr. 1, 1932; came to U.S., 1956, naturalized, 1976; s. Sheo and Mohan (Piyari) Shanker; m. Veera Saxena, Feb. 9, 1956; children: Rashmi, Amol, Varsha, Ashvin. BSc, Lucknow U., 1950, MSc, 1952, profl. cert. in German, 1954; post MS diploma, Inst. Nuc. Physics, Calcutta, India, 1955; PhD, Stanford U., 1963. Rsch. asst. Stanford U., 1956-60; mem. tech. staff Fairchild Semicondr. Co., Palo Alto, Calif., 1960-65; dept. head Sprague Electric Co., North Adams, Mass., 1965-69; mem. tech. staff RCA Labs., Princeton, N.J., 1969-71; pres., chmn. bd. Astro-Optics, Phila., 1972; pres. Internat. Sci. Co., Princeton Junction, N.J., 1973—. Disting. vis. scientist Centre de Récherches Nucléaires, Strasbourg, France, 1973, 77; sr. staff scientist, mgr. engring. Data Gen. Corp., Sunnyvale, Calif., 1975-80; mgr. process tech. Signetics Corp., Sunnyvale, 1980-81; Gould AMI scientist, dir. advanced process devel. Gould AMI Semicondrs., Santa Clara, Calif., 1981-87; dir. Ctr. for Integrated Electronics, prof. dept. elec. and computer system engring. Rensselaer Poly. Inst., Troy, N.Y., 1987-96, emeritus prof., 1996—; disting. vis. scientist Inst. Microelectronics, Stuttgart, Germany, 1993-94. Contbr. articles to semicondr. tech., optics, nuc. and high-energy physics to sci. jours.; patentee in field. Treas. pack 66 Boy Scouts Am., West Windsor, N.J., 1970-74. Recipient Disting. Citizen award State of N.J., 1975. Mem. IEEE (life, sr.), Stanford U. Alumni Assn. (life). Home: 4217 Pomona Ave Palo Alto CA 94306-4312 E-mail: thesaxena@aol.com.

SAXENA, BRIJ B. endocrinologist, biochemist, educator; PhD, India; DSc, U. Muenster, W.Ger.; PhD, U. Wis., 1961. Asst. prof. biochemistry and endocrinology N.J. Coll. Medicine., 1966-74; assoc. prof. biochemistry Cornell U. Med. Coll., N.Y.C., 1974—, prof. biochemistry, 1974—, prof. endocrinology, 1981—, dir. div. reproductive endocrinology, Harold and Percy Uris endowed prof. reproductive biology, 2000—. Contbr. 200 articles to profl. jours. Recipient Career Scientist award N.Y.C. Health Research Council; Upjohn research award; Campoz da Paz award. Fellow Royal Soc. Medicine (London); mem. Am. Soc. Biol. Chemists, AAAS, Endocrine Soc., Harvey Soc., Am. Physiol. Soc., Am. Chem. Soc. Office: Cornell U Med Coll 515 E 71st St Ste 412 New York NY 10021-4805 E-mail: brs2003@med.cornell.edu.

SAXENA, NARENDRA K. marine research educator; b. Agra, India, Oct. 15, 1936; came to U.S., 1969; s. Brijbasi Lal and Sarbati Saxena; children: Sarah Vasanti, Lorelle Sarita. Diploma Geodetic Engring., Tech. U., Hanover, Fed. Republic Germany, 1966; Dr. Tech. Scis., Tech. U., Graz, Austria, 1972. Research assoc. geodetic sci. Ohio State U., Columbus, 1969-74; asst. prof. U. Ill., Urbana, 1974-78, U. Hawaii, Honolulu, 1978-81, assoc. prof., 1981-86, prof., 1986-97, dept. chmn., 1994-97, prof., dir. Pacific Mapping program SOEST. Adj. research prof. Naval Postgrad. Sch., Monterey, Calif., 1984-87; co-chmn. Pacific Congresses on Marine Tech., Honolulu, 1984, 86, 88; pres. Pacon Internat. Inc., 1987—. Editor Jour. Marine Geodesy, 1976—. Mem. Neighborhood Bd., Honolulu, 1984. Fellow Marine Tech. Soc. (various offices 1974—); mem. Am. Geophys. Union, The Tsunami Soc. Office: U Hawaii Pacific Mapping Prog/SOEST 2525 Correa Rd HIG # 440 Honolulu HI 96822 E-mail: nsaxena@hawaii.edu.

SAXENA, PRASHANT, computer engineer; b. Mussoorie, Uttaranchal, India, July 27, 1969; s. Kailash Chandra and Savitri Saxena; m. Priti Johri. B of Elec. and Electronic Engring., Birla Inst. Tech. and Sci., Pilani, India, MSc in Computer Sci., 1991; PhD in Computer Sci., U. Ill., 1998. Staff engr. Strategic CAD Labs., Intel Corp., Hillsboro, Oreg., 2000—; sr. engr. Strategic CAD Labs, Intel Corp., 1998—2000. Mentor for acad. rsch. Semiconductor Rsch. Consortium, Research Triangle Park, 2000—, Design Sci. Tech. Com., Intel Corp., Santa Clara, 1999—; mem. tech. program com., session chair IEEE Internat. Symposium on Circuits and Sys., Phoenix, 2002—; demo chair Internat. Conf. on VLSI Design, Goa, India, 1999; tech. referee for peer-reviewed rsch. articles numerous internat. jours. and confs., 1994—; sub-editor, tech. reviewer IEEE press and John Wiley-Interscience Pubs. (for a compendium of signal integrity papers), 2001; tech. book manuscript reviewer computer sci. divsn. Prentice Hall Pubs., NJ; jour. proposal reviewer Oxford U. Press. Contbr. articles to profl. jours.; author: (book chpt.) Signal Integrity Issues in SoC Designs, 2001; co-author: VSIA Signal Integrity Specifications. Fellow univ.-wide grad. fellow, SUNY, Buffalo, 1991; grantee Rotary Found. grantee for outstanding student, 1987—91; scholar Nat. Talent Search scholarolarship, Govt. India, 1984—91, J. N.Tata Meml. scholar for higher edn. of Indians, Tata Ednl. Found., India, 1991, BITS merit scholar, Birla Inst. Tech. and Sci., 1986—91. Office: Intel Corp Strategic CAD Labs MS JF4-211 2111 NE 25th Ave Portland OR 97229 Business E-Mail: prashant.saxena@intel.com.

SAXENA, SUBHASH CHANDRA, mathematics educator, researcher, administrator; b. Etawah, India; came to U.S., 1959; s. Prem Narain and Hansmukh (Rani) S.; m. Pushpa Rani Kudesia; children: Anita, Anil. BA with honors, U. Delhi, India, 1952; MA, U. Delhi, 1954, PhD, 1958. Instr. Def. Acad. of India, Khadakvasla, 1958; sr. postdoctoral fellow Coun. Sci. and Indsl. Rsch., Delhi, 1958-59; asst. prof. maths. Atlanta U., 1959-60, assoc. prof., 1960-63, No. Ill. U., DeKalb, 1963-68, U. Akron, Ohio, 1968-73, U. S.C. (now Coastal Carolina U.), Conway, 1973-77, prof., 1977—, prof., chair, 1987-93, disting. prof., 1999-2000, disting. prof. emeritus, 2000—. Cons. Ednl. Testing Svc., 1997; advisor and cons. Ansal Inst. Tech., New Delhi, 2000. Author: Theory of Real Variables, 1972; biographer, contbr. Biog. Ency. Mathematicians; contbr. numerous articles to profl. jours. Recipient Disting. Tchg. award, U. S.C., 1985, Outstanding Tchr. award, Amoco Found., 1985; grantee, Rotary Internat. Mem. Am. Math. Soc., Math. Assn. Am. (sect. lectr. 1997-98, S.C. state dir. 2000—), Sigma Xi, Pi Mu Epsilon. Home: 4407 Green Bay Trl Myrtle Beach SC 29577-2651 Office: Coastal Carolina U Conway SC 29528-6054 Fax: 843-349-2344. E-mail: saxenas@coastal.edu., scsaxen@yahoo.com.

SAXER, RICHARD KARL, metallurgical engineer, retired air force officer; b. Toledo, Aug. 31, 1928; s. Alexander Albert and Gertrude Minnie (Kuebeler) S.; m. Marilyn Doris Mersereau, July 19, 1952; children: Jane Lynette, Robert Karl, Kris Renee, Ann Luette. Student, Bowling Green State U., 1946-48; BS, U. S. Naval Acad., 1952; MS in Aero. Mechanics Engring., Air Force Inst. Tech., 1957; PhD in Metall. Engring., Ohio State U., 1962; grad., Armed Forces Staff Coll., 1966, Indsl. Coll. Armed Forces, 1971. Commd. 2d lt. U.S. Air Force, 1952, advanced through grades to lt. gen., 1976; electronics officer, mech. officer (4th Tactical Support Sqadron, Tactical Air Command), Sandia Base, N.Mex., 1953-54; electronics and mech. officer, spl. weapons assembly sect. supr. (SAC 6th Aviation Depot Squadron), French Morocco, 1954-55; project engr. mech. equipment br. Air Force Spl. Weapon's Center, Kirtland AFB, N.Mex., 1957-59; project officer Nuclear Safety div., 1959-60; assoc. prof. dept. engring. mechanics Air Force Inst. Tech., 1962-66; asso. prof., dep. dept. head USAF Acad., 1966-70; comdr., dir. Air Force Materials Lab., Wright-Patterson AFB, Ohio, 1971-74; dep. for Reentry System Space and Missile Systems Orgn., 1974-77; dep. for aero equipment Aero. Systems Div., 1977-80, dep. for tactical systems, 1980, vice comdr., 1981-83; aero. systems div. dir. Def. Nuclear Agy., 1983-85, ret., 1985; pres. R.K. Saxer & Assocs., 1985-91; CEO Universal Tech. Corp., Dayton, Ohio, 1991—96. Research and tech. com. materials and structures NASA, 1973-74; chmn. planning group aerospace materials Interagy. Council Materials, 1973-74; mem. Nat. Mil. Adv. Bd., 1971-74, NATO adv. group for research and devel., 1973-74 Contbr. articles to profl. jours. Decorated Def. Disting. Svc. medal, Legion of Merit, Meritorious Service medal USAF, D.S.M., Joint Svc. Commendation medal, Air Force Commendation medal with 3 oak leaf clusters, Army Commendation medal U.S., Def. Superior Service medal, Cross of Gallantry with palm Vietnam, Def. Meritorious Service medal; recipient Disting. award for systems mgmt. Air Force Assn., 1979; Disting. Alumnus award Ohio State U., 1986. Mem. Air Force Assn., Am. Def. Preparedness Assn. (pres. Dayton 1977-78), Sigma Xi, Phi Lambda Epsilon, Alpha Sigma Mu, Masons, Shriners. Home: 215 Dalfaber Ln Springboro OH 45066-1571

SAXL, RICHARD HILDRETH, lawyer; b. Boston, June 3, 1948; BA, U. Pa., 1970; JD, Rutgers U., Camden, N.J., 1975. Bar: Conn. 1976, U.S. Dist. Ct. Conn. 1976, U.S. Ct. Appeals (2d cir.) 1977. Assoc. Jerry Davidoff, Westport, Conn., 1976-78; ptnr. Davidoff & Saxl, 1979-94; pvt. practice law offices Richard H. Saxl, 1994—; town atty. Fairfield, Conn., 1997—99, 2001—. Mem. Fairfield Town Plan and Zoning Commn., 1981-93, chmn., 1991-93; chair Fairfield Land Acquisition com., 1997; mem. Fairfield Charter Revision Commn., 1984-85, 92. Recipient Svc. award, Conn. Fedn. Planning and Zoning Agys., 1993, cert. of commendation, Conn. Jud. Dept. Mem. Conn. Bar Assn., Westport Bar Assn., Pequot Yacht Club. Democrat. Avocations: squash, astronomy. Home: 753 Sasco Hill Rd Fairfield CT 06430-6376 Office: 5 Imperial Ave Westport CT 06880-4302 E-mail: rhsaxl@aol.com.

SAXON, RANDALL LEE, pastor, author, educator; b. Waverly, N.Y., Oct. 28, 1947; s. Sherman Kenyon and Velma Marie (Dunning) S.; m. Diane Louise Kennedy, June 23, 1973 (div. Feb. 1985); children: Heather Marie, David Arthur; m. Anna Louise Clock, Mar. 15, 1986; children: Jennifer Elizabeth, Austin Todd. BA, Mansfield U., 1969; MDiv, Princeton Sem., 1973; certificate, Mansfield Coll., Oxford, England, 1980; D of Ministry, Drew U., 1992. Ordained to ministry Presbyn. Ch. U.S.A., 1973. Asst. pastor United Meth. Ch., Flemington, N.J., 1970-71; intern pastor Wattsburg (Pa.) Presbyn. Ch., 1971-72, East Greene Presbyn. Ch., Erie, Pa., 1971-72; asst. pastor Fewsmith Presbyn. Ch., Bellville, N.J., 1972-73; assoc. pastor Presbyn. Ch., Gettysburg, Pa., 1973-78; sr. pastor 1st Presbyn. Ch., Southampton, N.Y., 1978-86, Presbyn. Ch. of the Covenant, Port Arthur, Tex., 1986-91, 1st Presbyn. Ch., Wilmette, Ill., 1991-94, Peoria, 1994—; instr. parish nursing program OSF St. Francis Med. Ctr., 1995-99; instr. Inst. Learning in Retirement Bradley U., 1995—; instr. social scis. Ill. Ctrl. Coll., East Peoria, 1999—. Nat. chaplain Sigma Theta Epsilon, Mansfield, Pa., 1968-72; permanent clk. Presbytery of Carlisle, Camp Hill, Pa., 1975-77, Synod of the Trinity, Camp Hill, 1977-78; jour. clk. Presbytery of L.I., Commack, N.Y., 1980-84; mem. Presbytery of Great Rivers. Author: Voices in the Wilderness, 1985, Parables for People of God, 1992, Developing A Ministry of Evangelism With Baby Boomers in A Suburban Setting, 1992, Abraham Lincoln: The Man Beyond the Myth, 1999; also articles, poetry, hymns. Program dir. Camp Brule, Boy Scouts Am., Forksville, Pa., 1972; dir. Youth in Govt. Seminar, Harrisburg, Pa., 1977; v.p. Internat. Seamen's Ctr., Houston, 1987-89; chairperson City Task Force on Edn. Summit, Port Arthur, 1990-91; active Presbyn. Hist. Soc. Recipient cert. Shinnecock Indian Tribe, 1981; named an Outstanding Young Man of Am., Jaycees, 1971; Susquehanna Collegiate Inst. grantee, 1972. Mem. Acad. Parish Clergy, Am. Soc. Ch. History, Presbyn. Hist. Soc., Presbyn. Writers Guild, Scottish Soc. S.E. Tex. (pres. 1991-92), The Co. of Pastors, The Lincoln Party, The Lincoln Project, Abraham Lincoln Assn., Rotary (pres. 1977-78). Democrat. Avocations: numismatics, canoeing, white-water rafting, travel, gardening. Home: 3628 N Breckenridge Ct Peoria IL 61614-8034 Office: First Presbyn Ch 1101 Hamilton Blvd Peoria IL 61606-1522 E-mail: 1stpres@mtco.com.

SAXON, WOLFGANG ERIK GEORG, journalist; b. Leipzig, Germany, Sept. 5, 1930; arrived in U.S., 1952; s. Erich Otto and Klâre (Wochatz) Richter; m. Anna Forti, 1967. BS, Columbia U., 1954; postgrad., Columbia U. (Russian Inst.), 1960. Newspaper reporter, obituarist The New York Times, 1956—. With U.S. Army, 1954-56. Mem. The Silurians, Phi Beta Kappa. Avocations: reading, walking, travel. Office: The New York Times 229 W 43rd St New York NY 10036-3959 E-mail: www.saxon@nytimes.

SAXONHOUSE, GARY ROGER, economics educator, consultant; b. N.Y.C., June 21, 1943; s. Ernest George and Amy (Zweig) S.; m. Arlene Warmbrunn, June 28, 1964; children: Lilly Adaela, Noam Hans, Elena Kathryn. BA, Yale U., 1964, MA, 1966, MPhil, 1968, PhD, 1971. Acting instr. Yale U., New Haven, 1969-70; lectr. U. Mich., Ann Arbor, 1970-71, asst. prof. econs., 1971-75, assoc. prof., 1975-80, prof., 1980—, dir. Commn. on Comparative-Hist. Rsch. on Market Economies, 1980—. Vis. lectr. Harvard U., Cambridge, Mass., 1975; Henry Luce prof. comparative devel. Brown U., Providence, 1980-81; fellow Ctr. Advanced Study in Behavioral Sci., Stanford, Calif., 1984-85; cons. Coun. Econ. Advisers, Washington, 1989-90; disting. lectr. Assn. for Asian Studies, 1979; mem. adv. bd. Found. Advanced Info.and Rsch., Tokyo, 1987—, Inst. Fiscal and Monetary Policy, Tokyo, 1987—, Japanese Ministry Fin., Tokyo, 1987—, Rsch. Inst. Internat. Trade and Industry, Tokyo, 1988—, Japan Found., Tokyo, 1988—. Author: Comparative Technology Choice, 1988; editor Technique, Spirit and Form in the Making of Modern Economies, 1984, Law and Trade Issues of the Japanese Economy, 1986; contbr. articles to profl. jours. Mem. adv. panel on Am. competitiveness Office Tech. Assessment, U.S. Congress, Washington, 1981-82, mem. adv. panel on civilian uses space. 1984-85. Rsch. grantee NSF, 1979-81, 84-86, Ford Found., 1981-83. Mem. Am. Econ. Assn., Econ. History Assn. (nominating com. 1988—, editorial bd. 1990—), Com. on Japanese Econ. Studies (chmn. 1977—). Home: 2025 Vinewood Blvd Ann Arbor MI 48104-3613 Office: U Mich 611 Tappan St Ann Arbor MI 48109-1220

SAXTON, H. JAMES, congressman; b. Scranton, Pa., Jan. 22, 1943; s. Hugh R. and Helen M. (Billings) S.; m. Helen Jean Gadomski, June 9, 1965; children— Jennifer, James Martin BA, East Stroudsburg State Coll., 1965; postgrad. in elem. edn., Temple U., 1967-68. Tchr. Bordentown Pub. Schs., Bordentown, N.J., 1965-68; realtor Jim Saxton Realty Co., 1968-85; assemblyman N.J. State Assembly, Trenton, 1975-81; state senator N.J. State Senate, 1981-84; mem. U.S. Congress from 3rd N.J. dist., Washington, 1985—; mem. armed svcs. com., resources com., chmn. wildlife subcom., chmn. joint econ. com. Mem. travel and tourism caucus, maritime caucus, congl. port caucus environ. and energy study conf., Rep. study com., Stripers Ltd. (99th Congress); sec. N.J. Congl. Del., Washington, 1985-89. Active Boy Scouts Am., Burlington Council. Bordentown C. of C. Clubs: Leadership Found. N.J. Lodges: Elks. Office: US Ho of Reps 339 Cannon House Office Bldg Washington DC 20515-0001

SAXTON, LLOYD, psychologist, writer; b. Loveland, Colo., Sept. 28, 1929; s. Oliver George and Alice Augusta (Andersen) S.; m. Nancy Alison Roberts, Dec. 17, 1955; children: Perry Brent, Jay Ronald, Barbara Jean. AB in English, U. Calif., Berkeley, 1950, BS in Psychology, 1954; MS in Psychology, San Francisco State U., 1955; PhD in Psychology, U. of the Pacific, Stockton, Calif., 1957. Diplomate Am. Bd. Forensic Examiners (cert. 1996); lic. psychologist, Calif. Intern in clin. psychology Chidlren's Hosp., San Francisco, 1955-56; teaching fellow U. Pacific, 1955-57, instr. psychology, 1957-58, asst. prof. psychology, 1958-60; assoc. prof. psychology Am. Acad. of Asian Studies, 1960-62, prof. psychology, 1962-65; chmn. dept. psychology Coll. of San Mateo, Calif., 1965-75, prof. psychology, 1975-92; pvt. practice San Francisco/Larkspur, 1958—; emeritus, 1995. Author: Individual, Marriage and the Family, 1968, Individual, 9th edit., 1996; author/editor: A Marriage Reader, 1970, The American Scene, 1970. Mem. APA, AAAS, AAUP, Am. Assn. Marriage and Family Therapists, Western Psychol. Assn., Am. Coll. Forensic Examiners, Mensa, Am. Chess Fedn. Democrat. Avocations: chess, sailing, music, ballet, opera. Home and Office: 57 Hatzic Ct Larkspur CA 94939-1992.ital

SAXTON, MARY JANE, management educator; b. Syracuse, N.Y., Mar. 3, 1953; d. John Cook and Florence (Cooper) S.; m. Paul Hood. BA, SUNY, Cortland, 1975; MBA, U. Pitts., 1979, PhD, 1987. Counselor Methadone Mgmt. Svcs., Inc., N.Y.C., 1975-76; resident mgr. Crossroads Svcs., Inc., Jackson, Miss., 1976; outreach worker Jackson Mental Health Ctr., 1977-78; cons. Organizational Design Cons., Inc., Pitts., 1982-83, mktg. dir., 1984-86; asst. prof. mgmt. U. Houston, 1988-93; lectr. mgmt. U. Colo., Denver, 1994-97, U. Denver, 1994-96, Colo. Christian Coll., Denver, 1996; lectr. Met. State Coll., 1996-97; vis. assoc. prof. in strategy Norwegian Sch. Mgmt., Oslo, 1997-98, vis assoc. prof. in knowledge mgmt., 1999; orgnl. cons. Internat. Petroleum Cons. Assn., Inc., Evergreen, Colo., 1999—2002; vis. instr. U. Colo., Denver, 2000. Sabbatical researching Arab culture, Abu Dhabi, United Arab Emirates, 2001—01; cons. Wessex, Ctr. for Creative Comm., Kodak, Children's Hosp., Pullman Swindell, Westinghouse Elec. Corp.; lectr. in field; orgnl. cons. IPCA, Inc., Bergen, Norway. Co-editor: Gaining Control of the Corporate Culture, 1985; co-author: The Kilmann-Saxton Culture-Gap Survey, 1983; contbr. articles to profl. jours. Active Greater Houston Women's Found., 1991-93. U.S.-Soviet Joint Ventures grantee U. Houston, 1990. Mem. ASTD, Acad. of Mgmt., Inst. Ops. Rsch. and Mgmt. Svcs. Avocations: flying, sailing, reading, biking, movies. Home and Office: PO Box 1657 Evergreen CO 80437-1657

SAXTON, WILLIAM MARVIN, lawyer; b. Joplin, Mo., Feb. 14, 1927; s. Clyde Marvin and Lea Ann (Farnan) S.; m. Helen Grace Klinefelter, June 1, 1974; children: Sherry Lynn, Patricia Ann Painter, William Daniel, Michael Lawrence. AB, U. Mich., 1949, JD, 1952. Bar: Mich. Mem. firm Love, Snyder & Lewis, Detroit, 1952-53, Butzel, Long, Detroit, 1953—, dir., chmn., CEO, 1989-96, dir. emeritus, 1997—. Lectr. Inst. Continuing Legal Edn.; sec., bd. dirs. Fritz Broadcasting, Inc., 1983-97; mem. mediation tribunal hearing panel for 3d Jud. Dist. Mich., 1989—, 6th Jud. Dist., 1994—. Trustee Detroit Music Hall Ctr. Soc. for the Performing Arts, 1984-99; trustee Hist. Soc. U.S. Dist. Ct. (ea. dist.) Mich., 1992-95, pres., 1993-95. Recipient Distinguished award Mich. Road Builders Assn., 1987. Master of Bench Emeritus Am. Inn of Court; fellow Am. Coll. Trial Lawyers, Am. Bar Found., Am. Coll. Labor and Employment Lawyers, Mich. Bar Found.; mem. ABA, FBA, Detroit Bar Assn. (dir. 1974-79, Goodnow Pres.'s award 1996), Mich. Bar Assn. (atty. discipline panel, Disting. Svc. award 1998), Detroit Indsl. Rels. Rsch. Assn. (treas. 1980—, v.p. 1982, pres. 1984-85), Mich. Young Lawyers (pres. 1954-55), Am. Law Inst., Indsl. Rels. Rsch. Assn. Am. Arbitration Assn., U.S. 6th Cir. Ct. Appeals (life, mem. jud. conf., mem. bicentennial com.), Am. Inn Ct., Cooley Club, Renaissance Club, Detroit Golf Club (dir. 1983-89), Detroit Athletic Club. Office: Butzel Long 150 W Jefferson Ave Ste 900 Detroit MI 48226-4416

SAY, BURHAN, physician; b. Istanbul, Turkey, Feb. 26, 1923; came to U.S. 1951; s. Ethem Serif and Ayse Say; m. Elizabeth E. Jackson, Nov. 5, 1955; children: Ahmet Serif, Daniel Demir. MD, U. Istanbul, 1946. Diplomate Am. Bd. Pediatrics, Am. Bd. Med. Genetics. Asst. prof. pediatrics Hacettepe U., Ankara, Turkey, 1960-64, prof. pediatrics Turkey, 1964-73; clin. prof. of pediatrics U. of Okla./Tulsa Med. Coll., 1975—. Dir. H.A. Chapman Inst., Tulsa, 1982—; v.p. Children's Med. Ctr., Tulsa, 1988—. Contbr. articles to profl. jours. Pres. Am. Cancer Soc., Tulsa, 1980-90, Great Plains Genetics Soc., Tulsa, 1993. Lt. Turkish Army, 1946-48, Turkey. Fulbright scholar, Boston, 1966-68. Avocation: sports. Home: 6216 E 99th St Tulsa OK 74137-5503 Office: HA Chapman Inst Med Genetics Schusterman Health Scis Ctr 4502 E 41st St Tulsa OK 74135-6566 E-mail: Mbsay@aol.com.

SAY, CALVIN, state legislator; b. Feb. 1, 1952; m. Cora Say; children: Geoffrey, Jared. BEd, U. Hawaii at Manoa. Mem. state house State of Hawaii, 1976—; mgr. Kotake Shokai Ltd. Chmn. fin. com. Staste of Hawaii, mem. labor mgmt. com. Mem. Palolo Little League, Pop Warner, Hawaii Youth Symphony, Hawaii Sports Hall of Fame and Mus., Palolo Cmty. Coun., Honolulu Symphony Soc., Gov.'s Com. Commemorating the Chinese Bicentennial,; dir. Pacific Rim Found. Democrat. Office: Hawaii Ho Reps Hawaii State Capitol Rm 431 415 S Beretania St Honolulu HI 96813-2407*

SAY, CARLOS C. physician, surgeon; b. Philippines, Aug. 4, 1940; came to U.S., 1964; s. Felipe and Teresa Chua S.; m. Loretta Young, May 31, 1969; children: Brian Patrick, Janice Charlene. AA, U. Santo Thomas, Manila, 1959, MD, 1964; MS in Pub. Health, U. Mo., 1973. Intern Cambridge (Mass.) City Hosp., 1964-65; resident in gen. surgery The Carney Hosp., 1965-68; fellowship in surg. oncology Boston U. Med. Ctr., 1970-71; postdoctoral trainee NIH-Nat. Cancer Inst., 1971-73; chmn. dept. of clin. oncology Oak Forest (Ill.) Hosp., 1973-75; pvt. practice Atwater, Calif., 1975—. Staff physician Mercy Hosp., Merced, Calif., 1975—, Merced Cmty. Med. Ctr., 1975—, Bloss Meml. Dist. Hosp., Atwater, 1975—, Meml. Hosp. of Los Banos, Calif., 1990—. Contbr. articles to profl. jours. Fellow Am. Acad. of Family Physicians, Internat. Coll. of Surgeons, Am. Soc. of Abdominal Surgeons, Am. Coll. Emergency Physicians; mem. Merced Mariposa Med. Soc., Calif. Med. Assn., Am. Soc. of Clin. Oncology, Am. Assn. for Cancer Rsch., Am. Soc. of Gastrointestinal Endoscopy Am. Burn Assn., Am. Soc. of Enteral and Hyperalimentation Assn., Am. Assn. for Cancer Edn., U. Mo. Med. Sch. Alumni, Calif. Thracic Soc., Am. Acad. of Family Practice, N.Y. Acad. of Sci.

SAYAMA, HIROKI, researcher; DSc, U. Tokyo, 1999. Postdoctoral fellow New Eng. Complex Sys. Inst., Cambridge, Mass., 1999—2002; assoc. in rsch. Edwin O. Reischauer Inst. Japanese Studies Harvard U., 2000—01; asst. prof. U. Electro-Comm., Tokyo, 2002—. Overseas scholar Murata Overseas Scholarship Found., Japan, 1999-2001. Mem. IEEE, IEEE Computer Soc., Soc. for Math. Biology, Japanese Assn. for Math. Biology, Internat. Soc. for Artificial Life. Office: Univ Electro-Comm Dept Human Comm 1-5-1 Chofugaoka Chofu Tokyo 182-8585 Japan E-mail: sayama@hc.uec.ac.jp.

SAYATOVIC, WAYNE PETER, manufacturing company executive; b. Cleve., Feb. 8, 1946; m. Janice Elaine Zajac; children: Jason Scott, Jamie Elizabeth. BA in Econs., Syracuse U., 1967, MBA in Fin., 1969, fin. mgmt. program, 1969—72. Fin. and cost acctg. mgr. Lubriquip divsn. Houdaille Industries Inc., Solon, Ohio, 1972—88, contr. Hydraulics divsn. Buffalo, 1975-77, contr. Strippit divsn. Akron, 1977-79, treas. Ft. Lauderdale, Fla., 1979-86, v.p., treas., sec. Northbrook, Ill., 1986-88, IDEX Corp., Northbrook, 1988—, v.p. fin., CFO, sec., 1992-94, sr. v.p. fin., CFO, sec., 1994-98, sr. v.p. fin., CFO, 1998—. Mem. Mfrs.' Alliance for Productivity & Innovation (fin. coun.). Office: IDEX Corp 630 Dundee Rd Ste 400 Northbrook IL 60062-2745

SAYED, M. GARY, healthcare administrator, educator, scientist; BS in Nuclear Med. Sci., U. of Incarnate Word, San Antonio, 1985; MS in Radiochem., U. Iowa, 1989; PhD in Radiol. Scis., Med. Coll. Ohio, 1993. Med. health physicist U. Iowa, Iowa City, 1989-91; asst. prof. nuclear medicine U. Findlay, Ohio, 1992-97, asst. dir. Nuclear Medicine Inst., 1992-96, acting dir. Nuclear Med. Inst., 1997; assoc. prof. Thomas Jefferson U., Phila., 1998—, chmn. dept. diagnostic imaging, 1998—. Vis. prof. radiology Dokuz Eylul U., Izmir, Turkey, 1996; vis. prof. nuc. medicine Kuwait U., Kuwait, 2001—02; pres. Am. Bd. of Sci. in Nuc. Medicine. Editor: Nuclear Medicine Science Syllabus, 3d edit., 1999; guest editor: Radiologic Sci. and Edn. Jour. Recipient Leadership award Assn. Schs. of Health Professions, 1998; sr. Fulbright scholar, 1996. Fellow Am. Coll. Nuclear Medicine. Office: Thomas Jefferson U Dept Diagnostic Imaging 130 S 9th St Ste 1009 Philadelphia PA 19107-5233 E-mail: gary.sayed@mail.tju.edu.

SAYEED, USMAN AHMED, general engineer; b. Nellore, India, Nov. 15, 1939; came to U.S., 1970, naturalized, 1979; s. Mohammad Saiduddin and Zainab Begum; m. Gurdev Kaur Singh, Oct. 1, 1969; children— Iqbal, Siraj, Yusef. B.Sc. with honors, Andhra U., Waltair, India, 1959, M.Sc., 1960; M.Sc., Meml. U. Nfld., St. Johns, Can., 1970; Ph.D., U. Nebr., 1973; M.B.A., CUNY, 1979. Research asst. India Inst. Tech., Kharagpur, 1960; geologist Geol. Survey, Calcutta, India, 1961-68; research asst. Meml. U. Nfld., 1968-70; grad. teaching asst. U. Nebr., Lincoln, 1970-73; adj. asst. prof. Hofstra U., Hempstead, N.Y., 1974, 75; asst. prof. Fla. Internat. U., Miami, 1975-78; mining engr. IRS, Pitts., 1979-87, IRS, Louisville, Ky., 1987— . Contbr. articles to profl. publs. Fellow Geol. Assn. Can., Geol. Soc. India; mem. Am. Geophys. Union, Assn. Geologists for Internat. Devel., Sigma Xi. Democrat. Muslim.

SAYER, COLETTA KEENAN, gifted education educator; b. Cleve., July 4, 1950; d. Nicholas Charles and Coletta (Kuonen) Yawarsky; m. Mark Andrew Sayer, June 3, 1978; 1 child, Mark Martin. BA, St. Mary of the Wood Coll., 1972. Classroom tchr. Cath. Diocese of Cleve., 1972-76; learning disabilities specialist Brunswick (Ohio) Bd. Edn., 1976-77; classroom tchr. of gifted Houston Bd. Edn., 1988-91; tchr. ESL Benbrook Elem. Sch. Houston Ind. Sch. Dist., 1991-96; coord. gifted and talented Benbrook Elem. Sch., 1998—. Peer coord. Houston Ind. Sch. Dist., Algebra Initiative Fifth Grade. Houston Bus. Com. for Excellence in Edn. grantee, 1989. Mem. ASCD, Houston Classroom Tchrs. Assn. (pres. 1996—). Roman Catholic. Avocation: drama. Office: Benbrook Elem Sch 4026 Bolin Rd Houston TX 77092-4711 E-mail: csayer@houstonisd.org.

SAYER, RONALD J. composer, educator; b. Rochester, NY, Oct. 12, 1961; s. Barbara Sayer. B Music Edn., U. Mo., Kansas City, 1985; MEd, Tex. Wesleyan U., Ft. Worth, 2000—02. Vocal music instr. Lansing (Kans.) Unified Sch. Dist., 1985—97; artistic dir. Marshall (Mo.) Cmty. Chorus, 2000—; vocal music instr. Marshall H.S., 1997—, chmn. fine arts dept., 2000—. V.p. Mid-Missouri Fine Arts Coun., Marshall, 2002—. Mem. music com. St. Peter's Cath. Ch., Marshall, 1999—2002. Recipient Mo. Fine Arts Acad. Tchr. award, Mo. Fine Arts Acad.- S.W. Mo. State U., 2000, 2002, Sharon Murphy award for Dedication to Edn., Kans. NEA, 1996; scholar, U. Mo.-Kansas City, 1994. Mem.: Music Educators Nat. Conf., Am. Choral Directors Assn., Omicron Delta Kappa, Pi Kappa Lambda, Phi Mu Alpha Sinfonia. Home: 1017 S Ann Drive Marshall MO 65340 Office: Marshall Public Schs 805 S Miami Ave Marshall MO 65340

SAYERS, KEN W(ILLIAM), writer, consultant and public relations executive, web editor; b. N.Y.C., July 31, 1942; s. William Verey and Doris Edith (Weale) S.; m. Rose Mary Beirao, Aug. 20, 1965; children: Wendy Elizabeth, Matthew Verey. BA in Journalism, CCNY, 1965; postgrad., Columbia U., 1970. Dep. chief book br. Office Asst. Sec. of Def. for Pub. Affairs, Washington, 1967-69; mgr. rsch. and analysis DMS, Inc., Greenwich, Conn., 1969-72; mgr. rsch. and publs. Lulejian & Assocs., Inc., Falls Church, Va., 1972-74; mgr. internat. pub. affairs Am. Cyanamid Co., Wayne, N.J., 1974-77; various positions IBM Corp., 1977—. Pres. Halyard Ptnrs., Ridgefield, Conn., 1994—. Co-author: Anchors and Atoms, It Was a Very Good Year; author: Industrial Lasers; editor: Missiles and Spacecraft, World Aircraft Forecast; contbr. articles to profl. jours. Exec. officer Queens Nautical Cadets, Astoria, N.Y., 1963-65. Lt. USN, 1965-69. Decorated Joint Svc. Commendation medal. Home: 342 Limestone Rd Ridgefield CT 06877-2635 Office: IBM Corp Rt# 100 Somers NY 10589 E-mail: halyardp@ntplx.net.

SAYERS, MARTIN PETER, pediatric neurosurgeon; b. Big Stone Gap, Va., Jan. 2, 1922; s. Delbert Bancroft and Loula (Thompson) S.; m. Marjorie W. Garvin, May 8, 1943; children: Daniel Garvin Sayers, Stephen Putnam Sayers, Julia Hathaway Sayers Bolton, Elaine King Sayers Buck. BA, Ohio State U., 1943, MD, 1945; postgrad., U. Pa., 1948-51. Intern Phila. Gen. Hosp., 1945-46; resident in neurosurgery U. Pa. Hosps., Phila., 1948-51; practice medicine specializing in neurosurgery Columbus, Ohio, 1951—; mem. faculty Ohio State U., 1951-87, clin. prof. neurosurgery, 1968-87, emeritus, chief dept. pediatric neurosurgery, 1960-87. Cons. Bur. Crippled Children Services Ohio.; Neurosurgeon Project Hope, Ecuador, 1964, Ceylon, 1968, Cracow, Poland, 1979 Served as lt. jr. grade M.C., USN, 1946-48. Mem. Am. Assn. Neurol. Surgeons (chmn. pediatric sect.), Congress Neurol. Surgeons (pres.), Neurosurg. Soc. Am. (pres.), Am. Soc. Pediatric Neurosurgery, Soc. Neurol. Surgeons. Office: 931 Chatham Ln Columbus OH 43221-2417

SAYKIEWICZ-SAJKIEWICZ, JAN NAPOLEON, marketing educator; b. Lublin, Poland, June 10, 1939; came to U.S., 1987; s. Jan Sajkiewicz and Ewa Komorowska; m. Elzbieta Katarzyna Przetacznik, Aug. 27, 1966; children: Jan Rafal, Olaf Xawery, Mateusz Konstanty. MS in Econs., Ctrl. Sch. Planning & Stats., Warsaw, Poland, 1962, PhD, 1969; diploma in African studies, U. Warsaw, 1968; diploma, U. Calif., Berkeley, 1972. Cert. internat. tourism profl. Rsch. assoc. U. Calif., Berkeley, 1972-73; asst., assoc. prof. Ctrl. Sch. Planning & Stats., Warsaw, 1962-75; lectr. in mktg. Exec. Tng. Ctrs., 1969-88; assoc. prof. U. Warsaw, 1974-88; lectr., prof. Warsaw Acad. Arts, 1980-87; prof. Duquesne U. Sch. Bus. Adminstrn., Pitts., 1987—, L. Kozminski Acad. Entrepreneurship and Mgmt., Warsaw, 1998—. Vis. prof. Fordham U., N.Y.C., 1978, Duquesne U., Pitts., 1981, No. Jiaotong U., Beijing, 1997; Fulbright prof., 2000-2001; expert Internat. Labor Orgn., Geneva, 1982; vice-chmn., bd. dirs. Consumer Cooperative Enterprises, Warsaw, 1982-88; mem. Inter-Polcom, Chamber of Industry, Commerce, Warsaw, 1984-86; sec. gen., chief treas. Polish Mktg. Assn., 1974-81, exec. bd., 1985-88. Author: Concentration of Commercial Activities, 1972, Marketing Concept in Business Management, 1975, 2nd edit., 1976, 3rd edit., 1977, Management Systems in Integrated Capitalist Business, 1975; contbr. articles to profl. jours.; transl. profl. lit. Active Solidarity Movement, Poland, 1980-81; social and econ. coun., The Capital City of Warsaw, Poland, 1987-88. Vis. scholar U. Calif, Berkeley, 1972-73, Fordham U., N.Y., 1978, No. Jiaotong U., Beijing, 1997; Ford Found. fellow, 1972-73; Rsch. grantee U.S. Dept. Edn., 1993, 94; recipient Silver and Gold Crosses of Merit, Coun. of State, Poland, 1980, 82, Individual award for pedagogical performance Min. of Edn., Poland, 1981, Golden Mermaid Hon. Decoration for svc., Capital City of Warsaw, 1985. Fellow: Am. Acad. Mktg. Sci.; mem.: Polish Inst. Arts and Scis. in Am. (bd. dirs. 1995—97), Am. Mktg. Assn., Acad. Internat. Bus., Internat. Mgmt. Devel. Assn. (exec. v.p. 1997, pres. 2002, award 2001). Roman Catholic. Avocations: social studies, books, travel, cognac. Home: 5853 Douglas St Pittsburgh PA 15217-2101 E-mail: saykiewicz@duq.edu.

SAYLES, BRENDA CHRISTIAN, retired customer service administrator; b. Richmond, Va., May 18, 1961; d. George Anderson and Gloria (Leola) Christian; children: Xavier Lance, Jasmine Dionna1 stepchild Kimberly D. Student, John Tyler C.C., Chester, Va., Va. Commonwealth U. From clk., typist to quality control auditor Philip Morris USA, Richmond, Va., 1978—2000, consumer complaints specialist, 2000—02. Author: (poems) Feelings Within, 1997. Team capt. Jr. Achievement, Richmond, 1999—2001; participant Multiple Sclerosis Soc. Walkathon, 2000. Mem.: Internat. Mgmt. Coun. (registration chair divsn. conf. 2001, v.p. programs 2001—02). Baptist. Avocations: writing, poetry, travel, music.

SAYLES, CATHY A. lawyer; b. Kansas City, Mo., Sept. 8, 1960; d. Harold Richard and June A. Sayles. BA, U. Kans., 1982, JD, 1985. Bar: Kans. 1985, U.S. Dist. Ct. Kans. 1985, U.S. Ct. Appeals (8th and 10th cirs.) 1985. Assoc. Shamberg, Johnson, Bergman & Goldman, Overland Park, Kans., 1985-86, Couch & Pierce, Overland Park, 1986-89; sr. atty. for litigation Koch Industries, Inc., Wichita, Kans., 1989-95; legal cons., Kansas City, Mo., 1995-97; gen. counsel Ferrellgas, Inc., Liberty, 1997—. Mem. Phi Beta Kappa. Office: Ferrellgas Inc One Liberty Pla Liberty MO 64068

SAYLES, LEONARD ROBERT, management educator, consultant; b. Rochester, N.Y., Apr. 30, 1926; s. Robert and Rose (Sklof) S.; m. Kathy Ripin; children: Robert, Emily. BA with highest distinction, U. Rochester, 1946; PhD in Econs. and Social Sci, MIT, 1950. Asst. prof. Cornell U., 1950-53, U. Mich., 1953-56; prof. emeritus Grad. Sch. Bus. Adminstrn., Columbia U., 1956-91, prof. bus. adminstrn., 1962—, head div. indsl. relations and orgnl. behavior, 1960-72; adviser to adminstr. NASA, 1966-71; sr. rsch. scientist Ctr. for Creative Leadership, Greensboro, N.C., 1988-94. Disting. vis. lectr. McGill U., 1974; bd. govs. Center for Creative Leadership, 1984-88. Author: (with G. Strauss) The Local Union, 1953, Managerial Behavior, 1964, Human Behavior in Organizations, 1966, (with E. Chapple) Measure of Management, 1961, Behavior of Industrial Work Groups, 1958, Individualism and Big Business, 1963, (with W. Dowling) How Managers Motivate, 1971, (with M. Chandler) Managing Large Systems; Organizations for the Future, 1971, 2d edit., 1993, (with G. Strauss) Personnel, 4th edit, 1980, Managing Human Resources, 2d edit, 1981, Leadership, 1979, (with R. Burgelman) Inside Corporate Innovation, 1985, Managing in Real Organizations, 1989, The Working Leader, 1993, (with K. Ripin) Insider Strategies for Outsourcing Information Systems, 1999; mem. editorial bd. Human Orgn., 1957-62 Trustee Seacrest Sch., 1996-97. Fellow Am. Anthropol. Assn.; mem. Phi Beta Kappa. E-mail: LRSayles@aol.com.

SAYLES BELTON, SHARON, mayor, law educator; b. St. Paul, May 13, 1951; m. Steve Belton, Aug. 29, 1981; 3 children. Student, Macalester Coll., 1969-1973. Asst. dir. Minn. Program for Victims of Sexual Assault; parole officer Minn. Dept. Corrections; city coun. mem., 1983-93; coun. pres., 1989-93; mayor City of Mpls., 1994—2001; sr. fellow Roy Wilkins Ctr. Human Rels. and Social Justice U. Minn., 2001—. Pres., co- founder Nat. Coalition Against Sexual Assault; co-founder, pres. Harriet Tubman Shelter for Battered Women; trustee U.S. Conf. of Mayors, chair Youth Violence Task Forum; bd. dirs. Bush Found., Search Inst., Youth Coordinating Bd., Neighborhood Revitalization Program, Clean Water Partnership, Children's Healthcare and Hosp., Bush Found., U.S. Conf. Mayors, Nat. League Cities. Recipient Gertrude E. Rush Disting. Svc. award, Nat. Bar Assn., Rosa Parks award, Am. Assn. Affirmative Action . Office: U Minn Herbert Humphrey Inst Pub Affairs 301 19th Ave S Minneapolis MN 55455 E-mail: ssayles-belton@hhh.umn.edu.*

SAYLOR, CHARLES HORACE, lawyer; b. Bethlehem, Pa., Jan. 6, 1950; s. Howard James and Florence M. (Glasser) S.; m. Martha Louise Weaver, July 10, 1971; children: Amy Louise, Matthew Charles. BA, Pa. State U., 1971; JD, Dickinson Sch. Law, 1974. Bar: Pa. 1974, U.S. Dist. Ct. (mid. dist.) Pa. 1979. Law clk. Northumberland County Ct. Common Pleas, Sunbury, Pa., 1974-76; assoc. Wiest & Wiest, 1976-79; ptnr. Wiest, Wiest & Saylor, 1979-85, Wiest, Wiest, Saylor & Muolo, Sunbury, 1985-97, Wiest, Saylor, Muolo, Noon and Swinehart, Sunbury, 1998—2001; judge Court of Common Pleas, Northumberland County, Pa., 2002—. Solicitor Twp. of Rush, Pa., 1979-2001, Twp. of Point, Pa., 1983-2001, County of Northumberland, 1993-95; instr. Pa. State U., Schuylkill Haven, 1986. Asst. editor: Dickinson Law Rev., 1973, asst. editor: Northumberland (Pa.) Legal Jour., 1987—2001. Trustee Northumberland County Law Libr., 1986—, Priestley-Forsyth Meml. Libr., Northumberland, 1988-93, v.p., 1990-93; coach Am. Youth Soccer Assn., Northumberland, 1988-90; mem. com. YMCA, Sunbury, 1987-98, bd. dirs., 1991—, pres. of bd. dirs., 1997-98, chmn. sustaining campaign, 1992; asst. coach Girls Track and Field, Shikellamy H.S., 1992-93; profls. co-chair United Way, 2000-01. Mem. Pa. Bar Assn., Northumberland County Bar Assn. (sec.-treas. 1985-2000, pres. 2001), Pa. Trial Lawyers Assn. Republican. Roman Catholic. Avocations: running, golf. Home: 233 Honey Locust Ln Northumberland PA 17857-9679 Office: Northumberland County Courthouse 200 Market St Sunbury PA 17801

SAYLOR, HOWARD LEROY, JR. retired surgeon; b. Cogswell, N.D., July 25, 1917; s. Howard L. and Claire I. (Lyken) S.; m. Mary Ann Saylor, Apr. 1943 (dec. 1992); children: Mary Diane, Howard L. III, James C. AB, U. S.D., 1939, BS in Medicine, 1941; MD, Northwestern U., 1943. Diplomate Am. Bd. Surgery. Surg. resident Mayo Found., Rochester, Minn., 1947-50; active staff Huron (S.D.) Regional Med. Ctr., 1950-99, chief surg. com., chief of staff, 1950-96; clin. inst. surgery U. S.D. Med. Sch., Huron, 1954-90; ret., 1999. Cons. S.D. Crippled Children Hosp., Sioux Falls, 1980-86. Pres. C. of C., Huron, 1956-57; chair S.D. Welfare Commn., Pierre, 1966-72; mem. Govt. Hwy. Safety Com., Pierre, 1966-80; bd. dirs. Huron Coll., 1970-78. Capt. U.S. Army M.C., 1943-47, ETO. Decorated Bronze star; recipient Presidential citation U.S. Govt., 1978, C.B. Alford award S.D. Dept. Pub. Health, 1978. Fellow ACS; mem. S.D. State Med. Assn. (Cmty. Svc. award), Am. Soc. Gen. Surgery, Am. Legion, VFW. Republican. Episcopalian. Avocations: golf, hunting, sports, travel. Home: 1360 Ohio Ave SW Huron SD 57350-3526

SAYLOR, KATHLEEN MARIE, pediatric nurse practitioner; b. Suffern, N.Y., Dec. 4, 1956; d. Hans J. and Margaret M. (Brown) Wend; m. Robert A. Mohan, 1980 (dec. 1991); m. Richard Gary Saylor, Apr. 8, 1995. BS in Nursing, Duquesne U., 1978; MS in Nursing, U. Pa., 1988, CRNP, 1995. Post-masters cert. pediat. nurse practitioner, 1995. Nurse adult surg. staff Fitzgerald Mercy Hosp., Lansdown, Pa., 1978-80; nurse med. staff Children's Hosp. Phila., 1980-82, with short stay unit, 1982-83, primary nurse pediatric ICU, 1983-88; rehab. clin. nurse specialist Children's Rehab. Hosp., 1988-89; pediatric nursing instr. Roxborough Meml. Hosp., 1992-97; pediatric nurse practitioner Lehigh Valley Pediatric Assocs., Allentown, Pa., 1998—. Instr. basic cardiac life support Am. Heart Assn., Phila., 1987-90. Mem. Child Passenger Safety Project, Pa., 1986-88. Mem. AACN (workshop com. S.E. Pa. chpt. 1986-88, exec. bd. dirs. 1986), Am. Trauma Soc., Nurses Assn. Tchr. Edn. (mem. exec. com. 1994-96), Keystone Safety Belt Network, Sigma Theta Tau. Home: 3068 Bowers Mill Rd Pennsburg PA 18073-1904 Office: Lehigh Valley Pediatric Assocs 401 N 17th St Allentown PA 18104-5034

SAYLOR, PETER M. architect; b. Phila., July 26, 1941; s. Harry T. and Dorothy (Johnson) S.; m. Caroline Metcalf, Apr. 4, 1970; children: Thomas S., Elizabeth B. BArch, U. Pa., 1963, MArch, 1965. Registered arch., Iowa, Pa., N.J., Ind., Wis., Conn., Ohio, Minn. Architect Mitchell-Giurgola, Phila., 1967-70; ptnr. Dagit-Saylor Architects, 1970—. Design critic, juror U. Pa., 1975— ; bd. dirs. Found. for Architecture, Phila., 1980-90. Bd. dirs. Chestnut Hill Cmty. Assn., Phila., 1976—79, v.p., 1979; bd. dirs. All Saints Hosp., Wyndmoor, 1981—86, Cathedral Village Retirement Cmty., 1998—2001. Recipient various bldg. design award Fellow AIA (bd. dirs. Phila. chpt. 1973-82, chpt. pres. 1981-82); mem. Pa. Soc. Archs., Chestnut Hill Hist. Soc. (bd. dirs. 1988-95, pres. 1989-92), Phila. Soc. Preservation of Landmarks (bd. dirs. 1989-96, pres. 1993-94), Phila. Mus. Art (friends bd. dirs. 1990-93), Phila. Cricket Club (bd. dirs. 1985-91), Mask and Wig Club (pres. 1980-81, bd. dirs. 1970-84). Republican. Episcopalian. Office: Dagit-Saylor Archs 100 S Broad St Philadelphia PA 19110-1023 E-mail: psaylor@dagitsaylor.com.

SAYRAK, AKIN, economics educator; b. Bursa, Turkey, Apr. 10, 1969; came to U.S., 1994; BSc., Bogazici U., Istanbul, Turkey, 1994, MA, 1991; postgrad. studies in Fin., Econs., U. Tex., 1994—. Asst. instr. U. Tex., Austin, 1994—; asst. prof. U. Pitts., 1999—. Instr. U. Tex., Austin, 1996-97, Harvard U., Boston, 1998. Contbr. articles to Acad. Jours. Recipient Sabanci fellowship, Sabanci Holding Co., Istanbul, Turkey, 1988. fellowship U. Tex., 1996-98, Austin. Mem. Phi Kappa Phi. Avocations: photography, chess, guitar, motorcycle riding. E-mail address. Office: U Pitts Katz Grad Sch Bus Pittsburgh PA 15260 E-mail: asayrak@katz.pitt.edu.

SAYRE, DAVID, retired physicist; b. N.Y.C., Mar. 2, 1924; s. Ralph E. and Sylvia (Rosenbaum) S.; m. Anne Bowns, Dec. 26, 1947. BS, Yale U., 1944; MS, Auburn U., 1948; PhD, Oxford (Eng.) U., 1951. Staff mem. radiation lab. MIT, Cambridge, 1943-46; rsch. assoc. U. Pa., Phila., 1951-55; mathematician IBM Corp., N.Y.C., 1955-59, corp. dir. programming, 1959-62; mem. rsch. staff IBM T.J. Watson Rsch. Ctr., Yorktown Heights, N.Y., 1962-90, ret., 1990. Cons. U.S. Office Naval Rsch., London, 1951; mem. U.S.A. Nat. Com. for Crystallography, 1952-55, 81-84, vice chmn., 1984-86; vis. fellow All Souls Coll., Oxford U., 1972-73; guest scientist dept. physics SUNY, Stony Brook, 1980—; guest rschr. Brookhaven Nat. Lab., Upton, N.Y., 1983—; disting. guest prof. dept. chemistry Rutgers U., 1996-98. Co-author: Waveforms, 1947; editor: Computational Crystallography, 1983; co-editor: Structural Studies on Molecules of Biological Interest, 1983, X-Ray Microscopy II, 1988; contbr. numerous articles to profl. jours. Trustee Village of Head-of-the-Harbor, L.I., N.Y., 1975-95. Mem. Am. Crystallographic Assn. (treas. 1952-55, pres. 1983, Fankuchen award 1989) Episcopalian. Achievements include devel. of atomicity-based direct phasing method for x-ray crystallography, (with others) of first FORTRAN compiler and first virtual computer system; contbns. to x-ray microscopy; first observation (with others) of x-ray diffraction pattern from single biol. cell; extension of x-ray crystallographic methods into field of non-crystals.

SAYRE, EDWARD CHARLES, librarian; b. Longview, Wash., Aug. 15, 1923; s. Kenneth C. Sayre and Clare (Davis) Clingan; m. Virginia A. Hoy, June 9, 1951; children: Steven Anthony, Sabrina Karen. BA, Coll. of Gt. Falls, 1955; MA, U. Idaho, 1961; MLS, U. Md., 1968. Coord. libr. svcs. Thomas Nelson C.C., Hampton, Va., 1968-69; dir. Roswell (N.Mex.) Pub. Libr., 1969-70; cons. N.Mex. State Libr., Santa Fe, 1970-72; dir. Ctrl. Colo. Libr. System, Denver, 1972-78, Serra Coop. Libr. System, San Diego, 1978-79, Los Alamos (N.Mex.) County Libr. System, 1979-88; county adminstr. Los Alamos County, 1988-89; cons., 1976—. Contbr. articles to profl. jours. Mem. stat governing coun. Common Cause N.Mex. Home: 3 Timber Ridge Rd Los Alamos NM 87544-2317 E-mail: esayre4207@aol.com.

SAYRE, EDWARD VALE, chemist; b. Des Moines, Sept. 8, 1919; s. Edward Agnew and Audrey (Vale) S.; m. Virginia Nelle Rogers, Oct. 20, 1943. BS, Iowa State U., 1941; AM, Columbia U., 1943, PhD, 1949. Mgr. rsch. sect. Manhattan Dist. project Columbia U., 1942-45; rsch. chemist Eastman Kodak Rsch. Labs., Rochester, N.Y., 1949-52; sr. chemist Brookhaven Nat. Lab., Upton, 1952-84; rsch. phys. scientist Smithsonian Instn., Washington, 1984—. Dir. rsch. Museum Fine Arts, Boston, 1975-80, sr. scientist, 1980-84; sr. scientist Alexander von Humboldt Found., 1980; vis. lectr. Stevens Inst. Tech., 1955-61; adj. prof. fine arts Inst. Fine Arts, N.Y. U., 1960-74; disting. vis. prof. Am. U. Cairo, 1970; Regents prof. U. Calif., Irvine, 1972; mem. sci. adv. coun. Winterthur Mus. Contbr. numerous rsch. articles to profl. jours.; assoc. editor Archaeometry, 1969-93, Art and Archaeology Tech. Abstracts, 1970-87, Jour. Archaeol. Sci., 1971-77. Guggenheim fellow, 1969; recipient U.S. sr. scientist award Alexander von Humboldt Found., 1980-81, George von Hevesy medal, 1984, Alumni Disting. Achievement citation Iowa State U., 1996, Pomerance award Archaeol. Inst. Am., 1999. Fellow Internat. Inst. for Conservation of Hist. and Artistic Works, Am. Inst. for Conservation of Hist. and Artistic Works; mem. Am. Chem. Soc. Clubs: Cosmos. Home: Apt 616 1330 Massachusetts Ave NW Washington DC 20005-4152

SAYRE, E(NOCH) PHILLIP, retired political scientist, state official; b. Humboldt, Iowa, Apr. 19, 1926; s. Enoch Franklin and Grace Irene (Rusk) S.; m. Mary-Ellen Silverstone, May 25, 1957; children: Michael Franklin, Elisabeth Carol Sayre Lozinsky. BA, U. Wash., 1950; postgrad., Georgetown U., 1951-54. Campaign mgr. Congressman Henry M. Jackson and Senator Warren G. Magnuson, Skagit County, Wash., 1950; campaign staff Henry M. Jackson for U.S. Senate, 1953; adminstrv. asst. to Congressman John Lesinski, U.S. Ho. of Reps., Washington, 1954-56; ins. agt. State Mut. Life Assurance Co., 1956-62; staff assoc. J.D. Marsh & Assocs., Inc., 1962-64; dir. fin. planning, supr. ins. Capital Plans, 1964-68; v.p., registered prin. Diversified Planning Corp., 1968-70; adminstrv. analyst of office policy analysis, dept. legis. svcs. Md. Gen. Assembly, Annapolis, 1970-80, sr. adminstrv. analyst, 1980-96; ret., 1996. Staff dir. Md. Commn. on Intergovtl. Cooperation, 1974-78. Chmn. legis. com. Young Dems. D.C., 1954-56; co-founder Md. Com. for Fair Representation, 1960-62; chmn. issues com. We. Suburban Dem. Club Montgomery County, Md., 1962-64; mem. Md. Constl. Conv. Commn., 1965-67; co-chmn. Dem. Com. for Constn., Md., 1968; mem. steering com. Citizens for Proposed Constn. Md., 1968. With U.S. Army Air Svc. Corps, 1944-45. Recipient resolution Md. Ho. of Dels., 1963, 65, Young Dem. of Yr. award Young Dems. Md., 1965, Outstanding Civic Achievement award Young Dems. Montgomery County, 1966. Mem. Am. Soc. for Pub. Adminstrn., World Future Soc., Bannockburn Civic Assn., Bannockburn Cmty. Club, Washington Ethical Soc. Avocations: reading, futurist interests, walking, outdoors, nature. Home: 6809 Laverock Ct Bethesda MD 20817-4912 E-mail: epsayre@cs.com.

SAYRE, JOHN MARSHALL, lawyer, former government official; b. Boulder, Colo., Nov. 9, 1921; s. Henry Marshall and Lulu M. (Cooper) S.; m. Jean Miller, Aug. 22, 1943; children: Henry M., Charles Franklin, John Marshall Jr., Ann Elizabeth Sayre Taggart (dec.). BA, U. Colo., 1943, JD, 1948. Bar: Colo. 1948, U.S. Dist. Ct. Colo. 1952, U.S. Ct. Appeals (10th cir.) 1964. Law clk. trust dept. Denver Nat. Bank, 1948-49; asst. cashier, trust officer Nat. State Bank of Boulder, 1949-50; ptnr. Ryan, Sayre, Martin, Brotzman, Boulder, 1950-66, Davis, Graham & Stubbs, Denver, 1966-89, of counsel, 1993—; asst. sec. of the Interior for Water and Sci., 1989-93. Bd. dirs. Boulder Sch. Dist. 3, 1951-57; city atty. City of Boulder, 1952-55; gen. counsel Colo. Mcpl. League, 1959-63; prin. counsel No. Colo. Water Conservancy Dist. and mcpl. subdist., 1964-87, spl. counsel, 1987, bd. dirs. dist., 1960-64; former legal counsel Colo. Assn. Commerce and Industry. Lt. (j.g.) USNR, 1943-46, ret. Decorated Purple Heart; recipient William Lee Knous award U. Colo. Law Sch., 1999. Fellow Am. Bar Found. (life), Colo. Bar Found. (life); mem. ABA, Colo. Bar Assn., Boulder County Bar Assn. (pres. 1959), Denver Bar Assn., Nat. Water Resources Assn. (Colo. dir. 1980-89, 93-95, pres. 1984-86), Denver Country Club, Univ. Club, Phi Beta Kappa, Phi Gamma Delta, Phi Delta Phi. Home: 355 Ivanhoe St Denver CO 80220-5841 Office: Davis Graham & Stubbs 1550-17th St Ste 500 Denver CO 80202 E-mail: john.sayre@dgslaw.com.

SAYRE, LINDA DAMARIS, human resources professional; b. Washington, Nov. 26, 1945; d. Wallace Stanley and Kathryn Louise (McKnight) S. BA in English, Wells Coll., 1967; MA in Sociology, U. Sussex, Brighton, Eng., 1969; EdD in Adult and Continuing Edn., Rutgers U., 2002. Human resources specialist N.Y.C. Human Resources Adminstrn., 1967-68; rsch. assoc. Presdl. Campaign Gov. Nelson Rockefeller, N.Y.C., 1968; ednl. coord. Isabella Geriat. Ctr., 1970-72; rsch. assoc. N.Y.C. Mayor's Commn. on City Fins., 1973-75; project mgr. Urban Acad. for Mgmt., N.Y.C., 1976-80; internal and external tng. cons. Boston and N.Y.C., 1980-83; tng. cons. N.Y.C. Bd. of Edn., 1983-84; tng. and edn. dir. Gen. Hosp. Ctr., Passaic, N.J., 1984-87; dir. human rels. Bronx (N.Y.) Lebanon Hosp., 1987-90; external cons. Atlanta, N.Y.C., 1990-95; tng. & devel. mgr. BOC Gases, Murray Hill, N.J., 1995-99. Mem. steering com. Broadway Dems., N.Y.C., 1974-80, 93-96, pres., 1975, 77; coord. Carter Presdl. Campaign, N.Y. 20th Congl. Dist., 1976; bd. Westside Cares Food Voucher, N.Y.C., 1993-95. Mem.: ASTD (no. N.J. programs 1985—86, Atlanta chmn. nat. affairs 1991, nat. leadership design team), N.Y. ASTD (v.p. prof. edn. 1993, pres. 1994, past pres. 1995, co-chair adv. coun. 1996, nominating com. 1997—98, chair succession planning com. 1998, cmty. action team 1999). Democrat. Avocations: writing, community service. Home: 448 Riverside Dr New York NY 10027-6801

SAYRE, MATT MELVIN MATHIAS, lawyer; b. Seattle, Sept. 5, 1934; s. Melvin Edward and Ethyl Elizabeth (Mathias) S.; m. Sheri Teagle, Oct. 21, 1956; children: Jeffrey Mathias, Steven Michael, David Matthew. BA, U. Wash., 1956; JD, Gonzaga U., 1964. Bar: Wash. 1964, D.C. 1981, U.S. Dist. Ct. (we. dist.) Wash. 1964, U.S. Ct. Appeals (9th cir.) 1972, U.S. Supreme Ct. 1980. Law clk. Justice Robert T. Hunter, Olympia, Wash., 1964-65; asst. counsel Pacific Car & Foundry Co., Renton, 1965-66; ptnr. Mullavey, Hageman, Treece & Sayre, Seattle, 1966-69, McBride & Sayre, 1969-71; sole practice Seattle, 1971-94; sr. ptnr. Sayre Law Offices, 1994—. Judge pro tem King County Superior Ct., 1973-83, 89—; trustee King County Bar Found., 1985-88, 92-98. Bd. visitors Seattle Univ. Sch. Law, 1991—. Served to 1st lt. USAFR, 1957-60. Recipient Pro Bono Svc. award, 1988. Mem. ABA (Nat. Conf. Bar Pres.), Wash. Bar Assn. (spl. dist. counsel 1982-88, editorial adv. bd. 1986-89, chair BAR-PAC 1991-94, chair pub. rels. com. 1992-93), King County Bar Assn. (treas. 1982-85, trustee 1985-88, bench-bar delay reduction task force 1987-89, 2d v.p. 1988-89, 1st v.p. 1989-90, pres. 1990-91, Geisness award 1997), South King County Bar Assn., Rainier C. of C. (pres. 1977-78), Lions, Wash. Athletic Club, Useless Bay Golf and Country Club, Seattle Yacht Club (staff judge advocate 2000—), Beta Theta Pi, Phi Delta Phi. Office: Boren & Jefferson Bldg 1016 Jefferson St Seattle WA 98104-2435

SAYRE, ROBERT FREEMAN, English language educator; b. Columbus, Ohio, Nov. 6, 1933; s. Harrison M. and Mary (White) S.; (divorced); children— Gordon, Nathan, Laura; m. Hutha Refle, May 7, 1988. BA, Wesleyan U., Middletown, Conn., 1955; PhD, Yale U., 1962. Instr. English U. Ill., Urbana, 1961-63; Fulbright lectr. Lund (Sweden) U., 1963-65; faculty U. Iowa, 1965-72, prof. English, 1972-98, prof. emeritus, 1998—. Dir. inter-profl. seminars NEH, 1978, 79; Fulbright lectr. Montpellier, France, 1984; exch. prof. U. Copenhagen, 1988-89; mem. adv. bd. Leopold Ctr. for Sustainable Agr., 1994—, chair, 1996—. Author: The Examined Self: Benjamin Franklin, Henry Adams and Henry James, 1964, Adventures, Rhymes and Designs of Vachel Lindsay, 1968; Thoreau and the American Indians, 1977; editor: A Week on the Concord and Merrimac Rivers, Walden, The Maine Woods, Cape Cod (H.D. Thoreau), 1985, Take This Exit: Rediscovering the Iowa Landscape, 1989, New Essays on Walden, 1992, American Lives: An Anthology of Autobiographical Writing, 1994, Recovering the Prairie, 1999, Take the Next Exit, 2000; contbr. articles to profl. jours. Guggenheim fellow, 1973-74. Mem. Am. Studies Assn., MLA.

SAYRE, ROBERT MARION, ambassador; b. Hillsboro, Oreg., Aug. 18, 1924; s. William Octavius and Mary Sayre; m. Elora Amanda Moyhihan, Dec. 29, 1951; children: Marian Amanda, Robert Marion, Daniel Humphrey. BA summa cum laude, Willamette U., 1949; JD cum laude (Alexander Welborn Weddell Peace prize 1956), George Washington U., 1956; MA, Stanford U., 1960; LLD, Willamette U., 1965. Bar: D.C. 1956, U.S. Ct. Appeals 1956, U.S. Supreme Ct. 1962. Joined U.S. Fgn. Service, 1949; econ. adviser on Latin Am., dir. Truman Point 4 Program, 1950-52; mil. adviser, 1952-57; officer charge inter-Am. security affairs, 1955-57; polit. counselor embassy Lima, Peru, 1957-59; fin. attache embassy Havana, Cuba, 1960; exec. sec. Task Force Latin Am., State Dept., Kennedy's Alliance for Progress, 1961; officer charge Mexican affairs Task Force Latin Am., State Dept., 1961-63; dep. dir. Office Caribbean and Mexican Affairs, 1963-64; dir. Office Mexican Affairs, 1964; sr. advisor White House, 1964-65; sr. dep. asst. sec. Bur. Inter-Am. Affairs, Dept. State, 1965-68; acting asst. sec. Dept. State, 1968—; Am. ambassador to Uruguay, 1968-69, to Panama, 1969-74; sr. insp. Dept. State, 1974-75, insp. gen., 1975-78; ambassador to Brazil, 1978-81; chmn. U.S. Interdepartmental group on Terrorism, dir. Counter-terrorism and Emergency Planning Dept. State, 1981-84, sr. insp., 1985; ptnr. IRC Group, Inc., 1986-87; from adv. to U.S. rep. to under sec. for mgmt. Orgn. of Am. States, 1987-94; sr. assoc. Global Bus. Access, Ltd., Washington, 1995—; chair Open Forum Working Group on Internat. Econs. U.S. Dept. State, 1995-96. Sr. councilor Atlantic Coun. Washington Inst. Fgn. Affairs. Capt. AUS, WWII; col. Res., ret. Decorated Soc. Cross (Brazil); Cross of Balboa (Panama); recipient Outstanding Employee award Dept. State, 1952, Superior Honor awards, 1964, 75, Disting. Honor award, 1978, Outstanding Performance award, 1982-85, Presdl. Meritorious award, 1986, Fgn. Svc. Cup award, 1990, Sec.'s Cert. of Appreciation, U.S. Dept. State, 1996. Mem. Am. Acad. Diplomacy, Inter Am. Bar Assn., Inter Am. Dialogue, Atlantic Coun. Washington Inst. Fgn. Affairs, Cosmos Club, Dacor House, Blue Key, Phi Delta Theta, Phi Eta Sigma, Tau Kappa Alpha. Episcopalian. Home: 3714 Bent Branch Rd Falls Church VA 22041-1028 Office: Global Business Access Ltd 1825 I St NW Ste 400 Washington DC 20006-5415

SAYWELL, WILLIAM GEORGE GABRIEL, business development and management consultant; b. Regina, Sask., Can., Dec. 1, 1936; s. John Ferdinand Tupper and Vera Marguerite S.; m. Helen Jane Larmer; children: Shelley Jayne, William James Tupper, Patricia Lynn. BA, U. Toronto, 1960, MA, 1961, PhD, 1968; LLD (hon.), U. B.C., 1994, Simon Fraser U., 1997. Asst. prof. dept. East Asian studies U. Toronto, 1963-69, asst. prof., 1969-71, assoc. prof. RDt., 1971-82, prof., 1982-83, chmn. dept., 1971-76; prof. dept. history, pres., vice chancellor Simon Fraser U., Burnaby, B.C., Can., 1983-93; pres., chief exec. officer Asia Pacific Found. of Can., Vancouver, 1993-99; vice chmn. Intercedent Ltd., 1999—; chmn. Intercedent Ventures Ltd.; ptnr. Acad. Search Can. Ltd.; pres. William Saywell & Assocs., Vancouver, 1999—. Cons. in higher edn.; ptnr. Acad. Search Can.; sinologist and 1st sec. Can. Embassy, Beijing, 1972-73; dir. U. Toronto-York U. Ctr. Modern East Asia, 1974-75; prin. Innis Coll., 1976-79; vice provost U. Toronto, 1979-83; dir. Western Garnet Internat., Tokyo-Mitsubishi Bank (Can.). Author articles and revs. on Chinese affairs to profl. jours. Decorated Order of Can. Order of B.C. Office: 701 2095 Beach Ave Vancouver BC Canada V6G 1Z3

SAYYED, TAWFEEQ AMJADALI, radiologist; b. Pune, India, Jan. 17, 1968; came to U.S., 1985; s. Amjadali and Iffat S. Student, St. Vincent's Jr. Coll., Poona, India, 1983-85; MB BS, Poona U., Maharashtra, India, 1991. Intern St. Joseph Mercy Hosp., Pontiac, Mich., 1992-93; resident William Beaumont Hosp., Royal Oak, 1993-95, 95-99; fellow abdominal imaging U. Miami/Jackson Meml. Hosp., 1999-2000; radiologist Radiology Assocs. Ft. Lauderdale, Pompano Beach, Fla., 2000—. Mem. AMA, Am. Coll. Radiology, Am. Coll. Nuclear Medicine, Radiol. Soc. N.Am., Soc. Nuclear Medicine. Office: Radiology Assocs PA Fort Lauderdale 902 NE 1st St Ste 202 Pompano Beach FL 33060-6340

SAZAMA, GERALD WALTER, economist, educator; b. Milw., Apr. 10, 1937; s. Gerald Sylvester and Catherine Ann (Goetz) S.; children: Jennifer Katy, Andrew, Kenneth; m. Nancy B. McDowell. PhD, U. Wis., 1967. Assoc. prof. dept. econs. U. Conn., Storrs, 1966—. Cons. U.S. AID, Bolivia, 1968, Costa Rica, 1969, Nicaragua, 1975, Forensic Econs., Conn., 1985—. Contbr. articles to profl. jours. Cons. Conn. Conf. Municipalities, New Haven, 1972, Conn. AFL-CIO, Hartford, 1975-90. Fulbright-Hay Rsch. fellow U.S. Govt., Costa Rica, 1985, Social Sci. Rsch. Coun. Latin Am. fellow, Chile, 1967; grantee Conoco Corp., Fairfield, Conn., 1982. Mem. Am. Econ. Assn., Conn. Acad. Arts and Scis. Democrat. Mem. Soc. Of Friends. Avocations: wood carving, cross country skiing, hiking. Office: U Conn Dept Econs U-63 Storrs Mansfield CT 06269

SAZAMA, KATHLEEN, pathologist, lawyer; b. Sutherland, Nebr., May 8, 1941; d. Roger William and Esther Mary (Reitz) Paulman; m. Franklin Jed Sazama, Aug. 26, 1962; children: Clare Ann, Jill Patrice. BS, U. Nebr., 1962; MS, Am. U., 1969; MD, Georgetown U., 1976; JD, Cath. U. Am., 1990. Diplomate Am. Bd. Pathology; lic. pathologist Mich., Va., Md., D.C., Calif., Pa., Tex.; bar: Md. Intern and resident Georgetown U. Med. Ctr., Washington, 1976-78; resident NIH, Bethesda, Md., 1978-79; clin. asst. prof. pathology Uniformed Svcs. U. Health Scis., 1981-89; clin. affiliate Ferris State Coll., Big Rapids, 1985-86; chief lab. of blood bank practices FDA Ctr. for Biologics Evaluation and Rsch., Bethesda, 1986-89; cons. Ober, Kaler, Grimes & Shriver, Balt., 1989-90; assoc. med. dir. Sacramento (Calif.) Med. Found. Blood Ctr., 1990-92; asst. clin. prof. pathology U. Calif., Davis, 1990-92, assoc. prof., dir. clin. pathology, 1992-93; prof. pathology and lab. medicine Allegheny U. of the Health Scis., Phila., 1994-99; v.p. for faculty acad. affairs, prof. lab. medicine U. Tex./M.D. Anderson Cancer Ctr., Houston, 2000—. V.p. Bd. Met. Washington Blood Banks, Inc., 1981-84; pres.-elect bd. of Am. Assn. of Banks, 2002; speaker in field. Author: (with others) Stat: The Laboratory's Role, 1986; contbr. numerous articles to profl. jours. Comdr. USPHS, 1986-89. Fellow Coll. Am. Pathologists, Am. Soc. Clin. Pathologists; mem. AMA, ABA, Am. Assn. Blood Banks (bd. dirs.), Nat. Health Lawyers Assn., Phi Kappa Phi, Beta Beta Beta. Avocations: tennis, playing bridge. Address: Univ of Texas MD Anderson Cancer Center 1515 Holcombe Blvd # 201 Houston TX 77030-4009

SAZAWAL, VIJAY KUMAR, engineering executive; b. Srinagar, Kashmir, India, July 28, 1946; came to U.S., 1970; s. Chuni Lal and Chand Rani Sazawal; m. Meenakshi Sazawal, June 5, 1970; children: Priya, Vibha, Suraj Kumar. BSc, Inst. Tech., Varanasi, India, 1967; M in Tech., Coll. Tech., Bhopal, India, 1970; PhD, Mich. Tech. U., 1975. Sr. engr. Westinghouse Electric Corp., Madison, Pa., 1975-79, mgr. structural analysis, 1979-84, mgr. advanced reactor programs, 1984-86, mgr. sp-100 space power project, 1986-88, mgr. def. programs, 1988-92, mgr. govt. programs, 1993-95, dir. projects, 1995-98; v.p. Cogema Techs., Inc., Bethesda, Md., 1998-99; v.p. engrng. & tech. Cogema, Inc., 1999—. Adj. prof. U. Pitts., 1980-85. Mem. minority rights group UN Com. Human Rights, 1993—. Mem. ASME, Am. Nuc. Soc., Am. Acad. Mechanics, Sigma Xi. Avocations: public speaking, reading, boating.

SAZEGAR, MORTEZA, artist; b. Tehran, Iran, Nov. 11, 1933; s. Hassan Ali and Zahra (Frootan) S.; m. Patricia Jean Kaurich, July 13, 1959. BA, U. Tex., El Paso, 1955, BS, 1956; postgrad., Baylor U. Coll. Medicine, 1956-57, Cornell U., 1958-59. One man exhibitions include, Poindexter Gallery, N.Y.C., 1964, 67, 69, 71, 73, 75, 77, group exhibitions include, Detroit Inst. Arts, 1965, Chgo. Art Inst., 1965, Univ. Art Mus., U. Tex., Austin, 1965, 72, Whitney Mus. Am. Art, 1970, Cleve. Mus. Art, 1972, Corcoran Gallery Art, Washington, 1973, Tyler Sch. Art, Temple U., Phila., 1979; represented in permanent collections, Whitney Mus. Am. Art, N.Y.C., San Francisco Mus. Modern Art, Riverside Mus., N.Y.C., U. Mass., Amherst, Corcoran Gallery Art, Prudential Ins. Corp. Am., Mus. Contemporary Art, Tehran, Iran. Mem. Artists Equity Assn. Democrat. Address: 1223 Homeville Rd Cochranville PA 19330-1712

SAZHIN, SERGEY VICTOROVICH, electrochemist, researcher; b. Alma-Ata, Kazakhstan, USSR, Oct. 24, 1953; s. Victor Sergeevich and Vera Kuz'minichna Sazhin; m. Elena Mikhaylovna S., Mar. 20, 1976; children: Victoria Sergeevna, Tat'yana Sergeevna. MS with honors, Kiev (Ukraine) Poly. Inst., 1977, PhD, 1981. Rsch. engr. Kiev Poly. Inst., 1977; sr. engr. Inst. Gen. and Inorganic Chemistry, USSR Acad. Scis. Ukraine, Kiev, 1980-82, jr. rsch. scientist, 1982-84, sr. rsch. scientist, 1984-95; prin. rschr. Samsung Display Devices Co., Ltd., Suwon, Republic of Korea, 1995-98; sr. scientist, mgr. electroanalysis group Moltech Corp., Tucson, 1999-2000; mgr. Lithium Sys., prin. investigator Rayovac Corp., Madison, Wis., 2001—. Patentee in field; contbr. over 50 articles to profl. jours. and conf. procs. Recipient Bronze medal Exhbn. Nat. Economy Achievements USSR, 1982, Inventor award USSR, 1985, Samsung Display Devices Paper Contest, 1996. Achievements include development of advanced batteries. Mailing: 25 Laramie Ct Madison WI 53719 E-mail: sazhin@hotmail.com.

SAZIMA, HENRY JOHN, retired oral and maxillofacial surgery educator; b. Cleve., Dec. 25, 1927; s. Henry Charles and Frances (Masin) S.; m. Carol Ann Watson, Sept. 10, 1955; 1 child, Holly Ann Sazima Davani. BS, Case Western Res. U., 1948, DDS, 1953; grad. sch. medicine, U. Pa., 1956-57; grad. sch. edn., Chapman Coll., 1967-69. Diplomate Am. Bd. Oral and Maxillofacial Surgery. Chief maxillfacial div. Naval Support Act, Saigon, Republic of Viet Nam, 1969-70; chmn. dental dept. Naval Med. Ctr., Phila., 1971-73, San Diego, 1979-80; spl. asst. dentistry Sec. Def. Health Affairs, Washington, 1973-77; comdg. officer Naval Dental Ctr., Parris Island, S.C., 1977-79; dep. chief dental div. Bur. Medicine and Surgery, Washington, 1980-82; comdg. officer Nat. Naval Dental Ctr., Bethesda, Md., 1982-83; dir. resources div. Chief Naval Ops., Washington, 1983-84; dep. commdr. for readiness and logistics Naval Med. Command, 1984-87, ret. rear admiral, 1987; now clin. assoc. prof. oral and maxillofacial surgery Georgetown U. Med. Ctr.; exec. dir. Acad. Dentistry Internat., 1988-2000, exec. dir. emeritus, 2000—. Cons., lectr., rschr. in field. Co-author: Management of War Injuries, 1977; contbr. articles to profl. jours. Recipient Residents award St. Vincent Charity Hosp., 1957, Hillenbrand award Acad. Dentistry Internat., 2000. Fellow Am. Coll. Dentists, Assn. Oran and Maxillofacial Surgeons, Internat. Assn. Oral and Maxillofacial Surgeons, Acad. Dentistry Internat. (Blue Cloud award 1995); mem. Brit. Soc. Oral and Maxillofacial Surgeons, European Assn. Maxillofacial Surgery, Assn. Mil. Surgeons of U.S. (chmn. internat. com. 1984-86, Margetis award 1971), Internat. Coll. Dentists (dep. regent 1971-87), Hospitaller Order of St. John of Jerusalem, Hospitlar Knights of Malta, Omicron Kappa Upsilon, Delta Tau Delta, Psi Omega. Clubs: Mil. Order of CARABAO. Republican. Roman Catholic. Avocations: sports, tennis, music, travel. Home: 4924 Sentinel Dr Apt 105 Bethesda MD 20816-3506 E-mail: hjshome@mindspring.com.

SBAITY-KASSEM, FATIMA HASAN, political economist, researcher; b. Tripoli, Lebanon, Aug. 19, 1944; d. Hasan Abdelkader Sbaity and Asma Abdallah Karkanawi; m. Ziad Kassem Kassem, May 27, 1972 (dec. Mar. 1997); children: Hana, May, Ramzi. BBA, Am. U., Beirut, 1965, M in Devel. Adminstrn., 1970; M in Internat. Econs., Columbia U., 1991, MPhil in Internat. Rels., 1995, postgrad. Instr. Chweifat (Lebanon) Nat. Coll., 1965-69; chief women and devel. sect. UN-ESCWA/UNSESOB, Beirut, 1970—90; trade expert, internat. economist, 1990—. Contbr. chapters to books. Bd. dirs. CAWTAR, Tunis, 1999—. Mem. Am. Polit. Sci. Assn., Acad. Polit. Scis. Home: 10 Waterside Plz Apt 18F New York NY 10010 Office: UN Econ ESCWA Commn Western Asia PO Box 5749 New York NY 10163-5749 E-mail: kassemz@cyberia.net.lb., sbaity-kassem@un.org.

SBARBARO, ROBERT ARTHUR, banker; b. Bklyn., Jan. 24, 1933; s. John Vincent and Louise Olga (Perigone) S.; m. Kathleen Ann Noonan, Sept. 12, 1959; children— Robert, Paul, Nancy. BA, Wagner Coll., 1954, postgrad., 1977. CFP. Programming mgr. IBM, 1956-59; regional ops. mgr. Univac, 1959-65; asst. v.p., mgr. Computax Corp., N.Y.C., 1965-70; sr. v.p. Irving Trust Co., 1970-89; pres. SPAR Cons., Manasquan, N.J., 1990—. Mem. Montvale (N.J.) Recreation Commn., 1979-80; treas. Pascack Hills High Sch. Parents Assn., 1978-79; trustee Wagner Coll.; pres. Allington Towers Condo Assn., Hollywood, Fla., 1998, treas., 1999. With USN, 1954-56. Recipient Alumni Achievement award Wagner Coll., 1987—. Mem. Data Processing Mgmt. Assn., Am. Banking Assn., Data Security Inst., Internat. Assn. for Fin. Planning, K.C. Republican. Roman Catholic. Avocation: sports. Home and Office: 1541 Tanner Ave Manasquan NJ 08736-2217

SBUTTONI, KAREN RYAN, reading specialist; b. Albany, Sept. 9, 1953; d. Patrick Frederick and Virginia Mary Ryan; m. Michael James Sbuttoni, Aug. 9, 1975; children: Michael Louis, Ashley Ryan. BS in Bus. Edn., Buffalo State Coll., 1979; MS in Bus. Edn., SUNY, Albany, 1983, MS in Reading, 1991, cert. advanced study in reading, 1994. Cert. reading specialist K-12 and bus. edn. 7-12, N.Y. Tchr. Williamsville East H.S., Buffalo, spring 1979, East Irondequoit H.S., Rochester, 1979-81; reading specialist Albany Acad., 1992—. Tchg. asst. SUNY, Albany, 1992; mem. admissions com., curriculum com., 1999. Religious edn. tchr. St. Pius X Ch., Loudonville, N.Y., 1982-84. Mem. ASCD, Internat. Reading Assn., Nat. Coun. Tchrs. English. Avocations: skiing, walking, reading, cross-stitching.

SBUTTONI, MICHAEL JAMES, orthodontist, building contractor; b. Albany, N.Y., Aug. 6, 1953; s. Michael Francis and Mary Susan (Walsh) S.; m. Karen Sbuttoni, Aug. 9, 1975; children: Michael Louis, Ashley Ryan. BS, SUNY, Albany, 1975; DDS, SUNY, Buffalo, 1979; cert. in orthodontics,

Eastman Dental Ctr., Rochester, N.Y., 1981. Real estate salesman Tri City Realty-Albany Bd. Realtors, 1971—; bldg. contractor M. Sbuttoni Constrn., Albany, 1972-86; practice dentistry specializing in orthodontics Dr. Serling and Decker DDS. P.C., 1981—; pres. Eastern Broadcasting Group, 2002—. Bldg. contractor The Craftsmens Guild, Albany, 1987—; staff orthodontist St. Peter's Hosp., Albany, 1984—. Mem. ADA, Am. Coll. Dentists, Am. Assn. Orthodontists (coun. on govt. rels.), Internat. Coll. Dentists, Am. Assn. Lingual Orthodontists (charter), Dental Soc. State of N.Y. (pub. rels. 1985-88, coun. on edn. 1992-93), Angle Orthodontic Soc., 3d Dist. Dental Soc. (bd. dirs. 1985-89, v.p. 1987-88, pres. 1988-90, ADA rep. 1990-96), Kiwanis (fund raising dir. 1985-87), Elks, Northeastern Soc. of Orthodontists, Coun. on Govt. Rels. (chmn.), Angle Soc. of Orthodontists, Am. Assn. of Orthodontists. Republican. Roman Catholic. Avocations: marathon running, golf, skiing. Home: 92 Middlesex Ct Slingerlands NY 12159-9636 Office: Drs Serling & Decker DDS PC 1004 Western Ave Albany NY 12203-2743

SCACCHETTI, DAVID J. lawyer; b. Newark, July 13, 1956; s. Edmond and Evelyn Scacchetti; m. Marcia Ellen Gessiness, Aug. 31, 1985; children: Gabriella Elise, Olivia Beth. BA in Polit. Sci. with honors, U. Cin., 1978, JD, 1981. Bar: Ohio 1982, U.S. Dist. Ct. (so. dist.) Ohio 1982, U.S. Dist. Ct. (ea. dist.) Ky. 1986, U.S. Dist. Ct. Ariz. 1997. Atty. Edward J. Utz, Esq., Cin., 1982; sole practitioner, 1982-98; atty. Scacchetti & Scacchetti, 1998—. Mem. ATLA, Nat. Assn. Criminal Def. Lawyers, Greater Cin. Criminal Def. Lawyer Assn., Ohio Acad. Trial Lawyers, Ham. County Trial Lawyers Assn., Phi Beta Kappa. Avocations: writing, tennis, Tribal art, guitar, travel. Office: Scacchetti & Scacchetti 601 Main St Fl 3D Cincinnati OH 45202-2519

SCACCIA, DANTE M. lawyer; b. Rome, Oct. 11, 1925; s. Giovanni Battista and Ines (Biagioni) Scaccia; m. Dorothea B. Koch, June 6, 1954 (dec. Apr. 1982); children: Victoria Marie, Ronald Allen; m. Antonia Pizzari, Jan. 9, 1991. AB, Union Coll., 1945; LLB, Columbia U., 1949. Bar: N.Y. 1949. U.S. atty. U.S. Dept. Justice, Syracuse, 1961-65; pvt. practice, 1965—. Lt. comdr. USN, 1943-52. Decorated Bronze star. Mem. ABA, N.Y. State Bar Assn., Onondaga Bar Assn. Democrat. Roman Catholic. Avocations: hunting, fly-fishing, hiking, mountain climbing, canoeing. Home: 159 Brookside Ln Fayetteville NY 13066-1543 Office: Scaccia Law Firm 109 S Warren St Ste 402 Syracuse NY 13202-1758

SCAFETTA, JOSEPH, JR. lawyer; b. Chester, Pa., May 10, 1947; s. Giuseppe and Mary (Koslosky) S.; m. Teresa M. Talierco, July 4, 1986; 1 child, Joseph III. BS in Aero. Engring., Pa. State U., 1969; JD, U. Pitts., 1972; M in Patent Law, Georgetown U., 1973; MBA, George Washington U., 1983. Bar: Pa. 1972, U.S. Patent and Trademark Office 1973, D.C. 1978, Va. 1979, U.S. Supreme Ct. 1980, U.S. Ct. Appeals (fed. cir.) 1982. Legal rschr. Arent, Fox, Kintner, Plotkin et al, Washington, 1973; law clk. to presiding judge U.S. Dist. Ct. S.C., Columbia, 1973-74; assoc. Colton & Stone, Arlington, Va., 1975-77, Craig & Antonelli, Washington, 1977-78, Wigman & Cohen, Arlington, 1978-83, Wenderoth, Lind & Ponack, Washington, 1983-86, Cushman, Darby & Cushman, Washington, 1986-87; counsel Russell, Georges & Breneman, Arlington, 1987-91, Young & Thompson, Arlington, 1991-96; pvt. practice, 1996-98; counsel Oblon, Spivak, McClelland, Maier & Neustadt, 1999—. Voting mem. Nat. Commn. for Social Justice, 1995-97. Author: Book Review Copyright Handbook, 1979, The Constitutionality/Unconstitutionality of the Patent Infringement Statute, 1979, (with others) Patents on Microorganisms, 1980; editor: An Intellectual Property Law Primer, 1975; contbr. articles to profl. jours. Mem. Consumer Affairs Commn., Alexandria, Va., 1985-87; charter mem. Christopher Columbus Quincentenary Jubilee Com., 1990-93; chair Va. chpt. Commn. for Social Justice, 1987—; mem. Fairfax County Dem. Com., Falls Church, 1987-89; parliamentarian City Dem. Com., Alexandria, 1985-87. Recipient Robert C. Watson award Am. Patent Law Assn., 1975. Mem.: Patent and Trademark Office Soc., D.C. Bar Assn., Am. Intellectual Property Law Assn. (mem. pub. info. com. 1983—2001), Va. Bar Assn., Am. Arbitration Assn. (mem. comml. panel), ABA, Avanti Italiani (pres. Alexandria chpt. 1981—83), Grand Lodge Va. (state pres. 1993—95), Sons of Italy. Office: 1755 Jeff Davis Hwy Ste 400 Arlington VA 22202-3530

SCAFFIDI, JUDITH ANN, academic administrator; b. Bklyn., Aug. 2, 1950; d. Anthony William and Rose Virginia (Nocera) S. BA, SUNY, Plattsburg, 1972, MS, 1973; postgrad., Einstein Coll. Medicine, 1983; PhD (hon.), Internat. U. Bombay, 1993; HHD (hon.), London Inst. Applied Rsch., 1993. Cert. secondary edn. English. VISTA mem. ACTION, N.Y.C., 1976-77; coord. cultural resources Learning Leaders, 1977-80, tng. splst. in Bklyn., 1980—. Field supr., adj. faculty Coll. for Human Svcs., N.Y.C., 1984-86; adv. coun. chair Ret. Sr. Vol. Program in Bklyn., 1983-86; adv. bd. Ret. Sr. Vol. Program in N.Y.C., 1983-86. Acvive Am. Friends Svc. Com., 1994—. Recipient award for svcs. in promotion literacy Internat. Reading Assn. and Bklyn. Reading Coun., 1986, award for outstanding leadership Ret. Sr. Vol. Program, 1986, cert. of appreciation Mayor City of N.Y., 1991, cert. of appreciation for exceptional support and encouragement of volunteerism, 1998. Mem. NAFE, Cath. Tchrs. Assn. Bklyn. (del. sch. dist. 18, 1982-91), Internat. Platform Assn., World Found. Successful Women, Am. Biog. Inst. (rsch. bd. advisors 1992-93), Am. Biog. Inst. Rsch. Assn. (bd. govs. 1992—), Internat. Parliament for Safety and Peace (dep. mem. and diplomatic passport), Maisson Internat. de Intellectuels (Acad. MIDI), Cath. Alumni Club N.Y., Amnesty Internat. Roman Catholic. Avocations: foreign and domestic travel, reading, walking. Home: 2330 Ocean Ave Apt 3H Brooklyn NY 11229-3036 Office: Learning Leaders 352 Park Ave S Fl 13 New York NY 10010-1709

SCAFFIDI-WILHELM, GLORIA ANGELAMARIE, elementary education educator; b. Vineland, N.J., June 3, 1960; d. Joseph J. and Gloria Scaffidi; m. Andrew H. Wilhelm, Nov. 7, 1992; 1 child, Joseph Nicholas. BA summa cum laude, Glassboro State Coll., 1982. Cert. tchr. elem. edn., N.J. Tchr. 3rd grade St. Nicholas Sch., Egg Harbor City, NJ, 1982—85; 4th grade tchr. Charles L. Spragg Sch., 1986—2002. Advisor cheerleading club Egg Harbor City Schs., 1988-91, journalism club, 1989-93, staff mem. yearbook com., 1990-94, 96-97, editor sch. newspaper, 1989-94, 96-97, advisor pub. rels. sch. activities, 1989-94, 96-97. Named Tchr. of Yr., Egg Harbor City Schs., 1989-90. Mem. N.J. Edn. Assn., Kappa Delta Pi. Roman Catholic.

SCAFIDEL, JIM R. freelance/self-employed writer; b. Laurel, Miss., Aug. 14, 1942; s. Phillip and Clara Mae Scafidel; m. Beverly Gwen Robinson, Aug. 6, 1966. BA, Miss. State U., 1964; MA, U. Miss., 1966; PhD, U. S.C., 1976. Instr. Southwestern State Coll., Weatherford, Okla., 1966—68, Jacksonville (Ala.) State U., 1968—70; part-time tchr. U. Miss., University, 1972—82, U. S.C., Columbia, 1980—82; freelance writer Jackson, Miss., 1982—. Edn. cons. S.C. Nat. Corp., Columbia, 1977—78; newspaper columnist Clarion Ledger, Jackson, 1983—94. Co-editor: Anthology of Mississippi Writers, 1979; author: Northwest Glory, 1981, Wit's End, 1989. Home: 292 Park Lane Ct Jackson MS 39211 E-mail: jscafidel@jam.rr.com.

SCAGLIONE, CECIL FRANK, marketing executive, publisher; b. North Bay, Ont., Can., Dec. 2, 1934; came to U.S., 1967, naturalized, 1982; s. Frank and Rose (Aubin) S.; m. Mary Margaret Stewart, Nov. 11, 1954 (div. 1982); children: Cris Ann, Michael Andrew, Patrick Andrew (dec.); m. Beverly Louise Rahn, Mar. 25, 1983. Student, North Bay Coll., 1947-52, Ryerson Tech. Inst., Toronto, Ont., 1955-56, San Diego State U., 1979. Accredited Pub. Rels. Soc. Am. Fin. Writer Toronto Telegram, 1955; reporter Sarnia (Ont.) Observer, 1956-57; reporter, editor Kitchener-Waterloo (Ont.) Record, 1957-61; reporter, editor, analyst Windsor (Ont.) Star, 1961-67; writer, editor, photo editor Detroit News, 1967-71; reporter, assoc. bus. editor San Diego Union, 1971-80; mgr. corp. comm. Pacific Southwest Airlines, San Diego, 1981-83; sr. v.p. media rels. Berkman & Daniels, Inc., 1984-87; prin. Scaglione Mktg. Comm., 1987—. Pres., CEO, editor in chief Mature Life Features, 1990—. Founding editor-in-chief Aeromexico Mag., 1973; contbr. articles, columns and photographs to various publs. Mem. San Diego County Crime Commn. Recipient award B. F. Goodrich Can., Ltd., 1962, 66, San Diego Pub. Rels. Profl. of the Yr., 1995, Spl. Achievement award Nat. Assn. Recycling Industries, 1978; named Nat. Media Adv. SBA, 1980; Herbert J. Davenport fellow, 1977 U. Mo.; Can. Centennial grantee, 1966. Mem. San Diego Press Club (hon. life, past pres., awards 1978, 80, 84), Airline Editors Forum (awards 1982, 83), Soc. Profl. Journalists. Roman Catholic.

SCAGLIONE, LOUIS , III, music educator, conductor; b. Berwyn, Ill., June 7, 1969; s. Louis F. and Sharon L. Scaglione. BS Music Edn., U. Ill., 1992; M Music, Temple U., 1996. Cert. K - 12 Instnl. I in Music Pa., 1998, Spl. K - 12 Tchg. in Music Ill., 1992. Artistic dir. Arts at Andalusia, Andalusia, Pa., 1995—; conductor Phila. Young Artists Orch., 1997—; assoc. conductor Phila. Youth Orch., 1998—, exec. dir., 2001—; mem. faculty Temple U. Music Preparatory Divsn., Phila., 1998—. Trustee Andalusia Found., Andalusia, Pa., 2000—; dir. Pauls Found., Phila., 1998—. Mem.: Music Educators Nat. Conf., Am. Choral Dirs. Assn., Coll. Music Soc., Am. Symphony Orch. League (dir. youth orch. divsn. 2000—), Union League of Phila. (mem. house com. 2000—), Pi Kappa Lambda, Phi Eta Sigma, Kappa Delta Pi, Golden Key Soc. Office: Phila Youth Orch PO Box 41810 Philadelphia PA 19101 Personal E-mail: louisscag@aol.com. Business E-Mail: info@pyos.org.

SCAIRPON, SHARON CECILIA, retired information scientist; b. New Brunswick, N.J., May 7, 1946; d. Eric Christian and Erica Cecile Schreiber. Student, Trenton Jr. Coll., 1965-67; BSBA, Rider Coll., 1991. Various clerical postions E.R. Squibb & Sons, Princeton, N.J., 1967-87, sr. interlibr. loan and reference technician, 1987-88; lit. resource assoc., lan adminstr. Bristol-Myers Squibb, 1988-91, info. scientist, 1991—2001. Mem. ALA, Zonta (bd. dirs. Trenton 1990-91, 95—, chmn. various coms. 1991—, newsletter pub. 1995-99, 2nd v.p. 1999—), Sigma Iota Epsilon. Roman Catholic. Avocations: volunteer work, bicycling, reading, computers, yoga. Home: PO Box 5041 Trenton NJ 08638-0041

SCALA, JAMES, health care industry consultant, writer; b. Ramsey, N.J., Sept. 16, 1934; s. Edvigi and Lorene (Hendricksen) S.; m. Nancy Peters, June 15, 1957; children: James, Gregory, Nancy, Kimberly. BA, Columbia U., 1960; PhD, Cornell U., 1964; postgrad., Harvard U., 1968; LHD (hon.), Hofstra U., 1998. Cert. nutrition specialist. Staff scientist Miami Valley Labs., Procter and Gamble Co., 1964-66; head life scis., dir. fundamental rsch. Owens Ill. Corp., 1966-71; dir. nutrition T.J. Lipton Inc., 1971-75; dir. health scis. Gen. Foods Corp., 1975-78; v.p. sci. and tech. Shaklee Corp., San Francisco, 1978-85, sr. v.p. sci. affairs, 1986-87. Cons. Georgetown U. Med. Sch., U. Calif.-Berkeley extension. Author: Making the Vitamin Connection, 1985, The Arthritis Relief Diet, 1987, 1989, Eating Right for a Bad Gut, 1990, 1992, Eating Right for a Bad Gut, new edit., 1999, The High Blood Pressure Relief Diet, 1988, 1990, Look 10 Years Younger, Feel 10 Years Better, 1991, 1993, Prescription for Longevity, 1992, 1994, If You Can't/Won't Stop Smoking, 1993, The New Arthritis Relief Diet, 1998, 25 Natural Ways to Manage Stress and Avoid Burnout, 2000, 25 Natural Ways to Relieve Irritable Bowel Syndrome, 2000, 25 Natural Ways to Lower Blood Pressure, 2002; editor: Nutritional Determinants in Athletic Performance, 1981, New Protective Roles for Selected Nutrients, 1989; columnist: Dance mag.; contbr. With USAF, 1953-56. Disting. scholar U. Miami, Fla., 1977, Fla. Atlantic U., 1977. Mem. AAAS, Am. Inst. Nutrition, Am. Coll. Nutrition, Brit. Nutrition Soc., Sports Medicine Coun., Am. Soc. Cell Biology, Inst. Food Technologists, Astron. Soc. Pacific (bd. dirs., chmn. devel. coun.), Am. Dietetic Assn., Olympic Club (San Francisco), Oakland Yacht Club, Sigma Xi. Republican. E-mail: jscala2@attbi.com. *I am in awe of the incredible resiliency of living things, but most of all the human spirit.*

SCALA, MARILYN CAMPBELL, special education educator, writer, consultant; b. Lansing, Mich., June 25, 1942; d. Coral Edward and Eloise Campbell; children: Nicholas, Anne. BS Edn., U. Mich., 1964; MA Spl. Edn., Columbia U., 1967. Cert. elem. edn., spl. edn. tchr., N.Y. Tchr. physically handicapped Multi-Age, Port Chester, N.Y., 1964-66; tchr. spl. edn. PS 199, N.Y.C., 1966-69, Manhattan Sch. for Seriously Disturbed, N.Y.C., 1969-70; tchr. regular and spl. edn. Munsey Park Sch., Manhasset, N.Y., 1970-99. Cons. in field. Co-author: Three Voices: An Invitation to Poetry Across the Curriculum, 1995; author: Working Together: Reading and Writing in Inclusive Classrooms, 2001; contbr. articles to profl. jours. Avocations: reading, writing, travel, museum visits.

SCALES, JOHN THOMAS, state official; b. Cambridge, Mass., July 5, 1935; s. Frank and Louise Adelaide (Gifford) S. Cert.-qualified law libr. Libr. clk. Harvard U. Law Sch. Libr., Cambridge, Mass., 1955-58, Assn. Bar City N.Y., N.Y.C., 1958-60, NYU Sch. Law, N.Y.C., 1960-61; law libr. Paul, Weiss, Rifkind, Wharton & Garrison, 1961-69, Kelley, Drye & Warren, N.Y.C., 1969-71; editl. asst. N.J. Law Jour., Newark, 1971; reference libr. Seton Hall U., Law Sch. Libr., 1971; asst. law libr. Essex County Law Libr., 1972-80; tech. asst. legal activities State N.J. Bd. Pub. Utilities, 1981—. Roman Catholic. Avocations: opera, professional sports, public affairs. Home: 628 Arnold Ave Point Pleasant Beach NJ 08742-2531 Office: Bd Pub Utilities State NJ 2 Gateway Ctr Newark NJ 07102-5003 E-mail: john.scales@bpu.state.nj.us.

SCALES, RICHARD LEWIS, retired sales representative; b. Indpls., Nov. 16, 1928; s. Ortho Lorton and Nina L. (Julian) S.; m. E. Jean Rankin, Dec. 21, 1951; children: Richard, Allan, Anne. BSME, Purdue U., 1952. Rsch. and devel. engr. Bell Labs./Western Electric, Chgo., also Whippany, N.J., 1955-58; sales engr. Bodine Electric Co., Chgo., 1958-61; dist. sales mgr. Wabash (Ind.) Magnetics, 1961-66; founder, chmn. bd. (emeritus) Richard Scales Assocs., Wabash, 1966—, RSA Inc., Wabash, 1985—. Contbr. articles to mag. Elder, Presbyn. Ch. Lt. USNR, 1952-55, Korea; past pres. Wabash Rotary Club. Recipient Paul Harris award Rotary Internat. Republican. Avocations: computers, photography. Home: 550 Sommers Ave Wabash IN 46992-2021 E-mail: rscales@netusa1.net.

SCALESE, JOSEPH JAMES, III, pharmacist; b. Hagerstown, Md., Oct. 19, 1971; s. Joseph James Jr. and Melanie Ruth (Wyant) S.; m. Jenny Lynn McGrath, Nov. 5, 1994; children: Matthew Joseph, Andrew Robert. BS in Pharmacy, U. Md., 1994. Lic. pharmacist Md., W.Va. Staff pharmacist CVS Pharmacy, Jessup, Md., 1994-95, Middletown, 1995-96, Hagerstown, 1996-2000; pharmacy mgr. Weis Pharmacy, 2000—; clin. assoc. prof. U. Md. Sch. Pharmacy, 1999—. Adj. med. instr. Hagerstown Bus. Coll., 1996-99; lectr. CVS Pharmacy, Hagerstown, 1995-2000. Mem. Crestview Cmty. Assn., Boonsboro, Md., 1997; Healthwise coord., Hagerstown, 1998-2000; chmn. Boonsboro Park Bd., 2000—. Recipient Voice of Dem. award VFW, Howard County, Md., 1989. Mem. Am. Pharm. Assn., Md. Pharm. Assn., Sons of the Am. Legion, Phi Delta Chi. Democrat. Roman Catholic. Avocations: gardening, outdoor activities, cooking. Home: 108 Mason Pl Boonsboro MD 21713-2628

SCALETTA, PHILLIP JASPER, lawyer, educator; b. Sioux City, Iowa, Aug. 20, 1925; s. Phillip and Louise (Pelmulder) S.; m. Helen M. Beedle; children: Phillip R., Cheryl D. Kesler. BS, Morningside Coll., Sioux City, Iowa, 1948; JD, U. Iowa, 1950. Bar: Iowa 1950, U.S. Dist. Ct. Iowa 1950, Ind. 1966, U.S. Supreme Ct. 1968. Ptnr. McKnight and Scaletta, Sioux City, 1950-51; field rep. Farmers Ins. Group, Sioux City, 1951-54, sr. liability examiner, Aurora, Ill., 1954-60; br. claims mgr., Ft. Wayne, Ind., 1960-66; prof. law Purdue U., West Lafayette, Ind., 1966—; dir. profl. masters programs of the Krannert Grad. Sch. of Mgmt. Purdue U., 1987-90; of counsel with Mayfield & Brooks Attys. at Law, 1967—; arbitrator Panel of Arbitrators Am. Arbitration Assn. Co-author: Business Law and Regulatory Environments, 5th edit., 1996, Business Law Workbook, 5th edit., 1996, Foundations of Business Law and Legal Environment, 1986, 4th edit., 1997, Student Workbook and Study Guide, 1986, 4th edit., 1997; contbr. numerous articles to profl. jours. Mem. Ind. Gov's Commn. Individual Privacy, 1975. Recipient Best Tchr. of Yr. award Standard Oil Ind. Found., 1972, Outstanding Tchr. award Purdue U. Alumni Assn., 1974, Most Effective Tchr. award Krannert Grad. Sch. Mgmt. Purdue U., 1991. Mem. Am. Bus. Law Assn. (pres., Sr. Faculty Excellence award 1989), Tippecanoe County Bar Assn., Tri State Bus Law Assn. (past pres.), Midwest Bus. Adminstrn. Assn., Beta Gamma Sigma (bd. govs.). Office: Purdue U 511 Krannert Bldg West Lafayette IN 47907

SCALETTA, PHILLIP RALPH, III, lawyer; b. Iowa City, Dec. 18, 1949; s. Phillip Jasper and Helen M. (Beedle) S.; m. Karen Lynn Scaletta, May 13, 1973; children: Phillip, Anthony, Alexander. BSIM, MS, Purdue U., 1972; JD, Ind. U., 1975. Bar: Ind. 1975, U.S. Dist. Ct. Ind. 1975, Ill. 1993. Assoc. Ice Miller Donadio & Ryan, Indpls., 1975-81, ptnr., 1981—. Contbr. articles to profl. jours. Chmn. Ind. Continuing Legal Edn. Found., Indpls., 1989; mem. Environ. Quality Control Water Com., 1988-98. Mem. Ind. Bar Assn., Indpls. Bar Assn., Def. Rsch. Inst., Internat. Assn. Def. Counsel, Gyro Club Indpls. (v.p. 1992-93, pres. 1993-94, bd. dirs. 1990—). Avocations: golf, skiing, tennis. Home: 7256 Tuliptree Trl Indianapolis IN 46256-2136 Office: Ice Miller 1 American Sq Indianapolis IN 46282-0020

SCALF, JEAN A. KEELE, medical, surgical, geriatrics and home health nurse; b. Tullahoma, Tenn., Jan. 2, 1955; d. Sam Allen and Helen Virginia Keele; children: William Adam Keele, Mark Allen Scalf. AS, Motlow State Community Coll., Tullahoma, 1984, Cleve. State Community Coll., 1980. Staff and charge nurse Coffee Med. Ctr., Manchester, Tenn., 1985-86; staff nurse Elk Valley Home Health, Tullahoma, 1986-87; charge and staff nurse Bedford County Nursing Home, Shelbyville, Tenn., 1987-88; asst. dir. nursing Geriatrics Nursing Ctr., Heber Springs, Ark., 1990-93; geriatric psychiat. nurse Coffee Med. Ctr. Sr. Care, Manchester, Tenn., 1997; geriatric nurse Glen Oak sConvalesce Ctr., Shelbyville, 1999—. Owner, operator Jean's Feline & Canine Emporium , Tullahoma, Tenn., 1995—2001. Home: 441 Smith Ln Tullahoma TN 37388-6272

SCALI, VICTOR JOSEPH, emergency medicine physician; b. Darby, Pa., Feb. 23, 1948; s. Victor and Mary (DiPierro) S.; m. Lynn Karen Cunningham, Nov. 4, 1971; children: Victor III, Jeffrey, Kimberly Ann, Kristen. BA, Temple U., 1970; DO, Phila. Coll. Osteo. Medicine, 1980. Attending physician Barth Pavilion Hosp., Phila., 1986-89, Albert Einstein Med. Ctr., Phila., 1989-90; dir. Mercy Haverford Hosp., Havertown, Pa., 1990-93; attending physician Kennedy Health Systems, Stratford, N.J., 1993—, assoc. dir. residency in emergency medicine, 1993—, co-dir. residency combined emergency and internal medicine. Mem. affiliate faculty Am. Heart Assn., Phila., 1992-97; coord. Comlex II Nat. Bd. Osteo. Med. Examiners; bd. dirs. Found. for Osteo. Emergency Medicine. Contbr. articles to profl. jours. Capt. USAF, 1980—84. Decorated Def. Meritorious Svc. medal. Mem.: Soc. Acad. Emergency Physicians, Am. Coll. Osteo. Emergency Physicians (pres. 2002—, bd.dirs., reviewer jour. 2002), Am. Osteo. Assn., Phi Eta Sigma. Republican. Roman Catholic. Avocations: skiing, fishing, boating. Office: Kennedy Meml Hosps Univ Med Ctr 40 Laurel Rd E Stratford NJ 08084-1350 E-mail: scalicus@aol.com.

SCALIA, ANTONIN, United States supreme court justice; b. Trenton, N.J., Mar. 11, 1936; s. S. Eugene and Catherine Louise (Panaro) Scalia; m. Maureen McCarthy, Sept. 10, 1960; children: Ann Forrest, Eugene, John Francis, Catherine Elisabeth, Mary Clare, Paul David, Matthew, Christopher James, Margaret Jane. AB, Georgetown U., 1957; student, U. Fribourg, Switzerland, 1955—56; LLB, Harvard U., 1960. Bar: Ohio 1962, Va. 1970. Assoc. Jones Day Cockley & Reavis, Cleve., 1961—67; assoc. prof. U. Va. Law Sch., 1967—70, prof., 1970—74; gen. counsel Office Telecomm. Policy, Exec. Office of Pres., 1971—72; chmn. Adminstrv. Conf. U.S., Washington, 1972—74; asst. atty. gen. U.S. Office Legal Counsel, Justice Dept., 1974—77; prof. law U. Chgo., 1977—82; judge U.S. Ct. Appeals (D.C. cir.), 1982—86; justice U.S. Supreme Ct., Washington, 1986—. Vis. prof. Georgetown Law Ctr., 1977, Stanford Law Sch., 1980—81; vis. scholar Am. Enterprise Inst. , 1977. Editor: Regulation mag., 1979—82. Fellow Sheldon fellow, Harvard U., 1960—61. Office: US Supreme Ct Supreme Ct Bldg 1 1st St NE Washington DC 20543-0001*

SCALIA, ELIZABETH A. librarian; b. Thibodaux, La., July 12, 1972; d. Henry S. and Jane T. Webert; m. Bill R. Scalia. BS in Pharmacy, N.E. La. U., 1995; M of Libr. and Info. Sci.a, La. State U., 1999. Lic. Miss. Bd.harmacy Licensure Exam., La. Bd. Pharmacy Licensure Exam., Ala. Bd. Pharmacy Licensure Exam. Pharmacist Big B Pharmacy, Hanceville and Oneonta, Ala., 1995—96, K & B Pharmacy, Vicksburg, Miss., 1996—97; reference librn. State Libr. La., Baton Rouge, 1999—. Volunteer Capital Area Animal Welfare Society, Baton Rouge, 2001. Fellow Trustees Sect. fellow, La. Libr. Assn., 1999. Mem.: Health Scis. Libr. Assn. La., Beta Phi Mu (Beta Zeta chpt.), Rho Chi, Phi Kappa Phi. Avocation: cooking.

SCALLEN, THOMAS KAINE, broadcasting executive; b. Mpls., Aug. 14, 1925; s. Raymond A. and Lenore (Kaine) S.; m. Bille Jo Brice; children by previous marriage: Thomas, Sheila, Patrick, Eileen, Timothy and Maureen (twins). BA, St. Thomas Coll., 1949; JD, U. Denver, 1950. Bar: Minn. Asst. atty. gen. State of Minn., Mpls., 1950-55; sole practice, 1955-57; pres. Med. Investment Corp., 1957—, Internat. Broadcasting Corp., Mpls., 1977—; owner Harlem Globetrotters. Pres., exec. producer Ice Capades; chmn. bd. dirs. Century Park Pictures Corp., Los Angeles, chmn. bd. dirs. Blaine-Thompson Co., Inc., N.Y.C; chmn. Apache Plastics, Inc., Stockton, Calif. Served with AUS. Mem. World Pres. Orgn., Minn. Club, Calhoun Beach Club, L.A. Athletic Club. Clubs: University (St. Paul, Mpls.), Rochester (Minn.) Golf and Country, Edina (Minn.) Country, Athletic (Mpls.). Home: Heron Cove Windham NH 03087 Office: Internat Broadcasting Corp 80 S 8th St Ste 4701 Minneapolis MN 55402-2207

SCALZA, MARGARET T. publishing executive; b. Jersey City, May 27, 1936; d. Louis Patrick and Josephine M. (Cleary) Scalza; m. David Jenkins, Sept. 30, 1951 (div. 1962); children: Alison Brittain, Cynthia Higgins, Ann Jenkins Tunis Owner Towne House Restaurant, Hackettstown, N.J., 1963-65; pres. Kinsley Assocs., Inc., 1966—. Pub. purchasing guides, sch. directories, N.J., N.Y., Calif., Ill. Co-chmn. Northwestern N.J. divsn. U.S. Postal Customer Coun., 1978—. Mem. NAFE, Nat. Assn. Sch. Bus. Ofcls., North Ctrl. Jersy Assn. Realtors, Hackettstown Trade Assn. (sec.-treas., bd. dirs. 1963). Republican. Methodist. Avocations: cooking, sewing, reading, flower arranging, crabbing. Home: 9 House Wren Hackettstown NJ 07840-2815 Office: 4 Woodward Terr Hackettstown NJ 07840-4602

SCAMEHORN, JOHN FREDERICK, chemical engineer; b. York, Nebr., Oct. 26, 1953; s. Denver Alonzo and Mary Esther (Weber) S. BSChE, U. Nebr., 1973, MS, 1974; PhD, U. Tex., 1980. Registered profl. engr. Okla., Tex. Rsch. engr. Conoco, Ponca City, Okla., 1974-77; rsch. asst. U. Tex., Austin, 1977-80; rsch. engr. Shell Devel. Co., Houston, 1980-81; prof. U. Okla., Norman, Okla., 1981-92, Asahi glass chair, 1992—. V.p. Surfactant Assoc. Inc., Norman, 1987—; organizer 65th Annual Colloid and Surface Sci. Symposium, Norman, 1991; assoc. editr. Jour Am. Oil Chemists Soc., 1986-94. Editor: Phenomena in Mixed Surfactant Systems, 1986, Surfactant Based Separation Processes, 1989, Solubilization in Surfactant Aggregates, 1995; editl. bd. Jour. Surfactants Detergents, Separation Sci. Tech., Langmuir, Jour. Colloid Interface Sci., Colloidal Surfaces Bd. dirs. Opera Guild U. Okla., 1985-86. Recipient Cert. Appreciation ISEC Am. Chem. Soc., 1992. Mem. Am. Oil Chemists Soc. (mem. at large bd. 1990-96), Am. Chemical Soc. (chair spearations subdivsn. 1997). Republican. Achievements include development of new techniques in surfactant-based separation processes, pioneering development of micellar-enhanced ultrafiltration for wastewater/groundwater, clean-up. Office: U Okla 100 E Boyd St Norman OK 73019-1000 E-mail: scamehor@ou.edu.

SCAMMAN, FREDERICK L. retired tool and die maker; b. Haverhill, Mass., Sept. 4, 1920; s. Fred Llewellyn Scamman and Marion Clifford Smith; widowed; children: Andrea, Karen, Craig, Lisa. Cert., New Eng. Sch. Art; student, U. Las Vegas. Watchmaker Waltham (Mass.) Watch Co.; machinist United-Carr Co., Cambridge, Mass.; tool and die maker Boston Tool and Die Co., Newton, Polaroid Corp., Waltham. Tutor Missoula (Mont.) County Pub. Schs., 1988-99. With U.S. Army, 1942-45. Mem. VFW, Masons, Elks (life) Avocation: artist. Home: 1730 Dukes Ave Missoula MT 59808-5908

SCANDALIOS, JOHN GEORGE, geneticist, educator; b. Nisyros Isle, Greece, Nov. 1, 1934; s. George John and Calliope (Brouzos) Scandalios; m. Penelope Anne Lawrence, Jan. 18, 1961; children: Artemis Christina, Melissa Joan, Nikki Eleni. BA, U. Va., 1957; MS, Adelphi U., 1960; PhD, U. Hawaii, 1965; D.Sc. (hon.), Aristotelian U. Thessaloniki, Greece, 1986. Assoc. in bacterial genetics Cold Spring Harbor Labs., 1960-62; NIH postdoctoral fellow U. Hawaii Med. Sch., 1965; asst. prof. Mich. State U., East Lansing, 1965-70, assoc. prof., 1970-72; prof., head dept. biology U. S.C., Columbia, 1973-75; prof., head dept. genetics N.C. State U., Raleigh, 1975-85, disting. univ. research prof., 1985—. Mem. Inst. Molecular Biology and Biotechnology, Research. Ctr. Crete, Greece; vis. prof. genetics U. Calif., Davis, 1969; vis. prof. OAS, Argentina, Chile and Brazil, 1972; mem. recombinant DNA adv. com. NIH Author: Physiological Genetics, 1979; editor: Developmental Genetics, Advances in Genetics, Current Topics in Medical and Biological Research; co-editor: Isozymes, 4 vols., 1975, Monographs in Developmental Biology, 1968-86; molecular biology editor Physiol. Plant, 1988—. Served with USAF, 1957. Alexander von Humboldt travel fellow, 1976; mem. exchange program NAS, U.S.-USSR Fellow AAAS; mem. Genetics Soc. Am., Am. Soc. Biochemistry and Molecular Biology, Am. Genetic Assn. (pres.),

Soc. Devel. Biology (dir.), Am. Inst. Biol. Scis., Am. Soc. Plant Physiologists, N.Y. Acad. Scis., Sigma Xi. Office: NC State U Dept Genetics PO Box 7614 Raleigh NC 27695-0001 E-mail: jgs@unity.ncsu.edu.

SCANDARY, E. JANE, special education educator, consultant; b. Saginaw, Mich., Sept. 12, 1923; d. Leonard William and Reva Charlotte (Smith) Leipprandt; m. Theodore John Scandary; children: John S., Robert G. BA, Mich. State U., East Lansing, 1945, EdS, 1963, PhD, 1968; MEd, Wayne State U., 1951. Cert. secondary and spl. edn. tchr., Mich. Therapist speech and lang. Ann J. Kellogg Sch., Battle Creek, Mich., 1945-47; supr. speech therapy programs Wayne County Schs., Detroit, 1948-52; supr. programs for phys., hearing and visually impaired Ingham Intermediate Schs., Mason, Mich., 1960-78; spl. edn. cons. Mich. Dept. of Edn., Lansing, 1978-87, Livingston Intermediate Schs., Howell, Mich., 1987—. Rsch. assoc. Mich. State U., East Lansing, 1965-66, adj. prof., 1969-75, 81-82; mem. adv. com. China-U.S. Sci. Exchange Program Spl. Edn.; guest lectr. seminars spl. edn. Australia, Eng., Iran, Israel, Aruba, Germany, Scotland. Editor Chronicles newsletter, 1987—; contbr. articles to profl. jours. Vol. Mich. Hist. Mus., 1995—; chair futures com. Mich. Dept. Edn., 1992, editor, chair Task Force Futuresin Spl. Edn. 2000 AD and Beyond, 1992. 1st Chance Early Childhood grantee, 1972-78; recipient Resolution of Tribute Mich. State Senate, 1986; Scandary award for outstanding contbrs. early childhood edn. established in her name, 1990. Mem. Nat. Coun. Exceptional Children (field editor 1976-86, pres. div. physically handicapped 1982-83), Mid-Mich. Art Guild, World Future Soc. Avocations: painting, writing, reading, creative sewing.

SCANDURA, JOSEPH MICHAEL, cognitive scientist, software engineer; b. Bay Shore, N.Y., Apr. 29, 1932; s. Joseph and Lucy S.; m. Alice Baker, Aug. 13, 1960; children: Jeanne, Janette, Joseph, Julie. AB, U. Mich., 1953, MA, 1955; PhD, Syracuse U., 1962; postdoctoral, Stanford U., summer 1964, 68-69, U. Calif.-Berkeley, summer 1968, MIT, summer 1972; postgrad., U. Kiel, W.Ger., 1975, Inst. Ednl. Tech., Italy, summer 1978. Tchr. math., sci. White Plains, Bay Shore, 1953-56; instr. math., head wrestling coach Syracuse U., N.Y., 1956-63; asst. prof. edn., math. SUNY-Buffalo, 1963-64; research asst. prof. math. edn. Fla. State U., Tallahassee, 1964-66; dir. instructional systems, structural learning U. Pa., Phila., 1966-96; Fulbright prof. U. Koblenz & Dresden, 1998-99. Founder, chmn. Intelligent Micro Systems, Narberth, Pa., 1978-2002; chmn. bd. sci. advisors MERGE Rsch. Inst., 1973-2002; prin. investigator NIST Advanced Tech. Program Project on Automating Supply Chain; cons. jours., govt. agys., pub. cons., 1967—; cons. U.S. Office Edn., NSF, NAS, Tex. Instruments, Borg-Warner, U.S. Army; organizer, lectr., participant profl. confs., 1963—; dir. NATO Advanced Study Inst. on Structural Process Theories of Complex Human Behavior, 1977; coach undefeated Ea. Intercollegiate Wrestling Championship Team, 1963. Author: Mathematics - Concrete Behavioral Foundations, 1971, (with others) An Algorithmic Approach to Mathematics - Concrete Behavioral Foundations, 1971, Structural Learning I - Theory and Research, 1973, Problem Solving - A Structural Process Approach with Instructural Implications, 1977, (with A.B. Scandura) Structural Learning and Concrete Operations - An Approach to Piagetian Conservation, 1980, Cognitive Approach to Software Development, 1988, Prodoc (comprehensive suite of software devel. and maintenance tools), 1989, Cognitive Approach to Software Engineering and Re-engineering, 1991, ongoing projects; Flexys-customizable reengineering automation, Autobuilder-automated specification and implementation component based software while guaranteeing correctness, 1992—, NATO Advanced Study Inst., 1993, Automated Software Conversions and Re-engineering, 1993; contbr. 200 articles to profl. jours.; editor: Research in Mathematics Education, 1967, Structural Learning II - Issues and Approaches, 1976, (with C.J. Brainerd) Structural Process Models of Complex Human Behavior, 1978; developer, producer numerous computer-based instructional systems and software devel. systems; 4 software patents. Recipient Renssalaer award, 1949, Bausch and Lomb award, 1949, Nat. AAU Wrestling Champion and Outstanding Wrestler award, 1955; Fulbright scholar, 1975-76, 1998-99; U.S. Office Edn. fellow, 1978-79. Fellow: APA (chmn. E.L. Thorndike award com. 1974—79), Structural Learning Soc. (sr.; chmn. 1969—80, editor in chief Jour. Structural Learning 1976—90, chmn. 1985—88, Jour. Structural Learning and Intelligent Systems 1990—2001, chmn. 1995—, founder Tech., Instr., Cognition & Learning 2002—); mem.: IEEE, AAUP, Univ. Profs. for Acad. Order, Psychonomic Soc., Math. Assn. Am., Nat. Coun. Tchrs. Math. (past fed. funds com. chmn.), Am. Ednl. Rsch. Assn. (past com. chmn.), Assn. Computing Machinery, Phi Delta Kappa, Phi Eta Sigma, Phi Kappa Phi. Home: 1249 Greentree Ln Narberth PA 19072-1219 Office: U Pa Instructional Systems Philadelphia PA 19104 E-mail: scandura@scandura.com. *Accomodation to -- as well as leadership of -- groups, institutions and/or societies is an essential ingredient of success in most walks of life. There are circumstances, however, which require inner direction, whether developing a new scientific paradigm or standing firm against political pressures. Although vindication is rarely complete and often delayed, following one's best instincts yields its own rewards— perhaps the satisfaction of ultimately being proven right but more often simply knowing one did what had to be done.*

SCANIO, CHARLES JOHN VINCENT, chemist, consultant; b. Ann Arbor, Mich., June 23, 1940; s. Vincent A. and Georgette C. (Maulbetsch) S.; m. Kaaren Wellman, July 3, 1965; children: Erik W., Kurt C. BS in Chemistry, U. Mich., 1962; PhD, Northwestern U., 1966. Cert. profl. engr. Asst. prof. chemistry Iowa State U., Ames, 1966-72; staff chemist Pfizer, Inc., Groton, Conn., 1972-77; head process, research and devel. UpJohn Co., North Haven, 1977-84; corp. dir. research and devel. ChemDesign Corp., Fitchburg, Mass., 1984-86; exec. v.p. ChemSultants Internat., Inc., Winchendon, 1986-92; pres. Secant Chemicals, Inc., 1992—. Contbr. articles to profl. jours.; editor Jour. Radiation Curing, 1983. Mem. Planning and Zoning Commn., North Branford, Conn., 1983-84; v.p. Zoning Task Force, Winchendon, 1985-86, Indsl. Devel. Commn., Winchendon, 1985-90, Fin. Commn., Winchendon, 1989-90; mem. PCB Adv. Commn., 1990—; mem. Zoning Bd. Appeals, Winchendon, 1999—. Recipient Teaching award Iowa State U., 1969. Mem. Am. Chem. Soc., Chem. Soc. London, Sigma Xi. Republican. Achievements include 2 patents. Home and Office: PO Box 246 Winchendon MA 01475-0246 E-mail: cscanio@secantchemicals.com.

SCANLAN, CARLA R. researcher, educator; b. Medina, Ohio, Mar. 26, 1959; d. Ernest Charles and Lois Elinor Scanlan; m. Brian L. Johnson, Apr. 1, 2000. BS, U. Akron, 1985; MS, Ohio U., 1991, PhD, 2000; BA, U. Akron, 1981. Cost analyst Roadway Express, Akron, Ohio, 1986-88; psychology instr. Ohio U., Athens, 1991—2000; rschr., data analyst ILGARD Ohio U., 2000-01; asst. prof. psychology Marietta (Ohio) Coll., 2001—. John Houk grantee Ohio Univ. Mem. APA, Am. Psychol. Soc., Midwest Psychol. Assn., Soc. Judgment and Decision-making, Southeast Psychol. Assn. Avocations: physical fitness, cats, classical music. Home: 5 Cardinal Ln #5A Athens OH 45701 Office: 305 Erwin Hall 215 Fifth St Marietta OH 45750 E-mail: scanlanc@marietta.edu.

SCANLAN, ESTHER MEADER, psychiatric social worker; b. Providence, Jan. 21, 1932; d. Robert Osmond and Mary Lillian (Arnold) Meader; m. William Arthur Scanlan, Sept. 26, 1954 (div. June 1964); children: James Matthew, William Dustin, Julie Beth. BA, Bennington (Vt.) Coll., 1959; MSW, Simmons Sch. Social Work, Boston, 1965; MTS, Harvard Divinity Sch., 1991. Lic. social worker. Psychiat. social worker Boston City Hosp., 1965-68, Putnam Centre for Children, Roxbury, Mass., 1968-69, Children's Hosp., Boston, 1969-70, Somerville (Mass.) Mental Health Ctr., 1970-74; social worker Cath. Charities, Somerville, 1974-75; pvt. practice psychiat. social work Cambridge, Mass., 1975-96; psychiatric social workerhealth and edn. svcs. Addison Gilbert Hosp., 1998—. Mem. adv. council theological opprtunities program Harvard U., 1985—. One-woman shows include Simmons Coll., 1979, Hirshberg Gallery, 1979, Cambridge Pub. Libr., 1981, Sawyer Free Libr., 1998; (group shows) Simmons Coll., 1979, Muddy River Festival, 1985, Hirshberg Gallery, 1979, Cambridge Pub. Libr., 1981, Sawyer Free Libr., 1998, reader (poetry) Tufts Radio Sta., 1981. Vol. health and ednl. svcs. Fellow, NIMH, 1963—65. Democrat. Episcopalian. Avocations: swimming, needlepoint. Home and Office: 37 Washington St Apt 6 Gloucester MA 01930-3550

SCANLAN, JAMES PATRICK, philosophy and Slavic studies educator; b. Chgo., Feb. 22, 1927; s. Gilbert Francis and Helen (Meyers) S.; m. Marilyn A. Morrison, June 12, 1948. BA, U. Chgo., 1948, MA, 1950, PhD, 1956. Research fellow Inst. Philos. Research, San Francisco, 1953-55; instr. Case Inst. Tech., Cleve., 1955-56; from instr. to assoc. prof. Goucher Coll., Balt., 1956-68; prof., dir. Slavic Ctr. U. Kans., Lawrence, 1968-70; prof. Ohio State U., Columbus, 1971-91, dir. Slavic Ctr., 1988-91, prof. emeritus, 1992—. Vis. rsch. scholar Moscow State U., 1964-65, 69, 98, Acad. Scis. USSR, Moscow, 1978, 93, Russian State U. for the Humanities, 1995; fgn. vis. fellow Slavic Rsch. Ctr., Hokkaido U., Sapporo, Japan, 1987-88. Author: Marxism in the USSR, 1985, Dostoevsky the Thinker, 2002; editor: Historical Letters by Peter Lavrov, 1967, Soviet Studies in Philosophy, 1987—92, Russian Studies in Philosophy, 1992—97, Technology, Culture and Development: The Experience of the Soviet Model, 1992, Russian Thought After Communism, 1994; co-editor: Russian Philosophy, 1965, Marxism and Religion in Eastern Europe, 1976. Served with USMC, 1945-46. Woodrow Wilson Internat. Ctr. fellow, 1982; recipient Translation award Nat. Translation Ctr., 1967, Faculty Rsch. award Fulbright-Hays, 1982-83. Mem. Am. Philos. Assn., Am. Assn. Advancement Slavic Studies, Phi Beta Kappa. Home: 1000 Urlin Ave Apt 206 Columbus OH 43212-3324 E-mail: scanlan.1@osu.edu.

SCANLAN, JOHN DOUGLAS, foreign service officer, former ambassador; b. Thief River Falls, Minn., Dec. 20, 1927; s. Paul Douglas and Ruby (Bennes) S.; m. Margaret Anne Calvi; children: Kathleen, Michael, Malia, John. BA, U. Minn., 1952, MA in Russian Studies, 1955. Instr. U. Minn., 1955; Soviet research analyst U.S. Dept. State, Washington, 1956-58; third sec. Am. Embassy, Moscow, 1958-60, cultural attache Warsaw, 1961-65, second sec. Montevideo, 1966-67; prin. officer Am. Consulate, Poznan, Poland, 1967-69; sr. rep. to U.S. Dept. Defense, Washington, 1969-71; desk officer U.S.-Soviet bilateral relations, 1971-73; polit. counselor Am. Embassy, Warsaw, 1973-75; mem. state exec. seminar Washington, 1975-76; spl. asst. to Dir. Gen. of Fgn. Service, 1976-77; dep. dir. for Europe, USIA, 1977-79; dep. chief Mission in Belgrade, Yugoslavia, 1979-81; dep. asst. sec. of state for European affairs, 1981-82; fgn. affairs fellow Fletcher Sch. Law and Diplomacy, Tufts U., 1983-84; chmn. U.S. del. to Conf. on Security and Coop. in Europe, Cultural Forum Preparatory Conf., Budapest, 1984; amb. to Yugoslavia, Am. Embassy, Belgrade, 1985-89; dep. comdt. U.S. Army War Coll., Carlisle Barracks, Pa., 1989-91; sr. cons. East EUR, ICN Pharmaceutcals Inc. Mem. exec. bd. Project on Ethnic Rels.; mem. Ctr. Strategic and Internat. Studies U.S.- European-Poland Action Commn.; adv. coun. ABA Ctrl. and East European Law Initiative project, pres. U.S.-Yugoslavia Bus. Coun. Mem. Planning Commn., Falls Church, Va., 1972-73, City Council, 1975-79. Recipient Presdl. Meritorious Service award for Diplomacy, 1984. E-mail: ambscan@earthlink.net.

SCANLAN, MICHAEL, priest, academic administrator; b. Far Rockaway, N.Y., Dec. 1, 1931; s. Vincent Michael and Marjorie (O'Keefe) S. BA, Williams Coll., 1953; JD, Harvard U., 1956; MDiv, St. Francis Sem., Loretto, Pa., 1975; LittD (hon.), Coll. Steubenville, 1972; LLD (hon.), Williams Coll., Williamstown, Mass., 1978; PdD (hon.), St. Francis Coll., Loretto, Pa., 1987; STM, 3d Order Regular of St Francis, 1996. Ordained priest Roman Catholic Ch., 1964; Cross Pro Ecclesia et Pontifice, 1990. Acting dean Coll. Steubenville, Ohio, 1964-66, dean, 1966-69; rector pres. St. Francis Major Sem., Loretto, Pa., 1969-74; pres. Franciscan U. Steubenville, 1974-2000, chancellor, 2000—. Pres.(FIRE) Cath. Alliance for Faith, Intercession, Repentence and Evangelism, 1984—. Author: The Power in Penance, 1972, Inner Healing, 1974, A Portion of My Spirit, 1979, The San Damiano Cross, 1983, Turn to the Lord-A Call to Repentance, 1989, The Truth About Trouble, 1989, What Does God Want: A Practical Guide to Making Decisions, 1996, (with James Manney) Let the Fire Fall, 1997, The Holy Spirit: Holy Desire, 1998; chmn. editl. bd. New Covenant mag., 1985-92. Mem. Diocese of Steubenville Ecumenical Commn., 1964-69; bd. dirs. Rumor Control Ctr., Steubenville, 1968-69, C. of C., Steubenville, 1976-79; bd. trustees St. Francis Prep. Sch., Spring Grove, Pa., 1969-74; vice-chmn., bd. trustees St. Francis Coll., Loretto, Pa., 1969-74; trustee United Way, Steubenville, 1975-80; chmn. nat. svc. com. Cath. Charismatic Renewal, 1975-78. Staff judge adv. USAF, 1956-57. Named Sacrae Theologiae Magister Third Order Regular St Francis, 1996. Roman Catholic. Avocations: tennis, golf, skiing. Office: Franciscan U Office of Chancellor 1235 University Blvd Steubenville OH 43952-1796 *If you are going to change something, you've got to live on vision, before you live on reality. You have to be so inspired by the vision, that you keep telling everybody until it gets in them, and they start living it with you.*

SCANLAN, ROBERT MICHAEL, financial management company executive; b. Boston, May 2, 1936; s. Michael Henry and Grace Agnes (Thorne) S.; BS magna cum laude in Econs., Boston Coll., 1959, postgrad., 1963-66; cert. Stonier Grad. Sch. Banking, Rutgers U., 1968, Greater Boston Exec. Program, MIT, 1969; m. Joanne J. Radosta, Aug. 12, 1961; children— Robert M., Timothy J., Daniel F., Grace M. With Fed. Res. Bank Boston, 1959-69, asst. v.p.; pres., chief exec. officer Investment Cos. Services Corp., computer services to investment cos., Boston, 1969-79; pres., chief exec. officer Eagle Income Mgmt. Co., Inc., Boston, 1980-83; chmn., The Harborview Group Inc., Boston, 1985-89; exec. v.p., dir. Dean Witter Trust Co., 1989—, also bd. dirs.; pres., COO Dean Witter InterCapital Inc., 1993—, Dean Witter Svcs. Co. Inc., 1994—; pres., trustee Am. Liquid Trust, 1978-79; pres. ALT Mgmt. Corp., 1978-79; dir., prin. Cornerstone Fin. Services, 1976-79; trustee Keystone Employees Benefit Fund, 1974-79, The Carney Hosp. Found., 1983-89; mem. pension com. Keystone Retirement Equity Trust, 1974-79; mem. ops. com. Investment Co. Inst., 1970-79, chmn., 1973-75, chmn. broker/dealer subcom., 1971-72, chmn. electronic funds transfer adv. com., 1978—. Roman Catholic. Home: 21 S End Ave # P2X New York NY 10280-1044

SCANLAN, THOMAS CLEARY, publishing executive, editor; b. Birmingham, Mich., May 18, 1957; s. Thomas Matthew and Emily (Cleary) S.; m. Sally Sachs, June 20, 1981; children: Bridget C., Thomas M., Patrick J. BS, St. Louis U., 1979. Salesman Walter Heller Co., Chgo., 1979-82; pub., editor Surplus Record, Inc., 1982—. Office: Surplus Record Inc 20 N Wacker Dr Chicago IL 60606-2806

SCANLAN, THOMAS JOSEPH, college president, educator; b. N.Y.C., Mar. 5, 1945; s. Thomas Joseph and Anna Marie (Schmitt) S. BA in Physics, Cath. U. Am., 1967; MA in Math., NYU, 1972; PhD in Bus. Adminstrn., Columbia U., 1978. Prin. Queen of Peace High Sch., North Arlington, N.J., 1972-75; dir. fin., edn. N.Y. Province, Bros. of Christian Schs., Lincroft, 1978-81; vice chancellor Bethlehem (Israel) U., 1981-87; pres. Manhattan Coll., Bronx, N.Y., 1987—. Vice chmn. First Cova Life Ins. Co., 1993—; bd. dirs. Am. Coun. on Edn. Trustee Lewis U., Romeoville, Ill., 1987—, Commn. on Ind. Colls. & Univs., 2002, Assn. Cath. Colls. and Univs., 1994—. Recipient Pro Ecclesia et Pontifice medal, Pope John Paul II, Vatican City, 1986. Mem. Bros. of Christian Schs., Am. Coun. Edn., Assn. Cath. Colls. and Univs. (trustee 1994—), Assn. Am. Colls., Nat. Cath. Edn. Assn., Nat. Asns. Ind. Colls. and Univs., Nat. Collegiate Athletic Assn. (exec. com. & divsn. 1), Metro Atlantic Athletic Assn., Equestrian Order of the Holy Sepulchre of Jerusalem, Phi Beta Kappa, Beta Gamma Sigma. Avocations: golf, reading, movies. Office: Manhattan Coll Office of Pres Manhattan Coll Pky Bronx NY 10471-3913

SCANLIN, THOMAS F. pediatrician, researcher; b. Pa. married. MD, U. Pa., Phila., 1971. Intern in pediat. U. So. Calif. Med. Ctr., L.A., 1971—72, resident in pediat., 1972—73; clin. rsch. fellow Children's Hosp. Phila., Phila., 1973—75; prof. pediat. U. Pa., 1973—; dir. Cystic Fibrosis Ctr. Children's Hosp. Phila., 1973—, rsch. fellow, 1975—78. Fellow, Nat. Cystic Fibrosis Rsch. Found., 1973—75, NIH, 1975—78. Office: Childrens Hosp Phila 3516 Civic Ctr Blvd ARC 402G Philadelphia PA 19104-4318 Fax: (215 590-4298. E-mail: scanlin@email.chop.edu.

SCANLON, ANDREW, structural engineering educator; b. Bridge of Allan, Scotland, Apr. 16, 1944; BSc with honors, U. Glasgow, Scotland, 1966; PhD, U. Alta., Can., 1972. Civil engr. Pub. Works Can., St. John, N.B., Can., 1966-67; project engr. N.B. Devel. Corp., Fredericton, Can., 1967-68; teaching asst. U. Alta., Edmonton, Can., 1968-71; structural design engr. Duthie Newby and Assocs., 1971-73; structural divsn. head Reid, Crowther and Ptnrs. Ltd., 1973-78; sr. structural engr. structural evaluation sect. Constrn. Tech. Labs., Inc., 1978-80, mgr. analytical design sect., 1980-82; assoc. prof. civil engring. U. Alta., 1982-83, prof., 1983-87, Pa. State U., University Park, 1987—, dir. transp. structures program Pa. Transp. Inst., 1993—, assoc. dir. of Inst., 1999—, acting head dept., 1991. Recipient Le Prix P.L. Pratley award Can. Soc. Civil Engring., 1990. Fellow Am. Concrete Inst. Office: Pa State U 212 Sackett Bldg University Park PA 16802-1408

SCANLON, CHARLES FRANCIS, retired army officer, defense consultant, writer, publisher; b. Nashville, Jan. 31, 1935; s. Francis James Gordon and Dorothy Rose (Compton) S.; m. Barbara Jean Schoen, Oct. 9, 1954; children: Teri, Brett, Ashlyn, Kellie. BA in Polit. Sci., U. Fla., 1960; grad., Command and Gen. Staff Coll., Ft. Leavenworth, Kans., 1970, Naval War Coll., Newport, R.I., 1977; MA in Am. Studies, U. Hawaii, 1974; postgrad., Pa. State U., 1982, Harvard U., 1984, 92. Commd. 2d lt. U.S. Army, 1960, advanced through grades to maj. gen., 1988; chief collection U.S. Army Europe, Heidelberg, Germany, 1977-78; comdg. officer 66th Mil. Intelligence Brigade, Munich, 1978-80; chief ops. U.S. Army Intelligence and Security Command, Arlington, Va., 1980-82; exec. officer Dept. Army Asst. Chief Staff Intelligence, Washington, 1982-83; dep. commdr. gen. U.S. Army Intelligence and Security Command, Arlington, 1983-85; dir. estimates Def. Intelligence Agy., Washington, 1985-86, dir. attaches, 1986-90; comdg. gen. U.S. Army Intelligence and Security Command, Ft. Belvoir, Va., 1990-93; ret., 1993; pres. Internat. Security, Counterintelligence Cons. Svcs., Fairfax Station, Va., 1993—, Satellite Beach, Fla., 1993—. Author: The Attaches, 1997, Retribution, 1999. Decorated Def. D.S.M., Army D.S.M., Nat. Intelligence D.S.M., Legion of Merit with 3 oak leaf clusters, Bronze Star with 2 oak leaf clusters; elected to U.S. Mil. Intelligence Hall of Fame, 1995. Mem. Assn. U.S. Army, Nat. Mil. Intelligence Assn. (pres. 1974-76), 101st Airborne Divsn. Assn., Berlin U.S. Military Vets. Assn., Sigma Nu. Baptist. Avocations: boating, scuba diving, racquetball, soaring, reading. Home: 8036 Oak Hollow Ln Fairfax Station VA 22039-2627 also: 3220 River Villa Way Melbourne Beach FL 32951 Office: Apt 160 3220 River Villa Way Melbourne Bch FL 32951-3039

SCANLON, DOROTHY THERESE, history educator; b. Bridgeport, Conn., Oct. 7, 1928; d. George F. and Mazie (Reardon) S.; AB, U. Pa., 1948, MA, 1949; MA, Boston Coll., 1953; PhD, Boston U., 1956; postdoctoral scholar Harvard U., 1962-64, 72. Tchr. history and Latin Marycliff Acad., Winchester, Mass., 1950-52; tchr. history Girls Latin Sch., Boston, 1952-57; prof. Boston State Coll., 1957-82, Mass. Coll. Art, 1982-95, prof. emerita, 1995—; lectr. Cape Mus. Fine Arts, Dennis, Mass., 1997—. Recipient Disting. Svc. award Boston State Coll., 1979, Faculty Award of Excellence, Mass. Coll. Art, 1985, Faculty Disting. Service award, Mass. Coll. Art, 1987. Mem. Pan-Am. Soc., Latin Am. Studies Assn., Am. Hist. Assn., Orgn. Am. Historians, Am. Studies Assn., Am. Assn. History of Medicine, History of Sci. Soc., AAUP, AAUW, Phi Alpha Theta, Delta Kappa Gamma. Author: Instructor's Manual to Accompany Lewis Hanke, Latin America: A Historical Reader, 1974; contbr. Biographical Dictionary of Social Welfare, 1986. Home: 23 Mooring Ln Dennis MA 02638-2321 Office: Mass Coll Art Dept History 621 Huntington Ave Boston MA 02115-5801

SCANLON, EDWARD CHARLES, clinical psychologist; b. Bradford, Pa., Dec. 3, 1931; s. Edward John Scanlan and Martha (Karlous) Charles; m. Constance Morgan, May 19, 1962 (div. Jan. 1976); 1 child, Heather Marie. AB cum laude, SUNY, Buffalo, 1954; EdM, Harvard U., 1958, EdD, 1961; postgrad., Columbia U. Lic. psychologist, Pa. Assoc. prof. Lehigh U., Bethlehem, Pa., 1961-66; acad. dean Montgomery County C.C., Conshohoken, 1966-69; acting. dir. home sch. Wilkes Coll., Wilkes Barre, 1968-71; clin. psychologist dept. human svcs. mental health and mental retardation Northampton County Dept. Human Svcs., Easton, 1972—. Vis. prof. clin. psychology Clinic Mental Health and Mental Retardation, Pottsville, Pa., 1971-72. Capt. USAF, 1954-57. Thayer scholar Harvard U. Mem. APA, Pa. Psychol. Assn., Harvard Club of Phila., Lehigh Country Club, Masons, Phi Beta Kappa. Democrat. Anglican. Avocations: classic automobiles, psychoanalytic studies. Office: Bridal Path Woods D-2 Bethlehem PA 18017

SCANLON, GEORGE PATRICK, transportation services executive, accountant; b. Chgo., Sept. 29, 1957; s. George Patrick and Ann Marie (McInerney) S. BBA, U. Notre Dame, 1979; MBA, U. Miami, 1984. CPA, Ill., Fla. Sr. acct. Price Waterhouse, Chgo., 1979-82, sr. analyst corp. audit dept., 1982-84, mgr. corp. audit dept., 1984-85, sr. mgr. control analysis dept., 1985-87; sr. mgr. acquisition control Ryder System, Inc., Miami, Fla., 1987-88; div. controller, aviation leasing and svcs. div. Aviation Sales Co., Inc., 1988-90; dir. corp. acctg. Ryder Sys., Inc., 1990-91, group dir. audit svcs., 1991-93, group dir. corp. planning, 1993-95, v.p. corp. planning, 1995-97, sr. v.p. corp. planning, contr., 1997-2000; CFO Siesint, Inc., Boca Raton, Fla., 2000—01, DataCore Software Corp., Ft. Lauderdale, 2001—. Mem. Am. Inst. CPA's, Fla. Inst. CPA's. Clubs: Notre Dame (Miami) (bd. dirs. 1986-95, treas.). Roman Catholic. Home: 2742 Hampton Cir S Delray Beach FL 33445-7119 Office: DataCore Software Corp 6300 NW 5th Way Fort Lauderdale FL 33309 Fax: 561-638-4561. E-mail: gpscanlon@aol.com.

SCANLON, JANE CRONIN, mathematics educator; b. N.Y.C., July 17, 1922; d. John Timothy and Janet Smiley (Murphy) Cronin; m. Joseph C. Scanlon, Mar. 5, 1953 (div.); children: Justin, Mary, Anne, Edmund. Student, Highland Park Jr. Coll., 1939-41; BS, Wayne State U., 1943; MA, U. Mich., 1945, PhD, 1949. Mathematician Air Force Cambridge Research Center, 1951-54; instr. Wheaton Coll., Norton, Mass., 1954-55; asst. prof. Poly. Inst. Bklyn., 1957-58, asso. prof., 1958-60, prof., 1960-65; prof. math. Rutgers U., New Brunswick, N.J., 1965-91, prof. emerita, 1991—. Cons. Singer-Kearfott Div., Naval Research Lab. Office Naval Research Fellow Princeton, 1948-49; Horace H. Rockham Postdoctoral fellow U. Mich., 1950-51, Rutgers Research Council fellow, 1968-69, 72-73; NSF vis. professorship for women Courant Inst., NYU, 1984-85. Author: Fixed Points and Topological Degree in Nonlinear Analysis, 1964, Advanced Calculus, 1967, Differential Equations: Introduction and Qualitative Theory, 1980, 2d edit., 1994, Mathematics of Cell Electrophysiology, 1980, Mathematical Aspects of Hodgkin-Huxley Neural Theory, 1987; editor: Analyzing Multiscale Phenomena Using Singular Perturbation Methods, 1999. Mem. Am. Math. Soc., Soc. for Indsl. and Applied Math., Internat. Soc. Chronobiology. Home: 110 Valentine St Highland Park NJ 08904-2106 Office: Rutgers U Dept Math New Brunswick NJ 08903 E-mail: croninscanlon@erols.com.

SCANLON, LAWRENCE EUGENE, English language educator; b. Montclair, N.J., Sept. 12, 1927; s. Leo Dudley and Margaret Gertrude (Kennedy) S.; m. Anne Maxwell Sherrerd, Aug. 23, 1952; children: Lawrence Francis, Neal Patrick, Heidi Anne. BA, Wesleyan U., 1951; MA, Rutgers U., 1952; PhD, Syracuse U., 1958. Asst. prof. English Mount Holyoke Coll., South Hadley, Mass., 1958-63; prof. Hartford (Conn.) Coll. for Women, 1963-92. Author: First Came Commodore Perry, 1969, A Memorial of Ebensee, 1994, The Story He Left Behind Him Paddy the Cope, 1994. Justice of the peace Town of East Granby, Conn., 1970-72; v.p. Capital Region Libr. Coun., Hartford, 1970-74. With U.S. Army, 1945-46. Fulbright grantee, Austria, 1952-53, Japan, 1964-65, West Germany, 1980-81, summer grantee NEH, 1974. Avocations: writing, travel, investing. Home: 101 Holcomb St East Granby CT 06026-9531

SCANLON, MICHAEL J. real estate, food service and finance executive; b. Oak Ridge, Tenn., Nov. 7, 1954; s. Thomas Herbert and Marybelle (Johnston) S.; m. Margaret Taylor, Nov. 17, 1979; children: Erin H., Amy J. Student, Ball State U., 1977; cert., U. So. Carolina Real Estate Inst., 1983. Mgr. Craft House, Inc., Indpls., 1975-79; gen. mgr. Douglas Wilson Co., Greenville, S.C., 1979-81; pres. Gateway Realty, 1981-83; dir. ops. Merritt Properties, Inc., 1983-86, pres., 1986-88, CEO S.C., 1988—, Thomas & King Inc., Lexington, Ky., 1988—. Bd. dirs. S.C. Assn. Realtors, 1981; instr. Greenville Tech. Coll., 1981-84, curriculum adv. bd., 1982-85. Bd. dirs. Ky. Coun. on Child Abuse, Big Bros. Big Sisters, 1996—; trustee Georgetown Coll. Recipient Founders award Applebars Internat., 1992, Food Svc. Entrepreneur of Yr. Entrepreneur of Yr. Inc., Ky./So. Ind., 1995. Mem. Greenville Bd. Realtors (chmn. ethics com. 1981-83). Republican. Baptist. Home: 1224 Walnut Hill Chilesburg Rd Lexington KY 40515-9508 Office: Thomas & King Inc 249 W Main St Lexington KY 40507-1327

SCANLON, PATRICK JOSEPH, cardiologist, educator; b. Cleve., Jan. 30, 1938; m. Marianne McNamara, June 9, 1962; children: John, Susan, Kate, Beth, Margaret. Pre-medicine, Xavier U., Cin., 1955-58; MD, Loyala U., 1962. Diplomate Am. Bd. Internal Medicine, Am. Bd. Cardiovasc. Disease, Nat. Bd. Med. Examiners. Intern Cook County Hosp., Chgo., 1962-63; fellow in internal medicine Cleve. Clinic, 1963-65, fellow in cardiology, 1965-66; fellow in cardiology, asst. in medicine U. Colo. Med. Ctr., Denver, 1968-70; from asst. prof. to assoc. prof. medicine Loyola U. Med. Ctr., Maywood, Ill., 1970-79, prof., 1979—, dir. cardiopulmonary lab., 1970-78, dir. clin. cardiology, assoc. chief cardiology, 1978-82, chief sect. cardiology, 1982-93, co-dir.

cardiovasc. Inst., 1994-97. Hosp. ethics com. Stritch Sch. Medicine, 1983—. Contbr. over 300 articles and abstracts to med. jours., chpts. to books. Capt. med. corp. U.S. Army, 1966-68. Fellow Soc. Cardiac Angiography (sec. 1984-87, pres.-elect 1987-88, pres. 1988-89, chmn. nominating com. 1990-91, chmn. govt. rels. com. 1992-95), Am. Coll. Cardiology (gov. state of Ill. 1985-88, govt. rels. com. 1986-92, chmn. bd. govs. nominating com. 1988, database com. 1990-92, bd. trustees 1991-95, asst. sec. 1991-92, sec. 1992-95); mem. Am. Heart Assn. (v.p. Met. Chgo. chpt. 1989-90, pres.-elect 1990-91, pres. 1991-92, nominating and awards com. 1993-95) Avocations: golf, reading, travel. Office: Loyola U Med Ctr 2160 S 1st Ave Maywood IL 60153-3304

SCANLON, PETER JOSEPH, priest, university chaplain; b. Worcester, Mass., Sept. 2, 1931; s. Peter and Julia J. (O'Sullivan) S. AB, STB, St. Mary's Sem. and U., 1953, Licentiate in Sacred Theology, 1957. Ordained priest Roman Cath. Ch., 1957; cert. campus minister. Asst. pastor St. Mary's Parish, Southbridge, Mass., 1957-58; adminstr. St. Patrick's Parish, Rutland, 1958-61; Cath. chaplain Worcester (Mass.) Poly. Inst., 1961—; Bishop's vicar for coll. Roman Cath. Diocese of Worcester, Mass., 1969—; fire chaplain City of Worcester (Mass.) Fire Dept., 1971—. Diocesan bd. edn. Roman Cath. Diocese Worcester, Mass., 1969—; trustee Becker Coll., Worcester, 1971-2002, Aquinas Assn. Phi Kappa Theta, Worcester, 1975—. Recipient award to hon. alumnus Worcester (Mass.) Poly. Inst., 1985, award Becker Coll., 1990. Mem. Nat. Assn. Diocesan Dirs. of Campus Ministry, Cath. Campus Ministry Assn. Home: 44 Westwood Rd Shrewsbury MA 01545 Office: Campus Ministry Diocese Worcester PO Box 903 Worcester MA 01613-0903 E-mail: priest@wpi.edu.

SCANLON, PETER REDMOND, accountant; b. N.Y.C., Feb. 18, 1931; s. John Thomas and Loretta Dolores (Ryan) S.; m. Mary Jane E. Condon, Mar. 7, 1953; children: Peter, Barbara, Mark (dec.), Brian, Janet. BBA in Acctg., Iona Coll., 1952, LLD (hon.), 1992. CPA, N.Y. Mem. profl. staff Coopers & Lybrand, N.Y.C., 1956-66, ptnr., 1966-91, vice chmn., 1976-82, chmn., chief exec. officer, 1982-91, ret. chmn., 1991—. Hon. ptnr. N.Y.C. Partnership, 1991. Mem. fin. coun. Diocese of Palm Beach, 1995-2002. Lt. USN, 1952-56. Decorated Knight of Malta, Knight Holy Sepulchre; recipient Arthur A. Loftus award Iona Coll., 1974, Trustee award, 1990, Crain's N.Y. All Star award, 1990, Best in Class award Conf. Bd. Youth Edn., 1991. Mem.: AICPA, NY State Soc. CPAs, Jupiter Inlet Beach Club, NY Athletic Club. Roman Catholic.

SCANLON, ROSEMARY, economist; b. Dec. 25, 1939; d. Donald Angus McLennan and Mary Agnes (MacDonald) McLellan; m. Michael Scanlon, Apr. 24, 1966 (div. 1979); children: Sean Donald, Jennifer. AB, St. Francis Xavier U., N.S., 1959; MA (Ford Found. scholar), U. New Brunswick, 1960; PMD, Harvard Bus. Sch., 1981. Instr. econs. Coll. of William and Mary, Williamsburg, Va., 1960—63; asst. prof. Old Dominion U., Norfolk, 1963—65; econ. analyst Port Authority of NY and NJ, 1969—93, sr. economist for regional rsch., 1977—80, mgr. econ. devel. planning, 1980—83, chief economist, 1983—. Asst. dir. Planning and Devel. Dept., 1985; apptd. dep. state contr., N.Y.C., 1993—97; vis. rsch. fellow London Sch. Econs., 1997—2000; assoc. prof. econs. Real Estate Inst. NYU, 2001—; cons. urban and regional econs., 2000—; bd. dirs. Nova Scotia Power, Inc. Author: The Arts as an Industry in NY-NJ, 1983, The Arts as an Industry, 1993, The Regional Economy, 1993; author: (with others) Citiies in a Global Society, 1983; contbr. articles to profl. jours. Recipient Outstanding Achievement award, Exec. Dirs. award, 1987, de Luca award for lifetime achievement in econ. devel., 1999, Disting. Alumnus award, St. Francis Xavier U., 2001. Mem.: Nat. Coun. for Urban Econ. Devel. (bd. dirs. 1982—88). Home: 10 Clinton St Apt 9T Brooklyn NY 11201-2710 Office: 270 Broadway New York NY 10007-2306

SCANLON, TERRENCE MAURICE, public policy foundation administrator; b. Milw., May 1, 1939; s. Maurice John and Anne (Hayes) S.; m. Judy Ball, June 14, 1969; children: Michael Mansfield, Justin Ball, Brendan Hayes. BS, Villanova U., 1961. Staff asst. The White House, Washington, 1963-67; with SBA, 1967-69, Dept. of Commerce, Washington, 1969-83, mem. office Minority Bus. Enterprise, 1969-80, with Internat. Trade Adminstrn., 1980-81, with Minority Bus. Devel. Agy., 1981-83; mem. Consumer Product Safety Commn., 1983-89, vice chmn., 1983-84, chmn., 1985, 86-89; v.p., treas. The Heritage Found., 1989-91, v.p. corp. rels., 1991-94; chmn., pres. Capital Rsch. Ctr., 1994—. Am. Polit. Sci. Assn. Congl. fellow, 1967-68 Mem. Sovereign Mil. Order of Malta, University Club. Home: 4510 Dexter St NW Washington DC 20007-1115 Office: Capital Rsch Ctr 1513 16th St NW Washington DC 20036-1401 E-mail: tscanlon@capitalresearch.org.

SCANLON, VERA MARY, lawyer; b. Bklyn., June 23, 1968; d. Dennis P. and Alice (Keelty) S. AB, Columbia U., 1990; JD, Yale U., 1995. Bar: N.Y., N.J., U.S. Dist. Ct. (ea. and so. dists.) N.Y., U.S. Dist. Ct. N.J., Washington. Assoc. Hughes Hubbard & Reed LLP, N.Y.C., 1995-98; clk. to Hon. D. Dominguez U.S. Dist. Ct. Dist. P.R., San Juan, 1998; clk. to Hon. F. Block U.S. Dist. Ct. (ea. dist.) N.Y., Bklyn., 1998-2000; clk. to Hon. R. Katzmann U.S. Ct. Appeals (2d cir.), 2000—01; assoc. Beldock, Levine & Hoffman LLP, 2001—. Mem. Assn. Bar City N.Y., Alumni Assn. Jesuit Vol. Corps South, Marymount Sch. Alumnae Assn. Home: 224 89th St Brooklyn NY 11209-5612 E-mail: verascanlon@aya.yale.edu.

SCANNELL, WILLIAM EDWARD, aerospace company executive, consultant, psychologist; b. Muscatine, Iowa, Nov. 11, 1934; s. Mark Edward and Catharine Pearson (Fowler) S.; m. Barbara Ann Hoemann, Nov. 23, 1957; children: Cynthia Kay, Mark Edward, David Jerome, Terri Lynn, Stephen Patrick. BA in Gen. Edn., U. Nebr., 1961; BS in Engring., Ariz. State U., 1966; MS in Systems Engring., So. Meth. U., 1969; postgrad. in law, Western State U., 1977, 81-82; PhD, U.S. Internat. U., 1991. Commd. 2d lt. USAF, 1956, advanced through grades to lt. col., 1972; B-47 navigator-bombardier 98th Bomb Wing, Lincoln Air Force Base, Nebr., 1956-63; with Air Force Inst. of Tech., 1963-65, 68-69; chief mgmt. engring. team RAF Bentwaters, England, 1965-68; forward air contr. 20th Tactical Air Support Squadron USAF, Danang, Vietnam, 1970-71, program mgr. Hdqrs. Washington, 1971-74, staff asst. Office of Sec. Def., 1974-75, ret., 1975; account exec. Merrill Lynch, San Diego, 1975-77; program engring. chief Gen. Dynamics, 1977-79, engring. chief, 1979-80, program mgr., 1980-83; mgr. integrated logistics support Northrop Corp., Hawthorne, Calif., 1984-88, mgr. B-2 program planning and scheduling Pico Rivera, 1988-91; pres. Scannell and Assocs., Borrego Springs, 1991—. Author: The Nature of Motivation in Aerospace Executives, 1991. Cpl. USNG, 1952-54. Decorated DFC with three oak leaf clusters, Air medal with 11 oak leaf clusters, Vietnamese Cross Gallantry with palm, Meritorious Svc. medal. Mem. APA, Psi Chi. Republican. Roman Catholic. Home: 6130 Center Point Rd Fredericksburg TX 78624 E-mail: william@scannell.net.

SCAPERLANDA, MARIA DE LOURDES RUIZ, writer, journalist, author; b. Pinar del Río, Cuba, Aug. 13, 1960; came to U.S., 1962; d. Ignacio Manuel Ruiz and María de Jesus Páez Clausell; m. Michael Anthony Scaperlanda, Dec. 27, 1981; children: Christopher, Anamaría, Rebekah, Michelle. BA in Journalism, U. Tex., 1981; MA in Engish, U. Okla., 1997. News asst. The Daily Texan, Austin, 1979-80; pub. info. specialist Austin Parks and Rec., 1980-81; freelance writer Norman, Okla., 1981—; media coord. Cath. Diocese of Austin, 1983-84; mng. editor The Forum Mag., Austin, 1983-86; state corr. Tex. Cath. Press, 1990-94; sr. corr. Our Sunday Visitor, 1997-2000. Columnist Cath. Parent, 1998—, Cath. Practice Ezine, 1998-2000. Author: Their Faith Has Touched Us: The Legacies of Three Young Oklahoma City Bombing Victims, 1997, Edith Stein: St. Teresa Benedicta of the Cross, 2001, The Seeker's Guide to Mary2002; contbr. articles including Austin Mag., The Family, Columbia , New Convenant Mag., The Luth., Cath. Parent Mag. , U.S. Cath. Mag., Nat. Cath. Register, Cath. Twin Cir., St. Anthony Messenger, Cath. Digest, Our Sunday Visitor. Recipient Goldia D. Cooksey Meml. award for creative writing English dept. U. Okla., 1997; fellowship Salzburg seminar Am. Studies Ctr. Workshop, 1998. Mem.: Internat. Women's Writing Guild, Soc. Profl. Journalists (Excellence in Pub. Svc. Journalism 2d pl. award 2000), Am. Soc. Journalists and Authors, Cath. Press Assn. (Best News Report on Internat. Event 2nd Place 1994, Best Personality Profile 3rd Place 1996, Best Reporting on Local or State Matter 3rd Place 1996, 3rd Place 1996, Best Feature 2nd Place 1996, Best Campaign inthe Public Interest 2nd Place 1996, Best Reporting on Local or State Matter 3rd Place 1997, Best Campaign in Pub. Interest Hon. Mention 1997, Best Feature Hon. Mention 1997, Best Personality Profile 3rd Place 1998, Best Body of Work 1st Place 1999, Best Regular Column 1st Place 2001, Best Personality Profile 2d pl. in Mag. 2001, Best Personality Profile 2 pl. in Nat. Newspaper 2001, History/Biography Hon. Mention Book award 2002). Roman Catholic. Avocations: photography, music, art. Office: 3816 Waverly Ct Norman OK 73072-3218 E-mail: mscaperlanda@cox.net.

SCARANO-ILUTZI, DONNA LEE, community and business development executive; b. Newark, Apr. 23, 1952; d. Joseph and Rose (Giorella) Scarano; m. Anthony P. Ilutzi, June 20, 1993; 1 child, Liana. BA in Econs. and Acctg., Rutgers U., 1974; postgrad., U. Va., 1984. Asst. v.p., dept. mgr. Fidelity Union Bank, Newark, 1974-82; v.p. corp. and retail mktg. Core States, Pennington; v.p. cmty. devel. Nat. West/Fleet Bank, N.A., Jersey City, 1987-96; owner, cons. D. Scarano & Assocs., Livingston, N.J., 1996—. Mem. Gov.'s Cmty. Fin. Svcs. Adv. Bd. Dept. Banking; trustee, exec. com., mem. small and affordable housing loan com. N.J. Cmty. Loan Fund; bd. dirs. Bergen County Cmty. Action Program, The Cathedral Cmty. Devel. Corp.; bd. dirs., co-chair corp. adv. bd. State of N.J. Hispanic Ctr. for Policy, Rsch. and Devel.; mem. adv. coun. SBA, 1985. Scholar Rutgers U.; recipient Tribute to Women in Industry award YWCA, 1985, Nat. Bank Mktg. award, 1986, Excellence in Affordable Housing Financing award N.J. Gov. Whitman, 1995, Individual Housing Advocate of Yr. award N.J. Gov. Whitman, 1996, Leadership Am. award, 1998. Mem. Nat. Assn. Affordable Housing Lenders (bd. dirs.), Nat. Econs. Honor Soc., Nat. Journalism Honor Soc., Phi Beta Kappa. Avocations: public speaking, stock market, art collecting, Europe, gourmet cooking and entertaining. Office: D Scarano & Assocs 7 Vanderbilt Dr Livingston NJ 07039-6132

SCARBARY, OTIS LEE, lawyer; b. Macon, Ga., Feb. 4, 1952; s. Otis Thomas Jr. and Shirley (Tucker) S.; m. Donna Lynne Hughes, June 11, 1981; 1 child, Amanda Leigh. BA, Mercer U., 1974, JD, 1977. Bar: Ga., U.S. Dist. Ct. (mid. dist.) Ga. 1977, U.S. Ct. Appeals (11th cir.) 1981. Pvt. practice, Macon, 1977-83; asst. solicitor Bibb County, Office of Solicitor, 1983-96, solicitor-gen., 1996—. Mem. Ga. Assn. of Solicitors-Gen. (exec. bd. 1997—), Macon Bar Assn., State Bar of Ga. (govt. atty. involvement com.), W.A. Bootle Inn of Ct., Lions (exec. bd. Macon Evening Lions Club 1997-99), Order of Police. Democrat. avocations: jogging, diving, reading. Home: 110 Fredricksted Pl Macon GA 31204-1463 Office: Office of Solicitor-Gen Bibb County Cthouse Rm #504 Macon GA 31201 E-mail: odscarbary@cox.net., oscarbary@co.bibb.ga.us.

SCARBOROUGH, CHARLES BISHOP, III, broadcast journalist, writer; b. Pitts., Nov. 4, 1943; s. Charles Bishop and Esther Francis (Campbell) S.; m. Linda Anne Gross, Dec. 14, 1972; children: Charles Bishop IV, Elizabeth Anne; m. Anne Ford Uzielli, Oct. 2, 1982; m. Ellen Carol Ward, Sept. 25, 1994. BS, U. So. Miss., 1969. Prodn. mgr. Sta.-WLOX-TV, Biloxi, Miss., 1966-68; reporter, anchorman Sta.-WDAM-TV, Hattiesburg, 1968-69; reporter, anchorman, mng. editor Sta.-WAGA-TV, Atlanta, 1969-72; reporter, anchorman Sta.-WNAC-TV, Boston, 1972-74, NBC News, N.Y.C., 1974—. Author: (novels) Stryker, 1978, The Myrmidon Project, 1981, Aftershock, 1991. Served with USAF, 1961-65. Recipient awards for journalism AP (9), 1969-72, Emmy awards (25), 1974-2001, award Aviation/Space Writers Assn., 1977, 78, 88, UPI award for journalism N.Y. Press Club award, 1988, 89, Sigma Delta Chi award, Deadline Club award, Terry Anderson Journalism award Working Press Assn. N.J., 1992. Mem. Phi Kappa Phi. Office: NBC News 30 Rockefeller Plz Rm 723 New York NY 10112-0036

SCARBOROUGH, JOE, former congressman; b. Atlanta, Apr. 9, 1963; children: Joey, Andrew. BA, U. Ala., 1985; JD, U. Fla., 1990. Atty., 1990—; mem. U.S. Congress from 1st Fla. dist., Washington, 1995—2001. Mem. govt. reform com., judiciary com., armed svcs. com.; chmn. civil svc. subcom.; co-chmn. New Federalists; bd. dirs. Emerald Coast Pediat. Primary Care, Inc. Publisher The Fla. Sun. Mem. Fellowship Christian Athletes, Navy League (bd. dirs.), Rotary, Republican.*

SCARBOROUGH, JOHN SAMUEL, pharmacy, medicine and ancient history educator; b. St. Louis, Sept. 3, 1940; s. William John and Irene (Parish) S.; m. Lysa Gunlefinger, May 18, 1972 (div. Sept. 1990); children: Anne Elise, Isaac McKean; m. Yasemin Er, Dec. 27, 1990; 1 child, Amber Dilara. AB, BS in Zoology and History, Baker U., 1961, DHL (hon.), 1993; MA in Byzantine Studies, U. Denver, 1963; PhD in Ancient History-History Medicine, U. Ill., 1967; MA in Classics and History of Medicine, Oxford (Eng.) U., 1981. From asst. prof. to prof. U. Ky., Lexington, 1966-85; prof. history pharmacy-medicine, classics, ancient history U. Wis., Madison, 1985—. Author: Roman Medicine, 1969, 2d edit., 1976, Facets of Hellenic Life, 1976, Medical Terminologies: Classical Origins, 1992, 2d edit., 1998; editor, author: Symposium on Byzantine Medicine, 1985; editor Studies in Ancient Medicine, 1990—; contbr. articles to profl. jours. Fellow Wolfson Coll., Oxford U., 1981. Mem. Soc. for Ancient Medicine (pres., newsletter editor Lexington 1976-85, Madison 1985-87), Am. Inst. History of Pharmacy (bd. dirs., editor jour. 1985-87, Kremers award for hist. writing 1982), Byzantine Studies Conf. (governing bd. 1986-91), Am. Philol. Assn., Am. Assn. for History Medicine, Assn. Ancient Historians. Avocations: woodcarving, science fiction, classical music. Home: 25 Coronado Ct Madison WI 53705 Office: U Wis Sch Pharmacy 425 N Charter St Madison WI 53706

SCARBOROUGH, MARION KENNETH, real estate company executive; b. Celeste, Tex., Apr. 18, 1941; s. Marion H. and Knovis Elizabeth (Arnold) S.; m. Lynn Wilford Scarborough (div.); children: Valerie, Adam, Chris. BS, North Tex. State U., 1971, postgrad., 1976; postgrad., Inst. Orgn. Mgmt., 1981. Chmn., chief exec. officer Scarborough and Cotton Polit. & Pub. Affairs Consulting, Dallas, 1945-86; pres. Scarborough Rose Tekemktg. Co., Scarborough Prodns.; co-gen. ptnr. TV Album Ltd.; legis. aide Congressman Dale Milford, 1971-74; dist. aide Congressman Graham Purcell, 1968-71; dir. Learning Tree Mgmt. Systems Inc., LWS Communication, Wilford Scarborough Prodns. Contbr. articles to profl. jours. Mem. adv. bd. dirs. Yale Literary Mag.; mem. adv. bd. Heartwise Found.; bd. dirs. Swiss Ave. Counseling Ctr., Maverick Cinema Group; bd. advs. New Am. Patriots; bd. advs. Inst. Pub. Policy Research; mem. sustentation council Episcopal Found. for Drama; active Boy Scouts Am.; bd. regents Walden Prep. Sch.; chmn. bd. regents Scarborough Acad. Performing Arts. Served with U.S. Army, M.I., 1962-65. Mem. U.S. C. of C. (pub. affairs mgr. S.W. region 1974-83), Tex. C. of C. Execs. Assn. (Meritorious Service awards), N.Mex. C. of C. Execs. Assn. (Disting. Service award), Okla. C. of C. Execs. Assn., Mo. C. of C. Execs. Assn., Ark. C. of C. Execs. Assn., La. C. of C. Execs. Assn., Dallas Friday Group, Dallas Study Group, Dallas Bd. Realtors, Dallas 40, Dallas Rep. Mens, North Dallas C. of C., Waxahachie C. of C. Lodge: Rotary. Office: 6311 N Oconnor Blvd Ste 216 Irving TX 75039-3512 Address: Scarborough Land And Cattle 1030 W Pioneer Pkwy # 100 Arlington TX 76013-6331

SCARBOROUGH, MARION NICHOLS, nutritionist, recreational facility executive; b. Enosburg Falls, Vt., July 26, 1915; d. George Leonard and Clara May (Woodward) Nichols; m. Mat. Scarborough, Aug. 30, 1950 (dec. Mar., 1960); 1 child Mary Anne Scarborough O'Donnell Adams. ASS, Green Mountain Coll., Poultney, Vt., 1935; BS, Kans. State U., 1937; MPH, Harvard U., 1947. Chief dietitian Newton (Mass.) Wellesley Hosp., 1938-43, 182d Gen. Hosp., U.S. Army, 1943-45; nutritionist, author food exch. list U.S. Pub. Health Diabetes Sect., Boston, 1947-50; nutritionist Fla. Bd. Health, Jacksonville, 1950-52; owner Happy Acres Ranch, Inc., 1953—. Sec. Fla. Assn. Children Under Six ECA, 1965, pres., 1966, 67. Commd. officer USPHS, 1948-50. Mem. APHA, Am. Dietetic Assn., Am. Camping Assn., Nat. Assn. Edn. of Young Children. Episcopalian. Avocations: childrens' day care, summer camp. Home and Office: Happy Acres Ranch Inc 7117 Crane Ave Jacksonville FL 32216-9012

SCARBOROUGH, ROBERT HENRY, JR. enterpreneur; b. Hawkinsville, Ga., Mar. 12, 1923; s. Robert Henry and Janet Augusta (Burton) S.; m. Walterene Brant, July 1, 1946; children— Robert Henry, James Burton BS, U.S. Mcht. Marine Acad., 1944; BBA, U. Hawaii, 1969, MBA, 1971; MS, George Washington U., 1971, Armed Forces Staff Coll., 1963, Nat. War Coll., 1971. Commd. lt. (j.g.) USCG, 1949; advanced through grades to vice adm., 1978; chief Office of Ops. USCG, 1974-75, chief of staff, 1975-77, comdr. 9th Coast Guard Dist., 1977-78, vice comdt., 1978-82, ret., 1982; exec. dir. Navy League U.S., 1982-84; pres. Polaris Potomac Corp., 1985-96. Entrepreneur, 1996—. With USNR, 1942-49 Decorated DSM, Legion of Merit. Mem. Beta Gamma Sigma Office: 5547 37th St N Arlington VA 22207-1312

SCARBROUGH, CLEVE KNOX, JR. museum director; b. Florence, Ala., July 17, 1939; s. Cleve Knox and Emma Lee (Matheny) S. BS, U. No. Ala., 1962; MA, U. Iowa, 1967. Asst. prof. art history U. Tenn., 1967-69; dir. Mint Mus. Art, Charlotte, N.C., 1969-76, Hunter Mus. Art, Chattanooga, 1976—. Pres. N.C. Mus. Coun., 1976; bd. mem. adv. com. Tenn. Arts Commn., 1976-77, chmn. visual arts com., 1978—; mem. art selection com. TVA, 1983—, Provident Life Ins. Co., 1983—; cons. Mus. Assessment Program, 1984-94; grant evaluator Inst. Mus. Svcs., 1985-86; mem. art adv. com. First Tenn. Corp., 1991; lectr. Tenn. Gov.'s Conf. on the Arts, 1991. Compiler, editor: North Carolinians Collect, 1970, Pre Columbian Art of the Americas, 1971, Graphics by Four Modern Swiss Sculptors, 1972, British Paintings from the North Carolina Museum, 1973, Montain Landscapes by Swiss Artists, 1976. Mem. Chattanooga Landmark Com.; mem. City Planning Bd.; Bd. dirs. Chattanooga Conv. and Visitors Bur., 1977-79; advisor Chattanooga Cen. City Council, 1981-85, Tenn. State Mus., 1981, mem. Am. Federation of Arts Adv. Bd., 1987—. Served with USN, 1962-64. Mem. Am. Assn. Museums (accreditation vis. com. 1985-94), Southeastern Mus. Conf. (coun. 1976-80, 86-88, chmn. publs. com. 1979, rep. to Am. Assn. Mus.; bd. dirs. 1986-88), Rotary. Home and Office: Hunter Mus Art 1449 Stagecoach Rd Sewanee TN 37375

SCARBROUGH, ERNEST EARL, stockbroker, financial planner; b. Memphis, Jan. 7, 1947; s. Earl Carson and Mary Lillian (Keileber) S.; m. Cindy Cowley, Sept. 22, 1973; children: Michael E., William E. AA, Phoenix Coll., 1974; BA, Ottawa U., 1993; MBA, U. Phoenix, 1995; DBA in Fin., Nova So. U., 1999. CFP; cert. investment mgmt. analyst. Profl. pilot, airline transport rating, flight instr. various gen. aviation cos., Memphis and Phoenix, 1968-72; transp. analyst leasing and sales Rollins Leasing Co., Phoenix, 1971-73; cost analyst Ariz. Pub. Service Co., 1973-75; air traffic contr. FAA, Ariz. and Calif., 1975-81; account exec. E.F. Hutton & Co., Phoenix, 1982-83, asst. v.p., 1984-86, v.p., 1987; v.p., portfolio mgr. Prudential-Bache Securities, Inc., 1988-90; v.p. Esplanade Office Dean Witter Reynolds, 1990-95; mng. dir. investments, asst. br. mgr. Piper Jaffray, 1995-2000; 1st v.p. Prudential Securities, 2000—. Mem. adj. faculty Keller Grad. Sch. Mgmt., Phoenix and Mesa, 1995—97, U. Phoenix, Phoenix and Mesa, 1997—, Ariz. State U., 1999—, Thunderbird Grad. Sch. Internat. Mgmt., 2001—. Corp. chmn. Phoenix chpt. climb-the-mountain campaign Am. Cancer Soc., 1986; chmn. stewardship, vice-chmn. fin. Cross in Desert United Meth. Ch., Phoenix, 1987-88; bd. dirs. Sojourner Ctr., 1988-99, pres. bd., 1989-91, chmn. adv. bd., 1991-94; jr. achievement tchr. cons., 1992—. With USAF, 1966-70. Mem. Investment Mgmt. Cons. Assn., Am. Mgmt. Assn., Fin. Mgmt. Assn., Internat. Assn. for Fin. Planning, Internat. Assn. CFPs, Profl. Air Traffic Contrs. Orgn. (local pres. 1975-81), Ctrl. Ariz. Estate Planning Coun., Rotary (v.p. Phoenix chpt. 1987, pres.-elect 1988). Republican. Avocations: tennis, camping, hunting, flying, sailing. Home: 9409 N 17th Way Phoenix AZ 85020-2344 Office: Piper Jaffray 2525 E Camelback Rd Ste 900 Phoenix AZ 85016-4244

SCARBROUGH, FRANK EDWARD, government official; b. Knoxville, Tenn., Sept. 27, 1942; s. James L. and Anna Dale (Edwards) S.; 1 child, Elizabeth Anne. BS, U. Tenn., 1964; AM, Harvard U., 1966, PhD, 1971. Rsch. assoc. U. Bern, Switzerland, 1971-73; instr. U. Pa., Phila., 1973-76; chemist food additive rev. FDA, Washington, 1977-80, chief regulatory affairs staff, 1980-86, dep. dir. Office Nutrition, 1986-89, dir. Office Nutrition, 1989-92, dir. Office Food Labeling, 1992-97; U.S. mgr. dor codex alimentarius USDA, 1997—. Contbe. author: Food Labeling, 1994 Recipient award of merit FDA, 1985, Superior Svc. award USPHS, 1991, Disting. Svc. award HHS, 1993, Pres.'s Meritorious Exec. award, 2001. Mem. Am. Chem. Soc., Am. Soc. Clin. Nutrition, Inst. Food Technologists. Office: USDA 14th And Independence SW Washington DC 20250-0001 E-mail: eds942@hotmail.com., ed.scarborough@fsisusda.gov.

SCARBROUGH, GEORGE ADDISON, writer; b. Benton, Tenn., Oct. 20, 1915; s. William Oscar Scarbrough, Louise Anabel (McDowell) Scarbrough. BA, Lincoln Meml. U., 1947; MA, U. Tenn., Knoxville, 1954; postgrad., State U. Iowa, 1957. Tchr. secondary and higher edn. schs. Author: Tellico Blue, Invitation to Kim, 1990; contbr. articles to profl. jours. Recipient Bess Hokin award, Poetry, 2000, Mary Rugeley Ferguson award, Swanee Rev., 1960, James Still award, Coun. So. Lit., 2001; fellow Literary fellow, U. of South, 1941—43. Unitarian Universalist. Avocation: Avocations: travel, music and art, dictionaries. Home: 100 Darwin Ln Oak Ridge TN 37830

SCARBROUGH, SARA EUNICE, librarian, archivist, consultant; b. Houston, Jan. 8, 1933; d. George Washington Johnson and Frances Elizabeth Evans; m. Henry Lester Scarbrough Sr., July 5, 1953 (dec. Mar. 1993); children: Henry Lester Jr., Sarita. BA, Talladega Coll., 1953; MLS, U. Tex., 1968; PhD, Columbia State U., 1998. Cert. tchr., libr., media specialist, adminstr. Music tchr. Brazos County Pub. Schs., Bryan, Tex., 1954-58; English tchr. Edgewood Sch. Dist., San Antonio, 1958-62; head libr. Houston Ind. Sch. Dist., 1962-92; dir. Hope Resource Ctr., Houston, 1992—. Exec. bd. Friends of the Houston Pub. Libr., 1994-99. Author: History of a Black Family on the Brazos, 1998. Treas. West McGregor Civic Assn., Houston, 1995—96; pres. Women's Missionary Soc., 1994—97, pres. Sr. Adult Ministry, 1999. Named Churchman of the Yr., Good Hope Ch., Houston, 1993. Mem. AAUW, Tex. Libr. Assn., U. Tex. Alumni Assn., Order of the Ea. Star (worthy matron, Outstanding Contbn. award 1995), Zeta Phi Beta (Lambda Zeta chpt. exec. bd., sec., chmn. econ. devel. 1998, Outstanding Contbn. to Econ. Devel. award 1999). Avocations: music, traveling, genealogical research, bibliotherapy. Home: 3901 Fernwood Dr Houston TX 77021-1521

SCARDINO, MARJORIE MORRIS, publishing company executive; b. Flagstaff, Ariz., Jan. 25, 1947; d. Robert Weldon and Beth (Lamb) Morris; m. Albert James Scardino, Apr. 19, 1974; children: Adelaide Katherine Morris, William Brown, Albert Henry Hugh. BA, Baylor U.; JD, U. San Francisco. Ptnr. Brannen Wessels & Searcy, Savannah, Ga., 1976-85; pub. Ga. Gazette Pub. Co., 1978-85; pres. The Economist Newspaper Group, Inc., N.Y.C., 1985-93; chief exec. The Economist Group, London, 1993-97, Pearson P.L.C., London, 1997—. Non-exec. dir. Nokia Corp. Bd. dirs. Carter Ctr., The Bus. Coun., others. Office: Pearson PLC 80 Strand London WC2R ORL England

SCARF, HERBERT ELI, economics educator; b. July 25, 1930; s. Louis H. and Lena (Elkman) W.; m. Margaret Klein, June 28, 1953; children: Martha Anne Samuelson, Elizabeth Joan Stone, Susan Margaret Merrell. AB, Temple U., 1951; MA, Princeton U., 1952, PhD, 1954; LHD (hon.), U. Chgo., 1978. With RAND Corp., Santa Monica, Calif., 1954-57; asst., assoc. prof. stats. Stanford (Calif.) U., 1957-63; prof. econs. Yale U., New Haven, 1963-70, Stanley Resor prof. econs., 1970-78, Sterling prof. econs., 1979—. Vis. assoc. prof. Yale U., New Haven, 1959-60; dir. Cowles Found. Rsch. in Econs., Yale U., 1967-71, 1981-84, divsn. social sciences, 1971-72, 1973-74. Author: Studies in the Mathematical Theory of Inventory and Production, 1958, Computation of Economic Equilibria, 1973; editor: Applied General Equilibrium Analysis, 1984. Recipient Lanchester prize Ops. Rsch. Soc. Am., 1974, Von Neumann medal, 1983; named Disting. fellow Am. Econ. Assn., 1991. Fellow Econometric Soc. (pres. 1983); mem. NAS, Am. Acad. Arts and Scis., Am. Philos. Soc. Democrat. Jewish. Office: Yale U Cowles Found Rsch Econs PO Box 208281 New Haven CT 06520-8281 E-mail: herbert.scarf@yale.edu.

SCARF, MARGARET (MAGGIE SCARF), author; b. Phila., May 13, 1932; d. Benjamin and Helen (Rotbin) Klein; m. Herbert Eli Scarf, June, 1953; children: Martha Samuelson, Elizabeth Stone, Susan Merrell. BA, South Conn. State U., 1989. Contbg. editor New Republic, Washington, 1978—, Self Mag., N.Y.C., 1991—; writer-in-residence Jonathan Edwards Coll., 1995—. Assoc. fellow Jonathan Edwards Coll. Yale U., New Haven, 1979—; sr. fellow Bush Ctr. in Child Devel. and Social Policy, Yale U., 1991—; mem. adv. bd. Am. Psychiat. Press, Poynter Fellowship Journalism Yale U., 1995-96. Author: Meet Benjamin Franklin, 1968, Antarctica: Exploring the Frozen Continent, 1970, Body, Mind, Behavior, 1976 (Nat. Media award Am. Psychological Assn. 1977), Unfinished Business: Pressure Points in the Lives of Women, 1981, Intimate Partners: Patterns in Love and Marriage, 1987, Intimate Worlds: Life Inside the Family, 1996; contbr. numerous articles to jours. including N.Y. Times mag. and book rev., Psychology Today; TV appearances include: David Letterman Show, Oprah Wingrey Show, CBS News, Good

Morning Am., Today Show, Phil Donahue, numerous others. Recipient Nat. Media award Am. Psychol. Found., 1971, 74, 77, Conn. UN award Outstanding Conn. Women, 1987, cert. commendation Robert T. Morse Writers Competition Am. Psychiat. Assn., 1997, Disting. Svc. award Am. Psychiat. Assn., 1999, cert. of recognition N.Y. State Soc. Clin. and Social Work, 1998 ; grantee Smith Richardson Found., 1991-94; Ford Found. fellow, 1973-74, Neiman fellow Harvard U., 1975-76, Ctr. Advanced Study in Behavioral Scis. fellow, 1977-78, 85-86, Alicia Patterson Found. fellow, 1978-79. Mem. Conn. Soc. Psychoanalytic Psychologists, Am. Psychiat. Press (mem. adv. bd. 1992), Lawn Club, Elizabethans, PEN Writer's Assn. Avocations: reading, hiking, swimming. Office: Jonathan Edwards Coll Yale U 68 High St New Haven CT 06511-6643

SCARFF, HOPE DYALL, photographer; b. Mt. Pleasant, Iowa, Oct. 25, 1952; d. Charles and Marjorie (Hope) Dyall; m. David L. Scarff, Oct. 20, 1972; children: Misty Michelle, Shasta Shannon. Student, Southeastern Community Coll., Burlington, Iowa, 1973. Receptionist Dyall Photography, Mt. Pleasant, 1974-78, photographer, 1978—, mgr., 1978-80, owner, 1980—. Spkr. in field. Exhibited in group shows Epcot Ctr., Disneyworld, nat. convs. for Profl. Photographers Am., 1987—; portrait pub. in Eastman Kodak book The Portrait, Profl. Photographers of Am. Exhibit 95, 1996—. Recipient Top Portrait of a Woman award, 2001, Kodak Gallery award for excellence. Mem. Profl. Photographers Am., Am. Soc. Photographers, Profl. Photographers Iowa (One of Top 10 Photographers awards 1984, 88, 89, 90, Profl. Photographer of Yr. award 1988, 89, highest scoring portrait from Iowa for 1989, 96 conv., M. Photography degree 1990, Iowa Masters Silver Cup 1992, Iowa Master Photographer of Yr. 1996, 99, highest scoring portrait Iowa 96 Conv., One of Top Five Master Photographers 2000, Kodak Gallery award 2001), S.E. Iowa Assn. Photographers (pres. 1984), Mt. Pleasant C. of C., Mt. Pleasant Athletic Boosters Club. Republican. Methodist. Avocations: swimming, aerobics. Home: RR 3 Mount Pleasant IA 52641-9803 Office: Dyall Photography 123 N Main St Mount Pleasant IA 52641-2027 E-mail: davescar@interl.net.

SCARLATA, PAUL ANTHONY, oral surgeon; b. McKeesport, Pa., Apr. 3, 1935; s. Joseph Mario and Josephine Gloria (Battaglia) S.; m. Mary Jane Parks, June 15, 1963 (dec. 1982); children: Stephanie, Anthony, Christopher, Matthew, Sarah; m. Darla K. Hosler, May 27, 1988 (div. 1994). BS, U. Pitts., 1957, DDS, DMD, U. Pitts., 1961. Resident in oral surgery Western Pa. Hosp., Pitts., 1962-63, St. Luke's Hosp., N.Y.C., 1963-64; practice gen. dentistry and oral surgery Chambersburg, Pa., 1967—; chief dental svc. Chambersburg Hosp., 1974-76, 82-84. Treas. Franklin County (Pa.) Heritage, 1971—, pres., 1977-78; fgn. student exch. host Youth for Understanding. Capt., oral surgeon AUS, 1964—67, Mannheim, Germany. Recipient Buhl Planetarium Sci. award 1st prize Astronomy 6" Newtonian Reflector, 1952. Mem. ADA (life), Pa.Dental Assn., We. Pa. Assn., Gt. Lakes socs. oral surgeons, N.Y. Soc. Clin. Oral Pathologists, Am. Dental Soc. of Anesthetists, Cumberland Valley Dental Soc. (pres. 1982-83), Am. Legion (life). Clubs: Chambersburg, Antique Studebakers Club, Antique Auto Assn. (life mem.). Home: 3166 St Andrews Dr Chambersburg PA 17201-1465 Office: 421 Phoenix Dr Chambersburg PA 17201-2328 E-mail: tooth@pa.net., pars@pa.net.

SCARLATOS, PANAGIOTIS D. civil engineer, educator; b. Thessaloniki, Macedonia, Greece, Feb. 14, 1948; came to U.S., 1978; s. Dimitrios and Chrisoula (Kotsopoulos) S.; m. Evagelia Romanos, 1972; children: Dimitrios, Ioannis. Diploma in Civil Engring., Aristotle U., Thessaloniki, Greece, 1972, PhD in Civil Engring., 1981. Engr. Railroad Orgn., Thessaloniki, Greece, 1974; asst. engr. Hydraulic Lab. Aristotle U., Greece, 1975-80, sr. lectr., 1981-82; post-doctoral rsch. assoc. Ctr. Wetland Resources La. State U., Baton Rouge, 1982-83; rsch. assoc. La. Water Resources Rsch. Inst., 1984-85; water resources engr. So. Fla. Water Mgmt. Dist., West Palm Beach, 1985-89; assoc. prof. dept. ocean engring. Fla. Atlantic U., Boca Raton, 1989-96, prof., coord. civil engring. grad. program, 1996—2001, prof. dept. civil engring., 2001—. Contbr. 60 articles to profl. jours. 2nd lt. Greek Army. Recipient scholarship Inst. Nat. Scholarships, Greece, 1967-69, fellowship NATO, Greece-USA, 1978-79; Fulbright research scholar, summer 1992. Mem. ASCE, Am. Water Resources Assn., Internat. Assn. Hydraulic Rsch., Am. Geophsical Union. Republican. Greek Orthodox. Home: 10465 Avenida Del Rio Delray Beach FL 33446-2417 Office: Fla Atlantic U Dept Ocean Engring Boca Raton FL 33431

SCARLETT, PATRICIA LYNN, federal agency administrator; BA, MA in Polit. Sci., U. Calif., Santa Barbara. Joined Reason Pub. Policy Inst., 1979—, dir. rsch., 1985, mgr., 1989, exec. dir., v.p. rsch., pres., 2001—; asst. sec. policy, mgmt. and budget U.S. Dept. Interior, Washington, 2001—. Chair Inspection and Maintenance Rev. Com.; panelist Pay-as-You-Throw project EPA, 1995; tech. advisor N.Am. Integrated Waste Mgmt. Project Solid Waste Assn., 1995—96; bd. dirs. EarthShell Corp.; com. mem. Nat. Environ. Policy Inst.; sr. fellow Found. for Rsch. on Econs. and the Environment; environ. campaign advisor to George W. Bush; mem. Bush transition adv. team EPA. Contbr. articles to profl. jours. Bd. mem. Thoreau Inst. Office: US Dept Interior Policy Mgmt and Budget 1849 C St NW Washington DC 20240*

SCARLETT, RANDALL H. lawyer; b. Athens, Ohio, July 12, 1957; s. John Donald and Sherry (Richards) S.; m. Mary Anne Scarlett, Sept. 21, 1991; children: Randall Alexander, Christina Marie. BA, San Francisco State U., 1982; JD, Golden Gate U., 1985. Bar: Calif. 1988, U.S. Dist. Ct. (no. dist.) Calif. 1985, U.S. Dist. Ct. (ea. dist.) Calif. 1988, U.S. Dist. Ct. (so. and ctrl. dists.) Calif. 1995, U.S. Ct. Appeals (9th cir.) 1995, U.S. Supreme Ct. 1995. Ptnr. Belli, Belli, Brown, Monzione, Fabbro & Zakaria, San Francisco, 1989-93, Brown, Monzione, Fabbro, Zakaria & Scarlett, San Francisco, 1993-96, Brown, Fabbro & Scarlett, San Francisco, 1996—99, Scarlett Law Group, San Francisco, 1999—. Lectr. Mem. ATLA (sustaining, com. Traumatic Brain Injury Litigation Group), Consumer Attys. Calif. (sustaining), San Francisco Lawyers Assn., Bar Assn. San Francisco, Avocations: golfing, scuba diving. Office: Scarlett Law Group 3d Fl 857 Montgomery St San Francisco CA 94133

SCARLETT, TODD LEELAND, biology educator; b. Topeka, May 21, 1961; s. Jerrold Grant and Patty Jean Scarlett; m. Nancy Virginia Moyers, July 11, 1987; children: Benjamin Edward, David Grant. BS in Biology, S.W. Mo. State U., 1983; MS in Zoology, U. Ark., 1987; PhD in Zoology, Wash. State U., 1997. Tchr. asst. U. Ark., Fayetteville, 1984-86; tchr. sci. Kingston (Ark.) H.S., 1988-89; rsch. asst. Wash. State U., Pullman, 1991-93, tchr. asst., 1992-95; asst. prof. biology U. S.C., Lancaster, 1998—. Contbr. articles to sci. jours., including Jour. Wildlife Mgmt., The Condor. Mem. Ecol. Soc. Am., Am. Soc. Mammalogists, Am. Ornithologists Union, Animal Behavior Soc., S.C. Acad. Sci., S.C. Urban and Cmty. Forestry Coun. Avocations: mountain climbing, fly fishing, golf. Office: USCL PO Box 889 211 Bradley Lancaster SC 29721 E-mail: tlscarle@gwm.sc.edu.

SCARNE, JOHN, game company executive; b. Steubenville, Ohio, Mar. 4, 1903; s. Fiorangelo and Maria (Tamburro) S.; m. Steffi Kearney, 1956; 1 son, John Teeko. Student pub. schs., Guttenberg, N.J. Pres. John Scarne Games, Inc., North Bergen, N.J., 1950—. Gaming cons. Hilton Hotels Internat. Magician stage, screen and television; Author: Scarne on Dice, 1945, Scarne on Cards, 1950, Scarne on Card Tricks, 1950, Scarne on Magic Tricks, 1952, Scarne's New Complete Guide to Gambling, 1962, The Odds Against Me, 1967, Scarne's Encyclopedia of Games, 1973, The Mafia Conspiracy, 1976, Scarne's Guide to Casino Gambling; Scarne's Guide to Modern Poker; Contbr. to: World Book Ency, 1970, Ency. Brit, 1975. Cons. to U.S. Armed Forces, 1941-45. Named Man of Year for Police Chiefs of U.S., 1960 Office: Unit 312 2581 Countryside Blvd Clearwater FL 33761-3521

SCAROLA, JOHN MICHAEL, dentist, educator; b. N.Y.C., Nov. 18, 1934; s. Michael Fidelis and Filomena Mary (Turso) S.; m. Theodora Mary Marty, June 15, 1963; children: Michael A., John P., Stephen A., Robert M., Mary E. BS, Fordham Coll., 1956; DDS, Columbia U., 1960. Instr. Columbia Dental Sch., N.Y.C., 1962-68, asst. clin. prof., 1969-72, course dir. fixed partial dentures, 1969-72, assoc. clin. prof., 1973-86, course dir. prosthodontic elective, 1977-91, clin. prof., 1986—. Lectr., clin. prof. postgrad. prostodontics Columbia U., N.Y.C., 1986—, AEGD-Columbia U., N.Y.C., 1990-92, Luth. Med. Ctr., Bklyn., 1993—; cons. in prosthodontics Northport VA Hosp., East Northport, N.Y., 1970-91. Scoutmaster Boy Scouts Am., Port Washington, N.Y., 1976-78; chmn. spl. gifts Bishop's Annual Appeal, St. Peter's-Port Washington, 1977-78; Cath. Youth Orgn. sports coach St. Paul The Apostle, Brookville, N.Y., 1980-83; fundraising com. The Yard, Martha's Vineyard, Mass., 1990; concert com. Musician's Emergency Fund, N.Y.C., 1992. Lt. USNR, 1960-62. Fellow Am. Coll. Dentists (chmn. N.Y. sect. 1994, regent of Regency 1), N.Y. Acad. Dentistry (pres. 1989-90), Greater N.Y. Acad. Prosthodontics (dir. 1993-97); mem. Greater N.Y. Acad. Prosthodontics Found. (dir., pres. 1989-97), N.Y. Acad. Dentistry Endowment Fund (dir., pres. 1992-93). Republican. Roman Catholic. Avocations: golf, opera, classical music, gardening. Home: 83 Fruitledge Rd Glen Head NY 11545-3317 Office: 501 Madison Ave New York NY 10022-5602

SCAROLA, SUSAN MARGARET, lawyer; b. Elizabeth, N.J., Mar. 19, 1948; d. Anthony and Ruth (Cohen) S. BA cum laude, Thiel Coll., 1970; JD, Rutgers-State of U. of N.J., 1976. Bar: N.J. 1976, N.Y. 1985, Fla. 1993; cert. criminal trial atty., matrimonial law atty. Law sec. to Judge Triarsi, Superior Ct. of N.J., Elizabeth, 1976-77; asst. prosecutor Union County Prosecutor's Office, 1997-88; non-equity ptnr. Lomurro Davison Eastman & Munoz, Freehold, N.J., 1988-97; ptnr. Newman Scarola & Assoc., 1997—. Judge Mcpl. Ct., Twp. of Old Bridge, 1999—. Trustee Legal Aid Soc. of Monmouth County, 1992—, sec., 1998-2000, v.p. 2000—; committeewoman Old Bridge Dem. Com., 1995-99. Named Women of Yr. Women Lawyers in Monmouth County, 1994. Mem. Monmouth Bar Assn. (chair family law com. 1995-97), N.J. Bar Assn., Fla. Bar Assn., Middlesex County Bar Assn., Rutgers (Newark) Law Sch. Alumni (trustee 2000). Office: Newman Scarola & Assocs 64 W Main St Freehold NJ 07728-2142 E-mail: sscarola@monmouthlaw.com.

SCARPA, ANTONIO, medicine educator, biomedical scientist; b. Padua, Italy, July 3, 1942; s. Angelo and Elena (DeRossi) S. MD cum laude, U. Padua, 1966, PhD in Pathology, 1970; MA (hon.), U. Pa., 1978. Asst. prof. biochemistry, biophysics U. Pa., Phila., 1973-76, assoc. prof., 1976-80, prof., 1980-86, dir. biomed. instrumentation group, 1983-86; prof., chmn. dept. physiology and biophysics Case Western Res. U., Cleve., 1986—, dir. tng. ctr., program project, 1983—, prof. medicine, 1989—. Cons. study sect. NIH, Bethesda, 1984—, Am. Heart Assn., Dallas, 1986-91; pres., assoc. chair dept. physiology, 1993-94; vice chair Nat. Caucus Basic Sci. Presidents, Washington. Editor (books): Frontiers of Biological Energetics, Calcium Transport and Cell Function, Transport ATPases, Membrane Pathology, Membrane and Cancer Cells; editor (jours.) Archives Biochemistry and Biophysics, Cell Calcium, Biochemistry Internat., The Scientific Jour.; mem. editl. bd. Circulation Rsch., 1978-81, Biophys. Jour., 1979-82, Jour. Muscle Rsch., 1979—, Magnesium, 1982—, Physiol. Revs., 1982-90, FASEB Jour., 1987-92, Molecular Cellular Biochemistry, 1988—; contbr. numerous articles to profl. jours. Mem. Am. Soc. Physiologists, Am. Soc. Biol. Chemistry, Biophys. Soc. (exec. coun. 1980-83, 85-89, 94-97), U.S. Bioenergetics Group (program chmn. 1974-75, 82, 83, exec. officer 1985-90, assoc. chmn. dept. physiology, pres. 1993-95), Biophys. Soc. (treas. 1998—), Assn. Am. Med. Colls. (adminstrv. bd.), Federated Am. Soc. Exptl. Biologists (bd. dirs.). Avocations: farming, sailing, painting. Office: Case Western Reserve Univ Dept Of Physiology Cleveland OH 44106

SCARPELLI, VITO, adult education educator, administrator; b. Passaic, N.J., July 17, 1946; s. Peter and Celia (Pignataro) S.; m. JoAnn Motti, Aug. 23, 1970; children: Anthony, Michele. BA in Acctg. and Edn., Montclair State Coll., 1968; MA, Kean Coll., 1984; postgrad., St. Peters, Jersey City State U., Seton Hall U., Kans. State U. Prin. Roselle Park Mid. Sch., 1996—; supr. P. Scarpelli & Sons, Nutley, N.J., 1968-84; bus. adminstr. John J. Baum, Inc., Wayne; salesman Realty World-Monaco Realty, Nutley, 1980—; asst. track coach, tchr. jr. H.S. Belleville Bd. Edn., 1968-69; dir. adult edn. and summer programs Roselle Park (N.J.) Bd. Edn., 1984-96. Dir. Union County Summer Youth Employment and Tng., Roselle Park, 1986, asst. curriculum coord., 1992-96, dir. tech., 1993-96; adj. prof. Jersey City State Coll., 1993-96. Pres. Nutley Am. Little League, 1987-97; v.p. Nutley Basketball Assn.; past pres. Lincoln Sch. PTA. Mem. NEA, N.J. Bus. Edn. Assn., N.J. Edn. Assn., Roselle Park Edn. Assn., LERN, KC (grand knight 1976). Democrat. Roman Catholic. Avocation: fishing. Home: 81 Milton Ave Nutley NJ 07110-3017 Office: Roselle Park Bd Edn 510 Chestnut St Roselle Park NJ 07204-1928

SCARR, SANDRA WOOD, psychology educator, researcher; b. Washington, Aug. 8, 1936; d. John Ruxton and Jane (Powell) Wood; m. Harry Alan Scarr, Dec. 26, 1961 (div. 1970); children: Phillip, Karen, Rebbecca, Stephanie; m. James Callan Walker, Aug. 9, 1982 (div. 1994). AB, Vassar Coll., 1958; AM, Harvard U., 1963, PhD, 1965. Asst. prof. psychology U. Md., College Park, 1964-67; assoc. prof. U. Pa., Phila., 1967-71; prof. U. Minn., Mpls., 1971-77, Yale U., New Haven, 1977-83; Commonwealth prof. U. Va., Charlottesville, 1983-95, chmn. dept. psychology, 1984-90; CEO, chmn. bd. dirs. KinderCare Learning Ctr., Inc., 1995-97; ret., 1997. Mem. nat. adv. bd. Robert Wood Johnson Found., Princeton, N.J., 1985-91; coord. coun. psychology SUNY Bd. Regents, N.Y.C., 1984-92; prof. Kerstin Hesselgren, Sweden, 1993-94. Author: Race, Social Class and Individual Differences in IQ, 1981, Mother Care/Other Care, 1984 (Nat. Book award APA 1985), Caring for Children, 1989; editor Jour. Devel. Psychology, 1980-86, Current Directions in Psychol. Sci., 1991-95. Fellow Ctr. for Advanced Studies, Stanford U., Calif., 1976-77; grantee NIH, NSF, others, 1967-95. Fellow AAAS, APA (chmn. com. on human rsch. 1980-83, coun. of reps. 1984-89, bd. dirs. 1988-90, Award for Disting. Contbn. to Rsch. on Pub. Policy 1988), Am. Psychol. Soc. (bd. dirs. 1992—, pres. 1996-97, James McKeen Cattell award 1993); mem. Am. Acad. Arts and Scis. (coun. mem. 1995-2000), Behavior Genetics Assn. (pres. 1985-86, mem. exec. coun. 1976-79, 84-87), Soc. for Rsch. in Child Devel. (governing coun. 1974-76, 87-93, chmn. fin. com. 1987-89, pres. 1989-91), Internat. Soc. for Study of Behavioral Devel. (exec. bd. 1987-94). Avocations: dogs, gardening. Home: 77-6222 Kaumalumalu Dr Holualoa HI 96725-9757 E-mail: SandraScar@aol.com.

SCARRITT, RICHARD WINN, lawyer; b. Enid, Okla., Dec. 13, 1938; s. Nathan Spencer and Rilla Fayette (Winn) S.; m. Gloria June Gaba, Nov. 7, 1966 (div. Nov. 1971); m. Deborah Louise Guillemot, Sept. 3, 1986; 1 child, Nathan Spencer IV; ward, Samantha Jo Wickizer. BA, Okla. U., 1960; JD, Harvard U., 1963. Bar: Mo. 1963, U.S. Dist. Ct. (we. dist.) Mo. 1964, U.S. Supreme Ct. 1971. Assoc. Spencer, Fane, Britt & Browne, Kansas City, Mo., 1963-68, ptnr., chmn. real estate sect., 1969—. Guest lectr. real estate law U. Mo. Extension Ctr., Independence, 1966-68; mem. panel of arbitrators Am. Arbitration Assn.; chmn. standard forms com., mem. govt. affairs, zoning law and legis. coms. Met. Real Estate Bd. Greater Kansas City; panelist Plaza West Assn., Kansas City, 1971-78. Co-author: Missouri Real Estate Forms and Practice, 1988, supplements, 1989-98. Mem. Clay County Econ. Devel. Coun.; dir. Brookside Roller Hockey League, Kansas City Jr. Blades Amateur Hockey Assn. Fellow Am. Coll. Real Estate Lawyers (attys.' opinions com.); mem. ABA (real property, probate and trust law sect., loan documentation, real estate financing and comml. fin. svcs., environ. law com. subcom. energy law and real property, corp., banking and bus. law sect., comml. fin. svcs. com.), Mo. Bar Assn. (property law com., adv. coun., energy law com.), Kansas City Met. Bar Assn. (real estate law com., chmn. com. coun.), Lawyers Assn. Kansas City, Mo. C. of C., Kansas City Club, SAR, Mensa, Phi Delta Theta. Republican. Episcopalian. Avocations: photography, collecting art, electronics, computers, youth sports. Home: 825 W 53rd Ter Kansas City MO 64112-2327 Office: Spencer Fane Britt & Browne 1000 Walnut St Ste 1400 Kansas City MO 64106-2140 Fax: 816-474-3216. E-mail: rws@spencerfane.com.

SCARTELLI, JOSEPH PAUL, music therapy educator, dean; b. Scranton, Pa., May 4, 1952; s. Joseph Anthony and Angela Rose Scartelli; m. Frances Marie DiMaggio, June 15, 1974; children: Nicole, Joseph. BS in Music, Mansfield U., 1974; MusM in Music Therapy, U. Miami, Fla., 1977, PhD in Music Edn., 1981. Cert. music therapist. Tchr. Dade County Pub. Schs., South Miami, Fla., 1976-77; grad. tchg. fellow U. Miami, 1979-80, instr. music therapy, 1980-81; asst. prof. music Radford (Va.) U., 1981-87, assoc. prof. music, 1987-89, prof. music, 1989—, dean Coll. Visual and Performing Arts, 1988—. Mem. editl. bd. Jour. Music Therapy, 1996—, Arts in Psychotherapy, 1984—. Author monograph: Music and Self-Management, 1989; contbr. articles to profl. jours., chpts. to book. Bd. dirs. Radford U. Found., 1990—; bd. commrs. renovation project Dumas Music Ctr., Roanoke, Va., 1998—; bd. dirs. Va. Arts, Richmond, Va., 1992—; mem. City of Radford Arts and Events Commn., 1996—. Recipient Resolution of Recognition, Va. State Bd. Edn., 1999, Educator of Yr. award Radford C. of C., 2001. Mem. Am. Music Therapy Assn. (award of merit 1998), Assn. Performing Arts presenters, Internat. Coun. Fine Arts Deans. Avocations: music performance, golf, martial arts, tennis, carpentry. Home: 501 Randolph St Radford VA 24141 Office: Radford U Coll Visual/Performing Arts Radford VA 24142 E-mail: jscartel@radford.edu.

SCARVIE, WALTER BERNARD, clergyman; b. Story City, Iowa, July 23, 1934; s. Walter Bernard and Florence Emily (Thompson) S.; m. Korinne Mary Thompson, June 1, 1975; 1 child, Krista Ruth. BA, Luther Coll., Decorah, Iowa, 1956; BD, Luther Theol Sem., St. Paul, 1963; MA, Cath. U. Am., Washington, 1973, postgrad., 1973-79. Ordained to ministry Am. Luth. Ch., 1964. Pastor St. Peter Luth. Ch., St. Clair, Mich., 1964—67; campus pastor Luth. Campus Ministry of Washington, 1967—78; Protestant chaplain Georgetown U. Law and Med. Schs., 1978—81; pastor Cmty. of Christ, 1984—96, Our Saviors Luth. Ch., Milw., 1996—2001, Redeemer Luth. Ch., Hartford, 2001—02, Mt. Olive Luth. Ch., Mukwonago, 2002—. Rsch. cons. The Alban Inst., Washington, 1978-79; seminar leader, Washington, 1970-96. Editor Jour. Religious Concern, 1976; contbr. articles to religious jours. Active St. Clair (Mich.) Housing Commn., 1965-67, Friends of the Kennedy Ctr. for Performing Arts, Washington, 1971-96. With U.S. Army, 1957-58. Osterman fellow ea. dist. Am. Luth. Ch., 1975. Mem. NARAS, Milw. Luth. Coalition, Luth. Human Rels. Assn., Ctrl. City Chs. Bd., Milw. Innercity Congregations Allied for Hope. Office: Mt Olive Luth Ch 211 Main St PO Box 8 Mukwonago WI 53149-0008

SCARWID, DIANA ELIZABETH, actress; b. Savannah, Ga. d. Anthony and Elizabeth Scarwid. Grad., Am. Acad. Dramatic Arts, 1975; degree in Theater Arts, Acting, Pace U., 1975. Appeared in films including Pretty Baby, Honeysuckle Rose, Inside Moves, 1981 (Oscar award nomination Best Supporting Actress 1981), Mommie Dearest, Rumble Fish, Strange Invaders, Silkwood, Psycho III, Extremeties, Heat, Neon Bible, The Cure, Gold Diggers: The Secret of Bear Mountain, What Lies Beneath, The Angel Doll, A Guy Thing, 2002; TV films include Thou Shalt Not Kill, Studs Lonigan, Guyana Tragedy: The Story of Jim Jones, Desperate Lives, A Bunny's Tale, After the Promise, Night of The Hunter, Critical Choices, Bastard Out of Carolina, Angel of Pennsylvania Avenue, Truman (Emmy nomination 1996), If These Walls Could Talk, Ruby Bridges Story, also mini-series From the Earth to the Moon, 1998, Before He Wakes; theater prodns. include Key Exchange, Toronto, Can., A Thousand Clowns, Jupiter, Fla., Gethsemanie Springs, Mark Taper Forum, L.A., Spoon River Anthology, Ring 'round the Moon, N.Y.C., Nat. Shakespeare Conservancy, NY; (TV films) Down Will Come Baby, 1999, Dirty Pictures, 2000, Path to War, 2002 Avocations: reading, bicycle riding, crabbing from row boat, walking.

SCASTA, DAVID LYNN, forensic psychiatrist; b. Austin, Tex., Dec. 13, 1949; s. Albert Ray and Helen Pearl (Hennessy) S. BA, Baylor U., 1972, MD, 1977. Diplomate Am. Bd. Psychiatry and Neurology. Staff physician U. Houston, 1977-78; adminstr. Temple U. Med. Sch., Phila., 1982-83; resident in psychiatry Temple U. Hosp., 1982; dir. consultation svcs. Grad. Hosp., 1983-84; dir. outpatient programs Phila. Psychiat. Ctr., 1983-84; pvt. practice Grad. Hosp. Phila. Psychiat. Ctr., 1984-89; med. dir. Phila. Consultation Ctr., 1987-89; attending psychiatrist Hunterdon Med. Ctr., Flemington, N.J., 1989-98, chmn. dept. psychiatry, 1996-97; pvt. practice New Hope, Pa., 1989-98, forensic psychiatry, Princeton, NJ, 1998—; cons. Coordinated Med. Network, 1989—, dir. emotional recovery unit, 2002—. Clin. assoc. prof. dept. psychiatry Temple U. Med. Sch., Phila., 1983—. Editor Jour. of Gay & Lesbian Psychotherapy, 1987-98. Dist. rep. Rep. Party of Tex., Houston, 1977, precinct sec., 1975-77; bd. dirs. Phila. Bapt. Assn., mem. exec. com. Named Ginsberg Fellow Group for Advancement of Psychiatry, 1980-82. Fellow Am. Psychiat. Assn. (pres. Caucus of lesbian, gay and bisexual mems. 1996-97); mem. AMA, Assn. Gay and Lesbian Psychiatrists (pres. 1995-97, newsletter editor 1987-94), Am. Acad. Psychiatry and the Law, Am. Coll. Forensic Examiners. Republican. Avocations: skiing, antiques. Office: Ind Psychiat Svcs 115 Commons Way Princeton NJ 08540-1507

SCATENA, LORRAINE BORBA, rancher, women's rights advocate; b. San Rafael, Calif., Feb. 18, 1924; d. Joseph and Eugenia (Simas) de Borba; m. Louis G. Scatena, Feb. 14, 1960; children: Louis Vincent, Eugenia Gayle. *Father, Joseph de Borba, was born in Calheta, San Jorge, Azores Islands. Before the San Francisco earthquake of April 1906, he was a dairyman and part owner of the 2,200 acre Marin Land and Cattle Company at San Francisco harbor in Sausalito, California. Mother, Eugenia Simas, was born in Manadas, San Jorge Island. She immigrated to Bristol, Rhode Island, before going to Petaluma, California, where she worked in the silk mill until she married Joseph in 1922.Grandfather,Manuel Simas, traveled from the Azores Islands to California in the late 1850's for the Gold Rush. He stayed 17 years and then settled in Manadas,San Jorge is, built a two-story stone house, married and had a family of ten children. Husband, Louis G. Scatena, was born in Yerington on the present ranch. His father, Vincent Scatena, was born in Verciano, Italy, in 1879. His mother, Cheti Barsotti, was born in Galveston, Texas, where her family had a grocery store. They married in Italy and their son, Louis G., attended schools in Italy until he was twelve.* BA, Dominican Coll., San Rafael, 1945; postgrad., Calif. Sch. Fine Arts, 1948, U. Calif., Berkeley, 1956-57. Cert. elem. tchr., Calif. Tchr. Dominican Coll., 1946; tchr. of mentally handicapped San Anselmo (Calif.) Sch. Dist., 1946; tchr. Fairfax (Calif.) Pub. Elem. Sch., 1946-53; asst. to mayor Fairfax City Recreation, 1948-53; tchr., libr. U.S. Dependent Schs., Mainz am Rhine, Fed. Republic Germany, 1953-56; translator Portugal Travel Tours, Lisbon, 1954; bonding sec. Am. Fore Ins. Group, San Francisco, 1958-60; rancher, farmer Yerington, Nev., 1960-98. Hostess com. Caldecott and Newbury Authors' Awards, San Francisco, 1959; mem. Nev. State Legis. Commn., 1975; coord. Nevadans for Equal Rights Amendment, 1975-78, rural areas rep., 1976-78; testifier Nev. State Senate and Assembly, 1975, 77; mem. adv. com. Fleischmann Coll. Agr. U. Nev., 1977-80, 81-84; speaker Grants and Rsch. Projects, Bishop, Calif., 1977, Choices for Tomorrow's Women, Fallon, Nev., 1989. *The L.G. Scatena family owns and operates part of the Old Wilson Ranch in Mason Valley. After leasing, father Vincent bought the ranch in the early 1930's from second owner, Frank O. Stickney, a native of Maine, who built the New England style 11 room ranch house in 1916. It was the first in the area to have electricity supplied by a home plant of batteries. Stickney was a bank president and a member of the Nevada State Legislature and was an important factor in ranch management as was L.G.'s aunt, Paradisa Barsotti, who came from Verciano, Italy, in 1939. L.G. Scatena was in ranching all his life except for one year when he worked for the Bank of Italy in San Francisco. The ranch runs a herd of registered and commercial grade Herefords and Angus cattle; crops include alfalfa, potatoes, and grain.* Poetry presenter World Congress on Arts and Comm., Lisbon, Portugal, 1999, Washington, 2000, St. John's Coll.-Cambridge U., 2001, Vancouver, Can., 2002. Trustee Wassuk Coll., Hawthorne, Nev., 1984-87; mem. Lyon County Friends of Libr., Yerington, 1971—, Lyon County Mus. Soc., 1978—; sec., pub. info. chmn. Lyon County Rep. Ctrl. Com., 1973-74; mem. Marin County Soc. Artists, San Anselmo, Calif., 1948-53; charter mem. Eleanor Roosevelt Edn. Fund for Women and Girls, 1990, sustaining mem., 1992—; Nev. rep. 1st White House Conf. Rural Am. Women, Washington, 1980; participant internat. reception, Washington, 1980; mem. pub. panel individual presentation Shakespeare's Treatment of Women Characters, Nev. Theatre for the Arts, Ashland, Oreg., Shakespearean Actors local performance, 1977; mem. Nev. Women's History Project, U. Nev., 1996—; mem. pres.'s circle Dominican U. Calif., 1997--; mem. Bancroft Libr.'s coun. U. Calif., Berkeley, 2002--. Recipient Outstanding Conservation Farmer award Mason Valley Conservation Dist., 1992, Soroptimist Internat. Women Helping women award 1983, invitation to first all-women delegation to U.S.A. from People's Republic China, U.S. House Reps., 1979; Public Forum Travel grantee Edn. Title IX, Oakland, Calif., 1977; Internat. Biog. Ctr. (Cambridge) fellow World Lit. Acad., 1993. Mem. AAUW (Leaders Circle 1998--), Lyon County Ret. Tchrs. Assn. (unit pres. 1979-80, 84-86, v.p. 1986-88, Nev. State Outstanding Svc. award 1981, state conv. gen. chmn. 1985), Rural Am. Women Inc., AAUW (br. pres. 1972-74, 74-76, chair edn. found. programs 1983—, state conv. gen. chmn. 1976, 87, state sec. 1970-72, state legis. program chmn. 1976-77, state chmn. internat. rels. 1979-81, state pres. 1981-83, br. travelship, discovering women in U.S. history Radcliffe Coll. 1981, State Humanities award 1975, Future Fund Nat. award 1983, Lorraine Scatena endowment gift named in her honor for significant contbns. to AAUW Ednl. Found. 1997), Mason Valley Country Club, Italian Cath.

Fedn. (pres. 1986-88), Uniao Portuguesa Estado da Calif., Nat. Mus. of Women in Art (charter mem.; mem. mus. coun. 1999--). Roman Catholic. Avocations: writing, photography. Home: PO Box 247 Yerington NV 89447-0247

SCATES, ALICE YEOMANS, former government official, consultant; b. Pitts., Jan. 21, 1915; d. William E. and Georgiana L. (Lloyd) Yeomans. BS, State Tchrs. Coll., Glassboro, N.J., 1936; MEd, Duke U., 1949; EdD, George Washington U., 1963. Tchr. elem. sch., Haddon Heights, N.J., 1937-43; civilian personnel officer Sedalia Army Airfield, Mo., Greenfield Army Airfield, S.C., 1944-46; pers. tng. officer VA Ctr., Dayton, Ohio, 1947—48; rsch. assoc., dir. Am. Coun. on Edn. Staff for Office Naval Rsch. Projects, 1949-53; asst. dir. Nat. Home Study Coun., 1954; editor, rsch. asst. Office of Edn. HEW, 1955, rsch. analyst, coord. coop. rsch. program, 1956-64, program planning officer occupl. rsch. program, 1965-66, dir. basic rsch. br. secondary edn., 1967-69; program planning and eval. officer Nat. Ctr. Ednl. R & D, 1969-71; eval. specialist Office Program Eval., 1971-80; eval. officer Office of Mgmt. U.S. Dept. Edn., 1980-82, cons., 1982-91; mem. continuing care adv. com. Md. State Office on Aging, 1994-99. Contbr. articles to profl. jours.; editor: Life Line, 1998—. Mem. Nat. Continuing Care Residents Assn.; bd. dirs. Town Ctr. Cmty. Assn., Columbia, Md., 1997-2001. Capt. U.S. Army, 1943-46. Fellow AAAS; mem. LWV, Am. Sociol. Assn., Am. Ednl. Rsch. Assn., Adult Edn. Assn., Kappa Delta Pi, Phi Delta Gamma. Home and Office: Vantage House # 1006 5400 Vantage Point Rd Columbia MD 21044-2667 E-mail: ayscates@msn.com.

SCATES, ALLEN EDWARD, professional volleyball coach; BA, UCLA, 1961, MS, 1962. Coach volleyball UCLA, 1970—. Coached UCLA to 18 NCAA championships. Recipient All Time Great Coach awrd USA Volleyball, 1995; inducted Volleyball Hall of Fame, 1993, Calif. Beach Volleyball Hall of Fame, 1998; named AVCA Coach of Yr., 5 times, U.S. Olympic Com. Coach Yr., 1998. Office: UCLA Morgan Ctr PO Box 24044 Los Angeles CA 90024-0044 E-mail: ascates@athletics.ucla.edu.

SCATES, JENNIFER ANN, lawyer; b. Midland, Tex., Sept. 5, 1957; d. Marion (Braquet) S.; m. Timothy John Hayles, Apr. 30, 1988; 1 child, Richard Maxwell Scates Hayles. BA, U. St. Thomas, 1980; JD, Oklahoma City U., 1985. Bar: Tex. 1986. Pvt. practice, Houston, 1986-88, Austin, Tex., 1988—. Office: 5750 Balcones Dr Ste 207 Austin TX 78731-4269

SCATURRO, PHILIP DAVID, investment banker, university chancellor; b. Newark, Dec. 8, 1938; s. Charles and Rose (Montino) S. BA, Williams Coll., 1960; JD, MBA, Columbia U., 1963. Analyst Ladenburg, Thalmann & Co., Inc., N.Y.C., 1964-67; v.p. Sellin, Forbes & Smith, 1967, Allen & Co. Inc., N.Y.C., 1967-71, mng. dir., exec. v.p., 1977—; gen. ptnr. R&S Assocs., 1972-76; pvt. investor, 1976-77; chancellor New Sch U, 1999—. Bd. dirs. Opal Concepts, Inc., Anaheim, Calif., Wilmorite, Inc., Rochester, N.Y. Bd. dirs. Mass. Mus. Contemporary Art Found., Inc., North Adams; bd. dirs., mem. exec. com., chmn. fin. com., treas. N.Y.C. Opera; trustee, mem. exec. com., chmn. audit com., trustee New Sch. U. 1999—. Mem. Univ. Club (N.Y.C.), Century Assn. Avocations: opera, music, theatre, wine, fly fishing. Office: Allen & Co 711 Fifth Ave 9th Fl New York NY 10022-3111

SCAVARDA, DONALD ROBERT, composer, artist; b. Iron Mountain, Mich., June 18, 1928; m. Barbara Janet Regner, Nov. 13, 1965. MMus, U. Mich., 1953. Co-founder, organizer Once Festival Musical Premieres, Ann Arbor, Mich., 1960-65. Composer: Groups For Piano, 1959, Sounds for Eleven, 1961, (Haiku song cycle) In the Autumn Mountains, 1961, Matrix for Clarinetist (widely recognized as the pioneering work in discovery and development of clarinet multiphonics), 1962, (piano, clarinet, 8mm film) Landscape Journey, 1963, (film score for electronic realization) Greys, 1963, (multiple film projection and tape) Caterpillar, 1965; paintings include Chamber Music, 1997, Portrait of Helen P., 1998. Fulbright scholar, 1953; recipient 1st prize for Fantasy For Violin And Orchestra BMI Inc., 1954. Home: PO Box 1908 Ann Arbor MI 48106-1908

SCAVONE, EDMOND, retired surgeon; b. Italy, 1919; came to U.S., 1924; s. Giacomino and Serafina (Guarino) S.; m. Jane Frances Kennedy, Jan. 10, 1946 (dec. June 1996); children: Michael, John, Lawrence, Mary Ann, Gregory (dec.). BS, Loyola U., 1941; MD, U. Md., 1944. Bd. cert. gen. surgery. Roman Catholic.

SCEARCE, JANNA LUEBKEMANN, sales professional; b. Stuttgart, Ark., Oct. 23, 1960; d. Edward James and Theresa Frances (Sandor) Luebkemann; m. Marvin Wilson Scearce, Apr. 26, 1996. BS in Agri-Bus., U. Ark., 1983; postgrad., Ohio State U., 1985-86; MS in Agrl. Econs., U. Ark., 1986. Team leader, inventory auditor RGIS Inventory Specialists, Fayetteville, Ark., 1982-85, inventory auditor Columbus, Ohio, 1986, team leader, inventory auditor Memphis, 1986-93; asst. mgr. bakery Seessel's Supermarket, 1987-89; pricing coord. Seessel's Inc., 1989-90; coord. Tandy Learning Ctr. Radio Shack Computer Ctr., 1990; adminstr. bus. office Tandy Bus. System Sales, 1991-92; acct. exec. Tandy Corp., 1992-93; front-end mgr., baker mgr. Seessel's Supermarket, 1993-95; bakery mgr. trainee Wal-Mart, Dyersburg, Tenn., 1995-96; cellular/internet/computer sales specialist Electronic Comm. Sys., 1996—. Mem. newsletter staff Memphis PC Users Group, 1991-93. Den mother, dist. com. Boy Scouts Am., Fayetteville, 1982-85; youth Sunday sch. tchr., bd. dirs., pastor-parish rels. com., asst. pianist Bethesda United Meth. Ch., Halls, Tenn., 1994—; chmn. 1998 cookbook com., sec. Bethesda-Edith-Melville United Meth. Women, 1997-99. Recipient Disting. Svc. award Kiwanis, 1985, Disting. Svc. award Boy Scouts Am., Fayetteville, 1984. Mem. Am. Agrl. Econs. Assn., Alpha Zeta, Alpha Phi Omega. Democrat. Methodist. Avocations: computers, reading, music, gourmet cooking, traveling. Home: PO Box 86 Halls TN 38040-0086 Office: Electronic Comm Sys 640 I Hwy 51 Bypass East Dyersburg TN 38024 E-mail: janna.scearce@ecsis.net.

SCEATS, D(ONALD) JAMES, JR. neurological surgeon; b. Pueblo, Colo., Aug. 15, 1956; s. Donald James Sr. and Marsha (Marsh) S.; m. Deborah Ann Jalowiec, May 22, 1988 (div. Dec. 1994); children: Lindsey Anne, Hunter James, Benjamin James; m. Kristin Britt Olsen, June 29, 1996. BA in Chemistry summa cum laude, Whitman Coll., Walla Walla, Wash., 1978; MD with honors, U. Colo., 1982. Diplomate Am. Bd. Neurol. Surgery, Nat. Bd. Med. Examiners. Intern U. Colo., Denver, 1982-83; resident in neurol. surgery U. Fla., Gainesville, 1989; neurol. surgeon Colorado Springs (Colo.) Neurol. Assoc., 1989—. V.p. Colo. Springs Neurol. Assoc. Contbr. articles to profl. jours. Recipient Analytical Chemistry award Am. Chem. Soc., 1977. Mem. Am. Assn. Neurol. Surgeons, Congress Neurol. Surgeons, Colo. Med. Soc., Colo. Neurosurg. Soc. (v.p. 2001—), El Paso County Med. Soc., Phi Beta Kappa. Republican. Avocations: hunting, snowshoeing. Office: Colorado Springs Neurol 175 S Union Blvd Ste 310 Colorado Springs CO 80910-E-mail: djsceats@usa.net.

SCEDROV, ANDRE, mathematics and computer science researcher, educator; b. Zagreb, Croatia, Aug. 1, 1955; came to U.S., 1977, naturalized, 1987; s. Oleg and Mira (Petric) S.; m. Bonnie Carol Hoke, July 23, 1983. BA, U. Zagreb, 1977; MA, SUNY, Buffalo, 1979, PhD in Math., 1981. T.H. Hildebrandt asst. prof. rsch. U. Mich., Ann Arbor, 1981-82; asst. prof. U. Pa., Phila., 1982-88, assoc. prof., 1988-92, prof., 1992—. Vis. scholar U. Milan, 1982, McGill U., Montreal, 1985, U. Sydney, Australia, 1986, U. Catholique de Louvain, Louvain-La-Neuve, Belgium, 1988, U. Paris 7, 1992, Rijksuniv Utrecht, The Netherlands, 1993, CNRS Lab. de Math. Discretes, Marseille, France, 1995, Stanford U., 1995, Isaac Newton Inst. for Math. Scis., Cambridge, Eng., 1995, Mittag-Leffer Inst., Stockholm, 2001; vis. scientist Math. Scis. Inst. Cornell U., Ithaca, N.Y., 1987; vis. fellow SRI Internat., Menlo Park, Calif., 1995, Mittap-Leffler Inst., Stockholm, Sweeden, 2001; vis. assoc. prof. Stanford U., 1989-90; cons. Odyssey Rsch. Assocs., Ithaca, 1987, HP Labs., Palo Alto, 1990; vis. prof. Keio U., Tokyo, 1997; program chair IEEE Symposium on Logic in Computer Sci., Santa Cruz, Calif., 1992, mem. organizing com., 1992-97, mem. adv. bd., 1997—, program co-chair Math. Founds. Programming Semantics, New Orleans, 1999, mem. program com., 2001; mem. program com. Logical Found. Computer Sci., Tver, Russia, 1992, St. Petersburg, Russia, 1994, Linear Logic Tokyo '96, 1996, Computer Sci. Logic '98, Brno, Czech Republic, 1998, Typed Lambda Calculi and Applications L'Aquila, Italy, 1999, Category Theory in Computer Sci., Edinburgh, Scotland, 1999, Theoretical Aspects of Computer Software, Japan, 2001, IEEE Computer Security Found. Workshop, Nova Scotia, Canada, 2001; plenary spkr. 2d Croatian Math. Congress, Zagreb, 2000; invited spkr. Math. Founds. Programming Semantics, Oxford (Eng.) U., 1992, U. Colo., Boulder, 1996, Computer Sci. Logic, San Miniato, Italy, 1992, Internat. Summer Sch. Logic Computer Sci., Chambery, France, 1993, Proof and Computation, Marktoberdorf, Germany, 1993, Logic and Computer Sci. CIRM, Marseille-Luminy, France, 1994, Winter Sch. on Linear Logic and Applications, Lisbon, Portugal, 1995, 10th Internat. Congress on Logic, Philosophy and Methodology of Sci., Florence Italy, 1995, Linear Logic Meeting and Spring Sch., Tokyo, 1996, Linear Logic Workshop CIRM, Marseille-Luminy, France, 1998, Constructivism in Mathematics and Computing, The Netherlands, 1999, EEF summer sch. logical methods BRICS, Aarhus, Denmark, 2001, First Joint Internet Meeting between Am. Math Soc and Soc. Math de France, Lyon, 2001. Author: (with P. Freyd) Categories, Allegories; editor Math. Structures in Computer Sci., 1989—, Annals Pure Applied Logic, 1993—, Perspectives in Mathematical Logic book series, 1997—; contbr. articles and rsch. papers to profl. publs. Recipient Young Faculty award Nat. Scis. Assn. U. Pa., 1987; Rsch. grantee NSF, 1985—, Office Naval Rsch., 1988—. Fellow Japan Soc. for Promotion Sci. (sr.); mem. AAAS, Am. Math. Soc. (Centennial rsch. fellow 1993-94, mem. 1st joint internat. meeting with Soc. Math of France, Lyon, 2001), Assn. for Symbolic Logic (editor jours. 1988-93, chair nominating com. 1993, program com. 1988-90, coun. 1990-96, coordinating editor jours. 1994-96 exec. com. 1998-2001, program chair ann. meeting 2001), Assn. for Computing Machinery, Math. Assn. Am. Office: U Pa Dept Math 209 S 33rd St Dept Math Philadelphia PA 19104-6317 E-mail: andre@cis.upenn.edu.

SCEIFORD, MARY ELIZABETH, retired public television administrator; b. Erie, Pa., Nov. 30, 1932; d. William Michael and Ellen Elizabeth (Laffer) S. BA, Allegheny Coll., 1954; MS, Univ. Wis., 1960; PhD, Syracuse Univ., 1969. Cert. tchr. Pa., Wis., Ohio. Kindergarten tchr. Lakewood (Ohio) Pub. Schs., 1954-56; grade one/two tchr. Madison (Wis.) Pub. Schs., 1956-59; art tchr. Mt. Lebanon (Pa.) Pub. Schs., 1960-65; tv. tchr. WQED-TV, Pitts., 1965-66; art tchr. Mt. Lebanon Pub. Schs., 1966-67; assoc. dir. Sch. Svcs. WQED-TV, Pitts., 1969-74, dir. sch. svcs., 1974-75; assoc. dir. edn. and children's tv programs Corp. for Pub. Broadcasting, Washington, 1975-96; ret. Adv. bd. Nat. Pub. Broadcasting Archives, College Park, Md., 1993—. Contbr. articles to profl. jours. Bd. trustees Allegheny Coll., 1975—; USA rep. European Broadcasting Union Youth Group, Geneva, Switzerland, 1993-96. Mem. Am. Ednl. Rsch. Assn., ASCD, Assn. Ednl. Communications & Tech., Phi Beta Kappa, Pi Lambda Theta. Avocations: walking, swimming, gardening, piano, farm work.

SCELSA, JOSEPH VINCENT, sociologist, educator, university executive; b. N.Y.C., Dec. 7, 1945; s. Albert John and Katherine Mary S.; m. Joyce Ann Tisi, Nov. 13, 1981; 1 child, Jonathan. AA, LIU, 1966, BA, 1968; MA, CUNY, 1973, MSEd, 1984; MA, Columbia U., 1983, EdD, 1984. Cert. sch. counselor, N.Y. Counselor, tchr. N.Y.C. Bd. Edn., 1970-78, coord. career and occupational edn., 1979; coord. specialized counseling CUNY, 1979-81; pvt. practice counseling, N.Y.C., 1975—; lectr. grad. faculty Herbert H. Lehman Coll., CUNY, 1980—; dean Calandra Inst., CUNY, 1984—; prof. student pers. Queens Coll., CUNY, 1999, v.p., 2000. Consul gen. of Italy in N.Y. Active Coun. of 1000 nat. Italian-Am. Found.; past cive chair multi cultural adv. bd. N.Y.C. Bd. Edn., 1990-91; N.Y. State Mentoring Program Adv. Bd., 1990—; bd. dirs. Nat. Ethnic Coalition Orgns., 1990—, Coalition Italo-Am. Assn., 1986—; Italian Apostalate, N.Y., 1993. Decorated cavaliere Order of Merit Republic of Italy; recipient Disting. Alumni award LIU, 1985, Organizational Leadership award Coalition Italo-Am. Assns., Inc., 1988, Americus award Bronx Community Coll., 1989, Rolde Model award Club DaVinci, 1990, Inte I-A Student Assn. award, CUNY, 1991, Intergroup Rels. Chancellor's award, 1994, FIERI Leadership award, 1993, Philip Mazzei award, 1993, Ellis Island medal of honor, 1997, N.Y. State Govs. award for Excellence, 1999, Medal for 3d Millennium, 2000; named House of Savoy, 1997; Italian fellow John Jay Coll., 1993; inductee St. Lucy's Hall of Fame, 1996. Mem. Am. Counseling Assn., Am. Mental Health Counselors Assn. (cert. of recognition 1979, counselor of yr. 1983-84), Nat. Acad. Cert. Clin. Mental Health Counselors, Nat. Bd. for Cert. Counselors, Am.-Italian Hist. Assn., N.Y. State Mental Health Counselors Assn. (past pres., Outstanding Work award 1980), Ill. Club. Home: 41 Carwall Ave Mount Vernon NY 10552-1211 Office: CUNY Grad Ctr 33 W 42d St New York NY 10036-8003

SCEPER, DUANE HAROLD, lawyer; b. Norfolk, Va., Nov. 16, 1946; s. Robert George and Marion Eudora (Hynes) S.; m. Sharon Diane Cramer, July 4, 1981; stepchildren: Karin Stevenson, Diane Stevenson. BS in Law, Western State U., 1979, JD, 1980. Bar: Calif. 1982, U.S. Dist. Ct. (so. dist.) Calif. 1982. Field engr. Memorex/Tex. Instruments, San Diego, 1968-70; computer programmer, 1970-81; atty. Allied Ins. Group, 1981-85; sole practice, 1985-87; ptnr. Paluso & Sceper, 1987—. Cons. computers 1980—; lectr. estate planning various orgns. Patentee in field. Active Com. to Elect King Golden to Congress, San Diego, 1978. Served with USAF, 1965-68. Recipient Am. Jurisprudence award, 1979. Mem. ABA, San Diego County Bar Assn., Assn. Trial Lawyers of Am., Calif. Trial Lawyers Assn., San Diego Trial Lawyers Assn., Am. Subrogation Attys., Assn. of Ins. Def. Counsel, So. Calif. Def. Counsel, Air Commando Assn. (life), Delta Theta Phi. Democrat. Home: 2641 Massachusetts Ave Lemon Grove CA 91945-3149 Office: Paluso & Sceper 1010 2d Ave Ste 1350 San Diego CA 92101

SCERPELLA, ERNESTO GUILLERMO, physician researcher; b. Lima, Peru, Dec. 11, 1960; came to U.S., 1988; s. Juan Severino and Maria Doris (Porth) S.; m. Patricia Del Carmen Campos, Oct. 29, 1988; children: Ernesto Alessandro, Renato Patrizio. MD, Cayetano Heredia U., 1986. Resident internal medicine U. Miami, 1988-91, fellow spl. immunology, 1994-95, asst. prof. medicine, 1995—2000, assoc. prof., 2000—; fellow infectious disease U. Tex., Houston, 1991-94; med. rsch. specialist Pfizer Inc., 2001—. Mem. infection control com. Pub. Health Trust-Jackson Meml. Hosp., Miami, 1995-2000; instr. in histology Cayetano Heredia U., Lima, 1980-81. Author numerous scientific articles on areas related to infectious diseases and AIDS; sci. reviewer for several med. jours. Zeneca travel grant Nat. Found. for Infectious Diseases, 1993. Mem. ACP, AMA, Infectious Diseases Soc. of Am. (HIV/AIDS tng. program 1994), Panamerican Assn. of Infectious Diseases. Office: U Miami Sch Medicine 901 NW 17th St Ste D Miami FL 33136-1135

SCEUSA, NICHOLAS A. pharmacologist; b. Bklyn., July 22, 1948; s. Nicolo Sceusa and Mari Rita Anastasi; m. donna Lynn Klein, Feb. 23, 1973; children: Amanda, Nicholas. BS in Biology, Syracuse U., 1971; BS in Pharmacy, L.I. U., 1977; PharmD, U. Ill., Chgo., 1996. Pharmacist, N.Y. Sr. staff pharmacist King Khalid Univ. Hosp., Riyadh, Saudi Arabia, 1984-86, Tawam Hosp., Al Ain, United Arab Emirates, 1986-87; staff pharmacist II St. Luke's - Roosevelt Hosp., N.Y.C., 1987-90; staff pharmacist St. Clare's Hosp., 1990-95; dir. Gelsus Rsch. and Cons., 1997—. Author (with others): The Secret History of Italian-American Evacuation and Internment during World War II; contbr. articles to profl. jours. Advisor to Sch. Bd. Dist. 3, N.Y.C., 1996-98. Episcopalian. Achievements include patents for biofiltration and (Teorell-Meyer) dosage forms. Avocations: hunting, fishing, outdoors, science, invention. Home and Office: 145 W 96th St Ste 1A New York NY 10025-6449 Fax: (212) 280-1255. E-mail: gelsus@aol.com., nsceusa@gelsus.com.

SCHAAB, ARNOLD J. lawyer; b. Newark, 1939; s. Robert George and Pauline Schaab; m. Marcia Stecker, 1964 (div. 1978); children: Emily Diana, Genevieve; m. Patricia Caesar, 1981 (div. 1996); m. Susan McGlamery, 2000. BA, New Sch. U., 1962; LLB, Harvard U., 1965. Bar: N.Y. 1967, U.S. Dist. Ct. (so. and ea. dists.) N.Y. 1967. Assoc. Chadbourne & Parke, N.Y.C., 1966-69; ptnr. Anderson, Kill & Olick, 1969-78; sr. ptnr. Pryor, Cashman, Sherman & Flynn LLP, 1978—. Chmn. Literacy Ptnrs., Inc.; mem. exec. com. Shaker Mus. and Libr., Old Chatham, N.Y.; vis. com. Milano Grad. Sch. Mgmt. and Pub. Policy, New Sch. U. Fulbright scholar Law Faculty U. Paris. Fellow N.Y. Bar Found., Am. Bar Found.; mem. ABA (vice chair internat. fin. transactions com.), N.Y. State Bar Assn. (chmn. internat. law and practice sect., chmn. spl. com. free trade in the Ams., ho. of dels., fin. com., long range planning com., by-laws com.), Assn. Bar City N.Y. (com. internat. trade, com. fgn. and comparative law), Computer Law Assn., Univ. Club (treas., chmn. fin. com., chmn. audit com.), Doubles, Nat. Arts Club, Archaeol. Inst. Am., Bibl. Archaeology Soc. Office: Pryor Cashman Sherman & Flynn 410 Park Ave New York NY 10022-4441

SCHAACK, PHILIP ANTHONY, retired beverage company executive; b. Evanston, Ill., June 6, 1921; s. Harry Charles and Lora Mary (Colford) S.; m. Elizabeth Eberhart, Mar. 27, 1943; children: Susan, Laura, Betsy. Student, Northwestern U., 1943; LLD (hon.), Benedictine U., 1977. Vice-pres. Joyce Beverages/Chgo., 1957-60; v.p. Joyce Beverages/Ill., Joliet, 1960-63, exec. v.p., 1963-65, pres., 1965-85, dir. Retired ir. First Midwest Bank; past chmn., trustee Benedictine U., trustee emeritus; vice-chmn. nat. devel. coun. Sisters of Providence. With USN, 1942-45. Mem. Chgo. Golf Club, Innisbrook Golf Club, Minocqua Country Club, Timber Ridge Country Club. Republican. Roman Catholic. Home: 1480 Aberdeen Ct Naperville IL 60564-9797

SCHAAF, DOUGLAS ALLAN, lawyer; b. Green Bay, Wis., Nov. 18, 1955; s. Carlton Otto and Fern (Brunette) S.; m. Kathlyn T. Bielke, Feb. 23, 1988. BBA magna cum laude in Internat. Bus., St. Norbert Coll., DePere, Wis., 1978; JD, U. Notre Dame, 1981. Bar: Ill. 1981, Calif. 1987. Assoc. McDermott, Will & Emery, Chgo., 1981-84, Skadden, Arps, Slate, Meagher & Flom, 1984-89; ptnr. Paul Hastings, Janofsky & Walker, L.A., 1989—. Adj. faculty mem. John Marshall Law Sch., 1984-87. Atty. Chgo. Vol. Legal Services, 1984-87; bd. dirs. Orange County Alzheimer's Assn. Mem. Orange County Bar Assn. (chair tax sect. 1994-96). Office: Paul Hastings Janofsky & Walker 695 Town Center Dr Ste 1700 Costa Mesa CA 92626-7191 E-mail: dougschaaf@paalhastings.com.

SCHAAF, MARTHA ECKERT, author, poet, library director, musician, composer, educator, lecturer; b. Madison, Ind., Sept. 21, 1911; d. Frederick William and Julia (Richert) Eckert; m. Clarence William Schaaf, Dec. 27, 1941 (dec. 1987); 1 child, Susan Elizabeth Lee. AB with distinction, Ind. U., 1933; MLS, Columbia U., 1945; postgrad., Butler U., Ind. U. Lic. tchr. English, French, Spanish, music. Libr. dir. Twp. System, Crothersville, Ind., 1936-38; libr. music instr. Angola, 1938-39, Howe High Sch., Indpls., 1939-42; libr. dir. Reitz High Sch., Evansville, Ind., 1942; county libr. organizer County Brs. Libr., Columbus, Ga., 1943; hosp. libr. dir. Camp Van Dorn, Woodville, Miss., 1943-44; organized libr. Bulova Sch. for Disabled Vets., L.I., N.Y., 1944-45; organized bus. rsch. libr. Eli Lilly & Co., Indpls., 1946-50; rsch. libr. Wallace Collection Ind. Hist. Soc. Libr., 1958-61; dir. Pub. Libr., Pompano Beach, Fla., 1967-72. Pres. Ind. Spl. Libr. Assn., 1948. Author: Lew Wallace: Boy Writer, 1961, reprint, 2001, Duke Ellington: Music Master, 1975; contbg. author: War Paint and Wagon Wheels, 1968, reprint, 1999, Reading Incentive Series, 1969, The Nat. Library of Poetry; composer: The U.S.A. Way, Children of One Earth; contbr. articles to profl. jours. Named Valedictorian, Madison (Ind.) H.S., 1929; recipient History award DAR, 1930, C. of C. award Pompano Beach, Fla., 1970, Editor's Choice award Nat. Libr. Poetry award, 1995, Disting. Alumni award Ind. U., 1983. Mem. VFW, Nat. League Am. Pen Women (Svc. award Boca Raton br. 1995), Internat. Soc. Poets, Acad. Am. Poets, Mortar Board, Ind. U. Alumni Assn., Columbia U. Alumni Assn., Palm Bay Women's Club, Phi Beta Kappa, Pi Lambda Theta, Chi Omega (Found. award Theta Beta chpt.). Avocations: organ, choral direction, composing. Home: 1698 Sunny Brook Ln NE # G101 Palm Bay FL 32905-6540

SCHAAFSMA, POLLY DIX, archaeologist, researcher; b. Springfield, Vt., Oct. 24, 1935; d. Raymond Arthur and Mildred Elizabeth (Gafvert) Dix; m. Curtis Forrest Schaafsma, Sept. 28, 1958; children: Hoskinini Scott, Pieter Dix. BA, Mount Holyoke Coll., 1957; MA, U. Colo., 1962. Archaeologist Mus. N.Mex., Sante Fe, 1962-63, 94-96, project dir., 1966-67, rsch. assoc., 1985—; project dir. Utah State Pk. Commn. and Gov.'s Commn. on Historic Sites, Salt Lake City, 1970, N.Mex. State Planning Office, Santa Fe, 1971. Project dir. Nat. Pk. Svc., Grand Canyon National Park, Ariz., 1987; mem. blue ribbon panel adv. bd. Petroglyph Nat. Monument, Albuquerque, 1992-96; mem. adv. coun. Four Corners Sch. Outdoor Edn., Monticello, Utah, 1996—; mem. rev. com. The Rock Art Archive, Inst. Archaeology, UCLA, 1997—. Author: Rock Art of Navajo Reservoir, 1963, Early Navajo Rock Paintings, 1965, The Rock Art of Utah, 1971, 2d edit., 1994, The Rock Art in New Mexico, 1972, 2d edit., 1994, Indian Rock Art of the Southwest, 1980, Images in Stone, 1995; editor: Kachinas in the Pueblo World, 1994, Warrior, Shield and Star, 2000; contbr. articles to profl. jours. Mem. Am. Rock Art Rsch. Assn. (mem. adv. bd. 1985—), Soc. Am. Archaeology, Australian Rock Art Rsch. Assn. Office: Mus N Mex Mus Indian Arts and Culture PO Box 2087 Santa Fe NM 87504-2087

SCHAAL, PAMELA MARGUERITE, program evaluation analyst; b. Toledo, May 8, 1970; d. Peter Robert Schaal and Patricia Anne Olsson; m. Daniel Alexander Deresh. BA, U. Toledo, 1989—94, MA, 1994—97. Rsch. asst. intern The Urban Inst., Washington, 1997; rsch. asst. Assn. of Univ. Programs in Health Adminstrn., 1998; assoc. analyst COSMOS Corp., Bethesda, Md., 1998—2000; program evaluation analyst Legal Services Corp., OIG, Washington, 2000—02. Legis. intern Office of Rob Portman, U.S. Ho. of Reps., Washington, 1996; staff asst. Office of Mike DeWine, U.S. Senate, 1996. Mem.: Smithsonian Instn. Young Benefactor, Am. Eval. Assn., Am. Polit. Sci. Assn., Alpha Lambda Delta (life), Golden Key Nat. Honor Soc. (life; President 1992—93), Alpha Kappa Delta (life), Pi Sigma Alpha (life), Phi Alpha Delta (life). Avocations: travel, theater , photography, dancing. Office: Legal Services Corp OIG 750 First St NE 11th Fl Washington DC 20002-4250 Personal E-mail: pamela_schaal@yahoo.com. Business E-mail: pschaal@oig.lsc.gov.

SCHAAP, ALETTA JOHANNA, artist; b. Phila., June 20, 1948; d. Adolf and Ella Betsey Sanders S.; n. Patrick John Adrian Quinlan, July 4, 1982; children: Adriane, Alexander. AB with high honors, U. Mich., 1970; MFA, U. Puget Sound, 1973; MBA, UCLA, 1983. Assoc. dir. J. Paul Getty Trust, L.A., 1984-96; analyst FCA Am. Mortgage Corp., 1983; coun. mem. U.S. Holocaust Meml. Mus., Washington, 1997—. Mem. Am. Assn. Mus., Am. Crafts Coun., Internat. Coun. Mus. Democrat. Avocations: crafts, cultural events, exhibitions. Office: US Holocaust Meml Mus 100 Raoul Wallenberg Pl SW Washington DC 20024-2126

SCHAAR, SUSAN CLARKE, state legislative staff member; b. Lawrenceville, Va., Dec. 21, 1949; d. Garland Lewis and Frances Virginia (Matthews) Clarke; m. William Berkley Schaar Jr., Nov. 24, 1990. BA, U. Richmond, 1972. Engrossing clk. Senate of Va., Richmond, 1974, legis. rsch. analyst, 1974-77; asst. to the clk. Senate of Va., 1977-83; asst. clk. Senate Va., 1983-90, clk. of the Senate, 1990—. Exec. com. Nat. Conf. State Legis., 1999—, Mason's Manual Commn.; staff v.chmn. standing com. Nat. Conf. State Legis., 2002. Mem. YMCA Model Gen. Assembly Adv. com., Richmond, 1990—; trustee U. Richmond, 1990-94; pres. Richmond Club of Westhampton, 1988-90; mem. Spider Club Athletic Bd., Richmond, 1988-90; bd. assocs. U. Richmond, 1995—; govt. counselor Va. Girls State, bd. dirs., 2001—; staff vice chair legis. effectiveness com. Nat. Conf. of State Legislatures, 1996-98, chair, 1998-99. Mem. Am. Soc. Legis. Clks. and Secs. (mem. exec. com. 1995-99, sec.-treas. 1996, pres.-elect 1997, pres. 1997-98, past pres., 1998-99), Coun. on Preservation of Capitol Sq., Omicron Delta Kappa, Pi Sigma Alpha. Baptist. Office: Senate of Va PO Box 396 Richmond VA 23218-0396 E-mail: sschaar@sov.state.va.us.

SCHABELMAN, SERGIO EDUARDO, cardiologist, educator; b. San Juan, Argentina, Mar. 7, 1951; came to U.S., 1977; s. Moises and Dora (Roitman) S.; m. Florencia Iris Levinton, Nov. 9, 1974; children: Esteban, Andres. MD, Buenos Aires Nat. U., 1973. Diplomate Am. Bd. Internal Medicine. Internal medicine trainee Marcial Quiroga San Juan Hosp., San Juan, 1973-74; resident in cardiology Buenos Aires Argerich Hosp., 1974-77; fellow cardiology dept. Cardiovascular Rsch. Inst. U. Calif., San Francisco, 1977; fellow cardiovascular radiology Loma Linda (Calif.) U. Med. Ctr., 1978, instr. internal medicine, 1979; asst. prof. medicine cardiology sect., head invasive lab. La. State U., New Orleans, 1979-82; asst. to dir. Charity Hosp. Heart Sta., 1979-82; clin. asst. prof. cardiology La. State U., 1982—. Spkr. in field; contbr. articles to profl. jours. Fellow ACP, Am. Coll. of Cardiology; mem. Argentine Soc. Cardiology (assoc.; sec. Am. chpt. 1994-96), La. State Med. Soc., Orleans Parish Med. Soc. (emergency med. svcs. com. 1998—), N.Am. Soc. Pacing and Electrophysiology, Hispanic Am. Med. Assn. La. (sec. 1991-93, v.p. 1993-95), Ind. Physician Assn. New Orleans (bd. dirs. 1994-95), Hispanic Ind. Physician Assn. La. (bd. dirs. 1994-95). Home: 4033 Mouton St Metairie LA 70002-1303 Office: 3715 Prytania St Ste 203 New Orleans LA 70115-3766

SCHABERG, JOHN IRVIN, lawyer; b. St. Louis, Aug. 8, 1955; s. Irvin William Jr. and Hazel Mae (Matteson) S.; m. Denise Lynn Derickson, Sept. 26, 1981; children: Katherine Elizabeth, Caroline Marie, John Henry. BA, U. Tulsa, 1977; JD, U. Tex., 1980. Bar: Mo. 1980, Ill. 1981, U.S. Dist. Ct. (ea. dist.) Mo. 1981, U.S. Dist Ct. (no. dist.) Ill., U.S. Dist. Ct. (so. dist.) Ill. 1985. Assoc. Roberts & Heneghan, Inc., St. Louis, 1980-82, Hinshaw, Culbertson, Moelmann, Hoban & Fuller, Chgo., 1982-87, assoc., resident atty.-in-charge Belleville, Ill., 1985-87; prin. Roberts, Perryman, Bomkamp & Meives, P.C., St. Louis, 1988—. Editor notes and comments Am. Jour. Criminal Law, 1978-80; contbr. articles to legal jours. Mem. ABA (torts and ins. practice sect., sect. litigation), Mo. Bar Assn., Ill. State Bar Assn., Bar Assn. Met. St. Louis, St. Clair County Bar Assn., Ill. Assn. Def. Trial Counsel, Mo. Orgn. Def. Lawyers. Roman Catholic. Office: Roberts Perryman Bomkamp & Meives PC 1 Mercantile Ctr Ste 2300 Saint Louis MO 63101-1643 also: 23 Public Sq Ste 402 Belleville IL 62220-1627

SCHABNER, DAWN FREEBLE, artist, educator; b. Mercer, Pa., Jan. 30, 1933; d. Benjamin Frederick and Mary Emma (McElheny) Freeble; m. Donald Russell Schabner, Jan. 5, 1954; children: Donald Russell Jr., Dean Aaron. Student, Phila. Mus. Sch. Art, 1950-52; BA in Fine Arts with honors magna cum laude, Hofstra U., 1971; student, Cleve. Inst Art., 1952-53; MA in Liberal Studies, SUNY, Stony Brook, 1976. Designer Am. Greetings, Cleve., 1953; art educator Islip (N.Y.) Pub. Schs., 1967-95, Dowling Coll., Oakdale, N.Y., 1991—. One-woman shows include East Islip (N.Y.) Pub. Libr., 1977, 1988, Unitarian Bay Gallery, Bellport, N.Y., 1997, L-Art Gallery, Kiev, Ukraine, 1999, exhibited in group shows at Hofstra U., 1970, Patchogue-Medford Pub. Libr., 1983, East End Arts & Humanities Coun., Riverhead, N.Y., 1984, Islip Art Mus. Juried Exhibit, 1985, 1987, 1988, 1999, 2000, 2002, Suffolk County Legis. Bldg., Hauppage, N.Y., 1988, Bennington Coll., 1989, Goat Alley Gallery, Sag Harbor, N.Y., 1989, Canio's Books, Sag Harbor, 1990, South County Libr., Bellport, N.Y., 1991, The Parrish Art Mus., Southampton, N.Y., 1999, Stage Gallery, Merrick, N.Y., 2001; featured artist East End Arts and Humanities Coun., Riverhead, 1986, Clayton Liberatore Art Gallery, Bridgehampton, N.Y., 1994, 1995, 1997, 2001, 2002. Mem. Nat. League Am. Pen Women Inc., Met. Mus. Art, East End Arts Coun., Smithtown Twp. Arts Coun., Guild Hall. Avocations: golf, bicycling, weight training, reading, attending concerts & ballet.

SCHABOW, JOHN WILLIAM, accountant; b. Chgo., Mar. 30, 1937; s. William John and Mary V. (Brink) S.; m. Gail P. Ekren, Oct. 17, 1959; children: Robin, John R. Student, Davis Elkins Coll., 1955-58, Ariz. State U., 1972-74. Accredited tax advisor; accredited bus. acct.; accredited tax preparer. Cost clk. G.D. Searle, Skokie, Ill., 1958-60; acct. Sugarcreek Foods, Chgo., 1960-63, Arlington Park Rack Track, Chgo., 1963-65, G. Heiss & Assocs., Chgo., 1965-69, Murray & Murray CPA's, Phoenix, 1969-70, Wm. R. Schulz & Assocs., Phoenix, 1970-73; pres., owner John W. Schabow, Ltd., 1973—. Registered rep. H.D. Vest Investment Securities, Inc., Phoenix, 1985—, adv. bd. dirs. Mem. editorial adv. bd. Accounting Today, 1993—. Pres. Bellair Parks and Recreation Assn., 1999-2002; bd. dirs. Inst. for Partially Sighted, Phoenix, 1986-87, Phoenix Girls Choir, 1995-97; treas. Prescott Country Club Townhouse Assn. With U.S. Army, 1961-62. Recipient Acct. of Yr. award Nat. Soc. Accts., 2000. Mem.: Nat. Soc. Pub. Accts. (state dir. 1983—87, bd. govs. 1988—92, chmn. nat. affairs com. 1995—97, chmn. nominating com. 1997—98, right to practice com. 1999—2000, chmn. adminstrn. and fin. com. 1999—2000, chmn. right to practice com. 2000, bd. dirs. accreditation coun. of accountancy and taxation 2001—, chmn. ethics and grievance com.), Ariz. Soc. Practicing Accts. (pres. 1987—88, co-founder, co-chair legis. com. 1994—97). Republican. Lutheran. Avocation: golf. Home: 4440 W Bluefield Ave Glendale AZ 85308-1613 E-mail: jschabow49@hotmail.com.

SCHACHMAN, HOWARD KAPNEK, molecular biologist, educator; b. Phila., Dec. 5, 1918; s. Morris H. and Rose (Kapnek) S.; m. Ethel H. Lazarus, Oct. 20, 1945; children— Marc, David. BSChemE, Mass. Inst. Tech., 1939; PhD in Phys. Chemistry, Princeton, 1948; DSc (hon.), Northwestern U., 1974; MD (hon.), U. Naples, 1990. Fellow NIH, 1946-48; from instr. to asst. prof. U. Calif., Berkeley, 1948-54, assoc. prof. biochemistry, 1954-59, prof. biochemistry and molecular biology, 1959-91, chmn. dept. molecular biology, dir. virus lab., 1969-76, prof. emeritus, dept. molecular and cell biology, 1991-94, prof. grad. sch., 1994—. Mem. sci. coun. and sci. adv. bd. Stazione Zoologica, Naples, Italy, 1988—; cons. bd. sci. Meml. Sloan-Kettering Cancer Ctr., 1988—97; mem. sci. adv. com. Rsch. ! Am., 1990—; William Lloyd Evans lectr. Ohio State U., 1988; Carl and Gerty Cori lectr. Washington U. Sch. Medicine, 1993; faculty rsch. lectr. U. Calif., Berkeley, 1994; Alta. Heritage Found. for Med. Rsch. vis. prof. U. Alta., 1996; Wellcome vis. prof. in basic med. scis., 1999—2000; Walter C. MacKenzie lectr. Sch. Medicine U. Alta., Edmonton, Canada, 2001. Author: Ultracentrifugation in Biochemistry, 1959. Mem. bd. sci. counselors Cancer Biology and Diagnosis divsn. Nat. Cancer Inst., 1989-92; ombudsman in basic scis. NIH, 1994—. Lt. USNR, 1945-47. Recipient John Scott award, 1964, Warren Triennial prize Mass. Gen. Hosp., 1965, Alexander von Humboldt award, 1990, Berkeley citation for disting. achievement and notable svc. U. Calif., 1993, Theodor Svedberg award, 1998; Guggenheim Meml. fellow, 1956. Mem.: NAS (chmn. biochemistry sect. 1990—93, panelist sci. responsibility and conduct of rsch. 1990—92), AAAS (mem. com. on sci. freedom and responsibility 1998—, Sci. Freedom and Responsibility award 2000), Acad. Nat. Dei Lincei (fgn. mem.), Fedn. Am. Socs. for Exptl. Biology (pres. 1988—89, pub. affairs exec. com. 1989—, pub. svc. award 1994), Am. Soc. Biochemistry and Molecular Biology (pres. 1987—88, chmn. pub. affairs com. 1989—2000, Merck award 1986, Herbert A. Sober award 1994, pub. svc. award established in his name 2001 2001), Am. Chem. Soc. (Calif. sect. award 1958, award in chem. instrumentation 1962). Achievements include development of the ultracentrifuge as a tool for studying macromolecules of biological interest; studies on structure and function of a regulatory enzyme: Aspartate transcarbamylase. Office: U Calif Berkeley Dept Molecular Cell Bio 229 Stanley Hall # 3206 Berkeley CA 94720-3206

SCHACHNER, LAWRENCE ALAN, pediatric dermatologist; b. Mar. 3, 1945; s. Alex and Sarah (Rosenberg) S.; m Janet Smallberg, Dec. 21, 1970; children: Hollis, Adam. BS, Bklyn. Coll., 1965; MD, U. Nebr., 1972. Diplomate Am. Bd. Pediat., Am. Bd. Dermatology. Intern in pediat. Montefiore Hosp. and Med. Ctr., Bronx, N.Y., 1972-73, resident in pediat., 1973-75, chief resident in pediat., 1975-76, resident in dermatology, 1976-77; chief resident in dermatology N.Y.C. Hosps., Albert Einstein Coll. Medicine, Yeshiva U., 1977-78, Bronx Mcpl. Hosp. Ctr., 1977-78; from asst. prof. to assoc. prof. dermatology and pediat. U. Miami, Fla., 1978-89, prof. dermatology and pediat., 1989—, dir. M. Pediat. and M. Pediatric-Dermatology Confs., 1992—; chmn. U. Miami Med. Group, 1996—. Dir. divsn. pediat. dermatology U. Miami, 1978—; organizing com. Internat. Congress Pediat. Dermatology, 1989-92; cons. in field. Sr. editor: (with others) Pediatric Dermatology Textbook, 1987, 2d edit., 1995; contbr. articles to profl. jours. Mem. Am. Acad. Dermatology (task force on pediat. dermatology 1982-85), Am. Acad. Pediat. (db. dirs. pediat. dermatology sect. 1987—, chmn. 1992-95), Am. Soc. for Pediat. Dermatology (exec. bd. dirs. 1982-83, 86-96), Soc. for Pediat. Dermatology (v.p. 1982-83, 86-87, pres.-elect 1988-89, pres. 1989-90), Internat. Soc. Pediat. Dermatology (v.p. 1998—), Am. Dermatol. Assn., Soc. for Investigative Dermatology, Inc., Miami Dermatol. Soc., Miami Pediat. Soc., Fla. Dermatology Soc., Fla. Pediat. Soc., Nat. Ichthyosis Assn. (med. advisor), Dystrophic Epidermolysis Bullosa Rsch. Assn. (med. advisor, bd. dirs.). Avocations: fishing, tennis, reading, poker, sports. Office: U Miami Sch Medicine 1600 NW 10th Ave # R-250 Miami FL 33136-1090 E-mail: LSchachn@med.miami.edu.

SCHACHT, CATHERINE ANN, classical violinist, pianist, mezzo-soprano; b. Racine, Wis., Feb. 3, 1950; d. Wallis August and Doris (Carlson) S. MusB cum laude, U. N.Mex., 1983. Instr. music N.Mex. Acad. for Scis. and Math., Santa Fe, 1999-2000. Chamber music coach Elder Hostel, Jemez Springs, N.Mex., 1991-99; owner, pres. Desert Song Music. Composer: (art song) Once in a Song, 1991, (choral) Prayer for Choristers, 1991, (chant) Eagle Poem, 1992, Katy's Song, 1993, Song for a Women's Gathering, 1995, (song cycle) Passages, includes Baptismal Song, Wedding Vows, Song of Wholeness, In Memoriam, 1999; violinist with N.Mex. Symphony, Albuquerque, 1978-89, Opera Southwest, Albuquerque, 1982-89, San Juan Symphony, Durango, Colo., 1987—, Santa Fe (N.Mex.) Symphony, 1990—, New S.W. Symphony, Albuquerque, 1992, Ariz. Opera, 1996, Albuquerque Civic Light Opera, 1992—, concertmaster, 1996, others; singer with N.Mex. Symphony Chorus, 1990-91, Santa Fe Symphony Chorus, 1991-92, others; alto soloist Charpentier Midnight Mass Santa Fe Symphony, 1992; trumpet and piano recital Duo Classico Corrales Cultural Arts Coun., 1994; singer, guitarist (cassette rec.) Tonal Tapestry. Organist, pianist Rio Rancho Presbyn. Ch., 1991-99; violinist Terzetto String Trio; singer, guitarist Desert Song; min. music Messiah Luth. Ch., 1999—. Mem. Am. Fedn. Musicians (sec. 1988-90), Chamber Music Am. Democrat. Avocations: weaving, art history, interior decorating. Home: 3939 Rio Grande Blvd NW Albuquerque NM 87107-3147

SCHACHT, HENRY BREWER, electronics executive, director; b. Erie, Pa., Oct. 16, 1934; s. Henry Blass and Virginia (Brewer) S.; m. Nancy Godfrey, Aug. 27, 1960; children: James, Laura, Jane, Mary. BS, Yale U., 1956; MBA, Harvard U., 1962; DSc (hon.), DePauw U., 1982; MA (hon.), Yale U., 1988. Sales trainee Am. Brake Shoe Co., N.Y.C., 1956-57; investment mgr. Irwin Mgmt. Co., Columbus, Ind., 1962-64; v.p. fin. Cummins Engine Co., Inc., 1964-66, v.p., cen. area mgr. internat. London, 1966-67, group v.p. internat. and subsidiaries, 1967-69, pres., 1969-77, CEO, 1977-94, chmn., 1977-95; chmn., CEO, Lucent Techs., Murray Hill, NJ, 1995-98, interim CEO, 2000—02. Bd. dirs. AT&T, Chase Manhattan Corp., Chase Manhattan Bank N.A., Alcoa. Trustee emeritus The Culver Ednl. Found.; active Bus. Coun., Coun. Fgn. Rels.; mem. The Assocs., Harvard Bus. Sch., The Bus. Enterprise Trust; hon. trustee Brookings Instn., Com. Econ. Devel., Yale Corp.; chmn. trustees Ford Found.; sr. mem. Conf. Bd. With USNR, 1957-60. Mem. Tau Beta Pi. Republican. Office: Ford Foundation 320 E 43d St New York NY 10017-4890 also: Lucent Techs 600 Mountain Ave New Providence NJ 07974*

SCHACHT, HENRY MEVIS, writer, consultant; b. Pasadena, Calif., Feb. 28, 1916; s. Henry and Amelia (Claussen) S.; m. Mary Joan Turnbull, Dec. 30, 1937; children: Henry John, Linda Joan. BA, U. Calif., Berkeley, 1936. Info. specialist U. Calif., Berkeley, 1936-42; dir. agr. NBC, San Francisco, 1942-59, ABC, San Francisco, 1959-60; agrl. columnist San Francisco Chronicle, 1959-93. Dir. agrl. info. U. Calif., 1961-65; v.p. corp. relations, corp. sec. Calif. Canners & Growers, San Francisco, 1965-81; freelance writer, 1936—; cons. radio-TV to FAO of UN, Cairo, 1963, Mexico City, 1965, Tokyo, 1966; dir. Calif. Co. for Internat. Trade; dir. Agrl. Issues Ctr., U. Calif. Pres. U.S. Fruit Export Coun., 1972-75; exec. sec. Commn. Calif. Agr. and Higher Edn., 1993-95; adv. bd. Agrl. Issues Ctr. U. Calif., 1990—. Mem. Pub. Relations Soc. Am., Pub. Relations Roundtable San Francisco, Nat. Assn. Farm Broadcasters, Agrl. Relations Council, Nat. Canners Assn. (dir. 1966-81) Home: 60 Hiller Dr Oakland CA 94618-2351

SCHACHT, JOCHEN HEINRICH, biochemistry educator; b. Königsberg, Fed. Republic Germany, July 2, 1939; arrived in U.S., 1969; s. Heinz and Else (Sprenger) S.; m. Helga Hildegard Seidel, Jan..27, 1967; children: Miriam Helga, Daniel Jochen. BS, U. Bonn, Fed. Republic Germany, 1962; MS in Chemistry, U. Heidelberg, Fed. Republic Germany, 1965, PhD in Biochemistry, 1968. Asst. research chemist, Mental Health Research Inst. U. Mich., Ann Arbor, 1969-72, from asst. prof. to assoc. prof. biochemistry, Dept. Biol. Chemistry & Otolaryngology, 1973-84, prof., 1984—, chmn. grad. program in physiol. acoustics, 1981—; hon. prof. Med. Acad. of the Chinese PLA, Beijing, 1998. Vis. prof. Karolinska Inst., Stockholm, 1979-80; acting dir. Kresge Hearing Rsch. Inst., U. Mich., 1983-84, assoc. dir., 1989-99, dir., 2000—; mem. hearing rsch. study sect. USPHS, NIH, Nat. Inst. Neurol. and Communicative Disorders and Stroke, 1986-89, Task Force Nat. Strategic Rsch. Plan, Nat. Insts. Deafness and Communication Disorders, USPHS, NIH; hon. prof. Hunan Med. U., Changsha, China, 1999—, Tonghi Med. U., Wuhan, China, 1999—; guest prof. Fourth Mil. Med. U., Xian, China, 1999—. Mem. editl. bd. Hearing Rsch., 1990—; assoc. editor Audiology & Neuro-Otol., 1995—; contbr. more than 200 articles to profl. jours., book chpts., revs.; co-editor Neurochemistry of Cholinergic Receptors, 1974. Fogarty Sr. Internat. fellow NIH, 1979, Sen. J. Javitz Neurosci. investigator, 1984; recipient Chercheur Etranger rsch. award INSERM, Paris, 1986, 94, Animal Welfare award Erna-Graff Found., Berlin, 1987, Disting. Faculty Achievement award U. Mich., 1989, Employer of Yr. award Nat. Capital Assoc. Coop. Edn. and Gallaudet U., Washington. Mem. Am. Soc. Neurochemistry, Internat. Soc. Neurochemistry, Soc. for Neurosci., Assn. for Rsch. in Otolaryngology, Am. Soc. Biol. Chemists, Assn. Espanola de Audiologia Exptl. Avocations: photography, travel, birding. Office: U Mich Kresge Hearing Rsch Inst Ann Arbor MI 48109-0506

SCHACHT, RONALD STUART, lawyer; b. Stamford, Conn., Nov. 7, 1932; s. Saul Albert and Faye Dorothy (Gittleman) S.; m. Natalie Helene Goldman, June 17, 1956; children: Patti Ellen, Bonnie Anne, Cindy Joy. BS, U. Conn., 1954; LL.B., NYU, 1957, LL.M., 1960. Bar: N.Y. 1957, D.C. 1980. Tax atty. IRS, N.Y.C., 1957-62; assoc. Proskauer Rose, LLP, 1962-69, ptnr., 1969—, mng. ptnr., 1981-84, mem. exec. com., 1985-95. Lectr. Practising Law Inst., NYU Inst. Fed. Taxation; adj. asst. prof. Sch. Continuing Edn., NYU, 1970-72. Bd. dirs. Congregation Agudath Shalom, Stamford, 1968-73; mem. com. Fedn. Jewish Philanthropies, N.Y.C., 1972-80. Mem. N.Y. State Bar Assn., Assn. of Bar of City of N.Y., N.Y. County Lawyers Assn. (bd. dirs. 1977-83, chmn. ins. com. 1975-85), Newfield Swim Club (bd. dirs. 1967-70, pres. 1979), Phi Kappa Phi, Gamma Chi Epsilon. Democrat. Jewish. E-mail: rss6945@aol.com.

SCHACHT, RUTH ELAINE, nursing educator; b. Milw., Nov. 3, 1935; d. Paul Henry and Mavelle V. (Van de Kamp) Nickchen; m. Leonard L.Schacht, Nov. 17, 1962; children: Lisa, Lynette, Lori, Renee Terese. BSN, Marquette U., 1957, MSN, 1962. RN, Wis. Surg. head nurse Oconomowoc (Wis.) Meml. Hosp., 1957-60, day supr. staff nurse, 1970-86, staff pool nurse, 1986-96; mem. nursing faculty Marquette U., Milw., 1961-70, Cardinal Strich U., Milw., 1986-88, Waukesha County Tech. Coll., Pewaukee, Wis., 1988-98; ret., 1998. Cons., mem. nursing faculty Excelsior Coll., Albany, N.Y., 1988—. Mem. ANA, Waukesha Dist. Nurses Assn. (past pres., bd. mem.), Nat. League for Nursing, Wis. Nurses Assn. (past sec., mem. continuing edn. approval program com.). Home: 731 Browning Cir Oconomowoc WI 53066-4309

SCHACHTEL, BARBARA HARRIET LEVIN, epidemiologist, educator; b. May 27, 1921; d. Lester and Ethel (Neiman) Levin; m. Hyman Judah Schachtel, Oct. 15, 1941 (dec. Jan. 1990); m. Louis H. Green, Feb. 26, 1995; children: Bernard, Ann Mollie. Student, Wellesley Coll., 1939-41; BS, U. Houston, 1951, MA in Psychology, 1967; PhD, U. Tex., Houston, 1979. Psychol. examiner Meyer Ctr. for Devel. Pediats., Tex. Children's Hosp., Houston, 1967-81; instr. dept. pediats. Baylor Coll. Medicine, 1967-81, asst. prof. dept. medicine, 1982—. Asst. dir. biometry and epidemiology Sid W. Richardson Inst. for Preventive Medicine, Meth. Hosp., Houston, 1981-88, dir. quality assurance, 1988-93; ret., 1993; mem. instl. rev. bd. for human rsch. Baylor Coll. Medicine, Houston, 1981-87, 97—; mem. devel. bd. U. Tex. Health Sci. Ctr., Houston, 1987-97; mem. dean's adv. bd. Sch. Arch., U. Houston, 1987-89. Contbr. articles to profl. jours. V.p., bd. dirs. Houston-Harris County Mental Health Assn., 1966—67; vice-chmn. bd. mgrs. Harris County Hosp. Dist., Houston, 1974—90, chmn., 1990—92, bd. dirs., 1970—93; trustee Inst. Religion in Tex. Med. Ctr., 1990—, vice chmn., 2000—; sec. Bo Harris County Hosp. Dist. Found. Bd., 1993—; bd. dirs. Congregation Beth Israel, 1993—95, Planned Parenthood of Houston, Inc., 1994—2000, Houston Ind. Sch. Dist. Found., 1993—2001, Crisis Intervention, 1994—96. Named Great Texan of Yr., Nat. Found. for Ilietis and Colitis, Houston, 1982, Outstanding Citizen, Houston-Harris County Mental Health Assn., 1985; recipient Good Heart award B'nai Brith Women, 1984, Women of Prominence award Am. Jewish Com., 1991, Mayor's award for outstanding vol. svc., 1994. Mem. APA, APHA, Wellesley Club of Houston (pres. 1968-70). Avocations: golf, tennis, books. Home: 2527 Glen Haven Blvd Houston TX 77030-3511

SCHACHTER, EDWIN NEIL, medical educator; b. N.Y.C., May 10, 1943; s. Franz and Feiga (Zeltzman) S.; m. Deborah Chase, Nov. 15, 1969; children: Karen, Lauren. AB, Columbia U., 1964; MD, NYU, 1968. Intern Bellevue Hosp., 1968-69, resident, 1969-73; asst. prof. Yale U., New Haven, 1973-78, assoc. prof., 1978-84, med. dir. respiratory care, 1974-84; prof., med. dir. respiratory care Mt. Sinai Med. Ctr., N.Y.C., 1984—. Contbr. articles to profl. jours., chpts. to books. Bd. dirs. Lung Assn. N.Y., N.Y.C., 1994, pres., 1998, Nat. Assn. Med. Dirs. of Respiratory Care, Washington, 1990—92, Conn. Respiratory Assn., 1983; del. nat. coun. Am. Lung Assn., 2001. Lt. comdr. USN, 1970—72. Grantee Nat. Inst. Occpl. Safety and Health, 1987—. Fellow ACP, ACCP; mem. Am. Thoracic Soc., Am. Assn. Respiratory Care, Am. Physiol. Soc. Office: Mt Sinai Med Ctr 1 Gustave L Levy Pl New York NY 10029-6500 E-mail: neil.schachter@mssm.edu.

SCHACHTER, GUSTAV, economics educator; b. Botosani, Romania, May 27, 1926; s. Herman L. and Giselle (Gropper) S.; m. Francine Norma Lerner, Feb. 25, 1958; children: Livia, Levanto. BS, CCNY, 1954; MBA, NYU, 1956, PhD, 1962; DS, U. Lowell, Mass., 1975. Prodn. mgr. B&G, N.Y.C., 1951-61; lectr. CCNY, 1960-62, asst. prof., 1962-65, Northeastern U., Boston, 1966, assoc. prof., 1966-69, prof. econs., 1969—. Vis. prof. Bari (Italy) U., 1972-73; Siena (Italy) U., 1979-80, Inst. Applied Systems and Computer Sci.-Nat. Coun. Rsch., Rome, 1987; cons. Inst. Indsl. Reconstruction, Rome, 1989—. Author: The Italian South, 1965, The Economist Looks at Society, 1973, A MRIO for Italy, 1983; editor: Planning in Brazil, 1985. Fulbright grantee Rome, 1959-60, Italian Govt. rsch. grantee, 1959-60; Fulbright scholar, 1972-73, 79-80, Formez fellow, 1987; Fulbright Disting. Chair, Siena, Italy, 1994. Fellow Royal Econ. Soc.; mem. Am. Econ. Assn., Regional Sci. Assn., Econ. History Assn., N.E. Regional Sci. Assn. (pres. 1988-89). Home: 15 Thatcher St Brookline MA 02446-3575 Office: Northeastern U 360 Huntington Ave 301 Lake Hall Boston MA 02115

SCHACHTER, HINDY LAUER, public management educator; b. N.Y.C., May 8, 1945; d. George and Doris (Trenk) Lauer; m. Irving Schachter, Dec. 4, 1967; 1 child, Amanda. BA, Bklyn. Coll., 1966; MA, NYU, 1968; PhD, Columbia U., 1978. Asst. prof. Sch. Mgmt. N.J. Inst. Tech., Newark, 1979-85, assoc. prof. Sch. Mgmt., 1985-89, prof. pub. mgmt. Sch. Mgmt., 1989—. Trainer and workshop presenter in field. Author: Public Agency Communication, 1983, Frederick Taylor and The Public Administration Community, 1989, Reinventing Government or Reinventing Ourselves, 1997; sect. editor Pub. Adminstr. Quar., Pa., 1990—; mem. editl. bd. Pub. Adminstrn. Rev.; contbr. chpts. to books, articles to profl. jours. Recipient fellowship U.S. Office Edn., 1970-78, Lectr. Series grant GTE, 1984-85, Ednl. Devel. grants N.J. Dept. Higher Edn., 1985-87, 93, rsch. grant N.J. Dept. of Transp., 1995, 97, 2000, 02, U.S. Dept. Transp., 2001. Mem. Am. Soc. for Pub. Adminstrn. (exec. com. sect. for profl. devel. 1980-89, 97, chair sec. for profl. devel. 1982), Am. Polit. Sci. Assn. Jewish. Avocation: cycling. Office: NJ Inst Tech University Hts Newark NJ 07102

SCHACHTER, MYRON MARVIN, retired research chemist, engineer; b. Bklyn., Nov. 28, 1922; s. Mary (Deutsch) S.; m. Marilyn Bedell, Aug. 12, 1962; 1 child, Alana Diane. BS, CCNY, 1948; MA in Sci., Bklyn. Coll., 1962. Quality controller Kollsman Instrument Co., Elmhurst, N.Y., 1953-61; rsch. chemist FDA, Washington, 1961-83; innovative sci. engring. rschr. Chromalcarb Co., 1983—, innovative rschr., 1983—; quality auditor Hekimian Labs., Inc., 1989—. Patentee in field. Mem. AAAS, Am. Chem. Soc. Avocation: electronic instrument design and construction for scientific research. Home: 5215 Western Ave NW Washington DC 20015-2126 Office: Chromalcarb Co 5215 Western Ave NW Washington DC 20015-2126

SCHACHTER, OSCAR, lawyer, educator, arbitrator; b. N.Y.C., June 19, 1915; s. Max and Fannie (Javits) S.; m. Mollie Miller, Aug. 9, 1936 (dec. July 1980); children: Judith (Mrs. Albrecht Funk), Ellen (Mrs. John P. Leventhal); m. Muriel L. Sackler, June 14, 1982. BSS, Coll. City N.Y., 1936; JD, Columbia, 1939, LLD (hon.), 2000. Bar: N.Y. 1939. Editor-in-chief Columbia Law Rev., 1938-39; pvt. practice N.Y.C., 1939-40; atty. U.S. Dept. of Labor, Washington, 1940; chief nat. defense sect. in law dept. FCC, 1941; sect. of law com. and adviser on internat. communications Bd. of War Communications, 1941-42; prin., divisional asst., adviser on wartime econ. controls and on European liberated areas U.S. Dept. State, 1942-43; asst. gen. counsel UNRRA, 1944-46; drafting officer UNRRA council sessions, 1944-45; legal adv. UNRRA del. to USSR and Poland, 1945; legal counselor UN, 1946-52, dir. gen. legal div., 1952-66; dep. exec. dir., dir. studies UN Inst. for Tng. and Research, 1966-75; lectr. law Yale U. Law Sch., 1955-71; Carnegie lectr. Hague Acad. Internat. Law, 1963-82; Rosenthal lectr. Northwestern U. Law Sch., 1974; prof. Law Sch. and Faculty Internat. Affairs Columbia U., 1975—, Hamilton Fish prof. internat. law and diplomacy Law Sch. and Faculty Internat. Affairs, 1980-85, prof. emeritus Law Sch. and Faculty Internat. Affairs, 1985—. Vis. prof Harvard Law Sch., 1982; chmn. legal com. UN Maritime Conf., 1948; legal cons. UNESCO, 1948; past dir. Gen. Legal Div. of UN; served as legal adviser various internat. confs. and UN couns. and coms.; sec. legal adv. com. UN Atomic Energy Commn., 1946-47; vice chmn. Internat. Investment Law Conf., 1958; exec. sec. Internat. Arbitration Conf., 1958; mem. panel arbitrators Internat. Ctr. for Settlement of Investment Disputes, 1980-87; judge Ct. Arbitration in Canada-France Maritime Boundary dispute, 1989-92; expert advisor UN com. on transnational corps., 1990-93. Author: Relation of Law, Politics and Action in the U.N, 1964, Sharing the World's Resources, 1977, International Law in Theory and Practice, 1985, rev. edit., 1991; co-author: Across the Space Frontier, 1952, Toward Wider Acceptance of UN Treaties, 1971, International Law Cases and Materials, 1980, 3rd edit., 1993, United Nations Legal Order, 2 vols., 1995; contbr. articles and monographs on internat. law, internat. instns., legal philosophy, human rights, internat. peace and security, internat. resources to legal jours.; editor-in-chief Am. Jour. Internat. Law, 1978-84, hon. editor, 1985—; co-editor: Competition in International Business, 1981; editorial bd. Marine Policy. Bd. dirs. Internat. Peace Acad., 1970-82. Recipient Friedman award Columbia Law Sch., 1983, Carl Fulda award U. Tex. Law Sch., 1990, Columbia Law medal for excellence, 1991. Fellow Am. Acad. Arts and Scis., World Acad. Art and Sci.; mem. ABA, Am. Soc. Internat. Law (pres. 1968-70, hon. v.p., exec. coun., hon. pres. 1994-96, Manley Hudson medal 1981, Cert. of Merit for creative scholarship 1992), Coun. on Fgn. Rels., Inst. de Droit Internat. (v.p. 1991-93), Internat. Law Assn., Internat. Astronautical Acad., Phi Beta Kappa. Home: 11 E 86th St New York NY 10028-0501 Office: Columbia U Law Sch New York NY 10027

SCHACTER, BRENT ALLAN, oncologist, health facility administrator; b. Winnipeg, Man., Can., June 1, 1942; s. Irvin C. and Claire (Easton) S.; m. Sora Ludwig, Dec. 20, 1981; children: Isanne, Jennifer, Miriam. BSc, MD with honors, U. Man., 1965. Intern Winnipeg Gen. Hosp., 1965-66, jr. asst. resident, 1967-68; asst. resident in internal medicine Barnes Hosp., St. Louis, 1968-69; clin. fellow hematology Barnes Hosp. and Washington U., 1969-70; rsch. fellow, asst. in medicine U. Tex. Southwestern Med. Sch., Dallas, 1970-72; asst. prof. internal medicine U. Man., Winnipeg, 1972-77, assoc. prof. medicine, 1977-87, prof., 1987—; pres., CEO CancerCare Manitoba, 1993—. Lectr. in field; sci. officer grant panel C, Nat. Cancer Inst. Can., 1978, mem., 1979-82; mem. Man. Health Rsch. Coun. grant panel, 1982-84, 89-91, Coun. for Canadian Strategy for Cancer Contro, 2002-; adv. bd. Can. Porphyria Found., 1988—; mem. steering com. Can. Strategy For Cancer Control, 1999—2002, co-chair steering com., 2000—; mem. steering com. Can. Cancer Stats., 2000—. Contbr. numerous articles and abstracts to profl. jours. Bd. dirs. Nat. Cancer Inst. Can., 2000—. Recipient Med. Rsch. Coun. Can. Vis. Scientist award, 1986; fellow Muscular Dystrophy Assn., 1964, John S. McEachern Meml. fellow Can. Cancer Soc., 1969-70, Med. Rsch. Coun. Can. fellow, 1970-72, Nat. Cancer Inst. of Can. rsch. fellow, 1966-67; Isbister scholar, 1962, 63, Med. Rsch. Coun. Can. scholar, 1975-80. Fellow Royal Coll. Physicians; mem. AAAS, Royal Coll. Physicians and Surgeons of Can. (specialty com. in med. oncology 1985-94, bd. med. examiners in med. oncology 1987-90, specialty com. in hematology 1989-93, core com. mem. 1990-96, chmn. bd. examiners med. oncology 1990-93, mem. regional adv. com. Sask./Man. dist. 1992-97), Am. Fedn. for Clin. Rsch., Can. Soc. for Clin. Investigation (awards com. 1980-82, chmn. 1981-82), Am. Soc. Hematology, Can. Soc. Hematology, Am. Soc. Clin. Oncology, Can. Bone Marrow Transplant Group, Can. Assn. Provincial Cancer Agys., Can. Hemophilia Soc. (mem. clinic dirs. group 1990-93, sec-treas. 1991-93) Avocations: cross-country skiing, scuba diving, model railroading. Home: 224 Lamont Blvd Winnipeg MB Canada R3P 0E9 Office: CancerCare Manitoba 675 McDermot Ave Winnipeg MB Canada R3E 0V9 E-mail: brent.schacter@cancercare.mb.ca.

SCHACTER, DAVID MARTIN, judge; b. Toronto, Ont., Can., Sept. 14, 1941; came to the U.S., 1947, naturalized, 1951; s. Arnold and Elsie Schacter; m. Marcia Schacter, Dec. 28, 1968; 1 child, Danna. AA, L.A. Valley Coll., 1961; BA in English Lit., Calif. State U., Northridge, 1963, postgrad., 1964, Calif. Western U., 1965; JD, U. San Fernando Valley, 1968. Bar: Calif. 1968,

U.S. Dist. Ct. (ctrl. dist.) Calif. 1968, U.S. Ct. Appeals (9th cir.) 1969, U.S. Ct. Claims 1969, U.S. Customs Ct. 1969, Tax Ct. U.S. 1969, U.S. Supreme Ct. 1971. Dep. city atty. City of L.A., 1968-73, chief-appellate dept. and spl. prosecutions, 1972; sr. rsch. atty. Calif. Ct. Appeals, 1973-75; dep. city atty. City of Long Beach, 1975-81; commr. mcpl. ct. Santa Monica Jud. Dist., 1981-85; judge L.A. Superior Ct., San Fernando, Calif.; supervising judge North Valley Dist.; judge L.A. Superior Ct., Burbank, Calif. Mem. Atty. Gen. Adv. Bd. on Obscenity, 1972; mem. spl. com. to coordinate and investigate polluters County L.A., 1976; alt. co-chmn. legis. com. Nat. Conf. on the Blight of Obscenity, 1977; appt. mem. Mayor's ad hoc Tech. Adv. Com. on Crime Problems, Long Beach, 1977; mem. cts. and tech. com. Calif. Judges Assn., 1987; lectr. in field. Contbr. articles to profl. jours. and mags. Vol. Valley Village, Goodwill; pres. Alumni Assn. U. LaVerne, Coll. Law, San Fernando Campus, 1995-99. Recipient Nat. Merit award Zeta Beta Tau, 1968, Letter of Commendation, John S. Gibson, Jr., Pres., L.A. City Coun., 1970, Letter of Commendation, Walter F. Wilson, Environ. Mgmt. Dep., L.A. County, 1972, Letter Commendation, Frederick B. Hodges, M.D., Dir. Pub. Health for State Calif., 1973, Letter of Commendation, Archie D. Ross, Chief STate of Calif. Dept. Consumer Affairs, 1973, Letter Commendation, V.F. Hansen, Chief Intelligence Divsn., Dept. Treasury, So. Calif., 1973, award for legal counseling L.A. Police Dept. and Police Commn., 1973, others Mem. Shomrim Soc. So. Calif. Achievements include patent for method and apparatus for determiniing the location of information on magnetic tape. Avocations: photography, antique cameras, woodworking, auto repair, computer programming. Office: Burbank Superior Ct Dept A 300 E Olive Ave Burbank CA 91502

SCHAD, THEODORE MACNEEVE, science research administrator, consultant; b. Balt., Aug. 25, 1918; s. William Henry and Emma Margaret (Scheldt) S.; m. Kathleen White, Nov. 5, 1944 (dec. Aug. 1989); children: Mary Jane, Rebecca Christina; m. Margot Cornwell, March 19, 1995. BSCE, Johns Hopkins U., 1939. Registered profl. engr., D.C. Staff water resources engrng. U.S. Army C.E., U.S. Bur. Reclamation, Md., Colo., Oreg. Wash., 1939-54; prin. budget examiner water resources programs U.S. Bur. Budget, Exec. Office of Pres., 1954-58; sr. specialist engrng. and pub. works, dep. dir. Congl. Rsch. Svc., Libr. of Congress, 1958-68; staff dir. U.S. Senate Com. Nat. Water Resources, 1959-61; exec. dir. Nat. Water Commn., 1968-73; exec. sec. Environ. Studies Bd., 1973-77; dep. dir. Commn. Natural Resources, NAS, Washington, 1977-83; exec. dir. Nat. Ground Water Policy Forum, 1984-86; sr. fellow Conservation Found., Washington, 1986-; U.S. commr. Permanent Internat. Assn. Nav. Congresses, Brussels, 1963-70, commr. emeritus, 1987—. Cons. U.S. Senate Com. Interior and Insular Affairs, 1963, U.S. Ho. of Reps. Com. Sci. and Tech., 1962-65, U.S. Office Saline Water, 1965-67, A.T. Kearney, Inc., Alexandria, Va., 1979-80, Chesapeake Rsch. Consortium, 1984, Ronco Cons. Corp., 1986—, Gambia River Basin Devel. Commn., Dakar, 1986-87, Apogee Rsch. Corp., 1987—, Office Tech. Assessment, U.S. Congress, 1992-95. Contbr. articles to Ency. Brit. and profl. jours. Treas. Nat. Speleol. Found., 1961-65, trustee, 1965—; bd. dirs. Vets. Coop. Housing Assn., Washington, 1958-81, v.p., 1960-72. Recipient Meritorious Svc. award U.S. Dept. Interior, 1950, Icko Iben award Am. Water Resources Assn., 1978, Henry P. Caulfield medal, 1990, Woodrow Wilson award for disting. govt. svc. Johns Hopkins U., 1997. Fellow: ASCE (treas. Nat. Capital chpt. 1952—55, v.p. 1967, pres. 1968, Julian Hinds prize 1991); mem.: AAAS, U.S. Soc. on Dams, Internat. Commn. Irrigation and Drainage, Permanent Internat. Assn. Nav. Congresses (commr. emeritus), Nat. Acad. Pub. Adminstrn., Am. Acad. Environ. Engrs. (Gordon Maskew Fair award 2002), Am. Geophys. Union, Nat. Speleol. Soc., Am. Water Works Assn. (hon.), Am. Alpine Club, Seattle Mountaineers Club, Colo. Mountain Club (Denver), Cosmos Club, Potomac Appalachian Trail Club. Home: 4540 25th Rd N Arlington VA 22207-4102 Office: The Conservation Found 1260 24th St NW Washington DC 20037-1103

SCHAD, VICKI JEAN REYNOLDS, piano teacher; b. Machias, Maine, June 18, 1947; d. R. Bryce Reynolds and J. Rowena Towers; m. James K. Schad, July 17, 1970; children: Timothy James, Benjamin John. BS in Secondary Edn. with proficiencies in Music and Hist., Bob Jones U., 1969. Certified secondary edn. edr., Maine, Mich., APH, CCM. Town clk. Town of Vassalboro, Maine, 1974-96, voter registrar, 1996-99; owner, instr. Schad Piano Studio, North Vassalboro, 1980—; genealogist Maine State Archives, Augusta, 1988—; mins. coord. Hopeful Mins., Winslow, Maine, 1992-96; instr., facilitator, state coord. Maine Fellowship Christian Writers, China, 1996—. Dir. Kennebelles Chorus, Waterville, Maine, 1999. Mem. Primo piano II Stanley Hill Piano Quartet, Vassalboro, 1996—; author, rschr. Heart's Song, 1995, rev. edit., 2002, Doorway into History, 1999; author (devotionals): Daily Guideposts, 1988-90; author, editor: Some Early History of Lubec, Maine, 2001; contbr. The Town Line Newspaper; composer (music book) For Weary Souls, A Cool Retreat, 1999. Teen adv. Hopeful Mins. Winslow, Maine, 1996—; dir. Vassalboro Bible Study, 1999-. Mem. Nat. Guild Piano Tchrs. (Ctrl. Maine chairperson 1998-2001), Am. Coll. Musicians (Ctrl. Maine chairperson 1997-2001), Music Tchrs. Nat. Assn., Maine Music Tchrs. Assn., Ctrl. Maine Music Tchrs. Assn. (charter mem.), Assn. Personal Historians. Republican. Baptist. Avocations: poetry, genealogy, teaching, teen and adult counseling. Home and Office: Schad Piano Studio 180 S Stanley Hill Rd Vassalboro ME 04989 E-mail: jvschad@larck.net.

SCHADE, CHARLENE JOANNE, adult and early childhood education educator; b. San Bernardino, Calif., June 26, 1935; d. Clarence George Linde and Helen Anita (Sunny) Hardesty; m. William Joseph Jr., Apr. 12, 1958 (div., 1978); children: Sabrina, Eric, Camela, Cynthia; m. Thomas Byron Killens, Sept. 25, 1983. BS, UCLA, 1959. Tchr. dance and phys. edn. L.A. Unified Secondary Schs., Calif., 1959-63; dir., instr. (Kindergym) La Jolla YMCA, 1972-76; instr. older adults San Diego Cmty. Colls., 1977—, assoc. prof. continuing edn., 1997—; artist in residence Wolf Trap/Headstart, 1984-85. Workshop leader S.W. Dance, Movement and Acro-Sports Workshop, prime-time adult activities coord., 1988—, Am. Heart Assn., Arthritis Found., Am. Lung Assn., AAHPERD, S.W. Dist. AHPERD, Calif. Assn. Health, Phys. Edn., Recreation and Dance, Head Start, San Diego Assn. Young Children, Calif. Assn. Edn. Young Child, Calif. Kindergarten Assn., So. Calif. Kindergarten Assn., 1997, Assn. Childhood Edn. Internat., Nat. Pediat. Support Svcs., 1999, Calif. Dance Educators, 1999, IDEA Internat. Assn. Fitness Profls., San Diego C.C., Am. Soc. on Aging, Fourth Internat. Congress Phys. Activity, Aging and Sports, 1996, others; cons. to Calif. Gov.'s Coun. on Phys. Fitness and Sports, 1993—; feature guest Sta. KFMB and KPBS TV shows, San Diego, 1980-88; assoc. prof. San Diego C.C. Continuing Edn., 1997—; spl. advisor San Diego Coun. on Phys. Fitness and Sports, 1998—. Author: Move With Me From A to Z, 1982, Move With Me, One, Two, Three, 1988; co-author: Prime Time Aerobics, 1982, Muevete Conmigo, uno, dos, tres, 1990; co-writer: Guide for Physical Fitness Instructors of Older Adults, Grant Project, 1990, The Empowering Teacher, 1990, Handbook for Instructors of Older Adults, 1994. Bd. dirs. We Care Found., San Diego, 1977-79, Meet the Author programs San Diego County Schs., 1988—; founder SOLO, San Diego, 1981-83; adminstr., v.p. ODEM chpt. Toastmasters, San Diego, 1982; chmn. People with Arthritis Can Exercise com. San Diego chpt. Arthritis Found., 1994-95; trainer PACE instrs. Nat. Arthritis Found., 1995—. Grantee Video Showcase of Exercises for Older Adults, 1992-93. Mem. AAPHERD (workshop leader), Calif. Assn. Health, Phys. Edn., Recreation and Dance (workshop leader). Avocations: hiking, dancing, travel. Office: Exer Fun/Prime Time Aerobic 3089C Clairemont Dr #130 San Diego CA 92117-6802 E-mail: cschade@sdccd.cc.ca.us.

SCHADE, STEVEN ERNEST, conservator; b. Jamaica, N.Y., Mar. 24, 1958; s. Ernest Robert Schade, Dorothy Elaine Kowell; m. Catherine Scorsese, Mar. 14, 1999. Student advt. art, Nassau C.C., Uniondale, N.Y.; student, Southampton Coll. Sales real estate Merrill Lynch Realty, Franklin Square, NY, 1983—84; actor extra movie Sweet Liberty, Sag Harbor, 1984—85; broker real estate Thomas Zukas Real Estate, Water Mill, 1985—94; owner Steven E. Schade & Assocs., 1994—. Fundraiser Big Brothers-Big Sisters of L.I., NY, 1999—. Author: Contractor/Homeowner English-Spanish, 1998, Housekeeping English-Spanish, 1999; author: (screenplay) The Pool, 2002. Recipient Eagle Scout, Boys Scouts Am., 1976. Avocation: Avocations: motorcycles, surfing, sailing. Office: PO Box 2583 Southampton NY 11969

SCHADE, WILBERT CURTIS, education administrator; b. St. Louis, Jan. 4, 1945; s. Wilbert Curtis and Florence Mary (Allen) S.; m. Jacqueline Siewert, May 14, 1977; children: Benjamin Allen Siewert, Timothy Knorr Siewert. BA, U. Pa., 1967; AM, Washington U., St. Louis, 1970; PhD, Ind. U., 1986. Tchg. asst. dept. romance lang. Washington U., St. Louis, 1967-68; tchr. French St. Louis Priory Sch., 1970-71; assoc. instr. dept. French and Italian Ind. U., Bloomington, 1972-74, 76-80; tchr. French Webster Groves (Mo.) H.S., 1975-76; asst. dir. admissions Beloit (Wis.) Coll., 1980-83, assoc. dir. admissions, 1983-84; dir. coll. placement and dir. admissions Westover Sch., Middlebury, Conn., 1984-90; head upper sch. The Key Sch., Annapolis, Md., 1990-94, interim dir. devel., 1994-95; tchr. French, head lang. dept. Wasatch Acad., Mt. Pleasant, Utah, 1995-96, asst. headmaster for acad. affairs, 1996-2000; tchr., dir. of studies Internat. Seminar Series, Paris, 1999—. Lectr. in field. Co-editor: African Literature in its Social and Political Dimensions, 1983; mem. editl. bd. Jour. Coll. Admission, 2000—; contbr. articles to profl. jours. including World Lit. Written in English, Studies in 20th Century Lit. Active Anne Arundel County (Md.) Task Force on Year Round Edn., 1994-95, Utah State Office of Edn.'s Fgn. Lang. Instrl. Materials and Texbook Adv. Com., 1996-98. NEH Summer Inst. on African Am. Lit. and Film grant, 1994. Mem. Nat. Assn. Coll. Admission Counseling (presenter nat. conf. 1985), Rocky Mountain Assn. for Coll. Admission Counseling (exec. bd., chief assembly del. to Nat. Assn.), African Lit. Assn. (exec. com. 1979), Phi Delta Kappa. Mem. Soc. Of Friends. Avocation: tennis. Home: PO Box 3549 20 Malheur Ln Sunriver OR 97707

SCHADLE, WILLIAM JAMES, lawyer; b. Dubuque, Iowa, Aug. 4, 1932; s. John Paul and Helen Bernadine (Hird) S.; m. Jane Louise Cameron, Nov. 20, 1972. BA, U. Iowa, 1959; JD, Drake U., Des Moines, 1984. Bar: Iowa 1984. Gen. counsel Hettinga Equipment, Inc., Des Moines, 1984-87; assoc. Thomas J. Reilly Law Firm, P.C., 1987-89; pvt. practice, 1989-97; mng. atty. Drake Elderlaw project U. Law Sch., 1998—. With USN, 1952-56. Mem. Iowa State Bar Assn. Office: PO Box 35983 Des Moines IA 50315-0309

SCHADLER, FLORENCE ASHTON, artist, educator; b. Phila., Mar. 13, 1941; d. Clayton and Elva Elizabeth (Hodges) Ashton; m. Gary Lane Schadler, July 14, 1962 (dec. Apr. 1983); children: Cynthia Lynne, Craig Raymond; m. J.M. Harrison, May 25, 1990 (div. May 1998). BFA magna cum laude, Kutztown State U.; cert., Moore Inst. Art Phila. Art educator Parkland Sch. Dist., Allentown, Pa., Pa. State U., Allentown, Baum Sch. Art, Allentown, Jacksonville (Fla.) Art Mus., 1994-95; adj. prof. Fla. C.C. Jacksonville, 1995-97; prof. Mandarin (Fla.) Mid. Sch., 1996—. Exhibited in group shows at Cummer Mus., Jacksonville; represented in permanent collections. Mem. Fla. Watercolor Soc. (life), Jacksonville Watercolor Soc. (pres. 1994-95), Orange Park (Fla.) Fine Art Guild (v.p.), St. Augustine (Fla.) Art Assn., Kutztown U. Alumni Assn., Lehigh U. Alumni Assn. Republican. Roman Catholic. Home: 914 Bridgetown Pike Langhorne PA 19053-7218

SCHADOW, GUNTHER, medical information scientist; b. Frieburg, Germany, Feb. 19, 1969; s. W.G. Peter and Eva-Maria (Kleinert) S.; m. Dorothea Riemer, Aug. 7, 1993; children: Maria, Johannes. D Medicine, Free U., Berlin, 1999; MD, Humboldt U., Berlin, 1997; PhD, Free U., Berlin, 1999. Vis. assoc. scientist Regenstrief Inst. for Health Care & Ind. U. Sch. Medicine, Indpls., 1998-99, med. info. scientist, 1999—. Co-chair Health Level 7-Sig Secure Transactions, 1997-00, Orders-Observations Tech. Com., 2000—; adj. asst. prof. Ind. U. Sch. Medicine. Contbr. articles to profl. jours. Named W. Ed Hammond Vol. of Yr., Health Level 7, 1999. Mem. Am. Med. Informatics Assn., U. Senix Assn. Mem. Social Democratic Party of Germany. Lutheran. Office: Regenstrief Inst for Health Care 1050 Wishard Blvd Indianapolis IN 46202-2872

SCHADT, JAMES PHILLIP, investment and software executive; b. Saginaw, Mich., Aug. 7, 1938; s. Phillip Jr. and Jean D. (Cardy) S.; m. Barbara L. Soldmann, Aug. 16, 1959; children: Lauren C., Andrew F. BA, Northwestern U., 1960. With Procter & Gamble USA, 1960-65, Glendinning Cos., 1965-70, Squibb Corp., 1971-73, Pepsi Co., 1973-77, Sara Lee, 1977-80; pres., CEO Cadbury Schweppes Inc., 1981-91; dir., pres., COO Reader's Digest Assoc. Inc., Pleasantville, N.Y., 1991-94, pres., CEO, 1994—, chmn., pres., CEO, 1995-97; chair Dailey Capital Mgmt., L.P., Southport, Conn., 1997—; chmn. Mercator Software, Inc., Wilton, 2000—. Trustee Northwestern U. Mem. Blind Brook Club (Purchase, N.Y.), Chgo. Club, Am. Enterprise Inst. (trustee), Country Club of Fairfield, Conn., John's Island Club, Lotos Club N.Y.C. Home: 17 Owenoke Park Westport CT 06880-6834 Office: Mercator Software Inc 45 Danbury Rd Wilton CT 06897 also: Mercator Software 45 Danbury Rd Wilton CT 06897-0840

SCHAECHTER, MOSELIO, microbiology educator; b. Apr. 26, 1928; children: Judy, John. Student, Cen. U., Ecuador, 1947-49; MA, U. Kans., 1952; PhD, U. Pa., 1954. Postdoctoral fellow State Serum Inst., Copenhagen, 1956-58; from instr. to asst. prof. to assoc. prof. U. Fla., Gainesville, 1958-62; from assoc. prof. to disting. prof. dept. microbiology Tufts U., Boston, 1962-95, prof. emeritus, 1995—. Adj. prof. San Diego State U., 1995—. Editor: Molecular Biology Bacterial Growth, 1985, Escherichia coli and Salmonella Typhimurium, 1987, 95, Mechanisms of Microbiol. Disease, 1989, 92; author: In the Company of Mushrooms, 1997. Mem. Am. Soc. Microbiology (pres. 1985-86, chmn. internat. activities), Am. Soc. Med. Sch. Microbiology Chmn. (pres. 1984-85, chair internat. activities 1986-94), Soc. Gen. Microbiology, Boston Mycol. Club, Sigma Xi. Avocations: field mycology, hiking. Office: San Diego State U Dept Biology San Diego CA 92182 E-mail: mschaech@sunstroke.sdsu.edu.

SCHAEDE, RICHARD EDWIN, family practice physician; b. Thomasboro, Ill., Aug. 28, 1927; s. Mayo William and Opal Mae (Hutchison) S.; m. Ila Marlene Coffey, June 13, 1949; children: Pamela, Janet, Mark. BS in chemistry, U. Ill., 1949; BS in Medicine, U. Ill., Chgo., 1951, MD, 1953. Diplomate Am. Bd. Family Practice. Chief dept. internal medicine, cardiology, Shilling AFB, 1955-57; physician Chanute AFB, Rantoul, Ill., 1954-55; founder, pvt. practice Rantoul Clinic, 1957-80; assoc. dean medicine U. Ill., Champaign, 1972-78, assoc. prof. clin. medicine, 1978-86; dir. Christie Clinic Satellite, 1980-85; pvt. practice Marion, Ill., 1986—. Mem. faculty Parkland Coll., Champaign, 1970-72. Bd. dirs. Rantoul Elem. Sch. Bd., 1959-70; pres. Outlook T.B. Sanitorium Bd., 1959-69. Seaman first class USNR, 1945-46; capt. USAF, 1955-57. Fellow Am. Coll. Family Practice; mem. Rotary. Republican. Lutheran. Avocations: hunting, fishing. Home: 10242 Limb Branch Ln Marion IL 62959-6020 Office: 114 S Vicksburg St Marion IL 62959-1930

SCHAEFER, C. BARRY, railroad executive, lawyer, investment banker; b. Elizabeth, N.J., Feb. 23, 1939; s. Carl H. and Evelyn G. (Conk) S.; m. Carol Ann Craft, July 11, 1970; children: Sara Elizabeth, Susan Craft. BS in Engring., Princeton U., 1961; MS in Engring., U. Pa., 1962; LLB, Columbia U., 1965; MBA, NYU, 1970. Bar: N.Y. 1966, Nebr. 1972. With Kelley, Drye, Warren, N.Y.C., 1966-69; asst. gen. counsel Union Pacific Corp., 1969-72; western gen. counsel Union Pacific R.R. Co., Omaha, 1972-74, v.p., western gen. counsel, 1974-77, v.p. law, 1977-82; sr. v.p. planning and corp. devel. Union Pacific Corp., N.Y.C., 1984-88, exec. v.p. Bethlehem, Pa., 1988; sr. advisor Dillon Read & Co. Inc., 1989-91; mng. dir. The Bridgeford Group, 1992-97, Beacon Group, 1997-01, The Bridgeford Group, 2001—. Nat. bd. dirs. Jr. Achievement, Colorado Springs, Colo., 1986—. Mem. Racquet and Tennis Club (N.Y.C.), Round Hill Club (Greenwich, Conn.), Desert Mountain Club (Scottsdale, Ariz.).

SCHAEFER, CATHLEEN FRANCES, public relations executive; b. L.A., Feb. 11, 1961; d. Robert Edward and Vivian Kraut Thomas; m. Charles Joseph Schaefer Jr., Sept. 26, 1987; children: Allison Marie, Eric Joseph. BA in Comm. Studies, Calif. State U., Sacramento, 1984. With pub. rels. Dept. Energy Conservation, City of Roseville, Calif., 1984-88; pub. rels. acct. exec. McElroy Comms., Sacramento, 1988—. Pub. rels. cons. Am. Non-Smoker's Rights Found., Sacramento, 1999-2000, Driver Sober Sacramento, 1998-99; local organizer pub. rels. Calif. Wellness Found. Resources for Youth Silence the Violence Bus Tour, Sacramento, 1999; v.p. publicity, bd. dirs. Sacramento Valley chpt. Crohn's and Colitis Found. of Am., 1995—; treas. Harry Dewey PTA, Fair Oaks, Calif., 1999-2000; co-leader Girl Scouts of Am. Citrus Heights, 1998-2000; vol. Harry Dewey Elem. Sch., San Juan Sch. Dist., Fair Oaks, 1994—, Arcade Middle Sch., 2001-. Avocations: soccer, camping, skiing. Office: McElroy Comms 2410 K St Ste C Sacramento CA 95816-5002

SCHAEFER, CHARLES JAMES, III, advertising agency executive, consultant; b. Orange, N.J., Dec. 17, 1926; m. Eleanor Anne Montville, Apr. 8, 1961; 1 child, Charles James IV AB, Dartmouth Coll., 1948, M in Comml. Sci., 1949. V.p. Dickie-Raymond, 1952-67; sr. v.p. Metromedia, 1968-69; exec. v.p., treas. The DR Group, Boston, 1969-76, pres., 1976-87; exec. v.p., dir. Needham Harper Worldwide Inc., N.Y.C., 1984-87; chmn. bd. Marcoa DR Group, Inc., 1987-88; cons. Rapp Collins Marcoa, 1989-92; advt. cons., 1992—. Pres. Dartmouth Class of 1948, 1998-2000; trustee, mem. exec. com. Direct Mktg. Ednl. Found., 1983-89; campaign chairperson United Way Millburn-Short Hills, 1994, 95, trustee, 1991-98, 2000—. With USN, 1945-46. Mem. Direct Mktg. Assn. (chmn. awards com. 1971-76, Hall of Fame com. 1978-81, ethics com. 1981-86), Assn. Direct Mktg. Agys. (pres. 1980-82, gen. chmn. Caples awards 1985, Direct Mktg. Day N.Y. 1988, N.Y. Direct Marketer of Yr. award 1987, Silver Apple award 1989, contbr. to jour.), Dartmouth Club of N.Y. (pres. 1968-70), Lotos Club (bd. dirs. 1985-88, treas. 1987-88), Canoe Brook Country Club (Summit, N.J.). Home and Office: 307 Hobart Ave Short Hills NJ 07078-2207

SCHAEFER, CHRISTINA KASSABIAN, writer, genealogist; b. Meriden, Conn., May 31, 1954; d. Levon Harry and Lareine Alice (Kinstler) Kassabian; m. Douglas Eric Schaefer, May 1, 1981; children: Eric, Alice. BA in English, So. Conn. State Coll., 1975. V.p. Blue Sales, Inc., Guilford, Conn., 1977-81. Dir. Family Hist. Ctr., Annandale, Va., 1994-97. Author: The Center: Guide to Research in the National Capital Area, 1996, Guide to Naturalization Records of the United States, 1997, The Great War: Guide to the Service Records of All the World's Fighting Men and Volunteers, 1998, Genealogical Encyclopedia of the Colonial Americas: A Complete Digest of the Records of All the Countries of the Western Hemisphere, 1998, The Hidden Half of the Family: A Sourcebook for Women's Genealogy, 1999, Instant Information on the Internet/ A Genealogist's No-Frills Guide to the 50 States and the District of Columbia, 1999, Instant Information on the Internet: A Genealogist's No-Frills Guide to the British Isles, 1999. Vol. Boys Scouts Am., Springfield, Va., 1991—. Recipient 1st pl. literary award Conn. Soc. Genealogists, 1997, 1998; Selected for inclusion in Authors' Room of Libr. Va., 2000. Mem.: Bd. Cert. Genealogists.

SCHAEFER, DALE W. science educator; b. Willoughby, Ohio, May 17, 1941; s. George and Loretta Barbara Schaefer; m. Arlene Tellgren, Aug. 25, 1962; children: Jeanne, Joel. BS, Wheaton Coll., 1963; PhD, MIT, 1968. Postdoctoral fellow dept. physics MIT, Cambridge, Mass., 1968-70; rsch. assoc. IBM Watson Rsch. Lab., Yorktown Heights, N.Y., 1970-72; mem. tech. staff Sandia Nat. Labs., Albuquerque, 1972-80, dept. mgr., 1980-97; dean engrng. U. Cin., 1997-98, prof., 1997—. Sr. tech. advisor U.S. Dept. Energy, Washington. Contbr. articles to profl. jours. Trustee Colo. Christian U., Lakewood, 2000—, Christian Inn Ministries, Cin., 1998— Recipient Kodak prize, 1968, Rensselaer Sci. medal Rensselaer Poly. U., 1959. Fellow Am. Phys. Soc., Am. Inst. Chemists; mem. Am. Chem. Soc., Materials Rsch. Soc., Tau Beta Pi (eminent engr.). Avocations: hunting, skiing, golf. Home: 3323 Westside Ave Cincinnati OH 45208 Office: U Cin Dept Chem and Materials Engrng Cincinnati OH 45221-0012 Office Fax: 513-556-3773. E-mail: schaefdw@email.uc.edu.

SCHAEFER, FRANK WILLIAM, III, microbiologist, researcher; b. Dayton, Ohio, Sept. 1, 1942; s. Frank William Jr. and Irene Josephine (Krouse) S. BA, Miami U., Oxford, Ohio, 1964; MS, U. Cin., 1970, PhD, 1973. Rsch. assoc. parasitologist U. Notre Dame, South Bend, Ind., 1973-78; U.S. EPA EPA, Cin., 1978—. Mem. ASTM, AAAS, Am. Soc. Parasitology, Am. Soc. Microbiology, Am. Water Works Assn., Soc. Protozoologists, Sigma Xi. Home: 9948 McCauley Woods Dr Sharonville OH 45241-1489 Office: US EPA 26 Martin Luther King Dr Cincinnati OH 45268 E-mail: schaefer.frank@epa.gov.

SCHAEFER, GEORGE A., JR. bank executive; Pres., CEO Fifth Third Bancorp, Cin. Office: Fifth Third Bancorp Fifth Third Center 38 Fountain Square Plz Cincinnati OH 45263-0001*

SCHAEFER, GORDON EMORY, food company executive; b. 1932; married. BS, Marquette U., 1956. With Peat, Marwick, Mitchell & Co., 1955-59; treas. Pabst Brewing Co., Milw., 1965-72, v.p. adminstrn., 1972-75, v.p. ops., 1975-76, exec. v.p. ops., 1976-89, cons., 1980—, dir.; pres., dir. Krier Foods Inc., Belgium, Wis., 1981-85, Corrs Beverages, Chgo., 1985-86; dir. bus. devel. Lakeside Packing Co., Manitowoc, Wis., 1989-92; mng. dir. Robertson Assocs., Mfg. Europe Ltd., Cardiff, Wales, U.K., 1993-94. Bd. dirs. Fox Fin. Co., Grand Rapids, Mich., Berg Industries, Inc., Marshfield, Wis.; fin. and ops. cons.; owner, operator Schaefer's Orchards. Home: N27 W6567 Alyce St Cedarburg WI 53012 E-mail: schaefer1@milwpc.com.

SCHAEFER, HEINRICH C. retired anesthesiologist; b. Berlin, 1917; MD, U. Innsbruck, 1944. Diplomate Am. Bd. Anesthesiology. Intern St. Luke's Meth. Hosp., Cedar Rapids, Iowa, 1952-54; resident in anesthesiology Detroit Receiving Hosp., 1954-56; pvt. practice Detroit; sr. staff Henry Ford Hosp., 1991-96, Cottage Hosp., Grosse Pointe, Mich., 1976-96; ret., 1996. Mem. AMA, Am. Soc. Anesthesiologists.

SCHAEFER, HELENE G(ERALDINE), social services professional; b. Chgo., Apr. 4, 1948; d. Jerry and Helen (Hruska) Souta; m. Kenneth Schaefer (div.) June 4, 1972; children: Rebecca, Benjamin. BA, Valparaiso U., 1970; MA, Govs. State U., 1984. Registered social worker, Ill. Social worker Ill. Dept. of Children & Family Svcs., Chgo., 1970-76, Bodimetric Health Svcs., Hillside, Ill., 1984-86; counselor svc. dir. Crisis Ctr. For So. Suburbia, Worth, 1979-82; child protection investigator Ill. Dept. Children and Family Svcs., Chgo., 1987-93, supr., 1993—. Bd. dirs. Rainbow House Shelter for Battered Women; leader Girl Scouts of So. Cook County, Palos Heights, 1982-87. Mem. AAUW, Parent Faculty Assn., Chgo. Met. Battered, Women's Movement. Presbyterian. Avocations: camping, dancing, reading, traveling. Office: Ill Dept Children and Family Svcs 6201 S Emerald Dr Chicago IL 60621-2043 E-mail: h.schaefer@idcfs.state.il.usa.

SCHAEFER, HENRY FREDERICK, III, chemistry educator; b. Grand Rapids, Mich., June 8, 1944; s. Henry Frederick Jr. and Janice Christine (Trost) S.; m. Karen Regine Rasmussen, Sept. 2, 1966; children: Charlotte, Pierre, Theodore, Rebecca, Caleb. BS in Chem. Physics, MIT, 1966; PhD in Chem. Physics, Stanford U., 1969; Doctorate (hon.) , U. Plovdiv, Bulgaria, 1998, U. Sofia, 1999, Beijing Inst. Tech., 1999, Huntington Coll., Ind., 2002. From asst. prof. to prof. chemistry U. Calif., Berkeley, 1969-87; Graham Perdue prof., dir. Ctr. for Computational Quantum Chemistry U. Ga., Athens, 1987—. Apptd. Professeur d'Echange U. Paris, 1977, Gastprofessor Eidgenossische Technische Hochshule, Zurich, 1994, 95, 97, 2000, 02; Wilfred T. Doherty prof., dir. Inst. Theoretical Chemistry, U. Tex., Austin, 1979-80; lectr. in field. Contbr. more than 900 articles to profl. jours. including The Electronic Structure of Atoms and Molecules: A Survey of Rigorous Quantum Mechanical Results, 1972, Modern Theoretical Chemistry, 1977, Quantum Chemistry, 1983, A New Dimension to Quantum Chemistry, 1994; editor Molecular Physics, 1991-94, editor in chief, 1995—. Recipient Pure Chemistry award Am. Chem. Soc., 1979, Leo Hendrik Baekeland award, 1983, Schrödinger Medal, 1990, Centenary medal Royal Soc. Chemistry, London, 1992, Gold medal Camenius U., Bratislava, Slovakia, 2000; Sloan fellow, 1972, Guggenheim fellow, 1976-77; named one of 100 Outstanding Young Scientists in Am., Sci. Digest, 1984, named 3rd Most Highly cited chemist in world Science Watch, 1992. Fellow Am. Phys. Soc., Am. Sci. Affiliation; mem. Internat. Acad. Quantum Molecular Sci., Am. Chem. Soc. (chmn. divsn. phys. chemistry 1992), World Assn. Theoretically Oriented Chemists (pres. 1996—). Presbyterian. Office: U Ga Ctr Computational Quantum Chemistry Athens GA 30602 E-mail: hfsiii@uga.edu.

SCHAEFER, IRA MARC, music educator, musician; b. El Paso, Tex., July 5, 1968; s. Alan J. and Rhoda G. Schaefer; m. Jane P. L. Schaefer. MusB in Music Edn., SUNY, Fredonia, 1991; MEd in Sch. Adminstrn., Salem State Coll., 2000. Cert. music tchr. Mass., Conn., N.Y. Music tchr. Patchogue-Medford Schs., Patchogue, NY, 1991—92; condr. Cape Cod Conservatory, West Barnstable, Mass., 1992—2002; string tchr. Barnstable Pub. Schs., Hyannis, 1992—2001; bassist Cape Symphony Orch., Yarmouth Port, 1992—, Plymouth (Mass.) Philharm., 2000—; string tchr. Somerset (Mass.) Pub. Schs., 2001—. H.s. string orch. guest condr. Maine Music Educators Assn. Dist. II,

Portland, 2002; guest condr. R.I. String Tchrs. Assn., 2002. Mem.: ASTA with NSOA, MENC, Internat. Soc. Bassists, Sinfonia, Phi Mu Alpha. Home: 942 W Main St Centerville MA 02632 Office: Somerset Pub Schs Somerset MA 02726

SCHAEFER, JOHN FREDERICK, lawyer, educator; b. Detroit, Apr. 10, 1943; s. Gilbert Frederick and Mary Cathryn (Henderson) S.; m. Sharon Kathleen Chalmers, May 22, 1976; children: Kimberly Megan, Kelly Leigh, John Frederick, Charles Frederick. Student, U. Notre Dame, 1961-63; BA, Mich. State U., 1965, LLD, 1996; JD, Detroit Coll. Law, 1968. Bar: Mich. 1969. Ptnr. Buesser, Buesser, Snyder & Blank, Detroit, 1968-73, Williams, Schaefer, Ruby & Williams, Birmingham, 1973-89; propr. Law Firm of John F. Schaefer, 1989—. Adj. prof. domestic rels. Detroit Coll. Law, 1971—; instr. domestic rels. Mich. Jud. Inst., 1980-81; lectr. in field. Contbr. articles to legal jours. Trustee Detroit Coll. Law, Mich. State U., 1985—, William Beaumont Hosp., 2000; chair Detroit Coll. Law at Mich. State U. Found., 1995—; mem. ICLE Legal Edn. Inst. Fellow: Oakland Bar Found., Mich. State Bar Found. (jed. rev. com. 1997—), Am. Acad. Matrimonial Lawyers (pres. Mich. chpt. 1986—87), State Bar Mich. (family law com. 1972—73, com. on character and fitness 1972—75, coun. family law sect. 1974—, mem. fee abritration grievance bd. 1976—, chmn. 1978—79); mem.: Oakland County Bar Assn. (mem. character and fitness com. 1973, familyt law com. 1973—, chmn. com. 1974—77, cir. ct. com. 1985—88, bd. dirs. 1995—), Detroit Bar Assn. (friend of ct. and domestic rels. com. 1972—, chmn. com. 1975—76, mem. pub. adv. com. 1976—), ABA (family law sect. 1969—, jud. rev. com. 1997—). Roman Catholic. Office: Ste 320 380 N Old Woodward Ave Birmingham MI 48009-5347

SCHAEFER, MARILYN LOUISE, artist, writer, educator; b. Cedar Rapids, Iowa, Apr. 22, 1933; d. Henry Richard and Maria Augusta (Dickel) S. AA, Monticello Coll. for Women, 1953; BFA, Cranbrook Acad. Art, 1956, MFA, 1960; MA cum laude, U. Chgo., 1958; MA, St. John's Coll., Santa Fe, 1979. Rsch. asst. editor Encyclopaedia Britannica, Chgo., 1960-63; humanities editor Encyclopedia Americana, N.Y., 1964-68; acquisitions editor Litton Ednl. Pub., 1968-70; from instr. to prof. emeritus art and advt. design dept. N.Y.C. Tech. Coll. CUNY, 1970—. Contbg. editor Encyclopedia Americana, 1979—, Coll. Teaching jour., 1979. Contbr. articles to profl. publs. including Art and Auction mag., Art and Antiques mag., Am. Artist mag., Encyclopedia Americana, 1970—. Luce Found. postgrad. study fellow St. John's Coll., 1976-79; Ingram Merrill Found. grantee, 1983-84. Mem. AAUW, CUNY Acad. Arts and Scis. Home: 306 W 76th St New York NY 10023-8065 Office: NYC Tech Coll CUNY 300 Jay St Brooklyn NY 11201-1909

SCHAEFER, MARY ANN, health facility administrator, consultant; b. Chgo., May 18, 1942; d. Joseph and Mary A. (Kozyra) Strosnik; m. Robert Earl Schaefer, May 18, 1963; children: Debra Ann, Robert Joseph. Diploma in nursing, St. Francis Hosp. Sch. Nursing, Evanston, Ill., 1962; BA, Nat. Coll. Edn., Evanston, 1980; MBA in Health Svc. Mgmt., Webster U., 1990; MJ in Health Law, Loyola U., Chgo., 1993. Med. and surg. nurse Resurrection Med. Ctr., Chgo., 1962-79, charge nurse labor and delivery, 1978-79; coord. maternal child care Humana, Hoffman Estates, Ill., 1979-81; nurse mgr. labor and delivery Resurrection Med. Ctr., Chgo., 1981-91; mgr. Family Birthplace Resurrection Med. Ctr., 1991-98; cons., prin. M/B Assocs.-Consultants Perinatal Healthcare and Edn., Barrington, 1994-98; mgr. Maternal-Child Health Sherman Hosp., Elgin, Ill., 1998-00, dir. women's svcs., 2000—. Seminar leader on childbirth edn., legal issues in nursing. Contbr. to Motor Facilitation Handbook; editorial bd. Essentials publ., Resurrection Med. Ctr. Mem. Assn. Women's Health, Obstetric and Neonatal Nurses (cert. in inpatient obstetric nursing, instr. principles and practice electronic fetal monitoring), Nat. Perinatal Assn. Perinatal Assn. Ill. (exec. bd.). Home: 23370 N Juniper Ln Barrington IL 60010-2936

SCHAEFER, NANCY TURNER, artist, educator; b. Hamilton, Ohio, July 4, 1940; d. Edward and Leota (Taylor) Turner; m. Richard Burton Price, June 16, 1967 (div. July 1970); m. Donald Raymond Schaefer, July 6, 1970 (dec. Nov. 1990). BA in English and Art, Ea. Ky. U., 1965; postgrad., Cin. Art Acad., 1995—. Cert. tchr., Ky., Ohio, Va. Tchr. Boone County Bd. Edn., Florence, Ky., 1965-67, Rockingham County Bd. Edn., Harrisonburg, Va., 1967-69, Hamilton County Bd. Edn., Cin. and Greenhills, Ohio, 1969-86; pvt. tchr. art, instr. cmty. colls., Sarasota and Bradenton, Fla., 1986—. Demonstrator Palm Aire Artists Orgn., Sarasota, 1995; bd. dirs. Art League Manatee County. Works exhibited in two woman show Longboat Key (Fla.) Edn. Ctr., 1996, four woman show Art League of Manatee County, 1995 (Equal Merit award 1995), group shows Hilton Leech Studio, Sarasota, Fla., 1995 (1st honorable mention for mixed media 1995); represented in permanent collections Art League of Manatee County and many pvt. collections. Recipient numerous awards for paintings. Mem. Fla. Suncoast Watercolor Soc., Art League Manatee County (demonstrator 1995), Nat. Mus. Women in Arts (assoc.). Avocations: piano, gourmet cooking, calligraphy, cats, interior decorating.

SCHAEFER, PATRICIA, librarian; b. Ft. Wayne, Ind., Apr. 23, 1930; d. Edward John and Hildegarde Hartman (Hormel) S. MusB, Northwestern U., 1951; MusM, U. Ill., 1958; AMLS, U. Mich., 1963. With U.S. Rubber co., Ft. Wayne, 1951-52; sec. to promotion mgr. Sta. WOWO, Ind., 1952, sec. to program mgr., 1953-55; coord. publicity and promotion Home Telephone Co., 1955-56; sec. Fine Arts Found., 1956-57; libr. asst. Columbus (Ohio) Pub. Libr., 1958-59; audio-visual libr. Muncie (Ind.) Pub. Libr., 1959-86, asst. libr. dir., 1981-86, libr. dir., 1986-95. Chmn. Ind. Libr. Film Cir., 1962-63; treas. Ind. Libr. Film Svc., 1969-70, 83-85; mem. trustee adv. coun. Milton S. Eisenhower Libr., Johns Hopkins U.; mem. presdl. counsellors Johns Hopkins U., 1994—; bd. dirs. Franklin Elec. Co., Inc. Weekly columnist Libr. Lines, Muncie Evening Press, 1981-83; program annotator Muncie Symphony Orch. and Masterworks Chorale; contbr. articles to profl. jours. Bd. dirs. Muncie Symphony Assn., 1964-74, 85-91, Ctrl. City Bus. Assn., 1986-92, Ind. Inst. Tech., Ptnrs. for the Enhancement of Cmty. Coop., Ind. Humanities Coun., 1996—, Sta. WIPB-TV, 1997-2000, Muncie Ctr. for the Arts, 1999-2001; mem. adv. coun. Coll. Fine Arts, Ball State U.; mem. adv. com., bookshop dir. Midwest Writers Workshop, 1976-77; sec. Del. County Coun. for the Arts, 1978-79, pres., 1979-81, bd. dirs., 1985-86; mem. pres.'s coun. Berea Coll.; bd. dirs. Muncie YWCA, 1977-82, 85-89, 95-2001, treas. 1981-82, 88-89; bd. dirs. ARC, Hoosier Heartland chpt.; bd. govs. Minnetrista Cultural Ctr.; gen. chmn. Ind. Renaissance Fair, 1978-79; pres. Muncie Matinee Musicale, 1965-67; past pres. Ind. Film and Video Coun.; mem. adv. bd. Cmty. Found. Muncie and Delaware County; bd. dirs. Wapehani coun. Girl Scouts U.S., 1989-96; bd. govs. Minnetrista Cultural Ctr., 1998-2001; mem. pres.'s coun. Berea Coll., 1984-2001. Named Woman Achievement Pub. Svc., 1986; recipient Sagamore of the Wabash award Gov. State of Ind., Outstanding Libr. award Ind. Libr. Fedn., 1995, Cert. of Congrl. Recognition, 1995, Cert. of Achievement, Women's Coalition, 1996, Cert. of Appreciation, Masterworks Chorale, 1998. Mem. ALA, Ind. Libr. Assn. (pres. 1987-88), Nat. League Am. Pen Women (pres. Muncie br. 1974-78), Altrusa (pres. 1986-87, cmty. svc. award 2000), Art Students League, Riley-Jones Club, Del. Country Club, Delta Zeta, Mu Phi Epsilon. Republican. Roman Catholic. Home: 5400 W Deer Run Ct Muncie IN 47304-5775 E-mail: patschaefer@mindspring.com.

SCHAEFER, PATRICIA ANN, retired librarian; b. Lebanon, Ohio, Jan. 22, 1933; d. Riley Ray and Louise Collette (Fraher) Freeze; m. William H. Schaefer, Aug. 11, 1956; childen: Susan P., Nancy A., William H. III (dec.). BS, Miami U., Oxford, Ohio, 1954. Med. technologist Mercy Hosp., Hamilton, Ohio, 1954-58, Middletown (Ohio) Hosp., 1958-62; libr. Middletown City Schs., 1979-93; intermediate libr. McKinley Sch., 1982-93; ret., 1993. Active YMCA, pres., 1977-79; bd. dirs. Middletown Symphony, 1974-78, Arts in Middletown, 1983—, Middletown Symphony Women, 1992—, mem. exec. bd., 1995—, co-chmn. Luncheon Style Show, 1998-2001; hon. bd. dirs. Am. Cancer Soc., 1961—; chmn. legis. City Charter Rev. Com., 1970, charter revision com., 1989; residential chmn. United Way, 1976, residential-retiree chmn., 1990; chmn. Sch. Tax Levy, 1978; mem. Middletown City Commn., 1983-88; mem. exec. com. Ohio-Ky.-Ind. Regional Coun., 1986-88; mem. Bicentennial Com., Middletown; mem. Citizen's Adv. Com. for Miami U.; pres. Middletown Needy Youth Bd.; mem. adv. bd. Manchester Tech. Ctr., Drug Task Force Bd., Middletown Schs.; bd. dirs. Citizens Adv. Bd. Manchester Tech., 1991—, Middletown Fine Arts, 1993—, Dental Emergency Fund Area Children, 1994—; mem. Leadership Middletown Exec. Bd., Adminstrv. Bd. Meth. Ch.; sec. bd. dirs. Care View Home Health Bd., 2000; sec. bd. trustees First United Meth. Ch., 1999—; mem. exec. bd. United Meth. Women; co-chmn. Mary Alice Mack City Golf Tournament, 1998. Recipient Stuart Ives Service to Youth award, 1980; named Outstanding Woman of Butler County, 1997, hon. chmn. 1998 Charity Ball, Woman of Distinction, Soroptomists Internat., 2000. Mem. LWV (pres. 1962-63), PEO (pres. 1995—, co-chair state conv. 1997), Am. Soc. Clin. Pathologists, Registry Med. Technologists, Am. Bus. Women's Assn. (pres. 1961-62, Middletown C. of C., Browns Run Country Club, Sigma Sigma Sigma. Methodist. Home: 1909 Antrim Ct Middletown OH 45042-2901

SCHAEFER, RHODA PESNER, elementary school educator; b. Bronx, N.Y., Mar. 15, 1947; d. Herman Pesner; m. Alan Jacob Schaefer, Sept. 23, 1967; children: Ira Marc, Melissa Anne. BA, Dominican Coll., Orangeburg, N.Y., 1980; MA in Edn., SUNY, New Paltz, 1987; MA in Supervision and Adminstrn., Coll. New Rochelle, 1999. Cert. tchr., N.Y. Tchg. asst. East Ramapo Ctrl. Sch. Dist., Spring Valley, NY, 1984—87, tchr., 1987—; supr., dist. adminstr. Elmwood Elem. Sch., Monsey, 2000—. Instr. East Ramapo Tchrs.' Ctr., 1988—, instrnl. facilitator, 2000—; adj. prof. L.I. U., 1989—, SUNY, New Paltz, 1994—, Coll. of New Rochelle, N.Y.; mem. Hudson Valley Portfolio Project, 1993-96. Pres., officer PTA, Spring Valley, 1972—. Mem. ASCD, Internat. Reading Assn., N.Y. Reading Assn., Rockland Reading Coun., N.Y. Assn. for Computers and Tech. Edn., Nat. Coun. English Tchrs., Nat. Coun. for Social Studies, Delta Kappa Gamma. Office: Elmwood Elem Sch Robert Pitt Dr Monsey NY 10952

SCHAEFER, ROBERT ANTHONY, internist, gastroenterologist, educator; b. N.Y.C., Mar. 1, 1939; s. George John Schaefer, Regina Marie Farrell; m. Mary Jeanne Kreek, Jan. 24, 1970; children: Robert A. Jr., Esperance A.K. AB, Yale U., 1959; MD, Columbia U., 1963. Diplomate Am. Bd. Internal Medicine with subspecialty in gastroenterology. Intern, resident Vanderbilt U. Hosp., Nashville, 1963—65; resident in internal medicine U. Vt., 1967—68, chief resident, 1968—69; fellow gastroenterology N.Y.C., 1969—71; asst. prof. medicine Cornell U., Ithaca, 1971—77, clin. assoc. prof. medicine, 1977—99, assoc. prof. clin. medicine, 1999—. Lt. comdr. USNR, 1965—67. Fellow: Am. Coll. Gastroenterology; mem.: Am. Assn. for Study of Liver Disease, Am. Gastroenterology Assn. Mailing: 1175 York Ave New York NY 10021 Office: Weill Med Coll of Cornelll Univ 520 E 70th St New York NY 10021

SCHAEFER, ROBERT JOSEPH, counselor; b. Montreal, Que., Can., June 5, 1959; came to U.S., 1963; naturalized, 1990; s. Andreé and Marianne Schaefer. BAE, Fla. Atlantic U., 1993; MS in Mental Health Counseling, Nova Southeastern U., 2001. Benefits adminstr., employment interviewer L.A. Airport Hilton & Towers Hotel, 1983-85; personnel mgr. Doral Hotel, Miami Beach, Fla., 1985-87; personnel asst. Eagle Nat. Bank Miami, 1987-88; hotel asst. mgr., asst. front office mgr. Hyatt Regency Miami, 1988-90; reading lab. asst. Broward C.C., Hollywood, Fla., 1990-94; rsch. asst. Fla. Atlantic U., Davie, 1992-93; tchr. Miramar (Fla.) H.S., 1993-96; peer counseling coord. Westpine Mid. Sch., Sunrise, Fla., 1996—. Coord. Students Against Destructive Decision Making, Sunrise, 1996—, Student Mentoring Program, Sunrise, 1999—. Democrat. Roman Catholic. Avocations: running, weight lifting, reading, traveling. Office: Deerfield Beach High Sch 910 SW 15th St Deerfield Beach FL 33441 E-mail: platogemini@earthlink.net.

SCHAEFER, ROBERT KARL, research scientist; b. Abington, Pa., Nov. 17, 1955; s. Frank Adolf and Dorothy Marie Schaefer. BS in Physics cum laude, Wilkes Coll., 1977; MS in Physics, U. Del., 1980; PhD in Physics, Brandeis Univ., 1985. NRC rsch. fellow NASA/Goddard Space Flight Ctr., Greenbelt, Md., 1985-87; rsch. assoc. physics dept. Ohio State U., Columbus, 1987-89; rsch. scientist Bartol Rsch. Inst., Newark, 1989-97, Raytheon ITSS, Goddard Space Flight Ctr., Greenbelt, Md., 1998—. Contbr. articles to profl. jours. Mem. Am. Phys. Soc. Achievements include pioneering work on the cold plus hot dark matter model of galaxy formation; developed mathematical formalism for studying small density fluctuations in the early universe; invention of new techniques for choosing observing strategies and analysing data in cosmic microwave anisotropy experiments. Office: Code 664 Goddard Space Flight Ctr Greenbelt MD 20771-0001

SCHAEFER, ROBERT PAUL, software engineer; b. White Plains, N.Y., Oct. 7, 1958; s. William Paul and Dorothy (Herman) S.; m. Sheila Ann Birchander, Dec. 5, 1985; children: Gabrielle, Benjamin. BSEE, Clarkson Coll., Postdam, N.Y., 1980; BS, Boston U., 2002. Engr. Western Electric, North Andover, Mass., 1980-81; test engr. Burroughs, Piscataway, N.J., 1981-82; software engr. Lockheed Sanders, Nashua, N.H., 1982-2000, BAE Sys., 2000—. Instr. dept. computer sci. Daniel Webster Coll., Nashua, N.J., 1995—; software mgr. HF Surface Wave Radar, 1996; mem. Integration and Test Team, F22, 1997; mem. Integration and Test Team Common Missile Warning Sys., 1999. Author: (software) 45F/67 Built-In Test, 1985, LASCO Experiment, 1990; team leader (software) Star-MVP Processor, 1987, Microlook Cell Phone Geolocation, 1995. Mem. IEEE. E-mail: robert.p.schaefer@baesystems.com.

SCHAEFER, ROBERT WAYNE, banker; b. Balt., Feb. 28, 1934; s. Roland Elmer and Lillian (Reid) S.; m. Elaine Lennon, May 18, 1963; children: Linda, Karen. Student, Balt. City Coll., 1949-51; BS in Acctg., U. Balt., 1955; MBA in Fin., Loyola Coll., 1971. C.P.A., Md. With First Nat. Bank of Md., Balt., 1951-55, 59—, comptroller, 1961—, v.p., 1965-69, sr. v.p., 1969-73, exec. v.p., 1973-96; exec. dir. France-Merrick Founds., Balt., 1996—. Instr. accounting N.C. State Coll., 1956-58; instr. accounting, econs., taxes, credit Balt. chpt. Am. Inst. Banking, 1960-66, Investment Com. State of Md. Retirement System and Baltimore Fire, Police Retirement System. Mem. Balt. City Sch. Bd., 1973-75, Balt. City Bd. Fin.; bd. dirs., treas. Balt. Area United Fund, 1964-79; past bd. dirs. Balt. coun. Boy Scouts Am., Balt. chpt. ARC, Boys Latin Sch.; trustee, pres. Wesley Home for Aged; bd. dirs. Balt. City Aquarium, Roland Park Country Sch., Md. Gen. Hosp., Western Md. Coll., 1981-92, Lyric Theatre, 1985—, Enoch Pratt Libr., 1986-93, Ind. Coll. Fund Md., 1990—, Coun. on Econ. Edn., YMCA Ctrl. Md., 1992, U. Balt. 1st lt. USMCR, 1956-58. Mem.: Fin. Execs. Inst., Md. CPA Assn., Bank Adminstrn. Inst. (past pres., bd. dirs. Balt. chpt.), U. Balt. Found., U. Balt. Alumni Assn. (bd. dirs. 1972—), L'Hirondelle Club, Valley Country Club. Republican. Methodist (bd. dirs., mem. finance com.). Home: 5903 Meadowood Rd Baltimore MD 21212-2436 Office: France-Merrick Foundations 1122 Kenilworth Dr Ste 118 Baltimore MD 21204-2142 E-mail: rschaefer@france-merrickfdn.org.

SCHAEFER, STEVEN DAVID, head and neck surgeon, physiologist; b. L.A., Mar. 25, 1945; s. Glen Arthur and Alice (Malerstein) S.; m. Phyllis Lois Clark, July 1, 1977; 1 child, Jessica Leigh. BA, U. Calif., Berkeley, 1967; MD, U. Calif., Irvine, 1972. Diplomate Am. Bd. Otolarnyology. Asst. prof. U. Tex. Southwestern and U. Tex. Dallas, 1972-82, assoc. prof., 1982-86, prof., 1986-92; prof, dept. chmn. N.Y. Med. Coll., N.Y.C., 1992—, N.Y. Eye and Ear Infirmary, N.Y.C., 1992—. Author 4 books and 7 monographs; contbr. over 160 articles and abstracts to med. jours., chpts. to books. Dir. pub. edn. Tex. div., Am. Cancer Soc., Dallas, 1978-80. Named prin. investigator NIH, 1980-94. Fellow Am. Laryngol. Assn., Am. Acad. Otolaryngology (Honor award 1990), Am. Laryngol. Rhinol. and Otol. Soc.; mem. N.Y. Acad. Sci., Soc. Univ. Otolaryngologists (pres. 1992-93), NIH Divsn. Rsch. Grants. Office: NY Eye & Ear Infirmary 310 E 14th St New York NY 10003-4201

SCHAEFER, STEVEN J. lawyer; b. Watertown, Wis., July 21, 1951; m. Jacqueline Schaefer; 1 child Claire. BA in Econs., U. Wis., Madison, 1973; JD cum laude, U. Wis., 1977; MBA, Edgewood Coll., Madison, Wis., 1997. Bar: Wis. 1977, U.S. Dist. Ct. (we. dist.) Wis. 1977, U.S. Supreme Ct. 1980, U.S. Ct. Appeals (7th cir.) 1984. Assoc. Jacobs, Schacht & Olson, Beaver Dam, Wis., 1977—80; clk. U.S. Ho. Reps. Hon. Les Aspin, Washington, 1980; assoc. Thomas, Parsons, Schaefer & Bauman, S.C., Madison, Wis., 1981—84, Fox Law Offices, Madison, 1984—85, Fox, Fox, Schaefer & Gingras, S.C., Madison, 1985—90; ptnr. Gingras & Schaefer, S.C., 1990—92; pvt. practice, 1992—. Instr. Am. Inst. for Paralegal Studies, 1993—94, Coun. on Edn. in Mgmt., 1993—97, Edgewood Coll., 1998—, Undergrad. Bus. Program, 2000—; asst. city atty., Beaver Dam, 1977—80, Fox Lake, Wis., 1977—80. Mem. parks commn. City of Madison, 1981—86, mem. planning commn., 1982—85; mem. nursing bd. State of Wis., 1983—85; mem. R2 Zoning Code Adv. Com. City of Madison, 1997—99; bd. dirs. Univ. Ave. Daycare Ctr., Inc., Madison, 1987—88, Mendota Rowing club, Inc., Madison, 1999—2000, Wingra Rowing Regatta, Inc., Camp Randall Rowing Club, Inc. Mem.: ATLA, ABA, Dane County Bar Assn., Wis. Acad. Trial Lawyers, State Bar Wis. Home: PO Box 259206 Madison WI 53725-9206

SCHAEFER, SUSAN G. lawyer; b. Chgo., Feb. 15; d. Oscar and Sally Schaefer. BA and JD, UCLA. Rsch. atty. Superior Ct., L.A., 1968-71; atty. MCA, Inc. and Universal Studios, Universal City, Calif., 1971-73; bus. affairs exec. William Morris Agy., Beverly Hills, 1975-81; ptnr., head entertainment law dept. Hufstedler, Miller, Carlson & Beardsley, L.A., 1981-84; v.p. bus. and legal affairs Telepictures Prodns., Inc., 1984-86; prin. Law Offices of Susan G. Schaefer, Beverly Hills, Calif., 1984—. Author publs. Representing TV Writers: How to Negotiate a TV Movie Deal, 1991, Representation in the Entertainment Industry, 1992, L.A. Superior Ct. Writs and Receivers Policy and Procedural Manual, 1971; mem. adv. editorial bd. Entertainment Law Jour., 1981, 82. Named one of 50 most powerful female execs. Hollywood Reporter, 1994. Mem. Acad. TV Arts and Scis., Women in Film (bd. dirs. 1988-90), Los Angeles County Bar Assn. (chair intellectual property and entertainment law sect. 1982-83, trustee 1989-90), Century City Bar Assn. (pres. 1988, chair entertainment law sect. 1980-81, Governor's and Chairperson's award 1981, Spl. Achievement award 1982, Outstanding Svc. award 1989, bd. govs. 1981-91), Fin. and Adminstrv. Mgmt. Execs. in Entertainment (F.A.M.E.)(bd. dirs. 1994-96), Century City C. of C. (bd. dirs. 1988, Law Outstanding Achievement award 1990). Avocation: tennis. Office: 9601 Wilshire Blvd Ste 850 Beverly Hills CA 90210-5213

SCHAEFER, THEODORE PETER, chemistry educator, retired; b. Gnadenthal, Man., Can., July 22, 1933; s. Paul Jacob and Margarethe (Wiebe) S.; m. Nicola Caroline Sewell, Dec. 26, 1960; children: Catherine, Dominic, Benjamin. BS with Honors, U. Man., 1954, MS, 1955; D.Phil. (Shell scholar), Oxford (Eng.) U., 1958; D.Sc. (hon. causa), U. Winnipeg, 1982. Prof. chemistry U. Manitoba, Winnipeg, Can., 1958—, Univ. Disting. prof. Can., 1982-97, sr. scholar Can., 1997-2000, ret. Can., 2000; researcher NRC, Ottawa, Can., 1959, 62, Nat. Phys. Lab., Teddington, U.K., 1960, 65, Argonne Nat. Lab., Chgo., 1967, 68; sr. fellow, mem. grants com. NRC, Ottawa.; mem. council Nat. Scis. and Engring. Research Council, 1980-85. Contbr. articles on nuclear magnetic resonance to sci. jours. Recipient Herzberg award Spectroscopy Soc. Can., 1975. Fellow Chem. Inst. Can. (Noranda award 1973), Royal Soc. Can. Home: 210 Oak St Winnipeg MB Canada R3M 3R4 *Persistence can sometimes emulate perspicacity.*

SCHAEFER, WILLIAM DAVID, English language educator; b. Dighton, Mass., May 11, 1928; s. Louis and Elsie K. (Otterbein) S.; m. Josephine R. Lamprecht, Aug. 8, 1958; 1 dau., Kimberly. BA, NYU, 1957; MS, U. Wis., 1958, PhD, 1962. Mem. faculty UCLA, 1962-90, prof. English, 1970-90, chmn. dept., 1969-71, exec. vice chancellor, 1978-87. Author: James (BV) Thomson: Beyond the City, 1965, Speedy Extinction of Evil and Misery, 1967, Education Without Compromise: From Chaos to Coherence in Higher Education, 1990; contbr. articles to profl. jours., short stories to literary mags. Served with AUS, 1954-56. Fulbright fellow Eng., 1961-62 Mem. MLA (exec. dir. 1971-78). Home: 164 Stagecoach Rd Bell Canyon CA 91307-1044 Office: UCLA 405 Hilgard Ave Los Angeles CA 90095-9000 E-mail: wschae444@aol.com.

SCHAEFER, WILLIAM GOERMAN, lawyer; b. Kansas City, Mo., June 16, 1941; m. Sharon Saylor, Dec. 21, 1963; children: James, Kristen. BA, U. Kans., 1963; JD, Harvard U., 1966. Bar: Ill. 1966, D.C. 1978, Md. 1984. Ptnr. Sidley & Austin, Chgo. and Washington, 1966-74, 78-93; v.p., gen. counsel DeKalb Genetics Corp., Ill., 1974-77; spl. counsel Bechel Corp., Gaithersburg, Md., 1993-96; sr. v.p. corporate affairs Vertis, Inc., Balt., 1996-2000; cons., 2000—.

SCHAEFFER, ARTHUR CLYDE, television producer; b. Buffalo, June 8, 1928; s. Albert and Emma Ida (Kagelmacher) S.; m. Lucille Joan Jesall, June 13, 1953; children: Kim Hughes, Tracy L. Paladino, Darcy A. Zekas, Lisa J. Schaeffer. BA, U. Buffalo, 1953; MA, U. Calif. at San Diego, 1972. Producer, dir. WGR TV, Buffalo, 1961-65; exec. dir. KEBS Radio San Diego State U., 1965-66; adj. assoc. prof. Broadcasting Journalism Speech Dept., Buffalo, 1977-85; TV producer, dir. Buffalo State Coll., 1966—. Cons. in field. Producer, dir. TV play Dodo Bird, 1976, TV prodn. Now That My World Is Small, 1981; producer, dir. TV documentary including Play It Again Doc: Riviera Theatre, 1983, Buffalo Subway Series, 1983-85, Allentown Industries Employer of Handicapped, 1983, Visit To The Buffalo Zoo, 1983, Buffalo-150 Years Plus, 1983, Broadway Market, 1984. V.p., pres. NABET, Buffalo, 1961-63, United Univ. Professions, Buffalo, 1972-73; dist. chmn. Am. Field Svc., Western, N.Y., 1973-75. Cpl. USMC, 1946-51. Recipient 1st Pl. award Assn. Cinematic and Video Arts, 1990, Grant Alleged Offenders Program, 1988-89, Blue Pencil award Fed. Editors Assn., 1972, 1st Pl. award Regent Adv. Coun., 1976-79. Mem. United Univ. Professions (v.p. 1972-73), Phi Delta Kappa, AFT-CIO, Am. Legion, N.Y. State United Tchrs. Lutheran. Avocations: golf, white water rafting, travel, swimming, hiking, reading. Home: 116 Sunset Ter Tonawanda NY 14150-5560 Office: SUNY at Buffalo 1300 Elmwood Ave Buffalo NY 14222-1004

SCHAEFFER, BARBARA HAMILTON, retired rental leasing company executive, writer; b. Newton, Mass., Apr. 26, 1926; d. Peter Davidson Gunn and Harriet Bennett (Thompson) Hamilton; m. John Schaeffer, Sept. 7, 1946; children: Laurie, John, Peter. *Great-grandfather, Thomas Bennett, was an organist in St. Paul's Cathedral, London. Great-grandmother Bennett, founded and headed a dame's school in London. Grand-uncle, John Hamilton, left Wick, Scotland to become the first man to drive a herd of sheep over the Andes. He owned two-thirds of the Faulkland Islands. Father, Peter Davidson Gunn Hamilton, designed harbors, bridges and docks on four continents. Educated at Harvard, he is a past president of the American Society of Civil Engineers, and a contributor to the Encyclopedia Britannica. Mother, Harriet Bennett Hamilton, was a beloved elementary school teacher in Vermont, Massachusetts, New Jersey, and Guam.* Student, Skidmore Coll., 1943-46; AB in English, Bucknell U., 1948; postgrad., Montclair State U., 1950-51, Bank St. Coll. Edn., 1959-61, Yeshiva U., 1961-62. Cert. primary, secondary tchr. N.J. Dir. Pompton Plains Sch., N.J., 1959-62; adviser Episcopal Sch., Towaco, 1968-70; v.p. Deltona-DeLand Trolley, Orange City, Fla., 1980-81; pres. Monroe Heavy Equipment Rentals, Inc., 1981—; also Magic Carpet Travel, 1985-88. Cons., founder, pres. TLC Travel Club, Orange City, 1981-88; lectr. on children's art, 1959-70. Contbr. articles to profl. pubs. Mem. Small Bus. Devel. Regional Ctr. (Stetson U. chpt.), Nat. Trust Historic Preservation. Episcopalian. Avocations: restoring old homes, oil painting, piano, writing. Home: 400 Foothill Farms Rd Orange City FL 32763-5502

SCHAEFFER, CHARLES PERRY, newswriter, editor; b. Cumberland, Md., Mar. 20, 1926; s. Charles Perry and Dorothy Frances Schaeffer; m. Eliza Ann Riggins, June 16, 1950; children: Sally Ann Canepa, John, Jennifer Bartell. BA, U. Md., 1950. Writer U.S. Info. Agy., Washington, 1950—53; news picture writer UPI, N.Y.C., 1953—54; reporter Balt. Evening Sun, Balt., 1954—55, Am. Aviation Publs., 1955—61; science writer Newhouse Newspapers, Washington, 1961—65; writer, exec. editor Kiplinger Personal Fin. Mag. (formerly Changing Times) Kiplinger Washington Editors, Inc, 1966—89. Mem. profit sharing bd. Kiplinger Washington Editors. Author: (anthology) Esquire's World of Humor, 1964, Saturday Review's Phoenix Nest, 1965; contbr. articles to mags. Chmn. scout troop Walter Reed Army Med. Ctr., Silver Spring, Md., 1971—72; pres neighborhood Civic Assn., 1963—64; bd. dirs. Woodlin Elem. Sch., 1963—64. EM 3/C U.S. Navy, 1943—46, Pacific Theater of Operations. Decorated Phillippine Liberation Ribbon, 2 Stars USN, Pacific Theater Ribbon, Six Stars, Victory medal; recipient Blakeslee Nat. Sci. Writing award, Am. Heart Assn., 1965. Mem.: Soc. Profl. Journalists, Nat. Assn. Sci. Writers (life), Nat. Press Club (1st pl. consumer journalism 1987). Home: 6036 Chatsworth Ln Bethesda MD 20814 E-mail: schaeffer528@cs.com.

SCHAEFFER, LEONARD DAVID, healthcare executive; b. Chgo., July 28, 1945; s. David and Sarah (Levin) Schaeffer; m. Pamela Lee Sidford, Aug. 11, 1968; children: David, Jacqueline. BA, Princeton U., 1969. Mgmt. cons. Arthur Andersen & Co., 1969—73; dep. dir. mgmt. Ill. Mental Health/Devel. Disability, Springfield, 1973—75; dir. Ill. Bur. of Budget, 1975—76; v.p. Citibank, N.A., N.Y.C., 1976—78; asst. sec. mgmt. and budget HHS, Washington, 1978, adminstr. HCFA, 1978—80; exec. v.p., COO Student Loan Mktg. Assn., 1980—82; pres., CEO Group Health, Inc., Mpls., 1983—86;

chmn., CEO Blue Cross of Calif., Woodland Hills, 1986—96, WellPoint Health Networks Inc., 1992—. Bd. dir. Allergan, Inc., Irvine, Calif.; bd. councilors U. So. Calif. Sch. Policy, Planning & Devel., 1988—; bd. dir. exec. com. Blue Cross-Blue Shield Assn., Chgo., 1986—; mem. Congl. Prospective Payment Assessment Commn., 1987—93; mem. Pew Health Professions Com., Phila., 1990—93; chmn. bd. trustees Nat. Health Found., LA, 1992—2001; chmn. bd. dir. Nat. Health Care Mgmt., 1993—; mem. Coun. on the Econ. Impact of Health Sys. Change, 1996—; co-chair adv. coun. dept. of health care policy Harvard Med. Sch., 1998—; founding chmn. Coalition for Affordable and Quality Healthcare, 2000; bd. dirs. Allergan, Inc., Irvine, Calif.; bd. councilors U. So. Calif. Sch. Policy, Planning and Devel., 1988—; bd. dirs., exec. com. Blue Cross-Blue Shield Assn., Chgo., 1986—; mem. Congl. Prospective Payment Assessment Commn., 1987—93, Pew Health Professions Com., Phila., 1990—93; chmn. bd. trustees Nat. Health Found., L.A., 1992—2001; chmn. bd. dirs. Nat. Health Care Mgmt., 1993—; mem. Coun. on the Econ. Impact of Health Sys. Change, 1996—; co-chair adv. coun. dept. health care policy Harvard Med. Sch., 1998—; founding chmn. Coalition for Affordable and Quality Healthcare, 2000. Bd. gov. Town Hall of Calif., LA, 1989; bd. trustees The Brookings Inst., Nat. Health Mus., 2000—; bd. govs. Town Hall of Calif., L.A., 1989; bd. trustees The Brookings Inst., Nat. Health Mus., 2000—. Recipient Citation for Outstanding Svc., Am. Acad. Pediats., 1981, Disting. Pub. Svc. award, HEW, Washington, 1980; fellow, Kellogg Found., 1981—89, Internat. fellow, King's Fund Coll., London, 1990—. Mem.: Health Ins. Assn. Am. (chmn. 1999), Inst. of Medicine of NAS, Regency Club, Princeton Club, Cosmos Club. Office: Wellpoint Health Networks Inc 1 Wellpoint Way Thousand Oaks CA 91362-3893*

SCHAEFFER, PETER (PETER VIKTOR SCHAEFFER), urban and regional planning educator; b. Zurich, Switzerland, Aug. 26, 1949; s. Victor and Catharina M. (Sciuchetti) S.; m. Patricia Marie Dresler, June 1, 1976; 1 child, Joseph Victor. Licencitate in Econ., U. Zurich, 1975; MA in Econs., U. So. Calif., 1979, PhD in Econs., 1981. Asst. prof. urban and regional planning U. Ill., Urbana, 1981-88; assoc. prof. U. Colo., Denver, 1987-93, dir. urban and regional planning, 1988-93; prof., dir. divsn. resource mgmt. W.Va. U., Morgantown, 1993—. Vis. prof. Swiss Federal Inst. of Technology, Zurich, 1999-2000. Mem. editl. bd. Jour. Planning Edn. and Rsch., 1989—, Internat. Regional Sci. Rev., Jour. Planning Lit., 1996—; contbr. chpts. to books, articles to profl. jours. and books. Plan commr. City of Urbana, 1984-87; bd. dirs. Internat. Ctr. for Tourism Planning and Design, Denver, 1993-96; bd. dirs. Lightstone Found., Moyers, W.Va., 1995—, pres., 1997—. Mem. Am. Econ. Assn., Regional Sci. Assn. (treas. 1987-97), Am. Agrl. Econ. Assn., Labor Economists. Avocations: literature, history, hiking. Office: W Va U Div Resource Mgmt PO Box 6108 Morgantown WV 26506-6108 E-mail: Peter.Schaeffer@mail.wvu.edu.

SCHAEFFER, PETER NEAL, investment banking executive; b. Newark, Sept. 19, 1951; s. Jerome J. S. and Rosalind Susskind; m. Elisabeth Sue Harris, May 2, 1982; children: Justin Harris, Molly Rebecca. BS in Bus. Adminstrn. and Mktg., Drexel U., 1974. Merchandise v.p. R.H. Macy & Co., Inc., Newark, 1974-85; regional v.p. Bloomingdale's Divsn. Federated Dept. Stores, N.Y.C., 1985-90; exec. v.p. Steinbach's Divsn. Am. Retail Group, White Plains, N.Y., 1990-92; ptnr., assoc. dir. Johnson Redbook, N.Y.C., 1992-93; sr. v.p. Warburg Dillon Read, 1993-98; v.p. equity rsch. Donaldson, Lufkin & Jenrette, 1998-2000; mng. dir. Ernst & Young Corp. Fin., 2000—. Founder Essex Fells (N.J.) Edn. Found., 1994. Recipient N.Y. Doers award Dewars Scotch, 1990. Mem. Retail Analysts Group, Fells Brook Club (Essex Fells, N.J.). Jewish. Home: 1 Hillbury Rd Essex Fells NJ 07021-1405 Office: Ernst & Young 5 Times Sq New York NY 10036 E-mail: peter.schaeffer@eycf.com.

SCHAEFFER, REINER HORST, military officer, foreign language professional; b. Berlin, Fed. Republic Germany, Jan. 13, 1938; arrived in U.S., 1958; s. Immanuel Emil and Wilhelmine (Fahrni) Frei-Schaeffer; m. Cathy Anne Cormack, Apr. 6, 1966; 1 child Brian Reiner. Nat. cert., Bus. Sch., Thun, Switzerland, 1957; BGS in Bus., U. Nebr., 1970; MPA in Orgnl. Behavior, U. Mo., 1972; PhD in Fgn. Lang. Edn., Ohio State U., 1979. Commd. officer USAF, 1958, advanced through grades to lt. col.; instr. German, French USAF Acad., Colorado Springs, Colo., 1975-77, assoc. prof., 1979-81, chmn. German, 1981, dir. librs., 1982-86, prof., 1986-92, dir. Acad. Librs., 1986-92. Bd. dirs. Friends of AF Acad. Librs.; pres. Fgn. Lang. Ctr., Inc., 1999—2001; cons. Fgn. Langs., 2001—. Named Disting. Grad., Air Force Inst. Tech., 1979; recipient 5 Meritorious Svc. medals, 5 Air Force Commendation medals. Mem.: Am. Assn. Tchrs. German, Swiss Club (pres. Colorado Springs chpt. 1990—96, chmn.), Alpha Sigma Alpha, Pi Alpha Alpha. Republican. Avocation: Avocations: skiing, golfing, hiking, soccer. Home: 751 Babbling Brook Prescott AZ 86303 E-mail: swiss13@juno.com.

SCHAEFFER, ROBERT ALLEN, strategic communications consultant, educator, writer; b. Boston, Aug. 15, 1947; s. Daniel Monroe and Jean Doris (Gartenberg) S.; m. Elaine Christine Coughlin, Sept. 5, 1971; 1 child, Dario James. Student, MIT, 1965-69, 74-75. Asst. to pres. Royalton Coll., South Royalton, Vt., 1966, 67; rsch. asst. Publs. and Info. Ctr. Peace Corps, Washington, 1968; spl. asst. to v.p. MIT, Cambridge, Mass., 1969, instr. Edn. Rsch. Ctr., 1969-71; field sec. Mass. Polit. Action for Peace (MassPAX), 1971-72; organizer, lobbyist Citizens for Participation in Polit. Action (CP-PAX), Boston, 1972-77; legis. aide Sen. Jack H. Backman Mass. State Senate, 1978-84; rsch. dir. Joint Comm. on Human Svcs. and Elderly Affairs Mass. Gen. Ct., 1982-84; editorial writer Sta. WBZ-TV, Boston, 1984; cons., trainer, writer Pub. Policy Comms., Belmont, Mass., 1969-99, Sanibel, Fla., 1999—. Cons. ECIS, Cambridge, Mass., 1970-72, Tides Ctr. Project for Participatory Democracy, San Francisco, 1989—; mem. adj. faculty Antioch New Eng. Grad. Sch., Keene, N.H., 1987-93; trainer Ploughshares Fund, San Francisco, 1990-93; treas. Nat. Ctr. for Fair and Open Testing, Cambridge, Mass., 1985—. Author: (with J. Weiss and Barbara Beckwith) Standing Up to the SAT, 1989, (with Ann Beaudry) Winning Local and State Elections, 1986, (with Rochelle Lefkowitz) Community Jobs, 1981, Giving the Media Our Message, 1981, (with Barbara Beelar and Dick Cluster) Life After 2 1/2: Strategies to Fight Fiscal Chaos, 1981, (with others) Who Rules Boston, 1984, The Public Money Manager's Handbook, 1981, New Directions in Public Policy, 1977; co-editor: Developing the Public Economy, 1980; contbr. articles to profl. jours. Dir. Mass. Human Svc. Coalition, Boston, 1985-99, Ctr. for Social Justice, Boston, 1991-99, CPPAX Edn. Fund, Boston, 1985-91, 93-99; bd. dirs. Mass. Freeze, 1986-87; mem. pub. rels. adv. com. Mass. Office for Children, 1984-86; mem. exec. com. Mass. Freeze Voter, 1984-90; mem. media task force Mass. Nuclear Freeze Com., 1984-85; mem. community and social svc. task force Mayor Flynn Transition Team, 1983; mem. steering com. Mass. Citizens Caucus, 1972-74; mem. city budget task force Mel King for Mayor, 1983; mem. employment task force Mike Dukakis for Gov., 1982; mem. fin. com. Barney Frank for Congress, 1981-83; mem. referendum steering com. Citizens for Pub. Schs., 1982; mem. exec. com. Mass. Citizens Against the Death Penalty, 1981-86; mem. adv. bd. Civil Liberties Union Mass., 1981-83; bd. dirs. Policy Tng. Ctr., Inc., 1980-83; mem. adv. bd. Handicapped Constnl. Amendment, 1980; mem. exec. bd. Citizens for Participation in Polit. Action, 1978-87, budget dir., 1980-83; mem. nat. exec. bd. New Dem. Coalition, 1978-80; treas. Citizens Campaign for Open Legis., 1976-78; mem. planning com. Paul Guzzi for State Sec., 1974; regional dir. Movement for New Congress, 1970; campus coord. Boston area Vietnam Moratorium Com., 1970; mem. mgmt. bd. Back from the Brink De-alerting Campaign, 1999; treas. Seagate Homeowners Assn., 2001—. Recipient Book of Yr. award for teenagers, N.Y. Pub. Libr., 1989; Assoc. Univs. Inc. Trustees scholar, 1965-69. Democrat. Avocation: gardening. E-mail: bobschaeffer@earthlink.net.

SCHAEFFER-YOUNG, JUDITH, library director; b. York, Pa., Aug. 26, 1944; d. Robert Jackson and Helen Josephine (Chiappy) Schatz; m. Karl Schaeffer, Jan. 28, 1967 (div. Sept. 1981); children: Stephen Matthew, Elizabeth Chatten; m. Harrison H. Young Jr., Dec. 29, 1990. BA, Barnard Coll., 1966; MLS, Columbia U., 1968. part-time reference libr. Hewlett-Woodmere Pub. Libr., Hewlett, 1971-78; part-time reference libr. Chestnut Hill Hosp. Sch. Nursing, Phila., 1981-85; interim reference libr. Pa. State U., Abington, 1986. Editor std. catalog dept. H.W. Wilson Co., Bronx, N.Y., 1968-69; cataloger Hewlett-Woodmere (N.Y.) Pub. Libr., 1970-71, Merrick (N.Y.) Pub. Libr., 1972-78; sr. sch. libr. Chestnut Hill Acad., Phila., 1978-81; mgr. tech. svcs. Med. Coll. of Pa., 1981-83; libr. Sch. Nursing Albert Einstein Med. Ctr., 1983-86; coord. rsch. alerts Inst. for Sci. Info., 1986-89, mgr. editorial svcs., 1989-91; dir. med. libr. Wills Eye Hosp., 1991—. Cataloger St. Paul's Episcopal Ch., Phila., 1985—. Author: Index to Song Collections in the Hewlett-Woodmere Pub. Libr., 1974; contbr. articles to profl. jours. Bd. dirs. Friends of Glenside (Pa.) Libr., 1992—; mem. libr. com. St. Paul's Ch., Chestnut Hill, Pa., 1985—. Mem. Med. Libr. Assn., Acad. Health Info. Profls., Assn. Vision Sci. Librs. (sec.1996-97, chmn. 1998-99, treas. 2000—). Home: 529 Custis Rd Glenside PA 19038-2011 Office: Wills Eye Hosp 900 Walnut St Philadelphia PA 19107-5599 E-mail: young@hslc.org.

SCHAEFGEN, PHILIP P. business owner, insurance agent, real estate broker, consultant, certified public accountant; b. Memphis, Feb. 1, 1958; s. Harold W. Sr. and Gertrude S. BA, Memphis State U., 1980, postgrad., 1987; cert. in computers, State Tech. U., 1981. CPA, Tenn.; cert. tax preparer. Acct. Lewis Jones, CPAs, Memphis, 1976-77, Kenneth Miller, CPAs, Memphis, 1977-78; mng. ptnr. P.S. Enterprises, 1978-79; mgr. The Escapade, 1978-79; with Fed. Express Corp., 1980-95, sr. acct., 1983-85, sr. investment and security analyst, 1986-95; mng. ptnr. Schaefgen & Assocs., CPAs, 1980—; gen. ptnr. Schaefgen Investments, 1989—; owner Soft Source Sys., 1989—; contr. Tiger Internat. Ins. Ltd., 1993-94, v.p., 1993-95, sr. v.p., 1995—; pres. Perfect Green Landscaping, Inc., 1993-95; pres., CEO P. Schaefgen & Assocs., PC, 1995—; pres. SoftSource, Inc., 1997—; CEO, bd. dirs. Best Mortgage Inc., 1998; pres., CEO, bd. dirs. Small Bus. Solutions, Inc., 1999—. Bd. dirs. SoftSource, Inc., P. Schaefgen & Assocs. PC, Dock & Door Tech. Inc., Best Mortgage, Inc., Shelby County Soccer Complex, Inc.; v.p., treas., bd. dirs. adv. com. Shelby State C.C., Memphis; adj. lectr. U. Memphis. Contbr. articles to corp. newspaper. Active Suicide Prevention Ctr., Memphis 1976, Nat. Rep. Com.; pres. East Memphis Soccer Assn., 1995—; chmn. Tenn. Employers for Traffic Safety; treas. Shelby County Soccer Complex, Inc. Mem. AICPA, Soc. CPAs (tax divsn.), Nat. Soc. Tax Profls., Tenn. Assn. Pub. Accts., Tenn. Soc. CPAs, Jaycees (v.p. Memphis chpt. 1989—, bd. dirs. 1988, v.p. of month 1989, dir. of quarter 1988), KC (treas. Memphis chpt. 1984-92), Porsche Club Am. Republican. Roman Catholic. Avocations: golf, computers, investments. Home: PO Box 770235 Memphis TN 38177-0235

SCHAER, GARY STEVEN, account executive; b. Phila., Sept. 11, 1951; s. Gerald Bruce and Ethel Nesa S.; m. Donna J. Schaer, June 15, 1975; children: Jonathan Hillel, Jessica Rachel Kyla, Emanuelle Ruth. BA, Am. U., 1973. Accredited asset mgmt. specialist. Dir. univ. svcs. Am. Zionist Youth Found., N.Y.C., 1974-81; exec. dir. Am. Sephardi Fed., 1981-84; account exec. Shearson-Lehman, Short Hills, N.J., 1984-88; pension cons. Provident Mut., N.Y.C., 1988-92; v.p., account exec. Oppenheimer & Co., 1992-95, Gruntal & Co., LLC, N.Y.C., 1995—. Coun. pres., City of Passaic, N.J., 1995—; commr. Passaic County Vo-Tech., Wayne, N.J., 1999; trustee St. Mary's Hosp., Passaic, 1994—; commn. Passaic Housing Authority, 1991-95; pres. Hillel Acad., 1985-86, Chevra Kaoisha, chmn. 1987-88; co-chmn. Jewish Fedn. Super Sunday, 1986. Republican. Jewish. Office: Ryan Beck LLC 650 Madison Ave 10th Fl New York NY 10022 E-mail: schaerg@aol.com.

SCHAER, TERESA MCKINLEY, internist, geriatrician; b. L.A., Jan. 26, 1953; d. James B. and Pauline (Weimert) McKinley; m. David Harold Schaer, May 8, 1983 (div.); children: Daniel, Andrew. Student, Gonzaga U., Spokane, Washington, 1971-73; BS, U. Calif. San Diego, 1976, MD, 1981. Diplomate Am. Bd. Internal Medicine, Nat. Bd. Med. Examiners, Am. Bd. Geriatric Medicine. Intern, resident in internal medicine NYU Med. Ctr. Bellevue Hosp., N.Y.C., 1981-84; fellow in geriatric medicine George Washington U. Med. Ctr., Washington, 1984-86; chief divsn. geriatrics and med. dir. geriatric programs St. Peter's U. Hosp., New Brunswick, NJ, 1987—. Rsch. asst. biochemistry lab. U. Calif. San Diego, 1976-77, clin. assoc. prof. Robert Wood Johnson Med. Sch., Piscataway, N.J., 1988—; past mem. pub. and profl. edn. task force N.J. Bioethics Commn.; mem. ethics adv. com. Office of Ombudsman for Institutionalized Elderly; bd. trustees McCarrick Care Ctr., N.J. Health Decisions; ethics com., ethics policy subcom. chairperson ethics subcom. edn., ethics case review com., med. staff health com.; presenter, lectr. in field. Author: Psychiatric Care in the Nursing Home, 1996; contbr. articles to profl. publs. Vol., developer Hospice of San Diego, 1976-77. Fellow: ACP; mem.: AMA, N.J. Hosp. Assn. (coun. hosp. ops. bioethics com.), N.J. Med. Dirs. Assn. (pres.), Am. Med. Dirs. Assn., Gerontol. Soc. Am., N.J. Geriatric Soc., Am. Geriatric Soc., Med. Soc. N.J. (biomed. ethics com.). Avocations: reading, golfing, tennis. Office: St Peters Univ Hosp 254 Easton Ave New Brunswick NJ 08901-1766

SCHAER, WERNER, computer services executive; b. Olten, Switzerland, Sept. 23, 1940; came to U.S., 1966. s. Friedrich and Erna Helen (Kreuzberger) S.; m. Marisa Casseres, Dec. 20, 1965; children: Sara Elaine, William Ernest. Diplom in Elec. Engring., Fed. Inst. Tech., Zurich, Switzerland, 1962; MBA, Pepperdine U., 1975. Systems analyst Sperry Rand, Zurich, Geneva, Phila., Washington, 1963-66; dir., v.p. devel. Computer Sci. Corp. Infonet, El Segundo, Calif., 1969-77; pres. Computer Scis. Corp. Europe, S.Am., Brussels, 1978-82; sr. v.p. Computer Scis. Corp. Systems Div., Falls Church, Va., 1983-86; pres. Computer Scis. Corp. Network Integration Div., Herndon, 1987-95; corp. v.p. Telecomms. CSC, 1996—. Mem. IEEE, Armed Forces Communications and Electronics Assn., Zofingia Club (Aarau, Switzerland, pres. 1958). Avocations: violin, tennis, skiing. Home: 12206 Thoroughbred Rd Herndon VA 20171-2007 Office: Computer Scis Corp 3190 Fairview Park Dr Falls Church VA 22042-4510

SCHAFER, ALICE TURNER, retired mathematics educator; b. Richmond, Va., June 18, 1915; d. John H. and Cleon (Dermott) Turner; m. Richard Donald Schafer, Sept. 8, 1942; children: John Dickerson, Richard Stone. AB, U. Richmond, 1936, DSc, 1964; MS, U . Chgo., 1940, PhD (fellow), 1942. Tchr. Glen Allen (Va.) High Sch., 1936-39; instr. math. Conn. Coll., New London, 1942-44, asst. prof., 1954-57, asso. prof., 1957-61, prof., 1961-62; prof. math. Wellesley Coll., 1962-80, Helen Day Gould prof. math., 1969-80, Helen Day Gould prof. math. emerita, 1980—, affirmative action officer, 1980-82; prof. math. Marymount U., Arlington, Va., 1989-96; ret., 1996. Instr. U. Mich., Ann Arbor, 1945-46; lectr. Douglass Coll., New Brunswick, N.J., 1946-48; asst. prof. Swarthmore (Pa.) Coll., 1948-51, Drexel Inst. Tech., Phila., 1951-53; mathematician Johns Hopkins Applied Physics Lab., Silver Spring, Md., 1945; lectr. Simmons Coll., Boston, 1980-88, Radcliffe Coll. Seminars, Cambridge, Mass., 1980-85; U.S. chair postsecondary math. edn. U.S./China Joint Conf. on Edn., 1992, co-chair Citizen Amb. program People to People U.S. and China Joint Conf. on Women's Issues, 1995, session women in sci. and math. Contbr. articles on women in math. and other articles to math. jours. Recipient Disting. Alumna award Westhampton Coll., U. Richmond, 1977; NSF sci. faculty fellow Inst. for Advanced Study, Princeton, N.J., 1958-59. Fellow AAAS (math. sect. A nominating com. 1979-83, mem.-at-large 1983-86, chair-elect sect. A 1991, chair 1992, retiring chair 1993, Assn. for Women in Math. rep., 1993—), AAUP (chmn. nat. com. W 1980-83, mem. nat. coun. 1984-87), Am. Math. Soc. (chmn. postdoctoral fellowship com. 1973-76, affirmative action procedures com. 1980-82, chair com. on Human Rights of Mathematicians 1988-94), Soc. Indsl. and Applied Math., Am. Statis. Assn., Inst. Math. Stats., Nat. Coun. Tchrs. of Math. (chair com. on women 1976-81), Math Assn. Am. (adv. com. for Women and Math. program 1987-89, dir. fund raising 1989-92, lectr. 1982—, chair devel. com. 1988-92, Yueh-Gin Gung and Charles Y. Hu disting. svc. to math. award 1998), Internat. Congress Mathematicians (mem. fund raising com. 1986), Assn. for Women in Math. (pres. 1973-75, Alice T. Schafer Prize established 1989, chair fund raising com. 1992-94, leader math. del. women mathematicians to China 1990, Disting. Svc. award 1996), Emily's List (mem. majority coun.), Cosmos Club, Phi Beta Kappa, Sigma Xi, Sigma Delta Epsilon. Achievements include first study of singularities of space curves in projective differential geometry; research on undulation point of a space curve. Home: 1010 Waltham St Apt A404 Lexington MA 02421-8064

SCHAFER, CARL WALTER, investment executive; b. Chgo., Jan. 16, 1936; s. MacHenry George and Gertrude (Herrick) S.; 1 child, MacHenry George II. BA with distinction, U. Rochester, 1958. Budget examiner Budget Bur., Exec. Office Pres., Washington, 1961-64, legis. analyst, 1964-66, dep. dir. budget preparation, 1966-68, dir. budget preparation, 1968-69; staff asst. U.S. Ho. of Reps. Appropriations Com., 1969; dir. budget Princeton (N.J.) U., 1969-72, treas., 1972-76, fin. v.p., treas., 1976-87, lectr. indsl. adminstrn., 1975; prin. Rockefeller & Co., Inc., 1987-90; pres. Atlantic Found., Princeton, N.J., 1990—. Pres., CEO, Palmer Square Inc., 1979-81; trustee, treas. McCarter Theatre Co. Inc., 1974-76; co-chmn. N.J. Gov.'s Task Force on Improving N.J. Econ. and Regulatory Climate, 1982-83; chmn. investment adv. com. Howard Hughes Med. Inst., 1985-92; trustee Am. Bible Soc., 1987-92; trustee, dir. Roadway Corp., Frontier Oil Corp., Labor Ready, Inc., The UBS Paine Webber, Haring Loemer, European Investors and Guardian Groups of Mut. Funds, The Claremont Inst., Harbor Br. Inst. Inc., Hamilton and Co., The Johnson Atelier and Sch. Sculpture, The Banbury Fund; mem. internat. adv. coun. Wm. Sword & Co., Inc. Leadership Group. Bd. dirs. Jewish Guild for the Blind, 1988-96; chmn., investment com., William H. Donner Found. and Donner Can. Found., Amnesty Internat. Leadership Group. Mem. Phi Beta Kappa. Office: 66 Witherspoon St Ste 1100 Princeton NJ 08542-3226

SCHAFER, EDWARD T. former governor, real estate company executive; b. Bismarck, N.D., Aug. 8, 1946; s. Harold and Marian Schafer; m. Nancy Jones; children: Edward Thomas Jr., Ellie Sue, Eric Jones, Kari Jones. BSBA, U. N.D., 1969; MBA, Denver U., 1970. Quality control inspector Gold Seal, 1971-73, v.p., 1974, chmn. mgmt. com., 1975-78; owner/dir. H&S Distbn., 1976—; pres. Gold Seal, 1978-85, Dakota Classics, 1986—, TRIESCO Properties, 1986—, Fish 'N Dakota, 1990-94; gov. State of N.D., 1992-2000. Chmn. N.D. Micro Bus. Mktg. Alliance; pres. N.D. Heritage Group; adv. coun. Distributive Edn. Clubs of Am.; lectr. Hugh O'Brien Leadership Found.; counselor Junior Achievement; dir. Bismarck Recreation Coun.; trustee Missouri Valley Family YMCA; plankowner USS Theodore Roosevelt; ann. support com. Medcenter One Found.; mem. Bismarck State Coll. Found. Mem. NRA, Theodore Roosevelt Assn. (Theodore Roosevelt Medora Found., United Sportsman of N.D., U. N.D. Pres. Club, U. Mary Pres. Club, Bismarck-Mandan Rotary. Republican.*

SCHAFER, ELIZABETH DIANE, historian, writer; b. Opelika, Ala., Sept. 26, 1965; d. Robert Louis and Carolyn Louise (Henn) S. BA in History cum laude, Auburn U., 1986, MA in History of Sci. magna cum laude, 1988, PhD in History of Tech. magna cum laude, 1993; postgrad., Hollins Coll., 1996-98. Archivist Lee County Hist. Soc. Mus., 1988—. Ind. scholar, 1993—; presenter in field. Author: Beacham's Sourcebooks for Teaching Young Adult Fiction: Exploring Harry Potter, 2000; co-author: Women Who Made A Difference in Alabama, 1995; cons. editor Ency. of Sci., 1998; freelance editor various tech. docs.; editl. asst. Proceedings of the We. Soc. for French History, 1988-91, Nat. Forum: The Phi Kappa Phi Jour., 1990-91; contbr. History News Svc.; contbr. articles to profl. jours., encys., mags., chpts. to books. Recipient hon. mention poetry Writer's Digest, 1994 hon. mention children's non-fiction, 1997, children's non-fiction and fiction, 1998, Writer's Digest, Shirley Henn Meml. award Critical scholar, Hollins Coll., 1998. Mem. AAAS, AAUW, Am. Hist. Assn., Orgn. Am. Historians, Soc. History Tech., History Sci. Soc., Women's History Network, N.Y. Acad. Scis., So. Hist. Assn., Soc. Children's Book Writers and Illustrators, Children's Lit. Assn., Ala. Writer's Forum, Assn. Gravestone Studies, Lancaster Mennonite Hist. Soc., Lee County Hist. Soc. (life mem.), Auburn U. Alumni Assn. (life mem.), Descendants Mexican War Vets., United Daus. of the Confederacy, DAR (chmn. Light Horse Harry Lee's geneal. records com.), Daus. of Union Vets., Phi Alpha Theta (history hon.). Home and Office: PO Box 57 Loachapoka AL 36865-0057 E-mail: edschafer@reporters.net.

SCHAFER, EVA CADY, elementary school educator, musician; b. Seattle, May 7, 1918; d. Osman Horace and Hazel Bradley (Carpenter) Cady, m. Tillman Howard Schafer, June 7, 1942; children: Lyle, Steven, Martin, Gretchen, Hollace, Walter. BA in Zoology, UCLA, 1941, MA in Zoology, 1942. Tchr. San Diego Pub. Sch., 1941-49, Natural History Mus., San Diego, 1960; environ. coord. title 3 Mass. Audubon, Lincoln, 1967; sci. tchr. Concord (Mass.) Pub. Schs., 1969-82; tchr. adult edn. Concord and Bedford (Mass.) Pub. Schs., 1975-80. Played viola La Jolla Symphony, 1960-67; naturalist San Diego Mus. Natural History in orthitheology; played violin Sudbury Sayoyards Gilbert and Sullivan musicals, 1968; mem. Concord Music Club (pres., sec., treas., 1970; mem. Bedford Conservation Commn., Mass., 1998. Columnist Concord Pub. Schs. Bull., 1975-81; violist San Diego Symphony, 1956-68; prin. violist Concord (Mass.) Symphony, 1969-84; prin. 2nd violinist Waltham (Mass.) Philharmonic, 1984—. Co-dir. revolutionary music Concord (Mass.) Mus., 1981—; mem. Merrimack River Watershed Coun., Middlesex County, Mass., 1995—; camp dir. San Diego Girl Scouts USA, 1960-69. Recipient Arts Lottery award in music State of Mass., 1986, 87, 91. Mem. N.E. Antiquities Rsch. Assn., Bedford (Mass.) Garden Club (v.p. 1995-98, pres. 1998—), Sigma Alpha Iota. Avocations: music, gardening, organizing and leading nature walks, hiking. Home: Bedford, Mass. Died Oct. 4, 2001.

SCHAFER, GERARD THOMAS ROGER, lawyer; b. Pitts., Mar. 20, 1956; s. Francis John Schafer and Lucille L. Davis; m. Marie Teres Paulick, Dec. 18, 1982; children: Michael, Brett, Rachael, Matthew. BS, Pa. State U., 1978; JD magna cum laude, U. Pitts., 1982. Bar: Pa. 1982, Va. 1984; U.S. Dist. Ct. (ea. dist.) Pa. 1982, U.S. Dist. Ct. (ea. dist.) Va. 1984. Assoc. Tucker Arensberg P.C., Pitts., 1982-84, Clark & Stant, P.C., Virginia Beach, 1984-85; asst. atty. Office of the Commonwealth's Atty., 1985-88; assoc. John W. Brown, P.C., Chesapeake, Va., 1988; sole practice law Virginia Beach, 1989-95; ptnr. Schafer, Russo & Martin (formerly Schafer & Russo), 1996—. Mem. Va. Trial Lawyers Assn., Allegheny County Bar Assn. (award 1982), Order of the Coif. Avocations: sports, music. Office: Schafer Russo & Martin 4455 South Blvd Ste 310 Virginia Beach VA 23452-1159

SCHAFER, JOHN FRANCIS, retired plant pathologist; b. Pullman, Wash., Feb. 17, 1921; s. Edwin George and Ella Frances (Miles) S.; m. Joyce A. Marcks, Aug. 16, 1947; children— Patricia, Janice, James BS, Wash. State U., 1942; PhD, U. Wis., 1950. Asst. prof. to prof. plant pathology Purdue U., 1949-68; head dept. plant pathology Kans. State U., 1968-72; chmn. dept. plant pathology Wash. State U., Pullman, 1972-80; integrated pest mgmt. coordinator sci. and edn. USDA, 1980-81, acting nat. research program leader plant pathology Agrl. Research Service, 1981-82, dir. cereal rust lab., 1982-87, biol. sci. collaborator, 1987-95; ret., 1995. Vis. rsch. prof. Duquesne U., 1965-66; adj. prof. plant pathology U. Minn., 1982-92. Contbr. articles to profl. jours., chpts. to books. With AUS, 1942-46. Phi Sigma scholar, 1942. Fellow AAAS, Ind. Acad. Sci., Am. Phytopathol. Soc. (past pres.); mem. Am. Soc. Agronomy, Crop Sci. Soc. Am., Coun. for Agrl. Sci. and Tech. Achievements include identification of increased resistance to wheat leaf rust by genetic recombination; demonstration of probabilities of virulence to genetic resistance combinations, of tolerance as a mechanism of disease control, and of use of cultivaral diversity for disease protection; bred (with others) over 30 disease resistant cultivars of cereal crops, including Arthur wheat. Home: 4949 Snyder Ln Apt 108 Rohnert Park CA 94928-4834 E-mail: joyjac@msn.com.

SCHAFER, JOHN STEPHEN, poet; b. N.Y.C., Sept. 5, 1934; s. Stephen James and Siiri (Halmi) S.; m. Gertrud Rosa Fleischmann, June 14, 1958; children: Sylvia F., John Stephen, Karen D., Kristen H. BA, Rutgers U., 1956, MBA, 1963. Advt. research mgr. Union Carbide Corp., N.Y.C., 1959—65; rsch. mgr. Bus. Week, 1965—66; v.p. Opinion Rsch. Corp., Princeton, NJ, 1966—80; pres. Am. Econ. Found., Cleve., 1981—2002, trustee, 1975—2002; v.p., dir. Ams. for Competitive Enterprise System, Phila., 1970-82. Editor Linde Electric Welding Progress, 1959-62, ORC Pub. Opinion Index, 1968-72, AEF Straight Talk, 1981-82, Bellcore Exch., 1993-94. Polit. pollster Ed Clark for U.S. Pres., 1980; chmn. N.J. Libertarian party, 1983; nat. dir. U.S. Jaycees, 1965-66, v.p. N.J., 1964-65. Served to 1st lt. U.S. Army, 1957-59. Mem. Jr. Chamber Internat. (hon. life), Philosophean Soc., Scabbard and Blade, Delta Phi Alpha Presbyterian. Home: 114 Walton Palm Rd Panama City FL 32413-7311

SCHAFER, MATTHEW T. English language educator, coach; b. Indpls., May 23, 1970; s. Michael T. and Marianne (Grove) S. BS in Education, Ind. U., 1993. Lic. tchr., Ind. English tchr., wrestling coach Bishop Chatard H.S., Indpls., 1994-95, North Ctrl. H.S., Indpls., 1995—. Adj. instr. Ind. U., Bloomington. Contbr. nonfiction to local mags., poetry to nat. jours. Mem. Nat. Coun. Tchrs. English, USA Wrestling (Bronze Coach), Ind. State Wrestling Assn. Avocations: fishing, travel, writing, gardening. Office: North Central High School 1801 E 86th St Indianapolis IN 46240-2345 E-mail: matts@iquest.net., mschafer@msdwt.k12.in.us.

SCHAFER, MICHAEL FREDERICK, orthopedic surgeon; b. Peoria, Ill., Aug. 17, 1942; s. Harold Martin and Frances May (Ward) S.; m. Eileen M. Briggs, Jan. 8, 1966; children: Steven, Brian, Kathy, David, Daniel. BA, U.

Iowa, 1964, MD, 1967. Diplomate Am. Bd. Orthopedic Surgery. Intern Chgo. Wesley Meml. Hosp., 1967-68; resident in orthop. surgery Cook County Program, Northwestern U., Chgo., 1968-72; asst. prof. orthop. surgery Northwestern U., 1977—; Reyerson prof. and chmn. dept. orthopedic surgery; asso. attending orthopedic surgeon Northwestern Meml. Hosp., 1974—. Adj. staff Children's Meml. Hosp., Chgo., 1974—; cons. VA Lakeside Hosp., 1974—; panelist Bur. Health Manpower, HEW, 1976; sec.-treas. Orthop. Rsch. and Edn. Found.; attending orthop. surgeon Northwestern Meml. Hosp., 1980—, exec. dir. Back and Neck Inst. Contbr. articles to profl. jours. Maj. U.S. Army, 1973-74. Fellow Am. Orthopaedic Assn., Am. Acad. Orthopaedic Surgeons; mem. AMA, Am. Orthopedic Soc. Sports Medicine, Ill. Med. Soc., Chgo. Med. Soc., Scoliosis Rsch. Soc. Roman Catholic. Home: 1815 Ridgewood Ln W Glenview IL 60025-2205 Office: Northwestern U Med School Ste 910 645 N Michigan Ave Chicago IL 60611-2876 E-mail: m-schafer@nwu.edu.

SCHAFER, MILTON, composer, pianist, educator; b. N.Y.C., Sept. 24, 1920; s. Abraham and May (Meyerson) S.; div. 1974; 1 child, Nina Kathryn. Cert., Paris Conservatory, 1950; student, Am. Conservatory, Fontainbleu, France; pvt. study, Nadia Boulanger, Paris, 1949-50; BS, Juilliard Sch. Music, N.Y.C., 1952; MA, CCNY, N.Y.C., 1967; studied with, Alfred Mirovitch, Irwin Freundlich, Lonnie Epstein. Prof. music John Jay Coll., CUNY, N.Y.C., 1976-96. Lectr. music CCNY, N.Y.C., 1954—56; asst. to Frank Loesser Frank Music Pub., N.Y.C., 1956—58; mus. dir. Am. Theatre Wing, N.Y.C., 1962; mem. So. Hampton Poetry Workshop, 1997—. Piano recitals at Am. Embassy, Paris, 1949, Quaker Ctr. Internat., Paris, 1949, Town Hall, N.Y.C., 1950, 54; composer, lyricist: (children's song cycle) Mommy Gimme a Drinka Water, 1957 (recorded by Danny Kaye and televised by Nathan Lane with Boston Pops 1999), (Broadway musicals) Bravo Giovanni, 1962 (Tony award nomination for score), Drat! The Cat!, 1965 (voted Best Score of Yr. by Walter Kerr), He Touched Me, 1965 (recorded by Barbra Streisand), songs recorded by Peggy Lee, Sarah Vaughn, Jerry Vale, Eddie Fisher, Frank Pourcel, The Muppets; author: Practical Technique for Popular Piano Playing, 1947; author, composer adaptation Kate Simon's Bronx Primitive 1990 (staged reading at ASCAP 1998), (poem) The Hives of March, 1998; music critic High Fidelity, 1975, Music Jour., 1976-78. Staff sgt. USAAF, 1942-46. Co-winner Nat. Guild Piano Tchrs. Competition, N.Y.C., 1948. Mem. ASCAP, Dramatists Guild. Avocations: reading, yoga, swimming, travel, writing poetry. Home: 33 Riverside Dr New York NY 10023-8012 E-mail: mschafer@aol.com.

SCHAFER, PATRICIA DAY, physical education educator; b. Terre Haute, Ind., July 27, 1937; d. Charles Loran and Dorothy Pearl (McCool) Day; m. Dennis Meyer, Oct. 16, 1964 (div. Mar. 1975); children: Jennifer Jo Heerdink, Amy Kay Meyer. BS, Ind. State U., 1959, MS, 1964, MS, 1994, PhD, 1998. Cert. tchr. health, physical edn., recreation. Tchr. Flora High Sch., Ill., 1959-63; graduate asst. Ind. State U., Terre Haute, 1963-64; tchr. Speedway High Sch., Ind., 1964-65; asst. prof. Oakland City U., 1965-74, asst. prof./chairperson, 1984—; tchr. Pike County Schs., Petersburg, Ind., 1974-84. Instr. Am. Red Cross, 1957—. Leader 4-H Club, Princeton, Ind. 1985-88; umpire Summer League Softball, Oakland City, Ind., 1980-83; supr. Special Olympics, Oakland City, 1987-90 Recipient Realizing the Dream award Ind. Colls. and Univs. Ind., Inc., 1991. Mem. Am. Alliance Health, Physical Edn., Recreation and Dance, Ind. Assn. Health, Physical Edn., Recreation and Dance, Am. Assn. Tchr. Edn., ASCD, NAIA (voting delegate 1986, workshop leader 1986—), NCAA, DAR, Am. Quarter Horse Assn. (horseshow judge 1960—), Alpha Delta Kappa, Sigma Kappa. Meth. Avocations: raising, breeding and training registered quarter horses, swimming, camping, traveling. Home: RR 3 Box 259 Oakland City IN 47660-9371 Office: Oakland City University Lucretia St Oakland City IN 47660

SCHAFER, PHILIP NICHOLAS, physician assistant; b. Mt. Pleasant, Mich., Jan. 30, 1967; s. Donald N. and Shirley (TeVelde) S.; m. Carrie Lynn Sharrard, Sept. 12, 1992; children: Ashley Lynn, Hannah Marie. Paramedic cert., Delta Coll., 1991; physician asst. cert., AS, Kettering Coll., 1995. Physician asst. Otsego Meml. Hosp., Gaylord, 1995—. Mgr. Internet Medicine Forum for REMCEN. Fellow Soc. Emergency Medicine Physician Assts., Am. Acad. Physician Assts.; mem. Mich. Acad. Physician Assts. (bd. dirs.). Avocations: golf, computers. Office: Otsego Meml Hosp 825 N Center Ave Gaylord MI 49735-1560

SCHAFER, ROBERT LOUIS, agricultural engineer, researcher; b. Burlington, Iowa, Aug. 1, 1937; s. Marion Louis and Pansy (Head) S.; m. Carolyn Louise Henn, Aug. 1, 1959; 1 child, Elizabeth Diane. BS, Iowa State U., 1959, MS, 1961, PhD, 1965. Agrl. engr. Agrl. Rsch. Svc., USDA, Ames, Iowa, 1959-64, Auburn, Ala., 1964-95. Co-author: Advances in Soil Dynamics, 1994; contbr. articles to profl. jours. Fellow Am. Soc. Agrl. Engrs. (McCormick Case Gold medal 1997). Home: PO Box 189 Loachapoka AL 36865-0189 E-mail: rls@poka.laletk.com.

SCHAFER, RUTH ERMA, artist, educator; b. Thompson, Mo., Nov. 23, 1923; d. Lewis Maxwell and Ethel (Keller) Johnson; m. Paul Linzy Starlin (dec. Jan. 1987); children: Barbara Ann White, Larry David Starlin, Stephen Pual Starlin, Paula Lynn Norris, Randal Lee Starlin. Student, Art Sch. of Ft. Wayne, Ind. Bus. mgr. Chevrolet Dealership, Portland, Ind. Tchr. Portland Art Sch., 1964—68. Exhibitions include , Atlanta, Chgo., N.Y.C., Inpls., Ft. Wayne, Brown Country Art Guild. Leader Girl Scouts U.S., Boy Scouts Am., 4-H Club; head art booths Jay County Fairs; selected by Gov. Bowen of Ind. to serve as Ind. Arts Commn. cultural rep., 1967; tchr. Sunday sch. Ch. of Christ. Named Mother of the Yr., C. of C. Portland, 1957; recipient honored by Sen. Birch Bayh as one of the Ind. Artists, Washington, 1965. Mem.: Hoosier Salon, Nat. Endowment Arts (charter), Ind. Fedn. Art Clubs (pres. 1975—77, treas. 1971—75).

SCHAFER, SANDRA LEE, geriatrics nurse, educator; b. Fremont, Ohio, Nov. 2, 1949; d. Calvin H. and Norma Jean Gahn; m. Earl R. Schafer, Dec. 19, 1971; children: Jason Andrew, Matthew David. BSN, Capital U., 1971; MSN, Med. Coll. of Ohio, 1985. Cert. gerontol. nurse practitioner, Ga. Clin. nurse specialist Mercy Hosp., Toledo; asst. prof. U. Cmty. and Tech. Coll.; clin. instr. Brevard C.C., Cocoa, Fla.; dir. nursing Palm Bay (Fla.) Care Ctr.; collaborative nursing home practice Melbourne, Fla., 1991-96; gerontol. nurse practitioner HMO, Atlanta, 1996—. Mem. Ga. Nurses Assn., Sigma Theta Tau. Home: 40 Hunter's Trail Dallas GA 30157-9429 E-mail: sandy.schafer@kp.org.

SCHAFER, SHARON MARIE, anesthesiologist; b. Detroit, Mar. 23, 1948; d. Charles Anthony and Dorothy Emma (Schweitzer) Pokriefka; m. Timothy John Schafer, Nov. 12, 1977; children: Patrick Christopher, Steven Michael. BS in Biology, Wayne State U., 1971, MD, 1975; MBA in Practice Mgmt., Madonna U., 2000. Diplomate Am. Bd. Anesthesiology. Intern, resident Sinai Hosp. Detroit, 1975-78; pvt. practice anesthesiology Troy, Mich., 1988—. Mem. AMA, Am. Soc. Anesthesiologists. Roman Catholic. Home and Office: 5741 Folkstone Dr Troy MI 48085-3154

SCHAFER, THOMAS WILSON, advertising agency executive; b. Youngstown, Ohio, Sept. 12, 1939; s. Kenneth Charles and Clara Louise (Wilson) S.; m. Anne Kernwein, Jan. 22, 1972; children: Charles Kenneth, Bret Thomas. BA, Colgate U., 1962. Salesman Gen. Foods Corp., 1962-65; sr. ptnr. Tatham EURO RSCG Advt., Chgo., 1965-93; chmn. Schafer Rsch., Inc., Savannah, Ga., 1993—. Past dir. Off the Street Club. Mem. Chgo. Advt. Fedn. (past exec. v.p.) Clubs: The Landings Club. Office: Schafer Rsch Inc 5 Modena Rd Savannah GA 31411-2136

SCHAFF, BARBARA WALLEY, artist; b. Plainfield, N.J., May 6, 1941; d. Miron M. and Silvia S. (Solott) Walley; m. John A. Schaff, Apr. 10, 1963 (div. 1992); children: Elizabeth A., Joshua L. BA, Syracuse U., 1963; cert., Pa. Acad. Fine Arts, 1994; grad., China Nat. Acad. Fine Art, Hangzhou, 1994. Clay artist, Stockton, N.J., 1968-88; advisor to faculty BFA program Kean Coll., Union, 1987—; painter Phila., 1990—. Mem. adv. bd. Hunterdon Art Ctr., Clinton, N.J., 1988, 89; workshop leader, U.S. and Can. One-man shows include NJ State Mus, Trenton, 1985, Lee Sclar Gallery, Morristown, NJ, 1986, Howe Gallery, Kean Coll., Union, 1989, ITT Boston Sheraton, 1995, Thos. Moser Cabinetmakers, Phila., 1995, Ciboulette, 1997, So. Vt. Art Ctr., Manchester, 1997, NJ State Mus., Trenton, 1997, Questar Libr. , New Hope, Pa., 1998, Restaurant Phila. Mus. Art, 1999, Cafe Gallery, Phila., 1999, exhibited in group shows at Newark Mus., 1973, 1977, Morris Mus., Morristown, NJ, 1973, 1977, Carnegie Ctr., Princeton, NJ, 1984, Newman Galleries, Phila., 1986, Ednl. Testing Svc., Princeton, 1987, Monarch Title Nat. San Angelo Mus. Art, Tex., 1989, US Artists , Phila., 1992, 1993, China Nat. Acad. Fine Art, 1994, Morris Gallery Mus. Am. Art., Phila., 1994, Am. Drawing Biennial V Muscarelle Mus. Art, Williamsburg, Va., 1996, Restaurant Phila Mus. Art, 1996, 1999, Fellowship of Pa. Acad. Fine Arts, Woodmere Mus., 1996, Peng Gallery, Phila., 2000, others, Carspecker-Scott Gallery, Wilmington, Del., 2001—, Represented in permanent collections Linda Lee Aeter collection Art by Women, NJ State Mus, Trenton, Fuller Meml. Art Mus., Brockton, Mass., Pfizer Internat., NYC, Atlantic Richfield Corp., Phila., Towers Perrin, NYC, Independence Found., Phila., Temple U. Sch. Law, McGraw Hill, NYC, Chubb Corp., Warren, NJ, Sta. WHYY and WHYY-TV, Phila., Marriott Corp., Princeton, NJ, Prince Music Theater, Phila., BristolMeyers Squibb Co., Hopewell, NJ, commns., works featured in, . Recipient Medal of Excellence for promotion and design Art Dirs. Club N.J., 1986, medal for Outstanding Achievement, Long Beach Island Found. of the Arts and Scis., Harvey Aders, N.J., 1998, 99; fellow N.J. State Coun. on Arts, 1984-85, resident fellow Va. Ctr. Creative Arts, 1996, 98, 99, 2001. Mem. Fellowship of Pa. Acad. of Fine Arts (com. mem., exhibitor 1986, 87, 94, Mable Wilson Woodrow Meml. award 1994), Artist Equity, Nat. Arts Club. Avocations: gardening, cooking, music, sailing. Home: 1520 Spruce St Apt 906 Philadelphia PA 19102-4507 Office: Barbara Schaff Studio 314 Brown St Philadelphia PA 19123-2202

SCHAFF, MICHAEL FREDERICK, lawyer; b. Queens, N.Y., Nov. 14, 1957; s. Raymond and Norma S.; m. Robin Barbara Rose, Mar. 17, 1985; children: Rachel Lindsay, Aaron Jacob. BA, Rutgers Coll., New Brunswick, N.J., 1979; MBA, CUNY, 1982; JD, N.Y. Law Sch., N.Y.C., 1982; LLM, Boston U., 1983. Bar: N.Y. and N.J. 1982, Md. 1983, U.S. Dist. Ct. N.J. 1983, U.S. Dist. Ct. Md. 1983, U.S. Tax Ct. 1983. Assoc. Ober, Kaler, Grimes & Shriver, Balt., 1983-84, Greenberg, Dauber & Epstein, Newark, 1984-86, Wilentz, Goldman & Spitzer, Woodbridge, N.J., 1986-91, ptnr., 1991—. Mem. N.J. Legis. Com. for the Study of Pain Mgmt. Contbr. articles to profl. jours. Masters Rsch. fellow, Bernard M. Baruch Coll., 1980. Mem. Am. Health Lawyers Assn. (chair 2001—, vice chmn. physician's orgn. com. 1997-2001, newsletter editor 1997—), N.J. Bar Assn. (chair computer related law com. 1991-93, dir. health and hosp. law sect. 1996—, vice chair 1997-98, chair elect 1998-99, chair 1999-2000), Middlesex County Bar Assn. (chair health and hosp. law com. 1995—), Med. Group Mgmt. Assn., N.J. Med. Group Mgmt. Assn., N.J. Venture Club, Omicron Delta Epsilon. Office: Wilentz Goldman & Spitzer 90 Woodbridge Ctr Dr Woodbridge NJ 07095-1146 E-mail: Schafm@Wilentz.com.

SCHAFF, SHIRLEY LYNN, investment brokerage executive, insurance company executive; b. Mandan, N.D., May 10, 1971; d. Donald Frederick and Carla Ann (Wenger) S. Diploma, Mandan (N.D.) H.S. Rep. Mary Kay Cosmetics, Dallas; marketer First Select Brokers, West Palm Beach; mktg. dir. Universal Concepts; pres. Primary Fin. GP; marketer Am. Life, Fla. Mem. Palm Beach County Commn., Women's Life Underwriter, Palm Beach Life Underwriters, Nat. Life Underwriters. Republican. Roman Catholic. Avocations: golf, aerobics, water sports, traveling. Office: Primary Fin Group Ste 216 470 S Pin Oak Pl Longwood FL 32779-5925

SCHAFFER, CANDLER GARELD, conductor, hornist, educator; b. Takoma Park, Md., June 2, 1950; s. Henry Louis and June Georgette (Schweitzer) S. MusB, U. Miami, 1972; MEd, U. Md., 1977; MFA, U. Iowa, 1991, D Mus. Arts, 1992. Dir. orchestral studies Oreg. State U., Corvallis, 1982-85, Tex. Christian U., Ft. Worth, 1985-90; music dir., condr. Fla. Space Coast Philharm., Cocoa, 1995-99, Fla. Space Coast Pops, Cocoa, 1996-99, Wichita Falls (Tex.) Symphony Orch., 1996—, Wichita Falls Chamber Orch., 1998—. Mem. classical music selection panel Oreg. Arts Commn., 1984-85; grant cons. Irving (Tex.) Arts Coun., 1998; founder, bd. dirs. Camerata Winds Melbourne, Fla., 1994-96; co-founder, prin. condr. North Tex. Wind Symphony, Wichita Falls, 1997; adj. instr. horn Midwestern State U., 1996—. Bd. dirs. Willamette Arts Coun., Corvallis, 1983-85; mem. cultural execs. com. Brevard Cultural Alliance, Brevard County, Fla., 1995-96; co-founder, bd. dirs. Century Concerts, Wichita Falls, 1997-2000. Mem. Am. Symphony Orch. League, Am. Fedn. Musicians. Avocations: surfing, hiking, reading, yoga. bus. Home: 704 Greenwood Manor Cir West Melbourne FL 32904-1914 Office: Wichita Falls Symphony Orch Kemp Ctr for Arts 1300 Lamar Wichita Falls TX 76301 E-mail: schafferc1@aol.com., wfso@aol.com., conductorwfso@aol.com.

SCHAFFER, DAVID EDWIN, retired management systems executive; b. Nov. 3, 1929; s. Karl and Jeanette (Gotthelf) S.; m. Ariel Williams Sullivan, May 3, 1951; stepchildren: Adrienne Sullivan Smith, James W. Sullivan. Student, Wharton Sch. of U. Pa., 1948-49; BA, New Sch. for Social Rsch., 1959. Spl. edn. tchr. of emotionally disturbed children various schs. and hosps., 1954-65; br. mgr. 1st Westchester Nat. Bank, New Rochelle, N.Y., 1965-66; v.p. Longines-Symphonette Inc.; spl. asst. to chmn. bd. Longines Wittnauer Inc., Larchmont, N.Y., 1966-72; pvt. practice mgmt. cons. Franconia, N.H., 1973-77; v.p., dir. ops. Carroll Reed Ski Shops, Inc., 1978-80; ret. Instr. econs. Am. Inst. Banking, 1965-66. Moderator, Town of Franconia, 1973—, co-chmn. Frost Pl. com., founder, 1975—; bd. dirs. White Mountain Community Svcs., 1973-77; bd. dirs., past pres. No. N.H. Mental Health Services, 1975-77. Prodr. numerous record albums. With Signal Corps, AUS, 1951-53. Mem. Direct Mail Credit Assn. Am. (founding mem.), Asso. Retail Credit Men of N.Y.C., Direct Mail Assn. Am. (past chmn. subcom. on consumer affairs and regulatory agys.), Profile Club (pres., dir.). Democrat. Episcopalian. Home: River Rd Franconia NH 03580

SCHAFFER, DAVID IRVING, lawyer; b. N.Y.C., Oct. 17, 1935; s. Frank and Edith (Montlack) S.; m. Lois Ann Warshauer, June 16, 1957; children: Susan Edith, Eric Michael. BA, U. Pa., 1956; LL.B., Harvard U., 1959. Bar: N.Y. 1960. Assoc. Shearman & Sterling, N.Y.C., 1960-65; sec., counsel Yale Express System, Inc., 1965-66; sr. v.p., gen. counsel, sec. Avis, Inc., Garden City, N.Y., 1966-83; v.p., gen. counsel U.S. Surgical Corp., Norwalk, Conn., 1983-86; of counsel Meltzer, Lippe, Goldstein & Schlissel, LLP, Mineola, N.Y., 1986-89; ptnr. Meltzer, Lippe, Goldstein & Schlissel, P.C., 1989—. Past pres. Nassau County Legal Aid Soc., 1984-86. Bd. dirs. United Cmty. Fund, Great Neck, N.Y., 1980, Great Neck Estates Civic Assn., 1998—, L.I. Venture Group, 1988—. With USAR, 1960. Mem. ABA, N.Y. State Bar Assn., Nassau County Bar Assn., L.I. Software Assn., Harvard Club. Democrat. Home: 31 Amherst Rd Great Neck NY 11021-2910 Office: Meltzer Lippe El Al 190 Willis Ave Mineola NY 11501-2693 E-mail: dlefty35@aol.com., dschaffer@mdg.com.

SCHAFFER, EUGENE CARL, education educator; b. Phila., May 10, 1944; BA, Temple U., 1968, EdD, 1976. Dir. field experience Valparaiso U., Valparaiso, Ind., 1974-76; prof. curriculum and instrn. U. N.C., Charlotte, 1976-2000, chair dept. mid., secondary and K-12 edn., 1996-2000, chair curriculum and instrn. dept., 1994-96; prof., chair dept. edn. U. Md., Balt., 2000—. Co-author: Recent Advances in School Effects Research, 1994; contbr. articles to profl. jours. Recipient Fulbright scholarship, Japan rsch. fellowship. Mem. Am. Edn. Rsch. Assn., Phi Delta Kappa. E-mail: schaffer@umbc.edu.

SCHAFFER, JAMES MASON, foundation administrator; b. Detroit, Aug. 27, 1954; s. James Albert Schaffer and Patricia Jean (Mason) Tillman; m. Jennifer Lee Yoder, Aug. 27, 1988; children: Abigail, William. BA, Mich. State U., 1981; MPA, NYU, 1994. Ambudsman Covenant House, N.Y.C., 1981-83; dir. logistics, asst. to chmn. AmeriCares Found., New Canaan, Conn., 1983-86, 90-92; dir. devel. Emmaus House, N.Y.C., 1986-87, Legal Action Ctr. for Homeless, N.Y.C., 1987-88; mgr. resource devel. TechnoServe, Norwalk, Conn., 1988-90; dir. devel. Hole in the Wall Gang Fund, New Haven, 1992-96, St. Luke's Cmty. Svcs., Stamford, Conn., 1996-98; pres. The Schaffer Group, 1998—. Bd. dirs. Internat. Svc. Agys., Washington, 1988-92, Part of the Solution, Bronx; chmn. bd. dirs. Nat. Gardening Assn., Burlington, Vt.; mem. bd. advisors Outer Island, Stony Creek, Conn.; mem. adv. com. Domus Found.; mem. comms. com. Michael Bolton Found., Westport, Conn. Bd. dirs. Overseas Ministries Study Ctr., New Haven. With USAF, 1974-78. Mem. Nat. Soc. Fund Raising Execs., Phi Kappa Phi, Phi Alpha. Roman Catholic. Home: 32 Woodside Rd Guilford CT 06437-1801

SCHÄFFER, JUAN JORGE, mathematics educator; b. Vienna, Austria, Mar. 10, 1930; came to U.S., 1968; s. Daniel and Margarita (Lang) S.; m Inge Doris Kälbermann, Nov. 11, 1959; 1 child, Alejandro Alberto. MS in Physics, U. Pa., 1951; Ingeniero Indsl., U. Republic, Montevideo, Uruguay, 1953, Lic. mat., 1957; DSc in Elec. Engring., Swiss Fed. Inst. Tech., 1956; PhD in Math., U. Zurich, 1956. Prof. mechanics and math., dept. head Inst. Math. and Stats. U. Republic, 1957-68; prof. math. Carnegie-Mellon U., Pitts., 1968—, assoc. dean Mellon Coll. Sci., 1986-93. Sec. Inter-Am. Com. for Math. Edn., 1966-70; mem. exec. com. Nat. Commn. UNESCO, Montevideo, 1967-68. Co-author: Linear Differential Equations and Function Spaces, 1966, Arquímedes, 1969; author: Geometry of Spheres in Normed Spaces, 1976; contbr. numerous articles to math. jours. Guggenheim fellow, 1960. Mem. Am. Math. Soc., AAUP. Jewish. Achievements include development of concept of dichotomy in the global behavior of evolving systems. Office: Carnegie Mellon U Dept Math Sci Pittsburgh PA 15213 E-mail: js6n@andrew.cmu.edu.

SCHAFFER, RICHARD E(NOS), artist, registrar; b. Tucson, Nov. 25, 1955; s. Enos P. and Garnett Schaffer; children: Sara Nicole, Julie Ann. BFA, No. Ariz. U., 1979; MFA, U. Ariz., 1990. Gallery asst. Kay Bonfoey Art Gallery, Tucson, 1979-80; curatorial specialist U. Ariz. Mus. Art, 1980-96, asst. registrar, 1996-2001. Exhibits cons. Etherton-Stern Gallery, Tucson, 1990-92; treas. Dinnerware Artist Coop Gallery, Tucson, 1993-94; mus. rep. Tucson Assn. Mus., 1989-96; cons. GASP Gallery Learning Project, Tucson, 1991-96; adj. prof. dept. fine art U. Ariz., 1996-97; faculty Tucson Mus. Art Sch., 1997-99; mentor program and printmaking. One person shows include Dinnerware Gallery, 1993, Pima Coll. East Campus, 1994; exhibited in group shows Newton Art Ctr., Cambridge, Mass., 1993, Flandrau Sci. Ctr. and Cen. Arts, Tucson, 1996, Davis Gallery, 1997, Tucson Pima Arts Council Gallery, 1998. Recipient 3d Pl. award in printmaking Artquest 86 Internat., 1986. Mem. Nat. Assn. Mus. Exhbn., Mus. Computer Network.$D Avocations: hiking, nature walks. Home: PO Box 17694 Tucson AZ 85731-7694 Office: U Ariz Mus Art PO Box 210002 Tucson AZ 85721-0002 E-mail: reschaff@u.arizona.edu.

SCHAFFER, ROBERT (BOB SCHAFFER), congressman; b. Cin., July 24, 1962; s. Robert James and Florence Ann (Bednar) S.; m. Maureen Elizabeth Menke, Feb. 8, 1986; children: Jenniffer and Emily (twins), Justin, Sarah Mary. BA in Polit. Sci., U. Dayton, 1984; hon. doctorate in mgmt., Colo. Tech. U. Speechwriter republican caucus Ohio Gen. Assembly, 1984-85; legis. asst. State of Ohio, Columbus, 1985; majority adminstrv. asst. Colo. State Senate, Denver, 1985-87, mem., 1987-96, U.S. Congress from 4th Colo. dist., Washington, 1997—, mem. agr. com., edn. and workforce com., resources com. Mem. Rep. Policy Com., GOP Theme Team; commr. Colo. Advanced Tech. Inst., 1988—; proprietor No. Front Range Mktg. and Distbn., Inc. Mem. Mental Health Bd. Larimer County, 1986-87; mem. com. on human svcs. Nat. Conf. State Legislatures; campain co-chmn. Arnold for Lt. Gov.; Republican candidate for Lt. Gov. of Colo., 1994. Named Nat. Legislator of Yr., Rep. Nat. Legislators Assn., 1995, Taxpayer Champion, Colo. Union of Taxpayers, 1995, Bus. Legislator of the Yr. Colo. Assn. Commerce and Industry, Named Guardina Small Bus. Nat. Fedn. Ind. Bus.; recipient Spirit of Enterprise award U.S. C. of C. Mem. Jaycees (Mover and Shaker award 1989), KC. Roman Catholic. Avocations: backpacking, skiing, baseball, painting, reading. Home: 5027 Alder Ct Fort Collins CO 80525-5588 Office: US Ho Reps 212 Cannon Ho Office Bldg Washington DC 20515-0001

SCHAFFER, SETH ANDREW, lawyer; b. Bklyn., Jan. 7, 1942; m. Karen (Kiki) Cohn, Dec. 1, 1968; children: Amanda, Julia, James. BA in Econs. magna cum laude, Harvard U., 1963, LLB cum laude, 1967; postgrad., Cambridge (Eng.) U., 1964. Bar: N.Y. 1970, U.S. Dist. Ct. (so. dist.) N.Y. 1973, U.S. Ct. Appeals (2nd cir.) 1973, U.S. Supreme Ct. 1980. Tchr. math. and econs. York (Pa.) Country Day Sch., 1967-68; assoc. dir. Vera Inst. Justice, 1969-72; asst. U.S. atty. U.S. Dist. Ct. (so. dist.) N.Y., 1972-75; chief counsel Moreland Act Commn. on Nursing Homes, N.Y.C., 1975-76; of counsel Stanley S. Arkin, P.C., Attys. at Law, 1976-77; v.p., gen. counsel, sec. of univ. NYU, N.Y.C., 1977-93, sr. v.p., gen. counsel, sec., 1993—. Adj. prof. law NYU Sch. Law. Dir. Not for Profit Coordinating Com. N.Y., Nat. Ctr. Philanthropy and the Law, N.Y.C. Henry fellow Cambridge U., 1964. Mem. Nat. Assn. Coll. and Univ. Attys. (past pres.), Assn. of Bar of City of N.Y., Phi Beta Kappa. Home: 14 Washington Mews New York NY 10003-6608 Office: NYU 70 Washington Sq S New York NY 10012-1091

SCHAFFHAUSEN, ROBERT JOSEPH, retired structural engineer; b. Kansas City, Mo., June 12, 1926; s. Joseph John and Lorna Louise (Hahn) S.; m. Bette Fern Truskett, Apr. 22, 1951; children: Carol Ann, Cynthia Jean Hastings. BSCE, U. Mo., 1949; MS in Engring., U. Ala., 1976. Registered profl. engr., Ala. Jr. engr. Butler Mfg. Co., Kansas City, Mo., 1943-45, engr. Galesburg, Ill., 1949-52, plant product engr. Birmingham, Ala., 1952-66; regional engr. Am. Inst. Steel Constrn., 1966-79; pvt. practice, 1980-83; sr. engr. So. Bldg. Code Congress, 1983-91; ret., 1991—. Instr. U. Ala., Birmingham. Pres. Rotary, Hoover, Ala., 1984-85. With U.S. Army Air Corps, 1944-45. Named Ala. Vol. Yr. Prison Fellowship Ministries, 1989, Disting. Svc. award, 1996. Mem. ASCE, Ala. Soc. Profl. Engrs. United Methodist. Avocations: volunteering, swimming, photography, courier. Home: 3438 Ridgecrest Dr Hoover AL 35216-4410

SCHAFFMAN, KAREN HELEN, performing company executive; b. Hartford, Conn., Oct. 8, 1962; d. Marvin Nathan and Myrna Kaplan Schaffman. BA, U. Mass., 1985, European Dance Devel. Ctr., Arnheim, The Netherlands, 1991; PhD, U. Calif., Riverside, 2001. Tchr. Sch. New Dance & Theatre, Hannover, Germany, 1992-94; co-dir. Lower Left Dance Co., San Diego, 1995—; from tchg. assoc. to asst. prof. U. Calif., Riverside, 1996-99. Mentor Sushi Performance & Visual Arts, San Diego, 1998-00; guest lectr. U. Calif., Davis, 1999, 2000. Choreographer performance play by Hrostvita Von Gandersheim, Germany, 1993, San Diego Symphony Orch., 1993, World War II Meml., Germany, 1997. Vol. Am. Heart Assn., 1993-95, Sushi Performance & Visual Arts, San Diego, 1995—. Fellow Gluck Found., 1997-2000. Avocations: swimming, art, music, theatre, travel.

SCHAFFNER, BERTRAM HENRY, psychiatrist; b. Erie, Pa., Nov. 12, 1912; s. Milton and Gerta (Herzog) S. Student, Harvard U., 1928-29, 32-33; AB, Swarthmore Coll., 1932; MD, Johns Hopkins U., 1937; diploma, William Alanson White Inst., 1953. Diplomate Am. Bd. Psychiatry, Am. Bd. Neurology. Intern Johns Hopkins Hosp., Balt., 1937-38; resident in neurology Mt. Sinai Hosp., N.Y.C., 1938-39; resident in psychiatry Bellevue Hosp., 1939-40, N.Y. State Psychiat. Inst., N.Y.C., 1946-47; pvt. practice psychiatry and psychoanalysis, 1947—. Lectr. Sch. Nursing Cornell U., N.Y.C., 1950-60; mem. faculty, clin. supr. in psychotherapy William Alanson White Inst. Psychoanalysis, 1960—, med. dir. HIV svc., clin. supr. psychoanalysis, 1993—; cons., editor confs. Josiah Macy Jr. Found., 1949, 50, 51; cons. U.S. Children's Bur., 1946-47, Bur. Mental Health, V.I., 1954-60, World Fedn. Mental Health, 1958-68, others; mem. N.Y. County dist. bd. Com. on Gay and Lesbian Issues; cons. WHO, 1960-67; founder, exec. dir. U.S.-Caribbean Aid to Mental Health, Inc., 1960-68; organizer Biennial Caribbean Confs. for Mental Health, 1959-65; organizer, cons. Caribbean Fedn. for Mental Health, 1959-65; mem. rsch. study Pre-Soviet Russian Family in the Research in Contemporary Cultures, Columbia U., 1949-51. Mem. editl. bd. Jour. of Gay and Lesbian Psychotherapy, 1987—; author: Father Land: A Study of Authoritarianism in the German Family, 1948; contbr. numerous articles to profl. publs. Mem. acquisitions com. The Bklyn. Mus. of Art, 1995—; trustee Bklyn. Mus. of Art. Recipient Adolf Meyer award for Disting. Svc. on Behalf of Improved Care and Treatment of the Mentally Ill in the Caribbean, 1961. Fellow AMA (life), Am. Psychiat. Assn. (chmn. 1983-86, mem. com. on AIDS N.Y. County dist. br. 1989-99, life), Am. Acad. Psychoanalysis (life), Caribbean Psychiat. Assn.; mem. Group for Advancement of Psychiatry (chair internat. rels. com. 1960-65, chair com. on human sexuality 1987-98). Avocations: collecting Asian and Indian art. Home and Office: 220 Central Park S New York NY 10019-1417 E-mail: bertschmd@aol.com.

SCHAFFNER, CHARLES ETZEL, consulting engineering executive; b. N.Y.C., July 21, 1919; s. Louis C. and Christina (Etzel) S.; m. Olga T. Stroedecke, Feb. 13, 1943; children— Charles Etzel II, Linda Jean. B.C.E., Cooper Union, 1941, C.E., 1952; M.C.E., Bklyn. Poly. Inst., 1944; BSS.E., U. Ill., 1945, N.Y. U.; D.Sci (hon.), Iona Coll., 1983. Jr. engr. Moran Proctor, Freeman & Mueser, N.Y.C., 1941; instr. Cooper Union, 1941-44; mem. faculty

Bklyn. Poly. Inst., 1946-70, prof. engring., 1957-70, adj. prof., 1970-72, asst. dean, 1954-57, assoc. dean, 1957-58, dean, dir. planning, 1958-62, v.p. adminstrn., 1962-70; v.p. Syska & Hennessy, Inc., 1970-73, sr. v.p., 1973-76, exec. v.p., 1976-85, vice chmn., 1985-86, cons., 1987—, also dir. Chmn. nat. adv. bd. Summer Inst. Young Engring. Tchrs., 1959-63; mem. adv. panel NSF, 1960-70; chmn. exec. bd. N.Y.C. Bldg. Code Project, 1962-66; mem. panel 421.00 adv. to bldg. research div. Inst. Applied Tech., Nat. Bur. Standards, 1966-69; mem. bldg., constrn. adv. council Dept. Bldgs. City N.Y., 1966— ; mem. bldg. research adv. bd. NRC, 1972-79, vice chmn., 1973-77; chmn., 1977-78, Mayor's Bldg. and Constrn. Adv. Council, 1971-73; exec. dir. Mayor's Fire Safety Com., 1971-73; mem. N.Y.C. Constrn. Industry Advisory Council, 1973— ; v.p., bd. dirs. N.Y. Bldg. Congress, 1967-71, sec., 1971-75, chmn. govtl. affairs com., 1977-78, pres., 1979-83, chmn. council pres., 1983-87, chmn. council bus. and labor, 1987-88. Contbr. articles profl. jours. Commr. edn. dist., Locust Valley, N.Y., 1956-59, pres., 1958-59; commr. edn., pres. Central Dist. 3, Oyster Bay, N.Y., 1959-63; Trustee Cooper Union, 1975-78; trustee Cooper Union Research Found. Served with AUS, 1944-46. Named Outstanding Alumnus Cooper Union, 1966; Good Scout of Yr. Boy Scouts Am., 1979; recipient Disting. Alumnus award Poly. Alumni Assn., Alumnus of Year, 1972 Mem. Operation Democracy, ASCE (Civil Engr. of Year 1969), ASTM, Am. Arbitration Assn. (bd. arbitrators), Am. Soc. Engring. Edn. (v.p., gen. council 1965-67, v.p. fin. 1974-77, dir. 1965-67, 74-77, 78-81, pres. 1979-80), Nat. Inst. Bldg. Scis. (exec. com. consultative council 1978-82, dir. 1982-88), Engrs. Joint Council (dir. 1976-79), Am. Assn. Engring. Socs. (bd. govs. 1979-81, chmn. ednl. affairs council 1979-80), Am. Concrete Inst., N.Y. State Sch. Bds. Assn., N.Y. State Soc. Profl. Engrs. (dir. Nassau County chpt., Engr. of Year, Kings County chpt. 1968), Cooper Union Alumni Assn. (pres. 1973), Tau Beta Pi, Chi Epsilon, Omega Delta Phi. Clubs: Municipal, Nassau. Home and Office: Linden Farms Rd Locust Valley NY 11560

SCHAFFNER, CYNTHIA VAN ALLEN, writer, curator, lecturer; b. Washington, Jan. 28, 1947; d. James Alfred and Abigail Fifthian (Halsey) Van Allen; m. Robert Todd Schaffner, June 11, 1972; 1 child, Hilary Van Allen. BA, Western Coll., 1969; MAT, Simmons Coll., 1971; MA in History of Decorative Arts, Cooper Hewitt Smithsonian Instn., N.Y.C., 1999. Editor Mademoiselle mag., N.Y.C., 1972-79; dir. devel. Am. Acad. in Rome, 1987-89; curator Phila. Antiques Show, 1997-98; rsch. asst. Metropolitan Mus. Art, New York, 1999—; curator Halsey House, Southampton, N.Y., 1999—. Author: Discovering American Folk Art, 1991; co-author: Folk Hearts, 1984, American Painted Furniture, 1997; contbr. articles to popular mags. Co-chair Fall Antiques Show, N.Y.C., 1979-93; trustee Mus. Am. Folk Art, N.Y.C., 1980-95. Lisa Taylor fellow, 1995-96; Smithsonian Instn. Grad. Student fellow, 1998. Mem. Coll. Art Assn., Decorative Arts Soc., Cosmopolitan Club, Victorian Soc., Lenox Hill Hosp. Aux., Southampton Hist. Mus. (trustee 1996-2002). Avocations: canoeing, gardening, antiquing. Home: 850 Park Ave New York NY 10021-1845 E-mail: cvanschaf@aol.com.

SCHAFFNER, HOWARD SHELDON, lawyer; b. Chgo., Nov. 2, 1943; s. Irving and Frieda Schaffner; m. Gail Schaffner, July 14, 1970; children: Paula, Stacy. JD, John Marshall Law Sch., 1970. Bar: Ill. 1970. Asst. state's atty. Cook County States Atty.'s Office, Chgo., 1970-78; ptnr. Hofeld & Schaffner, 1978—. Mem. ABA, Ill. State Bar Assn., Ill. Trial Lawyers Assn. (bd. mgrs. 1980—; author Cont. Legal Edn. 1980—, Ill. Inst. Cont. Legal Edn. 1980, 83, 86), Ill. State Bar Assn. Office: Hofeld & Schaffner 30 N Lasalle St Ste 3120 Chicago IL 60602-2576

SCHAFFNER, KAREN ANN See FIELD, KAREN ANN

SCHAFFNER, ROBERT JAY, JR. nurse practitioner; b. Mechanicsburg, Pa., Feb. 25, 1949; s. Robert J. Sr. and Bertha May (Books) S.; m. Ellen Gail Hirsch, Sept. 7, 1974 (div.). BA in English and Edn., U. Mass., 1972; BSN, DD (hon.), SUNY, Albany, 1986; MS, U. Rochester, 1989; MBA, Simon Grad. Sch. Bus. Admin., 1992; PhD, Columbia State U., La., 1997. RN, N.Y., Mass.; cert. nurse practitioner and dietitian-nutritionist, N.Y. Head of math. Lear Sch. Inc., Miami, Fla., 1974-81; critical care nurse Strong Meml. Hosp. U. Rochester, N.Y., 1983-86, asst. clinician burn ICU, 1986-89, clin. specialist, nurse practitioner, 1990—; clin. assoc. faculty U. Rochester, 1992—; nurse practitioner J.L. Norris Clinic, Rochester, 1993—. Exec. com. profl. Nursing Orgn., Rochester, 1988-90, chair-elect, 1989; co-founder Men in Nursing Orgn., Rochester, chair, 1991-92, v.p. Am. Assembly, 1993-97, pres., 1997-98; mem. nursing faculty com. Regents Coll., 1992-97; presenter in field; CEO, RSA Assocs., 1986—. Author: poetry (A Best New Poet of 1988, Golden Poet award 1989, Poet of Merit, Am. Poetry Assn. 1989); contbr. articles to profl. jours. CPR instr., disaster action team vol., ARC, 1987—; blood pressure monitor ARC, Boston, 1982-83; mem. alumni bd. Regents Coll., 1992-96, 97-98, v.p., 1994-96. Decorated Imperial Cross of Charlemagne Prince of Saxony; named Internat. Citizen of Yr., Hutt River Province, 1996; recipient Eleanor Hall award, 1989, outstanding svc. award, Regents Coll., 1994, Genesee Valley Nursing Practice award, 1999, Nursing Innovation award, U. Rochester, 1998, Lee Cohen award, 1996; fellow Commonwealth Exec. Nurse fellow, 1989; scholar Mary Riddle scholar, Newton Wellesley Sch. Nursing, 1983. Mem. Am. Burn Assn., Am. Soc. Parenteral and Enteral Nutrition (nurse com. for Ross Pharm.), N.Y. State Nurses Assn., Am. Assembly for Men in Nursing, Genesee Valley Nurses Assn. (bd. dirs. 1995-97, Nurse Practice award 1999), U. Mass. Alumni Assn. (nominations com.), Sigma Theta Tau (chair fin. com. 1996-98, treas. 1998-2000, pres.-elect 2001, Rsch. in Practice award Epsilon Xi chpt. 1999). Avocations: painting, bicycling, windsurfing, weight lifting, motorcycling. E-mal. Home: 71 S Estate Dr Webster NY 14580-2809 Office: U Rochester Med Ctr 601 Elmwood Ave PO Box 667 Rochester NY 14603-0667 E-mail: Robert_Schaffner@urmc.rochester.edu.

SCHAFFNER, ROBERTA IRENE, retired medical, surgical nurse; b. Vero Beach, Fla., Oct. 5, 1926; d. Robert Wesley and Harriett Louise (Davis) Routh; m. David Leonard Schaffner, Apr. 25, 1947 (div. July 1975; dec.); children: Penny Routh S. (dec. July 1999), David Leonard II (dec. Jan. 1999). Mem. cadet nurse corps, Charity Hosp., New Orleans, La., 1944-45; ADA, Montgomery County C.C., Blue Bell, Pa., 1978; BSN, Gwynedd (Pa.) Mercy Coll., 1982, MSN, 1984. RN Pa. Med.-surg. nurse Chestnut Hill Hosp., Phila., 1978-2000, ret., 2000. Mem. delegation to study health care delivery sys., Moscow, Tbillisi, Azerbeijan, Kiev, 1981, Shanghai, Beijing, Nanjing, Hong Kong, 1984, Milan, Pisa, Bologna, Florence, Rome, Sorento, Naples, 1985. Cadet U.S. Nurse Corps, 1945. Mem. Oncology Nursing Soc., Sigma Theta Tau. Republican. Home: 1600 Church Rd Apt A214 Wyncote PA 19095-1929 E-mail: robertars4@aol.com.

SCHAFRICK, FREDERICK CRAIG, lawyer; b. Sept. 20, 1948; s. Rudolph Henry and Patricia Eleanor (Zemer) Schafrick; m. Sharon Lee Halpin, May 23, 1981; children: Michael Nile, Nathaniel Henry. AB, U. Mich., 1970, JD, 1973. Bar: D.C. 1973, U.S. Ct. Appeals (D.C. cir.) 1975, U.S. Supreme Ct. 1977. Law clk. U.S. Ct. Appeals (2d cir.), N.Y.C., NY, 1973—74; assoc., then ptnr. Shea & Gardner, Washington, 1974—. Editor (adminstrv.): (law rev.) Mich. Law Rev., 1973. Mem.: ABA, Order of Coif, Phi Beta Kappa. Democrat. Presbyterian. Home: 5416 Nebraska Ave NW Washington DC 20015-1350 Office: Shea & Gardner Ste 800 1800 Massachusetts Ave NW Washington DC 20036-1872

SCHAICH, WILLIAM L. physics educator; b. Springfield, Mass., Oct. 15, 1944; s. Wilbur Allison and Lillian Luella (Halfaker) S.; m. Georgia Jeann Loebrich, Dec. 23, 1966; children: Amy C., Lucy B. BS, Denison U., 1966; MS, Cornell U., 1968, PhD, 1970. Post doctoral fellow, Bristol, U.K., 1970-71; research asst. U. Calif., LaJolla, Calif., 1971-73; asst. prof. Ind. U., 1973-76, assoc. prof., 1976-80, prof., 1980—. Contbr. articles to profl. jours. Fellow Am. Physical Soc. Office: Ind U Swain Hall W Bloomington IN 47405 E-mail: schaich@indiana.edu.

SCHAIE, K(LAUS) WARNER, human development and psychology educator; b. Stettin, Germany (now Poland), Feb. 1, 1928; came to U.S., 1947, naturalized, 1953; s. Sally and Lottie Luise (Gabriel) S.; m. Coloma J. Harrison, Aug. 9, 1953 (div. 1973); 1 child, Stephan; m. Sherry L. Willis, Nov. 20, 1981. AA, City Coll., San Francisco, 1951; BA, U. Calif., Berkeley, 1952; MS, U. Wash., 1953, PhD, 1956; PhD (hon.), Friedrich-Schiller U., Jena, Germany, 1997. Lic. psychologist, Calif., Pa. Fellow Washington U., St. Louis, 1956-57; asst. prof. psychology U. Nebr., Lincoln, 1957-64, assoc. prof., 1964-68; prof. chmn. dept. psychology W.Va. U., Morgantown, 1964-73; prof. psychology, dir. Gerontology Rsch. Inst., U. So. Calif., 1973-81; Evan Pugh prof. human devel. and psychology, dir. Gerontology Ctr., Pa. State U., University Park, 1981—. Devel. behavior study sect. NIH, Bethesda, Md., 1970-72, chmn., 1972-74, chmn. human devel. and aging study sect., 1979-84, mem. expert panel in comml. airline pilot retirement, 1981, data and safety bd. shep project, 1984-91. Author: Developmental Psychology; A Life Span Approach, 1981, Adult Development and Aging, 1982, 5th rev. edit., 2002, Intellectual Development in Adulthood: The Seattle Longitudinal Study, 1996; editor: Handbook of Psychology of Aging, 1977, 5th rev. edit., 2001, Longitudinal Studies of Adult Development, 1983, Cognitive Functioning and Social Structure over the Life Course, 1987, Methodological Issues in Research on Aging, 1988, Social Structure and Aging: Psychological Processes, 1989, Age Structuring in Comparative Perspective, 1989, The Course of Later Life, 1989, Self-Directedness: Cause and Effects Throughout the Life Course, 1990, Aging, Health Behaviors and Health Outcomes, 1992, Caregiving Systems: Formal and Informal Helpers, 1993, Societal Impact on Aging: Historical Perspectives, 1993, Adult Intergenerational Relations: Effects of Societal Change, 1995, Older Adults Decision Making and the Law, 1996, Impact of Social Structures on Decision Making in the Elderly, 1997, Impact of the Workplace on Older Persons, 1998, Handbook of Theories of Aging, 1999, Mobility and Aging, 2000, Evolution of the Aging Self, 2000, Effective Health Behavior in the Elderly, 2002, Mastery and Control in the Edlerly,2002; editor Ann. Rev. Gerontology and Geriatrics, vol. 7, 1987, vol. 11, 1991, vol. 17, 1997; contbr. articles to profl. jours. Fellow APA (coun. reps. 1976-79, 83-86, Disting. Contbn. award, 1992), Gerontol. Soc. (Kleemeier award 1987, Disting. Mentorship award 1996), Am. Psychol. Soc.; mem. Psychometric Soc., Internat. Soc. Study Behavioral Devel. Unitarian Universalist. Avocations: hiking, stamps. Home: 425 Windmere Dr Apt 3A State College PA 16801-7670 Office: Pa State U Gerontology Ctr Dept Human Devel & Family Studies University Park PA 16802 E-mail: kws@psu.edu.

SCHAKE, LOWELL MARTIN, animal science educator; b. Marthasville, Mo., June 6, 1938; s. Martin Charles and Flora Olinda (Rocklage) S.; m. Wendy Anne Walkinshaw, Sept. 11, 1959; children: Sheryl Anne, Lowell Scott. BS, U. Mo., 1960, MS, 1962; PhD, Tex. A&M U., 1967. Asst. prof. Tex. A&M U., College Station, 1965-67, assoc. prof., 1969-72, prof., 1972-84, asst. prof., area livestock specialist Lubbock, 1967-69; prof., head animal sci. dept. U. Conn., Storrs, 1984-92; prof., chmn. animal sci. dept. Tex. Tech. U., Lubbock, 1992-95. Developer applied animal ethology program Tex. A&M U., 1970, New Eng. Biotech Conf. series, 1990, S.W. Beef Forum, 1993; chmn. Am. Registry of Profl. Animal Scientist Com. on Profl. Stds., 1988; chmn. Nat. Com. Exec. Officers of Animal Vet., Dairy and Poultry Sci. Depts., 1992; cons. Alpart, Kingston, Jamaica, 1975, U.S. Feeds Grain Coun., 1970-73, A.O. Smith Products Inc., 1968-92, Humphrey Land & Cattle Co., Dallas, 1980-86; lectr. in field. Author: Growth and Finishing of Beef Cattle, A Class Handbook, 1982; contbr. articles to profl. jours. Recipient Innovative Teaching award Tex. A&M U., 1978. Mem. Am. Soc. Animal Sci., Plains Nutrition Coun. (adv. bd. 1967-80, sec.-treas. 1994-95, founder), Nat. Assn. Colls. and Tchrs. Agr., Am. Registry Profl. Animal Scientists (dir. for Northeast 1987-89), Coun. for Agr. Sci. and Tech. World Conf. on Animal Prodn., Am. Soc. Dairy Sci., Gamma Sigma Delta. Clubs: Tiger (College Station) (pres.). Republican. Avocations: genealogy, fishing, gardening, outdoor work. Home: 13542 Carlos Fifth Ct Corpus Christi TX 78418-6913 E-mail: lschake@aol.com.

SCHAKOWSKY, JANICE, congresswoman; b. Chgo., May 26, 1944; d. Irwin and Tillie (Cosnow) Danoff; m. Harvey E. Schakowsky, Feb. 17, 1965 (div. 1980); children: Ian, Mary; m. Robert B. Creamer, Dec. 6, 1980; 1 stepchild, Lauren. BS, U. Ill., 1965. Cert. elem. tchr., Ill. Tchr. Chgo. Bd. Edn., 1965-67; organizer Ill. Pub. Action Coun., Chgo., 1976-85; exec. dir. Ill. State Coun. Sr. Citizens, 1985-90; mem. Ill. Ho. Reps., 1990-98; U.S. Congress from 9th Ill. dist., 1999—; mem. banking and fin. svcs. com., 1999—; mem. govt. reform com., 1999—. Bd. dirs. Ill. Pub. Action, 4 C's Day Care Coun., Evanston, Ill.; steering com. mem. Cook County Dem. Women, 1986-90; del. Nat. Dem. Conv., 1988; governing coun. Am. Jewish Congress, 1990—. Named Outstanding Legislator Interfaith Coun. for Homeless, 1993, Legislator of Yr. Ill. Nurses Assn., 1992, Ill. Assn. Cmty. Mental Health Agys., 1994, Coalition of Citizens with Disabilities and Ill. Coun. Sr. Citizens, 1993, Cmty. Action Assn., 1991, Champaign County Health Care Assn., 1992, Rookie of Yr. Ill. Environ. Coun., 1991. Mem. ACLU, NOW, Nat. Coun. Jewish Women, Ill. Pro-Choice Alliance, Evanston Mental Health Assn., Evanston Hist. Soc., Evanston Friends of Libr., Rogers Park Hist. Soc. Democrat. Jewish. Avocations: travelling, horsebackriding, reading. Home: 1101 Ridge Ave Evanston IL 60202-1231 Office: Ho of Reps 515 Cannon Ho Office Bldg Washington DC 20515-1309*

SCHALK, ROBERT PARTRIDGE, lawyer; b. Pueblo, Colo., June 20, 1931; s. Robert Louis and Elizabeth (Partridge) S.; m. Carolyn Ruthina Shusn, June 7, 1957; children: Steven Douglas, David Allen, Julie Dawn, Jeffrey Scott. BBA, U. Colo., 1953; JD, U. So. Calif., 1961; BBA, U. Colo., 1963. Bar: Calif. 1962; CPA, Calif., 1960; lic. real estate broker, Calif.; securities lic. Assoc. Millikan & Montgomery, L.A., 1961-63; tax lawyer L.H. Penney & Co., CPAs, San Francisco, 1963-67; pvt. practice law Santa Cruz, Calif., 1967—. Lt. USN, 1953-55. Office: 550 Water St Bldg F-3 Santa Cruz CA 95060-4131 Fax: 831-423-5419. E-mail: rbtschalk@aol.com.

SCHALL, ALVIN ANTHONY, federal judge; b. N.Y.C., Apr. 4, 1944; s. Gordon William and Helen (Davis) Schall; m. Sharon Frances LeBlanc, Apr. 25, 1970; children: Amanda Lanford, Anthony Davis. BA, Princeton U., 1966; JD, Tulane U., 1969. Bar: N.Y. 1970, U.S. Dist. Ct. (so. and ea. dists.) N.Y. 1973, U.S. Ct. Appeals (2d crct.) 1974, D.C. 1980, U.S. Dist. Ct. D.C. 1991, U.S. Ct. Appeals (D.C. crct.) 1991, U.S. Ct. Fed. Claims 1982, U.S. Ct. Appeals (fed. crct.) 1987, U.S. Supreme Ct. 1989. Assoc. Shearman & Sterling, N.Y.C., 1969—73; asst. U.S. atty. ea. dist. N.Y. Borough of Bklyn., 1973—78, chief appeals divsn., 1977—78; trial atty. civil divsn. U.S. Dept. Justice, Washington, 1978—87, sr. trial counsel, 1986—87, asst. to atty. gen., 1988—92; ptnr. Perlman & Ptnrs., 1987—88; judge U.S. Ct. Appeals (fed. cir.), 1992—. Office: 717 Madison Pl NW Washington DC 20439-0002

SCHALL, LAWRENCE DELANO, economics educator, consultant; b. Los Angeles, Nov. 5, 1940; s. Lee and Lillian (Seltzow) S.; m. Betty Jane Kay, Aug. 6, 1982; children: Michael Kay, Adam Kent. BA, UCLA, 1962; MA in Econs., U. Chgo., 1967, PhD in Econs., 1969. CPA, Wash. Sec.-treas. Permco Inc., Los Angeles, 1959-61; acting asst. prof. econs. U. Wash., Seattle, 1968-69, asst. prof., 1969-72, assoc. prof., 1972-76, prof., 1976—. Author: (with C. W. Haley) The Theory of Financial Decisions, 1972, 2d edit., 1979, Introduction to Financial Management, 1977, 6th edit., 1991, (with K. Henderson and R. May) Evaluating Business Ventures, 1982; contbr. articles to profl. jours. Recipient Bank of Am. Excellence award, 1983, Burlington No. Found. award, 1986, First Interstate Bank award, 1990, Andrew V. Smith award, U. Wash., 1992. Mem. Am. Econ. Assn., Am. Fin. Assn., Fin. Mgmt. Assn., Fin. Execs. Inst. Office: U Wash Sch Bus Adminstrn 261 Mackenzie Hall Dj # 10 Seattle WA 98195-0001

SCHALLAU, DONALD JOSEPH, writer; b. Williamsburg, Iowa, Apr. 18, 1944; s. Paul Raymond Schallau and Elsie Marie Boddicker. BA, U. Iowa, 1972, postgrad., 1986. Legal rschr. PJS Enterprises, Iowa City, 1973—89. Contbr. letters to jours.; editor, compiler: books Safety-Defect Recall Campaign Reports, 1986. Pres. Students for Eugene McCarthy for President, U. Iowa, Iowa City, 1968. Democrat. Roman Catholic. Avocations: foreign languages, poetry, Bible study in Greek and Hebrew. Home: Apt 201A 41 E Market St Iowa City IA 52245

SCHALLENKAMP, KAY, academic administrator; b. Salem, S.D., Dec. 9, 1949; d. Arnold B. and Jennie M. (Koch) Krier; m. Ken Schallenkamp, Sept. 7, 1970; children: Heather, Jenni. BS, No. State Coll., 1972; MA, U. S.D., 1973; PhD, U. Colo., 1982. Prof. No. State Coll., Aberdeen, S.D., 1973-88, dept. chair, 1982-84, dean, 1984-88; provost Chadron (Nebr.) State Coll., 1988-92, U. Wis., Whitewater, 1992-97; pres. Emporia (Kans.) State U., 1997—. Cons. North Ctrl. Assn., nursing homes, hosps. and ednl. instns. Contbr. articles to profl. jours. Commr. North Ctrl. Assn., 1995-99. Bush fellow, 1980; named Outstanding Young Career Woman, Bus. and Profl. Women's Club, 1976. Mem. NCAA (pres.'s coun. 2000—), Kans. C. of C. (bd. dirs. 2000—), Am. Speech and Hearing Assn. (cert.), Rotary. Avocation: martial arts. Office: Emporia State U 1200 Commercial St Emporia KS 66801-5087 E-mail: schallka@emporia.edu.

SCHALLER, ANTHONY JOSEF, technology management executive; b. Pitts., Nov. 17, 1957; s. Josef and Ruth Bridgette (Petschick) S.; m. Anna Marie Johnson (div. Nov. 1997); children: Kristofer, Derek. BS in Computer Sci. and Bus. Mgmt., U. Pitts., 1982; grad. degree computer sci., Carnegie-Mellon U., 1987. Mgr. sys. devel. Carnegie-Mellon U., Pitts., 1980-87; sr. mgr. applications engring. Ingres Corp., Alameda, Calif., 1988-91; dir. tech. mktg. MTI/SF2 Corp., Sunnyvale, 1991-92; dir. multidatabase sys. devel. MDL Info. Sys., Inc., San Leandro, 1992-93, dir. intersect project, 1993-94; pres., founder Intersect Software, Inc., Alameda, 1994-97; v.p. engring., chief tech. officer Open Object/Electric Classifieds, Inc., San Francisco, 1997-98; v.p. tech. Ticketmaster Online-CitySearch, Inc., Pasadena, Calif., 1998-99; sr. v.p. tech., chief tech. officer, COO RioPort.com, San Jose, 1999—. Bd. dirs. ZealMedia, Inc., L.A.; tech./mgmt. cons. Turnaround Mgmt. Assn., Alameda, 1998-99. Mem. Assn. for Computing Machinery (program devel. and spkr. liason/coord. Pitts. chpt. 1983-84, vice-chmn. Pitts. chpt. 1984-85, chmn. Pitts. chpt. 1985-86, Svc. Recognition award 1985, 86). Achievements include patent for system and methods for performing multi-source searches over heterogeneous databases. Avocations: skiing, physical fitness, travel, investment, reading. Home: 211 Encounter Bay Alameda CA 94502-7909 Office: RioPort.com 2895 Zanker Rd San Jose CA 95134-2101 Fax: 707-221-1598. E-mail: tony@schaller.net.

SCHALLER, BARRY R. judge; BA, Yale U., 1960, JD, 1963. Bar: Conn. 1963, U.S. Dist. Ct. Conn. 1963, U.S. Ct. Appeals (2nd cir.) 1964, U.S. Supreme Ct. 1966. Ptnr. Bronson & Rice, Attys., New Haven, 1963-74; judge Ct. of Common Pleas, Cir. Ct., 1974-78, Superior Ct., State Conn., 1978-92, Appellate Ct., State Conn., 1992—. Counsel to Ho. of Reps., 1969; mem. bd. pardons State of Conn., 1971-74, chair, 1973-74; mem. exec. com. Conn. Planning Com. on Criminal Adminstrn., 1972-74; chair Superior Ct. Benchbook Com., 1985-92; vis. lectr. Yale Coll., 1986, 88; clin. instr. evidence and trial practice Yale Law Sch., 1989—; vis. lectr., Quinnipiac Law Sch., 2002; adj. faculty Trinity Coll., Quinnipiac Law Sch.; lectr. W.Va. Magistrates Conf., 1990, Vt. Jud. Coll., 1992, Fla. Jud. Coll., 1993, 94, 96, 99, 2002, Ohio Jud. Coll., 1999, 2002, Mo. Jud. Coll., 2002, others; faculty Conn. Judges Inst., 1987-90; mem. Superior Ct. Jury Instrn. Com., 1989-92; mem. exec. com. Conn. Ctr. for Jud. Edn., 1989-92; active Superior Ct. Civil Case Mgmt. Task Force; mem. jud. evidence code drafting com. Author: A Vision of American Law: Judging Law, Literature, and the Stories We Tell, 1997, A Legal Prescription for Bioethical Ills, Quinnipiac Law Review, 2002; contbr. articles to profl. jours. Assoc. fellow Branford Coll.; adminstrv. co-sec. Yale Class of 1960; mem. adv. com. Fair Haven Mediation Bd., 19980-82; bd. dirs. Russian-Am. Rule of Law Project; mem. working groups Yale Bioethics Project; vestry mem., tchr. Trinity Ch., Branford, St. Andrew's Ch., Madison. Recipient book award Quinnipic Law Sch., 1997; Guggenheim fellow Yale Law Sch., 1975-76, 84, 85-86. Fellow Conn. Bar Found. (charter life, fellows adv. com.); mem. ABA (CEELI adv.), Conn. Bar Assn., Hartford County Bar Assn., New Haven County Bar Assn., Conn. Judges Assn. (dir. 1990-92), Am. Judges Assn., Am. Judicature Soc., Am. Law Inst., Yale Law Sch. Assn. (exec. com. 1990-92), Am. Inns of Ct. (bencher 1989-90), Conn. Russian-Am. Rule of Law Program (founder, co-chair), Phi Delta Phi. Office: Appellate Ct State Conn 95 Washington St Hartford CT 06106-4431

SCHALLER, GEORGE BEALS, zoologist; b. Berlin, May 26, 1933; s. Georg Ludwig S. and Bettina (Byrd) Iwersen; m. Kay Suzanne Morgan, Aug. 26, 1957; children: Eric, Mark. BS in Zoology, BA in Anthropology, U. Alaska, 1955; PhD in Zoology, U. Wis., 1962. Rsch. assoc. Johns Hopkins U., Balt., 1963—66; rsch. zoologist Wildlife Conservation Soc., Bronx, 1966—. Rsch. assoc. Am. Mus. Natural History Author: The Mountain Gorilla, 1963 (Wildlife Soc. award 1965), The Year of the Gorilla, 1964, The Deer and the Tiger, 1967, The Serengeti Lion, 1972 (Nat. Book award 1973), Golden Shadows, Flying Hooves, 1973, Mountain Monarchs, 1977, Stones of Silence, 1980, The Giant Pandas of Wolong, 1985, The Last Panda, 1993, Tibet's Hidden Wilderness, 1997, Wildlife of the Tibetan Steppe, 1998. Decorated Order of Golden Ark, The Netherlands, 1978; recipient Gold medal World Wildlife Fund, 1980, Explorers medal Explorers Club, 1990, Cosmos prize Japan, 1996, Tyler Environ. prize, 1997; Ctr. Advanced Study in Behavorial Scis. fellow Stanford U., 1962, fellow Guggenheim Found., 1971. Office: Wildlife Conservation Soc Bronx Park Bronx NY 10460 Business E-Mail: asiaprogram@wcs.org.

SCHALLER, JANE GREEN, pediatrician; b. Cleve., June 26, 1934; d. George and May Alice (Wing) Green; children: Robert Thomas, George Charles, Margaret May. AB, Hiram (Ohio) Coll., 1956; MD cum laude, Harvard U., 1960. Diplomate Am. Bd. Pediat., Am. Bd. Med. Examiners. Resident in pediat. Children's Hosp.-U. Wash., Seattle, 1960-63; fellow immunology Children's Hosp. U. Wash., 1963-65; faculty U. Wash. Med. Sch., 1965-83, prof. pediat., 1975-83; head divsn. rheumatic diseases Children's Hosp., Seattle, 1968-83; prof., chmn. dept. pediat., pediatrician-in-chief Tufts U. Sch. Medicine/New Eng. Med. Ctr., 1983-98; Karp prof. pediat. Tufts U. Sch. Medicine, Boston, 1983—, disting. prof., 1995—. Vis. physician Med. Rsch. Coun., Taplow, Eng., 1971-72; adj. prof. diplomacy The Fletcher Sch. Law and Diplomacy, Tufts U., 1998-2000. Contbr. articles to profl. jours. Bd. dirs. Seattle Chamber Music Festival, 1982-85; trustee Boston Chamber Music Soc., 1985—; mem. Boston adv. coun. UNICEF, tech. advisor UN Study on the Impact of Armed Conflict on Children, 1995-97; chmn., adv. com. children's rights divsn. Human Rights Watch, 1995—; mem. adv. com. Middle East divsn., 1998—; exec. com. Women's Commn. for Refugee Women and Children Internat. Rescue com., 1989-94, adv. coun. 1994—. Mem.: AAAS, Royal Coll. Pediats. U.K., Internat. Women's Forum, Mass. Women's Forum, Harvard U. Med. Sch. Alumni Coun. (v.p. 1977—80, pres. 1982—83), Physicians for Human Rights (exec. com. 1986—, founding pres. 1986—89), Com. Health in So. Africa (exec. com. 1986—92), Assn. Med. Sch. Pediat. Chmn. (exec. com. 1986—89, rep. to coun. on govt. affairs and coun. acad. socs.), New Eng. Pediat. Soc. (pres. 1991—93), Am. Coll. Rheumatology, Internat. Pediat. Assn. (pres.-elect 1998—2001, pres. 2001—04), Am. Acad. Pediat. (exec. com. sect. on internat. child health, head children's rights program, rep. to UNICEF), Am. Pediat. Soc., Soc. Pediat. Rsch., Inst. Medicine of NAS, Saturday Club, Tavern Club, Aesculapian Club (pres. 1988—89). Office: Floating Hosp for Children 750 Washington St # 8683 Boston MA 02111-1526

SCHALLER, MATTHEW FITE, architect; b. Denver, Nov. 28, 1953; s. Frank Henry and Jane (Fite) S.; m. Lavrette DeMandel, Nov. 23, 1991. Student, U. Colo., 1972-76; BS, U. Idaho, 1981, M in Engring., 1985. Registered arch.; real estate salesperson. Foreman Inter-Island Builders, Honolulu, 1978-80; custom home designer Idaho, Montana, Hawaii, 1980-85; rsch. engr. U. Idaho, Moscow, 1982-85; design assoc. Design Assocs., Hanalei, Hawaii, 1985-89; arch. Custom Home Designs, 1987; project mgr. Princeville Corp., Princeville, Hawaii, 1989-96. Pres. Princeville II Cmty. Assn., 1995—. Mem. ASCE, Tau Beta Phi. Avocations: golf, travel. Home and Office: PO Box 120 Hanalei HI 96714-0120

SCHALLERT, WILLIAM JOSEPH, actor; b. Los Angeles, July 6, 1922; s. Edwin Francis and Elza Emily (Baumgarten) S.; m. Rosemarie Diann Waggner, Feb. 26, 1949; children: William Joseph, Edwin G., Mark M., Brendan C. BA, UCLA, 1946. Co-founder, owner Circle Theatre, Hollywood, Calif., 1947-50. Appeared in motion pictures, TV, stage, radio, 1947—; movies include Lonely Are the Brave, Heat of the Night, Charley Varrick, Red Badge of Courage, Teachers; starred in TV series Patty Duke Show, 1963-66, Nancy Drew Mysteries, 1977-78, Little Women, 1979, The New Gidget, 1986-88, The Torkelson's, 1991-92; starred as judge in stage play and film The Trial of the Catonsville Nine, N.Y.C., Los Angeles, 1971 (Obie award 1971); recent TV movies include To Dance with Olivia, 1997; guest star ER, 1996, The Patty Duke Show Reunion, 1999; starred as Dr. Pangloss in Candide, L.A., 1995. Trustee Motion Picture and TV Fund, 1975—. With AUS, 1942-44; with USAAC, 1944-45. Fulbright fellow Brit. Repertory Theatre, 1952-53 Mem. ASCAP, SAG (pres. 1979-81, trustee pension and health plan 1983—, founder Com. for Performers with Disabilities 1981—, Ralph Morgan award 1993).

SCHALLY, ANDREW VICTOR, endocrinologist, researcher; b. Poland, Nov. 30, 1926; arrived in U.S., 1957; s. Casimir Peter and Maria (Lacka) Schally; m. Ana Maria Comaru, Aug. 1976. BSc, McGill U., Can., 1955, PhD in Biochemistry, 1957; 22 hon. doctorates. Research asst. biochemistry Nat. Inst. Med. Research, London, 1949—52; dept. psychiatry McGill U., Montreal, 1952—57; research assoc., asst. prof. physiology and biochemistry Coll. Medicine, Baylor U., Houston, 1957—62; assoc. prof. Tulane U. Sch. Medicine, New Orleans, 1962—67, prof., 1967—. Chief Endocrine Polypeptide and Cancer Inst. VA Med. Ctr., New Orleans; sr. med. investigator VA, 1973—99, disting. med. rsch. scientist, 1999—. Author several books; contbr. articles to profl. jours. Co-recipient Nobel prize for medicine, 1977; recipient Van Meter prize, Am. Thyroid Assn., 1969, Ayerst-Squibb award, Endocrine Soc., 1970, William S. Middletown award, VA, 1970, Ch. Mickle award, U. Toronto, 1974, Gairdner Internat. award, 1974, Borden award, Assn. Am. Med. Colls. and Borden Co. Found., 1975, Lasker Basic Rsch. award, 1975; fellow sr. rsch. fellow, USPHS, 1961—62. Mem.: AAAS, NAS, Acad. Sci. Mex., Acad. Sci. Russia, Acad. Sci. Hungary, Acad. Medicine Poland, Acad. Medicine Venezuela, Nat. Acad. Medicine Brazil, Mex. Acad. Medicine, Soc. Internat. Brain Rsch. Orgn., Internat. Soc. Rsch. Biology Reprodn., Soc. Exptl. Biol. Medicine, Soc. Biol. Chemists, Am. Physiol. Soc., Endocrine Soc. Home: 5025 Kawanee Ave Metairie LA 70006-2547 Office: VA Hosp 1601 Perdido St New Orleans LA 70112-1207

SCHALOW, FRANK HICKEY, philosopher, educator; b. Denver, Feb. 23, 1956; s. Berthold Erich and Frances Schalow. BA summa cum laude, U. Denver, 1978; MA, Tulane U., 1980, PhD, 1984. Vis. asst. prof. Loyola U., New Orleans, 1984-86, asst. prof., 1986-90, assoc. prof., 1990-92; lectr. Dillard U., 1993—; vis. assoc. prof. Xavier U., 1994-97, U. New Orleans, 1995—. Mem. editl. adv. bd. Auslegung U. Kans., Lawrence, 1983-97, Heidegger Studies U. Wis., LaCrosse, 2000—; mem. dissertation adv. bd. Union Inst., Cin., 1999—. Author: Imagination and Existence, 1986, Renewal of the Heidegger-Kant Dialogue, 1992, Language and Deed, 1998, Heidegger and the Quest for the Sacred, 2001; co-author: Traces of Understanding, 1990. Mem. Am. Philos. Assn., N.Am. Heidegger Conf. (sec. convenor 1992), S.W. Philosophy Soc. (exec. com. 1993), Phi Beta Kappa. Avocation: golf. Home: 7310 Freret St New Orleans LA 70118 Office: U New Orleans Lakefront Campus New Orleans LA 70148 E-mail: fschalow@uno.edu.

SCHANCK, PETER CARR, law educator; b. Chgo., May 9, 1938; s. Francis Raber and Kathryn (Short) S.; m. Sally Cessna, Aug. 10, 1960 (div. 1974); children— Christine, Brett, Derick, Julia; m. Karen Ushman, July 10, 1974. B.A., Dartmouth Coll., 1960; J.D., Yale U., 1963; M.L.S., U. Md., 1972. Bar: Conn. 1963. Legal specialist Library of Congress, Washington, 1965-71; head reference dept. law library U. Mich., Ann Arbor, 1974-78; assoc. prof. law, dir. law library U. Detroit, 1978-82; prof. law, dir. law library U. Kans., Lawrence, 1982— ; mem. adv. bd. Law Library Jour., 1984-86 , Legal Reference Services Quar., 1981-84. Author: A Guide to Legal Research, 1976, 2d edit., 1978; contbr. articles to profl. publs. Mem. Mich. Assn. Law Libraries (pres. 1979-80), Am. Assn. Law Libraries, Mid.-Am. Assn. Law Libraries (pres. elect 1987-89, pres. 1989—). Home: 1731 Indiana St Lawrence KS 66044-4049 Office: U Kans Law Sch Libr Green Hall Lawrence KS 66045-7577

SCHANDEL, SUSAN, professional sports team executive; Corp. controller Internat. Speedway Corp., Daytona Beach, Fla., 1992—96, CFO, 1996—, v.p. adminstrv. svcs. Office: ISC 1801 W International Speedway Blvd Daytona Beach FL 32114*

SCHANDELMEIER, CATHLEEN ANN, playwright, poet, producer; b. Chgo., Aug. 28, 1959; d. Dale Theodore and JoAnn Marie (Curren) S.; m. Peter Carl Bartels; children: Vincent James Peterson-Schandelmeier, Katrina Marie Bartels, Teodoro Schandelmeier Bartels, Katrina Marie Bartels. BA in Theater, Northeastern Ill. U., 1989. Tchr. Chgo. Children's Mus., 1996—97, 2002, Facets Multimedia Camp, 1998, Evanston Arts Camp, 2000, Irish Am. Heritage Ctr., 2001—. Poetry host Poetry on the Beach, Chgo., 1990—, artistic dir. Vince Charming Prodns., Chgo, 1991—; TV show Host, Venue, Chgo., 1992-93; artist in edn. Ill. Arts Coun.; presenter Chgo. Assn. for Edn. of Young Children, 1998, 2000; profl. artist Gallery 2828 Artshow Outbreak, 2001; film producer The Atruistic Alien, Childrens Film Festival, 2001, Potatoes Gone Bad, Heritage Ctr., 2001 (Best Narrative Film award Chgo. Youth Film and Video Festival 2002). Playwright: Sandy and the Circus, 1993, (grant IAC), Santa Girl, 1993 (Peace Mus. 1994), Mmm..Tatoo Screams of Love, 1994 (Adade Wheeler 1995), The Christmas Pageant-St Matthias, 1995, Beached, 1999, A Caribbean Cruise Ship Christmas, 2000 (grantee Ill. Arts Coun. 2000), Sidekick, 2000, The Adventures of Keaton the Cat, 2001; poet: (Anthologies of Poetry) Stray Bullets, 1991, Step Into the Light, 1992; author (book of poetry) Scream and I'll Believe You, 1993, (book of poetry and prose) Tattoo Screams of Love, 1997; also poetry in magazines and articles in Letter eX (Poetry News Mag.); coord. video for Internat. Soc. to Prevent Child Abuse and Neglect's World Congress, 1996 (100 Women Making a Difference award Today's Chgo. Woman Found. 1998); columnist: Chicago Parent, 1998; prodr.: (film short) The Altruistic Alien, 2001; editor: (poetry book) Best Chants, 2000 (Ill. Arts Coun. S.T.A.R. grant 2000); artist for Outbreak Visual Art Show, Gallery 2828, 2001; artist-in-residence, writer, illustrator The Lonely Lion, 2002. Pres. Children United for Strength, 1997; sponsor The 1997 Girl X Benefit; theater coord. Bucktown Arts Fest., 1997-99; founding dir. The Irish Arts Club, 2001-02. Recipient cert. of leadership in racial justice YWCA, DuPage County, Ill., 1994, spl. assistance grant Ill. Arts Coun., Chgo., 1994, 97, 2000; nominated for Adade Wheeler award Coll. of DuPage in Glen Ellyn, 1995; named Outstanding Local Leader in Peace, The Peace Mus., Chgo., 1994; grantee Ill. Arts Coun., 1997, 2000, 2001. Mem. Internat. Soc. to Prevent Child Abuse and Neglect, Guild Complex Literary Soc., Puppeteers of Am. Democrat. Avocations: skiing, stroller skating, bicycling, photography, reading. Home: 2044 W Arthur Ave Apt 3W Chicago IL 60645-5555 E-mail: petcat5@juno.com.

SCHANDER, MARY LEA, protective services official; b. June 11, 1947; d. Gerald John Lea and Marian Lea Coffman; m. Edwin Schander, July 3, 1971. BA, Calif. Luth. Coll., 1969; MA, UCLA, 1970. Staff aide City of Anaheim (Calif.) Police Dept., 1970-72, staff asst., 1972-78, sr. staff asst., 1978-80; with Resource Mgmt. Dept. City of Anaheim, 1980-82; asst. to dir. Pub. Safety Agy. City of Pasadena Police Dept., 1982-85, spl. asst. to police chief, 1985-88, adminstrv. comdr., 1988-92, police comdr., 1992—. Freelance musician; publisher Australian Traditional Songs, 1985, Songs in the Air of Early California, 1994; lectr. Calif. Luth. Coll.; instr. Calif. State U., Northridge, Pasadena City Coll., 2000-, Pasadena City Coll., 2000-; cons. City of Lodz, Poland, Internat. Assn. Chiefs of Police; speaker, panelist League of Calif. Cities, Pasadena Commn. on Status of Women; mcpl. mgmt. asst. CLEARS. Prodr.: (cable TV program) Traditional Music Showcase; contbr. articles in field to profl. jours. Bd. dirs. ARC, Rotary Club Pasadena, S.W. Chamber Music; instr. Bd. Corrections. Recipient Police Chief's Spl. award City of Pasadena, 1987, Women at Work Medal of Excellence, 1988, 2d Century Leadership award YWCA, 1998; Augustana fellow Calif. Luth. Coll., 1969. Mem. Internat. Assn. Chiefs of Police, Pasadena Arts Coun., L.A. Coun. Peace Officers, S.W. Chamber Music Soc. Home: PO Box 50151 Pasadena CA 91115-0151 Office: Pasadena Police Dept 207 N Garfield Ave Pasadena CA 91101-1791 E-mail: mschander@ci.pasadena.ca.us.

SCHANES, CHRISTINE, lawyer; b. Jersey City, Apr. 9, 1948; d. Steven Eli and Christine (Marra) S.; m. Ron Taylor; children: Christine Elizabeth, Patrick Steven. BA, U. San Diego, 1970; JD, Am. U., 1973; PhD, U. Notre Dame, 1975. Bar: calif. 1973, U.S. Dist. Ct. (cen., no. and so. dists.) Calif. 1973. Dep. atty. gen. Calif. Dept. Justice, Los Angeles, 1975-78; sr. atty. Atlantic Richfield Co., 1978-83; sole practice Santa Monica, Calif., 1983—. V.p., bd. dirs. Labor of Love Prodns., inc., 2001—. Co-dir. Nos Amis/Our Friends, Inc., Children Helping Poor and Homeless People, 1987—. Recipient Outstanding Achievement award Urban League, 1969. Mem. Calif. Bar Assn. Office: Children Helping Poor and Homeless People 2554 Lincoln Blvd Ste 522 Venice CA 90291-5082 E-mail: chphp@earthlink.net.

SCHANFARBER, RICHARD CARL, real estate broker; b. Cleve., June 11, 1937; s. Edwin David and Helen (Newman) S.; m. Barbara A. Berger, Dec. 21, 1958 (div. Sept. 1981); children: Edwin Jeffrey, Lori Jo, Tammy Joy. Grad., NYU, 1959. Lic. FCC broadcast engr. Pres. Erieview Realty, Gates Mills, 1961—, Miller Warehouse, Gates Mills, 1968—2001, ERI Travel Co., Gates Mills, 1974—2001, ERI Sales Co., Gates Mills, 1979—, Eastgate Travel Svcs., Gates Mills, Ohio, 1987—2001. Pres. Shaker Hts. (Ohio) Alumni Assn., 1986-97, chmn. bd., 1997–; pres. Cleve. Area Bd. Realtors, 1981, Cleve. Warehouseman Assn., 1977-79; chmn. City of Cleve. Landmarks Commn., 1984-2002 Mem. NRA (life), Nat. Assn. Realtors, Ohio Assn. Realtors, Cleve. Area Bd. Realtors. Avocation: real estate. Home: 6719 Sandalwood Dr Gates Mills OH 44040-9619 E-mail: richard@eri-group.com.

SCHANFIELD, FANNIE SCHWARTZ, community volunteer; b. Mpls., Dec. 25, 1916; d. Simon Zouberman and Mary (Schmilovitz) Schwartz; m. Melvin M. Stock, Oct. 27, 1943 (dec. Apr. 1944); 1 child, Moses Samuel Schanfield; m. Abraham Schanfield, Aug. 28, 1947; children: David Colman, Miriam Schanfield Kieffer. Student, U. Minn., 1962-75. Author: My Thoughts, 1996, Son, I Have Something to Tell You, 1997, Ma, I Wrote It Down, 1997, 20 April 44 WWII, 2001. Bd. dirs. Jewish Cmty. Ctr., Mpls., 1975-96, chairperson older adult needs, 1982-88; past pres. Bnai Emet Women's League, Mpls., 1988-90; rschr., advocate Hunger Hennepin County, Mpls., 1969-75; sec. Joint Religious Legis. Coalition; v.p., bd. dirs. Cmty. Housing Svc., Mpls., 1971-85. Recipient Citation of Honor, Hennepin County Commn., 1989, Lifetime Achievement award Jewish Comty. Ctr. Greater Mpls., 1995. Mem. NOW, Lupus Found. Minn., Internat. Soc. Poets, Hadassah (prs. 1967-69, Citation 1969). Jewish. Avocations: needlepoint, rug hooking, writing.

SCHANFIELD, MOSES SAMUEL, geneticist, educator; b. Mpls., Sept. 7, 1944; s. Abraham and Fanny (Schwartz) Schanfield; m. Patricia A. McCarthy. BA in Anthropology, U. Minn., 1966; AM in Anthropology, Harvard U., 1969; PhD in Human Genetics, U. Mich., 1971. Postdoctoral fellow in immunology U. Calif. Med. Ctr., San Francisco, 1971-74, rsch. geneticist, 1974-75; head of blood bank Milw. Blood Ctr., 1975-78; asst. dir. ARC, Washington, 1978-83; exec. dir. Genetic Testing Inst., Atlanta, 1983-85; lab. dir. Analytical Genetic Testing Ctr., Atlanta and Denver, 1985-2000; adminstr. Monroe County Pub. Safety Lab., Rochester, NY, 2000—02; prof., chair dept. forensic sci. George Washington U., 2002—. Adj. asst. prof. Med. Coll. Wis., Milw., 1976—78; adj. assoc. prof. George Washington U., Washington, 1979—83, Emory U., Atlanta, 1984—89, U. Kans., 1992—; affiliated faculty Colo. State U. Ft. Collins, 1992—2000; mem. Nat. Forensic DNA Rev. Panel, Nat. Inst. of Justice, 1996—2000; pres. 1st European-Am. Intensive Course in PCR, Split, Croatia, 1997; co-organizer 2d European-Am. Intensive Course in PCR, Dubrovnik, Croatia. Author, editor: book Immunobiology of the Erythrocyte, 1980, author, editor: book International Methods of Forensic DNA Analysis, 1996, contg. author: book Immunogenetic Factors and Thalassaemia of Hepatitis, 1975; contbr. articles to profl. publs. Recipient Gold medal, Latin Am. Congress Hemotherapy and Immunohematology, 1979, R&D 100 award, 1993. Fellow: Am. Acad. Forensic Sci.; mem.: Human Biology Coun., Am. Soc. Human Genetics, Am. Soc. Crime Lab. Dirs., Phi Kappa Phi. Achievements include discovery of of the biological function of GC protein as vitamin D transport protein; of 2 sources of errors in DNA sizings; detection of the presence of HIV in Africa in the 1950's. Office: Monroe County Pub Safety Labtr Pub Safety Bldg Rm 524 150 Plymouth Ave S Rochester NY 14614-2277 E-mail: mschanfield@netscape.net.

SCHANK, ROGER CARL, computer science and psychology educator; b. N.Y.C., Mar. 12, 1946; s. Maxwell and Margaret (Rosenberg) S.; children: Hana, Joshua. BS, Carnegie Inst. Tech., 1966; MA, U. Tex., 1967, PhD, 1969; MA (hon.), Yale U., 1976. Asst. prof. linguistics and computer sci. Stanford (Calif.) U., 1968-74; rsch. fellow Inst. Semantics and Cognition, Castagnola, Switzerland, 1973-74; assoc. prof. computer sci. Yale U., New Haven, 1974-76, prof. computer sci. and psychology, 1976-89, chmn. dept. computer sci., 1980-85; John Evans prof. computer sci., psychology and edn., founder Inst. for Learning Scis. Northwestern U., Evanston, Ill., 1989-2000, prof. emeritus, 2000—; chmn., chief tech. officer Cognitive Arts, N.Y.C., 1995—. Pres., chmn. bd. Cognitive Sys., Inc., New Haven, 1981-88; pres., chmn. Computeach, Inc., 1982-88. Author: Conceptual Information Processing, 1975, Dynamic Memory, 1982, (with others) Scripts, Plans, Goals and Understanding, 1977, Cognitive Computer, 1984, Explanation Patterns, 1986, The Creative Attitude, 1988, Tell Me A Story, 1990, reprinted with new forward, 1995, The Connoisseur's Guide to the Mind, 1991, Engines for Education, 1995, Virtual Learning: A Revolutionary Way to Build a Highly Skilled Workforce, 1997, Dynamic Memory Revisited, 1999, Coloring Outside the Lines, 2000, Scrooge Meets Dick and Jane, 2001, Designing World-Class E-learning, 2001; editor Cognitive Sci. Jour.; inventor computer programs. Recipient Disting. career prof., Carnegie Mellon U., Pitts., 2001. Mem. Cognitive Sci. Soc. (founder). Office: Cognitive Arts 115 E 57th St 10th Fl New York NY 10022 E-mail: schank@cognitivearts.com.

SCHANNEP, JOHN DWIGHT, brokerage firm executive; b. Newport News, Va., May 23, 1934; s. Dwight Bahney and Harriet Louise (Quinn) S.; m. Helen Ann Harris, June 21, 1958; children: John Barton, Dwight David, Timothy Michael, Marie Louise. BS, U.S. Mil. Acad., 1956. Commd. 1st lst. U.S. Air Force, 1956, resigned, 1960; acct. exec. Dean Witter Reynolds, Phoenix, 1960-68, v.p., resident mgr. Tucson, 1968-83, sr. v.p., 1983-89; ret. Pres. Tucson Stock/Bond Club, 1971-72; bd. dirs. SNEDCO. Author, pub. Schannep Timing Indicator and the Dow Theory Investment Timing Newsletter (available on Internet), 1980—. Pres. Big Bros. Tucson, 1972-74. Mem. Nat. Assn. Security Dealers (Ariz. committeeman and chmn. 1971-73), Tucson C. of C. (v.p. 1971), Pinetop Lakes Golf and Country Club (treas. 1990-91, pres. 1991-93), West Point Soc. (pres. 1967), Lions (pres. Phoenix chpt. 1966.) Republican. Home: 5191 E Hill Place Dr Tucson AZ 85712-1346

SCHANSTRA, CARLA ROSS, technical writer; b. Berwyn, Ill., Sept. 4, 1954; d. Caroles Schanstra and Heather Millar (Thomson) Alonso. BA, Western Ill. U., 1976; postgrad., U. Ill. Circle, Chgo., 1980-81. Assoc. editor Hitchcock Pub., Wheaton, Ill., 1976-80; assoc. product mgr. Advanced Systems, Inc., Elk Grove Village, 1980-81; tech. writer Profl. Computer Resources, Oak Brook, 1982; sr. tech. writer Lucent Techs. (formerly AT&T Bell Labs.), Naperville, 1982-99; info. devel. Visual Insights, 1999-2001; knowledge engr. ABN-AMRO Info. Tech. Svcs. Co., Chgo., 2001—. Freelance writer, 1980-85. Author: (stage plays) A Little Bit of Both, The Reversible Play, Survivors, Snakes and Apple Pie, It Should Be Obvious, Pastiche, The Model Home; contbr. articles to profl. jours. Violist DuPage Symphony, Glen Ellyn, Ill., 1984-87, 90-93, Elgin (Ill.) Symphonette, 1985-87. Mem. So. Tech. Comm. Assn. (award of excellence 1985), Dramatists Guild, Feminist Writers Western Suburbs (founder), Feminist Writers Guild Chgo. (adv. panel), Internat. Soc. Dramatists, Ill. Theatre Assn., Writers Workshop (co-founder), Village Theatre Guild. E-mail: Carla.Schanstra@abnamro.com.

SCHANUEL, STEPHEN H. mathematician, educator; b. Saint Louis, Mo., July 14, 1933; s. Arthur Edward Schanuel; children: Lynn Young, Jason. BA, Princeton U., 1955; MS, U. Chgo., 1959; PhD, Columbia U., 1963. Asst. prof. Johns Hopkins U., Balt., 1963—65; vis. scholar Inst. for Advanced Study, Princeton, NJ, 1965—66; asst. prof. Cornell U., Ithaca, NY, 1966—69, SUNY, Stony Brook, 1969—72, prof. Buffalo, 1972—. Author (with F.W. Lawvere): Conceptual Mathematics: A first introduction to Categories , 1997. Personal E-mail: schanuel@buffalo.edu.

SCHAPER, MARY L. financial services executive; b. Duluth, Minn., July 4, 1951; d. Norbert Henry and Lahja Mildred (Mykra) D. BA in Bus. Adminstrn., U. Minn., 1974; M in Mgmt. Adminstrn., Met. State U., 1987. With Norwest Info. Svcs., Inc., 1971-85; tech. contingency planner First Bank Sys., Inc., Mpls., 1985-87, tech. support supr., 1987-88, client mgr. human resource info. sys., 1988-89, sr. ops. project leader/officer, 1989-91, sr. project mgr., officer, 1991-92, MIS mgr., officer, 1992-93, sr. project mgr., asst. v.p., 1993-95; sr. bus. analyst fixed income Inter-Regional Fin. Corp., Inc., 1995-96; sr. bus. analyst process improvement Deluxe Corp., 1996-98; project mgr., bus. cons. Wells Fargo Home Mortgage, Inc., 1998-2000; bus. tech. cons. Wells Fargo Svcs. Co., 2000—. Mem. NAFE, Data Processing Mgmt. Assn., Minn. Women's Network. Avocations: piano, photography. Home: 8890 Montegue Ter Brooklyn Park MN 55443-3703 Office: Wells Fargo Svcs Co 255 Second Ave S Minneapolis MN 55479 E-mail: mary.schaper@wellsfargo.com.

SCHAPIRO, DONALD, lawyer; b. N.Y.C., Aug. 8, 1925; s. John Max and Lydia (Chaitkin) S.; m. Ruth Ellen Goldman, June 29, 1952 (dec. Aug. 1991); m. Linda N. Solomon, Oct. 10, 1993; children: Jane G., Robert A. AB, Yale U., 1944, LL.B., 1949. Bar: N.Y. 1949. Assoc. Paul, Weiss, Rifkind, Wharton & Garrison, N.Y.C., 1949-51; asst. chief counsel subcom. ways and means com. on adminstrn. revenue laws U.S. Ho. of Reps., Washington, 1951-52; assoc. Barrett, Smith, Schapiro, Simon & Armstrong, N.Y.C., 1952-55, partner, 1955-88; ptnr. Chadbourne & Parke, 1988—. Vis. lectr. law Yale U. Law Sch., 1949-78, 94-95, instr. law and econs., 1945-49. Mem. Order of Coif, Phi Beta Kappa, Phi Delta Phi. Home: 1035 5th Ave New York NY 10028-0135 Office: Chadbourne & Parke 30 Rockefeller Plz Fl 32 New York NY 10112-0129 E-mail: donald.schapiro@chadbourne.com.

SCHAPIRO, GEORGE A. electronics company executive; b. Richmond, Va., Mar. 21, 1946; s. Irwin Abraham and Jeanne (Goldman) S.; m. Jo Ann Katzman, Aug. 6, 1978; children: Rebecca Jeanne, Amy Elizabeth. BA, U. Va., 1967; MS in Indsl. Adminstrn., Carnegie-Mellon U., 1969. Fin. analyst data processing group IBM, Harrison, N.Y., 1968; product mktg. mgr. data sys. divns. Hewlett-Packard Co., Cupertino, Calif., 1969-74, med. electronics divsn. Waltham, Mass., 1974-76; pres., CEO Andros Inc., Berkeley, Calif., 1976-80, 90-91, Andros Analyzers, Inc., Berkeley, 1979-90, chmn. profl. bd. dirs., 1991—. Pres., CEO Hepatix Inc., Houston, Tex., 1992-93; pres., CEO U.S. Med. Instruments, Inc., San Diego, Calif., 1992-93; CEO Sonic Force, LLC, Burlingame, Calif., 1993-98; CEO Megabios, Inc., Burlingame, 1994; pres. Cardiac Mariners, Inc., Los Gatos, Calif., 1999-2000; guest lectr. Stanford U. Sch. Bus., U. Calif. at Berkeley Coll. Engring. and Extension Sch., Am. Mgmt. Assn. Seminar Series. Bd. dirs. Anesthesia Patient Safety Found. Mem. Assn. Computing Machinery, Assn. Advancement Med. Instrumentation, World Pres.'s Orgn. Democrat. Jewish. Home and Office: 3880 Ralston Ave Hillsborough CA 94010-6743

SCHAPIRO, JEROME BENTLEY, chemical company executive; b. N.Y.C., Feb. 7, 1930; s. Sol and Claire (Rose) S.; m. Edith Irene Kravet, Dec. 27, 1953; children: Lois, Robert, Kenneth. B.Chem. Engring., Syracuse U., 1951; postgrad., Columbia U., 1951-52. Project engr. propellents br. U.S. Naval Air Rocket Test Sta., Lake Denmark, N.J., 1951-52; with Dixo Co., Inc., Rochelle Park, 1954—; pres., 1966—. Lectr. detergent stds., drycleaning, care labeling, consumers stds., orgns., U.S., 1968—; U.S. del. spokesman on drycleaning Internat. Stds. Orgn.,Newton, Mass., 1971, Burssels, 1972, U.S. del. spokesman on dimensional stability of textiles, Paris, 1974, Ottawa, Can., 1977, Copenhagen, 1981; chmn. U.S. del. com. on consumer affairs, Geneva, 1974, 75, 76, spokesman U.S. del. on textiles, Pairs, 1974, mem. U.S. del. on care labeling of textiles, The Hague, Holland, 1974, U.S. del., chmn. del. coun. com. on consumer policy, Geneva, 1978, 79, 82, Israel, 1980, Paris, 1981, observer Internat. Std. Orgn./Consumer Com. on Policy meeting, Kyoto, Japan, 2000, Oslo, 2001; leader U.S. del. com. on dimensional stability of textiles, Manchester, Eng., 1984; fed. govtl. appointee to Industry Functional Adv. Com. on Stds., 1980-81; legal expert drycleaning techniques and procedures. Mem. Montclair (N.J.) Sch. Study Com., 1968-69; co-founder Jewish Focus, Inc., 1991, pub. Catskill/Hudson Jewish Star, 1991-98; v.p., treas. synagogue. 1st lt. USAF, 1952-53. Fellow ASTM (chmn. com. D-12 Soaps and Detergents 1974-79, mem. standing com. on internat. stds. 1980-84, hon. mem. award com. D-13 textiles); mem. AIChE, Am. Nat. Stds. Inst. (vice-chmn. bd. dirs. 1983-85, exec. com. 1979-81, 83-85, bd. dirs. 1979-85, fin. com. 1982-85, chmn. consumer coun. 1976, 79, 80, 81, mem. steering com. to advise Dept. Comerce on implementation GATT agreements 1976-77, mem. exec. stds. coun. 1977-79, intenat. stds. coun., chmn. internat. consumer policy adv. com. 1978-86), Am. Assn. Textile Chemists and Colorists (mem. exec. com. on rsch. 1974-77, chmn. com. on dry cleaning 1976-88, vice-chmn. internat. test methods com. 1982-86), Am. Chem. Soc., Stds. Engring. Soc. (cert.), Internat. Stds. Orgn. (mem. internat. stds. steering com. for consumer affairs 1978-81), Nat. Small Bus. Assn. (assoc. trustee 1983-85), Masons. Jewish. Home: PO Box 771 Wurtsboro NY 12790-0771 Office: 158 Central Ave PO Box 7038 Rochelle Park NJ 07662-7038

SCHAPPELL, ABIGAIL SUSAN, speech, language, hearing and massage therapist; b. York, Pa., May 25, 1952; d. Felix and Ann (Getty) DeMoise; m. Gery Mylan Schappell, Oct. 20, 1979; 1 child, Jonathan Michael. BS with Master's equivalency, Longwood Coll., 1974; postgrad., Bloomsburg U., 1975-77; cert., Lehmann Sch Massage and Muscle, 1991, East-West Sch. Massage Therapy, 1995—. Lic. speech-lang. pathologist, Pa. Speech-lang.-hearing specialist dept. pub. welfare Hamburg (Pa.) Ctr., 1975—. Judge deaf posters and essays Virginville (Pa.) Grange, 1990—, judge Pa. State Grange Conv., 1997, tchr. emergency pers. on communicating with deaf and hard of hearing, 1991, 92; leader demonstrations and workshops on sign lang. and dysphagia, non-verbal comms., active listening to various orgns., 1978—; instr. ARC; massage therapy; bd. dirs. Berks Deaf and Hard of Hearing Svcs., 2000-2003; presenter in field. Pub: (Boy Scouts Coun. manual), Scouting for the Handicapped, Hawk Mountain, 1981-82. Sign/del. to conf. Bible Sch. dir., mem. Zion's United Ch. of Christ, Windsor Castle, Pa., 1985—; rep. nat. triann. conv. Penn Laurel coun. Girl Scouts U.S., 1975; instr. ARC; vol. residential monitoring project Berks County ARC, 1998-99; bd. dirs. Berks Deaf and Hard of Hearing Svcs., 2000-03. Named Virginville Grange Cmty. Citizen of Yr., 1994—95, Outstanding Young Women of Am., 1984. Mem.: AAUW, Schuykill Haven Bus. and Profl. Women (Young Careerist local, dist. and state honors 1980—81, pres. 1983—84, asst. dir. dist. 9 Pa. 1997—99, dist. 9 dir. 1999—2001, state mentoring com. 2001—, dist. 9 parliamentarian 2002—, involvement on dist. and state level, presenter local, dist. and state level workshops, Eleanor Briner award as dist. 9 dir. 2000), Pa. Speech and Hearing Assn., Am. Assn. Mental Retardation (mem. Region 9 core com. for speech 1976, presenter at state conf. 1994, regional conf. 1995), Smithsonian Assocs., Yorktown chpt. DAR, Young Careerist Alumni Assn. (life), Hamburg Area Soccer Assn. (sec. 1989—94), Order Ea. Star (mem., chaplain Blue Mountain chpt. 1981, 1982). Republican. Avocations: massage, signing, music. Home: 531 S 4th St Hamburg PA 19526-1307 Office: Hamburg Ctr Old RR 22 PO Box 1000 Hamburg PA 19526

SCHAR, STEPHEN L. lawyer; b. Chgo., Oct. 19, 1945; s. Sidney and Lillian (Lieberman) Schar; m. Jessica S. Feit, Aug. 17, 1980; children: Scott Andrew, Elizabeth Loren. BA, U. Chgo., 1967; JD, DePaul U., 1970. Bar: Ill. 1970, U.S. Dist. Ct. (no. dist.) Ill. 1970. Assoc. Aaron, Aaron, Schimberg & Hess, Chgo., 1970-77, ptnr., 1977-80, Aaron, Schimberg, Hess, Rusnak, Deutsch & Gilbert, Chgo., 1980-84, Aaron, Schimberg, Hess & Gilbert, Chgo., 1984, Aaron, Schimberg & Hess, Chgo., 1984, D'Ancona & Pflaum, Chgo., 1985-98; mem. D'Ancona & Pflaum LLC, 1999—. Instr. estate planning Loyola U., Chgo., 1978—79. Bd. dirs. Jewish Children's Bur. Chgo., 1982—2001, pres., 1996—98, hon. dir., 2001—; pres. Faulkner Condominium Assn., Chgo., 1980—82, Carl Sandburg Village Homeowners Assn., Chgo., 1981—82. Mem.: Chgo. Estate Planning Coun., Chgo. Bar Assn. (pres. probate practice divsn. III 1979), Ill. Bar Assn. Home: 2155 Tanglewood Ct Highland Park IL 60035-4231 Office: D'Ancona & Pflaum LLC 111 E Wacker Dr Ste 2800 Chicago IL 60601-4209 E-mail: sschar@dancona.com.

SCHARF, PETER MARK, Sanskrit and Indian studies educator; b. New Haven, June 14, 1958; s. Roy Herbert and Candida Maria (Boccuzzi) S. BA in Philosophy, Wesleyan U., 1981; postgrad., Brown U., 1982-83; PhD in Sanskrit, U. Pa., 1990. Computer analyst, programmer, 1981-83; teaching asst. U. Pa., 1985-86, postdoctoral fellow in linguistics, 1990-91, 93, 94; lectr. in classics Brown U., Providence, 1994—2001, sr. lectr. in classics 2Providence, 2001—. Vis. lectr. religious studies U. Va., 1992; vis. lectr. in classics Brown U., Providence, 1992—94; presenter in field. Author: The Denotation of Generic Terms in Ancient Indian Philosophy: Grammar, Nyaya, and Mimamsa, 1996, Ramopakhyana: The Story of Rama in the Mahabharata, an independent-study reader in Sanskrit, 2002; designer computer program: Kramapatha: A Foreign Language Reader for the Sequential Unfoldment of Knowledge, 2000; contbr. articles to profl. jours. Outstanding High Sch. Sr.'s Semester scholar, 1976, Learn German in Germany scholar Goethe Inst., Berlin, 1998; Fgn. Lang. and Area Studies fellow, 1983-85, Jr. rsch. fellow Am. Inst. Indian Studies, 1986-88, Mellon grad. fellow, 1988-89, U. Pa. Dean's fellow, 1989-90, grantee Consortium for Lang. Tchg. and Learning, 1998, 2000, Am. Philos. Soc., 1998-99. Mem.: Am. Oriental Soc., Bhandarkar Oriental Rsch. Inst. (life). Avocations: chess, photography, transcendental meditation, mountain climbing. Office: Brown U Dept Classics PO Box 1856 Providence RI 02912-1856 E-mail: scharf@brown.edu.

SCHARF, ROBERT LEE, retired lawyer; b. May 13, 1920; s. Charles A. and Ethel Virginia (McNabb) S.; m. Jacqueline B. Scharf, Nov. 2, 1940; children: Bonnie Scharf Heald, Mary Ellen Pinero, Robert L. Jr. JD, Loyola U., 1948.

Bar: Ill. 1949, Calif. 1972; lifetime teaching credential Calif. C.C. With FBI, 1940-73; dep. city atty. City of L.A., 1973-84; atty. Mitsui Mfrs. Bank, L.A., 1984-85; ret., 1985; former part-time emeritus pro-bono atty. Mental Health Advocacy Office, L.A. Former L.A. County arbitrator; former pro-tem judge Small Claims Ct. 2d lt. U.S. Army, 1944-46. Mem. L.A. County Bar Assn., San Fernando Valley Bar Assn., Soc. Former FBI Agts.

SCHARF, WILLIAM, artist; b. Media, Pa., Feb. 22, 1927; s. Lester William and Ebba (Anderson) S.; m. Diana Denny, Mar. 11, 1947 (div. 1951); 1 child, William Denny; m. Sally Kravitch, Mar. 25, 1956; 1 child, Aaron Anderson. Student, Barnes Found., 1946-47; cert. in painting, Pa. Acad. of Fine Arts, 1947. Instr. Mus. Modern Art, N.Y.C., 1964, Sch. Visual Arts, N.Y.C., 1965-73, San Francisco Inst. Fine Arts, 1963, 66, 69, 74, 89. One-man shows include David Herbert Gallery, N.Y.C., 1960, 62, San Francisco Inst. Fine Arts, 1969, Neuberger Mus., Purchase, N.Y., 1976, High Mus., Atlanta, 1978, Armstrong Gallery, N.Y.C., 1987, U. Mich. Mus. Art, Ann Arbor, 1993, The Phillips Collection, Washington, 2000-2001, Frederick R. Weisman Mus., Malibu, Calif., 2001, P.S.I., MOMA, Queens, 2002; exhibited in group shows at Guggenheim Mus., N.Y.C., 1982, Hirschl-Adler Gallery, N.Y.C., 1980, Smith-Anderson Gallery, Palo Alto, Calif., Nat. Mus. Am. Art, Washington, 1987, 91, 92, Am. Acad. and Inst. Arts and Letters, N.Y.C., 1989, 91; represented in permanent collections Phila. Mus., Boston Inst. Contemporary Art, Bklyn Mus., Solomon r. Guggenheim Mus., N.Y.C., Newark Mus., Nat. Mus. Am. Art, Smith Coll. Mus., Northampton, Mass., Zimmerli Mus., Rutgers U., New Brunswick, N.J., U. Mich. Mus. art., Phillips Collection, Washington, The Neuroscis. Inst., San Diego, The High Mus., Atlanta, Colgate U. Trustee Rothko Found., N.Y.C., 1979-87; instr. Art Student's League, N.Y., 1987-99, 2001. With USAF, 1945-46. Emmlen Cresson fellow Pa. Acad. Fine Arts, 1948. Mem. Artist Equity Assn., Soc. of Illustrators.

SCHARFENBERG, MARGARET ELLAN, retired elementary educator; b. Lansing, Mich., Mar. 22, 1924; d. John Milton and Florence Lucille (Craig) Amiss; m. Howard Edward Scharfenberg, June 29, 1946; children: Ann Derr Scharfenberg White, Joan Carol Scharfenberg Anderson, John Howard Scharfenberg. Student, Oberlin Coll., 1942-44; BA, Mich. State U., 1946; MA in Teaching, Rollins Coll., 1966. Cert. tchr., elem. supr., Fla. Tchr. Hill Elem. Sch., Maitland, Fla., 1964-65, Cheney Elem. Sch., Orlando, 1965-66; reading lab. tchr. Richmond Heights Elem. Sch., 1966-68; supr. perceptual planning, oral clinician Orange County Schs., 1968-69; reading lab. tchr. Winter Park (Fla.) H.S., 1969-72; from perceptual trainer to exptl. reading lab. tchr. Gateway Sch., Orlando, 1972-74; tchr. of migrant children Zellwood (Fla.) Elem. Sch., 1974-93; ret., 1993. Pioneer white/black sch. staffing Richmond Heights Elem. Sch., 1966-68; dir. Learning Skills Profl. Ctr., Orlando, 1971-74; speaker numerous symposia and convs. in field, 1968—; cons. in field. Author, editor (newsletter) Paper Meeting, 1968-69, (perception package) Patterns for a Purpose, 1968-69; producer films on perceptual tng., 1968-69. Chaplain, Oleander Garden Cir., Lakes and Hills Garden Club, also past sec.; sec. Tangerine Garden Club; historian, past v.p. and pres. Women's Soc., Tangerine Cmty. Ch., also mem. choir; vol. Women of Hospice, Hospice Hope Chest; mem. Humane Soc. U.S.A. Named Tchr. of Yr., Zellwood Elem. Sch., 1993. Mem.: NEA, AAUW, Internat. Reading Assn. (sec. Orange County coun. 1965, pres. 1969), Rosicrucian Order (A.M.O.R.C.), Lions (staff mem. seminars on perception, recipient various certs. and plaques), Gamma Phi Beta (past pres. alumna group). Republican. Presbyterian. Avocations: reading, boating, gardening, animal study. Home: 6492 Dora Dr Mount Dora FL 32757-7064

SCHARFF, JOSEPH LAURENT, lawyer; b. New Orleans, Oct. 2, 1935; s. Joseph Roy and Celia Ray (Rosenhein) S.; m. Mary Susan Greulach, June 29, 1963; children: Catherine Elizabeth, Robert Laurent, Anne Victoria. BS in Journalism, Northwestern U., 1957; JD, Harvard U., 1964. Bar: D.C. 1965, U.S. Supreme Ct. 1970, U.S. Ct. Appeals (D.C. cir.) 1965, U.S. Ct. Appeals (2nd cir.) 1980, U.S. Ct. Appeals (5th cir.) 1973, U.S. Ct. Appeals (10th cir.); U.S. Ct. Claims 1965. From assoc. to ptnr. Pierson, Ball & Dowd, Washington, 1964-89; ptnr. Reed Smith Shaw & McClay, 1989-95, counsel, 1996. Mem. ABA (fair trial-free press com. 1973-76, com. reps. media 1985-95, co-chmn. 1989-92), Fed. Comm. Bar Assn., Soc. Profl. Journalists, Radio-TV News Dirs. Assn. (counsel 1965-95, Disting. Svc. award 1987, J. Laurent Scharff Legal Internship established 1996), Media Inst. First Amendment Adv. Coun. Home and Office: 12000 Turf Ln Reston VA 20191-2123

SCHARFF, MATTHEW DANIEL, immunologist, cell biologist, educator; b. N.Y.C., Aug. 28, 1932; s. Harry and Constance S.; m. Carol Held, Dec. 19, 1954; children: Karen, Thomas, David. AB, Brown U., 1954, DrMedSci (hon.), 1994; MD, NYU, 1959. House officer II and IV med. service Boston City Hosp., 1959-61; research asso. NIH, 1961-63; asst. prof. Albert Einstein Coll. Medicine, Yeshiva U., Bronx, N.Y., 1963-67, asso. prof., 1967-71, prof. dept. cell biology, 1971—, chmn. dept., 1972-83, dir. div. biol. scis., 1975-81; asso. dir. Cancer Center, 1975-86, dir., 1986-95, dep. dir., 1995—2002. Served with USPHS, 1961-63. Recipient Alumni Achievement award NYU Sch. Medicine, 1980, N.Y. Acad. Medicine medal, 1990, Commemorative award Albert Einstein Coll. Medicine, 1993, hon. Dr. Med. Sci., Brown U., 1994. Mem. Am. Assn. Immunologists (Mentoring Excellence award 1998), Am. Soc. Clin. Investigation, Nat. Acad. Scis., Am. Acad. Arts and Sci., Phi Beta Kappa, Sigma Xi, Alpha Omega Alpha. Office: Albert Einstein Coll Med Dept Cell Biology 1300 Morris Pk Ave Bronx NY 10461-1926

SCHARFF, MONROE BERNARD, investor relations consultant; b. Boston, Sept. 8, 1923; s. Bernard Wertheimer and Minette (Switzer) S.; m. Edwina Kuhn, June 30, 1949; children: Peter Bernard, Stuart Monroe. BA, Columbia U., 1948. V.p. Cold Cathode Corp., N.Y.C., 1951-56; pres. Monroe B. Scharff & Co., 1957—, Swofford & Scharff, N.Y.C., 1980-88; sr. cons. for investor rels. Doremus and Co. (merged with Swofford and Scharff), 1988—. Bd. dirs. Ingalls Assocs., Boston. Trustee Forman Sch., Litchfield, Conn., 1968—, Portland Mus. Art, 1985; bd. dirs. YMCA Greater N.Y., 1970-85, Found. for Blood Rsch., 1986—; mem. investor rels. adv. bd. Bentley Coll., 1995-99; dir.-at-large Boston chpt. Nat. Investor Rels. Inst; dir. PCA Great Performances; mem. adv. bd. River Tree Arts. 1st lt. USAF, 1943-46, 51-52. Mem. Arundel Yacht Club, Kennebunk River Club, Army and Navy Club, Cumberland Club, Downtown Club Boston. Republican. Avocations: skiing, sailing.

SCHARFFE, WILLIAM GRANVILLE, academic administrator, educator; b. Saginaw, Mich., Mar. 12, 1942; s. William Edward and Marion Kittie (Granville) S.; m. Mary Jo Whitfield, Sept. 4, 1965; children: Sue L., William W. BA, Mich. State U., 1965, MA, 1969, PhD, 1977. Tchr. English Webber Jr. High Sch., Saginaw, 1965-66; tchr. speech Arthur Hill High Sch., 1966-68; staff asst. for pers. Saginaw City Schs., 1968-73, dir. pers., 1977-94, dir. employee devel. and media ops., 1994-99; prin. Zilwaukee Jr. High Sch., Saginaw, 1973-74; asst. prin. North Intermediate Sch., 1974-75, 1975-77; dir. policy svcs. Mich. Assn. Sch. Bds., Lansing, 1999—. Adj. asst. prof. Mich. State U., East Lansing, 1977; pvt. practice pers. cons., Saginaw, 1978—; adj. lectr. Ctrl. Mich. U., Mt. Pleasant, 1987, Mich. State U., 1977, Saginaw Valley State U., 1991. Author: (children's book) Elfred Alanzo & Santa's Surprise, 1987. Bd. dirs. Japanese Cultural Ctr. and Tea House, Saginaw, 1986-97, pres., 1993-95. Recipient Key Man award United Way Saginaw County, 1978, Outstanding Svc. award, 1978. Mem. Mich. Assn. Sch. Pers. Assn. (sec., bd. dirs. 1988-90, pres., bd. dirs. 1992-93), Mich. Mid. Cities Pers. and Labor Rels. Task Force (pres. 1980-82), Soc. For Human Resource Mgmt., Exch. Club (Saginaw chpt. pres. 1981), Saginaw Club (pres. 1996-97), Phi Delta Kappa. Republican. Episcopalian. Avocations: writing, golf, photography, public speaking. Home: 2812 Adams Blvd Saginaw MI 48602-3103

SCHARFFENBERGER, ELIZABETH WATSON, classicist; b. Wheeling, W.Va., Sept. 14, 1957; d. William John and Elizabeth May (Fisher) S. AB, U. Chgo.; MA, MPhil, PhD, Columbia U. Instr. Clarkson U., Potsdam, N.Y., 1985-86, NYU, 1986-88; asst. prof. Wash. U., St. Louis, 1988-94; instr. NYU, 1997—. Vis. asst. prof. Barnard Coll., N.Y.C., 1996, Yale U., 1999, Columbia U., 1996, adj. assoc. prof., 1998—. Assoc. editor: Text & Presentation; Contbr. articles to profl. jours. Mem. Am. Philological Assn., Comparative Drama Conf. Office: Columbia U 617 Hamilton Hall New York NY 10027

SCHARLACK, RONALD STUART, medical device company executive; b. San Antonio, Nov. 26, 1945; s. Sheppard Abraham and Sylvia Thelma (Goldinger) S.; m. Elisabeth Thresher, Apr. 11, 1970; children: Jeremy, Daniel. BS in Mech. Engring., MIT, 1967, postgrad., 1971-73; MS in Mech. Engring., Stanford U., 1968; Progam in Mgmt. Devel., Harvard U., 1985. Cons. Kelsey Hayes Co., Romulus, Mich., 1968-71; project engr. No. Rsch. Engring. Corp., Cambridge, Mass., 1973-75; mgr. Mobol-Tyco Solar Energy Corp., Waltham, 1975-78, Thermo Electron Corp., Waltham, 1978-83; program mgr. Millipore Corp., Milford and Bedford, Mass., 1983-86; tech. licensing officer MIT, Cambridge, 1986-90; mgr. Chiron Diagnostics, Medfield, 1990-98; v.p., gen. mgr. Spire Corp., Bedford, 1998-2000; v.p. devel. Atlantis Components, Inc., Cambridge, 2000—. Contbr. articles to profl. jours.; 18 patents in field. Mem. Brookline (Mass.) Town Meeting. Mem. Soc. Biomaterials, Optical Soc. Am., Sigma Xi. Avocations: windsurfing, skiing, gardening. Home: 121 Colbourne Cres Brookline MA 02445-4571 Office: Atlantis Components Inc 270 Third St Cambridge MA 02142 E-mail: ron_scharlack@atlantiscomp.com.

SCHARLATT, HAROLD, management company executive; b. N.Y.C., Dec. 9, 1947; s. Bertram and Miriam Louise (Stone) S.; BEd, SUNY, 1969, MA in Liberal Studies, 1973; advanced cert. adminstrn. and supervision, Oxford U., 1975; m. Mary Moore, June 10, 1978. Tchr., in-service instr. N.Y., 1970-77; mgmt. devel. specialist Union Carbide Corp., N.Y.C., 1977, mgmt. devel. cons., 1978-80; regional dir. Vector Mgmt. Systems, Inc., Lexington, Ky., 1980-82; pres. Tng. and Devel. Assocs., Inc., Lexington, 1982—. Mem. Am. Soc. Tng. and Devel., Soc. Human Resource Mgmt., Human Resource Planning Soc., Assn. For Psychol. Type, Assn. For Quality and Participation. Office: 2220 Vinewood Rd Lexington KY 40515-1245

SCHARLEMANN, ROBERT PAUL, religious studies educator, clergyman; b. Lake City, Minn., Apr. 4, 1929; s. Ernst Karl and Johanna Meta (Harre) S. Student, Northwestern Coll., Watertown, Wis., 1946-49; BA, Concordia Coll. and Sem., St. Louis, 1952; BD, MDiv, Concordia Coll. and Sem., 1955; Dr. theol., U. Heidelberg (Germany), 1957. Ordained to ministry, Lutheran Ch., 1960. Instr. philosophy Valparaiso U., 1957-59; postdoctoral fellow Yale U., 1959-60; pastor Bethlehem Luth. Ch., Carlyle, Ill., 1960-62, Grace Luth. Ch., Durham, N.C., 1962-63; asst. prof. religion U. So. Calif., 1963-64, assoc. prof., 1964-66; assoc. prof. religion U. Iowa, Iowa City, 1966-68, prof., 1968-81; Commonwealth prof. religious studies U. Va., Charlottesville, 1981-97, prof. emeritus, 1997—. Fulbright-Hays prof. U. Heidelberg, 1975-76 Author: Thomas Aquinas and John Gerhard, 1964, Reflection and Doubt in the Thought of Paul Tillich, 1969, The Being of God, 1981, Inscriptions and Reflections, 1989, The Reason of Following, 1991, L'intemporel et l'eternel, 1993, Can Religion be Understood Philosophically?, 1995, The Mystical Correlate of Symbolic Appearing, 2001; editor Jour. of Am. Acad. Religion, 1980-85; contbr. articles to profl. jours. Fulbright scholar U. Heidelberg, 1955-57. Mem. Am. Acad. Religion, Am. Theol. Soc., Deutsche Paul-Tillich Gesellschaft, European Soc. Culture, Soc. for Philosophy of Religion.

SCHAROLD, MARY LOUISE, psychoanalyst, educator; b. Mar. 3, 1943; d. Walter John and Louise Helen (Hartmann) Baumgartner; m. William Ballew McCollum, Aug. 23, 1964 (div. 1981); m. Harry Karl Scharold, June 19, 1982; children: Margaret Louise, Walter Ballew. BA with highest distinction, U. Kans., 1964; MD, Baylor Coll. Medicine, 1968; postgrad., Topeka Inst. Psychoanalysis, 1981. Diplomate Am. Bd. Psychiatry and Neurology. Intern Meml. Bapt. Hosp., Houston, 1968-69; resident in psychiatry Baylor Coll. Medicine, 1969—72, chief resident, 1971-72; psychoanalyst, 1972—. Asst. prof. Baylor Coll. Medicine, Houston, 1973-76, asst. clin. prof., 1981-84, assoc. clin. prof., 1984—; dir. Baylor Psychiat. Clinic, Houston, 1973-76; co-dir. Rice U. Psychiat. Svc., Houston, 1981-82; asst. clin. prof. U. Kans. Sch. Medicine, Kansas City, 1977-81; tchg. assoc. Topeka Psychoanalytic Inst., 1984-86; tchg. analyst, Houston-Galveston Psychoanalytic Inst., 1986-90, tng. and supervising analyst, 1990—, v.p., 1994-96, pres., 1996-2001. Adv. bd. Leavenworth Mental Health Assn., Kans., 1977-81. Watkins scholar U. Kans., 1961-64. Fellow Am. Psychiat. Assn. (com. quality assurance 1986-87, chair Tex. peer rev. 1984-88); mem. Am. Psychoanalytic Assn. (cert. 1982, peer rev. com. 1985-90, prof. ins. commn. 1986-93, bd. profl. stds. 1994-2001, CME com. 1994-96, exec. coun. 1994-96, cert. com. 1995-98, preparedness and progress com. 1998—, chair preparedness and progress com. 2000—, coording com. bd. profl. stds. 2000—, bylaws com. 2001—), Am. Group Psychotherapy Assn., Ctr. Advanced Psychoanalytic Studies, Houston Psychiat. Soc. (v.p. 1984-85, pres.-elect 1985-86, pres. 1986-87), Houston-Galveston Psychoanalytic Soc. (sec.-treas. 1984-86, pres.-elect 1986-88, pres. 1988-90, alter councillor 1994-96), Houston Group Psychotherapy Soc. (adv. bd. 1984-85), Mortar Bd., Phi Beta Kappa, Delta Phi Alpha, Alpha Omega Alpha, Hilltopper, Pi Beta Phi Alumni Assn. Republican. Lutheran. Office: 2301 Westheimer Rd Houston TX 77098-1317 E-mail: mlscharold@mindspring.com.

SCHATKEN, NANCY LEAH, medical editor; b. N.Y.C., Jan. 7, 1938; d. Robert V. and Lillian Belle (Neff) S. BS, U. N.C., 1959; cert. med. tech., Albany Sch. Med. Tech., 1960. Med. tech., instr. various orgns., 1960-66; acting mng. editor med. jours. Harper & Row, N.Y.C., 1966-69; assoc. editor Med. World News-McGraw-Hill, 1969-70; owner, founder Mostly Med., 1970—, St. James, Barbados, 1978-98. Avocations: travel, reading, swimming, entertaining. E-mail. Address: 2677 Parkview Dr Hallandale FL 33009

SCHATKIN, ANDREW JAMES, lawyer; b. N.Y.C., Aug. 19, 1948; s. Sidney Bernhard and Amy Wheeler (White) S. AB in Classical Langs. cum laude, CUNY, 1969; MDiv, Princeton Theol. Sem., 1973; JD, Villanova U., 1976; diploma, U. Strasbourg, France, 1984; Cert. in Internat. Law, Acad. Internat. Law, The Hague, The Netherlands, 1985. Bar: N.Y. 1977, U.S. Dist. Ct. (so. and ea. dists.) N.Y. 1978, U.S. Dist. Ct. (no. dist.) N.Y. 1998, U.S. Ct. Claims 1991, U.S. Ct. Mil. Appeals 1991, U.S. Ct. Appeals (2d cir.) 1979, U.S. Ct. Appeals (fed. cir.) 1991, U.S. Supreme Ct. 1991. Dep. county atty. Nassau County Atty., Mineola, N.Y., 1977-81; assoc. Rivkin, Leff, Sherman and Radler, Garden City, 1981-82; pvt. practice Bayside, 1982-86; atty. Office of Hearings and Appeals, Social Security Adminstrn., New Haven, 1986-87; staff atty. criminal def. divsn. Legal Aid Soc., N.Y.C., 1987-94; pvt. practice Jericho, N.Y., 1994—. Author books and chpts. to books; contbr. over 130 articles to profl. jours. Named one of Outstanding Young Men of Am., 1979. Mem. ABA (criminal justice sect., family law sect., internat. law and practice sect., labor and employment law sect.), Nat. Assn. Criminal Def. Lawyers (scholarship 1994, 95), N.Y. State Assn. Criminal Def. Lawyers, N.Y. State Defenders Assn., N.Y. State Bar Assn., Suffolk County Bar Assn., Queens County Bar Assn., Nassau County Bar Assn. Republican. Lutheran. Avocations: reading, writing, classical music, travel, languages. Home: 21050 41st Ave Bayside NY 11361-1965 Office: 350 Jericho Tpke Jericho NY 11753-1317

SCHATKIN, MARGARET AMY, theology educator; b. N.Y.C., Apr. 29, 1944; d. Sidney and Amy (White) S. BA, CUNY, 1964; PhD, Fordham U., 1967; ThD, Princeton (N.J.) Theol. Sem., 1982. From asst. to assoc. prof. Boston Coll., Chestnut Hill, Mass., 1969—. Author: Fathers of the Church, 1985, Analecta Vlatadon, 1987; editor: Sources Chrétiennes, 1990. Woodrow Wilson Found. fellow, 1964, 67, NEH fellow, 1976, 83; grantee Mellon Found., 1980. Mem. U.S. Nat. Com. Byzantine Studies, Assn. Internat. d'Etudes Patristiques, The Hymn Society in the U.S. and Can. Democrat. Lutheran. Avocation: cycling. Home: 210 Lake Shore Rd Apt 1 Brighton MA 02135-6390 Office: Boston Coll 140 Commonwealth Ave Chestnut Hill MA 02467-3806

SCHATT, PAUL, newspaper editor; b. N.Y.C., Aug. 31, 1945; divorced; children: Suzannah, Andrew. BA with distinction Polit. Sci., English, Ariz. State U., 1967. Editor Ariz. Republic, 1964-66, reporter, 1965-74, urban affairs editor, 1974-75, asst. city editor, 1975-79, chief asst. city editor, 1979-82, asst. met. editor, 1985-86, met. editor, 1986-88, editor edit. pages, 1993—; asst. editor Ariz. Mag., 1981-82, editor, 1982-85; editor edit. pages Phoenix Gazette, 1988-93, The Ariz. Republic, 1993-97, assoc. editor, 1998—. Pres. 1st amendment coalition of Az., 1999; vis. lectr. Pub. Affairs Journalism, Ariz. State U., 1976—, instr. Mass. Comm. Dept., 1974-76; dir. Eugene C. Pulliam Fellowship. Phoenix program, 1990—; writing coach, 1989; del. Pre White House Conf. Librs., 1991, pres., Arizona Newspapers Assn., 2000—. V.p. Crisis Nursery, 1984-87, bd. dirs. 1980-87; exec. bd. Hospice of the Valley, 1980-87; pres. Friends of Phoenix Pub. Libr., 1985-86, bd. dirs. 1986—; bd. trustees 1st Amendment Congress, 1989—; bd. dirs. Ariz. Humanities Coun., 1999—; Dean's adv. bd., Arizona State U. Honors Coll., 1999—, adv. bd., Northern Arizona U. Sch. of Communications, 1999—, bd. dirs. Camelback Hosps. 1982-89, chmn. bd. dirs. 1986-87, Cactus Pine Coun. Girl Scouts Am., 1988-89, Sun Sounds Inc., 1982-89, Valley Leadership Inc., 1991—, alum. assn., 1985-89, Ariz. Zool. Soc., 1991—, Barrow Neurol. Found., 1991—, Kids Voting, 1991-93, Barry Goldwater Inst., 1991-93, Ariz. Club, 1991—. With Ariz. Nat. Guard, 1966-79. Recipient Montgomery award Outstanding Svc. to Community Friends of Phoenix Pub. Libr., 1989; profl. Journalism fellow Stanford U., 1970-71. Mem. Am. Soc. Newspaper Editors, Soc. Profl. Journalists (pres. Valley of Sun chpt. 1974-75, 83-84, exec. bd. 1988-92), Sigma Delta Chi (co-chair nat. convention 1974). Office: The Ariz Republic Editorial Dept 200 E Van Buren St Phoenix AZ 85004-2238 E-mail: paul.schatt@pni.com.

SCHATTSCHNEIDER, ADAM JAMES, music educator; b. Detroit Lakes, Minn., Mar. 24, 1966; s. Donald William and Marion Barbara Schattschneider; m. Kelly Jean Carlson; children: Leah Jaye, Haley Juleen. MusB, U. Minn., 1988; MusM, Ind. U., 1990, MusD, 1997. Prof. music, chair music dept. Bluffton (Ohio) Coll., 1991—. Leader workshops, master classes, adjudicator, Ohio, 1991—. Performer: CD Broken Boundaries, 2001. Mem.: Ohio Music Tchrs. Assn., Music Educators Nat. Assn., Music Tchrs. Nat. Assn. Avocation: fitness training. Office: Bluffton Coll 280 W College Ave Bluffton OH 45817-1196 Fax: 419-358-3323. E-mail: schatta@bluffton.edu.

SCHATTSCHNEIDER, DORIS JEAN, mathematics educator; b. N.Y.C., Oct. 19, 1939; d. Robert W. Jr. and Charlotte Lucile (Ingalls) Wood; m. David A. Schattschneider, June 2, 1962; 1 child Laura E. AB, U. Rochester, 1961; MA, Yale U., 1963, PhD, 1966. Instr. in math. Northwestern U., Evanston, Ill., 1964—65; asst. prof. U. Ill., Chgo., 1965—68; prof. Moravian Coll., Bethlehem, Pa., 1968—. Project dir. Fund for the Improvement of Post-Secondary Edn. U.S. Dept. Edn., 1991—93, 1995—97. Author: Visions of Symmetry, 1990; author: (with W. Walker) (books and models) M.C. Escher Kaleidocycles, 1977, 1987; co-author: (videos and activities) Visual Geometry Project, 1986—91, A Companion to Calculus, 1995; editor: Geometry Turned On, 1997, M.C. Escher's Legacy, 2002. Exhbn. curator Allentown Art Mus., 1979, Payne Gallery, 1987. Grantee NEH rsch. grantee, 1988—90. Mem.: Assn. for Women in Math., Am. Math. Soc., Math. Assn. Am. (editor 1980—85, gov. 1980—89, 1st v.p. 1994—96, Allendoerfer award 1979, Meritorious Svc. award 1991, Dist. Math. Tchg. award 1993), Pi Mu Epsilon (councillor 1990—96). Mem. Moravian Ch. Office: Moravian Coll Math Dept 1200 Main St Bethlehem PA 18018-6650 E-mail: schattdo@moravian.edu.

SCHATZ, CHARLOTTE ASNESS, artist, educator; b. Phila., Jan. 6, 1929; d. Zalman and Sara (Kaitz) Asness; m. Joseph Lewis Schatz, Apr. 10, 1949 (dec. Sept. 1979); children: Barbara J., Naomi H., Rachel E. BFA, Temple U., 1969, postgrad., 1978-79. Prof. Bucks County C.C., Newtown, Pa., 1973-98, prof. emeritus, 1998—. One-man shows include Jasuta Gallery, Phila., 2000, Conant Gallery Edn. Testing Svc., Princeton, N.J., 1999, Univ. City Sci. Ctr., Phila., 1993, Hicks Art Ctr., Newtown, 1986, Rider Coll., Lawrenceville, N.J., 1977, Stockton Coll., Atlantic City, N.J., 1976, Lehigh U., Bethlehem, Pa., 1975, Abington Art Ctr., Jenkintown, Pa., 1975, 91, Phila. Art Alliance, 1970; exhibited in group shows at Pictura Lucida Phila. Art Alliance, 2000, Rowan U., 1999, Borowsky Gallery, 1999, Pa. Treasures U. City Sci. Ctr., Phila., 1998, Tres Emeriti Hicks Art Ctr., Newtown, Pa., 1998, A Legacy Preserved James A. Michener Art Mus., Doylestown, Pa., 1998, Balch Inst. Ethnic Studies, Phila., 1997, Muse Gallery, Phila., 1995, 96, U. Delaware, Newark, 1994, Pa. State Mus., Harrisburg, 1993, City Govt. Ctr., Harrisburg, 1993, Moore Coll. Art, Phila., 1992, Galerie Nadeau, Phila., 1992, Cheltenham (Pa.) Art Ctr., 1992, Phillips Mill Assn., New Hope, Pa., 1992, Atelier Rachita, Paris, 1990, Crees Bldg., Corvallis, Oreg., 1990; represented in permanent collection James A. Michener Art Mus., Univ. City Sci. Ctr., Phila., Bucks County C.C. Leeway grantee for achievement in painting, 2000. Mem. Women's Caucus for Art (past pres. Phila. chpt.), Phila. Art Alliance (sculpture com. 1973-84). Home: 108 Glen Ln Elkins Park PA 19027-1760 Studio: 314 Brown St Philadelphia PA 19123-2202

SCHATZ, IRWIN JACOB, cardiologist, educator; b. St. Boniface, Man., Can., Oct. 16, 1931; came to U.S., 1956, naturalized, 1966; s. Jacob and Reva S.; m. Barbara Jane Binder, Nov. 12, 1967; children: Jacob, Edward, Stephen and Brian (twins). Student, U. Man., Can.), Winnipeg, 1951, MD with honors, 1956. Diplomate: Am. Bd. Internal Medicine. Intern Vancouver (B.C.) Gen. Hosp., 1955-56; resident Hammersmith Hosp., U. London, 1957, Mayo Clinic, Rochester, Minn., 1958-61; head sec. peripheral vascular disease Henry Ford Hosp., Detroit, 1961-68; asso. prof. medicine Wayne State U., 1968-71, chief sect. cardiovascular disease, 1969-71; assoc. prof., asso. dir. sect. cardiology U. Mich., 1972-73, prof. internal medicine, 1973-75; prof. medicine John A. Burns Sch. Medicine, U. Hawaii, 1975—, chmn. dept. medicine, 1975-90. Author: Orthostatic Hypotension, 1986; contbr. numerous articles to med. jours. Rockefeller Found. scholar, 1991. Master ACP (bd. govs. 1984-89, Laureate award Hawaii chpt. 1992); fellow Am. Coll. Cardiology (bd. govs. 1980-84); mem. Am. Heart Assn. (fellow coun. cardiology), Am. Fedn. Clin. Rsch., Asian-Pacific Soc. Cardiology (v.p. 1987-91), Accreditation Coun. for Grad. Med. Edn. (chmn. residence rev. com. internal medicine 1993-95), Hawaii Heart Assn. (pres.), Western Assn. Physicians, Am. Autonomic Soc. (chmn. bd. govs., pres. 1996-98), Pacific Interurban Club, Oahu Country Club. Jewish. Home: 4983 Kolohala St Honolulu HI 96816-5126 Office: 1356 Lusitana St Honolulu HI 96813-2421 E-mail: schatzi@hawaii.edu.

SCHATZ, LILLIAN LEE, playwright, molecular biologist, educator; d. Joseph Louis and Rose S. BA in Biology, SUNY, Buffalo, 1965, MA in Biology, 1970. Cert. h.s. tchr. biology, chemistry, gen. sci., N.Y., 1968. Rsch. asst. dept. biology SUNY at Buffalo, 1965-68, rsch. asst. dept. pharmacology Sch. Medicine, 1969; rsch. assoc. dept. biology SUNY, Buffalo, 1971-74; cancer rsch. scientist dept. viral oncology Roswell Park Meml. Inst., 1969-70; tchr. biology Kenmore East Sr. H.S., 1970-71; playwright, 1976—. Presenter workshop Rosa Coplon Jewish Home and Infirmary, Buffalo, N.Y., 1982, N.Y. State Community Theater Assn., 1982. Author: (plays) Solomon's Court, 1979, Neshomah, 1983, Bernie, 1985, The Jonah Men, 1991, For the Love of Jake, 2001; contbr. rsch. articles to sci. jours. Charter mem. B'not Israel Group, Hadassah, life mem. Recipient N.Y. State Regents Coll. Scholarship, 1961-65; semi-finalist Sergel Drama prize Ct. Theatre, U. Chgo., 1985, Nat. Play Award Competition Nat. Repertory Theatre Found., 1981; Playwriting fellow, N.Y. State Creative Artists Pub. Svc. fellow, 1980-81, Roswell Park Meml. Inst. fellow, 1962, Summer Sci. fellow. Avocations: art, genealogy.

SCHATZ, NORMA H. volunteer; b. N.Y.C., May 20, 1923; d. Arthur and Estelle (Rubin) Hirshon; m. S. Michael Schatz, Oct. 28, 1945; children: Andrew, Debra, Nathan, Donald. BA, Cornell U., 1944. Photo dept. asst. Harper's Bazaar, N.Y.C., 1943-44; prodn. rsch. Metro Goldwyn Mayer, 1944-45; personnel tng. Sage-Allen, Hartford, Conn., 1946-50. Trustee West Hartford (Conn.) Pub. Libr., 1962-65; mem., sec. bd. edn. City of West Hartford, 1965-70; mem. Conn. State Juvenile Justice Adv. Com., 1979—; steering com. Teen Pregnancy Prevention Coalition, 1989-99, Children in the Courts Com., 1988—; bd. dirs. Justice Edn. Ctr., 1987—, Conn. Voices for Children, 1996—; adv. bd. Prevent Child Abuse, Conn., 1993—, Voice of Conn. Youth, 1995-97, Office of Alternative Sanctions-Juvenile, 1997-2001; mem. Gov.'s Task Force on Abused Children, 1988-90. Recipient President's award Junior League of Hartford, Conn., 1987, Millie Victor award Parents Anonymous of Conn., 1989, Youth Advocate award Conn. Youth Svc. Assn., 1985, Judge Thomas Gill award Children in Placement/CASA, Hartford, Conn., 1993, Conn. Voices for Children's Citizen advocacy award, 2000. Jewish. Avocations: golf, grandchildren, travel. Home: 4 Hampton Pl Avon CT 06001-4554 also: 1932 Harbourside Dr # 247 Longboat Key FL 34228

SCHATZBERG, ALAN FREDERIC, psychiatrist, researcher; b. N.Y.C., Oct. 17, 1944; s. Emanuel and Cila (Diamond) S.; m. Nancy R. Silverman, Aug. 27, 1972; children: Melissa Ann, Lindsey Diamand. BS, NYU, 1965, MD, 1968; MA (hon.), Harvard U., 1989. Diplomate Nat. Bd. Med. Examiners, Am. Bd. Psychiatry and Neurology. Intern Lenox Hill Hosp., N.Y.C., 1968-69; resident in psychiatry Mass. Mental Health Ctr., Boston, 1969-72; clin. fellow in psychiatry Harvard Med. Sch., 1969-72, asst. prof. psychiatry, 1977-82, assoc. prof., 1982-88, prof., 1988-91; interim psychiatrist-in-chief McLean Hosp., Belmont, Mass., 1984-86, dir. depression rsch. facility, 1985—, svc. chief, 1982-84, 86-88; psychiatrist adv. panel Eli Lilly & Co., Indpls., 1986-93; clin. dir. Mass. Mental Health Ctr., Boston, 1988-91; Kenneth T. Norris, Jr. prof. psychiatry and behavioral scis. Stanford U., 1991—, chmn. dept. psychiatry and behavioral scis. Sch. Medicine, 1991—.

Cons. AMA Videoclinics, Chgo., 1979-83; mem. AMA/FAA panel on health regulations, Chgo., 1984-86; mem. NIH Biol. Psycholathology and Clin. Neuroscis. Intitial Rev. Group, 1991-95, chmn., 1993-94. Co-author: Manual of Clinical Psychopharmacology, 1986, 3d edit., 1997; contbr. more than 200 articles to profl. publs., chpts. to books; co-editor: Depression: Biology, Psychodynamics and Treatment, 1978, Hypothalamic-Pituitary-Adrenal Axis, 1988, Textbook of Psychopharmacology, 1995, 2d edit., 1998; mem. editl. bd. McLean Hosp. Jour., 1975-88, Jour. Psychiat. Rsch., 1986—, co-editor in chief, 2000—; mem. editl. bd. Integrative Psychiatry, 1990—, Harvard Rev. Psychiatry, 1992—, Archives of Gen. Psychiatry, 1995—, Psychoneuroendocrinology, 1995—, Annals Psychiatry, 1992—, Anxiety, 1993, Jour. Clin. Psychopharmacology, 1993—; assoc. editor-in-chief Depression, 1992—. Maj. USAF, 1972-74. Rsch. grantee NIMH, 1984-87, 94—, Poitras Charitable Found., 1985-93. Fellow APA, Am. Coll. Neuropsychopharmacology (coun. 1994-97, pres. 1999—), Am. Psychopath. Assn.; mem. Am. Coll. Psychiatrists, Mass. Psychiat. Soc. (coun. 1987-90), No. Calif. Psychiat. Soc. (v.p. 1997-99). Avocations: travel, theater, tennis, swimming, fine arts. Office: Stanford U Sch Medicine 401 Quarry Rd Rm 300 Stanford CA 94305-5717

SCHATZKI, GEORGE, law educator; b. 1933; AB, Harvard U., 1955, LLB, 1958, LLM, 1965. Prof. law u. Tex., Austin, 1965-79; dean U. Wash. Sch. Law, Seattle, 1979-82, prof., 1979-84; dean U. Conn. Sch. Law, Hartford, 1984-90, prof., 1994-2000; prof. law Ariz. State U., Tempe, 2000—. Vis. prof. law U. Pa., Phila., 1973-74, Harvard U., Cambridge, Mass., 1977-78; vis. lectr. law Yale U., New Haven, 1993, 96. Co-author: Labor Relations and Social Problems: Collective Bargaining in Private Employment, 1978, Labor and Employment Law, 1988, 3d edit., 2002. Fellow Tchg., Harvard U., 1963—65. Office: Ariz State U Coll Law PO Box 877906 Tempe AZ 85287-7906 E-mail: george.schatzki@asu.edu.

SCHAUB, GARY JOHN, JR. political scientist; b. Pitts., June 26, 1969; s. Gary John Schaub and Mary Ann Mendrolla. BS, Carnegie Mellon U., 1990; MA, U. Ill., 1992. Lectr. Chatham Coll., Pitts., 1999. Author: (with others) Compellence: Resuscitating the Concept, 1998. Recipient Hon. Mention, NSF, 1991-92; Andrew Carnegie Soc. scholar, 1990; MacArthur fellow in arms control, disarmament, and internat. security U. Ill., 1990-91; Merriam fellow in polit. sci. U. Ill., 1991-92; Owens fellow U. Pitts., 1993-94. Mem. Internat. Studies Assn. (Internat. Security Studies sect.), Am. Polit. Sci. Assn., Arms Control Assn. Avocations: aerobics, weight training. E-mail: schaub+@pitt.edu. Office: U Pitts 3E01 Posvar Hall Pittsburgh PA 15260 Fax: 412-648-2605.

SCHAUB, HARRY CARL, lawyer; b. Hazleton, Pa., Feb. 3, 1929; s. Harry J. and Lida M. (Fisher) S.; m. Kathryn Klindt Deans, Aug. 14, 1982; children: Lisa A., Irene Cannon, Christian K. BA, U. Pa., 1950; JD, Yale U., 1955; postgrad., Columbia U., 1962. Bar: Pa. 1955. Assoc. Montgomery, McCracken, Walker & Rhoads, Phila., 1955-62, ptnr., 1963-99, of counsel, 1999—. Consul Republic of Austria to State of Pa., 1978-84, consul gen., 1984—. Dir. Concerto Soloista Phila., 1997-99, Franklin Inn, 1998-2001; contbr. articles to profl. jours. V.p., bd. dirs. Luth. Ch. of Holy Communion, Phila., 1975-88; bd. dirs. YMCA Cen., Phila., 1986-91. Capt. U.S. Army, 1951-53. Decorated Golden Medal of Honor 1st Class (Austria), Grand Cross of Honor 1st class Austria; recipient Johann Strauss award, City of Vienna, 1979. Mem.: John Peter Zenger Law Soc. (founder, bd. dirs., pres. 1994—96), Mil. Order Fgn. Wars, Austrian Soc. Pa. (v.p., bd. dirs. 1981—97), Am. Coun. on Germany, Athenaeum of Phila., The Penn Club, Rittenhouse Club, Union League of Phila., Pi Gamma Mu, Phi Beta Kappa. Democrat. Lutheran. Home: 1420 Locust St Apt 7K Philadelphia PA 19102-4205 Office: Montgomery McCracken 123 S Broad St Fl 24 Philadelphia PA 19109-1099

SCHAUB, MARILYN MCNAMARA, religion educator; b. Chgo., Mar. 24, 1928; d. Bernard Francis and Helen Katherine (Skehan) McNamara; m. Thomas Schaub, Oct. 25, 1969; 1 child Helen Ann. BA, Rosary Coll., 1953; PhD, U. Fribourg, Switzerland, 1957; diploma, Ecole Biblique, Jerusalem, 1967. Asst. prof. classics and Bibl. studies Rosary Coll., River Forest, Ill., 1957-69; prof. Bibl. studies Duquesne U., Pitts., 1969-70, 73-01. Participant 8 archeological excavations, Middle East; hon assoc Am Schs Oriental Research, 1966—67, trustee, 1986—89; Danforth assoc, 1972—80; admin dir expedition to the Southeast Dead Sea Plains, Jordan, 1989—. Author: (book) Friends and Friendship for St. Augustine, 1964; translator (with H Richter): Agape in the New Testament, 3 vols, 1963—65. Mem.: Am Acad Religion, Cath Biblical Asn, Soc Biblical Literature. Democrat. Home: 25 Mckelvey Ave Pittsburgh PA 15218-1452

SCHAUBERT, DANIEL HAROLD, electrical engineering educator; b. Galesburg, Ill., Feb. 15, 1947; s. Robert Harold and Carolyn Virginia (Dunkle) S.; m. Joyce Marie Conard, June 15, 1968; 1 child, Karen Louise. BSEE, U. Ill., 1969, MS, 1970, PhD, 1974. Rsch. engr. U.S. Army Harry Diamond Labs., Adelphi, Md., 1977-80; rsch. engr., program mgr. U.S. Bur. Radiol. Health, Rockville, 1980-82; prof. elec. engring. U. Mass., Amherst, 1982—, dept. head elec. and computer engring., 1994-98. Patentee in field. 1st lt. U.S. Army, 1974-77. Fellow IEEE (Third Millennium medal), IEEE Antennas and Propagation Soc. (membership chair 1980-82, editor newsletter 1982-84, sec.-treas. 1984-88, v.p. 1998, pres. 1999). Office: U Mass Elec and Computer Engring Amherst MA 01003

SCHAUBLE, JOHN EUGENE, physical education educator; b. Paterson, N.J., Aug. 14, 1949; s. Charles Eugene and Rosemary (White) S.; children: Sarah, Angela. BA, Bemidji State U., 1973, BS, 1974; MA, U. Ala., 1984. Cert. tchr. health, phys. edn., K-12; cert. swimming coach/level 4; cert. aquatic mgr.; cert. pool operator, ARC water safety instr., lifeguard instr., waterfront lifeguard instr., first aid instr., CPR instr., water safety instr. trainer; cert. USAT&F level II. Northeast area dir. Phys. Fitness Inst. of Am., Albany, N.Y., 1974-75; head swim coach Lake Forest (Ill.) Swim Club, 1975-78; asst. swim coach/grad. asst. U. Ala., Tuscaloosa, 1978-79; head swim coach Palm Springs (Calif.) Swim Team, 1979-80; asst. swim coach Ft. Lauderdale (Fla.) Swim Team, 1980-82; aquatic dir., head swim coach Briarwood of Richmond Aquatic Club, Richmond, Va., 1982-83; head swimming coach, intramural coord. William Rainey Harper Coll., Palatine, Ill., 1983-85; boys/girls asst. swim coach Sch. Dist. 211, 1985-90; nat. coach Palatine Swim Team, 1983-92; head boys and girls swim coach Adlai E. Stevenson High Sch., Lincolnshire, Ill., 1990-96, aquatic coord., 1990—, asst. girls track and field coach, 1992-99, varsity cross-country coach, 1999—, boys distance track and field coach, 1999—. Head coach Patriot Aquatic Club, 1992-94, head coach sr. team, 1994-99; fund raising com. U.S. Swimming, Inc., Colorado Springs, Colo., 1990-94; coaches rep. Ill. Swimming, Inc., Aurora, 1990-94, bd. dirs., tech. planning com., others. Nominated Coach of Yr., Nat. Jr. Coll. Athletic Assn., Ft. Pierce, Fla., 1984; named Boys Sectional Coach of Yr., Ill. High Sch. Assn., 1992. Mem. Ill. Swimming Assn. (nominated Coach of Yr. coll. divsn. boys 1984), Nat. Interscholastic Swimming Coaches Assn., Am. Swimming Coaches Assn., Am. Coll. Sports Medicine, Nat. Strength and Conditioning Assn., AAPHERD, NEA. Republican. Roman Catholic. Avocations: computer, running, swimming, tennis, weight tng. Home: 608 Applegate Ln Lake Zurich IL 60047-2363 Office: 1 Stevenson Dr Lincolnshire IL 60069-2824

SCHAUDER, JOAN NORMA, secondary school educator, writer; b. N.Y.C., Apr. 5, 1951; d. Abe and Florence Hirschbein; m. Gary David Schauder. BA in Philosophy, Lehman Coll., N.Y.C., 1971, MA in Reading, 1975. Mem. faculty N.Y.C. Bd. Edn., N.Y.C., 1972—. Contbr. articles to popular mags. Mem. U.F.T., 1972—. Jewish. Avocation: antiques.

SCHAUDIES, JESSE P., JR. business executive; b. Knoxville, Tenn., Aug. 27, 1954; s. Jesse P. and Adele (Thompson) S.; m. Elizabeth D. Schaudies, Sept. 15, 1979; children: Jesse P. III, Frederick T., Deneen Adele. BA magna cum laude, Duke U., 1976; JD, Georgetown U., 1979. Ptnr. Troutman Sanders, Atlanta, 1979-94; mng. dir. gen. affairs, gen. counsel, sec. Randstad N.Am., 1994—. Mng. editor Am. Criminal Law Rev., 1978-79; contbr. articles to profl. jours. Mem. ABA, Ga. State Bar Assn. (labor sect., litigation sect.), Authors Ct. Ga. (charter), Industry Trade Assn. (officer), Internat. Lab. Orgn. (del.). Republican. Presbyterian. E-mail: schaudies@aol.com.

SCHAUER, CATHARINE GUBERMAN, public affairs specialist; b. Woodbury, N.J., Sept. 24, 1945; d. Jack and Anna Ruth (Felipe) Guberman; m. Irwin Jay Schauer, July 4, 1968; children: Cheryl Ann Schauer Crabb, Marc Cawin. AB, Miami-Dade Jr. Coll., 1965; BEd, U. Miami, 1967; postgrad., Mercer U., 1968; MPA, Troy State U., 1995. Writer Miami (Fla.) News, 1962-63; tchr. Dade County Schs., Miami, 1967-68; coord. pub. info. Macon (Ga.) Jr. Coll., 1968-69; writer Atlanta Jour., 1969-72; editor Ridgerunner, newspaper, Woodbridge, Va., 1973-75; pub. info. specialist U.S. Dept. Interior, Washington, 1980-82; writer Dept. Army, Ft. Belvoir, Va., 1982-84, chief prodn., design and editl. publs. divsn., 1984-85; head writer-editor S.E. region U.S. Naval Audit Svc., Virginia Beach, 1986; pub. affairs specialist, tech. rep. for vis. ctr. ops. NASA Langley, 1986-90, project mgr., chmn. 75th anniversary yr., 1991-92; with NASA Langley Rsch. Ctr., Hampton, Va., 1987-89, acting head Office Pub. Svcs., 1989, pub. affairs officer for space, 1993—, interpers. govt. assignment to prof. Embry Riddle Aero U. Daytona Beach, Fla., 2001—02. Columnist, writer Potomac News, Woodbridge, 1972-85; guest lectr. George Washington U. Grad. Sch.; apptd. mem. comm. program industry adv. bd. Embry-Riddle Aero. U., Dayton Beach, Fla., 2001—, bd. dirs. Sch. Comm. Contbr. articles to profl. jours. Historian, publicity chmn. PTO, Woodbridge, 1974; publicity chmn. Boy Scouts Am., Woodbridge, 1974-83, Girl Scouts U.S.A., Woodridge, 1974-79; bd. dirs. Congregation Ner Tamid, Woodbridge, 1984-85. Recipient Outstanding Tng. Devel. Support award U.S. Army, 1983, 1st place news writing award and 1st place for advt. design Fla. Jr. Coll. Press Assn., 1964, 1st place feature writing award, 1964, 1st place news writing award Sigma Delta Chi, 1965, 70th anniversary team NASA, 1988, Long Duration Exposure Facility Team award NASA, Combined Fed. Campaign Spl. award for Outstanding Svc. to Va. Peninsula, 1996, Discovery Team Excellence award NASA, 1998. Mem. Va. Press Women (1st place govt. mags. award 1991, 3d place govt. brochures award 1993, 1st place govt. media campaign award 1993, 2d place pub. svc. campaign award 1996, 1st place govt. pub. svc. campaign award 1996, 1st place pub. svc. campaign award 1997), Women in Comm., Nat. Fedn. Press Women (life, 1st place govt. mag. award 1991, 1st place govt. media campaign award 1993, 96, 1st place govt. internal comm. campaign award 1996, 3d place pub. svc. campaign award 1997), Internat. Assn. Bus. Communicators (1st place mktg. campaign award 1996, 1st place award of excellence for pub. svc. campaign 1996). Democrat. Office: 1063 Hampstead Ln Ormond Beach FL 32174-9286 E-mail: c.g.schauer@larc.nasa.gov.

SCHAUER, FRANZ PETER, civil and nuclear engineer, educator; b. Mankato, Minn., Nov. 29, 1932; s. Albert Franz and Marie Petrich (Nielsson) S.; m. Joan Laurie; children: Marie, Barbara, Franz, Jr., Lisa, Jill. BS, U.S. Mil. Acad., 1955; MSCE, MS in Nuclear Engring., Iowa State U., 1961, PhD, 1969. Cert. civil engr. Commd. 2d lt. U.S. Army, 1955, advanced through grades to col., 1980, ret., 1989; engr. U.S. Atomic Energy Commn., Germantown, Md., 1964-75; exec. U.S. Nuclear Regular Commn., Bethesda, 1975-82; prof. Minn. State U., 1982-93; pres. ADU Engring. Assn., Bethesda, 1994—. Engring. cons. Tex-La Power, Stone and Webster, Boston, 1987, Burns and Roe, N.Y.C., 1986, U.S. Army, Washington, 1984, Todd Shipbuilding, Washington, 1983. Author: Advances in Structural Dynamics, 1980. Trustee Christ Luth. Ch. Fellow Am. Soc. Civil Engrs. (several coms.); mem. IEEE Computer Soc., Am. Soc. Mech. Engrs. (several coms.), Phi Kappa Phi, Sigma Xi. Lutheran. Avocations: tennis, computers. Home: Unit 261 6860 Gulfport Blvd S Saint Petersburg FL 33707-2108 Office: PO Box 1423 Mc Lean VA 22101-1423 E-mail: franz1000@msn.com.

SCHAUER, FREDERICK FRANKLIN, law educator; b. Newark, Jan. 15, 1946; s. John Adolph and Clara (Balayti) S.; m. Margery Clare Stone, Aug. 25, 1968 (div. June, 1982); m. Virginia Jo Wise, May 25, 1985. AB, Dartmouth Coll., 1967, MBA, 1968; JD, Harvard U., 1972. Bar: Mass. 1972, U.S. Supreme Ct. 1976. Assoc. Fine & Ambrogne, Boston, 1972-74; asst. prof. law W.Va. U., Morgantown, 1974-76, assoc. prof., 1976-78, Coll. William and Mary, Williamsburg, Va., 1978-80, Cutler prof., 1980-83; prof. of law U. Mich., Ann Arbor, 1983-90; Frank Stanton prof. of 1st Amendment Kennedy Sch. of Govt., Harvard U., Cambridge, Mass., 1990—, acad. dean, 1997—. Vis. scholar, mem. faculty law Wolfson Coll. Cambridge (Eng.) U., 1977-78; vis. prof. Law Sch., U. Chgo., 1990; vis. fellow Australian Nat. U., 1993, 98; William Morton Disting. Sr. fellow in humanities Dartmouth Coll., 1991; vis. prof. law Harvard Law Sch., 1996, 97, 2000; Ewald Disting. vis. prof. law U. Va., 1996, vis. prof. govt. Dartmouth Coll., 1997; acad. dean, Frank Stanton prof. first amendment Kennedy Sch. Govt. Harvard U., Cambridge, 1997—; disting. vis. prof. law U. Toronto, 2000. Author: The Law of Obscenity, 1976, Free Speech: A Philosophical Enquiry, 1982 (ABA cert. merit 1983), Supplements to Gunther Constitutional Law, 1983-96, Playing by the Rules: A Philosophical Examination of Rule Based Decision-Making in Law and Life, 1991, The First Amendment: A Reader, 1992, 2d edit., 1995, The Philosophy of Law, 1995; editor: Legal Theory, 1995; contbr. articles to profl. jours. Mem. Atty. Gen.'s Commn. on Pornography, 1985-86. Served with Mass. Army N.G., 1970-71. NEH fellow, summer 1980, Guggenheim fellow, 2001-02. Fellow Am. Acad. Arts and Scis.; mem. Am. Philos. Assn., Am. Soc. for Polit. and Legal Philosophy (v.p. 1996-99), Assn. Am. Law Schs. (chmn. sect. constl. law 1984-86). Office: Kennedy Sch of Govt Harvard U Cambridge MA 02138 E-mail: fred_schauer@harvard.edu.

SCHAUER, JEFFREY EDWARD, surgeon; b. Milw., 1952; MD, U. Wis., 1977. Diplomate Am. Bd. Surgery. Intern U. Wis. Hosp., Madison, 1977-78, resident, 1978-82; pvt. practice surgeon Rockford., Ill., 1982—. Clin. asst. prof. surgery U. Ill. Coll. Medicine, Rockford, acting chmn., 2000—; attending surgeon Rockford Med. Hosp. Mem. ACS, Midwest Surg. Assn. Office: 1235 N Mulford Rd Rockford IL 61103 E-mail: jschauer@rhsnet.org.

SCHAUER, THOMAS ALFRED, insurance company executive; b. Canton, Ohio, Dec. 24, 1927; s. Alfred T. and Marie A. (Luthi) S.; m. Joanne Alice Fay, Oct. 30, 1954; children: Alan, John, David, Susan, William. BSc, Ohio State U., 1950. With Ind. Ins. Svc. Corp., 1964—, Ind. Benefit Svc. Corp., 1984—. Dir. Bank One, Akron, N.A., Ohio, 1991-97, mem. adv. bd., 1997-2000. Chmn. Joint Hosp. Blood Com., 1974; bd. dirs. McKinley Life Ins. Co., 1991-95; bd. dirs. Better Bus. Bur., Canton, 1970-81, chmn., 1979-80; bd. dirs. area YMCA, 1974-92, v.p., 1975-82, pres., 1982-84; trustee Canton Cemetery Assn., 1988-91, Stark County Blue Coats, 1987—; bd. dirs. Hosp. Bur. Cen. Stark City, 1972-78; vice chmn. bd. Aultman Hosp., 1981-84, chmn., 1984-87; chmn. Aultman Health Svcs. Assn., 1990-93; pres. Aultman Hosp. Found., 1987-90, trustee, 1971-98, trustee emeritus, 1998—; chmn. bd. JMS Found., 1968—; bd. dirs. United Way, 1974-84, pres., 1976-78; mem. distbn. com. Stark County Found., 1977-87, chmn. distbn. com., 1984-87, dir. Dime Bank, Canton, 1965-72, Ctrl. Trust Co. NE Ohio, N.A., 1972-91; adv. bd. Malone Coll., 1979-92; trustee Kent State U., 1980-88, trustee emeritus, 1988—, N.E. Ohio Univs. Coll. Medicine, 1983-88; past trustee Canton Urban League, Boys Village (Smithville, Ohio), Canton Art Inst., Buckeye Coun. Boy Scouts Am. Served with USNR, 1946-48. Recipient gold key award United Way Ctrl. Stark County, 1981, award of merit Canton C. of C., 1984, red triangle award Canton Area YMCA, 1985. Mem. Chartered Ins. Inst. London, Nat. Assn. Mfg., Am. Soc. CPCUs, Am. Soc. CLUs, Assn., Advanced Life Underwriters, Am. Risk and Ins. Assn., Am. Soc. Pension Actuaries, Stark County Accident and Health Underwriters (past pres.), Canton Club, Brookside Country Club, Atwood Yacht Club. Home: 1756 Dunbarton Ave NW Canton OH 44708-1807 Office: Millennium Ctr 200 Market Ave N Ste 100 Canton OH 44702 E-mail: tomschauer@att.net.

SCHAUER, WILBERT EDWARD, JR. lawyer, manufacturing company executive; b. Milw., Oct. 28, 1926; s. Wilbert Edward and Gertrude (Nickel) S.; m. Genevieve Stone, June 23, 1951; children— Jeffrey Edward, Constance Emily, Gregory Wilbert, Martha Ann, Jennifer Caroline. BBA, U. Wis., 1949, MBA, JD, U. Wis., 1950. Bar: Wis. 1950. Accountant Pub. Service Commn. Wis., 1950-52; with Rexnord, Inc., Milw., 1952-87, v.p. finance, treas., 1968-76, v.p. fin. and law, 1977-78, exec. v.p. fin. and adminstrn., 1978-86, vice chmn., 1986-87. Alderman, Brookfield, Wis., 1958-68; pres. Common Council, 1966-68. Mem.: Moorings Country Club, Westmoor Country Club (Brookfield, Wis.), Milw. Club. Home: 3215 Gulf Shore Blvd N Ph 4 Naples FL 34103-3920

SCHAUF, CAROLYN JANE, lawyer; b. Visalia, Calif., Sept. 30, 1946; d. William Powell and Mildred (Hudiburgh) Gateley; m. Jack Eldon Schuaf, Apr. 24, 1971; children: Christie, Jeffrey. JD, Western State Coll. Law, Fullerton, Calif., 1985. Bar: Calif. 1986. Pvt. practice, Downey, Calif., 1986—. Mem. SE Bar Assn., Los Angeles County Bar Assn. Office: 8301 Florence Ave Downey CA 90240-3936 E-mail: cjsattorney@yahoo.com.

SCHAUFENBUEL, BRADLEY JOHN, computer consultant, writer; b. Cedar Rapids, Iowa, Sept. 16, 1972; s. Robert Nicholas and Dianne Rose (Riha) S. AA, Kirkwood C.C., 1993; BA, U. No. Iowa, 1996; MBA, DePaul U., 2000. UNIX sys. adminstr. Iowa Rsch. and Edn. Network, Cedar Falls, Iowa, 1995; systems analyst MCI Telecom., Inc., Cedar Rapids, 1995; webmaster U. No. Iowa Coll. Edn., Cedar Falls, 1995; sr. cons. Andersen LLP, Chgo., 1996—. Dir. UpServe Techs., Inc., Chgo. Co-author: MCSE: Windows NT Server 4.0 for Dummies, 1998, MCSE: Windows NT Server in the Enterprise, 1998. Mem. IEEE, Internet Engring. Task Force, Internet Soc., Delta Mu Delta (sec. 1999—, Medallion award 1999). Republican. Roman Catholic. Avocations: hiking, reading, traveling, investing. Home: 5009 Cornell Ave Downers Grove IL 60515-4314 Office: Arthur Andersen LLP 330 N Wabash Ave Chicago IL 60611-3603 Fax: 312-507-1003. E-mail: bradley.j.schaufenbuel@us.andersen.com.

SCHAUFUSS, PETER, dancer, producer, choreographer, ballet director; b. Copenhagen, Denmark, Apr. 26, 1950; s. Frank Schaufuss and Mona Vangsaae S. Student, Royal Danish Ballet Sch. Apprentice with Royal Danish Ballet, 1965; soloist Nat. Ballet Can., 1967-68, Royal Danish Ballet, 1969-70; prin. with LFB, 1970-74, N.Y.C. Ballet, 1974-77, Nat. Ballet Can., 1977-83; artistic dir. London Festival Ballet (now English Nat. Ballet), 1984-90; ballet dir. Deutsche Oper Berlin, 1990-93, Royal Danish Ballet, 1994-95, Peter Schaufuss Balletten, 1997—; guest appearances in Can., Denmark, France, Germany, Italy, Japan, U.K., U.S.A., USSR, Austria, S.Am.; presented BBC TV series Dancer, 1984; numerous other TV appearances; created roles include Rhapsodie Espagnole, The Steadfast Tin Soldier (Balanchine), Phantom of the Opera (Petit), Verdi Variations, Orpheus (MacMillan); ballets produced include La Sylphide (London Festival Ballet, Stuttgart Ballet, Roland Petit's Ballet de Marseille, Deutsche Oper Berlin, Teatro Comunale Firenze, Vienna State Opera, Opernhaus Zurich, Teatro dell'Opera di Roma, Hessisches Staatstheater Wiesbaden, Ballet du Rhin, Royal Danish Ballet, Ballet West), Napoli (Nat. Ballet Can., Teatro San Carlo, Naples, English Nat. Ballet, formerly London Festival Ballet), Folktale (Deutsche Oper Berlin), Dances from Napoli (London Festival Ballet), Bournonville (Aterballetto), The Nutcracker (London Festival Ballet, Graz Opera Ballet, Deutsche Oper Berlin), Giselle (Deutsche Oper Berlin, Royal Danish Ballet), Tchiakovsky Trilogy (Deutsche Oper Berlin), Sleeping Beauty (Deutsche Oper Berlin), Swan Lake (Deutsche Oper Berlin); staging of Romeo and Juliet (Royal Danish Ballet); producer, choreographer (Royal Danish Ballet) Hamlet, 1996; new versions of Hamlet, Swan Lake, Sleeping Beauty, The Nutcracker, Romeo and Juliet (Peter Schaufuss Balletten); prodr., choreographer The King, Manden Der Onskede Sig En Havudsigt, 1999, Midnight Express (Peter Schaufuss Balletten), 2000, The 3 Presents (Kermessen in Bruges), 2000, Hans Christian Andersen, 2001. Decorated officer Order of the Crown (Belgium); recipient Solo award 2d Internat. Ballet Competition, Moscow, 1973, Star of the Yr. award Abendzeitung, Munich, 1978, Evening Std. award, 1979, Soc. of West End Theatres Ballet award (now Oliver), 1979, Manchester Evening News Theatre awards-dance, 1986, Lakerolprisen, Copenhagen, 1988, Berlin Co. award for best ballet prodn. Berlinerzeitung, 1991, Edinburgh Festival Critics prize, 1991,; named Knight of the Dannebrog, 1988. Office: Holstebro Hallen Ved Hallen 4 7500 Holstebro Denmark

SCHAULAND, MABEL DOROTHY, retired educator; b. Barnum Twp., Minn., Feb. 10, 1924; d. August Charles Schauland and Anna Marie (Madsen) S. BS cum laude, U. Minn., Duluth, 1949, MA, 1953; postgrad., U. Wis., 1967. Cert. spl. edn. tchr., elem. and secondary tchr. Tchr. Elem. Edn., Cloquet, Minn., 1949-54; 5th grade tchr. Duluth Lab. Sch. U. Minn., Duluth, 1954-65, instr. spl. edn., 1967-87, asst. prof., tchr., 1967-87, asst. prof., head dept., 1967-87. Pres. Epilepsy League of Lake Superior, United Cerebral Palsy, Port Cities com., Duluth; pres.-elect Friends of the Libr., Duluth, 1996. Named Woman of Yr. Duluth/Superior Port Cities, 1991, Hall of Fame City of Duluth, 1994. Mem. Duluth Woman's Club (pres.), Gen. Fedn. of Women's Club 20th Century (pres.), Women's Inst. (pres.), Gen. Fedn. Woman's Clubs (pres. 8th dist., parliamentarian). Lutheran. Avocations: reading, walking, skiing, swimming. Home: 100 Elizabeth St #604 Duluth MN 55803

SCHAUMANN, CAROLINE, language educator; b. Berlin, Sept. 7, 1969; came to U.S., 1991; d. Frank and Cora-Beate S.; m. Jeffrey Thomas Ransdell, June 30, 1997 (div. Aug. 1999). BA, Free U., Berlin, 1992; MA, U. Calif., Davis, 1994, PhD, 1999. Asst. prof. Middlebury (Vt.) Coll., 1999—. Author: Our Own Private Ezahlraum, 2000. Summer Seminar grant Ctr. for Advanced Holocaust Studies, 2000; Quadrille Ball scholar Office Internat. Edn., 1999. Mem. MLA, German Studies Assn., Am. Assn. Tchrs. German, Women in German. Avocations: rock climbing, mountaineering, running. Office: Middlebury Coll FIC Cook TL 15 Middlebury VT 05753 E-mail: cschauma@middlebury.edu.

SCHAUMBERG, TOM MICHAEL, lawyer; b. Amsterdam, The Netherlands, May 29, 1938; came to U.S., 1947; s. Ernest and Pollo Gertrud Schaumberg; m. Gail A. Greenberg, Aug. 25, 1963 (div.); children: Steven James, Lisa Jill, Erica Beth; m. Joan A. Rohrbeck, Oct. 14, 2000. BA, Yale U., 1960; LLB, Harvard U., 1963; postgrad., U. Frankfurt, Germany, 1964. Bar: Ohio 1964, D.C. 1968, U.S. Supreme Ct. 1972, Md. 1975, U.S. Ct. Appeals (fed. cir.) 1979. Atty. U.S. Fed. Trade Commn., Washington, 1964-67; assoc., ptnr. Gadsby & Hannah, 1968-74; ptnr. Rollinson & Schaumberg, 1974-78, Plaia & Schaumberg, Washington, 1978-86, Howrey & Simon, Washington, 1987-88; sr. ptnr. Adduci, Mastriani & Schaumberg, 1989—. Panelist U.S.-Can. Free-Trade Agreement, Washington, 1990-95. Contbr. articles to profl. periodicals. Mem. Dupont Cir. Citizens Assn., Washington, 1988—. Mem. Internat. Trade Commn. Trial Lawyers Assn. (pres. 1984-85, exec. com. 1987—). Office: Adduci Mastriani & Schaumberg 1200 17th St NW Fl 5 Washington DC 20036-3006 E-mail: Schaumberg@adduci.com.

SCHAUMBURG, DONALD ROLAND, art educator, ceramic artist; b. Oakland, Calif., Aug. 23, 1919; s. John J. and Ethel Florence (Gurney) S.; m. Darleen Jackson, Nov. 22, 1945; 1 child: Rhoda Jane Pertuit. BA in Art Edn., Calif. Coll. Arts and Crafts, 1941; MFA, Clare Coll., 1951; postgrad. advanced study, Pond Farm, Guerniville, Calif., 1957-59. Instr. Palamar Coll., San Marcos, Calif., 1946-49, Fine Arts Gallery, San Diego, 1952; tchr. La Jolla (Calif.) H.S., 1952-53; instr. San Diego State U., 1953; prof. art Ariz. State U., Tempe, 1953-88; dir. Payson (Ariz.) Art Ctr., summers 1967-70. Exhibited in group shows at 15th Nat. Syracuse (N.Y.) Bienniel, 1950, Mus. of Contemporary Crafts, N.Y., 1964, Mus. of Internat. Folk Art, Santa Fe, N.Mex., 1965, The U. Art Collections, Ariz. State U., Tempe, 1973, Nelson Art Ctr. Ariz. State U., Tempe, Phoenix Sky Harbour Airport Callery, 1999. With USN, 1942-45. Recipient 1st prize clay exhbn., Heard Mus., Phoenix, 1975; awards of merit Ariz. Crafts, Tucson, 1955-59. Mem.: Ariz. Designer Craftsmen (life; founder, Mary Soule award 1975). Avocations: gardening, fishing, travel, painting. Home: 5410 E Vernon Ave Phoenix AZ 85008-2622

SCHAUMBURG, HERBERT HOWARD, neurology educator; b. Houston, Nov. 6, 1932; m. Joanna Jane Austin; children: Barnabas Paul, Kristin Elizabeth. AB cum laude, Harvard Coll., 1956; MD, Washington U., 1960. Instr. in neurology Albert Einstein Coll. of Medicine, N.Y.C., 1964-67, asst. prof. neurology, 1967-69, assoc. prof. neurology, 1972-76, prof., 1976—, vice chmn., 1977-84, acting chmn., 1984-86, chmn., 1986—; instr. pathology Harvard Med. Sch., Boston, 1969-71. Mem. Am. Acad. Neurology, Am. Assn. Neuropathologists, Am. Neurol. Assn., Soc. Toxicology, Soc. Neurosci. Home: 616 King Ave City Island Bronx NY 10464 Office: Albert Einstein Coll Medicine 1300 Morris Park Ave Bronx NY 10461-1926

SCHAUPP, JOAN POMPROWITZ, trucking company executive, writer; b. Green Bay, Wis., Sept. 29, 1932; d. Joseph and Helen Elizabeth (VanderLinden) Pomprowitz; m. Robert James Schaupp, Sept. 4, 1956; children: Margaret Schaupp Siebert, Frederick, John Robert, Elizabeth Schaupp Sidles. BS cum laude, U. Wis., 1954; cert. in theology, St. Norbert Coll. Theol. Inst., 1979; MA, U. Wis., Green Bay, 1982; DMin, Grad. Theol. Found., 1996. Woman's editor Green Bay Press-Gazette, 1955-56; freelance writer Green Bay, 1957-75; sec.-treas., dir. L.C.L. Transit Co., 1962-70; dir. P & S Investment Co., 1982—, mgmt. cons., 1984-89, dir. strategic planning, 1992, vice chmn., 1994—. Pres. The Manna Co., Green Bay, 1992—; adv. com. Women's Ctr. St. Norbert Coll., 1999—. Author: Jesus Was a Teenager, 1972, Woman Image of Holy Spirit, 1975 (Thomas More Book award), Elohim: A Search for a Symbol for Human Fulfillment, 1995. Master gardener De Pere (Wis.) Beautification

Com., 1991-92; lector St. Francis Xavier Cathedral, Green Bay, 1991-92. Mem.: Nat. Press Club, Nat. Fedn. Press Women, Am. Acad. Religion, Franciscan Internat., Secular Franciscan Order (vice min. Assumption Province 1991—92), Equestrian Order of the Holy Sepulchre Jerusalem (lady grand cross), Soc. Bibl. Lit. Avocations: gardening, walking, swimming.

SCHAUSS, ALEXANDER GEORGE, psychologist, biomedical researcher; b. Hamburg, Fed. Republic Germany, July 20, 1948; came to U.S., 1953; s. Frank and Alla S.; m. Laura Babin; children: Nova, Evan. BA, U. N.Mex., 1970, MA, 1972; PhD, Calif. Coast U., 1992. State probation/parole officer 2nd Judicial Dist. Ct., Albuquerque, 1969-73; criminal justice planner Albuquerque/Bernalillo County Criminal Justice Planning Com., 1973-75; state asst. adminstr. dept. corrections State of S.D., Pierre, 1975-77; dir. Pierce County Probation Dept., Tacoma, 1977-78; tng. officer IV Wash. State Criminal Justice Tng. Commn., Olympia, 1978-79; dir. Inst. Biosocial Rsch. City Univ. Grad. Sch., Seattle, 1979-80; exec. dir. Am. Inst. Biosocial and Med. Rsch. Inc., Tacoma, 1980—, Am. Preventive Med. Assn., 1992-94, Citizens for Health, 1992-95; dir. Citizens for Health Edn., 1994-96; assoc. prof. behavioral scis. Nat. Coll. Naturopathic Medicine, Portland, 1996-97, clin. prof. natural products rsch. dept. rsch., 1998-99; assoc. prof. rsch. S.W. Coll. Naturopathic Medicine & Health Scis., Tempe, Ariz., 1995-96, rsch. dir., 1995-96, sr. dir. rsch. Scottsdale, 1996-97; clin. prof. natural products rsch. Nat. Coll. Naturopathic Medicine, 1998-99, adj. rsch. prof. botanical medicine, 1999—. Pres. Campaign To Label Genetically Engineered Foods, 1999—; mem. study group on health promotion WHO, Copenhagen, 1985; vis. lectr. pediats. The John Radcliffe Hosp., Oxford U., Eng., summer 1985; sec. coun. on food policy Nat. Assn. Pub. Health Policy, 1990-94, chmn., 1994-96; vis. scholar Kans. C.C. Consortium, 1982; vis. lectr. McCarrison Soc. Conf. at Oxford U., 1983; advisor Ministry Pub. Health for Thailand, 2000—; mem. presdl. adv. bd. Bastyr U., 1979-2000, S.W. Coll. Naturopathic Medicine, 1993-97; mem. devel. planning com., Office of Dietary Supplements, Office of Disease Prevention, NIH, Bethesda, 1996-99, mem. alternative medicine adv. coun. Office Alternative Medicine, NIH, 1997-99; chmn. safety com., compliance labeling integrity com. Nat. Nutritional Foods Assn., 1996—, mem. ComPLI, 1992—; chmn. ad hoc BSE Com. (Mad Cow's Disease), NNFA, 2001—. Author: Orthomolecular Treatment of Criminal Offenders, 1978, Diet, Crime and Delinquency, 1980, rev., 1995, Nutrition and Behavior, 1986, Nutrition and Criminal Behavior, 1990; co-author: Zinc and Eating Disorders, 1989, Eating for A's, 1991, Minerals, Trace Elements and Human Health, 1995, rev. edit., 1999, Anorexia and Bulimia, 1997, Cat's Claw (Una de Gato) Uncaria Tormentosa, 1996; editor-in-chief Internat. Jour. Biosocial and Med. Rsch., 1979—; reviewer U.S. Pharmacopeia Informational Monographs, 1998-99; mem. editl. bd. 14 jours. Master arbitrator Tacoma/Pierce County Better Bus. Bur., Tacoma, 1986-97; mem. Pierce County N. Area Transp. Adv. Coun., Tacoma, 1991-92; trustee Pierce County Pub. Safety Task Team, 1993, Nat. Inst. for Naturopathic Medicine, 1993-2000. Recipient Rsch. award Wacker Found., 1983-85, 88; fellow Am. Coll. Nutrition, 1986-87, Am. Orthopsychiat. Assn., 1980-95. Fellow N.Y. Acad. of Sci. (emeritus); mem. Am. Chem. Soc., Acad. Eating Disorders, Inst. Food Technologists, Am. Assn. Clin. Nutritionists, Consultants Assn. for Natural Products Industry (pres. 2000, bd. dirs. 2001—), Internat. Assn. Eating Disorders Profls. (pres. Citizens For Health 1995-97), Am. Found. Preventative Medicine (treas. 1992-93), Acad. Criminal Justice Scis., Am. Soc. Criminology, Brit. Soc. Nutritional Medicine (hon.), Soc. for Food Sci. and Tech., Inst. Food Technologists Soc. Food Scientists & Tech., Soc. Orthomolecular Health Medicine, Rotary (chmn. cmty. svcs. com. Tacoma chpt. 1989-90, chmn. civic affairs com. 1989-90, Vladivostok com. 1991-93, internat. exch. com. 1994-95, world cmty. svcs. com. 1996-97). Office: Am Inst for Biosocial and Med Rsch Inc Life Scis Divsn PO Box 1174 Tacoma WA 98401-1174

SCHAUT, JOSEPH WILLIAM, retired banker; b. Cleve., May 30, 1928; s. Francis Xavier and Emma Gertrude (Urmann) S.; m. Susan Stiver, Apr. 23, 1955; children: Deborah Anne Schaut Payne, Gregory F., Mary Theresa Schaut Bentley, Michael J. B in Social Sci. in Econs., Georgetown U., 1950, JD, 1953. Bar: D.C. 1953, U.S. Mil. Ct. Appeals 1953, U.S. Dist. Ct. D.C. 1953, U.S. Ct. Appeals (D.C. cir.) 1953, Ohio 1954. Tax analyst Republic Steel Corp., Cleve., 1953-60, asst. to sec., 1960-67, asst. sec., 1967-81, dir. corp. properties, 1976-84, corp. sec., 1981-84; bus. cons., 1984-85; sr. trust officer AmeriTrust Co. Nat. Assn., 1986-92, Soc. Nat. Bank, Cleve., 1992-93, v.p., 1993-96, Mellon Bank F.S.B., 1996-98; ret., 1998. Served to col. USAR, 1950-78. Recipient award Silver Beaver Greater Cleve. Coun., Boy Scouts Am., 1975 Mem. Am. Soc. Corp. Secs. (dir. 1976-79), Ohio State Bar Assn., Greater Cleve. Growth Assn., Delta Theta Phi, Pi Gamma Mu Roman Catholic.

SCHEAR, BETTY Z. engineering executive, consultant; b. Dayton, Ohio, Dec. 17, 1925; d. Jacob Zukerman and Esther (Groban) Litwack; m. Burt E. Schear, July 4, 1948; children: Abe, Martin, Edith, Jesse. BS in Engring., U. Cin., 1948; MBA, U. Dayton, 1968. Assoc. editor Gardner Pubs., Cin., 1948-50; adminstrv. mgr. Schear Family Practice, Dayton, 1952-85; cons., 1985—. Cons. Health Power, Inc., Columbus, Ohio, 1984-2000. One woman show U. Dayton, 1972. Mem. NSPE, NAFE, Nat. Mus. Women in the Arts (charter), Soc. Women Engrs., Am. Mgmt. Assn. Avocations: reading, art, travel, theater, music. Home: 4300 N Ocean Blvd # 8AB Fort Lauderdale FL 33308-5944 Home (Summer): Apt 4 927 Far Hills Ave Dayton OH 45419-3419

SCHECHNER, RICHARD, theater director, author, educator; b. Newark, Aug. 23, 1934; s. Sheridan and Selma Sophia (Schwarz) S.; m. Carol Martin; children: Samuel MacIntosh, Sophia Martin. BA, Cornell U., 1956; postgrad., Johns Hopkins U., 1957; MA, State U. Iowa, 1958; PhD, Tulane U., 1962. Asst. prof. theatre Tulane U., 1962-66, assoc. prof., 1966-67; prof. performance studies NYU, 1967-91, Univ. prof., 1991—; co-founder, co-dir. New Orleans Group, 1965-67; founder, dir. Performance Group, N.Y.C., 1967-80; founder, artistic dir. East Coast Artists, 1991—; Andrew H. White prof.-at-large Cornell U., 1999—. Hon. prof. Shanghai Theatre Acad., 1995—; prof. titular adj. Instituto Superior de Arte, Havana, Cuba; bd. dirs. Theatre Comms. Group, 1977-78; advisor Internat. Theatre Inst., 1975-77, Ctr. Performance Rsch., Aberwrystwich, Wales, 1993—; pres. Bunch of Exptl. Theatres, 1975, 77, Fulbright Theatre Discipline Com., 1988-91. Author: Public Domain, 1968, Environmental Theater, 1973 (with others) Theatres, Spaces, Environments, 1975, Essays on Performance Theory, 1977, 2d edit. 1988, (with others) Makbeth, 1977, The End of Humanism, 1982, Performative Circumstances, 1983, Betweeen Theater and Anthropology, 1985, (with Samuel MacIntosh-Schechner) The Englebert Stories: North to the Tropics, 1987, The Future of Ritual, 1993, Performance Studies--An Introduction, 2002; editor: Dionysus in 69, 1970; co-editor: Free Southern Theater, 1968, Ritual, Play, and Performance, 1976, By Means of Performance, 1990; gen. editor: (series) Worlds of Performance, 1993—, (with Lisa Wolford) Grotowski Sourcebook, 1997; editor: The Drama Rev., 1962-69, 85—, contbg. editor, 1971-85; adv. editor Jour. Ritual Studies, 1987—; dir. Dionysus in 69, 1968, Macbeth, 1969, Commune, 1970, The Tooth of Crime, 1972, Mother Courage, 1975, The Marilyn Project, 1975, Oedipus, 1977, Cops, 1978, The Balcony, 1979, The Red Snake, 1981, Richard's Lear, 1981, The Cherry Orchard, 1983, Prometheus Project, 1985, Don Juan, 1987, Tomorrow He'll Be Out of the Mountains, 1989, Ma Rainey's Black Bottom, 1992, Faust/Gastronome, 1993, The Oresteia, 1995, Three Sisters, 1997, Hamlet, 1999, Waiting for Godot, 2002.. Served with AUS, 1958-60. Recipient Modello prize, 1985, Contbns. to Theatre Spl. award New England Theatre Conf., 1991, Work in Theatre award Towson State U., 1991; grantee John D. Rockefeller 3d Fund, 1971-72, 76, Asian Cultural Coun., 1988, 95; Guggenheim fellow, 1976, Fulbright fellow, 1976, 83, N.Y. Inst. Humanities fellow, 1987-94, NEH sr. rsch. fellow, 1988, Am. Inst. Indian Studies, 1997; Humanities fellow Princeton U., 1992, Montgomery fellow Dartmouth Coll., 1998, Andrew A. White prof.-at-large Cornell U., 1999--. Office: NYU 721 Broadway 6th Fl Washington Sq New York NY 10003 E-mail: rs4@nyu.edu.

SCHECHTER, ARTHUR LOUIS, lawyer; b. Rosenberg, Tex., Dec. 6, 1939; s. Morris and Helen (Brilling) S.; m. Joyce Proler, Aug. 26, 1965; children: Leslie Schechter Karpas, Jennifer Schechter Rosen. BA, U. Tex., 1962, JD, 1964; postgrad., U. Houston, 1964-65. Bar: Tex. 1964, U.S. Dist. Ct. (ea. and so. dists.) Tex. 1966, U.S. Ct. Appeals (5th cir.), U.S. Supreme Ct. 1976; cert. Tex. Bd. Legal Specialization to Personal Injury Trial Law, 1964-. Pres. Arthur L. Schechter P.C., Houston, 1992-94, Schechter & Marshall, Houston, 1994-96; amb. U.S. to Commonwealth Bahamas, 1998-2000; atty. Schechter, McElwee & Shaffer, LLP, Houston, 2001—. Spkr. Marine Law Sem., 1983; spkr. in field. Contbr. to Law Rev., 1984. Bd. dirs. Theatre Under the Stars, Houston, 1972—78, Congregation Beth Israel, Houston, 1972—84, pres., 1982—84; bd. mem. Inst. Internat. Edn., 1996—98, S.E.A.R.C.H., 1996—98; pres. Am. Jewish Com., Houston, 1982—84, chmn. fgn. rels. com., chmn. United Jewish Campaign exec. com., chmn., 1993—94; pres. Jewish Fedn. Ctr. Houston, 1994—96; mem. Deans Coun. U. Tex. Law Sch.; mem. Houston Metro Bd., 2002; mng. trustee mem. fin. com. Dem. Nat. Com., 1992, fin. chmn. Tex. Clinton/Gore '96; vice chmn. Clinton/Gore Jewish Leadership Coun., 1996; v.p. exec. com. Nat. Jewish Dem. Coun., 1992; mem. Leadership Ctr. Dem. Senatorial Campaign Com.; mem. fin. coun. Nat. Dem. Orgn., 1979. Home: 19A West Ln Houston TX 77019-1007

SCHECHTER, CLIFFORD, financial executive, lawyer; b. N.Y.C., Feb. 14, 1958; s. Howard and Diana D. (Eiss) S.; children: Dana Ann, Adam Hillel, Talia Beth. BS summa cum laude, U. R.I., 1979; JD, Fordham U. Sch. Law, 1982; MBA, L.I. U., 1988. Bar: N.Y. 1983, U.S. Tax Ct. 1983, U.S. Supreme Ct. 1986, D.C. 1990, U.S. Dist. Ct. (so. and ea. dists.) N.Y. 1983; lic. gen. securities prin., fin. and ops. prin. Nat. Assn. Securities Dealers; CFP; registered investment advisor. Tax supr. Touche Ross & Co., Jericho, N.Y., 1982-86; sr. v.p., dir. taxes L.F. Rothschild & Co. Inc., N.Y.C., 1986-91, chief fin. officer, dir. adminstrn. and taxes, 1991-93; pres. Royal Fin. Svcs. Inc., San Diego, 1993-96; personal fin. counseling mgr. Ernst & Young, 1996-99; sr. v.p.,wealth strategist Bank of Am. Pvt. Bank, 1999—. Adj. prof. Adelphi U., Garden City, N.Y., 1983-91, Pace U., N.Y.C., 1991-93. Bd. dirs. P.A.D. Pub. Svc. Ctr., Washington, 1986-98, Congregation Chabad of Poway; trustee San Diego Hall of Champions, 2000—, v.p. 2001-. Recipient Uniroyal Found. Fellowship award, 1978, Am. Jurisprudence award Scholastic Excellence in Estate Planning, 1982. Mem. ABA, N.Y. State Bar Assn., D.C. Bar Assn., Bar Assn. Nassau County, Internat. Assn. Fin. Planning, Fin. Mgmt. Assn., Securities Industry Assn., Wall St. Tax Assn., Profl. Fraternity Assn. (bd. dirs. 1994-95, treas. 1995-96, pres.-elect 1996-97, pres. 1997-98, past pres. 1998-99), Phi Alpha Delta (internat. proctor 1986-88, marshal 1988-90, historian 1990-92, treas. 1992-94, internat. vice justice 1994-96, internat. justice 1996-98, dist. XV justice 1984-86, chmn. internat. adv. bd. 1998-2000, Outstanding Active mem. award 1982, Stan P. Jones Meml. award 1985, Outstanding Alumnus mem. Wormser chpt. 1982-85, Disting. Svc. Chapt. award 2002), Beta Gamma Sigma, Phi Kappa Phi. Republican. Jewish. Home: Unit 2009 11802 Paseo Lucido San Diego CA 92128 Office: Bank of America Private Bank 450 B St Ste 1700 San Diego CA 92101-8005 E-mail: padij@aol.com.

SCHECHTER, DONALD ROBERT, lawyer; b. N.Y.C., Feb. 24, 1946; s. Joseph and Katherine (Beer) S.; m. Roberta Sharon Horowitz, July 3, 1968; children: Elizabeth Anne, Sarah Marilyn. BA, Queens Coll., 1967; JD, Bklyn Law Sch., 1971. Asst. dist. atty. Queens County, Kew Gardens, N.Y., 1971-73; asst. atty. gen. organized crime task force City of N.Y., 1973-74; sole practice Forest Hills, N.Y., 1974—. Legal counsel Centro Civico Colombiano, Jackson Heights, N.Y., 1978—, Fedn. of Merchants and Profls. of Queens, Spanish Orgn., Jackson Heights, 1978—; hearing officer Family Ct., Queens County, Jamaica, N.Y., 1977; consumer counsel Civil Ct., Queens County, 1980. Mem. ABA, N.Y. State Bar Assn., Queens County Bar Assn. (chmn. lawyer placement), Nassau County Bar Assn., Audobon Soc., Sierra Club. Clubs: Glass Soc. Corvette, N.Y. Mets Dream Week. Lodges: KP. Democrat. Jewish. Avocations: antique automobiles, baseball, history, antiques. Office: Ste 1030 80-02 Kew Gardens Rd Kew Gardens NY 11415-3600

SCHECHTER, GAIL HELENE, association executive, educator; b. Bklyn., July 21, 1962; d. David and Irene (Lupu) S.; m. George Herman Sheppard, July 3, 1989 (separated); children: Julia, William. BA in History, Oberlin Coll., 1984; MA in Urban and Environ. Policy, Tufts U., 1990. Dir. organizing St. Nicholas Neighborhood Preservation Corp., Bklyn., 1984-87; landlord/tenant counselor Echo Housing, Hayward, Calif., 1988; program assoc. Ctr. for Neighborhood Tech., Chgo., 1990-92; asst. survey dir. Abt Assocs., 1992-93; exec. dir. Interfaith Housing Devel. Corp., Winnetka, Ill., 1993-97, Interfaith Housing Ctr. No. Suburbs, Winnetka, 1993—. Adj. instr. Kendall Coll., Evanston, Ill., 1994—. Rschr.: Strategies and Saints, 1992. Treas. Statewide Housing Action Consortium, Chgo., 2000—, bd. dirs., 1998—; pres. Citywide Task Force on Housing, N.Y.C., 1986-87; founder, bd. dirs. Chgo. Mut. Housing Network, 1993-95. Recipeint Golden Trowel award Statewide Housing Action Coalition, 2000, Champion of the Public Intrest award, 2001. Mem. LWV (bd. dirs. 1998-2000). Avocation: playing the clarinet. Office: Interfaith Housing Ctr of No Suburbs 620 Lincoln Ave Winnetka IL 60093 E-mail: gschechtr@aol.com.

SCHECHTER, HOWARD, lawyer; b. N.Y.C., Feb. 11, 1952; BA, NYU, 1972, JD, 1975. Bar: N.Y., U.S. Dist. Ct. (ea. and so. dists.) N.Y., U.S. Ct. Appeals (2d and 3d cirs.). Assoc. Schekter, Aber & Hecht, N.Y.C., 1975-79, Schekter, Aber & Rishty, N.Y.C., 1979-81; ptnr. Schechter, Aber, Rishty, Goldstein & Schechter, P.C., 1981-83; pvt. practice Law Offices of Howard Schechter, 1983-86; ptnr. Blodnick, Pomeranz, 1986-87, Schechter & Brucker P.C., N.Y.C., 1987—. Lectr. NYU Sch. Continuing Edn. Real Estate Profl. Programs, 1996—. Contbr. articles to profl. jours. Bd. dirs. N.Y. State Assn. Renewal and Housing Ofcls., Inc., 1979-84, parliamentarian, 1984-89; pres. Roslyn Hilltop Ednl. Found., Inc., 1994—. Mem. Nat. Assn. Housing Coops., N.Y. State Bar Assn., Coun. N.Y. Coops., Fedn. N.Y. Housing Coops., Assn. of Bar of City of N.Y., Phi Beta Kappa. Office: Schechter & Brucker PC 350 5th Ave Ste 4510 New York NY 10118-4585 E-mail: HSchechter@sblaw.com.

SCHECHTER, JOEL, magazine editor, writer, educator; b. Washington, June 21, 1947; s. Henry Bear and Ruth (Lindauer) S. BA, Antioch Coll., 1969; DFA, Yale U., 1973. Lit. advisor Am. Place Theater, N.Y.C., 1973-77; asst. prof. SUNY, Stony Brook, 1974-77; prof. Sch. Drama Yale U., New Haven, 1977-91; editor Theater Mag., 1977-91; prof. theatre arts San Francisco State U., 1992—. Polit. satire columnist New Haven Independent, 1988-90. Author: Durov's Pig, 1985, Satiric Impersonations, 1994, The Congress of Clowns, 1998, The Pickle Clowns, 2001, (play) The Complete Aristophanes, 1988. State senate candidate New Haven Green Party, 1988, 90. Fox fellow Yale U., Moscow, 1991. Mem. Lit. Mgrs. & Dramaturgs Am. (v.p. 1989—), Am. Soc. Theatre Rsch. Office: San Francisco State U Dept Theatre Arts 1600 Holloway Ave Dept Theatre San Francisco CA 94132-1722

SCHECHTER, STEPHEN L. political scientist; b. Washington, Nov. 28, 1945; s. William J. and Blossom (Rapaport) S.; m. Stephanie A. Thompson, Feb. 16, 1993; 1 child, Sarah J.; 1 stepdaughter: Kelly Anne Thompson. BA, Syracuse U., 1967; PhD, U. Pitts., 1972. Acting dir. Ctr. for Study of Federalism/Temple U., 1973-76; asst. to full prof. polit. sci. Russell Sage Coll., Troy, N.Y., 1977—; exec. dir. N.Y. State Commn. on Bicentennial of U.S. Constitution, 1986-90. Dir. Coun. for Citizenship Edn. Russell Sage Coll., N.Y., 1990—, dir. MAT/social studies program, 2001—; coord. We The People, 1992—; pres. N.Y. State Coun. on Social Edn., 1992-93; co-dir. civic edn. exch. program Civitas of Russia, 1994—; sr. rsch. advisor N.Y. State Commn. on the Capital Region, 1995-97; mem. Social Sci. Edn. Consortium, 1999; mem. adv. com. for participation in govt. N.Y. State Edn. Dept., 1999—. Co-editor: World of the Founders: New York Communities in the Federal Period, 1990, Contexts of the Bill of Rights, 1990, New York and the Union, New York and the Bicentennial, 1990; editor: Roots of the Republic: American Founding Documents Interpreted, 1990, others; contbr. articles to profl. jours., chpts. to books in field; editor: Social Sci. Record, 1993-96. Chmn. Rensselaer County Bicentennial Commn., 1991; commr. Albany City Charter Revision Commn., 1997-98; dir. Troy-Sage Homeownership Partnership, 1999—. Mem. Nat. Coun. Social Studies (state del. 1991), Internat. Assn. Ctrs. for Fed. Studies (co-founder 1976), Am. Polit. Sci. Assn., N.Y. State Acad. Pub. Adminstrn., others. Office: Russell Sage Coll 45 Ferry St Troy NY 12180-4115

SCHECHTER, STEVEN HART, neurologist; b. Detroit, Jan. 10, 1961; s. Ronald M. and Sheila (Weinbaum) S. BS, U. Mich., 1983; MD, U. Health Scis./Chgo. Med Sch., 1987. Diplomate Am. Bd. Psychiatry and Neurology. Intern Beaumont Hosp., 1987-88; resident Henry Ford Hosp., Detroit, 1988-91; fellow U. Mich., Ann Arbor, 1991-92; attending staff neurologist William Beaumont Hosp., West Bloomfield, Mich., 1992—; clin. asst. prof. neurology Wayne State U., Detroit, 1995—; pvt. practice West Bloomfield, 1992—. Office: Ste LL4 6900 Orchard Lake Rd West Bloomfield MI 48322-3405 E-mail: mdshs@yahoo.com.

SCHECHTER, WILLIAM SETH, pediatrician, anesthesiologist, educator; b. N.Y.C., Jan. 23, 1953; s. Harry and Anola (Satin) S. BA, Columbia U., 1976; MS, NYU, 1978; MD, SUNY, Buffalo, 1982. Diplomate Nat. Bd. Med. Examiners, Am. Bd. Pediatrics; diplomate in anesthesiology, critical care medicine and pain medicine Am. Bd. Anesthesiology. Pediatric intern Columbia U. Coll. Physicians and Surgeons, N.Y.C., 1982-83; resident in pediatrics Columbia-Presbyn. Med. Ctr., 1983-85, fellow in pediatric pulmonary medicine, 1985-86, resident in anesthesiology, 1986-88, fellow in pediatric anesthesia and critical care, 1988-89; asst. prof. anesthesiology and pediatrics Columbia U. Coll. Physicians and Surgeons, 1989-99, assoc. clin. prof. anesthesiology and pediatrics, 1999—. Instr. anesthesia Harvard Med. Sch., 1994-95; assoc. in anesthesia, dir. post-anesthesia care unit Children's Hosp., Boston, 1994-95; dir. pain medicine program Babies and Children's Hosp. N.Y., 1997; assoc. examiner Am. Bd. Anesthesiology. Office: Columbia U Coll Physicians and Surgeons 622 W 168th St New York NY 10032-3720 E-mail: ws5@columbia.edu.

SCHECHTERMAN, LAWRENCE, private chef, business consultant; b. Elizabeth, N.J., June 23, 1943; s. Josef and Sylvia (Berger) S.; children: Jill Laura, Danielle Sara, Gregory Jared. BA, U. Miami, Fla., 1966; JD, Suffolk U., 1969; LLM, NYU, 1973; AS in Culinary Arts, Art Inst. Ft. Lauderdale, 2001. Tax assoc. Coopers & Lybrand, N.Y.C., 1969-70; assoc. Bendit, Weinstock & Sharbaugh, Newark, 1970-72; pvt. practice East Brunswick, N.J., 1972-81; gen. counsel Equinox Solar, Inc., Miami, 1981-83; mem. Lawrence Schechterman, P.A., Boca Raton, Fla., 1983-93; pres. Ocean Cons. Group divsn. Securities Arbitration Recovery, Inc., 1993-97. Author: (books) In the Mood with Food, A Bachelor's Guide to Wooing Her with Food, 1998, 2000, 01; (poetry) New Dimensions: An Anthology of American Poetry, 1967, The Harmony of Silence, 2000, Touched by Grace, 1999, Touched by Love, 1999, Surrounded By Dreams, 1998, A Trusting Heart, 2000; contbr. articles to profl. jours. Mem. coun. Twp. of East Brunswick, NJ, 1976—80; pres. B'nai Torah Congregation of Boca Raton Inc., 1987—89, trustee, 1989—91. Mem.: B'nai B'rith Men's Lodge (co-founder Lodge 2935, charter pres. 1973—74). Office: 3151 Clint Moore Rd Apt 102 Boca Raton FL 33496-3346

SCHECK, FRANK FOETISCH, retired lawyer; b. Albuquerque, Apr. 9, 1923; s. Frank Henry and Ethel Jane (Garrett) S.; m. Jane Leonore Rembowski, Aug. 17, 1946; children: Christopher G., Jennifer J., Carl P. BS, Calif. Inst. Tech., 1948; LLB, Columbia U., 1951. Bar: N.Y. 1951, U.S. Dist. Ct. (so. dist.) N.Y. 1953, U.S. Ct. Appeals (2d cir.) 1959, U.S. Supreme Ct. 1959, U.S. Ct. Appeals (7th cir.) 1966, U.S. Ct. Appeals (D.C. and Fed. cirs.) 1983. Assoc. Pennie, Edmonds, Morton, Barrows & Taylor, N.Y.C., 1951-60; ptnr., Pennie, Edmonds, Morton, Taylor & Adams, N.Y.C., 1961-69; sr. ptnr. Pennie & Edmonds, 1970-91; retired, Pennie & Edmonds, 1991. With U.S. Army, 1942-45. Decorated Purple Heart. Mem. N.Y. Patent Law Assn. (dir. 1982-85, v.p. 1987-89, pres. elect 1989-90, pres. 1990-91). Conservative. Presbyterian. Home: 5 Linden Gate Ln Newport RI 02840-3334

SCHECK, ROXANE MARSHA, financial analyst; b. Freeport, Tex., Oct. 22, 1953; d. Donald Edward and Marlene June (Zulke) S. BS, Purdue U., 1975; M Mgmt., Northwestern U., 1977. Cert. cash mgr. Comml. banking officer 1st Nat. Bank in St. Louis, 1977-80; asst. dir. Mo. Health and Ednl. Facilities Authority, St. Louis, 1980-82; mgr. cash planning and banking Chromalloy Am. Corp., Clayton, Mo., 1982-84; sr. fin. analyst Nalco Chem. Co., Naperville, Ill., 1984-95; mgr. treasury ops. Andrew Corp., Orland Park, 1995-96. Fin. advisor Jr. Achievement, Naperville, 1987-88; cons. Mgmt. Assistance for Non-Profits, Chgo., 1990-92 Mem. Treasury Mgmt. Assn. Chgo. (acting edn. chmn. 1992, sec. 1992-93, treas. 1993-94, pres. 1994-95, pres. emeritus 1995-96). Address: 417 N Northwest Hwy Park Ridge IL 60068-3281

SCHECTER, BENJAMIN SETH, lawyer; b. Lexington, Ky., June 11, 1971; BA in English, SUNY, Geneseo, 1993; JD, U. Louisville, 1996. Bar: Ky. 1996, U.S. Dist. Ct. (we. dist.) Ky. 1997, U.S. Dist. Ct. (ea. dist.) Ky. 1999, U.S. Ct. Appeals (6th cir.) 2000. Assoc. Pike Legal Group, Shepardsville, Ky., 1996-97, Pedley Zielke & Gordinier, PLLC, Louisville, 1997—. Moot ct. negotiations team U. Louisville, 1996. Editor-in-chief Brandeis Brief Legal Mag., 1994-96; editor Jour. Law & Edn., 1994-96. Mem. ABA, Ky. Bar Assn., Louisville Bar Assn. Office: Pedley Zielke Gordinier & Pence 1150 Starks Bldg 455 S 4th St Ste 455 Louisville KY 40202-2508

SCHECTMAN, STEPHEN BARRY, pharmaceuticals company executive; b. Washington, Oct. 20, 1947; s. Samuel and Rae (Tarnef) S.; m. Barbara L. Butcher, Sept. 10, 1969 (div. May 1994); children: Christopher, Matthew. BS, Randolph Macon Coll., 1970; postgrad., U. Tenn., 1974. Pres., CEO Medvac Corp., N.Y.C., 1993-94; spl. cons. Medco Containment Svcs., Montvale, N.J., 1991-93; ptnr. Hudson BioCapital Corp., N.Y.C., 1993-96; sr. dir. Schering-Plough Pharms., Kenilworth, N.J., 1996—; v.p. Schering My Health Solutions, Inc., 2000—. Author (with others) Biomedical Innovation, 1980. Fellowship NIMH, NIH, 1969-73, postgrad. fellowship dept. physiology Georgetown U. Sch. of Medicine, 1975-76. Mem. AAAS, N.Y. Acad. Sci., Beta Beta Beta. Jewish. Home: 609 S Orange Ave #4d/5d South Orange NJ 07079-1063 Office: Schering-Plough Corp K53-A320 2000 Galloping Hill Rd Kenilworth NJ 07033-1328 E-mail: stephen.schectman@spcorp.com.

SCHEEDER, LOUIS, theater producer, director, educator; b. N.Y.C., Dec. 26, 1946; s. Louis W. and Julia H. (Callery) S. BA in English Lit., Georgetown U., 1968; postgrad., Sch. of Arts, Columbia U., 1968-69; MA in Performance Studies, NYU, 1995. Founder, dir. The Classical Studio NYU, 1991—; Master Tchr., Tisch Sch. of the Arts, NYU. Dir. NYU Tisch Sch. of the Arts, Shakespeare Ensemble, 1989-90; mem. adv. council Nat. Com. on Arts and Edn., 1977-82; mem. D.C. Commn. on Arts and Humanities, 1976-80; bd. advs. New Playwrights' Theatre of Washington, 1975-82; asst. stage mgr. Arena Stage, Washington, 1969-70; dir., producer Folger Theatre Group, Washington, 1973-81; cons. Ctr. for Renaissance and Baroque Studies U. Md., 1984-91; asst. dir. Royal Shakespeare Co. Stratford-Upon-Avon, Eng., 1988. Dir., prodr. plays including Creeps (Am. premiere), 1973, The Farm (Am. premiere), 1974, The Collected Works of Billy the Kid (Am. premiere), 1975, Henry V, 1976, The Fool (Am. premiere), 1976, Mummer's End (world premiere), 1977, Teeth 'n' Smiles (Am. premiere), 1977, Two Gentlemen of Verona, 1977, Mackerel (world premiere), 1978, Black Elk Speaks (tour), 1978, Richard III, 1978, Whose Life Is It Anyway? (Am. premiere), 1978, Richard II, 1978, As You Like It, 1979, Custer (Kennedy Ctr.), 1979, Charlie and Algernon (Kennedy Ctr.), 1980, Crossing Niagara (Am. premiere), 1981, Love's Labour's Lost, 1981; also dir. Broadway, Off Broadway, regional prodns. including (Broadway) Charlie and Algernon, 1980, (Off Broadway) Creeps, 1973, Passover, 1986, (Off-Off-Broadway) The Gettysburg Sound Bite, 1989, Brunch at Trudy and Paul's, 1990, The Christmas Rules, 1991, The Monkey Business, 1992; dir. All's Well That Ends Well, 1990; dance: dir. Near Ruins, Ruby, 1996, Let's Go Thundering, 1997, Give Us a Kiss, Johnny, 1998, Keeper, 1999; prodr. How I Got That Story (Off Broadway), 1982, Diamonds (Off Broadway), 1984, Today, I Am a Fountain Pen (Off Broadway), 1986; dir. Man. Theatre Ctr., 1982, 83, 84, Nat. Arts Ctr., Ottawa, Ont., Can., 1984, Hedda Gabler, Ctr. Stage, Toronto, 1985, Reg: Life in the Trees, GeVa Theatre, 1991; asst. dir. Broadway prodn. Carrie, 1988; author: (with Shane Ann Younts) All the Words on Stage: A Complete Pronunciation Dictionary for the Plays of William Shakespeare, 2002. Recipient Dixon award Georgetown U., 1968, Alumni Achievement award Georgetown U. Alumni Club Met. Washington, 1981, Mayor's Arts award, D.C., 1982, Acad. Excellence award NYU, 1995. Mem. Soc. Stage Dirs. and Choreographers (life), Episc. Actors' Guild (coun. 1990-96). Home: 7 Stuyvesant Oval New York NY 10009-1901 E-mail: louis.scheeder@nyu.edu., ls36@NYU.edu.

SCHEEL, MARK WESLEY, writer, retired library and information scientist; b. Emporia, Kans., Jan. 25, 1943; s. Dale A. and Ethyle L. (Hundertmark) Scheel. BA, U. Kans., 1967; postgrad., Emporia State U., 1976-77. Asst. field dir. ARC, U.S., Vietnam, Thailand, West Germany, Eng., 1968-72, field rep. Ft. Worth, 1973; English instr. Emporia (Kans.) State U., 1976; freelance writer, 1977—; info. specialist Johnson County Libr., Shawnee Mission, Kans., 1988-97; ret., 1998. Creative writing instr. Upward Bound, Emporia,

1986; essay contest judge Emporians Nuc. Disarmament, 1983; bd. dirs. Potpourri Publs. Co., Shawnee Mission; fiction contest judge Lansing Prison Writing Contest, Shawnee Mission, 1993. Author: (monograph) Death and Dying: Hemmingway's Predominant Theme, 1979, (book) A Backward View: Stories and Poems, 1998 (Coffin award, 1998); co-author: Of Youth and the River, 1993; contbr. articles to profl. jours. Precinct vol. Johnson County Reps., Shawnee Mission, 1996, 2000; vol. Friends of Libr., Emporia, 1978—88. Recipient Nostalgia Poetry award, Nostalgia Mag., 1990, 1st pl. award story contest, Emporia Gazette, 1983. Mem.: 5th St. Irregulars Writers Group (asst. editor 1992—93), Kans. Authors Club (J. Donald Coffin Meml. Book award 1998, 1st pl. award feature article 2001), Nat. Writers Union, Nat. Writers Assn. Methodist. Home: 5738 Maple Dr Mission KS 66202

SCHEEL, NELS EARL, financial executive, accountant; b. Spencer, Wis., Sept. 25, 1925; s. Roland Edward and Louise Ernestine Scheel; m. Elaine Marie Carlisle, Aug. 28, 1949; children: Thomas W., John E., Martha L., Mark A., Mary E. BS, Youngstown Coll., 1949; MBA, U. Pa., 1950. CPA, Ohio. Staff acct. Lybrand Ross Bros., Cleve., 1950-54; asst. controller Century Foods, Youngstown, Ohio, 1954-62; treas., controller The Bailey Co., Cleve., 1962-63, Golden Dawn Foods, Sharon, Pa., 1963-82; v.p., chief fin. officer Peter J. Schmitt Co., 1982-89; cons. to industry Columbiana, 1989—. Part-time faculty Youngstown (Ohio) State U., 1954—94; bd. mem. Sovereign Cirs., Inc., North Jackson, Ohio, 1992—2001, bd. chmn., 1995—99, sec.-treas., 1999—2001. Pres. Crestview Bd. Edn., Columbiana, Ohio, 1970-81. Staff sgt. AUS, 1943-46, PTO, hon. discharge. Mem. Am. Inst. CPA's, Ohio Soc. CPA's.

SCHEELE, PAUL DRAKE, former hospital supply corporate executive; b. Elgin, Ill., Aug. 6, 1922; s. Arthur R. and Helen M. (Christiansen) S. BA, Coe Coll., 1944; MBA, Harvard, 1947. With Am. Hosp. Supply Corp., 1947—; pres. Harleco div., Phila., 1966-68; group v.p. Am. Hosp. Supply Corp., 1968-70, exec. v.p., also pres. internat. group Ill., 1970-74, v.p., asst. to chmn. bd., 1974-81. Chmn. bd. trustees Coe Coll. Served to 1st lt., inf. AUS, 1943-46. Mem. Harvard Bus. Sch. Club, Harvard Club Fla., Econ. Club (Chgo.), Tau Kappa Epsilon, Pi Delta Epsilon.

SCHEELER, CHARLES, construction company executive; b. Balt., June 20, 1925; s. George F. and Catherine Louise (Seward) S.; m. Mary Katherine Scarborough, Aug. 22, 1953; children— Charles P., George D., Donald C. BS, U. Md., 1948, LL.B., 1952. Bar: Md. 1952; CPA, Md. With C. J. Langenfelder & Son., Inc., Balt., 1949—, exec. v.p., treas., 1974-77, pres., chief exec. officer, 1977-95. Chmn. bd. Rosedale Fed. Savs. & Loan Assn. Served with USN, 1943-46, PTO. Mem. AICPA, Md. Assn. CPAs. Office: 8427 Pulaski Hwy Baltimore MD 21237-3022

SCHEELER, JAMES ARTHUR, architect; b. Pontiac, Ill., Dec. 20, 1927; s. Aman B. and Jane (Steele) S.; m. Barbara Jean Lloyd, Sept. 2, 1950; children: James Erich, Carl Aman, Orissa Jane Elizabeth. BS with highest honors, U. Ill., 1951, MS, 1952; postgrad., U. Liverpool, 1952-53. Grad. asst. U. Ill., Urbana, 1950-52; draftsman-designer Lundeen & Hilfinger, Bloomington, Ill., 1952-53; designer Skidmore, Owings & Merrill, Chgo., 1955-59; partner Richardson, Severns, Scheeler & Assos., Inc., Champaign, Ill., 1959-65, v.p., treas., 1965-71; vice chmn. bd., dir. Prodn. Systems for Architects and Engrs., Inc., 1973-81. Vis. critic U. Ill., 1959-60 Mem. Plan Commn., Champaign, 1966— , chmn., 1969-71; mem. Champaign County Regional Planning Commn., 1967-71; bd. dirs. Nat. Center for a Barrier-Free Environment, 1978— , pres., 1981. Served with USN, 1946-47. Recipient various archtl. awards.; Francis J. Plym fellow, 1953-54; Fulbright fellow, 1953 Fellow AIA (treas. Ctrl. Ill. chpt. 1967-68, sec. 1968-69, pres. 1970-71, nat. dep. exec. v.p. 1971-76, pres. corp. 1974-78, exec. v.p. 1977-78, program devel. group exec. 1976-85, sr. exec. 1985-88, v.p. design practice group 1989, resident fellow 1990—), Internat. Union of Archs. Profl. Practice Commn. (sec. 1994—), Fedn. Colls. Archs. Republic Mex. (hon.), Royal Australian Inst. Architects; mem. Ill. Arts Coun. (archtl. adv. bd. 1966-71), Japan Inst. Architect (hon.), Montessori Soc. Champaign-Urbana (dir. 1964-66), Gargoyle, Scarab, Phi Kappa Phi, Lambda Chi Alpha, Lambda Alpha, Cosmos Club. Episcopalian. Address: 11179 Saffold Way Reston VA 20190-3824

SCHEER, GARY WERNER, electrical engineer; b. Rapid City, S.D., Sept. 11, 1954; s. Alfred Carl and Marcella Nadine (Caltvedt) S.; m. Karen Lynn Kradolfer, June 18, 1977; children: Nicole Rebecca, Lisette Megan. BSEE, Mont. State U., 1977. Registered profl. engr. Ind. automation cons., Bozeman, Mont., 1977; engr. project mgr., software supr. Mont. Power Co., Butte, 1977-84; mgr. tech. support and assessment Tetragenics Co., 1985-88, mktg.mgr., 1988-90; devel. engr. Schweitzer Engring. Labs., Inc., Pullman, Wash., 1990-92, engring. mgr., 1992-96, v.p. R&D, 1996-98, v.p. automation and engring. svcs., 1998-99, prodn. mgr. automation, 2000—. Trustee YMCA at Wash. State U., Pullman, 1992—; candidate for Mont. State Legislature, 1984. Inducted into Mont. Inventors Hall of Fame, 1988. Mem. IEEE, IEEE Computer Soc., IEEE Power Engring. Soc., Asns. Computing Machinery, Internat. Soc. Measurement Control. Achievements include patent for model 2 coder/decoder, patent for relay to relay communications. Home: 2000 NW Friel St Pullman WA 99163-3610 Office: Schweitzer Engring Labs 2350 NE Hopkins Ct Pullman WA 99163-5600 E-mail: garysc@selinc.com.

SCHEER, JULIAN WEISEL, business executive, author; b. Richmond, Va., Feb. 20, 1926; s. George Fabian and Hilda (Knopf) S.; m. Suzanne Fugler Huggan, Oct. 9, 1965; 1 child, Hilary Susannah; children by previous marriage: Susan, David Scott, George Grey. AB, U. N.C., 1950. Reporter Mid-Va. Publs., Richmond, 1939-43; asst. dir. Sports Info, UNC, 1947-53; pres. Scheer Syndicate, Chapel Hill, N.C., 1947-53; columnist, reporter Charlotte (N.C.) News, 1953-62; asst. adminstr. pub. affairs NASA, 1962-71; ptnr. Sullivan, Murray & Scheer, Washington, 1971-76; sr. v.p. corp. affairs LTV Corp., Dallas, 1976-93; ptnr. Murray, Scheer, Tapia and Montgomery, Washington, from 1993. Bd. dirs. several corps. Author: (children's books) Rain Makes Applesauce (Caldecott winner), Upside Down Day, By the Light of the Captured Moon, Thanksgiving Turkey, Tweetsie; free-lance writer, author. Adv. coun. Washington Coll.; bd. dirs. Sch. Journalism, U. N.C.; mem. nat. adv. com. 1st Flight Found.; bd. mem. John S. Mosley Found.; pres. Piedmont Environ. Coun. Found.; vice chmn. Piedmont Environ. Found.; bd. mem. Partnership for Warrenton Found., Fauquier County Indsl. Devel. Authority. Mem. Algonquin Soc., City Tavern Club, Sigma Delta Chi, Pi Lambda Phi. Home: Catlett, Va. Died Sept. 1, 2001.

SCHEER, LINDA CANFIELD, staff development specialist; b. Syracuse, N.Y., Oct. 16, 1942; d. Irving Rockwood Canfield and Gwendolyn Jane Bradley; m. Charles F. Scheer, Jr., Feb. 1, 1964 (div. 1975); children: Laurie Ann Oszczepinski, David Charles. BS in Elem. Edn., U. Conn., 1964. Cert. tchr. grades N-8, N.Y. Tchr. grade 1 Middletown (Conn.) Sch. Dist., 1964-65, Riverhead (N.Y.) Sch. Dist., 1965-66; founder, dir. Ecumenical Nursery Sch., Mattituck, N.Y., 1969-76; cert. tchr. L.I. Head Start, Greenport, 1976-78, site mgr., 1978-88, staff devel. coord. Patchogue, N.Y., 1988-92, site mgr., grant writer Shirley and Ctr. Moriches, 1992-95; tng./tech. assistance coord. NYU Quality Improvement Ctr. for Disabilities, N.Y.C., 1995—. Program reviewer Head Start Bur., Agy. for Children and Families, U.S. Dept. HHS, Washington, 1991-95; trainer Nassau County Assn. for the Edn. Young Children, Hempstead, N.Y., 1998; cons. in field. Avocations: reading, computing, camping, travel. Home: PO Box 198 Cutchogue NY 11935-0198 Office: NYU QIC-D 726 Broadway Fl 5 New York NY 10003-9502 Fax: 212-995-4562. E-mail: linda.scheer@nyu.edu.

SCHEER, MILTON DAVID, chemical physicist; b. N.Y.C., Dec. 22, 1922; s. Abraham and Lena (Brauner) S.; m. Emily Hirsch, June 23, 1945; children— Jessica, Richard Mark, Julia Rachel. BS, CCNY, 1943; MS, N.Y. U., 1947, PhD, 1951. Chemist Bd. Econ. Warfare, Guatemala, C. Am., 1943-44; research asst. N.Y. U., 1947-50; combustion scientist U.S. Naval Air Rocket Test Sta., Dover, N.J., 1950-52; phys. chemist U.S. Bur. Mines, Pitts., 1952-55; research scientist Gen. Electric Co., Cin., 1955-58; phys. chemist Nat. Bur. Standards, Washington, 1958-68, chief photochemistry sect., 1968-70, chief phys. chemistry div., 1970-77; dir. Center for Thermodynamics and Molecular Sci., Nat. Measurement Lab., 1977-80; research scientist chem. kinetics div. Ctr. for Chem. Physics, Nat. Measurement Lab., 1981-85; ptnr. McNesby & Scheer Research Assocs., 1985-89. Rsch. cons. U.S. Dept. Energy, Germantown, Md., 1990-94; vis. prof. U. Md., 1980-81; Fulbright scholar U. Rome, 1982-83. Contbr. numerous articles to profl. jours. Served with USN, 1944-46. Fellow Am. Inst. Chemists, AAAS; mem. Am. Chem. Soc., Am. Phys. Soc. Home: 15100 Interlachen Dr Apt 512 Silver Spring MD 20906-5605

SCHEER, R. SCOTT, physician; b. N.Y.C., Oct. 24, 1938; s. Leonard and Josephine (Holtschl) S.; m. Beverly Joan Henry Scheer, Dec. 27, 1940; children: Kirsten Leigh, Laura Lynn. AB, Cornell U., 1960; MD, SUNY, Buffalo, 1965. Diplomate Am. Bd. Radiology (cert.), Am. Bd. Nuc. Medicine (cert.), Nat. Bd. Med. Examiners (cert.). Intern Santa Barbara (Calif.) Cottage Hosp., 1965-66; resident Cornell Univ.-N.Y. Hosp., 1966, Phila. Gen. Hosp., 1968-71; staff radiologist Meth. Hosp., Phila., 1971-72; assoc. dir. radiology Coatesville (Pa.) Hosp., 1972-77; dir. dept. radiology Norristown (Pa.) State Hosp., 1973-93; dir., chief exec. officer Med. Imaging Svcs., Chester Springs, Pa., 1977—; dir. radiology Scranton (Pa.) Imaging Ctr., 1993-94; cons. radiologist Oxford Valley Imaging Ctr., 1992-95, mng. ptnr. Pa., 1995-97; dir. radiology Allied Med. Group, Phila., 1997—; dir. diagnostic imaging lab. Premier Rsch. Worldwide, 1998—; cons. radiologist Berwick (Pa.) Hosp., 2000—. Cons. radiol. expert, 1981—; attending radiologist Pottstown Meml. Med. Ctr., 1977-93; cons. in MRI, Fonar Corp., 1990-92; cons. radiologist U.S. Radiology Assocs., Bensalem, Pa., 1996-97; mem. med. bd. Foxexec. Health Exams. Internat., 2001—. Capt. U.S. Army Med. Corps, 1966-68. Recipient N.Y. State Regents Med. scholarship, 1961. Mem. AMA, Am. Coll. Radiology, Radiol. Soc. N.Am., Pa. Med. Soc., Pa. Radiol. Soc., Chester County Med. Soc., Am. Inst. of Ultrasound in Medicine, Pa. Coll. Nuclear Medicine, Union League of Phila., Valley Forge Mountain Racquet Assn. Republican. Presbyterian. Avocations: photography, gardening, tennis. Office: Med Imaging Svcs 1420 Conestoga Rd Chester Springs PA 19425-1901

SCHEERER, ERNEST WILLIAM, dentist; b. Wabash, Ind., May 18, 1932; s. Ernest William and Anna Lucille (Bahler) S.; m. Ingrid Elvy Yvonne, Sept. 28, 1973. BS, Purdue U., 1954; DDS, Ind. U., 1961. Intern The Queen's Hosp., Honolulu, 1961-62; assoc. Pvt. Dental Practice, 1963-65; owner Pvt. Solo Dental Practice, 1965-75; ptnr. Dental Adminstrn., 1975—; pres. Scheerer & West Dental Corp., 1978—. Chief Dept. Dentistry Queen's Hosp., Honolulu. Contbr. various clin. articles to profl. jours. Mem. Big Bros., Hawaii, 1968-74. Mem. Master Acad. Gen. Dentistry, Hawaii Acad. Gen. Dentistry (past pres.), Am. Coll. Dentists, ADA, Hawaii Dental Assn. (treas.), Internat. Acad. Gnathology, Pierre Fauchard Soc., Fedn. Dental Internat., Am. Equilibration Soc., Acad. of Osseointegration, Am. Acad. Esthetic Dentistry, O.K.U., Hawaii Med. Libr. (sec.), Elks. Mem. United Ch. of Christ. Club: Pacific. Avocations: tennis, travel, Hawaiian music. Office: Scheerer & West Inc 735 Bishop St Ste 211 Honolulu HI 96813-4884 E-mail: ewscheerer@aol.com.

SCHEETZ, ALLISON PAIGE, medical educator; b. Atlanta, Nov. 19, 1963; d. Bobby Reid Scheetz and Augusta Claire (Dunn) Sherrer; m. David Edwin Mathis, Feb. 13, 1993; children: Taylor Nicole Mathis, Morgan Lindsay Mathis. BA in Psychology, BS in Biology, Mercer U., 1986, MD, 1992. Diplomate Am. Bd. Internal Medicine, Adolescent Medicine. Intern Med. Ctr. Ctrl. Ga./Mercer U. Sch. Medicine, Macon, 1992-93, resident, chief resident in internal medicine, 1993-95, instr. medicine dept. internal medicine, 1995-96, asst. prof., 1996-2001, asst. program dir., 1996-00, dir. resident edn., 1996-00, instr. dept. pediats., 1996-99, asst. prof. dept. pediats., 1999—, clerkship dir., 2000—, assoc. prof., 2001—. Consulting physician Health South Rehab. Hosp., Macon, 1997—, med. dir. HealthSouth. Mem. ACP, AMA, Soc. Gen. Internal Medicine, So. Med. Assn., Soc. Adolescent Medicine, Bibb County Med. Soc., Mercer U. Sch. Medicine Alumni Assn. (bd. dirs. 1997-99), Alpha Omega Alpha. Republican. Baptist. Achievements include research on thiazolidinedione and on community acquired pneumonia. Office: Mercer Health Sys Dept Internal Medicine 707 Pine St Macon GA 31201-2106

SCHEETZ, SISTER MARY JOELLEN, English language educator; b. Lafayette, Ind., May 20, 1926; d. Joseph Albert and Ellen Isabelle (Fitzgerald) S. AB, St. Francis Coll., 1956; MA, U. Notre Dame, 1964; PhD, U. Mich., 1970. Tchr. English, Bishop Luers High Sch., Fort Wayne, Ind., 1965-67; acad. dean St. Francis Coll. (now U. St. Francis), 1967-68, pres. Ft. Wayne, Ind., 1970-93, pres. emeritus, English lang. prof. Ind., 1993—. Mem. Delta Epsilon Sigma. Office: U St Francis 2701 Spring St Fort Wayne IN 46808-3939 E-mail: jscheetz@sf.edu.

SCHEETZ, RAYMOND JOHN, SR. retired radiologist; b. Youngstown, Ohio, Sept. 27, 1914; MD, Ohio State U., 1940. Diplomate Am. Bd. Radiology. Intern St. Elizabeth Hosp., Youngstown, Ohio, 1940-41; fellow in radiology Mayo Found., Rochester, Minn., 1941-44; served with U.S. Army Med. Corps, 1945—47; with radiology dept. St. Elizabeth Hosp., 1947—78. Mem. AMA, Am. Coll. Radiology, Am. Roentgen Ray Soc.

SCHEFF, THOMAS JOEL, sociologist, educator; b. Wewoka, Okla., Aug. 1, 1929; s. Arthur C. and Sarah (Goldman) S.; children: Karl J., Robin A., Julie S. BS, U. Ariz., 1950; MA, U. Calif., Berkeley, 1953, PhD, 1960. Asst. prof. sociology U. Wis., Madison, 1960-64; prof. sociology U. Calif., Santa Barbara, 1965—. Author: Being Mentally Ill, 1966, 3rd edit., 1999, Catharsis in Healing, 1979, Microsociology, 1990; co-author: (with Suzanne Retzinger) Emotion and Violence, 1991, Bloody Revenge, 1994, Emotions the Social Bond, 1997. With U.S. Army, 1953-55. Mem. Am. Sociol. Assn. (chmn. sect. on sociology and emotions 1988-91), Pacific Sociol. Assn. (pres. 1996). Home: 3009 Lomita Rd Santa Barbara CA 93105-3319

SCHEFFING, DONALD GEORGE, county government administrator; b. St. Louis, July 31, 1946; s. Walter Eugene and Genieve Ester (Kreher) S.; m. Mary Helen Adler, Aug. 24, 1968; children: Robert Andrew, Ann Marie. BS in Bus. Adminstrn., U. Mo., St. Louis, 1972. Cert. facility mgr. Prodn. control mgr. Siegel Robert Inc., St. Louis, 1972-73; mgr. adminstrn. Wagner Electric, 1973-79; mgr. facilities & planning McDonnell Douglas, 1979-91; bldg. mgr. State Mo., 1991-94; facilities mgr. St. Louis County Govt., 1994—. Program dir. YMCA, 1978-82; t-ball coach Woerther Sch. PTO, 1978-82; com. chmn. Boy Scouts Am., 1983-84, scout master, 1984-86; softball coach Ballwin Athletic Assn., 1987, Affton Athletic Assn., 1988-89, Amateur Softball Assn., 1987-92, St. Ann Softball Assn., 1990-92. Recipient Man of Yr. award West Glen Woods Subdivsn., 1976, Scouter Tng. award Boy Scouts Am., 1983, Scouter Key award, 1985, named Order Arrow-Bortherhood, 1986. Mem. Internat. Facility Mgmt. Assn. (membership com. 1994-95, mem. svcs. chmn. 1995-96, treas. 1996-97, pres. 1997-98, past pres. 1998-2000), U. Mo.-St. Louis Alumni Assn., Delta Sigma Pi (sec., treas. 1970-72). Avocations: running, travel, gardening, golf, fishing. Home: 715 Lakeshore Manor Ct Wildwood MO 63038-2357 Office: St Louis County Govt 41 S Central Ave Saint Louis MO 63105-1719

SCHEFFLER, BARBARA JANE, statistician, business executive; b. Phila., May 2, 1951; d. David and Elaine B. (Rotghouse) Green; m. Stuart J. Scheffler, July 3, 1975. BS, Pa. State U., 1972, MS, 1973. Registered statistician. Biostatistician, sr. int. clin. info. Smith Kline Pharm., King of Prussia, Pa., 1973-78, mgr. clin. sci. adminstrn., 1985-87; v.p. clin. ops. USBiosci., Conshohocken, 1987-91, sr. v.p. clin. ops. and regulatory affairs, 1991-95, sr. v.p. project mgmt., 1995-96, sr.v.p. corp. and sci. affairs, 1996-98; pres. The Scheffler Group, Inc., 1999—. Cons. Oncon, Gaithersburg, Md., 1986—88; spkr., cons. Pa. State U., University Park, 1994—, chairperson Millennium Soc. Eberly Col. Sci., 2001; spkr., cons. Pa. State Math. Options Program, 1993—; bd. dirs., treas. Internat. Network Cancer Treatment & Rsch., 2000—; chmn. Millennium Soc. Pa. State U. Elberly Coll. Sci. , 2001—02. Fundraiser Am. Heart Assn., Villanova, Pa., 1995—96, Am. Diabetes Assn., Villanova, 1996, 1999. Fellow NSF, 1972—73. Mem.: AAAS, Planetary Soc., Healthcare Business women's Assn., Drug Info. Assn., Am. Soc. Clin. Oncology, Am. Statis. Assn., Phi Beta Kappa, Phi Kappa Phi. Home and Office: 540 Chandler Ln Villanova PA 19085-1204 Fax: 610-687-3382. E-mail: bobbischeffler@comcast.net.

SCHEFFLER, ECKART ARTHUR, publisher; b. Glauchau, Germany, June 8, 1941; came to U.S., 1963; s. Arthur Ernst and Marianne (Baltzer) S.; m. Hannelore Baustian, July 29, 1966; children: Thomas, Daniel. Bookseller Buchhändlerschule, Leipzig, Germany, 1955-58; bookstore mgr. Bücher-Binder, Stuttgart, Germany, 1959-62; v.p. Adler's Fgn. Books Inc., N.Y.C., 1963-72; v.p., gen. mgr. Walter de Gruyter Inc., Hawthorne, N.Y., 1972—. Served with USAR, 1964-69. Mem. Am. Assn. Pubs., Internat. Group of Sci., Tech. and Med. Pubs., Scholarly Pubs. Assn. Lodges: Rotary. Lutheran. Office: Walter de Gruyter 200 Saw Mill River Rd Hawthorne NY 10532-1523 E-mail: escheffler@degruyterny.com.

SCHEFFLER, ISRAEL, philosopher, educator; b. N.Y.C., Nov. 25, 1923; s. Leon and Ethel (Grünberg) S.; m. Rosalind Zuckerbrod, June 26, 1949; children: Samuel, Laurie. BA, Bklyn. Coll., 1945, MA, 1948; M.H.L., Jewish Theol. Sem., 1949; PhD (Ford fellow 1951), U. Pa., 1952; A.M. (hon.), Harvard U., 1959; D.H.L. (hon.), Jewish Theol. Sem., 1993. Mem. faculty Harvard U., 1952-92, prof. edn., 1961-62, prof. edn. and philosophy, 1962-64, Victor S. Thomas prof. edn. and philosophy, 1964-92, professor emeritus, 1992—, hon. research fellow in cognitive studies, 1965-66, co-dir. Research Ctr. for Philosophy of Edn., 1983-98, dir. Rsch. Ctr. Philosophy of Edn., 1998—. Fellow Center for Advanced Study in Behavioral Scis., 1972-73 Author: The Language of Education, 1960, The Anatomy of Inquiry, 1963, Conditions of Knowledge, 1965, Science and Subjectivity, 1967, Reason and Teaching, 1973, Four Pragmatists, 1974, Beyond the Letter, 1979, Of Human Potential, 1985, Inquiries, 1986, In Praise of the Cognitive Emotions, 1991, Teachers of My Youth, 1995, Symbolic Worlds, 1997; co-author: Work, Education and Leadership, 1995; editor: Philosophy and Education, 1958, 66; co-editor: Logic and Art, 1972; contbr. articles to profl. jours. Recipient Alumni award of merit Bklyn. Coll., 1967, Disting. Svc. medal Tchrs. Coll., Columbia, 1980, Benjamin Shevach award Boston Hebrew Coll., 1995; Guggenheim fellow, 1958-59, 72-73; NSF grantee, 1962, 65. Mem. Am. Acad. Arts and Scis., Am. Philos. Assn., Philosophy Edn. Soc., Nat. Acad. Edn. (charter), Philosophy of Sci. Assn. (prs. 1973-75), Charles S. Peirce Soc. (pres. 1998). Office: Harvard U PERC 14 Story St Cambridge MA 02138

SCHEFFLER, LEWIS FRANCIS, pastor, educator, research scientist; b. Springfield, Ohio, Oct. 13, 1928; s. Lewis Francis and Emily Louise (Kloker) S.; m. Willa Pauline Cole, Aug. 9, 1949 (div. 1978); children: Lewis F. Fischer, Richard Thomas, Gary Arlen, Tonni Kay; m. Mary Lee Smith, Apr. 18, 1978; stepchildren: Kimberly McCollum, Jeffrey McIlroy, Kerry Buell. BA in Liberal Arts, Cin. Bible Seminary, 1950; AA in Bus., Jefferson Coll., 1989; MAT, Webster U., 1989. Quality assurance Tectum Corp., Newark, 1954-57; rsch. group leader Owens-Corning Fiberglas, Granville, Ohio, 1957-64; tech. asst. to v.p. R&D and Engring., 1960-63; pres. Ohio Glass Fibers Cons., 1962-68; rsch. adminstr. Modiglas Fibers Corp., Bremen, Ohio, 1965-68; dir. R & D Flex-O-Lite Corp., St. Louis, 1968-71; pastor Christian Ch., 1972-75; police commns. Brentwood (Mo.) Police Dept., 1975-87; pastor Christian Ch., Potosi, Mo., 1988-89, Slater (Mo.) Christian Ch., 1989-93, Clark (Mo.) Christian Ch., 1996-99; asst. prof. English lang. and lit. Mo. Valley Coll., Marshall, 1989-94; adj. prof. theology Mo. Sch. Religion, 1993-97; adj. prof. English Moberly Area C.C., 1996-98; min. Ctrl. Union Cmty. Ch., Vaudalia, Mo., 1998—. Organizing co-chmn. aerospace composite materials com. ASTM, 1961; mem. exec. bd. Northwest Area Christian Ch., 1989-93; mem. Coun. of Areas of Mid-Am. Region Christian Ch., 1990-93; cons. and lectr. in field. Contbr. articles to profl. jours. Patentee in field. Money raiser United Appeal, chaplaincy Blessing Hosp., Quincy, Ill., 1974; vol. Ill. Divsn. Children and Family Svcs., 1972-75; sec. exec. com. N.W. Area Christian Ch. (Disciples of Christ), 1992-94. Mem. Medieval Acad. Am., Mo. Philol. Assn. Avocations: philosophy and pomology. Home: 701 Walnut St Laddonia MO 63352-1137 *Now and then, God has so touched people in such a way that, recognizing it, we think "So that's what God must be like!" and our ethical and moral sensitivities are heightened.*

SCHEFFLER, STUART JAY, lawyer; b. Phila., Oct. 9, 1950; s. Walter and Fritzy (Salkoff) S.; m. Barbara Jane Green, July 3, 1975. BA cum laude, Pa. State U., 1972, MPA, 1973; JD, Temple U., 1980. Bar: Pa. 1980, U.S. Dist. Ct. (ea. dist.) Pa. 1981, U.S. Ct. Appeals (3d cir.) 1983, U.S. Supreme Ct. 1986. Tchr. Sch. Dist. of Phila., 1974-75; claims authorizer Social Security Adminstrn., HEW, Phila., 1975-76, equal opportunity specialist Office of Civil Rights, 1976-77; paraprofessional Law Offices of Ronald A. Bell., Bala Cynwyd, Pa., 1978-80; assoc. Law Office of Robert B. Mozenter, Phila., 1980-81, Gekoski & Bogdanoff, Phila., 1981-82; ptnr. Rubin & Scheffler, Phila., 1982-84; sole practice, Phila., 1984-94; of counsel Solomon, Berschler, Warren & Schatz, P.C., Norristown, Pa., 1994—. Councilman Bakers Bay Condominium Assn., Phila., 1982; bd. dirs. Key West Coun. on the Arts, 1999—. Fellow Acad. of Advocacy, mem. ABA (tort and ins. practice, sports and entertainment, civil litigation sects.), Pa. Bar Assn. (legis. liaison, medico-legal coms.), Phila. Bar Assn., Am. Trial Lawyers Assn., Phila. Trial Lawyers Assn., Pa. Trial Lawyers Assn., Drug Info. Assn., Internat. Platform Assn., Phi Beta Kappa, Delta Sigma Rho, Tau Kappa Alpha, Zeta Beta Tau. Democrat. Club: Hartikvah Basketball Assn. (Phila.) (v.p. 1974—). Office: 522 Swede St Norristown PA 19401-4834

SCHEFFMAN, DAVID THEODORE, economist, management educator, consultant; b. Milaca, Minn., Dec. 1, 1943; s. David Theodore and Fern Virginia (Maas) Scheffman; m. Cathy Schutz, May 11, 1989; 1 child Christopher. BA, U. Minn., 1967; PhD, MIT, 1971. Lectr. Boston Coll., 1970-71; from asst. prof. to assoc. prof. Univ. Western Ont., London, Can., 1971-81; sr. economist FTC, Washington, 1979-82, dep. dir., 1983-86; prof., dir. Inst. Applied Econs. Concordia U., Montreal, Que., Can., 1982-83; dir., bur. econs. FTC, Washington, 1985-88; Justin Potter prof., prof. bus. strategy and mktg. Vanderbilt U., Nashville, 1989-99, prof. of bus. strategy and mktg., 1999—; dir. LECG, N.Y.C., 1993-2001, Bur. Econs., FTC, Washington, 2001—; prof. bus. strategy Cornell U., 2001—02. Adj. prof. Georgetown U. Law Ctr., Washington, 1986; lectr. Johnson Sch. Mgmt., Cornell U., 2001—; cons. Ont. Econ. Coun., Toronto, 1973-81, GM, 1977, Ctrl. Oil Inquiry, Ottawa, Ont., 1982-84, Ctrl. Govt., Ottawa, 1979-81, Can. Competition Tribunal, 1987-89, Can. Bur. Competition Policy, 1988-91, U.S. Sentencing Commn., 1988-89, PepsiCo, 1989-2000, Kraft Gen. Food, 1989-2001, PacifiCorp, 1989-93, NERA, 1991-93, Boeing, 1992-96, LECG, 1993-2001, Berwind Industries, Inc., 1993-95, Comm. Ctrl., Inc., Applied Innovation, Inc., TEC, 1995-98, Nortel, 1995, Coca Cola, 1996-98. Author: Speculation and Monopoly in Urban Development: Analytical Foundations, 1977, An Economic Analysis of Provincial Land Use Policies in Ontario, 1980, Social Regulation in Markets for Consumer Goods and Services, 1982, An Economic Analysis of the Impact of Rising Oil Prices on Urban Structure, 1983, Strategy, Structure, and Antitrust in the Carbonated Soft Drink Industry, 1992. Recipient Dissertation Fellowship award NSF, 1967-68; vis. scholar U. Minn., 1978. Mem. Am. Econ. Assn., Strategic Mgmt. Soc., Am. Mgmt. Assn., Am. Mktg. Assn. Office: Federal Trade Commn Bur Econs 6th and Pa Ave NW Washington DC 20580 E-mail: dscheffman@ftc.gov.

SCHEFMAN, ROBERT BANKLE, artist, educator; b. Detroit, May 23, 1952; s. Myron and Theda Bankle Schefman; m. Christine Unger Unger; children: Samantha, Nicolas. BFA, Mich. State U., 1973; MA, U. Iowa, 1976. Artist in residence Goddard Coll., Plainfield, Vt., 1980—80; vis. artist Sch. of Visual Arts, N.Y.C., 1982—82; studio course instr. Coll. For Creative Studies, Detroit, 1999—2002; dir., artist services ArtServe Mich., Southfield, 2000—01. Exhbn. Foley Sq., Fed. Plaza, N.Y.C., 1981, Ruggiero-Henis Gallery, N.Y.C., 1988; exhbn. Struve Gallery, Chgo., 1992; exhbnn Detroit Artist Market, 1995; exhbn. Detroit Inst. of Art, 1995, Art Students League, N.Y.C., 1998, Charach/Epstein Mus., West Bloomfield, 2000, Detroit Contemporary, 2000, Ford Arts Ctr., Dearborn, Mich., 2001; solo exhbn. Cornell Coll., Mt. Vernon, NY, 1976; solo exhbn. Saginaw Art Mus., Minn., 1979; solo exhbn. Ancient City of Troy, Truva, Canakkale, Turkey, 1982, Turkish Mission to the UN, N.Y.C., 1983, Aesthetic Arrest Gallery, N.Y.C., 1984; solo exhbn. Lemberg Gallery, Birmingham, Ala., 1991, Birmingham, 94, Charach/Epstein Mus., West Bloomfield, 1995; solo exhbn. Lemberg Gallery, Birmingham, Ala., 1997; solo exhbn. Birmingham/Bloomfield Art Ctr., Birmingham, Ala., 2000; solo exhbn. Robert Kidd Gallery, Birmingham, Ala., 2001; solo exhbn. Midland Ctr. Arts, Midland, 2002. Sculpture, sculpture , sculpture, sculpture , mural , sculpture. Grantee, Pollack-Krasner Found., 1995, Arts Found. of Mich., 1996, ArtServe Mich., 1999. Mem.: Nat. Soc. of Mural Painters. Personal E-mail: robertschefman@aol.com.

SCHEIB, GARRY L. hospital administrator; BS with honors, MBA, Lehigh U. V.p. network ops., mgr. rels. U. Pa. health sys., affiliated hosps.; with Am. Medicorp, Humana; pres. bus. group Mediq, Inc.; pres., grad. health sys. Rancocoas Hosp., 1990—93; pres. Rancocas Hosp., Zurbrugg Hosp. , 1997;

exec. dir. Hosp. U. Pa., 1999—; sr. v.p. hosp. ops. U. Pa. Health Sys. , 2002—. Pres. Burlington C.ofC.; mem. bd. dirs. various cmty. orgns. Office: Hosp U Pa 800 Spruce St Philadelphia PA 19107-6192*

SCHEIB, GERALD PAUL, fine art educator, jeweler, metalsmith; b. L.A., Dec. 26, 1937; s. Harry William and Olive Bauer (Cartwright) S.; m. Elizabeth Ann Galligan, Dec. 27, 1965 (div. 1978); children: Gregory Paul, Geoffrey Paul; m. Dedra Lynn True, Oct. l, 1983; l child, Adam True. AA, East L.A. Jr. Coll., 1959; BA, Calif. State U., L.A., 1962, MFA, 1968. Cert. life teaching credential in fine arts, secondary and coll. tchr., Calif. Secondary tchr. art L.A. Unified Sch. Dist., 1963-77; prof. fine art L.A. Community Coll. Dist., 1977-2001; ret., 2001; pres. faculty senate L.A. Mission Coll., San Fernando, Calif., l983-84. Bargaining unit rep., AFT Coll. Guild Local 1521; elected Arts and Letters chair L.A. Mission Coll., 1993; owner, mgr. Artificers Bench, Sylmar, Calif., 1976—; cons. to Edward H. Bohlin Co. Custom Silver Works, 1998. Mem. policy bd. The Calif. Arts Project, 1995-97; chair L.A. County Art Edn. Coun., 1997-98; plank owner U.S. Naval Meml., Washington; trustee L.A. Artcore, 2001. With USNR, 1955-97, ret. Recipient of tribute City of L.A., 1983, Citizen of Month award, Los Angeles County, l983, Cold War Cert. of Recognition, Sec. of Def., 2000. Mem. Calif. Art Edn. Assn. (membership chmn. 1985-87, pres.-elect 1989-91, pres. 1991-93, Calif.'s Outstanding Art Educator in Higher Edn. 1994-95), San Fernando Active 20-30 Club (pres. 1981-82), Nat. Assn. Scholars, Sons of Union Vets of Civil War, U.S. Naval Cryptologic Vets. Assn. Republican. Avocations: collecting antiques, creating custom jewelry. Office: 13356 Eldridge Ave Sylmar CA 91342-3200

SCHEIBE, KARL EDWARD, psychology educator; b. Belleville, Ill., Mar. 5, 1937; s. John Henry and Esther Julia (Friesen) S.; m. Elizabeth Wentworth Mixter, Sept. 10, 1961; children: David Sawyer, Robert Daniel. BS, Trinity Coll., 1959; PhD, U. Calif.-Berkeley, 1963; MA (hon.), Wesleyan U., 1973. Faculty mem. Wesleyan U., Middletown, Conn., 1963—, prof. psychology, 1973—, chmn. dept., 1973-76, 79-81, 86-88; v.p. Stonington Inst., 1984-91; dir. Saybrook Counseling Ctr., 1990—; prof. DUXX, Monterrey, Mex., 1995—. Vis. prof. U. So. Calif., 1974; dir. rev. panels NSF Sci. Profl. Devel. Program, 1975-81; cons. Am. Council Edn., 1975-81 Author: Beliefs and Values, 1970, Mirror, Masks, Lies and Secrets, 1979, Studies in Social Identity, 1983, Self Studies: The Psychology of Self and Identity, 1995, The Drama of Everyday Life, 2000. Trustee Trinity Coll., Hartford, Conn., 1977-83; moderator congregation First Ch. of Christ, Middletown, 1981-82. Woodrow Wilson fellow, 1959; NSF fellow, 1961; NIMH research grantee, 1964-68; Fulbright fellow Cath. U. Sao Paulo, Brazil, 1972-73, 84. Mem. Am. Psychol. Assn., Eastern Psychol. Assn., Conn. Acad. Arts and Scis., Phi Beta Kappa Congregationalist. Home: 11 Long Ln Middletown CT 06457-4046 Office: Wesleyan U Dept Psychology Middletown CT 06459-0001 E-mail: kscheibe@wesleyan.edu.

SCHEIBE, MARGARET HELEN, elementary school educator, librarian; b. Cloquet, Minn., July 26, 1946; d. Clarence E. and Elsie L. Scheibe. Diploma in edn., Lakehead U., 1970; BS, U. Wis., Superior, 1971, MEd, 1973; PhD, Walden U., 1989. Cert. tchr., Minn.; cert. media generalist, Minn. Asst. registrar U. Wis., Superior, 1979-84, counselor, fgn. student advisor, 1984-85; registrar Coll. St. Scholastica, Duluth, Minn., 1985-87, dir. media and tech. program, 1987-98; media dir. Proctor (Minn.) Pub. Schs., 1998—. Cons. Ind. Sch. Dist. 709, Duluth, 1996-98, mem. cmty. edn. bd., 1995-98; tchr. abroad St. Scholastica, Louisburg, County Mayo, Ireland, 1997; presenter Pictish Arts Soc., Dingwall, Scotland, 1994, Edinburgh, Scotland, 1995. Contbr. articles to profl. jours. Bd. dirs. WDSE Edn. Com., Duluth, 1995—. Fellow Blandin Found., 1995, Northland Found., 1996; grantee U.S. West, 1995-96. Mem. ALA, Minn. Ednl. Media Orgn., Internat. Soc. for Tech. in Edn., Phi Delta Kappa (historian 1996-98), Delta Kappa Gamma (past pres. 1994-96). Democrat. Avocations: reading, archeology, Celtic harp. Office: Proctor Pub Schs 131 9th Ave Proctor MN 55810-2741

SCHEIBEL, ARNOLD BERNARD, psychiatrist, educator, research director; b. N.Y.C., Jan. 18, 1923; s. William and Ethel (Greenberg) S.; m. Madge Mila Ragland, Mar. 3, 1950 (dec. Jan. 1977); m. Marian Diamond, Sept. 1982. BA, Columbia U., 1944, MD, 1946; MS, U. Ill., 1952. Intern Mt. Sinai Hosp., N.Y.C., 1946-47; resident in psychiatry Barnes and McMillan Hosp., St. Louis, 1947-48, Ill. Neuropsychiat. Inst., Chgo., 1950-52; asst. prof. psychiatry and anatomy U. Tenn. Med. Sch., 1952-53, assoc. prof., 1953-55, UCLA Med. Ctr., 1955-67, prof., 1967—, mem. Brain Rsch. Inst., 1960—, acting dir. Brain Rsch. Inst., 1987-90, dir., 1990-95. Cons. in field. Contbr. numerous articles to tech. jours, chpts. to books.; mem. editl. bd. Brain Rsch., 1967-77, Developmental Psychobiology, 1968—, Internat. Jour. Neurosci., 1969—, Jour. Biol. Psychiatry, 1968—, Jour. Theoretical Biology, 1980—; assoc. editor News Report, 1989—. Mem. Pres.'s Commn. on Aging, Nat. Inst. Aging, 1980—. Served with AUS, 1943-46; from lt. to capt. M.C. AUS, 1948-50. Guggenheim fellow (with wife), 1953-54, 59; recipient Disting. Svc. award Calif. Soc. Biomed. Rsch., 1998. Fellow Am. Acad. Arts and Scis., Norwegian Acad. Scis., Am. Psychiat. Assn. (life, Harriet and Charles Luckman Disting. Tchg. award 1997) AAAS; mem. Am. Neurol. Assn., Soc. Neuorosci., Psychiat. Rsch. Assn., Soc. Biol. Psychiatry, So. Calif. Psychiat. Assn. Home: 16231 Morrison St Encino CA 91436-1331 Office: UCLA Dept Neurobiology Los Angeles CA 90024 E-mail: scheibel@ucla.edu. *Intense personal tragedy can embitter life and choke off further personal creativity. It may also offer the opportunity to open new doors in the discovery of self. I am more aware than ever of my good fortune in having the opportunity to teach, to continue investigative work in the structure and function of the brain, and to give love and care to those who need it. I am more than ever convinced that loving and being loved is the greatest good that we can know, the state in which we most nearly fulfill our roles as human beings.*

SCHEIBEL, KENNETH MAYNARD, journalist; b. Campbell, Nebr., May 17, 1920; s. G. Alfred and Rachel Christine (Koch) S.; m. Helen Schmitt, May 14, 1955 (div. Sept. 1977); children: Victor Warren Schmitt, William Becker Schmitt, Kenneth Jr., Sally. Student, George Washington U., 1938-41; BA, U. Va., 1947, MA, 1949. Mag. salesman Periodical Pubs. Service Bur., Inc., 1935-38; reporter Internat. News Service, Washington, 1940-41, Wall St. Jour., Washington, 1949-51; Washington corr. Gannett Newspapers, 1951-63; syndicated columnist N.Am. Newspaper Alliance, 1963-64; chief Washington bur. Donrey Media Group, 1964-67; founder, bur. chief Washington Bur. News, 1967—; founder nat. syndicated column Washington Farm Beat, 1970-85. Washington corr. Wis. State Jour., 1963-66, LaCrosse (Wis.) Tribune, 1963-66, Billings (Mont.) Gazette, 1964-71, V.I. Network, 1966-67, Moline (Ill.) Daily Dispatch, 1967-68, Drovers' Jour., 1967-68, Newport News (Va.) Daily Press & Times Herald, 1969-71, Packer Pub. Co., 1964-74, Gasoline Retailer, 1966-67, Okla., Farmer Stockman; congl. corr. F-D-C Reports, 1975-77; Washington columnist Farm Jour., 1960-75; covered nat. polit. convs., campaigns; v.p. Fraser Assos. (public relations), Washington, 1976-79; Congl. broadcast interviewer. Contbr. nat. mags., newspaper syndicates. Incorporator War Meml. of Korea, Washington, 1981; editor Nat. Ctr. Fin. and Econ. Info., U.S.-Saudi Arabian Joint Econ. Commn., Riyadh, 1985-86; mem. Nat. Com. Korean War Meml., 1981. Capt. AUS, 1941-46, 755th Tank Bn., 1942-45, Europe, North Africa, Italy. Decorated Bronze star, U.S. Army Occupation medal, Combat Infantryman badge; co-recipient Croix De Guerre (France), Thoth award for excellence in pub. rels., 1980. Mem. Izaak Walton League Am., White House Corrs. Assn., Overseas Press Club of Am., Am. Radio Relay League, Sigma Chi. Clubs: Nat. Press (Washington) (financial sec., gov. 1969-73, vice chmn. bd. 1971), dir. Nat. Press Bldg. Corp. (Washington) (1973, v.p., pres. club and bldg. corp. 1974). Presbyterian. Home: 1325 18th St NW Apt 302 Washington DC 20036-6505 *The greatest sins are timidity and self indulgence, the greatest virtue is to love. Live each day, don't fret about yesterday or tomorrow. Enjoy the senses, learn from others, and never forget that both love and hate are returned.*

SCHEIBER, HARRY N. law educator; b. 1935; BA, Columbia U., 1955; MA, Cornell U., 1957, PhD, 1961; MA (hon.), Dartmouth Coll., 1965; D.Jur.Hon., Uppsala U., Sweden, 1998. Instr. to assoc. prof. history Dartmouth Coll., 1960-68, prof., 1968-71; prof. Am. history U. Calif., San Diego, 1971-80; prof. law Boalt Hall, U. Calif., Berkeley, 1980—. Chmn. jurisprudence and social policy program, 1982-84, 90-93, assoc. dean, 1990-93, 96-99; The Stefan Riesenfeld prof., 1991—; vice chair Univ. Academic Senate, 1993-94, chair 1994-95; dir. Earl Warren Legal Inst., 2002-; Fulbright disting. sr. lectr., Australia, 1983, marine affairs coord. Calif. Sea Grant Coll. Program, 1989-2000; vis. rsch. prof. Law Inst. U. Uppsala, Sweden, 1995, hon. prof. DiTella U., Buenos Aires, 1999; cons. Calif. Jud. Coun., 1992-93; acting dir. Ctr. for Study of Law and Soc., 1999-2001; co-dir. Law of the Sea Inst., 2002—; dir. Earl Warren Legal Inst., 2002—. Author: American Law and the Constitutional Order, 1978, 1988, The State and Freedom of Contract, 1998; co-author: Law of the Sea: The Common Heritage and Emerging Challenges , 2000, Inter-Allied Conflicts and Ocean Law (1945-1953), 2001, numerous others; editor: Yearbook of the California Supreme Court Historical Society, 1994—; contbr. articles to law revs. and social sci.jours. Chmn. Littleton Griswold Prize Legal History, 1985-88; pres. N.H. Civil Liberties Union, 1969-70; chmn. Project '87 Task Force on Pub. Programs, Washington, 1982-85; dir. Berkeley Seminar on Federalism, 1986-95; cons. judiciary study U.S. Adv. Commn. Intergovernmental Rels., 1985-88; dir. NEH Inst. on Constitutionalism, U. Calif., Berkeley, 1986-87, 88-91. Recipient Sea Grant Colls. award, 1981-83, 84-85, 86-2002; fellow Ctr. Advanced Study in Behavioral Scis., Stanford Calif., 1967, 71; Guggenheim fellow, 1971, 88; Rockefeller Found. humanities fellow, 1979, NEH fellow, 1985-86; NSF grantee 1979, 80, 88-89. Fellow U. Calif. Humanities Rsch. Inst., Am. Soc. for Legal History (hon., pres.-elect 2001—), Japan Soc. for Promotion of Sci. (invitational fellow); mem. Am. Hist. Assn., Orgn. Am. Historians, Agrl. History Soc. (pres. 1978), Econ. History Assn. (trustee 1978-80), Law and Soc. Assn. (trustee 1979-81, 96-99), Nat. Assessment History and Citizenship Edn. (chmn. nat. acad. bd. 1986-87), Marine Affairs and Policy Assn. (bd. dirs. 1991-96), Ocean Governance Study Group (steering com. 1991—), Internat. Coun. Environ. Law, Calif. Supreme Ct. Hist. Soc. (bd. dirs. 1993—, v.p. 1997-98). Office: U Calif Berkeley Law Sch Boalt Hall Berkeley CA 94720-2150 E-mail: scheiber@law.berkeley.edu.

SCHEIBER, STEPHEN CARL, psychiatrist; b. N.Y.C., May 2, 1938; s. Irving Martin and Frieda Olga (Schor) S.; m. Mary Ann McDonnell, Sept. 14, 1965; children: Lisa Susan, Martin Irving, Laura Ann. BA, Columbia Coll., 1960; MD, SUNY, Buffalo, 1964. Diplomate Am. Bd. Psychiatry and Neurology. Intern Mary Fletcher Hosp., Burlington, Vt., 1964-65; resident in psychiatry Strong Meml. Hosp., Rochester, N.Y., 1967-70; asst. prof. U. Ariz., Tucson, 1970-76, assoc. prof., 1976-81, prof., 1981-86; exec. sec. Am. Bd. Psychiatry and Neurology, Inc., Deerfield, Ill., 1986-89, exec. v.p., 1989—. Adj. prof. psychiatry Northwestern U., Chgo. and Evanston, 1986—, Med. Coll. Wis., Milw., 1986—. Co-editor: The Impaired Physician, 1983, Certification, Recertification and Lifetime Learning in Psychiatry, 1994; contbr. articles to profl. jours. Mem. med. adv. com. Casas de los Ninos, Tucson, 1974-86; mem. mental health adv. com. Tucson Health Planning Coun., 1974-75; med. student interviewer Office of Med. Edn., 1975; mem. Glenbrook (Ill.) North H.S. Boosters Club, 1988-91; treas. Robert E. Jones Found., 1988-96. Surgeon USPHS, 1965-67. Recipient Outstanding Tchr. award, U. Ariz., 1986, Lifetime Achievement award, SUNY, Buffalo, 1998; grantee Group Therapy Outcome Studies on Inpatient Svc., 1980, Dialysis and Schizophrenia Pilot Project, NIH, 1978. Fellow: Group for Advancement of Psychiatry (invited mem., chmn. mem. edn. com. 1987—91, bd. dirs., sec. 1993—97, pres.-elect 1997—99, pres. 1999—2001), Assn. Acad. Psychiatry (parliamentary sec. 1979—84, treas. 1984—88, pres.-elect 1988—89, pres. 1989—90), Am. Assn. Dirs. Psychiat. Residency Tng. (pres. 1981—82), Am. Coll. Psychiatrists (bd. regents 1992—2001, treas. 1995—2001), Am. Psychiat. Assn. (chmn. impaired physician com. 1985—88, cons. 1988—92); mem.: Oracle Heights Club (pres. 1983—84). Democrat. Jewish. Office: Am Bd Psychiatry & Neurology 500 Lake Cook Rd Ste 335 Deerfield IL 60015-5635

SCHEIBERG, SUSAN L. librarian; b. Chgo., Dec. 19, 1962; d. Steven M. Scheiberg, Margo Scheiberg. BA(hon.) , Ind. U., 1984; MA, UCLA, 1986; MS in Libr. Sci., U. Ky., 1997. Grad. rsch. libr. U. So. Calif., 1997—98, team leader, serials acquisitions, 1998—2001; head acquisitions and serials, coord. outreach and cost-ctr. svcs. RAND, Santa Monica, 2001—; assoc. dir. RAND Libr., 2002—. Editor: (book) NASIG 2001: A Serials Odyssey, 2001, Transforming Serials: The Revolution Continues, 2003; contbr. articles to profl. jours. Fellow Univ., UCLA, 1984-1987; grantee Bardin Endowment Rsch., U. So. Calif., 1998, 1999, 2000. Mem.: ALA (Tony B. Leisner grantee 1996), N.Am. Serials Interest Group (proceedings editor 2000—), Libr. Adminstrn. and Mgmt. Assn., Assn. Libr. Collections and Tech. Svcs., Am. Folklore Soc., Spl. Librs. Assn., Beta Phi Mu, Phi Beta Kappa. Business E-Mail: susanls@rand.org.

SCHEICH, JOHN F. lawyer; b. Bklyn., Aug. 6, 1942; s. Frank A. and Dorothy (O'Hara) S. BA, St. John's U., N.Y.C., 1963, JD, 1966; postgrad., John Marshall Law Sch., Chgo., 1968. Bar: N.Y. 1967, U.S. Ct. Internat. Trade Admission 1969, U.S. Dist. Ct. (ea. and so. dists.) N.Y. 1971, U.S. Ct. Appeals (2nd cir.) 1971, U.S. Supreme Ct. 1975, Pa. 1980. Spl. agt. FBI, U.S. Dept. Justice, Washington, 1966-69; asst. dist. atty. Queens County, Kew Gardens, N.Y., 1969-72; pvt. law practice, Richmond Hill, 1970-76, 79-91; ptnr. Raia & Scheich, P.C., 1976-79; sr. ptnr. Scheich & Goldsmith, P.C., Richmond Hill, Hicksville, N.Y., 1991-95, Scheich, Goldsmith & Dreishpoon, P.C, Richmond Hill, Hicksville, 1996—; mortgage settlement atty. GMAC, N.Y., 1996—. Lectr. estate planning Nat. Bus. Inst., 1994; mem. assigned counsel panel for indigent defendants in major felony and murder cases 9th and 11th jud. dists. N.Y. State Supreme Ct., Queens County, 1972—94; lectr. Lawyers in the Classroom, 1979—91; chmn. arbitration panel Civil Ct. City of N.Y., 1981—90; bd. dirs. Ra-Li Brokerage Corp., v.p., 1975—; mem. adv. bd. 1st Am. Title Ins. Co. Am., 1995—; mortgage settlement atty. Gen. Motors Acceptance Corp. N.Y. State, 1996—; trial judge student competition St. John's U. Sch. Law Civil Trial Inst. Student Competition, 1996—. Editor: Conashaugh Courier, 1989-92; mem. editorial bd., 1988-92; contbg. columnist, 1981-89. Mem. Com. for Beautification of East Norwich, Nassau County, L.I., N.Y., 1983—, bd. dirs., 1993-96, pres. 1996—; mem. Holy Name Soc. of Our Lady of Perpetual Help Ch., 1963—, sec., 1965-67, v.p., 1969-71, pres., 1971-73; bd. dirs. Conashaugh Lakes Cmty. Assn., Milford, Pa., 1981-90, organizing mem. Conashaugh Lakes Lot Owners interim com., 1977-81, sec. 1981-82, v.p. 1982-84, pres. 1984-86, past pres. 1986-88; mem. St. Edward the Confessor Sch. Bd., Syosset, N.Y., 1986-90; parish coun. Our Lady of Perpetual Help Roman Cath. Ch., 1976-82, pres. 1978-80, fin. com., adv. to pastor, 1970-82, chmn. fin. com., 1979-82; bd. dirs. Northslope II Homeowners Assn., Shawnee-on-Delaware, Pa., 1988-90, 92-94, 2000—, East Norwich Civic Assn., 1996—; mem. East Norwich Rep. Club, 1982—, bd. dirs. 1984-87, 93—, v.p. 1987-89, pres. 1989-93; nat. trust and estate assoc. Meml. Sloane Kettering Cancer Ctr., N.Y.C., 1994—; active Internat. Wine Ctr., 1985-96, St. Edward the Confessor Ch., Syosset, 1982—, St. Vincent Ch., Dingman Hills, Pa., 1977—, St. Dominic's Ch., Oyster Bay, N.Y., 1982— (apptd. pastor's adv. coun. on estate planning 1998, 99, 2000, 2001, 2002, mem. Legacy Soc. 1998, 99, 2000, 2001, Lincoln Ctr. Performing Arts, Inc., 1985—, Nat. Rep. Senatorial Com., 1988—, Bravo Soc., 1994—, Concern for Dying, 1984—, Sea Cliff Chamber Players, 1992-99; mem. Nassau County Rep. Com., Town of Oyster Bay, 1993—, St. John Vianney Roman Cath. Ch., St. Petersburg Beach, Fla., 1994—, Non-Resident Fellow, James Beard Found., NYC, 1995—, Performing Arts Ctr. Pinellas County, St. Petersburg, 1994—, Rep. Nat. Senate Adv. Coun., 1997—, Rep. Nat. Com. Chmn.'s Honor Roll, 1997 (cert. Achievement 1998), Pact, Inc. Ruth Eckerd Hall-Richard B. Baumgardner Ctr. for Performing Arts, Clearwater, Fla., 1995—; chmn. tri-centennial celebration com. Village of East Norwich, 1996-97; mem. Fransiscan Ctr. Guild, Tampa, Fla., 1996—, Tilles Ctr. Performing Arts, Inc., Long Island U., Brookville, N.Y., 1997—, adv. coun. estate planning St. Dominic's Ch., 1998, St. Dominic's Legacy Soc., 1998; bd. dirs. Northslope II Homeowners Assn., Shawnee-on-Del., Pa., 2000—; mem. Friends of the Arts, Locust Valley, L.I., N.Y., 1985—. Recipient J. Edgar Hoover award, 1967, award of appreciation, Civil Trial Inst., St. John's U. Sch. of Law, 1991, 95, Disting. Svc. award, 1992, cert. of appreciaiton Conashaugh Lakes Cmty. Assn., 1990, Dist. Svc. award Kiwanis Club, 1992, Cert. of Merit for Disting. Svc. award Nassau County Exec. Hon. Thomas Gulotta, 1989, Presdl. Order of Merit award Pres. George Bush, 1991, Order of Merit award Nat. Rep. Senatorial Com., 1994, Cert. Achievement, Rep. Nat. Com., 1998; named one of Best Trial Lawyers in the U.S., Town and Country Mag., 1985; non-resident fellow James Beard Found., N.Y.C., 1995—. Mem. ABA (cert. of appreciation Am. Bar Endowment 1992), ATLA, Pa. State Bar Assn., N.Y. State Bar Assn., Queens County Bar Assn., Nassau County Bar Assn., N.Y. State Trial Lawyers Assn., Criminal Cts. Bar Assn., Internat. Platform Assn., John Marshall Lawyers Assn. (bd. dirs. 1992—, pres. 1992-97, treas. 1997—), Soc. Former Spl. Agts. of FBI (nat. chpt., L.I. chpt.), N.Y. State Assn. Criminal Def. Lawyers, LeGal Law Assn. (bd. dirs. 2001—, bd. dirs. found. 1995-98, 2001—), St. John's Coll. Alumni Assn., Asst. Dist. Attys. Assn. Queens County, St. John's U. Sch. of Law Alumni Assn., St. John's Prep. Sch. Alumni Assn., Friends of the Arts of Nassau County, Inc., Cath. Lawyers Guild of Queens County, N.Y., KC, Brookhaven Wine Lovers Soc., East Norwich Civic Assn., Sun Island Assn. (bd. dirs. 2001-02), McCallen Soc., Phi Alpha Delta. Avocation: collecting fine wines. Home: 170 Sugar Toms Ln East Norwich NY 11732-1153 Office: Scheich Goldsmith & Dreishpoon PC 103-42 Lefferts Blvd South Richmond Hill NY 11419-2012 also: 109 Newbridge Rd Hicksville NY 11801-3908 also: 210 Conashaugh Trl Box 4042 Conashaugh Lakes Milford PA 18337

SCHEICK, LEIF ZEBEDIAH, radiation physicist; b. Cloumbus, OH, Oct. 13, 1970; s. John Theodore Scheick and Sandra Halleck. PhD, Clemson U., 1993—99. Sr. rschr. Jet Proplusion Lab., Pasadena, Calif., 1999—2002. Mem.: IEEE. Office: Jet Propulsion Lab 4800 Oak Grove Rd MS303-220 Pasadena CA 91109 Business E-Mail: Leif.scheick@jpl.nasa.gov.

SCHEIDECKER, JANE, management consultant, academic administrator; BA in Spanish, Eastern Mont. Coll., 1974; MA in Romance Linguistics, U. Wash., 1976; postgrad., U. Oreg., 1980-81; M in Internat. Mgmt., Thunderbird U., 1982. Instr. Lane C.C., 1974-80; tchr. Brookings Harbor H.S., 1974-80; tchr., owner Academia Rapididiom, 1974-80; instr. U. Wash., Seattle, 1974-80; program coord. Learning Resource Ctr. U. Oreg., 1980-81, co-dir. Univ. Forum, 1985-86, assoc. dean for devel., 1986-90; v.p., mgr. Tara Mgmt. Group, 1983-85; dir. Bus. Devel. Ctr. Lane C.C., 1990—; market cons., entrepreneur, 1976-98. Mem. editl. adv. bd. Oreg. Bus. Mag., 1991-95, 97-98. Mem. econ. com. Lane Coun. Govts., 1990—; bd. dirs. so. Willamette Rsch Corridor, 1990-97, U. Oreg. Mus. Natural History, 1990-92; appointee Riverfront Rsch. Park Commn., 1991—, Sister City Found., 1993-96. Heller Co. fellow. Fellow AAUW; mem. Assn. for Quality and Participation, Assn. Oreg. Entrepreneurs (founder, steering com.), Am. Assn. Women in Jr. and C.C.'s, Internat. Assn. Small Bus. Mgmt. Instrs., Women Entrepreneurs Oreg., Women's Mentoring Network (founding mem.), Rotary.

SCHEIDEGGER, KENT STEPHEN, lawyer; b. Arlington, Va., Dec. 31, 1953; s. Paul Francis and Elizabeth (Walker) S.; m. Lada Phasook, April 11, 1981. BS with honors, N.Mex. State U., 1976; JD with distinction, McGeorge Sch. Law, Sacramento, 1982. Bar: Calif. 1982, U.S. Ct. Appeals (9th cir.) 1985, U.S. Supreme Ct., 1987. Commd. nuclear research officer USAF, Sacramento, 1976, advanced through grades to capt., 1982, resigned, 1982; assoc. Neumiller & Beardslee, Stockton, Calif., 1983-84; gen. counsel Calif. Cooler Co., 1984-86; legal dir. Criminal Justice Legal Found., Sacramento, 1986—. Recipient William J. Schafer award for excellence in capital litigation Assn. Govt. Attys. in Capital Litigation. Mem. Federalist Soc. (bd. mem. Sacramento chpt., chmn.-elect criminal law practice group), McGeorge Alumni Assn. (Amicus lex scholar 1981), Order of the Coif. Republican. Office: Criminal Justice Legal Fdn 2131 L St Sacramento CA 95816-4924

SCHEIDLER, JAMES EDWARD, business executive; b. Chippewa Falls, Wis., Mar. 11, 1946; s. Clifford James and Mary Margaret (Roch) S.; m. Ellen Marie Swiontek, Aug. 23, 1970; children: Matthew, Nathan, Mary. BA in Econs. and History, U. Wis., Eau Claire, 1968, MA in Tchg. in History, 1975. Tchr., coach Campbellsport (Wis.) Sch. Dist., 1968-69, Reedsburg (Wis.) Sch. Dist., 1969-72; salesman IBM, Madison, Wis., 1973-78; salesman, mktg. mgr. WAF Inst. Raltech, 1978-85; nat. accounts and nat. sales mgr. Spacesaver Corp., Ft. Atkinson, Wis., 1985-92; mgr. plan devel. and govt. rels. Wis. Physican Svcs., Madison, 1992-96; v.p. Tiziani Enterprises, 1996-98; v.p. custom products Spectrum Industries, 2000—. Chmn. Madison Night at County Stadium, 1980-84; mem. steering com. Wis. Basketball Coaches All Star Game, Madison, 1983—; founder, chmn. Badger Classic, high sch. basketball tournament, Madison, 1986—; mem. Queen of Peace Sch. Bd., Madison, 1987-89; pres. Edgewood H.S. Athletic Assn., Madison, 1991—; bd. trustees Edgewood H.S., Madison, 1995—; pres. U. Wis. Basketball Boosters, 1977, 88. Named to Hall of Fame, Wis. Basketball Coaches, 1993. Mem. U. Wis.-Eau Claire Alumni Assn. (bd. dirs. 1989—, pres. 1996-97), Mendota Gridiron Club. Roman Catholic. Avocations: golf, reading, youth sports, music. Home: 21 Frederick Cir Madison WI 53711-1646

SCHEIDT, STEPHEN SLATON, internist, cardiologist; b. N.Y.C., Mar. 7, 1940; MD, Columbia P&S, 1965. Diplomate in internal medicine and cardiovascular diseases Am. Bd. Internal Medicine. Intern Montefiore Hosp., N.Y.C., 1965-66; resident in medicine Bellevue Hosp. - Columbia P&S, 1966-68; fellow in cardiology Cornell U., 1968-70; prof. clin. medicine N.Y. Hosp. - Cornell Med. Ctr. (now N.Y. Presbyn. Hosp.). Fellow: ACP, Am. Coll. Cardiology; mem.: Am. Heart Assn. Office: NY Hosp - Cornell MC 525 E 68th St New York NY 10021-4870

SCHEIDT, W. ROBERT, chemistry educator, researcher; b. Richmond Heights, Mo., Nov. 13, 1942; s. Walter Martin and Martha (Videtich) S.; m. Kathryn Sue Barnes, Aug. 9, 1964; children: Karl Andrew, David Martin. BS, U. Mo., 1964; MS, U. Mich., 1965, PhD, 1968; postdoctoral studies, Cornell U., 1970. Asst. prof. U. Notre Dame, Ind., 1970-76, assoc. prof., 1976-80, prof., 1980—, William K. Warren prof., 1999—. Vis. prof. U. Wash., Seattle, 1980, U. Paris (Orsay), France, 1991, U. Strasbourg, France, 1998; mem. review sect. Metallobiochemistry NIH, Bethesda, 1991-96. Contbr. articles to profl. jours. Fellow AAAS; mem. Am. Chem. Soc. (assoc. editor Chem. Revs. jour. 1980-85), Am. Crystallographic Assn., Biophys. Soc., Sigma X. Democrat. Office: U Notre Dame Dept Chemistry Notre Dame IN 46556 E-mail: scheidt.1@nd.edu.

SCHEIER, IVAN HENRY, volunteer, writer; b. Plattsburgh, N.Y., Jan. 7, 1926; s. Joel Henry and Melba Gottlob S. BA in Philosophy, Union Coll., 1948; MA in Psychology, McGill U., Montreal, 1951, PhD in Psychology, 1953. Vol. coord., project dir. Boulder County Juvenile Ct., 1965-69; interim dir. Vol. and Info. Ctr. of Boulder County, 1968; exec. dir. Nat. Info. Ctr. on Volunteerism, 1967-76; pres. Assn. Voluntary Action Scholars, 1973-74; chair Alliance for Volunteerism, 1975-76; pres. Yellowfire Press, 1981-89; dir. Ctr. for Creative Cmty., 1986-95; dreamcatcher-in-residence Voluntas Retreat Ctr., 1991-95; coord. Stillpoint Self-Help Healing Ctr., 1996—. Mem. faculty McGill U., 1950-51, U. Ill., 1953-58, Nat. Coll. Juvenile Justice, 1970, U. Colo. Vol. Mgmt. Cert. Program, 1973-87; mem. White House Conf. on Children and Youth, 1970, Nat. Adv. Commn. Criminal Justice Standards and Goals, 1971, Nat. Forum on Volunteerism, 1979-80; mem. adv. com. U. Colo. Vol. Mgmt. Cert. Program, 1973-77; sr. advisor Resource Devel., the Assn. for Vol. Adminstrn., 1979-80, Citizen Advocacy for Devel. Disabled, 1980-82, New Road Map Found., 1990—; mem. adv. bd. Madrid-Cerrillos Med. Clin., 1993-94; mem. youth volunteer leadership tng. project Sister Cities Internat., 1979-81. Author: Exploring Volunteer Space: The Recruiting of a Nation, 1980, Making Dreams Come True Without Much Money: The Midwifery of Dreams, 2000, When Everyone's a Volunteer, 1992, Images of the Future, 1994; pub., editor On Background, 1979-81, The Dovia Exchange, 1984-98, The Restless News, 1986-89, Ex Libris, 1987-90, Madrid Muse, 1991-95. Pres. emeritus Nat. Info. Ctr. on Volunteerism, 1979—; chair com. NAACP, Urbana, Ill., 1956-59; vol. various orgns., U.S., Can., 1963—; mem. Sierra Pride Com. Turning Point, Truth or Consequences, N.Mex., 1999—; mem. policy bd. Assn. Voluntary Action Scholars, 1971-74, Nat. Ctr. for Voluntary Action, 1971-76, Nat. Info. Ctr.on Volunteerism, 1971-79, Alliance for Volunteerism, 1974-77, Nat. Orgn. Victim Assistance, 1977-79, Partners, Inc., 1979-82; bd. dirs. Madrid, N.Mex. Landowners Assn., 1993-94. Recipient Nat. Meritorious Svc. award Nat. Coun. Juvenile Court Judges, 1971, Meritorious Svc. award Province of Ont., 1976, Leadership award Alliance for Volunteerism, Inc., 1976, Disting. Svc. award State of Miss., 1982, Nat. Cmty. Svc. award Nat. Assn. on Vols. in Criminal Justice, 1987, Lifetime Achievement award Denver Dirs. of Vols. in Agys., 1997. Mem. Assn. Vol. Adminstrn. (life, Nat. Disting. Svc. award 1984, editor Volunteer Adminstrn. 1979-81), Phi Beta Kappa. Avocations: tai chi, dancing, hiking, reading, gardening. E-mail: ivan@zianet.com.

SCHEIMAN, EUGENE R. lawyer; b. Bklyn., July 15, 1943; BA, L.I. U., 1966; JD cum laude, Bklyn. Law Sch., 1969. Bar: N.Y. 1970, U.S. Dist. Ct. (so. and ea. dists.) N.Y. 1971, U.S. Ct. Appeals (1st cir.) 1972, U.S. Ct. Appeals (5th cir.) 1973, U.S. Ct. Appeals (4th cir.) 1974, U.S. Supreme Ct. 1976, U.S. Ct. Appeals (2nd cir.) 1977, U.S. Ct. Appeals (fed. cir.), U.S. Ct.

Appeals (11th cir.) 1989, U.S. Ct. Appeals (3rd cir.) 1990. Shareholder Buchanan Ingersoll, N.Y.C. Rsch. editor Bklyn. Law Rev., 1968, editor-in-chief, 1969. Mem. ABA (sect. on individual rights and responsibilities, franchise forum), ATLA, N.Y. State Bar Assn., Assn. Bar. City of N.Y. (com. on profl. discipline), Philonomic Honor Soc. Office: Buchanan Ingersoll PC 140 Broadway New York NY 10005 E-mail: scheimaner@bipc.com.

SCHEIN, DANIEL, Internet company executive, photographer; b. Tex. m. Jill Schein. BA, George Washington U., 1992. Intern for Congressman Mickey Leland U.S. Ho. of Reps., Washington, 1989; photographer Reingold Studios, Houston, 1992—94; Web master City of Houston Contr.'s Office, 1999—, purchasing liaison Ala. DJ WRGW Radio, Washington, 1988—92. Contbr. photography and Articles, photography. Precinct capt. Dem. Party, Houston, 1988—90. Office: City of Houston Contr's Office 9th Fl 901 Bagby Houston TX 77002

SCHEINBERG, PERITZ, neurologist; b. Miami, Fla., Dec. 21, 1920; s. Mendel and Esther Dobrisch (Asch) S.; m. Chantal D'Adesky, Mar. 12, 1971; children: Philip Asch, Richard David, Marissa. AB in Chemistry, Emory U., 1941, MD, 1944. Diplomate: Am. Bd. Internal Medicine, Am. Bd. Psychiatry and Neurology. Intern Grady Hosp., Atlanta, 1944-45; resident in internal medicine and neurology Grady Hosp. and Duke U. Hosp., 1946-50; research asst. prof. physiology U. Miami Med. Research Unit, Miami, Fla., 1950-53, asso. prof. neurology, 1955-57, prof. neurology, 1957—; chmn. dept. neurology U. Miami Sch. Medicine, 1961—. Author, editor books in field.; contbr. articles to profl. jours. Served with M.C. USNR, 1945-46, 53-55. Fellow ACP, Am. Acad. Neurology; mem. Am. Neurol. Assn. (pres. 1981), Assn. Univ. Profs. Neurology (pres. 1977-78), Am. Heart Assn., Nat. Multiple Sclerosis Soc. (mem. med. adv. bd.) Democrat. Jewish. Office: U Miami Jackson Meml Med Ctr 1611 NW 12th Ave Miami FL 33136-1005

SCHEINDLIN, RAYMOND PAUL, Hebrew literature educator, translator; b. Phila., May 13, 1940; s. Irving and Betty (Bernstein) S.; m. Shira Ann Joffe, 1969 (div. 1981); children— Dov Baer, Dahlia Rachel; m. Janice C. Meyerson, 1986. BA, U. Pa., 1961; M.H.L., Jewish Theol. Sem., N.Y.C., 1963; PhD, Columbia U., N.Y.C., 1971. Ordained rabbi, 1965. Asst. prof. McGill U., Montreal, Que., Can., 1969-72; asst. prof. Cornell U., Ithaca, N.Y., 1972-74; assoc. prof. Jewish Theol. Sem. of Am., N.Y.C., 1974-85, prof. Hebrew lit., 1985—, provost, 1984-90; dir. Shalom Spiegel Inst. of Medieval Hebrew Lit., 1996—; rabbi Congregation Baith Israel Anshei Emes, Bklyn., 1979-82. Mem. publ. com. Jewish Publ. Soc., Phila., 1985-90; mem. internat. adv. com. Ctr. for Judaic Studies U. Pa., 1995—; mem. bd. acad. advisors Catalan Mus. Jewish Culture, Gerona, Spain, 1993—; mem. editl. com. Jewish Quar. Rev., 1995—. Translator: (novella) Of Bygone Days by Mendele Mokher Seforim, 1973, Jewish Liturgy: A Comprehensive History by Ismar Elbogen, 1993; author: Form & Structure in the Poetry of Al-Mu'tamid Ibn 'Abbad, 1974, 201 Arabic Verbs, 1978, Wine, Women, and Death: Medieval Hebrew Poems on the Good Life, 1986, The Gazelle: Medieval Hebrew Poems on God, Israel and the Soul, 1991, Chronicles of the Jewish People, 1996, The Book of Job, 1998, A Short History of the Jewish People, 1998, (libretto) Miriam and the Angel of Death, 1984; mem. editl. com. Prooftexts, 1988—, Edebiyat, 1992—, Studies in Muslim-Jewish Rels., 1992—; mem. editl. bd. Arabic and Mid. Ea. Lits., Medieval Iberia; co-editor The Literature of Al-Andalus, 2000. Guggenheim fellow, 1988, Annenberg Inst. fellow, 1993; sr. assoc. fellow Oxford Centre for Postgrad. Hebrew Studies. Fellow: Am. Acad. Jewish Rsch.; mem.: PEN Am. Ctr., Jewish Publ. Soc. (bd. dirs. 1987—93), Assn. Jewish Studies, World Union Jewish Studies, Soc. Judeo-Arabic Studies. Home: 420 Riverside Dr New York NY 10025-7773 Office: Jewish Theol Sem Am 3080 Broadway New York NY 10027-4650 E-mail: ibngabirol@aol.com.

SCHEINERT, JOEL L. lawyer; b. Bklyn., Feb. 12, 1937; s. Sidney and Ada Scheinert; m. Edie Scheinert, June 29, 1958; children: Howard, Phyllis. BS in Econs., U. Pa., 1957; JD, Harvard U., 1960. Assoc. Kreindler & Kreindler, N.Y.C., 1961-62; ptnr. Schwartz, Kobb & Scheinert, Nanuet, N.Y., 1962—. Legislator Rockland County, N.Y., 1974-77; chmn. bd. dirs. Monsey (N.Y.) Jewish Ctr., 1967-77; law chmn. Rockland County Dem. Ctr., 1972-73. Democrat. Jewish. Home: 59 S Parker Dr Monsey NY 10952 Office: Schwartz Kobb & Scheinert 404 E Rt 59 PO 220 Nanuet NY 10954 E-mail: sksattys@aol.com.

SCHEINESON, IRWIN BRUCE, insurance and investment company executive; b. Cin., Aug. 8, 1955; s. Julian and Joan (Klein) S.; married; children: Kate Marie, John Philip. BBA, U. Cin., 1978. Pres., prin. Lang-Kruke Fin. Group, Cin., 1978-97; agt. adv. liaison Community Mut. Ins. Co. (Blue Cross), 1978-80, Cen. Benefits Mut., Columbus, Ohio, 1986-88; pres. Gt. Am. Filter Co., Norwood, 1990-98; pres., CEO Planning Works, Ltd., 1997. Lectr. in field. Contbr. articles to profl. jours. Fund raiser Guilford Sch., Cin., 1985—. Mem. Internat. Assn. Fin. Planning, Nat. Assn. Health Underwriters, Nat. Assn. Life Underwriters (Nat. Sales Achievement award 1979), Cin. Assn. Health Underwriters (bd. dirs. 1984-87), Nat. Soc. CLUs and Chartered Fin. Cons., 2000 Top of the Table Million Dollar Roundtable, Crest Hills Country Club (bd. dirs. 1988-93). Republican. Jewish. Avocations: tennis, skiing, travel, golf, marathon running. Office: Planning Works Ltd Ste 250 11111 Montgomery Rd Cincinnati OH 45249-3305

SCHEINFELD, JAMES DAVID, travel agency executive; b. Milw., Nov. 11, 1926; s. Aaron and Sylvia (Rosenberg) S.; children from previous marriage: John Stephen, Shaina, Robert Alan; m. Elna Magnusson, 1994. BA in Econs. magna cum laude, U. Wis., 1949. With Manpower, Inc., 1948-78, salesman, Chgo., 1949-51, br. mgr., 1951-53, nat. sales mgr., Milw., 1953-56, dir. sales, corp. sec., 1956-59, v.p. sales, 1959-62, exec. v.p. mktg., 1962-65, exec. v.p. (sr.), chief ops. officer, 1965-76, v.p. spl. projects, 1976-78, mem. exec. com., bd. dirs., 1959-76, cons., 1978-84; exec. v.p., chief exec. officer, bd. dirs. Transpersonal, Inc., Any Task Inc., Manpower Argentina, Manpower Europe, Manpower Ltd. (U.K.), Manpower Australia, Manpower Japan, Manpower Germany GmbH, Manpower Norway, Manpower Denmark, Manpower Venezuela, 1966-76; pres. Travway Internat. Inc. - Funway Holidays, Funjet, 1976-81, Aide Svcs., Inc., Tampa, Fla., 1976-81; pres., chief exec. officer Travelpower Inc., 1976-84; sr. v.p. Carlson Travel Network, 1984—. Mem. Hickory Travel Systems Inc., 1977-85, bd. dirs., 1978-85, pres., 1980-82, pres. emeritus, 1982—. Contbr. articles to profl. jours. Chmn. Cancer Crusade Milwaukee County, 1970; bd. dirs. Sinai-Samaritan Med. Ctr., Better Bus. Bur. Milw., 1979-90, Found. for Santa Barbara City Coll., 1989—, pres., 1996-2000; trustee U. Wis. Milw. Found., 1981-91, emeritus trustee, 1991—; mem. bus. adv. bd. U. Wis.-Milw., 1987—; chmn. bus. adv. bd. Santa Barbara City Coll., 1988-92; dir. Santa Barbara Trust for Hist. Preservation, 1995—, v.p., 1998—; mem. Greater Milw. Com., 1984-97. With USNR, 1944-46. Mem. Nat. Assn. Temporary Svcs. (pres. 1975-76, bd. dirs. 1969-77), Univ. Club Milw., La Cumbre Country Club (Santa Barbara), Rotary Club of Montecito Calif. Home and Office: 129 Rametto Rd Santa Barbara CA 93108-2317 E-mail: jimscheinfeld1@cox.net. *I do not often walk or look back where my footprints are. I prefer to walk that part of the beach I have never walked before. I am a person who thinks more about tomorrow than yesterday . . . more about what can be done than what has been done . . . more about challenges than accomplishments. Looking back is helpful only if I can find a sign to help me in my future.*

SCHEINHOLTZ, LEONARD LOUIS, lawyer; b. Pitts., June 2, 1927; s. Bernard A. and Marie (Getzel) S.; m. Joan R. Libenson, Aug. 16, 1953; children: Stuart, Nancy, Barry. BA, U. Pa., 1948, MA, 1949; LLB, Columbia U., 1953. Bar: Pa. 1954, U.S. Ct. Appeals (3d cir.) 1959, U.S. Ct. Appeals (6th cir.) 1968, U.S. Supreme Ct. 1972, U.S. Ct. Appeals (4th cir.) 1973, U.S. Ct. Appeals (5th cir.) 1981, U.S. Ct. Appeals (11th cir.) 1991, U.S. Ct. Appeals (2d cir.) 1993. Assoc. Reed, Smith, LLP, Pitts., 1953—62, spl. ptnr., 1962—64, gen. ptnr., 1964—97, head labor dept., 1980—86, of counsel, 1997—. Dir. Am. Arbitration Assn., N.Y.C., 1980-96. Author: Exemption Under the Anti-Trust Laws for Joint Employer Activity, 1982, The Arbitrator as Judge and Jury: Another Look at Statutory Law in Arbitration, 1985. Vice chmn. Pa. AAA Fedn., Harrisburg, 1982-85 ; chmn. W. Pa. AAA Motor Club, 1979-82; trustee Montefiore Hosp., Pitts., 1976-79; bd. dirs. Nat. Aviary, 1999—; bd. dirs. United Jewish Fedn. Pitts., 1997-2000, Jewish Chronicle, Pitts., 1997-. Served with USN, 1945-46. Mem. ABA, Pa. Bar Assn., Allegheny County Bar Assn. Republican. Jewish. Home: 746 Pinoak Rd Pittsburgh PA 15243-1153 Office: Reed Smith LLP Mellon Sq 435 6th Ave Pittsburgh PA 15219-1886

SCHEINKMAN, JOSÉ ALEXANDRE, economics educator; b. Rio de Janeiro, Brazil, Jan. 11, 1948; s. Samuel and Sara (Lerner) S.; m. Michele Zitrin, Dec. 14, 1969; 1 child, Andrei Zitrin BA, U. Fed. Rio de Janeiro, 1969; MS, Instituto de Matematica Pura e Aplicado, Brazil, 1970; MA, U. Rochester, 1972, PhD, 1973; Docteur honoris causa, U. Paris-Dauphine, 2001. Asst. prof. econs. U. Chgo., 1973-76, assoc. prof., 1976-81, prof., 1981-86, Alvin H. Baum distin. prof. economics, 1987-99, chmn. econs. dept., 1995-98; v.p. Goldman, Sachs & Co., 1987-89; Theodore Wells '29 prof. econs. Princeton U., 1999—. Vis. prof. Instituto de Matematica Pura e Aplicado Brazil, 1979-80, Fundação Getulio Vargas, Brazil, 1979-80, U. Paris, 1985-94, Princeton (N.J.) U., 1998; Blaise Pascal rsch. prof., France, 2001; external prof. Sante Fe Inst., 1989—; Harry Johnson lectr. Royal Econ. Soc./Assn. Univ. Tchrs. in Econs., 1989; econs. adv. panelist Sloan Found., 1991-97. Editor: General Equilibrium Growth and Trade, 1975, Jour. Polit. Economy, Chgo., 1983-94; contbr. articles to profl. jours. NSF grantee. Fellow AAAS, Econometric Soc. Home: 161 Nassau St Princeton NJ 08542-7007 Office: Princeton U Dept Econs 307 Fisher Hall Princeton NJ 08544-1177 Fax: 609 258-4501. E-mail: joses@princeton.edu.

SCHEINMAN, LESLIE KASS, radio sales marketing executive; b. Flushing, N.Y., Oct. 27, 1953; d. R. Robert and Geraldine N. (Rothberg) Kass; m. William T. Scott, III, May 25, 1975 (div. Oct. 1981); m. Gerald Lynn Scheinman, July 1, 1984; children: Lee Jacob (dec.), Rachel Lee, Carly Rebecca. Student, Boston U.; BFA, U. R.I. Store mgr. McDonald's Corp., Raleigh, N.C., 1976-78; media dir. Martin J. Simmons Advt., Chgo., 1978-79; asst. dir. advt. Penta Investments, San Diego, 1979; account exec. Gemini II Advt., 1980; media planner, buyer Cole & Weber, L.A., 1980-83; account exec. McGavren Guild Radio, 1983-88, v.p. sales, 1988-90; v.p., dir. sales Schubert Radio Sales, 1991-92; v.p. The Interep Radio Store; v.p., regional mgr. Torbet Radio, 1992-94; local sales mgr. Sta. KEEY-FM/Minn., 1994-96, gen. sales mgr., 1996-99, KEEY-FM and KQQL-FM, 2000—. Bd. dirs. Am. Women in Radio and TV; cons. small advt. agys. Leader, organizer Young World Devel./Am. Freedom from Hunger Found., 1971; patron Los Angeles County Mus. Art, 1984— Boston U. scholar, 1971-72. Mem. NAFE, Advt. Industry Emergency Fund, Mortar Board. Jewish. Avocations: crafts, sculpture, sports.

SCHEINMAN, MELVIN MAYER, cardiologist, educator; b. Bklyn., Oct. 1, 1935; m. Margaret E. Krouse, Dec. 28, 1958; children— Ari Daniel, Elan, Aviva BA, Johns Hopkins U., 1956; MD, Albert Einstein Coll. Medicine, N.Y.C., 1960. Diplomate Am. Bd. Internal Medicine, Am. Bd. Cardiology. Asst. chief cardiology San Francisco Gen. Hosp., 1969-78; assoc. staff U. Calif. Med. Ctr., San Francisco, 1973—, assoc. prof. medicine, 1973-79, prof., 1979—, chief ECG and clin. cardiac electrophysiology, 1979—. Served as officer M.C., USAF, 1961-63 Fellow ACP, Am. Coll. Cardiology (regional bd. govs. 1981-83), Western Soc. Clin. Research; mem. Am. Heart Assn. (Paul Dudley White citation 1978, teaching scholar 1971-75), N.Am. Soc. Pacing and Electrophysiology Office: UCSF Cardiac Electrophysiology 500 Parnassus Ave San Francisco CA 94143-1354 E-mail: scheinman@medicine.ucsf.edu.

SCHEINMAN, STANLEY BRUCE, international financial executive, lawyer; b. N.Y.C., Nov. 13, 1933; s. Samuel and Sadie (Seiffer) S.; m. Susan L. Elstein (dec.); m. Janet L. Donnely, Dec. 30, 1975 (dec.); children: Catherine Amy, Anthony Paul, Sarah Jean, Norah Jane; m. Maria Shea Burke, Nov. 17, 2000. AB, Cornell U., 1954; MBA, CCNY, 1957; JD (Harlan Fisk Stone scholar), Columbia U., 1960. Bar: N.Y. 1960. Assoc. firm Cravath, Swaine & Moore, N.Y.C., 1960-62; capital projects officer, legis. programs staff coord. AID, Washington, 1962-64; sr. exec. officer Bur. Pvt. Enterprise, AID, 1982-83; v.p. fin. and adminstrn. svcs. industries div., also v.p., counsel internat. div. PepsiCo. Inc., 1965-70; v.p. fin. and adminstrn. pharm. divsn. Revlon, Inc., 1970-72; sr. v.p. MCI Comm., 1972-76; pres., COO FSC Corp., Pitts., 1976-81; pres. New Venture Capital Corp., Washington, 1984-85; prin. Re Venture Assocs., Salisbury, Conn., 1985-86; chmn., CEO Internat. 800 Telcom Corp., Geneva, 1987-88; pres., CEO Zurich Depository Corp., Manhasset, N.Y., 1988-89; exec. v.p. AMIF&S Ltd., N.Y.C., 1989-91; pres. IT Svc. Corp., Westport, Conn., 1991-92; v..p. ops. and bus. devel. EQ Corp., 1992-95; exec. v.p., CFO, Computer Products and Svcs. Inc., Wilton, Conn., 1995-96; pres., CEO TTC Internat. Ltd., London, 1996—. Mem.: ABA, Internat. Execs. Assn., Fin. Execs. Inst., Inst. for Dirs. (U.K.), Assn. Bar City NY, Brit.-Am. Club, Cornell Club, Fgn. Svc. Club, Paris-Am. Club. Home: 350 E 79th St Apt 33B New York NY 10021 Office: 43 Benbow House New Globe Walk London SE1 9DS England

SCHEINMAN, STEVEN JAY, medical educator; b. Monticello, N.Y., Oct. 22, 1951; married; 2 children. AB summa cum laude, Amherst Coll., 1973; MD cum laude, Yale U., 1977. Diplomate Am. Bd. Internal Medicine in Neprology, lic. physician N.Y., Conn. Resident internal medicine Yale-New Haven Hosp., 1977-80; chief resident internal medicine Upstate Med. Ctr., Syracuse, N.Y., 1980-81, fellow nephrology, 1981-83, Yale-New Haven Hosp., 1983-84; asst. prof. medicine SUNY Upstate Med. U., Syracuse, 1984-90, asst. prof. pharmacology, 1988-90, assoc. prof. medicine and pharmacology, 1990-94, prof. medicine and pharmacology, 1994—, chief nephrology divsn. dept. medicine, 1994—. Vis. scientist MRC Molecular Medicine Group, Royal Postgrad. Med. Sch. Hammersmith Hosp., London, 1992, London, 95; vis. scholar dept. biochemistry U. Oxford, 1985; attending physician U. Hosp., Syracuse, Crouse-Irving Meml. Hosp., Syracuse, VA Med. Ctr., Syracuse; dir. Nephrology Fellowship Program, 1993—; spkr. seminars, confs., orgns. Contbr. Recipient Lange award, Yale U. Sch. Medicine, 1976, Resident Merit award, ACP (Conn. chpt.), 1980, Nat. Rsch. Svc. award, NIH, 1981—83, clin. investigator award, 1985—90, Charles R. Ross Rsch. award, SUNY-Health Sci. Ctr., 1992, Pres.'s award for Excellence and Leadership in Rsch., SUNY Upstate Med. U., 2001; grantee, Nat. Inst. Arthritis Diabetes Digestive and Kidney Diseases, 1981—83, 1985—90, 1995—2002, Am. Heart Assn., 1985, 1988—90, 1990—91, 1992—95, 1995—97, NATO, 1995—98. Mem.: Assn. Subspecialty Profs., Nat. Kidney Found., Am. Heart Assn. Coun. on Kidney, Am. Soc. Bone and Mineral Rsch., Am. Physiol. Soc., Internat. Soc. Nephrology, Am. Soc. Nephrology (mem. editl. bd. Jour. 2000—), Am. Fedn. Med. Rsch., Am. Soc. Clin. Investigation, Phi Beta Kappa. Home: 24 University Ave Hamilton NY 13346-1326 Office: SUNY Upstate Med U 750 E Adams St Syracuse NY 13210-1834

SCHEIRING, MICHAEL JAMES, college official; b. Canton, Ohio, Oct. 11, 1949; s. Robert J. and Madonna L. (Geisigi) S.; m. Marcia L. Young, May 13, 1972; children: Kristy L., Lauren M. BA, Kent State U., 1971, MPA, 1972. Sect. supr. N.J. Dept. Treasury, Trenton, 1974-78; policy analyst to gov., 1978-80; dir. adminstrn. N.J. Dept. Community Affairs, 1980-82; dir. corp. budgeting N.J. Transit Corp., Newark, 1982-83; v.p. adminstrn. and fin. Thomas A. Edison Coll., Trenton, 1983—; exec. dir. Gov. Mgmt. Rev. Com., Gov.'s Office, N.J., 1990-93. Trustee N.J. Ednl. Computer Corp., 1984-90; trustee, comptroller Edison Found., Trenton, 1984—; mem. adv. bd. National Ctr. Productivity; pres. U.D. Dollars for Scholars Found.; chmn. Trenton Audit Commn.; mem. citizen's delegation to China; trustee Robert Wood Johnson U. Hosp. Hamilton. Contbg. author: N.J. Zero-Based Budgeting, 1979. Named Vol. of Yr. N.J. United Cerebral Palsy. Mem. ASPA (nat. coun., v.p. programs 1984, v.p. membership 1985, pres. 1987-89), Old Barracks Assn. (trustee, pres.), Rotary (pres.). Roman Catholic. Home: 2 Lotus Ln Trenton NJ 08648-3211 Office: Thomas Edison State Coll Trenton NJ 08625

SCHEITLIN, CONSTANCE JOY, real estate broker, accountant; b. Louisville, Nov. 21, 1949; d. Albert and Esther Joy (Sulzer) Kraus; m. Charles James Scheitlin, Sept. 11, 1982; 1 child, Brittany. Student, Bellarmine Coll., Louisville, 1971-72, U. Louisville, 1974-75, Spencerian Bus. Coll., Louisville, 1968. Lic. salesperson in real estate, Ky.; lic. real estate broker, Fla. Customer svc. rep. Chevron Oil Co., Louisville, 1968-77; acctg. asst. E. Bruce Neikirk, Atty., 1978; retail mgr. Stannye's Boutique, 1978-85; real estate sales person, 1970-85; real estate salesperson Venice, 1987-92; legal asst. Andrew Britton, Atty., 1986-92; real estate broker, mgr. Coldwell Banker, Venice, 1991-95; mgr. Coldwell Banker Residential Real Estate, 1995-96, regional mgr., property mgmt., 1996-97; mgr. acctg. Fla. Metro-NRT, Inc., Sarasota, 1997—. Treas. Stannye's Boutique, Louisville, 1983-85. Chmn. Metro United Way, Louisville, 1975-77; team capt. Greater Louisville Fund for the Arts, 1980-85; mem. South Venice Civic Assn., 1985—; chmn. So. Venice Road and Bridge Trustees, 1989-96. Mem. Venice Area Bd. Realtors (dir. 1992-95), Women's Coun. of Realtors (treas. 1988-89, pres. 1989-90), Sarasota Bd. Realtors. Avocations: golf, racquetball. Office: Coldwell Banker 5971 Cattleridge Blvd Sarasota FL 34232-6048 E-mail: cjscheitlin@comcast.net.

SCHELAR, VIRGINIA MAE, chemistry consultant; b. Kenosha, Wis., Nov. 26, 1924; d. William and Blanche M. (Williams) S. BS, U. Wis., 1947, MS, 1953; MEd, Harvard U., 1962; PhD, U. Wis., 1969. Instr. U. Wis., Milw., 1947-51; info. specialist Abbott Labs., North Chgo., Ill., 1953-56; instr. Wright Jr. Coll., Chgo., 1957-58; asst. prof. No. Ill. U., DeKalb, 1958-63; prof. St. Petersburg (Fla.) Jr. Coll., 1965-67; asst. prof. Chgo. State Coll., 1967-68; prof. Grossmont Coll., El Cajon, Calif., 1968-80; cons., 1981—. Author: Kekule Centennial, 1965; contbr. articles to profl. jours. Active citizens adv. coun. DeKalb Consol. Sch. Bd.; voters svc. chair League Women Voters, del. to state and nat. convs., judicial chair, election laws chair. Standard Oil fellow, NSF grantee; recipient Lewis prize U. Wis. Fellow Am. Inst. Chemists; mem. Am. Chem. Soc. (membership affairs com., chmn. western councilor's caucus, exec. com., councilor, legis. counselor, chmn. edn. com., editor state and local bulletins). Avocations: swimming, folk dancing.

SCHELBERT, HEINRICH RUEDIGER, nuclear medicine physician; b. Wuerzberg, Germany, Nov. 5, 1939; MD, U. Würzburg (Germany), 1964. Diplomate Am. Bd. Nuclear Medicine. Intern Mercy Med. Ctr., Phila., 1966-67, resident, 1967-68, 70-71; resident in cardiology U. Dusseldorf, Germany, 1971-72; fellow in cardiology, resident in nuclear medicine U. Calif., San Diego, 1968-69, asst. rsch. cardiologist, 1972-75, assoc. rsch. radiologist, 1975-76; hosp. assoc. UCLA Med. Ctr., 1977—; prof. radiol. scis. UCLA Sch. Medicine, 1980-90, prof. pharmacol. and radiol. scis., 1993—. Recipient Georg von Hevesy prize 2d Internat. Congress World Fedn. Nuclear Medicine and Radiation Biology, 1978, 3d Internat. Congress World Fedn. Nuclear Medicine and Radiation Biology, 1982. Fellow Am. Coll. Cardiology; mem. Am. Heart Assn. (disting. scientific achievement award 1989), Soc. Nuclear Medicine (Herrman L. Blumgart pioneer lectr. award 1989, George De Hevesy Nuclear Medicine Pioneer award 1998), German Soc. Nuc. Med. (hon.). Office: UCLA Sch Medicine Dept Molecular Med B2-985J Box 956948 Los Angeles CA 90095-6948

SCHELDE, PER, writer, educator; b. Copenhagen, Denmark, Sept. 23, 1945; came to U.S., 1978; s. Helge Jacob Schelde and Aase Schelde (Guldager Nielsen) Jacobsen. BA, CUNY, Queens, 1981; PhD, CUNY, 1985. Actor Svalegangen, Aarhus, Denmark, 1970-73, Fiolteatret, Copenhagen, 1974-77; asst. prof. York Coll., Jamaica, N.Y., 1985-90; actor St. George Theater, Grand Canyon Shakespeare Festival, Phoenix, 1996. Author: Ibsen's Forsaken Merman: Folklore in the Late Plays, 1988, Androids, Humanoids and Other Folklore Monsters: Science and Soul in Science Fiction Films, 1993; contbr. articles to profl. jours. Fellow Royal Anthropological Soc.; mem. Am. Anthropological Soc., Phi Beta Kappa. Avocations: reading, running, tennis. E-mail: per_schelde@qwest.net.

SCHELER, BRAD ERIC, lawyer; b. Bklyn., Oct. 11, 1953; s. Bernard and Rita Regina (Miller) S.; m. Amy Ruth Frolick, Mar. 30, 1980; children: Ali M., Maddie H., Zoey B. BA with high honors, Lehigh U., 1974; JD, Hofstra U., 1977. Bar: N.Y. 1978, U.S. Dist. Ct. (so. and ea. dists.) N.Y. 1978. Assoc. Weil, Gotshal & Manges, N.Y.C., 1977-81; sr. ptnr., chmn. bankruptcy and restructuring practice Fried, Frank, Harris, Shriver & Jacobson, 1981—. Rsch. editor Hofstra U. Law Rev., 1975-77. Treas., bus. mgr. Trustees of Gramercy Park, N.Y.C., 1979-87. Fellow Am. Coll. Bankruptcy; mem. ABA (bus. bankruptcy com. corp. banking and bus. law sect., creditors' rights com. litig. sect.), N.Y. State Bar Assn., Assn. Bar City of N.Y. (com. on bankruptcy and corp. reorgn. 1991-94), Sigma Alpha Mu (v.p. 1973). Jewish. Home: 94 Larchmont Ave Larchmont NY 10538-3723 Office: Fried Frank Harris 1 New York Plz Fl 23 New York NY 10004-1901 E-mail: Schelbr@ffhsj.com.

SCHELL, ALLAN CARTER, retired electrical engineer; b. New Bedford, Mass., Apr. 14, 1934; s. Charles Carter and Elizabeth (Moore) S.; m. Shirley T. Sardineer; children: Alice Rosalind, Cynthia Anne. BS, MSE.E., MIT, 1956, Sc.D., 1961; student, Tech. U. Delft, Netherlands, 1956-57. Research physicist Air Force Cambridge Research Labs., Bedford, Mass., 1956-76, Guenter Loeser Meml. lectr., 1965; dir. electromagnetics directorate Rome Air Devel. Ctr., Bedford, 1976-87; chief scientist Hdqrs. USAF Systems Command, 1987-92; chief scientist, dep. dir. sci. and tech. Hdqrs. USAF Materiel Command, 1992-94. Dir. Electro; vis. assoc. prof. MIT, 1974; chair dept. of elec. engring. adv. coun. U. Pa., 1992-94. Contbr. articles to profl. jours.; patentee in field (9). Served as lt. USAF, 1958-60. Recipient Fulbright award, 1956-57, Meritorious Exec. award U.S. Govt., 1989; NSF fellow, 1955-56, 60-61. Fellow IEEE (bd. dirs. 1981-82, editor IEEE Press 1976-79, Procs. of IEEE 1990-92), Antennas and Propagation Soc. of IEEE (pres. 1978, editor tran. 1969-71, John T. Bolljahn award 1966), Internat. Sci. Radio Union, Sigma Xi, Tau Beta Pi. E-mail: a.schell@ieee.org.

SCHELL, BRAXTON, lawyer; b. Raleigh, N.C., Feb. 24, 1924; s. Marshall H. and Margaret (Newsom) S.; m. Ann Cooper Knight, Mar. 30, 1951 (div. 1982); children: Braxton, Richard Knight, James Gray (dec.); m. Mary Rehill, Apr. 16, 1983. Student, N.C. State Coll., 1942-43; BS, U. N.C., 1948, JD with honors, 1951. Bar: N.C. 1951. Since practiced in, Greensboro; assoc. Smith, Moore, Smith & Pope, 1951-56; ptnr. Smith Moore Smith Schell & Hunter, 1956-85, Smith, Helms, Mullis, and Moore, 1986-87, Schell, Bray, Aycock, Abel & Livingston, 1987—. Gen. counsel, dir. Flagler Sys. and The Breakers Palm Beach, Inc. Assoc. editor: N.C. Law Rev. 1950-51. Chmn. Special Liason Tax Com. Southeastern Region, 1960-61; bd. dirs. N.C. Outward Bound Sch., 1975-88, chmn., 1977-80; trustee Outward Bound, Inc., 1978-81; bd. dirs. William R. Kenan Funds for Pvt. Enterprise, Arts and Engring., Tech. and Sci. and Ethics. Pilot USAAF, 1943-45. Fellow Am. Bar Found.; mem. ABA, N.C. Bar Assn., Greensboro Bar Assn., Order of Coif, Figure Eight Island Yacht Club, Greensboro Country Club (pres. 1971-72), Greensboro City Club (dir. 1980—), Phi Beta Kappa. Presbyterian. Home: 422B Fisher Park Cir Greensboro NC 27401-1615 Office: Schell Bray Aycock Abel & Living 1500 Renaissance Pla Greensboro NC 27420 E-mail: bschell@sbaal.com.

SCHELL, CATHERINE LOUISE, family practice physician; b. Niskayuna, N.Y., Jan. 27, 1948; m. Richard J. Rathe, Jan. 7, 1986. BA, Ind. U., 1970, MA, 1974; MLS, Simmons Coll., 1975; MD, Am. U. Caribbean, Montserrat, 1983. Diplomate Am. Bd. Family Practice; cert. CAQ Geriatrics. Libr. Calder Med. Libr., U. Miami, Fla., 1975-78; libr., dir. Mercy Hosp., Miami, 1978-79; libr. Miami-Dade C.C., 1978-80; intern Med. Coll. Ga., Rome, 1983; resident U. Wyo., Cheyenne, 1985-87; staff physician Vets. Hosp., 1986-88, Dept. of Army, U.S. Dept. Def., Ft. Devens, Mass., 1988-90, Vets. Hosp., Lake City, Fla., 1990-93, staff physician, fellow Gainesville, 1993-95; fellow in geriatrics U. Fla., 1993-95, fellow in geriatrics internal medicine, 1995, fellow geriatrics internal medicine, 1995; physician Dept. of Navy, 1995-96, locum tenens, 1996—; pres. Med. Decisions Software, Inc., 1999—. Tchr. ESL YMCA Internat., Taipei, Taiwan, 1970-71. Title IIB fellow Simmons Coll., 1974-75; Ford Found. grantee, Ind. U., 1969-70. Fellow Am. Acad. Family PRactice; mem. Acad. Health Sci., Med. Libr. Assn.

SCHELL, FARREL LOY, transportation engineer; b. Amarillo, Tex., Dec. 14, 1931; s. Thomas Phillip and Lillian Agnes (McKee) S.; m. Shirley Anne Samuelson, Feb. 6, 1955; children: James Christopher, Maria Leslyn Schell Peter. BS, U. Kans., 1954; postgrad., Carnegie-Mellon U., 1974. Registered profl. engr., Calif., Colo. Resident engr. Sverdrup & Parcel, Denver, 1957-61; project engr. Bechtel Corp., San Francisco, 1961-62, Parsons, Brinckerhoff-Tudor-Bechtel, San Francisco, 1962-67; mgr. urban transp. dept. Kaiser Engrs., Oakland, Calif., 1967-78; program dir. San Francisco Mcpl. Rwy I.C., 1978-80; project mgr. Houston Transit Cons., 1980-83, Kaiser Transit Group, Miami, 1983-85; mgr. program devel. Kaiser Engrs., Oakland, 1985-87; project mgr. O'Brien-Kreitzberg & Assocs., San Francisco, 1987-89; sr. project mgr. Bay Area Rapid Transit Dist., Oakland, Calif., 1989-2001. Dir./CEO Schelter Devel. Corp., Piedmont, Calif., 1982—. Contbr. articles to profl. jours. Chmn., bd. dirs. Achenbach Graphic Arts Coun. Lt. (j.g.) USN, 1954-57, PTO. Mem. ASCE, ASME, Nat. Soc. Profl. Engrs., Nat. Coun.

Engring. Examiners, Am. Planners Assn., Am. Pub. Transit Assn., Lakeview Club, Scarab Club, Pachacamac Club, Sigma Tau, Tau Beta Pi. Avocations: fly fishing, camping. Home: 24 York Dr Piedmont CA 94611-4123 E-mail: fschell@aol.com.

SCHELL, JAMES MUNSON, financial executive; b. Kalamazoo, Mar. 25, 1944; s. Frank John and Shirley I. S.; m. Susan O'Laughlin, Aug. 6, 1966; children: Karen, Michael, Ryan. BA, Vanderbilt U., 1966; MBA, Washington U., 1968. Dir. term and internat. financing Chrysler Fin. Corp., Troy, Mich., 1976-79, v.p., treas., 1980-81; v.p. domestic treasury Am. Express Co., N.Y.C., 1981-82; v.p. fin. resources Hertz Corp., 1982-83; v.p., chief fin. officer Clabir Corp., Greenwich, Conn., 1983-84; v.p., treas. Fairchild Industries, 1985-87; ind. fin. cons., 1987—. Bd. dirs. Jackson-Jordan Corp., CTI Industries, Country Home Bakers. Republican. Roman Catholic. Home: 40 Stony Brook Rd Darien CT 06820-4326 E-mail: jmsschell@aol.com.

SCHELL, JESSE NATHANIEL, interactive entertainment designer, juggler, circus performer; b. Denville, NJ, June 13, 1970; s. Anthony Schell, Susanne Fahringer; m. Nyra Munoz. BSCS, Rensselaer, Troy, NY, 1988—92; MSINI, Carnegie Mellon, Pittsburgh, PA, 1993—94. Entertainer Riverside Amusement Park, Agawam, MA, 1986—89; Software Engineer IBM, Kingston, NY, 1990—91; Writer / Director / Performer Juggler's Guild / Freihofer's Mime Circus, Springfield, MA, 1990—92; Member of Technical Staff Bell Communications Research, Piscataway, NJ, 1992—95; Creative Director Walt Disney Imagineering VR Studio, Glendale, CA, 1995—2002. Mem.: IGDA.

SCHELL, NORKA M. lawyer, consultant; b. Feira Santana, Bahia, Brazil, May 28, 1958; d. Agostino A. and Maria do Carmo Silva. BA, Coll. San Anthonio, Feira Santana, 1976; JD, Faculdde de Dirito, Gao.Valodares, 1984; LLM in Internt. Law, Golden Gate U., San Francisco, 1988. Paralegal Sindicato dos Metalungico, Ipatinga, 1983-84; atty. N.M. Da Silva Law Office, Ridgewood, N.J., 1989-95, pvt. practice Short Hills, 1995—. Pvt. practice, fgn. legal cons., Ridgewood, N.J., 1992-98. Mem. ATLA, San Francisco Bar Assn., N.Y. Bar Assn., Assn. Bar City N.Y. Avocations: sports, photography, travel, languages and music. Office: 60 Park Pl St Ste 530 Newark NJ 07102 E-mail: nmslaw@aol.com.

SCHELL, NORMAN BARNETT, physician, consultant; b. N.Y.C., May 25, 1925; s. Jack and Ada Sylvia (Rosen) S.; m. Lila Barbara Mendelsohn, Aug. 27, 1950; children: Martin, Judith, Steven. AB cum laude, NYU, 1946, MD, 1950; MPH, Harvard U., 1971. Diplomate Am. Bd. Pediats., Am. Bd. Preventive Medicine, Nat. Bd. Med. Examiners; lic. physician, N.Y. Rotating intern Beth Israel Hosp., N.Y.C., 1950-51; asst. resident in pediats. Mt. Sinai Hosp., 1951-52; clin. fellow in pediats. N.Y.-Cornell Med. Ctr., 1952-53; pvt. practice Jericho and Hicksville, N.Y., 1956-69; pub. health physician Nassau County Health Dept., Mineola, 1969-76, dep. commr., 1976-90. Asst. prof. preventive medicine SUNY, Stony Brook, 1974-90; pediat. cons. N.Y. State Health Dept., 1956-69, HEW Project Head Start, N.Y.C., 1968-75; emeritus pediat. staff Nassau County Med. Ctr. Author: Keys to Childhood Illnesses, 1992; contbr. articles to profl. jours. Lt. M.C., USN, 1953-55, capt. M.C., USNR, 1981-85. Recipient Physician Recognition award AMA, 1970, Grade 1A Health Officer N.Y. State Health Dept., 1973. Fellow Am. Acad. Pediats. (com. on sch. health 1971-77, citation com. on med. edn. 1977), Am. Coll. Preventive Medicine, N.Y. Acad. Medicine; mem. Am. Coll. Legal Medicine (assoc.), Nassau County Med. Soc. (chmn. sch. health com.), Harvard Club N.Y.C., West Point Club, Phi Beta Kappa. Avocations: photography, classical music, computer technology. Home and Office: 63 Birchwood Park Dr Jericho NY 11753-2238

SCHELL, PAUL E.S. former mayor; b. Fort Dodge, Iowa, Oct. 8, 1937; m. Pam Schell. BA, U. Iowa, 1960; JD, Columbia U., 1963. Pvt. practice, 1963-74; dir. dept. cmty. devel. City of Seattle, 1974-77, mayor, 1998—2001; pres., founder Cornerstone Columbia Devel. Co., 1979-87; commr. Port of Seattle, 1989-99, pres. commn., 1995-99; dean Architecture and Urban Planning U. Wash., 1992-95; strategic adv. & bus. developer NBBJ Archtl. Firm, Seattle, 2001—. Past bd. dirs. Intiman Theatre, A Contemporary Theater; past pres. Allied Arts; founder, active Cascadia Project; bd. dirs. Trade Devel. Alliance; mem. Friends of the Pike Place Market; sr. adv. & bd. mem. Columbia Hospitality, Seattle. Office: NBBJ 111 S Jackson St Seattle WA 98104 : Columbia Hospitality 2205 Alaskan Way Seattle WA 98121*

SCHELLENBERGER, ROBERT EARL, management educator and department chairman; b. Janesville, Wis., July 25, 1932; s. Ervin William and Adelaide Louise (Keller) S.; m. Linda Eula Todd, Dec. 30, 1961; children: Brian T., Keith W., Heidi L. BSBA, U. Wis., 1958, MBA, 1959; PhD, U. N.C., 1963. Personnel supr. Libby McNeill and Libby, Janesville, Wis., 1957-58; from asst. prof. to assoc. prof. chmn. div. stats. dept. bus U. Md., College Park, 1963-68; chair dept. mgmt. So. Ill. U., Carbondale, Ill., 1968-70, dir. planning Sch. Human Resources Devel., 1970-71, prof. mgmt., 1968-71; vis. prof., dir. program evaluation Babcock Grad. Sch. Mgmt., Wake Forest U., Winston-Salem, N.C., 1971-73; prof. dept. mgmt. Temple U., Phila., 1973-81, from chmn. dept. mgmt. to asst. to acad. vice chancellor, 1975-77; prof. decision scis. dept. East Carolina U., Greenville, N.C., 1981-2000, chmn. decision scis. dept., 1989-95. Pres. Md. Rsch. and Cons., Hyattsville, 1964-67; v.p. Ea. Acad. Mgmt., 1967; cons. Comml. Credit Corp., Balt., 1966. Author: Managerial Analysis, 1967, Policy Formulation, 1978, 2d edit., 1982; co-editor Jour. of Econs. and Bus., 1976; developer (software package) MANYSYM, 1965, 68, 78, 82, 86. Chmn. Utilities Com., Carbondale, 1970-72. Title IV NDEA fellow U. N.C., 1960-62, Earhart Jr. fellow U. Wis. Mem. Assn. for Bus. Simulation, SE Decision Scis. Inst., Decision Scis. Inst. (bd. dirs. 1974-77), Beta Gamma Sigma.

SCHELLHAAS, LINDA JEAN, toxicologist, consultant; b. South Haven, Mich., Apr. 27, 1956; d. Richard Louis and Virgene Frieda (Lietzke) Plankenhorn; m. Robert Wesley Schellhaas, May 27, 1990. BA in Biology, Albion Coll., 1978. Registered quality assurance profl. Pathology rsch. asst. Internat. R&D Corp., Mattawan, Mich., 1978-80; toxicology rsch. coord. Borriston Labs., Inc., Temple Hills, Md., 1980-84; quality assurance coord. Tegeris Labs., Inc., 1984-85; good lab. practice compliance specialist, staff scientist Dynamac Corp., Rockville, 1985-90; dir. quality assurance Pathology Assocs., Inc., Frederick, 1992-94; pres., regulatory compliance specialist Quality Reviews, Inc., Falling Waters, W.Va., 1990—. Instr. regulatory compliance tng. seminars, 1990—. Contbr. articles to profl. jours. Mem. Soc. Quality Assurance, Albion Coll. Fellows, Pi Beta Phi, Phi Beta Kappa. Avocations: sheep, goat and poultry husbandry, raising sheep-herding dogs, needlework, animal welfare. Office: Quality Reviews Inc 130 Traveller Rd Falling Waters WV 25419-9657

SCHELLING, THOMAS CROMBIE, economist, educator; b. Oakland, Calif., Apr. 14, 1921; s. John M. and Zelda M. (Ayres) S.; m. Corinne T. Saposs, Sept. 13, 1947 (div. 1991); children: Andrew, Thomas, Daniel, Robert; m. Alice M. Coleman, Nov. 8, 1991. AB, U. Calif., Berkeley, 1943; PhD, Harvard U., 1951. U.S. govt. economist, Copenhagen, Paris, Washington, 1948-53; prof. econs. Yale U., 1953-58, Harvard U., Cambridge, Mass., 1958-90; prof. econs. and pub. affairs U. Md., College Park, 1990—, disting. univ. prof., 1990—. Sr. staff mem. RAND Corp., 1958-59; chmn. rsch. adv. bd. Com. Econ. Devel., 1978-81, 84-85; mem. sci. adv. bd. USAF, 1960-64, def. sci. bd., 1966-70; mem. mil. econ. adv. panel CIA, 1980-85; trustee Aerospace Corp., 1984-93. Author: National Income Behavior, 1951, International Economics, 1958, The Strategy of Conflict, 1960, Arms and Influence, 1966, Micromotives and Macrobehavior, 1978, Choice and Consequence, 1984; co-author: Strategy and Arms Control, 1961. Recipient Frank E. Seidman Disting. award in polit. economy, 1977. Fellow Am. Acad. Arts and Scis., AAAS, Assn. for Pub. Policy Analysis and Mgmt., Am. Econ. Assn. (pres. 1991, Disting. mem. award); mem. NAS (rsch. award, 1993), Inst. Medicine, Ea. Econ. Assn. (pres. 1996). Office: Univ Md Sch Pub Affairs College Park MD 20742-0001 E-mail: ts57@umail.umd.edu.

SCHELLMAN, JOHN A. chemistry educator; b. Phila., Oct. 24, 1924; s. John and Mary (Mason) S.; m. Charlotte Green, Feb. 10, 1954; children: Heidi M., Lise C. AB, Temple U., 1948; MS, Princeton U., 1949, PhD, 1951; PhD (hon.), Chalmers U., Sweden, 1983, U. Padua, Italy, 1990. USPHS postdoctoral fellow U. Utah, 1951-52, Carlsberg Lab., Copenhagen, 1953-55; DuPont fellow U. Minn., Mpls., 1955-56, asst. prof. chemistry, 1956-58; assoc. prof. chemistry Inst. Molecular Biology, U. Oreg., Eugene, 1958-63, prof. chemistry, rsch. assoc., 1963—. Vis. Lab. Chem. Physics, Nat. Inst. Arthritis and Metabolic Diseases, NIH, Bethesda, Md., 1980; vis. prof. Chalmers U., Sweden, 1986, U. Padua, Italy, 1987. Contbr. articles to profl. jours. Served with U.S. Army, 1943-46 Fellow Rask-Oersted Found., 1954, Sloan Found., 1959-63, Guggenheim Found., 1969-70 Fellow Am. Phys. Soc.; mem. NAS, Am. Chem. Soc., Am. Soc. Biochemistry and Molecular Biology, Am. Acad. Arts and Scis., Biophys. Soc., Phi Beta Kappa, Sigma Xi. Democrat. Home: 780 Lorane Hwy Eugene OR 97405-2340 Office: Univ Oreg Inst Molecular Biology Eugene OR 97403 E-mail: john@molbio.uoregon.edu.

SCHELLNER, REINHARD ANTON, pharmaceutical company executive; b. Vienna, June 15, 1955; s. Hermann Godehard and Herta Maria (Poecherstorfer) S.; m. Susanne Katharina Krammer, Aug. 30, 1985; 1 child, Alwina Maria Eva. MS, Vienna U., 1979, PhD, 1982, MA in Agrl. Econs., 1983. Prof. biology and chemistry Ministry of Edn., Vienna, 1982-84; sr. product mgr. Ciba-Geigy Corp., 1984-87, regional mgr. Nairobi, Kenya, 1990-94, mng. dir. Manila, 1994-97; sales and distbn. mgr. SAPHAD, Riyadh, Saudi Arabia, 1987-89; asst. gen. mgr. SAPHAD, SACOM, 1989-90; pres., CEO, Novartis Healthcare, Manila, 1997-2000; gen. mgr. Bayer Corp., 2001—. Cons. Fed. Inst. Crop Protection, Vienna, 1975-79, U. Agriculture, Vienna, 1982-83. Contbr. articles to profl. jours. Cpl. Austrian Acad. Defense, 1983-84. Fulbright fellow Harvard U., 1979-81. Mem. AAAS, AMA, Pharm. and Healthcare Assn. Philipppines, Rotary. Roman Catholic. Avocations: travel, sports, reading. Home: Dasmariñas Village 1579 Cypress St 1200 Makati Manila Philippines Office: Bayer Philippines Canlubang Calamba 1229 Laguna 4028 Philippines Fax: 0063.2.844.2113. E-mail: raschellner@hotmail.com.

SCHELM, ROGER LEONARD, information systems specialist; b. Kingston, N.Y., July 29, 1936; s. Frederick G. and Elizabeth M. (Wojciehowski) S.; m. Gloria Mae Dutterer, June 13, 1958; children: Sandra Lee Kern, Theresa Jean Sollitto, Ginger Lisa Shah. BA in Polit. Sci., Western Md. Coll., 1958; MA in Pub. Adminstrn., Am. U., 1970; postgrad., U. Md., 1960-62. Analytic equipment programmer Nat. Security Agy., Ft. Meade, Md., 1958-60; computer cons. various cons. firms Balt. and Washington, 1960-68; mgr. army plans and programs Informatics Inc., Bethesda, Md., 1968; mgr. def. programs Automation Tech. Inc., Wheaton, 1968-69; dir. advanced planning Genasys Corp., Washington, 1969-71; mgr. info. systems Ins. Co. North Am., Phila., 1971-72, sect. mgr. computing ops., 1972-74; mgr. tech. services INA Corp., 1974-75; mem. spl. tech. projects INA Corp. merger with Conn. Gen. Ins. Co. to form CIGNA Corp. 1982, 1975-76, asst. dir. tech. services, 1977, asst. dir. spl. tech. projects, 1977-78, asst. dir. adminstrn., 1978-79, asst. dir. resource mgmt., data ctr. design, contingency planning, 1979-80; dir. corp. info. tech. now CIGNA Corp., 1981-82, dir. planning and control ops. div., 1982-83, v.p. strategic planning, systems div., 1983-84, v.p. applied research/expert systems, systems div., 1984-92; co-founder, pres. Schelm Internat., Inc., Cherry Hill, N.J., 1992—. Mem. adj. faculty Camden Coll., N.J., 1978-82; mem. Camden County EDP Adv. Com., 1980-82; mem. faculty Drexel U., Phila., 1983-95. Author: Ednl. Computer mag., 1982; mem. editl. adv. bd., author Small Sys. World mag., 1982-84; mem. editl. adv. bd. Spang-Robinson Report, 1986-87, Machine Intelligence News, 1987-93, AI Expert mag., 1985-88; cons. editor Expert Sys. Jour., 1987-91. Tech. advisor various sch. bds., colls., univs. and non-profit orgns. Served to capt. U.S. Army, 1959. Mem. Am. Assn. Artificial Intelligence, Assn. Computing Machinery (founder Delaware Valley chpt. vice. chmn., program chmn. 1983-84, chmn. 1984-85, founder Del. Valley Spl. Interest Group in Artificial Intelligence, 1985, vice chmn. 1985-87), World Future Soc. Home: 506 Balsam Rd Cherry Hill NJ 08003-3202

SCHELP, RICHARD HERBERT, mathematics educator; b. Kansas City, Mo., Apr. 21, 1936; s. Herbert and Ida Louise Schelp; m. Billie Marie Schelp, Dec. 20, 1958; children: Lisa Marie Martin, Richard John. BS in Math. and Physics, Ctrl. Mo. U., 1959; MS in Math., Kans. State U., 1961, PhD in Math., 1970. Assoc. mathematician applied physics lab. Johns Hopkins U., 1961-66; instr. math. Kans. State U., 1966-70; asst. prof. math. U. Memphis, 1970-74, assoc. prof. math., 1974-79, prof. math., 1979—. Chair spl. session Fifth Hungarian Combinatorics Conf., Keszthely, Hungary, 1976, First Japan Conf. Graph Theory and Application, 1986, First China-USA Conf. on Graph and Applications, 1986, Seventh Hungarian Combinatorics, Eger, 1987; chair session Probabilistic Workshop, Budapest, Hungary, 1998; vis. rschr. Hungarian Acad. Scis.-Math. Inst., 1985, 90, Lab. Rsch. and Info., U. Paris-Sud, 1993, Hungarian Acad. Scis.-Computer and Automation Inst., 1994; presenter in field. Mem. editl. bd. Jour. Graph Theory, 1981—, co-mng. editor, 1981-86; reviewer Math. Revs.; contbr. more than 130 articles to profl. jours. Named Outstanding Educators Am., 1975; recipient Disting. Alumnus award, Kans. St. U, 1999—2000, Bd. Visitors Eminent Faculty award, U. Memphis, 2001; fellow NSF, U. Mass., summer, 1968; grantee Internat. Rsch. and Exch. (travel), 1985, 1990, NSF, 1986—87, 1992—95, Nat. Security Agy., 1988—91. Mem. Am. Math. Soc. (organizer spl. session 1997), Math. Assn. Am., Inst. for Combinatorics and its Applications, N.Y. Acad. Sci. Home: 355 Leonora Dr Memphis TN 38117-2102 Office: Dept Math Scis Univ Memphis Memphis TN 38152-0001 E-mail: rschelp@memphis.edu.

SCHELSKE, CLAIRE L. limnologist, educator; b. Fayetteville, Ark., Apr. 1, 1932; s. Theodore J. and Ida S. S.; m. Betty Breukelman, June 2, 1957; children: Cynthia, John, Steven. AB, Kans. State Tchrs. Coll., Emporia, 1955, MS, 1956; PhD, U. Mich., 1961. Tchg. and rsch. asst. dept. biology Kans. State Tchrs. Coll., 1952-55, vis. instr., summer 1960; teaching fellow dept. zoology U. Mich., 1955-57; asst. prof. radiol. health dept. environ. health U. Mich. (Sch. Public Health); asst. research limnologist Gt. Lakes Research Div., Inst. Sci. and Tech., 1967-68, assoc. rsch. limnologist, 1969-71, rsch. limnologist, 1971-87; asst. dir. Gt. Lakes Research Div., Inst. Sci. and Tech. (Gt. Lakes Research Div.), 1970-72, acting dir., 1973-76, assoc. prof. limnology, dept. atmospheric and oceanic sci., 1976-87; assoc. prof. natural resources Sch. Natural Resources, 1976-86, prof., 1986-87; Carl S. Swisher prof. water resources U. Fla., Gainesville, 1987-2000, eminent scholar emeritus, 2001—. Research fellow Inst. Fisheries Research, Mich. Dept. Conservation, 1957-60; research assoc. U. Ga. Marine Inst., 1960-62; fishery biologist, supervisory fishery biologist, chief Estuarine Ecology Program, Bur. Comml. Fisheries, Radiobiol. Lab., Beaufort, N.C., 1962-66; adj. asst. prof. dept. zoology N.C. State U., Raleigh, 1964-66; tech. asst. Office Sci. and Tech., Exec. Office of Pres., Washington, 1966-67; cons. Ill. Atty. Gen., 1977-79; eminent scholar emer., 2001. Author: (with J.C. Roth) Limnological Survey of Lakes Michigan, Superior, Huron and Erie, 1973. Recipient Disting. Alumnus award Emporia State U. (formerly Kans. State Tchrs. Coll.), 1989, Edward S. Deevey Award for Outstanding Sci. Achievement, Fla. Lake Mgmt. Soc., 2000. Fellow AAAS, Am. Inst. Fishery Rsch. Biologists (regional and dist. dir. South-Cen. Gt. Lakes chpt. 1977-80); mem. Am. Soc. Limnology and Oceanography (sec. 1976-85, v.p. 1987-88, pres. 1988-90), Ecol. Soc. Am. (assoc. editor 1972-75), Internat. Assn. Gt. Lakes Rsch. (editl. bd. 1970-73, chmn. 20th Conf. 1977, assoc. editor 1984-93), Soc. Internat. Limnology (nat. rep. 1998). Home: 2738 SW 9th Dr Gainesville FL 32601-9003 Office: Dept Geol Sci Land Use and Environ Change Inst PO Box 112120 Gainesville FL 32611 E-mail: schelsk@ufl.edu.

SCHEMAN, L. RONALD, lawyer, professional society administrator; b. Aug. 9, 1931; s. Mac and Eleanor (Minkowitz) Scheman; children: Ann, Corinne, Jennifer, Daniel. BA with distinction cum laude, Dartmouth Coll., 1953; JD, Yale U., 1956. Bar: N.Y., 1956, D.C., 1979. Pvt. practice law, Hartford, Conn., 1957, N.Y.C., 1958-59; fellow Inter-Am. Cultural Conv., Brazil, 1959-61; atty. dept. legal affairs OAS, Washington, 1961-64, planning officer, 1968-70, asst. sec. gen. for mgmt., 1975-84; exec. dir. Pan Am. Devel. Found., 1964-68; pres. Porter Internat. Co., Washington, 1970-75; ptnr. Coudert Bros., 1984-85; exec. dir. Ctr. Advanced Studies of the Americas, 1985-87; ptnr. Kaplan, Russin and Vecchi, 1987-90, Heller, Rosenblatt and Scheman, 1990-93; U.S. exec. dir. Inter-Am. Devel. Bank, Washington, 1993-98; chmn. Internat. Fin. Group, Greenberg, Traurig, 1998-2000; secretariat Inter-Am. Commn. on Human Rights, 1961-64; dir. gen. Inter-Am. Agy. for Cooperation and Devel., 2000—. V.p. fin. Robert R. Nathan Assocs., 1974-75; pub. Soviet Bus. and Trade, 1973-75; dir. Vision mag., 1973-74; assoc. dir. Coun. of Ams., 1976—; adj. prof. internat. orgn. George Washington U., 1979-83. Author: Foundations of Freedom, 1966, The Inter-American Dilemma, 1988, The Alliance for Progress, A Retrospective, 1989; bd. editors Mng. Internat. Devel. quar., 1984-86; contbr. articles on internat. orgn. and inter-Am. affairs to profl. jours. Trustee Inter-Am. Bar Found., 1967-74; trustee Pan Am. Devel. Found., 1987-94, pres., 1976-83; chmn. Mus. of Americas Found., 1998—, Federal City Coun., 1998—; pres. Uruguay—U.S. C. of C., 1999-2000; mem. exec. com. Am. Jewish Com. of Washington; bd. dirs. East-West Trade Coun., 1974-75, Ctr. for Advanced Studies of the Ams., 1984-87. Decorated Order Bernardo O'Higgins (Chile), 1967, Russian Fedn., 1992. Mem. Washington Fgn. Law Soc. (bd. govs. 1965-67, pres. 1968), Am. Fgn. Law Assn. (v.p. 1971), Cosmos Club, Phi Beta Kappa. Home: 5002 50th Pl NW Washington DC 20016-4380 Office: Inter-Am Agy for Cooperation and Devel 1889 F St NW Washington DC 20006-4413

SCHEMMEL, RACHEL ANNE, food science and human nutrition educator, researcher; b. Farley, Iowa, Nov. 23, 1929; d. Frederic August and Emma Margaret (Melchert) Schemmel. BA, Clarke Coll., 1951; MS, U. Iowa, 1952; PhD, Mich. State U., 1967. Dietitian Children's Hosp. Soc., L.A., 1952-54; instr. Mich. State U., East Lansing, 1955-63, from asst. prof. to prof. food sci., human nutrition, 1967—. Author: Nutrition Physiology and Obesity, 1980; contbr. articles to profl. jours. Recipient Disting. Alumni award Mt. Mercy Coll., 1971, Borden award, 1986, Outstanding Alumni award U. Iowa, 1996, Mich. State U., 2002, Outstanding Achievement award Clarke Coll., 1997. Fellow: Am. Soc. Nutrition Scis.; mem.: Soc. for Nutrition Edn., Brit. Nutrition Soc., Am. Diet Assn. (pres. Mich. 1976—77, pres. Lansing 1960, Outstanding Dietetic Educator award 1988), Inst. Food Technologists, AAFCS (chair nutrition health and food mgmt. divsn. 1995—97, Outstanding Leader award 1998), Phi Kappa Phi (pres. 1994—95), Sigma Xi (pres. Mich. State U. chpt. 1983—84, Sr. Rsch award 1986). Roman Catholic. Home: 1341 Red Leaf Ln East Lansing MI 48823-1339 Office: Mich State U Dept Food Sci Nutrit East Lansing MI 48824 E-mail: schemmel@msu.edu.

SCHEMMER, BENJAMIN F. editor; b. Winner, S.Dak., Apr. 22, 1932; s. Clinton Henry and Minna Mathilda (Heese) S.; m. Cynthia Blythe Sweatt, Feb. 14, 1955 (dec.); 1 child, Clinton Howard; m. Lu Anne Kathryn Levens, Oct. 20, 1979. BS, U.S. Mil. Acad., 1954. Commd. 2d lt. U.S. Army, West Point, N.Y., 1954, 1st lt., 1957, various posts Inf. Sch., 2d Armored Div., 5th Inf. Div., resigned, 1957; customer liason mgr. The Boeing Co., Seattle, 1959-63, mgr. advanced systems planning Vertol div. Phila., 1963-64; dir. land force weapons systems Office Sec. of Def., Washington, 1965-67; editor Armed Forces Jour. Internat., 1968—. Cons. Dept. of Army, Washington, 1965; guest lectr. Nat. War Coll., Nat. Def. U., Washington, 1968—, Army War Coll., Carlisle Barracks, Pa., 1968—, Navy War Coll., Newport, R.I., USAF Spl. Ops. Sch., Maxwell AFB, Ala., Air War Coll., 1968—. Author: Almanac of Liberty, 1975, The Raid, 1976; contbr. articles to newspapers, mags., U.S. Naval Inst. Proceedings, others. Co-founder Col. Arthur D. Simons Scholarship Fund, Dallas, 1980; bd. visitors Def. Systems Mgmt. Coll.; bd. advisors Sch. Def. Journalism Boston U. Roman Catholic. Avocation: golf. Home: 2555 Pennsylvania Ave NW #503 Washington DC 20037

SCHEMNITZ, SANFORD DAVID, wildlife biology educator; b. Cleve., Mar. 10, 1930; s. David Arthur Schemnitz; m. Mary Margaret Newby, July 8, 1958; children: Ellen Kay, Steven, Stuart. Student, U. Wis., 1948-50; BS in Wildlife, U. Mich., 1952; MS in Wildlife, U. Fla., 1953; PhD in Wildlife, Olka. State U., 1958. Cert. wildlife biologist. Conservation aide State of Mich. Dept. Conservation, Ann Arbor, 1951-52; game research biologist State of Minn. Dept. Conservation, St. Paul, 1958-59; asst. prof. wildlife Pa. State U., University Park, 1960-61; prof. wildlife resources U. Maine, Orono, 1962-75; dept. head fish and wildlife sci. N.Mex. State U., Las Cruces, 1975-81, prof. wildlife scis., 1981—. Mem. resource adv. coun. Bur. Land Mgmt., N.Mex., 1996-99. Editor: Wildlife Management Techniques Manual, 1980; contbr. over 100 articles to profl. jours. Fulbright Prof. Council for Internat. Exchange Scholars, Kathmandu, Nepal, 1983, Kenya, 1990. Mem. Am. Soc. Mammalogists, The Wildlife Soc. (life, S.W. regional rep. 1979-80), Ecol. Soc. Am., Wilson Ornithol. Soc., N.Mex. Wildlife Fedn. (bd. dirs. 1983—), Sigma Xi. Home: 8105 Dona Ana Rd Las Cruces NM 88005-6305

SCHENCK, BENJAMIN ROBINSON, insurance consultant; b. N.Y.C., July 21, 1938; s. John T. and Harriet Buffum (Hall) S.; m. Sally V. Sullivan, Aug. 27, 1960; children: Steven T., Elizabeth F., Timothy S. BA, William Coll., Williamstown, Mass, 1960; LL.B., Harvard U., 1963. Bar: N.Y. 1964, Mass. 1978. Asst. counsel to gov. State of N.Y., Albany, 1963-66; assoc. Bond, Schoeneck & King, Syracuse, N.Y., 1966-68; dep. supt., 1st dep. sup. and supt. State of N.Y. Dept. Ins., N.Y.C., 1968-75; sr. v.p. Shearson Hayden Stone Inc., 1975-77, State Mut. Life Assurance Co. Am., 1977-86, exec. v.p., 1986-89; pres. Worcester Mut. Ins. Co., 1979-83, Cen. Mass. Health Care, Inc., Worcester, 1989-93. Home: 2400 Seabrook Island Rd Johns Island SC 29455-6505

SCHENCK, DAVID TUTTLE, elementary education educator, director; b. N.Y.C. s. Ferdinand and Anna (Tuttle) S.; m. Dorothy Hall, Oct. 4, 1952; children: David, Janet, Margaret, William. BBA, U. Mich., 1948; MEd, Emory U., 1958. Tchr. Rectory Sch., Pomfret, Conn., 1954-56, Camp Waya-Awi, Rangeley, Maine, 1954-57, Ga. Mil. Acad., Coll. Pk., 1958-59; founder, tchr., dir. The Schenck Sch., Atlanta, 1959—. Supr. pilot program adult dyslexics Schenck Sch., Atlanta, 1999—. Bd. dirs. The HAY (Hope Atlanta's Youth) Fund, 1994-99. With U.S. Army, 1942-45. Mem. Internat. Dyslexia Assn. (1st pres. Ga. br. 1990-91), Appalachian Trail Club. Democrat. Episcopalian. Avocations: hiking, painting, music. Home: 205 Ansley Villa Dr NE Atlanta GA 30324-4810 Office: The Schenck Sch 282 Mount Paran Rd NW Atlanta GA 30327-4698 Fax: 404-252-7615.

SCHENCK, JACK LEE, retired electric utility executive; b. Morgantown, W.Va., Aug. 2, 1938; s. Ernest Jacob and Virginia Belle (Kelley) S.; m. Rita Elizabeth Pietschmann, June 7, 1979; 1 son, Erik. BSE.E., BA in Social Sci., Mich. State U., 1961; MBA, NYU, 1975. Engr. AID, Tunis, Tunisia, 1961, Detroit Edison Co., 1962-63; engr., economist OECD, Paris, 1963-70; v.p. econ. policy analysis Edison Electric Inst., N.Y.C. and Washington, 1970-81; v.p., treas. Gulf States Utilities Co., Beaumont, Tex., 1981-92, sr. v.p., CFO, 1992-94. Cons. on electric utility restructuring and privatization in the former Soviet Union, 1994—. Mem. Internat. Assn. Energy Econs., Triangle Club, Eta Kappa Nu. Republican. E-mail: schenck1@aol.com.

SCHENCK, JOHN FREDERIC, physician; b. Decatur, Ind., June 7, 1939; s. John C. Schenck and Mildred Blosser; m. Jane Stark, Oct. 12, 1962 (div. 1982); children: Brooke, Kimberly, David; m. Susan J. Kalia, Oct. 8, 1994; 1 stepchild, Tania. BS in Physics, Rensselaer Poly. Inst., 1961, PhD in Physics, 1965; MD, Albany Med. Coll., 1977. Intern Albany (N.Y.) Med. Ctr. Hosp., 1977-78; staff scientist electronics lab GE, Syracuse, N.Y., 1965-73, staff mem., sr. scientist corp. R & D ctr. Schenectady, 1973—; assoc. prof. elec. engring. Syracuse U., 1970-73; mem. med. staff Ellis Hosp., Schenectady, 1981—. Adj. asst. prof. dept. radiology U. Pa., 1983-2000; chmn. Workshop on Advances in Magnetic Resonance Imaging Safety and Compatibility, McLean, Va., 1996. Contbr. articles to profl. jours; 15 patents in field of magnetic resonance imaging. Recipient S.S. Greenfield award Am. Assn. Physicists in Medicine, 1993; Nat. Merit Scholar, 1957-61; NSF fellow, 1962-63 Fellow Am. Phys. Soc.; mem. IEEE, AAAS, Internat. Soc. Magnetic Resonance in Medicine, N.Y. Acad. Scis., Sigma Xi. Home: 22 E Claremont Dr Voorheesville NY 12186-9104 Office: GE Global Rsch Bldg K1 NMR Schenectady NY 12309 E-mail: schenck@crd.ge.com.

SCHENDEL, DAN ELDON, management consultant, business educator; b. Norwalk, Wis., Mar. 29, 1934; s. Leonard A. and Marian T. (Koch) S.; m. Mary Lou Sigler, Sept. 1, 1956; children: Suzanne, Pamela, Sharon. BS in Metall. Engring., U. Wis., 1956; MBA, Ohio State U., 1959; PhD (Ford Found. fellow), Stanford U., 1963. With ALCOA, 1956, U.S. Civil Svc., 1959-60, SRI, 1963-65; prof. mgmt., dir. exec. edn. programs Purdue U., Lafayette, Ind., 1965-85; vis. prof. U. Mich., 1988-89, U. Chgo., 1990-91. Dean German Grad. Internat. Sch. Mgmt. and Adminstrn., Hannover, Germany; pres. Strat egic Mgmt. Assocs., Inc. Author: (with others) Strategy Formulation: Analytical Concepts, 1978, Divided Loyalties, 1980, Fundamental Issues in Strategy, 1994; editor: (with others) Strategic Management: A New View of Business Policy and Planning, 1979; founding editor Strategic Mgmt. Jour., 1980—. Served with USAF, 1956-59. Fellow Acad. Mgmt.; mem. Strategic Mgmt. Soc. (founding pres., exec. dir.), Lafayette Country Club, Univ. Club Chgo. Home: 1327 N Grant St West Lafayette IN 47906-2463 Office: Krannert Grad Sch Mgmt Purdue U West Lafayette IN 47907 E-mail: schendel@mgmt.purdue.edu.

SCHENDEL, STEPHEN ALFRED, plastic surgery educator, craniofacial surgeon; b. Mpls., Oct. 10, 1947; s. Alfred Reck and Jeanne Shirley (Hagquist) S.; children: Elliott, Mélisande. BA, St. Olaf Coll., Northfield, Minn., 1969; BS with high distinction, U. Minn., 1971, DDS, 1973; diplome asst. etranger with high honors, U. Nantes, France, 1980; MD, U. Hawaii, 1983. Diplomate Am. Bd. Plastic Surgery, Nat. Bd. Med. Examiners, Nat. Bd. Dental Examiners, Am. Bd. Oral and Maxillofacial Surgery (adv. com., bd. examiner 1991-95). Intern, then resident in oral and maxillofacial surgery Parkland Meml. Hosp., Dallas, 1975-79; resident in gen. surgery Baylor U. Med. Ctr., 1983-84, Stanford (Calif.) U. Med. Ctr., 1984-86, resident in plastic surgery, 1986-89, acting assoc. prof. surgery, 1989-91, assoc. prof., 1991-95, head div. plastic and reconstructive surgery, 1992—, dir. residency tng., 1992-98, chmn. dept. functional restoration, 1994—2002, prof., 1995—; head plastic surgery, dir. Craniofacial Ctr. Lucile Salter Packard Children's Hosp., Stanford, chief pediat. surgery, 1997—2002. Asst. to Dr. Paul Tessier, Paris, 1987-88; asst. dept. stomatology and maxillofacial surgery Centre Hospitalier Regional Nantes, 1979-80; mem. med. bd. Lucile Salter Packard Children's Hosp. at Stanford, 1991—. Assoc. editor Selected Readings in Oral and Maxillofacial Surgery, 1989—; mem. edtl. bd. Jour. Cranio-Maxillofacial Surgery; contbr. articles and abstracts to med. and dental jours., chpts. to books. Recipient Disting. Alumnus award St. Olaf Coll., 1993; Fulbright fellow, Nantes, 1979-80, Chateaubriand fellow Govt. of France, 1987-88. Fellow ACS, Am. Acad. Pediat.; mem. European Assn. Cranio-Maxillofacial Surgeons, Am. Soc. Pediat. Plastic Surgeons, Am. Assn. Plastic Surgeons, Soc. Baylor Surgeons (founding), Am. Cleft Palate-Craniofacial Assn., Am. Soc. Plastic and Reconstructive Surgeons (sec. 1996—), Am. Soc. Maxillofacial Surgeons (sec., pres. 2000-01), Assn. Acad. Chairmen Plastic Surgery, Zedplast (bd. dirs. 1993—), Omicron Kappa Upsilon. Avocations: fly fishing, painting and sculpture. Office: Stanford U Med Ctr NC 104 Divsn Plastic Reconstr Surg Stanford CA 94305

SCHENDEL, WILLIAM BURNETT, lawyer; b. 1948; BA, Swarthmore Coll., 1970; JD, Boston U., 1974. Bar: Alaska 1976, U.S. Dist Ct. Alaska (9th cir.), U.S. Supreme Ct. Ptnr. Schendel & Callahan, Fairbanks, Alaska, 1981—. Pres. Alaska Bar Assn. Mem. ABA, Alaska Bar Assn. (pres. 1998-99). Office: Schendel & Callahan 613 Cushman St Ste 200 Fairbanks AK 99701-4655

SCHENDEL, WINFRIED GEORGE, insurance company executive; b. June 19, 1931; came to U.S., 1952, naturalized, 1956; s. Willi Rudolf Max and Anna Margarete (Sassen) S.; m. Joanne Wiiest, Aug. 24, 1953; children: Victor Winfried, Bruce Lawrence, Rachelle Laureen. BS in Elec. and Indsl. Engring., Hannover-Stadthagen U., Hannover, Fed. Republic of Germany, 1952. Elec. draftsman Houston Lighting & Power Co., 1954-57; elec. draftsman, corrosion technician Transcontinental Gas Pipeline Co., Houston, 1957-59; elec. engr. Ken R. White Cons. Engrs., Denver, 1959-61; sales engr. Weco divsn. Food Machinery & Chem. Corp., various locations, 1961-64; ins. field underwriter N.Y. Life Ins. Co., Denver, 1964-66, asst. mgr., 1966-70, mgmt. asst., 1970-71, gen. mgr., 1971-77, mgr., 1979-85, field underwriter, 1985—; gen. agt. Woodmen Accident and Life Ins. Co., Ft. Collins, Colo., 1998—. Ind. gen. agt., Denver, 1978-79; ins. broker and adviser, 1979—. Instnl. rep., advancement chmn. Denver Area coun. Boy Scouts Am., Lakewood, Colo., 1968-72; precinct chmn. Rep. party, Jefferson County, Colo., 1976, 78; founder, life mem. Sister City Program, Lakewood, Colo.; chmn. adv. bd. ARC, Jefferson County, Colo., 1987-89; elder Presbyn. ch. Recipient Centurion award, 1966, Northwestern Region Leader Manpower Devel. award N.Y. Life Ins. Co., 1968, Salesman of Yr. award Jefferson County Salesman with a Purpose Club, 1983, Top awards ARC, 1988-89. Mem. Nat. Assn. Life Underwriters, Gen. Agts. and Mgrs. Assn. (Conf. Nat. Mgmt. award 1975), Colo. Life Underwriters Assn. (reg. v.p. Denver met. area 1989-90), Mile High Assn. Life Underwriters (pres. 1986-87, nat. com. 1988, 91), Lakewood C. of C. (pres. people-to-people, Trailblazer of Yr. award 1982, 83, Trail Boss of Yr. 1983), Lions, Edelweiss Club, Internat. Order Rocky Mountain Goats, N.Y. Life Star, Masons, Rotary (bd. dirs. Ft. Collins chpt., Paul Harris award 1995), Shriners. Home and Office: 925 Deerhurst Cir Fort Collins CO 80525-6919 Fax: (970) 206-9082.

SCHENK, QUENTIN FREDERICK, retired social work educator, mayor, psychologist; b. Fort Madison, Iowa, Aug. 25, 1922; s. Fred Edward John and Ida (Sabrowsky) S.; m. Patricia J. Kelley, Aug. 6, 1946 (div. Apr. 1970); children: Fred W. (dec. 1972), Patricia, Karl, Martha; m. Emmy Lou Willson, May 23, 1970. BA, Willamette U., 1948; MS, U. Wis., 1950, MS in Social Work, PhD, U. Wis., 1953. Lic. ind. clin. social worker, Wis.; cert. longterm care, Ariz. Asst. prof. social work U. Wis.-Madison, 1953-55, prof., chmn. extension social work, 1961-63; prof., former dean Sch. Social Welfare, Milw., 1962-68, prof. emeritus, 1990—; assoc. prof. U. Mo., 1955-61; project specialist Ford Found., 1968-71. Spl. cons. on urban mission in Africa United Presbyn. Ch., 1971— , World Council Chs., 1971— ; adviser to Haile Sellassie I U., Addis Ababa, Ethiopia, 1968-71; Alderman City of Cedarburg (Wis.), 1974-82, mayor, 1982-86 Author: (with Emmy Lou Schenk) Pulling Up Roots, 1978, Welfare Society and the Helping Professions, 1981; author sect. on Ethiopia, Welfare in Africa, 1987; contbr. articles, bulls., reports to profl. lit. Mem. Nat. Trust for Hist. Preservation, Wis. Hist. Preservation Negotiating Bd., 1975-76; chmn. bd. Guest House, Milw., 1987-89; mem. Sierra Club, Planned Parenthood, Unitarian Ch. S.E. Ariz. (v.p. 1999), ACLU, Dem. Party of Wis. Lt. USNR, 1942-46. Decorated Air medal with four gold stars, Disting. Flying Cross; recipient Presdl. citation Pres. Harry Truman, 1948. Mem. AAUP, Am. Sociol. Assn., Am. Assn. Ret. Persons, Coun. on Social Work Edn., Aircraft Owners and Pilots Assn., Nat. Audubon Soc., Nature Conservancy. Home: 3443 E Wild Rabbit Rd Hereford AZ 85615-9653 E-mail: schenk@theriver.com.

SCHENK, SUSAN KIRKPATRICK, business owner, nurse educator, consultant; b. New Richmond, Ind., Nov. 29, 1938; d. William Marcius and Frances (Kirkpatrick) Gaither; m. Richard Dee Brown, Aug. 13, 1960 (div. Feb. 1972); children: Christopher Lee, David Michael, Lisa Catherine; m. John Francis Schenk, July 24, 1975 (widowed Apr. 1995). BSN, Ind. U., 1962; postgrad., U. Del., 1973-75. RN, PHN, BCLS; cert. community coll. tchr., Calif.; cert. vocat. edn. tchr., Calif. Staff nurse, then asst. dir. nursing Bloomington (Ind.) Hosp., 1962-66; charge nurse Newark (Del.) Manor, 1967-69; charge nurse GU Union Hosp., Terre Haute, Ind., 1971-72; clin. instr. nursing Ind. State U., 1972-73; clin. instr. psychiatric nursing U. Del., Newark, 1974-75; psychiatric nursing care coord. VA Med. Ctr., Perry Point, Md., 1975-78; from nurse educator to cmty. rels. coord. Grossmont Hosp., La Mesa, Calif., 1978—91; dir. psychiat. svcs. Scripps Hosp. East County, El Cajon, 1991-97; nursing instr., adult edn. Grossmont Union H.S. Dist., La Mesa, 1996—. Tech. advisor San Diego County Bd. Supervisors, 1987; tech. cons. Remedy Home and Health Care, San Diego, 1988; expert panelist Srs. Speak Out, KPBS-TV, San Diego, 1988; guest lectr. San Diego State U., 1987. Editor: Teaching Basic Caregiver Skills, 1988; author, performer tng. videotape Basic Caregiver Skills, 1988. Mem. patient svcs. com. Nat. Multiple Sclerosis Soc., San Diego, 1986-89; bd. dirs. Assn. for Quality and Participation, 1989. Adminstrn. on Aging/DHHS grantee, 1988. Mem. Ind. U. Alumni Assn. (life), Calif. Coun. Adult Edn., Mensa, Sigma Theta Tau. Avocations: piano, gardening, reading. Home and Office: 9435D Carlton Oaks Dr Santee CA 92071-2582 E-mail: suesks@earthlink.net.

SCHENKEL, SUSAN, psychologist, educator, author; b. Wroclaw, Poland, Apr. 21, 1946; came to U.S., 1949; d. Leon and Siddi (Fiedleholz) S.; m. Alvin Helfeld, Apr. 8, 1984. BA, U. Wis., 1967; MA in Clin. Psychology, SUNY, Buffalo, 1970, PhD in Clin. Psychology, 1973. Lic. psychologist, Mass. Psychologist Fitchburg (Mass.) State Coll., 1972-75, instr. in psychology, 1973-74; staff psychologist div. of alcoholism Boston City Hosp., 1975-76; chief psychologist Cambridge (Mass.) Ct. Clinic, 1976-80; instr. in psychology dept. psychiatry Med. Sch. Harvard U., 1976-80; pvt. practice psychology Cambridge, 1976—; instr. in psychology U. Mass., Boston, 1978. Speaker in field. Author: Giving Away Success, 1984, German edit., 1986, Brazilian edit., 1988, rev. edit. 1991, Chinese edit., 1991; contbr. articles to profl. jours. USPHS fellow, 1967-70; N.Y. State Regents scholar, 1968-70; SUNY Rsch. Found. grantee, 1971-72. Mem. Am. Psychol. Assn., Mass. Psychol. Assn., Am. Soc. Tng. and Devel., Assn. for Advancement of Behavior Therapy.

SCHENKEL, SUZANNE CHANCE, retired natural resource specialist; b. Phila., Mar. 12, 1940; d. Henry Martyn Chance II and Suzanne (Sharpless) Jameson; m. John Lackland Hardinge Schenkel, June 15, 1963; children: John Jr., Andrew Chance. BS in Edn., Tufts U., 1962. Tchr. Roland Pk. Country Sch., Balt., 1962-65; exec. dir. Mass. Citizens' Com. for Dental Health, Springfield, 1981-83; pub., editor Women's Investment Newsletter, Longmeadow, Mass., 1985-89; pub. affairs officer USDA's Soil Conservation Svc., Amherst, 1990-93; resource conservationist conservation & ecosys. assistance divsn. USDA's Natural Resources Conservation Svc., Washington, 1993-97; ops. partnership liaison East Regional Office, Beltsville, Md., 1997—2002; ret., 2002. Staff Merchant Marine and Fisheries com. U.S. Ho. of Reps., Washington, 1993. Author Wetlands Protection and Management Act. Chmn. Longmeadow (Mass.) Conservation Commn., 1984-90; supr. Hampden County (Mass.) Conservation Dist., 1985-90; bd. dirs., v.p. League of Women Voters of Mass., Boston, 1974-85; exec. com. Water Supply Citizens' Adv. Com.; adv. bd. Water Resources Authority, Mass., 1979-90; bd. dirs. Alliance for Chesapeake Bay, 2001. Mem. Soil and Water Conservation Soc., Nat. Assn. Conservation Dists. Episcopalian. Avocations: golf, tennis, sailing. Home: 3519 Sherwood Blvd Delray Beach FL 33445 E-mail: suzanneschenkel@yahoo.com.

SCHENKEN, JERALD RUDOLPH, pathologist, educator; b. Detroit, Oct. 11, 1933; s. John Rudolph and Lucile (Jerald) S.; m. Charlotte Elizabeth Sutherland Parker, Aug. 8, 1959; children— John Rudolph II, Elizabeth Jerald Gray, Thomas Parker. B.A., Tulane U., 1954, M.D., 1958. Diplomate Am. Bd. Pathology, Spl. Comp. in Clin. Chemistry. Resident in pathology Charity Hosp., New Orleans, 1959-63, assoc. pathologist, 1963-65; pathologist Methodist and Children's Hosp., Omaha, 1965-74, dir. dept., 1974-88; pres. Pathology Ctr., P.C., Omaha, 1981— ; instr. Tulane U. Med. Sch., 1962-65; instr. U. Nebr. Coll. Medicine, 1965-67, asst. prof., 1967-72, assoc. prof., 1972-75, mem. grad. faculty, 1975— , clin. prof. pathology, 1975— ; clin. prof. pathology Creighton U. Sch. Medicine, Omaha, 1978— ; pres. Am. Bd. Pathology, 1983-84. Editor (with J.B. Fuller) Instrumentation Workshop Manual, 1967; (with others) Laboratory Instrumentation, 1980; Clinical Pathology Case Studies, 3d edit., 1975. Contbr. articles to profl. jours. Mem. Nebr. State Nursing Home Adv. Council, 1982-83; bd. dirs. Nebr. Meth. Hosp. Found., 1983— ; mem. pres.'s adv. council U. Nebr., 1984— ; vice-chmn. com. White House Conf. on Aging, 1981; mem. adv. com. Office of Tech. Assessment, 1984— ; candidate for Republican Congress, 1988; chmn. Nebr. Republican Party, 1991-95. Fellow Am. Soc. Clin. Pathologists, Coll. Am. Pathologists; mem. AMA (trustee 1985-94), Coll. Am. Pathologists (Pathologist of Yr. 1983, nat. legis. com. 1971-80, chmn. 1972-80), Am. Soc. Clin. Pathologists (chmn. council clin. chemistry 1969-71, commn. edn. 1982—), Nebr. Assn. Pathologists (pres. 1971-72), Met. Omaha Med. Soc. (exec. bd. 1982—, pres. 1987), Nebr. Med. Assn., AMA (vice-chmn. council legis. 1982-84, chmn. 1984-85), Am. Soc. Cytology, Internat. Acad. Pathology, Internat. Life Scis. Inst., Soc. Pediatric Pathology, Nebr. Assn. Commerce and Industry (bd. dirs. 1986-92), Omaha C. of C. (bd. dirs. 1982-85, v.p. govt. relations 1986-92), Alpha Omega Alpha. Republican. Episcopalian. Avocations: tennis; golf. Home: Omaha, Nebr. Died Dec. 14, 2001.

SCHENKER, ERIC, university dean, economist; b. Vienna, Austria, Feb. 24, 1931; came to U.S., 1939, naturalized, 1945; s. Adolph and Olga (Strauss) S.; m. Virginia Martha Wick, Apr. 14, 1963; children: David, Richard, Robert. BBA, CCNY, 1952; MS, U. Tenn., 1955; PhD, U. Fla., 1957. Asst. prof. Mich. State U., 1957-59; mem. faculty U. Wis.-Milw., 1959—, prof. econs., 1965—; dean U. Wis.-Milw. (Sch. Bus. Adminstrn.), 1976—, dean, prof. emeritus, 1997—; dir. Urban Research Center, 1974-76; assoc. dir. Center Great Lakes Studies, 1967-74, sr. scientist, 1974—; assoc. dean Coll. Letters and Scis., 1963-69. Bd. dirs. Am. Med. Bldgs., Ampco Metal, Pressed Steel; cons. in field. Author: The Port of Milwaukee: An Economic Review, 1967; co-author: Port Planning and Development as Related to Problems of U.S. Ports and the U.S. Coastal Environment, 1974, The Great Lakes Transportation System, 1976, Port Development in the United States, 1976, Maritime Labor Organizations on the Great Lakes-St. Lawrence Seaway System, 1978, Great Lakes Transportation System in the 80s, 1986; also monographs and articles. Sr. mem. Milw. Bd. Harbor Commrs., 1960-72, chmn., 1965-68; chmn. panel on future port requirements of U.S., Maritime Transp. Research Bd., Nat. Acad. Scis., 1973-76, chmn. panel on reducing tankbarge pollution, 1980-81; mem. pilotage adv. bd. to U.S. sec. transp., 1972-75; trustee Mt. Sinai Med. Ctr, 1984-88; mem. Econ. Progress Authority of Milw. Met. Sewerage Dist., 1983-88, Marine Bd., NAS, 1982-83, Gov.'s Coun. on Econ. Issues, 1983—. Served with AUS, 1952-54. Mem. Am. Econs. Assn., So. Econs. Assn., Phi Kappa Phi, Alpha Kappa Psi, Beta Gamma Sigma, Beta Alpha Psi. Home: 6792 N Melissa Ct Glendale WI 53209-3473 E-mail: esconinc@aol.com, Schenker@uwm.edu.

SCHENKER, LEO, retired utility company executive; b. Vienna, Austria, Jan. 3, 1922; came to U.S., 1952, naturalized, 1959; s. Max and Selda Lea (Podhorcer) S.; m. Alda R. Tinson, Jan. 20, 1949; children: Michael Gregory, Deborah Anne. BS with first class honors, U. London, 1942; MA in Sci. (Can. Inst. Steel Constrn. fellow), U. Toronto, 1950; PhD, U. Mich., 1954. Mng. dir. METAG Ltd., London, 1945-48; asst. rsch. engr. Hydro-Electric Power Commn. of Ont. (Can.), Toronto, 1948-52; rsch. assoc. U. Mich., Ann Arbor, 1952-54; with Bell Telephone Labs., 1954-87, various positions, dir. mil. electronic tech., 1968-71; dir. Loop Maintenance Systems Lab., 1971-80, exec. dir. Central Office Ops. div., 1980-83, exec. dir. network system planning div., 1983-84, exec. dir. tech. info. div., 1984-87. Adj. prof. electrical engring. Cooper Union, N.Y.C. Patentee communications tech. field. Served with RAF, 1942-45. Recipient Duggan medal Can. Inst. Steel Constrn., 1950 Fellow IEEE, Sigma Xi, Phi Kappa Phi. E-mail: lschen6161@aol.com.

SCHENKER, MARC BENET, preventive medicine educator; b. L.A., Aug. 25, 1947; s. Steve and Dosella Schenker; m. Heath Massey; children: Yael, Phoebe, Hilary. BA, U. Calif., Berkeley, 1969; MD, U. Calif., San Francisco, 1973; MPH, Harvard U., Boston, 1980. Instr. medicine Harvard U., Boston, 1980-82; asst. prof. medicine U. Calif., Davis, 1982-86, assoc. prof., 1986-92, prof., 1992—, chmn. dept. epidemiology and preventive medicine, 1995—. Fellow ACP; mem. Am. Thoracic Soc., Am. Pub. Health Assn., Soc. Epidemiologic Rsch., Am. Coll. Epidemiology, Soc. Occupl. Environ. Health, Internat. Commn. Occupl. Health, Assn. Tchrs. Preventive Medicine, Phi Beta Kappa, Alpha Omega Alpha. Office: Dept Epidemiology and Preventive Medicine TB 168 One Shields Ave Davis CA 95616-8638

SCHENKER, STEVEN, physician, educator; b. Poland, Oct. 5, 1929; came to U.S., 1943, naturalized, 1946; s. Alfred and Ernestyna S.; m. Sally Ann Wood, May 11, 1956; children: Julie C. Schenker Burn, Steven A., David S., Andrew G., Jennifer E. Schenker Campeggi; m. Jo Ann Neumann, Nov. 24, 1985. BA, Cornell U., 1951, MD, 1955. Intern Harvard Service-Boston City Hosp., 1955-56, resident in medicine, 1956-58; asst. prof. medicine U. Cin. Sch. Medicine, 1961-63; asst. prof. U. Tex., Southwestern Sch. Medicine, 1963-67, assoc. prof. medicine, 1967-70; prof. medicine, biochemistry, dir. div. gastroenterology Vanderbilt U. Sch. Medicine, Nashville VA Hosp., 1970-82; prof. medicine and pharmacology U. Tex. Sch. Medicine, San Antonio, 1982—, div. divsn. gastroenteroloty, 1982—2001. Chmn. study sect. Nat. Inst. on Alcohol Abuse and Addiction, 1980-83; chmn. study sects. VA, 1985-88. Editor: Hepatology, 1985-90. Contbr. numerous articles in field to profl. jours. Recipient Markle award, 1963; Career Devel. award NIH, 1968; Jurzykowski Found. for Research in Medicine award, 1979, Alcoholism Research Soc. award 1987. Mem. Am. Assn. for Study of Liver Diseases (pres. 1980, Disting. Svc. award 1997), Am. Soc. Clin. Investigation, Assn. Am. Physicians, Am. Gastroent. Soc., Am. Soc. Pharm. and Exptl. Therapeutics, Am. Soc. Clin. Nutrition, Internat. Soc. for Study of Liver Diseases, Alpha Omega Alpha. Home: 26025 Mesa Oak Dr San Antonio TX 78255-3533 Office: U Tex Med Sch San Antonio TX 78284 E-mail: schenkersj@aol.com.

SCHENKKAN, ROBERT FREDERIC, writer, actor; b. Chapel Hill, N.C., Mar. 19, 1953; s. Robert Frederic Sr. and Jean (McKenzie) S.; children: Sarah Victoria, Joshua McHenry. BA in Theatre Arts, U. Tex., 1975; MFA in Acting, Cornell U., 1977. Author: (plays) Final Passages, 1981, The Survivalist, 1982 (best of the fringe award Edinburgh Festival 1984), Tachinoki, 1987, Tall Tales, 1988 (Playwrights Forum award 1988, Best One Act Plays 1993), Heaven on Earth, 1989 (Julie Harris Playwright award Beverly Hills Theatre Guild 1989), The Kentucky Cycle, 1991 (Pulitzer prize for drama 1992, L.A. Drama Critics Circle Best Play award 1992, Penn Ctr. West award 1993, Best Play Tony award nominee 1993, Best Play Drama Desk award nominee 1993), Conversations with the Spanish Lady and Other One-Act Plays, 1993, The Dream Thief, 1998, Handler, 1999, The Marriage of Miss Hollywood and King Neptune, 2002, The Devil and Daniel Webster, 2002, (films) Crazy Horse, 1996, The Quiet American, 2002. Grantee Vogelstein Found., 1982, Arthur Found., 1988, Fund for New Am. Plays grantee 1990, Calif. Arts Coun. grantee, 1991. Mem. Writers Guild, Dramatists Guild, Actors Equity, SAG, Ensemble Studio Theatre.

SCHENKLER, BERNARD, lawyer; b. Trani, Italy, Aug. 25, 1948; s. Wolf and Nettie Schenkler; m. Ellen Haberman, Sept. 25, 1977; children: Alan, Sarah. BA, U. Pa., 1970; JD, Columbia U., 1973; diploma in mcpl. law, Rutgers U., 1991. Bar: N.Y. 1974, N.J. 1977, D.C. 1979, U.S. Ct. Appeals (2d cir.) 1975, U.S. Dist. Ct. (so. and ea. dists.) N.Y. 1975, U.S. Tax Ct. 1978, U.S. Ct. Mil. Appeals 1978, U.S. Ct. Appeals (3rd cir.), U.S. Dist. Ct. (no. and we. dists.) N.Y. 1980, U.S. Ct. Claims 1985, U.S. Ct. Internat. Trade 1985, U.S. Ct. Appeals (fed. cir.) 1990, U.S. Ct. Appeals (D.C. cir.) 1990, U.S. Ct. Appeals (4th cir.) 1991, U.S. Ct. Vets. Appeals 1990, U.S. Supreme Ct. 1980. Atty bus. law unit N.Y.C. Human Resources Adminstrn., 1973-76, exec. asst. to gen. counsel, 1977; assoc. Ravin, Sarasohn, Cook, Baumgarten & Fisch, West Orange, N.J., 1978-85; ptnr. Ravin, Sarasohn, Cook, Baumgarten, Fisch & Rosen, Roseland, 1986-2000; of counsel Orloff, Lowenbach, Stifelman & Siegal, P.A., 2000—. Author: Bankruptcy Aspects of Municipal Real Estate Taxation, 1991, Death and Bankruptcy, How the Probate and Bankruptcy Processes Interact, 1994, Close Encounters With the Bankruptcy Code, 1997. Mem. Randolph Twp. (N.J.) Bd. of Ethics, 1978-80. Mem. ABA, N.Y. State Bar Assn., N.J. State Bar Assn., Supreme Ct. N.J. (mem. dist. ethics com. Essex County 2001—), Essex County Bar Assn., D.C. Bar. Clubs: White Meadow Temple Men's Club (Rockaway, N.J.). Jewish. Avocations: karate (black belt), golf, astronomy. Office: Orloff Lowenbach Stifelman & Siegal PA 101 Eisenhower Pkwy Ste 29 Roseland NJ 07068-1082 E-mail: bs@olss.com.

SCHENKMAN, JOHN BORIS, pharmacologist, educator; b. N.Y.C., Feb. 10, 1936; s. Abraham and Theresa (Moses) S.; m. Deanna Owen, June 5, 1960; children: Jeffrey Alan, Laura Ruth. BA in Chemistry, Bklyn. Coll., 1960; PhD in Biochemistry, SUNY Upstate Med. Ctr., Syracuse, 1964. Postdoctoral fellow U. Pa. Johnson Found., Phila., 1964-67, Inst. Protein Research Osaka U., Japan, 1967-68, Inst. Toxicology Tübingen U., Germany, 1968; asst. prof. Yale U. Sch. Medicine, New Haven, 1968-71, assoc. prof., 1971-78; prof. pharmacology U. Conn. Health Ctr., Farmington, 1978-2000, head dept., 1978-87; dir. grad. program cellular and molecular pharmacology U. Conn., 1995-99, prof. emeritus, 2000—. Assoc. editor Drug Metabolism and Drug Interactions, 1988—, Xenobiotica, 1990—; mem. editl. bds.; contbr. articles to profl. jours. Served as sgt. U.S. Army, 1953-55. Research grantee NIH, NSF; recipient Research Career Devel award NIH, 1971-76. Mem. Am. Soc. Biochemists and Molecular Biologists, AM. Soc. Pharmacology Exptl. Therapeutics, Am. Med. Sch. Pharmacologists (councilor 1987-88). Jewish. Avocations: fishing, botany, wine making. Office: U Conn Sch Medicine Dept Pharm Farmington CT 06030-0001

SCHENTAG, JEROME JOHN, pharmacy educator; b. St. Clair, Mich., Jan. 25, 1950; s. John and Rose Schentag; m. Rita R. Sloan, June 26, 1976; 1 child, Annie. BS in Pharmacy, U. Nebr., 1973; D. Pharmacy, Phila. Coll. Pharmacy, 1975. Postdoctoral fellow SUNY, Buffalo, 1975-76, asst. prof. of pharmacy, 1976-81, assoc. prof., 1981-86, prof., 1986-2000. Dir. Clin. Pharmacokinetics Lab., Millard Fillmore Hosp., Buffalo. Editor: Applied Pharmacokinetics, 1981, 3d edit., 1992; contbr. articles to profl. jours. Am. Coll. Clin. Pharmacy fellow, 1985; recipient Disting. Young Alumni award Phila. Coll. of Pharmacy, 1989. Fellow Am. Assn. Pharm. Scientists; mem. Am. Soc. Microbiology. Office: U Buffalo Sch Pharms 543 Hochstetter Hall Buffalo NY 14260 E-mail: Schentag@Buffalo.edu.

SCHEPPS, VICTORIA HAYWARD, lawyer; b. Brockton, Mass., June 11, 1956; d. William George and Lucy Victoria (Mitcheroney) Hayward; m. Frank Schepps, Sept. 18, 1982; children: Frank IV, Lucia. BA, Suffolk U., 1977; JD, U. San Diego, 1981. Instr., Northeastern U., Boston, 1981-83; assoc. Hoffman & Hoffman, Boston, 1983-85, Mark J. Gladstone, P.C., 1985-87; Doktor, Hirschberg & Schepps, 1987-88, Schepps & Reilly, 1988-90; pvt. practice Law Office of Victoria Hayward Schepps, Stoughton, Mass., 1990—. Mem. Mass. Conveyancing Assn., Mass. Assn. Bank Counsel, Inc. Democrat. Roman Catholic. Office: 6 Cabot Pl Ste 9 Stoughton MA 02072-4625

SCHER, DAVID LEE, cardiac electrophysiologist; b. Freeport, N.Y., Jan. 8, 1957; s. Marlene S.; m. Ronni Michelle Frosch; children: Matthew, Jonathan, Carly. AB, Washington U., 1977; MD, U. Bologna, Italy, 1984. Diplomate Am. Bd. Internal Medicine, Am. Bd. Cardiovascular Diseases, Am. Bd. Cardiac Electrophysiology. Intern internal medicine Maimonides Med. Ctr., Bklyn., 1984-85, resident internal medicine, 1985-87, chief med. resident, 1987-88; cardiology fellow Phila. Heart Inst., 1988-90, cardiac electrophysiology fellow, 1990-91; dir. cardiac electrophysiology Polyclinic Medical Ctr., Harrisburg, Pa., 1991-99, Pinnacle Health Hosps., Harrisburg, 1999—. Clin. asst. instr. medicine SUNY Health Scis. Ctr. at Bklyn., 1987-88; clin. fellow in medicine U. Pa. Sch. Medicine, 1990-91; clin. asst. prof. medicine Pa. State U., 1991-98, clin. assoc. prof., 1998—. Author: (book chpt.) Current Management of Arrhythmias, 1991; contbr. articles to profl. jours. Named Outstanding Med. resident Maimonides Med. Ctr., 1986, 87. Fellow Am. Coll. Physicians, Am. Coll. Cardiology, Am. Coll. Chest Physicians; mem. North Am. Soc. Pacing and Electrophysiology, Am. Heart Assn. Avocations: golf, writing. Office: Associated Cardiologists PC 2808 Old Post Rd Harrisburg PA 17110

SCHER, HOWARD DENNIS, lawyer; b. Ft. Monmouth, N.J., Apr. 23, 1945; s. George Scher and Rita (Eitches) Zar; children: Seth Micah, Eli David. BA, Brandeis U., 1967; JD, Rutgers U., 1971. Bar: Pa. 1971, U.S. Dist. Ct. (ea. dist.) Pa. 1971, U.S. Ct. Appeals (3rd cir.) 1971, U.S. Supreme Ct. 1975. Asst. city solicitor City of Phila., 1971-73; assoc. Goodis, Greenfield, Henry & Edelstein, Phila., 1973-77, Montgomery, McCracken, Walker & Rhoads, Phila., 1977-80, ptnr., 1980-2001; shareholder Buchanan Ingersoll P.C., 2001—. Trustee Fedn. of Jewish Agys. of Greater Phila., 1994—; dir. Akiba Hebrew Acad., Merion, Pa., 1996-98; mem. pres.'s coun. Brandeis U.; chair Jewish Employment and Vocat. Svcs., 1998-02; chmn. com. Com. of Seventy, 2002. Fellow Am. Coll. Trial Lawyers, Internat. Acad. Trial Lawyers; mem. ABA, Pa. Bar Assn. (ho. of dels., chmn. fed. cts. com. 2001-02), Phila. Bar Assn., Brandeis U. Alumni Assn. (v.p. 1983-87). Home: 2222 Locust St Philadelphia PA 19103-5511 Office: Buchanan Ingersoll PC 11 Penn Ctr Ste 14th Fl 1835 Market St Philadelphia PA 19103 Fax: 215-665-8760. E-mail: scherhd@bipc.com.

SCHER, IRVING, lawyer; b. N.Y.C., July 22, 1933; s. Charles and Tillie (Ballenberg) S.; m. Amy Lynn Katz, June 8, 1985; 1 child, Sara Katz-Scher. BA, City Coll. N.Y., 1955; JD, Columbia U., 1962. Bar: N.Y. 1963. Assoc. Weil, Gotshal & Manges, N.Y.C., 1962-69, ptnr., 1969—. Adj. prof. NYU Sch. Law, 1972—; co-chmn. ann. anti-trust law inst. Practicing Law Inst., N.Y.C., 1976—; adv. bd. Antitrust and Trade Regulation Reports, 1980—. Author: Living With the Robinson-Patman Act, 2002; editor: Columbia Law Rev., 1960—61; revs. editor: , 1961—62, editor, co-author: Antitrust Advisor, 4th edit., 2001, editor, co-author: Antitrust Advisor, supplement, 2001; contbr. ; author: Living with the Robinson-Patman Act, 2001. Served as lt. USNR, 1955-59. Recipient Nat. Scholarship award, Columbia Law Sch., 1961—62; scholar Harlan Fiske Stone scholar, 1960—62, Gluck scholar, 1960—61. Mem.: ABA (chmn. antitrust law sect. 1988—89), N.Y. State Bar Assn. (chmn. antitrust law sect. 1980—81, Lifetime Achievement award 1998). Office: Weil Gotshal & Manges 767 5th Ave Fl Concl New York NY 10153-0119 E-mail: Irving.scher@weil.com.

SCHER, JORDAN MAYER, physician, psychiatrist, drug abuse specialist; b. Balt. s. Robert Samuel and Marye Kremen Scher; m. Jeanne Nonken, July 20, 1957 (div. June 1960); children: Jan. Jo, Jill, Gabhriel. BS, Wesleyan U., 1945; MD, U. Md., 1949; PhD, Neuropsychopharmacology, Northwestern U., 1957. Diplomate Am. Bd. Psychiatry and Neurology, Am. Bd. Med. Hypnosis, lic. physician Calif., N.Y., Md., Ill., Mich., Israel, cert. addiction specialist Am. Acad. Health Care Providers in Addiction Disorders. Resident and fellow in psychiatry U. Md. Psychiat. Inst., Balt., 1953—55; fellow in psychiatry NIMH, Bethesda; fellow in medicine, hypertension studies Cleve. Clinic Found.; rsch. psychiatrist NIMH, 1955-57; dir. narcotics project Cook County (Ill.) Jail and Criminal Ct., 1957—59; coor. undergrad. psychiatry Northwestern U. Med. Sch., 1957—60; pvt. practice psychiatry Chgo., 1957—79; cons.

Sheriff's Office and Cook County Jail, 1958—63; from asst. to assoc. prof. dept. neurology and psychiatry Northwestern U. Med. Sch., Chgo., 1960—63; dir. Chgo. Psychiat. Found. and Ontoanalytic Inst., 1960—70; prof. dept. neurology and psychiatry Northwestern U., 1963—65; dir. psychiat. svcs. Bd. of Health, 1963—65; exec. dir. Nat. Coun. Drug Abuse, Chgo., 1971—79; dir. sct. on psychiatry and religion Yeshiva Torat Israel, Jerusalem, 1972—74; exec. dir. Methadone Maintenance Inst., Chgo., 1972—79; advisor acupuncture Nat. Inst. Acupuncture and Herbal Medicine, Taiwan, 1974—; psychiatrist cons. Diaspora Yeshiva, Jerusalem, 1980—; pvt. practice psychiatry, 1982—. Vis. prof. Hebrew U., 1982-89; cons. psychiatry, Israel and numerous orgns.; rschr. in field; dir. Jerusalem Inst. Drug Abuse, 1980-85, Jerusalem House, Israel, 1989—; dir. drug abuse unit Ezrat Nashim; advisor on drugs and alcohol Min. of Health, Israel; commn. on addiction, chmn. Adult Subcom. on Drug Abuse, City of Jerusalem. Author: Narcotic Detoxification as Acute Induced Panic Disorder: Neuropsychopharmacological Causes, Treatment, and Implications, A Monograph, 1992, (with L. Appleby, J. Cumming) Chronic Schizophrenia, 1959, Theories of the Mind, 1963, Drug Abuse in Industry: Growing Corporate Dilemma, 1973; co-editor: (with M. Segal): Drugs and the Law, vol. 1, Perspectives in Drug Abuse, 1989; founder, editor The Jour. Existential Psychiatry, 1959-70; cons. Am. Psychiat. Assn. Jour., 1963-70, Jour. AMA, 1964-71; mem. editl. bd. Psychosomatics Jour., 1965-67, Human Context Jour., 1970-72, Medica Judaica Jour., 1971-72; editor, founder Nat. Coun. Drug Abuse Drug/Health Alert, 1972-79; co-editor: Perspectives in Drug Abuse, 1989; contbr. numerous articles to profl. jours.; patentee in field. Lt. USNR, 1949-57. Recipient Key to City of St. Louis, 1969, Wisdom award of honor, Wisdom Soc., 1972, Pawlowski Peace prize, 1974, Physician's Recognition award, AMA, 1975—99, DeQuincey prize in addiction rsch., 1993. Fellow AAAS, Royal Soc. Medicine, Am. Acad. Psychosomatic Medicine (program com.), World Med. Assn. (hon., U.S. com.), Comprehensive Medicine Assn., Am. Assn. Clin. and Exptl. Hypnosis, Nat. Acad. Religion and Mental Health, Am. Geriatric Soc., N.Y. Acad. Scis.; mem. AMA (cert. of merit for 50 yrs. dedicated svc. to med. profession 2002), Am. Coll. Forensic Psychiatry, Am. Acad. Psychiatry and Law, Am. Acad. Psychiatry in Alcohol and Drug Abuse, Am. Soc. Neuroimaging, Am. Soc. Addiction Medicine, Am. Soc. Addiction Psychiatry, Am. Ontoanalytic Assn. for Existential Psychiatry (founder), Am. Soc. Psychoanalytic Physicians, Inc., Am. Med. Soc. Alcoholism, Am. Acad. Orthomolecular Psychiatry, Am. Med. Record Assn., Am. Soc. Group Psychotherapy and Psychodrama, Chgo. Soc. Assn. Execs., Ill. Rehab. Assn., Nat. Rehab. Assn., Nat. Coun. Crime and Delinquency, Chgo. Assn. Commerce and Industry, Assn. Advancement of Psychotherapy, Am. Soc. Group Psychotherapy and Psychodrama, Am. Assn. Psychoanalytic Physicians, Assn. Advancement of Psychotherapy, Internat. Soc. Med. Hypnosis, Internat. Assn. Group Psychotherapy, Am. Psychiat. Assn., Am. Ontoanalytic Assn., Internat. Ontoanalytic Assn., Vienna Med. Psychol. Soc. (hon.), Assn. Am. Med. Colls., Am. Acad. Neurology, Washington Psychiat. Soc., Am. Humanistic Psychology Assn., Am. Acad. Psychotherapists, Am. Soc. Psychoanalytic Medicine, Am. Group Psychotherapy Assn., Psychosynthesis Rsch. Found., Soc. Advancement of Gen. Systems Theory, Soc. Sci. Study of Sex, Human Ecology Found., Soc. Biol. Psychiatry, Am. Soc. Photobiology, Ill. Med. Soc., Sigma Xi, Phi Delta Epsilon. Jewish. Avocations: Biblical/Jewish-Christian studies, archaeology, cosmology, paleoanthropological studies on the origin and evolution of human mind and communication.

SCHER, KAREN MARIA, illustrator, multimedia specialist, systems engineer; b. Summit, N.J., June 20, 1963; d. Anthony Carmen and Phyllis (Bursese) Dirienzo; m. David Brian Scher, May 15, 1993; children: Samuel Jude, Anya Marie. BA summa cum laude, Fairleigh Dickinson U., 1995. Silk screen designer Continental Screen Printing, N.Y.C., 1984; freelance illustrator, 1984—; graphic artist Bellcore, Piscataway, N.J., 1984-85; with NY Life Ins. Co., Lebanon; programmer Prudential-Bache Securities, Edison, 1987-88; info. ctr. cons. Supermarkets Gen. Corp., Woodbridge, 1988-90; programmer, ops. analyst Bell Atlantic, Madison, 1990-93, 1990-93, multimedia specialist, tech. staff, 1993-97; sys. engr. NCR-Internet Solutions, Iselin, N.J., 1997-99, Telcordia Technologies, Piscataway, 1999—, Internat. Internet Solutions, 2000—. Facilitator, author course Intro. to Internet and Mosaic, 1994. Recipient Don Bitger Ednl. Tech. award Bell Atlantic Ctr. for Networked Multimedia, 1994. Mem. Soc. for Applied Learning Tech., Phi Zeta Kappa. Office: Telcordia Technologies 444 Hoes Ln Piscataway NJ 08854-4104

SCHER, MONICA MARCIA See VETTEL, NIKI MARCIA

SCHER, ROBERT SANDER, instrument design company executive; b. Cin., May 24, 1934; m. Audrey Erna Gordon, Oct. 21, 1961; children: Sarahh, Alexander, Aaron. SB, MIT, 1956, SM, 1958, Diploma in Mech. Engring., 1960, ScD, 1963. Rsch. and teaching asst. MIT, Cambridge, Mass., 1957-62; control system engr. RCA, Hightstown, N.J., 1963-65; engring. mgr. Sequential Info. System, Elmsford, N.Y., 1965-71; tech. dir. Teledyne Gurley, Troy, 1971-78, v.p. engring., 1978-86, pres., 1986-92, Encoder Design Assocs., Clifton Park, 1993—. Co-author patent Linear Digital Readout, 1975. Mem. ASME, Optical Soc. Am. Jewish. Avocation: chamber music. Home: 2 Laurel Oak Ln Clifton Park NY 12065-4712 E-mail: bobscher@nycap.rr.com.

SCHER, STEVEN PAUL, literature educator, educator; b. Budapest, Hungary, Mar. 2, 1936; came to U.S., 1957, naturalized, 1963; Diploma in piano, Bela Bartok Conservatory of Music, Budapest, 1955; BA cum laude, Yale U., 1960, MA, 1963, PhD, 1966. Instr. German, Columbia U., N.Y.C., 1965-67; asst. prof. German, Yale U., New Haven, 1967-70, assoc. prof., 1970-74; prof. German and comparative lit. Dartmouth Coll., Hanover, N.H., 1974—, chmn. dept., 1974-80, 93-96, acting chmn. dept., 1982-83, Ted and Helen Geisel 3d Century prof. humanities, 1984-89, Daniel Webster prof. German and comparative lit., 2000—. Vis. prof. U. Paderborn, Fed. Republic Germany, summer 1980, Karl-Franzens-U. Graz, Austria, summer 1984; grant reviewer Guggenheim Found., NEH, Am. Council Learned Socs., others; cons. univ. presses and scholarly jours.; lectr. throughout world Author: Verbal Music in German Literature, 1968; editor: (with Charles McClelland) Postwar German Culture: An Anthology, 1974, 2d edit., 1980, Interpretationen: Zu E.T.A. Hoffmann, 1981, (with Ulrich Weisstein) Literature and the Other Arts. Proc. of IXth Congress of Internat. Comparative Lit. Assn., Innsbruck, vol. 3, 1981, Literatur und Musik. Ein Handbuch zur Theorie und Praxis eines komparatistischen Grenzgebietes, 1984, Music and Text: Critical Inquiries, 1992 (with Walter Bernhart and Werner Wolf) Word and Music Studies: Defining the Field, 1999; contbr. articles and essays to scholarly jours. Morse fellow, 1969-70; Humboldt fellow, 1972-73; Yale Coll. scholar, 1957-60, grad. fellow, 1960-62; DAAD grantee U. Munich, 1964-65 Mem. MLA (chmn. bibliography com. of div. lit. 1972-86), Am. Comparative Lit. Assn., Internat. Comparative Lit. Assn., Internat. P.E.N. Club Home: 6084 Dartmouth Hall Hanover NH 03755-3511 Office: Dartmouth College Dept German Studies 6084 Dartmouth Hall Hanover NH 03755-3511 E-mail: steven.p.scher@dartmouth.edu.

SCHERAGA, HAROLD ABRAHAM, physical chemistry educator; b. Bklyn., Oct. 18, 1921; s. Samuel and Etta (Goldberg) S.; m. Miriam Kurnow, June 20, 1943; children: Judith Anne, Deborah Ruth, Daniel Michael. BS, CCNY, 1941; A.M., Duke U., 1942, PhD, 1946, Sc.D. (hon.), 1961, U. Rochester, 1988, U. San Luis, 1992, Technion, 1993. Teaching, research asst. Duke U., 1941-46; fellow Harvard Med. Sch., 1946-47; instr. chemistry Cornell U., 1947-50, asst. prof., 1950-53, assoc. prof., 1953-58, prof., 1958-65, Todd prof. chemistry, 1965-92, Todd prof. chemistry emeritus, 1992—, chmn. dept., 1960-67. Vis. assoc. biochemist Brookhaven Nat. Lab., summers 1950, 51, cons. biology dept., 1950-56; vis. lectr. div. protein chemistry Wool Rsch. Labs., Melbourne, Australia, 1959; vis. prof. Soc. for Promotion Sci., Japan, Aug. 1977; mem. tech. adv. panel Xerox Corp., 1969-71, 74-79; mem. biochemistry tng. com. NIH, 1963-65, reviewers reserve, 1995-98; mem. rsch. career award com. NIGMS, 1967-71, NIH BBCA study sect. mem., 1998—; commn. molecular biophysics Internat. Union for Pure and Applied Biophysics, 1965-69, mem. commn. macromolecular biophysics, 1969-75, pres., 1972-75, mem. commn. subcellular and macromolecular biophysics, 1975-81; adv. panel molecular biology NSF, 1960-62; Welch Found. lectr., 1962, Harvey lectr., 1968, Gallagher lectr., 1968, Lemieux lectr., 1973, Hill lectr., 1976, Venable lectr., 1981; co-chmn. Gordon Conf. on Proteins, 1963; mem. coun. Gordon Rsch. Confs., 1969-71. Author: Protein Structure, 1961, Theory of Helix-Coil Transitions in Biopolymers, 1970; co-editor Molecular Biology, 1961-86; mem. editl. bd. Physiol. Chemistry and Physics, 1969-75, Mechanochemistry and Motility, 1970-71, Thrombosis Rsch., 1972-76, Biophys. Jour., 1973-75, Macromolecules, 1973-84, Computers and Chemistry, 1974-84, Internat. Jour. Peptide and Protein Chemistry, 1982-96, Jour. Peptide Rsch., 1997—; corr. PAABS Revista, 1971-73; mem. editl. adv. bd. Biopolymers, 1963—, Biochemistry, 1969-74, 85—, Structural Chemistry, 1989-93, Jour. Computational Polymer Sci., 1991-95, Jour. Biomolecular NMR, 1991—, Computational and Theoretical Polymer Sci., 1996-2000, Jour. Biomed. Sci., 1994—, Jour. Am. Chem. Soc., 1995-2000. Mem. Ithaca Bd. Edn., 1958-59; Bd. govs. Weizmann Inst., Israel, 1970-97; mem. staff Naval Research Lab. Project, Air Force OSRD Project, World War II. Fulbright, Guggenheim fellow Carlsberg Lab., Copenhagen, 1956-57, Weizmann Inst., Israel, 1963; NIH Spl. fellow Weizmann Inst., 1970; Fogarty scholar NIH, 1984, 86, 88-91; recipient Townsend Harris medal CCNY, 1970, Chemistry Alumni Sci. Achievements award, 1977, Kowalski medal Internat. Soc. Thrombosis and Haemostasis, 1983, Linderstrøm-Lang medal Carlsberg Lab., 1983, Internat. Soc. of Quantum Chemistry and Quantum Pharmacology award in Theoretical Biology, 1993, Stein & Moore award Protein Soc., 1995; named Hon. mem. Soc. Polymer Sci. Japan, 1995. Fellow AAAS, Biophys. Soc. (coun. 1967-70); mem. NAS, Am. Peptide Soc. (hon.), Am. Chem. Soc. (chmn. Cornell sect. 1955-56, mem. exec. com. div. biol. chemistry 1966-69, vice chmn. divsn. biol. chemistry 1970, chmn. divsn. biol. chemistry 1971, Eli Lilly award 1957, Nichols medal 1974, Kendall award 1978, Pauling award 1985, Mobil award 1990, Repligen award 1990, IBM award for computers in chem. and pharm. rsch. 1997, Hirschmann award in peptide chem., 1999), Am. Soc. Biol. Chemists, Am. Acad. Arts and Scis., N.Y. Acad. Scis. (hon. life), Hungarian Biophys. Soc. (hon.), Phi Beta Kappa, Sigma Xi, Phi Lambda Upsilon. Home: 212 Homestead Ter Ithaca NY 14850-6220 E-mail: has5@cornell.edu.

SCHERCH, RICHARD OTTO, minister, consultant; b. Balt., Nov. 21, 1926; s. Richard Leopold and Anna Elizabeth (Finger) S.; m. Janice Marie Halbgewachs, June 24, 1951; children: Richard Paul, Leslie Carol, Lisa Beth, Jeremy Thomas. BA, Gettysburg Coll., 1948; BD, Luth. Sch. Theology, Phila., 1951; PhD, Johns Hopkins U., 1959; D Ministry, Lancaster Theol. Sem., 1975; cert. in dispute resolution recognition, Capital U., 1993. Ordained to ministry Luth. Ch., 1951. Mission developer, Wichita, Kans., 1951-53; pastor Trinity Luth. Ch., Manhattan beach, Calif., 1953-57; asst. pastor 1st Luth. Ch., Balt., 1957-59; pastor St. Mark's Luth. Ch., Birdsboro, Pa., 1961-65, Zion Luth. Ch., Lebanon, 1965-71, Shiloh Luth. Ch., York, 1972-75, Christ Luth. Ch., Paramus, N.J., 1976-81; sr. pastor Emmanuel Luth. Ch., Venice, Fla., 1981-93; owner Bldg. Bridges Consultation Svcs., Sarasota, 1993—; mission developer Kansas City, Mo., 1959-61. Lectr. Chautauqua (N.Y.) Inst., 1963, 64, 65; instr. Johns Hopkins U., Balt., 1957-58, U. Balt., 1958-59; dir. Consult, Inc., Lebanon, Pa.; adj. faculty mem. Luther Coll., Teaneck, N.J., 1977-78, Bergen C.C., Paramus, 1979; chmn. profl. support com. Fla. Synod Luth. Ch. Am., Tampa, Fla., 1982-87, ptnr. in evangelism, Chgo., 1985-91; cons. Fla.-Bahamas Synod, 1993—, Episcopal Diocese of S.W. Fla., 1993—; faculty Interim Ministry Tng. Network, 1997—; interim ministry cons. Tng. Network, 1997—. Comdr. USNR, 1956-77. Mem. Internat. Transactional Analysis Assn., Rotary. Republican. E-mail: dickscherch@earthlink.net.

SCHERE, JEAN, researcher; b. Paris, Dec. 5, 1947; s. Robert Eugene Schere and Marie Rose Graillat; m. Danielle A. Cosson, Dec. 31, 1986; children: Constance, Elizabeth. BA, U. Pa., 1969, MBA in Mktg., 1972, PhD in Mgmt., 1981; MA in Internat. Law, Fletcher Sch., 1995. Lectr. mgmt. Wharton Bus. Sch., Phila., 1974—82; asst. prof. mgmt. Phila. Coll. Textiles, 1982—84; venture capitalist Inter Hotel, Montreal, Canada, 1987—91; asst. prof. econs. Tufts U., Medford, Mass., 1995—97; rsch. assoc. Fletcher Sch., 1997—2001. Dir. Sage, Phila., 1995—. U.S. del. Dem. Liberale, Paris, 2000—. Recipient Heizer award for best dissertation, Heizer Corp., 1982, Chevalier de L'Ordre, Nat. du Merite, 1998. Mem.: Aleps, Gesellschaft der Freunde von Bayreuth. Dl. Roman Catholic. Avocations: opera, swimming, skiing. Home: Apt 2 11 Edison Ave Medford MA 02155-5829 Office: Can Lodge 2 Grange Ter GY1 2BQ Guernsey Channel Islands E-mail: jschere@wanadoo.fr.

SCHERER, ANITA (ANITA STOCK), gerontologist, marketing consultant; b. Sept. 20, 1938; d. William John Stock and Gertrud Clara (Kaufmann) Bacher; m. Richard Phillip Scherer, Nov. 25, 1961; children: William Richard, Christopher Howard. Student, U. Cin., 1956-57; AB, Jones Bus. Coll., 1958; BA, Coll. Mount St. Joseph, 1999. Acct. sec. Northlich, Stolley Inc., Cin., 1978-79, acct. asst., 1979-80, asst. acct. mgr., 1980-81, acct. mgr., 1981-84, mktg. svc. assoc., 1984-89, mgr., 1989-97. Lectr. local schs., univs., Cin. 1980-93; adv. bd. mem. performing arts Coll. Mount St. Joseph, Ohio, 1974-80; mktg. cons. for the over 50 market; trustee Arts and Humanities Resource Ctr. for Older Adults, 1990—, chmn. bd., 1991-93. Co-editor: monthly newsletter Badge, 1967-72; designer assorted notepads, 1986. Corr. sec. Delhi Police Assn. Inc., Ohio, 1967—72; pres. Delhi Hills Cmty. Coun., 1974—75; v.p. adminstr. Stagecrafters, Cin., 1983—85, publicity chmn., 1984—89; mktg. bd. mem. Contemp. Arts Ctr., 1985—97; chmn. Advt./Graphic Arts div. Fine Arts Fund Campaign, 1988; docent Cin. Art Mus., 2002—; Lector Our Lady of Victory Roman Cath. Ch., Cin., 1972—. Winner nat. competition Am. Assn. Advt. Agys., 1980; recipient Outstanding Performance award Assn. Cmty. Theatres, Cin., 1983, Excellence in Acting award Ohio Cmty. Theatres Assn., 1984, Outstanding Achievement Gerontological Studies, Coll. Mount St. Joseph, 1999; first American to participate in Kalkriese dig, Germany, 1993, 95. Mem. Am. Mktg. Assn., Acad. Health Svcs. Mktg. (adv. bd. dirs. 1989-91), Cin. C. of C. (lectr. 1984-86). Avocations: travel, reading, medieval/renaissance history, community theater, archaeology. Home: 5511 Palomino Dr Cincinnati OH 45238-4143

SCHERER, FREDERIC MICHAEL, economics educator; b. Ottawa, Ill., Aug. 1, 1932; s. Walter King and Margaret (Lucey) S.; m. Barbara A. Silbermann, Aug. 17, 1957; children: Thomas, Karen, Christina. AB with honors, U. Mich., 1954; MBA with high distinction, Harvard U., 1958, PhD, 1963; D (hon.), Univ. Hohenheim, 1996. Asst. prof. Princeton (N.J.) U., 1963-66; prof. econs. U. Mich., Ann Arbor, 1966-72; chief economist FTC, Washington, 1974-76; prof. econs. Northwestern U., Evanston, Ill., 1976-82; Joseph Wharton prof. polit. economy Swarthmore (Pa.) Coll., 1982-89; Aetna prof. pub. policy and mgmt. Harvard U., Cambridge, Mass., 1989-2000, emeritus prof., 2000—. Vis. prof. Ctrl. European U., Prague, 1993-94; lectr. Princeton U., 2000—; Arthur Andersen disting. visitor U. Cambridge, U.K., 1997; Ludwig Erhard vis. prof. U. Bayreuth, 2000. Author: The Weapons Acquisition Process, 1964 (Lanchester prize 1964), Industrial Market Structure and Economic Performance, 1970, 3d rev. edit., 1990, The Economics of Multi-Plant Operation, 1975, Innovation and Growth, 1984, International High-Technology Competition, 1992, Competition Policies for an Integrated World Economy, 1994, Industry Structure, Strategy and Public Policy, 1996, New Perspectives on Economic Growth and Technological Innovation, 1999; co-author: Mergers, Sell-Offs and Economic Efficiency, 1987; mem. editl. bd. Jour. Indsl. Econs., 1982-89, Jour. Econ. Lit., 1989-2000. Mem. adv. panel NSF, Washington, 1980-83, U.S. Office Tech. Assessment, 1989-93, U.S. Bur. of the Census, 1997-2000. Sr. research fellow Internat. Inst. Mgmt., 1972-74, Am. Stats. Assn. Census fellow, 1989-90; Baker scholar Harvard U., 1957; grantee NSF, 1970, 79, 82; O'Melveny & Myers Centennial Rsch. grantee, 1989, Sloan Fedn. grantee, 1996. Mem. European Assn. for Rsch. in Indsl. Econs. (co-founder 1974), Internat. J.A. Schumpeter Assn. (pres. 1988-90), Am. Econ. Assn. (v.p. 1988), Indsl. Orgn. Soc. (pres. 1992), So. Econ. Assn. (v.p. 1990). Roman Catholic. Avocations: listening to music, musicology. Home: 601 Rockbourne Mills Ct Wallingford PA 19086-6779 E-mail: mike_scherer@harvard.edu.

SCHERER, GEORGE ROBERT, secondary education educator; b. Marion, Ill., Sept. 2, 1923; s. Herman Albert and Alice Madora (Bulliner) S.; m. Margaret Mary Brzozowski, Dec. 31, 1945; children: Marion, Anne Madora. BS in Piano, Juilliard Sch., N.Y.C., 1948; MMus in Piano, Roosevelt U., 1952; studied with Rudolph Ganz. Cert. elem. and secondary tchr., Ill. Tchr. Chgo. Bd. Edn., 1954-85. Profl. chorister Chgo. Symphony Orch. Chorus, 1965-70; instr. Fenger Jr. Coll., Chgo., 1971-73; Fenger H.S. Choir appeared 4 seasons with Chgo. Civic Symphony Orchestra, 1968-71. Composer music for chorus and piano; author: Scherer "A Genealogy", 1996. Recipient (with choir) 16 superior awards in city and state contests, 1960-75. Mem. Am. Guild of Music Artists, Juilliard Sch. Music Alumni Assn., Roosevelt U. Alumni Assn. Avocations: painting, genealogy, piano. Home: 17841 Anthony Ave Country Club Hills IL 60478-4724

SCHERER, HAROLD NICHOLAS, JR. electric utility company executive, engineer; b. Plainfield, N.J., Apr. 5, 1929; s. Harold Nicholas and Nora (McDonough) S.; m. Jane Neely, Sept. 6, 1952 (div.); children— Anne Scherer McConnell, Peter; m. Patricia Condon, May 4, 1974; stepchildren: James, John, Joseph, Jeffery Ludwig, Jean Ludwig Ransdell. BE, Yale U., 1951; MBA, Rutgers U., 1955. Registered profl. engr., N.J., Mass. Various engring. positions Pub. Service Electric and Gas Co., Newark, 1951-63, Am. Electric Power Service Corp., N.Y.C., 1963-68, asst. chief. elec. engr., 1968-69, chief elec. engr., 1969-73, v.p. elec. engr., 1973-82, sr. v.p. elec. engring. Columbus, Ohio, 1982-90, also dir., until 1990; pres. Commonwealth Electric Co., Wareham, Mass., 1990-93, Cambridge Electric Light Co., Canal Electric Co., Com/Steam Co., 1990-93. Bd. dirs. Commonwealth Electric Co., Cambridge Electric Light Co., Com/Steam Co., Commonwealth Svcs. Co., Canal Electric Co.; cons. utility mgmt. and engring., 1993—; mem. joint U.S.-USSR working group on power transmission, 1975-81, joint U.S.-Italy working group on power transmission, 1979-88; vice-chmn. Am. Nat. Stds., N.Y.C., 1985-87; v.p. U.S. Nat. Com., 1985-93, pres., 1993-99, chmn. U.S. tech. com. Internat. Conf. on Large High Voltage Electric Sys., 1985-91, internat. adminstrv. coun., 1988-99, internat. exec. com., 1993-99; mem. engring. rev. bd. Bonneville Power Adminstrn., 1984-94; chmn. elec. sys. and equipment com. Edison Electric Inst., 1989-90, pres. power engring. edn. found., 1992-96; chmn. blue-ribbon panel Pacific Coast Blackouts, Bonneville-Power Adminstrn., 1996-97; bd. dirs. N.Y. State Ind. Sys. Operator, 1998—. Contbr. articles to profl. jours. Pres. N.J. Jr. C. of C., 1960-61; councilman City of Plainfield, 1963-65; mem. Watchung (N.J.) Hills Regional H.S. Bd. Edn., 1970-72; pres. Woods at Josephinum Civic Assn., Worthington, Ohio, 1983-84. Recipient Clayton Frost award U.S. Jaycees, 1961, Young Man of Yr. award Plainfield Jaycees, 1963, Lifetime Achievement award T&D Mag., 1990. Fellow IEEE (v.p. power engring. soc. 1988-89, pres. 1990-91, William Habirshaw award for transmission and distbn. engring. 1986, Disting. Mem. award Internat. Conf. on Large High Voltage Electric Systems 1996, Hon. Mem. award Internat. Conf. on Large High Voltage Electric Systems 2000, Philip Sporn award U.S. ant. com. Internat. Conf. on Large High Voltage Electric Systems, 2002); mem. NAE, Yale Club N.Y.C., Tau Beta Pi, Beta Gamma Sigma. Home and Office: 467 Bay Ln Centerville MA 02632-3352 E-mail: schererhn@aol.com.

SCHERER, JOHN V. computing and instrumentation laboratory manager; b. Buffalo, Dec. 1, 1947; s. John V. and Anne V. (Duryea) S.; m. Marcia Susan Joslyn, Jan. 2, 1976. BSEE, SUNY, Buffalo, 1975, MSEE, 1978. Engr. Calspan/Arvin, Buffalo, 1975-81; mgr. R&D Eastman Kodak, Rochester, 1981—2000; CFO Inst. for Matching Person and Tech., Webster, 2000—. Sgt. U.S. Army, 1970-72. Avocations: fossil and mineral collecting, antique cars. Home: 486 Lake Rd Webster NY 14580-1055 E-mail: jscherer@aol.com.

SCHERER, KARLA, foundation executive, venture capitalist; b. Detroit, Jan. 13, 1937; d. Robert Pauli and Margaret (Lindsey) S.; m. Peter R. Fink, Sept. 14, 1957 (div. July 1989); children: Christina Lammert, Hadley McKenzie Tolliver, Allison Augusta Scherer; m. Theodore Souris, Sept. 5, 1992. Student, Wellesley Coll., 1954-55; BA, U. Mich., 1957; MA, U. Chgo., 1999. Chmn. Karla Scherer Found., Chgo., 1989—. Advisor on shareholders' rights; speaker on corp. governance to various univs. and profl. assns.; condr. workshops in field; leader only successful proxy contest of maj. U.S. publicly held corp., 1988; bd. dirs. R.P. Scherer Corp. Mem. vis. com. U. Chgo., Sch. for Humanities; former mem. bd. dirs. Cottage Hosp., Univ. Liggett Sch., Music Hall, Detroit League for Handicapped, Eton Acad.; former mem. adv. bd. Wellesley Coll; former mem. Rep. Dennis M. Hertel's Candidate Selection Com. for Armed Svcs. Acads.; mem. U. Mich. Ctr. for Edn. of Women Leadership Coun. Named Outstanding Woman Leader of Yr. Oakland U., 1990, one of Metro Detroit's Dynamic Women Women's Econ. Club, 1992; recipient Most Influential Women award Crain's Detroit Bus., 1997, Northwood Univ. 1997 Disting. Women award, Women of Achievements Courage award Mich. Women's Found., 1997. Mem. Am. Mgmt. Assn. (gen. mgmt. coun. for growing orgns.), Internat. Women's Forum, Chgo. Network, Country Club Detroit, Grosse Pointe Club. Office: 737 N Michigan Ave Ste 2330 Chicago IL 60611-2680

SCHERER, MARCIA JOSLYN, psychologist, researcher, educator; b. Buffalo, June 9, 1948; d. Alfred John and Marjorie (Greene) J.; m. John Vincent Scherer Jr., Jan. 2, 1976. BS, Syracuse U., 1970; MS, SUNY, Buffalo, 1977; MPH, PhD, U. Rochester, 1986. Cert. rehab. counselor. Editor Mental Health Assn., Buffalo, 1973-80; psychotherapist Erie County Dept. Mental Health, 1980-82; asst. prof. Nat. Tech. Inst. for Deaf, Rochester, N.Y., 1986-95, assoc. prof., 1995-96; pres., dir. Inst. Matching Person and Tech., Inc., 1997—; dir. consumer evaluations, sr. rsch. assoc. Ctr. Assistive Tech., Occupl. Therapy U. at Buffalo, 1996-98; assoc. prof. phys. medicine and rehab. U. Rochester Med. Ctr., 1997—. Asst. prof. psychology Eastman Sch. Music, Rochester, 1989-95; sr. rsch. assoc. Internat. Ctr. Hearing and Speech Rsch., Rochester, 1989—. Author: Communication in the Human Services: A Guide to Therapeutic Journalism, 1980, Living in the State of Stuck, 1993, Living in the State of Stuck, 3rd edit., 2000, (assessment instruments) Assistive Technology Device Predisposition Assessment, 1989, Educational Technology Predisposition Assessment, 1990; assessment instruments; author: (assessment instruments) Health Care Technology Predisposition Assessment, 1992, Matching Assistive Technology and Child, 1997; co-editor: Psychological Assessment in Medical Rehabilitation, 1995, Evaluating, Selecting and Using Appropriate Assistive Technology, 1996; mem. editl. bd.: Tech. and Disability, 1990—98, mem. editl. bd.: Disability and Rehab., 1998—; editor: Assistive Technology: Matching Device and Consumer for Successful Rehabilitation, 2002; contbr. articles to profl. jours. Dissertation grantee NSF, 1985; recipient Literary award Rho Chi Sigma, 1984; NIH grantee, 2000, 2002. Fellow APA, Am. Congress Rehab. Medicine (sec. 2002—); mem. AAUW (life, grantee 1983), Am. Edn. Rsch. Assn., Am. Bd. Med. Psychotherapy, Rehab. Engring. and Assistive Tech. Soc. N.Am. (bd. dirs. 1997-99), N.Y. Acad. Scis., Assn. Spinal Cord Injury Psychologists and Social Workers, Authors Guild Inc., Authors League Am. Inc., Chi Sigma Iota (life), Australian Rehab. and Assistive Tech. Assn. Methodist. Avocations: creative writing, boating, travel, fossils and minerals. Home and Office: 486 Lake Rd Webster NY 14580-1055 E-mail: impt97@aol.com.

SCHERER, ROBERT FREDERIC, management educator; b. Norwalk, Conn., Apr. 21, 1955; s. Bernard Louis and Helen B. (Bookbinder) S.; m. Susan Kay Sterling, July 28, 1984; 1 child, Evan Sterling. BA, Miami U., Oxford, Ohio, 1977; MA, U. Redlands, 1984; PhD, U. Miss., 1987. Supr. Transam. Life, L.A., 1978-80; mgr. Petersen Pub. Co., 1980-84; assoc. prof. mgmt., chmn. dept. Kennesaw (Ga.) State Coll., 1987—. Chair, assoc. prof. mgmt. Wright State U.; cons. Cobb County Juvenile Ct., Marietta, Ga., 1988—. Contbr. articles to profl. jours. Wal-Mart Free Enterprise fellow, 1990-91, Belinda A. Burns Faculty Scholar Wright State U., 1991—. Mem. Acad. Mgmt., U.S. Assn. for Sml. Bus. and Entrepreneurs (assoc. v.p. membership Individual Intrepreneurship div. 1989), Orgnl. Behavior Teaching Soc., Coun. on Employee Responsibilities and Rights (track chair 1990), Phi Kappa Phi, Beta Gamma Sigma. Democrat. Jewish. Avocations: hiking, fishing, music.

SCHERER, SUZANNE MARIE, artist, educator; b. Buffalo, Sept. 12, 1964; d. Robert Henry Scherer and Judith Louise Le Bar; m. Pavel Victorovich Ouporov, Oct. 25, 1991. AA, Broward C.C., 1984; BFA magna cum laude, Fla. State U., 1986; MFA summa cum laude, Bklyn. Coll., 1989; postgrad., Surikov State Art Acad., Moscow, 1989-91. Educator Bklyn. Mus., 1987-89, Newark Mus., 2000-01; profl. artist N.Y.C., 1989—. Guest lectr. Bklyn. Coll., 1992, Pa. Sch. Art and Design, Lancaster, 1996; artist-in-residence Lancaster Mus. and Pa. Sch. Art and Design, 1996; lectr. Lancaster Mus. Artist: The Trouble with Testosterone and Other Essays on the Biology of the Human Predicament, by Robert M Sapolsky, 1997, Bataille's Eye, 1997, The Basics of Buying Art, 1996, Monumental Propaganda, 1994, Genesis: A Living Conversation, 1996; artist (jour.) The Scis. 1995-97, (TV) Genesis: A Living Conversation, 1996, (radio) Radio Free Europe: Interview with Raya Vail, 1995, WBAI-FM: Interview with Charles Finch, 1994; solo exhbns. include Lancaster (Pa.) Mus. Art, 1996, H. Ferzt Gallery, N.Y.C., 1994, Ctrl. House of Artist-New Tretyakov Gallery, Moscow, 1991, Spaso House Gallery, Residence of Am. Amb., Moscow, 1991; group exhbns. include Bass Mus. Art, Miami Beach, Fla., 1996, Schmidt Bingham Gallery, N.Y.C., 1996, Kemper Mus. Contemporary Art, Kansas City, Mo., 1995, Smithsonian Instn., 1995,

Dalaenas Mus., Fawn, Sweden, 1995, Brit. Consulate, 1995, DeSaisset Mus., Santa Clara, Calif., 1994, N.Y. Acad. Scis., N.Y.C., 1996; pub. collections include N.Y. Pub. Libr., N.Y.C., Met. Mus. Art, N.Y.C., Harvard U. Fogg Art Mus., State Russian Mus., St. Petersburg, Binghamton (N.Y.) Art Mus., Ekaterinburg (Russia) Mus. Fine Art, Bob Blackburn's Printmaking Workshop Collection, N.Y.C., Lancaster Mus. Art, Min. Culture, Moscow, Russian Acad. Art, Moscow. Mem. Internat. Women's Orgn., Moscow, 1989-91. Grantee Internat. Rsch. and Exchs. Bd., 1989; Visual Arts Residency grantee Mid-Atlantic Arts Found., 1996. Democrat. Avocations: reading, visiting museums, collecting art and artifacts, photography. Home and Office: Scherer and Ouporov 594 16th St Brooklyn NY 11218-1201

SCHERER, VICTOR RICHARD, physicist, computer specialist, consultant, musician; b. Poland, Feb. 7, 1940; came to U.S., 1941; s. Emanuel and Florence B. Scherer; m. Gail R. Dobrofsky, Aug. 11, 1963; children: Helena Cecile, Markus David. BS magna cum laude, CCNY, 1960; MA, Columbia U., 1962; PhD, U. Wis., 1974. Health physics asst. Columbia U., N.Y.C., 1961-63; rsch asst. physics. dep. U. Wis., Madison, 1967-74; project assoc., project mgr. Inst. for Environ. Studies, World Climate-Food Rsch. Group, 1974-78; specialist computer systems U. Wis. Acad. Computing Ctr., 1978—; coord., sr. cons. Divsn. Info. Tech. U. Wis., Madison; concert pianist; tchr.; promoter contemporary composers. Researcher in particle physics, agroclimatology, soil-yield relationships and computer graphics; cons. on computer sys., electronic mail, geographic analysis, help desk and supercomputing applications. Fellow AEC, 1960-61. Mem. AAAS, Am. Phys. Soc., Am. Meteorol. Soc., Am. Soc. Agronomy, Assn. Computing Machinery, Nat. Computer Graphics Assn., Phi Beta Kappa, Sigma Xi. Office: U Wis-Madison Divsn Info Tech 1210 W Dayton St Madison WI 53706-1613

SCHERER, WILLIAM T. electrical engineer, educator; b. Trenton, NJ, Sept. 19, 1958; s. Christain F. and Joan S. Scherer; m. Amy Newcome Newcome, June 30, 1995. PhD, U. Va., 1985. Assoc. prof. U. Va., Charlottesville, 1993—. Tech. cons. numerous cos., Va., 1986—2002. Editor: (book) Intelligent Scheduling Systems, 1995. Mem.: IEEE (assoc. editor 1998—2002). Office: U Va 151 Engineer's Way Charlottesville VA 22904-4747 Office Fax: 434-982-2972. E-mail: wts@virginia.edu.

SCHERF, CHRISTOPHER N. trade association administrator; b. N.Y.C., Aug. 8, 1950; s. Richard Edward and Doris Margaret (Farley) S.; m. Diane Frances Koenig, Nov. 13, 1981; children: Casey Lyn, Donna Streit, Donald Makofske. BA, U. Md., 1972. Sports writer Hagerstown (Md.) Morning Herald, 1973, UPI, N.Y.C., 1973-77, The Courier-Jour., Louisville, 1977-78; mgr. media rels. N.Y. Racing Assn., Jamaica, 1978-82; dir. svc. bur. Thoroughbred Racing Assns. of N.Am., 1982-88, exec. v.p., 1988—, also bd. dirs. Md. Bd. dirs. TRA Enterprises, Inc.; mem. govt. affairs com. Am. Horse Coun., 1990; sec. Equibase Co. Co-author: Pro Basketball'76-'77, 1976, Pro Basketball '77-'78, 1977. Mem. Am. Soc. Assn. Execs. Office: Thoroughbred Racing Assns(TRA) Ste 1 420 Fair Hill Dr Elkton MD 21921-2573

SCHERF, DIETMAR (ALEC DONZI), publishing executive, artist, agent; b. Graz, Austria, June 12, 1961; came to U.S., 1990; s. Friedrich and Maria (Rosenberger) S.; m. Patricia Michaela Rech, Apr. 9, 1987; children: Alexander, Deborah, Daniel, David. Diploma, trade sch., Graz, 1979. CEO Handelshaus D. Scherf, Vienna, Austria, 1987-90; CEO, pres. Scherf, Inc., Las Vegas, Nev., 1990-2000, creative dir., 2001—. Author: Short Term Trading, 1990, (booklet) Ross Perot, 1992, I Love Me: Avoiding and Overcoming Depressions, 1998, The Consultant, 2000; composer, performer (CD) Nice to Meet Ya!, 1994. Avocations: swimming, movies, reading, contemporary art, Bible studies. Office: Scherf Inc PO Box 80180 Las Vegas NV 89180-0180 E-mail: ds@scherf.com.

SCHERICH, EDWARD BAPTISTE, retired diversified company executive; b. Inland, Nebr., Dec. 3, 1923; s. Clarence H. and Clara E. (Baptiste) S.; m. Hyacinth Rau, Aug. 11, 1945 (div. 1980); children: Carol, Eileen, John.; m. Antoinette Currera, 1981; 1 stepdau., Sylvia McNamara. BBA, Tulane U., 1948. Acct. Colo. Milling & Elevator Co., Denver, 1948-50; accountant, office mgr. Southdown, Inc., New Orleans, 1950-55, controller, 1955-69; v.p. finance, sec., treas. Southdown Sugars Inc., New Orleans, 1970-73; v.p., sec., treas. Southdown Land Co., 1971-75; sec.-treas. Southdown, Inc., Houston, 1975-78, v.p., sec., 1979-84, treas., 1980-83; ind. fin. cons., 1984—; pres. Valmax Inc., 1989—. Served in USNR, 1943-45. Mem. Beta Gamma Sigma. Home: 633 Brouilly Dr Kenner LA 70065-1101 Office: PO Box 641307 Kenner LA 70064-1307

SCHERICH, ERWIN THOMAS, civil engineer, consultant; b. Inland, Nebr., Dec. 6, 1918; s. Harry Erwin and Ella (Peterson) S.; student Hastings Coll., 1937-39, N.C. State Coll., 1943-44; B.S., U. Nebr., 1946-48; M.S., U. Colo., 1948-51; m. Jessie Mae Funk, Jan. 1, 1947; children— Janna Rae Scherich Thornton, Jerilyn Mae Scherich Dobson, Mark Thomas. Civil and design engr. U.S. Bur. Reclamation, Denver, 1948-84, chief spillways and outlets sect., 1974-75, chief dams br., div. design, 1975-78, chief tech. rev. staff, 1978-79, chief div. tech. rev. Office of Asst. Commr. Engring. and Rsch. Ctr., 1980-84; cons. civil engr., 1984— . Mem. U.S. Com. Internat. Commn. on Large Dams. Served with AUS, 1941-45. Registered profl. engr., Colo. Fellow ASCE; mem. NSPE (nat. dir. 1981-87, v.p. southwestern region 1991-93), Profl. Engrs. Colo. (pres. 1977-78), Jefferson County West C. of C. Republican. Methodist. Home and Office: 3915 Balsam St Wheat Ridge CO 80033-4449

SCHERMAN, SUSAN LOUISE, nurse; b. Hoboken, N.J., Apr. 20, 1953; d. Everett Harold and Louise Annetta (Becker) S.; m. John Alfred Pendenza, Oct. 6, 1979. Student, St. Mary Hosp. Sch. Nursing, 1974, Katharine Gibbs Secretarial Sch., N.Y.C., 1975; BA, Sch. Nursing and Health Edn. Jersey City Coll., 1978. RN, N.Y.; lic. real estate sales rep., N.J., 1994. Sr. staff NYU Med. Ctr., N.Y.C., 1974-78; nurse Christ Hosp., Jersey City, 1975-78; pub. health nurse Retarded Infants Svcs., Inc., N.Y.C., 1978-80; pub. health nursing supr. Hoboken Pub. Health Nursing Svc., N.J., 1980-83; nurse cons. N.Y. County Health Svcs. Rev. Orgn., N.Y.C., 1983-86; cons. risk mgmt. Bower & Gardner, 1986-91; nurse cons. Group Health, Inc., 1992; risk mgr. Jersey City Med. Ctr., 1992; sch. nurse/health edn. tchr. T. Roosevelt Sch., N.J., 1992-95; realtor Ray Fiore Real Estate, Hoboken, 1994; nurse cons. McAloon & Friedman, P.C. Attys., N.Y.C., 1995-2000; pediatric staff nurse div. devel. disabilities U. Medicine and Dentistry N.J., Newark, 2000—02; nurse paralegal Kasowitz, Benson, Torres & Friedman, LLP, N.Y.C., 2002—. Real estate agt. P.J. Miller Assocs., Secaucus, N.J.; condr., gen. mgr. The Robert Lawrence Orch., 1996—, prodr. CD, video, 1997; condr., gen. mgr. Susan Scherman Swing Band. Author: Community Health Nursing Care Plans: A Guide for Home Health Care Professionals, 1984, 2d edit., 2000; patentee in field. Mem. N.J. Bd. Realtors, Nat. Assn. Realtors, Hudson County Bd. Realtors, Soc. Scribes, Intravenous Nurses Soc., N.J. Bd. Realtors. Roman Catholic. Avocations: calligraphy, swimming, needlepoint, music, parasailing. Office: 1633 Broadway New York NY 10019-6799

SCHERMER, JUDITH KAHN, lawyer; b. N.Y.C., Feb. 28, 1949; d. Robert and Barbara Kahn; m. Daniel Woodrough Schermer; 1 child, Sarah Nicole. BA, U. Chgo., 1971; JD, William Mitchell Coll. Law, 1987. Bar: Minn. 1987, U.S. Dist. Ct. Minn. 1987. Advt. and promotion specialist U. Chgo. Press, 1971-75; systems analyst Allstate Ins. Co., Northbrook, Ill., 1975-78, Lutheran Brotherhood, Mpls., 1980-83; polit. aide Mpls. City Coun., 1986-87; ptnr. Schermer & Schermer, Mpls., 1987-99, Schermer & Guy, Mpls., 1999—. Assoc chair 5th Congl. dist., state exec. com. Dem. Farm Labor Party; pres. Minn. Consumer Alliance. Mem. ATLA, Minn. Trial Lawyers Assn. (bd. govs., chair legis. com., employment com. 1999—), Minn. State Bar Assn., Minn. Women Lawyers, Nat. Employment Law Assn. Home: 4624 Washburn Ave S Minneapolis MN 55410-1846 Office: Schermer and Guy Lumber Exch Bldg 10 S 5th St Ste 950 Minneapolis MN 55402-1006

SCHERMERHORN, KENNETH, music director; b. Schenectady, N.Y., Nov. 20, 1929; Music dir. Nashville Symphonic Orch., Nashville, 1983—. Office: Nashville Symphony Orch 2000 Glen Echo Rd Ste 204 Nashville TN 37215*

SCHERR, ALLAN LEE, computer scientist, executive, consultant; b. Balt., Nov. 18, 1940; s. Morris and Sarah (Kratzmar) S.; m. Marsha Kahn, Sept. 2, 1962 (div. 1974); children: Elise A., Stephanie L.; m. Linda Martin, June 8, 1980; 1 child, Katherine M. B.E.E., M.E.E., MIT, 1962, PhDE.E., 1965. Mgr. time sharing option (TSO) design System Devel. div. IBM, Poughkeepsie, N.Y., 1967-70, mgr. multiple virtual storage (MVS) project, 1971-74, mgr. distributed systems programming System Communications div. N.Y., 1977-80, dir. communications programming, 1980-81, dir. communications and applications systems corp. staff N.Y., 1981-83, dir. engring. and programming systems products div. White Plains, 1983-86, dir. integrated applications info. systems div. Milford, Conn., 1986-88, v.p. devel. and integration application systems div., 1988-89, application solutions dir. architecture and devel., Application Solutions Line Bus., 1990-91; v.p. tech. World Wide Cons. Practices IBM Cons. Group, 1991-93; ind. cons. bus. process engring., info. tech., tech. mgmt. Weston, 1993-94; sr. v.p. software engring. EMC Corp., Hopkinton, Mass., 1994-2000, sr. v.p. tech., new bus. devel., 2000—01; ind. cons., 2001—; chief tech. officer Mission Control Productivity, Inc., 2000—. Seminar leader Werner Erhard & Assocs., N.Y.C., 1982-90. Author: An Analysis of Time-Shared Computer Systems, 1966 (Grace Murray Hopper award Assn. Computing Machinery 1975); patentee in field. Mem. The Hunger Project, San Francisco, 1977. IBM fellow, 1984 Fellow IEEE; mem. Sigma Xi, Tau Beta Pi, Eta Kappa Nu Democrat. Home and Office: 18 Wyndclyffe Ct Rhinebeck NY 12572 E-mail: scherr@alum.mit.edu.

SCHERR, BARRY PAUL, foreign language educator; b. Hartford, Conn., May 20, 1945; s. Joseph and Helen Lillian (Shapiro) S.; m. Sylvia Egelman, Sept. 8, 1974; children: Sonia, David. AB magna cum laude, Harvard U., 1966; AM, U. Chgo., 1967, PhD, 1973. From acting asst. prof. to asst. prof. U. Washington, Seattle, 1970-74; from asst. prof. to prof. Russian, Dartmouth Coll., Hanover, NH, 1974—, chmn. dept. Russian, 1981-90, 96-97, chmn. program linguistics and cognitive sci., 1989-96, assoc. dean for humanities, 1997—2001, assoc. provost, 2001, provost, 2001—. Co-organizer Internat. Conf. Russian Verse Theory, 1987, Internat. Conf. Anna Akhmatova and the Poets of Tsarskoe Selo, 1989, Internat. Conf. Eisenstein at 100: A Reconsideration, 1998. Author: Russian Poetry: Meter, Rhythm and Rhyme, 1986, Maxim Gorky, 1988; co-trans. The Seeker of Adventure, Alexander Grin, 1989; mem. editorial bd. Slavic and East European Jour., 1978-88; co-editor: Russian Verse Theory: Procs. of the 1987 Conference at UCLA, 1987, ORUS! Studia litteraria Slavica in honorem Hugh McLean, 1995, A Sense of Place: Tsarskoe Selo and Its Poets, 1993, Twentieth-Century Russian Literature, 2000, Eisenstein at 100: A Reconsideration, 2001; co-translator, co-editor Maksim Gorky: Selected Letters, 1997; contbr. articles to profl. jours. Scholar Harvard Coll., 1963-66; fellow NDEA, 1966-69; grantee Internat. Rsch. and Exchange Bd., 1969-70, NEH, 1987, 89, U.S. Dept. Edn., 1987-89, Dartmouth Coll. Sr. Faculty, 1988; summer rsch. grantee Grad. Sch., Inst. Comparative and Fgn. Area Studies U. Wash., 1973. Mem. MLA (mem. exec. com. assoc. dept. fgn. langs. 1983-85, del. assembly 1986-88), Am. Assn. Advancement Slavic Studies, Am. Assn. Tchrs. Slavic and East European Langs. (pres. 1987-88, founder, past pres. No. New England chpt., numerous coms.). Office: Dartmouth Coll Russian Dept 44 N College St Hanover NH 03755-1801 E-mail: Barry.scherr@Dartmouth.edu.

SCHERR, LAWRENCE, physician, educator; b. N.Y.C., Nov. 6, 1928; s. Harry and Sophia (Schwartz) S.; m. Peggy L. Binenkorb, June 13, 1954; children: Cynthia E., Robert W. AB, Cornell U., 1950, MD, 1957. Diplomate Am. Bd. Internal Medicine (bd. dirs., sec.-treas. 1979-86). Intern Cornell Med. divsn. Bellevue Hosp. and Meml. Ctr., 1957-58, asst. resident, 1958-59, rsch. fellow cardiorenal lab., 1959-60, chief resident, 1960-61, co-dir. cardiorenal lab., 1961-62, asst. vis. physician, 1961-63, assoc. vis. physician, 1963-65, dir. cardiology and renal unit, 1963-67, assoc. dir., 1964-67, vis. physician, 1966-68; physician to out-patients N.Y. Hosp., 1961-63, asst. attending physician, 1963-66, assoc. attending physician, 1966-71, attending physician, 1971-2000; asst. attending physician, cons. Sloan-Kettering Cancer Ctr., 1962-71, 71-00. Chmn. dept. medicine North Shore Univ. Hosp., 1967-01, chmn. emeritus, 2001--, dir. acad. affairs, 1969-93, sr. v.p. med. affairs, 1993-2000; exec v.p. for med. and acad. affairs North Shore-Long Island Jewish Health System, 1998-2000, trustee; dean and sr. v.p. for acad. affairs, dir. Office of Cmty. Health and Pub. Policy, North Shore-L.I. Jewish Health Sys., 2000--; asst. in medicine Med. Coll. Cornell U., 1958-59; rsch. fellow N.Y. Heart Assn., 1959-60, instr. medicine, 1960-63, asst. prof., 1963-66, assoc. prof., 1966-71, David J. Greene disting. prof., 1971-96, assoc. dean, 1969-96; David J. Greene prof. medicine, assoc. dean NYU Sch. Medicine, 1996—; career scientist Health Rsch. Coun., N.Y.C., 1962-66; tchg. scholar Am. Heart Assn., 1966-67; pres. N.Y. State Bd. Medicine, 1974-75; bd. dirs. Nat. Bd. Med. Examiners, 1976-80; chmn. Accreditation Coun. for Grad. Med. Edn., 1988, N.Y. State Coun. on Grad. Edn., 1987-92. Contbr. articles to profl. jours. Lt. USN, 1950-53. Fellow N.Y. Acad. Medicine, Am. Heart Assn. (coun. on clin. cardiology), ACP (master, chmn. and gov. Downstate N.Y. region II 1975-80, regent 1980-86, chmn. bd. regents 1985-86; nat. pres.-elect 1986-87, pres. 1987-88, pres. emeritus, recipient Alfred Stengel Meml. medal); mem. AMA, Am. Fedn. Clin. Rsch., Harvey Soc., N.Y. Med. Soc., Nassau County Med. Soc., Assn. Am. Med. Colls., Am. Clin. and Climatologic Assn. Office: N Shore Univ Hosp Manhasset NY 11030 E-mail: scherr@nshs.edu., scherr@optonline.net.

SCHERRER, DEBORAH KING, computer software engineer; b. L.A., Apr. 28, 1946; d. Archie W. and Frances M. (Weibel) King; m. Philip H. Scherrer, June 24, 1967; children: Amanda Kathrine, Benjamin Douglas. BA, U. Calif. Berkeley, 1968, postgrad., 1968-70. Computer scientist, sci. programmer Lawrence Berkeley (Calif.) Lab., 1973-84; pres., software engr., project mgr. Mt. Xinu, Inc., Berkeley, 1984-94; project mgr. Stanford U., Palo Alto, Calif., 1996—. Sci. programmer Crimean Astrophys. Observatory, Crimea, USSR, summer 1975; pres. Carousel MicroTools, El Cerrito, Calif., 1982-84. Editl. adv. bd. Computing Sys. jour., 1988-96; editl. rev. bd. Unix Rev. mag., 1984-96; contbg. editor Unix, World mag., 1982-84; mem. editl. bd. Computer mag., 1995—; contbr. articles to profl. jours. Participant Project Astro Astron. Soc. of Pacific, Castro Valley, 1992—; project leader Astronomy 4-H, Castro Valley, 1990—; pres. Palomares Canyon Homeowners Assn., Castro Valley, 1993—. Recipient Acad. Driver award Unix Sys. Lab., 1993. Mem. IEEE Computing Soc. (tech. adv. bd. 1992—, bd. govs. 1997—), Usenix Assn. (pres., bd. dirs. 1980-92, Lifetime Achievement award 1996), Assn. Computing Machinery, Tri-Valley Stargazers. Avocations: astronomy, dressage, conservation activities. Home: 30261 Palomares Rd Castro Valley CA 94552-9638

SCHERRER, GEORGE M. electrical engineer; b. Shawneetown, Ill., Oct. 30, 1914; s. George Bernard and Susan Scherrer; m. Ruby Nance Scherrer; children: George M. Jr., Irene, Nancy, Joyce, Fred, Jamie BSEE, U. Ill., 1938; postgrad., Princeton U., 1944, MIT, 1945. Registered profl. engr. Farmer; ptnr. Scherrer Equipment Co., Inc.; mgr. Saline Valley Conservancy Dist.; tchr. physcis Washington U., St. Louis; prin. engr. Rural Electric Adminstrn., 1940-46; design and constrn. REA power lines A. Y. Taylor Co., 1938-40. Presenter in field. Bd. dirs. Ohio Valley Improvement Assn.; mem. Citizens Adv. Coun. Ohio Valley Commn., co-chmn.; chmn. bd. Cath. Shrine Pilgrimage, Inc., 1997-2000; bd. dirs. Camp Ondessonk, 1957—. Lt. (j.g.) USNR, 1943-46. Mem. IEEE, Am. Soc. Agrl. Engrs. (sr. mem., cert.), Nat. Cattlemens Assn., Ill. Farm Bur. Democrat. Roman Catholic.

SCHERSTEN, H. DONALD, retired oil company executive; b. Titusville, Pa., Nov. 6, 1919; s. H.J. and Clara (Brown) S.; m. Katherine Conley; 1 dau. by previous marriage, Sandra S. Hotard. BS, Temple U., 1941; postgrad., Tulsa U., 1946-48, Columbia U., 1955. With Creole Petroleum Corp. (affiliate Exxon Corp.), 1948-69, successively dist. field chief accountant Cabimas, Venezuela, coordinator procedures, fin. statements and audits, asst. controller, 1951-62, controller, 1962-69; gen. auditor Exxon Corp., N.Y.C., 1969-74, coordinator mdn., computers, systems, 1975-76; pres. H. Donald Schersten & Assocs. (Mgmt. Cons.), 1977—; v.p. fin. R.J. Reynolds Nabisco, 1976—78. Lic. real estate agt., 1985—; lic. mortgage broker, 1986-90. Pres. council Am. Ch. Caracas, 1960. Served to 1st lt. AUS, 1942-45. Named to Acct. Alumni Hall of Fame, Temple U., 1985. Mem. Am. Petroleum Inst. (chmn. audit com. 1974-76), Inst. Internal Auditors (cert.), U.S. Power Squadrons, USCG Aux. (comdr. 1983). Clubs: Internat. Safari Big Game Hunting, Toastmasters (past pres. Caracas chpt.), Los Rancheros Deep Sea Fishing. Avocations: champion/Classic Billfish Tourn. 1973, Cabo San Lucas, Mexico. Home: 4693 N Glebe Farm Rd Sarasota FL 34235-1806

SCHERZER, MARK P. lawyer; b. Bronx, N.Y., Apr. 24, 1951; s. Felix and Sylvia (Warman) S. BA, Haverford Coll., 1973; MA in Anthropology, U. Chgo., 1975; JD, Yale U., 1978. Bar: N.Y. 1979, U.S. Dist. Ct. (so. dist.) N.Y. 1979, U.S. Dist. Ct. (ea. dist.) N.Y. 1980, U.S. Ct. Appeals (6th cir.) 1985, U.S. Ct. Appeals (2d cir.) 1996. Assoc. Botein, Hays, Sklar & Herzberg, N.Y.C., 1978-80; pvt. practice, 1980-84, 90—; ptnr. Scherzer & Palella, 1984-90; legis. counsel New Yorkers for Accessible Health Coverage, 1994—. Contbr. to books on law. Mem. healthcare and ins. steering com. NEA, Washington, 1996-97; mem. nat. adv. bd. Artists health Ins. Resource Ctr., N.Y.C., 1997-98. Recipient Cmty. Svc. award, Lesbian and Gay Law Assn. of Greater NY, 1992. Democrat. Jewish. Office: 29 John St Ste 1103 New York NY 10038 E-mail: markscherzeresq@aol.com.

SCHETKY, LAURENCE MCDONALD, metallurgist, researcher; b. Baguio, The Philippines, July 15, 1922; s. Gerald Laurence and Ethyl Jane (McDonald) S.; m. Diane Heiskell, Dec. 12, 1977 (div. Feb. 1986); m. Karen Searles, July 12, 1986 (div. Oct. 1994); 1 child, Mark Christian; m. Margarita A. Smith, Oct. 27, 1995. BSChemE, Rensselaer Poly Inst., Troy, N.Y., 1943, MMetE, 1948, PhD, 1953. Registered profl. engr., Mass. Rsch. fellow MIT, Cambridge, 1953-59; v.p. rsch. Alloyd Electronics, Inc., 1959-63; dir. R & D Internat. Copper Rsch. Assn., Inc., N.Y.C., 1963-83; pres. Memory Metals, Inc., Stamford, Conn., 1983-86; v.p., chief scientist Memry Corp., Brookfield, 1987—. Editor: Beryllium Technology, 2 vol., 1966, The Metallurgy of Copper, 13 vols., 1966-83; author: (with others) Copper in Iron and Steel, 1982; contbr. over 100 articles to physics and metallurgy jours. With USN, 1944-46, PTO. Rsch. fellow Alcoa Corp., 1948-53. Fellow Am. Soc. Metals Internat. (life), Brit. Inst. Materials; mem. AIME (life). Democrat. Episcopalian. Achievements include 17 patents in Electron Beam Technology, Vapor Phase Deposition, Shape Memory Actuators, medical devices. Office: Memry Corp 3 Berkshire Blvd Bethel CT 06801-1037 E-mail: l.m_schetky@memry.com.

SCHETLIN, ELEANOR M. retired university official; b. N.Y.C., July 15, 1920; d. Henry Frank and Elsie (Chew) Schetlin. BA, Hunter Coll., 1940; MA, Tchrs. Coll., Columbia U., 1942, EdD, 1967. Playground dir. Dept. Parks, N.Y.C., 1940-42; libr. Met. Hosp. Sch. Nursing, 1943-44, dir. recreation and guidance, 1945-58, historian Alumnae Assn., 2000; coord. student activities SUNY, Plattsburgh, 1959-63, asst. dean students, 1963-64; asst. prof., coord. student personnel svcs. CUNY, Hunter Coll., 1967-68; asst. dir. student personnel Columbia U., Coll. Pharm. Scis., N.Y.C., 1968-69, dir. student personnel, 1969-71; assoc. dean students Health Scis. Ctr. SUNY, Stony Brook, 1971-73, asst. v.p. student svcs., 1973-74, assoc. dean students, dir. student svcs., 1974-85. Founding mem. Sea Cliff unit 300 Nassau County Auxiliary Police, Nassau NOW Women of Color Task Force. Contbr. articles to profl. jours. Recipient NOW Alliance PAC award, 1991, 1999, Lifetime Achievement award, Nassau NOW, 1992, Task Force Women of Color award, 1994. Mem.: So. Poverty Law Ctr., Wellesley Ctrs. Rsch. Women, Nat. Women's History Project, Women's Environment and Devel. Orgn., Nat. Women's Studies Assn., Nat. Assn. Women Edn., Nat. Mus. Women in the Arts. Home: 60 Hildreth Pl East Hampton NY 11937

SCHETTINO, MARIA CARMEN, preschool educator; b. N.Y.C., Mar. 12, 1949; d. Aniello and Mary Louise (Bove') S.; m. Albert Zezulinski (div. Apr. 1986); 1 child, Kerri; m. Michael J. Pulitano, June 24, 1989. A in Early Edn., SUNY, Farmingdale, 1969. Interviewer N.Y. State Planning Commn., Farmingdale, N.Y., 1969-70; Albany, 1970; asst. tchr. Alphabet Pre-Sch., 1971-72; tchr. art Montessori Sch., St. Thomas, V.I., 1975; substitute tchr. Miss Sue's Nursery Sch. and Kindergarten, Plainview, N.Y., 1975-80; asst. tchr. Bethpage (N.Y.) Nursery Sch., 1979-85, tchr., 1985-89, Kiddie Junction Pre-Sch. and Camp, Levittown, NY, 2000—. Coach Mid Island Gymnastics Sch., Hicksville, N.Y., 1986—, dir. presch. program, 1992-95; dir. M.A.T.S.S. Kids Gym, Syosset, N.Y., 1995-2000; gymnastics specialist 1st Class Child Care, Uniondale, N.Y., 1990. Fin. sec. Lantern Road Civic Assn., Hicksville, 1976. Mem. Early Childhood Ednl. Counsel. Democrat. Avocation: phys. fitness. Home: 90 Lantern Rd Hicksville NY 11801-6210 Office: Kiddie Junction Pre-Sch and Camp 3 N Village Green Levittown NY 11756

SCHEU, LYNN MCLAUGHLIN, scientific publication editor; b. Lancaster, Ohio, July 9, 1942; d. Franklin Neil and Carol Lois (Bigham) McLaughlin; m. Richard V. Scheu, Apr. 16, 1966; children: David Edward, Michael Patrick. BS, Auburn U., 1964; postgrad., Ohio State U., 1964-66. English, French tchr. Reynoldsburg (Ohio) H.S., 1966-70; adj. curator mollusks Mus. History & Sci., Louisville, 1978-85; editor Am. Conchologist, 1987—; tchr. English and French Franklin H.S., Frankfort, Ky., 2000—. Chairperson Lambis Group, 1996; mem. editl. adv. bd. Bailey Matthews Shell Mus. and Ednl. Found., Sanibel, Fla., 1988—. Editor (website) The Conchologist's Information Network (ConchNet). Mem. exec. bd. Friends of Libr., Louisville, 1989-95; mem. Mayor's Task Force on Librs., Louisville, 1988-89. Mem. Conchologists Am. (bd. dirs. 1987—). Avocations: shell collecting, fossils, landscape gardening, genealogy. Home and Office: 1222 Holsworth Ln Louisville KY 40222-6616 E-mail: amconch@mindspring.com.

SCHEUB, RICHARD HERMAN, photographer; b. Gary, Ind., Oct. 3, 1924; s. Frederick and Magdalene (Osterhus) S. BA, Valparaiso U., 1950; MA, Indiana U., 1953. Instr. William A. Wirt H.S., Gary, 1952-57, guidance counselor, 1958-64, libr., 1965-71; audio/visual dir. Lew Wallace H.S., 1972-89; freelance photographer Crown Point, Ind., 1975—. Cons. H.W. Wilson Jr. H.S. Catalog, N.Y.C., 1969-89; profl. rels. com. chmn. Ind. Sch. Media Personnel, Indianapolis, 1971-76, dir. bd., 1976-80. Exhibited in Field Mus., Chgo., 1970-80; designer (logo) Gary Assn. Sch. Media Personel, 1980; photographer (poster) 30th Anniversary Nat. Lakeshore, 1995; designer logo for Ind. Ret. Tchrs. Assn., 1999. Mem. Trinity Luth. Ch., Crown Point, 1974—, Save the Dunes, Michigan City, Ind., 1969—. Tec. sgt. U.S. Army, 1943-45. Mem. ALA (cons. booklist publ. 1970-75), Gary Assn. Sch. Media Personnel (pres. 1970-73), Miller Exch., Am. Legion, VFW. Avocations: golf, racquetball. Home: 3742 Cherry Hill Dr Crown Point IN 46307-8937

SCHEUCH, RICHARD, economist, educator; b. N.Y.C., July 15, 1921; s. William Allen and Marjorie (Tuller) S.; m. Fayette Van Alstyne Smith, Sept. 1, 1948; children: Evelyn Scheuch Lord, W. Allen II. AB, Princeton U., 1942, MA, 1948, PhD, 1952. Asst. in econs. Princeton U., 1946-50; mem. faculty dept. econs. Trinity Coll., Hartford, Conn., 1950-89, G. Fox and Co. prof. econs. emeritus, 1989—, vis. prof., 1990—. Elector Wadsworth Atheneum; trustee Watkinson Libr. Served with USNR, 1942-46. Woodrow Wilson fellow, 1946-47 Mem. Am. Econ. Assn., Indsl. Relations Research Assn., Internat. Indsl. Relations Assn. Clubs: Hartford Golf, Hyannis Port Yacht; Princeton (N.Y.C.). Unitarian Universalist. Home: PO Box 787 West Yarmouth MA 02673-0787

SCHEUER, DONALD WILLIAM, JR. educational administrator; b. Laurel, Miss., Jan. 11, 1944; s. Donald William Sr. and Billie Ruth (McKenzie) S.; m. Eileen Rose Flanagan, Dec. 21, 1968; children: Christopher, David, Jennifer, Kathryn, Geoffrey. BS in Edn., East Stroudsburg (Pa.) U., 1966; MS in Edn., Temple U., 1975. Cert. math. tchr., supr., Pa. Tchr. Phila. Sch. Dist., 1966-72, dept. chmn., 1972-77, supr., 1977-83; systems analyst Bucks County Community Coll., Newtown, Pa., 1983-87; dept. chmn. Abington (Pa.) Sch. Dist., 1987—. Past pres. Jenkintown Youth Activities, Jenkintown, Pa., 1982-84; pres. Del. Valley Swim League, Jenkintown, 1990-98. Recipient Presdl. award for excellence in math. teaching for Pa., 1990. Mem. Nat. Coun. Tchrs. Math. (com. chmn. 1982-83, 93—), Pa. Coun. Tchrs. Math. (pres. 1998—, chmn. contest com., Outstanding Svc. award 1980, 88), Nat. Coun. Suprs. Math. (v.p.), Pa. Coun. Suprs. Math. (pres. 1982-85), Assn. Tchrs. Math. Pa. Vicinity (pres., Outstanding Svc. award 1990). Republican. Roman Catholic. Avocations: cooking, golf. Home: 1332 Highland Ave Fort Washington PA 19034-1608 Office: Abington Sch Dist Abington PA 19001

SCHEUER, JAMES, physician, educator, researcher; b. N.Y.C., Feb. 21, 1931; s. Sidney Henry and Linda (Ullman) S.; m. Ruth Lucas, Dec. 15, 1961; children:Kim, Jeff, Greg. BA, U. Rochester, 1952; MD, Yale U., 1956. Diplomate in internal medicine and cardiovascular disease Am. Bd. Internal Medicine. Med. intern Bellevue Hosp., N.Y.C., 1956-57; NIH fellow in cardiology Mt. Sinai Hosp., 1957, 59, resident in internal medicine, 1958-60; rsch. fellow in internal medicine N.Y. Hosp.-Cornell Med. Ctr., 1962-63; rsch. assoc. Inst. for Muscle Disease, 1962-63; trainee in metabolism and nutrition Grad. Sch. Pub. Health/U. Pitts., 1963-64; from instr. to assoc. prof. medicine

U. Pitts. Sch. medicine, 1964-72; prof. medicine, assoc. prof. to prof. physiology Albert Einstein Coll. Medicine, Bronx, N.Y., 1972—; dir. divsn. cardiology Albert Einstein Coll. Medicine/Montefiore Med. Ctr, 1972-87, vice chmn. dept. medicine, 1980-87, Baumritter prof., chmn. dept. medicine, 1990-99; chmn. emeritus, 1999—. Lectr. and vis. prof. in field. Mem. editl. bd. Cardiology, 1970-75, Circulation Rsch., 1975-81, others; contbr. numerous articles to profl. jours. Recipient awards and grants in field; named one of Best Drs. in Castle County. Fellow ACP, Am. Coll. Cardiology; mem. AAAS, Assn. Am. Physicians, Assn. Profs. Medicine (exec. com. 1994—), Am. Fedn. for Clin. Rsch., Am. Heart Assn. (fellow coun. on circulation, coun. on clin. cardiology), Am. Physiol. Soc., Am. Soc. for Clin. Investigation, Assn. Univ. Cardiologists, Cardiac Muscle Soc., Ctrl. Soc. for Clin. Rsch., Internat. Soc. for Heart Rsch., N.Y. Acad. Sci., N.Y. Heart Assn., Soc. for Exptl. Biology and Medicine, N.Y. Cardiology Soc., Eastern Inter Urban Clin Club. Office: Albert Einstein Coll Med 1300 Morris Park Ave Bronx NY 10461-1926

SCHEUERMAN, ELEANOR JOYCE MILLER, medical association administrator; b. Jersey City, July 7, 1937; d. Lawrence Houseman and Bridie E.J. (Moran) M.; m. William Henry Scheuerman, Jr., Sept. 5, 1969; 1 child, Sheila Brigid. BS in Nursing, Seton Hall, 1959; MA in Pub. Health, N.Y.U., 1964. RN, N.J., Mass. Pvt. duty nurse Jersey City Med. Ctr., 1959-60; pub. health nurse Pub. Health Nursing Svc. of Jersey City, 1959-63, 66; health educator Acad. St. Aloysius, Jersey City, 1962-64; instr. sch. nursing Seton Hall Univ., South Orange, N.J., 1964-67; dir. Pub. Health Nursing Agy., Washington, 1967-93; head nurse Soldiers Home, Holyoke, Mass., 1994-95; charge nurse Anchorage Nursing Home, Shelburne, from 1996. Head nurse Hunterdon Devel. Ctr., Clinton, N.J., 1989-93; bd. dirs. Warren County Office on Aging, 1974-93, Legal Svc. of Warren County, 1976-77; med. and health staff chief Warren County Civil Def. and Disaster Control, 1979; info. and referral svc. area com. Warren County Human Svcs., 1985-91, adv. coun., 1983-91, chair protective svcs. com., 1984-91. Chair suprs.' workshop com. Home Health Assembly of N.J., 1974-75; adv. coun. for practical nursing Warren County Vocat. Tech. Sch., 1986-93; vol. Right to Read Program, Franklin Med. Ctr., Cmty. Meals Blessed Sacrament Parish. Mem. Nat. League for Nursing (bd. dirs. 1977-78), APHA, Am. Sch. Health Assn. (fellow 1965), Am. Nursing Assn. (pub. health sect., membership chair 1960, v.p. dist. 2 1962), N.J. State Nurses Assn. (membership chair 1965), Sigma Theta Tau. Home: Townshend, Vt. Died Aug. 11, 2001.

SCHEVE, MAY E. state legislator; b. St. Louis, June 27, 1964; d. Robert Anthony and May Ellen (Braun) S. BA, St. Louis U., 1987; postgrad., Webster U. Rep. Mo. State Ho. Reps. Dist. 98, 1991—. Committeewoman Gravois Twp. Dem. Club; chair, Mo. Dem. Party, 2002-. Mem. Women Legislators, Third Congl. Women's Club (sec.), Women's Dem. Forum, Alpha Gamma Delta, Kappa Beta Phi. Office: Mo Ho of Reps State Capitol Bldg 201 W Capitol Ave Rm 401A Jefferson City MO 65101-1556*

SCHEVILL, EDWARD, social services agency director; b. Boston, Jan. 16, 1948; s. William Edward Schevill and Barbara Lawrence. Student, Syraucse (N.Y.) U., 1965-68. Coord., dir. Epilepsy Self-Help, Tucson, 1977-88; dir., pres. Epilepsy Outreach Project, Inc., 1988—. Awards com., chair Dianne Lynn Anderson Meml. Award, Tucson, 1990—. Home: 922 N Campbell Ave Tucson AZ 85719-4915 Office: Epilepsy Outreach Project Inc 922 N Campbell Ave Tucson AZ 85719-4915

SCHEVILL, JAMES ERWIN, poet, playwright; b. Berkeley, Calif., June 10, 1920; s. Rudolph and Margaret (Erwin) S.; m. Margot Helmuth, Aug. 2, 1966; children (by previous marriage): Deborah, Susanna. BS, Harvard U., 1942; MA (ad eundem), Brown U.; LHD (hon.), R.I. Coll., 1986. Mem. faculty San Francisco State Coll., 1959-68, prof. English, 1968, dir. Poetry Center, 1961-68; prof. Brown U., 1969-85, prof. emeritus, 1985—. Reader various univs., insts., and orgns. Author: New and Selected Poems, 2000. Served to capt. AUS, 1942-46. Ford Found. grantee, 1954, 60-61, R.I. Com. on Humanities grantee, 1975; Fund Advancement Edn., 1953-54, Office for Advanced Drama Research fellow, 1957, Rockefeller fellow, 1964, Guggenheim fellow, 1981, McKnight fellow, 1984; recipient Performance prize Nat. Theatre Competition, 1945, 2d prize Phelan Biography Competition, 1954, 2d prize Phelan Drama Competition, 1958, William Carlos Williams award, 1965, Roadsted Found. award, 1966, Gov.'s award R.I., 1975, Best Story of Yr. award Ariz. Quart., 1977; story selected for O. Henry Awards Prize Stories, 1978; award in lit. Am. Acad. Arts and Letters, 1991; work commd. by Nat. Council Chs., 1956-61, Fromm Found., 1959, Trinity Repertory Co., R.I. Hosp., 1986, Providence Coll., 1986, Magdalena Group, 1992. Home: 1309 Oxford St Berkeley CA 94709-1424 Office: Brown U Dept English Providence RI 02912-0001

SCHEWE, DONALD BRUCE, archivist, library director; b. Cleve., Oct. 28, 1943; s. Norman Edward and Theodora (Robinson) S.; m. Charlene R. Wenz, June 10, 1965; children: Amanda Marie, Ann Elizabeth. BA, U. Nebr., 1964, MA, 1968; PhD, Ohio State U., 1971. Archivist Franklin D. Roosevelt Library, Hyde Park, N.Y., 1972-77, supervisory archivist, 1977-79, asst. dir., 1979-81; dir. Carter Presdl. Materials Project, Atlanta, 1981-86, Jimmy Carter Library, Atlanta, 1986-99, Ga. Dept. Archives and History, 2000. Editor: Franklin D. Roosevelt and Foreign Affairs, 1981. With U.S. Army, 1964-66, Vietnam, ret. lt. col. Mem. Assn. Records Mgrs. and Adminstrs., Soc. Ga. Archivists, Orgn. Am. Historians, Inst. of Cert. Records Mgrs. (pres. 1996-2000). Lodges: Rotary. Episcopalian.

SCHEXNAYDER, BRIAN EDWARD, opera singer, voice educator; b. Port Arthur, Tex., Sept. 18, 1953; s. Leonard and Dorothy (Carrier) S.; m. Sherri Scallan, Oct. 2, 1976. BA in Music, U. Southwestern La., 1976; postgrad., Juilliard Sch. Music, 1976-80. Vocal instr. Brian Schexnayder Vocal Studio, N.Y.C., 1995-97, Plano, Tex., 1997—. Performances with Met. Opera, N.Y.C., Paris Opera Co., Edmonton (Alta., Can.) Opera Co., New Orleans Opera Co., Santiago (Chile) Opera, Winnipeg (Man., Can.), St. Petersburg (Fla.) Opera, Jackson (Miss.) Opera Co., San Francisco Opera, Frankfurt Opera, Hamburg Staatsoper Opera, Oper der Studt Bonn, Spoleto (Italy) Festival of Two Worlds, Cin. Opera, Fla. Grand Opera. Mem. Am. Guild Musicians. Avocations: computers, billiards, remote control airplanes.

SCHEXNAYDER, CHARLOTTE TILLAR, state legislator; b. Tillar, Ark., Dec. 25, 1923; d. Jewell Stephen and Bertha (Terry) Tillar; m. Melvin John Schexnayder Sr., Aug. 18, 1946; children: M. John Jr., Sarah Holden, Stephen. BA, La. State U., 1944, postgrad., 1947-48. Asst. editor La. Agrl. Extension, Baton Rouge, 1944; editor The McGehee (Ark.) Times, 1945-46, 48-53; editor, co-publisher The Dumas (Ark.) Clarion, 1954-85, pub., 1985-99; mem. Ark. Ho. of Reps., Little Rock, 1985-99, asst. speaker pro tem, 1995—. Pres. Ark. Assn. Women, 1955, Nat. Newspaper Assn., Washington, 1991-92, Ark. Press. Assn., Little Rock, 1982, Nat. Fedn. Press Women, Blue Springs, Mo., 1977-78, Litte Rock chpt. Soc. Profl. Journalists, 1973; mem. pres.'s coun. Winrock Internat., 1990—; chmn. Dumas Area Cmty. Found., 2000-02. Editor: Images of the Past, 1991. 1st woman mem. Ark. Bd. Pardons and Parole, 1975-80; mem. Ark. Legis. Coun., 1985-92; bd. dirs. Women's Found. Ark., sec. 1999—; bd. dirs. Chicot-Desha Port Indsl. Com.; v.p. Desha County Mus., 1989—; dir. Dumas Indsl. Found., 1986—; mem. exec. com. Ark. Ctrl. Radiation Therapy Inst., 1991-92; mem. adv. bd. Ark. Profl. Women Achievement, 1992—; vice chair Ark. Rural Devel. Commn., 1991-96, chair 1996-97; mem. Winrock Internat. Adv. Coun., 1991—; founding incorporator Ark. Waterways Commn., 1996—, bd. dirs.; bd. visitors Manship Sch. Comm., La. State U., 1998—; bd. dirs. Main Street Ark., Hist. Preservation Alliance Ark.; mem. Ark. Transitional Employment Coun., 1999—; sec. Dumas Area Cmty. Fund, 2000—; bd. dirs. Enterprise Corp. for the Delta, 1999-2002, Dumas Main St., v.p.; bd. dirs. Historic Preservation Alliance Ark, 2000—; mem. Ark. Transitional Employment Assistance Bd., 2000. Named Disting. Alumnus Ark. A&M Coll., 1971, Woman of Achievement Nat. Fedn. Press Women, 1970, Outstanding Arkansan C. of C., 1986; recipient Ark. Profl. Women of Distinction award No. Bank, Little Rock, 1990, Emma McKinney award Nation's Top Cmty. Newspaper Woman, 1980, Journalist award Nat. Conf. of Christians and Jews, 1989, Lifetime Achievement award Nat. Fedn. Press Women, 1992, Outstanding Svc. award Ark. Assn. Elem. Prins., Disting. Svc. award Ark. Press Assn., 1993; named to La. State U. Alumni Hall of Distinction, 1994, Disting. Svc. award Internat. Soc. Weekly Newspaper Editors, 1996, Golden Svc. award Ark. Press Assn., 1996, State Leadership award Ark. Waterways Commn., 1996, Horizon award League Women Voters Ark., 1998; named one Top 100 Ark. Women, Ark. Bus., 1995, 96, 97, 98; named to Journalism Hall of Fame La. State U., 1998. Mem.: Ark. Delta Coun. (chmn. emeritus, v.p. Dumas Main St., mem. Main St. Ark. adv. bd.), Pi Beta Phi (Crest award 1992). Democrat. Roman Catholic. Home: 322 Court St Dumas AR 71639-2718 Office: PO Box 160 Dumas AR 71639-0160 E-mail: cts@seark.net.

SCHEXNAYDER, MYLES D. director; b. Donaldsonville, La., May 18, 1959; s. Carl Joseph Schexnayder and Gerry Malone; m. Brenda Joyce Hanson, Nov. 24, 1963. BA, La. Tech U., 1989. Instrumental music edn. Band dir. Ringgold H.S. Band, Ringgold, La., 1989—90, Arcadia (La.) H.S. Band, 1990—94, Neville H.S. Band, Monroe, 1994—97, Ouachita Parish H.S. Band, Monroe, 1997—. Musician: Euphonium Recital (Chairman''s Honor Recital, 1989). With USMC, 1978—82. Mem.: La. Music Edn. Assn., La. Band Assn., Nat. Band Assn., Music Educators N.C. Home: 2908 Hwy 151 Downsville LA 71234 Office: Ouachita Parish HS 681 Hwy 594 Monroe LA 71203

SCHEXNIDER, ALVIN J. academic administrator; b. Lake Charles, La., May 26, 1945; s. Alfred and Ruth Mayfield Schexnider; m. Virginia Y. Reeves. BA, Grambling State U., 1968; MA, Northwestern U., 1971, PhD, 1973. Asst. dir. pers. Owens-Ill. Inc., 1968; asst. prof. So. U., 1973-74, Syracuse U., 1974-77; sr. prof. Fed. Exec. Inst., 1977-79; assoc. dean Va. Commonwealth U., 1979-84, vice provost undergrad. studies, 1987-95; asst. vice chancellor U. N.C., Greensboro, 1984-87; chancellor, pres. Winston-Salem (N.C.) State U., 1996-00; dir. office health policy devel./sch. medicine Wake Forest U., 2000—. Fellow Inter-Univ. Seminar on Armed Forces and Soc., 1975—. Gov. commn. Va. Future, 1982-84; bd. visitors Va. State U., 1986-87; mem. Va. State Bd. Edn., 1990-94, N.C. econ. devel. bd., 1997-2000; bd. trustees Wachovia Funds; vice chair Gov.'s Adv. Commn. on Revitalization of Va.'s Cities. Sgt. AUS, 1968-70. Norman Wait Harris fellow, 1971-72, fellow Ford Found., 1972, Woodrow Wilson Found., 1973; named to Outstanding Young Men Am., U.S. Jaycees, 1978. Fellow Nat. Acad. Pub. Adminstrn.; mem. ASPA (pres. Va. chpt. 1983-84, J. Sargent Reynolds award 1980), Am. Polit. Sci. Assn., Nat. Conf. Black Polit. Sci., Alpha Phi Alpha, Sigma Pi Phi. Office: Wake Forest U Medical Ctr Blvd Winston Salem NC 27157-0001 E-mail: aschexni@wfubmc.edu.

SCHEY, JOHN ANTHONY, metallurgical engineering educator; b. Sopron, Hungary, Dec. 19, 1922; came to U.S., 1962; s. Mihaly and Hedvig Terez (Topfl) S.; m. Margit Maria Sule, Sept. 13, 1926; 1 child, John Francis. Diplome metall. engring., Tech. U., Sopron, 1946; PhD in Tech. Scis., Acad. Scis., Budapest, Hungary, 1953; D of Engring. (hon.), U. Stuttgart, 1987, U. Heavy Industry, Miskolc, Hungary, 1989. Cert. mfg. engr. Chief technologist Iron and Metal Works, Csepel, Hungary, 1947-51; reader Tech. U., Miskolc, Hungary, 1951-56; dept. head Brit. Aluminium Co. Research Labs., 1957-62; metall. advisor Ill. Inst. Tech. Research Inst., Chgo., 1962-68; prof. U. Ill., 1968-74, U. Waterloo, Ont., Can., 1974-88, disting. prof. emeritus Can., 1988. Resource person Niagara Inst., Ontario, 1980; course dir. Forging Industry Assn., Cleve., 1978; cons. to various corps. in U.S. and Can. Author: Tribology in Metalworking, 1983, Introduction to Manufacturing Processes, 3d edit., 2000; patentee in field. Recipient W.H.A. Robertson award Inst. Metals, 1966. Fellow Am. Soc. Metals, Soc. Mfg. Engrs. (Gold Medal award 1974); mem. Nat. Acad. Engring., fgn. mem. Hungarian Acad. Scis. Avocations: music, history, impact of technology on soc.

SCHIAFFINO, S(ILVIO) STEPHEN, retired medical society executive, consultant; b. Bklyn., Nov. 1, 1927; s. Stephen Anthony and Jane (DiDonato) S.; m. Josephine Rose Bovello, Apr. 25, 1954; children— Susan, Stephen. BS, Georgetown U., 1946, MS, 1948, PhD in Biochemistry, 1956. Research biochemist div. nutrition FDA, Washington, 1948-50, asst. br. chief div., 1954-60; mgr. chemistry dept. Hazelton Labs., Vienna, 1960-61; with NIH, 1961—; scientist adminstr. NIH (Nat. Cancer Inst.), 1961-64, asst. chief research grants rev. br., 1964-69, chief, 1969-72, asso. dir. for sci. rev., 1972-78, dep. dir. div. research grants, 1978-86; sr. sci. advisor office of extramural research and tng., office of dir. NIH, 1986-87; exec. officer, sci. officer Am. Soc. for Clin. Nutrition, Bethesda, Md., 1987-93; cons., 1993—. Cons. in field. Served with AUS, 1950-53. Recipient Superior Service award FDA, 1960, Superior Service award NIH, 1969 Mem. AAAS, Am. Soc. for Clin. Nutrition., Am. Soc. for Nutritional Scis.

SCHIAVO, GERALDINE ELIZABETH (GERI SCHIAVO), poet, screenwriter; b. Phila. d. Francis Anthony and Helen Nancy S. BA, Rugers U.; student, Performing Arts of N.J., The Actor's Lab., Phila., Weist-Barron Sch. TV. Cons. Ultima II Cosmetics, N.Y.C., 1981-85; realtor Old Colony, Moorestown, N.J., 1985-88; account exec. Success Pub., Hillside, 1986-88, Fragrances Du Monde, N.Y.C., 1987-88, Max Factor, L.A., 1989-90; freelance poet, screenwriter, 1990—; spl. event supr. Ritz Carlton, Phila., 1994-95. Contbr. poetry to Life Poems, An Anthology, 1996; author screenplays When Hearts Entwine, 1991, My Life in Boxes, 1993, Solitary Man, 1995, others. Vol. Am. Cancer Soc. South Jersey, 1995. State scholar State of N.J. Fellow Am. Film Inst. Democrat. Avocations: interior design, arts.

SCHIAVO, PASCO LOUIS, lawyer; b. Hazleton, Pa., June 21, 1937; s. Louis and Josephine (Cortese) S. BA, Lafayette Coll., 1958; JD, U. Pa., 1962. Bar: Pa. 1962, U.S. Dist. Ct. (mid. dist.) Pa. 1965, U.S. Ct. Appeals (3d cir.) 1972, U.S. Supreme Ct. 1970. Assoc. Laputka, Bayless, Ecker & Cohn, Hazleton, 1963-65; asst. dist. atty. Luzerne County, Wilkes-Barre, Pa., 1963-65; pvt. practice Hazleton, 1965—. Mem. disciplinary bd. Supreme Ct. Pa., Harrisburg, 1977-83. Contbr. articles to profl. jours. Pres. Luzerne County Commn. Econ. Opportunity, Wilkes-Barre, 1966-68. Mem. ABA, ATLA, Pa. Bar Assn., Luzerne County Bar Assn., Pa. Trial Lawyers Assn., Am. Judicature Soc., Nat. Bd. Trial Advocacy (diplomate, cert. civil trial advocate). Office: 199 N Church St Hazleton PA 18201-5874

SCHIAZZA, GUIDO DOMENIC (GUY SCHIAZZA), educational association administrator; b. Phila., May 17, 1930; s. Guido and Claudina (DiPrinzio) S.; m. Irmgard Heidi Reissmueller, May 15, 1954. BA, Pa. State U., 1952; postgrad., St. Joseph's U., 1954-55, Villanova U., 1954-55, Temple U., 1955-58. Cert. tchr., Pa.; cert. clinician, ednl. specialist, instructional specialist, sch. psychologist, guidance counselor, reading specialist. Speech therapist, lang. arts instr. Commonwealth of Pa., Dept. Edn., 1956-59; founder, clinician, instr., dir., bd. pres. Communicative Arts Ctr., Inc., Drexel Hill, Pa., 1958, Communication Skills Community Resources Ctr., Inc., Drexel Hill, 1958, 1964—; charter mem. exec. bd., bd. pres. United Pvt. Acad. Schs., Assn. of Pa., 1966—; exec. bd. govs., bd. chmn. The Accrediting Commn., 1971—. Charter mem. Pa. State Univ. Radio and TV Guild, University Park, Pa., 1951—; mem. legis. action com., Pa. State U., Univ. Park, 1988—; cons. communications skills, The Accrediting Commn., 1971—, United Pvt. Acad. Schs. Assn., Pa., 1966—. Founder, chmn., CEO Am. Ednl. Group, 1991—; chmn. CEO Internat. Ednl. Group, 1991—; CEO Cmty. Resources Ctr., Drexel Hill, 1991—, project coord. Energy Quest, 1992—; active Nat. Com. to Preserve Social Security and Medicare, Washington, 1986—, Am. Immigration Control Found., Monterey, Va., 1987—, English First, Springfield, Va., 1988—; mem. pres.'s coun. Rep. Nat. Com., 1989—, Nat. Rep. Senatorial Com., 1989—, Rep. Presdl. Task Force, 1989—; mem. Congrl. Legis. Agenda steering com. Empower Am., 1999. 1st Lt. Signal Corps, U.S. Army, 1952-54. Recipient Svc. award United Pvt. Acad. Sch. Assn. Pa., Monroeville, Pa., 1978, Disting. Achievement and Svc. award Bd. Govs. of the Accrediting Commn., Downington, Pa., 1980, Dr. Charles Boehm Edn. of Yr. award University Park, Pa., 1990, Loyal and Dedicated Svc. award The Accrediting Commn., 1974. Mem. NEA, Libr. Congress (chartered), Internat. Platform Assn., Pa. Edn. Assn., Jefferson Ednl. Found., World Affairs Coun. Phila., Heritage Found., Nat. Trust for Hist. Preservation, Nat. Congl. Club, Pa. State U. Nittany Lions Club, Pa. State U. Alumni Assn., Pa. State U. Football Lettermen's Club, Pa. State U. Varsity "S" Club. Republican. Roman Catholic. Avocations: music, home and garden design, automotive design, reading, golf. Office: The Accrediting Commn 436 Burmont Rd Drexel Hill PA 19026-3630

SCHIBLER, JOHN J. accountant; b. Canton, Ohio, Sept. 19, 1949; s. Lester Joseph and Irene Ann (Kocsis) S.; m. Susan Jude Moriarty, Sept. 14, 1973; children: Kathryn Ann, Jordan Michael. BBA, Kent State U., 1971; MBA, U. R.I., 1994. CPA, R.I. Staff acct. Ernst & Whinney, Canton, 1971-73, advanced staff acct., 1973-75, sr. acct., 1975-77, mgr., 1977-80, sr. mgr., 1980-84, ptnr., 1984-85, Cleve., 1985-89; sr. v.p. fin. R.I. Hosp., Providence, 1989-95; pres. Rhode Island Sound Enterprise, Ltd., Hamilton, Bermuda, 1991-99; sr. v.p. adminstrn., chief fin. officer Lifespan, Providence, 1995-99; pres. New Eng. Med. Ctr./ Ins. Co. Vermont, 1998-99; owner, pres. Harborview Cons., East Greenwich, RI, 1999—; instr. U. R.I., Providence, 2000—; sr. v.p., CFO Roger Williams Med. Ctr., 2001—. Pres. Canton Palace Theatre Assn., 1984, Cath. Cmty. League, Canton, 1986-88; treas. Buckeye Coun. Boy Scouts Am., 1987-89, treas. Narragansett Coun. Boy Scouts Am., 1991-94; trustee Providence Ronald MacDonald House, 1995-98, trustee Cmty. Prepatory Sch., 1996-2002. Recipient Dist. Svc. award Canton Jaycees, 1985, JCI Senatorship award, 1989. Mem. AICPA, R.I. Soc. CPAs, Healthcare Fin. Mgmt. Assn., Hosp. Assn., Nat. Avd. Coun., Fin. Execs. Inst., Quidnessett Country Club, Beta Gamma Sigma. Republican. Avocations: golf, reading, travel. Home: 62 Limerock Dr East Greenwich RI 02818-1643 Office: Harborview Cons PO Box 1711 East Greenwich RI 02818 also: U RI 825 Chalkstone Ave Providence RI 02908 E-mail: harborviewconsulting@worldnet.att.net., jjschilber@worldnet.att.net.

SCHICHLER, ROBERT LAWRENCE, English language educator; b. Rochester, N.Y., May 16, 1951; s. Alfred James and Elizabeth Johanna (Flugel) S. BA in English, SUNY, Geneseo, 1974, MA in English, 1978; PhD of English, Binghamton U., 1987. Writer, asst. administr. Artists-in-Residence Program, Rochester, N.Y., 1978-79; substitute tchr. City Sch. Dist., 1980-82; instr. English Talmudical Inst. Upstate N.Y., 1981-82, Binghamton (N.Y.) U., 1983-84; rsch. asst. Medieval and Renaissance Texts and Studies, Binghamton, 1985-86; adj. asst. prof. Rochester Inst. Tech., 1987-89; asst. prof. English Ark. State U., State University, 1989-94, assoc. prof., 1994-99, prof., 1999—. Adj. asst. prof. Monroe C.C., Rochester, 1987-89. Author: King of the Once Wild Frontier: Reflections of a Canal Walker, 1993; editor: Lady in Waiting: Poems in English and Spanish, 1994, Abstracts of Papers in Anglo-Saxon Studies, 1988—, Ctr. for Medieval and Early Renaissance Studies, Binghamton, 1986-94, Spillway Publs., Rochester, 1992—; asst. editor: Old English Newsletter, 1986-87, Mediaevalia, Binghamton, 1988-89; contbr. articles to profl. jours. Mem. Internat. Soc. Anglo-Saxonists, Medieval Acad. Am., Modern Lang. Assn. Am., Far West Popular Culture Assn., Am. Numismatic Soc., Am. Numismatic Assn. Home: Apt M1 726 Southwest Dr Jonesboro AR 72401-7045 Office: Ark State U Dept English and Philosophy State University AR 72467-1890 E-mail: rschich@mail.astate.edu., boonzither@hotmail.com.

SCHICK, EDGAR BREHOB, German literature educator; b. Phila., June 28, 1934; s. Claude Ernest and Martha Henrietta (Brehob) S.; m. Margaret Barbara Buehl, Feb. 12, 1938; children: Susanne, Christina. AB magna cum laude, Muhlenberg Coll., 1955; MA, Rutgers U., 1962, PhD, 1965. Asst. prof. German SUNY, Binghamton, 1963-68, asst. to pres. Albany, 1968-72, asst. prof., 1968-72; v.p. acad. affairs St. John Fisher Coll., Rochester, N.Y., 1972-78, exec. v.p., 1978-80, assoc. prof., 1972-80; pres. Nasson Coll., Springvale, Maine, 1980-83; provost, v.p. acad. affairs, prof. Eastern Ill. U., Charleston, 1984-87; exec. dir. Bd. Trustees, Md. State Univs. & Colls., Annapolis, 1987-88; vice chancellor for policy and planning U. Md. System, Adelphi, 1988-91; sr. fellow Am. Assn. State Colls. and Univs., 1991-94; cons. Assn. Governing Bds., 1993-95; interim v.p., dean St. Mary Coll., Lawrence, Kans., 1997-98; pres. Luther Inst., Washington, 1998—. Chmn. visitation team Mid. States Assn. Colls. and Schs., Phila., 1975-79; cons. IBM, Yorkville, N.Y., 1968, Nat. Luth. Campus Ministry, 1968-85, USAID, 1992-95. Author: Metaphorical Organicism in the Early Herder, 1971, Shared Visions of Public Higher Education Governance: Structures and Leadership Styles That Work, 1992, The "Local Board" in Multi-Campus Public Universities, 1994; contbr. articles on German lit. and higher edn. to profl. jours. Bd. dirs. United Way, 1981-82, Maine Ind. Colls. Assn., 1981-93, Deaton Hosp., Balt.; v.p. Christ Luth. Ch. Found., Balt.; mem. Accreditation Bd. for Engring. Tech.; pres. Oakleigh Forest Civic Assn. Fellow Univ. fellow, Rutgers U., New Brunswick, N.Y., 1962—63; grantee, Carnegie Found. Mem. Am. Assn. Higher Edn., Am. Assn. Univ. Adminstrs., Am. Assn. Tchrs. German, Assn. for Instl. Rsch., Soc. for Coll. and Univ. Planning, Thomas Mann Soc., Nat. Soc. Fund-Raising Execs. Lutheran. Home: 106 Quinn Rd Severna Park MD 21146-3015 E-mail: ebschick@erols.com.

SCHICK, HARRY LEON, investment company executive; b. N.Y.C., Oct. 24, 1927; s. Martin and Sadie (Spitz) S.; m. Eleanor Alter, Oct. 17, 1982; m. Inge Nussbaum, Oct. 12, 1964 (div. Nov. 1971); 1 child, Susan. AB magna cum laude, Bklyn. Coll., 1947; MS, Columbia U., 1948; postgrad., NYU, 1948-52. Securities analyst Sutro Bros., N.Y.C., 1948-52; asst. to pres. Clairdale Enterprises, Inc., 1953-66; mgr. arbitrage dept. First Manhattan Co., 1966-69, gen. ptnr., 1969-91, ltd. ptnr., 1992—. Lectr. Donaldson Sch. Orgn. and Mgmt., Yale U., New Haven, 1978-88, NYU Grad. Sch. Bus. Adminstrn., N.Y.C., 1977; lectr. in field. Bd. overseers Libr. of Jewish Theol. Sem.; trustee Washington Inst. for Near East Policy. Mem. Inst. Chartered Fin. Analysts, Am. Fin. Assn., Am. Econ. Assn., N.Y. Soc. Security Analysts (bd. dirs. 1975-76), Beta Gamma Sigma. Jewish. Home: 215 E 68th St Apt 15Y New York NY 10021-5726 Office: First Manhattan Co 437 Madison Ave New York NY 10022-7001

SCHICK, IRVIN HENRY, academic administrator, educator; b. Wilkes-Barre, Pa., Aug. 10, 1924; s. Irvin and Elizabeth (Valentine) S.; m. Marilyn Freeman, July 17, 1954 (dec. Aug. 1961); m. Marjorie Bletch Beach, Dec. 23, 1967; 1 child, Carolyn Patricia. Diploma, Bliss Elec. Sch., 1947; BEE with distinction, George Washington U., 1958; MSEE (NSF fellow), U. Md., 1961. Engring. asst. Jeddo-Highland Coal Co., Pa., 1942-43; instr. Bliss Elec. Sch., Washington, 1947-50; prof. math. and elec. engring., dept. head Montgomery Coll., Rockville, Md., 1950-65, dir. ext., 1965-67, dean adminstrn., 1967-75, adminstrv. v.p., 1975-78, prof. emeritus, adminstrv. v.p. emeritus, 1978—. Tchr., tutor, cons. indsl. cos., 1949—. Served with USAAF, 1943-46. Mem. AAUP, IEEE, Am. assn. Sch. Adminstrs., Internat. Platform Assn. , Md. State Tchrs. Assn., Montgomery County Edn. Assn., Bliss Elec. Soc. (bd. govs., past pres.), Tent Troupe Theatrical Orgn. (bd. govs.), Theta Tau, Sigma Tau (past pres.), Sigma Pi Sigma, Tau Beta Pi. Home: 105 Fleetwood Ter Silver Spring MD 20910-5512

SCHICK, MICHAEL WILLIAM, nonprofit organization executive; b. San Antonio, July 17, 1956; s. Lawrence Martin and Jeanne Frances (McCuen) S.; m. Diana Lynn McGinty, Mar. 14, 1988; children: Tiffany Michele, Jessica Diane. B in Media Arts with honors, U. S.C., 1979. Dir. prodns., asst. v.p. S.C. Savs. & Loan League, Columbia, 1978-81; dep. press sec. to U.S. Sen. Strom Thurmond Washington, 1981-85; sr. assoc. Civic Svc. Inc., 1985-2000; COO Justice Fellowship, 2000—01; dir. comm. U.S. Chamber of Commerce Inst. for Legal Reform, 2001—. Co-founder, chmn. First Monday Night, McLean, Va., 1981-94; Fourth Presbyn. Ch., Bethesda, Md., 1988—; chmn. Creative Living Internat., Reston, 1988—. C.S. Lewis fellow C.S. Lewis Inst., 1999-2000. Mem. Am. Assn. Polit. Conss., Washington Internat. Trade Assn. Republican. Avocations: golf, tennis, soccer, sailing, guitar. Home: 11560 Brass Lantern Ct Reston VA 20194-1221 Office: Justice Fellowship 1856 Old Reston Ave PO Box 97103 Washington DC 20090-7103 E-mail: mschick@justicefellowship.org.

SCHICK, PAUL K. hematologist; b. Bruno, Czechoslovakia, Oct. 12, 1932; came to U.S., 1939; s. Oskar and Vilma (Rushosky) S.; m. Barbara G. Pinsley, June 30, 1962; children: Darryl Richard, Jessica Ellen. Student, Tufts Coll.; DDS, Balt. Coll., 1957; MD, Boston U., 1961. Intern Kings County Hosp., Bklyn., 1961-62, resident in internal medicine, 1963-64; pvt. practice Manchester, Conn., 1965-69; fellow in hematology Montefiore Hosp., Bronx, N.Y., 1969-71; from asst. prof. medicine to assoc. prof. biochemistry Med. Coll. Pa., Phila., 1971-83; from assoc. prof. medicine to prof. Temple U. Sch. Medicine, 1979-88, prof. thrombosis, 1983-88; prof. medicine Jefferson Med. Coll., 1988—. Spkr. in field. Contbr. articles to profl. jours. Fellow ACP; mem. AAAS, Am. Fedn. in Cancer Rsch., Am. Soc. Hematology, Am. Soc. Physiology, Internat. Soc. Haemostasis and Thrombosis, Sigma Xi. Avocations: clarinetist, drawing, photography. Office: 221 Welsh Terrace Merion Station PA 19066

SCHICKLING, BARRY, editor, newspaper; b. Abington, Pa., Mar. 2, 1959; s. Harry III and Ruth Shirley (Spegal) S.; m. Jeanne Helen Kraft Keiser, July 26, 1985 (div. Jan. 1995). BA, Temple U., 1981. Sta. mgr. WCSD-FM, Warminster, Pa., 1979-82; west regional mgr. Comms. Team Inc., L.A., 1982-84; west regional office mgr. Siemens Audio, Hollywood, Calif., 1984-89; sports editor Daily Local News, West Chester, Pa., 1989-2000, mng. editor, 2000, editor, 2001—. Mng. editor Am. Dep. Sheriffs Assn., Houston,

1994-96; contbg. editor Deputy Sheriff Mag., 1999. Mem. AP Sports Editors, AP Mng. Editors, Soc. Profl. Journalists, Pa. Newspaper Assn., Pa. Soc. Newspaper Editors. Office: Daily Local News 250 N Bradford Ave West Chester PA 19382-2800 E-mail: editor@dailylocal.com.

SCHIDLOW, DANIEL, pediatrician, medical association administrator; b. Santiago, Chile, Oct. 23, 1947; m. Sally Rosen; children: David, Michael, Jessica. Grad., U. Chile, 1972. Diplomate Am. Bd. Pediatrics, Am. Bd. Pediatric Pulmonology; lic. in D.C., Pa., N.J. Rotating intern U. Chile Hosp., U. Chile Sch. Medicine, 1971-72, resident in internal medicine, instr. phys. diagnosis, 1972-73; resident, emergency rm. physician in pediatrics E.G. Cortes Hosp. Children, U. Chile, 1973-74; resident in pediatrics Albert Einstein Coll. Medicine Bronx (N.Y.)-Lebanon Hosp. Ctr., 1974-76; fellow pediatric pulmonary medicine St. Christopher's Hosp. for Children, Phila., 1976-78, chief sect. pediatric pulmonology dept. pediatrics, 1983-94, sr. v.p. clin. affairs, 1994—; from asst. to assoc. prof. pediatrics sch. medicine Temple U., 1978-90, prof., 1990-94, dep. chmn. dept. pediatrics, 1991-94; prof., sr. vice chmn. dept. pediatrics Allegheny U. of Health Scis., 1994-98, Med. Coll. Pa., Phila., 1994-98, Hahnemann Sch. Medicine, Phila., 1994-98; prof., acting chmn. dept. pediatrics MCP Hahnemann U. Sch. Medicine, 1998—; exec. v.p. med. and acad. affairs St. Christopher Hosp. for Children, 1998—; chmn. Dept of Ped. MCP Mahnemann U. Sch. Medicine, 1999—; physician-in-chief St. Christophers Hosp. for Children, 1999—. Sr. v.p. clin. affairs St. Christopher's Hosp. Children, 1978—, dir. fellowship tng. and edn. program sect. pediatric pulmonology, 1979-91, assoc. dir. pediatric pulmonary and cystic fibrosis ctr., 1981-83, med. dir. dept. respiratory therapy, 1982-88, project dir. Phila. pediatric pulmonary ctr., 1983-86, dir. cystic fibrosis ctr., 1983—, chair capital campaign com. dept. pediatrics, 1987, mem. exec. com. med. staff, 1988—, mem. various coms.; courtesy staff Lancaster (Pa.) Gen. Hosp., 1980-82; cons. divsn. rehab. Pa. Dept. Health, 1983—; mem. promotions com. dept. pediatrics sch. medicine Temple U., 1986—, chmn. com. appointments clin.-educator track 1991—; attending staff no. divsn. Albert Einstein Med. Ctr., 1987—; cons. Nat. Ctr. Youth Disabilities, 1987—; mem. med. adv. coun. Cystic Fibrosis Found., Bethesda, Md., 1987—, trustee, 1990—, med. dir. home care svcs., 1991—, various other positons; consulting staff Temple U. Hosp., 1988—; mem. organizing com. N.Am. Cystic Fibrosis Conf., 1990-93, co-chmn., 1992—; co-chmn. Nat. Concensus Conf. Pulmonary Complications Cystic Fibrosis, McLean, Va., 1992; mem. adv. bd. Phila. Parenting Assocs., 1992—. Reviewer Jour. Pediatrics, Am. Jour. Diseases Children, others. Named Illustrious Guest, City of LaPlata, Argentina, 1992. Fellow Am. Acad. Pediatrics (Pa. chpt., sect. diseases chest), Am. Coll. Chest Physicians (sect. cardiopulmonary diseases children); mem. AAAS, Am. Thoracic Soc. (mem. nominating com. 1993—), Am. Fedn. Clin. Rsch., Chilean Pediatric Soc. (hon.), Pa. Thoracic Soc., Ea. Soc. Pediatric Rsch., Phila. Pediatric Soc. Home: 315 N Bowman Ave Merion Station PA 19066-1523 Office: St Christopher's Hosp Chldn Office Med and Acad Affairs Erie Ave at Front St Philadelphia PA 19134

SCHIEB, PIERRE-ALAIN EDOUARD, economist; b. Marseille, France, Apr. 5, 1948; s. Edouard Auguste and Gabrielle (Crozat) S. LLD, Aix. en Provence U., France, 1970, DBA, 1974; MA, Sherbrooke U., Can., 1973; PhD, Strasbourg U., France, 1981. Assoc. prof. Paris U., 1970-82, 1982-85; dean Rouen Grad. Sch. Bus., France, 1985-91; v.p. Printemps Group, France, 1991-93; prin. adminstr. Orgn. for Econ. Coop. and Devel. (OECD), Paris, France, 1995—. Cons. BMD Internat., Strasbourg, 1976-81. Author: European Integration and Human Resource Management, 1989. Recipient Best Dissertation award, Inst. des Conseillers Adminstrn., 1974, Economics award Aix.en.Provence U., 1967. Mem. Sherbrooke Alumni Club. Office: OECD 2 rue Andre Pascal 75775 Paris Cedex 16 France

SCHIEBLER, GEROLD LUDWIG, pediatrician, educator; b. Hamburg, Pa., June 20, 1928; s. Alwin Robert and Charlotte Elizabeth (Schmoele) Schiebler; m. Audrey Jean Lincourt, Jan. 8, 1954; children: Mark, Marcella, Kristen, Bettina, Wanda, Michele. BS, Franklin and Marshall Coll., 1950; MD, Harvard U., 1954. Intern pediat. and internal medicine Mass. Gen. Hosp., Boston, 1954—55, resident, 1955—56; resident pediat. U. Minn. Hosp., Mpls., 1956—57, fellow pediatric cardiology, 1957—58, rsch. fellow, 1958—59; rsch. fellow sect. physiology Mayo Clinic and Mayo Found., 1959—60; asst. prof. pediatric cardiology U. Fla., 1960—63, assoc. prof., 1963—66, prof., 1966—92, Disting. Svc. prof., 1992—2000, adj. Disting. Svcs. prof., 2001—, chmn. dept. pediat., 1968—85, assoc. v.p. for health affairs for external rels., 1985—2000. Dir. divsn. Children's Med. Svcs. State of Fla., 1973—74. Author (with L.P. Elliott): The X-ray Diagnosis of Congenital Cardiac Disease in Infants, Children and Adults, 1968, 1979; author: (with L.J. Krovetz and I.H. Gessner) Pediatric Cardiology, 1979. Named Children's Med. Svcs. Pediatrician of Decade, Gov. Jeb Bush, 1999. Mem.: AMA (Benjamin Rush award 1993), AAAS, Fla. Med. Assn. (past v.p., bd. govs., pres. 1991—92), Fla. Heart Assn. (past pres.), Fla. Pediat. Soc. (exec. com.), Soc. Pediatric Rsch. (emeritus), Am. Coll. Cardiology, Am. Acad. Pediat. (Abraham Jacobi award 1993), Inst. Medicine NAS, Alpha Omega Alpha, Phi Beta Kappa. Home: 408 Beachside Villas Amelia Island Plantation Amelia Island FL 32034-6551

SCHIECK, FREDERICK W. federal agency administrator; m. Sara Schieck; 1 child Sara. B Fgn. Svc., Georgetown U.; MBA, Harvard U. Bd. trustees, v.p. exec. com. Pan-Am. Devel. Found.; with USAID; deputy adminstr. Agy. Internat. Devel., Washington, 2002—. With USAR. Office: USAID 1300 Pennsylvania Ave NW Washington DC 20523*

SCHIEFFER, BOB, broadcast journalist; b. Austin, Tex. m. Patricia Penrose; children: Susan, Sharon. BA in Journalism, Tex. Christian U. Reporter Ft. Worth Star-Telegram; news anchorman Sta. WBAP-TV, Dallas-Ft. Worth; with CBS News, 1969—, Pentagon corr., 1970-74, White House corr., 1974-79, chief Washington corr., 1982—; anchorman CBS Sunday Night News, 1973-74, Sunday edit. CBS Evening News, 1976—, Monday-through-Friday edits. Morning, 1979-80; co-anchorman CBS Morning News, from 1985; also participant CBS news spls. and spl. reports, including Peace and the Pentagon, 1974, Watergate-The White House Transcripts, 1974, The Mysterious Alert, 1974, 1976, Ground Zero, 1981; Democratic Nat. Conv., 1976; Republican Nat. Conv., Campaign '72; and mem. Emmy award-winning team CBS Evening News with Walter Cronkite, 1971; anchors Face the Nation CBS News, 1991—, chief Washington corr., 1975; co-anchor CBS Weekend News/Sunday News, N.Y.C. Author: (with Gary Paul Gates) The Acting President, 1989. Recipient various awards Sigma Delta Chi, various awards Tex. Associated Broadcasters, various awards AP Mng. Editors; co-recipient Emmy awards. Office: FACE THE NATION with Bob Schieffer 2020 M St NW Washington DC 20036-3304*

SCHIELE, PAUL ELLSWORTH, JR. education business owner, writer; b. Phila., Nov. 20, 1924; s. Paul Ellsworth Sr. and Maud (Barclay) S.; m. Sarah Irene Knauss, Aug. 20, 1946; children: Patricia Schiele Sommers, Sandra Schiele Kicklighter, Deborah Schiele Hartigan. AT, Temple U., 1949; BA, LaVerne U., 1955; MA, Claremont Grad. U., 1961; PhD, U.S. Internat. U., San Diego, 1970. Cert. sec. tchr., Calif. 1961. Tchr. sci. and math. Lincoln High Sch., Phila., 1956-57, Ontario (Calif.) Sch. Dist., 1957-65; math. and sci. cons. Hacienda La Puente U. Sch. Dist., Calif., 1965-75; asst. prof. Calif. State U., Fullerton, 1975-83; pres., owner Creative Learning Environments and Resources, Glendora, Calif., 1983—, cons. sci. curriculum, 1985—. Dir. title III project ESEA, 1974-75, cons. for project, 1975-77; cons. in field. Author: (student workbook) Beyond the Earth, 1969, Primary Science, 1972, 2d edit., 1976, (novel) Under Cover of Night, 1995, Chasing the Wild Geese, 1996, Deceptive Appearances, 1997; editor: A Living World, 1974, 2d edit., 1986; writer 9 sound filmstrips, model units for sci. and math. activity books, 10 sci. activities for L.A. Outdoor Edn. Program, 1980; editor 21 sci. and math. activity books, 1975-76; writer, co-dir. (TV) Marine Biology Series, 1970-71; contbr. munerous articles to profl. mags., 1960-85; writer and designer of 2 sci. ednl. games; designer in field. Apptd. adv. com. Sci. and Humanities Symposium Calif. Mus. Sci. and Industry, 1974; mem. State Sci. Permit Com., Tide Pools of Calif. Coast, 1974-75; mem. Friends of Libr., Friends Libr. Found. Mem. Internat. Platform Assn., Internat. Soc. Photographers, Glendora Hist. Soc., ABI Rsch. Assn. (bd. govs.), Calif. Elem. Edn. Assn. (hon.), Nat. PTA (hon.), Calif. Inter-Sci. Coun. (pres., chmn. 1971, 72), Elem Sch. Scis. Assn. (past pres., bd. dirs.), Paddlewheel Steamboating Soc. of Am., Phi Delta Kappa (chartered). Republican. Lutheran. Avocations: travel, etchings, art collecting, fencing. Home: 231 Catherine Park Dr Glendora CA 91741-3018

SCHIER, DONALD STEPHEN, language educator, educator; b. Ft. Madison, Iowa, Sept. 10, 1914; s. Francis and Marcella (Kenny) S. BA, State U. Iowa, 1936; MA, Columbia U., 1937, PhD, 1941. Mem. faculty State Tchrs. Coll., Bemidji, Minn., 1939-41, 41-42, Ill. Inst. Tech., 1946; mem. faculty Carleton Coll., Northfield, Minn., 1946-80, prof. French, 1953-80. Vis. prof. U. Wis., 1964-65; Brown tutor in French U. of South, Sewanee, Tenn., 1980-81 Author: Louis-Bertrand Castel, 1942; editor: (with Scott Elledge) The Continental Model, 1960, 2d edit., 1970; (Bertrand de Fontenelle), Nouveaux Dialogues des morts, 1965, rev. edit., 1974; translator: Letter on Italian Music (Charles de Brosses), 1978. Mem. selection com. Young Scholar Program, Nat. Found. Arts and Humanities, 1966-67. Served to capt. AUS, 1942-46. Mem. MLA, Am. Assn. Tchrs. French, Am. Soc. Eighteenth-Century Studies Home: 750 Weaver Dairy Rd Apt 1106 Chapel Hill NC 27514-1441

SCHIER, MARY JANE, science writer; b. Houston, Mar. 10, 1939; d. James F. and Jerry Mae (Crisp) McDonald; B.S. in Journalism, Tex. Woman's U., 1961; m. John Christian Schier, Aug. 26, 1961; children— John Christian, II, Mark Edward. Reporter, San Antonio Express and News, 1962-64; med. writer Daily Oklahoman, also Oklahoma City Times, 1965-66; reporter, med. writer Houston Post, 1966-84; sci. writer, univ. editor U. Tex. M.D. Anderson Cancer Ctr., 1984— . Recipient award Tex. Headliners Club, 1969, Tex. Med. Assn., 1972-74, 76, 78, 79, 80, 82 Tex. Hosp. Assn., 1974, 82, Tex. Public Health Assn., 1976, 77, 78, others. Mem. Houston Press Club Ednl. Found. (pres 1992—). Lutheran. Home: 9742 Tappenbeck Dr Houston TX 77055-4102 Office: 1515 Holcombe Blvd Houston TX 77030-4009

SCHIER, NEIL, lawyer, accountant; b. N.Y.C., Mar. 14, 1968; s. Lewis and Dorothy (Peretz) S. BA, U. N.C., 1989; MBA, Boston U., 1993; JD, Rutgers U., 1997. Bar: N.Y., N.J.; CPA. Tax staff KPMG, Short Hills, N.J.; sys. analyst, corp. acct. USRE, N.Y.C.; with Arthur Andersen, LLP, 1998-2000; v.p. Citibank, 2001—. Home: 15 Fairview Ave Apt 4 South Orange NJ 07079-2532 Office: Citibank 399 Park Ave New York NY 10043 E-mail: nschier@yahoo.com.

SCHIERINGA, PAUL KENNETH, special education educator, entertainer; b. Holland, Mich., Mar. 28, 1934; s. Peter and Mary (Van Kampen) Schieringa; m. Patti Ann Poling, Dec. 27, 1987. BA in Bus. Adminstrn., Hope Coll., 1957; MDiv, Founding Ch., Washington, 1963. Cert. nursing home adminstr., Ill. Quality control officer U.S. R.R. Retirement Bd., Chgo., 1957—61; entertainer, 1961—; med. mgr. hosps., nursing homes, mental health agencies, Chgo. and Ionia, Mich., 1971—87; theater adminstr. Croswell Opera House, Adrian, Mich., 1987—88; tchr. music/spl. edn./career edn. Guam Dept. Edn., Hagatna, 1991—2001. Cons. various nursing homes, Chgo., 1977—83, Betty's Learning Ctr., Upper Tumon, Guam, 1997—2001; mem. diabetes policy adv. bd. Mich. Dept. Pub. Health, Lansing, 1983—88; chairperson Citizens' Adv. Coun. for Southgate (Mich.) Mental Health Ctr., 1984—88. Composer: (songs) 23rd Psalm, 1972, He Cared So Much For Me, 1991, Lo, He Comes, 1992, It Still Took Calvary, 1997. Co-chair restoration adv. bd. Naval Air Sta., Hagatna, 1993—2001; bd. dirs. Friends of Guam Pub. Libr., 1996—2001. Named to Ancient Order of the Chamorri, Gov. of Guam, 2001. Avocations: writing childrens' books, World War II historian, organ, fishing. Home: 879 W 32d St Holland MI 49423

SCHIEROW, LINDA-JO, environmental policy analyst; b. Milw., Aug. 17, 1947; d. Joseph August Schierow and Ruth Eleanore (Beyersdorff) Heuer; 1 child, Katherine Irene. BS in Edn. with honors, U. Wis., 1969, MS in Land Resources, 1980, PhD in Land Resources, 1983. Cert. tchr., Wis. Tchr. elem. Cedarburg (Wis.) Pub. Schs., 1972-78; project assoc. Water Resources Ctr. U. Wis., Madison, 1985; asst. prof. U. Okla., Oklahoma City, 1985-88, rsch. fellow Norman, 1988; rsch. assoc. MIT, Cambridge, 1989-90; pvt. practice cons., 1990-91; policy analyst resources, sci. & industry U.S. Congress Congl. Rsch. Svc., Libr. of Congress, Washington, 1991-95, policy specialist resources, sci. & industry, 1995—. Cons. U.S.-Can. Internat. Joint Commn., Windsor, Ont., Can., 1985. Mem. editl. bd. RISK: Health, Safety & Environ., 1990—. Mem. Okla. State Groundwater Protection Strategy Com., Oklahoma City, 1985-88; bd. dirs. Ctr. for Cmty. Tech., Madison, 1983-84. Mem. Risk Assessment and Policy Assn. Democrat. Avocations: gardening, cooking. Office: Congl Rsch Svc Libr Of Congress Washington DC 20540-7450 E-mail: lschierow@crs.loc.gov.

SCHIESER, HANS ALOIS, education educator; b. Ulm, Germany, July 15, 1931; came to U.S., 1965; s. Alois and Anna (Stegmann) S.; m. Margret H. Schröer, June 6, 1962; children: Peter, Elisabeth. BA, Kepler Gymnasium, Ulm, 1952; MA in Philosophy, Passau, Fed. Republic Germany, 1959; EdM, Pedagogic Acad., Weingarten, Fed. Republic Germany, 1962; PhD, Loyola U., 1970. Head tchr. Pestalozzischule, Ulm, 1964-65; learning disabilities tchr. Jeanine Schultz Meml. Sch., Skokie, Ill., 1966-67; co-dir. Oak Therapeutic Sch., Evanston, 1967-70; from assoc. prof. to prof. edn. DePaul U., Chgo., 1969-91, prof. emeritus, 1991—. Cons. in field; program cons. Delphian Soc., L.A., 1977-90; rschr., tchr. in Germany, 1991—; active in tchrs. edn. Midwest Montessori Tchr. Tng. Ctr., Evanston, Ill.; guest prof. State U. Chelyabinsk, State Linguistic U., Irkutsk, Russia 1998–; ord. prof. Gustav-Siewerth-Akademie, Germany; prof. G. Siewerth Akademie (Germany). Author chpts. in books; contbr. articles to profl. jours.; adv. bd. Am. Edits. Sociology, Dushkin Pub. Group, 1985-91. Pres. N.Am. Family Svc. Found., Oak Lawn, Ill., 1974-91; bd. dirs. S.O.S. Children's Villages USA, Washington, 1986-94; pres. emeritus S.O.S. Children's Village Ill., Inc., Chgo.; bd. govs. Invest-in-Am. Nat. Found., Phila., 1988-90. Rsch. grant DePaul U., 1985-86, Rsch. sabbatical, 1989. Mem. Am. Ednl. Studies Assn., Nat. Soc. for Study of Edn., Philosophy of Edn. Soc. U.S.A., Soc. Educators and Scholars (bd. dirs. 1984-90), Am. Montessori Soc., Thomas More Gesellschaft/Amici Mori Europe, Phi Delta Kappa (pres. Zeta chpt., Chgo. 1973-75). Home: Veilchenweg 9 D-89134 Bermaringen Germany also: 400 E Main/6B/DJURI Evanston IL 60202 Office: DePaul U 2320 N Kenmore Ave Chicago IL 60614-3210 E-mail: prof_schieser@hotmail.com.

SCHIESS, BETTY BONE, priest; b. Cin., Apr. 2, 1923; d. Evan Paul and Leah (Mitchell) Bone; m. William A. Schiess, Aug. 28, 1947; children: William A. (dec.), Richard Corwine, Sarah. BA, U. Cin., 1945; MA, Syracuse U., 1947; MDiv, Rochester Ctr. for Theol. Studies, 1972. Ordained priest Episcopal Ch., 1974. Priest assoc. Grace Episc. Ch., Syracuse, N.Y., 1975; mem. N.Y. Task Force on Life and Law (apptd. by gov.), 1985—; chaplain Syracuse U., 1976-78, Cornell U., Ithaca, N.Y., 1978-79; rector Grace Episc. Ch., Mexico, 1984-89. Cons. Women's Issues Network Episc. Ch. in U.S., 1987—; writer, lectr., cons. religion and feminism, 1979—. Author: Take Back the Church, Indeed The Witness, 1982, Creativity and Procreativity: Some Thoughts on Eve and the Opposition and How Episcopalians Make Ethical decisions, Plumline, 1988, Send in the Clowns, Chrysalis, Journal of the Swedenborg Foundation, 1994, Cassandra in the Temple, Chrysalis, Journal of the Swedenborg Foundation, 1998; contbr. forward to book, A Still Small Voice! Women Ordination and the Church, Frederick W. Schmidt Jr., 1996. Bd. dirs. People for Pub. TV in N.Y., 1978, Religious Coalition for Abortion Rights; trustee Elizabeth Cady Stanton Found., 1979; mem. policy com. Coun. Adolescent Pregnancy; mem. N.Y. State Task Force Life and the Law, 1983-96. Recipient Gov.'s award Women of Merit in Religion, 1984, Ralph E. Kharas award ACLU Ctr., N.Y., 1986, Goodall disting. alumna award & Hills Sch., 1988, Human Rightes award Human Rights Commn. of Syracuse and Onondaga County, N.Y., 1989; inducted into Nat. Women's Hall of Fame, 1994. Mem. NOW (Syracuse), Internat. Assn. Women Ministers (dir. 1978 pres. 1984-87), Na'amat U.S. (hon. life), Mortar Bd., Theta Chi Beta. Democrat. Home and Office: 107 Bradford Ln Syracuse NY 13224-1901 Office: Episcopal Cmty Anabel Taylor Hall Cornell U Ithaca NY 14850 E-mail: bschies1@twcny.rr.com.

SCHIESS, WILLIAM ARNOLD, health services administrator, geriatrician; b. Syracuse, N.Y., Nov. 24, 1920; s. Walter Otto and Elsie Arlene (Olsen) S.; m. Betty Bone, Aug. 4, 1947; children: Richard, Sally. BA, Syracuse U., 1941, MD, 1943. Diplomate Am. Bd. Internal Medicine. Intern R.I. Hosp., 1944-45; fellow dept. physiology Syracuse U. Coll. Medicine, 1947, fellow dpet. pathology, 1947-48, resident in internal medicine, 1948-52; chief of medicine Crouse Hosp., Syracuse, 1957-84, v.p. med. affairs, 1987-90; med. dir. Cmty. Meml. Hosp., Hamilton, N.Y., 1990-96, Crouse Cmty. Ctr., Morrisville, 1996—. Capt. U.S. Army, 1944-46, Germany. Mem. Phi Beta Kappa, Alpha Omega Alpha. Democrat. Episcopalian. Avocation: fishing. Home: 107 Bradford Ln Syracuse NY 13224-1901

SCHIESSER, WILLIAM E, mathematician, researcher; s. Edward Valentine and Laura Virginia (Bauer) Schiesser; m. Dolores T Tubio; children: William Jr., Nathan. PhD, Princeton (N.J.) U., 1958. R.L. McCann prof. Lehigh U., Bethlehem, Pa., 1976—2002. Cons. Air Products and Chemicals, Trexlertown, Pa., 1975—2002. Educator (scientific software) Various titles, 1960; author: (books in scientific computation) The Numerical Method of Lines Integration of Partial Differential Equations, 1991; author: (with Silebi, C.A.) Dynamic Modeling of Transport Process Systems, 1992; author: (with Byrne G.D.) Recent Developments in Numerical Methods and Software for ODEs, DAEs and PDEs, 1992; author: Computational Mathematics in Engineering and Applied Science, 1994; author: (with Silebi, C.A.) Computational Transport Phenomena, 1997; author: (with others) Adaptive Method of Lines, 2001. First lt. Army, 1958—59, Aberdeen Proving Ground. Mem.: SIAM. Avocations: skiing, tennis. Office: Lehigh Univ Iacocca 0307 111 Research Dr Bethlehem PA 18015 Office Fax: 610-758-5057. Business E-Mail: wes1@lehigh.edu.

SCHIESSLER, ROBERT WALTER, retired chemical and oil company executive; b. Honesdale, Pa., Oct. 2, 1918; s. Walter A. and Josephine (Herzog) S.; m. Betty Hartman, June 5, 1939; children— Lynn Alice, Dale Ann; m. Florence Cutler, Aug. 16, 1968. BS, Pa. State U., 1939, PhD, 1944; MS, McGill U., 1941. Research chemist Gen. Electric Co., Schenectady, 1941; from instr. to asso. Prof. chemistry and dir. Am. Petroleum Inst. Research Pa. State U., 1942-55; chemistry and physics cons., 1946-55; tech. dir. Central Research div. Mobil Oil Co., Paulsboro and Princeton, N.J., 1950-60, mgr. central research div., asst. gen. mgr. research dept., 1960-62, gen. mgr. research dept., 1962-67; v.p. research Mobil Research & Devel. Corp., 1967-68; chmn., pres. Indsl. Reactor Labs., Inc., 1966-67; mgr. long-range planning Mobil Oil Corp., 1968-72, gen. mgr. real estate and land devel., 1972-83; chmn. Mobil Land Devel. Corp., 1972-83; pres. Sandvik, Inc., 1983-84. Chmn. bd. trustees Gordon Rsch. Conf., Inc., 1957; mem. bd. Am. Chem. Soc. Peroleum Rsch. Fund, 1955-59, 60-63; Rsch. chemist Can. govt., 1940-41. Co-Author: Chemistry of Petroleum Hydrocarbons, 1954; discoverer method for prodn. super-explosive used by U.S. and Can., World War II; identified hydrocarbon structure for super-lubricant Mobil 1. Recipient award in petroleum chemistry Am. Chem. Soc., 1953; named outstanding young man State Coll. of Pa., outstanding young man Jr. C. of C., 1952; recipient Wisdom award, 1970 Fellow Am. Inst. Chemists, AAAS (v.p. for chemistry, chmn. chemistry sect. 1960); mem. Am. Chem. Soc., AAUP, Sigma Xi, Phi Lambda Upsilon, Phi Eta Sigma. Home: 1500 Palisade Ave Fort Lee NJ 07024-5337

SCHIESSWOHL, CYNTHIA RAE SCHLEGEL, lawyer; b. Colorado Springs, Colo., July 7, 1955; d. Leslie H. and Maime (Kascak) Schlegel; m. Scott Jay Schlesswohl, Aug. 6, 1977; children: Leslie Michelle, Kristen Elizabeth. BA cum laude, So. Meth. U., 1976; JD, U. Colo., 1978; postgrad., U. Denver, 1984. Bar: Colo. 1979, Wyo. 1986, Ind. 1988, U.S. Dist. Ct. Colo. 1979, U.S. Ct. Appeals (10th cir.) 1984, U.S. Supreme Ct. 2000, Utah 2001, U.S. Dist. Ct. Utah 2001, cert.: (family mediator) 1992, (civil mediator) 1994. Rsch. clk. City Atty.'s Office, Colorado Springs, Colo., 1976; investigator Pub. Defender's Office, 1976; dep. dist. atty. 4th Jud. Dist. Colo., 1979-81; pvt. practice law Grand Junction, Colo., 1981-82, Denver, 1983-84; assoc. Law Offices of John G. Salmon P.C., 1984-85; pvt. practice Laramie, Wyo., 1985-88, Indpls., 1988-90; of counsel Rund & Wunsch, 1990—2000; dep. prosecuting atty. 53d Jur. Cir. Ind., 2000; pvt. practice Park City, Utah, 2001—. Guest lectr. Pikes Peak C.C., 1980; adj. prof. polit. sci. and speech Butler U., Indpls., 1993-99, spl. asst. to dean for pre-law, 1993-95, asst. dean for pre-profl. svcs., 1995-99. Advisor Explorer Law Post Boy Scouts Am., 1980—81; vol. Girl Scouts Am., 1993—94, Park City Mountain Resort, 2000—01, Canyons Resort, 2000—01, Leadership Park City, 2000; mem. Park City Singers, 2000—; hearing officer Wyo. Dept. Edn., 1987—88; vol. Project Motivation, Dallas, 1974; chairperson Wyo. Med. Rev. Panel, 1987; lectr. Ind. Pastor's Conf., Rethinking Prisons Conf., 1990, Econ. Edn. for Clergy Conf., 1991; trustee New Castle Cmty. Sch. Corp., 1998—2000, sec., 1999—2000, legis. liaison, 1999—2000; mem. exec. panel Henry County YMCA, 2000; ex officio mem. ch. devel. com. Ctrl. Rocky Mt. region Christian Ch. (Disciples of Christ), 1986—88; mem. evangelism commn. United Meth. Ch., 1987—88, fin. com. youth and music depts., 1979—81, lay del. Rocky Mountain Ann. Conf., 1986—87, acad. tutor youth programs, 1989—, Sunday sch. tchr., 1995—2000; mem. ch. and soc. com. Meridian St. United Meth. Ch., 1989—93, mem. refugee resettlement com., 1990—93; hon. pres. United Meth. Women, 1996—2000, mem. ch. choir, 1997—; bd. dirs. Art Ctr. and Art Assn. Henry County, 1997—2000, Arts-Kids, 2002—, Multicultural Alliance, 2002—. Named U. scholar So. Meth. U., 1973. Mem.: ABA (internat. law com.), Park City Bar Assn., Indpls. Bar Assn. (internat. law sect. ethics com. 1990—93), Am. Immigration Lawyers Assn. (sec. Ind. chpt. 1991—92, 1993—94, chpt. vice chair 1992—93, asylum liaison 1990—99, chpt. chair 1994—95, bd. govs. 1994—95, Utah chpt. vice chair 2002—), Colo. Bar Assn. (ethics com. 1984—85, long range planning com. 1985—88, chairperson 1986—87), Wyo. State Bar, Alpha Delta Pi, Alpha Lambda Delta, Pi Sigma Alpha (awards com. 1999—2000). Republican. Office: PO Box 981114 Park City UT 84098-1114

SCHIFF, ADAM BENNETT, congressman, lawyer; b. Framingham, Mass., June 22, 1960; s. Edward Maurice and Sherrill Ann (Glovsky) S.; m. Eve Schiff; 1 child, Alexa Marion BA, Stanford U., 1982; JD, Harvard U., 1985. Bar: Calif. 1986. Assoc. Gibson, Dunn & Crutcher, L.A., 1986; asst. U.S. atty. U.S. Atty.'s Office, 1987-93; mem. Calif. Senate, 1996-2000, U.S. Congress from 27th Calif. dist., Washington, 2001—; mem. judiciary com., internat. rels. com. Spl. assignment to Czechoslovakia, Justice Dept., Bratislava, 1992. Democrat. Avocation: writing fiction. Office: 437 Cannon HOB Washington DC 20515-0527 E-mail: congressman.schiff@mail.house.gov.

SCHIFF, DAVID TEVELE, investment banker; b. N.Y.C., Sept. 3, 1936; s. John Mortimer and Edith Brevoort (Baker) S.; m. Martha Elisabeth Lawler, May 11, 1963; children: Andrew Newman, David Baker, Ashley Reynolds. B.Engring., Yale U., 1958. Trainee Chem. Bank N.Y. Trust, N.Y.C., 1959-62; analyst Madison Fund, 1962; assoc., then partner Kuhn, Loeb & Co., 1963-77; vice chmn. Kuhn Loeb & Co. Inc., 1977; mng. dir. Lehman Bros. Kuhn Loeb Inc., N.Y.C., 1977-83, also dir.; mng. ptnr. Kuhn, Loeb & Co. (formerly KLS Enterprises), 1984—. Dir., vice chmn. Am. Crown Life Ins. Co., N.Y.C., 1981-95; bd. dirs. Crown Life Ins. Co., Toronto, 1971-92; mem. lower Manhattan adv. bd. Chem. Bank, 1977-85; bd. advisors Venture Capital Fund of Am., 1998—; mem. leadership coun. Yale Sch. Forestry and Environ. Studies, 2000—. Trustee, chmn. bd. Wildlife Conservation Soc.; trustee Met. Mus. Art, Citizens Budget Commn., N.Y.C., Greater N.Y. coun. Boy Scouts Am., 1965-91; trustee Beekman Downtown Hosp., 1966-82, chmn., 1975-79; trustee Brooks Sch., North Andover, Mass., 1972-90, treas., 1987-90; bd. govs. Yale U. Art Gallery, 1973-97, Fed. Hall Meml. Assn.; mem. adv. bd. dirs. Outward Bound, Inc., 1983-99; mem. Provident Loan Soc. N.Y.; bd. dirs. Am. Hosp. of Paris Found., N.Y.C., 1987. With U.S. Army, 1959. Mem. Econ. Club N.Y.C., Pilgrims U.S., Brook Club, Century Assn., River Club, Maroon Creek Club (Aspen, Colo.), Mill Reef Club (Antigua), Yale Club N.Y.C. Episcopalian. Home: 770 Park Ave New York NY 10021-4153 Office: 320 Park Ave 10th Fl New York NY 10022-6815

SCHIFF, DONALD WILFRED, pediatrician, educator; b. Detroit, Sept. 11, 1925; s. Henry and Kate (Boesky) S.; m. Rosalie Pergament; children: Stephen, Jeffrey, Susan, Douglas. Student, Wayne State U., 1943-44, Oberlin Coll., 1944-45; MD, Wayne State U., 1949. Diplomate Am. Bd. Pediatrics. Intern Detroit Receiving Hosp., 1949-50; resident in pediatrics U. Colo., 1954-55, chief resident in pediatrics, 1955-56; instr. U. Colo. Health Scis. Ctr., Denver, 1956-59, asst. clin. prof., 1959-69, assoc. clin. prof., 1969-78, clin. prof., 1978-87, prof., 1987—; pvt. practice Littleton (Colo.) Clinic, 1956-86, chmn. bd., 1973-79; med. dir. HMO Colo., Denver, 1980-86; med. dir. Child Health Clinic The Children's Hosp. Contbr. articles to profl. jours. Bd. dirs. Sch. Dist. VI, Colo., 1962; pres. Arapahoe Mental Health Clinic, Denver, 1968-70, bd. dirs., 1964-70; adv. coun. State of Colo. Medicaid, Denver, 1981—. With USN, 1944-46, USPHS, 1952-54, Turtle Mountain Indian Reservation, N.D. Recipient 25 Yrs. Teaching award U. Colo. Sch. Medicine, 1981. Mem. Am. Acad. Pediatrics (chmn. Colo. chpt. 1973-79, alternate dist.

chmn. 1977-81, chmn. dist. 8 1981-86, nat. pres. 1988-89), Rocky Mountain Pediatric Soc., Colo. Med. Soc. Home: 600 Front Range Rd Littleton CO 80120-4052 Office: The Childrens Hosp Child Health Clinic Box BO32 1056 E 19th Ave Denver CO 80218-1088

SCHIFF, EUGENE ROGER, medical educator, hepatologist; b. Cin., Jan. 3, 1937; s. Leon and Augusta (Miller) S.; m. Dana Kendall, Dec. 27, 1965; children: David, Lisa. BA, U. Mich., 1958; MD, Columbia U., 1962. Diplomate Am. Bd. Internal Medicine, Am. Bd. Gastroenterology, Nat. Bd. Med. Examiners. Intern and med. resident Cin. Gen. Hosp., 1962-64; med. resident Parkland Meml. Hosp., Dallas, 1966-67; USPHS postdoctoral fellow in gastroenterology Southwestern Med. Sch., U. Tex., 1967-69; asst. prof. medicine U. Miami (Fla.) Sch. Medicine, 1969-74, assoc. prof., 1974-78, prof., 1978—, chief div. hepatology, 1971—, dir. Ctr. for Liver Diseases, 1982—. Chief hepatology sect. VA Med. Ctr., Miami, 1971-97; chmn. adv. com. on gastrointestinal drugs FDA, Rockville, Md., 1983-85, 88-92, mem. adv. com. on blood safety, 1997—. Co-editor: Diseases of the Liver, 5th edit., 1982, 6th edit., 1987, 7th edit. 1993, 8th edit., 1998, Liver Transplantation, 3d edit., 2000. Bd. dirs. Am. Digestive Health Found., 1996-2001, chmn. digestive health initiative on viral hepatitis, 1996-2001. Lt. comdr. USPHS, 1964-66. Master: Am. Coll. Gastroenterology; fellow: ACP (gov. Fla. chpt. 1984—88), Royal Coll. Physicians; mem.: AMA, Am. Gastroenterology Assn. (chmn. Biliary disorders sect. 1993—95), Internat. Assn. for Study of Liver Diseases (councilor), Argentine Soc. Gastroenterology (hon.), Am. Bd. Internal Medicine (subsplty. bd. gastroenterology), Am. Assn. for Study of Liver Diseases (sec.-treas. 1991—96, councilor 1997—2002, pres.-elect 2000, pres. 2001). Jewish. Home: 9307 SW 123rd Ter Miami FL 33176-5060 Office: U Miami 1500 NW 12th Ave Ste 1101 Miami FL 33136-1052 E-mail: eschiff955@aol.com., eschiff@med.miami.edu.

SCHIFF, GARY STUART, academic administrator, educator, consultant; b. Bklyn., Mar. 27, 1947; s. Jacob and Lillian (Grumet) S.; children: Jeremy Jay, Rina Joy. BA, Bin Hebrew Lit., Yeshiva U., 1968; MA, Columbia U., 1970, Cert. in Middle East Studies, PhD, Columbia U., 1973; DHL (hon.), Gratz Coll., 1997. Asst. prof. Jewish studies and polit. sci. CUNY, 1973-76; dir. Mid. East affairs Nat. Jewish Cmty. Rels. Coun., N.Y.C., 1976-78; exec. asst. to pres. Acad. for Ednl. Devel., 1978-83; pres., prof. Middle East studies Gratz Coll., Melrose Park, Pa., 1983-97. Vis. prof. Balt. Hebrew U., 1997, Washington Coll., Md., 2000-2001; vis. asst. prof. polit. sci. Yeshiva U., 1973-77. Author: Tradition and Politics: The Religious Parties of Israel, 1977, The Energy Education Catalog, 1981; contbr. articles to profl. jours. Grantee NEH, Ford Found., Danforth Found., Woodrow Wilson Found., William Penn Found., Pew Charitable Trusts. Mem. Assn. of Colls. of Jewish Studies (bd. dirs.), Assn. for Israel Studies (v.p.), Coun. for Jewish Edn. (bd. dirs.), Assn. for Jewish Studies, World Jewish Congress (governing bd.), Am. Jewish Com. (N.Y. chpt. bd. dirs., Phila. chpt. communal affairs commn.). Avocations: cantorial music, boating, cats. Home: 29182 Ricks Landing Rd Kennedyville MD 21645-3306 E-mail: garygrant@aol.com.

SCHIFF, JAMES ANDREW, English educator; b. Cin., Dec. 6, 1958; s. Robert Cleveland and Adele Carol (Roehr) S.; m. Elizabeth Ann York, June 24, 1989; children: James Walker, Hayden Andrew. BA, Duke U., 1981; MA, NYU, 1985, PhD, 1990. Instr. English, NYU, N.Y.C., 1984-88; adj. asst. prof. U. Cin., 1989—. Bd. dirs. Channel 48, 1st Nat. Bank No. Ky. Author: Updike's Version, 1992, Understanding Reynolds Price, 1996, Critical Essays on Reynolds Price, 1998, John Updike Revisited, 1998. Bd. dirs. Cin. Merc. Libr., 1991—, Seven Hills Sch.; com. mem. Cin. Assn. for Blind, 1991—. Democrat. Home: 2 Forest Hill Dr Cincinnati OH 45208-1910

SCHIFF, JAYNE NEMEROW, underwriter; b. N.Y.C., Aug. 8, 1945; d. Milton E. Nemerow and Shirley (Kaplan) Wachtel; m. Albert John Schiff, Mar. 7, 1971; children: Matthew Evan, Kara Anne. BS in Bus., Marymount Coll., 1981; M in Profl. Studies in Elem. and Spl. Edn., Manhattanville Coll., 1995. Corporate sec., treas. Albert J. Schiff Assocs., Inc., N.Y.C., 1970-78; field underwriter Mut. N.Y. Fin. Svcs., Greenwich, Conn., 1973-90; freelance employee benefit cons., 1990-99; sr. account exec., contr. Nylex Benefits, Stamford, Conn., 1999—. Regional dir. mktg., MONY Fin. Services, N.Y.C., 1978-79; tutor HELP program Manhttanville Coll., 1996-2000. Bd. dirs. N.Y. League Bus. and Profl. Women, 1976-78, Temple Sinai, Stamford, Conn., 1979-84, N.Y. Ctr. Fin. Studies; leader Webelos Cub Scouts, 1977-78; treas. Ann. Mothers Bd. Benefit Greenwich Acad., 1988, upper sch. acquisitions chmn., 1989, chmn. spl. acquisitions Greenwich Acad. Benefit, 1990-91, chmn. advt., 1992; ESL tutor Lit. Vols. Am., ESL tutor, trainer, 1993; co-chair U. Rochester Parents Coun., 1993-96. Named Conn.'s Outstanding Young Woman, 1979. Mem. LWV, Am. Soc. Chartered Life Underwriters, N.Y. Ctr. Fin. Studies (bd. dirs.), N.Y.C. Life Underwriters Assn. (bd. dirs. 1977-78). Jewish. Avocations: sailing, knitting, playing piano, reading. Office: Clark Bardes Ptnrs 281 Tresser Blvd Stamford CT 06901-3284

SCHIFF, LAURIE, lawyer; b. Newark, Apr. 24, 1960; d. Norman Nathan and Claire Jane (Schott) S. BS in Law, Western State U., Fullerton, Calif., 1987, JD, 1988. Bar: Calif. 1989. Ptnr. Schiff Mgmt., Newport Beach, Calif., 1983-89; pvt. practice Schiff & Assocs., Irvine, 1989-91; ptnr. Schiff & Shelton, 1991—. Probation monitor State Bar Ct. Calif., 1991-97, spl. prosecutor, 1997—. Producer: (record album) Boys Just Want to Have Sex, 1984. Bd. dirs. Jewish Family Svcs. of Orange County, 1994—99. Mem. Orange County Bar Assn. (arbitrator 1995—), Am. Mensa, Am. Polocrosse Assn., Saddlebrook Polocrosse (treas. 1991), Am. Quarterhorse Assn., Internat. Cat Assn. (chair legis. com. 1995-97, 98-99, legal counsel 1999—, lic. splty. judge 2001—), Tonks West (v.p. 1994-96, pres. 1996-97), Tonkinese Breed Assn., Online Feline Fanciers (v.p. 1995-97, bd. dirs. 1997—), Intern. Politically Incorrect Cat Club (v.p. 1996—). Democrat. Jewish. Office: Schiff & Shelton 3700 Campus Dr Ste 202 Newport Beach CA 92660-2603 E-mail: lschiff@schiff-shelton.com.

SCHIFF, MARLENE SANDLER, entrepreneur; b. Great Barrington, Mass. d. Jack and Lena Yetta (Klein) Sandler; m. Haskel Schiff (dec. Feb. 1967), 1 child, Melissa Robin. BA, U. Mass., 1970; OPM, Harvard U., 1985. Founder, chief exec. officer, chmn. Transceiver East Inc., N.Y.C., 1971-88; founder, CEO, pres. MSS Assoc., Inc., 1995—. Founder, CEO, pres. MSS Assocs., Inc. Pub. Best of American Lifestyles mag./catalog, 1995-97. Eye adv. com. N.Y. Hosp./Cornell Med. Ctr., 1988—; adv. bd. dirs. Sol C. Schneider Entrepreneurial Ctr. of the Wharton Bus. Sch. U. Pa., 1989, chair, 1991-95; adv. bd. nutrition and fitness project Harvard U. Sch. Pub. Health. Mem. Com. of 200 (bd. dirs. 1989-91, N.E. regional chair 1989-91, C200 Found. bd, 1991-93), Am. Fedn. Arts (membership and spl. events com. 1990). Home: 950 5th Ave New York NY 10021-1741 Fax: 212-737-0100. E-mail: mssnyny@aol.com.

SCHIFF, MARTIN, physician, surgeon; b. Phila., July 16, 1922; s. Isidore and Cecelia (Miller) S.; m. Mildred Tepley, Jan. 5, 1946; children: Denise Schiff Simon, Michael, David BS, Pa. State U., 1943; MD, U. Calif.-Irvine, 1951. Intern L.A. County Gen. Hosp., 1950-51; gen. practice medicine specializing in bariatrics L.A., 1951—. Mem. staff Brotmam Meml. Hosp.; lectr. L.A. area community colls. Author: Eat & Stay Slim, 1972, Miracle Weight-Loss Guide, 1976, One-Day-At-A-Time Weight Loss Plan, 1980, (5 tapes) Weight Loss Plan for Health, Happiness & A Longer Life Span, 1982, The Thin Connection, 1986, Lose Unwanted Pounds Permanently Without Dieting/Trying/Playing Games, 1998, Weight Control-Fact or Fiction?, 1999, The Power of Your Will, 1999, Connections: Feelings and Emotions, 2000, YOU: A Guide to You and a Roadmap to Your Inner Being, 2002. Lt. USN, 1943-45, PTO Mem. AMA, Calif. Med. Assn., L.A. Med. Assn., Am. Soc. Weight Control Specialists Home: 1220 Corsica Dr Pacific Palisades CA 90272-4016 Office: 12900 Venice Blvd Los Angeles CA 90066-3510

SCHIFF, PETER GRENVILLE, venture capitalist; b. N.Y.C., Apr. 4, 1952; s. John M. and Edith (Baker) S.; m. Elizabeth Peters, June 25, 1976; children: Edward, James, Christie. BA, Lake Forest Coll., 1974; MBA, U. Chgo., 1976. With Chem. Bank, N.Y.C., 1976-80, E.M. Warburg, Pincus & Co., N.Y.C., 1980-83; founder, pres. Northwood Ventures, LLC, L.I., N.Y., 1983—. Trustee Lake Forest (Ill.) Coll., 1995—, Brooks Sch., North Andover, Mass., 1997—, N.Y. Racing Assn., Elmont, 1995—; advisor Wildlife Conservation Soc., Bronx, 1990—. Avocations: fishing, horse racing, skiing, art collecting. Office: Northwood Ventures 485 Underhill Blvd Syosset NY 11791-3434

SCHIFF, ROBERT, healthcare consulting company executive; b. N.Y.C., Jan. 7, 1942; s. Henry and Jeanette (Levine) S.; m. Adrianne Bendich, Aug. 16, 1964 (div. July 1979); children: Jorden, Debra; m. Joann McTaggart, Aug. 24, 1986. BS, CCNY, 1964; MS, Iowa State U., 1966; PhD, U. Calif., Davis, 1968. Asst. prof. anatomy Tufts U. Sch. Medicine, Boston, 1969-72; mgr. serology rsch. Hyland divsn. Baxter Labs., Costa Mesa, Calif., 1972-74; dir. R & D J.T. Baker Diagnostics, Bethlehem, Pa., 1974-77; dir. diagnostic R & D Hoffmann-LaRoche, Nutley, N.J., 1977-80; group v.p. Warner Lambert Co., Morris Plains, 1980-82; pres., CEO Schiff & Co., Inc., West Caldwell, 1982—. Del. Nat. Commn. for Clin. Lab. Stds., 1979-80; vice chmn. R & D Coun. N.J., 1980-82; bd. dirs. E.P.I. subs. E-Z-EM, Westbury, N.Y., 1991-98. Contbr. numerous articles to profl. jours.; patentee in field. Post Doctoral fellow U. Calif., Davis, 1969; Aid to Cancer Rsch. grantee, Mass., 1970. Mem. N.Y. Acad. Sci., Regulatory Affairs Profl. Soc. (cert.), Am. Soc. Quality Control (cert. quality auditor), Am. Assn. Clin. Chemistry, Brit. Inst. Regulatory Affairs, Parenteral Drug Assn., Sigma Xi. Avocation: licensed pilot. Office: Schiff & Co 1129 Bloomfield Ave West Caldwell NJ 07006-7123 E-mail: rschiff13@aol.com., schiffandcompany@aol.com.

SCHIFF, STEPHEN FRANK, urologic surgeon; b. Ft. Lee, Va., Sept. 22, 1956; s. Erwin Herbert and Charlene (Perlmutter) S.; m. Sharon May Perry, Sept. 10, 1989; children: Perry Tyler, Morgan Daniel. AB cum laude, Princeton U., 1978; MD, Ea. Va. Med. Sch., 1981. Diplomate Nat. Bd. Med. Examiners, Am. Bd. Urology; lic. physician, Pa., Mass., Conn., R.I. Surg. intern Hosp. U. Pa., Ea. Va. Grad. Sch. Medicine, 1981-82; radiology resident Ea. Va. Grad. Sch. Medicine, 1982-83; surg. resident Hosp. U. Pa., 1983-84; clin. fellow oncology Mass. Gen. Hosp./Am. Cancer Soc., 1985-86; resident urol. svc. Harvard Med. Sch./Mass. Gen. Hosp., 1984-87; med. dir. Renal Lithotripsy Ctr., Yale-New Haven Hosp., 1988-92; chief urology Yale U. Health Svcs., 1988-92, West Haven VA Med. Ctr., 1988-89; asst. prof. surgery sect. urology Yale Sch. Medicine, 1988-92; asst. clin. prof. surgery and urology Brown U. Sch. Medicine, Providence, 1992—. Clin. fellow dept. surgery Harvard Med. Sch., 1984-87, instr., 1987; asst. urology Harvard Med. Sch./Mass. Gen. Hosp., 1987; mem. Yale Trauma Group, Yale U. Sch. Medicine, faculty advisor, trainer urology teaching assocs. program, 1991-92, mem. Yale Comprehensive Cancer Ctr., 1990-92; mem. oper. rm. com. Yale-New Haven Hosp.; legis. com. med. adv. bd. Nat. Kidney Found. Conn.; vis. prof. dept. medicine St. Francis Hosp. and Med. Ctr., Hartford, Conn., 1990; mem. commn. on early detection R.I. Cancer Coun.; pres. med. staff RWMC and Meml. Hosp. of R.I. Contbr. articles to profl. jours. Clin. fellow Am. Cancer Soc., 1985; named Outstanding Young Man of Am., U.S. Jaycees, 1980. Fellow ACS; mem. AMA, Am. Assn. Clin. Urologists, Am. Urol.Assn., Endourological Soc., Mass.Med. Soc., N.Y. Acad. Scis., Mensa, Nat. Eagle Scout Assn., B'nai B'rith. Office: Urologic Surgeons New Eng 125 Corliss St # 2D Level Providence RI 02904-2611

SCHIFF, ZINA LEAH, violinist; b. Los Angeles, Apr. 25, 1953; d. Abraham and Rose Fay (Markin) S.; m. Ronald Lee Eisenberg; children: Avlana Kinneret, Cherina Carmel. BA, U. Calif., Berkeley, 1975; MA in Liberal Arts, La. State U., Shreveport, 1991. Soloist major Am. orchs.; performed in recitals and with orchs. Europe, Israel, Australia; guest artist Trogan Summer Music Festival, Switzerland, White Mountain Festival, Sewanee Music Festival; Mendocino Festival, Newport Music Festival. Solo violinist (film score) The Fixer; CD's include The Lark Ascending, 1989, Bach/Vivaldi, 1989, Korn Violin Concerto, 1997; Star (PBS-TV) Nova, What is Music, 1989; (CDs) King David's Lyre, 1996, Here's One, 1996, Cecil Burleigh--Works for Violin and Piano, 2002, Elijah's Violin, 2002, The Stradivarious Puzzle, 2002. Recipient Debut award Young Musicians Found., 1969, award San Francisco Symphony Found., 1970, Disting. Alumna award La. State U., 1997; named Outstanding Young Artist, Mus. Am., 1974, Top 10 Coll. Winner, Glamour mag., 1975; Martha Baird Rockefeller Fund grantee, 1972.

SCHIFFBAUER, WILLIAM G. lawyer; b. Columbia, S.C., Feb. 17, 1954; s. John R. and Jean A. Schiffbauer; m. Sarah L. Powers; children: J. William, Elisabeth, James Benjamin. BS, U. Nebr., 1976; JD, Creighton U., 1979; LLM, George Washington U., 1987. Bar: Nebr. 1979, U.S. Dist. Ct. Nebr. 1979, U.S. Ct. Claims 1982, U.S. Tax Ct. 1982, D.C. 1988. Counsel U.S. Senator J.J. Exon, Washington, 1979-85; ptnr. Groom & Nordberg, 1985-97, Schiffbauer Law Firm, Washington, 1997—. Mem. ABA, Nebr. Bar Assn., D.C. Bar Assn., Environ. Law Inst., Nat. Health Lawyers Assn., Omicron Delta Kappa. Democrat. Roman Catholic. Office: 1155 Connecticut Ave NW Ste 420 Washington DC 20036-4306

SCHIFFER, LOIS JANE, lawyer; b. Washington, Feb. 22, 1945; d. Benjamin and Clara (Goldberg) S. BA, Radcliffe Coll., 1966; JD, Harvard U., 1969. Bar: Mass. 1969, D.C. 1971, U.S. Supreme Ct. 1973. Legal svcs. lawyer Boston Legal Assistance Project, 1969-70; ct. law clk. D.C. Circuit Ct., Washington, 1970-71; assoc. Leva, Hawes, Symington, Martin, Oppenheimer, 1971-74; lawyer Ctr. for Law and Social Policy, 1974-78; chief gen. litigation sect. Land and Natural Resources div. U.S. Dept. Justice, 1978-81, spl. litigation counsel, 1981-84; gen. counsel Nat. Pub. Radio, 1984-89; ptnr. Nussbaum & Wald, 1989-93; acting asst. atty. gen. environ. and natural resources divsn. U.S. Dept. Justice, 1993-94, asst. atty. gen. environ. and natural resources divsn., 1994-2001; sr. v.p. for pub. policy Nat. Audubon Soc., 2001—02; ptnr. Baach, Robinson & Lewis, Washington, 2002—. Adj. prof. environ. law Georgetown U. Law Ctr., Washington, 1986—. Bd. dirs. Women's Legal Def. Fund, 1975-86, Am. Rivers, 1989-93, Keystone Ctr.; bd. dirs. ACLU/NCA, 1982-93, pres., 1988-90. Fellow Am. Bar Found.; mem. ABA, Am. Law Inst., Keystone Ctr. (bd. dirs.), Am. Bar Assn., Phi Beta Kappa. Democrat. Jewish. Avocations: reading, movies, hiking. Home: 4640 Brandywine St NW Washington DC 20016-4449 E-mail: lois.schiffer@baachrosinjon.com.

SCHIFFER, MICHAEL BRIAN, anthropologist, educator; b. Winnipeg, Man., Can., Oct. 4, 1947; came to U.S., 1953; s. Louie and Frances-Fera (Ludmer) S.; m. Annette Leve, Dec. 22, 1968; children: Adam Joseph, Jeremy Alan. BA in Anthropology summa cum laude, UCLA, 1969; MA, U. Ariz., 1972, PhD in Anthropology, 1973. Teaching asst. archaeol. field methods UCLA, spring 1969; student project supr. S.W. Expedition, Field Mus. Nat. History, summer 1969, rsch. asst., summer 1970, rsch. assoc., summer 1971; asst. prof. dept. anthropology U. Ark., 1973-75; teaching assoc. world prehistory U. Ariz., Tucson, 1972, teaching assoc. archaeol. interpretation, 1973, asst. prof. dept. anthropology, 1975-79, assoc. prof. dept. anthropology, 1979-82, prof., 1982—; dir. lab. traditional tech. dept. anthropology, 1984—. Archaeologist Phoenix dist. Bur. Land Mgmt., summers, 1980-81; dir. various archaeol. surveys and projects; vis. disting. archaeologist U. S.C., summer, 1977; vis. assoc. prof. U. Wash., summer 1979; vis. disting. prof. Ariz. State U., fall, 1982; cons. in field. Author: Behavioral Archeology, 1976, Formation Processes of the Archaeological Record, 1987, The Portable Radio in American Life, 1991, Technological Perspectives on Behavioral Change, 1992; co-author (with W. L. Rathje) Archaeology, 1982; editor: Advances in Archaeological Method and Theory, Vols 1-11, 1978-87, Selections for Students from Vols. 1-4, 1982; Archaeological Method and Theory, Vols. 1-5, 1989-93; co-editor: (books) Archaeology of US, 1981, Hohokam and Patayan: Prehistory of Southwestern Arizona, 1982, others; contbr. articles to profl pubs. Woodrow Wilson fellow, 1969-70. Fellow AAAS, Am. Anthrop. Assn.; mem. Soc. Am. Archaeology, Soc. Hist. Archaeology, Soc. Archeol. Scis., Soc. Hist. Tech., Phi Beta Kappa. Democrat. Jewish. Avocations: collecting old transistor radios, making pottery. Home: 2718 E 10th St Tucson AZ 85716-4750

SCHIFFER, RANDOLPH BRENTON, physician; b. Highland Park, Mich., May 25, 1948; s. Alfred Brenton and Dolores (Aspenson) S.; m. Lynn Scott Bickley, Sept. 18, 1982; children: Brenton B., Randolph T. BA, Yale U., 1969; MD, U. Mich., 1976. Diplomate Am. Bd. Psychiatry and Neurology. Asst. prof. psychiatry and neurology U. Rochester, N.Y., 1981-87, assoc. prof. psychiatry and neurology, 1987-92, prof. neurology psychiatry and environ. medicine, 1993-98; Vernon and Elizabeth Haggerton prof. neurology Tex. Tech U. Health Sci. Ctr., Lubbock, 1998—, chair dept. neuropsychiatry, 1998—. Author: The Medical Evaluation of Psychiatric Patients, 1988; co-editor: Neuropsychiatry, 1996. 1st lt. USMC, 1969-72, Vietnam. Mem. Am. Neuropsychiat. Assn. (bd. dirs. 1986-92), Am. Acad. Neurology, Am. Psychiat. Assn. (Falk fellow 1979-81). Home: 4515 11th St Lubbock TX 79416-4815 Office: Tex Tech U Health Scis Ctr Dept Neuropsychiat 3601 4th St Lubbock TX 79430-0001

SCHIFFMAN, GERALD, microbiologist, educator; b. N.Y.C., May 22, 1926; s. Samuel and Mollie (Brookner) S.; m. Lillian Ebert, July 12, 1951; children: Stewart, Howard. BA cum laude, NYU, 1948, PhD, 1954. Asst. prof. and disting. prof. microbiology Coll. Physicians and Surgeons, Columbia U., N.Y.C., 1960-63; asso. prof. dept. research medicine and microbiology U. Pa., Phila., 1963-70; prof. SUNY Health Sci. Ctr., Bklyn., 1970-97, disting. svc. prof., 1995-97, prof. emeritus, 1997. Cons. Contbr. articles to profl. jours. Served in U.S. Army, 1943-45, ETO. Decorated Bronze Star; recipient Nichols award, 1947; Atomic Energy fellow, 1948-52; NIH grantee, 1974-94. Mem. Am. Assn. Immunologists, Am. Chem. Soc., Am. Soc. Microbiology, AAAS, Harvey Soc., Soc. Complex Carbohydrates, Sigma Xi, Phi Beta Kappa, Mu Chi Sigma, Pi Mu Epsilon. Jewish. Office: 450 Clarkson Ave Brooklyn NY 11203-2056

SCHIFFMAN, HAROLD FOSDICK, Asian language educator; b. Buffalo, Feb. 19, 1938; s. Merl and Mathilda (Keller) S.; m. Marilyn Gail Hornberg, June 10, 1978; 1 son, Timothy Marc Rajendran. BA, Antioch Coll., 1960; MA, U. Chgo., 1966, PhD, 1969. Lectr. anthropology U. Calif.-Davis, 1966-67; asst. prof. U. Wash., Seattle, 1967-73, assoc. prof., 1973-78, prof. 1978-95, chmn. dept. Asian langs., 1982-87; prof. South Asian studies U. Pa., Phila., 1995-2000; acad. dir. Penn Lang. Ctr., Luce prof. lang. learning U. Pa. , 1995-2000, rsch. dir. Penn Lang. Ctr., 2000—; dir. Consortium for Lang. Policy and Planning, 2001—. Trustee Am. Inst. Indian Studies, Chgo., 1979-82; lang. dir. Southeast Asian Summer Studies Inst., 1992-93, mem. lang. adv. com., 1993-94. Author: A Grammar of Spoken Tamil, 1979, A Reference Grammar of Spoken Kannada, 1983, Linguistic Culture and Language Policy, 1996, A Reference Grammer of Spoken Tamil, 1999; co-editor: Dravidian Phonological Systems, 1975; co-author: Language and Society in South Asia, 1981. Pres. bd. dirs. Seattle Pro Musica (choral group), 1976-78; mem. Pacific Northwest Chamber Chorus, Seattle, 1983-87. Sr. fellow Am. Inst. Indian Studies, 1976, 78; grantee U.S. Office Edn., 1971, 74, 78, NEH, 1984-87, Smithsonian Inst., 1984-87, Fulbright Rsch., 1993-94. Mem. Assn. Asian Studies (S. Asia council 1982-85), Am. Inst. Indian Studies (trustee 1979-82), Soc. S. Indian Studies (sec.-treas. 1973-75), Internat. Assn. Tamil Research (v.p. 1987-89). Mem. Soc. Of Friends. Office: U Pa Dept South Asian Studies 820 Williams Hall Philadelphia PA 19104-6305 E-mail: haroldfs@ccat.sas.upenn.edn.

SCHIFFMAN, LOUIS F. management consultant; b. Poland, July 15, 1927; s. Harry and Bertha (Fleder) S.; m. Mina R. Hankin, Dec. 28, 1963; children: Howard Laurence, Laura Lea. BChemE, NYU, 1948, MS, 1952, PhD, 1955. Rsch. engr. Pa. Grade Crude Oil Assn., Bradford, 1948-50; tchg. fellow dept. chemistry NYU, 1950-54; rsch. chemist E.I. duPont de Nemours & Co., Wilmington, Del., 1954-56, Atlantic Refining Co., Phila., 1956-59; project leader, group leader, head corrosion sect. Amchem Products Inc., Ambler, Pa., 1959-70; pres. Techni Rsch. Assocs. Inc., Willow Grove, Pa., 1970—. Bd. dirs. Techno Ventures, Inc., Tecxchange.com; real estate developer: ptnr. Bay Properties Co., Bay Club Marina, Margate, N.J., Willow Grove (Pa.) Assocs.; pub., editor Patent Licensing Gazette, 1968—. World Tech., 1975—; panelist on forum patents and inventions Delaware Valley Industry, 1973; mem. adv. oversight com. NSF, 1975, moderator energy conf. ERDA, Washington, 1976, Las Vegas, 1977; mem. adv. group in small bus. R&D programs Dept. Def., 1980. Editor: (with others) Guide to Available Technologies, 1985; contbr. to Encyclopedia of Chemical Technology, 1967; contbr. articles to profl. jours.; patentee in field. Recipient Founders Day award NYU, 1956. Fellow Am. Inst. Chemists; mem. Am. Chem. Soc., N.Y. Acad. Scis., Lic. Exec.s Soc., Tech. Transfer Soc., Assn. Univ. Tech. Mgrs., Assn. Small Rsch. Cos. (editl. contbr. newsletter), Sigma Xi, Phi Lambda Upsilon. Home: 1837 Merritt Rd Abington PA 19001-4606 Office: Techni Rsch Assocs Inc PO Box 1036 Willow Grove PA 19090-0922

SCHIFFMAN, SUSAN STOLTE, medical psychologist, educator; b. Chgo., Aug. 24, 1940; d. Paul R. and Mildred (Glicksman) Stolte; m. Harold Schiffman (div.); 1 child, Amy Lise; m. H. Troy Nagle, July 22, 1989. BA, Syracuse U., 1965; PhD, Duke U., 1970. Lic. psychologist, N.C. Postdoctoral fellow Duke U., Durham, N.C., 1970-72, asst. prof., 1972-77, assoc. prof., 1978-83, full prof., 1983—. Cons., mem. adv. bd. Nestle, Vevey, Switzerland, 1990-98, Olfactory Rsch. Fund, N.Y.C., 1986—, and others. Author: Introduction to Multidimensional Scaling: Theory, Methods and Applications, 1981, Flavor Set-Point Weight Loss Cookbook, 1990. Nat. Inst. Aging grantee, 1972—. Mem. Assn. Chemoreception Scis., Internat. Behavioral Neurosci. Soc., Soc. for Neurosci. Office: Duke U Med Sch PO Box 3259 Durham NC 27710-0001 E-mail: sss@duke.edu.

SCHIFFMANN, ROBERT FRANK, research and development executive; b. N.Y.C., Feb. 11, 1935; s. Franz and Sophie (Bohling) S.; m. Marilyn Thelma Schneider, Aug. 20, 1987; children: Carla, Erica, Robert Franz. BS, Columbia U., 1955; MS, Purdue U., 1959. Rsch. scientist DCA Food Ind., N.Y.C., 1959-63; v.p. rsch. Nucleonics Corp. Am., Bklyn., 1963-64; sr. project mgr. DCA Food Ind., N.Y.C., 1964-71; ptnr. Bedrosian & Assocs., Alpine, N.J., 1971-78; pres. R.F. Schiffmann Assocs., N.Y.C., 1979—; chmn. Quiclave LLC, Chgo., 1994—. Patentee in field; contbr. articles to profl. jours., chpts. to books. Pres. Cadman Towers Cooperators Assn., Bklyn., 1970-73. Fellow, Internat. Microwave Power Inst., 1985; recipient Putnam award, Putnam Pub., 1973. Mem. Microwave Power Inst. (pres. 1973-83), Inst. Food Technologists (sci. lectr. 1988-91), Soc. Plastics Industry, N.Y. Acad. Sci., Sigma Xi. Avocations: trout fishing, piano. Office: RF Schiffmann Assocs 149 W 88th St New York NY 10024-2401

SCHIFFNER, CHARLES ROBERT, architect; b. Reno, Sept. 2, 1948; Robert Charles and Evelyn (Keck) S.; m. Iovanna Lloyd Wright, Nov. 1971 (div. Sept. 1981); m. Adrienne Anita McAndrews, Jan. 22, 1983. Student, Sacramento Jr. Coll., 1967-68, Frank Lloyd Wright Sch. Architecture, 1968-77. Registered architect, Ariz., Nev., Wis. Architect Taliesin Associated Architects, Scottsdale, Ariz., 1977-83; pvt. practice architecture Phoenix, 1983—. Lectr. The Frank Lloyd Wright Sch. of Architecture, 1994, 95. Named one of 25 Most Promising Young Americans Under 35, U.S. mag., 1979; recipient AIA Honor award Western Mountain Region, 1993, Western Home awards Sunset Mag., 1989, 91, AIA Ariz. Merit award, 1993 and numerous others. Home: 5202 E Osborn Rd Phoenix AZ 85018-6137 Office: Camelhead Office Ctr 2944 N 44th St Phoenix AZ 85018-7257

SCHIFFRIN, ANDRE, publisher; b. Paris, June 12, 1935; came to U.S., 1941; s. Jacques and Simone (Heymann) S.; m. Maria Elena de la Iglesia, June 14, 1961; children— Anya, Natalia BA summa cum laude, Yale U., 1957; MA with 1st class honors, Cambridge U., Eng., 1959. With New Am. Library, 1959-63; with Pantheon Books, Inc., N.Y.C., 1962-90, editor, then editor in chief, mng. dir., 1969-90; pub. Schocken Books subs. Pantheon Books Inc., 1987-90; pres. Fund for Ind. Pub., N.Y.C., 1990—; dir., editor in chief The New Press, 1990—. Vis. fellow Davenport Coll., 1977-79; vis. lectr. Yale U., 1977, 79; bd. dirs. The New Press, N.Y.C. Author: Edition sans Editeurs, 1999, The Business of Books, 2000; columnist Chronicle Higher Edn., 1998—; contbr. articles to profl. jours., including N.Y. Times Book Rev., Nation, New Republic. Mem. coun. Smithsonian Instn., 1969—; bd. dirs. N.Y. Coun. for Humanities, 1978—, mem. exec. com., 1979-80; bd. dirs. N.Y. Civil Liberties Union; mem. freedom to pub. com. Assn. Am. Pubs., 1976-78; mem. vis. com. history dept. Princeton U., 1978—; mem. freedom to read com. AAUP, 1985—; mem. U.S. cultural del. to Peoples Republic China, 1983, 87; mem. vis. com. grad. faculty The New Sch., 1995—. Mellon fellow Clare Coll., 1957, hon. scholar, 1959; hon. fellow Trumbull Coll., Yale U., 1979—; Fulbright travel grantee, 1958-59. Fellow N.Y. Inst. for the Humanities. Home: 250 W 94th St New York NY 10025-6954 Office: The New Press 450 W 41st St Rm 514 New York NY 10036-6814

SCHIFFRIN, MILTON JULIUS, physiologist; b. Rochester, N.Y., Mar. 23, 1914; s. William and Lillian (Harris) S.; m. Dorothy Euphemia Wharry, Oct. 10, 1942; children: David Wharry, Hilary Ann. AB, U. Rochester, 1937, MS, 1939; PhD cum laude, McGill U., 1941. Instr. physiology Northwestern U. Med. Sch., Chgo., 1941-45; lectr. pharmacology U. Ill. Med. Sch., 1947-57, clin. asst. prof. anesthesiology, 1957-61; with Hoffmann-La Roche, Inc.,

Nutley, N.J., 1946-79, dir. drug regulatory affairs, 1964-71, asst. v.p., 1971-79; pres. Wharry Rsch. Assn., Seattle, 1979—. Chmn. Everglades Health Edn. Ctr., 1986-87. Author: (with E.G. Gross) Clinical Analgesics, 1955; editor: Management of Pain in Cancer, 1957. Bd. dirs. Univ. Adult Day Ctr., 1993—; mem. adv. bd. Regional Ombudsman Program, 1998—, Residents Coun. Washington, 1998—. Capt. USAAF, 1942-46. Mem. Am. Med. Writers Assn. (bd. dirs. 1967-70, pres. N.Y. chpt. 1967-68, nat. pres. 1972-73), Am. Physiol. Soc., Internat. Coll. Surgeons, Am. Therapeutic Soc., Coll. Clin. Pharmacology and Therapeutics, Am. Chem. Soc. Home and Office: Unit 401 1001 2nd Ave W Seattle WA 98119-3560 E-mail: grampa@drizzle.com.

SCHIFLETT, MARY FLETCHER CAVENDER, retired health facility executive, researcher, educator; b. El Paso, Sept. 23, 1925; d. John F. and Mary M. (Humphries) Cavender: 1 son, Joseph Raymond. BA in Econs. with honors, So. Meth. U., 1946, BS in Journalism with honors, 1947; MA in English, U. Houston, 1971. Writer, historian Office Price Administrn., Dallas, 1946-47; asst. editor C. of C. Publs., 1947-48; bus. writer Houston Oil, 1948-49; market analyst Cravens-Dargan, Ins., 1949-52; bus. writer Bus. Week and McGraw-Hill Pub. Co., 1952-56; freelance writer in bus. econs., banking and ins., 1956-68; spl. projects coord. Ctr. for Human Resources, Houston, 1969-73; dir. publs. Energy Inst. U. Houston, 1974-78; sr. rsch. assoc. Inst. Labor and Indsl. Rels., 1973-80; mem. adj. faculty Coll. Architecture U. Houston, 1976-85; dir. Ctr. for Health Mgmt., Coll. Bus. Adminstrn., 1980-83; assoc. dir. rsch and planning Tex. (Houston) Med. Ctr., Inc., 1984, dir. spl. projects and pub. affairs, 1985-92, from asst. to assoc. v.p., 1993-98, v.p., 1998; ret., 1998. Bd. dirs. Third Ward Redevel. Coun., Houston Acad. Motion Pictures, Houston World Trade Assn. Author: (with others) Dynamics of Growth, 1977, Applied Systems and Cybernetics, 1981, The Ethnic Groups of Houston, 1984, Names and Nicknames of Places and Things, 1986. Bd. dirs. Friends Hermann Pk. 1995-02, adv. bd., 2002—, , mem. exec. com. 1996-2001, sec. bd. 1997-2001; pres. Houston Ct. Humanities, 1978-80; project dir. Houston Meets Its Authors I-IV, 1980-83; pub. program dir. Houston Internat. City, 1980-83. Named One of Houston's Women of Yr. YMCA, 1988. Mem.: AIA (profl. affiliate), Nat. Assn. Bus. Econs., Tex. Folklore Soc., World Future Soc., Internat. Coun. Indsl. Editors, Houston C. of C. (future studies com. 1975—84, small bus. coun. 1981—83), Friends of the Libr., Rotary Found. (com. mem. 2000—), River Oaks Rotary (bd. dirs. 1996, v.p. 1998—99, sec. 2001—02, pres.-elect 2002—, Outstanding Rotarian of Yr. 1998, Paul Harris fellow 1996), Downtown Club, Mortar Bd., Delta Delta Delta, Alpha Theta Phi, Theta Sigma Phi. Methodist. Office: Tex Med Ctr 406 Jesse H Jones Libr Bldg Houston TX 77030 E-mail: mfcs@swbell.net.

SCHIFRIN, LALO, composer; b. Buenos Aires, June 21, 1932; Student, Juan Carlos Paz and Olivier Messiaen.; PhD (hon.), RISD, 1989. Tchr. composition UCLA, 1970-71; guest condr. Israel Philharm, L.A. Philharm, L.A. Chamber Orch., Indpls. Symphony, Atlanta Symphony. Argentinian rep., Internat. Jazz Festival, Paris, 1955, formed own jazz group; composer for stage, modern dance, TV; with Dizzy Gillespie's band, 1962; film and TV composer, Hollywood, Calif., 1964—; compositions: (for ballet) Jazz Faust, 1963, (for orch.) Piano Concerto # 1, 1986, Cantos Aztecas, 1989, Concerto for guitar and orch., 1986, Concerto for double bass and orch., 1987, Three tangos for flute, harp and strings, 1987, Dance concertantes for clarinet and orch., 1990, Impressions for trumpet and orch., 1990, La Nouvelle Orleans Woodwind Quintet, 1991, Concerto # 2, 1992, Cantares Argentinos, 1992, Symphony # 1 for orch., 1993, Symphonic Impressions of Oman (recorded by London Symphony), 2001, (opera) The Trial of Louis XVI, 1988; theme for TV series Mission: Impossible (2 Grammy awards); film scores include The Cincinnati Kid, 1965, Cool Hand Luke, 1967, The Fox, 1968; film scores include Kelly's Heroes, 1970, W.U.S.A., 1970, Bullit, 1970, Dirty Harry, 1971, THX-1138, 1971, The Beguiled, 1971, Magnum Force, 1973, Enter the Dragon, 1973, The Four Musketeers, 1975, The Eagle Has Landed, 1977, Voyage of the Damned, 1976, Rollercoaster, 1977, Telefon, 1977, Boulevard Nights, 1979, The Concorde-Airport '79, 1979, Competition, 1981, Sudden Impact, 1984, The Sting II, 1985, The Fourth Protocol, 1987, Tango, 1996, Rush Hour, 1998, Rush Hour 2, 2001; TV series The Young-Lawyers, Mannix, 'Mission Impossible', Starsky and Hutch; writer orchestration for Grand Finale medley for Carreras, Domingo and Pavarotti, Rome, 1990, Dodger Stadium, 1994, Eiffel Tower, 1998, Yokohama, Japan, 2002; commd. Steinway Found piano concerto The Americas, selected by Nat. Symphony Orch., 1992. Recipient 4 Grammy awards, 1967, 1969, 1986, 6 Acad. award nominations Acad. Motion Picture Arts and Scis., 1966, 67, 75, 77, 80, 82, Walk of Fame award Hollywood C. of C.; chevalier de l'Ordre des Arts et des Lettres French gov. Office: care Brad Simon Orgn 122 E 57th St New York NY 10022

SCHIFTER, RICHARD, lawyer; b. Vienna, Austria, July 31, 1923; came to U.S., 1938; s. Paul and Balbina (Blass) S.; m. Lilo Krueger, July 3, 1948; children: Judith, Deborah, Richard P., Barbara, Karen BS in Social Sci. summa cum laude, CCNY, 1943; LLB, Yale U., 1951; DHL (hon.), Hebrew Union Coll., 1992. Bar: Conn. 1951, D.C. 1952, U.S. Supreme Ct. 1954, Md., 1958. Assoc. Fried, Frank, Harris, Shriver & Jacobson, Washington, 1951-57, ptnr., 1957-84; dep. U.S. rep. with rank of ambassador UN Security Council, N.Y.C., 1984-85; asst. sec. of state for human rights and humanitarian affairs Dept. State, Washington, 1985-92; U.S. rep. UN Human Rights Commn., Geneva, 1983-86, 93; spl. asst. to pres., counselor Nat. Security Coun., Washington, 1993-97, spl. adviser to Sec. of State, 1997-2001. Head U.S. del. Conf. on Security and Cooperation in Europe Experts Meeting on Human Rights, Ottawa, Ont., Can., 1985, Dem. Insts., Oslo, 1991; bd. dirs. U.S. Inst. Peace, 1986-92; mem. Congl. Commn. on Security and Cooperation in Europe, 1986-92. V.p., pres. Md. Bd. Edn., Balt., 1959-79; chmn. Md. Gov.'s Commn. on Funding Edn. of Handicapped Children, 1975-77, Md. Values Edn. Commn., 1979-83, Montgomery County Dem. Cen. Com., Md., 1966-70; del. Dem. Nat. Conv., 1968; bd. govs. Am. Jewish Com., 1992-93, 2001--, mem. exec. com., 2001--; chmn. Internat. Rels. Commn., 2001--; chmn. bd. dirs. Ctr. for Democracy and Reconciliation in Southeastern Europe, 2002--. With U.S. Army, 1943-46, ETO. Decorated Austrian Gt. Golden Decoration with starco, comdr. Order of the Romanian Star; recipient Disting. Svc. award, Sec. of State, 1992. Mem. Phi Beta Kappa. Democrat. Jewish. Home: 6907 Crail Dr Bethesda MD 20817-4723 E-mail: rschifter@aol.com.

SCHILD, RAYMOND DOUGLAS, lawyer; b. Chgo., Dec. 20, 1952; s. Stanley Martin and Cassoundra Lee (McArdle) S.; m. Ellen Arthea Carstensen, Oct. 24, 1987; children: Brian Christopher, Melissa Nicole. Student, U.S. Mil. Acad., 1970; BA summa cum laude, De Paul U., 1974, JD magna cum laude, 1982; M in Life Scis., Order of Essenes, 1996. Bar: Ill. 1982, U.S. Dist. Ct. (no. dist.) Ill. 1982, U.S. Ct. Appeals (7th cir.) 1982, Idaho 1989, U.S. Dist. Ct. Idaho 1989, U.S. Ct. Appeals (9th cir.) 1989, U.S. Supreme Ct. 1990. Assoc. Clausen, Miller, Gorman, Caffrey & Witous, Chgo., 1982-84; law clk. to chief judge law divsn. Cir. Ct. Cook County, 1984-85; assoc. John G. Phillips & Assocs., 1985-87, Martin, Chapman, Park & Burkett, Boise, Idaho, 1988-89; pvt. practice, 1989-90; pres. Martin, Chapman, Schild & Lassaw, Chartered, 1990-96; mng. assoc. prelitigation divsn. Litster Law Offices, 2001—. Dir. Behavioral Mgmt. Ctrs.; bd. dirs. Image Concepts Internat., Inc., Boise; lectr. on legal edn. ICLE and NBI, 1993-98. Co-host legal radio talk show KFXD, 1994; legal columnist Idaho Bus. Rev., 1988-96. Mem. adv. bd. Alliance for the Mentally Ill, Boise, 1991—, Parents and Youth Against Drug Abuse, Boise, 1991-92, Bethel Ministries; fair housing adminstr. Sauk Village (Ill.) Govt., 1987-88; instr. Ada County Youth Ct., Boise, 1992—. Schmitt fellow DePaul U., 1974; recipient award of merit Chgo. Law Coalition, 1987. Mem. ATLA, Idaho Trial Lawyers' Assn., Ill. State Bar Assn., Idaho State Bar Assn., Boise Estate Planning Counsel, Shriners (temple atty. 1994—, liaison Crippled Children's Hosp.), Masons (jr. steward 1992). Avocations: tennis, trombone, writing, music. Office: 6550 W Emerald Ste 108 Boise ID 83704

SCHILD, RUDOLPH ERNST, astronomer, educator; b. Chgo., Jan. 10, 1940; s. Kasimir A. and Anneliese (Schuricht) S.; m. Jane H. Struss, July 28, 1982. BS, U. Chgo., 1962, MS, 1963, PhD, 1966. Rsch. fellow Calif. Inst. Tech., Pasadena, 1966-69; scientific dir., 1.5m Telescope Program Smithsonian Astrophysical Obs., Amado, Ariz., 1969-74; astronomer Harvard-Smithsonian Ctr. for Astrophysics, Cambridge, Mass., 1974--. Lectr. Harvard U., 1975-83. Author: (slide set) The Electronic Sky: Digital Images of the Cosmos, 1985, (CD-ROM) Voyage to the Stars: The Rudy Schild Collection; contbr. over 100 articles to scholarly and profl. jours. Mem. Am. Astronomical Soc., Internat. Astronomical Union. Achievements include 2 patents; discovery of gravitational microlensing. Office: Ctr for Astrophysics 60 Garden St Cambridge MA 02138-1516 E-mail: rschild@cfa.harvard.edu.

SCHILDHAUS, SAM, political scientist, researcher; b. Basel, Switzerland, Sept. 27, 1944; came to U.S., 1952; s. Moses and Adele (Diener) S.; m. Liat Weiler, Apr. 25, 1990; children: Noam Annalee Weiler. BS, CCNY, 1966; PhD, Syracuse U., 1975. From tchg. asst. to asst. prof. SUNY, Syracuse U., 1968-1975; project dir. The Orkand Corp., Silver Spring, Md., 1975-1979; dir. divsn. evaluation Am. Health Planning Assn., Washington, 1979-1980; ind. cons., rschr. Silver Spring, 1980-83; mgr. health svcs. rsch., chief productivity mgmt. group Dept. Vet. Affairs, Washington, 1983-89; sr. policy analyst Exec. Office of the Pres. Office of Nat. Drug Control Policy, 1989-93; sr. rsch. scientist Nat. Opinion Rsch. Ctr. U. Chgo., 1993—. Cons., mem. task force Pres.'s Pvt. Sector Survey (Grace Commn.), Washington, 1982-83; rev. com. NIH, Bethesda, Md., 1981-82. Mem. Am. Polit. Sci. Assn. Office: Univ of Chgo NORC 1350 Connecticut Ave NW Washington DC 20036-1722 E-mail: schildhaus-sam@norcmail.uchicago.edu., evaluationresearch@hotmail.com.

SCHILDKRAUT, JOSEPH JACOB, psychiatrist, educator; b. Bklyn., Jan. 21, 1934; s. Simon and Shirley (Schwartz) S.; m. Elizabeth Rose Beilenson, May 22, 1966; children: Peter Jeremy, Michael John. AB summa cum laude, Harvard U., 1955; MD cum laude, Harvard Med. Sch., 1959. Intern medicine U. Calif. Hosp., San Francisco, 1959-60; resident in psychiatry Mass. Mental Health Center, Boston, 1960-63; dir. neuropsychopharmacology lab., 1967—98; founding dir., 1998—; sr. psychiatrist, 1967—; research psychiatrist NIMH, Bethesda, Md., 1963-67, cons., 1967-68; asst. prof. psychiatry Harvard Med. Sch., Boston, 1967-70, assoc. prof., 1970-74, prof., 1974—. Dir. psychiat. chemistry lab. Mass. Mental Health Ctr., 1977-98, founding dir., 1998-. Author: over 200 publ. including, Neuorpsychopharmacology and the Affective Disorders, 1970; editor: Depression and the Spiritual in Modern Art: Homage to Miró, 1996; editor-in-chief Jour. Psychiat. Rsch., 1982-92; mem. editorial bd. Psychophysiology, 1968-74, Jour. Psychiat. Rsch., 1968-82, Psychopharmacology, 1970-84, Sleep Revs., 1972-79, Communications in Psychopharmacology, 1974-81, Psychotherapy and Psychosomatics, 1974-91, Rsch. Communications in Psychology, Psychiatry and Behavior, 1976—, Jour. Clin. Psychopharmacology, 1980, Integrative Psychiatry, 1982-89, 91—, others. Bd. dirs. Med. Found., Boston, 1991-97 chair clin. rsch. com., 1994-96; trustee Mind/Body Med. Inst. Deaconess Hosp., Harvard Med. Sch., Boston, 1999-, chair sci. adv. bd., 1988-95. Served as surgeon USPHS, 1963-65. Recipient Anna-Monika Found. prize, 1967, Hofheimer award Am. Psychiat. Assn., 1971, hon. mention award, 1968; McCurdy-Rinkel prize No. New Eng. Dist. br. Am. Psychiat. Assn., 1969; William C. Menninger award ACP, 1978; Neuropsychiatry Classics; Lifetime Achievement award Soc. of Biological Psychiatry, 1996; Award for Rsch. in Mood Disorders The Am. Coll. of Psychiatrists, 1999. Mem. World Psychiat. Assn. (sec. sect. biol. psychiatry 1972-77), Psychiat. Research Soc., Am. Coll. Neuropsychopharmacology, Am. Psychiat. Assn., Am. Psychosomatic Soc., AAAS, Soc. Biol. Psychiatry, N.Y. Acad. Scis., Am. Psychopath. Assn., Am. Coll. Psychiatrists, Am. Soc. Pharmacology and Exptl. Therapeutics, Am. Soc. Neurochemistry, Group Without a Name, Assn. for Research in Nervous and Mental Disease, Collegium Internationale Neuropsychopharmacologicum, Soc. for Neurosci., Phi Beta Kappa. Home: 35 Jefferson Rd Chestnut Hill MA 02467-2341 Office: Mass Mental Health Ctr 74 Fenwood Rd Boston MA 02115-6113

SCHILLER, ALAN LEWIS, physician, educator; b. Feb. 12, 1943; AB, Bowdoin Coll., 1963; MD, Chgo. Med. Sch., 1967. Diplomate Bd. Anatomic Pathology. Intern Mass. Gen. Hosp., Harvard Med. Sch., N.Y.C., 1967-68, resident, fellow, 1967-71; from clin. instr. to asst. prof. Harvard Med. Sch., 1971-79, assoc. prof., 1979-86; Irene Heinz Given and John LaPorte Given prof., chmn. Mt. Sinai Sch. Medicine, N.Y.C., 1988—. Contbr. articles to profl. jours. Elected bd. trustees Nat. Space Biomed. Rsch. Inst., NASA. Comdr. USNR. Home: 1 Gustave L Levy Pl PO Box 1194 New York NY 10029-0313 Office: Mt Sinai Sch Medicine Dept Pathology 5th and 100th St New York NY 10029

SCHILLER, ARTHUR A. architect, educator; b. N.Y.C., July 23, 1910; s. Valentine and Rose (Bayer) S.; m. Anne O'Donnell, June 12, 1937; children: Valerie Schiller Schaefer, Virginia Schiller Waicul, Eileen Schiller Toomey. BArch, NYU, 1933; diploma, Beaux Arts Inst. Design, N.Y.C., 1935; MArch, MIT, 1939. Registered profl. architect, N.Y. Architect U.S. Govt., Washington, 1936-38, N.Y.C. Dept. Parks, 1938-47; chief architect Bd. Higher Edn., N.Y.C., 1947-51, dir. architecture and engring., 1951-67; coord. campus planning Queens Coll., 1967-73; adj. prof. N.Y. Inst. Technology, Old Westbury, 1973-91. Cons. Triboro Bridge Authority, N.Y.C., 1946; lectr. CCNY, 1957-67. Mayor Village of Plandome Manor, N.Y., 1965-87, trustee, 1960-65; trustee Sci. Mus. L.I. 1986—. Named Man of Yr. AARP, 1990, Sr. Citizen of Yr. Nassau County, State of N.Y., 1992 . Fellow AIA (pres. Queens chpt. 1957-58); mem. N.Y. State Assn. Architects (dir. 1959-60), Assn. Univ. Architects (emeritus), U.S. Power Squadron (comdr. 1961-62, budget dir. 1988-91), Elks (life). Avocations: boating, gardening, conducting defensive driving courses for older citizens. Home: 15 Luquer Rd Manhasset NY 11030-1015

SCHILLER, BRITT-MARIE CHRISTINA, philosophy educator; b. Uddevalla, Sweden, Apr. 29, 1947; d. Erik Gunnar and Ingvor Elvira Dalemar; m. Jerome Paul Schiller, May 11, 1984; 1 child, Eric Alexander. BA in Philosophy, U. Maine, Orono, 1976; PhD in Philosophy, Washington U., St. Louis, 1985; postgrad., St. Louis Psychoanalytic Inst., 2000—. Assoc. prof. philosophy Webster U., St. Louis, 1996—, chair dept. philosophy, 1998—. Grantee NEH, 1998. Office: Webster U Dept Philosophy 470 E Lockwood Ave Saint Louis MO 63119

SCHILLER, DONALD CHARLES, lawyer; b. Chgo., Dec. 8, 1942; s. Sidney S. and Edith (Lastick) S.; m. Eileen Fagin, June 14, 1964; children—Eric, Jonathan Student, Lake Forest Coll., 1960-63; JD, DePaul U., 1966. Bar: Ill. 1966, U.S. Dist. Ct. (no. dist.) Ill. 1966, U.S. Supreme Ct. 1972. Ptnr. Schiller, DuCanto & Fleck (formerly Schiller & Schiller and Schiller & DuCanto), Chgo., 1966—; lectr. in law U. Chgo. Law Sch. Chair domestic rels. adv. com. Cir. Ct. Cook County, 1993—2001, exec. com., 1986—93; lectr. in law U. Chgo. Law Sch., 2001—; spkr. profl. confs. Contbr. chpts. and articles to profl. publs. Mem. steering com. on juvenile ct. watching, LWV, 1980-81. Recipient Maurice Weigle award Chgo. Bar Found., 1978, Disting. Alumni award, DePaul U., 1988, various certs. of appreciation profl. groups: named One of Am.'s Best Divorce Lawyers, Town and Country, 1985, 98, The Nat. Law Jour., 1987, The Best Lawyers in Am., 1987—, One of Chgo's. Best Div. Lawyers, Crain's Chgo. Bus., 1981, Today Chgo. Woman, 1985, Inside Chgo. mag., 1988, Chgo. Sun Times, 2000. Fellow Am. Bar Found., Am. Acad. Matrimonial Lawyers (nat. chair continuing legal edn. 1993-94); mem. ABA (bd. govs. 1994-97, chmn. family law sect. 1985-86, Ill. State del. 1980-84, mem. Ho. of Dels. 1984—, editor-in-chief Family Law Newsletter 1977-79; mem. editorial bd., assoc. editor Family Adv. Mag. 1979-84, speaker at confs. and meetings), Ill. Bar Assn. (pres. 1987-88, chmn. family law sect. 1976-77, editor Family Law Bull. 1976-77, bd. govs. 1977-83, treas. 1981-84, v.p. 1984-86, chmn. various coms., lectr., incorporator and pres. Ill. State Bar Assn. Mutual Ins. Co., Inc. 1988-89), Chgo. Bar Assn., Am. Coll. Family Law Trial Lawyers (diplomate). Office: Schiller DuCanto & Fleck 200 N La Salle St Ste 2700 Chicago IL 60601-1098 E-mail: dschiller@sdflaw.com.

SCHILLER, FRANCIS, neurologist, medical historian; b. Prague, Czechoslovakia, Jan. 23, 1909; came to U.S., 1950; s. Friedrich and Luise (Mannheimer) S. MD, German U., Prague, 1933. Diplomate Am. Bd. Psychiatry and Neurology. With U. Calif. Med. Sch., San Francisco, 1951-79, clin. prof. neurology, 1972, emeritus prof, neurology, 1979; neurologist Kaiser Permanente Med. Group, 1953-78; cons. neurology Pub. Health Svc., 1978-81, VA Compensation & Pension, San Francisco, 1984—. Sr. lectr. history and health sci. U. Calif., San Francisco, 1962—. Author: Paul Broca, 1824-80, 1979, A Möbius Strip, 1981; contbr. articles to profl. jours. Fellow Am. Acad. Neurology, San Francisco Neurology Soc.; mem. Internat. Acad. History of Medicine, Bay Area History of Medicine Club (pres. San Francisco cht. 1975-76). Avocations: gardening, piano. Home: 2730 Wawona St San Francisco CA 94116-2866

SCHILLER, GERALD ALAN, writer; b. Phila., Feb. 13, 1936; s. Victor and Ida (Rosenbloum) S.; m. Esther Shoemaker, Aug. 24, 1957; children: Lisabeth, greg. BS in Edn., Temple U., 1957; MA in Cinema, UCLA, 1963. Cert. tchr., Calif. Tchr. Phila. Schs., 1957-58, L.A. Schs., 1960-91. Author: (novel) Deadly Dreams, 1996, Death Underground, 1999, (children's books) The Dog That Belonged to No One, 1998, Two Dogs, an Emperor, and Me, 1999, True Stories of Old California, 2001; script writer advt. and promotional videos and audio-visual prodns. for J.K. Lesser Prodns.; co-writer feature films The Red Fox, 1988, Wild Country, 1989; writer, dir. documentary films including The World Outside, Keaton: The Great Stone Face, 1980, Chaplin-A Character is Born, 1979; writer, dir. ednl. films; author articles and revs. With U.S. Army, 1959-60. Recipient Cine Golden Eagle award The World Outside, 1st prize Calif. State Coll. Film Festival, Blue Ribbon award Am. Film Festival, Chris award Columbus Film Festival, 2d prize Nat. Ednl. Film Festival, Tchr. of Yr. award L.A. Film Tchrs. Assn., 1990, others. Mem. Ventura County Writers Club (pres. 1997-99), Sisters in Crime, Small Pubs. Network, PEN. Jewish. Avocations: bicycling, book collecting, performing magician.

SCHILLER, HERBERT MILES, pathologist; b. N.Y.C., Mar. 19, 1943; s. Jack David and Dorothy (Coe) S.; m. Patricia Annette Fields, July 3, 1965; children: Anne Bothwell, Stephen Miles, Richard William. BS, Wake Forest Coll., 1964; MD, Bowman Gray Sch. Medicine, 1968; MA in History, Wake Forest U., 1987. Diplomate Am. Bd. Pathology, sub-bd. cytopathology. Assoc. pathologist St. Francis Hosp., Columbus, Ga., 1972-75, St. Lukes Hosp./McGuire Clinic, Richmond, Va., 1976-77; pathologist, lab. dir. Nat. Health Labs., Inc., Winston-Salem, N.C., 1977-95, v.p. anatomic pathology, 1994-95, Lab. Corp. of Am., Inc., Winston-Salem, 1995-96, pathologist, 1997—. Author: The Bermuda Hundred Campaign, 1988, Sumter is Avenged: The Siege and Conquest of Fort Pulaski, 1995; author, editor: Autobiography of Maj. Gen. Wm. F. Smith: 1861-64, 1989, A Captain's War: The Letters and Diaries of William H.S. Burgwyn 1861-65, 1994. Lt. comdr. USNR, 1969-79. Mem. Am. Soc. Clin. Pathologists, Coll. Am. Pathologists, Phi Beta Kappa, Alpha Omega Alpha. Avocation: U.S. civl war history. Office: Lab Corp of America 3908E Westpoint Blvd Winston Salem NC 27103-6719

SCHILLER, JAMES JOSEPH, lawyer; b. Cleve., July 1, 1933; s. Jacob Peter and Helen Elizabeth (Tosh) S.; m. Sara Brooke Wilson, Oct. 24, 1964; children: Charles A., Brooke V.G., Kristan W. BS, Case Inst. Tech., 1955; JD, U. Mich., 1961. Bar: Ohio 1962. Assoc. Marshman, Hornbeck & Hollington, Cleve., 1961-68; ptnr. Marshman, Snyder & Seeley, 1968-73, Zellmer & Gruber, Cleve., 1973-80, Weston, Hurd, Fallon, Paisley & Howley, Cleve., 1980-88, Porter, Wright, Morris & Arthur, Cleve., 1989-95, James J. Schiller & Assocs., Cleve., 1995—. Campaign mgr. John J. Gilligan for Gov. of Ohio, Cuyahoga County, 1970; campaign dir. U.S. Senator Howard M. Metzenbaum, Cleve., 1973; mem. Ohio Dem. Com., 1970-73; dep. registrar motor vehicles Dept. Hwy. Safety, Cuyahoga County, 1971-74; trustee Greater Cleve. Regional Transit Authority, 1985-87; vestryman Christ Episcopal Ch., Shaker Heights, Ohio, 1974-76, 90-93, clk., 1974-76, sr. warden, 1992-93; chmn. bd. suprs. ChristCh. Found., 1995—; trustee Recovery Resources, 1988—, chmn. bd. dirs., exec. com., 1994-96; trustee Ohio Ch. Orch., exec. com., 1996—; trustee Cleve. Ballet, 1997—. Lt. j.g. USNR, 1955-58. Recipient Cert. Commendation Bd. County Commrs., 1987. Mem. ABA, Ohio State Bar Assn. (ethics com. 1986-88), Cleve. Bar Assn., Rowfant Club (fin. com. 1988, coun. Fellowes 1990-91, 95—, advocate 1992-95, v.p. 1998-99, pres. 1999-2000), Union Club, Cleve. Skating Club. Avocations: sailing, skiing, restoring furniture. Home: 13415 Shaker Blvd Cleveland OH 44120-1586 Office: James J Schiller & Assocs 13224 Shaker Sq Ste 210 Cleveland OH 44120-2349

SCHILLER, JUSTIN GALLAND, antiquarian bookseller, researcher, editor; b. Bklyn., Sept. 10, 1943; s. S. Gary and Constance Audrey (Galland) S. BA in English Renaissance Lit., Ithaca Coll., 1965; postgrad., SUNY, Binghamton, 1965-66. Prin. Justin G. Schiller, Bklyn., 1960-69; pres. Justin G. Schiller, Ltd., N.Y.C., 1969—. Instr. hist. children's literature Rare Books Sch., Columbia U., 1984-89, U. Va., Charlottesville, 1996—; lectr. in field. Editor: (with A. Lurie) Garland's Classics in Children's Literature, 73 vols.; contbr. articles to Horn Book mag., Am. Book Collector, The Book Collector, others. Mem. coun. Bibliog. Soc. Am., 2001—. Mem Antiquarian Booksellers Assn. Am., Assn. Internat. de Bibliophilie, Am. Antiquarian Soc., Grolier Club. Home: 77 W Chestnut St Kingston NY 12401-5929 Office: Justin G Schiller Ltd Antiquarian Booksellers Ste 302 Rockefeller Ctr 1270 Ave of Amers New York NY 10020-1702 E-mail: jgs@childlit.com.

SCHILLER, LAWRENCE JULIAN, writer, motion picture producer, director; b. N.Y.C., Dec. 28, 1936; s. Isidore and Jean (Liebowitz) S.; children: Suzanne, Marc, Howard, Anthony, Cameron. BA, Pepperdine Coll., 1958. Photojournalist Life mag., 1959-69, Paris Match, 1960-69, London Sun. Times, 1960-69. Producer, dir.; (films) Hey, I'm Alive, The Winds of Kitty Hawk, Marilyn, Raid on Short Creek, An Act of Love, The Executioner's Song (Emmy award), Peter the Great (Emmy award), By Reason of Insanity, Margret Brourke-White Story, Plot to Kill Hitler, Double Jeopardy, Perfect Murder, Perfect Town, American Tragedy, Into the Mirror; author: Cape May Court House, Into the Mirror, American Tragedy, Perfect Murder, Perfect Town, Marilyn; collaborator: (with Albert Goldman) Lenny Bruce (with Eugene Smith) Minamata, (with Norman Mailer) The Executioner's Song (Pulitzer prize 1980), Oswald's Tale; (with O.J. Simpson) I Want To Tell You. Chmn. bd. dirs. Am.-Soviet Film Initiative, 1988; Am. del. Moscow Internat. Forum on Peace, 1987; mem. USSR-USA Bi-Lateral Talks, 1988. Recipient numerous awards in photojournalism Nat. Press Photographers Assn., Acad. award for The Man Who Skied Down Everest, 1975 Mem. Nat. Press Photographers Assn., Calif. Press Photographers Assn., Dirs. Guild of Am., Acad. of Motion Picture Arts and Scis. Democrat. Jewish.

SCHILLER, PIETER JON, venture capital executive; b. Orange, N.J., Jan. 14, 1938; s. John Fasel and Helen Roff (Roberts) S.; m. Elizabeth Ann Williams, Nov. 20, 1965; children— Cathryn Ann, Suzanne Elizabeth. BA in Econs. with honors, Middlebury (Vt.) Coll., 1960; MBA, NYU, 1966. Fin. analyst Merck & Co., Inc., N.Y.C., 1960-61; fin. analyst, asst. div. controller, dir. auditing, then asst. controller Allied Chem. Corp., N.Y.C. and Morristown, N.J., 1961-75, treas., 1975-79, v.p. planning and devel., 1979-83; Allied Corp. exec. v.p. diagnostic ops. Allied Health & Sci. Products Co., 1983-86; pres. subs. Instrumentation Lab., Lexington, Mass., 1983-86; gen. ptnr. Advanced Tech. Ventures, Waltham, 1986—. Bd. dirs. HealthShare Tech., Acton, Mass., Endius, Inc., Plainville, Mass., Purilens, Inc., Tampa, Fla., CytoLogix Corp., Cambridge, Mass., Synthon Corp., Monmouth Junction, NJ, Ardais Corp., Lexington, Mass. Chmn. bd. trustees Newark Boys Chorus Sch., 1976—78, pres. bd., 1974—76; trustee Colonial Symphony Soc., 1978—85, v.p., 1980—82, pres., 1982—83; active Morris Mus., Morristown, Concord (Mass.) Mus., 1994—96, v.p., 1996—2000; pres. Middlebury Coll. Alumni Assn., 1994—96; chmn. allocations com. United Way of Morris County, 1974—79, v.p. bd. dirs., mem. exec. com., 1979—80; trustee Morris Mus. Arts and Scis., 1980—83; bd. dirs. New Eng. Coun., Boston, 1983—86, Middlebury Coll. Alumni Assn., 1989—98, v.p., 1992—94. Mem. Fin. Execs. Inst. Republican. Episcopalian. Avocations: skiing, photography. Home: 18 S Meadow Rdg Concord MA 01742-3051 E-mail: pschiller@atvcapital.com.

SCHILLER, SOPHIE, artist, graphic designer; b. Moscow, Feb. 10, 1940; came to U.S., 1974; d. Samuel and Rebecca (Lagovier) Elinson; m. Mikhail Schiller, Apr. 29, 1960; 1 child, Maria. Student, Moscow State Art Sch., 1954-58; MA, Moscow Inst., 1964; cert. in graphic and book design, Mass. Coll. Art, 1977. Graphic artist Progress Pub. House, Moscow, 1964-70, Popular Sci. mag., Moscow, 1970-74; artist, graphic designer Boston, 1974—. Freelance graphic designer Harvard Press, Boston, M.E. Sharpe Pub., N.Y., Ginn Press, Simon & Schuster, Boston, Tech. Rev., MIT, Cambridge, Mass. One person shows include Galleria del Corso, Rome, 1974, Wennigar Gallery, Boston, 1977; exhibited in group shows Taganka Exhibit, Moscow, 1962, Moscow Artists Union, 1962, Am. Painters in Paris Exhbn., 1975, Unofficial Art from Soviet Union, Washington, 1977, Mariland Gallery, St. Mary's City, 1977, Bard Coll., N.Y., 1991, Rose Art Mus., Brandeis U., Boston, 1992, Tofias Gallery, Boston, 1994, Zimmerly Art Mus., Rutgers U., N.J., 1995; group shows include The Dorland-Haight Gallery, Milton, Can., 1993. Mem. Nat. Mus. Women in the Arts. Avocations: travel, hiking, collecting children's art. Home: 63 University Rd Brookline MA 02445-4532

SCHILLER, WILLIAM RICHARD, surgeon; b. Bennett, Colo., Jan. 14, 1937; s. Francis T. and Frances M. (Finks) S.; m. Beverlee Schiller; children from previous marriage: Julie, Lisa. BS, Drury Coll., Springfield, Mo., 1958; MD, Northwestern U., 1962. Diplomate Am. Bd. Surgery; cert. of added qualifications in surg. critical care, 1987, recertified in surg. critical care, 1994. Intern Passavant Meml. Hosp., Chgo., 1962-63; resident Northwestern U. Clin. Tng. Program, 1963-68; assoc. prof. surgery Med. Coll Ohio, Toledo, 1970-78; prof. surgery U. N.Mex, Albuquerque, 1978-83; dir. Trauma Ctr. St. Joseph's Hosp., Phoenix, 1983-89; dir. burn and trauma ctr. Maricopa Med. Ctr., 1989-98; prof. surgery So. Ill. U., Springfield, 1998—. Clin. prof. surgery U. Ariz. Health Sci. Ctr.; prof. surgery Mayo Grad. Sch. Medicine, Rochester, Minn. Contbr. chpts. to books, articles to profl. jours. Served as maj. M.C. U.S. Army, 1968-70, Vietnam. Fellow ACS; mem. Am. Assn. Surgery of Trauma, Cen. Surg. Assn., Western Surg. Assn., Soc. Surgery of Alimentary Tract, Am. Burn Assn., Internat. Soc. of Surgery. Republican. Home: 4505 Innis Brk Springfield IL 62707-6713 Office: So Ill Univ Med Sch Trauma Ctr Dept Surgery Box 19638 Springfield IL 62794-9638 E-mail: wschiller@siumed.edu.

SCHILLING, CURTIS MONTAGUE, professional baseball player; b. Anchorage, Nov. 14, 1966; m. Shonda Schilling; 1 child, Gehrig. Student, Yavapai Coll., Ariz. Selected by Boston Red Sox, 1986-88; traded Balt. Orioles, 1988-91, Houston Astros, 1991-92; pitcher Phila. Phillies, 1992-2000, Arizona Diamondbacks, 2000—. Recipient Lou Gehrig award Phi Delta Theta, 1996. Office: c/o Ariz Diamondbacks Bank One Ballpark 401 E Jefferson St Phoenix AZ 85004-2438*

SCHILLING, DON RUSSELL, electric utility executive; b. Greenburg, Ind., June 11, 1951; s. Cloyd H. and Ruth V. (Knarr) S.; m. Teri L. Edwards, July 14, 1973; children: Jaclyn, Christopher. BS in Elec. Engring., Purdue U., 1973; MS in Bus. Adminstrn., Ind. U., Fort Wayne, 1977. Registered profl. engr., Ind. Elec. engr. Ind. and Mich. Electric Co., Fort Wayne, 1973-79; asst. gen. mgr. Decatur County REMC, Greensburg, Ind., 1979-86, pres., gen. mgr., 1986—; sec.-treas. Hometown Energy LLC, 2001—. Pres. Ind. Rural TV, Inc., 1988-89. Mem. IEEE, Greensburg Area C. of C. (pres. 1994), Lions, Masons. Baptist. Avocations: woodworking. Office: Decatur County REMC PO Box 46 Greensburg IN 47240-0046 E-mail: dschilling@dcremc.com.

SCHILLING, EMILY BORN, editor, association executive; b. Lawton, Okla., Oct. 2, 1959; d. George Arthur and Sumiko (Nagamine) Born; m. Mark David Schilling, June 26, 1995. BS, Ball State U., 1981. Cert. coop. communicator Nat. Rural Electric Coop. Assn. Feature writer The News-Sentinel, Fort Wayne, Ind., 1981-83; wire editor The Noblesville (Ind.) Daily Ledger, 1983; staff writer Ind. Statewide Assn. Rural Electric Coops., Indpls., 1983-84, mng. editor, 1984-85, editor, 1985—. Author: Power to the People, 1985. Mem. Coop. Communicators Assn. (Michael Graznak award 1990), Internat. Assn. Bus. Communicators (award of excellence dist. 7 1985), Women's Internat. Network of Utility Profls. (pres. 1999, Mem. of Yr. 1999, Power award 1994), Nat. Electric Coops. Statewide Editors Assn. Office: Ind Statewide Assn RECs 720 N High School Rd Indianapolis IN 46214-3756

SCHILLING, FRANKLIN CHARLES, JR. retail management professional; b. Balt., Apr. 17, 1958; s. Franklin Charles and Shirley Jean (Whitehurst) S.; children: Franklin Charles III, Tyler Kyle. Student, Dundalk Community Coll., 1975-77. Dept. mgr. Santonis Market, Inc., Balt., 1976-80; store mgr. A&P Plus Food Stores, 1980-82; area supr. Southland Corp/7-Eleven, Suitland, Md., 1982-85; mgr. retail ops. Moore Oil Co./Makin' Tracks Stores, Washington, 1986, Besche Oil Co./Quik Shop Stores, Waldorf, Md., 1987-89; dist. mgr. Cloverland Greenspring Dairy/Royal Farm Stores, Balt., 1989-97, dir. ops., 1997-98, mktg. mgr., 1999—. Mem. Rep. Nat. Com. Lutheran. Avocations: reading, sports, music. Home: 1917 August Ave Baltimore MD 21222-3015 Office: Cloverland Dairies/Royal Farm Stores 3611 Roland Ave Baltimore MD 21211-2408

SCHILLING, FREDERICK AUGUSTUS, JR. geologist, consultant; b. Phila., Apr. 12, 1931; s. Frederick Augustus and Emma Hope (Christoffer) S.; m. Ardis Ione Dovre, June 12, 1957 (div. 1987); children: Frederick Christopher, Jennifer Dovre. BS in Geology, Wash. State U., 1953; PhD in Geology, Stanford U., 1962. Registered geologist, Calif.; cert. engring. geologist, Calif.; registered environ. assessor, Calif. Computer geophysicist United Geophys. Corp., Pasadena, Calif., 1955-56; geologist various orgns., 1956-61, U.S. Geol. Survey, 1961-64; underground engr. Climax (Colo.) Molybdenum Co., 1966-68; geologist Keradamex Inc., Anaconda Co., M.P. Grace, Ranchers Exploration & Devel. Corp., Albuquerque and Grants, N.Mex., 1968-84, Hecla Mining Co., Coeur d'Alene, Idaho, 1984-86, various engring. and environ. firms, Calif., 1986-91; prin. F. Schilling Cons., Canyon Lake, 1991—. Author: Bibliography of Uranium, 1976. Del. citizen amb. program People to People Internat., USSR, 1990-91. With U.S. Army, 1953-55. Fellow The Explorers Club; mem. Geol. Soc. Am., Am. Assn. Petroleum Geologists, Soc. Mining Engrs., Internat. Platform Assn., Adventurers' Club L.A., Masons, Kiwanis, Sigma Xi, Sigma Gamma Epsilon. Republican. Presbyterian. Avocation: track and field. Office: F Schilling Cons 30037 Steel Head Dr Canyon Lake CA 92587-7460 also: 14661 Myford Rd Ste C Tustin CA 92780-7205 E-mail: faschill@pacbell.net.

SCHILLING, JOHN MICHAEL, education director; b. L.A., Nov. 9, 1964; s. Gerard Joseph and Rose Carmen Schilling; m. Judith Marie Boylson, Jan. 8, 1994; children: John Joseph, Jordan Leigh. BA, U. San Diego, 1986; postgrad., Am. U., 1986. Rsch. supr. Rep. Nat. Com., Washington, 1987-91; spl. asst. Calif. Dept. Housing, Sacramento, 1991; dir. rsch. Benchmark Rsch., 1992; dir. ops. rsch. Rep. Nat. Com., Washington, 1993-94, dir. rsch., 1996-97; dep. chief staff Rep. Andrea Seastrand, 1995; chief policy and planning Ariz. Dept. Edn., Phoenix, 1997—. V.p. JMS Consulting, Alexandria, Va., Phoenix, 1995—. Republican. Roman Catholic. Avocations: sports, movies, music, politics. Home: 13103 Wheeler Way Herndon VA 20171-2353 E-mail: jmschilling@mindspring.com.

SCHILLING, JOHN RUSSELL, lawyer, retail executive; b. Huntington Park, Calif., Nov. 27, 1942; s. Alice S.; m. Susan Foster, Aug. 25, 1962 (div. Jan. 1976); children: Jennifer Susan, Lisa Ann, John Payton; m. Caroline Schilling, Aug. 20, 1976 (div. Dec. 1985); 1 child, Brice David; m. Sabrina Celeste August, Aug. 21, 1993; children: Elissia Jeanne, Chanel Marie, Chloe Celeste, Arianna Rachelle. BA, U. Calif., Santa Barbara, 1964; JD, UCLA, 1967. Bar: Calif. 1968; cert. family law, Nat. Bd. Trial Advocacy. Chief rsch. atty., 4th dist., divsn. II Ct. Appeals, San Bernardino, Calif., 1967-69; pvt. practice Orange County, 1969—. Lectr. in field; mem. Nat. Bd. Trial Advocacy, 2001. Trustee Santa Ana (Calif.) Unified Sch. Dist., 1971-75. Fellow Am. Acad. Matrimonial Lawyers (v.p. 1985—); mem. ABA (sect. child custody com. 1968—), Calif. State Bar Assn., Orange County Bar Assn. (sect. treas. 1984—), Robert A. Banyard Inn of Ct. (master bencher 1996—), Internat. Acad. of Matrimonial Lawyers. Office: 4675 MacArthur Ct Ste 590 Newport Beach CA 92660-8800 Fax: (949) 833-3883. E-mail: JRSchillingfamilylaw@earthlink.net.

SCHILLING, WARNER ROLLER, political scientist, educator; b. Glendale, Calif., May 23, 1925; s. Jule Frederick and Pauline Frances de Berri (Warner) S.; m. Jane Pierce Metzger, Jan. 27, 1951 (dec. Nov. 1983); children: Jonathan, Frederick. AB, Yale U., 1949, MA, 1951, PhD, 1954. Research fellow Center Internat. Studies, Princeton U., 1953-54; asst. prof. internat. relations Mass. Inst. Tech., 1957-58; mem. faculty Columbia, 1954—, prof. govt., 1967-73, James T. Shotwell prof. internat. relations, 1973—; dir. Inst. War and Peace Studies, 1976-86. Cons., occasional lectr. in field. Co-author: Strategy, Politics and Defense Budgets, 1962, European Security and the Atlantic System, 1973, American Arms and a Changing Europe, 1973; Contbr. numerous articles to jours. Served with USAAF, 1944-46. Guggenheim fellow, 1964-65; resident fellow Bellagio Study and Conf. Center, 1975 Mem. Internat. Inst. Strategic Studies, Council Fgn. Relations. Clubs: Leonia Democratic. Home: 496 Park Ave Leonia NJ 07605-1243 Office: 420 W 118th St New York NY 10027-7213

SCHILLINGER, EDWIN JOSEPH, physics educator; b. Chgo., July 14, 1923; s. Edwin Joseph and Marie (Wolf) S.; m. Carmelita Larocco, Aug. 27, 1949; children— Rosemarie, Mary, Ann, Edwin, Jerome, Elizabeth BS, DePaul U., 1944; MS, U. Notre Dame, 1948, PhD, 1950. Mem. faculty DePaul U., Chgo., 1950—, prof. physics, 1963-88, prof. emeritus, 1988—, chmn. dept., 1952-68, 76-79, dean Coll. Liberal Arts and Scis., 1966-70, acting dean, 1980-81. Ednl. cons. Served with AUS, 1944-46 Decorated Purple Heart; recipient merit award Chgo. Tech. Socs., 1976; AEC fellow, 1948-50 Fellow Am. Phys. Soc.; mem. AAAS, Am. Assn. Physics Tchrs., Sigma Xi Roman Catholic. Home: 7724 W Peterson Ave Chicago IL 60631-2246

SCHILLING-NORDAL, GERALDINE ANN, secondary school educator; b. Springfield, Mass., Feb. 4, 1935; d. Robert Milton and Helen Veronica (Ewald) Schilling; m. Reidar Johannes Nordal. BS, Boston U., 1956, MEd, 1957; postgrad., Springfield Coll., Anna Maria Coll. Tchr. art Agawam (Mass.) Jr. H.S., 1957-58, Agawam H.S., 1958—, K-12 art acad. coord., 1995-96, head art dept., 1970-95. Instr. oil painting univ. ext. course Agawam Night Sch., 1957-58; instr. creative arts Agawam Evening Sch., 1973-80. Active Agawam Town Report Com., 1967-77, Agawam Hist. Commn., 1979-87, Agawam Arts and Humanities Com., 1979-85, Agawam Minerva Davis Libr. Study Com., 1987-88, Agawam Cultural Coun., 1994-97; sec. Agawam Town Beautification Com., 1974-87; mem. town tchrs. rep. Agawam Bicentennial Com., 1975-77; chmn. 40th anniversary St. John the Evangelist Ch., Agawam, 1986, co-chmn. 50th anniversary com., 1996, mem. renovation com., 1983; decoration chmn. town-wide Halloween parties, Agawam, 1971-93; recruiter Miss Agawam Pageant; appeal vol. Cath. Charity, 1995-2002; mem. Agawam Cath. Womens Club, 1995—, banquet com., 1997, 99. Mem. NEA, Agawam Edn. Assn. (sec. 1970-74, 76-77, h.s. addition dedication com. 1998-99, scholarship com., 1997, Agawam Tchrs. Wall of Fame for 45 Yrs. Svc. 2002), Hampden County Tchrs. Assn., Mass. Tchrs. Assn., Mass. Art Edn. Assn., Nat. Art Edn. Assn., New Eng. Art Edn. Assn., Am. Assn. Ret. Persons, Mass. Cath. Order Foresters, West Springfield Neighborhood House Alumni Assn. (pres. 1966, advisor 1968), West Springfield H.S. Alumni Assn. (3d v.p. 1968-70, 1st v.p. 1970-71, pres. 1972-74), Boston U. Alumni Club Springfield Area (organizer area giving campaigns 1957-62, class agt. 1985—, mem. area scholarship com. 1995—), Am. Legion (life), Zeta Chi Delta (pres. 1955-56), Delta Kappa Gamma (Alpha chpt., art chairperson, reservation chmn. art work and hist. archives, hospitality 50th and 60th ann. com.). Office: Agawam Sr High Sch 760 Cooper St Agawam MA 01001-2177

SCHILLINGS, DENNY LYNN, history educator, grants manager; b. Mt. Carmel, Ill., June 28, 1947; s. Grady Lynn and Mary Lucille (Walters) S.; m. Karen Krek; children: Denise, Corinne. AA, Wabash Valley Coll., 1967; BEd, Ea. Ill. U., 1969, MA in History, 1972; MA in Adminstrn., Govs. State U., 1996; postgrad., Ill. State U., No. Ill. U. Grad. asst. dept. history Ea. Ill. U., Charleston, 1969; tchr. Edwards County High Sch., Albion, Ill., 1969-70, Sheldon (Ill.) High Sch., 1971-73, Homewood-Flossmoor (Ill.) High Sch., 1973—, grants and devel. mgr., 1994—. Participant, con. Atlantic Coun. U.S. and NATO, Washington, 1986, Internat. Soviet-U.S. Textbook Project Conf., Racine, Wis., 1987; moderator Soviet-U.S. Textbook Study: Final Report, Dallas, 1987; chair history content adv. com. Ill. Tchr. Certification Requirements Com. 1986; mem. Ill. State Bd. Edn., Com. to Establish Learner Outcomes, 1984, Joint Task Force on Admission Requirements Ill. State Bd. on Higher Edn., 1986—; mem. adv. com. for Jefferson Found. Sch. Programs, 1987-90, Ill. State Bd. Edn.'s Goals Assessment Adv. Com., 1987-90; chair Ill. Learning Standards Project, 1996-97. Author: (with others) Economics, 1986, The Examination in Social Studies, 1989, Links Across Time and Place: A World History, 1990, Illinois Government Text, 1990, Challenge of Freedom, 1990; author: The Living Constitution, 1991, 3d edit., 2002; co-editor: Teaching the Constition, 1987; reviewer, cons. for ednl. instns. and organizations; chair editorial bd. Social Edn., 1983; contbg. editor Social Studies Tchr., 1987-88. Mem. steering com. Homewood-Floosmoor High Sch. Found., 1983-84; elected bd. edn. Homewood Elem. Dist. 153, 1999—. Mem. NEA, Am. Hist. Assn. (James Harvey Robinson prize com. 1990-91), Ill. Coun. Social Studies (v.p. 1981, editor newsletter 1979-84, pres. 1983), Ill. Edn. Assn. (Gt. Lakes coord. com. 1982-83), Nat. Coun. Social Studies (publs. bd. 1983-86, bd. dirs. 1987-90, 94-96, exec. com. 1989-90, chair conf. com. 1989-90, pres. 1993-94, program planning com. 1989, 91), Phi Alpha Theta. Avocations: computers, reading. Home: 18447 Aberdeen St Homewood IL 60430-3525 Office: Homewood-Flossmoor High Sch 999 Kedzie Ave Flossmoor IL 60422-2248 E-mail: dschillings@hfhighschool.org.

SCHILSKY, RICHARD LEWIS, oncologist, researcher; b. N.Y.C., June 6, 1950; s. Murray and Shirley (Cohen) S.; m. Cynthia Schum, Sept. 24, 1977; children: Allison, Meredith. BA cum laude, U. Pa., Phila., 1971; MD with honors, U. Chgo., 1975. Diplomate Nat. Bd. Med. Examiners, Am. Bd. Internal Medicine (subspecialty med. oncology); lic. physician, Mo., Ill. Intern, resident medicine Parkland Meml. Hosp., Southwestern Med. Sch., Dallas, 1975-77; clin. assoc. medicine br. and clin. pharmacology br. Divsn. Cancer Treatment, Nat. Cancer Inst., Bethesda, Md., 1977-80, cancer expert clin. pharmacology br., 1980-81; asst. prof. dept. internal medicine U. Mo. Sch. Medicine, Columbia, 1981-84; asst. prof. dept. medicine U. Chgo. Pritzker Sch. Medicine and Michael Reese Med. Ctrs., 1984-86, assoc. prof. dept. medicine, 1986-89; assoc. dir. joint sect. hematology and med. oncology U. Chgo. and Michael Reese Med. Ctrs., 1986-89; assoc. prof. dept. medicine, assoc. dir. sect. U. Chgo. Pritzker Sch. Medicine, 1989-91, prof. dept. medicine sect. hematology-oncology, 1991—; dir. U. Chgo. Cancer Rsch. Ctr., 1991-99; chmn. Cancer and Leukemia Group B, Chgo., 1995—; assoc. dean clin. rsch. biol. scis. divsn. U. Chgo., 1999—. Vivian Saykaly vis. prof. oncology McGill U., 1992; sci. com. Internat. Congress on Anti-Cancer Chemotherapy, 2002; adv. panel on hematologic and neoplastic disease U.S. Pharmacopeial Conv., 1991-95; bd. dirs. Assn. Am. Cancer Insts., 1995-99; cancer ctr. support grant rev. com. Nat. Cancer Inst., NIH, 1992-95; expert panel on advances in cancer treatment, 1992-93; mem. Cancer Ctrs. Working Group, 1996-97; oncologic drugs adv. com. FDA, 1996-2000, chmn., 1999-2000; mem. NCI Clin. Trials Implementation com., 1997-98; bd. scientific advisors Nat. Cancer Inst., 1999—. Mem. editl. bd. Investigational New Drugs, 1988-95, Jour. Clin. Oncology, 1990-93, Contemporary Oncology, 1991-95, Jour. Cancer Rsch. and Clin. Oncology, 1991—, Seminars in Oncology, 1997—; assoc. editor Clin. Cancer Rsch., 1994—, Cancer Therapeutics, 1997-99, Cancer, 2000—; contbr. articles to profl. jours., chpts. to books. With USPHS, 1977-80. Recipient Spl. Advancement for Performance award VA, 1983, Fletcher Scholar award Cancer Rsch. Found., 1989; grantee VA, 1981-87, Am. Cancer Soc., 1983-86, 92-95, Ill. Cancer Coun., 1985-86, Michael Reese Inst. Coun., 1985-86, Nat. Cancer Inst., 1987, 88-90, Burroughs-Wellcome Co., 1987-88, NIH/Nat. Cancer Inst., 1988— Fellow ACP; mem. AAAS, Am. Soc. Clin. Oncology (chmn. pub. rels. com. 1994-96, bd. dirs. 2002-), Am. Assn. Cancer Rsch. (chmn. Ill. state legis. com. 1992—), Am. Fedn. Clin. Rsch. (senator Midwest sect. 1983-84, councilor 1983-86, chmn.-elect 1987-88, chmn. 1988-89), Am. Cancer Soc. (bd. dirs. Ill. divsn. 1997—), Am. Assn. Cancer Edn., Am. Soc. Clin. Pharmacology and Therapeutics, Ctrl. Soc. Clin. Rsch., N.Y. Acad. Scis., Assn. Am. Cancer Insts. (bd. dirs. 1995-99), Chgo. Soc. Internal Medicine, Sigma Xi, Alpha Epsilon Delta, Alpha Omega Alpha. Office: U Chgo Biol Scis Divsn 5841 S Maryland Ave Chicago IL 60637-1463 E-mail: rs27@midway.uchicago.edu.

SCHILT, ALEXANDER FRANK, academic administrator; b. Cheyenne, Wyo., Mar. 4, 1941; s. Louis Ford and Mary Alice (Linton) S.; m. Charlotte Frances Snyder, May 25, 1967 (div.); children: Paige Eileen, Kristen Rose. BA, U. Wyo., 1964; MA, Ariz. State U., 1966, PhD, 1969. Dir. residence Ariz. State U., Tempe, 1964-70; dean of students, assoc. prof. edn. Ind. U., New Albany, 1970-76, chancellor Richmond, 1976-80, U. Houston-Downtown, 1980-87; pres. Eastern Washington U., 1987-89; chancellor U. Houston System, 1989—. Bd. dirs. Ctrl. Houston, Inc., Greater Houston Partnership, Houston Industries, Inc., Houston Lighting and Power Co.; lectr. on urban univs. to profl. confs. Bd. dirs. St. Joseph Hosp. Mem. AAUP, Am. Coun. Edn., Am. Assn. State Colls. and Univs., Internat. Assn. Univ., Pres.'s (exec. com. 1993—), Interam. Univ. Coun. for Econ. and Social Devel. (pres. 1993—), Nat. Assn. of Sys. Heads, Nat. Assn. State Univs. and Land-Grant Colls., Petroleum Club, Houston Club, River Oaks Country Club. Roman Catholic. Office: U Houston System 1600 Smith St Fl 34 Houston TX 77002-7362

SCHIMBERG, A(RMAND) BRUCE, retired lawyer; b. Chgo., Aug. 26, 1927; s. Archie and Helen (Isay) S.; m. Barbara Zisook; children: Geoffrey, Kate. PhB, U. Chgo., 1949, JD, 1952. Bar: Ohio 1952, Ill. 1955, U.S. Supreme Ct. 1987. Assoc. Paxton & Seasongood, Cin., 1952-55; ptnr. Schimberg, Greenberger, Kraus & Jacobs, Chgo., 1955-65, Leibman, Williams, Bennett, Baird & Minow, Chgo., 1965-72, Sidley & Austin, Chgo., 1972-92, counsel, 1993-94; ret., 1994. Lectr. U. Chgo., 1953-54; gen. counsel Comml. Fin. Assn., 1978-94; past mem. editl. bd. Lender Liability News. Mng. and assoc. editor U. Chgo. Law Rev., 1951-52; contbr. articles to legal jours. Bd. dirs. U. Chgo. Law Sch. Alumni Assn., 1969-72; dir. vis. com. U. Chgo. Law Sch., 1980-83. Recipient Homer Kripke Lifetime Achievement award for contbns. to comml. fin. law, 1998. Mem. ABA (chmn. subcom. and charter mem. comml. fin. svcs. com.), Am. Coll. Comml. Fin. Lawyers (pres. 1994-95, bd. regents), Ill. Bar Assn. (chair comml. banking, bankruptcy sect. 1972-73), Chgo. Bar Assn. (chair ucc com., 1966, bd. mgrs. 1968-70, chair judiciary com. 1971-72), Law Club Chgo., Mid-Day Club, Lake Shore Country Club. Home: 132 E Delaware Pl Apt 5002 Chicago IL 60611-4944 Office: Sidley & Austin 55 W Monroe St Ste 2000 Chicago IL 60603-5008

SCHIMBERG, BARBARA HODES, organizational development consultant; b. Chgo., Nov. 30, 1941; d. David and Tybe Zisook; children from previous marriage: Brian Hodes, Valery Lodato; m. A. Bruce Schimberg, Dec. 29, 1984. BS, Northwestern U., 1962. Ptnr. Just Causes, cons. not-for-profit orgns., Chgo., 1978-86. Cons. in philanthropy, community involvement, and organizational devel., 1987—; Chgo. cons. Population Resource Ctr., 1978-82. Women's bd. dirs. Mus. Contemporary Art; bd. dirs., vice chmn. Med. Rsch. Inst. Coun., Michael Reese Med. Ctr.; bd. dirs., chmn. Midwest Women's Ctr.; trustee Francis W. Parker Sch.; bd. dirs. Women's Issues Network Found., 1991-98, pres., 1993-94; mem. adv. bd. Med. Rsch. Inst. Coun., Children's Meml. Hosp. Mem. ACLU (adv. com.). Office: 132 E Delaware Pl Apt 5002 Chicago IL 60611-4944

SCHIMEK, DIANNA RUTH REBMAN, state legislator; b. Holdrege, Nebr., Mar. 21, 1940; d. Ralph William and Elizabeth Julia (Wilmot) Rebman; m. Herbert Henry Schimek, 1963; children: Samuel Wolfgang, Saul William. AA, Colo. Women's Coll., 1960; student, U. Nebr., Lincoln, 1960-61; BA magna cum laude, U. Nebr., Kearney, 1963. Former tchr. and realtor; mem. Nebr. Legislature from 27th dist., Lincoln, 1989—; chmn. govt., mil. and vets. affairs com. Nebr. Legislature, 1993-94, 99—, vice chair urban affairs com., 1995-98. Dem. Nat. committeewoman, 1984-88; chmn. Nebr. Dem. Com., 1980-84, mem. exec. com., 1987-88; past pres., sec. bd. dirs. Downtown Sr. Ctr. Found., 1990-96; mem. exec. bd. Midwestern Legis. Conf., 1995-96, co-chair health and human svcs. com., 1995-96; exec. dir. Nebr. Civil Liberties Union, 1985; former bd. dirs. Nebr. Repertory Theater, Exon Found., 1997—; mem. adv. bd. Martin Luther Home, 1997—; chair Midwestern Legis. Conf. Coun. of State Govts., 2000-01; mem. Midwest Interstate passenger Rail Commn., 2001—; chair NCSL Task Force on Initiative and Referendum, 2001-02. Toll fellow, 1999; recipient Outstanding Alumni award U. Nebr., 1989, Tribute award YWCA, 1992, Friend of Psychology award N.E. Psychol. Assn., 1998, Woman of Yr. award Nova Chpt. Bus. & Profl. Women, 1999, Disting. Svc. award Nat. Guard Assn., 2000, Woman of Distinction award Soroptomists, 1999, Legis. of Yr. award N.E. Dental Hygienists Assn., 2001, Disting. Svc. award N.E. League of Municipalities, 2002, others. Mem. Nat. Conf. State Legislators Women's Network (bd. dirs. 1993-96, 1st vice chmn.), PEO, Soroptomists, Delta Kappa Gamma (hon.), Mortar Bd. (cmty. advisor 1998, hon.). Democrat. Unitarian Universalist. Home: 2321 Camelot Ct Lincoln NE 68512-1457 Office: Dist # 27 State Capital Lincoln NE 68509

SCHIMKE, DENNIS J. former state legislator; m. Olive Young, Dec. 1964 (dec. 1998); 3 children. BS, U. N.D., 1968, MS, 1972. Bison rancher, Coteau Hills, ND, 1987—; tchr. h.s. math. and physics LaMoure, N.D., 1975-2000; lectr. math. N.D. State U., 2001—; rep. Dist. 28 N.D. Ho. of Reps., 1991-93, rep. dist. 26, 1995-97, mem. edn. and agr. com., 1991—93, 1995—97. Founding bd. dirs. N.D. Buffalo Assn., 1991—95. Home: PO Box 525 Edgeley ND 58433-0525

SCHIMMEL, CLEO RITZ, civic worker; b. Canton, Ohio, Jan. 28, 1940; d. John Vail and Jesse (Roderick) Ritz; m. Paul R. Schimmel, Dec. 30, 1962; children: Kirsten Leah, Katherine Diane. AB, Ohio Wesleyan U., 1958-62. Cert. tchr. Ohio, Mass. Elem. tchr. Quincy (Mass.) Pub. Schs., 1962-63; adminstrv. asst. in counseling Counseling Ctr., Lexington, Mass., 1978-79; asst. dir. coop. edn. program Middlesex Coll., Bedford, 1979-80, instr. adult edn. Lexington, 1984-88; adminstrv. asst. Office of Pres., MIT, Cambridge, 1980-83. Substitute tchr., Cambridge Pub. Schs., 1964-66, Quincy Pub. Schs., 1964-66, Lexington Pub. Schs., 1977-79; interior design cons., 1985-88; program chmn. MIT Womens League, Cambridge, 1995—. Trustees Lexington Christian Acad., 1977-79, co-chmn. Ohio Wesleyan Alumae Sesquifest Celebration, Delaware, 1992-97; bd. govs., bd. overseers New Eng. Med. Ctr., Boston, 1992-98; chmn. Women's League MIT, 1992-95; benefactor Ohio Wesleyan U., 1999, MIT, 1999; chmn. La Jolla Farms Property Owners Assn., 2000—; mem. planning and devel. coun. Scripps Cancer Ctr., 2001—. Avocations: travel, reading, boating, painting. Home: 9822 La Jolla Farms Rd La Jolla CA 92037-1135 E-mail: cleo@paulschimmel.com.

SCHIMMEL, PAUL REINHARD, biochemist, biophysicist, educator; b. Hartford, Conn., Aug. 4, 1940; s. Alfred E. and Doris (Hudson) S.; m. Judith F. Ritz, Dec. 30, 1961; children: Kirsten, Katherine. AB, Ohio Wesleyan U., 1962; postgrad., Tufts U. Sch. Medicine, 1962-63, Mass. Inst. Tech., 1963-65, Cornell U., 1965-66, Stanford U., 1966-67, U. Calif., Santa Barbara, 1975-76; PhD, Mass. Inst. Tech., 1966; DSc (hon.), Ohio Wesleyan U., 1996. Asst. prof. biology and chemistry MIT, 1967-71, assoc. prof., 1971-76, prof. biochemistry and biophysics, 1976-92, John D. and Catherine T. MacArthur prof. biochemistry and biophysics, 1992-97; prof. Scripps Rsch. Inst. and The Skaggs Inst. for Chem. Biology, 1997-2001, Ernest and Jean Hahn prof. molecular biology and chemistry, 2001—. Mem. study sect. on physiol. chemistry NIH, 1975-79; indsl. cons. on enzymes and recombinant DNA; bd. dirs. Repligen Corp., Alkermes, Inc., Cubist Pharms., Inc., 1993-2002. Author: (with C. Cantor) Biophysical Chemistry, 3 vols., 1980; mem. editl. bd. Archives Biochemistry, Biophysics, 1976-80, Nucleic Acids Rsch., 1976-80, Jour. Biol. Chemistry, 1977-82, Biopolymers, 1979-88, Internat. Jour. Biol. Macromolecules, 1983-89, Trends in Biochem. Scis., 1984—, Biochemistry, 1989—, Accounts of Chem. Rsch., 1989-94, European Jour. Biochemistry, 1991-96, Protein Sci., 1991-94, Proc. Nat. Acad. Scis., 1993-99. Alfred P. Sloan fellow, 1970-72; recipient Emily M. Gray award Biophys. Soc., 2000. Fellow AAAS, Am. Acad. Arts and Scis. (chmn. Amory prize com. 1995-96); mem. NAS (class II biochemistry sect. rep. 1995-96), Am. Philos. Soc., Am. Chem. Soc. (Pfizer award 1978, chmn. divsn. biol. chemistry 1984-85) Am. Soc. for Biochemistry and Molecular Biology (chmn. nominating com. 1990, awards com. 1995-97), Ribonucleic Acid Soc. Office: The Scripps Rsch Inst 10550 N Torrey Pines Rd La Jolla CA 92037-1000

SCHIMMELBUSCH, WERNER HELMUT, psychiatrist; b. Vienna, Austria, Nov. 16, 1937; came to U.S., 1954; s. Hans Mowgli and Anneliese Martha (Koeppe) S.; m. Faye Karina Wrangel, Dec. 29, 1958 (div. Mar. 1967); m. Jeanette Ramona Dyal, Mar. 26, 1971; children: Andre Curt, Anne Ramona. MD, U. Wash., Seattle, 1962; psychiatrist, Yale U., 1968; adult psychoanalyst, Seattle Inst. Psychoanalysis, 1977, child psychoanalyst, 1992. Instr. Dept. Psychiatry and Behavioral Sci. U. Wash., Seattle, 1968-69; pvt. practice, 1969—. Clin. prof. U. Wash., Seattle, 1984—; tng. and supervising psychoanalyst Seattle Inst. Psychoanalysis, 1990—. Capt. U.S. Army, 1963-65. Mem. AMA, Am. Psychiatric Assn., Am. Psychoanalytic Assn., Seattle Psychoanalytic Soc. (pres. 1979-80, 94-96). Avocations: skiing, hiking, sailing. Office: 4033 E Madison St Seattle WA 98112-3104

SCHIMMELFENNIG, LADONA BETH, special education educator; b. Tulsa, Apr. 29, 1948; d. James Wyatt and Ladona Babe (Robertson) Holder; m. Bryan Anapuni Schimmelfennig, July 4, 1988; 1 child, Malia M. BS in Spl. Edn., U. Tulsa, 1969; MA in Edn., Pepperdine U., Malibu, Calif., 1976. Tchr. asst. Sarasota (Fla.) Head Start, 1968; spl. edn. tchr. S.E.C.O., Honolulu, 1969-70, Monroe Jr. High Sch., Tulsa, 1970-73, Honolulu Community Action prog., Project Head Start, 1973-76; spl. edn. coord. Oahu Head Start, Honolulu, 1976-77; dir. spl. edn. Govt. of Am. Samoa, Pago Pago, 1977-79; ednl. specialist II for emotionally handicapped Dept. Edn., Oahu, Hawaii, 1984; dist. edn. specialist II for spl. edn. Windward Oahu Dept. Edn., 1979—2002; mgmt. analysis and copliance specialist Hawaii Dept. Edn., Honolulu, 2002—. Dir. 1st Am. Samoa Spl. Olympics, 1978, 79. Contbr. articles to profl. jours. Bd. dirs., pub. rels. chmn. Hawaii Spl. Olympics, 1980-84; bd. dirs. Spl. Parent Info. Network, Wai Nani Way Hoeke; sec.-treas. Pacific Basin Consortium, 1977-79; adv. panel on edn. handicapped children Southwestern Reg. Deaf-Blind Ctr., 1977-79, others in past. Mem. Coun. for

Exceptional Children (chpt. pres. 1969), Nat. Assn. State Dirs. Spl. Edn., Nat. Info. for Spl. Edn. Mgmt., S.W. Deaf/Blind Assn. Avocations: aerobics, jogging, scuba diving, shopping. Home: 739 W Hind Dr Honolulu HI 96821-1805 Office: Hawaii Dept Edn Queen Liliuokalani Bldg 1390 Miller St Honolulu HI 96813

SCHIMMER, BARRY MICHAEL, rheumatologist; b. Newark, Jan. 7, 1945; s. Emanuel and Florence Pearl (Haflich) S.;m. Naomi Ann Raicer, May 24, 1970; children: Alexandra Tamar, Rebecca Tal. BA, Rutgers U., 1966; MD, Albert Einstein Coll. Medicine, Bronx, N.Y., 1970. Diplomate Am. Bd. Internal Medicine, subspecialty rheumatology. Intern Hosp. U. Pa., Phila., 1970-71, med. resident, 1971-73; clin. rsch. assoc. Harvard Med. Sch., Boston, 1973-75; clin. assoc. prof. medicine U. Pa. Sch. Medicine, Phila., 1978-95, 98—, Thomas Jefferson U., Phila., 1995-98, U. Pa. Sch. Medicine, Phila., 1998—; chief rheumatology sect. Pa. Hosp., 1978—. Chmn. grants and scholarship com. Arthritis Found., Ea. Ga. chpt., Phila., 1988-96; med. sec. rheumatology subspecialty bd. Am. Bd. Internal Medicine, Phila., 1990-98, mem., 1998—; chmn. grants and scholarship com. Harry R. Kellman Acad., Cherry Hill, N.J., 1984-91. Fellow: Am. Coll. Rheumatology, ACP; mem.: Pa. Osteoporosis Soc., Phila. Rheumatism Soc., Phi Beta Kappa, Alpha Omega Alpha. Avocations: classical music, opera. Office: Pa Rheumatology Assoc 822 Pine St Apt 1C Philadelphia PA 19107-6187

SCHINCK, AMELIE GINETTE, mathematician, educator; b. Montreal, Quebec, Canada, Jan. 8, 1976; arrived in U.S., 2002; d. Robert and Nicole Schinck; life ptnr. Craig Thomas Achen, June 25, 1978. M, Concordia U., Montreal, Can., 2002. Math. instr. Concordia U., Montreal, Canada, 2000—02, Mitchell C.C., Statesville, NC, 2002—. Grantee Number Theory Rsch. grant, 2000—02. Mem.: N.C. Tchr. Math., Am. Math. Soc., MAA. Avocations: photography, travel. Office: Mitchell Community College 500 Broad Street Statesville NC 28677 Personal E-mail: amelie@conninc.com. E-mail: aschinck@mitchell.cc.nc.us.

SCHINDEL, DONALD MARVIN, retired lawyer; b. Chgo., Jan. 5, 1932; s. Harry L. and Ann (Schiff) S.; m. Alice Martha Andrews, Apr. 24, 1960; children: Susan Yost, Judith Harris, Andrea Glickman. BS in Acctg., U. Ill., 1953; JD, U. Chgo., 1956. Ptnr. Sonnenschein, Nath & Rosenthal, Chgo., 1956-2000, ret., 2000. Author: Estate Administration and Tax Planning for Survivors, 1987, supplements, 1988-1996. Pres. United Way Highland Park-Highwood, Ill., 2000—, Congregation Beth Or, Deefield, 1983—85. Fellow Am. Coll. Trust and Estate Counsel; mem. Chgo. Estate Planning Coun. (Austin Fleming Disting. Svc. award 1999), ABA, Ill. Bar Assn., Chgo. Bar Assn. (chmn. probate practice com. 1981-82). Clubs: East Bank (Chgo.). Avocations: tennis, travel, photography, carpentry, running. Home: 636 Rice St Highland Park IL 60035-5012 E-mail: dmschindel@aol.com.

SCHINDELHEIM, FRANKLIN DAVID, special education guidance counselor; b. Bklyn., Nov. 11, 1946; BBA in Psychology, CCNY, 1968; MS in Counseling, L.I. U., 1972; MS in Adminstrn., Pace U., 1974. Instrumental and vocal music tchr. N.Y.C. Bd. of Edn., 1968-92, spl. edn. guidance counselor, 1992—. Exec. dir. Startime Dance and Performing Arts Ctrs. of N.Y. and N.J., 1978—; cons. in assertive discipline Lee Canter Assocs., Good Morning America, Good Day New York. Author: Training the Young Voice, 1990, N.Y.C. Board of Education Elementary Guidance Counselors Handbook, 1993; prodr. (TV show) Schools 2000. Mem. ASCD. Office: 2477 65th St Brooklyn NY 11204-4137

SCHINDERLE, ROBERT FRANK, retired hospital administrator; b. Mayville, Wis., Aug. 3, 1923; m. Elizabeth, June 23, 1949; children— David, Gary, Mary, Brian. BS, Marquette U., 1949; MS, Northwestern U., 1959. Asst. office mgr. Western Leather Co., Milw., 1949-51; mgr. bus. office St. Francis Hosp., Peoria, Ill., 1951-55; credit mgr. Mercy Hosp., Chgo., 1955-59, asst. to adminstr., 1957-58, controller, 1958-59, asst. adminstr., 1959-65, St. Joseph Hosp., Joliet, Ill., 1965-70, assoc. adminstr., 1970-71, adminstr., 1971-76, exec. dir., 1976-86; dir. corp. legis. affairs and devel. Franciscan Sisters Health Care Corp., Mokena, 1986-89, ret. Chmn. Areawide Hosp. Emergency Services Council. Bd. dirs. Region IX Health Systems Agy., Our Lady of Angels Retirement Home, Joliet, Joliet YMCA, St. Joseph Coll. Nursing, Joliet. Fellow Am. Coll. Hosp. Adminstrs.; mem. Am. Hosp. Assn., Ill. Hosp. Assn. (chmn. 1975-76), Catholic Hosp. Assn. (dir.), Ill. Cath. Hosp. Assn. (chmn. 1972-73) Lodges: Rotary, Elks, KC. Roman Catholic. Home: 408 W Newkirk Dr Plainfield IL 60544-1838

SCHINDLER, ALBERT ISADORE, physicist, educator; b. Pitts., June 24, 1927; s. Jonas and Esther (Nass) S.; m. Phyllis Irene Liberman, June 17, 1951; children— Janet Mae, Jerald Scott, Ellen Susan. BS, Carnegie Inst. Tech., 1947, MS, 1948, DSc, 1950. Research asst. Carnegie Inst. Tech., Pitts., 1947-50, research physicist, 1950-51; supervisory rsch. physicist Naval Rsch. Lab., Washington, 1951-75; assoc. dir. research for material sci. and component tech. Naval Research Lab., 1975-85; prof. materials engrng. and physics Purdue U., West Lafayette, Ind., 1985-92, cons., 1992-97, dir. Ind. Ctr. for Innovative Superconductor Tech., 1988-91, dir. Midwest Superconductivity Consortium, 1990-91; dir. div. materials rsch. NSF, Washington, 1988-90; chief scientist Office Naval Rsch., Arlington, Va., 1997-99; cons., 1999—. Cons. in field. Recipient E.O. Hulburt award Naval Research Lab., 1956, Nat. Capitol award for applied sci., 1962, Pure Sci. award Naval Research Lab.-Sci. Research Soc. Am., 1965, award Washington Acad. Scis., 1965, USN Disting. Achievement in Sci. award, 1975, Alumni Merit award Carnegie Mellon U., 1976, Sr. Exec. Service award Dept. Navy, 1983, Superior Pub. Svc. award Dept. Navy, 1999. Fellow Am. Phys. Soc.; mem. Sigma Xi. (dir.) Home: 6615 Sulky Ln Rockville MD 20852-4344

SCHINDLER, ANDREW J. tobacco company executive; b. Harrisburg, Pa., Aug. 1944; BA, Franklin and Marshall Coll; MBA, U. Pa. Dir. mfg. Nabisco Foods Co., Parsippany, N.J., 1987-88; with R.J. Reynolds Tobacco Co., Winston-Salem, N.C., 1974—, nat. mgr., sales pers., 1976-78, mgr. orgn. and mgmt. devel. Reynolds Industries parent co., 1978-79, dir. orgn. and mgmt. devel., 1979-82, plant mgr., 1982-87, v.p. pers., 1988-89, sr. v.p. ops., 1989-91, exec. v.p. ops., 1991-94, pres., COO, 1994-95, pres., CEO, 1995—, chmn., 1999—; chmn., CEO, R.J. Reynolds Tobacco Holdings, Inc., 1999—. Mem. adv. bd. Wachovia Bank N.C., N.A. Vice chmn. N.C. Emerging Tech. Alliance; bd. dirs. N.C. Sch. Arts Found., Winston-Salem Bus., Inc.; bd. visitors Wake Forest U. Bapt. Med. Ctr. Capt. U.S. Army, Vietnam. Office: RJ Reynolds Tobacco Holdings PO Box 2959 401 N Main St Winston Salem NC 27102-2866*

SCHINDLER, CHARLES ALVIN, microbiologist, educator; b. Boston, Dec. 27, 1924; s. Edward Esau and Esther Marian (Weisman) S.; m. Barbara Jean Francois, Jan. 14, 1955; children: Marian Giffin, Susan, Neal. BS in Biology, Rensselaer Poly. Inst., 1950; MS, U. Tex., 1956, PhD, 1961. Commd. officer USAF, 1951, advanced through grades to maj., 1965; asst. dir. for biology and medicine at atomic weapons tests Armed Forces Spl. Weapons Project, Camp Mercury, Nev., 1953; rsch. scientist USAF, 1954-68; tchr. Norman (Okla.) Pub. Schs., 1968-86; asst. prof. U. Okla., Flagler Coll., 1968-86; cons., sci. supr. Oklahoma City (Okla.) Sch. Dist., 1989-93. Cons. Mead Johnson Rsch. Ctr., Evansville, Ind., 1962-72. Contbr. articles to profl. jours. Coun. mem. Norman City Coun., Okla., 1976—81, 1983—85. Fellow Charles E. Lewis Fellowship Com., Austin, Tex., 1958; rsch. grantee NSF, Norman, 1972. Mem. Soc. Gen. Microbiology, Sigma Xi. Achievements include patents for on the bacteriolytic agent Lysostaphin; discovery of of purified and characterized lysostaphin. Home: 2000 Morgan Dr Norman OK 73069-6525 E-mail: schin@telepath.com.

SCHINDLER, JUDI(TH) (JUDITH KAY SCHINDLER), public relations executive, marketing consultant; b. Chgo., Nov. 23, 1941; d. Gilbert G. and Rosalie (Karlin) Cone; m. Jack Joel Schindler, Nov. 1, 1964; 1 child, Adam Jason. BS in Journalism, U. Ill., 1964. Assoc. editor Irving Cloud Publs., Lincolnwood, Ill., 1963-64; asst. dir. publicity Israel Bond Campaign, Chgo., 1965-69; v.p. pub. relations Realty Co. of Am., 1969-70; dir. pub. relations Pvt. Telecomm., 1970-78; pres. Schindler Comm., 1978—. Del. White House Conf. on Small Bus., Washington, 1980, 86; mem. adv. bd. Entrepreneurship Inst., Chgo., 1988-92. Bd. dirs. Family Matters Comty. Ctr.; mem. Chgo. bd. Roosevelt U.; leader luncheon coun. YWCA, Chgo., 1987, 89-90, 92; appointee small bus. com. Ill. Devel. Bd., 1988-89. Named Nat. Women in Bus. Adv. SBA, 1986, Chgo. Woman Bus. Owner of Yr., Continental Bank and Nat. Assn. Women Bus. Owners, 1989, Ill. Finalist Entrepreneur of Yr. award, 1991-92. Mem. Nat. Assn. Women Bus. Owners (pres. Chgo. chpt. 1980-81, nat. v.p. membership 1988-89), Small Bus. United of Ill., Publicity Club Chgo., Alpha Epsilon Phi. Office: Schindler Comm 500 N Clark St Chicago IL 60610-4288

SCHINDLER, KEITH WILLIAM, software engineer; b. Selma, Calif., May 27, 1959; s. George Junior and Doris Angelynn (Young) S. BSEE in Computer Sci. with honors, U. Calif., Berkeley, 1982. Programmer Summit Group, Berkeley, 1979-81; jr. programmer Control Data, Inc., Sunnyvale, Calif., 1983; assoc. mem. tech. staff Symbolics, Inc., Chatsworth, 1987-88; sr. mem. tech. support Graphics div. Symbolics, L.A., 1988-90; software engr. Sidley, Wright & Assoc., Hollywood, Calif., 1990-92; cons. Out-Takes, Inc., L.A., 1992-94; pres. Schindler Imaging Inc., Nipomo, Calif., 1997—. Tech. dir. Sidley-Wright & Assoc., Hollywood, 1990-92, Movie Time Cable Channel, Hollywood, 1990, Video Image, Marina Del Rey, Calif., 1990; cert. developer Apple Computer, Inc., 1991—, Truevision, Inc., 1990-93; developer software Out-Takes' Digital Photography System; dir. software applications devel. Pixera Corp., Los Gatos, Calif., 1997—, project leader, Cupertino, Calif., 1995-96. Patentee in field. Mem. Soc. Motion Picture and TV Engrs., Tau Beta Pi. Democrat. Avocations: mountain biking, hiking, chess, racquetball. Office: Schindler Imaging 741 Honey Grove Ln Nipomo CA 93444-5649

SCHINDLER, LAURA ANN, piano teacher, accompanist; b. St. Louis, Aug. 17, 1943; d. Francis Joseph and Alice Binkley (Hurtgen) Schindler; m. John Charles Noto, Dec. 27, 1986. BM cum laude, Fontbonne Coll., St. Louis, 1970; MAT, Washington U., St. Louis, 1972; student, Ecole Normale de Musique, Paris, 1973-74. Nat. cert. tchr. of music; cert. Orff Schulwerk, Mozarteum Acad., Salzburg, Austria. Organist, choir dir. St. John's Basilica, St. Louis, 1971-73; piano tchr. Cmty. Music Sch., 1971-73, St. Louis Inst. Music, 1972-73; accompanist Robert McFerrin, Sr., N.Y.C., Chgo.,Springfield, St. Louis, 1974-77; piano tchr., Orff instr. St. Louis Conservatory, 1974-82; pvt. piano tchr. and accompanist St. Louis, 1982—. Vocal accompanist Affiliate Artist Program, St. Louis, 1977; accompanist MTNA West. Ctr. Divsn. Auditions, St. Louis, 1979, Forest Park C.C. Chorus, 1980-82, Ethical Soc. Chorus, 1980-83, Washington U. Music Sch., 1970-72; adjudicator piano competitions, Mo. and Ill., 1978—; clinician Piano Tchr. Workshops, Mo./Ill., 1979—. Contbr. articles to profl. jours.; performer Today Show, NBC, 1976; performer, composer Am. Composers Concert, 1976; performer Rubinstein Music Club Meetings, 1997—, Benefit for Mo. Com. for Firearms Safety, 1982, Capella Soloists Sunset concerts, 1976, Bicentennial Horizons of Am. Music, 1976. Recipient Mid-Am. Disting. Ind. Piano Tchr. award N.W., 1997, Disting. Piano Tchr. award Cedarhurst Chamber Music and Beethoven Soc., 1992; Acad. fellow Washington U., 1970-72. Mem.: Piano Tchrs. Round Table (pres. 1999—2001), Musical Diversions Soc. (bd. dirs. 1995—), St. Louis Area Music Tchrs. Assn. (v.p. for programs 1986—88, pres. 1988—92, chair nominating com. 1996—2000), Rubinstein Music Club. Democrat. Mem. Ethical Soc. Avocations: travel, walking, reading, eastern European folk dancing, ballroom dancing. Home: 7567 Lindbergh Dr Saint Louis MO 63117-2173

SCHINDLER, WILLIAM STANLEY, retired public relations executive, consultant; b. Detroit, Jan. 4, 1933; s. William Henry and Katherine (Schilling) S. Student, Wayne State U., 1950-53. Sr. v.p. Campbell-Ewald Co., Warren, Mich., 1968-85; v.p. pub. rels. Detroit Med. Ctr., 1985-92; interim v.p. Wayne State U., Detroit, 1993. Cons. to bus., univs., and founds.; v.p. Sandusky Pub. Co., Mich. Editor: Progress Report-New Detroit, Inc, 1969. Past mem. Detroit Hist. Commn., Detroit Fire Commn.; chmn. Detroit CSC; past pres. Detroit Hist. Soc., Hist. Soc. Mich.; mem. Gov's. Sesquicentennial Commn., Peoria, Az. Fire Pension. Bd, Personnel Bd..; bd. dirs. Adult Well-Being Svcs., Sacred Heart Rehab. Ctr., Brush Park Devel. Authority, Harper Hosp. Aux. With U.S. Army. 1954-56. Decorated Commendation Medal with pendant. Mem. Pub. Rels. Soc. Am., Adcraft Club Detroit, Detroit Press Club, Sons Whiskey Rebellion, Recess Club, Univ. Club, Detroit Athletic Club, Prismatic Club, Box 12 Club, Heard Mus. Coun. Home: 8741 W Wescott Dr Peoria AZ 85382-8773

SCHINE, JEROME ADRIAN, retired accountant; b. Albany, Ga., Nov. 7, 1926; s. Nathan Benjamin and Celia (Hurwitz) S.; m. Marjorie Elizabeth Clark, July 11, 1955; 1 child, Michael Howard. Diploma, North Ga. Jr. Coll., Dahlonega, 1945; BSBA, U. Fla., 1949. CPA, Fla. Staff acct. M.A. Montenegro & Co., Tampa, Fla., 1949-52, ptnr., 1952-70, Arthur Young, Tampa, 1970-87. Cons., Tampa, 1987—; mem. Fla. Bd. Accountancy, 1982-89, chmn., 1984; pres. Nat. Assn. State Bds. Accountancy, 1989-90. Pres. Tampa Mus. of Art, 1985; v.p. Children's Ctr. Cancer and Dread Disease, Tampa, 1986-87; treas. Hillsborough County Charter Commn., Tampa, 1980; mem. Hillsborough County Local Govt. Commn., 1965. Cpl. U.S. Army Air Corps, 1945-47. Recipient Disting. Alumnus award Fisher Sch. Acctg., U. Fla., 1990, Van Rensselaer Pub. Svc. award Nat. Assn. State Bd. Accountancy, 1997. Mem. AICPA (mem. coun. 1973-80), Fla. Inst. CPAs (pres. 1973-74), Temple Terrace Golf and Country Club (pres. 1963). Republican. Jewish. Avocations: golf, history. Home: 444 Biltmore Ave Tampa FL 33617-7208

SCHINE, WENDY WACHTELL, foundation administrator; b. White Plains, N.Y., May 5, 1961; d. Thomas Schine and Esther Carole (Pickard) Scihne; children: Jameson Myer, Bradley Thomas, Davis Berndt. BA, Wellesley Coll., 1983; MA in Journalism, U. So. Calif., L.A., 1987. Legis. asst. U.S. House Reps., Washington, 1983-85; varied positions KCBS-TV, L.A., 1986-88; v.p. Joseph Drown Found., 1988—. Bd. dirs., co-chair L.A. Urban Funders, The Accelerated Sch., So. Calif. Assn. Philanthropy, U. So. Calif., Ctr. for Philanthropy and Pub. Policy, The John Thomas Dye Sch.; advisor Psychol. Trauma Ctr., L.A., 1988—98, Ctr. for Talented Youth, Glendale, Calif., 1989—98, Joseph Drown Found. Office: Joseph Drown Found Ste 1930 1999 Avenue Of The Stars Los Angeles CA 90067-6033 E-mail: wendy@jdrown.org.

SCHINK, FRANK EDWARD, electrical engineer; b. N.Y.C., May 14, 1922; s. Frank and Elizabeth (Kreps) S.; m. Barbara Jean McCally, Oct. 26, 1946; children: Stephen Frank, Thomas Ross. BEE, Bklyn. Poly. (now Poly. U. N.Y.), 1952, MEE, 1955. Registered profl. engr., N.Y., N.J. Elec. engr. George G. Sharp, Naval Architect, N.Y.C., 1940-43, 45, Anaconda Co., N.Y.C., 1946-59, Anaconda-Jurden Assocs., N.Y.C., 1959-61; sr. engr. M.W. Kellogg Co., 1961-62, Port Authority of N.Y. & N.J., N.Y.C., 1962-77, cons. engr., 1977-84, chief elec. engr., 1984-89; pvt. practice elec. cons. Cranford, N.J., 1989—. Mem. various coms. ELECTRO Confs., 1976-96, past bd. dirs.; mem. adv. coun. N.J. Union County Transp., Westfield, 1977-79; mem. Port Authority Maintenance Improvement coun., N.Y.C., 1979-80; mem. com. IEEE Vehicular Tech. Conf., 1993; lectr. seminars Internat. Elec. Exposition and Congress, 1986, 87, Power Engring. Soc. Chpts. Cong., 1996. Author/editor: Environmental Impact Assessment, 1977; contbr. articles to profl. jours. Pres. Brookside Civic Assn., Cranford, 1960-62; chmn. Cub Scout and Boy Scouts Troops, Cranford, 1960-65; capt. United Fund, Cranford, 1962; tchr. Am. Coun. for Emigres, N.Y.C., 1975. With U.S. Army, 1943-45, ETO. Fellow IEEE (vice chmn. region I 1986-87; chmn. N.Y. sect. 1984-85, vice chmn. 1982-84, treas. 1981-82, editor N.Y. sect. Monitor 1989-90, life mem. com. 1994-97; also various coms.); mem. IEEE Power Engring Soc. (ad com. 1978-87, exec. com. 1983-87, chpts. rep. 1976-80, chmn. Winter Power Confs., N.Y. 1990—), IEEE Industry Applications Soc. (coun. mem. 1977-90), Tau Beta Pi, Eta Kappa Nu. Republican. Methodist. Home and Office: 14 Middlebury Ln Cranford NJ 07016-1622

SCHINK, JAMES HARVEY, lawyer; b. Oak Park, Ill., Oct. 2, 1943; s. Norbert F. and Gwendolyn H. (Hummel) S.; m. Lisa Wilder Haskell, Jan. 1, 1972 (div. 1980); children— David, Caroline, Elizabeth; m. April Townley, Aug. 14, 1982 BA, Yale U., 1965, JD, 1968. Bar: Ill. 1968, Colo. 1982. Assoc. Sidley & Austin, Chgo., 1968; law clk. to judge U.S. Ct. Appeals, 1968-69; assoc. Kirkland & Ellis, 1969-72, ptnr., 1972—. Sustaining fellow Art Inst. Chgo. Mem. ABA, Ill. Bar Assn., Chgo. Bar Assn., Chgo. Club, Saddle and Cycle Club, Mid-Am. Club, Econ. Club of Chgo., Chgo. Yacht Club, Vail Racquet Club, Yale Club of Chgo., Racquet Club Chgo., Game Creek Club. Republican. Presbyterian. Home: 1530 N State Pkwy Chicago IL 60610-1614 Office: Kirkland & Ellis 200 E Randolph St Ste 6100 Chicago IL 60601-6436

SCHINNERER, ALAN JOHN, entrepreneur; b. Long Beach, Calif., June 8, 1925; s. Walter John and Esther Schinnerer; m. Barbara Elaine Daniger, Aug. 17, 1951 (div. Aug. 1971); children: Gregory, Scott, Brett, Vicky. AA, Long Beach City Coll., 1948; B of Elec. Engring., U. So. Calif., 1952, postgrad. law, 1956-57, postgrad. bus., 1958-59. Purchasing agt. McCulloch Corp., Los Angeles, 1952-56; systems engr. Hughes Aircraft Co., Culver City, Calif., 1956-59; sales engr. Gilfillan Corp., Los Angeles, 1959-61; mktg. specialist N.Am. Rockwell Corp., Downey, Calif., 1961-68; sr. project engr. Hughes Aircraft Co., El Segundo, 1968-74, dir. satellite tests, 1974-76, assoc. program mgr., 1976-84; pres., owner, founder Calif. Classic Boats, Inc., Long Beach, 1979—. Founding ptnr. Looking Glass Cellars, Murrieta, Calif., 1995—. Author: (catalog) Parts for Antique and Classic Chris-Craft, Dodge, Gar Wood and Hacker runabouts, 1979-2001. Bd. dirs. Antique Powercraft Hist. Soc., 1984-85. Served with USN, 1943-46, PTO. Mem. Antique and Classic Boat Soc. (founding pres. So. Calif. chpt. 1983-86), Gar Wood Soc., Riva Hist. Soc., Delta Tau Delta. Clubs: Chris-Craft Antique Boat, Porsche of Am., Tahoe Yacht, Sierra. Republican. Home: 5581 Ridgebury Dr Huntington Beach CA 92649-4825 Office: Calif Classic Boats 3267 E Grant St Signal Hill CA 90755-1212 E-mail: ajs@californiaclassicboats.com.

SCHIOWITZ, MARK F. surgeon; b. Wilkes-Barre, Pa., Oct. 30, 1952; s. Albert and Jean 9Fuerth) S.; m. Therese Greenfield, Oct. 23, 1994. BA, Franklin and Marshall Coll., 1974; MD, Jefferson Med. Coll., 1978. Diplomate Am. Bd. Surgery, cert. surg. critical care, 1988. Intern Albert Einstein Med. Ctr., Phila., 1978-79, resident in surgery, 1979-83; pvt. practice Wilkes Barre. Dir. surg. ICU, Wilkes-Barre Gen. Hosp., 1991—, chief sect. gen. surgery, 1993—, mem. med. exec. com., 1994-97, 2000—. Contbr. articles to profl. jours. Bd. dirs. EMS of N.E. Pa., pittston, 1991—. Fellow ACS (liaison physician commn. on cancer, 1997); mem. Soc. Critical Care Medicine, Am. Soc. for Parenteral & Enteral Nutrition, Am. Trauma Soc., Pa. Soc. Critical Care Medicine (exec. coun. 1999—). Office: Med Arts Bldg 35 W Linden St Ste 220B Wilkes Barre PA 18702-2619

SCHIPPER, MICHAEL, university official; b. N.Y.C., Nov. 26, 1942; s. Eddie and Gertrude S.; m. Janet Lynne Altmann, Nov. 1, 1947; children: Adam, Julie. AA, BS, U. Houston, 1964; MA, Bradley U., 1968; postgrad., Harvard U., 1986-90. Dir. human resources Choate Symms Health Svcs., Arlington, Mass., 1981-85, Marlbrough (Mass.) Hosp., 1985-87, Sts. Meml. Med. Ctr., Lowell, Md., 1991-94; v.p. human resources Lakeshore Hosp., Manchester, N.H., 1987-91; v.p. Roger Williams U., Bristol, R.I., 1994—. With USMC. Mem. Squantum Assn., Bristol Yacht Club, Masons (32 degree). Avocation: sailing. Home: 86 Kickemuit Ave Bristol RI 02809-4404 Office: Roger Williams U 1 Old Ferry Rd Bristol RI 02809-2921

SCHIRA, DIANA RAE, lawyer; b. Wausau, WI, Apr. 27, 1964; d. Ray Vernes and Alice LaVerne (Hasl) Deckelman; m. Jeffrey David Schira, June 20, 1992; children: Rae Hannah, Hazel Marie, Iris Lydia, Maximos Jeffrey. BA, U. Wis., Madison, 1986; JD, Marquette U., Milw., 1989. Bar: Wis. 1989, U.S. Dist. Ct. (ea. and we. dists.) Wis. 1989. Pvt. practice Schira Law Firm, S.C., Mosinee, Wis., 1989—. Mem. Phi Delta Phi. Democrat. Office: Schira Law Firm SC PO Box 266 1116 Western Ave Mosinee WI 54455-1535 E-mail: drsjds@mtc.net.

SCHIRBER, ANNAMARIE RIDDERING, speech and language pathologist, educator; b. Somerset County, N.J., Dec. 18, 1941; d. Pieter C. and Marie Louise (Kerk) Riddering; m. Eric R. Schirber, Aug. 25, 1960; children: Stefan Rene, Ashley Brooke. BA in Speech and Hearing Therapy, Rutgers U., 1964; MA in Edn. of Deaf and Hard of Hearing, Smith Coll., 1968; postgrad., Rutgers U., 1987-93. Cert. tchr. of deaf, hard of hearing, spl. edn., speech correctionist, speech-lang pathologist, N.J. Speech therapist Manatee County Bd. Edn., Bradenton, Fla., 1968-69; speech-lang. specialist Lawrence Twp. Pub. Schs., Lawrenceville, N.J., 1969—. Adj. instr. comm. dept. Trenton (N.J.) State Coll., 1983-87; vis. lectr. Rutgers U., New Brunswick, 1993. Author: Teaching Auditory Processing Skills to Children, 1994; co-author: (with Erica Winebrenner) Speech Activities for Children, 1994, Language Activities to Teach Children at Home, 1994. Mem. exec. com. Women's Coll. Symposium, Princeton, N.J., 1982-84; mem. nat. alumnae admissions com. Smith Coll., Northampton, Mass., 1984-86. Grantee Lawrence Twp. Bd. Edn., 1973, 89, 90, Lawrence Twp. Edn. Found., 1999, 2001. Mem. N.J. Speech-Lang. and Hearing Assn. (legis. com. 1996), Ctrl. Jersey Speech-Lang. and Hearing Assn. (exec. com. 1996—, v.p. 1985, pres. 1986-87), Princeton Area Smith Coll. Club (exec. com. 1996—, pres. 1998-2000). Home: 10 Sycamore Ln Skillman NJ 08558-2013 Office: Lawrence Twp Pub Shcs Princeton Pike Trenton NJ 08648 E-mail: aschirber@ltps.org.

SCHIRBER, JAMES EMMANUEL, retired physicist; b. Eureka, S.D., June 9, 1931; s. Leo E. and Adeline M. (Fautch) Schirber; m. Catherine A. Nolan, Aug. 22, 1955; children: Carol, Leo, Peter, Andrew, Mary Jane, Michael, Mark. BA, U. Minn., 1953; postgrad., MIT, 1954; PhD, Iowa State U., 1960. Rsch. assoc. Ames Lab., Iowa, 1960—61; fellow NAS-NRC, Bristol, England, 1961—62; mem. tech. staff, mgr. solid state rsch. Sandia Nat. Labs., Albuquerque, 1962—89, rsch. scientist, 1989—96; ret., 1996. Contbr. articles to profl. jours., chapters to books. Served to 1st lt. USAF, 1953—57. Fellow: AAAS, Am. Phys. Soc.; mem.: Sigma Xi. Roman Catholic. Achievements include research in in high pressure low temperature studies of Fermi surfaces and organic, fullerene and high temperature superconductors. Home: HC 89 Box 95 Hermosa SD 57744-9702 Personal E-mail: schirber@webtv.net.

SCHIRMEISTER, CHARLES F. retired lawyer; b. Jersey City, June 18, 1929; s. Charles F. and Louise P. (Schneider) S.; m. Barbara Jean Fredericks, Feb. 9, 1952; children: Pamela, Charles Bradford. BA, U. Mich., 1951; LLB, Fordham U., 1956. Bar: N.Y. 1956, U.S. Dist. Ct. (so. dist.) N.Y., U.S. Ct. Appeals (2d cir.), U.S. Supreme Ct. 1961. Asst. dist. atty. N.Y. County (N.Y.), 1956-61; assoc. Thelen, Reid & Priest, N.Y.C., 1961-71, ptnr., 1971-94. Deacon Cmty. Congrl. Ch., Short Hills, N.J.; trustee Ocean Grove (N.J.) Camp Meeting Assn. Capt. USMCR, ret., 1951-53. Mem. Univ. Club (N.Y.C.), Canoe Brook Country Club (Summit, N.J.), Sigma Alpha Epsilon. Republican. Avocations: tennis, oenology, golf. Home: 15 Beechcroft Rd Short Hills NJ 07078-1648

SCHIRMER, GINGER POMERANCE, small business owner; b. Columbus, Ga., Nov. 12, 1963; d. Warren Malcolm and Dorothy Labiner Pomerance; m. Edgardo Carlos Schirmer, Nov. 5, 1994; children: Gabrielle Rebecca, Alexis Nicole. BS, Ga. State U., 1987, MS, 1990; PhD, Auburn U., 1995. Reg. dietitian. Dietitian Carolina's Med. Ctr., Charlotte, 1987-90; asst. prof. Tex. Christian U., Ft. Worth, 1994-96; pres., dir. continuing edn. MED2000, Inc., Bedford, Tex., 1996—. Dir. CE Internat., Bedford, 1998-99. Author: Herbal Medicine, Women's Health & Stress Management, 1998, Successful Aging, 1999, Diabetes: An Emerging Epidemic, Children's Health, Functional Foods and Dietary Supplements, The Healthy Heart, Successful Weight Loss/Weight Management. Republican. Avocations: reading, exercising. Office: MED2000 Inc 1901 Central Dr Ste 608 Bedford TX 76021-5827 Fax: 817-354-1258. E-mail: med2000@ix.netcom.com.

SCHIRN, JANET SUGERMAN, interior designer; b. Jersey City; d. Oscar H. and Mary (Lustig) S.; 1 child, Martha. BFA, Pratt Inst.; MFA, Columbia U.; postgrad. in Architecture, U. Ill. Tchr. N.Y.C. Bd. Edn.; dir. N.Y.C. Bd. Adult Edn.; pres. Janet Schirn Design Group, Chgo., N.Y.C., 1950—; prin. The J S Collection, N.Y.C., 1978—. Adj. prof. So. Ill. U., 1991-92; mem. adv. bd. Du Pont Co., Monsanto, 1981-89, So. Ill. U., 1990-95; mem. adv. bd. interior arch. dept. Columbia Coll., Iowa State u. Contbr. articles to interior design mag. Bd. dirs. Washington Archtl. Forum, 1992-96, Chgo. Archtl. Assistance Ctr., 1975, pres., 1982; adv. bd. mem. Mundelein Coll. dept. interior architecture, 1978; mem. Met. Planning Coun., Chgo., 1980—, Art Resources Tchg., 1984-95—; mem. aux. bd. Sch. of Art Ins., Ill. Arts Alliance, 1992—. Recipient award Chgo. Lighting Inst., 1989, 92, 93, 95, 97, 98, Villeroy and Boch gold award, 1990, Designer mag. residential award, 1990, Edward Fields 1st prize Rug Design, 1981, 91, 1st prize project awards ASID, 1993, 95, 96, 98, 99, 2000, 01. Mem. UNESCO (steering com. tall bldgs. and urban habitat coun.), Am. Soc. Interior Designers (nat. pres. 1986, nat. treas. 1984, regional v.p. 1981, pres. Ill. chpt. 1977-78, nat. dir. 1979-83, chmn. pub. affairs 1989, Designer of Distinction 1998), Illuminating Engring. Soc., Am. Inst. Architects (nat. urban planning and design com. 1981-85), Chgo. Network, Internat. Fedn. Interior Designers (exec. bd. dirs. 1992-96). Home: 220 E Walton St Chicago IL 60611-1507 Office: Janet Schirn Design Group 401 N Franklin St Chicago IL 60610-4400 also: 521 5th Ave New York NY 10175-0003

SCHIRO-GEIST, CHRISANN, rehabilitation counselor; b. Chgo., Dec. 31, 1946; d. Joseph Frank and Ethel (Fortunato) Schiro; m. John J. Conway Sr., Oct. 26, 1985; children: Jennifer, Daniel; stepchildren: Patricia, Nicole, John Jr., Denise, Christine. BS, Loyola U., Chgo., 1967, MEd, 1970; PhD, Northwestern U., 1974. Registered psychologist, Ill.; Diplomate Am. Bd. Vocational Experts. Tchr. sci. Northbrook (Ill.) Jr. High Sch., 1967-70; dir. career counseling and placement Mundelein Coll., Chgo., 1972-74; counselor human devel. Regional Service Agy., Skokie, 1975-87; assoc. prof. psychology, rehab. counselor Ill. Inst. Tech., Chgo., 1975-87; full prof. rehab. U. Ill., Champaign-Urbana, 1987—, dir. Disability Rsch. Inst., 2000—. Co-author: Placement Handbook for Counseling Disabled Persons, 1982; author, editor: Vocational Counseling with Special Populations, 1990. Rsch. grantee Northwestern U., 1974; Region V Short-Term Tng. grantee Rehab. Svcs. Adminstrn., 1978-79, Long-Term Tng. grantee, 1983—, RSA grantee, 1988-91, 91-94, 93-96, 96—, 99—; Mary E. Switzer fellow NIDRR, 1989-90, VA, 1991-92, World Rehab. Fund fellow, 1993; co-grantee SSA, 2000—. Mem. APA, ACA, Nat. Rehab. Assn.(WF Faulkes award 2001), Nat. Coun. Rehab. Edn. (named Educator of Yr. 1987), Ill. Rehab. Counseling Assn. (pres. 1979-80), Coun. on Rehab. Edn. (pres. 1982-85, editor jour. 1986-92), Ill. Rehab. Assn. (pres. 1994), Kappa Beta Gamma Alumni Assn. (nat. officer). Office: U Ill Disability Rsch Inst 1207 S Oak St Champaign IL 61820-6901

SCHIRTZINGER, BARBARA ANN, systems analyst; b. Columbus, Ohio, July 2, 1959; d. Donald Kenneth and Joretta May (Kline) Jaynes; m. Philip William Schirtzinger, Mar. 5, 1984; 1 child, Frank William. Student, Columbus Paraprofl. Inst., 1983. Tape librarian, data svcs. clk. Highlights for Children, Columbus, 1979-80, computer operator, 1980-83, programmer analyst, 1983-87, database analyst/programmer, 1987-89, devel. coordination analyst, 1989, systems analyst, 1989-91, project leader, 1991-93, staff specialist, 1993—. Republican. Roman Catholic. Office: Highlights for Children 2300 W 5th Ave Columbus OH 43215-1053

SCHISGAL, MURRAY JOSEPH, playwright; b. N.Y.C., Nov. 25, 1926; s. Abraham and Irene (Sperling) S.; m. Reene Schapiro, June 29, 1958; children: Jane, Zachary. Student, Bklyn. Conservatory of Music, 1948, L.I. U., 1950; LLB, Bklyn. Law Sch., 1953; BA, New Sch. Social Research, 1959. Playwright, screenwriter and prodr. movies, TV and theatre. Author: The Typists and The Tiger, London, 1960, N.Y.C., 1963, Ducks and Lovers, London, 1961, Knit One, Purl Two, Boston, 1963, Luv (One of the Best Plays of 1964-65), London, 1963, N.Y.C., 1964, Fragments, Windows and other plays, 1965, Best Short Plays, 1981, 83, 85; contbr. to Best Short American Plays 1994-1995; original TV plays The Love Song of Barney Kempinski, 1966, Natasha Kovolina Pipishinski, 1976; off-Broadway Fragments, 1967, The Basement, 1967; Jimmy Shine, 1968, 69, Shooting Towards the Millinneum, 1997, Playtime, 1997; Broadway The Chinese, N.Y.C., 1970 (pub. in Best Short Plays of the World Theatre 1973), Dr. Fish, 1970, An American Millionaire, 1974, All Over Town, 1974 (pub. Best Plays 1974-75); screenplay The Tiger Makes Out, 1967, The Pushcart Peddlers, prod. off-off-Broadway, 1979 (pub. as The Pushcart Peddlers, The Flatulist and other plays); novel Days and Nights of a French Horn Player, 1980, Walter and the Flatulist; prod. off-Broadway The Downstairs Boys, 1980, The Songs of War, 1989; prod. regional theatre A Need for Brussels Sprouts, 1981, Play Time, Denver Ctr. Theatre, 1991, The Japanese Foreign Trade Minister, Cleve. Playhouse, 1992, 74 Georgia Ave., 1992, Circus Life, 1992; prod. Broadway Twice Around the Park, 1982; Other Plays, 1983, Closet Madness and Other Plays, 1984, Popkins, Paris, 1990, Play Time, 1991, The Songs of War, 1989; prod. Off Broadway The New Yorkers, 1984, Circus Life, 1995; prodr. Extensions, 1994; co-author: screenplay Tootsie (Winner Los Angeles Film Critics, N.Y. Film Critics, Nat. Soc. Film Critics, Writers Guild Am. award for best comedy); author Luv and Other Plays, 1983, The Rabbi and the Toyota Dealer, 1985, Jealousy, There are No Sacher Tortes in Our Society, 1985, Old Wine in a New Bottle, 1987, Road Show, 1987, Man Dangling, 1988, Oatmeal and Kisses, 1990, (with others) Best Short American Plays of 1991, 92-93, Sexaholics and Other Plays, 1995, Extensions, 1994, Circus Life, 1995, The Artist and The Model (Best Am. Short Play), 1994-95, Play Time (Published by Dramatists Play Svc., 1997), The Man Who Couldn't Stop Crying (Best Am. Short Plays, 1997-98); prodr. feature films A Walk on the Moon, 1999, (cable TV) The Devil's Arithmetic, 1999, Boys and Girls, 2000, Clubland, 2000. Recipient Vernon Rice award otustanding achievement off-Broadway Theatre, 1963; Outer Circle award Outstanding Theatre, 1963; named Outstanding Playwright, 1963. Office: care Arthur B Greene 101 Park Ave 26th Fl New York NY 10178-0002

SCHIZER, ZEVIE BARUCH, lawyer; b. Bklyn., Dec. 19, 1928; s. David and Bertha (Rudavsky) S.; m. Hazel Gerber, Aug. 23, 1962; children: Deborah Gail, Miriam Anne, David Michael. BA magna cum laude, NYU, 1950; JD, Yale U., 1953. Bar: N.Y. 1954, U.S. Dist. Ct. (so. and ea. dist.) N.Y. 1959, U.S. Ct. Appeals (2d cir.) 1959, U.S. Supreme Ct. 1959. Assoc. Guzik & Boukstein, N.Y.C., 1953-54; teaching fellow NYU Sch. Law, 1954-55; assoc. Philips, Nizer, Benjamin & Krim, N.Y.C., 1955-56, Aranow, Brodsky, Einhorn & Dann, N.Y.C., 1956-57; asst. counsel jud. inquiry Appellate Divsn. 2nd Dept., Bklyn., 1957-62; assoc. Hays, Porter, Spanier & Curtis, N.Y.C., 1963-68, ptnr., 1968-85; sec. United Aircraft Products, Inc., Dayton, Ohio, 1970-83; ptnr. Schizer & Schizer, N.Y.C., 1985—. Trustee Bklyn. Pub. Libr., 1966—, pres. 1985-88, N.Y. Young Dem. Club, N.Y.C., 1960-61; trustee East Midwood Jewish Ctr., Bklyn., 1991—. Mem. N.Y. County Lawyers Assn. (mem. profl. ethics com., mem. com. on profl. discipline), Phi Beta Kappa. Democrat. Jewish. Home: 1134 E 23rd St Brooklyn NY 11210-4519 Office: Schizer & Schizer 3 New York Plz New York NY 10004-2442 E-mail: zschizer@msn.com.

SCHLABACH, LELAND A. electrical engineer; b. Arthur, Ill., Sept. 12, 1931; s. Albert Edward and Pauline (Hershberger) S.; m. Lucille Anna Reagin, June 30, 1954 (div. Sept. 1976); children: Leon Arthur, Lou Ann, Larry Andrew; m. Helen Marie Lakly, May 23, 1981. BSEE, U. Ill., 1958; MSEE, U. Pitts., 1961, PhD, 1967. Design engr. Switchgear div. Westinghouse Electric Corp., Pitts., 1958-59, devel. engr. Rsch. Ctr., 1959-66, mgr. solid state inverters, 1967-69; engring. mgr. DC drives and systems Robicon Corp., 1969-94; cons. Indsl. Control Systems, Murrysville, Pa., 1995—. Mem. staff Boy Scouts Am., Pitts., 1967-74, CAP, Pitts., 1974-76. Staff sgt. USAF, 1950-54. Lamme scholar Westinghouse Electric Corp., 1966. Mem. IEEE (chmn. local Industry Applications Soc. chpt. 1975-76, contbr. conf. and transaction papers), AIME, Assn. Iron and Steel Engrs., Tau Beta Pi, Phi Kappa Phi, Eta Kappa Nu. Republican. Presbyterian. Achievements include 5 patents, 8 patents pending and 30 patent disclosures on alternating current motor drive control circuits. Home and Office: 4198 Gun Club Rd Murrysville PA 15668-9103

SCHLACHMAN, EDWIN, retired state agency administrator; b. N.Y.C., Oct. 12, 1933; s. Samuel and Ceil (Usdin) S.; m. June R. Ryan, May 15, 1966. BA, Rutgers U., 1957. Jr. pers. technician N.J. Dept. of Pers., Newark, 1960-63, pers. technician, 1963-68, sr. pers. technician, 1968-73, chief classification analyst, 1973-91, asst. regional administr., 1991, ret., 1991. Fin. ptnr. AU Investment Club, 1995. Mem. Internat. Pers. Mgmt. Assn., Am. Soc. for Pub. Adminstrn. (treas. No. N.J. chpt. 1984—), Am. Polit. Sci. Assn. Avocations: golf, hiking, swimming, photography, gardening. Home: 52 Victor Pl Hawthorne NJ 07506-1156

SCHLACHTER, GAIL ANN, publishing company executive; b. Detroit, Apr. 7, 1943; d. Lewis E. and Helen (Blitz) Goldstein; children: Eric, Sandra. BA, U. Calif.-Berkeley, Berkeley, 1964; MA in History, Edn., U. Wis.-Madison, 1966, MA in Libr. Sci., 1967; PhD in Libr. Sci., U. Minn., 1971; MPA, U. So. Calif., 1979. Asst. prof. U. So. Calif., L.A., 1971-74; libr. dept. head Calif. State U.-Long Beach, Long Beach, 1974-76; asst. libr. dir. U. Calif.-Davis, Davis, 1976-81; dir. serials ABC-Clio Info. Svcs., Santa Barbara, Calif., 1981-82, v.p. publs., 1982-83, v.p. gen. mgr., 1983-85; pres. Ref. Svc. Press, El Dorado, 1985—. Exec. dir. Info. Inst., Santa Barbara, 1981-82. Author: Library Science Dissertation, 1925-72, 1974, 1973-81, 83, Directory of Internships, 1975, Minorities and Women: A Guide to Reference Literature in the Social Sciences, 1976 (Choice's outstanding acad. book 1977), Directory of Financial Aids for Women, 1978, Service Imperative for Libraries, 1982, Directory of Financial Aids for Minorities, 1984, Reference Sources in Library and Information Services, 1984, How to Find Out About Financial Aid, 1987, Financial Aids for the Disabled, 1988, Financial Aid for Veterans Military and Their Dependents, 1988, Financial Aid for Study & Training Abroad, 1992, Financial Aid for Research & Creative Activities Abroad, 1992, College Students Guide to Merit & Other No-Need Funding, 1996, Money for Graduate Students in the Sciences, 1996, Money for Graduate Students in the Humanities, 1996, Back-to-School Money Book, 1996, Financial Aid for Native Americans, 1997, Financial Aid for Hispanic Americans, 1997, Financial Aid for African Americans, RPS Funding for Nursing Students & Nurses, 1998. Named Outstanding Prof. Libr. Sch. U. So. Calif., 1973; recipient Knowledge Industry Publs. award for Libr. Lit.; fellow U.S. Office Edn., 1968-71, Ford Found., 1966. Mem. ALA (editor RQ 1987—, councillor 1986—, v.p., pres. ref. and adult svcs. divsn. 1987, Isador Gilbert Mudge award 1992, Louis Shores-Oryx Press award 1997), Assn. Libr. and Info. Sci. Educators, Calif. Libr. Assn. (chpt. pres. 1977-78, bd. dirs. 1980—). Office: Reference Service Press 5000 Windplay Dr Ste 4 El Dorado Hills CA 95762 E-mail: findaid@aol.com.

SCHLACHTER, KATHLEEN, community health administrator, director; b. Bklyn. d. Joseph and Kathleen (Walsh) Connolly; children: Alfred Tria, Coral Hanson, Ian Tria. BSN, Hunter Coll., 1967; MS, Wagner Coll., 1984; MBA, Webster U., 2002. Supr. community health VNAB, Bklyn.; supr. home care St. Mary's Hosp.; dir. patient svcs. Kingsbrook Jewish Med. Ctr., St. Vincent's Hosp. Home Health Agy., N.Y.C.; adminstrn. dir. Home Health Agy. South Nassau Communities Hosp, Oceanside, N.Y.; dir. South Lake Home Health, Clermont, Fla. Mem. ANA (cert. nursing adminstrn.), NAHC (cert. hospice/homecare exec.), Sigma Theta Tau. E-mail: kschlach1@aol.com.

SCHLACHTMEYER, ALBERT STEPHEN, management consultant; b. Chgo., Jan. 2, 1942; s. Albert Stephen and Anne Velichko S.; m. Sandra Kay Spatz, Sept. 28, 1968; children: Laura Kathryn, Melissa Jean. BS, Northwestern U., 1963, postgrad., 1964-65. Asst. sales promotion mgr. Link-Belt co., Chgo., 1963-66; mgmt. cons. Towers, Perrin, Foster & Crosby, Inc., N.Y.C., 1966-69, Hewitt Assocs. LLC, Lincolnshire, Ill., 1969-99, hrmaven.com, Alexandria, Va., 1999—. Cert. instr., curriculum developer Am. Compensation Assn., Scottsdale, Ariz., 1986—. Co-author: (chpt.) Compensation, 1994. Reader Access 2000 (recordings of Smithsonian Inst. pubs. for the blind), Washington, 1998—; bd. dirs. Stamford (Conn.) Symphony Orch., 1983-89. With U.S. Army, 1965-71. Home: 124 Princess St Alexandria VA 22314-2325 E-mail: alschla@aol.com.

SCHLACKS, STEPHEN MARK, lawyer, educator; b. Pittsburg, Kans., Oct. 13, 1955; BA, Austin Coll., Sherman, Tex., 1978; MBA, U. Dallas, 1982; JD, Baylor U., 1986. Bar: Tex. 1987, U.S. Dist. Ct. (so. dist.) Tex. 1987, (no., ea. and we. dists.) Tex. 1988, U.S. Ct. Appeals (5th cir.) 1987, (8th cir.) 1989, U.S. Supreme Ct. 1990. In mgmt. Johnson & Johnson Products, Inc., Sherman, 1978-84; assoc. atty. Wetzel & Assocs., The Woodlands, Tex., 1986-92; ptnr. Hope, Causey & Schlacks, P.C., Conroe, 1992-96, Law Office of Stephen M. Schlacks, The Woodlands, 1996-99, Schlacks, Harrison & Cox PLLC, The Woodlands, 1999—. Adj. faculty North Harris County C.C., Houston, 1990—. Leon Jaworski scholar, 1984, Harcourt Brace Jovanovich scholar, 1986. Mem. Fed. Bar Assn., Montgomery County Bar Assn., Sigma Iota Epsilon, Pi Gamma Mu. Republican. Presbyterian. Home: 66 Racing Cloud Ct The Woodlands TX 77381-5203 Office: 2202 Timberloch Pl Ste 107 The Woodlands TX 77380-1163

SCHLADOR, PAUL RAYMOND, JR. insurance agent; b. Riverside, Calif., Oct. 16, 1934; s. Paul Raymond Sr. Schlador and Lois Geraldine (Burrus) Kaeding; m. Evangeline Kathern, Aug. 19, 1955; children: Debora Lynn TeSam, Cheryl Jean Bastian, Bonnie Kay Tucker. Student, San Diego City Jr. Coll., 1954-55, Ins. Industry, San Diego, 1960-62, Am. Coll., 1970-74. CLU. Agt. Bankers Life of Nebr., San Diego, 1959-63; agt./ mgr. Southwestern Life Ins. Co., 1959—; ind. agt. State Farm Ins. Co., 1978—. With USNG, 1952-60. Mem. San Diego Assn. Life Underwriters (pres. 1989-90, legis. v.p. 1988), Kiwanis Club El Cajon Valley. Republican. Methodist. Avocations: tennis, camping, sr. Olympic basketball. Home: 1267 Oakdale Ave # C El Cajon CA 92021-6454 Office: State Farm Ins 7800 University Ave # 1A La Mesa CA 91941-4928 also: BPOE Lodge # 1812 El Cajon CA 92021 E-mail: Ray.Schlador.B9EA@StateFarm.com.

SCHLAFER, DONALD HUGHES, veterinary pathologist; b. Sidney, N.Y., July 15, 1948; s. Donald Hughes and Mildred (Gamewell) S., Jr.; m. Judith Ann Appleton, Aug. 2, 1980; children: Nathan James, Russell Matthew. BS, Cornell U., 1971, MS, 1975; DVM, N.Y. State Coll. Vet. Medicine, Ithaca, 1974; PhD, Coll. Vet. Medicine, Athens, Ga., 1982. Diplomate Am. Coll. Vet. Pathologists, Am. Coll. Theriogenologists (exec. com. 1993-96), Am. Coll. Vet. Microbiologists. Gen. practice vet. medicine Guilderland Animal Hosp., Altamont, N.Y., 1975-77; resident dept. vet. pathology U. Ga., Athens, 1977-79; research pathologist USDA Plum Island Animal Disease Ctr., Greenport, N.Y., 1975-82; asst. prof. dept. vet. pathology Cornell U., Ithaca, 1982-88, assoc. prof., 1988-97, prof. comparative reproductive pathology, 1997—, dir. Bovine Research Ctr., 1982-91. Cons. in field, 1983— Contbr. articles to profl. pubs. Mem. AVMA, Soc. for Study of Reprodn., Soc. for Theriogenology (exec. com. 1993-96). Office: T6020 Coll Vet Medicine Cornell U Ithaca NY 14853

SCHLAFLY, HUBERT JOSEPH, JR. communications executive; b. St. Louis, Aug. 14, 1919; s. Hubert J. and Mary Ross (Parker) S.; m. Leona Martin, June 12, 1944. BSEE, U. Notre Dame, 1941; postgrad., Syracuse U., 1946-47. Electronics engr. Gen. Electric Co., Schenectady, 1941-44, Syracuse, 1946-47; project engr. radiation lab. MIT, 1944-45; dir. TV rsch. 20th Century-Fox Film Corp., N.Y.C., 1947-51; founder, v.p. Teleprompter Corp., 1951-74, pres., 1971-72, exec. v.p. tech. devel., 1972-74; pres. Transponder Corp., Greenwich, 1977-86; chmn., CEO Portel Services Corp., 1984-86; chmn., pres. Portel Services Network, Inc., 1987-91, chmn. bd., 1991-97, ret., 1998. Cons. in field; industry coord., chmn. exec. com., cable tech. adv. com. FCC, 1972—75; adviser com. telecomm. Nat. Acad. Engring.; adviser Sloan Commn. Cable Comms.; mem. engring. adv. coun. U. Notre Dame, 1977—2001, vice chmn., 1983, chmn., 84; bd. dirs., sec. Milbrook Corp., 1994—2001; lectr. in field. Author: Computer in the Living Room; patentee in field. Bd. govs. Milbrook Club, 1993-98. Recipient Engring. Honor award U. Notre Dame, 1976, Nat. Acad. TV Arts and Scis. Emmy award, 1992, 99, Discovery award Sacred Heart U., 2001. Fellow Soc. Motion Picture and TV Engrs.; mem. IEEE (Delmer Ports award 1979, life), Nat. Cable TV Assn. (chmn. standards com. 1965-69, chmn. domestic satellite com. 1971-73, chmn. future svcs. com. 1972, assns. com. 1981, Outstanding Tech. Achievements award 1974), Cable TV Pioneers, Electronic Industries Assn. (chmn. broadband cable sect. 1971-73, founding chmn. broadband communications com.), Soc. Cable TV Engrs. (sr.), Fairfield Found. (hon.); named Notre Dame alumni Man of Yr., 1992. Clubs: Rotary (pres. Greenwich club 1991-92), Knights of Malta, Knight St. Gregory the Great. Roman Catholic. Home and Office: 27 Orchard Dr Greenwich CT 06830-6711 E-mail: hschlafly@aol.com.

SCHLAFLY, PHYLLIS STEWART, author; b. St. Louis, Aug. 15, 1924; d. John Bruce and Odile (Dodge) Stewart; m. Fred Schlafly, Oct. 20, 1949; children: John F., Bruce S., Roger S., Phyllis Liza Forshaw, Andrew L., Anne V. BA, Washington U., St. Louis, 1944, JD, 1978; MA, Harvard U., 1945; LLD, Niagara U., 1976. Bar: Ill. 1979, D.C. 1984, Mo. 1985, U.S. Supreme Ct. 1987. Syndicated columnist Copley News Svc., 1976—. Pres. Eagle Forum, 1975—; broadcaster Spectrum, CBS Radio Network, 1973-78; commentator Cable TV News Network, 1980-83, Matters of Opinion sta. WBBM-AM, Chgo., 1973-75. Author, pub.: Phyllis Schlafly Report, 1967—; author: A Choice Not an Echo, 1964, The Gravediggers, 1964, Strike From Space, 1965, Safe Not Sorry, 1967, The Betrayers, 1968, Mindszenty The Man, 1972, Kissinger on the Couch, 1975, Ambush at Vladivostok, 1976, The Power of the Positive Woman, 1977, First Reader, 1994, Turbo Reader, 2001; editor: Child Abuse in the Classroom, 1984, Pornography's Victims, 1987, Equal Pay for Unequal Work, 1984, Who Will Rock the Cradle, 1989, Stronger Families or Bigger Government, 1990, Meddlesome Mandate: Rethinking Family Leav, 1991. Del. Rep. Nat. Conv., 1964, 1968, 1984, 1988, 1992, 1996, alt., 1960, 1980, 2000; 1st v.p. Nat. Fedn. Rep. Women, 1964—67; nat. chmn. Stop ERA, 1972—; mem. Ronald Reagan's Def. Policy Adv. Group, 1980, Commn. on Bicentennial of U.S. Constn., 1985—91, Adminstrv. Conf. U.S., 1983—86; pres. Ill. Fedn. Rep. Women, 1960—64; mem. Ill. Commn. on Status of Women, 1975—85. Recipient 10 Honor awards Freedoms Found., Brotherhood award NCCJ, 1975; named Woman of Achievement in Pub. Affairs St. Louis Globe-Democrat, 1963, one of 10 most admired women in world Good Housekeeping poll, 1977-90. Mem. ABA, DAR (nat. chmn. Am. history 1965-68, nat. chmn. bicentennial com. 1967-70, nat. chmn. nat. def. 1977-80, 83-95), Ill. Bar Assn., Phi Beta Kappa, Pi Sigma Alpha. Office: Eagle Forum 7800 Bonhomme Ave Saint Louis MO 63105-1906 E-mail: phyllis@eagleforum.org.

SCHLAGEL, DAVID MARK, academic administrator; b. Ortonville, Minn., Apr. 10, 1958; s. George Warren and Carolyn Mary (Lawson) S.; m. Rebecca Ellen Schmeichel, June 26, 1981; children: Sarah, Mark, Hannah, Paul, Esther, Joanna. BS in Aerospace Engring., U.S. Naval Acad., 1980; MS in Aeronautical Astronautical Engring, Stanford U., 1981; MS in Ednl. Adminstrn., Bob Jones U., 1994, EdS in Ednl. Adminstrn., 1995. Commd. ensign USN, 1980, advanced through grades to capt., 2000, main propulsion asst., elec. officer USS Lafayette, 1983-85, aide and flag lt. submarine group 2 Conn., 1985-87, engr. officer USS Dallas, 1987-90; divsn. dir. Naval Submarine Sch., Groton, Conn., 1990-93; commanding officer, exec. officer USNR, 1993—; sch. adminstr. Falls Baptist Acad., Menomonee Falls, Wis., 1995-99; dean Baptist Coll. of Ministry, 1998—; ch. adminstr. Falls Baptist Ch., 1999—; active duty Naval Tng. Ctr. Great Lakes, 2001—02. Bd. dirs. Wis. Assn. Christian Schs., Watertown, 1997-01. Author Preach the Word Mag., 1999. Recipient Meritorious Svc. medal (2 awards), Navy Commendation medal (six awards), Navy Achievement medal (2 awards); named Outstanding Young Men of Am., 1986. Mem. Baptist Ch. Avocations: reading, family activities. Home: N81w18428 Freedom Ct Menomonee Falls WI 53051-3505 Office: Baptist Coll Ministry N69w12703 Appleton Ave Menomonee Falls WI 53051-5215

SCHLAGEL, RICHARD H. philosophy educator; b. Springfield, Mass., Nov. 22, 1925; BS in Pre-Med cum laude, Springfield Coll., 1949; MA in Philosophy, Boston U., 1952, PhD, 1955. Instr. philosophy Coll. of Wooster, 1954-55; instr. Clark U., 1955-56; asst. prof. George Washington U., 1956-62, assoc. prof., 1962-68, prof., 1968—, chmn. dept., 1965-69, 70-71, 77-83, named Elton prof. philosophy, 1986, Elton prof. emeritus, 2001—. Sabbatical, Paris, with travel throughout Europe, 1962-63, 69-70, 76-77, 83-84, 90-91. Author: The Vanquished Gods: Science, Religion, and the Nature of Belief, 2001, From Myth to Modern Mind: A Study of the Origins and Growth of Scientific Thought, vol. 1, Theogony through Ptolemy, 1995, vol. 2, Copernicus through Quantum Mechanics, 1996; Contextual Realism: A Metaphysical Framework for Modern Science, 1986; contbr. articles and reviews to profl. jours. Borden Parker Browne fellow, 1953-54. Mem. AAUP, Am. Philos. Assn., Washington Philosophy Club (v.p. 1964-65, pres. 1965-66).

SCHLAGER, MAYNARD M(ORTON), psychologist, consultant; b. Winthrop, Mass., Apr. 3, 1928; s. Saul and Rose Schlager; m. Nathalie Lewin; children: Mason, Diane, David, Michael. BA, L.I. U., 1949; student, Yeshiva Ohr Yisroel, 1956, Mesivta Chaim Berlin, Jewish Theol. Sem., Jewish Inst. Religion, Hebrew Union Coll.; MA, Assumption Coll., 1976; D Ministry, Andover Newton Theol. Sch., 1978. Ordained rabbi, 1956; lic. psychologist, Mass.; accredited Coun. Nat. Register Health svc. and Providers in Psychology. Intern in clin. psychology U. Denver, 1952-54, Danvers State Hosp.-Tewksbury State Hosp.-Melrose-Wakefield Hosp., Mass., 1974-75; dir. Am. Counseling Ctrs., Peabody and Melrose, 1954—, dir. diet workshop div., 1985—. Supr. Worcester (Mass.) Pastoral Counseling Ctr., 1976-77. Author: Mixed Marriage, 1984; playwright (with Nathalie Schlager) Manhattan Mama, 1995, Crazy in Love, 2001. Acting chaplain USAF, 1950-54. Fellow Internat. Coun. Sex Edn. and Parenthood, Am. U., 1982. Mem. APA, Am. Assn. Marriage and Family Therapy (clin.), Mass. Assn. Marriage and Family Therapy, Mass. Psychol. Assn., Mixed Marriage Soc. U.S.A. (founder, bd. dirs. 1964—), Am. Legion (chaplain Malden 1978-83, Middlesex County 1983-85), Jewish War Vets. (vice comdr. 1965-66, Sugarman trophy 1966), B'nai B'rith (pres. Swampscott-Marblehead chpt. 1961-62, cert. of honor 1962), Masons. Home: 5190 Casa Real Dr Delray Beach FL 33484-6660 Office: Am Counseling Ctrs PO Box 811332 Boca Raton FL 33481 E-mail: docx6@juno.com.

SCHLAGETER, ROBERT WILLIAM, museum administrator; b. Streator, Ill., May 10, 1925; s. Herman Pete and Ida (Ladtkow) S.; divorced; children— David Michael, Robert William Diploma, Karl Ruprecht Univ., Heidelberg, Fed. Republic Germany, 1950; BA, U. Ill., 1950, MFA, 1957. Asst. prof. U. Tenn., Knoxville, 1952-58; dir. Mint Mus. Art, Charlotte, N.C., 1958-66; assoc. dir. Downtown Gallery, N.Y.C., 1966, Ackland Art Ctr., U. N.C., Chapel Hill, 1967-76; dir. Cummer Gallery Art, Jacksonville, Fla., 1976-92, dir. emeritus, 1992—. Fine arts cons. corp. and pvt. collecting, 1993—. Author: (exhbn. catalogue) Winslow Homer's Florida, George Inness' Florida, Martin Johnson Heade Florida, Robert Henri-George Bellows. Served with U.S. Army, 1943-45, ETO Home: 5201 Atlantic Blvd Apt 2 Jacksonville FL 32207-2473

SCHLAIKJER, STEPHEN ALLAN, foreign service officer; b. N.Y.C., Dec. 19, 1952; s. Jay Arthur Schlaikjer and Kathrina Elizabeth Pickens; m. Imoi Lee, June 4, 1977; children: Amena, Erica; 1 stepchild, Schuyler David. BA, Yale U., 1974. Deputy prin. officer U.S. Consulate Gen., Guangzhou, China, 1986-89; min. counselor econ. affairs U.S. Embassy, Beijing, China, 1990-93; counselor internat. econ. advairs U.S. Mission, Geneva, 1993-95; deputy prin. officer U.S. Consulate Gen., Hong Kong, 1995-98; dir. office Chinese & Mongolian affairs Dept. of State, Washington, 1998-2000; polit. advisor, chief naval ops. USN, 2000. Chmn. Guangzhou Am. Sch., 1986-88. Shanghai Am. Sch., 1982-83. Mem. Am. Fgn. Svc. Assn. Home: 11102 Sceptre Ridge Terr Germantown MD 20876

SCHLAM, MARK HOWARD, international marketing executive; b. Bklyn., Sept. 24, 1951; s. Murray J. and Sophia (Bonis) S. BSEE (N.Y. State Regents scholar), Poly. Inst. Bklyn., 1972, MSEE, 1973. Sales assoc. F.W. Madigan Real Estate Co., Flushing, N.Y., 1973-74; sales engr. Dayton T. Brown, Inc., Bohemia, 1975-77; sr. mktg. rep. advanced systems Sperry Marine Systems, Gt. Neck, 1977-80; pres. Mark H. Schlam Co. Internat., Melville, 1980—, MHSCO Internat. Corp., East Northport, 1987—. Assoc. editor Poly. Press, Bklyn., 1969-76. Asst editor: Computer Processing in Communications, 1970, Submillimeter Waves, 1971; assoc. editor Computers and Automata, 1971, Computer-Communications Networks and Teletraffic, 1972, Optical and Acoustical Micro-Electronics, 1975, Computer Software Engineering, 1976. Mem. Audio Engring. Soc., Acoustical Soc. Am., AIAA, Am. Soc. Naval Engrs., Armed Forces Communications and Electronics Assn., IEEE, Soc. Tech. Communication, Soc. Automotive Engrs., AAAS, Nat. Pilots Assn., Assn. Old Crows, Nat. Soc. Profl. Engrs., Realtors Nat. Mktg. Inst., Poly. Inst. N.Y. Alumni Assn. (assoc. dir. 1973—), Masons, Tau Delta Phi. Office: PO Box 97 East Northport NY 11731-0097 E-mail: mschlam@suffolk.lib.ny.us.

SCHLANG, DAVID, real estate executive, lawyer; b. N.Y.C., May 2, 1912; s. Alexander and Blanche (Cohen) S.; m. Arlene Roth, May 9, 1948. LLB, NYU, 1933. Bar: NY 1935, U.S. Dist. Ct. (so. dist.) NY 1940. Individual practice law, 1935-42; sec., pres. Schlang Bros. & Co., Inc., N.Y.C., 1945—. Trustee Brookdale Hosp., Bklyn., 1980—, vice chmn., 1983—, Linroc Nursing Home, 1993—; founding mem. U.S. Congl. Adv. Bd.; bd. dirs., vice chmn. Samuel Schulman Inst. Nursing and Rehab. of Brookdale Hosp., 1973—; bd. dirs. Legion Meml. Sq., Inc., 1983—. With AUS, 1942—45. Decorated Croix de Guerre with palm (France); recipient Conspicious Svc. award State of N.Y., 1965. Mem.: ABA, Real Estate Bd. N.Y., N.Y. County Lawyers Assn., N.Y. State Bar Assn., Criminal Investigation Divsn. Agts. Assn., Woodmere Club, Met. Club, U.S. Senatorial Club. Home: 737 Park Ave New York NY 10021-4256 Office: 67 Wall St New York NY 10005-3101 E-mail: schlang67@aol.com.

SCHLECKSER, JAMES HENRY, engineering executive, sales executive; b. Rahway, N.J., Sept. 16, 1962; s. Henry and Mary Ellen (Counihan) S.; m. Denise Priscille Bergeron, July 2, 1988. B of Chem. Engring., U. Del., 1984; MBA, U. Conn., 1988. Cert. engr.-in-tng., Del., quality mgr. ASQ. Product engr. Rogers Corp., Manchester, Conn., 1984-86; asst. corp. sec. R/MAT Inc., 1986-88; product supr. Rogers Corp., 1986-88; product mgr. J.M. Ney Electronics, Bloomfield, Conn., 1988-90; sales mgr. Ney Ultrasonics, 1990-92; dir. sales and engring. NEY Ultrasonics, 1992-95; pres. General Eastern, Woburn, Mass., 1995-2000; group v.p. Spirent Comm., 2000-01, pres., CEO Spirent-Hekimian divsn., 2001—. Chmn. Ultrasonic Industry Standards, Dayton, Ohio, 1994; bd. dirs. Gen. Eastern, Inc., Thermometrics Japan, Inc., Protimeter PLC and Modus Instruments, Inc., Hekimian Labs., Inc. Author:

(book chpt.) Modern Plastics Ency., 1988; contbr. articles to profl. jours. Chmn. Internat. Spl. Olympics, Bolton, Conn., 1995; exec. com. Canon Greater Hartford Open, Cromwell, Conn., 1988-94; dir. Hartford Jaycees, 1990-92, pres.; bd. dirs. Friends of Meml. Hall Libr., 1998-2001, pres. 1999-2001; bd. dirs. Jr. Achievement Capital Region, 2001-. Recipient Brownfield award Jaycees, 1989, State Champion Pub. Speaking, 1990. Mem. AIChE, Am. Soc. Quality (cert. quality mgr.), Soc. Automotive Engrs. (bd. dirs. local chpt. 1989). Home: 10804 Riverwood Dr Potomac MD 20854 E-mail: jimschleckser@att.net.

SCHLECT, CHRISTIAN, trade association administrator; b. Yakima, Wash., June 10, 1951; s. Don and Betty Schlect; m. Janet Fetsch; children: Emily, Frederick; children: Walter. BA in Polit. Sci., Wash. State U., 1973. Bar: Wash. 1977. Dep. pros. atty. County Prosecutor''s Office, Yakima, Wash., 1977—80; pres. N.W. Hort. Coun., 1980—. Chairman Coalition to Promote U.S. Agricultural Trade, Washington, 1995—2002. Chmn. Wash. Apple Edn. Found. Mem.: Univ. Club of Washington. Office: Northwest Horticultural Council 6 S 2d St Yakima WA 98901

SCHLEEDE, GLENN ROY, energy market and policy consultant; b. Lyons, N.Y., June 12, 1933; m. Sandra Christine Klafehn, Dec. 27, 1958; children: Kristen M., Kimberly J., Kendall E. BA, Gustavus Adolphus Coll., 1960; MA, U. Minn., 1968; advanced mgmt. program, Harvard U., 1987. Research asst. Indsl. Relations Ctr., U. Minn., Mpls., 1960-61; mgmt. intern, then contractor personnel specialist AEC, Argonne, Ill. and Germantown, Md., 1961-65; asst. chief div. natural resources U.S. Office Mgmt. and Budget, Exec. Office of Pres., Washington, 1965-72, exec. assoc. dir., 1981; dep. assoc. dir. Office of Policy Analysis, AEC, Germantown, 1972-73; assoc. dir. energy and sci. Domestic Council, The White House, Washington, 1973-77; sr. v.p. Nat. Coal Assn., 1977-81; pres. New Eng. Energy Inc., Westborough, Mass., 1982-92, also bd. dirs.; v.p. New Eng. Power Service Co., 1982-92, also bd. dirs.; v.p. New Eng. Electric System, 1986-92; pres., CEO, dir. Energy Market and Policy Analysis, Inc., Reston, Va., 1992—. Author numerous speeches, papers and congl. testimony on various nat. energy policy issues. Recipient Disting. Alumni in Bus. award Gustavus Adolphus Coll. Alumni Assn., St. Peter, Minn., 1987. Republican. Lutheran. Avocations: reading, travel, carpentry. Home: 1414 Hemingway Ct Reston VA 20194-1241 Office: Energy Market and Policy Analysis Inc PO Box 3875 Reston VA 20195-1875 E-mail: empainc@aol.com.

SCHLEGEL, BEVERLY FAYE, private club administrator; b. San Diego, May 15, 1950; d. Frederick Hugh and Fern (Bailey) Einhaus; m. Heinz Dieter Schlegel, Oct. 27, 1976; 1 child, Kailo Heinz. Student, Hollins Coll., 1990—. Cert. club mgr. Mgr. The Town Club of Salem, Va., Va., 1976-84, The Shenandoah Club, Roanoke, 1984—. Contbr. articles to profl. publ. Vol. Jr. Achievement; charter mem. Commonwealth Coun., 1996. Featured in Club Dir. mag., 1993, 2000. Mem.: Club Mgrs. Assn. Am. (cert., chap. liaison student chap. Va. Tech. 2001—, 2 Blue Ribbons 1993, Blue Ribbon 2001), Nat. Club Assn. (city coun. adv. bd. 1992—). Baptist. Avocations: writing, study of ancient history, church participation, Peruvian Paso horses. Home: 1109 Manteo Rd Montvale VA 24122-2592 Office: The Shenandoah Club Inc 24 Franklin Rd SW Roanoke VA 24011-2496

SCHLEGEL, CHRISTIAN BEAT, educator; b. St. Gallen, SG, Switzerland, Aug. 22, 1959; came to U.S., 1985. s. Alex Emil and Theres Agnes S.; m. Rhonda Denise Schlegel, Oct. 24, 1999; 1 child, Isabelle Brown. Student, ETH Zurich, 1979-84; MSEE, U. Notre Dame, 1985-87, PhD, 1985-88. Rsch. scientist ABB Corp., Baden, Switzerland, 1988-92; rsch. fellow U. So. Australia, Addaide, 1992-94; asst. prof. U. Tex., San Antonio, 1994-96; assoc. prof. U. Utah, Salt Lake City, 1996—. Cons. L3 Communications, Salt Lake City, 1997—; tech. program com. mem. various confs. Author: Trellis Coding, 1997; editor: IEEE Transactions on Communications, 1999. Recipient Nat. Sci. Found. Career award 1998. Sr. mem. IEEE. Avocations: climbing, skiing, poetry, psycology, languages. Office: Univ Utah Dept Elec Engring 50 S Campus Dr Salt Lake City UT 84112 E-mail: schlegel@ee.utah.edu.

SCHLEGEL, COLETTE SUE, musician; b. Hays, Kans., Apr. 2, 1960; d. Franklin Dale and Norma Jean Schlegel. MusB summa cum laude, B of Music Edn. summa cum laude, Fort Hays State U., 1982; postgrad., Syracuse U., 1982-83; MusM, SUNY, Binghamton, 1984; D of Musical Arts with honors, U. Kans., 1992. Choir dir., organist Temple Hesed, Scranton, Pa., 1984-86, Clarks Green (Pa.) United Meth. Ch., 1984-86; organist Ch. of the Epiphany, Sedan, Kans., 1986-87; choir dir., organist Blue Valley United Meth. Ch., Manhattan, 1987-90; organist, assoc. dir. St. Peter's United Ch. of Christ, Kansas City, Mo., 1990-93; dir. music/organist First United Meth. Ch., Decatur, Ill., 1993-95, First Presbyn. Ch., Corvallis, Oreg., 1995—. Dir. ch. music workshops U. Kans., 1989-90. Editor: Hymne au Soleil-Boulanger, 1998. Chair publicity com. Oreg. State U. Corvallis Symphony, 1996—98; mem. profl. concerns com. Salem Am. Guild Organists, 1996—2000; v.p. U. Kans., AGO, 1991—92; mem. exec. staff Scranton-Pocono Girl Scouts, 1985—86; dir. Skylake Choral Camp, Windsor, NY, 1982—83; mem. dist. worship com. United Meth. Ch., Decatur, 1993—95. Mem. Am. Guild of Organists, Pi Kappa Lambda, Phi Kappa Phi. Office: First Presbyn Ch 114 SW 8th St Corvallis OR 97333-4546

SCHLEGEL, DONALD MAX, retired surgeon; b. Staunton, Ind., 1923; AB, Ind. U., 1943, MD, 1945. Intern Wis. Gen. Hosp., Madison, 1945-46; fellow surg. rsch. Ind. U. Hosp., Indpls., 1949, resident surgery, 1949-53; surgeon Meth. Hosp.; ret., 1991. Clin. asst. prof. Ind. U. Sch. Medicine. Fellow ACS; mem. AMA. Home: 7445 Longleat Rd Indianapolis IN 46240-3678 E-mail: dmschlegel@aol.com.

SCHLEGEL, FRED EUGENE, lawyer; b. Indpls., July 24, 1941; s. Fred George and Dorothy (Bruce) S.; m. Jane Wessels, Aug. 14, 1965; children: Julia, Charles, Alexandra. BA, Northwestern U., 1963; JD with distinction, U. Mich., 1966. Bar: Ind. 1966. Assoc. lawyer Baker & Daniels, Indpls., 1966-72, ptnr., 1972—; vice chmn. Meridian St. Preservation Commn., 1975-90. Contbr. articles to profl. jours. Chmn. Indpls. Pub. Schs. Edn. Found., 1988-90; pres. Festival Music Soc., 1974-75, 79, 86-87; bd. dirs. Indpls. Symphony Orch., 1991—, Arts Coun. Indpls. Mem. ABA, Ind. Bar Assn., Energy Bar Assn., Northwestern U. Alumni Club Indpls. (pres. 1992-94). Republican. Presbyterian. Office: Baker and Daniels 300 N Meridian St Ste 2700 Indianapolis IN 46204-1782 E-mail: feschleg@bakerd.com.

SCHLEGEL, JOHN FREDERICK, management consultant, speaker, trainer; b. Ogden, Utah, Dec. 18, 1944; s. Max Joseph and Mary Georgia (Whittaker) S.; m. Priscilla Mary Hecht, Sept. 8, 1967. BS in Pharmacy, U. Pacific, 1967; D of Pharmacy, U. So. Calif., 1972, postdoctoral fellow, 1972-73, MS in Edn., 1980; ScD in Pharmacy (hon.) , Mass. Coll. Pharmacy, 1984, L.I. U., 1985. Lic. pharmacist, Calif., Nev.; cert. assoc. exec. Chief pharmacist U. So. Calif. Sch. Pharmacy, Los Angeles, 1967-73, dir. pharmacy admissions, 1973-75; dir. office student affairs Am. Assn. Colls. Pharmacy, Alexandria, Va., 1975-77, asst. exec. dir., 1977-81, exec. dir., 1981-84; chief exec. officer Am. Pharm. Assn., Washington, 1984-89; exec. v.p., chief exec. officer Am. Acad. Facial Plastic and Reconstructive Surgery, 1989-92; pres. Schlegel & Assocs., 1992—. Cons. to more than 300 profl. and trade assns., univs. and U.S. Govt. Contbr. over 100 articles on pharmacy, health care and assn. mgmt.; presenter in field. Nat. del. White House Conf. on Aging, Washington, 1981. Disting. alumnus U. So. Calif. Sch. Pharmacy, 1985, U. the Pacific Sch. Pharmacy, 1987. Fellow Am. Soc. Assn. Execs.; mem. Am. Soc. Assn. Execs., Am. Assn. Med. Soc. Execs., Fla. Soc. Assn. Execs., Phi Delta Chi (charter, bd. counsellors). Avocations: tennis, classical music, gardening. Office: 3390 Highlands Bridge Rd Sarasota FL 34235-6859 E-mail: jschlegel@comcast.net.

SCHLEGEL, JOHN P. academic administrator; b. Dubuque, Iowa, July 31, 1943; s. Aaron Joseph and Irma Joan (Hingtgen) S. BA, St. Louis U., 1969, MA, 1970; BDiv, U. London, 1973; DPhil, Oxford U., 1977. Joined Soc. of Jesus, 1963, ordained priest Roman Cath. Ch., 1973. From asst. prof. to assoc. prof. Creighton U., Omaha, 1976-79, asst. acad. v.p., 1978-82; dean Coll. Arts and Scis. Rockhurst Coll., Kansas City, Mo., 1982-84, Marquette U., Milw., 1984-88; exec. and acad. v.p. John Carroll U., Cleve., 1988-91; pres. U. San Francisco, 1991-2000, Creighton U., Omaha, 2000—. Cons. Orgn. for Econ. Devel. and Cooperation, Paris, 1975-76. Author: Bilingualism and Canadian Policy in Africa, 1979; editor: Towards a Redefinition of Development, 1976; contbr. articles to profl. jours. Mem. Milwaukee County Arts Coun., 1986—88, Mo. Coun. on Humanities, Kansas City, 1984; trustee St. Louis U., 1985—91, Loyola U., Chgo., 1988—95, Loyola U. New Orleans, 1995—98, St. Ignatius H.S., Cleve., 1990—91, Loyola Coll. in Md., 1992—98, Xavier U., 1998—; bd. dirs. Commonwealth Club Calif., Calif. Coun. on World Affairs, 1997—99. Oxford U. grantee, 1974-76; Govt. of Can. grantee, 1977-78. Mem. Am. Coun. on Edn., Bohemian Club, Univ. Club. Avocations: racquet sports, classical music, cooking, hiking. Office: Creighton U Office Pres 2500 Calif Plz Omaha NE 68178 E-mail: jpschlegel@creighton.edu.

SCHLEGEL, PETER NILES, urologist and educator; b. Malden, Mass., Feb. 17, 1958; s. Niles Matthew and Mary Patricia (McIntyre) S.; m. Suzanne Marie Bozzo, Sept. 14, 1991; children: Andrew Peter, Lucy Filice, Nicholas Halloran. AB, Hamilton Coll., 1979; MD, U. Mass., 1983. Diplomate Am. Bd. Urology, Nat. Bd. Med. Examiners; lic. physician, N.Y. Intern in gen. surgery and resident Johns Hopkins Hosp., Balt., 1983-85, resident, chief resident in urology, 1985-89, instr. urology, 1989; fellow-in-residence The Population Coun., N.Y.C., 1989-91, staff scientist, 1991—; asst. attending surgeon New York Hosp., 1991-96; assoc. attending surgeon N.Y. Hosp., 1996—; assoc. vis. physician Rockefeller U., 1991—; asst. prof. urology Cornell Med. Coll., 1991-96, assoc. prof. urology, 1996—, vice chmn. urology, 1999-2001, acting chmn., 2001—. Vis. prof. Austria, Israel, Indonesia, Saudi Arabia, Brazil, others; vis. fellow Royal Coll. Surgeons, 1993; co-dir. Ctr. for Male Reproduction and Microsurgery, Cornell Inst. for Reproductive Medicine, 2000—; lectr. in field. Contbr. numerous articles, abstracts to profl. jours., chpts. to books. Recipient Edwin Beer Program award N.Y. Acad. Medicine, 1996-98, New Investigator award Am. Found. for Urol. Disease, 1993-95, fellow, 1989-91; fellow Am. Cancer Soc., 1986-87, NIH, 1989-91; established Clinician award ESHRE, 1996. Mem.: Soc. for Study of Male Reprodn. (v.p.), Am. Urol. Assn., Soc. for Basic Urol. Rsch., Soc. for Study of Reprodn., Am. Soc. Andrology, Am. Soc. Reproductive Medicine, Alpha Omega Alpha. Roman catholic. Avocation: sailing. Office: New York Hosp Dept Urology 525 E 68th St Dept Urology New York NY 10021-4885 E-mail: pnschleg@med.cornell.edu.

SCHLEGELMILCH, REUBEN ORVILLE, electrical engineer, consultant; b. Green Bay, Wis., Mar. 8, 1916; s. Raymond Adolf and Emma J. (Schley) S.; m. Margaret Elizabeth Roberts, Aug. 22, 1943; children: Janet R., Raymond J., Joan C., Margaret Ann. BS in Elec. and Agrl. Engring., U. Wis., 1938; MS in Elec. and Agrl. Engring., Rutgers U., 1940; postgrad. in elec. engring., Cornell U., 1940-41, Poly Inst. Bklyn., 1947-51, U. Ill., 1941-42; SM in Indsl. Mgmt., MIT, 1955; postgrad. in elec. engring., Syracuse U., 1956-59, Fed. Exec. Inst., 1982. Registered profl. engr., N.J. Dir. rsch. and devel. Rome Air (Elec.) Devel. Ctr., N.Y., 1955-59; tech. dir. def./space Westinghouse Elec. Corp. Hdqrs., Washington, 1959-63; mgr. adv. tech. and missiles Fed. Sys. IBM, Owego, N.Y., 1963-68; gen. mgr., pres. Schilling Industries, Galesville, Wis., 1968-71; mgr. sys. design U.S. Army Adv. Sys. Concepts Agy., Alexandria, Va., 1971-74; mgr. gun fire control sys. Naval Sea Sys. Command, Washington, 1974-80; tech. dir. office R&D U.S. Coast Guard Hdqrs., 1980-86. Cons. in field, 1986—; govt. cons. electronics, Dept. Def. R & D Bd., 1949-54; indsl. cons. missile/space Aerospace Industries Assn., 1959-63; chmn. profl. sci. com. Rome Air Devel. Ctr., 1956-59; mem. nat. com. Engring. Mgmt. Inst. Elec. Engring., N.Y.C., 1956-59. Author tech. reports and articles; patentee target position indicator. Vol. Annandale Christian Cmty. for Action (Va.), 1973—; mem. winterset Civic Assn., Annandale, 1971—. Fellow Alfred P. Sloan Found. MIT, 1954-55. Mem. IEEE (sr. life, sec., vice chmn., chmn. 1956-59, Recognition award 1959), Am. Def. Preparedness Assn.(chmn. So. Tier Empire Post 1967-68, recognition award 1968), NSPE, N.Y. Acad. Scis., Soc. Sloan Fellows MIT, Mason, Rotary, Shriners. Home: PV203 7442 Spring Village Dr Springfield VA 22150-4444

SCHLEGER, PETER RALPH, corporate communications specialist, writer; b. N.Y.C., Apr. 7, 1944; s. Hans Emil and Susan Erna (Jacoby) S.; m. Batya Kahane, Apr. 29, 1975; children— Shane, Jesse. B.S. in Bus. Adminstrn., Boston U., 1965; M.B.A., Pace U., 1969; M.A., U. So. Calif., 1977. Bus. mgr. N.Y.C. Bd. Edn., Bronx, 1968-70; owner, operator Sandwich City, Tel Aviv, 1971-73; writer Baer/Joelson Prodns., 1975-76; dir. communications Barkers, Bronx, 1977-80; prin. Peter Schleger Co., N.Y.C., 1980— ; prodn. mgr. Fraternity Row, 1975; presenter various confs. Author screenplays The Assignment, 1975, Stanik & Catherine, 1976, Bridges, 1980; novel Tammuz Web, 1982. Contbr. articles to Tng. News and Tng. and Devel. Jour., Employee Benefits Jour., 1980-92, newspapers. Mem. Am. Soc. Tng. and Devel. (Communicator of Yr. 1981, exec. com. media div. 1981-83), Tau Kappa Epsilon. Democrat. Jewish. Lodge: Masons. Home: 780 W End Ave New York NY 10025-5573

SCHLEI, BERND ROBERT, physicist, researcher; b. Arolsen, Hessen, Germany, Dec. 28, 1963; s. Robert Schlei, Heidi Marlies Schlei; m. Uta Kleinhans, Sept. 3, 1987; children: Melissa Annika, Vincent Lennard, Emily-Marie, Jonathan David. Abitur, Christian Rauch Schule (Gymnasium), Arolsen, 1982; Dipl.-Phys., U. Marburg, Germany, 1990, Dr. rer. nat., 1994. Rsch. asst. U. Marburg, 1990—94; postdoctoral fellow Deutsche Forschungsgemeinschaft, 1994—95, 1995—96, Los Alamos (N.Mex.) Nat. Lab., 1996—99, tech. staff mem., 1999—. With Faehnrich (ROA), 1982—84. Home: 2410 Canyon Glen Los Alamos NM 87544 Office: Los Alamos Nat Lab PO Box 1663, MS B211 Los Alamos NM 87545 Business E-Mail: schlei@lanl.gov.

SCHLEICHER, DONALD, music director; Degree, U. Wis., Northwestern U.; studied with Gustav Meier, Simon Rattle, Seiji Ozawa, Maurice Abravanel, Roger Norrington, Joel Smirnoff, Leon Fleisher. Band dir. Williamsville (N.Y.) South High Sch., 1977-84; past mem. music faculty U. Wis., Stevens Point; past mem. conducting faculty U. Mich.; dir. orch. studies, condr. Univ. Symphony Orch., head grad. program in orch. conducting U. Ill.; music dir. Quad City Symphony Orch. Assn., Davenport, Iowa. Conducting fellow Tanglewood Music Ctr., 1993; music dir., prin. condr. Pine Mountain Music Festival, Mich., 1994—; condr. orchs. N.Y., Ala., Wis., Hawaii, R.I., Ill.; guest condr., resident Fla. State U., Ark. State U., U. Minn., U. Akron, Ohio U., U. Buffalo, Ithaca Coll., Ohio State U.; guest condr. orchs. Bridgeport, Conn., Tallahassee, Fla., Lansing, Mich., Ann Arbor, Mich., Southfield, Mich.past dir. Detroit Chamber Winds; guest condr. Chautauqua Festival, 1996, Taiwan Symphony Orch. Wind Ensemble; presenter conducting clinic at nat. convention Music Educators Nat. Conf., Kansas City, 1996. Condr. operas including La Boheme, Suor Angelica, Il Pagliacci, Susannah, The Barber of Seville, La Traviata, The Marriage of Figaro, Madama Butterfly, Carmen. Office: Quad City Symphony Orch PO Box 1144 Davenport IA 52805-1144*

SCHLEICHER, NORA ELIZABETH, banker, treasurer, accountant; b. Balt., Aug. 10, 1952; d. Irvin William and Eleanor Edna S.; m. Ray Leonard Settle Jr., July 27, 1985. AA cum laude, Anne Arundel Community Coll., 1972; BS summa cum laude, U. Balt., 1975. CPA, Md. Staff auditor Md. Nat. Bank, Balt., 1975-76, sr. staff auditor, 1976-77, supr. auditing dept., 1977-78; full charge acct. Wooden & Benson, CPA's, 1978-81; asst. to treas. First Fed. Savs. & Loan Assn., Annapolis, Md., 1981, asst. treas., 1982-83, v.p., 1984; v.p., treas. First Fed. Savs. & Loan Assn. (now First Annapolis Bank), 1984—. Bd. dirs., treas. Coll. Manor Community Assn. Mem. AICPA, Md. Assn. CPA's, Fin. Mgrs. Soc., Coll. Manor Community Assn. (bd. dirs., treas.). Methodist. Office: First Annapolis Savs Bank 1832 George Ave Annapolis MD 21401-4103

SCHLEIFER, JAMES THOMAS, history educator; b. Rochester, N.Y., Nov. 15, 1942; s. James E. Schleifer and Jeanette L. Kern; m. Alison Pedicord; children: Katharine, Margaret. Diploma, U. Paris, 1962-63; BA with honors, Hamilton Coll., 1964; MA, Yale U., 1966, MPhil, 1968, PhD, 1972. Grad. asst. in history Yale U., New Haven, 1966-68; instr. in history Coll. of New Rochelle, N.Y., 1969-73, asst. prof. history, 1973-76, assoc. prof. history, 1976-83, prof. history, 1983—, dir. Gill Libr., 1987-99, dean Gill Libr., 1999—. Vis. prof. Am. history U. Paris, 1986, Yale U., 1983-84, 95; vis. fellow history dept. Yale U., 1981-82; mem. French Nat. Commn. for Pub. of Complete Works of Alexis de Tocqueville, 1986— Author: The Making of Tocqueville's "Democracy in America", 1980, 2d edit. 2000, De la Démocratie en Amérique, 1992, The College of New Rochelle: An Extraordinary Story, 1994; contbr. chpts. to books, articles, revs. to profl. publs.; assoc. editor Tocqueville Rev./La Revue Tocqueville, 1985-95. Grantee Am. Philos. Soc., 1979, 85, Coll. New Rochelle, 1976, 81, 85, NEH, 1982-83; fellow Yale U., 1964-68, Am. Coun. Learned Socs., 1974-75, 81-82; recipient Merle Curti award Orgn. Am. Historians, 1981. Mem. ALA, Tocqueville Soc., Am. Hist. Assn., Orgn. Am. Historians, Westchester Acad. Libr. Dirs. Orgn. Home: 220 Alston Ave New Haven CT 06515-2038 Office: Coll of New Rochelle Castle Pl New Rochelle NY 10805

SCHLEIFER, THOMAS C. management consultant, author, lecturer; BS in Constrn. Mgmt., E. Carolina U., 1989, MS in Constrn. Mgmt., 1990; PhD, Herriot-Watt U., 1994. Owner Schleifer Bros., Inc., Hanover, N.J., 1964-75; owner, founder, pres., internat. cons. firm CMA Cons. Group, Morristown, 1976-86; dir. appropriate tech., vol. Habitat for Humanity, Americus, Ga., 1987-88; assoc. prof. Ariz. State U., Tempe, 1990-92; eminent scholar Del E. Webb Sch. Constrn., Ariz. State U., 1993-94; eminent scholar Del E. Webb Sch. Constrn. Ariz. State U., Tempe, 2001—. Vis. prof. East Carolina U., 1989-90; former chmn. continuing edn. com. Associated Gen. Contractors Am.; lectr. and presenter in field. Author: Construction Contractors' Survival Guide, 1990, Glossary of Suretyship and Related Terms, 1981; contbr. articles to profl. jours. Bd. advisors Habitat for Humanity Internat., 1989—. Mem. Am. Inst. Constructors (bd. dirs. 1990-93), Am. Arbitration Assn. (N.J. adv. coun. 1968-75), Am. Concrete Inst. (edn. com. 1972-76), Associated Gen. Contractors Am. (chmn. continuing edn. com. 1970-76), Assn. Advancement 3d World (internat. adv. coun. 1988-91). Home and Office: 5625 N 75th Pl Scottsdale AZ 85250-6471 E-mail: tschleifer.@aol.com.

SCHLEIN, BRUCE MAXWELL, pathologist; b. Jersey City, Jan. 28, 1937; s. David and Sylvia (Golub) S.; m. Alice Donner, Mar. 21, 1961; children: William Louis and Erik Alexander. BA, Columbia Coll., 1959; MD, SUNY, N.Y.C., 1963; postgrad. studies in Med. Mycology, Duke U., 1966. Diplomate Am. Bd. Pathology, Am. Bd. Cytopathology.; med. lic. S.C. Intern Duke U. Hosp., Durham, N.C., 1963-64, asst. resident in pathology, 1965-66, chief resident, instr., 1966-67; instr. bone pathology Columbia U., N.Y.C., 1968; instr. sch. med. tech. U.S. Pub. Health Svc. Hosp., Staten Island, N.Y., 1967-69; asst. prof. pathology Duke U. Med. Sch., Durham, 1969-71; assoc. prof. clin. pathology U. Ala. Sch. Medicine, Birmingham, 1971-73; pathologist Pathology Assocs. of Greenville, PA, S.C., 1973—; asst. prof. pathology Med. U. S.C., Charleston, 1973—; assoc. dir. labs. Greenville Meml. Hosp., 1973—. Dir. pathology assts. program Duke U., Durham, 1970; acting chief clin. pathology sect. VA Hosp., Birmingham, Ala., 1971-73, cons. in pathology VA, inspector Coll. of Am. Pathologists inspection and accreditation program; dir. labs. Greenville Hosp. Ctr., 1984-97; instr. photography Greenville County Mus. Art, Furman U. Photographer: exhbns. include Olden Photo Gallery, N.Y.C., Furman U., Greenville, N.C., Greeville Artists Guild Juried Exhibit, Anderson Art Ctr. Juried Exhibits, N.Y. Pub. Libr., U. N.C., Greensboro, Duke U. Student Union, and others. Bd. trustees and pres. Temple of Israel, Greenville, S.C., 1978-80; pres. Internat. Chamber Music Series, Greenville, S.C., 1996—. Lt. commdr. U.S. Pub. Health Svc., 1967-69. Fellow Am. Soc. Clin. Pathologists, Coll. Am. Pathologists (inspector); mem. AMA, S.C. Med. Assn., S.C. Soc. Pathologists, Greenville County Med. Soc., Avocations: photography, fishing. Office: Pathology Assocs Greenville 8 Memorial Hosp Ct Greenville SC 29605

SCHLEMOWITZ, JOEL, film studies educator, film director; b. Madison, Wis., Apr. 26, 1967; s. Abram and Carol Schlemowitz. BS, Ithaca Coll., 1989. Instr. The New Sch., N.Y.C., 1996—; adj. instr. The Cooper Union, 1998—; lectr. U. of the Arts, Phila., 1998—2000. Webmaster The Film-Makers' Coop., N.Y.C., 2000—. Dir.: (films) Moving Images - the Film-Makers' Cooperative relocates, 2001 (Hon. mention Thaw02 Film and Video Festival, 2002), Abrasions, 1990, Weeping Film, 1991, Übel, 1991, Unmeasured Prelude for Kerry Laitala, 1991, Jungian Conflicts, 1992, When He Leaves, 1993, Poem for the Past, 1993, Channeled Energies, 1993, Morris Engel Time Sculpture, 1994, Tombeau for Arnold Eagle, 1994, Doris' Garden, 1995, Angelbubble, 1995, Purple Candle Poem, 1995, Filmpoem for Wanda Phipps, Pillowbook, Weimar, 1995, Bagatelle in Neon, 1997, Eye Music, 1997, 1734, 1997, Invitation to a Voyage, 1997, Bacchanale, 1998, Incantation Documentation, 1998, Bagatelle Biologique, 2000, morning poem #40, 2001, Typeoclavecin Film, 2001, Reverie, 2001. Grantee filmmaking grantee, N.Y. State Coun. of the Arts, 2000, The Jerome Found., 1999. Home: 470 State St Brooklyn NY 11217 Personal E-mail: schlemoj@newschool.edu. E-mail: schlemoj@newschool.edu.

SCHLENDER, WILLIAM ELMER, management sciences educator; b. Sawyer, Mich., Oct. 28, 1920; s. Gustav A. and Marie (Zindler) S.; m. Lela R. Pullen, June 9, 1956 (dec. June 1983); m. Margaret C. Krahn, Mar. 3, 1987. AB, Valparaiso U., 1941; MBA, U. Denver, 1947; PhD, Ohio State U., 1955. With U.S. Rubber Co., 1941-43, 46; asst. prof., assoc. prof. bus. adminstrn. Bowling Green State U., 1947-53; asst. prof. bus. orgn., prof. Ohio State U., 1954-65, asst. dean, 1959-62; assoc. dean Ohio State U. (Coll. Commerce and Adminstrn.), 1962-63; prof. mgmt. U. Tex., 1965-68, chmn. dept., 1966-68; dean Cleve. State U. Coll. Bus. Adminstrn., 1968-75, prof. mgmt., 1975-76; Internat. Luth. Laymen's League prof. bus. ethics Valparaiso (Ind.) U., 1976-79, Richard E. Meier prof. mgmt., 1983-86, Richard E. Meier prof. emeritus, 1986—. Vis. assoc. prof. mgmt. Columbia U., 1957-58; vis. prof. mgmt. U. Tex., Arlington, 1981-82; cons. in field; bd. govts. Internat. Ins. Soc., 1972-90. Author: (with M.J. Jucius) Elements of Managerial Action, 3d edit, 1973, (with others) Management in Perspective: Selected Readings, 1965; Editor: (with others) Management in a Dynamic Society, 1965; Contbr. (with others) articles to profl. jours. Served with AUS, 1943-45. Decorated Bronze Star. Recipient Exec. Order Ohio Comodr. for outstanding contbn. to growth and devel. of state. Fellow Acad. Mgmt.; mem. Indsl. Rels. Rsch. Assn. (pres. N.E. Ohio chpt. 1971-72), Am. Legion, Tau Kappa Epsilon, Soc. for Case Rsch., Rotary, Beta Gamma Sigma, Sigma Iota Epsilon, Pi Sigma Epsilon, Alpha Kappa Psi, Phi Kappa Phi. Home: PO Box 446 Sawyer MI 49125-0446 Office: Coll Bus Adminstrn Valparaiso U Valparaiso IN 46383 E-mail: bschlend@aol.com. *I resolved long ago that where I worked and what I did would be guided not by prestige considerations, but by the answers to three questions: (1) Will my work allow me to grow by discovering and developing my capabilities? (2) Will it make a significant contribution to my profession and to the community? (3) Will I enjoy doing it? My career, and my personal philosophy, have these underlying guidelines.*

SCHLENOFF, ZEINA TAMER, language educator, literary critic; b. Zahle, Lebanon, Oct. 4, 1956; came to the U.S., 1984; d. Edouard Alexander Tamer and Georgette Salim Khoury; m. Joseph Bradbury Schlenoff, June 4, 1988; children: Natasha, Philip. BA, MA, Lebanese U., 1981; PhD, U. Mass., 1995. Adj. prof. Fla. State U., Tallahassee, 1996—. Vis. asst. prof. Am. U. of Beirut, 1998-2000, dir. Arabic summer program, 2000-01. Author: Le Bonheur Chez la Femme Colettienne, 1997. Founder, faculty advisor Fla. State U. Arabic Club, Tallahassee, 1996—. Recipient Fabriano (Italy) prize in art and painting, 1974. Mem. MLA, Women in French, Mid. East Studies Assn. Avocations: travel, reading, horticulture. Home: 6274 Hines Hill Cir Tallahassee FL 32312 Office: Dept Modern Langs Fla State U Tallahassee FL 32306 Fax: (850) 644-0524. E-mail: zschleno@mailer.fsu.edu.

SCHLENTZ, ROBERT JOSEPH, biomedical, electromagnetic compatibility, regulatory, reliability and safety engineer; b. Chgo., Dec. 9, 1940; s. Harold Joseph and Katherine (Dufalo) S.; m. Eileen Ellen Pride, May 10, 1969; children: Julie Joann, Karen Katherine. BS in Physics, DePaul U., 1963, MS in Physics, 1965. Registered profl. engr., Minn. Assoc. rsch. scientist U. Notre Dame, Ind., 1966-68; dept. mgr. electro magnetic compatibility, staff engr. Medtronic, Fridley, Minn., 1968-77; project engr. Maico Hearing Instruments, Edina, 1977-83; sr. specialist 3M (Minn. Mining & Mfg.), St. Paul, 1983—. Treas. Mpls. Dem. Farmer-Labor Com., Mpls., 1985-88. Mem. IEEE (sr., twin cities sect. chair), Minn. Soc. Profl. Engrs. (bd. dirs.). Roman Catholic. Avocations: music, science fiction, politics. Home: 3040 Buchanan St NE Minneapolis MN 55418-2251

SCHLEPP WEISKOPF, CONNIE ELIZABETH, artist, graphic artist; b. Denver, Nov. 18, 1956; d. Lawrence Carl and Joyce Angeline Schlepp. BA in Art and Edn., Western State Coll., 1977; postgrad., Regis Coll., 1988. Owner Creative Graphics, Gunnison and Arvada, Colo., 1979-82, 82—; fine artist, 1977—. Cons. numerous advt. firms, Denver, 1982-84. Illustrator: Environmental Impacts, 1982, The Gunnison Country, 1981; one-woman shows include Western State Coll., Gunnison, Colo., 1977, Gov.'s Park, Denver,

1984, 86, Schooners, Broomfield, Colo., 1982, 83, 84, 86, Blackdog Enterprises, Denver, 1986, Marlyn Design Internat. Galleries, Houston, 1987, Foothills Art Ctr., Golden, Colo., 1989, Rolling Hills Country Club, Golden, 1991, 92, 93, Keller Williams Realty, Westminter, Colo., 1997, Nat. Ctr. for Atmosphere Rsch., Boulder, 1998, South Fellowship, Littleton, Colo., 1998, Eccles Art Ctr., Ogden, Utah, 2001, Layton (Utah) Heritage, 2001; permanent collections Livingstone Gallery, Denver, 1993, Ariel Gallery, Soho, N.Y.C., 1989—, Marlyn Design Internat. Galleries, Houston, 1986—; group shows include Spring Art Expo, Gunnison, Colo., 1977, Brush & Palette Club, Grand Junction, Colo., 1981, Artists Alpine Holiday, Ouray, Colo., 1981, Black Forest Internat. Painting and Sculpture Exhibit, Colorado Springs, 1981, Foothills Energy Art Exhibit, Golden, 1982, The Frame Gallery, Aurora, 1984, Vail Arts Festival, 1985, 86, 88, 89, Nat. Watercolor Soc., L.A., 1987, 88, Allied Artists Am., N.Y.C., 1988, Am. Watercolor Soc., N.Y.C., 1988, Colo. State Fair, Pueblo, 1990, Cherry Creek Arts Festival, Denver, 1991, Autumn Expressions, Englewood, 1993, Parade of Homes, Castlerock, 1994, Spring Expressions, Littleton, 1997, 98, Colo. Watercolor Soc., Denver, 1994, CFFA, Littleton, 1995, Art of Women, Republic Plz., Denver, 1996, Landscape Cityscape, 1997, Eccles Art Ctr., Ogden, 2001, Am. Women Artists, Santa Fe, 2002, others. Mem. Colo. Artists Assn., Inc., Colo. Watercolor Soc., Utah Watercolor Soc., Allied Artists Am., Christian Fine Arts Assn., Foothills Artists Assn. Republican.

SCHLESINGER, ARTHUR, JR. (ARTHUR MEIER SCHLESINGER), writer, educator; b. Columbus, Ohio, Oct. 15, 1917; s. Arthur M. and Elizabeth (Bancroft) S.; m. Marian Cannon, 1940 (div. 1970); children: Stephen Cannon, Katharine Kinderman, Christina, Andrew Bancroft; m. Alexandra Emmet, July 9, 1971; 1 son, Robert Emmet Kennedy. AB summa cum laude, Harvard U., 1938, mem. Soc. of Fellows, 1939-42; postgrad. (Henry fellow), Cambridge (Eng.) U., 1938-39; hon. degrees, Muhlenberg Coll., 1950, Bethany Coll., 1956, U. N.B., 1966, New Sch. Social Rsch., 1966, Tusculum Coll., 1966, R.I. Coll., 1969, Aquinas Coll., 1971, Western New Eng. Coll., 1974, Ripon Coll., 1976, Iona Coll., 1977, Utah State U., 1978, U. Louisville, 1978, Northeastern U., 1981, Rutgers U., 1982, SUNY-Albany, 1984, U. N.H., 1985, U. Oxford, 1987, Akron U., 1987, Brandeis U., 1988, U. Mass., Boston, 1990, Hofstra U., 1991, Adelphi U., 1992, Dominican Coll., 1992, Mt. Ida Coll., 1993, Middlebury Coll., 1994, Roosevelt U., 1995, Lynn U., 1996, No. Ill. U., 1996, City U. N.Y., 1999, Harvard U., 2001, U. S.C., 2001, Miami U., 2001, Pa. State U., 2001. With OWI, 1942-43, OSS, 1943-45; assoc. prof. history Harvard U., 1946-54, prof., 1954-62; vis. fellow Inst. Advanced Study, Princeton, N.J., 1966; Schweitzer prof. humanities CUNY, 1966-95. Cons. Econ. Cooperation Adminstrn., 1948, Mutual Security Adminstrn., 1951-52; spl. asst. to Pres. of U.S., 1961-64; mem. jury Cannes Film Festival, 1964; mem. Adlai E. Stevenson campaign staff, 1952, 56; chmn. Franklin Delano Roosevelt Four Freedoms Found., 1983—; trustee Robert F. Kennedy Meml., Twentieth Century Fund.; adv. Arthur and Elizabeth Schlesinger Library. Author: Orestes A. Brownson, 1939, The Age of Jackson, 1945 (Pulitzer prize for history 1946), The Vital Center, 1949, (with R.H. Rovere) The General and the President, 1951, The Age of Roosevelt Vol. I: The Crisis of the Old Order 1919-1933, 1957 (Francis Parkman prize Soc. Am. Historians 1957, Frederic Bancroft prize Columbia U. 1958), The Age of Roosevelt Vol. II: The Coming of the New Deal, 1958, The Age of Roosevelt Vol. III: The Politics of Upheaval, 1960, Kennedy or Nixon: Does It Make Any Difference?, 1960, The Politics of Hope, 1963, (with John Blum) The National Experience, 1963, A Thousand Days, 1965 (Pulitzer prize for biography 1966, Nat. Book award 1966), The Bitter Heritage, 1967, The Crisis of Confidence, 1969, The Imperial Presidency, 1973 (Sidney Hillman Found. award 1973), Robert Kennedy and His Times, 1978 (Nat. Book award 1979), The Cycles of American History, 1986, The Disuniting of America, 1991, A Life in The 20th Century: I, Innocent Beginnings, 2000; contbr. articles to mags. and newspapers; film reviewer: Show mag., 1962-64, Vogue, 1967-72, Saturday Rev., 1977-80, Am. Heritage, 1981-82; editor: Harvard Guide to American History, 1954, Guide to Politics, 1954, Paths to American Thought, 1963, The Promise of American Life, 1967, The Best and the Last of Edwin O'Connor, 1970, History of American Presidential Elections 1789-1972, 1971, 1972-1984, 1986, The Coming to Power, 1972, The Dynamics of World Power: A Documentary History of United States Foreign Policy 1945-1973, 1973, History of U.S. Political Parties, 1973, Congress Investigates, 1975, Running for President, 1994; screenwriter: (teleplay) The Journey of Robert F. Kennedy. Served with AUS, 1945. Decorated comdr. Order of Orange-Nassau, The Netherlands, Ordem del Libertador, Venezuela, Order of St. Michael and St George, Gt. Britain; recipient gold medal in history and biography, Am. Acad. Arts and Letters, 1967, award for history, Ohio Gov., 1973, award in edn., Eugene V. Debs, 1974, Fregen Prize for Lit., Italy, 1983, award for internat. understanding, U. Thant, 1998, medal, Nat. Humanities1998, 1998; fellow, Guggenheim, 1946; grantee, Am. Acad. Arts and Letters, 1946. Mem. Am. Hist. Assn., Orgn. Am. Historians, Soc. Am. Historians (pres. 1989-92), Am. Acad. and Inst. Arts and Letters (pres. 1981-84, chancellor 1984-87), Am. Philos. Soc., Mass. Hist. Soc., Colonial Soc. Mass., Russian Acad. Scis., Franklin and Eleanor Roosevelt Inst. (co-chmn. 1983—), ACLU, Coun. Fgn. Rels., Ams. for Dem. Action (nat. chmn. 1952-54), Century Assn., Knickerbocker Club, Phi Beta Kappa. Democrat. Unitarian Universalist. Home: 455 E 51st St New York NY 10022-6474

SCHLESINGER, B. FRANK, architect, educator; b. N.Y.C., Sept. 17, 1925; s. Augustus and Ethel (Brower) S.; m. Draga A. Christy; children: Jeff, Nike, Katherine, Daniel, Christy Anna; 1 stepson, Frances L. Haley Jr. Student, Middlebury Coll., 1946-48; BS, U. Ill., 1950; MArch, Harvard U., 1954. Draftsman Hugh Stubbins Assocs., 1953-55, Marcel Breuer, 1955-56; pvt. practice architecture Princeton, N.J., 1956-59, Doylestown, Pa., 1959-69, Phila., 1969-71, Washington, 1971—. Instr. archtl. design U. Pa., 1957-60; vis. critic Columbia Sch. Architecture, 1962-63, U. Pa., 1965; KEA disting. prof. Sch. Architecture, U. Md., 1971, prof. architecture, 1971— With USNR, 1943-46. Wheelwright fellow Harvard U., 1963, Disting. Designer fellowship Nat. Endowment for the Arts, 1984; recipient design awards Pa. Soc. Archs., 1960-65, 69, 84, Bronze medal, 1965, Silver medal, 1973, Design awards Progressive Arch., 1966-67, 69, 72, 74, Design awards Interfaith Forum on Religion, Art and Arch., 1987, 92. Fellow AIA (Design awards Phila. chpt. 1960-61, 63-65, 68-69, No. Va. chpt. 1975, 2001, Washington chpt. 1990, 92, 95, Centennial medal Washington chpt. 2001); mem. Harvard Grad. Sch. Design Alumni Assn. (pres. 1971-73), Associated Harvard Alumni (dir. 1972). Address: 1015 33rd St NW Apt 806 Washington DC 20007-3538

SCHLESINGER, HARVEY ERWIN, judge; b. June 4, 1940; BA, The Citadel, 1962; JD, U. Richmond, 1965. Bar: Va. 1965, Fla. 1965, U.S. Supreme Ct. 1968. Corp. counsel Seabord Coast Line R.R. Co., Jacksonville, Fla., 1968-70; chief asst. U.S. atty. Mid. Dist. Fla., 1970-75, U.S. magistrage judge, 1975-91, U.S. Dist. judge, 1991—. Adj. prof. U. N. Fla., 1984-91; mem. adv. com. on Fed. Rules of Criminal Procedure to U.S. Supreme Ct., 1986-93; mem. Jud. Conf. Adv. Com. on Adminstrn. of Magistrate Judges Sys., 1996—, chmn., 1998—; chmn. U.S. Dist. Ct. Forms Working Group, Washington, 1983—, Jud. Ct. Ad hoc Com. on Long Range Planning, 1998—, Jud. Conf. Jud. Officers Resources Working Group, 1998-99, 11th Cir. Dist. Judges Assn., 1991—, sec.-treas. 1996- 97, v.p. 1997-98, pres.-elect. 1999-2001, pres. 2001—. Bd. dirs. Pine Castle Ctr. for Mentally Retarded, Jacksonville, 1970-87, pres., 1972-74, chmn. bd. dirs., 1973-74; trustee Pine Castle Found., 1972-76; trustee Congregation Ahavath Chesed, Jacksonville, 1970—, v.p., 1975-80, pres., 1980-82; v.p. S.E. Coun. Union Am. Hebrew Congregations, 1984-88; asst. commr. for exploring N. Fla. Coun. Boy Scouts Am., 1983-86, exec. com., 1986-98, adv. bd., 1998—; mem. Boy Scouts Am. Nat. Jewish Com. on Scouting, Irving, Tex., 1986-93; mem. Fla. Sesquicentennial Commn., 1995-96; trustee River Garden Home for Aged, 1982—, sec., 1985—; co-chmn. bd. govs. Jacksonville chpt. NCCJ, 1983—, presiding co-chmn. 1984-89, nat. bd. trustees, N.Y.C., 1986-93; trustee Jacksonville Cmty. Found., 2000—. Capt. JAGC U.S. Army, 1965-68. Recipient Silver Beaver award Boy Scouts Am., 1986, George Washington Medal Honor, Freedoms Found., Valley Forge, Pa., 1987, Silver Medallion Humanitarian award NCCJ, 1992, Founders award, Fed. Magistrate Judges Assn., 1999, William Green award for profl. excellence U. Richmond Law Sch., 2000, Jurist of Yr. award Am. Bd. Trial Advs., 2001. Mem. ABA (fed. rules of evidence and criminal procedure com. 1979-98, Nat. Conf. Spl. Ct. Judges, 1975-90, conf. newsletter editor, 1988-90, Nat. Conf. Fed. Trial Judges, 1990—, chmn. legislation com., 1996-97, Flascher award 1989), Va. Bar Assn., Fla. Bar Assn., Fed. Judges Assn., Jacksonville Bar Assn., Fed. Bar Assn. (pres. Jacksonville chpt. 1974, 75, 81-82), Am. Judicature Soc., Chester Bedell Am. Inns of Ct. (pres. 1992-96), Rotary (Paul Harris fellow, pres. S. Jacksonville club), Masons (past master, past venerable master, knights comdr. of Ct. Honour, 33 degree Scottish Rite bodies), Shrine. Office: 311 W Monroe St PO Box 1740 Jacksonville FL 32201-1740

SCHLESINGER, LEONARD ARTHUR, apparel company executive; b. N.Y.C., July 31, 1952; s. Joe and Edith (Smukler) S.; m. Phyllis Barbara Fineman, Dec. 23, 1972; children: Rebecca, Emily, Katharine. BA, Brown U., 1972; MBA, Columbia U., 1973; DBA, Harvard U., 1979. Mgr. Procter & Gamble, Green Bay, Wis., 1973-75; asst. prof., assoc. prof. bus. sch. Harvard U., Boston, 1978-85, prof. bus. adminstrn., 1988-98; exec. v.p., COO Au Bon Pain, Inc., 1985-88; sr. v.p. Brown U., 1998-99; exec. v.p., COO Limited Brands, 1999—. Bd. dirs. GC Companies, Chestnut Hill, Mass., 1997-00, Borders Group, Inc., Ann Arbor, Mich., 1995-00, Limited Brands, Columbus, Ohio, 1996—, Pegasystems, Inc., Cambridge, Mass., 1996-00. Editor: Human Resources Mgmt. Jour., Jour. Mgmt. Inquiry; contbr. 40 articles to profl. jours. Jewish. Avocation: travel, music, bicycling. Home: 12 Edge of Woods New Albany OH 43054 Office: Limited Brands 3 Limited Pkwy Columbus OH 43230-1467 E-mail: lschlesinger@limitedbrands.com.

SCHLESINGER, MILTON J. virology educator, researcher; b. Wheeling, W.Va., Nov. 26, 1927; s. Milton J. and Caroline (Oppenheimer) S.; m. Sondra Orenstein, Jan. 30, 1955. BS, Yale U., 1951; MS, U. Rochester, 1953; PhD, U. Mich., 1959. Rsch. assoc. U. Mich., Ann Arbor, 1953-56, 59-60; guest rsch. investigator Inst. Superiore di Sanita, Rome, 1960-61; rsch. assoc. MIT, Cambridge, 1961-64; asst. prof. virology Washington U. Sch. Medicine, St. Louis, 1964-67, assoc. prof., 1967-72, prof., 1972-99, chmn. exec. coun. divsn. biol. and biomed. scis., 1992-94, emeritus prof., 1999—. Vis. scientist Imperial Cancer Rsch. Fund, London, 1974-75; vis. scholar Harvard U., Cambridge, 1989-90, 95-96; mem. adv. panels Am. Heart Assn., Dallas, 1975-78, NSF, Washington, 1978-82; mem. sci. adv. bd. Friedrich Miescher Inst., Basel, Switzerland, 1988—, chmn., 1992-98; nat. lectr. Sigma Xi. 1991-93. Editor: Heat Shock, 1982, Togaviridae and Flaviviridae, 1986, Lipid Modification of Proteins, 1992, (monographs) The Ubiquitin System, 1988, Stress Proteins, 1990; mem. editl. bd. virology, 1975-92, Jour. Biol. Chemistry, 1982-87, Molecular and Cellular Biology, 1983-92. Bd. dirs. ACLU, St. Louis, 1966-72, Coalition for Environ., St. Louis, 1989-92. Fellow AAAS; mem. Am. Biol. Chemistry and Molecular Biology, Am. Soc. Microbiology, Am. Soc. Virologists, Am. Chem. Soc. Office: Dept Molecular Micro 8230 Washington U Med Sch 660 S Euclid Ave Saint Louis MO 63110-1010

SCHLESINGER, SANFORD JOEL, lawyer; b. N.Y.C., Feb. 8, 1943; s. Irving and Ruth (Rubin) Schlesinger; children: Merideth, Jarrod, Alexandra. BS in Govt. with hons., Columbia U., 1963; JD, Fordham U., 1966. Bar: N.Y. 1966, U.S. Dist. Ct. (so. and ea. dists.) N.Y. 1967, U.S. Ct. Appeals (2d cir.) 1968, U.S. Ct. Internat. Trade 1969, U.S. Tax Ct. 1993, U.S. Supreme Ct. 1978. Assoc. Frankenthaler & Kohn, NYC, 1966—67; asst. atty. gen. trusts and estates bur. charitable found. div. State of N.Y., 1967—69; ptnr. Rose & Schlesinger, 1969—81, Goldshmidt, Oshatz, Powsner & Saft, NYC, 1981—85; ptnr., head trusts and estates dept. Shea & Gould, 1985—93; ptnr., head wills and estates dept. Kaye Scholer LLP, 1993—, ptnr. co-chair family owned bus. practice group, 1993—. Adj. faculty Columbia U. Sch. Law, 1989-94; adj. prof. N.Y. Law Sch., 1978—; adj. prof. grad. program in estate planning U. Miami Grad. Sch. Law, 1995—; mem. estate planning adv. com. Practising Law Inst., 1990—; bd. advisors and contbrs. Jour. of S Corp. Taxation, 1989-96; lectr. in field; condr. workshops in field. Author: Estate Planning for the Elderly Client, 1984, Planning for the Elderly or Incapacitated Client, 1993; columnist, mem. editl. bd. Estate Planning mag., 1995—; contbr. articles to profl. jours. Mem. adv. bd. Inst. Fed. Taxation NYU, 1988-96, chmn., 1993-94; mem. legis adv. com. Scarsdale (N.Y.) Sch. Bd., 1981-83, mem. nominating com., 1979-82; pres. dist. 17 N.Y.C. Cmty. Sch. Bd., 1970-71; mem. fin. and estate planning adv. bd. Commerce Clearing House, 1988—; mem. adv. bd. Tax Hotline, 1997—. Fellow Am. Coll. Trust and Estate Counsel (chmn. Downstate N.Y. 2001—); mem. ABA (chmn. social security and other govt. entitlements com. 1990-91, chmn. probate and trust com.-estate planning, drafting charitable giving coms., 1992-94), Internat. Acad. Estate & Trust Law (Academician 1992—), Nat. Acad. Elder Law Attys., Bklyn. Bar Assn., Assn. of Bar of City of N.Y., N.Y. State Bar Assn. (treas. trusts and estates sect. 1991-92, sec. trusts and estates sect. 1992-93, chmn. trusts and estates sect. 1994-95, chmn. exec. com. 1st jud. dist. 1987-91, jour. bd. editors 1995—). Avocations: baseball, writing. Office: Kaye Scholer LLP 425 Park Ave New York NY 10022-3506

SCHLESINGER, STEPHEN CANNON, educator; b. Boston, Aug. 17, 1942; s. Arthur Meier and Marian (Cannon) S.; m. Judith Barbara Elster, Mar. 18, 1984; 1 child, Sarah Elizabeth. BA in Am. History and Lit. cum laude, Harvard U., 1964, JD, 1968; cert. study in European History, Cambridge U., 1965. Legal asst. to pres. N.Y. State Urban Devel. Corp., 1968; founder, editor The New Dem., 1969-72; speechwriter Dem. Presdl. Candidate George McGovern, 1972; staff writer TIME Mag., 1974-78; editorial writer, chief polit. corr. N.Y. Post, 1978; spl. asst. to Gov. Mario Cuomo, 1983-90; dir. for internat. orgns. N.Y. State Dept. Econ. Devel., 1990—94; vis. scholar Taub Urban Rsch. Ctr. NYU, 1995-97; spl. advisor UN Ctr. for Human Settlements, 1995-97; dir. World Policy Inst. at New Sch. U., N.Y.C., 1997—. With Gore Presdl. Campaign, 2000; mem. internat. election observer teams Nat. Dem. Inst., 1993, 90; teaching fellow in English composition Harvard U., 1968; adj. prof. in Am. politics New Sch. for Social Rsch., 1976-77; lectr. Royce Carlton Agy., 1984-88. Author: The New Reformers, 1975, Bitter Fruit: The Untold Story of the U.S. Coup in Guatemala, 1982; contbr. numerous articles and book revs. to profl. jours., mags. and newspapers; columnist: Boston Globe, 1973-74. Mem. Coun. Fgn. Rels., Roosevelt Inst., PEN, Author's Guild. Unitarian Universalist. Avocations: jogging, skiing, swimming, tennis. Home: 500 W 111th St Apt 4A New York NY 10025-1905 Office: World Policy Inst 66 5th Ave Fl 9 New York NY 10011 E-mail: schlesis@newschool.edu.

SCHLESINGER, STEPHEN LYONS, horticulturist; b. N.Y.C., July 24, 1940; s. Nathan and Gertrude (Lyons) S.; m. Barbara Bernthal, Feb. 17, 1963; children— Adam Lyons, Lauren Elizabeth. BA, Williams Coll., 1962; student, U. Paris, 1960-61; MA in French, Columbia U., 1964; cert. in landscape design, Rutgers U., 1995. Lectr. in French Hunter Coll., 1963-64; lectr. in French Columbia U., summers 1963-64; adminstrv. asst. John Simon Guggenheim Meml. Found., N.Y.C., 1965-67, asst. sec., 1967-70, assoc. sec., 1970-73, sec., 1973-88, spl. cons., 1988-89; ind. cons., 1989-90; assoc. dir., dir. maj. gifts The Corella and Bertram F. Bonner Found., Princeton, N.J., 1990-91; nurseryman Dubrow's Nurseries, Livingston, 1990-95; garden ctr. horticulturist, 1995-99; horticulturist Conduroso's Garden Ctr., Montville, N.J., 2000—. Woodrow Wilson fellow, 1962-63 Home: 17 Prospect Ter Montclair NJ 07042-3204 Office: Conduroso's Garden Ctr 96 River Rd Montville NJ 07045-9421 Fax: 973-263-2614.

SCHLESS, GUY LACY, endocrinologist; b. Phila., May 22, 1929; s. Robert A. (M.D.) and Bena Schless; m. Nancy Esther Halverson, July 19, 1952; children: Karina Halverson, Lauritis Halverson. BA, Stanford U., 1951; MD, Jefferson Med. Coll., Phila., 1955. Intern Meth. Hosp., Phila., 1955-56; resident and rsch. fellow in metabolism Pa. Hosp., 1956-58, asst. physician, 1959-68, assoc. physician, 1968-71, physician, 1971—, chief med. clinics, 1965-67, sr. Mellon fellow in medicine, 1962-63. Vis. fellow, hon. sr. registrar medicine Guy's Hosp., U. London, 1958-59, vis. rsch. fellow in medicine Med. Sch., 1962-70, hon. cons. in medicine, 1971-90, hon. vis. cons. in metabolic medicine, 1990—; instr. medicine U. Pa., 1962-64, assoc., 1964-68, asst prof. medicine, 1968-80, clin. assoc. prof. medicine, 1980-95, 97—; clin. assoc. prof. medicine Jefferson Med. Coll., Phila., 1995-97; fellow in medicine Am. Philos. Soc.; cons. in medicine 5th naval dist. U.S. Navy, 1965—; cons. in medicine U.S. Naval Regional Med. Ctr., Portsmouth, Va., 1965—; participant White House Conf. Food, Nutrition and Health, 1969. Contbr. articles on metabolism to profl. jours. Bd. dirs. Brit. Cathedrals and Hist. Chs. Found., Inc., v.p., 1997—. Served as lt. comdr. M.C., USNR, 1960-62. Fellow Royal Soc. Medicine (London), Phila. Coll. Physicians, Royal Soc. Health (London), Royal Soc. Arts (London) (Benjamin Franklin fellow), Am. Coll. Endocrinology; mem. ACP, Am. Diabetes Assn., Athenaeum of Phila., Victorian Soc. in Am. (dir., v.p. 1977, pres. 1984-90, pres. emeritus 1990—), Soc. Archtl. Historians. Republican. Home: 3926 Henry Ave Philadelphia PA 19129-1008 Office: Pa Hosp 304 Duncan Bldg 700 Spruce St Philadelphia PA 19106-4022 Fax: 215-829-3532.

SCHLESS, PHYLLIS ROSS, investment banker; d. Lewis H. and Doris G. Ross; m. Aaron Backer Schless, July 7, 1970; 1 son, Daniel Lewis Ross. Cert., Neighborhood Playhouse Sch. of Theatre, 1962, N.Y. Sch. Interior Design, 1964; BA in Econs., Wellesley Coll., 1964; MBA, Stanford U., 1966. Cert. theater prodns. Am. League Theater Owners and Prodrs. Assoc. internat. fin. Kuhn Loeb & Co., N.Y.C., 1966-70; fin. cons., 1971-73; sr. fin. analyst Trans World Airlines, N.Y.C., 1974-75; corp. fin., mergers and acquisitions Lazard Freres & Co., 1976-79; dir. mergers and acquisitions Am. Can Co., Greenwich, Conn., 1979-82; v.p. mergers and acquisitions Bear, Stearns & Co., N.Y.C., 1982-84; sr. v.p. corp. acquisitions Integrated Resources, 1984-85; chmn., chief exec. officer Ross Fin. Svcs. Group Inc., 1985—; supervisory dir. Merrill Lynch HYTS Funds, 1991-96. Bd. dirs. Calvery Hosp. Fund Bd., chair investment com., 1995-99; trustee A.E. Tinker Fund, 1993—; trustee Nat. Child Labor Com., 1981-95, chmn., 1992-94; trustee New World Found., 1986-92, chair fin. com., treas. 1988-92; bd. dirs. Stanford Bus. Sch. Club, N.Y., 1990—; adj. asst. prof. NYU, 1996—, Columbia U. Sch. Bus., 2001—; bd. dirs. Nat. Found. Tchg. Entrepreneurship, 1998—, chair N.Y. adv. bd., 2001—; adj. faculty N.Y. Inst. Fin., 2001. Pres. Greater Bridgeport Nat. Coun. Jewish Women, 1971-73, bd. dirs., 1974-75; bd. dirs. Girls Clubs Am., 1975-89, mem. exec. com., 1982-89, pres., 1984-86; bd. dirs. Pauline Koner Dance Co., 1979-81, So. Conn. Child Guidance Clinic, 1981-83, New Canaan United Way, 1981-83; treas. Wellesley Class '64, 1984-89. Mem. Univ. Club. Home: 12 E 86th St New York NY 10028-0506 Office: Ross Fin Svcs Group Inc 6th Fl 689 5th Ave Fl 8 New York NY 10022-3133

SCHLESSER, THOMAS PIPER, civil engineer; b. Oneida, N.Y., July 21, 1941; s. George Ernest and Lois Elizabeth (Piper) S.; m. Jane Abigail Simons, Apr. 24, 1964; children: Jane Hartwell, Julianna Piper. BSCE, Clarkson U., 1963; MSCE, Syracuse U., 1966. Registered profl. engr., Va., N.Y., N.J., Mass., Minn., N.H., Ill. Sr. lab analyst Newport News (Va.) Shipbuilding, 1967-69; sr. hyd. environ. engr. Stone & Webster Engring. Corp., Boston, 1969-74, asst. mgr. environ. engring. N.Y.C., 1974-84; dir. tech. svcs. Wehran Engring., Methuen, Mass., 1984-88; dir. engring. Truhan Engring., Boxborough, 1988-89; sr. project mgr. Stearns & Wheler, Cazenovia, N.Y., 1989-92; engring. mgr. IT Corp., O'Fallon, Mo., 1993—. Contbr. articles to profl. jours. V.p. Lions Club, Cazenovia, 1989-92. NDEA Title IV fellow, 1966. Mem. NSPE, Mass. SPE, Am. Acad. Environ. Engrs. (diplomat 1993—). Avocations: skiing, tennis, woodworking, golf, travel. Office: IT Corp 42 N Central Dr O'Fallon MO 63366-2336 Home: Apt D 12609 Sauterne Dr Saint Louis MO 63146-2533

SCHLESSINGER, BERNARD S. retired university dean; b. Toronto, Ont., Can., Mar. 19, 1930; came to U.S., 1938, naturalized, 1948; s. Morris and Eleanor Schlessinger; m. June Hirsch, Dec. 21, 1952; children: Rashelle, Jill, Joel. BS, Roosevelt U., 1950; MS, Miami U., Oxford, Ohio, 1952; PhD, U. Wis., 1955; M.L.S., U. R.I., 1975. Research chemist Am. Can Co., Barrington, Ill, 1955-56; dept. head Chem. Abstracts, Columbus, Ohio, 1958-66; info. researcher Olin Corp., New Haven, 1966-68; asst. dir. Library Sch., So. Conn. State Coll., 1968-74; prof. library sci. U. S.C., 1975-77; dean Library Sch. U. R.I., Kingston, 1977-82; prof. Sch. Libr. Sci. Tex. Woman's U., Denton, 1982-92; ret., 1992. Contbr. articles to profl. jours. Served with USAF, 1956-58. Named Outstanding Alumnus U. R.I. Grad. Library Sch., 1978 Mem. ALA, Tex. Library Assn., Sigma Xi, Phi Lambda Upsilon, Beta Phi Mu. Home: 15707 Hamilton St Omaha NE 68118-2339

SCHLEUNES, KARL A. history educator; b. Kiel, Wis., Apr. 21, 1937; s. Henry F. and Adelia Schluenes; m. Brenda Pursel, Aug. 15, 1964; 1 child Anna. BA, Lakeland Coll., Sheboygan, Wis., 1959; MA, U. Minn., 1961, PhD, 1965. Asst. prof. U. Ill., Chgo., 1965-71; assoc. prof. history U. N.C., Greensboro, 1971-85, prof., 1985—. Vis. prof. U. Cape Town, South Africa, 1999. Author: The Twisted Road to Auschwitz, 1970, 2d edit. 1990, Schooling and Society, 1989, Legislating the Holocaust, 2001. Grantee NEH, 1973, Univ. Rsch. Coun., 1973, 80, 89. 95. Mem. Am. Hist. Assn., German Studies Assn. Avocation: collecting books. Home: 117 S Tremont Dr Greensboro NC 27403 Office: U NC Dept History McIver Bldg Greensboro NC 27402-6170 E-mail: kaschleu@uncg.edu.

SCHLEUNING, JAY JAMES, reporter; b. N.Y.C. s. Carol Anita (Huber) S. AA, Valencia C.C., Orlando, Fla., 1992; BS in Telecom., U. Fla., 1994. Reporter, anchor WHCU/WYXL-FM, Ithaca, N.Y., 1990-91, WRUF-AM/WUFT-FM/WUFT-TV, Gainesville, Fla., 1992-94; bur. chief WTVY-TV, Dothan, Ala., 1994-96, WCTV-TV, Tallahassee, 1996-97, WVTM-TV, Birmingham, Ala., 1997-99; investigative reporter WANE-TV, Ft Wayne, Ind., 1999—2001; freelance reporter, 2001—. Finalist Green Eyeshade award, Soc. Profl. Journalists, 1997; named Hearst Broadcast scholar, 1993, Emmy award, NATAS, Cleve. chpt., 2002; recipient grand prize award, Nat. Broadcasting Soc., 1994, hon. mention investigative reporting, Ga. Associated Press, Atlanta, 1997, Green Eyeshade award for Best Non-Deadline Reporting, Soc. of Profl. Journalists, 1998, 2d place Best News Story, Ind. Broadcasters Assn., 2000, 1st place Best Investigative Report, Ind. AP, 2001, 2002, 2d place Best Enterprise Story, 2001; scholar, Radio-TV News Dirs. Found., 1993—94.

SCHLEUSE, WILLIAM, retired psychiatrist, psychoanalyst; b. Austin, Oct. 18, 1932; s. Louis W. and Oleta Vivian (Hedgpeth) S.; m. Virginia Walker, 1965 (div. 1977); children: Martin, Stuart, Paul; m. Doris Laird, Apr. 20, 1985. BA, U. Tex., 1953; MD, U. Tex. Med. Br., Galveston, 1957. Diplomate Am. Bd. Psychiatry and Neurology. Pvt. practice psychiatry and psychoanalysis, Houston, 1962-81, Austin, 1981-00; pres. med. staff Hedgecroft Hosp., Houston, 1966; ret., 2000. Photography exhibited in numerous shows, 1993—. Pres. Houston Psychiat. Soc., 1967, Austin chpt. Am. Assn. Individual Investors, 1992. Fellow Am. Psychiat. Assn. (life); mem. Am. Psychoanalytic Assn., Internat. Psychoanalytic Assn., San Antonio/Austin Psychoanalytic Soc. (pres. 1996-98), Austin Fine Art Photography Group (founding mem.), Phi Beta Kappa. Avocations: sailing, boating, fine-art photography. Home: 2803 Regents Park Austin TX 78746-7619

SCHLEUSENER, RICHARD AUGUST, college president; b. Oxford, Nebr., May 6, 1926; s. August William and Katherine Charlotte (Albrecht) S.; m. Elaine Emma Wilhelm, June 12, 1949; children: Kathryn Jeanne Schleusener Miller, Richard Dennis, Rand Lee, Debra Sue, Jeffrey Thomas. BS, U. Nebr., 1949, DSc (hon.), 1984; MS, Kans. State U., 1956; PhD, Colo. State U., 1958; postgrad., MIT, 1951-52. Rsch. engr. Colo. State U., 1958-64, dir. Inst. Atmospheric Sci.; prof., head dept. meteorology S.D. Sch. Mines and Tech., Rapid City, 1965-74, v.p., dean engring., 1974-75, acting pres., 1975-76, pres., 1976-86, Black Hills Regional Eye Inst. Found., 1987-96, ret., 1996. Cons. weather modification U.S. Dept. Interior, 1964—, U.S. Forest Svc., 1966—, UNESCO, 1971—, also pvt. firms. Contbr. articles to tech. jours. With USAF, 1950-55. Inductee S.D. Hall of Fame, 2000. Mem. Am. Meteorol. Soc., Am. Geophys. Union, Rotary, Sigma Xi, Beta Sigma Psi. Lutheran. Home: 315 S Berry Pine Rd Rapid City SD 57702-1923 E-mail: dickelaine@aol.com.

SCHLEUTER, SCOTT L. music educator; b. Madison, Wis., Jan. 19, 1973; s. Stanley L. and Lois J. Schleuter. MusB Edn., Ind. U., 1995, MusM, 2001—01. Cert. K-12 music tchr. Ind. Band dir. Bloomington (Ind.) H.S. North, 1995—99, Neuqua Valley H.S., Naperville, Ill., 2001—. Clarinettist Bloomington Symph. Orch., 1995—98, Bloomington Pops Orch., 1996—2001; adjudicator Ind. State Sch. Music Assn., Columbus, 1997—98; marching band drill writer Westfield (Ind.) H.S., 1996. Named to Tournament of Roses Parade, 1999; recipient Shell Lake Jazz Dir.'s scholarship, 1996. Mem.: Nat. Music Educators Conf., Ill. Music Educators Assn. Avocations: travel, hiking, skiing. Personal E-mail: sschleut@hotmail.com.

SCHLEY, WAYNE ARTHUR, political consultant; b. Hamilton, Mont., May 22; AA, Shasta Coll., 1960; BS, Sacramento State U., 1963; MS, Am. U., 1974; postgrad., U. Alaska, 1970, Harvard U. Cert. high sch. tchr. (lifetime), Calif. Dept. Edn. Tchr., admin. Placer H.S., Auburn, Calif., 1963-70; spl. asst. to Sen. Ted Stevens, Washington, 1971-77; staff dir. minority and majority subcom. civil svc. Post Office and Gen. Svcs., 1977-86; minority staff dir. Senate Com. on Rules and Adminstrn., 1987-92; commr. U.S. Postal Rate

Commn., 1992-95; cons. on legis. and postal issues, 1995—. Chmn. Calif. Teenage Reps., 1963-64; regional v.p. Calif. Young Reps., 1964-66, state sgt. at arms, 1966-67; mem. Placer County Rep. Ctrl. Com., 1965-70. Recipient Cert. of Achievement, JFK Sch. Govt. Harvard U., 1982. Home and Office: 614 Massachusetts Ave NE Washington DC 20002-6006

SCHLEY, WILLIAM SHAIN, otorhinolaryngologist; b. Columbus, Ga., Sept. 21, 1940; s. Frances Brooking Schley and Susie (Smith) Mathews. BA, Emory U., 1962, MD, 1966. Intern mixed surg. The Roosevelt Hosp., N.Y.C., 1966-67, resident in surgery, 1967-68; resident in otorhinolaryngology N.Y. Hosp.-Cornell Med. Ctr., 1970-73; clin. instr. otorhinolaryngology Cornell U. Med. Coll., 1972-75, clin. asst. prof., 1975-81, assoc. prof., 1982—, acting chmn. dept. otorhinolaryngology, 1988-94, chmn. dept. otorhinolaryngology, 1994—. Otorhinolaryngologist to putpatients with pvt. patient privileges N.Y. Hosp., 1973-75, asst. attending otorhinolaryngologist with pvt. patient privileges, 1975-81, assoc. attending, 1992—, acting otorhinolaryngologist-in-chief, 1988-94, otorhinolaryngologist-in-chief, 1994—; assoc. asst. surgeon otolaryngology Manhattan Eye, Ear, Nose and Throat Hosp., 1988-99; v.p. and sec. med. bd. N.Y. Hosp., 1994-97, pres., 1998-99; pres., v.p. med. bd. The N.Y. and Presbyn. Hosp., 1998, pres., 1998-99, mem. ex officio bd. trustees, 1998-99; mem. co-chmn. vis. day com. The N.Y. Hosp.-Cornell Med. Ctr., 1995-98; pres. N.Y. Hosp.-Cornell Med. Coll. Alumni Coun., 1996-98; course dir. Salzburg Cornell Med. Seminars, 1996—, steering com., 1999—. Author: (with others) Pulmonary Diseases of the Fetus Newborn and Child, 1978; contbr. numerous articles to profl. pubis. Vestry St. James Ch., N.Y.C., 1994-97; mem. ad hoc bd. visitors Emory U., 1994-95; bd. dirs. Health Advs. for Older People, 1997—, v.p., 2000—; mem. adv. bd. Sch. Medicine Emory U., 2000—, chmn. adv. bd., 2002--. Lt. comdr. USNR. Recipient The Emery medal, 2001. Fellow ACS (Manhattan dist. #2 com. on applicants 1991-97, Manhattan Credentials Com. 1991-99); mem. Am. Acad. Otolaryngology-Head and Neck Surgery, Med. Soc. State of N.Y., N.Y. State Soc. Otolaryngology-Head and Neck Surgery (exec. coun. 1974-80, dist. dir. 1980), County Med. Soc. N.Y., N.Y. Laryngol. Soc. (sec.-treas. 1981-84, v.p. 1984-85, pres. 1985-86), N.Y. Bronchoscopic Soc. (v.p. 1986-94, pres. 1994-97), N.Y. Clin. Soc. (v.p. 1998-99, pres. 1999-2000), Assn. Emory Alumni (bd. govs. 1990-97, pres.-elect 1993-94, pres. 1994-95), Omicron Delta Kappa. Episcopalian. Avocations: astronomy, ornithology. Home: 430 E 63d St Apt 5E New York NY 10021-7927 Office: NY Hosp Starr 541 525 E 68th St New York NY 10021-4885 E-mail: schley@med.cornell.edu.

SCHLEYER, TITUS KARL LUDWIG, dental educator; b. Schweinfurt, Germany, Aug. 13, 1963; came to U.S., 1989; s. Armin and Ulrike (Beisser) S. DMD, U. Frankfurt, Germany, 1987, PhD, 1989; DMD, Temple U., 1991, MBA, 1995. Lic. dentist, Pa. Assoc. prof. dentistry U. Pittsburgh, Pitts., 2002—. Assoc. editor Jour. ADA; contbr. articles to sci. publs. Capt. dental corps German Army, 1988-89. Rsch. grantee NLM/NIDCR, 1996—. Mem. IEEE, Am. Dental Edn. Assn., Am. Med. Informatics Assn., Foresight Inst., Assn. for Med. Informatics, Biometrics and Stats. Avocations: travel, kendo, mountain climbing. Office: Univ Pitts Sch of Dental Medicine 3501 Terrace St Pittsburgh PA 14218 E-mail: titus@pitt.edu.

SCHLICHT, JAMES P. lobbyist; b. Buffalo, Apr. 3, 1953; s. Kermit George and Mary Delores (Garvey) Schlicht; stepchildren: Rebecca L. Horst, Timothy R. Horst, Catherine L. Horst. BA in Social Scis. magna cum laude, St. Bonaventure U., 1975; MPA, Syracuse U., 1976. Mgmt. analyst U.S. Gen. Acctg. Office, Washington, 1976-78; budget specialist U.S. Office of Mgmt. and Budget, 1978-81; dir. govt. affairs Assoc. Builders and Contractors, 1981-84; ways and means counsel U.S. House of Reps., 1984-86; mgr. govt. relations Bristol Myers Squibb, 1986-90; dir. federal relations Johnson & Johnson, 1990-98; v.p. govt. affairs Astra Zeneca PLC, 1998—. Mem. bus. govt. relations coun., 1998—, health industry manufacturers govt. affairs com., 1990-97. Pres. Maxwell Sch. Alumni Assn., Washington, 1980. Recipient Outstanding Young Men of Am., 1982-84. Avocations: sailing. Office: Astra Zeneca PLC 1250 Eye St NW Ste 804 Washington DC 20005-5982

SCHLICHTEMEIER-NUTZMAN, SUE EVELYN, training consultant; b. Omaha, May 30, 1950; d. StuarTaylor and LaVera YVaughn (Conn) S.; m. Ronald E. Sorensen, Dec. 2, 1972 (div. Aug., 1984); m. Wade Edwin Nutzman, Aug. 27, 1988. BA in Journalism, U. Nebr., 1972, MA in Tng. and Devel., 1988, postgrad., 1989—. Advt. mgr. Burton Harpsichord Co., Lincoln, 1970-71; editorial asst. Nebr. Natural Resources Commn., 1971-72; editor Nebr. Personnel Dept., 1972-73; public info. specialist Governor's Budget Office, 1973-74; mental health cons. Mentl Health Ctr., 1974-81; tng. cons., keynote speaker, 1977—. Adj. advt. instr. U. Nebr., Lincoln, 1977-81, diversity instr., 1992—, orgn. cons., 1990—, dir. math camp, 1993—, team bldg. tnr. 1993—, motivational spkr. Author: Seeds of Change, 1985, Assertiveness Training, 1990, Help in the Aftermath, 1995; contbr. feature articles and reviews to newspapers and other pubs. Organist, youth music dir., trustee, historian, Nehawka (Nebr.) United Meth. Ch., 1985-93; dir. Community Youth Music Program, Nehawka, 1988-93; sec. Conestoga Found Bd., Murray, Nebr. 1988-92; treas. Conestoga Bd. Edn., Murray, 1988-92; project leader 4-H, 1993—; dir. Math Camp, 1993—; mem. steering com. Conestoga, 1994—; mem. Eastern Nebr. Regional Math Sci. Coalition, 1995—; many other civic and charitable roles as vol. Recipient fellowship U. Nebr., Lincoln, 1991-92. Mem. ASTD, Bus. and Profl. Women (keynote spkr. 1991-92), Missouri Valley Adult Edn. Assn., Adult and Continuing Edn. Assn. Nebr., Internat. Platform Speakers Assn., Am. Bus. Women's Assn. (keynote speaker 1993, tng. strategic planning cons., 1996, natl. keynotes, 1995-96), U. Nebr. Alumni Assn. (life). Democrat. Avocations: flower gardening, piano, art, reading, writing. Home and Office: Tng Plng Cons 3412 Mount Pleasant Dr Nehawka NE 68413-2424

SCHLICHTING, CATHERINE FLETCHER NICHOLSON, librarian, educator; b. Huntsville, Ala., Nov. 18, 1923; d. William Parsons and Ethel Loise (Breitling) Nicholson; m. Harry Fredrick Schlichting, July 1, 1950 (dec. Aug. 1964); children: James Dean, Richard Dale, Barbara Lynn. BS, U. Ala., 1944; MLS, U. Chgo., 1950. Asst. libr. U. Ala. Edn. Libr., Tuscaloosa, summers 1944-45; libr. Sylacauga (Ala.) H.S., 1944-45, Hinsdale (Ill.) H.S., 1945-49; asst. libr. Centre for Children's Books, U. Chgo., 1950-52; instr. reference dept. libr. Ohio Wesleyan U., Delaware, 1965-69, asst. prof., 1969-79, assoc. prof., 1979-85, prof., 1985—, curator Ohio Wesleyan Hist. Collection, 1986—, student pers. libr., 1966-72. Author: Introduction to Bibliographic Research: Basic Sources, 4th edit., 1983, Checklist of Biographical Reference Sources, 1977, Audio-Visual Aids in Bibliographic Instruction, 1976, Introduction to Bibliographic Research: Slide Catalog and Script, 1980; info. cons. (documentary) Noble Achievements: The History of Ohio Wesleyan 1942-1992, 1992, 150 Years of Excellence: A Pictorial View of Ohio Wesleyan University, 1992. Mem. adminstrv. bd. Meth. Ch., 1973-81, chmn. adminstrv. bd., 1985—, mem. coun. on ministries, 1975-81, chmn., 1975-77, trustee, 1999—. Recipient Algernon Sidney Sullivan award U. Ala., 1944, Hon. Alumna award Ohio Wesleyan U., 1997; Ohio Wesleyan U.-Mellon Found. grantee, 1972-73, 84-85; GLCA Tchg. fellow, 1976-77. Mem. ALA, Ohio Libr. Assn., Midwest Acad. Libr. Conf., Acad. Librs. Assn. Ohio (dir. 1984-86), AAUP (chpt. sec. 1967-68), United Meth. Women (pres. Mt. Vernon dist. 1994-97, newsletter editor 1998—), Ohio Wesleyan Woman's Club (exec. bd. 1969-72, 77-79, 81-84, pres. 1969-70, sec. 1977-78), History Club (pres. 1971-72, v.p. 1978-79) Fortnightly Club (pres. 1975-76, 87-88), Am. Field Svc. (pres. Delaware chpt. 1975-76), Kappa Delta Pi, Alpha Lambda Delta. Democrat. Home: 57 Willow Brook Way S Delaware OH 43015 Office: Ohio Wesleyan U La Beeghly Library Delaware OH 43015

SCHLICKAU, GEORGE HANS, cattle breeder, professional association executive; b. Haven, Kans., Nov. 2, 1922; s. Albert Rudulph and Florence Elsabe (Wittorff) S.; m. Lois Marie Ritthaler, Apr. 26, 1955; children: Bruce Alan, Susan Marie, James Darwin, Nancy Ann. Grad. high sch. Breeder registered Schlickau Hereford cattle, Haven, 1943—; pres. Reno County (Kans.) Hereford Assn., 1947-56, treas., 1956-58; dir. Reno County Cattleman's Assn., 1970-74, sec., 1970-71, treas., 1974; dir. Kans. Hereford Assn., 1955-71, 84-90, v.p., 1959, pres., 1960, 61; mem. organizing bd. Kans. Bull Test Sta., county committeeman Kans. Livestock Assn., 1960-75, bd. dirs., 1976-80, v.p. purebred coun., 1990-91, pres. purebred coun., 1992-93; bd. dirs. Am. Hereford Assn., 1969-75, v.p., 1973-74, pres., 1974-75; bd. dirs. Am. Nat. Cattleman's Assn., 1974-76; mem. fgn. trade com. Nat. Cattlemsn's Assn., 1990-93. Contbr. articles in field to profl. jours.; exhibitor, also winner numerous awards at major cattle shows across country; guest speaker, judge at numerous Hereford cattle events across country. Host ann. judging sch. and contest for Future Farmers Am. and 4-H youth, 1940-84; dir. Kans. Nat. Jr. Livestock Show, 1973—, sec., 1982-83, chmn., 1984-85, bd. govs., 1988—; bd. dirs. Haven State Bank, 1962—, Equus Beds Groundwater Mgmt. Dist. 2, 1975-79, Beef leader Haven 4-H Club, 1947-67; mem. Haven H.S. Bd., 1962-65, clk., 1964-65; mem. agrl. adv. com. Hutchinson (Kans.) Cmty. Jr. Coll., Kans., 1974-82; adv. Am. Jr. Hereford Assn., 1977-82; pres. Parent-Tchr. League Luth. Sch., 1979-80, 83-84; mem. zoning bd. City of Haven, 1985-88; bd. dirs. Ark Valley Electric Coop Assn., 1984-96, v.p., 1986-90, pres. 1990-93, Dist. IV Kans. Electric Coop., 1986-96, chmmn., 1992; bd. dirs. Kans. Coop. Coun., 1994-96; vice chmn. KACRE, 1992, chmn. 1993; adv. coun. mem. Arthur Capper Coop. Ctr., 1994-96. Recipient Am. Farmer Degree award Future Farmers Am., 1942, Reno County Outstanding Young Farmer award Hutchinson Jaycees, 1959, Kans. Hereford Herdsman of the Year award High Plains Jour., 1960, Soil Conservation award Kans. Bankers Assn., 1968, Hon. State Farmer Degree award Future Farmers Am., 1972, Kans. Hereford Breeder of Yr., 1976, Portrait Gallery Outstanding Livestock Breeder award Kans. State U. Block and Bridle Club, 1978, Reno County 4-H Family of Yr. award, 1987, Reno County Farm Focus Family award Hutchinson C. of C., 1989, Stockman of Yr. award Kansas Livestock and Meat Industry Coun., 1994; named Kans. Seedstock Producer of Yr. BIF, 1988; Kans Jr. Livestock Show dedicatory, 1991, Master Farmer, Master Farm Homemaker, 1991. Mem. Kans. Wheat Growers Assn., Kans. Farm Bur., Haven Industries, Inc., Kansas City (Kans.) Hereford Club, Kans. State U. Block and Bridle Club (hon. mem.), Haven Booster Club (sec. 1952-53, pres. 1954-56), Future Farmers Am. (mem. adv. com. Haven chpt. 1971—) Lutheran (mem. sch. bd. 1967-70, chmn. 1969-70; chmn. ch. bd. 8 yrs., chmn. congregation 1984-88, elder 1977-79). Home: 14506 S Victory Rd Haven KS 67543-7903

SCHLICKAU, LOIS MARIE, farmer; b. Arlington, Kans., Sept. 18, 1933; d. Otto W. and Maria Edna (Goering) Ritthaler; m. George Hans Schlickau, Apr. 26, 1955; children: Bruce, Susan Russell, James, Nancy Bernard. AA, Hutchinson C.C., 1953. Treas., v.p., pres. Kans. State Bd. Agr., 1986—93, Kans. State Fair Bd., 1986—94; mem. women's exec. com. Kans. Electric Coop., 1991—95, vice chmn. women's exec. com., 1994, 95; vice chmn. Kans. Value Added Ctr. Bd. , 1994—96, v.p., 1994; vice chmn. Kans. Fairs Assn. Bd., 1994—96, v.p., 1996; mem. Cong. Sam Brownback's Agrl. Adv. Bd., 1995—97, Senator Sam Brownback's Agrl. Adv. Bd., 1997—99, Cong. Jerry Moran's Exec. Adv. Bd., 1996—; mem., sec. Reno County Ext. Coun., Reno County Farm Bur., Nat. Cattle Women; mem. internat. agr. project adv. com. Kans. State U., mem. adminstrv. structure task force; mem. Kans. Vocat. Agr. Edn. Task Force. Charter mem., dir., parliamentarian, com. mem., v.p., pres. Am. Hereford Aux. Bd., 1978—83; charter mem., dir., com. mem., v.p., pres. Kans. Hereford Aux. Bd.; project leader Haven 4-H and Lucky H 4-H; past pres. Ladies of Congregation, past Sunday Sch. tchr., choir St. Paul's Luth. Ch.; former parent/tchr. league chmn. St. Paul's Luth. Sch.; local soc. pres. Luth. Women's Missionary League, 1994—96, local soc. sec., 2001—, com. chmn., zone v.p., sec., state bd. mem., v.p., parliamentarian, nat. bylaws com., 1995—99. Mem.: Hutchinson Hosp. Corp. Bd. (chmn. 2002), Kans. Tech. Enterprise (nat. livestock cmmodity chmn., nat. animal welfare com., LEAVEN award com., vice chmn. 1990—91), Reno Co. Hist. Soc. Bd. (dir. 1985—88, nat. conv. com. 1996, dir. 1996—, pres. 1998—2000, past pres. 2000—02, 1st v.p., parliamentarian, nat. legis. rep. 2001—, pres., v.p., sec.), Hutchinson Cmty. Found. Bd. (agri-bus. com., Kans. state fair com.). Avocations: reading, cooking, traveling. Home and Office: 14506 S Victory Rd Haven KS 67543

SCHLIEVE, HY C. J. school administrator; b. Mandan, N.D., Apr. 4, 1952; s. Calvin L. and Loretta L. (Johnson) S.; m. Terri Ann Hansen, Dec. 30, 1977; children: Derek, Aaron, Jessica. BA, N.D. State U., 1974, MS, 1984; EdD, Calif. Coast U., 1994. Tchr., coach Halliday (N.D.) Pub. Sch., 1974-75, Drake (N.D.) Pub. Sch., 1975-76, Montpelier (N.D.) Pub. Sch., 1976-81; prin. Unity Pub. Sch., Petersburg, N.D., 1981-83, Page (N.D.) Pub. Sch., 1983-85; supt. Wolford (N.D.) Pub. Sch., 1985-87, Garrison (N.D.) Pub. Schs., 1987-93; prin. Buhl Joint Sch. Dist. 412, Idaho, 1993-95, Oconto Falls Area Sch. Dist., Wis., 1995-99; supt. Ellendale (N.D.) Pub. Schs. #40, 1999—. Com. mem. NDASA Rsch. and Evaluation, Garrison, 1988-93; fiscal agt. Mo. Hills Consortium, McLean County, N.D., 1989-93; cons. asbestos Garrison Pub. Sch. Dist., 1987-93. Sec. Govtl. Affairs Com., Garrison, 1987-93; mem. Tourism Com., Garrison, 1988-92, Econ. Devel. Com., 1988-89. Recipient Nat. Superintendent of the Yr. awd., North Dakota, Am. Assn. of School Administrators, 1992. Mem. Nat. Assn. Secondary Sch. Prins. (prin. assessor tng. 1990), NSBA Fed. Policy Coords. Network. Avocations: golf, hunting, fishing, bowling, outdoor activities. Office: Ellendale Pub Schs PO Box 400 321 N 1st St Ellendale ND 58436 Home: 91 Prairieview Ellendale ND 58436-7401

SCHLIMME, JOAN MARIE, non-profit organization director; b. Coatesville, Pa., Feb. 5, 1941; d. Frederick Charles and Helen Maude (Thompson) S.; children: Harold Ray Young, Patti Jean Gillen, Kevin John Gillen. Student, Pa. State U., 1960-61, Arapahoe Coll., 1984-85. Sec., bookkeeper Gindy Mfg., Downingtown, Pa., 1958-62; adminstrv. asst. Lasko Metal Products, West Chester, 1962-65; secretarial supr. Roy F. Weston Environ., 1965-68; office mgr. DHR Systems, Paoli, Pa., 1968-71, Sigma Group, Paoli, 1971-75; gen. mgr. Stockton, Inc., Unionville, Pa., 1975-80; advt. coord. Holophane div. Manville, Denver and Newark, Ohio, 1981-87; exec. dir. Am. Trakehner Assn., Newark, 1988—. Editor newsletters, 1987-90; contbr. articles to profl. jours. Big sister Big Brothers, Newark, 1986-88, bd. dirs. 1988. Mem. U.S. Dressage Fedn., Mid-Ohio Dressage Assn., Rocky Fork Headley Hunt. Avocations: equestrian activities, fox collection, fox hunting. Address: 5060 Street Rd Oxford PA 19363-1049

SCHLINGER, WARREN GLEASON, retired chemical engineer; b. Los Angeles, May 29, 1923; s. William McKinley and Esther (Gleason) S.; m. Katharine S. Stewart, June 29, 1947: children: Michael S., Norman W., Sarah Lynne. BS, Calif. Inst. Tech., 1944, MS, 1946, PhD, 1949. Registered profl. engr., Calif. Instr. Calif. Inst. Tech., Pasadena, 1949-53; chem. engr. Texaco Inc., Montebello, Calif., 1953-61, supr. research, 1961-69, mgr., 1969-81, assoc. dir., 1981-87, ret. 1987; cons. 1987—. Contbr. numerous articles to profl. publs. Patentee in field. Fellow Am. Inst. Chem. Engrs. (Chem. Engring. Practice award 1981, So. Calif. sect. Tech. Achievement award 1976; Electric Power Research Inst. Achievement award 1985); mem. NAE, Am. Chem. Soc., Sigma Xi, Tau Beta Pi. Clubs: Jonathan (Los Angeles). Home: 3835 Shadow Grove Rd Pasadena CA 91107-2241

SCHLISKE, ROSALIND ROUTT, journalism educator, journalist; b. Ft. Worth, Jan. 30, 1950; d. Glenn Calvin and Ruth (Warth) Routt; m. Robert P. Schliske, Aug. 14, 1980. BA, Tex. Christian U., 1972; MA, U. Wyo., 1980, postgrad., 1984. Asst. news editor Wyo. Eagle, Cheyenne, 1972-73, news editor, 1973-76; dir. pub. info., prof. journalism Laramie County C.C., Cheyenne, 1976-84, prof. journalism, 1984—. Advisor Wingspan student newspaper, 1976— (Associated Collegiate Press Pacemaker award 1993, 94, 2000). Wyo. Ednl. Trust Fund grantee Wyo. C.C. Commn., 1991-92; recipient Keith L. Ware award U.S. Army, 1988, Excellence in Tchg. award Nat. Inst. Staff and Organal. Devel., Austin, Tex., 1995. Mem. Soc. Profl. Journalists (state pres. 1981-84, Spl. Achievement award 1982), Nat. Fedn. Press Women (prof. devel. com. 1993; various editing awards, Communicator of the Yr. 1998, runner-up Nat. Communicator of Achievement 2000), Women in Comm., Phi Kappa Pi. Democrat. Mem. Christian Ch. (Disciples Of Christ). Avocations: golf, gardening. Home: 5101 Yellowstone Rd Cheyenne WY 82009-4742 Office: Laramie County C C 1400 E College Dr Cheyenne WY 82007-3204 E-mail: schliske@lcc.cc.wy.us.

SCHLITT, WILLIAM JOSEPH, III, metallurgical engineer; b. Columbus, Ohio, June 12, 1942; s. William Joseph Jr. and Florence (McCall) S.; m. Anne Marie Ritchie, Apr. 1, 1994. BSMetE, Carnegie Inst. Tech., 1964; PhD in Metallurgy, Pa. State U., 1968. Registered profl. engr., Tex. Scientist Kennecott Minerals Co., Salt Lake City, 1968-75, sr. scientist, 1975-76, mgr. hydrometallurgy dept., 1977-81, prin. program mgr., 1981-82; process staff mgr. Brown & Root, Inc., Houston, 1982-83, mgr. tech., 1983-93, product line mgr. chems., 1993-94; mgr. process tech. metals engring. and constrn. divsn. Kvaerner, San Ramon, Calif., 1994-99, dir. metallurgy, 1999—. Mem. oversight com. soln. mining NSF, Socoro, N.Mex., 1977-79; mem. oversight com. smelter flue dust Environ. Prot. Agy., Butte, Mont., 1978-79; mem. internat. adv. bd. In Situ jour., N.Y.C., 1988—. Editor: In Situ Uranium Leaching and Ground Water Restoration, 1979, Leaching and Recovering Copper from As-Mined Materials, 1980 (Publ. Bd. Commendation 1981), Gold and Silver--Leaching, Recovery and Economics, 1981, Interfacing Technologies in Solution Mining, 1982 (Publ. Bd. Commendation 1983), Salts and Brines '85, 1985; assoc. editor: (handbook) SME Mining Engineering Handbook, 1992; contbr. more than 45 tech. articles to profl. jours., trade publs., and proc. volumes including Metall. Transactions B (Brit.) Sulphur, AIME Transactions, In Situ, Minerals and Metall. Processing. Pres. Ft. Bend County Kennel Club, Richmond, Tex., 1988-90. Trainee NSF, 1984-88. Mem. Soc. for Mining, Metallurgy & Exploration (bd. dirs. 1984-95, chmn. mining and exploration divsn. 1986-87, Arthur F. Taggart award 1999, Disting. mem. Class 2001), The Metall. Soc. (bd. dirs. 1982-83), Mining & Metallurgical Soc. Am., Can. Inst. Mining and Metallurgy, Sigma Xi, Tau Beta Pi, Phi Kappa Phi. Achievements include patents in field. Avocation: licensed dog show judge. Office: Kvaerner Davy Nonferrous Divsn 12657 Alcosta Blvd Ste 200 San Ramon CA 94583-4433 E-mail: joseph.schlitt@kvaerner.com.

SCHLITTER, STANLEY ALLEN, lawyer; b. Decorah, Iowa, Jan. 27, 1950; s. Joseph Everett and Lillian Helena (Helgerson) S.; m. Sheila Lynn Edwards, Sept. 24, 1977; children: Stephanie Anne, Joseph Allen, John Edward. BS, Iowa State U., 1972; JD, U. Iowa, 1977. Bar: Ill. 1977, U.S. Dist. Ct. (no. dist.) Ill. 1977, U.S. Ct. Appeals (7th cir.) 1981, U.S. Ct. Appeals (Fed. cir.) 1982, D.C. 1989. Assoc. Kirkland & Ellis, Chgo., 1977-84, ptnr., 1984-88, Washington, 1988-91, Jenner & Block, Chgo., 1991—. Mem. ABA, IEEE, Am. Intellectual Property Law Assn. Office: Jenner & Block One IBM Plaza Chicago IL 60611-3608

SCHLOEMANN, ERNST FRITZ (RUDOLF AUGUST), physicist, engineer; b. Borgholzhausen, Germany, Dec. 13, 1926; came to U.S., 1954, naturalized, 1965; s. Hermann Wilhelm and Auguste Wilhelmine (Koch) S.; m. Gisela Mattiat, June 19, 1955 (dec. 1990); children: Susan C., Sonia G., Barbara I.; m. Sally (Duren) Heafter, Nov. 5, 1994. BS, U. Göttingen, Fed. Republic of Germany, 1951, MS, 1953, PhD, 1954. With rsch. div. Raytheon Co., Lexington, Mass., 1955-94, electronics sys. divsn., 1994-95; ind. cons. Weston, 1995—. Cons. scientist, 1964-95; vis. assoc. prof. Stanford U., 1961-62; vis. prof. U. Hamburg, Germany, 1966. Assoc. editor: Jour. Applied Physics, 1974-76; contbr. numerous articles to profl. jours. Recipient T.L. Phillips award for Excellence in Tech., 1990. Fellow IEEE, Am. Phys. Soc., Sigma Xi. Democrat. Unitarian Universalist. Achievements include patents in field of magnetic materials and their application to microwave technology. Home and Office: 38 Brook Rd Weston MA 02493-1713 E-mail: schloemann@alum.mit.edu.

SCHLOERB, PAUL RICHARD, surgeon, educator; b. Buffalo, Oct. 22, 1919; s. Herman George and Vera (Gross) S.; m. Louise M. Grimmer, Feb. 25, 1950; children: Ronald G., Patricia S. Johnson, Marilyn A. Hock, Dorothy S. Hoban, P. Richard. AB, Harvard U., 1941; MD, U. Rochester, 1944. Intern U. Rochester Med. Sch., 1944-45, asst. resident, 1947-48, instr. surgery, 1952; rsch. fellow, resident Peter Bent Brigham Hosp., Boston, 1948-52; faculty U. Kans. Med. Ctr., Kansas City, 1952-79, prof. surgery, 1964-79, 88—, dean for rsch., 1972-79, dir. nutritional support svc., 1993—; prof. surgery U. Rochester (N.Y.) Med Ctr., 1979-88, adj. prof. surgery, 1988-90; surgeon Strong Meml. Hosp., 1979-88, dir. Surg. ICU, 1979-85, dir. surg. nutritional support service. Contbr. over 100 articles to profl. jours. Lt. (j.g.), M.C. USNR, 1944-45; to lt. 1953-55. Mem. AMA, ACS, AAAS, Am. Surg. Assn., Soc. U. Surgeons, Am. Physiol. Soc., Internat. Soc. Surgery, Ctrl. Surg. Assn., Am. Assn. for Surgery of Trauma, Am. Assn. Cancer Rsch., Biomed. Engring. Soc., Am. Inst. Nutrition, Am. Soc. Clin. Nutrition, Sigma Xi. Office: Dept Surgery U Kansas Med Ctr Kansas City KS 66160-0001

SCHLOESSLIN, MARK EDWARD, software quality engineer; b. Pitts., Apr. 2, 1955; s. Milton E. and Helen J. (Dugan) S. BS in Computer Sci., U. Pitts., 1978; MS in Computer Sci., U. Denver, 1995. Programmer/analyst NCR Corp., Dayton, Ohio, 1979-84; system safety engineer Martin Marietta, Denver, 1984-92, software quality engr. Colorado Springs, Colo., 1992-94, Lockheed Martin Denver Co., 1994—. Republican. Roman Catholic. Avocations: flying, guitar, swimming, aerobics.

SCHLOSBERG, THEODORE K. music educator; b. New Brunswick, N.J., Sept. 1, 1936; s. Ralph Schlosberg and Renee Aronson Schlosberg Sosin; m. Kathryn Sell Levine, Sept. 25, 1982; children: Lindsey Levine, Stephanie Levine Harvey; m. Natalie Berkowski, Aug. 14, 1959 (div. Feb. 1982); children: Susan Schlosberg McWilliams, Gail Schlosberg Sokoloff. BA in Music Edn., MusM, Trenton State Coll.; EdD in Creative Arts, Rutgers U. Music tchr. Plainfield Pub. Schs., 1960—67, Westfield Pub. Schs., 1967—96; founder, exec. dir. N.J. Workshop for Arts, 1972—. Dir. fine arts Lanark Camp, Maine, 1960—63; dir. Plainfield Sch. Music, 1960—68; dir. Plainfield Summer Music Workshop, 1964—67, Summer Music Workshop, Plainfield, 1964—67, Plainfield, 1997—, Workshop for Arts, Greenbrook, NJ, 1995, Recreation Dept. Music Workshops, Fanwood, NJ, 1995, Saturday Music Workshop, Plainfield, 1999—, Westfield Cmty. Ctr. Sr. Citizens Music Workshop, 2002. Recipient Faith in Westield award, Westfield C. of C., 1991, 2001, numerous grants. Home: 26 Scudder Rd Westfield NJ 07090 Office: NJ Workshop for Arts Inc 150-152 E Broad St Westfield NJ 07090

SCHLOSE, WILLIAM TIMOTHY, health care executive; b. West Lafayette, Ind., May 16, 1948; s. William Fredrick and Dora Irene (Chitwood) S.; m. Linda Lee Fletcher, June 29, 1968 (div. 1978); children: Vanessa Janine Schlose Hubert, Stephanie Lynn; m. Kelly Marie Martin, June 6, 1987; 1 child, Taylor Jean Martin-Schlose. Student, Bowling Green State U., 1966-68, Long Beach City Coll., 1972-75. Cert. tchr., Calif. Staff respiratory therapist St. Vincent's Med. Ctr., L.A., 1972-75; cardio-pulmonary chief Temple Cmty. Hosp., 1975-76; adminstrv. dir. spl. svcs. Santa Fe Meml. Hosp., 1976-79; mktg. and pub. rels. staff Nat. Med. Homecare Corp., Orange, Calif., 1979-81, Medtech of Calif., Inc., Burbank, 1981-84; regional mgr. Mediq Health Care Group Svcs., Inc., Chatsworth, 1984-88; pres. Baby Watch Homecare, Whittier, 1988-90, Tim Schlose and Assocs., Brea, 1990—. Staff instr., Montebello (Calif.) Adult Schs.; v.p. Naptime Diagnostics, Brea, 1990—. Author: Fundamental Respiratory Therapy Equipment, 1977; mem. editl. bd. RT, The Jour. Respiratory Car Practitioners, 1997—. With USN, 1968-72. Mem. Am. Assn. Respiratory Care, Calif. Soc. Respiratory Care (past officer), Nat. Bd. Respiratory Care, Nat. Assn. Apnea Profls., Am. Assn. Physicians Assts., L.A. Pediatric Soc., Calif. Perinatal Assn., Saleen Owners Enthusiasts Club, SVT Cobra Owner's Club So. Calif., Mustang Club Am., Saleen Mustang Owners Group (founder), SVTOA (charter dir. Calif. chpt.), Spl. Vehicle Team Owners Assn. (founder So. Calif. chpt.). Republican. Methodist. Avocations: boating, automobile racing, automobile restoration, wrist watch collecting, fly fishing. Office: Tim Schlose Assocs 747 S Brea Blvd Ste 36 Brea CA 92821-5379

SCHLOSS, CLAUDIA Z. investment executive; b. Geneva, Switzerland, Sept. 3, 1968; m. Patrick M. Schloss. BS Bus. Adminstrn., U. So. Calif., 1991. CFA. Dir. of fin. Cizeta Automobili USA, Inc. , L.A. , Calif., 1990—92; v.p. - equities Yaeger Capital Markets, 1992—96; assoc. v.p. - instl. sales Investment Advisers, Inc, Mpls., 1996—98; v.p. - dir. instl. mktg. Merrill Lynch Investment Mgrs., Los Angeles, Calif., 1996—2001; mktg. exec. Western Asset Mgmt., Pasadena, 2001—. Mem. Assn. For Investment Mgmt. & Rsch. , Charlottesville, Va., 1997—, L.A. Soc. of Fin. Analysts, L.A. , Calif., 1997—; program com. bd. mem. State Assn. of County Retirement Systems (CA), Sacramento, 1998—. Foster parent ChildReach, Worldwide, 1998. Mem.: L.A. Soc. Fin. Analysts, Assn. Investment Mgmt. and Rsch. Avocations: equestrian competition, travel, languages. E-mail: cschloss@westernasset.com.*

SCHLOSS, IRVING STEVEN, lawyer; b. N.Y.C., Feb. 3, 1945; s. Arthur and Bianca (Steinberger) S.; m. Christine Skeeles, June 28, 1970 (div. Mar. 1999); children: Tracy, David; m. Deborah V. Abildsoe, Nov. 21, 1999. AB magna cum laude, Harvard Coll., 1966; LLB, Yale U., 1970. Bar: Conn. 1972, U.S. Dist. Ct. Conn. 1972, U.S. Ct. Appeals (2d cir.) 1973, U.S. Tax Ct. 1985. Law clerk for Judge Spottswood Robinson, III (D.C. cir.) U.S. Ct. Appeals, Washington, 1970-71; ptnr. Tyler, Cooper & Alcorn, LLP, New Haven and Madison, 1976—. Co-author: Understanding TIAA-CREF: Planning for a Secure and Comfortable Retirement, 2000; bd. editors Tax Mgmt. Estates, Gift & Trust Jour.; contbr. articles to profl. jours. Bd. dirs. Guilford (Conn.) Free

Libr., 1986-92, Shoreline Found., Guilford, 1984-93, 97—, New Haven Symphony Orch., 1995-2001; vol. CPTV Auction, West Hartford, 1987-88; mem. Rep. Town Commn., Guilford, 1987-91. Recipient Man of Yr. award Guilford YMCA, 1990. Mem. ABA, Conn. Bar Assn. (chmn. sect. corps. and other bus. orgns. 1988-90, mem. exec. com. estates and probate sect. 1996—), Am. Coll. Trust and Estate Counsel, New Haven Conn. Bar Assn., Mory's Assn., Quinnipiack Club. Office: Tyler Cooper & Alcorn PO Box 1936 New Haven CT 06509-0906 E-mail: ischlos@attglobal.net., schloss@tylercooper.com.

SCHLOSS, NATHAN, retired economist; b. Balt., Jan. 14, 1927; s. Howard L. and Louise (Levi) S.; m. Rosa Montalyo, Mar. 1, 1958; children: Nina L., Carolyn D. BS in Bus., Johns Hopkins U., 1950. Buyer Pacific Coast gen. merchandise office Sears Roebuck & Co., Los Angeles, 1955-60; staff asst. econ. rsch. dept. Chgo., 1960-63; sr. market analyst corp. rsch. dept. Montgomery Ward & Co., 1963-65; rsch. mgr. real estate dept. Walgreen Co., 1970-72; v.p. rsch. and planning Maron Properties Ltd., Montreal, Que., Can., 1972-74; corp. economist, fin. analyst Real Estate Rsch. Corp., Chgo., 1974-88, sr. v.p., 1986-88, treas., chief fin. analyst, 1982-88; economist Office of Ill. Atty. Gen., 1988-97. Cons. in field, 1965-97. Contbr. articles on fin. and market analysis of real estate to profl. jours. Mem. Plan. Commn., village of Wilmette, Ill., 1975-77, tech. adv. com. on employment and tng. data Ill. employment and Tng. Coun., 1979-82, tech. adv. com. Ill. Job Tng. Coordinating Council, 1983-87; mem. com. on price indexes and productivity fgn. labor Bus. Rsch. Adv. Coun. of Bur. Labor Stats, Dept. Labor, 1979-88, chairperson, 1985-86, com. on employment and unemployment. Recipient Commendable Svc. Citation, Bur. Labor Stats., Dept. Labor, 1987. Mem. Am. Mktg. Assn., Nat. Assn. Bus. Economists, Ill. Econ. Assn., Lambda Alpha. Home and Office: 115 Hollywood Ct Wilmette IL 60091-3122

SCHLOSS, SAMUEL LEOPOLD, JR. retired food service executive, consultant; b. Montgomery, Ala., Mar. 30, 1926; s. Samuel Leopold and Amelia (Strauss) S.; m. Burke Hart Klein; children: Stephen, Alyce, Adam. BS in Indsl. Engring., Ga. Inst. Tech., 1947; MS in Indsl. Engring., Columbia U., 1948. Sec. Schloss and Kahn Inc., Montgomery, 1948-56, pres., 1956-86, chmn., 1986-94. Pres. Montgomery Acad., 1979-80, bd. dirs. emeritus, 1982; control bd. Montgomery Com. of One Hundred, 1984-86; bd. dirs. YMCA Metro Bd., Ctrl. Ala. Red Cross, 1996; chmn. 1997-99; past chmn. Montgomery chpt. Ala. Soc. Crippled Children and Adults. Capt. USAFR, 1960. Mem. Montgomery C. of C. (pres. 1983), Standard Club (pres. 1964), Capital City Club (bd. govs. 1977-80), Rotary (pres. 1972-73), Montgomery Country Club. Republican. Office: Religions Tower 60 Commerce St Ste 1210 Montgomery AL 36104-3562

SCHLOSSBERG, FRED PAUL, elementary education educator; b. N.Y.C., May 30, 1944; s. Alexander and Mae S.; divorced; 1 child, Elan. BSBA, Boston U., 1966; M of Phys. Edn., NYU, 1983. Tchr. elem. sch. N.Y.C. Bd. Edn., 1966—. Coach local basketball team, North Bellmore, N.Y., 1988—, local baseball team, North Bellmore, 1988-92. Vol. Alcoholics Anonymous, West Hempstead, N.Y., 1987-93; tutor Literacy Vols. Am. Democrat. Avocations: physical fitness, dealer of sports and non-sports cards, comic books and memorabilia, music, travel. Home: 3678 Ocean Ave Seaford NY 11783-3432

SCHLOSSBERG, JULIAN MAXIM, film producer, director, distributor; b. N.Y.C., Jan. 26, 1942; s. Louis and Charlotte (Bash) S. BA with honors, N.Y.U., 1964. Acct. exec. ABC, N.Y.C., 1964-66; v.p. theater div. Walter Reade Orgn., 1966-76; v.p. production. Paramount Pictures, 1976-77; pres. Castle Hill Prodns., 1978—. Rep. for Elia Kazan; producer's rep. for Dustin Hoffman, Elaine May, George C. Scott, and Robert Duvall; lectured in People's Republic China on the Motion Picture Ind., 1985; host syndicated radio program Julian Schlossberg's Movie Talk, 1974-80, also TV syndication 1982-83; pres. Quartet Films, Inc., 1984—; co-owner Gold Castle Records, Inc. Produced: (film) Hollywood Ghost Stories, 1985, Hollywood Uncensored, 1986, Going Hollywood: The War Years, Bad Girls, 1994, Widow's Peak, 1995; (Broadway theater) Nichols & May at the Rainbow Room, 1983, Mr. Gogol and Mr. Preen, 1991, Vita and Virginia, 1994, Death Defying Acts, 1995, Moscow Stations, 1995, Below the Belt, 1996, Cakewalk, 1996; (TV) Steve Allen's Golden Age of Comedy, 1987, All the Best, Steve Allen, 1987, Sex and Justice: the Anita Hill and Clarence Thomas Hearings, Slapstick Too, Eliz Kazan: A Director's Journey, Nichols and May: Take Two; Co-produced: (films) Ten From Your Show of Shows, 1973, Going Hollywood: The Thirties, 1983, In the Spirit, 1990; (theater) It Had to be You, 1981; co-producer, co-director: (film) No Nukes, 1980; (films) re-released The John Cassavetes Collections: A Woman Under of the Influence, Faces, The Killing of a Chinese Bookie, Shadows, 1991. Served with US Army, 1962. Mem. Am. Fedn. Television and Radio Artists. Clubs: Variety. Jewish. Office: Castle Hill Prodns 1414 Ave Of The Americas New York NY 10019-2514

SCHLOSSER, HERBERT S. broadcasting company executive; b. Atlantic City, Apr. 21, 1926; s. Abraham and Anna (Olesker) S.; m. Judith P. Gassner, July 8, 1951; children: Lynn C., Eric M. AB summa cum laude, Princeton, 1948; LL.B., Yale, 1951. Bar: N.Y. 1952. Assoc. firm Wickes, Riddell, Bloomer, Jacobi & McGuire, N.Y.C., 1951-54, Phillips, Nizer, Benjamin, Krim & Ballon, N.Y.C., 1954-57; with NBC, 1957-78; v.p., gen. mgr. Calif. Nat. Prodns., Inc. sub. NBC, 1960-61, dir. talent and program adminstrn., 1961-62, v.p. talent and program adminstrn., 1962-66; v.p. programs West Coast NBC, 1966-72; exec. v.p. NBC-TV Network, 1972-73, pres., 1973-74, mem. bd. dirs., 1973-78; pres. NBC, Inc., 1974-78, CEO, 1977-78; exec. v.p. RCA, 1978-85; sr. advisor broadcasting and entertainment Schroder & Co., Inc., N.Y.C., 1986—; sr. advisor, ind. cons. Salomon Smith Barney Inc. Pres. RCA cable sub. RCA, RCA Internat. Audio Visuals, Inc.; ptnr. Arts and Entertainment Cable Network, RCA/Columbia Home Video; bd. dirs. Ctrl. European Media Enterprises, Ltd., Data Broadcasting Corp., U.S. Satellite Broadcasting Co., Inc. Trustee Internat. Radio and TV Found., 1972-74; former mem. govs. Ford's Theatre Soc.; former trustee Nat. Urban League; chmn. bd. Am. Mus. of the Moving Image. With USNR, 1944-46. Recipient Humanitarian award NCCJ, 1974, Gold Brotherhood award, 1978 Mem. Assn. of Bar of City of N.Y., Am., N.Y. State bar assns., Council on Fgn. Relations, Acad. TV Arts and Scis., Advt. Council (past dir.), Yale Law Sch. Assn., Internat. Radio and TV Soc. (trustee 1973-74), Hollywood Radio and TV Soc. (trustee 1970-72), Phi Beta Kappa (pres. alumni assn. So. Calif. 1970-72, mem. Phi Beta Kappa assocs.). Clubs: Princeton (N.Y.). Office: Global Media and Entertainment 388 Greenwich St New York NY 10013-2375

SCHLOSSMAN, BERYL FERN, literature educator, writer; b. N.Y.C. d. Irwin Stanley and Linette (Kerzner) S. BA, Cornell U., 1976; postgrad., U. Paris VII, 1981; PhD, Johns Hopkins U., 1987. Mellon fellow U. Va., Charlottesville, 1988-90; asst. prof. Emory U., Atlanta, 1987-93; assoc. prof. Carnegie Mellon U., Pitts., 1993-2000, prof., 2000—. Author: The Orient of Style, 1991, Joyce's Catholic Comedy of Language, 1985, Angelus Novus, 1995, Objects of Desire: The Madonnas of Modernism, 1999; contbr. Fulbright scholar, 1998; Charlotte Newcombe fellow Wilson Found., 1985-86, ACLS fellow, 2001.

SCHLOSSMAN, JOHN ISAAC, architect; b. Chgo., Aug. 21, 1931; s. Norman Joseph and Carol (Rosenfeld) S.; m. Shirley Goulding Rhodes, Feb. 8, 1959; children: Marc N., Gail S. Mewhort, Peter C. Student, Grinnell Coll., 1949-50; BA, U. Minn., 1953, BArch, 1955; MArch, MIT, 1956. Registered architect, Ill. Archtl. designer The Architects Collaborative, Cambridge, Mass., 1956-57; architect Loebl Schlossman & Hackl and predecessors, Chgo., 1959-65, assoc., 1965-70, prin., 1970-98, cons. prin., 1998—. Bd. overseers Coll. Arch. Illinois Inst. Tech., Chgo.; founding bd. dirs. Chgo. Archtl. Assistance Ctr., 1974-79 Chmn. Glencoe Plan Commn., Ill., 1977-82; trustee Com. for Green Bay Trail, Glencoe, 1970-77, Chgo. Arch. Found., 1971-75, Graham Found. for Advanced Studies in Fine Arts, 1995-99, pres. 1999-2001; bd. dirs. Merit Music Program, Chgo., 1983-93, pres., 1988-90, hon. trustee 1996; governing mem. Chgo. Symphony Orch.; mem. founders coun. Field Mus., Chgo.; mem. zoning & planning com. Greater North Mich. Ave. Assn., Chgo., 2000-01; mem. Nat. Trust Coun., Nat. Trust for Hist. Preservation, Washington. Named dir. for life Young Men's Jewish Council, Chgo., 1971; Rotch travelling scholar, 1957; sustaining fellow Art Inst. Chgo. Fellow AIA (trustee ins. trust 1971-76, chmn. ins. com. 1974-75, v.p. Chgo. chpt. 1975, chmn. architects liability com. 1976, 80-82, hon. found. trustee 1995—), Archtl. Soc. of Art Inst. Chgo., Tavern Club (gov. 1986-88, v.p. 1990), The Club at Symphony Ctr., The Arts Club, Alpha Rho Chi, Office: Loebl Schlossman & Hackl 232 Mary St Winnetka IL 60093-1522

SCHLOSSMAN, MARK LOREN, physicist, physics educator; b. N.Y.C., Nov. 4, 1958; s. Irwin S. and Linette Schlossman; m. Binhua Lin, 1 daughter, Elizabeth Lin. Diploma, MIT, 1980; PhD, Cornell U., 1987. Post-doctoral fellow Harvard U., Boston, 1987-90; rsch. scientist U. Chgo., Chgo., 1990-94; assoc. prof. U. Ill., 1994—. Contbr. numerous articles to profl. jours. Mem. Am. Phys. Soc. Achievements include research in interfacial phenomena in soft condensed matter. Office: U Ill Dept Physics 845 W Taylor St Rm 2236 Chicago IL 60607-7056

SCHLOSSMAN, MITCHELL LLOYD, cosmetics and chemical specialties executive; b. N.Y.C., Dec. 30, 1935; s. Jack Lewis and Rae (Wernick) S.; m. Barbara Nadell, Dec. 24, 1956; childrn: David Scott, Edye Gail, Julie Ilene. BS, NYU, 1956; postgrad., Bklyn. Coll., 1956-59. Group leader Revlon, Inc., Bronx, N.Y., 1957-64; mgr. research and devel. Pfizer, Inc., Parsippany, N.J., 1964-69; dir. tech. ops. Paris Cosmetics, Inc., Jersey City, 1969-70; exec. v.p. Prince Industries Ltd., Linden, N.J., 1970-74; v.p. Emery Personal Products, 1974-78; pres. Tevco, Inc., South Plainfield, N.J., 1978-94, Presperse, Inc., South Plainfield, 1985—, also bd. dirs. Cons. Hibernia (N.J.) Labs., 1985—, Kobo Products, Inc., South Plainfiel Co-author: Chemical Manufacture of Cosmetics, 1974; contbr. articles to profl. and trade jours; patentee in field. Fellow Soc. Cosmetic Chemists (merit award 1971, chmn. N.Y. chpt. 1982—, bd. dirs. Eastern sect.), Am. Inst. Chemists; mem. Cosmetics, Toiletries, Fragrance Assn. (chmn. sci. program planning com. 1982—). Lodges: KP. Republican. Jewish. Home: 164 Dezenzo Ln West Orange NJ 07052-4127 Office: Kobo Products Inc 690 Montrose Ave South Plainfield NJ 07080-2602

SCHLOSSMAN, STUART FRANKLIN, physician, educator, researcher; b. N.Y.C., N.Y., Apr. 18, 1935; s. Abe and Pearl (Susser) Schlossman; m. Judith Seryl Rubin, May 25, 1958; children: Robert, Peter. BA magna cum laude, NYU, 1955, MD, 1958; MA, Harvard U., 1975. Intern in medicine med. divsn. III Bellevue Hosp., N.Y.C., 1958—59, asst. resident in medicine med. divsn. III, 1959—60; Nat. Found. fellow dept. microbiology Coll. Physicians Columbia U., 1960—62; asst. physician med. svc. Vanderbilt Clinic, Coll. Physician USPHS, Washington, 1960—62; Ward hematology fellow dept. internal medicine Sch. Washington U., St. Louis, 1962—63; rsch. assoc. lab. biochemistry Nat. Cancer Inst. USPHS, Washington, 1963—65; clin. instr. in medicine Sch. of Medicine George Washington U., 1964—65; assoc. in medicine, dir. blood bank Beth Israel Hosp., Boston, 1965—66; instr. Med. Sch. Harvard U., 1966—68, asst. physician, 1967—68, chief clin. immunology, 1971—73; physician Beth Israel Hosp., 1968—; from asst. to assoc. prof. medicine Harvard Med. Sch., 1968—77, prof., 1977—, Baruj Benacerraf prof. medicine, 1990—, chief divsn. tumor immunology and immunotherapy, 1973—; sr. physician Brigham and Women's Hosp., 1976—. Mem. editl. bd. Jour. of Immunology, 1969—74, Cellular Immunology, 1970—, Human Immunology, 1979—84, Clin. Immunology and Immunopathology, 1979—, mem. editl. bd.Hybridoma Hybridoma, 1980—, Cancer Investigation, 1981—, Stem Cells, 1981—, Cancer Revs., 1984, Internat. Jour. of Cell Cloning, 1983—86, mem. adv. bd. Cancer Treatment Reports, 1976—80, assoc. editor Human Lymphocyte Differentation, 1980—82; contbr. Recipient Solomon Berson Achievement award, 1984, Robert Koch prize and medal, 1984. Fellow: AAAS; mem.: Assn. Am. Physicians, Am. Soc. Clin. Investigation, Am. Soc. Immunologists, Am. Soc. Hematology, Inst. of Medicine of NAS, Alpha Omega Alpha. Office: Dana-Farber Cancer Inst Divsn Tumor Immunology 44 Binney St Mayer 557 Boston MA 02115-6084

SCHLOTFELDT, ROZELLA MAY, nursing educator, educator; b. DeWitt, Iowa, June 29, 1914; d. John W. and Clara C. (Doering) Schlotfeldt. BS, State U. Iowa, 1935; MS, U. Chgo., 1947, PhD, 1956; DSc (hon.), Georgetown U., 1972, Adelphi U., 1979, Wayne State U., 1983, U. Ill., Chgo., 1985, Kent State U., 1987, U. Cin., 1989, Case Western Res. U., 1996; LHD (hon.), Med. U. S.C., 1976. Staff nurse State U. Iowa, VA Hosp., 1935—39; instr., supr. maternity nursing (State U. Iowa), 1939—44; asst. prof. U. Colo. Sch. Nursing, 1947—48; asst., then asso. prof. Wayne State U. Coll. Nursing, 1948—55; prof., asso. dean Wayne State U. Coll. Nursing (Coll. Nursing), 1957—60; dean Frances Payne Bolton Sch. Nursing, Case Western Res. U., 1960-72, prof., 1960—82, prof., dean emeritus, 1982—95. Vis. prof. Rutgers U., 1984—89, 1990—95, U. Pa., 1985—86; spl. cons. Surgeon Gen.'s Adv. Group on Nursing, 1961—63; mem. nursing rsch. study sect. USPHS, 1962—66; mem. com. on nursing edn. facilities Nat. League for Nursing-USPHS, 1962—64; mem. com. on health goals Cleve. Health Coun., 1961—66; mem. Cleve. Health Planning and Devel. Commn., 1969—72; adv. com. divsn. nursing W.K. Kellogg Found., 1959—67; v.p. Ohio Bd. Nursing Edn. and Nurse Registration, 1970—71, pres., 1971—72; mem. Nat. Health Svcs. Rsch. Tng. Com., 1970—71; mem. supply and edn. panel Health Manpower Com., 1966—67; rev. com. Nurse Tng. Act, 1967—68; bd. visitors Duke U. Med. Ctr., 1968—70; mem. coun., exec. com. Inst. Medicine of NAS, 1971—75; mem. nat. adv. health svcs. coun. Health Svcs. and Mental Health Adminstrn., 1971—75; mem. def. adv. com. on women in svcs. Dept. of Def., 1972—75; bd. dirs., treas. Nursing Home Adv. and Rsch. Coun., 1975—96; mem. adv. panel Health Svcs. Rsch. Commn. on Human Resources, NAS, 1977—85; cons. Walter Reed Army Inst.; adv. coun. on nursing U.S. VA, 1965—69, chmn., 1966—69; mem. Yale U. Coun. Com. on Med. Affairs, 1981—86; mem. adv. bd. Scholarly Inquiry for Nursing Practice, 1987—96. Mem. editl. bd. Advances in Nursing Sci., Inquiry, 1982—85, Jour. Nursing Edn., 1982—91; contbr. articles. Bd. visitors Syracuse U., 1990—97. 1st lt. Nurse Corps U.S. Army, 1944—46. Named Living Legend, Am. Acad. Nursing, 1995; recipient Disting. Svc. award, U. Iowa, 1973, Case Western Res. U., 1991, N. Watts Lifetime Achievement award, 1995. Fellow: Nat. League Nursing, Am. Acad. Nursing (v.p. 1975—77); mem.: ANA (chmn. commn. on nurse edn. 1967—70, mem. com. for studying credentialling 1976—79, adv. com. W.K. Kellogg Nat. Fellowship program 1981—85), Sigma Theta Tau (nat. v.p. 1948—50, selection com., disting. lectr. program 1986—87, Founders award for creativity 1985, Henderson fellow 1985), Pi Lambda Theta. Home: Judson Manor 1089 E 107th St Cleveland OH 44106

SCHLOTTERBECK, WALTER ALBERT, manufacturing company executive, lawyer; b. N.Y.C., Dec. 22, 1926; s. Albert Gottlob and Maria Louise (Fritz) S.; m. Pauline Elizabeth Hoerz, Sept. 2, 1951; children— Susan, Thomas, Paul. AB, Columbia U., 1949, LL.B., 1952. Bar: N.Y. 1953. Counsel Gen. Electric Co. (various locations), 1952-87; v.p., corp. counsel Gen. Electric Co., N.Y.C., 1970-77, sec., 1975-76; gen. counsel Gen. Electric Co. (various locations), 1976-87, sr. v.p., 1977-87. Served with USNR, 1944-46. Home: 201 Overlake Dr E Medina WA 98039-5331

SCHLOTZHAUER, VIRGINIA HUGHES, parliamentary consultant; b. Washington , July 24, 1913; d. William and Secy Alice (Royston) Hughes; m. Elbert O. Schlotzhauer, May 16, 1936; children: Carol Schlotzhauer Hinds, Jean Schlotzhauer Sumner, Jude Schlotzhauer Wilson. AB in LS, George Washington U., 1934. Mem. libr. staff George Washington U., Washington, 1934; various clerical positions U.S. Govt., ARC, Washington, Phoenix, mid-1930s; cons. parliamentarian Washington, 1967—. Cons. Nat. Parliamentarian Edn. Project for Colls. and Univs. sponsored by Am. Inst. Parliamentarians funded by William Randolph Hearst Found., 1993-95; presenter seminars. Author: A Parliamentarian's Book of Limericks, 1984; (with others) Parliamentary Opinions, 1982, Parliamentary Opinions II, 1992; primary contbr./cons. column Parliamentary Jour.; contbr. articles to profl. publs. Mem. steering and bylaws coms., sec. Nominating Conv. for Endorsement of Candidates for Bd. Edn., Montgomery County, Md., 1966; election reporter ABC-LWV, Prince George's County, Md., 1970s; v.p., bylaws com. Planned Parenthood Am., Prince George's County, late 1960s and 70s; group leader, bd. dirs., sec., trustee Potomac Area coun. Camp Fire Girls, Md. and D.C. area, 1940s and 50s; participant nonpartisan and Dem. polit. campaigns; judge various contests Future Bus. Leaders Am., Washington, 1970s. Co-recipient (parliamentary book in Spanish) Las Asociaciones y Normas Procesales para sus Asambleas Deliberativas by Lcda Dominga Rivera-Rivera dedicated in her honor, 1996. Mem. AAUW (life, named gift Bethesda-Chevy Chase br. 1962, named gift Md. divsn. 1972), Am. Inst. Parliamentarians (cert. profl. parliamentarian, mem. adv. coun. or bd. dirs. 1966—, pres. D.C. chpt. 1966-68, opinions com. 1974-01, chmn. 1974-89, cons., name changed to Virginia Schlotzhauer D.C. chpt. 1984), Nat. Assn. Parliamentarians (ret. profl. registered parliamentarian), D.C. Assn. Parliamentarians (founding pres., 1st hon. pres., Achievement award 1976), Westerners. Avocations: travel, writing, poetry, gardening, Spanish language and culture. Home and Office: 9819 Indian Queen Point Rd Fort Washington MD 20744-6904

SCHLOZMAN, STEVEN C. psychiatrist; b. Kansas City, Kans., May 23, 1966; B of Arts and Scis., Stanford U., 1988; MD, Brown U., 1994. Staff child psychiatrist Mass. Gen. Hosp., Boston, 2000—; pvt. practice Cambridge, 2000—; lectr. edn. Harvard Grad. Sch. Edn., 1999—. Office: Mass Gen Hosp WACC-725 15 Parkman St Boston MA 02114 Office Fax: 617-726-7541. Business E-Mail: sschlozman@partners.org.

SCHLUETER, DAVID ARNOLD, law educator; b. Sioux City, Iowa, Apr. 29, 1946; s. Arnold E. and Helen A. (Dettmann) S.; m. Linda L. Boston, Apr. 22, 1972; children: Jennifer, Jonathan. BA, Tex. A&M U., 1969; JD, Baylor U., 1971; LLM, U. Va., 1981. Bar: Tex. 1971, Dec. 1973, U.S. Ct. Mil. Appeals 1972, U.S. Supreme Ct. 1976. Legal counsel U.S. Supreme Ct., Washington, 1981-83; assoc. dean St. Mary's U., San Antonio, 1984-89, prof. law, 1986—, Hardy prof. trial advocy, dir. trial advocacy, 2000—; reporter Fed. Adv. Com. on Criminal Rules, 1988—. Chmn. JAG adv. coun., 1974-75. Author: Military Criminal Justice: Practice and Procedure, 1982, 5th edit., 1999; (with others) Military Rules of Evidence Manual, 1981, 4th edit., 1997, Texas Rules of Evidence Manual, 1983, 6th edit., 2002, Texas Evidentiary Foundations, 1992, 2d edit., 1998, Military Evidentiary Foundations, 1994, 2d edit., 2000, Military Criminal Procedure Forms, 1997, Federal Evidence Tactics, 1997, Texas Rules of Evidence Trial Book, 2000; editor-in-chief: Emerging Problems Under the Federal Rules of Evidence, 3d edit., 1998; contbr. articles to legal publs. Maj. JAGC, U.S. Army, 1972-81. Fellow Am. Law Inst., Tex. Bar Found. (life), Am. Bar Found. (life); mem. ABA (vice-chmn. criminal justice sect. coun. 1991-94, vice-chmn. com. on criminal justice and mil. 1983-84, chmn. standing com. on mil. law 1991-92, mem. standing com. on armed forces law, chmn. editl. adv. bd., Criminal Justice Mag., 1989-91, 2000-), Tex. Bar Assn. Republican. Lutheran. Office: St Marys U Sch Law 1 Camino Santa Maria St San Antonio TX 78228-8500

SCHLUETER, ERIKA MANRIQUEZ, civil engineer, research scientist; b. Santiago, Chile; came to U.S., 1980; d. Javier Bustos Manriquez and Constantina Vilos Anso; m. Ross Donald Schlueter, May, 1981; children: Dietrich, Kurt. B of Civil Constrn., Cath. U., Santiago, 1980; postgrad., MIT, 1980-81, San Jose State U., 1983; MS in Civil Engring., U. Wash., 1986; PhD in Engring. Sci., U. Calif., Berkeley, 1995. Instr. continuing edn. Cath. U., Santiago, 1975-77, tchg. asst., 1976-77; hydrogeologist Celzac Co., 1978; med. asst. Stanford (Calif.) U. Med. Ctr., 1981, fin. aids analyst, 1981-82; homemaker Pleasanton, 1986-88; rsch. asst. Lawrence Berkeley Nat. Lab. U. Calif., Berkeley, 1988-95; rsch. scientist Lawrence Berkeley Nat. Lab. U. Calif., 1995—. Contbr. numerous articles to profl. jours. Fulbright fellow, 1980-81, Jane Lewis fellow, 1990-91. Mem. ASCE, Soc. Petroleum Engrs., Am. Geophys. Union, Soc. Exploration Geophysicists (Award of Merit 1994-95). Republican. Roman Catholic. Home: 780 Cragmont Ave Berkeley CA 94708-1345 Office: Lawrence Berkeley Nat Lab MS 44B 1 Cyclotron Rd Berkeley CA 94720-0001 E-mail: mag00net@ix.netcom.com.

SCHLUETER, JAMES WILLIAM, lawyer; b. Cin., June 5, 1947; s. Franklin Charles and Kathryn Elizabeth (Moore) S.; m. Diane Marilynn Vickery Schlueter, Apr. 7, 1977. BA, U. Cin., 1970; JD, Chase Coll. Law, Ky., 1974. Bar: Ohio 1974, U.S. Dist. Ct. (so. dist.) 1974, U.S. Supreme Ct. 1978. Ct. constable Common Pleas Ct. Hamilton County, Cin., 1970-74; atty. pvt. practice, 1975-93, West Union, Ohio, 1993—; magistrate Common Pleas Ct. Adams County, 1996—. Contbr. articles to profl. jours. Mem. Adams County Bar Assn., Cin. Bar Assn. Home: 505 Walt Allsgood Rd West Union OH 45693-9419 Office: Common Pleas Court PO Box 305 West Union OH 45693-0305

SCHLUETER, LINDA LEE, law educator; b. L.A., May 12, 1947; d. Dick G. Dulgarian and Lucille J. Boston; m. David A. Schlueter, Apr. 22, 1972; children: Jennifer, Jonathan. BA, U. So. Calif., 1969; JD, Baylor U., 1971. Bar: D.C. 1973, U.S. Supreme Ct. 1976, Ct. Mil. Appeals, 1990, Tex. 1997. Govt. rels. specialist hdqrs. U.S. Postal Svc., Washington, 1973-75; staff atty. Rsch. Group, Inc., Charlottesville, Va., 1979-81; pvt. practice Washington, 1981-83; asst. prof. law Sch. Law St. Mary's U., San Antonio, 1983-87, assoc. prof., 1987-90, prof., 1990-94. Presenter law Tex. Women Scholars Program, Austin, 1986, 87; bd. dirs Inst. for Comparative and Internat. Legal Rsch. Author: Punitive Damages, 1981-89, 4th edit., 2000, ann. suppls., Legal Research Guide: Patterns and Practice, 1986, 4th edit., 2000; editor Cmty. Property Jour., 1986-88, Cmty. Property Alert, 1989-90; editor Modern Legal Sys. Cyclopedia, 20 vols., 1990, ann. suppls. Mem. ABA, Bexar County Women's Bar Assn., San Antonio Conservation Soc., Order of Barristers, Phi Alpha Delta. Republican. Lutheran.

SCHLUMBERGER, ROBERT ERNEST, accountant; b. Pitts., Sept. 25, 1951; s. Ernest August Jr. and Barbara Ann (Rodler) S.; m. Mary Cecelia Leahy, Dec. 7, 1974; children: Jennifer Marie, Saralynne Cecelia. BS, Pa. State U., 1974. Mgr. Bradford House Restaurant, Punxsutawney, Pa., 1974-76, Latrobe, 1976-77, Butler, 1977-78; owner, acct. Schlumberger Bus. Svcs., 1978-88; pres., acct. Schlumberger Acctg. Svcs., Inc., Crystal River, Fla., 1988—. Registered rep. H.D. Vest Investment Securities, Inc., Las Colinas, Tex., 1986—; enrolled agt. IRS, 1983—. Mem. Nat. Soc. Accts., Nat. Fedn. Ind. Bus., Nat. Assn. Enrolled Agts. Republican. Lutheran. Avocations: airplanes, fishing, reading, swimming. Home: 720 N Dove Pt Crystal River FL 34429-5339 Office: Schlumberger Acctg Svcs Inc 6220 W Corporate Oaks Dr Crystal River FL 34429-8723

SCHLUSBERG, JULIAN SIMON, theater educator, theater director, writer; b. Mt. Vernon, N.Y., July 5, 1947; s. Herman and Esther Schlusberg; children: Jennifer Gelzinis. BS, So. Conn. State U., 1969, MS, 1975. Cert. English tchr.9-12 Conn. Tchr. theater and English Hamden (Conn.) Pub. Schs., 1969—99; artistic dir. Foote Summer Theater, New Haven, 1981—; dir. drama The Foote Sch., 2000—. Guest theater prodn. dir. So. Conn. State U., New Haven, 1984, New Haven, 85, New Haven, 2001, Cen. Conn. State U., New Britain, 1982, The Dandelion Players, Hamden, 1990, CET Opera Theater, Hamden, 1990, Hamden, 92, Hamden, 93, The Orange Players, Orange, 2000. Author: (book) Letters From the Prophets: A Theater Teacher's Memoir, 2001, Lessons For the Stage: An Approach to Acting, 1995; dir.: The Shadow Box by Michael Cristofer (New England Theatre Conference Moss Hart award , 1988), The Elephant Man by Bernard Pomerance (New England Theatre Conference Moss Hart award, 1984), The Crucible by Arthur Miller (New England Theatre Conference Moss Hart award, 1978). Named namesake of the Julian S. Schlusberg Theater Scholarship, The Hamden, Conn. Pub. Schs.; recipient The Mary Hunter Wolf award for excellence in the art and tchg. of theater, Long Wharf Theatre, 1997, Arts award for excellence and mastery in tchg. of theater, Arts Coun. Greater New Haven, 1996, Hamden Notable award for disting. svc. to cmty., Friends of the Hamden Libr., Dir. Outstanding H.S. Prodn. in Conn. award, Conn. Drama Assn. Festival, Ofcl. Citation for directing 20 prize-winning plays, Gov. John Rowland and Conn. Gen. Assembly, 1998. Mem.: Conn. Alliance for the Arts, Am. Alliance for Theater and Edn. (John C. Barner Nat. Theater Tchr. of Yr. 1988), New Eng. Theatre Conf., Conn. Arts Alliance (pres. 1979—81, Lifetime Achievement award 1999, Disting. Svc. award 1997). Office: The Foote Sch 50 Loomis Pl New Haven CT 06511 Personal E-mail: Julort@aol.com.

SCHLUSSEL, JOSEPH LAZAR, diamond dealer, publisher; b. Munkacs, Czechoslovakia, Apr. 19, 1935; came to U.S., 1951; s. Charles C. and Fanny Schlussel; m. Rose Ickowitz, June 16, 1960; children: Fay, Amy. Student, Bklyn. Coll., 1954-55, CCNY, 1956-59. Mgr. Gemcutters, N.Y.C., 1960-61; broker Diamond Dealers Club, 1961-69; pres. The Diamond Registry, 1969—. Editor and publisher The Diamond Registry Bulletin, 1969—; cons. Nat. Westminster Bank USA, E.A.B., Merchants Bank, Bankers Trust, Solomon Bros. Columnist Nat. Jeweler, 1978, Jewel Mag., 1988--; lectr. in field; guest on NBC Today, 1978; quoted in many major publs. as leading authority in field. Mem. Gemological Assn. Gt. Britain, Jewelry Industry Coun., Jewelers Vigilance Com., Jewelers Bd. of Trade, Diamond Dealers Club. Office: The Diamond Registry 580 5th Ave New York NY 10036-4701 Fax: 212-575-0722. E-mail: jschlussel@aol.com.

SCHLUTER, GERALD EMIL, economist; b. Carroll, Iowa, June 9, 1942; s. Emil and Violetta Marie (Witt) S.; m. Carolyn Jean Finnell, Apr. 27, 1968; 1 child, Deborah Jean. BS, Iowa State U., 1964, MS, 1966, PhD, 1971. Rsch. asst. econs. Iowa State U., Ames, 1964-66, rsch. assoc. econs., 1966-70; agrl. economist USDA Econ. Rsch. Svc., Washington, 1970-84, supervisory/sr. economist, 1984—. Econs. instr., Washington, 1983—, USDA Grad. Sch., Washington, 1979-83. Editor Agrl. Econs., 1984-87; author: (econs. series) Food & Fiber System, 1972; contbr. articles to profl. jours. Property com. Bethany Luth. Ch., Alexandria, Va., 1983-88; coach Lee-Mt. Vernon Soccer Assn., Alexandria, 1982-83. Mem. Am. Agrl. Econs. Assn., So Regional Sci. Assn. (coun. 1992-95), Am. Econ. Assn., Southern Econ. Assn., Western Agrl. Econs. Assn., Northeastern Agrl. and Resource Econs. Assn., Food Distbn. Rsch. Soc. Avocations: fishing, youth soccer, personal computers. Home: 3877 Manzanita Pl Alexandria VA 22309-1479 Office: USDA Econ Rsch Svc 1800 M St NW Rm 2122 Washington DC 20036-5802 E-mail: geraldschlter@aol.com.

SCHLUTER, PETER MUELLER, electronics company executive; b. May 24, 1933; s. Fredric Edward and Charlotte (Mueller) S.; m. Jaquelin Ambler Lamond, Apr. 18, 1970 (div. June 1990); children: Jane Randolph, Charlotte Mueller, Anne Ambler; m. Christine Moon Van Ness, Feb. 7, 1998. BME, Cornell U., 1956; postgrad., Harvard U. Grad. Sch. Bus. Adm, 1982. Sr. engr. Thiokol Chem. Corp., Brigham City, Utah, 1958-59; assoc. Porter Internat. Co., Washington, 1960-65, v.p., pres., treas., dir., 1966-70; pres., treas., dir. Zito Co., Derry, N.H., 1970-72; internat. bus. cons. Washington, 1972-74; v.p., dir. Buck Engrng. Co. Inc. (now Lab-Volt Sys., Inc.), Farmingdale, N.J., 1975, pres., CEO, dir., 1975—. Mem. Rep. Inaugural Book and Program Com., 1969; mem. cmty. adv. bd. Monmouth (N.J.) coun. Girl Scouts U.S.; mem. adv. coun. Monmouth U. Sch. Bus. Adminstrn.; bd. dirs. United Way of Monmouth County; trustee Monmouth Med. Ctr.; N.Am. rep., mem. presidium WORLDDIDAC, Bern, Switzerland, v.p., 1996—. Recipient Golden Osprey award So. Monmouth County C. of C., 1995. Fellow City and Guilds of London Inst. (hon.); mem. World Assn. Mfrs. and Distbrs. of Ednl. Materials (N.Am. rep.), Met. Club Washington, Rumson Country Club, Pi Tau Sigma. Home: 4 Quaker Ln Little Silver NJ 07739-1806 Office: PO Box 686 Farmingdale NJ 07727-0686

SCHLUTER, ROBERT ARVEL, physicist; b. Salt Lake City, Aug. 27, 1924; s. Arvel R. and Florence (Leach) S.; 1 child, Jonathan R. BS, U. Chgo., 1947, PhD, 1954. Rsch. assoc. U. Chgo. Inst. for Nuclear Studies, 1954; from instr. to asst. prof. MIT Lab. for Nuclear Studies, Cambridge, Mass., 1955-60; assoc. physicist Argonne (Ill.) Nat. Lab., 1961-72; prof. physics and astronomy Northwestern U., Evanston, Ill., 1961-92, emeritus, 1992—. Guest scientist Brookhaven (N.Y.) Nat. Lab., 1955-70, Lawrence Radiation Lab., U. Calif., Berkeley, 1958-60; guest appointee Aspen Inst. for Humanities, 1967. Contbr. chpts. to books. Served with Los Alomos, Manhattan Project, C.E., U.S. Army, 1943-46. Grantee AEC NSF, Dept. Energy, NASA, others. Mem. Am. Phys. Soc., Nat. Assn. Scholars. Achievements include first observation of K-Mesic X-rays, first measurement of Lambda Hyperon Magnetic Moment, first observation of 2d and 3d excited states of the proton; research in experimental hydrodynamics. Avocations: mountain climbing and exploration, study of history. Home: 241 N Vine St Apt 902E Salt Lake City UT 84103-1971 Office: Northwestern U Dept Physics and Astronomy 2145 Sheridan Rd Dept And Evanston IL 60208-0834 E-mail: schluter@northwestern.edu.

SCHLUTTER, LOIS COCHRANE, psychologist; b. Indpls., Oct. 18, 1953; d. Roy and Mavis (Wolfe) Cochrane; 1 child, Nathan Paul. BS, U. S.D., 1974, MA, 1975, PhD, 1978. Diplomate Am. Bd. Forensic Medicine, Am. Bd. Disability, Am. Bd. Psychol. Specialists; bd. cert. forensic examiner; Prepare/Enrich cert. counselor; sr. disability analyst and diplomate Am. Bd. Disability Analysts; lic. psychologist, Minn. Psychologist, asst. Neurol. Inst. and Pain Ctr., Sioux City, Iowa, 1975-77; staff Mpls. Psychotherapy Inst., St. Louis Park, Minn., 1978-80; with strategic planning Vail Place, Mpls. and Hopkins (Minn.), 1988-90; owner Schlutter & Assocs., St. Louis Park, Minn., 1994—. Bd. dirs. Vail Pl.; allied health staff, disability cons. Meth. Hosp., St. Louis Park, 1978—, mem. hospice adv. com., 1984—, mem. child abuse consortium, 1985-89; staff psychologist Sister Kenny Inst., Mpls., 1980-81; cons. Dept. Vocat. Rehab., St. Paul, 1984-93; supr. pastoral care AAPC, St. Louis Park, 1984-95; lectr. St. Mary's Hosp. and Coll., Mpls., 1984-90; psychologist, dir. Family Dynamics, St. Louis Park, 1980-94; owner Employee Assistance Programs; presenter in field; clin. adj. faculty Minn. Sch. Profl. Psychology, 1966—. Co-author: (play) The Extrapolator, 1968; contbr. articles to profl. jours. Mem. task force Vinland Nat. Ctr.; chmn. adult edn., Hopkins United Meth. Ch., 1988-91. Recipient rsch. grant Lederle Pharms., 1979. Fellow Am. Coll. Forensic Examiners; mem. APA, Mental Health Assn. Minn., Minn. Psychol. Assn., Am. Assn. Pastoral Counselors (profl. affiliate), Brookside Condominium Assn., Blvd. Condominium Assn., Internat. Platform Assn., Rotary, Twin West C. of C., Phi Beta Kappa (assoc.), Kappa Alpha Theta, Alpha Lambda Delta, Psi Chi. Avocations: reading, cooking. Office: Schlutter & Assocs 6200 Excelsior Blvd Ste 202 Saint Louis Park MN 55416-2734 E-mail: doclcs@yahoo.com.

SCHMALBECK, RICHARD LOUIS, university dean, lawyer; b. Chgo., Dec. 31, 1947; s. George Louis and Betty Jeanne Schmalbeck; m. Linda Michaels; children: Suzanne, Sabine. AB in Econs. with honors, U. Chgo., 1970, JD, 1975. Bar: Ohio 1975, D.C. 1977. Asst. to dir. and economist Ill. Housing Devel. Authority, Chgo., 1971-73; assoc. Vorys, Sater, Seymour & Pease, Columbus, Ohio, 1975-76; spl. asst. to assoc. dir. for econs. and govt. Office of Mgmt. and Budget, Washington, 1976-77; assoc. Caplin & Drysdale, 1977-80; assoc. prof. law Duke U., Durham, N.C., 1980-84, prof. law, 1984-90, 93—, vice chmn. acad. coun. NC, 1984—85, 2001—02; dean U. Ill. Coll. Law, Champaign, 1990-93. Assoc. editor U. Chgo. Law Rev., 1974-75; contbr. articles to profl. jours. Mem. ABA (articles editor jour. 1977-80), Am. Law Inst., Phi Beta Kappa. Office: Duke University Sch of Law PO Box 90360 Durham NC 27708-0360

SCHMALE, ALLEN LEE, financial services company executive; b. Addieville, Ill., Feb. 12, 1933; s. Arnold August and Leona Karoline (Becker) S.; m. Lorraine Marie Loyet, July 19, 1952; children: Judith Ann, Arnold August II, Michelle Lee, René Cerise, Allen Kent. CLU, ChFC. Salesman Western & So. Life Ins. Co., St. Louis, 1955-56, Monarch Life Ins. Co., St. Louis, 1956-58, Mass. Indemnity & Life Ins., St. Louis, 1958-65; pres. Schmale Fin. Svcs., Inc., Okawville, Ill., 1965-88, chmn., 1988—, also bd. dirs. Chmn. bd. dirs. Fin. Security Corp., PenFlex, Inc., Nashville, Ill.; bd. dirs. South Ctrl. Ill. Mass Transit. Trustee Village of Okawville, 1976-80, mem. bus. devel. com.; vice chmn. Washington County (Ill.) Rep. Com.; coord. Edgar for Gov., Ill., 1990, 94; pres. St. Peters Ch., 1975-77. Recipient Contbns. to Growth award Belleville (Ill.) Area Coll., 1977. Mem. Am. Soc. CLU and ChFC, East Side Life Underwriters (pres. 1971-72), Million Dollar Roundtable, Ill. Life Underwriters (bd. dirs. 1975-78), Nat. Assn. Life Underwriters (del. 1971), Estate Planning Coun. St. Louis, Okawville Comty. Club (pres. 1974-76). Republican. Avocation: golf. Address: Schmale Fin Services 9627 Wall St Nashville IL 62263-3416 E-mail: alschmale@finsvcs.com.

SCHMALENBERGER, JERRY LEW, pastor, religious studies educator; b. Greenville, Ohio, Jan. 23, 1934; s. Harry Henry and Lima Marie (Hormel) S.; m. Carol Ann Walthall, June 8, 1956; children: Stephen, Bethany Allison, Sarah Layton Wallace. BA, Wittenberg U., 1956, DDiv (hon.), 1984; MDiv, Hamma Sch. Theology, Springfield, Ohio, 1959, D of Ministry, 1976. Ordained to ministry Luth. Ch., 1959. Dir. Camp Mowana, Mansfield, Ohio, 1958-59; pastor 3d Luth. Ch., Springfield, 1959-61, 1st Luth. Ch., Bellefontaine, Ohio, 1961-66, sr. pastor Tiffin, 1966-70, Mansfield, 1970-79, St. John's Luth. Ch., Des Moines, 1979-88; pres. Pacific Luth. Theol. Sem., Berkeley, Calif., 1988-96, prof. parish ministry, 1988-99. Co-dir. Iowa Luth. Hosp. Min. of Health Program, Des Moines, 1986—88; Roland Payne lectr. Gbarnga Sch. Theology, Liberia, 1987; lectr. Luth. Theol. Sem., Hong Kong, 1994, Luth. Theol. Sem. , 1999—2002, The United Theol. Coll., Kingston, Jamaica, 1994, HKBP Sem., Sumatra, 1997; guest prof. The Augustana Hochschule, Germany, 1996, 99, 2001; guest lectr. Inst. Superior Evangelical Theol. Studies, Theol. Seminary, Argentina, 1998, Eccumenical Ctr., Montevideo, Uruguay, 1998; vis. faculty Moravian Theol. Seminary, Paramararibo, Surinam, 1998. Author: Lutheran Christians' Beliefs Book One, 1984, Book Two, 1987, Iowa Parables and Iowa Psalms, 1984, Saints Who Shaped the Church, 1986, Stewards of Creation, 1987, Nights Worth Remembering, 1989, The Vine and the Branches, 1992, Call to Witness, 1993, Plane Thoughts on Parish Ministry, 1994, Invitation to Discipleship, 1995, The Preacher's Edge, 1996, Preparation for Discipleship, 1998, These Will Preach, 1999, The Parables of Jesus and Their Flip Side, 2000, The Miracles of Jesus and Their Flip Side, 2001, Dear Friends and Family, 2001, The Preacher's Workbook, Cycle A, 2001, Cycle B., 2002; columnist Rite Ideas, 1987-88. Bd. dirs. Grand View Coll., Des Moines, 1980-88, Wittenberg U., Springfield, Ohio, 1974-87, Luth. Social Services of Iowa, 1980-87, chmn. pre fund drive, 1988; bd. dirs. Planned Parenthood of Mid-Iowa, Des Moines, 1987-88; dir. Evang. Outreach/Luth. Ch. Am., 1983-85; mem. Iowa Luth. Hosp. Charitable Trust, 1986-88; chair Com. for Homeless Fund, Des Moines, 1986. Named Outstanding Alumni Wittenberg U., 1965, Young Man of Yr. Tiffin Jaycees, 1965, Man of Yr. Bellefontaine Jaycees, Disting. Alumni award Trinty Sem., Columbus, 1989. Mem. NAACP, Acad. Preachers, Acad. Evangelists (organizer 1986—), Kiwanis, Rotary. Avocations: historical research and writing, travel, boating. Home and Office: 162 Pelican Loop Pittsburg CA 94565-2004 E-mail: jlschmalen@aol.com. *Personal philosophy: Not perfect, but forgiven, we find real life in living ours for others.*

SCHMALENSEE, RICHARD LEE, dean, economist, former government official, educator; b. Belleville, Ill., Feb. 16, 1944; s. Fred and Marjorie June (Veigel) S.; m. Edeth Diane Hawk, Aug. 19, 1967; children: Alexander Clayton, Nicholas Hawk. SB, MIT, 1965, PhD, 1970. From asst. prof. to assoc. prof. econs. U. Calif., San Diego, 1970-77; assoc. prof. applied econs. Sloan Sch. Mgmt. MIT, Cambridge, Mass., 1977-79, prof., 1979-86, prof. econs. and mgmt., 1986—, Gordon Y Billard prof., 1988-99; dir. MIT Ctr. for Energy and Environ. Policy Rsch., 1991-99; dep. dean Sloan Sch., 1996—98, John C Head III dean, 1998—. Bd. dirs. Internat. Securities Exch., Mass. Fin. Svcs.; mem. Pres.'s Coun. Econ. Advisers, 1989—91. Author: The Economics of Advertising, 1972, The Control of Natural Monopoly, 1979; co-author: Markets for Power, 1983, Economics, 1988, Paying with Plastic, 1999, Markets for Clean Air, 2000; co-editor: Handbook of Industrial Organization, 1989; mem. editl. bd. Jour. Indsl. Econs., 1981-89, Am. Econ. Rev., 1982-86, Internat. Jour. Indsl. Orgns., 1982-89, Jour. Econs. & Mgmt. Strategy, 1993-98, Jour. Econ. Perspectives, 1993-98. NSF grant, 1975-77, 81-83; Rsch. fellow U. Louvain, Belgium, 1973-74, 85. Fellow: AAAS, Econometric Soc.; mem.: Am. Econ. Assn. (nominating com. 1987, exec. com. 1993—95). Home: 20 Malia Ter Chestnut Hill MA 02467-1326 Office: MIT Sloan School of Mgmnt 50 Memorial Dr Rm E52-456 Cambridge MA 02142-1347

SCHMALER, TRACY ALICE, newspaper journalist, writer; b. Morristown, N.J., Sept. 23, 1972; d. Wayne Charles and Diane Marie Schmaler. BS in Mass Comm., Emerson Coll., 1994. News intern Boston Phoenix, 1994; staff reporter Berkshire Record, Great Barrington, Mass., 1994-96, Brattleboro (Vt.) Reformer, 1996-98, news wire editor, 1997-98; staff reporter Rutland (Vt.) Daily Herald, 1998—. Mentor Brattleboro Union H.S. Program, 1997. Recipient Spot News award New Eng. Press Assn., 1995. Mem. Soc. Profl. Journalists. Avocations: reading, snowboarding, tennis. E-mamil. E-mail: snowwhite@tds.net.

SCHMALL, VICKI LOUISE, gerentology; b. Spokane, Wash., Mar. 14, 1947; d. Grant Louis and Iona Grace (Taylor) Flagan; m. Rodney August Schmall, July 11, 1970. BS, Mont. State U., 1970; PhD, Oreg. State U., Corvallis, 1977. Instr. Wilsall (Mont.) Cons. Schs., 1969; tchg. asst., field supr. Oreg. State U., Corvallis, 1971—75, dir. program on gerontology, 1975—78; rsch. assoc. Applied Systems R&D, Beaverton, Oreg., 1977; spl. prof. gerontology Oreg. State U., Corvallis, 1978—94; coord. sr. series project Rural Devel. Ctr. Oreg. State U., 1991—92; pres., gerontology specialist Aging Concerns, West Linn, Oreg., 1994—. Curriculum developer, trainer Legacy Health Systems, Portland, Oreg., 1995—; cons. Oreg. Ctr. for Applied Scis., Eugene, 1998—; cons., trainer for older adult sensitivity Pfizer/Harrison Wilson, Parsippany, NJ, 1999—. Author: (Book) Home Sweet Home: How to Help Older Adults Live Independently, 1997 (Bronze award Nat. Mature Media, 1997), The Caregiver Helpbook: Powerful Tools for Caregiving, 2000; prodr.: (seven multi-media ednl. programs) When Dependency Inceases, 1985—90 (AARP and 2 other Nat. awards, 1992); developer (to nationally distributed tng./ednl. materials); contbr. 9 tng. guides, 4 ednl. games , 10 multipackage tng. programs, 3 videos, CD-Rom , over 125 articles , book chpts. and bulletins on age related issues and concerns. Mem. patient and family svcs. com. MS Soc. Oreg. chpt., Portland, 1998—; bd. dirs., several coms. Alzheimer's Assn.., Oreg., 1987—; bd. dirs. Willamette View CRC, 1995—. Named one of 100 most disting. alumni since founding, Mont. State U., 1993; recipient Achievement award, MS Soc. Oreg. chpt., Portland, 1994, Gloria Cavanaugh award, Am. Soc. on Aging, San Francisco, 2002. Fellow: Gerontol. Soc. Am.; mem.: Am. Coll. Health Care Adminstrs., Am. Soc. on Aging. Avocations: book club, investment group, outdoor activities, photo albums, reading. Home and Office: Aging Concerns 835 Marylhurst Cir West Linn OR 97068-1813 Home Fax: 503-636-7989.

SCHMALSTIEG, WILLIAM RIEGEL, retired Slavic languages educator; b. Sayre, Pa., Oct. 3, 1929; s. John William and Dorothy Augusta (Riegel) S.; m. Emily Lou Botdorf, Mar. 28, 1952; children: Linda, Roxanne. BA, U. Minn., 1950; postgrad., Columbia U., 1952; MA, U. Pa., 1951, PhD, 1956; PhD (hon.), Vilnius U., 1994. Instr. U. Ky., Lexington, 1956-59; asst. prof. Lafayette Coll., Easton, Pa., 1959-63; assoc. prof. U. Minn., Mpls., 1963-64; prof. Pa. State U., University Park, 1964—2002, head dept. Slavic langs., 1969-91. Mem. Internat. Commn. Balto-Slavic Linguistics, 1973—; appointed Edwin Erle Sparks prof. Slavic Lang., 1990. Author: (with L. Dambriunas and A. Klimas) An Introduction to Modern Lithuanian, 1966, 4th edit., 1990, 5th edit., 1993, reprinted as Beginner's Lithuanian, 1999, An Old Prussian Grammar, 1974, Studies in Old Prussian, 1976, Indo-European Linguistics, 1980, An Introduction to Old Church Slavic, 1976, 2d edit., 1983, A Lithuanian Historical Syntax, 1988; (with Warren Held and Janet Gertz) Beginning Hittite, 1988, A Student Guide to the Genitive of Agent in the Indo-European Languages, 1995, An Introduction to Old Russian, 1995, The Historical Morphology of the Baltic Verb, 2000; editor Gen. Linguistics, 1971-82; mem. editl. adv. bd. Jour. Indo-European Studies, Baltistica, Linguistica Baltica, Acta Linguistica Lithuanica, Archivum Lithuanicum, Lietuviu Kalbotyros Klausimai, Baltu Filologija. Served to 1st lt. U.S. Army, 1952-54. NEH grantee, 1978-79, Fulbright grantee and exch. scholar Acad. Scis., Vilnius, USSR, 1986; recipient Humanities medal Pa. State U., 1983, Friend of Lithuania award Knights of Lithuania, 1990, Lithuanian Govt. Mazvydas medal, 1997; named Disting. Alumnus Breck Sch., 1990. Mem. Assn. Advancement Baltic Studies (pres. 1982-84), Am. Assn. Tchrs. of Slavic and East European Langs. Episcopalian. Home: 814 Cornwall Rd State College PA 16801-1430 E-mail: wxsl@psu.edu.

SCHMALTZ, LAWRENCE GERARD, engineer, consultant; b. Belle Fourches, S.D., Feb. 11, 1957; s. Tony J. and Evalyn Marie (Kouf) S. BSCE, S.D. Sch. of Mines & Tech., 1979; postgrad., U. Phoenix; postgrad. in Remediation Engrng., Wright State U. Registered profl. engr., Fla. Engr. Skidmore, Owings & Merrill, Denver, 1979-82; project mgr. U.S. Dept. of Def., Rapid City, S.D., 1982-84; regional mgr. Waste Environ. Tech., Denver, 1986-87; project engr. Canonie Environ. Svcs., 1988; regional mgr. Burdco Environ., Inc., Longwood, Fla., 1988; v.p. Atcon, Inc., 1989-91; pres. CE Systems, Inc., 1989-95, A2L Techs., Inc., 1992—; adj. faculty U. North Fla., 1989-92; pres., CEO A2L Techs. Inc., 1992—; mng. prin. E-Net Ventures, LLC, 2000—. Gen. ptnr. LJS Properties, Rapid City, 1984-87; real estate broker Larry G. Schmaltz, Aurora, Colo., 1985-88; pres., cons. Dynamics Cons. & Mgmt., Aurora, 1986-88; instr., trainer in field; dir. Fla. Animal Health Found., 1996—. Bd. dirs. Cherry Creek Spl. Edn. Adv. Bd., Englewood, Colo., 1985; v.p. Adamo Properties Corp., 1995—. Mem. NSPE, Profl. Engrs. in Constrn., Fla. Engring. Soc., Fla. Environ. Auditors Assn., Nat. Registry of Environ. Profls., Nat. Groundwater Assn., Fla. Animal Health Found. (pres., bd. dirs. 1996—). Avocations: running, reading, scuba diving. Home: 1401 N Riverhills Dr Temple Terrace FL 33617 E-mail: larrys@a2ltechnologies.com.

SCHMALZ, CARL NELSON, JR. artist, educator, printmaker; b. Ann Arbor, Mich., Dec. 26, 1926; s. Carl Nelson and Esther Dorothy (Fowler) S.; m. Dolores Irene Tourangeau, Dec. 2, 1950; children: Stephen Theodore (dec.), Mathew Nelson, Julia Irene. AB, Harvard U., 1948, MA, 1949, PhD, 1958; MA (hon.), Amherst Coll., 1969. Teaching fellow in fine arts Harvard U., Cambridge, Mass., 1950-52; asst. prof. Bowdoin Coll., Brunswick, Maine, 1953-62; curator, asst dir. Walker Art Mus., 1953-62; asst. prof. Harvard U., 1960; prof. Amherst Coll., 1962-95, prof. emeritus, 1995—. Lectr. in field. Author: Watercolor Lessons from Eliot O'Hara, 1974, Watercolor Your Way, 1978, Finding and Improving Your Painting Style, 1986, paperback, 1992; exhibited in one-man shows including Cambridge (Mass.) Art Assn., 1948, Laing Gallery, Portland, Maine, 1955, Amherst (Mass.) Coll., 1963, U. Mass., 1965, W.C. Rawls Mus., Va., 1972, Concord (Mass.) Art Assn., 1974, Govt. House, Hamilton, Bermuda, 1979, Jones Library, Amherst, Mass., 1979, The Arlington, Kennebunkport, Maine, 1980, Harmon-Meek Gallery, Naples, Fla., 1987, 91, 92, 98, Gallery at 6 Deering St., Portland, Maine, 1987, 91, Fretz Gallery, Portland, 1987-88; exhibited in group shows including Jordan Marsh Co., 1947, 48, 50, 71-73, Colby Coll., 1958, Carnegie Inst., Pitts., 1963, FAR Gallery, N.Y.C., 1964-68, Am. Watercolor Soc., 1966, 68, 70, Bowdoin Coll. Mus., 1973, Balt. Watercolor Soc., 1976, Boston Atheneum, 1979, Watercolor U.S.A. Honor Soc., 1989, 91, Maine Art Gallery, 1991, Rolly-Michaux Gallery, Boston, 1995; represented in permanent collections: Signet Soc., Walker Art Mus., Brunswick, Maine, Jones & Laughlin Steel Corp., Diners Club Am., Kalamazoo Art Center, Hampshire Coll., Zanesville Art Inst., Blue Cross/Blue Shield, Philharmonic Ctr. for the Arts, Naples, Fla., Springfield (Mo.) Art Mus., Amherst Coll., Bowdoin Coll., Hampshire Coll., Kalamazoo Art Inst., Naples Philharm. Soc., Signet Soc., Springfield (Mo.) Art Mus.; work published in various pubs. including The Artist's Guide for Using Color, 1992, The Artist's Mag., 1994, Splash 3: Ideas and Inspirations, 1994. Mem. exec. bd. Interfaith Housing Corp., Amherst, 1966-76; pres. bd. trustees Amherst Day Sch., 1966-69; mem. Pelham Arts Lottery Coun., 1984-90; v.p. bd. dirs. Portland Mus. Art, 1957-62. Bacon fellow, 1951; recipient 1st prize watercolor Cambridge Art Assn. Ann., 1947, 1st prize for traditional watercolor Virginia Beach Boardwalk Show, 1965, South Mo. Trust purchase award Watercolor U.S.A., 1970, 1st prize watercolor 30th Ann. Kennebunk River Club Show, 1985, Purchase prize Watercolor U.S.A., 1997. Mem. The Signet Soc., Coll. Art Assn., Watercolor U.S.A. Honor Soc. Democrat.

SCHMALZ, ROBERT FOWLER, geology educator; b. Ann Arbor, Mich., May 29, 1929; s. Carl Nelson and Esther Dorothy (Fowler) S.; m. Barbara Ann Leetch, July 18, 1964; children: Timothy F., Dorothy L. AB with honors, Havard Coll., 1951; AM, Harvard U., 1954, PhD, 1959. Cert. profl. geologist. Rsch. asst. Harvard/W.H.O.I., Cambridge, Mass., 1957-58; asst. prof. Pa. State U., University Park, 1958-63, assoc. prof., 1963-69, prof. of geology, 1969-91, chmn. geology, 1971-74, undergrad. coord., 1974-77, prof. of geology emeritus, 1992—. Trustee Bermuda Biol. Sta., 1967-79; mem. adv. com. Appalachian Compact Users Radio Isotopes, University Park. Editor: Science Education in the United States, 1991, Environmental Radon, 1990; contbr. articles to profl. jours. Mem., vice chair, chair State Coll. Borough Water Authority, State College, 1978-98; mem. Univ. Area Joint Authority, 1998—. With U.S. Army, 1955-57. Recipient Wilson Teaching award Earth and Mineral Sci. Coll., 1969, Lindback Teaching award Pa. State U., 1970. Fellow AAAS, Geol. Soc. Am.; mem. Am. Assn. Petroleum Geologists (disting. lectr. 1977-78), Soc. Econ. Mineralogists and Petrologists, Pa. Acad. Sci., Explorers Club, Cosmos Club, Sigma Xi. Avocations: historical railroad operations, sailing. Home: 305 E Mitchell Ave State College PA 16803-3637 E-mail: rfs3@psu.edu.

SCHMALZRIED, MARVIN EUGENE, financial consultant; b. Dighton, Kans., Nov. 11, 1924; s. Carl D. and Marie M. (Bahm) S.; m. Jean Landino, Nov. 27, 1946; children— Darlene, Candace, Cynthia, Derek, Valerie, Rebecca. BBA, Northwestern U., 1949; LL.B., U. Conn., 1955. Bar: Conn. bar 1955; C.P.A., Conn. Acct. Webster, Blanchard & Willard, CPA's (named changed to Price Waterhouse & Co.), Hartford, Conn., 1950-55; contr., asst. treas. J.B. Williams Co., Glastonbury, 1955-57; treas., sec. Curtis 1000, Inc. (name changed to Am Bus. Products, Inc.), Atlanta, 1957-61; asst. to pres. Am. Home Products Corp., N.Y.C., 1961-63, comptroller, 1964-67, v.p., 1967-72, sr. v.p., 1972-84; pres. Venda Vid, Inc., 1986-90; sr. v.p. View-Master Ideal Group, Inc., 1987-90; exec. v.p. Strategics Inc., 1993-95. Recipient Gold medal Conn. Soc. C.P.A.'s, 1953 Mem. AICPA, ABA, Old Greenwich Friday Evening Reading Soc. (pres.) Clubs: Darien Country. Home and Office: 26 Cove Ave Norwalk CT 06855-2400

SCHMANDT, JURGEN AUGUSTINUS, public affairs educator; b. Mar. 2, 1929; PhD, U. Bonn, Germany, 1956. Prin. adminstr. sci. policy OECD, Paris, 1960-65; assoc. dir. program sci. and tech. Harvard U., Cambridge, Mass., 1965-71; prof. pub. affairs U. Tex., Austin, 1971—; dir. Ctr. Sustainable Devel. Houston Advanced Rsch. Ctr., The Woodlands, Tex., 1985—. Author: Acid Rain and Friendly Neighbors, 1988, The Regions and Global Warming, 1992, Scarce Water, 1998, Navigating the Waters of the Paso del Norte, 1999, Sustainable Development, 2000. Home: 11 Hull Circle Dr Austin TX 78746-3709 Fax: 281-363-7924. E-mail: jschmandt@harc.edu.

SCHMANDT-BESSERAT, DENISE, archaeologist, educator; b. Ay, France, Aug. 10, 1933; came to U.S., 1965, naturalized, 1970; d. Victor and Jeanne (Crabit) Besserat; m. Jurgen Schmandt, Dec. 27, 1956; children: Alexander, Christopher, Phillip. Ed., Ecole du Louvre, 1965. Rsch. fellow in Near Eastern Archaeology Peabody Mus. Harvard U., Cambridge, Mass., 1969-71; fellow Radcliffe Inst., 1969-71; asst. prof. Middle Eastern studies U. Tex., Austin, 1972-81, assoc. prof., 1981-88, prof., 1988—; acting chief curator U. Tex. Art Mus., 1978-79. Vis. assoc. prof. U. Calif., Berkeley, 1987-88; curator Legacy of the Middle East exhbn. Jeddah (Saudi Arabia) Hist. Preservation Dept. Author: Before Writing, 1992, How Writing Came About, 1996, History of Counting, 1999; adv. editor Tech. and Culture, 1978-92; mem. editl. bd. Written Communication, 1993-95, Visible Lang., 1985—, Explorations in Media Ecology, 2001, Ancient Adminstrn., 2001; contbr. articles to profl. jours. Recipient Kayden Nat. U. Press Book award, 1992, Robert W. Hamilton Author award, 1998; named in Am. Scientist, 1999; Wenner-Gren Found. grant, 1970-71, NEA grant, 1974-75, 77-78, ACLS grant, 1984, Deutscher Akademischer Austauschdienst grant, 1986, NEH grant, 1992; NEH fellow, 1979-80, U. Wis. Inst. for Rsch. in Humanities fellow,, 1984-85, USIA, Am. Ctr. Oriental Rsch. fellow, 1994-95, 97, 2001, Malone fellow 1997, 99. Mem. Am. Oriental Soc., Archeol. Inst. Am. (governing bd. 1983-89), Am. Anthropol. Assn., Am. Schs. of Oriental Rsch., Centro Internat. Rsch. Archeologiche Anthropologiche e Storiche (Rome). E-mail: dsb@mail.utexas.edu.

SCHMAUS, SIEGFRIED H. A. engineering executive, consultant; b. Muelheim/Ruhr, W. Ger., Dec. 23, 1915; s. Wilhelm Friedrich and Hedwig (Flader) S.; student Staatliche Ingineur Schule, Duisburg, W. Ger., 1940-41, Esslingen, W. Ger., 1945-46; m. A. Babette Schmid, Aug. 17, 1946. Apprentice-designer Demag A.G., Duisburg, 1930-36; designer/supr. Meissner, Cologne, W. Ger., 1936-38; designer aircraft engines Daimler-Benz A.G., Stuttgart, W. Ger., 1943-45; designer Fischer & Porter, Warminster, Pa., 1948-53, Ametek Inc., Sellersville, Pa., 1954-65; staff rsch. engr. Fischer & Porter, Warminster, 1966-80; pres. Sensor Devel. Inc., Broomall, Pa., 1977—, Sensor Rsch. Inc., Phila., 1980-90. Patentee in field. V.p. Friends Hist. Rittenhouse Town. Served with German Luftwaffe, 1938-42. Recipient Hess Ingenuity award, 1962. Mem. Franklin Inst. (sr., silver mem.), Instrument Soc. Am. (sr.), Am. Soc. Mfg. Engrs., German Soc. Pa. (v.p. 1984, Founders medal 1987, Officer's Cross of the Gov. of Germany 1988), Masons. Republican. Lutheran. Home and Office: 15 Spoonbill Rd Lantana FL 33462-4752

SCHMAUSS, STEPHEN ANTHONY, retired computer programmer; b. L.A., June 1, 1940; s. Kenneth and Doris (Armstrong) S. Student, UCLA, 1975, Mt. San Antonio Coll., 1989. Programmer Centaur Computer Sys., Glendale, Calif., 1970-75, Kaynar Industries, Fullerton, 1975-82; sr. systems programmer Shiley Inc., Irvine, 1982-94; ret., 1994. Adv. to bd. dirs. IBM; cons. J.P.L., Pasadena, Calif., 1975, FiServ, Spokane, Wash., 1994, U.S. 2000 Census, Pomona Data Capture Ctr. With USNR, 1957-63. Democrat. Avocations: boating, fishing, astronomy, flying.

SCHMECHEL, STEPHEN, physician; b. Butte, Mont., Feb. 2, 1968; s. Warren Paul and Patricia Anne Schmechel. BA, Carroll Coll., 1990; MD, U. Minn., 1997, PhD, 1999. Resident U. Wash., Seattle, 1998-2000, chief resident, 2000—; founder Rational Diagnostics, 2000—. Mem. Assn. Molecular Diagnostics, Assn. Clin. Lab. Physicians and Scientists, Am. Soc. Virology. Democrat. Roman Catholic. Office: U Wash 1959 Pacific St Seattle WA 98195

SCHMEHL MORLEY, SUSAN LINDA, fine arts educator; b. Sheffield, Mass., Aug. 29, 1949; BFA, U. Mass., Amherst, 1971; postgrad., Studio Art Ctr. Internat., Florence, Italy, Md. Inst. Coll. Art, 2000—. With Peace Corps, 1973-76; studio arts, Spanish tchr., 1976-97; chair of fine and performing arts Berkshire Sch., Sheffield, Mass., 1997-2000. Recipient Outstanding H.S. Tchr. award in Sculpture, U. Chgo., 1999, Nat. Sculpture Tchr. award, Internat. Sculpture Ctr., 2001, Outstanding H.S. Tchr. award, 2001, The Scholastic Art and Writing award recognition, 1998, 2000, Internat. Artist Residency, Jingdezhen Sanbao Ceramic Art Inst., China, 2002; fellow Art fellow, Skidmore College, 1994; scholar Fulbright Meml. Fund scholar, Japan, 2002. Mem.: Nat. Assn. Art Educators, Ind. Sch. Art Instrs. Assn. Home: 245 N Undermountain Rd Sheffield MA 01257 E-mail: slsmorley@yahoo.com.

SCHMEIDLER, NEAL FRANCIS, engineering executive; b. Hays, Kans., Feb. 29, 1948; s. Cyril John and Mildred Mary (Karlin) S.; m. Lorrinda Mary Brungardt, Jan. 31, 1950; children: Lori Ann, LaNette Renee, Lance Edward, LeAnna Karleen. BS in Math., Fort Hays State U., 1970; MS in Indsl. Engring., Kans. State U., 1973. Master engr. Trans World Airlines, Inc., Kansas City, Mo., 1973-78; chief indsl. engr. U.S. Dept. of the Army, Fort Carson, Colo., 1978-80; staff indsl. engr. U.S. Dept. of Agriculture, Washington, 1980-83; tech. dir. Tech. Applications, Inc., Alexandria, Va., 1983-86; v.p. engring. and tech. svcs. div. Standard Tech., Inc., Bethesda, Md., 1986-88; dir. indsl. engring. and ops rsch. svcs. Operational Technologies Svcs., Inc., Vienna, 1989-91; founder, pres. OMNI Engring. and Tech., Inc., McLean, 1989—. Dir. No. Va. Tech. Coun., 1993-95. Guest (radio talk show) Basically Business, 1991; contbr. articles to profl. jours. Mem. info. tech./telecommunications infrastructure com. Commonwealth of Va. Gov.'s Regional Econ. Devel. Adv. Couns., 1994. Named Sr. Engr. of Yr., D.C. Coun. of Engring. and Archtl. Socs., 1991; recipient Spl. Act or Svc. award U.S. Dept. of Army, 1980, Cert. Recognition, NASA, 1999. Mem. ABA (small bus. com. 1991-92), Inst. Indsl. Engrs. (sr., nat. capital chpt. bd. dirs. 1986-93, 97-99, 2001—, Award of Excellence 1982), Soc. for Work Sci. (dir. 1999—), Air Traffic Control Assn., Human Factors and Ergonomics Soc., Project Mgmt. Inst., Washington Acad. Scis. (bd. mgrs. 1993-96), Kappa Mu Epsilon, Sigma Pi Sigma. Office: OMNI Engring & Tech Inc 7921 Jones Branch Dr Ste 530 Mc Lean VA 22102-3336

SCHMELING, GARETH, classics educator; b. Algoma, Wis., May 28, 1940; married. BA, Northwestern Coll., 1963; MA (Knapp fellow), U. Wis., 1964, PhD (Knapp travelling grantee 1965-66, Univ. fellow 1967-68), 1968. Asst. prof. classics U. Va., 1968-70; assoc. prof. U. Fla., 1970-74, prof., 1974-93, chmn. classics, 1974—, chmn. humanities, 1974-76, dir. Center for Studies in Humanities, 1978-87, prin. investigator Humanities Perspectives on Professions, 1975-87, acting chmn. dept. philosophy, 1986-88, disting. prof., 1998—. Vis. prof. U. Colo., Boulder, 1992; panelist, research div. Nat. Endowment for Humanities, also mem. nat. bd. consultants. Translator and author Introduction: Cornelius Nepos: Lives of Famous Men, 1971; author: Petronius' Satyricon, 1971, Ovid's the Art of Love, 1972, Chariton and the Rise of Ancient Fiction, 1974, Homer's the Odyssey, 1974, A Bibliography of Petronius, 1977, Xenophon of Ephesus, 1980, Historia Apollonii Regis Tyri, 1988, The Novel in the Ancient World, 1996, Qui Miscuit Utile Dulci, 1998; contbr. numerous articles, revs. to profl. jours.; editor: Newsletter Petronian Soc. 1970—; editorial com.: U. Fla. Press Humanities Monographs, 1978—. Named 1 of 5 Tchrs. of Yr. for Arts and Scis. U. Fla., 1973; recipient Rome prize Am. Acad., 1977-78; U. Va. faculty fellow, summer 1969, summer 1970; U. Fla. fellow, summer 1971, summer 1974; Nat. Endowment for Humanities fellow, 1973-74; Am. Council Learned Socs. summer fellow, 1974; Am. Philos. Soc. grantee, 1970, 71, 72, 77-78, 84-85; U. Fla. grantee, 1977-78 Fellow Am. Acad. in Rome; mem. Am. Philol. Assn., Am. Classical League, Vergilian Soc., Classical Assn. of Middle West and South (sec.-treas. 1975-82, pres. 1985-86) Home: 320 NW 30th St Gainesville FL 32607-2524 Office: U Fla Dept Classics Gainesville FL 32611

SCHMELTZ, EDWARD JAMES, engineering executive; b. Newark, June 22, 1949; s. Edward Leo and Loretta (Pittman) S.; m. Donna Hoppi Schmeltz, Sept. 28, 1974; children: Leigh Erin Wildes, Erik Edward. BS, N.J. Inst. Tech., 1971; M Engring., Tex. A&M U., 1972. Registered profl. engr., N.Y., N.J., Conn., Tex. Rsch. asst. Tex. A&M U., College Station, 1971-72; coastal/ocean engr. F.R. Harris, Lake Success, N.Y., 1972-74; sr. coastal engr. PRC Harris, 1974-76; dept. mgr. PRC Engring., 1976-79, project mgr. N.Y.C., 1980-87; v.p., dep. dir. N.Y. ops. Frederic R. Harris, Inc., 1987-93, sr. v.p., dir. N.Y. ops., 1993-94, sr. v.p., dir. ports and harbors, 1994—, sr. v.p., dir. internat. ops., 1997—. Lectr. George Washington U., Lehigh U.; mem. Coastal Structures steering com., 1979, 83; mem. adv. bd. Albert Dorman Honors Coll., NJ Inst. Tech., 2002--. Contbr. articles to technical and profl. jours. Mem. Flood and Erosion Control Bd., Rep. Town Meeting, Greenwich, Conn., 1988—. Recipient Adm. Harris award Frederic R. Harris, Inc., N.Y.C., 1989. Fellow Soc. Am. Mil. Engring.; mem. ASCE, NSPE, Permanent Internat. Assn. Navigation Congresses, Moles. Roman Catholic. Avocations: golf, flying. Office: DMJM & Harris 605 3rd Ave New York NY 10158 E-mail: eschmeltz@frharris.com.

SCHMELTZ, SISTER MICHAELA, clinical social worker, chaplain; b. Bklyn., Aug. 16, 1924; d. Raymond Aloysius and Adele Virginia (Manning) S. BA, Immaculate Heart Coll., L.A., 1956; MSW, Cath. U. Am., 1960. Lic. clin. social worker, Calif. Social worker Guadalupe Ctr., Kansas City, Mo., 1948-53, 63-66, St. Augustine's Parish, Culver City, Calif., 1953-56, Cath. Youth Orgn., San Francisco, 1956-58, Bayside Ctr., San Diego, 1960-62, Cath. Charities, Vallejo, Calif., 1968-71; social worker, dir. Providence Hosp., Oakland, 1971-76; dir. social work St. Jude's Hosp., Fullerton, 1976-79; social worker various hosps. and home health agys., 1979-95; clin. social worker Modern Home Care, Monrovia, Calif., 1995—. Mem. adv. bd. Vol. Assn., Kansas City, 1951-53, Mental Health Assn., Vallejo, 1968-71, Sr. Cmty. Svcs., La Verne, Calif., 1992-94. Contbr. articles to various publs. Mem. Mexican-Am. Neighborhood Assn., Kansas City, 1948-53. Mem. NASW, Acad. Cert. Social Workers, Sisters of Social Svc., Oncology Social Workers, Nephrology Social Workers (western regional rep. 1973-76). Avocations: singing, hiking, candle making, various crafts. Office: Modern Home Care 602 E Huntington Dr Monrovia CA 91016-3600

SCHMELTZER, DAVID, lawyer; b. N.Y.C., Mar. 8, 1930; s. Harry Schmeltzer and Julia Hoffman Liebman; m. Louise Rose Levy, June 10, 1962; 1 child, Daniel Havram. BA, L.I. U., 1957; LLB, Bklyn. Law Sch., 1960. Bar: N.Y. 1961. Assoc. Charles Struckler Law Office, N.Y.C., 1960-61; mng. atty. Otterbourg, Steindler, Houston & Rosen, 1961-62; pub. counsel U.S. Maritime Adminstrn., Washington, 1962-66; atty. Dept. Commerce, 1966; asst. chief counsel Nat. Hwy. Traffic and Safety Ad, 1967-73; asst. gen. counsel Consumer Product Safety Commn., 1973-75, dep. gen. counsel, 1975-77, acting gen. counsel, 1976-77, dir. compliance, 1977-97; atty. Squire, Sanders & Dempsey, 1998-99; product safety cons. Bethesda, Md., 1999—. Instr. U. Md. Univ Coll., College Park, 1979-90; mng. dir. Inst. Safety Analysis, Rockville, Md., 1981; vice-chmn. Internat. Consumer Product Health and Safety Orgn., 1995, 96, mem. exec. com., 1995-97; contbr. papers and lectures for consumer safety orgns. for European Cmty. and Chinese nat. govt. and provincial govts. Avocation: tennis. Home: 9424 Garden Ct Potomac MD 20854-3964 Office: 7316 Wisconsin Ave Ste 214 Bethesda MD 20814-2973 E-mail: dschmeltze@aol.com.

SCHMELTZER, EDWARD, lawyer; b. N.Y.C., Aug. 22, 1923; s. Harry A. and Julia (Hoffman) S.; m. Elizabeth Ann Cooper, June 19, 1949; children: Henry Cooper, Elizabeth Sabine. BA, Hunter Coll., 1950; MA, Columbia U., 1951; JD, George Washington U., 1954. Bar: D.C. 1954, U.S. Supreme Ct 1958. Economist PHA, 1951-53; econ. cons., 1953-54; trial atty. Fed. Maritime Bd. Maritime Adminstrn., 1955-60; dir. bur. domestic regulation Fed. Maritime Commn., 1961-66, mng. dir., 1966-69; ptnr. Morgan, Lewis & Bockius, 1969-76, Schmeltzer, Aptaker & Shepard, 1976—. U.S. rep. 12th Diplomatic Conf. on Internat. Maritime Law, Brussels, 1967, 13th Diplomatic Conf., Brussels, 1968 Mem. bd. editors: Jour. Maritime Law and Commerce; Contbr. articles to profl. jours. Served with USAAF, 1943-46. Recipient Fed. Maritime Commn.; Distinguished Service award, 1969 Mem. Maritime Adminstrv. Bar Assn. (pres. 1971-73) Clubs: Cosmos (Washington). Home: 10412 Buckboard Pl Rockville MD 20854-3805 Office: The Watergate Ste 1000 2600 Virginia Ave NW Washington DC 20037-1905 E-mail: es@saslaw.com.

SCHMELTZER, JOHN CHARLES, financial writer; b. Davenport, Iowa, Sept. 30, 1945; s. J. Howard and Virginia Marie (Smith) S. BA, Wartburg Coll., Waverly, Iowa, 1967; MA, No. Ill. U., 1974. Reporter Davenport Times-Democrat, 1967, Lynchburg (Va.) News, 1968-69; dir. pub. rels. Doane Coll., Crete, Nebr., 1967-68; news editor Belvidere (Ill.) Daily Rep., 1971-72; reporter Chgo. Tribune Co./The Trib, Hinsdale, Ill., 1973-76; area editor Suburban Trib, 1976-82; reporter, asst. bur. chief Chgo. Tribune, 1982-88, bur. chief, 1988-91, fin. writer, 1991—. Instr. McHenry County Coll., Crystal Lake, Ill., 1970-74, Coll. of DuPage, Glen Ellyn, Ill., 1982-86. Recipient 1st place award for spot news photography Iowa AP, 1967, 1st place award for feature writing No. Ill. Newspaper Assn., 1972, for editl. writing, 1981, 1st place award for pub. svc. Ill. AP, 1984, Peter Lisagor award Bus. Journalism, 1993, 94. Mem. Nat. Assn. Hispanic Journalists, Soc. Am. Bus. Editors and Writers, Wartburg Coll. Alumni Assn., Soc. Profl. Journalists, Chgo. Headline Club. Lutheran. Avocations: golf, fishing. Home: 33 W Huron St Chicago IL 60610-3753 Office: Chgo Tribune 435 N Michigan Ave Chicago IL 60611-4066

SCHMELZ, BRENDA LEA, legal assistant; b. Washington, June 13, 1958; d. Edward G. and Wilma D. (Hektor) R.; m. Jan M. Schmelz, Oct. 7, 1978; children: Edward L., Brent T. Secretarial sci. cert. with honors, East Ctrl. Coll., Union, Mo., 1977. Sec., paralegal Mittendorf & Mittendorf, Union, 1976-83, Eckelkamp, Eckelkamp, Wood & Kuenzel, Washington, 1983—2002. Mem. legal secretarial adv. bd. East Ctrl. Coll., 1978, chmn., 1987; mem. legal secretarial adv. bd. State Fair C.C., 1995. Mem. Nat. Assn. Ct. Reporters, Nat. Assn. Legal Secs. (mem. certifying bd. 1997-2000, chmn. 1998-2000, Jett award 1999), Mo. Ct. Reporters Assn., Mo. Assn. Legal Secs. (pres. 1994-96, pres-elect 1992-94, v.p. 1986, 89-91, sec. 1984-86, 89-90, dir. pub. rels. 1987-89, parliamentarian 1998-99, Legal Sec. of Yr. 1987), Franklin County Legal Secs. (pres. 1989-92, Legal Sec. of Yr. 1986, 95), Union of Women Today, Phi Beta Kappa. Republican. Roman Catholic. Home: 1792 Oak Parc Union MO 63084-3607 Office: Eckelkamp Eckelkamp Wood & Kuenzel Bank of Washington Bldg Main & Oak Washington MO 63084

SCHMELZER, HENRY LOUIS PHILLIP, lawyer, financial company executive; b. Concord, Mass., Aug. 10, 1943; s. Frank Elden and Carroll (Blanning) S.; m. Cynthia E. Livingston, Sept. 28, 1978. BA, U. Maine, 1965; JD, George Washington U., 1968. Bar: Mass. 1971. Atty. State Mut. Life Assurance Co., Worcester, Mass., 1970-72; various positions New Eng. Securities Corp., Boston, 1972-90, pres., dir., 1991-92; v.p. New Eng. Mut. Life Ins. Co., 1983-87. Pres., trustee New Eng. Funds, 1992-98; bd. dirs. Maine Bank & Trust Co. Bd. overseers U.S.S. Constitution Mus.; mem. divsn. capital campaign steering com. Am. Cancer Soc. Capt. M.I., U.S. Army, 1968-70, Vietnam. Decorated Bronze Star with oak leaf cluster; recipient Vietnamese Cross for Gallantry. Fellow Kennedy Sch. Govt.; mem. Boston Com. on Fgn. Rels., Mt. Desert Is. Hist. Soc. (bd. dirs.), Mass. Hist. Soc. (bd. dirs.). Republican. Unitarian Universalist. Avocations: skiing, hiking, sailing, Italian language. Office: New Eng Funds LP 399 Boylston St Fl 10 Boston MA 02116-3305

SCHMEMANN, SERGE, journalist; b. Paris, Apr. 12, 1945; arrived in U.S., 1951; s. Rev Alexander and Juliana (Ossorguine) S.; m. Mary Schidlovsky, Sept. 13, 1970; children: Anne, Alexander, Nathalie. BA cum laude, Harvard U., 1967; MA, Columbia U., 1971; LittD (hon.), Middlebury Coll., 1995. Desk editor AP, N.Y.C., 1972-75, UN corr., 1975-77, South Africa corr., 1977-79, Moscow corr., 1979-80; Moscow bur. chief N.Y. Times, 1980-87, 91-95, Bonn bur. chief, 1987-90, Jerusalem bur. chief, 1995-98, dep. fgn. editor, 1998—2001, UN bur. chief, 2001—. Author: Echoes of a Native Land: Two Centuries of a Russian Village, 1997; contbr. articles to profl. publs. With U.S. Army, 1968-70, Vietnam. Recipient Hal Boyle award, Overseas Press Club, 1986, Pulitzer Prize for Coverage of German Reunification, 1991. Mem. Phi Beta Kappa. Avocations: piano, carpentry. Office: NY Times 229 W 43rd St New York NY 10036-3959 E-mail: serge@nytimes.com.

SCHMERLING, ERWIN ROBERT, counselor, retired physicist; b. Vienna, Austria, July 28, 1929; came to U.S., 1955, naturalized, 1962; s. Heinrich H. and Lily (Goldsmith) S.; m. Esther M. Schmerling, Apr. 5, 1957; children: Susan D., Elaine M. BA, Cambridge U., 1950, MA, 1954, PhD in Radio Physics, 1958; grad., Advanced Mgmt. Program, Harvard, 1969, Fed. Exec. Inst., 1975. Asst. prof. elec. engring. Pa. State U., University Park, 1955-60, assoc. prof., 1960-62, 63-64; staff scientist NASA-Hdqrs., Washington, 1962-63, program chief ionospheric physics, magnetospheric physics, space plasma physics, 1964-82; asst. dir. space and earth scis. Goddard Space Flight Ctr., NASA, Greenbelt, Md., 1984-86; chief data system scientist Office Space Science and Applications NASA Hdqrs., Washington, 1986-88; SAIS program scientist NASA, 1988-89; data system scientist solar system exploration div. NASA Hdqrs., 1989-90, program mgr. astrophysics data systems, 1991-94; counselor Svc. Corps of Retired Execs. (SCORE), 1995—. Mem. U.S. coms. III and IV Internat. Sci. Radio Union, 1985—, sec. U.S. Com. III, 1966-69, chmn., 1969-72; chmn. subcom. C1 Com. Space Rsch. (COSPAR), 1984-88; mem. Adv. Group Aerospace R&D, NATO, 1978-85; vis. scholar Stanford U., 1983; cons. RCA, Gen. Electric, 1959-62. Contbr. papers to profl. jours. Recipient medal for contbns. to internat. geophys. programs Soviet Geophys. Soc., 1985. Fellow IEEE (mem. wave propagation standards com.); mem. Am. Geophys. Union, AAAS, Sigma Xi. Home: 9917 La Duke Dr Kensington MD 20895-3140 E-mail: e.schmerling@rcn.com.

SCHMEROLD, WILFRIED LOTHAR, dermatologist; b. Munich, Germany, Dec. 30, 1919; came to U.S., 1956; s. Wilhelm and Frieda (Hinterwinkler) S.; m. Perlette J. Joers, 1962 (div. Apr. 1974); children: Klaus, John, Will, James, Susan, Paul, Carl, Mike, Tom, Marianne. Abiturient, Altes Realgymnasium, 1938; MD, U. Munich, 1945. Bd. cert. dermatologist, dermatopathologist. Intern U Munich Med. Faculty, 1945-46; asst. UN Hosp., Munich, 1946-50, Max Plank Inst., Munich, 1951-52, U. Erlangen, Germany, 1952-53, U. Munich, 1953-56; intern Fairview Park Hosp., Cleve., 1956-57; asst. U. Ill., Chgo., 1957-60, instr., 1960-75, clin. asst. prof., 1975—. Dermatologist pvt. practice, Carol Stream, Ill., 1959—, dermatopathologist, 1978—. Contbr. articles to profl. jours. Charter mem. founders club Ctrl. DuPage Hosp., Winfield, Ill., 1963. Fellow AMA, Am. Acad. Dermatology (life), German Dermatological Soc. (life), Am. Soc. Dermatopathology, Ill. Dermatological Soc., Ill. State Med. Soc., Chgo. Dermatological Soc. Roman Catholic. Avocations: opera, travel, anthropology, archaeology, history. Office: Mona Kea Med Park 507 Thornhill Dr # B Carol Stream IL 60188-2703

SCHMERSE, TRACI JO, financial services company executive; b. Rockford, Ill., Jan. 24, 1959; d. Paul Eugene and Barbara Jean (Nelson) Hutmacher; m. Mike Schmerse, May 10, 1986 (div. Jan. 1988). AS, Rock Valley Coll., Rockford, Ill., 1982; BS in Biology, Rockford Coll., 1985. Mktg. asst. Pioneer Fin. Svcs., Rockford, 1989-90, mktg. analyst, 1990-91, exec. adminstrv. asst., 1991—, asst. corp. sec., 1994-96, sr. mktg. liaison, 1996—. Office: Pioneer Fin Svcs Inc 304 N Main St Rockford IL 61101-1019

SCHMERTMANN, JOHN HENRY, civil engineer, educator, consultant; b. N.Y.C., Dec. 2, 1928; s. Johannes Conrad Schmertmann and Margaret Anna-Marie (Carstens) Schmertmann Ottesen; m. Pauline Anne Grange, Aug. 11, 1956; children: Carl, Gary, Neil, Joy. BSC.E., MIT, 1950; MSC.E., Northwestern U., 1954, PhD in Civil Engring., 1962. Registered profl. engr., Fla. Soils engr. Mueser Rutledge Cons. Engrs., N.Y.C., 1951-54; soils engr. C.E., U.S. Army, Wilmette, Ill., 1954-56; asst. prof. civil engring. U. Fla., Gainesville, 1956-62, assoc. prof., 1962-65, prof., 1965-79, adj. prof., prof. emeritus; prin. Schmertmann & Crapps, Inc., Gainesville, 1979-97, LoadTest Inc., Gainesville, 1991—, Office John H. Schmertmann Inc., Gainesville, 1997—. Postdoctoral fellow Norwegian Geotech. Inst., Oslo, 1962-63; vis. scientist div. bldg. research NRC Can., Ottawa Ont., 1971-72 Author numerous profl. papers Fellow ASCE (br. pres. 1972, Collingwood prize 1956, Norman medal 1971, State of the Art award 1977, Middlebrooks award 1981, Terzaghi lectr. 1989), Fla. Engring. Soc.; mem. Nat. Acad. Engring. Lutheran. Avocation: sport fishing. Office: Office John H Schmertmann Inc 4509 NW 23rd Ave Ste 19 Gainesville FL 32606-6570

SCHMERTZ, ERIC JOSEPH, lawyer, educator; b. N.Y.C., Dec. 24, 1925; married; 4 children. AB, Union Coll., 1948, LL.D. (hon.), 1978; cert., Alliance Francaise, Paris, 1948; JD, NYU, 1954. Bar: N.Y. 1955. Internat. rep. Am. Fedn. State, County and Mcpl. Employees, AFL-CIO, N.Y.C., 1950-52; asst. v.p., dir. labor tribunals Am. Arbitration Assn., 1952-57, 59-60; indsl. relations dir. Metal Textile Corp. subs. Gen. Cable Corp., Roselle, N.J., 1957-59; exec. dir. N.Y. State Bd. Mediation, 1960-62, corp. dir., 1962-68; labor-mgmt. arbitrator, N.Y.C., 1962—; mem. faculty Hofstra U. Sch. Bus., 1962-70; prof. Hofstra U. Sch. Law, 1970—, Edward F. Carlough disting. prof. labor law, 1981-98, dean Sch. Law, 1982-89, disting. prof. emeritus of law, 1998—; of counsel The Dweck Law Firm, N.Y.C., 1999—; commr. labor rels. City of N.Y., 1990-91. Scholar-in-residence Pace U. Sch. Law, 1998—; 1st Beckley lectr. in bus. U. Vt., 1981; bd. dirs. Wilshire Oil Co.; mem. N.Y. State Pub. Employment Rels. Bd., 1991-97; cons. and lectr. in field. Co-author: (with R.L. Greenman) Personnel Administration and the Law, 1978; contbr. chpts. to books, articles to profl. jours., to profl. law confs., seminars and workshops. Mem. numerous civic orgns. Served to lt. USN, 1943-46. Recipient Testimonial award Southeast Republican Club, 1969; Alexander Hamilton award Rep. Law Students Assn.; Eric J. Schmertz Disting. Professorship Pub. Law and Pub. Svc. established Hofstra Law Sch., 1993. Mem. Nat. Acad. Arbitrators, Am. Arbitration Assn. (law com., Whitney North Seymour Sr. medal 1984), Fed. Mediation and Conciliation Svc., N.Y. Mediation Bd., N.J. Mediation Bd., N.J. Pub. Employment Rels. Bd., Hofstra U. Club, Princeton Club. Office: The Dweck Law Firm 230 Park Ave Rm 416 New York NY 10169-0422 E-mail: schmertz@dwecklaw.com.

SCHMERTZ, MILDRED FLOYD, editor, writer; b. Pitts., Mar. 29, 1925; d. Robert Watson and Mildred Patricia (Floyd) S. B.Arch., Carnegie Mellon U., 1947; M.F.A., Yale U., 1957. Archtl. designer John Schurko, Architect, Pitts., 1947-55; assoc. editor Archtl. Record, N.Y.C., 1957-65, sr. editor, 1965-80, exec. editor, 1980-85, editor-in-chief, 1985-90. Vis. lectr. Yale Sch. Architecture, 1979— Editor, contbr.: New Life for Old Buildings, other books on arch. and planning; contbg. writer: Architectural Digest, 2000—. Bd. mgrs. Jr. League, City of N.Y., 1964-65; commr. N.Y. Landmarks Preservation Commn., 1988-91. Fellow AIA; mem. Archtl. League N.Y., Mcpl. Art Soc. N.Y., Century Assn. (N.Y.C.) Home and Office: 310 E 46th St New York NY 10017-3002

SCHMETTERER, JACK BAER, federal judge; b. Chgo., Apr. 11, 1931; s. Samuel and Gertrude (Schiff) Schmetterer; m. Joan L. Ruther, Mar. 18, 1956 (dec.); children: Laura, Mark, Kenneth; m. Barbara Friedman, Sept. 2, 2001. BA, Yale U., 1952, JD, 1955. Bar: Ill. 1956. Instr. polit. sci. Yale U., New Haven, 1954-55, U. Ga., 1957-58; ptnr. Schmetterer & Schmetterer, Chgo., 1958-63; asst. U.S. atty. U.S. Dist. Ct. (no. dist.) Ill., 1963-68, 1st asst. U.S. atty., 1968-70; ptnr. Freeman, Schmetterer, Freeman & Salzman, 1970-71; 1st asst. states atty. State's Atty. of Cook County, 1971-73; assoc., ptnr., head of litigation Gottlieb & Schwartz, 1973—85; U.S. bankruptcy judge U.S. Bankruptcy Ct. (no. dist.) Ill., 1985—. Vis. prof. dept. criminal justice U. Ill., Chgo., 1974-76. Bd. dirs. Cook County Ct. Watchers, Inc., until 1985, Better Govt. Assn., until 1985; former mem. Northbrook Village Bd., North Shore Mass Transit Dist. Bd. With U.S. Army, 1956-58. Mem.: John Howard Assn. (chairperson 1997—99, bd. mem.), Fed. Bar Assn. (pres. Chgo. chpt. 1993—94), Fed. Trial Judges Conf., ABA, Just the Beginning Found. (v.p.), Decalogue Soc., Mackey-Wigmore Inn of Ct., Lawyers Club of Chgo. Office: US Bankruptcy Ct # 600 219 S Dearborn St Apt 600 Chicago IL 60604-1702

SCHMETTERER, ROBERT ALLEN, advertising executive; b. N.Y.C., Nov. 23, 1943; s. Robert Mayer and Rosalie (Fernandez) S.; children: Adam, Tyler; m. Stacy Lynn Chiarello, Sept. 26, 1987. BS, Fairleigh Dickinson U., 1967, MBA, 1970. Sales promotion mgr. Brit. Motor Corp., Leonia, N.J., 1963-68; market research dir. Volvo, Rockleigh, 1968-71; v.p. market rsch. Scali, McCabe, Sloves Inc., N.Y.C., 1971-73, sr. v.p. dir. account service, 1974-79, exec. v.p., chief oper. officer, mng. dir., 1979-84; pres., chief exec. officer/worldwide HCM, N.Y.C. and Paris, 1984-87; pres., ptnr. Messner Vetere Berger McNamee Schmetterer, N.Y.C., 1987—97; chmn. & CEO Euro RSCG Worldwide, 1997—. Bd. dirs. N.Y.C. Partnership, 1987—. Mem. Advt. Club N.Y. (dir. 1983). Address: Euro RSCG Worldwide 350 Hudson St Fl 6 New York NY 10014-4504

SCHMETZER, ALAN DAVID, psychiatrist; b. Louisville, Sept. 3, 1946; s. Clarence Frederick and Catherine Louise (Wootan) Schmetzer; m. Janet Lynn Royce, Aug. 25, 1968; children: Angela Beth, Jennifer Lorraine. BA, Ind. U., 1968, MD, 1972. Diplomate am. Bd. Psychiatry and Neurology with added qualifications in addiction psychiatry and electroconvulsive therapy; diplomate Am. Psychotherapy Assn., Am. Bd. Forensic Med. Examiners. Intern Ind. U. Hosps., Indpls., 1972-73, resident, 1972-75; dir. clinics PCI, Inc., Anderson, Beech Grove, Kokomo, 1975-79; psychiat. cons. Cmty. Addiction Svcs. Agy., Indpls., 1975-80; instr. psychiatry in primary care Family Practice Residency Programs St. Francis Hosp., St. Vincent's Hosp. and Ind. U. Hosps., 1975-91; med. dir. Child Guidance Clinic of Marion County, 1980-81; chmn. psychiatry dept. St. Francis Hosp., Beech Grove, 1980-82; med. dir. Crisis Intervention Unit Midtown Mental Health Ctr., 1980-90, dir., 1990-96, med. dir., 1996-98; coord. emergency psychiat. svcs. Ind. U. Med. Ctr., Indpls., 1980-90, asst. prof. psychiatry, 1975-94, assoc. prof. psychiatry, 1994—2002, coord. psychiat. edn. of med. students, 1989-95, asst. chmn. dept. psychiatry, 1993-96, dir. psychiat. edn., 1995-97, asst. chmn. edn. dept. psychiatry, 1997—, dir. psychiatry residency tng., 1998—, dir. addiction psychiatry residency tng., 1999—, prof. psychiatry, 2002—; chief psychiatry Wishard Meml. Hosp., 1990-98. Primary psychiat. cons. Ind. Dept. of Mental Health, 1988-89; med. dir. Ind. Divsn. Mental Health, 2001—. Contbr. articles to profl. jours. Maj. Ind. N.G., 1972-79. Decorated Army Commendation medal; recipient Residents award for outstanding teaching, 1985, 90, 97, Roeske Excellence in Teaching award, 1992, Med. Student Psychiatry Clin. Teaching award, 2000. Fellow Am. Psychiat. Assn. (distinq.), Am. Ortho-psychiat. Assn.; mem. AMA (Physicians Recognition award 1978—), Ind. Med. Assn., Indpls. Med. Soc., Ind. Psychiat. Soc. (pres. 1989-90, 97-98), Am. Orthopsychiat. Assn., Am. Acad. Clin. Psychiatry, Univ. Faculty Club Indpls. (v.p. 1999-2000, pres. 2000-01), Athenaeum Turnverein Club, Alpha Phi Omega, Phi Beta Pi, Psi Chi, Alpha Epsilon Delta. Presbyterian. Office: Dept Psychiatry 541 Clinical Dr # Cl292 Indianapolis IN 46202-5233 E-mail: aschmetz@iupui.edu.

SCHMID, ALFRED ALLAN, economist; b. Dawson, Nebr., Mar. 12, 1935; s. Alfred E. and Florence A. Schmid; m. Alice B. Todd, 1956 (dec.); children: Elizabeth, John; m. Kay A. McDevitt, 1985. BS, U. Nebr., 1956; MS, U. Wis., 1957, PhD, 1959. Asst. prof. Mich. State U., East Lansing, 1959-64, assoc. prof., 1964-68, prof., 1968-98, Univ. Disting. prof., 1998—. Vis. scholar Resources for the Future, Washington, 1964-65; mem. World Bank Mission to Romania, 1993. Author: Property, Power and Public Choice, 1978, 2d edit., 1987, (Chinese trans. 1999) Law and Economics, 1980, Benefit-Cost Analysis, 1989; editor: Beyond Agriculture and Economics, 1997; mem. edit. bd. Land Econs., 1969-71, Jour. Econ. Issues, 1972-75, Am. Jour. Agrl. Econs., 1978-80. Mem. East Lansing Planning Commn., 1973-75. Mem. Am. Agrl. Econs. Assn. (Quality of Comm. award 1992), Am. Econs. Assn., Assn. for Evolutionary Econs. Avocations: travel, writing. Office: Mich State Univ Dept Agr Econs East Lansing MI 48824 E-mail: schmid@msu.edu.

SCHMID, ANDREW MICHAEL, JR. advertising executive; b. Nanticoke, Pa., Aug. 19, 1957; s. Andrew Michael Sr. and Shirley Mae (Lasher) S.; m. Cindy L. Seiwell, Oct. 14, 1995. AAS in Comm. Design cum laude, Luzerne County C.C., 1977; BFA in Comm. Design, Kutztown State Coll., 1979. Designer, artist Conner Comml. Co., Bloomsburg, Pa., 1979-80; owner Schmid Advt., 1980—. Adj. prof. Bloomsburg State Coll., 1983-84. Bd. dirs. Ronald McDonald House, Danville, Pa., v.p. bd. dirs., 1999—. Recipient Addy Certs. of Merit and Excellence Am. Advt. Fedn., 1986. Republican. Roman Catholic. Avocation: painting.

SCHMID, FRANK ANDREAS, economist; b. Hermaringen, Germany, May 11, 1962; came to U.S., 1993; s. Hans Andreas and Maria Margarethe Schmid; m. Irene Evelyn Hinz, July 19, 1985 (div. Nov. 1991). Dipl.-Volkswirt, U. Gottingen, Germany, 1988; Dr.rer.pol., U. Luneburg, Germany, 1991, Dr.habil., 1996. Asst. prof. U. Vienna, 1991-94; lectr. U. Luneburg, Germany, 1996—2002, prof. fin. Germany, 2002; sr. economist Fed. Res. Bank, St. Louis, 1997—. Vis. prof. fin. U. Osnabruck, Germany. 1st lt. German Navy, 1981-83. Rsch. grantee Deutsche Forschungsgemeinschaft, Bonn, Germany, 1995-97; sr. rsch. fellow Fin. Inst. Ctr., U. Pa., Phila., 1995-97; vis. scholar U. Pa., Fin. Dept., 1993-94, postdoctoral scholar Free U., Berlin, Germany, 1994-95. Lutheran. Avocation: distance running. Office: Fed Res Bank 411 Locust St Saint Louis MO 63102 E-mail: mail@frankschmid.com.

SCHMID, HARALD HEINRICH OTTO, biochemistry educator, academic director; b. Graz, Styria, Austria, Dec. 10, 1935; Came to U.S., 1962; s. Engelbert and Annemarie (Kletetschka) S.; m. Patricia Caroline Igou, May 21, 1977. MS, U. Graz, 1957, LLD, 1962, PhD, 1964. Rsch. fellow Hormel inst. U. Minn., Austin, 1962-65, rsch. assoc., 1965-66, asst. prof., 1966-70, assoc. prof., 1970-74, prof., 1974—. Cons. NIH, Bethesda, Md., 1977—; acting dir. Hormel inst. U. Minn., 1985-87, exec. dir., 1987-01; faculty mem. Mayo Med. Sch., Rochester, Minn., 1990—. Mng. editor Chemistry and Physics of Lipids, Elsevier Sci. Publs., Amsterdam, The Netherlands, 1984-01; contbr. numerous articles to profl. jours. Rsch. grantee NIH, 1967—. Mem. AAAS, Am. Soc. Biochemistry and Molecular Biology, Am. Chem. Soc., The Oxygen Soc. Avocations: yacht racing, downhill skiing, classical music. Home: 2701 2nd Ave NW Austin MN 55912-1195 Office: U Minn Hormel Inst 801 16th Ave NE Austin MN 55912-3679

SCHMID, JOHN HENRY, JR. lawyer; b. Erie, Pa., May 11, 1944; s. John Henry Sr. and Margery (St. Lawrence) S.; m. Carol Christine Imig, July 1, 1967; children: Christine Catherine, Heidi Imig. BA, Beloit Coll., 1966; JD, U. Wis., 1969. Bar: Wis. 1969, U.S. Dist. Ct. (we. dist.) Wis. 1969, U.S. Ct. Appeals (7th cir.) 1993, U.S. Supreme Ct. 1993. Sr. ptnr. Axley Brynelson, Madison, Wis., 1969—. Emergency med. technician Village of Maple Bluff, Madison, 1977-84, trustee, 1985-89. Mem. Assn. Def. Trial Attys., Civil Trial Counsel Wis. Avocations: fishing, golf, travel. Home: 802 Farwell Dr Madison WI 53704-6034 Office: Axley Brynelson 2 E Mifflin St Madison WI 53703-2889

SCHMID, LYNETTE SUE, child and adolescent psychiatrist; b. Tecumseh, Nebr., May 28, 1958; d. Mel Vern John and Janice Wilda (Bohling) S.; m. Vijendra Sundar, June 13, 1987; children: Jesse Christopher Mikaéle, Eric Lynn Kalani, Christina Elizabeth Ululani. BS, U. Nebr., 1979; MD, U. Nebr., Omaha, 1984; postgrad., U. Mo., 1984-89. Diplomate Am. Bd. Med. Examiners, Am. Bd. Psychiatry and Neurology. Child and adolescent psychiatrist Fulton (Mo.) State Hosp., 1990-91, Mid-Mo. Mental Health Ctr., Columbia, Mo., 1991-96; owner Fairview Motel, Kemmerer, Wyo., 1996—. Clin. asst. prof. psychiatry U. Mo., Columbia, 1990-96. Contbr. articles to profl. jours. Mem. Am. Psychiat. Assn., Am. Acad. Child and Adolescent Psychiatry, Ctrl. Mo. Psychiat. Assn. (sec.-treas. 1992-93, pres.- elect 1993-94, pres. 1994-95), U. Nebr. Alumni Assn., Phi Beta Kappa, Alpha Omega Alpha. Republican. Avocations: walking, reading, studying scripture.

SCHMID, MICHAEL R. chemical engineer, consultant; b. Geneva, Switzerland, May 18, 1934; s. Robert Schmid and Hilda Aurora Forsberg; m. Mary Elizabeth Cronin, Feb. 20, 1965; children: Elizabeth Beatrice Schmid, Susan Forsberg Schmid Mitchell, Robert Glenn Schmid. BSChemE, MIT, 1957; postgrad., Newark Coll. Engring., 1962-64, Rutgers U., 1964. Registered profl. engr., D.C. Tech. supt. FMC Corp., Pocatello, Idaho, 1957-75; tech. mgr. Fluor Corp., Irvine, Calif., 1975-78; program mgr. Atlantic Rsch. Corp., Alexandria, Va., 1983-86, Summit Techs. Inc., Springfield, 1986-89; tech. dir. ABB, Pine Bluff, Ark., 1989-91; dir. Tamco Power Ptnrs., Williamsport, Pa., 1992-95; cons. Michael R. Schmid P.E., Independence, Va., 1995—. Mem. organizing com. Process Equipment Reliability Data Inst., N.Y.C., 1988-89. Contbr. articles to profl. jours.; patentee in field. Mem. AIChE, Am. Chem. Soc., Ancient Order Nobles of Mystic Shrine, Loyal Order of Moose. Republican. Methodist. Avocations: participating in large and small singing groups, church, adult education. E-mail: schmid@alum.mit.edu.

SCHMID, RUDI (RUDOLF SCHMID), internist, educator, academic administrator; b. Switzerland, May 2, 1922; arrived in U.S., 1948, naturalized, 1954; s. Rudolf and Bertha (Schiesser) Schmid; m. Sonja D. Wild, Sept. 17, 1949; children: Isabelle S., Peter R. BS, Gymnasium Zurich, 1941; MD, U. Zurich, 1947; PhD, U. Minn., 1954. Intern U. Calif. Med. Center, San Francisco, 1948—49; resident medicine U. Minn., 1949—52, instr., 1952—54; research fellow biochemistry Columbia U., 1954—55; investigator NIH, Bethesda, Md., 1955—57; assoc. medicine Harvard Med. Sch., 1957—59; asst. prof. Harvard U., 1959—62; prof. medicine U. Chgo., 1962—66, U. Calif., San Francisco, 1966—91, prof. emeritus, 1991—, dean Sch. Medicine, 1983—89, assoc. dean internat. rels., 1989—95. Cons. to U.S. Army surgeon gen. USPHS; hon. prof. Peking Union Med. Coll., Shanghai Second Med. U., Xian U. of Med. Sci., Jillin U. Medicine. Mem. med. editl. bd.: Blood, 1962—75, mem. med. editl. bd.: Jour. Clin. Investigation, 1965—70, mem. med. editl. bd.: Gastroenterology, 1965—70, mem. med. editl. bd.: Jour. Investigative Dermatology, 1968—72, mem. med. editl. bd.: Annals Internal Medicine, 1975—79, mem. med. editl. bd.: Procs. Soc. Exptl. Biology and Medicine, 1974—84, mem. med. editl. bd.: Chinese Jour. Clin. Scis., Jour. Lab. Clin. Medicine, 1991—, mem. med. editl. bd.: Hepatology Rsch., 1993—, hon. editor-in-chief: World Jour. Gastroenterology, 1996—, cons. editor: Gastroenterology, 1981—86. With Swiss Army, 1943—48. Master: ACP; fellow: AAAS, Royal Coll. Physicians, N.Y. Acad. Scis.; mem.: NAS, German-Am. Acad. Coun. (exec. com. 1992—99), Leopoldina, Swiss Acad. Med. Scis. (mem. senate), Am. Assn. Study Liver Disease (pres. 1965), Am. Gastroenterol. Assn., Am. Soc. Hematology, Am. Soc. Biol. Chemistry and Molecular Biology, Am. Soc. Clin. Investigation, Assn. Am. Physicians (pres. 1986, 1986), Am. Acad. Arts and Scis., Internat. Assn. Study Liver (pres. 1980—82, 1982). Achievements include research in biochemistry, metabolism of hemoglobin, heme, prophyrins, bile pigments, liver and muscle. Home: 211 Woodland Rd Kentfield CA 94904-2631 Office: U Calif Med Sch Office Dean PO Box 0410 San Francisco CA 94143-0410 E-mail: schmidr@medsch.ucsf.edu.

SCHMIDER, MARY ELLEN HEIAN, American studies educator, academic administrator; b. Chippewa Falls, Wis., Apr. 17, 1938; d. A. Bernard and Ellen Dagmar (Gunderson) Heian; m. Michael Heaton Leonard, June 16, 1962 (div. Oct. 1969); 1 child, William Gunerius Leonard; m. Carl Ludwig Schmider, June 17, 1970; 1 child, Dagmar Heian Schmider. BA in English Lit. magna cum laude, St. Olaf Coll., Northfield, Minn., 1960; MA in English Lit., U. So. Calif., 1962; PhD in Am. Studies, U. Minn., 1983. Mem. founding faculty in English, Calif. Luth. Coll., Thousand Oaks, 1961-64; instr. dept. English U. Vt., Burlington, 1964-70; instr. univ. writing program U. R.I., South Kingston, 1973-77; grad. asst. dept. rhetoric U. Minn., Mpls., 1975-76; dir. continuing edn./cmty. svcs. Moorhead (Minn.) State U., 1977-86, dean grad. studies and grad. faculty, 1983-95; U.S. Fulbright lectr. Lanzhou U., China, 1997. Bd. dirs. Luth. Brotherhood, Mpls., 1988-2001; mem. bd. higher edn. and schs. Evang. Luth. Ch. in Am., Chgo., 1987-95; mem. bd. pensions Luth. ch. in Am., Mpls., 1982-87; certificate coll. mgmt. Carnegie Mellon U., 1987; lectr. U. Maryland, U. Coll., Europe, Heidelberg, Germany, 2000—. Author biog. sketches Biog. Dictionary of Social Welfare. Mem. exec. comm. Minn. Humanities Commn., St. Paul, 1983-89, chair, 1987-88. Bush Leadership fellow, 1987. Mem. U.S. Fulbright Assn., Am. Studies Assn., Phi Beta Kappa, Phi Kappa Phi. Lutheran. Avocation: swimming, design, music, internat. travel, family activities.. Home: 7701 180th St Chippewa Falls WI 54729-6440

SCHMIDHAMMER, ROBERT HOWARD, environmental executive, engineering consultant; b. Altoona, Pa., May 13, 1931; s. Leo Anselm and Audrey Norma (Dibert) S.; m. Elaine Carol Jones, Dec. 18, 1954 (dec. Nov., 1986); children: Linda K., Raymond J.; m. Patricia M. Burgess, Feb. 29, 1996. BSME/ BSCE, Finlay Engring. Coll., Kansas City, Mo., 1958; grad. studies Engring. & Constrn. Mgmt., Various Schs., 1960-72. Constrn. mgr., consulting engr. Developers and individuals, different locations, 1960-87; sr. project mgr. Marcor Environ. Corp., Rochester, N.Y., 1987-90; engring. cons., environ. svcs. AAC Contracting, Inc., 1990-2001; pres., cons. RHS Assocs., LLC, 2001—. Cons. pvt. practice, Rochester, 1990—; bd. dirs. 3 non-pub. corps. Contbr. articles to environ. jours. Bd. dirs. various civic orgns. With USAF, 1950-53, Korea. Mem. Rochester Engring. Soc. (fin. cons.), Rochester Host Lions Club (pres., dir.), Rochester C. of C., Assn. Facilities Engrs., Cert. Hazardous Materials Mgr. (Finger Lakes chpt.), Construction Specifications Inst. (dir.), VFW, Am. Legion, Bldg. Owners and Mgmt. Assn. Republican. Roman Catholic. Avocations: travel, community service work. Home: 36 Rogers Ave Rochester NY 14606-1827 Office: AAC Contracting Inc Engring and Environ Svcs Rochester NY 14611 E-mail: rhls@frontiernet.net.

SCHMIDHAUSER, JOHN RICHARD, political science educator; b. N.Y.C., Jan. 3, 1922; s. Richard J. and Gertrude (Grabinger) S.; m. Thelma Lorraine Ficker, June 9, 1952; children: Steven, Paul, Thomas, John C., Martha, Sara, Susan. BA with honors, U. Del., 1949; MA, U. Va., 1952, PhD, 1954. Instr. U. Va., 1952-54; prof. constl. law U. Iowa, 1954-64, prof. polit. sci., 1967-73, U. So. Calif., 1973-92, prof. emeritus, 1993—. Mem. 89th Congress 1st dist. Iowa.; research fellow Research Inst. on Jud. Process, Social Sci. Research Council, 1958; sr. fellow law and behavorial scis. U. Chgo. Law Sch., 1959-60; Talbot vis. prof. govt. U. Va., 1982-83. Author: The Role of Supreme Court as Final Arbiter in Federal-State Relations, 1789-1957, 1958, The Supreme Court; Its Politics, Personalities and Procedures, 1960, Constitutional Law in the Political Process, 1963, (with Berg) The Supreme Court and Congress, 1972, (with Berg and Hahn) American Political Institutions and Corruption, 1976, (with Totten) Whaling in Japan-U.S. Relations, 1978, Judges and Justices, 1979, Constitutional Law in American Politics, 1984, Comparative Judicial Politics, 1987; contbr. chpt. to book; also numerous articles in jours. Chmn. Citizens Action Com. for Fair Representation in Iowa Legislature, 1961; dist. chmn. Operation Support Pres. Kennedy and Johnson, 1961—; chmn. Johnson County Dem. Ctrl. Com., 1961-64; del. Iowa Dem. Convs., 1956, 58, 60, 62; mem. Dem. Nat. Com. Alumni Coun., 1986—; chmn. Santa Barbara, Calif. Dem. Ctrl. Com., 1991-92; mem. exec. com. Los Padres chpt. of the Sierra Club, 1992-96; sec. Santa Barbara Dem. League, 1993-96. With USNR, 1941-45, PTO. Recipient Raubenheimer award U. So. Calif., 1991, Golden Key award for Comparative Rsch, 1991. Mem. Iowa City Mgr. Assn. (bd. reps. 1956-59, chmn. handbook revision 1958), Internat. Polit. Sci. Assn. (chmn. research com. for comparative jud. studies 1980-88), Am. Polit. Sci. Assn., Western Polit. Sci. Assn. (v.p., program chmn. 1980-81, pres.-elect 1981-82), AAUP (sec.-treas. State U. Iowa 1958-59, mem. com. on relationship fed. and state govt. to higher edn., mem. exec. com. U. So. Calif. chpt. 1983-92), Humanities Soc., Raven Soc., Phi Beta Kappa, Phi Kappa Phi. Unitarian (chmn. Iowa City Soc. Men's Club 1960-61). Avocation: French horn. Home: 726 Arbol Verde St Carpinteria CA 93013-2508 *For the young today the opportunity for a good education puts them at the threshold of great opportunities. I encourage them to enjoy that with the same spirit that my generation experienced.*

SCHMIDLI, KEITH WILLIAM, vocational education administrator, educator, researcher; b. Niagara Falls, N.Y., Oct. 11, 1952; s. Duane Irving and Jennie Mary (Schultz) S.; m. Jaquline Barbara Irish, May 27, 1978 (div. Jan. 3, 1982). AA in Liberal Arts and Scis., Niagara County C.C., Sanborn, N.Y., 1972; journeyman cert. auto/diesel mechanics, Trott Vocat. Sch., 1982; BS in Vocat. Tech. Edn. summa cum laude, SUNY, Buffalo, 1992, MS in Edn. summa cum laude, 1993; PhD magna cum laude, U. Buffalo, 1999; MBA, DBA, Cambridge State U., 2000, 01. Cert. tchr., N.Y.; cert. career devel. facilitator; cert. coord. for diversified coop. work-study programs. Maintenance mechanic, operating engr., machinist Gt. Lakes Carbon Corp., Niagara Falls, N.Y., 1973-82; owner, mgr. Apt. Rental Units, 1975-88; mechanic Tracy-Luckey Co. Inc., Andalusia, Ala., 1984-85; mechanic, operating engr. Niagara Falls Country Club, Lewiston, N.Y., 1985-86; millwright Custom Maintenance, Buffalo, 1986-87; pipefitter John Martin Plumbing, Niagara Falls, 1987; engring. technician Precious Plate, 1987-90; grad. adminstrv. asst. SUNY Coll., Buffalo, 1993-94, asst. prof., 1999—; adminstr. Niagara County C.C., Sanborn, N.Y., 1995-96. Faculty selection com. Dept. Tech. SUNY, Buffalo, 1992-94; tchg./curriculum cons. LaSalle Sr. H.S., Niagara Falls, 1992—; grad. student selection com. U. Buffalo, 1994-95, rsch. symposium com., 1994-95, acad. stds. com., 1995-99. Author: Increasing Enrollment in Secondary Vocational Eduction Programs Through Teacher-Based Promotion, 1993, Career Education: Exploring the Unfinished Agenda of Providing Applied Practical Knowledge and Skills Needed in a Changing Economy, 1999, Career Readiness and Employers' Expectations, 2000; contbr. articles to profl. jours. Vol., donor Red Cross Western N.Y., Buffalo, 1991-95; vol. Am. Heart Assn., Buffalo, 1996, Dept. Comty. Edn./Resource Devel., Niagara Falls, 1992. Mem. ASCD, ASME, Assn. Study of Higher Edn., Coun. Exceptional Children, Am. Soc. Quality, Soc. Mfg. Engrs., Libr. Congress Assoc., Am. Mus. Natural History, Postal Commemorative Soc., Alpha Sigma Lambda (charter pres. 1993-94), Kappa Delta Pi. Avocations: guitar playing, songwriting, camping, hunting, home remodeling. Home: 209 Sabre Park Niagara Falls NY 14304-1754 Office: SUNY Coll at Buffalo 109 Bacon Hall Buffalo NY 14222 E-mail: schmidkw@buffalostate.edu., schmidkw@juno.com.

SCHMIDLY, DAVID J. university president, biology educator; b. Levelland, Tex., Dec. 20, 1943; m. Janet Elaine Knox, June 2, 1966; children: Katherine Elaine, Brian James. BS in Biology, Tex. Tech U., 1966, MS in Zoology, 1968; PhD in Zoology, U. Ill., 1971. From asst. prof. to prof. dept. wildlife fisheries scis. Tex. A&M U., College Station, 1971-82, prof., 1982-96, head dept. wildlife, 1986-92, CEO, campus dean Galveston, 1992-96; chief curator Tex. Coop. Wildlife Coll., College Station, 1983-86; v.p. Tex. Inst. Oceanography, 1992-96; v.p. rsch. and grad studies, dean grad. sch., tech. transfer Tex. Tech U., Lubbock, 1996—, prof. biol. scis., 1996—, pres., 2000—. Cons. Nat. Park Svc., Wildlife Assocs., Walton and Assocs., Continental Shelf Assn., LGL; lectr. in field; press adv. com. Tex. A&M U., 1983-96; charter mem. Tex. A&M U. Faculty Senate, 1983-85, chmn. Scholarship Com., 1978-82. Author: The Mammals of Trans-Pecos Texas including Big Bend National Park and Guadalupe Mountains National Park, 1977, Texas Mammals East of the Balcones Fault Zone, 1983, The Bats of Texas, 1991, The Mammals of Texas, 1994, Texas Natural History: A Century of Change, 2002; contbr. articles to profl. jours. Trustee Tex. Nature Conservancy, 1991—; mem. adv. bd. Ft. Worth Zoo, 2000. Recipient Dist. Prof. award Assn. Grad. Wildlife and Fisheries Scis., 1985, Donald W. Tinkle Rsch. Excellence award Southwestern Assn. Naturalists, 1988, Diploma Recognition La Universidad Autonoma de Guadalajara, 1989, La Universidad Autonoma de Tamaulipas, 1990. Fellow Tex. Soc. Sci. (bd. dirs. 1979-81); mem. AAAS, Am. Soc. Mammalogists (life, editor Jour. Mammalogy 1975-78), Am. Inst. Biol. Scis. (bd. dirs. 1993—, coun. affiliate socs. 1989—), Am. Naturalist, Soc. Marine Mammalogy (charter mem.), Soc. Systematic Zoology, The Wildlife Soc. Soc. Conservation Biology, Nat. Geog. Sci. Soc., S.W. Assn. Naturalists (life mem., bd. govs. 1980-86, 91—, pres. 1981, trustee 1986—), Tex. Mammal Soc. (pres. 1985-86), Assn. Systematic Collections (bd. dirs.), Chihuahuan Desert Rsch. Inst. (v.p. bd. scientists 1982—, bd. dirs. 1991), Mexican Soc. Mammalogists, Sigma Xi (v.p. 1986-87, pres. 1987-88), Disting. Scientist award 1991), Coun. Pub. Univ. Pres. and Chancellors (exec. com. 2000), Golden Key, Beta Beta Beta, Phi Sigma, Phi Kappa Phi. Home: 4607 9th St Lubbock TX 79416 Office: Tex Tech U PO Box 42005 Lubbock TX 79409-2005 E-mail: david.schmidly@ttu.edu.

SCHMID-SCHOENBEIN, GEERT WILFRIED, biomedical engineer, educator; b. Albstadt, Baden-Wurttemberg, Germany, Jan. 1, 1948; came to U.S., 1971; s. Ernst and Ursula Schmid; m. Renate Schmid-Schoenbein, July 3, 1976; children: Philip, Mark, Peter. Vordiplom, Liebig U., Giessen, Germany, 1971; PhD in Bioengring., U. Calif., San Diego, 1976. Staff assoc. dept. physiology Columbia U., N.Y.C., 1976-77, sr. assoc., 1977-79; asst. prof. dept. applied mechs. & engring. scis. U. Calif., San Diego, 1979-84, assoc. prof., 1984-89, prof., 1989-94, prof. dept. bioengring., 1994—. Editor: Frontiers in Biomechanics, 1986, Physiology and Pathophysiology of Leukocyte Adhesion, 1994; author more than 220 rsch. reports. Recipient Melville medal ASME, 1990, Ratschow medal European Soc. Phlebology, 1999. Fellow Am. Inst. for Med. and Biol. Engring., Am. Heart Assn.; mem. Biomed. Engring. Soc. (pres. 1991-92), Am. Microcirculatory Soc., European Microcirculatory Soc., Am. Physiol. Soc. Achievements include bioengineering research on cardiovascular disease, microcirulation, and lymphology. Office: U Calif San Diego Dept Bioengineering La Jolla CA 92093-0412

SCHMID-SCHONBEIN, GEERT WILFRIED, biomedical engineer, educator; b. Albstadt, Germany, Jan. 1, 1948; came to the U.S., 1971; s. Ernst and Ursula Schmid; m. Renate Elisabeth Schmid-Schonbein, July 3, 1976; children: Philip, Mark, Peter. MS, U. Calif. San Diego, La Jolla, 1973, PhD, 1976. Staff assoc. Columbia U., N.Y.C., 1976-77, sr. staff assoc., 1977-79; asst. prof. U. Calif. San Diego, La Jolla, 1979-84, assoc. prof., 1984-89, prof. 5, 1989—. Founding fellow Am. Inst. Med. and Biol. Engring., Washington, 1991. Editor: Physiology and Pathophysiology Leukocyte Adhesion, 1995; contbr. articles to profl. jours. Cadent sgt. Bundeswehr, 1967-69. Recipient Melville medal ASME, 1990, Ratchow medal European Soc. Phlebology, Bremen, Germany, 1999; named hon. mem. Am. Venous Forum, San Diego, 1992; founding fellow Am. Inst. Med. and Biol. Engring., Washington, 1991. Fellow Am. Heart Assn., Am. Physiol. Soc., Biomed. Engring. Soc. (sr., pres. 1991-92); mem. World Coun. on Biomechanics, Microcirculatory Soc. (coun. mem. 1990-93), N.Am. Soc. Biorheology (pres. 1998-99). Avocation: hiking. Office: U Calif San Diego Dept Bioengring 9500 Gilman Dr La Jolla CA 92093-0412

SCHMIDT, ARTHUR, film editor; Editor: (films) (with Jim Clark) Marathon Man, 1976, The Last Remake of Beau Geste, 1977, Coal Miner's Daughter, 1980 (Academy award nomination best film editing 1980), The Escape Artist, 1982, Firstborn, 1984, The Buddy System, 1984, (with Harry Keramidas) Back to the Future, 1985, Fandango, 1985, (with Gib Jaffe) Ruthless People, 1986, Who Framed Roger Rabbit?, 1988 (Academy award best film editing 1988), (with Keramidas) Back to the Future II, 1989, (with Keramidas) Back to the Future III, 1990, (with Dov Hoenig) The Last of the Mohicans, 1992, Death Becomes Her, 1992, (with Jim Miller) Addams Family Values, 1993, Forrest Gump, 1994 (Academy award best film editing 1994), The Birdcage, 1996, (with Hoenig, Mark Stevens, Don Broschu) Chain Reaction, 1996, Contact, 1997, Primary Colors, 1998, What Lies Beneath, 1999, Cast Away, 2000. Office: Motion Picture & Video Editors Guild Local 776 7715 W Sunset Blvd Ste 220 Los Angeles CA 90046-3912

SCHMIDT, ARTHUR IRWIN, steel fabricating company executive; b. Sept. 9, 1927; s. Louis and Mary (Fliegel) S.; m. Mae Rosman, July 25, 1950; children: Jerrold, Cynthia, Elizabeth, Richard. Student, Colo. A&M Coll., 1946-47; BS in Aero. Engring., U. Ill., 1950. Sec. Rosman Iron Works, Inc., Franklin Park, Ill., 1950-86; pres. Rosman-Schmidt Steel Corp., 1986-00. With USNR, 1944-46, 51-52. With USNR, 1944—46, with USNR, 1947—52. Mem. B'nai Brith (trustee, past pres. Lincolnwood chpt.). Home: 1901 Somerset Ln Northbrook IL 60062-6067

SCHMIDT, B. JUNE, education educator; b. Alleghany County, Pa., Dec. 26, 1932; d. Ralph F. and Elizabeth M. (Gottschall) Hoffman; m. Richard E. Schmidt, Sept. 3, 1956; children: Amy Elizabeth, Stephen F. BBA, U. Pitts., 1956; MS, Va. Poly. Inst., 1959, EdD, 1974. Tchr. Montgomery County (Va.) Schs., 1959-62; free-lance writer Blacksburg, Va., 1963-68, 69-71; instr. Radford U., Redford, 1968-69; grad. rsch. asst. Va. Poly. Inst. and State U., Blacksburg, 1971-74, from asst. to prof., 1979-98; prof. emeritus, 1998—; supr. bus. edn. Va. Dept. Edn., Radford, 1974-79. Vis. scholar Inst. Edn. Rsch., Jyvaskyla, Finland, 1992; rschr. Nat. Ctr. Rsch. in Vocat. Edn., U. Calif., Berkeley, 1988-97. Named Collegiate Tchr. of Yr., Nat. Bus. Edn. Assn., 1991, Tchr. Educator of Yr., So. Bus. Edn. Assn.; recipient John Robert Gregg award McGraw Hill Pub., 1992; U. Coun. for Vocat. Edn. vis. scholar, 1994-95 Mem. Am. Vocat. Edn. Rsch. Assn. (pres. 1991, chair editl. bd. jour. 1989), Delta Pi Epsilon (pres. 1996-97, editor jour. 1988-89). Office: Va Poly Inst & State U Coll of Edn Blacksburg VA 24061-0254 E-mail: schmidtj@v1.edu.

SCHMIDT, BARNET MICHAEL, communications and electronic engineer; b. New Milford, N.J., June 30, 1958; s. Frank Lowell and Lee (Fishkin) S. BSEE, BS Computer Sci., Stevens Inst. Tech., 1980, MSEE, 1985. Cert. comml. pilot/instrument. Electronic engr. Cessna Aircraft Co., Boonton, N.J., 1980-81; sr. sys. engr. Timeplex Corp., Unisys Co., Woodcliff Lake, 1981-85; tech. staff, cons. AT&T Bell Labs., Holmdel, 1985-90; tech. staff Bell Comms. Rsch. (now Telcordia Technologies, Inc.), Piscataway, NJ, 1990—95; tech. staff network transmission sys. lab. Lucent Technologies Bell Labs., Holmdel, N.J., 1995-99; sr. tech. staff data arch. divsn. AT&T Corp. R&D, Middletown, NJ, 1999—2000; mem. tech. staff network ops. sys. engring. lab Lucent Tech., 2000—02; project engr., comm. sys. analysis BAE Sys. Inc., Totowa, NJ, 2002—. Cons. engr. Computer Scis. Corp., El Segundo, Calif., 1986-90. 3 Patents in field. Mem. IEEE (sr.). Achievements include invention of neural-network based intelligent systems for isolating hidden troubles in telecommunications networks; novel adaptive filter synthesis techniques, statistical signal identification methods, multiplanar image correlation, parallel image processing systems; development of optimal SONET network architectures and routing methods; robust fault tolerant optical transmission sys. and network surveillance sys., dense wavelength division multiplexing system developing; performance analysis and tuning of communications networks and operational support systems, wireless network modulation error correcting codes. Office: BAE Sys Inc Rm 11A52 164 Totowa Rd Totowa NJ 07474-0975 E-mail: barnetschmidt@lucent.com.

SCHMIDT, BERLIE LOUIS, soil and water conservation research administrator; b. Treynor, Iowa, Oct. 2, 1932; s. Hans Frederick and Louisa Amalie (Guttau) S.; m. Joanne Doris Bruning, Sept. 4, 1954 (dec. Apr. 1982); children: Brian, Luanne Schmidt Code, Kevin, Kimberly Schmidt Nelson, Christy Schmidt Mash; m. Bonnijane G. Mehlhop, June 14, 1986. BS, Iowa State U., 1954, MS, 1959, PhD, 1962. Soil scientist Soil Conservation Svc. USDA, Council Bluffs, Iowa, 1954-57; grad. rsch. assoc. Iowa State U., Ames, 1957-62; asst. prof. agronomy Ohio State U., Wooster, 1962-65, assoc. prof., 1965-69, prof., assoc. chmn. dept. agronomy Columbus, 1969-75, prof., chmn. dept. agronomy, 1975-86, prof., coord. Conservation Tillage Systems Program, 1986-87, prof. emeritus, 1987—; nat. program leader, soil and water rsch. Coop. State Rsch., Edn. and Extension Svc., USDA, Washington, 1987-99; ret., 1999. Program dir. Nat. Rsch. Initiative Competitive Rsch. Grants Program, 1994-97. Editor: Determinants of Soil Loss Tolerance, 1982; contbr. articles to sci. jours. Elder Worthington United Presbyterian Ch., Worthington, Ohio, 1983. With U.S. Army, 1954-56, PTO. Fellow Am. Soc. Agronomy, Ohio Acad. Sci., Soil Sci. Soc. Am.; mem. Soil and Water Conservation Soc. Am. (Outstanding Mem. award All-Ohio chpt. 1977), Internat. Soc. Soil Sci., Coun. Agrl. Sci. and Tech. Republican. Home: 6117 Turvey Loop E Dublin OH 43016-8791 E-mail: berboni614@aol.com.

SCHMIDT, CHARLES EDWARD, lawyer; b. N.Y.C., Oct. 6, 1951; s. Donald J. and Yanina S. (Giera) S.; children: John Charles, Michael Joseph. AB cum laude, Boston Coll., 1972; JD, Fordham U., 1975. Bar: N.Y. 1976, U.S. Supreme Ct. 1982. Law clk. Lilly Sullivan & Purcell, P.C., N.Y.C., 1973-76, assoc., 1976-84, Donovan Maloof Walsh & Kennedy, N.Y.C., 1984-86; ptnr. Kennedy & Lillis, 1986-93, Kennedy Lillis Schmidt & English, 1993—. Mem. N.Y. State Bar Assn., Maritime Law Assn., Assn. Average Adjusters U.S. (assoc.). Roman Catholic. Home: 255 W 108th St Apt 8D1 New York NY 10025-2926 Office: Kennedy Lillis Schmidt & English 100 Maiden Ln Ste 402 New York NY 10038-4816 E-mail: cschmidt@klselaw.com.

SCHMIDT, CHAUNCEY EVERETT, banker; b. Oxford, Ia., June 7, 1931; s. Walter Frederick and Vilda (Saxton) S.; m. Anne Garrett McWilliams, Mar. 3, 1954; children: Carla, Julia, Chauncey Everett. BS, U.S. Naval Acad., 1953; MBA, Harvard U., 1959. With First Nat. Bank, Chgo., 1959-76, v.p., gen. mgr. br. London, Eng., 1965-68, v.p. for Europe, Middle East, Africa, 1968-69, sr. v.p., 1969-72, exec. v.p., 1972, vice chmn. bd., 1973, pres., 1974-76; chmn. bd., chief exec. officer, dir. Bank of Calif. N.A., San Francisco, 1976—; chmn. bd., pres., chief exec. officer, dir. BanCal Tri-State Corp., 1976—. Dir. Amfac, Inc., Honolulu; mem. Adv. Council Japan-U.S. Econ. Relations; adv. bd. Pacific Rim Bankers Program. Exec. bd. and pres. San Francisco Bay Area council Boy Scouts Am.; council SRI Internat.; bd. dirs. Bay Area Council; bd. govs. San Francisco Symphony; trustee U.S. Naval War Coll. Fedn., Newport, R.I. Served with USAF, 1953-56. Mem. Assn. Res. City Bankers, Am. Bankers Assn., Internat. Monetary Conf., Calif. Bankers Clearing House Assn. (dir.), Calif. Roundtable (dir.), Japan-Calif. Assn. Clubs: Comml. (Chgo.); Bankers (San Francisco), Bohemian (San Francisco). Home: 40 Why Worry Ln Woodside CA 94062-3654 Office: Ste 140 525 Middlefield Rd Menlo Park CA 94025

SCHMIDT, CHERYL A. ZEISE, community health nurse; b. Green Bay, Wis., May 17, 1952; d. Richard F. and Darlene L. (Van Ess) Zeise; m. Dennis L. Schmidt, June 12, 1976; children: Heather, Andrew, Nick, Michael. ADN, Madison Area Tech. Coll., Wis., 1978; student, U. Wis., Stout, U. Wis. Extension; BSN summa cum laude, Marian Coll., Fond du Lac, Wis., 1997. Cert. in ambulatory care nursing. Staff nurse St. Mary's Hosp. Med. Ctr., Madison, 1978-80, Meth. Health Ctr., Madison, 1980-87; nursing coord. Meriter Retirement Svcs., 1987-94; acute care l-tel. triage nurse Group Health HMO, 1988-98, allergy nurse clinician, 1991-98, family practice nurse clinician, 1998—. Particpant in Robert Wood Johnson Found. Teaching Nursing Home, Meth. Health Ctr., Madison; rsch. specialist Ctr. for Health Sys. Rsch. and Analysis, Comprehensive Health Edn. Support Systems, U. Wis. Madison, 1998; lectr. in field. Past leader Boy Scouts Am., Girl Scouts U.S.A.; past project leader Dane County 4-H; past docent art in classroom

Huegel Elem. Sch.; classroom vol. Lakeview Elem. Sch.; libr. vol. Blackhawk Mid. Sch., 1991-93; coord. Tough Love Parent Support Group, 1997. U.S. Leadership grantee U. Wis., Stout. Mem. AAACN, Am. Acad. Asthma, Allergy and Immunology, Assn. Asthma Educators, Nurses Christian Fellowship. Office: Group Health East Clinic 5249 E Terrace Dr Madison WI 53718 E-mail: czschmidt@lycos.com.

SCHMIDT, CLAUDE HENRI, retired research administrator; b. Geneva, Switzerland, May 6, 1924; came to U.S., 1935; s. Roger Auguste Schmidt and Lucette (Henriette) Wuhrman; m. Melicent Esther Hane, June 25, 1953; children— Valerie Lynn, Jeffrey Allan AB, Stanford U., 1948, MA, 1950; PhD, Iowa State U., 1956. With Agrl. Rsch. Svc., USDA, 1956-88; rsch. entomologist Orlando, Fla., 1956-62; project leader Fargo, N.D., 1964-67; br. chief Beltsville, Md., 1967-72; area dir. N. Cen. region Fargo, 1972-82; lab. dir., 1982-88; acting dir. Red River Valley Agrl. Rsch. Ctr., 1988; collaborator, 1988-94; with Cass County Vector Control Dist., 1994—. Entomologist IAEA, Vienna, Austria, 1962-64; sec. Nat. Mosquito Fish and Wildlife Commn., Washington, 1968-72 Editor Leafy Spurge News, 1994—; contbr. articles to profl. jours. Mem. state legis. com. AARP, N.D., 2000—; mem. Fargo Sr. Commn., 2001—. With AUS, Signal Corps 1942-46, to 1st lt. Med. Service Corps, 1950-53. Fellow Washington Acad. Sci., AAAS; mem. Am. Mosquito Control Assn. (pres. 1981-82), Am. Chem. Soc., Entomol. Soc. Am., Nat. Assn. Ret. Fed. Employees (pres. N.D. fedn., 1988-89). Lodges: Elks. Republican. Home: 1827 3rd St N Fargo ND 58102-2335

SCHMIDT, CYRIL JAMES, librarian; b. Flint, Mich., June 27, 1939; s. Cyril August and Elizabeth Josephine S.; m. Martha Joe Meadows, May 22, 1965; children: Susan, Emily. BA, Cath. U. Am., 1962; MSLS, Columbia U., 1963; PhD, Fla. State U., 1974. Asst. bus. and industry dept. Flint Pub. Library, 1963-65; reference librarian Gen. Motors Inst., Flint, 1965; asso. librarian S.W. Tex. State U., San Marcos, 1965-67; head undergrad. libraries, asst. prof. Ohio State U., 1967-70; dir. libraries SUNY, Albany, 1972-79; also mem. faculty SUNY (Sch. Library and Info. Sci.); univ. librarian Brown U., Providence, 1979-81; exec. v.p. Rsch. Libraries Group, Stanford, Calif., 1981-89; prin. cons. Schmidt & Assocs., Palo Alto, 1989—; univ. prof. San Jose (Calif.) State U., 1992—. Author papers in field. Libr. Svcs. Act fellow, 1962-63, Higher Edn. Act fellow, 1970-72 Mem. ALA, ACLU, Pi Sigma Alpha, Beta Phi Mu. Home: 244 Forest Ave Palo Alto CA 94301-2510 Office: San Jose State U 1 Washington Sq San Jose CA 95192-0001 E-mail: schmidtc@sjsuvm1.sjsu.edu.

SCHMIDT, DANIEL EDWARD, IV, lawyer, commercial arbitrator; b. N.Y.C., Dec. 17, 1946; s. Daniel Edward III and Mary (Mannion) S.; m. Gail Kennedy, Sept. 5, 1980; children: Kathryn Kennedy, Michael Kennedy. BA, St. Lawrence U., 1971; postgrad., New Sch., 1972; JD, St. John's U., 1975. Bar: N.Y. 1976; cert. arbitrator. From asst. counsel to assoc. gen. counsel Prudential Property & Casualty, Holmdel, N.J., 1975-81, assoc. gen. counsel, divsn. head, 1981-82; v.p., assoc. gen. counsel, asst. sec. Prudential Reins Co., Newark, 1982-84; dir., v.p., gen. counsel, corp. sec. Scor U.S. Group, 1984-86, dir., sr. v.p., gen. counsel, corp. sec., 1986-89; dir., exec. com., sr. v.p., gen. counsel, corp. sec. Sorema N.A. Group, 1989-94, dir., exec. com., exec. v.p., group gen. counsel, 1995-99, dir. exec. com., group exec. v.p., chief legal officer, 1999-2000; dep. gen. mgr., gen. counsel, corp. sec. Sorema Internat. Holding, N.V., Netherlands, 1993-96; U.S. counsel Groupama, France, 1996-2000; cons. Sorema NA Group, 2000—. Pvt. practice comml. arbitrator, umpire, Little Silver, N.J., 1987—; reins. lectr., 1986—; pres., 1999-2002, chmn. 2002—, bd. dirs. ARIAS (U.S.), N.Y.C. Mem. editl. bd. Arias- U.S. Quar. Presiding judge Ecclesiastical Trial Ct., 1999—2000, Episcopal Diocese of N.J., 1997—; bd. dirs., exec. com. ARC, Monmouth County, Shrewsbury, NJ, 1981—84. With U.S. Army, 1967—70. Mem. ABA, Am. Arbitration Assn. (panel comml. arbitrators, roster of umpires), N.Y. Bar Assn., Assn. Internat. Droit des Assureurs (U.S. chpt.), Bamm Hollow Country Club, Desert Mountain Club. Episcopalian. Avocations: cycling, golf, skiing. Home and Office: Dispute Resolution Svcs Internat 628 Little Silver Point Rd Little Silver NJ 07739-1737 E-mail: dschmidt4@comcast.net.

SCHMIDT, DEREK, state legislator; b. Independence, Kans., Jan. 23, 1968; m. Jennifer Shaw, May 23, 1998. Student, Independence C.C.; B, Kans. U., 1990; M in Internat. Politics, U. Leicester, Eng., 1992; JD, Georgetown U., 1996. Bar: Kans. 1996, D.C. 1996. Mem. legis. staff Senator Nancy Kassebaum, 1992—96; gen. counsel, legis. dir. Senator Chuck Hagel, 1996—98; asst. atty. gen. State of Kans., 1999; legis. liaison, spl. counsel to Kans. Gov. Bill Graves, 2000; pvt. practice Scovel, Emert, Heasty & Chubb, Independence; mem. Kans. Senate from 15th dist., Topeka, 2001—, chmn. agr. com. Trustee Leadership Kans., ea. Kans. br. Nat. Multiple Sclerosis Soc.; active Am. Coun. Young Polit. Leaders. Ralph Kirchner scholar U. Leicester. Mem. Rotary. Republican. Office: PO Box 747 Independence KS 67301

SCHMIDT, DIANE JOY, photographer, author, educator; b. Lake Forest, Ill., Oct. 10, 1953; d. John and Miriam (Friedman) S. BA in Lit., Prescott (Ariz.) Coll., 1974; BFA, R.I. Sch. Design, 1976; MA, U. N.Mex., 2002. Pvt. practice, Chgo., 1977—, Chgo. and Ariz., 1992—, Chgo., Ariz., N.Mex., 1998—; grad. fellow U. N.Mex., 1999, instr. English creative writing and composition, 2001—02. Photography dept. faculty Columbia Coll., 1991-92; photog. and publs. cons. Northwestern U., U. Chgo., U. Ariz., Shimer Coll, Diné Coll.; pres., CEO Secure Magic Cane, Inc., 2000. Author, photographer: The Empire of Hell, 1981, Night Moves, 1984, Dishing It Out, 1986, Amen Corners: Chicago's Storefront Churches, 1987, Mother's Table, 1989, I Am a Jesse White Tumbler, 1990, WISE, 1996; photographer: Abstract Relations, 1980, The Chicago Exhibition, 1985, Street Level, A Journey Along Milwaukee Avenue, 1988, Where's Chimpy, 1988, Glass Acts, 1990, Signs, 1995, Navajo Psychology, 1997; co-dir. Elders Album Project, 1994; contbr. articles to profl. jours. Organizer Operation Family Photo, USO, 1991. Recipient Childrens Reading Round Table, 1988, 89, IABC Silver Quill award, 1994, PIX Photo Dist. News Digital Photo award, 1996, Arts Genesis Vol. of Yr. award, 1994, Health Edn. Sci. Comm. award, 1996; Arts Midwest fellow Nat. Endowment for Arts, 1988.

SCHMIDT, EDWARD CRAIG, lawyer; b. Pitts., Nov. 26, 1947; s. Harold Robert and Bernice (Williams) S.; m. Elizabeth Lowry Rial, Aug. 18, 1973; children: Harold Robert II, Robert Rial. BA, U. Mich., 1969; JD, U. Pitts., 1972. Bar: Pa. 1972, U.S. Dist. Ct. (we. dist.) Pa. 1972, U.S. Ct. Appeals (3d cir.) 1972, U.S. Ct. Appeals (D.C. cir.) 1975, U.S. Supreme Ct. 1981, U.S. Ct. Appeals (9th cir.) 1982, U.S. Ct. Appeals (4th cir.) 1982, U.S. Ct. Appeals (6th cir.) 1987, U.S. Ct. Appeals (2d cir.) 1992, U.S. Ct. Appeals (4th cir.) 1994. Assoc. Rose, Schmidt, Hasley & Di Salle, Pitts., 1972-77, ptnr., 1977-90, Jones, Day, Reavis & Pogue, Pitts., 1990—2001, Thompson Coburn LLP, Washington, 2002—. Mem. adv. com. Superior Ct. Pa., 1978-80; NITA instr. Duquesne U., 1998-99. Co-editor: Antitrust Discovery Handbook-Supplement, 1982; asst. editor: Antitrust Discovery Handbook, 1980; contbr. articles to profl. jours. Bd. dirs. Urban League, Pitts., 1974-77, NITA instr., Duquesne U., 1998, 99. Mem. Supreme Ct. Hist. Soc., Pa. Bar Assn., D.C. Bar Assn., Allegheny County Bar Assn. (pub. reos. com. coun. civil litigation sect. 1977-80), Internat. Acad. Trials Lawyers, Acad. Trial Lawyers Allegheny County (bd. govs. 1980), Western Res. Acad. Alumni Assn. (trustee 1998—). Clubs: Rolling Rock (Ligonier, Pa.), Duquesne (Pitts.), Longue Vue (Pitts.) Republican. Office: Thompson Coburn LLP 6th Fl 1909 K St NW Washington DC 20006-1167 Home: 159 Washington St Pittsburgh PA 15218-1351

SCHMIDT, FREDERICK ALLEN, research scientist, consultant; b. Cin., Dec. 26, 1930; s. Charles Louis and Elfrieda (Vetter) Schmidt; m. Barbara Jane Westhoff, Oct. 20, 1951; children: Frederick Louis, John Robert, Mark Edward, Cheryl Ann. BS in Chemistry, Xavier U., 1951. Jr. chemist Iowa State U. Ames Lab., 1951—54, jr. rsch. assoc., 1954—56, assoc. metallurgist, 1957—71, metallurgist, 1971—77, sr. metallurgist, 1977—86, prin. metallurgist, 1986—93, scientist emeritus, 1993—. Cons. in field, 1993—96. Contbr. chapters to books, articles to profl. jours. Recipient Svc. award, NASA/AIAA Tech. Com. Space Processing, 1980, R&D 100 award, R&D Publ., Chgo., 1990, Annual Fed. Lab. Consortium Excellence in Tech. Transfer award, 1990. Mem.: AIAA, Am. Inst. Mining, Metallurgical and Petroleum Engrs., Am. Soc. for Metals. Republican. Roman Catholic. Achievements include patents for concerning the preparation, refining and recovery of various refractory and rare earth alloys. Avocations: hunting, fishing, golf, skeet shooting, wine making. Home: 211 20th St Ames IA 50010 Office: Ames Lab Iowa State Univ 221 MD Bldg Ames IA 50011

SCHMIDT, GEORGE, physicist, educator; b. Budapest, Hungary, Aug. 1, 1926; s. Laszlo Schmidt and Katalin Wellisch; m. Katalin Varkonyi, June 26, 1955; children: Franklin R., Ronald W. Diploma in Elec. Engring., Tech. U., Budapest, 1950; PhD in Physics, Hungarian Acad. Scis., Budapest, 1956; M in Engring., Stevens Inst. Tech., 1961. Sr. lectr. Israel Inst. Tech., Haifa, Israel, 1957-58; asst. prof. Stevens Inst. Tech., Hoboken, N.J., 1959-61, assoc. prof., 1961-63, prof. physics, 1963-83, George Meade Bond prof. physics and engring. physics, 1983-92, prof. emeritus, 1992—. Vis. prof. U. Wis., 1965, UCLA, 1972-73; vis. scientist Culham Labs., Culham, Eng., 1965, Ecole Polytechnique, Paris, 1979-80; cons. Sci. Applications Inc., Washington, 1981—, Poly. U. of N.Y., 1984—, Berkeley Assocs., Washington, 1985. Author: Physics of High Temperature Plasmas, 1966, 2nd rev. edit., 1979; contbr. sci. articles to profl. jours. Recipient Research award Stevens Inst. Tech., 1961. Fellow Am. Phys. Soc.; mem. N.Y. Acad. Scis. Office: Stevens Inst of Tech Dept Of Physics Hoboken NJ 07030 E-mail: gschmidt@stevens-tech.edu.

SCHMIDT, GLENN NORBERT, special education educator; b. LaCrosse, Wis., Sept. 19, 1949; s. Norbert John and Arlene Louise Schmidt; m. Kristine Kay Hoover, Jan. 15, 1972; 1 child John Charles. BA, U. Wis., Madison, 1971; MS in Edn., U. Wis., LaCrosse, 1976. Tchr. LaCrosse Home for Children, 1974—77; spl. edn. tchr. Sun Prairie (Wis.) Pub. Schs., 1977—. Mem. adv. panel on spl. edn. State Supt. of Schs., Madison, Wis., 1998—2001; Dem. Nat. Conv. L.A., 2000. Grantee Fulbright Meml. Fund, Japan, 1998. Mem.: NEA (alt. dir., Washington 2001—, del. Edn. Internat. Gen. Assembly, Costa Rica, Stockholm and Washingto 1989—98), Wis. Edn. Assn. Coun. (bd. dirs. 1995—), Sun Prairie Edn. Assn. (pres. 1990—). Democrat. Avocations: golf, travel, writing for periodicals. Home: 227 North St Sun Prairie WI 53590 Office: Sun Prairie Pub Schs 230 W Klubertane Dr Sun Prairie WI 53590

SCHMIDT, GORDON PEIRCE, artistic director; Former dancer; resident choreographer Ballet Chgo., 1990-95; artistic dir. Grand Rapids (Mich.) Ballet, 1999—. Office: Grand Rapids Ballet Co 341 Ellsworth Ave Grand Rapids MI 49503-4045*

SCHMIDT, HAROLD EUGENE, real estate company executive; b. Cedar Rapids, Iowa, Oct. 12, 1925; s. Alfons W. and Lillie (Schlegel) S.; m. Lucy Hermann, Apr. 13, 1957; children: Harold, Sandra. BS in Civil Engring, U. Iowa, 1949; MS in San. Engring, MIT, 1953. Research and devel. engr. Chgo. Pump Co., 1949-51; engr. A.B. Kononoff, Miami, Fla., 1956-58; with Gen. Devel. Corp., 1958-82, v.p. utilities, asst. v.p. ops., 1967-72, v.p., 1972-81, v.p. community div., 1973-81, sr. v.p., 1981-82; pres. Gen. Devel. Utilities Inc., 1972-82, Kingsway Properties, Inc., 1982—. Dir. Port Charlotte Bank, Fla. Served to capt. USAF, 1951-56. Mem. Sigma Xi, Chi Epsilon. Home and Office: 12313 SW Kingsway Cir Arcadia FL 34269-8734

SCHMIDT, HARVEY MARTIN, economic forecaster, educator, financial consultant; b. Chgo., Sept. 15, 1925; s. Joseph David and Dorothy Schmidt; m. Barbara Bebe Bloom, Nov. 25, 1961; children— Ellen Louise, Jay Stephen, Gregg Arthur. Student U. So. Calif., 1943; B.A. magna cum laude, Woodbury U., 1947. Assoc. prof. bus. Woodbury U., 1947-48; pvt. practice acctg., Los Angeles, 1948-80; cons. mgmt., taxes and fins., Los Angeles, 1965-82; econ. forecaster, internat. lectr., investment lectr. on Audio Tapes, 1989—, Investment lectr. on Internat. Cruise Ships, 1992, fin. cons. Pacific Palisades, 1982—; pres. Harvey Schmidt Mgmt. Inc., 1983— pres. Med-Plan Operators, 1969-89; pres. Kit Travel, 1987—. With USCG, 1943-44. Life Master, U.S. Contract Bridge League, 1960—. Internat. Platform Assn., Exch. Club (pres. local chpt. 1953-56), Bruin Athletic Club of UCLA. Contbr. articles to profl. jours.

SCHMIDT, HERMAN J. former oil company executive; b. Davenport, Iowa, Feb. 26, 1917; s. Herman and Lillian (Beard) S.; m. Eileen Carpenter, Dec. 20, 1967; children: Paul David, Sarah Louise. AB, U. Iowa, 1938; JD, Harvard U., 1941. Bar: N.Y. 1943. With Cravath, Swaine & Moore, 1941-44, 47-51; tax counsel Socony Mobil Oil Co. Inc. (now Mobil Corp.), N.Y.C., 1951-55, adminstrv. asst. to gen. counsel, 1955, assoc. gen. counsel, 1955-56, gen. counsel, 1956-59, exec. v.p., 1959-74, vice chmn., 1974-78, dir., 1957-78; pres. Mobil Internat. Oil Co., 1959-63. Bd. dirs. H.J. Heinz Co. Former chmn. bd. trustees Am. Enterprise Inst.; hon. life trustee U. Iowa Found. Served to 1st lt. M.I. Corps, AUS, 1944-47. Mem. Harvard Law Rev. Assn., Blind Brook Club (Ryebrook, N.Y.), Phi Beta Kappa, Phi Gamma Delta. Home: 15 Oakley Ln Greenwich CT 06830-3025

SCHMIDT, JAMES CRAIG, retired bank executive; b. Peoria, Ill., Sept. 27, 1927; s. Walter Henry and Clara (Wolfenbarger) S.; m. Jerrie Louise Bond, Dec. 6, 1958; children: Julie, Sandra, Suzanne. Student, Ill. Wesleyan U., 1945, 48-50, Ph.B. in Bus. Adminstrn, 1952; postgrad., U. Ill. Coll. Law, 1950-52; JD, DePaul U., 1953. Spl. agt. Fidelity & Deposit Co., Chgo., 1956-58; with Home Fed. Savs. & Loan Assn., San Diego, 1958-67; asst. sec. bus. and transp. State of Calif., 1967-69; vice-chmn., pres. Gt. Am. Bank, San Diego, 1969-88. Pres. Conf. Fed. Savs. and Loans of Calif., 1974-75; mem. Calif. Toll Bridge Authority, 1969-74; mem. Calif. State Transp. Bd., 1972-78; past chmn. San Diego Bal. Commn. Task Force. Pres. San Diego Holiday Bowl Football Game, 1986; bd. dirs. San Diego Internat. Sports Coun., San Diego Hwy. Devel. Assn. Mem. Calif. Bar Assn., Ill. Bar Assn., Calif. League Savs. Instns. (chmn. 1986-87), Calif. C. of C. (bd. dirs. 1987-90), U.S. Savs. Instn. League (exec. com. 1983-86), San Diego East County C. of C. (bd. dirs.), Catfish Club, Sigma Chi, Phi Delta Phi. Office: 8383 Center Dr Ste J La Mesa CA 91942-2913 Fax: 619-469-5927.

SCHMIDT, JANIS ILENE, elementary education educator; b. Wyandot County, Ohio., Feb. 4, 1930; d. Floyd Dale and Edith June (Clark) Herbert; m. William Frederick Schmidt, Aug. 27, 1950; children: Lon William, Randy Floyd. BS, Findlay Coll., 1968; MEd, Ashland Coll., 1986. Cert. elem. tchr., Ohio. Elem. tchr. Wharton (Ohio) Elem., 1950-52, Upper Sandusky (Ohio) Schs., 1967—. Author: Improvement of Retention, 1986. Officer Beta Usando Literary Club, Upper Sandusky, 1993; mem. Wyandot Meml. Hosp. Guild, 1980-95, North Salem Luth. Ch. Tchr., officer, 1950—, Tri-G Mothers League, 1953-80. Jennings scholar The Martha Holden Jennings Found., Ohio, 1969-73. Mem. Internat. Reading Assn. (com. chmn. 1990). Republican. Lutheran. Avocations: golf, boating, bicycling, gardening, sewing. Home: 569 N Warpole St Upper Sandusky OH 43351-9332 Office: East Sch 401 3rd St Upper Sandusky OH 43351-1105

SCHMIDT, JOANNE (JOSEPHINE ANNE SCHMIDT), language educator; b. N.Y.C., June 7, 1950; d. Joseph William and Maria Esther (Morazzani) S. BA, Chestnut Hill Coll., Phila., 1972; MA, U. Va., 1974, PhD, 1980. Tchg. asst. U. Va., Charlottesville, 1973-76, Lycée Marie Curie, Sceaux, France, 1976-77; lectr. U. Va., Charlottesville, 1977-79; asst. prof. Cedar Crest Coll., Allentown, Pa., 1981-84, Calif. State U., Bakersfield, 1984-88, assoc. prof., 1988-94, prof., 1994—, chair dept., 1998—. Freelance translator, Bklyn., 1979-81, Allentown, Pa., 1981-84, Bakersfield, Calif., 1984—. Author: (book) If There Are No More Heroes There Are Heroines: A Feminist Critique of Corneille's Heroines, 1987, (jour.) San Jose Studies, 1987, (poetry book) (author as Teresita Bosch) Portraits, 1991; assoc. editor: (jour.) Coll. Tchg., 1985-89. V.p. Women, Inc., Allentown, 1983-84; pub. spkr. Alliance Against Family Violence, Bakersfield, Calif., 1985-90. Fulbright Hays grantee Fed. Govt., 1976-77, Affirmative Action grantee Calif. State U., 1985, 87, 91. Mem. MLA, NOW, Am. Assn. Tchrs. of French, Nat. Women's Studies Assn., Calif. Lang. Tchrs. Assn., Delta Kappa Gamma. Democrat. Avocations: carpentry, golf, creative writing, family history, oral history. Office: Calif State U Modern Langs & Lit Dept 9001 Stockdale Hwy Bakersfield CA 93311-1022

SCHMIDT, JOHN GERHARD, neurologist, educator, researcher; b. Rock Springs, Wyo., Oct. 17, 1956; s. Gerhard Daniel and Phillys Elaine (Score) S.; m. Lenore Ann Ilg, May 2, 1987; children: Kirstin, Joseph, Rebecca. BS in Phys. Scis., Colo. State U., 1980; MD, U. Minn., 1985. Diplomate Am. Bd. Psychiatry and Neurology, Nat. Bd. Med. Examiners. Intern in internal medicine Med. Coll. Wis. Affiliated Hosps., Milw., 1985-86, resident in neurology, 1986-88, chief resident, 1988-89; fellow in neurorehab. Burke Rehab. Ctr., Cornell U. Med. Coll., White Plains, N.Y., 1989-90; med. dir. PremierCare Neurorehab. Ctr., St. Louis, 1990-93; instr., dir. divsn. neurologic rehab. dept. neurology St. Louis U., 1990-93; dir. stroke rehab. Souers Stroke Inst., St. Louis, 1991-93; sr. instr. dept. neurology U. Rochester (N.Y.) Sch. Medicine and Dentistry, 1993-95, asst. prof. neurology, 1995—2001; asst. prof. rehab. U. Rochester (N.Y.) Sch. Medicine, 1997—2001, assoc. prof. neurology and rehab., 2001—; assoc. attending neurologist Strong Hosp. U. Rochester, 1998—; attending neurologist dept. phys. medicine and rehab. St. Mary's Hosp., 1993—, med. dir., 1993-96, secondary appointment, asst. prof. of rehab., 1997—2001. Mem. cardiovascular health care team Preferred Care, 1999—; mem. ethics com. Unity Health Systems; presenter in field. Contbg. author: Comprehensive Neurologic Rehabilitation, Vol. 5: Orthotics in Neurologic Rehabilitation, 1992, Neurotrauma, 1996; contbr. articles and abstracts to med. jours. Bd. dirs., med. dir. PRALID (People Rebldg. and Living in Dignity), Rochester, 1994-2000, treas., 1998-2000; mem. stroke edn. com. Am. Heart Assn., St. Louis, 1991-93; mem. Operation Stroke, Am. Stroke Assn., 2000—, chair subcom. rehab. and recovery Genesee Valley chpt. Recipient Burke award Winifred Masterson Burke Found., 1990, lifetime achievement award N.Y. Easter Seals Soc., 1994; Army and Navy ROTC scholar, 1975-79; NSF fellow Colo. Sch. Mines, 1974 Mem. Am. Acad. Neurology, Am. Soc. Neurorehab. (cert.), Phi Kappa Phi. Lutheran. Avocations: fishing, skiing, mountain climbing, photography. Office: Unity Health Sys Rehab Program 89 Genesee St Rochester NY 14611-3201 E-mail: schmidtjohng@netscape.net.

SCHMIDT, JOHN RICHARD, agricultural economics educator; b. Madison, Wis., July 3, 1929; s. Oscar John and Alma Theodora (Ula) S.; m. Rosemary Pigorsch, Oct. 7, 1951; children: Janet, Deborah, Allen. BS, U. Wis., 1951, MS, 1953; PhD, U. Minn., 1960. Asst. prof. agr. econs. U. Wis., Madison, 1956-61, assoc. prof., 1961-65, prof., 1965-95, prof. emeritus, 1995—, chmn. dept., 1966-70; owner, mgr. JRS Computing Svcs., 1995—. Farm mgmt. cons. Am. Farm Bur. Fedn., Chgo., 1962; cons. Banco de Mexico, 1972-84, IBRD (World Bank), 1973-94; Agrl. Devel. Bank Iran, 1974-76; mem. adv. bd. Internat. Devel. Inst., 1983; faculty Salzburg Seminar, 1983, 85. Contbr. articles to tech. jours., also monographs, bulls. Bd. dirs. U. Wis. Credit Union, 1968-77, pres., 1969-75; mem. com. Wis.-Upper Mich. Synod Sem., 1972-75, mem. ch. coun. 1967-69, 72-75, pres. 1974-75. Mem. Rotary (pres. Madison West 1994-95), Delta Theta Sigma (nat. sec. 1962-64), Gamma Sigma Delta (pres. Wis. chpt. 1975). Lutheran. Home: 106 Frigate Dr Madison WI 53705-4426 Office: JRS Computing Svcs 6601 Grand Teton Plz Ste 4 Madison WI 53719-1049 E-mail: jrschmi1@facstaff.wisc.edu.

SCHMIDT, JOSEPH DAVID, urologist; b. Chgo., July 29, 1937; s. Louis and Marian (Fleigel) S.; m. Andrea Maxine Herman, Oct. 28, 1962. BS in Medicine, U. Ill., 1959, MD, 1961. Diplomate Am. Bd. Urology. Rotating intern Presbyn. St. Luke's Hosp., Chgo., 1961-62, resident in surgery, 1962-63; resident in urology The Johns Hopkins Hosp., Balt., 1963-67; faculty U. Iowa Coll. Medicine, Iowa City, 1969-76, U. Calif., San Diego, 1976—, prof., head div. urology, 1976—, vice-chmn. dept. surgery, 1985-97. Cons. U.S. Dept. Navy, San Diego, 1976—; attending urologist Vets. Affairs Dept., San Diego, 1976—; assoc. dir. for clin. rsch. U. Calif. San Diego Cancer Ctr., 1997-98. Author, editor: Gynecological and Obstetric Urology, 1978, 82, 93. Capt. USAF, 1967-69. Recipient Francis Senear award. U. Ill., 1961 Fellow Am. Coll. of Surgeons; mem. AMA, Am. Urol. Assn. Inc., Alpha Omega Alpha. Avocations: collecting antique medical books, manuscripts. Office: U Calif Med Ctr Divsn Urology 200 W Arbor Dr San Diego CA 92103-8897 Fax: 619-543-6573.

SCHMIDT, JOSEPH W. lawyer; b. Jeffersontown, Ky., July 6, 1946; s. A.W. and Olivia Ann S.; m. Angela Petchara Apiradee, Dec. 20, 1969; children: Narissa Ann, Suriya Christine. BA in Psychology, Bellarmine Coll., 1969; AB in Commerce, U. Md., Bangkok, 1972; JD, Columbia U., 1975. Bar: N.Y. 1976. Law clk. to presiding judge U.S. Dist. Ct. (so. dist.), N.Y., 1975-76; assoc. Breed, Abbott & Morgan, N.Y.C., 1976-83, ptnr., 1983-93, Whitman Breed Abbott & Morgan, 1993-96, Coudert Bros., N.Y.C., 1996—. Adminstrv. editor Columbia Jour. of Law and Social Problems, 1974-75. Woodrow Wilson fellow, 1968; Harlan Fiske Stone scholar, 1975. Mem. ABA, Assn. of Bar of the City of N.Y., N.Y. Bar Assn., Am. Coll. Investment Counsel. Avocations: skiing, reading. Office: Coudert Bros 1114 Ave Of The Americas New York NY 10036-7710 E-mail: schmidtj@coudert.com.

SCHMIDT, JULIUS, sculptor; b. Stamford, Conn., June 2, 1923; s. Louis Frank and Susie (Koment) S.; m. Carolyn Marsha Wolf (div.); children: Ania J., Ianos; m. Mary Katherine Powers, 1981 (div.); 1 child, Araan J. Student, Okla. A&M U., 1950-51; BFA, Cranbrook Acad. Art, 1952, MFA, 1955; student, Ossip Zadkine, Paris, 1953, Accademia di Belle Arti, Florence, Italy, 1954. Chmn. sculpture dept. Kansas City Art Inst., 1954-59, R.I. Sch. Design, 1959-60, U. Calif.-Berkeley, 1961-62, Cranbrook Acad. Art, 1962-70, U. Iowa, Iowa City, 1970-93; ret., 1993. Exhibited in 39 one-man shows 1953—; group shows include Allen Meml. Art Mus., Oberlin, Ohio, 1958, Arts Club of Chgo., Mus. Modern Art, N.Y.C., 1960, Whitney Mus., 1960-63, Gallerie Claude Bernard, paris, 1960, Guggenheim Mus., 1962, San Francisco Mus. Art, 1962, Phila. Art Alliance, 1963, Battersea Park, London, 1963, Sai Paolo Bienal, Brazil, 1963, White House Festival of Arts, Washington, 1965, Bienale Middleheim, Belgium, 1971; represented in permanent collections Nelson Gallery-Atkins Mus., Kansas City, Mo., Art Inst., Chgo., Mus. Modern Art, N.Y.C., Mus. U. Nebr., Whitney Mus. Art, N.Y.C., Krannert Art Mus., Urbana, Ill., Washington, U., Walker Art Center, Mpls., Albright-Knox Mus., Buffalo, Detroit Inst. Art, U. Calif. Art Mus., Cranbrook Acad. Art, Mich., Princeton Mus. Art, Hirschhorn Mus., Washington, Numerous others. Served with USNR, World War II. Decorated Air medal (2); recipient Lifetime Achievement award in sculpture edn. Internat. Sculpture Ctr., 1998; Guggenheim fellow, 1963-64. Address: 5 Highview Knl NE Iowa City IA 52240-9149 E-mail: jfeschmidt@earthlink.net.

SCHMIDT, KARL A. lawyer; b. Stockton, Calif., Sept. 18, 1947; BS, U. Calif., Berkeley, 1969, JD, 1974. Bar: Calif. 1974. Mem. Parker, Milliken, Clark, O'Hara & Samuelian, L.A. Contbr. Retaliation Matters, to L.A. Daily Jour. Ann. Employment Update, 1997. Mem. ABA. Office: Parker Milliken Clark O Hara & Samuelian 333 S Hope St Ste 2700 Los Angeles CA 90071-1449

SCHMIDT, KARL M., JR. political science educator; b. Utica, N.Y., Mar. 19, 1917; s. Karl Marx and Jennie Christina (Greenia) S.; m. Josephine Ruth Leighton Smith, Mar. 7, 1934 (div. Dec. 1942); 1 child, Karl Michael; m. Mary Erma Murphy, Apr. 3, 1943; children: Jill Sheryl Fowler, Glen Mark. AB, Colgate U., Hamilton, N.Y., 1948, MA, Johns Hopkins U., Balt., 1950, PhD, 1951. Asst. prof. govt. and econs. Union Coll., Schenectady, 1951-57; vis. prof. polit. sci. U. Hawaii, Honolulu, 1964-65; assoc. prof. polit. sci. Syracuse (N.Y.) U., 1957-70, prof. polit. sci. and pub. adminstrn., 1971-85, prof. emeritus, 1985—. Sr. resident adviser Pakistan Adminstrv. Staff Coll., Lahore, Pakistan, 1960-62, 67; rsch. cons. N.Y. State Dept. Audit and Control, Albany, 1956-57. Author: Henry A. Wallace: Quixotic Crusade, 1948, 1960; editor: American National Government in Action, 1965, Am. State and Local Government in Action, 1966, American Government in Action: National State and Local, 1967. Pres. Camillus (N.Y.) Dem. Club, 1964, 66; Co-chmn. Onon County McGovern for Pres., Syracuse, 1972, Profs. and Physicians for Humphrey, Syracuse, 1968; chmn. Town Planning Bd., Clayton, N.Y., 1988-90. With USCG, 1942-46. Mem. AAUP, Am. Polit. Sci. Assn., Am. Soc. Pub. Adminstrn., N.Y. State Polit. Sci. Assn., Sigma Nu. Democrat. Unitarian Universalist. Avocations: boating, apple-growing, grape-growing. Home: 16643 Rainbow Shores Dr Clayton NY 13624-2153

SCHMIDT, KATHLEEN MARIE, lawyer; b. Des Moines, June 17, 1953; d. Raymond Driscoll and Hazel Isabelle (Rogers) Poage; m. Dean Everett Johnson, Dec. 21, 1974 (div. Nov. 1983); children: Aaron Dean, Gina Marie; m. Ronald Robert Schmidt, Feb. 7, 1987. BS in Home Econs., U. Nebr., 1974; JD, Creighton U., 1987. Bar: Nebr. 1987, U.S. Dist. Ct. Nebr. 1987, U.S. Ct. Appeals (8th cir.) 1989, U.S. Supreme Ct. 1991. Apprentice printer, journeyman Rochester (Minn.) Post Bull., 1978-82; dir. customer info. Cornhusker Pub. Power Dist., Columbus, Nebr., 1982-83; artist Pamida, Omaha, 1983; offset artist Cornhusker Motor Club, 1983-84; assoc. Lindahl O. Johnson Law Office, 1987-88; pvt. practice, 1988-90; ptnr. Emery, Penke, Blazek & Schmidt, 1990-91; pvt. practice, 1992—. Atty. in condemnation procs.

Douglas County Bd. Appraisers, Omaha, 1988-99, Sarpy County Bd. Appraisers, Omaha, 1999—; presenter Nebr. Sch. Bd. Assn., 1991, 92. Mem. Millard Sch. Bd., Omaha, 1989-96, treas. 1991, 92; mem. strategic planning com. Millard Sch. Dist., 1990; mem. Omaha Mayor's Master Plan Com., 1991-94. Named hon. mem. Anderson Mid. Sch., Omaha, 1991; recipient Award of Achievement, Nebr. Sch. Bd. Assn., 1991, 94. Mem. Nebr. Bar Assn., Omaha Bar Assn. (spkrs. bur. 1992—), Nat. Sch. Bd. Assn. (del. federal rels. network 1991-96, cert. recognition 1991). Republican. Lutheran.

SCHMIDT, KLAUS DIETER, management consultant, university administrator, marketing and management educator; b. Eisenach, Germany, May 8, 1930; came to U.S., 1949, naturalized, 1952; s. Kurt Heinrich and Louise (Kruger) S.; m. Lynda Hollister Wheelwright, June 29, 1950; children: Karen, Claudia. BA in Econs., U. Calif., Berkeley, 1951; MBA, Stanford U., 1953; PhD in Bus. Adminstrn., Golden Gate U., 1978. Buyer, jr. mdse. mgr. Broadway Hale, 1952-54; sales mgr. Ames Harris Neville Co., 1954-56, ops. mgr., 1956-57; gen. mgr. Boise Cascade Corp., 1957-60; pres., chmn. bd. Kimball-Schmidt Inc., San Rafael, Calif., 1960-73, chmn. subs. Kalwall Pacific, 1962-67, chmn. subs. AFGOA Corp., 1966-69; asst. prof. mgmt. and mktg. San Francisco State U., 1970-75, assoc. prof. mgmt., 1975-80, prof. mgmt. and mktg., 1989-85, chmn. dept., 1979-85, prof. emeritus, 1989—, assoc. dean emeritus Sch. Bus., 1985-88; chmn. Schmidt Cons. Group, Brooklin, Maine, 1988—. Dir. Ctr. for World Bus., 1976-88, dir. U.S.-Japan Inst., 1981-88, editor-in-chief Sch. Bus. Jours., 1980-88; U.S. negotiator for Pres. Carter White House on Afghanistan issue, 1980-88; mem. Dept. Commerce Dist. Export Council, 1982-88; rsch. cons. SRI Internat. Author: (20 booklet series) Doing Business In ..., Stanford Rsch. Inst., 1978-80. Mem. Univ. Club (San Francisco), Alpha Delta Phi, Beta Gamma Sigma. Republican. Office: PO Box 269 Brooklin ME 04616-0269

SCHMIDT, KLAUS FRANZ, advertising executive; b. Dessau, Germany, May 25, 1928; came to U.S., 1951; naturalized, 1957; s. Franz and Elfriede (Klamroth) S.; m. Gisela Garbrecht, June 19, 1954; children: Dagmar Schmidt Etkin, Ena Schmidt Reynen. Student, Coll. of Journalism, Aachen, Germany, 1947-48, Sch. of Design and Printing, Bochum, Germany, 1948-50; BA, Wayne State U., 1956. Printer, compositor, 1948-56; type dir. Mogul Williams & Saylor, N.Y.C., 1956-59, Doyle, Dane, Bernbach, N.Y.C., 1959-61, Young & Rubicam, N.Y.C., 1961-68, v.p., dir. print ops., 1968-75, v.p., dir. creative support, 1975-85, sr. v.p., mgr. prodn. svcs., 1985-91; advt./graphic arts cons., 1991—. Co-organizer Vision Congress Internat. Ctr. for Communications Arts & Scis., N.Y.C., 1965, 67, 69, 77; chmn., bd. trustees Internat. Ctr. Typographic Arts, N.Y.C. 1969-70. Author: Signs of the Times, 1997; Am. editor Der Druckspiegel, 1957-64; contbg. editor Print Mag., 1968-01, The Dunn Report, 1991-95. Recipient Typomundus award, 1964, Internat. Book Exhbn. award, Leipzig, Germany, 1965. Mem. Print Advt. Assn. (chmn. N.Y. chpt. 1969-71, nat. sr. v.p. 1971-75), Am. Assn. Advt. Agys. (chmn. subcom. on phototypography 1969-75), Digital Distbn. of Advt. to Publ. Assn. (vice chmn. 1991-95), N.Y. Type Dirs. Club (pres. 1984-86, awards 1962, 64-66, 68, 69), N.Y. Art Dirs. Club (v.p. 1984-86), Advt. Prodn. Club (pres. 1982-84), Gravure Advt. Coun. (chmn. 1970-72). Home and Office: 549 Munroe Ave Sleepy Hollow NY 10591-1333

SCHMIDT, L(AIL) WILLIAM, JR. lawyer; b. Thomas, Okla., Nov. 22, 1936; s. Lail William and Violet Kathleen (Kuper) S.; m. Diana Gail (div. May 1986); children: Kimberly Ann, Andrea Michelle; m. Marilyn Sue, Aug. 11, 1990; stepchildren: Leland Darrell Mosby, Jr., Crystal Rachelle Mosby. BA in Psychology, U. Colo., 1959; JD, U. Mich., 1962. Bar: Colo. 1962, U.S. Dist. Ct. Colo. 1964, U.S. Tax Ct. 1971, U.S. Ct. Appeals (10th cir.) 1964. Ptnr. Holland & Hart, Denver, 1962-77, Schmidt, Elrod & Wills, Denver, 1977-85, Moye, Giles, O'Keefe, Vermeire & Gorrell, Denver, 1985-90; of counsel Hill, Held, Metzger, Lofgren & Peele, Dallas, 1989-94; pvt. practice law Denver, 1990-2001; ptnr. Schmidt & Horen LLP, 2001—. Lectr. profl. orgns. Author: How To Live-and Die-with Colorado Probate, 1985, A Practical Guide to the Revocable Living Trust, 1990; contbr. articles to legal jours. Pres. Luth. Med. Ctr. Found., Wheat Ridge, Colo., 1985-89; pres. Rocky Mountain Prison and Drug Found., Denver, 1986—; bd. dirs. Luth. Hosp., Wheat Ridge, 1988-92, Bonfils Blood Ctr. Found., 1995—, Planned Giving Adv. Group of Nat. Jewish Hosp., Denver, 1996-98, St. Joseph Hosp. Found., 1999—; planned giving advisor Aspen Valley Med. Found., 1997—; mktg. and gifts adv. com. The Denver Found., 1998—. Fellow Am. Coll. Trust and Estate Counsel (Colo. chmn. 1981-86); mem. ABA, Am. Judicature Soc., Denver Estate Planning Coun., Rocky Mtn. Estate Planning Coun. (founder, pres. 1970-71), Greater Denver Tax Counsel Assn., Am. Soc. Magicians, Denver Athletic Club, Phi Delta Phi. Republican. Baptist. Avocation: magic. Office: 1050 17th St Ste 1700 Denver CO 80265-2077 also: Law Offices Robert L Bolick Ltd 6060 Elton Ave Ste A Las Vegas NV 89107-0100 E-mail: estpln@aol.com.

SCHMIDT, LAWRENCE KENNEDY, philosophy educator; b. Rochester, N.Y., Oct. 2, 1949; s. Paul Frederick Schmidt and Rebecca Jane Gilford; m. Monika Reuss, Sept. 2, 1984; 1 child, Kassandra Gaya Reuss-Schmidt. BA, Reed Coll., 1972; MA, U. N.Mex., 1978; PhD, U. Duisburg (Germany), 1983. Instr. Philosophy U. Duisburg, Duisburg, 1979-83, U. N.Mex., Albuquerque, 1984; asst. prof. Philosophy Hendrix Coll., Conway, Ark., 1984-89, chair dept. Philosophy, 1987-92, 96-98, 2000—, assoc. prof. Philosophy, 1989-99, prof. philosophy, 1999—. Bd. dirs. Marshall T. Steel Ctr. for the Study of Religion and Philosophy. Author: (book) The Epistemology of H-G Gadamer, 1985, 2d edit., 1987; editor: (book) The Specter of Relativism, 1995, Language and Linquisticality in Gadamer's Harmeneutics, 2000; translator: (book) Hans-Georg Gadamer on Education, Poetry, and History, 1992; contbr. articles to profl. jours. Fulbright scholar, Duisburg, 1977-79, Fulbright sr. scholar Heidelberg, 1999; faculty rsch. grantee Hendrix Coll., 1985, 88, 91, 93, 96, 99. Mem. AAUP (pres. Hendrix chpt. 1987-91, 95-97, 99—), Ark. Philos. Assn., Am. Philos. Assn., Phi Beta Kappa. Avocations: travel, skiing, hiking. E-mail: schmidt@Hendrix.edu.

SCHMIDT, LEEANNE, artist; b. Dayton, Ky., June 13, 1940; d. Douglas Walter and Marian Brown; m. Edward Schmidt; children: Douglas, Eric. BS, U. Cin., 1962, MFA, 1992. Tchr. Gov.'s Inst. for Talented and Gifted, Miami U., 1997, U. Cin., 1991-92, 94, 96, 97, No. Ky. U., Highland Heights, 1992-96, Cairo Am. Coll., 1998, U. Calif., San Diego, 1999; vis. artist Art Acad. Cin., 1997, instr., 1998; vis. artist Morehead State U., 1997, U. Louisville, 1996, Thomas More Coll., Crestview Hills, Ky., 1996, U. Cin., 1996, numerous others; curator Summerfair, Inc., Cin., 1997, Images Gallery, Cin., 1995, others. One-person shows linclude: The Marta Hewett Gallery, Cin., 1997, Morehead State U., Ky., 1997, Gallery 292, N.Y.C., 1997, Gallery of So. Photographers, New Orleans, 1996, Miami U., Oxford, Ohio, 1996, U. Louisville, 1996, Lycoming Coll., Williamsport, Pa., 1996, others; groups exhbns. include Huntington Mus. Art, W.Va., 1997, Swann Galleries, N.Y.C., 1997, Wellington B. Gray Art Gallery, E. Carolina U., Greenville, 1997, Bank One Gallery, Louisville, 1997, Art Acad. of Cin., 1997, Marta Hewett Gallery, Cin., 1992-96, Gallery for So. Photographers, New Orleans, 1996, U. Minn., Mpls., 1996, numerous others; selected books and catalogues include: Nudes 2, 1997, Signs, 1997, Eros, 1996, Love, Flesh, and Water, 1996, Horizons, 1996, Body of Evidence, 1995, The Myth and Madness of Ophelia, 2001, others; corp. commns. include No. Ky. U., 1993; selected pub. collections include: The Bibliotek Nationale, Paris, J.B. Speed Art Mus., Louisville, Ogden Coll., New Orleans, Dayton Art Inst., Ohio, Cin. Art Mus., Cin. Bell Corp. Collections, U. Louisville; works collected in numerous pvt. collections; represented by Gallery 292, N.Y.C. Artist Profl. Devel. grantee Ky. Arts Coun., Frankfort, 1997, 98; recipient scholarships U. Cin., 1990-92, Kodak Educator scholarship, Palm Beach Workshops, Boca Raton, Fla., 1994, fellowships Ky. Found. for Women, Louisville, 1996, Al Smith Artist Fellowship, Frankfort, 1994, Wolfstein Travel fellowship U. Cin., 1991, others; recipient exhbn. awards that include: Inst. Nacional de Bellas Artes, San Miguel de Allende, Mexico, 1995, Hunter Mus. of Am. Art, Chattanooga, 1995, Louisville Visual Art Assn., 1993, 94, others.

SCHMIDT, LYNDA WHEELWRIGHT, psychotherapist; b. Beijing, July 29, 1931; came to the U.S., 1931; d. Joseph Balch and Jane Byers (Hollister) Wheelwright; m. Klaus Dieter, May 8, 1930; children: Karen Clay, Claudia Lewis. BA, U. Calif., Berkeley, 1965, MSW, 1968. Cert. Jungian analyst; bd. cert. diplomate Am. Bd. Examiners Clin. Social Work. Staff psychiat. social worker Pacific Med. Ctr., San Francisco, 1968-71; pvt. practice psychotherapy and Jungian analysis, 1971-87, Brooklin, Maine, 1985—. Tng. analyst CG Jung Inst., San Francisco, 1978—; mem. certifying com. CG Jung Inst., San Francisco, 1980-84; cons. and lectr. in field. Author: Time Out of Mind: Trekking the Hindu Kush, 1978, The Long Shore, A Psychological Experience of the Wilderness, 1991; contbr. articles to profl. jours. Fellow Calif. Soc. Clin. Social Workers; mem. NASW, Acad. Cert. Social Workers, Inc., CG Jung Inst. (chair certifying com. 1980-84), Alpha Phi Sorority. Democrat. Avocations: reading, horseback riding, travel, music. Home and Office: PO Box 269 Brooklin ME 04616-0269

SCHMIDT, MAARTEN, astronomy educator; b. Groningen, Netherlands, Dec. 28, 1929; came to U.S., 1959; s. Wilhelm and Antje (Haringhuizen) S.; m. Cornelia Johanna Tom, Sept. 16, 1955; children: Elizabeth Tjimkje, Maryke Antje, Anne Wilhelmina. BSc, U. Groningen, 1949; PhD, Leiden U., Netherlands, 1956; ScD, Yale U., 1966. Sci. officer Leiden Obs., The Netherlands, 1953-59; postdoctoral fellow Mt. Wilson Obs., Pasadena, Calif., 1956-58; mem. faculty Calif. Inst. Tech., 1959-95, prof. astronomy, 1964-95, exec. officer for astronomy, 1972-75, chmn. div. physics, math. and astronomy, 1975-78, mem. staff Hale Obs., 1959-80, dir. Hale Obs., 1978-80, emeritus prof. astronomy, 1996—. Co-winner Calif. Scientist of Yr. award, 1964 Fellow Am. Acad. Arts and Scis. (Rumford award 1968); mem. Am. Astron. Soc. (Helen B. Warner prize 1964, Russell lecture award 1978), NAS (fgn. assoc., recip. James Craig Watson Medal, 1991), Internat. Astron. Union, Royal Astron. Soc. (assoc., Gold medal 1980) Office: Calif Inst Tech 105 24 Robinson Lab Pasadena CA 91125-0001

SCHMIDT, MARK JAMES, state public health official; b. Milw., July 16, 1955; s. Warren J. and Carolyn Juel (Gissing) S.; m. Janet M. Schmidt, Oct. 5, 1991; children: Andrew T., Rachel M., Malia D.; stepchildren: Nathan A. and Aaron M. Stotts. BA, U. Wis., Eau Claire, 1977; MSc., Ill. State U., 1978. Dir. debate U. No. Iowa, Cedar Falls, 1978-79; dir. comm. Ill. Rep. Party, Springfield, 1979-83; asst. adminstr. driver svc. dept. Office of the Sec. State, Ill., 1983-87, asst. to dir., driver svc. dept., 1987-91; dir. pub. affairs Ill. Dept. Ctrl. Mgmt. Svcs., 1991-95; asst. dir. Ill. Dept. Pub. Health, Springfield, 1995-2000, acting dep. dir. Office of Health and Wellness, 1999-2000, dep. dir. Office of Health Promotion, 2000—. Guest lectr. cert. program in health policy Am. Osteo. Assn., 1997; guest lectr. Ill. Pub. Health Leadership Inst., 1999—2000, Leadership Springfield Conf., 1999, 2000; guest lectr. polit. comm. Ill. State U., Normal, 1980; guest lectr. social mktg. U. Ill., Springfield, 2001—02; cons. 6th Congl. Dist. Rep. Com., Lombard, Ill., 1985—90; rep. Ill. Drivers Lic. Compact Com., Falls Church, Va., 1987—91; mem. Ill. Rural Health Assn.; bd. dirs. Ill. Rural Ptnrs., Inc., 1995—2000, co-chmn. pub. sector, 1997—99; chair Rural Transp. Task Force, 1997—; mem. Ill. Rural Ptnrs. Telecomm. Commn., 1999—; keynote spkr. conf. on managed care Coop. Extension Svc., 1996; keynote spkr. Ill. Rural Poverty Conf., 1998, SIV Cancer Prevention and Control Conf., 2002; leader, mentor Mid-Am. Regional Pub. Health Leadership Inst., 1999—; chair Springfield Pub. Health and Safety Strategy Group, 1999—; mem. panel advisors Mayor Karen Hasarn, Springfield; chair Ill. Adoption Registry Adv. Coun., 1999—2001; staff Gov.'s Domestic Preparedness Conf., 2001; lectr. tobacco prevention and control Ill. Sch. Health Days, 2001; spkr. in field; guest lectr. cert. program in health policy cancer control conf. So. Ill. U., 2002. Editor: Driver's Handbook (annual) Rules of the Road, 1984-91; editor Driver Svcs. Dept. newsletter, 1988-91, Rural Health News, 1999-2000; contbg. editor: Lyme Disease Handbook for Physicians, 1997, Management and Treatment of Lyme Disease, 1998; co-editor tng. manual for local bds. of health; contbr. articles to profl. jours. Debate strategist Fahner for Atty. Gen. Ill., 1982, Bertini for Congress, Chgo., 1982; advisor Richard Austin for Congress, Springfield, 1984; designer local advt. Al Salvi for Sec. of State of Ill., 1998; health care developer George Ryan for Gov. of Ill., 1998; coord. Citizens for Jim Edgar, Springfield, 1985-91; sr. staff, Ill. gubernatorial transition team, 1990-91; stage mgr. 1999 Ill. Gubernatorial Inauguration; chmn. pub. info. subcom. Ill. Comml. Drivers License Program, 1989-91; media coord. Lincoln Land C.C. Trustee Campaign, 1997; mem. local advance staff George W. Bush for Pres., 1999-2000; mem. long range planning com. 1st United Meth. Ch., Springfield; mem. Food and Nutrition Work Group, Ill. Farm Bill Task Force, 2001. Recipient Gov. Adminstrs. Recognition award Ill. Primary Health Care Assn., 1997, Presdl. award for Outstanding Contbn. Ill. Rural Health Assn., 1999. Fellow: Ill. Pub. Health Leadership Inst.; mem.: Ill. Pub. Health Assn., Order Ea. Star (chmn. Grand chpt. info. com. 2001—02), Masons. Republican. Methodist. Home: 37 Meander Pike Chatham IL 62629-1569 Office: Ill Dept Pub Health 535 W Jefferson St Springfield IL 62702-5058 E-mail: mschmidt@idph.state.il.us.

SCHMIDT, MARTHA BUBECK, educator, counselor; b. Cadott, Wis., Sept. 28, 1912; d. Karl Christian and Lydia Sarah (Keller) Bubeck; m. Eugene Milton Schmidt, Sept. 11, 1943; children: Eugene Karl, Fredric John. BS, U. Wis., Stout, 1934; MPhil, U. Wis., Madison, 1947, M in Psychology and Behavioral Studies, 1959. Tchr. home econs. Barron (Wis.) High Sch., 1934-37; supr. student teaching U. Wis., Stout, 1937-38; state supr. home econs. edn. Wis. State Bd. Vocat. Edn., Madison, 1938-48; instr. adult evening sch. Madison Area Tech. Coll., 1949-69; guidance counselor Madison Met. Schs., 1959-79; coord. AARP and Wis. Ret. Tchrs. Assn., Madison, 1986-90; state chmn. health/long term care action group AARP, Wis., 1990-99, coord. health advocacy svcs., 1991-2001. Founder Future Homemakers of Am., 1943, past advisor; condr. fgn. study programs, Europe, Asia, Australia, 1971-88. Bd. dirs. Madison Oakwood Retirement Ctr., 1983-89, mem. resident care com., 1992—; com. mem. Wis. Legis. Study Elderly Abuse, 1985-88. Recipient Disting. Educator award, U. Wis., Stout, 1998. Mem.: AAUW, AARP, Mental Health Assn./Wis. Coalition Aging Groups (regional bd.), Valparaiso U. Guild (state pres. 1981—85), Luth. Women Missionary League, Nat. Honor Soc. Home Econs., Wis. Ret. Tchrs. Assn. (rec. sec. 1983—89, bd. dirs. 1990—2002), Madison Civics Club, Rotary (Sr. Svc. award 1998). Lutheran. Avocation: volunteering. Home: 3709 Zwerg Dr Madison WI 53705-5229

SCHMIDT, PATRICIA JEAN, special education educator; b. Cleve., June 15, 1941; Cert. applied lab. tech., Cuyahoga C.C., Cleve., 1967; student, IIT Tech. Coll., 2000—. Lic. student driver instr. Lab. sect. supr. Meridia Euclid (Ohio) Hosp., 1968-74; gen. lab. technician, 1974-94; student driving instr. Cleve., 1994-2000. Tutor deaf students in coll. math.; designer including vet.'s memls. Author: A Manual of Disciplines for Interpreters of the Deaf; composer, vocal and stage presentation coach; sculptor and designer. Active voter registration Rep. Party. Recipient Acad. award Math. Assn. Am., Washington, 1959. Mem. Nat. Assn. of the Deaf, Nat. Head Injury Found., Sweet Adeline Internat. Avocations: writing, stamp collecting, reading. Home: PO Box 43123 Cleveland OH 44143-0123

SCHMIDT, PAUL JEFFREY, federal government official; b. Hinsdale, Ill., Feb. 2, 1960; s. Robert Herman and Shirley Ann Schmidt; m. Brenda Sue Schmidt, May 28, 1983; children: Brandon, Kelly. BS in Acctg., So. Ill. U., 1982, MBA, 1983. CPA, Ill. Asst. dir. U.S. GAO, Chgo., 1983—. Mem. Met. Planning Coun., 1999—. Mem. AICPAs, Ill. Soc. CPAs. Avocations: power lifting, reading, family. Office: US GAO 200 W Adams Ste 700 Chicago IL 60606 E-mail: schmidtpj@gao.gov.

SCHMIDT, PAUL JOSEPH, physician, educator; b. N.Y.C., Oct. 22, 1925; m. Louise Kern Fredericks, June 18, 1953; children: Damien, Matthew, Thomas, Maria. BS, Fordham U., 1948; MS, St. Louis U., 1952; MD, NYU, 1953. Diplomate Am. Bd. Pathology, Nat. Bd. Med. Examiners. Intern St. Elizabeth's Hosp., Boston, 1953-54; staff assoc. Nat. Microbiol. Inst., Bethesda, Md., 1954-55; chief blood bank dept. NIH, 1955-74, asst. chief clin. pathology dept., 1963-65; sr. asst. surgeon USPHS, 1954, advanced through grades to med. dir., 1964-74; assoc. clin. prof. pathology, then clin. prof. Georgetown U., Washington, 1965-75; dir. S.W. Fla. Blood Bank, Inc., Tampa, 1975-90, pres., 1987-90; head transfusion medicine Transfusion Medicine Acad. Ctr., 1991—; prof. pathology U. South Fla., Tampa, 1975—. Cons. com. on Blood, AMA, 1964-69; tech. adv. Blood Transfusion Rsch. div. US Army, 1966-74; res. adv. com. Blood Program, ARC, 1967-73; com. Human Rsch. ARC, 1968-74; council on Immunohematology, Am. Soc. Clin. Pathologists, 1968-74; com. Anticoagulant Solutions, NRC-Nat. Acad. Sci., 1968-70; com. Plasmapheresis, NRC-Nat. Acad. Sci., 1969-70; com. Blood Bank Programs, N.Y.C., 1969-70; com. Component Therapy, NRC-Nat. Acad. Sci., 1969; com. standards, Am. Assn. Blood Banks, 1970-85 (chmn. 1981-85); Task Force on Blood Banking, Dept. HEW, 1972-73; adv. com. Blood Diseases and Resources, Nat. Heart Lung Blood Inst., 1975-79; cons. to surgeon gen. U.S. navy, 1976; dir. clin. svcs. ARC Blood Svcs., San Juan, P.R., 1993-95; clin. prof. pathology U. P.R., 1993-2001, Koppisch lectr., 1994; Molthan Meml. lectr. Pa. Assn. Blood Banks, 1995; DeGowin lectr. U. Iowa, 1997. Editor: Progress in Transfusion and Transplantation, 1972; mem. editl. bd. Transfusion, 1968—, Annals Clin. Lab. Sci., 1971-74, Blood, 1976-77; contbr. articles to profl. jours.; described etiology of renal failure after hemolytic blood transfusion reactions, 1967, Rh null disease, 1967. Mem. svc. and rehab. com. Fla. div. Am. Cancer Soc., 1976-84; bd. dirs. ARC, Tampa, 1978-83 (v.p. 1980); com. Transfusion Medicine, Coll. Am. Pathologists, 1981-92; bd. dirs. Am. Blood Commn., 1985-87; adv. com. Blood Products, FDA, 2000—. Served with U.S. Army, 1944—46. Recipient Jour. Club Rsch. award NYU, 1952, Silver medal Spanish Red Cross, 1960, Emily Cooley award Am. Assn. Blood Banks, 1974, John Elliott award, 1993. Fellow Coll. Am. Pathologists (emeritus); mem. Am. Assn. Blood Banks (pres. 1987-88), Internat. Soc. Blood Transfusion, Fla. Assn. Blood Banks (pres. 1980-81), Cosmos Club, Rotary. Roman Catholic. Office: Fla Blood Svcs 10100 9th St N Saint Petersburg FL 33716

SCHMIDT, PAUL WICKHAM, lawyer; b. Milw., June 25, 1948; s. Edmund Julian and Barbara (Wickham) S.; m. Cathryn Ann Piehl, June 27, 1970; children: Thomas Wickham, William Piehl, Anna Patchin. BA cum laude, Lawrence U., 1970; JD cum laude, U. Wis., 1973. Bar: Wis. 1973, U.S. Dist. Ct. (we. dist.) Wis. 1973, U.S. Supreme Ct. 1982, D.C. 1988. Atty. advisor Bd. Immigration Appeals, Washington, 1973-76; gen. atty. office of gen. counsel Immigration and Naturalization Service, 1976-78, acting gen. counsel, 1979-81, 86-87, gen. counsel, 1978-87; assoc. Jones, Day, Reavis & Pogue, 1987-89, ptnr., 1990-92; mng. ptnr. Fragomen, Del Ray & Bernsen, PC, 1993-95; chmn. Bd. of Immigration Appeals, Falls Church, Va., 1995-2001, mem., 2001—. Mem. Bd. of Immigration Appeals. Mem. ABA, Internat. Assn. Refugee Law Judges (coun. mem.), D.C. Bar Assn., Wis. Bar Assn., Fed. Bar Assn. (immigration sect.). Avocations: crew volunteer, gardening, camping, history. Home: 711 S View Ter Alexandria VA 22314-4923 Office: Bd Immigration Appeals Skyline Tower 5107 Leesburg Pike Ste 2400 Falls Church VA 22041-3234 E-mail: paul.schmidt@usdoj.gov.

SCHMIDT, PETER GUSTAV, shipbuilding industry executive; b. Tumwater, Wash., Dec. 3, 1921; s. Peter G. and Clara Louise (Muench) S.; m. Elva Mary Ingalls, Dec. 3, 1945; children: Mimi Schmidt Fielding, Jill Schmidt Crowson, Janet Schmidt Mano, Hans. BSME, U. Wash., 1948; MS in Naval Architecture and Marine Engring., U. Mich., 1950. Naval architect Nat. Steel Shipbldg. Corp., San Diego, 1950-52, Carl J. Nordstrom/P. Spaulding, Seattle, 1952-53; pres. Marine Constrn. & Design Co., 1953—, Astilleros Marco Chilena Ltd., Santiago, Chile, 1960—, Marco Peruana S.A., Lima, Peru, 1965—, Campbell Industries, San Diego, 1979-99, Campbell Ship Design & Engring., Seattle, 2000—. Author papers on fishing gear and vessels. Served to lt (j.g.) USN, 1942-45, PTO. Recipient Puget Sound's Maritime Man of Yr. award Puget Sound Press Assn., 1975, Naval Arch. and Marine Engring. Merit award U. Mich., 1996. Mem. Soc. Naval Architects and Marine Engrs., Wash. State Boatbuilders Assn. (pres. 1956-58), Alpha Delta Phi. Avocations: competitive sailing, classical music. Office: Marine Constrn & Design 2300 W Commodore Way Seattle WA 98199-1226

SCHMIDT, RAYMOND PAUL, naval career officer, historian, government official; b. Western, Nebr., Sept. 14, 1937; s. Reuben Edward and Angeline Agnes (Kudlik) S.; m. Roberta Ruth Schrom, June 11, 1961; 1 child, Douglas Craig. B in Edn., History and Social Sci., U. Nebr., 1958; postgrad., U. Md., 1960-62, The Am. U., 1975-81; M in History, U. Wis., 1966. Instr. math. and social sci. Sr. High Sch., Bellevue, Nebr., 1958-59; ensign USN, 1959, advanced through grades to capt., 1981, historian, archivist Naval Security Group Command, 1968-81, sr. congl. security policy rev. officer, Naval Intelligence, 1981-82, sr. res. forces advisor Dept. Def., 1982-88, head Navy info. security policy, 1988-98, mgr. declassification program, 1998-00; cons., 2000—; history instr. James Madison Meml. High Sch., Madison, Wis., 1966-68. Mem. U.S. Nat. Disclosure Policy Com. Team, Japan, Thailand, 1989, Germany, 1991, leader, Albania, 1995. Author: (with others) Naval Officers Guide, 1983, And I Was There, 1985; contbr. articles to profl. jours. Pres. North Ashburton Citizens Assn., Bethesda, Md., 1982—; Merit badge counselor Boy Scouts Am., 1974-93; info. officer U.S. Naval Acad., Annapolis, Md., 1978-93; spkr. Pearl Harbor Symposium Adm. Nimitz Found., Tex., 1991, symposium moderator, 1992; active Montgomery County Planning Bd. Citizens Adv. Com., Md., 1989-94; mem. Ret. Pers. Adv. Coun. for the Naval Dist. Washington. Named Hon. Admiral Great Navy of State of Nebr., 1983. Mem. DAV (life), Nat. Assn. Ret. Fed. Employees, Nat. Classification Mgmt. Soc. (editor Viewpoints 1991-96), Nat. Trust Hist. Preservation, Am. Hist. Assn., U.S. Naval Inst. (life, contbr.), Nat. Assn. Uniformed Svcs. (life), Res. Officers Assn. (life), Ret. Officers Assn. (life), Naval Res. Assn. (life, sec./treas. 1966-68), U. Nebr. Alumni Assn. (life), Naval Intelligence Profls., U.S. Naval Cryptologic Vets. Assn., Colonial Williamsburg Found., Phoenix Soc. Unitarian Universalist. Home: 6205 Lone Oak Dr Bethesda MD 20817-1743

SCHMIDT, RENÉ R. music educator, organist, choirmaster; b. Glencoe, Minn., Sept. 17, 1952; s. Victor John and Ruth M. (Goodeman) S. BA in Music, Luther Coll., 1974; Master of Music Organ and Harpsichord, So. Meth. U., 1978; PhD in Musicology, U. North Tex., 1992. Music instr. Dallas Ind. Sch. Dist., 1978-81, 85—. Adj. music faculty So. Meth. U., 1980, U. North Tex., 1995; mus. instr. St. Philip's Cath. Sch., 1991-92, Skidmore Coll. U. without Walls, fall 1992, 93; dir. children's chorus Lyric Opera Dallas, summer 1990; dir. Dallas Boys Choir, 1989-91, accompanist, asst. dir., 1986-89; organist Christ Episcopal Ch., Dallas, 1976—, choirmaster, 1976—; lectr. summer sch. English Organ Music Cleve. Lodge, Dorking, Eng., 1979; presenter papers in field. Mem. Am. Guild Organists (Dallas chpt., dir. edn. com. 1990-93, exec com. 1987-93, steering com. nat. conv. Dallas 1993-94, dir. recital series com. 1994—), Am. Musicological Soc., Tex. Mus. Educators Assn. Home: 715 Parkmont St Dallas TX 75214-4925

SCHMIDT, RICHARD MARTEN, JR. lawyer; b. Winfield, Kans., Aug. 2, 1924; s. Richard M. and Ida (Marten) S.; m. Ann Downing, Jan. 2, 1948; children: Eric, Gregory, Rolf (dec.), Heidi. AB, U. Denver, 1945, JD, 1948. Bar: Colo. 1948, D.C. 1968. Dep. dist. atty., City and County of Denver, 1949-50; mem. firm McComb, Zarlengo, Mott & Schmidt, Denver, 1950-54; ptnr. Schmidt & Van Cise (and predecessor), 1954-65; gen. counsel USIA, 1965-68; of counsel Cohn and Marks, Washington, 1969—. Counsel spl. agrl. investigating subcom. Counsel Am. Soc. Newspaper Editors, 1968—; mem. Gov.'s Coun. Local Govt., Colo., 1963-64; chmn. Mayor's Jud. Adv. Com., Denver, 1963-64, Gov.'s Supreme Ct. Nominating Com., 1964-65; mem. Gov.'s Oil Shale Adv. Com., 1963-65, Colo. Commn. on Higher Edn., 1965; mem. bd. Nat. Press Found., 1993—. Trustee U. Denver (life). Mem. ABA (chmn. standing com. on assn. comms. 1969-73, chmn. forum com. on comms. 1979-81, co-chmn. nat. conf. lawyers and reps. of media 1984-89, mem. commn. on lawyer advt. 1964-68), Colo. Bar Assn. (gov.), Denver Bar Assn. (pres. 1963-64), D.C. Bar Assn., Cosmos Club (Washington). Episcopalian. Home: 115 5th St SE Washington DC 20003-1123 Office: Cohn and Marks 1920 N St NW Ste 300 Washington DC 20036-1622 E-mail: rms@cohmarks.com.

SCHMIDT, RICHARD ALOYSIUS, aerospace engineer; b. St. Paul, Apr. 3, 1923; s. Henry Robert and Florence Caroline (Pfeiffer) S.; m. Martha Allyne Cooper, May 21, 1949; children: Carroll Ann, Catherine Jeanne. B of Aero. Engring., U. Minn., 1946; postgrad., UCLA, 1958. Tech. dir. Rocket Propulsion Lab., Edwards AFB, Calif., 1951-60; chief launch support Hdqrs. NASA, Washington, 1960-64; program dir. Dept. Def., 1964-79; pres. Beasley Electric Corp., Ripley, Ohio, 1979-83; v.p. Lutsky Baird Corp., L.A., 1983-84; cons. Springfield, Va., 1985—. Lt. col. USAF Res. Assoc. fellow AIAA (chmn. test facility com. 1958-60); mem. Am. Rocket Soc. (pres Antelope Valley sect. 1956-58). Avocations: golf, skiing, soaring, big game hunting. Home and Office: 7903 Jansen Ct Springfield VA 22152-2410

SCHMIDT, RITA, retired library media specialist; b. Tacoma, Aug. 9, 1947; d. Robert V. and Ann Regine (Minette) Westermark; m. Guy Douglas Schmidt, June 29, 1972. BA, Knox Coll., 1969; MSLS, Case Western Res. U., 1970. Cert. tchg., sch. adminstrn., Mont. Libr. cataloger Trenton Pub. Libr., 1970-71; libr. media specialist Great Falls (Mont.) Pub. Schs., 1971—2001. Part-time instr. Coll. Great Falls, 1973-76. Chair, mem. Mont. Libr. Svcs. Adv. Coun., Helena, Mont., 1983-84, 85-89; mem. Project Excellence Sch. Accreditation

Stds., Helena, 1988-89. Recipient scholarship Mountain Plains Libr. Assn., 1985. Mem. ALA (coun. 1986), Mont. Edn. Assn. (bd. dirs. 1989-90), Great Falls Edn. Assn. (v.p. 1988-90, Silver Key award 1983, 84, 85, 89, 90, 94, 98), Mont. Libr. Assn. (pres. 1983-84). Democrat. Home: 3721 7th Ave N Great Falls MT 59401-2222

SCHMIDT, ROBERT, retired mechanics and civil engineering educator; b. Ukraine, May 18, 1927; came to U.S., 1949, naturalized, 1956; s. Alfred and Aquilina (Konotop) S.; m. Irene Hubertine Bongartz, June 10, 1978; children: Ingbert Robert. *Robert's father Alfred Schmidt was an Austrian army lieutenant, and was wounded and taken prisoner during World War I. He escaped from the POW camp in Shadrinsk, Siberia, in 1917, was recaptured and avoided execution by escaping again. However, for some inexplicable reason, he stayed in Ukraine, later becoming a teacher of German. With the outbreak of military hostilities in 1941, he was arrested by Soviet militia and marched eastward with hundreds of thousands of other political prisoners ahead of the fast approaching German armies. He perished somewhere near Poltava. Only through the printed word can I memorialize his decency and tragic short life.* Student, UNRRA-Univ., Munich, 1946-47, Technische Hochschule Karlsruhe, Germany, 1947-49, Vorpruefung; BS, U. Colo., 1951, MS, 1953; PhD, U. Ill., 1956. Tech. draftsman, Kalisch, Poland, 1943-45; rsch. asst. U. Ill., 1953-56, asst. prof. mechanics, 1956-59; assoc. prof. U. Ariz., Tucson, 1959-63; prof. mechanics and civil engring. U. Detroit, 1963-99, chmn. civil engring. dept., 1978-80; ret., 1999. Lectr. Oakland U., 1997-98; rschr. in linear and nonlinear theory of elasticity, theories of arches, plates, and shells, and approximate methods of analysis. Editor: Indsl. Math., 1969—; book reviewer Applied Mechanics Rev., Indsl. Math. Jour.; contbr. numerous articles to profl. jours. With C.E., U.S. Army, 1951-52. Grantee NSF 1960-78. Mem. AAUP, ASCE, ASME (cert. recognition 1972), Am. Acad. Mechanics (a founder), Indsl. Math. Soc. (pres. 1966-67, 81-84, 1st Gold award 1986), Sigma Xi. Avocations: biosophy, walking, bicycling, swimming.

SCHMIDT, ROBERT CHARLES, JR. finance executive; b. Oklahoma City, Apr. 2, 1942; s. Robert Charles and Francis Laura (Schiele) S.; m. Susan G. Dietz-Felbinger, Nov. 8, 1974; children: Laura Stewart, Elizabeth Berry Saldebar. BA, Westminster Coll., Fulton, Mo., 1964; postgrad., U. Okla., 1972, London Grad. Sch. Bus. Studies, 1974-76. Exec. trainee First Nat. Bank in St. Louis, 1967-68, comml. banker, 1968-74, v.p., mgr. client services div., 1974-76; v.p. treasury ops. Am. Express Co., N.Y.C., 1976-81, dep. treas., 1981-86; chmn. bd. Am. Express Export Credit Corp., 1982-86; group v.p., gen. mgr. Nat. Data Corp., Atlanta, 1986-88, exec. v.p., 1988-89, Capital Guaranty Corp., San Francisco, 1989-91; pres. Tampsco Enterprises, Inc., St. Louis, 1993; ptnr. The Whitelaw Group, 1994-96; pres. SCM Group, Inc., 1996—. Cons. City of N.Y., 1977 Loaned exec. United Fund, St. Louis, 1973; trustee Congl. Summer Assembly Edn. Fund, 1993—; Served with U.S. Army, 1965—67; dir. Crystal Lake Assn., The Endowment for Experimental Arch., Ltd. Decorated Army Commendation medal; recipient cert. of merit USO, 1966, Alumni Achievement award Westminster Coll., 1977 Mem. Treas. Group (chmn. 1982-83), Noonday Club (St. Louis), Crystal Downs Country Club (Frankfort, Mich.), Beta Theta Pi Republican. Episcopalian. Office: 230 S Bemiston Ave Ste 300 Saint Louis MO 63105-1907

SCHMIDT, ROBERT MILTON, physician, scientist, educator, administrator; b. Milw., May 7, 1944; s. Milton W. and Edith J. (Martinek) S.; children Eric Whitney, Edward Huntington. AB, Northwestern U., 1966; MD, Columbia U., 1970; MPH, Harvard U., 1975; PhD in Law, Medicine and Pub. Policy, Emory U., 1982; MA, San Francisco State U., 1999. Diplomate Am. Bd. Preventive Medicine. Resident in internal medicine Univ. Hosp. U. Calif.-San Diego, 1970-71; resident in preventive medicine Ctrs. Disease Control, Atlanta, 1971-74; commd. med. officer USPHS, 1971; advanced through grades to comdr., 1973; dir. hematology div. Nat. Ctr. for Disease Control, Atlanta, 1971-78, spl. asst. to dir., 1978-79, inactive res., 1979—; clin. asst. prof. pediatrics Tufts U. Med. Sch., 1974-86; clin. asst. prof. medicine Emory U. Med. Sch., 1971-81, clin. assoc. prof. community health, 1976-86; clin. assoc. prof. humanities in medicine Morehouse Med. Sch., 1977-79; attending physician dept. medicine Wilcox Meml. Hosp., Lihue, Hawaii, 1979-82, Calif. Pacific Med. Ctr., San Francisco, 1983—; dir. Ctr. Preventive Medicine and Health Research, 1983—, dir. Health Watch, 1983—; sr. scientist Inst. Epidemiology and Behavioral Medicine, Inst. Cancer Research, Calif. Pacific Med. Ctr., San Francisco, 1983-88; prof. hematology and gerontology, dir. Ctr. Preventive Medicine and Health Rsch., chair health professions program San Francisco State U., 1983-99, prof. medicine, 1983—, prof. emeritus, Calif. State U. Sys., 1999—; founding dir. Health Watch Internat., 1994—, CEO, pres. Cons. WHO, FDA, Washington, NIH, Bethesda, Md., Govt. of China, Mayo Cline, Rochester, Minn., Northwestern U., Evanston, Ill., Chicago, U. R.I., Kingston, Pan Am. Health Orgn., Inst. Pub. Health, Italy, Nat. Inst. Aging Rsch. Ctr., Baltimore, U. Calif., San Diego, U. Ill., Chicago, Columbia U., N.Y.C., Harvard U., Johns Hopkins U., U. Chgo., UCLA, U. Calif. Berkeley, Brown U., Providence, U. Calif., San Francisco, Stanford U., Boston, Emory U., Atlanta, Duke U., NC, U. Tex., Houston, Ariz. State U., U. Hawaii, Honolulu, U. Paris, U. Geneva, U. Munich, Heidelberg U., U. Frankfurt, U. Berlin, Cambridge (Eng.) U., U. Singapore, others; vis. rsch. prof. gerontology Ariz. State U., 1989—90; mem. numerous sci. and profl. adv. bds., panels, coms. Mem. editorial bd. Am. Jour. Clin. Pathology, 1976-82, The Advisor, 1988—, Generations, 1989—, Contemporary Gerontology, 1994—, Alternative Therapies in Health and Medicine, 1995—, Aging Today, 1997—; book and film reviewer Sci. Books and Films, 1988—, many other jours.; author: 17 books and manuals including Hematology Laboratory Series, 4 vols., 1979-86, CRC Handbook Series in Clinical Laboratory Science, 1976—; assoc. editor: Contemporary Gerontology, 1993—; contbr. more than 300 articles to sci. jours. Alumni regent Columbia U. Coll. Physicians and Surgeons, 1980—. Northwestern U. scholar, 1964-66; NSF fellow, 1964-66; Health Professions scholar, 1966-70; USPHS fellow, 1967-70; Microbiology, Urology, Upjohn Achievement, Borden Rsch. and Virginia Kneeland Frantz scholar awards Columbia U., 1970; recipient Am. Soc. Pharmacol. and Exptl. Therapy award in pharmacology, 1970, Commendation medal USPHS, 1973, Meritorious Performance and Profl. Promise award, 1989, Student Disting. Teaching and Svc. award Pre-Health Professions Student Alliance, 1992, Leadership Recognition awards San Francisco State U., 1984-89, 91-96, Meritorious Svc. award, 1992. Fellow: ACPM, AAAS (med. scis. sect.), ACP (commentator ACP Jour. Club/Annals of Internal Medicine 1993—), Internat. Soc. Hematology, Am. Soc. Clin. Pathology, Am. Coll. Preventive Medicine (sci. com.), Am. Geriatrics Soc., Royal Soc. Medicine (London), Gerontol. Soc. Am.; mem.: APHA, AMA, Calif. Coun. Gerontology and Geriatrics, Nat. Assn.Advisors for Health Professions, Internat. Health Evaln. Assn. (v.p. for Ams. 1992—94, bd. dirs. 1992—, pres. 1994—96), Calif. Med. Assn., San Francisco Med. Soc., N.Y. Acad. Scis., Am. Soc. Aging (editl. bd. 1990—, Dychtwald Pub. Speaking award 1991), Am. Soc. Microbiology, Assn. Tchrs. Preventive Medicine (edn. com., rsch. com.), Am. Coll. Occupl. and Environ. Medicine, Calif. Coun. Gerontology and Geriatrics, Am. Assn. Med. Informatics, Nat. Assn. Advisors for Health Professions (bd. dirs.), Am.Assn. Blood Banks, Acad. Clin. Lab. Physicians and Scientists, Internat. Soc. Thrombosis and Hemostasis, Am. Soc. Hematology, Internat. Commn. Standardization in Hematology, Am. Assn. Med. Informatics (chair prevention and health evaln. informatics WG), Nat. Gallery of Art (Washington), Columbia U. Club No. Calif., Northwestern U. Club. No. Calif., Harvard Club (N.Y. and San Francisco) (N.Y. and San Francisco), Golden Key (hon. faculty mem.), Army and Navy Club, Circle Club, Cosmos Club (mem. art com. 1997—), Knights of Malta, Sigma Xi, Phi Beta Kappa. Home: Whaleship Plaza 25 Hinckley Walk San Francisco CA 94111-2303 Office: Health Watch Med Ctr PO Box 7999 San Francisco CA 94120-7999 Fax: 415-956-8950. E-mail: rmschmidtmd@aol.com.

SCHMIDT, RODNEY ALBERT, computer science educator, retired; b. Bronxville, N.Y., Dec. 10, 1945; s. Rodney Albert and Janet Garner (Allen) S.; 1 child, Melanie Kayser. BSEE, MIT, 1966; MSEE, Stanford U., 1968, PhDEE, 1971; MA in Psychology, U. Denver, 1998, D of Psychology, 2000. Mgr. computer sci. Electromagnetic Systems Labs, Sunnyvale, 1971-76; systems engr., asst. prof. U. Denver, 1976-78; mgr. software engring. Denelcor, Inc., Denver, 1978-82; asst. prof. U. Colo., 1982-87, assoc. chmn. computer sci., 1986-87; assoc. prof. Colo. Sch. Mines, Golden, 1987-92; retired, 1992; intern VA Med. Ctr., Coatesville, Pa., 1999-2000. Cons. ESL Inc., Sunnyvale, 1976-78, Robot Def. Systems, Thornton, Colo., 1983-84, Syntronics Venture, Toronto, 1985. Contbr. articles to profl. jours. Named Outstanding Researcher in Elec. Engring and Computer Sci., U. Colo., 1986, 87. Mem. APA, Nat. Acad. Neuropsychologists, Tau Beta Pi (faculty advisor 1986-87).

SCHMIDT, RONALD HANS, architect; b. Hoboken, N.J., Sept. 9, 1938. BArch., Syracuse U., 1961. Sr. designer Skidmore, Owings & Merrill, N.Y.C., 1963-68; ptnr., dir. archtl. design Grad. Partnership, Newark, 1968-81; pres., chief exec. officer Ronald Schmidt & Assocs., P.A., Englewood, N.J., 1981—. Chmn. Bergen County (N.J.) Econ. Devel. Corp.; mem. bd. regents Felician Coll.; mem. exec. com. Network of Opportunity. Recipient numerous awards. Office: 222 Grand Ave Englewood NJ 07631-4352 E-mail: rschmidt@RSAaia.com.

SCHMIDT, RUSSEL ALAN, II, sales executive; b. Stuttgart-Bad Canstatt, Germany, Nov. 18, 1953; Came to U.S., 1954. s. Russell Allen and Phyllis (Coty) S.; m. Christie Ellen Duncan, Oct. 18 1975; children: Rachel Lea, Russell Alan III. BS, U. Minn., 1984. Lic. federal communications commn. gen. radiotelephone operator; cert. Motorola Effective Presentations, Successful Negotiator. Pres. Electronic Engring. Inds. Co., St. Paul, 1971-77, Dis-Com Inc., St. Paul, 1978-81; sales engr. Motorola Inc., Mpls., 1984-85, dist. sales engr., 1985-86, dist. sales mgr.(IBM), 1987-89, sr. account sales mgr. (IBM), 1989-93, sr. acct. sales mgr., 1993-95, market devel. mgr., 1995—. Bd. dirs. Dis-Com Inc. 1978-81; chief TV engr. Renewal Internat. Inc., St. Paul, Minn., 1984-87; pres. Forefront Devel., Inc., 2001; chief mgr. R&C Schmidt Properties LLC; v.p. Essential Bus. Svcs. Roseville, 2001. Published (music CD) Living In Laodicea, 1999. Mem. Nat. Small Bus.Assn.; St. Paul Chamber Commerce, North Suburban Chamber Commerce, Mpls. Chamber Commerce, North Oaks Golf Club. Republican, Lutheran Avocations: small business or real estate ventures, non-fiction reading, computer programming, travelling. Office: Motorola Semiconductor Products 5620 Smetana Dr Minnetonka MN 55343-9611

SCHMIDT, RUTH ANN, academic administrator emerita; b. Mountain Lake, Minn., Sept. 16, 1930; d. Jacob A. and Anna A. (Ewert) S. BA, Augsburg Coll., Mpls., 1952; MA, U. Mo., 1955; PhD, U. Ill., 1962; LLD, Gordon Coll., 1987. Asst. prof. Spanish Mary Baldwin Coll., Staunton, Va., 1955-58, SUNY-Albany, 1962-67, assoc. prof., 1967-78, dean of humanities, 1971-76; prof. and provost Wheaton Coll., Norton, Mass., 1978-82; pres. Agnes Scott Coll., Decatur, Ga., 1982-94, pres. emerita, 1994—. Interim pres. Lyon Coll., 1998; chair Women's Coll. Coalition, 1986-88. Author: Ortega Munilla y sus novelas, 1973, Cartas entre dos amigos del teatro, 1969. Trustee Gordon Coll., Wenham, Mass., 1980-86, Lyon Coll., 1993-2001; bd. dirs. DeKalb C. of C., 1982-85, Atlanta Coll. Art, 1984-94; mem. exec. com. Women's Coll. Coalition, 1983-88; v.p. So. Univ. Conf., 1993. Named Disting. Alumna Augsburg Coll., 1973 Mem. Assn. Am. Colls. (dir. 1979-82, treas. 1982-83), Soc. Values in Higher Edn., Am. Coun. Edn. (commn. on women in higher edn. 1985-88), AAUW, Assn. Pvt. Colls. and Univs. Ga. (pres. 1987-89), Internat. Women's Forum, Young Women's Christian Assn. Acad. Women Achievers. Democrat. Presbyterian.

SCHMIDT, RUTH A(NNA) M(ARIE), geologist; b. Bklyn., Apr. 22, 1916; d. Edward and Anna M. (Range) S. AB, NYU, 1936; MA, Columbia U., 1939, PhD, 1948. Cert. profl. geologist. Geologist U.S. Geol. Survey, Washington, 1943-56, dist. geologist Anchorage, 1956-63; prof., chmn. geology dept. U. Alaska, 1959-84; cons. geologist, 1964—. Lectr. Elder Hostels Alaska Pacific U., Anchorage, 1988—89, U. Alaska, Anchorage, 1994; coord. Engring. Geol. Evaluation Group, Alaskan 1964 Earthquake, Anchorage, 1964; environ. cons. Trans Alaska Pipeline Office of Gov., Anchorage, 1975—76. Editor: Alaska geology field trip guide books, 1984, 89; contbr. articles to profl. jours. Trustee, pres. Brooks Range Libr., Anchorage, 1979-91; bd. dirs., com. chmn. Anchorage Audubon Soc., 1989-98; mem. exec. bd., chmn. various coms. Alaska Cen. Environment, Anchorage; mem. adv. coun. Alaska Mus. Natural History, 1999—. Fellow AAAS, Arctic Inst. N.Am. (bd. govs. 1983-94), Geol. Soc. Am.; mem. Am. Inst. Profl. Geologists (charter), Am. Assn. Petroleum Geologists, Internat. Geol. Congress (del.), Alaska Geol. Soc. (hon. life mem., bd. dirs. 1993-95), Sigma Xi. Avocations: photography, gardening, hiking.

SCHMIDT, SANDRA JEAN, secondary school educator; b. Limestone, Maine, Mar. 21, 1955; d. Dale Laban and Marie Audrey (Bailey) Winters; m. Lee Lloyd Schmidt, Oct. 20, 1973; children: Colby Lee, Katrina Leesa. AA summa cum laude, Anne Arundel Community Coll., 1987; BS summa cum laude, U. Balt., 1990. CPA, Md. Enlisted U.S. Army, 1973, traffic analyst, 1973-85, resigned, 1985; auditor Md. State Office of Legislative Audits, Balt., 1990-93; fin. analyst Md. Ins. Adminstrn., 1993-2000; tchr. math. Baltimore City Pub. Schs., 2000—. Tutor Anne Arundel County Literacy Coun., Pasadena, Md., 1990-97; mentor U. Balt., 1991; host family Am. Intercultural Student Exchange, 1992-98. Mem.: Md. Coun. Tchrs. Math., Nat. Coun. Tchrs. Math., U. Balt. Alumni Assn., Phi Theta Kappa, Beta Gamma Sigma, Alpha Chi. Republican. Baptist. Home: 7716 Pinyon Rd Hanover MD 21076-1585 E-mail: beadmaniac@hotmail.com.

SCHMIDT, SARA MARIE, food services educator; b. Joliet, Ill., Aug. 7, 1970; d. Frank Bertram Jr. and Ruth Irene (Kemper) S. BA in English, Eastern Ill. U., 1992, student, 1992-93; cert. in adult literacy tchg., Nat.-Louis U., 1998; M in Adult Edn., Nat.-Louis Univ., 2001. Registrar Am. Acad. Computer Tng. and Tech., Rolling Meadows, Ill., 1996-97; faculty sec. Coll. Arts and Scis., National Louis U., Chgo., 1997-2000; adminstrv. asst. Columbia Coll., 2000—02; instr. Cooking and Hospitality Inst. Chgo., 2002—. Adj. instr. Roosevelt U., 2000—, MacCormac Coll., 2001. Mem.: Kappa Delta Pi, NADE, Sigma Tau Delta. Avocation: fiction writing. E-mail: Sara_Schmidt@excite.com.

SCHMIDT, SHERI LYNN, band director; b. Kalamazoo, Dec. 21, 1969; d. Robert LaDuke and Judith LaDuke; m. Darin Schmidt, Mar. 29, 1993. B Music Edn., Western Mich. U., 1992; M Music Edn., VanderCook Coll. of Music, 1999. Cert. tchr. Asst. dir. bands Pennfield Schs., Battle Creek, Mich., 1992—98; dir. bands Shakamak Schs., Jasonville, Ind., 1998—2001; band dir. Lakeview Schs., Battle Creek, Mich., 2001. Flute tchr., Battle Creek, 1985—2001. Mem.: Music Educator's Nat. Conf., Mich. Sch. Band and Orch. Assn. (treas. Dist. 8 1995—98). Presbyterian. Avocations: photography, yoga.*

SCHMIDT, SKIP FRANCIS, writer; b. Jonesboro, Ark., Oct. 26, 1960; s. Eugene Francis and Jean Anne (Holman) S.; m. Katherine Glaude, May 23, 1987 (div. 1990). AA, Meramec Coll., 1990. Playwright: Kaleidoscope, 1995. Mem. Poetry Soc. Am. Avocations: historical research, gourmet cooking. Home: 7401 Zephyr Pl Apt 1 Maplewood MO 63143-2027 E-mail: skipfs@juno.com.

SCHMIDT, STANLEY EUGENE, retired speech educator; b. Harrington, Wash., Dec. 14, 1927; s. Otto Jacob and Ella Genevieve (Wilson) S.; m. Jayne Brown; children: Randall Lee, Stephen Douglas. BS in Edn., U. Idaho, 1956; MEd in Adminstrn., U. Oreg., 1958; MA in Speech, Wash. State U., 1975. Supt., tchr., coach Rose Lake (Idaho) Sch. Dist. #35, 1949-55; forensics coach, speech tchr., dir. forensics Jefferson H.S., Portland, Oreg., 1955-65; dir. forensics Portland C.C., 1965-93, lead speech instr., 1979-82, subject area chmn., 1986-90; adj. prof. speech U. Portland, 1987-93; ret., 1993. Parliamentarian faculty senate, 1975-80. Co-author anthology: The Literature of the Oral Tradition, 1963. Chmn., precinct committeeman Rep. Party, Kootenai County, Idaho, 1951-53; mem. Easter Seal Soc.; pres. Kootenai County Tchrs. Assn., 1953-54, North Idaho Edn. Assn., 1954-55, Oreg. Speech Assn., 1960-61, Oreg. C.C. Speech Assn., 1971-72. Recipient Excellence award U.S. Bank, Portland, 1993, Merit award N.W. Forensic Assn., 1992, Faculty Merit award Portland C.C., 1984. Mem.: Oreg. Ret. Tchrs. Assn, Am. Rose Soc., Portland Rose Soc., Tualatin Valley Shrine Club (pres. 1994), Scottish Rite (pres. 2002—), Royal Ark Mariners, Royal Order Scotland, York Rite Sovereign Coll., Red Cross of Constantine (dir. of the work 1989—2001, recorder 1993—97, sovereign 2000—01, St. Laurence Conclave), Order of Ea. Star (Worthy Patron 1970), Knights Templar, Cryptic Masons of Oreg. (grand orator 1994—95, illustrious master 1997), Masons (worshipful master 1984—85, dist. dep. 1986—90, jr. grand deacon 1990—91, jr. grand steward 1991—92, grand orator 1992—93), Royal Rosarian. Baptist. Avocations: rose gardening, stamps, coins, fishing, sports. Home: 5460 SW Palatine St Portland OR 97219-7259

SCHMIDT, STEPHEN CHRISTOPHER, agricultural economist, educator; b. Isztimer, Hungary, Dec. 20, 1920; came to U.S., 1949, naturalized, 1965; s. Francis Michael and Anne Marie (Angeli) S.; m. Susan M. Varszegi, Dec. 20, 1945; children— Stephen Peter, David William. Dr.Sc., U. Budapest, Hungary, 1945; PhD, McGill U., Montreal, Que., Can., 1958. Asst. head dept. Hungary Ministry Commerce, Budapest, 1947-48; asst. prof. U. Ky., Lexington, 1955-57, Mont. State U., Bozeman, 1957-59, U. Ill., Urbana-Champaign, 1959-63, assoc. prof., 1963-70, prof. agrl. mktg. and policy, 1970-91, prof. emeritus, 1991—. Fulbright grantee Bulgaria, 1992-93; Ford Found. fellow, 1959; Agrl. Devel. Coun. grantee, 1966, U. Man. Rsch. fellow, 1968-69, Ford Found. rsch. grantee, 1973, 74, Whitehall found. grantee, 1979, Internat. Inst. Applied Systems Analyses (Laxenburg, Austria) rsch. scholar, 1976-77, USDA Intergovtl. Personnel Act grantee, 1983-84. Mem. Am. Agrl. Econs. Assn. (award 1979), Internat. Assn. Agrl. Economists, Am. Assn. Advancement Slavic Studies, Ea. Econ. Assn., Sigma Xi, Gamma Sigma Delta. Office: 1301 W Gregory Dr Urbana IL 61801-9015 E-mail: scschmid@uiuc.edu.

SCHMIDT, TED, talent agent, entertainment producer; b. N.Y.C., July 13, 1957; s. Otto F. and Lila (Raffa) S.; m. Lori Thompson; children: Kara Ashley, Joslyn Janelle, Evan Graham. BSBA in Fin., U. Fla., 1979. Gen. mgr. Peter Duchin Orch.; v.p. Duchin Entertainment, N.Y.C., 1979-87; pres. Ted Schmidt & Assocs., Inc., N.Y.C. and Vero Beach, Fla., 1987—. Entertainment producer Va. Gov.'s Inaugural Ball; pres. Dorsey Bros. Orch., Inc., Fla. Pops; founder Fla. Pops Orch.; pres. and founder Am. Swing Orchestra. Prodr. Salute to Frank Sinatra, Salute to Ella Fitzgerald. Office: 901 Winding River Rd Vero Beach FL 32963-2548

SCHMIDT, TERRY LANE, health care executive; b. Chgo., Nov. 28, 1943; s. LeRoy C. and Eunice P. Schmidt; children: Christie Anne, Terry Lane II. BS, Bowling Green State U., 1965; MBA in Health Care Adminstrn, George Washington U., 1971; D, U.S.C., 2001. Resident in hosp. adminstrn. U. Pitts. Med. Center, VA Hosp., Pitts., 1968-69; adminstrv. asst. Mt. Sinai Med. Center, N.Y.C., 1969-70; asst. dir. Health Facilities Planning Council of Met. Washington, 1970-71; asst. dir. dept. govtl. relations A.M.A., Washington, 1971-74; contract lobbyist and govtl. rels. Wash. Reps. in Health, 1974-87; pres. Terry L. Schmidt Inc. Physician Svcs. Group, San Diego, 1987-99, Washington Actions on Health, 1975-79; partner Washington Coun. Medicine and Health, 1979-81; pres. Recreational Enterprises, Inc., Washington, 1977-78; v.p. Crisis Communications Corp. Ltd., 1982-90; pres. Med. Cons. Inc., 1983-84, Ambulance Corp. Am., La Jolla, Calif., 1984-87; exec. dir., chief operating officer Emergency Health Assocs. P.C., Phoenix, 1989-91, Charleston Emergency Physicians, Inc., S.C., 1990-94, Joplin Emergency Physican Assocs., 1991-92, Big Valley Med. Group, 1991-92, Blue Ridge Emergency Physicians, P.C., 1992-94, Berkeley Emergency Physicians, P.C., 1992-94; chmn., pres. Univ. Inst., 1992—; asst. dir. Dept. of Emerg. Med., Med. U.S.C., 1999—. Bd. dirs., Univ. Inst., 1997—, lectr., instr. dept. health svcs. adminstrn. George Washington U., 1969-83, preceptor, 1975-84; adj. prof. grad. sch. Pub. Health San Diego State U., 1996—, preceptor, 1989—, guest lectr. health care adminstrn. Nat. U. San Diego, 1992-93; guest lectr. Bus. Adminstrn. U.S. Internat. U., San Diego, 1994—; instr. Nat. Naval Sch. Health Care Adminstrn., 1971-73; faculty Civil Svc. Commn. Legis. Insts., 1972-76; fac. Am. Assn. State Colls. and U. Health Tng. Insts., 1975-78; mem. adv. com. ambulatory care standards Joint Commn. Accreditation of Hosps., 1971-72, pres., Recreational Enterprises, Inc., Wash., 1977-78, guest lectr., Coll. of Med. & dept. Health Admin. & Pol., Med. U.S.C., 1998-99, preceptor, 1999—, assoc. prof., Coll. of Health, Med. U.S.C., 1999—. Author: Congress and Health: An Introduction to the Legislative Process and the Key Participants, 1976, A Directory of Federal Health Resources and Services for the Disadvantaged, 1976, Health Care Reimbursement: A Glossary, 1983; mem. editl. adv. bd. Nation's Health, 1971-73; contbr. articles to profl. jours. Bd. dirs. Nat. Eye Found., 1976-78. Mem. Med. Group Mgmt. Assn., Health Care Fin. Mgmt. Assn., Assn. Venture Capital Groups (bd. dirs. 1984-89), Amer. Coll. of Health Execs., Amer. Coll. of Med. Prac. Exec., Assn. of Univ. Progs. in Health Admin., San Diego Venture Group (chair 1984-87), Univ. Club (life), Natl. Rep. Club (life), Nat. Dem. Club (life), Capitol Hill Club (life), Alpha Phi Omega (pres. Bowling Green alumni chpt. 1967-70, sec.-treas. alumni assn. 1968-71). Office: Terry L Schmidt Inc Ste 113 611 7770 Regents Rd San Diego CA 92122-1967

SCHMIDT, THOMAS JOSEPH, JR. lawyer; b. New Haven, Jan. 16, 1945; s. Thomas Joseph and Rosemary (O'Shaughnessy) S.; m. Linda Diane Crider, Nov. 16, 1974; children: Elizabeth Anne, Thomas Joseph III, Karen Diana. AB, Xavier U., 1967; JD, U. Cin., 1970. Bar: Ohio 1970, U.S. Ct. Mil. Appeals 1970. Commd. 2d lt. U.S. Army, 1967, advanced through grades to capt., 1969-75; legal officer U.S. Army Corps Engrs., Ft. Hayes, Ohio, 1967-68, Ft. Knox, Ky., 1969-70; atty. U.S. Army JAGC, Ft. Benning, Ga., 1971-75; asst. counsel Midland Enterprises Inc., Cin., 1975-77, assoc. gen. counsel, 1977-83, gen. counsel, 1983-87, gen. counsel, sec., 1987-95, v.p., gen. counsel and sec., 1995—. Republican. Roman Catholic. Office: Midland Enterprises Inc 300 Pike St Cincinnati OH 45202-4222

SCHMIDT, VIVIEN ANN, political scientist, educator; b. N.Y.C., , , Nov. 19, 1949; d. Edith Diane Kurzweil and Charles Schmidt, Robert Kurzweil (Stepfather); m. Jolyon Michael Howorth. BA, Bryn Mawr Coll., 1971; MA, U. Chgo., 1973, PhD, 1981. Prof. U. Mass., Boston, 1979—98, Boston U., 1998—2002. Vis. prof. Institut d'Etudes Politiques, Paris, 0200—2002; vis., Fulbright fellow Nuffield Coll., Oxford U., Oxford, England, 2001—02; vis. prof. Max Planck Inst. for the Study of Societies, Cologne, Germany, 1998—99, European U. Inst., Florence, Italy, 1999—2000, U. of Lille, France, 1995—96; dir. Ctr. for Democracy and Devel., McCormack Inst., U. of Mass., Boston, 1994—98, European Studies Program, U. of Mass., Boston, 1993—98. Author: (book) The Futures of European Capitalism, 2002; editor (co-editor): Welfare and Work in the Open Economy (2 volumes), 2001; author: From State to Market? The Transformation of French Business and Government, 1996, Democratizing France, 1990 (Mention d'Honneur, Gaston Defferre Prize Ceremony, 1992). Named Chevalier in the Order of the Palmes Académiques, French Govt., 1994; named to Jean Monnet Professorship, European Union Commn., 2001—; recipient Fulbright European Union Rsch. Award, Fulbright Commn., 2001—02. Mem.: Internat. Polit. Sci. Assn., Am. Polit. Sci. Assn. (exec. com. European sect. 2000—03), European Union Studies Assn. (chair exec. com. 1999—2001). Avocation: photography, skiing, travel. Office: Boston U 152 Bay State Rd Boston MA 02215 Office Fax: 617-353-9290.

SCHMIDT, WALDEMAR ADRIAN, pathologist, educator; b. L.A., Aug. 22, 1941; s. Waldemar Adrian and Mary Charlotte (Parker) S.; m. Karmen LaVer Bingham, Feb. 1, 1963; children: Rebecca, Sarah, Waldemar, Diedrich. BS, Oreg. State U., 1965; PhD, MD, U. Oreg., 1969. Intern U. Oreg. Hosps. and Clinics, Portland, 1969-70, resident, 1970-73; pathologist LDS Hosp., Salt Lake City, 1973-77; prof. pathology U. Tex. Med. Sch., Houston, 1977-91, Oreg. Health and Scis. U. , Portland, 1991—; chief pathology and lab. medicine svc. Oreg. Health and Scis. U. and VA Med. Ctr., 1997—2001, vice chair pathology, 1997—2001. Author: Principles and Techniques of Surgical Pathology, 1982; editor Cytopathology Annual, 1991-94, Revs. in Pathology-Cytopathology, 1994-99. Asst. scoutmaster Boy Scouts Am., Houston, 1982-91. Maj. U.S. Army, 1970-76. Fellow Am. Soc. Clin. Pathologists, Coll. Am. Pathologists; mem. Internat. Acad. Cytology, Sigma Xi, Alpha Omega Alpha. Avocations: photography, silviculture, apiculture. Office: U Oreg Health and Scis U Sch Medicine Dept Pathology 3181 SW Sam Jackson Park Rd Portland OR 97201-3098

SCHMIDT, WAYNE WALTER, law association executive; b. St. Louis, Feb. 8, 1941; s. Warren W. and Geneva N. (Walker) S.; children: Andrew M., Nancy K. Diploma in English and comparative law, City of London Coll., 1963; BA, U. N.Mex., 1964; JD, Oklahoma City U., 1966; LLM, Northwestern U., 1974. Bar: N.Mex. 1966, Ill. 1968, D.C. 1970, N.Y. 1982. Dir. police legal advisor program Northwestern U., 1968-70; counsel Internat. Assn. Chiefs of Police, 1970-73; exec. dir. Am. for Effective Law Enforcement, Inc., Chgo., 1973—; pres. Pub. Safety Pers. Rsch. Inst., 1974—, Govt. Employment Rsch. Inst., Inc., 1986-89, Lauterbrunnen Properties, 1990-93; dir. Comprehensive Ensurers Market Syndicate, Inc., 1984-91, 93-94, Capital Exch. Mgmt., Inc., 1988-91. Cons. Uniform Code of Criminal Procedure. Co-author: Legal Aspects of Criminal Evidence, 1978, Introduction to Criminal Evidence, 1982, Introduction to Criminal Evidence and Court Procedure, 1987, 3d edit. 1995;

editor Fire and Police Pers. Reporter, 1975—, Pub. Employment Health Law and Benefits, 1986-89, Fire and Police Ann. Case Digest, 1984—. Served with U.S. Army, 1966-67. Mem. ABA (liaison to criminal justice coun. 1973—), Internat. Assn. Chiefs of Police (vice chair legis. com. 1988—). Office: Am Effective Law Enforcement Legal Ctr 841 W Touhy Ave Park Ridge IL 60068-3351 E-mail: aele@aol.com.

SCHMIDT, WILLIAM ARTHUR, JR. lawyer; b. Cleve., Oct. 2, 1939; s. William Arthur and Caroline (Jäger) S.; m. Gerilyn Pearl Smith, Sept. 30, 1967; children: Deborah, Dawn, Jennifer. BSBA, Kent State U., 1962; JD, Cleve. State U., 1968. Bar: Ohio 1968, Ill. 1990. Contract specialist NASA-Lewis, Cleve., 1962-66, procurement analyst, 1967-68; atty. Def. Logistics Agy., Alexandria, Va., 1968-73; assoc. counsel Naval Sea Sys. Command, Arlington, 1973-75; procurement policy analyst Energy R & D Adminstrn., Germantown, Md., 1975-76; sr. atty. U.S. Dept. Energy, 1976-78, counsel spl. projects Oak Ridge, Tenn., 1978-83; judge Agr. Bd. Contract Appeals, Washington, 1983-87; judge Bd. Contract Appeals HUD, 1987; chief legal counsel Fermilab, Batavia, Ill., 1987-92; gen. counsel Univ. Rsch. Assn., Inc., Washington, 1992—. Co-author: (NASA handbook) R & D Business Practices, 1968. Founder/dir. M&O Contractor Attys. Assn.; dir. Spotsylvania Crime Solvers. Mem. Fed. Bar Assn. (past pres. East Tenn. 1978-83, 25 Yr. Svc. award 1994), Ill. Bar Assn., Bd. Contract Appeals Judges Assn. (dir.-sec. 1986-88), Sr. Execs. Assn., Delta Theta Phi (dist. chancellor 1978-83), Sigma Chi. Republican. Lutheran. Avocations: classic cars, M-1 carbines. Home: 11729 Collinwood Ct Fredericksburg VA 22407-7115 Office: Univ Rsch Assn Inc 1111 19th St NW Ste 400 Washington DC 20036-3627

SCHMIDT, WILLIAM C. chemical company executive; b. Niles, Mich., Sept. 27, 1938; s. Felix A. and Anna (Reifschneider) S.; m. Bethany Ann Boyd, Dec. 17, 1966; 1 child, Craig W. BBA, U. Mich., 1960, MBA, 1961. Cert. Mgmt. Acct. Various acctg. positions Dow Chem. Co., Midland, Mich., 1961-73; controller Dow Chem. Pacific Ltd., Hong Kong, 1973-78; area controller Dow Chem. Co., Midland, Mich., 1978-82, asst. corp. controller, 1982-98; v.p., chief fin. officer DowElanco, Indpls., 1989-98. Dir. Wolverine Bank, F.S.B., 1998—. Dir. Midland Hosp., 1982-89, 98—, chmn. bd., 1986-88; bd. dirs. Mid-Mich. Health Corp., 1983-89, 2001—, chmn. bd., 1986-88; treas., bd. dirs. Indpls. Symphony Orch., 1992-98; dir. West Midland Family Ctr., 2000—. Cpl. U.S. Army, 1962-64. Mem. Inst. Mgmt. Accts., Inst. Cert. Mgmt. Accts. (regent 1985-89), Am. Indsl. Health Coun. (treas. 1986-87), Fin. Execs. Inst., Ind. C. of C. (bd. dirs. 1992-98). Presbyterian. Home: 5908 Londonberrie Ct Midland MI 48640-6965

SCHMIDT, WILLIAM MAX, management consultant, business executive; b. Danville, Pa., Nov. 23, 1947; s. Frank Wilhelm and Doris Savilla (Maurer) S.; m. Marylea O'Reilly, Sept. 20, 1980. BS, U. Pa., 1969; MBA, Northwestern U., 1971. Mktg. specialist Moody's Investors Svc., Inc., N.Y.C., 1971-72; cons. William E. Hill & Co. Inc., N.Y.C, 1972-74; product supr. Internat. Paper Co., N.Y.C., 1974-79; dir. market analysis U.S. Industries, Inc., Stamford, Conn., 1979-82, mgr. corp. devel., 1982-84; dir. corp. mktg. Combustion Engring., Inc., 1984-86, v.p. mktg., planning Union, N.J., 1986-91; pres. Pragmatics, Basking Ridge, NJ, 1991—2000; global dir. mktg. Gemplus Corp., Montgomeryville, Pa., 2000—. Author: (newsletter) Think Again, 1995. Bd. dirs. Curbing Hunger, Inc., Basking Ridge, N.J., 1995—; adv. Jr. Achievement, N.Y.C., 1976-78. Mem. TAPPI, Exec. Forum, Strategic Leadership Forum, Univ. Club, Sons of the Revolution, Wharton Club (N.Y.C.), Sigma Chi. Republican. Mem. United Ch. of Christ. Avocations: tennis, astronomy, canoeing, community service, numismatics. Home: 46 Quincy Rd Basking Ridge NJ 07920-2245 Office: Gemplus Corp 101 Park Dr Montgomeryville PA 18936 E-mail: billprag@worldnet.att.net.

SCHMIDT-BOVA, CAROLYN MARIE, career and technical school administrator; b. Jacksonville, Fla., Sept. 1, 1948; d. Leonard Stephen and Marianne Vesta (Ruscher) S.; m. Edward W. Bova. EdB, SUNY, Buffalo, 1980, MEd, 1981; cert. advanced study, SUNY, Brockport, 1988. Cert. tchr., N.Y., SDA Work Study Coord. Instr. Erie Bd. Coop. Edn. Svcs., Lancaster, N.Y., 1977-82, Orleans-Niagara Bd. Coop. Ednl. Svcs., Medina, 1982-88. Adj. instr. SUNY, Buffalo, 1988—, student adv.; cons. N.Y. Dept. Edn., Albany, 1982—, facilitator, 1982—85, regional resource person, 1985—91; bd. dirs. Inst. for Curriculum Advancement; mem. adv. com. Sch. Dist. Reorganization Ctrl. Western Regional Study; regional rep. N.Y. State Alternative Sch. Educators Adminstrn. Leader Girl Scouts U.S.A., Buffalo; trustee Skills-USA. Tchr. Intern award Tchrs. Ctr., Lockport, N.Y., 1989; N.Y. Disting. Occupational edn. award, 1991. Mem.: ASCD, United Univ. Profls., Sch. Adminstrs. Assn. N.Y. State, N.Y. State Tchr. Educators, N.Y. State Tchrs. Vocat. Assn., N.Y. State Alternative Edn. Assn. (regional rep.), Career and Tech. Clubs Am. (advisor, Advisor of Yr. N.Y. State 1994—95, Buffalo State Coll. Career Tech. Edn. Excellence award 1995—96), Am. Career and Tech. Assn., Am. Career and Tech. Skills Edn. Adminstrs., So. Poverty Law Ctr., Buffalo State Coll. Alumni, Nefane Hist. Soc., Western N.Y. Women in Adminstrn., Iota Lambda Sigma, Epsilon Pi Tau, Phi Delta Kappa. Home: 5894 Fisk Rd Lockport NY 14094-9224 Office: Orleans-Niagara Bd Ednl Svc 3181 Saunders Settlement Rd Sanborn NY 14132-9487

SCHMIDT-NIELSEN, BODIL MIMI (MRS. ROGER G. CHAGNON), physiologist, educator; b. Copenhagen, Denmark, Nov. 3, 1918; came to U.S., 1946, naturalized, 1952; d. August and Marie (Jorgensen) Krogh; m. Knut Schmidt-Nielsen, Sept. 20, 1939 (div. Feb. 1966); children: Astrid, Bent, Bodil; m. Roger G. Chagnon, Oct. 1968. DDS, U. Copenhagen, 1941, DOdont, 1946, DPhil, 1955; DS (hon.), Bates Coll., 1983; MD (hon.), U. Aarhus, Denmark, 1997. Faculty Duke, Durham, N.C., 1952-64; prof. biology Case Western Res. U., Cleve., 1964-71, chmn. dept., 1970-71, adj. prof., 1971-74; trustee Mt. Desert Island Biol. Lab., Maine, research scientist, 1971-86, exec. com., 1978-85, v.p., 1979-81, pres., 1981-85. Adj. prof. Brown U., Providence, 1971-75, dept. physiol. U. Fla., Gainesville, 1986—; mem. tng. grant com. NIGMS, 1965-71 Author: August and Marie Krogh, Lives in Science, 1995, Danish edit., 1997; editor: Urea and the Kidney, 1970; assoc. editor Am. Jour. Physiology: Regulatory, Integrative and Comparative Physiology, 1978-81. Trustee Coll. of Atlantic, Bar Harbor, Maine, 1972-92. Recipient Career award NIH, 1962-64, John Simon Guggenheim Meml. fellow, 1952-53; Bowditch lectr., 1958, Jacobaeus lectr., 1974. Fellow AAAS (de. coun. 1977-79), N.Y. Acad. Scis., Am. Acad. Arts and Scis.; mem. Am. Physiol. Soc. (coun. 1971-77, pres. 1975-76, Ray G. Daggs award 1989, Orr Reynolds award 1994, August Knogh lectr. 1994, Berliner award 1998), Soc. Exptl. Biology and Medicine (coun. 1967-71). Achievements include research, publs. on biochemistry of saliva, water metabolism of desert animals, urea excretion, peristalsis of renal pelvis and concentrating mechanism, comparative kidney physiology, comparative physiology of excretory organs. Home: 4426 SW 103rd Ct Gainesville FL 32608-7146 Office: U Fla Dept Physiology Gainesville FL 32605 E-mail: Bodilmi@aol.com.

SCHMIDT-NIELSEN, KNUT, physiologist, educator; b. Norway, Sept. 24, 1915; came to U.S., 1946, naturalized, 1952; s. Sigval and Signe Torborg (Sturzen-Becker) Schmidt-N. Mag. Scient., U. Copenhagen, 1941, Dr. Phil., 1946; Dr. Med. (hon.), U. Lund, Sweden, 1985; D in Philosophy (hon.), U. Tondheim, Norway, 1993. Research fellow Carlsberg Labs., Copenhagen, 1941-44, Carlsberg Labs. (U. Copenhagen), 1944-46; research assoc. zoology Swarthmore (Pa.) Coll., 1946-48; docent U. Oslo, Norway, 1947-49; research assoc. physiology Stanford U., 1948-49; asst. prof. Coll. Medicine, U. Cin., 1949-52; prof. physiology Duke U., Durham, N.C., 1952—, James B. Duke prof. physiology, 1963—; Harvey Soc. lectr., 1962; Regents' lectr. U. Calif. at Davis, 1963; Brody Meml. lectr. U. Mo., 1962; Hans Gadow lectr. Cambridge (Eng.) U., 1971; vis. Agassiz prof. Harvard, 1972. Wellcome vis. prof. U. S.D., 1988; mem. panel environmental biology NSF, 1957-61; mem. sci. adv. com. New Eng. Regional Primate Center, 1962-66; mem. nat. adv. bd. physiol. research lab. Scripps Instn. Oceanography, U. Calif. at San Diego, 1963-69, chmn., 1968-69; organizing com. 1st Internat. Conf. on Comparative Physiology, 1972-80; pres. Internat. Union Physiol. Scis., 1980-86, mem. U.S. nat. com. 1966-78, vice chmn. U.S. nat. com., 1969-78; mem. subcom. on environmental physiology U.S. nat. com. Internat. Biol. Programme, 1965-67; mem. com. on research utilization uncommon animals, div. biology and agr. Nat. Acad. Scis., 1966-68; mem. animal resources adv. com. NIH, 1968; mem. adv. bd. Bio-Med. Scis., Inc., 1973-74; chief scientist Scripps Instn. Amazon expdn., 1967. Author: Animal Physiology, 3d. edit, 1970, The Physiology of Desert Animals; Physiological Problems of Heat and Water, 1964, How Animals Work, 1972, Animal Physiology; Adaptation and Environment, 1975, 5th edit., 1997, Scaling: Why is Animal Size So Important?, 1984, The Camel's Nose: Memoirs of a Curious Scientist, 1998; sect. editor Am. Jour. Physiology, 1961-64, 70-76; editor Jour. Applied Physiology, 1961-64, 70-76; mem. editorial bd. Jour. Cellular and Comparative Physiology, 1961-66, Physiol. Zoology, 1959-70, Am. Jour. Physiology, 1971-76, Jour. Applied Physiology, 1971-76, Jour. Exptl. Biology, 1975-79, 83-86; cons. editor: Annals of Arid Zone, 1962—; hon. editorial adv. bd. Comparative Biochemistry and Physiology, 1962-63; chief editor News in Physiol Scis., 1985-88, cons. editor, 1988—; contbr. articles to sci. publs. Guggenheim fellow, 1953-54; grantee Office Naval Rsch., 1952-54, 58-61, UNESCO, 1953-54, Office Q.M. Gen., 1953-54, Office Surgeon Gen., 1953-54, NIH, 1955-86, NSF, 1957-61, 59-60, 60-61, 61-63; recipient Rsch. Career award USPHS, 1964-85, Internat. prize for biology Japan Soc. for the Promotion of Sci., 1992, Disting. Svc. medal Smithsonian Instn., Nat. Zool. Park, 1998; recipient N.C. award in sci., 1999. Fellow AAAS, N.Y. Acad. Sci., Am. Acad. Arts and Scis.; mem. NAS, N.C. Acad. Sci. (Poteat award 1957), Am. Physiol. Soc., Am. Soc. Zoologists (chmn. div. comparative physiology 1964), Soc. Exptl. Biology, Royal Danish Acad., Acad. Scis. (France) (fgn. assoc.), Royal Norwegian Soc. Arts. and Sci., Norwegian Acad. Scis. and Letters, Physiol. Soc. London (assoc.), Royal Soc. London (fgn.); hon. mem. Soc. Integrative & Comparative Biology, Harvey Soc., Zool. Soc. London, Deutsche Ornitologengesellshaft. Office: Duke U Dept Biology PO Box 90338 Durham NC 27708-0338

SCHMIEL, DAVID GERHARD, clergyman, religious education administrator; b. Cedarburg, Wis., Dec. 10, 1931; s. Gerhard August and Frieda Helena (Labrenz) S.; m. Shirley Ann Friede, July 6, 1957; children: Mark, Peter, Steven, Daniel, Julia. BA, Northwestern Coll., 1953; ThD, Concordia Sem., 1967. Pastor St. Paul's Luth. Ch., Gresham, Nebr., 1958-60, Onalaska, Wis., 1960-62; prof. St. Paul's Coll., Concordia, Mo., 1962-70; prof., dean Concordia Coll., St. Paul, 1970-81; dir. instrn. Concordia Sem., St. Louis, 1981-82; pres. Concordia Coll., Ann Arbor, Mich., 1983-91; dir. theol. edn. svc. Luth. Ch.-Mo. Synod, St. Louis, 1991-93; pres. Concordia Theol. Sem., Ft. Wayne, Ind., 1993-95, ret., 1995. Author: Via Propria and Via Mystica...Gerson, 1969. Found. for Reformation Rsch. Jr. fellow, Southeastern Inst. for Medieval and Renaissance Studies, Jr. fellow, 1965, 66, 68.

SCHMIO, STEVEN R. mechanical engineer, educator; b. Chgo., Nov. 24, 1964; s. Karl Josef and Martha Teres (Trautendorfer) Schmid; m. Shelly Anne Petronis. BS in Mech. Engring., Ill. Inst. Tech., 1986; MS in Mech. Engring., Northwestern U., 1989, PhD, 1993. Engr. Triodyne, Inc., Niles, Ill., 1986—92; from asst. to assoc. prof. Notre Dame (Ind.) U., 1993—. Co-author: Fundamentals of Machine Elements, 1999, Manufacturing Engineering and Technology, 2001, Manufactuing Proc. Eng. Materials, 2002. Sec. Schaebische Untrshtangs-Verein, Chgo., 1992—. Recipient Newkirk award, ASME, 2000, Parsons award, Soc. Mfg. Engrs., 2000. Office: U Notre Dame 377 Fitzpatrick Hall Notre Dame IN 46556

SCHMIT, LUCIEN ANDRÉ, JR. structural engineer; b. N.Y.C., May 5, 1928; s. Lucien Alexander and Eleanor Jessie (Donley) S.; m. Eleanor Constance Trabish, June 24, 1951; 1 son, Lucien Alexander, III. BS, MIT, 1949, MS, 1950. Structures engr. Grumman Aircraft Co., Bethpage, N.Y., 1951-53; rsch. engr., aeroelastic and structures lab. MIT, 1954-58; asst. prof. engring. Case Inst. Tech., 1958-60, assoc. prof., 1961-63, prof., 1964-70; prof. engring. and applied sci. UCLA, 1970-91, Rockwell prof. aerospace engring. emeritus, 1991—. Sci. adv. bd. USAF, 1977-84. Contbr. articles on analysis and synthesis of structural systems, finite elements methods, design of fiber composite components and multidisciplinary design optimization to profl. jours. Fellow AIAA (Design Lecture award 1977, Structures, Structural Dynamics and Materials award 1979, Multidisciplinary Design Optimization award 1994, Walter J. and Angeline H. Crichlow Trust prize 1999), ASCE, Am. Acad. Mechanics; mem. NAE. Home: 545 3rd Ave S Edmonds WA 98020-4103 E-mail: schmit13@attbi.com.

SCHMITT, DIANA MAE, elementary education educator; b. Dubuque, Iowa, Jan. 19, 1950; d. Raymond J. and Marie Arlen Schmitt. BA, U. Iowa, 1972; MA, Clarke Coll., Dubuque, 1981; postgrad., U. Wyo. 6th grade tchr. Shelby County Sch. Dist., Shelby, Iowa, 1972-73; 4th and 5th grade tchr. Dist. 200, Woodstock, Ill., 1973-76; rural sch. tchr. Albany County Sch. Dist., Laramie, Wyo., 1976-83, 1st, 3d, 5th and 6th grade tchr., 1983-98; chmn. outdoor classrm. devel. Indian Paintbrush Elem., 1992—. Mem. rev. com. for excellence in sci. edn., adv. com. Western Edn. Adv. Com. for Wyo., 1989; tchr. sci. methods for elem. sch. U. Wyo., 1990-91; mem. Higher Edn. Grant Reading State Com., 1994; participant Sci. Grasp, 1990, Inst. Chemical Edn. Fundamental, 1992; presenter 1st Soviet-Am. Sci. Conv., Moscow, 1991; mem. workshop on water, Nat. Geog. Soc., 1993; presenter NSTA nat. and regional convs., state Wyo. Interdisciplinary Conf. convs., No. Iowa Beginning Reading conf. Recipient Delta award, 1993; named Dist. Exemplary Sci. Tchr., 1986-87; Wyo. Game and Fish grantee, 1993-95, Nat. Geog. Soc. grantee, 1997. Mem. NEA, Internat. Reading Assn., Nat. Sci. Tchrs. Assn., Wyo. Sci. Tchrs. Assn. (sec.), Alpha Delta Kappa (pres.). Home: 5737 Southview Rd Laramie WY 82070-6801 Office: Indian Paintbrush 1653 N 28th St Laramie WY 82072-9200 E-mail: msdmschmitt@yahoo.com.

SCHMITT, GEORGE FREDERICK, JR. materials engineer; b. Louisville, Nov. 3, 1939; s. George Frederick and Jane Limbird (Hurst) S.; m. Ann Cheatham, July 31, 1965; 2 children. BS, U. Louisville, 1962, MS, 1963; MBA, Ohio State U., 1966. Chief integration and ops. divsn. Air Force Rsch. Lab. USAF Materials Directorate, Wright Patterson AFB, Ohio, 1966—; advanced engring devel. mgr. USAF Materials Lab., 1986-90, chief plans and programs br. Wright AFB, 1989-90, asst. chief nonmetallic materials divsn., 1990-96. Guest lectr. U. Dayton, 1970, 95, Cath. U., 1973, U. Mich., 1975. Contbr. articles to profl. jours. Mem. Kettering (Ohio) Civic Band, 1965—, Affiliate Socs. Coun. Dayton, 1972-81; mem. Dayton Philharm Chorus, 1999—, Dayton Letter Carriers Band, 2000—. 1st lt. USAF, 1963-66. Named Fed. Profl. Employee of Yr., Dayton, 1972, One of Ten Outstanding Engrs., Engrs. Week, 1975; recipient Air Force Meritorious Civilian Svc. award, 1994, Burton award for svc., Playhouse South Cmty. Theater, 1998, Tech. Transfer award, Fed. Lab. Consortium, 2001. Fellow Soc. for Advancement Materials and Process Engrs. (Best Paper award 1973, nat. sec. 1975-76, nat. membership chmn. 1977-79, nat. v.p. 1979-81, nat pres. 1981-82, chmn. long-range planning com. 1983-87, trustee 1991—, chmn. Internat. SAMPE Symposium 1996, chmn. SAMPE Trophy com. 1998—), AIAA (assoc., materials tech. com.); mem. ASTM (rec. sec. 72-75, chmn. com. on erosion and wear 1976-79, chmn. liaison subcom. 1979-83, award of merit 1981), Am. Chem. Soc., Affiliate Socs. Coun. Dayton (chmn. 1978-79). Republican. Lutheran. Home: 1500 Wardmier Dr Dayton OH 45459-3354 Office: AFRL Materials and Mfg Directorate MLO Wright-Patterson AFB 2977 P St Bldg 653 Dayton OH 45433-7733 E-mail: george.schmitt@wpafb.af.mil.

SCHMITT, HOWARD STANLEY, minister; b. Waterloo, Ont., Can., Oct. 19, 1933; came to U.S., 1971; s. Delton Howard and Beulah (Weber) S.; m. Dorothy Jean West, May 20, 1960; children: Valerie Jean Schmitt Jones, Jeffrey Howard. B Theology, Toronto Bible Coll., Ont., Can., 1963. Ordained to ministry Mennonite Ch., 1963. Pastor Wanner Mennonite Ch., Cambridge, Ont., 1960-71, Calvary Mennonite Ch., Ayr, 1964-69, S. Union Mennonite Ch., West Liberty, Ohio, 1971-83; hosp. chaplain Mary Rutan Hosp., Bellefontaine, 1983-85; dir. devel. Adriel Sch., West Liberty, 1985-86; pastor Bay Shore Mennonite Ch., Sarasota, Fla., 1986-95, Sharon Mennonite Ch., Plain City, Ohio, 1995—. Sec. Mennonite Conf. Ont., Cambridge, 1970-71; overseer Ohio Conf. Mennonites, West Liberty, 1972-78, 84-86; moderator Southeast Mennonite Conf., Sarasota, 1989-92; mem. Mennonite Ch. Gen. Bd., 1991-95. Vice chair Mary Rutan Hosp. Bd., 1978-83; sec. Plain City Ch. Fellowship, 1997—. Recipient 13 Yrs. Svc. award Vol. Chaplains Group, Mary Rutan Hosp., 1985. Mem. Sarasota Mennonite Mins. Fellowship (past sec., chmn.), Plain City Pastors' Fellowship, Ctrl. Ohio Mennonite Pastor Peer Group, Ohio Conf. Mennonites Coun. E-mail: howjean@prodigy.net.

SCHMITT, JOHN FRANCIS, lawyer; b. Indpls., Dec. 27, 1950; s. Herman Louis and Amelia Agnes (Sustarsich) S.; m. Regina Ann Louden, Jan. 15, 1969 (div. Feb. 1975); 1 child, Michael Joseph; m. Julie Ann Zellers, Aug. 11, 1979 (div. May 14, 1986); m. Deborah Ann Everton, Sept. 17, 1987. AB in Polit. Sci. with distinction, Ind. U., 1976, JD, 1979. Bar: Ind. 1979, U.S. Dist. Ct. (so. dist.) Ind. 1979, U.S. Ct. Appeals (7th cir.) 1982. Dep. auditor of state State of Ind., Indpls., 1976-78; assoc. Lewis, Bowman, St. Clair & Wagner, 1979-83, ptnr., 1984—. Pres. Ind. Young Dems., 1975-76. Mem. ABA, Ind. State Bar Assn., Indpls. Bar Assn., Assn. Trial Lawyers Am., Ind. Trial Lawyers Am., AFL-CIO Lawyers Coordinating Com. Avocations: guitar, bicycling, golf, tennis, fishing. Home: PO Box 348 Trafalgar IN 46181-0348 Office: Lewis Bowman St Clair & Wagner 501 Indiana Ave Ste 200 Indianapolis IN 46202-6146

SCHMITT, JOHN PATRICK, lawyer; b. Hempstead, N.Y., Oct. 23, 1956; s. William Jude and Janet Patricia (Hurley) S.; m. Sylvia Yvonne Picard, Mar. 10, 1979; children: Emily, Patrick, Daniel, Peter. AB, Georgetown U., 1977; JD, Fordham U., 1980. Bar: N.Y. 1981. Assoc. Lord Day & Lord, N.Y.C., 1980-82, Patterson, Belknap, Webb & Tyler LLP, N.Y.C., 1983-88, ptnr., 1989—. Mem. ABA, N.Y. State Bar Assn., Assn. of Bar of City of N.Y. Democrat. Roman Catholic. Office: Patterson Belknap Webb & Tyler LLP 1133 Avenue Of The Americas Fl 22 New York NY 10036-6731 E-mail: jpschmitt@pbwt.com.

SCHMITT, KARL MICHAEL, retired political scientist; b. Louisville, July 22, 1922; s. Edward Peter and Mary Ann (Iula) S.; m. Grace Bernadette Leary, June 18, 1949; children: Karl, Edward, Barbara, William, Michael. BA, Cath. U. Am., 1947, MA, 1949; PhD, U. Pa., 1954. Teaching asst. U. Pa., 1948-50; instr. history Niagara U., 1950-54, asst. prof., 1954-55; research analyst U.S. Dept. State, 1955-58; asst. prof. dept. govt. U. Tex., 1958-63, assoc. prof., 1963-66, prof., 1966-91, prof. emeritus, 1991—, chmn., 1975-80. Vis. prof. U. Calif., Los Angeles, summer 1959, Nat. War Coll., 1970-71; vis. sr. fellow U. Manchester, Eng., 1988-89; cons. Dept. of State, 1962-70 Author: Communism in Mexico; A Study in Political Frustration, 1965, Mexico and the United States, 1821-1973: Conflict and Coexistence, 1974, others. Contbr. articles to profl. jours. Served with U.S. Army, 1943-45. Decorated Purple Heart. Mem. Tex. Cath. Hist. Assn. (pres. 1976-77). Roman Catholic. Home: 2603 Pinewood Ter Austin TX 78757-2136 Office: U Tex Dept Govt Austin TX 78712

SCHMITT, NATALIE CROHN, theatre educator; b. Chgo., Aug. 10, 1936; d. Nathan N. and Lera Christina C. BA, U. Chgo., 1958, MA, 1961; PhD, Stanford U., 1968. Asst. prof. U. Ill., Chgo., 1968-72, assoc. prof. theatre, 1972-88, prof. theatre, 1988-99, prof. English, 1992-99, prof. emeritus, 1999—. Dir. theatre Brown U., Providence, 1961-63, U. Ill., 1968-98; founder Looking Glass Theater, Providence, 1962, dir., 1962-65; vis. assoc. prof. Stanford (Calif.) U., 1985. Author: Actors and Onlookers, 1990; contbr. articles to profl. jours. Sr. fellow Humanities Inst., U. Ill., 1983, NEH, 1984, 1996-97, assoc. fellow Stanford U., 1996-97. Mem. Assn. Soc. Theatre Rsch. (exec. com. 1999—, fin. com. 2000—), Assn. Theatre Higher Edn. (conf. planner 1992, chair theatre rsch. project 1973-74, dir. project, regional advisor 1975-78). Avocation: ballet. Office: U Ill Dept Performing Arts 1040 W Harrison M/C 255 Chicago IL 60607 E-mail: nschmitt@uic.edu.

SCHMITT, PETER HARLAN, educator; b. Miami, Fla., Dec. 2, 1958; s. Walter Gordon and Evelyn S. BA cum laude, Amherst Coll., 1980; MFA, U. Iowa, 1983. Asst. editor Am. Welding Soc., Miami, Fla., 1983-85; editor Club Publ., 1985-86; lectr. English U. Miami, Coral Gables, 1986—. Mem. Acad. Am. Poets, Acad. Am. Poets, Assn. Literaty Scholars & Critics. Avocations: tennis, music, collecting rare books. Office: U Miami Box 248145 Coral Gables FL 33124 E-mail: pschmittfl@aol.com.

SCHMITT, RALPH GEORGE, manufacturing company executive; b. Tarrytown, N.Y., Aug. 8, 1944; s. Alfons George and Otillie Lucie (Mehler) S.; m. Kathleen OShaughnessy; children: Ralpha Scott, Carrie Lee, Kurt Ryan. BS, MIT, 1966, MS, 1967, U. Calif., 1970. Engr. McDonnell Douglas, Huntington Beach, Calif., 1967-70, Rockwell Internat., Downey, 1970-72; pres., chmn. bd. TPG Industries, L.A., 1972-74; gen. mgr. Columbia Yacht divsn. Whittaker Corp., Chesapeake, Va., 1975-76; v.p. ops., dir. R&G Sloane Mfg. Co., L.A., 1976-83; dir. mgr.-plastics Sweetheart Products Group Ft. Howard Paper Co., Wilmington, Mass., 1983-86; v.p., gen. mgr. PHI, City of Industry, Calif., 1986-90; v.p. ops. Dowty Aerospace, L.A., 1991-93, Applied Sys. divsn. York (Pa.) Internat., 1993-96, v.p. product engring. and mfg. tech., 1996-99; v.p., gen. mgr. Airside Products, 1999-2000, Chillers, 2000—02. Mem. Soc. Concurrent Product Devel. (adv. bd. dirs. 2002—), MIT Alumni Assn. (nat. selection com. 1991-93, class v.p., ednl. counselor), Tau Beta Pi, Sigma Xi, Sigma Gamma Tau, Sigma Alpha Epsilon. Home: 1730 Wyndham Dr York PA 17403-5913 E-mail: ralph.schmitt@suscom.net.

SCHMITT, ROBERT LEE, computer scientist; b. Astoria, N.Y., Oct. 1, 1948; s. Edward and Margaret Louise (Gleason) S.; m. Elsy Evagelene Burnett, June 1999; stepchildren: Eric Jason Marin, Alexis Michelle Marin. AAS in Data Processing, SUNY, Farmingdale, 1972; student, Hofstra U., 1972-73; BS in Computer Sci., SUNY, Stony Brook, 1974, MS in Computer Sci., 1975; postgrad., U. Md., 1979-80, 94-96; grad. diploma in strategic sci., U.S. Naval War Coll., 1991. Cert. computer programmer, data processor. Computer programmer U.S. Army Environ. Hygiene Agy., Aberdeen Proving Ground, Md., 1976; data systems programmer Dept. Def., Ft. George G. Meade, 1976-78, data systems analyst, 1978-83, computer systems analyst, 1983-85, sr. computer systems analyst, 1985-86, computer scientist, 1986-89, sys. acquisition mgr., 1989-94, dep. dir. for tech. fellow, 1994-95, sr. computer scientist, 1995-96, stds., tng. and verification engr., 1996-97, systems engr., 1997-99, yr. 2000 compliance mgr., 1999, sys. arch. implementation engr., 2000-01, sys. engr., 2001—. With Va. Summer Inst. for Math. Tchrs., 1995-96, dir. 1996-2000. With USNR, 1968-79. Home: 3002 Viburnum Pl Olney MD 20832-3073 Office: 9800 Savage Rd Fort George G Meade MD 20755-6000 E-mail: rls48@msn.com.

SCHMITT, ROLAND WALTER, retired academic administrator; b. Seguin, Tex., July 24, 1923; s. Walter L. and Myrtle F. (Caldwell) S.; m. Claire Freeman Kunz, Sept. 19, 1957; children: Lorenz Allen, Brian Walter, Alice Elizabeth, Henry Caldwell. BA in Math, BS in Physics, U. Tex., 1947, MA in Physics, 1948; PhD, Rice U., 1951; DSc (hon.), Worcester Poly. Inst., 1985, U. Pa., 1985; DCL (hon.), Union Coll., 1985; DL (hon.), Lehigh U., 1986; DSc (hon.), U. S.C., 1988, U. Tech. De Compeigne, 1991; DL (hon.), Coll. St. Rose, 1992, Russell Sage, 1993, Hartford Grad. Ctr., 1995, Ill. Inst. Tech., 1996, Rensselaer Polytechnic Inst., 1997. With GE, 1951-88, R & D mgr. phys. sci. and engring., 1967-74, mgr. energy sci. and engring. R & D, 1974-78, v.p. corp. R & D, 1978-82, sr. v.p. corp. R & D, 1982-86, sr. v.p. sci. and tech., 1986-88, ret., 1988; pres. Rensselaer Poly. Inst., Troy, N.Y., 1988-93; ret., 1993. Bd. dirs. Blasch Precision Ceramics, Reveo Corp., VRex, GlobalSpec.com, Logical Net, Value Innovations; chair adv. bd. NYSTAR; bd. advisors LearnLinc, 1996-2000; tech. adv. bd. Chrysler Corp., 1990-93; tech. adv. coun. Mobil Corp., 1997-99; mem., past pres. Indsl. Rsch. Inst., 1978-88; energy rsch. adv. bd. U.S. Dept. Energy, 1977-83; mem. Nat. Sci. Bd., 1982-94, chmn., 1984-88; chmn. CORETECH, 1988-93; mem. Com. on Japan, NRC, 1988-90, Comml. Devel. Ind. Adv. Group, NASA, 1988-90; exec. com. Coun. on Competitiveness, 1988-93; chmn. NRC Panel on Export Controls, 1989-91; mem. Dept. Commerce Adv. Commn. on Patent Law Reform, 1990-92; adv. bd. Oak Ridge Nat. Lab., 1993-98; chair Rev. NATO Sci. program, 1998; mem. NRC panel rev. state dept. use sci. tech. and health, 1999—; chmn. Motorola's Sci. Adv. Bd., 1995-99; chmn. rsch. priority panel for NRC Future of Space Sci., 1994-95. Trustee N.E. Savs. Bank, 1978-84; bd. advisors Union Coll., Schenectady, 1981-84, Argonne Univs. Assn., 1979-82, RPI, 1982-88; bd. govs. Albany Med. Ctr. Hosp., 1979-82, 88-90; bd. dirs. Sunnyview Hosp. and Rehab. Ctr., 1978-86, Coun. on Superconductivity for Am. Competitiveness, 1987-89; mem. exec. com. N.Y. State Ctr. for Hazardous Waste Mgmt., 1988-89; chmn. Office of Tech. Assessment adv. panel on industry and environment; mem. Nat. Commn. Ill. Inst. Tech., 1993-94; chair NSF Acad. Rsch. Fleet Rev., 1998-99. With USAAF, 1943-46. Recipient RPI Community Svc. award, 1982, award for disting. contbns. Stony Brook Found., 1985, Rice U. Disting. Alumni award, 1985, IRI Medalist award, 1989, Royal Swedish Acad. of Engring. Sci., 1990, Arthur M. Bueche award Nat. Acad. of Engring., 1995, N.Y. State Bus. Coun.'s Corning award, 2001; named Fgn. Assn. of Engring. Acad. of Japan, U. Albany Found. Acad. Laureate, 1997; named to Jr. Achievement Capital Region Bus. Hall of Fame, 1996; inducted RPI Hall of Fame, 1999. Fellow AAAS, IEEE (Centennial medal 1984, Engring. Leadership award 1989, Founders medal 1992, Hoover medal 1993), Am. Phys. Soc. (Pake award 1993), Am. Acad. Arts and Scis.; mem. NAE (coun.), Am. Inst. Physics (chmn. 1993-98), Coun. Sci. Soc. Pres.

(chair 1993-97), N.Y. Acad. Scis. (pres. coun. 1993—), Dirs. Indsl. Rsch., Rensselaer Alumni Assn. (Disting. alumni award 1993), Eta Kappa Nu (eminent mem.) Office: PO Box 240 Rexford NY 12148-0240

SCHMITT, STEPHEN RICHARD, electronics engineer; b. Phila., July 31, 1948; s. Robert Diehl and Janet Olive (Lawson) S.; m. Suzanne Marie Sachs, Oct. 9, 1981. BSc, Brown U., 1971; MSE, U. Pa., 1978. Registered profl. engr., Pa. Engr. Stone & Webster Engring. Corp., Cherry Hill, N.J., 1978-79, The Franklin Inst., Phila., 1980-81, Naval Air Devel. Ctr., Warminster, Pa., 1981-89; electronics engr. Hanscom AFB, 1989—. Served with USN, 1971-76. Mem. IEEE, Masons. Independent. Episcopalian. Home: 962 Depot Rd Boxboro MA 01719-1119 Office: AFSC/ESC/SR Hanscom AFB MA 01731

SCHMITT, WILLIAM ALLEN, lawyer; b. Louisville, Aug. 29, 1909; s. Michael Joseph and Naoma Katherine Schmitt; m. Dorothy S. Turner, June 12, 1936 (dec. Feb. 1998); 1 child, Selene S. Kaelin. Student, U. Louisville, 1933. Bar: Ky. 1936, U.S. Dist. Ct. (we. dist.) Ky. 1936, N.C. 1997. Pvt. practice law, Louisville, 1936—; assoc. atty. Schmitt & Schmitt, 1936-60; judge Jefferson County Probate Ct., 1962-70; alcohol beverage control adminstr. Jefferson County Govt., 1962-70; law ptnr. Schmitt & Sandmann, 1968-74; pvt. practice law, 1974—, Jamestown, N.C., 1997—. Author: Kentucky Probate, 1980, 2nd edit., 1997; contbr. articles to profl. jours. Election poll judge various gen. elections, Louisville; active Muir Chapel United Meth. Ch.; pres. Wildwood Country Club, 1964, Legal Aid Soc., Louisville, 1968. Lt. USN, 1944-46. Inductee Ky. Tennis Hall of Fame, 1993. Mem. ABA, ATLA, Am. Arbitration Assn. (arbitration panelist 1983—, cert. mediator 1995—), Nat. Assn. Securities Dealers (arbitration panelist 1990—, cert. mediator 1994—), Am. Coll. Trust and Estate Counsel (state chmn. 1978-83), Ky. Bar Assn. (life, spkr. at seminars and convs. 1960-80, pres. 1970-71, probate com. 1970-86, chmn. 1977-81, trustee 1971-86, chmn. 1978-86, clients indemnity fund), N.C. State Bar Assn., N.C. State Bar, Fla. Acad. Cert. Mediators, Louisville Bar Assn. (spkr. at seminars 1960-80, pres. 1966, chmn. probate com. 1974-79, various meritorious svc. awards 1966-75). Avocation: tennis. Home: 109 Sagewood Rd Jamestown NC 27282-9489 Office: PO Box 997 Jamestown NC 27282-0997 also: 500 Ky Home Life Bldg 239 S 5th St Louisville KY 40202-3213 E-mail: waschmitt@northstate.net.

SCHMITT, WILLIAM GERARD, magazine editor, journalism educator; b. Flushing, N.Y., Feb. 17, 1957; s. William Thomas and Eileen Schmitt; m. Eileen Rita Schmitt, Sept. 29, 1990; 1 child, Mary. BA, Fordham U., 1978; MPA, Princeton U., 1981; cert. in theol. studies, Georgetown U. Copy editor, reporter Gannett Westchester Newspapers, Yonkers, N.Y., 1978-79; sr. editor Metals Week, N.Y.C., 1981-85; mng. editor, Washington bur. chief Am. Metal Market, Washington, 1986-89, 93-98; assoc. editor Kiplinger Washington Letter, 1989-92; sr. editor Chem. Week Assocs., N.Y.C., 1998—. Adj. prof. L.I. U., Bklyn., 1999—, Fordham U., Bronx, 2001. Contbr. articles to Editor & Publisher, Quill Mag. Mem. Soc. Profl. Journalists, Assn. for Edn. in Journalism and Mass comm., N.Y. Fin. Writers Assn., Nat. Press Club, Secular Franciscan Order, KC. Roman Catholic. Avocations: music, songwriting. Home: 111 Hauxhurst Ave #1 Weehawken NJ 07086 E-mail: billgerards@aol.com.

SCHMITT, WILLIAM HOWARD, cosmetics company executive; b. Sterling, Ill., Oct. 27, 1936; s. Alfred William and Katherine Henrietta (Skow) S.; m. Antionette Marie Payne, Mar. 22, 1960; children: Hilary Ann, Andrea Kay, Joseph Michael. BS in Pharmacy, Drake U., 1958. Rsch. assoc. G.D. Searle, Skokie, Ill., 1963-66; assoc. dir. rsch. Alberto Culver, Melrose Park, 1966-71; dir. product devel. Chesebrough-Pond's USA, Trumbull, Conn., 1971-74; dir. internat. Unilever HPC (formerly Chesebrough-Pond's Inc.), 1974-83, group dir. R&D, 1983-85, v.p. R&D, 1985-89, Uniliver-H.P.C. USA, sr. v.p. R&D, 1989—. Mem. sci. adv. commn. Cosmetics, Toiletry and Fragrance Assn., Washington, 1984—. Author: (with others) An Overview of World-Wide Regulatory Programs, 1984; editor: Cosmetics and Toiletries Industry, 1992, 2nd edit., 1996 (Cosmetic Industry Buyers Soc. award 1996); patentee in toiletry and cosmetics field. Bd. dirs. Sense of Smell Fund, N.Y.C., 1998. Lt. USAF, 1959-62. Mem. Soc. Cosmetic Chemists, Am. Assn. for Dental Rsch. Avocations: boating, hunting, fishing. Office: Unilever HPC 40 Merritt Blvd Trumbull CT 06611-5413 E-mail: willilam.schmitt@unilever.com.

SCHMITTER, CHARLES HARRY, electronics manufacturing company executive, lawyer; b. Paterson, N.J., Feb. 4, 1928; s. Charles and Jennie (Schoe) S.; m. Margaret Ann Roose, Oct. 24, 1964 (dec. Dec. 1989). AB magna cum laude, Rutgers U., 1948; JD, Columbia, 1953. Bar: N.Y. bar 1956, Mich. bar 1960. Asso. atty. firm Cravath, Swaine & Moore, N.Y.C., 1955-59; asst. sec. Ford Motor Co., 1959-64; corp. sec. Sperry Rand Corp. (now Unisys Corp.), N.Y.C., 1964-87, ret., 1987. Served with AUS, 1953-55. Mem. Am. Bar Assn., Am. Soc. Corp. Secretaries, Phi Alpha Delta, Theta Chi. Clubs: Rockefeller Center Luncheon (N.Y.C.). Home: 420 E 51st St New York NY 10022-8014

SCHMITZ, BARBARA, art preservationist; b. Cin., 1936; AM, U. Chgo., 1960; MA, PhD, NYU, 1981. Contbr. series of illustrated catalogs of major collections of Islamic paintings including Islamic Manuscripts, N.Y. Pub. Libr., 1992, Islamic and Indian Manuscripts and Paintings, Pierpont Morgan Libr., 1996; co-author: (with Z.A. Desai) Mughal and Persian Painting and Illustrated Manuscripts in the Raza Library, Rampur (U.P.), 2002; editor, contbr.: After the Great Mughals: Painting in Delhi and the Regional Courts in the 18th-19th Centuries, 2002. Fulbright grantee, 1992-93, 97-98, grantee Indira Gandhi Nat. Ctr. for the Arts, New Delhi, 1995, Am. Inst. Indian Studies, 1998-99. E-mail: barbaraschmitz65016@yahoo.com.

SCHMITZ, CHARLES EDISON, evangelist; b. Mendota, Ill., July 18, 1919; s. Charles Francis Schmitz and Lucetta Margaret (Foulk) Schmitz Kaufmann; m. Eunice Magdalene Ewy, June 1, 1942 (dec. Mar. 26, 2000); children: Charles Elwood, Jon Lee; m. Irene I. Cords Walter, Jan. 1, 2001. Student, Wheaton Coll., 1936-37, 38, 39; BA, Wartburg Coll., Waverly, Iowa, 1940; BD, Wartburg Theol. Sem., Dubuque, Iowa, 1942, MDiv, 1977. Ordained to ministry Am. Luth. Ch., 1942. Founding pastor Ascension Luth. Ch., L.A., 1942-48, Am. Evang. Luth. Ch., Phoenix, 1948-65; dir. intermountain missions, founding pastor 14 Evang. Luth. Parishes, Calif., Ariz., N.Mex., Fla., 1942-89; evangelist Am. Luth. Ch., Mpls., 1965-73; sr. pastor Peace Luth. Ch., Palm Bay, Fla., 1973-89; pastor-at-large Am. Evang. Luth. Ch., Phoenix, 1989—. Charter mem. Navajo Luth. Mission, Rock Point, Ariz., 1960—; chmn. Greater Phoenix Evangelical Ministers Assn., 1998-99; pastoral advisor Ariz. Luth. Outdoor Ministry Assn., Prescott, 1958-65, 89—; Kogudus Internat. Retreat master and chaplain, Fla., Berlin and Marbach, Germany, 1990; mem. transition team Fla. Synod, Evang. Luth. Ch. Am., 1985-89. Author: Evangelism for the Seventies, 1970; co-author: ABC's of Life, 1968; assoc. editor Good News mag., 1965-71. Founder, chmn. Ariz. Ch. Conf. on Adult and Youth Problems, 1956-65; vice chmn. synod worship & ch. music com. Am. Luth. Ch., Mpls., 1960-66; chmn. Space Coast Luth. Retirement Ctr., Palm Bay, Fla., 1985-89; chaplain Ariz. chpt. Luth. Brotherhood, 1991-2000. Named Citizen of Yr., Palm Bay C. of C., 1979. Mem. Nat. Assn. Evangelicals, Greater Phoenix Assn. of Evangelicals (pres.), German Am. Nat. Congress (nat. chaplain 1970), Lions (life mem., officer Phoenix and Palm Bay clubs 1952—, Ariz. Dist. 21A chaplain 1994-95, Melvin Jones fellow 1995), Kiwanis (bd. dirs. L.A. chpt. 1942-48). Republican. Home: 12444 W Toreador Dr Sun City West AZ 85375-1926 *The truly modern person today who, like the scribes of old, would aspire to fulfillment in leadership would do well to remember Jesus' words: "Therefore every scribe who has been trained for the Kingdom of Heaven is like the master of a household who brings out of his treasure what is new and what is old." (Matt. 13:52).*

SCHMITZ, CLARENCE T. investment company executive; Exec. v.p., CFO Jefferies Group Inc., L.A.; mng. dir. Golenberg Schmitz Capital Ptnrs., LLC, 2000—. Office: Golenberg Schmitz Capital Ptnrs LLC Ste 970 11100 Santa Monica Blvd Los Angeles CA 90025-3384

SCHMITZ, DENNIS MATHEW, English language educator; b. Dubuque, Iowa, Aug. 11, 1937; s. Anthony Peter and Roselyn S.; m. Loretta D'Agostino, Aug. 20, 1960; children— Anne, Sara, Martha, Paul, Matthew. BA, Loras Coll., 1959; MA, U. Chgo., 1961. Instr. English Ill. Inst. Tech., Chgo., 1961-62, U. Wis., Milw., 1962-66; asst. prof. Calif. State U., Sacramento, 1966-69, assoc. prof., 1969-74, prof., 1974-99; ret., 1999. Poet-in-residence, 1966-99. Author: We Weep for Our Strangeness, 1969, Double Exposures, 1971, Goodwill, Inc., 1976, String, 1980, Singing, 1985, Eden, 1989, About Night: Selected and New Poems, 1993, The Truth Squad, 2002. Recipient Discovery award Poetry Center, N.Y.C., 1968; winner First Book Competition Follett Pub. Co., 1969; di Castagnola award Poetry Soc. Am., 1986; Shelley Meml. award Poetry Soc. Am., 1987; NEA fellow, 1976-77, 85-86, 92-93, Guggenheim fellow, 1978-79. Mem. PEN, Assoc. Writing Programs. Roman Catholic.

SCHMITZ, DOLORES JEAN, primary education educator; b. River Falls, Wis., Dec. 27, 1931; d. Otto and Helen Olive (Webster) Kreuziger; m. Karl Matthias Schmitz Jr., Aug. 18, 1956; children: Victoria Jane, Karl III. BS, U. Wis., River Falls, 1953; MS, Nat. Coll. Edn., 1982; postgrad., U. Minn., Mankato, 1969, U. Melbourne, Australia, 1989, U. Wis., Milw., 1989, Carroll Coll., 1990, Cardinal Stritch Coll., 1990. Cert. tchr., Wis. Tchr. Manitowoc (Wis.) Pub. Schs., 1953-56, West Allis (Wis.) Pub. Schs., 1956-59, Lowell Sch., Milw., 1960-63, Victory Sch., Milw., 1964, Palmer Sch., Milw., 1966-84, 86-94, unit leader, 1984-86; ret., 1994. Co-organizer Headstart Tchg. Staff Assn., Milw., 1968; insvc. organizer Headstart and Early Childhood, Milw., 1969-92; pilot tchr. for Whole Lang., Hi-Scope and Math. Their Way, 1988-93; bd. dirs. Curriculum Devel. Ctr. of Milw. Edn. Ctr., 1993-94. Author: (curriculum) Writing to Read, 1987, Cooperation and Young Children (ERIC award 1982), Kindergarten Curriculum, 1953. Former supporter Milw. Art Mus., Milw. Pub. Mus., Milw. County Zoo, Whitefish Bay Pub. Libr., Riveredge Nature Ctr.; vol. fgn. visitor program Milw. Internat. Inst., 1966-94, holiday folk fair, 1976-94, Earthwatch, 1989; lobbyist Milw. Pub. Sch. Bd. and State of Wis., 1986-93; coord. comty. vols., 1990-94. Grantee Greater Milw. Ednl. Trust, 1989. Mem. NEA (life), ASCD, Milw. Kindergarten Assn. (rec. sec. 1986-93), Nat. Assn. for Edn. of Young Children, Tchrs. Applying Whole Lang., Wis. Early Childhood Assn., Milw. Tchrs. Ednl. Assn. (co-chmn. com. early childhood 1984-86), Assn. for Childhood Edn. Internat. (charter pres. Manitowoc chpt. 1955-56), Milw. Educating Computer Assn., Alpha Psi Omega. Roman Catholic. Avocations: bicycling, nature, world travel. Home: 1355 Pinellas Bayway S Apt 22 Tierra Verde FL 33715-2140 E-mail: dolintv@aol.com. *Like a very old song said-Accentuate the POSITIVE, eliminate the negative,and don't mess with Mr. In-Between. Life is better for you and everyone around you if these "rules" are followed. Success=If it is to be, it is up to me. I can.*

SCHMITZ, EDWARD HENRY, retired distribution company executive; b. Glenbeulah, Wis., June 21, 1929; s. John Charles and Angeline Ann (Gundrum) S.; m. Janyth Lanier, Dec. 26, 1959; stepchildren: Janyth Lynn, Leslee; children: Robert, Ellen. BS in Bus. Adminstrn., Bryant Coll., 1955. Cert. purchasing mgr. Mgr. purchasing and traffic Hooker Glass Co., Chgo., 1961-65; materials mgr. API Industries, 1965-71; purchasing mgr. G&W Electric Co., Blue Island, Ill., 1971-92; mgr. transp. svcs. Chgo. Tube and Iron Co., 1992-98, ret., 1998. Cons. engr. A. Proudfoot, Chgo., 1957-60; mem. U.S. Procurement Del. to U.S.S.R., 1990. Served with U.S. Army, 1951-53. Apptd. adm. Gt. Navy of Nebr., 1977. Mem. Purchasing Mgmt. Assn. (bd. dirs. Chgo. chpt. 1971-73, 83-85), Nat. Assn. Purchasing Mgmt. (dist. chmn. 1980-90, asst. nat. chmn. 1989-91, nat. chmn. 1991-93), Am. Prodn. and Inventory Control soc., Traffic Men's Assn. of Chgo. (bd. dirs. 1994-98). Avocation: canoeing. Home: 1928 Calla Dr Joliet IL 60435-8522

SCHMITZ, EUGENE GERARD, engineer; b. Brackenridge, Pa., Sept. 17, 1929; s. Wienand Gerard and Florence Marie (Grimm) S.; student Phoenix Coll., 1946-48, Ariz. State U., 1959-63; m. Anna May Lee, May 3, 1952; children: Joyce Marie, Michael Paul, Carol Ann, John David, Eugene Jr. Dist. mgr. Field Enterprise Ednl. Corp., Phoenix, 1955-59; designer, engr. Motorola Inc., Scottsdale, Ariz., 1961-67; project engr. space and re-entry systems div. Philco-Ford Co., Palo Alto, Calif., 1967-70; engring. program adminstr. Memorex Equipment Co., Santa Clara, Calif., 1970-71; plant mgr. Tijuana (Mex.) ops. Philco-Ford, 1971-72; engring. cons. FMC Corp., San Jose, Calif., 1972-75; staff cons. engr. Stetter Assos., Inc., Palo Alto, 1975-80, Schmitz Engring. Assocs., 1980-82, 1986—; sr. project engr. Ordnance div. FMC Corp., 1982-86; instr. electronic design Middlton Inst., Phoenix, 1965-66. Served with U.S. Army, 1948-55. Registered profl. engr., Calif. Mem. Soc. Mfg. Engrs. (cert.). Republican. Home and Office: 302 Shuksan Way PO Box 401 Everson WA 98247-0401 E-mail: eugeneschmitz@hotmail.com., sergent1948@excite.com., sgt51korea@yahoo.com.

SCHMITZ, FRANCIS DAVID, lawyer; b. Milw., July 13, 1950; s. Joseph Francis and Helen Julia (Rudzik) S.; m. Elizabeth Ann Brinker, Dec. 12, 1975; children: Sarah, Catherine. BA, St. Norbert Coll., 1972; MBA, So. Ill. U., 1975; JD, Marquette U., 1983. Bar: Wis. 1983, U.S. Dist. Ct. (ea. and we. dists.) Wis. 1983, U.S. Ct. Appeals (7th cir.) 1985. Law clk. to judge U.S. Ct. Appeals (7th cir.), Chgo., 1983-84; asst. U.S. atty. for ea. dist. Wis. U.S. Dept. Justice, Milw., 1984—, chief criminal divsn., 1993-96, chief econ. crimes, 1996-98, chief civil divsn., 1999—2001. First asst. U.S. Atty., 2002-. Capt. U.S. Army, 1973-80, col. USAR, 1980-2002. Mem. State Bar Wis., Habitat for Humanity. Roman Catholic. Avocations: flyfishing, golf. Office: Office US Atty 517 E Wisconsin Ave Milwaukee WI 53202-4500

SCHMITZ, JOHN ANTHONY, systems analyst; b. Louisville, July 26, 1955; s. Melvin Anthony and Elizabeth Ann (Jonas) S.; m. Reina Aguila, Apr. 30, 1985; children: Elizabeth, Christopher. BA, Marquette U., 1978. Cert. MCSE. Gen. clk. Fed. Res. Bank of Chgo., Milwaukee Branch, Wis., 1978, check processor, 1979, printer ops., 1979; check processor Fed. Res. Bank L.A., 1979-80, clk. files and old records, 1980-82, cash vault custodian, 1982-86, mail supr., 1986-87, computer analyst, 1988-91, supervising system analyst, 1991—. Avocations: martial arts (3rd degree Black Belt), home computer installations and consulting. Home: 1305 N Aileron Upland CA 91784 Office: Federal Res Bank San Fransisco L A Branch 950 S Grand Ave Los Angeles CA 90015-1422

SCHMITZ, JOSEPH E. federal agency administrator; Grad. with distinction, U.S. Naval Acad., 1978; JD, Stanford U., 1986; grad., Naval Inspector Gen. Sch., Army Inspector Gen. Sch. Inspector gen. Dept. Def., Arlington, Va., 2001—; commd. USN; capt. USNR; spl. asst. to Atty. Gen. U.S. Hon. Edwin Meese III; law clk. to Hon. James L. Buckley U.S. State Ct. Appeals D.C. cir.; sr. leadership positions USNR, dep. sr. inspector for Naval Res. Intelligence program. Adj. prof. law Georgetown U. Law Ctr., 1995—; mem. steering com. Washington Lawyers chpt. Federalist Soc. for Law and Pub. Policy Studies. Mem.: Sovereign Mil. Order Malta. Office: Dept Def Inspector Gen 400 Army Navy Dr Arlington VA 22202-4704

SCHMITZ, LARRY W. management consultant, computer professional; b. Plymouth, Wis., Dec. 4, 1942; s. Lawrence A. and Marcella L. Schmitz; m. Nancy L. Schmitz; children: Michelle, Renee, Amy. BBA, U. Wis., Whitewater, 1965. Cert. computer profl.; cert. mgmt. cons. Sys. analyst Trane Co., LaCrosse, Wis., 1965-67; data processing mgr. Tenneco Automotive, Racine, 1967-73; sr. mgr. Price Waterhouse, Milw., 1973-80; exec. officer info. tech. cons. Schenck & Assocs. S.C., Appleton, Wis., 1980—. Divsn. chmn. United Way, Appleton; chmn. Gov.'s task force on small bus., Madison, Wis., 1983. Mem. Assn. Info. Tech. Profls. (pres. 1999), North Shore Golf Club (treas. 1990—). Republican. Roman Catholic. Avocations: golf, fishing, sports cars. Office: Schenck & Assocs SC PO Box 1739 Appleton WI 54912-1739

SCHMITZ, ROBERT ALLEN, publishing executive, investor; b. Chgo., Jan. 19, 1941; s. John and Lee (Zeal) S.; m. Jenny Ann Quest, Aug. 23, 1969 (div.); m. Judith Mair Grey, Oct. 25, 1997; children: Alexander, Nicholas, Lara, Maximilian. BA with distinction, U. Mich., 1963; MBA, MIT, 1965. Asst. to pres. Lima (Peru) Light and Power Co., 1965-67; acquisition analyst W.R. Grace Co., N.Y.C., 1967-69; asst. to chmn. N.W. Industries, 1969-70; prin. McKinsey & Co., Inc., 1970-82; v.p. books Dow Jones & Co., 1982-88; chmn., pres., chief exec. officer Richard D. Irwin, Inc., Homewood, Ill., 1983-89; pres., founder Quest Capital Ltd., 1989—; investment cons. Soros Fund Mgmt., 1990-92; mgn. dir., sr. ptnr. Trust Co. of the West, 1993-97; mng. dir., founder. Quest Turnaround Advisors, 1999—; chmn., founder Headline Media Group, 2001—. Mem. adv. bd. Coll. Commerce De Paul U., Chgo., 1985—; bd. dirs. Adams Rite Sabre, Inc., Glendale, Calif., Superior Fireplace Co., Fullerton, Calif., Houston Foods Co., Chgo., Archibald Candy Co., Chgo., US Media Group, Inc., Crystal City, Mo., Ctrl. Valley Publ., Merced, Hobby Products Co., Inc., Penrose, Colo., Automated Bar Controls, Vacaville, Calif., Spectran Techs., Inc., Sturbridge, Mass. Pres. Cultural Arts Ctr. Found., Homewood, Ill. Mem. Assn. Am. Pubs. (chmn. higher edn. divsn. 1989), Nature Conservancy (trustee N.Y. state chpt.). Office: Quest Capital Ltd 37 Purchase St Rye NY 10580

SCHMITZ, ROGER ANTHONY, chemical engineering educator, academic administrator; b. Carlyle, Ill., Oct. 22, 1934; s. Alfred Bernard and Wilma Afra (Aarns) S.; m. Ruth Mary Kuhl, Aug. 31, 1957; children: Jan, Joy, Joni BS in Chem. Engring., U. Ill., 1959; PhD in Chem. Engring., U. Minn., 1962. Prof. chem. engring. U. Ill., Urbana, 1962-79; Keating-Crawford prof. chem. engring. U. Notre Dame, Ind., 1979—, chmn. dept. chem. engring., 1979-81, dean engring., 1981-87, v.p., assoc. provost, 1987-95. Cons. Amoco Chems., Naperville, Ill., 1966-77; vis. prof. Calif. Inst. Tech., Los Angeles, 1968-69, U. So. Calif., Los Angeles, 1968-69 Contbr. articles to profl. jours. U.S. Army, 1953—55. Fellow, Guggenheim Found., 1968. Mem. Nat. Acad. Engring., Am. Inst. Chem. Engrs. (A.P. Colburn award 1970, R.H. Wilhelm award 1981), Am. Chem. Soc., Am. Soc. for Engring. Edn. (George Westinghouse award 1977) Roman Catholic. Home: 16865 Londonberry Ln South Bend IN 46635-1444 Office: U Notre Dame 301 Cushing Hall Notre Dame IN 46556 E-mail: schmitz.1@nd.edu.

SCHMITZ, SHIRLEY GERTRUDE, marketing and sales executive; b. Brackenridge, Pa., Dec. 19, 1927; d. Wienand Gerard and Florence Marie (Grimm) S. BA, Ariz. State U., 1949. Tchr., guidance counselor Mesa (Ariz.) H.S., 1949-51; area mgr. Field Enterprises Ednl. Corp., Phoenix, 1951-52, dist. mgr., 1952, regional mgr., 1953-55, br. mgr. Montreal, 1955-61, nat. supr. Chgo., 1961-63, asst. sales mgr., 1963-65, nat. sales mgr., 1965-70; v.p., gen. sales mgr. F.E. Compton Co. divsn. Ency. Brit., 1970-71, exec. v.p., dir. sales, 1971-73; pres. CHB Port-A-Book Store, Inc., 1973-76; gen. mgr. Bobbs-Merrill Co., Inc., Indpls., 1976-82; v.p. sales U. S. Telephone Comms. of Midwest, Inc., 1982-83; exec. v.p. sales and market devel. Entertainment Publs. Corp., Birmingham, Mich., 1983-89, sr. v.p. mktg. and sales Troy, 1989-92. Prin. S.G. Schmitz and Assocs., Chgo., 1992—; bd. advisors, founder Ctr. Advancement of Small Bus., Ariz. State U. Sch. Bus.; mem. pres.'s cabinet capital fund raising campaign Ariz. State U.; bd. dirs. Enterprise Network, Inc. Recipient Elizabeth Cutter Morrow award Internat. Bd. YWCA, 1978, Disting. Achievement award Ariz. State U., 1995, Angel award Ariz. chpt. Nat. Assn. Women Bus. Owners, 1996, Nat. Bus. Achievement award Beta Gamma Sigma, 1998, Impact for Enterprising Women award, 2001. Home: 93 Miller Rd Hawthorn Woods IL 60047-1395 Office: SG Schmitz and Assocs Scottsdale AZ 85259-3651 E-mail: reysgs@aol.com.

SCHMITZ, WIDO FRIEDRICH, sales consulting executive; b. Bonn, Germany, Dec. 15, 1927; s. Maximilian and Paula (Klein) S.; Engr., Tech. U., 1951; LL.D. (hon.), Tech. Inst. Applied Research, London, 1971; m. Ellinor Nebelung, Jan. 21, 1966; 1 dau., Angelica. Sales mgr. F.P. Hamberger GmbH, 1945-50; self-employed cons. in Munich, 1950-65, Washington, 1965-70; pres., chmn., partner Washington Mgmt. & Devel. Corp., McLean, Va.; mgmt. cons. numerous internat., multinat. corps.; dir. cos. in Germany, Italy, France, Switzerland and U.S.; with Internat. Cons. Enterprises Inc., mktg. cons. for airlines, McLean. Club: International (Washington). Lodge: Rotary (hon.). Inventor blind landing systems, solar powered traffic signs, waterproof wall plaster. Office: Internat Intelligence Agy Corp One Tampa City Ctr Ste 2530 Tampa FL 33602-5163

SCHMOLKA, LEO LOUIS, law educator; b. Paris, Apr. 25, 1939; came to U.S., 1944; s. Francis and Irene S.; m. Lucille J. Schoenbaum, July 29, 1965; children— Andrew, Gregory. AB, Dartmouth Coll., 1960; LL.B., Harvard U., 1963; LL.M., NYU, 1971. Bar: N.Y. 1964. Assoc. Weil, Gotshal and Manges, N.Y.C., 1964-71, ptnr., 1971-81, of counsel, 1981—; adj. asst. prof. law NYU Sch. of Law, 1971-75; adj. assoc. prof. law NYU Law Sch., 1975-76, adj. prof., 1977-80, assoc. prof., 1981-84, prof., 1985—, mem. faculty, dir. IRS/NYU continuing profl. edn. program, 1987—. Cons. U.S. Treasury Dept. Office Tax Policy, Washington, 1994-95, Am. Law Inst., 1979-86, U. Miami (Fla.) Estate Planning Inst., 1976-80; vis. adj. prof. law U. Miami Sch. Law, 1977, 80, U. San Diego Sch. Law, 1999; vis. lectr. continuing legal edn. various univs. and tax insts., 1973—. Contbr. articles to legal jours. Fellow Am. Coll. Trust and Estate Counsel; mem. ABA, N.Y. State Bar Assn. (chmn. com. on income taxation estates and trusts 1973-75, estate and gift tax 1976-77, mem. exec. com. tax sect. 1978), Internat. Acad. Estate and Trust Law (academician). Office: NYU Sch Law 40 Washington Sq S Rm 430 New York NY 10012-1099 E-mail: schmolka@optonline.net.

SCHMOLL, HANS JOACHIM, internal medicine, hematology, oncology educator; b. Hannover, Germany, June 21, 1946; s. Johannes and Edeltraut (Schneider) S. MD, Med. U. Hannover, 1970, PhD, 1982. Rsch. assoc. Med. U., Hannover, 1971-84, prof. medicine and hematology-oncology, 1984-95; prof. medicine and hematology, chair hematology/oncology Martin Luther U., Halle-Wittenberg, Germany, 1996—. Author, editor: Kompendium Intern Onkologie, 1986, 3d edit., 1999 (German award 2001). Recipient German Cancer award, 2001, Sci. award, German Assn. Med. Oncologists, 1998. Home: Ludwig Barnay Strasse 9 D-30175 Hannover Germany Office: Martin Luther Univ Dept Hematol/Oncol Int Med IV D-06120 Halle Germany

SCHMOLL, HARRY F., JR. lawyer, educator; b. Somers Point, N.J., Jan. 20, 1939; s. Harry F. Sr. and Margaret E. S.; m. Rita L. Miescier, Aug. 29, 1977. BS, Rider Coll., 1960; JD, Temple U., 1967. Bar: Pa., D.C. 1969, N.J. 1975. With claims dept. Social Security Adminstrn., Phila., 1960-67; staff atty. Pa. State U., State College, 1968-69, instr. criminal justice University Park, 1969-74; regional dir. Pa. Crime Commn., State College, 1969-70; campaign aide U.S. Senator Hugh Scott, Harrisburg, Pa., 1970; pvt. practice law State College, 1970-74, Manahawkin, NJ, 1975-96; prof. criminal justice, bus. law Burlington County Coll., Pemberton, 1974—2002; pres. elect edn. assn., 1992-93, 96-97; pres. edn. assn., 1993-94, 97-98. Judge mcpl. ct., Stafford Twp., 1982-85. Author: New Jersey Criminal Law Workbook, 1976, 2nd edit., 1979, Absecon Diary of Margie Roth, 1933-37, 2000. Former gen.counsel German Heritage Coun. N.J., Inc.; mem. Barnegat Twp. Rent Control Bd., 1991, Barnegat Twp. Zoning Bd., 1994; mem. fund distbn. com. United Way of Burlington County, N.J., 1987—; trustee H.B. Smith Indsl. Village Conservacny, 1988—; mem. Stafford Twp. Com., 1979-81; dep. mayor, 1979. Mem. Pa. Bar assn., N.J. Bar Assn., German-Am. Club So. Ocean County (past pres.), Tri-State Jazz Soc. (bd. dirs.). E-mail: HarrySchmoll2@comcast.net.

SCHMUDDE, LEE GENE, corporate lawyer; b. Harvey, Ill., Apr. 13, 1950; s. Kenneth H. and Jean E. (Alexander) S.; m. Mariann Verscharen, June 25, 1976; 1 child, Leighanne K. BA summa cum laude, Cornell Coll., Mount Vernon, Iowa, 1972; JD, Duke U., 1975. Bar: Fla. 1975, U.S. Dist. Ct. (ctrl. dist.) Fla. 1975. Law clk. to Chief Judge Joseph P. McNulty 2d Dist. Ct. Appeals, Lakeland, Fla., 1975-76; atty. Peterson, Myers, Lake Wales, 1976-78; v.p. legal and environ. affairs Walt Disney World Co., Orlando. Lectr. ABA, Fla. Bar, Orange County Bar Assn., Def. Lawyers Assn. Contbr. articles to Fla. Bar Jour. Bd. dirs., treas. Fla. Symphony Orch., Orlando, 1997; bd. dirs. Children's Home Soc., 1981-85; mem. adv. bd. Jr. Achievement, 1995—; chmn. Fla. Self-Ins. Guaranty ASsn., 1985, 93, bd. dirs., 1985—. Mem. Fla. Bar Assn. (lectr.), Am. Zoo and Aquarium Assn., U.S. C. of C. (Outstanding Young Man of Am. 1975), Fla. C. of C. (jud. and tort reform adv. bd. 2000—), Fla. Assn. Self-Insurers (bd. dirs. 1984-85), Ctrl. Fla. Hist. Soc. (bd. dirs. 2000—), Phi Beta Kappa. Avocations: tennis, basketball, sport fishing. Office: Walt Disney World Co PO Box 10 000 Lake Buena Vista FL 32830-1000

SCHMULTS, EDWARD CHARLES, lawyer, corporate and philanthropic administrator; b. Paterson, N.J., Feb. 6, 1931; s. Edward M. and Mildred (Moore) S.; m. Diane E. Beers, Apr. 23, 1960; children: Alison C., Edward M., Robert C. BS, Yale U., 1953; JD, Harvard U., 1958. Bar: N.Y. 1959, D.C. 1974. Assoc. White & Case, N.Y.C., 1958-65, ptnr., 1965-73, 77-81; gen. counsel Treasury Dept., Washington, 1973-74, undersec., 1974-75; dep. counsel to Pres. U.S., 1975-76; dep. atty. gen. of U.S. Dept. Justice, Washington, 1981-84; sr. v.p. external rels., gen. counsel GTE Corp., Stamford, Conn., 1984-94. Lectr. securities laws. Bd. dirs. GreenPoint Fin. Corp., Germany Fund, Ctrl. European Equity Fund, Deutsche Asset Mgmt. VIT Funds; chmn. bd. trustees Edna McConnell Clark Found. Served to 1st lt. USMC, 1953-55; capt. USMCR. Mem. Am. Bar Assn., Assn. Bar City N.Y., Adminstrv. Conf. U.S. (council 1977-84), Sakonnet Golf Club, Met. Club.

SCHMUTZ, CHARLES REID, university foundation executive; b. Youngstown, Ohio, Jan. 26, 1942; s. Charles Edward and Alice Mae (Bliss) S.; m. Judith Rhodes Seiple, June 19, 1965; children: Charles Reid Jr., Andrew Edward, Jill Caroline. AB in Econs., Brown U., 1964. Lab. technician The Standard Slag Co., Youngstown, 1964-65, direct salesman Cleve., 1965-69, mktg. and prodn. scheduler Youngstown, 1969-73, mktg. and indsl. engr., 1973-85, gen. mgr., v.p. ops., 1985-89; pres. Youngstown State U. Found., 1989—. Bd. dirs. StanCorp., Youngstown. Bd. dirs. Youngstown Playhouse, Jr. Achievement Mahoning Valley. Named to Hall of Fame, Ohio Aggregates Assn., 1990. Mem. Rotary. Methodist. Avocations: golf, tennis.

SCHMUTZHART, BERTHOLD JOSEF, sculptor, educator, art and education consultant; b. Salzburg, Austria, Aug. 17, 1928; came to U.S., 1958, naturalized, 1963; s. Berthold Josef and Anna (Valaschek) S. Student, Acad. for Applied Art, Vienna, Austria, 1956. Cert. fed. tchr., Austria. Prof. Wekschulheim Felbertal, Salzburg, 1951-58; sculptor Washington, 1959-60; tchr. Longfellow Sch., Bethesda, Md., 1960-63; prof., chmn. dept. sculpture Corcoran Sch. Art, Washington, 1963-94, prof. emeritus, 1994—; lectr. Smithsonian Instn., 1968-84. One-man shows include Fredericksburg Gallery Fine Art, Va., 1967-73, Franz Bader Gallery, Washington, 1978, 81, 83, 86, 88; group shows include Nat. Collection Fine Arts, Washington, 1961-70, High Mus. Art, Atlanta, 1965, Ark. Art Ctr., Little Rock, 1966, Birmingham Mus. Art, Ala., 1967, Hirschhorn Mus. and Sculpture Garden, Washington, 1981, Nat. Gallery Modern Art, New Delhi, 1990; represented in permanent collections Hirschhorn Collection; designer fountain, Gallery of Modern Art, Fredericksburg, 1967; author: The Handmade Furniture Book, 1981; contbr. articles to profl. jours. Fine arts panelist D.C. Commn. for Arts, 1973-79; chmn. bd. Market Five Gallery, Washington, 1978-82; bd. dirs. Franz Bader Gallery, Washington, 1981-86; trustee Arts for the Aging, Inc., Washington, 1990—; chmn. Franz and Virginia Bader Fund, 1991—. Recipient 1st prize Washington Religious Arts Council, 1960, for sculpture, Little Rock, 1966, Louisville, 1968, Silver medal Audubon Soc., Washington, 1971 Mem. Guild for Religious Architects, Artists Equity Assn. (pres. D.C. chpt. 1973-75), AAUP, Am. Austrian Soc. (pres. 1968-70, exec. com.), Soaring Soc. Am. Home: 32 Layline Ln Fredericksburg VA 22406-4061 E-mail: bschmutzha@aol.com.

SCHNABEL, ECKHARD JOHANNES, theologian, educator; b. Stuttgart, Germany, May 9, 1955; s. Paul and Elsbeth (Blattner) S.; m. Barbara Cornelia Duerrschmidt, Sept. 11, 1981; children: Mirjam, Benjamin. ThM, FETA, Basel, Switzerland, 1979; PhD, U. Aberdeen, Scotland, 1983. Asst. prof. N.T. Asia Theol. Sem., Manila, The Philippines, 1985-88; lectr. Wiedenest Bible Coll., Bergneustadt, Germany, 1989-94; head N.T. dept. German Theol. Sem., Giessen, Germany, 1994-98; assoc. prof. N.T. Trinity Internat. U., Deerfield, Ill., 1998—. Exec. com. Arbeitskreis für evangelikale Theologie, Germany, 1991-98. Author: Law and Wisdom From Ben Sira to Paul, 1985, Inspiration und Offenbarung, 1986, Das Reich Gottes als Wirklichkeit und Hoffnung, 1993, Sind Evangelikale Fundamentalisten?, 1995, Die Gemeinde des neuen Bundes, 1996, Jesus and the Beginnings of the Mission to the Gentiles, 1994, Studium des Neuen Testaments, 2 vols., 1999-2000, Urchristliche Mission, 2002; contbr. articles to profl. jours. Mem. Soc. N.T. Studies, Tyndale Fellowship, Soc. of Bibl. Lit., Evangelical Theol. Soc., Inst. for Bibl. Rsch. Office: Trinity Internat U Half Day Rd Deerfield IL 60015 E-mail: eschnabel@trin.edu.

SCHNABEL, ROBERT VICTOR, retired academic administrator; b. Scarsdale, N.Y., Sept. 28, 1922; s. Frederick Victor and Louise Elizabeth (Frick) S.; m. Ellen Edyth Foelber, June 7, 1946; children: Mark F., Philip P. Student, Concordia Sem., St. Louis, 1943-45; AB, Bowdoin Coll., 1944; MS, Fordham U., 1951, PhD, 1955; LLD (hon.), Concordia Coll., 1988. Tchr. St. Paul's Sch., Ft. Wayne, Ind., 1945-49; prin. St. Matthew's Sch., N.Y.C., 1949-52; assoc. supt. edn. Central Dist., Luth. Ch.-Mo. Synod, 1952-56; asst. prof. philosophy Concordia Sr. Coll., Ft. Wayne, 1956-60, assoc. prof., 1960-65, prof., acad. dean, 1966-71; pres. Concordia Coll., Bronxville, N.Y., 1971-76; acad. v.p., dean Wartburg Coll., Waverly, Iowa, 1976-78; pres. Valparaiso (Ind.) U., 1978-88. Cons. Luth. Edn. Conf. N.Am., 1977-88. Contbr. articles to profl. jours. Mem. AAUP, Luth. Acad. Scholarship, Assoc. Colls. Ind., Nat. Assn. Ind. Colls. and Univs., Rotary, Phi Delta Kappa. Office: Valparaiso Univ 23 Huegli Hall Valparaiso IN 46383

SCHNACK, HAROLD CLIFFORD, lawyer, retired; b. Honolulu, Sept. 27, 1918; s. Ferdinand J. H. and Mary (Pearson) S.; m. Gayle Hemingway Jepson, Mar. 22, 1947 (dec. Feb. 1998); children: Jerrald Jay, Georgina Schnack Hankinson, Roberta Schnack Poulin, Michael Clifford. BA, Stanford U., 1940, LLB, 1947. Bar: Hawaii 1947. Dep. prosecutor City and County Honolulu, 1947-48; gen. practice with father F. Schnack, 1948-60; pvt. practice Honolulu, 1960-86. Pres. Harcliff Corp., 1961—, Schnack Indsl. Corp., 1969-73, Instant Printers, Inc., 1971-81, Koa Corp., 1964—, Nutmeg Corp., 1963-89, Global Answer System, Inc., 1972-78; pres., treas. Golden Rainbow, Inc. (Pasta Chef), Reno, 2001—. Pres. Goodwill Industries of Honolulu, 1971-72. Mem. Outrigger Canoe Club, Phi Alpha Delta, Alpha Sigma Phi. Office: 817 A Cedar St PO Box 3077 Honolulu HI 96802-3077

SCHNAITMAN, WILLIAM KENNETH, finance company executive; b. Talbot County, Md., May 12, 1926; s. William and Catherine Almeda (Cheezum) S.; m. Beverly June Marshall, July 13, 1963. Student, Strayer Bus. Sch., Balt., 1943. Clk. Comml. Credit Co., Balt., 1946-70, asst. sec., 1970-72, treas., 1972-75, dir. cash mgmt., 1976-87, ret., 1987. With AUS, 1944-46, ETO. Home: 12520 Wye Landing Ln Wye Mills MD 21679-2050

SCHNAKENBERG, DONALD G. financial administrator; b. Queens, N.Y., Dec. 6, 1939; s. Herman G. and Rose (Conte) S. BS in Acctg., Bklyn. Coll., 1960; MBA in Mgmt. with honors, Pace U., 1969. Acct. Rosen, Futterman & Berylson CPA's, N.Y.C., 1960-62; sr. acct. Fluhr, Massen & Light CPA's, 1963; tax examiner N.Y. State Tax Commn., 1963-65; acct. N.Y.C. Housing and Redevel. Bd., 1965-67; sr. acct. N.Y.C. Bd. Edn., 1967-68, N.Y.C. Housing and Redevel., N.Y.C., 1968; prin. budget examiner Bur. of Budget Office of Mayor, 1968-76; fin. dir. N.Y.C. Coun., 1976-89; chief fin. officer Lower Eastside Svc. Ctr., N.Y.C., 1989-90, Promesa Inc., Bronx, 1990-91, cons., 1991-93; CFO Am. Chess Found., N.Y.C., 1993-94; cons., 1994—. Mem. Am. Mgmt. Assn., Govt. Fin. Officers Assn., JFK Dem. Club, Manhattan Chess Club. Democrat. Roman Catholic. Avocations: opera, classical music, chess, reading, football. Home: 12335 82nd Rd Apt 7K Kew Gardens NY 11415-1624 E-mail: dschnak@excite.com.

SCHNAKENBERG, LORI ANN, secondary school educator; b. Carbondale, Pa., Jan. 2, 1976; BS in English Edn., Pensacola Christian Coll., 1998, MS in English Edn., 2001. Tchr. English, bus. Twin Tiers Bapt. High Sch., Breeseport, NY, 1998—99; tchr. English, computer sci. Twin City Christian Sch., Lunenburg, Mass., 2001—. Mem.: English First, Internat. Reading Assn., Nat. Coun. Tchrs. of English. Office: Twin City Christian Sch 194 Electric Ave Lunenburg MA 01426

SCHNALL, EDITH LEA (MRS. HERBERT SCHNALL), microbiologist, educator; b. N.Y.C., Apr. 11, 1922; d. Irving and Sadie (Raab) Spitzer; m. Herbert Schnall, Aug. 21, 1949; children: Neil David, Carolyn Beth. AB, Hunter Coll., 1942; AM, Columbia U., 1947, PhD, 1967. Clin. pathologist Roosevelt Hosp., N.Y.C., 1942-44; instr. Adelphi Coll., Garden City, N.Y., 1944-46; asst. med. mycologist Columbia Coll. Physicians and Surgeons, N.Y.C., 1946-47, 49-50; instr. Bklyn. Coll., 1947; mem. faculty Sarah Lawrence Coll., Bronxville, N.Y., 1947-48; lectr. Hunter Coll., N.Y.C., 1947-67; adj. assoc. prof. Lehman Coll., City U. N.Y., 1968; hon. curator N.Y. Botanical Garden, 1968; asst. prof. Queensborough Community Coll., City U. N.Y., 1967, assoc. prof. microbiology, 1968-75, prof., 1975—; adminstr. Med. Lab. Tech. Program, 1985—. Vis. prof. Coll. Physicians and Surgeons, Columbia U., N.Y.C., 1974; advanced biology examiner U. London, 1970—. Editor: Newsletter of Med. Mycology Soc. N.Y., 1969-85; founder, editor Female Perspective newsletter of Queensborough Community Coll. Women's Club, 1971-73. Mem. Alley Restoration Com., N.Y.C., 1971—; mem. legis. adv. com. Assembly of the State of N.Y., 1972; mem. Cmty. Bd. 11, Queens, N.Y., 1974-98, 3d vice-chmn., 1987-92, 2d vice chmn., 1992-97; public dir. of bd. dirs. Inst. Continuing Dental Edn. Queens County, Dental Soc. N.Y. State and ADA, 1973-97. Rsch. fellow NIH, 1948-49; faculty rsch. fellow, grantee-in-aid Rsch. Found. of SUNY, 1968-70; faculty rsch. grant Rsch. Found. City U. N.Y., 1971-74. Mem. AAAS, Internat. Soc. Human Animal Mycology, Am. Soc. Microbiology (coun., N.Y.C. br. 1981—, co-chairperson ann. meeting com. 1981-82, chair program com. 1982-83, v.p. 1984-86, pres. 1986-88), Med. Mycology Soc. N.Y. (sec.-treas. 1967-68, v.p. 1968-69, 78-79, archivist 1974—, fin. advisor 1983-97, pres. 1969-70, 79-80, 81-82), Bot. Soc. Am., Med. Mycology Soc. Americas, Mycology Soc. Am., N.Y. Acad. Scis., Torrey Bot. Club (N.Y. State), Queensborough Community Coll. Women's Club (pres. 1971-73, N.Y.C.), Sigma Xi, Phi Sigma. Home: 21406 29th Ave Flushing NY 11360-2622

SCHNAPF, ABRAHAM, aerospace engineer, consultant; b. N.Y.C., Aug. 1, 1921; s. Meyer and Gussie (Schaeffler) S.; m. Edna Wilensky, Oct. 24, 1943; children: Donald J., Bruce M. BSME, CCNY, 1948; MSME, Drexel Inst. Tech., 1953. Registered profl. engr., N.J. Devel. engr. on lighter-than-air aircraft Goodyear Aircraft Corp., Akron, Ohio, 1948-50; mgr. fire control system def. electronics RCA, Camden, N.Y., 1950-55, mgr. airbourne navigation system, aerospace weapon system, 1955-58; program mgr. TIROS/TOS weather satellite systems RCA Astro-Electronics, Princeton, N.J., 1958-70, mgr. satellite programs, 1970-79, prin. scientist, 1979-82; cons. Aerospace Systems Engring., Willingboro, 1982—. Lectr., presenter on meteor. satellites, space tech., communication satellites. Sgt. USAF, 1943-46. Recipient award Nat. Press Club Washington, 1975, award Am. Soc. Quality Control-NASA, 1968, Pub. Svc. award NASA, 1969, cert. of appreciation U.S. Dept. Commerce, 1984, RCA David Sarnoff award; inducted into Space Tech. Hall of Fame, 1992; named to 5000 Personalities of the World, named Internat. Man. of Yr. 1992-93. Fellow AIAA; mem. Am. Astro. Soc., Am. Meterol. Soc., Space Pioneers, N.Y. Acad. Scis. (mem. think tank week sessions 1980's), N.J. Arbitration Soc. Address: PO Box 160 Willingboro NJ 08046

SCHNAPP, ROGER HERBERT, lawyer, consultant; b. N.Y.C., Mar. 17, 1946; s. Michael Jay and Beatrice Joan (Becker) S.; m. Candice Jacqueline Larson, Sept. 15, 1979; 1 child, Monica Alexis. BS, Cornell U., 1966; JD, Harvard U., 1969; postgrad. Pub. Utility Mgmt. Program, U. Mich., 1978. Bar: N.Y. 1970, U.S. Ct. Appeals (2d cir.) 1970, U.S. Supreme, 1974, U.S. Dist. Ct. (so. dist.) N.Y. 1975, U.S. Ct. Appeals (4th and 6th cirs.) 1976, U.S. Ct. Appeals (7th cir.) 1977, U.S. Dist. Ct. (so. dist.) N.Y. 1975, U.S. Dist. Ct. (no. dist.) Calif. 1980, U.S. Ct. Appeals (8th cir.) 1980, Calif., 1982, U.S. Dist. Ct. (cen. dist.) Calif. 1982, U.S. Ct. Dist. (ea. dist.) Calif., 1984. Atty. CAB, Washington, 1969-70; labor atty. Western Electric Co., N.Y.C., 1970-71; mgr. employee rels. Am. Airlines, 1971-74; labor counsel Am. Electric Power Svc. Corp., 1974-78, sr. labor counsel, 1978-80; indsl. rels. counsel Trans World Airlines, 1980-81; sr. assoc. Parker, Milliken, Clark & O'Hara, L.A., 1981-82; ptnr. Rutan & Tucker, Costa Mesa, Calif., 1983-84, Memel, Jacobs, Pierno, Gersh & Ellsworth, Newport Beach, 1985-86, Memel, Jacobs & Ellsworth, Newport Beach, 1986-87; pvt. practice, 1987—. Bd. dirs. Dynamic Constrn., Inc., Laguna Hills, Calif., 1986—; commentator labor rels. Fin. News Network; commentator Sta. KOCN Radio, 1990-91; commentator employment law Orange County Register; lectr. Calif. Western Law Sch., Calif. State U.-Fullerton, Calif. State Conf. Small Bus.; lectr. collective bargaining Pace U., N.Y.C.; lectr. on labor law Coun. on Edn. in Mgmt.; N.E. regional coord. Pressler for Pres., 1979-80. Author: Arbitration Issues for the 1980s, 1981, A Look at Three Companies, 1982; editor-in-chief Indsl. and Labor Rels. Forum, 1964-66; columnist Orange County Bus. Jour., 1989-91; contbr. articles to profl. publs. Mem. Bus. Rsch. Adv. Coun. U.S. Dept. Labor; trustee Chapman U., 1991-95. Mem. Calif. Bar Assn. (chmn.), Labor Law Consulting Group, Calif. Bd. of Legal Specialization, Balboa Bay Club, The Ctr. Club (chmn. membership com.), Club 33. Republican. Jewish. Office: PO Box 9049 Newport Beach CA 92658-1049 E-mail: rhs@schnapp.com.

SCHNARE, ROBERT EDEY, JR. library director; b. Morristown, N.J., Dec. 31, 1944; s. Robert Edey and Olive Margaret (Flatt) S.; m. MaryKay Wise, Aug. 29, 1970; 1 child, Katharine Grace. BA, William Paterson Coll., 1967; MLS, U. Pitts., 1968; MA, U. Conn., 1971. Reference libr. history dept. Conn. State Libr., Hartford, 1968-73; head spl. collections U.S. Mil. Acad. Libr., West Point, N.Y., 1973-86; libr. dir. U.S. Naval War Coll., Newport, R.I., 1986—. Chmn. Consortium of R.I. Acad. and Rsch. Librs., Providence, 1991-93; bd. dirs. New Eng. Libr. Network, 1998—; chmn. edn. and tng. com. R.I. Preservation Planning Grant, 1991-92; del. White House Conf. on Libr. and Info. Svcs., 1990-91; chmn. preservation working group New England Libr. Network, 1992-2000; mem. adv. com. N.E. Documents Conservation Ctr., 1994-2001; mem. com. on mgmt. Anne S.K. Brown Mil. Collection, 1987—; mem. Mid-Atlantic Archivist Conf., 1973—; mem. preservation working group Fed. Libr. Info. Ctr. Com., 1991—, co-chair, 1999—. Co-author: Bibliography of Preservation Literature 1983-1996, 2001; book awarded Soc. of Amer. Archivists Best Preservation Publication, 2002; publ. editor Conservation Adminstrn. News, 1979-87, mem. editl. bd., 1987-94; contbr. articles to profl. jours., chpt. to book; compiler Union List of Mil. Edn. Coordinating Com. Library Resources, 1994. Chmn. gifted adv. coun. Providence Bd. Edn., 1990-92; chmn. stewardship St. Martin's Episcopal Ch., Providence, 1990; vol. Providence schs., 1992—. Named Disting. Grad., William Paterson Coll., 1985; recipient Disting. Svc. award Conservation Adminstrn. News, 1987, 94, Dept. of the Army's Comdr.'s award for civilian svc. U.S. Mil. Acad., 1987, Navy Dept.'s Meritorious Civilian Svc. award Naval War Coll., 1995. Mem. ALA (chmn. William Young Boyd Mil. Novel award jury 1997-98, 2001, 2002), Spl. Librs. Assn., Assn. for Study Conn. History, New Eng. Archivists, R.I. Hist. Soc. (mem. libr. com. 1999—). Office: US Naval War Coll Libr 686 Cushing Rd Newport RI 02841-1207

SCHNATTERLY, MICHAEL DEAN, priest; b. Hays, Kans., Oct. 9, 1955; s. Harry Lee Schnatterly and Toya Ann Abbatiello; m. Clare Lorelle Inman, July 21, 1984; children: Ansel Jack, Eric Elias. BA in Theatre, Furman U., 1979; MDiv, Seabury-Western Theol. Sem., 1989. Ordained to ministry Episcopal Ch. as deacon, 1989, as priest 1989. Curate Christ Ch., St. Michaels, Md., 1989-92; rector Emmanuel Episcopal Ch., Opelika, Ala., 1992-96, St. Edwards Episcopal Ch., Mount Dora, Fla., 1996—2001, St. Francis Episc. Ch., Greensboro, NC, 2001—. Examining chaplain, commn. on ministry Diocese of Easton, Md., 1990-92, chmn. youth com., 1991-92; del. Nat. Episcopal Youth Event, Missoula, Mont., 1990; del. Province III youth network Episcopal Ch., 1989-92. Mem. Bay 100 Youth Task Force, St. Michaels, 1989-92, Talbot County AIDS Task Force, Easton, 1990-92; organizer St. Michaels Forum on Drugs in the Community, 1990; active Nat. Episcopal AIDS Coalition; bd. dirs. Child Advocacy Ctr. of East Ala., 1994-96, Lee County AIDS Outreach, 1994-96; cubmaster Mount Dora Cubscout Pack 19, 1999—; chmn. Habitat for Humanity Task Force, Diocese of Ctrl. Fla., 1999—. Recipient Cotton Meml. award Seabury-Western Theol Sem., 1989; Muriel Mount Joy Miller-Hart Trust grantee, 1986. Mem. Mensa, Order St. Helena (assoc.), Liturgical Conf., Rotary (v.p. St. Michaels Club 1990-91, pres. elect 1991-92, bd. dirs. Opelika club 1995-96). Office: St Edwards Episcopal Ch 3506 Lawndale Dr Greensboro NC 27408 Home: PO Box 39383 Greensboro NC 27438-9383 E-mail: stedwrd@aol.com. *Religious folk are often viewed as hypocrites who point accusing fingers at others, saying, "Thou shall not..." Jesus Christ challenges us to a new ethical life which calls others to His positive and forgiving model with the words, "Blessed are those who...".*

SCHNAUS, PETER, musical history educator; b. Berlin, Apr. 17, 1936; s. Kurt and Ilse (Grünbaum) S.; m. Ursula Grünbaum, Dec. 22, 1967; children: Christian, Andrea, Susanne. Assessor, Studienseminar Hannover, Germany, 1968; PhD, U. Freiburg, Germany, 1976. Tchr. Hannover H.S., 1966-70; asst., tchr. Musikhochschule, Hannover, 1970-82, prof. music history, 1982—. Mem. Senat Musikhochschule, Hannover, 1979-99, spkr. dept. instrumental edn., 1979-2001, v.p., 1986-90. Author: E.T.A. Hoffmann als Beethoven—Rezensent der Allgemeinen Musikalischen Zeitung, 1977; editor, author: Europäische Musik in Schlaglichtern, 1990; contbg. author: Kunst und Kultur, Vols. 3, 4 and 5, 1998-99; contbr. articles to profl. jours. Home: 4 Mendelssohnstrasse D-30173 Hannover Germany

SCHNEBELEN, PIERRE, resort planner and developer, consultant; b. Mulhouse, Alsace, France, June 10, 1935; s. Emile and Renee (Gingelwein) S.; children: Stephanie, Mathieu; m. Francois E. Roetynck, June 1, 1985; children: Yvan, Sophie, Wendy, Thomas. Diploma in engring., Ecole Nat. d'Arts et Metiers, Paris, 1958; MS, MIT, 1960. With Mobil Oil Internat., N.Y.C., 1961; founder, chief exec. officer SEFCO, 1965-73, Soc. des Telepheriques de la Grande Motte, 1967-87, SEGMO, 1974-88; founder, pres. SEPARFI, SEGMO IMMOBILIER; founder, dir. Soc. de reprentacoes et de participacoes, Sao Paulo, Brazil, 1977—; pres., chief exec. officer Piersen SA, 1989—; founder, pres. P.S.I. Resorts, Paris, 1988—. Founder, pres. Soc. des telepheriques de Valfrejus, 1983-88, societa delle Funivie del Frejus, 1983-88; founder, dir. SEGMO Vacances; CEO West Rock Assocs. LLC, Boise, Idaho, 1998—; pres., CEO Athlon Fin. Corp., L.A., 1995—. Avocations: skiing, tennis, squash. Home: 820 El Oro Ln Pacific Palisades CA 90272-2813 Office: Athlon Resorts 1801 Ave Of Stars Los Angeles CA 90067-5902

SCHNEBLE, ALFRED WILLIAM, III, lawyer; b. Dayton, Ohio, Nov. 4, 1956; s. A. William and Marijane (Spitler) S. BS, Marquette U., 1978; JD, Ohio No. U., 1981. Bar: Ohio 1981, Fla. 1983. Staff atty. James W. Knisley Co., Dayton, 1981-83; pvt. practice, 1983-85; prin. Alfred W. Schneble III Co. LPA, 1986-2000; shareholder, pres. Schneble, Cass & Assoc. Co., LPA, 2000—. Mem. Ohio Bar Assn., Fla. Bar Assn., Dayton Bar Assn., Ohio Acad. Trial Lawyers. Republican. Roman Catholic. Office: 11 W Monument Ave #402 Dayton OH 45402

SCHNECK, JEROME M. psychiatrist, medical historian, educator; b. N.Y.C., Jan. 2, 1920; s. Maurice and Rose (Weiss) S.; m. Shirley R. Kaufman, July 24, 1943. AB, Cornell U., 1939; MD, SUNY, Bklyn., 1943. Diplomate Am. Bd. Psychiatry and Neurology, Am. Bd. Psychotherapy. Intern Interfaith Med. Ctr., 1943; psychiat. staff Menninger Clinic, Topeka, 1944-45; chief psychiatry and sociology dept. Fort Missoula, Mont., 1946, Camp Cooke, Calif., 1947; mem. psychiat. staff L.I. Coll. Hosp., 1947-48, Kings County Hosp., 1948-70, SUNY Hosp., Bklyn., 1955-70; assoc. vis. psychiatrist Kings County Hosp., 1949-70; mem. psychiat. staff State U. Hosp., Bklyn., 1955-70; pvt. practice N.Y.C., N.Y.C., 1947—; attending psychiatrist St. Vincent's Hosp. and Med. Ctr. N.Y., 1970—, hon. sr. psychiatrist, 1990—. Psychiat. cons. VA Regional Office, 1947-48, N.Y. State Dept. Social Svcs., 1977-83, N.Y. State Dept. Civil Svc., 1978-84, N.Y. State Office Ct. Adminstrn., 1978-85, N.Y. State Dept. Edn., 1981-83; dir. Mt. Vernon Mental Hygiene Clinic, 1947-52; assoc. chief psychiatrist Westchester County Dept. Health, 1949-50, cons., 1951-52; clin. instr. L.I. Coll. Medicine, 1947-50; clin. assoc. SUNY Coll. Medicine, Bklyn., 1950-53, asst. prof., 1955-58, assoc. prof., 1958-70; supervising psychiatrist Community Guidance Svcs., 1955-70; cons. coun. on mental health AMA, 1956-58; cons. NBC, 1962, Ctr. Rsch. in Hypnotherapy, 1964-70; vis. lectr. N.Y. Med. Coll.-Met. Hosp., 1965; faculty and fellow Am. Inst. Psychotherapy and Psychoanalysis, 1970-85. Author: Hypnosis in Modern Medicine, 1953, 2d edit., 1959, Spanish lang. edit., 1962, 3rd edit., 1963, Studies in Scientific Hypnosis, 1954, A History of Psychiatry, 1960, The Principles and Practice of Hypnoanalysis, 1965 (Best Book award Soc. For Clin. and Exptl. Hypnosis 1965); editor: Hypnotherapy, Hypnosis and Personality, 1951; author over 400 med. and sci. publs., book chpts., articles; mem. bd. editors: Personality: Symposia on Topical Issues, 1960-61, Jour. Integrative and Eclectic Psychotherapy, 1986-89; contbg. editor Psychosomatics, 1961-75; mem. editorial bd. Voices—The Art and Science of Psychotherapy, 1965; features editor The Interne, 1942, co-editor, 1943. Lt. U.S. Army Field Arty. Res., 1939-42; capt. M.C. AUS, 1945-47. Recipient Shirley R. Schneck award to physician making significant contbns. to devel. of med. hypnosis, 1970, Clarence B. Farrar award for history of Am. psychiatry rsch. Clarke Inst. Psychiatry, U. Toronto, 1976, Roy M. Dorcus award for best clin. paper on hypnosis, 1981, Spl. Presdl. award for lifetime contbns. to lit. on sci. hypnosis, 1986. Fellow AAAS, APA, Am. Med. Authors, Acad. Psychosomatic Medicine, Am. Psychiat. Assn. (life), Am. Soc. Clin. Hypnosis (life), Soc. for Clin. and Exptl. Hypnosis (life, founder, founding pres. 1949-56, exec. coun. 1949—, assoc. editor jour. 1953—, Award of Merit 1955, Gold medal 1958, Bernard B. Raginsky award 1966, Shirley Schneck award 1970, Roy M. Dorcus award 1980, Spl. Presdl. award 1986), Am. Acad. Psychotherapists (co-founder, v.p. 1956-58), Am. Med. Writers Assn., Am. Soc. Psychoanalytic Physicians (founding fellow, bd. dirs. 1958-62), Internat. Soc. Clin. and Exptl. Hypnosis (co-founder, bd. dirs. 1958-68, founding fellow), Internat. Acad. Eclectic Psychotherapists (charter fellow); mem. AMA, N.Y. Acad. Scis., Soc. Acad. Achievement (charter), Soc. Apothecaries London, Inst. Practicing Psychotherapists, Pan Am. Med. Assn. (v.p. sect. clin. hypnosis 1960-65, N.Am. v.p. 1966), N.Y. Soc. Med. History (exec. com. 1956-62), Am. Bd. Med. Hypnosis (founder, pres. 1958-60, life bd. dirs.), Inst. Rsch. in Hypnosis Inc. (bd. dirs., bd. editors 1957-70), Am. Assn. History Medicine, History of Sci. Soc., Assn. Advancement Psychotherapy (charter) Can. Med. History Assn., N.Y. Soc. for Clin. Psychiatry (chmn. com. on history of psychiatry), Charles F. Menninger Soc., Internat. Soc. Hypnosis (hon. life mem.), Brit. Soc. Med. Hypnosis (hon.), Internat. Soc. Hypnosis (hon. life mem.), Sigma Xi. Address: 26 W 9th St New York NY 10011-8971

SCHNECK, PAUL BENNETT, computer scientist; b. N.Y.C., Aug. 15, 1945; s. Irving and Doris (Grossman) S.; m. Marjorie Ann Axelrod, Feb. 5, 1967; children: Phyllis Adele, Melanie Jane. BS, Columbia U., 1965, MS, 1966; PhD, NYU Courant Inst. Math. Scis., 1979. Computer scientist Inst. for Space Studies, N.Y.C., 1970-76; program mgr. Goddard Space Flight Ctr., Greenbelt, Md., 1976-79, asst. to dir., 1979-80, chief info. extraction div., 1980-81, asst. dir., 1981-83; head info. sci. div. Office of Naval Rsch., Arlington, Va., 1983-85; founding dir. Supercomputing Rsch. Ctr., Bowie, Md., 1985-93; chief scientist Inst. Defense Analyses, 1993; fellow Mitre Corp., McLean, Va., 1993-96, dir. info. sys. and fellow, 1994-96, Mitretek Systems, Inc., McLean, 1996-97; v.p. tech. and sys. devel. MRJ Tech. Solutions, Fairfax, 1997-98, v.p. info. analysis solutions, 1998-2000, Veridian Info. Solutions, 2000; v.p., chief tech. officer Veridian Corp., 2001. Vice chmn. bd. Nat. Info. Tech. Ctr., 1993, chmn. bd., CEO, 1994, exec. com., 1994-97; mem. adv. bd. Inst. Computational Sci. and Informatics, George Mason U., 1995-2000; mem. adv. bd. computer scis. U. Md., College Park, 1989-95, Johns Hopkins U., Balt., 1998-2000; tchr. Columbia U., Johns Hopkins U., U. Md. Author: Supercomputer Architecture, 1987; contbr. articles to Ency. of Computer Sci. and Tech., Ann. Rev. of Computer Sci., Ency. Phys. Sci. and Tech. Yearbook. Fellow IEEE, Assn. for Computing Machinery; mem. Brit. Computer Soc., Engring. Coun. (chartered engr., Eng.). Achievements include management of Massively Parallel Processor project, 1980-81; design and implementation of the science supervisory operating system in use at NASA from 1968-83, on the IBM 360/95 and 370/165, and the Amdahl 470/V6, V7; and of the vector/parallel compiler; inventor: System for Controlling Access and Distribution of Digital Property; patentee in field. Office: Veridian Corp 1200 S Hayes St Arlington VA 22202

SCHNECK, STUART AUSTIN, retired neurologist, educator; b. N.Y.C., Apr. 1, 1929; s. Maurice and Sara Ruth (Knapp) S.; m. Ida I. Nakashima, Mar. 2, 1956; children— Lisa, Christopher. BS magna cum laude, Franklin and Marshall Coll., 1949; MD, U. Pa., 1953. Diplomate Am. Bd. Psychiatry and Neurology (bd. dirs., sec. 1990-91, v.p. 1991-92, pres. 1992-93). Intern Hosp. U. Pa., Phila., 1953-54; resident in medicine U. Colo. Med. Center, Denver, 1954-55, 57-58, resident in neurology, 1958-61; instr. neurology U. Colo. Sch. Medicine, 1959-61; instr. neuropathology Columbia U., N.Y.C., 1961-63; vis. fellow in neurology Vanderbilt Clinic, Columbia-Presbyn. Med. Center, 1961-63; asst. prof. neurology and pathology U. Colo., 1963-67, assoc. prof., 1967-70, prof., 1970-95, assoc. dean clin. affairs Sch. Medicine, 1984-89, emeritus prof., 1996—. Cons. Fitzsimons Army Hosp., VA, Nat. Jewish Hosp.; pres. med. bd. Univ. Hosp., Denver, 1983-89, bd. dirs., 1989-90; mem. benefits adv. bd. U. Colo., 1999—, v.p. retired faculty assn. health sci. ctr., 1998-99, pres., 1999-2001. Contbr. articles to profl. jours. Served with USAF, 1955-57. USPHS fellow, 1961-63 Mem. Am. Acad. Neurology, Am. Assn. Neuropathologists, Am. Neurol. Assn., Univ. Srs. Assn. (chmn. bd. dirs. 1997-2002), Rocky Mountain Stroke Assn. (bd. dirs. 1998—), Colo. Personalized Edn. Physicians (bd. dirs. 1999—), Alpha Omega Alpha (bd. dirs. 1979-89, treas., pres. 1990-93, edit. bd. 1994—).

SCHNEEBERGER, HELEN HAYNES, artist, consultant; b. Ky., May 14, 1923; d. Garland Griffin and Wilma Hazel (Horsley) H.; m. Frederick John Schneeberger, Oct. 11, 1946; children: Frederick J. III, Craig Garland, Kimberly E. Student, U. Tenn., 1957-58; BA, Atlanta Sch. Art, 1969; postgrad., LaRomita Sch. Art, Terni, Italy, 1988, Inst. Art, San Miguel Allende, Mex., 1991. Tchr. Decatur (Ga.) Fine Arts Program, 1974-91. Co-founder Coker Creek (Tenn.) Artists, 1965-93; visual arts adv. bd. Dekalb County Schs., Decatur, 1976-80. One-woman shows include Night Gallery, Cleveland, Tenn., 1988, Creative Arts Gallery, Dalton, Tenn., 1990, Cultural Arts Gallery, Douglasville, Ga., 1998; group shows include traveling show in West Germany (selected by Pres. Jimmy Carter), 1979, Atlanta Artists Show (Govt. J. Frank Harris's office), 1979, Italian govt. show in hill towns out of Rome,

1979, others; illustrator: Making Watercolor Sing, 1986, Peachtree Bouquet, 1987; permanent collections include West Ga. Coll. Art, Carrollton, King and Spalding Law Firm, Ga., Coca Cola, Columbus (Ga.) Mus. Arts and Scis., Dalton Mus. Fine Arts, Dr. Nicholas Bath, Decatur, Ga., Gordon Jackson, Dunwoody, Ga., Felleppe Tella, Mayor of Sulmona (Italy), Mayor Maynard Jackson, Atlanta, Jack and Mary Gracie, Isle of Skye, Scotland. Active Ga. Rep. Party, 1998, Nat. Rep. Party, 1998. Named one of Outstanding Women in the Arts in Ga., 1987; recipient PEN Women of Am. Artist of Yr. award, 1998. Mem. Ga. Watercolor Soc., Ky. Watercolor Soc., Ala. Watercolor Soc., So. Watercolor Soc. Republican. Mem. Coop. Bapt. Fellowship. Home: 1982 Tall Tree Dr NE Atlanta GA 30324-2724

SCHNEEGURT, MARK ALLEN, microbiologist, researcher; b. Bklyn., Jan. 18, 1962; s. Errol and Elaine Francis (Sacks) S. BS, Rensselaer Poly. Inst., 1984, MS, 1985; PhD, Brown U., 1989. Postdoctoral rsch. scientist Dow Elanco, Greenfield, Ind., 1989-91; postdoctoral fellow Purdue U., West Lafayette, 1992-96; rsch. asst. prof. U. Notre Dame, 1996-2000; asst. prof. Wichita (Kans.) State U., 2000—. Contbr. articles to profl. jours. Recipient Nat. Rschr. Svc. award NIH, 1987; Nat. Merit scholar, 1980, N.Y. State Regents scholar, 1980. Mem. Am. Soc. Plant Physiologists, Am. Soc. for Microbiology, The Planetary Soc., Sigma Xi (Rsch. grant 1988). Jewish. Achievements include research in microbial biochemistry and physiology, cyanobacteria and applied environmental microbiology. Office: Wichita State U Dept Biol Sci Box 26 Wichita KS 67260-0026 E-mail: maschnee@twsu.edu.

SCHNEEMAN, BARBARA OLDS, nutritionist, educator; m. Paul Schneeman; 1 child Eric. BS in Food Sci. and Tech., U. Calif., Davis, 1970; PhD in Nutrition, U. Calif., Berkeley, 1974. NIH postdoctoral fellow gastrointestinal physiology Children's Hosp., Oakland, Calif., 1974-76; asst. prof. nutrition dept. nutrition and food sci. & tech. U. Calif., Davis, 1976-82, assoc. prof. nutrition, 1982-86, prof. nutrition, nutritionist, 1986—, prof. dept. internal medicine divsn. clin. nutrition, 1986—, assoc. dean Coll. Agrl. and Environ. Scis., 1985-88, chair dept. nutrition, 1988-93, dean Coll. Agrl. and Environ. Scis., 1993-99, dir. programs. divsn. agr. and natural resources, 1993-99. Pres., bd. dirs. Dannon Inst., 1996—; vis. scientist Cardiovascular Rsch. Inst., U. Calif., San Francisco, 1991-92; lectr. women in sci. series Coll. St. Catherine, St. Paul, 1987; adv. dir. Blue Cross Calif., 1992-95; mem. dietary guidelines for Ams. adv. com. to Secs. of Agr., Health and Human Svcs., 1989-90, 94-95; mem. expert panel on food safety and nutrition Inst. Food Technologists, 1985-91; mem. external adv. bd. Post Ctr. for Nutrition and Health, 1989-90; councilor Soc. for Exptl. Biology and Medicine, 1988-91. Assoc. editor Jour. Nutrition, 1991-94; contbg. editor Nutrition Revs., 1982-90; editl. bd. Jour. Nutrition, 1982-87, Procs. for Soc. Exptl. Biology and Medicine, 1985-91, Acad. Press: Food Sci. and Nutrition, 1988—. Fellow NDEA, U. Calif., Berkeley; food sci. scholar; recipient Outstanding Cmty. Svc. award Tierra del Oro coun. Girl Scouts U.S., 1995, Future Leaders award for rsch. Nutrition Found., 1978-80, Samuel Cate Prescott award for rsch. Inst. Food Tech., 1985, Farma Food Internat. Fibre prize, Copenhagen, 1989, Ethel Austin Martin disting. lectr. on Human Nutrition, S.D. State U., 1999. Mem. AAAS, Inst. Food Technologists (sec.-treas. nutrition divsn. 1988-89), Am. Physiol. Soc., Am. Inst. Nutrition (treas. 1989-92), Am. Heart Assn. (fellow arteriosclerosis coun.). Office: U Calif Davis Dept Nutrition Davis CA 95616

SCHNEEWIND, ELIZABETH HUGHES, social worker; b. Chgo., May 11, 1940; d. Everett Cherrington and Helen (MacGill) Hughes; m. Jerome Borges Schneewind, 1963; children: Sarah, Rachel, Hannah. BA in Philosophy, U. Chgo., 1959; MA in Philosophy, Brown U., 1962; MSW, U. Md., 1985; postgrad., Yale U., 1962-63. ACSW, LCSW-C; cert. German translator. Program evaluator Coll. Human Svcs, N.Y.C., 1976-77; rsch. asst. Fordham U. Gerontology Ctr., N.Y., 1977-80; field supr. N.Y.C. Dept. Aging Foster Grandparent Program, 1980-82; social worker Levindale Geriatric Ctr., Balt., 1985-88, Johns Hopkins Hosp., Balt., 1988; social worker, asst. dir. older adult svcs. Jewish Family Svcs., 1988-2000; project mgr. Pro Bono Counseling Project, 2002; specialist social work Baltimore City Commn. on Aging, 2002—. Presentor in field. Pres. Balt. Washington Soc. Psychogeriatrics, 1987-89; mem. exec. bd. Alzheimer's Assn., Balt. chpt. 1986-92; v.p. Women in Urban Crisis, Pitts., 1972-73; bd. mem. Balt. Crisis Response, Md. Gerontol. Assn., Timothy House, Handel Choir of Balt. Mem. NASW, Brit. Soc. Authors, Am. Translators Assn. Democrat. Avocations: chamber music, singing. Home: 325 Woodlawn Rd Baltimore MD 21210-2308 E-mail: jbs1@jhu.edu.

SCHNEEWIND, JEROME BORGES, philosophy educator; b. Mt. Vernon, N.Y., May 17, 1930; s. Jerome John and Charlotte (Borges) S.; m. Elizabeth G.R. Hughes, Feb. 23, 1963; children: Sarah, Rachel, Hannah. BA, Cornell U., 1951; MA, Princeton U., 1953, PhD, 1957. Instr. philosophy U. Chgo., 1957-60, Princeton U., 1960-61; asst. prof. Yale U., 1961-63; asso. prof. philosophy U. Pitts., 1964-68, prof., 1968-75, dean Coll. Arts and Scis., 1969-73; v.p., provost Hunter Coll., CUNY, 1975-81; prof. philosophy Johns Hopkins U., Balt., 1981—, chmn. dept., 1981-91. Philosophy adviser Ency. Americana, 1967-98; mem. adv. bd. sci. tech. and values program NEH, 1975-78; mem. Coun. for Phil. Studies, 1975-80. Author: Backgrounds of English Victorian Literature, 1970, Sidgwick's Ethics and Victorian Moral Philosophy, 1977, The Invention of Autonomy, 1998; editor: Moral Philosophy From Montaigne to Kant, 1990; mem. editl. bd. Victorian Studies, 1968-75, The Monist, 1969-76, Am. Philosophy Quar., 1975-77, Philos. Studies, 1975-78, Jour. of History Ideas, 1985—, pres. bd. dirs., 1988-2000; contbr. articles on ethics and history of ethics to publs. Served with Signal Corps, AUS, 1954-56. Mellon postdoctoral fellow, 1963-64; Guggenheim fellow, 1967-68; Am. Council Learned Socs. grantee, 1973; NEH sr. fellow, 1974, Ctr. for Advanced Study in the Behavioral Scis., 1992-93. Fellow AAAS; mem. Am. Philos. Assn. (exec. com. Ea. divsn. 1964-67, chmn. com. on teaching philosophy 1973-78, nominating com. 1986-88, v.p. Ea. divsn. 1994-95, pres. 1995-96, chmn. bd. officers, 1999-2002). Office: Philosophy Dept Johns Hopkins U Baltimore MD 21218 E-mail: jbs1@jhu.edu.

SCHNEIDER, ADAM JASON, neurologist, neurophysiologist; b. Bklyn., May 5, 1966; s. Larry and Linda Schneider; m. Deborah Schneider; children: Andrew, Rachel. BS in Biol. Scis. summa cum laude, SUNY, Stony Brook, 1988; MD, Albert Einstein Coll. Medicine, 1992. Resident neurology L.I. Jewish Med. Ctr., New Hyde Park, N.Y., 1993-96, chief resident neurology, 1995-96, fellow neuromuscular disease/emg., 1996-97; acad. full time attending neurology divsn. Maimonides Med. Ctr., Bklyn., 1997-99; neurologist, neurophysiologist Pro Health Care Assocs., Lake Success, N.Y., 1999—. Mem. N.Y. State Med. Soc. (media and publs. com. 1997—), Am. Assn. of Electrodiagnostic Medicine, Myasthenia Gravis Alliance, Am. Acad. of Neurology, Phi Beta Kappa. Avocations: baseball, meteorology. Office: Pro Health Care Assocs 2800 Marcus Ave New Hyde Park NY 11042-1052

SCHNEIDER, ADAM LOUIS, management consultant; b. N.Y.C., Mar. 7, 1956; s. George Mitchell and Ruth (Rubinstein) S.; children: Jason, Dana, Evan. BS, MIT, 1978; MBA, Columbia Bus. Sch., N.Y.C., 1980. Ind. cons. Nat. Found./March of Dimes, White Plains, N.Y., 1975-80; cons. Booz, Allen & Hamilton, N.Y.C., 1980-81; mgr. systems devel. Goldman Sachs & Co., 1981-83; ptnr. Deloitte & Touche, 1983-91; mng. dir. Chancellor Capital Mgmt., 1991-95; ptnr. Deloitte Cons., N.Y.C., 1995—. Contbr. articles to profl. jours. Mem. Nat. Investment Co. Svc. Assn., Fin. Svcs. Assn. (lectr.), Bank Administrn. Inst. (lectr.), Am. Bankers Assn. (lectr.). Avocations: sailing, photography, car collecting. Home: 104 Browning Rd Short Hills NJ 07078-1143 Office: Deloitte Cons 25 Broadway New York NY 10004

SCHNEIDER, ADELE GOLDBERG, librarian, educator; b. N.Y.C., May 13, 1924; d. Abraham and Anna (Levy) Goldberg; m. Noel Schneider, Jan. 1, 1950; children: Adam Matthew, Tracy Lynn. BA, Bklyn. Coll., 1945; MLS, Pratt Inst., 1965; MA, L.I. Univ., 1971. Field interview Gallup Poll, N.Y.C., 1941-48; social worker N.Y.C. Dept. Social Svcs., 1949-52; editor Bklyn. Coll. Alumni Quar., 1961-65; instr. Kingsborough C.C./CUNY, 1965-70, asst. prof. dept. libr., 1970-72, assoc. prof., 1972-88, prof., 1988-92, prof. emeritus, 1992—. Contbr. articles to profl. jours. Recipient lifetime achievement award Bklyn. Coll., 2000. Mem. ALA, Libr. Assn. CUNY, N.Y. Tech. Svcs. Librs., Beta Phi Mu. Home: 124 Oxford St Brooklyn NY 11235-2311 Office: 2001 Oriental Blvd Brooklyn NY 11235-2333

SCHNEIDER, ALLAN STANFORD, biochemistry, neuroscience and pharmacology educator, biomedical research scientist; b. N.Y.C., Sept. 26, 1940; s. Harry and Edith (Gonsky) S.; m. Mary-Jane Beekman Tunis, Dec. 14, 1968; children: Henry Seth, Joseph Benjamin B.Chem. Engring., Rensselaer Poly. Inst., 1961; MS, Pa. State U., 1963; PhD, U. Calif.-Berkeley, 1968. Chem. engr. E.I. du Pont de Nemours & Co. Exptl. Sta., Wilmington, Del., 1963-64; postdoctoral fellow Weizmann Inst. Sci., Rehovot, Israel, 1969-71; staff fellow NIH, Bethesda, Md., 1971-73; assoc. Sloan-Kettering Inst. Cancer Research, N.Y.C., 1974-80, assoc. mem., 1980-85; asst. prof. Cornell U. Grad. Sch. Med. Scis., 1974-80, assoc. prof. biochemistry, 1981-83, assoc. prof. cell biology and genetic, 1983-85, chmn. biochemistry unit Sloan-Kettering div., 1982-83; assoc. prof. pharmacology and toxicology Albany (N.Y.) Med. Coll., 1985-86, prof. pharmacology and toxicology, 1986-94, prof. pharmacology and neurosci., 1995—, dir. grad. studies, 1987-91. Adjunct prof. Biomedical Sci., Sch. of Public Health, St. U. N.Y., Albany, 1987—; vis. prof. Weizmann Inst. Sci., Rehovot, Israel, 1987; vis. rsch. scholar U. Bergen, Norway, 1989, 95; vis. rsch. scholar, U. of Melbourne, Australia, 1998. Contbr. chpts to books, sci. articles to profl. jours. Rsch. grantee Am. Cancer Soc., 1980-83, Am. Heart Assn., 1977-82, 90-93, NIH, 1982-93, 2001—, NSF, 1977-79, 1997-2002, Cystic Fibrosis Found., 1980-82; established investigator Am. Heart Assn., 1977-82. Mem. Biophys. Soc., Soc. Neurosci., Soc. of Gen. Physiologist, Am. Heart Assn. (coun. on basic sci. 1977-95), Phi Lambda Upsilon, Tau Beta Pi (internat. com. for chromaffin cell biology 1987-93). Achievements include first isolation and characterization of chromaffin cells of the adrenal gland now widely used as a model neuronal cell culture system; determination of the relation between cytosolic calcium signals and neurohormone (adrenaline) secretion, relevant to cellular mechanism of hormone and neurotransmitter release; spectroscopic characterization of protein structure in situ in biomembranes and cells; theoretical and experimental analysis of optical activity spectra of turbid biological suspensions; research on neurochemistry of adrenal chromaffin cells, regulation of cell calcium and hormone and neurotransmitter release; mechanisms of nicotine dependence and fetal nicotine syndrome and effects of maternal smoking on fetal brain development. Office: Ctr for Neuropharmacology & Neurosci Albany Med Coll MC 136 Albany NY 12208 E-mail: schneia@mail.amc.edu.

SCHNEIDER, ARTHUR PAUL, retired videotape and film editor, author; b. Rochester, N.Y., Jan. 26, 1930; s. Mendell Phillip and Frieda (Bl) S.; m. Helen Deloise Thompson, June 5, 1954; children: Robert Paul, Lori Ann. Student, U. So. Calif., 1953. With NBC, 1951-68, film and videotape editor, 1953-60, developer double system method of editing video tape, 1958; pres. Burbank (Calif.) Film Editing, Inc., 1968-72, Electronic Video Industries Inc., 1977-79; supr. video tape editing Consol. Film Industries Inc., Hollywood, Calif., 1972-76, editorial supr., 1980-83; pvt. practice editing, 1983-88. Cons., lectr., author. Film and tape editor all: Bob Hope shows, 1951-67; supr. NBC kinescope and video tape editors (1966-67); video tape editor: Laugh-In Series, 1967-68; video tape editor: Comedy Shop Series, 1977-80; post-prodn. cons. to Video Systems and Broadcast Engring. mag.; video tape editor: TV series Sonny & Cher, 1973, Sonny Comedy Revue, 1974, Tony Orlando and Dawn, 1974, Hudson Bros., summer, 1974, Dean Martin Series, 1975-76, Mickey Mouse Club Series, Walt Disney Prodns., 1976, Redd Foxx Series, 1977; (author: Electronic Post Production and Videotape Editing, 1989 (pub. in Chinese 1995), Electronic Post Production Terms and Concepts, 1990; contbg. author: Association of Cinema and Video Laboratores (ACVL) Handbook, 5th edit., 1995, Focal Guide to Electronic Media CDRom Version, 1998, Jump Cut: Memoirs of a Pioneer Television Editor, 1997; oral history interview for Acad. TV Arts and Scis. Found. Archive of Am. TV First 50 Yrs., 2001; contbr. articles to publs. in field. Recipient Broadcast Preceptor award San Francisco State U., 1975; named hon. Ky. Col. Mem. Acad. Television Arts and Scis. (Emmy nominations and Emmy award for video tape editing 1966, 68, 73, 84, gov. 1977-80, sec. 1980-81), Am. Cinema Editors (life, Life Achievement award 1999), Soc. Motion Picture and TV Engrs., Delta Kappa Alpha (life). Home: PO Box 156 Fish Camp CA 93623-0156 E-mail: art156@sierratel.com.

SCHNEIDER, ARTHUR SANFORD, physician, educator; b. Los Angeles, Mar. 24, 1929; s. Max and Fannie (Ragin) S.; m. Edith Kadison, Aug. 20, 1950; children: Jo Ann Schneider Farris, William Scott, Lynnellen. BS, UCLA, 1951; MD, Chgo. Med. Sch., 1955. Diplomate Am. Bd. Internal Medicine, Am. Bd. Pathology. Intern, Wadsworth VA Hosp., Los Angeles, 1955-56, resident, 1956-59, chief clin. pathology sect., 1962-68; mem. faculty UCLA, 1961-75, clin. assoc. prof., 1971-75; chair dept. clin. pathology City of Hope Med. Ctr., Duarte, Calif., 1968-75; prof., chair dept. clin. pathology Whittier Coll., 1974-75; prof., chair dept. pathology Chgo. Med. Sch., 1975—; chief lab. service VA Med. Ctr., North Chicago, Ill., 1975-86, chief lab. hematology, 1986-94. Contbr. numerous chpts. to books and articles to med. jours. Served to capt. M.C., USAF, 1959-61. Fellow ACP, Coll. Am. Pathologists, Am. Soc. Clin. Pathologists; mem. AAUP, AMA, Internat. Acad. Pathology, Am. Assn. for Investigative Pathology, Assn. Pathology Chairs, Acad. Clin. Lab. Physicians and Scientists, Am. Soc. Hematology, Am. Assn. Blood Banks, Am. Soc. Clin. Rsch., Ill. Med. Soc., Lake County Med. Soc., Sigma Xi, Alpha Omega Alpha, Phi Delta Epsilon. Office: Chgo Med Sch 3333 Green Bay Rd North Chicago IL 60064-3037 Fax: 847-578-5002. E-mail: arthur.schneider@finchcms.edu.

SCHNEIDER, BARBARA CARVER, world affairs executive; b. Ft. Sill, Okla., Apr. 19, 1938; d. George Allen and Barbara Ellen (Bristol) Carver; m. William Henry Schneider, Aug. 31, 1957 (dec. May 1994); children: Michael, Allen, Catherine, Patricia. BSBA, George Mason U., 1980; grad., Rep. Nat. Com. Campaign Mgmt. Coll., 1981. Sales agt. Routh Robbins Realtor, McLean, Va., 1968; exec. sec. to v.p. Decision Making Info., Arlington, 1980-81; dir. adminstrn. Nat. Rep. Senatorial Com., Washington, 1981-82; exec. dir. World Affairs Coun. San Antonio, 1995—. Bd. dirs. Nat. Coun. World Affairs Orgns., Washington, 1996—. Mem. steering com. Assocs. of Bapt. Hosp. Sys., San Antonio, 1995—; cmty. outreach chair, bd. trustees Cancer Ctr. Coun., San Antonio, 1996—; bd. dirs. Any Baby Can Alliance, San Antonio, 1990-91, Tex. Mil. Inst., San Antonio, 1994—, Soc. for Preservation of Hist. Ft. Sam Houston, San Antonio, 1994—, Morningside Ministries, 1999; co-chmn. San Antonio Sr. Olympics, 1990-92; pres., devel. chmn. Bexar County Women's Ctr., San Antonio, 1991-92, 92-93; co-chair parade sect. mil. Battle of Flowers Assn., San Antonio, 1993, chair parade sect. antique cars, 1994, judges com., 1995, meeting chmn., 1996-97; bd. dirs. ARC, San Antonio chpt., 1987-95, sec., 1991-92, chmn.-elect., 1992-93, chmn., 1993-94; bd. dirs. USO San Antonio and Ctrl. Tex., 1988—, v.p., 1991-93, pres., 1993-95; v.p. Alamo City Rep. Women, San Antonio, 1992-93, pres., 1993-95; chmn. U. Tex. Walk for Women's Athletics, San Antonio, 1996. Recipient Outstanding Civilian Svc. medal Dept. Army, 1989, Cmty. Leadership award Prudential Healthcare, 1996; named Hon. chmn. Nat. Sr. Sports Classic, 1994. Mem. AAUW, Women in Comm. (Headliner/Pub. Endeavor award 1997), Oaks Club San Antonio, Greater San Antonio C. of C., Rotary, Kappa Gamma Alumni Assn. (pres. 1990-91). Roman Catholic. Avocations: reading, volunteerism, running marathons. Home: 69 Granburg Cir San Antonio TX 78218-3031 Office: World Affairs Coun San Antonio 40 NE Loop 410 Ste 608 San Antonio TX 78216-5869 E-mail: wacofsa@aol.com.

SCHNEIDER, BENJAMIN, psychology educator; b. N.Y.C., Aug. 11, 1938; s. Leo and Rose (Cohen) S.; m. H. Brenda Jacobson, Jan. 29, 1961; children: Lee Andrew, Rhody Yve. BA, Alfred U., 1960; MBA, CUNY, 1962; PhD, U. Md., 1967. Lic. psychologist, Md. Asst. prof. adminstrv. scis. and psychology Yale U., New Haven, 1967-71; prof. psychology-mgmt. U. Md., College Park, 1971-79, prof. psychology and mgmt., 1982—; John A. Hannah prof. orgnl. behavior Mich. State U., East Lansing, 1979-82. V.p. Orgnl. and Pers. Rsch., Inc.; vis. prof. Inst. Adminstrn. and Enterprise, U. Aix-Marseille, 1993, 99, 2001, Peking U., 1989, Tuck Sch. Bus. Adminstrn., Dartmouth Coll., 1999. Author: (with D.T. Hall) Organizational Climates and Careers, 1973, Staffing Organizations, 1976, 2d edit. (with N. Schmitt), 1986; (with F.D. Schoorman) Facilitating Work Effectiveness, 1988, Organizational Climate and Culture, 1990, (with D.E. Bowen) Winning the Service Game, 1995; mem. editl. rev. bd. Jour. Applied Psychology, 1988-98, 2002—, Internat. Jour. Svc. Industry Mgmt., 1989—, Jour. Svc. Rsch., 1998—, Orgnl. Behavior and Human Decision Processes. Fulbright grantee, 1973-74 Fellow APA, Am. Psychol. Soc., Soc. for Indsl. and Orgnl. Psychology (pres. 1984-85, Disting. Sci. Contbns. award 2000), Acad. Mgmt. (pres. orgnl. behavior div. 1982-83), Orgnl. and Personnel Rsch., Inc. (v.p., cons. to mgmt.). Home: 10519 Tuckerman Heights Cir Rockville MD 20852-7410 Office: U Maryland Dept Psychology College Park MD 20742-0001 E-mail: ben@psyc.umd.edu.

SCHNEIDER, CALVIN, physician; b. N.Y.C., Oct. 23, 1924; s. Harry and Bertha (Green) S.; m. Elizabeth Gayle Thomas, Dec. 27, 1967. AB, U. So. Calif., 1951, MD, 1955; JD, LaVerne (Calif.) Coll., 1973. Intern L.A. County Gen. Hosp., 1955-56, staff physician, 1956-57; pvt. practice medicine West Covina, Calif., 1957—. Staff Inter-Community Med. Ctr., Covina, Calif. With USNR, 1943-47. Republican. Lutheran.

SCHNEIDER, CARL EDWARD, law educator; b. Exeter, N.H., Feb. 23, 1948; s. Carl Jacob and Dorothy (Jones) S.; m. Joan L. Wagner, Jan. 6, 1976. BA, Harvard Coll., 1972; JD, U. Mich., 1979. Curriculum specialist Mass. Tchrs. Assn., Boston, 1972-75; law clk. to judge U.S. Ct. Appeals (D.C. cir.), Washington, 1979-80; law clk. Potter Stewart U.S. Supreme Ct., 1980-81; asst. prof. law U. Mich., Ann Arbor, 1981-84, assoc. prof. law, 1984-86, prof. law, 1986—, prof. internal medicine, 1998—, Chauncey Stillman prof. ethics, morality and practice of law; vis. prof. U. Tokyo, 1998. Author: The Practice of Autonomy: Patients, Doctors and Medical Decisions, 1998, (with Margaret F. Brinig) An Invitation to Family Law, 1996; editor: (book) The Law and Politics of Abortion, 1980, Family Law in Action: A Reader, 1999 (with Margaret F. Brinig & Lee E. Teitelbaum), Law at the End of Life: The Supreme Court and Assisted Suicide, 2000; contbr. articles to profl. jours. Fellow Am. Council of Learned Socs., Ford Found., 1985, Hastings Ctr.; life fellow Clare Coll., Cambridge. Mem. Order of Coif. Office: U Mich Law Sch 801 Monroe St Ann Arbor MI 48109-1210

SCHNEIDER, CARL WILLIAM, lawyer; b. Phila., Apr. 27, 1932; s. Nathan J. and Eleanor M. (Milgram) S.; m. Mary Ellen Baylinson; children: Eric, Mark, Adam, Cara BA, Cornell U., 1953; LLB magna cum laude, U. Pa., 1956. Bar: Pa. 1957. Law clk. U.S. Ct. Appeals (3d cir.), Phila., 1956-57; sr. law clk. U.S. Supreme Ct., Washington, 1957-58; assoc. Wolf, Block, Schorr and Solis-Cohen LLP, Phila., 1958-65; ptnr. Wolf, Block, Schorr and Solis-Cohen, 1965-2000, of counsel, 2000—. Spl. advisor divsn. corp. fin. SEC, Washington, 1964; lectr. securities law U. Pa., 1968-70, vis. assoc. prof., 1978-81, acting dir. Ctr. for Study Fin. Instns.; bd. editors and advisors Rev. Securities and Commodities Regulations. Author: SEC Consequences of Corporate Acquisitions, 1971, Pennsylvania Corporate Practice and Forms: The Wolf, Block, Schorr and Solis-Cohen Manual, 1997; also numerous articles; mem. editl. adv. bd. Securities Regulation and Law Report. Bd. dirs. Foun. of Jewish Families and Children's Svc., Abramson Ctr. for Jewish Life; chmn. bd. dirs. Jewish Family and Children's Svc. of Greater Phila.; trustee Long Beach Island Found. of the Arts and Scis., Loveladies, NJ. Mem. ABA, Pa. Bar Assn., Phila. Bar Assn. (chmn. sect. corp. banking and bus. law 1972), Am. Law Inst. (life). Home: 235 Linden Dr Elkins Park PA 19027-1341

SCHNEIDER, CAROL ANN, staffing services company executive; d. Glenn William and Beatrice Helen Kluth; m. Leon A. Schneider, Feb. 4, 1961; children: Paul, Joel, Neil. BEd in Bus. Edn., U. Wis., Whitewater, 1958; postgrad., U. Wis., 1971-74. Lic. secondary bus. educator, Wis., vocat. bus. educator, Wis.; cert. pers. cons.; sr. prof. in human resources. Bus. divsn. chair Milw. Area Tech. Coll.-North, Mequon, Wis., 1969-80, Port Washington (Wis.) Vocat., Tech. and Adult Sch., 1969-80; founder, CEO, chair of the bd. SEEK, Inc., Grafton, Wis., 1971—. Founder, mgr. The Schneider Co., LLC, Grafton, 1996—, ITech Profls., LLC, Grafton, 1998—, Guardian HealthStaff, LLC, 2002; past pres. Wis. Assn. Staffing Svcs.; presenter in field. Fund raising chair St. Joseph's Ch.; founder, past co-chair Workforce 2010; founder, co-chair Ozaukee County Transp. Mgmt. Assn.; former bd. mem. Ozaukee County Econ. Devel. Corp.; bd. mem., capitol campaign mem. B.A.B.E.S. Recipient Celebrate Success award Wis. Women Entrepreneurs, 1993, named Outstanding Citizen, Grafton C. of C., Nat. Employer of Yr., Coun. for Exceptional Children Divsn. on Career Devel. and Transition, 1998, Outstanding Bus. of Yr., Grafton Area C. of C., 1998, Wis. Welfare-to-Work Small Bus. Person of Yr., U.S. Small Bus. Adminstrn., 1999; named Woman of Yr. Wis. Women Entrepreneurs, 2000. Mem. FOCUS (founder, past pres., past v.p.), Am. Staffing Assn. (nat. temporary help week regional chair), Wis. Assn. Pers. Svcs. (past pres.), Washington/Ozaukee County Pers. Mgmt. Assn. (past pres.), Ind. Bus. Assn. Wis. (past bd. dirs., past pres., past v.p. state programs, past welfare reform chair, Mem. of Yr. award 1999). Republican. Roman Catholic. Avocations: community service, playing piano, reading, politics. Office: SEEK Inc PO Box 148 Grafton WI 53024-0148

SCHNEIDER, CHARLES IVAN, newspaper executive; b. Chgo., Apr. 6, 1923; s. Samuel Hiram and Eva (Smith) S.; m. Barbara Anne Krause, Oct. 27, 1963; children: Susan, Charles I. Jr., Kim, Karen, Traci. BS, Northwestern U., 1944. Indsl. engr., sales mgr., v.p. mktg. and sales Curtis-Electro Lighting Corp., Chgo., 1945-54, pres., 1954-62, Jefferson Electronics, Inc., Santa Barbara, Calif., 1962-64; pres. 3 sub., v.p., asst. to pres. Am. Bldg. Maintenance Industries, Los Angeles, 1964-66; group v.p. Times Mirror Co., 1966-88, ret.; pvt. investor and cons., 1988—. Bd. dirs. Jeppesen Sanderson, Inc., Denver, Graphic Controls Corp., Buffalo, Regional Airports Improvement Corp. Bd. regents Northwestern U., Evanston, Ill.; trustee, past pres. Reiss-Davis Child Study Center, L.A.; bd. govs., past pres. The Music Ctr.; trustee the Menninger Found.; pres. St. John's Hosp. and Health Ctr. Found., Santa Monica, Calif. Served with AUS, 1942-44. Mem. Chief Execs. Orgn. (past pres., bd. dirs.). Clubs: Standard (Chgo.); Beverly Hills Tennis (Calif.); Big. Ten of So. Calif. Avocations: tennis, squash, music, reading. Home: 522 N Beverly Dr Beverly Hills CA 90210-3318 *An individual's growth and success as a manager are in direct proportion to his or her ability to develop, motivate and lead able, capable people.*

SCHNEIDER, CHRISTIAN CLAUS, veterinarian, researcher, investment company executive; b. Ingolstadt, West Germany, Oct. 20, 1964; s. Rolf-Dieter and Ingrid Schneider; m. Caecilia Schneider, Dec. 30, 1997. DVM, U. Munich, 1992, PhD in Vet. Sci., 1995; MBA, Pa. State U., 1999. Doctoral rsch. fellow Boehringer-Mannheim, Penzberg, Germany, 1992—94, postdoctoral rsch. fellow Germany, 1995; sr. rsch. scientist CENTOCOR Diagnostics, Malvern, Pa., 1995—98; new product planning mgr. CENTOCOR Inc., 1998—99, external rsch. mgr., 1999—2000; investment mgr. Polytechnos Venture Ptnrs., Munich, 2000—01, ptnr., 2002—. Contbr. articles to sci. and profl. jours. Recipient Golden award Pharmacia Sweden, London, 1993, Outstanding Young Scientist award, 1993; grantee Hanns-Seidel Found., Munich, 1993-95. Mem. Am. Assn. Clin. Chemistry, German Vet. Assn., Internat. Acad. Assembly. Avocations: sailing, mountaineering, skeet shooting, hiking. Office: Polytechnos Venture Ptnrs GmbH Promenade Platz 12 80333 Muenchen Germany E-mail: christian.schneider@polytechnos.com.

SCHNEIDER, CINDY E(LAINE) (LONES), financial advisor; b. Springfield, Ohio, Nov. 27, 1960; d. James K. Lones and Catherine May (Dellinger) Oldfield; children: Natasha May, Matthew W.; m. Brian J. Schneider, Nov. 27, 1999. AAS in Electronic Engring., AAS in Acctg., Columbus State C.C., 1993. HVAC electronic control tech. Creative Control Designs, Inc., Columbus, 1993—96. Owner Schneider's Tax and Bookkeeping Svc., Columbus, 1992—; ptnr. Oldfield's Baby Items, 2000—. Mem. Nat. Assn. Tax Profls., Am. Inst. Profl. Bookkeepers, WIBC. Republican. Avocations: pencil drawing, reading, bowling, electronics, philosophy. Office: Rear Bldg 1632 Harrisburg Pike Columbus OH 43223-3614 E-mail: taxprocindy@aol.com.

SCHNEIDER, CLARA GARBUS, dietitian, nursing consultant; b. Paterson, N.J., Sept. 2, 1955; d. Edward George and Constance (Murray) Garbus; m. Philip John Schneider, July 22, 1978; children: Amy L., Stephen P. BS, U. Del., 1977; MS, U. Md., 1979; postgrad., Marymount U., 1995-97. RN, Va.; registered dietitian. Nutritionist Woman, Infant and Children Feeding Program, Leesburg, Va., 1980-81, Barney Sr. Svcs., Washington, 1982-83; cons. dietitian Sharon Nursing Home, 1984-85, NAS, Washington, 1985; cons. Nat. Assn. WIC Dirs., Balt., 1990; cons. dietitian J.B. Johnson Nursing Ctr., Washington, 1990-93, Am. Inst. for Cancer Rsch., Washington, 1987—, Higher Horizons Head Start, Fairfax, Va., 1985-93, Arlington (Va.) Cmty. Action Program, 1985-98; nurse-dietician Inova/Vis. Nurses Assn., 1996—2001, INOVA Alexandria Diabetes Ctr., 2001—. Employment exch. coord. for dietitians D.C. Dietetic Assn., 1985-98; cons. dietitian Hospice Vis. Nurses Assn. No. Va., 1993-97. Author: Diabetic's Brand Named Food

Exchange Handbook, 1991; contbr. articles to profl. jours. Active Girl Scouts U.S., Arlington, 1989-95, Boy Scouts Am., 1992-98. Mem. Am. Dietetic Assn. Avocations: tennis, bike riding, skiing. Home and Office: 263 N Bryan St Arlington VA 22201-1418

SCHNEIDER, CYNTHIA PERRIN, ambassador, art historian, educator; b. Pa., Aug. 16, 1953; m. Thomas J. Schneider; 2 children. BA in Fine Arts magna cum laude, Harvard U., 1977, PhD in Fine Arts, 1984. Asst. curator European paintings Mus. Fine Arts, Boston, unitl 1984; asst. prof. art history Georgetown U., Washington, 1984-90, assoc. prof., 1990—; amb. to The Netherlands Am. Embassy, The Hague, 1998-2001. Lectr. on Rembrandt and Dutch art in U.S. and Europe. Author: Rembrandt's Landscapes, 1990; organizer, writer (catalog) Rembrandts Landscapes: Drawings and Prints, Nat. Gallery Art, Washington, 1990; contbr. articles to profl. jours. Former vice-chmn. President's Com. on Arts and Humanities, mem. steering com. for Creative Am. and millenium planning group, also chmn. fed. design subcom.; corrd. arts policy Clinton-Gore Campaign, 1992; past bd. dirs. Nat. Mus. Women in Arts, Australian-Am. Leagership Dialogue. Home: 17201 Norwood Rd Sandy Spring MD 20860 Office: US Embassy Lange Voorhout 102 The Hague Netherlands

SCHNEIDER, DAN W. lawyer, consultant; b. Salem, Oreg., Apr. 28, 1947; s. Harold Otto and Frances Louise (Warner) S.; m. Nancy Merle Schmalzbauer, Mar. 29, 1945; children: Mark Warner, Edward Michael. BA cum laude, St. Olaf Coll., 1969; JD, Willamette U., 1974; LLM, Columbia U., 1975. Bar: Oreg. 1974, D.C. 1978, Ill. 1987. Trial atty. U.S. Dept. Justice Antitrust, Washington, 1975-79; dep. assoc. dir. U.S. SEC, 1979-86; gen. ptnr. Schiff Hardin & Waite, Chgo., 1986-95; name ptnr. Smith Lodge & Schneider, 1995-98; ptnr. Hopkins & Sutter, 1998-2000; internat. ptnr. Baker & McKenzie, 2000—. Bd. dirs. NygaarArt, Northfield, Minn. Contbr. articles to profl. jours. Trustee, sec. Ill. Acad. Fine Arts, Chgo., 1990-98; mem. adv. bd. Steensland Art Mus., Northfield, 1990—; mem. adv. bd. Hallie Ford Mus. Art, Salem, Oreg., 1999—. Recipient 1st prize Nathan Burkan Law Essay Competition ASCAP, N.Y., 1974, Christie award Securities Transfer Assn., 1987. Mem. Met. Club. Chgo., Monroe Club, Plaza Club. Avocations: art collecting, art writing, music composition. Office: Baker & McKenzie 1 Prudential Plz 130 E Randolph St Ste 3700 Chicago IL 60601-6342 E-mail: dan.w.schneider@bakernet.com.

SCHNEIDER, DANIEL MAX, law educator; b. Cin., Sept. 13, 1948; s. Meyer R.and Berenice R. (Hecht) S.; children: Anna, Claire. AB, Washington U., St. Louis, 1970; JD, U. Cin., 1973; LLM, NYU, 1976. Bar: Ohio 1973, N.Y. 1978, Ill. 1992. Law clk. to presiding judge U.S. Dist. Ct. (so. dist.) Ohio, Columbus, Ohio, 1973-75; assoc. LeBoeuf, Lamb, Leiby & MacRae, N.Y.C., 1977-81, Murphey, Young & Smith, Columbus, 1981-84; prof. No. Ill. U., DeKalb, 1984—. Vis. prof. Washington U. Sch. Law, 1988, U. Wis. Law Sch., 1996, Fla. State U. Coll. Law, 2001, Washington U. Sch. Law, 2001. Author: Taxation of Dividends and Corporate Distributions, 1995; co-author: Federal Tax Aspects of Corporate Reorganizations, 1988; contbr. articles to profl. jours. Yale U. Law Sch. research fellow, 1976-77. Mem. Am. Law Inst. Office: No Ill Univ Coll Law Dekalb IL 60115

SCHNEIDER, DANIEL SCOTT, pediatric cardiologist; b. Mitchell, S.D., July 17, 1953; s. Robert George and Lois Irene (Theis) S.; m. Lisa Anne Magri, Oct. 22, 1988; children: Elizabeth, Emily, Luisa, Robert, Daniel. BS, Creighton U., 1975, MD, 1979. Diplomate Am. Bd. Pediat., Am. Bd. Pediat. Cardiology. Commd. ensign USN, 1979, advanced through grades to comdr., 1992; pediat. cardiologist Childrens Hosp. of the Kings Dau., Norfolk, Va., 1992—. Gen. bd. dirs. Cath. Charities of Hampton Rds., 1999—. Named Tchr. of Yr. Portsmouth Naval Hosp. Pediat. Residents, 1992; recipient Faculty Tchg. award Children's Hops. of Kings Daus., 2001. Mem. tidewater Down Syndrome Assn. (profl. adv. 1993—), Alpha Sigma Nu, Alpha Omega Alpha. Roman Catholic. Office: Childrens Hosp the Kings Daus 601 Childrens Ln Norfolk VA 23507-1910 E-mail: schneids@chkd.com.

SCHNEIDER, DAVID PAUL, SR. church administrator; b. Kansas City, Mo., Dec. 18, 1954; s. Paul Edward and Frances Nell (Keeney) S.; m. Sally Faye Narramore, Dec. 20, 1980 (div. June 1983); 1 child, Phillip Andrew; m. Christine Maria Hafner, Nov. 27, 1998; 1 child, John Paul. Student, La. State U., 1981-82, Oral Roberts U., 1987-89, St. Vladimir's Seminary, 1989-90. Sec., treas. Orthodox Ch. in Am. Diocese of N.Y. and N.J., Bronxville, 1990—2001; pres., CEO Schneider Martial Arts, Inc., Johnson City, Tex., 2002—. Avocations: history, humanities, karate, scuba diving, auxiliary police service. Office: Schneider Martial Arts Inc 1199 Ranch Rd 3232 Johnson City TX 78636

SCHNEIDER, DENNIS EUGENE, manufacturing company executive; b. Bellevue, Ohio, Dec. 27, 1957; s. Vernon Edwin and Marquerite Mary (Best) S.; m. Sandra Lynn Seavolt, June 26, 1982; children: Elaina Amanda, Alexander Nikita. BS, Bowling Green State U., 1981; MBA, Rockford Coll., 1995. Buyer Teledyne Continental Aviation and Engring. Co., Toledo, 1981-84; div. purchasing mgr. Tappan Appliances, Mansfield, 1984-85; corp. purchasing mgr. Marathon Electric Mfg. Corp., Wausau, Wis., 1985-88; materials mgr. Pacific Sci. Corp., Rockford, Ill., 1988-90; group materials mgr. Case Corp., Racine, Wis., 1990-93, ops. mgr., 1993-95, dir. global logistics, 1995-97, dir. supply chain Europe, Africa and Middle East, 1997; v.p. supply chain Allied Signal, Tempe, Ariz., 1998-2000; sr. v.p. supply chain and ops. World Kitchens, Elmira, NY, 2000—02; v.p. global ops. Stanley Tool Works, East Greenwich, RI, 2002—. Vol. Toledo Bid Bros./Big Sisters, 1982-85. Mem. Am. Prodn. and Inventory Control Soc., Nat. Assn. Purchasing Mgmt., Coun. Logistics Mgmt., Internat. Platform Assn., Ducks Unltd., Am. Chesapeake Club, KC. Republican. Roman Catholic. Avocations: history, dog tng., music, backpacking, wildlife art. Home: 213 Lincoln Rd Horseheads NY 14845-2267 Office: Stanley Tool Works Briggs Dr East Greenwich RI 02818

SCHNEIDER, DENNIS RAY, microbiology educator and executive; b. Sinton, Tex., June 10, 1952; 2 children. BA with honors, U. Tex., 1974, PhD, 1978. Post-doctoral fellow Behringwerke AG, Marburg/Lahn, West Germany, 1978-79; postdoctoral fellow U. Mo. Med. Sch., Columbia, 1980-81; rsch. microbiologist New England Nuc., North Billerica, Mass., 1981-82; dir. R & D Austin (Tex.) Biol. Lab., 1982-88; adj. assoc. prof. U. Tex., Austin, 1986—; dir. R & D devel. Micro-Bac Internat., 1988-94, v.p. Round Rock, Tex., 1994—. Author: Bioremediation: A Desktop Manual for the Environmental Professional; contbr. chpt. to Microorganism Adaptation to Host Defense. Grantee NASA, 1988, 92, 93. Mem. AAAS, Am. Soc. for Microbiology, Mensa, Profl. Assn. Dive Instrs. Avocations: scuba diving, writing. Office: Micro-Bac Internat 3200 N I H 35 Round Rock TX 78681-2410 E-mail: drdiver@mail.utexas.edu.

SCHNEIDER, DONALD FREDERIC, banker; b. N.Y.C., Nov. 12, 1939; s. Charles and Lillian S.; m. Mary Patricia McCafferty, Sept. 7, 1963; children—Laurie, John. BS, Lehigh U., 1961; MBA, N.Y. U., 1968. Mgmt. trainee Marine Midland Bank, N.Y.C., 1961-65, asst. sec., 1965-68, asst. v.p., 1968-69, v.p., 1969-79, 1st Nat. Bank Chgo., 1979-87; fin. cons. Cigna Individual Fin. Svcs. Co., Chgo., 1987; v.p. Irving Trust Co./Bank of N.Y., 1987-90, Citibank N.A., N.Y.C., 1990-96; MMS Assocs., Inc., 1997-99; retired, 1999. Mem. corp. trust activities com. Am. Bankers Assn., fiduciary and securities ops. exec. com. Mem. Am. Soc. Corporate Secs. (pres. Chgo. region 1987), Securities Transfer Assn. Home and Office: 13 Linton Ct Pinehurst NC 28374-9751 E-mail: donschneider@nc.rr.com.

SCHNEIDER, DUANE BERNARD, English literature educator, publisher; b. South Bend, Ind., Nov. 15, 1937; s. William H. and Lillian L. (Pitchford) S.; m. Crystal J. Gips; children: Jeffrey, Eric, Lisa, Emily. BA, Miami U., Oxford, Ohio, 1958; MA, Kent State U., 1960; PhD, U. Colo., 1965. Instr. engring. English U. Colo., 1960-65; asst. prof. English Ohio U., Athens, 1965-70, assoc. prof., 1970-75, prof., 1975-98, chmn. Faculty Senate, 1981-83, chmn. dept. English, 1983-86, prof. emeritus, 1998—; dir. Ohio U. Press, 1986-95; part-time faculty New Sch. U., N.Y.C., 2000—. Editor, pub. Croissant & Co., 1968-2002. Author: (with others) Anais Nin: An Introduction, 1979. Mem. Thomas Wolfe Soc. (trustee, pres. 1979-81). Home: 40 Daniel St Slingerlands NY 12159-9758

SCHNEIDER, EDGAR ROLF GOTTFRIED, retired mathematician, application developer, writer; b. Bklyn., Apr. 9, 1932; s. Richard Bernhard Grunewald and Sylvia Goldberg, Nathan Schneider; m. Sally Jane Mitchell, Oct. 3, 1959 (div.); children: Elisabeth Sutter, Christian, Eric; m. Alexandra Khan Kazan, June 26, 1999. BA, City Coll. of N.Y., 1954; MA, The Am. U., Washington, 1970. Mathematician, sci. computer programmer The Svc. Bur. Corp., N.Y.C., 1959—63, L.A., 1963—66, IBM Corp., Bethesda, Md., 1966—70, Warminster, Pa., 1974—75, Owego, NY, 1975—82. Spkr. Autism Soc. Fla., Fort Lauderdale, 1996—. Author: (novels) Discovering My Autism, 1999, Living the Good Life with Autism, 2002. Singer Fla. Philharmonic Chorus, Fort Lauderdale, 1974—2001. 2nd lt. U.S. Army, 1954—58. Mem.: Phi Beta Kappa, Sigma Xi. Democrat. Roman Catholic. Avocation: mathematics, science, art, music, photography, goumet cooking, small-bore rifle target shooting, history, literature, philosophy. Personal E-mail: hansachsthegreat@juno.com.

SCHNEIDER, EDWARD LEE, botanic garden administrator; b. Portland, Oreg., Sept. 14, 1947; s. Edward John and Elizabeth (Mathews) S.; m. Sandra Lee Alfarone, Aug. 2, 1968; children: Kenneth L., Cassandra L. BA, Ctrl. Wash. U., 1969, MS, 1971; PhD, U. Calif., Santa Barbara, 1974. From asst. to assoc. prof. botany S.W. Tex. State U., San Marcos, 1974-84, prof., 1984-94, chmn. biology dept., 1984-89, dean sci., 1989-92; pres., CEO Santa Barbara (Calif.) Botanic Garden, 1992—. Author: The Botanical World, CEOs and Trustees--Building Working Partnerships; contbr. articles to profl. jours. Bd. dirs. Ctr. for Plant Conservation. Recipient Presdl. Rsch. award S.W. Tex. State U., 1986, Disting. Alumnus award Ctrl. Wash. U., 1996; grantee NSF, 1980, 90. Fellow Tex. Acad. Sci. (pres. 1992-93); mem. Internat. Water Lily Soc. (bd. dirs., sec. 1989-96, inducted into Hall of Fame, Award of Appreciation 1997), Bot. Soc. Am. (bd. dirs., Award of Merit 1998), Am. Assn. Bot. Gardens and Arboreta (bd. dirs.), Internat. Pollination Congress, Nat. Coun. Deans, Am. Assn. Mus. (assessment program adv. com.). Home: 1140 Tunnel Rd Santa Barbara CA 93105-2134 Office: Santa Barbara Botanic Garden 1212 Mission Canyon Rd Santa Barbara CA 93105-2126 E-mail: eschneider@sbbg.org.

SCHNEIDER, EDWARD LEWIS, medicine educator, research administrator; b. N.Y.C., June 22, 1940; s. Samuel and Ann (Soskin) S. BS, Rensselaer Poly. Inst., 1961; MD, Boston U., 1966. Intern and resident N.Y. Hosp.-Cornell U., N.Y.C., 1966-68; staff fellow Nat. Inst. Allergy and Infectious Diseases, Bethesda, Md., 1968-70; research fellow U. Calif., San Francisco, 1970-73; chief, sect. on cell aging Nat. Inst. Aging, Balt., 1973-79, assoc. dir., 1980-84, dep. dir., 1984-87; prof. medicine, dir. Davis Inst. on Aging U. Colo., Denver, 1979-80; dean Leonard Davis Sch. Gerontology U. So. Calif., L.A., 1986—, exec. dir. Ethel Percy Andrus Gerontology Ctr., 1986—, prof. medicine, 1987—, William and Sylvia Kugel prof. gerontology, 1989—. Sci. dir. Buck Ctr. for Rsch. in Aging, 1989-98; cons. MacArthur Found., Chgo., 1985-93, R.W. Johnson Found., Princeton, N.J., 1982-87, Brookdale Found., N.Y.C., 1985-89. Editor: The Genetics of Aging, 1978, The Aging Reproductive System, 1978, Biological Markers of Aging, 1982, Handbook of the Biology of Aging, 1985, 95, 96, Interrelationship Among Aging Cancer and Differentiation, 1985, Teaching Nursing Home, 1985, Modern Biological Theories of Aging, 1987, The Black American Elderly, 1988, Elder Care and the Work Force, 1990, A Secure Old Age: Financing Long-Term Care, 1998. Med. dir. USPHS, 1968—. Recipient Roche award, 1964. Fellow Gerontology Soc., Am. Soc. Clin. Investigation; mem. Am. Assn. Retired Persons, U.S. Naval Acad. Sailing Squadron (coach 1980-86). Office: U So Calif Andrus Gerontology Ctr Los Angeles CA 90089-0001 E-mail: eschneid@usc.edu.

SCHNEIDER, EDWARD MARTIN, retired physician; b. Cleve., May 12, 1922; s. Sol S. and Beatrice Hilda (Sicherman) Schneider; m. Jane H. Einstein, June 18, 1950 (dec. Aug. 2001); children: Douglas A., Robert S.1 stepchild Donald E. Deutsch. Student, Northwestern U., 1940-43; MD, U. Cin., 1946. Diplomate Am. Bd. Internal Medicine. Intern Mt. Sinai Hosp., Cleve., 1946-47, asst. resident medicine, 1947-48, sr. asst. resident medicine, 1950-51; fellow in medicine Cin. Gen. Hosp., 1951-52; asst. prof. of medicine U. Okla. Sch. Medicine, Oklahoma City, 1952-57; sr. physician gastroenterology Miner's Meml. Hosp. Assn., McDowell, Ky., Beckley, W.Va., 1957-61; chief of medicine Cameron Meml. Hosp., Bryan, Ohio, 1961-62; chief medical rsch. sect. Upjohn Co., Kalamazoo, 1962-67; pvt. practice Woodland Hills, Calif., 1968-81. Author 17 rsch. papers. Capt. M.C., AUS, 1948-50. Fellow Am. Coll. Physicians, Am. Coll. Gastroenterologists; mem. Assn. Mil. Surgeons (life), Am. Assn. Study Liver Disease (emeritus), Soc. of Sigma Xi. Avocations: ham radio operating, music appreciation. Home: 1521 Lake Forest Dr Charlottesville VA 22901 E-mail: edwardmd@sprintmail.com.

SCHNEIDER, EDWIN KAHN, research scientist; b. Philadelphia, Pa., May 6, 1948; s. Abraham and Edna May Schneider; m. Penelope Lee Ganzel, Aug. 5, 1980; children: Andrew Ganzel, Thomas Schmidt. PhD, Harvard Univ., Cambridge, MA, 1970—75; AB, Harvard, Cambridge, MA, 1966—70, MS, 1970—75. Postdoctoral rsch. assoc. MIT, Cambridge, Mass., 1974—77; nato postdoctoral fellow Reading U., Reading, England, 1977—78; rsch. fellow/rsch. assoc. Harvard U., Cambridge, Mass., 1978—83; prin. rsch. scientist MIT, 1984—84; assoc./sr. rsch. scientist U. of Md., College Park, Md., 1984—93; sr. rsch. scientist Ctr. for Ocean-Land-Atmosphere Studies, Calverton, 1993—. Author: (peer-reviewed journal articles) J. Atmos. Sci., Mon. Wea. Rev., J. Climate, ICARUS, J. Geophys. Res., Quart. J. Roy. Met. Soc., PAGEOPH, Climate Dyn., Annales Geophysicae, J. Phys. Oceanogr., Bull. Amer. Meteor. Soc., Global and Planetary Change, (book chapter) Climate Change: An Integrated Perspective (Open University), (articles in reference book) Encyclopedia of Global Environmental Change (Wiley). Fellow NATO Postdoctoral Fellowship, NATO, 1977-1978, Fellowships For Grad. Edn., NSF, 1970-1972; grantee Money For And Computer Resourses For Rsch., Nsf, Noaa, Nasa, Doe, Epri, 1985-2002; scholar Nat. Merit Scholarship, 1966-1970. Mem.: Royal Meteorol. Soc., Am. Geophys. Union, Am. Meteorol. Soc. Achievements include research in Hadley circulation, El Nino/Southern Oscillation, atmospheric and oceanic dynamics, climate change. Avocations: orchestral violinist, orchestral violinist. Office: Center for Ocean-Land-Atmosphere Studies 4041 Powder Mill Rd Suite 302 Beltsville MD 20705

SCHNEIDER, ELAINE CAROL, lawyer, researcher, writer; b. Mpls., Aug. 28, 1957; d. Allan William and Deborah G. Schneider; m. William Mack Olivé, Oct. 10, 1987 (div. July 1996); 1 child Vanessa Inez Olivè ; m. G.R. Smith, Jan. 2, 2002. BA, U. Minn., 1979; JD, William Mitchell Coll. Law, St. Paul, 1982. Bar: N.Mex. 1984, Minn. 1998, D.C. 1999. Assoc. Settles, Kalamarides & Assocs., Anchorage, 1982, Dickson, Evans & Esch, Anchorage, 1982; legal rschr. John Hanson, 1983, 1983; acct. rep. Westlaw Svcs., Inc., Albuquerque, 1984, sales rep. New Orleans, 1985-86; libr. sales rep. West Pub. Co., Spokane, Wash., 1986-87, reference atty. St. Paul, 1988-97, product mgr., 1997-2001; pvt. practice Mpls. Ethics adv. bd. N.Mex. Bar, Albuquerque, 1984-85; midwest regional conf. com. Am. Immigration Lawyers Assn., 2000. Author: Substantive Judicial Law Outline of Habeas Corpus, 1984, What They Don't Teach You in the Bar Review Course, 1991, Challenging an Incredibility Finding on Appeal, An Incredibility Paradigm, 2001; mem. law rev. staff : William Mitchell Coll. Law, 1980—81. Atty. immigration and naturalization law Minn. Advocates for Human Rights, Refugee and Immigrant Project. Recipient Vol. Pro Bono Atty. award, 15th Ann. Minn. Advocates for Human Rights, 1999. Mem. Phi Beta Kappa. Avocations: ventriloquism, skiing, swimming, travel, languages. Office: 701 4th Ave S Ste 500 Minneapolis MN 55415-1810 E-mail: avocatecs@aol.com.

SCHNEIDER, EUGENE SAUL, retired microbiologist, laboratory administrator; b. N.Y.C., Apr. 28, 1920; s. Isreal and Gertrude (Mendelsohn) S.; m. Bertha Gollan, Feb. 18, 1945; 1 child, Myles Gordon. BS in Microbiology, Cornell U., 1942. Cert. med. technologist, microbiologist. Microbiologist 50th Gen. Hosp., 1942-45, Morrisania City Hosp., Bronx, N.Y., 1946; rsch. microbiologist Coll. Phys. and Surg., N.Y.C., 1946; microbiologist Tacoma Gen. Hosp., 1946-48; lab. dir. Pierce County Hosp., Tacoma, 1948-52, St. Helens Med. Labs., Tacoma, 1952-68, Nat. Health Labs., Kent, Wash., 1985-92, Meridian Valley Lab., Kent, 1992—. Founding pres. Wash. State Soc. Med. Tch., 1947-48, Wash. Soc. AMTs, 1963-66; mem. Stae Commn. on Alcoholism. Contbr. articles to profl. jours.; presenter in field. Mem. Tacoma Coun. on Alcoholism, 1961-75. 1st lt. U.S. Army, 1949-52. Recipient Disting. Citizen award, Olympia, Wash., 1972, Order of Golden Microscope, AMT, 1963. Mem. Anaerobic Soc. of the Ams. Democrat. Jewish. Avocations: painting, model railroading. Home: 6810 Opal Ln SW Tacoma WA 98498-6410 Office: Meridian Valley Clin Lab 515 W Harrison St Kent WA 98032-4403

SCHNEIDER, FRANK DAVID, family physician; b. Brookline, Mass., Aug. 12, 1961; s. Morris I. and Shirley R. (Freedman) S.; m. Peggy S. Lorton, Aug. 14, 1993; children: Michael, Brian, Daniel, Allison. BA, Boston U., 1983, MD, 1987; MS in Pub. Health, U. Mo., 1992. Diplomate Am. Bd. Family Practice; lic. physician N.C., Tex. Intern Duke U., Fayetteville, NC, 1987—88, resident in family practice, 1988—90; acad. fellow, clin. instr. dept. family and cmty. medicine U. Mo., Columbia, 1990—92; asst. prof. U. Tex. Health Sci. Ctr., San Antonio, 1992—98, dir. med. student edn. dept. family practice, 1993—99, assoc. prof., 1999—, residency dir., 1999—2002. Mem. staff Univ. Hosp., San Antonio, 1992, U. Mo. Hosp. and Clinics, Columbia, 1990, Santa Rosa Hosp., 1997; lectr. in field. Contbr. articles on family violence and med. edn. to profl. jours. Am. Acad. Family Physicians Found. grantee, 1994, HHS grantee, 1995, 98, 2000; recipient Tex. Acad. Family Physicians Rsch. award, 1996. Mem.: AMA (nat. adv. coun. violence & abuse 2001—, chair edn. com.), Tex. Med. Assn., Bexar County Med. Soc., Tex. Acad. Family Physicians (exec. com. 1997—, pres.-elect 2002—), Soc. Tchrs. Family Medicine (edn. com. 1987—2001, chmn. group on fellowship tng. 1991—93, chmn. group on violence edn. 1996—2000, family medicine curriculum project adv. com. 2001—), Am. Acad. Family Practitioners (commn. on pub. health 2001—), Assn. Am. Med. Colls. (group on edn. affairs 1998—). Office: U Tex Health Sci Ctr Dept Family Practice 7703 Floyd Curl MSC 7795 San Antonio TX 78229-3900 E-mail: fschneider@uthscsa.edu.

SCHNEIDER, FRANZ, investment counsel; b. N.Y.C., July 3, 1947; s. Franz and Elizabeth (Burns) S.; children: Franz Emerson, Andrew Oliver. AB, Harvard Coll., 1969, MPA, 1995, ALM in Psychology, 1999. Pvt. investor, N.Y.C., 1969-78; investment banker F. Eberstadt & Co., Inc., 1978-79; pres. Calif. Power & Light, San Francisco, 1979-84; investment adviser Marblehead, Mass., 1985-86; v.p., sr. trust officer First Nat. Bank, Ipswich, 1987-91; investment counsel Marblehead, 1991—; rsch. assoc. in psychopharmacology Harvard Med. Sch., McLean Hosp., Belmont, Mass., 1999—. Mem. Eastern Yacht Club, Royal Bermuda Yacht Club, Transpacific Yacht Club. Republican. Avocation: ocean racing. Office: 9 Harbor View Marblehead MA 01945 E-mail: franz69@post.harvard.edu.

SCHNEIDER, GEORGE, internist, endocrinologist; b. Boston, Oct. 29, 1939; s. Morris and Doris (Saslavsky) S.; m. Patricia Marian Seymour, Aug. 2, 1964; children: Andrew Gordon, Pamela Robin. AB, Harvard U., 1961; MD, Tufts U., Boston, 1965. Diplomate Am. Bd. Internal Medicine, Am. Bd. Internal Medicine in Endocrinology and Metabolism. Intern Bellevue Hosp., N.Y.C., 1965-66, asst. resident, 1966-67; assoc. resident Strong Meml. Hosp., Rochester, N.Y., 1969-70; fellow Yale U. Sch. of Medicine, New Haven, 1970-72; pvt. practice endocrinology Roseland, NJ, 1980—; chief endocrinology VA Hosp., East Orange, 1972-80, Beth Israel Med. Ctr., Newark, 1980—, St. Barnabas Med. Ctr., Livingston, 1994—. Med. dir. diabetes treatement ctr. Beth Israel Hosp., Newark, 1986-99. Contbr. over 36 articles to profl. jours., 1970-90 Lt. cmmdr. USPHS, 1967-69. Fellow ACP, Am. Coll. Endocrinology; mem. AMA, Acad. Medicine of N.J., Am. Diabetes Assn., Endocrine Soc., Alpha Omega Alpha. Avocations: tennis, travel, water sports, fishing, fine dining. Office: 204 Eagle Rock Ave Roseland NJ 07068-1718

SCHNEIDER, GEORGE T. obstetrician-gynecologist; b. New Orleans; s. George Edmond Schneider and Erna Marie Kraft; 1 child, Lynne Schneider Cantrell. Diploma, U. Heidelberg, Fed. Republic Germany, 1938; BS, Tulane U., 1941, MD, 1944. Intern Touro Infirmary, New Orleans, 1944-45, resident ob-gyn, 1945-47, U.S. Naval Hosp., Creat Lakes, Ill., 1947-48; vice chmn. Ochsner Med. Instns., New Orleans, 1960-86, cons., 1986—. Prof. ob-gyn Sch. Medicine, La. State U., New Orleans, 1965—. Contbr. articles to profl. jours. Bd. dirs. Assn. Internat. Edn., Houston, 1984—, YMCA New Orleans, 1985—, Am. Cancer Soc. La. Lt. USNR, 1945. Recipient Cert. of Merit Cancer Soc. El Salvador, 1980; named hon. counsul Honduras, 1988. Fellow ACS, Am. Coll. Ob-Gyn; mem. Ob-Gyn Soc. New Orleans (past pres.), Internat. Soc. Reproductive Medicine (past pres.), Hospitaliers Order St. Lazarus. Presbyterian. Office: Ochsner Med Instns 1514 Jefferson Hwy New Orleans LA 70121-2429 Fax: 504-842-4141. E-mail: g.t.schneidermd@aol.com.

SCHNEIDER, GEORGE WILLIAM, retired aircraft design engineer; b. Riley, Kans., Aug. 17, 1923; s. George William and Helen Juanita (Carey) S.; m. Marguerite Ann Bare, May 7, 1945 (div. Oct. 1977); children: Peggy Diane Schneider Tsolakopolous, Donald Lynn; m. L. Elaine Phillips, Oct. 22, 1977. Student, Wichita State U., 1952-58; BSME in Design, Kans. State U., 1962. Designer Ling Temco Vought, Dallas, 1962-65; lead designer 727 Boeing Airplane Co., Renton, Wash., 1965-66, lead designer 747 Everett, 1966-72, designer 707, 727, 737, AWACS Renton, 1972-75; designer DeHavilland Dash 7 Boeing Airplane Co., Toronto, Ont., Can., 1975-77; design engr. Boeing Airplane Co., Morgantown, W.Va., 1977-79, lead designer 757 Renton, 1980-81, sr. design engr. Oak Ridge, Tenn., 1981-83; ret., 1983. Vice chmn. Nat. Agenda Bd., 1995-96. Author books, articles, reports in field. Chmn. com. Explorer scouts Boy Scouts Am., Seattle, 1966-68. Mem. ASME (regional chmn. history and heritage 1991, regional nat. agenda bd. 1992-94, sec. nat. agenda bd. 1994-95, editor Dixie News regional news bull., chmn. govtl. rels. Greenville sect. 1990—, chmn. Greenville sect. 1989-93, chmn. awards and hons.), S.C. Coun. of Engring. Soc. (sec., treas. 1992-93, v.p. 1993-94, pres. 1994-95). Avocations: science, photography, travel, woodworking, fishing. Home: 211 Roper Mount Rd Ext Greenville SC 29615-4826

SCHNEIDER, GRETA, economist, speaker, author, security consultant; b. Bklyn. Student, Bklyn. Conservatory of Music, 1961—66; BA, MA, CUNY, 1975, MA, 1976. Writer, cons., Pitts., 1972-73; cons. Flushing, N.Y., 1973-85; sr. writer, cons. Buck Cons. Inc., N.Y.C., 1985-86; chmn., CEO Schneider Cons. Inc., 1986-90; pvt. cons. Greta Schneider Cons., 1991—; prin. Schneider Consulting Group, 1996—. Lectr. The Learning Annex, 1995-96, 2002, Seminar Ctr., N.Y.C., 1998-, others; advisor Am. Women's Econ. Devel. Corp., 1988—; adv. bd. Women's Profl. Coun., 1998; guest mem. discussion Reuters Bus. Report, 1998; mem. Women's Econ. Round Table , 1998; mem. Profl. Women's Adv. Bd., 1998; spkr. in field. Author: Exploding the Bankruptcy Mystique, 1993, Holistic Bankruptcy, 1998, 2002. Mem. Little Theatre Group, Marathon Cmty. Ctr., Little Neck, N.Y., 1980-83; founder, pres. Bankruptcy Anonymous, 1996; mem. Bklyn. Conservatory of Music, 1961-66. Cambridge Biographical Inst. fellow, 1993. Mem. AFTRA, Nat. Assn. Women Bus. Owners, Nat. Assn. Bus. Communicators, Internat. Platform Assn. (spkr. 2001), Employee Assistance Profls. Assn., Soc. Human Resource Mgmt., U.S. C. of C., Writers Guild Am., Rotary. Avocations: chef, pilot, tennis, chess, speech coach. Office: 130 W 30th St New York NY 10001-4004

SCHNEIDER, HAROLD LAWRENCE, lawyer; b. N.Y.C., June 24, 1942; s. Milton and Florence (Haimowitz) S.; m. Sandra Berkowitz, Aug. 3, 1974; children: Mara Susan, Douglas Howard. BS, CCNY, 1964; JD, Fordham U., 1967; LLM, NYU, 1968. Bar: N.Y. 1967. Ptnr. Kirkpatrick & Lockhart LLP, N.Y.C. Lectr. continuing legal edn. programs and bus. seminars. Editor Fordham Law Rev., 1967; contbr. articles to profl. jours. Mem. ABA, N.Y. State Bar Assn., N.Y.C. Bar Assn. Jewish. Avocations: sports memorabilia, reading, music, antiquing. Home: 305 E 86th St Apt 4J New York NY 10028-4702 Office: Kirkpatrick & Lockhart LLP Ste 4500 1251 Avenue Of The Americas New York NY 10020-1190

SCHNEIDER, HOWARD, lawyer; b. N.Y.C., Mar. 21, 1935; s. Abraham and Lena (Pincus) S.; m. Anne Evelyn Gorfinkle; children— Andrea Rose, Jeffrey Winston AB, Cornell U., 1956, JD with distinction, 1959. Bar: N.Y. 1959, D.C. 1976. Assoc., then ptnr. Stroock & Stroock, N.Y.C., 1959-75; gen. counsel Commodity Futures Trading Commn., Washington, 1975-77, Rosenman & Colin, N.Y.C., 1977—. Contbr. articles to profl. jours. Served to capt. USAR, 1956-66 Mem.: Assn. Bar of City of N.Y. (chmn. com. 1982—86), ABA (chmn., com. on regulation of futures and derivative insts. 1997—2001). Republican. Jewish. Home: 830 Park Ave New York NY 10021-2757 Office: Rosenman & Colin 575 Madison Ave New York NY 10022-2585 E-mail: hschneider@rosenman.com.

SCHNEIDER, JAMES JOSEPH, military theory educator, consultant; b. Oshkosh, Wis., June 18, 1947; s. Joseph Edward and Virginia Gertrude Schneider; m. Peggy L. Spees, July 28, 1973 (dec. May 1976); m. Claretta Virginia Burton, Nov. 11, 1984; children: Kevin, Jason, Jenifer, Julie. BA, U. Wis., Oshkosh, 1973, MA, 1974; PhD, U. Kans., 1992. Planning evaluator Winnegago County, Oshkosh, 1978-80; ops. rsch. analyst Tng. and Doctrine Command Analysis Ctr., Ft. Leavenworth, Kans., 1980-84; prof. mil. theory Sch. Advanced Mil. Studies U.S. Army Command and Gen. Staff Coll., 1984—. Adj. assoc. prof. history Russian and East European Studies Ctr., U. Kans., 1994—; vis. assoc. prof. philosophy St. Mary Coll., Leavenworth, Kans., 2000. Author: (monograph) Exponential Decay of Armies in Battle, 1985, The Structure of Strategic Revolution, 1994; also numerous articles. With U.S. Army, 1965-68, Vietnam. Recipient medal for civilian achievement Dept. Army, 1989, superior civilian svc. award, 2001, Bronze Order of St. George, U.S. Cav. Assn., 1990 Mem. Am. Hist. Assn., Mil. Ops. Rsch. Soc., Alpha Pi chpt. Phi Beta Delta. Office: U S Army Command/Gen Staff Coll Sch Advanced Mil Studies Fort Leavenworth KS 66027

SCHNEIDER, JAN, retired obstetrics and gynecology educator; b. Prague, Czechoslovakia, Dec. 10, 1933; came to U.S., 1963, naturalized, 1967; s. Evzen and Erika S.; m. Sandra Wilson, May 20, 1961; children— Hana, Donald, Kathryn, Jonathan. M.B., U. London, 1957; M.P.H., U. Mich., 1967. Prof. ob-gyn, chief obstetric service dept. ob-gyn U. Mich. Med. Sch., Ann Arbor, 1963-77; prof., chmn. ob-gyn. Med. Coll. Pa. and Hahnemann U., Phila., 1978-97, assoc. dean, 1997-99; ret., 1999. Editor: (with R. J. Bolognese and R. H. Schwarz) Perinatal Medicine, 2d edit, 1981. Fellow Am. Coll. Obstetricians and Gynecologists, Soc. Perinatal Obstetricians, Am. Gynecol. and Obstet. Soc., Phila. Obstet. Soc. Presbyterian.

SCHNEIDER, JANE HARRIS, sculptor; b. Trenton, N.J., Jan. 2, 1932; d. Leon Harris and Dorothy (Perlman) Rosenthal; m. Alfred R. Schneider, July 25, 1953; children: Lee, Jeffry, Elizabeth. BA, Wellesley Coll.; postgrad., Columbia U., Coll. New Rochelle. Exhibitions include in numerous group and solo shows June Kelly Gallery, 1988, 1990, 1993, 1995, 1997, 2000, 2001, Collaborative Concepts, Cold Spring, N.Y., 1998—99, 2001, Nassau County Mus. Fine Art, Roslyn, N.Y., 1988, Alternative Mus., N.Y.C., 1985, Phila. Art Alliance, 1984, Atrium Gallery, St. Louis, 1993, 1996, 1997, 1999, exhibitions include in numerous group and solo shows, 2001, exhibitions include in numerous group and solo shows Bill Bace Gallery, 1992, Triplex Gallery, N.Y.C., 1991, Rockland Ctr. for Arts, West Nyack, N.Y., 1990, Hudson River Mus., Yonkers, N.Y., 1989, Sculpture Ctr., N.Y.C., 1988, Quietude Gardens Gallery, East Brunswick, N.J., 1997, 1998, Isis Conceptual Lab., West Branch, Iowa, 1997, 1998, Interch. Ctr., 2001, Gallery 128, N.Y.C., 1999—2001, many others, Represented in permanent collections Fine Arts Mus. L.I., Davis Mus. and Cultural Ctr., Wellesley, Mass., Paterson (N.J.) Mus., N.J. State Mus., Trenton, Ark. Art Ctr., Little Rock, Neuberger Mus., Purchase, N.Y., Kutztown (Pa.) U., Munson-Williams Proctor Inst., Utica, N.Y. Avocations: swimming, gardening, fabricating furniture. Studio: 75 Grand St New York NY 10013-2235 E-mail: jhsart@earthlink.net.

SCHNEIDER, JANET M. arts administrator, curator, painter; b. N.Y.C., June 6, 1950. d. August Arthur and Joan (Battaglia) S.; m. Michael Francis Sperendi, Sept. 21, 1985. BA summa cum laude, Queens Coll., CUNY, 1972; spl. study fine arts Boston U. Tanglewood Inst., 1971. With Queens Mus., Flushing, N.Y.C., 1973-89, curator, 1973-75, program dir., 1975-77, exec. dir., 1977-89. Collections arranged include: Sons and others, Women Artists See Men (author catalog), 1975, Urban Aesthetics (author catalog), 1976, Masters of the Brush, Chinese Painting and Calligraphy from the Sixteenth to the Nineteenth Century (co-author catalog), 1977, Symcho Moszkowicz: Portrait of the Artist in Postwar Europe (author catalog), 1978, Shipwrecked 1622, The Lost Treasure of Philip IV (author catalog), 1981, Michaelangelo: A Sculptor's World (author catalog), 1983, Joseph Cornell: Revisited (author catalog), 1992, Blueprint for Change: The Life and Times of Lewis H. Latimer (co-author catalog), 1995. Chmn. Cultural Instns. Group, N.Y.C., 1986-87; mem. N.Y.C. Commn. for Cultural Affairs, 1991-93; bd. dirs. N.Y.C. Partnership, 1987-88, Gallery Assn. N.Y. State 1979-81; exec. dir. Cultural Inst. Group, 1995—. Mem. Artists Choice Mus. (trustee 1979-82), Am. Assn. Mus., Phi Beta Kappa.

SCHNEIDER, JAYNE BANGS, retired school librarian; b. Cin., Nov. 9, 1950; d. Neil Kendrick and Edith (Dilworth) Bangs; m. James R. Bronn, June 9, 1973 (div. 1979); m. Arthur Schneider, July 11, 1986; 1 stepdaughter, Heather. BS in Elem. Edn., Ea. Ky. U., 1973; MA in Libr. Sci., Spaulding U., 1978. Tchr., 1st & 2d grades Fort Thomas (Ky.) Pub. Schs./Ruth Moyer Elem., 1973; libr. Lassiter Middle Sch., Ky., 1973-2000. Presenter Nat. Middle Sch. Assn., St. Louis, 1988, Denver, 1989, Assn. of Ind. Media Educators, 1992. Mem. Ky. Hist. Soc., Friends of the Libr.; co-capt. Block Watch. Recipient Outstanding Media Librarian award Jefferson County, 1998; named Superstar Ky. Ednl. TV; Owen Badgett grantee Louisville Community Grant, 1988. Mem. NEA, ALA, AASL, PTSA (life), Nat. Mid. Sch. Assn., Jefferson County Sch. Media Assn. (treas. 1982-83, sec. 1991-92, newsletter editor 1992-93, pres.-elect 1993-94, pres. 1994-95, nomination chairperson 1996-97, bd. dirs. 1997-2000, named Jefferson County's Outstanding Sch. Media Librarian 1998), Ky. Sch. Media Assn. (bd. dirs. 1994-95, 97-98). Presbyterian. Avocations: genealogy, collecting antique glass, knitting. Home: 2553 Kings Hwy Louisville KY 40205-2646 E-mail: jaynesch@aol.com.

SCHNEIDER, JOAN, public relations company executive; BA, Boston U., 1972; postgrd., Harvard U. Pres. Schneider & Assocs., 1980—. Office: 240 Newbury St Boston MA 02116-3609

SCHNEIDER, JOANNE, artist; b. Lima, Ohio, Dec. 4, 1919; d. Joseph and Laura (Office) Federman; m. Norman Schneider, May 15, 1941; children— Melanie Schneider Tucker, Lois Schneider Oppenheim. B.F.A., Syracuse U., 1941. One-man shows John Heller Gallery, N.Y.C., 1954, 55, 57, 58, Tirca Karlis Gallery, Provincetown, Mass., 1963, Frank Rehn Gallery, N.Y.C., 1965, 66, 69, 72, 75, Elaine Benson Gallery, Bridgehamton, N.Y., 1972, 74, 79, 85, St. Mary's Coll., St. Mary's City, Md., 1978, Alonzo Gallery, N.Y.C., 1978, Discovery Art Gallery, Clifton, N.J., 1978; group shows include Whitney Mus., N.Y.C., Pa. Acad. Arts, Corcoran Galleries, Washington, Toledo Mus., U. Nebr., Everson Mus., Syracuse, N.Y.; represented in permanent collections Met. Mus. Art, N.Y.C., Colby Coll., Syracuse U., Butler Inst., St. Mary's Coll., U. Notre Dame, Guild Hall, East Hampton, N.Y. Recipient Audubon Artists Stanley Grumbacher Meml. award, 1972 Address: 35 E 75th St New York NY 10021-2761 *A life spent in pursuit of creative expression is a fuller, more satisfying life.*

SCHNEIDER, JOHN ARNOLD, business investor; b. Chgo., Dec. 4, 1926; s. Arnold George and Anna (Wagner) S.; m. Elizabeth C. Simpson, Oct. 20, 1951; children: Richard Ward, William Arnold, Elizabeth Anne. BS, U. Notre Dame, 1948. Exec. assignments with CBS-TV in, Chgo. and N.Y.C., 1950-58; v.p., gen. mgr. sta. WCAU-TV, Phila., 1958-64; sta. WCBS-TV, N.Y.C., 1964-65; pres. CBS TV Network, 1965-66, CBS/Broadcast Group, 1966-69, 71-77; exec. v.p. CBS, Inc., 1969-71, sr. v.p., from, 1977; pres., chief exec. officer MTV Networks, Inc., 1979-84. Trustee, mem. exec. com. U. Notre Dame; trustee Com. for Econ. Devel. Served with USNR, 1943-46. Mem.: Indian Harbor Yacht. Roman Catholic. Home: 155 Clapboard Ridge Rd Greenwich CT 06831-3304

SCHNEIDER, JULIA, library director; b. St. Joseph, Mo., Feb. 17, 1947; d. Lewis Wilber and Rosella Thompson; m. Thomas Edwin Schneider, Jan. 31, 1975; children: Jedd Christian, Jeremy Adam, Jacob Martin. AA, Mo. Western State Coll., 1967; BA, N.W. Mo. State U., 1969; MA, U. Mo., 1971. Cataloger St. Joseph Pub. Libr., 1969-70; acquisitions libr. Mo. Western State Coll., St. Joseph, 1971-75, tech. processes libr., 1975-83, coord. tech. svcs., 1983-90, libr. dir., 1990—. V.p. Mo. Libr. Network Corp., St. Louis, 1998—2001, pres., 2001—; treas. MOBIUS Consortium, Columbia, Mo., 1998—2001. Mem. St. Joseph Area Literacy Coalition, 1994—; mem. fund drive steering com. Allied Arts Assn., St. Joseph, 1991—; vol. United Way, St. Joseph, 1990—. Mem. Mo. Libr. Assn. (pres. 1994), The Runcie Club, Bus. and Profl. Women (pres. 1998, 99), Delta Kappa Gamma, Beta Phi Mu. Methodist. Avocations: antiques, music, organ. Home: 4908 NE County Line Rd Saint Joseph MO 64505-9329 Office: Mo Western State Coll 4525 Downs Dr Saint Joseph MO 64507-2246

SCHNEIDER, KAREN BUSH, lawyer, educator; b. Lansing, Mich., Mar. 17, 1951; d. Gerard Joseph and Emily Virginia (Szoka) Bush; 1 child, Emily Margaret. BA magna cum laude, U. Notre Dame, 1973, JD, 1976. Bar: Mich. 1976, U.S. Dist. Ct. (we. dist.) Mich. 1976, U.S. Dist. Ct. (ea. dist.) Mich. 1981. From assoc. to ptnr. Foster, Swift, Collins & Smith P.C., Lansing, 1976-88; ptnr. White, Schneider, Young & Chiodini, P.C., Okemos, Mich., 1988—, pres., 1994—97, 1999—2001. Adj. prof. Thomas M. Cooley Law Sch., Lansing, 1985—, vis. prof., 1988-89; mem. jud. qualifications com. State Bar Mich., 1987-91; arbitrator, Mich. Employment Rels. Commn., 1990—. Contbr. legal briefs to profl jours., quarterly articles to Greater Lansing Bus. Monthly mag., Lansing. Mem. adv. coun. Wharton Ctr., 2001—. Recipient Frederick Griffiths award for Tchg. Excellence, Thomas M. Cooley Law Sch., 2000. Fellow Mich. State Bar Found.; mem. Am. Arbitration Assn. (labor arbitrator 1985—), Ingham County Bar Assn. (bd. dirs., sec. 1982-83, pubs. com. 1983-85, chmn. pubs. com. 1984-85), Am. Lung Assn. Mich. (bd. dirs. 1985-89, chmn. pers. com. 1986-89), U. Notre Dame Alumni Assn. of Lansing (sec. 1979-80, pres. 1980-81, pub. rels. officer 1981-82, v.p. 1983-85), Capital Area Humane Soc. (bd. dirs. 1984-90, corr. sec. 1984, rec. sec. 1985, fundraising chmn. 1985-90, pres. 1986), State Bar of Mich. (continuing edn. com. 1997—, Biennial Diana award for profl. and cmty. svc. 1999). Roman Catholic. Avocations: fitness swimming, gourmet cooking. Home: 16717 Thorngate Rd East Lansing MI 48823-9772 Office: White Schneider Young & Chiodini PC 2300 Jolly Oak Rd Okemos MI 48864-3546 E-mail: Kschneider@wsbyc.com.

SCHNEIDER, KIRK J. psychologist, writer, psychologist, educator; b. Cleve., July 27, 1956; s. Murray Harold Schneider and Laura Siegal; m. Jurate Elena Raulinaitis, Sept. 17, 1989. BA in Psychology, Ohio State U., 1978; MA in Psychology, West Ga. Coll., 1979; PhD in Psychology, Saybrook Inst., 1984. Lic. psychologist Mass., Calif. Suicide prevention staff Columbus Mental Health Ctr., 1977—78; family therapy trainee Ohio State U., 1978—79; counseling intern West Ga. Coll., 1978—79, grad. tchg. asst., 1978; adv. psychology trainee N.E. Cmty. Mental Health Ctr./Fairhill Psychiat. Hosp., East Cleveland, Ohio, 1979—80; intern, supervisee InterLogue-James F.T. Bugental, PhD, Santa Rosa, Calif., 1980—83; post-doctoral trainee Massillon (Ohio) State Hosp., 1984—85; staff psychologist Human Resources Inst., Norton, Fall River, Mass., 1985—87; pvt. practice, founder Ctr. for Existential Therapy, San Francisco, 1987—. Staff psychologist Ctr. for Nutritional Rsch., Quincy, Mass., 1987—88; mem. crisis counseling team Merrill-Lynch & Co., Boston, 1988; staff psychologist South Shore Coun. on Alcohol, Quincy, 1988—89; pres. Existential-Humanistic Inst., San Francisco, 1999—2001, instr., 1997—; adj. faculty Lesley Coll., Cambridge, 1986—90, Bentley Coll., Waltham, Mass., 1989, Union Inst., Cin., 1989—90, Calif. Sch. Profl. Psychology, Berkeley, Alameda, 1990—96, The Profl. Sch. Psychology, San Francisco, 1992, Saybrook Grad. Sch., San Francisco, 1995—, Calif. Inst. Integral Studies, San Francisco, 1996—, clin. supr., 1990—; adj. faculty Ctr. for Humanistic Studies, Detroit, 2001—; spkr. in field. Author, editor: The Paradoxical Self: Toward an Understanding of Our Contradictory Nature, 1990, author, editor: Horror and the Holy: Wisdom-teachings of the Monster Tale, 1993, author, editor: The Psychology of Existence: An Integrative, Clinical Perspective, 1995, author, editor: The Handbook of Humanistic Psychology: Leading Edges in Theory, Research, and Practice, 2001; contbr. chapters to books, articles to profl. jours. Pres. Existential-Humanistic Inst., San Francisco, 1999—. Fellow: APA; mem.: AAAS, Assn. for Humanistic Psychology. Office: Saybrook Grad Sch 450 Pacific St San Francisco CA 94133

SCHNEIDER, LAZ LEVKOFF, lawyer; b. Columbia, S.C., Mar. 15, 1939; s. Philip L. and Dorothy Harriet (Levkoff) S.; m. Ellen Linda Shiffrin, Dec. 12, 1964; 1 child, David Allen. BA, Yale U., 1961, LLB, 1964; LLM, NYU, 1965. Bar: D.C. 1965, N.Y. 1965, Fla. 1970. Assoc. Fulton, Walter & Duncombe, N.Y.C., 1965-67, Roseman, Colin Kaye Petschek Freund & Emil, N.Y.C., 1967-69, Kronish, Lieb, Weiner, Shainswit & Hellman, N.Y.C., 1969-70; ptnr. Ruden Barnett McClosky & Schuster, Ft. Lauderdale, Fla., 1970-80, Sherr, Tiballi, Fayne & Schneider, Ft. Lauderdale, 1986-91, Berger Singerman, Ft. Lauderdale, 1991—; pvt. practice, 1980-86. Bd. dirs. Ocean Biochem. Inc. Grad. editor Tax Law Rev., 1964-65. Exec. com. Fla. regional bd. Anti Defamation League, 1972—. Mem. Fla. Bar Assn., Broward County Bar Assn. (chmn. sect. corp. bus. and banking law 1978-80), Yale Club (pres. 1977-79). Jewish. Office: 350 E Las Olas Blvd Ste 1000 Fort Lauderdale FL 33301-4215 E-mail: Lschneider@bergersingerman.com., lazsch@att.net.

SCHNEIDER, MAHLON C. lawyer; b. 1939; BA, U. Minn., 1962, LLB, 1964. Bar: Minn. 1965. Atty. Green Giant Co., 1980, Pillsbury, 1980-84, v.p., gen. counsel foods divsn., 1984-89; corp. atty. Geo. A. Hormel & Co., Austin, Minn., 1989-90, v.p., gen. counsel, 1990-99, sr. v.p. external affairs, gen. counsel, 1999—. Office: Hormel Foods Corp 1 Hormel Pl Austin MN 55912-3680

SCHNEIDER, MARK, political science educator; b. N.Y.C., Oct. 28, 1946; s. Irving and Ida (Schwartz) S.; m. Susan Roth, June 27, 1986; children: Johanna, Elizabeth. BA, Bklyn. Coll., 1967; PhD, U. N.C., 1974. vis. scholar Russell Sage Found., 1997-98. Asst. prof. polit. sci. U. Mich., Ann Arbor, 1973-74, SUNY, Stony Brook, 1974-78, assoc. prof., 1978-85, prof., 1985—, chmn. dept., 1986—. Fulbright sr. lectr., India, 1980-81. Author: The Competitive City, 1989, Public Entrepreneurs, 1995, Choosing Schools, 2000; contbr. articles to profl. jours. Mem. Am. Polit. Sci. Assn. (v.p. 2000-01), Midwest Polit. Sci. Assn. Office: SUNY Dept Polit Sci Stony Brook NY 11794-0001

SCHNEIDER, MARK LEWIS, government official; b. Newark, Dec. 31, 1941; s. Benjamin and Ruth (Kobran) S.; m. Susan Gilbert, June 20, 1965; children: Aaron Mitchell, Miriam Beth. AB in Journalism with honors, U. Calif., Berkeley, 1963; MA in Polit. Sci., San Jose State Coll., 1965; LLD (hon.), Am. U., 2000. Reporter UPI, San Francisco, 1963-64, San Francisco News Call Bull., 1965; vol. Peace Corps, El Salvador, 1966-68; reporter Washington Daily News, 1969-70; mem. staff U.S. Senate Judiciary Subcom., 1970-71; legis. asst. to Sen. Edward M. Kennedy, 1971-77, 80-81; dep. asst. sec. for human rights Dept. State, Washington, 1977-79; mem. del. UN Gen. Assembly, 1978, UN Human Rights Commn., 1979; coordinator policy planning, sr. advisor Pan Am. Health Orgn., 1981-93; adminstr. for Latin Am. and Caribbean U.S. AID, 1993-99; dir. The Peace Corps, 1999-2001; sr. v.p. Internat. Crisis Group, Washington, 2001—. Lectr. Kennedy Inst. Politics, Harvard U., 1976; adj. prof. Georgetown U., 1996. Bd. dirs. Internat. Human Rights Law Group, 1981-92. Fulbright fellow, 1976; Recipient George W. Eastman medal for pub. svc. U. Rochester, 2000. Mem. Am. Polit. Sci. Assn., Latin Am. Studies Assn. Democrat. Jewish. Home: 3517 Tilden St NW Washington DC 20008-3122

SCHNEIDER, MARTIN AARON, photojournalist, ecologist, engineer, writer, artist, TV director, filmmaker, public advocate, educator, university instructor, lecturer, inventor; b. N.Y.C., Sept. 23, 1926; s. Morris and Florence (Frohlich) S. Student, Stuyvesant Science, 1941-44; BC, CUNY, 1953. Editor Nocturne; artist, 1941—; photographer, 1954—. Photojournalist Life, Time, Newsweek, Sports Illustrated, N.Y. Times, NBC-TV, Ency. Britannica, Mpls. Tribune, Handball Illustrated, Time Annual Year in Review, Grolier Ency., Crowell-Collier Ency., NBC Startime, Variety, Time-Life: Ecology, Saturday Review of Literature, 1960—; ecologist, USPHS, U.S. Senate, U.S. EPA, N.Y.C.EPA, N.Y. State Dept. Environ. Conservation, N.Y.C. Dept. Air Pollution, 1964—; product safety engineer, designer, builder, crash-safety, pollution and radiation monitoring, multi-alternate fuel, laboratory vehicle, stereotactic radiosurgery: safer therapy delivery collimator, 1967—, instr., lectr. NYU, Cornell U., Ithaca, NY, New Sch. Social Rsch., N.Y.C., SUNY, Albany, Cooper Union for Advancement of Sci. and Art, N.Y.C., CUNY, Iowa U., lectr. in field, 1969—; pub. advocate, N.Y.C. Health Dept., N.Y. State Health Dept., N.Y. State Dept. Environ. Conservation, Gov. Rockefeller's State Study Commission for N.Y.C. (Scott Commission), U.S. District Ct., N.Y. Supreme Ct.; People of N.Y.C., N.Y.C. Council, N.Y. Attorney General, 1970—. TV news guest NBC Today, CBS, ABC, FOX, PBS, 1970—; radio news guest NBC, CBS, NPR, 1970; TV and radio commentator, NBC, CBS, ABC, PBS, Fox, 1970—; author: Breath of Death, 1972, Consumer Genocide: Censored Survival Kit 1992; The Schneider Tapes, 1996, War Against War, ed. 1996, Crash Genocide: Millions Killed by Suppressed 75 mph Safety, 1997, The Food You Eat--Eats You: How to Get Safe Food in same Stores at Same Price, 1998; co-author: NBC Startime, 1963, America-Photographic Statements, 1972, Eye of Conscience, 1974; dir., prodr., writer, videographer, cinematographer (TV documentaries) Environment Crusade, CBS, 1970, The Poisoned Air, CBS, 1970, Killers of the Environment, NBC, 1971, Censorship of Pollution Solutions by Media and Government, PBS, 1974, No Justice for Victims-Criminals Only, 1992; contbr. N.Y. Times, Ency. Britannica, Macmillan Ency. of Photographic Artists, N.Y. Village Voice "Whole Earth Ranger: Ecology's Batman", New World Or No World (Frank Herbert) 1970—; photography exhibited at Mus. Modern Art, N.Y.C., 1958—, George Eastman House Mus., Rochester, N.Y., 1963, 64—, Libr. Congress, 1970, Smithsonian Instn., 1972—, Art Inst. Chgo., 1973—, Whitney Mus., N.Y.C., 1978—; permanent exhibit includes N.Y. Mus. of TV and Radio; painting exhibited at Guggenheim Mus., N.Y.C., 1943; film exhibited at Am. Mus. Natural History, N.Y.C., 1969-72, network TV guest appearances; dir. documentaries. Served with U.S. Army Paratroopers, 1944-46, PTO. Fellowship grantee Creative Artists Pub. Svc., 1977, 78; recipient TV Franny Consumer Advocacy award, 1974, for work that was a basis for the first Clean Air Act of 1970. Jewish. Office: 545 8th Ave Ste 401 New York NY 10018 *Where millions are endangered where my work makes a difference--despite gunfire, vehicle sabotage, seizure of home and all possessions, censorship--there is no dream for me in moving mere mountains, but only in moving man to move himself.*

SCHNEIDER, MARY LOUISE, retired elementary education educator; b. Waterville, Wash., Oct. 17, 1918; d. John Steve and Alice Ray (Jones) S. *Her Great-grandfather, Gothard Schneider, who was born in Germany in 1808, then immigrated to the U.S., in July 1857. Grandfather, John Schneider, who was born in Germany then immigrated to the U.S. in July 1857 with his parents. Her Grandmother, Mary Krueger was born in Riga, Russia, May 1, 1869. Her maternal ancestors were descendents of Nathaniel Pendleton, a minister, and Phillip Pendleton, a schoolmaster who in about 1674 left Norfolk, England to settle in Virginia in America.* BA in Edn., Holy Names Coll., 1940. Cert. elem. tchr., Wash. Tchr. Mud Springs/Douglas County, Mansfield, Wash., 1941-42; elem. tchr. Mansfield Sch. dist., Douglas County, 1942-43, Waterville (Wash.) Sch. Dist., Douglas County, 1943-49, Lewis and Clark Elem. Sch., Wenatchee, 1949-60; spl. reading tchr. H.B. Ellison Jr. High, 1960-62, Orchard Jr. High, Wenatchee, 1962-67; lang. arts tchr. Pioneer Jr. High, 1967-77; retired, 1977. Author lang. arts learning packages for students, 1967; co-author: Name on the Schoolhause, 1989. Vol. Am. Heart Assn., Wenatchee, 1975-90, Am. Cancer Soc., Wenatchee, 1975-88. Recipient Cert. of Recognition, Wash. State Ct. Cath. Daus. of the Ams., 1970, 72, 74. Mem.: AAUW (treas. 1973—75), PEO (pres. 1980—82, 1988—90), Chelan-Douglas County Sch. Retirees Assn. (com. chmn. 1989—90), Cath. Daus. of the Ams. (state pres. 1984—86, nat. evangelization chmn. 1986—88, local ct. pres. 1958—60, 1999—2001, author Wash. State Ct. of Cath. Daus. 1988). Avocation: sewing.

SCHNEIDER, MATTHEW ROGER, lawyer; b. N.Y.C., Nov. 7, 1948; s. Theodore David Schneider and Rosalind (Schwartz) Werner; m. Marjorie Ann Friedlander, Mar. 6, 1976; children: Adam Benjamin, Emily Beth. BA, Cornell U., 1970; student, Georgetown U., 1971; JD, Cath. U., Washington, 1974. Bar: D.C. 1976, U.S. Dist. Ct. D.C., 1994. Staff asst. U.S. Senate Jud. Com., Washington, 1973-74; counsel U.S. Senate Govt. Ops. Com., 1974-77; spl. asst. Office of Sec. Def., 1977-79; dir. legis. affairs SEC, 1979-81, sr. counsel, divsn. corp. fin., 1981-82; chief of staff U.S. Senator Jeff Bingaman, 1983-85; prin. Law Office Matthew Schneider, 1985-87; ptnr. Willkie, Farr & Gallagher, 1987-95, Garvey, Schubert & Barer, 1996-98; mng. dir. D.C. office Garvey, Shubert & Barer, Washington, 1998—. Bd. dirs. Nat. Epilepsy Found., 2000—, mem. exec. com., 2001—; Bd. dirs Capitol Hill Hosp., Washington, 1987—95, chmn. govt. and legal affairs com., 1997—. Avocations: physical fitness training, singing, guitar. Office: Garvey Schubert & Barer 5th Fl 1000 Potomac St NW Ste 5 Washington DC 20007-3501

SCHNEIDER, MAX ALEXANDER, physician, educator; b. Buffalo, June 29, 1922; s. Henry Nathanial and Ruth Irene (Alexander) S.; life ptnr. Ronald F. Smelt. MD, SUNY, 1949. Cert. Am. Soc. Addiction Medicine; diplomate Am. Bd. Med. Examiners. Residency internal medicine Buffalo Gen. Hosp., 1950-52, internship, 1949-50; instr. in medicine SUNY, Buffalo, 1953-64; fellow Harvard Med. Sch., Boston, 1952-53; clinical assoc. prof. Univ. Calif., Irvine, 1989-96; medical dir. Beverly Manor/Care Hosp., Orange, Calif., 1969-76; clinical prof. U. Calif., Irvine, 1996—; edn. dir. chem. dependency recovery svcs. St. Joseph Hosp., Orange, Calif., 1976-88, medical dir., 1988-97; dir. of edn. Positive Action Ctr. Chapman Med. Ctr., 1997—. Cons. N.Am. Rockwell, 1970—80; mem. sci. adv. bd. Am. Coun. Drug Addiction, 1993—99; mem. drug abuse adv. com. FDA, 1993—96, chair, 1996—97, cons., 1997—2001; chair Ruth Fox Meml. Endowment Fund Am. Soc. Addiction Medicine, 1995—; bd. chair Nat. Coun. Alcpolism and Drug Dependency, 1999—2000; pres. Med. Edn. and Rsch. Found., 1981—. Contbr. numerous articles to profl. jours.; lectr. in field. Recipient Disting. Svc. award Jr.C of C., Buffalo, 1956, Citation for Civic Svc., City Anaheim, 1981, Disting. Svc. award Nat. Assn. State Alcohol & Drug Abuse., 1985, Disting. Cmty. Svc. award Elections Com. Orange County, 1986, Man of Yr. award Orange County Cultural Pride, 1992, Disting. Svc. award Am. Soc. Addiction Medicine, 1993, Silver Key award Nat. Coun. Alcoholism & Drug Dependence, 1993, Physician of Yr. award Orange County Medical Assn., 1995, Disting. Svc. award Pasadena Coun. Alcoholism & Drug Dependence, 1996, John Wallace Life-Time Achievement award Merrill Scott Symposium on Alcoholism, 1997, and numerous others. Fellow Am. Coll. Addiction Treatment Adminstrs., Am. Soc. Addiction Medicine (pres. 1985-87), Calif. Soc. Addiction Medicine (pres. 1983-85); mem. AMA, ACP, Am. Soc. Internal Medicine, Calif. Medical Assn., Orange County Calif. Jewish. Avocations: travelling, organizing trips to foreign countries, classical music, opera. Office: Max A Schneider MD Inc 3311 E Kirkwood Ave Orange CA 92869-5211 Fax: (714) 639-0987. E-mail: masmdinc@aol.com.

SCHNEIDER, NANCY JO, education educator; b. Monett, Mo., July 11, 1962; d. Floyd Laverne and Patricia Ann (House) A.; m. Bradley Stephen Schneider, Apr. 7, 1998. BEd, S.W. Mo. State U., 1984, MEd, 1988, EdS, 1989; EdD, U. Mo. Columbia, 1994. Cert. tchr., adminstr. Tchr. Springfield (Mo.) Pub. Schs., 1985-92; grad. asst. U. Mo. Columbia, 1992-93; asst. prin. Wentzville (Mo.) R-IV Sch. Dist., 1993-97, prin, 1997-99; assoc. prof. edn., coord. elem. student tchg. Lindenwood U., St. Charles, Mo., 1999—. Participant Mo. Leadership Acad., St. Louis, 1997—, Vision West, Wentzville, 1996-97. Mem. NAESP, Mo. Assn. Elem. Sch. Prins., West PTA. Baptist. Office: Lindenwood U 209 S Kingshighway St Saint Charles MO 63301-1693

SCHNEIDER, NANCY REYNOLDS, pathologist, educator; b. Schenectady, N.Y., July 27, 1942; d. Charles Philip Jr. and Ruth Louise (Taylor) Reynolds; m. John Stanley Schneider, July 13, 1968. BA, Ohio Wesleyan U., 1963; MA, U. Mich., 1964; MD, PhD, Cornell U., 1981. Diplomate Am. Bd. Pathology, Am. Bd. Med. Genetics; lic. Tex. Bd. Med. Examiners. Resident in pathology U. Tex. Southwestern Med. Ctr., Dallas, 1982-85, asst. instr. pathology, 1986, instr. pathology, 1986-87, asst. dir. hemotherapy dept., 1986-87, asst. prof. pathology, 1987-92, dir. cytogenetics lab., 1987—, assoc. prof. pathology, 1992-97, prof. pathology, 1997—. Attending staff physician Parkland Meml. Hosp., Dallas, 1986—. Contbr. articles to profl. jours. and chpt. to book. Mem. AMA, AAAS, Am. Soc. Clin. Pathologists, Am. Soc. Human Genetics, Tex. Genetics Soc., Coll. Am. Pathologists, Phi Beta Kappa. Office: Univ Tex Southwestern Med Ctr Dept Pathology 5323 Harry Hines Blvd Dallas TX 75390-7208

SCHNEIDER, NICHOLAS MCCORD, planetary scientist, educator, textbook author; b. Appleton, Wis., Dec. 17, 1956; s. Ben Ross Jr. and Mackay (McCord) S. BA in Physics and Astronomy, Dartmouth Coll., 1979; PhD in Planetary Sci., U. Ariz., 1988. Assoc. prof. lab. for atmospheric & space physics and dept. of astrophysical & planetary scis. U. Colo., Boulder, 1990—. Recipient Presdl. Young Investigator award NSF, 1991. Mem. Am. Astron. Soc. (divsn. for planetary scis.), Am. Geophys. Union, Internat. Astron. Union, Astron. Soc. of the Pacific. Office: U Colo Lab Atmospheric Space Physics 392 UCB Boulder CO 80309-0392

SCHNEIDER, PAM HORVITZ, lawyer; b. Cleve., Nov. 29, 1951; m. Milton S. Schneider, June 30, 1973; 1 child, Sarah Anne. BA, U. Pa., 1973; JD, Columbia U., 1976. Bar: N.Y. 1977, Pa. 1979. Assoc. White & Case, N.Y.C.,

1976-78, Drinker Biddle & Reath LLP, Phila., 1978-84, ptnr., 1984-2001; founding ptnr. Gadsden Schneider & Woodward LLP, King of Prussia, Pa., 2001—. Contbr. articles to profl. jours. Fellow Am. Coll. Trust and Estate Counsel (past regent); mem. ABA (past chair, real property probate and trust law sect.), Internat. Acad. Estate and Trust Law (academician). Office: Gadsden Schneider & Woodward LLP The Merion Bldg 700 S Henderson Rd Ste 345 King Of Prussia PA 19406 E-mail: pschneider@gsw-llp.com.

SCHNEIDER, PAUL, consultant; b. N.Y.C., May 3, 1934; s. Joe and Rose (Tannenbaum) S.; m. Rosalie Lubin, June 2, 1957; children: Aimie, Robert, Marc. BS, CCNY, 1956; MS, Yale U., 1958; PhD, NYU, 1961. Rsch. chemist IITRI, Chgo., 1961-62; rsch. scientist, asst. prof. NYU, N.Y.C., 1962-65; rsch. dir. Pfizer Diagnostics, 1965-69; dir. chem. ops. Bayer Diagnostics (formerly Technicon Corp.), Tarrytown, N.Y., 1969-75; dir. quality assurance & regulatory affairs Boehringer-Manheim, Indpls., 1975-81; dir. reagent ops. MetPath Labs., Teterboro, N.J., 1981-84; dir. quality assurance & regulatory affairs Datascope Corp., Montvale, 1984-93; cons. Schneider Assocs., Inc., Red Bank, 1993—, Boynton Beach, Fla., 1993—, 1993—. Inventor and patentee in field. Mem. Regulatory Affairs Profl. Soc. Home and Office: 12672 Coral Lakes Dr Boynton Beach FL 33437-4192 also: 19 Morford Pl Apt 8A Red Bank NJ 07701-1059 E-mail: paul@schneider-inc.com., Paul.Schneider@aya.yale.edu.

SCHNEIDER, PAUL, writer; b. Passaic, N.J., Aug. 4, 1923; s. Solomon Peter and Rose (Levine) S.; m. Margaret Flood Perrin, Apr. 10, 1951; children: Peggy Lee, Peter Lincoln, Ann. BA, Harvard U., 1945. Writer, N.Y.C., Hollywood, Calif., 1954-91; staff writer Universal City Studios, North Hollywood, 1967-74; head writer Love of Life CBS Studios, N.Y.C., 1974-76. Writer: (TV) Star Trek, 1954-85, Bonanza, 1954-85, Marcus Welby, M.D., 1954-85, (movies) The Looters, 1957, Ride the Wind, 1966, (plays) Effigy, 1983, Acrimonious, 1962. Mem. Writers Guild Am. (chmn. violence com. 1980-81), Harvard Alumni Assn., Dems. for Action. Avocations: hiking, mountain trails, travel, Zen. Home: PO Box 65 Idyllwild CA 92549-0065

SCHNEIDER, PHYLLIS LEAH, writer, editor; b. Seattle, Apr. 19, 1947; d. Edward Lee Booth and Harriet Phyllis (Ebbinghaus) Russell; m. Clifford Donald Schneider, June 14, 1969; 1 child, Pearl Brooke BA, Pacific Luth. U., 1969; MA, U. Wash., 1972. Fiction, features editor Seventeen Mag., N.Y.C., 1975-80; mng. editor Weight Watchers Mag., 1980-81; editor YM mag., 1981-86. Author: Parents Book of Infant Colic, 1990, Kids Who Make a Difference, 1993, Straight Talk on Women's Health: How to Get the Health Care You Deserve, 1993, Hot Health Care Careers, 1993, What Kids Like To Do, 1993; contbr. The Parents Answer Book, 1998. Recipient Centennial Recognition award Pacific Luth. U., 1990. Democrat. Episcopalian.

SCHNEIDER, RICHARD A. lawyer; b. Bklyn., Mar. 10, 1954; s. Robert Thomas and Nancy Ann (James) S.; m. Helen D. Schroll; children: Heather Elizabeth, Kristin Anne. Student, U.S. Naval Acad., 1975-77; BA, Auburn U., 1978; JD, Mercer U., 1981. Bar: Ga. 1981, U.S. Ct. Appeals (11th cir.), U.S. Supreme Ct. 1991. Litigator King & Spalding, Atlanta, 1981-88, ptnr., 1988—. Bd. dirs. UNICEF, Atlanta, 1991—. With USN, 1973-77. Mem. 191 Club, Atlanta Soc. Avocations: writing, songwriting. Home: 1014 Brookhaven Ln NE Atlanta GA 30319-4702 Office: King & Spalding 191 Peachtree St SW Atlanta GA 30303-3637

SCHNEIDER, RICHARD GRAHAM, lawyer; b. Bryn Mawr, Pa., Aug. 2, 1930; s. Vincent Bernard and Marion Scott (Graham) S.; m. Margaret Peter Fritz, Feb. 15, 1958; children: Margaret W., Richard Graham, John F. BA, Yale U., 1952; JD, U. Pa., 1957, MLA, 2001. Bar: Pa. 1958. Assoc. Dechert Price & Rhoads, Phila., 1957-66, ptnr., 1966-95; of counsel, 1995—. Case editor U. Pa. Law Rev., 1956-57. Trustee Baldwin Sch., Bryn Mawr, 1971-79; trustee Episcopal Acad., Merion, Pa., 1976-83. 1st lt. USAF, 1952-54, PTO. Mem. ABA, Pa. Bar Assn., Phila. Bar Assn., Order of Coif, Merion Cricket Club, Merion Golf Club (sec. 1997—), Yale Club (pres. 1966-68). Republican. Presbyterian. Office: Dechert Price & Rhoads 4000 Bell Atlantic Tower 1717 Arch St Lbby 3 Philadelphia PA 19103-2713 E-mail: gladwyue@aol.com.

SCHNEIDER, RICHARD T(HEODORE), optics research executive, engineer; b. Munich, July 29, 1927; came to U.S., 1961; s. Wilhelm and Martha E. (Hofmann) S.; m. Lore M. Reinhard, May 16, 1950; children: Ursula M. Schneider Long, Richard W. Diploma in physics, U. Stuttgart, Fed. Republic of Germany, 1958, PhD, 1961. Registered profl. engr. Calif. Teaching asst. U. Stuttgart, 1958-61; sect. chief Allison div. Gen. Motors Corp., Indpls., 1961-65; assoc. prof. U. Fla., Gainesville, 1965-68, prof., 1968-88, prof. emeritus, 1988-90; pres. Eye Rsch. Lab., Inc., Alachua, Fla., 1984-90; chief scientist RTS Labs., Inc., 1984-92. Cons. Allison div. Gen. Motors Corp., Indpls., 1965-67; IPA assignment Eglin AFB, Ft. Walton Beach, Fla., 1983; liaison scientist USN Office Naval Rsch., London, 1975. Editor: Uranium Plasmas, 1971; patentee in field; contbr. articles to profl. jours. Recipient Medal for Exceptional Sci. Achievement, NASA, 1975, Outstanding Tech. Achievement award, Fla. Engring. Soc., 1978. Mem. Internat. Soc. for Optical Engring., Sigma Xi, Tau Beta Pi (Eminent Engr. 1970). Avocation: flying airplanes. Home: 12903 NW 112th Ave Alachua FL 32615-6520 Office: Eye Rsch Lab 1663 Technology Ave Alachua FL 32615-9499

SCHNEIDER, RICHARD WILLIAM, academic administrator; b. July 31, 1946; m. June 8, 1968. BS in Engring. cum laude, U.S. Coast Guard Acad., 1968; MA in Liberal Studies, Wesleyan U., 1972; PhD, U. Del., 1985. Ensign USCG, 1968, advanced through grades to RADM, 1993; navigator, gunnery officer, deck dept. head USCGC, Dallas, 1968-70; chief navigation sect. Officer Candidate Sch., Yorktown, Va., 1970-72; asst. dean academics, asst. prof. physics U.S. Coast Guard Acad., 1973-77; exec. officer Coll. Marine Studies U. Del., 1977-85; v.p. rsch. Drexel U., Phila., 1985, v.p., chief fin. officer, 1986, acting v.p. acad. affairs, 1986-88, sr. v.p., 1990-92; pres. Norwich U., Northfield, Vt., 1992—. Lectr. Paoli Tech. Enterprise Ctr., 1985, U. Del., 1984, Swarthmore Coll., 1984, meeting Nat. Coun. Univ. Rsch. Adminstrs., 1984, U. Del. Rsch. Park, 1982. Contbr. articles on total quality mgmt. to various publs. Recipient personal citation Joint Resolution Del. Legislature, 1980; named an Outstanding Young Man of Am., Jaycees, 1978. Home: 63 Central St Northfield VT 05663-5757 Office: Norwich U Office of Pres Northfield VT 05663

SCHNEIDER, RITA JOYCE, property management company executive, real estate broker, mortgage broker; b. Bklyn., June 22, 1932; d. Joseph George and Mary (Cohen) Rothkopf; m. Arthur B. Schneider, Oct. 18, 1953 (dec. Feb. 1995); children: Linda Ellen, Debra Carol. Degree in Comml. Art, Pratt Inst., 1953; BA in Acctg., Bklyn. Coll., 1954. Contr. Central Funding Co., Bklyn., 1973-80; owner, contbr. Riteway Mgmt. Inc., Coral Sprigns, Fla., 1980-86; realtor Riteway Internat. Realty Corp., 1985-86, ERA Regal Internat. Realty Inc.; realtor, mortgage broker Regal Fin. Svcs. and LCAM Regal Assn Svcs., Coral Springs, 1986-94, mortgage broker, sr. loan officer contr., 1995—. Cons. in field. Active Cancer Soc., Bklyn., 1954-73, March of Dimes, Bklyn., 1960-70. Recipient 1st art award City of N.Y., 1950. Mem. Nat Bd. Realtors, North Broward Bd. Realtors, Fla. Assn. Mortgage Brokers, Nat. Real Estate Assn., Fla. Assn. Cmty. Mgrs. (lic), Cmty. Assn. Inst. Democrat. Jewish. Avocations: reading, dancing, swimming. E-mail: reejay@aol.com.

SCHNEIDER, ROBERT ANDREW, social worker, educator, psychotherapist, educator; b. Balt., Aug. 4, 1958; s. Andrew G. and Mary L. Schneider. BA, U. Md., Balt., 1975, MSW, 1989, PhD, 1995. Lic. ind. social worker. Pvt. practice, Storm Lake, Iowa; asst. prof. Buena Vista Coll., 1996—99; assoc. prof. U. No. Iowa, Cedar Falls, 1999—. Contbr. over 70 articles to health-related jours.; author: Statistics for Social Workers, 1999; editor: Jour. Nephrology Social Work, 1999—2002. Bd. dirs. Am. Cancer Soc., Waterloo, Iowa, 2000. Pvt. USMC. Grantee, U. No. Iowa, 1999, 2001. Mem.: Am. Assn. Psychoanalysis (assoc.), Federalist Soc. Roman Catholic. Avocations: musical composition, Tae Kwon Do (black belt). Home: 101 Maplewood Rd #10 Cedar Falls IA 50613 Office: U No Iowa 34 Sabin Hall Cedar Falls IA 50614-0405 E-mail: robert.schneider@uni.edu.

SCHNEIDER, ROBERT JAY, oncologist; b. Miami, Fla., May 31, 1949; s. Irving and Ethel (Pack) S.; m. Barbara Cunningham, June 1, 1974; children: Matthew, Kirsten. Student, Washington U., 1967-69; BA cum laude, Boston U., 1971; MD, Albert Einstein Coll. Medicine, N.Y.C., 1975. Diplomate Am. Bd. Internal Medicine, Am. Bd. Oncology; lic. physician, N.Y. Intern, jr. and sr. resident internal medicine Bronx Mcpl. Hosp., N.Y.C., 1975-78; fellow med. oncology Meml. Sloan-Kettering Cancer Ctr., 1978-80, adj. attending physician/cons. dept. medicine, 1981—; asst. prof. medicine N.Y. Med. Coll., Valhalla, 1980-81. Clin. instr. medicine Cornell U. Med. Coll., 1978-80; jr. clin. faculty fellow Am. Cancer Soc., 1980-81; mem. N.Y. Met. Breast Cancer Group, 1990—; cons. cancer program No. Westchester Hosp. Ctr., Mt. Kisco, N.Y., 1981-82; mem. staff Westchester County Med. Ctr., Valhalla, N.Y., No. Westchester Hosp. Ctr., Mt. Kisco, Meml. Sloan-Kettering Cancer Ctr., N.Y.C. Contbr. articles to profl. jours. Mem. adv. bd. Cancer Care, Inc. Conn., 1997-99. Recipient Clin. Fellowship award Am. Cancer Soc., 1978-79. Mem. Am. Soc. Clin. Oncology, Westchester County Med. Soc., N.Y. State Med. Soc., Woodway Country Club. Republican. Presbyterian. Achievements include research in detection and treatment of early breast cancer, the human spirit in the fight against cancer, salvage chemotherapy with etoposide, ifosfamide and cisplatin in refractory germ cell tumors. Office: 101 S Bedford Rd Ste 202A Mount Kisco NY 10549-3456

SCHNEIDER, ROBERT KERRY, electric utility engineer; b. Bremerton, Wash., Jan. 11, 1949; s. Emil Kerry and Glady Elizabeth (Anderson) S.; m. Carol Anne Pfeiffer, Aug. 28, 1971; children: Steve, Jeff. BS in Physics, U. Wash., Seattle, 1971; MS in Nuclear Engring., U. Wash., 1973, MBA, 1976. Cert. profl. engr., Wash., Calif., Ala. Engr. Bechtel Power Corp., San Francisco, 1971-72; dir. power mgmt. Snohomish Co. Pub. Utility Dist., Everett, Wash., 1977-87; sr. cons. CH2M Hill, Bellevue, 1987-95; v.p./mgr. D. Hittle & Assocs., Inc., Lynnwood, 1995—. Vis. com. adv., U. Wash. Mech. Engring. Dept., 1994—. Mem. Am. Soc. Mech. Engrs. (Disting. Svc. award, 1999, mem. bd. govt. rels. 1996-2002, v.p. region VIII, coun. mem. affairs, 1993-96, western Wash. sect. chmn., 1984-85), Puget Sound Engring. Coun. (pres. 1990-91). Avocation: skiing. Office: D Hittle and Assocs Inc PO Box 6755 Lynnwood WA 98036-0755 Fax: 425-744-1253. E-mail: schneiderr@asme.org.

SCHNEIDER, SHARON M. systems administrator, information technologist; b. Detroit, Mar. 15, 1958; d. Peter and Mary S.; m. Wesley A. Comes, May 23, 1987. BS, Kutztown U., 1990; MS, MSIS, Drexel U., 1998. Reference and info. asst. Bucks County Free Libr., Doylestown, Pa., 1988-94; computer sys. tech. Cedar Crest & Muhlenberg Colls., Allentown, 1994-95; sys. adminstr., info. technologist Cedar Crest Coll., 1995—. Mem. ALA, IEEE Computer Soc., Am. Soc. Info. Sci., Assn. Computing Machinery, World Future Soc.

SCHNEIDER, SOL, electronic engineer, consultant, researcher; b. N.Y.C., Feb. 24, 1924; s. David and Naomi F. Schneider; m. Rhoda B. Schneider, Apr. 16, 1950; children: Sandra E., Barry. BA, CUNY Bklyn. Coll., 1946; MS, NYU, 1949. Supervisory physicist U.S. Army Electronics Tech. and Devices Lab., Ft. Monmouth, N.J., 1948-80, chief pulse power and plasma devices, 1956-80; cons. Army Rsch. Office, 1980-85, U.S. Army Pulse Power Ctr., Ft. Monmouth, 1982-98, SRI, Internat., Menlo Park, Calif., 1983-91, Vitronics, Inc., Eatontown, N.J., 1987-96, Berkeley Rsch. Assocs., Springfield, Va., 1996—2002, U.S. Army Rsch. Lab., Adelphi, Md., 1997—2002. Adj. prof. Southwestern Ctr. for Elec. Engring. Edn., St. Cloud, Fla., 1980-86; mem. USN Pulsed Power Tech. Adv. Group, Washington, 1978-80, SDIO Pulsed Power Tech. Adv. Group, 1983-93, Adv. Group on Electronic Devices, Dept. Def., Washington, 1970-80. Contbr. articles to profl. jours.; holder 15 patents. With U.S. Army, 1942-46, ETO. Recipient award Sec. Army, 1963, U.S. Army R&D Achievement award Dept. Army, 1963, 78, Army Sci. award, 1978. Fellow IEEE (life; chmn./editor symposium proc. 1957-80, chmn. emeritus internat. power modulator symposium 1981-2001, co-chmn. high voltage workshop 1989-90, exec. com. 1991-2001, High Voltage award 1991, Germeshausen award 1992); mem. Am. Phys. Soc. (exec. com. gaseous electronics conf. 1961-66, sec. 1964, exec. com. electron and atomic physics divsn. 1965-66). Home: 100 Arrowwood Ct Red Bank NJ 07701-6717

SCHNEIDER, STEPHEN HENRY, climatologist, environmental policy analyst, researcher; b. N.Y.C., Feb. 11, 1945; s. Samuel and Doris C. (Swarte) S.; married, 1995; 2 children from previous marriage. BS, Columbia U., 1966, MS, 1967, PhD in Mech. Engring./Plasma Physics, 1971; DSc (hon.), N.J. Inst. Tech., 1990, Monmouth Coll., 1991. NAS, NRC rsch. assoc. Goddard Inst. Space Studies NASA, N.Y.C., 1971-72; fellow advanced study program Nat. Ctr. Atmospheric Research, Boulder, Colo., 1972-73, scientist, dep. head climate project, 1973-78, acting leader climate sensitivity group, 1978-80, head visitors program and dep. dir. advanced study program, 1980-87, sr. scientist, 1980-96, head interdisciplinary climate systems sect. Colo., 1987-92; prof. biol. scis. dept., sr. fellow Inst. Internat. Studies Stanford (Calif.) U., 1992—, prof. civil and environtl. engring. dept. (courtesy). Affiliate prof. U. Corp. Atmospheric Rsch. Lamont-Doherty Geol. Obs., Columbia, U., 1976-83; mem. Carter-Mondale Sci. Policy Task Force, 1976; Clinton-Gore sci. advisor, 1992, 96; sci. advisor, interviewee Nova Sta. WGBH-TV, Planet Earth, Sta. WQED-TV; mem. internat. sci. coms. climatic change, ecology, energy, environ. edn., food and pub. policy; expert witness congl. coms.; mem. Def. Sci. Bd. Task Force on Atmospheric Obscuration; lead author Intergovernmental Panel on Climate Change Working Group I, 1995-96; coord. lead author Working Group II, 1998—; mem. core writing team Synthesis Report, 2000—. Author: (with Lynne E. Mesirow) The Genesis Strategy: Climate and Global Survival, 1976; (with Lynne Morton) The Primordial Bond: Exploring Connections Between Man and Nature Through Humanities and Science, 1981, (with Randi S. Londer) The Coevolution of Climate and Life, 1984, Global Warming: Are We Entering the Greenhouse Century?, 1989; (with W. Bach) Interactions of Food and Climate, 1981; (with R.S. Chen and E. Boulding) Social Science Research and Climate Change: An Interdisciplinary Appraisal, 1983; (with K.C. Land) Forecasting in the Social and Natural Sciences, 1987; (with P. Boston) Scientists on Gaia, 1990; editor-in-chief: The Encyclopedia of Climate and Weather, 1996, Laboratory Earth: The Planetary Experiment We Can't Afford to Lose, 1997; editor: Climatic Change, 1976—; contbr. articles on theory of climate, influence of climate on soc., relation of climatic change to world food, population, energy, development and environ. policy issues, environ. aftereffects of nuclear war, carbon dioxide greenhouse effect, pub. understanding sci., environ. edn. Recipient Louis J. Battan Author's award Am. Meteorol. Soc., 1990, Mary B. Ansari Ref. Work award Geosci. Info. Soc., 1997; named one of 100 Outstanding Young Scientists in Am. by Sci. Digest, 1984; MacArthur Found. Prize fellow John D. and Catherine T. MacArthur Found., 1992. Fellow AAAS (Westinghouse award 1991), Scientists Inst. for Pub. Info.; mem. U.S. Assn. Club Rome, Am. Meteorological Soc., Am. Geophysical Union, Fedn. Am. Scientists, Soc. Conservation Biology, Soc. Ecol. Economics., Acad. Europae (fgn.), Ecol. Soc. Am., NAS (elected, 2002). Office: Stanford U Dept Biol Scis Stanford CA 94305-5020

SCHNEIDER, STEVEN PHILIP, aerodynamics educator; b. Chgo., Aug. 4, 1960; s. Philip Walter and Barbara Jean (Brilla) S.; m. Lynette Diane Brown, Aug. 24, 1985; children: Ariel, Kaitlyn. BS with honor, Calif. Inst. Tech., 1981, MS in Aeronautics, 1984, PhD in Aeronautics, 1989. Engr., scientist Naval Ocean Systems Ctr., San Diego, 1981-83; rsch. fellow Calif. Inst. Tech., Pasadena, 1989; asst. prof. Sch. Aero. and Astronautical Engring., West Lafayette, Ind., 1989-95, assoc. prof., 1995—. Presenter in field. Contbr. articles and abstracts to profl. jours. Achievement Rewards for Coll. Scientists scholar, 1986-87. Fellow AIAA (assoc.); mem. Am. Phys. Soc. (fluid dynamics div. 1983—). Avocations: backpacking, bicycling. Office: Purdue U Airport Aerospace Scis Lab West Lafayette IN 47906

SCHNEIDER, THOMAS AQUINAS, surgeon, educator, retired surgeon; b. St. Charles, Mo., Dec. 22, 1934; s. Vincent Augustine and Anna Maria (Marheineke) Schneider; m. Joyce Elaine Diehr, June 7, 1958; children: Lisa, Thomas, Dawn, Tracy. BS, Loras Coll., 1954; MD, St. Louis U., 1958. Diplomate Am. Bd. Surgery. Resident surgery St. Louis City Hosp., 1958—63; pvt. practice St. Charles, 1963—2001; ret., 2001. Clin. instr. St. Louis U., 1966—91, asst. clin. prof., 1991—; med. dir. vascular lab. St. Joseph Health Ct., St. Charles, 1991—, dir. trauma svc., 1981—91. Fellow: ACS; mem.: St. Louis Vascular Soc. (pres. 1993—95), St. Louis Surg. Soc. (councilor 1988—91, v.p. 1996—97), Mo. Com. on Trauma, Hodgen Club (pres. 1988), Alpha Omega Alpha. Roman Catholic. Avocations: golf, music, history.

SCHNEIDER, THOMAS PAUL, non-profit agency administrator; b. June 5, 1947; s. Milton and Gloria (Bocaner) S.; m. Susan G. Stein, May 31, 1987; children: Rachel Jenny, Daniel Joshua. BA with honors, JD, U. Wis., 1972. U.S. atty. U.S. Dist. Dist. Ct. (ea. dist.) Wis., Milw., 1993-2001; exec. dir. youth svcs. COA Youth & Family Ctrs., 2001—. Mem. Wis. Bar Assn. Democrat. Jewish. Office: COA Youth & Family Ctrs 909 E North Ave Milwaukee WI 53212 E-mail: tomcoa@execpc.com.

SCHNEIDER, THOMAS RICHARD, hospital administrator; b. Cin., July 16, 1944; s. Richard Arthur and Janet (Tingley) S.; m. Judith Ann Johnson, June 10, 1967; children: Gregory Thomas, Marcia Kay, Jill Elise. BS in Bus. Adminstrn., Miami U., Oxford, Ohio, 1966; MHA, U. Minn., 1968. Asst. adminstr. Meml. Hosp. of South Bend, Ind., 1971-77, Ft. Hamilton-Hughes Meml. Hosp., Hamilton, Ohio, 1977-82, assoc. adminstr. 5, 1982-84, assoc. adminstr., chief oper. officer, 1984-85, v.p. ops. and profl. svcs., 1985-91; adminstr. Shriners Hosp. for Children, Shreveport, La., 1992—. Chmn. health careers Greater Cin. Hosp. Coun., 1983-90; mem. adv. bd. Xavier U. Ctr. for Health Mgmt. Edn., Cin., 1985-91; trustee Cmty. Blood Ctr., Dayton, Ohio, 1985-91. Trustee, 1st v.p. YMCA of Hamilton-Fairfield, 1990; chmn. city charter comms. com. City of Hamilton, 1990; chmn. pub. svc. div. United Way of Hamilton-Fairfield, 1988-90. Mem. Med. Svc. Corps. USN, 1968-71. Recipient disting. svc. award YMCA, 1982, great American family award of honor, 1990, proclamation Mayor and City Coun. of Hamilton, 1992. Fellow Am. Coll. Healthcare Execs.; mem. Rotary Internat., Masons, Shriner. Republican. Methodist. Avocations: fishing, golf, boating, reading, clowning. Home: 535 Northpark Dr Bossier City LA 71111-2241 Office: Shriners Hosp 3100 Samford Ave Shreveport LA 71103-4289

SCHNEIDER, VALERIE LOIS, speech educator; b. Chgo., Feb. 12, 1941; d. Ralph Joseph and Gertrude Blanche (Gaffron) S. BA, Carroll Coll., 1963; MA, U. Wis., 1966; PhD, U. Fla., 1969; CAS, Appalachian State U., 1981. Tchr. English and history, dir. forensics and drama Montello (Wis.) H.S., 1963-64; instr. speech U. Fla., Gainesville, 1966-68, asst. prof. speech, 1969-70, Edinboro (Pa.) State Coll., 1970-71; assoc. prof. speech East Tenn. State U., Johnson City, 1971-76, prof. speech, 1976-97. Instr. newspaper course Johnson City Press Chronicle, 1979, Elizabethton Star, Erwin Record, Mountain City Tomahawk, Jonesboro Herald and Tribune, 1980; mem. investor panel USA Today, 1991-92. Editor East Tenn. State U. evening and off-campus newsletter, 1984-91; assoc. editor Homiletic, 1974-76; columnist Video Visions, Kingsport Times-News, 1984-86; book reviewer Pulpit Digest, 1986-90; contbr. articles to profl. jours. Chmn. AAUW Mass Media Study Group Com., Johnson City, 1973-74. Recipient Creative Writing award Va. Highlands Arts Festival, 1973, award Kingsport Times News, 1984, 85, Tri-Cities Met. Advt. Fedn., 1983, 84, hon. life mem. Tenn. Presbyn. Women, 2000; named Danforth assoc., 1977; finalist Money mag. contest, 1994, Writer's Digest contest, 2000. Mem.: AAUW (v.p. chpt. 1974—75, pres. 1975—76), Tenn. Basic Skills Coun. (exec. bd. 1979—80, v.p. 1980—81, pres. 1975—76), Religious Speech Comm. Assn. (Best Article award 1976), Tenn. Speech Comm. Assn. (exec. bd. 1974—77, publs. bd. 1974—78, pres. 1977—78), So. Speech Comm. Assn., Speech Comm. Assn. (Tenn. rep. to states adv. coun. 1974—75), Mensa, Presbyn. Women (hon.; life mem.), Johnson City Book Club (pres. 2001—), Bus. and Profl. Women's Club (chpt. exec. bd. 1972—73, v.p. 1976—77), Pi Gamma Mu, Phi Delta Kappa, Tau Kappa Alpha, Delta Sigma Rho. Presbyterian. Home: 3201 Buckingham Rd Johnson City TN 37604-2775 Office: East Tenn State U PO Box 23098 Johnson City TN 37614-1310

SCHNEIDER, WESLEY CLAIR, marketing communications company executive; b. Chgo., May 2, 1953; s. Clair A. and Ruth (Jenks) S.; m. Jeanie A. Tomaino, Nov. 23, 1990. BA magna cum laude, Ill. Wesleyan U., 1975. Sales rep. confectionery div. Am. Home Products, Chgo., 1975-77; midwest regional sales mgr. confectionery & snacks div. Beatrice Foods, Denver, 1977-78, mktg. analyst, 1978-80; product mgr. Tootsie Roll Industries, Chgo., 1980-85, mgr. internat. mktg., 1985-88; v.p., gen. mgr. Marden-Kane, inc., 1988-91; pres., owner Creative Mktg. Comm., Inc., 1991—. Bd. dirs. Wesleyan Co., Inc., Chgo.; speaker Inst. for Internat. Rsch. and Promotion Mktg. Assn. Am., N.Y.C., 1991. Patentee in field. Cubmaster Boy Scouts Am., Chgo., 1991; fin. chmn. Twp. Reps.; mem., chair candidates slating subcom. Kenilworth Citizens Adv. Com.; bd. dirs. Kenilworth Assembly Hall Soc., 2001—. Recipient Best Design award retail food category Nat. Flexible Packaging Assn., 1979, Indian statue Point of Purchase Advt. Inst., 1986, 87, U.S. Senatorial Medal of Freedom, 1999. Mem. Am. Def. Preparedness Assn., Exec. Club Chgo. (comms. com.) Internat. Platform Assn., Masons, Shriners, Sigma Chi. Episcopalian, Vestry, 1998. Avocations: running, fishing, hockey, reading. Office: Creative Mktg Comm Inc 980 North Michigan Ave Ste 1400 Chicago IL 60611

SCHNEIDER, WILLIAM, JR. commissioner; PhD, NYU, 1968. Assoc. dir. for nat. security and internat. affairs Office Mgmt. Budget; under sec. state for security assistance, sci. and tech. U.S. Dept. Def., 1982—86, chmn. def. sci. bd.; pres. Internat. Planning Svcs., Inc.; commr., co-chair aerospace global issues Aerospace Commn. Chmn. Pres. Gen. adv. Com. on Arms Control and Disarmament, 1987—93; cons. in field. Office: Aerospace Commn Crystal Gateway One 1235 Jefferson Davis Hwy Ste 940 Arlington VA 22202-3283*

SCHNEIDER, WILLIAM GEORGE, former life insurance company executive; b. Shenandoah, Iowa, Jan. 18, 1919; s. Fred M. and Abba F. (Ferguson) S.; m. Phyllis Welch, Mar. 28, 1943; children— Stephen F., Richard W. BA, State U. Iowa, 1940; postgrad., N.Y. U. With Met. Life Ins. Co., 1940-41, 45-46; with Bankers Life Co. (now named Prin. Fin. Group), Des Moines, 1946-84; sr. v.p. Bankers Life Co., 1970-82, exec. v.p., 1982-84, ret., 1984. Served with AUS, 1941-45. Fellow Soc. Actuaries; mem. Am. Acad. Actuaries, Phi Beta Kappa. Clubs: Des Moines, Des Moines Golf and Country. Republican. Home: 3662 Ingersoll Ave Apt 414 Des Moines IA 50312-3422

SCHNEIDER, WILLIAM GEORGE, chemist, research consultant; b. Wolseley, Sask., Can., June 1, 1915; s. Michael and Phillipina (Krauschaar) S.; m. Jean Purves, Sept. 2, 1940; children: Judith Schneider Saunders, Joanne Schneider Spurrier. B.Sc., U. Sask., 1937, M.Sc., 1939, D.Sc., 1969; PhD, McGill U., 1941, D.Sc., 1970; D.Sc. (hon.), York U., 1966, Meml. U., 1968, McMaster U., 1969, Laval U., 1969, Moncton U., 1969, U. N.B., 1970, U. Montreal, 1970, Acadia U., 1976, U. Regina, 1976, Ottawa U., 1978; LL.D., U. Alta., 1968, Laurentian U., 1968. Head phys. chemistry sect., div. chemistry NRC Can., Ottawa, Ont., 1946-63, dir. div. pure chemistry, 1963-65, v.p., 1965-67, pres., 1967-80; research cons., 1980—. Author: (with J.A. Pople, H.J. Bernstein) High Resolution Nuclear Magnetic Resonance, 1959; contbr. articles to profl. jours. Decorated Order of Can., 1977 Fellow Royal Soc. Can. (Henry Marshall Tory medal), Royal Soc. London, Chem. Inst. Can. (medal 1969, Montreal medal 1973); mem. Internat. Union Pure and Applied Chemistry (pres. 1983-85) Office: Unit # 2 65 Whitemarl Dr Ottawa ON Canada K1L 8J9

SCHNEIDER, WILLIAM JAMES, retired plastic and reconstructive surgeon; b. Miami, Fla., Dec. 19, 1943; s. James William and Reva (Gross) S.; m. Rebecca Jo Phillips, June 10, 1967; children: James Carter, Jason Christopher, Brian Phillips. BS, Stetson U., 1966; MD, Vanderbilt U., 1970. Cert. Am. Bd. Plastic Surgery. Intern surgery U. Fla., Gainesville, 1970-71, resident surgery, 1971-72, 1970-72, Emory U., Atlanta, 1972-75, rsident plastic surgery, 1975-77; pvt. practice, Knoxville, Tenn., 1977-99; ret., 1999. Chief dept. surgery East Tenn. Children's Hosp., Knoxville, 1982, Ft. Sanders Regional Med. Ctr., Knoxville, 1986. Author chpts. in several books; contbr. articles to profl. jours. Pres. Westborough Neighborhood Assn., Knoxville, 1986; coach, commr. West Knoxville Youth Baseball, 1978-85. Fellow Am. Coll. Surgeons; mem. Southeastern Soc. Plastic & Reconstructive Surgeons, Tenn. Soc. Plastic & Reconstructive Surgeons (pres. 1988-90), Am. Soc. Plastic & Reconstructive Surgeons, Am. Soc. for Aesthetic Plastic Surgery, Knoxville Surg. Soc. (pres. 1985), Knoxville Acad. Medicine. Methodist. Avocations: photography, hiking. Home: 8101 Osler Ln Knoxville TN 37909-2130

SCHNEIDER, WILLYS HOPE, lawyer; b. N.Y.C., Sept. 27, 1952; d. Leon and Lillian (Friedman) S.; m. Stephen Andrew Kals, Jan. 21, 1979; children: Peter, Josefine. AB, Princeton U., 1974; JD, Columbia U., 1977. Bar: N.Y. 1978, U.S. Dist. Ct. (ea. and so. dists.) N.Y. 1978, U.S. Tax Ct. 1979. Law clk. to hon. Jack B. Weinstein U.S. Dist. Ct. (ea. dist.) N.Y., Bklyn., 1977-78;

assoc. Paul, Weiss, Rifkind, Wharton & Garrison, N.Y.C., 1978-83, Kaye Scholer LLP, N.Y.C., 1983-87, 1987—. Contbr. articles to profl. jours. Mem. ABA, N.Y. State Bar Assn., Assn. of Bar of City of N.Y. Home: 320 W End Ave New York NY 10023-8110 Office: Kaye Scholer LLP 425 Park Ave New York NY 10022-3506

SCHNEIDER-CRIEZIS, SUSAN MARIE, architect; b. St. Louis, Aug. 1, 1953; d. William Alfred and Rosemary Elizabeth (Fischer) Schneider; m. Demetrios Anthony Criezis, Nov. 24, 1978; children: Anthony, John and Andrew. BArch, U. Notre Dame, 1976; MArch, MIT, 1978. Registered architect, Wis. Project designer Eichstaedt Architects, Roselle, Ill., 1978-80, Solomon, Cordwell, Buenz & Assocs., Chgo., 1980-82; project architect Gelick, Foran Assocs., 1982-83; asst. prof. Sch. Architecture U. Ill., 1980-86; exec. v.p. Criezis Architects, Inc., Northfield, Ill., 1986—. Graham Found. grantee MIT, 1977, MIT scholar, 1976-78; Prestressed Concrete Inst. rsch. grantee, 1981. Mem. AIA, Chgo. Archtl. Club, Chgo. Women in Architecture, Am. Solar Energy Soc., NAFE, Jr. League Evanston, Evanston C. of C. Roman Catholic. Avocations: tennis, swimming. Office: 1775 Winnetka Ave Ste 100 Northfield IL 60093-3386

SCHNEIDER-KISSELEV, KATE MARIE, economist; b. Boston, Oct. 24, 1972; d. Edmond Joseph and Elaine Marie (Callahan) Schneider; m. Alexei Mikhailovich Kisselev, Oct. 14, 1994. BS in Fgn. Svc./Econs. magna cum laude, Georgetown U., 1994. Fundraiser Georgetown U. Alumni House, Washington, 1990-91; rsch. asst. U.S. Dept. State, 1991-94; drill instr. Russian lang. Georgetown U., 1993-94; intern Aset Cons., 1994; rsch. asst. Fed. Res. Bank N.Y., N.Y.C., 1994-95, asst. economist, 1995-96, economist, 1996—. Nat. Merit scholar, 1990. Mem. Phi Beta Kappa, Phi Alpha Theta. Republican. Avocations: softball, running, flute, reading.

SCHNEIDERMAN, IRWIN, lawyer; b. N.Y.C., May 28, 1923; s. Meyer and Bessie (Klein) S.; m. Roberta Haig, Nov. 28, 1966; 1 child, Eric T. BA, Bklyn. Coll., 1943; LLB cum laude, Harvard U., 1948; DHL (hon.), Bklyn. Coll., 1993. Bar: N.Y. 1949, D.C. 1952. Assoc. Cahill Gordon & Reindel, N.Y.C., 1948-59, ptnr., 1959-89, sr. counsel, 1990—. Spl. cons. to chmn. SEC, 1981-82, mem. adv. com. on tender offers, 1983. Trustee Bklyn. Coll. Found., 1983—; chmn. N.Y.C. Opera, 1993—; bd. dirs. WNYC Radio, 1989—, City Ctr. Music and Drama, Inc., 1990—, N.Y.C. NARAL, 1990—, Lincoln Ctr. for Performing Arts, Inc., 1994—; pres. N.Y.C. NARAL Found., 1998--. Lt. (j.g.) USNR, 1943-46. Mem. Harvard Club. Home: 203 E 72nd St New York NY 10021-4568 Office: Cahill Gordon & Reindel 80 Pine St Fl 17 New York NY 10005-1790

SCHNEIDEWIND, NORMAN FLOYD, information scientist, educator; b. San Francisco, Apr. 22, 1928; s. Walter Schneidewind and Freida Anderegg; children: Molly Crowe, Philip Schneidewind. BSEE, U. Calif., Berkeley, 1951; PhD, U. So. Calif., 1966, MS in Operational Rsch., 1970; MS in Computer Sci., San Jose State U., 1983, MSEE, 1989. Computer cons. in pvt. practice, Pebble Beach, Calif., 1951-71; prof. info. scis. Naval Postgrad. Sch., Monterey, 1971—. Contbr. articles to profl. jours. Fellow IEEE (gen. chair on internat. conf. on software maintenance 1983, 96, 2000); mem. Eta Kappa Nu, Tau Beta Pi, Sigma Xi. Home: 2822 Raccon Tr Pebble Beach CA 93953 Office: Naval Postgrad Sch Code IS/SS Monterey CA 93943

SCHNEIDLER, JON GORDON, lawyer; b. Seattle, Oct. 22, 1938; s. J. Gordon and Mary Louise (Bartholomew) S.; m. Linda Gilmore White, June 27, 1964 (div. June 1988); children: Kristina Richards, Jolie Wolcott, Andrew Schneidler, Peter Schneidler; m. Elizabeth Ann Nairn, Apr. 2, 1989; 1 stepdaughter: Jessica Albright. BA, U. Wash., 1962, JD, 1968. Bar: Wash.; U.S. Ct. Appeals (9th Cir.), U.S. Dist. Ct. (we. dist.) Wash. CEO Schneidler Industries, Inc., Seattle, 1968-70; ptnr. Cartano, Botzer & Chapman, 1970-86; dir., CEO 4100 Assocs., 1989—. Sec. Transiplex Internat., Inc., Seattle; mem. adv. bd. Pacific Legal Found., Sacramento; trustee Ehrlich Donnan Found., Seattle. Co-author: (book) Real Property Deskbook, 1981, 2d edit. 1986; patentee Air Structure Systems, 1969. Bd. dirs. North Kitsap Sch. Bd., Poulsbo, Wash., 1984, Friends of Youth, Renton, Wash., 1974; founder, dir. Tchr. of Yr. Found., Poulsbo, 1988—. 1st lt. USAF, 1962-66. Decorated Air Force Commendation medal; recipient Baker scholar George F. Baker Foun., 1957-60. Fellow Paul Harris Found.; mem. ABA (bus. law sect., comml. lease com.), Wash. State Bar Assn., King County Bar Assn., Coll. Club (trustee, treas. 1998-2002), Rotary. Avocations: fly fishing, competitive bridge, sailing, gardening. Office: 999 3rd Ave Ste 4100 Seattle WA 98104-4084

SCHNEIDMAN, BARBARA SUE, psychiatrist; b. Mpls., Jan. 18, 1944; d. Norman Reuben and Mildred (Roberts) S.; m. William McAllister. BA, U. Minn., Mpls., 1966, MD, 1970; MPH, U. Wash., 1974. Diplomate Am. Bd. Psychiatry and Neurology. Resident ob-gyn. U. Wash., Seattle, 1972-74, dir. gynecology, 1974-78, resident in psychiatry, 1978-81, cons. primary care, 1981-88; pvt. practice, 1981-93; cons. Sexual Assault Ctr., 1981-93, Cen. Area Mental Health, Seattle, 1990-92; assoc. v.p. Am. Bd. Med. Specialties, Evanston, Ill., 1993-98; dir. divsn. of medical edn. liaison and outreach AMA, 1998—2002, v.p. med. edn., 2002—. Mem., chair Wash. State Bd. Med. Examiners, 1982-93; pres. Fedn. State Med. Bds., 1991-92. Mem. AMA, Am. Psychiat. Assn., Ill. State Med. Assn., Ill. Psychiat. Soc. Avocation: bicycling. Office: AMA 515 N State St # 7170 Chicago IL 60610-4325 Fax: 312-464-5830.

SCHNEITER, GEORGE MALAN, golfer, development company executive; b. Ogden, Utah, Aug. 12, 1931; s. George Henery and Bernice Slade (Malan) S.; m. JoAnn Deakin, Jan. 19, 1954; children: George, Gary, Dan, Steve, Elizabeth Ann, Michael. B in Banking and Fin., U. Utah, 1955. With 5th Army Championship Golf Team, U.S. Army, 1955-56; assoc. golf pro Hidden Valley Golf Club, Salt Lake City, 1957; golf pro Lake Hills Golf Club, Billings, Mont., 1957-90, sec., 1957-61, pres., 1964-90, Schneiter Enterprises, Sandy, Utah, 1974—; developer Schneiter's Golf Course, 1973—, and subdiv., 1961—; player PGA tour, 1958-78, Sr. PGA tour, 1981—. Missionary So. State Mission, LDS Ch., 1951-52. Served with U.S. Army, 1955-56. Named winner, Utah sect. Sr. Championship, Wyo., Open Super Sr. Championshio, Salt Lake City Parks Tournament, Vernal Brigham Payson Open, Yuma Open, Utah Sr. PGA Chamption, Utah Super Sr. Championshio, World Pro Am., Kona, Hawaii, Ft. Carsopn Golf Champion; fellow Banking & Fin. fellow, First Security Bank Utah, 1953. Mem. PGA, Salt Lake City C. of C., Intermountain Golf Course Supertaints Assn. Achievements include over 30 hole in ones. also: 8968 S 1300 E Sandy UT 84094 Office: 2009 Brassy Dr Las Vegas NV 89142-2033 Fax: (702) 457-7065.

SCHNELL, GEORGE ADAM, geographer, educator; b. Phila., July 13, 1931; s. Earl Blackwood and Emily (Bernheimer) S.; m. Mary Lou Williams, June 21, 1958; children: David Adam, Douglas Powell, Thomas Earl. BS, West Chester U., 1958; MS, Pa. State U., 1960, PhD, 1965; postdoctoral study, Ohio State U., 1965. Asst. prof. Coll. SUNY, New Paltz, 1962-65, assoc. prof., 1965-68, prof. geography, 1968-99, founding chmn. dept., 1968-94, prof. emeritus, 1999—. Adj. prof. SUNY; vis. assoc. prof. U. Hawaii, summer, 1966; cons. cmty. action programming, 1965 ; manuscript reader, cons. to several pubs., 1967—; founder, founding bd. dirs. Inst. for Devel., Planning and Land Use Studies, 1986-96; cons. Mid-Hudson Pattern for Progress, 1986, Open Space Inst., 1987, Mid-Hudson Regional Econ. Devel. Coun., 1989, Urban Devel. Corp., 1989-90, 93, Tech. Devel. Ctr., 1991, Catskill Ctr., 1991, Ednl. Testing Svc., 1993-94, 96, 97; consulting editor Exams Unltd., Albany, N.Y., 1995-99; founding mem. exec. bd. dirs. Hudson Valley Study Ctr., 1995-98; cons. several depts. geography, 1988—, Pa. Geographic Alliance, 1999; presenter in field. Author: (with others) The Local Community: A Handbook for Teachers, 1971, The World's Population, Problems of Growth, 1972, Pennsylvania Coal: Resources, Technology, Utilization, 1983, West Virginia and Appalachia: Selected Readings, 1977, Hazardous and Toxic Wastes: Technology, Management and Health Effects, 1984, Environmental Radon: Occurrence, Control and Health Hazards, 1990, Natural and Technological Disasters: Causes, Effects and Preventive Measures, 1992, Conservation and Resource Management, 1993, Medicine and Health Care into the 21st Century, 1995, Forests: A Global Perspective, 1996, (with M.S. Monmonier) Ecology of the Wetlands and Associated Systems, 1998, (with M.S. Monmonier)Renewable Resources: Trends and Prospects, 2002; co-author: (with M.S. Monmonier) The Study of Population: Elements, Patterns, Processes, 1983, Map Appreciation, 1988; editor: (with G.J. Demko and H.M. Rose) Population Geography: A Reader, 1970; contbr. articles to profl. jours. Appt. mem. local bds. and coms. Town and Village of New Paltz, and New Paltz Ctrl. Sch. Dist., 1965—; elder Reformed Ch. of New Paltz; Rep. committeeman Town of Gardner, Ulster County, N.Y., 2000-01. With AUS, 1952-54. Recipient Excellence award N.Y. State/United Univ. Professions, 1990; Disting. Alumnus award West Chester U., 1994. Mem. Assn. Am. Geographers, Pa. Geog. Soc. (mem. editl. bd. Pa. Geographer, Disting. Geographer award 1994), Pa. Acad. Sci. (assoc. editor jour. 1988—), Nat. Coun. for Geographic Edn. Home: 29 River Park Dr New Paltz NY 12561-2636 Office: SUNY at New Paltz Dept Geography 75 S Manheim Blvd New Paltz NY 12561-2400

SCHNELL, PATRICIA LENORE, military officer; b. Maywood, Ill., Aug. 28, 1975; d. Richard Michael and Jean Marie Cesak. AA Criminology, Fayetteville Tech. C.C., Fayetteville, N.C., 1999; BS Psychology, Campbell U., 2001. Lic. FAA comml. and instrument helicopter and pvt. pilot fixed wing. Aviator US Army, Fort Rucker, Ala., 1997—. Tchg. asst., resident asst. Ill. State U., Bloomington, 1994—97. Mem.: Army Aviation Assn. Am. (pres.), Pi Beta Phi. Avocations: working out, travel, flying, scuba diving, sky diving. Home: 1340 Andrus Ave Downers Grove IL 60516 Address: 22 Somerset Pkwy Daleville AL 36322-2200

SCHNELL, ROBERT LEE, JR. lawyer; b. Mpls., Sept. 20, 1948; s. Robert Lee and Dorothy Mae (Buran) S.; m. Jacqueline Irene Husak, Dec. 19, 1969 (div. Aug. 1988); children: Robert Lee III, Elizabeth Anne, Jennifer Irene; m. Julie Ann Bemlott, Sept. 29, 1989; children: Helen Bridget, Michael Henry. BA cum laude, Princeton U., 1970; JD magna cum laude, Harvard U., 1974. Bar: Minn. 1974, U.S. Dist. Ct. Minn. 1974, U.S. Ct. Appeals (8th cir.) 1975, U.S. Supreme Ct. 1990. Assoc. Faegre & Benson, Mpls., 1974-81, ptnr., 1982—. Bd. dirs. United Way of Mpls., 1992-93. Office: Faegre & Benson 2200 Wells Fargo Ctr 90 S St Ste 2200 Minneapolis MN 55402-1109

SCHNELL, ROGER THOMAS, business owner, retired state official and career officer; b. Wabasha, Minn., Dec. 11, 1936; s. Donald William and Eva Louise (Barton) S.; m. Barbara Ann McDonald, Dec. 18, 1959 (div. Mar. 1968); children: Thomas Allen, Scott Douglas. A in Mil. Sci., Command and Gen. Staff Coll., 1975; A in Bus. Administn., Wayland Bapt. U., 1987. Commd. 2d lt. Alaska N.G., 1959, advanced through grades to col., 1975, shop supt., 1965-71, personnel mgr., 1972-74, chief of staff, 1974-87, dir. logistics, 1987; electrician Alaska R.R., 1955-61, elec. foreman, 1962-64; dir. support personnel mgmt. Joint Staff Alaska N.G., 1988-92, ret.; personnel mgr. State of Alaska, 1992, asst. commr. dept. mil. and vets. affairs, 1992-95, dep. commr. dept. mil. and vets. affairs, 1995-98; owner RTS Enterprises, Anchorage, 1999—. Prin., owner RTS Enterprises, 1999—; adv. bd. state joint armed svc. com. State of Alaska, 2001—. *Roger Schnell has over 25 years of progressively responsible experience in state and federal government senior management and executive levels. As Chief of Staff, Alaska Army National Guard, he directed staff expansion of the organization from 2,200 employees to over 3,000. From 1988-1991, as director of personnel management, he administered expansion of full time work force from 850 to over 1,350. In 1992, Roger was appointed Chief of Staff, Department of Military and Veterans Affairs. As Deputy Commissioner, 1995, he was responsible for daily operations of 8 divisions with over 4,500 personnel and $150 million budget. In 1999, Roger retired as State Official and opened A-1 Preventive Health care/RTS Enterprises.* Chmn. pastor parish rels. com. Meth. 1st Ch., 2001—02; bd. dirs. Meth. Trust Fund; chmn. Alaska Nat. Guard Mus. Trust Fund, 2001—. Mem. Fed. Profl. Labor Relations Execs. (sec. 1974-75), Alaska N.G. Officers Assn. (pres. 1976-78, bd. dirs. 1988—), Assn. U.S. Army (corp.), NG Assn. U.S. (life, retiree rep. from Alaska 1993—), Am. Legion, Amvets, Elks. Republican. Methodist. Avocations: travel, photography. Home and Office: Huntwood Park Estates 6817 Queens View Cir Anchorage AK 99504-5203 E-mail: rogertschnell@gci.net., rtschnellenterprises@gci.net.

SCHNELL, RONALD OTTO, art educator, art collections director; b. Stuttgart, W.Ger., July 1, 1929; came to U.S., 1958; s. Otto Franz and Frieda Maria (Woehrle) S.; m. Ruthanne Delong, June 19, 1958; children: David, Inge. BA, Schickhardt-Realgymnasium, Stuttgart, 1949; MA, State Acad. Fine Arts, Stuttgart, 1952, MFA, 1953; MA, Tuebingen U., 1957, postgrad., 1958; cert. Los Angeles County Art Inst., 1959. State diploma for art edn. and German, Baden-Wuerttemberg. Asst. prof. Tougaloo Coal., Miss., 1959-64, assoc. prof., 1964-70, prof. art, 1970—, curator art collections, 1965-82, dir. art collections, 1982—; adj. prof. Jackson State U., Miss., 1970, 73, 74. Painter; author catalogues Tougaloo Coll. art collections, 1978. Participant City Spirit, Jackson Arts Alliance, 1979, 80; co-dir. Tougaloo Coll.-Miss. Mus. Art Coop, Jackson, 1978-85. Howard fellow in painting, Brown U., Providence, 1960; recipient Merril F. Ingram award in painting, 1964, Griot award, SE Conf. Afro-Am. Studies, 1984, award for Dissemination Afro-Am. Art, Miss. Cultural Arts Coalition, Jackson, 1984; NEH fellow, 1984. Mem. Coll. Art Assn., Miss. Mus. Art. Home: Tougaloo Coll Tougaloo MS 39174

SCHNELL, RUSSELL CLIFFORD, atmospheric scientist, researcher; b. Castor, Alta., Can., Dec. 12, 1944; s. Henry Emmanuel and Anna (Traudt) S.; m. Suan Neo Tan, May 25, 1974; children: Alicia, Ryan. BSc with distinction, U. Alta. (Can.), Edmonton, 1967; BSc, Meml. U., St. John's, Nfld., Can., 1968; MSc, U. Wyo., 1971, PhD, 1974. Research scientist U. Wyo., Laramie, 1971-74, Nat. Ctr. Atmospheric Research and NOAA, Boulder, Colo., 1974-76; dir. Mt. Kenya study World Meteorol. Orgn. div. UN, Nairobi, Kenya, 1976-78; research scientist U. Colo., Boulder, 1979-82, dir. Arctic Gas and Aerosol Sampling Program, 1982-92, fellow Coop. Inst. Research in Environ. Scis., 1985-92; dir. Mauna Loa Observatory, Hilo, Hawaii, 1992-98, NOAA Observatory Ops., Boulder, Colo., 1998—. Mem. aerobiology com. Nat. Acad. Sci., 1976-79; cons. UN, Geneva, 1977-80, Shell Devel., Modesto, Calif., 1978-79, Holme, Roberts & Owen, 1990-92; mem. adv. bd. Frost Tech., Norwalk, Conn., 1983-85; bd. dirs. TRI-S Inc., Louisville, Colo., Magee Sci., Editor Geophys. Research Letters, Arctic Haze Edit., 1983-84; discovered bacteria ice nuclei, 1969; patentee in field; contbr. articles to profl. jours. Chmn. Boulder Coun. Internat. Visitors, 1983-85. Rotary Internat. fellow, 1968-69. Mem. Am. Geophys. Union, AAAS, Am. Meteorol. Soc. (cert. cons. meteorologist), Internat. Assn. Aerobiology, Soc. Cryobiology, Sigma Xi, Sigma Tau. Avocations: travel (80 countries), real estate investing, public speaking, flying. Office: 325 Broadway St Boulder CO 80305-3337 E-mail: rschnell@cmdl.noaa.gov.

SCHNELLE, HELMUT OTTO, educator; b. Cologne, Germany, Feb. 28, 1932; s. Karl and Elisabeth (Hulser) S.; m. Marlene Schneyder, Dec. 19, 1958; children: Daniele, Andreas. Diploma in physics, U. Bonn, 1957, PhD, 1961; PhD honoris causa (hon.) , U. Bielefeld, Germany, 2000. Rsch. coord. U. Bonn, 1960-65, rsch. asst., 1965-68; prof. linguistics Tech. U., Berlin, 1968-75; prof. U. Bochum, Germany, 1975-97, prof. emeritus Germany, 1997—. Mem. Acad. Europaea, London. Home: Schattbachstr 17 D-44801 Bochum Germany Office: U Bochum D-44780 Bochum Germany

SCHNELLE, KARL BENJAMIN, JR. chemical engineering educator, consultant, researcher; b. Canton, Ohio, Dec. 8, 1930; s. Karl Benjamin and Kathryn Emily (Hollingsworth) S.; m. Mary Margaret Dabney, Sept. 8, 1954; children: Karl Dabney, Kathryn Chappell. BS, Carnegie Mellon U., 1952, MS, 1957, PhD, 1959. Registered profl. engr., Tenn. Chem. engr., shift foreman Organics area Pitts. Plate Glass Co., New Martinsville, W.Va., 1952-54; asst. prof. chem. engring. Vanderbilt U., 1958-61, assoc. prof., 1961-64, assoc. prof. environ. and air resources engring., 1967-70, prof., 1970-80, chmn. div. socio-technol. systems, 1972-75, chmn. environ. and water resources engring., 1975-76, chmn. environ. engring. and policy mgmt. dept., 1976-80, chmn. chem. engring. dept., 1980-88, prof. chem. and environ. engring., 1980—; Alexander Heard disting. svc. prof., 1995-96. V.p. ECCE, Nashville, 1983-88, pres., 1989—; mem. Air Pollution Control Bd., State Tenn., 1978-82, 82-87; Fulbright prof. U. Liege, Belgium, 1977; invited prof. Universite Catholique de Louvain, Belgium, 1982; vis. prof. chem. engring. Danish Tech. Inst., Lyngby, Denmark, 1988-89. Fellow AICE; mem. Air and Waste Mgmt. Assn., Instrument Soc. Am., Am. Soc. Engring. Edn., Am. Soc. Environ. Engrs., Sigma Xi, Phi Kappa Phi, Tau Beta Pi. Office: Vanderbilt U VU Station B 351604 Nashville TN 37235-1604 E-mail: schnelk2@ctrvax.vanderbilt.edu.

SCHNELLE, PHILLIP DAVID, electrical engineer, consultant; b. Orange, Tex., Feb. 29, 1952; s. Philip Davis and Mary (Lyons) Schnelle; m. Janie Lou Wilson, June 17, 1972; children: Brandy Glennon, Elisabeth Miller, Phillip. MSEE, U. Del., Newark, 1975. Registered Profl. Engr. , Tex., 1982. Cons. DuPont Engring. Project Group, Wilmington, Del., 1974—80; sr. cons. DuPont Engring. Services Divsn., Beaumont, Tex., 1980—85; prin. cons. DuPont Engring. Tech., Wilmington, Del., 1985—. Lyme disease activist London Britian Twp., Landenberg, Pa., 1990—. Recipient Engring. Excellence Award, DuPont Co., 2001. Mem.: ISA. Achievements include research in dynamic modeling, advanced control applications (regulatory and MPC), data modeling (neural networks MVS and TSA)and interfaces between SPC and APC (Lab Feedback Control and Performance Monitoring). Avocations: fishing, sailing.

SCHNEPS, JACK, physics educator; b. N.Y.C., Aug. 18, 1929; s. Elias and Rose (Rephen) S.; m. Lucia DeMarchi, Mar. 11, 1960; children: Loredana, Melissa, Leila. BA, N.Y. U., 1951; MS, U. Wis., 1953, PhD, 1956. Asst. prof. physics Tufts U., 1956-60, asso. prof., 1960-63, prof., 1963—, chmn. dept. physics, 1980-89, Vannevar Bush chair, 1995—. Vis. scientist European Orgn. Nuclear Research, Geneva, Switzerland, 1965-66; lectr. Internat. Sch. Elementary Particle Physics, Yugoslavia, 1968; vis. research fellow Univ. Coll., London, Eng., 1973-74; vis. prof. Ecole Polytechnique, Palaiseau, France, 1982-83, The Technion, Haifa, Israel, 1989-90, Coll. de France, Paris, 1997. Contbg. author: Methods in Subnuclear Physics, Vol. IV, 1970; editor Proc. of Neutrino 88, 1989; contbr. articles to profl. jours. NSF postdoctoral fellow U. Padua, Italy, 1958-59 Fellow Am. Phys. Soc.; mem. European Phys. Soc., AAUP, Phi Beta Kappa, Sigma Xi. Home: 3 Foxcroft Rd Winchester MA 01890-2407 Office: Dept Physics Tufts U Medford MA 02155 E-mail: jschneps@tufts.edu.

SCHNITZER, ARLENE DIRECTOR, art dealer; b. Salem, Oreg., Jan. 10, 1929; d. Simon M. and Helen (Holtzman) Director; m. Harold J. Schnitzer, Sept. 11, 1949; 1 child, Jordan. Student, U. Wash., 1947-48; BFA (hon.), Pacific NW Coll. Art, 1988. Founder, pres. Fountain Gallery of Art, Portland, Oreg., 1951-86; exec. v.p. Harsch Investment Corp., 1951—. Apptd. to Oreg. State Bd. Higher Edn., 1987-88; former bd. dirs. Oreg. Symphony Assn., v.p. Oreg. Symphony; former bd. dirs. U.S. Dist. Ct. Hist. Soc.; bd. dirs. Boys and Girls Club, 1988—; mem. Gov.'s Expo '86 Commn., Oreg.; mem. exec. com., former bd. dirs. Artquake; former mem. adv. bd. Our New Beginnings; past bd. dirs. Artists Initiative for a Contemporary Art Collection; former trustee Reed Coll., 1982-88; mem. exec. com. bd. dirs. N.W. Bus. Com. for Arts., 1992-97; former trustee, mem. exec. com. Oreg. Health Scis. Univ. Found.; campaign chair campaign for women's helath Oreg. Health Sci. Found., 2000—; mem. arts acquisition and collections com. Portland Art Mus.; mem. Nat. Com. for the Performing Arts, Kennedy Ctr., 1995—; past adv. bd. Svc. to Children and Families Orgn., 1995-97; bd. trustees Oreg. Jewish Cmty. Found., 1996-97; mem. Nat. Coun. Fine Arts Mus. San Francisco, 1995—; bd. dirs. Oreg. Hist. Soc., 1999-2000. Recipient Aubrey Watzek award Lewis and Clark Coll., 1981, Pioneer award U. Oreg., 1985, Met. Arts Commn. award, 1985, White Rose award March of Dimes, 1987, Disting. Svc. award Western Oreg. State Coll., 1988, Oreg. Urban League Equal Opportunity award 1988, Gov.'s award for Arts, 1987, Woman of Achievement award YWCA, 1987, Disting. Svc. award U. Oreg., 1991, SAFECO Art Leadership award ArtFair/Seattle, 1994, Portland First Citizen award Portland Met. Assn. Realtors, 1995, Tom McCall Leadership award, 1995; honored by Portland Art Assn., 1979, Northwest Bus. Com. for the Arts, 1997, Arts Champions, 1997. Mem. Univ. Club, Multnomah Athletic Club, Portland Golf Club. Office: Harsch Investment Properties 1121 SW Salmon St Ste 400 Portland OR 97205-2092

SCHNITZER, DAVID, advertising executive; b. San Antonio, Mar. 21, 1970; s. Stephen and Barbara Schnitzer. BS in Advt., U. Tex., 1992. New bus. team GSD&M Advt., Austin, Tex., 1990-92; assoc. account mgr. Hal Riney & Ptnrs./Angotti, Thomas, Hedge, N.Y.C., 1992-94; sr. account mgr. DDB Needham/Focus Agy., Dallas, 1994-98; sr. mktg. mgr. GTE Internetworking, 1998-99; pres. Martech Consulting Group, 1998—. Chair Am. Jewish Com.-Perspectives, Dallas, 2000-01. Mem. Assn. Internet Profls., Ex-Students Assn. U. Tex. Austin (life). Office: Martech Consulting Group Ste 100 25 Highland Park Village Dallas TX 75205 Office Fax: 214-352-6791. E-mail: david@martechconsulting.com.

SCHNITZER, IRIS TAYMORE, financial management executive, lawyer; b. Cambridge, Mass., Aug. 3, 1943; d. Joseph David and Edith (Cooper) Taymore; m. Stephen Mark Schnitzer, Sept. 10, 1966. BA in Econs., Boston U., 1967; JD, Mass. Sch. Law, 1996. Bar: Mass. 1996; lic. real estate broker, life ins. advisor, life ins. and health ins. broker; registered rep. NASD; CFP; CLU; cert. in fin. counseling, advanced pension planning. Real estate broker Woods Real Estate, Braintree, Mass., 1968; real estate broker, property mgr. Village Gate Realty, Brockton, 1969; agt. Prudential Ins., Boston, 1970-73, Northwestern Mutual Life, Boston, 1973—78, supr. edn. and advanced underwriting, 1976—78; fin. planning cons. Iris Taymore Schnitzer Assocs., 1973-79; trainer fin. planners Gerstenblatt Co., Newton, 1978-79; founder, CEO The Fin. Forum, Inc., Boston, 1979-91; CEO TFF, Inc. at the Chase Exchange, N.Y.C., 1980—83; prin. I&S Assocs., Boston, 1991; v.p. Fleet Pvt. Clients Group, 1993-2000; pvt. practice Law Office of Iris Taymore Schnitzer, 2000—. Bd. dirs., clk. Mister Tire, Inc., Abington, Mass.; arbitrator Nat. Assn. Securities Dealers Regulation, Inc., 1992—. Contbr. articles to profl. jours. Chair credit com., bd. dirs. Mass. Feminist Fed. Credit Union, Cambridge, Mass., 1975-77; bd. dirs. Ledgewood, Brookline, Mass., 1967-70, LWV, Brockton, Mass., 1968-70, NOW, Boston, 1972-73; bd. govs. Women's City Club, Boston, 1976-80; pres. Mass. divsn. Women's Equity Action League, 1977-79; life mem. Navy League U.S.; treas., bd. dirs. Festival of Light and Song, 1989-92; bd. dirs. Achievement Rewards for Coll. Scientists, Boston, 1991-95; steering com. Fleet Bank of Mass. United Way, 1994-95; chair task group to establish Girls' Bank of Patriots' Trail Girl Scout Coun., 1996-98; overseer Boston Lyric Opera, 1999—. Named one of Best Fin. Planners in the U.S., Money Mag., 1987, to Mutual Funds Panel, Sylvia Porter's Personal Fin. Mag., 1988, 89. Fellow Mass. Bar Found., Am. Assn. Individual Investors (pres. Boston chpt. 1987-89, bd. dirs. 1985-95); mem. ABA, Mass. Bar Assn., Boston Bar Assn., Boston Estate Planning Coun., Boston Club. Republican. Avocations: sailing, gardening, interior and fashion design, animals, classical music. Office: Law Office of Iris Taymore Schnitzer 65 E India Row Boston MA 02110-3308

SCHNITZER, ROBERT C. theater administrator; b. N.Y.C., Sept. 8, 1906; s. Louis and Clara (diBilliani) S.; m. Marcella Abels Cisney, June 7, 1953. Grad., Horace Mann Sch. for Boys, 1923; AB, Columbia U., 1927. State dir. Del., asst. dep. nat. dir. Fed. Theatre Project, 1936-39; exec. dir. Civic Theatre, Kalamazoo, 1939-40; faculty Vassar Coll., 1941-42, Smith Coll., 1942-43, Columbia U. Sch. Dramatic Arts, 1948-54. Cons. Martha Graham Sch. Dance, Rollins Sch. Theatre, Randall Sch. Theatre, Dramatic Workshop of New Sch., Denver Red Rocks Theatre, Utah Centennial, 1945-49; vets. counselor Nat. Theater Conf., 1945-46; gen. mgr. ANTA Exptl. Theatre, 1946-47, Cheryl Crawford Prodns., 1952-53, Gilbert Miller Prodns., 1953-54, Am. Nat. Theatre and Acad. Internat. Cultural Exch., 1954-60; gen. mgr. overseas tour Theatre Guild Am. Repertory Co., 1960-61; exec. dir. Profl. Theatre Program U. Mich., Ann Arbor, prof. theatre arts, 1961-73, prof. emeritus and exec. dir. emeritus, 1974—; co-founder, exec. dir. Univ. Resident Theatre Assn., 1969-74, cons., 1974—; del. U.S. Nat. Conf. on UNESCO, 1953-57, 1st Inter-Am. Conf. Exch. Persons, 1958; vis. theatre expert German Fgn. Office Cultural Exch. Program, 1965; cons. to pres. U. Bridgeport for Coll. Fine Arts, 1975-87; disting. vis. prof. U. Miami, Fla., 1980, U. Bridgeport, Conn., 1981; co-founder Westport Arts Ctr., 1984, interim pres., 1985, v.p., 1986, chmn. bd., 1987-89, chmn. emeritus, 1989—; mem. Fulbright selection com. theatre arts, 1955-59, Mich. Coun. Arts, 1961-73; hon. bd. dirs. Westport/Weston Arts Coun., 1969-84; mem. Weston Town Commn. for Arts, 1997—. Stage mgr., actor, Theatre Guild, Walter Hampden, Katherine Cornell, other Broadway cos., 1927-36; owner, dir., Robin Hood Summer Theatre, Arden, Del., 1933-40; gen. mgr. U.S. participation, Denmark Hamlet Festival, Elsinore, 1949, 1st Am. Ballet Theatre tour, Europe, 1950, U.S. ofcl. participation, Berlin Festivals, 1951-53, U.S. participation, Congress Cultural Freedom Festival, Paris, 1952, U.S. Salute to France, Paris, 1955; arranged visits to U.S., Greek Nat. Theatre, 1952, Yugoslav Nat. Folk Ballet, 1956, Shanta Rao East Indian Dance Co., 1957; Contbr. articles in field to various publs. Mem. Weston (Conn.) Commn. Arts, 1995—. Served with ARC, 1943-45, CBI. Recipient Pres.'s Citation U. Mich., 1971, Arts Mgmt. Career award for svcs. to Am. theater, 1971, Sidney Howard award, 1951; Rockefeller Found. grantee, 1948; grad. fellow in theater adminstrn. named in his honor U. Mich., 1974; Robert C. Schnitzer theater memorabilia collection established at George Mason U. Mem. Coll. Fellows of Am. Theatre (life), Actors Equity

Assn., Am. Nat. Theatre and Acad., Assn. Theatrical Press Agts. and Mgrs., Nat. Coun. Arts and Govt., Nat. Theatre Conf., Theatre Libr. Assn., U.S. Inst. Theatre Technicians, The Players Club (bd. dirs. 1997—), The Century Club. Home: 1332 Edgehill Stamford CT 06902-2145

SCHNITZLEIN, HAROLD NORMAN, anatomy educator; b. Hannibal, Mo., Aug. 29, 1927; s. Harold Daniel and Martha Anna (Wilhelm) S.; m. Harriett Elizabeth Scheidker, June 2, 1949; children: Jan Elizabeth, Paul Norman, Daniel Richard, Thomas Harry. AB, Westminster Coll., Fulton, Mo., 1950; MS, St. Louis U., 1952, PhD, 1954. USPHS fellow Dept. Anatomy St. Louis U., 1951-54; instr. anatomy U. Ala., Birmingham, 1954-57, asst. prof., 1957-62, assoc. prof., 1962-70, prof., 1970-73; chmn., prof. anatomy U. S. Fla. Coll. Medicine, Tampa, 1973-78, prof., 1978-85, prof. anatomy and radiology, 1985-93, prof. anatomy, radiology, neurology, 1985-93; clin. prof. radiology U. Diagnostic Inst., 1993-94, prof. emeritus anatomy, 1995—. Coeditor: Correlative Comparative Anatomy Vertebrate Tel., 1982, Imaging Anatomy: Head and Spine, 2d edit., 1990. Sgt. USAAF, 1946-47. E-mail: hschnitzlein@aol.com.

SCHNOBRICH, ROGER WILLIAM, lawyer; b. New Ulm, Minn., Dec. 21, 1929; s. Arthur George and Amanda (Reinhart) S.; m. Angeline Ann Schmitz, Jan. 21, 1961; children: Julie A. Johnson, Jennifer L. Holmers, Kathryn M. Kubinski, Karen L. Holetz. BBA, U. Minn., 1952, JD, 1954. Bar: Minn. 1954. Assoc. Fredrikson and Byron, Mpls., 1956-58; pvt. practice, 1958-60; ptnr. Popham Haik, Schnobrich & Kaufman, 1960-97, Hinshaw & Culbertson, Mpls., 1997—. Bd. dirs. numerous corps., Mpls. With U.S. Army, 1954-56. Mem. ABA, Minn. Bar Assn., Hennepin County Bar Assn., Order of Coif, Law Rev. Roman Catholic. Avocations: family, jogging, reading, golf. Home: 530 Waycliff Dr N Wayzata MN 55391-1385 Office: Hinshaw & Culbertson 3100 Piper Jaffray Tower 222 S 9th St Minneapolis MN 55402-3389 E-mail: rschnobrich@hinshawlaw.com.

SCHNOLL, HOWARD MANUEL, investment banking and managed asset consultant; b. Milw., June 6, 1935; s. Nathan P. and Della (Fisher) S.; m. Barbara Ostach, Dec. 3, 1988; children: Jordan, Terry, Jeffrey, Robert, Tammy, Daniel. BBA, U. Wis., 1958. CPA, Wis.; cert. mgmt. cons.; registered investment advisor. Mng. ptnr. Nankin, Schnoll & Co., S.C., Milw., 1966-86; mng. ptnr., bd. dirs. BDO Seidman, 1986-90; pres., chief oper. officer Universal Med. Bldgs., L.P., Milw., 1990, also bd. dirs.; pres. Howard Schnoll & Assocs., 1991; mng. dir. Grande, Schnoll & Assocs., 1992-93; exec. mng. dir., COO Glaisner, Schilffarth, Grande & Schnoll, Ltd., 1993-98; exec. v.p., treas., bd. dirs GS2 Securities, Inc., 1998-99; sr. v.p. B.C. Ziegler and Co., 1999—. Bd. dirs. Milw. World Festival, Inc., 1968—, City of Festivals Parade, Milw., 1983-89, Aurora Health Care Ventures, Milw. Heart Rsch. Found., Milw. Heart Inst., Arthritis Found.; pres. Milw. Coun. on Alcoholism and Drug Dependance, 1993—, bd. dirs.; pres., treas. Am. Heart Assn., Milw., 1978-82; capt. United Way, Milw., 1985; mem. Greater Milw. Com. Nat. Found. Ileitis and Colitis, Milw. chpt. Served to sgt. U.S. Army, 1956-63. Mem.: AICPA, Brynwood Country Club (bd. dirs., treas., pres. 1988—2000), Acct. Computer Users Tech. Exchange, Wis. Inst. CPAs, B'nai Brith (pres. 1960—62). Jewish. Avocations: golf, tennis. Office: BC Ziegler & Co 250 E Wisconsin Ave Ste 2000 Milwaukee WI 53202-4298 E-mail: hschnoll@ziegler.com.

SCHNOOR, JEFFREY ARNOLD, lawyer; b. Winnipeg, Man., Can., June 22, 1953; s. Toby and Ray (Kass) S. BA, U. Man., 1974, LLB, 1977. Bar: Man. 1978. Assoc. McJannet Weinberg Rich, Winnipeg, 1977-84, ptnr., 1984-86; exec. dir. Man. Law Reform Commn., 1986-97; dir. criminal justice policy Man. Dept. Justice, 1998—2002, exec. dir. policy devel. & analysis, 2002—. Pres. Fedn. Law Reform Agys. Can., 1995-98; del. Uniform Law Conf. Can., 1986—, exec. com. 1995-2001, chair civil sect., 1996-97, v.p., 1998-99, pres., 1999-2000. Trustee United Way of Winnipeg, 1990-97, 99—, exec. com., 1990-97, 2001— treas., 1991-92, pres., 1994-95, cmty. rels. com. 1995-98, chmn. 1996-97, chair United Way 2005 com., 1997-98, hon. solicitor, 2001—, chmn. 211 implementation com., 2001-; mem. R&D 2000 steering com., United Way of Can., 1995-98; bd. dirs. Winnipeg Libr. Found., 1997-2001; Man. Voluntary Sector Coun., 2001-. Named Queen's Counsel Govt. of Man., 1992; recipient Chair's award of distinction United Way of Can., 1997. Mem. Law Soc. Man. (lectr. bar admission course 1981-96), Man. Bar Assn. (governing coun. 1988-96, life mem.), Can. Bar Assn. (legis. and law reform com. 1994-2000, 2001— vice-chair 1997-2000, chair 2001—). Avocations: travel, languages, performing arts, fitness. Home: 2245 West Taylor Blvd Winnipeg MB Canada R3P 2J5 Office: Policy Development & Analysis 1210-405 Broadway Winnipeg MB Canada R3C 3L6 E-mail: jschnoor@gov.mb.ca.

SCHNUDA, DANIEL NASR, internist, pathologist; b. Luxor, Egypt, Dec. 20, 1938; came to U.S., 1961; s. Daniel Schnuda; children: Charles, Peter. MB, MD, Faculty of Medicine, Cairo, 1959; MSc, Ohio State U., 1966. diplomate Am. Bd. Pathology. Resident in pathology Ohio State U., Columbus, 1963—66, mem. faculty, 1966—67; rsch. fellow immunology Toronto (Can.) Western Hosp., 1967—68; rsch. fellow electron microscope Banting Inst. U. Toronto, 1968—71; asst. prof. pathology Wayne State U., Detroit, 1971—76; chmn. dept. pathology, dir. of labs. Edgewater Hosp. Mazel Med. Ctr., Chgo., 1976—79; assoc. prof. Chgo. Med. Sch., 1977—81; pres. N.W. Internal Medicine S.C., Palatine, Ill., 1981—; attending physician N.W. Cmty. Hosp., Arlington Heights, 1983—, med. dir., leader, 1996—; attending physician Good Shephard Hosp., Barrington, 1989—, St. Alexis Hosp., 1981. Pres. Chgo. Internat. Corp. Ltd., 1987—. Contbr. articles in molecular and cellular immunology to profl. jours.; patentee in field. CEO Internat. Med. Coun. Ill., 1996—; founder "Crops for the World", 1998; founding bd. dirs. Assn. Am. Physicians and Surgeons, 1998. Fellow Coll. Am. Pathologists; mem. AMA, ACP, Ill. State Med. Soc. (del. 1988—), Chgo. Med. Soc. (coun. mem. 1988—, pres. Irving Park br. 2002—) Achievements include work conducting agriculture projects to convert desert land to fertile land, achieved in the Egyptian desert and the Chinese desert using newly invented patented product "fertile desert." Avocation: growing desert crops to alleviate hunger in 3d world countries.

SCHNUR, ROBERT ARNOLD, lawyer; b. White Plains, N.Y., Oct. 25, 1938; s. Conrad Edward and Ruth (Mehr) S.; children: Daniel, Jonathan. BA, Cornell U., 1960; JD, Harvard U., 1963. Bar: Wis. 1965, Ill. 1966. Assoc. Michael, Best & Friedrich, Milw., 1966-73, ptnr., 1973—. Chmn. Wis. Tax News, 1983-90; adj. prof. tax law U. Wis. Law Sch., 1988—. Capt. U.S. Army, 1963-65. Fellow Am. Coll. Tax Counsel; mem. ABA, Wis. Bar Assn. (chmn. tax sect. 1986-88), Milw. Bar Assn. Home: 3093 Timber Ln Verona WI 53593 Office: Michael Best Friedrich 100 E Wisconsin Ave Ste 3300 Milwaukee WI 53202-4108 E-mail: raschnur@mbf-law.com.

SCHOBER, MYRON JEROME, newspaper editor and publisher; b. Marion, N.D., June 23, 1942; s. John M. and Marie Louise Schober; m. Darlene J. Anderson, Sept. 1, 1963; children: John Mark, David J. PhB, U. N.D., 1966, postgrad., 1971. With pub. info. dept. U. N.D., Grand Forks, 1962-64; editor Lamoure (N.D.) Chronicle, 1969-70; comm. dir. Rocky Mountain Farmers Union, Denver, 1971-77; mgr., sec. Mont. Farmers Union, Gt. Falls, 1977-78; editor, pub., owner Tri-County Record, Rushford, Minn., 1978—. Former lobbyist for agr., Colo., Wyo., N.Mex. and fed. govt.; active in cmty. devel., edn. and arts; performer cmty. theater. 1st lt., inf. U.S. Army, 1966-69, Vietnam. Mem. Nat. Press Photographers Assn., Soc. Profl. Journalists (past pres. Colo.), Minn. Newspaper Assn., Lions. Democrat. Lutheran. Avocations: theater, music, photography, community volunteering. Office: Tri-County Pub Inc 300 S Mill St Rushford MN 55971-8824 E-mail: tricopub@rushford.net.

SCHOBER, THOMAS GREGORY, lawyer; b. Waukesha, Wis., Aug. 17, 1948; s. Theodore Michael and Rosalie (Blando) S.; m. Patricia Ann Farrell, Jan. 17, 1981; children: Wendy, Sara, Sarah, Sonya, Christy, Marc. BS, Marquette U., 1970, JD, 1972. Bar: Wis. 1973, U.S. Dist. Ct. (ea. and we. dists.) Wis. 1973, U.S. Tax Ct. 1976. Mng. ptnr., atty. Schober & Radtke, S.C., New Berlin, Wis., 1973-96, Schober Schober & Mitchell, S.C., New Berlin, 1996—. Prof. acctg. U. Wis., Waukesha, 1975-77; prof. law Marquette Law Sch., Milw., 1977-81; mem. adv. bd. Luth. Social Svcs., Milw., 1983-86; bd. dirs. Stepping Stones Child Devel. Ctr., New Berlin, 1998-99. Airport commr. Waukesha County Airport Commn., 1994—. With Wis. N.G., 1970-76. Republican. Lutheran. Avocation: pilot. Office: Schober Schober & Mitchell SC 16845 W Cleveland Ave New Berlin WI 53151-3532 E-mail: tgs@schoberlaw.com.

SCHOBERT, MELODY A. educator, counselor educator; b. Creston, Iowa, May 8, 1953; d. Joseph C. and Donna J. Schobert; divorced; children: Arlen D. Chase, Benjamin M. MusB, Iowa State U., 1976, M in Counselor Edn., 1987; PhD in Counselor Edn., U. Iowa, 2000. Lic. counselor 7-12, tchr. K-12 music, 7-12 secondary tchr., postsecondary counselor, postsecondary psychology tchr., Iowa. Student devel. specialist William Penn Coll., Oskaloosa, Iowa, 1987-90; acad. advisor III Iowa State U., Ames, 1990-2000; asst. prof. U. Memphis, 2000—. Presenter in field. Performer, River City Concert Band. Mem. ACA, Am. Assn. for Counselor Edn. and Supervision, Tenn. Counseling Assn., Am. Coll. Pers. Assn., West Tenn. Counseling Assn., Tenn. Assn. for Counselor Edn. and Supervision (pres.-elect). Avocations: musical groups, counted cross-stitch. Office: U Memphis 100 Ball Hall Memphis TN 38152 E-mail: mschobrt@memphis.edu.

SCHOCHET, BARRY P. health care executive; b. N.Y.C., Mar. 13, 1951; s. George and Freda Schochet. BA in Zoology, U. Maine, 1973; MA in Health Care Adminstrn., George Washington U., 1975. Asst. adminstr. Doctors Hosp., Hollywood, Fla., 1975-76, Cypress Community Hosp., Pompano Beach, 1976-77, adminstr., 1977-78, exec. dir., 1978-79; asst. regional v.p. Nat. Med. Enterprises, St. Petersburg, 1979-80, asst. v.p. Los Angeles, 1980-81, v.p. ops. Tampa, Fla., 1981-83, sr. regional v.p., 1984-87, sr. divisional v.p., 1987-89, exec. v.p., 1989-91, sr. exec. v.p. and COO Santa Monica, Calif., 1991-93; pres., COO Hosp. Group Nat. Med. ENT, 1993-95; vice chmn. Tenet Healthcare, Dallas, 1996—. Mem. Am. Hosp. Assn., Fedn. Am. Health Care Systems (bd. govs. 1985—, bd. dirs. 1989—, chmn. 2000), Am. Coll. Health Care Execs., Fla. League Hosps. (bd. dirs. 1981—, chmn. 1988-89), bd. dir. Healthcare leadership coun., 1999—. Office: Tenet Healthcare 13737 Noel Rd Dallas TX 75240*

SCHOCHOR, JONATHAN, lawyer, educator; b. Suffern, N.Y., Sept. 9, 1946; s. Abraham and Betty (Hechtor) S.; m. Joan Elaine Brown, May 31, 1970; children: Lauren Aimee, Daniel Ross. BA, Pa. State U., 1968; JD, Am. U., 1971. Bar: D.C. 1971, U.S. Dist. Ct. D.C. 1971, U.S. Ct. Appeals (D.C. cir.) 1971, Md. 1974, U.S. Dist. Ct. Md. 1974, U.S. Supreme Ct. 1986. Assoc. McKenna, Wilkinson & Kittner, Washington, 1970-74, Ellin & Baker, Balt., 1974-84; ptnr. Schochor, Federico & Staton, 1984—. Lectr. in law; expert witness to state legis. Editor-in-chief: Am. U. Law Rev., 1970—71. Mem. ABA, ATLA (state del. 1991, state gov. 1992-95), Am. Bd. Trial Advs. (membership com. 1994—), Am. Bd. Trial Advs., Am. Judicature Soc., Md. State Bar Assn. (spl. com. on health claims arbitration 1983), Md. Trial Lawyers Assn. (bd. govs. 1986-87, mem. legis. com. 1985-88, chmn. legis. com. 1986-87, sec. 1987-88, exec. com. 1987-92, v.p. 1987-88, pres.-elect 1989, pres. 1990-91), Balt. City Bar Assn. (legis com. 1986-87, spl. com. on tort reform 1986, medicolegal com. 1989-90, cir. ct. for Balt. City task force-civil document mgmt. sys. 1994-95), Bar Assn. D.C., Internat. Platform Assn., Phi Alpha Delta. Office: Schochor Federico & Staton PA 1211 Saint Paul St Baltimore MD 21202-2783

SCHOCK, MARTIN IRVING, oncologist; b. Cleve., Sept. 7, 1938; s. Abraham G. and Shirley S.; m. Carole Klugerman, June 24, 1967; children: Pamela E., Joseph L., Abby G. BA, Cornell U., 1960; MD, Northwestern U., 1964. Diplomate Am. Bd. Internal Medicine, Am. Bd. Med. Oncology. Chief of medicine North Detroit Gen. Hosp., 1975, 85-92; chief of oncology Macomb Hosp. Ctr., Warren, Mich., 1980-96; treas. Holy Cross Hosp. Physician Orgn., Detroit, 1995-97; pvt. practice Warren, 1971—; chief of medicine Greater Detroit Med. Ctr., 1997-99; chief of oncology, vice chief of medicine St. John's N.E. Cmty. Hosp., 2001—. Capt. USAF, 1968-70. Mem. Am. Soc. Clin. Oncology, Am. Soc. Hematology, Mich. State Med. Soc., Michigan Soc. Oncology, Blood Club, Oakland County Med. Soc., Phi Delta Epsilon (pres. grad. club 1976-77). Avocations: tennis, travel, music. Office: 11900 E 12 Mile Rd Ste 205 Warren MI 48093-3400 E-mail: shockdoc12@aol.com.

SCHOCK, ROBERT NORMAN, geophysicist; b. Monticello, N.Y., May 25, 1939; s. Carl Louis and Norma Elizabeth (Greenfield) S.; m. Susan Esther Benton, Nov. 28, 1959; children: Pamela Ann, Patricia Elizabeth, Christina Benton. BS, Colo. Coll., 1961; MS, Rensselaer Poly. Inst., 1963, PhD, 1966; postgrad., Northwestern U., 1963-64. Cert. Calif. state wine judge. Jr. geophys. trainee Continental Oil Co., Sheridan, Wyo., 1960; jr. geologist Texaco In., Billings, Mont., 1961; teaching asst. Rensselaer Poly. Inst., Troy, N.Y., 1961-63, research asst., 1964-66; research assoc. U. Chgo., 1966-68; sr. research scientist Lawrence Livermore Nat. Lab., U. Calif., 1968—, group leader high pressure physics, 1972-74, sect. leader geoscis. and engring., 1974-76, div. leader earth scis., 1976-81, head dept. earth scis., 1981-87, energy program leader, 1987-92, dep. assoc. dir. for energy, 1992-98, sr. fellow Ctr. Global Security Rsch., 1998—. Pres. Pressure Sys. Rsch. Inc.; mem. faculty Chabot Coll., 1969-71; dir. Alameda County Flood Control and Water Conservation Dist., 1984-86; mem. adv. panel on geoscis. U.S. Dept. Energy, 1985-87; chair adv. com. U. Calif. Energy Inst., 1992-98; mem. rsch. adv. com. Gas Rsch. Inst., Chgo., 1995-2001; chmn. World Energy Coun., London, Study Group Energy Tech. in 21st Century, 1999—. Mem. editl. bd. Rev. Sci. Instruments, 1975-77; assoc. editor Jour. Geophys. Rsch., 1978-80; bd. assoc. editors 11th Lunar and Planetary Sci. Conf., 1980; mem. adv. bd. Physics ans Chemistry of Minerals, 1983-97; rsch. and publs. on high pressure physics, solid state physics, physics of earth interior, rock deformation, energy R&D and energy policy. Fulbright sr. fellow U. Bonn (Germany), 1973; vis. research fellow Australian Nat. U. Canberra, 1980-81 Mem. AAAS, Am. Geophys. Union, Sigma Xi, Commonwealth of Calif. Club, Cosmos Club (Washington). Office: Lawrence Livermore Nat Lab PO Box 808 Livermore CA 94551-0808 E-mail: schock1@llnl.gov.

SCHOCK, WILLIAM WALLACE, pediatrician; b. Huntingdon, Pa., Aug. 15, 1923; s. Clarence and Mabel (Decker) S.; m. Doris Ann Wilson, July 1, 1944; 1 child, William Wallace, Jr. MD, Temple U., 1947. Intern Conemaugh Valley Meml. Hosp., Johnstown, Pa., 1946-48; resident Women AFB, Cheyene, Wyo., 1951-52; pvt. practive medicine Huntingdon, 1948-50; pediatrician Warren AFB Hosp., 1951-52; chief outpatient svc. USAF, Cheyenne, Wyo., 951-52; pvt. practice medicine specializing in pediatrics Huntingdon, 1952—. Pediatrician J. C. Blair Meml. Hosp.; local pub. health pediatrician. Pres. Huntingdon chpt. Am. Cancer Soc., 1955-57; bd. dirs. local chpt. Am. Heart Assn., 1955-62; mem. Am. Security Coun., Rep. Nat. Com., 2d Amendment Found. With AUS, 1942-45, USAF, 1950-52. Recipient Wisdom award Leon Gutterman, Wisdom Hall of Fame, 1970. Fellow Royal Soc. Health; mem. AMA, Pa. Med. Soc., Huntingdon County Med. Soc. (past pres.), Med. Alumni Assn. Temple U., Am. Assn. Mil. Surgeons U.S., Am. Acad. Pediatrics (assoc.), Internat. Platform Assn., Phi Rho Sigma, Huntingdon Country Club, Heidelburg Country Club (Altoona, Pa.), U.S. Senatorial Club, Rotary. Republican. Presbyterian. Home and Office: RR 2 Box 69 Huntingdon PA 16652-9115

SCHODER, WENDELL LOUIS, lawyer; b. Battle Creek, Mich., July 11, 1926; s. Harold Maurice and Hildred Angeline (Baird) S.; m. Helen Marie Bauman, Feb. 3, 1951; children: Patrice Schoder Emmerson, Robert, Gerald, Martha Schoder Terry, Mary Collins, David. Student, Georgetown U., 1946-47; JD, U. Detroit, 1951. Bar: Mich. 1951, U.S. Dist. Ct. (we. dist.) Mich. 1953. Sole practice, Battle Creek, 1951-64; cir. ct. commr. Calhoun County, Marshall, Mich., 1954-60, asst. pros. atty., 1960-64, probate judge, 1965-84; of counsel Holmes, Mumford, Schubel, Norlander & Macfarlane, Battle Creek, 1984-88. Instr. law Kellogg Community Coll., Battle Creek, 1974-79; lectr. in field. Contbr. articles to profl. jours. Apptd. Mich. Mental Health Adv. Council, Lansing, 1975-77; chmn. Mich. Mental Health Research, Lansing, 1975-77; pres. Goodwill Industries/Family Services, Battle Creek, 1969-70. Served with U.S. Army, 1944-46. Recipient Mental Health Services award VA, 1981, Commendation Chief Atty. VA, 1984; Snyder-Kok award Mental Health Assn. for Mich., 1983. Mem. Mich. Bar (chmn. probate and estate planning council 1987-88), Calhoun County Bar Assn. (pres. 1963-64), Mich. Assn. Probate Judges. Clubs: Exchange (pres. 1973-74) (Battle Creek). Lodges: K.C. (4 degree). Republican. Roman Catholic. Home and Office: 251 Martha Dr Battle Creek MI 49015-3805 E-mail: w.hschoder@attbi.com.

SCHOECK, RICHARD J(OSEPH), English and humanities scholar, poet; b. N.Y.C., Oct. 10, 1920; s. Gustav J. and Frances M. (Kuntz) S.; m. Reta R. Haberer, 1945 (div. 1976); children: Eric R., Christine C., Jennifer A.; m. Megan S. Lloyd, Feb. 19, 1977. MA, PhD, Princeton U., 1949. Instr. English Cornell U., 1949-55; from asst. prof. to assoc. prof. U. Notre Dame, 1955-61; prof. English U. Toronto, 1961-71; head dept. English St. Michael's Coll., 1965-70; prof. vernacular lit. Pontifical Inst. Mediaeval Studies, Toronto, 1964-71; dir. rsch. activities Folger Shakespeare Libr., also dir. Folger Inst. Renaissance and 18th Century Studies, 1970-74; adj. prof. English Cath. U. Am., 1972; prof. English, medieval and renaissance studies U. Md., 1974-75; prof. English and humanities U. Colo., Boulder, 1975-89, prof. emeritus, 1987—, chmn. dept. integrated studies, 1976-79; chmn. comparative lit., 1983-84; prof. Anglistik Univ. Trier, 1987-90, head dept. (Geschäftsführer), 1988-89; adj. prof. English U. Kans., Lawrence, 1990—. Vincent J. Flynn prof. letters Coll. St. Thomas, 1969; vis. prof. Princeton U., 1964, U. Dallas, 1985; vis. fellow Inst. Advanced Studies in Humanities, Edinburgh, 1984-85; vis. scholar Corpus Christi Coll., Oxford, 1994, Wolfson Coll., Oxford, 1997; fellow Assn. Advancement Edn., 1952-53, Yale U., 1959-60, Can. Coun. 1967-68, Ctr. for the Book, Brit. Libr., 1995-96; cons. NEH: bd. dirs. Natural Law Inst. U. Notre Dame; advisor Italian Acad. for Advanced Studies in Am., 1993. Author: The Achievement of Thomas More, 1976, Intertexuality and Renaissance Texts, 1984, Erasmus Grandescens, 1988, (poems) A Raging Against Chaos, 1989, The Eye of a Traveller, 1992, The Knights Book, 1993, My Hiroshima, 1997, Laureutian Codicit, 2001, Childhood of Old Age, 2001; Erasmus of Europe, Vol. I, The Making of a Humanist, 1467-1500, 1990, Vol. II The Prince of Humanists, 1501-1536, 1993; contbr. numerous articles, papers, revs. to jours. and mags.; editor: Delehaye's Legends of the Saints, 1961, Editing 16th Century Texts, 1966, Roger Ascham: The Scholemaster, 1966, Shakespeare Quar., 1972-74, Acta Conventus Neo-Latini Bononiensis, 1985; gen. editor: The Confutation of Tyndale, 3 vols., 1973; co-editor: Voices of Literature, 2 vols., 1964, 66, Chaucer Criticism, 2 vols, 1960, 61, Style, Rhetoric and Rhythym: Essays by M.W. Croll, 1966, Acta Conventus Neo-Latini Torontonensis, 1991; former gen. editor: Patterns of Literary Criticism; spl. editor Canada vol. Rev. Nat. Literatures, 1977, Sir Thomas Browne and the Republic of Letters, 1982, A Special Number of English Language Notes, 1982; gen. editor (series) Renaissance Masters, 1992—; mem. editl. bds. profl. jours. Served with U.S. Army, 1940-46. Guggenheim Found. fellow, 1968-69, Fulbright fellow, 1983; recipient Centennial medal U. Colo., 1976, Falconer Madan award Bibliographical Soc., London, 1997; co-recipient 1st prize Mellen Poetry Competition, 1997; grantee Can. Coun., UNESCO, Am. Coun. Learned Socs., U. Toronto, U. Colo. Fellow Royal Soc. Can., Royal Hist. Soc.; mem. Internat. Assn. Neo-Latin Studies (pres. 1976-79), MLA, Renaissance Soc. Am., PEN (N.Y.), Internat. Assn. U. Profs. English. Home: 232 Dakota St Lawrence KS 66046-4710 E-mail: schoeck@midusa.net. *More than a thousand years ago Bede summed up what are for me the principles of my professional career: I have always thought it fitting to learn and to teach and to write.*

SCHOEFFEL, GEORGIA B. secondary education educator; b. St. Louis, July 17, 1944; d. George Otis Blockburger and Alene Rosemary Ketterer Dwyer; m. Kent Edward Schoeffel, Jan. 2, 1965; children: Stacey Ann, Kullin Edward. BA, St. Louis U., 1967; MAT, Webster U., St. Louis, 1976. Cert. tchr. English, drama and speech, Mo. Tchr. St. Louis Pub. Schs., 1967-98, instrnl. coord., 1998—. Mem. adv. coun. Gateway Writing Project, St. Louis, 1991—, co-dir., 1988-92. Co-author: (manual) In-Service Guide for Writing with Computers, 1987. Mem. Bi-Partisan Health Cabinet, St. Louis, 1994; campaign worker Gloria Weber for State Rep., St. Louis, 1994-96; fundraiser Ch. 9 PBS, St. Louis, 1976-82. Recipient Tchr. of Yr. award St. Louis Pub. Schs., 1990; S.W. Bell grantee, 1988. Mem. ASCD, Nat. Coun. Tchrs. English, Action Rsch. Collaborative, Greater St. Louis English Tchrs. Assn. (adv. bd. 1997-2000), Delta Kappa Gamma. Avocations: reading, cooking, travel, needlepoint. Home: 9822 Antonia Dr Saint Louis MO 63123-4004 Office: St Louis Pub Schs 801 N 11th St Saint Louis MO 63101-1471

SCHOEFFLER, MAX S. usability design consultant; b. Berlin, Dec. 2, 1928; came to U.S., 1939; s. Nathan and Bertha (Schlussel) S.; m. Jessica C. Tanner, Aug. 11, 1957 (div. 1979); m. Judith E. Burgis, May 30, 1982; children: Dan, Matthew, Steven, Michael, Cynthia, Louis. BS, Rutgers U., 1950; PhD, MA, Ind. U., 1954; MA, U. Mich., 1958. Lectr. Ind. U., Bloomington, 1952-56; sr. rsch. assoc., lectr. U. Mich., Ann Arbor, 1956-60; mem. staff, supr. Bell Labs., Holmdel, N.J., 1960-85; cons. MaxTech Consulting, Inc., Matawan, 1985—. Patentee in field. Contbr. articles to profl. jours. Fellow APA, APS; mem. Human Factors Soc., Psychonomic Soc. Avocations: bridge, camping, pottery. Office: 17 Kenwood Ln Matawan NJ 07747-3711 E-mail: maxsch@optonline.net.

SCHOEFFMANN, RUDOLF, consulting engineer; b. Linz, Austria, May 25, 1926; s. Rudolf and Anna (Hartl) S.; m. Herta Buttinger, Apr. 20, 1954; children: Monika M.B., Margit M.A., Rudolf M.G. Ing., Engring. Sch. Linz, 1944; Dipl.Ing., Tech. U. Vienna, Austria, 1951. Constructor Vôest, Linz, 1951-55, constrn. group leader, 1955-65, mgr., 1959-65, divsn. mgr., 1965-72; cons. Allis Chalmers Corp., Milw., 1972-81; dir. and cons. Rokop-Davy, Stockton, Eng., 1980-82; pvt. cons. engr. Linz, 1973—. Contbr. articles to profl. jours. Recipient Silver Cross of Merit, Pres. of Austria, 1969. Mem. Club of Engrs. and Architects, Chamber of Cons. Engrs., Golf Club of Linz. Roman Catholic. Achievements include 18 patents. Avocations: golf, skiing, swimming, chess.

SCHOELL, WILLIAM ROBERT, editor, author; b. N.Y.C., Nov. 30, 1951; s. William Theodore and Caroline (baumann) S. BA, Castleton (Vt.) State Coll., 1973. Exec. editor Quirk's Revs., N.Y.C., 1979—, Macabre Newsletter, N.Y.C., 1979—; v.p. Quirk-Schoell Enterprises, 1990—. Author: Stay Out of the Shower!, 1985, Saurian, 1987, The Dragon, 1988, The Pact, 1989, Fatal Beauty, 1990, Comic Book Heroes of the Screen, 1993, The Films of Al Pacino, 1995, Magic Man: Life and Films of Steven Spielberg, 1998, The Rat Pack, 1998, Martini Man: The Life of Dean Martin, 1999, Heartbreaker: The Dorothy Dandridge Story, 2002, Remarkable Journeys: The Life of Jules Verne, 2002. Avocations: classical music, opera, swimming, travel, films. Office: PO Box 117 Village Station New York NY 10014-0117

SCHOEM, ALAN HOWARD, lawyer; b. Washington, Dec. 18, 1946; s. David and Lillian S.; m. Hazel Schoem, Jan. 4, 1970; children: Cara Beth, Scott Robert. BA, U. Md., 1968; JD, Am. U., 1972. Bar: D.C. 1972, Md. 1973, U.S. Ct. Appeals D.C. 1973, U.S. Supreme Ct. 1980. Atty. GAO, Washington, 1972-73; atty. Office of Gen. Counsel, Consumer Product Safety Commn., 1973-79, asst. gen. counsel Bethesda, Md., 1979-87, dir. div. adminstrv. litigation, 1987-94. Legis. fellow to U.S. Senator Paul Wellstone, Washington, 1992; atty., advisor to chmn. Ann Brown Consumer Product Safety Commn., 1994-96; exec. asst. Office of Compliance, 1996-97, dir., 1997—. Pres. Stonebridge Homeowners Assn., North Potomac, Md., 1985-86, Lakewood Elem. Sch. PTA, Rockville, Md., 1986-88; v.p. T.S. Wooton High Sch. PTSA, Rockville, 1988-91, cluster coord., 1989-91. Democrat. Jewish. Avocation: reading. Home: 14809 Rolling Green Way North Potomac MD 20878-4202 Office: Consumer Product Safety Com 4330 E West Hwy Bethesda MD 20814-4408 E-mail: aschoem@cpsc.gov.

SCHOEN, ALLEN HARRY, retired aerospace engineering executive; b. N.Y.C., Mar. 10, 1936; s. Harry Alfred and Dorothy Julia (Browne) S.; m. Patricia Alice O'Madigan, June 1, 1958 (div. 1989); children: Theresa Mary, James Allen, Karen Linda; m. Lauria Juliette Trahan, Feb. 14, 2001. SB in Aero. Engring., MIT, 1958, postgrad., 1989. Aerodynamicist Douglas Aircraft Co., Santa Monica, Calif., 1958-61, United Aircraft Co., Farmington, Conn., 1961-66; with Boeing Helicopters, Phila., 1966-98, tech. mgr., 1980-84, dir. tech., 1984-86, dep. tech. dir. V-22 Osprey joint program, 1986-88, dir. preliminary design, 1988-92, dir. devel. engring., 1992-95, dir. devel. program, 1995-98; ret., 1998. Aero. adv. com. NASA, Washington, 1985-90. Patentee propulsion sys.; contbr. articles to profl. jours. Fellow AIAA (assoc.), Am. Helicopter Soc. (hon., pres. Phila. chpt. 1983-84, v.p. Mideast region 1986-88, dir.-at-large 1988-90, Paul E. Haueter meml. award 1999). Republican. Episcopalian. Avocations: photography, gardening, woodworking, woodcarving.

SCHOEN, CAROL BRONSTON, retired English language educator; b. Plainfield, N.J., May 14, 1926; d. Harry E. and Yetta (Cohen) Bronston; m. Andrew J. Schoen, June 26, 1949 (div.); children: Douglas, Sarah. BA, Radcliffe, 1948; MA, Columbia U., 1963, PhD, 1968. Lectr. Lehman Coll.

CUNY, N.Y.C., 1968-75, asst. prof., 1975-85, assoc. prof., 1986-91; ret., 1991. Author: The Writing Experience, 1978, Anzia Yezierska, 1982, Sara Teasdale, 1986, Thinking & Writing in College, 1986. Democrat. Jewish.

SCHOEN, CHARLES JUDD, service executive; b. Owatonna, Minn., Sept. 6, 1943; s. John Nicholas and Dorothy Georgine (Jacobson) S.; m. Birgitta Marianne Haggren, Dec. 15, 1972; 1 child, Vanja Karina. BA, U. Minn., 1965. Stockbroker Harris, Upham and Co., Mpls., 1967-70; with Litton Industries, Sydney, Australia, 1970-71; gen. mgr. Westinghouse Electric, Mpls., 1971-77; pres. Westco Security, Wayzata, Minn., 1977—, Automatic Alarm Corp., Wayzata, 1986-95; pres., chmn. Westec Security Products, Plymouth, 1993—. Bd. chmn. SpyderNet, Minn., 1993—. Past pres. Wayzata Hist. Soc. With USN, 1966-67 Mem. Assn. Former Intelligence Officers. Office: Westco Security 401 Lake St E Wayzata MN 55391-1667

SCHOEN, DIANE HOHMAN, dental hygienist; b. Balt., Mar. 26, 1949; d. Eugene R. and Mary Jane (Crist) Hohman; m. Ronald M. Schoen, June 5, 1976. BS in Dental Hygiene, U. Md., Balt., 1976, MS in Dental Hygiene, 1991. Registered dental hygienist, Md., Pa., N.J., N.Y.; cert. BLS. Dental hygienist pvt. practice Joseph D. Stephens, D.D.S., Sykesville, Md., 1976-86; dental hygienist intramural faculty practice U. Md. Dental Sch., Balt., 1986-91, instr. dept. oral health care, 1987-88, clin. instr. dept. periodontics, 1989-90, clin. instr. dept. dental hygiene, 1989-91; dental hygienist pvt. practice Lawrence Passarrelli, Ridgewood, N.J., 1991-98; clin. instr. dept. gen. and hosp. dentistry U. Medicine and Dentistry N.J., Newark, 1992-95, clin. asst. prof. dept. gen. and hosp. dentistry, 1995-98, assoc. prof. dept. gen. dentistry and cmty. health, 1998—. Dir. divsn. cmty. health, U. Medicine and Dentistry, 1999—; cons. Dept. HHS, USPHS, N.Y.C., 1992-95, Vancouver C.C., B.C., 1992; presenter in field. Co-author: A Workbook for Periodontal Instrumentation, 1993, Contemporary Periodontal Instrumentation, 1996; contbr. articles to profl. jours. Mem. Am. Dental Hygienists Assn., Am. Dental Edn. Assn., N.J. Dental Hygienists Assn., Bergen County Dental Hygiene Assn., Internat. Assn. Dental Rschrs. Office: N.J. Dental Sch 110 Bergen St Newark NJ 07103-2400 E-mail: schoend@umdnj.edu.

SCHOEN, HOWARD FRANKLIN, computer programmer, analyst; b. N.Y.C., Jan. 4, 1946; s. Sohl and Celia (Permut) S.; m. Althea Shepherd, June 15, 1986. BS, U. Pitts., 1965; PhD, CUNY, 1975. Fellow Mt. Sinai Sch. Medicine, N.Y.C., 1975-79; asst. prof. Downstate Med. Ctr., 1979-89; sr. programmer, analyst US Servis (formerly Micro Healthsystems, Inc.), Somerset, N.J., 1989-92, project team leader, 1992-99; sr. applications programmer, analyst McKesson HBOC (formerly US Servis), 1999-2000; programmer/analyst Verizon Comms., 2000—. Contbr. articles to profl. jours. Chmn. Libertarian Party of Somerset and Middlesex Counties, Edison, N.J., 1988-92, 2001--, sec., 1992-95, treas., 1996-2001; steering com. Libertarian Party N.J., 1988-91, 96-97, candidate for U.S. Congress, 1988, 90; mem. Separation Sch. State Alliance. Mem. N.Y. Acad. Sci., Nat. Assn. Parliamentarians, Forth Interest Group. Achievements include development of instrumentation used in studying ion (salt) transport across epithelial cell membranes; demonstration of simple physical mechanism for ion transport in frog skin epithelium; demonstration of mechanisms for hormone and drug action. E-mail: Howard.F.Schoen@Verizon.com.

SCHOEN, REM, investment executive; b. N.Y.C. s. Harry L. and Rita (Connors) S. BS, Trinity Coll., Burlington, Vt., 1951. Registered rep. Bache & Co., N.Y.C., 1956-61; instl. sales Gruntal & Co., 1961-65; v.p., ptnr., dir. instl. sales Pressman, Frohlich & Frost, Inc., N.Y.C., 1965-74; allied mem. N.Y. Stock Exchange; with Bernard Herold & Co., Inc., N.Y.C., 1974-77, Hamershlag, Kempner & Marks, N.Y.C., 1978-80; v.p. North East Securities, 1980-82; sr. account exec. Smith Barney Harris Upham, 1982-84, Gruntal & Co. (formerly Herzfeld & Stern), N.Y.C., 1984—. Fin. adviser to banks in Paris, Milan, Geneva. Author: Childhood Poems, 1972. Vol. Lighthouse, N.Y. Assn. for Blind; fund chmn. ex-officio, trustee Trinity Coll. of Vt. Home: 225 E 70th St New York NY 10021-5211 Office: Gilford Securities 850 Third Ave New York NY 10022 Fax: 212-826-9738.

SCHOEN, RICHARD MELVIN, mathematics educator, researcher; b. Celina, Ohio, Oct. 23, 1950; s. Arnold Peter and Rosemary (Heitkamp) S.; m. Doris Helga Fischer-Colbrie, Oct. 29, 1983; children: Alan, Lucy. BS, U. Dayton, 1972; PhD, Stanford U., 1976. Lectr. U. Calif.-Berkeley, 1976-78, prof. math., 1980-85; asst. prof. Courant Inst. NYU, 1978-80; prof. math. U. Calif.-La Jolla, 1985-87, Stanford U., 1987—. Contbr. articles to profl. jours. Fellow NSF, 1972, Alfred P. Sloan Found., 1979, MacArthur Found. prize, 1983, Bôcher prize, 1989. Mem. Am. Acad. Arts and Scis., Am. Math. Soc., Nat. Acad. Sci. Democrat. Office: Stanford U Mathematics Dept Stanford CA 94305

SCHOEN, STEVAN JAY, lawyer; b. N.Y.C., May 19, 1944; s. Al and Ann (Spevack) S.; m. Cynthia Lukens; children: Andrew Adams, Anna Kim. BS, U. Pa., 1966; JD, Cornell U., 1969; MPhil, Cambridge U. (Eng.), 1980. Bar: N.Mex. 1970, N.Y. 1970, U.S. Supreme Ct. 1076, U.S. Tax Ct. 1973, U.S. Ct. Internat. Trade 1982. Dir. Vista law recruitment OEO, Washington, 1970-71; atty. Legal Aid Soc. of Albuquerque, 1971-73; chief atty. N.Mex. Dept. Health and Social Svcs., Albuquerque, 1973-77; ptnr. Brennan, Schoen & Eisenstadt, 1979-88, Stevan J. Schoen PA, 1989-2001, Crider, Bingham & Hurst, P.C., 2001—; probate judge Sandoval County, 1990-98. Arbitrator NYSE; mem. N.Mex. Supreme Ct. Appellate Rules Com., 1982-92; chmn. rules com. Com. on Fgn. Legal Cons., 1993, N.Mex. Supreme Ct. Com., Probate Ct. Rules and Forms, 1998-2002, Jud. Edn. Planning com.; mem. Children's Code Rules Com., 1976-78. Mem. Mayor's Albuquerque Abd. Com. on Fgn. Trade Zone, 1992-94; v.p. Placitas Vol. Fir Dept., 1974-86; bd. edn. Bernalillo Pub. Sch. Dist., 1996-97. Recipient Cert. for Outstanding Svc. to Judiciary, N.Mex. Supreme Ct., 1982, Outstanding Svc. award N. Mex. Supreme Ct., 1992, Cert. of Appreciation, N.Mex. Sec. of State, 1980, Pro Bono Pub. Svc. award, 1989, Cert. of Recognition Legal Aid, 1994, award Las Placitas Assn., 1996, Outstanding Pub. Svc. N.Mex State Senate, 1998. Mem. Am. Judges Assn. (ho. of dels. 1999-2002), Nat. Coll. Probate Judges, State Bar N.Mex. (past chmn. real property, probate and trust sect. 1989, Outstanding Contbn. award 1989, task force on regulation of advt. 1990-91, past chmn. appellate practice sect. 1991, past chmn. internat. law sect. 1991-92, commn. on professionalism 1992-95, organizing com. U.S.-Mex. law inst. 1992), N.Mex. Probate Judges Assn. (chmn. 1993-99, award 1998, N.Mex. state bar bench and bar rels. com. chair 2000—, vice chair sr. lawyers sect.), Oxford-Cambridge Soc. N.Mex. (sec.), M.Mex. Assn. Counties (adv. bd. 1995-98). Home: 2 Hillside Dr Placitas NM 87043-9156 Office: 3908 Carlisle Blvd NE Ste A Albuquerque NM 87107-4829 Fax: 505-888-2806. E-mail: schoenstevanj@aol.com.

SCHOEN, WILLIAM JACK, financier; b. Los Angeles, Aug. 2, 1935; s. Jack Conrad and Kathryn Mabel (Stegmayer) S.; m. Sharon Ann Barto, Oct. 1, 1966; children: Kathryn Lynn, Karen Anne, Kristine Lea, William Jack. BS in Fin. magna cum laude, U. So. Calif., 1960, MBA, 1963. Mktg. mgr. Anchor Hocking Glass Co., 1964-68; v.p. sales and mktg. Obear-Nester Glass Co., 1968-71; pres. Pierce Glass Co., Port Allegheny, Pa., 1971-73; pres., chief exec. officer, dir. F.&M. Schaefer Brewing Co., N.Y.C., 1973-81; now chmn., pres. Wilshar Mgmt. Co. Inc., Naples, Fla., 1981—; chmn. Health Mgmt. Assocs. Inc., 1983—, also bd. dirs. Bd. dirs. Horace Mann Ins. Co. Contbr. to indsl. publns. Served with USMC, 1953-56, Korea. Mem. Naples Yacht Club, Port Royal Club, Quail Creek Country Club, Phi Kappa Phi. Republican. Lutheran.

SCHOENBERG, APRIL MINDY, nursing administrator; b. Nassau, N.Y., June 2, 1955; d. Robert and Eleanor (Marks) Christian; m. Gerald Duggan, 1979 (div.); children: Lance, Craig, Danielle; m. Bruce Schoenberg; 1 child, Michael. BSN, Long Island U., 1978. Intravenous cert., 1994, cen. line intravenous cert., 1995; cert. Nassau Fire Commn. Head nurse Sunrise Manor Nursing Home, Bayshore, N.Y., 1982-87; unit coord. East Neck Nursing Ctr., Babylon, 1987-89; dir. nursing svcs., asst. dir. nursing svcs. Oceanside (N.Y.) Care Ctr., 1988-91; PRI nurse, medicare nurse, rehab. coord., MDST coord. Ctrl. Island Health Care, Plainview, N.Y., 1993-95; reviewer, monitor restraints and psychoactive medications Quality of Care Mgmt., N.Y.C., 1995—; RN discharge planner Northshore Hosp. Plainview (N.Y.), 1995—. Asst. info. Tumor Registry Northshore Hosp., Manhasset, N.Y., 1975. Assoc. mem. Am. Mus. Natural History; sponsor Child Reach, 1984—. Mem. N.Y. State Nurses Assn., Multiple Sclerosis Soc., Nat. Trust Hist. Preservation, The Nature Conservancy Soc. Avocations: puzzles, bowling, racquetball, reading, speed walking.

SCHOENBERG, COCO, sculptor; b. Paris, May 3, 1939; came to U.S., 1941; d. Heinz Ernst and Kathe (Gassman) Oppenheimer; m. Bernard Schoenberg, Aug. 11, 1963 (dec. Apr. 1979); children: Nara, Jonathan Alexander, Amanda; m. William G. Swartchild III, June 5, 1988. BS in Lit., Sci. and Arts, U. Mich., 1961; MA in Art, Columbia U., 1964. Tchr. handicapped children Steven Sch., N.Y.C., 1962-63; assoc. in pottery for occupational therapy Columbia Tchrs. Coll., 1963; studio potter, tchr., lectr. various cities, N.Y., 1965—. Chmn. N.J. Designer Craftsman, New Brunswick, 1983-85; coord. Ctr. Crafts Fair-Old Ch., Demarest, N.J., 1983-84, ACC Craft Fair, Balt., 1985-2002, West Springfield, 1985-94; juror Lincoln Ct. Craft Fair, N.Y.C., 1985, Art Rider Craft Fairs, N.Y.C., 1986, Sta. WBAI Craft Fair, N.Y.C., 1989; commd. by Gulick Group, 1988, Harrison, Star Weiner and Beitler Advt., N.Y.C., 1989; juror Am. Craft Exposition, 1992. Two-person shows include Latitude, Greenwich, Conn., Handworks Gallery, Manchester, Vt.; exhibited in group shows at Montclair (N.J.) Mus., Bergen Mus., Paramus, N.J., Morris Mus., Morristown, N.J., Noyes Mus., Oceanville, N.J., Mus. Am. Jewish History, Phila., High Mus., Atlanta, Craft and Folk Mus., L.A., Brockton (Mass.) Mus., Summit (N.J.) Art Ctr., Campbell Mus., Arts Annual 1996 State Mus. of N.J., Hamburg Mus. 100th Anniversary Celebration, 1996 Juror in Clay for the Accraft Shows, and various other galleries, ACC craft fairs and stores; represented in collections of Art Inst. chgo., Hamburg (Germany) Mus. N.J. State Coun. on the Arts grantee 1983-84; recipient Innovative Sculpture award Texaco, 1982, purchase award Noyes Mus., 1986, highest award for crafts Craft Concepts, 1986, Juror's award Summit Art Ctr., 1985, Mamoroneck Artist Guild award, 1984, Charlotte Simons Glicksman Meml. award, 1983, merit award in ceramics N.Y.C. Artist/Craftsmen of N.Y., 1987, Most Innovative Use of Medium award Toshiko Tokaezu, 1994. Avocation: horseback riding. Home: 119 Erledon Rd Tenafly NJ 07670-2503

SCHOENBERG, DAVID ARTHUR, business educator; b. N.Y.C., Oct. 28, 1946; s. Saul and Lillian (Etkin) S.; m. Janet M. Baecker, June 4, 1972; children: Neil, Rachel. BS, CCNY, 1967; MPhil, Yale U., 1971, PhD, 1977; MPS, New Sch. for Social Rsch., 1989. Lectr. U. Conn., Storrs, 1977; asst. prof. U. Puerto Rico, Rio Piedras, 1977-78; post-doctoral assoc. Lehigh U., Bethlehem, Penn., 1978-80; asst. prof. Med. U. S.C., Charleston, 1980-81; spl. projects mgr. Hardach Travel, Inc., N.Y.C., 1982-85; instr. N.Y. Food and Hotel Mgmt. Sch., 1985-86; asst. prof. LaGuardia C.C., Long Island City, N.Y., 1986-89, assoc. prof., 1989-93, prof., 1993—. Advisory bd. mem. Acad. Travel and Tourism, N.Y.C., 1991—; cons. Universidad Autonoma de Santo Domingo, Dominican Rep., 1993—. Contbr. articles to profl. jours. Recipient Acad. Splist. grant USIA, 1992. Mem. Soc. Travel and Tourism Educators (bd. dirs., 1992-94), Internat. Soc. Travel and Tourism Educators, N.Y. State Hospitality and Tourism Assn. (bd. dirs., 1991-93), Pacific Asia Travel Assn. (bd. dirs. N.Y. chpt. 1998-99), Am. Soc. Travel Agts. Office: LaGuardia CC 31-10 Thomson Ave Long Island City NY 11101

SCHOENBERG, MARK GEORGE, government agency administrator; b. Bklyn., Nov. 22, 1947; s. Abraham Arthur and Ruth Millie (Dunn) S. BA, Columbia U., 1971, postgrad., 1972-73, N.C. State U., 1971-72. Research asst. NIMH-sponsored project at N.C. State U., Raleigh, 1971-72; asst. to pres. Key Electric Ltd., Glen Oaks, N.Y., 1973-76, gen. mgr. Los Angeles, 1976; asst. to pres. Kalsan Electric, Hempstead, N.Y., 1977; asst. mgr. Lincoln Inn, Rockville Ctr., 1978; expert, cons. EPA, Washington, 1978; assoc. dir. U.S. Regulatory Council, 1979-82; exec. dir. Regulatory Info. Service Ctr., 1982-99; sr. advisor to dep. adminstr. Gen. Svcs. Adminstrn., 1999—. Mem. Train Collectors Assn., Lionel Collectors Club Am. Avocations: healthy gourmet cooking, early music, wine collecting. Office: Gen Svcs Adminstrn (MI) 18th & F Sts NW Washington DC 20405-0001

SCHOENBERGER, JAMES EDWIN, retired federal agency administrator; b. Dayton, Ohio, Sept. 7, 1947; s. Harry Robert and Elizabeth Jane Schoenberger; m. Aura Victoria Montana, June 24, 1977; children: David, Eric. BSCE, Purdue U., 1969; MBA, Harvard U., 1971. V.p. ops. for midwestern housing developer Herman Devel. Group, Indpls., 1971-74; various positions New Communities Adminstrn. and with sec. HUD, Washington, 1974-77, assoc. dep. asst. sec., 1981-83; dir. land utilization Peabody Coal Co., St. Louis, 1977-81; sr. v.p. ops. The Investment Group, Washington, 1983-86; gen. dep. asst. fed. housing commr. HUD, 1987-89, assoc. gen., dep. asst. sec., 1990-97, ret., 1997. Roman Catholic. Avocations: computers, gardening.

SCHOENBERGER, STEVEN HARRIS, physician, research consultant; b. Cleve., Nov. 26, 1950; s. Stanford L. and Irene (Gold) S. BA, Tulane U., 1972; MD, U. Autonoma Guadalajara, Mex., 1976. Diplomate Am. Bd. of Urology. Asst. prof. Tulane U. Sch. Medicine, New Orleans, 1983—. Rsch. assoc. Delta Regional Primate Rsch. Ctr., Covington, La., 1983-85; chmn. laser com., Lawrence and Meml. Hosp., New London, Conn., 1989—, rsch. cons. Pfizer Med. Group, Groton, Conn., 1989—. Fellow ACS, Am. Soc. Laser Medicine and Surgery; mem. Soc. Univ. Urologists, N.Y. Acad. Scis., New Eng. Escadrille. Office: 3 Shaws Cv Ste 206 New London CT 06320-4968

SCHOENBORN, BENNO P. biophysicist, educator; b. Basel, Switzerland, May 2, 1936; came to U.S., 1955; s. Wilhelm and Maria (Dobler) S.; m. Catherine Cowie Kay, Oct. 26, 1962. BA, UCLA, 1958; PhD, U. New South Wales, Australia, 1962; DSc (hon.), N.J. Inst. Tech., 1982. Teaching fellow U. New South Wales, Sydney, 1958-61; postdoctoral fellow U. Calif., San Francisco, 1962-63, asst. prof. dept. pharmacology, 1964-66, assoc. prof. dept. pharmacology and biochemistry, 1967; biophysicist dept. biology Brookhaven Lab., Upton, N.Y., 1968-74, sr. biophysicist dept. biology, 1974-92, assoc. chmn. dept. biology, 1984-90; head ctr. structural biology, 1984-91; sr. fellow Los Alamos (N.Mex.) Nat. Lab., 1992—; adj. prof. biochemistry Columbia U., N.Y.C., 1978-93. Vis. scientist Molecular Biology Lab., Cambridge, Eng., 1964-66; adj. scientist biophysics SUNY, Stony Brook, 1988-92; vis. prof. biophysics U. New South Wales, Sydney, Australia, 2002--; mem. editorial bd. Biophys. Jour., 1977-80; mem. Reactor Safety Com., 1972-79. Editor: Neutrons in Biology, 1976, 84, 96; contbr. articles to profl. jours.; patent in multilager monochromator, 1975. Recipient E.O. Lawrence award Dept. of Energy, 1980. Mem. Nat. Com. for Crystallography, Biophys. Soc. (coun. mem. 1976-79). Republican. Avocation: sailing. Home: 816 Stagecoach Dr Santa Fe NM 87501-1144 E-mail: schoenborn@lanl.gov.

SCHOENBUCHER, BRUCE, health physicist; b. Dec. 15, 1943; s. Albert King and Alice Elizabeth (Thomson) S.; m. Patty Jo Parry, Feb. 3, 1965 (div. Feb. 1980); children: Teresa Marie Schoenbucher Abbey, Bonnie Lynn Schoenbucher Mendoza; m. Nancy Lippincott, Jan. 3, 1987; 1 child, Carly Cramer Cutler. BS in Radiation Protection Engring., Tex. A&M U., 1977, MS in Nuclear Engring., 1982. Lic. med. physicist, Tex.; cert. healthcare safety profl. Health physicist nuclear sci. ctr. Tex. A&M U., College Station, 1971-75, health physicist Coll. Vet. Medicine, 1977-79; mgr. radiation safety programs U. Tex. Med. Br., Galveston, 1980-88, asst. dir. environ. health and safety, 1984-88, radiation safety officer, dir. environ. health and safety, 1988—; radiation safety officer Burn Inst Shriners Hosp. for Crippled Children, 1991—. Presenter in field. Contbr. articles to profl. publs. With USN, 1962-71. Mem. APHA, Health Physics Soc. (med. sect. exec. bd. 1993-96, mem. pub. info. com. 1981-84, chmn. 1982-84), South Tex. Chpt. Health Physics Soc. (chmn. ad hoc com. on licensure of med. physicists 1988-89, chmn. fin. com. 1986-88, treas. 1980-85, pres-elect 1985-86, pres. 1986-87), Am. Assn. Physicists in Medicine, Am. Biol. Safety Assn., Am. Soc. Safety Engrs., Laser Inst. Am., Nat. Fire Protection Assn., Tex. Safety Assn., Galveston C. of C., U.S. Coast Guard Auxilliary, Phi Kappa Phi, Sigma Nu Epsilon, Tau Beta Pi. Office: U Tex Med Br 301 University Blvd Galveston TX 77555-5302 E-mail: bschoenb@utmb.edu.

SCHOENE, KATHLEEN SNYDER, lawyer; b. Glen Ridge, N.J., July 24, 1953; d. John Kent and Margaret Ann (Bronder) Snyder. BA, Grinnell Coll., 1974; MS, So. Conn. State Coll., 1976; JD, Washington U., St. Louis, 1982. Bar: Mo. 1982, Ill. 1983. Head libr. Mo. Hist. Soc., St. Louis, 1976-79; assoc. Peper, Martin, Jensen, Maichel & Hetlage, 1982-88, ptnr., 1989-98, Armstrong Teasdale LLP, St. Louis, 1998—. Bd. dirs. Legal Svcs. of Eastern Mo. Author: (with others) Missouri Corporation Law and Practice, 1985, Missouri Business Organizations, 1998; contbr. articles to profl. jours. Trustee Grinnell (Iowa) Coll., ex officio voting mem., 1991-93; bd. dirs. Jr. League St. Louis, 1995-96, Leadership Ctr. Greater St. Louis, 1995-96, FOCUS St. Louis, 1996-2001, exec. com., 1997-99; active St. Louis Forum, 1997—, Herbert Hoover Boys and Girls Club, St. Louis, 1999—. Mem. ABA, Nat. Conf. Bar Founds. (trustee 1996-2000, pres. elect 1997-98, pres. 1998-99), The Mo. Bar (bd. govs. 1997-99, chair bus. law com. 2000—), Ill. State Bar Assn., Bar Assn. Met. St. Louis (treas. 1991-92, sec. 1992-93, v.p. 1993-94, pres.-elect 1994-95, pres. 1995-96, chair small bus. com. 1987-88, exec. com. 1988-96, chair bus. law sect. 1988-89, mem. exec. com. young lawyers sect. 1988-90), St. Louis Bar Found. (bd. dirs. 1994-2000, v.p. 1995-96, pres. 1996-98). Home: 7824 Cornell Ave Saint Louis MO 63130-3701 Office: Armstrong Teasdale One Metropolitan Sq Saint Louis MO 63102 E-mail: kschoene@armstrongteasdale.com.

SCHOENEBERGER, MARLIES LUISE, alcohol/drug abuse services professional, gerontologist; b. Wemmetsweiler, Saarland, Germany, Dec. 27, 1947; d. Nikolaus Andreas and Katharina Regina Schoeneberger. BA summa cum laude, Spalding U., 1991; MA, U. Ky., 1994, PhD magna cum laude, 2000. Cert. gerontology, postgrad. cert. in med. behavioral sci.; women's studies. Health educator Ctr. on Drug and Alcohol Rsch., U. Ky., Lexington, 1996—99, rsch. analyst, 1999—2000, rsch. coord., 2000—02; asst. project dir. NDRI, Denver, 2002—. Contbr. Mem.: NAHOF Nat. Assn. of HIV over Fifty, So. Gerontol. Soc., Gerontol. Soc. Am. Home: 9888 E Vassar Dr # I-203 Denver CO 80231-5906 Office: 1642 S Parker Rd #309 Denver CO 80231 E-mail: schnmarlies@aol.com.

SCHOENER, GEORGE FRANCIS, JR. lawyer; b. Phila., Oct. 17, 1954; s. George Francis Sr. and Irene Louise (Nocito) S.; m. Patrice Irene Cipressi, Nov. 24, 1984; children: Michael James, Kristin Elizabeth, Stephen Christopher. BS, Rensselaer Poly. Inst., 1975; JD, Villanova U., 1978. Bar: Pa. 1978, U.S. Dist. Ct. (ea. dist.) Pa. 1978, U.S. Ct. Appeals (3d cir.) 1983, U.S. Supreme Ct. 1987; bd. cert. civil trial advocate Nat. Bd. Trial Advocacy. Assoc. Kessler & Sorin P.C., Phila., 1978-81, M. Mark Mendel Ltd., Phila., 1981-86, shareholder, 1986-95; atty. George F. Schoener Jr., P.C., 1995—. Seminar presenter in the field. Author: (with M.D. Zingarini and R.B. Goss) Civil Trial Procedures in Pennsylvania, 1992; co-author: Two New Products Liability Courses, 1995, Products Liability Practice Update, 1996, Products Liability Update, 1997, 4th edit., 2001. Mem. ABA, FBA, Assn. Trial Lawyers Am., Pa. Bar Assn., Phila. Bar Assn., Pa. Trial Lawyers Assn., Phila. Trial Lawyers Assn., Justinian Soc., Nat. Italian-Am. Bar Assn. Avocation: long distance running. Office: Eight Penn Center Ste 1301 1628 John F Kennedy Blvd Philadelphia PA 19103-2199 Fax: (215) 564-9187. E-mail: gfs@schoenerlaw.com.

SCHOENER, THOMAS WILLIAM, zoology educator, researcher; b. Lancaster, Pa., Aug. 9, 1943; BA, Harvard Coll., 1965, PhD, 1969. Asst. prof. Harvard Coll., Cambridge, Mass., 1972-73, assoc. prof., 1973-75, U. Wash., Seattle, 1975-76, prof., 1976-80, U. Calif., Davis, 1980—, chairperson sect. evolution and ecology divsn. biol. scis., 1993-99. Mem. editl. bd. dirs. Oecologia, 1984-93; past mem. editl. bd. Evolution, Am. Naturalist, Sci., Acta Oecologia; contbr. chpts. to books, articles to profl. jours. Recipient MacArthur prize Ecol. Soc. Am., 1987; grantee NSF, 1975—, Nat. Geog. Soc.; jr. fellow Harvard U., 1969-72; Guggenheim fellow, 1992-93. Mem. NAS, Am. Acad. Arts and Scis., Am. Ornithologists Union (elective), Am. Soc. Naturalists, Ecol. Soc. Am., Am. Soc. Ichthyologists and Herpetologists, Cooper Ornithol. Soc., Wilson Ornithol. Soc., Am. Arachnological Soc., Bahamas Nat. Trust, Soc. Study of Amphibians and Reptiles. Avocations: weight lifting; reading. Office: U Calif Sect Evolution Ecology Davis CA 95616

SCHOENFELD, DAVID ALAN, statistician, educator; b. Ft. Monmouth, N.J., Apr. 19, 1945; s. Robert Louis Schoenfeld and Helene Flapan; m. Ellen Maurine Beeks, Dec. 30, 1973; children: Heather, Elizabeth, Jonathan. BA, Reed Coll., 1967; MA, U. Oreg., 1968, PhD, 1974. Postdoctoral fellow Stanford (Calif.) U., 1974—75; rsch. asst. SUNY, Buffalo, 1975—77; from asst. to assoc. scientist Dana-Farber Cancer Inst., Boston, 1977—84; from asst. prof. to assoc. prof. Sch. Pub. Health Harvard U., 1977—86, prof. dept. biostatistics, 1999—, assoc. prof. dept. medicine Med. Sch., 1985—88, prof. biostatistics, 1998—; dir. Biostatistics Ctr. Mass. Gen. Hosp., 1985—. Editor: (book) Aids Clinical Trials, 1995. Fellow: Americal Statis. Assn.; mem.: Assn. of GCRC Statisticians, Internat. Statis. Inst., Biometric Soc., Inst. of Math. Stats. Avocation: skiing. Home: 41 Brook Rd Sharon MA 02067 Office: Mass Gen Hosp 50 Staniford St Boston MA 02114 Office Fax: 617-724-9878. Personal E-mail: david@schoenfeld.com. E-mail: dschoenfeld@partners.org.

SCHOENFELD, DIANA LINDSAY, photographer, educator; b. Knoxville, Tenn., Sept. 3, 1949; d. David Lindsay and Martha Jane (Zigler) S. Student, Fla. Presbyn. Coll., 1967-69, U. Neuchâtel, Switzerland, 1969-70; B in Visual Arts in Art and Art History, Ga. State U., 1972; MA in Studio Art, U. N.Mex., 1974, MFA in History, Practice of Photography, 1984. Instr. Rio Hondo Coll., Whittier, Calif., 1975-76, Coll. of Redwoods, Eureka, 1976-85; vis. asst. prof. U. Nebr., Lincoln, 1985, U. Mich., Ann Arbor, 1986-87; vis. asst. prof., guest curator U. Hawaii at Manoa, Honolulu, 1987, 88-89; vis. asst. prof. U. Oreg., Eugene, 1994; vis. lectr., artist in residence Ohio State U., Columbus, 1996-97; instr. art studies in Am. West Ohio Wesleyan U., Mont. State U., Bozeman, 1999; lectr. Humboldt State U., 1999—. Diversity cons. Calif. Arts Project, 1995-96, instr./participant summer insts. and visual arts wokshops for tchrs., 1994—; rep. Calif. Arts Project Leadership Acad., 2002; rep. Calif. Arts Project Leadership Acad., 2002; exhbn. curator and co-curator Rio Hondo Coll., Clarke Mus., Coll. of Redwoods, Ohio State U., U. Hawaii, Maine Photog. Workshops, Rockport, others, 1975—; exhbn. dir./juror Coll. of Redwoods with Eureka C. of C., 1983; presenter on art and rehab., instns. including U.S. HHS, Soc. for Photog. Edn., U. Mich., Nat./Internat. Head Injury Conf., Family Survival Project San Francisco, Sta. KOLN-TV, Lincoln, 1983, other univs., head injury orgns., 1983—; lectr. U. Hawaii, Claremont Coll., Pomona, Calif., nat. conf. Soc. for Photog. Edn., New Orleans, 1990, Humboldt State U., Arcata, Calif., 1999, 2000; juror Humboldt Cultural Ctr., Eureka, Calif., 1999; juror photography exhbn. Humbolt County Fair, Ferndale, Calif., 2002; instr., 2000; cons. Redwood Arts Project, Klamath-Trinity Schs., Calif., 2001, 02; actor, Castle Rock Prodns., 2001; spkr., presenter in field, including Matble Hist. Soc., Petolia, Calif., 2001; juror photography exhbn., Humboldt County Fair, Ferndale, Calif., 2002. Author, curator exhbn. and illus. catalog with essay Symbol and Surrogate: The Picture Within, 1989-90; artist, author, presenter autobiog. exhbn. Fractures and Severances: Patient as Artist, 1982-84, 84—; artist: Illusory Arrangements, 1978; exhibited photog. still life compositions Rhythmic Arrangements, San Francisco Mus. Modern Art, 1980 (print awards 1978, 79), landscape photography Serenity Studies, Albuquerque Mus. Art., Humboldt Bay Nat. Wildlife Refuge, Loleta, Calif., 2001-2002, color photographs Vietnam Veterans' State Memls. West of Miss., illustrated brochure Diana Schoenfeld: Landscape and Memory, sponsored by Humboldt State U. and First St. Gallery, 1999; artist (exhbns.) Office Extended Edn., Humboldt State U., Arcata, Calif., Humboldt Bay Nat. Wildlife Refugee, 2001-02, 2002, Morris Graves Mus. Art, Eureka, Calif., 2002; documentary photographer Schoolhouse Odyssey, 1995—, (presenter and exhibitor 2001), interviewed by KHSU radio, Arcata, Calif., 2000, 2001; Refuge Views: Humboldt Bay Nat. Wildlife Refuge, Lofeta, Calif.,2002, Morris Graves Museum of Art, Eureka, Calif., 2002; exhibited in group shows, most recently at 1st St. Gallery, Eureka, Calif., 1999, Alinder Gallery, Gualala, Calif., 1992, 93, 95, Art Ctr., Eureka, 1992, Ink People Gallery, Eureka, 1992, Solomon-Dubnick Gallery, Sacramento, 1994, Tokyo Inst. Polytechnics, 1995, Ohio State U., 1996, B.C. Space, Laguna Beach, Calif., 1997, Internat. Ctr. Photography, N.Y.C., 1997, Humboldt State U., Arcata, Calif., Internat. Photography Hall of Fame and Mus. Okla. City, 1999-2000, Thonson Invitational Show, Morris Graves Mus. Art, Eureka, Calif., 2000; numerous one-woman shows at Humboldt Bay Nat. Wildlife Regue Welcome Ctr., Loleta, Calif., 2001-02, Travel Advantage, Eureka, Calif., 1999, Art Ctr., 1991, Orange Coast Coll., Costa Mesa, Calif., 1991, A.G. Edwards, Eureka, 1992, Ambiance, Eureka, 1993, Iris Inn, Eureka, 1994, Redwood Arts Project, Arcata, Calif., 1996, Humboldt State U., 1997, 98, Players' Theatre, Ukiah, Calif., 1997, 1st St. Gallery, Humboldt. State U., Eureka, 1999, others, 1974-90; represented in many collections, including Houston Mus. Art, Ctr. Creative Photography, Tucson, Ariz., Graham Nash Collection, Barrow Neurol. Inst., Phoenix, Avon Collection, Mus. Contemporary Photography, Chgo., L.A. Ctr. for Photog. Studies, Nat. Mus. Women in Art, Washington,

San Francisco Mus. Modern Art, Princeton U., Laguna Beach Mus. Art, Ohio Wesleyan U., pvt. collections, others; creator CD-ROM multimedia presentation Schoolhouse Odyssey. Exploring Remote, Rural and Ghost Schools-A Photographer's Notes, 1998. Vol. Women's Resource Ctr., Eureka, 1996, Lewis Rathburn Wellness Ctr., Asheville, N.C., 1997. Selected for Gov. of Ga. Honors Program in Art, Wesleyan Coll., summer 1966; Marion Crowe scholar Atlanta Press Photographers Assn., 1971; Nat. Endowment for Arts Emerging Artist fellow/grantee, 1980; recipient Reva and David Logan award for New Writing in Photography, Boston U., 1985, Discovery award Art of Calif. jour., 1992. Mem. Soc. for Photog. Edn., Friends of Photography (presenter). Avocations: carpentry and construction, camping, hiking, writing, gardening. Home and Office: PO Box 596 Wildbird Ln Loleta CA 95551-0560

SCHOENFELD, ELINOR RANDI, epidemiologist; b. N.Y.C., Apr. 9, 1956; d. Samuel and Helen (Goldstein) S.; m. Eric Gottesman, 1998. BS, SUNY, Stony Brook, 1977; MS, SUNY, Buffalo, 1980, PhD, 1988. Clin. assoc. Columbia U. Sch. Pub. Health, N.Y.C., 1980-82; data mgr. cmty. oncology program Hackensack (N.J.) Med. Ctr., 1982-83; rsch. affiliate Roswell Park Cancer Inst., Buffalo, 1984-85, cancer rsch. scientist, 1985-88; epidemiology cons. Joel Bernstein, MD Otolaryngology, 1984-89; rsch. scientist SUNY Sch. Medicine, Stony Brook, 1988-93, rsch. instr., 1989-90, asst. prof., 1990-98, rsch. assoc. prof. preventive medicine, 1998—, dir. ops., 1992—, sr. rsch. scientist, 1993—, rsch. assoc. prof. opthalmology, 1998—. Epidemiology cons. Univ. Hosp., Stony Brook, 1990-92; dir. Suffolk County Diabetes Study, 1992-99; mem. admissions com. SUNY, Buffalo, 1985-87; presenter, invited speaker in field. Author: Applications of Diffusion Theory to Cancer Care in the United States: 1972-81, 1990, (with others) On Diabetes, Breast and Skin Cancers, Cataracts, Diabetic Retinopathy, Otitis Media, Myopia, Clinical Trials, Osteoporosis, 1988-2002; contbr. articles to profl. jours. Bd. dirs. Essential Needs for Srs. Efforts, Inc., N.Y.C., 1995-97; mem. health svcs. rsch. working group Nat. Eye Inst., 1997; mem. nat. health adv. com. Hadassah USA, 1998—. Predoctoral fellow NYU, 1977-78, Epidemiology Program fellow U. Minn., 1980, fellow in cancer epidemiology Columbia U., 1980-82; Nat. Cancer Inst. grantee NIH, 1987-88, 95—; Nat. Eye Inst. grantee, NIH, 1992—; Carol Baldwin Fund grantee, 2001—. Mem. APHA, Am. Diabetes Assn., Soc. Clin. Trials, Soc. Behavioral Medicine, Assn. for Rsch. in Vision and Ophthalmology, Soc. for Epidemiologic Rsch. Jewish. Office: SUNY Stony Brook Sch Med Dept Prev Med Stony Brook NY 11794-0001 E-mail: eschoenfeld@notes.cc.sunysb.edu.

SCHOENFELD, HANNS-MARTIN WALTER, accounting educator; b. Leipzig, Germany, July 12, 1928; came to U.S., 1962, naturalized, 1968; s. Alwin and Lisbeth (Kirbach) S.; m. Margit Frese, Aug. 10, 1956; 1 child, Gabriele. MBA, U. Hamburg, Fed. Republic Germany, 1952, DBA, 1954; PhD, U. Braunschweig, Fed. Republic Germany, 1966. Pvt. practice acctg., Hamburg, 1948-54; bus. cons. Europe, 1958-62; faculty accountancy U. Ill., Champaign/Urbana, 1962—, prof. acctg., bus. adminstrn. Urbana, 1967—, Weldon Powell prof. acctg., 1976, 80-81, H. T. Scovill prof. acctg., 1985-94; prof. emeritus, 1994—; dir. Office of West European Studies, 1982-84. Lectr., cons. in bus. and acctg., Eng., Belgium, Austria, Denmark, Brazil, Mex., Germany, Poland, Indonesia, Japan, Switzerland, Hungary, Czechoslovakia, 1962—; vis. prof. Econ. U. Vienna, Austria, 1984—, Handelshochschule, Leipzig, Germany, 1996—. Author: numerous books including Management Dictionary 2 vols., 4th edit, 1971, Cost Accounting, 8th edit, 1974-95, Management Development, 1967, Cost Terminology and Cost Theory, 1974, (with J. Sheth) Export Marketing: Lessons from Europe, 1981, (with H.P. Holzer) Managerial Accounting and Analysis in Multinational Enterprises, 1986, (with L. Noerreklit) Resources of the Firm, 1996. With German Army, 1944-45. Recipient Dr. Kausch prize for internat. integration of acctg. U. St. Gall, Switzerland, 1996. Mem. Am. Acctg. Assn. (chmn. internat. sect. 1976-77), Acad. Acctg. Historians (v.p. 1976-77, pres. 1978-79, Hour Glass award for best book publs. 1975), Acad. Internat. Bus., German Profs. Bus. Adminstrn., German Assn. Indsl. Engring., European Acctg. Assn., Coun. of European Studies, Internat. Assn. for Acctg. Edn. and Rsch., Beta Gamma Sigma, Beta Alpha Psi. Home: 1014 Devonshire Dr Champaign IL 61821-6620 Office: U Ill Dept Acctg Wohlers Hall W 1206 S 6th St Champaign IL 61820-6915

SCHOENFELD, HARRIS, cardiologist; b. N.Y.C., Feb. 16, 1940; MD, SUNY, Douwnstate, 1971. Diplomate Am. Bd. Internal Medicine, Am. Bd. Cardiology. Intern U. Chgo. Hosps., 1965-66; resident in medicine Mayo Clinic, Rochester, Minn., 1966-67; resident UCLA Med. Ctr., 1967-68; fellow in cardiology Cornell U., N.Y.C., 1968-70; dir. cardiology Motion Picture Hosp., 1984—, Med. Ctr., Tarzana, Calif., 1985-93; assoc. prof. medicine UCLA. Mem. AMA, Nat. Assn. Pacing and Electrophysiology, Los Angeles County Heart Assn., Los Angeles County Med. Assn. E-mail: dochs007!aol.com. Office: Cardiol Consults Med Group 18370 Burbank Blvd Tarzana CA 91356-2804

SCHOENFELD, LAWRENCE JON, real estate developer, asset lender; b. L.A., Nov. 30, 1945; s. Donald and Trudy (Libizer) S.; m. Carol Sue Gard, Aug. 24, 1969. AA, L.A. Valley Coll., Van Nuys, Calif., 1963; BBA, Wichita State U., 1969, MSBA, 1970; grad., Army Med. Acad., 1976, US Army Command/Gen Staff Coll., Ft. Leavenworth, Kans., 1988. Cert. tchr., Calif.; life lic. jr. coll. tchg. credential, Calif.; lic. real estate broker (cert.) developer, Calif. Asst. treas. Advance Mortgage, L.A., 1970-72; v.p. ops. Unigem Internat., 1972-98; pres. C. & L. Schoenfeld Investments Inc., Manhattan Beach, Calif., 1998—. Bd. dirs. The Schoenfeld Constrn. Co., South Star Wours, Uniorr Corp., Execucentre-West, Schoenfeld & Co., Customer Ground Handling Svc. Corp.; co-developer Los-Osos Mini Storage Co., Los Osos, Calif., Bay Osos,, 1984, Bay Osos Mini Storage Co., 1984, El Mercadero World Trade Show, Guatemala, 1986, 97, Santiago, 1987, Bahai, 1988, Paraguay, 1989, El Mercado, Costa Rica, 1990, Panama City, 1995, Manaus, 1996, Guayaquil, 1998, Los Osos Mini Storage Co., Quito, 1991, Santa Cruz, 1993, Ecuador, 1998, Uruguay, 1999, Punta del Este, 1999, Fortaleza, Brazil, 2000, San Jose, Costa Rica, 2002; pres. Accents on Beverly Hills, 1991, Accents at the Biltmore, Santa Barbara, 1995, Accents on Newport Beach, 1996, Accents on San Francisco Travelers Centrury Club, 2001, The Regis, L.A. Mem. Improvement Commn., Hermosa Beach., Calif. 1976-78. Served to maj. Med. Svc. Corps, U.S. Army, 1970-72; lt. col. USAR, 1972—. Recipient Humanitarian award, Richstone Found., 2001. Mem. South Am. Travel Assn., World Trade Assn. (assoc.), Town Hall, Wichita State U. Alumni Assn. (nat. dist. rep., mem. coun. 1992—), Res. Officers Assn., Brit. Am. C. of C., Skal Internat., Travelers Century Club, Navy Golf Club, Palos Verdes Golf Club. Jewish. Office: 224 5th St Manhattan Beach CA 90266-5710 also: 8405 Pershing Dr Ste 301 Playa Del Rey CA 90293-7861 Fax: 310-318-7106. E-mail: lccorp@earthlink.net.

SCHOENFELD, MICHAEL P. lawyer; b. Oct. 17, 1935; s. Jack and Anne Schoenfeld; m. Helen Schorr, Apr. 3, 1960; childrne: Daniel, Steven, Tracy. BS in Acctg., NYU, 1955; LLB, LLD, Fordham U., 1958. Bar: N.Y. 1959, U.S. Supreme Ct. 1963. Coun. Am. Home Assurance Co., N.Y.C., 1958-62; ptnr. Schoenfeld & Schoenfeld, Melville, N.Y., 1959—. V.p. Interstate Brokerage Corp., 1965-84, pres., 1984-90; ptnr. Melville Realty Co., 1977-90; legal adv. various bus. orgns. V.p., trustee Temple Beth David, Commack, N.Y., 1972-75; chmn. Cmty. Action Com. of Dix Hills and Commack, 1970-72, Dix Hills Planning Bd., 1972-74; treas. Dix Hills Rep. Club, 1976-80; mem. Huntington (N.Y.) Zoning Bd. Appeals, 1980-91, chmn., 1986-89. Recipient United Jerusalem award Israel Bond Drive, 1977, City of Hope Svc. award, George Bacon award Fordham Law Sch. Mem. N.Y. State Bar Assn., Suffolk County Bar Assn. Home: 14 Clayton Dr Dix Hills NY 11746-5517 Office: 999 Walt Whitman Rd Melville NY 11747-3007

SCHOENFELD, ROBERT LOUIS, biomedical engineer; b. N.Y.C., Apr. 1, 1920; s. Bernard and Mae (Kizelstein) S.; m. Helene Martens, Jan. 22, 1944 (div. 1965); children: David, Joseph, Paul; m. Florence Moskowitz, Dec. 11, 1965 (dec. 1989); children: Nedda, Bethany; m. Shulamith Stechel, July 8, 1990. BA, Washington Square Coll., 1942; BSEE, Columbia U., 1944; MEE, Poly. Inst. Bklyn., 1949, DEE, 1956. Rsch. assoc. Columbia U. Med. Sch., N.Y.C., 1947-51; rsch. fellow Sloan Kettering Cancer Rsch. Inst., 1951-56; assoc. prof. Poly. Inst. Bklyn., 1957—59; biomed. engr. Rockefeller U., N.Y.C., 1957—59, from asst. prof. to assoc. prof., 1957-90, prof. emeritus, 1990—. Contbr. articles to profl. jours. Lt. Signal Corps, U.S. Army, 1944-46, ETO. Fellow IEEE (mem. editl. bd. 1965-75, Centennial medal 1985), Am. Inst. for Med. and Biol. Engring. Democrat. Jewish. Achievements include pioneering application of computer automation to biological laboratory experiments. Office: Rockefeller U 1230 York Ave New York NY 10021-6399 E-mail: RLS@mail.rockefeller.edu.

SCHOENFELD, WALTER EDWIN, manufacturing company executive; b. Seattle, Nov. 6, 1930; s. Max and Edna Lucille (Reinhardt) S.; m. Esther Behar, Nov. 27, 1955; children— Lea Anne, Jeffrey, Gary. BBA, U. Wash., 1952. Dir. Reading Railroad, 1964—68; Vice pres., dir. Sunshine Mining Co., Kellogg, Idaho, 1964-69, First N.W. Industries, Inc. (Seattle Super Sonics), 1968-79; chmn. bd., pres. Schoenfeld Industries, Inc. (diversified holding co.), 1968-93; vice chmn., acting pres., CEO, Vans, Inc., 1993-97, chmn., bd. dirs., 1997—. Ptnr. Seattle Mariners Baseball Club, 1977-81, Seattle Sounders Soccer Club, 1974-79; bd. dirs. Hazel Bishop Cosmetics. Bd. dirs. Wash. China Rels. Coun., 1980—, Sterling Recreation Orgn., 1985-90; chmn. Access Long Distance of Washington; bd. govs. Weizmann Inst. Sci., Rehovot, Israel, 1980—; trustee Barbara Sinatra Children's Ctr., Eisenhower Hosp., Rancho Mirage, Calif., 1990—. With AUS, 1952-55, Korea. Recipient various service awards. Mem. Chief Execs. Orgn. (v.p., bd. dirs. 1987-93), Rainier Club, Tamarisk Country Club (Rancho Mirage, Calif.), Mission Hills Country Club, Glendale Country Club (Bellevue, Wash.), Alpha Kappa Psi. Office: 999 3rd Ave Ste 3800 Seattle WA 98104-4023

SCHOENHALS, KATHERINE VIOLA, social worker; b. Detroit, June 3, 1935; d. Anthony Andrew and Claire Elizabeth (Burkhardt) Fodell; m. Donald Eugene Schoenhals; children: Martin, Juliann. BA, U. Mich., 1957, MA, 1963, Oakland U., 1980, PhD, 1991. Cert. tchr. K-12 reading; secondary permanent tchg. cert.; sch. social work approval, Mich. Tchr. h.s. Berkley (Mich.) Schs., 1957-58, Romulus (Mich.) Schs., 1958-60; sch. social worker Bloomfield Hills (Mich.) Schs., 1960-61, 64-69, Walled Lake (Mich.) Schs., 1971-73, Birmingham (Mich.) Schs., 1978-96; tutor, counselor State of Mich. Rehab. Svcs., Pontiac, 1994—. Cons., rschr. Head Start/High Scope, Southfield, Mich., 1997; part-time faculty Schoolcraft C.C., Livonia, Mich., 1997-98; cons. Hamilton (Mich.) Pub. Schs., 1994-95, Bloomfield Hills Assn. for Gifted and Talented, 1978-81; curriculum planning cons. Birmingham Schs., 1984-94; rschr. Southfield (Mich.) Schs./Head Start, 1997; tutor, tchr., trainer, cons. Sarasota Literacy Coun., 1999; asst. artistic dir. Historic Spanish Point, 1999; presenter in field. Editor: (book) Shadows of Blackhawk, 1996. Vol. tutor, reading cons. Baldwin Ctr., Pontiac, 1995; advisor Maple Clinic Adv. Bd., Birmingham, Mich., 1986—; storyteller Birmingham Storytelling Guild, 1994—; pres. PTA, Bloomfield Hills, 1977-78; co-leader Girl Scouts of Am., Bloomfield Hills, 1973-74; mem., vol. Emily's List, Dem. Party, Episcopal Women's Club. Regents Alumni scholar U. Mich., 1953-57. Mem. AAUW (vol.), ACLU (vol.), NEA (Birmingham rep. pers. sect. 1961—), Internat. Reading Assn. (world conf. presenter 1992), Am. Ednl. Rsch. Assn., Sch. Social Workers Assn. of Am., Mich. Sch. Social Worker Presenters (state conf. presenter 1992), Mich. Edn. Assn., Birmingham Edn. Assn. Democrat. Episcopalian. Avocations: reading, needlework/crafts, golf, walking/exercise, gardening. Home: 4320 S Willoway Ct Bloomfield Hills MI 48302

SCHOENHARD, WILLIAM CHARLES, JR. health care executive; b. Kansas City, Mo., Sept. 26, 1949; s. William Charles S. and Joyce Evans (Thornsberry) Bell; m. Kathleen Ann Klosterman, June 3, 1972; children: Sarah Elizabeth, Thomas William. BS in Pub. Adminstrn., U. Mo., 1971; M of Health Adminstrn. with honors, Washington U., St. Louis, 1975. V.p., dir. gen. svcs. Deaconess Hosp., St. Louis, 1975-78; assoc. exec. dir. St. Mary's Health Ctr., 1978-81; exec. dir. Arcadia Valley Hosp., Pilot Knob, 1981-82, St. Joseph Health Ctr., St. Charles, St. Joseph Hosp. West, Lake St. Louis, 1982—86; exec. v.p., COO SSM Health Care, St. Louis, 1986—. Adv. bd. dirs. Firstar Bank, 1998-2001; regent Mo.-Gateway area Am. Coll. Healthcare Execs., 1997-2001. Contbr. articles to profl. jours. Mem. fin. com. Cath. Health Assn. U.S., 1999—; mem. adv. bd. St. Louis chpt. Lifeseekers, St. Louis, 1985—94; mem. bd. mgrs. Kirkwood-Webster (Mo.) YMCA, 1990—96, sec., 1996; mem. healthcare adv. bd. Sanford Brown Colls., 1992—94; del. Am. Hosp. Assn. Regional Policy Bd., 1999—; bd. trustees Mo. Hosp. Assn., 1999—, chmn., 2002—; mem. Greater St. Louis divsn. bd. dirs. Am. Heart Assn., 2001—; bd. dirs. St. Andrews Mgmt. Svcs., Inc., 1994—2002, Mid Am. Transplant Svcs., 1995—, Lindenwood U., 1997—, Civic Entrepreneurs Orgn., 1997—2000, Greater St. Louis Boy Scouts Am., 1997—, Benedictine Health Sys., 2002—; pres. Shaw Neighborhood Improvement Assn., St. Louis, 1979—80. With USN, 1971—72, Vietnam. Fellow Am. Coll. Health Care Execs. (bd. govs. 2002—); mem. VFW, Am. Legion, U.S. Navy League, Phi Eta Sigma, Pi Omicron Sigma, Delta Upsilon, Delta Sigma Pi. Roman Catholic. Avocations: reading, walking. Home: 420 Fairwood Ln Saint Louis MO 63122-4429 Office: SSM Health Care 477 N Lindbergh Blvd Saint Louis MO 63141-7832

SCHOENING, RUTH IRENE, retired music educator, musician; b. Moline, Ill., Mar. 23, 1922; d. Karl John and Cora Irene (Reynolds) Wilhelmsen; m. Raymond Edward Schoening, Apr. 28, 1945; children: Stephen Ray, Carol Irene Haertel, John Edward. MusB Edn., U. Wis., 1945, MusM, 1979. Cert. music tchr. Pvt. piano instr., Racine, Wis., 1945—; music instr. Racine Christian Sch., 1960-75; workshop presenter Music Educators Nat. Confs., 1975-82; instr. music U. Wis.-Parkside, Racine, 1985-90, 95, 98. Author, editor: From Sound to Symbol, 1969, Can You Do This?, 1984, Shortcuts for the Older Beginner, 1987. Organist Luth. Ch. Resurrection, Racine, 1960—; accompanist Racine Symphonic Chorus, 1987-98; vol. accompanist Racine Pub. Schs., 1983-93, Park High Sch. Concert Choir, 1998—; active vol. Christian Coalition, Chesapeake, Va., 1990—, nat. and state Rep. coms., 1993—. Mem. Am. Guild Organists, Music Tchrs. Nat. Assn. Avocations: reading, walking, computers, entertaining. Home: 923 Illinois St Racine WI 53405-2223 E-mail: golfray1@alynk.com.

SCHOENL, WILLIAM JAMES, history educator; b. Buffalo, Feb. 15, 1941; s. William and Erma Osborne Schoenl; m. Linda Volker, May 14, 1966; children: Karen Schoenl Carpenter, Lauren Schoenl van Loon, Mark William. BS in Math., Canisius Coll., 1963; MA in History, Columbia U., 1964, PhD in History, 1968. Prof. humanities Mich. State U., East Lansing, 1968-89, prof. history, 1989—. Mem. com. on rsch. Am. Soc. Ch. History, Chgo., 1988-93. Author: Intellectual Crisis in English Catholicism, 1982, C.G. Jung, 1998; editor: Major Issues in Jung, 1996, New Perspectives on the Vietnam War, 2002; author of poetry. Mem., chair disbursement com. for dire needs overseas St. John Student Parish, East Lansing, Mich., 1971—. Rsch. grantee Nat. Endowment for the Humanities, Washington, 1970, Am. Philos. Soc., Phila., 1975, global competence grantee Mich. State U., East Lansing, 1993. Mem. Ctr. for Jung Studies Detroit (trustee 1991-94), Kiwanis Club Okemos (chair internat. iodine deficiency disorders project 1994-98, chair Salvation Army project 1996-2002, chair human and spiritual values com. 1999-2002). Avocations: fishing, walking, traveling, cross-country skiing, reading mysteries. Home: 2643 Roseland East Lansing MI 48823 Office: Mich State Univ Dept History East Lansing MI 48824

SCHOENRICH, EDYTH HULL, internal and preventive medicine physician; b. Cleve., Sept. 9, 1919; d. Edwin John and Maud Mabel (Kelly) Hull; m. Carlos Schoenrich, Aug. 9, 1942; children: Lola, Olaf. AB, Duke U., 1941; MD, U. Chgo., 1947; MPH, John Hopkins U., 1971. Diplomate Am. Bd. Internal Medicine, Am. Bd. Preventive Medicine. Intern John Hopkins Hosp., Balt., 1948-49, asst. resident medicine, 1949-50, fellow medicine, 1950-51, chief resident, pvt. wards, 1951-52; asst. chief, acting chief dept. chronic and cmty. medicine Balt. City Hosp., 1963-66; dir. svc. to chronically ill and aging Md. State Dept. Health, 1966-74; dir. divsn. pub. health adminstrn. Sch. Pub. Health, John Hopkins U., 1974-77, assoc. dean acad. affairs, 1977-86, dir. part time profl. programs and dep. dir. MPH program, 1986—, prof. dept. health policy and mgmt., 1974—, joint appointment medicine, 1978—. Contbr. articles to profl. jours. Trustee Friends Life Care Cmty., 1984—, Kennedy-Krieger Inst., Balt., 1985—, Vis. Nurses Assn., 1990-95, Md. Home and Cmty. Care Found., 1995—. Recipient Stebbins medal John Hopkins U., 1989, Disting. Med. Alumna award, 1997. Fellow ACP, Am. Coll. Preventive Medicine; mem. APHA, Assn. Tchrs. Preventive Medicine, Med. and Chirurg. Soc. Md., Balt. City Med. Soc., Phi Beta Kappa, Alpha Omega Alpha, Delta Omega. Avocations: gardening, music, theater, swimming. Home: 1402 Boyce Ave Baltimore MD 21204-6512 Office: Johns Hopkins Univ Sch Pub Health 615 N Wolfe St Baltimore MD 21205-2103 E-mail: eschoenr@Jhsph.edu.

SCHOENROCK, TRACY ALLEN, airline pilot, aviation consultant; b. Oshkosh, Wis., Jan. 11, 1960; s. Elder Roy and Shirley Mae (Rutz) S.; m. Kathleen Mary Neumann, Oct. 8, 1983; children: Amanda Beth, Veronica Grace, Shannon Traci. BS in Geography summa cum laude, U. Wis., Oshkosh, 1982. Charter pilot Basler Airlines, Oshkosh, 1977-82; pilot Simmons Airlines, Marquette, Mich., 1982-84, Northwest Airlines, St. Paul, 1984—; owner charter operation. Lutheran. Avocations: golf, travel, flying, electronics. Home and Office: 1345 Maricopa Dr Oshkosh WI 54904-8150

SCHOETTGER, THEODORE LEO, city official; b. Burton, Nebr., Sept. 2, 1920; s. Frederick and Louise Cecelia (Gierau) S.; m. Kathlyn Marguerite Hughey, June 3, 1943; children— Gregory Paul, Julie Anne. BS in Bus. Adminstrn. with Distinction, U. Nebr., 1948. C.P.A., Calif. Sr. acct. Haskins & Sells, Los Angeles, 1948-55; controller Beckman Instruments, Inc., Fullerton, Calif., 1955-58, corp. chief acct., 1958-60; treas. Docummun Inc., Los Angeles, 1960-77; fin. dir. City of Orange, Calif., 1977-93. Mem. fin. com., treas., bd. dirs. Childrens Hosp. Served to lt. USNR, 1942-45. Mem. Calif. Soc. CPA's (nat. dir., v.p., past pres. Los Angeles chpt.), Fin. Execs. Inst., Mcpl. Fin. Officers Assn., Beta Gamma Sigma, Alpha Kappa Psi. Clubs: Jonathan, Town Hall. Methodist. Home: 2235 Sunset Rdg Mckinleyville CA 95519-4095

SCHOETTLER, GAIL SINTON, former ambassador; b. Los Angeles, Oct. 21, 1943; d. James and Norma (McLellan) Sinton; children: Lee, Thomas, James; m. Donald L. Stevens, June 23, 1990. BA in Econs., Stanford U., 1965; MA in History, U. Calif., Santa Barbara, 1969, PhD in History, 1975. Businesswoman, Denver, 1975-83; exec. dir. Colo. Dept. of Personnel, 1983-86; treas. State of Colo., 1987—95, lt. gov., 1995-99. U.S. amb. World Radio Comm. Conf., Istanbul, 1999-2000; bd. dirs. AspenBio, Inc., CancerVax Corp. Active Douglas County Bd. Edn., Colo., 1979-87, pres., 1983-87; trustee U. No. Colo., Greeley, 1981-87; pres. Denver Children's Mus., 1975-85; dir. Aspen Bio, Inc., CancerVax Corp.; bd. dirs. Nat. Jewish Hosp., Gunnison Ranchland Conservation Legacy, Colo. Conservation Trust. Decorated Chevalier, French Legion of Honor; recipient Disting. Alumna award U. Calif., Santa Barbara, 1987, Trailblazer award AAUW, 1997, Childrens Advocacy award Colo. Soc. Sch. Psychologists, 1997. Mem. Internat. Women's Forum (mem. bd. dirs. 1981-89, pres. 83-85), Women Execs. in State Govt. (bd. dirs. 1981-87, chmn. 1988), Leadership Denver Assn. (bd. dirs. 1987, named Outstanding Alumna 1985), Nat. Congress Lt. Govs., Stanford Alumni Assn. Democrat.

SCHOETZ, DAVID JOHN, JR. colon and rectal surgeon, educator; b. Milw., Oct. 29, 1948; s. David John and Beverly (Rogers) S.; m. Ruthanne Brennan, Mar. 25, 1972; children: Elizabeth Anne, David John III. BA, Coll. of Holy Cross, 1970; MD, Med. Coll. Wis., Milw., 1974. Diplomate Am. Bd. Surgery, Am. Bd. Colon and Rectal Surgery (sr. examiner 1996—). Resident in surgery Boston U. Med. Ctr., 1974-81; resident in colon/rectal surgery Lahey Clinic Med. Ctr., Burlington, Mass., 1981-82, staff colon-rectal surgeon, 1982—, chmn. dept. colon-rectal surgery, 1987—; prof. surgery Med. Sch. Tufts U., Boston, 1999—. Fellow ACS (commn. on cancer 1998—), Am. Soc. Colon and Rectal Surgeons (sec. 1999—). Office: Lahey Clinic Med Ctr 41 Mall Rd Burlington MA 01803-4521

SCHOFIELD, ANTHONY WAYNE, judge; b. Farmington, N.Mex., Mar. 5, 1949; s. Aldred Edward and Margueriete (Knudsen) S.; m. Rebecca Ann Rosecrans, May 11, 1971; children: Josie, Matthew Paul, Peter Christian, Addie, Joshua James, M. Thomas, Jacob L., Daniel Z. BA, Brigham Young U., 1973, JD, 1976. Bar: Utah 1976, U.S. Dist. Ct. Utah 1976, U.S. Ct. Appeals (7th and 10th cirs.) 1977. Law clk. to hon. judge A. Sherman Christansen U.S. Dist. Ct. Utah, Salt Lake City, 1976-77; assoc. Ferenz, Bramhall, Williams & Gruskin, Agana, Guam, 1977-79; pvt. practice American Fork, Utah, 1979-80; assoc. Jardine, Linebaugh, Brown & Dunn, Salt Lake City, 1980-81; mem., dir. Ray, Quinney & Nebeker, Provo, Utah; judge 4th Jud. Dist. Ct., 1993—. Bishop Mormon Ch., American Fork, 1985-88; commr. American Fork City Planning Commn., 1980-85; trustee American Fork Hosp., 1984-93. Mem. Cen. Utah Bar Assn. (pres. 1987, 91). Avocations: photography, music. Office: 125 N 100 W Provo UT 84601-2849

SCHOFIELD, JAMES ROY, computer programmer; b. Reedsburg, Wis., Aug. 16, 1953; s. G. C. Schofield and Margaret (Collies) Tverberg. BA, Carleton Coll., 1976. Programmer Brandon Applied Systems, San Francisco, 1977-78, Rand Info. Systems, San Francisco, 1979-83; systems programmer IBM, San Jose, 1983-91; programmer Office of Instnl. Rsch./U. Calif., Berkeley, 1991-94, Datis Corp., San Mateo, Calif., 1994-95, Compuware Corp., Los Gatos, 1995-96, Pacific Bell, San Ramon, 1996—2001, SBC Comms., San Ramon, 2002. Mem. Assn. for Computing Machinery, Assn. for Computing Machinery Spl. Interest Group in Computers and Soc., Phi Beta Kappa. Avocations: guitar, reading, swimming. Home: PO Box 25143 San Mateo CA 94402-5143 Office: SBC Comms 2600 Camino Ramon San Ramon CA 94583-5099

SCHOFIELD, ROBERT E(DWIN), history educator, academic administrator; b. Milford, Neb., June 1, 1923; s. Charles Edwin and Nora May (Fullerton) S.; m. Mary-Peale Smith, June 20, 1959; 1 son, Charles Stockton Peale. AB, Princeton U., 1944; MS, U. Minn., 1948; PhD, Harvard U., 1955. Research asst. Fercleve Corp. and Clinton Labs., Oak Ridge, 1944-46; research assoc. Knolls Atomic Power Lab., Gen. Electric Co., 1948-51; asst. prof., then assoc. prof. history U. Kans., Lawrence, 1955-60; mem. faculty Case Western Res. U., Cleve., 1960-79, prof. history of sci., 1963-72, Lynn Thorndike prof. history of sci., 1972-79; prof. history Iowa State U., Ames, 1979-93, prof. emeritus, 1993—, dir. grad. program history tech. and sci., 1979-92. Mem. Inst. Advanced Study, 1967-68, 74-75; Sigma Xi nat. lectr., 1978-80 Author: The Lunar Society of Birmingham, 1963, Scientific Autobiography of Joseph Priestley: Selected Scientific Correspondence, 1966, Mechanism and Materialism: British Natural Philosophy in an Age of Reason, 1970, (with D.G.C. Allan) Stephen Hales: Scientist and Philanthropist, 1980, The Enlightenment of Joseph Priestley: A Study of His Life and Work from 1733 to 1773, 1997. Served with AUS, 1945-46. Fulbright fellow, 1953-54; Guggenheim fellow, 1959-60, 67-68 Fellow Am. Phys. Soc., Royal Soc. Arts; mem. History of Sci. Soc., Soc. History Tech., Midwest Junto History of Sci., Am. Soc. 18th Century Studies, Acad. Internat. d'Histoire des Scis. (corr.) Home: 44 Sycamore Rd Princeton NJ 08540-5323

SCHOGGEN, PHIL H(OWARD), psychologist, educator; b. Tulsa, Aug. 28, 1923; s. Walter B. and Emma F. (Alexander) S.; m. Maxine F. Spoor, June 28, 1944; children: Leida, Christopher, Ann, Susan. AB in Psychology, Park Coll., 1946; MS, U. Kans., Lawrence, 1951, PhD in Psychology, 1954. Asst. prof. psychology U. Oreg., 1957-62, asso. prof., 1962-66; prof., chmn. dept. psychology George Peabody Coll., 1966-75; prof. York U., Toronto, Ont., Can., 1975-77; prof. human devel. and family studies N.Y. State Coll. Human Ecology, Cornell U., 1977-90, prof. emeritus, 1990—, chmn. dept., 1977-82. Author: (with R. G. Barker) Qualities of Community Life, 1973; Behavior Settings: A Revision and Extension of Roger G. Barker's Ecological Psychology, 1989. Served with USNR, 1944-46, 50-51. Mem. APA. Home: 121 Vossland Dr Nashville TN 37205-3617 E-mail: schoggph@comcast.net.

SCHOLDER, FRITZ, artist; b. Breckenridge, Minn., Oct. 6, 1937; Student, Wis. State Coll., 1956-57; AA, Sacramento City Coll., 1958; BA, Sacramento State Coll., 1960; MFA, U. Ariz., 1963, DFA (hon.), 1985, Ripon Coll., Wis., 1984, Concordia Coll., Minn., 1986; HHD (hon.), Coll. Sante Fe; DFA (hon.), U. Wis., Superior, 1993. Teaching asst. art Univ. Ariz., 1962-64; instr. art history, advanced painting Inst. Am. Indian Arts, 1964-69; artist in residence Dartmouth Coll., 1973; guest artist Santa Fe Art Inst., 1987, Okla. Art Inst., 1980-81, 88, Am. U., Washington, 1990. One-man shows: Crocker Art Gallery, Sacramento, 1959, Coll. Santa Fe, 1967, Roswell (N.Mex.) Art Center, 1969, Tally Richards Gallery Contemporary Art, Taos, N.Mex., 1971, 73, 75, 78, 79, St. John's Coll., Santa Fe, 1972, Cordier & Ekstrom, N.Y.C., 1972, 74, 76, 78, 90, Gimpel & Weitzenhoffer, N.Y.C., 1977, Graphics 1 and 2, Boston, 1977, Smith Andersen Gallery, Palo Alto, Calif., 1979, Plains Mus., Moorhead, Minn., 1980, 1981-89, Scottsdale Center for Arts, 1981, Tucson Mus. Art, 1981, Weintraub Gallery, N.Y.C., 1981, ACA Galleries, N.Y.C., 1984, 86, Sena Galleries West, Santa Fe, N.Mex., 1986, 87, Louis Newman Galleries, L.A., 1985, 87, 90-94, Schneider Mus. Art, Ashland, Oreg., 1990, Alexander Gallery, N.Y., 1991, Riva Yares Gallery, Scottsdale, Ariz., 1992, 94, Thorne-Sagendorph Art Mus. Keene, 1996, Phoenix Art Mus., 1997, Scottsdale Mus. Art, 1998; exhibited group shows: Carnegie Art Inst., Butler Inst. Am. Art, Calif. Palace of Legion of Honor, Houston Mus. Fine Arts, Dallas Mus. Fine Arts, San Francisco Mus. Art, Denver Art Mus., Ft. Worth Art Center, Basel Art 5, Linden Mus., Stuttgart, Philbrook Art Center, Oakland Art Mus., Tucson Art Center, N.Mex. Art Mus., Edinburgh Art Festival, Museo de Bellas Artes, Buenos Aires, Biblioteca Nacional, Santiago, Chile, Mus. voor Land-en-Volkenkunder, Rotterdam, Amerika Haus, Berlin Festival, Center for Arts of Indian Am., Washington, Yellowstone Art Center, Nat. Mus. Modern Art, Tokyo, Kyoto, Japan, also other fgn. and Am. shows, Smithsonian tour, Bucharest, Berlin, London, Ankara, Madrid, Belgrade, Athens, 1972-73; represented in permanent collections: Mus. Modern Art, N.Y.C., Art Inst. Chgo., Center Culturel Americain, Paris, Art Gallery Toronto, NEA, Houston Mus. Fine Arts, Boston Fine Arts Mus., Milw. Art Mus., Portland (Oreg.) Art Mus., Dallas Mus. Fine Arts, Bur. Indian Affairs, Mus. N.Mex., Smithsonian Instn., Bklyn. Mus., Phoenix Art Mus., San Diego Fine Arts Gallery, Okla. Art Center, Brigham Young U., Heard Mus., Phoenix, Bibliotheque Nat., Paris, San Francisco Mus. Art, Hermitage Mus., Leningrad, others; Included in: American Prints and Printmakers; Subject of: PBS film Fritz Scholder, 1976, PBS film Fritz Scholder, An American Portrait, 1983, PBS film Fritz Scholder, Painting the Paradox, 1998; author: Fritz Scholder Lithograph, 1975, 1983, Scholder/Indians, Fritz Scholder, Rizzoli, Fritz Scholder, Paintings and Monotypes, Afternoon Nap, 1991, Live Dog/Evil God, 1992, Fritz Scholder, A Survey of Paintings, 1993, Remnants of Memory, 1993, Fritz Scholder's Book of Symbols for Children, 1994, Fritz Scholder, Thirty Years of Sculpture, 1994, Rot/Red, 1995, Flirting with Possessions, 1997, Icons & Apparations, 1997, Last Portraits, 2001; guest artist Santa Fe Art Inst., 1987, Taos Inst. Art, 1990, Am. U., Washington, 1990. Recipient Ford Found. purchase award, 1962, 1st prize W.Va. Centennial Exhbn., 1973, purchase prize 13th S.W. Print Drawing Show, 1963, Hallmark purchase award, 1965, 1st prize Scottsdale Indian Nat., 1966, Grand prize Washington Biennial Indian Show, 1967, Grand prize Scottsdale Indian Nat., 1969, jurors award S.W. Fine Arts Biennial, 1970, 71, 72, prize in painting Am. Acad. and Inst. Arts and Letters, 1977, award in painting AAAL, 1977, internat. prize in lithography Intergrafiks, Berlin, 1980, 90, N.D. Gov.'s award in arts, 1981, N.Mex. Gov.'s award, 1983, Societaire Salon d'Automne, Paris, 1983, Golden Plate award Am. Acad. Achievement, 1985, Third prize Intergrafiks, 1990, Laird Leadership award in the arts U. Wis., Stevens point, 1995, Visionary award Inst. Am. Indian Arts, Gov.'s Arts award, Ariz., 2002; named Artist of the Yr. Scottsdale Arts Coun., 1998; John Hay Whitney fellow, 1962-63. Address: 118 Cattletrack Rd Scottsdale AZ 85250 E-mail: fritzscholder@earthlink.net. *I Believe in Art, Love, and the Unknown.*

SCHOLEFIELD, PETER GORDON, health agency executive; b. Newport, Wales, June 26, 1925; emigrated to Can., 1947, naturalized, 1952; s. Tom and Margaret (Bithell) S.; m. Erna Mary Cooper, Sept. 29, 1951; children— David, John, Paul. B.Sc., U. Wales, 1944, M.Sc., 1946, D.Sc., 1960; PhD, McGill U., Montreal, Que., Can., 1949. From research fellow to prof. biochemistry McGill U., 1949-65, dir. cancer research unit, 1965-69; asst. exec. dir. Nat. Cancer Inst. Can., Toronto, 1969-80, exec. dir., 1980-91, spl. adviser to chief exec. officer, 1991-92; dir. grants and awards Alta. Heritage Found. for Med. Rsch., Edmonton, 1992-94; coord. acad. affairs Samuel Lunenfeld Rsch. Inst. Mt. Sinai Hosp., Toronto, 1994-99; mem. adv. bd. Inst. Neurosics. Mental Health and Addiction Can. Insts. Health Rsch., 2001—. Chair rsch. policy com., bd. dirs. Alzheimer Soc. of Can., 1994-2000; mem. health adv. com. Alta. Heritage Found. Med. Rsch, 1994-99; bd. dirs., program adv. com. Ont. Neurotrauma Found., 1999—. Home: 2010 Islington Ave # 1503 Etobicoke ON Canada M9P 3S8 E-mail: peter.scholefield@sympatico.ca.

SCHOLER, SUE WYANT, state legislator; b. Topeka, Oct. 20, 1936; d. Zint Elwin and Virginia Louise (Achenbach) Wyant; m. Charles Frey Scholer, Jan. 27, 1957; children: Elizabeth Scholer Truelove, Charles W., Virginia M. Scholer McCal. Student, Kans. State U., 1954-56. Draftsman The Farm Clinic, West Lafayette, Ind., 1978-79; assessor Wabash Twp., 1979-84; commr. Tippecanoe County, Lafayette, Ind., 1984-90; state rep. Dist. 26 Ind. Statehouse, Indpls., 1990—. Asst. minority whip, 1992-94, Rep. whip, 1994-2000, asst. Rep. leader, 2001—; mem. Tippecanoe County Area Plan Commn., 1984-90; chmn. Midwestern legis. conf. CSG, 1998. Bd. dirs. Crisis Ctr., Lafayette, 1984-89, Tippecanoe Arts Fedn., 1990-99, United Way, Lafayette, 1990-93; mem. Lafayette Conv. and Visitors Bur., 1988-90. Recipient Salute to Women Govt. and Politics award, 1986, United Sr. Action award, Outstanding Legislator award, 1993, Small Bus. Champion award, 1995, Ind. Libr. Fedn. Legislator award, 1995, Disting. Legislator award Nat. Alliance for Mentally Ill, 1997, Friend of Cmty. Action award, 1999. Mem. Ind. Assn. County Commrs. (treas. 1990), Assn. Ind. Counties (legis. com. 1988-90), Greater Lafayette C. of C. (ex-officio bd. 1984-90), LWV, P.E.O., Purdue Women's Club (past treas.), Kappa Kappa Kappa (past pres. Epsilon chpt.), Delta Delta Delta (past pres. alumnae, house corp. treas.). Republican. Presbyterian. Avocations: golf, needlework, reading. Home: 807 Essex St West Lafayette IN 47906-1534 Office: Indiana Statehouse 200 W Washington Indianapolis IN 46204

SCHOLES, EDISON EARL, army officer; b. McCaysville, Ga., Aug. 16, 1939; s. Alvin L. and Marie (Plemmons) S.; m. Elva E. Bussey, June 4, 1961; children: Juana Kimberly Scholes, Tracy Michele Scholes Heller, Michael Lee. BS in Physics cum laude, No. Ga. Coll., 1961; MS in Ops. Rsch., Naval Postgrad. Sch., 1970; postgrad., Army War Coll., 1980, Harvard Def. Policy Seminar, 1991. Commd. 2d lt. U.S. Army, 1961, advanced through grades to maj. gen., 1991; comdr. A Detachment, 10th Spl. Forces Group, 1st Spl. Forces U.S. ArmyEurope, 1963-66; comdr. Co. D, 2d Bn.(Abn.), 8th Cav., 1st Cav. Divsn. U.S. Army, Republic of Vietnam, 1967-68, comdr. 1st Bn., 23d Inf., 2d Inf. Divsn. Republic of Korea, 1976-77, comdr. 2d Tng. Bn., Sch. Brigade, U.S. Army Inf. Sch. Ga., 1978-79, comdr. 1st Inf. Tng. Brigade, U.S. Army Infantry Tng. Ctr., 1983-85, dep. commanding gen. chief of staff 3d U.S. Army/U.S. Army Cen. Command Ft. McPherson, 1986-88, asst. divsn. comdr. 82d Airborne Divsn. Ft. Bragg, N.C., 1988-89, chief of staff XVIII Airborne Corps, 1989-90, chief of staff joint task force-south, Op. Just Cause, 1989-90, dep. commanding gen. XVIII Airborne Corps, Operation Desert Shield/Desert Storm Saudi Arabia, Iraq, 1990-91, dep. commanding gen. XVIII Airborne Corps, 1991-93; dep. comdr. Allied Land Forces, S.E. Europe NATO, 1993-95; program gen. mgr. Saudi Arabia N.G. Modernization Program, Vinnell Arabia, 1995—. Decorated Dept. Def. Disting. Svc. medal, Army Disting. Svc. medal with oak leaf cluster, Silver Star, Legion of Merit with oak leaf cluster, Bronze Star with V device and 4 oak leaf clusters, Purple Heart with oak leaf cluster, 6 Air medals, Army Commendation medal with V device and oak leaf cluster, Armed Forces Expeditionary medal, Vietnam Svc. medal with 6 campaign stars, Southwest Asia Svc. medal with 3 campaign stars, Combat Infantry badge, Expert Infantry badge, Army Gen. Staff badge, Meritorious Svc. medal, Nat. Def. Svc. medal with oak leaf cluster, Kuwait Liberation medal; Cross of Gallantry with Silver and Bronze Stars and Palm (Republic of Vietnam), S.W. Asia Svc. medal with 3 stars; numerous other domestic and foreign awards and skill badges. Mem. 82d Airborne Divsn. Assn., Spl. Forces Assn. (chpt. XXXIV), U.S. Army Ranger Assn., Assn. of U.S. Army, Spl. Ops. Assn., VFW. Baptist. Avocations: running, reading, camping, fishing.

SCHOLES, ROBERT THORNTON, physician, research administrator; b. Bushnell, Ill., June 24, 1919; s. Harlan Lawrence and Lura Zolene (Camp) S.; m. Kathryn Ada Tew, Sept. 3, 1948; 1 child, Della. *Wife Kathryn, MS 1944 University of Iowa, is a registered dietitian who taught at Cornell and did nutrition research at Harvard and Rochester. She is a cofounder-treasurer of the Bioresearch Ranch, Inc. Daughter Delia, PhD 1990 University of Washington in Epidemiology, is currently an associate scientific investigator in reproductive health research at Group Health Cooperative of Puget Sound. She is also Affiliate Assoiate Professor in Epidemiology at the University of Washington and is the recipient, as principal investigator or Co-PI, of research grants from NIH and CDC. Son-in-law Ed Newbold is a Seattle wildlife artist who also devotes time, talent and money to many worthy conservation causes.* Student, Knox Coll., 1937-38; BS, Mich. State U., 1941; MD, U. Rochester, 1950; postgrad., U. London, 1951-52, U. Chgo., 1953. Intern Gorgas Hosp., Ancon, C.Z., 1950-51; lab. asst. dept. entomology Mich. State U., 1940-41; rsch. asst. Roselake Wildlife Exptl. Sta., 1941; rsch. assoc. Harvard U., 1953-57; served to med. dir. USPHS, 1954-71; med. officer, dep. chief health and sanitation divsn. U.S. Ops. Mission, Bolivia, 1954-57, chief health and sanitation divsn. Paraguay, 1957-60; internat. health rep. Office of Surgeon Gen., 1960-62; br. chief, rsch. grants officer, acting assoc. dir. Nat. Inst. Allergy and Infectious Diseases, NIH, Bethesda, Md., 1962-71; cofounder, pres. The Bioresearch Ranch, Inc., Rodeo, N.Mex., 1977—. Cons. Peace Corps, 1961, Hidalgo County Med. Svcs., Inc., 1979-99, N.Mex. Health Sys. Agy., 1980-86, N.Mex. Health Resources, Inc., 1981-93, Luna County Charitable Found., 1993—. Contbr. articles to profl. publs. Capt. USAAF, 1942-45. Commonwealth Fund fellow, 1953. Mem. AAAS, AMA, APHA, Am. Ornithologists Union, N.Y. Acad. Sci., Sembot Hon. Soc. Achievements include research, writing and field test of first health survey indices detailing anthropological parameters; institution of first country wide malaria control project in Paraguay. Home and Office: PO Box 117 Rodeo NM 88056-0117 E-mail: scholes@vtc.net.

SCHOLFIELD, ARLENE R. social worker; b. Coldwater, Mich., July 3, 1944; d. Carl D. and Nina Mae (Doolittle) Mitchell. BSW, Western Mich. U., 1984, MSW, 1988. Cert. qualified social worker. Clin. social worker Coldwater Regional Psychiat. Hosp. Therapist individual, group and family Fairweather Cons. Mem. NASW, Acad. Cert. Social Workers. Home: 5770 Wildflower St # 82 Kalamazoo MI 49009-8149

SCHOLL, BELINDA K. librarian; b. Killeen, Tex., Oct. 26, 1957; d. Burton Thomas King and Alice Rose Coghlan-King; m. Timothy J. Scholl, May 31, 1980. MusB in Piano cum laude, Southwestern U., 1979; MusM in Piano Pedagogy, Tex. Christian U., 1987; MSLS, U. North Tex., 1992. Music dir. Rochester (N.Y.) Acad. Performing ARts, 1981-85; tchg. asst. in piano and theory Tex. Christian U., Ft. Worth, 1985-87; organist, accompanist Genesis United Meth. Ch., 1987-93; librarian, cataloger Hotho & Co., 1994-97; head librarian S.W. Christian Sch., 1997—. Mem. regional librarians' forum Ednl. Svc. Ctr., Ft. Worth, 1997—. Contbr. articles to profl. jours. V.p. Southbrook Neighborhood Assn., 1990-92; judge local and state piano contests and festivals, 1993—. Mem. ALA, Tex. Libr. Assn., Am. Coll. Musicians (judge 1997—), Nat. Guild Piano Tchrs. (co-chair Ft. Worth 1993—), Phi Kappa Lambda. Methodist. Avocations: theater, concerts, antiquing, reading, family and friends. Home: 7928 Regency Ln Fort Worth TX 76134-5017 Office: SW Christian Sch 6801 Dan Danciger Rd Fort Worth TX 76133-4903

SCHOLL, DAVID ALLEN, former federal judge, lawyer; b. Bethlehem, Pa., Aug. 20, 1944; s. George Raymond and Beatrice Roberta (Weaver) S.; m. Cynthia Ann Schuler Vetere, June, 1966 (div. 1972); m. Portia Elizabeth White, May 26, 1973; children: Tracy, Xavier; 1 stepchild, Sierra Milan. AB, Franklin & Marshall Coll., 1966; JD, Villanova U., 1969. Bar: Pa. 1969, U.S. Dist. Ct. (ea. dist.) 1970, U.S. Ct. Appeals (3d cir.) 1971, U.S. Tax Ct. 1975, U.S. Supreme Ct. 1975. Staff atty. Community Legal Services, Inc., Phila., 1969-73, 77-80; exec. dir. Delaware County Legal Assistance Assn., Chester, Pa., 1973-76; mng. atty. Lehigh Valley Legal Services, Bethelehem, Allentown, 1980-86; judge U.S. Bankruptcy Ct., Phila., 1986-94, chief judge, 1994-99, judge, 1999-2000. Bd. dirs. Phila. Vols. for Indigent Program, 1988—94, Consumer Bankruptcy Assistance Project, 1992—98, 2000—. Recipient Joseph Harris award Ba'Hais of Lehigh Valley, Bethelehem, 1984, Vol. of Yr. award Temple LEAP Program, 1997. Mem. Pa. Bar Assn. (chairperson consumer law commn., 1983-86), Northampton County Bar Assn. Avocations: baseball, rock music. Office: Ste 309 200 E State St Media PA 19063 Fax: 610-566-1002. E-mail: judgescholl@redemptionlawcenter.com.

SCHOLL, JUDITH LOIS, lawyer; b. N.Y.C., Nov. 2, 1949; d. Harry and Deena (Isreal) Teitelbaum; m. Frederick William Scholl, May 23, 1978. B.A., SUNY, 1971; J.D., Bklyn. Law Sch., 1974; LL.M., NYU, 1979. Bar: N.Y. 1976, U.S. Dist. Ct. (so. dist.) N.Y. 1981. Assoc. prof. law Del. Law Sch., Wilmington, 1975-79; contracts coordinator, adminstr. Optical Info. System, Exxon Enterprises, Inc., Elmsford, N.Y., 1977-79; assoc. prof. law Touro Law Sch., N.Y.C., 1980— ; v.p., gen. counsel, gen. mgr., dir. Godenoll Tech. Corp., Yonkers, N.Y., 1980— ; tutor Kingston Study group for disadvantaged, N.Y., 1968-69; atty. pro bono publico court case, N.Y.C., 1981-82, executor and trustee of charitable estate and trust, 1984— . Named Outstanding Tchr., Del. Law Sch. Students, Wilmington, 1976. Mem. Order of Barristers, ABA, Westchester Women's Bar Assn., Phi Alpha Delta. Home: 2575 Palisade Ave Bronx NY 10463-6101 Office: Codenoll Tech Corp 1086 N Broadway Yonkers NY 10701-1107

SCHOLLANDER, WENDELL LESLIE, JR. lawyer; BS, U. Pa., 1966, MBA, 1968; postgrad., Stetson U., 1969-70; JD, Duke U., 1972. Bar: N.C. 1977, Tenn. 1972, Fla. 1987. With Container Corp. Am., Fernandina, Fla., 1968-69; assoc. Miller, Martin, Chattanooga, 1972-75; asst. counsel R.J. Reynolds Industries, Inc., 1975-78, assoc. counsel, 1978-79, sr. assoc. counsel, 1979-82, sr. counsel, 1982-85; gen. counsel RJR Archer, Inc., Winston-Salem, N.C., 1979-85; of counsel Finger, Parker & Avram, 1985-87; ptnr. Schollander, 1987—. Gen. counsel Splty. Tobacco Council, 1985-87. Mem. ABA, N.C. Bar Assn., Forsyth County Bar Assn., Mensa, SAR, Phi Delta Phi, Kappa Sigma. Presbyterian. Office: 2000 W 1st St Ste 509 Winston Salem NC 27104-4225

SCHOLLER, THOMAS PETER, lawyer, accountant; b. Big Rapids, Mich., Aug. 15, 1937; s. Clarence Leo and Ruth Winona (Williams) S.; m. Marcia Kay Harman, June 25, 1960; children: Susan, Mark, Katrina, Laura, Emily. BS in Acctg., Ferris State U., 1959, LLD (hon.), 1984; LLB, U. Mich., 1962. CPA, Mich. Staff acct. Arthur Andersen & Co., Detroit, 1962-63, sr. acct., 1963-66, tax mgr., 1966-72, tax ptnr., 1972-91, dir. tax div. Grand Rapids, Mich., 1982-85, 88-91; of counsel Smith, Haughey, Rice & Roegge, 1992-97; dir. planned giving Archdiocese Detroit, 1997—. Contbr. articles to profl. jours. Taxation adv. com. Walsh Coll., 1972—92; trustee Ferris State U., Big Rapids, 1978—83, chmn., 1988; trustee Grand Rapids Art Mus., 1989—95, Ferris Found., 1999—; bd. dirs. Planned Giving Roundtable S.E. Mich., 2002—. Republican. Roman Catholic. Avocations: golf, swimming. Office: Archdiocese Detroit 1234 Washington Blvd Detroit MI 48226-1825 E-mail: scholler.tom@aod.org.

SCHOLSKY, MARTIN JOSEPH, priest; b. Stafford Spring, Conn., Jan. 16, 1930; s. Sigmund Felix and Mary Magdalen (Wysocki) S. BA, St. John's Sem., 1952, MA in History, 1956; MA in Classical Greek, Cath. U. of Am., 1966. Ordained priest Roman Cath. Ch., 1956. Asst. pastor St. Peter's Ch., Hartford, Conn., 1956-61; prin. St. Peter's Sch., 1956-58; instr. St. Thomas Sem., Bloomfield, Conn., 1961-67, admissions dir., 1965-67; vocations dir. Archdiocese of Hartford, 1967-78; chaplain Newington (Conn.) Children's Hosp., 1961-78; weekend asst. St. Mary's Ch., Newington, 1961-78; pastor St. Bartholomew Ch., Manchester, Conn., 1978-90; dean Manchester Deanery, 1989-91; spiritual dir. St. Thomas Aquinas High Sch., New Britain, Conn., 1991-92. Weekend asst. St. Francis of Assis Ch., South Windsor, Conn., 1991-92; instr. Holy Apostle's Sem. & Coll., Cromwell, Conn., 1988-94; pastor St. Mary's Ch., East Hartford, Conn., 1992—. Contbr. articles to profl. jours. Home: 36 Griswold St Manchester CT 06040-3928 Office: St Marys Ch East East Hartford CT 06108 *Conscience is not our own personal feelings about things; rather, it is our innate awareness of the rightness and wrongness of our deeds as God sees them, an awareness, often denied, that still remains the measure by which God will ultimately judge us all.*

SCHOLTEN, MENNO NICO, mortgage banker; b. Assen, Drenthe, Netherlands, June 18, 1943; came to U.S., 1949; s. Nico Menno and Hennie (Nienhuis) S.; m. Susan Sumnar, Aug. 11, 1973; 1 child, Paul Menno. BArch., U. Calif., Berkeley, 1967; MBA, DePaul U., 1980. Registered architect. Architect various, including Skidmore, Owings & Merrill, others, Chgo., 1968-78, Knight Architects, Engrs. and Planners, Chgo., 1978-81, 1989-92; asst. v.p. constrn. lending adminstr. First Nat. Bank of Chgo., 1981-85; v.p. real estate group First Tex. Savs., Dallas, 1985-87; mgr. constrn. lending Household Internat. (Household Bank), Prospect Heights, Ill., 1992-94; pres. The Mesu Group, Ltd., Evanston, 1995—. Bd. dirs. Global Med. Relief Program. Patentee chair design, 1979. Bd. dirs. Global Med. Relief Program. Recipient award of merit Chgo. Assn. of Commerce and Industry and Internat. Trade Club of Chgo., 1979. Mem. AIA (Chgo. chpt.), Am. Guild Organists (bd. dirs., treas. 1991-99), Calif. Scholarship Fedn. (life mem.), Delta Mu Delta., Intl. Platform Assn., Mortgage Bankers of Am., Rotary Internat. Inst. Mgmt. Cons. Avocations: tennis, skiing. Home: 3521 Central St Evanston IL 60201-4915

SCHOLTZ, JAMES CHARLES, library director, consultant; b. Freeport, Ill., Nov. 23, 1956; s. Clyde E. and Margaret E. Scholtz; m. Susan D. Scholtz, Sept. 15, 1979; children: Benjamin, Aaron. AA, Highland C.C., Freeport, Ill., 1976; BA, Ill. State U., 1978; MLS, No. Ill. U., 1982. Libr. asst. Highland C.C., 1980-82; libr. dir. Colo. Northwestern C.C., Rangely, 1982-84; YA/AV libr. Decatur (Ill.) Pub. Libr., 1984-86; multitype cons. No. Ill. Libr. Sys., Rockford, 1986-92; AV head, assoc. dir. Elkhart (Ind.) Pub. Libr., 1992-94; libr. dir. Yankton (S.D.) Cmty. Libr., 1994—. Author: Developing and Maintaining Video in Libraries, 1989, Video Acquisitions and Cataloging: A Handbook, 1996, Video Policies and Procedures for Libraries, 1991; editor: (with Sally Mason) Video for Libraries, 1988; contbr.: Video Collection Development in Multitype Libraries, 1994, 2d edit., 2001; contbr. chpts. to books, articles to profl. jours. and newsletters.; contbg. editor Librarian's Video Rev., 1987-90; mem. editl. bd., reviewer, Video Rating Guide for Libraries, 1989-94. Named MCI Cybrarian of Yr., 1998. Mem. Sertoma, Rotary. Democrat. Methodist. Avocations: tennis, barbershop singing, scuba diving, pottery, basketball. Home: 112 Sunset St Yankton SD 57078 Office: Yankton Cmty Library 515 Walnut St Yankton SD 57078 E-mail: jscholtz@sdln.net.

SCHOLTZ, ROBERT ARNO, electrical engineering educator; b. Lebanon, Ohio, Jan. 26, 1936; s. William Paul and Erna Johanna (Weigel) S.; m. Laura Elizabeth McKeon, June 16, 1962; children: Michael William, Paul Andrew. BSEE, U. Cin., 1958; MSEE, U. So. Calif., 1960; PhD, Stanford U., 1964. Co-op student Sheffield Corp., Dayton, Ohio, 1953-58; MS and PHD fellow Hughes Aircraft Co., Culver City, Calif., 1958-63, sr. staff engr., 1963-78; prof. U. So. Calif., L.A., 1963—. Vis. prof. U. Hawaii, 1969, 78; cons. LinCom Corp., L.A., 1975-81, Axiomatix Inc., L.A., 1980-86, JPL, Pasadena, 1985, Tech. Group, 1987-89, TRW, 1989, Pulson Comm., 1992-93, Colley-Godward, Palo Alto, 1994-97, Time Domain Corp., 2000—. Co-author: Spread Spectrum Comm., 3 vols., 1984, Spread Spectrum Communications Handbook, 1994, Basic Concepts in Information Theory and Coding, 1994; contbr. articles to profl. jours. (recipient Leonard G. Abraham award 1983, Donald G. Fink award 1984, Sr. Paper award Signal Processing Soc. 1992, Comm. Soc. Fred Ellersick Paper award 1997, Mil. Comms. Conf. award 2001). Pres. South Bay Community Concert Orgn., Redondo Beach, Calif., 1975-79. Fellow IEEE (bd. govs. info. theory group 1981-86, bd. govs. communication soc. 1981-83, chmn. fin. com. NTC 1977, program chmn. ISIT 1981). Office: U So Calif Comm Scis Inst Dept Elec Engring Los Angeles CA 90089-2565 E-mail: scholtz@usc.edu.

SCHOLZ, CHRISTOPHER HENRY, geophysicist, writer; b. Pasadena, Calif., Feb. 25, 1943; s. Joseph George and Elizabeth (Ochsner) S.; m. Paula Hanna, May 19, 1962 (div. 1978); children: Erich Frederich, Adrienne Louise; m. Yoshiko Yanagisawa, Feb. 8, 1986; 1 child, Morika Tsujimura. BS, U. Nev., 1964; PhD, MIT, 1967. Rsch. fellow Calif. Inst. Tech., Pasadena, 1967-68; rsch. assoc. Lamont-Doherty Geol. Obs., Columbia U., N.Y.C., 1968-70, sr. rsch. assoc., 1970—, assoc. prof. geology, 1971-75, prof., 1975—. Author: The Mechanics of Earthquakes and Faulting, 1990, Fieldwork: A Geologist's Memoir of the Kalahari, 1997; contbr. articles on earthquakes, deformation of the earth, mech. properties of rock to profl. jours. A.P. Sloan fellow, 1975-77; C.I. Green fellow, 1980-81. Fellow Am. Geophys. Union; mem. Seismol. Soc. Am., Médaille du Collége de France.

SCHON, ALAN WALLACE, lawyer, actor; b. Mpls., Nov. 27, 1946; s. Hubert Adelbert and Jennie (Jamieson) S.; m. Linda Kay Long, June 14, 1969; 1 child, Cynthia Anne. BA, U. Minn., 1969; JD, William and Mary Coll., 1973; grad. Command & Gen. Staff Coll., U.S. Army, 1984. Bar: Minn. 1973, U.S. Dist. Ct. Minn., Alaska 1986, U.S. Dist. Ct. Alaska, U.S. Ct. Appeals (9th cir.) 1988, Va. 1995. Prin. Schon Law Office, Fairbanks, Alaska, 1986-94; owner, pub. Nordland Pub. Co., Hampton, Va., 1991-94; dep. city atty. mcpl. bonds, environ. law, pub.-pvt. econ. devel. funding environ. law City of Hampton, 1994-99. Nationwide environ. group mgr. Delphi Info. Network, Gen. Videotex Corp., Cambridge, Mass., 1991-94; ind. assoc. Pre-Paid Legal Svcs. Inc., 1999—. Author, pub. EnvironLaw, 1991-94; editor William and Mary Law Rev., 1970-73; stage, film and TV actor; screenwriter: Operation Desert Fire, 1997, Operation Firestorm, 1998. Dir. Alaska State Fair, Fairbanks, 1987-91, Fairbanks Light Opera Theater, Fairbanks, 1991-94; dir., v.p. bus. and fin. Williamsburg (Va.) Players Theater, 2000—; dir., sec. Riding for Am., Inc., 1993-97; dir. Interior Alaska Econ. Devel. Ctr., 1993-94. Maj. U.S. Army, 1974-86. Mem. Fairbanks C. of C. (chmn. environ. concerns com. 1992-94). Avocations: outdoor sports, arts. Home and Office: 389 River Forest Rd Virginia Beach VA 23454-3288

SCHON, ISABEL, library science specialist, educator; b. Mexico City, Jan. 19; d. Oswaldo and Anita S.; m. Richard R. Chalquest, Oct. 7, 1977; 1 child: Vera. Attended, U. Nat. Autonoma de Mex., 1967-70; BS cum laude, Mankato State U., 1971; MA in Elem. Edn., Mich. State U., 1972; PhD in Edn., U. Colo., 1974. Founding dir. ednl. media ctr. Am. Sch. Found., Mexico City, 1958-72; ednl. evaluator sch. bus. adminstrn. Nat. U. Mex., 1972; evaluator bilingual ednl. materials U. Colo., 1973; asst. prof. dept. ednl. tech. and libr. sci. Ariz. State U., Tempe, 1974-79, assoc. prof., 1979-83, prof. reading edn. and libr. sci., 1983-89; Barahona Ctr. for study of books in Spanish for children and adolescents Calif. State U., San Marcos, 1989—, prof. edn., 1989—. Vis. prof. U. Ams., Mex., 1972, Am. Schs., Guayaquil and Quito, Ecuador, 1971; adminstrv. asst. Materials Dissemination Ctr. Kettering Found., 1966; evaluator libr.-media ctrs., 1960-72, evaluator Southwestern Coop. Ednl. Lab., Albuquerque, 1967, Nat. Indigenous Inst., Chiapas, Mex., 1972; cons. bilingual-bicultural edn. Mex., Argentina, Chile, Venezuela, Spain, Ecuador, U.S., 1971—; editl. cons. Macmillan Pub. Co., 1985, 87, Holt, Rinehart and Winston Inc., 1994, Harcourt Brace & Co., 1997—, Monterey Bay Aquarium, 1997—; columnist Booklist, 1989—; mem. adv. bd. Santillana Pub. Co., 1991-94, Parents' Choice, 1989—; mem. lang. adv. bd. Scholastic Inc., 1992-94. Author: A Hispanic Heritage: A Guide to Juvenile Books about Hispanic People and Cultures, 1991, Books in Spanish for Children and Young Adults, 1993, Contemporary Spanish-Speaking Writers and Illustrators for Children and Young Adults: A Biographical Dictionary, 1994, Tito Tito: Rimas, adivinanzas y juegos infantiles, 1994, Latino Heritage: A Guide to Juvenile Books about Latino People and Cultures, 1995, Introduccion a la literature infantil y juvenil, 1996, A Guide to the Best Juvenile Books about Latino People and Cultures, 1997, Recommended Books in Spanish for Children and Young Adults 1991-95, 1997, 1996-99, 2000, also others; contbr. chpts. to 9 books; contbr. over 400 articles to profl. jours.; mem. editl. bd. The Reading Tchr., 1998—, The New Advocate, 1995—, PBS Svc. para la familia, 1997—; contbg. Spanish editor Sch. Libr. Jour., 1984-87; referee, reviewer Sch. Libr. Media Quarterly, 1993-95; reviewer Libr. Sci. Annual, 1986—, Am. Edn. Rsch. Jour., 1983-85, Jour. Nat. Assn. Bilingual Edn., 1982-85, NEH, 1981—. Judge libr. essay contest San Diego Pub. Libr., 1998, 99, Arroz con Leche Children's Lit. Contest, 1994—, Nat. Libr. Writing Competition Am. Libr. Assn., 1977; chair internat. bd. books for young people Asahhi Reading Promotion Award Com., 1997—. Grantee Ariz. State U., 1974-75, 75-76, 77-78, 79-80, 81-82, 82-83, 85-86, Santillana Pub. Co., 1992, Office Edn. Dept. Health, Edn., Welfare, 1978-79, Ariz. Dept. Edn., 1980-81, Am. Libr. Assn., 1982-83, Ariz. State Libr. Assn., 1983-84, 84-85; recipient U.S. Role Model in Edn. award U.S. Mex. Found 1992, Women's Book award Women's Nat. Book Assn., 1987, Herbert W. Putnam Honor award Am. Libr. Assn., 1979, Grolier Found. award, 1986, Denali Press award, 1992. Avocation: tennis. Office: Calif State U Barahona Ctr Study Books in Spanish for Children San Marcos CA 92096-0001 Fax: 760-750-4073. E-mail: ischon@csusm.edu.

SCHONAUER, ANNE MILLER, music educator; b. Houston, July 29, 1965; d. George Louquet and Marilyn Ann (Rhoades) Miller; m. Paul Richard Schonauer, July 2, 1988 (div. June 2001); children: Paul David, Joanna Louquet. BA in Music, BMusEd, Southwestern Okla. State U., 1987; MA, 1991; PhD in Music Edn., U. Okla., 2002. Cert. music tchr., Okla., Tex., Ala., Ga. Tchr. band 5-6 Dallas Ind. Schs., 1988-89; tchr. gen. music, K-5 Norman (Okla.) Pub. Schs., 1991—96; vis. instr. U. Okla., 1997—99; tchr. gen. music K-6 Moore Pub. Schs., Okla., 1999—. Mem. NEA, Orgn. of Am. Kodaly Educators, Music Edn. Nat. Conf. Office: Plaza Towers Elem 852 SW 11th St Moore OK 73160

SCHONBERG, ALAN ROBERT, management recruiting executive; b. N.Y.C., Oct. 23, 1928; s. Julius and Evelyn (Guzik) S.; m. Carole May Kreisman, Dec. 27, 1975; children: William, Evelyn, David, Jeffrey. Nat. sales mgr. Majestic Specialties, Inc., Cleve., 1953-63; pres. Internat. Personnel, Inc., 1963-65; chmn. Mgmt. Recruiters Internat., Inc., 1965-98, 1998—2000, chmn. emeritus, 2001—. Pres., bd. dirs. Jewish Vocat. Service, Cleve., 1983—; trustees Mt. Sinai Hosp. (now Mt. Sinai Found.), Cleve., bd. dirs. Cleve. Jewish News; gen. chmn. Welfare Fund Campaign; trustee Am. Jewish Commn., Mt. Sinai Med. Ctr., Hebrew Immigrant Aid Soc. Named one of Cleve.'s 86 Most Interesting People, Cleve. Mag., 1986, Man of Yr. local chpt. Orgn. through Rehab. and Tng., 1996, Entrepreneur of Yr. Inc. Mag., Merrill Lynch Ernst & Young, 1995; recipient Human Rels. award Cleve. chpt. Am. Jewish Com., 1998. Mem. Internat. Franchise Assn., Internat. Confederation Pvt. Employment Agys. Assns., Am. Mgmt. Assn., Assn. Human Resource Cons. (chmn. 1980—), Org. for Rehab. and Training (ORT), Assn. Am.-Israel C. of C. (pres.), Ohio Israel C. of C. (co-chmn.), Jewish Family Svcs. Assn. (v.p., pres. 1998-2002). Avocation: world travel. E-mail: aschonberg@adelphia.net.

SCHONBRUN, MICHAEL K. health facility administrator, consultant; b. N.Y.C., Jan. 26, 1948; s. Arnold Laurance and Madeline (Courland) Schonbrun; m. Michelle I. Fredson, June 6, 1971 (div. Dec. 1998); 1 child Ethan F. ; m. Susan E. Juroe, Feb. 17, 2001. BA, Yale U., 1969; JD, U. Pa., 1973. Bar: Ohio 1973, Colo. 1975. Asst. to gov. Ohio Gov.'s Office, Columbus, 1973—74, Colo. Gov.'s Office, Denver, 1974—75; asst. dir. Colo. Dept. Health, 1976—78; pres., CEO Nat. Jewish Hosp., 1979—91; sr. v.p. Blue Cross/Blue Shield of Colo., 1991—93; exec. v.p. Vitas Healthcare Corp. Inc., Miami, Fla., 1994—95; pres. Schonbrun & assocs., Boulder, Colo., 1995—97; founder, pres., CEO Balfour Sr. Care, 1997—. Chmn. Young Pres.'s Orgn. Healthcare Focus Forum, Dallas, 1999—2001; bd. dirs. Colo. Assn. Housing and Svcs., Denver, United Bank of Denver, 1985—91; mem. leadership coun. Assisted Living Fedn. Am., Washington, 1999—. Contbr. Chmn. Rocky Mountain Alzheimers Assn., 2002, Denver Met. Air Quality Coun., 1985—89; mem. Internat. Med. Corp., L.A., 1996—2000. Democrat. Jewish. Avocation: Avocations: travel, running, tennis, reading fiction, movies. Home: 1735 19th St #56 Denver CO 80202 Office: Balfour Senior Care 1855 Plaza Dr Louisville CO 80027-2325

SCHÖNEMANN, PETER HANS, psychology educator; b. Pethau, Fed. Republic Germany, July 15, 1929; came to U.S., 1960, naturalized, 1965; s. Max Paul Franz and Hertha Anna (Kahle) S.; m. Roberta Dianne Federbush, Jan. 29, 1962; children: Raoul Dieter, Nicole Deborah. Vordiplom in Psychologie, U. Munich, 1956; Hauptdiplom in Psychologie, U. Goettingen, 1959; PhD, U. Ill., 1964. Thurstone postdoctoral fellow U. N.C., 1965-66; asst. prof., then assoc. prof. Ohio State U., 1966-69; postdoctoral fellow Ednl. Testing Service, Princeton, N.J., 1967-68; vis. prof. Technische Hochschule, Aachen, Fed. Republic Germany, 1981; mem. faculty Purdue U., 1969—, prof. psychology, 1971-2001, emeritus, 2001—. Vis. prof. Univs. Munich, Bielefeld and Braunschweig, 1984-85, Nat. Taiwan U., 1992, 96, 97. Author papers in field. Recipient Found. for the Advancement of Outstanding Scholarship award, Taiwan, 1996. Mem. Soc. Multivariate Exptl. Psychology. Office: Dept Psychol Scis Purdue U Lafayette IN 47907 E-mail: phs@psych.purdue.edu.

SCHONFELD, GUSTAV, medical educator, researcher, administrator; b. Mukacevo, Ukraine, May 8, 1934; came to U.S., 1946; s. Alexander Schonfeld and Helena Gottesmann; m. Miriam Steinberg, May 28, 1961; children: Joshua Lawrence, Julia Elizabeth, Jeremy David. BA, Washington U., St. Louis, 1956, MD, 1960. Diplomate Am. Bd. Internal Medicine. Intern. Bellevue Med. Ctr. NYU, 1960-61, resident in internal medicine, 1961-63; chief resident in internal medicine Jewish Hosp., St. Louis, 1963-64; from NIH trainee in endocrinology & metabolism to prof. Washington U., 1964—2002, Samuel B. Schechter prof. medicine, 2002—; rsch. assoc. Cochran VA Hosp., 1965-66, clin. investigator, 1968-70, cons. in internal medicine, 1972—; rsch. flight med. officer USAF Sch. Aerospace Medicine, Brooks AFB, Tex., 1966-68; from asst. physician to asst. physician Barnes Hosp., St. Louis, 1972—99; physician Barnes Jewish Hosp., 1999—; clin. instr. medicine Harvard U. Med. Sch., Boston, 1970-72; assoc. prof. metabolism and human nutrition, asst. dir. Clin. Rsch. Ctr. MIT, Cambridge, 1970-72. Mem. rsch. com. Mo. Heart Assn., 1978-80; expert witness working group on atherosclerosis Nat. Heart, Lung and Blood Inst., 1979, Nat. Diabetes Adv. Bd., 1979; mem. endocrinologic and metabolic drugs adv. com. USPHS, FDA, 1982-86; mem. nutrition study sect. NIH, 1984-88, spl. reviewer metabolism study sect.; mem. adult treatment guidelines panel Nat. Cholesterol Edn. Program, 1986; mem. Consensus Devel. Conf. on Triglyceride, High Density Lipoprotein and Coronary Heart Disease, 1992; cons. Am. Egg Bd., Am. Dairy Bd., Inst. Shortening and Edible Oils, Ciba-Geigy, Sandoz, Fournier, Parke-Davis, Bristol-Meyers Squibb, Monsanto/Searle. Past editor: Atherosclerosis, past mem. editl. bd.: Jour. Clin. Endocrinology and Metabolism, past mem. editl. bd.: Jour. Clin. Investigation, past mem. editl. bd.: Jour. Lipid Rsch., past assoc. editor: Circulation. Recipient Berg Prize in Microbiology, 1957, 58, Faculty/Alumni award Washington U., 1995; named Physician honoree Am. Heart Assn. Mo. Affiliate, 1995; grantee MERIT status NIH. Fellow ACP, AAAS; mem. Assn. Am. Physicians, Am. Soc. for Clin. Investigation, Am. Physiol. Soc., Am. Soc. Biol. Chemists, Am. Inst. Nutrition, Am. Diabetes Assn., Am. Heart Assn. (program com. coun. on atherosclerosis 1977-80, 86-88, nat. com. 1980-84, pathology rsch. com. 1980-83, budget com. 1991, awards com. 1992), Endocrine Soc., Alpha Omega Alpha. Office: Washington U Sch Medicine Box 8046 660 S Euclid Ave Saint Louis MO 63110-1010 E-mail: gschonfe@im.wustl.edu.

SCHONFELD, JOEL, lawyer; b. N.Y.C., Jan. 12, 1935; s. Samuel P. and Ruth (Rottenberg) S.; m. Lori M. Dean, 1967; children: Robert, Chelsea. BA, Adelphi U., 1956; LLB, JD, Bklyn. Law Sch., 1959. Bar: N.Y. 1960. Ptnr. Schonfeld & Weinstein LLP, N.Y.C., 1995—. Trustee Adelphi U., Garden City, N.Y., 1963-68; bd. dirs. Gift of Life, Inc., Manhasset, N.Y., 1995-97, sec., 1996-97, v.p., 1998—. Paul Harris fellow, 1995, 97. Mem. Nassau County Bar Assn., Kings County Bar Assn., L.I. Yacht Club (Babylon, N.Y.), Rotary (sec. Bklyn. 1995, treas. 1997). Home: 82 Dune Rd Island Park NY 11550 Office: Schonfeld & Weinstein LLP 63 Wall St New York NY 10005-3001

SCHONFELD, WALTER TIBOR, retired jewelry importer, writer; b. Vienna, Austria, May 14, 1917; came to U.S., 1951; s. Ferdinand Schonfeld and Irma Pollatschek; m. Beth Bond Valentine, Sept. 22, 1990. Student, Charles U., Prague, Czechoslovakia, 1939. Prosecutor War Crimes Trials, Nuremberg, Germany, 1945-49; case editor War Crimes Case Trials, Germany, 1949—51; importer Sterling, Sheffield, London, 1952-56; jewelry salesman Balt., 1957-75; freelance writer Onancock, Va., 1976-88; writer, author Onley, 1989—. Author: Nazi Madness Highlighted in Nuremberg. Mem. Country Yacht Club. Republican. Presbyterian. Home: PO Box 536 Onley VA 23418-0536 E-mail: lilbuff@visinet.com.

SCHONFELD, WAYNE BRENT, gastroenterologist; b. Miami Beach, Fla., Aug. 29, 1951; s. Abe and Beryl (Rose) S.; m. Felice Sue Krizner, June 19, 1977; children: Mark Brian, Scott Andrew. BS, U. Miami, 1973, MD, 1977. Resident in internal medicine U. Miami, Fla., 1977-79, resident in neurology, 1979-80, chief resident, 1980-81, fellow in gastroenterology, 1981-83; pvt. practice Hollywood, Fla., 1983—. Author: Controversies in Gastroenterology, 1984, Bockus Text of GI, 1984. Fellow ACP, Am. Coll. Gastroenterology; mem. Am. Gastroeneterol. Soc., Am. Soc. for Gastrointestinal Endoscopy, Fla. Gastrointestinal Soc., Phi Kappa Phi, Alpha Omega Alpha. Avocations: electronics, amateur radio. Office: Gastroenterology Cons PA 4700 Sheridan St Hollywood FL 33021-3420

SCHONFELD, WILLIAM ROST, political science educator, researcher; b. N.Y.C., Aug. 28, 1942; s. William A. and Louise R. (Rost) S.; m. Elena Beortegui, Jan. 23, 1964; children: Natalie Beortegui, Elizabeth Lynn Beortegui. Student, Cornell U., 1960-61; BA cum laude with honors, NYU, 1964; MA, Princeton U., 1968, PhD, 1970. Research asst. Princeton U., 1966-69, research assoc., 1969-70, vis. lectr., 1970; asst. prof. polit. sci. U. Calif.-Irvine, 1970-75, assoc. prof., 1975-81, prof., 1981—, dean Sch. Social Scis., 1982—; sr. lectr. Fond. Nat. de Sci. Politique, Paris, 1973-74; researcher Centre de Sociologie des Organisations, 1976-78. Author: Youth and Authority in France, 1971, Obedience and Revolt, 1976, Ethnographie du PS et du RPR, 1985 Recipient Disting. Teaching award U. Calif.-Irvine, 1984, Disting. Faculty Lectureship award for tchg., 1998, Daniel G. Aldrich Disting. Univ. Svc. award, 2000-01, Lauds & Laurels Extraordinarious award, 2002; Fulbright fellow Bordeaux, France, 1964-65; Danforth grad. fellow, 1964-69; Fulbright sr. lectr. Paris, 1973-74; NSF-CNRS Exchange of Scientists fellow Paris, 1976-78; Ford Found. grantee France, Spain, 1978-79; finalist Prof. Yr. Council for Advancement and Support of Edn., 1984; Lauds & Laurels Extraordinarious award, U. Calif. Alumni Assn., 2002. Mem. Am. Polit. Sci. Assn., Assoc. Francaise de Sci. Pol., Phi Beta Kappa. Office: U Calif Sch Social Scis Irvine CA 92697-0001

SCHONHOFF, ROBERT LEE, marketing and advertising executive; b. Detroit, May 24, 1919; s. John Clement and Olympia Regina (Diebold) S.; m. Kathleen O'Hara, Dec. 24, 1971; children: Rita, Elise, Robert. Student, Wayne State U., 1940-41. Artist J.L. Hudson, 1939-42; v.p. advt. and mktg. Dillard Dept. Stores, Little Rock & San Antonio, 1963-77; owner R.L. Schonhoff Advt. and Mktg., San Antonio, 1977-83, Ad Graphics, AMC Printers Inc. Former ltd. ptnr. New Orleans Saints football team; mem. faculty Bus. Sch., St. Mary's U., 1975-81; bd. dirs. Groos Bank, San Antonio. Permanent deacon Roman Cath. Ch., San Antonio Diocese. 1st lt. USAF, 1942-46. Mem. Am. Mktg. Assn. (founding dir. San Antonio chpt.). Home: 501 Hillside Dr San Antonio TX 78212-1737 Office: 1520 Contour Dr Ste 101 San Antonio TX 78212-1200

SCHONHOLTZ, GEORGE JEROME, orthopaedic surgeon; b. Bklyn., June 9, 1930; s. Morris and Rose (Stofsky) S.; m. Joan S. Hirsch, Aug. 21, 1951; children: Margot, Steven, Barbara. BA, NYU, 1950; MD, N.Y. State U., 1954. Diplomate Am. Bd. Orthopaedic Surgery, Nat. Bd. Med. Examiners. Intern, resident gen. surgery and orthopaedic surgery Walter Reed Gen. Hosp., Washington, 1954-59; asst. chief orthopaedic surgery Martin Army Hosp., Ft. Benning, Ga., 1960-63, asst. dir., dir. med. edn., 1962, 63; instr. human biology Am. U. Undergrad. Sch., 1962, 63; asst. clin. prof. orthopaedic surgery Howard U., Washington, 1964-66, Georgetown U., Washington, 1966-67, George Washington U., Washington, 1968-95; pvt. practice Silver Spring, Md., 1964-95. Orthopaedic cons. VA Hosp., Martinsburg, W.Va., 1964-68; civilian cons. orthopaedic surgery Walter Reed Army Hosp., Washington, 1968-95; chief orthopaedic surgery Holy Cross Hosp., Silver Spring, 1971-74, chmn. infection control com., 1975-76; v.p. med. and dental staff Washington Adventist Hosp., 1988-89, mem. fin. com., 1988-94; rep. Coun. of Musculoskeletal Soc., 1987-90. Author: Arthroscopy of the Shoulder, Elbow and Ankle, 1986, An Atlas of Arthroscopic Surgery of the Knee, 1988. Maj. U.S. Army, 1960-64. Mem. AMA, ACS, Am. Acad. Orthop. Surgery (mem. resolutions com. 1989-95), Am. Coll. Physician Educators, Soc. Mil. Orthop. Surgeons, Internat. Arthroscopy Assn., Ea. Orthop. Assn. (bd. incorporators, bd. dirs. 1970-79), Arthroscopy Assn. N.Am. (pres. 1988-89, bd. dirs. 1983-90), Montgomery County Med. Soc., Med. and Chirurgical Faculty Md., Washington Orthop. Soc. (pres. 1969), Internat. Soc. Knee, Am. Acad. Orthop. Surgery. Republican. Avocation: golf. E-mail: G_Schonholtz@aol.com.

SCHONHOLTZ, JOAN SONDRA HIRSCH, banker, civic worker; b. N.Y.C., Sept. 8, 1933; d. Joseph G. and Mildred (Klebanoff) Hirsch; m. George J. Schonholtz, Aug. 21, 1951; children: Margot Beth, Steven Robert, Barbara Ellen. Student, Vassar Coll., 1950-52; BA, Barnard Coll., 1954; postgrad., Am. U., 1963. Chmn. bd. dirs., founding mem. Grand Bank (formerly) 1st Women's Bank of Md., Rockville, 1976-2001. Chmn. FWB Bancorp, Rockville, 1982—98, Grand Bank Inc.; bd. dirs. Century Bank. Pres. Ft. Benning Med. Wives, Ga., 1962—63; sec. Montgomery County Women's Med. Aux., Md., 1968; bd. dirs. Svc. Guild of Washington, 1968—77, sec., 1969—70, pres., 1975—77; bd. dirs. Pilot Sch. for Blind Multiple Handicapped Children, Washington, 1968—77, Strathmore Hall Arts Ctr., North Bethesda, Md.; spl. gifts chmn. Montgomery County Cancer Soc., 1968, 1969; mem. Washington Adv. Coun. on Deaf-Blind Children, 1972—74; chmn. Friends of Washington Adventist Hosp., Takoma Park, Md., 1993—94. Recipient Outstanding Svc. award, Svc. Guild of Washington, 1969. Mem.: Barnard Club, Vassar Club. Republican. Jewish. Home: 32 Beman Woods Ct Potomac MD 20854-5481 E-mail: g.schonholtz@aol.com.

SCHONHORN, HAROLD, chemist, researcher; b. N.Y.C., Apr. 2, 1928; s. Benjamin and Dorothy (Gitlin) S.; m. Esther Matesky, Jan. 17, 1954; children: Deborah, Jeremy. BS, Bklyn. Coll., 1950; PhD, N.Y. Polytech. U., 1959. Mem. tech. staff Bell Labs., Murray Hill, N.J., 1961-84; v.p. R & D Polyken Tech. div. Kendall Co., Lexington, Mass., 1984-93; pres. Schonhorn Consultants, 1993—. Contbr. over 100 articles to profl. jours. Pres. B'nai B'rith Lodge, Summit, N.J., 1970. With U.S. Army, 1953-55, Korea. Mem. Am. Chem. Soc. Achievements include 15 patents. Fax: (617) 738-4742.

SCHONWETTER, RONALD SCOTT, physician, educator; b. Miami Beach, Fla., Apr. 24, 1958; s. Morris Jack and Joyce (Trager) S.; m. Rita A. Nemitoff, Mar. 2, 1986; children: Sara Wendi, Rachel Elana, Jonathan Harris. BA in Chemistry and Psychology with high honors, Emory U., 1979; MD, U. South Fla., 1984. Diplomate Am. Bd. Internal Medicine, Nat. Bd. Med. Examiners, Am. Bd. Geriat. Medicine. Intern Baylor Coll. Medicine, Houston, 1984-85, resident in primary care internal medicine, 1985-87; fellow geriat. medicine Baylor Coll. Medicine and VA Med. Ctr., 1987-89; asst. prof. medicine divsn. geriatric medicine, dept. internal medicine, coll. medicine U. South Fla., Tampa, 1989-94, assoc. prof. medicine, dir. divsn. geriat. medicine, 1994-2000, prof. medicine divsn., geriatric medicine, 2000—; assoc. med. dir. LifePath Hospice, 1989-92, med. dir., 1992—; med. dir. palliative care clinic Hospice Hillsborough, Inc., 1993-97; med. dir. Univ. Village Nursing Ctr., 1989-94; staff physician Tampa Gen. Hosp. Skilled Nursing Facility, 1989—. Vice chmn. Am. Bd. Hospice and Palliative Medicine, 1996-99, chmn., 1999-2001; presenter in field. Contbr. articles to profl. jours. Recipient New Investigator award Am. Geriatric Soc. and Merck U.S. Human Health, 1994. Fellow ACP, Am. Geriatrics Soc. (mem. ethics com. 1992—); mem. Am. Med. Dirs. Assn. (cert. med. dir.), Nat. Hospice Orgn. (coun. hospice profls. 1994—, rsch. award 1999), Gerontol. Soc. Am., Am. Acad. Hospice and Palliative Medicine (bd. dirs. 2000—). Jewish. Office: U South Fla Coll Medicine Dept Internal Medicine Divsn Geriatric Medicine 12901 Bruce B Downs Blvd Tampa FL 33612-4742

SCHOOLAR, JOSEPH CLAYTON, psychiatrist, pharmacologist, educator; b. Marks, Miss., Feb. 28, 1928; s. Adrian Taylor and Leah (Covington) S.; m. Betty Jane Peck, Nov. 2, 1960; children— Jonathan Covington, Cynthia Jane, Geoffrey Michael, Catherine Elizabeth, Adrian Carson AB, U. Tenn., Knoxville, 1950, MS, 1952; PhD, U. Chgo., 1957, MD, 1960. Diplomate Am. Bd. Psychiatry and Neurology. Chief drug abuse research TRIMS, Houston, 1966-72; assoc. prof. U. Tex. Grad. Sch. Biomed. Scis., 1968—; prof. psychiatry Baylor Coll. Medicine, 1975—, prof. pharmacology, 1974—, chief div. psychopharmacology, 1973-82; dir. Tex. Research Inst. Mental Scis., 1972-85. Mem. Nat. Bd. Med. Examiners' Task Force on Drug Abuse and Alcoholism, 1982— ; mem. Drug Abuse Adv. Com., FDA, Washington, 1983-85, chmn., 1984; chmn. profl. needs planning task force Nat. Inst. Drug Abuse, Washington, 1977— Editor: Current Issues in Adolescent Psychiatry, 1973, Research and the Psychiatric Patient, 1975, The Kinetics of Psychiatric Drugs, 1979, Serotonin in Biological Psychiatry - Advances in Biochemical Psychopharmacology, 1982. Cons. Parents' League Houston, 1972-74; mem. coordinating com. Citizens Mental Health Service, Houston, 1976; mem. acad. com. for study of violence Houston Police Dept., 1979; bd. dirs. Can-Do-It, Houston, 1982— . Served with U.S. Army, 1945-47, to 1st lt. USAR, 1950-62. Recipient Eugen Kahn award Baylor Coll. Medicine, Houston, 1964, Alumni award for Disting. Svc., U. Chgo., 1995, Psychiat. Excellence award Tex. Soc. Psychiat. Physicians, 1995. Fellow Am. Psychiat. Assn., Am. Coll. Psychiatrists; mem. Am. Coll. Neuropsychopharmacology, Collegium Internationale NeuroPsychopharmacologicum, Am. Soc. Pharmacology and Exptl. Therapeutics. Episcopalian. Home: 1111 Hermann Dr Unit 17E Houston TX 77004-6930 Office: Baylor Coll Medicine One Baylor Pla PO Box 25302 Houston TX 77265-5302

SCHOOLER, CARMI, psychologist, sociologist, researcher; b. N.Y.C., Oct. 4, 1933; s. Samuel S.; m. Nina H. Rosenberg, June 22, 1956; children: Jonathan, Lael. BA, Hamilton Coll., 1954; PhD, NYU, 1959. Rsch. psychologist Lab. Socio-environ. Studies, Bethesda, Md., 1959-85, acting chief, 1985-97; chief sect. socio-environ. studies NIMH, 1997—. Japan Soc. Promotion of Sci. fellow, 1985, Disting. Invited Rsch. fellow Japanese Min. Edn., 1990. Fellow Am. Psychol. Soc.; mem. Sociol. Rsch. Assn., Psychonomic Soc. Home: 1731 34th St NW Washington DC 20007 Office: Sect Socio-environ Studies 7550 Wisconsin Ave Bethesda MD 20892-9005 Fax: (301)402-0621. E-mail: carmi.schooler@nih.gov.

SCHOOLER, STEVEN JAMES, lawyer; b. Pullman, Wash., Apr. 30, 1955; s. Arnold and Iris S.; m. Marsha Mae Mansfield, June 9, 1955; 1 child, Sarah. BA in Econs., George Washington U., 1973; JD, U. Mich., 1981. Bar: Wis. 1981, U.S. Dist. Ct. (ea. and we. dists.) Wis. 1981, U.S. Ct. Appeals (7th cir.) 1981. Atty. Axley Brynelson, Madison, Wis., 1981-89, Lawton & Cates, S.C., Madison, 1989-2000; exec. dir. Transitional Housing Inc., 2001—. Chair, chair elect individual rights sect. Wis. State, Madison, 1994-96; pres., bd. dirs. Ctr. Pub. Representation, Madison, 1998—. Co-author: Law of Damages, 1988, Wisconsin Civil Procedures Before Trial, 1996; co-editor: Wisconsin Civil Forms Manual, 1995. Mem. adminstrv. coun. First United Meth. Ch., pres., 1993-96; bd. dirs. U. Wis. Madison Campus Ministries, sec., 1986-87; bd. dirs. Transitional Housing, Inc., Madison, 1991-99. Mem. Order of Coif, Phi Beta Kappa. Office: Transitional Housing Inc 1490 Martin St Madison WI 53713-1140

SCHOOLEY, CAROLINE NAUS, retired laboratory supervisor; b. San Francisco, Feb. 15, 1932; d. George Mortimer and Ruth Raymond (Lange) Naus; m. John Campbell Schooley, Aug. 8, 1953; children: Diana, Karen, Peter. BA, U. Calif., Berkeley, 1954, MA, 1958. Rsch. asst. zoology dept. U. Calif., Berkeley, 1953-54, 56-59; staff rsch. assoc. R.D. Ogg Electron Microscope Lab., 1967-83, supr., 1983-93; rsch. assoc. Oak Ridge Inst. Nuclear Studies, 1955. Fellow AAAS; mem. Microscopy Soc. Am. (coun. 1985-88, coord. Project MICRO), Am. Soc. Cell Biology, No. Calif. Soc. Electron Microscopical (sec. 1974-77), Royal Microscopy Soc. Home: PO Box 117 Caspar CA 95420 E-mail: schooley@mcn.org.

SCHOOLEY, DOLORES HARTER, entertainment administrator; b. Nora Springs, Iowa, May 2, 1905; d. Amil A. and Elizabeth (Sefert) Zemke; m. Leslie J. Harter, June 5, 1934 (dec. 1963); m. Charles Earl Schooley, Apr. 1, 1966. BE, BA, U. Colo., 1927; MA, Northwestern U., 1931. Tchr. high sch. Consol. Schs., Johnstown, Colo., 1927-28, Byers, Colo., 1928-29, Clayton, Mo., 1931-34; theatrical makeup artist, 1937-86; instr. theatrical makeup dramatic clubs, N.J. Theatre League; lectr., demonstrator theatrical makeup, dramatic and women's clubs, high schs., N.J. and N.Y. area, 1937-53; nat. officer, entertainer, dir. internat. entertainment project for mil. posts Phi Beta Nat. Profl. Fraternity for Creative & Performing Arts, 1951-61; cons. radio broadcast series Sta. WNYC, N.Y., 1962-65; dir. community rels. Wingspread Summer Theatre, Colon, Mich., 1955; co-chmn. Valley Shore Community Concerts, Conn., 1958-61, artist mgr., 1959—; founder, pres. Berkshire Hills Music and Dance Assn., Conn., 1970-78; mem. Music Mountain Corp., Falls Village, Conn., 1975-81. Trustee Sharon (Conn.) Creative Arts Found., 1970-73; hon. trustee Bar Harbor Maine Festival, 1968-80; founder, pres. Wingspread Found., Conn. 1977—; mem. adv. bd. Community Found. of Henderson County, N.C., 1990-93; trustee Brevard (N.C.) Music Ctr., 1990-93. Mem. Montclair (N.J.) Dramatic Club (chmn. and instr. makeup), Rehearsal Club (program chmn.), Montclair (N.J.) Women's Club (dir. plays, chmn. drama dept.), Sharon (Conn.) Women's Club, Sharon Rep. Women's Club (pres. 1982-85), Sharon Country Club, Hendersonville (N.C.) Country Club, Alpha Omicron Pi., Phi Beta (nat. profl. fraternity for peforming arts). Congregationalist. Address: PO Box 746 Hendersonville NC 28793-0746

SCHOOLEY, ROBERT T. medical educator; b. Denver, Nov. 10, 1949; s. Robert Enoch and Lelia Francis (Barnhill) S.; m. Constance Benson; children: Kimberly Dana, Elizabeth Kendall. BS, Washington and Lee U., 1970; MD, Johns Hopkins U., 1974. Diplomate Am. Bd. Internal Medicine. Intern Johns Hopkins Hosp., Balt., 1974-75, resident, 1975-76; clin. assoc. lab. clin. investigation Nat. Inst. Allergy & Infectious Disease, NIH, Bethesda, Md., 1976-77, chief clin. assoc. lab. clin. investigation, 1977-78, med. officer lab. clin. investigation, 1978-79; from instr. to assoc. prof. medicine Harvard Med. Sch., Boston, 1979-90; prof. medicine U. Colo., Denver, 1990—. Sect. chief internal medicine Mass. Eye and Ear Infirmary, Boston, 1980-85, cons. infectious diseases Harvard U. Health Svcs., Cambridge, Mass., 1982-90. Mem. editl. bd.: Antimicrobial Agts. and Chemotherapy, 1987—2000, mem. editl. bd.: Biotherapy, 1987—95, mem. editl. bd.: Jour. Acquired Immune Deficiency Syndromes, 1988—, mem. editl. bd.: Clin. and Diagnostic Lab. Immunology, 1992, assoc. editor: Clin. Infectious Diseases, 2002—; contbr. articles to profl. jours. Mem. Bonfils-Stanton Found. Clin. and rsch. fellow Infectious Disease Unit, Mass. Gen. Hosp., Boston, 1979-81; rsch. fellow Medicine Harvard Med. Sch., 1979-81; recipient Bonfils-Stanton award for sci. and medicine. Fellow Infectious Disease Soc. Am.; mem. AAAS, Am. Assn. Immunologists, Am. Soc. Clin. Investigation, Assn. Am. Physicians, Omicron Delta Kappa. E-mail: robert.schooley@uchsc.edu.

SCHOOLMAN, ARNOLD, neurological surgeon; b. Worcester, Mass., Oct. 31, 1927; s. Samuel and Sarah (Koffman) Schulman; m. Gloria June Feder, Nov. 22, 1963; children: Hugh Sinclair, (Jill) Annette. Student, U. Mass., 1945-46; BA, Emory U., 1950; PhD, Yale U., 1954, MD, 1957. Diplomate Am. Bd Neurol. Surgery, Nat. Bd. Med. Examiners. Intern U. Calif. Hosp., San Francisco, 1957-58; resident in neurol. surgery Columbia-Presbyn. Med. Ctr., Neurol. Inst. N.Y., N.Y.C., 1958-62; instr. neurol. surgery U. Kans. Sch. Medicine, Kansas City, 1962, asst. prof. surgery, 1964; assoc. prof. U. Mo. Sch. Medicine, 1976; chief sect. neurosurgery Research Med. Ctr., 1982; dir. Midwest Neurol. Inst., 1982-83. Patentee (20) in field. Served with USN, 1946-48. Fellow ACS (mem. Mo. chpt.); mem. AMA, Mo. State Med. Assn., Kansas City Med. Soc., Kansas City Neurosurg. Soc. (pres. 1984-85), Kansas City Neurol. Soc., Rocky Mountain Neurosurg. Soc., Am. Assn. Neurol. Surgeons, AAAS, Mo. Neurol. Soc., Internat. Coll. Surgeons, Congress Neurol. Surgeons, Brit. Royal Soc. Medicine, Phi Beta Kappa, Sigma Xi. Avocation: pilot. Home: 8705 Catalina St Shawnee Mission KS 66207-2351 Office: 5350 W 94th Ter Ste 104 Shawnee Mission KS 66207-2520

SCHOOLS, CHARLES HUGHLETTE, banker, lawyer; b. Lansing, Mich., May 24, 1929; s. Robert Thomas and Lillian Pearl (Lawson) S.; m. Rosemarie Sanchez, Nov. 22, 1952; children: Charles, Michael. BS, Am. U., 1952, MA, 1958; JD, Washington Coll. of Law, 1973; LLD, Bethune-Cookman U., 1973. Dir. phys. plant Am. U., 1952-66, owner, 1957—, Gen. Security Co., Washington, 1969—. Chmn., pres. Consol. Ventures Ltd.; pres., chmn. bd. McLean Bank (Va.), 1974— , Instl. Environ. Mgmt. Services; chmn. bd. Harper & Co.; chmn., pres. Community Assos. of Va., Associated Real Estate Mgmt. Services; dir. Computer Data Systems Inc., DAC Devel. Ltd., Am. Indsl. Devel. Corp., Intercoastal of Iran; mem. Met. Bd. Trades. Pres. McLean Boys' Club; bd. dirs. D.C. Spl. Olympics, Nat. Kidney Found.; trustee Bethune Cookman Coll., Western Md. Coll., Randolph Macon Acad. With USAAF, 1946-47, USAF, 1947-48. Mem. Va. C. of C., Profl. Businessman's Orgn., Georgetown Club of Washington, Touchdown Club of Washington, Univ. of Washington Club, Washington Golf and Country Club, Pisces Club (Washington), Halifax Club (Daytona Beach, Fla.), Masons, Alpha Tau Omega. Democrat. Office: 1313 Dolley Madison Blvd Mc Lean VA 22101-3926 Home: 458 S Beach St Ormond Beach FL 32174-7034

SCHOON, DORIS VIVIEN, ophthalmologist; b. Luverne, Minn., Dec. 31, 1928; d. Jacob and Esther Viola (Hansen) S. BA, U. Minn., 1950, MD, 1954; MSEE, Calif. State U., 1991. Diplomate Am. Bd. Ophthalmology. Intern Kings County Hosp., Bklyn., 1954-55; physician Embudo Presbyn. Hosp., N.Mex., 1955-57; resident in clin. pathology U. Colo. Med. Ctr., Denver, 1957-58; gen. practice medicine Anaheim, Calif., 1958-61; resident in ophthalmology L.A. Eye and Ear Hosp. at Hollywood Presbyn. Hosp., 1961-64; ophthalmologist Anaheim, 1965-75; dir. Electrophysiology Lab. of Ophthalmology Dept. U. Calif., Irvine, 1978-97; pvt. practice electrophysiology related to vision, 1997—; assoc. prof. clin. ophthalmology U. Calif., Irvine, 1997—. Physician Long Beach Vets. Hosp., 1998—. Fellow Am. Acad. Ophthalmology; mem. IEEE, Am. Women's Med. Assn., Internat. Soc. Clin. Electrophysiology in Vision, Soc. of Women Engrs., Order Eastern Star. Republican. Presbyterian. Achievements include research in field of using fast random stimuli to obtain electroretinograms and visually evoked potentials. also: Electrophysiology Lab Eye Clinic 2d Fl Pavilion II UCI MC 101 The City Dr Orange CA 92868 E-mail: doris_schoon@juno.com.

SCHOONHOVEN, RAY JAMES, retired lawyer; b. Elgin, Ill., May 24, 1921; s. Ray Covey and Rosina Madeline (Schram) (White) S.; m. Marie Theresa Dunn, Dec. 11, 1943; children: Marie Kathleen "Kamie", Ray James, Jr., Pamela Suzanne, John Philip, Rose Lynn. BSC., U. Notre Dame, 1943; JD, Northwestern U., 1948. Bar: Ill. 1949, U.S. Supreme Ct. 1954, D.C. 1973, U.S. Ct. Mil. Appeals 1954. Assoc. Seyfarth, Shaw Fairweather & Geraldson,

Chgo., 1949-57; ptnr. Seyfarth, Shaw Fairweather & Geraldson now Seyfarth Shaw, 1957-92; ret. Chief rulings and ops. br. Wage Stabilization Bd. Region VII, Chgo., 1951-52 Book rev. editor: Ill. Law Rev., 1948. Served to lt.comdr. USNR, 1942-62. Mem. ABA, Ill. State Bar Assn., Chgo. Bar Assn., D.C. Bar Assn., Chgo. Athletic Assn., Univ. Club. Chgo., Fed. Bar Assn., Order of Coif. Republican. Roman Catholic. Home: 1182 Lynette Dr Lake Forest IL 60045-4601 Office: Seyfarth Shaw 55 E Monroe St Ste 4200 Chicago IL 60603-5863 *I work hard to preserve our free enterprise system and, hopefully, to make such contribution to our society that it is better for my having been a part of it.*

SCHOONMAKER, L. CRAIG, political organization executive; b. Teaneck, N.J., Dec. 20, 1944; s. Ernest Tappan Schoonmaker and Gertrude Wilson Wynne. BA, CUNY, 1971. Pres. Homosexuals Intransigent!, Newark, 1969—; chmn. Expansionist Party of the U.S., 1977—. Author: (webpage) Homepage of the Expansionist Party of the U.S., 1997; author, webmaster (newsletter, mag., webpage) Homosexuals Intransigent!/Mr. Gay Pride, 1969. Roman Catholic. Avocations: pool (8-ball), traveling, history. Home: 295 Smith St Newark NJ 07106

SCHOONMAKER, SAMUEL VAIL, III, lawyer; b. Newburgh, N.Y., Sept. 1, 1935; s. Samuel V. Jr. and Catherine (Wilson) S.; m. Carolyn Peters, Sept. 18, 1965; children: Samuel V. IV, Frederick P. BA magna cum laude, Yale U., 1958, JD, 1961. Bar: Conn. 1961, U.S. Dist. Ct. Conn. 1961, U.S. Dist. Ct. (so. and ea. dist.) N.Y. 1964, U.S. Ct. Appeals (2d cir.) 1964, U.S. Supreme Ct. 1965. Assoc. Cummings & Lockwood, Stamford, Conn., 1961-70, co-mng. ptnr., 1987-90, mng. ptnr., 1990-94, chmn. exec. com., 1987-96; founder, pres. Schoonmaker George & Colin, P.C., Greenwich, 1996—. State trial referee Conn. Superior Ct., 1989; pres. Schoonmaker Family Assn., New Paltz, N.Y., 1975-77. Sr. topical editor Conn. Bar Jour., 1977-81; mem. editl. bd. Fairshare and Am. Jour. Family Law, 1992—; contbr. articles to profl. jours. Chmn. Conn. Child Support Commn., 1984-86; mem. Conn. Family Support Com., 1986-90; mem. Darien (Conn.) Rep. Town Com., 1974-76, rep. town meeting, 1990-98; pres. Youth Tennis Found. New Eng., Needham, Mass., 1975-77; pres. New Eng. Lawn Tennis Assn., 1977-79 (Man of Yr. award 1979); pres., trustee Huegenot Hist. Soc., 1999—. Fellow Am. Acad. Matrimonial Lawyers Conn. (bd. mgrs., Disting. Svc. award 1988), Internat. Acad. Matrimonial Lawyers, Am. Bar Found.; mem. ABA (chmn. family law sect. 1982-83), Conn. Bar Assn. (chmn. family law sect. 1971-74), Conn. Bus. and Industry Assn. (bd. dirs. 1993-98), S.W. Conn. Bus. and Industry Assn. (bd. dirs. 1990-97), Pub. Defenders Assn. (chmn.), Wee Burn Country Club (Darien, Conn., asst. sec.), Yale Club (N.Y.C.), Phi Beta Kappa. Avocation: tennis, platform tennis. Home: 231 Old Kings Hwy S Darien CT 06820-5931 Office: Schoonmaker George & Colin PC PO Box 5059 81 Holly Hill Ln Greenwich CT 06831-5059

SCHOONMAKER POWELL, THELMA, film editor; b. 1940; m. Michael Powell, 1984 (dec. 1990). Editor: (films) Who's That Knocking at My Door, 1968, Woodstock, 1970 (Academy award nomination best film editing 1970), Raging Bull, 1980 (Academy award best film editing 1980), The King of Comedy, 1983, After Hours, 1985, The Color of Money, 1986, The Last Temptation of Christ, 1988, New York Stories (Life Lessons), 1989, Good-Fellas, 1990 (Academy award nomination best film editing 1990), Cape Fear, 1992, The Age of Innocence, 1993, A Personal Journey with Martin Scorsese Through American Movies, 1995, Casino, 1995 (Am. Cinema Editors nomination best film editing 1995), Kundun, 1997, Bringing Out The Dead, 1999, Il Mio Viaggio in Italia, 2000, Gangs of New York, 2002. Office: Cappa Prodns 445 Park Ave Fl 7 New York NY 10022-2606

SCHOONOVER, AMY JO, English educator, poet; b. Glen Ellyn, Ill., Apr. 25, 1937; d. John Dale Schoonover and Alice R. Fletcher; m. Boyd W. McCarty, Aug. 23, 1957 (div. Jan. 1972); children: Michael, Deborah, Dale; m. Samuel J. Zook, Jr., July 15, 1972. BA in English, Wittenberg U., 1969; MA in English, W.Va. U., 1982, PhD in English, 1993. Adj. prof. English, speech, humanities Urbana (Ohio) U., 1986-88, 91—; adj. prof. Clark State C.C., Springfield, Ohio, 1989-90. Author: Sonnet Sampler, 1979, New & Used Poems, 1988, Greatest Hits, 2001, The Blue Tree: new sonnets, 2000; editor: Study and Writing of Poetry, 2d edit., 1996, author poems; contbr. articles and book revs. to profl. jours. Mem. Soc. for the Study Midwestern Lit., Nat. Fedn. State Poetry Socs. (bd. mem., contest chmn. 1977-96, pres. 1996-98), Ohio Poetry Assn. (various positions including pres. and editor), Ohio Poetry Day Assn. (bd. mem., contest chmn. 1975-87, 99—, treas. 1987-99, Ohio Poet of Yr. 1988). Home: 3520 State Rte 56 Mechanicsburg OH 43044

SCHOONOVER, BRENDA B. ambassador; BA, Morgan State U., Balt.; postgrad., Howard U. Vol. Peace Corps, The Phillipines, 1961, adminstr. Office Talent Search Washington, assoc. dir. Tanzania, dir. sch. partnership program; affirmative action officer Govt of Arlington County, Va.; with Fgn. Svc., U.S. Dept. State, Manila, Colombo, Sri Lanka, Tunis, Tunisia, with Bur. Near East and South Asia, Washington, 1978-88, chief pers. Bur. European and Can. Affairs, 1988-91; adminstrv. officer, dept. dir. Office Joint Adminstrv. Svcs. Am. Embassy, Brussels, 1992-96; mem. Sr. Seminar, U.S. Dept. State, 1996-97; Capstone fellow Nat. Def. U., Washington, 1997; U.S. amb. to Togo, Am. Embassy, Lome, Togo, 1998-2000; amb.-in-residence Chapel Hill, NC, 2000—01; dep. chief of mission, min. counselor Am. Embassy, Brussels, 2001—. Recipient Order of the Mono award The Togalese Govt., 2001. Office: American Embassy PSC 82 Box 002 APO AE 09710 Brussels 09710Belgium E-mail: RCSchoon2@aol.com.

SCHOONOVER, JACK RONALD, retired judge; b. Winona, Minn., July 23, 1934; s. Richard M. and Elizabeth A. (Hargeisheimer) S.; m. Ann Marie Kroez, June 18, 1965; children: Jack Ronald, Wayne J. Student, Winona State Coll., 1956-58; LLB, U. Fla., 1962. Bar: Fla. 1962. Atty. Wotitzky, Wotitzky & Schoonover, 1962-69, Schoonover, Olmsted & Schwarz, 1969-75; spl. asst. state's atty. State of Fla., 1969-72; city atty. City of Punta Gorda, Fla., city judge, 1973-74; judge 20th Jud. Cir. Ct., Ft. Myers, Fla., 1975-81, 2d Dist. Ct. Appeal, 1981-97, chief judge, 1990-92, ret., 1997. Atty. Charlotte County Sch. Bd., 1969-75, Charlotte County Zoning Bd., Charlotte County Devel. Authority; mem. unauthorized practice law com. 12th Jud. Cir., mem. grievance com. 20th Jud. Cir.; adj. prof. Edison C.C.; tchr. Charlotte County Adult Edn. Assn. Served with USAF, 1952-56. Home and Office: 14380 Olde Hickory Blvd Fort Myers FL 33912-0816

SCHOONOVER, JEAN WAY, public relations consultant; b. Richfield Springs, N.Y. AB, Cornell U., 1941. With D-A-Y Pub. Rels., Ogilvy & Mather Co., N.Y.C., 1949-91, D-A-Y Pub. Rels. Inc. and predecessor, N.Y.C., 1949—; owner, pres. Dudley-Anderson-Yutzy Pub. Rels. Inc. and predecessor, 1970—, chmn., 1984-88; merger with Ogilvy & Mather, 1983; sr. v.p. Ogilvy & Mather U.S., 1984-91; vice chmn. Ogilvy Pub. Relations Group, 1986-91; ind. cons., 1992—; pres. YWCA of the City of N.Y., 1994-98. Mem., historian, Pub. Rels. Seminar; mem. USDA Agribus. Promotion Coun., 1985-86. Trustee Cornell U., 1975-80; mem. Def. Adv. Com. on Women in Svcs., 1987-89. Named Advt. Woman of Yr. Am. Advt. Fedn., 1972, one of Outstanding Women in Bus. & Labor, Women's Equity Action League, 1985; recipient Matrix award, 1976, Nat. Headliner award, 1984, N.Y. Women in Comm., 1976, Leadership award Internat. Orgn. Women Bus. Owners, 1980, Entrepreneurial Woman award Women Bus. Owners N.Y., 1981, Women of Distinction award Soroptimists Internat. N.Y., 1995, Achievement award LWV of N.Y.C., 1997. Mem. Women Execs. in Pub. Rels. N.Y.C. (pres. 1979-80), Pub. Rels. Soc. Am., Pub. Rels. Soc. N.Y. (pres. 1979), Womens Forum, Women's City Club. Home and Office: 25 Stuyvesant St New York NY 10003-7505

SCHOONOVER, MARGARET See LEFRANC, MARGARET

SCHOPP, DAVID L. music educator; b. Tyrone, Pa., Oct. 1, 1965; s. David A. and Lee A. Schopp; m. Beth L. Rogers, June 24, 2000; 1 child Maxwell. BS in Music Edn., Pa. State U., 1987. Music tchr. Tredyfrin-Easttown, Devon, Pa., 1987—88; band dir. Norristown (Pa.) Area HS, 1988—99, Hatboro-Horsham (Pa.) HS, 1999—. Recipient Gift of Time award, Am. Family Inst., 1990, 1992. Mem.: Music Educators Nat. Conf., Pa. Music Educators Assn. Office: Hatboro Horsham HS 899 Horsham Rd Horsham PA 19044 E-mail: dschopp@hatboro-horsham.org.

SCHOPPA, ELROY, accountant, financial planner; b. Vernon, Tex., Aug. 25, 1922; s. Eddie A. and Ida S.; m. Juanita C. Young, Aug. 11, 1956 (div.); children: Karen Marie, Vickie Sue. BBA, Tex. Tech. U., 1943; postgrad. Law Sch., U. Tex., 1946-47; MA, Mich. State U., 1950. CPA, Tex., Calif.; cert. real estate broker; cert. ins. agt. Mem. faculty Tex. Tech. U., Lubbock, 1943, U. Tex., Austin, 1946-47, Mich. State U., East Lansing, 1947-50; auditor GM Corp., 1950-56; dir. systems and procedures Fansteel Metall. Corp., 1956-59; gen. auditor Consol. Electro Dynamics Corp., 1959-60; auditor, sr. tax acct. Beckman Inst. Inc., Fullerton, Calif., 1960-70; pres. Elroy Schoppa Acctg. Corp., La Habra, 1960—. Fin. planner Nat. Assn. Stock Dealers; bd. dirs., chmn. Mexican Ventures, Inc. (dba Baja BUDs, Del Norte); cons. to bus. CEO, pres., founder The Schoppa Family Found., 1999—; treas. La Habra Devel. Corp.; organizer, pres., 4-H Club, Vernon, Tex.; adviser Jr. Achievement, Waukegan, Ill.; bd. dirs. Klein Ctr. for Prevention of Domestic Violence; asst. football and basketball coach, Manzanola, Colo.; coach Am. Girls Sport Assn., La Habra. Served with USN, 1942-46, USNR, 1946-62. Mem. Calif. Soc. CPAs, USS LSM/LSMR Orgn., Phoenix Club (Anaheim, Calif.), Alpha Phi Omega, Theta Chi. Republican. Lutheran. Avocations: hunting, fishing, camping, traveling. Office: 801 E La Habra Blvd Ste B La Habra CA 90631-5531

SCHOPPMANN, MICHAEL JOSEPH, lawyer; b. N.Y.C., May 17, 1960; s. Fred Richard and Dorothy Ann (Wood) S.; m. Marlene Elizabeth Macbeth, Nov. 21, 1987; children: Michael, Steven. BS, St. John's U., 1982; JD, Seton Hall U., 1985. Bar: N.J. 1985, U.S. Dist. Ct. N.J. 1986, U.S. Supreme Ct. 1992, D.C. 1993, N.Y. 1994. Assoc. Baker Garber Duffy & Baker, Hoboken, N.J., 1985-87; counsel Johnstone Skok Loughlin & Lane, Westfield, 1987-90; prin. Kern Augustine Conroy & Schoppmann, Bridgewater, 1990—. Author, editor: (text) Basic Health Law, 1993; author: New Legal Threats in Managed Care, New Criminals for the Millenium?, Physician Unions - The Myth and One Potential Truth. Mem. ATLA, N.J. Bar Assn. (chmn. adminstrv. law sect. 1994-98), N.Y. State Bar Assn., D.C. Bar Assn., Somerset County Bar Assn. Office: Kern Augustine Conroy & Schoppmann 1120 Us Highway 22 Ste 8 Bridgewater NJ 08807-2972 E-mail: schoppmann@drlaw.com.

SCHOPPMEYER, MARTIN WILLIAM, education educator; b. Weehawken, N.J., Sept. 15, 1929; s. William G. and Madeleine M. (Haas) S.; m. Marilyn M. Myers, Aug. 9, 1958; children: Susan Ann, Martin William. BS, Fordham U., 1950; Ed.M., U. Fla., 1955, Ed.D., 1962. Tchr. Fla. pub. schs., 1955-59; instr., then asst. prof. U. Fla., 1960-63; assoc. prof., then prof. edn. Fla. Atlantic U., Boca Raton, 1963-68, dir. continuing edn., 1965-67; mem. faculty U. Ark., Fayetteville, 1968—, prof. edn., 1971-93, univ. prof., 1993—99, univ. prof. emeritus, 1999—, program coord. for ednl. adminstrn., 1983-90. Mem. Nat. Adv. Coun. Edn. Professions Devel., 1973-76; exec. sec. Ark. Sch. Study Coun., 1976—; evaluator instructional tng. program Nat. Tng. Fund, 1978; bd. dirs. Women's Ednl. and Devel. Inst., 1977-80, Nat. Sch. Devel. Coun., sec., 1989-90, v.p. 1990, pres., 1990-92; mem. oversight com. South Conway (Ark.) County Sch. Dist.; mem. state commn. to study effect of Amendment 59 to Ark. Constn.; cons. Lake View U. Huckabee, 1994-2002. Author books, monographs, articles in field. Mem. president's coun. Subiaco Acad., 1984-90; chmn. Subiaco Sch. Bd., 1990-93, mem., 1993-97. With U.S. Army, 1951-53, Korea. Recipient numerous fed. grants. Mem. NEA, Ark. Edn. Assn. (past chpt. pres.), Ark. Assn. Ednl. Adminstrs., KC, Rotary, Kappa Delta Pi, Phi Delta Kappa, Delta Tau Kappa. Roman Catholic. Home: 2950 Sheryl Ave Fayetteville AR 72703-3542 E-mail: MSCHOPPMEYER@aol.com. *The only really sound investment for a family, a community, or a society is that money spent for the education of its youth.*

SCHOR, EDWARD LEWIS, physician; b. Denver, Aug. 14, 1944; s. Manny and Marjorie (Lewis) S.; m. Delynn Irene Harrison, Oct. 21, 1988. AB, Washington U., St. Louis, 1966; MD, Chgo. Med. Sch., 1970; postgrad., Johns Hopkins U., 1981-83. Intern, resident Baylor Coll. of Medicine, Houston, 1970-72; pediatric resident Johns Hopkins Hosp., Balt., 1972-73; faculty Johns Hopkins U., 1973-81; med. dir. Chesapeake Health Plan, 1976-81; faculty U. N.Mex., Albuquerque, 1983-87; program dir. Kaiser Family Found., Menlo Park, Calif., 1987-90; dir. Functional Outcome program New Eng. Med. Ctr., Boston, 1990-95; med. dir., dir. Ctr. pub. policy Iowa Dept. Pub. Health, 1995—2002; asst. v.p. The Commonwealth Fund, N.Y.C., 2002—. Clin. faculty Stanford U., 1988-90, U. Iowa, Iowa City, 1995-2002; faculty Tufts U., Boston, 1990-95. Editor: Caring for Your School-Age Child, 1999; mem. editl. rev. bd. Jour. Devel. and Behavioral Pediatrics, 1993—; mem. editl. bd. Pediatrics, 1996-, Healthy Kids, 1996-2001, Johnson & Johnson Pediat. Inst., 1993-97, others. Fellow Am. Acad. Pediat. (com. on early childhood, adoption and dependent care 1984-90, chmn. 1992-96, chmn. task force on family 1997-2000); mem. Ambulatory Pediat. Assn. (bd. dirs. 1985-88, Mead-John vis. prof. 1981). Office: Commonwealth Fund 1 E 75th St New York NY 10021

SCHOR, JOSEPH MARTIN, pharmaceutical executive, biochemist; b. Bklyn., Jan. 10, 1929; s. Aaron Jacob and Rhea Iress (Kay) S.; children: Esther Helen, Joshua David, Gideon Alexander, Eric, Neil; m. Laura Sharon Strumingher, June 14, 1992. BS magna cum laude, CCNY, 1951; PhD, Fla. State U., 1957. Sr. rsch. chemist Armour Pharm. Co., Kankakee, Ill., 1957-59, Lederle Labs., Pearl River, N.Y., 1959-64; dir. biochemistry Endo Labs., Garden City, 1964-70; head dept. biochemistry DuPont and Endo Labs., 1970-77; v.p. sci. affairs Forest Labs., N.Y.C., 1977-94, sr. v.p. sci. affairs emeritus, 1995—. Editor, contbr.: Chemical Control of Fibrinolysis-thrombolysis, 1970. Contbr. articles to profl. jours. Patentee in field. USPHS fellow, 1955-57. Fellow Am. Inst. Chemists (cert. prof. chemist); mem. Am. Chem. soc. (chmn. Nassau County subsect. 1971-72), Internat. Soc. on Thrombosis and Hemostasis, N.Y. Acad. Scis., AAAS, Phi Beta Kappa, Sigma Xi. Home: 28 Meleny Rd Locust Valley NY 11560-1221 E-mail: joseph.m.schor@verizon.net.

SCHOR, LAURA STRUMINGHER, historian; b. N.Y.C., June 24, 1945; d. David Charles and Esther Rachel (Pearl) Gross; children: Eric Alain, Neil Remy; m. Joseph Martin Schor, June, 1992. BA, Queens Coll., CUNY, 1967; MA, U. Rochester, 1970, PhD, 1974. Asst. prof. SUNY, Fredonia, 1973-79; assoc. prof., dir. women's studies U. Cin., 1979-85, prof., vice provost, 1985-89; prof., provost, v.p. acad. affairs Hunter Coll., CUNY, N.Y.C., 1989-98; exec. dir. Hadassah, The Women's Zionist Orgn. of Am., Inc., 1998-2000; dir. CUNY Honors Coll., 2001—. Author: Women and the Making of the Working Class, 1979, What Were Little Boys and Girls Made Of?, 1984, The Odyssey of Flora Tristan, 1988, Les Jolies Femmes d'Edouard de Beaumont, 1994. Mem. Internat. Soc. for Study European Ideas, Am. Hist. Assn., French Hist. Assn., Phi Beta Kappa.

SCHOR, LAURENCE, lawyer; b. Bklyn., May 3, 1942; s. Julius and Ruth (Zackowitz) S.; m. Susan Leslie Gurevitz, Dec. 26, 1965; children: Meredith Nan, Joseph Sanford, Wendy Claire, Samuel Julius. BBA, So. Meth. U., 1963; JD, U. Tex., 1966; LLM, George Washington U., 1972. Bar: Tex. 1966, D.C. 1971, Md. 1993.; U.S. Ct. Appeals (D.C., 4th, 5th, 11th cirs.). Atty. NASA, Huntsville, Ala., 1966-68; asst. gen. counsel NASA support U.S. Army C.E., Washington, 1968-70; assoc. Sellers, Conner & Cuneo, 1970-73; from assoc. to ptnr. Max E. Greenberg, Trayman, Cantor, Reiss & Blasky, 1974-80; ptnr. Schnader, Harrison, Segal & Lewis, 1981-91, ptnr.-in-charge, 1986-88; mem. Miller & Chevalier, 1991-93; ptnr. Smith, Somerville & Case, LLC, 1993-96, McManus, Schor, Asmar & Darden, LLP, Washington, 1997—. Lectr. George Washington U., others. Author: The Right to Stop Work, 1991; author: (manual) Delays, Suspensions and Acceleration, Workplace Safety and Health in the 1990's, 1992; author: Claims Against Bonding Companys, Construction Contractors' Handbook of Business and Law, 1992, How to File a Federal Contract Claim, 1998; co-author: Suing a Government: Special Considerations for Book Construction Disputes: Representing the Contractor, 3d edit., 2001; author, editor 50 State Lien and Bond Laws, 1993—2001, Vol. 3 Form Book rewrite, 2000, editor update, 2001; contbr. chapters to books. Founder, pres. Manor Lake Civic Assn., Montgomery County, 1969-71; precinct chmn. Montgomery County Dems., 1972-76; mem. D.C. City Coun. Procurement Reform Task Force, 1995-96. Mem. ABA (chmn. region III pub. contract law sect., 1982-88, chmn. constrn. com. 1986-90, sect. budget and fin. 1990-95), D.C. Bar Assn. (chmn. divsn. 10 govt. contracts and litigation, 1981-85), Fed. Bar Assn., Am. Coll. Constrn. Lawyers (founder, bd. govs., treas. 1996-2000, pres. elect 2000, pres. 2001-02), B'nai B'rith Youth Orgn (adult adv. bd. 2001-02), Phi Alpha Delta (pres. T.C. Clark chpt. 1965-66). Jewish. Avocations: reading, travel. Home: 7021 Mountain Gate Dr Bethesda MD 20817-3913 Office: McManus Schor Asmar & Darden LLP 1301 Connecticut Ave NW Fl 6 Washington DC 20036-1815 E-mail: lschor@msdalaw.com.

SCHOR, STANLEY SIDNEY, mathematical sciences educator; b. Phila., Mar. 3, 1922; s. Joseph and Dorothy (Abrams) S.; m. Irene Sternberg, June 19, 1949; children— Mark, Robin, Randi. AB, U. Pa., 1943, AM, 1950, PhD, 1952; certificate, U. Cin., 1944. Instr. U. Pa., Phila., 1950-53, asst. prof. stats., 1953-58, assoc. prof., 1958-64, dir. Nat. Periodic Health Exam. Research Group, 1958-64; dir. dept. biostats. AMA, Chgo., 1964-66; prof. biostats. Chgo. Med. Sch., 1964-66; prof., chmn. dept. biometrics Temple U. Med. Sch., 1966-75, adj. prof., 1975-85. Vis. prof. Tel Aviv U., 1973-74, Med. Coll. Pa., 1979; exec. dir. Cbards, Merck Sharp & Dohme, West Point, Pa., 1975-91; clin. prof. Hahnemann Med. Sch., 1975-85; cons. in field. Author: Fundamentals of Biostatistics, 1968; mem. editorial staff Jour. Trauma, 1955-91, Jour. AMA, 1964-91, Chest, 1966-91; contbr. articles to profl. jours. Served with AUS, 1943-46. Recipient Career Achievement award Pharm. Rsch. and Mfrs. Am., 1996, Stanley S. Schor fellowship in biostatistics U. N.C. and Merck. given in his honor. Fellow Am. Public Health Assn., Am. Statis. Assn. (Career Achievement award), Phila. Coll. Physicians; mem. AAUP, Biometric Soc., Royal Soc. Health, Pi Gamma Mu. Home: 3912 S Ocean Blvd Apt 1105 Highland Beach FL 33487-3336

SCHOR, SUZI, lawyer, psychologist; b. Chgo., Feb. 1, 1947; d. Samuel S. and Dorothy Helen (Hineline); 1 child, Kate. BSBA, Ind. U., 1964; JD, Northwestern U., 1970, U. Palmer's Green, London, 1971; PhD in Fine Arts (hon.), U. Nev., PhD in Clin. Psychology, 1989, Kensington U., 1989. Bar: Ill., 1971. Pvt. practice, L.A., 1971-80; v.p. legal affairs Little Gypzy Mgmt., Inc., Beverly Hills, Calif., 1980—; trust officer, pvt. fiduciary svcs. Bank of Am., L.A. Mem. Pres.'s Coun. on Alcoholism. Author: 13th Step to Death, 1995; contbg. author Wine and Dine Mag.; contbr. articles to profl. jours. Bd. dirs. Nat. Ctr. for Hyperactive Children, L.A., 1989-91, sec. Rainbow Guild Cancer Charity, L.A., 1985-89, ind. cons. Jewish Legal Aid, L.A., 1988—; campaign coord. advisor Dem. Nat. Campaign, L.A., 1990, 94, 2000; donor mem. L.A. Coun. on World Affairs. Recipient Poet of Yr. award Nat. Libr. and Assn. of Poetry, 1995, 98. Mem. ABA (criminal justice com. 1994), AAUW, NAA-DAC, CAADAC, L.A. Breakfast Club (chmn. entertainment 1988-90), Rotary, Mensa, Beverly Hills Bar Assn., Century City Bar Assn. Jewish. Avocations: singing, skiing, writing.

SCHORE, NILES, lawyer; b. N.Y.C., Mar. 27, 1950; s. Harold G. and Hilda (Werner) S.; m. Anne Dunlap Vaughan, May 18, 1979. BS, U. Pa., 1971; JD, George Washington U., 1975. Bar: Pa. 1975, Ga. 1980. Co.-dir., mng. atty. Keystone Legal Svcs., Clearfield, Pa., 1981-82; dir. Elderly Law Project, Phila., 1983-88; staff atty. Pa. Health Law Project, Chester, 1988-89; counsel, exec. dir. Urban Affairs and Housing Commn., Pa. Senate, Harrisburg, 1989-94, counsel, exec. dir. Pub. Health and Welfare Commn., 1995—. Chmn. consumer com. Pa. Intragovtl. Coun. on Long Term Care, Harrisburg, 1988-89; mem. Atty. Gen.'s Task Force on Violence Against the Elderly, Harrisburg, 1987-88; mem. children, families and health com. Assembly on State Issues, Nat. conf. State Legislatures, 1993—; bd. dirs. Del. Valley Child Care Coun., 1997-2001; outstanding policy advocate Ctr. for Advocacy in the Rights and Interests of the Elderly, 1977-97; mem. Atty. Gen.'s Task Force on Protection of Older Pennsylvanians, 1998-99; lectr. Pa. Bar Inst., 1999. Author: An Advocate's Guide to Medical Assistance Eligibility in Pennsylvania, 2d edit., 1988; author: Analysis of a Rulemaking: Standing Committees, 1999. Bd. trustees The Green Tree Sch., 2000—. Mem. Pa. Bar Assn. Democrat. Jewish. Home: 2519 Hillcrest Rd Drexel Hill PA 19026-1333 Office: Pa Senate Main Capitol Bldg Rm 543 Harrisburg PA 17120

SCHORE, ROBERT, social worker, educator, consultant; b. N.Y.C., July 29, 1934; married, three children. Student, Mesivta Tifereth Jerusalem, N.Y.C., 1947-48; BA, CCNY, 1955; MS, Columbia U., 1959; cert. advanced study, SUNY, New Paltz, 1985. Diplomate Clin. Social Work, NASW; cert. social worker, impartial hearing officer, supr. sch. social workers, N.Y. Social worker Dept. Social Svcs./Child Placement Svcs., N.Y.C., 1956-58, Edwin Gould Found., N.Y.C., 1959-63; supr. with NIMH dem. project Shield Inst., Bronx, N.Y., 1963-65; sch. social worker N.Y.C. Bd. Edn., 1965-91; pvt. practice West Nyack, N.Y., 1992-95. Psychotherapist Ind. Consultation Ctr., Bronx, 1967, Rockland County Mental Health Ctr., Monsey, N.Y., 1968-69; rsch. assoc., editor, writer /NIMH demo project Nathan Kline Inst., Orangeburg, N.Y., 1968-85, 98—; instr. CCNY, 1966; field instr. NYU, 1970-73; adj. prof. Rockland C.C., Suffern, N.Y., 1993-97; impartial hearing officer N.Y. State Edn. Dept., 1992-2000; faculty Ctr. for Study of Issues in Pub. Mental Health, Orangeburg, N.Y., 1999—. Supr., cons. Vol. Counseling Svc., New City, N.Y., 1992-94. Mem. Am. Fedn. Tchrs., United Fedn. Tchrs., Acad. Cert. Social Workers, Am. Radio Relay League, Crystal Radio Club, Radio Amateur Civil Emergency Svcs., N.Y. Disaster Preparedness Comm., Jewish War Vets. (chaplain post 425). Jewish. Avocations: photography, music, violin, piano, amateur radio. Office: PO Box 276 Monsey NY 10952-0276

SCHORER, SUKI, ballet teacher; b. Boston; d. Mark and Ruth (Page) S.; 1 child, Nicole. Studied with, George Balanchine. Dancer San Francisco Ballet, 1956-59, N.Y.C. Ballet, 1959-72; prin. dancer N.Y.C. Ballet Co., 1968-72, artistic assoc. lecture demonstration program, 1972-95; mem. faculty Sch. Am. Ballet, 1972—, Brown Found. sr. faculty chair, 1998—. Internat. guest tchr. and lectr. specializing in Balanchine tng. and technique; artist dir., tchr. on Balanchine Essays (videos). Author (monograph) Balanchine Pointework, 1995, Suki Schorer on Balanchine Technique, 1999 (de la Torre Bueno prize 2000); created roles in Balanchine's Harlequinade, Don Quixote, Midsummer Night's Dream, Jewels, La Source, Raymonda Variations; repertory included prin. roles in Apollo, Serenade, Concerto Barocco, Symphony in C, La Somnambula, Stars and Stripes, Tarantella, Valse Fantaisie, The Nutcracker, Brahams Schoenberg, La Valse, Western Symphony, Ivesiana, Divertimento # 15, Ballet Imperial, others. Recipient Disting. Tchr. in Arts award Nat. Found. Advancement in Arts, 1997, award Dance mag., 1998. Office: Sch of Am Ballet 70 Lincoln Center Plz New York NY 10023-6548

SCHORLING, WILLIAM HARRISON, lawyer; b. Ann Arbor, Mich., Jan. 7, 1949; s. Otis William Schorling and Ruthann (Bales) Schorling Moorehead; m. Lynne Ann Newcomb, June 1, 1974; children: Katherine Pearce, Ann Oury, John Roberts. BA cum laude, Denison U., 1971; JD cum laude, U. Mich., 1975. Bar: Pa. 1975, U.S. Ct. Appeals (3d cir.) 1977, N.J. 1998, Del. 2001. Ptnr. Eckert, Seamans, Cherin & Mellott, Pitts., 1984-89, Klett Rooney Lieber & Schorling, PC, Pitts., 1989—. Lectr. Pa. Bar Inst., Harrisburg, 1983—, Comml. Law League, N.Y.C., 1984—, Profl. Edn. Systems, Inc., Eau Claire, Wis., 1986—, Southwest Legal Found., Dallas, 1994—; founders' coun. Comml. Fin. Assn. Edn. Found., 1991—; bd. dirs. Consumer Bankruptcy Assistance Project. Contbr. articles to profl. jours. Trustee Pa. Acad. Fine Arts. Fellow Am. Coll. Bankruptcy, Am. Bar Found.; mem. ABA (bus. law section coun. 2000—, chmn. bus. bankruptcy com. 1996-99, lectr. 1988—), Am. Banker Inst. (lectr. 1994—), Phila. Bar Assn. (lectr. 1996—), E. Dist. Bankruptcy Conf., Pa. Bar Assn. (lectr. 1983—), Allegheny County Bar Assn. (chmn. bankruptcy and comml. law sect. 1991), The Com. of Seventy (vice chair), Longue Vue Club, Duquesne Club, Pyramid Club, Pa. Soc., Bedens Brook Club. Presbyterian. Home: 12 Scudder Ct Pennington NJ 08534-2325 Office: Klett Rooney Lieber & Schorling 2 Logan Sq Fl 12 Philadelphia PA 19103-2707

SCHORNACK, JOHN JAMES, accountant; b. Chgo., Nov. 22, 1930; s. John Joseph and Helen Patricia (Patrickus) S.; m. Barbara Anne Lelli, June 5, 1965; children: Mark Boyd, Anne Marguerite Schornack Trueman, Erin Keeley Schornack Dickes, Tracy Bevan Schornack Power. BS, Loyola U., 1951; MBA, Northwestern U., 1956; grad., Advanced Mgmt. Program, Harvard Bus. Sch., 1969. With Ernst & Young (formerly Arthur Young & Co.), 1955-91, partner, 1964-91; firm dir. personnel Ernst & Young LLP (formerly Arthur Young & Co.), N.Y.C., 1966-71, asst. mng. ptnr. N.Y.C. office, 1971-72, mng. ptnr., 1972-74, mng. ptnr. Chgo. office, 1976-85, mng. ptnr. Midwest region, vice chmn., 1985-91; mem. mgmt. com. Arthur Young & Co. Mgmt. com. Arthur Young & Co.; vice chmn., mng. ptnr. Midwest region Ernst & Young, 1989-91; bd. dirs., chmn. Ernst & Young Found., 1981-91; chmn., bd. dirs. North Shore Bancorp, Inc., 1992-, Wintrust Fin. Corp., 1996-. Pres. Chgo. Youth Ctrs., 1979-95; bd. govs. Chgo. Symphony, 1979-85, trustee, 1985—, life trustee; vol. United Way, 1975-92, dir., 1989-92; vis. adv.

com. sch. accountancy DePaul U., 1980-83; mem. Loyola U. Citizens Bd., 1977-94, chmn., 1993-94; mem. adv. com. Northwestern U. Grad. Sch. Mgmt., 1967-91; coun. U. Chgo. Grad. Sch. Bus., 1982-91; bd. dirs. Met. Planning Coun., 1992-95; trustee Kohl Children's Mus., 1994—, Lyric Opera, 1984-92, Cath. Theol. Union, 1992-97, Graham Found., 1992-98; trustee Barat Coll., 1983-98, life trustee, 1999-2001, vice chmn., 1985-90, chmn., 1990-97; trustee St. Francis Hosp., 1986-97, vice chmn., 1991-94; trustee Night Ministry, 1998—. Recipient Order of the Sacred Treas., Emperor of Japan, 1999. Mem. AICPA, Am. Acctg. Assn., Ill. Soc. CPA's, Midwest-Japan Assn. (chmn. 1983-99), Japan Am. Soc., 410 Club, Tavern Club, Chgo. Club, Glen View Club, Ocean Club, The Little Club. Home: 314 Regent Wood Rd Northfield IL 60093-2762 Office: Ernst & Young LLP Great Lakes Reg Office 233 S Wacker Dr Chicago IL 60606-6306 E-mail: northdel@aol.com.

SCHORR, ALAN EDWARD, librarian, publisher; b. N.Y.C., Jan. 7, 1945; s. Herbert and Regina S.; m. Debra Genner, June 11, 1967; 1 son, Zebediah. BA, CUNY, 1966; MA, Syracuse U., 1967; postgrad., U. Iowa, 1967-71; MLS, U. Tex., 1973. Tchr., rsch. asst. dept. history U. Iowa, 1967-70; govt. publs. and map libr., asst. prof. Elmer E. Rasmuson Libr., U. Alaska, 1973-78; assoc. prof., dir. libr. U. Alaska, Juneau, 1978-84; prof., dean univ. libr. Calif. State U., Fullerton, 1984-86; pres. The Denali Press, Juneau, 1986—. Freelance indexer and bibliographer; vis. lectr. Birmingham (Eng.) Poly., 1981; mem. Alaska Ednl. Del. to China, 1975. Author: Alaska Place Names, 1974, 4th edit., 1991, Directory of Special Libraries in Alaska, 1975, Government Reference Books, 1974-75, 1976, 1976-77, 1978, Government Documents in the Library Literature 1909-1974, 1976, ALA RSBRC Manual, 1979, Federal Documents Librarianship 1879-1987, 1988, Hispanic Resource Directory, 1988, 3d edit., 1996, Refugee and Immigrant Resource Directory, 1990, 92, 94; editor: The Sourdough, 1974-75, Directory of Services for Refugees and Immigrants, 1987, 3d edit., 1993, Guide to Smithsonian serial publs., 1987 ; book reviewer, columnist: S.E. Alaska Empire, 1979-82, L.A. Times; contbr. articles to profl. jours. Mem. Auke Bay (Alaska) Vol. Fire Dept., 1978—81, Juneau Borough Libr. Adv. Com., 1981—82, Juneau Borough Cemetery Adv. Com., 1980—81, Am. Book Awards Com., 1980; chmn. program evaluation com., former chmn. facilities com., former chmn. policy com. to v.p. Juneau Bd. of Edn., 2000—; Mem. Juneau Bd. Edn., 1991-94, 95-97, 97-00, 2000—. Mem. ALA (mem. reference and subscription books rev. com. 1975-86, mem. reference and adult svcs. divsn. publs. com. 1975-77, Nat. Assn. Hispanic Publs., Mudge citation commn. 1977-79, 84-86, Dartmouth Coll. Medal Commn., Governing Coun. 1977-84, mem. Dewey medal com. 1984-85, Denali Press award), Alaska Libr. Assn. (mem. exec. bd. 1974-75, mem. nominating com. 1977-79), Pacific N.W. Libr. Assn. (rep. publs. com. 1973-75), Assn. Coll. and Rsch. Librs. (mem. publ. com. 1976-80), Spl. Librs. Assn. (assoc. editor geography and map divsn. bull. 1975-76), Soc. for Scholarly Pub., Internat. Assn. Ind. Pubs (bd. dirs. 1990-92), Pub. Mktg. Assn., Alaska State Employees Fed. Credit Union (bd. dirs. 1997—, treas. 2001-2002, vice chmn., 2002--), PEN Ctr. USA West, Amnesty Internat., Explorers Club N.Y., Wash. Athletic Club (Seattle). Office: Denali Press PO Box 1535 Juneau AK 99802

SCHORR, ALVIN LOUIS, social worker, educator; b. N.Y.C., Apr. 13, 1921; s. Louis and Tillie (Godiner) S.; m. Ann Girson, Aug. 21, 1948; children—Jessica Lee, Kenneth L., Wendy Lauren. BSS, CCNY, 1941; MSW, Washington U., St. Louis, 1943; DHL, Adelphi U., 1975. With Family Service No. Va., 1956-58; family life specialist Office Commr. Social Security, 1958-62; vis. prof. London (Eng.) Sch. Econs., 1962-63; acting chief long range research Social Security Adminstrn., 1963-64; dir. research and planning Office Econ. Opportunity, 1965-66; dep. asst. sec. Dept. Health, Edn. and Welfare, 1967-69; prof. social policy, dir. income maintenance project Brandeis U., 1969-70; dean Grad. Sch. Social Work, N.Y.U., 1970-73; gen. dir. Community Service Soc. N.Y., 1973-77; vis. prof. Cath. U. Am., 1977-79; Leonard W. Mayo prof. Case Western Res. U., 1979-92, Leonard W. Mayo prof. emeritus, 1992—. Fulbright sr. rsch. scholar, 1962-63; vist. prof. Hebrew U., Jerusalem, 1986, Fla. Internat. U., 1995, N.Mex. State U., 1996; vis. scholar London Sch. Econs., 1991-92. Author: Filial Responsibility in the Modern American Family, 1961, Slums and Social Insecurity, 1963, Social Services and Social Security in France, 1964, Poor Kids, 1966, Explorations in Social Policy, 1968, Children and Decent People, 1974, Jubilee for Our Times, 1977, Thy Father and Thy Mother, 1980, Common Decency: Domestic Policies After Reagan, 1986, Economic Development in Cleveland: A Dissenting View, 1991; The British Personal Social Services: An Outside View, 1992, Passion and Policy: A Social Worker's Career, 1997, Welfare Reform: Failure and Remedies, 2001. Recipient Disting. Service in Social Welfare award Washington U. Alumni Assn., 1969, Michael Schwerner award, 1972, Lifetime Achievement award Ohio Assn. Social Workers, 1998. Fellow Nat. Acad. Social Ins.; mem. Phi Beta Kappa. Home: 1701 E 12th St Apt 14tw Cleveland OH 44114-3206 Office: Case Western Res U Mandel Sch Appl Social Sci Cleveland OH 44106

SCHORR, BRIAN LEWIS, lawyer, business executive; b. N.Y.C., Oct. 5, 1958; s. Philip I. and Hannah Schorr; m. Amy B. Horowitz, 1984; 2 children. BA magna cum laude, MA, Wesleyan U., Middletown, Conn., 1979; JD, NYU, 1982. Bar: N.Y. 1983, D.C. 1985, U.S. Supreme Ct. 1988. Assoc. Paul, Weiss, Rifkind, Wharton & Garrison, N.Y.C., 1982-90, ptnr., 1991-94; exec. v.p., gen. counsel Triarc Cos., Inc., 1994—. Mem. bd. advisors Jour. Ltd. Liability Cos., 1994-98; lectr. CLE programs. Author: Schorr on New York Limited Liability Companies and Partnerships, 1994; contbr. articles to legal jours. Vice pres. Bronx (N.Y.) H.S. Sci. Endowment Fund, Inc. Mem. ABA, N.Y. State Bar Assn., Assn. Bar City N.Y. (chmn. com. on corp. law 1993-96, co-chmn. joint drafting com. N.Y. ltd. liability co. law), Tri Bar Opinion Com., Bronx H.S. Sci. Alumni Assn. (trustee). Office: Triarc Cos Inc 280 Park Ave New York NY 10017-1216

SCHORR, DANIEL LOUIS, broadcast journalist, author, lecturer; b. N.Y.C., Aug. 31, 1916; s. Louis and Tillie (Godiner) S.; m. Lisbeth Bamberger, 1967; children: Jonathan, Lisa. BSS, CCNY, 1939; hon. doctorate, Kalamazoo Coll., Columbia Coll., Chgo., Wilkes U., Nebr. Wesleyan U., L.I. U., Brandeis U., Spartus Coll., Bates Coll., Haverford Coll. Asst. editor Jewish Telegraphic Agy., 1934-41; news editor ANETA (Netherlands) News Agy. in N.Y., 1941-43; freelance corr. N.Y. Times, Christian Sci. Monitor, London Daily Mail, 1948-53; Washington corr. CBS News, also spl. assignments L.Am. and Europe, 1953-55; reopened CBS Moscow Bur., 1955; roving assignments U.S. and Europe, 1958-60; chief CBS News Bur., Germany, Ctrl. Europe, 1960-66; Washington corr. CBS, 1966-76; Regents prof. U. Calif., Berkeley, 1977; columnist Des Moines Register-Tribune Syndicate, 1977-80; sr. Washington corr. Cable News Network, 1980-85; sr. analyst Nat. Pub. Radio, 1985—. Author: Don't Get Sick in America!, 1971, Clearing the Air, 1977, Forgive Us Our Press Passes, 1999, Staying Tuned, 2001. With U.S. Army, 1943-46, 47. Decorated officer Orange Nassau (The Netherlands), Grand Cross of Merit (Germany); recipient citations of excellence for radio-TV reporting Soviet Union Overseas Press Club, 1956, Best TV Interpretation of Fgn. News award 1963, ACLU and other awards for pub. suppressed Congsl. intelligence report, Emmy awards for coverage of Watergate, 1972, 73, 74, Peabody award for lifetime of uncompromising reporting of highest integrity, 1992, George Polk award for radio commentary L.I. U., 1994, Disting. Svc. award Am. Soc. Journalism and Mass Comm., 1994, Golden Baton award for lifetime achievement A.I. DuPont Columbia U., 1996; inducted in Hall of Fame Soc. Profl. Journalists, 1991, Comms. Hall of Fame CCNY, 1999. Mem. Am. Acad. Arts and Scis. (elected), Coun. on Fgn. Rels. N.Y.C., Nat. Press Club. E-mail: dschorr@npr.org. *Journalism, for more than 60 years, has been both profession and outlook on life. I have always felt myself the observer and nonparticipant, the quintessential outsider. I have pursued the sense of things behind the appearance of things, the meaning behind the manipulation. I have fought, with dubious success, against the blurring of the media line between reality and fantasy.*

SCHORR, LAWRENCE MARTIN, civil engineer, environmental engineer; b. Phila., Apr. 29, 1959; s. Norman and Rosalie Natalie (Goldberg) S.; m. Debra Lynn Geiger, May 28, 1989; children: Elizabeth Stephanie, Lauren Meredith. BSCE, Pa. State U., 1981; MS in Systems Mgmt., U. So. Calif., 1988; MS in Environ. Engring., U. Houston, 1996. Registered profl. engr., Va., Tex. Commd. 2d lt. U.S. Army, 1981, advanced through grades to capt., 1985, ret., 1991; commd. capt. USAR, 1991, promoted to lt. col., 1999; platoon leader 94th engr. bn. U.S. Army, Darmstadt, Fed. Republic Germany, 1981-83, constrn. officer Fed. Republic Germany, 1983-84, intelligence/tng. officer Fed. Republic Germany, 1984; project officer U.S. Army C.E., Kansas City, Kans., 1984-87; logistics officer 1st engr. bn. U.S. Army, Ft. Riley, 1987-89, co. comdr., 1989-90, maintenance/logistics officer, 1990-91; served 1st Infantry Dvsn. Desert Shield/Storm, S.E. Asia; subcontract specialist Brown & Root, Inc., Houston, 1991-96, area mgr., project engr., 1996-98; mgr. divsn. project and constrn. mgmt. Infrastructure Assocs., 1998—2000; mgr. dept. constrn. mgmt. United Engrs., Inc., 2000—. Sec. Manhattan (Kans.) Jewish Congregation, 1989-90. Decorated Bronze Star, 1991; recipient Marshall award ROTC & Marshall Soc., 1981. Fellow Soc. Am. Mil. Engrs. (sec. Flint Hills post 1985-87, vice chmn. readiness com. Houston post 1992—, bd. dirs. Houston post 1998-2001, pres.-elect 2001, pres. 2002); mem. NSPE, ASCE, Tex. Soc. Profl. Engrs., Scabbard & Blade, Chi Epsilon. Avocations: skiing, reading, bicycling, exercise, carpentry. Home: 91 N Cochrans Green Cir The Woodlands TX 77381-6208

SCHORR, LISBETH BAMBERGER, child and family policy analyst, author, educator; b. Munich, Jan. 20, 1931; d. Fred S. and Lotte (Krafft) Bamberger; m. Daniel L. Schorr, Jan. 8, 1967; children: Jonathan, Lisa. BA with highest honors, U. Calif., Berkeley, 1952; LHD (hon.) , Wilkes U., 1991, U. Md., 1994; LHD (hon.) , Bank St. Coll. Edn., 1999, Wheelock Coll., 2000, Lewis & Clark Coll., 2001. Med. care cons. U.A.W. and Community Health Assn., Detroit, 1956—58; asst. dir. Dept. Social Security AFL-CIO, Washington, 1958—65; acting chief CAP Health Svcs., OEO, 1965—66; chief program planning Office for Health Affairs, OEO, Washington, 1967. Cons. Childrebn's Def. Fund, Washington, 1973—79; scholar-in-residence Inst. of Medicine NAS, 1979—80; chmn. Select Panel on Promotion Child Health, 1979—80; adj. prof. maternal and child health U. N.C., Chapel Hill, 1981—85; lectr. social medicine Harvard U. Med. Sch., 1984—; dir. project on effective interventions Harvard U., 1988—; nat. coun. Alan Gutmacher Inst., 1974—79, 1982—85; pub. mem. Am. Bd. Pediat., 1978—84; vice chmn. Found. for Child Devel., 1978—84, bd. dirs., 1976—84, 1986—94; mem. coun. Nat. Ctr. for Children in Poverty, 1987—96; mem. children's program adv. com. Edna McConnell Clark Found., 1987—97; bd. dirs. Pub. Edn. Fund Network, 1991—93; co-chair Roundtable on Comprehensive Cmty. Initiatives Aspen Inst., 1992—; mem. bd. on children and families NAS, 1993—95; mem. Nat. Commn. State and Local Pub. Svcs., 1992—94; mem. task force on young children Carnegie Corp., 1992—94; mem. sec.'s adv. com. Head Start quality and expansion, 1993—94; mem. nat. selection com. Ford Found./Kennedy Sch. Awards for Innovations in Am. Govt., 1998—. Author: Within Our Reach: Breaking the Cycle of Disadvantage, 1988, Common Purpose: Strengthening Families and Neighborhoods to Rebuild America, 1997. Co-chmn. Boundaries task force Harvard Children's Initiative, 1998—2000; mem. Brookings Children's Roundtable, 1999—; bd. dirs. Nat. Student Partnerships, 2001, Eureka Cmtys., 1995—, Civic Ventures, 1997—99. Recipient Dale Richmond Meml. award, Am. Acad. Pediat., 1977, 9th ann. Robert F. Kennedy Book award, 1989, Nelson Cruikshank award, Nat. Coun. Sr. Citizens, 1990, Porter prize, 1993, PASS award, Nat. Coun. on Crime and Delinquency, 1997, Marian F. Langer award, Am. Orthopsychiat. Assn., 1999, Empatheia award, Vols. of Am., 1999. Mem.: Nat. Acad. on Social Ins., Inst. Medicine NAS, Phi Beta Kappa. Home: 3113 Woodley Rd NW Washington DC 20008-3449 E-mail: lisbeth_schorr@hms.harvard.edu.

SCHORR, MARTIN MARK, forensic examiner, psychologist, educator, screenwriter; b. Sept. 16, 1923; m. Dolores Gene Tyson, June 14, 1952; 1 child, Jeanne Ann. Student, Oxford (Eng.) U., 1945-46; AB cum laude, Adelphi U., 1949; postgrad., U. Tex., 1949-50; MS, Purdue U., 1953; PhD, U. Denver, 1960; postgrad., U. Tex. Diplomate in psychology, Am. Bd. Profl. Disability Cons., Am. Bd. Forensic Examiners, Am. Bd. Forensic Medicine; lic. clin. psychologist. Chief clin. psychol. svcs. San Diego County Mental Hosp., 1963-67; clin. dir. human services San Diego County, 1963-76; pvt. practice San Diego, 1962—. Forensic examiner superior, fed. and mil. cts., San Diego, 1962—; prof. abnormal psychology San Diego State U., 1965-68; chief dept. psychology Center City (Calif.) Hosp., 1976-79; cons. Dept. Corrections State of Calif., Minnewawa, 1970-73, Disability Evaluation Dept. Health, 1972-75, Calif. State Indsl. Accident Commn., 1972-78, Calif. Criminal Justice Adminstrn., 1975-77, Vista Hill Found., Mercy Hosp. Mental Health, Foodmaker Corp., Convent Sacred Heart, El Cajon, FAA Examiner; lectr. S.D. Police Acad. Author: Death by Prescription, 1988; author short stories. Recipient award for aid in developing Whistle Blower Law Calif. Assembly, 1986, Man of Yr. award, 1995. Fellow Internat. Assn. Social Psychiatry, Am. Coll. Forensic Examiners (life); mem. AAAS, PEN, APA, Am. Acad. Forensic Scis. (qualified med. evaluator), Internat. Platform Assn., World Mental Health Assn., Mystery Writers Am., Nat. Writers Club, Mensa.

SCHORR, MARVIN G. technology company executive; b. N.Y.C., Mar. 10, 1925; s. Samuel and Fannie (Smolen) S.; m. Rosalie Yorshis, Dec. 22, 1957; children: Eric Douglas, Susan Ellen. BS, Yale U., 1944, MS, 1947, PhD, 1949. Rsch. asst., instr. Yale U., New Haven, 1946-47; project dir. physics and electronics divsn. Tracerlab, Inc., 1940-51; exec. v.p., treas. Tech/Ops., Inc., Boston, 1951-62, CEO, 1962-88, chmn., 1988—. Spl. cons. USAF, 1951-52; dir. Mass. Tech. Devel. Corp., 1973-76, chmn. bd., 1976-83; dir. Ealing Corp., 1965-76, Hysil Mfg. Co., 1965-78, Dynamics Research Corp., 1978-85, Helix Tech. Corp., Costar Corp. Mem. nuclear engring. adv. com. Lowell Inst. Tech., 1958-68; trustee Park Sch., 1974-80; trustee Am. Coll. Greece, 1970-82, chmn. exec. com., 1980-82, hon. trustee, 1982—; trustee New Eng. Deaconess Hosp., 1972—, vice chmn. bd., 1978-81, chmn., 1981-86. Served with U.S. Army, 1944-46. Fellow AAAS; mem. IEEE, Ops. Rsch. Soc. Am., Am. Phys. Soc., Young Pres. Orgn. (chmn. New Eng. chpt. 1967-68), Boston Com. Fgn. Rels., The Forty-Niners, World Bus. Coun., Chief Execs. Orgn., Internat. Bus. Ctr.-Chief Exec. Officers Round Table, Explorers Club, Cosmos Club (Washington), Harvard Club, St. Botolph Club, Union Club, Yale Club (Boston and N.Y.C.), Longwood Cricket Club (Brookline, Mass.). Home: 330 Beacon St Boston MA 02116-1153

SCHORR, PHILIP IRVING, real estate developer; b. N.Y.C., Dec. 27, 1925; s. Morris Schorr and Beckie Wohl; m. Hannah Schwartz, Aug. 28, 1955; children: Brian, Beth. BA, NYU, 1946, MPA, 1947, PhD, 1974. Cert. real estate broker N.Y. Housing mgr. N.Y. Housing Authority, N.Y.C., 1947—48; gen. mgr. Braislin, Porter & Wheelock, 1958—60; pres. Relocation & Mgmt. Assocs., 1960—, Rental & Mgmt. Assocs., N.Y.C., 1963—, Devel. & Mgmt. Assocs., N.Y.C., 2001—; assoc. prof., dept. pub. adminstrn. L.I. U., C.W. Post Campus, Brookville, L.I., NY, 1978—85, prof., dept. pub. adminstrn., 1985—98, prof. emeritus, 1998—. Pres. NYU Sch. Pub. Adminstrn., N.Y.C., 1967—68; exec. bd. N.Y.C. Housing and Planning Coun., 1990—. Author: Planned Relocation, 1975; editor: Critical Cornerstones of Public Administration, 1985. Bd. dirs. Kimmel Found., L.I., NY, 2001—. Pvt. U.S. Army, 1944—45. Recipient Presdl. award for Exemplary Cmty. Svc., Pres. Reagan, 1986. Mem.: ASPA, Nat. Assn. Schs. Pub. Adminstrn. Avocations: cross country skiing, hiking, travel, music. Home: 149-05 ee Ave Flushing NY 11354 Office: Rental & Mgmt Assocs Corp 215 E 164th St Bronx NY 10456 Fax: 718-538-2407. E-mail: philipschorr@aol.com.

SCHORR, S. L. lawyer; b. N.Y.C., Feb. 19, 1930; s. Charles and Clara (Lerech) S.; m. Eleanor Daru, Mar. 23, 1956; children: Lewis, Andrew, Emily, Roberta. Student, L.I. U., 1948-50; LLB, Bklyn. Law Sch., 1953. Bar: N.Y. 1955, Ariz. 1962, U.S. Dist. Ct. Ariz. 1962, U.S. Supreme Ct. 1979. Planning commr. Pima County, Tucson, 1959-62; asst. city mgr., 1962-63; ptnr. Lewis and Roca, 1988—. Co-chair Continuing Legal Edn. Seminar on Ballot Box Zoning, U. Ariz., 1991, Ariz. State Bar Continuing Legal Edn. Seminar on Land Use Regulation and Litigation, 1977, 86, 89, 95. Bd. dirs. Pima Coll., 1966-67, Pima County Real Estate Rsch. Coun., 1997—, So. Ariz. Leadership Coun., 1997—; mem. Commn. on Improved Govtl. Mgmt., Tucson, 1974-77, Gov.'s Econ. Planning and Devel. Adv. Bd., Phoenix, 1983-85; chmn. Gov.'s Task Force on Seriously Mentally Ill, Phoenix, 1989-91. Mem. Ariz. Bar Assn., Pima County Bar Assn. Democrat. Office: Lewis Roca 1 S Church Ave Ste 700 Tucson AZ 85701-1611

SCHORR, TIMOTHY BRIAN, music educator, concert pianist; b. Belleville, IL, Nov. 4, 1966; s. Paul Emil Schorr, Marilyn Louise Schorr, Anne Schorr (Stepmother). Doctor of Musical Arts in piano performance, University of Cincinnati College-Conservatory of Music, Cincinnati, OH, 1990—97, Master of Music in piano performance, 1988—90; Bachelor of Music with honors in piano performance, Eastern Illinois University, Charleston, IL, 1984—88. Assistant Professor of Music & Coordinator of Applied Piano and Pedagogy Viterbo University, La Crosse, WI, 1999—2002; Instructor Lutheran Summer Music, 1998—2002; Lecturer University of Cincinnati College-Conservatory of Music Preparatory Department, Cincinnati, OH, 1992—97; Coach-Accompanist Cincinnati Opera, 1997—99, Dayton Opera, Dayton, 1997; Organist St. Peter & Paul United Church of Christ, Cincinnati, 1998—99, Oakley Baptist Church, Cincinnati, 1994—98; Director of Music Lutheran Campus Ministry, 1998—92; Organist First Presbyterian Church, Charleston, IL, 1987—88. Musician, concert pianist and collaborative artist, performances as a piano soloist, profl. accompanist and chamber musician; guest artist masterclasses and recitals, musician live radio and TV broadcasts, presenter workshops in field. Musician: (Performances as a piano soloist) Performances as a professional accompanist & chamber musician, 2002, Music competitions & auditions, Weill Recital Hall at Carnegie Hall. Mem.: Phi Mu Alpha Sinfonia, College Music Society, Music Teachers National Association, Wisconsin Music Teachers Association (Chair, Community Outreach 2001—02), La Crosse Area Music Teachers Association (Vice President 2001—02). Avocation: travel, running, yoga, reading, music, theatre. Office: Viterbo University 815 South 9th Street La Crosse WI 54601 Business E-Mail: TBSchorr@viterbo.edu.

SCHORR-LESNICK, BETH, gastroenterologist, internist; b. N.Y.C., Oct. 18, 1960; d. Philip Irving and Hannah Schorr; m. Charles Schorr Lesnick, June 5, 1985; children: Emily, Ariel. BS, Yale U., 1981; MD, Mt. Sinai Sch. Medicine, 1985. Intern, resident Montefiore Hosp., Bronx, 1988-90; fellow N.Y. Med. Coll., Valhalla, 1990; internist, gastroenterologist Laser Med. Assocs., N.Y.C., 1990-91; asst. prof. medicine, assoc. attending Beth Israel Med. Ctr., 1991-99; attending St. John's Riverside Hosp., Yonkers, NY, 2000—, Dobbs Ferry (NY) Cmty. Hosp., 2000—; asst. prof. medicine Albert Einstein Coll. Medicine, 1990—. Contbr. articles to profl. jours. Mem. sch. bd. Shaarei Tikvah Synagogue, Scarsdale, N.Y., 1993—. Fellow ACP, Am. Coll. Gastroenterologists (women in gastroenterology com. 1990—, pub. rels. com. 1998—); mem. Am. Gastroenterol. Assn., Am. Soc. Gasteroinitestinal Endoscopy, N.Y. Soc. Gastrointestinal Endoscopy. Office: 623 Warburton Ave Hastings On Hudson NY 10706

SCHORR-RIBERA, HILDA KEREN, psychologist; b. N.Y.C., May 2, 1942; d. Leon and Rosa Schorr-Ribera; m. Ira Eli Wessler, Aug. 6, 1971; children: Mike, Daniel. BA, Hunter Coll., 1963; MEd, U. No. Fla., 1982; PhD, U. Pitts., 1988. Lic. psychologist, Pa.; diplomate Am. Bd. Forensic Examiners; diplomate, fellow Am. Bd. Med. Psychotherapists and Psychodiagnosticians; diplomate Am. Bd. Forensic Medicine, Am. Acad. Experts in Traumatic Stress; cert. in clin. hypnosis. Psychotherapist South Hills Interfaith Ministries, Bethel Park, Pa., 1989-92, Profl. Psychol. Assn. of Greater Pitts., 1992; pvt. practice psychologist Pitts., 1993—. Child therapist Forbes Hospice, 1993—; group facilitator of adult wellness group and children's support groups Burger King Cancer Caring Ctr., Pitts., 1989—, Allegheny Hospice, Pitts., 1994—96; psychol. evaluator Washington (Pa.) County Ct., 1993—, Allegheny County Ct., Pitts., 1995—98; cons. psychologist to sch. dists. Allegheny and Washington Counties. Author: (with others) Educating the Child With Cancer, 1993. Keynote spkr. on illness and bereavement to profl. assns., hosps., schs. and agys., Pitts., 1989—. Mem. APA, Internat. Soc. Hypnosis, Am. Soc. Clin. Hypnosis, Am. Acad. Experts in Traumatic Stress, Am. Counseling Assn., Am. Coll. Forensic Examiners, Pa. Psychol. Assn., Greater Pitts. Psychol. Assn. Avocations: music, bilingual activities, reading, walking, traveling. Office: 117 Ridgeway Ct Pittsburgh PA 15228-1729 E-mail: schorrribera@yahoo.com.

SCHORSCH, ISMAR, clergyman, Jewish history educator; b. Hannover, Germany, Nov. 3, 1935; m. Sally Korn; children: Jonathan, Rebecca, Naomi. BA, Ursinus Coll., 1957; MA, Columbia U., 1961, PhD, 1969; MHL, Jewish Theol. Sem. Am., 1962; LittD , LittD , Hebrew Union Coll., 2002. Ordained rabbi, 1962. Instr. Jewish Theol. Sem., N.Y.C., 1964-68; asst. prof. Jewish Theol. Sem. Am., 1970-72, assoc. prof., 1972-76, prof., 1976—, dean Grad. Sch., 1975-79, provost, 1980-84; chancellor, 1986—; asst. prof. Jewish history Columbia U., N.Y.C., 1968-70. Bd. dirs. Leo Baeck Inst., 1976, mem. exec. com., 1980, pres., 1985-86, 90—, mem. editorial bd. of yearbook, 1987; participant symposium Spirit and Nature: Religion, Ethics and Environ. Crisis, Middlebury Coll.; organizer Nat. Religious Partnership for the Environment. Author: From Text to Context: The Turn to History in Modern Judaism, 1994, (monograph) Sacred Cluster: The Core Values of Conservative Judaism, 1995; contbr. articles to Judaism, also other profl. publs. Chaplain U.S. Army, 1962-64. Recipient Clark F. Ansley award Columbia U. Press, 1969; NEH fellow, 1979-80 Fellow Am. Acad. Jewish Rsch. Office: Jewish Theol Sem 3080 Broadway New York NY 10027-4650

SCHORSKE, CARL EMIL, historian, educator; b. N.Y.C., Mar. 15, 1915; s. Theodore A. and Gertrude (Goldschmidt) S.; m. Elizabeth Gilbert Rorke, June 14, 1941; children: Carl Theodore, Anne (Mrs. J. L. Edwards), Stephen James, John Simon, Richard Robert. AB, Columbia U., 1936; MA, Harvard U., 1937, PhD, 1950; DLitt (hon.), Bard Coll., 1982, Clark U., 1983, New Sch. Social Rsch., 1986, Miami U., 1987, Monmouth Coll., 1994, Princeton U., 1997; DPhil (hon.), U. Salzburg, 1986, U. Graz, 1996. Prof. history Wesleyan U., Middletown, Conn., 1946-60; prof. history U. Calif.-Berkeley, 1960-69, Princeton U., 1969-80, emeritus, 1980—. Author: (with Hoyt Price) The Problem of Germany, 1947, German Social Democracy 1905-17, 1955, Fin-de-Siècle Vienna, 1980, Thinking with History, 1998. Lt. (j.g.) USNR, 1943-46; with OSS, 1941-46. Recipient Austrian Cross of Honor for arts and scis., 1979, Pulitzer prize for gen. nonfiction, 1981, Grand prize for cultural edn. City of Vienna, 1985, Harvard Centennial medal, 1999; named Officer, French Order Arts and Letters, 1987, Great Silver medal of Honor, Austria, 1996, Gold Cross of Honor, City of Vienna, 2000; MacArthur fellow, 1981-86. Fellow Royal Acad. Fine Arts Netherlands (hon.); mem. Am. Acad. Arts and Scis., Austrian Acad. Scis. (corr.), Am. Hist. Assn. (council 1964-68, Disting. Scholar award 1992), Ctr. Advanced Study Behavioral Sci., Inst. Advanced Study., Getty Ctr. Home: 106 Winant Rd Princeton NJ 08540-6738 E-mail: schorske@princeton.edu.

SCHOSS, MAXIMILLIAN, surgeon; b. Bucharest, Romania, May 6, 1926; came to U.S., 1952; s. Fanny Schoss; m. Sadie W. Warren, June 30, 1957; children: Felicia, Johanna, Ethan. MD, U. Bucharest, 1950. Diplomate Am. Bd. Surgery. Pvt. practice gen. surgery, Roselle and Elizabeth, N.J., 1957-91; former med. examiner Union County, Elizabeth, 1966-86; pres. med. staff St. Elizabeth Hosp., 1980-82; dir. divsn. surgery Elizabeth Gen. Med. Ctr., 1980-90, clin. dir.dept. surgery, 1991—2002. Fellow ACS; mem. N.J. Soc. Surgeons.

SCHOTLAND, DONALD LEWIS, retired medical educator, neurologist; b. Orange, N.J., Sept. 21, 1930; s. Joseph Henry and Elsie (Block) S.; m. Estherina Shems, Jan. 11, 1976; children: John, Thomas, Peter. AB, Harvard U., 1952, MD, 1957; spl. student, MIT, 1955-56; MA (hon.), U. Pa., 1973. Diplomate: Am. Bd. Psychiatry and Neurology. Intern U. Ill. Research and Edn. Hosp., 1957-58; asst. resident in neurology Columbia Presbyn. Med. Center, N.Y.C., 1958-61, asst. neurologist, 1961-65, asst. attending neurologist, 1965-66; asst. in neurology Coll. Physicians and Surgeons, Columbia U., N.Y.C., 1960-61, vis. fellow in neurology, 1961-64, assoc. in neurology, 1964-66, asst. prof. neurology, 1966-67; assoc. prof. Sch. Medicine, U. Pa., Phila., 1967-72, prof., 1972-98, prof. emeritus, 1998—. Speaker profl. confs., U.S., Can., Italy, Japan, China, France, Israel, Finland; dir. Henry M. Watts, Jr. Neuromuscular Disease Rsch. Ctr., 1974-90. Editor: Diseases of the Motor Unit, 1982; contbr. articles, papers to profl. publs. Served to 1st lt. USAR, 1958-65. NIH postdoctoral fellow, 1961-64; recipient Research Career Devel. award, 1966-67, various grants NIH and Muscular Dystrophy Assn. Fellow Coll. of Physicians of Phila.; mem. Am. Acad. Neurology, Am. Neurol. Assn., Phila. Neurol. Soc., Muscular Dystrophy Assn. (sci. adv. com. 1974-86, chmn. fellowship com. 1974-86, chmn. 6th Internat. Conf. 1980). Home: 1310 Wyngate Rd Wynnewood PA 19096-2455 Office: Hosp of Univ Pa 3400 Spruce St Philadelphia PA 19104-4206 E-mail: dlschotl@mail.med.upenn.edu.

SCHOTT, CHERYL SUZANNE, health educator; b. Phila., Feb. 8, 1972; d. George Frederick and Virginia Roberta (Cooper) Schott. BA, U. Richmond, Va., 1994; MPH, U. Mich., 1998. Assoc. coord. Learning in Cmty. Settings, U. Richmond, 1993-94; VISTA vol. Dorchester County Health Dept., Cambridge,

Md., 1994-96; program devel. cons. Inter-Networks Multi Svc. Ctr., Detroit, 1997; evaluation cons. Flint (Mich.) Action Cmty. Econ. Devel. Corp., 1997—; rsch./instrnl. asst. U. Mich. Sch. Pub. Health, Ann Arbor, 1997—. Prevention specialist CDC Pub. Health Prevention Svc., 1998—2001; asthma program specialist Mich. Pub. Health Inst., 2001—. Co-author, editor: African American Health in Michigan, 1997; editl. asst. Health Edn. Behavioral Jour., 1998. Bd. dirs. VA COOL, Richmond, 1991—93; mem. Dorchester County Underage Drinking Prevention Coalition, Cambridge, Md., 1996; pub. health prevention specialist Ctrs. for Disease Control and Prevention, 1998—2001. Mem.: Phi Beta Kappa. Lutheran. Avocations: photography, hiking, biking. Office: Mich Dept Cmty Health PO Box 30195 3423 N ML King Jr Blvd Lansing MI 48909 E-mail: csschott@hotmail.com.

SCHOTT, CLIFFORD JOSEPH, lawyer; b. Newark, July 28, 1926; s. Clifford J. and Sally V. (Donnelly) S.; m. Nancybelle MacDonnell, July 22, 1951; children: Christylee, Clifford, Sally, Steven, Craig. Student, Upsala U., 1949-51; grad., U. Miami, 1952, JD, 1954. Bar: Fla. 1955, U.S. Dist. Ct. (so. dist.) Fla. 1956, U.S. Ct. Appeals (5th cir.) 1959, U.S. Ct. Appeals (11th cir.) 1981, U.S. Tax. Ct. 1973, Fla. RR and Pub. Utilities Commn. 1963, U.S. Supreme Ct. 1968. Assoc. Holladay & Swann, Miami, Fla., 1955-56; ptnr. Hastings, Thomas & Sheppard, 1956-57; asst. gen. counsel Dade County Port Auth., 1957-60; atty., negotiator Eastern Airlines, Inc., 1960-63; assoc. Carver, Langston & Massey, Lakeland, Fla., 1963-66; ptnr. Wendel & Schott, 1966-68; pvt. practice, 1968-83; sr. ptnr. Schott & Dale, P.A., 1983-89; pvt. practice Fla., 1989-99; ret., 1999—. Mcpl. judge City of Lakeland, 1967-68; asst. county solicitor County of Polk, Bartow, Fla., 1967-69. Pres., Polk County Assn. Retarded Children, Lakeland, 1966-67, com. chmn., 1967; counsel Ch. of the Resurrection, Lakeland; bd. dirs. St. Joseph's Sch., Lakeland, 1973. With USAAF, 1944-46, ETO. Mem. ABA, ATLA, Fla. Bar Assn., Lakeland Bar Assn., Polk County Trial Lawyers Assn. (adv. com. 1983—), Fla. Def. Lawyers Assn. (bd. dirs. 1985—), 10th Judicial Cir. Bar, Lakeland C. of C. (aviation adv. com.), Am. Legion (judge adv. 1978), Rotary (pres. 1969-70), KC (dep. grand knight 1973), Phi Alpha Delta. Republican. Roman Catholic. Avocations: tennis, fishing, squash, travel, reading. Home: 111 Florida Shores Blvd Daytona Beach Shores FL 32118-5629

SCHOTT, JOHN ROBERT, international consultant, educator; b. Rochester, N.Y., Jan. 30, 1936; s. John and Ellen (Waite) S.; m. Diane Elizabeth Dempsey, June 19, 1963; children: Elizabeth Anne (dec.), Jennifer, Jared Reed, George Kermit Alexander. BA magna cum laude, Haverford Coll., 1957; postgrad., Oxford U., 1957-59; PhD, Harvard U., 1964. Resident tutor in govt. Eliot House, Harvard Coll., Cambridge, Mass., 1960-64; inst. polit. sci. Wellesley (Mass.) Coll., 1964-66; policy planning specialist AID, Washington, 1966-67; chief Title IX div. AID, 1967-68; vis. prof. polit. devel. Fletcher Sch. Law & Diplomacy, Tufts U., Medford, Mass., 1968-70; sr. v.p. Thunderbird Grad. Sch. Internat. Mgmt., Phoenix, 1970-71; cons. internat. affairs Francestown, N.H., 1971-74; pres. Schott & Assocs., Inc., Jaffrey Center, 1974-93. Mem. U.S. Del. World Assembly Internat. Secretariat for Voluntary Service, New Delhi, 1967; advisor Office Prime Minister Royal Thai Govt., Bangkok, 1978-80, Minister Cooperatives Govt. of Indonesia, Jakarta, 1983-84; research asst. spl. appointment The Brookings Inst., Washington, 1960-61 Author: Kenya Tragedy: European Colonization in East Africa, 1964, Frances' Town: History of Francestown, N.H., 1972, 98, A Five-Year Comprehensive Plan for Development of Agricultural Cooperatives in Thailand, 1979, Recana-Komprehensip Pengembangan Kud, Jakarta, Indonesia, 1985, also various govt. reports and articles in profl. jours. and regional publs.; editor: An Experiment in Integrated Rural Development, 1978. Mem. Bd. of Selectmen, Francestown, N.H., 1975-78; trustee Spaulding Youth Ctr., Tilton, N.H., 1971-82, 85-89, pres. bd. trustees, 1972-75; trustee Internat. Inst. Rural Reconstrn., N.Y.C., 1979-89, mem. exec. com., 1985-89, bd. trustees N.H. Pub. Radio, 1990-96, chmn., 1993-95; mem. spl. study commn. Coop. Extension Svc. State of N.H., 1980-81, also mem. scenic and cultural by-ways com., 1993-96; forestry rep. County Extension Coun., Hillsboro County, N.H., 1979-82; pres. N.H. Timberland Owner's Assn., 1989-90, bd. dirs., 1988-91; chmn. N.H. chpt. The Nature Conservancy, 1990-93, hon. trustee, 1993—, chmn. N.H. Timber-Tourism Coalition, 1990-94; vice-chmn, Foresters Lic. Bd. State of N.H., 1990-95; bd. trustees Cheshire Med. Ctr., 1992-94, RiverMead Retirement Cmty., Peterborough, N.H., 1992-2000, chmn., 1996-2000; mem. bd. overseers cmty. econ. devel. program So. N.H. U., 1997-2001, chmn., 1997-2000; trustee Sharon Arts Ctr., 2001--. Rotary Found. fellow, 1957-58, Coslett Found. fellow, 1958-59, Harvard Arts & Scis. fellow, 1959-60, Fulbright scholar, 1962-63; recipient award for svc. to humanity Haverford (Pa.) Coll., 1999. Mem. Am. Forestry Inst. (cert. tree farmer). Home and Office: Schott & Assocs 617 Mountain Rd PO Box 660 Jaffrey NH 03452-0660

SCHOTT, JOHN WILLIAM, psychiatrist; b. LaSalle, Ill., July 2, 1940; s. Joseph William and Anne Marie Schott; m. Sarah Purdy, June 4, 1966; children: Anne Rutherford, Hannah Elizabeth, Lilly Hamilton. AB, Johns Hopkins U., 1962; MD, Harvard U., 1966. Clin. dir. Dorchester Mental Health, Boston, 1970-73, Westboro (Mass.) State Hosp., 1973-75; chmn. dept. psychiatry Leonard Morse Hosp., Natick, Mass., 1975-91, MetroWest Med. Ctr., Framingham & Natick, 1991—; clin. instr. Harvard Med. Sch., Boston, 1991—; portfolio mgr. Steinberg Global Asset Mgmt., 1993—. Treas. AEMS Corp., Natick, 1990—; pres. Cochituate Enterprises, Natick, 1991—. Author: Mind Over Money, 1998; assoc. editor Jour. of Psychology and Fin. Markets, 2000—; writer, publisher The Schott Letter, 1983—. Dir. Learning Ctr. Deaf Children, Framingham, 1977—; chmn. bd. trustees Dover (Mass.) Ch., 1978-80. Mem. Am. Psychoanalytic Assn., Am. Psychiat. Assn., Mass. Med. Soc., Boston Psychoanalytic Soc. (treas. 1983-90, chmn. bd. trustees 1986-90), East Chop Tennis Club, East Chop Beach Club. Mem. United Ch. of Christ. Avocations: croquet, chess, gardening. Home: 120 Centre St Dover MA 02030-2411 Office: Leonard Morse Hosp 67 Union St Natick MA 01760-6089

SCHOTTENFELD, DAVID, epidemiologist, educator; b. N.Y.C., Mar. 25, 1931; m. Rosalie C. Schaeffer; children: Jacqueline, Stephen. AB, Hamilton Coll., 1952; MD, Cornell U., 1956; MS in Pub. Health, Harvard U., 1963. Diplomate Am. Bd. Internal Medicine, Am. Bd. Preventive Medicine. Intern in internal medicine Duke U., Durham, N.C., 1956-57; resident in internal medicine Meml. Sloan-Kettering Cancer Ctr., Cornell U. Med. Coll., N.Y.C., 1957-59; Craver fellow med. oncology Meml. Sloan-Kettering Cancer Ctr., 1961-62; clin. instr. dept. pub. health Cornell U., N.Y.C., 1963-67, asst. prof. dept. pub. health, 1965-70, assoc. prof. dept. pub. health, 1970-73, prof. dept. pub. health, 1973-86; John G. Searle prof., chmn. epidemiology sch. pub. health U. Mich., Ann Arbor, 1986—, prof. internal medicine, 1986—. Vis. prof. epidemiology U. Minn., Mpls., 1968, 71, 74, 82, 86; W.G. Cosbie lectr. Can. Oncology Soc., 1987. Editor: Cancer Epidemiology and Prevention, 1982, 2d edit., 1996; author 9 books; contbr. more than 200 articles to profl. jours. Served with USPHS, 1959-61. Recipient Acad. Career award in Preventive Oncology, Nat. Cancer Inst., 1980-85. Fellow AAAS, ACP, Am. Coll. Preventive Medicine, Am. Coll. Epidemiology, Armed Forces Epidemiology Bd.; mem. soc. Epidemiologic Rsch. (pres. 1998—), Phi Beta Kappa. Office: U of Mich Sch Pub Health Dept Epidemiology 109 Observatory St Ann Arbor MI 48109-2029 E-mail: daschott@umich.edu.

SCHOTTER, ANDREW ROYE, economics educator, consultant; b. N.Y.C., June 6, 1947; s. I. Harvey and Sara (Rothstein) S.; m. Anne Howland, June 7, 1970; children: Geoffrey, Elizabeth. BS, Cornell U., 1969; MA, PhD, NYU, 1974. Asst. prof. Syracuse (N.Y.) U., 1974-75, NYU, 1975-81, assoc. prof., 1981-86, prof., chmn. econs. dept., 1989-93, 96-99, chmn. C.V. Starr Ctr. for Applied Econs., 1986-89, dir. Ctr. for Experiential Social Sci., 2001—. Vis. asst. prof. Cornell U., Ithaca, 1974-75; vis. prof. U. Venice, 1993, U. Amsterdam; cons. Gulf & Western Corp., N.Y. 1987, Pegalis & Wachsman, Great Neck, N.Y., 1987-88, Nat. Econ. Rsch. Assocs., White Plains, N.Y., 1989—. Author: Economic Theory of Social Institutions, 1981, Free Market Economics: A Critical Appraisal, 1985, 2d edit., 1990, Microeconomics: A Modern Approach, 1993, 3d edit., 2000; mem. editl. bd.: Am. Econ. Rev., 1995—, Exptl. Econs., 1997; assoc. editor: Games and Econ. Behavior; spl. editor: Exptl. Econs. Grantee Office of Naval Rsch., 1980-85, NSF, 1988-90, 97—; recipient Kenan Enterprise award, 1993. Mem. Am. Econ. Assn., Econometric Soc., Econ. Sci. Assn. (pres.-elect 1997), Cane Theory Soc. Office: NYU Dept Econs 269 Mercer St New York NY 10003-6633

SCHOULTZ, LARS, political scientist, educator; b. San Gabriel, Calif., Aug. 23, 1942; s. Ture Wilhelm and Bernice (Bowie) S.; m. Jane Volland, Jan. 18, 1969; children: Nils Gibson, Karina Anne. BA, Stanford U., 1964, MA, 1966; PhD, U. N.C., 1973. Prof. Miami U., Oxford, Ohio, 1973—77, U. Fla., Gainesville, 1977—79; William Rand Kenan Jr. prof. polit. sci. U. N.C., Chapel Hill, 1979—. Author: Human Rights and U.S. Policy Toward Latin America, 1981, National Security and U.S. Policy Toward Latin America, 1987, The Populist Challenge, 1983, Beneath the United States, 1998. Sgt. U.S. Army, 1966-67. MacArthur fellow in internat. peace and security MacArthur Found., 1990-91, Fulbright fellow, Rockefeller Found. fellow, Ford Found. fellow, Social Sci. Rsch. Coun., Woodrow Wilson fellow, 1994-95, Nat. Humanities Ctr. fellow, 1999-00. Mem. Latin Am. Studies Assn. (pres. 1991-92, v.p. 1990-91). Democrat. Home: 250 Glandon Dr Chapel Hill NC 27514-3816 Office: U NC Inst Latin Am Studies Chapel Hill NC 27599-0001 E-mail: Schoultz@unc.edu.

SCHOUMACHER, BRUCE HERBERT, lawyer; b. Chgo., May 23, 1940; s. Herbert Edward and Mildred Helen (Wagner) S.; m. Alicia Wesley Sanchez, Nov. 4, 1967; children: Liana Cristina, Janina Maria. BS, Northwestern U., 1961; MBA, U. Chgo., 1963, JD, 1966. Bar: Nebr. 1966, U.S. Dist. Ct. Nebr. 1966, Ill. 1971, U.S. Dist. Ct. (no. dist.) Ill. 1971, U.S. Ct. Appeals (7th cir.) 1979, U.S. Supreme Ct. 1982, U.S. Ct. Fed. Claims 1986. Assoc. Luebs, Tracy & Huebner, Grand Island, Nebr., 1966-67, McDermott, Will & Emery, Chgo., 1971-76, ptnr., 1976-89, Querrey & Harrow, Ltd., Chgo., 1989—. Instr. bus. adminstrn. Bellevue Coll., Nebr., 1967-70; lectr. U. Md., Overseas Program, 1970. Author: Engineers and the Law: An Overview, 1986; contbg. author: Construction Law, 1986, Construction Law Handbook, 1999; co-author: Successful Business Plans for Architects, 1992; contbr. articles to profl. jours. Served to capt. USAF, 1967-71, Vietnam. Decorated Bronze Star, 1971. Fellow Am. Coll. Constrn. Lawyers; mem. ABA, AIA (profl. affiliate), Nebr. Bar Assn., Ill. State Bar Assn. (ad hoc com. large law firms 1992-98, chmn. membership and bar activities com. 1988-89, coun. ins. law sect. 1986-91, mem. spl. com. on computerized legal rsch. 1986-87), Chgo. Bar Assn. (chmn. fed. civil procedure com. 1982-83), Def. Rsch. Inst., Ill. Assn. Def. Trial Counsel, Chgo. Bldg. Congress (bd. dirs. 1985—, sec. 1987-89, 95—, v.p. 1989-91), Soc. Ill. Constrn. Attys., Western Soc. Engrs. (assoc.), The Lawyers Club of Chgo., Tower Club (Chgo.), Univ. Club Chgo., Pi Kappa Alpha, Phi Delta Phi. Republican. Methodist. Office: Querrey & Harrow Ltd 175 W Jackson Blvd Ste 1600 Chicago IL 60604-2827

SCHOW, TERRY D. state official; b. Ogden, Utah, Dec. 14, 1948; s. Hugh Stuart Sloan and Minnie Aurelia (Ellis) Mohler; m. June Hansen, Feb. 14, 1973; children: Amy, Jason. AD, Honolulu C.C., 1975; BA, Chaminade U., 1975. Cert. in mgmt., Utah. Spl. and criminal investigator State of Utah, Ogden, 1976-83, lead investigator, 1984-92; investigator Fed. Govt., Salt Lake City, Denver, 1983-84; mgr. State of Utah, Ogden, 1992—99, state dir. vets. affairs, 2001—. Active Gov.'s Coun. on Vets. Issues, 1989—, chmn., 1990—; mem. State of Utah Privatization Policy Bd., 1989-92; chmn. 1st Congressional Dist. Utah Rep. Party, 1982-83, state exec. com., 1982-83; chmn. legis. dist Weber County Rep. Party, Ogden, 1987-91, 93—; trustee Utah's Vietnam Meml., Salt Lake City, 1988—; leader Boy Scouts Am., Ogden, 1985—; citizens' adv. com. Ogden City Neighborhood Redevel., 1996-2000. Sgt. U.S. Army, 1967-70, 72-76, Vietnam. Decorated Bronze Star, Combat Inf. Badge; recipient Championship Team Trophy Pistol U.S. Army, 1975. Mem. DAV (life, Weber chpt. 4, comdr. 1994, state comdr. 1995—), NRA (life), VFW, AL (comdr. Ogden post 9 1996-97, state comdr. 1999—), Utah Peace Officers Assn., Utah Pub. Employees Assn. (bd. dirs. 1988-89, v.p. 1989-92, pres. 1992-93, chmn. Ogden Valley dist.), Kiwanis (Ogden chpt. pres. 1992-93, pres. Layton chpt. 1985-86, Kiwanian of Yr. 1982-83, lt. gov. divsn. 3 ut/ld dist. Kiwanis internat. 1995—, homeless vets. fellow Ogden 1992-2000, Weber County vets. meml. com. 1994—). Republican. Mem. Lds Ch. Avocations: woodworking, photography, scouting. Home: 4045 Bona Villa Dr Ogden UT 84403-3203 Office: State Utah Divsn Vets Affairs rM 5223 125 S State Salt Lake City UT 84138

SCHOWALTER, JOHN ERWIN, child and adolescent psychiatry educator; b. Milw., Mar. 15, 1936; s. Raymond Phillip and Martha (Kowalke) S.; m. Ellen Virginia Lefferts, June 11, 1960; children: Jay, Bethany. BS, U. Wis., Madison, 1957, MD, 1960. Diplomate Am. Bd. Psychiatry and Neurology (com. on cert. in child psychiatry 1983-85, chmn. 1986-87, bd. dirs. 1993-2000, chmn. com. added qualifications forensic psychiatry 1993-97); cert. in adult and child psychiatry also psychoanalysis. Intern in pediatrics Yale-New Haven Hosp., 1960-61; asst. resident in psychiatry Cin. Gen. Hosp., 1961-63; fellow in child psychiatry Yale Child Study Ctr., 1963-65; psychiatrist Mental Hygiene Clinic U.S. Army, Ft. Ord, Calif., 1965-67; asst. prof. Yale U. Child Study Ctr., New Haven, 1967-70, assoc. prof. Sch. Medicine, 1970-75, dir. tng., 1971-96, prof. pediatrics and psychiatry, 1975-89, chief child psychiatry, 1982-90, dir. child psychiatry clin. svcs., 1990—, Albert J. Solnit prof. child psychiatry and pediatrics, 1989—, interim chmn., 2001—. Mem. publ. com. Yale U. Press., 1992-97; mem. sci. adv. bd. Sophia Found. Med. Rsch., Rotterdam, The Netherlands, 1984-89; dir. mental health and substance abuse Yale Preferred Health Plan, 1995-99. Co-author: The Family Handbook of Adolescence, 1979; contbr. numerous articles, book revs.; mem. editl. bd. Pediatrics, 1976-81, Children's Health Care, 1977—, Jour. Am. Psychoanalytic Assn., 1978, Pediatrics in Rev., 1978-85; asst. editor: Jour. Am. Acad. Child and Adolescent Psychiatry, 1988-97; co-editor: Yearbook Psychiatry and Applied Mental Health, 1988-97. Capt. U.S. Army, 1965-67. Fellow Am. Acad. Child and Adolescent Psychiatry (sec. 1985-87, pres. 1989-91, Simon Wile award 1996, mem. fin. planning com. 2000—), Am. Coll. Psychiatrists (chair Laughlin fellowship com. 2000-01, chair membership com. 2002—), Am. Acad. Pediatrics; mem. Am. Pediatric Soc., Am. Psychoanalytic Assn. (cert. adult and child), Group for Advancement Psychiatry (life fellow, com. on child psychiatry 1981, bd. dirs. 1989-91, pres. 1993-95, chair life fellowship com. 2000—), Assn. for Care of Children's Health (pres. 1984-86), AMA (residency rev. com. for psychiatry 1983-87, 89-94), Soc. Profs. Child Psychiatry (pres. 1984-86), Western New Eng. Inst. Psychoanalysis (mem. faculty in child psychoanalysis 1984—, pres. 1986-88), Conn. Med. Soc., New Haven Med. Soc., Conn. Coun. Child Psychiatrists (pres. 1979-81), Benjamin Rush Soc. (sec., treas. 1998-99, v.p. 1999-2000, pres. 2000-2002), DARE Am. (mem. sci. adv. panel), others, Sigma Xi. Lutheran. Home: 256 Ives St Hamden CT 06518-2200 Office: Yale U Child Study Ctr PO Box 207900 230 S Frontage Rd New Haven CT 06520-7900

SCHOWALTER, WILLIAM RAYMOND, college dean, educator; b. Milw., Dec. 15, 1929; s. Raymond Philip and Martha (Kowalke) S.; m. Jane Ruth Gregg, Aug. 22, 1953; children: Katherine Ruth, Mary Patricia, David Gregg. BS, U. Wis., 1951; postgrad., Inst. Paper Chemistry, 1951-52; MS, U. Ill., 1953, PhD, 1957; PhD (hon.), Inst. Nat. Poly. Lorraine, France, 1996. Asst. prof. dept. chem. engring. Princeton U., 1957-63, assoc. prof., 1963-66, prof., 1966-86, Class of 1950 prof. engring. and applied sci., 1986-89, acting chmn. dept. chem. engring., 1971, chmn. dept. chem. engring., 1978-87, assoc. dean Sch. Engring. and Applied Sci., 1971-77, class of 1950 prof. engring. and applied sci. emeritus, 2000—; dean Coll. Engring. U. Ill., Urbana, 1989-2001, dean, prof. emeritus, 2001—; Mobil prof. chem. engring. Nat. U. Singapore, 1998, sr. advisor to vice-chancellor, 2001—. Sherman Fairchild disting. scholar Calif. Inst. Tech., 1977-78; vis. fellow U. Salford, Eng., 1974; vis. sr. fellow Sci. Rsch. Coun., U. Cambridge, Eng., 1970; cons. to chem. and petroleum cos.; editl. adv. bd. McGraw-Hill Pub. Co., 1964-92; co-chmn. Internat. Seminar for Heat and Mass Transfer, 1970; vis. com. for chem. engring. MIT, 1979-87, Lehigh U., 1980-87; mem. vis. com. Sch. Engring., Stanford U., 1990-2001; evaluation panelist Ctr. Chem. Engring. Nat. Bur. Standards, 1982-88, chmn., 1986-88; mem. commn. engring. and tech. sys. NRC, 1983-88; engring. rsch. bd., 1984-86, com. on chem. engring. frontiers; adv. coun. chem. engring. Cornell U., 1983-91; adv. coun. Sch. Engring., Rice U., 1986-92; adv. com. Ill. Inst. Tech., 1992-97; adv. coun. Coll. Engring., U. Calif., Berkeley, 1997-2001, Coll. Engring. U. Mich., 1997-2001, Carnegie Inst. Tech., 1999-2001; acad. adv. bd. Sematech Corp., 1992-2001; internat. adv. panel Nat. U. Singapore, 1996; Reilly lectr. in chem. engring. U. Notre Dame, 1985, Van Winkle lectr. in chem. engring. U. Tex., Austin, 1986, David M. Mason lectr. chem. engring. Stanford U., 1987; bd. dirs. Champaign (Ill.) Nat. Bank, 1991-95, BankIll. Trust Co., 1996-98; mem. fellowship program Packard Found. Sci. Adv. Panel, 1998—; adv. coun. Sch. Engring., Princeton U., 1999—. Author: Mechanics of Non-Newtonian Fluids, 1978; co-author: Colloidal Dispersions, 1989; mem. editl. com. Ann. Rev. Fluid Mechanics, 1974-80, Internat. Jour. Chem. Engring., 1974-94, Indsl. and Engring. Chemistry Fundamentals, 1975-78, Jour. Non-Newtonian Fluid Mechanics, 1976-2001, AIChE Jour., 1979-83; contbr. articles to profl. jours. Mem. Ill. Gov.'s Sci. Adv. Com., 1989-96. Served with U.S. Army, 1953-55. Decorated officier des Palmes Académiques (France), 1995; recipient Disting. Svc. citation Coll. Engring., U. Wis., Madison, 1983; Guggenheim fellow, 1987-88. Fellow AIChE (William H. Walker award 1982, bd. dirs. 1992-94), NAS (class membership com. 2000, 2002), Am. Acad. Arts and Scis.; mem. Am. Soc. Engring. Edn. (Lectr. award chem. engring. divsn. 1971, exec. com. engr. deans coun. 1992-95, vice-chair, engring. deans coun. pub. policy com. 1998, chair engring. deans coun. pub. policy com. 1999-2001), NAE (awards com. 1986-88, chmn. 1987, acad. adv. bd. 1991-94, chmn. 1992-94, coun. 1994-2000, Draper Award com. 2001-2002), Am. Chem. Soc., Soc. Rheology (exec. com. 1977-79, v.p. 1981-83, pres. 1983-85, Bingham medal 1988), Sigma Xi, Tau Beta Pi, Phi Lambda Upsilon, Phi Eta Sigma. Home: 1846 Maynard Dr Champaign IL 61822-5268

SCHRADE, ROBERT WARREN, classical pianist, educator; b. Walden, N.Y., Dec. 2, 1924; s. Louis J. and Elizabeth M. (Eitner) S.; m. Rolande M. Young, Dec. 21, 1949; children: Robelyn, Rhonda Lee, Rolisa M., Randolph R.A., Rorianne C. MusB, MusM, Manhattan Sch. Music, 1948. Mem. piano faculty Manhattan Sch. of Music, N.Y.C., 1949-56, 68-89; mem. music faculty, artist-in-residence Chapin sch., 1948-89; pres., artistic dir. Sevenars Concerts, Inc., Worthington, Mass., 1976—. Lectr. in field. Appeared in frequent piano concerts, N.Y.C., Europe, including Carnegie Hall, Lincoln Ctr., 1977, 81, 86, with Schrade Family Pianists, 1980-93, Lincoln Ctr., N.Y.C., 2000; soloist symphony orchs. throughout Europe and South Pacific; ann. solo concerts Sevenars Music Festival, Sevenars Music Festival, Worthington, Mass., Berkshires; featured on radio and TV shows including PM Mag. film, NBC Today Show, Radio New Zealand; 50th anniversary of N.Y. adult debut Liederkranz Found. (Town Hall), N.Y.C; featured in Lifetime TV film, 2000. Cpl. USAAC, 1942-45. Avocations: tennis, fishing. Home: 30 East End Ave New York NY 10028-7053 Address: Rte 112 at Ireland St S Worthington MA 01098

SCHRADE, ROLANDE MAXWELL YOUNG, composer, pianist, educator; b. Washington, Sept. 13; d. Harry Robert and Isabelle Martha (Maxwell) Young; m. Robert Warren Schrade, Dec. 21, 1949; children: Robelyn, Rhonda Lee, Rolisa, Randolph, Rorianne. Pupil, Harold Bauer, N.Y.C., Vittorio Giannini; student, Manhattan Sch. Music, Juilliard Sch. Music. Debut as concert pianist Town Hall, N.Y.C., 1953, Nat. Gallery, Washington, 1954; concert pianist Constitution Hall, 1972; founder, dir. ann. performances Sevenars Concerts, Inc., Worthington, Mass., 1968—, music dir., 1975—, also broadcasts, 1984, 85; recitalist Radio Sta. WGMS-FM, Washington; mem. music faculty Allen-Stevenson Sch., N.Y.C., 1968-89; co-founder, v.p., treas. Sevenars Music House, Inc., 1968—. Concerts include Lincoln Ctr., Alice Tully Hall, 1980, 93, Sevenars Concerts, Inc., 1968—, Lincoln Ctr., 2000; Lifetime T.V. film tour, N.Z., 1982, 84; featured NBC Today Show with Schrade family pianists, 1993; named to Steinway Piano Co. Global Artist List; appearances PM Mag., TV film, 1980-81; composer, pub., recs. of more than 100 songs; albums include America 76, Original and Traditional Songs for Special Days, 1988; editor: songs of Carrie Jacobs Bond, Boston Music Co.; TV feature film with Schrade Family Pianists, 1997; performed in Schrade-James Family Concert Lincoln Ctr., N.Y.C., 2000 Mem. ASCAP, DAR (Bicentennial award 1972), Mut. Artists Mgmt. Alliance (founder, bd. dirs.). Episcopalian. Home and Office: 30 East End Ave Ste 3A New York NY 10028-7053 Office: Sevenars Concerts Ireland St S at Rte 112 Worthington MA 01098

SCHRADER, ALFRED EUGENE, lawyer; b. Nov. 1, 1953; s. Louis Clement and Helen Mae (Eberz) S.; m. Debra Susanne Britt-Garrett, Aug. 12, 1997. BA in Polit. Sci. magna cum laude, Kent State U., 1975; JD, Ohio State U., 1978. Bar: Ohio 1978, U.S. Dist. Ct. (no. dist.) Ohio 1978, U.S. Ct. Appeals (6th cir.) 1985, U.S. Supreme Ct. 1985. Dep. clk. Summit County Clk. of Cts., Akron, 1972-74; pvt. practice law, 1978—; spl. counsel Bath Twp., Ohio, 1980-92, 95-98. Spkr. Akron Bar Assn. Akron Univ. Sch. Law CLE Seminars. Trustee Springfield Twp., Ohio, 1973-2001, pres., 1975, 79, 82, 88, 90, 95-96, 2000-01; v.p. Springfield-Akron Joint Econ. Devel. Dist., 1995-97, pres., 1997-2000; mem. adv. com. Cmty. Devel. Block, Summit County, 1985-97, Twinsburg Twp. tax abatement counsel, 1994—, Summit County Annexation Com., 1981-85; mem. Summit County Jail Study Commn., 1983, 84; mem. adv. bd. Springfield Schs., 1975; acting law dir. City of Streetsboro, Portage County, Ohio, 1997; rep. numerous twps. State of Ohio on land use planning, annexation, revenue sharing, zoning and local govt. law matters. Mem. ATLA, Akron Bar Assn. (v.p. legis. com. 1981-82, v.p. local govt. sect. 1992-93, chair local govt. sect. 1993-95, v.p. continuing legal edn. com. 2001--), Ohio Acad. Trial Lawyers, Ohio Bar Assn., Summit County Twp. Assn. (exec. com. 1983-2001), Ohio Twp. Assn., Risk Mgmt. Authority (bd. dirs. 1996-2001, sec. 1997-2000, pres. 2000-01), Nat. Assn. Town and Twp. Attys. (bd. dirs. Ohio chpt. 1986, sec. 1987-93, v.p. 1993-97). Democrat. Roman Catholic. Fax: 330 762 2255. Home: 3344 Brunk Rd Akron OH 44312-3710 Office: Schrader Romanoski Stevenson and Grant 441 Wolf Ledges Pky Ste 400 Akron OH 44311-1039 Fax: (330) 762-2255. E-mail: attysrsg@aol.com.

SCHRADER, ANDREW ROBERT, music educator; b. Torrance, Calif., Sept. 15, 1977; s. Milton James and Norma Jean Schrader. BA Music Edn., U. of Ill. at Urbana-Champaign, Urbana, Illinois, 1999. Performer/musician Springfield Mcpl. Band, Springfield, Ill., 2002—; music educator/band dir. Calvary Acad., 2001—; music educator Springfield Pub. Schools, 2000—01; pvt. instrumental instr. Torrance, CA and Champaign and Springfield, 1995—. Dir./clinician Calvary Band Camp, Springfield, Ill., 2002. Recipient Bronze Tablet Recipient, U. of Ill., 1999; scholar Music Performance Scholarship, 1995-1999. Mem.: Music Educator's Nat. Conf. Avocations: music, sports, movies. Office: Calvary Academy 1730 West Jefferson Springfield IL 62702

SCHRADER, BRADLEY, physicist; BS in Nuc. Engring., Idaho State U., 1982, postgrad., 1998—; MS in Indsl. Safety, U. Idaho, 1992. Radiol. engr. Newport News (Va.) Shipbuilding, 1985—87; adv. engr. Bechtel Idaho Health Physics, Idaho Falls, 1988—. Author: (software program) Radiological Safety Analysis, 2001. Mem.: Am. Nuc. Soc., Health Physics Soc. Office: INEEL PO Box 1625 Idaho Falls ID 83415-2503

SCHRADER, HENRY CARL, retired civil engineer, consultant; b. Jan. 5, 1918; s. Henry Fred and Helene (Arkenberg) S.; m. Marium Warner, Aug. 22, 1942; children: Henry Carl, Gary Warner. BSCE, U. Ill., 1940, MSCE, 1959; diploma, Indsl. Coll. Armed Forces, Ft. McNair, D.C., 1962. Registered profl. engr., Ill., Va., Md., Pa., N.C. Commd. 2d lt. U.S. Army, 1940, advanced through grades to maj. gen., 1971; dist. engr. Corps of Engrs., Okinawa, Ryukus Island, 1962-64; chief sys. analyst Office Chief Staff Dept. Army, Washington, 1966-67, dir. mgmt. info. sys., 1967-70; comdr. 18th Engr. Brigade, Vietnam, 1970-71, Computer Sys. Command, Ft. Belvoir, Va., 1971-73; ret., 1973; prin. mktg. Dalton Dalton Newport, Washington, 1973-84; v.p. URS Dalton, 1984-86, URS (Greiner, Inc. (formerly URS Cons., Inc.), Virginia Beach, Va., 1986-97. Specialist high speed ground transp. systems, 1978-98. Decorated Air Medal with 2 clusters, Disting. Svc. medal with cluster, Legion of Merit with 3 clusters; recipient Engr. of Yr. award Dept. Civil Engring., U. Ill., 1971. Fellow ASCE, Soc. Am. Mil. Engrs. (dir. 1979-86); mem. NSPE, High Speed Ground Transp. Assn. (bd. dirs. 1982-98, chmn. membership com. 1985-97), Nat. Assn. Uniformed Svcs. Assn., Ret. Officers Assn., Bethesda Country Club (dir. 1983-86). Republican. Episcopalian. Fax: (301) 299-1695.

SCHRADER, KEITH WILLIAM, mathematician; b. Neligh, Nebr., Apr. 22, 1938; s. William Charles and Gail (Hughes) S.; m. Carol Jean Taylor, Dec. 26, 1960; children: Jeffrey, Melinda. BS, U. Nebr., 1959, MS, 1961, PhD, 1966; postgrad., Stanford U., 1961-63. Engr. Sylvania Co., Mountain View, Calif., 1962-63; asst. prof. dept. math U. Mo.-Columbia, 1966-69, assoc. prof., 1969-78, prof., 1978-79, chmn. dept. math. prof., 1979-82, 85-88, prof. dept. math., 1988—. Bd. dirs. Schrader Inst. Early Learning, Columbia, 1970-83; mem. Planning And Zoning Commn., 1980-90. NASA grantee, 1967-68; NSF grantee, 1969-70 Mem. Am. Math. Soc., Sigma Xi, Sigma Phi Epsilon Office: Dept Math U Mo Columbia MO 65211-0001 E-mail: keiths99k@netscape.net.

SCHRADER, LAWRENCE EDWIN, plant physiologist, educator; b. Atchison, Kans., Oct. 22, 1941; s. Edwin Carl and Jenna Kathryn (Tobiason) S.; m. Elfriede J. Massier, Mar. 14, 1981 BS, Kans. State U., 1963; PhD, U. Ill., 1967; grad., Inst. Ednl. Mgmt., Harvard U., 1991. Asst. prof. dept. agronomy U. Wis., Madison, 1969-72, assoc. prof., 1972-76, prof., 1976-84; prof., head dept. agronomy U. Ill., Urbana, 1985-89; dean Coll. Agr. and Home Econs. Wash. State U., Pullman, 1989-94, prof. dept. horticulture, 1994—. Chief competitive rsch. grants office Dept. Agr., Washington, 1980-81; trustee, treas. Agrl. Satellite Corp., 1991-94. Contbr. chpts. to books, articles to profl. jours. Active Consortium for Internat. Devel., 1989-94, chair fin. com., vice chair exec. com., 1990-92, trustee 1989-94; mem. exec. com. Coun. Agrl. Heads of Agr., 1992-94. Capt. U.S. Army, 1967-69. Recipient Soybean Researchers Recognition award 1983, Disting. Service award in Agriculture Kansas State U., 1987; Romnes Faculty fellow U. Wis., 1979 Fellow AAAS (steering group sect. agr. 1991-95, chair-elect sect. on agr., food and renewable resources 1995-96, chmn. 1996-97, past chmn. 1997-98, coun. mem. 1997-98), Am. Soc. Agronomy, Crop Sci. Soc. Am.; mem. Internat. Soc. for Hort. Sci., Am. Soc. for Hort. Sci., Am. Soc. Plant Biologists (sec. 1983-85, pres.-elect 1986, pres. 1987), Am. Chem. Soc., Coun. for Agrl. Sci. and Tech., Blue Key, Sigma Xi, Gamma Sigma Delta, Phi Kappa Phi, Phi Eta Sigma, Alpha Zeta (named to Centennial Honor Roll 1997). Methodist. Home: 3504 Crestview Rd Wenatchee WA 98801-9668 Office: Wash State U Tree Fruit Rsch & Extension Ctr 1100 N Western Ave Wenatchee WA 98801-1230 E-mail: schrader@wsu.edu.

SCHRADER, MICHAEL EUGENE, columnist, editor; b. Jersey City, Apr. 3, 1938; s. Eugene Charles and Anne Veronica (Kane) S. BA in Latin, NYU, 1961, MA in English, 1963; postgrad., UCLA, 1965-67, 68-69, Trinity Coll., Dublin, 1967-68, U. Copenhagen, Denmark, 1970. Asst. editor Macmillan Co., N.Y.C., 1962-64; teaching asst. U. Ill., Urbana, 1964-65; teaching asst., rsch. asst. UCLA, 1965-67, 68-69; sr. copy editor Dell Pub. Co., N.Y.C., 1971-72; copy chief Sat. Rev. mag., 1972-76, Penthouse mag., N.Y.C., 1976-82; assoc. editor Med. Econs. mag., Oradell, N.J., 1982; sr. copy editor Woman's World mag., Englewood, 1983-84; book reviewer, sr. copy editor Nation's Restaurant News, N.Y.C., 1985—. Columnist: From the Bookshelf, in Nation's Restaurant News, 1988—. Friend of Bobst Libr., Soc. of Torch, NYU, 1994—, established Anne Kane Schrader Cookbook and Nutrition Collection. Recipient Danish Marshall award U. Copenhagen, 1970; Fulbright scholar, 1967-68. Fellow James Beard Found. (judge food and beverage book awards 1991-94); mem. Soc. of the Torch (charter), Internat. Assn. Culinary Profls. Democrat. Roman Catholic. Avocations: reading fiction and poetry, growing house plants, travel, movies, theater. Home: 30 Waterside Plz Apt 33H New York NY 10010-2627 Office: Lebhar-Friedman Inc Nation's Restaurant News 425 Park Ave New York NY 10022-3549 E-mail: Mschrade@nrn.com.

SCHRADER, RICHARD JAMES, English language educator; b. Canton, Ohio, Aug. 24, 1941; s. A.W. and Margaret Louise (Karcher) S. BA, U. Notre Dame, 1963; MA, Ohio State U., 1965, PhD, 1968. Asst. prof. English, Princeton (N.J.) U., 1968-75, John Witherspoon Bicentennial preceptor, 1972-75; prof. English, Boston Coll., Chestnut Hill, Mass., 1975—. Author: God's Handiwork: Images of Women in Early Germanic Literature, 1983, Old English Poetry and the Genealogy of Events, 1993, H.L. Mencken: A Descriptive Bibliography, 1998; editor: The Reminiscences of Alexander Dyce, 1972, Arator's On the Acts of the Apostles, 1987, H.L. Mencken: A Documentary Volume, 2000; mem. editl. bd. Menckeniana: A Quar. Rev., 1999—; contbr. articles. to profl. jours. Grantee Mellon Found., 1980-81, NEH, summer 1995; Helms fellow, 2002. Mem. Medieval Acad. Am., Assn. for Lit. Scholars and Critics, Mencken Soc., Soc. for Am. Baseball Rsch., New Chaucer Soc. Roman Catholic. Avocations: book collecting, genealogy, baseball. Office: Boston Coll Dept English Chestnut Hill MA 02467 E-mail: richard.schrader@bc.edu.

SCHRADER, ROBERT WESLEY, judge; b. Cheyenne, Wyo., Feb. 3, 1944; s. Marvin Glen and Bertha Lorene (Winingar) S.; m. Betty Ann Pruter, June 14, 1964; children: Christina Lynn, Tashana Dee. AA in Mortuary Sci., San Francisco Mortuary Sci., 1965; BSBA, U. Wyo., 1967, JD, 1979. Bar: Wyo., 1978, U.S. Dist. Ct. Wyo., 1978 U.S. Ct. Appeals (10th cir.), 1979, U.S. Supreme Ct., 1991. Assoc. Omohundro & O'Brien, Buffalo, 1978-80; pvt. practice Schrader Law Office, 1980-84; ins. commr. State Wyo., Cheyenne, 1984-86; pvt. practice Schrader Law Office, 1986-92; dist. ct. commr. 1st Jud. Dist., 1987—. Justice of the peace, Johnson County, Wyo., 1980-84; dist. ct. commr. 4th Jud. Dist., Johnson County, 1981-84; pres., bd. mem. Attention Homes, Inc., Cheyenne, 1983-98; pres. Scottish Rite Found., Cheyenne, 1992—. Heels, Cheyenne Frontier Days, 1979—; Wyo. races officer Wyo. Emergency Mgmt. Agy., Cheyenne, 1991-97. Capt. U.S. Army, 1967-70, Vietnam, lt. col. USAFR ret. 1994. Decorated three Meritorious Svc. medals USAF, Combat Med. badge U.S. Army, Vietnam, 1968. Mem. VFW Post 11454 (adv.), Burns Lodge 41 AF&AM (past master), Scottish Rite Bodies, York Rite Bodies, Korein Shrine (chief clown), Shrine Circus (sec.-treas.), Phi Epsilon Phi, Sigma Phi Epsilon. Republican. Episcopalian. Avocations: flying, raising quarter horses, clowning, hunting, amateur radio. Home: 607 Monte Carlo Dr Cheyenne WY 82009-2050 Office: First Jud Dist Ct Dist Ct 309 W 20th St Cheyenne WY 82001-3601

SCHRADY, DAVID ALAN, civilian military employee, educator; b. Akron, Ohio, Nov. 11, 1939; s. Marvin G. and Sheila A. (O'Neill) S.; m. Mary E. Hilt, Sept. 1, 1962; children: Peter, Patrick, Matthew. BS, Case Inst. Tech., 1961, MS, 1963, PhD, 1965. Prof., chmn. Naval Postgrad. Sch., Monterey, Calif., 1974-76, dean acad. planning, 1976-80, provost and acad. dean, 1980-87, prof. ops. rsch., 1988—, Disting. prof., ops. rsch. educator, 1995—. Vis. prof. Cranfield Inst. Tech./Royal Mil. Coll. of Sci., Shrivenham, Eng., fall 1987-spring 88. Contbr. articles to profl. jours. Recipient Goodeve medal Ops. Rsch. Soc., U.K., 1992. Fellow Mil. Ops. Rsch. Soc. (pres. 1978-79, Wanner Meml. award 1984); mem. Ops. Rsch. Soc. Am. (pres. 1983-84, Kimball medal 1994), Internat. Fedn. Ops. Rsch. Socs. (hon. treas. 1988-97), Inst. Mgmt. Scis. Avocation: guitar, motor sports. Office: Naval Postgrad Sch Dept Ops Rsch Monterey CA 93943-5000

SCHRAG, ADELE FRISBIE, business education educator; b. Cynthiana, Ky., May 7, 1921; d. Shirley Ledyard and Edna Kate (Ford) S.; m. William Albert Schrag, Apr. 6, 1963; 1 stepchild, Marie Carol. BS, Temple U., 1942; MA, N.Y. U., 1944, PhD, 1961. Tchr. Manor Twp. High Sch., Millersville, Pa., 1942-43, Downingtown (Pa.) Sr. High Sch., 1943-50; instr., asst. prof. Temple U. Sch. Bus. and Pub. Adminstrn., Phila., 1950-60; prof. bus. edn. and vocat. edn. Coll. Edn., 1960-85, sr. prof. edn., 1985-88, prof. emeritus, 1988—. Vis. lectr. N.Y. U.; cons. Phila. Community Coll., 1967-82 Editor: Business Education for the Automated Office, 1964; author: (with Estelle L. Popham and Wanda Blockhus) A Teaching-Learning System for Business Education, 1975, How to Dictate, 1981, Office Procedures Update, 1982, (with Robert Poland) A Teaching System for Business Subjects, 1988; contbr. articles to profl. jours., chpts. to books. Trustee Meth. Hosp., 1981—85, Sun Cities Symphony Assn., 1988—93, Habitat for Humanity of West Valley, 1994—, co-pres., 1999—2001; trustee Habitat for Humanity Ariz., 1999—. Recipient Profl. Panhellenic award, 1963; Kensington High Sch. Alumnae award, 1972 Mem. Soc. Automation in Bus. Edn. (pres. 1969-73, dir. 1974), Nat. Assn. Bus. Tchr. Edn. (pres. 1983-84), Bus. Edn. Certification Council, Phi Gamma Nu (nat. treas. 1952-54, nat. sec. 1954-56), Delta Pi Epsilon (policy commn. for bus. and econ. edn. 1975-78, dir. research found. 1978-83, pres. research found. 1983). Home: 14515 W Granite Valley Dr # 644 Sun City West AZ 85375-6021 E-mail: afs107@earthlink.net.

SCHRAG, EDWARD A., JR. lawyer; b. Milw., Mar. 27, 1932; s. Edward A. and Mabel Lena (Baumbach) S.; m. Leslie Jean Israel, June 19, 1954; children: Amelia Marie Schrag Prack, Katherine Allison Schrag Roberts, Edward A. III (dec.). BS in Econs, U. Pa., 1954; JD, Harvard, 1960. Bar: Ohio 1961. Assoc., then firm partner, now of counsel Vorys, Sater, Seymour and Pease, Columbus, 1960—. Sec. Ranco Inc., 1972-87; trustee Lake of Woods Water Co., 1972-91; mem. Ohio div. Securities Adv. Com. Mem. Downtown Area Com., 1970-74. Served to lt. (j.g.) USNR, 1954-57. Mem. ABA, Ohio Bar Assn. (chmn. corp. law com. 1986-88, chmn. securities regulation subcom., spl. com. bus. cts., bd. govs., corp. counsel sect., chmn. 1991-93), Columbus Bar Assn., Columbus Area C. of C., Navy League, Alpha Tau Omega, Beta Gamma Sigma, Phi Sigma Alpha, Pi Gamma Mu. Clubs: Capital, Crichton, Ohio State U. Pres.'s. Episcopalian. Home: 9400 White Oak Ln Westerville OH 43082-9606 Office: Vorys Sater Seymour & Pease PO Box 1008 52 E Gay St Columbus OH 43216-1008

SCHRAG, PETER, editor, writer; b. Karlsruhe, Germany, July 24, 1931; came to U.S., 1941, naturalized, 1953; s. Otto and Judith (Haas) S.; m. Melissa Jane Mowrer, June 9, 1953 (div. 1969); children: Mitzi, Erin Andrew; m. Diane Divoky, May 24, 1969 (div. 1981); children: David Divoky, Benaiah Divoky; m. Patricia Ternahan, Jan. 1, 1988. AB cum laude, Amherst Coll., 1953. Reporter El Paso (Tex.) Herald Post, 1953-55; asst. sec., asst. dir. publs. Amherst Coll., 1955-66, instr. Am. Studies, 1960-64; asso. edn. editor Sat. Rev., 1966-68, exec. editor, 1968-69; editor Change mag., 1969-70; editor at large Saturday Rev., 1969-72; contbg. editor Saturday Review/Education, 1972-73; editorial adv. bd. The Columbia Forum, 1972-75; editorial bd. Social Policy, 1971—; contbg. editor More, 1974-78, Inquiry, 1977-80, The Am. Prospect, 1995—; editorial page editor Sacramento Bee and McClatchy Newspapers, 1978-96, contbg. editor, 1996—. Vis. lectr. U. Mass. Sch. Edn., 1970-72; fellow in profl. journalism Stanford U., Palo Alto, Calif., 1973-74; lectr. U. Calif. at Berkeley, 1974-78, 90—; Pulitzer Prize juror, 1988-89 Author: Voices in the Classroom, 1965, Village School Downtown, 1967, Out of Place in America, 1971, The Decline of the Wasp, 1972, The End of the American Future, 1973, Test of Loyalty, 1974, (with Diane Divoky) The Myth of the Hyperactive Child, 1975, Mind Control, 1978, Paradise Lost: California's Experience, America's Future, 1998; contbr. articles. Mem. adv. com. Student Rights Project, N.Y. Civil Liberties Union, 1970-72; mem. Com. Study History, 1958-72; trustee Emma Willard Sch., 1967-69; bd. dirs. Park Sch., Oakland, Calif., 1976-77, Ctr. for Investigative Reporting, 1979-81, Ed Source, 1998—; bd. visitors Claremont Grad. Sch.; mem. bd. advisors Pub. Policy Inst. Calif. Guggenheim fellow, 1971-72; Nat. Endowment for Arts fellow, 1976-77 Office: 5835 Colton Blvd Oakland CA 94611-2204 E-mail: pschrag@sacbee.com.

SCHRAG, PETER EDWARD, physician; b. Beirut, May 10, 1938; came to U.S., 1938; s. Karl and Ilse (Szamatolski) S.; m. Minna S., 1962 (div. 1982); children: Daniel, Deborah, Jonathan; m. Jeanette S., Sept. 14, 1985. AB, Harvard U., 1959, MD, 1964—66. Intern, resident Columbia U. div. Bellevue Hosp., N.Y.C., 1964-66; resident Columbia U. divsn. Harlem Hosp., 1968-70; asst. prof. Columbia U., 1971-85; assoc. in medicine Lenox Hill Hosp., 1985—; assoc. med. dir. Met Life Ins. Co., 1988-93, med. dir., 1993—. Contbr. article to Am. Jour. Lung Disease. Fellow Am. Coll. Phycians; mem. AMA. Office: Met Life Ins Co 1 Madison Ave New York NY 10010-3603

SCHRAG, PHILIP GORDON, law educator; b. Chgo., Apr. 12, 1943; s. Louis Phillip and Lala D. (Fineman) S.; m. Emily Shiling, June 7, 1964 (div. Aug. 1985); children: David, Zachary; m. Lisa Gabrielle Lerman, Dec. 29, 1985; children: Samuel Lerman, Sarah. AB, Harvard U., 1964; LLB, Yale U., 1967. Bar: N.Y. 1967, D.C. 1981. Asst. counsel NAACP Legal Def. & Edn. Fund Inc., N.Y.C., 1967-70; consumer adv. City of N.Y., 1970-71; assoc. prof. law Columbia U., N.Y.C., 1971-73, prof. law, 1973-77; dep. gen. counsel ACDA, Washington, 1977-81; prof. law Georgetown U., 1981—. Cons. Consumer Protection Bd., N.Y., 1975, Carter-Mondale Transition Planning, 1976, Gov.'s Adv. Coun., P.R., 1970. Author: Counsel for the Deceived, 1972, Behind the Scenes: The Politics of a Constitutional Convention, 1985, A Well-Founded Fear: The Congressional Battle to Save Political Asylum in America, 2000. Del. Statehood Constnl. Conv., D.C., 1982; chair Consumer's Adv. Coun., N.Y.C., 1968-70.

SCHRAGE, ROSE, educational administrator; b. Montelimar, France, Apr. 15, 1942; came to U.S., 1947; d. Abraham and Celia (Silbiger) Levine; m. Samuel Schrage, Dec. 12, 1935 (dec. 1976); children: Abraham, Leon. BRE, Beth Rivkah Tchrs. Sem., Bklyn., 1968; Paralegal, Manpower Career Devel. Agy., Bklyn., 1973; MS, L.I. U., 1975; Advanced Cert. Ednl. Adminstrn., Bklyn. Coll., 1983. Cert. sch. dist. adminstr., guidance counselor, tchr., asst. prin. Sec., N.Y.C., 1964-68; police adminstrv. aide N.Y.C. Police Dept., 1974-75; coordinator state reading aid program Sch. Dist. 14, Bklyn., 1977-78, project dir. Title VII, 1978-81, asst. dir. reimbursable fed. and state programs, 1981-85, dist. bus. mgr., 1985-94, asst. prin., 1994—99, spl. edn. instruction specialist, adminstr., 1999—. Chmn. N.Y.C. Bd. Edn. IMPACT Com., Bklyn., 1986—. Author (poem): Never Again, 1983; contbg. editor Chai Today; contbr. articles on current affairs and concerns to profl. jours. Del. Republican. Jud. Conf., 1968; founder, pres Concerned Parents, Bklyn., 1977; radio co-host Israeli War Heroes Fund-Radiothon, Bklyn.; family counselor local social agys., Bklyn.; co-founder cmty. vol. ambulance Hatzalah, 1977. Recipient Cert. of Appreciation as vol. regional coord. N.Y. State Mentoring Program N.Y. Gov. Cuomo, 1991. Mem. Am. Assn. Sch. Adminstrs., Assn. Orthodox Jewish Tchrs. (v.p. exec. bd.), N.Y. State Assn. Sch. Bus. Ofcls., N.Y.C. Assn. Sch. Bus. Ofcls., Coun. Suprs. and Adminstrs. Avocations: tennis, needlepoint, piano, reading, communal activities.

SCHRAGER, MINDY RAE, software company professional; b. Paterson, N.J., Jan. 18, 1958; d. Julius Maxwell and Miriam (Max) S.; m. Jim Flannery, 1993. BA, Dickinson Coll., 1979; MBA, Babson Coll., 1981. Cons. Nolan Norton & Co., Lexington, Mass., 1981-86; mgr. Logos Corp., Dedham, 1986-87; resource ctr. supr., customer satisfaction mgr., dir. quality Motorola ISG, Mansfield, 1987-95; dir. quality, dir. bill payment ops., dir. project mgmt. Fidelity Investments, Boston, 1995-99; sr. program mgr., sr. mgr. programs office Ascential Software, Westboro, 1999—. Co-author: Non Product Quality: The Cornerstone for Success, Continuous Improvement of the Selling Process. Mem. NAFE, Am. Soc. Quality (founder, chmn., bus. process improvement com.), Assn. for Rsch. and Enlightenment, Assn. Quality and Participation (co-founder Boston chpt.). Avocation: gardening. Home: 10 Magnolia Pointe Ashland MA 01721-2529 Office: Ascential Software 50 Washington St Westborough MA 01581-1013

SCHRAM, MARTIN JAY, journalist; b. Chgo., Sept. 15, 1942; s. Marlo Joseph and Charleene Janice (Fidler) S.; m. Patricia Stewart Morgan, May 23, 1964; children— Kenneth Marlo, David Morgan. BA, U. Fla., 1964. Reporter The Miami (Fla.) News, 1964-65; reporter Newsday, Garden City, N.Y., 1965-67, mem. Washington bur., 1967-69, White House corr., 1969-73, chief Washington bur., sr. editor paper, 1973-79; writer on the presidency Washington Post, 1979-81, nat. affairs writer, 1981-86; assoc. editor, editor Sunday edits. Chgo. Sun-Times, 1986-87; asst. mng. editor, editor Sunday edits. Rocky Mountain News, Denver, 1987-88; commentator Cable News Network, 1988-98; nat. editor Washingtonian Mag., 1988-90; polit. columnist United Feature Syndicate, Newspaper Enterprise Assn., 1989-94, Scripps Howard News Svc., Washington, 1994—; news story edit., columnist Fox News, 1998-2000. Fellow Gannett Ctr. for Media Studies, Columbia U., 1985-86; guest scholar Woodrow Wilson Internat. Ctr., 1990-91. Author: Running for President, A Journal of the Carter Campaign, 1976, Running for President: 1976, The Carter Campaign, 1977; (with others) The Pursuit of the Presidency, 1980, The Great American Video Game: Presidential Politics in the Television Age, 1987, Speaking Freely, 1995; co-editor: Mandate for Change, 1993. Recipient James Wright Brown Meml. award Sigma Delta Chi, 1965, Lowell Mellet award Pa. State U., 1988. Office: Scripps Howard News Svc 1090 Vermont Ave NW Ste 1000 Washington DC 20005-4906

SCHRAM, PENINNAH, communication educator, storyteller; b. New London, Conn., Dec. 28, 1934; d. Samuel Eli and Dora Manchester; m. Irving Schram, Dec. 7, 1958 (dec. Feb. 1967); children: Rebecca, Michael. BA in Speech and Theatre, U. Conn., 1956; MA in Speech and Theatre, Columbia U., 1968. Instr. Iona Coll., New Rochelle, N.Y., 1967-69; instr. Stern Coll. Yeshiva U., N.Y.C., 1969-74, asst. prof. speech and drama, 1974-85, assoc. prof., 1985—, assoc. prof. David J. Azrieli Grad. Sch. Jewish Edn., 1988—. Spkr., presenter numerous confs., festivals, symposia. Author, editor: A Teaching Guide to Elijah's Violin and Other Jewish Fairy Tales, 1985; author: The Big Sukkah, 1986, Jewish Stories One Generation Tells Another, 1987, Tales of Elijah the Prophet, 1991, Ten Classic Jewish Children's Stories, 1998, Stories Within Stories: From the Jewish Oral Tradition, 2000, The Chanukah Blessing, 2000; co-author: Eight Tales for Eight Nights: Stories for Chanukah, 1990; editor: Chosen Tales: Stories Told by Jewish Storytellers, 1995; storyteller: (audio CD) The Minstrel and the Storyteller: Stories and Songs of the Jewish People; contbg. author: Who Says? Essays on Pivotal Issues in Contemporary Storytelling, 1995; contbr. The Storyteller's Companion to the Bible: Old Testament Wisdom, 1994; contbr. articles to profl. publs. including Jewish Book World, Nat. Storytelling Jour., Melton Jour., Pedagogic Reporter. Recipient Disting. Svc. award Jewish Braille Inst., 1976, Hadassah Myrtle Wreath award Eastern Pa. Region of Hadassah, 1990, Covenant award Covenant Found., 1995, Cir. of Excellence award Nat. Storytelling Network, 1999. Mem. Phi Beta Kappa, Kappa Delta Pi. Home: 525 W End Ave New York NY 10024-3207

SCHRAM, RONALD BYARD, lawyer; b. Detroit, Sept. 7, 1942; s. Byron Canby and Mary Louise (Byard) S.; m. Carol Lorraine Anderson, July 19, 1969; children: Laura Mary, Alison Leigh. BA, Dartmouth Coll., 1964; MA in Econs., Cambridge U., England, 1966; JD, U. Mich., 1969, LLM, 1970, SJD, 1971. Bar: Mass. 1970. Assoc. Ropes & Gray, Boston, 1970-78, ptnr., 1978—. Trustee Dartmouth Coll., Hanover, N.H., 1981-92, Dartmouth-Hitchcock Med. Ctr., Lebanon, N.H., 1983-93, New Eng. Sports Mus., Cambridge, Mass., 1984-1999, Derby Acad., Hingham, Mass., 1982-89, ctrl. New Eng. chpt., Nat. Multiple Sclerosis Soc., Waltham, Mass., 2002—. Keasbey Found. fellow, Phila., 1964-66; George M. Humphrey fellow in law econ. policy, U. Mich. Law Sch., Ann Arbor, 1969-70. Mem. Boston Bar Assn., Am. Acad. Hosp. Attys., Phi Beta Kappa. Office: Ropes & Gray 1 International Pl Boston MA 02110-2624 E-mail: rschram@ropesgray.com.

SCHRAM, SANFORD FRANCIS, political science educator; b. Newark, Jan. 18, 1949; s. Harold Harvey and Lillie (Schneider) S.; m. Joan Sweeney, Aug. 18, 1973; children: Ryan, Jonathan. BA, St. Lawrence U., Canton, N.Y., 1971; MA, SUNY, Albany, 1973, PhD, 1979. Instr. govt. Nasson Coll., Springvale, Maine, 1976-77; asst. prof. polit. sci. SUNY, Potsdam, 1977-83, assoc. prof., 1983-89, chairperson dept. polit. sci., 1984-88; vis. assoc. prof. pub. affairs Lafollette Inst. Pub. Affairs, 1986-87,. 93-94; assoc. prof. Macalester Coll., St. Paul, 1989—, chairperson dept. polit. sci., 1992-93. Author: Words of Welfare, 1995; ann. rev. co-editor Publius; contbr. articles to profl. jours. Named Disting. Alumnus, Rockefeller Coll., SUNY, Albany, 1988. Mem. Am. Polit. Sci. Assn., Midwest Polit. Sci. Assn., So. Polit. Sci. Assn. Democrat. Home: 215 Fairview Ave S Saint Paul MN 55105-1501 Office: Macalester Coll 1600 Grand Ave Saint Paul MN 55105-1801

SCHRAM, SUSAN GALE, agriculturist, consultant; b. Grand Rapids, Mich., June 19, 1948; d. Paul Gerard and Dorothy Maxine (Putnam) S. BS, Mich. State U., 1970, MA, 1973; PhD, U.Md. Tchr. Lansing (Mich.) City Schs., 1970; mem. child care staff Hawthorn Ctr. Psychiat. Facility, Northville, Mich., 1971-72; rsch. asst. U. Mich., Ann Arbor, 1973; county extension agt. Grand Haven, Mich., 1975-76; state program leader Coop. Extension Svc., East Lansing, 1976-80; exec. sec. Joint Council on Food and Agrl. Scis. U.S. Dept Agr., Washington, 1980-82; sr. rsch. assoc. Ctr. for Policy Rsch., Bethesda, Md., 1982-83; dir. rsch. & devel. LBS Internat., 1983-84; cons. Office Sec. Agr. for Pub. Liason, Washington, 1984; staff Office Internat. Programs U. Md., 1985-86; spl. asst. to assoc. v.p. for agrl., 1987-88; spl. asst. to vice chancellor, 1988-90; asst. dir. fed. rels. for internat. programs Nat. Assn. State Univs. and Land Grant Colls., 1990-92; food and agrl. coord., dep. dir. Wash. ops. Consortium for Internat. Earth Sci. Info. Network, 1992-99; dep. dir. Wash. ops., 1996-99; pres. TBR Internat., Inc., Washington, 1999—2001; exec. dir. Partnership to Cut Hunger in Africa, 2000-2001; v.p. ACDI/VOCA, 2001—. Author handbooks, books and papers in field. V.p. Potowmac Overlook Condominiums, Washington, 1985. Recipient Exemplary Svc. award Asst. Sec. of Agr. for Sci. and Edn., 1982; named Mich. Regional Young Career Woman of Yr., Bus. and Profl. Women, 1976; grantee rural devel. Title V, 1977. Mem. Assn. Internat. Agriculture and Rural Devel. (pres. 1997-98, Disting. Svc. award 1999), Nat. Policy Assn., Phi Kappa Phi, Omicron Nu, Kappa Alpha Theta. Congregationalist. Avocation: photography. Home: 1001 26th St NW Apt 708 Washington DC 20037-1604 Office: ACDI/VOCA 50 F St NW Ste 1075 Washington DC 20001

SCHRAMEK, TOMAS, ballet dancer, educator; b. Bratislava, Czechoslovakia, Sept. 11, 1944; emigrated to Can., 1968, naturalized, 1973; s. Hans and Valeria (Neudorfer) S. BFA, Acad. Mus. and Theatre Arts, Bratislava, 1968. Mem. Sluk, Slovakia folk dance ensemble, 1959-68, prin. dancer, 1964-68; dancer Nat. Ballet Can., 1969-71, soloist, 1971-73, prin. dancer, 1973-91, prin. character artist, ballet master, 1991—. Mem. Actors Equity Assn., Assn. Can. TV and Radio Artists. Home: 125 Rose Park Dr Toronto ON Canada M4T 1R6 Office: Nat Ballet Canada 470 Queens Quay West Toronto ON Canada M5V 3K4 E-mail: tomasch@rogers.com.

SCHRAMM, ALICIA LARRIMORE, writer; b. Washington, Aug. 9, 1932; d. Charles Harry and Alice Virginia (Larrimore) S. BA, Barnard Coll., 1954; MA, Columbia U., 1956; cert., U. Paris, 1973. Cert. tchr. Md., N.Y. Tchr. Bd. Edn., Montgomery County, Md., 1955-56, tchr., coord., curriculum writer, dean N.Y.C., 1956-83; ret., 1983. Active spl. materials ESL programs Bd. Edn., N.Y., 1957-83, curriculum writer, 1978-82; coord. native lang. arts, 1979-80. Author, illustrator: The Secret of Ajidamo, 1995, Baker's Dozen, 1996; performed with M.S. Hodgson Sch. Ballet, 1939-48; appeared in shows and pageants; performed with dance and drama groups at Columbia U.; contbr. to art shows, 1950, 60-64. Active com. to approve new readers Recording for the Blind, N.Y.C., 1974—82; past vice comdr., ednl. trainer, divsn. staff officer, pub. affairs liaison USCG Aux. flotilla 5-3, 1983—; cert. mem. Senator Roy M. Goodman's Legis. Adv. Com., 1998; mem. Humane Soc. U.S., Squirrel Lovers Club, Nat. Zoo, Smithonian Inst./Am. Indian Mus. Columbia U. grantee, 1965. Mem. Barnard in Washington Alumnae Club. Avocations: environment, travel, wild and domestic animals, especially squirrels, cancer awareness and cures.

SCHRAMM, BERNARD CHARLES, JR. retired advertising agency executive; b. Balt., Jan. 23, 1928; s. Bernard C. and Juliet Marie (Barranger) Schramm; m. Florence Mae Fangman, 1950; children: Stephanie Schramm McDaniel, Carol Schramm Molander, Bernard Charles III, Claudia Schramm Smith. Grad., Balt. Poly. Inst., 1946. Prodn. mgr. Van Sant, Dugdale & Co., Balt., 1946-52; media dir. AWL Advt., 1952-55; dir. prodn. Henry J. Kaufman Assocs., Washington, 1955-58; exec. v.p. Avalon Hill Co., Balt., 1958-64; v.p. Cargill, Wilson & Acree Advt., Richmond, Va., 1964-68; pres. William Cook Advt. Inc. (now William Cook Mktg. Comm.), Jacksonville, Fla., 1968-89, chmn. bd., 1989-97; ret., 1997. Bd. dirs. Otis F. Smith Found., chmn., 1991—97. Mem. exec. com., v.p. United Way N.E. Fla., 1982-87, bd. dirs., 1982-93; bd. dirs. N.E. Fla. chpt. ARC, 1976-89, chmn., 1980-81; bd. dirs. Fla. C.C. Found., 1976-89. Mem.: Am. Assn. Advt. Agys. (chmn. Fla. coun. 1984—85, So. Region Bd. of Govs. 1988—92, chmn. 1989, nat. bd. dirs., agy. mgmt. com. 1989—92), Jacksonville Area C. of C., San Jose Club, Rotary Club. Republican. Roman Catholic. Avocations: golf, reading, spectator sports, hunting. Home: 12856 Bay Plantation Dr Jacksonville FL 32223-0784

SCHRAMM, PAUL HOWARD, lawyer; b. St. Louis, Oct. 6, 1933; s. Benjamin Jacob and Frieda Sylvia (Goruch) S.; m. Sue-Ann Batson; children: Scott Lyon, Dean Andrew, Thomas Edward, Jeremy Arthur Savran. AB, U. Mo., 1955, JD, 1958. Bar: Mo. 1958, U.S. Dist. Ct. (ea. dist.) Mo. 1963, U.S. Ct. Appeals (8th cir.) 1967, U.S. Tax Ct. 1970, U.S. Supreme Ct. 1972, U.S. Dist. Ct. (ea. dist.) Wis., 1988. Ptnr. Schramm & Schramm, St. Louis, 1959-61, Schramm & Morganstern, St. Louis, 1970-76, Schramm, Pines & Marshall, St. Louis, 1977-79, Schramm, Newman, Pines & Freyman, St. Louis, 1979-82, Schramm, Pines & Spewak, St. Louis, 1983-85, Schramm & Pines, L.L.C., St. Louis, 1985-2000, Edwards, Singer, Schramm, Watkins & Spoeneman, L.L.P., St. Louis, 2000—. Pros. atty. City of Ellisville, Mo., 1973-77; judge Ellisville mcpl. div. St. Louis County Cir. Ct., 1977-83; teaching faculty trial advocacy Harvard Law Sch., 1991. Mem. Bar Assn. Met. St. Louis (exec. com. 1976-77, chmn. county sect. 1976-77), St. Louis County Bar Assn. (chmn. lawyers reference service 1971, cir. ct. jud. com. 1970), Phi Delta Phi. Clubs: University (St. Louis). Avocations: music, sports, reading. Home: 7507 Byron Pl Saint Louis MO 63105-2703 Office: Edwards Singer Schramm Watkins & Spoeneman LLP 1600 Clayton Ctr 120 S Central Ave Ste 1600 Saint Louis MO 63105-1798

SCHRAND, RICHARD HENRY, broadcaster, writer; b. Cin., Nov. 1, 1957; s. Edward August and Jane Marie (Scheib) S.; m. Deborah Fortner, 1979 (div. 1985); 1 child, Cynthia Lanette; m. Sharon Lynn Lassandro, Dec. 24, 1986; children: Courtney Lynne, Richard Jr., Brandon Ian. Student, Ohio State U., 1975-76, No. Ky. U., 1976-77. Intern Sta. WCPO-TV, Cin., 1971-75; producer Sta. WKRC-TV, 1975-79; pub. affairs dir., reporter, anchor Sta. WCSC-TV, Charleston, S.C., 1979-83; actor Phila. Experiment, L.A., 1984; asst. promotion dir. Sta. WLWT-TV, Cin., 1983-86; spl. projects coord. Sta. KXAS-TV, Dallas/Ft. Worth, 1986-87; mgr. media svcs. NBC TV Network, Burbank, Calif., 1987-89; pres. Cyn-Court Enterprises, 1989-91; mktg. dir. Sta. WPTA-TV, Ft. Wayne, Ind., 1991-92; v.p., gen. mgr. Branson (Mo.) Broadcasting Corp., 1992-95; dir. spl. projects/nat. media, graphics and advt. creator Jim Owens & Assocs., 1995-98; gen. mgr. Jim Owens Radio, Inc., Nashville, 1995-98; pres. GRFX ByDesign, 1996—; v.p. Komodo Studios, L.A., 1999-2000; instr. computer graphics and web design Nossi Coll. Art, Nashville, 2001—. Instr., spkr. Graphic Design Tour, 2000—, computer design Nossi Coll. Art, 2001—; demonstrator 3D software Sig Graph, MacWorld, 2001—. Author: Canoma Visual Insight, 2000, 3D Creature Workshop vol. 2, 2000, Macromedia Web Design Handbook, 2000, Adobe Golive 5F/X & Design, 2000, Adobe Live Motion Visual Jumpstart, 2000, Adobe Photoshop 6 Visual Jumpstart, 2000, Poser 4 Pro Pack F/X & Design, 2001, Final Cut Pro 3: The Complete Reference, 2002, The Vue D'Esprit Book, 2002; contbr.: Pixels: 3D Book, 1999, Mastering Pixels: 3D, 2001; webmaster Crook & Chase Theater, Middle Tenn. LightWave Users Group, Nossi Coll. of Art. Bd. dirs. Project Graduation, Dallas/Ft. Worth, 1986-87; mem. Muscular Dystrophy Assn., Charleston, 1980-83; publicist Housing Now, L.A., 1988. Recipient Regional Emmy award NATAS, 1975, award Broadcast Promotion and Mktg. Exec., Seattle, 1992. Avocations: guitar, writing, singing, golf. E-mail: rschrand@grfxbydesign.com.

SCHRANDT, CURTIS LEON, lawyer, securities analyst, financial advisor; b. Van Nuys, Calif., Nov. 21, 1957; s. Edward Leon and Ethel Jeannine (Thompson) S. BS in Bus. Mgmt. summa cum laude, U. Utah, 1992, BA in Bus. Fin., 1993; JD cum laude, Quinnipiac U. Sch. Law, 1996. Bar: Conn. 1996, N.Y. 1998, D.C. 1999; CFA. Owner Friends-Exotic Pets, Salt Lake City and Orem, Utah, 1978-89; mgr. ZCMI Dept. Stores, Salt Lake City, 1991-93; ptnr. Hersh & Fowler-Cruz, White Plains, N.Y., 1996-98; owner Law Offices of Curtis Schrandt, Stratford, Conn., 1998—. CLS Enterprises, Stratford, 1996—. Fin. chmn. Hersh & Fowler-Cruz, 1996-98. Mng. editor Quinnipiac Law Rev., 1995-96 (Disting. Svc. award 1996). Mem. ABA, Conn. Bar Assn., N.Y. Bar Assn., D.C. Bar Assn. Office: Law Offices Curtis Schrandt 803 Stratford Ave Stratford CT 06615-6350 Fax: 530-463-9223. E-mail: cschrandt@lawyer.com.

SCHRANK, SHIRLEY ANN, artist; b. Nunda, N.Y., Jan. 30, 1933; d. Ward Donald and Norma Mae (Kelley) Crane; m. John Roberts McKalip Jr., Oct. 8, 1966 (dec. May 1974); children: Catherine, William Ward; m. William Thomas Schrank, Nov. 24, 1976 (dec. Aug. 1993). Degree in nursing, U. Rochester, 1954, BSN, 1960, MS in Nursing Edn., 1961. Staff nurse dept. psychiatry U. Rochester, N.Y., 1954-56, team leader dept. medicine, 1956-60; instr. in pediatric nursing Genesee Hosp., Rochester, 1960-61; staff nurse eye surgery Children's Hosp. San Francisco, 1961; nurse pvt. duty surg. patients Presbyn. Med. Ctr., San Francisco, 1962; instr. medicine, surg. and ICU nursing Samuel Merritt Hosp. Sch. Nursing, Oakland, Calif., 1963-67, ret., 1967. With The Sculpture Group Gallery, Danville, Calif., 1995—, East Bay Women Artists, Oakland, Calif., 1993-99. Stephen min., Stephen tchg. leader, choir. Mem.: AAUW, Calif. Watercolor Assn. Republican. Presbyterian. Avocations: camping, traveling, singing, needlepoint. Home: 609 Maureen Ln Pleasant Hill CA 94523-2719 E-mail: shirleyschrank@earthlink.net.

SCHRANS, THOMAS, consumer products company executive; b. Gent, Belgium; BSEE, U. Gent, 1987; MSEE, Calif. Inst. Tech., Pasadena, 1988, PhD in Elec. Engring., 1994. Postdoctoral fellow IBM Corp., Hawthorne, NY, 1994—95; scientist Ortel Corp., Alhambra, Calif., 1995—98, sr. scientist, 1998—2000; tech. mgr. product devel. Agere Sys., Irwindale , 2000—. Fellow Fellowship, Belgian Am. Ednl. Found., 1987. Mem.: IEEE, Calif. Inst. Tech. Alumni Assn. (life). Office: Agere Sys 4920 Rivergrade Rd Baldwin Park CA 91706

SCHREADLEY, RICHARD LEE, writer, retired newspaper editor; b. Harrisburg, Pa., Jan. 3, 1931; s. Harry Leroy and Flora Rebecca (McQuilken) S.; m. Doris Arlene Sheaffer, Dec. 18, 1952; 1 child, Rhys Leroy. BA, Dickinson Coll., 1952; MA, Tufts U., 1968, MAL.D., 1969, PhD, 1972. Reporter The News and Courier, Charleston, S.C., 1975; asso. editor The Evening Post, 1975-76, editorial page editor, 1976-77, editor, 1977-81; exec. editor The Evening Post and The News and Courier, 1981-88; assoc. editor and sr. writer mil. and polit. affairs The News and Courier, 1989. Author: From the Rivers to the Sea, The United States Navy in Vietnam, 1992, Virtue and Valor, The Washington Light Infantry in Peace and in War, 1996. Chmn. Fgn. Affairs Forum of Charleston, 1987-88, mem. steering com., 1989. Served to comdr. USN, 1949-52, 56-73. Mem. Navy League, Ret. Officer Assn., Washington Light Infantry, German Friendly Soc. Charleston, Army-Navy Club of Washington, Country Club of Charleston. Home: 812 Clearview Dr Charleston SC 29412-4511 E-mail: rlschreadley@charleston.net.

SCHRECK, ROBERT A., JR. lawyer; b. Buffalo; BS in Bus. Adminstrn., Georgetown U., 1974; MBA, Northwestern U., 1975, JD, 1978. Bar: Ill. 1978. Ptnr. McDermott, Will & Emery, Chgo., 1978—. Mem. ABA. Office: McDermott Will & Emery 227 W Monroe St Ste 4400 Chicago IL 60606-5096 E-mail: rschreck@mwe.com.

SCHRECK, SCOTT JEFFREY, university program director, aerodynamicist; b. Coon Rapids, Iowa, Mar. 11, 1959; s. Paul Douglas and Mildred Mary (Friedman) S.; m. Christine Lucy Boyajian, Sept. 22, 1990. BS, USAF Acad., 1981; MS, Air Force Inst. Tech., 1983; PhD, U. Colo., 1989. Commd. capt. USAF, 1981—; football coach USAF Acad., Colorado Springs, 1981-82, program mgr., researcher Frank J. Seiler Rsch. Lab., 1989—; systems intergration engr. Wright Patterson AFB Strategic Systems Program Office, Dayton, Ohio, 1983-86.

SCHRECKENGAST, WILLIAM OWEN, lawyer; b. Greenwood, Ind., Oct. 14, 1926; s. Vernon Edward and Marthena O. (Mullinix) S.; m. Helen Margaret Sheppard, Nov. 11, 1949 (div.); children: Pamela, Sandra, James, John; m. Virginia Thompson, Mar. 14, 1990. LLB, Ind. U., 1956. Bar: Ind. 1956, U.S. Ct. Appeals (7th cir.) 1956, U.S. Dist. Ct. (so. dist.) Ind. 1956, U.S. Supreme Ct. 1967. Ptnr. Kitley, Pontius & Schreckengast, Beech Grove, Ind., 1957-59, Kitley & Schreckengast, Beech Grove, 1959-63, 78-82, Kitley, Schreckengast & Davis, Beech Grove, 1963-78, Schreckengast & Lovern, Indpls., 1982-88, Schreckengast Lovern & Helm, Indpls., 1988—. Chmn. Ind. campaign John Walsh for Sec. of State, Indls., 1958; chmn. ward Beech Grove Dems., 1958-60. Served to 1st sgt. U.S. Army, 1944-46, PTO. Mem. ABA, Ind. Bar Assn. (bd. mgrs. 1973-74, pres. citation 1974, pres. trial lawyer sect. 1977-78), Ind. Def. Lawyers Assn. (diplomat), Am. Judicature Soc., Nat. Inst. Trial Advocacy (teaching faculty 1980-85), Platform Soc. Clubs: Hillview Country (Franklin, Ind.). Lodges: Masons. Republican. Avocations: golf, flying. Home: 8026 Singleton St Indianapolis IN 46227-2568 Office: Schreckengast Lovern & Helm 8007 S Meridian St Ste 1 Indianapolis IN 46217-2922

SCHRECKER, ELLEN WOLF, historian, educator, editor; b. Phila., Aug. 4, 1938; d. Edwin II and Margaret Dannenbaum Wolf; m. John E. Schrecker, Feb. 18, 1962 (div. Mar. 1979); children: Michael Franz, Daniel Edwin; m. Marvin E. Gettleman, Aug. 28, 1981. BA, Radcliffe Coll., 1960, MA, 1962; PhD, Harvard U., 1974. Preceptor expository writing Harvard U., Cambridge, Mass., 1975-81; adj. asst. prof. history NYU, N.Y.C., 1983; program officer N.Y. Coun. for the Humanities, 1984-85; lectr. dept. history Princeton (N.J.) U., 1985-87; prof. history Yeshiva U., N.Y.C., 1987—. Adj. prof. Columbia U., N.Y.C., 1996. Author (with J. Schrecker): Mrs. Chiang's Szechwan Cookbook, 1976; author: The Hired Money, 1979; author: (with Craig Kaplan) Regulating the Intellectuals, 1983; author: No Ivory Tower: McCarthyism and the Universities , 1986, The Age of McCarthyism: A Brief History with Documents, 1994, Many Are the Crimes: McCarthyism in America, 1998; editor: Academe, 1998—2002. Chair N.Y. local chpt. Nat. Writers Union, N.Y.C., 1985-87; treas. Scholars, Artists and Writers for Social Justice, N.Y.C., 1996-98. Fellow Bunting Inst., Radcliffe Coll., Cambridge, 1977-78, rsch. fellow Harry S. Truman Libr., Independence, Mo., 1987, fellow Nat. Humanities Ctr., Research Triangle Park, 1994-95. Mem. AAUP, PEN, Am. Hist. Assn., Orgn. Am. Historians (program com. mem. 1995). Home: 771 W End Ave Apt 7D New York NY 10025-5538 E-mail: schreckr@ymail.yu.edu.

SCHRECKINGER, SY EDWARD, advertising executive, consultant; b. Bklyn., Jan. 10, 1937; s. Robert and Bessie (Gable) S.; m. Linda Fiarman, Mar. 4, 1962; children: Jamie Fran, Jon Gary. B.F.A., Pratt Inst., 1958. Art dir. Sudler and Hennesey, N.Y.C., 1958-61; sr. art dir. Marschalk Co., 1961-63; group supr. Grey Advt., 1963-66; v.p., assoc. creative dir. Hicks & Greist, 1966-69; sr. v.p., assoc. creative dir. Young & Rubicam Inc., 1969-88; advt. and mktg. cons. Oceanside, NY, 1988—2002; advt.-mktg. dir. Magnificent Muffin Corp., 1995—. Recipient Lion Venice Internat. Film Festival, 1972, Andy Ad Club, N.Y., 1965, 86, award Internat. Bus. Assn., Best award Hollywood Radio & TV Soc., 1971, Clio Am. TV Comml. Festival, 1967, 72, 82, 85, Effy, 1985. Jewish.

SCHREFFLER, NEIL FRANKLIN, lawyer; b. Danville, Pa., June 24, 1947; s. Franklin Harold and Lera Emma (Sheddy) S.; children: Elizabeth Ann Dollinger, Sept. 12, 1992; children: Gabrielle Freia, Franklin Henry. BBA, The Coll. of Ins., N.Y.C., 1970; JD, Syracuse U., 1973. Bar: N.Y. 1974, U.S. Dist. Ct. (ea. and so. dists.) N.Y. 1975, U.S. Dist. Ct. (no. dist.) 1992. Atty. Mony, N.Y.C., 1973-74; assoc. Lanzone & Assocs., 1974-77, Lester Schwab Katz & Dwyer, N.Y.C., 1977, Lipsig Sullivan & Liapakis, N.Y.C., 1977-79, Fuchsberg & Fuchsberg, N.Y.C., 1979-81; pvt. practice, 1981-88; ptnr. Schreffler & Gitlin, 1988—. Advocate Nat. Coll. Advocacy, Washington, 1996—; mem. Million Dollar Advocates Forum, 1995—; sec. Small Law Firm Mgmt. Com.-City Bar, N.Y.C., 1996—. Assoc. editor: Syracuse Law Rev., 1972. Mem. ATLA (sustaining, mem. M Club 1996—, sec. small office practice sect., editor sect. newsletter, mem. ATLA-PAC task force, mem. pub. edn. com.), Nat. Employment Lawyers Assn., N.Y. State Trial Lawyers Assn. (dir., sustaining mem. 1997—, membership com.), N.Y. County Lawyers Assn. (Supreme Ct. com., labor rels. and employment law com.), Rockland County Bar Assn., Trial Lawyers for Pub. Justice, N.Y. Athletic Club (sec. law com. 1995-97). Democrat. Avocations: opera, tennis, fly fishing, skiing. Home: 35 Rome Ave Apt 1B Bedford Hills NY 10507-2342 Address: Schreffler & Gitlin 60 E 42nd St Rm 2001 New York NY 10165-2099

SCHREFLER, BERNHARD ARIBO, civil engineering educator; b. Merano, Italy, Oct. 4, 1942; s. Ludwig and Eleonora (Tirler) Schrefler; m. Chantal Marie Saint-Blancat, Sept. 30, 1971; 1 child Lorna. Degree in civil engring., U. Padua (Italy), 1967; PhD, U. Wales, Swansea, 1984, DSc, 1992; PhD (hon.) , St. Petersburg State Tech. U., 1999, Tech. U. Lodz, Poland, 2002. Asst. lectr. in constrn. sci. U. Padua, 1969-70, asst. prof. structural mechanics, 1970-80, lectr. in computational mechanics, 1973-80, prof. structural mechanics, 1980-89, prof. constrn. sci., 1989—. Dir Inst Structural Mechs Univ Padua, 1988—96, dir dept structural and transp eng, 1996—2000; mem sci adv bd Int Ctr Numerical Methods Eng, 1993—; secy gen Int Ctr Mech Scis, 2000—. Author 22 books; mem. editl. bd. European Jour. Mechs., 1995—2000; mem. editl. bd.: Internat. Jour. Comm. in Applied Numerical Methods, Internat. Jour. Computer Applications in Tech., Internat. Jour. Numerical Methods in Engring., Jour. Mechanics Composite Materials and Structures , mem. editl. bd.: Jour. Engring. Analysis and Design, Computers and Structures, Archives Computational Methods in Engring. (handbook series) Theory and Engring. Applications Computational Methods, mem. editl. bd.: Computer Methods in Applied Mechanics and Engring., 2001. Fellow: Int Asn Computational Mechs (mem exec coun 2000—); mem.: Int Union Theoretical and Applied Mechs (mem cong comt 1998—, mem exec coun cong comt 2000—), Padua Acad Scis, Humanities and Arts, NY Acad Scis, European Solids Mechs Conf Comt (chmn 2001—), Euroscience, European Community Computational Methods in Applied Scis (mem mng coun 1993—94, bur mem 1996—), Rèunion Int des Labs d'Essais et Techerches sur les Matèriaux et Constrns, Italian Group Computational Mechs (coord 1995—2000), Rotary Padova. Avocations: tennis, skiing, mountaineering. Home: Via Cappelli 7 35123 Padua Italy Office: Dept Constrn & Transp Via Marzolo 9 35131 Padua Italy Fax: 39 049 827 5604. E-mail: bas@caronte.dic.unipd.it.

SCHREIBER, ALAN HICKMAN, lawyer; b. Muncie, Ind., Apr. 4, 1944; s. Ephriam and Clarrisa (Hickman) S.; m. Phyllis Jean Chamberlain, Dec. 22, 1972; children: Jennifer Aline, Brett Justin. Student, DePauw U., 1962-64; BS in Bus., Ind. U., 1966, JD, 1969. Bar: Fla. 1971, U.S. Dist. Ct. (so. dist.) Fla. Asst. State Atty.'s Office, Ft. Lauderdale, Fla., 1971-76; pub. defender 17th Jud. Cir., 1976—. Cons. Fla. Bar News on Criminal Law, 1982; lobbyist for indigent funding, Fla., 1980—; apptd. to Supreme Ct. Com. on Racial and Ethic Bias; co-chair Chiles-MacKay task force on criminal justice. Contbr. articles to profl. jours. Mem. Dem. Exec. Com., Ft. Lauderdale, 1980; mem. Plantation Dem. Club, 1983; campaign chmn. Goldstein for Atty. Gen. Fla., 1982. Named Young Dem. of Yr., Broward County Young Dems., 1980; Man of Yr., Jewish War Vets., 1982; recipient B'nai B'rith Pub. Servant award, 1990, Dem. of Yr. award 2000, Harry Galkin Meml. award 2002. Mem. Fla. Bar Assn., Broward County Bar Assn., ABA, Nat. Legal Aid Defenders Assn., Phi Alpha Delta. Home: 885 Orchid Dr Fort Lauderdale FL 33317-1221 Office: 201 SE 6th St Fort Lauderdale FL 33301-3303

SCHREIBER, AVERIL ELSPETH, retired retirement home administrator; b. London, Apr. 15, 1933; d. William John and Mary Brynhilde (Richardson) Stephenson; m. Gary Lee Pielemeier, June 21, 1957 (div. 1980); children: Ashley Lee, Heidi Ann; m. Robert Edwin Schreiber, July 4, 1981; stepchildren: Shey, Lana, Deborah, Robert William, Matthew. BA, U. Chgo., 1953. Program coord. Sr. Citizens Ctr. Greater Mpls., 1968-73; site coord. Title VII Nutrition Program, LaGrange, Ill., 1973-74; activity dir. S.W. Suburban Ctr. on Aging, 1974-77; dir. title VII nutrition program Feed Our Older DeKalb, Ill., 1977-80; adminstr. Barb City Manor for City of DeKalb's Housing Commn., 1980-95, ret., 1995. Cons. to author Terrence Edgar, Canton, Mo., 1984, for People of the Manor, 1984. Recipient Woman of Accomplishment award City of DeKalb. Mem. Altrusa Internat. (sec. DeKalb/Sycamore 1983-84, corr. sec. 1990-92). Avocations: gardening, choir, attendance at opera and symphony concerts. Home: 29500 Glidden Rd Kingston IL 60145-8338

SCHREIBER, BARBARA, artist; b. Balt., Mar. 25, 1953; d. Francis Ralph and Lillian (Silverman) Schreiber; m. M. William Ribarsky, Apr. 16, 1983; 1 child, Dinah Jan. Student, Atlanta Coll. Art, 1976; BFA, Md. Inst. Coll. Art, Balt., 1977. Employment counselor Ga. State U., Atlanta, 1977-80; conservation tech./writer Atlanta Cyclorama Conservation, 1980-82; asst. editor Art Papers, 1982-83; adminstrv. asst. Nexus Contemporary Art Ctr., 1983-85; op-ed illustrator Atlanta Jour. & Constn., 1990—91; assoc. editor Art Papers, Atlanta, 1985-97. Grants panelist, site evaluator Ga. Coun. for Arts, Atlanta, 1997—; columnist Art Papers, 1998—. (one-woman shows) Shedspace Exhbn. series , Atlanta, 2001, Sandler Hudson Gallery, Atlanta , 1991, 1998, 2000, 2001, Nexus Contemporary Art Ctr., Atlanta, 1994, (exhibitions) Ruby Green, Nashville, Tenn. , 2002, Eyedrum, Atlanta, 2002, Gallery at Green Street, Boston, Mass., 1998, PS1 , N.Y.C. , 1998, Bunde, Germany, 1997, Amerika Haus, Magdeburg, Berlin, Cologne, Hamburg, Munich, Frankfurt, Germany , 1996—97, artist/print collaborator Rolling Stone Press, 1995, (permanent collections) CGR Advisors, Atlanta, Chase Banking Corp. , N.Y.C., King and Spalding , Atlanta, Mus. Contemporary Art Ga., Nexus Contemporary Art Ctr. , Brenau U., Gainesville, Ga., Telfair Mus., Savannah, Ga. , others , columnist Art Papers, 1998—, (one-woman shows) Atlanta Contemporary Art Ctr., 2003, Mus. of Contemporary Art. Mem. artists' adv. bd. City Gallery at Chastain, 1990-93. Recipient award, Ga. Women in the Visual Arts, Silver medal for best column/nonprofit category, GAMMA awards Ga. Assn. Mags., 2001, Md. Senatorial scholarship, 1975—77; grantee, Ga. Coun. for the Arts, 1981, 1990, Dept. Cultural Affairs, 1981; scholar, Ford Found., 1975—77. Avocations: dancing, vocal music, hiking. Home and Office: 2429 King Arthur Cir NE Atlanta GA 30345-2117

SCHREIBER, BERTRAM MANUEL, mathematics educator; b. Seattle, Nov. 4, 1940; s. Isador and Amy (Hurwitz) S.; m. Rita Ruth Stusser, June 30, 1963; children: Susannah M. Schreiber Bechhofer, Deborah H. Schreiber Shapiro, Abraham D., Elisabeth T. Schreiber Seigel. BA, Yeshiva U., 1962; MS, U. Wash., 1966, PhD, 1968. Asst. prof. Wayne State U., Detroit, 1968-71, assoc. prof., 1971-78, prof., 1978—, chair dept. math., 1987-90. Vis. prof. Hebrew U., Jerusalem, 1975, 2000, Mich. State U., East Lansing, 1982-83, Nat. U. Singapore, 1992, U. New South Wales, Australia, 1992, Indian Statis. Inst., 1993, Tata Inst. Fund Res., Bombay, 1993, Bar Ilan U., 1993, Tel Aviv U., 1993, U. Utrecht, The Netherlands, 1993, U. Wroclaw, Poland, 1993, U. Paris VII, 1999, U. Granada, Spain, 1999-2000, U. Wash., Seattle, 2000. Contbr. articles to profl. jours. NSF grantee, 1968-87; Sci. and Engring. Rsch. Coun. Gt. Britain fellow U. Edinburgh, Scotland, 1976. Mem. Am. Math. Soc., Math. Assn. Am., Israel Math. Union, Edinburgh Math. Soc. Achievements include research in the fields of harmonic analysis, topological groups, and probability theory. Office: Wayne State U Dept Math Detroit MI 48202

SCHREIBER, DAVID M. lawyer, judge; b. Kansas City, Mo., Aug. 13, 1937; s. William and Hinda Gold Schreiber; m. Adrienne Rennie Ehre, May 31, 1959; children: Beth F., Kathy L. JD, LLB, U. Ariz., 1962; cert. jud. devel. adminstrv. law, Nat. Jud. Coll., 1997. Bar: Ariz., 1962, Nev., 1968, U.S. Ct. Appeals (9th cir.), 1978, U.S. Dist. Ct., 1968, U.S. Supreme Ct., 1972. Pvt. practice, Tucson, 1962-64; hearings officer, referee Indsl. Commn. Ariz., Phoenix, 1964-67; asst. v.p., house counsel First Western Savings & Loan, Las Vegas, Nev., 1967-69; chief dep. pub. defender Clark County Pub. Defenders Office, 1969-71; chief dep. dist. atty., counsel Nev. Juvenile Ct., 1971-76; pvt. practice, 1976-92; adminstrv. law judge State of Nev., Dept. Motor Vechiles and Pub. Safety, 1992—. Chmn. Cmty. Devel. Adv. com., Clark County, Nev., 1995-96. Recipient Law Enforcement Commendation medal Nat. Soc. Sons Am. Revolution, 1995 Mem. Nat. Assn. Adminstrv. Law Judges. Avocations: classical music, collecting art, politics. Home: 3310 Brookfield Dr Las Vegas NV 89120-1969 Office: State Nev Dept Motor Vechiles 2701 E Sahara Ave Las Vegas NV 89104-4119

SCHREIBER, EILEEN SHER, artist; b. Denver, 1925; d. Michael Herschel and Sarah Deborah (Tannenbaum) Sher; m. Jonas Schreiber, Mar. 27, 1945; children: Jeffrey, Barbara, Michael. Student, U. Utah, 1942-45, NYU ext., 1966-68, Montclair (N.J.) State Coll., 1975-79; also pvt. art study. Exhibited Morris Mus. Arts and Scis., Morristown, N.J., 1965-73, N.J. State Mus., 1969, Lever House, N.Y.C., 1971, Paramus (N.J.) Mus., 1973, Newark Mus., 1978, 1991-92, Am. Water Color Soc., Audubon Artists, N.A.D. Gallery, N.Y.C., Pallazzo Vecchio Florence, Italy, Art Expo 1987, 1988, India Mus., 1994, 95, Athens (Greece) Mus., 1996, 97; represented in permanent collections Tex. A&M U., Telesoft Inc., Phoenix, State of N.J., Morris Mus., Seton Hall U., Bloomfield (N.J.) Coll., Barclay Bank of Eng., N.J., Somerset Coll., NYU, Morris County State Coll., Broad Nat. Bank, Newark, Ind. Cmty. Bank, Consulting Actuaries, Internat., IBM, Am. Tel. Co., RCA, Johnson & Johnson, Champion Internat. Paper Co., Sony, Mitsubishi, Celanese Co., Squibb Corp., Nabisco, Nat. Bank Phila., Data Control, Ind. Cmty. Bank, Sperry Univac, Ga. Pacific Co., Pub. Svc. Co. N.J., Diane Levine Gallery, Boston, S.W. Gallery, Long Beach Island, N.J., others; also pvt. collections. Recipient awards N.J. Watercolor Soc., 1969, 72, 1st award in watercolor Hunterdon Art Ctr., 1972, Best in Show award Short Hills State Show, 1976, Tri-State Purchase award Somerset Coll., 1977, Art Expo, N.Y.C., 1987, 88, numerous others. Mem. Nat. Assn. Women Artists (chmn. watercolor jury, Collage award 1983, Marian Halpren Meml. award 1995), Nat., N.Y. Artists Equity, Printmaker Coun. Visual Artists (1st award in printmaking 1996), Women Visual Artists (Fla.). Home: 22 Powell Dr West Orange NJ 07052-1337 Office: 1011 Atlantic Ave Beach Haven NJ 08008

SCHREIBER, GEORGE RICHARD, association executive, writer; b. Ironton, Ohio, July 4, 1922; s. George Joseph and Marie Frances (Heitzman) S.; m. Veva Jeanette Hopkins, May 14, 1945; children— Susan (Mrs. Arlan Shorey), George, Ellen (Mrs. Norman Hodge). AB, St. Joseph's Coll., Rensselaer, Ind., 1943, L.H.D., 1974; MA, U. Chgo., 1944. Exec. editor Billboard mag., 1945-60; editor, pub. Vend mag., 1946-66; editorial dir. Billboard Publs., 1966-70; pres., chief exec. officer Nat. Automatic Mdsg. Assn., Chgo., 1970-88, pres. emeritus, 1988—; pres., chief exec. Sunrise Books, 1994—. Mem. staff and faculty U. Chgo., 1944-46 Author: Verses from the River Country, 1941, What Makes News, 1943, Automatic Selling, 1954, A Concise History of Vending in the U.S.A, 1965, revised 2d edit., 1990, Millenium edit., 1999, The Bobby Baker Affair— How to Make Millions in Washington, 1964, Vending For Investors-How to Spot Phony Deals, 1994, 2d edit., 1996; contbg. author: Handbook of Modern Marketing, 1986. Chmn. Glenview (Ill.) Plan Commn., 1962-64, mayor, 1964-67; chmn. Region 1, Chgo. Area Transp. Study Group, 1962-63; bd. dirs. Rockefeller Meml. Chapel, U. Chgo., 1944-45; trustee St. Joseph's Coll., 1964—, chmn., 1970-76, life trustee, 1978—. Recipient Jesse H. Neal award for editorial achievement, 1964; dedication of St. Joseph's Coll. (Ind.) G. Richard Schreiber Dept. Humanities, 1987. Mem. The Authors Guild Inc., Am. Bus. Press (editorial bd.), Assn. Econs. Council, Am. Soc. Assn. Execs., Tavern Club, Internat. Club, Tower Club. Home: 735 Ravine Ave Lake Bluff IL 60044-2625 E-mail: vevaj@aol.com.

SCHREIBER, HANS, pathology educator; MD, DMSc in Exptl. Pathology-Radiology, U. Freiburg, Germany, 1969; PhD in Immunology, U. Chgo., 1977. Mem. rsch. staff Oak Ridge (Tenn.) Nat. Lab., 1970-73; med. intern Moabit U. Hosp., Berlin, 1973-74; Nat. Cancer Inst. fellow in immunology U. Chgo., 1974-77, asst. prof. pathology, 1977-81, assoc. prof., 1982-85, prof., 1986—. Vis. prof. dept. genetics U. Calif., Berkeley, 1983-84. Contbr. articles to Nature, Procs. NAS USA, Sci., Jour. Exptl. Medicine, Jour. Immunology, Cancer Rsch., Jour. Cell. Biochemistry, Current Opinion in Immunology, Ann. Rev. Immunology, Transplantation, Annals N.Y. Acad. Scis., Clin. Immunology and Immunopathology, European Jour. Immunology, Immunity, also others; contbr. chpts. to books. Recipient fellow German Nat. Fellowship Found., 1966-70; faculty scholar Gould Found., 1980; Individual Nat. Rsch. Svc. award Nat. Cancer Inst., 1975-77, Rsch. Career Devel. award, 1978-83. Achievements include patent for development of device. Office: U Chgo 5841 S Maryland Ave # 1089 Chicago IL 60637-1463

SCHREIBER, HARRY, JR. management consultant; b. Columbus, Ohio, Apr. 1, 1934; s. C. Harry and Audrey (Sard) S.; m. Margaret Ruth Heinzman, June 12, 1955; children: Margaret Elizabeth Schreiber Yeager, Thomas Edward, Amy Katherine Schreiber Garcia. BS, MIT, 1955; MBA, Boston U., 1958. CPA, N.Y. Acct. truck and coach divsn. Gen. Motors Corp., Pontiac, Mich., 1955; instr. MIT, 1958-61; pres. Data-Service, Inc., Boston, 1960—64, Harry Schreiber Assocs., Wellesley, 1964; mgr., nat. dir. merchandising cons. Peat, Marwick, Mitchell & Co., N.Y.C., 1964—70, ptnr. Chgo., 1970-75; chmn. bd. Close, Martin, Schreiber & co., 1975-83; ptnr. Deloitte Haskins & Sells, 1983-85; chmn. bd. Harry Schreiber & Assocs., Ltd., 1985—. Mem. staff Work Simplification Conf., Lake Placid, N.Y., 1959-60; Tobe retailing lectr. Harvard Bus. Sch., 1963; lectr. indsl. engring. Northeastern U., 1958-61; lectr. info. sys. Babson Coll., 1962; lectr. Bridgeport Engring. Ins., 1962, Western Mich. U., 1975. Pub., Retail Working Papers, 1991—. Treas., Emmanuel Episcopal Ch., Chestertown, 1999—. 1st lt. AUS, 1956—58. Mem. Am. Inst. Indsl. Enrs. (chmn. data processing divsn. 1964-66, chpt. v.p. 1961, 65, chmn. retail industries divsn. 1976-78), Com. Internat. Congress Transp-.Confs., Assn. for Computing Machinery, Assn. for Sys. Mgmt., Inst. Mgmt. Scis., Retail Rsch. Soc., Retail Fin. Execs., Nat. Retail Fedn. (retail sys. specifications com., acctg. stds. com.), Food Distbn. Rsch. Soc. (dir. 1972-78, pres. 1974), Japan-Am. Soc. Chgo., MIT Faculty Club, Hidden Creek Country Club (Reston, Va.), Chester River Yacht and Country Club (Chestertown, Md.), Army and Navy Club (Washington), Plaza Club (Chgo.). Republican. Home: 105 High St Chestertown MD 21620-1515 E-mail: HarrySchreiber@compuserve.com.

SCHREIBER, JAMES RALPH, obstetrician, researcher; b. Rosebud, Tex., May 29, 1946; s. Lester B. and Jane Elinore (Hodges) Schreiber; m. Mary Celia Schmitt, Aug. 16, 1968; children: Lisa, Joseph, Laura, Cynthia. BA, Rice U., 1968; MD, Johns Hopkins U., 1972. Diplomate Am. Coll. Ob-gyn., Am. Bd. Reproductive Endocrinology. Intern. ob-gyn. U. So. Calif. Los Angeles County Hosp., 1972-73, resident ob-gyn., 1973-74, 76-78; fellow reproductive endocrinology NIH, Bethesda, Md., 1974-76; asst. prof. ob-gyn U. Calif., San Diego, 1978-82; assoc. prof. U. Chgo., 1982-87, prof., 1988-91; prof., chmn. dept. Washington U., St. Louis, 1991—. Contbr. articles to profl. jours. Grantee, NIH, 1978—. Mem.: Soc. Gynecologic Investigation. Home: 22 Frontenac Estates Saint Louis MO 63131-2600 Office: Washington U Sch Medicine Dept Ob-Gyn 4911 Barnes Hospital Plz Saint Louis MO 63110-1003 E-mail: schreiberj@msnotes.wustl.edu.

SCHREIBER, KURT GILBERT, lawyer; b. Milw., Aug. 22, 1946; s. Raymond R. and Mildred L. (Kleist) S.; m. Nelda Beth Van Buren, May 3, 1974; children— Katharine Anne, Matthew Edward AB in Econs., Cornell U., 1968; JD, U. Mich., 1971. Bar: Wis. 1971, Tex. 1979, Tenn. 1997. Internat. atty. Tenneco Internat. Holdings Co., London, 1974-78; atty. Tenneco Inc., Houston, 1978-80; 2d v.p., asst. gen. counsel Am. Gen. Corp., 1980-83, v.p., gen. counsel, 1983-84, sr. v.p., gen. counsel, 1984-93, sr. v.p., corp. sec.,

1993-94; pvt. practice, 1994-96; exec. v.p., gen. counsel Direct Gen. Corp., Nashville, 1996-98, pres., 1998—. Fellow Tex. Bar Found.; mem. ABA, Wis. Bar Assn., Tex. Bar Assn., Tenn. Bar Assn., Cumberland Club. Home: 524 Turtle Creek Dr Brentwood TN 37027-5617

SCHREIBER, MAE NYUHA, librarian; b. Wahiawa, Hawaii, May 3, 1941; d. Bert Kyuske and Masako Miyashiro Nyuha; m. Karl J.Schreiber, Aug. 29, 1964; children: Tanya, Erich, John, Michael. BS in Edn., Ohio State U., 1963; MLS in Libr. and Info. Sci., Simmons Coll., 1988. Ref. libr. U. Akron, Ohio, 1989-92, asst. prof. bibliog., 1992-97, assoc. prof. bibliog., 1998—. Author: International Trade Sources: A Research Guide; contbr. articles to profl. jours. Mem. ALA, AAUP, Assn. Coll. and Rsch. Librs. (chair racial and ethnic diversity com. 1998-2000), Govt. Documents Round Table, Women in Higher Edn. (v.p. Akron chpt. 2000-01), Govt. Documents Round Table of Ohio (sec./treas. 1996-98). Office: Univ Akron Bierce Libr 315 Buchtel Ave Akron OH 44325-1709 E-mail: mael@uakron.edu.

SCHREIBER, MARVIN MANDEL, agronomist, educator; b. Springfield, Mass., Oct. 17, 1925; s. William and Florence Schreiber; m. Phyllis E. Altman, Dec. 18, 1949; 1 child, Michelle. BS, U. Mass., 1950; MS, U. Ariz., 1951; PhD, Cornell U., 1954. Asst. prof. dept. agronomy Cornell U., Ithaca, N.Y., 1954-59; assoc. prof. dept. botany and plant pathology Purdue U., West Lafayette, Ind., 1959-73—, prof., 1973—; rsch. agronomist Agrl. Rsch. Svc. USDA, 1959—. Fellow AAAS, Am. Soc. Agronomy, Weed Sci. Soc. Am.; mem. Internat. Weed Sci. Soc. (pres. 1979-81), Controlled Release Soc., Coun. Agrl. Sci. and Tech., Sigma Xi. Avocations: golf, gardening. Office: Dept Botany & Plant Pathology Purdue U Lilly Hall Life Scis West Lafayette IN 47907

SCHREIBER, PAUL SOLOMON, lawyer; b. Krakow, Poland, Mar. 29, 1941; came to U.S., 1949; s. John and Betty (Silber) S.; m. Joan A. Perlmutter, Mar. 20, 1971; children: Douglas Arun, Stacey Lauren. BS, CCNY, 1963; LLB, NYU, 1966, LLM, 1967; postgrad., U. Paris, 1967-68. Bar: N.Y. 1966. Assoc. Marshal, Bratter, Greene, Allison & Tucker, N.Y.C., 1969-76, ptnr., 1976-82, Kramer, Levin, Naftalis, Nessen, Kamin & Frankel, N.Y.C., 1982-94, Shearman & Sterling, N.Y.C., 1994—. Bd. dirs. Harbor Trust Co., Hoboken, N.J., 1985-92. Editor: Annual Survey Am. Law; co-author articles, papers and revs. Pres. Park Ave. Synagogue, N.Y.C., 1985—; bd. dirs. Am. Friends of the Rambam Med. Ctr., N.Y.C., 1989-99, N.Y.C. chpt. Nat. Multiple Sclerosis Soc., 1991—, Sch. for Strings, 1994-96; bd. overseers Rabbinical Sch. Jewish Theol. Sem., 1995-96. Arthur Garfield Hayes fellow; Ford Found. fellow. Democrat. Jewish. Office: Shearman & Sterling 599 Lexington Ave Fl C2 New York NY 10022-6069

SCHREIBMAN, THELMA RABINOWITZ, psychotherapist, educator; b. N.Y.C., July 29, 1945; d. Philip and Gussie (Lubowsky) Rabinowitz; divorced; children: Andrea Rudolph, Jill Schreibman. BA, Coll. of New Rochelle, 1984; MSW, Fordham U., 1989; postgrad., Riverdale Sch. Modern Psychoanalysis. Cert. social worker N.Y. Coord. Albert Einstein Hosp., Bronx, N.Y., 1977-84; adminstr. Goldwater Meml. Hosp., N.Y.C., 1984-96; pvt. practice psychotherapist Bronx and New Rochelle, N.Y., 1984—; adj. prof. Coll. of New Rochelle, 1990—. Analyst, tng. supr. Riverdale Sch. Modern Psychotherapy, Bronx, 1985-95. Mem. NASW, N.Y. State Med. Staff Adminstrs. Avocations: photography, swimming. Home: 463 Pelham Rd New Rochelle NY 10805-2240

SCHREIER, CARL ALAN, writer, publisher; b. Lewistown, Mont., June 2, 1956; s. John Ambrose and Goldie (Thomas) S. BS, U. Mont., 1979; postgrad., U. Wyo., 1980, U. Utah, 1981. Mgr. Yellowstone Nat. Park, 1976-80, naturalist, 1979-81, 87-89; dir. Wyo. Waterfowl Trust, Cody, 1985-87; pub. Homestead Publishing, Moose, Wyo., 1981—. Leader African Wildlife, Nairobi, Kenya, 1980-81. Author: Yellowstone Explorers Guide, 1982, A Field Guide to Yellowstone's Geysers, 1992, A Field Guide to Wildflowers, 1996, Banff-Jasper Explorers Guide, 1999. Bd. dirs. Wyo. Ctr. for the Book. Office: Homestead Pub PO Box 193 Moose WY 83012-0193 also: Denver CO 80203 also: San Francisco CA 94114

SCHREIER, PETER, tenor; b. Meissen, Germany, July 29, 1935; Ed., Dresden Hochschule für Musik, Germany. With Dresden State Opera, Germany, 1959-63, Berlin Staatsoper, Germany, 1963. Appearances include Vienna State Opera, Salzburg Festival, La Scala, Milan, Sadler's Wells, London, Met. Opera, N.Y.C., Teatro Colon, Buenos Aires; recital debut London, 1978; debut as conductor, 1969; has conducted recordings of several choral works by J.S. Bach and Mozart. Office: Kammersänger Calberlastr 13 D-01326 Dresden Germany

SCHREINER, ALBERT WILLIAM, physician, educator; b. Cin., Feb. 15, 1926; s. Albert William and Ruth Mary (Neuer) S.; m. Jean Tellstrom, Dec. 12, 1953; 1 child, David William. BS, U. Cin., 1947, MD, 1949. Diplomate Am. Bd. Internal Medicine. Clin. investigator VA Hosp., Cin., 1957-59, chief med. service, 1959-68, dir. dept. internal medicine, 1968-93; dir. resident program internal medicine Christ Hosp., 1978-87; mem. faculty U. Cin. Coll. Medicine, 1955—, assoc. prof. medicine, 1962-67, prof. internal medicine, 1967-98, emeritus prof. internal medicine, 1998—; attending physician Cin. Gen. Hosp., 1957—. Cons. to med. dir. Gen. Electric, 1987-96; med. dirs. United Home Care Hospice, 1993-99, United Home Care Agy. Contbr. articles to profl. jours. Bd. dirs., chmn. health com. Cmty. Action Commn., 1968-71; trustee Drake Meml. Hosp., 1975-78, Leukemia Found. Southwest Ohio, Cancer Control, Am. Cancer Soc., bd. dirs. Hamilton County unit, 1990; bd. dirs., chair profl. affairs com. United Home Care Agy., 1998; bd. dirs. Gamble Inst. Med. Rsch., Cin., 1991-96, Signo O The Cross Housing for the Homeless, 2001-. Fellow: ACP; mem.: Am. Soc. Clin. Rsch. Program Dirs. Internal Medicine, Assn. Program Dirs. Internal Medicine, Clin. Soc. Internal Medicine (pres. 1979—80), Ohio Soc. Internal Medicine (trustee 1978, sec.-treas. 1981—85, v.p. 1982—83, pres. 1984—85), Ohio Med. Assn., Am. Fedn. Clin. Rsch., N.Y. Acad. Scis., Am. Cancer Soc. (bd. dirs. Hamilton County unit 1990—92), Am. Leukemia Soc. (med. adv. exec. bd.), Phi Beta Kappa, Sigma Xi. Roman Catholic. Home: 8040 S Clippinger Dr Cincinnati OH 45243-3248 Office: 2139 Auburn Ave Cincinnati OH 45219-2906

SCHREINER, HELEN ANN, special education educator; b. Lancaster, Pa., Oct. 1, 1949; AA, York Coll. of Pa., 1969; B of Edn., Millersville U., 1971, MEd, 1979. Cert. , spl. edn. tchr., supr., Pa. Tchr. Solanco Sch. Dist., Quarryville, Pa., 1971—. Adult edn. tchr./GED, Intermediate Unit 13, Lancaster, Pa., 1974-78. Recipient mini-computer grant, Intermediate Unit 13, 1983. Mem. Coun. for Exceptional Children, Assn. for Retarded Citizens, Learning Disabilities Assn., United Comml. Travelers, Phi Delta Kappa, Pi Lambda Theta, Fraternal Order of Police. Democrat. Roman Catholic. Avocations: travel, collecting menus from restaurants. Home: 5 Bentley Ln Lancaster PA 17603-6203 Office: Solanco Sch Dist 585 Solanco Rd Quarryville PA 17566-9615

SCHREINER, JOHN CHRISTIAN, economics consultant, software publisher; b. Los Angeles, Nov. 2, 1933; s. Alexander and Margaret S.; m. Marie Nielsen, June 19, 1967; children: Christian Alexander, Carl Arthur, Elizabeth, Nathan Alexander. BSM.E., U. Utah, 1958; MBA, Harvard U., 1960; PhD, UCLA, 1970. Chartered fin. analyst. Design engr. Eimco Corp., Salt Lake City and N.Y.C., 1957-59; credit exec. James Talcott, Inc., N.Y.C. and Boston, 1960-65; lectr. mgmt. U. Utah, 1965-66; mem. faculty Grad. Sch. Mgmt., U. Minn., Mpls., 1969-84, chmn. dept. fin. and ins., 1973-74, 76-81; pres. The Sebastian Group, Inc., 1984—. Dir. Deluxe Corp.; cons. to corps. and govt. agys. Co-author: Executive Recruiting: How Companies Obtain Management Talent, 1960; contbr. articles to profl. jours. Mem. Fin. Execs. Inst., Fin. Analysts Fedn., Tau Beta Pi, Phi Kappa Phi. Republican. Mem. Ch. Jesus Christ of Latter-day Saints (missionary, Ger. 1953-56). Club: Harvard Bus. Sch. Minn. Office: The Sebastian Group Inc 5730 Duluth St Minneapolis MN 55422-4000

SCHRENK, GARY DALE, foundation executive; b. San Jose, Calif., Apr. 29, 1949; s. Robert Shepard and Katherine Mildred (Grant) S.; m. Rhonda Lynn King, Oct. 9, 1981 (div. Jan. 1989); children: Stephen, Kristen, James. BA in Comm., Am. U., 1970; M in Nonprofit Mgmt., Regis U., 2002. TV dir. WTOP (now WUSA), Washington, 1971-73, KBTV (now KUSA), Denver, 1973-75; with Denver Area Boy Scouts Am., 1975-80; regional dir. St. Jude Children's Rsch. Hosp., Memphis, 1980-83; dir. devel. Denver Art Mus., 1983-85; asst. dir. devel. The Children's Hosp., Denver, 1985-87; pres. North Colo. Med. Ctr. Found., Greeley, 1987—. Dir., instr. Fast Start Course, 1985—; pres. Monfort Children's Clinic, Greeley, 1994-2001 Pres. Vision Together, Weld County, Colo., 1994-95; chmn., founding dir. Weld Citizen Action Network, 1995-98, 2000—; founding dir. First Steps Weld County, 1993-99; chmn. Weld Cmty. Health Coalition, 1992-98; chmn. pub. support com. Team Colo. ARC, 1997—. Recipient Disting. Citizen award Highlanders, Denver, 1974. Mem. Assn. Fundraising Profls. (mem. nat. found. bd. 1998—, nat. assembly 1994-98, bd. dirs. Colo. chpt. 1979-2000, pres. 1984), Colo. Assn. Nonprofit Orgns. (founding dir. 1987-92), Rotary, Greeley Country Club, Tahosa Alumni Assn. (past pres., past chair). Methodist. Avocation: golf. Home: 4956 13th St Greeley CO 80634-2215 Office: North Colo Med Ctr Found 1801 16th St Greeley CO 80631-5154 E-mail: gary.schrenk@bannerhealth.com.

SCHRENKO, LINDA C. state agency administrator; b. July 24, 1949; m. Frank Schrenko; 1 child, Katherine. BA in Elem. Edn., Augusta Coll., 1972, EdS in Adminstrn. and Supervision, 1986; MEd in Counseling, Ga. So. U., 1982. Tchr. 7th grade Richmond County (Ga.) Schs., 1972-74; tchr. 5th grade South Columbia (Ga.) Elem., 1974-76, tchr. Title I grades 1-6, 1976-77, tchr. 2nd grade, 1977-81, asst. prin., 1984-86; tchr. gifted program grades K-3 Columbia County Schs., 1981-82; counselor Evans Middle Sch., Columbia County, 1982-84; prin. South Columbia (Ga.) Elem., 1986-90; tchr. gifted program grades K-3 Columbia County Schs., 1981-82; counselor Evans Middle Sch., Columbia County, 1982-84; nat. and internat. edn. cons., 1990-94; supt. schs. Ga. Dept. Edn., Atlanta, 1994—. Bd. dirs. Coun. Sch. Performance, Edn. Commn. of States, Ga. Child Care Coun., Ga. Pub. Telecomm. Commn.; lectr. in field. Author: Teaching in the Learner Centered School. Past pres. Ctrl. Savannah Regional Area Humane Soc.; mem. Columbia County Humane Soc.; past pres. Columbia County Fedn. Republican Women; mem. Ga. Republican Found., Women Who Win.; mem. Kiokee Bapt. Ch., Appling, Ga. Named one of 100 Most Powerful and Influential People in Ga., Ga. Trend Mag., 1995-96. Mem. ASCD, Profl. Assn. Ga. Educators, Ga. Assn. Elem. Sch. Prins., Phi Delta Kappa.

SCHRETER, CAROL ANN, social worker, gerontologist, writer; b. Balt., Nov. 1, 1947; d. A. Harvey and Phyllis (Kolker) S.; m. Jonas J. Fendell, Aug. 12, 1984 (dec. 1994). BA, U. Pa., 1969; MSW, Temple U., 1973; PhD in Social Work, Bryn Mawr (Pa.) Coll., 1983. Caseworker Md. Dept. Welfare, Balt., 1969-70; therapist psychiatry dept. Temple Hosp., Phila., 1970-71; sr. social worker Waxter Ctr. for Sr. Citizens, Balt., 1973-79; freelance writer and researcher, 1976—. Coord. found. funds Assoc. Jewish Charities, Balt., 1983-86; cons. Balt. City Area on Aging, 1982, Shared Housing Resource Ctr., Phila., 1981-84, Elvirita Lewis Found., Calif., 1986-91, Grantmakers in Aging, Flint, Mich., 1986-91, Retirement Rsch. Found., Park Ridge, Ill., 1990-91; cons. AARP, 1992—. Co-editor: Allies and Adversaries: the Impact of Managed Care on Mental Health Services, 1994, Managing Care, Not Dollars: the Continuum of Mental Health Services, 1996; contbr. articles to profl. jours. and consumer mags. Home and Office: 1905 Dixon Rd Baltimore MD 21209-3507 E-mail: cschreter@earthlink.net.

SCHREUR, BARBARA, computer science educator; b. Neuendettelsau, Germany, Jan. 4, 1944; came to U.S., 1952; d. Franz and Elsbeth (Gasner) Fischer; m. Julian Jay Schreur, June 4, 1966; children: Alex, George. BA, Manhattanville Coll., 1964; MA, U. Ariz., 1969; PhD, Fla. State U., 1979. Physicist CBS Labs., Stamford, Conn., 1965-66; grad. assist. U. Ariz., Tucson, 1967-70; tchr. Valdosta (Ga.) H.S., 1971-74; grad. assist. Fla. State U., Tallahassee, 1974-80; asst. prof. Tex. A&M U., Kingsville, Tex., 1980-86, assoc. prof., 1986-97, prof., 1997—. Cons. Coastal Bd. Coun. of Govts., Corpus Christi, Tex., 1990—93. Recipient presentation of shuttle hardware and software, NASA, 1996—98, software engrng. initiative, NASA, Huntsville, Ala., 1998—2002, software reuse libr., NASA, 2000—02; fellow Summer faculty fellow, 1993, 1994, 1995. Mem. IEEE, Am. Computing Machinery, Tex. Acad. Sci, Am. Astron. Soc. (divsn. Dynamical Astronomy). Avocations: reading, golf. Home: 555 Elizabeth Ave Kingsville TX 78363-6741 Office: Tex A&M U-Kingsville MSC 192 Kingsville TX 78364-0192 E-mail: bschreur@ieee.org.

SCHREURS, BRIAN FREDERICK, editor, publisher; b. Wakefield, Mass., June 4, 1974; s. Stephen Frederick and Susan Jeanette (Clement) S. BS in Journalism, W.Va. U., 1997. Pres. Coltrane Prodns., Midland, Va., 1989—; tech. editor Silver Chips, Silver Spring, Md., 1990-92; reporter, columnist The Daily Athenaeum, Morgantown, 1993-96; promotion designer WCLG AM/FM, W.Va., 1997; editor-in-chief The Inn Times, Washington, 1997; editor State Tax One Disc, Arlington, Va, 1998-2000; tech. editor Sci. Applications Internat. Corp., Vienna, 2000—. Author: S.H.A.L.T.: The Book, 1990, The Hot Rodder's Quck Reference, 1995, Insert Stupid Catchphrase Here, 1997, Hodge Podge, 1997, Loose Ends, 1998. Patrolman Morgantown Police Res., 1996. With U.S. Army, 1995-97. Mem. NRA, Soc. Profl. Journalists, Sports Car Club of Am. Avocations: hot rodding, target shooting, amateur racing. Office: SAIC 1953 Gallows Rd Vienna VA 22182

SCHREYER, LESLIE JOHN, lawyer; b. N.Y.C., Apr. 11, 1946; s. Oscar and Greta (Loebl) S.; m. Judith Camps, Sept. 25, 1994; 1 child, Gabrielle. BA, Columbia U., 1967; LLB, Yale U., 1970; LLM in Taxation, N.Y.U., 1977. Bar: N.Y. 1971. Assoc. Chadbourne & Parke, N.Y.C., 1970-78, ptnr., 1978-81, 83—; dep. internat. tax counsel U.S. Treasury Dept., 1981-83; gen. counsel GLG Ptnrs. Svcs. Ltd., 2000—, also bd. dirs. Adj. assoc. prof. law NYU, 1990-97; cons. Am. Law Inst., Fed. Income Tax Project on Internat. Aspects of U.S. Income Taxation, 1983-91. Author: (with others) Foreign Tax Credit, 1980; contbr. numerous articles to profl. jours. Bd. dirs. The Poster Soc., N.Y.C., 1985-93, 910 Park Ave Corp., 1993-94. Mem. ABA, Internat. Bar Assn., Internat. Fiscal Assn., N.Y. State Bar Assn., Assn. of Bar of City of N.Y., Phi Beta Kappa. Republican. Home: 60 E End Ave New York NY 10028-7907 Office: Chadbourne & Parke 30 Rockefeller Plz Fl 31 New York NY 10112-0129 E-mail: leslie.j.schreyer@chadbourne.com., les@glgpartners.com.

SCHREYER, WILLIAM ALLEN, retired investment firm executive; b. Williamsport, Pa., Jan. 13, 1928; s. William L. and Elizabeth (Engel) S.; m. Joan Legg, Oct. 17, 1953; 1 child, DrueAnne Frazier. BA, Pa. State U., 1948. With Merrill Lynch, Inc. and predecessors, N.Y.C., 1948-93; CEO Merrill Lynch & Co., 1984-92, chmn., 1985-93; chmn. emeritus, 1993—. Portfolio dir. Marbo, Inc. Trustee Ctr. for Strategic and Internat. Studies, Pa. State U., 1986—, chmn. bd. trustees, 1993-96. With USAF, 1955-56. Mem. Econ. Club N.Y., River Club, Links Club, Saturn Club, Springdale Golf Club, Bedens Brook Club, Eldorado Country Club, Georgetown Club, Met. Club, Old Baldy Club, Nassau Club, The Carnegie Club at Skibo Castle, Knights of Malta. Roman Catholic. Office: Merrill Lynch & Co Inc 800 Scudders Mill Rd Plainsboro NJ 08536-1606

SCHRIBMAN, SHELLEY IRIS, database engineer, consultant; b. Weehawken, N.J., July 29, 1944; d. George and Mildred (Kamen) Shulman; m. Marshall Melvin Schribman, Aug. 26, 1979. BFA cum laude, Art Inst. Chgo., 1966; MBA, Simmon Coll. Grad. Sch. Mgmt., 1982. Asst. dir. Advanced Inst. Devel. Am. Repertory Theatre, N.Y.C., 1970-71; ptnr. Sir Charles Cleaning Co., Boston, 1982-83; owner SIS Internat., 1984-87; database developer (freelance), 1995-2000; sys. analyst Dept. Pub. Health, 2000—. Cons. Boston Computer Soc., 1995-96, Catchpole Corp., Wellesley, Mass., 1996-97, Ptnrs. In Home Care Inc., Missoula, Mont., 1996-97; designer, developer Shulman Bankruptcy Program, 1998-99 Pres. Orgn. for Rehab. Through Tng., Boston, 1986-88; mem. LWV, Boston (housing specialist 1989-91, pres. 1990-91, nat. credentials chairperson 1991-92). Mem. Belmont Dramatic Club, Alumni Theatre, Lexington Players. Jewish. Avocations: acting, composing music. Home: 8 Whittier Pl Boston MA 02114-1402 Office: Dept Public Health 250 Washington St Fl 5 Boston MA 02108-4619 E-mail: shelleyischribman@rcn.com., Shelley.Schribman@state.ma.us.

SCHRICK, JERRY L. minister; b. Riverside, Calif., Dec. 29, 1959; s. Marvin and Patricia Mae (Taitt) S.; m. Debra Lynn Schrick, July 23, 1983; children: Rebecca, Andrea, Catherine, Jeremiah. BA, Christian Heritage Coll., El Cajon, Calif., 1984; postgrad., Dallas Theol. Sem., 1984-89; MDiv, Biola U., LaMirada, Calif., 1991. Lic. to ministry, Bapt. Ch., 1992. Min. Calvary Cmty. Ch., Beaumont, Calif., 1992—. Officer, bd. trustees S.W. Bapt. Conf., West Covina, Calif., 1997-2000, chmn., 2002-, chair ch. svcs. coord. com., 1994-95; reserve chaplain Riverside County Fire Dept., 1995-97. Co-author: (booklet) Guidelines for Designing HIV/AIDS Policy for the Local Church, 1995. Republican. Avocations: singing, reading. Office: Calvary Cmty Church 1252 Beaumont Ave Beaumont CA 92223-1506

SCHRICKER, ETHEL KILLINGSWORTH, retired business management consultant; b. Hagerstown, Md., July 22, 1937; d. Lloyd Granville and Ethel Mull; children: Jeanne, Lori, Jerri. BA in Mgmt., Hood Coll., 1994. Vol. Literacy Coun., Frederick, 1976-84, Dept. Social Svcs., Frederick, 1984; active Frederick County Commn. for Women, 1996, Nat. Presbyn. Ch., Washington. Named Bus. Woman of Yr., 1991, Frederick Bus. and Profl. Women. Mem. Assn. Sch. Bus. Ofcls. (chairperson seminar devel. com. 1990-94, dir. emeritus 1999-2000), Frederick County Assn. Adminstrv. and Supervisory Pers. 1987-94, Frederick County C. of C., Frederick County Advt. Fedn. 1995-97, Rotary Club of Carroll Creek (pres. 1999-2000), Toastmasters Internat. (area gov. 1991-92, pub. rels. 1991-93, v.p. pub. rels. 1995-97). Avocations: photography, bicycling, watercolor. Home: PO Box 15 Frederick MD 21705-0015

SCHRIEFFER, JOHN ROBERT, physics educator, science administrator; b. Oak Park, Ill., May 31, 1931; s. John Henry and Louise (Anderson) Schrieffer; m. Anne Grete Thomsen, Dec. 30, 1960; children: Anne Bolette, Paul Karsten, Anne Regina. BS, MIT, 1953; MS, U. Ill., 1954, PhD, 1957, ScD, 1974, Tech. U., Munich, 1968, U. Geneva, 1968, U. Pa., 1973, U. Cin., 1977, U. Tel Aviv, 1987, U. Ala., 1990. NSF postdoctoral fellow U. Birmingham, England, Niels Bohr Inst., Copenhagen, 1957—58; asst. prof. U. Chgo., 1958—59; asst. prof., then assoc. prof. U. Ill., 1959—62; prof. U. Pa., Phila., 1962—79, Mary Amanda Wood prof. physics, 1964—79; Andrew D. White prof. at large Cornell U., 1969—75; prof. U. Calif., Santa Barbara, 1980—91, Chancellor's prof., 1984—91, dir. Inst. for Theoretical Physics, 1984—89; Univ. prof. Fla. State U., Tallahassee, 1992—, Univ. Eminent Scholar prof., 1995—, chief scientist Nat. High Magnetic Field Lab., 1992—. Pres.'s com. Nat. Medal of Sci., 1996—. Author: Theory of Superconductivity, 1964. Recipient Comstock prize, NAS, 1968, Nobel prize for Physics, 1972, John Ericsson medal, Am. Soc. Swedish Engrs., 1976, Alumni Achievement award, U. Ill., 1979, Nat. medal of Sci., 1984; fellow Guggenheim, Copenhagen, 1967, Los Alamos Nat. Lab., Exxon faculty, 1979—89. Fellow: Am. Phys. Soc. (v.p. 1994, pres.-elect 1995, pres. 1996, past pres. 1997, Oliver E. Buckley solid state physics prize 1968); mem.: NAS (coun. 1990—), Acad. Sci. USSR, Royal Danish Acad. Scis. and Letters, Am. Acad. Arts and Scis. Office: Fla State Univ NHMFL 1800 E Paul Dirac Dr Tallahassee FL 32310-3748*

SCHRIER, ARNOLD, historian, educator; b. N.Y.C., May 30, 1925; s. Samuel and Yetta (Levine) S.; m. Sondra Weinshelbaum, June 12, 1949; children— Susan Lynn, Jay Alan, Linda Lee, Paula Kay. Student, Bethany Coll., W.Va., 1943-44, Ohio Wesleyan U., 1944-45; BS, Northwestern U., 1949, MA, 1950, PhD (Social Sci. Research Council fellow, Univ. fellow), 1956. Asst. prof. history U. Cin., 1956-61, assoc. prof., 1961-66, prof., 1966-95, dir. grad. studies history, 1969-78, Walter C. Langsam prof. modern European history, 1972-95; Walter C. Langsam prof. history emeritus, 1995—. Vis. asst. prof. history Northwestern U., Evanston, Ill., 1960; vis. assoc. prof. history Ind. U., Bloomington, 1965-66; vis. lectr. Russian history Duke U., 1966; disting. vis. prof. U.S. Air Force Acad., 1983-84; dir. NDEA Inst. World History for Secondary Sch. Tchrs., U. Cin., 1965; Am. del. Joint U.S.-USSR Textbook Study Commn., 1989. Author: Ireland and the American Emigration, 1958, reissued, 1970, paperback edit., 1997, The Development of Civilization, 1961-62, Modern European Civilization, 1963, Living World History, 1964, rev., 1993, Twentieth Century World, 1974, History and Life: the World and Its People, 1977, rev., 1993, A Russian Looks at America, 1979. Pres. Ohio Acad. History, 1973-74, Midwest Slavic Conf., 1980. Served with USNR, 1943-46, 52-54. Recipient Disting. Svc. award Ohio Acad. History, 1992; Am. Council Learned Socs. fgn. area fellow, 1963-64 Mem. World History Assn. (v.p. 1986-88, pres. 1988-90). Home: 10 Diplomat Dr Cincinnati OH 45215-2073 Office: Univ Cincinnati Dept History Mail Location 373 Cincinnati OH 45221-0001 E-mail: arnsond@aol.com.

SCHRIER, RUTH, artist, educator; b. Bklyn., May 20, 1924; d. Morris And Bella (Balopole) Feinman; m. Aaron Schrier, Feb. 20, 1963; children: Tina, Paul. BA, Calif. State U., Northridge, 1962; MFA, U. So. Calif., 1970. Art tchr. Clark Jr. High, Glendale, Calif., 1962-63, Glendale C.C., 1963-70; prof. Calif. State U., Northridge, 1970-95. One-woman shows include Mcpl. Art Gallery, L.A., 1976, Faculty Ctr., Calif. State U., Northridge, 1978, Oviatt Libr., 1982, Gallery II, 1984, N. Gallery, 1993, Homestead Savings, Sausalito, Calif., 1978, Glendale C.C., 1979, Office Chancellor, Long Beach, Calif., 1979, Orlando Gallery, 1999, Sherman Oaks, Calif., 1996; exhibited in group shows at Fine Arts Main Gallery, Calif. State U., Carnegie Mus., 1998, Northridge, 1979, Ariz. Show, 1983, Descanso Gardens Hospitality Ho., La Canada, Calif., 1984, Encino (Calif.) Ter. Ctr., 1987, Creative Arts Ctr., Burbank, Calif., 1993. Home: 7127 Goodland Ave North Hollywood CA 91605-5028

SCHRIER, SHEILA SUE, social worker; b. Cleve., Jan. 22, 1943; d. Samuel Z. and Dorothy (Gordon) Desatnik; m. Michael I. Schrier, June 27, 1965; children— Bethany, Daniel. B.A., Calif. State U.-Los Angeles, 1966; Caseworker, Urban League, Syracuse, N.Y., 1975-77, Salvation Army, 1977-78, ARC, Los Angeles, 1978— . Mem. Nat. Assn. Social Workers. Home: 1912 Monon St Los Angeles CA 90027-3202 Office: ARC Arc 9200 Ate St South Gate CA 90280 also: 2700 Wilshire Blvd Los Angeles CA 90057-3202

SCHRIER, STANLEY LEONARD, hematologist, educator; b. N.Y.C., Jan. 2, 1929; s. Harry and Nettie (Schwartz) S.; m. Peggy Helen Pepper, June 6, 1953; children: Rachel, Leslie, David. AB, U. Colo., 1949; MD, Johns Hopkins U., 1954. Diplomate Am. Bd. Internal Medicine (chmn. subsplty. bd. hematology). Intern Osler Med. Service, Johns Hopkins Hosp., 1954-55; resident U. Mich., Ann Arbor, 1955-56, U. Chgo. Hosp., 1958-59; sr. asst. surgeon USPHS, 1956-58; instr. medicine Stanford Sch. Medicine, Calif., 1959-60, asst. prof. medicine, 1960-63, assoc. prof., 1963-72, prof. medicine, 1972-95, chief divsn. hematology, 1968-94. Vis. scientist Weizmann Inst., Rehovot, Israel, 1967-68; vis. prof. Oxford U., Eng., 1975-76, Hebrew U., Jerusalem, 1982-83 John and Mary Markle scholar, 1961; recipient Kaiser award Stanford U., 1972, Kaiser award Stanford U., 1974, 75, David Rytand award, 1982, Eleanor Roosevelt Union Internationale Contre le Cancer award 1975-76, Albion Walter Hewlett award, 1996. Fellow ACP; mem. Am. Soc. Hematology (v.p. 2002), Am. Physiol. Soc., Soc. Exptl. Biology and Medicine, Am. Soc. Clin. Investigation, Western Assn. Physicians, Assn. Am. Physicians. Democrat. Jewish. Office: Stanford U Sch Medicine CCSR 1155 269 Campus Dr Palo Alto CA 94305-5156 E-mail: sschrier@leland.stanford.edu.

SCHRIER, STEVEN ROBERT, television producer, director; b. Kalamazoo, Oct. 31, 1950; s. Clarence Martin and Evelyn Marian (VanderSalm) S. BA, Western Mich. U., 1973; MA, Northwestern U., 1974. Media dir., TV prodr. State of Mich. Dept. Cmty. Health, Kalamazoo, 1974—2002. Dir. pvt. video prodn., Kalamazoo, 1974—. Recipient Media award Mental Health Assn. Mich., 1985. Mem. Soc. Motion Picture & TV Engrs. Avocations: world travel, cars.

SCHRIER-POLAK, CAROL, lawyer; BA, Brandeis U., 1967; postgrad., Wayne State U., 1967-68; MSW, SUNY, Buffalo, 1969; JD, Temple U., 1977. Bar: Va. 1983, Pa. 1977. Assoc. planner rsch. and planning divsn. Cmty. Coun. Atlanta, 1969-72, project coord. child care planning project, 1972-73; exec. dir. Coun. for Children, Inc., Atlanta, 1972-74, Support Ctr. for Child Advocates Inc., Phila., 1977-83; legal cons. ABA/Nat. Resource Ctr. for Child Advocacy and Protection, Washington, 1983-84; sole practitioner Alexandria, Va., 1984-88; atty. Bean, Kinney & Korman, P.C., Arlington, 1988—, ptnr., 1990—. Mediator, 1994—; faculty Va. State Bar, Va. Trial Lawyers and local bar assns.; mem. child support quadrenneal rev. panel Commonwealth of Va. Co-editor: Making Financial Decisions when Divorce Occurs: A Virginia Guide, 1993; editor legal manuals; contbr. articles to profl. jours. Bd. dirs. Legal Svcs. No. Va., 1991-97; bd. dirs. Mental Health Assn. No. Va., 1989-92. Fellow Am. Acad. Matrimonial Lawyers (sec.-treas. Va. chpt. 1999-2001, v.p. 2001—); mem. ABA, D.C. Bar Assn., Va. Bar Assn. (mem. family law bd. govs. 1990-94, mem. faculty professionalism course 1999-2002), Fairfax Bar Assn. (bd. dirs. 1993—, sec. 1995-96, pres. 1997-98). Office: Bean Kinney & Korman 2000 14th St N Ste 100 Arlington VA 22201-2552

SCHRIESHEIM, ALAN, research administrator; b. N.Y.C., Mar. 8, 1930; s. Morton and Frances (Greenberg) Schriesheim; m. Beatrice D. Brand, June 28, 1953; children: Laura Lynn, Robert Alan. BS in Chemistry, Poly. Inst. Bklyn., 1951; PhD in Phys. Organic Chemistry, Pa. State U., 1954; DSc (hon.) , No. Ill. U., 1991; PhD (hon.) , Ill. Inst. Tech., Chgo., 1992; Laureate, Lincoln Acad., 1996. Chemist Nat. Bur. Standards, 1954—56; with Exxon Rsch. & Engring. Co., 1956—83, dir. corp. rsch., 1975—79; gen. mgr. Exxon Engring., 1979—83; sr. dep. lab. dir., COO Argonne Nat. Lab., 1983—84, lab. dir., CEO, 1984—96, dir. emeritus, 1996—; prof. chemistry dept. U. Chgo., 1984—96, lectr. Bus. Sch., 1996—; prin. Washington Adv. Group, 1996—. Karcher lectr. U. Okla., 1977; Hurd lectr. Northwestern U., 1980; Rosensteil lectr. Brandeis U., 1982; Welsh Found. lectr., 87; com. svc. NRC, 1980—; vis. com. chemistry dept. MIT, 1977—82; mem. vis. com. mech. engring. and aerospace dept. Princeton (N.J.) U., 1983—87, mem. vis. com. chemistry dept., 1983—87; mem. Pure and Applied Chemistry Com.; del. to People's Republic of China, 1978; mem. Presdl. Nat. Commn. on Superconductivity, 1989—91, U.S.-USSR Joint Commn. on Basic Sci. Rsch., 1990—93; mem. U.S. nat. com. Internat. Union Pure and Applied Chemistry, 1982—85; mem. magnetic fusion adv. com. Divsn. Phys. Scis. U. Chgo. Magnetic Fusion adv. com. to U.S. DOE, 1983—86; mem. Dept. Energy Rsch. Adv. Bd., 1983—85, Congl. Adv. Com. on Sci. and Tech., 1985—96; mem. vis. com. Stanford (Calif.) U., U. Utah, Tex. A&M U., Lehigh U.; bd. govs. Argonne Nat. Lab., 1984—96; mem. adv. com. on space sys. and tech. NASA, 1987—93; mem. nuc. engring. and engring. physics vis. com. U. Wis., Madison; mem. Coun. Gt. Lakes Govs. Regional Econ. Devel. Commn., 1987—, rev. bd. Compact Ignition Tomamak Princeton U., 1988—91; advisor Sears Investment Mgmt. Co., 1988—89; bd. dirs. HEICO, Smart Signal Corp.; adv. bd. Batterson Venture Ptnrs., Influx, UHV Aluminum, Valley Indsl. Assn., Coun. on Superconductivity for Am. Competitiveness; mem. State of Ill. Commn. on the Future of Pub. Svc., 1990—92; co-chair Indsl. Rsch. Inst. Nat. Labs./Industry Panel, 1984—87; mem. Nat. Acad. Engring. Adv. Commn. on Tech. and Soc., 1991—92, Sun Electric Corp. Bd., 1991—92, U.S. House of Reps. subcom. on Sci.-Adv. Group on Renewing U.S. Sci. Policy, 1992—96, Chgo. Acad. Scis. acad. coun., 1994—; mem. adv. bd. Chemtech; mem. sr. action group on R&D investment strategies Ctr. for strategic and Internat. Studies, 1995; bd. vis. Astronomy and Astrophysics Pa. State U., 1995—. Adv. bd.: Chemtech, 1970—85, editl. bd.: Rsch. & Devel., 1988—92, editl. bd.: Superconductor Industry, 1988—95; patentee in field. Mem. spl. vis. com. Field Mus. of Natural History, Chgo., 1987—88; trustee The Latin Sch. of Chgo., 1990—92; adv. bd. WBEZ Chicagoland Pub. Radio Cmty., 1990—96; mem. Conservation Found. DuPage County, 1983—96, Econ. Devel. Adv. Commn. of DuPage County, 1984—88, Ill. Gov.'s Commn. on Sci. and Tech., 1986—90, Inst. for Ill. Coun. Advisors, 1988—, Ill. Coalition Bd. Dirs., 1989—, Inst. for Ill. Adv. Rev. Panel, 1986—88, NASA Sci. Tech. Adv. Com. Manpower Requirements Ad Hoc Rev. Team, 1988—91, Ill. Sci. and Tech. Adv. Com., 1989—, chmn., 1997; mem. U. Ill. Engring. Vis. com., Urbana-Champaign, 1986—95; trustee Tchrs. Acad. for Math. and Sci. Tchrs. in Chgo., 1990—96; bd. visitors astronomy and astrophysics Pa. State U., 1995—; bd. dirs. LaRabida Children's Hosp. and Rsch. Ctr., 1987—95, Children's Meml. Hosp., Children's Meml. Inst. for Edn. and Rsch. Recipient Outstanding Alumni Fellow award, Pa. State U., 1985, laureate, Lincoln Acad. Ill., 1996, Disting. fellow, Poly. U., 1989. Fellow: AAAS (coun. del. chem. sect. 1986—92, sci. engring. and pub. policy com. 1992, standing com. audit 1992, bd. dirs. 1992—96, selection com. to bring FSU scientists to ann. mtg. 1995—), N.Y. Acad. Scis.; mem.: AIChE (award com. 1992—), NAE (adv. com. tech. and soc. 1991—92, mem. program adv. com. 1992—94, chair study fgn. participation in U.S. R&D 1993—96, NRC com. on dual use tech. 1996—97, com. to assess policies and practices of Dept. of Energy to design, ma 1998—99), Ctr. Strategic and Internat. Studies (sr. action group 1995—96), Indsl. Rsch. Inst. (fed. adv. com. to Fed. Sci. and Tech. Com. 1992—96, co-chmn. Nat. Labs. Indsl. Panel 1984—87, sr. action group on R&D Investment Strategies), Am. Nuc. Soc., Am. Petroleum Inst. (rsch. coord. coun.), Nat. Conf. Advancement Rsch. (conf. com. 1985—, site selection com. 1994, conf. com. 50th ann. 1996), Am. Mgmt. Assn. (R&D coun. 1988—), Am. Chem. Soc. (joint bd. com. on sci. 1983—87, chmn. petroleum divsn. 1983—91, councilor, com. on chemistry and pub. affairs 1983—91, petroleum chemistry award 1969, 1995—96), Econ. Club, Comml. Club, Cosmos Club, Carleton Club (bd. govs. 1992—), Phi Lambda Upsilon, Sigma Xi. Home: 1440 N Lake Shore Dr Apt 31ac Chicago IL 60610-5927 Office: Argonne Nat Lab 9700 S Cass Ave Argonne IL 60439-4803

SCHRIEVER, BERNARD ADOLPH, management consultant; b. Bremen, Germany, Sept. 14, 1910; came to U.S., 1917, naturalized, 1923; s. Adolph Niholaus and Elizabeth (Milch) S.; children: Brett Arnold, Dodie Elizabeth Schriever Moeller, Barbara Alice Schriever Allan. BS, Tex. A&M U., 1931; MSM.E., Stanford U., 1942; D.Sc. (hon.), Creighton U., 1958, Rider Coll., 1958, Adelphia Coll., 1959, Rollins Coll., 1959; D.Aero. Sci. (hon.), U. Mich., 1961; D.Eng. (hon.), Bklyn. Poly. Inst., 1961; LL.D. (hon.), Loyola U., Los Angeles, 1960. Commd. 2d lt. U.S. Army Air Force, 1938; advanced through grades to gen. U.S. Air Force, 1961; comdr. ICBM Program, 1954-59, AFSC, 1959-66; ret., 1966; chmn. bd. Schriever & McKee, Washington, 1971-87; cons. B.A. Schriever, 1987—. Decorated D.S.M., D.S.M. with oak leaf cluster, Legion of Merit, Air medal, Purple Heart; named to Aviation Hall of Fame, 1980; recipient Forrestal award, 1987, Nat. Air and Space Mus. Trophy Lifetime Achievement award, 1996. Hon. fellow AIAA; mem. NAE, Am. Astron. Soc., Air Force Assn. Clubs: Burning Tree. Home: 4501 Dexter St NW Washington DC 20007-1116 Office: 1101 30th St NW Ste 200 Washington DC 20007-3769

SCHRIEVER, FRED MARTIN, management consultant, financial investor; b. N.Y.C. s. Samuel and Sara S.; m. Cheri G. Spatt; children: Melissa Ann, Elizabeth Ellen. BME, Poly. U. N.Y., 1956, MME, 1958. Registered profl. engr., N.Y., Wash.; cert. mgmt. cons. Chief engr. divsn. Sperry Corp., N.Y.C., 1956-64; ptnr. Booz, Allen and Hamilton, N.Y.C. and Washington, 1964-71; chmn., pres. RCG Internat. Inc., N.Y.C., 1971-96. Investor and cons. in field; dir. Nat. Exec. Svc. Corps., 1998—, Hagler Bailly Inc., 1996-2000. Fellow Inst. of Dirs., Inst. Mgmt. Consultants U.K.; mem. ASME, Inst. Mgmt. Cons., Chemists Club. Home: PO Box 32 Westport CT 06881-0032

SCHRIFT, ALAN DOUGLAS, philosophy educator; b. Bklyn., Mar. 2, 1955; s. Leonard Joel and Joan (Gash) S.; m. Jill Lynn Davis, June 2, 1984. BA, Brown U., 1977; MA, Purdue U., 1980, PhD, 1983. Asst. prof. philosophy Purdue U., West Lafayette, Ind., 1983-85, Clarkson U., Potsdam, N.Y., 1985-87; from asst. prof. to assoc. prof. philosophy Grinnell Coll., Iowa, 1987-98, prof., 1998—, chmn. dept. philosophy, 1994-2000, dir. Ctr. for Humanities, 2000—. Author: Nietzsche and the Question of Interpretation: Between Hermeneutics and Deconstruction, 1990, Nietzsche's French Legacy: A Genealogy of Poststructuralism, 1995; editor: The Hermeneutic Tradition: From Ast to Ricoeur, 1990, Transforming the Hermeneutic Context: From Nietzsche to Nancy, 1990, The Logic of the Gift: Toward an Ethic of Generosity, 1997, Why Nietzsche Still? Reflections on Drama, Culture, and Politics, 2000; editor ann. Nietzsche issue Internat. Studies in Philosophy, 1998—; mem. editl. bd. Jour. History of Philosophy, New Nietzsche Studies. Fellow Am. Coun. Learned Socs., 1985, Grinnell Coll., 1990, Oreg. Humanities Ctr., 1991. Mem. Am. Philos. Assn., N.Am. Nietzsche Soc. (chmn. program com. 1997—), Internat. Assn. Philosophy Lit., Soc. Phenomenology Existential Philosophy, Nietzsche Soc. Avocations: travel, photography. Home: 1032 Chatterton St Grinnell IA 50112-1734 Office: Dept Philosophy Grinnell Coll Grinnell IA 50112 Fax: 641-269-4414. E-mail: schrift@grinnell.edu.

SCHRIMSHER, JOANNE JOHNSON, professional counselor; b. Miami, May 23, 1944; d. Alfred Peter and Patricia (Pearson) Johnson; m. Geoffrey Schrimsher, Dec. 21, 1964; children: John Alfred, Jana. BS in Home Econs., Tex. A&I U., 1964; MS in Counseling and Human Devel., Troy State U., 1979, EdS in Sch. Counseling, 1980. Lic. profl. spl. edn. counselor, profl. edn. diagnostician. Home econs. tchr. William Adams H.S., Alice, Tex., 1964-66, Sharyland (Tex.) H.S., 1967-68; home econs. and substitute tchr. Panama Canal Co., 1974-77; psychometrist, counselor Wiregrass MHMR and Family Life Ctrl., Dothan and Ft. Rucker, Ala., 1979; cons. Region III Edn. Svc. Ctr., Victoria, Tex., 1980-82; ednl. diagnostician Region III ESC, 1982-86, edn. diagnositicia, LPC (ECI), 1988—. Worship com. St. Mark's Meth. Ch., 1981-86. Mem. Tex. Counseling Assn., Tex. Ednl. Diagnosticians Assn., Tex. Assn. for Play Therapy, Victoria African Violet Soc. (pres.), Victoria Christian Svc. Assn. (bd. dirs. 1981-85), Assn. for Play Therapy. Office: Region III ESC 1905 Leary Ln Victoria TX 77901-2899

SCHROCK, DONALD E. communications executive; BSEE, U. Ill.; MSEE, degree in bus. adminstrn., Ariz. State U. Various positions Motorola Semiconductor; v.p., divsn. gen. mgr. Burr-Brown Corp.; past v.p. ops Applied Micro Circuit Corp.; past group v.p., divsn. mgr. Hughes Aircraft Co. Office: Corp Hdqs Qualcomm Inc 5775 Morehouse Dr San Diego CA 92121 Office Fax: 858-658-2100.

SCHROCK, EDWARD L. (ED SCHROCK), congressman, former state senator; b. Middletown, Ohio, Apr. 6, 1941; m. Judith Schrock. BA, Alderson Broaddus Coll., 1964; MA, Am. U., 1975. Commd. ensign USN, 1964, advanced through grades to capt., retired, 1988; investment broker, 1989-95; mem. Va. State Senate, 1996-2001, mem. gen. laws com., mem. local govt. com., mem. privileges & elections com., mem. transp. com.; mem. U.S. Congress from 2d Va. dist., 2001—; mem. armed svcs. com., budget com., govt. reform com., small bus. com. Republican. Baptist. Office: 128 Cannon House Office Bldg. Washington DC 20515*

SCHROCK, RICHARD ROYCE, chemistry educator; b. Berne, Ind., Jan. 4, 1945; m. Nancy F. Carlson, 1971; children: Andrew, Eric. BA, U. Calif., 1967; PhD, Harvard U., 1971; postdoctorate, Cambridge U., Eng., 1971-72. Rsch. chemist E.I. du Pont de Nemours & Co., Wilmington, Del., 1972-75; asst. prof. MIT, Cambridge, 1975-78, assoc. prof., 1978-80, prof. chemistry, 1980-89, Frederick G. Keyes prof. chemistry, 1989—. Contbr. articles to profl. jours. Recipient Bailar medal, U. Ill., 1998, Sir Geoffrey Wilkinson medal, Royal Soc. Chemistry, 2002. Mem. AAAS, Am. Chem. Soc. (award organometallic chemistry 1985, Harrison Howe award 1990, Humboldt award 1994, award inorganic chemistry 1996, Arthur C. Cope Scholar award 2001), NAS. Office: MIT Dept Of Chemistry Cambridge MA 02139 E-mail: rrs@mit.edu.

SCHROCK, ROBERT D., JR. orthopaedic surgeon, educator; b. Omaha, Aug. 6, 1938; s. Robert D. and Elizabeth Winslow (Wetherbee) S.; m. Carolyn Gorthy, May 30, 1964; children: Robert D. III, Suzanne Bartlett Schrock Kelley. AB, Princeton U., 1960; MD, Cornell U., 1964. Cert. Am. Bd. Orthopadic Surgery. Instr. dept. orthopaedics U. Wash. Sch. Medicine, Seattle, 1969-70; clin. asst. prof. dept. orthopaedics U. Rochester (N.Y.) Sch. Medicine and Dentistry, 1972—. Pres. Genesee Valley chpt. Arthritis Found., Rochester, 1989-91 (Nat. Vol. award 1991, Zaia award 1993), Rochester Acad. Medicine, 1991-92. Author: (with others) Operative Surgery, 1976; contbr. articles to profl. jours. Cub master, Webelos leader Cub Scouts, Pittsford, N.Y., 1973-78 (Long House award 1977); elder Third Presbyn. Ch., Rochester, 1984-87. Maj. U.S. Army, 1970-72. Fellow ACS Coll. Surgeon, Am. Acad. Orthopaedic Surgeons, Am. Acad. Cerebral Palsy and Devel. Medicine, Am. Orthopaedic Foot and Ankle Soc., Rochester Acad. Medicine (co-chair com.); mem. Med. Soc. State N.Y. (com. mem.). Presbyterian. Avocations: tennis, photography, sailing. Home: 8 Stonegate Ln Pittsford NY 14534-1914 Office: Greater Rochester Orthopaed 220 Linden Oaks Ste 100 Rochester NY 14625-2839

SCHROCK, SIMON, retail executive; b. Oakland, Md., Dec. 28, 1936; s. Noah and Cora (Burkholder) S.; m. Eva Lena Yoder, June 7, 1959 (dec. Apr. 1962); m. Pauline Yoder, Sept. 29, 1963; children: Janice Yvonne, Eldon Laverne, Ivan Dale. With Eastern States Farm Supply Co., Oakland, Md., 1957-59, Children's Hosp., Washington, 1959-61, Copp Properties, Washington, 1961-75; pres. Choice Books of No. Va., Fairfax, 1975—. Chmn. Lighthouse Lit., 1976—. Author: Get on With Living, 1976, Price of Missing Life, 1981, One-Anothering, 1986, Vow-Keepers Vow-Breakers, A Smoother Journey, 1994, What Shall The Redeemed Wear, 2001, Where Has Integrity Gone, 2001; contbr. articles to ch. jours. Bishop Faith Christian Fellowship, Catlett, Va., 1981—. Avocations: traveling, writing, biking. Office: 110100 Piper Ln Bristow VA 20136

SCHROCK, THEODORE R. surgeon; b. Berne, Ind., Oct. 21, 1939; s. N.J. and M.A. Schrock; married. AB, U. Calif., San Francisco, 1961, MD, 1964. Diplomate Am. Bd. Surgery. Intern U. Calif. Hosps., San Francisco, 1964-65, resident, 1965-67, 69-71; fellow Mass. Gen. Hosp., Boston, 1967-69; chmn. dept. surgery U. Calif. San Francisco Med. Ctr., 1993-99, J. Englebert Dunphy prof. surgery, 1998—, assoc. dean clin. svcs., chief med. officer, 1999—. Fellow ACS; mem. Am. Gastroenterological Assn., Am. Soc. Colon and Rectal Surgery, Am. Soc. Gastroenterological Endoscopy, Am. Surg. Assn., Soc. Surgery Alimentary Tract. Office: UCSF Campus Box 0296 500 Parnassus Ave San Francisco CA 94143-0296 Fax: 415-353-2765. E-mail: ted.schrock@ucsfmedctr.org.

SCHRODER, DIETER KARL, electrical engineering educator; b. Lübeck, Germany, June 18, 1935; came to U.S., 1964; s. Wilhelm and Martha (Werner) S.; m. Beverley Claire Parchment, Aug. 4, 1961; children: Mark, Derek. BSc, McGill U., Montreal, Que., Can., 1962, MSc, 1964; PhD, U. Ill., 1968. Sr. engr. research and devel. sect. Westinghouse Electric Corp., Pitts., 1968-73, fellow engr., 1973-77, adv. engr., 1977-79, mgr., 1979-81; prof. elec. engring. Ariz. State U., Tempe, 1981—. Researcher Inst. Solid-State Physics, Freiburg, Fed. Republic Germany, 1978-79. Author: Advanced MOS Devices, 1987, Semiconductor Material and Device Characterization, 1998; patentee in field; contbr. articles to profl. jours. Fellow IEEE (life, disting. nat. lectr. 1993-2002); mem. Electrochem. Soc., Sigma Xi, Eta Kappa Nu. Mem. Baha'i Faith. Home: 10572 E Firewheel Dr Scottsdale AZ 85255-1911 Office: Ariz State U Dept Elec Engring Tempe AZ 85287-5706

SCHRÖDER, HARALD BERTEL, aerospace industry executive; b. Stockholm, Dec. 31, 1924; s. Bertel and Selma Katarina (Kraepelien) S.; m. Kjerstin Sjögren, Mar. 7, 1949; children: Göran, Hans, Henrik. M in Aeronautics Engring., Swedish Royal Inst. Tech., Stockholm, 1948. Developmental engr. SAAB-Scania AB, Linköping, Sweden, 1957-62, program mgr. SAAB Viggen Fighter Program Sweden, 1962-68, v.p. aircraft sector Sweden, 1971-83; sr. v.p. SAAB aircraft div., gen. mgr. SAAB-Aircraft div., 1983-87; exec. v.p. SAAB-Scania AB, Linköping, Sweden, 1987-91; pres. Industry Group JAS AB, 1980-91; adviser to pres. Saab Mil. Aircraft, 1991-95; chmn. Novator AB, 1999—. Bd. dirs. Aero. Rsch. Inst. Sweden, 1987-91. Mem. Royal Swedish Acad. War Scis., Swedish Assn. Def. Industries (pres. 1987-89, bd. dirs. 1986-91), Swedish Aerospace Industries Assn. (pres. 1991-94), European Aerospace Industries Assn. (v.p. 1992-94). Home: Banergatan 53 11522S Stockholm Sweden

SCHRODER, JACK SPALDING , JR. lawyer; b. Atlanta, July 10, 1948; s. Jack Spalding Sr. and Van (Spalding) S.; m. Karen Keyworth, Sept. 1, 1973; children: Jack Spalding III, James Edward. BA, Emory U., 1970; JD, U. Ga., 1973. Bar: Ga. 1973, U.S. Dist. Ct. (no. dist.) Ga. 1973, U.S. Ct. Appeals (5th cir.) 1973, U.S. Ct. Appeals (11th cir.) 1982. Assoc. Alston & Bird, Atlanta, 1973-78, ptnr., 1978—. Author: Credentialing: Strategies for a Changing Environment/BNA's Health Law and Business Series, 1996; co-editor, contbg. author: Georgia Hospital Law manual, 1979, 84,92. Bd. dirs. Rsch. Atlanta, 1996-2000, pres., 1999; participant Leadership Ga., Atlanta, 1986. United Way (chmn. legal divsn.), Atlanta, 1980. Mem. ABA (vice chmn. medicine and law com. 1989-90), Am. Health Lawyers Assn. (bd. dirs. 1994-99, chmn. med. staff and physician rels. com. 1991-94, vice chair hosps. and health systems law inst. 2001--), Ga. Acad. Healthcare Attys. (pres. 1981-82), State Bar Ga. (bd. govs. 1987-89), Atlanta Coun. Younger Lawyers (pres. 1977-78), Atlanta Bar Assn. (pres. 1982-83), Atlanta Bar Found. (pres. 1991-95). Office: Alston & Bird 1 Atlantic Ctr 1201 W Peachtree St NW Atlanta GA 30309-3424 E-mail: jschroder@alston.com.

SCHROEDER, ALBERT JOHN, retired pediatrician; b. Mpls., Aug. 31, 1919; BA, U. Minn., 1941, BS, 1943, MD, 1944. Diplomate Am. Bd. Allergy and Immunology, Am. Bd. Pediats. Intern U.S.N.V.H., San Diego, 1944-45; resident in pediats. U. Minn. Hosp., Mpls., 1946-48; fellow in pediat. allergy Boston Children's Hosp., 1970-72; mem. staff Fairview Southdale Hosp., Edina, Minn.; clin. assoc. prof. pediats. Med. Sch. U. Minn., 1978-90; ret. Fellow Am. Acad. Allergy and Immunology, Am. Acad. Pediats., Am. Coll. Allergists and Immunologists, AMA. Home: 7220 York Ave S #212 Edina MN 55435-4462

SCHROEDER, ALFRED CHRISTIAN, electronics research engineer; b. West New Brighton, N.Y., Feb. 28, 1915; s. Alfred and Chryssa (Weishaar) S.; m. Janet Ellis, Sept. 26, 1936 (dec.); 1 dau., Carol Ann Schroeder Castle.; m. Dorothy Holloway, Nov. 21, 1981. BS, MS, MIT, 1937. Mem. tech. staff Sarnoff, Inc., Princeton, N.J., 1937-2000; ret. Contbr. articles to profl. jours. Recipient RCA Lab. awards, 1947, 50, 51, 52, 57, 70 Fellow IEEE (Vladimir Zworykin award 1971); mem. AAAS, Optical Soc. Am., Soc. Motion Picture and TV Engrs. (David Sarnoff Gold medal 1965), Soc. Info. Display (Karl Ferdinand Braun prize 1989), Sigma Xi. Mem. Soc. Of Friends. Achievements include 75 patents for color TV products including shadow mask tube. Home: Pennswood Village Apt B22 Newtown PA 18940-2401

SCHROEDER, ARNOLD LEON, mathematics educator; b. Honolulu, May 27, 1935; s. Arnold Leon and Wynelle (Russell) S.; m. Maybelle Ruth Walker, Nov. 9, 1956; children: Steven, Michael, Wendy. BS in Math., Oreg. State U., 1960, MS in Stats., 1962; postgrad., UCLA, 1964, U. So. Calif., 1965. Prof. emeritus math./stats. Long Beach (Calif.) C.C., 1962—. Computer cons. McDonnell-Douglas Corp., 1966-74, statis. researcher and tutoring on Soc. Sci., Bio-Med, and Bus. Mgmt. using SPSS, Minitab, and Lin. Prog. Applications; dir. Schroeder's Statis. Svcs. Author: statistics/Math Note's for Colleges, 1986—. Chmn. bd. elders Grace Bible Ch., South Gate, Calif., 1985-92. With USAF, 1953-57. Mem. Am. Bowlers Tour (life). Home and Office: 5481 E Hill St Long Beach CA 90815-1923 E-mail: alschroeder@charter.net.

SCHROEDER, CAROLINE THERESA, non-profit association administrator; b. Phoenix, June 14, 1971; d. Milton Robert and Mary Barbara (Murphy) S. BA magna cum laude, Brown U., 1993. Resident counselor Brown U., Providence, 1990-92; libr. coord. Sarah Doyle Women's Ctr., 1992-93; program coord. St. Mark's Luth. Ch., San Francisco, 1993—; sch. supr. East Bay Conservation Corps/Summer Svc., Oakland, Calif., 1993. Active vol. various women's ctrs. Mem. NOW, Phi Beta Kappa. Democrat. Avocation: horsemanship. Home: 2615 Sarah Ave Durham NC 27707-1939

SCHROEDER, DONALD J. orthopedic surgeon; b. Omaha, Nov. 5, 1938; s. Francis A. and Maire L. (Schlueter) S.; m. Patricia A. Speer, Feb. 11, 1962 (div. June 1980); children: Cynthia, Douglas; m. Carol E. Schaan, Aug. 20, 1983. BS, Creighton U., 1960, MD, 1964. Diplomate Am. Bd. Orthopedic Surgery. Intern Detroit Receiving Hosp., 1964-65; resident in orthopedic surgery Wayne State U., Detroit, 1964-71; resident with affiliate hosp. Shriners Hosp., St. Louis, 1969-70; attending surgeon Sacred Heart Gen. Hosp., Eugene, Oreg., 1971—2001; resident orth. surgery Wayne State U.; attending surgeon Sacred Heart Gen. Hosp., Eugene, Oreg., 1971—. Pres. Marist Found., Eugene, 1993. Smith Kline fellow, 1964. Fellow Am. Acad. Orthopedic Surgeons; mem. AMA (alt. del. 1993-98, del., 1998—), Oreg. Med. Assn. (pres. 1993-94), Lane County Med. Soc. (pres. 1987-88), Western Orthopedic Assn., Am. Bd. Forensic Medicine (vice chair, chair 2000—), Alpha Omega Alpha. Republican. Roman Catholic. Avocation: buffalo ranching. Office: 1180 Patterson St Eugene OR 97401-3619

SCHROEDER, DONALD PERRY, retired food products company executive; b. Danville, Ill., Nov. 2, 1930; s. Donald Joseph and Pauline Hannah (Critchfield) S.; m. Barbara Ann Engle, Jan. 6, 1951; children: Patricia Ann Schroeder Capizzi, Helen Schroeder Marrano, Jeffrey Joseph. Student, Purdue U., 1949, Stanford U., 1982. Mgr. Schroeders I.G.A. Supermarket, Danville, 1950-57; specialist retail meat J.M. Jones Co., Champaign, Ill., 1957-59, mgr. retail zone, 1959-62, dir. meat ops., 1962-67; dir. customer services Olean (N.Y.) Wholesale Grocery Co., 1967-70; nat. dir. meat Ind. Grocers Alliance, Chgo., 1970-74; dir. meat ops. Fleming Cos., Inc., Topeka, 1974-83, v.p. meat., produce ops. Oklahoma City, 1983-88, v.p. meat ops., 1988-89, ret., 1989. Chmn. meat council Ind. Grocers Alliance, Chgo., 1962-87. Bd. dirs. Big Bros./Sisters Greater Oklahoma City, 1984-87, North Side YMCA, Oklahoma City, 1988-90. Mem. Nat. Livestock and Meat Bd. (universal meat cut identity com. 1970-73), United Fresh Fruit and Vegetable (bd. dirs. 1984-87). Republican. Roman Catholic. Avocations: yard and garden work, golf, fishing. Home: 5 Charnela Ln Hot Springs National Park AR 71909-3030

SCHROEDER, DOUGLAS FREDRICK, architect; b. Omaha, June 12, 1935; s. Walter Elmer and Ellen Ruth (Niles) S.; m. Joanne Vlecides, July 5, 1980. B.Arch., U. Mich., 1959. Registered Architect, Ill., N.C., Mich. Designer, draftsman C.F. Murphy Assocs., Chgo., 1959-63; architect, sr. architect Skidmore, Owings & Merrill, 1964-67; architect, ptnr. Schroeder, Yamamoto & Schreiber, 1968-69; ptnr. Hinds & Schroeder, Ltd., 1972-74; propr. Douglas Schroeder Assocs., 1974-83, 93—; ptnr. Siegel & Schroeder, P.C., 1983-91; dir. SGA Planning and Constrn. Cons. Co. div. Goforth Group, 1991-93; v.p. Yacht Harbor Mgmt. Co., South Haven, Mich., 1983-88. Dir. Inland Architect Mag. Contbr. articles to profl. jours. Bd. dirs. Chgo. Archtl. Assistance Ctr., 1982-84; chmn. Mass. Transp. Crisis Com., Chgo., 1973, Ill. Futures Forum, 1976-77; pres. Ill. Planning and Conservation League, Chgo., 1971-74. Named Outstanding Alumnus Lake Superior State U., 1971. Fellow AIA; mem. Am. Arbitration Assn. (arbitrator) Clubs: Cliff Dwellers (dir. 1971-74). Unitarian Universalist. Home: 700 W Irving Park Rd Apt 4A Chicago IL 60613-3133 Office: Douglas Schroeder Assocs Arch & Planners 980 N Michigan Ave Ste 1277 Chicago IL 60611-4523 E-mail: dschroeder@dsa-architects.com.

SCHROEDER, EDMUND R. lawyer; b. N.Y.C., Feb. 6, 1933; s. Robert C. and Rose A. (Garramone) S.; m. Elaine P. Diserio, Jan. 21, 1961; children: Edmund Jr., Christopher, Elizabeth. AB cum laude, Harvard U., 1953, LLB, 1958. Assoc. Archibald R. Graustein, N.Y.C., 1958-61, Root, Barrett, Cohen, Knapp & Smith, N.Y.C., 1961-67; ptnr. Barrett Knapp Smith & Schapiro, 1967-88, Lord Day & Lord/Barrett Smith, N.Y.C., 1988-94, Cadwalader, Wickersham & Taft, N.Y.C., 1994-2000, sr. counsel, 2000—. Mem. adv. com. Commodity Futures Trading Commn. on Definition and Regulation of Market Instruments, 1975-76. Contbr. articles to profl. jours. Bd. dirs. Orch. St. Luke's N.Y.C., 1987—, chmn. exec. com., 1993-95; trustee The United Way of Scarsdale-Edgemont, 1990-92; mem. Scarsdale Bd. Edn., 1976-79; co-founder, 1st chmn. Edn. Through Music, Inc., N.Y.C., 1991—; trustee Hoff-Barthelson Music Sch., Scarsdale, 1974—, chmn. bd., 1986-90, hon. chmn., 1990—; trustee The Nat. Guild Cmty. Schs. Arts, Englewood, N.J., 1992-96; bd. advisors Sacred Heart/Mt. Carmel Sch. for Arts, Mt. Vernon, 1995-97; arbitrator Am. Arbitration Assn., Nat. Futures Assn. Mem.: ABA (chmn. com. futures regulation 1981—85), N.Y. State Bar Assn. (com. comty. and futures law and regulation 1996—), Bar Assn. City of N.Y. (founder, 1st chmn. com. futures regulation 1976—). Office: Cadwalader Wickersham & Taft 100 Maiden Ln New York NY 10038-4818 E-mail: edmund.schroeder@cwt.com.

SCHROEDER, EDWARD JAMES, lawyer; b. Abilene, Tex., June 29, 1947; s. Edward and Alice (Dufour) S. BA, McMurry Coll., 1970, MA, Hardin-Simmons U., 1973; postgrad., U. Louvain, Belgium, 1973; JD, St. Mary's U., San Antonio, 1979. Bar: Tex. 1979, U.S. Dist. Ct. (no. dist.) Tex. 1980, U.S. Ct. Appeals (5th cir.) 1981, U.S. Dist. Ct. (we. dist.) Tex. 1981, U.S. Tax Ct. 1997. Assoc. Trueheart McMillan, San Antonio, 1979-80, Westbrook & Goldston, San Antonio, 1980-81; ptnr. Westbrook Schroeder, 1981-83; pvt. practice, 1983—. Pres. Kidney Found., San Antonio, 1983-85. Mem. San Antonio Bar Assn., Club Giraud (bd. dirs.), Friends of the McNay.

SCHROEDER, EDWIN MAHER, law educator; b. New Orleans, June 25, 1937; s. Edwin Charles and Lucille Mary (Maher) S.; m. Marietta Louise DeFazio, Aug. 1, 1936; children: Edwin Charles II, Jonathan David, Margaret Louise. AA, St. Joseph Sem., St. Benedict, La., 1957; PhB, Gregorian U., Rome, 1959; JD, Tulane U., 1964; MS, Fla. State U., 1970. Bar: Mass. 1964. Asst. prof. law U. Conn., 1965-68; asst. prof., asst. law libr. U. Tex., 1968-69; asst. prof. Fla. State U., 1969-71, assoc. prof., 1971-75, prof., 1975—, dir. Law Libr., 1969—, asst. dean Coll. Law, 1979-83, assoc. dean Coll. Law, 1983-93. Mem. ABA, Am. Assn. Law Librs. (v.p. Southwestern chpt. 1983-84, pres. 1984-85), Order of Coif, Beta Phi Mu. Roman Catholic. Home: 806 Middlebrooks Cir Tallahassee FL 32312-2439 Office: Fla State U Coll Law Law Libr Tallahassee FL 32306-1600 E-mail: eschroed@law.fsu.edu.

SCHROEDER, ERIC PETER, lawyer; b. Floral Park, N.Y., July 20, 1970; s. Fredric G. and Linda M. Schroeder. BA, Duke U., 1992; JD, Vanderbilt U., 1996. Bar: Ga. 1997, U.S. Dist. Ct. (no. dist.) Ga. 1997, U.S. Ct. Appeals (11th cir.) 1998. Law clk. Hon. William C. O'Kelley, U.S. Dist. Ct. (no. dist.) Ga., Atlanta, 1996-97; atty. Powell, Goldstein, Frazer & Murphy, 1997—. Mem. planning com. Ga. Bar Media Jud. Conf., 1999, 2000. Articles editor Vanderbilt Law Rev., 1995-96; mem. editl. bd. INTA The Trademark Reporter,

2000-01. Active Boys and Girls Club of Am., Atlanta, 1998-01; vol. Ga. Vol. Lawyers for the Arts, Atlanta, 1998; lawyer Anti-Defamation League, Atlanta, 1998. Mem. Atlanta Bar Assn., U.S. Copyright Soc., Internat. Trademark Assn., Order of Coif, Lamar Inn of Ct. Home: 977 North Ave Atlanta GA 30306-4701 Office: Powell Goldstein Frazer & Murphy 191 Peachtree St Atlanta GA 30303 E-mail: eschroeder@pgfm.com.

SCHROEDER, FRED ERICH HARALD, humanities educator, educator; b. Manitowoc, Wis., June 3, 1932; s. Alfred William and Sissel Marie (Lovell) S.; m. Janet June Knope, Aug. 21, 1954; 1 child, Erich Karl. BS, U. Wis., 1960; MA, U. Minn., 1963, PhD, 1968. Elementary sch. tchr. various locations, Wis., 1952-60; asst. prof. English U. Minn., Duluth, 1968-71, assoc. prof. English, 1971-74, prof. behavioral sci., 1977-82, prof. humanities, 1974-96, dir. Ctr. for Am. Studies, 1986-87, dir. Inst. Interdisciplinary Studies, 1987-90, dir. dept. humanities and classics, 1989-90, dir. grad. liberal studies, 1992-95, prof. emeritus, 1996—. Author: Joining the Human Race: How To Teach Humanities, 1972, Outlaw Aesthetics: Arts and the Public Mind, 1977; editor Interdisciplinary Humanities (formerly Humanities Edn. jour.), 1983-95, assoc. editor, 1995—; editor 5000 Years of Popular Culture, 1980, 20th Century Popular Culture in Museums and Libraries, 1981, Front Yard America: The Evolution and Meanings of a Domestic Vernacular Landscape, 1993; lectr., writer Nat. Humanities Series, 1969-71. Mem. Minn. Humanities Commn., 1985-90. Woodrow Wilson Nat. Found. fellow, 1960-61, dissertation fellow 1963; NEH scholar, 1969-70; Inst. for Human Values in Medicine fellow, 1976. Mem. Am. Culture Assn. (pres. 1984-87), Nat. Assn. Humanities Edn. (pres. 1987-89, exec. sec.-treas. 1989-96), Am. Assn. for State and Local History (seminar instr. 1978-82), Popular Culture Assn. Avocations: collecting art, woodworking, gardening. Home: 5756 N Shore Dr Duluth MN 55804-9660 E-mail: fschroed@d.umn.edu.

SCHROEDER, GERALD FRANK, state supreme court justice; b. Boise, Idaho, Sept. 13, 1939; s. Frank Frederick and Josephine Ivy (Lucas) S.; m. Carole Ann McKenna, 1967; children: Karl Casteel, Erich Frank. BA magna cum laude, Coll. of Idaho (now Albertson Coll. of Idaho), 1961; JD, Harvard U., 1964. Bar: Idaho 1965. Assoc. Moffatt, Thomas, Barrett & Blanton, Boise, 1965—66; pvt. practice, 1966—67; asst. U.S. atty. Dept. Justice, 1967—69; judge Ada County Probate Ct., 1969—71; magistrate State of Idaho, 1971—75; dist. judge U.S. Dist. Ct. (4th dist.) Idaho, 1975—95; justice Idaho Supreme Ct., 1995—. Instr.Boise Bar Rev. Boise Bar Rev., 1973—; adj. faculty law Boise State U., 1986—95; former mem. Gov. Coun. on Crime and Delinquency. Author: Idaho Probate Procedure, 1971, (Novel) Triangle of the Sons-Phenomena, 1983; contbr. Adminstrv. and dist. judge 4th dist. State of Idaho, 1985—95; Bd. dirs. Boise Philharm. Assn., 1979—81. Fellow Toll fellow, Nat. Coun. State Govt., 1990. Mem.: Idaho Bar Assn., Boise Racquet and Swim Club (pres. bd. dirs. 1991—93).

SCHROEDER, HAROLD KENNETH, JR. U.S. magistrate judge; b. Buffalo, Aug. 6, 1936; s. Harold Kenneth and Margaret Mary (Mescall) S.; m. Jean Louise Benbenek, Aug. 20, 1958; children: Mary Margaret, Mark, Keith, Kurt, Jennifer. BS, Canisius Coll., 1958; JD, U. Buffalo, 1961; ML, Georgetown U., 1962. Bar: N.Y. 1961, D.C. 1961, U.S. Dist. Ct. (we. dist.) N.Y. 1961, Fla. 1979, U.S. Ct. Appeals (2nd cir.) 1981. Trial atty. U.S. Dept. Justice, Washington, 1962-63; spl. asst. U.S. Atty. D.C., 1962-63; U.S. Atty. Western Dist. N.Y. U.S. Dept. Justice, Buffalo, 1969-72; ptnr. Hodgson, Russ, Andrews, Woods & Goodyear, 1963-69, sr. ptnr., 1972-2000. Chmn. fed. merit selection panel U.S. Magistrate Judge We. Dist. N.Y., 1989, 92, 94, 98; chmn. Author: (with others) Law and Tactics in Federal Criminal Cases, 1964. V.p. Orchard Park, N.Y. Ctrl. Sch. Dist., 1972-76, Buffalo Sem., 1972-88. E. Barrett Prettyman fellow Georgetown U., 1961; recipient Disting. Alumnus award U. Buffalo Law Sch., 1996. Fellow Am. Coll. Trial Lawyers; mem. Western N.Y. Def. Trial Lawyers Assn. (Def. Trial Lawyer of Yr. 1996), Erie County Bar Assn. Avocation: tennis. Home: 3872 Baker Rd Orchard Park NY 14127-2031 Office: US Courthouse 68 Court St Buffalo NY 14202-3405 E-mail: kenneth_schroeder@nywd.uscourts.gov.

SCHROEDER, HARRY WILLIAM, JR. physician, scientist; b. Mpls., Oct. 1, 1952; s. Harry Williams Sr. and Maria de los Angeles (Melendez) S.; m. Dixie Lee Douglas, Nov. 24, 1979; children: Harry William III, Elena, Jeannette. BS, Tex. A&M U., 1974; PhD, Baylor Coll. Medicine, 1979, MD, 1981. Vis. fellow Yale U., New Haven, 1980; intern, then resident in internal medicine U. Ky., Lexington, 1981-84; sr. fellow med. genetics U. Wash., Seattle, 1984-88; rsch. assoc. Howard Hughes Med. Inst., 1986-88; asst. prof. medicine and microbiology U. Ala., Birmingham, 1988-93, assoc. prof. medicine & microbiology, 1993-98, prof. medicine µbiology, 1998—. RJR Nabisco scholar in immunology, 1989. Fellow Am. Coll. Med. Genetics (founder 1993), Molecular Medicine Soc.; mem. AAAS, Am. Soc. Human Genetics, Am. Fedn. Med. Rsch., Am. Assn. Immunologists, Clin. Immunology Soc., So. Soc. for Clin. Investigation, Am. Coll. Rheumatologists, Kunkel Soc. Office: WTI 378 1530 3rd Ave S Birmingham AL 35294-0002 E-mail: harry.schroeder@ccc.uab.edu.

SCHROEDER, HERMAN ELBERT, scientific consultant; b. Bklyn., July 6, 1915; s. Henry W. and Caroline (Schmidt) S.; m. Elizabeth Barnes, June 13, 1938; children: Nancy Schroeder Tarczy, Edward L., Peter H., Martha L. Schroeder Lewis. AB summa cum laude, Harvard, 1936, A.M., 1937, PhD, 1939. With E.I. du Pont de Nemours & Co., Wilmington, Del., 1938-80, asst. dir. R&D, 1957-63, dir. R&D, 1963-80; pres. Schroeder Sci. Svcs., Inc., 1980—. Sci. cons. Met. Mus. Art, N.Y.C., Smithsonian Instn., Winterthur Mus. Mem. Chester County Sch. Bd., Unionville, Pa., 1950-56; pres. Assn. Harvard Chemists, 1955-56; mem. vis. com. Harvard Chemistry Dept., 1960-72; mem. sci. adv. com. Winterthur Mus.; trustee, chmn. research com. U. Del. Research Found., 1976-84, former v.p. Recipient award Internat. Inst. Synthetic Rubber Producers, 1979, Lavoisier medal DuPont, 1992, Disting. Achievment award PolyPrep, N.Y.C., 1997. Mem. AAAS, Am. Chem. Soc. (Charles Goodyear medal 1984), N.Y. Acad. Scis., Phi Beta Kappa, Alpha Chi Sigma. Home and Office: 74 Stonegates 4031 Kennett Pike Greenville DE 19807-2033 E-mail: herzschro@aol.com. *A life in industrial research has been for me both challenging and rewarding. Forces which impel me are largely the compulsion to look for the new, to change for the better, be it by finding better ways to do things or by inventing products to make the world function better. Gratifyingly, these often make the world aesthetically more pleasant and sometimes cleaner. I am concerned by the growing hostility of society to science and to developments that ensure a more comfortable life and safer food and energy than would otherwise be possible.*

SCHROEDER, HORST WILHELM, food products executive; b. Schwerin, Germany, May 5, 1941; m. Gisela I. Kammin; 1 child, Bernd; stepchildren: Ralph, Isabel Lange. MBA, U. Gottingen, Hamburg, Fed. Republic Germany, 1965. Sr. auditor Price Waterhouse, Hamburg, 1966-70; fin. contr. Kellogg Co. of West Germany, Bremen, 1970-71, dir. fin., 1971-76, mng. dir., 1976-81; pres., chief exec. officer Kellogg Salada Can., Toronto, 1981-83; pres. Kellogg Internat., Battle Creek, Mich., 1983-86, Kellogg N.A., Battle Creek, 1986-88; exec. v.p. Kellogg Co., 1988, pres., chief oper. officer, 1988—. Mem. adv. bd. J.L. Kellogg Grad. Sch.; Bd. of govs. St. Joseph Acad. of Food Mktg., Phila., 1986-88; mem. com. external affairs U. Ill., Chgo., 1987-88. Mem. Am. Health Found. (bd. dirs. 1987—), KC (pres. 1988—, bd. dirs. 1989—). Avocations: golf, tennis. Office: Am Italian Pasta Co 1000 Italian Way Excelsior Springs MO 64024

SCHROEDER, JOHN H. university chancellor; b. Twin Falls, Idaho, Sept. 13, 1943; s. Herman John and Azalia (Kimes) S.; m. Sandra Barrow; children: John Kimes, Andrew Barrow. BA, Lewis and Clark Coll., Portland, Oreg., 1965; MA, U. Va., 1967, PhD, 1971. Instr. history U. Wis., Milw., 1970-71, asst. prof., 1971-76, assoc. prof., 1976-86, prof., 1986—, Am. Coun. on Edn. fellow, 1982-83, assoc. dean, 1976-82, asst. to vice chancellor, 1982-85, acting vice chancellor, 1985-87, vice chancellor, 1987-90, chancellor, 1990-98, U. Wis. sys. prof., 1998—. Louis M. Sears Meml. lectr. Purdue U., 1978. Author: Mr. Polk's War: American Opposition and Dissent, 1973, The Commercial and Diplomatic Role of the American Navy 1829-1861, 1985, Matthew C. Perry: Antebellum Sailor and Diplomat, 2001. V.p. bd. dir. John Michael Kohlers Arts Ctr.; bd. dir. Wis. Hist. Soc. Recipient Edward and Rosa Uhrig award U. Wis.-Milw., 1974, Disting. Teaching award AMOCO/U. Wis.-Milw., 1975. Mem. Orgn. Am. Historians, Soc. for History of Early Republic, Soc. for History Am. Fgn. Rels., Rotary. Office: U Wis Dept History PO Box 413 2310 E Hartford Ave Milwaukee WI 53211-3165 E-mail: jhs@uwm.edu.

SCHROEDER, JOYCE KATHERINE, state agency administrator, research analyst; b. Moline, Ill., Apr. 1, 1951; d. Reinhold J. and Miriam-May Schroeder. BS in Math., U. Ill., 1973, MA in Ops. Rsch., 1978. Underwriter, programmer, Springfield, Ill., 1973-76; ops. rsch. analyst Ill. Dept. Transp., 1976-78, data analyst, 1978-80, team leader, fatal accident reporting sys., 1980-83, mgr. safety project evaluation, 1983-92, mgr. accident studies and investigation, 1992—. Sys. engring. del. to China China Assn. for Sci. and Tech., 1986; mem. staff Driving While Intoxicated Adv. Coun. and Task Force, State of Ill., 1983-86, 89-92, Gov. Task Force on Occupant Protection, 1988-90, Ill. Traffic Safety Info. Sys. Coun., 1993-95. Vol. Animal Protective League, Springfield; leaderbd. co-chairperson LPGA Rail Classic, Springfield, 1983-87; amb. of goodwill Lions of Ill. Found., 1993, trustee, 1995-99. Lions Clubs Internat. Melvin Jones fellow, 1993, Lions of Ill. Found. fellow, 1995. Mem.: Past Dist. Gov. Assn. (sec.-treas. 1993—), Lions of Ill. Endowment Fund (trustee 1998—99, coord. memls. and endowments 1999—2002), Lions Club (dist. gov. Ill. 1992—93, state membership coord. 1994—96, Melvin Jones fellow 1993), Springfield Lincoln Land Lions Club (charter pres. 1988—90, news editor 1995—, treas., 1993-95, 2002-), Lions of Ill. Found. (amb. goodwill 1993, trustee 1995—99, treas. found. bd. 1996—97, v.p. found. bd. 1997—98, chmn. long range planning com. 1997—, pres. found. bd. 1998—99, policy ad hoc com. 1999—), Kappa Delta Pi, Phi Kappa Pi. Avocations: dogs, travel, music, sports, humanitarian service. Office: Ill Dept Transp 3215 Executive Park Dr Springfield IL 62703-4514 E-mail: jks999@juno.com.

SCHROEDER, LEILA OBIER, retired law educator; b. Plaquemine, La., July 11, 1925; d. William Prentiss and Daisy Lavinia (Mays) Obier; divorced; 1 child, James Michael Cutshaw; m. Martin Charles Schroeder Jr., Sept. 19, 1969. BA, Newcomb Coll., 1946; MSW, La. State U., 1953, JD, 1965. Bar: La. 1965. Exec. dir. Evangeline Area Guidance Ctr. La. Dept. Hosps., Lafayette, 1955-57, dir. social services dept. East La. State Hosp. Jackson, 1957-60, cons. psychiat. social work Baton Rouge, 1960-61; research assoc. La. State U., 1965-68, asst. prof., 1968-73, assoc. prof., 1973-80, prof., 1980-96; ret., 1996. Author: The Legal Environment of Social Work, 1982, The Legal Environment of Social Work, 1995; contbr. articles to profl. jours. Fellow Am. Orthopsychiat. Assn.; mem. ABA, Nat. Assn. Social Workers, Acad. Cert. Social Workers, La. State Bar Assn., Baton Rouge Bar Assn. Home: 4336 Oxford Ave Baton Rouge LA 70808-4651

SCHROEDER, MARY MURPHY, federal judge; b. Boulder, Colo., Dec. 4, 1940; d. Richard and Theresa (Kahn) Murphy; m. Milton R. Schroeder, Oct. 15, 1965; children: Caroline Theresa, Katherine Emily. BA, Swarthmore Coll., 1962; JD, U. Chgo., 1965. Bar: Ill. 1966, D.C. 1966, Ariz. 1970. Trial atty. Dept. Justice, Washington, 1965—69; law clk. to Hon. Jesse Udall Ariz. Supreme Ct., 1970; mem. Lewis and Roca, Phoenix, 1971—75; judge Ariz. Ct. Appeals, 1975—79, U.S. Ct. Appeals (9th cir.), Phoenix, 1979—2000, chief judge, 2000—. Vis. instr. Ariz. State U. Coll. Law, 1976—78. Contbr. articles to profl. jours. Mem.: ABA (Margaret Brent award 2001), Am. Judicature Soc., Am. Law Inst. (coun. mem.), Fed. Bar Assn., Ariz. Bar Assn., Soroptimists. Office: US Ct Appeals 9th Cir US Courthouse Ste 610 401 W Washington St SPC-56 Phoenix AZ 85003-2156 Fax: (602) 322-7329. E-mail: mary_schroeder@ca9.uscourts.gov.

SCHROEDER, PATRICIA SCOTT, trade association administrator, retired congresswoman; b. Portland, Oreg., July 30, 1940; d. Lee Combs and Bernice (Lemoin) Scott; m. James White Schroeder, Aug. 18, 1962; children: Scott William, Jamie Christine. BA magna cum laude, U. Minn., 1961; JD, Harvard U., 1964. Bar: Colo. 1964. Field atty. NLRB, Denver, 1964-66; practiced in, 1966-72; mem. faculty U. Denver, 1969-72, C.C. Denver, 1969-70, Regis Coll., Denver, 1970-72; hearing officer Colo. Dept. Personnel, 1971-72; mem. 93d-104th Congresses from 1st Colo. dist., Washington, 1973-96; co-chmn. Congl. Caucus for Women's Issues, 1976-96; dir. New Solutions for a New Century, Inst. for a Civil Soc.; prof. Woodrow Wilson Sch. of Pub. and Internat. Affairs Princeton U., NJ, 1997; pres., CEO Assn. Am. Pubs., Washington, 1997—. Mem. Ho. Reps., ranking minority mem. judiciary subcom. on the Constitution, Nat. Security Com.; dean Congl. Women; chair Ho. Select Com. Children, youth and Families, 1991—93. Author: (book) Champion of the Great American Family, 1989, 24 Years of House Work and the Place is Still a Mess: My Life in Politics, 1998. Mem. adv. bd. Casey Family Grants Program. Named to Nat. Women's Hall of Fame, 1995. Congregationalist. Office: Assn Am Publishers 50 F St NW Fl 4 Washington DC 20001-1530

SCHROEDER, RANDALL LEE, librarian; b. Waverly, Iowa, Sept. 4, 1959; s. Duane Roy and Mary Ellen (Mueller) S.; m. Lenore Ann Kuehn, July 23, 1983; children: Lukas, Nikolaus. BA, Wartburg Coll., 1982; MA in Libr. & Info. Sci., U. Iowa, 1988. Ref. libr. Augustana Coll., Rock Island, Ill., 1988-95; info. literacy libr. Wartburg Coll., Waverly, Iowa, 1995—. Reviewer Libr. Jour., 1992—; part-owner Green Bay Packers, 1997—. Spkr., presenter Wartburg Spkrs. Bur., Waverly, 1996—; trustee Waverly Pub. Libr. Bd., 1998—, v.p., 2000-01, sec., 2001-. Mem. ALA, Iowa Libr. Assn., Iowa Acad. and Coll. Rsch. Librs., Acad. and Coll. Rsch. Librs. Democrat. Lutheran. Avocations: bicycling, German history, ancient musical instruments, books, baseball. Home: 323 6th St NW Waverly IA 50677-2438 Office: Wartburg Coll Robert and Sally Vogel Libr Waverly IA 50677 E-mail: schroederr@wartburg.edu.

SCHROEDER, RITA MOLTHEN, retired chiropractor; b. Savanna, Ill., Oct. 25, 1922; d. Frank J. and Ruth J. (McKenzie) Molthen; m. Richard H. Schroeder, Apr. 23, 1948 (div.); children— Richard, Andrew, Barbara, Thomas, Paul, Madeline. Student, Chem. Engring., Immaculate Heart Coll., 1940-41, UCLA, 1941, Palmer Sch. of Chiropractic, 1947-49; D. Chiropractic, Cleve. Coll. of Chiropractic, 1961. Engring.-tooling design data coordinator Douglas Aircraft Co., El Segundo, Santa Monica and Long Beach, Calif., 1941-47; pres. Schroeder Chiropractic, Inc., 1982-93; dir. Pacific States Chiropractic Coll., 1978-80, pres. 1980-81. Recipient Palmer Coll. Ambassador award, 1973. Parker Chiropractic Research Found. Ambassador award, 1976, Coll. Ambassador award Life West Chiropractic Coll. Mem. Internat. Chiropractic Assn., Calif. Chiropractic Assn., Internat. Chiropractic Assn. Calif., Assn. Am. Chiropractic Coll. Presidents, Council Chiropractic Edn. (Pacific State Coll. rep.), Am. Pub. Health Assn., Royal Chiropractic Knights of the Round Table. Home: 8701 N State Highway 41 Spc 18 Fresno CA 93720-1010 Office: Schroeder Chiropractic Inc 2535 N Fresno St Fresno CA 93703-1831

SCHROEDER, ROLF ROBERT, chemical engineer; b. Cleve., July 19, 1934; s. August C.G. and Adele A. (Siemer) S.; m. Gail A. Erickson, Feb. 5, 1956 (div. Jan. 1986); children: Mark, Susan, Eric; m. Joyce M. Wilkins, Oct. 5, 1989. BS in Chem. Engring., Ill. Inst. Technology, Chgo., 1956, MS, 1961, PhD, 1963; MBA, La. State U., 1977. Sr. engr. Esso Rsch. & Devel. Labs., Baton Rouge, 1963-69; sr. analyst Esso Internat., N.Y.C., 1969-71; dir. rsch. Howe-Baker Engrs., Tyler, Tex., 1971-75; engring. assoc. Exxon Rsch. & Devel. Labs., Baton Rouge, 1975-86; prin. engr. Kerr McGee Oil Co., Oklahoma City, 1987-90; advanced sr. refining engr., tech. mgr. Marathon Ashland Petroleum Co., Garyville, La., 1990—. Home: 3127 E Lakeshore Dr Baton Rouge LA 70808-2852

SCHROEDER, ROXANN JEAN, scientific writer, consultant; b. Baraboo, Wis., Feb. 6, 1961; d. Norman Eugene and Florence E. Schroeder; m. Sean Francis Craig, June 27, 1992; 1 child, Ciara Craig. BS in Zoology, U. Wis., Madison, 1983; MS in Biology, U. Houston, 1988; PhD in Cell and Devel. Biology, SUNY, Stonybrook, 1996. Post-doctoral rschr. U. Calif., Davis, 1997-98; mng. editor MethodsFinder Biosys, Phila., 1998-2000; cons. sci. comm. Schroeder Sci. Comm., Arcata, Calif., 2000—. Editor: (web newsletter) MethodsNews, 1999; contbr. articles to web. Travel grantee Endocrine Soc., 1988. Mem. AAAS, AAUW, Am. Med. Writers Assn., Sigma Xi (Excellence in Rsch. award 1991). E-mail: roxannschroeder@hotmail.com.

SCHROEDER, STEVEN ALFRED, medical educator, foundation administrator; b. N.Y.C., July 26, 1939; s. Arthur Edward and Norma (Scheinberg) Schroeder; m. Sally B. Ross, Oct. 21, 1967; children: David Arthur, Alan Ross. BA, Stanford U., 1960; MD, Harvard U., 1964; LHD (hon.) , Rush U., 1994; DSc (hon.) , Boston U., 1996, U. Mass. Med. Ctr., 1997, Georgetown U., 2000, Med. Coll. Wis., 2002. Diplomate Am. Bd. Internal Medicine. Intern and resident in internal medicine Harvard Med. Svc., Boston City Hosp., 1964—66, 1968—70; asst. prof., then assoc. prof. George Washington Med. Ctr., Washington, 1971—76; vis. prof. St. Thomas' Hosp. Med. Sch., London, 1982—83; prof. medicine, chief div. gen. internal medicine, mem. Inst. Health Policy Studies U. Calif., San Francisco, 1976—90; pres., CEO Robert Wood Johnson Found., Princeton, NJ, 1990—; clin. prof. medicine U. of Medicine and Dentistry N.J., 1990—. Conv. various govtl. and philanthropic health orgns.; chair internat. adv. com. faculty medicine Ben Gurion U., Israel. Sr. editor: Current Med. Diagnosis and Treatment, 1987—93, mem. editl. bd.: New Eng. Mag.; contbr. numerous articles to profl. jours. Mem. U.S. Prospective Payment Assessment Commn., 1983—88; bd. overseers Harvard Coll., 2000—; mem. IOM Coun.; bd. dirs. Am. Legacy Found., 2000—, vice chair, 2001—. Master: ACP; mem.: APHA, Soc. Gen. Internal Medicine (past pres.), Inst. Medicine, Assn. Am. Physicians, Physicians for Social Responsibility, Alpha Omega Alpha, Phi Beta Kappa. Office: Robert Wood Johnson Found PO Box 2316 Princeton NJ 08543-2316

SCHROEDER, TODD DAVID, accountant; b. Sioux Falls, S.D., Nov. 29, 1968; s. Keith Harm and Beverly Delores (Behr) S. BA in Acctg., Buena Vista Coll., 1991. CPA, Iowa. Sr. auditor Blue Cross Blue Shield of Iowa, Des Moines, 1991-94; asst. dir. reimbursement Girling Health Care, Inc., Austin, Tex., 1994—. Mem. AICPA, Tex. Soc. CPAs, Iowa Soc. CPAs, Young Men's Bus. League. Republican. Presbyterian. Avocations: golf, running, bicycling, sailing. Home: PO Box 925931 Houston TX 77292-5931 Office: Girling Health Care Inc 4902 Grover Ave Austin TX 78756-2629 Address: PO Box 925931 Houston TX 77292-5931

SCHROEDER, WILLIAM ARTHUR, law educator; b. Chgo., Mar. 19, 1943; s. Arthur C. Schroeder; children: Elizabeth, Matthew, David, Sara, John. BA, U. Ill., Champaign, 1966, JD, 1969; LLM, Harvard U., 1977. Bar: Mass. 1972, Mo. 1990, U.S. Supreme Ct. 1978. Instr. law Boston Coll., 1970-71; practicing atty. various firms, Mass., 1972-80; assoc. prof. law U. Ala., Tuscaloosa, 1980-84; prof. law So. Ill. U., Carbondale, 1984—. Vis. prof. law U. Mo.-Columbia, 1983; Washington U. 1991, 99. Co-author: Alabama Evidence, 1987, 3d edit., 2000; author: Missouri Evidence, 1992, 2d edit., 1999, 2000, Missouri Courtroom Handbook, 1999, 2000, 2001, 2002; contbr. articles to profl. jours. Mem. ABA, Harvard Club of St. Louis, Lions. Home: 2914 Kent Dr Carbondale IL 62901 Office: So Ill U Lesar Law Bldg Carbondale IL 62901

SCHROEDER, W(ILLIAM) WIDICK, religion educator; b. Newton, Kans., Nov. 12, 1928; s. William Fredric and Irene (Widick) S.; m. Gayle Eadie, Sept. 1, 1956; children: Scott David, Carla Gayle. BA, Bethel Coll., 1949; MA, Mich. State U., East Lansing, 1952; BDiv, Chgo. Theol. Sem., 1955; PhD, U. Chgo., 1960; DD (hon.), Chgo. Theol. Seminary, 1995. Ordained to ministry Congl. Christian Ch., 1955. Instr. Mich. State U., East Lansing, 1953-54, U. Chgo., 1958-60; from asst. prof. to prof. religion and society Chgo. Theol. Sem., 1960-94, prof. emeritus, 1994—. Vis. fellow Mansfield Coll., Oxford, Eng., 1966; vis. lectr. Yale U., 1970; vis. scholar Ctr. for Process Studies, Claremont, Calif., 1976; vis. lectr. in ethics and soc. Divinity Sch. U. Chgo., 1967-71, 76; editor Rev. of Religious Rsch., 1964-69. Author: (with Victor Obenhaus) Religion in American Culture: Unity and Diversity in a Midwestern County, 1964; Cognitive Structures and Religious Research, 1970; (with Victor Obenhaus, Larry A. Jones and Thomas P. Sweetser) Suburban Religion: Churches and Synagogues in the American Experience, 1974; (with Keith A. Davis) Where Do I Stand? Living Theological Options for Contemporary Christians, 1973, rev. edit., 1975, 3d edit., 1978; Flawed Process and Sectarian Substance: Analytic and Critical Perspectives on the United Church of Christ General Synod Pronouncement, Christian Faith: Economic Life and Justice, 1990; Toward Belief: Essays in the Human Sciences, Social Ethics, and Philosophical Theology, 1996; co-editor: (with Philip Hefner) Belonging and Alienation: Religious Foundations for the Human Future, 1976; (with Gibson Winter) Belief and Ethics: Essays in Ethics, the Human Sciences and Ministry in Honor of W. Alvin Pitcher, 1978; (with John B. Cobb, Jr.) Process Philosophy and Social Thought, 1981; (with Perry LeFevre) Spiritual Nurture and Congregational Development, 1984, Pastoral Care and Liberation Praxis: Essays in Personal and Social Transformation, 1986, Creative Ministries in Contemporary Christianity, 1991; (with Franklin I. Gamwell) Economic Life: Process Interpretations and Critical Responses, 1988; co-editor Studies in Religion, Society and Personality, Center for the Scientific Study of Religion, 1972-2001. Mem. Religious Rsch. Assn. Home: 6315 Longwood Rd Libertyville IL 60048-9447 *The aims of existence are aesthetic satisfaction and intensity of feeling. In facilitating these aims, the Divine Reality is the locus of potentiality, the mediator of experience, the evoker of feeling and the ultimate recipient of all that has become.*

SCHROEN, FRANCES BRANT, police department administrator; b. Salt Lake City, July 21, 1945; d. Albert Lynn and Julia (Rees) Brant; m. John Richard Schroen, May 19, 1979; 1 child, Joseph Thomas. Student, U. Utah. Research technician Geneol. Soc., Salt Lake City, 1963-65; exec. sec. Lang Wang Equipment Co., Salt Lake City, 1969-70; sec. E-Systems, 1971-72; legal sec., 1981-82; supr., examiner Salt Lake City Police Dept., 1972—; cons. in document examination for local and state police agys. Utah; handwriting specialist, lectr. pvt. bus., local and community orgns.; owner Am. Writs. Contbr. articles to profl. pubs. Treas. Salt Lake City Ctr./World Messianity, 1984—. Internat. Graphoanalysis Soc. scholar, 1984. Mem. Ind. Assn. Document Examiners, World Assn. of Document Examiners, Nat. Assn. Female Execs., Utah Bus. Women, Sigma Alpha Gamma. Avocations: racquetball, horseback riding, weight lifting. Office: Salt Lake City Police Dept 450 S 300 E Salt Lake City UT 84111-3202

SCHROER, BERNARD JON, industrial engineering educator; b. Seymour, Ind., Oct. 11, 1941; s. Alvin J. and Selma A. (Mellencamp) S.; m. Kathleen Dittman, July 5, 1963; children: Shannon, Bradley. BSE, Western Mich. U., 1964; MSE, U. Ala., 1967; PhD, Okla. State U., 1972. Registered profl. engr., Ala. Mech. designer Sandia Labs., Albuquerque, 1962-63; engr. Teledyne Co., Huntsville, Ala., 1964-67, Boeing Co., Huntsville, 1967-70, Computer Sci. Corp., Huntsville, 1970-72; dir. Johnson Ctr. U. Ala., 1972-91, prof., 1991—, chmn. dept. indsl. and sys. engring., 1991-94, assoc. v.p. rsch., 1994—. Mem. adv. coun. Energy Dept., Montgomery, Ala., 1980-86; bd. dirs So. Solar Energy Ctr., Atlanta, 1980-83; mem. gov.'s cabinet State of Ala., Montgomery, 1982; exec. dir. Ala. Automotive Mfrs. Assn., 2000—. Author: Modern Apparel Manufacturing Systems and Simulation, 1991; contbr. articles to profl. jours. Named Outstanding Engr., Robotics Internat., 1986, Outstanding Engr., So. Tech. Coun., 1987; recipient summer traineeship NSF, 1971. Fellow: Inst. Indsl. Engrs. (pres. 1972, 1986, Outstanding Engr. 1973, 1977); mem.: Soc. Computer Simulation. Lutheran. Home: 716 Owens Dr SE Huntsville AL 35801-2034 Office: U Ala Huntsville AL 35899-0001 E-mail: schroerb@email.uah.edu.

SCHROER, JANE HASTINGS, nurse practitioner; b. Pender, Nebr., Aug. 24, 1947; d. John Dean and Florence (Meier) Hastings; m. Ronald L. Schroer, May 13, 1967; 1 child, Patricia Schroer Kennedy. LPN, Antonian Sch. Prac. Nursing, Carroll, Iowa, 1966; Diploma, St. Joseph Sch. Nursing, Sioux City, Iowa, 1980; BS, Westmar Coll., LeMars, Iowa, 1985; Women's Health Care Nurse Practitioner, S.W. Med. Ctr./U. Tex., Dallas, 1990. Nurse practitioner, cardiac catheterization lab. Marian Health Ctr., Sioux City, 1980-85; nurse practitioner Chandler, Ariz., 1991-93, STD Clinic, Austin, Tex., 1994-95, Round Rock, 1995-96; founder, owner Lone Star Med. Reimbursement, 1997-99; ret., 2000. Republican. Roman Catholic. Avocations: scrapbooking, travel, collecting angels, cookbooks and Bobbsey Twins books. Home: 21204 Derby Day Ave Pflugerville TX 78660

SCHROFF, LOIS GRUNWELL, artist, color researcher; b. Arlington, Va., Apr. 5, 1924; d. William T. and Grace B. Grunwell; m. Roy P. Spaulding, Mar. 6, 1944 (div. 1954); children: Candyce, Roy; Frank A. Schroff, Jr., July 10, 1954 (div. 1962); children: Frank, Guy Schroff. AS, No. Va. C.C., 1969. Lic. real estate sales assoc., comml. real estate sales assoc., Va. Pres. Color Rsch. Ctr., Reston, Va., 1972-77, Chalice Ctr. for Art, Herndon, 1978-94, Seaside Studio, Virginia Beach, 1995—; owner, mgr. Newlight Books, Herndon, 1970—. Author: Experiencing Color Between Darkness and Light, 1985, The

Archangel Michael, 1990, Creator Video Spirit in Watercolor, 1992, Color, its Relationship to Soul and Sprit, 2002; exhibited in group shows Waterford (Va.) Art Group, 1973 (1st in watercolor award 1973), Vienna Soc. Artists, Tysons Corner, Va., 1974 (Best in Show award 1974), Internat. Icarus, Nags Head, N.C., 1995, Seaside Art Gallery, Nags Head, 1996, Visions Gallery, Virginia Beach, Va., 1996, Portsmouth (Va.) Mus., 1996,Virginia Watercolor Soc., annual juried show, Abingdon, Va.; In permanent collection at U.S. Embassy, Tegucigalpa, Honduras, pvt. collections in U.S., Can. and Switzerland. Mem. Chesapeake Bay Watercolorists, Christians in Visual Arts, Va. Watercolor Soc., Soc. Layerists in Multi-Media, Inst. Noetic Scis. Avocations: singing, dancing, swimming, painting, watercolor instruction. Office: Seaside Studio 6501A Atlantic Ave Virginia Beach VA 23451-2014

SCHROFFNER, WERNER GEORG, internist, endocrinologist; b. Salzburg, Austria, June 28, 1939; came to U.S., 1964; s. Paul and Walburga S.; m. Aileen Sueko Nakanishi, Aug. 27, 1966; children: Ingrid Chiemi, Mark Georg, Stefan Paul. MD, U. Innsbruck, Austria, 1963. Mem. staff Queen's Med. Ctr., Honolulu, 1993—, chief staff, 1993-94; pvt. practice, 1993—. Fellow ACP, Am. Coll. Endocrinologists; mem. Am. Assn. Clin. Endocrinology, German Soc. Endocrinology, Endocrine Soc. Avocations: violin, classical music, reading, travel, tennis. Office: 1380 Lusitana St Ste 902 Honolulu HI 96813-2448

SCHROLL, EDWIN JOHN, retired secondary educator, stage director; b. Watertown, N.Y., Feb. 14, 1941; s. Clarence Edwin and Frances Lucille (Snyder) S. BS, Lyndon State Coll., 1966; MS, Oswego State U., 1971. Cert. tchr. N.Y. English tchr. jr. h.s. Watertown (N.Y.) Sch. System, 1966-67; English tchr. h.s. Belleville (N.Y.) Cen. Sch., 1967-71, Massena (N.Y.) Cen. Sch., 1971-96, drama and speech tchr., 1988-96, drama coach, 1975-96, forensics coach; ret., 1996. Engr., announcer, programmer Pathways to Peace program Sta. WNCQ, Watertown, 1967-92; dir. Family History Ctr., Watertown, N.Y. Cinematographer, writer, narrator, prodr. (documentaries) The United States: A Bicentennial Tour, 1976, Europe on $100 a Day, 1986; cinematographer: (TV) Wish You Were Here in Cape Vincent, 2000, Partying, 1989; co-author: Standard Operations Procedures and Duties of a Desk Clerk, 1963, Wish You Were Here in Cape Vincent, 2000; prodn. supr. (hist. pageant) 1,000 Seasons, 2001; dir. various high sch. prodns.; actor various community prodns. Bd. dirs. Youth in Action, 1993-94; active Nat. Family Opinion, 1991—; state advocate Ednl. Theatre Assn., 1996; del. Citizens Ambassador Program of People to People Internat. Theatre Edn. Delegation to China, 1996; active Cape Vincent Arts Coun., 1997—, Gravelly Point Players, 1997—, Breakwater Art Gallery, 1997—. Mem. Nat. Geog. Soc., Ednl. Theatre Assn., Archaeology Inst. Am., Am. Film Inst., Nat. Trust Hist. Preservation, Cinerama Preservation Soc. Republican. Mem. Lds Ch. Avocations: stamp and coin collecting, gardening, historical research, genealogy, travel. Home: PO Box 216 143 S Murray St Cape Vincent NY 13618 Office: Massena Sch System 290 Main St Massena NY 13662-1901 E-mail: edschroll@tds.net.

SCHROM, ELIZABETH ANN, educator; b. Princeton, Minn., June 7, 1941; d. Raymond Alois and Grace Eleanor (Hayes) S. Student, U. Minn., 1960; BA, St. Scholastica Coll., Duluth, Minn., 1963; postgrad., Princeton U., 1965; MEd, Temple U., 1972; MLS, Drexel U., 1974; postgrad., NYU, 1981, Russian Temple U., 1983. Tchr. Strandquist (Minn.) H.S., 1963-64, Hutchinson (Minn.) H.S., 1964-65, Peace Corps, Ankara, Turkey, 1965-67, Phila. Sch. Dist., 1968-80; children's libr. Laurel (Del.) Pub. Libr., 1983; writer Ontonville Ind., Ontanville, Ind., 1983—. Mem. Jewish Com. on Middle East, Washington, 1988-90, 93, Nat. Coun. Returned Peace Corps. Vols., Washington, 1989-99, Nat. Taxpayers Union, Washington, 1988-92; mem. bd. policy Liberty Lobby, Washington, 1989-2000 Populist. Roman Catholic. Avocations: writing, cooking, history, travel. Home: RR 2 Box 206 Ortonville MN 56278-9784

SCHROPFER, DAVID WALDRON, pharmaceutical executive, educator, consultant; b. Plainfield, N.J., Oct. 27, 1939; s. Frank Jeremiah and Edna Mae (Mueller) S.; m. Gloria Weaver, Aug. 10, 1963; children: Suzanne, David Jr., Kathleen. BS, NYU, 1961; postgrad., Hunter Coll., 1972-74. Asst. product mgr. Procter and Gamble, Cin., 1961-63; account exec. Ted Bates, N.Y.C., 1963-65; sr. account exec. Ogilvy and Mather, 1965-68; v.p., mgmt. supr. SSC&B, 1969-72, D'Arcy McManus and Masius Inc., N.Y.C., 1973-75; exec. v.p. James Neal Harvey, Inc., 1976-79; exec. v.p., ptnr. Griffin-Bacal, Inc., 1979-81, Mike Sloan, Inc., Miami, Fla., 1980-82; pres., CEO Knudsen Moore Schropfer Advt., Inc., Stamford, Conn., 1983-88; pres. DWS Assocs., Inc., 1988-95, EnviroDerm Pharms., Inc., Louisville, 1995—. Adj. prof. Fla. Internat. U., Miami, 1982; lectr. U. Mass., Amherst, 1985-86, U. New Haven, 1985, Providence Coll., 1987. Author: What Every Account Executive Should Know About Marketing Plans, 1990, Fundamentals of Marketing: Basic Concepts and Applications, AMA, 1990. Bd. dirs. Jr. Achievement, Miami, 1982-83; bd. dirs. ARC, Stamford, 1984-90, chmn., 1987-89; chmn. Charter Revision Commn., Stamford, 1986-87; mem. Stamford Bd. Fin., 1987-93; candidate U.S. Ho. of Reps. from 4th Congl. Dist., 1992; vol. exec. Internat. Exec. Svc. Corp. Mem. Am. Assn. Advt. Agys. (lectr. 1982-85), Am. Mktg. Assn., Am. Mgmt. Assn. (lectr. 1984—). Roman Catholic. Office: EnviroDerm Pharm Inc PO Box 32370 Louisville KY 40232-2370

SCHROPP, JAMES HOWARD, lawyer; b. Lebanon, Pa., June 20, 1943; Work e-mail: schroja@ffhsj.com. s. Howard J. and Maud E. (Parker) S.; m. Jo Ann Simpson, Sept. 4, 1965; children: James A., John C., Jeffrey M., Jeremy M. BA, U. Richmond, 1965; JD, Georgetown U., 1973. Bar: D.C. 1973, U.S. Supreme Ct. 1980. Asst. gen. counsel SEC, Washington, 1973-79; ptnr. Fried, Frank, Harris, Shriver & Jacobson, 1979—. Adj. prof. Georgetown U., Washington, 1982-86; mem. faculty Na.t Inst. for Trial Advocacy. Mem. ABA (discovery com. litigation sect. 1984-86, tender offer litigation subcom. corp. banking and bus. law sect. 1985-86, task force on broker-dealer compliance supervisory procedures 1987-89). Office: Fried Frank Harris Shriver & Jacobson 1001 Pennsylvania Ave NW Washington DC 20004-2505

SCHROPP, TOBIN, lawyer; b. 1962; BS in Fgn. Svc., Georgetown U., 1984, JD, 1987, LLM in Taxation, 1991. Bar: 1987. V.p., gen. counsel Peter Kiewit Sons' Inc., Omaha. Office: Peter Kiewit Sons Inc 1000 Kiewit Plaza Omaha NE 68131

SCHROTE, JOHN ELLIS, retired government executive; b. Findlay, Ohio, May 6, 1936; s. Millard L. and Alberta (Ellis) S.; m. Rachel Daly, Mar. 2, 1957; children: James D., Gretchen Schrote Kent. BS in Agr., Ohio State U., 1958; MBA, Xavier U., 1964. Buyer-expediter McGraw Constrn. Co., Middletown, Ohio, 1958-59; buyer Armco Corp., 1959-66; adminstrv. asst. Congressman D.E. Lukens, Washington, 1967-71; prin. asst. dir. OEO, 1971-72; spl. asst. to sec. USDA, 1972-77, nat. rep. congl. com., 1977-79; adminstrv. asst. Congressman F.J. Sensenbrenner, Jr., 1979—81; acting asst. sec. USDA, 1981-82; dep. dir. presdl. pers. office The White House, 1982-83; exec. v.p. Bishop Bryant & Assocs., Washington, 1983-84; adminstrv. asst. Congressman F.J. Sensenbrenner, Jr., 1984—89; asst. to sec. and dir. congl. affairs Dept. Interior, 1989, dep. asst. sec. policy mgmt. and budget, 1989-91, asst. sec. policy mgmt. and budget, 1991-93; retired, 1993. Mem. Nat. Policy Forum, The Environ. Policy Coun., 1994-96, N.C. Seafood Indsl. Park Authority, 1994-97; mem. Currituck County Econ. Devel. Bd., 1994—, chmn., 1996-99; mem. Currituck County Rep. Exec. Com., 1993-97, 3d Dist. Rep. Exec. Com., 1994-97, N.C. State Rep. Exec. Com., 1994-97; mem. Currituck County Ext. Svc. Adv. Leadership Coun., 1994-2000, chmn., 1996-97; bd. dirs. Currituck County 4-H Found., 1994-2000; mem. Ocean Hills Property Owners Assn., 1996-98, treas., 1997-2000, v.p., 1996-97; commr. Northeastern N.C. Regional Econ. Devel. Commn., 1997—. Mem. Reagan-Bush Alumni Assn., Bush-Quayle Alumni Assn. Episcopalian. Home: PO Box 209 Corolla NC 27927-0209

SCHROTH, PETER W(ILLIAM), lawyer, management and law educator; b. Camden, N.J., July 24, 1946; s. Walter and Patricia Anne (Page) S.; children: Laura Salome Erickson-Schroth, Julia James. AB, Shimer Coll., 1966; JD, U. Chgo., 1969; M in Comparative Law, U.Chgo., 1971; SJD, U. Mich., 1979; postgrad., U. Freiburg, Fed. Republic Germany, Faculté Internationale pour l'Enseignement de Droit Comparé; MBA, Rensselaer Poly. Inst., 1988; DHL, Shimer Coll., 2000; MSc, Sch. Oriental and African Studies, 2000. Bar: Ill. 1969, N.Y. 1979, Conn. 1985, Mass. 1990; solicitor Supreme Ct. England and Wales 1995. Asst. prof. So. Meth. U., 1973-77; fellow in law and humanities Harvard U., 1976-77, vis. scholar, 1980-81; assoc. prof. N.Y. Law Sch., 1977-81; prof. law Hamline U., St. Paul, 1981-83; dep. gen. counsel Equator Bank Ltd., 1984-87; v.p., dep. gen. counsel Equator Holdings Ltd., 1987-94, v.p., gen. counsel, 1994-2000. Adj. prof. law U. Conn., 1985-86, Western New Eng. Coll., 1988—, adj. prof. of mgmt. Rensselaer Poly. Inst., 1988-98, prof., 1999—, dir. Ctr. for Global Bus. Studies, 2000—. Author: Foreign Investment in the United States, 2d edit., 1977; (with Stiefel) Products Liability: European Proposals and American Experience, 1981, Doing Business in Sub-Saharan Africa, 1991; bd. editors Am. Jour. Comparative Law, 1981-84, 91—; mem. editl. bd. Conn. Bar Jour., 1988—, sr. editor, 1993-2000, editor-in-chief, 2000—; mem. editl. bd. N.Y. Internat. Law Rev.; mem. editl. rev. bd. Jour. Bus. in Developing Nations, 1996-2000, editor, 2000—; contbr. articles to profl. jours. Mem. ABA (editor in chief ABA Environ. Law Symposium 1980-82), Am. Soc. Comparative Law (bd. dirs. 1978-84, 91—), Am. Fgn. Law Assn., Internat. Bar Assn., Internat. Law Assn. (com. multinat. banking), Acad. Internat. Bus., Conn. Civil Liberties Union (bd. dirs. 1985-92), Environ. Law Inst. (assoc.), Columbia U. Peace Seminar (assoc.), Hartford Club (bd. govs. 1995-98), Am. Corp. Counsel Assn. (pres. Conn. chpt.1997-2000), Conn. Bar Assn. (chair sect. of internat. law 1997-2000). Office: Rensselaer Poly Inst Lally Sch Mgmt and Tech 275 Windsor St Hartford CT 06120-2910

SCHROTH, THOMAS NOLAN, editor; b. Trenton, N.J., Dec. 21, 1920; s. Frank David and Loretta (Nolan) S.; m. Colette Streit, May 1, 1948 (div. 1958); 1 child, Valerie; m. Patricia Wiggins, Sept. 27, 1958; children: Jennifer, Amy, Anne. Student, Tuck Sch. Bus. Adminstrn., 1942; AB, Dartmouth Coll., 1943. Reporter Time, Washington, 1946-47, UPI, Boston, 1947-48; reporter, news editor Bklyn. Eagle, 1948-51, mng. editor, 1951-55; editorial adviser Magnum Photos, Inc., N.Y.C., 1955; exec. editor, pub. Congl. Quar. Inc. and Editorial Research Reports, Washington, 1955-68; founder, editor Nat. Jour. Ctr. Polit. Rsch., 1969-70; communications adviser Pub. Broadcasting Environment Ctr., 1970-71; asst. dir. pub. affairs for communications EPA, 1970-71, cons., 1972; exec. editor The Ellsworth (Maine) American, 1972-77; co-pub.-editor (with Patricia Schroth) Maine Life Mag., Sedgwick, 1977-81; editorial cons. U. Maine, Bangor, 1976-90; mng. editor South-North News Svc., Hanover, N.H., 1987-91; co-pub. New Leaf Pubs., Sedgwick, Maine, 1990—. Mem. Am. Press Inst. Seminar for Mng. Editors, 1953, Regional Transp. Adv. Com., 1996-99. Editor: Congress and the Nation, 1946-64--A Review of Government and Politics in the Postwar Years; editor Improving the U. of Maine trustee's pamphlet. Elected selectman Town of Sedgwick, 1989-94, moderator 1995—; bd. dirs. Blue Hill (Maine) Meml. Hosp., 1978-93, Bangor Symphony Orch., 1981-87, Blue Hill Concert Assn., 1991—; bd. dirs., v.p. Island Nursing Home, Deer Isle, Maine, 1985—; mem. Maine State Dem. Com., Augusta, 1985-92, 97—; bd. dirs. Downeast Transp., Inc., 1993—; del. Maine Dem. Nat. Conv., 2000. 1st lt. Army Airways Comm. Sys., USAAF, WWII. Mem. Sigma Delta Chi. Avocations: gardening, walking, music. Home and Office: 50 Benjamin River Rd Sedgwick ME 04676-9729

SCHROTT, NORMAN, retired clinical social worker; b. N.Y.C., Jan. 26, 1938; s. Walter Quido Otto and Anna (Klein) S.; m. Janet Ann Cupolo, July 25, 1964. BA in Sociology, Cleve. State U., 1972; MS in Social Planning and Adminstrn., Case Western Res. U., 1976. Lic. Ind. Social Worker, Ohio. Adminstrv. specialist div. social svcs. Cuyahoga County Welfare Dept., Cleve., 1972-74, foster care specialist, 1976-79, child abuse supr., 1979-80, protective svcs. supr., 1980-2000. Served with U.S. Army, 1962-65. Grantee State of Ohio, 1974-76. Mem. Acad. Cert. Social Workers, Nat. Geog. Soc., Greater Cleve. Orchid Soc., Westshore Orchid Soc., Nat. Audubon Soc., Am. Orchid Soc., Kiwanis Club. Home: 25925 Lake Rd Cleveland OH 44140-2563

SCHROY, IDA JEAN, mental health nurse; b. Watertown, N.Y., Dec. 21, 1927; d. Milton Russell and Ethel Minerva Lee; m. Robert Thomas Schroy, Jan. 1, 1949; children: Robert Russell, David Alan. Diploma in nursing, Mercy Hosp., Watertown, N.Y., 1948; BSN, C.W. Post Coll., Brookville-Westbury, N.Y., 1975; MSN, Adelphi U., 1978. Staff nurse Queens Gen. Hosp., Jamaica, N.Y., 1948-51, Huntington (N.Y.) Hosp., 1951-57; head office nurse Drs. Gordon, Kagan, Schwager, Huntington, 1957-68; indsl. nurse Macys Dept. Store, Bay Shore, N.Y., 1968; staff nurse, head nurse U.S. VA Med. Ctr., Northport, 1968-85, psychotherapist Mental Health Clinic, 1985-89; pvt. practice, 1989—. Sec. ELYC, Northport, 1983-85. With U.S. Cadet Nurse Corps, 1945-48. Mem. Network of N.Y. Clin. Nurse Specialists (vice chairperson 1988-96), Eatons Light Yacht Club. Methodist. Avocations: treasure hunting, water sports, bowling, bridge. Home and Office: 136 Eatons Neck Rd Northport NY 11768-1110 E-mail: ischroy@suffolk.lib.ny.us.

SCHROYER, MICHAEL KEVIN, critical care nurse and hospital administrator; b. Kewanee, Ill., Sept. 14, 1959; s. Jesse Wayne and Shirley Ann (Brown) S.; m. Joy Anne, June 20, 1987; children: Tiffany Marie, Rebecca Ann, Adam Michael. Diploma, Moline Pub. Hosp. Sch. Nursing, 1980; BSN, Loyola U., 1984; MSN, Seton Hall U., 1987; postgrad., Rush U., 1990-91. Cert. nursing adminstr., hosp. adminstr. Nurse mgr., CCU, ICU, PICU, CCFP Jersey Shore Med. Ctr., Neptune, NJ; assoc. dir., critical care nursing Hyde Park Hosp., Chgo.; adminstrv. dir., transplant svcs. Rush-Presbyn./St. Lukes Med. Ctr.; adminstrv. coord., v.p. cardiovascular and med./surg. svcs. United Med. Ctr., Moline; adminstrv. leader, v.p. Regional CardioLife Ctr., Tenet Brookwood Med. Ctr., Birmingham, Ala., 1993-96; v.p. clin. svcs. MedCath McAllen (Tex.) Heart Hosp., 1996-98, MedCath Dayton (Ohio) Heart Hosp., 1998-2000, interim CEO, 2000, v.p. ops./COO, 2000—01; pres. / CEO Okla. Heart Hosp., Oklahoma City, 2001—; cons. The Rielly Group, Denver, 2001—. Author: Emergency Nursing, 1989, Nursing Spectrum, 1989, Comprehensive Nursing Care Plans, 1995. Former bd. dirs. Rock Island County chpt. Am. Heart Assn. Mem.: AACN, Am. Heart Assn. (bd. dirs. Oklahoma City chpt.), Am. Assn. Med. Cardiovasc. Adminstrs., Am. Coll. Healthcare Execs., Sigma Theta Tau. Office: Okla Heart Hosp 4050 W Memorial Rd Oklahoma City OK 73120 Business E-Mail: mschroyer@okheart.com.

SCHRYVER, BRUCE JOHN, safety engineer; b. Newark, Aug. 14, 1944; s. Francis Henry and Ann Laura (Hart) S.; m. Lorraine Patricia Simodis, Oct. 8, 1966 (div.); children: Holly Lynn, Wendy Marie; m. Laura Lee Davis, Mar. 17, 2000. BA in Occupational Safety and Health, Western States U., 1984, MS in Safety Mgmt., PhD in Safety Mgmt., Western States U., 1989. Cert. safety profl.; cert. products safety mgr.; cert. hazard control mgr.; cert. hazardous materials mgr.; cert. healthcare safety profl. Inspector Lansing B. Warner Inc., Chgo., 1968-69; engrng. rep. Glens Falls Ins. Co., Newark, 1969; safety dir. Hillside Metal Products, 1969-70; loss prevention specialist Warner Ins. Group, Chgo., 1970-79, regional loss control mgr., 1979-82, nat. loss control coordinator, 1982-85; mgr., asst. v.p. loss control svcs. Ins. Co. of the West, San Diego, 1990—; v.p. loss control svcs. ICW Group, 1990—, v.p. mcpl. law enforcement svcs., 1992—. Inventor Emergency Light Mount, 1971. Mem. Town of Clay (N.Y.) Pub. Safety Com., 1976-78, Beacon Woods East Homeowners Assn., Hudson, Fla., 1979-85, Meadowridge Homeowners Assn., La Costa, Calif., 1986-98, Harbor Pointe Homeowners Assn., 1999—; cons. Town of Clay Police Dept., 1975-78. With USCG, 1964-68. Recipient letter of appreciation Town of Clay, 1977, cert. of appreciation DAV, 1968, Golden State award, 1990. Mem. Am. Soc. Safety Engrs., Soc. Fire Protection Engrs., Nat. Safety Mgmt. Soc., Vets. Safety, Nat. Fire Protection Assn., San Diego Safety Coun., Calif. Conf. Arson Investigators. Republican. Roman Catholic. Avocations: auto racing, boating, photography, electronics. Home: 803 Spindrift Ln Carlsbad CA 92009-3740 Office: ICW Group 11455 El Camino Real San Diego CA 92130-2088 E-mail: BSchryver@lcwgroup.com.

SCHUBEL, JERRY ROBERT, marine science educator, scientist, university dean; b. Bad Axe, Mich., Jan. 26, 1936; s. Theodore Howard and Laura Alberta (Gobel) S.; m. Margaret Ann Hostetler, June 14, 1958; children: Susan Elizabeth, Kathryn Ann. BS, Alma Coll., 1957; MA in Tchg., Harvard U., 1959; PhD, Johns Hopkins U., 1968; DSc (hon.), Mass. Maritime Acad., 1997. Rsch. assoc. Chesapeake Bay Inst., Johns Hopkins U., Balt., 1968-69, rsch. scientist, 1969-74, adj. rsch. prof., assoc. dir., 1973-74; dir. Marine Sci. Rsch. Ctr. SUNY, Stony Brook, 1974-83, dean, leading prof., 1983-94, acting dir. Waste Mgmt. Inst., 1985-87, provost, 1986-89, dir. COAST Inst., 1989, Disting. Svc. prof., 1994-95, prof. emeritus, 1995—; pres. emeritus, CEO New England Aquarium, Boston, 1994—2001; vis. prof. Wash. Coll., Chestertown, Md., 2002—. Hon. prof. East China Normal U., Shanghai, 1985—; sec. exec. com. Commn. on Food, Environ. and Renewable Resources, 1993, chair steering com., 1994; mem. governing bd. Regional Marine Rsch. Program, Greater N.Y. Bight, 1993-94. Author: The Living Chesapeake, 1981, The Life and Death of the Chesapeake Bay, 1 986; (with H.A. Neal) Solid Waste Management and the Environment, 1987, Garbage and Trash: Can We Convert Mountains Into Molehills?, 1992; editor: (with B.C. Marcy Jr.) Power Plant Entrainment, 1978; (with others) The Great South Bay, 1991; sr. editor Coastal Ocean Pollution Assement News, 1981-86; co-editor in chief Estuaries, 1986-88; mem. editl. bd. CRC Revs. in Aquatic Scis.; contbr. articles to profl. jours. Mem. adv. bd. Environ. Sci. Com. Outer Continental Shelf, Minerals Mgmt. Scs., 1984-86, chmn., 1986; bd. dirs. N.E. Area Remote Sensing Sys., 1983-85, L.I. Incubator Corp.; v.p. L.I. Forum for Tech., 1989-92; chair Mass. Outfall Monitoring Task Force, 1995-98; mem. sci. adv. bd. EPA, 1996-98; commr. Nat. Rsch. Coun.'s Commn. on Engrng. Tech. Sys., 1996—; mem. vis. com. dept. ocean engrng MIT, 1995—; trustee Natural Heritage Insts., 1995—; mem. Boston Artery Bus. Bd. Dirs., 1994—; mem. Boston Mcpl. Rsch. Bur. Bd. Dirs., 1994—; mem. Annenberg Challenge Adv. Com., 1995—; hon. trustee Sci. Mus. L.I., 2000—. Recipient L.I. Sound Am. Environ. Edn. award, 1987, Stony Brook U. medal, 1989, Matthew Fontaine Maury award, 1990, Ben Gurion U. medal, 1993, sci. achievement award Sci. Mus. L.I., 2000; Alfred P. Sloan fellow, 1959; Wheaton Coll. Disting. fellow, 2000. Mem. NAS (mem. marine bd. 1989-94, mem. exec. com. 1990, vice chair 1991-94, chair 1992-94, com. on Coastal Ocean 1989-93), Nat. Assn. State Univ. and Land Grant Colls. (bd. dirs. marine divsn., chmn. 1986-88), L.I. Environ. Coun., L.I. Marine Resources Adv. Coun. (chair 1990-94), L.I. Rsch. Inst. (bd. dirs. 1992-94), L.I. Environ.-Econ. Roundtable (co-chair 1991-92), Suffolk County Recycling Commn., (chmn. 1987-88), Estuarine Rsch. Fedn. (v.p. 1982-83, pres. 1985-87), N.Y. Sea Grant Inst. (chmn. governing bd. 1988-90, mem. gov.'s task force on coastal resources 1990-91), The Nature Conservancy (trustee L.I. chpt. 1991-94), Franklin Electronic Pubs. (bd. dirs. 1991—), Taproot (bd. dirs. 1988-93, vice chair 1990-93), Sigma Xi, Phi Sigma Pi. Avocation: photography. Office: New England Aquarium Central Wharf Boston MA 02110-3399 E-mail: jschubel@neaq.org.

SCHUBERT, BARBARA SCHUELE, retired performing company executive; b. Cleve., Feb. 21, 1939; d. William Edward and Mildred Marianne (Matousek) Schuele; m. John Dwan Schubert, June 15, 1963; children: William Edward, Christopher John, David Matthew. BS in Social Scis., John Carroll U, 1962, MA in English, 1967; MEd, 1980. Cert. secondary tchr., elem. remedial reading tchr., Ohio. Tchr. Sch. on Magnolia, Cleve., 1980-82, Ruffing Montessori, Cleve., 1982-83; tchr. English U. Sch., Chagrin Falls, Ohio, 1983-86; gen. mgr. Ohio Ballet, Akron, 1987-90, assoc. dir., 1990-99; ret. Bd. trustees Ohio Ballet, 1974-87, 91-99. Bd. dirs. John Carroll U., 1990—; trustee Benjamin Rose Inst., 1999—, Boys Hope Girls Hope, 2001. Mem.: Cleve. Skating. Roman Catholic. E-mail: BJSchubert@earthlink.net.

SCHUBERT, BLAKE H. lawyer, investor; b. Wheeling, W.Va., Apr. 21, 1939; s. John Arnold and Esther Elizabeth (Masters) S.; m. Carol Jean Cramp, Jan. 13, 1962; children: Cheryl Lynn, Charles Bradley, Elisabeth Anne. BA, Ohio Wesleyan U., 1961; JD, U. Chgo., 1964. Bar: Ill. 1964, U.S. Dist. Ct. (no. dist.) Ill. 1968, U.S. Tax Ct. 1994. Atty., Brunswick Corp., Chgo., 1964-68; asst. group counsel FMC Corp., Chgo., 1968-73; gen. counsel Dresser Tool Group, Chgo., 1973-79; chmn. Schubert Securities Corp., Oak Park, Ill., 1979-84, Inter-Am. Investments, Inc., Oak Park, 1980—; gen. ptnr. Investment Trust Ltd., St. Petersburg, Fla., 1981-91, Inter-Am. Fund, Oak Park, 1982-91, Inter-Am. Fund I, Oak Park, 1982-91, Inter-Am. Fund II, Oak Park, 1984-89; chmn. Compath Video Corp., Oak Park, 1984-85; lectr. Am. Inst. Banking, 1965, Chgo. Inst. Fin. Studies, 1984-85. Chmn. 1st United Ch. Endowment Fund, Oak Park, 1975-80, Park Forest Co-op. (Ill.), 1966-70; mem. Chgo. Bd. Options Exch., 1979-83. Recipient Bancroft-Whitney Prize U. Chgo., 1964. Author: The Well-Kept Secrets of Investing, 1982. Home and Office: 522 Linden Ave Oak Park IL 60302-1659

SCHUBERT, E. FRED, electrical engineer, educator; b. Stuttgart, Germany, Feb. 8, 1956; came to U.S., 1985; s. Konrad and Martha Ruth (Reichert) S.; m. Jutta Maria Lukai, Feb. 22, 1980; children: Anne F., Martin F., Ursula V. Diploma in Engrng. with honors, U. Stuttgart, 1981, D in Engrng. with honors, 1986. Rsch. assoc. Max Planck Inst., Stuttgart, 1981-85; tech. staff, prin. investigator AT&T Bell Labs., Murray Hill, N.J., 1985-95; prof. dept. elec. and computer engrng. Ctr. for Photonics Rsch., Boston U., 1995—2002; constellation chmn., prof. Rensselaer Poly. Inst., Troy, 2002—. Author: Doping in III-V Semiconductors, 1993; editor: Delta Doping of Semiconductors, 1996; patentee in field. Postdoctoral fellow AT&T, 1985-87; recipient Alexander von Humboldt Rsch. prize, 2000, Discover Mag. award, 2000. Fellow IEEE, Internat. Soc. Optical Engrng., Am. Phys. Soc., Optical Soc. Am.; mem. Verein Deutscher Elektrotechniker (lit. prize 1994), Material Rsch. Soc. Roman Catholic. Achievements include several patents involving doping of III-V semiconductors and several patents on high efficiency light emitting diodes. Home: 49 Angela St Canton MA 02021-2251 Office: Rensselaer Poly Inst. Dept Elec Computer and Sys Engrng 110 8th St Boston MA 12180

SCHUBERT, FRANK NICHOLAS, Historian; b. Washington, June 3, 1943; s. Max and Elizabeth Schubert; m. Irene Louise Schubert, May 29, 1969; 1 child, Max Edward. BA, Howard U., 1965; MA, U. Wyo., 1970; PhD, U. Toledo, 1977. Historian Joint History Office Office of the Chmn., Joint Chiefs of Staff, Washington, 1977—. Guest lectr. Janos Pannonius U., Pecs, Hungary, spring 2000. Author: Buffalo soldiers, Braves and the Brass, 1993, On the Trail of the Buffalo Soldiers, 1995 (Outstanding Ref. Book of Yr. Choice 1995), Black Valor, 1997. Capt. U.S. Army, 1965-68, Vietnam. Avocations: stamp collector, brewer, cyclist. Home: 8505 Cherry Valley Ln Alexandria VA 22309 Office: Joint Chiefs of Staff Office of Chmn Joint History Office Washington DC 20318-9999 E-mail: theschuberts@earthlink.net.

SCHUBERT, GLENDON, political scientist, educator; b. Oneida, N.Y., June 7, 1918; s. Glendon Austin and Agnes (Rogers) S.; m. Elizabeth Josephine Neal (dec. 1949); children: Frank, James; m. Elizabeth Harris (div.); children: Susan, Kathleen, Robin; m. Natalie Klavans, 1999. AB, Syracuse U., 1940, PhD, 1948. Mem. faculties Syracuse U., 1946-48, UCLA, 1948-49, Howard U., 1949-50, Rutgers U., 1950-51, Franklin and Marshall Coll., 1951-52, Mich. State U., 1952-67, U. Minn., 1955; William Rand Kenan Jr. prof. polit. sci. U. N.C. at Chapel Hill, 1967-68; Univ. prof. York U., 1968-70; Univ. prof. polit. sci. U. Hawaii, 1970-2000, emeritus prof., 2000—; rsch. prof. polit. sci. So. Ill. U. at Carbondale, 1986-91. Fulbright lectr. U. Oslo, Norway, 1959-60; fellow Center for Advanced Study in Behavioral Scis., 1960-61; sr. scholar in residence Center for Cultural and Tech. Interchange Between East and West, U. Hawaii, 1963-64, 65; Fulbright-Hays research scholar, Netherlands, 1977; NSF faculty fellow U. Groningen, Netherlands, 1977-78; NATO sr. fellow, U.K.; fellow Netherlands Inst. Advanced Study Humanities and Social Sci., Wassenaar, Netherlands, 1978-79 Author 30 books; assoc. editor for biosocial behavior The Behavioral and Brain Sci., 1979—; adv. editor Jour. Social and Evolutionary Systems, 1980—; assoc. editor Politics and the Life Scis., 1980-90; contbr. articles to profl. jours. in biobehavioral and polit. sci., jud. behavior and politics, and pub. policy. Served with Signal Intelligence U.S. Army, 1942-46. Decorated Bronze Star; recipient Regents' medal and award for excellence in research U. Hawaii, 1975 Mem. Internat. Soc. Polit. Psychology, Am. Polit. Sci. Assn. (past mem. exec. coun., Career Lifetime Achievement award 1999), Assn. Polit. Life Scis. (past pres., Lifetime Career Achievement award 1994), Internat. Soc. Human Ethology, Phi Beta Kappa. E-mail: nklavans@yahoo.com.

SCHUBERT, GUENTHER ERICH, pathologist; b. Mosul, Iraq, Aug. 17, 1930; s. Erich Waldemar and Martha Camilla (Zschitzschmann) Schubert; children: Frank, Marion, Dirk. MD, University, Heidelberg, Germany, 1957; pvt. docent in pathology, University, Tuebingen, Germany, 1966. Asst. med. dir. University Tuebingen, Fed. Republic of Germany, 1966-76; prof. pathology, 1972; head Inst. Pathology, Wuppertal, Fed. Republic of Germany, 1976-96; chair of pathology U. Witten-Herdecke, Fed. Republic of Germany, 1985-96. Co-author: Coloratlas of Cytodiagnosis of the Prostate, 1975, Pathologie, 1984, 1997, Endoscopy of the Urinary Bladder, 1989, Textbook of Pathology, 1981, 1987. Mem. Wissenschaftlicher Beirat, Bundesarztekammer, Bonn, Germany, 1976—85; pres. Medizinisch Naturwissenschaftliche Gesellschaft, Wuppertal, 1984—85, Onkologischer Schwerpunkt, Wuppertal, 1985—93, OSP Bergisch-Land, 1992—95, Bergische Arbeitsgemeinschaft fur Gastroenterologie, Wuppertal, 1987—88, 1990—91, 1994—95. Mem.: N.Y. Acad. Scis., Internat. Acad. Pathology, Deutsche Gesellschaft fur Urologie,

Deutsche Gesellschaft fur Nephrologie, Deutsche Gesellschaft fur Pathologie, Lions. Avocations: music, diving, photography. Office: Inst of Pathology Am Anschlag 71 42113 Wuppertal Germany

SCHUBERT, JEANNE, artist; b. Harlan, Ky., June 2, 1932; d. Lewis Marion and Bertha Faye (Paul) Conklin; m. Robert Breckenridge Stroup, Feb. 5, 1953 (dec. May 1954); 1 child, Robert Breckenridge; m. Robert Buxton (div. 1967); 1 child, Beverly Buxton; m. Robert Kenyon Schubert, Apr. 25, 1970. Student, Cumberland Coll., Williamsburg, Ky., 1951, Rollins Coll., Winter Park, Fla., 1974, Art Students' League, N.Y.C., 1984. Mortgage clk. Orlando (Fla.) Fed. Savs., 1962-76; real estate broker Orlando; co-owner, creator Art Works Orlando, 1993-96. Mem./exhibitor Orlando Mus. Art, 1972—, Dayton Beach Mus., 1972—, Arts on Douglas, New Smyrna Beach, Fla., 1995—, Albertson-Peterson Gallery, Winter Park, 1990-99. One woman shows include Lighthouse Gallery, Tequesta, Fla., Orlando Mus Art Assocs., Valencia C.C., Orlando, LeMoyne Ctr. for Visual Arts, Tallahassee, Melvin Gallery, Lakeland, U. Ctrl. Fla., Orlando, Vero Beach (Fla.) Ctr. for the Arts, Osceola Ctr. for Arts, Kissimmee, Fla., Gallery Contemporanea, Hot Springs, Ark., Brevard Art Ctr. and Mus., Melbourne, Fla., Melvin Gallery, Fla. So. Coll., Albertson-Peterson Gallery, First Union Tower, Orlando, Arts on Douglas, New Smyrna Beach; exhibited in group shows at Orlando Mus. Art, 1984, 87, 88, 92, Barbara Gilman Gallery, Miami, Miami-Dade Coll., 1986, North Miami Mus. Art, Salmagundi Club, N.Y., Fla. Gulf Coast Art Ctr., Belleaire, 1986, U. Ctrl. Fla., 1987, Harmon Gallery of Am. Art, Sarasota, Fla., Crealde Art Ctr. Gallery, Winter Park, , Mus. Arts and Sci., Daytona Beach, Daytona Beach Art Ctr., Epcot Ctr., Lake Buena Vista, 1994-2001, Soc. of the Four Arts, West Palm Beach, 1997-2001; works in permanent collections at Maitland Art Ctr., Rollins Coll., Valencia C.C., Mus. Arts and Scis., Walt Disney World, Flagship Banks, Melbourne, Gen. Mills Corp., Orlando, Hyatt Regency Corp., Orlando, City Hall, Orlando, Barnett Bank of Fla., Jacksonville, Orange County Courthouse, Shands Hosp., Gainesville, Mayo Clinic, Jacksonville, Baker & Hostetler, Orlando, Akerman, Senterfitt & Eidson, Orlando, Holland and Knight, Orlando, City Orlando Collections Orange County Collection, others. Bd. dirs. Maitland (Fla.) Art Ctr., 1972—. Art Svcs. Coun. Art grant. Mem. Fla. Watercolor Soc., Fla. Artist Group (area rep. 1985-2001). Home: 1426 Magnolia St New Smyrna Beach FL 32168

SCHUBERT, RICHARD FRANCIS, consultant; b. Trenton, N.J., Nov. 2, 1936; s. Yaro and Frances Mary (Hustak) S.; m. Virginia Thomas Austin, Sept. 15, 2000; children: Robyn, David. BA cum laude, Eastern Nazarene Coll., 1958; LLB, Yale U., 1961. Bar: Pa. 1962, U.S. Supreme Ct 1972. Arbitration atty. Bethlehem Steel Corp., Pa., 1961-66, asst. mgr. labor relations, 1966-70; exec. asst. to undersec. labor Washington, 1970; gen. counsel labor, 1971-73; dep. sec. labor, 1973-75; asst. to v.p. indsl. relations Bethlehem Steel Corp., 1973, asst. v.p. public affairs, 1975-77, v.p. public affairs, 1977-79, pres., 1979-80, vice chmn., 1980-82; pres., CEO ARC, 1982-89, Points of Light Found., 1990-95. Bd. dirs. Weirton Steel, Mgmt. Tng. Corp. Bd. dirs. Nat. Alliance Bus.; sr. v.p. EXCN; chmn. emeritus Internat. Youth Found., Biorelease Inc., Nazarene Compassionate Ministries; vice chmn. Peter F. Drucker Found.; chmn. Nat. Job Corps Assn. Mem.: Ctr. Excellence in Govt., Coun. on Fgn. Rels., Northampton County Bar Assn., Pa. Bar Assn., Ea. Nazarene Alumni Assn. (pres. 1969—73), Phi Alpha Delta. Mem. Ch. of Nazarene. Home: 6615 Madison McLean Dr Mc Lean VA 22101-2425 Office: Ste 701 Crystal Gateway 4 1213 Jefferson Davis Hwy Alexandria VA 22202 E-mail: rfs@iyfnet.org.

SCHUBERT, WILLIAM G. federal agency administrator; m. Gail Marlene Becker; 2 children. Grad., U.S. Maritime Acad. Unltd. master lic. any oceans USCG. Master/offshore installation mgr. Global Marine Drilling; pres. Internat. Trade and Transp., Inc., Houston; offshore industry expert to maritime adminstrn. U.S. Dept. Transp., Washington, 1986—90, regional rep. maritime adminstrn., 1990—95, adminstr. to maritime adminstrn., 2001—. Co-founder U.S. Exporters Competitive Maritime Coun., 1998. Commd. officer USNR. Office: US Dept Transp Maritime Adminstrn 400 7th St SW Washington DC 20590*

SCHUBERT, WILLIAM HENRY, curriculum studies educator; b. Garrett, Ind., July 6, 1944; s. Walter William and Mary Madeline (Grube) S.; children by previous marriage: Ellen Elaine, Karen Margaret; m. Ann Lynn Lopez, Dec. 3, 1977; children: Heidi Ann, Henry William. BS, Manchester Coll., 1966; MS, Ind. U., 1967; PhD, U. Ill., 1975. Tchr. Fairmount, El Sierra and Herrick Schs., Downers Grove, Ill., 1967-75; clin. instr. U. Wis., Madison, 1969-73; tchg. asst., univ. fellow U. Ill., Urbana, 1973-75, asst. prof. Chgo., 1975-80, assoc. prof., 1981-85, prof., 1985—, coord. secondary edn., 1979-82, coord. instrnl. leadership, 1979-85, dir. grad. studies Coll. Edn., 1983-85, coord. grad. curriculum studies, 1985—, coord. edn. studies, 1990-94, 96—, chair area curriculum and instrn., 1990-94. Vis. assoc. prof. U. Victoria (B.C., Can.), 1981; disting. vis. prof. U. S.C., 1986; presenter in field. Author: (with Ann Lopez) Curriculum Books: The First Eighty Years, 1980; Curriculum: Perspective, Paradigm and Possibility, 1986; (with Edmund C. Short and George Willis) Toward Excellence in Curriculum Inquiry, 1985, (with J. Dan Marshall and James T. Sears) Turning Points in Curriculum: A Contemporary American Memoir, 2000; editor: (with Ann Lopez) Conceptions of Curriculum Knowledge: Focus on Students and Teachers, 1982, (with George Willis) Reflections from the Heart of Educational Inquiry: Understanding Curriculum and Teaching Through the Arts, 1991, repub., 2001, (with William Ayers) Teacher Lore: Learning From Our Own Experience, 1992, repub., 1999, (with George Willis, R. Bullough, C. Kridel, J. Holton) The American Curriculum: A Documentary History, 1993; assoc. editor, editl. bd. Ednl. Theory; former mem. editl. bd. Ednl. Studies; former cons. editor Phenomenology and Pedagogy; adv. bd. Teaching Edn., Pi Lamda Theta Pubs., 1995—, Jour. Curriculum and Supervision; editl. bd. Curriculum and Teaching, emeritus editl. bd., Jour. Curriculum Theorizing, 1999—; editor: book series Student Lore, 1990—; cons. editor Jour. Curriculum Discourse and Dialogue; mem. adv. bd. Jour. Critical Issues in Curriculum and Instrn., 2000—; contbr. over 200 articles and chpts. to profl. pubs.; presenter in field. Mem. Internat. Acad. Edn. (elected 1997), Profs. of Curriculum (factotum 1984-85), Soc. for Study of Curriculum History (founding mem., sec.-treas. 1981-82, pres. 1982-83), Am. Ednl. Rsch. Assn. (chmn. creation and utilization of curriculum knowledge 1980-82, program chmn. curriculum studies divsn. 1982-83, sec. Divsn. B 1989-91, v.p. 2000-01), Am. Assn. Colls. for Tchr. Edn., John Dewey Soc. (bd. dirs. 1986-95, chair awards com. 1988-90, co-chair lectures commn. 1989-91, pres.-elect 1990-91, pres. 1992-93), ASCD (steering com. of curriculum com. 1980-83, publs. com. 1987-90, internat. polling panel 1990—), Am. Ednl. Studies Assn., World Coun. for Curriculum and Instrn., Soc. for Profs. of Edn. (exec. bd. 1997-88, pres.-elect 2000-01, pres. 2001—), Nat. Soc. for Study of Edn., Inst. Dem. in Edn., Masons, Scottish Rite, Phi Delta Kappa, Phi Kappa Phi (pres. U. Ill.-Chgo. chpt. 1981-82). Office: U Ill Coll Edn M/C 147 1040 W Harrison St Chicago IL 60607-7129 E-mail: schubert@uic.edu.

SCHUCH, CYNTHIA SILLECK, nurse; b. Oceanside, N.Y., Oct. 31, 1956; AAS, SUNY, Morrisville, 1976; cert. in Cardiovascular Nursing, Meth. Hosp., Houston, 1978; BS in Nursing, U. Ala., 1984, MS in Nursing, 1985. RN, N.Y., Va., Ala., Calif. Staff nurse, relief charge nurse, postoperative surgical nurse Meth. Hosp., Houston, 1976-77, staff nurse ICU, 1977-78, cardiovascular nurse specialist, 1978-79; staff nurse ICU U. Va. Hosp., Charlottesville, 1979; staff nurse, relief charge nurse U. Ala. Hosp., Birmingham, 1979-80, scrub nurse, circulating nurse, 1980-83, staff nurse CICU, 1983-84, charge nurse CICU, 1984-86; staff nurse CICU Sutter Meml. Hosp., Sacramento, 1986-89, clin. specialist cardiac surgery unit, 1989—. Vol. instr. cardiac maintenance YMCA Shades Valley Br., Birmingham, 1984; instr. family night CPR, Sacramento, 1987—, BCLS instr., 1986—, ACLS instr., 1988—. Mem. Am. Assn. Critical Care Nurses (Houston-Gulf chpt. 1976-79, Greater Birmingham chpt. 1985-86, Sacramento chpt. 1986—), Phi Theta Kappa, Phi Kappa Phi, Sigma Theta Tau.

SCHUCK, EDWIN GEORGE, JR. lawyer; BS cum laude, Columbia U., 1967, MBA, JD cum laude, Columbia U., 1970. Bar: N.Y. 1971, Calif. 1980, U.S. Tax Ct., U.S. Ct. Fed. Claims, U.S. Supreme Ct. With Sullivan & Cromwell, N.Y.C., 1970-76, Donovan Leisure Newton & Irvine, N.Y.C. and L.A., 1976-80, ptnr., 1980-83, Sidley & Austin, L.A., 1983-87, Munger, Tolles & Olson, L.A., 1987-95; atty. pvt. practice, 1996—. Adj. prof. U. San Diego, 1987; lectr. in field. Contbr. articles to profl. jours. Pres. Bradbury Estates Assn., 1991-92, 94-96, Bradbury Cmty. Svcs. Dist., 1996; mem. Bradbury City Coun., 1996; mayor City of Bradbury, 1998. Mem. Calif. State Bar (taxation sect. vice chair, mem. exec. com. 1987-89, chair corp. tax com. 1992-93, chair 2d ann. meeting Calif. Tax Bar 1992), N.Y. State Bar Assn. (com. reorgn. corp. taxation, partnerships & U.S. tax problems of fgn. persons), L.A. County Bar Assn. (chair taxation sect. 1988-89, chair income tax com. 1985-87, chair corp. tax com. 1994-95), Internat. Fiscal Assn., Internat. Bar Assn. (spkr., presenter), Assn. Tax Counsel. Office: 626 Wilshire Blvd Ste 900 Los Angeles CA 90017-2922

SCHUCK, PETER HORNER, lawyer, educator; b. N.Y.C., Apr. 26, 1940; s. Samuel H. and Lucille (Horner) S.; m. Marcy Cantor, June 26, 1966; children: Christopher, Julie. BA with honors, Cornell U., 1962; JD cum laude, Harvard U., 1965, MA, 1969; LLM, NYU, 1966; MA (hon.), Yale U., 1982. Bar: N.Y. State 1966, D.C. 1972. Practiced law, N.Y.C., 1965-68; teaching fellow in govt. Harvard U., 1969-71; cons. (Center for Study of Responsive Law), Washington, 1971-72; dir. Washington office Consumers Union, 1972-77; dep. asst. sec. for planning and evaluation HEW, Washington, 1977-79; vis. scholar Am. Enterprise Inst. for Public Policy Research, 1979; assoc. prof. law Yale U., 1979-81, prof., 1981-86, Simeon E. Baldwin prof. law, 1986—, dep. dean, 1993-94. Vis. prof. Georgetown U. Law Ctr., 1986-87, NYU Law Sch., fall 1994, N.Y. Law Sch., spring 1997, 98, 99 Author: The Judiciary Committees, 1975, Suing Government, 1983, Citizenship Without Consent, 1985; co-author: Agent Orange on Trial, 1986, enlarged edit., 1987, Citizens, Strangers and In-Betweens: Essays on Immigration and Citizenship, 1998, The Limits of Law: Essays on Democratic Governance, 2000; editor: Tort Law and the Public Interest, 1991, Foundations of Administrative Law, 1994; co-editor: Paths to Inclusion, 1998; contbr. articles and revs. to profl. and popular publs. Guggenheim fellow, 1984-85; recipient Silver Gavel award ABA, 1987. Jewish. E-mail: peter.schuck@yale.edu.

SCHUCK, THOMAS ROBERT, lawyer, farmer; b. Findlay, Ohio, Feb. 7, 1950; s. Robert Damon and Katherine Margaretta (Beynon) S. BA, DePauw U., 1972; MA, U. Kent, U.K., 1974; JD, Harvard U., 1976. Bar: Ohio 1976, U.S. Dist. Ct. (no. dist.) Ohio 1977, U.S. Dist. Ct. (so. dist.) Ohio 1979, Ariz. 1990, U.S. Ct. Appeals (6th cir.) 1978, U.S. Ct. Appeals (9th cir.) 1991, U.S. Ct. Appeals Armed Forces, 2000. Law clk. U.S. Dist. Ct., Cleve., 1976-79; assoc. Taft, Stettinius & Hollister, Cin., 1979-87, ptnr., 1987—; owner, operator Rural Hill Farm. Participant Ohio Bench Bar Conf., Columbus, 1990, 91, Glenmoor Justice Inst., 2000; barrister Am. Inn of Ct., 1986-87, LEAD Clermont, 1997-98; mem. bar exam com. U.S. Dist. Ct. (so. dist.) Ohio; mem. merit panel for bankruptcy judge selection U.S. Ct. Appeals Sixth Cir., 1998. Contbg. author: Aids and the Law, 2d edit. 1992; contbr. articles to profl. jours. Trustee Mental Health Svcs. East, Inc., Cin., 1985-91; sec. bd. trustees Joy Outdoor Edn. Ctr., Inc., 1999—; mem. Clermont County Mental Health Bd., Batavia, Ohio, 1992-2000, vice chair, 1997-2000; mem. Clermont County Mental Retardation Developmental Disabilities Levy Steering Com., 1996, bd. trustees, 2000—, vice chmn., 2002—, vice chair, 2002—; mem. May Festival Assocs., Cin., 1984-86; spl. gifts com. Cin. Art Acad., 1987; mem. WGUC Radio Cmty. Bd., 1984-86. Rotary Internat. Found. grad. fellow, 1972, 73. Mem. FBA (pres. Cin. chpt. 1994-95, v.p. 6th cir. 1996-99, nat. sec. 2001-2002, nat. treas. 2002-03, nat. membership chair 1997-99, govt. rels. com.), Potter Stewart Am. Inn of Ct. (barrister 1986-87), U.S. Rowing Assn. (asst. referee), Harvard Club Cin. (pres. 1995-96), Camargo Hunt Club, Ohio Soc. (sec.), Soc. Bacchus Am., Masons, Phi Beta Kappa, Delta Chi, Phi Eta Sigma, Sigma Delta Chi. Republican. Methodist. Avocations: reading, photography. Home: PO Box 615 189 State Route 133 Felicity OH 45120 Office: Ste 1800 425 Walnut St Cincinnati OH 45202-3957

SCHUCKIT, MARC ALAN, psychiatry educator, researcher; b. Milw., Mar. 5, 1944; s. Samuel Bernard and Lillian (Ginsberg) S.; m. Judith Schrinsky, July 2, 1967; children: Dena Leigh, Jordan Daniel. BS, U. Wis., 1965; MD, Wash. U., 1968. Diplomate Am. Bd. Psychiatry, Am. Bd. Neurology. Intern Cedars-Sinai Hosp., L.A., 1968-69; resident Wash. Univ., St. Louis, 1969-71; chief resident in psychiatry U. Calif., San Diego, 1971-72, asst. prof. psychiatry, 1974-75, prof., 1978—; spl. asst. alcohol studies USN Naval Health Research Ctr., 1972-74; dir. alcohol and drug abuse inst. U. Wash., Seattle, 1975-78; dir. alcoholism research ctr. VA Hosp., San Diego, 1978—. Author: Drug and Alcohol Abuse, 4th edit., 1995, Educating Yourself about Alcohol and Drugs: A People's Primer, 1995; editor Jour. of Studies in Alcohol, 1994—; contbr. some 350 articles to psychiat. jours. Recipient Diego's Young Man of Yr. award Friendly Sons of St. Patrick, 1982, Disting. Rschr. award Rsch. Soc. Alcoholism, 1993, Isaacson award Internat. Soc., 1994, Margaret Cork award Nat. Assn. Children Alcoholics, 1996. Fellow Am. Psychiat. Assn. (Hofheimer award 1972), Am. Coll. Neuropsychopharmacology; mem. Research Soc. Alcoholism, Internat. Soc. Biomed. Research in Alcoholism, Am. Med. Soc. on Alcoholism. Avocations: recorder playing, walking, racquetball. Office: VA Med Ctr 3350 La Jolla Village Dr # 116A San Diego CA 92161-0002

SCHUDEL, HANSJOERG, international business consultant; b. Wald, Switzerland, Sept. 27, 1937; s. Rene and Alice S. Ed., Coll. Bus. Adminstrn., Zurich, Switzerland. With Byk-Gulden, Konstanz, Germany and Sao Paulo, Brazil, 1962-69, Hicksville, N.Y., 1964-69; pres., chief exec. officer, dir. Stinnes Corp., N.Y.C., 1971-83; exec. officer Stinnes A.G., Muelheim, Fed. Republic of Germany, 1978-83; rep. for the Americas First Arab Pacific Corp. Ltd., Chappaqua, N.Y., 1984—. Mem. German-Am. C. of C. (bd. dirs. 1976-83), Internat. World Travelers Club, Swiss Soc., Confrerie de la Chaine des Rotisseurs, Order des Coteaux de Champagne, Foothills Assn. (bd. dirs., pres.). Office: First Arab Pacific Corp Ltd PMB 307 1275 4th St Santa Rosa CA 95404-4056

SCHUDER, JOHN CLAUDE, biomedical engineer; b. Olney, Ill., Mar. 2, 1922; s. Charles Claude Schuder and Louise Ella Muench; m. Retha Elizabeth Sumner, July 23, 1946; children: Linda Lee Brown, Charles Wayne, Jonna Elizabeth. BSEE, U. Ill., 1943; MSEE, Purdue U., 1951, PhD, 1954. Jr. engr. Westinghouse Rsch., East Pittsburgh, Pa., 1943-44; from instr. to asst. prof. Purdue U., West Lafayette, Ind., 1949-56; assoc. prof. Doane Coll., Crete, Nebr., 1956-57; fellow, asst. prof. U. Pa., Phila., 1957-60; from assoc. prof. to prof. emeritus U. Mo. Sch. Medicine, Columbia, 1960—. Cons. Hewlett-Packard, Medtronics, GE, Physio Control, NIH, others. Mem. editl. bd. PACE, 1991—; contbr. numerous articles to profl. jours. Peace activist, anti-death penalty activist Columbia Fellowship of Reconciliation, local and nat., 1960—. Recipient numerous grants NIH, Am. Heart Assn., Mo. Heart Assn., others. Mem. AAUP, IEEE Engring. in Medicine and Biology Soc. (life), Am. Soc. Artificial Internal Organs, Sigma Xi. Mem. Soc. Of Friends. Achivements include research on experimental rationale for waveforms used in cardiac defibrilators; devel. of transcutaneous energy transformer used with implanted artificial hearts. Home: 105 Manor Dr Columbia MO 65203-1727 Office: U Mo DC011.00 Cardiothoracic Surgery Columbia MO 65212-0001 E-mail: schuderj@health.missouri.edu.

SCHUDER, RAYMOND FRANCIS, lawyer; b. Wickford, R.I., Dec. 27, 1926; s. Rollie Milton and Selma (Ball) S.; m. Betty Jo Williams, Mar. 14, 1948; children: Gregg Williams, Glen Arva. AB, Emory U., 1949, JD, 1951. Bar: Ga. 1951. With Trust Co. Ga., Atlanta, 1951-54; assoc. firm Wheeler Robinson & Thurmond, Gainesville, Ga., 1954-59; pvt. practice law, 1959-70, 76-96; ptnr. Schuder & Brown, 1971-76. Mcpl. ct. judge Gainesville, 1956-60, 73-75; magistrate ct. judge, 1985—, sr. magistrate, 2001—. Supr. Upper Chattahoochee Soil and Water Conservation Dist., 1971-74; CEO, bd. dirs. Charles Thompson Estes Found., Inc., Gainesville. Cpl. USMCR, 1944-50; 1st lt. USAR, 1950-56, ret. Mem. State Bar Ga. (gov. 1966-70), Gainesville-Northeastern Bar Assn. (pres. 1969-70), Am. Legion, VFW, Elks. Methodist. Home: 2224 Riverside Dr Gainesville GA 30501-1232 Office: 2224 Riverside Dr Gainesville GA 30501-1232 E-mail: xrfs@charter.net.

SCHUELE, DONALD EDWARD, physics educator; b. Cleve., June 16, 1934; s. Edward and Mildred (Matousek) S.; m. Clare Ann Kirchner, Sept. 5, 1956; children: Donna, Karen, Melanie, Judy, Rachel, Ruth. BS, John Carroll U., Cleve., 1956, MS, 1957; PhD, Case Inst. Tech., 1962. Instr. physics and math. John Carroll U., 1956-59; part-time instr. physics Case Inst. Tech., 1959-62, instr., asst. prof., assoc. prof., 1962-70; mem. tech. staff Bell Telephone Labs., 1970-72; assoc. prof. physics Case Western Res. U., 1972-74, prof., 1974—, dean undergrad. coll., 1973-76, chmn. dept. physics, 1976-78; vice dean Case Inst. Tech., 1978-83, v.p. for undergrad. and grad. studies, 1983-84, dean, 1984-86, prof. physics, 1986-88, dean math. and natural sci., 1988-89, Albert A. Michaelson prof. physics, 1989—, acting chmn. elec. engring. and applied physics, 1992-93. Cons. in field. Co-editor: Critical Revs. in Solid State Scis, 1969-84; contbr. articles to profl. jours.; patentee in field. Mem. adv. bd. St. Charles Borromeo Sch., 1970-72; pres. Seed Found., 1986-89; trustee St. Mary's Sem., 1980-93; mem. Olympic Sports Equipment and Tech. Com., 1982-93; trustee Newman Found., 1983—, Northeastern Ohio Sci. Fair, 1983—; mem. Diocesan Pastoral Coun., 1992-94; active Rep. Presdl. task force. Recipient Disting. Physics Alumnus award John Carroll U., 1983; NSF Faculty fellow, 1961-63; Sam Givelber fellow Case Alumni Assn., 2001. Mem.: North Coast Thermal Analysis Soc., Am. Assn. Physics Tchrs., Am. Phys. Soc. (vice chair Ohio sect. 1995—96, chair 1996—97), Newman Apostolate, Case Alumni Coun. (life; treas. 1992, 3d v.p. 2001—02), Tau Beta Pi, Sigma Xi, Alpha Sigma Nu. Republican. Roman Catholic. Achievements include patents fluid pressure device, impact wrench torque calibrator, detection of wear particles and other impurities in industrial fluids, electrical oil analysis instrument. Home: 4892 Countryside Rd Cleveland OH 44124-2513 Office: Case Western Res U 10900 Euclid Ave Cleveland OH 44106-1712 E-mail: des3@po.cwru.edu.

SCHUELER, GERALD JOSEPH, technical writer, systems analyst, counselor; b. Darby, Pa., Oct. 29, 1942; s. Charles Carroll and Bertha Julia (Fadgen) S.; m. Betty Jane Sherlin, Aug. 17, 1963; children: Diane Sue, Joseph Carroll, Andrew Tyson, Crystal Ann. BS, U. Md., 1965; MS in Adminstrn., Ctrl. Mich. U., 1991; PhD, Capella U., Minn., 1996, 98. Lic. profl. counselor, D.C. Test dir. U.S. Army Test and Evaluation Command, Aberdeen Proving Ground, Md., 1965-75, ops. rsch. analyst, 1975-94; tech. writer Harford Writers Group, Aberdeen, Md., 1984—; sys. analyst Quantum Rsch. Internat., Bel Air, 1999—. Co-owner Shellay, Aberdeen, 1964-99, Creative Sales & Svc., Aberdeen, 1975—; cons. Compucats Computer Store, Aberdeen, 1982-1989. Author: Enochian Magic, 1984, Enochian Physics, 1988; co-author: Coming into the Light, 1989, Angels Message to Humanity, 1996. Leader/com. mem. Boy Scouts Am., Aberdeen, 1974-80; officer Friends of Harford County Libr., Aberdeen, 1975—; county leader Harford County 4-H Club, Aberdeen, 1978-95. Mem. Am. Counseling Assn., Internat. Assn. Transpersonal Psychology, Noetic Inst. Dem. Avocations: computers, reading, crafts. E-mail: jerry@schuelers.com.

SCHUELER, JOHN R. newspaper executive; b. Grosse Point, MI; BA, W. Mich. U. With Miami Herald, Miami, Fla.; pres. New England Newspapers; v.p. consumer mktg. & circulation The Orange County Register, Santa Ana, Calif., 1991, exec. v.p. & gen. mgr. 1992-95, pres., COO, 1995-98; publisher Star Tribune, Mpls., 1998—2001; pub. Los Angeles Daily News, 2001—. Office: Los Angeles Daily News 21221 Oxnard St PO Box 4200 Woodland Hills CA 91367*

SCHUELKE, JOHN PAUL, religious organization administrator; b. Benton Harbor, Mich., Nov. 5, 1934; s. Alwin E. and Martha M. (Schoeneberg) S.; m. Noreta H. Petersen, Sept. 9, 1956; children: Alvin, Mary, Sheryl, Brian. BS in Acctg., U. Wyo., 1957; LLD (hon.), Concordia U., Irvine, Calif., 1983. CPA. From acct. to sr. acct. Colo. Interstate Gas Co., Colorado Springs, 1957-63; staff acct. Arthur Anderson & Co., Denver, 1963-64; mgr. fin. control Colo. Interstate Corp., Colorado Springs., 1964-67, dir. fin. control, 1967-71; adminstrv. v.p. mfg. divsn. Marsh Instrument Co. subs. Colo. Mfg. Corp., Skokie, Ill., 1971-72; exec. officer bd. dirs., CAO Luth. Ch.-Mo. Synod, St. Louis, 1972-98, ret., 1999. Former chmn. Concordia Asia Ednl. Found.; lectr. in field. Asst. scoutmaster Boy Scouts Am., Colorado Springs; governing bd. Luth. Svcs. in Am.; former mem. governing bd. Luth. Coun.-USA, com. Luth. Coop.; mem. Faith Luth Ch., Woodland Park; mem. bd. for human care ministries Luth. Ch.-Mo. Synod. Recipient God and Country award Eagle Scout. Mem. Alpha Kappa Psi, Gamma Delta (former pres.). Avocations: traveling, fishing, reading.

SCHUELLER, THOMAS GEORGE, lawyer; b. Budapest, Hungary, Oct. 4, 1936; came to U.S., 1938; s. Herbert H. and Edith (Geiringer) S.; m. Sandra Burke, Sept. 3, 1960 (div. Apr. 1982); children: Katherine, Matthew, John. AB cum laude, Amherst Coll., 1958; LLB, Harvard U., 1962. Bar: N.Y. 1963. Salesman Gen. Mills. Inc., Utica, N.Y., 1958-59; assoc. Hughes Hubbard & Reed, N.Y.C., 1962-69, ptnr., 1969—. Bd. dirs., sec. Ballet Hispanico, N.Y.C., 1987-2001. Mem. ABA, Assn. of Bar of City of N.Y., Phi Beta Kappa. Home: 335 W 70th St New York NY 10023-3525 Office: Hughes Hubbard & Reed 1 Battery Park Plz 12th Fl New York NY 10004-1482 also: 108 Fairchild Rd Sharon CT 06069-2440 E-mail: schuelle@hugheshubbard.com.

SCHUESSLER, CINDY SANDLIN, lawyer, judge; b. Florence, Ala., Feb. 19, 1951; d. James Harold Sr. and Sarah Nell Sandlin; m. John M. Schuessler, Mar. 14, 1971; 1 child, Christopher Warren. BA, U. North Ala., 1975; JD, Cumberland Sch. Law, 1978. Bar: Ala. 1978, U.S. Dist. Ct. (no. dist.) Ala. 1978. Assoc. Engel, Hairston, Birmingham, Ala., 1978-79, Peck & Slusher, Florence, 1980-83; ptnr. Schuessler & Sandlin, 1983—. Instr. Faulkner U., Florence, 1985-88; mcpl. prosecutor, Town of Killen, Ala., 1983-94, city atty., 1989—; mcpl. judge Town of Rogersville, Ala., 1988—. Pres. Harlan Sch. PTA, Florence, 1988-90; chmn. bd. trustees Highland Bapt. Ch., Florence, 1989—; mem. grant com. United Way, florence, 1989-91. Mem. Ala. State Bar Assn., Ala. Mcpl. Judges Assn. (pres. 1992-93), Lauderdale County Bar Assn., Phi Kappa Phi, Phi Alpha Delta. Avocations: travel, swimming, reading. Office: Schuessler & Sandlin 225 W Alabama St Florence AL 35630-5515

SCHUESSLER FIORENZA, ELISABETH, theology educator; b. Tschanad, Romania, Apr. 17, 1938; parents German citizens; d. Peter and Magdalena Schuessler; m. Francis Fiorenza, Dec. 17, 1967; 1 child, Chris. MDiv, U. Wuerzburg, Germany, 1962; Lic. Theol., U. Wuerzburg, 1963; DrTheol, U. Muenster, Germany, 1970. Asst. prof. theology U. Notre Dame, South Bend, Ind., 1970-75, assoc. prof., 1975-80, prof., 1980-84; instr. U. Muenster, 1966-67; Talbot prof. N.T., Episcopal Div. Sch., Cambridge, Mass., 1984-88; Krister Stendahl prof. Divsn. Scripture and Interpretation Harvard U., 1988—. Harry Emerson Fosdick vis. prof. Union Theol. Sem., N.Y.C., 1974-75; guest prof. U. Tuebingen, Federal Republic of Germany, 1987, Cath. Theol. Faculty Luzern, Switzerland, 1990; Stiftungs prof. Humboldt U., Berlin, 1997; Ernst Troeltsch prof. U. Heidelberg, Germany, 1999. Author: Der Vergessene Partner, 1964, Priester für Gott, 1972, The Apocalypse, 1976, Invitation to the Book of Revelation, 1981, In Memory of Her, 1983, Bread not Stone, 1984, Judgement or Justice, 1985, Revelation: Vision of a Just World, 1991, But She Said - Feminist Practices of Biblical Interpretation, 1992, Discipleship of Equals: A Critical Feminist Ekklesialogy of Liberation, 1993, Jesus: Miriam's Child and Sophia's Prophet, Critical Issues in Feminist Christology, 1994, Sharing Her Word, 1998, Rhetoric and Ethic The Politics of Biblical Studies, 1999, Jesus and the Politics of Interpretation, 2000, Wisdon Ways: Introducing Feminist R.Mical Interpretation, 2001; editor: Searching the Scriptures, 2 vols, 1993, 94, The Power of Naming, 1996; founding co-editor Jour. Feminist Studies in Religion; also editor other works. Mem.: Am. Acad. Arts and Scis., Soc. Bibl. Lit. (past pres.), Am. Acad. Religion. Office: Harvard Div Sch 45 Francis Ave Cambridge MA 02138-1911

SCHUETT, CAROL ANN, travel industry business analyst; b. Columbus, Wis., May 12, 1967; d. Arnold Joseph and Marilyn Delores (Krejcsi) S. BA in Internat. Bus. with honors, Augsburg Coll., 1996; postgrad., U. St. Thomas, 1997—. Travel agt. AAA, Mpls., 1986-88, Am. Express, Mpls., 1988-91, team leader, 1991-97; bus. analyst Northwest Airlines, 1997—. Mem. NAFE, AAUW, Delta Mu Delta. Avocations: travel, reading, hiking, writing. Home: 6833 Bloomington Ave Richfield MN 55423-2661

SCHUETTE, CHARLES A. lawyer; b. Columbus, Ind., Feb. 24, 1942; BBA, U. Okla., 1964, JD, 1967. Bar: Okla. 1967, Fla. 1970, U.S. Supreme Ct. 1979, U.S. Dist. Ct. (so. dist.) Fla. 1982, U.S. Dist. Ct. (mid. dist.) Fla. 1982. Chmn., CEO Akerman, Senterfitt & Eidson P.A. Fellow Am. Bar Found.; mem. ABA, Fla. Bar, Okla. Bar Assn., Dade County Bar Assn. Office: Akerman Senterfitt & Eidson PA 1 SE 3rd Ave Fl Miami FL 33131-1700

SCHUETZENDUEBEL, WOLFRAM GERHARD, engineering executive; b. Germany, Feb. 17, 1932; came to U.S., 1958; s. Gerhard Egon and Kaethe (Warmbier) S.; m. Ingeborg Jutta Lesch, Dec.15, 1960. BME, Tech. U. Berlin, 1956, MME, MS in Power Engring., 1958; DSc in Nuclear Engring., U. Beverly Hills, L.A., 1979. Registered profl. engr., Calif. Asst. mgr. boiler engring. dept. Riley Stoker Corp., Worcester, Mass., 1958-61; sect. mgr. systems devel. Combustion Engring., Inc., Windsor, Conn., 1961-68; various tech. mgmt. positions Gen. Atomic Co. (subs. Gulf Oil Corp.), San Diego, 1968-79; dir. utilities Solvent Refined Coal Internat., Inc. (subs. Gulf Oil Corp.), Denver, 1979-81, Gulf Oil Corp., Houston, 1981-82; pres. Endyne Internat., Inc., 1982-84; v.p. engring. and technology, sr. v.p. ops. Blount Energy Resource Corp., Montgomery, Ala., 1984-91; v.p. Montenay Internat. Corp., Miami, Fla., 1991—. Fgn. corr. Resch Verlag, Munich, 1975—; bd.dirs. W&E Umwelttechnik A.G., A Previous Blount Co., Zurich, Switzerland, 1986-89. Patentee in field; author, co-author, translator tech. and sci. works. Fellow ASME (past chmn. nuclear heat exchanger com.); mem. Nat. Assn. Corrosion Engrs. (cert. corrosion specialist), Assn. German Profl. Engrs., Assn. Energy Engrs. (sr. mem.), Cogeneration Inst., Integrated Waste Svcs. Assn., Solid Waste Assn. N.Am. Home: 801 Timberlane Rd Pike Road AL 36064-2208 Office: Birwelco-Montenay Inc 3225 Aviation Ave Miami FL 33133-4741 E-mail: wolframgs@aol.com.

SCHUG, KENNETH ROBERT, chemistry educator; b. Easton, Pa., Aug. 27, 1924; s. Howard Lester and Marion Henry (Hulbert) S.; m. Miyoko Ishiyama, June 13, 1948; children: Carey Tyler, Carson Blake, Reed Porter. Student, Johns Hopkins U., 1942-43; BA, Stanford U., 1945; PhD, U. So. Calif., 1955. Instr. Seton Hall Coll., South Orange, N.J., 1948-50; research assoc. U. Wis.-Madison, 1954-56; instr. Ill. Inst. Tech., Chgo., 1956-59, asst. prof., 1959-65, assoc. prof., 1965-75, prof. chemistry, 1975—, chmn. dept. chemistry, 1976-82, 85-87, 89-90, assoc. chair dept. biol. chem. phys. sci., 1999-01. Project dir. Chgo. Area Health and Med. Careers Program, 1979—; project co-dir. Sci. and Math. Initiative for Learning Enhancement, 1985—; project dir. Howard Hughes Med. Inst. Undergrad. Biol. Scis. Program, 1992-97; cons. Argonne (Ill.) Nat. Lab., 1960-62. Co-author: Eigo Kagoku Ronbun no Kakikata, 1979; contbr. articles to profl. jours. Trustee Michael Reese Health Plan, Chgo., 1976-91, Michael Reese Trust, 1991—; bd. dirs. Hyde Park Consumers Coop. Soc., 1982-94. Fulbright scholar, 1964-65; grantee in field Mem. Am. Chem. Soc. (dir., officer Chgo. sect. 1978-84). Home: 1466 E Park Pl Chicago IL 60637-1836 Office: Ill Inst Tech Div Chemistry IIT Ctr Chicago IL 60616 E-mail: schug@lit.edu.

SCHUH, ANNA MARIE, human resources professional; b. Evergreen Park, IL, Oct. 5, 1945; d. Edwin Emil Bernardy and Frances Rose Kouba; m. Daniel Robert Schuh, Nov. 28, 1970; children: Peter Edwin, Justin Daniel, Elizabeth Frances. BA, U. Ill., 1971, PhD, 1997; MS, DePaul U., 1974. Chief compliance and classification br. U.S. Office Pers. Mgmt., Chgo., 1976-82, area mgr., 1982-87, dir. Chgo. oversight divsn., 1987-97, asst. dir. oversight Washington, 1997—2001; vis. asst. prof. DePaul U., Chgo., 2001—02; asst. prof. Roosevelt U., 2002—. Adj. lectr. human resource mgmt. Roosevelt U., Chgo., 1988-94, DePaul U., Chgo., 1988-94, George Mason U., Fairfax, Va., 2001—. Author: Timing Successful Policy Change, 2000; contbr. chpt. to: Empowerment in Chicago, 1998. Mem. fin. com. Village of University Park, Ill., 1984-97. Mem. Am. Soc. Pub. Adminstrn., Internat. Pers. Mgmt. Assn., Phi Kappa Phi. Office: Roosevelt U Sch Policy Studies 430 S Michigan Ave Rm 752 Chicago IL 60605

SCHUH, FRANK JOSEPH, drilling engineering company executive, consultant; b. Columbus, Ohio, Feb. 3, 1935; s. Sebastian and Elizabeth (Zorn) S.; m. Alice Virgene Kasler, June 16, 1956; children: Dwain Joseph, Michael James, Barbara Ann. BS in Petroleum Engring., MS in Petroleum Engring., Ohio State U., 1956. Registered profl. engr., Ohio. Drilling and rsch. engr. Atlantic Refining Co., Tex., La., 1956-62; mem. drilling engring. staff, dir. engring. Atlantic Richfield Co., Dallas, 1962-82, mgr. drilling rsch., sr. advisor Plano, Tex., 1982-86; v.p. Enertech Engring. & Tech., Dallas, 1986-87; pres. Drilling Tech., Inc., Plano, 1987—; v.p. Supreme Resources Corp., Dallas, 1988-92. Founder, 1st pres. Drilling Engring. Assn., Dallas, 1983-85. Author: Drilling Equations, 1975; patentee horizontal drilling, high pressure drilling system, continuous heavy oil production process, 30 other patents. Precinct, region chmn. Rep. Party, Dallas, 1964-74; vol. bldg. com. Mary Immaculate Ch., Dallas, 1965-66; mem. tech. engring. and devel. com. Ocean Drilling Program, Bryan, Tex., 1980—. Recipient outstanding achievement in field of engring. award Nat. Engrs. Coun., 1980, Robert Earl McConnell award Am. Inst. Mining Engrs., 1994, Ohio State Univ. Coll. of Engring. Benjamin G. Lamme Meritorious Achievement medel, 1995. Mem. NAE, Soc. Petroleum Engrs. (nat. bd. dirs. 1983-86, Drilling Engring. award 1986, Disting. Mem. award 1989), Am. Petroleum Inst. (chmn. com. 6, 1985-88, svc. citation 1986), Am. Assn. Drilling Engrs., Soc. Ind. Profl. Earth Scientists, Petroleum Engrs. Club (pres. 1974-75), Ohio State U. Alumni Club (pres. 1968-69), Dallas-Ft. Worth Oilman's Club (handicapper 1973-86). Avocations: golf, sailing. Office: Drilling Tech Inc 5808 Wavertree Ln Ste 1000 Plano TX 75093-4513

SCHUH, G(EORGE) EDWARD, university dean, agricultural economist; b. Indpls., Sept. 13, 1930; s. George Edward and Viola (Lentz) S.; m. Maria Ignez, May 23, 1965; children: Audrey, Susan, Tanya. BS in Agrl. Edn, Purdue U., 1952, DAgr (hon.), 1992; MS in Agrl. Econs., Mich. State U., 1954; MA in Econs, U. Chgo., 1958, PhD, 1961; prof. (hon.), Fed. U. Vicosa, Brazil, 1965; hon. doctorate, Purdue U., 1992. From instr. to prof. agrl. econs. Purdue U., 1959-79; dir. Center for Public Policy and Public Affairs, 1977-78; dep. undersec. for internat. affairs and commodity programs Dept. Agr., Washington, 1978-79, chair bd. for internat. food and agrl. devel., 1995—; prof. agrl. and applied econs., head dept. U. Minn., Mpls., 1979-84; dir. agr. and rural devel. World Bank, Washington, 1984-87; dean Humphrey Inst. for Pub. Affairs U. Minn., 1987—96; Orville and Jane Freeman Endowed chair Humphrey Inst. for Pub. Affairs, U. Minn., 1996—; regents prof. U. Minn., 1998—. Program advisor Ford Found., 1966-72; sr. staff economist Pres.'s Coun. Econ. Advisors, 1974-75; bd. on agr. NRC, 1998—; trustee Internat. Food Policy Rsch. Inst., 1997—. Author, editor profl. books; contbr. numerous articles to profl. publs. Served with U.S. Army, 1954-56. Fellow AAAS, Am. Acad. Arts and Scis., Am. Agrl. Econs. Assn. (Thesis award 1962, Pub. Rsch. award 1971, Article award 1975, Policy award 1979, Publ. of Lasting Value award 1988, bd. dirs. 1977-80, pres.-elect 1980-81, pres. 1981-82); mem. Internat. Assn. Agrl. Econs., Am. Econ. Assn., Brazilian Soc. Agrl. Economists. Office: Humphrey Ctr U Minn 301 19th Ave S Minneapolis MN 55455-0429 E-mail: geschuh@hhh.umn.edu.

SCHUH, JOHN HOWARD, higher education educator, academic administrator; b. Cleve., July 29, 1947; s. Howard John and Elfreide Marie (Wachcic) S.; m. Linda Kay Rezin, June 30, 1973; 1 child, Kimberly Chrisette. BA, U. Wis., Oshkosh, 1969; M in Counseling, Ariz. State U., 1972, PhD, 1974. Resident complex dir. Ariz. State U., Tempe, 1970-72, asst. dir. housing, adj. prof., 1972-78; dir. residence life Ind. U., Bloomington, 1978-82, asst. dean, assoc. prof., 1982-84, assoc. dean, assoc. prof., 1985-87, assoc. dean students, prof. edn., 1985-87; assoc. v.p. student affairs Wichita State U., 1987-97, prof. counseling and sch. psychology, 1987-97; prof. higher edn. Iowa State U., 1997—, chair dept. ednl. leadership and policy studies, 1998—. Cons. to colls. and univs., 1977—; presenter to profl. cons. Editor: Programming and Activities in College and University Residence Halls, 1977; (with G.S. Blimling) Increasing the Educational Role of Residence Halls, 1981, A Handbook for Student Group Advisers, 1984, Enhancing Relationships with the Student Press, 1986, A Handbook for Student Group Advisers, 2d edit., (with G.D. Kuh and E.J. Whitt) Involving Colleges, (with M.L. Upcraft) Assessment in Student Affairs, (with N.W. Dunkel) Advising Student Groups and Organizations, (with A.M. Hoffman and R.H. Fenske) Violence on Campus, (with E.J. Whitt) Creating Successful Partnerships Between Academic and Student Affairs; gen. editor New Directions for Student Svcs.; assoc. editor Jour. of Coll. Student Devel.; contbr. articles to profl. jours., chpts. to books. Bd. dirs. NASPA Found., 2002—. Served to maj. USAR, 1973. Recipient Outstanding Rsch. award, Am. Coll. Pers. Assn. Commn. III, 1983, 1984, Contbn. to Knowledge award, Annuit Coeptis award, Sr. Scholar award, Presdl. Svc. award, ACPA Diamond Honoree, 1999, Contbn. to Lit. or Rsch. award, NASPA, Pillar of the Profession award, 2001, S. Earl Thompson award, Assn. of Coll. and Univ. Housting Officers Internat., 1999; scholar Fulbright scholar, 1994. Mem. Assn. Coll. Housing Officers (exec. bd. 1977-81, 85-87, chmn. legis. issues 1983-85), Am. Coll. Pers. Assn. (mem. media editl. bd. 1979-87, media bd. 1985-88, govtl. rels. com. 1984-85, Commn. III dir. 1979-82, commn. XII directorate 1987—), Nat. Assn. of Student Pers. Adminstrs. (bd. dirs. 1992-93, 99-2000, chair ann. conf. 2000), North Ctrl. Assn. Cons. Evaluator Corps. Home: 1706 Amherst Dr Ames IA 50014-3927 Office: Iowa State U N243 Lagomarcino Hl Ames IA 50011-0001 E-mail: Jschuh@iastate.edu.

SCHUH, MARTHA SCHUHMANN, mathematics educator; b. Boston, Oct. 12, 1941; d. Reinhardt and Betsy (Hancock) Schuhmann; 1 child, Erika. BA in Math., Oberlin Coll., 1962; MA in Math., U. Ill., 1963. Tchr. math. Sandburg High Sch., Orland Park, Ill., 1964-66, Centennial High Sch., Champaign, 1966-71; lectr. in math. U. Wis., Stevens Point, 1971-75; tchr., math. dept. chair Baraboo (Wis.) Jr. High Sch., 1976-82; assoc. prof. math. U. Wis. Ctr., Manitowoc, 1982—. Mem. Math. Assn. Am., Am. Math. Assn. Two-Yr. Colls., Nat. Coun. Tchrs. Math., Wis. Math. Coun. Home: 1118 Fairmont Ln Manitowoc WI 54220-2712 Office: U Wis Viebahn St Manitowoc WI 54220 E-mail: mschuh@uwc.edu.

SCHUHART, ANNE DASHLEY (SUSAN SCHUHART ZITO), actress; b. Rochester, N.Y., June 10, 1947; d. Richard Quinabert and Aynn (Miller) Schuhart; m. Frank John Zito, June 23, 1984. B.A. in English and Drama, Nazareth Coll., 1969. Asst. to Robert and Barbara Taylor Bradford, Bradford Enterprises, N.Y.C., 1981; v.p. Bradford Enterprises, 1991; corp sec., dir. Gemmy Prodns., Inc. Asst. to exec. producer miniseries "To Be the Best", CBS, 1992, "Remember", NBC, 1993, Everything to Gain, CBS, 1996, Love in Another Town, CBS, 1997, Her Own Rules, CBS, 1998, A Secret Affair, CBS, 1999. Appeared in Hold Me!, Phila., 1978, Vanities, Chgo., 1979. Recipient Comdrs. award Nat. Catholic Theatre Conf., 1965. Mem. AFTRA, N.Y. Celebrity Assts. Democrat. Roman Catholic. Office: Bradford Enterprises 450 Park Ave New York NY 10022-2605

SCHUISKI, LARRY LEROY, information scientist, consultant; b. L.A., Jan. 5, 1950; s. Leroy Hillis Duitsman and Charleen Edna (Nelson) Sager; m. Larissa Schuiski, June 17, 1988. BS in Physics with honors, U. Washington, 1972. Architect Boeing Computer Svcs., Seattle, 1978-88; dir. Trident Sys., San Francisco, 1988-92, View Star Corp., Alameda, Calif., 1993-95; v.p. Moore Document Solutions, Lake Forest, Ill., 1995-97; sr. cons. The Concours Group, Kingwood, Tex., 1997-99; sr. v.p. Attachmate corp., Bellevue, Wash., 1999—.

SCHUK, LINDA LEE, legal assistant, business educator; b. Scott Field, Ill., July 19, 1946; d. Frank A. Schuk and Jessie (Bumpass) Stearns; divorced; 1 child, Earl Wade. BBA, U. Tex., El Paso, 1968. Lic. life and health ins. agt., Tex. Acct., traffic mgr. Farah Mfg. Co., El Paso, 1970-71; adminstrv. asst. Horizon Corp., 1971-76; adminstrv. asst. in charge office ops. Foster-Scwartz Devel. Corp., 1976-78; legal sec. Howell and Fields, 1978-80; supr. Southland Corp., San Antonio, Waco, El Paso, 1980-83, sales mgr. San Antonio, 1983-84, dist. mgr., 1984-87; dist. supr. E-Z Mart Convenience Stores, 1987-89; legal asst. Brock & Brock, 1989—. Instr. San Antonio C.C., 1989—. Mem. NAFE. Democrat. Baptist. Avocation: music. Home: 11903 Parliament St Apt 324 San Antonio TX 78216-2451 Office: Brock & Brock 803 E Mistletoe Ave San Antonio TX 78212-3524 E-mail: ischuk@yahoo.com.

SCHUKER, ELEANOR SHEILA, psychiatrist, educator; b. N.Y.C., Jan. 3, 1941; d. Louis Aaron and Millicent (Milchman) S.; m. Alan Melowsky, Dec. 26, 1974; 1 child, Julie. BA, Swarthmore Coll., 1961; MD, Columbia U., 1965; cert. in psychoanalytic medicine, Columbia U. Ctr. for Psychoanalytic Training and Rsch., 1975. Diplomate Am. Bd. Psychiatry and Neurology. Intern Mt. Sinai Hosp., N.Y.C., 1965-66; resident in psychiatry N.Y. State Psychiat. Inst., Columbia U., 1966-69; attending psychiatrist Columbia U. Health Svc., 1969-90; co-dir. psychiat. emergency svcs. St. Luke's Hosp., 1970-72, founder, dir. rape intervention program, 1977-80, assoc. attending psychiatrist, 1978-99; collaborating psychoanalyst Columbia U. Psychoanalytic Ctr., 1975-85, training and supervising analyst, 1985—; mem. exec. com. Columbia U., 1996-99, asst. clin. prof. psychiatry, 1980-90, assoc. clin. prof. psychiatry, 1990—. Cons. Women's Counseling Project, N.Y.C., 1974-89. Editor: (with Nadine Levinson) Female Psychology: An Annotated Psychoanalytic Bibliography, 1991; contbr. articles to profl. jours. Fellow Am. Psychiat. Assn.; mem. Am. Psychoanalytic Assn. (cert., alt. del. to exec. coun. 1986-93), Assn. for Psychoanalytic Medicine (pres. 1995-97, George E. Daniels Merit award 1999), Alumni Assn. Columbia Psychoanalytic Ctr. (pres. 1978-80). Office: 150 W End Ave Apt 26A New York NY 10023-5743

SCHUL, BILL DEAN, psychological administrator, author; b. Winfield, Kans., Mar. 16, 1928; s. Fred M. and Martha Mildred (Miles) S.; m. Virginia Louise Duboise, Aug. 3, 1952; children: Robert Dean, Deva Elizabeth. BA, Southwestern Coll., 1952; MA, U. Denver, 1954; PhD, Am. Internat. U., 1977. Reporter, columnist Augusta (Kans.) Daily Gazette, 1954-58, Wichita (Kans.) Eagle-Beacon, 1958-61; youth dir. under auspices Kans. Atty. Gen., 1961-65; state dir. 7th Step Found., Topeka, 1965-66; mem. staff Dept. Preventive Psychiatry, Menninger Found., 1966-71; dir. cons. Ctr. Improvement Human Functining, Wichita, 1975—. Psychologist Ctr. Human Devel., Wichita. Mng. editor The Register, Oxford, Kans., 1988—; author: (with Edward Greenwood) Mental Health in Kansas Schools, 1965, Let Me Do This Thing, 1969, (with Bill Larson) Hear Me, Barabbas, 1969, How to Be An Effective Group Leader, 1975, The Secret Power of Pyramids, 1975, (with Ed Pettit) The Psychic Powre of Pyramids, 1976, Pyramids: The Second Reality, 1979, The Psychic Power of Animals, 1977, Psychic Frontiers of Medicine, 1977, Animal Immortality, 1990, Life Song, 1995, Synchronize Your Brain, 1997, Wayward Angel, 1988. Bd. dirs. Recreation Commn., Topeka, United Funds, Topeka, Acadic Inst., Trees for Life; v.p. Pegasus Way; pres. Intraface Corp., 1989—; mem. adv. bd. Clayton U. With USN, 1945-46. Recipient John H. McGinnis Meml. award Nonfiction, 1972, Am. Freedom Found. award, 1966, Spl. Appreciation award Kans. State Penitentiary, 1967. Mem. Acad. Parapsychology and Medicine, Kans. Coun. Children and Youth (pres. 1965-66), Assn. Strenghtening higher Realities and Aspirations of Man (pres. 1970-71), Smithsonian Instn., Lions (pores. 1957). Address: 7233 192d Rd Winfield KS 67156-9803 E-mail: schul@kcisp.net. *Personal philosophy: While the purpose of life may include joy and contentment, I believe that the primary goal of life is learning. Considering life as a school allows us to assign reason and direction to our successes and failures, that every experience can contribute to our growth as long as it is used to expand our awareness and increase our will.*

SCHULBERG, BUDD, author; b. N.Y.C., Mar. 27, 1914; s. Benjamin P. and Adeline (Jaffe) S.; m. Virginia Ray, July 23, 1936 (div. 1942); 1 dau., Victoria; m. Victoria Anderson, Feb. 17, 1943 (div. 1964); children: Stephen, David; m. Geraldine Brooks, July 12, 1964 (dec. 1977); m. Betsy Anne Langman, June 9, 1979; children: Benn Stuart, Jessica A. Student, Deerfield Acad., 1931-32; AB cum laude, Dartmouth Coll., 1936, LLD, 1960; LittD, Long Island U., 1983; DHL, Hofstra U., 1987, Five Points Coll., 2001. Boxing editor Sports Illustrated; pres., prodr. Schulberg Prodns. Founder, dir. Watts Writers Workshop, L.A., 1965—; founder, chmn. Frederick Douglass Creative Arts Ctr., N.Y.C., 1971—. Screenwriter, Hollywood, 1936-39; writer "The Schulberg Report", Newsday Syndicate; author: What Makes Sammy Run?, 1941, The Harder They Fall, 1947, The Disenchanted, 1950, Some Faces in the Crowd, 1953, Waterfront, 1955 (Christopher award 1955), Sanctuary V, 1969, The Four Seasons of Success, 1972, Loser and Still Champion: Muhammad Ali, 1972, Swan Watch, 1975, Everything that Moves, 1980, Moving Pictures: Memories of a Hollywood Prince, 1981, Love, Action, Laughter and Other Sad Tales, 1990, Sparring with Hemingway: And Other Legends of the Fight Game, 1995; editor: From the Ashes: Voices of Watts, 1967; screenwriter: (films) (with Samuel Ornitz) Little Orphan Annie, 1938, (with F. Scott Fitzgerald) Winter Carnival, 1939, (with Dorothy Parker) Weekend for Three, 1941, (with Martin Berkeley) City without Men, 1943, Government Girl, 1943, On the Waterfront, 1954 (Academy award best original story and screenplay 1954, N.Y. Critics award 1954, Fgn. Corrs. award 1954, Screen Writers Guild award 1954, Venice Festival award 1954), A Face in the Crowd, 1958 (German Film Critics award 1957), Wind across the Everglades, 1958, (teleplays) The Pharmacist's Mate, 1951, Paso Doble. A Question of Honor, A Table At Ciro's; playwright: The Disenchanted: A Play in Three Acts, 1958, What Make's Sammy Run?, 1959, (musical) Senor Discretion Himself, 1985, (play in 2 acts) The Disenchanted, 1999, On the Waterfront, 2001; contbr. to Sports Illustrated, Life, N.Y. Times Book Rev., Esquire, Newsday Syndicate, Los Angeles Times Book Rev., N.Y. Times Sunday Mag., Playboy, The New Yorker. Bd. dirs. Westminster Neighborhood Assn., L.A., 1965-68, Inner City Cultural Ctr., L.A., 1965-68; mem. nat. adv. commn. on black participation John F. Kennedy Ctr. for Performing Arts; trustee Humanitas Prize. Lt. (j.g.) USNR, 1943-46, assigned to OSS. Awarded Army Commendation Ribbon for gathering photog. evidence of war crimes for Nuremberg Trial, 1945-46; recipient Susie Humanitarian award B'nai B'rith, Image award NAACP, Journalism award Dartmouth Coll., Merit award Lotos Club., L.A. Community Svc. award, 1966, B'hai Human Rights award, 1968, spl. award for Watts Writers Workshop, New Eng. Theater Conf., 1969, Amistad award, award for work with black writers Howard U., Prix Literaire, Deauville Festival 1989, World Boxing Assn. Living Legend award, 1990, Westhampton Writers Lifetime Achievement award, 1989, Southampton Cultural Ctr. 1st Annual Literature award, 1992, Heritage award Deerfield Acad., 1986. Mem. Dramatists Guild, ASCAP, Authors Guild N.Y.C. (mem. council), ACLU, Writers Guild East (mem. coun.), Boxing Writers Am. (A. J. Liebling award 1997), P.E.N., Sphinx (Dartmouth), The Players Club, Yale/Dartmouth Club, Phi Beta Kappa. Address: Mr Mickey Freiberg Ache Literary Agy 4727 Wilshire Blvd Los Angeles CA 90064 also: Ms Mirian Altshuler 53 Old Post Rd N Red Hook NY 12571 E-mail: bschul@optonline.com.

SCHULBERG, JAY WILLIAM, foundation official; b. N.Y.C., July 17, 1939; s. Perry and Esther (Eagle) S.; m. Kathryn Carmel Nicholson, Sept. 18, 1968. BS (Founder's Day award 1961), NYU, 1961. With Seagram's Inc., 1962, Grumman Aircraft Co., 1963-66, Foote, Cone & Belding Inc., 1967-68, Ogilvy & Mather, Inc., N.Y.C., 1968-87, exec. v.p., head creative dept., 1985-87, also mem. U.S. coun. dirs., 1988-99; vice chmn., chief creative officer, bd. dirs. Bozell Worldwide, N.Y.C., 1987—99; office of chmn., also bd. dirs. Bozell, operating bd.; creative dir. Outdoor with Found. for A Better Life, 2000—. Bd. dirs. Ogilvy & Mather Worldwide, chmn., exec. com. Author: The Milk Mustache Book; creator advt. campaigns for Am. Express, Bahamas, TWA, Maxwell House Coffee, Country Time, Gen. Foods, Duracell, Hardees, Brit. Tourism, Hershey's, Huggies, Merrill Lynch, N.Y. Times, Excedrin, Milk "Mustache", Tyco, USAF, Mass. Mut., Vanity Fair, Vassrette, others. Developed Big Apple campaign, N.Y.C. With AUS, 1962. Recipient Art Dirs. Club awards, One Show awards, Andy awards, Addy awards, Cannes, Hollywood Festival awards, 6 David Ogilvy awards; named Creative Dir. of Yr. Adweek Mag., 1986. Mem. The One Club, Internat. Rescue Com. (bd. dirs.).

SCHULDT, EVERETT ARTHUR, engineer, consultant; b. Newark, Oct. 29, 1938; s. Arthur John and Ruby Ellen (Warner) S.; m. Georgiana Louise Benson, Sept. 24, 1960; children: David Arthur, Carl Everett. BSME, Rensselaer Poly. Inst., 1960. Lic. profl. engr., Ohio, Calif., Fla., Washington. Mfg. mgr. Procter & Gamble Co., N.Y.C., 1960-70, engr. Cin., 1970-72, group leader, 1972-76, sr. engr., 1976-85, tech. section head, 1985-93; ret., 1993. Mem. Am. Soc. of Mech. Engrs., Am. Inst. of Chemical Engrs., Natl. Soc. of Profl. Engrs., Am. Welding Soc., Soc. of Naval Architects & Marine Engrs., Am. Boat & Yacht Coun., Nat. Marine Mfrs. Assn. Republican. Presbyterian. Avocation: sailing. Home and Office: 2442 NW Market St # 514 Seattle WA 98107-4137

SCHULER, ALISON KAY, lawyer; b. West Point, N.Y., Oct. 1, 1948; d. Richard Hamilton and Irma (Sanken) S.; m. Lyman Gage Sandy, Mar. 30, 1974; 1 child, Theodore. AB cum laude, Radcliffe Coll., 1969; JD, Harvard U., 1972. Bar: Va. 1973, D.C. 1974, N.Mex. 1975. Assoc. Hunton & Williams, Richmond, Va., 1972-75; asst. U.S. atty. U.S. Atty.'s Office, Albuquerque, 1975-78; adj. prof. law U. N.Mex., 1983-85, 90, 98—; ptnr. Sutin, Thayer & Browne, Albuquerque, 1978-85, Montgomery & Andrews, P.A., Albuquerque, 1985-88; sole practice, 1988—. Bd. dirs. Am. Diabetes Assn., Albuquerque, 1980—85, chmn. bd. dirs., 1984—85; bd. dirs. June Music Festival, 1980—95, pres., 1983—85, 1993—94; bd. dirs. Albuquerque Conservation Trust, 1986—90, N.Mex. Osteo. Found., 1993—96; chairperson Albuquerque Com. Fgn. Rels., 1984—85; mem. N.Mex. Internat. Trade and Investment Coun., Inc., 1986—; chartered org. rep. troop 444 Boy Scouts Am., 1997—, mem. nominating com., mem.-at-large dist. com. Sandia dist., 1998—, dist. vice chmn., 1999—2001, v.p. Great S.W. coun., 2001—; mem. coun. St. Lukes Luth. Ch., 1976—80, 1982—84, 1991—96, v.p., 1978—80, 1982—84, pres., 1994—95. Recipient Award of Merit, Sandia Dist., 2000, Tng. award, 2000, Wood Badge, 2001. Mem. Fed. Bar Assn. (coord.), ABA, Va. Bar Assn., N.Mex. Bar Assn. (chmn. corp., banking and bus. law 1982-83, bd. dirs. internat. and immigration law sect. 1987-95, chmn. 1993-94), Harvard U. Alumni Assn. (mem. fund campaign, regional dir. 1984-86, v.p. 1986-89, chmn. clubs com. 1985-88, chmn. communications com. 1988-91), Radcliffe Coll. Alumnae Assn. Bd. Mgmt. (regional dir. 1984-87, chmn. comms. com. 1988-91), Harvard-Radcliffe Club (pres. 1980-84). Home: 632 Cougar Loop NE Albuquerque NM 87122-1808 Office: 4300 San Mateo Blvd NE Ste B380 Albuquerque NM 87110-8401 E-mail: akschuler@aol.com.

SCHULER, RICHARD EDWARD, economics educator, consultant; b. Allentown, Pa., Nov. 22, 1937; s. Edward John and Clare May (Moyer) S.; m. Mary Patricia Callaghan, May 12, 1962; children: Richard E. Jr., Anne E., Judith M. BE, Yale U., 1959; MBA, Lehigh U., 1969; MA, PhD, Brown U., 1972. Registered profl. engr., Pa. Engr., mgr. Pa. Power and Light Co., Allentown, Pa., 1959-67; sr. energy economist Battelle Meml. Inst., Columbus, Ohio, 1968-69; dir., Office Rsch., N.Y. State Dept. Pub. Svc., Albany, N.Y., 1977-78; commr., deputy chmn. N.Y. State Pub. Svc. Commn., 1981-83; prof. econ. and civil engring. Cornell U., Ithaca, 1972—. Vis. prof. Fuqua Sch. Mgmt., Duke U., Durham, N.C., 1987; chmn. adv. panel study increased competition in elec. supply U.S. Office Tech. Assessment, Washington, 1987-89; vis. scholar Ctr. for Ops. Rsch. and Econometrics, Louvain-la-Neuve, Belgium, 1988; dir. N.Y. State Solid Waste Combustion Inst., 1988-93, Cornell Inst. for Pub. Affairs, Ithaca, N.Y., 1995-2001; mem. bd. trustees Cornell U., Ithaca, 11194-98; bd. dirs. NYISU, Schenectady, N.Y.; sr. fellow Cornell Ctr. for Environment, 1992—; vis. fellow dept. ecology and evolutionary biology Princeton U., 1994; cons. World Bank, numerous regulatory bodies, ind. and utilities, 1976—. Co-author: The Future of Electrical Energy, 1986; mem. editl. bd. Jour. Indsl. Ecology, 1995—; contbr. numerous articles to profl. jours. Named one of twelve Stars of State Govt., Washington Monthly, 1982. Mem. Am. Econ. Assn., Regional Sci. Assn. Democrat. Office: Cornell U 422 Hollister Hall Ithaca NY 14853-3501

SCHULER, ROBERT HUGO, chemist, educator; b. Buffalo, Jan. 4, 1926; s. Robert H. and Mary J. (Mayer) S.; m. Florence J. Forrest, June 18, 1952; children: Mary A., Margaret A., Carol A., Robert E., Thomas C. BS, Canisius Coll., Buffalo, 1946; PhD, U. Notre Dame, 1949. Asst. prof. chemistry Canisius Coll., 1949-53; assoc. chemist, then chemist Brookhaven Nat. Lab., 1953-56; staff fellow, dir. radiation research lab. Mellon Inst., 1956-76, mem. adv. bd., 1962-76; prof. chemistry, dir. radiation research lab. Carnegie-Mellon U., 1967-76; prof. chemistry U. Notre Dame, Ind., 1976—, dir. radiation lab., 1976-95, dir. emeritus, 1995—, John A. Zahm prof. radiation chemistry, 1986—; Raman prof. U. Madras, India, 1985-86. Vis. prof. Hebrew U., Israel, 1980. Author articles in field. Recipient Curie medal Poland, 1992. Fellow AAAS; mem. Am. Chem. Soc., Am. Phys. Soc., Chem. Soc., Radiation Research Soc. (pres. 1975-76), Sigma Xi. Clubs: Cosmos. Office: U Notre Dame Radiation Lab Notre Dame IN 46556 E-mail: schuler.1@nd.edu.

SCHULER, ROBERT JORDAN, English educator, writer; b. San Mateo, Calif., June 25, 1939; s. Edward Peter and Georgia Ruth Schuler; m. Carol Florence Schuler, Sept. 7, 1963; children: Sally, Edward Anthony, Michael. BA in Polit. Sci. with honors, Stanford U., 1961; MA in Comparative Lit., U. Calif., Berkeley, 1965; PhD in English, U. Minn., 1989. Instr. English Menlo Coll., Menlo Park, Calif., 1965-67; instr. humanities Shimer Coll., Mt. Carroll, Ill., 1967-77; prof. English U. Wis.-Stout, Menomonie, 1978—. Hormel prof. U. Wis.-Stout, 1995-96. Author: Seasonings, 1978, Axle of the Oak, 1978, Where is Dancers' Hill?, 1979, Morning Raga, 1980, Origins, 1981, The Red Cedar Scroll, 1981, Music for Monet, 1985; Floating Out of Stone, 1982 (award Coun. Wis. Writers 1983), Grace, 1995, Red Cedar Suite, 1999; Journeys Toward the Mind, 1995; contbr. numerous poems to lit. jours. Bd. dirs. Shimer Coll. Assn., Waukegan, Ill., 1997—; dir. film series Menomonie Pub. Libr., 1997—; mem. land use planning com. Twp. of Menomonie, 1999—. Pub. grantee Ill. Arts Coun., Chgo., 1976, 77, Nat. Endowment for the Arts, Washington, 1978; fellow Danforth Found., 1969-70, lit. fellow (poetry) Wis. Arts Bd., Madison, 1997; recipient New Works award Wis. Arts Bd., 1999. Mem. Phi Kappa Phi. Avocations: cross-country skiing, hiking, gardening. Home: E4549 479th Ave Menomonie WI 54751 Office: Dept English U Wis-Stout Menomonie WI 54751 E-mail: schulerr@uwstout.edu.

SCHULER, ROBERT LEO, appraiser, consultant; b. Cin., June 15, 1943; s. Del D. and Virginia D. (Heyl) S.; m. Shelagh J. Moritz, Aug. 11, 1962; children: Robert C., Sherry L. V.p. Comprehensive Appraisal Service, Cin., 1977—. Bd. dirs. Hamilton County Regional Planning Commn., Cin., 1987-88; mem. exec. com., past pres. OKI Regional Coun. Govts., Cin., 1981-92. Councilman City of Deer Park, Ohio, 1979-86; trustee Sycamore Twp., 1988-92; Ohio state rep. 36th dist., 1993—2000; active Scarlet Oaks Bus. Adv. Coun. Mem. Cin. Bd. Realtors, Ohio Assn. Realtors, Jaycees (v.p.), Nat. Assn. Independent Fee Appraisers, Appraisal Inst. Republican. Roman Catholic. Home: 3648 Jeffrey Ct Cincinnati OH 45236-1544 Office: 3648 Jeffrey Ct Cincinnati OH 45236-1544

SCHULER, THEODORE ANTHONY, retired civil engineer, retired city official; b. Louisville, July 1, 1934; s. Henry R. and Virginia (Meisner) S.; m. Jane A. Bandy, July 29, 1979; children: Marc, Elizabeth, Eric, Ellen. BCE, U. Louisville, 1957, M in Engring., 1973. Registered profl. engr., Tenn. Design constrn. engr. Brighton Engring. Co., Frankfort, Ky., 1960-65; design engr. Hensley-Schmidt Inc., Chattanooga, 1965-68, assoc. mem., 1969-73, sr. assoc. mem., 1973-75, prin., asst. v.p., head Knoxville office, 1975-81; chief planning engr. engring. dept. City of Knoxville, 1981-96; ret., 1996. Served to lt. (j.g.) USNR, 1957-60. Fellow ASCE. Home: 5907 Adelia Dr Knoxville TN 37920-5801 E-mail: Tschu30447@aol.com.

SCHULER, WALTER E. lawyer; b. Memphis, Sept. 8, 1962; s. James D. and Clare A. Schuler. BBA magna cum laude, U. Memphis, 1993; JD cum laude with cert. in health law with hons., St. Louis U., 1996. Bar: Tenn. 1996, U.S. Dist. Ct. (Western Dist.) Tenn. 1996, U.S. Ct. Appeals (6th cir.), 1998. Assoc. The Bogatin Law Firm, PLC, Memphis, 1996—. Contbr. articles to profl. jours., chpt. to book. Sgt. (E-5), U.S. Army, 1985-90, staff sgt. (E-6) USAR, 1990-93. Recipient Commendation Medal-1st Oak Leaf Cluster, U.S. Army, 1989, Army Achievement Medal-2nd Oak Leaf Cluster, 1989, Nat. Def. Svc. Med., 1992. Mem. Am. Health Lawyers Assn., ABA, Tenn. Bar Assn., Memphis Bar Assn. Office: Bogatin Law Firm PLC Ste 300 International Place Dr Memphis TN 38120

SCHULHOF, MICHAEL PETER, entertainment, electronics company executive; b. N.Y.C., Nov. 30, 1942; s. Rudolph B. and Hannelore (Buck) S.; m. Paola Nissim, Apr. 17, 1969; children: David Kenneth, Jonathan Nissim. BA, Grinnell Coll., 1964, DSc (hon.), 1990; MS, Cornell U., 1967; PhD (NSF fellow), Brandeis U., 1970. Lic. comml. pilot. Am. research fellow Brookhaven Nat. Lab., Uptown, N.Y., 1969-71; asst. to v.p. mfg. CBS Records, Inc., N.Y.C., 1971-73, mem. exec. com., bd. dirs., 1987—; gen. mgr. bus. products div. Sony Corp., 1973-77, v.p., 1977-78, sr. v.p., 1978-86; pres. Sony Industries, 1978-86; chmn. Digital Audio Disc Corp., Terre Haute, Ind., 1986-96; pres. Sony Software Corp., 1991-96; pres., CEO Sony Corp. Am., 1993-95. Chmn. bd. dirs. Quadriga Art Inc., 1980—, World On Line, 1998—99; bd. dirs. Sony Corp., Japan, Sony Corp. Am., Sony Pictures Entertainment, Materials Rsch. Corp., JFAX, CBS/Sportsline; chmn. Sony Music Entertainment, Comml. Electronics, 1998—; chmn., CEO Global Tech. Investments, 2001—. Contbr. articles to profl. jours. Patentee audio disc apparatus, 1986. Trustee Brandeis U., 1990—, Lincoln Ctr. for Performing Arts, Inc., N.Y.C., The Brookings Instn., Washington; bd. dirs. Ctr. on Addiction and Substance Abuse at Columbia U., N.Y.C.; mem. investment and svcs. policy adv. com. to U.S. Trade Rep.; active Coun. Fgn. Rels. NSF fellw Brandeis U. Mem. Am. Phys. Soc. (dir. 1978), Computer and Bus. Equipment Mfrs. Assn. (dir.), Am. Radio Relay League, Aircraft Owners and Pilots Assn., Guggenhiem Mus., Whitney Mus., Harmony Club, Gipsy Trail Club, East Hampton Tennis Club, Profile Club, Fenway Golf Club, Atlantic Golf Club. Office: 375 Park Ave New York NY 10152-0002

SCHULHOFER, STEPHEN JOSEPH, law educator, consultant; b. N.Y.C., Aug. 20, 1942; s. Joseph and Myrelle S.; m. Laurie Wohl, May 28, 1975; children: Samuel, Jonah. AB, Princeton U., 1964; LLB, Harvard U., 1967. Bar: D.C. 1968, U.S. Dist. Ct. (ea. dist.) Pa. 1973, U.S. Supreme Ct. 1973. Law clk. U.S. Supreme Ct., Washington, 1967-69; assoc. Coudert Freres, Paris, 1969-72; prof. law U. Pa., Phila., 1972-86; prof. U. Chgo., 1986—. speedy trial reporter U.S. Dist. Ct., Wilmington, Del., 1975-80; cons. U.S. EPA, Washington, 1977-78, U.S. Sentencing Commn., Washington, 1987-94. Author: Unwanted Sex: The Culture of Intimidation and the Failure of Law, 1998; Prosecutorial Discretion and Federal Sentencing Reform, 1979. Editor: Criminal Law and its Processes, 1983, 89, 95; contbr. articles to profl. jours. Trustee, Community Legal Services, Inc., Phila., 1981-86. Walter Meyer grantee Am. Bar Found., 1984. Mem. ACLU (Ill. bd. dirs. 1993-97), Law and Soc. Assn. Office: NYU Law Sch 40 Washington Sq S New York NY 10012

SCHULHOFF, KAREN L. information specialist; b. Long Island City, N.Y., Dec. 11, 1959; d. Edward and Eleanor (Gillespie) S. MLS, CUNY, 1993. Tng. program coord. Chem. Bank, N.Y.C., 1983-90; libr. Katharine Gibbs Sch., 1990-92; cons. Pfizer, 1993-2001; info. specialist, rschr. Bear, Stearns Investment Banking, 2001—. Mem. NAFE, Am. Mgmt. Assn. Roman Catholic. Office: Bear Stearns Investment Banking 245 Park Ave New York NY 10167

SCHULIAN, JOHN (NIELSEN SCHULIAN), screenwriter, author; b. L.A., Jan. 31, 1945; s. John and Estella Katherine (Nielsen) S.; m. Paula Lynn Ellis, Aug. 20, 1977 (div. Oct. 1984). BA, U. Utah, 1967; MS, Northwestern U., 1968. Copy editor Salt Lake City Tribune, 1968; reporter Balt. Evening Sun, 1970-75; sportswriter Washington Post, 1975-77; sports columnist Chgo. Daily News, 1977-78, Chgo. Sun-Times, 1978-84, Phila. Daily News, 1984-86; staff writer Miami Vice, Universal City, Calif., 1986-87, story editor, 1987, The Slap Maxwell Story, North Hollywood, 1987-88; exec. story editor TV series Wiseguy, Hollywood, 1988-89; co-producer TV series Midnight Caller, Burbank, Calif., 1989-90, supervising producer, 1990-91; co-exec. producer TV series Reasonable Doubts, Burbank, Calif., 1991-92; creative cons. TV series The Untouchables, L.A., 1992-93; co-exec. producer TV series Hercules, Universal City, Calif., 1994-96; co-creator Xena: Warrior Princess, 1995; assoc. prodr. (documentary) Ben Johnson: Third Cowboy on the Right, 1996; co-exec. prodr. (TV series) Lawless, 1996-97; consulting prodr. (TV series) JAG, 1999-2000; exec. prodr. (TV series) The Outer Limits, Vancouver, Can., 2000-01; culture columnist MSNBC.com, 2001—02; co-exec prodr. (TV series) Tremors, Universal City, Calif., 2002—. Spl. contbr. Sports Illustrated, 1998—. Author: Writers' Fighters and Other Sweet Scientists, 1983; contbg. editor Panorama mag., 1980-81; syndicated columnist UP Syndicate; commentator Nat. Pub. Radio, 1985-86; cons. The Reader's Catalog, 1989; contbr. articles to N.Y. Times, Playboy, Gentlemen's Quar., The National, L.A. Times; included in The Best Am. Sports Writing, 1994. Mem. Pacific Coast League Hist. Soc. With U.S. Army, 1968-70. Recipient Nat. Headliners Club award, 1980, Column Writing award AP Sports Editors, 1979, 82, Best Sports Stories award, 1983, 84, Nat Fleischer Excellence in Boxing Journalism award Boxing Writers Assn. Am., 1985. Mem. Writers Guild Am., Phi Beta Kappa. Office: Endeavor Talent Agy 9701 Wilshire Blvd 10th Fl Beverly Hills CA 90212 E-mail: jschulian@aol.com.

SCHULING, MARK RICHARD, lawyer; b. Furstenfeldbruk, Germany, June 6, 1955; came to U.S., 1957; s. Richard Charles and Dorraine Faye S.; m. Eliza Jane Ovrom, Sept. 4, 1982; children: Charles Mark, Matthew Arthur. BA in Social Scis., Drake U., 1976, JD, 1980. Bar: U.S. Dist. Ct. (no. and so. dists.) Iowa 1982, U.S. Ct. Appeals (8th cir.) 1983; CPA, Iowa. Asst. atty. gen. Atty. Gen. State Iowa, Des Moines, 1980-84; assoc. Brick, Gentry Law Firm, 1984-87; prin. Brick, Gentry, Bowers, Swartz, Stoltze, Schuling & Levis, PC, 1987—. Dir. Des Moines Sch. Dist., 1996—, v.p., 1999-2000, pres., 2000-01; exchange dir. Friendship Force Des Moines. Mem. Iowa State Bar Assn., Polk County Bar Assn., Iowa Soc. CPA's, Greater Des Moines C. of C. (dir. 1996-2000), Order of Barristers. Democrat. Congregationalist. Avocations: biking, hiking, reading, golfing. Home: 500 Glenview Dr Des Moines IA 50312-2526 Office: Brick Gentry Bowers Swartz Stoltze Schuling & Levis PC 550 39th St Ste 200 Des Moines IA 50312-3529

SCHULLER, DAVID EDWARD, cancer center administrator, otolaryngologist; b. Cleve., Oct. 20, 1944; m. Carole Ann Hauss, June 24, 1967; children: Rebecca, Michael. BA, Rutgers U., 1966; MD cum laude, Ohio State U., 1970. Diplomate Am. Bd. Otolaryngology 1975. Intern dept. surgery U. Hosps. Cleve., 1970-71; resident dept. otolaryngology Ohio State U., Columbus, 1971-72; resident dept. surgery U. Hosps. Cleve., 1972-73; fellow head and neck surgery Pack Med. Found. with John Conley, N.Y.C., 1973; resident dept. otolaryngology Ohio State U. Hosps., Columbus, 1973-75; fellow head and neck oncology and facial plastic and reconstructive surgery U. Iowa, Iowa City, 1975-76; trustee Ohio Cancer Found, 1988—; from clin. instr. to prof. and chmn. dept. otolaryngology The Ohio State U., Columbus, 1971—; dir. Am. Bd. Otolaryngology, 1988—2000; dir. Comprehensive Cancer Ctr., Columbus, 1997—; prof. sect. oral biology, Coll. Dentistry The Ohio State U., 1990—; dir. Arthur G. James Cancer Hosp. & Richard J. Solove Rsch. Inst., Columbus, 1988—; chair dept. otolaryngology Ohio State U., 1990—; pres. American Board of Otolaryngology, 2000—. Mem., chmn. various coms. Ohio State U. Hosps. and Coll. Medicine, 1976—; dir. CCC head and neck oncology program Ohio State U., 1977—, hosps. physician flr. coord. 10th flr., 1977-82, dir. laser-microsurgery teaching and rsch. lab., 1987-88; mem. various coms. Grant Hosp., 1980-84; mem. Accreditation Coun. for the Grad. Med. Edn. Residency Review Com. for Otolaryngology, 1985—, chmn., 1988—; vis. prof., lectr., ACS prof. clin. Oncology, 1989-94. numerous instns. Author: (books) (with others) Otolaryngology-Head and Neck Surgery-4 Vols., 1986, Textbook of Otolaryngology-7th Edit., 1988, Otolaryngology-Head and Neck Surgery-Update I, 1988, Musculocutaneous Flaps in Head and Neck Reconstructive Surgery, 1989, Otolaryngology-Head and Neck Surgery Update II, 1990, Otorinolaringologia-Cirugia de Cabeza y Culleo, 1991, Otolaryngology-Head and Neck Surgery-4 Vols., 1992; contbr. chpts. to books and articles to profl. jours.; mem. editorial bd. New Horizons in Otolaryngology/Head and Neck Surgery, 1982-87, The Laryngoscope, 1986—, Am. Jour. Otolaryngology, 1988—, Facial Plastic Surgery Internat. Quar. Monographs, 1992—; mem. rev. bd. Jour. Head and Neck Surgery, 1985—; mem. editorial rev. bd. Otolaryngology-Head and Neck Surgery, 1990—; reviewer New Eng. Jour Medicine, 1992—. Recipient Cert. of Appreciation, Scioto Meml. Hosp., 1982, Edmund Prince Fowler award Triological Soc., 1984; Henry Rutgers scholar Rutgers U., 1965-66; grantee Nat. Cancer Inst., 1980-88, 90-97, Bremer Found., 1982-83, 87-88, Photomedica Inc., 1986-89, Upjohn Co., 1986-90, others. Mem. AMA (mem. rev. panel Archives of Otolaryngology-Head and Neck Surgery 1984—), Am. Cancer Soc. (mem. instl. grant rev. com. 1980—, chmn. rehab. com. Franklin County unit 1981-82, mem. profl. edn. com. 1981—, chmn. 1982-85, v.p. 1982-83, pres. 1986, 87, trustee Ohio divsn. 1988—), Am. Assn. Cosmetic Surgeons, Am. Acad. Facial Plastic and Reconstructive Surgery (mem. rsch. com. 1977-82, chmn. residency rels. com. 1982-85, mem. program com. 1982-85, v.p. mid. sect. 1983-87, chmn. by-laws com. 1988-90, treas. 1988-90, Honor award 1989), Am. Coll. Surgeons, Am. Cleft Palate Assn., Assn. Am. Cancer Insts., Am. Soc. Head and Neck Injury, Am. Acad. Otolaryngology Head and Neck Surgery (mem. editorial bd. self-instructional package program 1982—, del. bd. govs. 1982-87, Honor award 1983), Am. Soc. Laser Medicine and Surgery, Am. Laryngological, Rhinological, Otological Soc., Inc., Am. Laryngological Assn., Am. Soc. Clin. Oncology (mem. program com. 1989—), Am. Assn. Cancer Researchers, Am. Soc. Head and Neck Surgery (mem. coun. 1983-86, chmn. scholastic and fellowship award com. 1984-86, mem. profl. rels. and pub. edn. com. 1989—), Southwest Oncology Group (chmn. head and neck com. 1983—), Collegium ORLAS, Ohio State Med. Assn. (pres. sect. otolaryngology 1987—), Ohio Soc. Otolaryngology (pres. 1985, 86, 87), Acad. Medicine of Columbus and Franklin County, Columbus E.E.N.T. Soc., Franklin County Acad. Medicine (mem. profl. rels. com. 1982—), Head and Neck Intergroup (vice-chmn. 1984-86, chmn. 1986-89), Assn. Rsch. Otolaryngology, Ohio State U. Med. Alumni Soc. (class rep. 1980—, v.p. 1987-88, pres. 1989-90), Med. Forum, Med. Review Club, Order of Hippocrates (charter), Alpha Omega Alpha. Office: 456 W 10th Ave Columbus OH 43210-1240 also: Ohio State Univ Comp Cancer Ctr 300 W 10th Ave Columbus OH 43210-1240*

SCHULLER, DIANE ETHEL, allergist, immunologist, educator; b. Bklyn., Nov. 27, 1943; d. Charles William and Dorothy Schuller. AB cum laude with honors in Biology, Bryn Mawr Coll., 1965; MD, SUNY, Bklyn., 1970. Diplomate Am. Bd. Allergy & Immunology, Am. Bd. Pediatrics, Nat. Bd. Med. Examiners. Intern, resident in pediats. Roosevelt Hosp., Bklyn., 1970-72; resident in allergy Cooke Inst. Allergy, 1972-74; assoc. in pediatrics Geisinger Med. Ctr., Danville, Pa., 1974-78, dir, dept. pediat. allergy, immunology & pediat. diseases, 1978-95; asst. clin. prof. pediats. Hershey Med. Coll. Pa. State U., 1974-79, assoc. clin. prof., 1979-88; clin. prof. Jefferson Med. Coll., Phila., 1989-95; dir. pediat. allergy, immunology, pulmonology Pa. State U./Hershey Med. Coll., 1995—, prof. pediats., 1995—. Bd. dirs. Ctrl. Pa. Lung and Health Assn.; bd. dirs., exec. com. Am. Lung Assn. Pa., sec., 1992—; chmn. Susquehanna Vly. Lung Assn., 1983—; scholarship com. Bryn Mawr Club, N.Y., 1970-75; Columbia-Montour Home Health Svcs. Adv. Group Profl. Personnel, 1975-95. Editl. bd. Annals of Allergy, Asthma and Immunology. Recipient physician's recognition award AMA, 1973-76, 74-76, 75-78, 79-82, 83-86, 87-90, 91-94, 95-98, 1999-2002. Fellow AAP (exec. com. 1998—), Am. Coll. Allergy Asthma and Immunology (2d v.p. 1988, bd. regents 1989-92, exec. com. 1990-93, v.p. 1992-93, pres.-elect 1993-94, pres. 1994-95), Am. Assn. Clin. Immunology and Allergy (regional dir., exec. com.), Joint Coun. Allergy and Immunology (bd. dirs. 1986-95, treas. joint coun. 1991-93), Am. Acad. Allergy and Immunology; mem. Am. Assn. Cert. Allergists, Pa., N.Y. State Allergy Soc., N.Y. State Med. Soc., N.Y. County Med. Soc. Office: Milton S Hershey Med Coll Pa State U Hershey PA 17033

SCHULLER, GERALD DIEDRICH THOMAS, electrical engineer; b. Neuenstein, Germany, Oct. 8, 1961; s. Thomas Schuller and Renate Mingers-Schuller. MS, Tech. U. Berlin, 1989; PhD, U. Hannover, Germany, 1997. Intern AEG, Berlin, 1987, Hahn-Meitner-Inst., Berlin, 1988-89; rsch. asst. Tech. U. Berlin, 1990-92; tchg. asst. Ga. Inst. Technology, Atlanta, 1993; rsch. asst. U. Bonn, Germany, 1994, U. Hannover, 1995—, Bell Labs., Lucent Techs., Murray Hill, N.J., 1998—, Fraunhofer Inst., Ilmenau, Germany, 2002—. Inventor in field; contbr. articles to profl. jours. Mem. IEEE, Deutscher Amateur Radio Club. Avocation: amateur radio. Home: Leopoldstr 13 99089 Erfurt Germany Office: Fraunhofer Inst Am Ehrenberg 8 98693 Ilmenau Germany E-mail: schuller@emt.iis.fhg.de.

SCHULLER, GUNTHER ALEXANDER, composer; b. N.Y.C., Nov. 22, 1925; s. Arthur E. and Elsie (Bernartz) S.; m. Marjorie Black, June 8, 1948; children: Edwin Gunther, George Alexander. Student, St. Thomas Choir Sch., N.Y.C.; MusD (hon.), Manhattan Sch. Music, 1987, Northeastern U., 1967, U. Ill., 1968, Colby Coll., 1969, Williams Coll., 1975, Cleve. Inst. Music, 1977, New Eng. Conservatory Music, 1978, Rutgers U., 1980, Manhattan Sch. Music, 1987, Oberlin Coll., 1989. Tchr. Manhattan Sch. Music, 1950-63; head composition dept. Tanglewood, 1963-84; pres. New Eng. Conservatory of Music, 1967-77; artistic dir. Berkshire Music Center, Tanglewood, 1969-84, Festival at Sandpoint, 1985—; founder, pres. Margun Music Inc., 1975, GM Recs., 1980. French horn player, Ballet Theatre, then prin. horn player, Cin. Symphony Orch., 1943-45, prin. French horn, Met. Opera Orch., 1945-59, Contours #1 for Horn, 1945; composer: Quartet for Four Double Basses, 1947, Fantasy for Unaccompanied Cello, 1951, Recitative and Rondo for Violin and Piano, 1953, Music for Violin, Piano and Percussion, 1957, Contours, 1958, Woodwind Quintet, 1958, Seven Studies on Themes of Paul Klee, 1959, Spectra, 1960, Six Renaissance Lyrics, 1962, String Quartet No. 2, 1965, Symphony, 1965, opera The Visitation 1966, opera Fisherman and His Wife, 1970, Capriccio Stravagante, 1972, The Power Within Us, 1972, Tre Invenzioni, 1972, Three Nocturnes, 1973, Four Soundscapes, 1974, Concerto No. 2 for Orch., 1975, Triplum II, 1975, Horn Concerto No. 2, 1976, Violin Concerto, 1976, Diptych for organ, 1976, Sonata Serenata, 1978, Contrabassoon Concerto, 1978, Deaï for 3 orchs., 1978, Trumpet Concerto, 1979, Octet, 1979, Eine Kleine Posaunenmusik, 1980, In Praise of Winds (Symphony for Large Wind Orch.), 1981, Symphony for Organ, 1982, Concerto Quaternio, 1983, Concerto for Bassoon and Orch., 1984, Farbenspiel (Concerto No. 3 for Orch.), 1985, On Light Wings (piano quartet), 1984; author: Horn Technique, 1962, Early Jazz: Its Roots and Development, 1968, Musings: The Musical Worlds of Gunther Schuller, 1985, The Swing Era, 1989; premiere of Symphony for Brass and Percussion, Cin., 1950, Salzburg Festival, 1957, Dramatic Overture, N.Y. Philharm., 1956, String Quartet, Number 1 Contemporary Arts Festival, U. Ill., 1957, String Quartet Number 3, 1986, Concertino for Jazz Quartet and Orch, Balt. Symphony Orch., 1959, Seven Studies on Themes of Paul Klee, Ford Found., commn., Minn. Symphony, 1959, Spectra, N.Y. Philharm. 1960, Music for Brass Quintet, Coolidge Found., Library of Congress, 1961, Concerto No. 1 for Orch, Chgo. Symphony Orch., 1966, Triplum, N.Y. Philharm. commd. Lincoln Center, 1967, Aphorisms for Flute and String Trio commd, Carlton Coll. Centennial, 1967, Eine Kleine Posaunenmusik, 1980, In Praise of Winds, 1983, Concerto Quaternio, N.Y. Philharm., 1983, Duologue for Violin and Piano, Library of Congress, 1984, Farbenspiel, Berlin Philharm., 1985, Concerto for Viola and Orch., 1985, String Quartet No. 3, 1986, Chimeric Images, 1988, Concerto for String Quartet and Orchestra, 1988, Concerto for Flute and Orchestra, 1988, On Winged Flight: A Divertimento for Band, 1989, Chamber Concerto, 1989, Concerto for Piano Three Hands, 1989, Phantasmata for Violin and Marimba, 1989, 5 Impromptus Eng. Horn and String Quartet, 1989, Impromptus and Cadenzas, 1990, Hommage à Rayechla for 8 cellos/or multiples thereof, 1990, A Trio Setting for clarinet, violin, piano, 1990, Violin Concert No. 2, 1991, Sonata Fantasia for piano, 1992, Ritmica Melodia Armonia for orchestra, 1992, Of Reminiscences and Reflections for orchestra, 1993 (Pulitzer Prize for music 1994), Brass Quintet No. 2, 1993, The Past is in the Present for orchestra, 1994, Sextet for left hand piano and woodwind quintet, 1994, Concerto for organ and orchestra, 1994, Mondrian's Vision, 1994, Magnificat and Nuncdimittis (choir), 1994, Lain out for it (jazz ensemble), 1994, Brass Quintet No. 2, 1994, Rush Hour an 23d, 1994, Blue Dawn into White Heat (concert band), 1995, An Are Ascending, 1996, Guggenheim fellow, 1962, 63, MacArthur fellow, 1991; recipient Creative Arts award Brandeis U., 1960, Deems Taylor award ASCAP, 1970, Alice M. Ditson Conducting award, 1970, Rodgers and Hammerstein award, 1971, Friedheim award, 1988, William Schuman award Columbia U., 1989, Down Beat Lifetime Achievement award, 1993, Pulitzer prize in music, 1994, BMI Lifetime Achievement award, 1994, Gold medal Am. Acad. Arts and Letters, 1997, Order of Merit Cross Fed. Republic Germany, 1997, Max Rudolf award, 1998; named Composer of Yr., Mus. Am., 1995; inductee Am. Classical Music Hall of Fame, 1998. Mem. Nat. Inst. Arts and Letters, Am. Acad. Arts and Scis. Address: 167 Dudley Rd Newton Center MA 02459-2830

SCHULMAN, ALAN MICHAEL, small business owner; b. Chgo., Feb. 5, 1946; s. Aaron and Anne Schulman; m. Barbara Picard, May 27, 1984; 1 child, Jeffrey. BBA, Roosevelt U., 1968. Salesman Dictaphone Corp., Chgo., 1968-69; sales engr. Boston Gear, 1969-70; mgr. Imperial Packaging, 1970-71; owner A.M.S. Distbg., Skokie, Ill., 1971-77; owner, pres. Greater Distbn. Svcs., Glenview, 1977-90, The Battery Bank div. Jalco, Inc., Glenview, 1982-92, Glentronics Inc., Glenview, 1989—. Host tv gardening program. Author (newspaper column) Gardening Information, 1980; host numerous TV fishing programs; contbr. articles on battery to nat. mags.; patentee in field; subject of mag., newspaper articles; appearances in nat. radio program Home Improvement U.S.A.; inventor in field. Named to Freshwater Fishing Hall of Fame for world record catch. Mem. Entrepreneurs Network. Clubs: Men's Garden of North Shore (Highland Park) (pres. 1984-85). Achievements include inventing basement watchdog pumps, socklight drawer lights, timely lighting care, plant light. Avocations: gardening, fishing, photography. Office: 1150 Willis Ave Wheeling IL 60090-5817

SCHULMAN, DAVIDA WEINBERG, artist, educator, graphic designer; b. Chgo., May 12, 1946; d. Sol and Dorothy (Shulman) Weinberg; m. Lawrence Stuart Schulman, Mar. 27, 1966; children: Kenneth S., Robert L. BA in Plastic and Graphic Art, U. Ill., Chgo., 1969; MS in Painting, Ill. State U., 1994, MFA in Painting, 1996. Cert. tchr., Ill. Adj. faculty Benedictine U., Lisle, Ill., 1996-97, Elgin (Ill.) C.C., 2000—, Oakton C.C., Des Plaines, Ill., 2001—. Artist, tchr., painter, printmaker. Recipient Norris award 1996, Vt. Studio Ctr. fellowship, 1999, award Watercolor USA Springfield Art Mus., 1999. Mem. Coll. Art Assn., Artists of Rogers Park (editor, writer newsletter 1998-2000).

SCHULMAN, ELLIOTT A. neurologist, educator, researcher; b. Buffalo, Mar. 17, 1947; s. Morris Schulman and Rose (Axlerod) S.; m. Bonnie S. Merion, Oct. 24, 1982; children: David, Andrew. BA, SUNY, Buffalo, 1969, MD, 1974. Diplomate Am. Bd. Neurology and Psychiatry. Fellow NIH, Bethesda, Md., 1978-79; mem. neurology staff, asst. prof. Temple U., Phila., 1979-82; co-dir Comprehensive Headache Ctr., 1984-96; dir. Ctr. for Headache Mgmt., Upland, 1996—; assoc. prof. neurology Hahnemann Sch. Medicine, Phila., 1996—. Nat. lectr. Contbr. articles to profl. jours. Fundraising chmn. Crossroads Sch. Fellow ACP, Am. Acad. Neurology, Am. Assn. for Study of Headache (vol.). Avocations: exercising, reading. Office: Ctr for Headache Mgmt 1 Medical Center Blvd Chester PA 19013-3902 E-mail: Eschul6641@home.com.

SCHULMAN, HAROLD, obstetrician, gynecologist, perinatologist; b. Newark, Oct. 26, 1930; m. Rosemarie Vincenti; childrne: Stanley H., Sandra C., Gina M. BS, U. Fla., 1951; MD, Emory U., 1955. Diplomate Am. Bd. Ob-Gyn., Am. Bd. Maternal and Fetal Medicine; registered diagnostic med. sonographer. Intern Jackson Meml. Hosp., Miami, Fla., 1955-56, resident, 1958-61; instr. dept. ob-gyn. U. Miami (Fla.) Sch. Medicine, 1961; instr., asst. prof. dept. ob-gyn. Temple U. Sch. Medicine, Phila., 1961-65; asst. prof. dept. ob-gyn. Albert Einstein Coll. Medicine, Bronx, 1965-67, assoc. prof., 1968-71, prof., 1971—, acting dept. chmn., 1972-73, chmn., 1973-80; assoc. dir. dept. ob-gyn Bronx Mcpl. Hosp. Ctr., 1967-70, dep. dir., 1970-72; chmn. dept. ob-gyn. Winthrop U. Hosp., Mineola, N.Y., 1984-93; prof. ob-gyn SUNY, Stony Brook, 1984-93; chmn. dept. ob-gyn. Lawnwood Regional Med. Ctr., Ft. Pierce, FL, 1995-2000. Contbr. articles to profl. pubs. Served to capt. U.S. Army, 1956-58. Am. Cancer Soc. fellow, 1959-60; USPHS trainee, 1965-66 Fellow ACOG (vice chmn. Dist. II 1972-75); mem. Bronx County Obstet. Soc. (pres. 1974), AAAS, Obstet. Soc. (sec. 1978-80, pres. 1982-83), N.Y. Obstetrical Soc., Soc. Maternal Fetal Medicine, Am. Gynecologic and Obstetric Soc., Am. Gynecol. Obstetrics, N.Y. Obstetics Soc. (pres. 1982), Phi Beta Kappa, Alpha Omega Alpha; hon. mem. Miami Ob-Gyn. Soc., South Atlantic Obstetricians and Gynecologists Soc., Buffalo Gynecologic and Obstetric Soc. (E.G. Winkler meml. lectr.), Croatian Ultrasound Soc. (hon.). Democrat. Jewish. E-mail: TippingtheScales@xlibris.com.

SCHULMAN, JACQUE-LYNNE AMANN, information scientist; b. Balt. children: Joshua, Jonathan. BA in Sociology, George Washington U., Washington, 1972; MSLS, Cath. U. Am., Washington, 1973; MA in Social Orgn., George Washington U., Washington, 1981. Head reference and online svcs. George Washington U. Med. Ctr., Washington, 1973-81; information specialist Pergamon Internat., McLean, Va., 1981-83; asst. head reference Nat. Libr. Medicine, Bethesda, Md., 1984-85, head collection access sect., 1984-85, tech. info. specialist, 1987—. Mem. editl. bd. Med. Libr. Assn., Chgo., 1983-85; editor Intercom, 1979—. Mem. AAAS, D.C. Libr. Assn. (pres. 1985-86, disting. svc. award 1997). Office: Nat Libr Medicine MeSH sect 8600 Rockville Pike Bethesda MD 20894-0001 E-mail: schulman@hlm.nih.gov.

SCHULMAN, MARK ALLEN, market research company executive; b. Phila., Nov. 15, 1945; s. Morris and Ida (Dunn) S. AB, Washington Coll., Chestertown, Md., 1967; MA, U. Wis., 1968; PhD, Rutgers U., 1980. Dir., div. experimental studies U. Md. Ea. Shore, Princess Anne, Md., 1972-75; sr. project dir. Eagleton Inst. Poll Rutgers U., New Brunswick, N.J., 1975-77; sr. v.p. Louis Harris and Assocs., Inc., N.Y.C., 1977-81; pres. Schulman, Ronca & Bucuvalas, Inc., 1981—. Mem. bd. visitors and govs. Washington Coll., 1999—; bd. dirs. New Sch. Univ. Jazz Program, 1997—. Mem. Am. Assn. Pub. Opinion Rsch. (pres. N.Y. chpt. 1994-95, sec./treas. 1997-98, conf. chair 1999-2000, pres.-elect 2001—), Coun. of Am. Survey Rsch. Orgns. (bd. 2000—). Office: Schulman Ronca & Bucuvalas Inc 145 E 32nd St New York NY 10016-6055

SCHULMAN, MELVIN LOUIS, food processing company executive; b. Balt., Nov. 5, 1921; s. Louis and Rose (Kasofsky) S.; m. Zelma Jean Sharff, Nov. 8, 1953; children: Stuart, Karen, Alan, Glen. BA, U. Cin., 1947. Plant employee Food Spltys. Co., Cin., 1947-53, plant mgr., 1953-60, v.p., 1960-71, pres., 1971-91, chmn., CEO, 1991—. Pres. Soc. Preservation Music Hall, Cin., 1996—; bd. dirs. Inst. Learning in Retirement, U. Cin., 1992—, Am. Classical Music Hall of Fame, 1999; trustee emeritus U. Cin. Found., 1990—; bd. overseers Hebrew Union Coll., Cin., 1984—; trustee Corbett Found., 1997—. Republican. Jewish. Avocations: boating, travel, motorcycling. Home: 7201 Fair Oaks Dr Cincinnati OH 45237-2921

SCHULMAN, ROBERT, journalist; b. N.Y.C., July 7, 1916; s. Samuel and Rebecca (Yuster) S.; m. Eleanor Langham, Feb. 17, 1943 (div. May 1974); 1 child, Rebecca Schulman McIntyre; m. Louise Tachau, Nov. 4, 1976. BS, NYU, 1936; MS in Journalism, Columbia U., 1937; Hon. Alumnus, U. Louisville, 1996. Reporter Post-Dispatch, St. Louis, 1937-38; program dir. Community Chest, 1938-40; features writer, columnist Star-Times, 1940-42,

46-51; staff corr. Time-Life Mags., Chgo., 1951-53; spl. features dir. King Broadcasting, Seattle, 1959-69; news bur. chief, Pacific N.W. Time-Life Mags., 1953-59; mag. writer, commentator WHAS-TV and Radio, Louisville, 1968-74; press critic, columnist Courier-Journal and Times, 1974-81; exec. dir. Ctr. for Humanities U. Louisville, 1984—. Exec. dir. Design for Washington, Seattle, 1967-68; bd. dirs. Soc. Profl. Journalists, Louisville, 1969—. Author: (biography) John Sherman Cooper: Global Kentuckian, 1976. Bd. dirs. Family and Children's Agy., Louisville, 1986-95;, nat. bd. dirs. Family Assn. of Am., Seattle, 1962-65. Capt. Air Transport Command, 1942-46. Mem. Sigma Delta Chi (Disting. Editl. award/TV 1972). Jewish. Avocations: swimming, exercising, reading, theatre, movie and concert-going. Home: 3917 Elfin Ave Louisville KY 40207-2021 Office: U Louisville Gardiner Hall Louisville KY 40292-0001

SCHULMAN, SIDNEY, neurologist, educator; b. Chgo., Mar. 1, 1923; s. Samuel E. and Ethel (Miller) S.; m. Mary Jean Diamond, June 17, 1945; children— Samuel E., Patricia, Daniel. BS, U. Chgo., 1944, MD, 1946. Asst. prof. neurology U. Chgo., 1952-57, asso. prof., 1957-65, prof., 1965-75, Ellen C. Manning prof., div. biol. scis., 1975-93, Ellen C. Manning prof. emeritus, 1993—. Served with M.C. AUS, 1947-49. Mem. Am. Neurol. Assn., U. Chgo. Med. Alumni Assn. (pres. 1968-69), Chgo. Neurol. Soc. (pres. 1964-65) Home: 5000 S East End Ave Chicago IL 60615-3140 Office: U Chgo Divsn Biol Scis CLI L633 (MC 5080) 5841 S Maryland Ave Chicago IL 60637

SCHULMEYER, G(EORGE) GORDON, information systems executive, consultant; b. Balt., July 15, 1940; s. Theodore George and Eva (Gunzelman) S.; m. Jane Frances Florin, Aug. 20, 1960; children: Bonnie Kay, Gordon James, Sean Gordon. BS in Math., Loyola Coll., Balt., 1962, MBA in Mgmt., 1972; JD, U. Balt., 1966. Cert. in data processing Inst. for Cert. of Computer Profls. Software analyst and programmer Westinghouse Electronic Systems, Balt., 1961-68; program mgr. various satellite programs Westinghouse Electronics Systems, 1968-74, mgr. Iran project Balt. and Iran, 1974-77; software quality assurance mgr. Westinghouse Electronic Systems, Balt., 1977-78; quality assurance mgr. Morroccan project Westinghouse Electronics Systems, Balt., Calif., Morocco, 1979-80, mgr. software quality engrng. Balt., 1982-85, mgr. software engrng. for C3I and Comml. Divs., 1985-92; dep. mgr. software engrng. dept. Electronic Systems, 1993—. Prin. Pyxis Systems Internat., Inc., 1987; adj. instr. Johns Hopkins U., Balt., 1993. Author: (books) Computer Concepts for Managers, 1985, Handbook of Software Quality Assurance, 1987, rev. 2nd edit. 1992, 3d edit., 1999, Zero Defect Software, 1990, Total Quality Management for Software, 1993, Verification and Validation of Modern Software-Intensive Systems, 2000; contbr. articles to profl. jours., presented papers at sci. confs. and symposiums. Recipient Shingo prize 1st pl., Utah State U., 1993. Mem. IEEE Computer Soc., Greater Md. Software Process Improvement Network (founder). Republican. Roman Catholic. Avocation: filmology. Home: 5215 Grenock Dr Lothian MD 20711-2801 Office: Pyxis Systems Internat Ste 121 1120C Benfield Blvd Millersville MD 21108 E-mail: ggordons@erols.com., pyxis@pyxisinc.com.

SCHULNER, KEITH ALAN, lawyer, business owner; b. Burbank, Calif., Aug. 4, 1966; s. Lawrence Mayor and Diane Bebe (Goldstein) S.; m. Debbie Dennison, July 28, 1991; children: Eliana, Marissa. BA, UCLA, 1989; JD, Loyola U., 1992; MBA, Pepperdine U., 2000; M.Dispute Resolution, Straus Inst.Dispute Resolution, 2000. Bar: Calif. 1992. Owner Law Offices of Keith A. Schulner & Assocs., Camarillo, Calif., 1997—, lawyer mgr., 1992—; pub. defender L.A. County Pub. Defender's Office, Van Nuys, 1992; prin. Medinfo, L.A., 2000—. Mentor Loyola U. Law Sch., 1997—; guest lectr. U. Calif., Santa Barbara; mem. dispute resolution bd. Ford Motor Co.; mediator, prin. for mediator, L.A., 2000—; pres. Gold Coast Bruins, 2000-01, Ventura County Bruins, 2001—; tchr. grad. students Pepperdine U., 2001—. Mem. task force com. Jewish Fedn. Coun., 1997—; chairperson Havurah com. Temple Adat Elohim, 1997-98, brotherhood pres.; mentor, entertainment chairperson Fulfillment Fund, 1995-2000. Mem. Calif. State Bar Assn. (mediator, arbitrator 1997—), Calif. County Bar Assn. (mediator, arbitrator 1997—), Jerome H. Berenson Inns of Ct., Camarillo C. of C., Sigma Phi Epsilon. Office: 4826 Parma Drive Oak Park CA 91377-6325 E-mail: jd_mba_mdr_mediator@uclalumni.net.

SCHULSINGER, MICHAEL ALAN, data processing executive; b. Springfield, Ohio, Dec. 2, 1952; s. Gerald Morton and Dolores Mae (McLendon) S. AS, SUNY, Albany, 1977, BS, 1985; BA, Wittenberg U., 1984. Technician Dimension Electronics, Dayton, Ohio, 1977-78; electronics technician Yellow Springs (Ohio) Instrument Co., 1978-79, 80-81; lab. technician Scripps Inst. Oceanography U. Calif., San Diego, La Jolla, 1979; electronics technician Nu-Tech Industries, Inc., Trotwood, Ohio, 1981-82; project dir. Clark County Hist. Soc., Springfield, 1983; editor Scott Pub. Co., Sidney, Ohio, 1985; facilities supr. Inst. Comm. and Media Arts Antioch Coll., Yellow Springs, 1986-87; designer Analytical Rsch., 1988-89, Huntington Instruments Inc., Yellow Springs, 1989-99; analyst Allied Signal (now Honeywell), Urbana, Ohio, 1999—. Editor Australasian Informer, 1977-78, Scott Stamp Monthly, 1985. Treas. Citizen's Arcade Alliance, Springfield, 1986-87; planning officer Clark County Civil Def., 1970-71; vol. disaster relief ARC, 1993—, disaster chmn. local chpt., 1998—; spl. projects coord. Clark County Emergency Mgmt. Agy., 1998—. Recipient Staff award Clark County Civil Def., 1972; named Vol. of Yr., Clark County chpt. ARC, 1996; grantee Ohio Humanities Coun., 1983. Mem. AAAS, Ind. Radio Assn., Inc. (pres. 1993, sec. 1994-97, pres. 1998, v.p. 1999), N.Y. Acad. Scis. Democrat. Jewish. Avocations: philately, shortwave and amateur radio. Home: 1002 Woodlawn Ave Springfield OH 45504-2140 Office: Allied Signal 240 W Twain Ave Urbana OH 43078-1059

SCHULT, DAIN LESLIE, broadcast executive, consultant; b. Atlanta, Mar. 29, 1954; s. Ronald Dains and Sara Juanita (Denman) S.; m. Constance Lynn Prichard, Nov. 18, 1978 (div. Sept. 1986); children: Dain Leonard, Robert Harlston; m. Sherry Lynn Ringle, Oct. 11, 1987. AS in Comml. Music, Rec., Ga. State U., 1977. Cameraman, prodr. Sta. WATV, College Park, Ga., 1968-72; booking agt. Circus Maximus, East Point, 1972-74; announcer, dir. training Sta. WRAS-FM, Atlanta, 1973-75; announcer, dir. rsch. Sta. WQXI-AM-FM, 1975-80; pres., founder Radioactivity Inc., 1977-97; gen. mgr. Sta. WFOM, Marietta, Ga., 1980-81; program mgr. Sta. WHVE-FM, Sarasota, Fla., 1981-82; pres., founder Radioactivity Promotions Inc., Atlanta, 1986-88; co-owner, COO Radioactivity Broadcast Group, 1988-89; v.p., COO Sunbelt Radio Group, Inc., 1989-91, also part owner, 1989-92; pres., COO So. Radio, Inc., 1992-94; pres., CEO Equicom, Inc. dba Tex. Eagle Radio Networks, Atlanta, 1994-95, Austin, Tex., 1996-98; pres., chmn., CEO Am. Comm. Enterprises, Inc., 1998-2000; chmn., CEO Am. Radio Empire, Inc., 1998—. Cons. Interax, Atlanta, 1986-90, The TYFG Co., Atlanta, 1986—; developer Mgmt. for Profit svc. Author: (trade publs.) Billboard, 1981, The Pulse of Broadcasting, 1987, Roll Away the Stone, 1989, Radio Manager, 1991, Grandpa's Road-The History of the N.C. and St.L Railway, 2001; columnist: Radio World, 1992—; editor: The Radio Guide, 1983; inventor in field. Charter mem. Bd. Disting. Alumni Sta. WRAS-FM, Ga. State U., Atlanta, 1991. Recipient Freedom award Freedom Found., 1964, Sustaining Mem. award Clearwater Jaycees, 1981, Disting. Alumni award Ga. State U. Mem. Nat. Assn. Broadcasters (assoc.), NARAS (co-degree), Tex. Assn. Broadcasters. Avocations: American history, model railroading, walking. Fax: 815 352-2889. E-mail: dstrr@aol.com.

SCHULTE, ALFONS FRIEDRICH, physicist, educator; b. Wulmeringhausen, Germany, Aug. 8, 1954; s. Josef B. and Veronika T. Schulte; m. Cinderella G. Gayoso, Apr. 17, 1990. Dipl. in Physics, Tech. U. Munich, 1980, Dr.rer.nat. in Physics, 1985. Rsch. assoc. Tech. U. Munich, 1985; rsch. assoc., rsch. asst. prof. U. Ill., Champaign, 1986-88; vis. scientist IBM Almaden Rsch. Ctr., San Jose, 1989-90; asst. prof. Physics Ctr. Rsch. on Electrooptics and Lasers U. Ctrl. Fla., Orlando, 1990—, assoc. prof. Physics Ctr. Rsch. on Electrooptics and Lasers. Vis. scientist Los Alamos Nat. Lab., 1998. Contbr. articles to profl. jours. Mem. Am. Phys. Soc., Biophys. Soc., Deutsche Physikalische Gesellschaft. Achievements include research in biomolecular physics, disordered systems. Office: Univ of Cen Fla Dept Physics Orlando FL 32812

SCHULTE, BRUCE JOHN, lawyer; b. Burlington, Iowa, June 27, 1953; s. James Andrew and Julia Germaine (Van Dale) S.; m. Mary E. Guest, July 1984 (div. Feb. 1995); children: James, John; m. Catherine Tobben, 2001. BA in Am. Studies, U. Notre Dame, 1975; JD, U. Iowa, 1978. Bar: Iowa 1978, U.S. Dist. Ct. (so. dist.) Iowa 1979, U.S. Ct. Appeals (8th cir.) 1982, Minn. 1988, U.S. Dist. Ct. Minn. 1988, Ill. 1989. Law clk. Justice K. David Harris Supreme Ct. Iowa, Des Moines, 1978-79; ptnr. Dailey, Ruther, Bauer, Schulte & Hahn, Burlington, Iowa, 1979-87; atty. Bennett, Ingvaldson & McInerny, Mpls., 1988; gen. counsel Blackwood Corp., St. Paul, 1988-89; publs. editor Nat. Inst. for Trial Advocacy-U. Notre Dame, Ind., 1989-91; asst. dean pub. affairs Chgo. (Ill.) Kent Coll. Law, 1991-94; dep. dir. assoc. rels. West Pub., Eagan, Minn., 1995-97; dir. mktg., v.p. acad. consulting Performance Comm. Group, Chgo., 1997-2001. Key person com. ATLA, 1984-88; mem. commn. on jud. dists. Supreme Ct. Iowa, 1987-88; publs. com. Nat. Law Firm Mktg. Assn., 1993-94. Author: Persuasive Expert Testimony, 1990, Laser Disc Technology in the Courtroom, 1990; editor: Cases and Materials on Evidence, 1991, Modern State and Federal Evidence, 1991, Problems and Cases for Legal Writing, 1991. Mem. state ctrl. com. Iowa Dem. party, 1984-88; devel. com. Frances Xavier Ward Sch., Chgo., 1993—; mem. cmty. task force Chgo. (Ill.) Downtown Circulator Project, 1994-96; v.p. pub. affairs U. Notre Dame Alumni Class of 1975. Notre Dame scholar U. Notre Dame, Ind., 1971-72; recipient Spectra award Internat. Assn. Bus. Communicators, 1993, Silver Trumpet, Publicity Club Chgo., 1994. Mem. ABA (mem. tech. com. lawyers conf. jud. adminstrn. divsn. 1995—, vice chair task force on image of judiciary 2000—), Ill. Bar Assn. (mem. standing com. legal edn. and admission to bar 1993-97), Chgo. Bar Assn. (mem. law office tech. com. 1995-97), Assn. Am. Law Schs., Chgo. Pub. Rels. Forum (treas. 1997), Notre Dame Club Chgo. (co-chair Hesburgh Forum com. 1993-98, trustee 1995-98, sec. 1997-98), Nat. Soc. Fundraising Profls. (cert. fundraising profl., Midwest conf. steering com. 1997-99), Execs. Club of Chgo. (co-chair standing com. on edn. and pub. svc.). Avocations: sailing, choir, gardening, skiing. Home: 816 Main St Evanston IL 60202-1706 E-mail: brucejschulte@aol.com.

SCHULTE, DAVID MICHAEL, investment banker; b. N.Y.C., Nov. 12, 1946; s. Irving and Ruth (Stein) S.; m. Patricia Gordon, Sept. 5, 1999; children: Michael B., Katherine F. BA, Williams Coll., 1968; postgrad., Exeter Coll., Oxford (Eng.) U., 1968-69; JD, Yale U., 1972. Bar: D.C. 1973. Law clk. to Mr. Justice Stewart, U.S. Supreme Ct., 1972-73; spl. asst. to pres. N.W. Industries, Inc., Chgo., 1973-75, v.p. corp. devel., 1975-79, exec. v.p., 1979-80; sr. v.p. Salomon Bros., Chgo., 1980-84; mng. ptnr. Chilmark Ptnrs., 1984—. Editor-in-chief: Yale Law Jour., 1971-72. John E. Moody scholar Exeter Coll., Oxford U., 1968-69. Mem. Washington Bar Assn., Chgo. Club, Racquet Club, Bryn Mawr Country Club, Vineyard Golf Club. Office: Chilmark Ptnrs 875 N Michigan Ave Ste 3460 Chicago IL 60611-1957

SCHULTE, FREDRICK STEVEN, accountant; b. Dayton, Ohio, Nov. 16, 1942; s. John W. and Eleanor L. Schulte; m. Sharon K. Arnold, June 30, 1962; children— Curtis W., Gretchen L. B.B.A. in Acctg., U. Tex.-Austin, 1971. C.P.A., Tex. Vice pres., controller Tracor, Inc., Austin, 1966— ; dir. M Bank, North Austin. Mem. Nat. Assn. Accts. (past nat. v.p., mem. exec. com.). Roman Catholic. Office: Tracor Inc 6500 Tracor Ln Austin TX 78725-2000

SCHULTE, GREGORY ALAN, art educator; b. Bad Constadt, Germany, Apr. 12, 1964; arrived in U.S., 1964; BFA, U. Wis., 1987, MFA in Drawing and Painting, 1991. Instr. Madison (Wis.) Area Tech. Coll., 1987; tchg. asst. U. Wis., 1988—91; asst. prof. Utah State U., Logan, 1991—97, assoc. prof. drawing and painting, 1997—. Exhibitions include over 60 solo and group shows nationally. Fellow NEA regional, Western States Arts Fedn., 1994, Utah Arts Coun., 2001; grantee, 1994, 1996. E-mail: schulte@cc.usu.edu.

SCHULTE, JEFFREY LEWIS, lawyer; b. N.Y.C., July 24, 1949; s. Irving and Ruth (Stein) S.; m. Elizabeth Ewan Kaiser, Aug. 13, 1977; children: Andrew Riggs, Ian Garretson, Elizabeth Alexandra. BA, Williams Coll., 1971; postgrad., Harvard U., 1971-72; JD, Yale U., 1976. Bar: Pa. 1978, Ga. 1993. Law clk. to hon. John J. Gibbons U.S. Ct. Appeals (3d cir.), Newark, 1976-77; assoc. Schnader, Harrison, Segal & Lewis, Phila., 1977-84, ptnr., 1985-92, founding ptnr. Atlanta, 1992-98, exec. com., 1994-98; ptnr. Morris, Manning & Martin, 1998—. Nat. steering com. lawyers com. to end "Pay-to-Play." Contbr. articles to profl. jours. Trustee Ga. Shakespeare Festival, 1997-99; bd. dirs. North Ardmore (Pa.) Civic Assn., pres., 1990; bd. dirs. Main Line YMCA, chmn., 1989-91. Mem.: ABA, Bus. and Tech. Alliance, Atlanta Venture Forum, Atlanta Bar Assn. (chmn. comm. and media rels. com.), Phila. Bar Assn., State Bar Ga., Pa. Bar Assn., Weekapaug Tennis Club, Yale Club of Ga. (bd. dirs. 1996—, pres. 2000—01, chmn. of bd. 2001—02), Weekapaug Yacht Club R.I., Williams Club N.Y.C., Williams Club Atlanta, Marion Cricket Club, Phi Beta Kappa. Office: Morris Manning & Martin Atlanta Financial Center 3343 Peachtree Rd NE Ste 1600 Atlanta GA 30326-1044 E-mail: jls@mmmlaw.com.

SCHULTE, PATRICK JOSEPH, not-for-profit developer, not-for-profit fundraiser; b. Grosse Pointe, Mich., Jan. 11, 1965; s. Eugene J. Schulte; m. Susan R. Rousseau, June 25, 1996; children: Frances, Sydney. BA in Comm., Mich. State U., 1998. Cert. Nat. Planned Giving Inst. 2001. Dir. of advancement Detroit Cath. Ctrl. H.S., Redford, Mich., 1998—. Co-founder Chgo. Cares, Inc, 1991.

SCHULTE, STEPHEN CHARLES, lawyer; b. Evanston, Ill., June 26, 1952; s. George John and Mary Ruth (Lamping) S.; m. Kathleen Ann O'Donnell, Sept. 4, 1982; children: Kate, Maureen, John. BA magna cum laude, St. Louis U., 1973, JD, 1976. Bar: Ill. 1976, U.S. Dist. Ct. (no. dist.) Ill. 1976, U.S. Ct. Appeals (7th cir.) 1991. Atty. Perz & McGuire, Chgo., 1976-83; ptnr. Winston & Strawn, 1983—. Founder, bd. dirs. Greater Orgn. for Less Fortunate (GOLF), Chgo., 1982—; fundraiser for Maryville Acad.; mem. Glenview Park Dist. Commn., 1989—, v.p., 1991-92, 98-99, pres., 1992-93, 99-2000. Mem. ABA, Ill. State Bar Assn., Chgo. Bar Assn., Ill. Trial Lawyers Assn., Ill. Assn. Def. Trial Counsel, Chgo. Vol. Legal Svcs., Nat. Legal Aid Defender Assn., Phi Beta Kappa. Avocations: basketball, baseball, golf, music, travel. Home: 941 Club Cir Glenview IL 60025-3101 Office: Winston & Strawn 35 W Wacker Dr Ste 4200 Chicago IL 60601-1695 E-mail: sschulte@winston.com.

SCHULTE, STEPHEN JOHN, lawyer, educator; b. N.Y.C., July 7, 1938; s. John and Marjorie (Fried) S.; m. Patricia Walker, June 6, 1962 (div.); children: Susan Jean, Jeffrey David, Elizabeth Ann; m. Margaret Van Doren Cook, Mar. 12, 1975. BA, Brown U., 1960; JD, Columbia U., 1963. Bar: N.Y. 1964. Assoc. Lowenstein, Pitcher, Hochkiss & Parr, N.Y.C., 1963-66, Fried, Frank, Harris, Shriver & Jacobson, N.Y.C., 1966-69; founding ptnr. Schulte Roth & Zabel LLP, 1969—. Adj. prof. law Benjamin N. Cardozo Law Sch., 1992—2000, vice chmn. bd. dirs., 1995—2000, bd. dirs., 1992—; adj. prof. law Columbia U., 2000—, Fordham U., 1992—97; lectr. securities law field; panelist various forums. Life trustee Choate Rosemary Hall Sch., Wallingford, Conn., 1982—, chmn. investment and fin. com., 1984-85, chmn. devel. com., 1985-86, chmn. nominating com., 1986-89, chmn. bd. trustees, 1990-95. Mem. ABA, N.Y. State Bar Assn. (com. on securities regulation), Assn. of Bar of City of N.Y. (chmn. com. on securities regulation 1998-2000), Norfolk Country Club. Office: Schulte Roth & Zabel LLP 919 3rd Ave New York NY 10022-4774

SCHULTE, TIMOTHY J. psychologist, counselor, educator, consultant; b. Phillipsburg, N.J., Aug. 21, 1959; s. Milton Robert Schulte and Carolyn Annette Swartz; m. Carolene Faye Schmidt, July 16, 1983; children: Michael Andrew, Philip Jon. BA, U. Ill., Chgo., 1984, MA, EdS, James Madison U., 1995, PsyD, 1999. Lic. counselor, marriage and family therapist; lic. clin. psychologist, profl. counselor. Social work Dept. Social Svcs., Harrisonburg, Va., 1987-90, social work supr., 1990-94; child therapist Cmty. Svcs., 1994-96, Kuely Ruan Assocs., Staunton, Va., 1997-99; owner Broadway (Va.) Family Counseling, 1997—; asst. prof. James Madison U., Harrisonburg, 1999—. Cons. Harrisonburg Pediatrics, 2000; mem. adv. bd. Impact Child/Parent, Harrisonburg, 1992-93, Rockingham Social Svcs., Harrisonburg, 1990-94; adminstrv. bd. Harrisonburg Social Svcs., 1990-94. Bd. dirs. First Step, Harrisonburg, 1993-94. Mem. ACA, APA, Va. Counseling Assn., Va. Psychol. Assn., Marriage and Family Therapists, Chi Sigma Iota. Mennonite. Avocation: woodworking.

SCHULTENOVER, DAVID GEORGE, theology educator; b. Sauk Rapids, Minn., Aug. 19, 1938; s. Isadore Joseph and Frances Ludwina (Ohmann) S. BS in Chemistry, Spring Hill Coll., 1963; MS in Organic Chemistry, Loyola U., Chgo., 1966; PhD in Hist. Theology, St. Louis U., 1975. Joined Soc. of Jesus, Roman Cath. Ch., 1956. Mng. editor Theology Digest, St. Louis U., 1968-70; asst. prof. theology Marquette U., Milw., 1974-78; asst. dir. novices Jesuit Novitiate, St. Paul, 1978-83; assoc. prof. theology Creighton U., Omaha, 1984-94, prof. theology, 1994—. Adj. asst. prof. Creighton U., 1979-84; Wade rsch. scholar Marquette U., 2001—. Author: George Tyrrell: In Search of Catholicism, 1981 (Alpha Sigma Nu Book award 1981), A View from Rome: On the Eve of the Modernist Crisis, 1993; contbr. articles to profl. jours.; book rev. editor, Theol. Studies, Marquette U., 2000—. Deutscher Akademischer Austauschdienst (DAAD)-Fulbright fellow, Tübingen, Germany, 1973-74, NEH fellow, Rome, other Western European locations, 1984-85; Wade scholar Marquette U., 2001-2002. Mem. Am. Acad. Religion, Am. Soc. Ch. History, Cath. Theol. Soc. Am., Alpha Sigma Nu. Office: Marquette U Theology Dept Coughlin Hall 100 607 N 13th St Milwaukee WI 53233 E-mail: david.schultenover@marquette.edu.

SCHULTE SHIELDS, MARY ANN, finance executive; b. Phoenix, Feb. 6, 1953; d. Walter Barry and Norma Gladys (Caffey) S. BSBA, U. So. Calif., 1975, MBA, 1989. Mgr. acctg. Coldwell Banker, L.A., 1975-78; contr. Adams, Ray and Rosenberg, Inc. (now The William Morris Agy.), Century City, Calif., 1978-81; co-owner Marwal, Inc., L.A., 1976-82; contr., CFO DNA Group, Inc., Pasadena, Calif., 1982-86; CFO Sukut Constrn., Inc., Santa Ana, 1986-99, bd. dirs., 1998-2000; asset mgr. Chandler Real Properties, 1999-2000. Cons. Mikeselle DeKorff, L.A., 1981-82, Hollywood (Calif.) H.S., 1986-87; cons., bd. dirs. Inner Ear Prodns., L.A., 1983-85; guest speaker Am. Soc. Women Accts., Inland Empire Women in Bus. Conf., 1994, Assoc. Gen. Contractors, L.A., Riverside, San Bernardino, San Diego and Orange Counties. Assoc. producer (documentary film) Echoes of The Ozarks, 1989; speaker in field. Staff leader drop-out prevention program Hollywood H.S., 1986; bd. dirs., chair fin. com. STOP GAP; mem. joint budget task force City of Santa Ana, 1991-92; mem. adv. bd. Orange County Acad. Decathlon; chair vendor subcom. to master creditors com. Orange County Bankruptcy; chair County of Orange Govt. Practices Oversight Com.; mem. County of Orange Blue Ribbon Com., 2000. Named Bus. Woman of Yr. Orange County, 1996. Mem. U. So. Calif. Commerce Assocs., Alpha Chi Omega. Republican. Roman Catholic. Avocations: musical theater, travel, piano, entertaining, wheelchair tennis.

SCHULTHEIS, EDWIN MILFORD, dean, business educator; b. N.Y.C., Apr. 15, 1928; s. Milford Theodore and Lillian May (Hill) S.; m. Joan Edna Bruckner, June 23, 1956. BS, Hofstra Coll., 1950; MBA, NYU, 1958, EdD, 1972. Officer mgr., sales rep. Topton Rug Mfg. Co., N.Y.C., 1950-54; area mgr., trainer Mobil Oil Co., 1954-62; coord. distributive edn. North Babylon (N.Y.) Pub. Schs., 1962-88, chmn. bus. mktg. and indsl. edn. depts., 1988-91; prof. bus. adminstrn. SUNY, Farmingdale, 1970-91; asst. prof. edn. NYU, 1973—; dir. edn. Syracuse (N.Y.) U., 1973-78; chmn. dept. bus. adminstrn. Five Towns Coll., Seaford, N.Y., 1991-92, divsn. chmn. bus. and tech. Dix Hills, 1992-98, dean instrn., 1993-98, dep. dean of faculty, 1993-98, assoc. dean, 1996-97, prof. emeritus, 1998—. Test writer, cons. N.Y. State Dept. Edn., Albany, 1965—; textbook reviewer McGraw-Hill Book Co., N.Y.C., 1967-69; cons. Cornell U., 1975; dist. adviser Distributive Edn. Clubs N.Y., 1970, bd. govs., trustee, 1975-78; mem. curriculum adv. coun. Suffolk County (N.Y.) Distributive Edn. Assn., 1967—. Author: Modern Petroleum Marketing, 1971, Content and Structure of Belief-Disbelief Systems, 1972. Elder Presbyn. Ch., U.S.A. Named N.Y. State Tchr. of Yr., 1976, Outstanding Tchr. in N.Y. State, 1978; recipient Outstanding Svc. award Distributive Edn. Clubs N.Y., Suffolk County Distributive Edn. Assn., Tchr. Excellence award N.Y. State, 1980, Citation for Excellence in Edn. Gov. Mario Cuomo N.Y., 1991, Citation Excellence in Teaching Babylon Twp., 1991. Mem. Acad. Mgmt., Am. Petroleum Inst., Am. Security Coun., Suffolk County Assn. Distributive Edn. Tchrs. (mem. exec. bd. 1962-74), N.Y. State (pres. 1975-78), L.I. Distributive Edn. Assns. (hon. life, exec. bd. 1972-75), N.Y. State Occupl. Edn. Assn. (v.p. 1975-78), L.I. Bus. Edn. Chmns. Assn. (hon. life, exec. bd. 1972-75), N.Y. State Occupl. Edn. Assn. (v.p. 1975-78), L.I. Bus. Edn. Chmns. Assn. (hon. life), Distributive Edn. Clubs Am. (regional leader 1972-75, hon. life 1991), Bellport (N.Y.) Golf Club, Phi Delta Kappa, Kappa Delta Pi, Sigma Alpha Lambda, Phi Sigma Eta. Presbyterian (ordained ruling elder). Home: 14 Thorn Hedge Rd Bellport NY 11713-2616

SCHULTHEISS, EMILY EKONEN, management consultant, writer; b. Oklahoma City, Feb. 6, 1949; d. Tauno Otto and Dorothy Guhlstorf Ekonen; m. Arthur Howard Schultheiss (dec. Aug. 9, 2000). BBA, U. Okla., 1971; MS, LaRoche Coll., 1985. Human resources generalist Westinghouse Electric Corp., Norman, Okla., 1971—77, human resources supr. Boston, 1977—80, human resources mgr. Norman, 1980—81, mgr. orgn. devel. Pitts., 1981—83, mgr. corp. tng., 1983—95; v.p. Impact Strategy Assocs., 1996—97; sole proprietor Thriving Sys., 1997—. Mem. resource team Evang. Luth. Ch. Am. S.W. Pa. Synod, Pitts., 1996—. Author: (Book) Optimizing the Organization, 1988, Day by Day: A Journey Toward Thriving, 1998. V.p. Northland Pub. Libr. Found. Bd., Pitts., 1998—2002. Lutheran. Avocations: music, quilting, reading. Office: Thriving Systems PO Box 97121 Pittsburgh PA 15229 Personal E-mail: thriver@earthlink.net. Business E-Mail: thriver@earthlink.net.

SCHULTIS, GAIL ANN, library director; b. Freeport, Ill., May 12, 1951; d. Richard C. and Ida G. Schultis. BA, Cornell Coll., 1973; MLS, U. Mo., 1976; MA, U. Tex., San Antonio, 1989. Reference libr. U. Tex., San Antonio, 1976-79, El Paso, 1979-84, 89, head access svcs., 1984-88; reference libr. Park Coll., Parkville, Mo., 1989-96, dir. libr. sys., 1996—. Co-author: Best Self-Help & Self-Awareness Books, 1995. Mem. ALA, Am. Hist. Assn., Orgn. Am. Historians. Home: 10307 NW 57th Ter Parkville MO 64152-3396 Office: Park Univ Libr 8700 NW River Park Dr Parkville MO 64152-4358 E-mail: aschultis@mail.park.edu.

SCHULTZ, ALBERT BARRY, engineering educator; b. Phila., Oct. 10, 1933; s. George D. and Belle (Seidman) S.; m. Susan Resnikov, Aug. 25, 1955; children: Carl, Adam, Robin BS, U. Rochester, 1955; M.Engring., Yale U., 1959, PhD, 1962. Asst. prof. U. Del., Newark, 1962-65; asst. prof. U. Ill., Chgo., 1965-66, assoc. prof., 1966-71, prof., 1971-83; Vennema prof. U. Mich., Ann Arbor, 1983-99. Contbr. numerous articles to profl. jours. Served to lt. USN, 1955-58 Rsch. Career award NIH, 1975-80; Javits Neurosci. Investigator award NIH, 1985-92 Mem. NAE, Internat. Soc. for Study Lumbar Spine (pres. 1981-82), ASME (chmn. bioengring. div. 1981-82, H.R. Lissner award 1990), Am. Soc. Biomechanics (pres. 1982-83, Borelli award 1996), U.S. Nat. Com. on Biomechanics (chmn. 1982-85), Phi Beta Kappa

SCHULTZ, ARTHUR JOSEPH, JR. retired trade association executive; b. Detroit, June 20, 1918; s. Arthur Joseph and Olive U. (Beauchesne) S.; m. Barbara Farnan, Aug. 20, 1942; children: Arthur, Robert, William, Barbara, John, Karen. Student, U. Detroit, 1937-39, Naval Line Sch., 1947-48, Naval War Coll., 1956-57, Brookings Inst., 1962. Commd. ensign USN, 1940, advanced through grades to capt., 1950, comdg. officer Com. Strike/S. NATO Italy, 1959-61, comdg. officer Naval Air Sta. Grosse Ile, Mich., 1961-63, ret., 1963; pres. Chrysler Corps. subs., Highland Park, Mich., 1971-75; dep. adminstr. VA, Washington, 1975-77; pres. Steel Shipping Container Inst., Union, N.J., 1977-89; ret., 1989. V.p. Detroit Aviation Commn., 1968-77; bd. dirs. United Way Union County, Elizabeth, N.J., 1981-85, sec.-treas., 1983-85; chmn. Hazardous Materials Adv. Com., Washington, 1984-85. Decorated Navy Cross; recipient Meritorious Svc. award VA, 1977. Mem. Am. Soc. Assn. Execs., Soc. Automotive Engrs., Mil. Order World Wars, St. Andrew Soc. Sarasota (pres.), Boca Royale Golf and Country Club (Fla.). Republican. Roman Catholic. Home: 55 Cayman Isles Blvd Englewood FL 34223-1832

SCHULTZ, ARTHUR LEROY, clergyman, educator; b. Johnstown, Pa., June 14, 1928; s. Elmer Albert Robert and Alice Lizetta (Flegal) S.; m. Mildred Louise Stouffer, Nov. 29, 1948; children: Thomas Arthur, Rebecca Louise. BA, Otterbein Coll., 1949; MDiv, United Theol. Sem., 1952; MEd, U. Pitts., 1955, PhD, 1963. Sr. min. Albright United Meth. Ch., Pitts., 1952-56; dir. pub. rels. Otterbein Coll., Westerville, Ohio, 1956-65, adj. prof. religion and philosophy, 1990-98; pres. Albright Coll., Reading, Pa., 1965-77, Ashland (Ohio) Coll., 1977-80; exec. dir. Cen. Ohio Radio Reading Svc., Columbus, 1980-84; parish min. Ch. Master United Meth., Westerville, 1984-89; min. of visitation Ch. Messiah United Meth., 1991—2002. Pres. Pa. Assn. Colls. & Univs., Harrisburg, 1974-75. Trustee Reading Hosp., 1967-77, Wyoming Sem., Kingston, Pa., 1971-80; v.p. Found. for Ind. Colls. Pa., Harrisburg, 1972-73; pres. Pa. Coun. on Alcohol Problems, Harrisburg, 1968-76; pres. Westerville (Ohio) Hist. Soc., 1986-89, Westerville Area Ministerial Assn.,

1992-93. Named Outstanding Young Man of the Year Jr. C. of C., Westerville, Ohio, 1960. Mem. Brookstone Cmty. Assn. (sec. bd. trustees 1994-99, v.p. 1999-2000), Rotary (charter pres. 1959, dist. gov. 1965-66, dist. sec.-treas. 1982-93), Masons, Shriners, Torch Club. Republican. Methodist. Avocations: collecting post cards, golf, tennis, travel. Home: 151 Sandstone Loop Westerville OH 43081-4599

SCHULTZ, ARTHUR WARREN, communications company executive; b. N.Y.C., Jan. 13, 1922; s. Milton Warren and genevieve (Dann) S.; m. Elizabeth Carroll Mahan, 1949 (div. 1987); children: Arthur Warren, John Carroll (dec.), Julia Hollingsworth; m. Susan Keefe, 1988. Grad., U. Chgo.; DLitt (hon.), Rosary Coll. With Foote, Cone & Belding Comms., Chgo., 1948-82, v.p., 1957-63, sr. v.p., dir., 1963-69, exec. v.p., 1969, chmn. bd., CEO, 1970-81, chmn. exec. com., CEO, 1981-82; dir. Chgo. Sun-Times Co.; vice chmn. Chgo. Sun-Times Newspaper Co., 1989-94. Lectr. in field. Author: In Praise of America's Collectors; editor Caring for Your Collections. Pres. Cook County Sch. Nursing, 1963-64, Welfare Coun. Met. Chgo., 1965-67; mem. bus. adv. coun. Urban League Chgo., 1971-82; chmn. Nat. Com. to Save Am.'s Cultural Collections, 1990-94; mem. Pres.'s Com. Arts and Humanities, 1984-93; bd. dirs. Chgo. Crime Commn., 1965-71, Cmty. Fund Chgo., 1966-67, Better Bus. Bur., 1970-78, Lyric Opera Chgo., 1967-77, Chgo. Coun. Fgn. Rels., 1977-86, Chgo. Pub. TV, 1978-82, Chgo. Central Area Com., 1978-82; mem. millennium Com. to Save Am.'s Treasures, 1998; trustee YWCA, 1962-74, Calif. Coll. Arts & Crafts, 1985-87; trustee Art Inst. Chgo., 1975—, chmn. bd., 1981-84; trustee U. Chgo., 1977—, Santa Barbara Mus. Art, 1988—, pres., 1989-92. 1st lt. USAF, 1943-45. Recipient Alumni Svc. award U. Chgo., 1986. Mem. Am. Assn. Advt. Agys. (dir. 1968-71, 74-76, chmn. Chgo. coun. 1964-65, chmn. Ctrl. region 1970-71), Comml. Club, Valley Club (Montecito, Calif.), Delta Kappa Epsilon. Episcopalian. Home and Office: 2072 China Flat Rd Santa Barbara CA 93108-2211

SCHULTZ, BARBARA MARIE, financial advisor; b. Chgo., Sept. 9, 1943; d. Edwin and Bernice (Barstis) Legner; m. Ronald J. Schultz Sr., May 1, 1965; 1 child, Ronald J. Student, Prairie State Coll., Chicago Heights, Ill. Fin. planner Metlife Fin. Svcs., N.Y.C., 1981-2001; fin. advisor Morgan Stanley Dean Witter, 2001—02; agt., investment advisor rep. Country Ins. and Fin. Svcs., Palos Heights, Ill., 2002—. Qualifier Met. Life Leaders Conf., 1990. Fellow Nat. Assn. Life Underwriters (edn. chmn. 1988-91, nat. quality award Robert L. Rose award 1990), Life Underwriters Tng. Coun. (chmn. 1986-88, citation 1987), South Cook County Assn. Life Underwriters (edn. chmn. 1988-91). Roman Catholic. Avocations: boating, aerobics, golfing. Office: Country Ins and Fin Svcs 15040 S Ravinia Ste 49 Orland Park IL 60462

SCHULTZ, CARL HERBERT, real estate management and development company executive; b. Chgo., Jan. 9, 1925; s. Herbert V. and Olga (Swanson) S.; m. Helen Ann Stevenson, June 6, 1948; children: Mark Carl, Julia Ann. BS in Gen. Engring., Iowa State U., 1948. With Schultz Bros. Co., 1948—, mdse. mgr. and store planner, 1962-70, v.p. Lake Zurich, Ill., 1968-72, pres., 1972-2000; chmn., 2000—; pres. Ill. Schultz Bros. Co., Ind. Schultz Bros. Co., Iowa Schultz Bros. Co., Wis. Schultz Bros. Co.; chmn. Schultz Bros. Co., 2000—. Mem. Lake Bluff (Ill.) Zoning Bd. Appeals, 1976-85, chmn., 1978-85. Served with U.S. Army, 1944-46. Mem. Lake Zurich Indsl. Coun. (sec. 1976), Assn. Gen. Mdse. Chains (dir. 1975-86, exec. com. 1983-86, chmn. nat. conv. 1982), Ill. Retail Mchts. Assn. (dir. 1984-89), Wis. Retail Fedn. (dir. 1981-89) Clubs: Bath and Tennis (Lake Bluff). Presbyterian. Home: 701 E Center Ave Lake Bluff IL 60044-2607 Office: 785 Oakwood Rd Ste 102S Lake Zurich IL 60047-1549

SCHULTZ, CAROLE LAMB, community volunteer; b. Corning, N.Y., May 14, 1946; d. Arthur Martin and Jane Ursula (Oehler) Lamb; m. John Charles Schultz, July 13, 1968; children: David Michael, Geoffrey Brian. BS in Math. magna cum laude, St. Lawrence U., Canton, N.Y., 1968. Systems engr. IBM, Williamsport, Pa., 1968-71. Invited attendee Gov.'s Cong. of Bus./Edn. Partnerships, Harrisburg, Pa., 1991. Helped establish Children's Hands-on Mus., Children's Discovery Workshop, 1979-88. Treas. Jr. League Williamsport, Inc., 1980-82, cmty. v.p., 1985-86, pres.-elect, 1986-87, pres., 1987-88; area II coun. mem. Assn. Jr. Leagues Internat., Inc., 1988-90, chair nominating com., 1989-90; NE regional coun. United Way Am., 1993—; pers. chair Faxon-Kenmar United Meth. Ch., Williamsport, 1991-92; trustee St. Lawrence U., 1988—, chair honors com., 1994—; ednl. tech. adv. com. Williamsport Area Sch. Dist., 1994—; 2d v.p., sec., divsn. chair, planning mem. Lycoming United Way, Williamsport, 1991—, vice-chair campaign 1992, chair campaign 1993; candidate Williamsport Area Sch. Bd., 1989; panelist Leadership Lycoming, 1987, mentor, 1990—; chair steering com. Lycoming County Sch.-to-Work Partnership, 1995—; cmty. adv. bd. Williamsport-Lycoming Found., 1995—; bd. govs. Cmty. Arts Ctr. Recipient Lycoming County Brotherhood award, 1996, Lycoming United Way award 1997. Mem. AAUW (program v.p. 1973-75, pres. 1975-77, treas. Pa. conv. 1973, 85, Woman of Yr. 1981), Williamsport-Lycoming C. of C. (chair edn. subcom. on partnerships 1991-92), Lycoming Bus.-Edn. Coalition (exec. com., steering com., co-chair task force on skills/curriculum), Phi Beta Kappa. Methodist. Avocations: swimming, travel, music, art, French. Home: 300 Upland Rd Williamsport PA 17701-1852

SCHULTZ, CAROLYN JOYCE, nursing educator; b. Johnstown, Pa., Aug. 26, 1949; d. Robert Charles and Marion Elizabeth (Beatty) Miller; children: Melissa Lynn, Allison Marie. ADN, Mt. Aloysius Coll., 1972; BSN, Indiana U. Pa., 1979; MSN, W.Va. U., 1984, postgrad., 1997—. RN, Pa. Staff nurse Conemaugh Valley Meml. Hosp., Johnstown, 1975-94, faculty Sch. of Nursing, 1984-92; clin. rsch. nurse Laurel Highlands Cancer Program, 1992-94; with Pa. State Nursing Faculty, 1998, Mt. Aloysius Coll. Nursing Faculty, 1998-00; staff nurse UPMC Lee Regional, 2000—. Mem. faculty St. Francis Coll., Loretta, Pa., 1983-84; chair svc. and rehab. com., bd. dirs. Johnstown unit Am. Cancer Soc., 1985-94, Cambria dist. dir., Johnstown, 1992-94. Recipient Vol. of Yr. award Am. Cancer Soc., 1990. Home: 330 Phillips St Johnstown PA 15904-1226 E-mail: coco120208@aol.com.

SCHULTZ, CLARENCE JOHN, minister; b. Morris Twp., Wis., Aug. 4, 1937; s. Clarence John Sr. and Ella Mae (Feavel) S.; m. Doroland Kay King, Aug. 24, 1957 (dec. Jan. 1974); children: Sharon Kay Braun, Susan May Schultz Rogers; m. Martha Ann Aylor, Apr. 5, 1975. BS, Bryan Coll., 1960. Ordained to ministry Conservative Congl. Ch., 1961. Min. 1st Congl. Ch., Herreid, S.D., 1961-66, Immanuel Evang. Congl. Ch., Sheboygan, Wis., 1966-77, Hope Congl. Ch., Superior, 1977-83, Zion Evang. Ch., Scottsbluff, Nebr., 1983-89, 1st Congl. Ch., Buffalo Center, Iowa, 1989-92, Kenosha, Wis., 1992-98, St. Lucas Cmty. Ch., Lake Elmo, Minn., 1998—. Mem. Conservative Congl. Christian Conf. (rec. sec. 1973-82, v.p. 1994-96, pres. 1996-99, Rocky Mountain area rep. 1987-89, endorser of chaplains 1988-2000, mem. credentials com. 1988—), Rotary (ch. chaplain com. 1993-95). Avocations: amateur radio, golf. Home and Office: 1195 Manning Ave N Lake Elmo MN 55042-9607 E-mail: stlucas@attbi.com., stlucas2000@netzero.net.

SCHULTZ, DAVID A. political science educator, editor, writer, lawyer; b. Binghamton, N.Y., June 28, 1958; s. Fred L. and Margaret (Schuh) S.; m. Helene Levy, Sept. 10, 1982. BA, SUNY, Binghamton, 1980, MA, 1986, Rutgers U., 1982; PhD, U. Minn., 1989, JD, 1998. Bar: Minn. 1998. Dir. code enforcement City of Binghamton, 1982-84; planner Opportunities for Broome, Binghamton, 1984-86; prof. Gustavus Adolphus Coll., St. Peter, Minn., 1989-91, Trinity U., San Antonio, 1991-94, U. Minn., Mpls., 1995; prof. polit. sci. U. Wis., River Falls, 1996-99; prof. Hamline U. Grad. Sch. Pub. Adminstrn., 1999—. Adj. prof. Sch. of Law U. Minn., 1999—; editor Peter Lang Pub., N.Y.C., 1994—; lobbyist Common Cause Minn., St. Paul, 1994-99, pres., 1994-99. Author, editor: Law and Politics: Unanswered Questions, 1994, : Leveraging the Law, 1998, : The Politics of Civil Service Reform, 1998; author: Inventors of Ideas, 1997, Jurisprudential Vision of Justice Antonin Scalia, 1996, It's Show Time! Media, Politics and Popular Culture, 2000, Encyclopedia of American Law, 2002, Money, Politics and Campaign Finance Reform in the States, 2002, Social Capital: Critical Perspectives on Community and Bowling Alone, 2002. V.p. Minn. Civil Liberties Union, Mpls., 1995, South Tex. ACLU, San Antonio, 1993-94. Mem. AAUP (pres. chpt. 1993-94). Avocations: tennis, running, cooking, gardening. Home: 1120 Saint Clair Ave Saint Paul MN 55105-2846 Office: Hamline U Grad Sch Pub Adminstrn MS-A1710 Saint Paul MN 55104 E-mail: DSchultz@hamline.edu.

SCHULTZ, DAVID ANDREW, political science educator; b. Binghamton, N.Y., Jan. 28, 1958; s. Fred L. and Margaret (Schuh) S.; m. Helene Levy, Sept. 10, 1982. BA, Harpur Coll., Binghamton, 1980; MA, Rutgers U., 1982, SUNY, Binghamton, 1986; PhD, U. Minn., 1989. Dir. code enforcement City of Binghamton, 1982-84; planner Opportunities for Broome, Binghamton, 1985-86; asst. prof. Polit. Sci. Gustavus Adolphus Coll., St. Peter, Minn., 1989-91, Trinity U., San Antonio, 1991-94; adj. prof. polit. sci. U. Minn., St. Paul, 1994-95; asst. prof. dept. polit. sci. U. Wis., River Falls. Bd. dirs. Hampden Park Foods. Author: Property, Power and American Democracy, 1992, An Introduction to American Government through Microcase, 1992, A Short History of the U.S. Civil Service, 1991; editor: Law and Politics: Unanswered Questions, 1994, The Juris Prudential Vision of Justice Antonin Scalia, 1996. Mem. ACLU (bd. dirs. San Antonio chpt. 1992-93, case com. Minn. chpt. 1988-91, bd. dirs., treas. Minn. chpt.), common Cause (bd. dirs., state pres.).

SCHULTZ, DENNIS BERNARD, lawyer; b. Detroit, Oct. 15, 1946; s. Bernard George and Madeline Laverne (Riffenberg) Schultz; m. Andi Lynn Leslie, Apr. 18, 1967; 1 child Karanne Anne. BS, Wayne State U., 1970; JD, Mich. State U., 1977. Bar: Mich. 1977, U.S. dist. Ct. (ea. and we. dists.) Mich., U.S. Ct. Appeals (6th cir.), U.S. Dist. Ct. (we. dist.) Pa. V.p. Barkay Bldg. Co., Ferndale, Mich., to 1976; law clk. Hon. George N. Bashara, Mich. Ct. Appeals, Detroit, 1977; shareholder Butzel Long, 1978—. Editor: Detroit Coll. Law Rev., 1977. Scholar Detroit Coll. Law Alumni Assn., 1976, Mich. Consol. Gas Co., 1977. Mem.: Mich. Bar Assn., Detroit Bar Assn. Republican. Roman Catholic. Avocations: boating, bicycling, golf.

SCHULTZ, DOUGLAS GEORGE, art museum director; b. Oakland, Calif., Oct. 3, 1947; s. Leon H. and Teresa (deMonte) S. AB, U. Calif., Berkeley, 1969, MA in History of Art, 1972; grad., Inst. Arts Adminstrn., Harvard U., 1971. Summer intern Nat. Gallery of Art, Washington, 1970; curatorial intern Albright-Knox Art Gallery, Buffalo, 1972, asst. curator, 1973-75, asso. curator, 1975-76, curator, 1977-79, chief curator, 1980-83, dir., 1983—. Adj. prof. art history SUNY, Buffalo, 1975-79; mem. adv. bd. Arts Council of Buffalo and Erie County 1975— Office: Albright-Knox Art Gallery 1285 Elmwood Ave Buffalo NY 14222-1096

SCHULTZ, EILEEN HEDY, graphic designer; b. Yonkers, N.Y. d. Harry Arthur and Hedy Evelyn (Morchel) S. BFA, Sch. Visual Arts, 1955. Staff artist C.A. Parshall Studios, N.Y.C., 1955-57; editorial art dir. Paradise of the Pacific, Honolulu, 1957-58; graphic designer Adler Advt. Agy., N.Y.C., 1958-59; art dir. Good Housekeeping Mag., 1959-82, creative dir. advt. and sales promotion, 1982-86; creative dir. Hearst Promo, 1986-87; pres. Design Internat., N.Y.C., 1987—. Creative dir. The Depository Trust Co., 1987-99. Art dir., editor, designer, 50th Art Directors Club Annual, 1973; columnist: Art Direction, 1969—. Dir. Sch. Visual Arts, N.Y.C., 1978— ; trustee Sch. Art League, 1978—; advisor Fashion Inst. Tech., 1979—; adv. commn. N.Y.C. Cmty. Colls., 1979—. Named Yonkers Ambassador of Good Will to Netherlands, 1955; recipient Outstanding Achievement Sch. Visual Arts Alumni Soc., 1976, Sch. Art League Youth award, 1976. Mem. Art Dirs. Club (pres. 1975-77), Soc. Illustrators (pres. 1991-93), Joint Ethics Com. (chmn. 1978-80), Am. Inst. Graphic Arts, Soc. Publ. Designers, Type Dirs. Club.

SCHULTZ, ELAINE CAROL, social worker, consultant; b. Manitowoc, Wis. d. Webster H. and Fern (Lienau) Krueger; m. Robert Schultz, Aug. 18, 1962; children: John, Daniel. BS, U. Wis., 1961, MS in Social Work, 1964. Cert. ICSW. Social worker Wis. Div. of Corrections, Madison, 1964-65; adoptions worker, intake supr. Wis. Div. for Children and Youth, 1965-67; exec. dir. Middleton (Wis.) Youth Coun. Crisis Intervention, 1975-88; psychotherapist Luth. Social Svcs., Madison, 1988—; ret. Preceptor U. Wis., Madison, 1986, 87. Mem. NASW. Home: 2211 Mayflower Dr Middleton WI 53562-2718

SCHULTZ, ESTALENE, music educator; b. Dec. 2, 1924; MusB, North Tex. State U., 1946; postgrad., Midwestern State U., So. Meth. U. Tchr. music Henrietta (Tex.) Ind. Schs., Tex. Ind. Schs., Era; pvt. music tchr. Henrietta. Celloist Wichita Falls Symphony Orch. Organist, choir dir. United Meth. Ch.; organist Trinity Episcopal; coun. rep. Head Start, 1997-98; mem. Tex. Silver Haired Legis., 1997—; bd. dirs. Sr. Citizens Clay County, 1998—; cert. lay reader Meth. Ch. Mem. Clay County Ret. Tchrs. Assn. (pres. 1996-98), Tex. Music Tchrs. Assn., United Meth. Women's Assn. (pres. 1998—).

SCHULTZ, EVELYN ECALE, artist; b. Chgo., Nov. 28, 1931; d. George Ecale and Marie Elise Bauermeister; m. Robert Frank Schultz, Dec. 19, 1925; children: Kenneth M., Robin C. Brower, Karen M. Rantis, Jennifer B. Kaiser, Erik K., Steven E., Jason Robert. Attended, U. Ill., 1949-54, Coll. DuPage, Glen Ellyn, Ill., 1995—2002, numerous art workshops. Owner, operator ECALE Studio, Villa Pk., Ill., 1997—2002; represented by Ill. Artisans Shop, Chgo., Wallscapes Gallery, Elmhurst Art. Mus. Gallery, DuPage Art Gallery and Sch., Coll. of DuPage, Glen Ellyn, Ill. Del. W. Suburban Fine Arts Alliance, Oakbrook Terrace, Ill., 1995-97; judge U. Ill., Coop. Ext. Svc., DuPage County, Triton Coll., River Grove, Ill., Naperville Art League, Ill., Henry Hyde Congressional Art Exhbn., Elmurst Art Mus., local guilds and leagues, others. One-woman shows include Loyola Med. Ctr., Maywood, Ill., Navy Pier, Chgo., Hinsdale (Ill.) Libr., DuPage Gallery, Wheaton, Ill., Wallscapes Gallery, Elmhurst, Riverside Art Exhbn., Elmhurst Art Mus., Coll. DuPage, Ill., Firstar Bank, Elmhurst, West Suburban Bank, Villa Park, exhibited in group shows at Chgo. Cultural Ctr., 1999, Elmhurst Art Mus., 1999, Ill. State Profl. Art Exhbn., Springfield, ICARUS, Nags Head, N.C., St. Charles Art and Music Festival, Ill., numerous juried art shows and nat. and internat. exhbns., Represented in permanent collections Neville Mus., Green Bay, Wis., Elmhurst Art Mus., Beverly Art Ctr. Mus., Chgo., Drury Ln. Theater, Oakbrook, Ill., DuPage County Bar Assn., Wheaton, Pegasus Assocs., Chgo., Elk Grove Village Libr., Villa Park Libr., Elmhurst Mcpl. Bldg., Coll. of DuPage, numerous other pub. and pvt. collections; subject of numerous articles: in newspapers, mags. Mem. exec. bd. Elmhurst Art Mus., 1998—99; v.p. Sr. Art Network Chgo., 2002. Named Best of Show, Beverly Arts Ctr., Chgo., 1999, DuPage Art League and Gallery, Sr. Art Network, Chgo., Bloomingdale Art Mus., Ill., Addison Art Guild, Ill., Elmhurst Artists Guild, 1997; recipient Grumbacher medallion and award of excellence, No. Colo. Art Assn., 1998, Gold medallion award, Merit award, Ill. Watercolor Exhbn., 1999, 1st pl. Christian Art Exhbn., Coll. DuPage, 1997, 1998, 3d pl. award, Grumbacher Gold medallion exhbn. in nat. shows, numerous other nat. and internat. awards. Signature mem. Water Color Soc. (Midwest, Ga., Mont., Pa., Tex., Ill., Niagara Frontier, We. Colo., La., Okla., Ky.), Taos Soc. Watercolorist; mem. Watercolor Soc. (assoc. mem., Phila., W. Tex., La., Colo., Ky., Ala.), Art Inst. Chgo., Elmhurst Artists Guild (hon. life, pres. 1995-2000), Addison Art Guild, Chgo. Artists Coalition, Sr. Art Network (v.p. 2002), DuPage Art League. Roman Catholic. Avocations: opera, German studies, museum studies, travel, books. Home: 550 Edgewood Ave Elmhurst IL 60126-4140 Studio: 320 Ardmore Villa Park IL 60181 E-mail: ecalestudio@aol.com.

SCHULTZ, FRANKLIN M. retired lawyer; b. Cin., June 16, 1917; s. Max and Goldie (Wise) S.; m. Jean Carol Barnett, Apr. 5, 1946 (dec. 1981); children: William B., John M., Katherine, Caroline; m. Virginia B. Henderson, Sept. 4, 1983 BA, Yale U., 1939, LLB, 1942. Bar: Ohio 1947, D.C. 1954, Mass. 1985, U.S. Supreme Ct. 1954. Atty. Fed. Power Commn., 1946-47; assoc. prof. Sch. Law, Ind. U., Bloomington, 1947-53; with firm Purcell & Nelson, Washington, 1953-80, ptnr., 1957-80, Reavis & McGrath, Washington, 1980-85; lawyer-in-residence Sch. Law, Washington and Lee U., 1985, vis. prof., 1991-94, ret., 1994; vis. prof. Sch. Law, U. Iowa, 1986-90. Lectr. Sch. Law, George Washington U., 1958-59; vis. prof. Sch. Law, U. Va., 1975; mem. ednl. appeal bd. U.S. Dept. Edn., 1974-82. Contbr. articles to profl. jours. Trustee Nantucket Land Coun., 1992—. Served to capt. AUS, 1942-46. Decorated Bronze stars. Mem. ABA (mem. council adminstrv. law sect. 1966-69, chmn. 1970-71, del. ho. of dels. 1972-74), D.C. Bar (gen. counsel 1977-79, mem. legal ethics com. 1976-81), Am. Law Inst., Am. Bar Found., Adminstrv. Conf. U.S. (council 1980-82) Home: 1953 Marthas Rd Alexandria VA 22307-1966 E-mail: FMSchultz@aol.com.

SCHULTZ, FREDERICK HENRY, investor, former government official; b. Jacksonville, Fla., Jan. 16, 1929; s. Clifford G. and Mae (Wangler) S.; m. Nancy Reilly, Aug., 1951; children: Catherine G., Frederick H., Clifford G., John R. BA, Princeton U., 1951; postgrad., U. Fla. Sch. Law, 1954-56. With Barnett Nat. Bank, Jacksonville, 1956-57; owner, operator investment firm, from 1957; mem. Fla. Ho. of Reps., 1963-70, speaker of the house, 1968-70; chmn. bd. Barnett Investment Svcs., Inc.; dir. Barnett Banks Inc., to 1979; vice chmn. bd. govs. Fed. Res. System, Washington, 1979-82. Bd. dirs. Wickes Lumber Co. Served to lt. U.S. Army, 1952-54, Korea Decorated Bronze Star Roman Catholic. Office: PO Box 1200 Jacksonville FL 32201-1200

SCHULTZ, GERALD ALFRED (JERRY SCHULTZ), chemical company executive; b. Lockport, N.Y., Jan. 22, 1941; s. Alfred Henry and Lucy Vivian (Proctor) S. ;m. Barbara Joan Beals, July 13, 1962; 1 child, Amy Lynn Schultz-Kessler. AAS, Erie County Tech. Inst., Buffalo, 1961; BA in Chemistry, SUNY, Buffalo, 1969; postgrad., Harvard U., 1979. Rsch. technician Occidental Chem. Corp., Niagara Falls, N.Y., 1961-63; rsch. engr. Nat. Gypsum Co. Inc., Buffalo, 1963-66; from chemist, devel. mgr., gen. mgr. to v.p. Akzo Chems., Burt, N.Y. and Chgo., 1966-86; CEO, VanDeMark Inc. subs. Groupe SNPE, Lockport, NY, 1986—. Contbr. articles to profl. jours; patentee in field. Fund raiser United Way, Newfane, N.Y., 1982-84; treas., bd. dirs. Newfane Intercommunity Meml. Hosp., 1980-84; bd. dirs. ARC, Lockport, N.Y., 1980-84, 97-2000; mem. United Way Ea. Niagara Allocations Com., 1994-97. Mem. Am. Chem. Soc., Soc. Plastic Engrs., Soc. Plastics Industry (bd. dirs. 1974-76), Organic Peroxide Prodn. Safety Divsn. (chmn. 1974-76), Synthetic Organic Chem. Mfrs. Assn. (bd. dirs. 1991-94), Soc. Plastics Engrs., N.Y. State Bus. Coun., N.Y. State Chem. Alliance, Lockport Indsl. Coun. (treas. 1991-98), Ea. Niagara C. of C. (bd. dirs. 1992-95), Lockport Town and Country Club (bd. dirs. 1995-96), Tuscawara Club, Olcott Yacht Club (past commr. 1975), Legends Town and Country Club. Republican. Episcopalian. Avocations: golf, gardening, computers, boating. Home: 6953 Chestnut Ridge Rd Lockport NY 14094-3429 Office: VanDeMark Inc One North Transit Rd Lockport NY 14094 E-mail: g.schultz@snpe.com.

SCHULTZ, HARLEY, consulting company executive; b. N.Y.C. s. William and Rose Diane Schultz. MBA, NYU, 1981. Pres. Harley Schultz & Assocs., Cons. in Mktg., Mgmt. and Internet Bus. Devel., Scarsdale, N.Y., 1987—. Mem. various charitable orgns. Avocations: sailing, golf, French literature, 19th-Century art, classical music. Office: Harley Schultz & Assocs 130 Garth Rd # 250 Scarsdale NY 10583-3750 E-mail: harleyschultz@consultant.com.

SCHULTZ, HARRY PERSHING, chemistry researcher, retired educator; b. Racine, Wis., Mar. 9, 1918; s. Harry Carl and Agnes (Olson) S.; m. Pearle Marie Henriksen, Sept. 25, 1943; children: Stephanie Schultz Buehler, Tor, Alison Schultz Mohns. BS summa cum laude, U. Wis., 1942, PhD, 1946. Rsch. chemist Nat. Def. Rsch. Coun., 1942-45, Merck & Co., Inc., Rahway, N.J., 1946-47; mem. faculty U. Miami, Coral Gables, Fla., 1947-91, prof. chemistry, 1952-84, chmn. chemisty dept., 1972-84, prof. emeritus, 1984—; rsch. chem. topology Big Horn, Wyo., 1991—. Vis. lectr. U. Wis., Madison, summer 1958; vis. prof. Mich. State U., East Lansing, summers 1960, 62; mem. adv. bd. Jour. Chem. Info. and Computer Scis., Washington, 1995-99. Author: (with Popp) Organic Chemical Preparation, 1964, (with Schultz) Sir Isaac Newton, 1972, (with others) Topology in Chemistry, 2001; contbr. numerous articles to profl. jours. Mem. Planning Commn., South Miami, Fla., 1951-55. Grantee NIH, Walter Reed Army Inst. Rsch., Phi Beta Kappa, Sigma Xi, Phi Lambda Upsilon, Phi Kappa Phi, among othrs. Mem. Am. Chem. Soc. (chmn. Fla. sect. 1964, gen. chmn. 153rd nat. conf. 1967, councilor 1974-77, Fla. award 1986), Lions Club. Avocations: swimming, Civil War memorabilia. Home: PO Box 262 Big Horn WY 82833

SCHULTZ, HELEN WELKLEY, marriage and family therapist, minister; b. Rochester, N.Y., Apr. 29, 1939; d. Russell Edward Sr. and Helen Elizabeth (Mater) Welkley; m. Leroy Benjamin Schultz, June 16, 1963; children: Mary Beth, Leroi George, Helen Susan, Rachel Anne. BA, MacMurray Coll., 1961; MDiv, Asbury Theol. Sem., 1965; MA, Syracuse U., 1974. Min. Cheningo United Meth. Ch., Truxton, N.Y., 1965-80; asst. min. Christ Covenant Ch., 1980—; marriage and family therapist Onondaga Pastoral Counseling Ctr., Syracuse, N.Y., 1972-82, St. Andrew's Episcopal Ch., Syracuse, 1982—, Meml. Bapt. Ch., Cortland, N.Y., 1982—. Workshop presenter in field. Troop leader Girl Scouts U.S.A., 1957—, mem. program com. Ctrl. N.Y. coun., mem. wider opportunities com., gold award com.; chaplain Boy Scouts Am., 1997—, unit comdr. Baden Powell coun., 1998—; mem. Gospel Crusade Ministerial Assn. Recipient Appreciation pin Ctrl. N.Y. Girl Scout Coun., Syracuse, 1994. Mem. Am. Assn. for Marriage and Family Therapy (clin.), Gospel Crusade Ministerial Assn. Republican. Avocations: quilting, sewing, backpacking-camping, canoeing, gardening. Home and Office: 5458 Dog Hollow Rd Truxton NY 13158-3163

SCHULTZ, HOWARD, entrepreneur, professional basketball team owner; BS, No. Mich. U., 1975. V.p. Hammarplast; founder, chmn., & chief global strategist Starbucks Corp., 1987—; chmn. & owner Seattle Supersonics, 2001—. Office: Seattle Supersonics 351 Elliott Ave W Ste 500 Seattle WA 98119*

SCHULTZ, JAN ROGER, computer scientist, software engineer; b. Detroit, Jan. 24, 1942; s. Pierce Schultz and Clara Ruth (Cantor) Diamant; m. Sue Diane Burton, Nov. 25, 1989. BS, U. Ill., Champaign, 1962; MS, U. Ill., 1964. Rsch. assoc. Dept. Medicine Case Western Res. U., Cleve., 1966-68; asst. prof, engring, bus. adminstrn. and computer sci. U. Vt., Burlington, 1976-78, rsch. assoc., dir. computer devel. PROMIS lab. Dept. Medicine, 1969-80; dir. programming and application devel. Promis Info, Systems, Inc., South Burlington, Vt., 1981-86; owner, prin. JRS Computer Cons., Burlington, 1987-90; dir. bus. and info. svc. Univ. Health Ctr., Inc., Vt., 1991-94; pres., sr. v.p. engring. and devel. Step Soft, Inc., 1994-97; dir. devel. IDX Systems Corp., 1997—. Site visitor Can. Govt. Health, 1972, Ill. Regional Med. Program, Chgo., 1975; programmer, music mentor workstas., 1989. Contbr. chpts. to books. Mem. Burlington Econ. Devel. Coun., Burlington, 1982-83; chmn. Burlington Electric Commn., 1985, commr., 1984-90; bd. dirs. Burlington Revolving Loan Fund Bd., 1983-84; mem. com. in info. tech. workforce needs Nat. Rsch. Coun., 1999-2000. Grantee Nat. Ctr. for Health Svcs. Rsch., 1967-75. Mem. Assn. Computing Machinery. Avocations: bicycling, cross country skiing, electronic music, reading. Home: 17 Bayview St Burlington VT 05401-4017 Office: 1400 Shelburne Rd Burlington VT 05403-7754 E-mail: schultzj@acm.org.

SCHULTZ, JANE SCHWARTZ, health research administrator; b. N.Y.C., July 28, 1932; d. Jacob and Helene (Rosenthal) Schwartz; m. Jerome Samson Schultz, Sept. 1, 1955; children: Daniel S., Judith Schultz Nyquist, Kathryn Schultz Hubbard. BA in Chemistry cum laude, CUNY, 1953; MSChemE, Columbia U., 1955; MS in Human Genetics, U. Mich., 1968, PhD, 1970. Rsch. scientist USDA Forest Products Lab., Madison, Wis., 1955-58; sci. tchr. Pearl River (N.Y.) High Sch., 1958-64; sr. rsch. investigator dept. immunohaematology U. Leiden, Holland, 1971-72; geneticist, prin. investigator VA Med. Ctr., Ann Arbor, Mich., 1972-83; asst. prof., then assoc. prof. dept. human genetics U. Mich., 1975-83; asst. dean curriculum, then asst. dean student affairs U. Mich. Med. Sch., 1979-83; chief divsn. program dev. and rev. VA, Washington, 1977-79; chief genetics and transplantation biology br. Nat. Inst. Allergy and Infectious Diseases/NIH, Bethesda, Md., 1983-88; dir. rsch. adminstrn. health scis., assoc. prof. pathology U. Pitts., 1988-93, rsch. integrity officer, 1991-92; dir., CEO Biomation Ltd., Pitts., 1993—; rsch. assoc. chem engr. U. Pitts., 1993-94, 96—; rsch. dir./exec. dir., dir. spl. projects Nat. Disease Rsch. Interchange, Phila., 1994—. VA liaison rep. genetics study sect. NIH, Bethesda, 1973-77; com. mem. Fed. Interagy. Com. on Recombinant DNA Rsch., Bethesda, 1977-83; VA rep. nat. Insts. Gen. Med. Scis. Coun. /NIH, Bethesda, 1979-83; mem. Organ Tranplantation task force Med. Scis. Coun., NIH, Bethesda, 1985-86; advisor NASA/Ames, 2001-02. Contbr. over 30 rsch. papers to peer-reviewed jours.; contbr. book revs. to profl. jours. Grantee NIH/Nat. Cancer Inst., 1975-78, NIH/Nat. Ctr. for Rsch. Resources, 1999-03; recipient Pub. Health Svc. Spl. Achievement award NIAID, 1988. Mem. Am. Soc. Human Genetics, Genetics Soc. Am., Am. Assn. Immunologists, Am. Soc. Histocompatibility and Immunogenetics, Soc. Rsch. Adminstrs., Phi Beta Kappa. Office: Nat Disease Rsch Interch 1880 Jfk Blvd Philadelphia PA 19103-7422

SCHULTZ, JANET K. nursing consultant, business executive; b. Rochester, N.Y., Jan. 23, 1944; d. Charles T. and Madelyn (Daley) Schultz. BSN with distinction, Ind. U., Indpls., 1968; MSN, Ind. U., 1980. Chmn. operating rm. and allied areas nursing Ind. U. Hosps., Indpls., 1971-76; asst. dir. edn. Assn. Operating Rm. Nurses, Denver, 1976-81; dir. edn. and profl. svcs. Baxter

Healthcare Corp., McGaw Park, Ill., 1981-88; v.p. profl. svcs. AMSCO, Pitts., 1988-96; pres. Jan Schultz & Assocs., Roswell, Ga., 1996—2002; v.p. program devel. Med Ascend, Inc., Atlanta, 1998-99; prodn. mgr. Health-Stream, Inc., Denver, 2002—. Participant internat. consultation on health care associated infections in urology WHO, 1999-2000; lectr. in field; cons. in field. Editl. adv. bd. OR Manager, 1985-98, contbg. editor, 2001—; editl. adv. bd. OR Reports, 1992—; bi-monthly columnist OR Manager, 1997—; contbr.: Design of Special Care Facilities in Hospitals, 1981, Perioperative Patient Care, 1983, 3rd edit., 1994, Sterilization Technology for the Health Care Facility, 1993, 2d edit., 1997, Disinfection, Sterilization and Prservation, 5th edit., 2001, Perioperative Services, 2001. Mem. Nurse Cons. Assn. (pres. 1984-88, bd. dirs. 1989-91), ANA, Assn. Operating Rm. Nurses (mem. environ. issues com. and audiovisual com. 1995-96, nat. environ. liaison 1997-99, Jerry G. Peers award Disting. Svc. 1997), Assn. for Advancement of Med. Instrumentation (bd. dirs. 1991-98, mem. sterilization stds. com., co-leader U.S. del. 1994-98), Am. Hosp. Assn. (EPA task force on chlorofluorocarbon use in healthcare 1988-89), Health Industry Mfrs. Assn. (chmn. sterilization and packaging subcom. 1994-96), Sigma Theta Tau. Office: 2170 S Parker Rd Ste 140 Denver CO 80231 E-mail: jsassoc@msn.com.

SCHULTZ, JEFFREY ERIC, optometrist; b. Cleve., Jan. 28, 1948; s. Albert I. and Lenore (Aster) S.; m. Jane Steinman; children: Brian David, Amy Robin. BS in Zoology, Ohio State U., 1970, OD, MS in Physiol. Optics, 1974. Lic. optometrist, Ohio, Fla. Rsch. asst. Ohio State U. Coll. Optometry, Columbus, 1970-74, clin. instr., 1974-75; gen. practice optometry Cleve., 1975—. Contbr. articles to profl. jours. Nikon scholar. Mem. Ohio Optometric Assn. (continuing edn. com. 1976—, chmn. sports vision com. 1977-79, keyman com. 1984—, coord. zone 2 PAC 1989—, peer rev. and quality assurance com. 1992—, Optometric Recognition award 1978), Fla. Optometric Assn., Am. Optometric Assn. (Optometric Recognition award 1980, 82—, charter mem. contact lens sect. 1982—, mem. sports vision sect. 1983—), Am. Acad. Optometry (v.p. Cleve. chpt. 1991—), Nat. Eye Rsch. Found., Coun. Sports Vision, Vision Conservation Inst., Better Vision Inst., Ohio Contact Lens Soc., Cleve. Optometric Assn. (trustee 1985—, pres. 1989-91), Cmty. Eye Care Assocs. (pres. 1994-95, sec.-treas. 1995—), Masons, Beta Sigma Kappa, Phi Eta Sigma. Avocations: philately, fine art collecting. Office: 5706 Turney Rd Cleveland OH 44125-3971 also: 5555 Mayfield Rd Lyndhurst OH 44124-2913 E-mail: info@myeyedoc.net.

SCHULTZ, JOEL SIDNEY, architect; b. Buffalo, Feb. 3, 1945; s. Raymond Abraham and Emilia (Citron) S.; m. Betty Krul, Aug. 18, 1968; children: Andrea Schultz Schelowitz, Jennifer. AAS, Erie C.C., Buffalo, 1965; BArch, Kans. State U., 1970. Registered architect, Fla.; lic. gen. contr., Fla. Pres. J.S. Schultz Architect, Boca Raton, Fla., 1975—; v.p. Tropic Coast Bldg. and Design, Inc. Mem. constrn. rev. com. City of Coral Springs, 1993-99, chmn. code enforcement bd., 1987-99. Recipient Guild for Excellence in Mktg., Fla. Atlantic Bldrs. Assn., 1987, Pinnacle award, 1991, Cert. of Recognition City of Ft. Lauderdale, 1989, Fame award Bldrs. Assn. South Fla., 1991. Jewish. Office: 7630 NW 6th Ave Boca Raton FL 33487-1320

SCHULTZ, JOHN L. writer, educator; b. Columbia, Mo., July 28, 1932; s. Gerard Frederick William and Jennie Lee (Brumley) S.; m. Anne Bray, Dec. 10, 1963 (div. Nov. 1975); children: Timothy, Susan; m. Betty E. Shiflett, May 9, 1992. Student, U. Mo., 1950-51, U. Iowa, 1951-53, U. Chgo., 1955-56, 58-59. Direct mail mgr. U. Chgo. Press, 1959-60; dir. mail cons. Free Press, Chgo., 1960-62, Aldine Pub. Co., Chgo., 1962-65, Quadrangle Books, Chgo., 1965-67; story workshop classes, 1965-70; chair English and writing Columbia Coll., 1967-86, chair fiction writing, 1986-95, prof. emeritus, 1995—. Pres. The Story Workshop Inst., Chgo., 1997—, F Mag., Inc., Chgo., 1967—; cons. John Schultz Assocs., Chgo., 1986—, Schultz Group, Inc., 2000—; pub. Ga. Rev., Ohio Rev., Chgo. Tribune Law Rev. Author: The Tongues of Men, 1969, No One Was Killed, 1969, The Chicago Conspiracy Trial, 1993, Writing From Start to Finish, 1982, 90, 97; contbg. editor Evergreen Rev., N.Y.C., 1969-73; featured in PBS prodn. Daley: The Last Boss, 1996, A&E prodn. The Chgo. Conspiracy Trial, 1994, BBC radio drama The Chgo. Conspiracy Trial, 1993, Court TV The Chicago Conspiracy Trial, 1999, Jury in Politicized Trials. Cpl., M.C., U.S. Army, 1953-55, Korea. Ill. Arts Coun. fellow, 1983-84. Mem. MLA, Assoc. Writing Programs, Nat. Coun. Tchrs. English, Coll. Composition and Comms. Avocations: running, hunting, archery, rock climbing, travel, theater. Office: Columbia Coll Chicago 600 S Michigan Ave Chicago IL 60605-1900 Home: 8 Wellbrock Hts San Rafael CA 94903-3785 E-mail: jschu10054@aol.com.

SCHULTZ, KAREN ROSE, clinical social worker, author, publisher, speaker; b. Huntington, N.Y., June 16, 1958; d. Eugene Alfred and Laura Rose (Palazzolo) Squeri; m. Richard S. Schultz, Apr. 8, 1989; children: Carlos, Sarah Rose. BA with honors, SUNY, Binghamton, 1980; MA, U. Chgo., 1982. Lic. clin. social worker, Ill. Unit dir., adminstr. Camp Algonquin, Ill., 1981; clin. social worker United Charities Chgo., 1982-86; social worker Hartgrove Hosp., Chgo., 1986-87; pvt. practice, Oak Brook, Ill., 1987—. Owner, founder Inner Space pub. Co., 1993; trainer, speaker various groups, schs. and orgns., 1988-89; group leader Optifast Program, Oak Park and Aurora, Ill., 1989-90; instr. social work Morraine Valley C.C., Palos Hills, Ill., 1989-90; instr. eating disorders Coll. of Dupage, Glen Ellyn, Ill., 1990-92, tchr. intuition and counseling, 1995—. Author: The River Within, 1993, Shelter in the Forest, 1998, Flashes of Brilliance, 2002; editor, contbg. author: The River Within newsletter, 1989—. Mem. NASW (registered, diplomate), Acad. Cert. Social Workers, Nat. Spkrs. Assn., Profl. Spkrs. Ill., Toastmasters Interant., Women Entrepreneurs DuPage. Avocations: creative writing, aerobics, yoga, personal growth. Office: 900 Jorie Blvd Ste 234 Oak Brook IL 60523-3841

SCHULTZ, KATHLEEN STEFANI, lawyer; b. Detroit, May 23, 1951; d. Andrew Earl and Letty Marie Stefani; m. W. Dennis Schultz, June 13, 1976; children: Kathleen Marie, John Andrew. BA, U. Mich., 1973; JD, Detroit Coll. Law, 1978. Bar: Mich., U.S. Dist. Ct. Mich., U.S. Ct. Claims. Assoc. atty. Martin J. Smith, Atty. at Law, Eastpointe, Mich., 1978-81; ptnr. Smith and Schultz, 1981-2000, Smith, Schultz and Huget, LLP, Eastpointe, 2000—. Mediator Macomb County Cir. Ct., Mt. Clemens, Mich., 1995—. Treas., Com. to Re-elect Judge Martin J. Smith, Eastpointe, 1978—. Mem. Macomb County Bar Assn., State Bar Mich. (dist. character and fitness com.). Roman Catholic. Avocations: family activities, reading, water sports. Office: Smith Schultz and Huget LLP 24405 Gratiot Ave Eastpointe MI 48021-3306 E-mail: kschultz23@aol.com.

SCHULTZ, KENNETH CARL, antiques dealer; b. Hoboken, N.J., July 16, 1938; s. Arthur Edgar and Edna Caroline S. BA, Jersey City State Coll., 1960. Tchr. fifth grade Bd. Edn., Union City, N.J., 1960-61; window display artist B. Altman & Co., N.Y.C., 1962-69; display dir. Fortunoff's, 1969-73; self employed antiques dealer Hoboken, 1973—. Owner, pub., writer Steamship Catalogues, 1980—. Lutheran. Avocations: collecting motion picture costumes and memorabilia. Office: Box M 753 Hoboken NJ 07030

SCHULTZ, LOUIS EDWIN, management consultant; b. Foster, Nebr., Aug. 8, 1931; s. Louis Albert and Lula Pusey (Cox) S.; m. Mary Kathleen Peck, Mar. 3, 1962; children: Kurt Michael, Kristen Leigh. BSEE, U. Nebr., 1959; MBA, Pepperdine U., 1974. Mktg. mgr. Bell & Howell, Pasadena, Calif., 1962-70; dir. mktg. Cogar Corp., Utica, N.Y., 1970-71; product mgr. Pertec Corp., L.A., 1971-73; gen. mgr. Control Data Corp., Mpls., 1973-84; founder Process Mgmt. Internat., Inc., 1984, pres., 1984-99; ptnr., mng. dir. Bluefire Ptnrs., 1999—. Bd. dirs. CorCom Cos., Inc., Mpls., PMI Ltd, 1995-98; adv. bd. Inst. for Productivity Through Quality, U. Tenn., Knoxville, 1982-84; ptnr. CorCom Cos., Inc., 1997-99, ptnr.-mng. dir., Bulefire Ptrns. Author: Managing in the Worldwide Competitive Society, 1984, Quality Management Philosophies, 1985, Profiles in Quality, 1994; co-author: Quality Handbook for Small Business, 1994, Deming, The Way We Knew Him, 1995. Mem. Gov.'s Commn. on Productivity, St. Paul, 1986; chmn. Wirth Park Tree Restoration Com., Mpls., 1983; mem. Productivity Planning Com., St. Paul, 1985—. Staff sgt. USMC, 1952-54; advisor to Deming Forum, 1985—; judge Minn. Quality award, 1992. Recipient Profl. Partnership award U. Minn., 1987. Mem. Am. Soc. Performance Improvement (bd. dirs. 1984-89, outstanding svc. award), Minn. Coun. for Quality (bd. dirs. 1987-97), Human Sys. Mgmt. (editl. bd.), Asia-Pacific Orgn. Quality Control (life), Toastmasters Internat. Republican. Methodist. Office: Bluefire Ptnrs 150 S 5th St Ste 1300 Minneapolis MN 55402-4213 E-mail: lschultz@bluefirepartners.com.

SCHULTZ, LOUIS MICHAEL, advertising agency executive; b. Detroit, Aug. 24, 1944; s. Henry Richard and Genevieve (Jankowski) S.; children: Christian David, Kimberly Ann; m. Diane Lee; stepchildren: Vince, Andrea, Frank. BA, Mich. State U., 1967; MBA, Wayne State U., 1970. Staff Campbell-Ewald, Warren, Mich., 1967-74, v.p. group dir., 1975-77, sr. v.p., assoc. dir., 1977-82, group sr. v.p., 1982-83, exec. v.p., 1984-87, Lintas: USA, 1987-94; chmn. Lintas: WW Media Coun., 1991; mem. devel. council IPG, N.Y.C., 1984—; pres., CEO CE Comm., 1994—; vice chmn. Campbell-Ewald, 1998-99; chmn., CEO Initiative Media N.Am., L.A., 2000—; chmn. Initiative Media WW, 2000. Advisor, Detroit Renaissance Com., 1981-84. With USAR, 1967-73. Mem. NATAS, Am. Women in Radio and TV, Am. Mktg. Assn., Detroit Advt. Assn., Promotion Mktg. Assn. (bd. dirs. 1999), Ad Club N.Y. (bd. dirs.), Adcraft Club, Old Club, Hidden Valley Club, Longboat Key Club, Detroit Athletic Club, Am. Advt. Fedn. (bd. dirs.), Forest Lake Country Club, Renaissance Club, Detroit Athletic Club. Episcopalian. Avocations: golf; tennis; travel. Home: 5011 Elmgate Dr Orchard Lake MI 48324-3014 Office: Initiative Media 5700 Wilshire Blvd Ste 400 Los Angeles CA 90036-3639

SCHULTZ, LOUIS WILLIAM, retired judge; b. Deep River, Iowa, Mar. 24, 1927; s. M. Louis and Esther Louise (Behrens) S.; m. D. Jean Stephen, Nov. 6, 1949; children: Marcia, Mark, Paul. Student, Central Coll., Pella, Iowa, 1944-45, 46-47; LLB, Drake U., Des Moines, 1949. Bar: Iowa. Claims supr. Iowa Farm Mut. Ins. Co., Des Moines, 1949-55; partner firm Harned, Schultz & McMeen, Marengo, Iowa, 1955-71; judge Iowa Dist. Ct. (6th dist.), 1971-80; justice Iowa Supreme Ct., 1980-93; county atty. Iowa County, 1960-68; ret., 1993. Served with USNR, 1945-46. Mem. Am. Bar Assn., Iowa Bar Assn. (bd. govs.), Iowa Judges Assn. (pres.)

SCHULTZ, MARVIN E. historian, educator; b. Albuquerque, Oct. 8, 1949; s. Marvin and Elizabeth Schultz; life ptnr. Shelia Kaye Jenkins. BA, Angelo State U., San Angelo, Tex., 1971; MA, SW Tex. State U., San Marcos, 1984; PhD, Tex. Christian U., Fort Worth, 1994. Asst. instr. history SW Tex. State U., San Marcos, 1980—84, instr. history, 1984—85; tchg. fellow Vanderbilt U., Nashville; adj. instr. history Vol. State CC, Gallatin; tchg. asst. Tex. Christian U., Fort Worth, Tex., 1990—94; lectr. in Tex. history U. of Tex. at Dallas, Richardson, 1994; dir. Ctr. for Am. Culture and History in Edn., Malvern, Ark., 1999—; instr. history Ouachita Tech. Coll., 1994—. Hist. cons., editor Applied Acad. Svcs., Fort Worth, Tex., 1990—92; jr. rsch. fellow Tex. State Hist. Assn., Austin, Tex., 1983—84; prodn. mgr. On With the Show, Austin, Tex., 1972—79. Editor: U. S. History Documents, 1996; contbr. articles and revs. to profl. jours., chapters to books. Commr. plus one City Parks Commn., Malvern, Ark., 2001—; mem. Garvan Woodland Garden, Hot Springs, 2001—. Recipient Kent Trinkle Book Collecting award, Friends of the Tex. Christian U. Libr., 1991. Fellow: Grady McWhiney Rsch. Found.; mem.: Hot Spring County Hist. Assn., Ark. Hist. Assn., Friends of the Malvern/Hot Spring County Libr. (life), So. Hist. Assn., Alpha Chi. Avocations: gardening, travel, public history. Office: Ouachita Tech Coll One College Circle Malvern AR 72104 E-mail: mschultz@otcweb.edu.

SCHULTZ, NANCY REILLY, artist; b. N.Y.C., July 20, 1930; d. John Francis and Eunice Genevieve (Crowley) Reilly; m. Frederick Henry Schultz, Aug. 11, 1951; children: Catherine, Frederick, Clifford, John Reilly. BA, Smith Coll. for Women, 1951; BFA, U. North Fla., 2000. Pres. The Smash Tennis Shop, Inc., Jacksonville, Fla., 1976-86; chmn. Schultz, Barrett Interiors, Inc. Chmn. Duval County Mothers March, March of Dimes, 1958-59; mem. adv. bd. Women's Bd. Jacksonville Wolfson Children's Hosp. at Bapt. Med. Ctr.; chmn. Docents Cummer Mus. Art, 1968-70; caseworker Family Counseling Ctr., Jacksonville, 1961-62; vol. worker Cmty. Pub. TV, Am. Cancer Soc.; chmn. fund raising Symphony Show House, 1972; met. bd. dirs. YMCA of Fla.'s First Coast, 1988; trustee U. North Fla. Found., 1989—, mem. exec. com., 1992-96. Mem. Jr. League of Jacksonville, Phi Kappa Phi (U. N.Fla. chpt.). Democrat. Roman Catholic. Home: 505 Lancaster St Jacksonville FL 32204-4143 Office: 118 W Adams St Ste 3B Jacksonville FL 32202-3800

SCHULTZ, PATRICIA BOWERS, vocal music educator, performer; b. Gomer, Ohio, Apr. 26, 1941; d. Paul Edward and Blodwen (Watkins) Bowers; m. Charles Albert Schultz; children: Todd Matthew, Vaughn Andrew, Cynthia Cinnamon. BS in Edn., French & Music, Miami U., Oxford, Ohio, 1963; MEd in Counseling, U. Ill., 1964; D of Musical Arts in Vocal Performance, U. Mo-Kansas City, 1984. Music educator, counselor Northmont Pub. Schs., Dayton, Ohio, 1964-66; French educator Bowling Green (Ohio) H.S., 1967-68; performer freelance USA and Europe, 1969—; instr. music and French Dickinson (N.D.) State U., 1972-74; instr. voice Ctrl. State U., Wilberforce, Ohio, 1975-76; dir. choral activities Savannah (Mo.) H.S., 1979-80; prof. music N.W. Mo. State U., Maryville, 1981—. Dir. music First United Meth. Ch., Maryville, 1977—88; tour mgr. Jenny Lind Ensemble, 1978—; musical dir. N.W. MO. State U., Maryville, 1981—, Internat. Enrichment, London, 2000, vis. faculty mem., 02; adjudicator Nat. Assn. Tchrs. of Singing, Mo. H.S. Activities Assn. Accomplishments in music include author, lead role in music drama Encore for Jenny Lind, 1976— (London Premiere 1992); conductor choral music Welsh Gymanfoedd Ganu, 1989— (Nat. Selection 1993); Coloratura soprano recitals and concerts throughout U.S.; soloist European tour Cin. Symphony, 1969; presentator Am. Assn. Higher Edn. Teaching Learning & Tech. Conf., 1997. Pres. Univ. Women, Maryville, 1978-79; first judge of vocal competition Nat. Glenn Miller Scholarship Competition, Clarinda, Iowa, 1992, 94, 2001; pres. Faculty Senate N.W. Mo. State U., 1993-95; organizer, charter mem. Mo. Assn. Faculty Senates, Springfield, Mo., 1993-94. Named Faculty Fellow Mo. Coordinating Bd. for Higher Edn., Jefferson City, 1997-98, Outstanding Alumnae Conservatory of Music, U. Mo.-Kansas City, 1990; grantee Mo. State Coun. on Arts, 1991-95. Mem. AAUW, Am. Assn. Higher Edn., Am. Coun. on Edn./Nat. Identification Program, Nat. Assn. Tchrs. Singing (Teacher of regional state and chpt. winners in Mo., Nebr. and eight state region 1986, 88, 90, 92, 97, 98), Am. Choral Dirs. Assn., Coll. Music Soc. Avocations: gardening, reading, travel. Home: 1004 W Cooper St Maryville MO 64468-2005 Office: NW Mo State Univ Dept Music 800 University Dr Maryville MO 64468-6015 E-mail: pbschul@mail.nwmissouri.edu.

SCHULTZ, PAUL NEAL, electronic publishing executive; b. Evanston, Ill., Nov. 3, 1957; s. Edward Delfus and Loretta Mae (Fraine) S.; m. Robin Lyn Davis, May 27, 1989; children: Kyle Neal, Caitlyn McKenzie, Sophie Davis. BS in Bus. & Mktg., No. Ill. U., 1979. Territory mgr. Burroughs Corp., Chgo., 1979-81; sr. mktg. rep. Mead Data Cen., 1981-84, br. mgr., 1984-90, nat. sales dir. LEXIS Document Svcs. divsn., 1990—; pres. LexisNexis Document Solutions, 2001—. Cons. ABA Law Office of Future Com., Chgo., 1985, 86; speaker Chgo. Bar Assn. Tech. Com., Chgo., 1986, 87, 88. Mem. Credit Mgrs. Assn., Comml. Fin. Assn. (adv. bd. dirs.), Equipment Lessors Assn., Western Assn. Equipment Lessors. Roman Catholic. Avocations: golf, fishing, hunting, skiing. Home: 285 S Valley Rd Barrington IL 60010-4748 Office: 135 S La Salle St Dept 2200 Chicago IL 60674-1000

SCHULTZ, PHILIP, poet; b. Rochester, N.Y., Jan. 6, 1945; s. Samuel Benjamin and Lillian Bedina Schultz; m. Monica Banks, Jan. 28, 1995; childre: Elias, August. BA, San Francisco State U., 1967; MFA, U. Iowa, 1971. Poet-in-residence Kalamazoo (Mich.) Coll., 1971-72; writer-in-residence Newton (Mass.) Coll. of Scared Heart, 1973-74; adj. tchr. liberal arts Tufts U., Somerville, Mass., 1973-74; writing tchr. U. Mass., Boston, 1973-75; founder, dir. grad. dept. creative writing NYU, 1978-88. Adj. prof. creative writing Columbia U., N.Y., 1973-75; founder, dir. The Writers Studio. N.Y.C., 1985—. Author: LIKE Wings, 1978, DEEP Within in the Ravine, 1984, My Guardian Angel Stein, 1986, The Holy Worm of Praise, 2002; contbr. poetry to various publs. Vol. tchr. poetry to troubled children Columbia-Presbyn. Hosp., 1986-87, Coalition for Homeless. Fellowship in poetry N.Y. Found. for Arts, 1985, N.Y. State Coun. for the Arts, 1976, 80, Fulbright fellow to Israel Hebrew U., 1983-84; recipient Levinson prize Poetry mag., 1996-97, Am. Acad. and Inst. Arts and Letters award, 1979. Mem. Pen Am. Ctr. (events com., membership com. 1979-81), Poetry Soc. of Am. (bd. govs.), Acad. Am. Poets (Lamont award), Poets House. Democrat. Jewish. Avocations: reading, running. Home: 88 Osborne Ln East Hampton NY 11937-2207 Office: The Writers Studio 78 Charles St Apt 2R New York NY 10014-2661 *I place clarity and precision above all else in my work, and if these are the modes of expression, honesty of feeling provides the substance as well as the goal. I believe the art of good writing takes place in the art of revision, which, if taxing, often enough gives me the time to get to the heart of the matter. I choose to write about only those things which I feel most passionate about: the particular circumstances of my life.*

SCHULTZ, RICHARD CARLTON, plastic surgeon; b. Grosse Pointe, Mich., Nov. 19, 1927; s. Herbert H. and Carmen (Huebner) S.; m. Pauline Zimmermann, Oct. 8, 1955; children: Richard, Lisa, Alexandra, Jennifer. McGregor scholar, U. Mich., 1946-49; MD, Wayne State U., 1953. Diplomate Am. Bd. Plastic Surgery. Intern Harper Hosp., Detroit, 1953-54, resident in gen. surgery, 1954-55, U.S. Army Hosp., Fort Carson, Colo., 1955-57; resident in plastic surgery St. Luke's Hosp., Chgo., 1957-58, U. Ill. Hosp., Chgo., 1958-59, VA Hosp., Hines, Ill., 1959-60; practice medicine specializing in plastic surgery Park Ridge, 1961-96; retired, 1996; clin. asst. prof. surgery U. Ill. Coll. Medicine, 1966-70, assoc. prof. surgery, 1970-76, prof., 1976-96, head div. plastic surgery, 1970-87; pres. med. staff Luth. Gen. Hosp., Park Ridge, 1977-79. Vis. prof. U. Pitts., 1972, U. Miss., 1973, U. Pisa, Italy, 1974, Jikei U. Coll. Medicine, Tokyo, 1976, Ind. U., 1977, U. Helsinki, 1977, U. N.Mex., 1978, U. Milan, 1981, So. Ill. Sch. Medicine, 1982, Tulane U. Med. Sch., 1983, Shanghai 2d Med. Coll., 1984, U. Guadalajara (Mex.), 1986, Gazi U., Turkey, 1988, U. Coll. Medicine Tsuksba, Japan, 1996, Taegu (Korea) U., 1996; participant, guest surgeon Physicians for Peace, Turkey and Greece, 1988, Israel and Occupied Ters., 1990, Egypt, 1991, Lithuania, Estonia, 1993 (team leader); leader citizen amb. People to People Internat. Del. Plastic Surgeons to Albania & Russia, 1994, del. leader, Tibet and China, 1998. Author: Facial Injuries, 1970, 3d edit., 1988, Maxillo-Facial Injuries from Vehicle Accidents, 1975, Outpatient Surgery, 1979. Mem. sch. bd., Lake Zurich, Ill., 1966-72, pres., 1968-72; pres. Chgo. Found. for Plastic Surgery, 1966— . Served to capt. M.C., AUS, 1955-57. Recipient research award Ednl. Found. Am. Soc. Plastic and Reconstructive Surgery, 1964-65, Med. Tribune Auto Safety award, 1967, Robert H. Ivy award, 1969, Disting. Sci. Achievement award Wayne U. Coll. Medicine Alumni, 1975; Sanvenero-Rosselli award, 1981; Fulbright scholar U. Uppsala, Sweden, 1960-61 Fellow ACS (pres. local commn. on trauma 1985-87); mem. Am. Assn. Plastic Surgeons (trustee 1990-91), Am. Soc. Plastic and Reconstructive Surgeons, Midwestern Assn. Plastic Surgeons (pres. 1978-79), Chgo. Soc. Plastic Surgeons (pres. 1970-72), Midwestern Assn. Plastic Surgeons (pres. 1978-79), Am. Soc. Maxillofacial Surgeons (pres. 1988-89, award of honor 1986), Am. Assn. Automotive Medicine (pres. 1970-71, A. Merkin award 1982), Am. Cleft Palate Assn., Am. Soc. Aesthetic Plastic Surgery, Tord Skoog Soc. Plastic Surgeons (pres. 1971-75), Can. Soc. Plastic Surgery, Chilean Soc. Plastic Surgery (corr.), Japanese Soc. Plastic Surgery (corr.), Cuban Soc. Maxillofacial Surgery (corr.), Korean Soc. Plastic Surgery. Office: PO Box 357 Northport MI 49670-0357 Home: PO Box 357 Northport MI 49670-0357

SCHULTZ, RICHARD DALE, national athletic organization executive; b. Grinnell, Iowa, Sept. 5, 1929; s. August Henry and Marjorie Ruth (Turner) S.; m. Jacquilyn Lu Duistermars, June 26, 1949; children: Robert Dale, William Joel, Kim Marie. BS, Ctrl. Coll., Pella, Iowa, 1950; EdD (hon.), Ctrl. Coll., 1987; LLD (hon.), Wartburg Coll., 1988, Alma Coll., 1989, Luther Coll., 1991; PhD (hon.), U.S. Sports Acad., 1993; LLD (hon.), Daniel Webster Coll., 1997, Gettysburg Coll., 1998. Head basketball coach, athletic dir. Humboldt (Iowa) High Sch., 1950-60; freshman basketball coach U. Iowa, Iowa City, 1960-62, head baseball coach, assoc. basketball coach, 1962-70, head basketball coach, 1970-74, asst. v.p., 1974-76; dir. athletics and phys. edn. Cornell U., Ithaca, N.Y., 1976-81; dir. athletics U. Va., Charlottesville, 1981-87; exec. dir. NCAA, Mission, Kans., 1987-94; pres. Global Sports Enterprises, 1994-95; exec. dir. U.S. Olympic Com., Colorado Springs, Colo., 1995-2000; chmn. Mktg. Assocs. Internat., 2000—. Mem. honors ct. Nat. Football Found. and Hall of Fame, Nat. Basketball Hall of Fame, 1992; chmn. bd. NCAA Found., 1989; organizer Iowa Steel Mill, Inc.; bd. trustees Gettysburg Coll., 1996—. Author: A Course of Study for the Coaching of Baseball, 1964, The Theory and Techniques of Coaching Basketball, 1970; Contbr. articles to mags. Bd. dirs. Fellowship of Christian Athletes, 1986, chmn., 1990; chmn. Multiple Sclerosis, 1974-75; mem. Knight Found. Commn. on Intercollegiate Athletics, 1990—; mem. adv. com. on svc. acad. athletic programs Def. Dept. Recipient Disting. Alumni award Ctrl. Coll., Pella, 1970, 98, Lifetime Svc. award U. Iowa, 1994, Corbett award Nat. Assn. Collegiate Dirs. Athletics, 1994, medal of honor Ellis Island, 1997, Disting. Alumni award Ctrl. Coll., 1998, Casey award, 1999, Pres. and Mrs. Bush Cmty. Impact award 1999; mem. Basketball Hall of Fame Honor Ct., 1992, Sportsman of Yr. award Marine Corp., 1997; inducted into Iowa Baseball Hall of Fame, 1993. Mem. Nat. Assn. Coll. Basketball Coaches, Ea. Coll. Athletic Assn. (mem. exec. com. 1980-81), Am. Basketball Coaches Assn. (Award of Honor 1994), Am. Football Coaches Assn. (lifetime membership award 1995). Home: 3670 Twisted Oak Cir Colorado Springs CO 80904-4720 Office: 10975 Benson 12 Corporate Woods Ste 55 Overland Park KS 66210 E-mail: dschultz@maisports.com.

SCHULTZ, RICHARD MICHAEL, biochemistry educator, researcher; b. Phila., Oct. 28, 1942; s. William and Beatrice (Levine) S.; m. Rima M. Lunin, Mar. 7, 1965; children: Carl M., Eli J. BA, SUNY, Binghamton, 1964; PhD, Brandeis U., 1969. Rsch. fellow Harvard U. Med. Sch., Boston, 1969-71; asst. prof. Loyola U. Stritch Sch. of Medicine, Maywood, Ill., 1971-78, assoc. prof., 1978-84, prof., 1984—, chmn. dept. molecular and cellular biochemistry, 1984-2000. Mem. adv. med. bd. Leukemia Rsch. Found., Chgo., 1987-91. Contbr. articles to profl. jours. and chpts. to books. Recipient Rsch. grants NIH. Achievements include in vivo evidence for the role of protease enzymes and their inhibitors in regulating tumor cell metastasis, oncogene pathways in metastasis, obtaining evidence on the nature of the transition-state in enzyme catalysis.. Office: Divsn Molecular & Cellular Biochemistry Loyola U Sch Medicine Maywood IL 60153 E-mail: rschult@lumc.edu.

SCHULTZ, RICHARD OTTO, ophthalmologist, educator; b. Racine, Wis., Mar. 19, 1930; s. Henry Arthur and Josephine (Wagoner) S.; m. Diane Haldane, Sept. 29, 1990; children: Henry Reid, Richard Paul, Karen Jo. BA, U. Wis., 1950, MS, 1954; MD, Albany Med. Coll., 1956; MSc, U. Iowa, 1960. Diplomate Am. Bd. Ophthalmology. Intern, Univ. Hosps., Iowa City, 1956-57, resident in opthalmology, 1957-60; chief ophthalmology sect. div. Indian health USPHS, Phoenix, 1960-63; practice medicine specializing in ophthalmology, 1963; NIH spl. fellow in ophthalmic microbiology U. Calif., San Francisco, 1963-64, clin. assoc., 1963-64, research assoc., 1963-64; assoc. prof., chmn. dept. ophthalmology Marquette U. Sch. Medicine (now Med. Coll. Wis.), Milw., 1964-68, prof., chmn., 1968-97, prof. ophthalmology, 1997—2000, prof. emeritus, 2000—. Mem. nat. adv. eye coun. NIH, 1984-88; cons. VA regional ctr. Milw. Children's, Columbia, Froedert and hosps., Milw. Contbr. articles to profl. jours. Served with USPHS, 1960-63. Fellow: ACS, Am. Ophthalmol. Soc., Am. Acad. Ophthalmology; mem.: Milw. Acad. Medicine, Med. Soc. Milwaukee County, Oxford Ophthalmol. Congress (Eng.), Rsch. to Prevent Blindness, N.Y. Acad. Scis., Assn. Rsch. Vision and Ophthalmology, Milw. Ophthal. Soc., Assn. Univ. Profs. Ophthalmology. Home: 13070 W Bluemound Rd 107 Elm Grove WI 53122-1973 Office: MCW Eye Inst 925 N 87th St Milwaukee WI 53226-4812 E-mail: roschulz@mcw.edu.

SCHULTZ, RUTH ANNE, home economics educator, parenting educator, consultant; b. Oneida, N.Y., Jan. 27, 1953; d. Herman Lyon and Anna Marie (Jarvis) S. BS, Cornell U., 1975; MS, Syracuse U., 1982; postgrad., Plattsburgh State U., 1986, 89, L.I. U., 1990—. Cert. tchr., N.Y.; cert. in family and consumer scis. Tchr. home econs. Phelps-Clifton Springs (N.Y.) Cen. Schs., 1975-77, adult educator, 1976-77, 93; home econs. tchr. Fabius (N.Y.)-Pompey Cen. Schs., 1977-82; tchr. home econs. Chittenango (N.Y.) Ctrl. Schs., 1982—, adviser family, cmtys. & career leaders Am., 1986—, mem. bldg. planning team, 1994-97. Parenting educator Cornell Coop. Extension, Madison County, Morrisville, N.Y., 1985—; cons. N.Y. Dept. Edn., 1988-96. Primary author curriculum materials. Community rep. Madison County Head Start Policy Coun., Morrisville, 1985-88; chmn. program com. Cornell Coop. Extension, Madison County, 1990-92, Long Range Planning Com.; bd. dirs. Community Action Program of Madison County. Recipient N.Y. State Edn. Dept. Region 7 Disting. Occupational Educator ward, 1990. Mem. ASCD, N.Y. State Future Homemakers Am. (trustee, vice chmn.), Home Econs. Edn. Assn. (v.p. 1988-90, pres.-elect 1990-91, pres. 1991-93, past pres. 1993-94), N.Y. State Home Econs. Tchrs. Assn. (pres. 1986-88, state conv. chmn. 1989-90, 96, legis. co-chmn. 1989-90), N.Y. State Home Econs. Assn. (elem., secondary and adult chmn. 1989-93, New Achiever award 1988, Tchr. of Yr.

award 1989), Am. Home Econs. Assn. (nat. leadership com. 1989-91), Ctrl. N.Y. Home Econs. Tchrs. Assn. (Tchr. of Yr. award 1985), N.Y. State Occupl. Edn. Assn. (affiliate v.p. 1986-88, state conv. chmn. 1988-89, 93, 95, regional rep. 1994—, state pres. 1997—, policy coun. mem. region I, Disting. Svc. award 1990), Nat. Assn. Vocat. Home Econs. Tchrs. (spl. award of merit 1991), Am. Vocat. Assn. (Region I Vocat. Tchr. of Yr. award 1994). Democrat. Roman Catholic. Home: RR 3 Cazenovia NY 13035-9803 Office: Chittenango Mid Sch 1732 Fyler Rd Chittenango NY 13037-8522

SCHULTZ, STANLEY GEORGE, physiologist, educator; b. Bayonne, N.J., Oct. 26, 1931; s. Aaron and Sylvia (Kaplan) S.; m. Harriet Taran, Dec. 25, 1960; children: Jeffrey, Kenneth. AB summa cum laude, Columbia U., 1952; MD, N.Y. U., 1956. Intern Bellevue Hosp., N.Y.C., 1956-57, resident, 1957-59; research assoc. in biophysics Harvard U., 1959-62, instr. biophysics, 1964-67; assoc. prof. physiology U. Pitts., 1967-70, prof. physiology, 1970-79; prof., chmn. dept. physiology U. Tex. Med. Sch., Houston, 1979-96, prof. dept. internal medicine, 1979—, prof. dept. integrative biol. pharm. physiology, 1997—, vice chmn., 1999—, Fondren chair in cell signalling, 1999—. Cons. USPHS, NIH, 1970—; mem. physiology test com. Nat. Bd. Med. Examiners, 1974-79, chmn., 1976-79 Editor Am. Jour. Physiology, Jour. Applied Physiology, 1971-75, Physiol. Revs., 1979-85, Handbook of Physiology: The Gastrointestinal Tract, 1989-91—; mem. editl. bd. Jour. Gen. Physiology, 1969-88, Ann. Revs. Physiology, 1974-81, Current Topics in Membranes and Transport, 1975-81, Jour. Membrane Biology, 1977—, Biochim. Biophys. Acta, 1987-89; assoc. editor Ann. Revs. Physiology, 1977-81; assoc. editor News in Physiol. Scis., 1989-94, editor, 1994—; contbr. articles to profl. jours. Served to capt. M.C. USAF, 1962-64. Recipient Research Career award NIH, 1969-74; overseas fellow Churchill Coll., Cambridge U., 1975-76 Mem. AAAS, Am. Heart Assn. (estab. investigator 1964-68), Am. Physiol. Soc. (councillor 1989-91, pres.-elect 1991-92, pres. 1992-93, past pres. 1993-94), Fed. Am. Soc. Exptl. Biology (exec. bd. 1992-95), Biophys. Soc., Soc. Gen. Physiologists, Internat. Cell Rsch. Orgn., Internat. Union Physiol. Scis. (chmn. internat. com. gastrointestinal physiology 1977-80, chmn. U.S. nat. com. 1992-98), Assn. Am. Physicians, Am. Assn. Ob-Gyn. (hon. fellow), Assn. Chmn. Depts. Physiology (pres. 1985-86), Sigma Xi, Phi Beta Kappa. Home: 4955 Heatherglen Dr Houston TX 77096-4213

SCHULTZ, SUSAN MARIE, special education educator; b. Buffalo, June 29, 1957; d. Henry E. and Dorothy C. Mechlinski; m. Thomas L. Schultz, Aug. 18, 1979; children: Jacob, Jessica, Alexander. AAS, Erie C.C., Orchard Park, N.Y., 1977; BS in Elem. Edn., SUNY, Buffalo, 1979, MS in Spl. Edn., 1982; CAS in Ednl. Adminstrn., SUNY, Brockport, 1996; postgrad., U. Rochester, 1996—. Cert. sch. dist. adminstr., sch. adminstr. and supr., N.Y. Tchr. Our Lady Help of Christians, Cheektowaga, N.Y., 1980-82; tchr., team leader Cantalician Ctr. for Learning, Amherst, 1982-84; staff devel./parent resource team Assn. for Retarded Children, Cheektowaga, 1985-88; tchr. Bornhava Specialized Learning Ctr., Amherst, 1988-94, program dir., 1994-96; tchr. Pembroke Ctrl. Sch. Dist., Corfu, N.Y., 1996; prin. Cantalician Ctr. for Learning, Amherst, 1996—2002; coord. com. for spl. edn. Grand Island (N.Y.) Ctrl. Sch. Dist., 2002—. Mem. legis. task force Western N.Y. Devel. Disabilities Planning Coun., 1997—, mem. edn., com., 1994—. Bd. dirs. United Cerebral Palsy Assn. Western N.Y., 1990-92, program svcs., 1989-96; mem. Pembroke Ctrl. Schs. Shared Decision Making Team, recorder of minutes/sec., 1998—, bldg. planning team, 1999—. Recipient Cert. of Appreciation, United Cerebral Palsy Assn., 1992. Mem. ASCD, Am. Edn. Rsch. ASsn. Roman Catholic. Home: 9170 S Lake Rd Corfu NY 14036-9578 Office: Grand Island Ctrl Sch Dist 1100 Ransom Rd Grand Island NY 14072 E-mail: susan_schultz@gris.wnycric.org

SCHULTZ, T. PAUL, economics educator; b. Ames, Iowa, May 24, 1940; s. Theodore W. and Esther (Werth) S.; m. Judith Hoenack, Sept. 16, 1967; children: Lara, Joel, Rebecca. BA, Swarthmore Coll., 1961; PhD, MIT, 1966; MA (hon.), Yale U., 1974. Cons. Joint Econ. Com., Washington, 1964; researcher econs. dept. Rand Corp., Santa Monica, Calif., 1965-72, dir. population research, 1968-72; prof. econs. U. Minn., Mpls., 1972-75, Yale U., New Haven, 1974—, dir. Econ. Growth Ctr., 1983-96. Cons. World Bank, Rockefeller Found., InterAm. Devel. Bank; mem. com. on population NAS, Washington, 1987-89, 90-93. Author: Structural Change in a Developing Country, 1971, Economics of Population, 1981; editor: (books) The State of Development Economics, 1988, Investment In Women's Human Capital, 1995, (periodical) Research in Population Economics, 1985, 88, 91, 96; assoc. editor Jour. Population Econs., 1991—, Econ. of Edn. Rev., 1993—, China Econ. Rev., 1994—. Mem. commn. on behavioral scis. and edn. Nat. Rsch. Coun., 1997—. Fellow: AAAS (population resources environ. com. 1985—89, nomination com. 1987—90); mem.: Econ. Rsch. Forum for Arab Countries (trustee 1993—2001), European Soc. for Population Econs. (bd. dirs., pres. 1997), Soc. for Study Social Biology (bd. dirs. 1986—89), Internat. Union for Sci. Study Population, Population Assn. Am. (bd. dirs. 1979—81), Econometrics Soc., Am. Econ. Assn. Office: Yale U Econ Growth Ctr PO Box 208269 27 Hillhouse Ave New Haven CT 06520-8269 E-mail: paul.schultz@yale.edu.

SCHULTZ, VICTOR M. physician; b. Pitts., Aug. 14, 1932; s. Irvin and Rose (Reiss) S. BS, Kent (Ohio) State U., 1955; MD, Ohio State U., Columbus, 1958. Diplomate Am. Bd. Dermatology. Pvt. practice, Santa Monica, Calif., 1965—. Fellow Am. Acad. Dermatology, Pacific Dermatologic Assn.; mem. AMA, Am. Coll. Physicians, Calif. Med. Assn., L.A. County Med. Assn. Avocations: skiing, tennis, golf, music, swimming. Office: 2461 Santa Monica Blvd Santa Monica CA 90404-2049

SCHULTZ, VICTORIA L. entertainer, music teacher; b. Kansas City, Mo., May 12, 1952; d. Kenneth Leroy and Russie Juanita (McIntosh) S. BMusic, U. Mo., Kansas City, 1975; M Music, Drake U., 1977. Opera coach, accompanist, prof. piano U. Ctrl. Fla., Orlando, 1977-80; prof. voice and piano Valencia C.C., 1980-86; music dir. Pine Castle (Fla.) Ctr. of the Arts, 1983-84; pianist, harpist Hyatt Regency Grand Cypress, Orlando, 1984-96; pianist Altamonte Springs (Fla.) Hilton and Towers, 1985-89; pianist, harpist Caruso's Palace, Orlando, 1990-94; harpist Sergio's Restaurant, 1994-95. Adj. prof. voice Rollins Coll., Winter Park, Fla., 1991-92; entertainer Walt Disney World, Orlando, 1996—; adj. prof. harp U. Ctrl. Fla., Orlando, 1998—; pvt. tchr. and freelance entertainer, Fla., 1980—. Composer: (music for piano and voice) Set of Songs, 1979; composer/arranger : music CD Orange Blossom Tale, 1996, arranger/performer : music CDs Harp Dreams, 1997, arranger/performer : music CDs Harp Favorites, 1998, arranger/performer : music CDs Soothing Harp, 1999, composer, harpist: CD Harp Meditation for Chakra Attunement, 2001; author: (textbook) You Can Play the Harp , 2002. Sponsor, Riverside Musicale Jr. Music Club, Orlando, 1991—; entertainer fund raising events for AHA, Am. Cancer Soc., Muscular Dystrophy, Am. Diabetes Assn.; artist-in-residence Fla. Hosp. Recipient Nat. 1st Place award Encore Prodns. Talent Competition, 1985, 86, State Young Artist 1st prize Fla. Fedn. Music Clubs, 1976, Silver medal Internat. Piano Rec. Competition, Am. Coll. Musicians, 1978. Mem. Ctrl. Fla. Musicians Assn. (local 389), Am. Harp Soc., Fla. Harpers and Friends (1st Place Composition award 2002, People's Choice award 2002), Ctrl. Fla. Music Tchrs. Assn. (recital chmn. 1999-2000), Orlando Music Club (founding mem.), Nat. Music Tchrs. Assn., Scottish Harp Soc. of Am. Democrat. Avocations: reading, movies, going to concerts, shopping. Home: 848 River Cove Ave Orlando FL 32825-8107 Office: Harpspun Prodns PMB 306 425 S Chickasaw Trl Orlando FL 32825-7852

SCHULTZ-ROSS, ROY ANDREW, forensic psychiatrist, educator, writer; b. Chgo., May 15, 1961; s. Leslie Schultz and Phyllis Joan (Rudnick) Ross. BA in Humanities, Johns Hopkins U., 1983; MD, Jefferson Med. Coll., 1987. Lic. psychiatrist, Hawaii, N.C., Calif. Resident in psychiatry U. N.C. Hosps., Chapel Hill, 1987-90; fellow in forensic psychiatry Harvard/Mass. Mental Health, Boston and Bridgewater, Mass., 1990-91, psychiatrist, inst., 1991-92; asst. prof. U. Hawaii, Honolulu, 1992-96, assoc. prof., 1996-97, assoc. clin. prof., 1997—. Psychiatrist Hawaii State Hosp., Kaneohe, 1992-97; cons. and spkr. in field. Author: Looking into the Eyes of a Killer: A Psychiatrist's Journey Through the Murderer's World, 1998; contbr. articles to Jour. Forensic Sci., Hosp. and Cmty. Psychiatry, Bull. Am. Acad. Psychiatry and Law, Jour. Psychotherapy Practice and Rsch., Am. Jour. Psychotherapy. Mem. Task Force on Individuals with Mental Illness in the Criminal Justice System, Honolulu, 1992-94. Mem. Am. Acad. Psychiatry and Law (program com. 1994-96), Am. Psychiatric Assn., Assn. for Advancement of Philosophy and Psychiatry. Achievements include research in mental illness in legal issues. Office: PO Box 556 Honaunau HI 96726

SCHULZ, BRADLEY NICHOLAS, lawyer; b. Staten Island, N.Y., July 1, 1959; s. George Robert Jr. and Mary Jane (Fazakerley) S. BA, Wake Forest U., 1981; JD, N.Y. Law Sch., 1984. Bar: N.Y. 1985, N.C. 1985, N.J. 1985, U.S. Dist. Ct. (ea. dist.) N.C. 1985, U.S. Dist. Ct. (so. dist.) N.Y. 1985. Assoc. Mast, Tew, Armstrong & Morris, P.A., Smithfield, N.C., 1984-85; ptnr. Mast, Schulz Mast Mills & Stem, P.A., 1986-97, mng. ptnr., 1998—. Chmn. Young Republicans, Johnston County, Smithfield, 1988. Hankins scholar Wake Forest U., 1977-8l, N.Y. Law Sch. scholar, l98l-84. Mem. ABA, N.C. Bar Assn., N.Y. Bar Assn., N.J. Bar Assn., N.C. Acad. Trial Lawyers, Johnston County Bar Assn., Theta Chi Fraternity. Republican. Episcopalian. Avocations: yachting, sailing, skiing. Home: 946 Debro Rd Kenly NC 27542-9725 Office: Mast Schulz Mast Mills & Stem PA PO Box 119 Smithfield NC 27577-0119 E-mail: Brad@mastschulz.com.

SCHULZ, HELMUT WILHELM, chemical engineer, environmental executive; b. Berlin, July 10, 1912; came to U.S., 1924; s. Herman Ludwig Wilhelm and Emilie (Specka) S.; m. Colette Marie Francoise Prieur, Mar. 6, 1954; children: Raymond A., Caroline P., Roland W., Robert B., Thomas F. BS, Columbia U., 1933, ChE, 1934, PhD, 1942. Rsch. engr. to mng. dir. Union Carbide Corp., Charleston, W.Va., 1934-69; spl. asst. to dir. def. rsch. and engrng. U.S. Dept. of Def., Washington, 1964-67; spl. asst. to U.S. commr. of edn. U.S. Dept. of Edn., 1971; sr. rsch. scientist, adj. prof. Columbia U., N.Y.C., 1972-85; chmn., CEO Dynecology, Inc., Harrison, N.Y., 1974—. Contbr. articles to profl. jours. Mem. N.Y.C. Mayor's Sci. and Tech. Adv. Coun., 1973-74; bd. dirs. Charleston Symphony Orch., 1956-62, Am. Cancer Soc., W.Va., 1954-58; chmn. W.Va. Atomic Energy Commn., Charleston, 1962-64. Grantee in field. Fellow AIChE; mem. N.Y. Acad. Scis., Am. Chem. Soc. (emeritus), N.Y. Yacht Club, Cosmos Club. Achievements include patents; centrifugation cascade for enrichment of fissionable uranium isotope; high acceleration rocket motor; tar-free, slagging coal/waste gasifier; enhanced oil recovery process; synthesis of ethanol from ethylene and steam; waste-to-energy conversion processes, and 60 others. Home: 611 Harrison Ave Harrison NY 10528-1406 E-mail: hwschulz@msn.com.

SCHULZ, JOHN JOSEPH, communications educator; BA in Journalism, U. Mont., 1962; MPhil, Oxford U., 1979, DPhil, 1981; student, Nat. War Coll., Washington, 1985-86. Newswriter, reporter Voice of Am. News, Washington, 1971-72, corr. Hong Kong, 1972-74, bur. chief Tokyo, 1974-77; commentator BBC, London, 1977-79; coverage editor Voice of Am., 1979-82; deputy dir. Voice of Am. News Divsn., 1982-84; South Asia corr. Voice of Am. News, Islamabad, Pakistan, 1987-89; thinktank analyst Oxford Analytica, 1977-79, 84-88; prof. Nat. War Coll., Washington, 1989-91; sr. corr. Voice of Am. News, 1984-87, 91-92; assoc. dir. publs. The Arms Control Assn., 1992-95; prof. internat. comms. Coll. Comms. Boston U., 1995-97, 2000—, chair dept. mass. comms., advt., and pub. rels., 1997-2000; editor Arms Control Today, 1992-95. Presenter in field. Editor-in-chief Global Beat Syndicate, 2002—; contbr. articles to profl. jours. With USAF, 1963-71. Decorated 3 DFC, silver star, air medals, gallantry crosses, USAF; recipient disting. alumni award U. Mont., 1995. Office: Coll Communications 640 Commonwealth Ave Boston MA 02215-2422 E-mail: jjschulz@bu.edu.

SCHULZ, JUERGEN, art history educator; b. Kiel, Germany, Aug. 18, 1927; came to U.S., 1938; s. Johannes Martin Askan Schulz and Ilse (Lebenbaum) Hiller; m. Justine Hume, Sept. 1951 (div. 1968); children: Christoph (dec.), Ursula, Catherine; m. Anne Markham, May 19, 1969; 1 child, Jeremy. BA, U. Calif., Berkeley, 1950; PhD in History of Art, U. London, 1958. Reporter San Francisco Chronicle, 1950-51; copy editor UPI, London, 1952-53; from instr. to prof. history of art U. Calif., 1958-68; prof. Brown, Providence, 1968-90, Andrea V. Rosenthal prof. history art and architecture, 1990-95; Samuel H. Kress prof. Nat. Gallery of Art, 2000-2001. Mem. Inst. for Advanced Study, Princeton, N.J., 1971-72. Author: Venetian Painted Ceilings of the Renaissance, 1968, Printed Plans and...Views of Venice, 1971, La cartografia tra scienza e arte, 1990; also articles. Staff sgt. U.S. Army, 1945-48. Decorated grande ufficiale Ordine della Stella della Solidarieta della Repubblica Italiana; Guggenheim fellow, 1966-67. Mem. Ateneo Veneto, Centro Internaz. di Studi di Architettura A. Palladio. Office: Brown U Dept History Art and Architecture PO Box 1855 Providence RI 02912-1855

SCHULZ, KEITH DONALD, corporate lawyer, writer; b. Burlington, Iowa, Dec. 20, 1938; s. Henry Carl and Laura Iral (Bowlin) S.; m. Emily Brook Roane, Apr. 19, 1985; children: Keith Jr., Sarah, Christine, Stefan. BA, U. Iowa, 1960, JD, 1963. Bar: Iowa 1963, Ill. 1966, Wis. 1990. Dep. Sec. of State, State of Iowa, Des Moines, 1965-66; atty. AT&T, Chgo., 1966-67; sec., gen. counsel Borg-Warner Acceptance Corp., 1967-74; asst. gen. counsel Borg-Warner Corp., 1974-84, v.p., gen. counsel, 1984-88; of counsel Bell, Boyd & Lloyd, 1988—. Chmn., CEO Downtown Ptnrs., Inc., 1995-96. Author: (novel) Keepers of the River; contbr. articles to Harvard Bus. Rev., Jour. for Corp. Growth. Chmn. bd. dirs. Vol. Legal Svcs. Found., Chgo., 1984-91; bd. dirs. Southeast Iowa Symphony Orch., pres., 1998-2000, Heritage Trust Found. Mem. Iowa Bar Assn., Chgo. Bar Assn. (chmn. corp. law depts. com. 1983-84), Wis. Bar Assn., Assn. of Gen. Counsel, Am. Soc. Corp. Secs., Law Club of Chgo. Clubs: University, Economic (Chgo.). Avocations: tennis, bicycling, skiing. Office: Bell Boyd & Lloyd 70 W Madison St Ste 3300 Chicago IL 60602-4284 E-mail: KDons@aol.com.

SCHULZ, LAURA JANET, writer, retired secretary; b. Alba, Tex., Aug. 12, 1931; d. Joseph Clifton and Laura Oza (Carruth) English; m. Gordon Robert Schulz, Dec. 4, 1953; children: LeAnn Clarinda Schulz Barclay, Peggy Gaynell Schulz Lingbloom. Grad. h.s., Denison, Tex., 1948. Sec. history dept. Tex. Christian U., Ft. Worth, 1948-49; continuity editor Sta. KDSX, Denison, 1949-51; clk., typist Perrin AFB, Sherman, Tex., 1951-55; acctg. clk. England AFB, Alexandria, La., 1955; sec. Emile R. Jardine, CPA, Stockton, Calif., 1957-59; tchr. Little Meth. Pre-Sch., Lodi, 1968-69; sec. Heather, Sanguinetti, Caminata & Sakai, CPAs, Stockton, 1983-92; sec., feature writer, photographer Lodi (Calif.) Dist. C. of C., 1993-97. Author: Katy's Children, 1990, Little Rocky's True Adventures, 1991, Depot Days, 1999. Hon. life mem. Wesleyan Svc. Guild Trinity Meth. Ch., Denison, 1955—, Calif. Congress of PTA, 1984—; pres. PTA Needham Sch., Lodi, 1968-70; leader Camp Fire, Lodi, 1974-82; vol. advisor, tchr. Grapevine Newspaper Vinewood Sch., Lodi, 1974-82; tchr. First United Meth. Ch., Lodi, 1961-80, circle chair. Recipient Appreciation award Vinewood Sch., Lodi Unified Sch. Dist., 1974-82. Mem. Nat. League Am. Pen Women, Sierra Club. Democrat. Methodist. Avocations: photography, reading, walking, camping, nature. Home: 1910 W Tokay St Lodi CA 95242-3440

SCHULZ, LAWRENCE A. lawyer; b. Buffalo, Jan. 5, 1941; BA, SUNY, Buffalo, 1966, JD, 1969. Bar: N.Y. 1970, U.S. Dist. Ct. (we. dist.) N.Y. 1970, U.S. Ct. Appeals (2d cir.) 1972, U.S. Supreme Ct. 1974, U.S. Ct. Appeals (4th cir.) 1982, U.S. Dist. Ct. (no. dist.) N.Y. 1990. Pvt. practice, Orchard Park, N.Y. Confidential asst. to appellate divsn. 4th Dept., 1975-81; mem. N.Y. State Jury Selection Uniform Rules Task Force, 1977, Chief Judge's Drafting Com. Ct. Adminstrn. Stds. and Policies, 1977-78. Revision editor New York Appellate Practice, 1994, 95. With USN, 1958-62. Mem. N.Y. State Bar Assn. (com. cts. appellate jurisdiction, legis. policy com.), Erie County Bar Assn. (appellate practice com., practice and procedure in city, county and state cts. com., comml. and bankruptcy com.), Monroe County Bar Assn.

SCHULZ, MARIANNE, accountant; b. East Orange, N.J. d. Clifford W. Schulz; m. James A. Willits, Dec. 29, 1991; children: Lukas James, Laura Christine. BA in Bus., U. Wash., 1979. Cert. mgmt. acct. Contr. Farwest Spl. Products, Bellevue, Wash., 1974-88; acct. Lakeside Industries, 1988—. Mem. Inst. Mgmt. Accts. (bd. dirs. 1990-92, v.p. 1992-93).

SCHULZ, MICHAEL, physicist; b. Petoskey, Mich., July 14, 1943; s. Helmuth Martin Walter and Annette Elaine Marie (Steimel) Schulz. BS in Physics, Mich. State U., 1964; PhD in Physics, MIT, 1967. Physicist Nat. Bur. Stds., Washington, 1964—65; mem. tech. staff Bell Tel. Labs., Murray Hill, NJ, 1967—69; from staff scientist to sr. scientist The Aerospace Corp., El Segundo, Calif., 1969—93; staff physicist Lockheed Martin Advanced Tech. Ctr., Palo Alto, 1993—. Co-author (with L. J. Lanzerotti): (book) Particle Diffusion in the Radiation Belts, 1974; contbr. articles to profl. jours. Recipient Outstanding Alumnus award, Coll. Natural Sci., Mich. State U., 1983; fellow Grad. fellow, NSF, 1964—67; scholar Alumni Disting. scholar, Mich. State U., 1961—64. Fellow: Am. Phys. Soc.; mem.: European Geophys. Soc., Am. Geophys. Union (sec. for magnetospheric physics 1980—84). Home: 1037 Twin Oak Ct Redwood City CA 94061-1818 Office: Lockheed Martin Adv Technology Ctr Dept L9-42 Bldg 255 3251 Hanover St Palo Alto CA 94304-1187

SCHULZ, MICHAEL JOHN, fire and explosion analyst, consultant; b. Milw., Oct. 7, 1958; s. John F. and JoAnn E. (Carlson) S.; children: Kari L., Brian M. BS in Fire and Safety Engring. Tech., U. Cin., 1996; grad., U.S. Fire Adminstrn. Acad. Cert. fire and explosion investigator; cert. fire protection specialist; cert. fire investigation instr.; cert. fire svc. instr. II; cert. Can. fire investigator. Fire investigator Cedarburg (Wis.) Police Dept., 1979-90; capt., fire investigator Cedarburg (Wis.) Fire Dept., 1981-90; sr. staff expert John A. Kennedy & Assoc., Hoffman Estates, Ill., 1990-2000; pres. M.J. Schulz Assocs., Inc., 2000—. Cons. U.S. Fire Adminstrn.; instr. fire tech. and police sci. depts. Milw. (Wis.) Area Tech. Coll.; instr. fire sci. tech. dept. William Rainey Harper C.C.; lectr. in field. Author: Manual for the Determination of Electrical Fire Causes, 1988, Guide for Fire and Explosion Investigations, 1992, 95, 98. Recipient Common Coun. Commendation, City of Cedarburg, Wis., 1986; named Firefighter of Yr., Ozaukee County Assn. Fire Depts., 1985. Mem. ASTM, Nat. Assn. Fire Investigators (bd. dirs. 1987—, nat. cert. bd. 1987—, chmn. edn. com., editor The Nat. Fire Investigator, Man of Yr. 1991), Nat. Fire Protection Assn. (tech. com. on fire investigations 1985—, fire svc. sect., sect. rep. tech. com. on fire investigations 1985-92, sec. rep. nat. conf. on fire investigation instrn., mem. bd. dirs. fire sci. and tech. educators sect.), Fire Marshal's Assn. N.Am. (assoc.), Nat. Inst. Bldg. Scis. (reviewing mem. fire rsch. sub-com.), Bldg. Ofcls. and Code Adminstrs. Internat., Soc. Automotive Enmgrs., Human Factors and Ergonomics Soc., So. Bldg. Code Congress Internat., Internat. Bldg. Code Ofcls., Internat. Assn. Arson Investigators (John Charles Wilson scholarship award 1982), Ill. Chpt. Internat. Assn. Arson Investigators, Internat. Soc. Fire Svc. Instrs., Am. Soc. Safety Engrs., Nat. Conf. Fire Investigation Instrn. (bd. dirs.), Wis. Soc. Fire Svc. Instrs., Ky. Cols. Republican. Lutheran. Avocations: amateur radio, flying. E-mail: mjschulz@mjschulz.com.

SCHULZ, RALPH RICHARD, publishing consultant; b. N.Y.C., June 5, 1928; s. Harry and Margaret (Faecher) S.; m. Joyce S. Woolf, Sept. 9, 1951; children: Laura Stern, Barbara Tejerina, Susan. BS in Chemistry, CCNY, 1950. Asst. editor McLean-Hunter Pub. Co., Toronto, Can., 1950; assoc. editor McGraw-Hill Pub. Co., N.Y.C., 1951-60, mng. editor Chem. Week, 1960-68, editor-in-chief, 1968-73; dir. McGraw-Hill World News, 1973-76; v.p. editorial dept. McGraw-Hill Pubs. Co., 1976-84; sr. v.p. McGraw-Hill, Inc., 1985-92; pub. cons., 1992—; mng. dir. DeSilva & Phillips Inc., N.Y.C., 1994-2001. Adj. prof. Grad. Sch. Bus. Adminstrn., Fordham U., 1990-97. Author to numerous mag. on bus. and sci. Trustee Correspondents Fund, N.Y.C., 1979—; bd. dirs. Bus. Press Ednl. Found., N.Y.C., 1986-99, McGraw-Hill Found., N.Y.C., 1987-92, Copyright Clearance Ctr., N.Y.C., 1983-92. Petty officer USN, 1946-48. Recipient Honor award for disting. svc. in journalism Ohio U., 1972, Jesse H. Neal Editorial Achievement cert. of merit Am. Bus. Press, 1972. Mem. Am. Soc. Mag. editors (exec. com. 1984-88), Overseas Press Club Am. (bd. dirs. 1969-73), Nat. Press Club, Players Club (bd. dirs. 1974-78), Silurians, Sigma Delta Chi. E-mail: d5sag@aol.com.

SCHULZ, RAYMOND ALEXANDER, medical marketing professional, consultant; b. Paris, June 2, 1946; s. Helmut W. and Colette (Prieur) S.; m. Dixie Lee Suzanne Specht, Apr. 9, 1977 (div. Dec. 1990); children: Christopher, William; m. Casey Elizabeth Watson, Apr. 10, 1999; 1 child, Francis John. BA in Physics, W.Va. U., 1970; MS in Computer Sci., Columbia U., N.Y.C., 1975. Sr. programmer Meml. Sloan Kettering Cancer Ctr., N.Y.C., 1972-74; program coord. Neurol. Inst. Columbia Presbyn. Hosp., 1974-76; engring. mgr. EMI Med. Systems, Northbrook, Ill., 1976-78; product mgr. Johnson & Johnson (Technicare), Solon, Ohio, 1978-80; group product mgr. Siemens Corp., Iselin, N.J., 1980-82; mktg. mgr. Toshiba Am. Med. Systems (formerly Diasonics MRI), South San Francisco, 1983-92; dir. mktg. Voxel, Laguna Hills, Calif., 1992-98; v.p. mktg. and customer support Voxel, Inc., Provo, Utah, 1999—2000; prin. RA Enterprises, San Mateo, Calif., 2001—02; v.p. mktg. and sales Scanis, Inc., Foster City, 2002—. Bd. dirs. Dynecology, Harrison, N.Y.; presenter in field. Contbr. articles to Life mag. and profl. jours. Mem. St. Matthews Ch., San Mateo, Calif. Recipient first prize Roentgen Centenary Congress, 1995, Best Paper prize Am. Assn. Neurosurgeon/Cong Neurosurg. Brain Tumor Meeting, San Francisco, 2000. Mem. Am. Assn. Physicists in Medicine, N.Y. Acad. Scis., Internat. Soc. Magnetic Resonance in Medicine, Med. Mktg. Assn., Larchmont Yacht Club, Commonwealth Club Calif., Eta Kappa Nu. Avocations: skiing, running, hiking, swimming, mountainbiking. E-mail: ras257@columbia.edu.

SCHULZ, ROBERT ADOLPH, management educator, management consultant; b. Long Branch, N.J., Aug. 20, 1943; s. Robert Adolph and Anna Elizabeth (Fuga) S. BA in Math., St. Vincent Coll., Latrobe, Pa., 1965; BS in Mech. Engring., U. Notre Dame, 1966; MBA, U. Pitts., 1967; PhD in Bus. Adminstrn., Ohio State U., 1971. Rsch. asst. Tech. and Bus. Svcs., Ohio State U., Columbus, 1967-68; teaching asst. dept. mktg. Ohio State U., 1968-70; sr. assoc. Mgmt. Horizons, Inc., Columbus, 1970-71; dir. tech. edn. Mgmt. Horizons Data Systems, 1971-72, dir. edn., 1972-73; assoc. prof., Faculty of Mgmt. U. Calgary, Alta., Can., 1973-88, acad. dir. petroleum land mgmt. Can., 1983—, prof. mgmt. Can., 1988—. Coord. tchg. devel. office U. Calgary, Alta., 1991-98; pres. Scenario Mgmt. Cons. Ltd., Calgary, 1987—; bd. dirs. Wi-Lan, Inc. Chmn. align to 21st century task force Calgary Econ. Devel. Authority, 1989-92, bd. govs., 1994-96; chmn. coord. com. Calgary Cath. Diocese Synod, 1990-94, co-chmn. Synod implementation com., 1994-2001; bd. dirs. Calgary Sponsor and Refugee Soc., 1981-83. 3M Tchg. fellow, 1987; recipient awards for teaching and coaching acad. teams, Hon. Life Mem. award U. Calgary Students' Union, 1991, City of Calgary award for edn., 1995. Mem. Soc. for Teaching and Learning in Higher Edn., Can. Assn. Petroleum Landmen (hon.), Order of the U. Calgary, Beta Gamma Sigma. Roman Catholic. Avocations: golf, basketball, jogging. Home: 24-1815 Varsity Estates Dr NW Calgary AB Canada T3B 3Y7 Office: U Calgary Faculty of Mgmt Calgary AB Canada T2N 1N4

SCHULZ, SANDRA E. secondary art educator; b. Dallas, July 2, 1963; d. Lionel Leigh and Ida Maria Johanna Schulz. BS in Art Edn., Tex. Woman's U., 1985, MFA in Sculpture, 1990. Cert. tchr. art all levels, Tex. Clk. and advt. Bartos Inc., Dallas, 1982-90; art tchr. 7th and 8th grades Harry Stone Middle Sch., 1990-91; art tchr. 9-12th grades Thomas Jefferson H.S., 1992—. Art club sponsor, robotics team sponsor Thomas Jefferson H.S., Dallas. Chair publicity and decoration Tex. Cultural Partnership, Dallas, 1994-2001; publicity chair Am. Czech Culture Soc., Dallas, 1992-2001. Recipient Brookhaven Coll. Pyramid award for tchg., 2001, Tex. Senate Excellence award for outstanding tchrs. Mem. Nat. Art Educators Assn., Tex. Art Educators Assn., Dallas Art Educators Assn. (publicity chair 1996-98), Sculpture Assn. (sec. 1993-95), Dallas Rotary Club, 2002. Lutheran. Avocations: camping, fishing, gardening, music, electric trains. Home: 415 Woodhaven Blvd Duncanville TX 75116-2443 Office: Thomas Jefferson HS 4001 Walnut Hill Ln Dallas TX 75229-6239

SCHULZ, TAMELA J. social worker; BA in Social Work and Psychology, U. Dubuque, 1980; MSW, U. Ill., 1985. Lic. clin. social worker, Ill. Intake worker/adult svcs. worker Janet Wattles Mental Health Ctr., Rockford, Ill., 1980-83; social svc. cons. Med. and Surg. Assoc. of Park Ridge (Ill.), S.C., 1985-91. Recipient Mark Hale award for scholarship Univ. Ill. Sch. of Social Work, Urbana, 1985. Mem. NASW (qualified clin. social worker), Acad. Cert. Social Workers.

SCHULZ, WALTER KURT, accountant, information technology consultant; b. Hamburg, Germany, Apr. 9, 1940; came to U.S., 1970; s. Richard and Karla (Halm) S.; m. Beth Ann Edwards, June 21, 1972; children: Alec, Elli, Peter, Andrew, Heidi. MBA, U. Münster, Germany, 1969; M in Acctg., Ohio State U., 1972. Auditor Dr. Kaase, CPA, Bad Oeynhausen, Germany, 1966-71; systems analyst United Airlines, Chgo., 1973-77; v.p. fin. Eickhoff-Nat. Corp., Pitts., 1977-79; div. controller Mobay Corp., 1979-86; owner Infotek/Euronet, Inc., Charlotte, N.C., 1986—; cons. Penske Nascar Racing, Charlotte Hornets.

Cons. Westinghouse Corp., Mercy Hosp., Pitts, Charlotte Hornets. Lt. German Air Force, 1960-63. Mem. Am. Mgmt. Assn., Assn. MBA Execs. Republican. Avocation: flying. Home: 301 Sardis Rd N Charlotte NC 28270-2245 E-mail: wkschulz@compuserve.com.

SCHULZ, WILLIAM FREDERICK, human rights association executive; b. Pitts., Nov. 14, 1949; s. William F. and Jean Smith; m. Beth Graham, 1993. AB, Oberlin Coll., 1971; MA, Meadville/Lombard Theol. Sch., 1973, DMin, 1975, DDiv, 1987; MA, U. Chgo., 1974; DHL, Nova Southea. U., 1995. Minister First Parish Unitarian Universalist, Bedford, Mass., 1975-78; dir. social responsibility Unitarian Universalist Assn., Boston, 1978-79, exec. v.p., 1979-85, pres., 1985-93; exec. dir. Amnesty Internat. USA, 1994—. Bd. trustees Meadville/Lombard Theol. Sch., 1996—, chair 2000—. Author: Finding Time and Other Delicacies, 1992, In Our Own Best Interest: How Defending Human Rights Benefits Us All, 2001, Making the Manifesto: The Birth of Religious Humanism, 2002; (editor, contbr.): Transforming Words: Six Essays on Preaching , 1984; editor, contbr.: 2d edit., 1996. Named Humanist of Yr., Am. Humanist Assn., 2000. Mem. ACLU, Unitarian Universalist Mins. Assn., Coun. Fgn. Rels. Democrat. Home: 10 Castle Harbor Rd Huntington NY 11743-1209

SCHULZ, WILLIAM HENRY, transportation executive; b. Glen Cove, N.Y., Dec. 16, 1956; s. Henry C. and Elizabeth A. Schulz; m. Janet L. Goldstein. BA, U. Calif., Santa Barbara, 1979. Pres. sec. Calif. Dept. Ins., L.A., 1991-94; dep. pub. affairs dir. Dept. Trans., Washington, 1994-99, pub. affairs dir., 1999-2000; v.p. corp. comms. Amtrak, 2000—. Office: Amtrak 60 Massachusetts Ave NE Washington DC 20002-4285

SCHULZE, ARTHUR EDWARD, biomedical engineer, researcher; b. Richmond, Tex., Nov. 22, 1938; s. Arthur Dorwin and Ida (Bockhorn) S.; m. Sharon Kay Havemann, Sept. 2, 1962; children: Keith E., Mark A. BSEE, U. Tex., 1962, MSEE, 1963; MS Biomed. Sci., U. Tex., Houston, 1968. Registered profl. engr., Tex. Sr. aerosystems engr. Gen. Dynamics, Ft. Worth, 1963-67; rsch. assoc. U. Tex. Grad. Sch. Biomed. Scis., Houston, 1967-68; mgr., biomed. engr. SCI Systems, Inc., 1968-74; v.p. Telecare, Inc., 1974-79; gen. mgr. Tex. Sci. Corp., 1979-81; dir. R & D Narco Bio-Systems, 1981-84, pres., 1984-86; v.p. Lovelace Sci. Resources, Inc., Houston, 1986-92; pres. Healthcare Tech. Group, 1993—. Contbr. articles to sci. publs. Mem. IEEE, Aerospace Med. Assn., Assn. Advancement Med. Instrumentation, AAAS, Biomed. Technology Club. Avocations: photography, beekeeping. Home: 1819 Half Moon Dr Wharton TX 77488-9449 Office: Healthcare Tech Group 625 N Fulton St Wharton TX 77488-3941 E-mail: schulze@neosoft.com.

SCHULZE, ERIC WILLIAM, lawyer, legal publications editor, publisher; b. Libertyville, Ill., July 8, 1952; s. Robert Carl and Barbara (Mayo) S. BA, U. Tex., 1973, JD, 1977. Bar: Tex. 1977, U.S. Dist. Ct. (we. dist.) Tex. 1987, U.S. Ct. Appeals (5th cir.) 1987, U.S. Dist. Ct. (ea. and so. dists.) Tex. 1988, U.S. Dist. Ct. (no. dist.) Tex. 1989, U.S. Supreme Ct. 1989; bd. cert. civil appellate law Tex. Bd. Legal Specialization, 1990—. Rsch. asst. U. Tex., Austin, 1978; legis. aide Tex. Ho. of Reps., Austin, 1979-81; editor Tex. Sch. Law News, Austin, 1982-85; assoc. Hairston, Walsh & Anderson, Austin, 1986-87; ptnr. Walsh, Anderson, Brown, Schulze & Aldridge, Austin, 1988—, mng. ptnr., 1993—; editor Tex. Sch. Adminstrs. Legal Digest, Austin, 1986-92, co-pub., 1991—, mng. editor, 1992—. Editor: (legal reference books) Texas Education Code Annotated, 1982-85; editl. adv. com. West's Edn. Law Reporter, 1996—. Del. Tex. State Democratic Conv., 1982, Travis County Dem. Conv., 1982, 84, 86. Recipient Merit award for pubs. Internat. Assn. Bus. Communicators-Austin br., 1983, Merit award for authorship Coll. of State Bar Tex., 1992. Mem. Fed. Bar Assn., Am. Bar Assn., Tex. Bar Assn., Travis County Bar Assn., Bar Assn. of 5th Cir., Defense Rsch. Inst., Nat. Council Sch. Attys., Tex. Council Sch. Attys., Edn. Law Assn., Toastmasters (pres. Capital City chpt. 1995). Home: 3416 Mount Bonnell Cir Austin TX 78731-5745 Office: Walsh Anderson Brown Schulze & Aldridge PO Box 2156 Austin TX 78768-2156

SCHULZE, FRANZ, JR. art critic, educator; b. Uniontown, Pa., Jan. 30, 1927; s. Franz and Anna E. (Krimmel) S.; m. Marianne Gaw, June 24, 1961 (div. 1975); children: F. C. Matthew, Lukas; m. Stephanie Mora, 1992. (div. 1996). Student, Northwestern U., 1943; PhB, U. Chgo., 1945; BFA, Sch. Art Inst. Chgo., 1949, MFA, 1950; postgrad., Acad. Fine Arts, Munich, Germany, 1956-57. Instr. art Purdue U., 1950-52; chmn. dept. art Lake Forest (Ill.) Coll., 1952-58, artist-in-residence, 1958-61, prof. art, 1961—, Hollender prof. art, 1974-91; art critic Chgo. Daily News, 1962-78, Chgo. Sun-Times, 1978-85. Adj. prof. U. Ill., Chgo., 1996; Chgo. corr. in art Christian Sci. Monitor, 1958-62; art and arch. critic The Chicagoan, 1973-74; mem. vis. com. dept. art U. Chgo., 1974—. Author: Art, Architecture and Civilization, 1969, Fantastic Images: Chicago Art Since 1945, 1972, 100 Years of Chicago Architecture, 1976, Stealing Is My Game, 1976, Mies van der Rohe: A Critical Biography, 1985, The University Club of Chicago: A Heritage, 1987, Mariotti, 1988; editor: Mies van der Rohe: Critical Essays, 1989, Mies van der Rohe Archive, 1993; co-editor Chicago's Famous Buildings, 1993, Philip Johnson: Life and Work, 1994, A. James Speyer, Architect, Curator, Exhibition Designer, 1997, The Farnsworth House, 1997, (with Rosemary Cowler and Arthur Miller) Thirty Miles North, 2000; contbg. editor Art News, 1973—, Inland Architect, 1975-94; corr. editor Art in Am., 1975—. Trustee Ragdale Found., Lake Forest, 1981— . Recipient Harbison award for tchg. Danforth Found. of St. Louis, 1971, Excellence in Architecture award Ill. Inst. Tech., 1999; Adenauer fellow, 1956-57; Ford Found. fellow, 1964-65; Graham Found. for Advanced Studies in the Fine Arts fellow, 1971, 81, 93; NEH fellow, 1982, 88; Skidmore Owings & Merrill Found. fellow, 1983; recipient Disting. Svc. award Chgo. Phi Beta Kappa Soc., 1972; Hon. Mention Hitchcock Book award Soc. Archtl. Historians, 1987. Mem. AAUP, Coll. Art Assn. (bd. dirs. 1983-86), Archives Am. Art (adv. com.), Soc. Archtl. Historians. Office: Lake Forest Coll Dept Art Lake Forest IL 60045 E-mail: schulze@lfc.edu.

SCHULZE, RICHARD HANS, engineering executive, environmental engineer; b. Buffalo, May 28, 1933; s. Hans Joachim and Lucy (Kawczynska) S.; m. Jacqueline Van Luppen, Nov. 2, 1967 (div. Aug. 1979); children: Richard Hans Jr., Linda, John; m. Enika Grooters, Aug. 29, 1987. BSME, Princeton U., 1954; MBA, Northwestern U., 1958. Registered profl. engr., Tex. Rsch. analyst U.S. Steel Corp., Pitts., 1958-60; chief engr. G&H Rsch. and Devel., McKeesport, Pa., 1960-62; cons. Mgmt. and Mktg. Inst., N.Y.C., 1962-63, Ill. Inst. Tech. Rsch. Inst. mgmt. consulting divsn., N.Y.C., 1963-64; market analyst plastics divsn. Mobil Chem. Co., 1964-66; market devel. mgr. Mobil Chem. Co. (now PACTIV), Jacksonville, Ill., 1966-68, dist. sales mgr. Dallas, 1967-71; pres. Ecology Audits, Inc. (Core Labs.), 1971-74; pres., CEO, Trinity Cons., Inc., 1974-97, chmn. bd. dirs., 1997—, CEO, 2001—. Instr. over 200 short courses on dispersion modeling of air pollutants throughout world; vis. lectr. air quality Princeton U., 1998. Contbr. articles to Jour. of Air and Waste Mgmt. Assn., Atmospheric Environ., others; presented papers at sci. symposiums, seminars, confs. Mem. Dallas Symphony Assn., Mus. Art; bd. dirs. Dallas Opera, 1993—; elder Preston Hollow Presbyn. Ch., 1996-98; commr. to Grace Presbytery, 1996-98. Lt. (j.g.) USNR, 1954-56. Mem. ASME, TAPPI (air quality com.), Am. Acad. Environ. Engrs. (diplomate, trustee 2001—), Am. Chem. Soc., Am. Meteorol. Soc., Air and Waste Mgmt. Assn. (bd. dirs. 1986-89, 90-93, v.p. 1988-89, 1st v.p. 1990-91, pres. 1991-92, past pres. 1992-93, chmn. honors and awards com. 1996-97, vice chmn. planning com. 1999-2000), Soc. Petroleum Engrs. (chmn. environ. health and safety award com. 1994-95), Soc. for Risk Analysis, Verein Deutscher Ingenieure, Assn. Francaise des Ingénieurs et Techniciens Environ., Inst. Profl. Environ. Practice (qualified environ. profl., trustee 1993-95), Emissions Mktg. Assn., European Assn. for the Sci. of Air Pollution. Home: 7619 Marquette St Dallas TX 75225-4412 Office: Trinity Cons Inc 12801 N Central Expy Ste 1200 Dallas TX 75243-1791

SCHULZE, RICHARD M. retail electronics company executive; b. 1941; With No. States Sales Co., 1962-66; founder, chmn. Besy Buy Co., Inc., Eden Prairie, Minn., 1967—, CEO, 1967—2002. Office: Best Buy Co 7075 Flying Cloud Dr Eden Prairie MN 55344-3538*

SCHUMACHER, ANN, artist, educator; b. Kansas City, Mo., Jan. 28, 1946; d. George Davis and Mary Alice (Matchette) S.; m. Meir Shillor, Apr. 22, 1995. Student, Inst. for European Studies, Vienna, Austria, 1966-67; BA in Humanities, Kans. State U., 1968; diploma in Croatian lang., U. Zagreb, Croatia, 1969; MA in Internat. Rels., George Washington U., 1971; MFA in Textiles, Cranbrook Acad. Art, Bloomfield Hills, Mich., 1985. Head fgn. desk Croatia Cancer Soc., Zagreb, 1971-76; studio artist, translator, 1977-83; assoc. prof. art Berea (Ky.) Coll., 1985-95; full-time studio artist, 1995-2000. Lectr. Ohio State U., Lima, 1995, Ann Arbor (Mich.) Fiberarts Guild, 1996, Cranbrook Acad. Art, 1997, Mich. Handweavers' Guild, Detroit, 1997, 2000, Handweavers' Guild, Kalamazoo, 1997, Ctr. Creative Studies, Detroit, Woodland Weavers & Spinners Guild, Grand Rapids, Mich., 1999, Arts/Culture, Michigan, 2000; artist-in-residence Avondale Schs., Auburn Hills, 1996, Harrington Elem. Sch., Pontiac, Mich., 1997, Robert Frost Elem. Sch., Pontiac, 1998, Alcott Elem. Sch., Pontiac, Mich., 2000; condr. tapestry workshops Deemer House, Smicksburg, Pa., 1996, Detroit Inst. Art, 1996, Paint Creek Ctr. for Arts, Rochester, Mich., 1996, Imagine/Render Ctr., Oxford, Mich., 1996, Arrowmont Sch. Arts & Crafts, Gatlinburg, Tenn., 1997, Ctr. for Fiber Arts, Tarrytown, N.Y., 1997, Fiber Festival, Hastings, 1999, Mich. League Handweavers, Ontonville. Contbr. articles to profl. publs.; one-woman shows include Smokvin List Gallery, Groznjan, Croatia, 1978, Ulrich Gallery, Zagreb, 1981, Dars Gallery, Zagreb, 1983, East Hall Gallery, Ann Arbor, 1987-88, U. Ky. Art Mus., Lexington, 1987, Doris Ullman Gallery, Berea. 1987, 95, Worthington (Ohio) Arts Coun., 1989, Paint Creek Ctr. for Arts, 1996, Guild Gallery, Ann Arbor, 1996, Ctr. Regional d'Art Textile, Angers, France, 1999; exhibited in numerous group shows, including Hiestand Gallery, Miami U., 1988, Syntex Gallery, Palo Alto, Calif., 1991, Intimate Gallery, Ft. Collins, Colo., 1991, BASF Carpet Fibers, Dalton, Ga., 1991, 93, 95, Headley-Whitney Mus., Lexington, 1993, Hearst Ctr. for Arts, Cedar Falls, Iowa, 1993, Corvallis (Oreg.) Arts Ctr., 1994, 96, Textile Mus., Taichung, Taiwan, 1994, Pitts. Ctr. for Arts, 1995, 97, Wichita (Kans.) Ctr. for Arts, 1995, U. Ky. Art Mus., 1995, Ctr. for Visual Arts, Denton, Tex., 1995, Holter Mus. Art, Helena, Mont., 1995, 98, Tucson Mus. Art, 1995, Sullivan County Mus., Hurleyville, N.Y., 1996, Sandra Blain Gallery, Gatlinburg, Tenn., 1997, Canton (Ohio) Mus. Art, 1997, Fiberart Internat., Pitts., 1997, Muse of the Millennium, Nordic Heritage Mus., Seattle, 1998, Fiber Celebrated, Lincoln Ctr., Ft. Wilson, Colo., 1999, Woven Image: 20th Cent. Tapestry, Ukrainian Inst. Modern Art, Chgo., Grateful Threads, Delaplaine Visual Arts Ctr., Frederick, 1999, Am. Tapestry Alliance Bayeux Gallery, Denver, Jean Pail Slusser Gallery, Ann Arbor, Mich., Basilica of Assumption, Cincinnati, Ohio, Ella Sharp Museum, Jackson, 2000; exhbn. Fibuarts Internat., Pitts., 2001, Creative Arts Ctr., St. Charles, Ill., Texlile Ctr. of Minn., St. Paul, Fiber Celebrated, Hogan, Utah, 2001, Craft Forms, Wayne, Pa., 2001, Am. Tapestry Alliance, Richard Art Gallery, Vancouver, Can., 2002, Zoller Gallery, University Park, Pa., 2002, Convergence 2002, Vancouver (1st pl. award), JC Epstein Gallery, West Bloomfield, Mich., 2002, Alfred Berkowitz Gallery, Dearborn, Mich., 2002 (Best of Show). Recipient poster award Yugoslav Exhbn. Tapestries, 1982, 3d prize Salina (Kans.) Art Ctr., 1982, 1st runner-up Mose Pijade award Croatian Assn. Applied Arts and Design, 1982, 2d place award Focus: Tapestry of S.E., 1983, juror's commendation BASF 6th Nat. Fiber Arts Show, 1993, hon. mention Wichita Nat. 1995, award of excellence Am. Tapestry Alliance, 1995, Handweavers' Guild Am. award, 1997; Quaker Goodwill fellow, Croatia, Hungary, summer 1968, Fulbright-Hays fellow, India, 1987, Indo-Am. fellow, India, 1989-90, fellow in visual arts Ky. Found. for Women, 1992, 94; scholar George Washington U., 1969-71; grantee Cranbrook Acad. Art, 1983-85, Banff Art Ctr., 1985, Mich. Coun. for Arts and Cultural Affairs, 1997-2000; Dorcas Stevens award for handweaving/1st place 2D award, Fiber Celebration, Estes Park, Colo., 1998; recipent of Best of Show award, TLD Design Ctr., Westmont, Ill., 2001; Residency fellow Ragdale Found., 1997, 98; ArtServe Mich. Artist residency, 2000, third place award Mich. Ann. XXIX, Detroit, 2000. Avocation: foreign travel. Home: 3743 Eaton Gate Ln Auburn Hills MI 48326-3893 E-mail: annschumacher_2000@yahoo.com.

SCHUMACHER, CYNTHIA JO, retired elementary and secondary education educator; b. Sebring, Fla., Sept. 24, 1928; d. Floyd and Espage S. BA, Fla. State U., 1950, MA, 1951; MS, Nova U., 1978; postgrad., Fla. State U., 1968-69. English tchr. Grady County Sch. System, Cairo, 1951-53; elem. tchr. Brevard County Sch. System, Melbourne, Fla., 1953-55; elem. tchr., curriculum generalist, secondary tchr. Lake County Schs., Tavares, Fla. area, 1955-85; retired, 1985. Mem. Edn. Standards Commn., Fla., 1980-85, Quality Instrn. Incentives Coun., Fla., 1983-84. Author: (poetry) Seeds from Wild Grasses, 1988, Creekstone Crossings, 1993, Soul Candles, 1998, Wellspring Legacies, 2000; (poetry and stories) Butterfly Excursions, 1996; (children's books) Colorful Character, 1998, Searching for S, 1998. Pres. League of Women Voters of Lake County, 1989-91; mem. Lake Conservation Coun., The Nature Conservancy, Habitat for Humanity of Lake County. Named Fla. Tchr. of Yr., Fla. Fedn. Women's Clubs, 1966, Lake County Tchr. of Yr., Lake County Sch. Sys., 1985, East Cen. Fla. Tchr. of Yr. finalist, State of Fla., 1986; recipient Good Egg award, Leesburg Area C. of C., 1991, Lifetime Achievement award, Fla. Edn. Assn. United, 2000. Mem. Lake County Edn. Assn. (pres. 1971-72, cons. 1985—). Democrat. Roman Catholic. Avocations: environ. support activities, gardening, creative writing, macrobiotic cooking.

SCHUMACHER, H(ARRY) RALPH, internist, rheumatologist, medical educator, researcher; b. Montreal, Feb. 14, 1933; s. H. Ralph and Dorothy (Shreiner) S.; m. Elizabeth Jean Swisher, July 13, 1963; children: Heidi Ruth, Kaethe Beth. BS, Ursinus Coll., 1955; MD, U. Pa., 1959. Intern Denver Gen. Hosp., 1959-60; resident in medicine Wadsworth VA Hosp., L.A., 1960-62, fellow in rheumatology, 1962-63, Robert B. Brigham Hosp. and Harvard U. Med. Sch., Boston, 1965-67; chief arthritis-immunology ctr. VA Med. Ctr., Phila., 1967—; faculty mem. U. Pa. Sch. Medicine, 1967—, prof. medicine, 1979—, acting arthritis divsn. chief, 1978-80, 91-95, prof. orthopaedics, 1998—. Vis. scholar NIH, 1994-99; lectr. in field. Author: Gout and Pseudogout, 1978, Essentials of a Differential Diagnosis of Rhematoid Arthritis, 1981, Rheumatoid Arthritis, 1988, Case Studies in Rheumatology for the House Officer, 1989, Atlas of Synovial Fluid and Crystal Identification, 1991, A Practical Guide to Synovial Fluid Analysis, 1991, The Spondylarthropathies, 1998, Classic Papersin Rheumatology, 2001; editor: Primer on Rheumatic Disease, 1981—97, Jour. Clin. Rheumatology, 1994—; mem. editl. bd. Jour. Rheumatology, 1973—, Arthritis and Rheumatism, 1981—88, Revue du Rhumatisme (now Joint, Bone, Spine), 1992—, Internat. Jour. Clin. Practice, 1992—, New European Rheumatology, 1993—, Asian Pacific League Against Rheumatism Jour. Rheumatology, 1997—, Current Rheumatology Reports, 1999—, Indian Jour. Rheumatology, 2000—, Portuguese Jour. Rheumatology, 2000—; mem. editl. bd. Resident and Staff Physician, 2001—; contbr. articles to profl. jours. Pres. Eastern Pa. chpt. Arthritis Found., 1980-82; chmn., founder Phila. Garden Tours, 1987—; bd. dirs. Hemochromatosis Rsch. Found., 1984—, Am. Bd. Med. Advancement China, 1983-99. With M.C. USAF, 1963-65. Recipient VanBreeman award The Netherland Rheumatism Soc., 1988, Philip Hench award Assn. Mil. Surgeons, 1986, Hollander award Arthritis Found., 1996, Alumnus of Yr. Ursinus Coll, 1995, Sports Hall of Fame, 1997; Deposition VA grantee, 1967-95, NIH grantee, 1981, 94—. Fellow ACP; mem. AAAS, Am. Coll. Rheumatology (master; pres. Southeastern region 1981-82, Klemperer lectr. 2002), Phila. Rheumatism Soc. (pres. 1980), Phila. Electron Microscopy Soc. (chmn. 1975-76), Rheumatism Soc. Mex., Rheumatism Soc. Australia, Rheumatism Soc. Colombia, Rheumatism Soc. Chile, Rheumatism Soc. Republic of China, Rheumatism Soc. Argentina, Med. Soc. Argentina, Slovak Soc. Rheumatology, Fedn. Clin. Rsch. Office: Hosp U Pa 8 Penn Tower 3400 Spruce St Philadelphia PA 19104-4206 also: VA Med Ctr 151K Univ and Woodland Aves Philadelphia PA 19104 E-mail: schumacr@mail.med.upenn.edu. *I try to teach meticulous observation and questioning of dogma both in daily care of patients and in laboratory investigation of the poorly understood rheumatic diseases.*

SCHUMACHER, HENRY JEROLD, museum administrator, former career officer, business executive; b. Torrance, Calif., June 17, 1934; s. Henry John and Rene (Wilcox) S.; m. Barbara Howell, Aug. 24, 1958; children: Sheri Lynn, Henry Jerold II. Student, Stanford U., 1953; BS, U.S. Mil. Acad., 1957; MS, Northeastern U., Boston, 1965; MBA, Auburn U., 1977. Commd. lt. U.S. Army, 1958, advanced through grades to maj. gen., 1982; army attaché Moscow, 1969-71; chief communications ops. Vietnam, 1971-72; exec. officer Office Chief of Staff, 1972-75; comdr. U.S. Army Communications Command, Panama, 1977-79; dir. network integration, Office Asst. Chief of Staff Automation and Communications, Dept. Army, 1979-81; comdr. The White House Communications Agy., Washington, 1981-82; chief U.S. Army Signal Corps, 1981-83; ret., 1983; sr. v.p. Visa Internat., 1983-86; chief oper. officer Fuel Tech., Inc., Stamford, Conn., 1986-87; pres. IMM Systems, Phila., 1987-89; exec. v.p. Cylink Corp., Sunnyvale, Calif., 1990-95; exec. dir. Hiller Mus. of No. Calif. Aviation History, Redwood City, 1995-98; mng. gen. ptnr. Distributed Syss. Ptnrs., 1999—. Decorated Def. D.S.M., D.S.M., Legion of Merit. Home: 156 Normandy Ct San Carlos CA 94070-1519 E-mail: jerry57@attbi.com.

SCHUMACHER, JON LEE, lawyer; b. Rochester, N.Y., Feb. 28, 1937; s. Howard Alexander and Ruth S.; m. Katherine Truesdell, Apr. 22, 1967; children: Sara Wolff, Howard Alexander II. AB, Princeton U., 1959; JD, U. Va., 1964. Bar: N.Y. 1964. With Nixon Peabody LLP and predecessor firms, Rochester, 1964—; mem. mgmt. com. Nixon, Hargrave, Devans & Doyle, 1986-90, mng. ptnr., 1988-90. Co-author Charitable Giving and Solicitation. Bd. dirs., officer Rochester Area Found., Inc., 1987-94, United Way, 1986—; pres. estate planning Coun. Rochester, 1986-87. Fellow Am. Coll. Trusts and Estate Counsel; mem. N.Y. State Bar Assn. (exec. com. trusts and estates law sect. 1985-88, 94—, chmn. 1997, chmn. estate planning com. 1992-94), Monroe County Bar Assn. (found. pres. 1995-97), Country Club of Rochester, Genesee Valley Club. Republican. Presbyterian. Avocations: walking, opera. Home: 550 Allens Creek Rd Rochester NY 14618-3406 Office: Nixon Peabody LLP Clinton Sq PO Box 31051 Rochester NY 14603-1051 E-mail: jschumacher@nixonpeabody.com.

SCHUMACHER, JON WALTER, accountant, educator; b. Quincy, Ill., Jan. 11, 1955; s. Harold Herman and Mina Ruth (Zierk) S.; m. Diana Irene Andrews, Sept. 6, 1980; children: Lisa, Roberta. BS in Bus. Adminstrn., Calif. Poly. State U., San Luis Obispo, 1977. Tax/cost acct. Guy F. Atkinson Co., South San Francisco, Calif., 1977-79; mine acct. Pathfinder Mines, Inc., Jeffrey City, Wyo., 1979-80; cost engr. Stauffer Chem. Co. Wyo., Green River, 1980-84; mine acct. Summitville Cons. Mining Co., Del Norte, Colo., 1984-86; sr. acct. Kenneth Leventhal & Co., L.A., 1986-87; CFO Southwest Wyo. Rehab. Ctr., Rock Springs, 1987—. Asst. Vol. Income Tax Assistance Program, San Luis Obispo, 1976; v.p. Luth. Ch. Mission, Jeffrey City, 1980-81; helper Rock Springs (Wyo.) Food Bank, 1989. Recipient Disting. Leadership award Am. Biog. Inst.; named to Outstanding Young Men of Am., 1989. Mem. Assn. Retarded Citizens, Sweetwater Econ. Devel. Assn. Avocations: bicycling, guitar, model railroading, softball. Office: Southwest Wyo Rehab Ctr 4509 Foothill Blvd Rock Springs WY 82901-4367

SCHUMACHER, LARRY P. health facility administrator; b. Waseca, Minn., Apr. 26, 1959; s. James H. and Judith A. (Voight) S.; m. Casey A. Hager, June 26, 1982; children: Matthew, Nicholas, Nathan, Mark. Diploma, Burge Sch. Nursing, 1980; BSN, S.W. Mo. State U., 1983; MS in Nursing, Ind. U., 1985. RN, Iowa; cert. nursing adminstr. advanced, 1989. Dir. critical care and med. nursing Rsch. Med. Ctr., Kansas City, Mo.; v.p. nursing and anesthesia St. Joseph Mercy Hosp., Mason City, Iowa; v.p. patient care svcs. Mercy Hosp.; v.p. patient svcs., chief nursing officer North Iowa Mercy Health Ctr. Sr. vp. clin. integration, chief nursing officer, COO North Iowa Mercy Health Network; exec. v.p., COO Mercy Med. Ctry., Des Moines. Mem. ANA, Nat. League Nursing, Am. Orgn. Nurse Execs. Home: 6775 River Bend Dr Johnston IA 50131-1308 E-mail: lschumacher@mercydesmoines.org.

SCHUMACHER, MICHAEL JOHN, allergist; b. London, 1936; MBBS, U. Melbourne, Australia, 1960. Diplomate Am. Bd. Allergy and Immunology, Am. Bd. Pediatrics. Resident in pediat. Royal Children's Hosp., Melbourne, 1963-66; resident in allergy and clin. immunology Nat. Jewish Hosp., Tucson, 1969-72; fellow in immunology Inst. Med. Rsch., Melbourne, 1977-79; mem. staff Univ. Med. Ctr., Tucson, 1979—; chief allergy/immunology, assoc. prof. U. Ariz. Coll. Medicine, 1979—, prof., 1996—. Mem. Am. Acad. Allergy & Immunology. Office: Univ Ariz Health Sci Ctr Pediat 1501 N Campbell Ave Tucson AZ 85724-0001

SCHUMACHER, NANCY CARLISLE, writer; b. Tex., July 18, 1938; d. William Bass Thornton and Mary Wyrelle Roberts Beall; children: Norma Jane, Malinda Lea, JoAnna Lynn. AA in Edn., Lon Morris Jr. Coll., 1958; BS in Edn., Tex. Women's U., 1962. Cert. acct. Acct. U.S. Marines, Pearl Harbor/Camp Smith, Hawaii, 1965; file clk./receptionist U. Minn., Mpls., 1983-84; cons. Mary Kay Cosmetics, 1997—2002. Lectr. Epilepsy Found., Mpls., 1977-95. Author: The Special Children: A Mother's Point of View, 1977, Epilepsy, A Personal Approach, 1985; contbr. articles to profl. jours. Sec./newsletter person Hale Hoopika, NWCA, Barber's Point, Hawaii, 1972-76, Bloomington (Minn.) Assn. Children With Learning Disabilities, 1977-83; sec. Bloomington Archtl. Barrier Com., 1979-84; mem. Nat. Arts for the Handicapped, Minn., 1978. Mem. Am. Epilepsy Soc., Am. Med. Writer's Assn., Am. Med. Illustrators Assn. Episcopalian. Avocations: photography, drawing. Home and Office: 148 Everit St New Haven CT 06511 Fax: 203 865 2471. E-mail: Nschu38@aol.com.

SCHUMACHER, PAUL MAYNARD, lawyer; b. Columbus, Nebr., Apr. 4, 1951; s. Maynard Mathew and Rita Bell (Jarosz) S.; m. Michele Suzanne Gassé, June 26, 1976; children: Nicole Suzanne, Kristen Paulette. AA, Platte Coll., 1971; BS, Fort Hays U., 1973; JD, Georgetown U., 1976. Bar: Fla. 1976, Nebr. 1977, U.S. Dist. Ct. Nebr. 1977. Mem. staff U.S. Senate, Washington, 1974-76; sole practice Miami, Fla. and Columbus, 1976—; v.p. Community Lottery Systems, Inc., Columbus, 1990-92, pres., 1992—. V.p. Megavision Corp., Columbus, 1976—. Treas. prin. Rep. campaign com. U.S. Senate Candidate, Lincoln, Nebr., 1978-79; atty. Platte County, Columbus, 1979-87; chmn. Platte county Reps., 1988-94; mem. Nebr. Rep. State Ctrl. Com., 1994-96, 2000—; CEO Lotto Nebr., 1992—; CEO Cmty. Internet Sys., Inc., 1995-98, bd. dirs., 1995—. Mem. Nebr. Bar Assn., Fla. Bar Assn., Platte County Bar Assn. (pres. 1992-93), N.Am. Gaming Regulators Assn. (internat. gaming com.), Nat. Republican small bus. adv. council, Rotary, Elks. Roman Catholic. Avocation: physics. Home: 6255 Meyer Rd Columbus NE 68601-8044 Office: PO Box 122 Columbus NE 68602-0122 E-mail: pschumac@megavision.com.

SCHUMACHER, PHILIP GERARD, fundraising executive; b. Green Bay, Wis., Mar. 5, 1949; s. Peter John and June Elizabeth (Umberham) S.; m. Elizabeth Lucille Burke, Aug. 15, 1972 (div. Apr. 1985); children: Nicholas Philip, Eric Peter. BA, St. Norbert Coll., 1971; MA, St. Mary's U. Minn., 1974. Cert. fund raising exec. Tchr., coach Premontre H.S., Green Bay, 1971-73; assoc. dean students St. Mary's U. Minn., Winona, 1973-75, dir. residential life, 1975-77, v.p. student affairs, 1977-85; v.p. Maly & Co., 1985-87; dir. devel. Gundersen Med. Found., La Crosse, Wis., 1987-89; v.p. The Metanoia Group, Winona, 1989-90; dir. devel. St. Mary's U. Minn., 1989-90, v.p. instnl. advancement, 1990-93; exec. dir. devel. Gundersen Med. Found., La Crosse, 1993-96; grad. faculty St. Mary's U. Minn., 1994—; exec. dir. Gundersen Luth. Med. Found., LaCrosse, 1996—. Editor: Memoirs of Jean Pierre Schumacher, 1975. Vol. Minn. Pvt. Coll. Found., St. Paul, 1987-97; bd. dirs. Winona Cath. Schs., 1989-95; mem. nat. bd. visitors St. Mary's U. Minn., Winona, 1993—; bd. dirs. Riverfront, Inc. Mem. Assn. Fundraising Profls. (chpt. pres. 1993-95, nat. nominating com. 1997, nat. bd. dirs., vice chair member svcs., exec. com.), Winona Country Club, La Crosse Club, Rotary (com. mem.). Roman Catholic. Avocations: tennis, travel. Office: Gundersen Luth Med Found 1836 South Ave La Crosse WI 54601-5429 E-mail: pschumac@gundluth.org.

SCHUMACHER, ROBERT BOYCE, transit consultant, civil engineer; b. N.Y.C., Feb. 15, 1917; s. Ernest and Graycie (Boyce) S.; m. Eva H. Jasie, Feb. 20, 1948; 1 child, George, 1 stepchild, Edward Jasie. BSCE, Cooper Union, 1942; MSCE, Polytechnic, 1957; MS in Urban Planning, Columbia U., 1967. Registered profl. engr., N.Y. Engr. office design and field supervision heavy indsl. cons. various pvt. cons. firms, 1936-43, 46-56; civil engr., asst. to gen. mgr., asst. supt. structure dept. N.Y.C. Transity Authority, 1956-61; transp. planning engr. N.Y. State Office Transp., 1961-68; supr. inspectors of track & structures r.r. divsn. N.Y. State Pub. Svc. Commn., 1968-69; dir. mass transit planning N.Y.C. Dept. Transp., 1969-87; apptd. MTA Citizens Adv. Coun., 1985—; cons. transp. planning, 1987—. Home: 311 Packman Ave Mount Vernon NY 10552-1613

SCHUMACHER, ROBERT DENISON, banker; b. Evanston, Ill., Dec. 16, 1933; s. Frank Ade and Dorothy Ormonde (Hilton) S.; m. Mary Ann Montgomery, Aug. 25, 1956; children— Stephen Michael, Jeffrey Hilton. BA, Williams Coll., 1956; postgrad., Grad. Bus. Sch. N.Y. U., 1957-59; P.MD, Harvard Bus. Sch., 1966. With Irving Trust Co., N.Y.C., 1956-89, sr. v.p., 1977-89, mgr. adminstrv. services, 1987-89, ret., 1989. Treas. Calvary, Holy

Communion and St. George's Episcopal Ch., 1976-79, warden, 1980-86, 89-93, 2001—; trustee The Church Club, 1993—, treas., 1994-99. Mem. The Church Club. Republican. Home: 431 E 20th St New York NY 10010-7502 E-mail: rschumach@aol.com.

SCHUMACHER, STEPHEN JOSEPH, lawyer, educator; b. L.A., Feb. 5, 1942; s. Joseph Charles and Theresa Isabel (Flynn) S.; m. Jeanne Keller Schumacher, Sept. 29, 1990; children by previous marriage: William Scott, Stacey Elizabeth. AB, U. So. Calif., 1963; JD, Hastings Coll. Law, U. Calif., 1967; LLM in Taxation, NYU, 1969. Bar: Calif. 1968. Assoc. Stephens, Jones, LaFever & Smith, L.A., 1967-68, Wenke, Kemble & Burge, 1970-73; ptnr. Wenke, Taylor, Schumacher & Evans, Santa Ana, Calif., 1974-79, Schumacher & Evans, Costa Mesa, 1979-87; sole practice Orange County, 1987—. Instr. real estate taxation U. Calif.-Irvine, 1980-83. Bd. dirs. Orange County Opportunities Industrialization Ctr., 1973-75. Mem. ABA, Calif. Bar Assn., Orange County Bar Assn., Balboa Bay Club. Office: 4340 Campus Dr Ste 100 Newport Beach CA 92660-1812 E-mail: sjschu42@hotmail.com.

SCHUMACHER, SUSAN LOUISE, underwriter; b. Nashville, June 30, 1943; d. Robert Lynn and Elsie (Keiter) Vetters; m. Stanley Eversole Schumacher, Sept. 9, 1967. BA, Butler U., 1967. FLMI, FALU. Actuarial clk. Indpls. Life Ins. Co., 1964-67, Midland Mut. Life Ins. Co., Columbus, Ohio, 1967-74; sr. underwriter Nationwide Life Ins. Co., 1974-78, Puritan Life Ins. Co., Providence, 1978-80; sec. Pikeville (Ky.) Coll., 1980-81; re-ins. underwriter Lincoln Nat. Life Ins. Co., Millburn, N.J., 1981-87; underwriter Guardian Life Ins. Co., Bethlehem, Pa., 1987—. Avocations: knitting, walking, reading, travel. Home: 4606 Cheryl Dr Bethlehem PA 18017-8705

SCHUMACHER, THERESA ROSE (TERRY SCHUMACHER), singer, musician, legal assistant; b. Muskegon, Mich. d. Boles and Marguerite (Lassard) Pietkiewicz; m. Glenn O. Schumacher, 1968 (div. 1988); children: Pamela Harrington Boller, Daniel Mark Harrington. BS in Sociology, Fairmont State Coll., 1975. Mem. adv. com. W.Va. Dept. Agr. Active W.Va. U. Symphony Choir, 1988—, 93 Fairmont State Coll. Choir; musician with spl. knowledge of music from 1735-1850, Nat. Park Svcs., 1989—; appeared on W.Va. Pub. Radio. Mem. Bus. And Profl. Women Assn., W.Va. Poetry Soc., Morgantown, W.Va. Poetry Soc., W.Va. Writers, West Augusta Hist. Soc. W.Va. Avocations: special knowledge of cacti and succlents, storytelling, writing poetry, country and folk music. Home: PO Box 162 Mannington WV 26582-0162

SCHUMACHER, WILLIAM JACOB, retired army officer; b. Scranton, Pa., Apr. 15, 1938; s. Jacob and Kathryn Isabel (Williams) S.; m. Sandra Dee Caryl, July 23, 1960; children: Caryl Lee, Leslie Karen. BSEE, Lafayette Coll., 1960; MS in Aerospace Engring., Pa. State U., 1970. Commd. 2d lt. U.S. Army, 1960, advanced through grades to brig. gen., 1989; asst. prof. dept. engring. U.S. Mil. Acad., West Point, N.Y., 1970-73; student Def. Systems Mgmt. Coll., Ft. Belvoir, Va., 1975; asst. project mgr. Office of Project Mgr., Rock Island (Ill.) Arsenal, 1976-78; asst. mgr. conventional ammunition and guided missiles div. Cannon Arty. Weapons System, Picatinny (N.J.) Arsenal, 1978-81; comdg. officer Iowa Army Ammunition Plant, Burlington, 1981-83; student U.S. Army War Coll., Carlisle, Pa., 1983-84; project mgr. for Hellfire Missile U.S. Army Missile Command, Huntsville, Ala., 1984-87; program exec. officer Close Combat Missiles, 1987-88, Fire Support, Huntsville, 1988-90; dep. ammunition, asst. sec. army rsch., devel., acquisition Hdqrs. Army Materiel Command, Washington, 1990-92; dep. comdg. officer Strategic Def. Command, Huntsville, 1992; retired, tech. cons. Garber Internat. Assoc., Inc., Arlington, Va., 1992; gen. mgr. strategic systems Martin Marietta, 1992-96; exec. v.p. Bunyard Enterprises, Inc., Alexandria, 1996-2000; private cons., 2000—. Mem. Assn. U.S. Army, Nat. Def. Indsl. Assn., Phi Kappa Phi. Avocations: swimming, gardening, book collecting.

SCHUMACKER, RANDALL ERNEST, educational psychology educator; b. Oakes, N.D., May 26, 1951; s. Ernest and Helen (Jackson) S.; m. Joanne Cummins, July 24, 1952; children: Rachel Ann, Jamie Maureen. AA, William Rainey Harper Jr. Coll, Palatine, Ill., 1970; BS, Western Ill. U., 1972; MS, So. Ill. U., 1978, PhD, 1984. Rsch. asst. So. Ill. U., Carbondale, 1980-84, assoc. dir. computing, 1984-87; asst. prof. U. North Tex., Denton, 1988-90, assoc. prof., 1991-97, prof. ednl. tech. and rsch., 1998—. Adj. prof. med. edn. U. North Tex. Health Scis. Ctr., 1996—; vis. prof. So. Ill. U., 1980-84; vis. scholar U. Chgo., 1996; cons. Tex. Acad. Math. & Sci., Denton, 1993, Carrollton-Farmers Br., Tex., 1991-94, Profl. Devel., 1989-92; presenter in field. Author: Beginners Guide to Structural Equation Modeling, 1996, Advanced Structural Equation Modeling: Issues and Techniques, 1996, Interaction and Non-Linear Effects in Structural Equation Modeling, 1998, Understanding Statistical Concepts Using S-Plus, 2001, New Development and Technologies in Structural Equation Modeling, 2001; editor Structural Equation Modeling: A Multidisciplinary Jour., 1994-98; editor Multiple Linear Regression Viewpoints, 1998—; editor emeritus Structural Equation Modeling, 1999—; contbr. articles to profl. jours. Mem. Am. Psychol. Assn., Am. Ednl. Rsch. Assn., S.W. Ednl. Rsch. Assn., Am. Statis. Assn., Nat. Coun. Measurement Edn. Republican. Lutheran. Avocations: sailing, golf. Office: U North Tex Coll Edn PO Box 311337 Denton TX 76203-1137 E-mail: rschumacker@unt.edu.

SCHUMAKER, WILLIAM THOMAS, retired insurance company executive; b. Phila., Apr. 14, 1925; s. William John and Julia Ida Schumaker. BSc, Drew U., Madison, N.J., 1964, DD, 1980. Ordained to ministry Meth. Ch., 1974. V.p. New Amsterdam Casualty Co., Phila., 1947-59; gen. mgr. P.L.M. Ins. Co., 1959-79; min. Cortez (Pa.) United Meth. Ch.; chmn. Julia Ida Schumaker Found. Instr. Surety Bonds Ins. Soc. Phila., 1950-52; mem. adv. bd. P.L.M. Ins. Co., Phila., 1954-59. City ofcl. 34th ward City of Phila., 1955. Staff sgt. U.S. Army, 1943-46. Nat. acctg. fellow New Amsterdam Casualty Co., Phila., 1955, Paul Harris fellow Rotary of Nfld., Pa., 1990. Mem. Mensa. Avocations: antiques, stamp collecting. Home: 2978 Montgomery Tr Murrells Inlet SC 29576-8207 E-mail: karpadopol@aol.com.

SCHUMAN, GERALD EUGENE, soil scientist, researcher; b. Sheridan, Wyo., July 5, 1944; s. George and Mollie (Michael) S.; m. Mabel F. Kaisler, Mar. 27, 1965; children: William G., Kara L. BS in Soil Sci., U. Wyo., 1966; MS in Soil Sci., U. Nev., 1969; PhD in Agronomy, U. Nebr., 1974. Cert. profl. soil scientist. Soil scientist USDA Agrl. Rsch. Svc., Reno, 1966-69, Lincoln, Nebr., 1969-75, Cheyenne, Wyo., 1975-77, soil scientist, rsch. leader, 1977-98, soil scientist, 1998—. Reclamation cons. HKM Assocs., Billings, Mont., 1986-88; vis. fellow U. Westrn Australia, 1996-97. Co-editor: Reclaiming Mine Soils, 1987, symposium proc. Soil and Overburgen in Reclamation, 1983; contbr. articles to profl. jours., book chpts. Mem., pres., elder, trustee Our Savior Luth. Ch., Cheyenne, 1975—. Recipient Profl. of Yr. award Orgn. Profl. Employees of USDA, 1988; named Outstanding Alumnus, Coll. Agr., U. Wyo., 2000. Fellow: Soc. Range Mgmt. (Man of the Range award Wyo. sect. 1993, Outstanding Achievement award 1995), Soil and Water Conservation Soc. (bd. dirs. 1986—89, commendation 1980), Am. Soc. Agronomy (cert.), Soil Sci. Soc. Am.; mem.: Internat. Soil Sci. Soc., Am. Soc. Surface Mining and Reclamation (nat. exec. com. 1991—93, pres. 1992—93, Reclamation Rsch. award 1991). Avocations: fishing, hunting, traveling. Office: High Plains Grasslands Rsch Sta 8408 Hildreth Rd Cheyenne WY 82009-8809

SCHUMAN, MITCHELL A. ophthalmologist; b. Staten Island, N.Y., Apr. 25, 1952; BA, NYU, 1972; MD, N.Y. Med. Coll., 1975. Diplomate Am. Bd. Ophthalmology. Pvt. practice, Staten Island, N.Y., 1980—. Office: 1122 Richmond Rd Staten Island NY 10304-2402

SCHUMAN, PATRICIA GLASS, publishing company executive, educator; b. N.Y.C., Mar. 15, 1943; d. Milton and Shirley Rhoda (Goodman) Glass; m. Alan Bruce Schuman, Aug. 30, 1964 (div. 1973); m. Stanley Robert Epstein, June 14, 1997. AB, U. Cin., 1963; MS, Columbia U., 1966. Libr. trainee Bklyn. Pub. Libr., 1963-65; tchr. libr. Brandeis High Sch., N.Y.C., 1966; asst. prof. libr. N.Y. Tech. Coll., Bklyn., 1966-71; assoc. editor Sch. Libr. Jour., N.Y.C., 1970-73; sr. editor R.R. Bowker Co., 1973-76; pres. Neal-Schuman Pubs., 1976—. Vis. prof. St. John's U., Queens, N.Y., 1977-79, Columbia U., N.Y.C., 1981-90, Pratt Inst., 1993-2000, Syracuse U., 1997—; cons. N.Y. State Coun. on Arts, 1987, Office Tech. Assessment, U.S. Congress, 1982, 84, Coord. Coun. Lit. Mags., N.Y.C., 1987, NEH, 1980, Temple U., 1978-80; bd. visitors Sch. Libr. and Computer Studies Pratt Inst., 1987—; juror Best of Libr. Lit., 1980-88; mem. adv. bd. Sch. Libr. and Info. Studies, Queens Coll., 1989-91. Author: Materials for Occupational Education, 1973, 2d edit., 1983 (Best Edn. Book award 1973), Library Users and Personnel Needs, 1980, Your Right to Know: The Call to Action, 1993; editor: Social Responsibilities and Libraries, 1976; mem. editorial bd. Urban Acad. Libr., 1987-89, Multicultural Review, 1991-95; contbr. articles to profl. jours. Bd. dirs. Women's Studies Abstracts, Albany, N.Y., 1970-74, Pratt Inst. Sch. of Libr. and Info. Studies, 1993—, Ctr. for Publ., NYU, 1996—; mem. Com. To Elect Major Owens to U.S. Congress, 1983, N.Y.C. Mayor's Com. for N.Y. Pub. Ctr., 1984-85; pres. Met. Reference and Resources Coun./Met. N.Y. Libr. Coun. Recipient Fannie Simon award Spl. Librs. Assn., 1984, Disting. Alumni award Columbia U., 1992; U.S. Office Edn. fellow, 1969. Mem. ALA (councillor 1971-79, 84-88, exec. bd. 1984-88, 90-93, treas. 1984-88, chmn. legis. com. 1989-90, 94-96, chmn. internat. rels. com. 1998, 99, chmn. Libr. Advocacy NOW!, v.p., pres.-elect 1990-91, pres. 1991-92, Disting. Coun. Svc. award 1979, 88, Equality award 1993, hon. mem. Black Caucus, appreciation award 1993, Freedom to Read Found. Honor Roll 1999, Lippincott award for disting. svc. 2001), N.Y. Libr. Assn., Assn. for Libr. and Info. Sci. Edn., Spl. Librs. Assn . Office: Neal-Schuman Pubs Inc 100 Varick St New York NY 10013-1506 E-mail: pgs@neal-schuman.com.

SCHUMAN, STANLEY HAROLD, epidemiologist, educator; b. St. Louis, Dec. 29, 1925; married, 1952; 8 children. MD, Wash. U., St. Louis, 1948; MPH, U. Mich., 1960, DrPH, 1962; LLD (hon.), Clemson U., 1996. Diplomate Am. Bd. Pediatrics. Intern Jewish Hosp., St. Louis, 1948-49; resident Children's Hosp., 1950-51, Grady Hosp., 1953; clin. instr. pediatrics, sch. medicine Wash. U., 1954-59; from asst. prof. to prof. epidemiology, sch. pub. health U. Mich., Ann Arbor, 1962-73; prof. epidemiology in family practice, coll. medicine Med. U. S.C., Charleston, 1974—2002, prof. pediatrics, 1976—2002, prof. emeritus, 2002—. Med. dir. Agromedicine Program, Clemson and Med. U. S.C., 1984—. Author: Epidemiology, 1986, Environmental Epidemiology for the Busy Clinician, 1997, AG-MED, Rural Practitioner's Guide, 1997, User's Guide to Agromedicine, 2000; editor-in-chief Jour. Agromedicine, 1994—. Recipient Gov.'s Palmetto award for pub. svc., 2000, Man of Yr. award in S.C. Agr., Progressive Farmer Mag., 2000. Mem. Am. Epidemiol. Soc., Soc. Epidemiol. Rsch., Coun. Agrl. Sci. Tech., Am. Physicians' Poetry Assn., Sigma Xi. Achievements include research on pesticide health effects; field trials with young drivers; epidemiology in family practice; cancer of the esophagus, health effects of heat stress, fireant anaphylaxis, agricultural and occupational medicine. Home: 1019 Scottland Dr Mount Pleasant SC 29464-3612 Office: Med U SC Agromedicine Program 171 Ashley Ave Charleston SC 29425-0001

SCHUMANN, ALICE MELCHER, medical technologist, educator, sheep farmer; b. Cleve., Sept. 1, 1931; d. John Henry and Marian Louise (Clark) M.; m. Stuart McKee Struever, Aug. 21, 1956 (div. June 1983); children: Nathan Chester, Hanna Russell; m. John Otto Schumann, July 3, 1985. BS, Colby Coll., New London, N.H., 1953. Cert. tchr.; cert. med. technologist. Rschr. Lakeside Hosp., Cleve., 1953-54, Bambridge (Ohio) Schs., 1954-55, Shalersville (Ohio) Schs., 1955-56, Richtnior Sch., Overland, Mo., 1956-57; tchr. sci. Tonica (Ill.) H.S., 1956-58, Morton Grove (Ill.) H.S., 1958—60, U. Chgo. Lab Sch., 1960-65; co-founder Ctr. for Am. Archeology, dir. flotation rsch. U. Chgo. Campus, Kampsville, Ill., 1957-71, head supplies distbn., dir. food svcs. dept.; head mailing dept. Found. for Ill. Archeology, Evanston and Kampsville, 1971-83; sheep farmer, wool processor Gravel Hill Farm, Kampsville, 1983—. Vol. Mt. Sinai Hosp., Cleve., 1948-49; tchr. Title I Dist. 40, Kampsville, 1970-71. Recipient Beverly Booth award Colby Coll., 1953, 1st prize for hand spun yarn DeKalb County Fair, Sandwich, Ill., 1987, 88. Mem. Precious Fibers Found., Natural Colored Wool Growers Assn., Farm Bur. of Calhoun County. Avocations: wool growing, custom wash and spinning wool and cotton, knitting, raising Great Pyrenees guard dogs for sheep, gardening. Home and Office: Gravel Hill Farm RR 1 Box 121A Kampsville IL 62053-9720

SCHUMANN, DEBRAOH KAY, construction company executive; b. Tomball, Tex., Apr. 22, 1957; d. Erwin Herman Joe and Agnes Marie Mazac Seydler; m. Jerome A. Schumann, July 11, 1970; children: Richard Peter, Jerome Jr. AS, San Antonio Coll., 1994. Owner Double-D Cedar Yard, New Braunfels, Tex., 1983, Schumann Constrn., New Braunfels, 1945—. Inventor auto windshields, children's gameboards; author of short stories. Recipient Editor's Choice award Nat. Libr. Poetry, 1998. Mem. The McNay Arts, Toastmasters, Women's Power Group for CEO's, NAFE. Avocations: deer hunting, writing mysteries, golfing, fishing, hiking. Home: 403 River Bend Dr New Braunfels TX 78130-8964

SCHUMANN, J. PAUL, federal agency administrator; b. Kansas City, Mo., Dec. 10, 1937; s. Fred and Miriam E. (Penzotti) S.; m. Olva Kimmel Dorris, Dec. 23, 1960; 1 child, Robert Reynold. BA, MA, U. Miss., 1960; cert., Indsl. Coll. Armed Forces, 1966; PhD, U. Okla., 1982. Instr. polit. sci. Jacksonville (Ala.) State U., 1961-64; intelligence officer Missile and Space Intelligence Ctr., Huntsville, Ala., 1964-91, sr. intelligence officer, 1991-99, sr. intelligence analyst, 1999—. Adj. asst. prof. U. Ala., Huntsville, 1981—2001; pres. Tenn dept. Coun. on Am's Mil. Past, Huntsville, 1981—82. Contbr. articles to profl. jours. V.p. external affairs Jaycees, Jacksonville, 1963-64. Recipient achievement medal for civilian svc. U.S. Army, 1992, letter of commendation South Korean Def. Intelligence Agy., 1992; Dept. Def. scholar, 1971-72. Mem. Nat. Mil. Intelligence Assn., Am. Polit. Sci. Assn., Phi Alpha Theta, Phi Kappa Psi (treas. 1957-58), Pi Sigma Alpha. Avocations: military history, collecting books. Home: 8204 Willowbrook Cir SE Apt A Huntsville AL 35802-3335 E-mail: sch@msic.dia.mil.

SCHUMER, CHARLES ELLIS, senator; b. Brooklyn, N.Y., Nov. 23, 1950; s. Abraham and Selma (Rosen) S.; m. Iris Weinshall, 1980; children: Jessica Emily, Alison. BA magna cum laude, Harvard U., 1971, JD with honors, 1974. Bar: N.Y. 1975. Mem. staff U.S. Senator Claiborne Pell, 1973; assoc. Paul, Weiss, Rifking, Wharton and Garrison, 1974; mem. N.Y. State Assembly, 1975-80, chmn. subcom. on city mgmt. and governance, 1977, chmn. com. on oversight and investigation, 1979; mem. 97th-98th Congresses from 16th N.Y. Dist., 99th-105th Congresses from 10th (now 9th) N.Y. dist., Washington, 1985-98; mem. Banking & Fin. Svcs. Com.; ranking minority mem. jud. subcom. on crime; senator 106th Congress, N.Y., 1998—, senate com. on banking, housing and urban affairs, mem. judiciary and rules and adminstrn. Mem. B'nai Brith, Phi Beta Kappa. Democrat. Jewish. Office: US Senate 313 Hart Office Bldg Washington DC 20515-0001*

SCHUMM, STANLEY ALFRED, geologist, educator; b. Kearny, N.J., Feb. 22, 1927; s. Alfred Henry and Mary Elizabeth (Murdock) S.; m. Ethel Patricia Radli, Sept. 3, 1950; children: Brian Murdock, Mary Theresa, Christine Ann. BA, Upsala Coll., 1950; PhD, Columbia U., 1955. Research geologist U.S. Geol. Survey, Denver, 1955-67; prof. geology Colo. State U., Ft. Collins, 1967-86, Univ. disting. prof., 1986-98, acting assoc. dean, 1973-74, prof. emeritus, 1998—; prin. geomorphologist Mussetter Engring., 1995—. Vis. prof. U. Calif., Berkeley, 1959-60, U. Witwatersrand, South Africa, 1975; fellow U. Sydney, Australia, 1964-65, U. New South Wales, 1988; vice chmn. U.S. Nat. Com. Quaternary Rsch., 1967-70, 75-82; dist. vis. scientist U. tex., 1970; vis. lectr. numerous univs. in U.S., vis. scientist N.Z., Europe, Can., Venezuela, Brazil; vis. scientist Polish Acad. Sci., 1969; cons. to govt. agys., engring. firms; prin. geomorphologist, dir. Water Engring. Tech., Davis, Calif., and Ft. Collins, Colo., 1980-91; sr. assoc. Ayres Assocs., Ft. Collins, 1991-2000; prin. investigator rsch. projects NSF, 1969-92, Colo. Agrl. Expt. Sta., 1970-75, Army Rsch. Office, 1970-80, 82-93, Office Water Rsch. and Tech., 1974-83, Nat. Park Svc., 1975-77, Fed. Hwy. Adminstrn., 1978-80, Soil Conservation Svc., 1980-85, NASA, 1984-88, Smithsonian Inst., 1986-87, Can. Internat. Devel. Agy., 1991-92. Author: The Fluvial System, 1977, To Interpret the Earth, 1991; co-author: Incised Channels, 1984, Geomorphology, 1985, Experimental Fluvial Geomorphology, 1987, Active Tectonics and Alluvial Rivers, 2000; editor: United States Contribution to Quaternary Research, 1969, River Morphology, 1972, Slope Morphology, 1973, Drainage Basin Morphology, 1977, Physical Geography of W.M. Davis, 1980, The Variability of Large Alluvial Rivers, 1994; contbr. chpts. to sci. books, articles to profl. jours. Served with USNR, 1944-45. Recipient Disting. Alumnus award Upsala Coll., 1980, L.W. Durrell award Colo. State U., 1980, Linton award Brit. Geomorphology Rsch. Group, 1981, Warren prize NAS, 1986, Outstanding Paper award Soc. Sedimentary Geology, 1996; Harkness fellow U. Canterbury, N.Z., 1983; fellow Japanese Soc. for Advancement of Sci., 1983, Dept. Agr., Republic of South Africa, 1984, Australian Nat. U., 1988; named honor scientist Colo. State U. chpt. Sigma Xi, 1986, Frost lectr. U. Hull, 1999. Fellow AAAS, Geol. Soc. Am. (asso. editor 1973-75, vice chmn. geomorphology div. 1978-79, chmn. 1979-80, Kirk Bryan award 1979, Disting. Career award 1997); mem. Am. Geophys. Union (Horton award 1958, assoc. editor 1973-75), ASCE, Internat. Geog. Union, Assn. Am. Geographers, Internat. Assn. Quaternary Research, Am. Quaternary Assn. (councillor), Sigma Xi (pres. Colo. State U. chpt. 1987-88, honor scientist 1987). Home: 1308 Rollingwood Ln Fort Collins CO 80525-1946 also: Mussetter Engring 1730 S College Ave Fort Collins CO 80525-1073 E-mail: stans@mussei.com.

SCHUNDLER, BRET DAVIS, former mayor; b. Colonia, N.J., Jan. 14, 1959; s. Hans Otto and Gertrud (Droop) S.; m. Lynn Greenfield, Aug. 10, 1985; children: Shaylin Annedore, Hans Otto. Student, U. Haifa, Israel, 1980; BA in Sociology cum laude, Harvard U., 1981. Exec. asst. U.S. Congressman Roy Dyson, Washington, 1982-83; campaign organizer Gary Hart for Pres., 1983-84; instl. sales assoc. Salomon Bros., N.Y.C., 1984-87, C.J. Lawrence, N.Y.C., 1987-90; self-employed fin. mgr. Jersey City, 1990-92; mayor Jersey City, 1992—2001. Pres. Downtown Coalition of Neighborhood Assns., Jersey City, 1989; co-founder, co-chair Jersey City Coalition for Fair Taxation; Republican nominee for Gov. of N.J., 2001; elder Old Bergen Ch., 1989—. Republican. Presbyterian. Avocations: travel, boating, reading. Home: 299 Varick St Jersey City NJ 07302-4021 Office: 355 2nd St Jersey City NJ 07302

SCHUNK, MAE, state official; b. Greenwood, Wis., May 21, 1934; m. William Schunk; 1 child. BS in Elem. Edn., U. Wis., Eau Claire; MS in Gifted/Talented Edn., U. St. Thomas. Curriculum specialist, asst. prin., elem. tchr. various pub. schs.; enrichment specialist Phalen Lake Elem. Sch., St. Paul; lt. gov. State of Minn., 1999—. Mem. Minn. Exec. Coun.; chair Capitol Area Archtl. Planning Bd.; co-chair The Minn. Alliance with Youth, the NetDay Minn. Program, Minn. Office of Citizenship and Vol. Svcs. Avocations: flower and vegetable gardening, creative cooking and baking, stained glass, watercolor painting, fishing. Office: Office of Lt Governor 130 State Capitol Saint Paul MN 55155-0001*

SCHUNK, ROBERT WALTER, space physics research administrator; b. N.Y.C. BS, NYU, 1965; PhD in Phys. Fluids, Yale U., 1970. Fellow space physics Inst. Sci. and Tech., U. Mich., 1970-71; rsch. assoc. geophysicist Yale U., 1971-73; rsch. assoc. space physics U. Calif., San Diego, 1973-76; assoc. prof. Utah State U., Logan, 1976-79, prof. physics, 1979—. Mem. Com. Solar Terrestrial Rsch., Geophys. Rsch. Bd., Nat. Acad. Sci., 1979-82, Nat. Ctr. Atmospheric Rsch. Computer Divsns. Adv. Panel, 1980-83; prin. invester Solar Terrestrial Theory Program, 1980—. Assoc. editor Jour. Geophys. Rsch., 1977-80. Recipient Gov.'s Medal Sci. & Tech., Utah, 1988. Fellow Am. Geophys. Union; mem. AAAS. Home: Utah State U Ctr Atmospheric Space Logan UT 84322-4405

SCHUNKE, HILDEGARD HEIDEL, accountant; b. Indpls., Nov. 24, 1948; d. Edwin Carl and Hildegard Adelheid (Baumbach) S. BA, Ball State U., Muncie, Ind., 1971, MA in German/English, 1973, MA in Acctg., 1975. CPA, Ind., Calif. Exch. tchg. grad. asst. Padagogische Hochschule, Germany, 1971-72; tchg.ing grad. asst. in German and acctg. Ball State U., 1972, 74-75, asst. prof. acctg., 1975-78; investing rschr. Family Partnership, Muncie, 1977-83; staff acct. Am. Lawn Mower Co., 1984-88, G&J Seiberlich, CPAs, St. Helena, Calif., 1988-89, R.A. Gullotta, MBA, CPA, Sonoma, 1989-90; plant acct. Napa (Calif.) Pipe Corp., 1990—2001; software engr. Napa Oreg. Steel Mills, Napa, Calif., 2002—. ESOL instr. Napa County Project Upgrade, 1988-92; ticketing and refreshments com. North Bay Philharm. Orch., Napa, 1988—, North Bay Wind Ensemble, Napa, 1988— ; mem. TC 207 Tag Team. Mem. AICPA, Calif. Soc. CPAs (continuing edn. instr. Redwood City 1990, bd. dirs. East Bay chpt. 1998-2000), Inst. Internal Auditors, Am. Soc. for Quality. Avocations: gardening, transcribing, translating and reading German. Home: 1117 Devonshire Ct Suisun City CA 94585-3343 Office: Oregon Steel Mills 1025 Kaiser Rd Napa CA 94558-6257 E-mail: hschunke@Concentric.net.

SCHUPAK, DONALD, merchant banker, strategic planner, lawyer; b. N.Y.C., Apr. 2, 1943; s. Sidney and Helen (Smith) S.; m. Leslie Silverman, June 21, 1964 (div. 1981); children: Andrew, Jessica; m. Cynthia Saul, Nov. 19, 1981; children: Amanda, Philip Nicholas. BA, Syracuse U., 1964, JD, 1966; LLM in Taxation, NYU, 1970. Bar: N.Y. Assoc. various law firms, N.Y.C., 1966-70; ptnr. Schupak, Rosenfeld, Fishbein, et al, 1970-82; chmn. bd., chief exec. officer Donald Schupak and Co., Inc., 1982—, Safety Harbor Corp., N.Y.C., 1985-90. Vice chmn. Horn and Hardart Co., N.Y.C., 1977-88, chmn. bd., chief exec. officer, pres., 1988—. Mem. Assn. of Bar of City of N.Y., N.Y. Bar Assn., Phi Kappa Phi, Order of Coif. Clubs: Rombout Hunt (Hyde Park, N.Y.). Office: Danskin Inc 530 7th Ave New York NY 10018 also: Hardart Cons Co 730 5th Ave New York NY 10019-4105 also: Learn2.com Inc 1311 Mamaroneck Ave White Plains NY 10605

SCHUPAK, LESLIE ALLEN, public relations company executive; b. Spokane, Wash., Apr. 5, 1945; s. Leo and Henrietta (Neumann) S.; m. Dianne Barbara Goldin, June 23, 1968; 1 child, Adam J. BS, Boston U., 1967, MS, 1971. Asst. to pres., account exec. Sperber Assocs., Inc., Boston, 1968-69; account supr. Wilcox & Williams, N.Y.C., 1969-70; v.p., mgr. Daniel J. Edelman, Inc., 1970-72; mng. ptnr. Kanan, Corbin, Schupak & Aronow, Inc., 1972—. Pres. Whippoorwill Lake Property Owners Assn., Chappaqua, N.Y., 1984-88; chmn. exec. com. Coll. Comm., Boston U., 1997-2002. With U.S. Army, 1968-73. Mem.: Golf Writers of Am. Assn., Nat. Investor Rels. Inst., Donald Ross Soc., Met. Golf Writers Assn. (bd. dirs. 2002), Met. Golf Assn. (exec. com.), U.S. Golf Assn. (comms. com.), Desert Mountain Club (Scottsdale, Ariz.), Metropolis Country Club (White Plains, N.Y.). Avocations: golf; tennis. Home: 11342 E Salero Dr Scottsdale AZ 85262 Office: KCSA Worldwide 800 2nd Ave New York NY 10017-4709 E-mail: lschupak@kcsa.com.

SCHUPBACH, ROSA LECHNER, retired economist; b. Zurich, Switzerland, June 19, 1928; arrived in U.S., 1959, naturalized, 1966; d. Florian and Marie (Ozeler) Lechner; m. Edmund W. Schupbach, Dec. 27, 1967 (dec.). BS, Columbia U., 1967, MA, 1968, MEd, 1981. Jr. economist Caltex Petroleum Corp., N.Y.C., 1967—67; economist, legal asst. Anderson Russell Kill & Olick, 1971—77; rsch. asst. to prof. Fritz Machlup Dept. Econs. NYU, 1979—83; with Nat. Bur. Econ. Rsch., 1983—90; ret., 1990. Aux. police officer N.Y.C. Police Dept., 1980—; pres. East 74th St. Block Assn., 1980—. Mem.: NY Acad. Scis. Home: 20 E 74th St New York NY 10021-2654

SCHUPP, ANASTASIA LUKA, retired lawyer; b. Chgo. d. Joseph Anthony and Anastasia Maria (Romel) Luka; m. William Schupp, Apr. 20, 1968 (div. June 1994); 1 child, William Joseph. BS in Social Sci., Loyola U., 1966, JD, 1977; MA, U. Mich., 1968; Jagellonian, U. Sum., Poland, 1993. Bar: Ill. 1982, U.S. Supreme Ct. 1994. Law libr. Seyfarth, Shaw, Fairweather & Geraldson, Chgo., 1979-82; ptnr. Flader & Haces, 1982-85; pvt. practice, 1986—2001; assoc. Hyatt Legal Svcs., 1985—86, ret., 2001. Lectr. Chgo. Bd. Realtors, 1988—89, Robert Morris Coll., Orland Park, Ill., 1992, East West U. Chgo., 1992, Montay Coll., Chgo., 1994—95, acad. coun., 1994—95. Editor: An Ethnic Christmas, 1982; (newsletter) The Overture, 1980-81; contbr. articles to profl. jours. Vol. Chgo. Vol. Legal Svcs., 1991—95; arbitrator Chgo. Archdiocese, 1994—2000; atty. coord. Com. to Elect Richard J. Owens for Judge, Chgo., 1993—94. Recipient Honorable Mention Polish Arts Club, 1996. Mem.: Advs. Soc. (historian 1985—87), Chgo. Bar Assn., Womens Bar Assn. Ill. (chair com. 1982—95), First Cath. Scouak Ladies Assn., Chgo. Artists Coalition, Polish Arts Club of Chgo. (bd. dirs. 1999—2002). Democrat. Roman Catholic. Avocations: writing, exhibiting artist. Home: 5425 S Richmond St Chicago IL 60632

SCHUPP, PAUL EUGENE, mathematician, educator; b. Cleve., Mar. 12, 1937; s. Paul Eugene and Venna Marie Schupp; m. Elva Stewart, June 14, 1984 (div. June 14, 1984); 1 child Jerome Oliver William. BA, Case Western Res. U., 1959; PhD, U. Mich., 1966. Asst. prof. U. Wis., Madison, 1966—67, U. Ill., Urbana, 1968—71, assoc. prof., 1971—75, prof., 1975—, assoc. mem. Ctr. for Advanced Study, 1976—77. Vis. prof. U. London, 1982, U. Paris VII, 1984—92, U. Singapore, 1982, U. Bordeaux, 1984, 96; exch. vis. USA-USSR Nat. Acads. Sci. Exch. Program, 1982. Fellow, John Simon Guggenheim

Found., 1977—78. Mem.: Am. Math. Soc. Greek Orthodox. Home: 2007 Vawter Urbana IL 61801 Office: U Ill Dept Math Urbana IL 61801 Fax: 217-333-9576. E-mail: schupp@math.uiuc.edu.

SCHUPP, RONALD IRVING, clergyman, missionary; b. Syracuse, N.Y., Dec. 10, 1951; s. George August and Shirley Louise (Mitchell) S. Ordained ministry, The Old Country Ch., 1972; ordained Bapt. Ministry, 1976. Cert. Moody Bible Inst., 1986, 1988, Emmaus Bible Coll., 1996, 1997, Ctr. Biblical Counseling, 2001, Henry George Sch. of Soc. Sci.. Chgo., 2002; Advanced Cert. Evang. Tng. Assn., 1992. Missionary, asst. pastor The Old Country Ch. Inc., Chgo., 1972-76; missionary Solid Rock Bapt. Ch., 1976-89, Marble Rock Missionary Bapt. Ch. (Ch.-Lic. Pastoral Coun.) , Chgo., 1990—; field organizer and staff person Nite Pastor, 1972—78; Southern Culture Exchange, 1973—76; Alt. Christian Training Sch. Chgo., 1974—78; The Great Am. Coffeehouse, 1976—78; Chgo. Area Conf. on Hunger and Malnutrition, 1974—78. Asst. dir. Uptown Community Orgn, Chgo, 1974—76; dir. Chgo. Action Ctr, 1978—80; mem. Chgo. Clergy and Laity Concerned, 1981—87; Rep. Chgo. Welfare Rights Organ., 1986—88. Mem. Chgo. Coalition for the Homeless, 1988—99, vol. organizer, 1988—94, mem. empowerment adv. com., 1991—94; mem. steering com. 1st Congl. Dist. Ministerial Assn., 1993—95, chair housing com., 1993—95; Mem. Am. Assn. Christian Counselors , 2001—. Named Wa-Kin-Ya-Wicha-Ho Thunder Voice by trad. Lakota Elders, 1993, Kiyuyakki Northern Lights by Inuit Elder Etok, 1994; recipient Letter of Commendation, Chgo. Fire Dept., 1983, appreciation award, West Englewood United Orgn. / Clara's House Shelter, Chgo., 1992. Mem.: North Am. Shortwave Assn., AARP (life). Democrat. Avocation: radio. Home and Office: 6412 N Hoyne Ave Apt 3A Chicago IL 60645-5655 *Look inward to see your soul, look outward to serve God and humanity.*

SCHUR, MAXINE ROSE, marketing consultant, children's author; b. San Francisco; BA in Theater Arts, U. Calif., Berkeley, 1971; MA in Liberal Arts, Stanford U., 1999. Author: Hannah Szenes: A Song of Light, 1986 (Nat. Jewish Book award, 1986), 1999, The Circlemaker, 1994, The Marvelous Maze, 1995, When I Left My Village, 1996 (Sydney Taylor award, Joan Sugarman award), Sacred Shadows, 1997 (Nat. Jewish Book award finalist), The Peddler's Gift, 1999 (Sydney Taylor award). Mem. Soc. Am. Travel Writers, Soc. Children's Book Writers and Illustrators, Author's Guild. E-mail: mschur@promethod.com.

SCHUR, PETER HENRY, internist; b. Vienna, Austria, May 9, 1933; came to U.S., 1939; s. Max and Helen (Kraus) S.; m. Susan Dorfman, Sept. 3, 1963 (div. 1984); children: Diana, Erica. BS, Yale U., 1955; MD, Harvard U., 1958. Diplomate Am. bd. Internal Medicine, Am. Bd. Allergy and Clin. Immunology and Lab. Clin. Immunology. Intern, then resident Bronx (N.Y.) Mcpl. Hosp., 1958-62; postdoctoral fellow Rockefeller U., N.Y.C., 1964-67; instr., then assoc. prof. Harvard Med. Sch., Boston, 1967-81, prof. medicine, 1981—; sr. physician Robert B. Brigham Hosp., 1967-81, dir. clin. labs., 1970-81; dir. Clin. Immunology Lab. Brigham and Women's Hosp., 1981—; sr. physician, dir lupus clinic & rsch. Brigham & Women's Hosp., 1981—. Bd. dirs. Lupus Found. Am., Washington, 1979-89, pres. Mass. unit, 1989-93; bd. dirs. Arthritis Found., Atlanta, 1980-85. Editor: Clinical Management of Systemic Lupus Erythematosus, 1983, 2d edit., 1996; co-author: In Search of the Sun, 1989; editor Arthritis and Rheumatism, 1990-95, Up to Date in Rheumatology, 1995—; contbr. over 180 articles to med. and sci. jours. Capt. U.S. Army, 1962-64. Grantee NIH, 1967—, Lupus Found., 1975—. Fellow ACP; mem. Am. Soc. Clin. Investigation, Assn. Am. Physicians, Am. Coll. Rheumatology, N.Y. Acad. Sci. Office: Brigham and Womens Hosp 75 Francis St Boston MA 02115-6106

SCHUR, WALTER ROBERT, physician; b. Webster, Mass., June 17, 1914; s. Robert O. and Alma L. (Gatzke) S.; m. Delta Jean Newman, June 17, 1944; children: Paul, David, Jonathan, Ruth, Timothy, Peter, Stephen, Mary, Joel, Daniel, Rhoda. Student, Valparaiso U., 1931-34; MD, Middlesex U.Sch. of Med., 1940. Resident Milford (Del.) Meml. Hosp., 1940-41, Grace Hosp., Cleve., 1942-43; intern Luth. Hosp., 1941-42; pvt. practice Oxford, Mass., 1944—. Bd. dirs., pres. Doctors Hosp., Worcester, Mass., chmn. bd., 1978-87; bd. dirs. AdCare Hosp., 1987—, chmn. bd. dirs., 1987-91, Atlantic dist. Luth. Ch.-Mo. Synod, 1978-87, mem., sec. edn. com., missions com., 1960-77, mem. stewardship com., youth com., edn. com., 1951-57, chmn. edn. com. Atlantic dist., 1954-57, mem. commn. on mission and minitry in ch., named Dist. Layman of Yr., 1966, chmn. com. on ministry Atlantic dist., 1970; bd. dirs. Luth. Assn. Works of Mercy, assn. Evang. Luth. Chs.; bd. dirs. Valparaiso U., 1969-99, sec., 1984-99; pres., scholarship chmn. N.E. dist. Luth. Laymen's League, 1957; vice chmn. Luth. Hour Oper. Com., 1958, chmn., 1959-61; New Eng. bd. dirs. Assn. Evang. Luth. Chs., 1977-87, trustee East Coast Synod, 1977-87, mem. nat. bd. dirs., 1979-88; mem. coun. New Eng. Synod Evang. Luth. Ch. Am., 1988-94; bd. dirs., vice chmn. French River Edn. Ctr., 1985—; mem. Oxford Sch. Com., 1961-86, Mass. Commn. on Christian Unity; assoc. charter mem. Park Ridge Ctr., 1986. Recipient award of merit Internat. Luth. Laymen's League, 1963, Soli Deo Gloria award New Eng. Synod, Evang. Luth. Ch. Am., 1994. Fellow Am. Acad. Gen. Practice, Am. Acad. Family Physicians (charter); mem. AMA, Mass. Med. Soc., Worcester Dist. Med. Soc., Am. Geriatrics Assn., New Eng. Ob-gyn. Soc., Valparaiso U. Alumni Assn. (past pres.), Luth. Acad. for Scholarship (bd. dirs. 1977-86), Concordia Hist. Inst., New Eng. Luth. Hist. Soc. (charter), Internat. Platform Assn., New Eng. Huguenot Soc., Rotary (past pres.). Home: 168 Charlton St Oxford MA 01540-2008 Office: 367 Main St Oxford MA 01540-1746

SCHURE, ALEXANDER, university chancellor; b. Can., Aug. 4, 1920; s. Harry Joshua and Bessie (Ginsberg) S.; m. Dorothy Rubin, Dec. 8, 1943 (dec. June 1981); children: Barbara, Matthew, Louis, Jonathan; m. Gail Doris Strollo, Sept. 12, 1984. AST in Elec. Engring, Pratt Inst., 1943; BS, CCNY, 1947; MA, NYU, 1948, PhD, 1950, EdD, 1953; D in Engring. Sci. honoris causa, Nova U., 1975; DSc, N.Y. Inst. Tech., 1976; LLD, Boca Raton Coll., 1976, LI U., 1983; LHD, Columbia Coll., Calif., 1983; D of Pedagogy, N.Y. Chiropractic Coll., 1985. Asst. dir. Melville Radio Insts., N.Y.C., 1945-48; pres. Crescent Sch. Radio and TV, Bklyn., 1948-51, Crescent Electronics Corp., N.Y.C., 1951-55; founder, pres., CEO N.Y. Inst. Tech., Bklyn., 1955—82, chancellor, CEO, 1982-91, chancellor emeritus, 1991—; pres., CEO, chancellor The Univ. Fedn., Inc., 1995—; founder Computer Graphics Lab NY Inst. Tech., 1970-91; chancellor, CEO Nova U., 1970-86; mem. Fla. State Bd. Ind. Colls. and Univs., 1991—; pres. Vidbits, Inc., 1992, N.Y. Coll. for Wholistic Health Edn. and Rsch., Syosset, L.I., NY, 2000—. Cons. N.Y. State Dept. Edn., U.S. Office Edn., UNESCO; mem. Regents Regional Coordinating Council for Post-Secondary Edn. in N.Y.C., 1973—; mem., 1st inductee Nassau County Consortia on Higher Edn., L.I., 1971—, Alfred P. Sloan Found. adv. com. for expanding minority opportunities in engring., 1974; rep. to Nat. Assn. State Adv. Council, 1975—; chmn. N.Y. Title IV Adv. Council, 1975-77; mem. steering com. L.I. Regional Adv. Council, 1974—; chair Regents Adv. Council on Learning Techs., 1986-88; mem., trustee exec. com. Commn. Ind. Colls. and Univs.; mem. adv. council learning technologies N.Y. State Dept. Edn., 1982—; mem. Accreditation Task Force for Council on Postsecondary Accreditation/SHEEBO Project on Assessing Long Distance Learning Via Telecommunications (Project ALLTEL), 1982—; mem. N.Y. State Motion Picture and TV adv. bd., chairperson tech. com.; dir. numerous research projects; expert witness Ho. Reps. com. of Commn. on Sci. and Astronautics; mem. adv. coun. Fla. State Bd. Ind. Colls. and Univs.; vis. tech. exec. Hofstra U., L.I., N.Y., 1998, 99. Author and-or editor textbooks, film producer; designer automatic teaching machine; built one of first computer-controlled anthropomorphic speech devices, 1959; contbr. articles to tech. publs.; patentee in field. Pres. bd. dirs., trustee L.I. Ednl. TV Coun., Garden City; bd. dirs. Coun. Higher Ednl. Instns., N.Y.C., 1973-83; pres. The Univ. Fedns., Fla., 1995--. Served with Signal Corps AUS, 1942-45. 1st inductee Fine Arts Mus. of Long Island's Computer Hall of Fame, 1986. Mem. IEEE (L.I. sect. Gruenwald award 1988), N.Y. Acad. Sci., Am. Inst. Engring. Edn., N.E.A., Electronic Industries Assn. (chmn. task force curriculum devel.), Phi Delta Kappa, Delta Mu Delta, Eta Kappa Nu. E-mail: schure1ufi@aol.com. *The world is an ever changing, ever challenging reality, filled with opportunities for individual fulfillment and success. A positive philosophy toward life does much to make the realization of individual potential an actuality.*

SCHURE, MATTHEW, college president; b. N.Y.C., May 26, 1948; s. Alexander and Dorothy (Rubin) S.; m. Judith Z. Birchman, Aug. 12, 1973; children: Jared, Deborah. BA magna cum laude with high honors in Psychology, Queens Coll., 1969; MA, Columbia U., 1970, MPH, PhD, Columbia U., 1976. Lic. psychologist, N.Y. Mem. faculty N.Y. Inst. Tech., Old Westbury, 1969—, research assoc., instr., asst. prof., assoc. prof. behavioral scis., 1969-70, counselor, 1970-72, assoc. dir. Human Resources Devel. Ctr., 1973-77, assoc. dean acad. assessment, 1977-78, dir. Human Resources Devel. Ctr., 1978-81, pres., 1982—. Dep. provost, chmn. dept. community medicine N.Y. Coll. Osteo. Medicine, 1981-91. Author: Hannah's Trial: Our Triumph Over Infertility, 1981; contbr. articles and papers in field to profl. pubs. Trustee Commn. on Ind. Colls. and Univs., 1983-86, St. Barnabas Hosp., 1993-99, L.I. Regional Adv. Coun. on Higher Edn.; chmn. bd. trustees N.Y. State Higher Edn. Svcs. Corp., 1993-96; mem. N.Y. State Coun. on Problem Gambling, 1995; chmn. program com. Pvt. Industry Coun., Town of Oyster Bay; vice chair L.I. Works Coalition, 1999—. Mem. APA, Nassau County Psychol. Assn., Am. Assn. Colls. of Osteo. Medicine (chair, bd. govs.), Phi Beta Kappa. Office: NY Inst Tech PO Box 8000 Old Westbury NY 11568-8000

SCHURGIN, ROBERT DANIEL, television producer; b. Boston, June 10, 1968; s. Stanley Melvin and Judith Ann S.; m. Katherine Cassandra Conover, July 4, 1993; 1 child, Henry. BA in English Lit., Skidmore Coll., 1990. Prodr. Oliver Prodns., Washington, 1991-94; sr. prodr. New River Media, 1994-99, v.p. prodn., 1999-2001, COO, 2001—02. Supv. producer (television documentary) The Measured Century, 2000; producer, dir. (documentary) Omnibus: Television's Golden Age, 1999. Mem. Assn. Ind. Video and Filmmakers, Internat. Documentary Assn.

SCHURMAN, DAVID JAY, orthopedic surgeon, educator; b. Chgo., Apr. 25, 1940; s. Shepherd P. and Dorothy (Laskey) S.; m. Martha Ellen Rocker, Mar. 8, 1967; children: Hilary Sue, Theodore Shepherd. BA, Yale U., 1961; MD, Columbia U., 1965. Intern Baylor U., Houston, 1965-67; resident in gen. surgery Mt. Sinai Hosp., N.Y.C., 1966-67; resident in orthop. surgery UCLA, 1969-72; asst. rsch. surgeon UCLA Med. Sch., 1972-73; asst. prof. orthopedic surgery Stanford Med. Sch., 1973-79, assoc. prof., 1979-87, prof., 1987—. Acting chief divsn. orthop. surgery Stanford U. Med. Ctr., 1990-93, fellowship dir. total joint replacement, 1983—, fellowship dir. sports medicine, 1992-95, dir. orthop. rsch. lab., 1973—. Capt. USAF, 1967-69. Fellow NIH, 1972-73; grantee NIH, 1976-96; recipient Top Dr. award, San Francisco Mag. Mem. Am. Orthopaedic Assn. (bd. dirs. 1994-95), Clin. Orthopaedics and Related Rsch. (bd. dirs. 1994-00), Assn. Bone and Joint Surgeons (v.p. 1996-97, pres. 1997-98). Office: Stanford U Sch Medicine R144 Divsn Orthop Surgery 300 Pasteur Dr Palo Alto CA 94304-2203

SCHURMEIER, HARRIS MCINTOSH, aeronautical engineer; b. St. Paul, July 4, 1924; m. Bettye Jo, 1949; children: Harris Jr., Sydne, Dennis, Alan. BSME, Calif. Inst. Tech., 1945, MS in Aeronautcial Engring., 1948, Profl. Engr. in Aeronautics, 1949. Sr. rsch. engr. jet propulsion lab Calif. Inst. Tech., 1949-53, chief wind tunnel sect., 1953-56, chief aerodynamics divsn., 1956-58, dep. program mgr. sgt. missile, 1958-59, mgr. systems divsn., 1959-62, project mgr. Ranger, 1962-65; project mgr. Mariner Mars 69, 1965-69, Voyager, 1970-76; asst. lab dir. energy and tech. application Calif. Inst. Tech., 1976-81, assoc. dir. def. and civil programs, 1981-85; cons., 1985—. Mem. rsch. steering com. manned space flight NASA, 1959, rsch. adv. com. missile and space vehicle aerodynamics, 1960-62, com. project. mgmt., 1980-81; chmn. W. M. Keck Obs. Project Review Bd., 1986-95, Galileo Project Standing Review Bd., 1986-95, Soaring Soc. Am. Tech. Bd., 1989-94; Von Karman lectr. Am. Inst. Aeronaut and Astronaut, 1975. Served with USN, 1942—47. Recipient Exceptional Sci. Achievement medal NASA, 1965, Exceptional Svc. medal, 1969, Dist. Svc. medal, 1981, Astronaut Engr. award Nat. Space Club, 1965, 81. Fellow AIAA; mem. AAAS, NAE, Supersonic Tunnel Assn (chmn. 1954-56), Sigma Xi.

SCHURTER, RICHARD ALLEN, secondary school history educator; b. Pekin, Ill., Oct. 27, 1954; s. Henry K. and Helen V. (Adcox) S.; m. Vicki L. Stuber, June 21, 1975; children: Paul R., Michael A. BS in Edn., Greenville Coll., 1978; MS in Edn., Ill. State U., 1991. Tchr. Vandalia (Ill.) H.S., 1978-79; carpenter Ken Stuber Constrn., Tremont, Ill., 1979-81, R.A. Cullinan, Tremont, 1981-82; store mgr. Mcdonald's Corp., Pekin, Ill., 1982-83; adminstr. Hopedale (Ill.) Med. Complex, 1983-85; history tchr., chair dept. Pekin H.S., 1985—. Mem. adv. bd. Pekin Schs. Subject Area Com., 1994-97, Learning Cmty. 2000 Grant, Pekin, 1997-99. Supr. Tremont (Ill.) Township, 1989—; H.S. tchr. Northfield Christian Fellowship, 1990—, youth group advisor, 1993—. Ill. Tech. grantee, 1999-2000. Mem. ASCD, Christian Educators Assn. Avocations: camping, mountain biking, road biking, hiking, reading. Home: PO Box 422 Tremont IL 61568-0422 Office: Pekin Cmty H S 1903 Court St Pekin IL 61554 E-mail: rschurter@hotmail.com.

SCHURZ, FRANKLIN DUNN, JR. media executive; b. South Bend, Ind., May 22, 1931; s. Franklin Dunn and Martha (Montgomery) S.; m. Robin Rowan Tullis, Nov. 22, 1975 (div. 1985). AB, Harvard U., 1952, MBA, 1956, A.M.P., 1984. Exec. asst. South Bend Tribune, 1956-60, dir., 1971-76, sec., 1970-75, assoc. pub., 1971-72, editor, pub., 1972-82, exec. v.p., 1975-76, pres., 1976-82; asst. pub. Morning Herald and Daily Mail, Hagerstown, Md., 1960-62, pub., 1962-70, editor, 1966-70; pres. Schurz Communications, Inc., 1982—, treas., 1983-89. Bd. dirs. Atlantic Salmon Fedn., MSTV, CSPAN.. Chmn. Ind. Arts Commn., 1979-81; bd. regents St. Marys Coll., Notre Dame, Ind., 1977-83; chmn. adv. coun. Coll. Arts and Letters Notre Dame U., 1980-82; bd. dirs. Ind. Endowment Ednl. Excellence Inc., Indpls., 1987-90; mem. pres.'s coun. Ind. U., Bloomington, 1988-94; bd. dirs. C-Span, 1997—, MSTV, 2001—. 2d lt. U.S. Army, 1952-54. Recipient Presdl. Award of Merit Nat. Newspaper Assn., 1965, Frank Rogers award Rotary, South Bend, 1980 Mem. Am. Press Inst. (bd. dirs. 1985-94), AP (chmn. audit com. 1979-84), Chesapeake AP Assn. (past pres.), Md.-Del.-D.C. Press Assn. (past pres.), Hoosier State Press Assn. (past pres.), Newspaper Advt. Bur. (past bd. dirs.), South Bend Mishawaka Area C. of C. (pres. 1980-82), Am. Soc. Newspaper Editors, Am. women in Radio and TV (Found. hon. trustee 1996—), Inland Press Assn., Inst. Newspaper Fin. Execs. (past pres.), South Bend Country Club, Nat. Press Club, Soc. Profl. Journalists, MSTV (bd. dir. 2001-), C-SPAN (bd. dir. 1997-). Presbyterian. Home: 1329 Erskine Manor Hl South Bend IN 46614-2186 Office: Schurz Communications Inc 225 W Colfax Ave South Bend IN 46626-1000

SCHURZ, SCOTT CLARK, journalist, publisher; b. South Bend, Ind., Feb. 23, 1936; s. Franklin Dunn and Martha (Montgomery) S.; m. Kathryn Joan Foley, Aug. 5, 1967; children: Scott Clark, Alexandra Carol, John Danforth. BA, Denison U., 1957; LHD (hon.), Ind. U., 2000. Asst. instr. U. Md., 1957-58; adminstrv. asst. South Bend Tribune, 1960-66; circulation cons. Imperial Valley Press, El Centro, Calif., 1966; pres. Hoosier Times, Inc.; dir., v.p. Schurz Comms., Inc.; pub., editor-in-chief Martinsville (Ind.) Reporter-Times, Ind., Bloomington Herald-Times, Bedford Times-Mail, Mooresville The Times, Beech Grove Southside Times; pres. Kiva Telecomm., Inc. Pres., Bloomington Boys' Club, 1970-71, Jr. Achievement Monroe County, 1971-73; bd. dirs. United Way Monroe County, 1979-81, Cmty. Found. Area Arts Coun. Served with U.S. Army, 1958-60. Mem. World Assn. Newspapers (bd. dirs.), Internat. Newspaper Mktg. Assn. (pres. 1986, treas. 1997—), Inland Daily Press Assn. (pres. 1989), Newspaper Assn. Am. (bd. dirs. 1992-95), Inter-Am. Press Assn. (bd. dirs. 1995—), Hoosier State Press Assn. (pres. 1989, 97), World Press Freedom Com. (exec. com.), Internat. Press Inst., Newspaper Advt. Bur. (bd. dirs. 1987-92), Newspaper Assn. Am. Found. (pres.). Republican. Presbyterian. Office: Hoosier Times Inc 1900 S Walnut St Bloomington IN 47401-7720

SCHUSSHEIM, JOAN LANA, mathematician, educator; b. Montreal, Can., Aug. 4, 1940; d. Irving and Gertrude Yares; m. Arnold Schussheim, June 1, 1963; children: Abigail, Adam. AB in Math. magna cum laude, CUNY, 1961, MS in Edn., 1974. Tchr. math. enrichment lab. Roslyn Pub. Schs., 1974—76; tchr. remedial math. lab. Great Neck (NY) Pub. Schs., 1977—. Adj. prof. Hofstra U., Hempstead, NY, 1998; presenter at workshops and confs. in field. Contbr. articles to profl. jours. Mem.: Great Neck Tchrs. Assn., Nat. Coun. Tchrs. Math. Avocations: choral singing, reading, travel, piano, golf. Home: 24 Russell Woods Rd Great Neck NY 11021-4633 Office: Lakeville Sch 47-27 Jayson Ave Great Neck NY 11020

SCHUSSLER, IRWIN, psychiatrist, educator; b. Bklyn., Nov. 14, 1943; s. Jack and Fannie Yetta (Blank) S.; m. Myra Yvette Paget, June 26, 1966; children: Jeffrey Mitchell, Doreen Robyn, Kimberly Beth, Howard, Brian. BS, Bklyn. Coll., 1964; DO, Chgo. Coll. Osteopathic Medicine, 1968. Diplomate Am. Bd. Psychiatry and Neurology, Am. Bd. Gen. Psychiatry and Child Psychiatry, Am. Osteopathic Bd. Neurology and Psychiatry, Am. Bd. Sexology. Intern Interboro Gen. Hosp., Bklyn., 1968-69; resident in gen. psychiatry U. Fla. Coll. Medicine, Gainesville, 1972-74, asst. prof. psychiatry and pediatrics, 1976-77, dir. in-patient psychotherapy, 1976-77, fellow in child and adolescent psychiatry, 1974-76; fellow in human sexual medicine U. Pa., Phila., 1975; practice medicine specializing in psychiatry Ft. Worth, 1977-79; clin. assoc. prof., vice chmn. dept. psychiatry North Tex. State U. Health Scis. Ctr., Tex. Coll. Osteo. Medicine, 1979—. Pres. bd. dirs. Osteo. Med. Ctr. Tex., med. dir. psychiatry dept.; bd. dirs. Health Care Tex., Mental Health Assn.; pres. Osteo. Health Sys. of Tex. Contbr. articles to profl. jours. Bd. dirs. Mental Health Assn. Fellow Am. Coll. Neuropsychiatry, Am. Coll. Sexology; mem. Am. Psychiat. Assn., Am. Acad. Child Psychiatrists, Am. Acad. Clin. Psychiatrists, Am. Assn. Sex Educators, Counselors and Therapists, Tex. Soc. Psychiat. Physicians (pres. Tarrant County chpt.), Am. Osteo. Assn., Tex. Osteo. Med. Assn., Fla. Osteo. Med. Assn., Masters and Johnson Found. Jewish. Home: 3712 Myrtle Springs Rd Fort Worth TX 76116-9213 Office: Psychiat Cons Ft Worth 3704 Mattison Ave Fort Worth TX 76107-2619

SCHUSTER, BERTRAM, recruiter, management consultant, publisher; b. N.Y.C., Jan. 7, 1940; s. Harry and Lillian (Grossfield) S.; m. Zohara Teena Glassman, Mar. 16, 1980. BA, CUNY, 1986; postgrad., U. Pa. Sales dir. Franklin Mint, Franklin Center, Pa., 1971-74; nat. dir. AMR Internat., N.Y.C., 1974-77; pub., COO Vital Mag., Chgo., 1977-79; v.p. Morgan Stanley Dean Witter, 1980-86; mng. dir. Robbins Trading Co., 1986-91; pub., COO Futures Mag., Cedar Falls, Iowa, 1992-94; mgmt. cons. George S. May Internat., Inc., Park Ridge, Ill., 1994-96; pub., CEO Traveler Pub. Corp., Chgo., 1996—; ptnr. DHR Internat., 1998—. Author: The Insider's Edge, 1985; contbr. articles to profl. pubs. Bd. dirs. Winston Tower 1 Condominiums, pres., 1997-99. With U.S. Army, 1963-69. Mem. Managed Futures Trade Assn. (founding bd. dirs. 1985-88). Avocations: reading, music, race car driving, photography, swimming. Home: 6933 N Kedzie Ave Apt 316 Chicago IL 60645-2891 Office: DHR Internat Inc 10 S Riverside Plz Ste 2220 Chicago IL 60606-3703 E-mail: bschuster@dhrintl.net.

SCHUSTER, CARLOTTA LIEF, psychiatrist; b. N.Y.C., Sept. 16, 1936; d. Victor Filler and Nina Lincoln (Rayevsky) Lief; m. David Israel Schuster, Sept. 2, 1962; 1 child, Amanda. BA, Barnard Coll., 1957; MD, NYU, 1964. Cert. Am. Bd. Psychiatry and Neurology; cert. addiction psychiatry. Intern Lenox Hill Hosp., N.Y.C., 1964-65; resident St. Luke's Hosp., 1965-68; fellow Inst. Sex Edn., U. Pa., Phila., 1968-69; instr. N.Y. Med. Coll., N.Y.C., 1969-72; asst. attending Met. Hosp., 1969-72; assoc. attending St. Luke's-Roosevelt Hosp. Ctr., 1972-95; staff psychiatrist Silver Hill Hosp., New Canaan, Conn., 1972-95; clin. assoc. instr. Columbia U., N.Y.C., 1990-95. Chief substance abuse svc. Silver Hill Hosp., New Canaan, 1976-95; clin. faculty dept. psychiatry Sch. Medicine NYU, 1995—; dir. Recovery Clinic Bellevue Hosp., N.Y.C., 1995—. Author: Alcohol and Sexuality, 1988; co-author: Chapter in Advances in Alcohol and Substance Abuse, 1987; contbr. chpt. Mental Health in the Workplace, 1993. Mem. Am. Psychiat. Assn., Am. Med. Soc. on Addictions, Am. Acad. Addiction Psychiatry. Democrat. Jewish. Avocations: cooking, attending concerts, opera, films. Office: 207 E 30th St New York NY 10016-8230 E-mail: carlotta_schuster@msn.com.

SCHUSTER, DAVID J. entomologist, researcher; b. Memphis, Aug. 29, 1947; s. Michael I. and Jaunita F. Schuster; m. Jan M. Dreiling, Jan. 23, 1971; children: Brian, Scott, Amy. AS, Hutchinson Jr. Coll., 1967; BS, MS, Kans. State U., 1970; PhD, Okla. State U., 1973. Asst. prof. U. Fla., Bradenton, 1975—80, assoc. prof., 1980—85, prof., 1985—. Recipient Ann. Rsch. award, Fla. Fruit and Vegetable Assn., 1985. Mem.: S.C. Entomol. Soc., Ga. Entomol. Soc., Fla. State Hort. Soc. (Coun. Tomato Rsch. award 1981, 1984, 1990), Fla. Entomol. Soc. (pres. 1986—87, Achievement award for Rsch. 1989, Entomologist of Yr. 1993), Entomol. Soc. Am. (Excellence in Integrated Pest Mgmt. award, S.E. br. 2002). Republican. Roman Catholic. Avocations: fishing, hunting, photography. Office: Univ Fla GCREC 5007 60th St E Bradenton FL 34203 Office Fax: 941-751-7639. E-mail: dschuster@mail.ifas.ufl.edu.

SCHUSTER, E. ELAINE, lawyer; b. Oklahoma City, June 8, 1936; d. John Otto and Eula Delone (Campbell) Schuster. AB, Sweet Briar Coll., 1958; MA in Econs. and Fin., U. Okla., 1961, JD, 1968. Bar: Okla. 1968, U.S. Dist. Ct. (we. dist.) Okla. 1969, U.S. Dist. Ct. (no. dist.) Okla. 1981, U.S. Dist. Ct. (ea. dist.) Okla. 1991, U.S. Ct. Appeals (10th cir.) 1969. Prof. econs. Southeastern State U., Durant, Okla., 1961-65; assoc. Whitten & Whitten, Oklahoma City, 1968-71; asst. dist. atty. Oklahoma County, 7th Dist., 1972-78; ptnr. Jones, Schuster & Flaugher, Oklahoma City, 1978-82; prin. E. Elaine Schuster, P.C., 1982—. Lectr. in field. Mem. Oklahoma County Bd. Adjustment, 1978-97, chmn., 1984-97; citizen mem. profl. liaison com. City of Oklahoma City, 1980—; mem. bd. edn. Metro Area Career Tech. Sch. Dist., 1982—, Oklahoma City, pres., 1984-85, 91-93, 98-2000; mem. ch. bd. University Pl. Christian Ch., 1982-86, 89-92, elder, 1989-92, trustee, 1992; deacon, bd. dirs. Crown Heights Christian Ch., 2001—; bd. overseers Sweet Briar Coll., 1986-90; founding bd. dirs. Nat. Kidney Found. Okla., 1969-82. Named Outstanding Bus. Woman of Okla., Town Club of Bus. and Profl. women, 1986, Hon. All State Sch. Bd., Okla. State Sch. Bds. Assn., 1999, One of Fifty Women Making a Difference, Okla. Jour. Record, 1997, 2001; grantee GE, U. Va., 1963. Mem. Okla. Bar Assn. (del. 1996-97, 2000-01, alt. del. 1998-99), Oklahoma County Bar Assn. (bench and bar com. 1994-95, long range planning com. 1995-97, CLE com. 1999-2001, bd. dirs. 1997-2000), AAUW (br. pres. 1978-80, Okla. divsn. bd. 1969-75, 81-83, 85-87, Polished Diamond award S.W. Ctrl. Region 1987), Sweet Briar Coll. Alumnae Assn. (bd. dirs. 1986-90, 96-2001, region IX dir. 1996-2001), Kappa Beta Pi, Delta Kappa Gamma (hon.). Avocations: hiking, photography, travel. Office: Heritage Law Ctr 515 NW 13th St Oklahoma City OK 73103-2203 E-mail: eschuster@icnet.net.

SCHUSTER, ELAINE, civil rights professional; b. Detroit, Sept. 26, 1947; d. William Alfred and Aimee Isabelle (Cote) LeBlanc; m. James William Schuster, Sept. 6, 1969; 1 child, Cambrian James. BA, Wayne State U., 1972, postgrad., 1974-75, paralegal cert., 1991. Asst. payments Mich. Dept. Social Svcs., Detroit, 1972-73; rights rep. Mich. Dept. Civil Rights, 1973-80, 82-87, 90, asst. dir. div., 1987-90, supr., 1993-97, dir. Svc. Ctr., 1997-99, contract coord., 1999—; ct. adminstr. Chippewa-Ottawa Conservation Ct., Bay Mills, Mich., 1980-82; quality assurance coord. State Mental Health Facility, Southgate, 1991-93; acting interim dir. Mich. Indian Commn., Detroit, 1995. Author: Critique, An Indian Tours Michilimackinac, 1981; contbr. articles and poems to mags. and profl. jours. Bd. dirs. Tri-County Native Ams., Warren, Mich., 1982-89, sec. Native Am. Sesquicentennial subcom., Mich., 1987; mem. Linking Lifetimes, mentor program for Native Am. youth, 1992-93; sec., newsletter editor various civic orgns.; also other polit. and civic activities. Native Am. fellow Mich. State U., 1989. Mem. NAACP (housing com. S. Oakland br. 2000), ACLU (bd. dirs. Union-Oakland county 1987-88). Democrat. Avocations: exploring local historical and natural places of interest, historical re-enactment, research, fitness. Office: Mich Dept Civil Rights Cadillac Pl Ste 3-600 3054 W Grand Blvd Detroit MI 48202

SCHUSTER, GARY FRANCIS, public relations executive; b. Detroit, Jan. 26, 1942; s. Dwayne Alger and Mary Elizabeth (Cullen) S.; m. Barbara Anne Leopold, Aug. 30, 1968 (dec. Sept. 1999); children— Rory Anne, Reid Patrick. BS in Journalism/Psychology, Wayne State U., 1966. Gen. assignment reporter Royal Oak (Mich.) Tribune, 1966-68; gen. assignment reporter Detroit News, 1968-70, state capital corr., 1970-74, bur. chief, 1974-75, chief asst. city editor Detroit, 1975-76, city editor, 1976-77, news editor, 1977-78, Washington Bur. chief, 1978-85, White House corr., 1978-85, CBS News, 1985-86; pvt. practice media cons., 1986-87; v.p. corp. rels. Union Pacific Corp., 1987-2000; sr. v.p. comms. Cambridge Technology Ptnrs., 2000-2001, Novell, 2001—. Mem. White House Corrs. Assn. (pres. 1985-86). E-mail: gary.schuster@novell.com.

SCHUSTER, MARVIN MEIER, retired physician, educator; b. Danville, Va., Aug. 30, 1929; s. Isaac and Rosel (Katzenstein) S.; m. Lois R. Bernstein, Feb. 19, 1961; children: Roberta, Nancy, Cathy. BA, BS, U. Chgo., 1951, MD, 1955. Diplomate Am. Bd. Internal Medicine. Intern Kings County Hosp., Bklyn., 1955-56; resident Balt. City Hosps., 1956-58, Johns Hopkins Hosp.,

Balt., 1958-61; founder divsn. digestive disease Balt. City Hosps.; Janssen, Strauss Halbreich prof. emeritus medicine and psychiatry Johns Hopkins U. Sch. Medicine, Balt., 1976-97, chief digestive disease divsn.; dir. Marvin M. Schuster Ctr. for Digestive and Motility Disorders. Author: Gastrointestinal Disorders: Behavioral and Physiological Basis for Treatment; Keeping Control: Understanding and Managing Fecal Incontinence; editor: Gastrointestinal Motility Disorders, 1981, Atlas of Gastrointestinal Motility, 1st edit. 1994, 2d edit. 2002; mem. editl. bd. Gastroenterology, 1978-81, Gastrointestinal Endoscopy, 1979-81, Psychosomatics, 1979—, Am. Jour. Gastroenterology, 1993—; contbr. chpts. to textbooks and articles to profl. jours. Bd. dirs. Beth El Congregation, 1961-76, Am. Cancer Soc., 1975—, pres., 1984-86; chmn. med. adv. bd. Balt. Ostomy Assn., 1966—; chmn. phys. divsn. Assoc. Jewish Charities, 1961-76. Recipient St. George Disting. Svc. award Am. Cancer Soc., 1979. Fellow ACP, Am. Psychiat. Assn., Am. Gastroent. Assn. (master; chmn. audiovisual com. 1975-78); mem. AAUP, Am. Soc. Gastrointestinal Endoscopy (governing bd. 1975-78), Am. Coll. Gastroenterology (master, pres. 1996), Am. Physiol. Soc. Democrat. Jewish. Achievements include research on gastrointestinal motility and application of biofeedback to gastrointestinal control. Home: 10 Red Cedar Ct Baltimore MD 21208-6305

SCHUSTER, PHILIP FREDERICK , II, lawyer, writer; b. Denver, Aug. 26, 1945; s. Philip Frederick and Ruth Elizabeth (Robar) S.; m. Barbara Lynn Nordquist, June 7, 1975; children: Philip Christian, Matthew Dale. BA, U. Wash., 1967; JD, Willamette U., 1972. Bar: Oreg. 1972, U.S. Dist. Ct. Oreg. 1974, U.S. Ct. Appeals (9th cir.) 1986, U.S. Ct. Appeals (D.C. cir.) 2001, U.S. Supreme Ct. 1986. Dep. dist. atty. Multnomah County, Portland, Oreg., 1972; title examiner Pioneer Nat. Title Co., 1973-74; assoc. Buss, Leichner et al, 1975-76; from assoc. to ptnr. Kitson & Bond, 1976-77; pvt. practice, 1977-95; ptnr. Dierking and Schuster, 1996—; adj. prof. law Lewis & Clark Coll., 2002. Arbitrator Multnomah County Arbitration Program, 1985—; student mentor Portland Pub. Schs., 1988—. Author: The Indian Water Slide, 1999; contbg. author OSB CLE Publ., Family Law; contbr. articles to profl. jours. Organizer Legal Aid Svcs. for Community Clinics, Salem, Oreg. and Seattle, 1969-73; Dem. committeeman, Seattle, 1965-70; judge Oreg. State Bar and Classroom Law Project, H.S. Mock Trial Competition, 1988—. Mem. ABA, ATLA, NAACP (exec. bd. Portland, Oreg. chpt. 1979-98), ACLU, Multnomah Bar Assn. (Vol. Lawyers Project), Internat. Platform Assn., Alpha Phi Alpha. Avocations: river drifting, camping, swimming, walking, writing. Office: 3565 NE Broadway St Portland OR 97232-1820 E-mail: schuster@pcez.com. *Hard work and perseverence are the keys to accomplishing any goal. Protecting and nurturing our children and our environment are life's most noble goals. Success is the pursuit of these goals.*

SCHUSTER, ROBERT CONRAD, consulting engineer; b. St. John, Wash., July 17, 1935; s. Robert Charles and Alma Lydia (Schierman) S.; m. Marcia Sue Delaplain, Oct. 1, 1960; children: Robert Calvin, Douglas Westfield, Scott Alan. BSCE, Wash. State U., 1957. Registered profl. engr., Wash. Various positions Wash. State Dept. Transp., Seattle, 1958-67, dist. reconaissance engr. Yakima, 1967-70, dist. location engr., 1970-75, dist. adminstr., 1975-85, asst. sec. hwys. Olympia, 1985-89; engr. Sverdrup Civil, Inc., Bellevue and Olympia, Wash., 1990-99, Costa Mesa, Calif. Mem. Wash. Road Jurisdiction Com., 1985-89, Wash. Transp. Improvement Bd., 1988-89. Recipient Silver Beaver award Boy Scouts Am., 1984. Fellow ASCE. Methodist. Avocations: backpacking, golf, hunting. Office: Civil Inc 711 Capitol Way S Ste 700 Olympia WA 98501-1230

SCHUSTER, ROBERT PARKS, lawyer; b. St. Louis, Oct. 25, 1945; s. William Thomas Schuster and Carolyn Cornforth (Daugherty) Hathaway; 1 child, Susan Michele. AB, Yale U., 1967; JD with honors, U. Wyo., 1970; LLM, Harvard U., 1971. Bar: Wyo. 1971, U.S. Ct. Appeals (10th cir.) 1979, U.S. Supreme Ct. 1984, Utah 1990. Dep. county atty. County of Natrona, Casper, Wyo., 1971-73; pvt. practice law, 1973-76; assoc. Spence & Moriarity, 1976-78; ptnr. Spence, Moriarity & Schuster, Jackson, Wyo., 1978—. Trustee U. Wyo., 1985-89; Wyo. Dem. nominee for U.S. Ho. of Reps., 1994; polit. columnist Casper Star Tribune, 1987-94; pres. United Way Natrona County, 1974; bd. dirs. Dancers Workshop, 1981-83; chair Wyo. selection com. Rhodes Scholarship, 1989-98; mem. bd. visitors Coll. Arts and Scis., U. Wyo., 1991-2000; mem. Dem. Nat. Com., 1992-2000; chair Wyo. Pub. Policy Forum, 1992-98; mem. Wind River Reservation Econ. Adv. Coun., 1998-99. Ford Found. Urban Law fellow, 1970-71. Mem. ABA, ATLA, Wyo. Trial Lawyers Assn. Home: PO Box 548 Jackson WY 83001-0548 Office: Spence Moriarty & Schuster 15 S Jackson St Jackson WY 83001

SCHUTH, MARY MCDOUGLE, interior designer, educator; b. Kansas City, Mo., Jan. 19, 1942; d. William Darnall and Marie DeArmond (Meiser) McDougle; m. Howard Wayne Schuth, Sept. 4, 1965; 1 child, Andrew Wayne. BS in Interior Design, Comm., Northwestern U., 1964; cert. basic mgmt., U. Mo., 1966. Lic. interior designer, La. Interior designer Cottington's Interiors, Glen Ellyn, Ill., 1964-65, Robnett-Putman Interiors, Columbia, Mo., 1966-67, Nu-Idea Furniture Co., New Orleans, 1973, Maison Blanche, New Orleans, 1974-75, Mary M. Schuth Interior Design, Metairie, La., 1977—; instr. interior design divsn. continuing edn. U. New Orleans, 1973-97; instr. interior design non credit program Tulane U., 1998. Judge model homes U.S. Homes, Mandeville, La., 1978, Mandeville, 80; bd. dirs. Interior Design Adv. Com., Delgado Coll., New Orleans, 1981—2000; mem. Alpha Chi Omega Frat. housing rev. com., 1991—96; guest lectr. Delta Queen Steamboat Co., 1995—2001; lectr. ASID Super Campus for Longue Vue Home and Garden Tour, New Orleans, 2002. Co-author: cookbook From the Privateers' Galley, 1980; design work featured in profl. jours.; contbr. to Metairie Mag., 1993-94. Recipient 3rd place Batik Design Juried Art Show Columbia (Mo.) Art League, 1969. Mem. AIA (profl. affiliate), Am. Soc. Interior Designers (profl.), New Orleans Old Garden Rose Soc., Alpha Chi Omega Alumnae Club (New Orleans).

SCHUTT, ALLAN JACKSON, retired medical oncologist; b. Defiance, Ohio, Mar. 7, 1932; m. Ann H. Schutt, Sept. 8, 1956 (div. Mar. 1988); 1 child, John C.; m. Marcia L. Schutt, June 2, 1990. BA, Bowling Green State U., 1954; MD, Ohio State U., 1958. Diplomate Am. Bd. Internal Medicine, Am. Bd. Gastroenterology, Am. Bd. Med. Oncology. Intern Toledo Hosp., 1958-59; fellow in internal medicine and gastroenterology Mayo Found., Rochester, Minn., 1961-65; mem. staff Fargo (N.D.) Clin., 1965-69; assoc. prof. oncology Mayo Med. Sch., Rochester, 1969-94; locum tenens, 1994-99; ret. Bd. dirs. Bristlecome Home Care and Hospice, Frisco, Colo., 1997-2000. Mem. AMA, Am. Gastroenterol. Assn., Am. Assn. for Cancer Rsch., Am. Soc. Clin. Oncology, Optimists (pres. Breckenridge club 1996-98). Republican. Presbyterian. E-mail: SchuttAJ@aol.com.

SCHUTT, WALTER EUGENE, lawyer; b. Cleve., July 27, 1917; s. Erle Minchin and Elizabeth (Eastman) S.; m. Dorothy Louise Gilbert, Apr. 18, 1942 (dec. Mar. 2000); children: Gretchen Sue, Stephen David, Elizabeth Ann, Robert Barclay; m. Virginia Varley, Nov. 2, 2001. AB, Miami U., Oxford, Ohio, 1939; JD, U. Cin., 1948. Bar: Ohio 1948, U.S. Dist. Ct. (so. dist.) Ohio 1953, U.S. Supreme Ct. 1962, U.S. Tax Ct. 1983, U.S. Ct. Appeals (6th cir.) 1986. Pvt. practice, Wilmington, Ohio, 1948—; city solicitor, 1950-53. Mem. Wilmington Bd. Edn., 1958-65; chmn. Clinton County chpt. ARC, 1951-53; Wilmington chmn. Cin. Symphony Orch. Area Artists Series, 1969-71; trustee Wilmington Coll., 1962-74, sec. 1966-74; trustee Quaker Hill Found., Richmond, Ind., 1970-75, Friends Fellowship Cmty. Inc., 1986-93; rep. U.S. preparations com. 6th Internat. Assembly World Coun. of Chs., 1982. 1st lt. USAAF, 1943-46. Decorated DFC; recipient Disting. Svc. award Wilmington Jr. C. of C., 1953. Mem. Am. Bar Assn. (arms control and disarmament com. 1977-80), Ohio State Bar Assn., Clinton County Bar Assn. (past pres.), World Peace Through Law Ctr. Mem. Soc. of Friends (presiding clk. Friends United Meeting 1978-81, rep. to bd. Nat. Coun. Chs. of Christ 1985-96, presiding clk. Friends com. on nat. legis. 1984-87), Rotary. Home: 3043 W State Route 73 Wilmington OH 45177-9287

SCHUTTA, HENRY SZCZESNY, neurologist, educator; b. Gdansk, Poland, Sept. 15, 1928; came to U.S., 1962, naturalized, 1967; s. Jakub and Janina (Zerbst) S.; m. Henryka Kosmal, Apr. 29, 1950; children— Katharine, Mark, Caroline. M.B., BS, U. Sydney, Australia, 1955, MD, 1968. Jr. resident, then sr. resident St. Vincent's Hosp., Sydney, 1956-58; acad. registrar, house physician Nat. Hosp. Nervous Diseases, London, 1958-62; neurologist Pa. Hosp., Phila., 1962-73; asso. prof. neurology U. Pa. Med. Sch., 1963-73; prof. neurology, chmn. dept. SUNY Downstate Med. Center, Bklyn., 1973-80; prof. U. Wis. Med. Sch., 1980-98, chmn. dept. neurology, 1980-95, prof. emeritus, 1999; prof. neurology U. Ariz., Tucson, 2001—. Achievements include research on bilirubin encephalopathy, cerebral edema, degeneration and regeneration of muscle, history of medicine. Home: 35 Mountain View Ln PO Box 4692 Tubac AZ 85646 Office: U Hosp 600 Highland Ave Madison WI 53792-0001 E-mail: hsschutta@aol.com.

SCHUTTE, RICHARD DAVID, diversified financial services company executive; b. Corona, Calif., Sept. 25, 1954; s. Richard A. and Cory M. Schutte; m. Karen M. Schutte, Sept. 8, 1984; children: Laura M., Michael R. BBA in Acctg., U. Wis., Eau Claire, 1976. CPA. Audit. mgr. Ernst & Young, Milw., 1976-83; contr. Hytek Internat. Corp., Brookfield, 1983-86; asst. contr. Autotrol Corp., Milw., 1986-89; v.p. fin., CFO Manu-Tronics Inc., Kenosha, 1989-2000; CFO Accutec, Oak Creek, 2000—01, Microelectronic Modules Corp., New Berlin, 2001—. Mem. AICPA, Wis. Inst. CPAs, Kenosha Area Bus. Alliance, Fin. Execs. Inst. (bd. dirs. 1992-95, treas. 1996, sec. 1997, v.p. 1998, pres. 1999), Kenosha Health Care Ptnrs., Inc. (bd. dirs. 1994-95, treas. 1994, pres. 1995), Assn. for Corp. Growth. Avocations: reading, golf. Home: 2954 W Briarwood Dr Franklin WI 53132-9145 Office: Microelectronic Modules Corp 2601 S Moorland Rd New Berlin WI 53151 Office Fax: 414-761-1870. E-mail: rds@execpc.com.

SCHUTTER, DAVID JOHN, banker; b. Erie, Pa., Apr. 21, 1945; s. Donald John and Ruth Margaret (Hilbert) S. m. Ellen Carol Hoffman, June 18, 1967; children: David, Erica. BS with honors and distinction, Pa. State U., 1967; postgrad., Mich. State U., 1967-68, Ohio State U., 1973-75; cert., Stonier Grad. Sch. Banking, 1981. Asst. v.p. Huntington Nat. Bank, Columbus, Ohio, 1973-80; v.p. Ameritrust Co., Cleve., 1980-81, v.p., mgr. asset based lending dept., 1981-86, sr. v.p. secured lending div., 1986-89, dep. sr. loan adminstr., 1989-90, sr. cred. pol. off., 1990-92; sr. v.p., regional credit exec. Soc. Nat. Bank, 1992-94; exec. v.p., chief credit officer, 1994-97; exec. v.p., sr. lending officer Key Bank NA, Cleve., 1997—; exec. v.p., chief credit officer Key Corp., 2000—. Pres. AT Comml. Corp., 1986-96; panelist Robert Morris Assocs., Cleve., 1981, 93, mem., 1986—, Cleve. Bar Assn., 1986. Served to capt. U.S. Army, 1968-72. Mem. Nat. Comml. Fin. Assn. (bd. dirs. 1986—), Key Bank (dir., mem. exec. com., 2000—), Beta Gamma Sigma, Omicron Delta Epsilon. Office: Key Bank NA 127 Public Sq Cleveland OH 44114-1216 E-mail: david_schutter@keybank.com.

SCHUTZ, DONALD FRANK, geochemist, environmental corporate executive; b. Orange, Tex., Sept. 22, 1934; s. Theodore J. and Mildred Irene S.; m. Beatriz Valera, May 18, 1958; children: Delfino, Celita. BS in Geology cum laude, Yale U., 1956, PhD in Geology, 1964; MA in Geology, Rice U., 1958. Research staff geologist Yale U., New Haven, 1963-64; mgr. nuclear geochemistry dept. Teledyne Isotopes, Westwood, N.J., 1968-70, v.p., 1970-75, pres., 1975-93; engring. group exec. Teledyne, Inc., 1989-92; chief scientist Teledyne Environ. Systems, 1992-93; gen. mgr. Teledyne Brown Engring. Environ. Svcs., 1993—; v.p. Teledyne Environ., Inc., 1996-99; pres. Geonuclear, Inc., 1999—. Low level waste adv. com. N.J. Dept. Environ. Protection, Trenton, 1988-90; chmn. com. on radioactive materials N.J. BIA, Trenton, 1980-88. Pres. Children's Aid and Adoption Soc. N.J. Inc., Bogota, 1976-95, Am. Amateur Judo Found., River Vale, N.J., 1979-89; bd. visitors Berry Coll., 1985—; bd. dirs. Yale U. Alumni Fund, 1989-94; co-chmn. Children's Aid and Family Svcs. Inc., 1995-96, bd. dirs. emeritus, 2000—. Recipient Antarctic Service medal U.S. Congress, 1964. Mem.: Am. Assn. Engring. Soc. (engrs. forum on sustainable devel. 1995—), Am. Nuc. Soc. (chmn. no. N.J. sect. 1988—89, pub. policy com. 1991—96, coord. climate change and sustainable devel. activities UN 1994—, chair 1995—96, vice chair 2000—01, chair 2001—02, spl. com. on environ. coop. 2001—, bd. dirs.), Greening Earth Soc., Am. Assn. Radon Sci. and Tech. (life; pres. 1986—89, treas. 1990—95), Yale Sci. and Engring. Alumni Assn. (bd. dirs. Bergen County and vicinity chpt. 1989—), Sigma Xi. Office: Geonuclear Inc PO Box 163 Orangeburg NY 10962 E-mail: donald.schutz@aya.yale.edu.

SCHUTZ, JOHN ADOLPH, historian, educator, former university dean; b. L.A., Apr. 10, 1919; s. Adolph J. and Augusta K. (Gluecker) S. AA, Bakersfield Coll., 1940; BA, UCLA, 1942, MA, 1943, PhD, 1945. Asst. prof. history Calif. Inst. Tech., Pasadena, 1945-53; assoc. prof. history Whittier (Calif.) Coll., 1953-56, prof., 1956-65; prof. Am. history U. So. Calif., L.A., 1965-91, chmn. dept. history, 1974-76, dean social scis. and communication, 1976-82. Author: William Shirley: King's Governor of Massachusetts, 1961, Peter Oliver's Origin and Progress of the American Rebellion, 1967, The Promise of America, 1970, The American Republic, 1978, Dawning of America, 1981, Spur of Fame: Dialogues of John Adams and Benjamin Rush, 1980, 2001, A Noble Pursuit: A Sesquicentennial History of the New England Historic Genealogical Society, 1995, Legislators of the Massachusetts General Court, 1691-1780, 1997; joint editor: Golden State Series; contbg. author: Spain's Colonial Outpost, 1985, Generations and Change: Genealogical Perspectives in Social History, 1986, Making of America: Society and Culture of the United States, 1990, rev. edit., 1992, Encyclopedia Britannica. Trustee Citizens Rsch. Found., 1985—99; mem. Neighborhoodwatch, L.A., 1999—. NEH grantee, 1971; Sr. Faculty grantee, 1971-74; U. Calif. fellow, 1944-45. Mem. Am. Hist. Assn. (pres. Pacific Coast br. 1972-73, sec.-treas. 1951-88, 95-96), Am. Studies Assn. (pres. 1974-75), Mass. Hist. Soc. (corr.), New Eng. Hist. Geneal. Soc. (trustee 1988-2000, trustee emeritus 2001—, editor, author intro. book Boston Merchant Census of 1789, 1989, rec. sec. 1995—), Colonial Soc. Mass. (corr.). Home and Office: 1100 White Knoll Dr Los Angeles CA 90012-1353 E-mail: jschutz@rcj.usc.edu. *The excitement of collegiate activities makes each year an adventure in learning and a renewal of one's youth.*

SCHUTZ, ROBERTA MARIA (BOBBI SCHUTZ), social worker; b. Smithtown, N.Y., July 19, 1962; d. Robert N. S. and Janice (Sharpe) Taylor. BS, U. Utah, 1988, MSW, 1996. Lic. clin. social worker, Divsn. Occupl. and Profl. Licensing, Utah. Intern Salt Lake Rape Crisis Ctr., 1987-88, VA Med. Ctr., 1992, East Valley Mental Health, 1994-95, Obs. & Assessment. Divsn. Youth Corrections, 1995-96; behavior/employment specialist Columbus Cmty. Ctr., Salt Lake City, 1986-88; skills instr. Project TURN/Possibilities, 1987-90; indsl. unit supr. South Valley Tng. Co., Sandy, 1988-90; case mgr. Office Social Svcs./Divsn. Svcs. People with Disabilities, Midvale, 1990-91; DD/MR home & cmty.-based waiver specialist Dept. Human Svcs./Renevue Mgmt. Unit, Salt Lake City, 1991-93; case mgr. Dept. Human Svcs./Divsn. Svcs. People with Disabilities, Murray, 1993-96, social worker, 1996-97, Utah State Prison Dept. of Corrections, Draper, 1997—. Mem. Nat. Health Svc. Corps Utah State Prison, 2000—02. Author of poems. Mem.: NASW (Utah PACE com. 1995—, Utah bd. dirs. 1995—2000, Salt Lake City rep. 1996—98), Am. Assn. Mental Retardation (Utah bd. dirs. 1996—98). Democrat. Avocations: running, stamp collecting, reading, writing poetry. Office: Dept Corrections Utah State Prison PO Box 250 Draper UT 84020-0250 E-mail: bschutz@utah.gov.

SCHUTZIUS, LUCY JEAN, retired librarian; b. Cin., Dec. 27, 1938; d. Gregory Girard and Harriet Elsa (Wiggers) Wright; m. Paul Robert Wilson, Aug. 25, 1962 (div. 1968); 1 child Ellen Field ; m. William Carl Schutzius, Dec. 12, 1976; stepchildren: Christopher Matthew, Catharine Alexander, John Benedict, Margaret Elizabeth. BA in French, Middlebury Coll., 1960; MLS, U. Ill., 1963. Tech. libr. Chanute AFB, Rantoul, Ill., 1963-65; libr. Coll. Prep. Sch., Cin., 1969-74; pub. svcs. libr. Raymond Walters Coll., 1974-79, dir. libr., 1979-92, sr. libr., 1988—2001, sr. libr. emerita, 2001—. Access svcs. libr. U. Cin. Coll. Engring., 1992—2001. Mem.: Friends of Univ. Librarians. Home: 3444 Stettinius Ave Cincinnati OH 45208-1204 E-mail: lucy.wilson@uc.edu.

SCHUTZIUS, MARY JANE, volunteer activist; b. St. Louis, Mar. 12, 1931; d. Francis Xavier and Margaret Mary (Lavin) Krekeler; m. Robert Edward Schutzius, Dec. 11, 1969; children: Mary Jane Schutzius Horvath, Ann Marie Schutzius. AB in English, Fontbonne Coll., St. Louis, 1952; MA in Psychology, So. Ill. U., Edwardsville, 1979. Caseworker Mo. Divsn. Welfare, St. Louis, 1952-55; claims rep. Social Security adminstrn., Clayton, Mo., 1955-61; lay vol. Papal Vols. for L.Am., La Paz, Bolivia, 1961-68; tng. and devel. specialist Dept. of the Army, St. Louis, 1969-70; talk show host WGNU, 1986-95. Translator: (book) On the Holy Mountaintop, 1981; editor Diaspora quar., 1981-84; co-editor St. Louis W.I.L.P.F. Bull., 1995-97. Co-chair Women's Internat. League for Peace and Freedom, St. Louis, 1997—2001; mem. Bolivian Soc. St. Louis, treas., 1987—2001; pres. Ch. Women United, 1988—90, Mo. State Ch. Women United, 1992—96. Named Valiant Woman, Ch. Women United, 1991; named to Outstanding Young Women of Am., 1965; honoree Mo. Women's Network, 1997. Mem.: Missourians for Single Payer East (chair 1996—97, sec. 1998—99), Missourians for Single Payer (sec. 1997—99, vice-chair 2001—), Mo. Alliance for Campaign Reform (treas. 1996—2001), Fedn. Christian Ministries (pres. 1984—88), Women's Internat. League for Peace & Freedom. Roman Catholic. Home: 3150 Newgate Dr Florissant MO 63033-6218 E-mail: rschutz1@prodigy.net.

SCHUUR, DIANE JOAN, vocalist; b. Tacoma, Dec. 10, 1953; d. David Schuur. Ed. high sch., Vancouver, Wash. Singer: (albums) Pilot of My Destiny, 1983, Deedles, Schuur Thing, 1986, Timeless (Grammy award for female jazz vocal , 1986), Diane Schuur and the Count Basie Orchestra (Grammy award for female jazz vocal, 1987), Talkin' 'Bout You, 1988, Pure Schuur, 1991 (#1 on Billboard contemporary jazz chart, 1991, nominated for Grammy award , 1991), In Tribute, 1992, Love Songs, 1993 (Grammy nomination, Best Traditional Vocal, Grammy nomination for The Christmas Song); singer: (with B.B. King) Heart to Heart, 1994 (No. 1 on Billboard contemporary jazz chart); singer: Love Walked In, 1996, Blues For Schuur, 1997, The Best of Diane Schuur, 1997, Music Is My Life, 1999, Friends for Schuur; singer: (with Maynard Ferguson) 'Swingin' for Schuur, 2001; singer: (performances) White House, Monterey Jazz Festival, Hollywood Bowl, Carnegie Hall, Moscow Symphony, (tours) Japan, Far East, Near East, South Am., Europe, South Africa. Recipient 1st Ella Fitzgerald ann. award Montreal Jazz Festival, 1999, Helen Keller Personal Achievement award Am. Found. for Blind, 2000. E-mail: cantor15@aol.com. *"There is no plateau that can't be reached, no obstacle that can't be overcome if you believe in yourself and your higher power".*

SCHUUR, ROBERT GEORGE, lawyer; b. Kalamazoo, Dec. 5, 1931; s. George Garrett and Louise Margaret (DeVries) S.; m. Susan Elizabeth White, Sept. 28, 1968; children— Arah Louise Adele, Jeremiah Donald Garrett. A.B., U. Mich., 1953, LL.B., 1955. Bar: Mich. 1955, N.Y. 1956. Assoc. Reid & Priest, N.Y.C., 1955-65, ptnr., 1966— . Served with USN, 1956-58. Mem. ABA, N.Y. State Bar Assn., Assn. of Bar of City of N.Y., Phi Beta Kappa. Club: University (N.Y.C.). Home: 163 E 82nd St New York NY 10028-1856 Office: Reid & Priest 40 W 57th St Fl 28 New York NY 10019-4097

SCHUYLER, JANE, fine arts educator; b. Flushing, N.Y., Nov. 2, 1943; d. Frank James and Helen (Oberhofer) S. BA, Queens Coll., 1965; MA, Hunter Coll., 1967; PhD, Columbia U., 1972. Asst. prof. art history Montclair State Coll., Upper Montclair, N.J., 1970; assoc. prof. C.W. Post Coll., L.I. Univ., Greenvale, N.Y., 1971-73, adj. assoc. profl, 1977-78; coord. fine arts, asst. prof. York Coll., CUNY, Jamaica, 1973-77, 78-87, assoc. prof., 1988-92, prof. 1993-96, prof. emerita 1996—. Author: Florentine Busts: Sculpted Portraiture in the Fifteenth Century, 1976; contbr. articles to profl. jours. Mem. fine arts com. Internat. Women's Arts Festival, 1974-76; pres. United Cmty. Dems. of Jackson Heights, 1987-89. N.Y. Columbia U. summer travel and rsch. grantee, 1969; recipient PSC-CUNY Rsch. award, 1990-91. Mem. Coll. Art Assn., Nat. Trust for Hist. Preservation, Renaissance Soc. Am. Roman Catholic. Home: 35-37 78th St Jackson Heights NY 11372

SCHUYLER, MICHAEL ROBERT, librarian; b. Denver, May 21, 1949; s. Robert Julius and Mary Eugenia (Russell) S.; m. Virginia Pauline Gardner, June 5, 1977 (dec. Jan. 1995); 1 child, Linnea Gardner; m. Carol Jean Rice, May 21, 1996. BA, U. Wash., 1971, ML, 1974. CNE. Adult services librarian Kitsap Regional Library, Bremerton, Wash., 1977-81, chief, support services, 1981—; info. systems analyst Zimmerman & Assoc., Poulsbo, Wash., 1980-81. Juror Am. Book awards, 1981; cons. in field, 1981—. Author: (software) Readability, 1973, Member Tender, 1985, Now What? How to Get Your System Up and Keep It Running, 1988, Librarian's Guide To PC Management, 1990, Dial-In, 1991, An Annual Guide to Library On Line Public Access Catalogs In North America, The Systems Librarian Guide to Computers, 1990; reviewer Libr. Jour., 1977-84; columnist The Bit Bucket, 1985; editor, pub. Systems Libr. and Automation Rev., 1986-89; assoc. editor Computers in Librs., 1989; contbr. articles to profl. jours. Named MCI Cybrarian of Yr., 1998. Mem. Wash. Library Assn. (sec. 1979-81), ALA. Home: 11254 Fieldstone Ln NE Bainbridge Island WA 98110-4282 Office: Kitsap Regional Libr 1301 Sylvan Way Bremerton WA 98310-3498 E-mail: michael@krl.org.

SCHUYLER, ROBERT L. anthropologist, archaeologist; b. New Haven, Sept. 13, 1941; BA, U. Ariz., 1964; MA, U. Calif., Santa Barbara, 1968; PhD, U. Calif., 1974. Registered profl. archaeologist. Lectr. U. Md., College Park, 1969-70; instr. City Coll. N.Y., N.Y.C., 1970-74, asst. prof., 1974-79; assoc. prof., assoc. curator U. Pa., Phila., 1980—. Editor: Historical Archaeology: A Guide to Substantive and Theoretical Contributions, 1978, Archaeological Perspectives on Ethnicity in America: Afro-American and Asian American Culture History, 1980; founding editor North Am. Archaeologist, 1979-82. Mem. Soc. Historical Archaeology (pres. 1982), Coun. for Northeast Historical Archaeology (pres. 1980). Democrat. Office: Univ Pa Museum 33rd and Spruce Sts Philadelphia PA 19104 E-mail: schuyler@sas.upenn.edu.

SCHWAAB, RICHARD LEWIS, lawyer, educator; b. Oconomowoc, Wis., Nov. 15, 1945; s. Thomas L. and Phyllis N. (Lord) S.; m. Lynn Louise Howie; children: Amy, William, Andrew, Matthew. BSChemE, U. Wis., 1967; JD with honors, George Washington U., 1971, LLM in Internat. Law with highest honors, 1979. Bar: Va. 1971, U.S. Dist. Ct. (ea. dist.) Va. 1979, U.S. Supreme Ct. 1980, U.S. Ct. Appeals (fed. cir.) 1982, D.C. 1998. Ptnr. Stepno, Schwaab & Linn, Arlington, 1974-78, Schwartz, Jeffrey, Schwaab, Mack, Blumenthal & Evans, P.C., Alexandria, 1978-88; ptnr. in charge, chair dept. intellectual property Foley & Lardner, Washington, 1988-99, ptnr., 1999—. Lectr. law George Washington U., 1978-88, George Mason U., 1989—. Max Planck Inst. Fgn. and Internat. Patent, Copyright and Competition Law fellow, 1971-72. Co-author Patent Practice, 6 vols., 1976-99, International Patent Law: EPC & PCT, 3 vols., 1978; Intellectual Property Protection for Biotechnology Worldwide, 1987; contbr. articles to profl. jours. Mem. ABA, Am. Intellectual Property Law Assn., Va. State Bar (gov. 1974-78), Am. Soc. Internat. Law, Internat. Patent and Trademark Assn., Internat. Fedn. Indsl. Property Attys., Christian Legal Soc., Phi Kappa Phi, Tau Beta Pi. Home: 34205 Nashotah Rd Nashotah WI 53058-9534 Office: Foley & Lardner 3000 K St NW Ste 500 Washington DC 20007-5143 E-mail: rschwaab@foleylaw.com.

SCHWAB, ANDREAS, science educator; b. Offenbach, Germany, Feb. 9, 1964; MBA, Ea. Ill. U., 1987; Dipl. UfM, Mannheim U., Germany, 1991; PhD, U. Wis., 2000. Tchg. and rsch. asst. U. Wis., Madison, 1993—99; asst. prof. U. Miss., Oxford, 1999—2001, La. State U., Baton Rouge, 2001—. Office: Louisiana State U Baton Rouge LA 70803

SCHWAB, ARTHUR JAMES, lawyer; b. Pitts., Dec. 7, 1946; s. Earl Walter and Helen Alice (Gascoine) S.; m. Karen Jenny, Sept. 2, 1967; children: John Arthur, Ellen Katherine, David Earl. Student, Muskingum Coll., 1964-65; AB, Grove City Coll., 1968; JD, U. Va., 1972. Bar: Pa. 1972, N.J. 1985, U.S. Dist. Ct. (we. dist.) Pa. 1972, U.S. Dist. Ct. (ea dist.) Pa. 1978, U.S. Dist. Ct. (no. dist.) Ohio 1979, U.S. Dist. Ct. S.C. 1980, U.S. Dist. Ct. N.Mex. 1981, U.S. Dist. Ct. Mass. 1984, U.S. Dist. Ct. N.J. 1984, U.S. Ct. Appeals (3d cir.) 1972, U.S. Ct. Appeals (11th cir.) 1982, U.S. Ct. Appeals (4th cir.) 1982, U.S. Ct. Appeals (8th cir.) 1991, U.S. Ct. Appeals (9th cir.) 1995, U.S. Supreme Ct. 1975. Ptnr. Reed, Smith, Shaw and McClay, Pitts., 1973-90; ptnr., chair of litigation Buchanan Ingersoll, 1990-99, chief counsel complex litig., 2000—. Mem. faculty Grove City Coll., U. Va. Trial Advocacy Program. Mem. editorial bd. Va. Law Rev., Sch. Law U. Va., Charlottesville, 1972. Bd. dirs. Grove City (Pa.) Coll. Mem. Pa. Bar Assn. (past chair civil litigation sect.), Acad. Trial Lawyers Allegheny County (past mem. bd. dirs.), Allegheny County Bar Assn., (past chair civil litigation sect.), Am. Inns of Ct. (past pres. Pitts. chpt.), Duquesne Club. Republican. Presbyterian. Home: 3000 Old Orchard Ct Gibsonia PA 15044-6072 Office: Buchanan Ingersoll One Oxford Ctr 301 Grant St Fl 20 Pittsburgh PA 15219-1410

SCHWAB, CHARLES R. brokerage house executive; b. Sacramento, 1937; m. Helen O'Neill; 5 children. , Stanford U., 1959, postgrad., 1961. Formerly mut. fund mgr., Marin County, Calif.; founder brokerage San Francisco, 1971; now chmn., CEO Charles Schwab & Co., Inc. Author: How to be Your Own Stockbroker, 1984. Republican. Office: Charles Schwab & Co Inc 101 Montgomery St San Francisco CA 94104-4175*

SCHWAB, EILEEN CAULFIELD, lawyer, educator; b. N.Y.C., Feb. 11, 1944; d. James and Mary (Fay) Caulfield; m. Terrance W. Schwab, Jan. 4, 1969; children: Matthew Caulfield, Catherine Grimley Welykoridko, Claire Gillespie. BA, Hunter Coll., 1965; JD, Columbia U., 1971; BA magna cum laude. Bar: N.Y. 1972, U.S. Dist. Ct. (so. and ea. dists.) N.Y. 1975, U.S. Ct. Appeals (2d cir.) 1975, U.S. Tax Ct. 1980, U.S. Ct. Appeals (10th cir.) 1993. Assoc. Poletti Friedin, N.Y.C., 1971-72, Hughes Hubbard & Reed, N.Y.C., 1972-75, Davis Polk & Wardwell, N.Y.C., 1975-81; dep. bur. chief Charities Bur., Atty. Gen. of N.Y., 1981-82; counsel Sidley Austin Brown & Wood (formerly Brown & Wood), N.Y.C., 1983—; ptnr. Sidley Austin Brown & Wood LLP, 1984. Adj. prof. N.Y. Law Sch. Trustee Cath. Communal Fund; chair planned gifts, bequests and endowment com. Archdiocese of N.Y.; mem. planned giving adv. com. Mus. of Modern Art, Met. Mus. Art, Cen. Park Conservancy; trustee Cooke Ctr. Learning & Devel. Fellow Am. Coll. Trust and Estate Counsel; mem. N.Y. State Bar Assn., Phi Beta Kappa. Democrat. Roman Catholic. E-mail: eschwab@sidley.com.

SCHWAB, FRANK, JR. management consultant; b. Brookline, Mass., Dec. 19, 1932; s. Frank Sr. and Phyllis (Robinson) F. BA, Rutgers U., 1952; MBA, Harvard Bus. Sch., 1956. Cert. mgmt. cons. Internal auditor Champion Paper, Inc., Hamilton, Ohio, 1956-57, mgmt. engr. Pasadena, Tex., 1957-58; cons., assoc. Booz Allen & Hamilton, N.Y.C., 1958-65; dir. trans. planning Planning Rsch. Corp., L.A., 1965; pres., CEO F.R. Schwab & Assocs., N.Y.C., 1965-82; pres., co-CEO Fenvessy & Schwab, 1982-87; pres., CEO, Anderson & Schwab, 1987—. Bd. dirs. Sugarland Oil Corp., N.Y.C., mfrs. and svcs. divsn. Nat. Mining Assn., Washington. Trustee Nat. Mining Hall of Fame and Mus., Leadville, Colo., 1992—. 1st lt. U.S. Army, 1952-54, Korea. Decorated Nat. Def. Svc. medal, Korean Svc. medal with bronze star, Commendation ribbon with medal pendant, UN Svc. medal. Mem. Inst. Mgmt. Cons. (pres. N.Y. chpt. 1975-77), Am. Arbitration Assn. (panel arbitrator), Mil. Order Fgn. Wars (vet. companion), Maidstone Club, Union Club, River Club, King Coal Club, Army and Navy Club. Republican. Avocation: tennis. Office: Anderson & Schwab Inc 444 Madison Ave New York NY 10022-6903 Fax: (212) 755-9576. E-mail: fschwab@andersonschwab.com.

SCHWAB, GEORGE DAVID, social science educator, author; b. Nov. 25, 1931; s. Arkady and Klara (Jacobson) S.; m. Eleonora Storch, Feb. 27, 1965; children: Clarence Boris, Claude Arkady, Solan Bernhard. BA, City Coll. N.Y., 1954; MA, Columbia U., 1955, PhD, 1968. Lectr. Columbia Coll., N.Y.C., 1959, CUNY, 1960-68; asst. prof. history, 1968-72; assoc. prof. history, 1973-79; prof., 1980—2000; prof. emeritus, 2001—. Mem. Columbia U. Seminar on History of Legal and Polit. Thought and Institutions; dir. Conf. History and Politics CUNY; with Nat. Com. Am. Fgn. Policy. Author: Dayez: Beyond Abstract Art, 1967, Enemy oder Foe, 1968, Switzerland's Tactical Nuclear Weapons Policy, 1969, The Challenge of the Exception: An Introduction to the Political Ideas of Carl Schmitt, 1970, 2nd edit., 1989, Appeasement and Detente, 1975, 81, Carl Schmitt: Political Opportunist?, 1975; translator: The Concept of the Politcal with Comments by Leo Strauss (Carl Schmitt), 1976, 96, Legality and Illegality as Instruments of Revolutionaries in Their Quest for Power, Remarks Occasioned by the Outlook of Herbert Marcuse, 1978, The German State in Historical Perspective, 1978, Ideology: Reality or Rhetoric, 1978, Ideology and Foreign Policy, 1978, 81, The Decision: Is the American Sovereign at Bay?, 1978, State and Nation: Toward a Further Clarification, 1980, American Foreign Politics at the Crossroads, 1980, Carl Schmitt: Through a Glass Darkly, 1980, From Quantity and Heterogeneity to Quality and Homogeneity: Toward a New Foreign Policy, 1980, Toward an Open-Society Bloc, 1980, Eurocommunism: The Ideological and Political Theoretical Foundations, 1981, American Foreign Policy at the Crossroads, 1982, A Decade of the National Committee on American Foreign Policy, 1984, trans. Political Theology: Four Chapters on the Concept of Sovereignty (Carl Schmitt), 1985, 88, The Destruction of a Family, 1987, Elie Wiesel: Between Jerusalem and New York, 1990, The Broken Vow, The Good Obtained, 1991, Thoughts of a Collector, 1991, Carl Schmitt Hysteria in the United States, 1992, Contextualizing Carl Schmitt's Concept of Grossraum, 1994; (translation) The Leviathan in the State Theory of Thomas Hobbes (Carl Schmitt), 1996, Carl Schmitt, A Note on a Qualitative Authoritarian Bourgeois Liberal, 2000, The National Committee on American Foreign Policy's Focus on Russia, 2000; editor Am. Fgn. Policy Interests; series Global Perspectives in History and Politics. Trustee, pres. mem. exec. com. Nat. Com. Am. Fgn. Policy. Recipient Ellis Is. medal of honor. Mem. Coun. on Fgn. Rels. Office: Nat Com Am Fgn Policy 320 Park Ave New York NY 10022-6815 E-mail: ncafp@aol.com.

SCHWAB, GLENN ORVILLE, retired agricultural engineering educator, consultant; b. Gridley, Kans., Dec. 30, 1919; s. Edward and Lizzie (Sauder) S.; married; children: Richard, Lawrence,Mary Kay. BS, Kans. State. U., 1942; MS, Iowa State U., 1947, PhD, 1951; postdoctoral, Utah State U., 1966. Registered profl. engr., Ohio. Instr. to prof. agrl. engring. Iowa State U., Ames, 1947-56; prof. agrl. engring. Ohio State U., Columbus, 1956-85, ret., 1985, prof. emeritus Ohio, 1985—. Co-author: Soil and Water Conservation Engineering, 4th edit., 1993, Agricultural and Forest Hydrology, 1986, Soil and Water Management Systems, 4th edit., 1996; contbr. articles to profl. jours. Served to capt. U.S. Army, 1942-46. Fellow Am. Soc. Agrl. Engrs. (bd. dirs. soil and water div. 1976-78, Hancock Brick and Tile Drainage Engr. 1968, John Deere medal 1987), ASTM, Soil and Water Conservation Soc. Am., Am. Geophys. Union, Internat. Commn. Irrigation and Drainage. Avocations: rock polishing, wood working, photography, traveling. Home: 2637 Summit View Rd Powell OH 43065-8446

SCHWAB, GRACE S. state legislator; m. Steven Schwab; 3 children. BS, postgrad., Mankato State U. Mem. Minn. State Senate, 2000—, mem. crime prevention com., edn. com., transp. com., E-12 edn. budget divsn. com., taxes com., income and sales tax budget divsn. com. Home: 1858 Greenwood Dr Albert Lea MN 56007 Office: 151 State Office Bldg Saint Paul MN 55155-1206 E-mail: sen.grace.schwab@senate.leg.state.mn.us.

SCHWAB, HAROLD LEE, lawyer; b. N.Y.C., Feb. 5, 1932; s. Harold Walter and Beatrice (Braverman) S.; m. Rowena Vivian Strauss, June 12, 1953; children: Andrew, Lisa, James. BA, Harvard Coll., 1953; LLB, Boston Coll., 1956. Bar: N.Y. 1957, U.S. Ct. Mil. Appeals 1958, U.S. Dist. Cts. (so. and ea. dists.) N.Y. 1967, U.S. Dist. Ct. (no. dist.) N.Y. 1974, U.S. Dist. Ct. (we. dist.) N.Y. 1988, U.S. Dist. Ct. Conn. 1995, U.S. Dist. Ct. (ea. and we. dists.) Ark. 2000, U.S. Ct. Appeals (2d cir.) 1971, U.S. Ct. Appeals (D.C. cir.) 1986, U.S. Ct. Appelas (11th cir.) 1988, U.S. Ct. Appeals (5th cir.) 1991, U.S. Supreme Ct. 1971. V.p. H.W. Schwab Textile Corp., N.Y.C., 1959-60; assoc. Emile Z. Berman & A. Harold Frost, 1960-67, ptnr., 1967-74; sr. ptnr. Lester Schwab Katz & Dwyer, 1974—. Lectr. N.Y. Jud. Seminars, N.Y. State Bar Assn., N.Y. County Lawyers Assn. Contbr. articles to legal jours.; mem. editl. bd. Jour. Products and Toxics Liability, 1976-96. Served to lt. col. USAFR. Fellow Internat. Acad. Trial Lawyers; mem. ABA, ASTM, SAE, Assn. Advancement of Automotive Medicine, Product Liability Adv. Coun., N.Y. State Bar Assn. (chmn. trial lawyers sect. 1980-81, editor sect. newsletter 1981-84), Am. Bd. Trial Advs. (pres. N.Y. chpt. 1982-83), Fedn. Ins. and Corp. Counsel (v.p. 1979-80), N.Y. State Trial Lawyers Assn., Def. Assn. N.Y., Harvard Club N.Y., Downtown Assn. Home: 205 Beach 142 St Neponsit NY 11694 Office: Lester Schwab Katz & Dwyer 120 Broadway Fl 38 New York NY 10271-0071

SCHWAB, HERMANN CASPAR, banker; b. N.Y.C., Jan. 8, 1920; s. Hermann Caspar and Ruth (Bliss) S.; m. C. Meteer Shanks, July 5, 1955; children: Henry R., Lesley Schwab Forman, Margery Schwab Weekes, Stuart Taylor, George Bliss, Katharine Lambard Schwab Kimmick. Grad., St. Marks Sch., 1937, Yale U., 1941. With Hanover Bank, 1941-44, 46-55, asst. sec., 1949-53, asst. v.p., 1953-55; ptnr. Dick & Merle Smith, 1956; v.p. Empire Trust Co., 1957-66, sr. v.p., 1965-66; with Bank N.Y., 1966-67; sr. v.p. Schroder Trust Co., N.Y.C., 1967-73, dir., 1970-73; pres., dir. Cheapside Dollar Fund Ltd., 1970-88; sr. v.p. Schroder Capital Mgmt. Inc., 1973-84, cons., 1984-88. Chmn., dir. Schroder Capitol Funds Inc., 1988-98, trustee dir., 1998—. Mayor Oyster Bay Cove, N.Y., 1973-85, trustee, 1965-98; trustee St. Lukes-Roosevelt Hosp. Ctr., 1969-99. 2d lt. inf., AUS, 1943-46. Mem. Piping Rock Club (Locust Valley, N.Y.). Home: 34 Northern Blvd Oyster Bay NY 11771-4105

SCHWAB, HOWARD JOEL, judge; b. Charleston, W.Va., Feb. 13, 1943; s. Joseph Simon and Gertrude (Hadas) S.; m. Michelle Roberts, July 4, 1970; children: Joshua Raphael, Bethany Alexis. BA in History with honors, UCLA, 1964, JD, 1967. Bar: Calif. 1968, U.S. Dist. Ct. (cen. dist.) Calif. 1968, U.S. Ct. Appeals (9th cir.) 1970, U.S. Supreme Ct. 1972. Clk. legal adminstrn. Litton Industries, L.A., 1967-68; dep. city atty., 1968-69; dep. atty. gen. State of Calif., 1969-84; judge Mcpl. Ct. L.A. Jud. Dist., 1984-85; judge Superior Ct. Superior Ct. L.A. County, L.A., 1985—. Mem. faculty Berkeley (Calif.) Judicial Coll., 1987—. Contbr. articles to profl. jours. Recipient CDAA William E. James award Calif. Dist. Atty.'s Assn., 1981. Mem. San Fernando Valley Bar Assn. (Appreciation award as Judge of Yr. 2002_, Inn. of Ct., Phi Alpha Delta. Democrat. Jewish. Avocations: history, book collecting. Office: LA Superior Ct 900 3rd St San Fernando CA 91340-2935

SCHWAB, JAMES CHARLES, urban planner; b. Oceanside, N.Y., Dec. 20, 1949; s. Charles Francis and Hazel Dorothy (Waters) S.; m. Jean Catlett, June 8, 1985; children: Jessica, Anna. BA in Polit. Sci., Cleve. State U., 1973; MA in Urban & Regional Planning, MA in Journalism, U. Iowa, 1985. Purchasing agt. Kaufman Container Co., Cleve., 1973-75; rsch. assoc. No. Ohio Project on Nat. Priorities, 1975-76; sales rep. Met. Life Ins. Co., Willoughby Hills, Ohio, 1976-78; exec. dir. Iowa Pub. Interest Rsch. Group, Iowa City, 1979-81; rsch. asst. Legis. Extended Assistance Group, 1982-85; asst. editor Am. Planning Assn., Chgo., 1985-90, sr. rsch. assoc., 1990—. Author: Raising Less Corn and More Hell, 1988, Industrial Performance Standards for a New Century, 1993, Deeper Shades of Green, 1994; author, prin. investigator: Planning for Post-Disaster Recovery and Reconstruction, 1998, Planning and Zoning for Concentrated Animal Feeding Operations, 1998; editor Zoning News, 1990—, Environment and Devel., 1992-96; contbr. articles to profl. publs. Chmn. Environ. Concerns Working Group, Met. Chgo. synod Evang. Luth. Ch. Am., 1989—; chmn. Task Force on Care of Creation, Region 5, Dubuque, Iowa, 1992-93; mem. ch. coun. Augustana Luth. Ch., Chgo., 1990-93; co-leader Luth. Environ. Network of the Synods, 1997—. Mem. Soc. Midland Authors (bd. dirs., newsletter editor 1990-95, membership sec. 1995-97, chmn. non-fiction awards 1995-96, chmn. biography awards 2000-02, pres. 1997-99, treas. 1999-2001), Soc. Environ. Journalists, Soc. Profl. Journalists, Investigative Reporters and Editors, Am. Planning Assn., Am. Inst. Cert. Planners. Lutheran. Avocations: travel, reading history, health club workouts, ethnic restaurants. Home: 1755 N Campbell Ave Chicago IL 60647-5205 Office: Am Planning Assn 122 S Michigan Ave Ste 1600 Chicago IL 60603-6190 E-mail: jschwab@planning.org.

SCHWAB, JOHN JOSEPH, psychiatrist, educator; b. Cumberland, Md., Feb. 10, 1923; s. Joseph L. and Eleanor (Cadden) S.; m. Ruby Baxter, Aug. 4, 1945; 1 dau., Mary Eleanor. BS, U. Ky., 1946; MD, U. Louisville, 1946; MS in Physiology (Med. fellow), U. Ill., 1949; postgrad., Duke U., 1951-52, U. Fla., 1959-61. Diplomate: Nat. Bd. Med. Examiners. Intern Phila. Gen. Hosp., 1947-48; resident medicine Louisville Gen. Hosp., 1949-50; edn. officer med. coll. U. Yokohama, 1952-54; internist, psychosomaticist Holzer Clinic, Gallipolis, Ohio, 1954-59; resident psychiatry U. Fla. Hosp., 1959-61; NIMH Career tchr. U. Fla., Gainesville, 1962-64, mem. faculty, 1961-73, prof. psychiatry and medicine, 1967-73, dir. cons. liaison program, 1964-67, resident tng. dir., 1965-71; prin. investigator Fla. Health Study, 1969-74; prof., chmn. dept. psychiatry and behavioral scis. Sch. Medicine U. Louisville, 1973-91, prof. psychiatry, 1991-93, prof. emeritus, 1993—, assoc. dir. clin. psychopharm. rsch., 1991—. Chmn. epidemiologic studies rev. com. Ctr. for Epidemiologic Studies, NIMH, 1973-75, cons. psychiatry br., 1975-92; cons. Old Order Amish Study of Depression, 1978—; vol. vis. lectr. Howard U., 1992; ann. vis. lectr. U. Würzburg, Germany, hon. faculty, 1992—; vis. prof. El-Azar U., Cairo, 1991; prin. investigator LSVL Family Health Study, 1982—; dir. U. Fla. Coll. Med. Program: History and Philosophy of Medicine, 1965-72. Author: Handbook of Psychiatric Consultation, 1968; also articles; co-author: Sociocultural Roots of Mental Illness: An Epidemiologic Survey, 1978, Social Order and Mental Health, 1979; assoc. editor Psychosomatics, 1965-86; co-editor: Man for Humanity: On Concordance V. Discord in Human Behavior, 1972, Social Psychiatry, vol. 1, 1974, The Psychiatric Examination, 1974, first author Family Mental Health History, Epidem, Clinical Health Issues, 1993, first author Family Functioning: The General Living Systems Research Model, 2000; co-edited 9 books, 11 Monographs, and over 250 articles. Capt. USAMC, 1949-54. Recipient Disting. Mental Health award Mental Health Assn. Ky., 1992. Fellow Am. Coll. Psychiatrists (regent 1977-79), Collegium Internat. Neuro-Psychopharmacologicum, World Assn. Social Psychiatry, AAAS, Am. Psychiat. Assn. (chmn. council research and devel. 1974-75); mem. AMA, Acad. Psychosomatic Medicine (exec. 1965-72, pres. 1970-71), Group for Advancement Psychiatry (bd. dirs. 1985-87), So. Assn., Jefferson County Med. Soc., Ky. Psychiat. Assn., Am. Assn. Social Psychiatry (pres. 1971-73), Alpha Omega Alpha, (Outstanding Performance award for Affirmative Action U. Louisville 1986), World Assn. Soc. Psychiatry (internat. adv. com., Rome, 1991), Psychiatrists for Better Psychiat. (pres. 1990-99), U. of the World (co-chair health, edn. com. 1992-98). Achievements include research on applicability of psychiatric concepts to general medicine, sociocultural aspects of mental illness; establishing guidelines for identification and management of medical patients with illnesses complicated by emotional stress; epidemiology of mental illness; depression and the family; clinical psychopharmacology, historical and epidemiologic perspectives on the family. Home: 6217 Innes Trace Rd Louisville KY 40222-6008

SCHWAB, PAUL JOSIAH, psychiatrist, educator; b. Waxahachie, Tex., Jan. 14, 1932; s. Paul Josiah and Anna Marie (Baeuerle) S.; m. Martha Anne Beed, June 8, 1953; children: Paul Josiah III, John Conrad, Mark Whitney. BA, North Ctrl. Coll., 1953; MD, Baylor U., 1957. Diplomate Am. Bd. Psychiatry and Neurology. Intern Phila. Gen. Hosp., 1957-58; clin. assoc. Nat. Cancer Inst., Bethesda, Md., 1958-60; resident in internal medicine U. Chgo., 1960-62, resident psychiatry, 1962-65, chief resident, 1965, clin. instr. psychiatry, lectr. psychiatry, 1968-74, assoc. prof., 1974-79; clin. assoc., 1979-86; clin. assoc. prof., 1986—2002; dir. residency tng. U. Chgo., 1976-79, dir. in-patient unit and day treatment program, 1975-79; pvt. practice Naperville, Ill., 1965—; cand. Chgo. Psychoanalytic Inst., 1970-72. Clin. instr. dept. psychiatry U. Ill., Chgo., 1965-66. Contbr. articles to profl. jours. Bd. trustees North Ctrl. Coll., chair liaison com., 1983—, vice-chmn. acad. and student affairs com., 1983-92, vice chair admissions, fin. aid and student devel., 1992-95; pres. North Ctrl. Coll. Alumni Assn., 1979-80. Recipient Outstanding Alumnus, North Ctrl. Coll., 1983, Gael D. Swing award, 2001. Fellow: Am. Psychiat. Assn. (life Nancy C.A. Roeske award 1991); mem.: Am. Soc. Clin. Psychopharmacology, Alpha Omega Alpha. Democrat. Methodist. Home and Office: 1200 Tall Oaks Ct Naperville IL 60540-9494 E-mail: pauljschwab@earthlink.net.

SCHWAB, SUSAN CARROLL, dean; BA in Polit. Economy, Williams Coll., 1976; MA in Devel. Policy, Stanford U., 1977; PhD in Pub. Adminstrn., George Washington U., 1993. U.S. trade negotiator Office of U.S. Trade Rep., Washington, 1977-79; trade policy officer U.S. Embassy, Tokyo, 1980-81; chief economist, legis. asst. for internat. trade for Senator John C. Danforth, 1981-86, legis. dir., until 1989; asst. sec. commerce, dir. gen. U.S. and Fgn. Comml. Svc. Dept. Commerce, 1989-93; with corp. strategy office Motorola, Inc., Schaumburg, Ill., 1993-95; dean U. Md. Sch. Pub. Affairs, College Park, 1995—. Office: U Md Sch Pub Affairs College Park MD 20742-0001

SCHWAB, TERRANCE W. lawyer; b. Pitts., May 19, 1940; m. Eileen Caulfield, Jan. 4, 1969; children: Matthew Caulfield, Catherine Grimley, Claire Gillespie. BA magna cum laude, Harvard U., 1962; LLB cum laude, Columbia U., 1966. Assoc. Milbank, Tweed, Hadley & McCloy, N.Y.C., 1966-70, Kelley, Drye & Warren, N.Y.C., 1970-74, ptnr., 1975-96; sr. v.p., gen. counsel global fin. and investment banking The Sanwa Bank Ltd. (now UFJ Bank Ltd.), 1996—. Lectr. various profl. orgns. Assoc. editor: Law Practice of Alexander Hamilton, 1964-1980; contbr. articles to profl. jours. Trustee, sec. Caramoor Ctr. for Music and Arts, Katonah, N.Y., 1971—; trustee Sch. of Convent of Sacred Heart, N.Y.C., 1987-93, chmn., 1990-93. Mem. ABA, N.Y. State Bar Assn., Assn. of Bar of City of N.Y., Harvard Club. Office: UFJ Bank Ltd 55 E 52nd St Fl 24 New York NY 10055

SCHWAB, THERESE MATHES, nursing educator; b. Detroit, Sept. 18, 1935; d. Charles Joseph and Wilhelmina (Kengel) Mathes; m. Francis Schwab, Aug. 29, 1964 (div. 1990); children: Mary, Karen, Jodie, Charles. BS in Nursing, Barry U., 1957; MPH in Nursing, U. Minn., 1965; MS in Edn., No. State U., 1975; PhD, Walden U., 1981. Pub. health nurse Washtenaw County Health Dept., Ann Arbor, Mich., 1959-62; nursing coord. Regional Med. Program, Omaha, 1968-73; assoc. prof. U. Wyo., Laramie, 1975-86, U. Tex. Health Sci. Ctr., San Antonio, 1986-95, Tex. A&M U., Laredo, 1995-96, U. Tex., Brownsville, 1996-97, Ea. Mich. U., Ypsilanti, 1997-98; with Ea. Mich. U.-AAUP, 1998-2001. Contbr. articles to profl. jours. Recipient Ellogen Meritorious Teaching award, 1986. Mem.: ANA, Sigma Xi. Home: 5922 Wexford Brook San Antonio TX 78240 E-mail: tschwab1@satx.rr.com.

SCHWABE, GEORGE BLAINE, III, lawyer; b. Tulsa, Oct. 10, 1947; s. George Blaine Jr. and Marguerite Irene (Williams) S.; m. Jann Lee Schoonover, July 28, 1972; 1 child, George Blaine IV. BBA, U. Okla., 1970, JD, 1974. Bar: Maine 2001, U.S. Ct. Appeals (10th cir.) 1974, Okla. 1974, U.S. Dist. Ct. (we. dist.) Okla. 1974, U.S. Dist. Ct. (no. dist.) Okla. 1985, U.S. Dist. Ct. (ea. dist.) 1998, U.S. Supreme Ct. 1991, Maine 2001. From assoc. to ptnr. Crowe & Dunlevy, Oklahoma City, 1974-82; ptnr., dir. Mock Schwabe, Waldo, Elder, Reeves & Bryant, 1982-96; shareholder, dir. Gable Gotwals Mock Schwabe, 1996-98; member Mock, Schwabe, Waldo, Elder, Reeves & Bryant, 1998—. Adj. prof. law Oklahome City U.; lectr. in field. Capt. USAR. Fellow Am. Coll. Bankruptcy; mem. ABA (bus. bankruptcy com. sect. bus. law), Okla. Bar Assn., Bankruptcy and Reorganization Sect. (pres. 1987-88, bd. dirs. 1985—), Okla. City Golf & Country Club, Rotary. Republican. Mem. Christian Ch. Avocation: golf, snow and water skiing, tennis.. Office: Mock Schwabe et al 2 Leadership Sq 14th Fl 211 N Robinson Ave Oklahoma City OK 73102-7109 E-mail: gschwabe@mswerb.com.

SCHWABE, JOHN BENNETT, II, lawyer; b. June 14, 1946; s. Leonard Wesley and Hazel Fern (Crouch) Schwabe. AB, U. Mo., Columbia; JD, U. Mo., Columbia, 1970. Bar: Mo. 1970, U.S. Dist. Ct. (we. dist.) Mo. 1970, U.S. Ct. Mil. Appeals 1971, U.S. Supreme Ct. 1973; ordained minister. Pvt. practice, Columbia, Mo., 1974—96, St. Louis, 1984—96. Mem. N. Am. Boxing Fedn., 1997—; minister, founder John Schwabe Ministries. Capt. JAGC USAF, 1970—74. Mem.: Lawyers Assn. St. Louis, Boone County Bar Assn. (sec. 1977—79), Am. Legion, Phi Delta Phi. Methodist. Office: John B Schwabe II Law Firm Schwabe Bldg 2 E Walnut St Columbia MO 65203-4163

SCHWABER, EVELYNE ALBRECHT, psychiatrist; b. Vienna, Austria, Sept. 17, 1934; d. Henry and Augusta Albrecht; m. Jules R. Schwaber, Apr. 29, 1956; children: Carl S., Jeff M., Mitchell S., Glen I.A. AB, Radcliffe Coll., Cambridge, Mass., 1955; MD, Albert Einstein Coll. Medicine, Bronx, N.Y., 1959. Faculty Boston Psychoanalytic Inst., 1973—; tng. and supervising analyst Psychoanalytic Inst. New Eng. East, Needham, Mass., 1983—. Speaker in field. Author: more than 60 publs. on aspects of clinical listening with translations published in several foreign languages. Recipient Jour. prize, Am. Psychoanalytic Assn., 1985, Samuel G. Hibbs award Am. Psychiatric Assn., 1992. Mem. Psychoanalytic Soc. of New Eng., East, Boston Psychoanalytic Inst. and Soc., Am. Psychoanalytic Soc. (cert.), Am. Psychiatric Assn., Internat. Psychoanalytical Assn., Mass. Med. Soc., Norfolk Dist. Med. Soc., New Eng. Coun. of Child Psychiatry. Avocations: grandparenting, music.

SCHWADE, JAMES GARY, radiation oncologist; b. Milw., Dec. 14, 1946; s. Leonard and Esther S.; m. Karyn Karl, July 4, 1982; children: Loryn, David, Jonathan. AB cum laude, Washington U., St. Louis, 1969; MD, Med. Coll. Wis., Milw., 1973. Diplomate Am. Bd. Med. Examiners, therapeutic radiology Am. Bd. Radiologists. From intern to resident in radiaton oncology U. Calif., San Francisco, 1973-77, chief resident radiaiton oncology, 1976-77, instr., 1977-78; acting head radiology sect. radiation oncology br. divsn. cancer treatment, Nat. Cancer Inst., Bethesda, Md., 1978-81; assoc. clin. prof therapeutic radiology U. Miami (Fla.) Sch. Medicine, 1981-87, prof., chmn. dept radiation oncology, 1987-94; assoc. dir. clin. rsch. program Sylvester Cancer Ctr., Miami, 1989-94; med. dir. radiation oncology AMI Palmetto Gen. Hosp., Oncology Treatment Ctr., 1994-95; dir. radiation oncology, Gamma Knife unit Miami Neuro Sci. Ctr., Health South Doctor's Hosp., Coral Gables, 1994—; sr. v.p. for medicine and sci. Proton Therapy Corp. of Am., 1995-97; chmn., CEO Quality Oncology, Ft. Lauderdale, Fla., 1994-98. Spl. asst. for radiation oncology, cancer therapy evaluation program, Divsn. Cancer Treatment, Nat., Cancer Inst., Bethesda, 1977-78; cons. Nat. Naval Med. Ctr., Bethesda, 1978-81; chief dept. radiation oncology, med. dir. regional cancer treatment ctr., Baptist Hosp. Miami, 1981-87; chief radiation oncology svc. Jackson Meml. Hosp., VA Hosp., UMHC/SCCC, Miami, 1981-87; lectr. and presenter in field. Contbr. articles to profl. jours., chpts. to books; assoc editor Internat. Jour. of Radiation Oncology, Biology, Physics, 1991-97; revewer ASTRO, Sci. Program 1989-92, Internat. Jour. Oncology. Mem. Am. Cancer Soc., chmn. task force on prostate cancer, Fla. Divsn, mem. rsch. peer rev. subcom; chmn. spl. com. and Fla. com. for Health Care Reform, 1991-92; mem. adv. coun. on radiation protection, Fla., HRS, 1985-94, vice chmn. 1988-90, chmn. subcom. on emergency preparedness; chmn. Nat. Assn. for Proton Therapy, 1992. Recipient Order of Red Sword, Am. Cancer Soc., Dade County Unit, Fla., 1988—; grantee Alpha Therapeutic Corp., Inter Am. Pharms. Ltd., Radiation Therapy Oncology Group, Nat. Cancer Inst. Fellow Am. Coll. Radiology; mem. AMA, Fla. Med. Assn., Dade County Med. Assn., Fla. Radiol. Soc. (legis. com. 1984), Am. Radium Soc., Coun. of Affiliated Regional Radiation Therpy Socs. (counselor-at-large Am. Coll. of Radiology ann. mtg. 1988), Am. Soc. for Therapeutic Radiology and Oncology, Fla. Soc. Clin. Oncology (bd. dirs. 1988-91, legis., legal and ethics com. 1989-90). Home: 10201 Sabal Palm Ave Coral Gables FL 33156 Office: 9130 S Dadeland Blvd Ste 1528 Miami FL 33156 Fax: 305-670-2259. E-mail: drschwade@aol.com.

SCHWAKE, TORSTEN, chiropractor; b. Barsinghausen, Germany, Apr. 11, 1963; came to U.S., 1969; s. Werner and Antje (Heine) S.; m. Heidi A. Schubert, Dec. 7, 1996; 1 child, Katarina. AS, Orange County C.C., Middletown, N.Y., 1983; D in Chiropractic, Life Chiropractic Coll., Marietta, Ga., 1987. Assoc. Broadway Office Chiropractic, Newburgh, N.Y., 1987-88; clinic dr. United Chiropractic Clinic, Nashville, 1988-89; pvt. practice Newburgh, 1989—. Mem.: Network Holistic Health, Internat. Chiropractic Assn., Am. Back Soc., Found. Chiropractic Edn. and Rsch., Citizens Against Drug Impaired Drivers, C. of C. Orange County, Scenic Hudson, Chi Rho. Lutheran. Avocations: hiking, mountain biking, basketball, volleyball, traveling. Office: 20 Starrow Dr Newburgh NY 12550-3015 E-mail: Tors10@aol.com.

SCHWALB, HARRY, artist; b. Pitts., July 2, 1924; s. Adolf and Maria (Bruder) Schwalb; m. Myrna Kline, Dec. 28, 1958 (div. May 1989); 1 child, Adam. Student, Pa. State U., 1940-42; BS summa cum laude, U. Pitts., 1947, MA, 1949. Creative dir. Fisher Sci. Co., Pitts., 1951-93; U.S. corr. ARTnews Mag., N.Y.C., 1988—. Editor The Lab. Mag., Pitts., 1960-93; art critic Pitts. Mag., 1977-95; dean Ivy Sch. Profl. Art, Pitts., 1970-72; juror, curator and cons. for arts orgns. in U.S. and Can. Illustrator: Of Long Ago, 1949, A Western Journal, 1951; one man shows include Collectors Gallery, N.Y.C., 1960, Arnot Art Gallery, Elmira, N.Y., 1962, Carnegie Mus. Art, Pitts., 1965, Westmoreland Mus. Am. Art, Greensburg, Pa., 1965, 99, Mendelson Gallery, Pitts., 1995, 98; represented in permanent collections Carnegie Mus. Art, Westmoreland Mus. Am. Art. Recipient Critical Writing Silver medal U. Kans., 1990, Golden Quill award Pitts. Press Club, 1990-95; ann. Harry Schwalb award established in 1996 Pitts. Mag. Avocations: lecturing, writing essays. Home and Office: 166 N Dithridge St Pittsburgh PA 15213-2647

SCHWALBE, MARY ANNE, nonprofit committee executive; b. N.Y.C., Mar. 31, 1934; d. Alfred Goldsmith and Emily (Goetz) Buck; m. Douglas Schwalbe, Dec. 5, 1959; children: Douglas, William, Nina. BA, Radcliffe Coll., 1955; cert., London Acad. Music & Dramatic Art, 1956. Asst. dir. Theatre Comm. Group, N.Y.C., 1962-65; dir. admissions Radcliffe Coll., Cambridge, Mass., 1971-75; asst. dean admissions Harvard/Radcliffe, 1975-79; dir. coll. counseling Dalton Sch., N.Y.C., 1979-85; head upper sch. Nightingale-Bamford Sch., 1985-90; staff dir. Women's Comm., 1990-94; staff liaison Internat. Rescue Com., 1994—. Chair adv. bd. Refugee Women Coun., N.Y.C., 1995—. Elder Madison Ave. Presbyn. Ch., N.Y.C., 1985—; bd. dirs. Marymount Manhattan Coll., N.Y.C., 1991—, Searac, Washington, 1992—, Brearley Sch., N.Y.C., 1994—. Recipient Gayle Wilson award Nat. Assn. Coll. Admissions Counselors, 1985, Harvard U. Alumni award, 1993, Leadership award Marymount Manhattan Coll., 1995. Office: Internat Rescue Com 122 E 42nd St New York NY 10168-0002

SCHWALLIE, DANIEL PHILLIP, legal consultant; b. Canton, Ohio, Mar. 9, 1955; s. Paul C. and Margaret Kailey (Livingston) S.; children: Halden Reid, Kailey Justine. BA magna cum laude, Kalamazoo Coll., 1977; MA, U. Iowa, 1982, PhD, 1984; JD cum laude, Case Western Res. U., 1991. Bar: Ohio 1991. Asst. prof. econs. Case Western Res. U., Cleve., 1984-91; assoc. Thompson, Hine & Flory, 1991-93; cons. Hewitt Assocs. LLC, Lincolnshire, Ill., 1993-95, Independence, Ohio, 1995—. Cons. to law firms, Cleveland Heights, Ohio, 1989-90; grant proposal reviewer NSF, Washington, 1987-88. Author: The Impact of Intergovernmental Grants on the Aggregate Public Sector, 1989; articles referee Oxford (Eng.) Econ. Papers, 1988, Pub. Fin. Quar., New Orleans, 1988-91; contbr. articles to profl. jours. Recipient Am. Jurisprudence award Lawyers Coop. Pub. Co. and Bancroft-Whitney Co., 1987. Mem. ABA, Phi Eta Sigma, Omicron Delta Epsilon, Beta Gamma Sigma. Avocations: photography, gourmet cooking, jogging, dogs. Office: Hewitt Assocs LLC 5005 Rockside Rd Independence OH 44131

SCHWALM, FRITZ EKKEHARDT, biology educator; b. Arolsen, Hesse, Germany, Feb. 17, 1936; came to U.S., 1968; s. Fritz Heinrich and Elisabeth Agnes (Wirth) S.; m. Renate Gertrud Streichhahn, Feb. 10, 1962; children—Anneliese, Fritz-Uwe, Karen PhD, Philipps U., Germany, 1964; Staatsexamen, Philipps U., 1965. Educator boarding sch., Kiel, Fed. Republic Germany, 1956-57; lectr. Folk Universitetet, Stockholm, Sweden, 1959-60; research assoc. U. Witwatersrand, Johannesburg, South Africa, 1966-67, U. Notre Dame, South Bend, Ind., 1968-70; asst. prof., then assoc. prof. Ill. State U., Normal, Ill., 1970-82; assoc. prof. biology, then prof., chair dept. Tex. Woman's U., Denton, 1982-2001, dir. Animal Care Facility, 1990-2001, chmn. pro tem grad. coun., 1991-92, prof. emeritus, 2001—. Coord., chmn. S.W. Conf. for Devel. Biology, Denton, 1985, 90, 96. Author: (monograph) Insect Morphogenesis, 1988; contbr. articles to profl. jours. Vice pres. PTA, Normal, 1975 Fellow Anglo-Am. Corp. South Africa, 1966, 67; NATO advanced research fellow, Freiburg, Fed. Republic Germany 1977. Mem.: Phi Kappa Phi (chpt. pres. 1993—96). Home: 1116 Linden Dr Denton TX 76201-2721 Office: Tex Woman's U Biology Sci Rsch Lab Denton TX 76204 E-mail: fschwalm@msn.com.

SCHWAM, MARVIN ALBERT, graphic design company executive; b. Newark, Apr. 18, 1942; s. Meyer and Fannie (Lerman) S.; m. Jeanette Fein, June 13, 1964; children; Frederic, Matthew. BFA, Cooper Union, 1964. Staff artist Domerus & Co., 1964-66; mgr. Flowerental Corp., N.Y.C., 1966-68; pres. M. Schwam Floralart, 1968-76; exec. v.p., bd. chmn. Florenco Foliate Systems Corp., 1975-88; pres., chmn. bd. Am. Christmas Decorating Svc., Inc., 1989—. Res. Marc Shaw Graphics, Inc., N.Y.C., Florenco Graphics Systems, Inc.; exec. v .p. Display Arts Worldwide, 1975-88; pres. Creative Animations, Inc., 1988-90; creative dir., v.p. Rennoc Animations, Inc., 1988-90; pres. Almar Comm., Ltd., 1990-94, Sayso Comm., Ltd., 1990-95, Gay Entertainment TV, Inc., 1992-99, Forma Studio Gallery, 1999—; chmn. bd., pres. Union Sq. Ceramic Ctr., 2002. Industry chmn. March of Dimes, 1975-78, pres. bd. dirs. Happi Found for Austic People, N.Y.C.; trustee Nat. Found. Jewish Genetic Diseases; patron Young Adult Inst. and Workshop, Inc.; co-chmn. restaurant, hotel and entertainment industry lincheon Boy Scouts Am., 1988-96; chmn. benefit com. Plan Internat. USA, 1991-92; pres. Union Square Ceramic Ctr., 2002--. Recipient award of merit for svc. to GM Corp., 1978, award for Highlight of Christmas Citibank/Citicorp Ctr., 1978, Disting. Svc. award Coler Hosp., 1982-86, Sr. Citizens of Roosevelt Island. Mem. Mcpl. Art Soc. N.Y., Am. Mus. Natural History, Alumni Assn. Cooper Union (2d Century Soc. fellow), Internat. Platform Assn. Achievements include designer largest artificial Christmas tree in U.S., Radio City Music Hall, N.Y.C., 1979; decorator Pulitzer Fountain, N.Y.C., 1979-80 Christmas season; chief designer Town Sq., New Orleans, Christmas, 1981, Albany Tricentennial, 1986; interior landscape designer La. State Pavillion World's Fair, New Orleans, 1984. Home: 7 E 17th St New York NY 10003-1913 Office: Am Christmas Decorations Inc 1135 Bronx River Ave Bronx NY 10472- E-mail: marvinschwam@aol.com.

SCHWAN, DAVID PAUL, radio broadcaster; b. East Chicago, Ind., Aug. 22, 1956; s. Paul Hugo Schwan and Martha Lee Helen Reinhardt Schwan. Student, Purdue U.-Calumet, Hammond, Ind., 1974-75; BA, Ball State U., 1978. Program host WBST Radio, Muncie, Ind., 1977-78; news anchor, reporter WJOB Radio, Hammond, 1978-81; news prodr. WCFL Radio, Chgo., 1981-82; news anchor, reporter, prodr. WFYR Radio/RKO Network, 1982-86; news anchor, prodr. WGN Radio/Tribune Radio Networks, 1986-91; news anchor Ill. Radio Network, 1989—2002; program host Ill. Byways, 1993—2002; prodr. Eye of Ill. radio program, 1993—2002. Host radio program Illinois Byways, 1993—; prodr. radio program Eye on Illinois, 1993—; author (novel) In Good Time, 2002; contbr. articles to Route 66 mag. Program annotator, mem. Chgo. Businessmen's Orch., 1992—. Mem. AFTRA, Ill. News Broadcasters Assn. Avocations: music, music history, American history, travel, physical fitness. Home: 1169 S Plymouth Ct # 610 Chicago IL 60605 Office: Ill Radio Network 430 W Erie # 505 Chicago IL 60610 E-mail: DSCHWAN@prodigy.net.

SCHWAN, HERMAN PAUL, electrical engineering and physical science educator, research scientist; b. Aachen, Germany, Aug. 7, 1915; came to U.S., 1947, naturalized, 1952; s. Wilhelm and Meta (Pattberg) S.; m. Anne Marie DelBorello, June 18, 1949; children: Barbara, Margaret, Steven, Carol, Cathryn. Student, U. Goettingen, 1934-37; PhD, U. Frankfurt, 1940; Habilitation in physics and biophysics, 1946; DSc (hon.), U. Pa., 1986, U. Kuopio, Finland, 2000, U. Graz, Austria, 2001. Rsch. scientist, prof. Kaiser Wilhelm Inst. Biophysics, 1937-47, asst. dir., 1945-47; rsch. scientist USN, 1947-50; prof. elec. engring., prof. elec. engring. in phys. medicine, assoc. prof. phys. medicine U. Pa., Phila., 1950-83, Alfed F. Moore prof. emeritus, 1983—, dir. electromed. divsn., 1952-73, chmn. biomed. engring., 1961-73, program dir. biomed. engr. tng. program, 1960-77. Vis. prof. U. Calif., Berkeley, 1956, U. Frankfurt, Germany, 1962, U. Würzburg, Germany, 1986-87; lectr. Johns Hopkins U., 1962-67, Drexel U., Phila., 1983-90; W.W. Clyde vis. prof. U. Utah, Salt Lake City, 1980; 10th Lauristan Taylor lectr. Nat. Council Radiation Protection and Measurements, 1986; Fgn. sci. mem. Max Planck Inst. Biophysics, Germany, 1962—; cons. NIH, 1962-90; chmn. nat. and internat. meetings biomed. engring. and biophysics, 1959, 61, 65; mem. nat. adv. council environ. health HEW, 1969-71; mem. coms. NAS-NRC, 1968-87. Co-author: Advances in Medical and Biological Physics, 1957, Therapeutic Heat, 1958, Physical Techniques in Medicine and Biology, 1963; editor: Biol. Engring, 1969; co-editor: Interactions Between Electromagnetic Fields and Cells, 1985; mem. editorial bd. Environ. Biophysics, IEEE Transactions Med. Biol. Engring., Jour. Phys. Med. Biol., Nonionizing Radiation, Bioelectromagnetics; contbr. articles to profl. jours. Recipient Citizenship award Phila., 1952, 1st prize AIEE, 1953, Achievement award Phila. Inst. Radio Engring., 1963, Rajewsky prize for biophysics, 1974, U.S. sr. scientist award Alexander von Humboldt Found., 1980-81, Biomed. Engring. Edn. award Am. Soc. Engring. Edn., 1983, d'Arsonval award Bioelectromagnetics Soc., 1985. Fellow IEEE (chmn. and vice-chmn. nat. profl. group biomed. engring. 1955, 62-68, Morlock award 1967, Edison medal 1983, Centennial award 1984, Phila. Sect. award 1991, Millenium medal 2000), AAAS, Am. Inst. Med. and Biol. Engring.; mem. Nat. Acad. Engring., Am. Standards Assn. (chmn. 1961-65), Biophys. Soc. (publicity com., council, constn. com.), German Biophys. Soc. (hon.), Soc. for Cryobiology, Nordic (Scandinavian) Bioimpedance Club (hon.), Internat. Fedn. Med., and Biol. Engring. (Otto Schmitt award 2000), Bioelectromagnetics Soc., Biomed. Engring. Soc. (founder, dir. 1968-71), Sigma Xi, Eta Kappa Nu. Achievements include discovery of counterion relaxation; dielectric spectroscopy of cells and tissues; nonlinearity law of electrode polarization; research on nonionizing radiation biophysics; fundamentals electromagnetic bioengineering; first standard for safe exposure to electrical fields; development of biomedical engineering and education. Home: 99 Kynlyn Rd Wayne PA 19087-2849 Office: U Pa Dept Bioengring D2 Hayden Hall Philadelphia PA 19104 E-mail: hschwan@seas.upenn.edu.

SCHWANAUER, FRANCIS, philosopher, educator; b. Zsámbék, Hungary, Jan. 20, 1933; came to U.S., 1959; s. Georg and Maria (Keller) S.; m. Johanna Maria Koelln, Sept. 29, 1957; children: Stephan Michael, Miriam Frances. Maturum, Ulrich von Hutten Gymnasium, Korntal, Germany, 1954; PhD, U. Stuttgart, Germany, 1959. Asst. prof. Lebanon Valley Coll., Annville, Pa., 1960-62, U. Maine, Orono, 1962-65, U. So. Maine, Portland Gorham, 1965-67, assoc. prof., 1967-72, prof., 1972—. Author: Truth is a Neighborhood with Nothing in Between, 1977, Those Fallacies by Slight of Reason, 1978, No Many is not a One (For the Case is Comparison), 1981, The Flesh of Thought is Pleasure or Pain, 1982, To Make Sure is to Cohere, 1982, Philosophical Fact and Paradox, 1987, Fables from the Fox, 1991; abstracts, 1997, 98, 99, 2000, 01, 02; contbr. articles to profl. publs. Grantee John Anson Kittredge Ednl. Fund, 1991, 93. Mem. New England Philos. Assn., Internat. Platform Assn. Democrat. Roman Catholic. Avocation: fishing. Home: 4 Woodmont St Portland ME 04102-2709

SCHWANDA, TOM, religious studies educator; b. E. Stroudsburg, Pa., Oct. 23, 1950; s. Theodore Frank and Madlyn Betty (Backensto) S.; m. Grace Elaine Dunning, July 30, 1977; children: Rebecca Joy, Stephen Andrew. Student, Worcester Polytechnic Inst., 1968-69; BA in Econ., Moravian Coll., 1969-72; student, Gordon-Conwell Sem., 1972-74; MDiv, New Brunswick Sem., 1975; DMin, Fuller Theol. Sem., 1992. Ordained to ministry Reformed Ch. in Am., 1975. Pastor Wanaque (N.J.) Reformed Ch., 1975-87; pastor congl. care Immanuel Reformed Ch., Grand Rapids, Mich., 1987-92; interim sr. pastor Remembrance Reformed Ch., 1992-93; rsch. fellow H. Henry Meeter Ctr. for Calvin Studies Calvin Coll., 1993-95; instr. spirituality and worship Bethlehem Ctr. for Spirituality, 1993—; dir. Reformed Spirituality Network, 1992—; assoc. for spiritual formation Reformed Ch. in Am., 1995-99; prof. spiritual formation Reformed Bible Coll., Grand Rapids, Mich., 1999—. Organizer, convener Gathering Reformed Spirituality, 1993, 94, 95, 97, 99, 2001; chair spirituality com. Synod of Great Lakes, 1989-2000, mem. Christian discipleship com., 1988-94; mem. ch. life, evangelism, missions com. South Grand Rapids Classics, chair, 1992; mem. commn. on worship Reformed Ch. in Am., 1978-94; mem. care of students com. Passaic Classis, 1975, 87, chair, 1978, 83-86, pres., 1979; adj. prof. spirituality and spiritual direction and worship Fuller Theol. Sem., San Francisco Theol. Sem., No. Bapt. Theol. Sem., Western Theol. Sem., Columbia Theol. Sem., Charlotte, Orlando, Reformed Theol. Sem., Charlotte. Author: Celebrating God's Presence: The Transforming Power of Public Worship, 1995; contbr. articles to religious jours.; author poetry; manuscript reader, evaluator religious pub. co. Established, managed Wanaque Cmty. Food Pantry, 1977-87; vol. Domestic Crisis Ctr., Grand Rapids, 1988—; bd. dirs. Nat. Inst. Rehabilitation Engring., Hewitt, N.J., 1984—, pres. bd. dirs., 1986—. Recipient Barnabas award Iglesia Cristiana Ebenezer, 1987. Mem. Czechoslovak Soc. Arts and Sci., Czechoslovak Hist. Conf., Soc. for Study of Christian Spirituality. Avocations: running, landscaping, genealogy/family history. Home: 6125 Capitan Dr SE Grand Rapids MI 49546-6721 Office: Reformed Bible Coll 3333 E Beltline Ave NE Grand Rapids MI 49525-9781 E-mail: tschwanda@reformed.edu.

SCHWANK, JOHANNES WALTER, chemical engineering educator; b. Zams, Tyrol, Austria, July 6, 1950; came to U.S., 1978; s. Friedrich Karl and Johanna (Ruepp) S.; m. Lynne Violet Duguay; children: Alexander Johann, Leonard Friedrich, Hanna Violet, Rosa Joy. Diploma in chemistry, U. Innsbruck, Austria, 1975, PhD, 1978. Mem. faculty U. Mich., Ann Arbor, 1978—, assoc. prof. chem. engring., 1984-90, acting dir. Ctr. for Catalysis and Surface Sci., 1985-90, prof., interim chmn. dept. chem. engring., 1990-91, assoc. dir. Electron Microbeam Analysis Lab., 1990—2000; chmn. dept. chem. engring., 1991-95; prof. chem. engring. U. Mich., Ann Arbor, 1995—. Vis. prof. U. Innsbruck, 1987-88, Tech. U. Vienna, 1988; cons. in field. Patentee bimetallic cluster catalysts, hydrodesulfurization catalysts and microelectronic gas sensors; contbr. over 125 articles to sci. jours. Fulbright-Hays scholar, 1978. Mem. Am. Chem. Soc., Am. Inst. Chem. Engrs., Mich. Catalysis Soc. (sec.-treas. 1982-83, v.p. 1983-84, pres. 1984-85). Home: 5633 Meadow Dr Ann Arbor MI 48105-9368 Office: U Mich Dept Chem Engring 2300 Hayward St Ann Arbor MI 48109-2136 E-mail: schwank@umich.edu.

SCHWANTES, CARLOS ARNALDO, history educator, consultant; b. Wilmington, N.C., Mar. 7, 1945; s. Arnaldo and Frances (Casteen) Schwantes; m. Mary Alice Dassenko, Sept. 4, 1966; children: Benjamin, Matthew. BA, Andrews U., 1967; MA, U. Mich., 1968, PhD, 1976. From instr. to prof. Walla Walla Coll., College Place, Wash., 1969-85; prof. history U. Idaho, Moscow, 1984—2002; St. Louis Merc. Libr. endowed prof. transp. studies U. Mo., St. Louis, 2001, 2002—. Consult TV History Idaho, 1988. Author: (book) Coxey's Army: An Amercian Odyssey, 1985, The Pacific Northwest: An Interpretive History, 1989, In Mountain Shadows: A History of Idaho, 1989, Railroad Signatures Across the Pacific Northwest, 1993; author or ed: 7 other books, mem ed bd: Pacific NW Quart, 1982—97, mem ed bd: Idaho Yesterdays, 1987—2002, mem ed bd: Forest and Conservation History, 1988—95, mem ed bd: Pacific Hist Rev, 1991—95; contbr. articles to profl jours. Fellow NEH, 1982—83, Research, Idaho Humanities Coun, 1989—90; grantee, Idaho State Bd Educ, 1990—91. Mem.: Idaho State Hist Soc, Lexington Soc, Mining Hist Asn (coun 1990—94), Western Hist Asn, Orgn Am Historians, Am Hist Asn (pres Pacific Ct br 1999—2000). Republican. Seventh Day Adventist. Avocations: photography, backpacking. E-mail: cmschwantes@aol.com.

SCHWANTES, ROBERT SIDNEY, international relations executive; b. Beetown Township, Wis., July 11, 1922; s. Kurt John and Lillian Ellen (Walker) S.; m. Marion Laura Miles, July 15, 1943; children: Virginia, Janet, Ingrid. AB summa cum laude, Harvard U., 1943; MA, U. Colo., 1947; PhD, Harvard U., 1950. Instr. in history Harvard U., Cambridge, Mass., 1950-52; Carnegie resch. fellow Coun. on Foreign Rels., N.Y.C., 1952-54; various positions The Asia Found., San Francisco and Tokyo, 1954-66, dir. of programs San Francisco, 1966-69, v.p. for programs, 1969-84, exec. v.p., 1984-88; vis. rsch. scholar Hoover Inst., Stanford, 1988—. Mem. Am. adv. com. Japan Found., Tokyo, 1984-86, vis. History lectr. Harvard U., 1958. Author: Japanese and Americans, 1955, What Did You Do in the War, Daddy?, 1998; contbr. articles to profl. jours. Vestryman St. Paul's Episcopal Ch., Burlingame, Calif., 1993-95. Lt. (j.g.), USNR, 1942-46, PTO. Assn. Asian Studies, World Affairs Coun. No. Calif., Japan Soc. No. Calif. Democrat. Avocations: reading, travel. Home: 1432 Benito Ave Burlingame CA 94010-5550

SCHWARCZ, HENRY PHILIP, geologist, educator; b. Chgo., July 22, 1933; s. Arthur and Zita Elizabeth (Strauss) S.; m. Molly Ann Robinson, Dec. 20, 1964; 1 child, Joshua Arthur AB, U. Chgo., 1952; M.Sc. in Geochemistry, Calif. Inst. Tech., 1955, PhD in Geology, 1960. Rsch. assoc. E. Fermi Inst., U. Chgo., 1960-62; prof. geology McMaster U., Hamilton, Ont., Can., 1962—, chmn., assoc. mem. dept. anthropology Can., 1998—, univ. prof. Can., 1996-99, prof. emeritus Can., 1999—. Mem. assoc. com. on meteorites NRC of Can., 1978-86; vis. fellow Clare Hall Coll. Cambridge U., 1991-92, Australian Nat. U., 1995; vis. prof. Hebrew U., Jerusalem, 1992; assoc. mem. dept. anthropology U. Toronto, 1993—; mem. panel refs. Rivista di Antropologia (Roma). Assoc. editor Geochimica et Cosmochimica Acta, 1984-96, Jour. Human Evolution, 1994—, Geoarchaeology, 1994—; mem. editorial bd. Jour. Archaeol. Sci., 1986—; contbr. articles to profl. jours., chpts. to books. Fulbright fellow, Pisa, Italy, 1968-69, Killam fellow Can. Coun., 1993—. Fellow Royal Soc. Can., Geol. Soc. Am. (Archeol. Geol. Div. award 1991, Fryxell award 1999); mem. Geochem. Soc., Lithoprobe NSERC 1991—), Am. Quaternary Assn., Acad. III Sci. (mem. coun.), Geol. Soc. Am. (chmn. archeol. geol. divsn.), Sigma Xi (disting. lectr. 2000-01). Avocations: playing violin, drawing, painting, cooking. Office: McMaster U Sch Geography and Geology Hamilton ON Canada L8S 4M1 E-mail: schwarcz@mcmaster.ca.

SCHWARCZ, STEVEN LANCE, law educator, lawyer; b. N.Y.C., Nov. 10, 1949; s. Charles and Elinor Schwarcz; m. Susan Beth Kolodny, Aug. 24, 1975; children: Daniel Benjamin, Rebekah Mara. BS summa cum laude in Aero. Engring., NYU, 1971; JD, Columbia U., 1974. Bar: N.Y. 1971, U.S. Dist. Ct. (so. dist.) N.Y. 1975. Assoc. Shearman & Sterling, N.Y.C., 1974-82, ptnr., 1983-89; ptnr., chmn. structured fin. Kaye, Scholer, Fierman, Hays & Handler, 1996—; prof. Duke U. Sch. Law, Durham, N.C., 1996—; spl. counsel Kaye, Scholer, Fierman, Hays & Handler, 1996—; faculty dir. Duke Global Capital Markets Ctr. Adj. prof. law Yeshiva U., Benjamin N. Cardozo Sch. Law, N.Y.C., 1983-92; vis. lectr. Yale Law Sch., 1992-96; lectr. Columbia Law Sch., 1992-96. Contbr. articles to profl. jours. Chmn. Friends of the Eldridge St. Synagogue, N.Y.C., 1979-96, Legis. Drafting Rsch. Fund. George Granger Brown scholar, 1971; NSF grantee in Math., 1969. Fellow Am. Coll. Comml. Fin. Lawyers; mem. Am. Law Inst., Assn. of Bar of City of N.Y. (environ. law com. 1975-78, nuc. tech. com. 1979-81, sci. and law com. 1985—, chmn. 1987-90), Am. Law and Econs. Assn., Tau Beta Pi, Sigma Gamma Tau. Jewish. Office: Duke U Sch Law Box 90360 Science Dr & Towerview Rd Durham NC 27708 E-mail: schwarcz@law.duke.edu.

SCHWARCZ, SUSAN KOLODNY, lawyer; b. N.Y.C., Feb. 4, 1954; d. Armand and Elaine (Witkin) Kolodny; m. Steven L. Schwarcz, Aug. 24, 1975; children: Daniel, Rebekah. BA cum laude, Barnard Coll., 1975; postgrad. in social work, Columbia U., 1975-76; JD, Yeshiva U., 1979. Bar: N.Y. 1980, N.C. 1997. Pleadings atty. U.S. Fidelity & Guaranty Co., N.Y.C., 1980-81; pvt. practice Great Neck, N.Y., 1981-85, Scarsdale, 1985—, Chapel Hill, N.C., 1997—. Moot ct. judge Duke U. Sch. Law, 1998—2000; instr. Durham Tech. C., 1999—, Duke U. Sch. Bus., summer, 2002. Mem. Friends Eldridge Street Synagogue, N.Y.C., 1982—; mem. polit. action com. Jewish Action Com., N.Y.C., 1986—; mem. Commn. on Chapel Hill Pub. Arts Commn., 1998—. Mem. Westchester County Bar Assn. (family law com. 1985-97), Westchester Law Guardians Assn., N.C. Bar Assn., Orange County Bar Assn., Sierra Club. Avocations: travel, Asian philosophy and antiques. Office: 109 Boxwood Pl Chapel Hill NC 27517-6503

SCHWARCZ, VERA, history educator; d. Elmer and Katherine Savin; m. Jason Wolfe, July 31, 1983; children: Elie, Esther. BA in French Lit. and Oriental Religions, Vassar Coll., 1969; MA in East Asian Studies, Yale U., 1971; PhD in Chinese History, Stanford U., 1977. Instr. Stanford (Calif.) U., 1973; lectr. Chinese history Wesleyan U., Middletown, Conn., 1975-77, asst. prof. Chinese history, 1975-83, assoc. prof. history, 1983-87, prof. history, 1987—, chair East Asian studies, 1985-88, 94-96. Dir. Mansfield Freeman for East Asian Studies, 1987-88, 94-96; exch. scholar Beijing U., 1979-80, vis. scholar, 1983, 86, 89; vis. scholar Ctr. de Documentation sur la Chine Contemporaine, Paris, 1985, DAO Assn., Cluj, Romania, 1993, Miskenot Sha'ananim, Jerusalem, 1991; vis. prof. East Asian studies Hebrew U., Jerusalem, 1996-97; mem. editl. bd. History and Theory, 1981-84, 96-99, China Rev. Internat., 1994—; bd. dirs. Sino-Judaic Inst., 1993-96; presenter, referee for various jours. in field. Author: Long Road Home: A China Journal, 1984, Chinese Enlightenment: Intellectuals, and the Legacy of the May Fourth Movement in Modern China, 1986, Zhongguo de qimeng yundong, 1989, Time for Telling Truth is Running Out: Conversations with Zhang Shenfu, 1992, Bridge Across Broken Time: Chinese and Jewish Cultural Memory, 1998, co-editor: China: Inside the People's Republic, 1972; contbr. articles, revs., poetry and fiction to profl. publs. Fellow Danforth Found., 1971-73, NDFL, 1973-74, NAS, 1979-80, Guggenheim Found. fellow, 1989-90, Great River Arts Inst. poetry fellow, 2000, founders fellow AAUW, 1988-89, faculty fellow Ctr. for Humanities Wesleyan U., 1988; grantee AAUW, 1974-75, Am. Philos. Soc., 1985, Am. Coun. Learned Socs., 1978, 96; finalist Nat. Jewish Book award in History, 1999; recipient Wesleyan Writers Conf. Poetry scholarship, 1999. Mem. Assn. for Asian Studies (coun. on confs. 1989—, mem. Levenson prize com. 1991-92, chair 1992-93), New Eng. Assn. for Asian Studies (pres. 1988-89). Home: 42 Seneca Rd West Hartford CT 06117-2245 Office: Wesleyan U History Dept Middletown CT 06459-0001 Fax: 860-685-2781.

SCHWARTZ, AARON ROBERT, lawyer, former state legislator; b. Galveston, Tex., July 17, 1926; s. Joseph and Clara (Bulbe) S.; m. Marilyn Cohn, July 14, 1951; children: Richard Austin, Robert Allen, John Reed, Thomas Lee. Pre-law student, Tex. A&M U., 1948; JD, U. Tex., 1951. Bar: Tex. 1951. Mem. Tex. Ho. of Reps., 1955-59, Tex. Senate, 1960-81, past chmn. rules, jurisprudence and natural resources coms. Chmn. Tex. Coastal & Marine Coun., U.S. Coastal States Orgn.; adj. prof., legis. and costal mgmt. law, Bates Law Sch., U. Houston. Contbr. articles to profl. jours. Mem. emeritus exec. com. Galveston Bay Fond.; apptd. to Tex. Oil Spill Oversight Commn., 1993. Served with USN, 1944-46, 2d lt. USAFR, 1948-53. Recipient conservation and legis. awards, Outstanding Citizen award Galveston Jr. C. of C., 1981, Man of Yr., People of Vision award Galveston chpt. Soc. for Prevention of Blindness, 1986, Disting. Service award Nat. Hurricane Conf., Tex. Coastal Mgmt. Adv. Com., 1987, Lifetime Coastal Achievement award, 1997. Mem. Tex. State Bar Assn., Galveston County Bar Assn. Democrat. Jewish. Address: 1122 Colorado St Apt 2102 Austin TX 78701-2142 E-mail: ars71726@aol.com.

SCHWARTZ, ALAN E. lawyer, director; b. Detroit, Dec. 21, 1925; s. Maurice H. and Sophia (Welkowitz) S.; m. Marianne Shapero, Aug. 24, 1950; children: Marc Alan, Kurt Nathan, Ruth Anne. Student, Western Mich. Coll., 1944-45; BA with distinction, U. Mich., 1947; LLB magna cum laude, Harvard U., 1950; LLD, Wayne State U., 1983, U. Detroit, 1985. Bar: N.Y. 1951, Mich. 1952. Assoc. Kelley, Drye & Warren, N.Y.C., 1950-52; mem. Honigman, Miller, Schwartz & Cohn, Detroit, 1952—. Spl. asst. counsel N.Y. State Crime Commn., 1951; bd. dirs. Pulte Corp. Editor: Harvard Law Rev., 1950. Dir. Detroit Symphony Orch.; v.p., bd. dirs. United Found.; bd. dirs. Detroit Renaissance, New Detroit, Jewish Welfare Fedn. Detroit, Wayne State Univ. Found.; trustee Cmty. Found. for Southeastern Mich., Interlochen Arts Acad.; adv. mem. Arts Commn., City of Detroit; mem. investment com. Krespe Found. Served as ensign Supply Corps, USNR, 1945-46. Recipient Mich. Heritage Hall of Fame award, 1984, George W. Romney award for lifetime achievement in volunteerism, 1994, Max M. Fisher Cmty. Svc. award, 1997. Mem. Mich. Bar Assns. Clubs: Franklin Hills Country; Detroit, Economic (dir.). Office: Honigman Miller Schwartz & Cohn 2290 1st National Bldg Detroit MI 48226

SCHWARTZ, ALAN GIFFORD, sport company executive; b. N.Y.C., Nov. 7, 1931; s. Kevie Waldemar and Vera (Isaacs) S.; m. Roslyn Smulian, Sept. 6, 1958; children: Steven, Andrew, Sally, Elizabeth. BS, Yale U., 1952; MBA, Harvard U., 1954. Ptnr. Gifford Investment Co., Chgo., 1954—; CEO Tennis Corp. of Am., 1969—, chmn. bd., 1974—. Dir. Firstar Bank Ill., Comtrex Systems, Inc., Mt. Laurel, N.J.; trustee Roosevelt U., 1994—, Inst. European & Asian Studies, 1993—; v.p. U.S. Tennis Assn., 1994—. Contbr. articles to profl. jours.; editorial cons. Club Industry mag., 1985—. Bd. dirs. Grad. Sch. of Bus., Duke U., Durham, N.C., 1977—, McCormick Boys and Girls Club, 1989—. Elected to Club Industry Hall of Fame, 1987. Mem. Standard Club of Chgo., Exec. Club. Chgo. Jewish. Avocations: travel, tennis. Office: Tennis Corp of Am 3611 N Kedzie Ave Chicago IL 60618-4513

SCHWARTZ, ALAN LEIGH, pediatrician, educator; b. N.Y.C., Apr. 25, 1948; s. Robert and Joyce (Goldner) S.; m. Judith Child, June 22, 1974; 1 child, Timothy Child. BA, PHD in Pharmacology, Case Western Res. U., 1974, MD, 1976. Diplomate Am. Bd. Pediatrics. Intern Children's Hosp., Boston, 1976-77, resident, 1976-78, fellow Dana Farber Cancer Inst., 1978-80; instr. Harvard Med. Sch., 1980-81, asst. prof., 1981-83, assoc. prof., 1983-86; prof. pediatrics, molecular biology and pharmacology Washington U. Sch. Medicine, St. Louis, 1986—, chmn. dept. pediatrics, 1995—; chmn. faculty practice plan Washington U., 1999—2001. Vis. scientist MIT, Boston, 1979-82; mem. sci. adv. bd. Nat. Inst. Child Health and Human Devel., NIH, Bethesda, Md., 1988-94; investigator Am. Heart Assn. Alumni Endowed Prof. Pediats. Wash. U. Sch. Medicine, 1987-97, Harriet B. Spoehrer Prof. Pediats., 1997—. Mem. Inst. Medicine of NAS. Office: Washington U Sch Medicine Dept Pediatrics Box 8116 One Children's Pl Saint Louis MO 63110-1093

SCHWARTZ, ALAN MARSHALL, radiologist; b. Bklyn., June 27, 1944; s. Harry and Elsa Schwartz; m. Mary Jane Weimann, Jan. 13, 1968 (div. Oct. 1997); m. Stephanie Blair Andrew Schwartz, June 15, 2000; children: Evan, Alexander. MD, Tufts U., 1969. Diplomate Am. Bd. Radiology. Radiologist New Eng. Med. Ctr., Boston, 1975—83, Morton Hosp. & Med. Ctr., Taunton, 1993—. Med. dir. radiation tech. program C.C. R.I., Lincoln, 1991—; med. dir. NEMY, Mass., 1999—. Contbr. articles to profl. jours. Treas. Selectmans Campaign, Cohasset, Mass., 1978. Lt. comdr. USN, 1973—75. Mem.: Mass. Med. Soc. (alt. del. 1970), Radiol. Soc. N.Am., Am. Coll. Radiology, Alpha Omega Alpha. Jewish. Avocations: golf, travel, painting. Office: Taunton Radiology Assoc 88 Washington St Taunton MA 02780

SCHWARTZ, ALAN VICTOR, advertising agency executive; b. Detroit, July 12, 1948; s. Seymour and Adeline (Goldstein) S.; children: Stacy Ilana, Andrew Robert. BS with honors, Lehigh U., 1970; MBA with highest honors, Cornell U., 1972. CPA, N.Y. Mgr. Price Waterhouse, Huntington, N.Y., 1972-79; v.p., dir. fin. control Doyle Dane Bernbach, N.Y.C., 1979-81; v.p., CFO, Bernard Hodes Group, 1981-84, sr. v.p., chief oper. and fin. officer, 1984-87, exec. v.p., COO, 1987—2001, pres., CEO, 2002—, 2002—. Bd. mgrs. Evans Tower, treas. 1991-92, pres. 1991-92. Campaign vice chmn. United Way L.I., 1978. Mem. Nat. Assn. Accts. (various directorships, treas.), N.Y. State Soc. CPAs, Lehigh Alumni Assn. (pres. L.I. chpt. 177-79, treas. 1975-77). Office: Bernard Hodes Group 220 E 42d St New York NY 10017

SCHWARTZ, A(LBERT) TRUMAN, chemistry educator; b. Freeman, S.D., May 8, 1934; s. Albert and Edna Kaufman Schwartz; m. Beverly Beatty, Aug. 12, 1958; children: Ronald Eric, Katherine Schwartz Herrmann. BA, U. S.D., 1956, Oxford (Eng.) U., 1958, MA, 1960; PhD, MIT, 1963; DSc, U. S.D., 1991. Rsch. chemist Procter & Gamble Co., Cin., 1963-66; asst. prof. Macalester Coll., St. Paul, 1966-72, assoc. prof., 1972-78, prof., 1978-83, DeWitt Wallace prof., 1983—, dean faculty, 1974-76, chair dept. chemistry, 1980-88, 94-95. Vis. rschr. U. Lund, Sweden, 1968, U. Mass., Amherst, 1972-73; vis. prof. U. Wis., Madison, 1979-80, U. S.D., 2000; hon. vis. prof. U. York, Eng., 1994; dep. dir. tchr. preparation and enhancement NSF, Washington, 1986-87. Author: Chemistry: Imagination and Implication, 1973; sr. author: Chemistry in Context: Applying Chemistry to Society, 1994, 2nd edit., 1997; co-editor: Motion Toward Perfection: The Achievement of Joseph Priestley, 1970; contbr. articles to profl. jours. Mem. selection com. Rhodes Scholarship Trust, 1963—, sec. Minn. and Midwest dist. coms., 1993-2001. Recipient Catalyst award in chem. edn. Chem. Mfrs. Assn., 1982, Coll. Sci. Tchr. of Yr., Minn. Sci. Tchrs. Assn., 1988; Rhodes scholar Rhodes Trust, Oxford U., 1956-58. Fellow AAAS; mem. Am. Chem. Soc. (chair divsn. chem. edn. 1989, chair Minn. sect. 1992-93, mem. various coms., Conn. Sect. award 1991, Brasted award 1996, James Flack Norris award 1997). Avocations: music, photography, travel, cooking. Home: 68 Otis Ave Saint Paul MN 55104 Office: Macalester Coll 1600 Grand Ave Saint Paul MN 55105-1801 E-mail: schwartz@macalester.edu.

SCHWARTZ, ALFRED, university dean; b. Chgo., Jan. 8, 1922; s. Isadore and Lena (Ziff) S.; m. Delle Weiss, Aug. 26, 1945; children: Reid Mitchell, Karen Ruth. B.Ed., Chgo. Tchrs. Coll., 1944; MA in Polit. Sci., U. Chgo., 1946, PhD in Ednl. Adminstrn., 1949. Tchr. Chgo. pub. schs., 1944-45; contact officer VA, 1946; instr. U. Chgo. Lab. Sch., 1946-50; assoc. prof. edn. Drake U., 1950-56, U. Del.; also exec. sec. Del. Sch. Study Council, 1956-58; dean (Univ. Coll.); prof. Coll. Edn., Drake U., 1958-85, dean, 1964-79, 80-84, dean emeritus, 1985; acting v.p. acad. adminstrn. Coll. Edn., Coll. Edn., 1979-80; cons., 1985—. Adviser Iowa Dept. Pub. Instrn.; mem. coordinating bd. Nat. Council Accreditation for Tchr. Edn.; chmn. tchr. edn. and adv. com. Iowa Dept. Pub. Instrn. Author: (with Harlan L. Hagman) Administration in Profile for School Executives, 1954, (with Stuart Tiedeman) Evaluating Student Progress, 1957, (with Willard Fox) Managerial Guide for School Principals, 1965. Mem. Gov.'s Commn. State-Local Relations, pres. condo assn., 1987-97. Mem. World Council on Curriculum and Instrn., Iowa Assn. Colls. for Tchr. Edn. (pres., exec. sec.), Am. Profs. for Peace in Middle East, Am. Ednl. Research Assn., Iowa Edn. Assn., NEA, Phi Delta Kappa, Kappa Delta Pi. Home: 3450 3rd Ave Apt 511 San Diego CA 92103-4939

SCHWARTZ, ALLEN G. federal judge; b. Bklyn., Aug. 23, 1934; s. Herbert and Florence (Safier) S.; m. Joan Ruth Teitel, Jan. 17, 1965; children: David Aaron, Rachel Ann, Deborah Eve. BBA, CCNY, 1955; LLB, U. Pa., 1958. Bar: N.Y. 1958. Asst. dist. atty. Office of Dist. Atty., N.Y. County, 1959-62; assoc. firm Paskus Gordon & Hyman, N.Y.C., 1962-65; ptnr. firm Koch Lankenau Schwartz & Kovner, 1965-69, Dornbush Mensch Mandelstam & Schwartz, N.Y.C., 1969-75; mem. Schwartz & Schreiber, P.C., 1975-77; corp. counsel City of N.Y., 1978-81; mem. Schwartz Klink & Schreiber, P.C., 1982-87; ptnr. Proskauer Rose Goetz & Mendelsohn, N.Y.C., 1987-94; judge U.S. Dist. Ct. (so. dist.) N.Y., 1994—. Mem. ex officio N.Y.C. Bd. Ethics, 1978-81; pro bono sports commr. City of N.Y., 1982-83. Research editor: U. Pa. Law Rev., 1957-58. Recipient Award of Achievement, Sch. Bus. Alumni, Soc. of the City Coll., 1981, Hogan-Morganthau Assocs. award, 1980, Corp. Coun. ann. award, 1995, Frank S. Hogan Assocs. award, 1995, Pres.'s medal Baruch Coll., 2001. Office: US Courthouse 500 Pearl St Rm 1350 New York NY 10007-1316 E-mail: allen_g._schwartz@nysd.uscourts.gov.

SCHWARTZ, ALLEN MARVIN, production company executive; b. Chgo., Jan. 3, 1932; s. Herman and Shirley (Cohen) S.; m. Jayne Mary Knoerzer, Oct. 3, 1963; children: Scott, Jill, Wendy. Student, U. Wis., 1953. Performer, dir. Sta. WKOW-TV, Madison, Wis., 1953-54, 56-57; dir., producer CBS-TV, Chgo., 1957-64; pres. Schwartz and Wallace Prodns., 1964-68; v.p., exec. producer Polaris Prodns., Los Angeles, 1968-76; freelance producer CBS, ABC, NBC, 1976-78; sr. v.p. TV prodns. Dick Clark Prodns., 1978—. TV producer, dir. The World of Andrew Wyeth, 1968 (Emmy award); TV producer: Golden Globe Awards, 1997-2001, Beyond Belief Acad. Country Music Awards, American Music Awards, 1976—, TV Bloopers & Practical Jokes, 1981-97; prodr., dir. Acad. Awards Spl. Segments; prodr. Emmy Awards, 1996, Daytime Emmy Awards, 1991-97, 2001-02. Served with U.S. Army, 1954-56. Recipient Ohio State U. award, 1968, Chgo. Film Festival award, 1968, Iris award Nat. Assn. TV Program Execs., Los Angeles, 1971. Mem. Zeta Beta Tau. Home: 9707 Arby Dr Beverly Hills CA 90210-1203 Office: Dick Clark Prodns 3003 W Olive Ave Burbank CA 91505-4538 E-mail: aldcp@aol.com.

SCHWARTZ, ALVAN ROBERT, retired neurologist, consultant, sculptor, author, photographer; b. Springfield, Mass., Nov. 23, 1933; s. Jacob and Edna Schwartz; m. Janice Ellen Segal, Feb. 21, 1960; children: Larry Wayne, David Lee, Susan Beth. AB, Dartmouth Coll., 1955; MD, Tufts U., 1959; postgrad., Sch. Mus. Fine Arts, Boston, 1978, 79, 2001. Diplomate Am. Bd. Psychiatry and Neurology. Intern R.I. Hosp., Providence, 1959-60; resident in internal medicine Hartford (Conn.) Hosp., 1960-61; resident in neurology Lemuel Shattuck Hosp., Jamaica Plain, Mass., 1961-62, Tufts New Eng. Med. Ctr., Boston, 1962-63, Boston City Hosp., 1963-64; pvt. practice Beverly, Mass., 1964-99; brain cons. Neuropsychology Svc., Inc., 1999—. Cons. in neurology Walter Reed Gen. Hosp., Washington, 1968-69; dir. Multiple Sclerosis Regional Clinic North Shore, Beverly, 1977-99; mem. med. adv. bd. Mass. chpt. Nat. Multiple Sclerosis Soc., Waltham, 1994-99; electroencephalographer, evoked potential interpreter, founder Neurodiagnostic Ctr., Beverly Hosp., 1981-99. Author: Travel-At Its Best, 1978; co-author: Understanding Multiple Sclerosis, 1988, Living with Multiple Sclerosis, 1994;Exhibited in group shows at Mast Cove Gallery, Kennebunkport, Maine, 1987, Mass. Transp. Bldg., Boston, 1991, The Beverly Hosp., Mass., 1991, 1994, Blossoms by M Gallery, Beverly Farms, Mass., 1998, Mingo Gallery, Beverly, 1999, Russian and Am. Art Festival, Marblehead, Mass., 2001, landscape design. Sponsor Multiple Sclerosis Night at the Pops, Boston, 1994-98; philanthropic founder Arthur Feinstein "55 Meml. Award for Outstanding Work in English, Dartmouth Coll., Hanover, N.H., 1984-99. Recipient Best of Show award, 1991, 94, People's Choice and regional awards for sculpture Tufts Assoc. Health Plan, Beverly, 1991, 3d prize Marblehead (Mass.) Arts Assn., 1984, Pres.'s award Guild Beverly Artists, 1994. Mem. Mass. Med. Soc. (chmn. neurology sect. 1983-84), Mass. Neurology Assn. (founder, pres. 1982-84). Avocations: travel, landscape design, photography, cycling, physical conditioning. Office: Neuropsychology Svc 100 Cummings Ctr Ste 431J Beverly MA 01915-5990 Fax: 978-922-6717.

SCHWARTZ, ANNA JACOBSON, economic historian; b. N.Y.C., Nov. 11, 1915; married; four children. BA, Barnard Coll., 1934; MA, Columbia U., 1935, PhD, 1964; LittD (hon.), U. Fla., 1987, Emory U., 2000; ArtsD (hon.), Stonehill Coll., 1989; LLD (hon.), Iona Coll., 1992, Rutgers U., 1998; LHD (hon.), CUNY, 2000; LLD (hon.), Williams Coll., 2002. Rschr. USDA, 1936, Columbia U. Social Sci. Rsch. Coun., 1936-41; sr. rsch. staff Nat. Bur. Econ. Rsch. Inc., N.Y.C., 1941—. Instr. Bklyn. Coll., 1952, Baruch Coll., 1959-60; adj. prof. econs. grad. CUNY, 1967-69, grad. sch. CUNY, 1986—, NYU Grad. Sch. Arts and Sci., 1969-70; hon. vis. prof. City U. Bus. Sch., London, 1984—; hon. fellow Inst. of Econ. Affairs, London, 1998. Mem. editorial bd. Am. Econ. Rev., 1972-78, Jour. Money, Credit and Banking, 1974-75, 84—, Jour. Monetary Econs., 1975—, Jour. Fin. Svcs. Rsch., 1993—; contbr. articles to profl. jours. Disting. fellow Am. Econ. Assn., 1993; hon fellow Inst. Econ. Affairs, London. Mem. Western Econ. Assn. (pres. 1987-88). Office: Nat Bur Econ Research 365 Fifth Ave 5th Fl New York NY 10016-4309

SCHWARTZ, ANTHONY, veterinary surgeon, educator; b. Bklyn., July 30, 1940; s. Murray and Miriam Sarah (Wittes) S.; m. Claudia Rosenberg, July 21, 1963; children: Thomas Frederick, Eric Leigh. Student, Mich. State U., 1957-58; DVM, Cornell U., 1963; PhD, Ohio State U., 1972. Diplomate Am. Coll. Vet. Surgeons (bd. of regents 1989-92). Gen. practice vet. medicine, Huntington, N.Y., 1963-66; resident in surgery Animal Med. Ctr., N.Y.C., 1968-69, Ohio State U., Columbus, 1969-70, asst. prof., head sect. small animal surgery, 1973; asst. prof. then assoc. prof. comparative medicine Yale U. Sch. Medicine, New Haven, 1973-79; assoc. prof. then prof., chmn. dept. surgery, assoc. dean Tufts U. Sch. Vet. Medicine, Boston, 1979-89, assoc. dean clin. edn., 1989-93, prof., chmn. dept. surgery, assoc. dean academic affairs, 1993-97, assoc. dean for acad. and outreach programs, 1997—. Cons. U.S. Surg. Corp., Norwalk, Conn., 1975—; mem. Bd. Tufts Animal Expo LLC, program dir., 1999—; mem. vet. adv. bd. PetPlace.com, 2000—. Author: (with others) Small Animal Surgery, 1989, Complications in Small Animal Surgery, 1996; editl. bd. Vet. Surgery, 1987-90, Jour. Investigative Surgery, 1987-98; assoc. editor: Textbook of Small Animal Surgery, 1985; contbr. articles to profl. jours. Capt. U.S. Army Vet Corps., 1966-68. Recipient 1st prize N.Y. State Vet. Med. Soc., 1963; Robert Wood Johnson Health Policy fellow, Washington, 1988-89; NIH grantee, 1975-84. Mem.: AAAS, AVMA (legis. planning com. 1989—92, coun. on govt. affairs 1992—97), Mass. Vet. Med. Assn. (animal welfare com. 1990—98, chmn. 1990—91), Nat. Acads. of Practice, Assn. Am. Vet. Med. Colls. (Washington, exec. dir., treas. 1992—93), Phi Kappa Phi, Sigma Xi. Democrat. Jewish. Office: Tufts U Sch Vet Medicine 200 Westboro Rd North Grafton MA 01536-1895 E-mail: Anthony.Schwartz@tufts.edu.

SCHWARTZ, ARTHUR, social worker; b. Brockton, Mass., July 10, 1927; s. Morris and Esther C. Schwartz; m. Ruth May Silverstein, Jan. 30, 1955; children: Elizabeth, David Morris. BA, Northeastern U., Boston, 1951; MS in Social Svc., Boston U., 1953; PHD, Columbia U., 1965. Case worker Jewish Bd. Guidance, Bklyn., 1953-55, CCNY, 1955-59; rsch. assoc. YM-YWHAs of Greater N.Y., 1960-63; asst. prof. Sch. Social Work, Rutgers U., New Brunsville, 1963-66; assoc. prof. U. Chgo., Chgo., 1966-82; prof. Sch. Social Work, U. Hawaii, Honolulu, 1982-83, U. Md., Balt., 1983-94; scholar-in-residence Widener U., Chester, Pa., 1994-99; lectr. U. Pa., 1997—. Author: Social Casework: A Behavioral Approach, 1975, The Behavior Therapies, 1982, Depression: Theories & Treatment, 1993. Mem. NASW, AAUP. Democrat. Jewish. Home: 2401 Pennsylvania Ave Apt 10b24 Philadelphia PA 19130-3037 Office: U Pa 1 University Mews Philadelphia PA 19104-4756

SCHWARTZ, ARTHUR GERALD, microbiology educator; b. Balt., Mar. 13, 1941; s. Paul and Rose (Goldfinger) S.; m. Karen Jean Bantley, Mar. 27, 1988; 1 child, Daniel Paul. BA, Johns Hopkins U., 1961; PhD, Harvard U., 1968. Postdoctoral fellow Sir William Dunn Sch. Pathology U. Oxford, Eng., 1968-71; postdoctoral fellow dept. cell biology Albert Einstein Coll. Medicine, N.Y., 1971-72; investigator Fells Rsch. Inst. Temple U. Sch. Medicine, Phila., 1972—, asst. prof. microbiology, 1972-77, assoc. prof. microbiology, 1977-85, prof. microbiology, 1985—. Patentee method for prophylaxis of obesity and steroids useful as anti-cancer and anti-obesity agts. Jane Coffin Childs Meml. Fund for Med. Rsch. fellow, 1968. Mem. Phi Beta Kappa. Office: Temple U Sch Medicine Fels Inst Cancer Rsch 3400 N Broad St Philadelphia PA 19140-5104

SCHWARTZ, ARTHUR JAY, lawyer; b. Atlanta, May 28, 1947; s. William B. Jr. and Sonia (Weinberg) S.; m. Joyce Straus, Aug. 12, 1972; children: Tracy Jill, Allison Jaye. BA, U. N.C., 1969; JD, Emory U., 1972. Bar: Ga. 1972, U.S. Dist. Ct. (no. dist.) Ga. 1972, U.S. Ct. Appeals (5th and 11th cirs.) 1972. Ptnr. Smith, Gambrell & Russell L.L.P., Atlanta, 1972—, chmn. exec. com., mng. ptnr., 1988-89, 92-93, 96-97, fin. ptnr., 1998—. Sec. Lamin Art, Inc., Chgo., 1984—, also bd. dirs. Mem. Emory Law Sch. Coun., 1997—2001; bd. dirs. Am. Jewish Com., Atlanta, 1982—84, The Temple, Atlanta, 1983—85, 1994—, treas., 1998—2000, v.p., 2000—02, pres., 2002—. With USAR, 1970—72. Mem. Am. Technion Soc. Atlanta (v.p., bd. dirs. 1980-87), Soc. Internat. Bus. Fellows, Buckhead Club (bd. dirs. 1987-97). Avocations: hunting, running, golf, boating. E-mail: JSchwartz@sgrlaw.com.

SCHWARTZ, AUBREY EARL, artist, educator; b. N.Y.C., Jan. 13, 1928; s. Louis and Clara S. Student, Art Students League, Bklyn. Mus. Art Sch. , 1969-94; prof. emeritus Harpur Coll., SUNY, Binghamton, 1994—. Prof. art Harpur Coll., SUNY, Binghamton, 1969— One-man shows Grippi Gallery, N.Y.C., 1958, Art U.S.A., N.Y. Coliseum, N.Y.C., 1959, Contemporary Graphic Art, U.S. State Dept., 1959, group shows include Whitney Mus. Am. Art, N.Y.C., 1957, Binghamton Univ. Art Mus., 1997; represented in permanent collections Nat. Gallery Art, Washington, Bklyn. Mus. Art, Phila. Mus. Art, Library Congress, Washington, Art Inst. Chgo. Recipient 1st prize for graphic art Boston Arts Festival 1960; Guggenheim fellow, 1958-60; Tamarind fellow, 1960; N.Y. State CAPS fellow, 1973-74 Home: PO Box 6 Afton NY 13730-0006

SCHWARTZ, BARRY FREDRIC, lawyer, diversified holding company executive; b. Phila., Apr. 16, 1949; s. Albert and Evelyn (Strauss) S.; m. Sherry L. Handsman, Mar. 21, 1985; children: Fanny Rose, Abraham David. AB cum laude, Kenyon Coll., 1970; JD, Georgetown U., 1974. Bar: Pa. 1974, Ill. 1974, N.Y. 1992, U.S. Dist. Ct. (ea. dist.) Pa. 1974, U.S. Dist. Ct. (no. dist.) Ill. 1975, U.S. Dist. Ct. (so. dist.) N.Y. 1992, U.S. Ct. Appeals (7th cir.) 1977, U.S. Ct. Appeals (3d cir.) 1978, U.S. Ct. Appeals (4th cir.) 1979, U.S. Ct. Appeals (6th cir.) 1981, U.S. Supreme Ct. 1981, N.Y. 1992. Assoc. Sachnoff, Schrager, Jones & Weaver, Chgo., 1974-76; ptnr. Wolf, Block, Schorr & Solis-Cohen, Phila., 1976-89; exec. v.p. gen. counsel MacAndrews & Forbes Holdings, Inc., N.Y.C., 1989—. Trustee Kenyon Coll.; mem. adv. coun. Westchester Holocaust Commn., 2000–; mem. Adv. Com. for Justices of the Comml. divsn. Supreme Ct., New York County, 1999–. Home: 16 Brookside Park Greenwich CT 06831-5316 Office: MacAndrews & Forbes Holdings Inc 35 E 62nd St New York NY 10021-8032

SCHWARTZ, BERNARD, physician; b. Toronto, Can., Nov. 12, 1927; s. Samuel and Gertrude Schwartz; children: Lawrence Frederick, Karen Lynne, Jennifer Carla, Ariane Samara MD, U. Toronto, 1951; MS, State U. Iowa, 1953, PhD, 1959. Intern U. Hosps., State U. Iowa, 1951-52, resident ophthalmology, 1951-54; research fellow U. Iowa, 1954-58; asst. prof. to assoc. prof. Downstate Med. Center fo State U. N.Y., 1958-68; prof. ophthalmology Tufts U., 1968-93, chmn. dept., 1968-90, prof. emeritus ophthalmology, 1993—. Author: Syphilis and the Eye; Editor in chief of: Survey of Ophthalmology, 1968— , Comprehensive Ophthalmology Update, 1998— ; Contbr. articles to profl. jours. Fellow Am. Acad. Ophthalmology, ACS; mem. Assn. Rsch. in Ophthalmology, New Eng. Ophthalmol. Soc., N.Y. Acad. Medicine, N.Y. Acad. Scis., Soc. Française D'Ophthalmologie, Sigma Xi. Home: 180 Beacon St Boston MA 02116-1408 Office: 20 Park Plz Ste 535 Boston MA 02116-4301 E-mail: glaucomares@mva.net.

SCHWARTZ, BERNARD JULIAN, lawyer; b. Edmonton, Alberta, Can., July 29, 1960; came to U.S., 1982; s. Sol and Anne (Motkovich) S. BA, U. Alberta, 1981; JD, McGeorge Sch. Law, 1986. Bar: U.S. Supreme Ct. 1991. Atty. Ropers, Majeski, San Francisco, 1987-88, Riverside County Pub. Defenders, Riverside, Calif., 1988-89; pvt. practice, 1990—. Coach Riverside County H.S. Mock Trial Team, 1990, 96, 97. Mem. Calif. Attys. Criminal Justice, Calif. Pub. Defenders Assn., Riverside County Bar Assn., Criminal Cts. Bar Assn. (pres.).

SCHWARTZ, BRENDA KEEN, lawyer; b. Ft. Smith, Ark., Dec. 5, 1949; d. James Pritchard and Era Erline (Jones) Denniston; m. Dean Edward Keen, June 23, 1973 (dec. June 1990); 1 child, Duncan Denniston Keen; m. Sylvan Schwartz, Jr., Apr. 26, 1992. BA, U. Houston, 1972, JD magna cum laude, 1975. Bar: Tex. 1975, U.S. Dist. Ct. (so. dist.) Tex. 1975. Assoc. Haynes & Fullenweider, P.L.C., Houston, 1975-79, v.p., ptnr., 1979-87; ptnr., officer Wallis & Keen, P.C., 1988-92; prin. Brenda Keen Schwartz P.C., 1992—. Contbr. articles to legal publs. Fellow Am. Acad. Matrimonial Lawyers (pres. Tex. chpt. 1996-97), Tex. Acad. Family Law Specialists (pres. elect 2002—), Tex. Bar Found., Houston Bar Found.; mem. State Bar Tex. (family law coun. 1989-93). Roman Catholic. Office: 1800 Bering Dr Ste 690 Houston TX 77057-3169

SCHWARTZ, CARL EDWARD, artist, printmaker; b. Detroit, Sept. 20, 1935; s. Carl and Verna (Steiner) S.; m. Kay Joyce Hofmann, June 18, 1955 (div.); children: Dawn Ellen, Cari Leigh; m. Frieda Nelson, Oct. 17, 1982 (div.); m. Dinah Lee Wilson, Jan. 20, 1996. BFA, Art Inst. Chgo. Sch.-U. Chgo., 1957. Past tchr. art , Chgo., N. Shore Art League, Suburban Fine Arts Center, Deerpath Art League; faculty art Edison C.C., Fla. Gulf Coast U. One-man shows include, South Bend (Ind.) Art Center, Feingarten Gallery, Chgo., 1960, Bernard Horwich Center, Chgo., Covenant Club, Chgo., Barat Coll., Chgo. Pub. Library, Alverno Coll., 1020 Art Center, Rosenberg Gallery, Peoria (Ill.) Art Guild, 1977, Ill. State Mus., 1977 Ill. Inst. Tech., 1978, Miller Gallery, Chgo., 1979, Union League Club, Chgo., 1982, Art Inst. Rental and Sale Gallery, Chgo., 1982, Horwich Gallery, Chgo., 1983, Lake Forest (Ill.) Coll., 1983, Campanile-Capponi Contemporary Gallery, Chgo., 1987, Nagata Gallery, Ft. Myers, Fla., 1988, Jan Cicero Gallery, Chgo., 1990, Neopolitan Gallery, Naples, Fla., 1996, 97; numerous group shows include 9th Ann. Michigana Exhbt, Detroit (Cloetingh and Deman award 1959), Hyde Park Art Center, Chgo., 1960 (5th Ann. Jury Exhbn. prize), Spectrum Exhbn. '63, Chgo. (1st prize), New Horizons Exhbt, Chgo., 1960 (Joseph Shapiro award), Nat. Design Center, Chgo., 1965 (New Horizons in Painting 1st prize), 3d Ann. Chgo. Arts Competition, 1962 (1st prize), Union League Club, Chgo., 1967 (2d prize), N. Shore Art League Ann. Drawing and Print Show, Chgo., 1965 (1st prize), Artists Guild Chgo., 1965 (prize), McCormack Pl., Chgo., 1965 (1st prize), Detroit Art Inst., 1965 (Commonwealth prize), Park Forest (Ill.) Art Exhbn, 1969 (Best of Show), 14th Ann. Virginia Beach (Va.) Show, 1969 (Best of Show), Suburban Fine Arts Center, Highland Park, Ill., 1970 (prize), 15th Ann. Virginia Beach Show, 1970 (prize), 32d Ann. Artists Guild, Chgo., 1970 (2d prize), N. Shore Art League Print and Drawing Show, 1970 (prize), 16th Ann. Virginia Beach Show, 1971 (2d prize), Ill. State Fair, 1972 (prize), Artists Guild Chgo., 1972 (1st prize), 17th Ann. Virginia Beach Exhbt, 1972 (1st prize), Artists Guild 50th Fine Art Exhbn., Chgo., 1973 (prize), Dickinson State U., 1973 (prize), N. Shore Art League Print Exhbn, 1973 (prize), Lakehurst Exhbt, 1974 (prize), Union League Art Exhbt, 1974 (1st prize), Artists Guild Fine Arts Exhbn., 1974 (best of Show), Bluegrass Painting Exhbn, Louisville, 1975 (award), Union League Art Exhbn, 1976 (prize); represented in permanent collections, Brit. Mus., London, Smithsonian Inst., Washington, Art Inst. Chgo., K. Van Ella, Chgo., Weatherburn Gallery, Naples. Home: 6150 Briarwood Ter Fort Myers FL 33912-4204 *I am a painter of light. I'm intrigued and fascinated with form. To me, there are two worlds-the one we all live in, and the one that I create. Painting is the discipline by which I constantly rediscover both of these worlds.*

SCHWARTZ, CHARLES, JR. federal judge; b. New Orleans, Aug. 20, 1922; s. Charles and Sophie (Hess) S.; m. Patricia May, Aug. 31, 1950 (dec.); children: Priscilla May, John Putney. BA, Tulane U., 1943, JD, 1947. Bar: La. 1947. Ptnr. Guste, Barnett & Little, 1947-70; practiced in New Orleans, until 1976; ptnr. firm Little, Schwartz & Dussom, 1970-76; dist. counsel Gulf Coast dist. U.S. Maritime Adminstrn., 1953-62; judge U.S. Dist. Ct. (ea. dist.) La., New Orleans, 1976-91, sr. judge, 1991—. Mem. Fgn. Itelligence Surveillance Ct., 1992-98; prof. Tulane U. Law Sch., 1977-99; lectr. continuing law insts., 1974-75; mem. Jud. Conf. Com. U.S. on implementation of jury system, 1981-85; mem. permanent adv. bd. Tulane Admiralty Law Inst., 1984—. Bd. editors Tulane Law Rev. Pres. New Orleans unit Am. Cancer Soc., 1956-57; v.p., chmn. budget com. United Fund Greater New Orleans Area, 1959-61, trustee, 1953-65; bd. dirs. Cancer Assn. Greater New Orleans, 1958— , pres., 1958-59, 72-73; bd. dirs. United Cancer Council, 1963-85, pres., 1971-73; mem. com. on grants to agencies Community Chest, 1965-87; men's adv. com. League Women Voters, 1966-68; chmn. com. admissions of program devel. and coordination com. United Way Greater New Orleans, 1974-77; mem. comml. panel Am. Arbitration Assn., 1974-76; bd. dirs. Willow Wood Home, 1979-85, 1989-92; bd. mgrs. Touro Infirmary, 1992—; trustee Metairie Park Country Day Sch., 1977-83; mem. La. Republican Central Com., 1961-76; mem. Orleans Parish Rep. Exec. Com., 1960-75, chmn., 1964-75; mem. Jefferson Parish Rep. Exec. Com., 1975-76; del. Rep. Nat. Conv., 1960, 64, 68; mem. nat. budget and consultation com. United Community Funds and Coun. of Am., 1961; bd. dirs. Community Svcs. Coun., 1971-73. Served to 2d lt. AUS, 1943-46; maj. U.S. Army Res.; ret. Mem. La. Bar Assn. New Orleans Bar Assn. (legis. com. 1970-75), Fed. Bar Assn., Fgn. Rels. Assn. New Orleans (bd. dirs. 1957-61), 5th Cir. Dist. Judges Assn. (pres. 1984-85), Lakewood Country Club (bd. dirs. 1967-68, pres. 1975-77). Office: 219 Northline Metairie LA 70005-4447

SCHWARTZ, CHARLES PHINEAS, JR. financial and business consultant, lawyer; b. Chgo., Apr. 23, 1927; s. Charles Phineas and Lavinia Duffy (Schulman) S.; m. Joan Straus, Aug. 12, 1954 (div. 1971); children: Alex, Ned, Debra, Emily; m. Susan Lamm Hirsch, Dec. 18, 1976. AB, U. Chgo., 1945; LLB, Harvard U., 1950. Bar: Ill. 1950, N.Y. 1951, U.S. Supreme Ct. 1955. Assoc. Szold & Brandwen, N.Y.C., 1950-52; rsch. assoc., teaching fellow Harvard U. Law Sch., Cambridge, Mass., 1952-56; pvt. practice Chgo., 1956-61; ptnr. Straus, Blosser & McDowell, 1961-67; fin. and bus. cons., 1967-75, 93—; pres., chief exec. officer Champion Parts Inc., Oak Brook, Ill., 1975-86, chmn. bd., chief exec. officer, 1986-92, chmn. emeritus, 1992—. Dir. CMP Industries, Albany, N.Y. Trustee, officer Hull House Assn., Chgo., 1958-70; dir., officer Chgo. Fedn. Settlements, 1972-79; dir., officer, pres. Friends of the Parks, Chgo., 1982—; dir., officer, pres. Hyde Park Coop. Soc., 1962-68; pres. U. Cho. Lab. Schs. Parents Assn., 1970-72, 75-77; trustee KAM Isaiah Isrel Congregation, 1975-85; bd. dirs. Chgo. Hearing Soc., 1996—. Served with USNR, 1945-46. Recipient Boulton Meml. award for disting. bus. statesmanship and dedicated service rendered to the entire auto parts rebuilding industry Automotive Parts Rebuilders Assn., 1987. Mem. ABA, Motor Equipment and Mfrs. Assn. (dir. 1977-81), Automotive Pres. Coun., Heavy Duty Bus. Forum, Automotive Sales Coun., Soc. Automotive Engrs., Automotive Parts Rebuilders Assn. (dir., officer, chmn. 1988—), Chgo. Coun. Lawyers, Heavy Vehicle Maintenance Group (officer 1994—), Quadrangle Club (Chgo.), Harvard Club (N.Y.C.). Clubs: Quadrangle (Chgo.); Harvard (N.Y.C.). Jewish. E-mail: charles2@aol.com.

SCHWARTZ, CHARLES WALTER, lawyer; b. Brenham, Tex., Dec. 27, 1953; s. Walter C. and Annie (Kuehn) S.; m. Kay Anne Kern, Sept. 24, 1996. BS, U. Tex., 1975, MA, 1980, JD, 1977; LLM, Harvard U., 1980. Bar: Tex. 1977; bd. cert. civil appellate law Tex. Bd. Legal Specialization. Law clk. U.S. Ct. Appeals (5th cir.), Austin, Tex., 1977-79; assoc. Vinson & Elkins L.L.P., Houston, 1980-86, ptnr., 1986—. Contbr. articles to law revs. Fellow: Coll. of State Bar of Tex., Houston Bar Found. (life), Tex. Bar Found. (life); mem.: ABA, Tex. Law Rev. Assn., Am. Law Inst., Bar Assn. of 5th Cir., State Bar Tex. (former chmn. griveance com. 1993—99, bd. dirs. 2000—, mem. exec. com. 2001—, chmn. 2002—). Home: 2154 Chilton Rd Houston TX 77019 Office: Vinson & Elkins LLP 2300 First City Tower 1001 Fannin St Houston TX 77002-6760 E-mail: cschwartz@velaw.com.

SCHWARTZ, CHERIE ANNE KARO, storyteller, writer; b. Miami, Fla., Feb. 24, 1951; d. William Howard and Dorothy (Olesh) Karo; m. Lawrence Schwartz, Aug. 12, 1979. BA in Lit., The Colo. Coll., 1973; MA in Devel. Theater, U. Colo., 1977. Tchr. English, drame, mime, creative writing, speech coach South High Sch., Pueblo, Colo., 1973-76; tchr. English and drama Rocky Mountain Hebrew Acad., Denver, 1981-83; full-time profl. storyteller throughout N.Am., 1982—. Storyteller, docent, tchr. tng., mus. outreach Denver Mus. Natural History, 1982—; trainer, cons., performer, lectr, keynote speaker various orgns., synagogues, instns., agys., confs. throughout the country, 1982—; co-founder, chairperson Omanim b'Yachad: Artists Together, Nat. Conf. Celebrating Storytelling, Drama, Music and Dance in Jewish Edn., Denver, 1993. Storyteller: (audio cassette tapes) Cherie Karo Schwartz Tells Stories of Hanukkah from Kar-Ben Books, 1986, Cherie Karo Schwartz Tells Stories of Passover From Kar-Ben Books, 1986, Miriam's Trambourine, 1988, Worldwide Jewish Stories of Wishes and Wisdom, 1988; storyteller, actor: (video tape) The Wonderful World of Recycle, 1989; author: (books) My Lucky Dreidel: Hanukkah Stories, Songs, Crafts, Recipes and Fun for Kids, 1994, A Worldwide Celebration, 2000, The Kids' Catalog of Passover, 2000; co-author: (with Barbara Rush) The Kids' Catalog of Passover, Circle Spinning: Jewish Turning and Returning Tales, 2002; author numerous stories in anthologies of Jewish lit., including Chosen Tales, Because God Loves Stories, Reading Between the Lines, Grey Heroes, Elder Tales from Around the World. Title III grantee State of Colo. Edn., Pueblo, 1975-76. Mem. Coalition for Advancement of Jewish Edn. (coord. Jewish Storytelling Conf. 1989-98, coord. Nat. Jewish Storytelling Network 1994-97), Nat. Assn. for Preservation and Perpetuation of Storytelling, Nat. Storytelling Assn., Rocky Mountain Storytelling Guild, Rocky Mountain Storytellers Conf. (performer, tchr.), Spellbinders (tchr., nat. bd. dirs.). Democrat. Jewish. Home: 996 S Florence St Denver CO 80247-1952 E-mail: schwartstory@earthlink.net.

SCHWARTZ, DANIEL BENNETT, artist; b. N.Y.C., Feb. 16, 1929; s. Bennett Henry and Lillian (Blumenthal) S.; m. Judith Nancy Kass, June 12, 1955 (div. 1980); 1 child, Claudia Bennet. Grad., High Sch. of Music and Art, N.Y.C., 1946; student, Art Students League, 1946, Y. Kuniyoshi; BFA, R.I. Sch. Design, 1949. Instr. pvt. painting class, 1965-81, 90-95, Parsons Sch. Design, 1983. One man shows include Davis Galleries, N.Y.C., 1955, 56, 58,

60, Hirschl & Adler Galleries, N.Y.C., 1963, Maxwell Galleries, San Francisco, 1964, Babcock Galleries, N.Y.C., 1967, F.A.R. Galleries, N.Y.C., 1970, Armstrong Galleries, N.Y.C., 1985, 87, Hammer Galleries, N.Y.C., 1994, Hudson River Gallery, Dobbs Ferry, N.Y., 2001; exhibited in group shows at Albany Inst. History and Art, Am. Fedn. Arts, Butler Inst. Am. Art, Libr. of Congress, Nat. Acad. Design, Pa. Acad. Fine Art, Whitney Mus. Art, Collection Nat. Portrait Gallery, Munson-Williams-Proctor Inst., Bates Coll., British Mus., Century Assn., others; subject of various articles. Louis C. Tiffany Found. grantee, 1956, 60; recipient Purchase prize Am. Acad. Arts and letters, 1964, 84, 11 Gold medals Soc. Illustrators, N.Y.C., 1960-85, Obrig prize for painting Nat. Acad. Design, 1990, winner 1st Benjamin Altman Figure prize, 1992; named to Soc. of Illustrators Hall of Fame, 2002. Mem. NAD, Century Assn. Avocation: jazz piano. Home and Office: 48 E 13th St New York NY 10003-4631 E-mail: danbensch@aol.com.

SCHWARTZ, DANIEL C. lawyer; b. Pa., 1943; AB, Stanford U., 1965; JD, George Washington U., 1969. Bar: D.C. 1969. Asst. to dir. Bur. Competition, FTC, Washington, 1973-75, asst. dir. evaluation, 1975-77, dep. dir., 1977-79; gen. counsel Nat. Security Agy., 1979-81; ptnr. Bryan Cave LLP. Mem. ABA. Office: Bryan Cave LLP 700 13th St NW Fl 7 Washington DC 20005-5921 E-mail: dcschwartz@bryancave.com.

SCHWARTZ, DANIEL JOEL, education administrator; b. Buffalo, Apr. 23, 1957; s. Tobias Louis and Helen Wilma (Silverstein) S.; m. Charla Beth Reinganum, June 7, 1987; children: Rachel Mara, Ilyana Rose. BA, U. Conn., 1980; MEd, Lesley Coll., 1994; postgrad., Nat. Louis U. Cert. secondary history tchr., Mass. Exhibit producer Conn. Humanities Coun., Hartford, 1979-81; vocat. instr. Gen. Dynamics Shipyard, Quincy, Mass., 1981-85; history tchr. Brookline (Mass.) H.S., 1987-89, New Perspectives Sch., Brookline, 1987-88, Boston Pub. Schs., 1988-90; dir. edn. USS Constitution Mus., Boston, 1990-93; asst. prin. Peabody Sch., Cambridge, Mass., 1993-94, Carleton W. Washburne Sch., Winnetka, Ill., 1994-98, prin., 1998—. Mem. educators bd. People and Places Program, Boston, 1990-94; adj. faculty Nat. Louis U., 1998-2001. Photographer: Guide to Quincy Market, 1980; author curriculum, monograph in field. Grantee Conn. Humanities Coun., 1979, Mass. Culutral Coun., 1991, 92, Mass. Charitable Mechanics Assn., 1991, 92, Lowell Inst., 1990, 91, 92, Jeremiah E. Burke High Sch., 1989. Avocations: woodworking, photography. Home: 530 Audubon Pl Highland Park IL 60035-1204 Office: Carleton W. Washburne Sch 515 Hibbard Rd Winnetka IL 60093-1600 E-mail: schwartd@nttc.org.

SCHWARTZ, DONALD, chemistry educator; b. Scarsdale, N.Y., Dec. 27, 1927; s. Harry A. and Ethel S.; m. Lois Schwartz, Sept. 8, 1948; children: Leanne, Mark W., Scott B., Bradley F. BS, U. Mo., 1949; MS, Mont. State U., 1951; PhD, Pa. State U., 1955. Program dir. NSF, 1966-68; asso. dean Grad. Sch., Memphis State U., 1968-70; dean advanced studies Fla. Atlantic U., Boca Raton, 1970-71; v.p., acting pres. State U. N.Y., Buffalo, 1971-74; chancellor Ind. U.-Purdue U., Ft. Wayne, Ind., 1974-78; chancellor, prof. U. Colo., Colorado Springs, 1978-83, prof., 1983-93, prof. emeritus, 1993—. Cons. in field. Author papers structure of coal and organo-titanium compounds, also on higher edn. Bd. dirs. Colorado Springs Osteo. Found., 1985—. Served with USCG, 1945. Research fellow AEC, 1953-55; N.Y. State fellow, 1947-48 Mem. Am. Chem. Soc., AAAS, Sigma Xi, Phi Lambda Upsilon, Phi Delta Kappa. Clubs: Rotary, Shriners. Home: 21 Sanford Rd Colorado Springs CO 80906-4219 E-mail: lolodo@msn.com. *Each can become all that he or she is capable of being through education, hard work and compassion for other human beings. This I believe.*

SCHWARTZ, DONALD FRANKLIN, communication scientist; b. Jamestown, N.D., 1935; m. Lois Carolyn Schwartz, June 26, 1965; children: Daria, Karin, Marc. BS, N.D. State U., 1957, MS, 1961; PhD, Mich. State U., 1968. Asst. dir. pub. rels. N.D. State U., Fargo, 1959-66, chmn. social scis., 1969-71, chmn. comm., 1967-79; instr. comm. Mich. State U., East Lansing, 1966-67; vis. scientist U.S. Dept. Agr., Washington, 1979-80; prof. comm. Cornell U., Ithaca, N.Y., 1980-98, chmn. dept., 1980-85, dir. undergrad. studies, 1995-98, prof. emeritus, 1998—. Vis. scholar U. N.Mex., 1994. Contbr. articles to profl. jours. Recipient Outstanding Svc. award Future Farmers Am., 1976, Svc. award USDA, 1980, A.D. White Prof. of Yr. award, 1993. Mem. AAUP, Internat. Comm. Assn. (sec., pub. rels. interest group 1992-93), Am. Acad. Mgmt., Am. Soc. Pers. Adminstrn. (chpt. pres. 1976-77), Pub. Rels. Soc. Am. (nat. faculty advisor student assn. 1989-90, vice-chair educators sect. 1992, Pres.'s Citation for Leadership 1990, nat. ednl. affairs com. 1993-96). Roman Catholic. Office: Cornell U Dept Communication 331 Kennedy Hall Ithaca NY 14853-4203 E-mail: dfs9@cornell.edu.

SCHWARTZ, DONALD LEE, lawyer; b. Milw., Dec. 8, 1948; s. Bernard L. and Ruth M. (Marshall) S.; m. Susan J. Dunst, June 5, 1971; children: Stephanie Jane, Cheryl Ruth. BA, Macalester Coll., 1971; JD, U. Chgo., 1974. Bar: Ill. 1974. Assoc. Sidley & Austin, Chgo., 1974-80, ptnr., 1980-88, Latham & Watkins, Chgo., 1988—. Chmn. Ill. Conservative Union, 1979-81, bd. dirs. 1977-85. Served with U.S. Army, 1971-77. Mem. ABA (uniform comml. code com., comml. fin. svcs. comm.), Ill. Bar Assn. (sec. coun. banking and bankuprtcy sect. 1982-83), Chgo. Bar Assn. (chmn. comml. law com. 1980-81, fin. insts. com. 1982-83), Ivanhoe Country Club, Sea Pines Country Club, Colleton River Country Club, Met. Club. Republican. Episcopalian. Avocation: golf. Home: 191 Park Ave Glencoe IL 60022-1351 Office: Latham & Watkins Ste 5800 Sears Tower Chicago IL 60606 E-mail: Donald.schwartz@lw.com.

SCHWARTZ, EDWARD ARTHUR, lawyer; b. Boston, Sept. 27, 1937; s. Abe and Sophie (Gottheim) S.; m. Sheila Kauffman, Apr. 5, 1997; children: Eric Allen, Jeffrey Michael. AB, Oberlin Coll., 1959; LLB, Boston Coll., 1962; postgrad., Am. U., 1958-59, Northeastern U., 1970; postgrad. exec. program, Stanford U., 1979. Bar: Conn. 1962, Mass. 1965. Legal intern Office Atty. Gen. Commonwealth of Mass., 1961; assoc. Schatz & Schatz, Hartford, Conn., 1962-65, Cohn, Reimer & Pollack, Boston, 1965-67; v.p., gen. coun., sec. Digital Equipment Corp., Maynard, Mass., 1967-88; pres. New Eng. Legal Found., Boston, 1990-98. Vis. prof. law Boston Coll., 1986, adj. prof., 1987-89 bd. dirs. SatelLife Corp.; bd. advisors Buffalo Hill Hist. Ctr. Editor Boston Coll. Indsl. and Comml. Law Rev, 1960-62, Ann. Survey Mass. Law, 1960-62. Trustee Rural Land Found. Home: 62 Todd Pond Rd Lincoln MA 01773-3808

SCHWARTZ, EDWARD LESTER, retired lawyer; b. N.Y.C., July 13, 1910; s. Alexander and Serene (Brown) S.; m. Edna B. Smith, July 31, 1941 (dec.); 1 child, Andrea Helen Saiet. BA, CCNY, 1931; JD, Harvard U., 1934. Bar: N.Y. 1935, Mass. 1939. Pvt. practice, N.Y.C., 1935-39, Boston, 1939-90. Lectr. law Boston U., Northeastern U., Suffolk U., New Eng. Law Inst., Mass. Continuing Legal Edn. Inst.; asst. atty. gen. State of Mass., 1970-75; commr. Nat. Conf. Commrs. on Uniform Laws (life); chmn. spl. com. Uniform Securities Act, spl. com. Landlord/Tenant Relationship Act; Mass. commr. Interstate Coop., 1949-74. Author: Lease Drafting in Massachusetts, 1961, updated 1996; contbr. articles to profl. jours. Mem. ABA, Am. Law Inst. (life), Am. Judicature Soc., Boston Bar Assn., Mass. Bar Assn. (lectr.), Scribes, New Eng. Law Inst. (exec. com.), Mass. Continuing Legal Edn. (bd. dirs.). Home: 17 Ledgewood Rd Weston MA 02493-1423

SCHWARTZ, ELI, economics educator, writer; b. N.Y.C., Apr. 2, 1921; s. Israel and Tillie (Shapiro) S.; m. Renee S. Kartiganer, Aug. 29, 1948; children: Pamela F., Alan G. BS, Denver U., 1943; MA, U. Conn., 1948; PhD, Brown U., 1952. Instr. U. R.I., Kingston, 1947-48; asst. instr. Brown U., Providence, 1948-51; chief regional economist Office Price Stblzn., Boston, 1951-53; lectr. Mich. State U., East Lansing, 1953-54; asst. prof. econs. Lehigh U., Bethlehem, Pa., 1954-58, assoc. prof., 1958-62, prof., 1962-91, Charles Macfarlane prof. econs., 1978-91, chmn. dept. econs., 1978-84, ret., 1991; cons. econs. and fin., expert witness Schwartz-Aronson Assocs., 1965—. Author: Corporate Finance, 1962, Trouble in Eden, 1980; editor: Managing Municipal Finance, 1980, 83, 87, 96, Restructuring the Thrift Industry, 1989, Theory and Application of the Interest Rate, 1993. With U.S. Army, 1943-46, ETO. Recipient sr. teaching Lehigh U., 1972; Earhart Found. grantee, 1978 Mem. Am. Econs. Assn., Am. Fin. Assn., Nat. Assn. Forensic Econs. (founding mem.). Jewish. Home: 3185 W Cedar St Allentown PA 18104-3441 Office: Lehigh U Dept Econs Rauch Ctr 621 Taylor St Dept Econs Bethlehem PA 18015-3107 *If I have achieved any success it is because I am interested in the subject matter of my field. I am fortunate to enjoy reading, teaching, consulting and writing.*

SCHWARTZ, ELIEZER LAZAR, psychologist, educator; b. Arad, Romania, Dec. 14, 1947; came to U.S., 1974; s. George and Elka (Rothchild) S.; m. Susan Ellen Lorge; children: Dafna, Michal, Amitai. BA in Psychology, Hebrew U., Jerusalem, Israel, 1973; MS in Psychology, Ill. Inst. Tech., 1975, PhD in Psychology, 1977. Cert. clin. psychologist, Ill. Psychologist, chief svc. Chgo.-Read Mental Health Ctr., 1979-80; core faculty Ill. Sch. Profl. Psychology, Chgo., 1981—. Clin. psychologist Ray Graham Assn. for Handicapped, Elmhurst, Ill., 1981-89; dir. clin. svcs. Michael Solomon Psychology Ctr., Chgo., 1989-91; instr. Northwestern U., Evanston, Ill., summers 1988—; dir. neuropsychology Brownstone Ctr., Chgo., 1991-92; cons. Jewish Vocat. Svcs., Chgo., 1983-84, 91-92, North Suburban Spl. Edn. Orgn., Arlington Heights, Ill., 1985-91, Grant Hosp., Chgo., 1991-95; dir. clin. tng. Ill. Sch. Profl. Psychology, 1996-97, dean, prof., 1997—. Author: (with others) Severe Developmental Disabilities, 1987, The Mental Status Exam, 1989; contbr. articles to profl. jours. Mem. APA, ASCD, Ill. Psych. Assn., Coun. for Exceptional Children. Jewish. Avocations: reading, listening to classical music. Office: 20 S Clark St Chicago IL 60603

SCHWARTZ, ELLIOTT SHELLING, composer, author, music educator; b. Bklyn, Jan. 19, 1936; s. Nathan and Rose (Shelling) S.; m. Dorothy Rose Feldman, June 26, 1960; children: Nina, Jonathan. AB, Columbia U., 1957, MA, 1958, EdD, 1962. Instr. music U. Mass., Amherst, 1960-64; from asst. prof. music to assoc. prof. Bowdoin Coll., Brunswick, Maine, 1964-75, prof. music, 1975—. Vis. prof. music Ohio State U., Columbus, 1988-92; vis. composer Trinity Coll. Music, London, 1967, U. Calif. Coll. Creative Studies, Santa Barbara, 1970, 73, 74; composer, pianist, commentator British Broadcast Corp, London, 1972, 74, 78, 83; vis. research musician Center Music Expt., La Jolla, Calif., 1978-79; disting. vis. prof. Ohio State U., 1985-86; music cons. Holt, Rinehart & Winston, Random House, Oxford Univ. Press, Schirmer Books, N.Y.C., 1977—; vis. fellow Robinson Coll., Cambridge U., U.K., 1993-94, 99. Composer: Island, 1970 (Internat. Gaudeamus prize 1970), Chamber Concertos I-IV, 1977-81, Extended Piano, 1980, Dream Music With Variations, 1983, Four Ohio Portraits, 1986, Memorial in Two Parts, 1989, Elan, 1990, Rows Garden, 1993, Equinox, 1994, Timepiece, 1994, Chiaroscuro, 1995, Reflections, 1995, Rainbow, 1996, Tapestry, 1996, Alto Prisms, 1997, Vienna Dreams, 1998, Kaleidoscope, 1999, Jack O'Lantern, 2000, Mehitabel's Serenade, 2000; author: Electronic Music: A Listener's Guide, 1973, Music: Ways of Listening, 1982, (with Daniel Godfrey) Music Since 1945: Issues, Materials and Literature, 1993; editor: (with Barney Childs) Contemporary Composers on Contemporary Music, 1967, rev. edit., 1998; contbr. articles to profl. jours. Nat. Endowment for Arts composition grantee, 1974, 76, 82; Rockefeller Found. residence fellow Bellagio, Italy, 1980, 89; MacDowell Colony resident fellow, 1965, 66; Yaddo residence fellow, 1977; recipient Maine State award Maine Commn. Arts and Humanities, 1970, McKim Commn., 1986 Mem.: Am. Composers Alliance (governing bd. 1994—2000), Am. Soc. Univ. Composers (nat. coun. 1968—72, nat. chmn. 1983—88), Coll. Music Soc. (nat. coun. 1982—88, pres. 1988—90), Am. Music Ctr. (v.p. 1981—87). Home: PO Box 451 South Freeport ME 04078-0451 Office: Bowdoin Coll Dept Music Brunswick ME 04011 E-mail: eschwart@bowdoin.edu.

SCHWARTZ, ESTAR ALMA, lawyer; b. Bklyn., June 29, 1950; d. Henry Israel and Elaine Florence (Scheiner) Sutel; m. Lawrence Gerald Schwartz, June 28, 1976 (div. Dec. 1977); 1 child, Joshua (dec.); m. James Frances Edward Stuart, Sept. 25, 1999 (div. Aug. 2001). JD, NYU, 1980. Mgr., ptnr. Scheiner, Scheiner, DeVito & Wytte, N.Y.C., 1966-81; fed. govt., social security fraud specialist DHHS, OI, OIG, SSFIS, 1982-83; pensions Todtman, Epstein, et al, 1983-85; office mgr., sec. Sills, Beck, Cummis, 1985-86; office mgr., bookkeeper Philip, Birnbaum & Assocs., 1986-87; office mgr., sec. Stanley Posses, Esq., Queens, N.Y., 1989-90. Owner Estaris Paralegal Svc., Flushing, N.Y., 1992—, Sutel Creative Mgmt. Agy., Flushing, 1999—. Democrat. Jewish. Avocations: needlepoint, horseback riding, tennis, bowling, writing children's stories. Home and Office: 67-20 Parsons Blvd Apt 2A Flushing NY 11365-2960 E-mail: sutel@email.com., sutelmmgmt@aol.com.

SCHWARTZ, GAIL GARFIELD, communications executive; b. Medina, N.Y., July 21, 1934; d. Edward and Barbara (Munson) Garfield; children: Jennifer, James, Daniel. BA, Smith Coll., 1955; M in Urban Planning, NYU, 1969; PhD, Columbia U., 1972. Commr. N.Y. State Pub. Svc. Commn., 1985-92, dept. chmn., 1985-92; v.p., dir. pub. policy and govt. affairs Teleport Comm Group Inc, N.Y.C., 1992-98, dir. policy AT&T network svcs., 1998-99; telecom. cons., 2000—. Mem. adv. bd. CUNY Ctr. on Comm., N.Y., 1989—. Author: Being Number One, 1980, Advanced Industrialization and the Inner Cities, 1981, The Work Revolution, 1984; editor Econ. Devel. Quar., 1985—; contbg. editor, editl. advisor Telecom. Report Internat., 2000—; mem. editl. bd. Telematies, 1988-92; mem. editorial adv. com. X-Change Mag. Mem. White House Conf. on Balanced Nat. Growth, 1978; mem. Landmarks Adv. Commn., Village of Mamaroneck, 1991-93, chmn., 1992. Mem. Nat. Assn. Regulatory Utility Commrs. (fin. and tech. com. 1985-86, comms. com. 1986-92), Nat. Rsch. Coun. (transp. rsch. bd., com. on Nat. Urban Policy), Am. Econ. Assn., Assn. for Local Telecomms. Svcs. (bd. dirs.). Democrat. Avocations: tennis, sailing. Office: Apt 5N 215 E 68th St New York NY 10021-5720

SCHWARTZ, GARRY ALBERT, advertising executive; b. Toledo, Jan. 4, 1949; s. Albert Theodore Otto and Ethel Anna (Weiler) S. BA in Speech, Adrian Coll., 1971; MA in Communication, Bowling Green State U., 1972; postgrad., Ind. U., 1974. Creative dir. S & L Advt. & P.R., Toledo, 1976-78; instr. U.S. Savings League Inst., 1977; conf. leader Aeroquip Corp., Jackson, Mich., 1978-79, sales promotion supr., 1979-87, advt. display mgr., 1987-88, sr. writer, producer, video, pub. rels., 1988-89, advt. prodn. supr., 1989-91; sr. copywriter Donald L. Arends, Inc., Oak Brook, Ill., 1992-96, Alexander Mktg. Svcs., Inc., Grand Rapids, Mich., 1996—. Mem. Lambda Iota Tau, Iota Beta Sigma, Pi Kappa Delta. Avocations: painting, stamp collecting. Home: 2045 Wyndham Hill Dr NE Grand Rapids MI 49505-6353 Office: Alexander Mktg Svcs Inc PO Box 601 Grand Rapids MI 49516-0601

SCHWARTZ, GERALD, public relations and fundraising agency executive; b. N.Y.C., June 22, 1927; s. George and Martha F. S.; m. Felice P. Schwartz, June 25, 1950; children: Gary R., Gregg R., Wendy L. Student, N.C. State U., 1944-45; AB, U. Miami, Fla., 1949, BS, 1950, postgrad., 1966-67. Staff writer Miami Herald, 1941-44; publicity dir. U.S. Army in Europe, 1946-48; editor Miami Beach Sun, 1950-51; fund raising and pub. rels. counselor Miami, 1952-58; press sec. to Gov. Nebr., 1959—60; exec. v.p. Bar-Ilan U., Ramat Gan, Israel, 1960-61; prin. Gerald Schwartz Agy., Miami, Fla., 1962—. Exec. vice-chmn. South Shore Hosp. and Med. Ctr., Miami Beach, Fla., 1989—. Editor, pub. Jewish Herald Newspaper, 1999-2000; editor, pub. emeritus Jewish Star-Times, 2000—. Dep. chmn. Dem. Midwest Conf., 1958-60; pres. Am. Zionist Fedn. So. Fla., 1970-73, 86-92; nat. v.p. Am. Zionist Fedn., 1985-89, 91-93; pres. Pres.'s coun. Zionist Orgn. Am., 1983-85; bd. dirs. Temple Emanu-El of Greater Miami, Papanicolaou Cancer Rsch. Inst., Miami, 1962-80; vice chmn. Urban League of Greater Miami, 1983-87; vice chmn. City of Miami Beach Planning Bd., 1953-55; bd. dirs. Greater Miami Symphony, 1982-87, Miami Beach Taxpayers Assn., 1988-89; pres. Civic League Miami Beach, 1985-87; nat. chmn. Friends of Pioneer Women/Na'amat, 1984-98; pres. Greater Miami chpt. Assn. Welfare of Soldiers in Israel, 1983-86; chmn. City of Miami Beach Hurricane Def. Com., 1978-86, 90-97; trustee South Shore Hosp. and Med. Ctr., Miami, 1987—; vice chmn. South Shore Med. Ctr. Found., 1989—; bd. govs. Barry U., 1985-86; chmn. Econ. Devel. Coun. City of Miami Beach, 1985-91; bd. dirs. Crimestoppers of Dade County, 1991-94; bd. dirs. administrv. com. Jewish Nat. Fund of Am., 1995—, v.p. Greater Miami region, 1996-97; mem. exec. bd. State of Israel Bonds Orgn., 1996—. Served with U.S. Army, 1944-46. Recipient Jerusalem Peace award State of Israel Bonds, 1978, Jerusalem 3000 award State of Israel, 1996. Mem. Pub. Rels. Soc. Am. (accredited; treas. So. Fla. chpt. 1962-64), Am. Pub. Rels. Assn. (pres. chpt. 1960-61), Am. Assn. Polit. Cons., Nat. Assn. Fund Raising Execs. (pres. chpt. 1977-78), Miami Beach Taxpayers Assn. (bd. dirs. 1994-2000), Miami Internat. Press Club (bd. dirs. 1991-99), Miami Beach C. of C. (v.p. 1978-80, 81-84, 86-87, pres.-elect 1988-90, trustee 1990—), Lead and Ink, Tiger Bay Club (pres. 1986-88), Prime Minister's Club of State of Israel (Greater Miami chmn. 1997—), B'nai B'rith (pres. lodge 1964-66), Theta Omicron Pi, Omicron Delta Kappa, Alpha Delta Sigma (pres. 1965-67), Zeta Beta Tau. Office: Gerald Schwartz Agy Ste 505 600 Alton Rd Miami FL 33139-5502

SCHWARTZ, GERALD WILFRED, financial executive; b. Winnipeg, Man., Can., Nov. 24, 1941; s. Andrew O. and Lillian Arkin (Leith) S.; m. Heather Reisman, May 15, 1982; children: Carey, Jill, Andrea, Anthony. B.Commerce, U. Man., 1962, LLB, 1966; MBA, Harvard U., 1970. V.p. Estabrook & Co., Inc., N.Y.C., 1970-73, Bear Stearns & Co., N.Y.C., 1973-77; pres., dir., mem. exec. com. CanWest Capital Corp., Winnipeg, 1977-83; chmn., pres., CEO ONEX Corp., Toronto, 1984—. Bd. dirs. Sky Chefs Inc., Celestica Internat. Holdings Inc., Bank of N.S. Bd. dirs. Can. Coun. Christians and Jews; vice chmn., bd. dirs., gov., mem. exec. com. Mt. Sinai Hosp. of Toronto; dir. bd. of assocs. Harvard Bus. Sch.; trustee Simon Wiesenthal Ctr.; mem. adv. coun. Dancer Transition Ctr.; nat. bd. dirs. Ben-Gurion U. of the Negev. With RCAF, 1958. Office: Onex Corp 161 Bay St 49th Fl PO Box 700 Toronto ON Canada M5J 2S1

SCHWARTZ, GLORIA PUDICK, foundation administrator; b. N.Y.C., Aug. 19, 1945; d. Joseph and Gertrude Pudick; m. Michael B. Schwartz, Aug. 11, 1968; 1 child, Jean Paul. BA, Bklyn. Coll., 1967, MS in Edn., 1969. Elem. sch. tchr. N.Y.C. Pub. Schs., 1967-68; libr. asst. County Day Sch., New Orleans, 1969-71; devel. coord. WSEC-Pub. TV, Springfield, Ill., 1988-90; exec. dir. Springfield Jewish Fedn., 1990—. Radio commentator news program WSSR-Nat. Pub. Radio Affiliate, 1983-87. Mem. nat. exec. com. Nat. Jewish Cmty. Rels. Adv. Coun., N.Y.C., 1982-85; chair small fedn. exec. coun. United Jewish Cmtys., N.Y.C., 1998-2000; bd. dirs. Springfield Human Rels. Coun., 1987-90, Springfield Internat. Rels. Coun., 1992-98, Mini-O'Beirne Crisis Nursery, Springfield, 1989-91. Recipient Nat. Young Leadership award Coun. Jewish Fedns., 1979, Star of David award Israel Bond, 2001. Avocations: cooking, reading. Office: Springfield Jewish Fedn 2815 Old Jacksonville Rd Ste 103A Springfield IL 62704 E-mail: sjf@springnet1.com.

SCHWARTZ, GORDON FRANCIS, surgeon, educator; b. Plainfield, N.J., Apr. 29, 1935; s. Samuel H. and Mary (Adelman) S.; m. Rochelle DeG. Krantz, Sept. 5, 1959; children— Amory Blair, Susan Leslie AB, Princeton U., 1956; MD, Harvard U., 1960; MBA, U. Pa., 1990. Intern N.Y. Hosp.-Cornell Med. Ctr., N.Y.C., 1960-61; resident in surgery Columbia-Presbyterian Med. Ctr., 1963-68; instr. surgery Columbia U., 1966-68; assoc. in surgery U. Pa., Phila., 1968-70; dir. clin. services Breast Diagnostic Ctr., Jefferson Med. Coll., 1973-78, asst. prof. surgery, 1970-71, assoc. prof., 1971-78, prof., 1978—. Practice medicine specializing in surgery and diseases of breast, Phila., 1968—; founder, chmn. acad. com. Breast Health Inst., 1990—; edtl. bd. The Breast Jour., 1994—. Author: (with R.H. Guthrie, Jr.) Reconstructive and Aesthetic Mammoplasty, 1989, (with Douglas Marchant) Breast Disease: Diagnosis and Treatment, 1981; mem. editl. bd. The Breast-Ofcl. Jour. of the European Soc. of Mastology, 1996—, Cancer, 1997—; co-editor Seminars Breast Disease, 1997; mem. editl. bd. ONE, Oncology Econs., 1999—; contbr. some 185 articles to profl. jours. Mem. Pa. Gov.'s Task Force on Cancer, 1976-82; mem. breast cancer task force Phila. chpt. Am. Cancer Soc.; mem. clin. investigation rev. com. Nat. Cancer Inst., 1992-95. Served to capt. AUS, 1961-63. NIH Cancer Control fellow, 1968-69 Mem. ACS, AMA, AAUP, Assn. for Acad. Surgery, Allen O. Whipple Surg. Assn., Soc. Surg. Oncology, Internat. Cardiovasc. Soc., Soc. for Surgery Alimentary Tract, John Jones Surg. Soc., Am. Soc. Clin. Oncology, Soc. for Study Breast Diseases (pres. 1981-83), Soc. Internat. Senologie (treas. 1982-90, v.p. 1990-92, sci. com. 1992—), Am. Soc. Breast Surgeons, N.Y. Acad. Scis., Am. Soc. Artificial Internal Organs, Am. Radium Soc., Philadelphia County Med. Soc. (chmn. com. on econs. 1999-2000, bd. dirs. 1999-2000), Italian Soc. Senology (hon.), Greek Surg. Soc. (hon.), The Phila. Club, Union League, Princeton Club Phila. (pres. 1989-91), Princeton Club (N.Y.C.), Princeton Terrace Club, Nassau Club, Phi Beta Kappa, Sigma Xi, Alpha Omega Alpha, Nu Sigma Nu. Republican. Jewish. Office: 1015 Chestnut St Ste 510 Philadelphia PA 19107-4305 E-mail: gordonschwartz@yahoo.com.

SCHWARTZ, GREGORY JOHN, lawyer, business and investments transactions specialist; b. Rochester, Pa., Oct. 10, 1958; s. Louis Frederick and Helene (Kardasz) S.; m. Ann Elizabeth Salazar, Aug. 20, 1988. BA in Govt. and Politics cum laude, U. Md., 1981; JD, Cath. U. Am., 1985; postgrad., Georgetown U., 1990-93. Bar: Md. 1986, U.S. Dist. Ct. Md. 1986, D.C. 1987. Assoc. Williams and Huffman, Chevy Chase, Md., 1985-87, Conroy, Fitzgerald, Ballman and Dameron, Gaithersburg, 1987-90; mng. ptnr. Gregory J. Schwartz, Profl. Law Corp., Washington, 1990-2000; ret., 2000. Contbr. articles to profl. jours. Mem. ABA (former program Ctrl. and Ea. European Law Initiative), Md. Bar Assn., D.C. Bar Assn., Montgomery County Bar Assn., Washington Fgn. Law Soc. (former bd. dirs., rapporteur), Suburban Md. Internat. Trade Assn. (former pres. and bd. dirs.), Internat. Trade Networking Group of Washington (founder), Jaycees (bd. dirs. and legal counsel Washington br. 1987-90), Lowry Alumni Investors Club, Phi Alpha Delta, Sigma Alpha Epsilon, Omicron Delta Kappa, KC. Avocations: horsemanship, tennis, golf, magic, flying. Office: International Sq 1825 I St NW Ste 400 Washington DC 20006-5415 E-mail: BizDealmaker@aol.com., gsesquire@aol.com.

SCHWARTZ, HERBERT FREDERICK, lawyer; b. Bklyn., Aug. 23, 1935; s. Henry and Blanche Theodora (goldberg) S.; m. Gail Lubets, Jan. 23, 1960; children: Wendy Helene, Karen Anne, Peter Andrew; m. Nan Budde Chequer, Mar. 13, 1987; stepchildren: Elizabeth Guthrie, Anne Hamilton, Laura Dunham. BSEE, MIT, 1957; MA in Applied Econs., LLB, U. Pa., 1964. Assoc. Fish & Neave, N.Y.C., 1964-70, jr. ptnr., 1970-71, ptnr., 1972—, mng. ptnr., 1985-91. Lectr. law U. Pa., Phila., 1980-89, adj. prof., 1990—. Mem. adv. bd. PTC Jour., Washington, 1983; author: Patent Law and Practice, Federal Judicial Center, 1988, 2d edit., 1995, Bureau of National Affairs, 2d edit., 1996, 3d edit., 2001; co-author: Principles of Patent Law, 1998, 2d edit., 2001; contbr. articles to profl. jours. Vice-chmn. Jr. Yacht Racing Assn. of L.I. Sound, 1985-88. 1st lt. U.S. Army, Signal Corps, 1957-59. Mem. U.S. Trademark Assn., Assn. of Bar of City of N.Y., Am. Intellectual Property Lawyers Assn., N.Y. Intellectual Property Lawyers Assn. (pres. 1999-2000), Am. Coll. Trial Lawyers, Am. Bar Found., Am. Law Inst., Order of Coif, N.Y. Yacht Club, Riverside Yacht Club, Cruising Club of Am. Avocation: racing and cruising sailboats. Home: 24 Cherry Tree Ln Riverside CT 06878-2629 Office: Fish & Neave 1251 Avenue Of The Americas Fl 50 New York NY 10020-1105

SCHWARTZ, HERBERT S. surgical oncology educator; b. Chgo., July 22, 1955; BS, U. Ill., Chgo., 1977; MD, U. Chgo., 1981. Diplomate Am. Bd. Orthopaedic Surgery (test task force 1998—). Resident in orthopaedic surgery U. Chgo., 1981-86; fellow in orthopaedic oncology Mayo Clinic, Rochester, Minn., 1986-87; asst. prof. surg. oncology Vanderbilt U., Nashville, 1987-93, assoc. prof., 1993-97, prof., 1997—. Chief orthopaedic surgery VA Med. Ctr., Nashville, 1992—. Contbr. over 50 articles to cancer and orthopaedic jours. Fellow ACS, Am. Acad. Orthopaedic Surgeons, Am. Orthopaedic Assn. (chmn. Hatcher fellow 1999-00), Phi Beta Kappa. Achievements include patent for spinal nail. Office: Vanderbilt U T-4323 MCN Dept Orthopaedics Rehab Nashville TN 37232-2550 E-mail: herberts.schwartz@mcmail.vanderbilt.edu.

SCHWARTZ, HERMAN, law educator; b. Bklyn., Dec. 19, 1931; s. Jacob and Rose S.; m. Mary Cahn Schwartz, Nov. 20, 1960; 1 child, Susan C.S. Levin. AB, Harvard Coll., 1953; JD, Harvard U., 1956. Bar: N.Y., 1957. Prof. of law SUNY, Buffalo, 1963-77; chmn. designate Commn. of Corrections/N.Y. State, Albany, 1975-76; chief counsel subcom. U.S. Senate, Washington, 1977-78; chief counsel revenue sharing U.S. Treasury, 1978-79; chief counsel U.S. Senate Antitrust Subcom., 1979-80; prof. of law Am. U., 1982—. Cons. U.S. Agy. for Internat. Devel., Washington, 1995—; self-employed writer Cen.-Ea. Europe. Author: (book) Packing the Courts, 1988, the Struggle for Constitutional Justice in Post-Communist Europe, 2000; editor: (book) The Burger Years, 1988, others. Probono civil rights lawyers Am. U. Law Sch., Buffalo, 1982—, ACLU, Washington, 1963—, others. Recipient citation City of Buffalo, 1977. Mem. Am. Law Inst. Jewish. Avocations: reading, concerts. Office: Am Univ Law Sch 4801 Massachusetts Ave NW Washington DC 20016-8196 E-mail: Hschwar@wcl.American.edu.

SCHWARTZ, HOWARD WYN, business/marketing educator, consultant; b. Mpls., June 12, 1951; s. Jerry Schwartz and Geraldine (Berg) Brooks; m. Jeannie Marie Holtzmann, Aug. 2, 1975; children: Abigail Jorene, Rachel Elizabeth. BA cum laude, U. Minn., 1973, MBA, 1982, MEd, 1999. Acct. Med. Sch., U. Minn., 1973-77, bus. mgr. dept. neurology, 1977-79, adminstr. found. edn. dept., 1979-82, assoc. to chmn. dept. radiology, 1982-99; chmn. bus./mktg. edn. dept. Robbindale-Cooper H.S., New Hope, Minn., 1999—. Adj. instr. dept. radiology U. Minn., 1982—; pres. Bus. Mgmt. Svcs., Golden Valley, Miss., 1979—; lectr., author topics in bus./mktg. edn., 2000—. Editor-in-chief: RADWORKS Workload Measurement Manual, 1985-87; editor: Radiology Management, 1985-87, Purchasing the Radiology Information System, 1991, Current Concepts in Radiology Management, 1991; contbr. articles to profl. jours. Mem. Cystic Fibrosis Found., Minn., 1980—; chmn. Human Rights Commn., Robbinsdale, 1982-84; sec. Coord. Coun. Minority Concerns, 1984-85; chmn. imaging tech. adv. com. Univ. Hosp. Consortium, 1989-92; dir. Univ. Hosp. Consortium Svcs. Corp., 1990-92, Nat. Summit on Manpower, 1989-92; treas. Tech. Learning Campus Site Coun., Dist. 281, 1990-91, chmn. Bond Referendum campaign, 1995; pres. Armstrong H.S. Parent Assn., Dist. 281, 1991-92. Fellow Am. Healthcare Radiology Adminstrn. (regional pres. 1986-87, nat. pres. 1988-89, sec. edn. found. 1990-91, bd. dirs. edn. found. 1993-95, 97-98, Outstanding Author award 1990, 93, 96, Midwest Region Disting. Mem. award 1991, Gold award 1991); mem. Radiologists Bus. Mgrs. Assn., Delta Kappa Epsilon. Home: 7400 Winnetka Heights Dr Golden Valley MN 55427-3549 Office: PO Box 27405 Minneapolis MN 55427-0405 E-mail: Schwa006@ix.netcom.com, howard_schwartz@rdale.k12.mn.us.

SCHWARTZ, HOWARD ALAN, periodontist; b. Paterson, N.J., Dec. 27, 1944; s. Samuel and Ruth (Dimond) S.; m. Rita Blumenthal, Dec. 29, 1968; children: Andrew David Schwartz, Steven Austin Schwartz. BS, Fairleigh Dickinson U., 1967, DDS, 1970; cert. in periodontology, Georgetown U., 1972. State Dental Lic. N.J., N.Y., Mass., Pa., Md., Washington. Clin. instr. in periodontics Georgetown U., 1970-72; chief resident Periodontal Section Dept. Dentistry Veteran's Adminstrn. Hosp., Washington, 1972; asst. prof. Periodontics and Oral Medicine Fairleigh Dickinson U. Sch. Dentistry, Hackensack, N.J., 1972-73, part time clin. asst. prof. Periodontics and Oral Medicine, 1973-79, part time clin. assoc. prof. Periodontics and Oral Medicine, 1979-87, part time clin. prof. Periodontics and Oral Medicine, 1987-89; pvt. practice Periodontics and Oral Medicine, 1972—. Author: (with W.A. Gibson) Immunofluorescent Demonstration of IgG, IgM, and IgA in Human Dental Plaque, (with others) Histochemical Localization of Selected Dehydrogenases in Frozen Sections of Human Dental Plaque, (with others) Salvary Composition as related to Dental Calculus Formation in Humans. Mem. Dentist's Div. Com., Hon. Cabinet, United Jewish Community of Bergen County, 1984-85. Fellow Am. Coll. Dentists, Internat. Coll. Dentists. Fellow Acad. Dentistry Internat.; mem. ADA, Am. Acad. Periodontology, N.J. Dental Assn. (trustee, treas. 1994-96, v.p. 1996-97, pres.-elect 1997-98, pres. 1998-99), Internat. Assn. Dental Rsch., Northeastern Soc. Periodontists, Am. Acad. Oral Medicine, N.J. Soc. Periodontists (pres. 1978-79), Bergen County Dental Soc. (pres. 1989-90), Am. Coll. Dentists, Internat. Coll. Dentists, Acad. Dentistry Internat. Jewish. Avocations: running, photography, computers. Home: 10 Wood Hollow Trail Saddle River NJ 07458-1346 Office: 97 N Dean St Englewood NJ 07631-2806 E-mail: pemodds@aol.com.

SCHWARTZ, ILENE, psychotherapist; b. Phila., June 19, 1942; d. Israel Gerson and Jean Schiffman. BS, Temple U., 1970; MEd, Antioch U., 1990. Crisis counselor, Phila., 1972-82; pvt. practice counseling, 1972-84. Cons., crisis counselor in field; instr. psychology and edn., 1974-79; designer, writer, crafts coord. for children. Mem. ACA, AAUW, Freud Friends.

SCHWARTZ, IRVING DONN, architect; b. Chgo., June 11, 1927; s. Simon S. and Rose P. S.; children: Charles, Linda. BS, U. Ill., 1949, BS in Architecture, 1965, MS in Architecture, 1972. Registered architect, Ill., Ind., Fla., D.C., Ohio, Ga., Ala., Calif., N.H., Va., Md., Pa, Tenn., La., N.J., Tex., Mo., N.C., S.C., Ark. Chief standard cost and indsl. engring. Lanzit Corrugated Box Co., Chgo., 1950-53; pres. Kaufman, Inc., Champaign, Ill., 1953-60; v.p. Hart Mirror Plate Co., Grand Rapids, Mich., 1953-60; asso. Richardson, Severns, Scheeler & Assos., Inc., Champaign, 1960-71; pres. IDS, Inc., 1971-83, ADI, Dallas, 1983-86, IDS/B, Inc., Dallas, 1986—. Prof. architecture Grad. Sch. Architecture, U. Ill., 1976-83; assoc. prof. design U. North Tex.; cons. in field. Mem. Champaign County Devel. Council; mem. Model Community Coordinating Council, Champaign; co-chmn. bldg. com. Mercy Hosp.; bd. frat. affairs U. Ill.; bd. dirs. United Fund. Served to 2d lt. U.S. Army, 1945-47. Recipient archtl. design research award, graphic design citation Progressive Architecture mag., 1974, Gold Key Design award Hospitality Mag., 1994, John Robinson award, 2001. Fellow Am. Soc. Interior Designers (treas. 1976, nat. pres. 1978, Louis Tregre award 1992, Nat. design award 1983); mem. AIA (Design award 1983), Nat. Council Archtl. Registration Bds., Nat. Council Interior Design Qualifications (bd. dirs., pres. 1980), Tex. Assn. Interior Design (pres. 1993). Clubs: Standard (Chgo.). Home: 4928 Briarwood Pl Dallas TX 75209-2004 Office: IDS/B Inc 2777 N Stemmons Fwy Ste 1650 Dallas TX 75207-2502

SCHWARTZ, IRVING LEON, physician, scientist, educator; b. Cedarhurst, N.Y., Dec. 25, 1918; s. Abraham and Rose (Doniger) S.; m. Felice T. Nierenberg, Jan. 12, 1946; children: Cornelia Ann, Albert Anthony, James Oliver. AB, Columbia U., 1939; MD, NYU, 1943. Diplomate Am. Bd. Internal Medicine. Intern, then asst. resident Bellevue Hosp., N.Y.C., 1943-44, 46-47; NIH fellow physiology NYU Coll. Medicine, 1947-50; Am. Physiol. Soc. Porter fellow, also Gibbs meml. fellow in clin. sci. Rockefeller Inst., 1950-51, Am. Heart Assn. fellow, 1951-52, asst., then assoc., 1952-58; asst. physician, then assoc. physician Rockefeller Inst. Hosp., 1950-58; sr. scientist Brookhaven Nat. Lab., Upton, NY, 1958-61, rsch. collaborator, 1961—97; attending physician Brookhaven Nat. Lab. Hosp., 1958-97; Joseph Eichberg prof. physiology, dir. dept. U. Cin. Coll. Medicine, 1961-65; dean grad. faculties Mt. Sinai Med. and Grad. Schs., CUNY, 1965-80, prof. physiology and biophysics, chmn. dept., 1968-79, exec. officer biomed. scis. doctoral program, 1969-72, Dr. Harold and Golden Lamport disting. prof., 1979-98; dir. Ctr. Peptide and Membrane Research Mt. Sinai Med. Ctr., 1979-87; dean emeritus Mt. Sinai Grad. Sch. Biol. Scis., 1980—. Contbr. articles to sci. publs. Pres. Life Scis. Found., 1962-98, pres. emeritus, 1998--. Served from 1st lt. to capt., M.C. AUS, 1944-46. Recipient Solomon A. Berson Med. Alumni Achievement award NYU Sch. Medicine, 1973. Fellow ACP; mem. Am. Physiol. Soc., Soc. Exptl. Biology and Medicine, Am. Soc. Clin. Investigation, Am. Fedn. Clin. Rsch., Biophys. Soc., Endocrine Soc., Harvey Soc., Soc. for Neurosci., Am. Heart Assn., John Jay Assocs. Columbia Coll., AAAS, N.Y. Acad. Sci., N.Y. Acad. Medicine, Sigma Xi, Alpha Omega Alpha. Home: 1120 5th Ave # 14B New York NY 10128-0144 Office: Mt Sinai Med Ctr Grad Sch Biol Scis Box 1022 100th St & 5th Ave New York NY 10029 also: Brookhill Group 501 Madison Ave 18th Fl 10022 *The excitement and stimulation that comes from a productive collaboration with other people has been a major source of satisfaction in my life. I feel privileged to have had the opportunity to interact with a wide range of imaginative and inspiring colleagues, students and friends, including my wife of 50 years, whose extraordinary career emphasized the importance of idealism, commitment, persistence and a felicitous blending of focus and flexibility.*

SCHWARTZ, IRWIN H. lawyer; b. Bklyn., Mar. 25, 1948; s. Julius and Sylvia (Holzman) S.; m. Barbara T. Granett, July 3, 1971; 1 child, Matthew Lane. BA, Bklyn. Coll., 1968; JD, Stanford U., 1971. Bar: Calif. 1972, Washington 1972, U.S. Ct. Appeals (9th cir.) 1972, U.S. Supreme Ct. 1977. Asst. U.S. atty. U.S. Dist. Ct. (we. dist.) Wash., Seattle, 1972-74, exec. asst. U.S. atty., 1974-75, fed. pub. defender, 1975-81; pvt. practice, 1981—. Fellow Am. Coll. Trial Lawyers, Am. Bd. Criminal Lawyers; mem. ABA (criminal justice sect. coun. 1991-94. 2002--), Nat. Assn. Criminal Def. Lawyers (pres. 2001-02), Wash. Athletic Club (Seattle). Avocations: photography, woodworking. Office: 710 Cherry St Seattle WA 98104-1925 E-mail: ischwartz@compuserve.com.

SCHWARTZ, JAMES PETER, real estate broker; b. Bridgeport, Conn., Oct. 30, 1919; s. Joseph and Stephanie (Tischler) S.; m. Natalie Postol, Mar. 12, 1944; 1 child: Joseph William. Reporter Bridgeport Times-Star, 1940-41; reporter, photographer Bridgeport Post, 1942-43, 45-49; pres. Jay James Inc., Fairfield, Conn., 1949-70; owner James P. Schwartz & Assocs., Bridgeport, 1970—. Dir. Lafayette Bank & Trust Co., 1965-85, Lafayette Bancorp, 1985-88, Lafayette Am. Bank & Trust Co., 1992-93. Contbg. editor Photog. Trade News, 1960-70. Treas. Greater Bridgeport Bd. Realtors, 1974-77, sr. v.p., 1978, pres., 1979; pres. Barnum Festival Soc., 1975-76; ringmaster Barnum Festival, 1979; justice of peace, 1970-96; mem. Easton (Conn.) Zoning Bd. Appeals, 1971-76; police commr., Easton, 1976-90, chmn. bd. police commrs., 1986-88; bd. dirs. Bridgeport divsn. Am. Cancer Soc., 1977-94; bd. assocs. U. Bridgeport, 1962-94. With AUS, 1943-45. Named Man of Yr. dept. sociology U. Bridgeport, 1962, Realtor of Yr. award Greater Bridgeport Bd. Realtors, 1979. Mem. Fairfield Bd. Realtors, Nat. Assn. Realtors (bd. dirs.), Conn. Assn. Realtors (treas. 1981-82, pres. 1984-85), Masons, Corinthian Lodge. Home: Embassy Towers 2625 Park Ave Unit 10P Bridgeport CT 06604-1348

SCHWARTZ, JANE LINKER, social worker, nurse; b. Tampa, Fla., Sept. 4, 1925; d. Sydney Linker and Sadie Friedman; m. Lawrence Schwartz (div. 1976); children: Karen, Joel, David. BS, Russell Sage Coll., 1948; MSW, U. Wash., 1967; M in Nursing, 1973; PhD, Union Inst., 1982. Diplomate Am. Bd. Examiners Clin. Social Work; lic. clin. social worker Acad. Cert. Social Workers, Fla. Clin. social worker Navy Regional Med. Ctr., Guam, U.S.A., 1983-84; pvt. practice Honolulu, 1985-89; clin. social worker, psychotherapist VA Med. Ctr., Tampa and Miami, Fla., 1989-90; pvt. practice Miami, 1990-94; clin. social worker Eglin (Fla.) AFB, 1994-95; clin. social worker, psychotherapist Emerald Coast Psychol. Care, Ft. Walton, Fla., 1995—. Author: The Psychodynamics of Patient Care, 1972, Vulnerable Infants-A Psychosocial Dilemma, 1977. 2nd lt. U.S. Army Nurse Corp, 1948-49. Mem. ANA (registered profl. nurse, cert. psychiat. and mental health nurse), NASW, Sigma Theta Tau. Democrat. Jewish. Avocations: swimming, reading, computer writing. Home: 4471 Luke Ave # D Destin FL 32541-3575 Office: Emerald Coast Psychiat Care Fort Walton Beach FL 32548

SCHWARTZ, JEFFREY BYRON, lawyer; b. Phila., Dec. 3, 1940; s. Carl Sidney and Tessie Claire (Cohen) S.; m. Joan S. Weinman, Aug. 4, 1963; children: Kevin, Jill. BS, Pa. State U., 1962; JD, U. Pa., 1965; MBA, Am. U., 1967. Bar: Pa. 1965, D.C. 1968, La. 1969. Staff acct. Price Waterhouse & Co., Washington, 1962; trial atty. SEC, 1965-68; sr. atty. New Orleans Legal Assistance, 1968-70; gen. counsel Nat. Tenants Orgn., Washington, 1970-73; litigation atty. Nat. Health and Environ. Law Project, 1971-74; chief counsel Pa. Dept. Health, Harrisburg, 1974-79; ptnr. Berman & Schwartz, King of Prussia, Pa., 1979-85; sr. ptnr. Wolf, Block, Schorr & Solis-Cohen, Phila., 1985-92; ptnr. Cohen, Shapiro, Polisher, Shiekman & Cohen, 1992-95, Fox Rothschild, O'Brien & Frankel, LLP, Phila., 1995-99; sr. legal advisor USAID Assistance Program Bulgarian Securities and Stock Exch. Commn., 1999—; atty. J. Schwartz & Assocs., 2000—; v.p., gen. counsel Crossover Med. Tech., 2000—. Guest lectr. on welfare and health law U. Pa. Sch. Law, Tulane U. Law Sch., Wayne State U. Law Sch. and Georgetown U. Law Sch.; instr. Catholic U. Am. Law Sch., 1972-73; course planner Pa. Bar Inst., 1980—. Contbr. articles to profl. jours. Reginald Heber Smith fellow, 1968-70. Mem. Am. Soc. Hosp. Attys., Am. Health Lawyers Assn. (dir.), Pa. Soc. Hosp. Attys. (pres. 1983-85, bd. dirs. 1983-89), Hosp. Attys. Southeastern Pa., Am. Pub. Health Assn. (chmn. health law com. 1978-81), Pa. Bar Assn., D.C. Bar Assn. Democrat. Jewish. Home: 10 Radcliff Rd Bala Cynwyd PA 19004-2631

SCHWARTZ, JEFFREY SCOTT, lawyer; b. N.Y.C., Aug. 2, 1959; s. Philip Harold and Carolyn Annette (Stern) S.; m. Lynette Pam Vigdor, Dec. 23, 1984; children: Michelle Renee, Joel Benjamin. BA, SUNY, Oneonta, 1981; JD, Western State U. Coll. Law, San Diego, 1984. Bar: Calif. 1987, U.S. Dist. Ct. (so. dist.) Calif. 1987, U.S. Supreme Ct. 1997, D.C. 1998. Legal asst. Law Office William O'Connell, San Diego, 1983-87, assoc., 1987-88; pvt. practice, 1988-99; CEO, pres. ionUS.com Corp., 1999—. Chmn. legal clinic San Diego State U., San Diego City Coll., San Diego County Bar Assn., 1987—, vice chmn. Pub. Info. and Rels. com., 1991. Mem. ABA, State Bar Calif. (advisor gen. practice sect., author Criminal Justice Jour. 1983), San Diego County Bar Assn. (chmn. call for action 1989, 91-97), ATLA, Calif. Trial Lawyers Assn., San Diego Trial Lawyers Assn., Delta Theta Phi (supreme ct. justice 1987-95, Percy J. Power award 1987, Wiley W. Manuel award for legal svcs. 1990). Democrat. Jewish. Office: 5703 Oberlin Dr Ste 108 San Diego CA 92121 E-mail: jschwartz@ionus.com

SCHWARTZ, JOAN LAM, computer graphics consultant, writer, artist; b. Phila., Dec. 19, 1928; d. Alfred C. and Sara (Maybaum) Lam; m. Arthur J. Schwartz, Sept. 17, 1952; children: Charles, Dona. BArch, U. Pa., 1951; MA in Adminstrn., Antioch U., 1983; postgrad., Northrop U., 1984. Cert. community coll. instr., Calif. Archtl. designer Pullinger, Stevens, Bruder and Assocs., Phila., 1951-52; pvt. practice, 1952-75; acct. exec. Fahnestock and Co., N.Y. Stock Exch., 1975-80; rsch. cons. The Rand Corp., Santa Monica, Calif., 1982-83; rsch. analyst Info. Displays, Inc., L.A., 1984-85, Info. Internat., Inc., Culver City, Calif., 1985; computer graphics cons. L.A., 1985—. One man shows Barzansky Galleries, N.Y.C., 1966, 68; represented in mus. collections; contbr. articles to profl. jours. Recipient nat. 3d prize Beaux Arts Inst. Design, 1949, Benedictine award, 1967, honorable mention Corel Draw Internat. Design Contest, 1991, Excellence award Corel Internat. Design Contest, 1993. Mem.: Siggraph, Assn. Computing Machinery. Democrat. Avocations: golf, photography, bridge, travel. Home and Office: 154 Windsor Ln New Brighton MN 55112-3311

SCHWARTZ, JOAN RUTH, writer; b. Newark, June 27, 1938; d. Benjamin S. and Leah Pines Teitel; m. Allen G. Schwartz, Jan. 17, 1965; children: David, Rachel, Deborah. BA, Rutgers U., 1960; MA, U. Chgo., 1961. Editl. positions U. Chgo. Press, 1961, Columbia U. Press, N.Y.C., 1962, Macmillan Pub. Co., N.Y.C., 1962—63, The Free Press, N.Y.C., 1963—66; editor, 1966—73. Co-author: Mitchel London's Gracie Mansion Cookbook, 1989, David's Delicious Weight-Loss Program, 1990, David's Delicious Weight-Loss Program, reissued in soft cover as David's Lose Weight Permanently, Reduce Your Cholesterol, and Still Eat 97% of the Food You Love Diet, 1991, Memories of a Cuban Kitchen, 1992, Cooking Provence, 1994, Bobby Flay's Bold American Food, 1994, French Food/American Accent, 1996, From My Kitchen to Your Table, 1998, Boy Meets Grill, 1999, Matthew Kenney's Big City Cooking, 2002; author: The Greenmarket Cookbook, 2000, Macaroni and Cheese, 2001. Jewish.

SCHWARTZ, JOEL LAWRENCE, oral pathology educator; b. N.Y.C., Nov. 12, 1951; s. Arthur and Rae (Topaz) S.; m. Roberta Rdunitsky, June 14, 1973; 1 child, Lori. DMD, Tufts Sch. Dentistry, 1976; DMS, Harvard Med. Sch., 1981. Lic. oral pathologist and dentist, Mass., Md., D.C. Postdoctoral fellow Harvard Med. Sch., Boston, 1976-80, asst. prof., 1982-88, assoc. prof., 1988—; dir. rsch. Coll. Dentistry, Howard U., Washington, 1996—. Cons. Cardiospectrum, Providence, 1991; reviewer study sects. NIH. Assoc. editor Jour. Nutrition Immunology, 1991; contbr. articles to profl. jours., including Oral Maxillofacial Surgery, JADA, Nutrition and Cancer. NIH grantee, 1981—. Mem. AAAS, Am. Assn. Cancer Rsch., Acad. Oral Pathology, Nutritional Oncology Adjuvant Therapy (v.p.), Boston Cancer Rsch. Soc. Jewish. Achievements include demonstration that carotenoids and alpha tocopherols can prevent and inhibit the growth of various cancers; that B-carotene, a carotenoid, can induce the expression of novel proteins. Office: Howard Univ Coll Dentistry 600 W St NE Washington DC 20002-1241

SCHWARTZ, JOHN NORMAN, health care executive; b. Watertown, Minn., Dec. 13, 1945; s. Norman O. and Marion G. (Tesch) S. BA, Augsburg Coll., Mpls., 1967; MHA, U. Minn., 1969. Adminstrv. resident Luth. Hosp. and Med. Ctr., Wheat Ridge, Colo., 1968-69; asst. adminstr. St. Luke's Hosp., Milw., 1969-73, med. adminstr., 1973-75, v.p., 1975-84; sr. v.p. and chief oper. officer Good Samaritan Med. Ctr., 1984-85, pres. and chief exec. officer, 1985-88; exec. v.p. Aurora Health Care Inc., 1988-89; gen. mgr. SmithKline Beecham Clin. Labs., Schaumburg, Ill., 1989-90; chief exec. Trinity Hosp. of Advocate Health Care, Chgo., 1991—. Bd. dirs. Samaritan Health Plan, Milw., 1984-89. Bd. dirs. Gt. Lakes Hemophilia Found., Milw., 1975-89, S.E. Chgo. Devel. Commn., 1996—, East Side Bank, 1998—; Gov.'s appointee to Coun. on Hemophilia and Related Blood Disorders, Madison, 1978; mem. Sullivan Chamber Ensemble, Milw., 1975-84, South Chgo. YMCA, 1993—. Recipient Bd. Mem. of Yr. award Great Lake's Hemophilia Found., 1986, Outstanding Cmty. Leadership award Stony Island C. of C., 1996, Am. Hosp. Assn. Cir. of Distinction award, 1999; named Exec. of Yr. Coun. on Health and Human Svcs. Ministry, 1999. Fellow Am. Coll. Healthcare Execs. (regent 1993-99, Regent's award for sr. exec. leadership 1999). Lutheran. Avocations: jogging, photography, music, choral singing. Office: Trinity Hosp 2320 E 93rd St Chicago IL 60617 E-mail: john.schwartz@advocatehealth.com.

SCHWARTZ, JOHN HOWARD, poultry science and extension educator; b. Gettysburg, Pa., Nov. 26, 1948; s. John W. and Stella B. (Brown) S.; m. Kathryn A. Bentz, Sept. 21, 1986; children: Kathryn A., John L. BS, Pa. State U., 1970, MEd, 1975; PhD, Colo. State U., 1985. Diplomate Am. Coll. Animal Physiology. 4-H extn. agt. Pa. State U., West Chester, 1970-75, agrl. extn. agt. Gettysburg, 1975-83; rsch. asst. Colo. State U., Ft. Collins, 1983-84; exec. v.p. Colo. Quality Rsch., 1984-85; asst. prof. Clemson (S.C.) U., 1986-88; poultry extn. agt. Pa. State U., Lancaster, 1988-91, county extension dir., from 1991. Assoc. Thurmond Inst., Clemson, 1987. Mem. Nat. Assn. County Agrl. Agts. (Achievement award 1979), Poultry Sci. Assn., Coun. Agrl. Sci. and Tech., Pa. Poultry Fedn., Masons, Phi Kappa Phi, Gamma Sigma Delta, Alpha Tau Alpha. Home: York, Pa. Died Aug. 20, 2001.

SCHWARTZ, JOHN J. association executive, consultant; b. New Rochelle, N.Y., Aug. 28, 1919; s. Edwin Benner and Marjorie Helen (James) S.; m. Katharine S. Sprackling, Jan. 6, 1942; children: Christopher Louis. Grad. high sch., New Rochelle; student, Mercersburg Acad., 1938. Campaign dir. John Price Jones Inc., N.Y.C., 1946-50; dir. pub. relations and fund raising Travelers Aid Soc. N.Y., 1950-55; dir. devel. Community Service Soc., 1955-57, Near East Found., N.Y.C., 1957-60; v.p. G.A. Brakeley & Co. Inc., 1960-61; dir. devel. Fgn. Policy Assn., 1962-64; founding pres. Greater N.Y. Nat. Soc. of Fund Raising Execs., 1964; asst. v.p. for crusade Am. Cancer Soc., N.Y.C., 1964-66; exec. dir. Am. Assn. Fund Raising Counsel, 1966-68, exec. v.p., 1968-72, pres., 1972-87. Founding bd. mem. Ind. Sector, Washington, 1980-85, mem. com. to measurably increase giving; mem., former pres. Com. on Nat. Ctr. for Charitable Stats.; spl. cons. to Com. on Pvt. Philanthropy and Pub. Needs., 1973; chair pvt. adv. group Nat. Assn. Attys. Gen. Model Law Project. Author: Modern American Philanthropy; A Personal Account, 1993. Mem. adv. bd. mgmt. fund-raising cert. program NYU; mem. adv. coun. Grad. Sch. Mgmt. and Urban Professions, New Sch. Social Rsch.; active formation of 5 borough coalitions Daring Coals for Caring Soc., N.Y.C., 1987; cons. Ind. U. Ctr. on Philanthropy, 1988—91, Cmty. Counselling Serv. Co., Inc., 1988—91; pres. Nat. Philanthropy Day, 1988—90, mem. hon. com., 1981; pres. Friends of Westport Libr., 1995—98; bd. dir.-at-large USA World Fund Raising Coun., 1993; bd. dirs. Norwalk Sr. Ctr., 2001—. Capt. PTO USAF, 1941—46. Recipient Disting. Profl. Service to Philanthropy award Am. Assn. Fund-Raising Counsel, N.Y., 1976, Outstanding Agy. Profl. award United Way Am., Alexandria, 1982, Henry A. Rosso Lifetime Achievement in Ethical Fundraising award Ind. U. Ctr. on Philanthropy, 1997. Mem.: Assn. Fund Raising Profls. Fairfield County (bd. dirs. emeritus), Am. Asn. Ret. Persons (bd. dir. Andrus Found. 1983-90), Fairfield County Asn. Fundraising Profls. (bd. dir. 1992-2000, bd. dir. emeritus 2000-02), Nat. Soc. Fund Raising Execs. (bd. dirs. 1964-90, past pres.), Nat. Charities Info. Bur. (bd. dirs. 1978-94), VFW, Princeton Club (N.Y.C.), 501C-3 Soc. Democrat. Unitarian Universalist. Avocations: writing history, ship models. E-mail: jschwarz227@aol.com.

SCHWARTZ, JONATHAN RALPH, psychiatrist; b. N.Y.C. s. Jack Schwartz and Elinor Ruth Landau; m. R. Lisa Sheiman, Dec. 23, 1984; children: Noah, Nicholas, Molly. BA, Cornell U., 1968; MD, U. Pitts., 1972. Intern U. Wis., Madison, 1972-73; resident Mt. Sinai Hosp., N.Y.C., 1977-80; pvt. practice, 1980-92, C.L.M. Behavioral Health, Derry, N.H., 1992-98, Riverbend Mental Health, Concord, 1998—. Asst. prof. Mt. Sinai, N.Y.C., 1982-92. Contbr. articles to profl. jours. With USPHS, 1972-75. Mem. Am. Psychiat. Assn., Am. Assn. for Geriatric Psychiatry, Soc. for Sex Therapy and Rsch. Avocations: tennis, music, gardening. Office: Concord Hosp 250 Pleasant St Concord NH 03301-2598

SCHWARTZ, JOSEPH, retired container company executive; b. N.Y.C., Apr. 22, 1911; s. Nathan and Ida (Estrich) S.; m. Hazel Shapiro, Dec. 25, 1932; children— Arlene Schwartz Bornstein, Linda Schwartz Rosenbaum Grad., high sch. Ptnr. Mut. Paper Co., Lynn, Mass., 1928-38; treas. Allied Container Corp., Hyde Park, 1938-56; pres., treas. Allied Container Corp., Dedham, 1956-84. Chmn. bd. Cargal, Ltd., Lod Israel; ret. v.p. Union Camp Corp., Wayne, N.J. Fellow Brandeis U. Home: 3960 Oaks Clubhouse Dr Apt 307 Pompano Beach FL 33069-3645

SCHWARTZ, JOSEPH, English language educator; b. Milw., Apr. 9, 1925; s. Alfred George and Mary (Brandt) S.; m. Joan Jackson, Aug. 28, 1954; 1 son, Adam. BA, Marquette U., 1946, MA, 1947; PhD, U. Wis., 1952. Teaching asst. Marquette U., Milw., 1946-47, instr., 1947-48, 50-54, asst. prof., 1954-59, assoc. prof., 1959-64, prof., 1964-90, chmn. dept. English, 1963-75, prof. emeritus, 1990—. Teaching fellow U. Wis., 1948-50; Chmn. region X Woodrow Wilson Nat. Fellowship Found., 1967-73; pres. bd. edn. Archdiocese of Milw., 1977-79 Author: A Reader for Writers, 3d edit., 1971, Perspectives on Language, 1963, Province of Rhetoric, 1965, Poetry: Meaning and Form, 1969, Hart Crane: A Critical Bibliography, 1970, Hart Crane: A Descriptive Bibliography, 1972, Exposition, 2d edit., 1971, Hart Crane: A Reference Guide, 1983; sr. editor: Renascence Mag., 1978—. Recipient Distinguished Alumni award Marquette U. Sch. Speech, 1967, Outstanding Tchr. award Marquette U., 1974; Ford Found. grantee, 1956; Am. Council Learned Socs. grantee, 1972, 89; HEW grantee, 1966, 67 Mem. Nat. Coun. Tchrs. English (nat. dir. 1965-68), Modern Lang. Assn., Midwest Modern Lang Assn. (exec. com. 1973-76), Fellowship of Cath. Scholars (bd. dirs. 1987-90), Conf. on Christianity and Lit. (bd. dirs. 1987-90), Phi Beta Kappa, Alpha Sigma Nu (hon.). Republican. Roman Catholic. Home: 8516 W Mequon Rd # 112 Thiensville WI 53097-3100 Office: Marquette U PO Box 1888 Renascence Helfaer Bldg Milwaukee WI 53201-1888

SCHWARTZ, JOSEPH HERSH, surgeon, educator; b. L.A., Feb. 26, 1956; MD, Harvard U., 1982. Diplomate Am. Bd. Surgery, Am. Bd. Surg. Critical Care. Intern SUNY-Downstate, Bklyn., 1982-83; surg. resident New England Deaconess Hosp., Boston, 1983-88; resident in pediatric critical care medicine Mass. Gen. Hosp., 1985; chief surg. resident New England Deaconess Hosp., 1988; fellow in gastroenterol. surgery Ohio Digestive Disease Inst., Columbus, 1991-92; active staff Deaconess Waltham (Mass.) Hosp., 1993—, Newton (Mass.)-Wellesley Hosp., 1994—; courtesy staff Beth Israel Deaconess Med. Ctr., Boston, 1993—, Norwood (Mass.) Hosp., 1995—. Clin. instr. surgery Harvard U., Boston, 1993—. Fellow ACS; mem. AMA, Am. Soc. Parental Enteral Nutrition, Soc. Critical Care Medicine, Soc. Am. Gastrointestinal Endoscopic Surgeons, Am. Soc. Gen. Surgeons. Office: Twinbrook Surgical Assocs 20 Hope Ave Ste 207 Waltham MA 02453-2717

SCHWARTZ, JOYCE GENSBERG, pathologist; b. San Antonio, July 24, 1950; d. Frank and Sara Gensberg; m. Alan R. Schwartz, July 17, 1977. BA, U. Tex., Austin, 1971, MA, 1972; MD, U. Tex., San Antonio, 1980. Speech pathologist N.E. Ins. Sch. Dist., San Antonio, 1971-73, vet. asst., 1973-74; resident in pathology U. Tex. Health Sci. Ctr., 1980-84, mem. faculty pathology, 1984-96; med. dir. southern region Quest Diagnostics, Irving, 1996—2000; chief lab. officer Quest Diagnostics , Teterboro, NJ, 2000—. Pres. P.I. Nixon Hist. Libr., 1991-92. Recipient Presdl. Tchg. award, 1991, Piper Prof. award, 1992; named San Antonio Women's Hall of Fame, 1995. Mem. AMA, Coll. Am. Pathologists (regional commr.), Tex. Soc. Pathologists (sec. 1994-96), Dallas Med. Assn., Women's Faculty Assn. (pres. 1988-89), San AntonioSoc. Pathologists (pres. 1988-89), Phi Kappa Phi, Alpha Omega Alpha. Jewish. Office: Quest Diagnostics 1 Malcolm Ave Teterboro NJ 07608

SCHWARTZ, JUDITH, interior designer; b. N.Y., Apr. 29, 1942; d. Joseph and Blanche (Kirsch) Rosensweig; m. Stanley Schwartz, June 9, 1963; children— Blair, Kim. B.S., Finch Coll., 1963; degree N.Y. Sch. Design, 1965; student Sorbonne, Paris, 1961. N.Y. rep. Better Home Furniture Co., N.C., 1965-67; prin., designer J.R.S. Interiors, Inc., N.Y.C., 1967— ; designer showcase work Scalamandré Fabrics, N.Y.C., 1981, 83. Contbr. articles to profl. jours.; design work pub. in trade mags. Expeditor Dept. of Consumer Affairs, N.Y.C., 1980; active fund raising activities Jr. League Yeshivah U., N.Y.C., 1978; nat. pres. Yeshiva U. Women's Orgn., 1977-79. Named Woman of Yr. Park E. Cultural Ctr., 1985, Woman of Distinction, Yeshivah U., 1980. Mem. Am. Soc. Interior Designers, Am. Womens Econ. Devel., Nat. Home Fashion League. Avocations: antiques; music; opera.

SCHWARTZ, JUDY ELLEN, cardiothoracic surgeon; b. Mason City, Iowa, Oct. 5, 1946; d. Walter Carl and Alice Nevada (Moore) S. BS, U. Iowa, 1968, MD, 1971; M.P.H., Johns Hopkins U., 1996. Diplomate Am. Bd. Surgery, Am. Bd. Thoracic Surgery, Am. Bd. Med. Mgmt.; cert. physician exec. Cert. Commn. Med. Mgmt. Intern Nat. Naval Med. Ctr., Bethesda, Md., 1971-72, gen. surgery resident, 1972-76, thoracic surgery resident, 1976-78, staff cardiothoracic surgeon, 1979-82, chief cardiothoracic surgeon, 1982-83; chmn. cardiothoracic surg. dept. Naval Hosp., San Diego, 1983-85, quality assurance program dir., 1985-88. Exec. office Rapidly Deployable Med. Facility Four, 1986-88; asst. prof. surgery Uniformed Svcs. Univ. Health Sci., Bethesda, 1983-99; sr. policy analyst quality assurance Profl. Affairs and Quality Assurance, 1988-90, dep. dir. quality assurance, 1990; dir. clin. policy Health Svcs. Ops., Washington, 1990-94; head performance evaluation and improvement Nat. Naval Med. Ctr., 1994-99; cardiothoracic speciality cons. to naval med. command U.S. Navy, Washington, 1983-84; Dept. Def. rep. to Joint Commn. Accreditation Health Care Orgn. task force on info. mgmt., 1990-93, chmn. 1991-93, task force on IMS Tech., 1993-94; chmn. info mgmt. workshop Fed. Health Care Study Commn.'s Corrd. Fed. Health Care, 1993; corp. med. dir. Medctr. One Health Systems, 1999—, N.Dak. Dept. Corrections & Rehab., 1999-, VPMA Medcenter One, 2000; mem. bd. dir. SCCI; bd. trustees Medcenter One Health Sys., 1999-; mem. adv. com. BCBS Care Mgmt., 1999-. Contbr. articles to various publs. Mem. nat. physician's leadership coun. VHA, 2000; bd. trustees St. Vincent's Nursing Home, 2001—. Fellow Am. Coll. Cardiology, Am. Coll. Surgeons (com. allied health pers. 1985-91, exec. com. 1987-91, accreditation review com. edn. physician asst. 1988-94, treas. accreditation review com. 1991-93, sr. mem. com. allied health pers. 1991-94); mem. AMA, Am. Thoracic Soc., Am. Med. Women's Assn., Am. Mgmt. Assn., Am. Coll. Physician Execs. Office: Medcenter One Health Systems PO Box 5525 300 N 7th St Bismarck ND 58506-5525 E-mail: medicaldirector@mohs.org.

SCHWARTZ, KENNETH ERNST, communications executive; b. Detroit, July 12, 1922; s. Bernath and Sadie (Weiss) S.; m. June Henry; m. 2d, Eileen Frances Lamb, Dec.13, 1969; children: Joshua, Sarah. Grad., U.S. Merchant Marine Acad., 1944, Am. Acad. Dramatic Arts, 1944-46. Producer/dir. Great Lakes Drama Festival, Saginaw, Mich., 1951-53; gen. mgr. Weil & Co., Detroit, 1953-55; producer/director Northland Playhouse, Southfield, Mich., 1955-69; deck officer U.S. Merchant Marine, 1969-71; freelance film producer/writer, 1971-73; pres. Cutting Edge Enterprises, Inc., Easy Edit, V & W Sound Rec., Inc., N.Y.C., 1973-89, U.S. Editing Systems and Kenedit Film Svcs., N.Y.C., 1989—. Pres. U.S. Editing Systems, N.Y.C.; dir. Midwest Alliance Summer Theatres, Detroit. Asst. producer (Broadway prodn.) Raisin in the Sun, 1959; co-producer (Broadway prodn.) Once There Was a Russian, 1961; assoc. producer (motion picture) Popcorn, 1990; co-author (film): Snapshots, 1973. Served to lt. USNR, 1944-47. Recipient Key to City of Detroit. Mem. B'nai B'rith Cinema, Radio, TV. Jewish. Office: Kenedit Film Svcs 630 9th Ave New York NY 10036-3708

SCHWARTZ, KENNETH STUART, surgeon; b. N.Y.C., Apr. 3, 1948; BS in Engring. Scis., SUNY, Stony Brook, 1970; MS in Biomed. Engring., U. Fla., Gainesville, 1972; MD, Albert Einstein Coll. Medicine, 1977. Diplomate Am. Bd. Surgery; lic. MD, Calif., N.Y. Resident in surgery Montefiore Hosp., Bronx, N.Y., 1977-81; fellow U. So. Calif., 1981-82; pvt. practice N.Y.C., 1982—. Adj. asst. prof. N.Y. Coll. Podiatric Medicine, 1993; assoc. prof. surgery N.Y. Coll. Osteopathic Medicine, 1992; clin. asst. prof. surgery N.Y. Med. Coll., 1982—; chief surgery St. Barnabas Hosp., Bronx, 1987, pres. med. staff, 1990-92; chief vascular surgery sect. White Plains Hosp. Med. Ctr., 1995; chmn. surgery N.Y. United Hosp., 2001. Fellow ACS; mem. Am. Med. Soc., N.Y. Cardiovascular Soc., Ea. Vascular Soc., Westchester County Med. Soc., Sigma Xi, Tau Beta Pi. Office: Vascular Surg Assocs 14 Harwood Ct Ste 326 Scarsdale NY 10583-4122 E-mail: avgraft@hotmail.com.

SCHWARTZ, LAWRENCE, aeronautical engineer; b. N.Y.C., Nov. 30, 1935; s. Harry and Fanny (Steiner) S.; m. Cherie Anne Karo, Aug. 12, 1979; children: Ronda, Daran. SB in Aero. Engring., SM in Aero. Engring., MIT, 1958; postgrad., Ohio State U., 1960, U. Dayton, 1962-63; PhD in Engring., UCLA, 1966. Registered profl. engr., Colo., Calif. Electronics design engr. MIT Instrumentation Lab., Cambridge, 1959; aerospace engr. Wright-Patterson AFB, Wright-Patterson AFB, Ohio, 1962-63; mem. tech. staff Hughes Aircraft Co., Culver City, Calif., 1963-65, staff engr., 1965-67, sr. staff engr., 1967-72, sr. scientist, 1972-79, chief scientist lab., 1979-93, tech. mgr., 1985-87, chmn., tech. adv. bd., 1987-88, prin. scientist/engr., 1993-97, Raytheon Systems Co., Aurora, Colo., 1997-98, sr. prin. engr., 1999, engring. fellow, 1999, Raytheon Co. (formerly Raytheon Systems Co.), Aurora, 2000—. Cons., tchr. in field. Contbr. articles to profl. jours. With USAF, 1959-62. Mem. IEEE, AAAS, N.Y. Acad. Scis., Sigma Xi, Sigma Gamma Tau, Tau Beta Pi. Home: 996 S Florence St Denver CO 80247-1952 Office: 16800 E Centretech Pky Aurora CO 80011-9046 E-mail: lschwart@ieee.org.

SCHWARTZ, LEON, foreign language educator; b. Boston, Aug. 22, 1922; s. Charles and Celia (Emer) S.; m. Jeanne Gurtat, Mar. 31, 1949; children—Eric Alan, Claire Marie. Student, Providence Coll., 1939-41; BA, UCLA, 1948; certificat de phonetique, U. Paris, 1949; MA, U. So. Cal., 1950, PhD, 1962. Tchr. English, Spanish and Latin Redlands (Calif.) Jr. High Sch., 1951-54; high sch. tchr. Spanish and French, 1954-59; prof. French Calif. State U., Los Angeles, 1959-87, chmn. dept. fgn. langs. and lit., 1970-73, prof. emeritus, 1987—. Author: Diderot and the Jews, 1981. Served as 2d lt. USAAF, 1942-45. Decorated Air medal with 5 oak leaf clusters; recipient Outstanding Prof. award Calif. State U. L.A., 1976 Mem. Am. Assn. Tchrs. French, Modern and Classical Lang. Assn. So. Calif., Am. Soc. 18th Century Studies, Société Diderot, Calif. State U. L.A. Emeriti Assn. (pres. 1998-2000), Phi Beta Kappa, Phi Kappa Phi, Pi Delta Phi, Sigma Delta Pi, Alpha Mu Gamma. Office: Calif State U Dept Modern Langs and Lit Los Angeles CA 90032 E-mail: l_schwar@pacbell.net.

SCHWARTZ, LEONARD JAY, lawyer; b. San Antonio, Sept. 23, 1943; s. Oscar S. and Ethel (Eastman) S.; m. Sandra E. Eichelbaum, July 4, 1965; 1 child, Michele Fay. BBA, U. Tex., 1965, JD, 1968. Bar: Tex. 1968, Ohio 1971, U.S. Supreme Ct. 1971, U.S. Dist. Ct. (no., ea., wes. and so. dists.) Tex., U.S. Dist. Cts. (no. and so. dists.) Ohio, U.S. Dist. Ct. Nebr., U.S. Ct. Appeals (5th, 6th, 7th and 11th cirs.). Assoc. Roberts & Holland, N.Y.C., 1968-70; ptnr. Rigely, Schwartz & Fagan, San Antonio, 1970-71; staff counsel ACLU of Ohio, Columbus, 1971-74; ptnr. Schwartz & Fishman, 1974-79; elections counsel to sec. of state State of Ohio, 1979-80; ptnr. Waterman & Schwartz and successor firms, Austin, Tex., 1981-85; mng. dir. Schwartz & Eichelbaum, PC, Austin and other cities, 1985-99, 2000—, shareholder Austin, various locations, 1985—. Gen. counsel various sch. dists., cities and counties; adj. prof. law U. Tex. Sch. Law, Austin; labor and employment law cons. and sch. law Tex. Assn. Sch. Adminstrs; condr. workshops in field; mem. com. on fed. judiciary rels. Tex. Bar. Contbr. articles to profl. jours. Mem. chancellor's coun. U. Tex. Sys.; mem. U. Tex. Pres.'s Assocs., Littlefield Soc., Sch. of Law Keeton Fellows. Recipient Outstanding Tchg. Quiz Master award U. Tex. Sch. Law, 1968. Fellow Tex. Bar Found.; mem. ABA, FBA, Tex. Bar Assn., Bar Assn. 5th Cir., Phi Delta Phi. Democrat. Jewish. Office: Schwartz & Eichelbaum PC 4201 W Parmer Ln Ste 100 Austin TX 78727 Fax: 512-472-2599. E-mail: lschwartz@edlaw.com.

SCHWARTZ, LILLIAN FELDMAN, artist, filmmaker, art analyst, writer, nurse; b. Cin., July 13, 1927; d. Jacob and Katie (Green) Feldman; m. Jack James Schwartz, Dec. 22, 1946; children: Jeffrey Hugh, Laurens Robert. RN, U. Cin., 1947; Dr. honoris causa, Kean Coll., 1988. Nurse Cin. Gen. Hosp., 1947; head supr. premature nursery St. Louis Maternity Hosp., 1947-48; cons. AT&T Bell Labs., Murray Hill, N.J., 1968-97; pres. Computer Creations Corp., Watchung, 1989—; cons. Bell Communications Research, Morristown, 1984-92, Lucent Technologies/Bell Labs. Innovations, 1996—2001. Artist-in-residence Sta. WNET, N.Y.C., 1972-74; cons. T.J. Watson Rsch. Lab. IBM Corp., Yorktown, N.Y., 1975, 82-84; vis. mem. computer sci. dept. U.. Md., College Park, 1974-80; adj. prof. fine arts Kean Coll., Union, N.J., 1980-82, Rutgers U., New Brunswick, N.J., 1982-83; adj. prof. dept. psychology NYU, N.Y.C., 1985-86, assoc. prof. computer sci.; guest lectr. Princeton U., Columbia U., Yale U., Rockefeller U.; mem. grad. faculty Sch. Visual Arts, N.Y.C., 1990—; dir. team from Rutgers U. to create world's first computer-generated 3-D model of Leaning Tower of Pisa to test structures, 1999; invited com. mem. info. tech. and creativity NAS, 2000-01; invited juror L'Oreal/Color/Internat., 2000-01. Co-author: The Computer Artist's Handbook; contbd. articles to profl. jours including Scientific Am., 1995; contbr. chpts. to books, also Trans. Am. Philos. Soc., vol. 75, Part 6, 1985; one-woman shows of sculpture and paintings include Columbia U., 1967, 68, Rabin and Krueger Gallery, Newark, 1968; films shown at Met. Mus., N.Y.C., Franklin Inst., Phila., 1972, U. Toronto, 1972, am. Embassy, London, 1972, L.A. County Mus., Corcoran Gallery, Washington, 1972, Whitney Mus., N.Y.C., 1973, Grand Palais, Paris, Musee Nat. d'Art Moderne, Paris, IBM, (digital print show) Bklyn. Mus. Art, 2001, and others; dir.: Save the Leaning Tower. Recipient numerous art and film awards, Emmy award Mus. Modern Art, 1984, Computer Graphics World Smithsonian awards for virtual reality, art analysis, inventing computer medium for art and animation, 1993; named Outstanding Alumnus, U. Cin., 1987; grantee Nat. Endowment for Arts, 1977, 81, Corp. Pub. Broadcasting, 1979, Nat. Endowment Composers and Librettists, 1981. Fellow World Acad. of Art and Sci.; mem. NATAS, Am. Film Inst., Info. Film Prodrs. Am., Soc. Motion Picture and TV Engrs., Internat. Sculptors Assn., Centro Studi Pierfrancescani (Sansepolcro, Italy, founding mem.). Achievements include pioneer in use of computers as art media; commd. to create computer poster and TV comml. for opening New Mus. Modern Art, 1984; discovered identities of the Mona Lisa, hidden surface, 1987, and identified steps DaVinci made in transforming Isabella, Duchess of Aragon, into the Mona Lisa using his own features as the model, 1993; discovered perspective used by DaVinci in The Last Supper, 1988; identified time of day and tree of thorns in Piero della Francesca's Resurrection; discovered Elizabeth I is model for Martin Droeshout engraving of Shakespeare, 1991; performed first transmission of computer drawing between U.S. and Germany, 1990; used morphing algorithms to determine Leonardo's creative decision-making steps in transforming the Duchess of Aragon into the Mona Lisa using his own features to segue; discovered method Leonardo used to create his Grotesques, 1994; discovered new Renaissance illusion of another figure in a painting of Christ, 1996, rediscovered Renaissance illusion published in visual computer, 1997, Satan-like figure in Leonardo's Munich "Madonna", 1998; created with Professor Madara Ozot and PhD candidate Zheng Zhou, first computer-generated 3D model of the Leaning Tower of Pisa to test the structure, 1999. *I have always been provoked by and concerned with the mechanical and technological world around me. I enjoy experimenting with traditional media and combining them with technology today. For example, I used computers as an art medium when computers were solely programmed for scientific purposes. By using the computer to understand the creative process I have made clear the intent of the great masters and applied their decision-making steps to my own work. The excitement in creating is to discover and to make a new world. My present success was achieved in part by being able to make new rules and not be hindered by old or obvious solutions.*

SCHWARTZ, LISA M. (LISA SHEPARD), research and development chemist; b. Cherry Point, N.C. d. Luverne M. and Janet M. Shepard; m. Alan J. Schwartz. BS in Chemistry/Geology, S.W. Mo. State U.; MS in Analytical Chemistry, Ind. U. Assoc. instr. Ind. U., Bloomington, rsch. assoc.; rsch. and devel. chemist Applied Labs., Columbus, Ind. Contbr. articles to profl. jours. Recipient 1st place geology presentation, Mo. Acad. Scis., Outstanding Pres. award, Mo. ARK Cir. K. Internat.; scholar Presidential and Nat. Merit, SMSU, Springfield, Mo. Mem. Am. Chemical Soc. Avocations: music, cooking, crafts, reading, travel.

SCHWARTZ, LITA LINZER, psychologist, educator; b. Jan. 14, 1930; d. Aaron Jerome and Dorothy Claire Linzer; m. Melvin Jay Schwartz, June 18, 1950 (div. 1983); children: Arthur Lee, Joshua David, Frederic Seth. AB, Vassar Coll., 1950; EdM, Temple U., 1956; PhD, Bryn Mawr Coll., 1964. Diplomate Am. Bd. Forensic Psychology, Am. Bd. Profl. Psychology; lic. psychologist, Pa. Part-time instr., counselor Pa. State U., Abington, 1961-66, from asst. prof. ednl. psychology to assoc. prof., 1966-76, prof., 1976-93, disting. prof., prof. women's studies, 1993-95, disting. prof. emerita, 1995—. Pvt. practice, 1964—; cons. in field. Author: American Education, 1969, 74, 78, Educational Psychology, 1972, 77, The Exceptional Child: A Primer, 1975, 79, Exceptional Students in the Mainstream, 1984, (with Natalie Isser) The American School and The Melting Pot, 1985, 89, (with Natalie Isser) The History of Conversion and Contemporary Cults, 1988, Alternatives to Infertility: Is Surrogacy the Answer?, 1991, Why Give Gifts to the Gifted?: Investing in a National Resource, 1994, (with Florence W. Kaslow) The Dynamics of Divorce, 1987; editor: Mid-Life Divorce Counseling, 1994, (with Florence W. Kaslow) Painful Partings: Divorce and Its Aftermath, 1997, (with Phil Rich) The Healing Journey Through Divorce, 1999; editor: Psychology and the Media: A Second Look, 1999, (with N. Isser) Endangered Children: Neonaticide, Infanticide, Filicide, 2000; contbr. numerous articles to profl. jours., chpts. to books. Recipient Humanitarian award N.Y. Philanthropic League, 1973, Christian R. and Mary F. Lindback award, 1982, Outstanding Tchr. award Pa. State U. Coll. Edn. Alumni, 1982. Fellow: APA; mem.: Ethnic Studies Assn. Delaware Valley (co-chair program com. 1986—88), Acad. for Conflict Resolution (evaluation com. child study mediation project Delaware Valley), Assn. Family and Conciliation Cts., Internat. Coun. Psychologists (bd. dirs. 1995—96), Am. Bd. Forensic Psychology, Psi Chi. Office: Pa State U Abington Coll Abington PA 19001 E-mail: lls2@psu.edu.

SCHWARTZ, LLOYD, music critic, poet; b. N.Y.C., Nov. 29, 1941; s. Sam and Ida (Singer) S. BA, Queens Coll., N.Y.C., 1962; MA, Harvard U., 1963, PhD, 1976. Classical music editor Boston Phoenix, 1977—; dir. creative writing U. Mass., Boston, 1982—, 1990—; classical music critic Fresh Air Nat. Pub. Radio, Phila., 1987—. Prof. English U. Mass., Boston, 1986—. Author: (poems) These People, 1981, Goodnight, Gracie, 1992, Cairo Traffic, 2000, (play) These People: Voices for the Stage, 1990; editor: Ploughshares, 1979, Elizabeth Bishop and Her Art, 1983; actor The Spider's Web, 1975-82; dir. These People: Voices for the Stage, 1990, (operas) L'Heure Espagnol (Ravel), 1972, Mavra (Stravinsky), 1973. Recipient Pulitzer prize for criticism, 1994; NEA creative writing fellow in poetry, 1990. Mem. PEN (exec. com. New Eng. chpt. 1983-98) PEN Am., Poetry Soc. Am., MLA, New Eng. Poetry Club. Avocations: collecting old recordings, books. Home: 27 Pennsylvania Ave Somerville MA 02145-2217 Office: Boston Phoenix 126 Brookline Ave Boston MA 02215-3920

SCHWARTZ, LLOYD MARVIN, newspaper and magazine correspondent, broadcaster; b. Bklyn., Mar. 6, 1923; s. Philip and Celia W. Schwartz; m. Doris Grossman, May 19, 1946; children: Ellen, Philip, Laura. BA, NYU, 1944. NYU corr. N.Y. Times, 1942-44; news editor, writer Trade Union Courier, 1943-44; reporter Lima (Ohio) News, 1945; reporter, The White House corr. Fairchild Publs., Washington, 1945-65, Washington bur. chief, 1965-88; Congl. corr. Fairchild News Service, 1977-88; panelist, news broadcaster Voice of Am., AFL-CIO, Fairchild Broadcast News and WJR-Detroit; Congl. corr. Van Dahl Publs., Albany, Oreg., 1980-90, mem. Senate and Ho. of Reps. Press Galleries, 1946—; Congl. corr. Linn's Stamp News, Sidney, Ohio, 1990-92. Cons. Rsch. Inst. of Am. Docent, historian Newseum, 1997—2001, Pope-Leighey House, 2001—, Carlyle House, 2002—. Democrat. Jewish. E-mail: lloydmschwartz@att.net.

SCHWARTZ, LOIS C. instructional technologist, consultant; b. N.Y.C., Aug. 15, 1935; d. Arthur H. and Dorothy (Blaine) S. Student, London Sch. Econs., 1955-56; BA cum laude, U. Mich., 1957. Editl. asst. Harry N. Abrams, Inc., N.Y.C., 1957-59; assoc. prodr. radio, tv dept. Jewish Theol. Sem., 1959-62; editl. coord. Book of Knowledge Grolier, Inc., 1962-64; audiovisual prodr. Harcourt Brace, 1965-67; v.p. Sterling Inst. Innovative Instrn. Inc., 1967-72; pres. ESPRIT Cons. Corp., 1972-99. Author: No Experience Necessary, 1967; contbr. article to Northeast Tng. News. Bd. dirs. Victor Herbert Found., Inc., 1988—, Am. Opera Projects, Inc., N.Y.C., 1994-02. Mem. Internat. Soc. Performance Improvement (chair N.Y. chpt. 1980-82), Opera Am. Avocations: opera, book collection, spectator sports, swimming, cats. Home: 299 W 12th St Apt 9F New York NY 10014-1826 E-mail: lcschwar@umich.edu.

SCHWARTZ, LOUIS WINN, ophthalmologist; b. Pa., Apr. 19, 1942; s. Edward and Sylvia Beatrice (Winn) S.; m. Linda Weinberg, June 14, 1964; children: Joanne Karen, Geoffrey Paul. AB, Bowdoin Coll., 1963; MD, Jefferson Med. Coll., 1967. Diplomate Am. Bd. Ophthalmology. Intern Phila. Gen. Hosp.-U. Pa., 1967-68; resident in ophthalmology Wills Eye Hosp., Phila., 1970-73; ophthalmologist Ophthalmic Assocs., Lansdale, 1973—; attending surgeon Wills Eye Hosp. Glaucoma Svc., Phila., 1984—; clin. assoc. prof. ophthalmology Jefferson Med. Coll., 1984—; sec.-treas. Wills Eye Hosp., 1998-2000, v.p., 2000—02, pres., 2002—. Chief ophthalmology North Penn Hosp., 1995—. Co-author: Laser Therapy of Anterior Segment, 1988, 7 other books; assoc. editor Contact Lens Assn. Ophthalmology Jour., 1988; contbr. articles to profl. jours. Recipient Honor award Am. Acad. Ophthalmology, 1988. Mem. AMA, Am. Glaucoma Soc., Pa. Acad. Ophthalmology, InterCounty Ophthalmol. Soc. (pres. 1985-86), Ophthalmic Club Phila. (pres. 1985-86). Office: Ophthalmic Assocs 1000 N Broad St Lansdale PA 19446-1138

SCHWARTZ, MARINA MALIA, insurance company official, dancer; b. Paterson, N.J., May 22, 1944; d. Jacob J. and Anne (Pochna) Blokker. BA in Psychology, Calif State U., L.A., 1973, MA in Psychology, 1976; postgrad., Loyola U., L.A. Claim adjustor State Compensation Ins. Fund, L.A., 1966-70; claim supr. Firemans Fund Ins. Co., 1970-76; rehab. supr. Fremont Ins. Co., 1976-77, Intracorp, Anaheim, Calif., 1977-79; sr. claim supr. ITT Hartford, Honolulu, 1979-99; workers compensation specialist Kalama Svcs., 1999-2000. Vol., bd. dirs. UN Assn.-USA, Honolulu, 1981—; bd. dirs. Neighborhood Bd., Kahuluu, Hawaii, 1981-83, Ewa, Hawaii, 1983-85; vol. Hawaii coun. Girl Scouts U.S.A., 1983—, bd. dirs., 1992-94; mem., vol. Hist. Hawaii, 1980—. Mem. AAUW, LWV (bd. dirs. 1998-99), Nature Conservancy, Hawaii Acad. Rec. Arts. Democrat. Avocations: travel, reading, dancing. E-mail: marina@hale.schwartz.ms.

SCHWARTZ, MARSHALL ZANE, pediatric surgeon; b. Mpls., Sept. 1, 1945; s. Sidney Shay and Peggy Belle (Lieberman) S.; m. Michele Carroll Walker, Oct. 16, 1971; children: Lisa, Jeffrey. BS, U. Minn., 1968, MD, 1970. Diplomate Am. Bd. Surgery, Am. Bd. Pediatric Surgery. Intern N.Y. Hosp., N.Y.C., 1970-71; resident in gen. surgery U. Minn., Mpls., 1971-73, 75-76, rsch. fellow, 1974-75; jr. resident in pediatric surgery Children's Hosp. Med. Ctr., Harvard Med. Sch., 1973-74, sr. resident in pediatric surgery, 1976-77, chief resident in pediatric surgery, 1977-78; instr. Med. Sch. Harvard U., Boston, 1978-79; asst. in surgery Childrens Hosp. Med. Ctr., 1978-79; asst. prof. Med. Br. U. Tex., Galveston, 1979-81, assoc. prof., 1981-83, chief. pediatric surgery, 1980-83; assoc. prof. U. Calif., Davis, 1983-86, prof., 1986-92, chief pediatric surgery, 1983-92, vice chmn. faculty Sch. Medicine, 1990-91, chmn. faculty Sch. Medicine, 1991-92; prof. surgery and pediatrics George Washington Sch. Medicine, 1992-96; surgeon-in-chief, chmn. dept. pediatric surgery Children's Nat. Med. Ctr., Washington, 1992-96; assoc. med. dir., vice chmn. dept. surgery Dupont Hosp. for Children, Wilmington, Del., 1996—; prof. surgery and pediatrics, vice-chmn. dept. surgery Thomas Jefferson U., 1996—. Mem. editl. bd. Jour. Pediat. Surgery, 1988—, Jour. ACS, 1999—. Vice chmn. Bd. of Childrens Faculty Assocs., Childrens Nat. Med. Ctr.; bd. dir. Am. Pediat. Surg. Assn., 2001—; pres. bd. dir. Sacramento Children's Hosp. Found., 1990—92; chmn. bd. dir. Delaware Valley Transplant Program, 2000—. Recipient Basil O'Connor Rsch. award March of Dimes Found., 1981, Young Investigator award NIH, 1982, Found. for Children Rsch. award, 1982, James W. McLaughlin award U. Tex., 1983, ASPEN-Rhodes Rsch. award, 1999, Rsch. award Am. Colon and Rectal Surg. Assn., 2000. Fellow: ACS; mem.: Pacific Assn. Pediat. Surgeons (pres. 1997—98), Am. Pediat. Surg. Assn. (bd. dirs.), Soc. Surgery Alimentary Tract, Am. Pediatric Surg. Assn. (bd. govs.), Soc. Univ. Surgeons, Am. Surg. Assn. Jewish. Avocations: skiing, fishing, wood working. Office: Dupont Hosp for Children 1600 Rockland Rd Wilmington DE 19803-3607 E-mail: mschwart@nemours.org.

SCHWARTZ, MARTIN ARNOLD, geriatrician, educator; b. , Oct. 22, 1951; MD, N.Y. Med. Coll., 1975. Diplomate Am. Bd. Internal Medicine added qualifications in geriat. Asst. prof. Drake Ctr.-U. Cin. Sch. Medicine, 1990-97; pvt. practice.

SCHWARTZ, MARTIN LERNER, physician; b. Newport News, Va., 1945; PhD in Biochemistry, Duke U., 1972, MD, 1973. Resident U. N.C., Chapel Hill, 1973-77; mem. staff Bess Kaiser Hosp., Portland, Oreg., 1977-96, Providence-St. Vincent's Hosp., Portland, 1996—. Home: 7824 NW Blue Pointe Ln Portland OR 97229-9105 Office: 3550 N Interstate Ave Portland OR 97227-1196 E-mail: martin.l.schwartz@kp.org.

SCHWARTZ, MARVIN, lawyer; b. Phila., Nov. 3, 1922; s. Abe and Freda (Newman) S.; m. Joyce Ellen Sidner, Sept. 7, 1947; children: Daniel Bruce, Pamela Louise Pier. LL.B., U. Pa., 1949. Bar: Pa. 1950, N.Y. 1951, D.C. 1955. Law sec. to judge U.S. Ct. Appeals, 3d Circuit, Phila., 1949-50; law sec. to Justice Burton U.S. Supreme Ct., Washington, 1950-51; assoc. Sullivan & Cromwell, N.Y.C., 1951-60, ptnr., 1960-92, sr. counsel, 1993—. Mediator U.S. Dist. (so. dist.) N.Y., N.Y. Supreme Ct. Comml. Divsn.; arbitrator Am. Arbitration Assn., N.Y. Stock Exch., Nat. Assn. Securities Dealers. Spl. master appellate divsn. 1st dept. Supreme Ct. N.Y.; chmn. Zoning Bd. of Adjustment, Alpine, N.J., 1966-74; mem. Planning Bd., Alpine, 1966-67; bd. overseers emeritus U. Pa. Law Sch.; bd. dirs. Waterbury Found. With Signal Corps U.S. Army, 1943-46. Mem. ABA, N.Y. Bar Assn., D.C. Bar Assn., Am. Coll. Trial Lawyers (sec. 1986-88, bd. regents 1981-86, chmn. Downstate N.Y. com. 1976-78), Am. Law Inst. (adviser complex litigation project), Univ. Club (N.Y.C.), Litchfield (Conn.) Country Club. Democrat. Jewish. Office: Sullivan & Cromwell 125 Broad St Fl 28 New York NY 10004-2489 E-mail: mvnsch@aol.com.

SCHWARTZ, MELVIN, physics educator, laboratory administrator; b. N.Y.C., Nov. 2, 1932; s. Harry and Hannah (Shulman) Schwartz; m. Marilyn Fenster, Nov. 25, 1953; children: David N., Diane R.;1 child Betty Lynn. AB, Columbia U., 1953, PhD, 1958, DSc (hon.) , 1991. Assoc. physicist Brookhaven Nat. Lab., 1956—58; mem. faculty Columbia U., N.Y.C., 1958—66, prof. physics, 1963—66, Stanford U., Calif., 1966—83, cons. prof., 1983—91; chmn. Digital Pathways, Inc., Mountain View, Calif., 1970—91; assoc. dir. high energy and nuclear physics Brookhaven Nat. Lab., Upton, NY, 1991—94; prof. physics Columbia U., N.Y.C., 1991—94, I.I. Rabi prof. physics, 1994—. Co-discoverer muon neutrino, 1962. Weizmann Inst. Sci. Recipient Nobel prize in Physics, 1988, John Jay award, Columbia Coll., 1989, Alexander Hamilton medal, Columbia U., 1995; fellow Guggenheim, 1968. Fellow: Am. Phys. Soc. (Hughes award 1964); mem.: NAS. Home: PO Box 5068 Ketchum ID 83340-5068 Office: Columbia U Dept Physics New York NY 10027 E-mail: melschw@cox-internet.com.

SCHWARTZ, MICHAEL ALAN, physician; b. N.Y.C., Dec. 13, 1944; s. David Henry and Ray Schwartz; m. Joan Kay Clayton, Jan. 12, 1979; children: Dana, David, Elizabeth. AB, Princeton, 1965; MD, Cornell U., 1969. Intern, medicine N.Y. Hosp., Cornell, 1969-70, resident, psychiatry Cornell, Westchester, 1970-74; clin. assoc. NIMH, Washington, 1972-74; asst. prof. psychiatry Cornell Med. Coll., N.Y.C., 1974-76; assoc. to prof. of psychiatry N.Y. Med. Coll., 1976-92; prof. dept. psychiatry Case Western Res. U., Cleve., 1992—, vice chmn. dept. psychiatry, 1992-96. Plenary spkr. symposium on advances in neurosci. Decade of the Brain, WHO, Chinese Psychiat. Assn. Editor: (with Manfred Spitzer, Christoph Mundt, Friedrick Uehlein) Phenomenology, Language, and Schizophrenia, 1992, (with John Sadler and Osborn Wiggins) Psychiatric Diagnostic Classification, 1994; mem. editl. bd. Comprehensive Psychiatry, 1992—; assoc. editor Philosophy, Psychiatry, Psychology, 1993—; mem. internat. adv. bd. L'Evolution Psychiatrique, 1997—; mem. internat. editl. bd., sect. editor Phenemenology and Psychiatry, 1997—; contbr. articles to numerous sci. jours. Recipient Egner-Stiftung prize Dr-Margrit Egneér-Stiftung Found., 1998, Exemplary Psychiatrist award Nat. Alliance for the Mentally Ill, 2000. Fellow Am. Psychopathol. Assn., Am. Psychiat Assn., Am. Psychopath Assn.; mem. Ind. Psychiat. Assn. of Russia (hon.), Soc. Italiana per la Psicopatologia (hon.), World Psychiat. Assn. (sec. sect. on religion and psychiatry 1996—), Gesellschaft Philosophie und Wissenschaften der Psyche. Home: 34650 Cedar Rd Gates Mills OH 44040-9787 Office: Univ Hosps of Cleve Dept Psychiatry 11100 Euclid Ave Cleveland OH 44106-1736 E-mail: mas1@concentric.net.

SCHWARTZ, MICHAEL AVERILL, pharmacy educator, consultant; b. N.Y.C., Aug. 4, 1930; s. Ralph M. and Minnie (Bezner) S.; m. Marilyn Ettinger, Nov. 24, 1954 (div. Apr. 1987); children: Lori N., Sharon M.; m. Karan Ann Burt, Jan. 25, 1992. BS, Bklyn. Coll. of Pharmacy, 1952; MS, Columbia U., 1956; PhD, U. Wis., 1959. Lic. pharmacist, Fla. Mil. svc. pharmacist Tokyo Army Hosp., 1952-54; fellow Am. Found. Pharm. Edn., 1956-59; sr. rsch. scientist Bristol Labs., Syracuse, N.Y., 1959-63; from asst. prof. to prof. pharmaceutics SUNY, Buffalo, 1963-78; dean coll. of pharmacy

U. Fla., Gainesville, 1978-96, prof., dean emeritus, 1996—. Dean coll. pharmacy SUNY, Buffalo, 1970-76; cons. Bristol-Myers Co., 1968-78, Acad. PHarm. Scis., 1984-86, Ala. Pharm. Assn., 1986, Ctr. for Pharm. Scis. and Tech. U. Ky., 1986, U. Cin. Coll. Pharmacy, 1989-90, St. Louis Coll. Pharmacy, 1989-90, Mass. Coll. Pharmacy, 1995-97, Am. Assn. Colls. of Pharmacy, 1994, Nat. Pharmacy Cholesterol Coun., 1996, Am. PHarm. Assn. Found., 1997, Fla. Pharmacy Assn., 1996-97, La. Bd. Regents, 1997; bd. dirs. ANDRX Corp. Contbr. articles to profl. jours., chpts. to books. Bd. dirs. Gainesville Jewish Appeal. Recipient Disting. Alumnus award Arnold and Marie Schwartz Coll. Pharmacy and Health Scis., 1992. Fellow AAAS (pharm. scis. sect. com. 1978-81), Am. Pharm. Assn. (trustee 1982-84, trustee found. 1985-94), APhA Acad. Pharm. Scis. (founding mem. Higuchi Rsch. prize com., chair strategic planning com. 1984-86, Hugo H. Schaefer award 1995, Achievement award 1986), Am. Assn. Pharm. Scientists (chmn. strategic planning com. 1986-87); mem. Am. Soc. Health Sys. Pharmacists, Am. Assn. Colls. of Pharmacy, Fla. Pharmacy Assn., Rho Chi. Office: U Fla Coll Pharmacy PO Box 100496 Gainesville FL 32610-0496 E-mail: mike@cop.ufl.edu.

SCHWARTZ, MICHAEL LEE, financial planner, consultant; b. Chgo., Dec. 8, 1945; s. Harry and Charlotte (Rose) S.; m. Patricia Helen Chapman, Jan. 15, 1972; children: Scott Daniel, Michelle Lynn. CFP, CFdC, RFC, CSA; certified Benefits Instr. Field engr. Storage Tech. Corp., Chgo., 1973-76; v.p. AMS Life Ins. Co., Bridgeview, Ill., 1976-81; pres. Wealth Masters Inc., Rolling Meadows, 1981—. Instr. Morraine Valley Community Coll., Worth, Ill., 1985-87, St. Xavier Coll., Chgo., 1986-87, Prairie State U., Chicago Heights, Ill., 1987. Mem. Nat. Coun. on the Aging, 1991-93. Mem. Inst. CFPs, Internat. Assn. of Registered Fin. Cons., Soc. Cert. Sr. Advisors, Colo. Assn. of Chartered Fid. Cons. Avocations: amateur radio, racquet ball, traveling. Office: Ste 300 6635 S Dayton St Englewood CO 80111-6119

SCHWARTZ, MICHAEL LEE, computer software engineer; b. Buffalo, Nov. 7, 1950; s. Robert Donald and Annette S.; m. Bonni Lynne Jacobs, Dec. 30, 1978; children: Jeremy L., Melody L. BA in Math. Sci./Elec. Engring., M in Elec. Engring., Rice U., 1973. Software programmer, analyst Tex. Instruments, Houston and Austin, 1973-79; engr. Sperry/Honeywell, Phoenix, 1979—. Recipient Life Giver Pheresis Donor award United Blood Svcs., 1992. Mem. Assn. Computing Machinery (voting, treas. Phoenix chpt. 1991—), AzTec Freenet (supporter). Jewish. Office: Honeywell 5353 W Bell Rd Glendale AZ 85308-3900 E-mail: schwartz@acm.org.

SCHWARTZ, MICHAEL ROBINSON, health facility administrator; b. St. Louis, Mar. 18, 1940; s. Henry G. and Edith C. (Robinson) Schwartz; m. Kathleen Nowicki, Dec. 9, 1989; children from previous marriage: Christine, Richard. AB, Dartmouth Coll., 1962; MHA, U. Minn., 1964. Asst. in adminstrn. Shands Tchg. Hosp., Gainesville, Fla., 1966-67, asst. dir., 1967-68, assoc. dir., 1968-73; assoc. adminstr. St. Joseph Mercy Hosp., Pontiac, Mich., 1973-76, pres., 1976-85; exec. v.p. Mercy Health Svcs., Farmington Hills, 1985-96, COO, 1988-96; exec. v.p. Ea. Mich. region Sisters of Mercy Health Corp., 1991-92; pvt. practice Birmingham, Mich., 1996—. Non-resident lectr. U. Mich., 1982—93; cons. prof. Oakland U., 1980—88; asst. prof. hosp. adminstrn. U. Fla., 1967—73; pres. Eastern Mich. Regional Bd. Sisters of Mercy Health Corp., 1976—79; v.p. Lourdes Nursing Home, 1981—84, United Way-Pontiac/North Oakland, 1982—84; treas. Oakland Health Edn. Program, 1978—79; coms. Blue Cross/Blue Shield of Mich., 1978—86, chair hosp. contingent to participating hosp. agreement adv. com., 1989—96; bd. dirs. Vis. Nurse Assn., Inc., 1997—, treas., 1998—99, vice chair, 1999—2000, chair, 2000—02; chmn. bd. dirs., pres. Accord Ins. Co. Ltd., 1983—88; chmn. bd. dirs. Mercy Health Plans, 1986—96, Venzke Svc. Co., 1983—88, pres., 1983—84; chmn. bd. dirs., pres. Venzke Ins. Co. Ltd., 1988—96; mem. audit and fin. com. Am. Healthcare Sys., 1988—92; mem. S.E. Mich. Hosp. Coun., chmn. pub. rels. com., 1983—85; mem. Commonfund Healthcare Coun., 1999—; trustee Sisters of Mercy Health Corp., 1991—93, sec. bd. trustees, 1993. Mem. charitable trust Sisters of Mercy, Regional Cmty. Detroit, 1999—. With U.S. Army, 1964—66. Fellow: Am. Coll. Healthcare Execs. (mem. exec. com. higher edn. 1990—93, Mich. Regent's award 1992); mem.: Comprehensive Health Planning Coun. (com. mem. 1976—81), Am. Healthcare Sys. Risk Retention Group (bd. dirs. 1990—91), Mich. Hosp. Assn. (at-large rep. corp. bd. 1990—96, exec. com. 1992—96), Pontiac Urban League (pers. com. 1979). E-mail: swrtzmk@aol.com.

SCHWARTZ, MILES JOSEPH, cardiologist; b. Richmond, Va., Aug. 7, 1925; s. Hugo and Ella (Kramer) Schwartz; m. Margery Baer Irish, June 7, 1956 (div. 1972); children: Elizabeth, James, Margaret; m. Katherine Rush, May 26, 1980. BS, Queens Coll., 1947; MD, N.Y.U., 1951. Diplomate Am. Bd. Internal Medicine, Am. Bd. Cardiovasc. Disease. Intern Mt. Sinai Hosp., N.Y.C., 1951-52, resident, 1953-54, Bronx (N.Y.) VA Hosp., 1952-53, fellow, 1954-55, asst. med. sect. chief, 1956-58; resident, then chief resident St. Luke's Hosp. Ctr., N.Y.C., 1955-56, from asst. attending physician to assoc. cardiologist, 1959-69, chief hypertension clinic, 1959-81, attending physician, dir. cardiography, 1970-98, clin. dir. pvt. med. svc., 1974-78, assoc. dir. medicine, 1978-84, dir. clin. cardiology tng. program, 1966—97, assoc. dir. divsn. cardiology, 1987—97; acting dir. divsn. cardiology St. Luke's/Roosevelt Hosp., 1995—96; pres. Williamsburg Healthcare Consortium, 2001—. Cons. Sharon (Conn.) Hosp., 1976—91; prof. clin. med. emeritus, spl. lectr. in medicine Columbia U. Coll. P&S, N.Y.C., 1998. With USNR, 1944—46. Fellow: ACP, Am. Heart Assn., Am. Coll. Cardiology; mem.: Phi Beta Kappa, Alhpa Omega Alpha. Jewish. Avocations: travel, history, bioethics, medical education. Home: 217 W Queens Dr Williamsburg VA 23185-4918 E-mail: mjschwartz@tni.net.

SCHWARTZ, MISCHA, electrical engineering educator; b. N.Y.C., Sept. 21, 1926; s. Isaiah and Bessie (Weinstein) S.; m. Lillian Mitchnick, June 23, 1957 (div.); 1 son, David; m. Charlotte F. Berney, July 12, 1970. B.E.E., Cooper Union, 1947; M.E.E., Poly. Inst. Bklyn., 1949; PhD in Applied Physics (Sperry Gyroscope grad. scholar), Harvard U., 1951. Project engr. Sperry Gyroscope Co., 1947-52; mem. faculty Poly. Inst. Bklyn., 1952-74, prof. elec. engring., 1959-74, head dept., 1961-65; prof. elec. engring. and computer sci. Columbia U., N.Y.C., 1974-88, Charles Batchelor prof. elec. engring., 1988-96, Charles Batchelor prof. emeritus, 1996—. dir. Ctr. for Telecommunications Research, 1985-88. Part-time tchr. Adelphi Coll., 1951-52, CCNY, 1952; cons. radiation physicist Montefiore Hosp., N.Y.C., 1954-56; vis. prof. sys. sci. dept. UCLA, 1964; vis. prof. dept. elec. engring. and computer sci. Columbia U., 1973-74; vis. prof. dept. electronic and elec. engring. U. Coll., London, 1995; vis. prof. dept. elec. and computer engring. U. Calif., San Diego, 1997; chmn. Commn. C, U.S. Nat. Com. Internat. Union Radio Sci., 1977-80; vis. scientist IBM Rsch., 1980, 94, NYNEX Sci. and Tech., 1986; vis. mem. tech. staff AT&T Bell Labs., 1995; cons. in field. Author: Information Transmission, Modulation and Noise, 4th edit., 1990, (with L. Shaw) Signal Processing, 1975, Computer Communication Network Design and Analysis, 1977, Telecommunications Networks, 1987, Broadband Integrated Networks, 1996; editor, contbr.: Communication Systems and Techniques, 1966, reissued, 1995. Trustee Gt. Neck Libr., 1997-2001, pres., 1998, 99. Served with AUS, 1944-46. NSF sci. faculty fellow, 1965-66; recipient Disting. Vis. award Australian-Am. Ednl. Found., 1975, Vis. Scientist award Nippon Tel. & Tel., 1981, Tchg. award Columbia U., 1984, Gano Dunn award Cooper Union, 1986, Mayor's award for excellence in tech., City of N.Y., 1995; finalist Mayor's Awards for Excellence in Sci. & Tech., City of N.Y., 1992. Fellow AAAS, IEEE (chmn. adminstrv. com. profl. group info. theory 1964-65, bd. dirs. 1978-79, bd. govs. Comm. Soc. 1973-79, v.p. 1982-83, pres. 1984-85, Edn. medal 1983, IEEE Centennial Hall of Fame 1984, Region 1 award for leadership in mgmt. Ctr. for Telecom. Rsch. 1990, Edwin Armstrong award for contbns. to telecomm. 1994, Millennium medal 2000); mem. NAE, AAUP (chpt. pres. 1970-72), Assn. for Computing Machinery, Sigma Xi, Tau Beta Pi, Eta Kappa Nu (eminent mem. 1999). Home: 66 Maple Dr Great Neck NY 11021-1928 Office: Columbia U Schapiro CEPSR Rm 806 New York NY 10027 E-mail: schwartz@ctr.columbia.edu., mcschw66@aol.com.

SCHWARTZ, MURRAY MERLE, federal judge; b. 1931; BS, Wharton Sch. U. Pa., 1952; LLB, U. Pa., 1955; LLM, U. Va., 1982. Part-time referee in bankruptcy Dist. of Del., 1969-74; judge U.S. Dist. Ct. Del., 1974-85, chief judge, 1985-89, sr. judge, 1989—. Author: The Exercise of Supervisory Power by the Third Circuit Court of Appeals, 1982. Mem. Del. State Bar Assn. Office: US Dist Ct Lockbox 44 844 N King St Wilmington DE 19801-3519

SCHWARTZ, NEENA BETTY, endocrinologist, educator; b. Balt., Dec. 10, 1926; d. Paul Howard and Pauline (Shulman) S. AB, Goucher Coll., 1948, DS. (hon.), 1982; MS, Northwestern U., 1950, PhD, 1953. From instr. to prof. U. Ill. Coll. Medicine, Chgo., 1953-72, asst. dean for faculty, 1968-70; prof. physiology Northwestern U. Med. Sch., Chgo., 1973-74; Deering prof. Northwestern U., Evanston, 1974—99, chmn. dept. biol. scis., 1974-78, acting dean, Coll. Arts and Scis., 1996-97, prof. emeritus, 2000—. Contbr. chpts. to books, articles to profl. jours. NIH research grantee, 1955— Fellow: AAAS (exec. bd. 1998—2002); mem.: Soc. for Neurosci., Am. Physio. Soc., Soc. for Study of Reprodn. (dir. 1975—77, exec. v.p. 1976—77, pres. 1977—78, Carl Hartman award 1992), Endocrine Soc. (v.p. 1970—71, mem. coun. 1979—83, pres. 1982—83, Disting. Educator award 1998, Williams award 1985), Am. Acad. Arts. Scis. Home: 1511 Lincoln St Evanston IL 60201-2338

SCHWARTZ, NORMAN B. humanities educator, consultant; b. Brooklyn, Ny, Feb. 13, 1932; s. Joseph Harry Schwartz and Bertha Goldberg; m. Delia Tyvand Schwartz; children: David, Deborah, Michael, Jonathon. BA, philosophy, CUNY, New York, 1958—58; MA, Anthropol., U. Penn., Philadelphia, 1955—60; PhD, Anthropol., U. Penn., 1968. Instr. Middlebury Coll., Middlebury, Vt., 1962—68; prof. Univ. Del., Newark, 1968—. Cons. Conservation Internat., Washington, 1992—96, World Bank, Washington, 1999—2001. Author: (book) A Milpero of Peten, Guatemala, Forest Society. Recipient Phi Beta Kappa, CUNY, 1958. Fellow: Soc. for Applied Anthropology, Am. Anthrop. Assn. Office: Univ Delaware Dept Anthropol Newark DE 19716 Office Fax: 302-831-4002. E-mail: nbsanth@udel-edu.

SCHWARTZ, NORMAN BENJAMIN, theatre director; b. N.Y.C., July 27, 1933; Student, NYU, 1950-54. Pres. Charing Cross Sound, Inc., L.A., 1980-93; artistic dir. Santa Barbara (Calif.) Actors Theatre, Inc., 1998—. Author: Acting: A String of Beads, 1995. Recipient Motion Picture Sound Editors Golden Reel award, 1977. Mem. Acad. Motion Picture Arts and Scis., Brit. Film Acad. Office: Santa Barbara Actors Theatre Inc 1050 The Fairway Montecito CA 93108 E-mail: ilprof@cox.net.

SCHWARTZ, PERRY LESTER, information systems engineer, consultant; b. Bklyn., July 29, 1939; s. Max David and Sylvia (Weinberger) S.; m. Arlene Metz, Jan. 24, 1960; 3 children. BEE, CUNY, 1957-62; MS in Indsl. Engring. and Computer Sci., NYU, 1967. Registered profl. engr., N.J., profl. planner, N.J.; cert. mediator and arbitrator, expert witness comm. Microwave engr. Airbourne Inst. Lab., Deer Park, N.Y., 1962-63; ITT Fed. Labs, Nutley, N.J., 1963-64; program mgr. Western Electric Co., N.Y.C., 1964-69; dept. head RCA, Princeton, N.J., 1970-71; dir. engring. Warner Comms. Inc., N.Y.C., 1972-74; cons. engr. Intertech Assocs., Freehold, N.J., 1974—. Adj. faculty CCNY, 1962-71, Ocean County Coll., Toms River, N.J., 1981-83, Rutgers U., New Brunswick, N.J., 1984-87; lectr. N.J. Dept. Edn., 1994, 95. Mem. steering com., trustee Intelligent Bldgs. Found., 1982-89. Mem. IEEE (sr.), Am. Cons. Engrs. Coun., Nat. Soc. Profl. Engrs., Nat. Assn. Radio and Telecom. Engrs. (sr. mem. charter mem., cert. master engr. in wire and RF, Cert. of Distinction 1994-95), Cons. Engrs. Coun. N.J., N.Y. Acad. Sci., Zeta Beta Tau (chpt. founder 1958), K. P. Office: Intertech Assoc 77-55 Schanck Rd Ste B-9 Freehold NJ 07728 E-mail: ps@intertechassociates.com.

SCHWARTZ, PETER EDWARD, physician, gynecologic oncology educator; b. N.Y.C., Mar. 28, 1941; s. Bernard and Marcia (Firkser) S.; m. Arlene Harriet Eigen, Aug. 18, 1966; children: Bruce, Andrew, Kenneth. BS, Union Coll., Schenectady, N.Y., 1962; MD, Yeshiva U., N.Y.C., 1966; MA (hon.), Yale U., 1985. Diplomate Am. Bd. Ob-Gyn., Am. Bd. Gynecol. Oncology. Surg. intern U. Ky. Med. Ctr., Lexington, 1966-67; resident in ob-gyn. Yale-New Haven Hosp., 1967-71; fellow in gynecol. oncology U. Tex. M.D. Anderson Hosp., Houston, 1973-75; asst. prof. Yale U. Sch. Medicine, New Haven, 1975-80, assoc. prof., 1980-85, prof., 1985—, now vice chmn. dept. ob-gyn., 1992—. Maj. USAF, 1971-73. John Slade Ely Prof. of obstetrics and gynecology at Yale U. (hon. chair). Office: Yale U Sch Medicine Dept Ob-Gyn 333 Cedar St Dept Ob New Haven CT 06510-3289

SCHWARTZ, RANDY KEN, mathematics educator; b. Washington, Aug. 30, 1956; s. Hyman Alex Schwartz and Clare Louise Carp. BA in Math., Dartmouth Coll., 1977; MA in Math., U. Mich., 1979. Computer programmer Logicon, Inc., Merrifield, Va., 1974-77; adj. instr. Washtenaw C.C., Ann Arbor, Mich., 1979-84; instr. Cleary Coll., Ypsilanti, 1981-84; prof. Schoolcraft Coll., Livonia, 1984—. Author: Test Bank for Elementary Linear Algebra, 1994, 2000; editor (newsletter) Repast, 1999—; contbr. articles to profl. jours. Mem. Am. Math. Soc., Math. Assn. of Am., Assn. for Computing Machinery, Ann Arbor Track Club, Culinary Historians of Ann Arbor (editor 1999-2002), Phi Beta Kappa. Avocations: running, poetry, blues music, cooking. Home: 2222 Fuller Ct #1101A Ann Arbor MI 48105-2316 Office: Schoolcraft Coll 18600 Haggerty Rd Livonia MI 48152-2696 E-mail: rschwart@schoolcraft.cc.mi.us.

SCHWARTZ, RENEE GERSTLER, lawyer; b. Bklyn., June 18, 1933; d. Samuel and Lillian (Neulander) Gerstler; m. Alfred L. Schwartz, July 30, 1955; children: Carolyn Susan, Deborah Jane. AB, Bklyn. Coll., 1953; LLB, Columbia U., 1955. Bar: N.Y. 1956, U.S. Dist. Ct. (so. and ea. dists.) N.Y. 1956, U.S. Ct. Appeals (2d cir.) 1956, U.S. Dist. Ct. D.C. 1983, U.S. Supreme Ct. 1986. Assoc. Botein, Hays & Sklar, N.Y.C., 1955-64, ptnr., 1965-89, Kronish, Lieb, Weiner & Hellman, N.Y.C., 1990—. Bd. dirs. New Land Found., N.Y.C., 1965—. Mem. Bar Assn. City of N.Y. Home: 115 Central Park W New York NY 10023-4153 Office: Kronish Lieb Weiner & Hellman 1114 Avenue Of The Americas New York NY 10036-7703 E-mail: rschwartz@kronishlieb.com.

SCHWARTZ, RICHARD BRENTON, English language educator, university dean, writer; b. Cin., Oct. 5, 1941; s. Jack Jay and Marie Mildred (Schnelle) S.; m. Judith Mary Alexis Lang, Sept. 7, 1963; 1 son, Jonathan Francis. AB cum laude, U. Notre Dame, 1963; AM, U. Ill., 1964, PhD, 1967. Instr. English U.S. Mil. Acad., 1967-69; asst. prof. U. Wis.-Madison, 1969-72, assoc. prof., 1972-78, prof., 1978-81; assoc. dean U. Wis.-Madison (Grad. Sch.), 1977, 79-81; prof. English, dean Grad. Sch., Georgetown U., Washington, 1981-98, interim exec. v.p. for main campus academic affairs, 1991-92; interim exec. v.p. for the main campus Georgetown U., 1995-96; prof. English, dean Coll. Arts and Sci. U. Mo., Columbia, 1998—. Mem. exec. bd. Ctr. Strategic and Internat. Studies, 1981-87. Author: Samuel Johnson and the New Science, 1971 (runner-up Gustave O. Arlt prize), Samuel Johnson and the Problem of Evil, 1975, Boswell's Johnson: A Preface to the Life, 1978, Daily Life in Johnson's London, 1983, Japanese edit., 1990, After the Death of Literature, 1997, Nice and Noir: Contemporary American Crime Fiction, 2002, (novels) Frozen Stare, 1989, The Last Voice You Hear, 2001, After the Fall, 2002, Into the Dark, 2002, (short stories) The Biggest City In America, 1999 (Choice Mag. citation); editor: The Plays of Arthur Murphy, 4 vols., 1979, Theory and Tradition in Eighteenth-Century Studies, 1990; contbr. articles to profl. jours. Served to capt. U.S. Army, 1967-69. Decorated Army Commendation medal; recipient Presdl. medal Georgetown U., 1998; Nat. Endowment Humanities grantee, 1970, 87; Inst. for Research in Humanities fellow, 1976; Am. Council Learned Socs. fellow, 1978-79; H.I. Romnes fellow, 1978-81. Mem. Mystery Writers Am., Johnson Soc. So. Calif., Johnson Soc. of London, Am. Soc. Eighteenth-Century Studies, Coun. Grad. Schs., N.E. Assn. Grad. Schs. (exec. com. 1986-88), Assn. Grad. Schs. in Cath. Univs. (exec. com. 1984-87), Assn. Literary Scholars and Critics, Nat. Assn. Scholars, N.Am. Conf. Brit. Studies, Jefferson Club, Mosaic Soc., Alpha Sigma Nu, Alpha Sigma Lambda. Roman Catholic. Home: 5800 Highlands Pkwy Columbia MO 65203-5125 Office: U Mo Coll of Arts and Sci 317 Lowry Hall Columbia MO 65211-6080 E-mail: SchwartzRB@missouri.edu.

SCHWARTZ, RICHARD DERECKTOR, sociologist, educator; b. Newark, Apr. 26, 1925; s. Selig and Tillie (Derecktor) S.; m. Emilie Zane Rosenbaum, June 30, 1946; children: David, Margaret Jane, Deborah. BA, Yale U., 1947, PhD in Sociology, 1952; LL.D. (hon.), Am. Internat. Coll., 1977. Research fellow Inst. Human Relations, Yale, 1951-54, instr., asst. prof. sociology and law, 1953-61; faculty Northwestern U., Evanston, 1961-71, prof. sociology, 1964-71, prof. sociology and law, 1966-71; dir. Council Intersocietal Studies, 1965-70, co-dir. law and social sci. program, 1967-70; dean, provost Faculty of Law and Jurisprudence, State U. N.Y. at Buffalo, 1971-76; Ernest I. White rsch. prof. law Syracuse U., 1977—. Adviser Nat. Conf. Commrs. on Uniform State Laws, 1968-70, ABA, 1979-83; mem. com. law enforcement and adminstrn. of justice NAS, 1975-85; fellowship referee Russell Sage Found., 1970-77, NEH, 1972-77, NSF, 1978-81; mem. bd. edn., Orange, Conn., 1954-61; mem. exec. com. Am. Friends Svc. Com., Middle Atlantic Region, 1987-92; chmn. Am. Coalition for Middle East Dialogue, 1990-93; exec. dir. NESCO, 1995—. Author: (with others) Society and the Legal Order, 1970, Criminal Law, 1974, Handbook of Regulation and Administrative Law, 1994, Unobtrusive Measures, 2000; founding editor: Law and Soc. Rev., 1966-69. Served with USNR, 1943-45. Ctr. for Advanced Study in Behavioral Scis. fellow, 1989-90. Fellow AAAS, Am. Acad. Polit. and Social Sci.; mem. ABA (nonprofl. legal edn. com. 1986-89), Am. Sociol. Assn., Law and Soc. Assn. (pres. 1972-75) Jewish. Home: 15 Clarmar Rd Fayetteville NY 13066-1603 Office: Syracuse U Coll Law Syracuse NY 13244-0001 *I believe that we could create a better way of life if we structured society to encourage-rather than to penalize-altruism. Although I have not yet contributed much toward achieving such a society, the effort to do so has been satisfying.*

SCHWARTZ, RICHARD FREDERICK, electrical engineering educator; b. Albany, N.Y., May 31, 1922; s. Frederick William and Mary Hoyle (Holland) S.; m. Ruth Louise Feldman, Oct. 25, 1945 (div. Oct. 1977); children: Kathryn Gail, Frederick Earl, Karl Edward, Eric Christian, Frieda Diane; m. Margaret Camp Boes, May 29, 1982. BEE, Rensselaer Poly. Inst., Troy, N.Y., 1943, MEE, 1948; PhD, U. Pa., 1959. Registered profl. engr., Pa., Mich. Instr. Rensselaer Poly. Inst., Troy, 1946-48; engr. Radio Corp. Am., Camden, N.J., 1948-51; instr. U. Pa., Phila., 1951-53, rsch. assoc., 1953-59, asst. prof. electrical engring., 1959-62, assoc. prof. electrical engring., 1962-73; prof. elec. engring. Mich. Tech. U., Houghton, 1973-85, dept. head, 1973-79; prof. elec. engring. SUNY, Binghamton, 1985-95, prof. emeritus, 1995—; pvt. practice Endicott, N.Y., 1999—. Vis. asst. prof. U. Mich., Ann Arbor, 1960; cons. Pa. Bar Assn. Endowment, Armstrong Cork Co., Am. Electronics Labs., Inc., IBM, RCA, City of Phila., GE. Co-author: The Eavesdroppers, 1959; contbr. 40 papers to various pubs. Active Delaware County Symphony, Pa., 1967-72, Keeweenaw Symphony Orch., Houghton, 1973-85, Vestal Cmty. Band, 1993—, Ctr. for Tech. and Innovation, Endicott, N.Y., 1995—; mem. exec. bd. Broome County Peace Action, 1995—, mem. exec. bd., sec. bd., 1998-2001; active Broome County Interfaith Caregivers, 1997—; mentor Schs. to Careers Partnership. 1995—. With U.S. Army, 1942-46. Fellow Acoustical Soc. Am.; mem. IEEE (sr., life, vice chmn. Binghamton sect. 2000—), AAAS (life), NSPE (life), Am. Soc. Engring. Edn. (life), N.Y. Soc. Profl. Engrs. (life, Broome chpt., bd. dir. 2000-, treas. 2001-02, Engr. of Yr. 1995, Contbns. to Edn. award 1996), Audio Engring. Soc. (life), Catgut Acoustical Soc., Found. for Engring. Edn. Inc.(bd. dirs. 2000—. sec. 2001—), Order of the Engr., Sigma Xi, Eta Kappa Nu, Tau Beta Pi. Democrat. Unitarian Universalist. Achievements include patents for tuning sys., 1954, oscillator frequency control, 1954, transistor amplifier with high undistorted output, 1954. Home and Office: 2624 Bornt Hill Rd Endicott NY 13760-8231

SCHWARTZ, RICHARD HARVEY, pediatrician; b. Bklyn., July 6, 1938; s. Hy and Ruth (Marshak) S.; m. Rose Lynne Hass, May 29, 1960; children: Lisa, Keith, Keira. BA, George Washington U., 1960; MD, Georgetown U., 1965. Diplomate Am. Bd. Pediat., Am. Soc. Addiction Medicine. Intern U.S. Army, 1965-66, resident in pediat., 1969-71; pvt. practice, Vienna, 1972—. Contbr. articles to profl. jours. Maj. U.S. Army, 1965-69. Mem. AMA (Outstanding Contbn. in Adolescent Medicine award 1990), Am. Acad. Pediatrics (rsch. award 1989). Jewish. Avocations: walking, travel. Office: Advanced Pediatrics 115 Park St SE Vienna VA 22180-4653

SCHWARTZ, RICHARD JOHN, electrical engineering educator, researcher; b. Waukesha, Wis., Aug. 12, 1935; s. Sylvester John and LaVerne Mary (Lepien) S.; m. Mary Jo Collins, June 29, 1957; children: Richard, Stephen, Susan, Elizabeth, Barbara, Peter, Christopher, Margaret. BSEE, U. Wis., 1957; SM, MIT, 1959, ScD, 1962. Mem. tech. staff Sarnoff Rsch. Labs. RCA, Princeton, N.J., 1957-58; instr. MIT, Cambridge, 1961-62; v.p. Energy Conversions, Inc., 1962-64; assoc. prof. Purdue U., West Lafayette, Ind., 1964-71, prof., 1972—, head dept., 1985-95, dean engring., 1995—2001, dir. Optoelectronic Ctr., 1986-89. Co-dir. Nano Tech. Ctr. Purdue U., W. Lafayette, Ind.; cons. solar cells, 1965—. Contbr. chpts. to books, articles to profl. jours. Served to 2nd lt. U.S. Army, 1957-58. Recipient Disting. Svc. medal U. Wis., 1989, Centennial medal, 1991. Fellow: IEEE (William R. Cherry award 1998); mem.: Nat. Elec. Engring. Dept. Heads Assn. (bd. dirs.). Achievements include development of high intensity solar cells, of surface charge transfer device, and of numerical models for solar cells. Office: Purdue U 1285 ElectricalEngring West Lafayette IN 47907

SCHWARTZ, ROBERT M. lawyer; b. Phila., Aug. 6, 1940; s. Nathan and Miriam (Albus) S.; m. Karen Leaf, Feb. 11, 1966; children: Eric, Lauren. BS, Pa. State U., 1962; JD, Villanova U., 1965. Bar: Pa. 1965, U.S. Ct. Appeals (3rd cir.) 1965. Law clk. to presiding justice Common Pleas Ct. Montgomery County, Norristown, Pa., 1965; v.p., assoc. counsel Commonwealth Land Title Ins. Co., Phila., 1969-73; ptnr. in charge bus. dept., mem. exec. com. White and Williams, 1973—. Spkr. in field. Mem. regional exec., chmn. com. civil rights com., regional bd. trustees Anti-Defamation League, vice chmn., 1997-99; bd. dirs., mem. facilities and legal coms. Police Athletic League. Mem. Phila. Bar Assn. (chmn. real property com. 1981, exec. bd. real property sect. 1983-89, 91, 2002, chmn. real property sect. 1986), Am. Coll. Real Estate Lawyers (Best Lawyers in Am. award 1989-2002), Am. Coll. Mortgage Attys., Am. Land Title Assn. (leader's counsel group 1993—), Order of Coif. Republican. Jewish. Avocations: bridge, tennis. Office: White and Williams 1650 Market St Fl 18 Philadelphia PA 19103-7395

SCHWARTZ, ROBERT ALLEN, dermatologist, educator; b. Oakland, Calif., June 30, 1947; s. Jack and Bertha Schwartz; m. Camila Krysicka Janniger, Dec. 29, 1984; 1 child, Edmund Jack Janniger. AB, U. Calif., Berkeley, 1969, MPH, 1970; MD, N.Y. Med. Coll., 1974. Diplomate Am. Bd. Dermatology. First year house officer in medicine St. Mary's Hosp., San Francisco, 1974-75; dermatology resident U. Cin. Coll. Medicine, 1975-77; chief resident in dermatology Roswell Park Meml. Inst., Buffalo, 1977-78; asst. prof. dermatology U. Ariz. Coll. Medicine, 1978-80; asst. prof. dept. dermatology U. Calif. Sch. Medicine, San Francisco, 1980-83; assoc. prof., head dermatology UMD-N.J. Med. Sch., Newark, 1983-88; prof., head dermatology N.J. Med. Sch., 1988—. Prof. pediatrics, pathology and preventive medicine UMD-N.J. Med. Sch., Newark, 1995—. Author: Skin Cancer Recognition and Management, 1988; contbr. over 100 chpts. to books; asst. editor Jour. Medicine; cons. editor Jour. Surg. Oncology; mem. editl. adv. bd. Am. Family Physicians, Cutis, others; contbg. editor Dermatologic Surgery; contbr. numerous articles to med. jours. Recipient hon. award Polish Acad. Dermatology, 1994. Mem. Lithuanian Soc. Dermatology (hon.). Roman Catholic. Office: U Medicine and Dentistry NJ NJ Med Sch 185 S Orange Ave Newark NJ 07103-2757 E-mail: roschwar@umdnj.edu.

SCHWARTZ, ROBERT G. physician; b. Mineola, N.Y., Feb. 14, 1951; s. Irving Bernard and Lillian (Bendel) S.; m. Joan Forman, Apr. 24, 1954; children: Stephanie Rebecca, Jonathan Alan. MD, Emory U., 1976. Diplomate Am. Bd. Internal Medicine, Am. Bd. Gastroenterology. Intern categorical internal medicine La. State U. Med. Ctr., Shreveport, 1976-77, resident in internal medicine, 1977-79; fellow in gastroenterology U. Conn. Affiliated Program, 1979-81; pvt. practice Manchester, Conn., 1981—. Treas. Manchester PHO, 1994—; sec., treas. MHS, PC, IPA, Manchester, 1996—. Fellow Am. Coll. Gastroenterology; mem. Am. Gastroent. Assn., Am. Soc. Gasteoent. Endoscopy, Ea. Conn. Health Network Physician Hosp. Orgn. (treas.). Address: 360 Tolland Tpke Ste 2C Manchester CT 06040-1759

SCHWARTZ, ROBERT GEORGE, retired insurance company executive; b. Czechoslovakia, Mar. 27, 1928; came to U.S., 1929, naturalized, 1935; s. George and Frances (Antoni) S.; m. Caroline Bachurski, Oct. 12, 1952; children: Joanne, Tracy, Robert G. BA, Pa. State U., 1949; MBA, NYU, 1956. With Met. Life Ins. Co., N.Y.C., 1949-93, v.p. securities, 1962-70, v.p., 1970-75, sr. v.p., 1975-78, exec. v.p., 1979-80, vice chmn. bd., 1980-83, chmn. investment com., 1980-93, chmn. bd., 1983-93, chmn. bd., pres., chief exec. officer, 1989-93. Bd. dirs. Lowe's Cos., Inc., North Wilkesboro, N.C., Horatio Alger Assn. Trustee Com. for Econ. Devel. With U.S. Army, 1950—52. Mem.: Sky Club, Alpha Chi Rho. Office: MetLife Bldg 200 Park Ave Ste 5700 New York NY 10166-0005

SCHWARTZ, ROBERT JOHN, landscape contractor, landscape designer; b. Elkhorn, Wis., June 14, 1954; s. Robert Knilans and Mary Cosella (Fleming) S. 2 BS degrees cum laude, U. Wis., Stevens Point, 1976; AA in Landscape

Design ad hoc, U. Minn., 1985; AA, Calif. Poly. Inst., Pomona. Lic. landscape contractor, Calif., Nev. Real estate broker, salesman McKy-Ellis Realtors Madison Wis., Janesville, Wis., 1979-80; sole proprietor Teutonic Landscapes Co., Milw., 1982-85, Rancho Cucamonga, Calif., 1985-88, Rialto, 1989-96, Las Vegas, Nev., 1996—. Supporter St. Joseph's Indian Sch., Chamberlain, S.D., 1986—, Mercy Home for Boys and Girls, Chgo., 1986—, Asian Relief, Inc., Riverdale, Md., 1986—, So. Poverty Law Ctr., Montgomery, Ala., 1991-93; active The Heritage Found., Washington, 1992—, The Wall of Liberty Nat. Found., Washington, 1993—, Am. Conservative Union, Washington, 1993—. Recipient City Hall Coun. citations City of Claremont, Calif., 1986-87, City of Upland, Calif., 1989. Democrat. Avocations: para-sailing, traveling, ancient and medieval European Armaments collecting. Home and Office: 1750 S Rainbow Blvd Ste 11 Las Vegas NV 89146-2950 Address: 9709 Double Rock Dr Las Vegas NV 89134

SCHWARTZ, ROBERT MARC, psychology educator; b. N.Y.C., Feb. 6, 1948; s. Jacob Louis and Ruth Zelda Schwartz; children: Aleksandr, Spenser. BA in Psychology/Anthropology cum laude, U. Calif., Irvine, 1969; MA in Psychology, U. B.C., Vancouver, Can., 1970, PhD in Psychology, 1972. Instr. in psychology Rio Hondo Coll., Whittier, Calif., 1974-88; owner Schwartz Svcs., Henderson, Tenn., 1982—; instr. in psychology Jackson (Tenn.) State C.C., 1994—. Adj. asst. prof. psychology U. Memphis, 1997—, U. Tenn., Martin, 1999—. Contbr. numerous articles to profl. jours. Asst. scoutmaster Boy Scouts Am., Henderson, 1996—. NIMH postdoctoral fellow, 1972, Rockefeller U. rsch. fellow, 1973. Home: 620 Pleasant Springs Rd Henderson TN 38340-7453 E-mail: drbobnet@cs.com.

SCHWARTZ, ROBERT PAUL, pediatric endocrinologist; b. Lakeland, Fla., Sept. 29, 1941; s. Sydney and Edythe (Racz) S.; m. Rebecca Chambers, Apr. 29, 1965; children: Sharon, Michael. BS, U. Fla., 1964, MD, 1968. Diplomate Am. Bd. Pediatrics, Nat. Bd. Med. Examiners. Intern, resident Charlotte (N.C.) Meml. Hosp., 1968-70; fellow in pediat. endocrinology Duke U. Med. Ctr., Durham, N.C., 1970-71, 73-74; asst. chmn. dept. pediats. Carolinas Med. Ctr., Charlotte, 1974-92; prof., chief pediat. endocrinology Wake Forest U. Sch. Medicine, Winston-Salem, NC, 1992—. Mem. Residency Rev. Com. Pediats., 1991-96, vice-chair, 1994-96. Mem. editl. bd. Jour. Pediatrics, 1996—. Mem. Am. Acad. Pediats. (chair endocrine sect. 1996-99), Am. Bd. Pediats., N.C. Pediat. Soc. (pres. 1987-89), Am. Diabetes Assn., Ambulatory Pediat. Assn., Endocrine Soc., Lawson Wilkins Pediat. Endocrine Soc. Office: Wake Forest U Sch Medicine Med Ctr Blvd Winston Salem NC 27157-0001 E-mail: rschwrtz@wfubmc.edu.

SCHWARTZ, ROBERT TERRY, industrial design executive; b. Irvington, N.J., Sept. 29, 1950; s. Edward Herman and Harriet Selma (Rosenstein) S.; m. Carol Fawn Mullenix, July 27, 1975; children: Zachary Jacob, Allison Lizabeth. BFA, Kansas City Art Inst., 1973; M of Indsl. Design, R.I. Sch. Design, 1975. Red Cross project dir. R.I. Sch. Design, Providence, 1975-76; head indsl. design/architecture Red Cross Nat. Hdqrs., Washington, 1976-88; dir. sci. and tech. Health Industry Mfrs. Assn., 1988-90; exec. dir., COO Worldesign Found., Great Falls, Va., 1990-96, Indsl. Designers Soc. Am., Great Falls, 1990-99; dir. indsl. design Motorola, Inc., Ft. Lauderdale, Fla., 1999—. Provider expert testimony before Congress, 1994, commencement address, Kansas City Art Inst., 1995; sr. tech. advisor to Peoples Republic of China, UN, 1998. Contbr. chpts. to books, articles to profl. jours.; presenter in field; holder 5 patents, 1 trademark. Recipient Project of Merit award Indsl. Design Mag., 1985, Cert. of Achievement, ARC, 1988, Louis B. Tiffany award ARC, 1987, numerous others; Nat. Endowment for the Arts grantee, 1984, 92, 94; EPA grantee, 1992. Mem. Indsl. Designers Soc. Am. (Personal Recognition award 2000). Avocations: Edison antiquities collecting, sailing. Office: Motorola Inc Rm 11-9G5 8000 W Sunrise Blvd Fort Lauderdale FL 33322-4170 E-mail: ebs025@email.mot.com.

SCHWARTZ, ROBERT WILLIAM, management consultant; b. N.Y.C., Oct. 23, 1944; s. Edward and Bertha R. S.; m. Gail Beth Greenbaum, Mar. 18, 1967; children: Jill, Evan. BS, Cornell U., 1967; postgrad., SUNY, Albany, 1970. Assoc. IBM, 1967-68; cons. Peat, Marwick, Mitchell & Co., Albany, 1970-71; v.p. Security Gen. Svcs., Inc., Rochester, N.Y., 1971-73; v.p. fin. and adminstrn. Gardenway Mfg. Co., Troy, 1973-77; exec. v.p. United Telecommunications Corp., Latham, 1977-79, pres., 1980-82, also bd. dir.; pres., chmn. Winsource, Inc., Albany, 1982-85, Schwartz Heslin Group, Inc., 1985—. Bd. dirs. Docucon, Inc., San Antonio, GoZPay.com, Inc., Troy, N.Y., LBO Capital Corp., Detroit; N.Y. State Zone Capital Corp, Albany, 6ozpay.com, Inc., N.Y. State Industries for Disabled; adj. prof. Rochester Inst. Tech., 1971-73, U. Albany, SUNY Albany, 1998—. Bd. dirs. United Cerebral Palsy of Capital Dist., 1973—; trustee Newman Found., Rensselaer Poly. Inst., 1974-78, Gov. Clinton coun. Boy Scouts Am., SUNY Found. Mem. Am. Mgmt. Assn., Esarco Internat., N.Am. Tel. Assn., Assn. for Systems Mgmt., Ft. Orange Club, Econ. Club, Corenell Club (N.Y.C.). Republican. Home: 2 Myton Ln Albany NY 12204-1310 Office: 8 Airport Park Blvd Latham NY 12110-1441

SCHWARTZ, ROGER ALAN, judge; b. N.Y.C., May 2, 1945; s. George Martin Ronald and Claire Marie (Dorsch) S.; 1 child, Julia Claire. BA, Muhlenberg Coll., 1967; JD, Temple U., 1973, M in Labor Law, 1976, MPA, 1979; disting. grad., U.S. Army Command and Gen. Staff Coll.; MA in History summa cum laude, U. Scranton, 1997; postgrad., Marywood U., 1997—. Bar: Pa. 1973, N.Y. 1982, D.C. 1976, U.S. Dist. Ct. (ea. dist.) Pa. 1973, U.S. Ct. Appeals (3d cir.) 1976, U.S. Mil. Appeals 1981, U.S. Ct. Appeals (Fed cir.) 1986, U.S. Supreme Ct, 1976. Personnel mgmt. specialist CSC, Phila., 1973-74, asst. appeals officer, 1974-78; sr. adminstrv. judge U.S. Merit Systems Protection Bd., 1979-89; adminstrv. law judge Social Security Adminstrn., Wilkes-Barre, Pa., 1989—. Arbitrator Phila. Ct. Common Pleas, 1973-89; asst. prof. Inst. for Paralegal Tng., Phila., 1976-77; adj. prof. history Keystone Coll., La Plume, Pa. With U.S. Army, 1968-70, Vietnam, Persian Gulf War, 1990; col. JAGC Res., ret. Decorated Legion of Merit, Bronze Star, Purple Heart, Nat. Svc. medal with svc. star, Meritorious Svc. medal with one oak leaf cluster, Meritorious Achievement medal with 1 oak leaf cluster, Army Commendation medal with 4 oak leaf clusters. Mem. ABA, Phila. Bar Assn., Am. Judicature Soc., Am. Arbitration Assn., Res. Officers Assn. (Pa. state sec. 1996-97), Assn. Adminstrv. Law Judges (v.p. region III), Rotary (bd. dirs. Wilkes Barre chpt. 1999-2000). Avocations: piano, computers, billiards. Office: Social Security Adminstrn Office Hearings & Appeals 7 N Wilkes Barre Blvd Wilkes Barre PA 18702-5249 E-mail: rogschwa@infi.net.

SCHWARTZ, ROSEMARY, fundraiser; b. Vinton, Iowa, July 21, 1953; d. Kenneth Wilbert and Berniece June Schwartz; m. Lynn Lee Duitsman, Apr. 14, 1979 (dec. July 1998). BA, U. No. Iowa, Cedar Falls, 1996, postgrad.; MA, U. No. Iowa, 2002. Owner Hitchin Post, Garrison, Iowa, 1983-93; customer svc. supr. Hawkeye Cmty. Action Program, Cedar Rapids, 1997; dist. mgr. Am. Diabetes Assn., 1997—2001; owner Event Innovations, Mt. Auburn, Iowa, 2002—. Bd. mem. Benton County Bd. of Health; sec. Iowa 2d Dist. Dem. Ctrl. Com., Waterloo, 1997—2000; Dem. candidate Iowa Ho. of Reps., 2000, 2002. Mem. AAUW, Nat. Soc. Fund Raising Execs. (bd. dirs. 1999—). E-mail: rosemary@netins.net.

SCHWARTZ, SAMUEL, retired chemical company executive, business consultant; b. Moose Jaw, Sask., Can., Nov. 12, 1927; came to U.S., 1951, naturalized, 1965; s. Benjamin and Rose (Becker) S.; m. Margaret Patterson, Feb. 20, 1956; children: Michael R., Thomas R., David C., Janet C. BA, U. Sask., 1948, B in Commerce, 1950; MBA, Harvard U., 1953. Research assoc. Harvard Bus. Sch., Boston, 1953-57; with Conoco Inc., 1957-83, sr. v.p. coordinating and planning Conn., 1974-75, sr. v.p. corp. planning, 1975-78, sr. v.p. adminstrv., 1978-80, group sr. v.p. adminstrv., 1980-83; sr. v.p. adminstrv. E.I. duPont de Nemours & Co., Wilmington, Del., 1983-87, sr. v.p., corp. plans dept., 1987-88. Dir. Conoco Inc. Consol. Coal Co., 1981-88. Trustee Inst. for the Future, Menlo Park, Calif., 1975-92, Henry du Pont Winterthur Mus., Winterthur, Del., trustee, 1984—, chmn., 1994-97. E-mail: samnmarg@aol.com.

SCHWARTZ, SANDY, publishing executive; Exec. v.p., gen. mgr. The Austin Am.-Statesman Cox Newspapers, Inc., 1996—2000; v.p. & gen. mgr. Atlanta Journal-Constitution, 2001—. Office: Atlanta Journ-Const. PO Box 4689 Atlanta GA 30302*

SCHWARTZ, SERGIU, concert violinist, conductor, educator; b. Bucharest, Romania, Dec. 16, 1957; came to U.S., 1981; m. Diana R. Schwartz. Student, Rubin Acad. Music, Tel Aviv, 1972, MA, 1977; dipl. profl. studies, Hochschule für Musik, Hannover, Germany, 1978; dipl. premier prix artist, Guildhall Sch. London, 1981; dipl. profl. studies, Juilliard Sch., N.Y.C., 1985; studies with Stefan Gheorghiu, Romania, Rami Shevelov, Israel and Germany, Yfrah Neaman, London, Dorothy DeLay, N.Y.C., Sandor Vegh, Felix Galimir, Sergio Celibidache. Concert violinist Joanne Rile Artists Mgmt., Phila., 1983—; artist faculty Conservatory Sch. Music, Lynn U., Boca Raton, Fla., 1991—. Prof. violin Wells Cathedral Sch., Bath, Eng., 1979-81, Pimlico Sch. Music, London, 1979-81, E. Kaufman Cultural Ctr., N.Y.C., 1985-86; vis. artist Fla. Internat. U., Miami, 1995-96; prin. guest condr., music advisor Ashdod Chamber Orch. Israel; instr. master classes at various instns., including Eastman Sch. Music, San Francisco Conservatory, U. Tex., Austin, Interlochen Arts Acad., UCLA, Oberlin Conservatory, Idyllwild Arts Acad., LaGuardia (N.Y.) Sch. Performing Arts, Jerusalem Acad. Music, Royal Acad. Music, London, Reina Sofia Acad. Music, Madrid, master courses in Romania and Bulgaria; judge internat. violin competitions in France, Spain, Italy, Mexico, U.S. and Russia. N.Y. debut at Carnegie Recital Hall; London debut at Wigmore Hall; N.Am. debut at Mus. Fine Arts, Montreal, Que., Can.; soloist with over 200 orchs., Europe, Israel, and U.S., including Dresden Staatskapelle, Jerusalem Symphony, London Symphony, Sarajevo, Dresden, and Slovak Philharms., European Cmty. Chamber Orch., Fla. Philharm., Grant Pk. Festival Orch., Chgo., also numerous ensembles; performances with condrs., including Sergiu Comissiona, James udd, Peter Maag, Giuseppe Sinopoli, Bruno Weil; concert hall performances at Lincoln Ctr., 92nd St. Y, N.Y., Kennedy Ctr., Washington, Barbican Hall, Queen Elizabeth Hall, others; guest artist internat. music festivals, including Aspen, Newport, Interlochen (U.S.), Israel, Switzerland, Finland, Eng., France, Romania, Bulgaria; radio and TV broadcasts for BBC, Nat. Pub. Radio, CNN; recording artist for Vox, Gega-New, Naxos, Arcobaleno, CRS Records, Discover/Koch Internat. Solo Recitalist fellow Nat. Endowment for Arts, 1985; award recipient Artists Internat. Competition, N.Y., Am.-Israel Cultural Found., 1975, Nat. Found. for Advancement of Arts; major prizes at internat. violin competitions. Address: care Joanne Rile Artists Mgmt 801 Old York Rd Ste 212 Jenkintown PA 19046-1611

SCHWARTZ, SHARON LINDA, publisher, writer, educator; b. Honesdale, Pa., Aug. 25, 1948; d. Joseph F. and Elizabeth (Daniels) S.; 1 child, Jay L. BS, Bloomsburg U., 1970; MS, Marywood Coll., 1973. Cert. K-8 elem. edn. tchr., 8-12 math. tchr., Pa. Tchr. Wayne Highlands Sch. Dist., Honesdale, 1970-79; editor Holt, Rinehart Winston, N.Y.C., 1979-83; freelance writer/editor, 1983—; editl. dir. Nichols Schwartz Pub., Honesdale, 1990—. Author: Mathematics Dictionary and Handbook, 1993. Mem. Nat. Coun. Tchrs. Math., Nat. Coun. Suprs. Math., Math. Soc. Am. Avocations: skiing, horseback riding.

SCHWARTZ, SHERRY LYNN ANKER, vocational education educator; b. St. Paul, Sept. 7, 1952; d. E. Howard and Donna E. (Hartman) A.; m. Robert P. Schwartz, Aug. 22, 1975; children: David Paul Anker Schwartz, Clarissa Louise Anker Schwartz. BS with high distinction, U. Minn., 1978, MA, 1984, PhD, 1989. Mgr., trainer Marriott Corp., Mpls., 1975-78; instr., coord. Normandale C.C., Bloomington, Minn., 1978-82; v.p. tng. Anker, Inc., Mpls., 1982-85; instr. U. Minn., St. Paul, 1985-89, asst. prof. vocat. edn., 1989—. Sr. cons. Key Cons., Mpls., 1989—. Contbg. author: Emerging Social and Political Trends in Vocational Education, 1990; contbr. articles to profl. publs. Mem. Parent Assn., Murray Jr. High Sch., St. Paul, 1988-90, Cen. High Sch., St. Paul, 1990—; mem. sch. bd. St. Anthony Park Elem. Sch., St. Paul, 1982-88. Lutheran. Avocation: gardening. Home: 1505 Grantham St Saint Paul MN 55108-1449 Office: Univ Minn 420 VoTech Bldg 1954 Buford Ave Saint Paul MN 55108-1062

SCHWARTZ, SHIRLEY E. chemist, researcher; b. Detroit, Aug. 26, 1935; d. Emil Victor and Jessie Grace (Galbraith) Eckwall; m. Ronald Elmer Schwartz, Aug. 25, 1957; children: Steven Dennis, Bradley Allen, George Byron. BS, U. Mich., 1957, Detroit Inst. Tech., 1978; MS, Wayne State U., 1962, PhD, 1970. Asst. prof. Detroit Inst. Tech., 1973-78, head divsn. math. sci., 1976-78; mem. rsch. staff BASF Wyandotte (Mich.) Corp., 1978-81, head sect. functional fluids, 1981; sr. staff rsch. scientist GM Rsch., Warren, Mich., 1981-99; materials engr. GM Powertrain, 1999—. Contbr. articles to profl. jours.; patentee in field. Recipient Gold award Engring. Soc. Detroit, 1989, Life Achievement award Soc. Women Engrs., 1999; inducted U.S. Nat. Acad. of Engring., 2000. Fellow Soc. Automotive Engrs. (Excellence in Oral Presentation award 1986, 91, 94, Arch T. Colwell Merit award 1991, Lloyd L. Withrow Disting. Spkr. award 1995), Soc. Tribologists and Lubrication Engrs. (treas. Detroit sect. 1981, vice chmn. 1982, chmn. 1982-83, chmn. wear tech. com. 1987-88, bd. dirs. 1985-91, assoc. editor 1989-90, contbg. editor 1989—, Wilbur Deutsch award 1987, P.M. Ku award 1994), Soc. Automotive Engrs.; mem. Soc. Tribologists and Lubrication Engrs., Am. Chem. Soc., Soc. In Vitro Biology, Mich. Women's Hall of Fame (lifetime achievement award 1996), Women of Wayne (headliners award 2000), U.S. Nat. Acad. Engring., Mensa, Classic Guitar Soc. Mich., U.S. Power Squadrons, Detroit Navigators, Sigma Xi. Lutheran. *I've spent a number of very pleasant hours trying to make water behave like oil and alcohol behave like gasoline—a quest not much different from that of the ancient alchemists, who also spent their time trying to convert one substance to another.*

SCHWARTZ, STEPHAN ANDREW, entrepreneur, writer; b. Cin., Jan. 10, 1942; s. Abraham Leon and Bertha Culbertson (Watson) S.; m. Katherine Rowland, Jan. 6, 1965 (div. 1979); 1 child, Catherine Rowland; m. Hayden Oliver Gates, July 10, 1982; 1 stepchild, Lea Daniel Meyers. Student, U. Va. Founder, chmn., rsch. dir. The Mobius Soc., L.A., 1977—; pres. S. A. Schwartz & Assocs., 1992—. Gen. ptnr. V-Partners, Inc.; chmn. Clearlight TV Prodns., L.A.; former vis. prof. John F. Kennedy U.; adv. bd. PHOENIX: New Directions in the Study of Man; sr. fellow Philos. Rsch. Soc.; cons. to oceanographer USN; spl. asst. rsch. and analysis Chief Naval Ops.; co-inventor ThighMaster; mem. bd. advisors Global Inst. Network N. Inst., Aura Comms. Sys., Inc.; cons. in field. Editor: Seapower Magazine; author: The Secret Vaults of Time, 1978, The Alexandria Project, 1980, 1983, Psychic Detectives, 1987; author: (with others) Stories From Omni, 1984; contbr. over 47 publications to profl. jours.; screenwriter spl. presentations and documentaries. Bd. dirs. World Children's Transplant Found., 1992—. Fellow Royal Geog. Soc.; mem. Internat. Soc. for Subtle Energies and Energy Medicine (bd. dirs., editor Subtle Energies Jour.,), Soc. for the Anthropology of Consciousness (past pres., founding mem.), Soc. for Hist. Archaeology, Calif.-Russia Trade Assn. (bd. dirs.), Explorer's club. N.Y. Avocations: reading, scuba diving, canoeing, sailing, hiking. Home: 9899 Santa Monica Blvd # 444 Beverly Hills CA 90212-1672 also: 4470 W Sunset Blvd Ste 339 Los Angeles CA 90027-6305

SCHWARTZ, STEPHEN LAWRENCE, composer, lyricist; b. N.Y.C., Mar. 6, 1948; s. Stanley Leonard and Sheila Lorna (Siegel) S.; m. Carole Ann Piasecki, June 6, 1969; children— Scott Lawrence, Jessica Lauren. Student, Juilliard Sch. Music, 1960-64; BFA, Carnegie-Mellon U., 1968. Works include: title song for play and film Butterflies Are Free, 1969; (theatre) music and new lyrics Godspell, 1971, Pippin, 1972, The Magic Show, 1974, The Baker's Wife, 1976, Children of Eden, 1991, four songs, adaptation and direction Working, 1978, music for 3 songs Personals, 1985, (with Leonard Bernstein) English texts for Leonard Bernstein's Mass, 1971, lyrics Rags, 1986, (films) Pocahontas, 1995 (Acad. award for best original score 1996, Acad. award for best original song 1996), The Hunchback of Notre Dame, 1996; (music and lyrics) The Prince of Egypt, 1998 (Acad. award for best original song 1999); (TV, music and lyrics) Geppetto, 2000, (juvenile) The Perfect Peach, 1977, The Trip, 1983, (recording) Reluctant Pilgrim, 1997, Uncharted Territory, 2001. Recipient Drama Desk awards, 1971, 78, Grammy awards, 1971, 96, Golden Globe award, 1996, Broadcast Film Critics award, 1999. Mem. ASCAP, Nat. Acad. Rec. Arts and Scis., Am. Motion Picture Arts Soc.

SCHWARTZ, STEPHEN BLAIR, retired information industry executive; b. Chgo., Oct. 19, 1934; s. Herbert S. and Gertrude Schwartz; m. Nancy Jean Astrof, Dec. 18, 1955; children: Debra Lee Schwartz Zaret, Susan Beth Schwartz Derene BS in Indsl. Engring., Northwestern U., 1957. With IBM Corp., 1957-92; various mgmt. positions, dir. product programs Harrison, N.Y., to 1977; v.p. Systems Communications div., 1977-81; v.p. Armonk, 1982-90; v.p. Am. Far East Corp. subs. IBM Corp. Tokyo, 1982-84; pres., CEO Satellite Bus. Systems, McLean, Va., 1984; v.p., asst. group exec. Telecommunications, 1985-86; v.p., pres. Systems Products Div., 1986-88; v.p., gen. mgr. Application Bus. Systems, 1988-90; sr. v.p. market driven quality Stamford, Conn., 1990-92. Adv. bd. Niagara Mohawk Power Corp., MFRI, Inc. Mem. PGA Nat. Golf Club (Palm Beach Gardens, Fla.). Republican. Jewish.

SCHWARTZ, STEPHEN WAYNE, critical care, emergency and recovery room nurse; b. Alva, Okla., July 4, 1957; s. Arthur Gregory and Fern Marie (Burns) S. Cert. EMT, Phoenix Community Coll., 1982; LPN, Maricopa Tech. Community Coll., 1986, ADN, 1987; AAS in Electro-neuro Diagnostics, Phoenix Coll., 1992. RN, Ariz. EMT Ariz. Ambulance & Rescue, Mesa; LPN orthopedic and psychiatry Maricopa Med. Ctr., Phoenix; RN John C. Lincoln Hosp., Med Pro, Inc., Phoenix, Phoenix Bapt. Hosp., Health Temp, Inc., Phoenix.

SCHWARTZ, STEVE WENDELIN, physician; b. Bethesda, Md., May 16, 1955; s. Wallace John and Gwynne June (Lingenfelter) S. AB in Chemistry summa cum laude, Duke U., 1977, MD, 1981. Diplomate Am. Bd. Family Practice. Rotating intern Med. U. S.C., Charleston, 1981-82, resident in family practice, 1982-84; emergency rm. physician Coastal Emergency Svc., 1985-86; family physician Carolina Health Care, Myrtle Beach, S.C., 1984—; CEO Cactus Internat., Inc. Data processing dir. HMI, 1984—; pres. Unitrerds Software Corp., 1989—; rschr. Symbol Theory; programmer langs. Columnist SCO World Mag.; contbr. articles to profl. jours. Del. ann. meeting N.C. Med. Soc., 1980; participant Intramural Soccer, 1977-80; mem. Intramural Track, 1980, Blacknall Meml. Presbyn. Ch., 1977-80; coord. Boy Scouts Phys. Exam. Program, 1983; vol. cmty. health care project for poor East End Cmty. Health Ctr.; tchr. seminars on alcoholism for drug edn. project Holistic Medicine Group, 1980; Bible study coord. Valley of Achor. With USAF. 1973-75. First Place Durham Open Chess Tournament, 1974; recipient Grand Strand Leadership, 1986. Fellow Am. Acad. Family Physicians; mem. AMA (Physicians Recognition award 1986), So. Med. Assn., Horry County Med. Soc., Phi Beta Kappa, Upsilon Pi Epsilon. Avocations: chess, soccer. Home: 100 Lands End Blvd Apt 310 Myrtle Beach SC 29572-7005 Office: Carolina Health Care 4605 Hwy 17 Byp S Myrtle Beach SC 29577-6681

SCHWARTZ, STEVEN, corporate executive; b. Bklyn. BS in Acctg., Bklyn. Coll., 1972; MBA in Taxation, St. John's U., 1975. CPA, N.Y. Tax acct. R.E.A. Express Inc., N.Y.C., 1973-75; acct. Loeb & Troper, 1975, Kornbluh, Sirkin Ritter CPA's, N.Y.C., 1975-77; v.p. A. Flohr Co., Pelham, N.Y., 1977—. Pres., owner Steven Schwartz CPA, Riverdale, N.Y., 1979—. Mem. AICPA, N.Y. CPA's. Office: 630 W 246th St Ste 224 Bronx NY 10471-3632

SCHWARTZ, STEVEN MARK, marketing executive; b. Phila., Feb. 26, 1948; s. Edward and Erika (Schneier) S.; m. Paula Mae Levine, May 15, 1979; 1 child, Roger. AB magna cum laude, Bowdoin Coll., 1970; MFA in Writing, Columbia U., 1973. Writer, account exec. Schneider & Rich Assocs., N.Y.C., 1973-76; sr. account exec. Richard Weiner Inc., 1976-78; account supr., v.p. The Rowland Co., 1978-79; project mgr. exec. communications GE, Fairfield, Conn., 1979-83, mgr. exec. communications, 1983-84; v.p. corp. communications Interleaf Inc., Cambridge, Mass., 1984-86, v.p. mktg. programs and communications, 1986-88, v.p. mktg., 1989-90; pres. Schwartz Comms. Inc., Waltham, 1990—. Trustee Bowdoin Coll. Mem. Appalachian Mountain Club (bd. dirs.), Phi Beta Kappa, Theta Delta Chi. Republican. Avocations: hiking, kayaking. Office: Schwartz Communications Inc 230 3rd Ave Waltham MA 02451-7528*

SCHWARTZ, STEVEN SCOTT, orthodontist; b. Bklyn., Sept. 11, 1959; s. Jack W. and Harriet Schwartz; m. Amy L. Zuker, Mar. 24, 1990; children: Aaron M., Nathaniel P., Eli S. BA magna cum laude, SUNY, Buffalo, 1981; DDS, SUNY, Stony Brook, 1985; MMSc, Harvard U., 1989. Rsch. assoc. Forsyth Dental Ctr., Boston, 1989-90; clin. asst. prof. SUNY, Stony Brook, 1990—; orthodontist pvt. practice, Wantagh, N.Y., 1990—. Contbr. articles to profl. jours.; patentee in oral medicine. Regents scholar SUNY, 1977-81, 81-85. Mem. ADA, Am. Assn. Dental Rsch., Am. Assn. Orthodontists, Nassau County Dental Soc. (pub. and profl. rels. com. 1996—), Internat. Assn. Dental Rsch., Phi Beta Kappa. Avocations: music, basketball. Office: 3341B Park Ave Wantagh NY 11793-3716

SCHWARTZ, SUSAN R. reporter; b. Plattsburg, N.Y., May 1, 1970; d. Steven Greenberg and Marsha Beth Schwartz. Bachelor's Degree, U. Colo., 1992. Reporter Portsmouth (Ohio) Daily Times, 1993—96, Press Enterprise, Bloomsburg, Pa., 1996—. Recipient 2nd place award Divsn. IV Spot News Ongoing News, Pa. Newspaper Pubs. Assn., 1997, 2nd place award Divsn. Investigative Reporting, 1999, 1st place award Divsn. Spot News, 2001. Mem.: Soc. Profl. Journalists (Pa. Project Sunshine chair 2000—). Jewish. Avocations: kayaking, hiking, medieval music. Home: 226 E Fifth St Bloomsburg PA 17815 Office: Press Enterprise 3185 Lackawanna Ave Bloomsburg PA 17815

SCHWARTZ, TERI J. clinical psychologist, educator; b. N.Y.C., Dec. 30, 1949; d. Jerome and Shirley Ruth (Dushkind) Kraus; m. Raymond C. Schwartz; children: Rachel, Michael, Daniel. BA, Queens Coll., 1971; MS, C.W. Post Ctr., 1974; MA, New Sch. for Social Rsch., 1977, PhD, 1980. Diplomate in psychopharmacology and psychol. assessment, evaluation and testing Am. Bd. Psychol. Spltys., diplomate in psychopharmacology Internat. Coll. Prescribing Psychologists and Prescribing Psychologists Register, diplomate Nat. Registry Neurofeedback Providers, Am. Acad. Experts in Traumatic Stress. Staff psychologist to chief psychologist New Hope Guild, Howard Beach, NY, 1985—2001, 1982—85; staff psychologist Queens Child Guidance Ctr., Flushing, N.Y., 1985-88; staff psychotherapist Adelphi Univ.-Postdoctoral Psychotherapy Ctr., Garden City, 1984—; pvt. practice, clin. psychologist Briarwood and Floral Park, 1984—; asst. prof. Queens Coll., 1998-00; clin. supr. Steinway Family and Child Svcs., 2001—; adj. assoc. prof. John Jay Coll. Criminal Justice, 2001—. Adj. clin. supr. Yeshiva U., Bronx, N.Y., 1987—, C.W. Post Ctr., L.I. U., 1995; clin. supr. Adelphi U., Garden City, 1991—, assoc. clin. prof., 1992—; supr. child therapy tng. program New Hope Guild, Bklyn., 1994—; adj. assoc. prof. Queens Coll., CUNY, 1995—. Mem. exec. bd. Briarwood (N.Y.) Civic Assn., 1984-90; adv. bd. Queens Cmty. Mental Health Ctr. and Area D Subcom.-Queens Hosp. Ctr., Jamaica, N.Y., 1984-89. Fellow Am. Coll. Forensic Examiners; mem. Am. Acad. Experts in Trumatic Stress, N.Y. State Psychol. Assn., Nassau County Psychol. Assn., Queens County Psychol. Assn. Avocations: painting, gourmet cooking.

SCHWARTZ, THEODORE B. physician, educator; b. Phila., Feb. 14, 1918; s. William F. and Fanny (Farkas) S.; m. Genevieve Etta Bangs, Jan. 9, 1948; children: Richard, Steven, Michael, David, Jonathan, Thomas. BS, Franklin and Marshall Coll., 1939; MD, Johns Hopkins U., 1943. Diplomate Am. Bd. Internal Medicine (bd. govs., 1970-78, sec.-treas., 1976-78). Intern Osler Clinic, Johns Hopkins Hosp., 1943-44; asst. resident medicine Salt Lake City Gen. Hosp., 1946-47, resident medicine, 1947-48; fellow medicine Duke U. Med. Sch., 1948-50, asso. medicine, asst. prof. medicine, 1950-55; dir. sect. endocrinology and metabolism Rush-Presbyn.-St. Luke's Med. Center, Chgo., 1955-82, attending physician, 1960—; chmn. dept. medicine Rush-Presbyn.-St. Lukes's Med. Center, 1970-82; cons. endocrinology Hines (Ill.) VA Hosp., 1956-71, Great Lakes Naval Hosp., 1960-74; prof. medicine U. Ill. Coll. Medicine, 1960-71; prof., chmn. dept. medicine Rush Med. Coll., 1971-82; prof. medicine U. Wash., Seattle, 1982-96; chief med. services VA Med. Ctr., Boise, 1982-86. Mem. Am. Bd. Med. Spltys., 1972-79; cons. endocrinology 1997—. Editor: Yearbook of Endocrinology, 1964-86, endocrinology article Ency. Brit., 1985— ; contbr. articles to profl. jours. Bd. dirs. Boise Art Mus., 1984-92. Served with M.C. AUS, 1944-46. Decorated Bronze Star. Fellow ACP (publs. com. 1973-78, chmn. subcom. on aging 1982-85, mem. health and pub. policy com.), Am. Assn. Clin. Endocrinology (hon.), Am. Coll. Endocrinology (hon.); mem. Assn. Program Dirs. Internal Medicine (councilor 1978-80), Am. Fedn. Clin. Rsch., Am. Diabetes Assn., Diabetes Assn. Greater Chgo. (bd. dirs.), Am. Soc. Clin. Investigation, Am. Clin. and Climatol. Assn., Am. Thyroid Assn., Endocrine Soc., Ctrl. Clin. Rsch. Club, Ctrl. Soc. Clin. Rsch., Chgo. Soc. Internal Medicine (pres. 1966-67), Phi Beta Kappa, Alpha Omega Alpha. Address: 200 Lee St Evanston IL 60202-1450

SCHWARTZ, THEODORE FRANK, lawyer; b. Clayton, Mo., Aug. 14, 1935; s. Ben and Mary (Roufa) S.; m. Barbara Jean Rader, Aug. 30, 1959; children: Michael D., Kenneth R. JD, Washington U., St. Louis, 1962. Bar: Mo. 1967, D.C. 1972, Calif. 1974, N.Y. 1981, Fla. 1994; U.S. Dist. Ct. (ea. dist.) Mo. 1962, U.S. Ct. Appeals (8th cir.) 1963, U.S. Dist. Ct. (so. dist.) Ind. 1968, U.S. Dist. Ct. (so. dist.) Tex. 1971, U.S. Ct. Appeals (5th cir.) 1971, U.S. Ct. (cen. dist.) Calif. 1978, U.S. Ct. Appeals (7th cir.) 1979, U.S. Ct. Appeals (2d, 10th and 11th cirs.) 1980, U.S. Ct. Appeals (9th cir.) 1981, U.S. Supreme Ct. 1981. Assoc. Charles M. Shaw, Clayton, 1962-64; ptnr. Ackerman, Schiller & Schwartz, 1964-74; sole practice, 1975—. Mem. ABA, Assn. Trial Lawyer Am., Mo. Assn. Trial Lawyers, Am. Judicature Soc., Nat. Assn. Criminal Def. Lawyers. Home: 597 Purdue Ave Saint Louis MO 63130-4136 Office: 130 S Bemiston Ave Ste 700 Clayton MO 63105-1928 E-mail: theodore@gtw.net.

SCHWARTZ, VICTOR ELLIOT, lawyer, educator; b. N.Y.C., July 3, 1940; AB summa cum laude, Boston U., 1962; JD magna cum laude, Columbia U., 1965. Bar: N.Y. 1965, Ohio 1974. Law clk. to judge So. Dist. N.Y., 1965-67; from asst. to assoc. prof. law U. Cin., 1967-72, prof., 1972-79, acting dean, 1973-74; vis. prof. U. Va. Law Sch., 1970-71; adj. prof. law U. Cin., 1985—; ptnr. firm Crowell & Moring, Washington, 1980—2001; sr. ptnr. firm Fed. Interagy. task Force on Products Liability, 1976; ptnr., chair firm's pub. policy group Shook Hardy & Bacon, Washington, 2001—. Bd. visitors U. Cin. Sch., 1998—; gen. counsel, bd. dirs. Am. Tort Reform Assn.; chmn. Civil Justice Task Force, Am. Legis. Exch. Coun.; adj. prof. law Georgetown U., 1987—; chmn. Dept. of Commerce Task Force on Product Liability and Accident Compensation, 1977-80. Author: Comparative Negligence, 1974, 3d edit., 1994; (with Prosser and Wade) Cases and Materials on Torts, 1976, 10th edit., 2000, How to Prepare for the Multi-State Bar Examination, 1977, Products Liability: Cases and Trends, 1987, Products Liability: Asset Trends, 1988, (with Lee and Kelly) Multistate Legislation, 1985; editor: Columbia Law Rev., 1965; prin. draftsman: Model Uniform Product Liability Act. Recipient Sec. of Commerce award for disting. svc., Burton award for best law rev. writing in U.S.; named One of 100 Most Influential Attys. in U.S., Nat. Law 3, 1994, 97. Mem. ABA (chmn. products liability com. 1979, uniform laws com. 1981, torts and ins. practice sect.), Am. Law Inst. (life, adv. com. Restatement Third of Torts), Phi Beta Kappa. Office: Shook Hardy & Bacon LLP 600 14th St NW Ste 800 Washington DC 20005-2004 *The greatest joys in life are found in one's relationships, be it business, romance or friendship, with other people.*

SCHWARTZ, WALTER RICHARD, obstetrician/gynecologist, retired; b. Lancaster, Wis., Jan. 2, 1931; MD, U. Wis., 1955. Diplomate Am. Bd. Ob/gyn. Intern St. Josephs Hosp., Marshfield, 1955-56; resident in ob/gyn. Milw. County Hosp., 1958-61; staff West Allis Hosp., Wis., 1961—, Sinai Samaritan Hosp., 1961—, Elmbrook Meml. Hsop., 1971—; assoc. clin. prof. ob/gyn. Med. Coll. Wis., 1976—. Fellow Am. Coll. Obstetricians/Gynecologists, Am. Coll. Surgeons; mem. AMA, ACOG, Ctrl. Assn. Obstetricians and Gynecologists.

SCHWARTZ, WILLIAM, lawyer, educator; b. Providence, May 6, 1933; s. Morris Victor and Martha (Glassman) S.; m. Bernice Konigsberg, Jan. 13, 1957; children: Alan Gershon, Robin Libby. AA, Boston U., 1952, JD magna cum laude, 1955, MA, 1960; postgrad., Harvard Law Sch., 1955-56; LHD (hon.), Hebrew Coll., 1996, Yeshiva U., 1998. Bar: D.C. 1956, Mass. 1962, N.Y. 1989. Prof. law Boston U., 1955-91, Fletcher prof. law, 1968-70, Roscoe Pound prof. law, 1970-73, dean Sch. of Law, 1980-88, dir. Ctr. for Estate Planning, 1988-91; univ. prof. Yeshiva U., N.Y.C., 1991—; of counsel Swartz & Swartz, 1973-80; v.p. for acad. affairs, chief acad. officer Yeshiva U., N.Y.C., 1993-98; counsel Cadwalader, Wickersham and Taft, N.Y.C., Washington, Charlotte, London, 1988—; mem. faculty Frances Glessner Lee Inst., Harvard Med. Sch., Nat. Coll. Probate Judges, 1970, 77, 78, 79, 88; gen. dir. Assn. Trial Lawyers Am., 1968-73; reporter New Eng. Trial Judges Conf., 1965-67; participant Nat. Met. Cts. Conf., 1968; dir. Mass. Probate Study, 1976—; chmn. spl. com. on police procedures City of Boston, 1989, 91. Bd. dirs. UST Corp., chmn. of co., 1993-94, chmn. bd. dirs., 1996-2000; bd. dirs. Viacom Inc., Viacom Internat. Inc.; chmn. compensation com., mem. adv. com. WCI Steel, Inc., Ambient; mem. legal adv. bd. N.Y. Stock Exch. Author: Future Interests and Estate Planning, 1965, 77, 81, 86, Comparative Negligence, 1970, A Products Liability Primer, 1970, Civil Trial Practice Manual, 1972, New Vistas in Litigation, 1973, Massachusetts Pleading and Practice, 7 vols., 1974-80, Estate Planning and Living Trusts, 1990, The Convention Method: The Unused Amending Superhighway, 1995, Jewish Law and Contemporary Dilemmas and Problems, 1997, Does Time Heal All Wrongs?, 1999, others; note editor: Boston U. Law Rev., 1954-55; property editor: Annual Survey of Mass. Law, 1960—; contbr. articles to legal jours. Rep. Office of Pub. Info., UN, 1968—73; chmn. legal adv. panel Nat. Commn. Med. Practice, 1972—73; examiner of titles Commonwealth of Mass., 1964—; spl. counsel Mass. Bay Transp. Authority, 1979; pres. Fifth Ave. Synagogue, N.Y.C., 1997—2001, hon. pres., 2001—; bd. dirs. Kerry Found.; trustee Hebrew Coll., 1975—, Salve Regina U., Yeshiva U. Recipient Homer Albers award Boston U., 1955, John Ordronaux prize, 1955; Disting. Service award Religious Zionists Am., 1977; William W. Treat award; William O. Douglas award. Fellow Am. Coll. Probate Counsel; mem. ABA, Am. Law Inst., Mass. Bar Assn. (chmn. task force tort liability), N.Y. State Bar Assn., Assn. Bar City N.Y., Nat. Coll. Probate Judges (hon. mem.), Phi Beta Kappa. Office: 100 Maiden Ln New York NY 10038-4818 *I have been guided by the maxim: "Ideals are like stars. You cannot touch them with your hands, but like the seafaring man, if you choose them as your guide and follow them, you will reach your destiny.".*

SCHWARTZBERG, DAVID B. chemical industry executive; b. N.Y.C., Feb. 8, 1946; s. Morris and Anne S.; m. Susan R. Schwartzberg, Nov. 25, 1967; children: Robert, Mindy, Frank, Lauren. BSChE, Polytechnic Inst. of N.Y., 1967; MBA, Fairleigh Dickinson U., 1973. Gen. mgr. indsl. chem. divsn. M&T Chems., Inc., Woodbridge, N.J., 1988-89; gen. mgr. plastic additives divsn. Elf Atochem NA (name now Atofina Chems. Inc.), Phila., 1989-90, pres. mineral products divsn., 1990-93, v.p. performance products, 1993-95, v.p. remediation, 1995-98, v.p., health, environ. and safety, 1998—. Adv. bd. Hazardous Substance Mgmt. Rsch. Ctr., Newark, N.J., 1996—. Office: Atofina Chems Inc 2000 Market St Philadelphia PA 19103-3231

SCHWARTZBERG, JOANNE GILBERT, physician; b. Boston, Nov. 30, 1933; d. Richard Vincent and Emma (Cohen) Gilbert; m. Hugh Joel Schwartzberg, July 7, 1956; children: Steven Jonathan, Susan Jennifer. BA magna cum laude, Radcliffe Coll., 1955; MD, Northwestern U., 1960. Diplomate Am. Bd. Quality Assurance and Utilization Rev. Physicians. Founder, med. dir. Chgo. Home Health Svc., 1972-95; founder, v.p., med. dir. Suburban Home Health Svc., Chgo. area, 1975—87; clin. asst. prof. preventive medicine and community health U. Ill. Coll. Medicine, 1985—. Dir. Aging and Cmty. Health AMA, 1990—; pres. Inst. Medicine of Chgo., 1994—95, bd. dirs., 1990—2000; co-chair Ill. Health and Social Svc. Caucus to the White House Conf. on Aging, 1995. Contbr. articles to profl. jours. Mem. Cmty. Adv. Bd. Joint Youth Devel. Commn. and Health Planning Com., Chgo., 1963-67; pres. Near North Montessori Sch., Chgo., 1972-75, bd. dirs., 1970-83; del. White House Conf. on Aging, 1995. Recipient Mayor's citation, City of Chgo., 1963, Physician of Year award, Nat. Assn. Home Care, 1988, Henry P. Russe citation, Inst. Medicine Chgo. & The Rush Presbyn. St. Luke's Med. Ctr., 2001. Mem.: Alexander Graham Bell Assn. for Deaf (bd. dirs. 1984—90, gen. chmn. internat. conv. 1986, chmn. internat. parents orgn. 1988—90), Am. Geriatrics Soc, Chgo. Med. Soc., Ill. Med. Soc., Ill. Geriatrics Soc. (pres. 1990—92), Am. Coll. Med. Quality, Am. Acad. of Home Care Physicians (pres. 1992—94, founding bd. dirs. 1987—, Physician of Yr. 1994). Jewish. Home: 853 W Fullerton Ave Chicago IL 60614-2412 Office: 515 N State St Chicago IL 60610-4325

SCHWARTZBERG, JOSEPH EMANUEL, geographer, educator; b. Bklyn., Feb. 5, 1928; s. Philip and Frances (Lefkowitz) S. m. Monique Elisabeth Ribaux, Dec. 19, 1963 (div. Oct. 1998); children: Philip, Paul. BA, Bklyn. Coll., 1949; MA, U. Md., 1951; PhD, U. Wis., 1960. Geographer U.S. Army Map Svc., Brookmont, Md., 1949-51; soldier U.S. Army, Heidelberg, Germany, 1951-53; asst. prof. geography and South Asian studies U. Pa., Phila., 1960-64; assoc. prof. U. Minn., Mpls., 1964-70, prof., 1970—2001. Vis. prof. Jawaharlal Nehru U., New Delhi, India, 1979-80. Author: Occupational Structure and Level of Economic Development in India: A Regional Analysis, 1960; co-author, editor: A Historical Atlas of South Asia, 1978, 92, The History of Cartography, Vol. 2, Books 1 and 2, 1992, 94. Pres. Minn. chpt. World Federalist Assn., 1976-79, 96-99, nat. bd. dirs., 1996--. Mem. Assn. Am. Geographers, Assn. Asian Studies, Am. Geographic Soc., Acad. Coun UN Sys., Amnesty Internat., Minn. Alliance of Peacemakers. Home: 5492 Bald Eagle Blvd E White Bear Lake MN 55110-1100 Office: U Minn Dept Geography Minneapolis MN 55455 E-mail: schwa004@tc.umn.edu.

SCHWARTZBERG, MARTIN M. chemical company executive; b. N.Y.C., Dec. 10, 1935; s. Morris H. and Anne C. (Steskanin) S.; m. Florence M. Bloom, Sept. 22, 1957; children: Steven E., Michael C., Scott A. B ChemE, NYU, 1956; MBA, Wayne State U., 1965. Asst. to div. mgr. Pennwalt Corp., Phila., 1969-72, mgr. mktg. service, 1972-74, asst. to chief exec. officer, 1974-76, mng. dir. chems. Europe, 1976-78, mng. dir. splt. chems., 1978-80, pres. agrichems. div., 1980-85, pres. inorganic chems. div., 1985, v.p. chems., 1985-87, sr. v.p. chems., 1987-89; group pres. Elf Atochem N.Am., Inc. (formerly Pennwalt Corp.), 1990-94, ret., 1995. Bd. dirs. Camden County chpt. ARC. Served with U.S. Army, 1959. Mem. Sigma Iota Epsilon. Avocations: volleyball, golf. E-mail: martyflor@aol.com.

SCHWARTZBERG, ROGER KERRY, osteopath, internist; b. Bklyn., Mar. 30, 1948; s. Erwin and Edna (Kuchlik) S.; m. Linda Lurie, July 1, 1972 (div. Nov. 1974); m. Vicki Ann Davis, Nov. 28, 1976; children: Jeremy Dylan, Joshua Ryan. BA in Psychology, Syracuse U., 1970; DO, Mich. State U., 1973. Diplomate Am. Acad. Osteopathic Internists. Intern, sr. asst. surgeon USPHS Hosp., S.I., N.Y., 1973-74; med. resident Southeastern Med. Ctr., North Miami Beach, Fla., 1974-77, chief resident, 1975-77; pvt. practice Seminole, 1977—. Active staff Univ. Gen. Hosp., Seminole 1978-97, chmn. dept. internal medicine, 1981-82, governing bd. 1981-86, 88-97, vice chmn. 1986, 88-97, Pinellas Community Hosp., Pinellas Park, Fla., 1980-96, chief of staff, 1985-86, Seminole Hosp. and Women's Ctr., Seminole, 1989-96; adj. clin. faculty U. New Eng. Coll. Osteo. Medicine, Biddeford, Maine, 1985—; clin. asst. prof. internal medicine, 1987—, Nova Southeastern Univ. Coll. of Osteopathic Medicine, 1987—; clin. asst. prof. internal medicine Kirksville (Mo.) Coll. Osteo. Medicine, 1989—; mem. active staff Suncoast Osteo. Hosp., Largo, Fla., 1982—, Largo Med. Ctr. Hosp., 1990—, St. Petersburg Gen. Hosp., 1991—; clin. assoc. prof. coll. osteo. medicine U. Health Scis., 1992—. Named Educator of Yr. Met. Gen. Hosp., Pinellas Park, Fla., 1985. Fellow Am. Acad. Osteo. Internists (certification bd. 1990); mem. Am. Osteo. Assn., Am. Assn. Physician Specialties, Am. Coll. Osteo. Internists, Fla. Osteo. Med. Assn. (trustee 1985-89), Pinellas County Osteo. Med. Soc. (trustee 1985-89, gov. 1989-90, v.p. 1991-96). Jewish. Avocations: photographer, singing, keyboards. Office: Oakhurst Med Clinic 13020 Park Blvd Seminole FL 33776-3639

SCHWARTZEL, CHARLES BOONE, lawyer; b. Louisville, Jan. 4, 1950; s. Charles Joseph and Rosemary Jane (Redens) S.; m. Rose Marie Carlisi, June 20, 1980; children: Sally Ann, Charles Gerard. BA, Vanderbilt U., 1972; JD, U. Tex., 1975. Bar: Tex. 1975. Atty. Vinson & Elkins L.L.P., Houston, 1975-98, ptnr., 1983-98; pvt. practice, 1998—. Contbr. articles to profl. jours. Councilman City of West University Place, Tex., 1985-89. Fellow Am. Coll. Trust and Estate Counsel; mem. Tex. Bar Assn. Roman Catholic. Office: Attorney at Law 1010 Lamar St Ste 1520 Houston TX 77002-6315

SCHWARTZHOFF, JAMES PAUL, foundation executive; b. Waukon, Iowa, June 24, 1937; s. Harold J. and Mary (Regan) Schwartzhoff; m. Mary Lou Hess, Apr. 23, 1960; children: Tammara, Eric, Stephanie, Mark, Laurie, Michelle, Steven. B, U. Iowa, 1962. Asst. chief auditor Wis. Dept. Tax, Madison, 1962-67; mgr. treas. dept. Mead Johnson and Co., Evansville, Ind., 1967-69; v.p., treas., investment officer Kettering Found., Dayton, Ohio, 1969—. Chmn., treas. bd. Pastoral Counseling Ctr., Dayton, 1975-81; treas. Ohio River Rd. Runners, Dayton, 1986-87; spkr. nat. investment confs. Past treas. Nat. Issues Forums Inst., Coun. Pub. Policy Edn., Ctr. for Community and Ednl. Devel.; mem. Donor's Forum Ohio Fin. Com., 1990-92; mem. investment com. U. Dayton; adv. com. JMB Endowment and Found. Realty Funds, 1991-94. Cpl. U.S. Army, 1957-59. Mem. AICPA, Found. Fin. Officers Group, Southern Ohio Pension Fund Group. Avocations: bicycling, running, photography, woodworking, skiing. Office: Kettering Found 200 Commons Rd Dayton OH 45459-2799

SCHWARTZKOPFF, IVO S. investment banker; b. Frankfurt am Main, Germany, 1962; JD, Goethe U., Frankfurt, 1986, PhD, 1996; MBA, Pa. State U., 1991. Bar: Germany 1989. Assoc. Goldman, Sachs & Co., N.Y.C., 1991-92, Frankfurt, 1992-95, exec. dir., 1995-2000; mng. dir. Deutsche Bank AG, 2001—. Cons. on real estate devel., Frankfurt, 1986-91. Author: International Tax Law, 1997. Avocations: music, numerous sports. Office: Deutsche Bank AG Taunusanlage 12 60262 Frankfurt Germany

SCHWARTZMAN, DAVID, economist, educator; b. Montreal, Que., Can., Apr. 22, 1924; came to U.S., 1954, naturalized, 1964; s. Joseph and Jeannette (Zurick) S.; m. Gertrude Schneiderman, June 17, 1951; children— Michael, Jason, Paul. BA, McGill U., 1945; postgrad., U. Minn., 1945-46; PhD, U. Calif. at Berkeley, 1953. Lectr. McGill U., 1948-51; economist Dominion Bur. Statistics, 1951-53, United 5[009b] to $1.00 Stores, Can., 1953-54; instr. Columbia, 1954-58; asst. prof. N.Y. U., 1958-60; assoc. prof. New Sch. for Social Research, N.Y.C., 1960-64; prof. New Sch. for Social Rsch., 1964—, chmn. dept. econs., 1966-69, 76, 83-84. Mem. staff Nat. Bur. Econ. Research, 1963-69; prof. environ. medicine and community health state U. N.Y. Downstate Med. Center, part-time, 1969-70; Cons. Royal Commn. on Farm Machinery, Ottawa, Can., 1968-70, U.S. Bur. Census, 1973, anti-trust div. U.S. Dept. Justice, 1973, U.S. Council on Wage and Price Stability, Exec. Office of Pres., 1975-76; adj. mem. Com. on Trade Regulation, N.Y. County Lawyers' Assn., 1976-85; Bd. advisors Inst. Health Economics and Social Studies, 1976-80 Author: Oligopoly in the Farm Machine Industry, 1970, Decline of Service in Retail Trade, 1971, The Expected Return from Pharmaceutical Research, 1975, Innovation in the Pharmaceutical Industry, 1976, Games of Chicken: Four Decades of Nuclear Policy, 1988, Economic Policy: An Agenda for the Nineties, 1989, The Japanese Television Cartel: A Study Based on Matsushita v. Zenith, 1993, Black Unemployment: Part of Unskilled Unemployment, 1997; contbr. articles to profl. jours. Mem. Am. Econ. Assn. Home: 285 Central Park W New York NY 10024-3006 Office: New Sch for Social Rsch Dept Econs 65 5th Ave Dept Econs New York NY 10003-3003

SCHWARTZOTT, CAROL ANN, artist, educator; b. Jamaica, N.Y., Jan. 9, 1945; d. George Paul and Lucille (Savino) Sotak; m. Peter E. Schwartzott, Aug. 1965; children: Jennifer, Gretel, Peter. BS in Art Edn., SUNY, Buffalo, 1965, MA in Anthropology and Fine Art, 1990. Instr. SUNY, 1988-90, Niagara County C.C., Sanborn, N.Y., 1988-95; tchr. drawing and design pub. schs., Webster, 1965—66, Niagara Falls, 1966—67. One-woman shows include Castellani Mus. Art, Niagara U., Lewiston, N.Y., Daemon Coll. Gallery, Buffalo, Lamoreaux Landing & Wine Cellars, Lodi, N.Y.; exhibited in group shows, including Nat. Mus. Women in Arts, Washington, Montclair (N.J.) Mus. Art, Nat. Book Mus. South Africa, Johannesburg, Honolulu Acad. Art, Ctr. for Book Arts, U. Ala., Tuscaloosa, Galleria Mesa, Ariz., Mus. Contemporary Crafts, N.Y.C., DeCordova Mus., Lincoln, Mass., Carnegie Mellon Inst., Pitts., Denver Mus. Fine Arts, Albright-Knox Mems. Gallery, Buffalo; represented in permanent collections Art Scholars Libr., Nat. Galley Art, Washington, Victoria and Albert Mus., London, Joseph Cornell Study Ctr., Smithsonian Inst., Washington, Libr. and Rsch. Ctr., Nat. Mus. Women in Arts, Yale U. Libr., Sachner Rare Book Archives, Miami, Fla., Toronto (Ont., Can.) Pub. Libr., Rare Book Ctr., Oberlin Coll., Jack Ginsberg Rare Book Libr., Forest Town, South Africa, Fine Print Libr., Rochester (N.Y.) Inst. Tech.; artist Booksowks, 1989-2002. Home: 1000 Irish Settlement Rd Freeville NY 13068

SCHWARTZTOL, HOLLY WECHSLER, psychologist; b. Washington, Dec. 20, 1946; d. James Arthur and Nancy (Fraenkel) Wechsler; m. Robert Ira Schwartzol, Nov. 16, 1975; children: Laurence, Andrew. BA, Finch Coll., 1968; MA, C. W. Post Coll., 1971; PhD, U. Miami, 1981. Instr. psychology C. W. Post Coll., Greenvale, N.Y., 1971; tchr. Yorktown High Sch., Yorktown Heights, 1971-73; sch. psychologist Dade County Schs., Miami, Fla., 1973-84; pvt. practice holistic psychology, 1983—; Reiki master, trainer radiant heart therapy. Adj. asst. prof. counseling psychology U. Miami, 1984-85; co-founder, co-dir. Miami Inst. Clin. Hypnosis, 1986-93; co-founder, dir. Miami Inst. Expanding Light, 1993-96. Author: (with James A. and Nancy F. Wechsler) In a Darkness, 1972, 2d edit., 1988. Reiki master, trainer and practitioner of radiant heart therapy. Mem. Dade County Psychol. Assn. (pres. 1988), Fla. Psychol. Assn., Am. Psychol. Assn., Am. Soc. Clin. Hypnosis (bd. dirs. 1998-99, pres.-elect 1999-2000, pres. 1999—), South Fla. Soc. for the Study Multiple Personality and Dissociative Disorders (bd. dirs. 1989, pres. 1991). Office: 806 S Douglas Rd Ste 560 Coral Gables FL 33134-3157

SCHWARTZWALD, ROBERT S. language educator; b. Winnipeg, Manitoba, Can., Apr. 27, 1955; s. Martin H. Schwartzwald, Clara Schwartzwald. BA, U. Manitoba, 1975; MA, U. Toronto, 1977; PhD, Laval U., 1986. From instr. to assoc. prof. U. Mass., Amherst, 1982—97, prof., 1997—. Dir. Ctr. for Crossroads in Study of Americas Five Colleges, Inc., Amherst, 1998—. Co-author: Fictions de l'identitaire au Québec, 1991; contbr. Grantee Focus grant, NEH, 2000, Aid to Scholarly Publ., Social Sci. and Humanities Rsch. Coun. Can., 2001, Program for Internat. Rsch. Linkages, Internat. Coun. Can. Studies, 1997. Mem.: Modern Lang. Assn., Assn. Can. Studies in U.S., Am. Coun. Quebec Studies (pres. 1987—90), Nat. Trust for Hist. Preservation. Office: Dept French & Italian Studies Univ Mass Amherst MA 01003

SCHWARY, RONALD LOUIS, motion picture producer; b. The Dalles, Oreg., May 23, 1944; s. Mitchell Louis and Lorraine (Ablan) S.; children: Brian L., Neil L. BS, U. So. Calif., 1967. Pres. Schwary Enterprises, L.A., 1985—. Prodr. (motion pictures) Ordinary People, 1980 (Golden Globe award 1981, Acad. award 1981), Absence of Malice, 1981, Tootsie, 1982, A Soldier's Story, 1984, Batteries Not Included, 1987, Havana, 1990, Scent of a Woman, 1992, Cops and Robbersons, 1994, Sabrina, 1995, Mirror Has Two Faces, 1996, Meet Joe Black, 1997, Random Hearts, 1999; (TV series) Tour of Duty, 1987, Now and Again, 1999. Mem. Dirs. Guild Am. Republican. Roman Catholic.

SCHWARZ, A. DAVID, III, real estate broker; b. Houston, Apr. 29, 1948; children: A. David IV, Blake B. BBA in Acctg., U. Tex., 1970. Lic. comml. real estate broker, Tex. Salesman Arnold K. Altsuler & Assocs., Houston, 1970-72, Fontana, Murrell & Polydoros, Houston, 1973-76; pres. A. David Schwarz III, Inc., 1977—; exec. v.p., dir. sales REOC Property Svcs., 1996-99; broker assoc. McDade, Smith, Gould, Johnston & Co., 2001—. Mem. divsn. adv. com. Am. Cancer Soc., Houston, 1987-91; pres. Rotary Club of Houston Found., 1997-99, chmn. bd. 1999-2000). Mem. Soc. Indsl. and Office Realtors (sec.-treas. Houston Gulf Coast chpt. 1987, v.p. 1988, pres. 1989), Nat. Assn. Realtors (John E. Wolf Citizenship Cup 1989, comml. svcs. com. 1988-91), Tex. Assn. Realtors, Houston Assn. Realtors (bd. dirs. 2001—), Rotary Club of Houston (dir. 1982-84, sgt. of arms 1985-86, treas. 1986-87, v.p., pres. elect 1991-92, pres. 1992-93, dir. 1994, Lombardi award exec. com. 1978-89, gen. chmn. 1987), Houston Realty Breakfast Club. Home: 727 Bunker Hill Rd Apt 56 Houston TX 77024-4443 Office: McDade Smith Gould Johnston & Co # 56 5005 River Way # 310 Houston TX 77056 Home Fax: (713) 365-0861. E-mail: adavidschwarz@cs.com.

SCHWARZ, BARBARA RUTH BALLOU, elementary school educator; b. East Orange, N.J., Aug. 8, 1930; d. Robert Ingram Ballou and Ruth Edna Sweeney; m. Eugene A. Schwarz, Jr., Dec. 24, 1954 (div. 1977); children: Ruth Ellen, Eugene A. III. BS, Trenton State Coll., 1952. Tchr. West Orange N.J. Schs., 1952-54, Franklin Sch., Ft. Wayne, Ind., 1955-56, Parliament Place Sch., North Babylon, N.Y., 1965-91. Trustee welfare trust fund North Babylon Tchrs. Orgn., N.Y., 1988-91. Vol. Safe Home, Suffolk County Coalition Against Domeestic Violence, Bayshore, N.Y., 1979-90; sec. Victims Info. Bur., Suffolk, 1987-88, v.p., 1989-90, pres. bd. dirs., 1990-94, regional bd. dirs., 2002--, rep. to Women's Equal Rights Coalition, Suffolk County Human Rights Commn., 1989-94; mem. adv. bd. Suffolk County Women's Svcs., 1990-96, vice-chair, 1991-93; rep. LD 14 Suffolk County Women's Adv. Commn., 2001--; bd. dirs. Suffolk Abortion Rights Coun., 1992-96; mem. Suffolk-Nassau Abortion Def., 1991-94; pub. affairs com. Planned Parenthood Suffolk County, 1990-92; mem. Long Islanders for Fairness and Equality 1994-97; mem. subcom. Islip Presbyn. Ch. on Legis. Com. of N.Y. State Coalition Against Domestic Violence, 1999—; steering com. Save Our Svcs., Long Island, 1998—. Women's History Month Community Svc. honoree Town of Babylon, 1997. Mem. AAUW (mem. v.p. Islip area br. 1982-84, pres. 1984-88, legis. chair 1988-93, mem. com. promoting individual liberties Nassau-Suffolk dist. VI 1989-91, pro-choice coord. N.Y. state 1990-92, rep. to women on job task force 1986-98, chair dist. VI inter-br. 1991-92, chair N.Y. state pub. policy 1992-96, rep. on L.I. and N.Y. State Pro-Choice Coalitions, chair N.Y. state voter edn. campaign, 1995-98, assoc. pub. policy com. 1996-98, L.I. Achievement award 1996), N.Y. State Ret. Tchrs. Assn., Western Suffolk Ret. Tchrs. Assn., Coalition Ret. Tchrs. L.I., North Babylon Tchrs. Orgn. (retirees chpt.). Republican. Avocations: lobbying, reading, handcrafts, gourmet cooking, volunteer activities. Home: 23 Wyandanch Ave Babylon NY 11702-1920

SCHWARZ, BERTHOLD ERIC, psychiatrist; b. Jersey City, Oct. 20, 1924; s. Berthold Theodore D. and Thyra I.W. (Ericson) S.; m. Ardis Marilyn Peterson, Jan. 22, 1955; children: Lisa Thyra, Eric Rolf. AB, Dartmouth Coll., 1945; MD, NYU, 1950; MS, Mayo Grad. Sch. Medicine, 1957. Intern Mary Hitchcock Meml. Hosp., Hanover, N.H., 1950-51; psychiatrist, researcher pvt. practice, Montclair, N.J., 1955-82; Mayo Found., Rochester, Minn., 1951-55; psychiatrist, researcher pvt. practice, Vero Beach, Fla., 1982—. Cons. Essex County Hosp. Ctr., Cedar Grove, N.J., 1965-82, Med. Correctional Assn., Ossining, N.Y., 1960-72; exec. dir. Internat. Psychosomatics Inst., Mountain Lakes, N.J., 1995—. Contbr. articles to med. jours. With USNR, 1943-45. Fellow AAAS, Am. Psychiat. Assn., Am. Soc. Psychical Rsch., Am. Geriatric Soc. Republican. Avocations: UFOs, paranormal aspects, swimming, walking. Home: 1070 Reef Rd Apt 305 Vero Beach FL 32963-4342 Office: 642 Azalea Ln Vero Beach FL 32963-1832 E-mail: ardisps@aol.com.

SCHWARZ, DANIEL ROGER, English literature educator; b. Rockville Centre, N.Y., May 12, 1941; s. Joseph Alexander and Florence (Rimler) S.; m. Marcia Mitson, Sept. 1, 1963 (div. 1986); m. Marcia Jacobson, 1998; children: David K., Jeffrey C. BA, Union Coll., 1963; MA, Brown U., 1965, PhD, 1968. Asst. prof. Cornell U., Ithaca, N.Y., 1968-74, assoc. prof., 1974-80, prof., 1980—, dir. undergrad. studies in English, 1976-82, Stephen H. Weiss Presdl. fellow, 1999—. Disting. vis. Cooper prof. U. Ark., Little Rock, 1988; vis. Citizen's prof. lit. U. Hawaii, 1992-93; vis. eminent scholar U. Ala., Huntsville, 1996; U.S. Info. Svc. vis. scholar Australia, 1993, Cyprus, 1999; dir. Summer Seminars for Coll. Tchrs. on Modernism, NEH, 1984, 86, 88, 90, 93, Summer Seminars for Secondary Tchrs. on James Joyce, 1985, 87, 89, 91. Author: Rereading Conrad, 2001, Imagining the Holocaust, 1999, Reconfiguring Modernism: Explorations in the Relationship Between Modern Art and Modern Literature, 1997, Narrative and Representation in the Poetry of Wallace Stevens, 1993, The Case for a Humanistic Poetics, 1991, The Transformation of the English Novel, 1890-1930, 1989, rev. edit., 1995, Reading Joyce's Ulysses, 1987, rev. edit., 1991, The Humanistic Heritage: Critical Theories of the English Novel from James to Hillis Miller, 1986, rev. edit., 1989, Conrad: The Later Fiction, 1982, Conrad: Almayer's Folly to Under Western Eyes, 1980, Disraeli's Fiction, 1979; editor: The Secret Sharer (Joseph Conrad), 1997, The Dead (James Joyce), 1994; co-editor: Narrative and Culture, 1994. Bd. mem. Freeville Planning Bd., 1968-74, Freeville Zoning Bd., 1968-74. Recipient Russell Disting. Tchg. award Cornell U., 1998; grantee Am. Philos. Soc., 1981, NEH, 1984-91, 93. Mem. MLA, Internat. Narrative Soc. (pres. 1990-91), James Joyce Soc., Phi Beta Kappa. Jewish. Avocations: travel, tennis, museums, theater. Home: 925 Mitchell St Apt 3 Ithaca NY 14850-4991 Office: Cornell U 242 Goldwin Smith Hall Ithaca NY 14853-3201 E-mail: drs6@cornell.edu.

SCHWARZ, EGON, humanities and German language educator, writer, literary critic; b. Vienna, Austria, Aug. 8, 1922; arrived in U.S., 1949, naturalized, 1956; s. Oscar and Erna S.; m. Dorothea K. Klockenbusch, June 8, 1950; children— Rudolf Joachim, Caroline Elisabeth, Gabriela Barbara. PhD, U. Wash., 1954; Hon. Doctorate, U. Vienna, 1997. Mem. faculty Harvard U., 1954-61; mem. faculty dept. Germanic langs. and lit. Washington U., St. Louis, 1961—, prof. German, 1963—, Rosa May Disting. Univ. prof. in the Humanities, 1975-93, prof. emeritus, 1993—. Vis. prof. U. Hamburg, Fed. Republic Germany, 1962-63, U. Calif., Berkeley, 1963-65, Middlebury Coll., 1969, U. Calif.-Irvine, 1977, U. Tübingen, 1986; William Evans prof. U. Otago, Dunedin, N.Z., 1984; Disting. scholar Ohio State U., Columbus, 1987, U. Graz, Austria, 1989, 93, U. Siegen, 1993-94. Author: Hofmannsthal und Calderon, 1962, Joseph von Eichendorff, 1972, Das verschluckte Schluchzen-Poesie und Politik bei Rainer Maria Rilke, 1972, Keine Zeit für Eichendorff:

Chronik unfreiwilliger Wanderjahre; an autobiography, 1979, revised and expanded, 1992, Dichtung, Kritik, Geschichte: Essays zur Literatur 1900-1930, 1983, Literatur aus vier Kulturen: Essays und Besprechungen, 1987, Ich bin Kein Freund allgemeiner Urteile uber ganze Volker: Essays uber osterreischische, deutsche und judische literatur, 2000, Die japanische Mauer: Uhgewohnliche Reisegeschichten, 2002, also numerous other books. Recipient Joseph von Eichendorff medal, 1986, Austrian Medal of Honor for Arts and Scis., 1991, Alexander von Humboldt prize for fgn. scholars, 1995; Guggenheim fellow, 1957-58, Fulbright fellow, 1962-63, sr. fellow NEH, 1970-71, fellow Ctr. for Interdisciplinary Studies, Bielefeld, Germany, 1980-81; grantee Am. Coun. Learned Socs., 1962-63. Mem. MLA, Am. Assn. Tchrs. German, German Acad. Lang. and Lit. (hon.). Home: 1036 Oakland Ave Saint Louis MO 63122-6565 Office: Washington U German Dept Saint Louis MO 63130 E-mail: gabrielas@aol.com. *When I was young, heroic phantasies were closer to my heart than ethical ones, desires of self-fulfillment stronger than the hopes for an equitable world. Today my horizon is broader in that I wish for a society where personal satisfactions are not achieved at the expense of others, where the earth which one generation inherits is not left more depleted to the next, a society which does not coerce other societies.*

SCHWARZ, EITAN DANIEL, psychiatrist; AB, Cornell U., 1965; MD, Johns Hopkins U., 1969. Intern Boston City Hosp., 1969-70; resident in psychiatry U. Chgo., 1970-73, chief resident, 1972-73, fellow in child psychiatry, 1972-73; chief fellow in child psychiatry Michael Reese Hosp., Chgo., 1973-75; clin. asst. prof. U. Chgo., 1976-83; asst. prof. Northwestern U. Med. Sch., Chgo., 1988—. Sr. attending physician Northwestern Health Coll.; head divsn. child/adolescent psychiatry, head divsn. pediat. psychiatry Evanston (Ill.) Hosp., 1988—96. Contbr. sci. papers; developer computer programs. Fellow Am. Acad. Child and Adolescent Psychiatry, Am. Psychiat. Assn. Avocations: fitness, cello, computer. Office: 735 St Johns Ave Highland Park IL 60035-4649

SCHWARZ, EKKEHART RICHARD JOHANNES, architect, urban designer; b. Stettin, Germany, Sept. 12, 1938; came to U.S., 1970; s. Walter and Barbara Elisabeth (Doberman) S.; m. Elaine Carmella Wong, Sept. 12, 1982; children: Elisabeth Barbara Alicia, Patricia Kathrina. Diploma in architektur, T.U. Berlin, 1969; MArch, U. Calif., Berkeley, 1971. Registered architect, N.Y., N.J., Conn., Ariz. Draftsman Hans Scharoun, West Berlin, Fed. Republic Germany, 1964, J.P. Kleihues, Architect, West Berlin, 1970; urban design cons. The Architects Renewal Com. in Harlem, N.Y.C., 1972; urban designer Urban Design sect. NYC Dept. of Transp., 1972, architect-in-charge Urban Design sect., 1977-84, dir. Office of Urban Design, 1984-86; prin. Ekkehart Schwarz Architect P.C., N.Y.C., 1987—. Mem. Tribeca Community Orgn., N.Y.C., 1984. Mem. AIA, Am. Inst. Cert. Planners. Lutheran. Office: 28 Hubert St New York NY 10013-2041

SCHWARZ, FRED, lawyer, ophthalmic plastic surgeon; b. Trenton, N.J., Dec. 13, 1939; s. Ferdinand and Laura Schwarz. BSEE, Lafayette Coll., 1961; MD, N.J. Coll. Medicine and Dentistry, 1970; MBA, Winthrop U., 1991; JD, Fla. Sch. Law, 1999. Diplomate Nat. Bd. Med. Examiners. Bar: Fla. 2000. Project engr. Astro div. RCA, Princeton, N.J., 1961-66; intern Robert Packer Hosp., Sayre, Pa., 1970-71; resident Guthrie Clinic Ophthalmology/Robert Packer Hosp., 1971-74; Heed fellowship in ophthalmic plastic and reconstructive surgery U. Pa. Med. Sch./Temple Med. Sch./Hahnemann Med. Sch., Phila., 1974-75; pvt. practice law Columbia, SC, 1975—. Vice chief med. staff Providence Hosp., Columbia, 1984, chief med. staff, 1985; cons. Dorn VA Hosp., Columbia, 1975—, Moncrief Hosp., Columbia, 1975-89. Contbr. numerous articles to sci. engring. and med. publs., 1962—. Heed (Found.) Ophthalmic fellow, Chgo., 1975. Fellow Am. Coll. Legal Medicine; mem. AMA, S.C. Med. Soc., S.C. Ophthalmology Soc., Ctrl. S.C. Ophthalmology Soc. (pres. 1983), Soc. Heed Fellows, Fla. Bar. Roman Catholic. Avocations: tennis, skiing, model trains, computers. Home: 10120 Two Notch Rd Ste 2108 Columbia SC 29223-4395 Office: Drs Schwarz and Milne PA 1655 Brabham Ave Ste 100 Columbia SC 29204-2039 E-mail: fschwarzmdjd@docemail.com.

SCHWARZ, FREDERICK A.O., JR. lawyer; b. N.Y.C., Apr. 20, 1935; s. Frederick August Otto and Mary Delafield (DuBois) S.; m. Marian Ladd, June 19, 1959; children: Frederick August Otto III, Adair L., Eliza Ladd; m. Frederica Perera, May 11, 1996. BA in History magna cum laude, Harvard Coll., 1957, LLB magna cum laude, 1960; LLD (hon.), N.Y. Law Sch., 1987, CUNY, 1993. Bar: N.Y. 1961, U.S. Dist. Ct. (so. dist.) N.Y. 1963, U.S. Ct. Appeals (2nd cir.) 1978, U.S. Ct. Appeals (9th cir.) 1972, U.S. Ct. Appeals (10th cir.) 1973, U.S. Supreme Ct. 1973. Law clk. to chief judge J. Edward Lumbard U.S. Ct. of Appeals, 2d Circuit, 1960-61; asst. commr. for law revision Govt. of No. Nigeria, 1961-62; assoc. firm Cravath, Swaine & Moore, N.Y.C., 1963-68, ptnr., 1969-75, 1976-81, 87—; chmn. N.Y.C. Charter Revision Commn., 1989; corp. counsel City of N.Y., 1982-86; chief counsel Senate Select Com. on Intelligence, 1975-76. Speaker in the field. Author: Nigeria: The Tribes, The Nation, or the Race, 1966; Editor Harvard Law Sch. Law Review. Contbr. articles to profl. jours. Chmn. Fund for the City of N.Y., 1977-81, 87-97; pres. Vera Inst. Justice, 1978-81, chmn. 1987-98; mem. bd. overseers Harvard U., 1977-83; mem. Com. to Visit Harvard Coll., N.Y.-N.J. Citizens Commn. on AIDS; trustee Experiment in Internat. Living, 1965-82; bd. dirs. NAACP Legal Def. Fund. Constl. Edn. Found., Manhattan Bowery Corp., 1970-81, Lawyers for the Public Interest, 1976-81, FAO Schwarz, 1970-85; chair leadership N.Y. Adv. Coun., 1989—; trustee Nat. Resources Def. Coun., 1987-92, chmn., 1992—, Legal Action Center, 1973-81, N.Y.C. Criminal Justice Agy., 1977-81, Town Sch., 1972-80, Am. Com. on Africa, 1965-79, Milton Acad., 1960's, NAACP Legal Def. Fund, Constitutional Edn. Found., William Nelson Cromwell Found.; trustee The A Theater Found., 1992—. Recipient Liberty award Lambda Legal Def. and Edn. Fund, 1987, The Louis Lefkowitz award Fordham Urban Law Jour. 1990, Civic Leadership award Citizens Union City of N.Y., 1990, The Whitney North Seymour Pub. Svc. award Fed. Bar Coun., 1991., Fellow N.Y. Bar Found.; mem. ABA, Assn. of Bar of City of N.Y. (mem. exec. com. 1986-90, coun. on criminal justice, chmn. juvenile justice com. 1980-81, chmn. nominating com. 1983, Cardozo lectr. 1991), Am. Law Inst., Harvard Law Sch. Assn. of N.Y.C. (pres. 1983-84), N.Y. State Bar Assn., N.Y.C. Bar Assn. Office: Ste 2003 Washington County Courthouse Washington PA 15301 also: Cravath, Swain & Moore 825 8th Ave Fl 38 New York NY 10019-7475

SCHWARZ, GERARD, conductor, musician; b. Weehawken, N.J., Aug. 19, 1947; m. Jody Greitzer, June 23, 1984; children: Alysandra, Daniel, Gabriella, Julian. BS, MA, Juilliard Sch., 1972; DFA (hon.), Fairleigh Dickinson U., Seattle U.; DMus (hon.), U. Puget Sound. Trumpet player Am. Symphony Orch., 1965-72, Am. Brass Quintet, 1965-73, N.Y. Philharm., 1973-77; trumpet player, guest condr. Aspen Music Festival, 1969-75, bd. dirs., 1973-75; music dir. Erick Hawkins Dance Co., 1967-72, SoHo Ensemble, 1969-75, Eliot Feld Ballet Co., N.Y.C., 1972-78, Music Sch. Princeton (N.J.) U., N.Y. Chamber Symphony, 1977—, L.A. Chamber Orch., 1978-86, White Mountains (N.H.) Music Festival, 1978-80, Music Today at Merkin Concert Hall, N.Y.C., 1988-89; music advisor Mostly Mozart Festival, Lincoln Ctr., 1982-84, music dir., 1984—. Music advisor Seattle Symphony, 1983-84, prin. condr., 1984-85, music dir., 1985—; mus. dir. Royal Liverpool Philharm. Orch., 2001—; artistic advisor Tokyu Bunkamura's Orchard Hall, Japan, 1994—; mem. faculty Juilliard Sch., N.Y.C., 1975-83, Mannes Coll. Music, 1973-79, Montclair (N.J.) State Coll., 1975-80; guest condr. various orchs. including Phila. Orch., L.A. Philharm., St. Louis, Buffalo, Detroit, San Francisco, Atlanta, Houston, Pitts., Minn., Jerusalem Symphony, Israel Chamber Orch., Moscow Philharm., Moscow Radio Orch., Orch. Nat. de France, Paris, London Symphony Orch., Frankfurt Radio, Stockholm Radio, Helsinki Philharm., Ensemble InterContemporain, Monte Carlo Philharm., Nat. Orch. Spain, English Chamber Orch., London Symphony, Scottish Chamber Orch., City of Birmingham (Eng.) Symphony, Nouvel Orchestre Philharmonique, Sydney (Australia) Symphony, Melbourne (Australia) Symphony, Orchestre Nat. de Lyon, France, Orchestre Philharm. de Montpellier, France, Washington Opera, Da Capo Chamber Players, 20th Century Chamber Orch., Chamber Music Soc. Lincoln Ctr., San Francisco Opera, Seattle Opera, Tokyu Bunkamura, Japan, Residentie Orch. of The Hague, The Netherlands, St. Louis Symphony, London Mozart Players, Kirov Orch., St. Petersburg, Russia, Tokyo Philharm., Royal Liverpool (Eng.) Philharm., Vancouver (Can.) Symphony Orch., City of London Symphonia, Evian Festival in France. Rec. artist Columbia, Nonesuch, Vox, MMO, Desto, Angel, Delos Records; record: Seattle Symphony 1994-95 Season, 1995, New Japan Philharmonic, 1998. Bd. dirs. Naumburg Found., 1975—. Recipient award for concert artists Ford Found., 1973, Grammy award nominee, Mumms Ovation award, Record of Yr. awards, Ditson Condrs. award Columbia U., 1989; named Condr. of Yr., Musical Am. Internat. Directory of Performing Arts, 1994.

SCHWARZ, GLENN VERNON, newspaper editor; b. Chgo., Nov. 24, 1947; s. Vernon Edward and LaVerne Louise (Schuster) S.; m. Cynthia Frances Meisenhoelder, June 17, 1984; 1 child, Chloe. BA, San Francisco State U., 1970. Sports writer San Francisco Examiner, 1970—87, sports editor, 1988—2000, San Francisco Chronicle, 2000—. Fundraiser San Francisco Zoological Soc., 1987—. Mem. AP Sports Editors, Baseball Writers Assn. Am. (bd. dirs. 1986-87). Avocation: nature travel. Office: San Francisco Chronicle 901 Mission St San Francisco CA 94103

SCHWARZ, J(AMES) CONRAD, psychology educator; b. Hartford, Conn., Sept. 19, 1936; s. William Merlin and Violet May (List) S.; m. Lois J. Stonebraker, 1956 (div. 1981); m. Carolina A.B. Herfkens, Oct. 12, 1984. BS, Pa. State U., 1958; MA, Ohio State U., 1961, PhD, 1963. Lic. clin. psychologist, Conn.; cert. psychologist, N.Y. Rsch. asst. Pa. State U., 1957-58; psychol. trainee Chillicothe (Ohio) VA N.P. Hosp., 1958-60; psychol. intern Columbus (Ohio) VA Out-Patient Clinic, 1960-61; instr. psychology Bowling Green (Ohio) State U., 1962-64, asst. prof., 1964-65; asst. prof., mem. teaching faculty grad. tng. Syracuse U, 1965-70, assoc. prof., 1970-72; assoc. prof., mem. teaching faculty grad. tng. program U. Conn., Storrs, 1972-75, prof., mem. teaching faculty grad. tng. program, 1975—; pvt. practice clin. psychology Mansfield Ctr., Conn., 1973-94, North Windham, 1995-96. Asst. field assessment officer Peace Corps Tng. Programs, 1967-68; clin. psychology cons. VA Out-Patient Clinic, Syracuse, 1968-72, Onodaga Co. Mental Health Clinic, Syracuse, 1969-72; with Windham Pub. Schs.-Project Self-Search, 1974-76; cons. Ea. Conn. Mental Health Group, 1974-83, Bermuda Govt., Child Devel. Project, 1979-82, Optimum Resource, Inc., Software for Learning Disabled Children. Author: Deck-a-Dot Manual: An Educational Card Game Program to Develop Arithmetic Readiness, 1970; If This Is Love, Why Do I Feel So Insecure?, 1989, 90, Teacher's Manual for Optimum Resource Reading Program, 1991; cons. editor Devel. Psychology, 1981-84; co-developer The Optimum Resource Reading Program, 1991; contbr. articles to profl. jours. USPHS fellow, 1958-59, 61-62; grantee Nat. Lab. Early Childhood Edn. Ctr. Syracuse U., 1968-71, NIMH, 1978-83, 84-85, Nat. Inst. Alcohol Abuse and Addiction, 1986-89, U. Conn. Rsch. Found., 1985-87. Mem. APA (div. clin., family psychology), Sigma Xi, Phi Beta Kappa, Psi Chi, Phi Eta Sigma, Phi Kappa Phi. Avocations: tennis, landscape gardening. Office: U Conn Dept Psychology 406 Babbidge Rd Storrs Mansfield CT 06269-9025

SCHWARZ, LOUIS JAY, financial advisor; b. Chgo., May 15, 1946; s. Milton Joseph and Anita (Holtshutz) S.; m. Doris Ethel Fowler, May 31, 1969; children: Jovialis Ona, Iris Nana, Janis Anna. BA, Gallaudet U., 1968; postgrad., Ill. Inst. Tech., 1968-69, U. Md., 1970-72. CFP; registered fin. cons.; registered investment advisor. Tchr. Ill. Sch. for Deaf, Jacksonville, 1969-70; tax preparer Income Tax Svc. for the Deaf, Silver Spring, Md., 1971—; chemist U.S. Geol. Survey, Reston, Va., 1970-85; agt. Nat. Fraternal Soc. of Deaf, Mt. Prospect, Ill., 1975-93; owner, fin. planner Schwarz Fin. Concepts, Silver Spring, 1983—; pres. Giuntoli & Schwarz, Inc., Gaithersburg, Md., 1987-91. Stockbroker Integrated Resources Equity Corp., N.Y.C., 1984-89; cons. instr. Nat. Ctr. for Fin. Edn., San Francisco, 1986—; pres. Met. Wash. Telecom. Directory for the Deaf Inc., Silver Spring, 1988—; registered rep. Royal Alliance Assocs., Inc., N.Y.C., 1989—; adj. prof. Gallaudet U. Sch. Mgmt. 1993-94, 97—. Author: (with L. Dunton) About Your Future, 1988; columnist NAD Broadcasters, 1984-95, Silent News, 1984-95, Deaf Nation, 1996-2000, Newswaves, 1996-2000, Deaf Digest, 1999-. Active Nat. Assn. of Deaf, 1972—, Md. Assn. of Deaf, 1972—, Montgomery County Assn. Deaf, 1990—; consumer adv. C&P Tel. Co., 1981-84; bd. dirs. Telecommunications for Deaf Inc., 1976-82; commr. Montgomery County Commn. for Handicapped Individuals, 1979-83; adv. coun. Telecommunications Exch. of the Deaf, Inc., 1981-87. Named Top Prodr., Nat. Fraternal Soc. of Deaf, 1979, 83, Outstanding Handicapped Fed. Employee, U.S. Dept. Interior, 1974, 77; recipient Internat. Yr. of Disabled Persons Honor award U.S. Dept. Interior, 1981, Montgomery County Coun. Bus. Svc. award, 1988, 89, Knight of Flying Fingers award Nat. Assn. Deaf, 1990, 92, Disting. Svc. award Md. Assn. Deaf, 1993, Bus. of Yr. award Montgomery County Assn. of Deaf, 1997, Cmty. Svc. award Md. Assn. Deaf, 2001. Mem. Nat. Deaf Bus. Inst., Inc. (bd. dirs. 2001—), Internat. Assn. Registered Fin. Cons., Fin. Planning Assn., Deaf and Hard of Hearing Entrepreneurs Coun. (pres. 1993-96, bd. dirs. 1989-96). Jewish. Avocations: photography, swimming, cycling, hiking, gardening. Office: Schwarz Fin Concepts 814 Thayer Ave Ste 301 Silver Spring MD 20910-4500 E-mail: wswlouis@moneysigns.com.

SCHWARZ, MICHAEL, lawyer; b. Brookline, Mass., Oct. 19, 1952; s. Jules Lewis and Estelle (Kosberg) S.; m. Rebecca Handy; 1 child, Patrick Joshua Charles. BA magna cum laude, U. No. Colo., 1975; postgrad., U. N.Mex., 1977, JD, 1980; reader in Negligence Law, Oxford U., 1978; diploma in Legal Studies, Cambridge U., 1981. Bar: N.Mex. 1980, U.S. Dist. Ct. N.Mex. 1980, U.S. Ct. Appeals (10th, D.C. and Fed. cirs.) 1982, U.S. Ct. Internat. Trade 1982, U.S. Tax Ct. 1982, N.Y. 1987, U.S. Supreme Ct. 1983; cert. U.S.A. hockey coach, advanced level. Vol. VISTA, Albuquerque, 1975-77; rsch. fellow N.Mex. Legal Support Project, 1978-79; supr. law Cambridge (Eng.) U., 1980-81; law clk. to chief justice Supreme Ct. N.Mex., Santa Fe, 1981-82; pvt. practice, 1982—. Spl. pros. City of Santa Fe, 1985, spl. asst. atty. gen., 1986-88; mem. west editl. adv. com. Social Security Reporting Svc., 1983-95; mem. N.Mex. Supreme Ct. Com. Profl. Responsibility, 1990—, chmn., 1998—. Author: New Mexico Appellate Manual, 1990, 2d edit., 1996; contbr. articles to profl. jours. Vice-dir. Colo. Pub. Interest Rsch. Group, 1974; scoutmaster Great S.W. Area coun. Boy Scouts Am., 1977—79; mem. N.Mex. Acupuncture Lic. Bd., 1983; level 2 referee, head coach Squirt Gold Trailrunners; coaching level USA Hockey. Recipient Cert. of Appreciation Cambridge U., 1981, Nathan Burke Meml. award, 1980, N.Mex. Supreme Ct. Cert. Recognition, 1992, 93, 95, N.Mex. Supreme Ct. Cert. Appreciation Outstanding Svc. to Legal Sys., 2001. Mem.: ACLU, ATLA, ABA (10th cir. editor 1998, litigation com. on profl. responsibility, mem. Ctr. Profl. Responsibility, litigation com. on pretrial practice and discovery), N.Mex. State Bar (chmn. 1990—91, bd. dirs. employment law sect. 1990—96, family law sect. bd. 1999—2001), Bar Assn. U.S. Dist. Ct. Dist. N.Mex. (1st judical dis. bar assoc. pres. 1990—91), Santa Fe Trailrunners Hockey Assn. (bd. dirs. 2001—02). Home and Office: PO Box 1656 Santa Fe NM 87504-1656 E-mail: barristr@nm.net.

SCHWARZ, PAUL WINSTON, judge; b. Sacramento, Sept. 24, 1948; s. Egon Ferdinand and Louise (Fulcher) S.; m. Virginia Adams, July 12, 1987; children: Austin Winston, Julie Adams. BA in Philosophy, Calif. State U., San Jose, 1971; JD, Santa Clara U., 1974. Bar: Pa. 1975, U.S. Supreme Ct. 1978, D.C. Ct. Appeals 1987, Va. 1992. Commd. 2d. lt. U.S. Army, 1971, advanced through grades to lt. col., 1992; corp. counsel Oracle Corp., Bethesda, Md., 1992-93; sec., v.p. and corp. counsel Oracle Complex Systems Corp., Arlington, Va., 1992-93; counsel McAleese & Associates, P.C., Washington, 1993-94; apptd. U.S. adminstrv. law judge, 1994. Author: A Roadmap into the World of Federal Contracts, 1989. Decorated Legion of Merit, U.S. Army Gen. Staff Badge award. Mem. ABA (chmn. com. on pub. contract law gen. practice sect. 1991, vice-chmn. judiciary com. 1995), Army and Navy Country Club, Army and Navy Club Washington D.C., Nat. Soc. SAR. Episcopalian. Avocations: swimming, pistol. Home: 5336 Sugar Hill Dr Houston TX 77056-2028

SCHWARZ, RALPH JACQUES, retired engineering educator; b. Hamburg, Germany, June 13, 1922; naturalized, 1944; s. Simon J. and Anna (Schoendorff) S.; m. Irene Lassally, Sept. 9, 1951; children: Ronald Paul, Sylvia Anne. BS, Columbia U., 1943, MS, 1944, PhD, 1949; postgrad., Poly. Inst. Bklyn., 1944-45, N.Y. U., 1946-47. Registered profl. engr., N.Y. Mem. faculty Columbia U., 1943-92, prof. elec. engring., 1958-92, chmn. dept., 1958-65, 71-72, assoc. dean acad. affairs Faculty Engring. and Applied Sci., 1972-75, acting dean, 1975-76, 80-81, vice dean, Thayer Lindsley prof., 1976-92, Thayer Lindsley prof. emeritus, 1992—; cons. systems analysis, communications and noise theory, 1945—. Vis. assoc. prof. UCLA, 1956; adviser Inst. Internat. Edn., 1952-65; vis. scientist IBM Research Center, 1969-70 Author: (with M.G. Salvadori) Differential Equations in Engineering Problems, 1954, (with B. Friedland) Linear Systems, 1965. Bd. dirs. Armstrong Meml. Research Found.; trustee Associated Univs., Inc., 1980-92. Fellow IEEE (chmn. circuit theory group 1963-65, Centennial medal 1984); mem. Communications Soc. (bd. govs.), Am. Soc. Engring. Edn., AAAS, Sigma Xi, Tau Beta Pi, Pi Mu Epsilon, Eta Kappa Nu. Home: 1270 North Ave # 5G New Rochelle NY 10804-2601 Office: Columbia U Engring Sch 116th St And Broadway New York NY 10027 E-mail: rjs613@aol.com.

SCHWARZ, RICHARD HOWARD, obstetrician, gynecologist, educator; b. Easton, Pa., Jan. 10, 1931; s. Howard Eugene and Blanche Elizabeth (Smith) S.; m. Patricia Marie Lewis, Mar. 11, 1978; children by previous marriage: Martha L., Nancy Schwarz Tedesco, Paul H., Mary Katherine Schwarz Murray. MD, Jefferson Med. Coll., 1955; MA (hon.), U. Pa., 1971. Diplomate Am. Bd. Ob-Gyn. (examiner 1977-95). Intern, then resident Phila. Gen. Hosp., 1955-59; prof. U. Pa., Phila., 1963-78; prof., chmn. Downstate Med. Ctr., Bklyn., 1978-90, dean, v.p. acad. affairs, 1983-89, provost, v.p. clin. affairs, 1988-93, interim pres., 1993-94, prof. ob.-gyn., 1990-96, disting. Svc. prof. ob.-gyn. emeritus, 1996; chmn. ob.-gyn. N.Y. Meth. Hosp., 1996—; prof. ob.-gyn. Cornell U. Med. Coll., N.Y.C., 1996—. Obstetrical cons. March of Dimes Birth Defects Found., 1995— Author: Septic Abortion, 1968. Editor: Handbook of Obstetric Emergencies, 1984, mem. editorial bd. jour. Ob-Gyn., Milw., 1983-87; contbr. articles to profl. jours. Bd. dirs. March of Dimes, N.Y.C., 1985-95. Capt. USAF, 1959-63. Fellow Royal Coll ObGyn, 1999; mem. Am. Coll. Obstetricians and Gynecologists (chmn. dist. 2 1984-87, v.p. 1989-90, pres. elect 1990-91, pres. 1991-92). Republican. Presbyterian. Office: NY Meth Hosp 506 6th St Brooklyn NY 11215-3645 E-mail: ris9002@nyp.org.

SCHWARZ, RONALD PAUL, gastroenterologist; b. N.Y.C., July 9, 1952; s. Ralph J. and Irene (Lassally) S.; m. Mina Lea Levin, May 4, 1980; 1 child, Jonathan. BA, Yale Coll., 1973; MD, Cornell U., 1977. Diplomate Am. Bd. Internal Medicine, Am. Bd. Gastroenterology. Resident internal medicine, fellow gastroenterology U. N.C., Chapel Hill, 1977-83; pvt. practice Raleigh (N.C.) Med. Group, 1983—. Recipient Leadership award Triangle chpt. Crohns and Colitis Found. of Am., 1996. Fellow Am. Coll. Gastroenterology. Avocation: photography. Office: Raleigh Med Group 3521 Haworth Dr Raleigh NC 27609-7216

SCHWARZ, WOLFGANG, psychologist; b. Stuttgart, Germany, Oct. 30, 1926; came to U.S., 1934, naturalized, 1940; s. Mole and Edith (Gutstein) S.; m. Cynthia Mae Johnson, Sept. 12, 1949 (div.); children: Amy Maria, Casey Andrew, Darcy Lynn, Priscilla Anne, Lydia Beth, Emily Jane; m. Susan Decker, 1976; children: Jaime Bartholomew, Noah. AB, NYU, 1948, AM, 1949, PhD, 1956. Diplomate Am. Bd. Profl. Psychology. Intern Bellevue Med. Ctr., N.Y.C., 1949-51; chief psychology Rip Van Winkle Med. Found., Hudson, N.Y., 1951-53; dir. psychology Hillcrest Med. Ctr., Tulsa, 1953-56, Hollywood Presbyn. Hosp., L.A., 1956-58; cons. psychology Cedars Lebanon Hosp., 1956-58; spl. cons. D.C. Govt., 1959-61, NIH, Bethesda, Md., 1962-64; dir. psychol. rsch. Mass. Dept. Mental Health, Boston and Malden, 1965-68; individual practice clin. psychology Tulsa, 1953-56, Beverly Hills, Calif., 1956-59, Washington, 1959-63, Malden and Concord, Mass., 1963-73, Mt. Kisco, N.Y., 1973—. Lectr. U. Tulsa, 1953-54, L.A. State Coll., 1956-57; asst. prof. Howard U., 1961; assoc. prof. George Washington U., 1961-62; vis. rsch. asst. Harvard Psychiatry Lab., 1966-68; prof. Malden Hosp., 1968-71; cons. No. Westchester Hosp., 1974—, United Hosp., 1975—, Four Winds Hosp., 1975-80; cons. psychology Peace Corps, Mass., 1969—. Author: A Survey of the Mental Health Facilities in the Disctict of Columbia, 1961; contbr. articles to profl. jours. and chpt. to book. Mem. exec. com. Mayor's Model City Program, Malden, 1967-68. With USNR, 1945-46. Recipient Founder's Day award NYU, 1956, Individual award USPHS/NIH, 1960-64. Mem. APA, N.Y. Psychol. Assn., Mass. psychol. Assn., Washington Soc. Hist. of Medicine (exec. com. 1963-64), N.Y. Acad. Scis., Psi Chi, Beta Lambda Sigma. Home: 81 Paulding Dr Chappaqua NY 10514-2818 Office: 101 S Bedford Rd Mount Kisco NY 10549-3439

SCHWARZER, WILLIAM W, federal judge; b. Berlin, Apr. 30, 1925; came to U.S., 1938, naturalized, 1944; s. John F. and Edith M. (Daniel) S.; m. Anne Halbersleben, Feb. 2, 1951; children: Jane Elizabeth, Andrew William. AB cum laude, U. So. Calif., 1948; LLB cum laude, Harvard U., 1951. Bar: Calif. 1953, U.S. Supreme Ct. 1967. Teaching fellow Harvard U. Law Sch., 1951-52; asso. firm McCutchen, Doyle, Brown & Enersen, San Francisco, 1952-60, ptnr., 1960-76; judge U.S. Dist. Ct (no. dist.) Calif., San Francisco, 1976—; dir. Fed. Jud. Ctr., Washington, 1990-95. Sr. counsel Pres.'s Commn. on CIA Activities Within the U.S., 1975; chmn. U.S. Jud. Conf. Com. Fed.-State Jurisdiction, 1987-90; mem. faculty Nat. Inst. Trial Advocacy, Fed. Jud. Ctr., All-ABA, U.S.-Can. Legal Exch., 1987, Anglo-U.S. Jud. Exch., 1994-95, Salzburg Seminar on Am. Studies; disting. prof. Hastings Coll. Law U. Calif. Author: Managing Antitrust and Other Complex Litigation, 1982, Civil Discovery and Manadatory Disclosure, 1994, Federal Civil Procedure Before Trial, 1994; contbr. articles to legal publs., aviation jours. Trustee World Affairs Coun. No. Calif., 1961-88; chmn. bd. trustees Marin Country Day Sch., 1963-66; mem. Marin County Aviation Commn., 1969-76; mem. vis. com. Harvard Law Sch., 1981-86. Served with Intelligence, U.S. Army, 1943-46. Fellow Am. Coll. Trial Lawyers (S. Gates award 1992), Am. Bar Found.; mem. ABA (Meador Rosenberg award 1995), Am. Law Inst., San Francisco Bar Assn., State Bar Calif., Coun. Fgn. Rels. Office: 450 Golden Gate Ave San Francisco CA 94102-3661

SCHWARZKOPF, GLORIA A. education educator, psychotherapist; b. Chgo., Apr. 20, 1926; m. Alfred E. Grossenbacher. BE, Chgo. State U., 1949, ME in Libr. Sci., 1956. Cert. nat. recovery specialist, reality therapist; libr. sci. endorsement; cert. hypnotherapist; cert. nat. forensic counselor; nat. cert. domestic violence counselor. Tchr. Chgo. Bd. Edn., 1949-91, inservice trainer in substance abuse, 2001, 1990—91; co-therapist ATC outpatient unit Ingalls Meml. Hosp., Chgo., 1981-86; recovery specialist Interaction Inst., Evergreen Park, 1993-95; quality assurance evaluation Ill. State Bd. Edn., 1997-2000; ct. watcher Cook County, 1994—2002. Instr. Govs. State U., University Park, Ill., 1987, University Park, 91, South Suburban Coll., South Holland, Ill., 1991, Prairie State Coll., Chicago Heights, Ill., 1993, Chicago Heights, 96; with CP5 Project Assist Program, 2000—02. Columnist Peoples Choice Weekly, 1991-93. Citizens Amb. Program del. to Russia and Czechoslovakia, 1996; sch. quality assurance reviewer Ill. State Bd. Edn., 1997-99; ct. watcher, 1995-2002; presenter in field of alcoholism. Recipient Sci. Tchr. of Yr. award, 1976, Svc. Recognition award, 1985, IMSA Recognition award, 1988; grantee Chgo. Pub. Sch., 1981. Mem. NEA, Nat. Assn. Forensic Counselors, Sci. Tchrs. Assn., Ill. Alcoholism Counselors Alliance, Nat. Alcoholism Coun., Am. Assn. Hypnotherapists, Am. Assn. Behavioral Therapists, Soc. of Am. for Recovery (nat. cert. recovery specialist). Home: 2216 W 91st St Chicago IL 60620-6238

SCHWARZROCK, SHIRLEY PRATT, writer, lecturer, educator; b. Mpls., Feb. 27, 1914; d. Theodore Ray and Myrtle Pearl (Westphal) Pratt; m. Loren H. Schwarzrock, Oct. 19, 1945 (dec. 1966); children: Kay Linda, Ted Kenneth, Lorraine V. BS, U. Minn., 1935, MA, 1942, PhD, 1974. Sec. to chmn. speech dept. U. Minn., Mpls., 1935, instr. in speech, 1946, team tchr. in creative arts workshops for tchrs., 1955-56, guest lectr. Dental Sch., 1967-72, asst. prof. (part-time) practice administrn. Sch. Dentistry, 1972-80; tchr. speech, drama and English Preston (Minn.) H.S., 1935-37; tchr. speech, drama and English, dir. dramatics Owatonna (Minn.) H.S., 1937-39; tchr. creative dramatics and English, tchr.-counselor Webster Groves (Mo.) Jr. H.S., 1939-40; dir. dramatics and tchr.-counselor Webster Groves Sr. H.S., 1940-43; exec. sec. bus. and profl. dept. YWCA, Mpls., 1943-45; tchr. speech and drama Covent of the Visitation, St. Paul, 1958; editor pro-tem Am. Acad. Dental Practice Adminstrn., 1966-68. Guest tchr. Coll. St. Catherine, St. Paul, 1969; vol. mgr. Gift Shop, Eitel Hosp., Mpls., 1981-83, Edina Cmty. Resource Pool, 1992-95; cmty. citizen mem. planning, evaluating, reporting com. Edina Pub. Sch. Sys., 1993-96; tutor for reading, writing, and speaking, 1993-96; cons. for dental med. programs Normandale C.C., Bloomington, Minn., 1968; cons. on pub. rels. to dentists, 1954-96; guest lectr. to various dental groups, 1966-95; lectr. Internat. Congress on Arts and Comm., 1980, Am. Inst. Banking, 1981; condr. tutorials in speaking and profl. office mgmt., 1985-96; owner Shirley Schwawrzrock's Exec. Support Svc., 1989-99; cons. to mktg. comm. mgr. Ergodyne Corp., St. Paul, 1991-92; freelance editor med. support bus., 1992. Author: (books) (series) Coping With Personal Identity, Coping With Human

Relationships, Coping With Facts and Fantasies, Coping With Teenage Problems, 1984; individual book titles include: Do I Know the "Me" Others See?, My Life-What Shall I Do With It?, Living With Loneliness, Learning to Make Better Decisions, Grades, What's So Important About Them, Anyway?, Facts and Fantasies About Alcohol, Facts and Fantasies About Smoking, Food as a Crutch, Facts and Fantasies About the Roles of Men and Women, You Always Communicate Something, Appreciating People-Their Likenesses and Differences, Fitting In, To Like and Be Liked, Can You Talk With Someone Else?, Coping With Emotional Pain, Some Common Crutchees, Parents Can Be a Problem, Coping With Cliques, Crises Youth Face Today, Effective Dental Assisting, (with L.H. Schwarzrock) 1954, 59, 67, (with J.R. Jensen) 1973, 78, 82, (with J.R. Jensen, Kay Schwarzrock, Lorraine Schwarzrock) 1990, Workbook for Effective Dental Assisting, 1968, 73, 78, 82, 90; (with Donovan F. Ward) Effective Medical Assisting, 1969, 76, Manual for Effective Assisting, 1969, 76; (with C.G. Wrenn) The Coping With Series of Books for High School Students, 1970, The Coping With Manual, 1973, Contemporary Concerns of Youth, 1980; contbr. articles to profl. jours. Pres. Univ. Elem. Sch. PTA, 1955-56; vol. judge Minn. State Hist. Day Program, 1994-98. Fellow Internat. Biog. Assn.; mem. Minn. Acad. Dental Practice Adminstrn. (hon.), Authors Guild, Minn. Hist Soc., Minn. Geneal. Soc., Zeta Phi Eta (pres. 1948-49), Eta Sigma Upsilon. Home: 7448 W Shore Dr Edina MN 55435-4022 *Growing up as a latch key child, challenged to accomplish adult tasks accompanied by "You can do it, kid", provided me with the ability to face challenges from scrubbing floors to delving deeply into reseach. Assured that there is a solution to every problem, I absorbed the knowledge and skills my professors taught, developed my creativity and spiritual awareness, and learned to listen sensitively and compassionately. This training enabled me to draw forth creative expression from adolescents, respond to their many needs, and to develop adults' communication skills in numerous settings.*

SCHWARZTRAUBER, SAYRE ARCHIE, former naval officer, maritime consultant; b. Zion, Ill., June 23, 1929; s. Archie Douglas and Eleanor Miriam (Sayrs) S.; m. Beryl Constance Stewart, June 27, 1953; children: Sayre Archie, Beryl Ann, Heidi, Holly. BS cum laude, Maryville Coll., 1951; MA, Am. U., 1964, PhD, 1970. Commd. ensign USN, 1952, advanced through grades to rear adm., 1976; comdr. River Squadron 5, Vietnam, 1968-69, U.S.S. Decatur guided missile destroyer, 1970-71, Navy Recruiting Area 4, 1974-76; dep. chief staff Supreme Command Atlantic (NATO), 1976-79; co-dir. U.S.-Spanish Combined Staff, Madrid, 1979-81; dir. Inter-Am. Def. Coll., Washington, 1981-83; ret., 1983; apptd. rear adm. U.S. Maritime Svc., 1984. Mem. Sec. of Navy Adv. Com., 1986-90; nat. and internat. lectr. strategic naval and maritime matters, 1973—. Author: The Three-Mile Limit of Territorial Seas, 1972, Schwarztrauber, Stewart and Related Families, 1995; editor Mass. Maritime Mag., 1987-90; contbr. articles, essays and revs. to profl. jours. Ruling elder Presbyn. Ch. U.S.A., 1965-86. Decorated Def. Disting. Svc. Medal, Legion of Merit, Cross of Gallantry (Vietnam), Gran Cruz de Merito (Spain); recipient Alfred Thayer Mahan award Navy League, 1974. Mem. SAR (pres. Cape Cod chpt. 1993-95, state reg. and genealogist 1992—, state pres. 1998-99, nat. trustee 1999-2000), Gamewardens of Vietnam, Nat. Geneal. Soc., U.S. Naval Inst., Am. Legion, Masons (adjutant Aleppo Temple), VFW, Mil. Order World Wars, Mensa, Travelers' Century Club, Phi Kappa Phi, Pi Gamma Mu, Pi Sigma Alpha, Theta Alpha Phi. Home and Office: PO Box 589 Osterville MA 02655-0589

SCHWEBEL, MILTON, psychologist, educator; b. Troy, N.Y., May 11, 1914; s. Frank and Sarah (Oxenhandler) S.; m. Bernice Lois Davison, Sept. 3, 1939; children: Andrew I., Robert S. AB, Union Coll., 1934; MA, SUNY, Albany, 1936; PhD, Columbia U., 1949; Cert. in Psychotherapy, Postgrad. Ctr. Mental Health, N.Y.C., 1958. Lic. psychologist, N.Y., N.J.; diplomate Am. Bd. Examiners Profl. Psychology. Asst. prof. psychology Mohawk Champlain Coll., 1946-49; asst. to prof. edn., dept. chmn., assoc. dean NYU, 1949-67; dean, prof. Grad. Sch. Edn., Rutgers U., New Brunswick, N.J., 1967-77; prof. Grad. Sch. Applied and Profl. Psychology, 1977-85, prof. emeritus, 1985—. Vis. prof. U. So. Calif., U. Hawaii; postdoctoral fellow Postgrad. Ctr. Mental Health, N.Y.C., 1954-58, lectr. psychology, 1958-60; cons. NIMH, U.S., state and city depts. edn., ednl. ministries in Europe, Asia, univs. and pub. schs.; pvt. cons. psychologist and psychotherapist, 1953—; disting. cons. & faculty Saybrook Grad. Sch. & Rsch. Ctr., 1999—. Author: A Guide to a Happier Family, 1989, Personal Adjustment and Growth, 1990, Student Teachers Handbook, 3d edit., 1996, Interests of Pharmacists, 1951, Health Counseling, 1953, Who Can Be Educated?, 1968, Remaking America's Three School System: Now Separate and Unequal, 2002; editor: Mental Health Implications of Life in the Nuclear Age, 1986, Facilitating Cognitive Development, 1986, Promoting Cognitive Growth Over the Life Span, 1990, Behavioral Science and Human Survival, 1965, The Impact of Ideology on the I.Q. Controversy, 1975; editor Peace & Conflict: Jour. Peace Psychology, 1993-2000; co-editor Bull. Peace Psychology, 1991-94; mem. editl. bd. Am. Jour. Orthopsychiatry, Readings in Mental Health, Jour. Contemporary Psychotherapy, Jour. Counseling Psychology, Jour. Social Issues, others. Mem. sci. adv. bd. Internat. Ctr. for Enhancement of Learning Potential, 1988—; trustee Edn. Law Ctr., 1973-81, Nat. Com. Employment Youth, Nat. Child Labor Com., 1967-75, Union Exptl. Colls. and Univs., 1976-78; pres. Nat. Orgn. for Migrant Children, 1980-85; pres. Inst. of Arts and Humanities, 1984-95. Served with AUS, 1943-46, ETO. Met. Applied Rsch. Coun. fellow, 1970-71. Fellow APA, Am. Psychol. Soc., Am. Orthopsychiatry Assn., Soc. Psychol. Study Social Issues, Jean Piaget Soc. (trustee), Am. Ednl. Rsch. Assn., N.Y. Acad. Scis., Psychologists for Social Responsibility (pres.), Inst. Arts and Humanities Edn. (pres.), Sigma Xi. Home: Apt 17L 1050 George St New Brunswick NJ 08901-1068 Office: Rutgers U Grad Sch Applied and Profl Psychology 152 Frelinghuysen Rd Piscataway NJ 08854-8020 E-mail: mschwebe@rci.rutgers.edu.

SCHWEBEL, RENATA MANASSE, sculptor; b. Zwickau, Germany, Mar. 6, 1930; came to U.S., 1940, naturalized, 1946; d. George and Anne Marie (Simon) Manasse; m. Jack P. Schwebel, May 10, 1955; children: Judith, Barbara, Diane. BA, Antioch Coll., 1953; MFA, Columbia U., 1961; student, Arts Students League, 1967-69. Cartographer Ecostate Inc., Ridgewood, N.J., 1949; display artist Silvestri Inc., Chgo., 1950-51; asst. Mazzolini Art Found., Yellow Springs, Ohio, 1952. One-woman shows include Columbia U., 1961, Greenwich Art Barn, Conn., 1975, Sculpture Ctr., N.Y.C., 1979, Pelham Art Ctr., N.Y., 1981, New Rochelle Libr. Gallery, 1980, Outdoor Installations Katonah Gallery, 1986, 1989, Berman/Daferner Gallery, N.Y.C., 1992—93, exhibitions include Stamford Mus., Conn., 1967, 1996, Hudson River Mus., Yonkers, N.Y., 1972, 1974, Wadsworth Atheneum, Hartford, 1974, Silvermine Art of the Northwest U.S.A. Anns., 1972, 1976, 1980, 1995, 1998, Silvermine Gallery, 1986, 1991, 2000, 2001, 2002, New Britain Mus. Am. Art, Conn., 1974, Sculptors Guild Anns., 1974—, Imprimatur Gallery, St. Paul, 1985, 1986, Bergen County Mus., N.J., 1983, Sculpture Ctr., 1978—88, Katonah Gallery , N.Y., 1986—90, Cast Iron Gallery, N.Y.C., 1991, 1993, Kyoto (Japan) Gallery, 1993, traveling show exhibitions, , , Represented in permanent collections S.W. Bell, Columbia U., Colt Industries, Am. Airlines, Comcraft Industries, Nairobi, Grüber Haus, Berlin, Mus. Fgn. Art, Sofia, Bulgaria. Bd. dirs. Fine Arts Fedn., N.Y., 1985-87; trustee Sculpture Ctr., 1980-88, chmn. exhbn. com., 1986-88; adv. bd. Pelham Art Ctr., 1982. Mem.: Artists Equity NY, Silvermine Guild, Conn. Soc. Women Artists, Conn. Acad. Fine Arts, Audubon Artists (Chaim Gross award 1980, Medal of Honor 1982, Rennick award 1986, 1990, 1992, 1995), Nat. Assn. Women Artists (Willis Meml. prize 1974, Medal of Honor 1981, Paley Meml. award 1979), Sculptors Guild (bd. dirs. 1975—94, 1995—, pres. 1980—83), Katonah Gallery (artist mem. 1986—90), Ams. for Peace Now (bd. dirs. 1991—2001), Antioch Coll. Assn. (bd. dirs. 1971—77). Home: 10 Dogwood Hills Pound Ridge NY 10576-1508 E-mail: RENATA99M@aol.com.

SCHWEBEL, STEPHEN MYRON, judge, arbitrator; b. N.Y.C., Mar. 10, 1929; s. Victor and Pauline (Pfeffer) S.; m. Louise Ingrid Nancy Killander, Aug. 2, 1972; children: Jennifer, Anna. BA in Govt. magna cum laude with highest honors in govt., Harvard U., 1950; postgrad., Cambridge (Eng.) U., 1950-51; LLB, Yale U., 1954; LLD (hon.), Bhopal (India) U., 1983, Hofstra U., 1997, U. Miami, 2002. Bar: N.Y. 1955, U.S. Supreme Ct. 1965, D.C. 1976. Dir. UN hdqrs. office World Fedn. UN Assns., 1950-53; lectr. Am. fgn. policy various univs. U.S. Dept. State, India, 1952; research, drafting asst. to Trygve Lie for writing of In the Cause of Peace, 1953; assoc. White & Case, N.Y.C., 1954-59; asst. prof. law Harvard U., Cambridge, Mass., 1959-61; asst. legal advisor U.S. Dept. State, Washington, 1961-66, dep. legal advisor, 1973-81; exec. dir. Am. Soc. Internat. Law, 1967-72; Burling prof. internat. law Sch. of Advanced Internat. Studies, Johns Hopkins U., 1967-81; pres. Adminstrv. Tribunal, IMF, 1994—; judge Internat. Ct. Justice, The Hague, The Netherlands, 1981-2000, v.p., 1994-97, pres., 1997-2000; jurist-in-residence John's Hopkins Sch. Adv. Internat. Studies, 2000-01. Hon. fellow Cambridge U. Ctr. for Rsch. in Internat. Law, 1983—; mem. bd. electors Whewell Professorship in Internat. Law U. Cambridge, 1983—; hon. bencher Gray's Inn, London, 1998—; numerous others, 1948—; spl. rep. Micronesian claims U.S. Dept. State, 1966—71; legal adv. U.S. del. 16th-20th and 4th Spl. Gen. Assemblies UN; U.S. assoc. rep. Internat. Ct. Justice, 1962, U.S. dep. agt., 1979, U.S. counsel, 1980; U.S. rep., chmn. U.S. del. to 1st session UN Spl. Com. on Principles Internat. Law concerning friendly rels. and coop. among states, Mexico City, 1964; US rep. numerous other UN coms.; pres. So. Blue Fin Tuna Arbitration, 2000, Eritrea-Yemen Arbitration Tribunal, 1998—2000; mem. Eritrea-Ethiopia Boundary Commn., 2001—; mem. panels arbitrators and conciliators Internat. Ctr. Settlement of Investment Disputes World Bank , 2000—; cons. Ford Found., 1990; chmn. supr. bd. Telders Internat. Law Moot Ct. Competition, The Hague, The Netherlands, 1993—98; chmn. Hauser Scholars Selection Bd., N.Y.U. Law Sch., 1997—2000; vis. lectr. in field. Author: The Secretary-General of the United Nations, 1952, International Arbitration: Three Salient Problems, 1987, Justice in International Law, 1994; editor: The Effectiveness of International Decisions, 1971; mem. editorial bd. Am. Jour. Internat. Law, 1967-81, hon. mem., 1996—; chmn. editorial adv. com. Internat. Legal Materials, 1967-73. Frank Knox fellow Harvard U., 1950-51, Hallows Jud. fellow Marquette U. Law Sch., 2000; recipient Gherini prize Yale Law Sch., 1954, medal of Merit, 1997, Pres. medal Johns Hopkins U., 1992, Harold Weill medal NYU, 1992, Wolfgang Friedmann award Columbia U., 1998. Mem. ABA, Am. Soc. Internat. Law (exec. v.p. 1967-73, hon. v.p. 1982-95, hon. pres. 1996-2001, Manley O. Hudson medal 2000), Internat. Law Assn., Inst. Droit Internat., Coun. Fgn. Rels., Acad. of Experts (v.p. 1995—), Harvard Club (N.Y.C.), Athenaeum (London), Cosmos Club (Washington), Phi Beta Kappa. Avocation: music. Office: 6th Fl 1001 Pennsylvania Ave NW Washington DC 20004 E-mail: judgeschwebel@aol.com.

SCHWEBLER, STEPHEN, retired chemist; b. Flemington, N.J., Dec. 5, 1928; s. Philip and Elizabeth (Pratscher) S.; m. Marian Finch, May 3, 1953; children: Bradley Stephen, Susan Elizabeth, Nancy Carol. AS, Columbia-Greene C.C., Hudson, N.Y., 1974; BS, SUNY, Saratoga, 1982. With Marshall's Chrysler-Plymouth, Ravena, N.Y., 1953-56; owner/mgr. Steve's Auto Svc., Coxsackie, 1956-58; svc. mgr. Jackson & Boone Chrysler-Plymouth, West Coxsackie, 1958-66; sr. lab. technician N.Y. State Dept. Health, Albany, 1966-72, N.Y. State Dept. Environ. Conservation, Albany, 1972-85; phys. chemist N.Y. State Office Gen. Svcs., 1985-88, specification writer, 1988-90, N.Y. State Thruway Authority, Albany, 1990-94; ret. Deacon New Baltimore Ref. Ch., N.Y., 1985-90; rsch. vol. Greene County Hist. Soc., West Coxsackie, 1996—. Democrat. Reformed Ch. Achievements include developing first confirmatory test for the birth defect, galactosemia, by paper chromatography; research in improved methods of sewage treatment and toxic substance monitoring of all bodies of water in N.Y. state. Avocations: musical keyboard performance, computer music arrangement, genealogy, motorcycling, bowling. Home: 3931 Rt 51 Hannacroix NY 12087-9708 E-mail: SSchwebler@cs.com.

SCHWED, PETER, author, retired editor and publisher; b. N.Y.C., Jan. 18, 1911; s. Frederick and Bertie (Stiefel) S.; m. Antonia Sanxay Holding, Mar. 6, 1947; children: Katharine Holding (Mrs. Eric F. Wood), Peter Gregory, Laura Sanxay (Mrs. Michael Sirico), Roger Eaton. Grad., Lawrenceville (N.J.) Sch., 1928; student, Princeton, 1929-32. Asst. v.p. Provident Loan Soc. N.Y., 1932-42; with Simon & Schuster, Inc., N.Y.C., 1946-84, v.p., exec. editor, 1957-62, exec. v.p., 1962-66, pub. trade books, 1966-72, chmn. editorial bd., 1972-82, editorial chmn. emeritus, 1982-84, dir., 1966-72. Author: Sinister Tennis, 1975, God Bless Pawnbrokers, 1975, The Serve and the Overhead Smash, 1976, Hanging in There, 1977; (with Nancy Lopez) The Education of a Woman Golfer, 1979, Test Your Tennis IQ, 1981, Turning the Pages, 1984, Overtime: A 20th Century Sports Odyssey, 1987, How to Talk Tennis, 1988, Quality Tennis after 50...Or 60...Or 70...Or..., 1990, The Common Cold Crusade: A Novel Not to be Sneezed At, 1994, Plum to Peter: Letters of P.G. Wodehouse to his Editor, 1996, Say, Could That Lad Be I?, 1998; compiler: The Cook Charts, 1949; editor: (with H.W. Wind) Great Stories From the World of Sports, 1958; (with Allison Danzig) The Fireside Book of Tennis, 1972; contbr. articles to jours. Trustee Lawrenceville Sch., 1968-72. Capt. F.A. AUS, World War II. Decorated Bronze Star, Purple Heart. Mem. Authors Guild, Century Assn. Democrat. Home: 151 W 86th St New York NY 10024-3401 *I suppose my guiding principle has been to face up to problems and difficult situations as immediately as I can, even if taking more time to think about them might have resulted in better ideas and actions. But an honest, un-Machiavellian handling of matters, without putting them off while brooding about them, has always struck me as effective when I do it, and appealing when others do. I try to carry this principle through with everyone, from my wife and children, through my associates, to community affairs. It gives me a reputation ranging from bluntness to rudeness with those whose favorite I may not be, but I would hope one of respect and admiration with those about whom I care.*

SCHWEDLER, JILLIAN MARIE, political science educator; b. Warren, Mich., Feb. 9, 1966; d. Marvin Charles and V. Diana (Keller) S.; m. Joel Allan Sherman, Nov. 14, 1992. BA, NYU, 1988, MA, 1992, PhD, 2000. Program officer Civil Soc. Project, N.Y.C., 1992-95; asst. prof. dept. govt. and politics U. Md., College Park, 2000—. Chair bd. dirs. MERIP/Mid. East Report, Washington. Author: Toward Civil Society in the Middle East, 1995, Islamist Movements in Jordan, 1997; mem. editl. bd. New Eng. Jour. Polit. Sci. Internat. rsch. fellow Social Sci. Rsch. Coun., Jordan & Yemen, 1995, Fulbright fellow, 1996-97, Am. Inst. Yemeni Studies fellow, 1997. Mem. Am. Polit. Sci. Assn., Mid. East Studies Assn., Law and Soc. Assn., Internat. Studies Assn. Avocations: scuba diving, dance, travel. Home: 131 Sprague Rd Scarsdale NY 10583-6347 Office: U Md Dept Govt and Politics 3140 Tydings Hall College Park MD 20742-7215 Fax: 301-314-9690. E-mail: jschwedler@gvpt.umd.edu.

SCHWEDT, RACHEL ELAINE, librarian; b. Lockport, N.Y., Dec. 2, 1944; d. Richard Thomas and Una May Traver; m. Ronald Anthony Schwedt, Feb. 3, 1967; children: Julie Lynn, Alan Ernest. BA, Roberts Wesleyan Coll., 1967; MLS, SUNY, Geneseo, 1979. Libr. Frewsburg (N.Y.) Ctrl. Sch., 1969-85; adminstrv. asst. Regent U., Virginia Beach, Va., 1986-88; libr. Lynchburg (Va.) Christian Acad., 1989-92, Liberty U., Lynchburg, 1992—. Spkr. various tchr. convs. Author: Core Collection for Small Libraries, 1997, Contemporary Christian Authors, 2000, A Guide to Poetry for Adolescents, 2001; author (newsletter) Libr. News, 1992-97. Tchr. various chs.; singer various choral groups. Mem. Assn. Christian Schs. Internat. (accreditation teams 1994-98). Avocations: reading, antiques, music, interior design, gardening. Home: 4052 Fort Ave Lynchburg VA 24502 Office: Libr Univ 1971 University Blvd Lynchburg VA 24502 E-mail: Spanky519@juno.com.

SCHWEGMAN, MONICA JOAN, artist; b. Hamilton, Ohio, Apr. 19, 1958; d. David Michael and LaVerne Henrietta (Mergy) Kiley; m. Craig Alfred Schwegman, Oct. 6, 1978; children: Craig, Sarah. Student, U. Cin., 1976-78; AAS, Brookdale C.C., 1978; postgrad., Kansas City Art Inst., 1990. Mgmt. trainee coll. coop. Marshall Fields, Chgo., 1977-78; decorator, cons. Sears, Toms River, N.J., 1985-88; artist, owner studio and gallery Lampasas, Tex., 1990-94. Chmn. Keystone Art Alliance, Lampasas, 1991-94; art dir. Theatre for Lampasas, 1993-94. Exhibited in group shows at Gallery One, 1993, Marble Falls, Tex., Found Art, Lampasas, 1992, KBUO TV Set Design, Austin, Tex., 1992, Breckenrdige Fine Arts Ctr., 1992, Pasillo De Artes Gallery, Austin, 1992, Contemporary Art Exhibit, Lampasas, 1991, Gannon U., Erie, Pa., Erie, Barnes & Noble, Erie, Springhill, Erie, Erie Art Mus., 1997, 99, Beacon Gallery, 1999, Kada Gallery, 1999, Erie Art Mus. Spring Show, 1999; solo shows A Woman's Touch, Erie Art Mus. Frame Shop Gallery, 1999, Schuster Gallery, Gannon U., Erie, Pa., 2000. Instr. art City of Lampasas/Sparts, 1993. Mem. Lampasas C. of C. (mem. tourism com. 1993). Republican. Roman Catholic. Avocations: reading, exercise.

SCHWEICHLER, MARY ELLEN, childhood education educator, consultant; b. Buffalo, Oct. 19, 1931; d. Joseph John and Teresa Mary (McVey) Carter; (div. May 1973); children: Michele, Richard, Maria Regina, Beth, David. Cert. Indsl. and Labor Rels., Cornell U., 1983; BS magna cum laude, SUNY, Buffalo, 1986, postgrad. studies, 1986—. Cert. early childhood edn. Postulant and tchr. Missionary Servants Blessed Trinity Pre-Sch., Phila., 1950-51; tchr., adminstr., founder Southtowns Pre-Sch. Devel., Blasdell, N.Y., 1975-82; asst. doord. dept. surgery 3d yr. student program SUNY, Buffalo, 1982-84, asst. to chair Health and Behavioral Scis., 1984-88. Lectr. early childhood edn. Orchard Pk. (N.Y.) Sch. Dist., 1975-82, SUNY Buffalo, 1975-82; cons. early childhood edn. Day Care Assn. Resource Ctr., Buffalo, 1987—. Contbr. articles profl. publs.; author numerous poems. Vol. Head Start, Lackawanna, N.Y., 1970-75, P.R. Teen Ctr., Lackawanna, 1970-72; mem. Orchard Pk. Enrollment and Bldg. Utilization Com., 1982, Orchard Pk. Edn. Adv. Bd., 1988, Nat. Multiple Sclerosis Soc., 1990—, Found. for Internat. Cooperation, 1965-69, Christian Family Movement, 1962-70, U-U Task Force on Domestic Violence, 1993—; founding mem. West N.Y. chpt. Reyes Syndrome Found., 1979-83; ombudsman ARC, Buffalo, 1989—; workshop leader Career Devel. Ctr. for Women in Govt., Albany, N.Y., 1982-84; trainer Smoking Cessation Am. Lung Assn., Buffalo, 1984-86. Recipient Appreciation award, Orchard Park Sch. Bd., 1988. Mem. Women's Auxiliary Am. Physical Therapy Assn. (founder, pres. 1965-72), Nardin Acad. Alumni (bd. dirs. 1965-70), Alpha Sigma Lambda (sec. 1987—). Unitarian Universalist. Avocation: reading. Home: Masonic Home Village 260 Masonic Home Dr Apt 202 Masonic Home KY 40041-9011

SCHWEICKART, JIM, advertising executive, broadcast consultant; b. Toledo, June 25, 1950; s. Norman Marvin and Anne Belle (Cress) S.; m. Deborah J., Aug. 14, 1971; children: Jennifer, Kimberly, Stephen. BA in Polit. Sci, Taylor U., Upland, Ind., 1972. News anchor, announcer Sta. WCMR, Elkhart, Ind., 1967-71; news anchor, disc jockey Sta. WWHC, Hartford City, 1971-72; gen. mgr. Sta. WTUC, Taylor U., 1971; news dir. Sta. WCMR, Elkhart, 1972-74; news anchor Sta. WOWO, Fort Wayne, Ind., 1974-78, Sta. KDKA, Pitts., 1978-79; gen. mgr. Sta. WBCL-FM, Fort Wayne, 1979-85; owner advt. agy., broadcast cons., 1984—. Bd. dirs. Christians for Polit. Alternatives; adv. bd. Taylor U., Fort Wayne campus. Republican. Baptist. Office: 3452 Stellhorn Rd Fort Wayne IN 46815-4630

SCHWEICKERT, RICHARD JUSTUS, psychologist, educator; b. Madison, Wis., July 19, 1946; s. Carl E. and Marie E. (Dilzer) S.; m. Carolyn M. Jagacinski, Dec. 27, 1980; children: Patrick, Kenneth. BS in Math., U. Santa Clara, 1968; MA in Math., Ind. U., 1972; PhD in Psychology, U. Mich., 1979. Statistician Bellevue Psychiatric Hosp., N.Y.C., 1969-71; asst. prof. Purdue U., West Lafayette, Ind., 1978-83, assoc. prof., 1984-91, prof., 1992—. Adv. panel on human cognition & perception NSF, 1993-96. Author: (with others) Handbook of Human Factors, 1987; editor Jour. Math. Psychology; assoc. editor Psychol. Bull. and Rev., 1993-98; mem. editl. bd. Jour. Exptl. Psychology; Learning, Memory and Cognition, 1985-89, 91-94, Jour. Math. Psychology, 1986-94; contbr. articles to profl. jours. Grantee NSF, 1981-84, 92-2000, NIMH, 1983-89. Fellow AAAS, Am. Psychol. Soc.; mem. Soc. for Math. Psychology (pres. 1990-91, bd. dirs.), Psychonomic Soc., Informs. Office: Purdue U Dept Psychol Scis Lafayette IN 47907

SCHWEIGERT, JACK F. lawyer; b. July 26, 1947; s. Charles Arthur and Alma Mae S.; m. Valerie Bavero, 1981; children: Carly, Scott. BS in Econs., U. Gannon, 1969; JD, U. Akron, 1974. Bar: Hawaii 1975, U.S. Ct. Appeals (9th cir.) 1975, U.S. Ct. Appeals (4th cir.), U.S. Claims Ct. 1977, Ct. Internat. Trade, Customs Ct. Pvt. practice, Honolulu, 1975—. Co-author: Medical Malpractice, 1986; appeared in numerous TV, newspaper, mag. stories. Past pres. and dir. Pauoa Cmty. Assn.; republican Mayoral candidate, Honolulu, 1980, libertarian Mayoral candidate, Honolulu, 1992. With U.S. Army, 1969-71. Mem. Honolulu Lions Club (immediate past pres., dir. 1990—, Melvin Jones award 1997-98), Phi Alpha Delta. Independent. Office: The Lawyers Bldg 550 Halekauwila St Ste 309 Honolulu HI 96813-5035 Fax: 808-533-7490. E-mail: conlawjack@cs.com.

SCHWEIKART, DEBORA ELLEN, lawyer; b. Belfonte, Pa., Apr. 14, 1971; d. Kenneth Earl and Catherine Joyce (Seaman) S. BA in Russian Lang. and Lit., U. Pitts., 1992, JD, 1996; MBA, U. Miami, 2001. Bar: Pa. Rsch. asst. U. Pitts. Sch. Law, 1994-96, teaching asst., 1994-95, Pa. Govs. Sch. Internat. Studies, Pitts., 1994-96; atty. Peterson Cons., 1997; jud. clk. N.Mex. Ct. Appeals, 1997-99; energy industry analyst Fed. Energy Regulatory Commn. Contbr. articles to profl. publs. Scholar Internat. Christian Youth Exch., Ronde, Denmark, 1989, Am. Coun. Tchrs. Russian, 1992, Internat. Women's Club, 1992, U. Pitts., 1996; Emery Means Findley, Jr. Grad. fellowship, 1999, Patrick J. Cesarano scholar, 2000. Mem. Dona Anna County Bar Assn. (treas. 1998). Avocations: dance, hiking. Address: Apt 304 8500 16th St Silver Spring MD 20910-2927

SCHWEIKER, MARK S. governor; b. Bucks County, Pa., Jan. 31, 1953; s. John and Mary S.; m. Katherine Schweiker; children: Brett, Eric, Kara. BS, Bloomsburg U., 1975; MA in Adminstrn., Rider U., 1983. Merrill Lynch; McGraw Hill; supr. Middletown Twp., 1979; commr. Bucks County, Pa., 1987-94; elec. lt. gov., 1994; reelected, 1998; lt. gov., pres. of the Senate, chmn. of the bd. of pardons Commonwealth of Pa., 1995—2001; former chmn. prime coun., chmn. local govt. adv. coun., chmn. gov.'s exec. coun. recycling devel. & waste reduction, dir. Pa. weed and seed program, gov., 2001—. Former chmn. Dela. Valley Regional Fin. Authority. Former bd. dirs. Bucks County United Way. Recipient Alumnus of Yr. Bloomsburg U., 1990, Outstanding Svc. to Conservation award Nature Conservancy Pa. Branch, 1993, Tech. Advocate of Yr. Tech. Coun. Ctrl. Pa., 1996, Outstanding Achievement award Citizens Against Govt. Waste, 1997, Commitment to Excellence in Local Govt. award Pa. Economy League, 1998. Office: 225 Main Capitol Building Harrisburg PA 17120*

SCHWEIKER, RICHARD SCHULTZ, trade association executive, former senator, former cabinet secretary; b. Norristown, Pa., June 1, 1926; s. Malcolm Alderfer and Blanche (Schultz) S.; m. Claire Joan Coleman, Sept. 10, 1955; children: Malcolm C., Lani, Kyle, Richard S. Jr., Lara Kristi. BA, Pa. State U., 1950; D of Pub. Svcs. (hon.), Temple U., 1970; D.Sc. (hon.), Georgetown U., 1981. Bus. exec., 1950-60; mem. 87th-90th congresses from 13th Dist. Pa., mem. house armed services and govt. ops. coms.; U.S. senator from Pa., 1969-80; mem. appropriations com., ranking mem. Labor-HEW subcom., ranking mem. health and human resources com., ranking mem. health subcom.; sec. HHS, 1981-83; pres. Am. Council Life Ins., Washington, 1983-94. Chmn. Partnership for Prevention, 1991—97. Alt. del. Nat. Rep. Conv., 1952, 56, del., 1972, 80; designated v.p. candidate with Reagan for Pres. of U.S., 1976. Served with USNR, World War II. Recipient Disting. Alumnus award Pa. State U., 1970, Dr. Charles H. Best award Am. Diabetes Assn., 1974, Outstanding Alumnus of Yr. award Phi Kappa Sigma, 1982, Gold medal Pa. Assn. Broadcasters, 1982, Nat. Outstanding Svc. award Headstart, 1983, Pub. Svc. Gold medal Surgeon Gen. U.S., 1988, Govt. Achievement award Juvenile Diabetes Found., 1990, Disting. Achievement award Nat. Coun. on Aging, 1991, John Newton Russell award Nat. Assn. Life Underwriters, 1992; named Outstanding Young Man of Yr., Jr. C. of C., 1960. Mem. Phi Beta Kappa.

SCHWEIKERT, EDGAR OSKAR, dentist; b. Heidelberg, Germany, Aug. 30, 1938; came to U.S., 1972; s. Oskar and Priska (Zehr) S.; m. Mary Lou Como, Apr. 7, 1969; 1 child, Marisa. Degree, Hamburg Dental Sch., 1966; Dr. Med. Dentistry, U. Munich, 1969. Lic. dentist, Calif., N.Y. Dentist, U.S. Army, Frankfurt, Fed. Republic Germany, 1969-72; gen. practice dentistry, L.A., 1972-73, Bklyn., 1973—; lectr. in field. Author Multiple Cantilevers in Fixed Prosthesis, 1988, Spanish edit., 1990; contbr. articles to profl. jours. Served as capt. German Air Force, 1967-69. Mem. ADA, German Dental Assn., Second Dist. Dental Assn., Bay Ridge Dental Soc., Guild Dental Craftsmen. Home and Office: 429 77th St Brooklyn NY 11209-3205

SCHWEIKERT, NORMAN CARL, retired musician; b. Los Angeles, Oct. 8, 1937; s. Carl Albert and Hilda (Meade) S.; m. Sally Hardin Haizlip, July 22, 1961; 1 son, Eric Carl. Mus.B. performer's certificate in horn, Eastman Sch. Music, 1961. Teaching assoc. Northwestern U., 1973-75, assoc. prof. (part-time), 1975-98; horn instr. Nat. Music Camp, Interlochen, 1967; curator Leland B. Greenleaf Collection Mus. Instruments, Interlochen, 1970-71 Successively 4th, 2d and 3d horn with, Rochester Philharmonic, Civic and

Eastman-Rochester symphonies, 1955-62, 64-66, instr. horn, mem., Interlochen (Mich.) Arts Quintet, Interlochen Arts Acad., 1966-71, 1st horn, Rochester Chamber Orch., 1965-66, Midland (Mich.) Symphony Orch., 1969-71, 1st horn, soloist, Northwestern Mich. Symphony Orch., 1966-71, Chgo. Little Symphony, tours, 1967, 68, asst. 1st horn, soloist, Chgo. Symphony Orch., 1971-75, 2d horn, Chgo. Symphony Orch., 1975-97; appearances with, Eastman Chamber Orch., Rochester Bach Festival, Aspen Festival Orch., Moravian Music Festival, Alaska Festival, Peninsula Music Festival, Rochester Brass Quintet, Canterbury Wind Quintet, Westchester Brass Quintet, Eastman Wind Ensemble, Chgo. Symphony Winds, Quadrangle Chamber Players, Washington Island Music Festival; soloist, New Japan Philharmonic, rec. artist for, Mercury, Columbia, Everest, C.R.I., Capitol. Mark Ednl., London-Decca, DGG, RCA Victor records, Sheffield Lab, Koch; recitals, also lecture demonstrations.; Contbr. articles to profl. jours. Served with AUS, 1962-64. Recipient certificate of merit City Chgo., 1971 Mem. Internat. Horn Soc. (hon., chmn. organizing com., sec.-treas. 1970-72, adv. coun. 1972-76), Am. Mus. Instrument Soc., Phi Mu Alpha Sinfonia (life alumni mem.), Pi Kappa Lambda. Home: RR 1 Box 40-s Washington Island WI 54246-9708

SCHWEITZER, GEORGE KEENE, chemistry educator; b. Poplar Bluff, Mo., Dec. 5, 1924; s. Francis John and Ruth Elizabeth (Keene) S.; m. Verna Lee Pratt, June 4, 1948; children: Ruth Anne, Deborah Keene, Eric George. BA, Central Coll., 1945, ScD in Philosophy, 1964; MS, U. Ill., 1946, PhD in Chemistry, 1948; MA, Columbia U., 1959; PhD in History, NYU, 1964. Asst. Central Coll., 1943-45; fellow U. Ill., 1946-48; asst. prof. chemistry U. Tenn., 1948-52, assoc. prof., 1952-58, prof., 1960-69, Alumni Distinguished prof., 1970—. Cons. to Monsanto Co., Proctor & Gamble, Internat. Tech., Am. Cyanamid Co., AEC, U.S. Army, Massengill, CTI-Siemens; lectr. colls. and univs.; mem. adv. bd. East Tenn. Hist. Soc. *Achievements include chemical expertise in solvent extraction, ion exchange, lanthanide chemistry, stable isotope concentration, radiochemistry, inductively-coupled plasma mass spectroscopy, the chemical implementation of positron-emission tomography and history and philosophy of science. Genealogical expertise in Revolutionary War, War of 1812, Civil War, Georgia, Kentucky, Illinois, Indiana, Massachusetts, Maryland, Missouri, New Jersey, New York, North Carolina, Ohio, Pennsylvania, South Carolina, Tennessee, Virginia, Germany, Ulster Ireland, migration routes, immigration and emigration records, settlement patterns, and tracing ancestors back across the Atlantic Ocean. Theological expertise in science and religion, religious epistemology, comparative religion, American colonial and frontier religion.* Author: Radioactive Tracer Techniques, 1950, The Doctorate, 1966, Genealogical Source Handbook, 1992, Civil War Genealogy, 1993, Tennessee Genealogical Research, 1981, Kentucky Genealogical Research, 1981, Revolutionary War Genealogy, 1982, Virginia Genealogical Research, 1982, War of 1812 Genealogy, 1983, North Carolina Genealogical Research, 1983, South Carolina Genealogical Research, 1984, Pennsylvania Genealogical Research, 1985, Georgia Genealogical Research, 1987, New York Genealogical Research, 1988, Massachusetts Genealogical Research, 1989, Maryland Genealogical Research, 1991, German Genealogical Research, 1992, Ohio Genealogical Research, 1994, Indiana Genealogical Research, 1996, Illinois Genealogical Research, 1997, Missouri Genealogical Research, 1997; also 170 articles. Faculty fellow Columbia U., 1958-60. Mem. Am. Chem. Soc., Am. Philos. Assn., History Sci. Soc., Soc. Genealogists, Phi Beta Kappa, Sigma Xi. Home: 407 Ascot Ct Knoxville TN 37923-5807

SCHWEITZER, LOREN MARCUS, computer programmer; b. Ft. Worth, Jan. 3, 1966; s. Leonard and Rose-Marie (Gustafson) S. BA in Econs., U. Tex., 1989. Analyst Nat. Asset Placement Corp., Dallas, 1995-96; programmer I Daily Data Inc., 1996-98; programmer II Blockbuster Inc., 1999, Bank Am., Dallas, 2000—. Mem. Delphi Developers Dallas, 1999—. Home: 14902 Preston Rd # 404-313 Dallas TX 75254-9191 E-mail: lorens@airmail.net.

SCHWEITZER, PAMELA BIFANO, psychiatric and mental health nurse practitioner; b. Detroit, Apr. 18, 1958; d. Daniel Frank and Roberta Rosemary (Hudson) Bifano; m. Jeffrey William Schweitzer, June 10, 1989; children: Elizabeth Gabrielle, Katherine Eleanore, Christopher Daniel. ADN, Henry Ford C.C., Dearborn, Mich., 1980; BSN, Madonna U., 1986; MS, U. Mich., 1991. RN, Mich.; cert. nurse practitioner, Mich.; cert. clin. specialist adult psychiat. and mental health nursing, ANCC. RN, charge nurse, preceptor Sinai Hosp. Detroit, 1980-83, Henry Ford Hosp., Detroit, 1983-86; mental health nurse, case mgr. Washtenaw County Cmty. Mental Health Ctr., Ann Arbor, Mich., 1986-87; rsch. nurse, clin. care coord. U. Mich. Psychiat. Hosps., 1987-91, clin. nurse specialist, 1991—. Pvt. practice as cognitive and behavioral therapist, Ann Arbor, 1993-96; panic disorder trainer NIMH and Soc. Edn. & Rsch. Psychiat. Nursing, Midwestern region, 1993-95; state clusters convener Kellogg and Coalition Psychiat. Nursing Orgns., Mich., 1994; adj. lectr. divsn. of acute, critical and long-term care programs U. Mich. Sch. of Nursing, 1996—. Editor: (with others) Nursing Diagnosis Handbook: A Guide to Planning Care, 2d edit., 1994, 4th edit., 1999; contbr. articles to profl. publs. Parent rep. to bd. dirs. U. Mich. Child Care Ctr., Ann Arbor, 1993-2000. Mem. Am. Psychiat. Nurses Assn., Anxiety Disorders Assn. Am. (profl. mem.), Mich. Nurses Assn. (chair advance practice coun. 1996-97), Internat. Soc. Psychiat.-Mental Health Nurses (midwestern region), Sigma Theta Tau (Rho chpt.). Home: 3200 Appleridge Dr Ann Arbor MI 48103 Office: U Mich Anxiety Disorders Program 1500 E Medical Center Dr Ann Arbor MI 48109-0118 E-mail: schweitz@umich.edu.

SCHWEITZER, THEODORE GOTTLIEB, III, United Nations administrator; b. Hannibal, Mo., Aug. 28, 1942; s. Theodore Gottlieb Jr. and Dorothy Lois (Burnett) S. Cert. in French Lang., U. Paris, 1968; BA, U. Iowa, 1970, MA, 1974; student, Hanoi (Vietnam) Fgn. Langs. U., 1992-94. Cert. Thai Lang. Am. Univ. Alumnae Assn., Bangkok, 1976, profl. tchr., Iowa. Tchr., librarian Lewis County Schs., Ewing, Mo., 1971-73; head librarian Internat. Sch., Bangkok, 1974-76; info. officer U.S. Army, Udorn, Thailand, 1974-76; dir. media services Am. Sch., Teheran, 1976-77, dir. media svcs. Isfahan, Iran, 1977-78; refugee officer UN HCR, Geneva and Bangkok, 1979—. Founder S.E. Asia Rescue Found., Ft. Walton Beach, Fla., 1981—, Hanoi Fgn. Langs. U., 1992-94. Author: (with Malcolm McConnell) Inside Hanoi's Secret Archives-Solving the MIA Mystery, 1995. Spl. rep. to Vietnam, Office of the Sec. of Def., Washington, 1992-94. With USAF, 1959-62. Recipient Award of merit SOS Boat people Com., San Diego, 1982, replica of Nobel Peace Prize, UN High Commr. for Refugees, 1981. Mem. Mensa, BPOE. Republican. Baptist. Avocations: writing, reading, scuba diving, photography, private pilot. Home: Ste 486 8635 W Sahara Ave Las Vegas NV 89117-5858 Office: UN High Commr for Refuges Palais Des Nations Geneva Switzerland E-mail: ted@searescue.org.

SCHWEIZER, EDWARD SOWERS, insurance agency owner; b. Houston, May 6, 1938; s. John Mel Jr. and Alicia Lucille (Sowers) S.; m. Suzan Lee Peterson, June 20, 1964; children: Edward Jr., Sally, Elizabeth. Degre superieur, U. Paris, 1957; BA, Occidental Coll., 1961; MA, Pepperdine U., 1978. Cert. surface warfare officer USN. Owner ESS Ins. Svcs., Chesapeake City, Md., 1989—. Mem. bd. Laguna Beach Pageant of the Masters; mem. adv. bd. San Diego Found., 1998-2000, Orange County Register Grants Bd., Santa Ana, Calif., 1998-99. Commr. City of Mission Viejo, 1990-92, 97-2000, Parks and Recreation Com., Chesapeake City, 2000—. Capt. USN, 1962-88. Decorated Meritorious Svc. medal. Mem. Ret. Officers Assn., Res. Officers Assn., Surface Navy Assn. (life), Naval Res. Assn., KC (Grand Knight 1989-90), Navy League of the U.S. (life). Republican. Roman Catholic. Avocations: civic affairs, fine art, international traveling, running, skiing, scuba diving. Home: 204 Bohemia Ave Chesapeake City MD 21915-0711 E-mail: edandsuzan1@juno.com., capted99@go.com.

SCHWEIZER, KARL WOLFGANG, historian, writer; b. Mannheim, Fed. Republic Germany, June 30, 1946; came to U.S., 1988; s. Ernest Schweizer; m. Elizabeth Wild, 1969; 1 child, Paul. BA in History, Wilfrid Laurier U., Can., 1969; MA, U. Waterloo, Can., 1970; MA, PhD, Cambridge U., 1976. Prof. history Bishop's U., Lenoxville, Que., Can., 1976-88, chmn. dept. Can., 1978-79, 82-84, 86; prof., chmn. humanities dept. N.J. Inst. Tech., Newark, 1988-93, prof. history dept. social sci. and policy studies, 1993—, chmn. dept. humanities and social scis., 2000—; assoc. Ctr. for Study of Global Change Rutgers U., 1995—. Grad. faculty Rutgers U., 1993—; vis. lectr. U. Guelph, Can., 1978-80; rsch. assoc. Russian Rsch. Ctr., Ill., 1979-80, 99; acad. visitor London Sch. Econs., 1986, 94, vis. scholar, 1986-87, Queens U., Ont., Can., 1986-87; vis. fellow Darwin Coll., Cambridge, 1987, 94, Princeton U., 1994, Yale U., 1994; vis. prof. dept. polit. sci. Rutgers U., 1997—. Author: The Art of Diplomacy, 1983, Lord Bute: Essays in Reinterpretation, 1988, England, Prussia and the Seven Years War, 1989, Frederick the Great, William Pitt and Lord Bute, 1991; co-author (with J. Osborne): Cobbett in His Times, 1990; author: Lord Chatham, 1993, Francois de Callieres: Diplomat and Man of Letters, 1995, Statesmen, Diplomats and the Press, 2002, War, Politics and Diplomacy: The Anglo Prussian Alliance, 1756-1763, 2001, Seeds of Evil: The Gray/Snyder Murder Case, 2001; co-author: The Origins of War in Early Modern Europe, 1987, The War of the Spanish Succession, 1994, British Prime Ministers, 1997, Hanoverian Britain and Empire, 1998; editor: The Devonshire Political Diary, 1757-1762, 1982, Diplomatic Thought 1648-1815, 1982, Warfare and Tactics in the 18th Century, 1984; co-editor: Essays in European History 1648-1815 in Honour of Ragnhild Hatton, 1985, Politics and the Press in Hanoverian Britain, 1989; editor: Herbert Butterfield: Essays on the History of Science, 1998; contbr. articles to profl. jours. Mem. NJ Gov.'s Adv. Panel on Higher Edn. Restructuring, 1994; nominee Rep. Senatorial Inner Cir., 1998; trustee NJ Literary Hall of Fame, 1988—92. Recipient thesis defence award Can. Coun., 1976, travel awards Peterhouse Coll., 1971-73, Adelle Mellen prize for outstanding contbn. to scholarship Edwin Mellen Press, 1989, Author's award N.J. Writer's Conf., 1993, Tchg. award N.J. Inst. Tech., 2000; fellow U. Waterloo, 1969-70, Province of Ont., 1969-70, Can. Coun., 1970-75; named Wilfred Laurier Proficiency scholar, 1966-69; rsch. grantee Bishop's U., 1977, 78, 80, 82, 83, postdoctoral rsch. grantee Can. Coun., 1977-78, 82-83, grantee Inter-Univ. Ctr. for European Studies, 1978, 81, conf. grantee S.S.H.R.C., 1985; travel grantee NEH, 1991, N.J. Com. for Humanities, 1988-1992. Fellow Royal Hist. Soc.; mem. Internat. Commn. on History of Internat. Rels., Hist. Soc., Cambridge Hist. Soc., North American Conf. on Brit. Studies, Can. Assn. Scottish Studies, Can. Assn. 18th Century Studies, N.Y. Acad. Sci., Avocations: music, writing, reading. Home: 37 Lenape Trl Chatham NJ 07928-1812 Office: Dept Social Scis and Policy Studies NJ Inst Tech Newark NJ 07102

SCHWEIZER, KENNETH STEVEN, physics educator; b. Phila., Jan. 20, 1953; s. Kenneth Paul and Grace Norma (Fischer) S.; m. Janis Eve Pelletier, Oct. 18, 1986; children: Gregory Michael, Daniel Patrick. BS, Drexel U., 1975; MS, U. Ill., 1976, PhD, 1981. Postdoctoral rsch. assoc. AT&T Bell Labs., Murray Hill, N.J., 1981-83; sr. mem. tech. staff Sandia Nat. Labs., Albuquerque, 1983-91; prof. materials sci. engrng. and chemistry U. Ill., Urbana, 1991—, prof. chem. engrng., 1998—, G. Ronald and Margeret H. Morris prof. materials sci., 2001—. Contbr. articles to profl. jours. Recipient Sandia award for Excellence, 1990, R&D 100 award, 1992, Award for Scientific Achievement in Materials Chemistry DOE, 1996, Burnett Tchg. award, 1997, Everitt Tchg. award, 2002. Fellow Am. Phys. Soc. (John H. Dillon medal 1991); mem. Am. Chem. Soc., Soc. Rheology, Sigma Xi, Pi Mu Epsilon. Office: U Ill Dept Materials Sci Engring 1304 W Green St Urbana IL 61801-2920 E-mail: kschweiz@uiuc.edu.

SCHWEIZER, PAUL DOUGLAS, museum director; b. Bklyn., Nov. 26, 1946; s. Alvin Charles and Marie Gertrude (Scholtz) S.; m. Jane Kulczycki, June 10, 1978. BA, Marietta Coll., Ohio, 1968; MA, U. Del., 1975, PhD, 1979; postgrad. Mus. Mgmt. Inst., U. Calif., Berkeley, 1990. Instr. art history St Lawrence U., Canton, N.Y., 1977-78; asst. prof. St. Lawrence U., 1978-80; curator St. Lawrence U. (Brush Gallery), 1977-78; dir. St. Lawrence U., 1979-80; dir. and chief curator Munson-Williams-Proctor Arts Inst. Mus. Art, Utica, 1980—; adj. prof. art history Pratt at Munson-Williams-Proctor, 2000—. Mem. vis. com. Picker Art Gallery, Colgate U., 1999—. Author exhbn. catalog; contbr. articles to profl. jours. Bd. dirs. Remington Art Mus., Ogdensburg, N.Y., 1979-80; bd. dirs. Williamstown (Mass.) Regional Art Conservation Lab., 1981-92, pres., 1988-92. Rsch. grantee Nat. Endowment for Arts, 1978. Mem. Coll. Art Assn., Assn. Art Mus. Dirs., N.Y. State Assn. Art Mus. (trustee 1993-95), Mus. Assn. N.Y. (councilor 1995—), Gallery Assn. of N.Y. (bd. dirs. 1996—, pres. 1999), Otsego Sailing Club, Alpha Sigma Phi, Omicron Delta Kappa. Office: Munson-Williams-Proctor Arts Inst Mus Art 310 Genesee St Utica NY 13502-4799 E-mail: pschweiz@mwpi.edu.

SCHWELB, FRANK ERNEST, appellate judge; b. Prague, Czechoslovakia, June 24, 1932; came to U.S., 1947; s. Egon and Caroline (Redisch) S.; m. Taffy Wurzburg, Apr. 9, 1988. BA, Yale U., 1949-53; LLB, Harvard U., 1958. Bar: N.Y. Ct. Appeals 1958, U.S. Dist. Ct. (so. and ea. dists.) N.Y. 1960, U.S. Ct. Appeals (2d cir.) 1961, U.S. Supreme Ct. 1965, U.S. Ct. Appeals (4th cir.) 1968, D.C., D.C. Ct. Appeals, U.S. Dist. Ct. D.C. 1972. Assoc. Mudge, Stern, Baldwin & Todd, N.Y.C., 1958-62; trial atty. Civil Rights Div. U.S. Dept. Justice, Washington, 1962-79, chief eastern sect., 1969, chief housing sect., 1969-79, spl. counsel for litigation, 1979; spl. counsel rev. panel on new drug regulation HEW, 1976-77; assoc. judge Superior Ct. D.C., 1979-88, D.C. Ct. Appeals, Washington, 1988—. Instr. various legal edn. activities. Contbr. articles to profl. jours. With U.S. Army, 1955-57. Recipient Younger Fed. Lawyer award, Fed. Bar Assn., 1967. Mem. Bar Assn. D.C., World Peace Through Law Ctr., World Assn. Judges, Czechoslovak-Am. Orgns., De Tocqueville Soc., Order of the Battered Boot. Avocations: tennis, table tennis, sports, Gilbert and Sullivan operettas, Shakespeare. Home: 4879 Potomac Ave NW Washington DC 20007-1539 Office: DC Ct Appeals 500 Indiana Ave NW Washington DC 20001-2138 E-mail: fschwelb@dcca.state.dc.us.

SCHWEMIN, JOSEPH, retired pharmacist; b. Blackwell, Okla., Aug. 14, 1922; s. Joseph Julian and Julia Ann (Grapes) S.; m. Bettye Mae Wright, June 12, 1943 (div. Aug. 1966); children: Sue, Mary, Joe; m. Louise Elizabeth Williams, Feb. 22, 1969; children: Julie, Joey. BS in Pharmacy, Southwestern Okla. State U., 1948. Registered pharmacist, Okla., Ark. Mgr. Madding Drug, Houston, 1950-51; owner Pharmacy, 1952-53, Vern Drug, Tulsa, 1955-75, J-Bar-J Ranch, Talihina, Okla., 1961-70; dir. Okla. State Bd. Pharmacy, Oklahoma City, 1965-89. Sgt. USMC, 1942-45, PTO. Recipient Hygeia award A.H. Robins Bowl, 1962, Disting. Alumni award Southwestern Okla. State U., 1981, Pharmacy Disting. Alumni award, 1976, Spl. Recognition award 1974, Outstanding Contbn. Pharmacy award, 1971, Gaffney Bldg. Mortgage Retirement Drive award Okla. Pharmacy Heritage Found., 1996. Mem. Nat. Assn. Bds. Pharmacy (pres. 1973, chmn.), An. Assn. Colls. Pharmacy (chmn. Dist. 6), Southwestern Okla. State U. Pharmacy Alumni Found. (pres. 1978-98), Tulsa C. of C., Lions Club (dist. gov. 3-0 1961-62), Beta Tau Beta (past pres.), Beta Tau Beta Fraternity Alumni (past pres.). Democrat. Roman Catholic. Avocations: golf, fishing. Home: 5025 NW 26th St Oklahoma City OK 73127-1750

SCHWENDEMAN, KENNETH DAVID, government official, consultant; b. Pensacola, Fla., June 10, 1958; s. Allyn Nelson Bransby, Oct. 11, 1980 (div. Aug. 28, 1988); children: James Russell, Douglas Clayton; m. Louise Anderson, Nov. 25, 1994. BBS in Fn., Eastern Ky. U., 1979, MBA, 2000. Comd. 2d lt. U.S. Army, 1980, platoon leader, staff officer 2-69 armor bat. Ga., 1980-86, co. and troop comdr. 1st inf. divsn. 3d brigade Boeglingen, Germany, 1986-90, recruitint co. comdr. Houston Recruiting Bat. Houston, 1990-92, advanced through grades to maj., 1992, strategic logistics planner Office Dep. for Ops. Germany, 1992-96, counter-terrorism ops. OIC Office Prog. Mgr. Saudi Arabia NG Riyadh, 1996-97; ret., 1997; prin. asst. to comdr. Dept. Criminal Justice Tng. Ky. Justice Cabinet, Richmond, 1997-99, dir. divsn. adminstrn., 1999—. Mem. Ky. Soc. Pub. Adminstrs. (cert. pub. mgr.), ASPA, Ky. Soc. Cert. Pub. Mgrs.(Outstanding Project award 1999), Soc. Human Resource Mgrs., Ky. Women's Law Enforcement Network, Ky. Law Enforcement Meml. Found. (sec.-treas. 1999—), Richmond C. of C. (chairperson membership directory 2001—, chairperson membership dr. 2000-01). Roman Catholic. Avocations: gardening, piano, fishing, restoring antique automobiles. Office: Ky Dept Criminal Justice Tng 521 Lancaster Rd Richmond KY 40475-3102 E-mail: kschwendeman@docjt.jus.state.ky.us.

SCHWENDEMAN, PAUL WILLIAM, lawyer; b. Chgo., Apr. 7, 1945; s. Oscar and Edna Dorothy (Ellis) S.; m. Shirley Anne Starke; children: Paul A., John E., Thomas D. BA in Econs., Carleton Coll., 1966; MSJ, Northwestern U., 1967; JD, Duquesne U., 1978. Bar: Pa. 1978. Mgr. divsn. ops. Greater Waterbury (Conn.) C. of C., 1971-75; v.p. Greater Pitts. C. of C., 1975-78; assoc. Kirkpatrick & Lockhart, Pitts., 1978-84, ptnr., 1984—. Lt. USNR, 1971. Office: Kirkpatrick & Lockhart 1500 Oliver Building Bldg Pittsburgh PA 15222-2312

SCHWENDIMAN, STEPHEN GLENN, lawyer; b. Freeport, Ill., Apr. 2, 1948; s. Glenn and Helen (Snow) S.; m. Carolee Kulinsky, Sept. 3, 1971; children: Larah, Stephen, Karissa, Jeremy. BA, Brigham Young U., 1972; JD, U. Utah, 1975. Bar: Utah 1975. Asst. atty. gen. Utah, Salt Lake City, 1975—. Divsn. chief, 1983-89. Voting dist. vice chmn. Rep. Com., Salt Lake City, 1982-84, voting dist. chmn., 1988-90; scoutmaster, Boy Scouts Am., 1981-84, roundtable commr. Evergreen dist., 1980-84, asst. dist. commr., 183-85, dist. commr., 1985-89, dist. chmn., 1990-94, nat. jamboree scoutmaster, 1989, 97, dist. merit award, 1981, Silver Beaver award, 1990. Mem. Utah Bar Assn. Mem. Lds Ch. Office: Utah Atty Gen 160 E 300 S Salt Lake City UT 84111-2316

SCHWENK, JAMES LEE, minister, educator; b. Reading, Pa., May 6, 1965; s. Donald and Patricia (Finefrock) S.; m. Loretta Jean Friends, Feb. 20, 1988; two children. BS, United Wesleyan Coll., 1986; MDiv, Evang. Sch. Theology, Myerstown, Pa., 1991; MPhil, Drew U., 1996, PhD, 1999. Pastor Manbeck's Evang. Congl. Ch., Schuylkill Haven, Pa., 1986-92; assoc. pastor Blvd. Evang. Congl. Ch., Allentown, 1992-95; pastor Grace Evang. Congl. Ch., Columbia, 1995-98; asst. prof. ch. history Evang. Sch. Theology, Myerstown, 1998-01, assoc. prof., 01—. Adj. faculty Coll. St. Francis, Joliet, 1997—, Messiah Coll., Grantham, Pa., 1998—. Pres. Columbia Area Ministerium, 1997-98; bd. dirs. Schuylkill County Fair Assn., 1989-92, assoc., 1987-99, pres., 1998-99. Mem. Am. Acad. Religion, Evang. Theol. Soc., Am. Soc. Ch. History, Nat. Rifle Assn., N. Am. Hunting Club. Home: 214 W Bahney Ave Myerstown PA 17067-1201 E-mail: jschwank@evangelical.edu.

SCHWENKE, ROGER DEAN, lawyer; b. Washington, Oct. 18, 1944; s. Clarence Raymond and Virginia Ruth (Gould) S.; m. Carol Lynne Flenniken, Nov. 29, 1980; 1 child: Matthew Robert; stepchildren: Tracy L. Wolf Dickey, Mary M. Wolf. BA, Ohio State U., 1966; JD with honors, U. Fla., 1969. Bar: Fla. 1970. Instr. Coll. Law U. Fla., Gainesville, 1969-70; assoc. Carlton Fields, P.A., Tampa, Fla., 1970-74, ptnr., 1975—; adminstr., dept. head Real Estate, Environ. and Land Use Dept., 1978—99. Adj. prof. Coll. Law, Stetson U., St. Petersburg, Fla., 1979-80; mem. faculty U. Miami Coll. of Law Master of Law's in Real Estate Devel. Program, 1994-96. Author chpt. in Environmental Regulation and Litigation in Florida, 1987, chpt. in Florida Real Property Complex Transactions, 1997, 2000; contbr. articles to profl. jours., chpt. to book. Mem. diocesan coun. Episc. Diocese SW Fla., 1978-86, mem. standing com., 1989-92, chief judge Eccles. Ct., 1996—. Recipient Gertrude Brick Law Rev. prize U. Fla., 1969. Fellow Am. Coll. Real Estate Lawyers (bd. govs. 1985-88), Am. Law Inst.; mem. ABA (standing com. on environ. law 1980—, coun. real property sect. 1988-95, liaison), Fla. Bar Assn., Air & Waste Mgmt. Assn., Order of Coif, Greater Tampa C. of C. (chmn. environ. coun. 1980-81), Tampa Club. Democrat. Office: Carlton Fields PO Box 3239 Tampa FL 33601-3239 Fax: 813-229-4133. E-mail: rschwenke@carltonfields.com.

SCHWENN, LEE WILLIAM, retired medical center executive; b. Morrisonville, Wis., Dec. 23, 1925; s. LeRoy William and Vivian Mae (Kramer) S.; m. Glenna Edith Mehne, Jan. 16, 1947; 1 son, William Lee. BS, U. Wis., 1948; M.P.H., U. N.C., 1956. Tchr. pub. schs., Appleton, Wis., 1948-52; teaching cons. Wis. Health Dept., 1952-53; adminstrv. asst. Madison (Wis.) Health Dept., 1953-57; adminstrv. cons. U.S. Children's Bur., Atlanta Regional Office, 1957-58; adminstr. USPHS, Washington, 1958-66; assoc. dir. D.C. Dept. Health, 1966-70, D.C. Dept. Human Resources, 1970-71; exec. v.p. Maimonides Med. Center, Bklyn., 1971-88, pres., 1988-89, spl. cons. Bd. Trustees, 1989-96. Recipient Distinguished Pub. Service award D.C. Govt., 1970 Mem. Delta Omega. Home: 1007 Westminster Dr Greensboro NC 27410-4551

SCHWENSEN, DAVID EDWARD, writer, columnist, talent coordinator; b. Lorain, Ohio, June 19, 1953; s. Edward and Arlys Schwensen; m. Debbie Baker; children: Kevin Hanley, Paul. BS, Bowling Green State U., 1976. Talent coord. TelAmerica /The Improv, L.A., 1991—93; owner Dave Schwensen Entertainment, Vermilion, Ohio, 1993—. Motivational spkr., humorist Dave Schwensen Entertainment, Vermilion, 1993—. Author: (Book) How To Be A Working Comic: An Insider's Guide To A Career In Stand-Up Comedy, 1998; columnist: newspaper columns Entertainment, 1993, columnist: syndicated humor column Something To Laugh About, 1999. Mem.: Am. Assn. for Therapeutic Humor. Home and Office: David Schwensen Entertainment PO Box 318 Vermilion OH 44089 Home Fax: 440-967-2634; Office Fax: 440-967-2634. Personal E-mail: DSEntertainment@centurytel.net. Business E-Mail: DSEntertainment@elvis.com.

SCHWERDT, LISA MARY, English language educator; b. Coral Gables, Fla., Feb. 7, 1953; d. Henry G. and Dilys Doris (Bandurske) S. BS, Fla. Internat. U., 1973, BA, 1977; MA, Purdue U., 1979, PhD, 1984. Cert. secondary educator English, spl. edn., Fla. Tchr. English, Green Sch. English, Tokyo, 1973-75; tchr. spl. edn. Carol City (Fla.) Elem. Sch., 1975-77; grad. instr. Purdue U., West Lafayette, Ind., 1977-85; asst. prof. U. North Ala., Florence, 1985-89; adj. lectr. U. Ctrl. Fla., Orlando, 1989-90, Rollins Coll., Winter Park, Fla., 1989-90; prof. English, California U. Pa., 1990—, interim assoc. dean, 1995-98. Author: Isherwood's Fiction, 1989; contbr. articles and book revs. to profl. jours. Mem. Sierra Club, Pitts., 1990-98, Planned Parenthood, Pitts., 1986-94. Grantee Purdue Found., 1982; recipient Excellence in Teaching award Purdue U., 1979, 81. Mem. MLA, Coll. English Assn., Nat. Assn. Scholars, Nat. Coun. Tchrs. English, N.E. MLA, Pa. Coll. English Assn., Soc. for the Study of Narrative Lit., Soc. for Health and Human Values. Unitarian Universalist. Home: 5337 California Ave Bethel Park PA 15102-3821 Office: California U of Pa Dept English California PA 15419 E-mail: schwerdt@cup.edu.

SCHWERDTFEGER, CARL RICHARD, real estate executive; b. Chgo., Nov. 29, 1940; s. Carl Heintz and Lucille Evelyn Schwerdtfeger; m. Carol Elizabeth Schwerdtfeger, Oct. 29, 1960; children: Caren, C. Richard. BA, McKendree Coll., Lebanon, Ill., 1963; MS, U. Wis., Platteville, 1968. Cert. tchr., Ill.; lic. real estate broker, Ill., Wis., Iowa; lic. real estate instr. and cert. mediator, Ill. Social worker Ill. Pub. Aid, East St. Louis, 1963; tchr. DeLand-Weldon Pub. Schs., Weldon, Ill., 1963-64; head dept. social studies Elizabeth (Ill.) Pub. Schs., 1964-84; v.p. mktg. Greater Rockford (Ill.) Aviation, 1985; dir. info. svcs. U Wis., Platteville, 1985-87; real estate sales McCoy Real Estate, Galena, Ill., 1987-88; pres., CEO Old Northwest Land Co., Inc., 1989—. V.p. Realtors Land Inst., Springfield, Ill. Editor/author: (view book) UW-Platteville, 1985; project historian Find and Restore Apple River Fort, 1994—. Dem. candidate for U.S. Congress from 16th Ill. Dist., 1982, 84; mem. state ctrl. com. Ill. Dem. Party, 1986, 94; v.p. Ill. Hist. Soc., Springfield, 1975. Named Outstanding History Tchr., Ill. State Hist. Soc., 1972, Outstanding Tchr., Daus. Colonial Wars, 1974; named to Outstanding Young Men of Am., 1972. Mem. Nat. Assn. Realtors, Freeport/Galena Area Assn. Realtors (pres. 1995), Ill. Assn. Realtors (v.p. 2000), Aircraft Owners and Pilots Assn., NRA, Masons, Dubuque Sailing Club, Julian Dubuque Yacht Club. Methodist. Avocations: sailing, flying, scuba diving, training horses, restoring sports cars. Home: 1126 Scales Mound Rd Elizabeth IL 61020 Office: Old Northwest Land Co Inc 5140 W Us 20 Galena IL 61036-9393

SCHWERDTNER, FREDERICK HOWARD, retired police commander, lawyer; b. Chgo., Oct. 13, 1949; s. Fred and Lydia (Tatz) S.; m. Julie Anne Carramusa, Oct. 21, 1990; 1 child, Sarah Elizabeth. BS, Loyola U., Chgo., 1973, JD, 1989; MBA with distinction, DePaul U., 1983. Bar: Ill. 1989, U.S. Dist. Ct. (no. dist.) Ill. 1989. Officer Oak Park (Ill.) Police Dept., 1973-93, commdr., 1989-93; pres. DuPage County Vets. Assistance Commn., 1998. Contbr. articles to profl. jours. Tutor inner city high sch. students, Chgo., 1988. With USMC, 1965-69, Vietnam. Mem. ABA, Fraternal Order Police, Marine Corps League (Band of Bros. Detachment), Ill. State Bar Assn., Chgo. Bar Assn., DuPage County Bar Assn., Viet-Now (DuPage County chpt.), Beta Gamma Sigma. Republican. Lutheran. Avocations: hiking, tennis, racquetball, golf. Address: 39 W Wrightwood Ave Glendale Heights IL 60139-2485

SCHWERIN, HORACE S. marketing research consultant; b. N.Y.C., Jan. 18, 1914; s. Paul and Rose (Lewis) S.; m. Lorraine Roth, June 14, 1941 (div. Dec. 1969); children— Barbara, Bruce; m. Enid May Highton, Apr. 28, 1973. BS, Lafayette Coll., 1935; MA, London U., 1936; MS, U. Paris, 1937. Gen. mgr., research dir., cons. N.Y. advt. agys., 1936-41; pres. Research Analysts, Inc., 1946; chmn. bd. Schwerin Research Corp., N.Y.C., Toronto, London, Hamburg, to 1968; chmn., pres. Horace Schwerin & Assos., Englewood Cliffs, N.J., 1968-72; dir. marketing devel. Campbell Soup Co., Camden, 1972—, v.p. market planning Canned Food div., 1977-82, mktg. strategy cons., 1982—; CEO, chmn. Schwerin Murphy, Inc., 1991-98; ret., 1998. Author: (with Henry H. Newell) Persuasion in Marketing, 1981; also articles on market research, nutrition, use of govt. data bases. Served as capt. U.S. Army, 1946. Decorated Legion of Merit with oak leaf cluster; inducted into Market Rsch. Coun. Hall of Fame, 1992. Mem. Am. Mktg. Assn., Market Rsch. Coun., Can. Club (N.Y.C.), Penn Club (N.Y.C.). Methodist. Home: 5D Toll Gate Of Moorestown 633 E Main St Moorestown NJ 08057-3059 Office: 633 E Main St Moorestown NJ 08057-3059 E-mail: hschwerin@comcast.net.

SCHWERIN, KARL HENRY, anthropology educator, researcher; b. Bertha, Minn., Feb. 21, 1936; s. Henry William and Audrey Merle (Jahn) S.; m. Judith Drewanne Altermatt, Sept. 1, 1958 (div. May 1975); children: Karl Frederic, Marguerite DelValle; m. Partha Louise Hake Buell, Jan. 25, 1979; stepchildren: Tamara, Brent, Taryn. BA, U. Calif., Berkeley, 1958; PhD, UCLA, 1965. Instr. Los Angeles State Coll., 1963; asst. prof. anthropology U. N.Mex., Albuquerque, 1963-68, assoc. prof., 1968-72, prof., 1972-2001, asst. chmn. dept. anthropology, 1983-85, chmn. dept. anthropology, 1987-93, prof. emeritus, 2001—. Prof. invitado Inst. Venezolano de Investigaciones Cientificas, Caracas, 1979. Author: Oil and Steel Processes of Karinya Culture Change, 1966, Antropologia Social, 1969, Winds Across the Atlantic, 1970; editor: Food Energy in Tropical Ecosystems, 1985; contbr. articles to profl. jours. V.p. Parents without Ptnr., Albuquerque, 1976-77. Grantee Cordell Hull Found., Venezuela, 1961-62, N.Y. Zool. Soc., Honduras, 1981; Fulbright scholar Cañar, Ecuador, 1969-70, Paris, 1986; founded Karl H. Schwerin Fellowship in Ethnology. Fellow Am. Anthropol. Assn.; mem. Am. Ethnol. Soc., Am. Soc. Ethnohistory (pres. 1975), Southwestern Anthropol. Assn. (co-editor Southwestern Jour. Anthropology 1972-75), N.Mex. Cactus and Succulent Soc. (v.p. 1970-71), Internat. Congress of Americanists (35th-40th, 43d, 46th, 48th, 49th, 50th), Sigma Xi (chpt. pres. 1980-81). Avocations: photography, gardening, hiking, camping, cycling. Office: U NMex Dept Anthropology Albuquerque NM 87131-0001 E-mail: schwerin@unm.edu.

SCHWERIN, SUZANNE KENNY, civic volunteer; b. Plainfield, N.J., Oct. 11, 1933; d. William Francis and Adelaide (Bride) Kenny, Jr.; m. Clarence M. Schwerin III; children: Michael Francis, Tara Ann Innes, Noel Marie, Merrill Louise. AS, Bennett Coll., 1953; student, C.W. Post Coll., 1970, 71. Vol. Achilles Club (orgn. for disabled); mem. Harvard/Outward Bound Adv. Program; expeditionary learning adv. bd. New Am. Schs. Design Corp.; bd. dirs. Fund for the City of N.Y.; adv. bd. Joan and Arnold Saltzman Community Svcs. Ctr.; bd. trustees Hofstra U.; bd. advisors Outward Bound U.S.A., also past trustee and exec. mem.-at-large; founder, past chmn. Mobilized Community Resources; past advisor Nassau House; past bd. exec. com., v.p. Health and Welfare Coun., Nassau County; mem. Jr. League, 1957-80, bd. dirs. 1960-67. Recipient Disting. Svc. award North Shore Jr. League, 1968. Mem. Quogue Field Club (tennis com.), Westhampton Country Club, The Wintergreen Club (past bd. dirs.), The Creek, Inc. Avocations: tennis, paddle tennis, canoeing, golf, whitewater rafting. Home: 200 E 57th St New York NY 10022-2860

SCHWERING, FELIX KARL, electronics engineer, researcher; b. Cologne, Nordrhein-Westfalen, Federal Republic of Germany, June 4, 1930; came to U.S., 1964; s. Felix Bernhard and Maria (Heinrichs) S. BS, U. Aachen, Federal Republic of Germany, 1951, Diplom-Ingenieur, 1954, PhD, 1957. Asst. prof. U. Aachen, Federal Republic of Germany, 1956-58; electronic scientist U.S. Army R & D Labs., Fort Monmouth, N.J., 1958-61; project leader AEG-Telefunken, Ulm, Federal Republic of Germany, 1961-64; rsch. scientist U.S. Army Communication Electronics Command (CECOM), Fort Monmouth, N.J., 1964-96, ret., 1996, guest rschr., 1996—. Vis. lab. assoc. U.S. Army Rsch. Office, Rsch. Triangle, N.C., 1984-85; vis. prof. N.J. Inst. Tech., Newark, 1986—, Rutgers U., New Brunswick, N.J., 1973-87, Monmouth U., 1996—. Author: (with others) Millimeter Wave Antennas, 1988; author and editor (with others) Microwave Antennas, 1989; mem. editorial bd. Microwave and Optical Tech. Letters, 1988—; contbr. over 30 articles to profl. jours.; patentee in field. Fellow IEEE (Best Paper award Antennas and Propagation Soc. 1961, 82), Internat. Sci. Radio Union, Am. Geophys. Union, Armed Forces Comm. Electronics Assn., Sigma Xi. Roman Catholic. Office: US Army Comm Elec Command Amsel Rd St # WL Fort Monmouth NJ 07703 E-mail: schwerin@mail1.monmouth.army.mil.

SCHWERS, DOROTHY JEAN, retired music educator; b. Youngstown, Ohio, Mar. 4, 1928; d. Russel P. and Florence Wilma (Davis) Donahue; m. William G. Schwers, Dec. 29, 1951 (dec. Apr. 1998); children: Russell A., William A. BS in Music Edn., Youngstown (Ohio) State U., 1950; MM in Music Edn., Kent (Ohio) State U., 1980. Cert. tchr. music edn. Ohio. Vocal music tchr. grades 1-8 Austintown (Ohio) Local Schs., 1950-57, vocal music tchr. grades 5-8, 1965-92; pvt. vocal and piano tchr. Austintown, 1992—. Bd. elections Judge of Precinct, Mahoning County, Youngstown, Ohio, 1998-2001; women's com. for children's concerts Youngstown Symphony Orch., 1992—. Mem. Youngstown Area Fedn. of Womens Clubs Inc. (pres. 2000—), Sigma Alpha Iota Internat. (pres. 1988-95 (Sword of Honor, Rose of Honor, Rose of Dedication), Gamma Epsilon chpt. (bd. dirs. 1990-95), Delta Kappa Gamma. Republican. Avocations: music, reading, needlework. Home: 4253 Wedgewood Dr Youngstown OH 44511

SCHWERT, G(EORGE) WILLIAM, III, finance educator, educator; b. Durham, N.C., Jan. 26, 1950; s. George William Jr. and Margaret (Houlton) S.; m. Camille Matthews, Dec. 19, 1970 (div. 1983); 1 child, Lisa Margaret; m. Patricia Michel, Dec. 23, 1983; children: Michael William, Andrew Patrick. AB in Econs. with honors, Trinity Coll., 1971; MBA, U. Chgo., 1973, PhD in Fin., 1975. Asst. prof. Grad. Sch. Bus. U. Chgo., 1975-76; asst. prof. to prof. Simon Sch. Bus. U. Rochester, N.Y., 1976-86, Gleason prof. fin., 1986-98, Disting. U. prof., 1998—. Chmn. Knollwood Cons. Group, Inc., Rochester, 1987—. Co-editor Jour. Fin. Econs., 1979-86, 89-95, adv. editor, 1986-89, mng. editor 1995—; assoc. editor Jour. of Fin., 1983-2000, Jour. Monetary Econs., 1984—; contbr. articles to econs. jour. Recipient Smith-Breeden Disting. Paper prize Jour. Fin., 1990, Graham and Dodd plaque Fin. Analysts Jour., 1990. Mem. Am. Fin. Assn. (bd. dirs. 1987-89), Am. Econs. Assn., Econometrics Soc., Am. Statis. Assn. (chair bus. econs. sect. 1990-91). Avocations: tennis, boating, fishing, golf. Home: 71 Knollwood Dr Rochester NY 14618-3512 Office: U Rochester W E Simon Grad Sch Bus Adminstrn Rochester NY 14627

SCHWETMAN, JOHN WILLIAM, retired English language professional educator; b. Boston, Jan. 27, 1942; s. Herbert DeWitt and Mary Jean (Knight) S.; m. Jenny Lynn Noe, Apr. 15, 1962; children: Sondra Paige, Melinda Sue. BA in English, Baylor U., 1963, MA in English, 1965; PhD in English, U. Kans., Lawrence, 1974. Asst. instr. Baylor U., Waco, Tex., 1963-65; instr. Cen. Mo. State Coll., Warrensburg, 1965-68; asst. instr. English Kans. U., 1969-72; asst. prof. and prof. Sam Houston State U., Huntsville, Tex., 1972-2001, ret., 2001. Author: Advanced Composition, 1976; contbr. articles to profl. jours. Mem. Medieval Acad. Am., Internat. Soc. of Anglo-Saxonists, S. E. Medieval Assn. (bd. dirs. 1987-90, pres. 1995-97). Democrat. Avocations: birding, backpacking. Home: 281 Elkins Lk Huntsville TX 77340-7307

SCHWIEBERT, DEBORAH JOHNSON, marketing executive; b. Moline, Ill., Apr. 26, 1952; d. Robert B. and Ruth E. Cronin; m. Mark W. Schwiebert, Oct. 10, 1987. BA in English, St. Mary's Coll., 1974. Dealer mgmt. rep. John Deere co., East Moline, Ill., 1975-77, territory mgr., 1977-85; mktg. cons. John Deere Info. Systems, 1985-91, mgr. quality assurance, 1991-93; project mgr., product safety mktg. Deere & Co., Moline, 1993-97, divsn. mgr. retail customer, 1997-98, mgr. Deere.com, 1998—. Deere & Co. Credit Union, 1996—. Mem. St. Mary's Coll. Alumni (pres. 1998—, bd. dirs. 1994—, bd. trustees 1998—). Roman Catholic. Avocations: reading, travel. Home: 3913 14th St Rock Island IL 61201-6016 Office: Deere & Co 400 19th St Moline IL 61265-1373

SCHWIEDEREK, WILLIAM NEIL, engineering executive; s. Joseph Schwiederek and Kathleen Garland Harper; m. Joanne Marie Schmidt, Oct. 30, 1964; children: Emily, Grace. BS in Mech. Engring. Tech., Thomas A. Edison State Coll., 1989. Cert. energy mgr., NICET cert. in fire protection engring. tech. Sr. svc. account engr. Siemens Bldg. Techs., Inc., Pine Brook, NJ, 1986—90, svc. ops. supr., 1990—93, svc. ops. mgr., 1993—. Mem.: Nat. Fire Protection Assn., Assn. Energy Engrs., Am. Soc. Heating, Refrigerating and Air Conditioning Engrs., Blessed Sacrament Drum and Bugle Corps. Lutheran. Avocations: coaching soccer, trumpet. Office: Siemens Building Techs Inc 19 Chapin Rd PO Box 704 Pine Brook NJ 07058 Personal E-mail: schwdrk@optonline.net. E-mail: bill.schwiederek@sbt.siemens.com.

SCHWIER, ANN STRANQUIST, economics educator; b. St. Louis; d. E. Alvin and Katherine (Hemp) Stranquist; m. Jerome F. Schwier, June 2, 1948 (dec.); 1 child, Charles. BS, St. Louis U., 1944, MA, 1949, PhD, 1952. Assoc. Bee Angel & Assocs., St. Louis, 1945-48; instr. St. Louis U., 1948-51, lectr., 1953-60; ptnr. Inland Rsch., 1953-60; from lectr. to prof. So. Ill. U., Edwardsville, 1960-90, ret., 1990. Translator, editor: Vilfredo Pareto's Manual of Political Economy, 1972; founder, book rev. editor Jour. Econs., 1994—. Mem. Am. Mktg. Assn. (former chpt. pres.), Am. Econs. Assn., Am. Statis. Assn. (former chpt. pres.), Mo. Valley Econ. Assn. (former pres.), Hist. Econ. Soc. Home: 4440 Lindell Blvd Apt 1601 Saint Louis MO 63108-2442

SCHWIER, PRISCILLA LAMB GUYTON, television broadcasting company executive; b. Toledo, Ohio, May 8, 1939; d. Edward Oliver and Prudence (Hutchinson) L.; m. Robert T. Guyton, June 21, 1963 (dec. Sept. 1976); children— Melissa, Margaret, Robert; m. Frederick W. Schwier, May 11, 1984. B.A., Smith Coll., 1961; M.A., U. Toledo, 1972. Pres. Gt. Lakes Comms., Inc., 1982-97; vice chmn. Seilon, Inc., Toledo, 1981-83, also dir. Contbr. articles to profl. jours. Trustee Wilberforce U., Ohio, 1983—, Planned Parenthood, Toledo, 1979-83, Maumee Valley Country Day Sch., Toledo; bd. dirs. N.W. Ohio Hospice, 1991-98, Episcopal Ch., Maumee, Ohio, 1983—, Pub. Broadcasting Found. of N.W. Ohio, 2002-; bd. trustees Toledo Hosp., Maumee Country Day Sch., 1986-92; pres. Edward Lamb Found., 1987—. Democrat. Episcopalian. Home and Office: 345 E Front St Perrysburg OH 43551-2131

SCHWIMMER, SIGMUND, food enzymologist; b. Cleve., Sept. 20, 1917; s. Solomon and Sarah (Brown) S.; m. Sylvia Klein, Dec. 18, 1941; children— Susan, Elaine. Student Ohio State U., 1935-36; B.S., George Washington U., 1940; M.S., Georgetown U., 1941, Ph.D., 1943. From lab. asst. to research chemist USDA, Washington and Berkeley, Calif., 1936-62; adj. prof. biology Calif. Inst. Tech., Pasadena, 1963-65; chief research biochemist USDA, Berkeley, 1966-72, collaborator emeritus, 1975— ; adj. prof. dept. nutritional scis. U. Calif.-Berkeley, 1985-87; sr. expert biochemistry UN Indsl. Devel. Orgn., Haifa, Israel, 1973-74; cons. food enzymology, Berkeley, 1980— ; lectr. dept. biotech. food engring. Israel Inst. Tech., Haifa, 1973; vis. scientist Food Industry Rsch. and Devel. Inst., Hsinchu, Taiwan, 1992. Contbr. articles to profl. jours.; editor, Biochem. Sci. Biotech., Cambridge, Eng., 1983—, Trends in Biochemistry, Trends in Biotechnology, 1983—, Jour. Food Biochemistry, 1977-98; author: Source Book of Food Enzymology, 1982 (Jour. Assn. Coll. and Research Librarians award 1983). Fellow John S. Guggenheim, NSF; recipient Superior Service award USDA, 1949, 59, Lifetime Achievement award, 1993, Agrl. and Food Chemistry Divsn. award Am. Chem. Soc., 1996. Fellow Inst. Food Technologists; mem. Am. Soc. Biochemistry Molecular Biology, Sigma Xi. Office: Western Regional Ctr USDA 800 Buchanan St Berkeley CA 94710-1105 also: U Calif Dept Nutritional Sci Berkeley CA 94720-0001

SCHWIND, MICHAEL ANGELO, law educator; b. Vienna, Austria, July 2, 1924; came to U.S., 1951; s. Siegfried and Sali (Salner) S. JD, U. Central, Ecuador, 1949; LL.M. in Internat. Law, NYU, 1953, LL.B., 1957. Bar: Ecuador 1949, N.Y. 1957, U.S. Supreme Ct. 1967. Pvt. practice, N.Y.C., 1957-69; Lectr. law NYU Sch. Law, 1959-63, adj. asst. prof., 1963-64, assoc. prof., 1964-67, prof., 1967-94, prof. emeritus, 1994—. Dir. Inter-Am. Law Inst., Inst. Comparative Law, NYU Sch. Law, 1967-71. Bd. editors Am. Jour. Comparative Law, 1971-97. Mem. Am. Assn. Comparative Study Law (bd. dirs. 1971-2000), Am. Fgn. Law Assn. (bd. dirs. 1980-83, 84-87, 88-91, 93-96, 97-2000, v.p. 1983-84, 91-93, 96-97, 2000—). Office: NYU Sch Law 40 Washington Sq S Rm 321 New York NY 10012-1005 E-mail: schwindm@juris.law.nyu.edu.

SCHWING, MARK DAVID, artist; b. Ann Arbor, Mich., Aug. 2, 1957; s. Richard Schwing and Joan Baker. Student, Parsons Sch. Design, N.Y.C., 1975-80. Represented by Sherry Washington Gallery, Detroit. Gallery vol. Detroit Inst. Arts, 1993-96; mem. exhbn. com. Detroit Focus Gallery, 1996-98. One-man shows include Sixth Street Gallery, 1984, Urban Inst. for Contemporary Art, 1989, Willis Gallery, 1990, 1st Unitarian-Universalist Ch., 1997, Millers Artist Supplies Co., 1999, A.C., T. Gallery, 2001, Birmingham Unitarian Church, 2002; exhibited in group shows at Detroit Focus Gallery, 1983, 89, 98, Detroit Artists Mkt., 1985, 88, Galaxy Hut, 1997, A.C., T. Gallery, 1998-2002, Swann Gallery, 1998, Sherry Washington Gallery, 2000; completed Time Capsule 2098, 1998. Vol. Travelers Aid Soc., Detroit, 1989; mem. ACLU. Mem. The Detroit Inst. Arts, The Artists Coop., Urban Inst. for Contemporary Arts. Democrat. Unitarian-Universalist. Office: Painting Etc 459 Prentis St Apt B3 Detroit MI 48201-1262 E-mail: bluskyart@hotmail.com.

SCHWINN, DONALD EDWIN, environmental engineer; b. N.Y.C., July 18, 1935; BS in Civil Engring., The Cooper Union, 1957; MS in Sanitary Engring., MIT, 1959. Diplomate Am. Acad. Environ. Engrs. Sanitary engr. Dorr-Oliver Inc., Stamford, Conn., 1957-62, Metcalf & Eddy, Boston, 1962-66, exec. engr., 1966-70, v.p., 1970-74; ptnr. Stearns & Wheler, Cazenovia, N.Y., 1974-88, sr. ptnr., 1988-98, cons. wastewater, 1998—. Mem. US/USSR joint tech. commn. external utility systems HUD, Washington, 1979-85. Sr. author: U.S. EPA Process Design Manual for Upgrading Wastewater Treatment Plants, 1974; contbg. author: U.S. EPA Process Design Manual for Nitrogen Control, 1992; co-editor: WEF Manual of Practice for Design of Municipal Wastewater Treatment Plants, 1998; contbr. articles to profl. jours. Co-chmn. Cazenovia Youth Soccer Program 1980-85; mem. Cazenovia Conservation Commn., 1984-93, St. James Music Ministry, Cazenovia, 1990—; dir. Three Bays Preservation Inc., Osterville, Mass., 1999—. Recipient Arthur Sidney Bedell award Water Pollution Control Fedn., 1974, 1st award Consulting Engrs. Coun. N.Y., 1977, Chmn.'s award Water Pollution Control Fedn., 1988. Mem. ASCE (life), Water Environ. Fedn. (life), N.Y. Environ. Assn. (life; Kenneth Allen award 1985). Achievements include invention and development of cyclical nitrogen removal process for removal of nitrogen from sewage. E-mail: deschwinn@att.net.

SCHWINN, STEVEN DAVID, lawyer, mediator; b. Dayton, Ohio, Sept. 15, 1969; s. David Ronald and Marilyn Esther (Durst) S.; m. Sandra Gutek, May 26, 1995. BA, Mich. State U., 1992; JD, The Am. U., 1995. Bar: Mich. 1995. Asst. gen. counsel Peace Corps, Washington, 1995-99; assoc. dir. legal rsch., writing program George Washington Univ., 1999—. Adj. prof. law Am. U., 1996-99; mediator D.C. Superior Ct., 1996—. Vol. lawyer Washington Legal Clinic for Homeless, 1995—. Home: 11204 Edson Park Pl # 8 Bethesda MD 20852 E-mail: sschwinn@main.nlc.gwv.edu.

SCHWISTER, JAY EDWARD, portfolio manager; b. Milw., Apr. 16, 1962; s. Jerome Charles and Carol Christina (Keeler) Schwister; m. Sara M. Schlaudecker; 1 child Katharine Claire. BS in Fin. cum laude, Marquette U., 1984. Chartered fin. analyst. Sr. investment officer First Wis. Trust Co., Milw., 1984-87; sr. v.p., sr. portfolio mgr. Putnam Investments, Boston, 1987—. Fin. com. mem. Hills Bd. Trustees, Wayland, Mass., 1990—; pres. coun. Marquette U., Milwaukee, Wis., 1990—. Chmn. fund raising com. Marquette U. Alumni Fund, Boston, 1989—. Mem. Assn. for Investment Mgmt. and Rsch., Boston Security Analysts Soc., Inc., Bond Analysts Soc., Inc., Beta Gamma Sigma. Avocations: golf, tennis, travel, woodworking, music. Home: 83 Hillside Dr Wayland MA 01778-3826 Office: Putnam Investments 1 Post Office Sq Fl 7 Boston MA 02109-2106

SCHWOERER, JOHN ARNOLD, mechanical engineer; b. Phila., Apr. 9, 1954; s. Frank and Lois Katherine (Green) S.; m. Virginia Mary Tierney, Apr. 13, 1991; children: Emma Anne, Charles Francis. AB in Physics, Dartmouth Coll., 1976; MSME, MIT, 1979, ScDME, 1985. Engr. transient/control analysis GE Aircraft Engines, Lynn, Mass., 1984-87, staff engr. transient/controls, 1987-93; staff engr. screw compressor Carrier Carlyle Compressor, Syracuse, N.Y., 1993-95; sr. engr. technology Jacobs Vehicle Systems, Bloomfield, Conn., 1995-99, prin. engr., analysis team leader, 1999—. Software cons. Neutron Products, Inc., Dickerson, Md., 1974-83; engring. cons. Carrier Carlyle Compressor, Syracuse, 1996-97. Contbr. articles to profl. jours. including Advances in Cryogenic Engring., AIAA Jour. of Energy, Symposium on the Engring. Aspects of MHD; patentee in field. Mem. ASME, Soc. of Automotive Engrs. Achievements include developing real-time simulation approach for digital control development at GE Aircraft Engines; developed approach for performance rating of screw compressors; developed state-of-the-art hydraulic simulation capability and lead the selection and customization of engine performance analysis software at Jacobs Vehicle Systems for the design of new technology diesel engine retarding and variable actuation systems. Avocations: home improvement projects, swimming, tennis, small sailboat racing, cross-country skiing. Office: Jacobs Vehicle Systems 22 E Dudley Town Rd Bloomfield CT 06002-1440 E-mail: jschwoerer@jakebrake.com.

SCHWYN, CHARLES EDWARD, accountant; b. Muncie, Ind., Oct. 12, 1932; s. John and Lela Mae (Oliver) S.; m. Mary Helen Nickey, May 25, 1952 (dec.); children: Douglas, Craig, Beth; m. Madelyn Steinmetz, June 26, 1993. BS, Ball State U., 1957. CPA, Calif., D.C. With Haskins & Sells, Chgo., Orlando, Fla., 1958-67; mgr. Deloitte, Haskins & Sells, Milan, Italy, 1967-70, San Francisco, 1970-80; with Deloitte, Haskins & Sells (now Deloitte & Touche), Oakland, Calif., ptnr. in charge, 1980-92, ret., 1992. Bd. dirs. Jr. Ctr. Art and Sci., 1982-89, pres., 1987-88; bd. dirs., trustee Oakland Symphony, 1982-86, 89-91; bd. dirs. Oakland Met. YMCA, 1984-89, Oakland Police Activities League, 1981-91, Joe Morgan Youth Found., 1982-91, Summit Med. Ctr., 1989-94, 96-99, Marcus A. Foster Ednl. Inst., 1986-95, pres., 1991-93; bd. dirs. Greater Oakland Internat. Trade Ctr., 1996-97; mem. adv. bd. Festival of Lake, 1984-89, U. Oakland Met. Forum, 1991-99; co-chmn. Commn. for Positive Change in Oakland Pub. Schs., 1989-91; mem. campaign cabinet United Way Bay Area, 1989; bd. regents Samuel Merritt Coll., 1993-2001, chmn. bd. regents, 1996-2001; chief of protocol, City of Oakland, 1996-97; mem. Calif. Coun. of the Oakland Mus. of Calif. Found., 1997—; docent Pt. Sur Hist. Lighthouse, 2000—; bd. dirs. Monterey Symphony, 2001--, Ctrl. Coast Lighthouse Keepers, 2001--. With USN, 1952—56. Recipient Cmty. Svc. award Kiwanis Club, Orlando, Fla., Cert. Recognition Calif. Legis. Assembly, 1988, Ctr. for Ind. Living award, Oakland Bus. Arts award for outstanding bus. leader Oakland C. of C., 1992; honoree Schwyn Endowment fund for cancer rsch. Bay Area Tumor Inst., 1998; date of job retirement honored in his name by Oakland mayor; named Knight Order of St. John of Jerusalem Knights Hospitaller. Mem. AICPA (coun. 1987-90), Oakland C. of C. (chmn. bd. dirs. 1987-88, exec. com. 1982-89), Oakland Met. C. of C., pres., 1996, Calif. Soc. CPAs (bd. dirs. 1979-81, 83-84, 85-87, pres. San Francisco chpt. 1983-84), Nat. Assn. Accts. (pres. Fla. chpt. 1967), Sons in Retirement (treas. 2001—), Claremont Country Club (treas., bd. dirs. 1989-97), Lakeview Club (bd. govs. 1987-92), Oakland 100 Club (pres. 1994), Rotary (bd. dirs. Oakland club 1986-88, 91-92, treas. 1984-86, pres. 1991-92), Golf Club at Quail Lodge (bd. dirs. 2000-02). E-mail: ceschwyn@aol.com.

SCHY, GAY, artist, investor; b. Greenwich, Conn., July 10, 1937; d. Ralph Morrel and Dorothy (Abrams) Griswold; m. John Craver (div. 1974); 1 child, Linda Craver; m. Charles W. Torrey, July 22, 1979. BS, U. Chgo., 1959, MSW, 1964; MA, San Jose State U., 1989, MFA, 1990. Social worker Santa Clara County, San Jose, Calif., 1970-80, pvt. practice, Los Gatos, 1980-86; artist Santa Cruz, 1986—; represented by Fredrick Spratt Gallery, San Jose. Bd. dirs. San Jose State Sch. Art and Design, 1988-92; advisor, bd. dirs. San Jose Inst. for Contemporary Art, 1990—. Vol. Habitat for Humanities, Santa Cruz, 1991—, U. Calif. Santa Cruz Arbor, 1996—. Avocations: gardening, bicycling, reading, travel, swimming. Home: 3040 Pleasant Valley Rd Aptos CA 95003-9716

SCIABARRA, CHRIS MATTHEW, political scientist; b. Bklyn., Feb. 17, 1960; s. Salvatore Charles and Ann (Michalopoulos) S. BA, NYU, 1981, MA, 1983, PhD, 1988. Vis. scholar dept. politics N.Y.U., 1989—. Author: Ayn Rand: The Russian Radical, 1995, Marx, Hayek and Utopia, 1995, Total Freedom: Toward a Dialectical Libertarianism, 2000; co-editor: Feminist Interpretations of Ayn Rand Studies, 1999; founding co-editor The Jour. of Ayn Rand Studies, 1999—; contbg. editor: Critical Rev., 1987—. Bd. dirs. Canarsie AWARE, Inc., Bklyn., 1993-00. Herbert Lehman fellow, 1981-85, Charlotte Newcombe Found. fellow, 1987-88, O'Boyle fellow Inst. for Humane Studies, 1990-91, Earhart Found. fellow, 1990-92, 96. Mem. MLA, Am. Polit. Sci. Assn., Am. Philosophical Assn., Joseph H. Park History Hons. Soc. (award 1980), Omicron Delta Epsilon, Phi Beta Kappa. Avocations: music, film history, pop culture. Home and Office: 1840 W 5th St Brooklyn NY 11223-2638

SCIALLIS, GABRIEL FRANK, dermatologist; b. Trenton, Apr. 15, 1944; s. Gabriel Frank and Mary Margaret Sciallis; m. Mary Margaret Osborn, Aug. 25, 1972; children: Gabriel Frank III, Michael Joseph, Andrew Peter, Margaret Kelly. BA, Rutgers U., 1966; MD, George Washington U., 1970. Diplomate Am. Bd. Dermatology. Intern George Washington U. Hosp., 1970-71; fellow in dermatology Mayo Clinic, Rochester, Minn., 1974; Med. Sch. instr. Georgetown U., Washington, 1974-76; pvt. practice Mercerville, N.J., 1976-2000; staff cons. dept. dermatology Mayo Clinic, Rochester, Minn., 2000—. Bd. dirs. Lawrenceville (N.J.) Property Casualty, Med. Inter-Ins. Exch., Lawrenceville, 1977-99. Contbr. articles to profl. jours. Lt. comdr. USN, 1974-76. Fellow AMA, Soc. Dermatologic Surgery, Soc. for Investigative Dermatology, Acad. Dermatology; mem. Internat. Soc. Dermatology, Dermatol. Soc. N.J. (pres. 1993-94), Mercer County Med. Soc. (pres. 1991), Minn. Dermatol. Assn., Minn. Med. Assn., Phi Beta Kappa, Alpha Omega Alpha. Avocations: music, guitar, golf. E-mail: sciallis.gabriel@mayo.edu.

SCIAME, DONALD RICHARD, computer systems analyst, dentist; b. Bklyn., Sept. 10, 1945; s. Mario and Ruth Marie (Kozell) S.; m. Kathy Ann Thamann, Mar. 17, 1987. AB, Rutgers U., 1967; DMD, N.J. Coll. Medicine & Dentistry, 1971; MAPA, U. N.Mex., 1984; cert. locksmith, electronic security, NRI Schs., 1988. Dep. chief svc. unit dental program USPHS Indian Hosp., Whiteriver, Ariz., 1971-73, chief svc. unit dental program Sacaton, 1973-76, Santa Fe, 1976-88; systems analyst USPHS Area Office, Albuquerque, 1988-90; dir. div. info. mgmt. svcs. USPHS-IHS Area Office, 1990-98; ret., 1998. Contbr. articles to profl. jours. Mem. ADA, Internat. Coll. Dentists, Soc. Am. Magicians, Psi Omega Dental Fraternity, N.J. Dental Sch. Alumni Assn., Am. Culinary Fedn. Home: 1914 Conejo Dr Santa Fe NM 87505-6108 E-mail: donsciame@mail.com. *Personal philosophy: Moving from bites to bytes.*

SCIAME, JOSEPH, university administrator; b. Bklyn., Sept. 9, 1941; s. Joseph and Sophie (Pintacuda) S. EdB, St. John's U., 1971. Fin. aid officer, asst. to dean of admissions St. John's U., Jamaica, N.Y., 1967-71, dir. fin. aid, 1971-82, dean fin. aid, 1982, v.p. fin. aid and student svcs., 1982-94, v.p. for govt. and cmty. rels. NY, 1994—2002, v.p. for cmty. rels., 2002—. Mem. Gov. Commn. on Sch. Achievement, 1971—, chairperson, 1993—; pres. N.Y. Assn. Student Fin. Aid Adminstrn., 1980-82, Ea. Assn. Student Fin. Aid Adminstrn., 1986-87. Chmn. bd. ethics Town of North Hempstead, N.Y., 1984—; nat. chmn., bd. dirs. Garibaldi-Meucci Mus., N.Y., 1987-93, 97-99, pres., CEO, 1999-2002; mem. Providence Rest Found., 1995—; bd. dirs. St. John's Prep, 1996—; bd. mem. Queens Symphony Orch., 2000—, Boy Scouts Am., 2000—, v.p. membership, 2001—; bd. mem. Holocaust Resource Ctr., 2002—. Decorated cavaliere del Merito della Repubblica Italiana, Cavaliere Ufficiale Order Merit House of Savoy; recipient Lifetime Membership award Ea. Assn., 1995, Achievement award N.Y. State Fin. Aid Adminstrs., 1982, Congl. Record award, 1979, 91, 93, 94, 95. Mem. Nat. Assn. Student Fin. Aid Adminstrs. (chmn. 1987-88, Disting. Svc. award 1988, Leadership award 1994), Assn. Equestrian Order Holy Sepulchre (knight grand cross 1991, knight invested 1980), Order Sons of Italy in Am. (lodge pres. 1974-75, state pres. 1993-97, nat. v.p. 1997—), Futures in Edn. Found. (vice chair 1991-93, chair 1994-97), Jamaica C. of C. (bd. dirs.), Queens Symphony Orch. (bd. dirs.), Boy Scouts Am.(v.p. membership com. 2001—), Holocaust Rejourne Ctr. (bd. dirs.). Roman Catholic. Avocations: walking, cooking, gardening, reading, lecturing. Home: 6 Jones St New Hyde Park NY 11040-1616 also: Trout Ln Southampton NY 11968 Office: St John's Univ Off Vp Cmty Rels 8000 Utopia Pky Jamaica NY 11439-0001 Fax: 718-990-1920. Business E-mail: sciamej@stjohns.edu.

SCIANCE, CARROLL THOMAS, chemical engineer; b. Okemah, Okla., Feb. 16, 1939; s. Carroll Elmer and Winifred (Black) S.; m. Anita Ruth Fischer, Jan. 30, 1960; children: Steven, Frederick, Thomas, Erica. BS in Chem. Engring., U. Okla., 1960, M in Chem. Engring., 1964, PhD, 1966. With E.I. duPont de Nemours & Co., Inc., 1966-95, planning mgr. nylon intermediates divsn., petrochem. dept. Del., 1978-80, tech. mgr., 1980-83, dir engring.

rsch., engring. dept., 1983-87, prin. cons. corp. rsch. and devel. planning divsn., 1987-89; mgr. petroleum products R&D divsn. Conoco, Inc., 1989-93; dir. environ. tech. partnerships ctrl. R&D dept. DuPont, 1993-95; pres. Sci. Cons. Svcs., Inc., 1995—. Sr. lectr. U. Tex., Austin, 1996—; mem. Travis County (Tex.) Appraisals Rev. Bd., 1999—; mem. math. scis. and edn. bd. NRC, 1987-89; mem. adv. bd. for chem. sci. and tech. NIST, 1988-94. Served as officer USAR, 1961-63. Fellow AIChE (bd. dirs. material engring. and scis. divsn. 1986-92, chmn. new tech.com. 1990-92, govt. rels. com. 1993-96); mem. Fedn. Materials Socs. (v.p. 1988-92, pres. 1993-94), Am. Chem. Soc. (mem. environ. R&D com. 1995-99), N.Y. Acad. Scis., Sigma Xi. Home: 16658 Forest Way Austin TX 78734-1110

SCIANNA, IRENE F. film company executive; b. Newark, Feb. 22, 1942; d. Louis Flaxman and Evelyn (Schwartz) Livenstein; m. Cosimo J. Scianna, June 12, 1971; children: Paul Sebastian, Stephanie Ann. Student, U. Cin., 1960; graduate, Lat. Am. Inst., 1962. Owner Jeanirene Ltd., N.Y.C., 1986-2000; co-founder, owner Cosimo's Studio, Inc., 1972—; owner, sponsor Sweet Dreams, A Film. Co., Inc., 1995-97. Pres. South Orange (N.J.) Neighbors, 1981-82, Glass House Coop., N.Y.C., 1989-91, treas. 1988-89; chairperson fundraising Midnite Madness, South Orange, N.J., 1992; bd. dirs. Youth Employment Svcs., 1990-91. Mem. Dir. Guild of Am. (1st asst. dir. 1991—), Assn. Indep. Comml. Producers. Office: Cosimo and Company 435 W 19th St New York NY 10011-3803 E-mail: IScianna@aol.com.

SCIANNAMEO, FRANCO LUDOVICO ORLANDO, music educator; b. Maglie, Apulia, Italy, Aug. 5, 1942; came to the U.S., 1968; s. Donato and Noemi (De Donno) S.; m. Louise G. Cavanaugh, Oct. 26, 1984; 1 child, Nicholas. Diploma (prof. music), Conservatorio Santa Cecilia, Rome, 1963; MA in Hist. Musicology, MA in Cultural Studies, U. Pitts., 1996. Solo player I Solisti di Roma, Rome, 1963-68; prof. music Nazionale Academia Santa Cecilia, 1967; faculty The Hartford (Conn.) Conservatory, 1968-79; assoc. concertmaster Ft. Worth Symphony, 1980-83; dir. publs. L.F.S. Publs., Inc., Ann Arbor, Mich., 1984-89; faculty Carnegie Mellon U., Pitts., 1990—. Faculty The Chautauqua (N.Y.) Instn., 1996—. Author: Scoring Fellini, 1996, Giacinto Scelsi, 1998, Filippo Traetta, 1998, Roman Soundtrack, 1999; editor The Violexchange, 1986-92; editor sheet music Rarities for Strings, 1970-86. Office: Carnegie Mellon Univ Sch Music 5000 Forbes Ave Pittsburgh PA 15213-3890

SCIARRA, JOHN J. physician, educator; b. West Haven, Conn., Mar. 4, 1932; s. John and Mary Grace (Sanzone) S.; m. Barbara Crafts Patton, Jan. 9, 1960; children: Vanessa Patton, John Crafts, Leonard Chapman. BS, Yale U., 1953; MD, Columbia U., N.Y.C., 1957, PhD, 1963. Asst. prof. Columbia U., N.Y.C., 1964-68; prof., dept. head U. Minn. Med. Sch., Mpls., 1968-74; prof. Northwestern U. Med. Sch., Chgo., 1974—; chmn. ob-gyn Northwestern Meml. Hosp., 1974—. Editor Gyn-Ob Reference Series, 1973—, Internat. Jour. Gyn-Ob, 1985—. V.p. med. affairs Chgo. Maternity Ctr., Chgo., 1974—. Fellow ACS, Am. Coll. Ob-Gyn. (chmn. internal affairs com. 1985-89); Internat. Fedn. Gyn-Ob. (pres. 1991-94, pres. Supporters Assn. 1994-2000); mem. Assn. Profs. Gyn-Ob. (sec. 1976-79, pres. 1980-81), Am. Assn. Maternal and Neonatal Health (pres. 1980-89), Coun. Resident Edn. in Ob-Gyn., Am. Fertility Soc. (Hartman award 1965, bd. dirs. 1971-73), Assn. Profs. Gyn-Ob. Med. Edn. Found. (sec.-treas. 1987-91, pres. 1991-93), Ctrl. Assn. Ob-Gyn. (trustees 1986-90, pres. 1990-91), Chgo. Gynecol. Soc. (pres. 1990-91), Internat. Soc. Gynecol. Endoscopy (v.p. 1997-99, pres. 1999-2001), Internat. Acad. Human Reprodn., Yale Club N.Y.C., Carleton Club (Chgo.). Avocation: photography, food, wine. Office: Northwestern U Med Sch 333 E Superior St Chicago IL 60611-3015 E-mail: jsciarra@nmh.org.

SCIBA, JOANN, social worker; b. Manistee, Mich., Oct. 19, 1946; d. Raymond Peter and Bernardine Alice (Wroblewski) Sciba. Student, Muskegon Bus. Coll., 1964-66; BS, Ferris State U., 1969; MSW, Western Mich. U., 1982. Cert. AIDS educator. Tchr. North Muskegon (Mich.) High Sch., 1969-70; caseworker Muskegon County Dept. Social Svcs., Muskegon, 1970-76, child welfare specialist, 1976-88; med. social work cons. Mich. Dept. Social Svcs., 1988-97; client adv. L&S Assocs., Okemos, Mich., 1997—. Vol. United Way, Muskegon, 1985-86; H-PAC mem. March of Dimes, Grand Rapids, Mich., 1988-92; program chmn. Friends of Norton Shores Libr., Muskegon, 1990-94, Muskegon Area AIDS Resource Svcs., 1993—, West Mich. AIDS Forum, Grand Rapids; bd. dirs. Cmty. AIDS Coun. West Ctrl. Mich., chmn. pub. policy com., 1994-96. Recipient Cert. of Recognition, NASW, 1986, McClees award, Muskegon Area AIDS Resource Svcs., 2001. Mem. Mich. Coun. Social Svcs. Workers. Democrat. Avocations: travel, theater, corresponding with pen friends, swimming, reading. Home and Office: 665 Lake Forest Ln Apt R12 Muskegon MI 49441-4785 E-mail: rubyred42@attbi.com.

SCIFRES, DONALD RAY, semiconductor laser, fiber optics and electronics company executive; b. Lafayette, Ind. m. Carol Scifres. BS, Purdue U., 1968; MS, U. Ill., 1970, PhD, 1972; Doctorate (hon.) , Purdue U., 2001. Rsch. and tchg. asst. U. Ill., Urbana, 1968-72; rsch. fellow, area mgr. Xerox Corp., Palo Alto, Calif., 1972-83; founder, pres., CEO SDL, Inc., San Jose, 1983-2001, dir., 1983-2001, chmn., 1992-2001; co-chmn., chief strategy officer JDS Uniphase Corp., 2001—. Nat. lectr. IEEE Quantum Electronics Soc., 1979 Bd. editors Jour. Fiber and Integrated Optics, 1978; mem. editorial adv. bd. Photonics Spectra, 1992—; contbr. articles to tech. jours.; patentee in field. Recipient Disting. Engring. Alumni award, Purdue U., 1990, Outstanding Elec. Engr. award, 1992, Engring. Alumni award, U. Ill., 1991, Alumni Honor award, 1993, Distinction in Photonics award, Laurin Pub. Co., 1999, The Rank prize, Royal Soc. Medicine, 2001; fellow U. Ill., 1968, Gen. Telephone and Electronics, 1970—72. Fellow IEEE (Jack Morton award 1985, 3d Millenium award 2000), IEEE Lasers and Electro-Optics Soc. (pres. 1992, Engring. Achievement award 1994), Optical Soc. Am. (Edward H. Land medal 1996); mem. Am. Phys. Soc. (George E. Pake prize 1997), Lasers and Electro-Optics Mfg. Assn. (bd. dirs. 1992—, sec. 1994, pres. 1996), Nat. Acad. Engring., Tau Beta Pi, Eta Kappa Nu, Phi Eta Sigma. Office: SDL Inc 80 Rose Orchard Way San Jose CA 95134-1356

SCIMECCA, JOSEPH ANDREW, sociologist, educator; b. N.Y.C., Aug. 26, 1940; s. Francis and Frances (Mula) S.; m. Elsie M. Lundberg, Nov. 23, 1968; children: Kirsten, Faith. BA, Hunter Coll.-CUNY, 1962; MA, NYU, 1965, PhD, 1972. Instr. Upsala Coll., East Orange, N.J., 1966-68; lectr. Herbert H. Lehman Coll., Bronx, N.Y., 1968-69; asst. prof. U. Maine, Orono, 1969-70, disting. prof., 1970; assoc. prof. SUNY-Albany, 1970-77; prof., chmn. dept. sociology George Mason U., Fairfax, Va., 1977-87, 96—, dir. Ctr. for Conflict Analysis and Resolution, 1987-90. Author: (with Roland Damiano) Crisis at St. John's, 1968, The Sociological Theory of C. Wright Mills, 1977, Education and Society, 1980, Society and Freedom, 1995. Mem. Am. Sociol. Assn., Am. Soc. Criminology, Eastern Sociol. Soc., Soc. Study Social Issues, Assn. for Humanist Sociology (v.p. 1982-83, pres. 1987-88). Democrat. Lutheran. Home: 11391 Bantry Ter Fairfax VA 22030-5411 Office: George Mason U 4400 University Dr Fairfax VA 22030-4422

SCIOCCHETTI, PAUL VINCENT, lawyer; b. Schenectady, N.Y, Mar. 1, 1961; s. Augusto Julius and Josephine (DeLeonardis) S. BA, Siena Coll., 1983; JD, Pace U., 1986. Bar: N.Y. 1987, U.S. Dist. Ct. (no. dist.) N.Y. Assoc. Parisi, DeLorenzo, Gordon, Pasquariello & Weiskopf, P.C., Schenectady, 1986-87, Capasso Burns & Massaroni, Schenectady, 1987-90; pvt. practice, 1990-94; of counsel Donald Zee, P.C., Albany, 1995-97; pvt. practice, 1997—. Mem. panel arbitrators Am. Arbitration Assn., Syracuse, N.Y., 1987—, Schenectady County Arbitration Commn., 1987—; mem. Ctrl. Park Music Stage Task Force, 1999. Bd. dirs. Hispanic Cmty. Coalition, Electric City Music Festival, Inc., 1990-94, Boys and Girls Club Am., 1993-94; chmn. Com. for Preservation of Schnectady County Parks (Adopt-a-Park), 1990-95; Mayfair com. Residential Opportunities, Inc., 1996-97. Mem. ATLA, N.Y. State Trial Lawyers Assn., N.Y. State Bar Assn. (entertainment, arts and sports law sect. exec. com. 1991—), Schenectady County Bar Assn., Pace U. Alumni Assn. (chmn. Capital Dist. chpt. 1988-89), Nat. Italian Am. Found. (founder, co-chair greater capital dist./upstate N.Y. chpt.), N.Y. State Assn. (small law firm task force 1996). Roman Catholic. Office: 201 Nott Ter Schenectady NY 12307-1025 Home: 122 Dedhem Post Dr Schenectady NY 12303-5274

SCIOLARO, CHARLES MICHAEL, cardiac surgeon; b. Kansas City, Kans., July 5, 1958; s. Gerald Michael and Charleen Gwen Sciolaro; m. Vicki Lynn Mizell, Sept. 29 BA in Biology and Chemistry magna cum laude, Mid Am. Nazarene Coll., 1980; MD magna cum laude, U. Kans., Kansas City, 1984. Diplomate Am. Bds. Gen. Surgery, Thoracic and Cardiac; lic. Ariz., Calif., La., Fla., Kans.; cert. advanced cardiac life support, advanced cardiac life support instr., advanced trauma life support, Calif. x-ray supr. and operator, transesophageal echocardiography. Intern gen. surgery Tucson hosps. surg. program U. Ariz., 1984-85, resident gen. surgery, 1985-86, 87-89, chief resident gen. surgery, 1989-90; biochemistry rsch. fellow U. Kans., Kansas City, 1978-79; instr. surgery Loma Linda U. Med. Ctr., Tucson, 1991-92; staff physician St. Francis Cabrini Hosp., Alexandria, La., 1993-96, Rapides Regional Med. Ctr., Alexandria, 1993-96; instr. surgery Loma Linda (Calif.) U. Med. Ctr., 1991-93; physician divsn. cardiac, thoracic and vascular surgery MacArthur Surg. Clinic, Alexandria, 1993-96, Kanza Multispecialty Clinic, Kansas City, 1996—; staff physician Providence Med. Ctr., 1996—, Bethany Med. Ctr., 1996—. Emergency rm. physician, cons. Nat. Emergency Corp., Tucson, 1986-87; part-time emergency care attendent Veteran's Med. Ctr., Tucson, 1985-89, Cigna Urgent Care, 1985-89; with divsn. cardiac, thoracic and vascular surgery MacArthur Surg. Clin., Alexandria, 1993-96. Author: (manuscripts) Aortic Coarctation in Infants, 1991; researcher, lectr. and presenter in field. Mem. ACS, AMA, Am. Coll. Cardiologists, Am. Coll. Chest Physicians, La. Med. Soc., Kans. Med. Soc., Wyandotte Med. Soc., Rapides Med. Soc., Southea. Surg. Congress, Soc. Thoracic Surgery, Internat. Soc. Intraoperative Cardiovasc. Ultrasound, Internat. Coll. Surgons, Kans. Med. Soc., Wyandotte County Med. Soc., Internat. Platform Assn., Am. Heart Assn. (bd. dirs. Kansas City chpt.), Phi Delta Lambda. Republican. Avocations: photography, golf, softball. Office: Kanza 8919 Parallel Pky Ste 555 Kansas City KS 66112 E-mail: csciol@dnamail.com.

SCIPIO, L(OUIS) ALBERT, II, former aerospace science engineering educator, architect, military historian; b. Juarez, Mex., Aug. 22, 1922; s. Louis Albert and Marie Leona (Richardson) S.; m. Katherine Ruth Jones, Aug. 15, 1942; children: Louis Albert, Karen R. BS, Tuskegee Inst., 1943; B.Civil Engring., U. Minn., 1948, MS, 1950, PhD, 1958. Archtl. draftsman McKissack & McKissack, Tuskegee, Ala., 1943; instr. Tuskegee Inst., 1946; designer Long & Thorshov, Mpls., 1948-50; lectr. U. Minn., 1950-59; research physicist Hughes Aircraft Co., Culver City, Calif., 1954; Fulbright prof. Cairo U., Giza, Egypt, 1955-56; assoc. prof. mechanics Howard U., Washington, 1959-61; Fulbright prof. Cairo U., Giza, Egypt, 1955-56; dir. grad. studies for engring. and architecture, prof. aerospace engring. Howard U., Washington, 1967-70, Univ. prof. space scis., 1970-87, Disting. Univ. prof. emeritus, 1987—; prof. phys. scis. U. P.R., Mayaguez, 1961-63; prof. aerospace engring. U. Pitts., 1963-67; pub. Roman Publs., Silver Springs, Md., 1981—; cons. in field. Author Compendium of Aircraft Stress Analysis and Design, 1956 Author: Principles on Continua with Applications, 1966, Structural Design Concepts, 1967, E.M. Collar Insignia, 1907-1926, 1981, Last of the Black Regulars, 1983, With the Red Hand Division, 1985, The 24th Infantry at Fort Benning, 1986, Pre-War Days at Tuskegee, 1987, The Collar Disk Story (1907-1999), 1999. Bd. visitors Air Force Inst. Tech., 1979-83. Served with AUS, 1943-46. Mem. N.Y. Acad. Scis., Internat. Assn. Bridge and Structural Engrs., Soc. Natural Philosophy, AIAA, AAAS; mem. Am. Phys. Soc.; mem. NSPE, Co. of Mil. Historians, Coun. on Am. Mil. Past, Phi Beta Kappa, Sigma Xi, Alpha Kappa Mu, Pi Mu Epsilon, Sigma Pi Sigma, Sigma Gamma Tau, Pi Tau Sigma. Home: 12511 Montclair Dr Silver Spring MD 20904-2053

SCIRE, FRANK JACKSON, retired radar scientist; b. Bklyn., July 15, 1928; s. Marco and Marianna (Bianco) S.; m. Jacqueline Deleranko, June 21, 1958; children: Marianne, Mark, Paul. BSEE, Pratt Inst., 1952; MSEE, NYU, 1958; PhD, Polytech. Inst. Bklyn., 1967. Tech. staff Bell Telephone Labs., N.Y.C., 1952-54; mgr. missile electronics Maxson Electronics, N.Y.C., Great River, N.Y., 1954-63; dept. head advanced radar systems Sperry, Unisys, Paramax, Great Neck, 1963-93. Radar scientist rep. U.S. on NATO Adv. Bd. for NIAG-16, Washington and N.Y.C. at NATO Countries, 1985-86; advanced radar tech. coord. Unisys Tech. Transfer Team, Great Neck, N.Y., 1990-92; radar cons. for defense and air traffic, Unisys and Alcott, N.Y., 1993-94. Contbr. articles to profl. jours. Tutor calculus and stats., for referred coll. students, Melville, N.Y., 1970-80; asst. soccer coach St Elizabeth Parish, Melville, N.Y., 1979; asst. baseball coach Little League, Huntington, N.Y., 1981. Mem. IEEE, Mus. Natural History, Sigma Xi, Tau Beta Pi. Republican. Roman Catholic. Achievements include patents on missile guidance, hi-radar visibility in the presence of clutter and jamming, electronic scanning; provided radar solution to USAF for the DEW line detection, tracking, identification of low-flying hostile aircraft by incorporating simultaneously hi data rates with long dwell times; designed and developed a mobile solid state radar capable of extracting aircraft space, time data over land or sea in a sustained severe clutter-jamming environment. Home and Office: Advanced Radar Consulting 19 Saxon St Melville NY 11747-1303

SCIRICA, ANTHONY JOSEPH, federal judge; b. Norristown, Pa., Dec. 16, 1940; s. A. Benjamin and Anna (Sclafani) Scirica; m. Susan Morgan, May 6, 1966; children: Benjamin, Sarah. BA, Wesleyan U., 1962; JD, U. Mich., 1965; postgrad. Fulbright Scholar, Central U., Caracas, Venezuela, 1966. Bar: Pa. 1966, U.S. Dist. Ct. (ea. dist.) Pa. 1984, U.S. Ct. Appeals (3d cir.) 1987. Ptnr. McGrory, Scirica, Wentz & Fernandez, Norristown, Pa., 1966—80; asst. dist. atty. Montgomery County, 1967—69; mem. Pa. Ho. of Reps, Harrisburg, 1971—79; judge Montgomery County Ct. Common Pleas, Pa., 1980—84, U.S. Dist. Ct. (ea. dist.) Pa., Phila., 1984—87, U.S. Ct. Appeals (3d cir.), 1987—. Chmn. Pa. Sentencing Commn., 1980—85. Scholar Fulbright scholar, Ctrl. U., Caracas, Venezuela, 1966. Mem.: ABA, Montgomery Bar Assn., Pa. Bar Assn. Roman Catholic. Office: James A Byrne Courthouse 601 Market St Rm 2100 Philadelphia PA 19106-1715*

SCISM, DANIEL REED, lawyer; b. Evansville, Ind., Aug. 27, 1936; s. Daniel William and Ardath Josephine (Gibbs) S.; m. Paula Anne Sedgwick, June 21, 1958; children: Darby Claire, Joshua Reed. BA, DePauw U., 1958; JD, Ind. U., 1965. Bar: Ind. 1965, U.S. Dist. Ct. (so. dist.) Ind. 1965, U.S. Ct. Appeals (7th cir.) 1967, U.S. Supreme Ct. 1976. Reporter Dayton (Ohio) Jour.-Herald, 1958-59; editor Mead Johnson & Co., Evansville, 1961; first assoc., then ptnr. Roberts, Ryder, Rogers & Scism and predecessor firms, Indpls., 1965—86; ptnr. Barnes & Thornburg, 1987—. Cons. Ind. Personnel Assn., 1984—. Treas. Marion County chpt. Myasthenia Gravis Found., Indpls., 1970; v.p. Marion County Mental Health Assn., Indpls., 1970-71; pres. The Suemma Coleman Agy., Indpls., 1973-74; bd. dirs. Ind. Humanities Coun., 1995-2000, chmn. bd., 1997-98; trustee Indpls. Mus. Art, 2001—; pres. Persimmon Woods Homeowners Assn., 2001-02. With U.S. Army, 1959—62. Edwards fellow Ind. U., 1964. Mem. ABA, Ind. Bar Assn., Indpls. Bar Assn., Ind. State C. of C. (social legis. com. 1970-80). Clubs: Indpls. Athletic; Woodland Country (bd. dirs. 1984-88, sec. 1998-99) (Carmel, Ind.). Methodist. Home: 10909 300 Yard Dr Fishers IN 46038-9306 Office: Barnes & Thornburg 11 S Meridian St Indianapolis IN 46204-3535

SCITOVSKY, ANNE AICKELIN, economist, researcher; b. Ludwigshafen, Germany, Apr. 17, 1915; arrived in U.S., 1931, naturalized, 1938; d. Hans W. and Gertrude Margarete Aickelin; 1 child Catherine Margaret. Student, Smith Coll., 1933—35; BA, Barnard Coll., 1937; postgrad., London Sch. Econs., 1937—39; MA in Econs., Columbia U., 1941. Mem. staff legis. reference svc. Libr. of Congress, 1941—44; mem. staff Social Security Bd., 1944—46; with Palo Alto (Calif.) Med. Found./Rsch. Inst., 1963—, chief health econs. div., 1973—94, sr. staff scientist, 1994—. Lectr. Inst. Health Policy Studies, U. Calif., San Francisco, 1975—94; mem. Inst. Medicine of NAS, Nat. Acad. Social Ins., Pres.'s Commn. for Study of Ethical Problems in Medicine and Biomed. and Behavioral Rsch., 1979—82, U.S. Nat. Com. on Vital and Health Stats., 1975—78, Health Resources and Svcs. Adminstrn., AIDS adv. com., 1990—94; cons. HHS, Inst. Medicine Coun. on Health Care Tech. Assessment, 1986—90. Home: 161 Erica Way Portola Valley CA 94028-7439 Office: Palo Alto Med Found Rsch Inst Ames Bldg 795 El Camino Real Palo Alto CA 94301-2302 E-mail: ascitovsky@aol.com.

SCIUCHETTI, DALE, municipal official; b. Kellogg, Idaho, Feb. 15, 1940; BA, Whitworth Coll., Spokane, Wash., 1962; MBA, U. Wash., 1964. Cert. mcpl. fin. adminstr. Lead analyst Boeing, Seattle, 1962-68; asst. chief acct. Cowles Pub., Spokane, 1968-70; tchr. Gonzaga U., 1970-73; field auditor City of Spokane, 1973-74, retirement specialist, 1974-75, retirement dir., 1975-82, treas., 1982—. Recipient Nat. Svc. award Mcpl. Treasurers of U.S. and Can., 1997. Mem. Wash. Mcpl. Treasurer's Assn. (pres. 1993), Wash. Fin. Officers Assn. (charter), Profl. Fin. Officer. Office: 808 W Spokane Falls Blvd Spokane WA 99201-3345 E-mail: dsciuchetti@spokanecity.org.

SCIVALLY, BART MURNANE, accountant, auditor; b. Oklahoma City, Mar. 13, 1944; s. Louis Frensley and Mary Helen (Boadway) S.; divorced; children: Amy D., Robyn M., Louis Francis. BS in Bus. Adminstrn., U. Ark., 1969. CPA Ark. Auditor Div. of Legis. Audit, Little Rock, 1968-73, audit supr., 1974—. Named Acct. of Yr. U. Ark., 2000. Mem.: AICPA, Assn. Govt. Accts. (cert. govt. fin. mgr. 1995). Roman Catholic. Office: Div of Legis Audit 172 State Capitol Little Rock AR 72201-1033 E-mail: bscivally@lapo.state.ar.us.

SCLAFANI, ANTHONY PAUL, plastic surgeon, educator, biomedical researcher; b. Bklyn., Oct. 3, 1963; BA, Columbia U., 1985; MD, U. Pa., 1989. Diplomate Am. Bd. Otolaryngology, Am. Bd. Facial Plastic and Reconstructive Surgery. Intern in gen. surgery Beth Israel Med. Ctr., N.Y.C., N.Y., 1989-91; resident in otolaryngology, head and neck surgery N.Y. Eye and Ear Infirmary, 1991-95, assoc. prof., dir. facial plastic surgery, 1996—; fellow in facial plastic and reconstructive surgery St. Louis U. Sch. Medicine, 1995-96; pvt. practice, N.Y.C., N.Y., 1996—, Chappaqua, 1998—. Assoc. editor: Facial Plastic Surgery, Facial Plastics Clins. N.Am.; contbr. articles to profl. jours. Fellow ACS, Am. Acad. Facial Plastic and Reconstructive Surgery (Sir Harold Delf Gillies award 1996, Tresley award 2002); mem. Am. Acad. Otolaryngology and Head and Neck Surgery, Am. Soc. for Laser Medicine and Surgery. Office: NY EE Infirm/Facial Pl Surg Dept Otolaryng/Head Neck 310 E 14th St 6th Fl New York NY 10003-4201 also: 59 S Greeley Ave Chappaqua NY 10514-3321 also: 1130 Second Ave Ste 110 New York NY 10021 E-mail: drsclafani@nyfacialsurgery.com.

SCLAR, DAVID ALEXANDER, medical policy educator; b. Columbus, Ohio, Dec. 31, 1954; B Pharmacy cum laude, Wash. State U., 1985; PhD in Pharmacy and Bus. Adminstrn., U. S.C., 1988. Boehringer Ingelheim scholar Wash. State U. Coll. Pharmacy, Pullman, 1992—, Boeing Disting. prof. health policy and adminstrn., 1999—. Advisor U.K. Dept. Health and Social Svcs., China Bur. of Drugs and Biologicals, U.S. Senate Select Com. on Aging; mem. FDA Rev. Com. on pharm. mktg. practice. Mem. editl. bd. Formulary; editor: Clin. Therapeutics; contbr. articles to profl. jours. Grantee in field. Mem. Am. Assn. Pharm. Scientists, Am. Pharm. Assn., Am. Soc. Hosp. Pharmacists, Am. Pub. Health Assn., Am. Assn. Colls. of Pharmacy, Assn. Health Svcs. Rsch. Office: Coll of Pharmacy Wash State Univ Pullman WA 99164-0001 E-mail: sclar@mail.wsu.edu.

SCLAROFF, STAN, computer science educator; b. Mt. Holly, N.J., Nov. 13, 1961; BA, Tufts U., 1984; MA, PhD, MIT, 1995. Programmer Portable Software, Cambridge, Mass., 1983-84; software engr. Schlumberger (Applicon), Billerica, 1984-89; rsch. asst. MIT Media Lab., Cambridge, 1989-94; asst. prof. computer sci. Boston U., 1995-2001, assoc. prof., 2001—. Mem. tech. adv. bd. Salient Stills, Inc., Mass., 1998—. Assoc. editor IEEE Trans. on Pattern Analysis and Machine Intelligence, 2000—; co-inventor finite element for image morphing and alignment. Recipient Young Investigator award U.S. Office Naval Rsch., 1996, Faculty Early Career Devel. Award NSF, 1996. Office: Boston U Dept Computer Sci 111 Cummington St Boston MA 02215

SCLATER, JAMES STANLEY, music educator, composer, musician; b. Mobile, Ala., Oct. 24, 1943; parents Athur Lee and Naomi Bell Sclater, Naomi Bell Sclater; m. Ann Judy Davis; children: Patricia. BMus, U. So. Miss., 1966, MMus, 1967; Dr. Mus. Arts, U. Tex., 1970. Prof. music Miss. Coll., Clinton, 1970—. Composer: (music for voice, chorus, band, orch.) Visions, 1973 (Ostwald Prize, 1974), (orchestral work) Concerto for Orchestra, 1989 (Music Award, Mississippi Institute of Arts and Letters, 1990), (choral/orchestral work) Witness to Matters Human and Divine, 1995, (piano sonata) Piano Sonata, 1975 (Bicentennniel performance at Kennedy Center, 1976), (organ and brass) Images of Southern Religion, 2000 (American Guild of Organists commission, 2001). Bd. dirs. Miss. Inst. of Arts and Letters, Jackson, 1999—2002. Named Disting. Prof. of the Yr., Miss. Coll., 1997. Mem.: ASCAP (Serious Music awards 1991-2001). Avocation: photography. Office: Mississippi College Box 4021 Clinton MS 39058 Home Fax: 601-925-3945; Office Fax: 601-925-3945. Personal E-mail: sclater@mc.edu. Business E-Mail: sclater@mc.edu.

SCLOVE, STANLEY LOUIS, statistics educator; b. Charleston, W.Va., Nov. 25, 1940; s. Abraham Bernard Sclove and Dorothy Ruth (Gold) Broh; m. Suzan Tash, June 14, 1962 (div. Mar. 1983); children: Sarabeth, Benjamin; m. Caryl L. Wertheimer, Sept. 30, 1990; 1 child, Aaron Joseph. AB, Dartmouth Coll., 1962; PhD, Columbia U., 1967. Math. statistician USPHS, Cin., Summers 1962-64; rsch. assoc. Stanford U., Palo Alto, Calif., 1966-68, vis. asst. prof., 1971-72; asst. prof. stats. Carnegie-Mellon U., Pitts., 1968-72; assoc. prof. U. Ill., Chgo., 1972-81, prof., 1981—; vis. assoc. prof. Northwestern U., Evanston, Ill., 1980-81. Statis. cons. for various firms; expert witness in fed. ct.; contracted prin. investigator USAF Office Scientific Rsch., 1978, Office of Naval Rsch., 1980-82, Army Rsch. Office, 1982-85. Co-author: (with T.W. Anderson) Introductory Statistical Analysis, 1974, An Introduction to the Statistical Analysis of Data, 1978, 86; author of numerous articles in field. Mem. exec. bd. Friends of Libr., Highland Park, Ill., 1976-77; saxophonist, historian Highland Park Pops Jazz/Dance Band, 1976—. Mem. Am. Statis. Assn. (bd. dirs. Chgo. chpt. 1976, program chmn. risk assessment sect. 1993-95), Classification Soc. (bd. dirs. 1993-95), Inst. Math. Stats., Inst. for Ops. Rsch. and Mgmt. Scis. Avocations: play clarinet, saxophone and flute, tennis. Office: U Ill Dept Info and Decisions Scis 601 S Morgan St # C294 Chicago IL 60607-7100

SCOATES, WESLEY MARVIN, mining company executive; b. Jacksonville, Fla., Apr. 21, 1938; s. Harry William and Orlene (Buffkin) S.; m. Patty Ann Flora, 1958 (div. 1969); children: Teresa, Lesa, Leslie, Randall; m. Anneliese Marie Knorlein, May 11, 1970; children: Stephen, Cherry. B in Mech. Engring., U. Dayton, 1962; MBA, Fla. Internat. U., 1983. Commd. 2d lt. U.S. Army, 1962, advanced through grades to lt. col., 1982, artillery officer Okla., 1962-65; mech. engr. U.S. Army Corps of Engrs., Jacksonville, 1965-66; artillery officer U.S. Army, Republic of Vietnam, Republic of Korea, Federal Republic of Germany, 1968-76, refrad Republic of Vietnam, Republic of Korea, Federal Republic of Germany, 1975; project engr. U.S. Gypsum Co., Jacksonville, 1966-67; div. chief City of Jacksonville, 1976-78; asst. equipment supt. Metro Dade County, Miami, Fla., 1978-79; asst. service mgr. Kelly Tractor Co., 1979-81; maintenance supt. Vulcan Materials Co., 1981-87, area mgr., 1987-91; equipment mgr. Lowell Dunn Co., 1991-92; ops. mgr. Ind. Aggregates, Inglis, Fla., 1992-93; dir. mining ops. Marcona Ocean Industries Ltd., Jacksonville, 1993—2000; mining cons., 2001—. Ret. U.S. Army, 1999; CGSOC instr. USAR Sch., 1979-88. Contbr. articles to army logistician mag. With USAR, 1975-90. Decorated Bronze Star with oak leaf cluster, Air medal, Army Commendation medal with oak leaf cluster, Meritorious Svc. medal. Mem. Acad. Polit. Sci., Coun. on Fgn. Rels., Am. Def. Preparedness Assn., Am. Assn. Individual Investors, Sunshine Via De Cristo (lay dir.), Ret. Officers Assn. Republican. Methodist. Avocations: fishing, singing, photography. E-mail: wscoates@bellsouth.net.

SCOBLIC, J. PETER, editor; b. N.Y.C., July 29, 1974; s. Joseph Michael and Barbara Scoblic. BA, Brown U., 1997. Editor-in-chief Brown Jour. World Affairs, Providence, 1994-96; rsch. dir. Hedrick Smith Prodns., Bethesda, Md., 1998-99; editor Arms Control Today, Washington, 1999—. Home: 1808 Connecticut Ave NW Washington DC 20009-5729 Office: Arms Control Today 1726 M St NW Washington DC 20036-4502

SCOFIELD, DAVID WILLSON, lawyer; b. Hartford, Conn., Oct. 17, 1957; s. Leslie Willson and Daphne Winifred (York) S. AB, Cornell U., 1979; JD, U. Utah, 1983. Bar: Utah 1983, U.S. Dist. Ct. Utah 1983, U.S. Dist. Ct. Ariz. 1993, U.S. Dist. Ct. Hawaii 1995, U.S. Ct. Appeals (10th cir.) 1990, U.S. Ct. Appeals (9th cir.) 1995, U.S. Supreme Ct. 1996, U.S. Ct. Claims, 1997. Assoc. Parsons & Crowther, Salt Lake City, 1983-87, Callister, Duncan & Nebeker, Salt Lake City, 1987-89, ptnr., 1989-92; founding ptnr. Parsons, Davies, Kinghorn & Peters, 1992-96, pres., 1996-97. Mem. adv. com. on Utah rules of civil procedure Utah Supreme Ct., 2002—. Author: Trial Handbook for Utah Lawyers, 1994; mem. Utah Law Rev., 1981-83; contbr. articles to legal jours. Bd. dirs. Westminster Coll. Found., 1994-96, chmn. cultivation com., 1995-96. Named to Outstanding Young Men of Am., 1986. Mem. ABA, Assn. Trial Lawyers Am., Utah Trial Lawyers Assn., Salt Lake County Bar Assn., Zeta Psi. Congregationalist. Avocations: American history, writing, sports. Home: 2331 Scenic Dr Salt Lake City UT 84109-1432 Office: Parsons Davies Kinghorn & Peters 185 S State St Ste 700 Salt Lake City UT 84111-1550 E-mail: dws@pdkplaw.com.

SCOFIELD, GORDON LLOYD, mechanical engineer, educator; b. Huron, S.D., Sept. 29, 1925; s. Perry Lee and Zella (Reese) S.; m. Nancy Lou Cooney, Dec. 27, 1947; children: Cathy Lynn, Terrence Lee. B.M.E., Purdue U., 1946; M.M.E., U. Mo., Rolla, 1949; PhD in M.E, U. Okla., 1968. Instr. mech. engring. S.D. State Coll., Brookings, 1946-47; successively grad. asst., instr., asst. prof., asso. prof., prof. U. Mo., Rolla, 1947-69; prof., head mech. engring.-engring. mechs. dept. Mich. Technol. U., Houghton, 1969—80; disting. prof. mech. engring. S.D. Sch. Mines and Tech., Rapid City, 1981-88, asst. v.p. for acad. affairs, 1981-83, v.p., dean engring., 1984-86; pres. S.D. Sch. Mines and Tech. Found., 1982-90. Cons. U.S. Naval Ordnance Test Sta., China Lake, Calif., 1956-71; bd. dirs. Accreditation Bd. for Engring. and Tech., 1994-2000; cons. to industry. Served with USNR, 1943-46. NSF sci. faculty fellow, 1966-67; recipient alumni achievement award U. Mo., Rolla, 1975 Mem. ASME, Soc. Automotive Engrs. (pres. 1977, Excellence in Engring. Edn. award, 1999), Am. Soc. Engring. Edn., Sigma Xi, Tau Beta Pi, Pi Tau Sigma, Phi Kappa Phi. Home: PO Box 1085 Rapid City SD 57709-1085 *Satisfaction comes from sharing achievements. By acknowledging and sharing the importance of others in our success it is possible to accomplish more that is worth remembering.*

SCOFIELD, LOUIS M., JR. lawyer; b. Brownsville, Tex., Jan. 14, 1952; s. Louis M. and Betsy Lee (Aiken) S.; children: Christopher, Nicholas, Emma. BS in Geology with highest honors and high distinction, U. Mich., 1974; JD with honors, U. Tex., 1977. Bar: Tex. 1977, U.S. Dist. Ct. (ea. and so. dists.) Tex., U.S. Ct. Appeals (5th cir.) 1981, U.S. Supreme Ct. 1984. Ptnr. Mehaffy & Weber, Beaumont, Tex., 1982—. Spkr. CNA Ins., Dallas, Jefferson County Ins. Adjusters, S.E. Tex. Ind. Ins. Agts., Gulf Ins. Co., Dallas, Employers Casualty Co., Beaumont, Tex. Employment Commn., Jefferson County Young Lawyers Assn., Jefferson County Bar Assn., South Tex. Coll. of Law, John Gray Inst., Lamar U., 1991, Tex. Assn. Def. Counsel, 1991; cert. arbitrator Nat. Panel of Consumer Arbitrators; arbitrator BBB; presenter Forest Park H.S., Martin Elem. Sch., St. Anne's Sch. Contbr. articles to profl. jours.; columnist Jefferson County Bar Jour. Patron Beaumont Heritage Soc., John J. French Mus.; bd. dirs. Beaumont Heritage Soc., 1983-84, mem. endowment fund com., 1988; chmn. lawyers divsn. United Appeals Campaign, 1984; grand patron Jr. League of Beaumont, 1989, 90. Fellow: State Bar of Tex. (mentors com. 1995), Tex. Bar Found. (life); mem.: ABA (contbg. editor newsletter products, vice chmn.gen liability and consumer laws com.), Jefferson County Bar Assn. (disaster relief project 1979, outstanding young lawyer's com. 1980), Am. Judicature Soc., Def. Rsch. Inst., Tex. Assn. Defense Counsel (dir. at large 1986—87, v.p. 1987—89, adminstrv. v.p. 1989—90, program chmn. San Diego 1989), Assn. Defense Trial Attys. (chmn. Tex. membership com., chmn. Ctrl. U.S. region 2000—, exec. coun. 1999—2002), Beaumont County Country Club, Phi Beta Kappa. Democrat. Episcopalian. Avocations: golf, reading, fishing. Home: 4790 Littlefield St Beaumont TX 77706-7748 Office: Mehaffy & Weber PO Box 16 Beaumont TX 77704-0016

SCOFIELD, PAUL, actor; b. Jan. 21, 1922; m. Joy Parker; 2 children. Trained, London Mask Theatre Drama Sch., Birmingham Repertory Theatre, 1941, 43-46, Stratford-on-Avon, Shakespeare Meml. Theatre, 1946-48, Arts Theatre, 1946, Phoenix Theatre, 1947. With H.M. Tennent, 1949-56; assoc. dir. Nat. Theatre, 1970-71. Has appeared in Adventure Story, Chekhov's Seagull, Anouilh's Ring Round the Moon, Gielgud's prodn. Much Ado About Nothing, Charles Morgan's The River Line, Richard II, The Way of the World, Venice Preserved, Time Remembered, A Question of Fact, Hamlet, Power and the Glory, Family Reunion, A Dead Secret, Expresso Bongo, The Complaisant Lover, A Man For All Seasons, Stratford Festival, Ont., Can., 1961, Coriolanus, Don Armado, N.Y., 1961-62, A Man for All Seasons, London, 1962-63, King Lear, N.Y.C., Moscow and Ea. Europe, 1964, Timon, 1965, Staircase, 1966, The Government Inspector, 1967, Macbeth, 1968, The Hotel in Amsterdam, 1968, Uncle Vanya, 1970, The Captain of Kopenik, 1971, Rules of the Game, 1971, Savages, 1973, The Tempest, 1974, 75, Dimetos, 1976, Volpone, 1977, The Madras House, 1977, The Family, 1978, Amadeus, 1979, Othello, 1980, Don Quixote, 1982, A Midsummer Night's Dream, 1982, I'm Not Rappaport, 1986-87, Heartbreak House, 1992, John Gabriel Borkman, 1996; films: The Train, 1962, A Man For All Seasons (Oscar and N.Y. Film Critics award, Moscow Film Festival and Brit. Film Acad. awards), King Lear, 1970, Scorpio, 1972, Bartleby, 1980, A Delicate Balance, A Potting Shed, 1981, If Winter Comes, 1981, Song at Twilight, 1982, Come into the Garden Maud, 1982, 1919, 1985, Anna Karenina, 1984, Mr. Corbett's Ghost, 1986, The Attic, 1987, Why the Whales Came, 1989, Henry V, 1990, Hamlet, 1990, UTZ, 1991, Quiz Show, 1994, Martin Chuzzlewit, 1994, The Little Riders, 1995, The Crucible, 1996, CD of King Lear, 2001, Almeida Theatre prodn. of I Take Your Hand in Mine, 2001. Decorated comdr. Brit. Empire; decorated Companion of Honour, 2001. Address: The Gables Balcombe Sussex RH17 6ND England

SCOFIELD, RODERICK ARTHUR, meteorologist, researcher, educator; b. Louisville, Ky., Dec. 3, 1942; s. Edward Harold and Hortense Alice (Gillespie) S.; m. Eileen Joyce Wiedmar, Aug. 22, 1964; children: Michelle Eileen, Matthew Roderick, Brett Edward. BS in Physics, U. Louisville, 1964; MS in Meteorology, U. St. Louis, 1969, PhD in Meteorology, 1973. Rschr. Nat. Weather Svc., Silver Springs, Md., 1972-74; rschr. flood prediction, precipitation forecaster Nat. Environ. Satellite Data Information Svc., Camp Springs, 1974—. Cons. Project Atmosphere, Washington, 1984—; tchr. meteorol. enhancement program. Contbr. articles to profl. jours. including Monthly Weather Review, Remote Sensing Review, Bull. Am. Meteorol. Soc., Am. Geophys. Union Newsletter. Recipient bronze medal NOAA, 1989, medal Weather Bureau of Taiwan, 1992, gold medal for outstanding rsch. and leadership in developing flash flood forecasting techniques using satellite data Dept. Commerce, 1999; named U. Louisville Arts and Scis. Alumni Fellow of Yr., 2000; fellow Univ. Louisville Arts and Sci. Alumni, 2000. Fellow: Am. Meteorol. Soc. (Reichelderfer award 1999, bronze awards for edn. and tng. flash flood forecasting techniques 1999, bronze award for edn. and tng. flash flood forecasting techniques 2001); mem.: Am. Geophys. Union, Nat. Weather Assn. (pres.-elect 1999, pres. 2000, outstanding contbns. award 1986), Sigma Xi. Episcopalian. Achievements include the development of a neural network (expert system) algorithm that uses geostationary and polar microwave date for diagnosing flash floods around the world. Home: 8850 Lowell Rd Pomfret MD 20675-3110 Office: NOAA Science Ctr 5200 Auth Rd Suitland MD 20746-4304 E-mail: roderick.scofield@noaa.gov., cbstorm@aol.com.

SCOGIN, TROY POPE, publishing company executive, accounts executive; b. Manchester, Ala., Oct. 31, 1932; s. James David and Thelma Katie (Helton) S.; m. Katie Elizabeth Bates, May 26, 1956; children: Norma Kay, Joyce Marie. BA, Howard Coll., 1955; MDiv, So. Baptist Theol. Seminary, Louisville, 1959; MA, Samford U., 1972. Ordained to ministry Baptist Ch., 1956. Pastor West Port (Ky.) Baptist Ch., 1956-58, Providence Baptist Ch., Bellevue, Ohio, 1958-61; chaplain/capt. USAF, Lincoln, Nebr., 1961-64; pastor Sycamore (Ala.) Baptist Ch., 1964-65; sales rep. Houghton Mifflin Co., Boston, 1965-74, regional mgr., 1974-89, spl. asst. to exec. v.p. coll. div., 1989-90, v.p., 1984—, nat. accounts exec., 1990-92; pastor Ross Ave. Bapt. Ch. Intercity Mission, Dallas, 1993-98; prof. Wake Tech. C.C., Raleigh, N.C., 1998—. Adv. bd. dirs. Ross Ave. Ctr.; faculty Eastfield Coll., 1992-98; bd. trustees St. Johns MCC. Chmn. bd. deacons Ross Avenue Bapt. Ch., Dallas, 1991. Mem. Am. Mgmt. Assn., Am. Soc. Tng. Devel., Nat. Coun. Tchrs. English, Tex. Jr. Coll. Tchrs. Assn., N.C. C.C. Faculty Assn., Phi Kappa Phi, Omicron Delta Kappa (nat. leadership fraternity pres. 1954), Alpha Phi Omega (nat. svc. fraternity pres. 1952). Democrat. Avocations: bowling, swimming, fishing, tennis, golf. Home: 7202 Hidden Ridge Dr Apt 104 Raleigh NC 27613-3967 E-mail: tpopes@aol.com. *Accomplishment of goals requires setting priorities. Anything worth doing is worth doing well. To determine what is worthwhile decide if it is right, if it is needed, and if it is worth the cost.*

SCOGLAND, WILLIAM LEE, lawyer; b. Moline, Ill., Apr. 2, 1949; s. Maurice William and Harriet Rebecca S.; m. Victoria Lynn Whitham, Oct. 9, 1976; 1 child, Thomas. BA magna cum laude, Augustana Coll., 1971; JD cum laude, Harvard U., 1975. Bar: Ill. 1975, U.S. Dist. Ct. (no. dist.) Ill. 1975. Assoc. Wildman, Harrold, Allen & Dixon, Chgo., 1975-77, Hughes Hubbard & Reed, Milw., 1977-81; from assoc. to ptnr. Jenner & Block, Chgo., 1981—. Author: Fiduciary Duty: What Does It Mean?, 1989; co-author Employee Benefits Law, 1987. Mem. Phi Beta Kappa, Omicron Delta Kappa. Republican. Office: Jenner & Block One IBM Plz Fl 4000 Chicago IL 60611-7603

SCOGNO, STACIE JOY, financial services company executive; b. Camden, N.J., Dec. 5, 1957; d. Albert Joseph Scogno and Josephine Geovanni Fiorello. AAS, Bay State Coll., Boston, 1978; BS in mgmt., Boston Coll., 1986; cert. of mgmt. and spl. scis., Harvard Ext. Sch., 1994. Software sys. cons., owner North Shore Svcs., Boston, 1984-88; tech. cons. Lotus Devel. Corp., 1988-90; mgr. MIS Blackwell Sci. Publs., 1990-93; product design analyst Thomson Fin. Corp., 1993-95; sr. cons. The Hunters Group, 1995-96; N.E. regional mgr. nat. fin. systems Coopers & Lybrand, 1997—, co-dir. Natl. PeopleSoft Ctr. of Excellence, 1996—, dir. east region, 1998-99, dir. global programme office, 1999-2001; v.p. profl. svcs. Paradigm Tech., 2001—. Notary pub. Commonwealth of Mass., 1980—. Trustee Action Dance Theater, treas., 1980-91; bd. dirs. Friends of City Sq., Charlestown, Mass., 1996—. Avocations: triathlons, body building. Office: 30 S 17th St Philadelphia PA 19103-4001

SCOLAMIERO, PETER, retired artist; b. Aug. 12, 1916; Grad., Newark Sch. Fine & Indsl. Arts, 1937; postgrad., The New Sch., N.Y.C. Owner photography studio, N.Y.C., 25 years. One man shows include N.Y.C. Met. Mus. Invitation Show, 1952, Barron Arts Ctr., 1998, Johnson & Johnson Gallery, New Brunswick, 1995; exhibited in group shows at: Kresge Gallery, Rabin & Krueger Gallery, N.Y.C., Montclair Mus., N.J., Newark Pub. Libr. Collection; represented in photography publs. Photo Graphics, Camera Geijutsu, 1960, Photography of the World, 1961, Life Library of Photography-The Studio, 1971, Popular Photography Photo Annual. Recipient Purchase award Bklyn. Mus., 1950. Address: 623 Cricket Ln Woodbridge NJ 07095-1545

SCOLARO, ANTHONY JON, urban planner, consultant; b. Detroit, Feb. 27, 1959; s. Anthony and Angela (Mangiapane) S.; m. Linda Jean Calabro, Sept. 21, 1991. BA in English, Wayne State U., 1984; M of Urban Planning, NYU, 1997. Cert. planner. Sr. planner Edwards and Kelcey Inc., Morristown, N.J., 1993—. Mem. AICP. Office: Edwards and Kelcey Inc PO Box 1936 299 Madison Ave Morristown NJ 07962-1936 E-mail: ascolaro@ekmail.com.

SCOLES, CLYDE SHELDON, library director; b. Columbus, Ohio, Apr. 14, 1949; s. Edward L. and Edna M. (Ruddock) S.; m. Diane Francis, July 14, 1976; children: David, Kevin, Karen, Stephen. BS, Ohio State U., 1971; MLS, U. Mich., 1972. Librarian Columbus Pub. Library, 1972-74; library dir. Zanesville (Ohio) Pub. Library, 1974-78; asst. dir. Toledo-Lucas County Pub. Library, 1978-85, dir., 1985—. Adj. lectr., libr. bldg. cons. U. Mich.; v.p. bd. dirs. Read for Literacy. Mem. ALA, Ohio Libr. Assn., Ohio Libr. Coun., Toledo C. of C., Com. of 100, Maumee Hist. Soc. Clubs: Torch (Toledo). Lodges: Rotary.

SCOLES, EUGENE FRANCIS, law educator, lawyer; b. Shelby, Iowa, June 12, 1921; s. Sam and Nola E. (Leslie) S.; m. R. Helen Glawson, Sept. 6, 1942; children— Kathleen Elizabeth, Janene Helen. AB, U. Iowa, 1943, JD, 1945; LLM, Harvard U., 1949; JSD, Columbia U., 1955. Bar: Iowa 1945, Ill. 1946. Assoc. Seyfarth-Shaw & Fairweather, Chgo., 1945-46; asst. prof. law Northeastern U., 1946-48, assoc. prof., 1948-49, U. Fla., 1949-51, prof., 1951-56, U. Ill., Champaign, 1956-68, Max Rowe prof. law, 1982-89, prof. emeritus, 1989—; vis. prof. McGeorge Law Sch. U. Pacific, Sacramento, 1989-92; prof. U. Oreg., 1968-82, dean Sch. Law, 1968-74, disting. prof. emeritus, 1982—. Vis. prof. Khartoum U., Sudan, 1964-65. Author: (with H.F. Goodrich) Conflict of Laws, 4th edit., 1964, (with R.J. Weintraub) Cases and Materials on Conflict of Laws, 2d edit., 1972, (with E.C. Halbach, Jr., R.C. Link, P.G. Roberts) Problems and Materials on Decedents' Estates and Trusts, 6th edit., 2000, Problems and Materials on Future Interests, 1977, (with P. Hay, P.J. Borchers, S.C. Symeonides) Conflict of Laws, 3d edit., 2000; contbr. articles to profl. jours.; notes and legislation editor Iowa Law Rev., 1945; reporter Uniform Probate Code Project, 1966-70; mem. joint editorial bd. Uniform Probate Code, 1972— Mem. ABA, Soc. Pub. Tchrs. Law, Am. Law Inst., Ill. Bar Assn., Assn. Am. Law Schs. (pres. 1978), Order of Coif Office: U Oreg Sch Law 1515 Agate St Eugene OR 97403-1221 E-mail: escoles@law.uoregon.edu.

SCOLESE, CHRISTOPHER, federal agency administrator; BSEE, SUNY, Buffalo; MSEE, George Washington U. EOS program mgr., dep. dir. flight programs and projects for earth sci. Goddard Space Flight Ctr., 1987; dep. assoc. adminstr. Office Space Sci. NASA, Washington; sr. analyst Gen. Rsch. Corp., McLean, Va. With USN, 1978—83. Recipient Presdl. Rank award of meritorious exec. Fellow: AIAA (assoc.; mem. astrodynamics com., chmn. nat. capitol sect. guidance navication and control tech. com., Young Engr./Scientist of Yr. award nat. capitol sect.); mem.: IEEE, Tau Beta Pi, Eta Kappa Nu. Office: NASA Hdqrs Mail Code S 300 E St SW Washington DC 20546

SCOLL, EULALIE ELIZABETH, writer, researcher; b. Vancouver, Wash., Mar. 6, 1920; d. Frederick and Elizabeth (Williamson) Laws; m. James Leslie Hildebrand; children; James, Frederick. BS, Women's U. Tex., 1941; MS, Salve Regina U., 1989, PhD, 1996. Engring. draftsman for Dr. Urey Manhattan Project, N.Y.C.; high fashion designer. Interior decorator. Author: The Role and Abuse of Women as Portrayed in Three Dostoevsky's Major Novels, 1989, Nietzsche Journal of Antichrist Tibetan Buddhism Versus Christianity, 1991, Dostoevsky's Sonya and Martha: Fiction and Reality, 1996. Mem. AAUW, Am. Assn. Advancement Slavic Studies, Nat. Trust for Historic Preservation, Nat. Mus. Women in the Arts, Am. Soc. Phys. Rsch., Inc., The Authors Guild, Inc., Newport Preservation Soc., Newport Hist. Soc., Asian Soc., Naval War Found., Internat. Dostoevsky Soc., Bailey's Beach Oldest Beach Club Am. Home: Cave Cliff 11 Chastellux Ave Newport RI 02840-3811

SCOLLARD, DAVID MICHAEL, research pathologist; b. N.D. s. Denzil and Audrey Scollard; m. Fredrikke Skinsnes Scollard, June 24, 1971; children: Winston, Darikka. BA, St. Olaf Coll., 1969; BS in Medicine, U. N.D., 1971; MD, PhD, U. Chgo., 1975. Diplomate Am. Bd. Pathology. Med. resident U. Hawaii, Honlulu, 1975-76; lectr. pathology U. Hong Kong, 1976-81; asst. prof. pathology U. Ill. Med., Chgo., 1981-84; field dir. leprosy rsch. project U. Ill., Chiang Mai, Thailand, 1981-84; asst. prof. pathology U. Hawaii Sch. Medicine, 1984-88, assoc. prof. pathology, 1988-92; chief rsch. pathology Nat. Hansen's Disease Ctr., Baton Rouge, 1993—. Adj. prof. La. State U. Sch. Vet. Medicine, Baton Rouge, 1993—, La. State U. Sch. Medicine, New Orleans, 1993—. Guest editor Hawaii Med. Jour., 1989; author: (with others) Handbook of Animal Models, 1999; contbr. articles to profl. jours.; interviewed for TV documentaries on leprosy. Fulbright fellowship Fulbright Commn., 1990. Mem. Am. Soc. for Investigative Pathology, Am. Soc. of Microbiologists, Internat. Acad. of Pathology, Am. Assn. Immunologists, Internat. Leprosy Assn. Office: Nat Hansens Disease Programs at LSU Skip Bertman Dr Baton Rouge LA 70803 E-mail: dscoll1@lsu.edu.

SCOLLARD, PATRICK JOHN, hospital executive; b. Chgo., Apr. 20, 1937; s. Patrick J. and Kathleen (Cooney) S.; m. Gloria Ann Carroll, July 1, 1961; children: Kevin, Maureen, Daniel, Thomas, Brian. BS in Econs., Marquette U., 1959; grad. sr. exec. program, MIT, 1976. With Equitable Life Assurance Soc. U.S., N.Y.C., 1962-79, asst. v.p., 1969-71, v.p., personnel dir., 1971-75, v.p. corp. adminstrv. svcs., 1975-79; sr. v.p. Chem. Bank, 1979-80, exec. v.p., 1980-87, chief adminstrv. officer, 1987-92; pres., CEO St. Francis Hosp., Roslyn, N.Y., 1992-99; pres. Scollard Assocs. LLC, Garden City, 1999—. Bd. dirs. Work in Am.; regional adv. bd. Chase Manhattan Corp. Bd. dirs. Curaspan, Inc., St. Francis Hosp., Woodstock Theol. Ctr. Office: Scollard Assocs LLP 1461 Franklin Ave Garden City NY 11530-1648

SCOMMEGNA, ANTONIO, physician, educator; b. Barletta, Italy, Aug. 26, 1931; came to U.S., 1954, naturalized, 1960; s. Francesco Paola and Antonietta (Maresca) S.; m. Lillian F. Sinkiewicz, May 3, 1958; children: Paola, Frank, Roger. BA, State Lyceum A. Casardi, Barletta, 1947; MD, U. Bari (Italy), 1953. Diplomate: Am. Bd. Obstetrics and Gynecology, also sub-bd. endocrinology and reprodn. Rotating intern New Eng. Hosp., Boston, 1954-55; resident obstetrics and gynecology Michael Reese Hosp. and Med. Center, Chgo., 1956-59, fellow dept. research human reprodn., 1960-61, research asso., 1961; fellow steroid tng. program Worcester Found. Exptl. Biology, also Clark U., Shrewsbury, Mass., 1964-65; asso. prof. obstetrics and gynecology Chgo. Med. Sch., 1965-69; mem. staff Michael Reese Hosp. and Med. Center, 1961—, attending physician obstetrics and gynecology, 1961—, dir. sect. gynecologic endocrinology, 1965-81; dir. ambulatory care obstetrics and gynecology Mandel Clinic, 1968-69, chmn. dept., 1969-89; attending, chief svc. U. Ill. Chgo. Hosp. and Med. Ctr., 1989-98; trustee Mandel Clinic, 1977-80; prof. dept. ob-gyn. Pritzker Sch. Medicine, U. Chgo., 1969-89; prof., head dept. ob-gyn. Coll. Medicine, U. Ill. Chgo., 1989-98. Author numerous articles in field. Fulbright fellow, 1954-55 Fellow Am. Coll. Obstetricians and Gynecologists, Endocrine Soc., Chgo. Inst. Medicine, Am. Gynecol. and Obstet. Soc.; mem. AMA, Ill., Chgo. med. socs., Am. Fertility Soc., Chgo. Gynecol. Soc. (sec. 1976-79, pres. 1981-82), Soc. Study Reprodn., AAAS, Soc. for Gynecologic Investigation. Home: 1023 W Vernon Park Pl Apt E Chicago IL 60607-3447 E-mail: anmis@uic.edu.

SCONYO, PHILIP, engineering consultant; b. Phila., Dec. 14, 1951; s. Joseph J. and Susie A. (Minghinelli) S.; m. Coleen A. Murphy, Apr. 3, 1972; children: Pamela, Diana. BEE, Villanova U., 1973. Registered profl. engr. N.J., Pa., Del. Md., Mass., N.C. Field engr. Factory Mut. Enging. Assocs., Phila., 1974-76; sr. engr. Phila. Mfrs. Mut. Ins. Co., Valley Forge, Pa., 1977-85; unit engring. mgr. Arwkwright Mut. Ins. Co., Malvern, 1985-87; pres. Phiscon Enterprises Inc., Audubon, N.J., 1987—. Candidate for commr., Borough of Audubon, 1989. Mem. Soc. Fire Protection Engrs., Nat. Fire Protection Assn., Burlington County Firemarshals Assn., Order Sons of Italy, Audubon PTA. Avocations: racquetball, golf, tennis, needlework. Home and Office: Phiscon Enterprises Inc 213 S Davis Ave Audubon NJ 08106-1115 E-mail: phiscon@snip.net.

SCOONES, BEATRICE WEISS, accountant, lawyer; b. Detroit, Dec. 28, 1945; d. Ernest Walter Weiss and Hilda Elizabeth (Seiter) Andrus; m. Jeffrey Kimball Hall, Dec. 27, 1966 (div. Nov. 1972); 1 child, Shaleen Hall Scoones Wunrow; m. Louis Charles Scoones, June 11, 1975. BA, So. Meth U., 1968, JD, 1985. Bar: Tex. 1985; CPA, Tex.; cert. tchr., Tex. Cost acct. Republic Nat. Bank, Dallas, 1979-80, Chaparral Steel Co., Midlothian, Tex., 1980-83; clk., assoc. Bradford & Snyder, Dallas, 1984-87; acct., atty. in pvt. practice, Cedar Hill, Tex., 1987—. Contr. Pizza Inn franchises, 1985-96, Longhorn Bar-B-Que, Cedar Hill, 1992—; owner, mgr. Baskin-Robbins franchises, 1967-82.

SCORSESE, MARTIN, film director, writer; b. Flushing, N.Y., Nov. 17, 1942; s. Charles and Catherine (Cappa) S.; m. Laraine Marie Brennan, May 15, 1965 (div.), 1 daughter: Catherine Terese Glinora Sophia; m. Julia Cameron, 1975 (div.), 1 daughter: Dominica Elizabeth; m. Isabella Rosellini, Sept. 29, 1979 (div. 1983); m. Barbara DeFina, Feb. 9, 1985. BS in Film Communications, NYU, 1964, MA in Film Communications, 1966. Faculty asst., then instr. film NYU, N.Y.C., 1963-70. Films include: (dir.): The Big Shave, 1968 (also writer), Who's That Knocking at My Door?, 1968, (also writer, assoc. prodr., actor), Boxcar Bertha, 1972 (also actor), Mean Streets, 1973 (also co-writer, actor), Alice Doesn't Live Here Anymore, 1975, Taxi Driver, 1976 (also actor, Palme d'Or Cannes Internat. Film Festival), New York, New York, 1977, The Last Waltz, 1978, Raging Bull, 1980, The King of Comedy, 1983 (also actor), After Hours, 1985, The Color of Money, 1986, The Last Temptation of Christ, 1988, New York Stories (Life Lessons), 1989, GoodFellas, 1990 (also co-writer), Cape Fear, 1991, The Age of Innocence, 1993 (also co-writer), Casino, 1995 (also writer), Kundun, 1997, With Friends Like These, 1998, Bringing Out the Dead, 1999, The Gangs of New York, 2000, AFI's 100 Years...100 Movies, 1998, (TV) Dolce Cinema, I1, 1999, The Muse, 1999; (prodr.): The Grifters, 1990, Mad Dog and Glory, 1993, Clockers, 1995 (also exec. prodr.), Casino, 1995; (exec. prodr.): Naked in New York, 1994, Grace of My Heart, 1996; documentaries include: (editor): Woodstock, 1970 (also asst. dir.), Elvis on Tour, 1973; (assoc. prodr.): Medicine Ball Caravan, 1971; (dir.): Street Scenes 1970, 1970, Italianamerican, 1974, American Boy: A Profile of Steven Price, 1979, Man in Milan, 1990; co-dir. (documentary) A Personal Journey with Martin Scorsese Through American Movies, 1997; other film appearances include: Cannonball, 1976, Pavlova: A Woman for All Seasons, 1983, 'Round Midnight, 1986, Akira Kurosawa's Dreams, 1990, Guilty by Suspicion, 1991, Quiz Show, 1994, Search and Destroy, 1995 (also prodr.), (TV films) La Memoire Retrouvee, 1996, (exec, prodr.) Kicked in the Head, 1997, The Hi-Lo Country, 1998. Recipient Edward L. Kingsley Found. award, 1963-64, 1st prize Rosenthal Found. awards Soc. Cinemetologists, 1964, 1st prize Screen Producer's Guild, 1965, 1st prize Brown U. Film Festival, 1965, also others; named Best Dir. Cannes Film Festival, 1986. Office: Jeff Dooley Starr & Co 350 Park Ave Fl 9 New York NY 10022-6022 also: Artists Management Group 9465 Wilshire Blvd Ste 519 Beverly Hills CA 90212-2604

SCORSINE, JOHN MAGNUS, lawyer; b. Rochester, N.Y., Dec. 3, 1957; s. Frank and Karin (Frennby) S.; m. Susan Nauss, May 31, 1980 (div.); m. Theresa A. Burke, Dec. 17, 1988; 1 child, Jennifer E. BS, Rochester Inst. Tech., 1980; JD, U. Wyo., 1984. Bar: Wyo. 1984, U.S. Dist. Ct. Wyo. 1984, U.S. Ct. Appeals (10th cir.) 1989, U.S. Army Ct. Criminal Appeals 1995. Part-time deputy sheriff Monroe County (N.Y.), 1978-80; police officer Casper (Wyo.) Police Dept., 1980-81; intern U.S. Atty. Office, Cheyenne, Wyo., 1983-84; pvt. practice Rock Springs, 1984-85; ptnr. Scorsine and Flynn, 1986; prin. Scorsine Law Office, 1986-95; commr. Dist. and County Court, 1986-95; dep. chief of staff for mil. support Wyo. Nat. Guard, 1995—. Ptnr. Sunset Advt., 1987-89; chmn. bd. dirs. Youth Home Inc., Rock Springs, 1987-88; treas. Sweetwater County Cmty. Corrections Bd., 1990-95; mem. Nat. Ski Patrol, 1976-97, Wyo. Bd. of Parole, 1998—. Leader Medicine Bow Ski Patrol, Laramie, Wyo., 1983; legal advisor Rocky Mountain divsn. Nat. Ski Patrol, 1984; asst. patrol leader White Pine Ski Area, Pinedale, Wyo., 1986; avalanche advisor Jackson Hole Snow King Ski Patrol, 1987-96, avalanche instr. 1993-96; sect. chief Teton sect. nat. Ski Patrol, 1991-94, mem. Eldore Ski Patrol, 1996-97; mem. Sweetwater County Search and Rescue, 1989-95, tng. officer, 1993-95; mem. Sweetwater County Emergency Dive Team, 1990-95, mem. Sweetwater County Fire Dept., 1992-94, Reliance Vol. Fire Dept., 1994-95; lt.k, training officer Laramie Cmty. Fire Dist. #6 and Burns Ambulance Svc., 1995-98, treas./sec. bd. dirs. 1997-98, Am. N. Peary Land expdn., 1989; scoutmaster Boy Scouts Am., 1987-93, 96-98, 4H leader, 1997—; pres. Sweetwater County Vol. Fire Assn., 1993-94; mem. Laramie County Sch. Dist. #2 accreditation panel; dir. emergency svcs. Wyo. Civil Air Patrol, 1998—, comdr. Wyo. wing, 1999—. Maj. JAG, USAR , 1991—; bd. dirs., sec. Burns Cmty. Ambulance, 1997-99. Recipient Yellow Merit star Nat. Ski Patrol, 1993, Fritch Volunteerism award, 1993, Armed Forces Outstanding Vol. Svc. medal, Gibb Wilson award CAP, 2002. Mem. ABA, Wyo. State Bar, Wyo. Trial Lawyers Assn., Assn. Am. Trial Lawyers, Rock Springs C. of C., Res. Officers Assn. (nat. councilman 1993—, state pres. 1994), Rotary. Democrat. Lutheran. Avocations: rock climbing, backpacking, hunting, scuba, karate. Office: Wyo Nat Guard 5500 Bishop Blvd Cheyenne WY 82009-3320 E-mail: john.scorsine@wy.ngb.ermy.mil.

SCORZA, LARI MARIE, physician; b. Monongahela, Pa., Oct. 5, 1969; d. Pete and Gertrude Scorza. BS in Pre-Medicine, Pa. State U., 1991; MD, U. Pitts., 1994. Cert. Am. Bd. Radiology. Resident in internal medicine U. Pitts. Med. Ctr., 1994-96; resident in diagnostic radiology Western Pa. Hosp., Pitts., 1996-2000, women's imaging fellow, 2000—01. Mem. med. staff radiation safety com. Western Pa. Hosp., 1998-2001, physician adv. subcom., 1999-2001. Contbr. articles to profl. jours. Vol. Assn. Retarded Citizens, Western Pa. Mem. AMA, Am. Coll. Radiology, Am. Roentgen Ray Soc., Radiologic Soc. N.Am., Gamma Phi Beta, Golden Key Nat. Honor Soc., Alpha Epsilon Delta, Phi Lambda Epsilon. Democrat. Roman Catholic. Avocations: golfing, swimming, reading, photography. Office: Western Pa Dept Radiology 4800 Friendship Ave Pittsburgh PA 15224-1722 Home: 5171 Bronson Dr Lewiston NY 14092-2003 E-mail: larired@aol.com.

SCORZA, SYLVIO JOSEPH, religion educator; b. Zürich, Switzerland, Mar. 21, 1923; came to U.S., 1929; s. Joseph Peter and Helena Christina (Kopp) S.; m. Phyllis Joan VanSetters, June 6, 1952; children: Christine Marie, Philip Joseph, John Forrest. AA, Woodrow Wilson Jr. Coll., 1942; AB, Hope Coll., 1945; BD, Western Theol. Sem., Holland, Mich., 1953; ThD, Princeton Theol. Sem., 1956; PhD, U. Ill., 1972. Ordained to ministry Ref. Ch. in Am., 1955. Stated supply pastor Hickory Bottom Charge, Loysburg, Pa., 1957-58; prof. religion Northwestern Coll., Orange City, Iowa, 1959-90, prof. emeritus, 1990—. Vis. prof. Lancaster (Pa.) Theol. Sem., 1956-57, Western Theol. Sem., Holland, Mich., 1958-59; v.p. Ref. Ch. in Am., N.Y.C., 1988-89, pres., 1989-90, moderator, exec. com., 1990-91; mem. Iowa Bd. Law Examiners, 1997—. Co-editor: Concordance to the Greek and Hebrew Text of Ruth, The Computer Bible, Septuagint series, Vols. XXX, XXX-B, 1988-89; contbr. articles to profl. jours. County del. Iowa Dems., Ft. Dodge, 1984. Recipient Disting. Alumnus award Hope Coll., 1989, Homecoming Honors award Northwestern Coll. N Club, 1990, Handicapped Person of Siouxland award Siouxland Com. for the Handicapped, 1990, Gov.'s award Iowa Commn. of

Persons with Disabilities, 1990, Victory award Nat. Rehab. Hosp., 1991, Disting. Alumnus award Western Theol. Sem., 2002. Mem. Internat. Orgn. for Septuagint and Cognate Studies, Smithsonian Instsn., Nat. Geog. Soc., Iowa State Chess Assn. (v.p. 1984-85, dir. postal tournament 1987-97). Avocations: chess, bridge. Home and Office: 520 2nd St SW Orange City IA 51041-1728 E-mail: scorza@nwciowa.edu.

SCOTCH, BARRY MARTIN, lawyer; b. Newark, Aug. 2, 1939; s. Philip and Clara (Blecher) S.; m. Barbara Katz, May 2, 1970; children: Adam Michael, Matthew Laurence, Molly Claire. AB, Columbia U., 1961, JD, 1964. Bar: N.J. 1965, U.S. Ct. Mil. Appeals 1967, U.S. Supreme Ct. 1969, N.H. 1974, U.S. Ct. Appeals (1st cir.) 1982. Assoc. atty. Teltser, Byrne & Greenberg, East Orange, N.J., 1965-66, Baker, Garber, Chazen & Duffy, Hoboken, 1966-69, Canter & Chazen, Jersey City, 1969-70; atty. Barry M. Scotch, Esq., Hackensack, N.J., 1970-74, Scotch Law Office, Manchester, N.H., 1974-84; atty., ptnr. Scotch & Zalinsky, NH, 1984—2001; ptnr. Backus Meyer Solomon Law Firm, 2001—. Pres. Cystic Fibrosis Found., Manchester, 1977-78; pres., bd. dirs. Temple Adath Yeshurun, Manchester, 1986-93; judge advocate Merrimack Valley Naval League, Manchester, 1984—; sec., bd. dirs. N.H. Assn. Blind, Concord, 1982-93; treas. bd. dirs. Jewish Fedn. Manchester, 1998-2000; v.p., 2000-02. Lt. comdr. USNR, 1965. Mem. ATLA, N.H. Bar Assn., N.H. Trial Lawyers Assn., Def. Rsch. Inst. Republican. Jewish. Home: 21 Garrison Dr Bedford NH 03110-5911 Office: Backus Meyer Solomon 116 Lowell St Manchester NH 03104 E-mail: bscotch@backusmeyer.com.

SCOTT, A. HUGH, lawyer; b. Auckland, New Zealand, Jan. 10, 1947; came to U.S., 1957; s. John E. and Leona (Lacey) S.; m. Susan Campbell, Dec. 3, 1946; 1 child, Matthew Campbell. BA, Williams Coll., 1968; JD, Columbia U., 1974. Bar: Mass. 1974, U.S. Dist. Ct. Mass 1975, U.S. Ct. Appeals (1st cir.) 1975, U.S. Supreme Ct. 1982. Asst. U.S. atty. U.S. Atty.'s Office, Boston, 1978-83; assoc. Choate, Hall & Stewart, 1975-78, 83-85, ptnr., 1986—. Author: Computer and Intellectual Property Crime: Federal and State Law, 2001. Lt. (j.g.) USNR, 1968-71. Democrat. Unitarian Universalist. Home: 10 Cazenove St Boston MA 02116-6205 Office: Exchange Pl 53 State St Boston MA 02109-2804 E-mail: ahs@choate.com.

SCOTT, A. TIMOTHY, lawyer, business executive; b. Natchez, Miss., Feb. 16, 1952; s. John William and Patricia (O'Reilly) S.; m. Nancy E. Howard, June 7, 1976; children: Kevin Howard, Brian Howard. BA in Psychology, Stanford U., 1974, JD, 1977. Bar: Calif. 1977, U.S. Tax Ct. 1978. Assoc. then ptnr. Agnew, Miller & Carlson, L.A., 1977-83; assoc. Greenberg, Glusker, Fields, Claman & Machtinger, 1983; ptnr. Sachs & Phelps, 1983-91; mem. Heller, Ehrman White & McAuliffe, 1991-96, of counsel, 1996-99; sr. v.p., tax counsel Pub. Storage, Inc., Glendale, Calif., 1996—. Speaker in field. Note editor Stanford Law Rev., 1976-77; contbr. article to profl. publs., chpt. to book. Mem. ABA, L.A. County Bar Assn. (chmn. real estate taxation com. 1988-91, exec. com., taxation sect. 1989-91), Order of Coif. Democrat. Avocations: volleyball, gardening, Calif. wine, contemporary art, skiing. Office: Pub Storage Inc 701 Western Ave Glendale CA 91201-2349 E-mail: tscott@publicstorage.com.

SCOTT, ADAM, telecommunications consultant, educator, clergyman; b. Devizes, Wiltshire, Eng., May 6, 1947; s. Fraser and Bridget Penelope (Williams) S.; m. Oona MacDonald Graham, Sept. 30, 1978. BA, Oxford (Eng.) U., 1968, MA, 1972; MSc, City U., London, 1979. Barrister, Eng. and Wales, 1972; ordained priest Anglican Ch., 1976. Intellectual property lawyer, Eng., 1972-80; corp. planner Brit. Telecomms., London, 1981-86, dir. pvt. office, 1986-88, dir. internat. affairs, 1988-92, cmn. BT Apparatus, 1992-94, divsn. dir., 1994-97. Fellow Salzburg Seminar, 1983; hon. curate St. Michael's, Blackheath Park, Eng., 1975—; speaker in field. Columnist Jour. of the Lawyers Christian Fellowhip; contbr. chpt. to book, articles to profl. jours. Mem. U.K. del. CSCE, London, 1989; trustee BT Benevolent Fund, 1984-94; fellow Brit.-Am. Project, 1989—; dean Woolwich Episcopal Area, 1990-2000; mem. Appeal Tribunals U.K. Competition Commn., 2000—. Decorated Territorial decoration (U.K.); U. St. Andrews fellow. Fellow IEE; mem. Cannons. Avocations: opera, gardening, walking, aerobics. Home: 19 Blackheath Park Blackheath London SE3 9RW England Office: U St Andrews/The Scores St Katharine's West St Andrews, Fife KY16 9AL Scotland

SCOTT, ADRIENNE, social worker, psychotherapist; b. N.Y.C. BA, Finch Coll., 1957; postgrad., NYU, 1958-62, MA in English, 1958; MSW, Adelphi U., 1988. Mem. English faculty Fordham U., N.Y.C., 1966-68; editor-in-chief Blueboy Mag., Miami, Fla., 1974; editor "M" Mag., N.Y.C., 1976; mem. English faculty NYU, 1958-65; pres. Googolplex Video, N.Y.C., 1981-86; clin. social worker Mt. Sinai Hosp., 1988-93, Stuyvesant Polyclinic, N.Y.C., 1993-95. Presenter Nat. Methadone Conf., 1992. Author: Film as Film, 1970; contbg. editor Menstyle Mag., 1995; contbr. articles to numerous mags., including Vogue, Interview, N.Y. mag.; pioneer in fashion video; videographer documentaries; performance artist in Robert Wilson's King of Spain, 1973. Mem. exec. com. Adopt-An-AIDS Rschr. Program Rockefeller U.; nat. co-chairperson Gay Rights Nat. Lobby, 1976. Mem. NASW (cert.), AAUW, Assn. for Psychoanalytic Self Psychology, Am. Psychoanalytic Assn. (assoc.). Home: 165 E 66th St New York NY 10021-6132 Office: 7 Patchin Pl New York NY 10011-8341 E-mail: freudnut@aol.com.

SCOTT, ALAN EDWARD, music educator; b. Fresno, Calif., Sept. 21, 1975; s. Dorothy Stiles Scott. MusB, U. of the Pacific, 1997. Band dir. Stockton (Calif.) Unified Sch. Dist., 1997—. Mem.: Music Educator's Nat. Conf. Republican. Avocations: tennis, golf, computer game design. Home: PO Box 7309 Stockton CA 95267

SCOTT, ALASTAIR IAN, chemistry educator; b. Glasgow, Scotland, Apr. 10, 1928; came to U.S., 1968; s. William and Nell (Newton) S.; m. Elizabeth Wilson Walters, Mar. 4, 1950; children: William Stewart, Ann Walker. BSc, Glasgow U., 1949, PhD, 1952, DSc, 1964; MA (hon.), Yale U., 1968; DSc (hon.), U. Coimbra, Portugal, 1990, U. Pierre & Marie Curie, Paris, 1992. Lectr. organic chemistry Glasgow U., 1957-62; prof. U. B.C., Vancouver, 1962-65, Sussex (Eng.) U., 1965-68, Yale U., 1968-77; disting. prof. Tex. A&M U., 1977-80; prof. dept. chemistry U. Edinburgh, Scotland, 1980-82; Davidson prof. sci. Tex. A&M U., 1982—2001, Welch & Barton chair in chemistry, 2002—. Cons. in field. Author: Interpretations of Ultraviolet Spectra of Natural Products, 1964; contbr. articles to profl. jours. Recipient Rsch. Achievement award, Am. Soc. Pharmacognosy, 1993, Robert A. Welch award in chemistry, 2000, Disting. Tex. Scientist of Yr. award, Tex. Acad. Sci., 2002. Fellow: Royal Soc. Edinburgh (Royal medal 2001), Royal Soc. (Bakerian lectr. 1996, Davy medal 2001); mem.: Tex. Acad. Sci. (Tex. Scientist of Yr. 2002), Japan Pharm. Soc. (hon.), Chem Soc. (Corday-Morgan medal 1964, Centenary lectr. 1994, Tetrahedron prize for creativity in organic chemistry 1995, Natural Products Rsch. award 1996), Am. Chem. Soc. (Ernest Guenther award 1976, A.C. Cope scholar 1992, Nakanishi prize 2003). Office: Tex A&M U Dept Chemistry College Station TX 77843-0001

SCOTT, ALEXANDER ROBINSON, engineering association executive; b. Elizabeth, N.J., June 15, 1941; s. Marvin Chester and Jane (Robinson) Scott; m. Angela Jean Kendall, July 17, 1971; children: Alexander Robinson, Jennifer Angela, Ashley Kandall. BA in History, Va. Mil. Inst., 1963; MA in Personnel and Counseling Psychology, Rutgers U., 1965. Sales mgr. Hilton Hotels, 1967-70; meetings mgr. Am. Inst. Mining Engrs., N.Y.C., 1971-73; exec. dir. Minerals, Metals and Materials Soc., 1973—. With U.S. Army, 1965—67. Decorated Bronze Star. Mem.: Am. Soc. Assn. Execs. Republican. Baptist. Home: 107 Staghorn Dr Sewickley PA 15143-9506 Office: TMS 184 Thorn Hill Rd Warrendale PA 15086-7514 E-mail: TMSgeneral@tms.org.

SCOTT, ALICE HOLLY, retired librarian; b. Jefferson, Ga. d. Frank D. and Annie D. (Colbert) Holly; m. Alphonso Scott, Mar. 1, 1959; children—Christopher, Alison AB, Spelman Coll., Atlanta, 1957; M.L.S., Atlanta U., 1958; PhD, U. Chgo., 1983. Librarian Bklyn. Pub. Library, 1958-59; br. librarian Chgo. Pub. Library, 1959-72, dir. Woodson Regional Library, 1974-77, dir. community relations, 1977-82, dep. commr., 1982-87, asst. commr., 1987-98; ret., 1998. Doctoral fellow, 1973 Mem. ALA (councilor 1982-85), Chgo. Spelman Club, DuSable Mus., Chgo. Urban League Democrat. Baptist.

SCOTT, ANNE BYRD FIROR, history educator; b. Montezuma, Ga., Apr. 24, 1921; d. John William and Mary Valentine (Moss) Firor; m. Andrew Mackay Scott, June 2, 1947; children: Rebecca, David MacKay, Donald MacKay. AB, U. Ga., 1941; MA, Northwestern U., 1944; PhD, Radcliffe Coll., 1958; LHD (hon.), Lindenwood Coll., 1968, Queens Coll., 1985, Northwestern U., 1989, Radcliffe Coll., 1990, U. of the South, 1990, Cornell Coll., 1991. Congressional rep., editor LWV of U.S., 1944-53; lectr. history Haverford Coll., 1957-58, U. N.C., Chapel Hill, 1959-60; asst. prof. history Duke U., Durham, N.C., 1961-67, assoc. prof., 1968-70, prof., 1971-80, W.K. Boyd prof., 1980-91, W.K. Boyd prof. emerita, 1992—, chmn. dept., 1981-85; Gastprofessor Universität, Bonn, Germany, 1992-93. Vis. prof. Johns Hopkins U., 1972-73, Stanford U., 1974, Harvard U., 1984, Cornell Coll., 1993, Williams Coll., 1994, U. Miss., 2000; Times-Mirror scholar Huntington Libr., 1995; vice chmn. Nat. Humanities Ctr., 1991-98; mem. adv. com. Schlesinger Libr. Author: The Southern Lady, 1970, 25th anniversary edit., 1995, (with Andrew MacKay Scott) One Half the People, 1974, Making the Invisible Woman Visible, 1984, Natural Allies, 1991; editor: Jane Addams, Democracy and Social Ethics, 1964, The American woman, 1970, Women in American Life, 1970, Women and Men in American Life, 1976, Unheard Voices, 1993; mem. editl. bd. Revs. in Am. History, 1976-81, Am. Quar., 1974-78, Jour. So. History, 1978-84; contbr. articles to profl. jours. Chmn. Gov.'s Commn. on Status of Women, 1963-64; mem. Citizens Adv. Council on Status of Women U.S., 1964-68; trustee Carnegie Corp., 1977-85, W.W. Ctr. for Scholars, 1977-84; chmn. bd. dirs. Nat. Cmty. Investment Fund, 1996—. AAUW fellow, 1956-57; grantee NEH, 1967-68, 76-77, Nat. Humanities Ctr., 1980-81; grad. medal Radcliffe Coll., 1986, Duke U. medal, 1991, John Caldwell medal N.C. Humanities Coun., 1994; fellow Ctr. Advanced Study in Behavioral Sci., 1986-87; Fulbright scholar, 1984, 92-93. Mem. Am. Antiquarian Soc., Orgn. Am. Historians (exec. bd. 1973-76, pres. 1983, Disting. Pub. Svc. award 2002), So. Hist. Assn. (exec. bd. 1976-79, pres. 1989), Soc. Am. Historians, Phi Beta Kappa. Democrat. Office: Duke U Dept History Durham NC 27708 E-mail: ascott2@email.unc.edu., ascott@acpub.duke.edu.

SCOTT, BARBARA JUNE, editor, writer; b. Cuba, Mo., Oct. 5, 1948; d. Robert Earl Wayne and Eula Mae Stowell; m. Michael Dennis Scott; m. Stephen Wesley Hill. BA in English, Mo. So. Coll., 1972; postgrad., Stanford U., 1983; cert. film prodn., Mass Media Inst., Stanford U., 1983. Sr. sales rep. McGraw-Hill, Inc., San Diego, 1984—91; writer O.r.e.a., Tulsa, 1994—95; freelance writer, editor Scott Creative Comm., Grand Rapids, Mich., 1991—2002; acquisitions editor Honor Books, Tulsa, 1998—2000; editor Zondervan, Grand Rapids, 2000—. Author: (novels) Sedona Storm, 1994, Secrets of the Gathering Darkness, 1996, (book) God's Little Book of Proverbs, 1999, God's Little Book of Blessings, 2002; contbr. book, ; editor: (book) Merry Christmas, 1999, E-Mail from God for Teens, 1999, God's Little Instruction Book for Leader, God's Little Instruction Book for Parents, 1999, Cheapskates Little Instruction Book, What My Dog Has Taught Me About Life, 1999; : God's Little Devotional Book for Teachers, 1999, (books) God's Little Devotional Book for Mothers/Couples/Teens, 2000, (book) The Christmas Lizard, 2000 (ECPA Silver medallion, 2001), A Gift from St. Nicholas, 2001, More E-Mail from God for Teens, 2001, At Home with God, 2001, Lily Series (fiction and non-fiction), 2001, (biography series) Today's Heroes, 2002, Sports Heroes, (book) The Legend of the Valentine, 2002, I Am a Promise, 2002, Dr. Devo's Lickety-Split Devotions, 2002, NIrV Kid Reference Library, 2002. Avocations: reading, walking, travel. Office: Zondervan 5300 Patterson Ave SE Grand Rapids MI 49530 Office Fax: 616-698-3326. Business E-Mail: barbara.scott@zondervan.com.

SCOTT, BETSY SUE, lawyer; b. Chgo., July 3, 1951; d. Leo and Regina Mackta; m. Thomas Jefferson Scott Jr., Apr. 25, 1981; children: Elspeth Watts, Marghuerita Taylor, Thomas Jefferson Scott III. Cert. in French lang., U. Paris, 1971; BA, Hamilton Coll., 1972; JD, Cumberland Coll., 1976. Bar: Pa. 1976, N.Y. 1980, D.C. 1984. Trust adminstr. Mfrs. Hanover Trust, N.Y.C., 1976-78; assoc. Fink, Weinberger et al, 1978-80; employee benefits officer 1st Va. Bank, Falls Church, 1982-83; mem. Hill, Betts & Nash, Washington, 1983-85; sole practice, litigation cons., 1985-86; employee benefits atty., Pension and Welfare Benefits Adminstrn. U.S. Dept. Labor, 1986-90; atty. Office Fgn. Assets Control, U.S. Treasury Dept., 1990—. Translator French-English litigation, Washington, 1985—. Mem. Great Falls Womens Club, River Bend Golf and Country Club. Republican. Avocations: sailing, fencing, gardening. Office: US Treasury Dept Office Fgn Assets Control 1500 Pennsylvania Ave NW Washington DC 20220-0001

SCOTT, BRIAN DAVID, lawyer; b. Spokane, Wash., Sept. 30, 1946; s. Dick E. and Helene L. (Johnson) S.; m. Lynita G. Muzzall, Sept. 9, 1972; children: D. Alexander, Rachel E., S. Andrew. BA, U. Wash., 1968; JD, U. Wis., 1972. Bar: Wis. 1972, Wash. 1972, U.S. Dist. Ct. (we. dist.) Wash. 1972, U.S. Dist. Ct. (we. dist.) Wis. 1972. Asst. atty. gen. Wash. State Atty. Gen.'s Office, Seattle, 1972-74; assoc. Jackson, Ulvestad, Goodwin, Grutz, 1974-81; ptnr. Goodwin, Grutz & Scott, 1981-96, Grutz, Scott & Kinney, Seattle, 1996-99, Grutz, Scott, Kinney & Fjelstad, Seattle, 1999—. Mem. ATLA, Wash. Trial Lawyers Assn., Wash. Athletic Club. Democrat. Avocations: boating, skiing, travel. Home: 158 Prospect St Seattle WA 98109-3750 Office: Grutz Scott Kinney & Fjelstad 600 University St Ste 1928 Seattle WA 98101-4178 E-mail: scott@gskf-law.com.

SCOTT, BRIAN WALTER, management consultant; b. Melbourne, Victoria, Australia, Apr. 23, 1935; s. Walter and Dorothy Ada (Ransom) S.; m. Dorothy Yvonne Allen, Aug. 15, 1959; children: David, Mark, Jennifer, Susan. B of Econs., Sydney (Australia) U., 1955; MBA, Stanford U., 1959; D of Bus. Adminstrn., Harvard U., 1963. Asst. prof. U. So. Calif., Los Angeles, 1961-62; cons. mgmt. W.D. Scott and Co. Pty. Ltd., Sydney, 1963-69, dir., 1969-74, mng. dir., 1974-79, chmn., 1979-85; dep. chmn. A.C.I. Internat. Ltd., 1985-86, chmn., 1986-88; dir., mgmt. rev. Edn. Portfolio, New South Wales, 1988-90. Chmn. Mgmt. Frontiers Pty. Ltd., Sydney, Found for Devel. Cooperation Ltd., Brisbane; bd. dirs. ANZ Banking Corp. Ltd., Melbourne, Liquid Air Australia Ltd., Melbourne, James N. Kirby Found. Ltd. Chmn. Trade Devel. Coun., Canberra, 1984-90, chmn. Australian-Korean Found, 1992-2000; chmn. coun. Knox Grammar Sch., Sydney, 1981-89, Australia-Asean Bus. Coun., Canberra, 1980-82; mem. governing bd. Asian Inst. Mgmt., Manila, 1990—; co-chmn. Australia-Korea Forum, 1989-91. Named Officer, Order of Australia, 1985; recipient Australian Mfrs. Export Coun. award, 1989. Fellow Inst. Dirs. Australia (fed. pres. 1982-86), Internat. Acad. Mgmt., Australian Inst. Mgmt., Inst. Mgmt. Cons.; mem. Trade Policy Rsch. Ctr. (coun. mem. 1985-90), Sydney U. (senate 1990-95), Royal Sydney Yacht Squadron Club, Am. Club (Sydney). Avocations: reading, travel. Home: #4 2-6 Russell Ave Lindfield NSW 2070 Australia Office: Mgmt Frontiers Pty Ltd 118 Alfred St Milsons Pt North Sydney NSW 2061 Australia E-mail: mfed@mgtfrontiers.com.au.

SCOTT, BYRON ALTON, professional basketball coach, former professional basketball player; b. Ogden, Utah, Mar. 28, 1961; m. Anita Scott; children: Thomas, Londen. Student, Ariz. State U., 1979-85. With L.A. Lakers, 1983-93, 96-97; shooting guard Indiana Pacers, Indpls., 1993-95, Vancouver Grizzlies, 1995-96; asst. coach Sacramento Kings, Sacramento, 1998-00; head coach New Jersey Nets, East Rutherford, N.J., 2000—. Mem. NBA Championship Team, 1985, 87, 88. Office: New Jersey Nets 405 Murray Hill Pkwy East Rutherford NJ 07073-2136*

SCOTT, CATHERINE DOROTHY, librarian, information consultant; b. June 21, 1927; d. Leroy Stearns Scott and Agnes Frances (Meade) Scott Schellenberg. AB in English, Cath. U. Am., 1950, MS in Libr. Sci., 1955. Asst. libr. Export-Import Bank U.S.A., Washington, 1951-55, Nat. Assn. Home Builders, 1955-62, reference libr., 1956-62; founder, chief tech. libr. Bellcomm, Inc., subs. AT&T, Washington, 1962-72; chief libr. Nat. Air and Space Mus. Smithsonian Instn., 1972-82, chief libr. Mus. Reference Ctr., 1982-88, sr. reference libr., 1989-95; info. cons., 1995—. Bd. visitors Cath. U. Am. Libr. Sci. Sch. and Librs., 1984-93; presdl. appointee, mem. Nat. Commn. Libr. and Info. Sci., 1971-76. Editor: International Handbook of Aerospace Awards and Trophies, 1980, 81; guest editor: Aeronautics and Space Flight Collections, 1985, in Spl. Collections, 1984. Vice-chmn. D.C. Rep. Com., 1960-68; mem. platform com. Rep. Nat. Com., 1964, sec., 1968; del. Rep. Nat. Conv., San Francisco, 1964, Miami, Fla., 1968. Named to Hon. Order Ky. Cols., 1968; recipient Sec.'s Disting. Svc. award Smithsonian Instn., 1976, Alumni Achievement award Cath. U. Am., 1977, Century Circle, 1998—, Disting. Fed. Svc. Nat. Commn. Libr. and Info. Sci. medal, 1985. Mem. Spl. Librs. Assn. (pres. Washington chpt. 1973-74, 92-93, cons. 1976-89, chmn. aerospace divsn. 1980-81, bd. dirs. 1986-89, 91-94, awards com. 1990-91, pres.-elect 1991-92, immediate past pres. 1993-94, chair assn. awards and honors 1994-95, 98-99, chmn. cons. com. 1994-98, anniversary com. aerospace divsn. 1995, convenor ret. caucus 1997-99, conf. program facilitator Indpls. 1998, Mpls. 1999, Phila. 2000, San Antonio 2001, L.A., 2002, Hall of Fame award 1996, , Disting. Svc. award 1982, 96-97, Mem. of Yr. 1994), Spl. Librs. Assn., Legacy Club, Am. Soc. Assn. Execs. (internat. round table), Nat. Mus. Women in Arts, Internat. Fedn. Libr. Assns. (del. 1976, 83, 85, 88-89), Friends of Cath. U. Librs. (founder, pres. 1984-88, exec. coun. 1984-96, sustaining mem. 1998—), Cath. U. Am. Devel. Com., Cent. Club, Nat. Fedn. Rep. Women, League Rep. Women D.C. (bd. dirs. 1995-97, nominating com. 1996-97, contbg. mem. 1999—), Capital Yacht Club. Fax: (202) 488-9223..

SCOTT, CHARLES DAVID, chemical engineer, consultant; b. Chaffee, Mo., Oct. 24, 1929; s. Charles Perry and Alma Gertrude (Kendall) S.; m. Alice Reba Bardill, Feb. 11, 1956; children: Timothy Charles, Mary Alice, Lisa Ann. BS in Chem. Engring., U. Mo., 1951; MS in Chem. Engring., U. Tenn., 1961, PhD, 1966. Registered profl. engr., Tenn. Devel. engr. Union Carbide Corp., Oak Ridge, 1953-57; rsch. engr. Oak Ridge Nat. Lab., 1957-73, sect. chief, 1973-76, assoc. divsn. dir., 1976-83, rsch. fellow, 1983-86, sr. rsch. fellow, 1987-94; dir. bioprocessing rsch. and devel. ctr., 1991-94; engirng. R&D cons. Oak Ridge, 1994—. Adj. prof. chem. engring. U. Tenn., Knoxville. Contbr. articles to profl. jours.; patentee in field. 1st lt. AUS, 1951-53. Recipient U.S. Dept. Energy E.O. Lawrence award, 1980, U. Tenn. Nathan W. Doughtery award, 1987, U. Mo. Honor award, 1988, David Perlman award Am. Chem. Soc., 1994; Union Carbide Corp. fellow, 1983; Martin Marietta Sr. Corp. fellow, 1987. Mem. Am. Chem. Soc. (chmn. separation sci. subdivsn.), Am. Assn. Clin. Chemistry (chmn. com. advanced analytical concepts, nat. award 1980), Am. Inst. Chem. Engrs. (bd. dirs.), Nat. Acad. Engring., Sigma Xi, Alpha Chi Sigma. Lutheran.

SCOTT, CHARLES LEWIS, photojournalist; b. Grayville, Ill., Aug. 18, 1924; s. Marvin Joseph and Prudence (Blood) S.; m. Jane Turner, Jan. 14, 1945 (dec. 1983); children— Lyntha Ann, Thomas Marvin; m. Martha McDonald, Aug. 23, 1986. BS in Journalism, U. Ill., 1948; MS, Ohio U., 1970. Photographer Champaign-Urbana (Ill.) Courier, 1946-50, chief photographer, 1953-56; photographer Ill. Natural History Survey, 1946-51, Binghamton (N.Y.) Press, 1951-53; asst. picture editor Milw. Jour., 1956-58; picture editor, 1958-66; graphics dir. Chgo. Daily News, 1966-69; instr. Sch. Journalism, Ohio U., Athens, 1969-70, asst. prof., 1971-72, asso. prof., 1972-74, 76-77, prof., 1977—; dir. Sch. Visual Communication, 1978-95, prof. emeritus visual comm., 1995; picture editor Chgo. Tribune, 1974-76; dir. photography Rocky Mountain News, Denver, 1987-88; ret., 1995. Served with U.S. Navy, 1942-45. Decorated D.F.C., Air medal (3); recipient numerous awards in regional and nat. news photo contests. Mem. Nat. Press Photographers Assn. (charter mem., Newspaper Photographer of Yr. 1952, Editor of Yr. 1966, Joseph Sprague Meml. award 1975, Robin F. Garland Educator award 1979), Soc. Profl. Journalists, Ohio News Photographers Assn. (Lifetime Achievement award 1995). Presbyterian. Home: 8559 Lavelle Rd Athens OH 45701-9190

SCOTT, CHARLOTTE H. business educator; b. Yonkers, N.Y., Mar. 18, 1925; d. Edgar B. and Charlotte Agnes (Palmer) Hanley; m. Nathan Alexander Scott, Jr., Dec. 21, 1946; children: Nathan Alexander Scott, Leslie Kristin Scott Ashamu. AB, Barnard Coll., 1947; postgrad., Am. U., 1949-53; MBA, U. Chgo., 1964; LL.D., Allegheny Coll., 1981. Research asso. Nat. Bur. Econ. Research, N.Y.C., 1947-48; economist R.W. Goldsmith Assos., Washington, 1948-55, U. Chgo., 1955-56, Fed. Res. Bank, Chgo., 1956-71, asst. v.p., 1971-76; prof. bus. adminstrn. and commerce, sr. fellow Tayloe Murphy Inst., U. Va., Charlottesville, 1976-86; prof. commerce and edn. U. Va., 1986-98, prof. emeritus, 1998—. Bd. dirs. Atlantic Rural Expn., Inc.; mem. adv. bd. NationsBank Charlottesville, 1991-93; mem. nat. adv. bd. coun. SBA, 1979-82; mem. consumer adv. coun. bd. govs. FRS, 1979-82, vice chmn., 1980-81, chmn., 1981-82. Mem. editorial bd. Jour. Retail Banking, 1978-85, Jour. Internat. Assn. Personnel Women, 1981-85; contbr. articles to profl. jours. Pres. women's bd. Chgo. Urban League, 1967-69; mem. Va. Commn. on Status of Women, 1982-85, Gov.'s Commn. on Va.'s Future, 1982-85, Gov.'s Commn. on Efficiency in Govt., 1985-87; treas. Va. Women's Cultural History Project, 1982-85; bd. dirs. Boys and Girls Club of Charlottesville/Albemarle; governing bd. Charlottesville/Albemarle Found., 1993—; mem. adv. bd. Ash Lawn-Highland Mus.; treas. Episcopal Diocese, Coun. Region XV, 1999—. Mem. Internat. Assn. Personnel Women (v.p. mems.-at-large 1980-82), Assn. Study of Higher Edn., Va. Assn. Econs., Acad. Mgmt., Barnard Coll./Columbia U. Alumnae Assn. (bd. dirs. 1977-81, trustee 1977-81). Episcopalian. Home: 1419 Hilltop Rd Charlottesville VA 22903-1226 Office: U Va McIntire Sch Commerce Monroe Hall Charlottesville VA 22903

SCOTT, CHARLOTTE PATRICIA, artist; b. Apr. 23, 1927; BA, U. Manitoba, Winnipeg, Can., 1949. Cert. rescue scuba diver and underwater photographer. Asst. prin. Hartney Sch. Syc., Man., 1948-49; social worker Children's Aid Soc., Detroit, 1951-53; tchr. Southfield (Mich.) Sch. Sys., 1954-55. Exhibited paintings in Adirondacks Nat. Watercolor Exhbn., N.Y., Southeastern Watercolor Competition, Fla.; works published in numerous mags., books. Recipient Outstanding Achievement in Photography award Internat. Marine Photo Contest, 1988; awards Nikonos Shootout Internat. Underwater Photography Competitions. Mem. Fla. Watercolor Soc. (signature life mem.). Home: 743 24th Sq Vero Beach FL 32962-1336 E-mail: patscott@mindspring.com.

SCOTT, CHRISTOPHER G. metallurgical engineer, researcher; b. Poughkeepsie, N.Y., Aug. 12, 1956; s. Donald C. Scott, Virginia J. Scott; m. Juanita A. Talbert; children: Kristen, Caitlin. BA in Biology, Bowdoin Coll., 1978; BSMetE, U. Ill., Chgo., 1984, MS in Metallurgy, 1988. Rsch. engr. The Lubrizol Corp., Wickliffe, Ohio, 1987—92, group leader, 1992—99, prin. rsch. engr., 1999—. Mem. editl. bd.: ASTM Jour. Testing and Evaluation, 1995—; contbr. articles to profl. jours. Trustee, head deacon The Word of God Cmty. Ch., Canton, 1995—2002. Mem.: ASM International (local chpt. chmn. 1992—94, reviewer ASM Handbook Vol. 3 1991—92, Scholarship award 1983). Avocations: reading, racquetball, spectator sports. Office: The Lubrizol Corp 29400 Lakeland Blvd Wickliffe OH 44092 Office Fax: 440-347-4713. Business E-Mail: cgs@lubrizol.com.

SCOTT, CONCETTA CIOTTI, artist, art educator; b. Phila., Jan. 17, 1927; d. Giulio J. Ciotti and Adelina D'Andrea; m. Pierre Brutsche Scott, Apr. 20, 1963; children: Elizabeth Ann, Christopher John. Assocs. Degree, Moore Coll. Art and Design, 1951; student, The Embroiders Guild Am., INc., 1967—78, No. Va. C.C., Woodbridge, Va., 1988. Graphics designer/illustrator, freelance artist various advt. agys. and dept. stores, Phila., 1946—54; art tchr. grades 1-12 Melrose Acad., Melrose Park, 1951—54; designer ads/direct mail The Hecht Co., Washington, 1954—56; designer, art dir. Woodward and Lothrop Stores, 1956—63; freelance artist Alexandria, McLean, Va., 1963—66; art tchr. St. Luke's Sch., McLean, 1974—75; art tchr., cons. The Montessori Sch. McLean, 1975—98. McLean rep. Fairfax County Coun. of the Arts, Annandale, Va., 1988—93. Cover-illustrations, rhyme and play book, one-woman shows include Brookside Gardens Gallery, Wheaton, Md., 1989, The Charles Sumner Sch. Mus., Washington, 1990, The Manor House Gallery, Green Spring, Alexandria, Va., 1991, Nat. Inst. Health Galleries, Bethesda, Md., 1992, GTE Govt. Sys. Corp., Chantilly, Va., 1993, Barry Gallery, Marymount U., Arlington, Va., 1994, The Asman Gallery, NBC-TV Studios, Washington, 1995, The Clin. Ctr. Galleries, NIH, Bethesda, Md., 1996, La Vignette, Dinan, Brittany, France, 1999, Gallery West, Goodwin House West, Falls Church, Va., 1999, The Asman Gallery, NBC-TV Studios, Washington, 2000, Gallery Walk, Goodwin House, East, Alexandria, Va., 2000, The Manor House Gallery, Green Spring, 2001, two-persons shows, , internat. exhbn., , , exhibitions include Nat. League Am. Pen Women, Roanoke, Va., 1985, Furman U., S.C., 1987, Fells Point Gallery, Balt., 1994, 1997, 1998, 1999, numerous group shows including, exhibited in group shows at Va. Watercolor Soc., Martinsville, Va., 2000, Phila. Watercolor Soc., Atlantic City, 2000, McLean Art Club, Emerson Gallery, 2000, Arts Coun. Fairfax, Annandale, Va., 2000, Balt. Watercolro Soc., Bethesda, Md., 2001, Va. Watercolor Soc., Richmond, 2001, Washington Water Color Assn., Bethesda, 2001, Ctrl. Va. Watercolor Guild, Charlottesville, 2001, Berryville-Clarke County Coun., Millwood, Va., 2001, Art League/Torpedo Factory, Alexandria, 2001, Phila. Watercolor Soc., The

Am. Coll., Bryn Mawr, Pa., 2001. Vol. art tchr. grades 1-3 Churchill Rd. Sch., McLean, 1972; aide 4H Club, McLean, Great Falls, 1973—75; vol. mail and phones Dem. Party, Washington, 1960. Recipient Distinctive Merit award, Art Dirs. Club Washington, 1961, 1962, 1963, grant, artist residency, Les Amis de La Grande Vigne, 1999; fellow P.P. Morris Grad. fellow, Moore Coll. Art and Design, Phila., 1951. Mem.: Nat. League Am. Pen Women (art editor 1980—82, biennial conv. chmn. 1983—84), Vienna Arts Soc., Fairfax Art League, The Art League, Miniature Arts Soc. Fla., Miniature Painters, Sculptors and Gravers Soc. Washington, McLean Art Club (show chmn. 1977), Potomac Valley Watercolorists (publicity/telephone 1996—98), Washington Water Color Assn. (show chmn. 1996—2001, show co-chmn. 2002—), Balt. Watercolor Soc. (signature), Phila. Water Color Soc. (signature), Va. Watercolor Soc. (art bd. 1993, signature, awards com.). Roman Catholic. Avocations: photography, reading, music, opera. Home: 1111 Dead Run Dr Mc Lean VA 22101

SCOTT, DALE ALLAN, major league umpire; b. Springfield, Oreg., Aug. 14, 1959; s. Jesse Lee and Betty Ann (Potts) S. AS, Lane C.C., 1979. Radio disc jockey Sta. KBDF, Eugene, Oreg., 1976-81; minor league umpire various orgns., 1981-85; umpire Am. League, 1986-99, World Series, 1998, 2001, Major League Baseball, 2000—, All Star Game, 1993, 2001. Ofcl. Lane County Baseball Umpire Assn., 1975-81, Lane County Basketball Ofcls. Assn., 1977-85, Portland Basketball Assn., 1986-96, Lane County Football Ofcls. Assn., 1978-88, H.S. football Portland Football Ofcls. Assn., 1989-96; instr. Golden State Umpire Camp, 1991—. Democrat. Office: Office of Commr of Baseball 245 Park Ave New York NY 10167-0002

SCOTT, DALE PHILLIP, minister; b. Fresno, Calif., Dec. 25, 1955; s. Kenneth Milton and Zoe Zane (Schmuke) S.; m. Kimberly Joyce Bohigian, Nov. 18, 1978; children: Taylor Zane, Rachel Leigh. BA in Religion, Calif. State U., Fresno, 1978; MDiv, Princeton Theol. Sem., 1982; grad. Fuqua Internat., Christian Sch. Comm. Ordained to ministry Presbyn. Ch., 1982. Program coord. Calvin Crest Conf., Oakhurst, Calif., 1978-80; intern Boonton (N.J.) Presbyn. Ch., 1980-81; chaplain Princeton (N.J.) Nursing Home, 1981-82; assoc. minister edn. Webster Groves Presbyn. Ch., Webster Grove, Mo., 1982-90; assoc. minister evangelism Second Presbyn. Ch., Bloomington, Ill., 1990-92, Good Shepherd Presbyn. Ch., Bartlesville, Okla., 1992—. Del. Nat. Youth Workers Conf., 1982, 84, 87, Presbyn. Ch. U.S.A. Gen. Assembly, 1993. Co-chmn. Centennial Parade, 1995-97; distbn. com. chair United Way, 1998, 99, 2000. Named Theologian of the Yr., Huguenot Soc., 1981. Mem. Daybreak Rotary (charter). Republican. Office: Good Shepherd Presbyn Ch 801 SE Washington Blvd Bartlesville OK 74006-4424

SCOTT, DARCY L. artist; b. Waterbury, Conn. BS, Mich. State U., 1978. Artist, West Bloomfield, Mich., 1989—. One-woman shows include Cary Gallery, Rochester, Mich., 1999, exhibited in group shows at Buckham Gallery, Flint, Mich., 1999, Univ. Art Gallery, Mt. Pleasant, Mich., 1999, Mt. Clemens (Mich.) Art Ctr., 2001. Recipient Madonna Alldredge award for landscape, Rocky Mt. Nat. Exhbn., Foothills Art Ctr., 2001, Juror's award, Showcase Gallery, 2001, NWWS Nat. Exhbn., 2001, Silver medal, Pikes Peak Internat. Exhbn., 2001. Mem.: Ala. Watercolor Soc. (signature), Detroit Inst. Arts, Ga. Watercolor Soc. (juror 1999, signature), Tex. Watercolor Soc. (signature), Watercolor Honor Soc., Mich. Watercolor Soc. (bd. dirs. 1998—, patron 1999—2002).

SCOTT, DAVID CLINTON, research scientist; b. Brighton, Colo., Sept. 5, 1960; s. Robert Glenn and Janice Elizabeth (Smith) S.; m. Dana Jungschaffer, Aug. 7, 1988; children: Clinton P., Alexander J., Eric O. BA, U. Colo., 1986; PhD, U. So. Calif., 1993. R & D chemist ICI, Hawthorn, Calif., 1987-88; rsch. asst. chemistry dept. U. So. Calif., L.A., 1988-93; rsch. scientist Jet Propulsion Lab, Pasadena, Calif., 1993-2000; sr. mem. tech. staff Atmospheric Scis., 2000—. Contbr. articles to profl. jours. Mem. AAAS, Am. Geophys. Union, Am. Chem. Soc., Applied Optics, Phi Beta Kappa. Avocations: mountain biking, running, swimming, skiing, hiking. Office: Jet Propulsion Lab M/S 183-401 4800 Oak Grove Dr Pasadena CA 91109

SCOTT, DAVID IRVIN, minister; b. Yakima, Wash., Dec. 5, 1947; s. Jack Phillip and Betty Lucille (Paronto) S.; m. Jill Louise Baker, June 23, 1982 (div. May 1991). AA, Monterey Peninsula Coll., Calif., 1975. Accredited resident mgr., Inst. Real Estate Mgmt., 1987. Courier Gallery Hawaii, Inc., Honolulu, 1981; acting resident mgr. Fairway Gardens, 1981; resident mgr. Waimalu Park, 1981-83, Waikiki Skyliner, Honolulu, 1983-84, Bishop Gardens, Honolulu, 1985-86, Plaza Landmark, Honolulu, 1986-88, Westlake Apts., Honolulu, 1988, Fairway Gardens, Honolulu, 1988-94. Condo mgmt. cons.; pres. Inner Man Ministries Mem. Alpha Gamma Sigma. Avocations: vocalist, archery, billiards, fishing, community theater. Office: Inner Man Ministries PO Box 2141 Pearl City HI 96782-9141 E-mail: chosnstone@msn.com. *Jesus is the way, the truth, and the life: no man comes to the Father, but by Him JN 14:6.*

SCOTT, DAVID KNIGHT, physicist, university administrator; b. North Ronaldsay, Scotland, Mar. 2, 1940; married, 1966; 3 children. BSc, Edinburgh U., 1962; DPhil in Nuclear Physics, Oxford U., 1967. Rsch. officer nuclear physics lab. Oxford U., 1970-73; rsch. fellow nuclear physics Balliol Coll., 1967-70, sr. rsch. fellow, 1970-73; physicist Lawrence Berkeley Lab. U. Calif., 1973-75, sr. scientist nuclear sci., 1975-79; prof. physics, astronomy and chemistry Nat. Superconducting Cyclotron Lab. Mich. State U., East Lansing, 1979-93; Hannah disting. prof. physics, astronomy and chemistry Mich. State U., 1979-86, assoc. provost, 1983-86, provost, v.p. acad. affairs, 1986-92; Hannah Disting. prof. learning, sci. and soc. Nat. Superconducting Cyclotron Lab. Mich. State U., 1992-93; chancellor U. Mass., Amherst, 1993—2001. Fellow Am. Phys. Soc. Office: U Mass 251 Lederle Amherst MA 01003 E-mail: dkscott@chancellor.umass.edu.

SCOTT, DAVID MICHAEL, pharmacy educator; b. St. Paul, July 5, 1949; s. David Marvin and Cecelia (Ventura) S.; m. Patti L. Anderson, May 1, 1976; children: Michael, Justin, Nathan. BS, U. Minn., 1972, MPH, 1982, PhD, 1987. Lic. pharmacist, Minn. Pharmacy intern United Hosps., St. Paul, 1972-73, staff pharmacist, 1973-75; pharmacy dir. Cmty.-Univ. Health Care Ctr., Mpls., 1975-84; clin. instr. pharmacy U. Minn., 1975-86; assoc. dir. orthop. rsch. St. Paul Ramsey Med. Ctr., 1984-86; asst. prof. U. Nebr. Med. Ctr., Omaha, 1986-95, assoc. prof., 1996—. Project epidemiologist Toward a Drug-Free Nebr., Nebr. Dept. Edn., Lincoln, 1989-94; mem. Springville Elem. Sch. Drug Abuse, Omaha, 1988-97; faculty advisor Acad. Student Pharmacists, APHA, Omaha, 1994—. Contbr. articles to sci. jours. Coach Keystone Little League, Omaha, 1991-94; bd. dirs. Butler-Gast YMCA, Omaha, 1992-96; vice chmn. bd. dirs., 1994-95; chmn. Nebr. PACT (Pulling Am. Cmtys. Together) Sch. Truancy Task Force, Lincoln, 1994-97. Grantee Am. Assn. Colls. Pharmacy, Alexandria, Va., 1995-97, U.S. Dept. Edn., Washington, 1996-97, U.S. Dept. Health and Human Svcs. Health Resources and Svcs. Adminstrn., 2000—. Mem. APHA (mem. program com. 1991-93), Am. Assn. Colls. of Pharmacy (mem. program com. 1990-92, grant 1995-97), Internat. Soc. Pharmacoepidemiology (mem. program com. 1992-97), Nat. Cmty. Pharmacists Assn. (faculty liaison 1987—), Internat. Soc. Pharmacoeconomics and Outcomes Rsch. Avocations: jogging, softball, golf, reading, basketball. Home: 5305 Raven Oaks Dr Omaha NE 68152-1750 Office: U Nebr Med Ctr Coll Pharmcy 986045 Nebr Med Ctr Omaha NE 68198-6045 E-mail: dscott@unmc.edu.

SCOTT, DAVID RODICK, lawyer, legal educator; b. Phila., Dec. 30, 1938; s. Ernest and Lydia Wister (tunis) S.; m. Ruth Erskine Wardle, Aug. 20, 1966; children: Cintra W., D. Rodman. AB magna cum laude, Harvard U., 1960, JD, 1965; MA, Cambridge U., 1962. Bar: Pa. 1966, D.C. 1977, U.S. Dist. Ct. (ea. dist.) Pa. 1966, U.S. Ct. Appeals (3rd cir.) 1966, U.S. Ct. Appeals (D.C. cir.) 1977, U.S. Supreme Ct. 1977. Law clk. to assoc. justice Supreme Ct. Pa., Phila., 1965-66; assoc. Pepper, Hamilton & Scheetz, 1966-69, 72-76; asst. dist. atty. City of Phila., 1970-72; sr. trial atty. criminal divsn. U.S. Dept. Justice, Washington, 1976-80; chief counsel, acting dir. Office Govt. Ethics, 1980-84; univ. counsel Rutgers U., New Brunswick, N.J., 1984—. Acting dir. U.S. Office Govt. Ethics, 1982-83; tchr., lectr. in law Cath. U. Am., Washington, 1977-81, Inst. Paralegal Tng., Phila., 1970-74; instr. faculty of arts and scis. Rutgers U.; lectr. in field. Contbr. chpts. to textbooks, articles to profl. jours. Trustee United Way Greater Mercer County, 1990—, Princeton Area Cmty. Found., Inc., 1991—; bd. mgrs. Episc. Acad., Merion, Pa., 1970-74. Keasbey Found. fellow, 1960-62. Mem ABA, Pa. Bar Assn., Nat. Assn. Coll. and Univ. Attys. (bd. dirs. 1993-96), Am. Friends Cambridge U. (head N.J. chpt. 1987-93). Home: 255 Russell Rd Princeton NJ 08540-6733 Office: Rutgers U Office of Univ Counsel Winants Hall New Brunswick NJ 08901 E-mail: scott@oldqueens.rutgers.edu.

SCOTT, DAVID WARREN, statistics educator; b. Oak Park, Ill., July 16, 1950; s. John V. and Nancy (Mellers) S.; m. Jean Charlotte Madera, June 15, 1974; children: Hilary Kathryn, Elizabeth Alison, Warren Robert. BA, Rice U., 1972, MA, PhD, Rice U., 1976. Asst. prof. Baylor Coll. Medicine, Houston, 1976-79, Rice U., Houston, 1979-80, assoc. prof., 1980-85, chmn. statistics dept., 1990-93; vis. prof. Stanford U., Palo Alto, Calif., 1985-86. Vis. prof. Dept. Def., Ft. Meade, Md., 1993-94, 99-2000. Author: Multivariate Density Estimation, 1992; mem. editl. bd. John Wiley & Sons Probability and Stats. Series, 1994—; past editor jour. Computational Stats. and Jour. Statis. Scis.; editor Jour. Computational and Graphical Stats., 2000—; contbr. articles to profl. publs. Mem. applied and Theoretical stats. com. Nat. Rsch. Coun., 2001-03. Grantee NASA, 1982-84, Office Naval Rsch., 1985-93, NSF, 1993—. Fellow Internat. Stats. Inst., Inst. Math. Stats., Am. Statis. Assn. (assoc. editor jour. 1983-94); mem. Inst. Math. Statis. (cons.). Avocations: woodworking, hiking, family. Home: 4143 Marlowe St Houston TX 77005-1953 Office: Rice U Dept Stats 6100 Main St # Ms-138 Houston TX 77005-1827 E-mail: scottdw@rice.edu.

SCOTT, DAVID WINFIELD, artist, museum consultant; b. Fall River, Mass., July 10, 1916; s. Benjamin David and Edith May (Romig) S.; m. Tirsa Lilia Saavedra, July 10, 1947 (dec. Jan. 1986); children: Tirsa Margaret, Edith Elizabeth; m. Doris Jean Fitch White, Aug. 19, 1988. AB, Harvard Coll., 1938; MA, Claremont Grad. Sch., 1940, MFA, 1951; PhD, U. Calif., Berkeley, 1960; DFA, Corcoran Sch. Art, 1991. Instr. art Riverside (Calif.) Jr. Coll., 1940-41; from lectr. to prof. Scripps Coll., Claremont, Calif., 1947-63; dir. Nat. Collection Fine Art, Washington, 1964-69; planning officer Nat. Gallery Art, 1969-84; acting dir. Corcoran Gallery Art, 1990; artist, cons. pvt. practice, Whitehaven, Md., 1991—. Cons. in field. Capt. USAF, 1945. Mem. Cosmos Club. Home: 2764 Whitehaven Rd Quantico MD 21856-2507

SCOTT, DEBBIE ANN, recreational facility executive; b. Washington, Mar. 22, 1956; d. Dewey L. and Udra L. Barnwell; m. Jeffery W. Scott, Nov. 1, 1980; children: Amy Beth, Brennan Marshall. BA in Psychology, U. New Orleans, 1984; M in Gerontology, Baylor U., 1987; M in Religious Edn., Southwestern Bapt. Sem., 1989. Youth and children dir. Corace Temple Bapt., Waco, Tex., 1984-87; activity coord. Asbury Meth. Village, Gaithersburg, Md., 1988-90; activity dir. Wayside Farm Nursing, Akron, Ohio, 1990; social worker Laural Lake Retirement, Hudson, 1990-95; children and sr. adult dir. Colonial Ave Bapt., Roanoke, Va., 1999—. Avocations: crafts, sewing. Office: Colonial Ave Bapt 6143 Colonial Ave Roanoke VA 24018

SCOTT, DEBORAH EMONT, curator; b. Passaic, N.J. d. Harold and Rhoda (Baumgarten) Emont; m. George Andrew Scott, June 4, 1983; children: Meredith Suzanne, Diana Faith. BA, Rutgers U., Livingston Coll., 1973; MA, Oberlin Coll., 1979. Asst. curator Allen Meml. Art Mus., Oberlin, Ohio, 1977-79; curator collections Memphis Brooks Mus. Art, 1979-83; curator The Nelson-Atkins Mus. Art, Kansas City, 1983—, chief curator, 1998—. Project dir. Kansas City Sculpture Pk., 1986-01. Author: (catalogue) Alan Shields, 1983, (essay) Jonathan Borofsky, 1988, (essay) Judith Shea, 1989, (interview) John Ahearn, 1990, (essay) Gerhard Richter, 1990, (essay) Kathy Muehlemann, 1991, (essay) Nate Fors, 1991, (essay) Julian Schnabel, 1991, (essay) Louise Bourgeois, 1994, (essay) Joel Shapiro, 1995, (essay) Lewis deSoto, 1996, (catalogue) Ursula von Rydingsvard, 1997; contbr.: Celebrating Moore: Works from the Collection of the Henry Moore Foundation, Selected by David Mitchinson, 1998, Modern Sculpture at The Nelson-Atkins Museum of Art: An Anniversary Celebration, 1999; (CD ROM) Masterworks for Learning: A College Collection Catalogue, Allen Memorial Art Museum, Oberlin College, 1998. Office: Nelson-Atkins Mus Art 4525 Oak St Kansas City MO 64111-1818

SCOTT, DONALD MICHAEL, educator; b. L.A., Sept. 26, 1943; s. Bernard Hendry and Barbara (Lannin) S.; m. Patricia Ilene Pancoast, Oct. 24, 1964 (div. June 1971); children: William Bernard, Kenneth George. BA, San Francisco State U., 1965, MA, 1986. Cert. tchr. Calif. Tchr. Mercy High Sch., San Francisco, 1968-71; park ranger Calif. State Park System, Half Moon Bay, 1968-77; tchr. adult div. Jefferson Union High Sch. Dist., Daly City, Calif., 1973-87; dir. NASA-NPS Project Wider Focus, 1983-90; dir. Geo.S. Spl. Projects Wider Focus, San Francisco, 1990—, also bd. dirs. Daly City; nat. park ranger/naturalist Grant-Kohrs Ranch Nat. Hist. Site, Deer Lodge, Mont., 1987-88; nat. park ranger pub. affairs fire team Yellowstone Nat. Park, 1988; nat. park ranger Golden Gate Recreation Area, 1988-92. Rsch. subject NASA, Mountain View, Calif., 1986-90; guest artist Yosemite (Calif.) Nat. Park, 1986; nat. park ranger Golden Gate Nat. Recreation Area, Nat. Park Svc., San Francisco, 1986, nat. park svc. history cons. to Bay Dist., 1988-94; adj. asst. prof. Skyline Coll., 1989-94, Coll. San Mateo, 1992-94; aerospace edn. specialist NASA/OSU/AESP, 1994; state rep. AESP, 1999-; cons. Friends of Ea. State Penitentiary Project, Phila., 1993. Contbr. articles, photographs to profl. jours., mags., chpts. to books. Pres. Youth for Kennedy, Lafayette, Calif., 1960; panelist Community Bds. of San Francisco, 1978-87; city chair Yes on A com., So. San Francisco, San Mateo County, Calif., 1986; active CONTACT Orgn., 1991—, bd. dirs. 1995—; mem. edn. working group Case for Mars VI, Boulder, 1996. Mem. Nat. Assn. for Interpretation (founding mem.), Yosemite Assn. (life), Wider Focus, Friends of George R. Stewart, Nat. Sci. Tchrs. Assn., Nat. Coun. of Tchrs. of Math., Internat. Tech. Edn. Assn., Planetary Soc. (charter mem.), Mars Soc. (founding), Orange County Space Soc., Mars Soc. Ednl. Task Force. Avocations: photography, hiking, camping, travel. Home and Office: NASA Ames Rsch Ctr MS 253 2 Moffett Field CA 94035-1000

SCOTT, DOROTHY, writer; b. Rochester, Pa., July 21, 1951; d. Mildred Boettner and James Frantz; m. Thomas C.H. Scott, June 10, 1978; 1 child Margaret 1 child T.A. Malcolm. BA, U. Pitts., 1973. Asst. editor Learning Rsch. & Develop. Ctr., U. Pitts., 1973—79; manuscript editor Eye Rsch. Inst. Retina Found., Boston, 1979—81; freelance med. copy editor Pitts., 1981—86; project mgr., editor Physicians World, Secaucus, NJ, 1987—88; mng. editor Health Learning Sys., Lyndhurst, 1988—89; med. editor Discovery Internat., Deerfield, Ill., 1990—91, dir. edit. svcs., 1991—95, sr. mng. med. editor, 1995—2001; sr. med. writer CPE Comm., Chgo., 2001—. Mem.: Am. Med. Writers Assn. Episcopalian. Avocations: bead work, singing.

SCOTT, DOUGLAS WILLIAMS, architect; b. Troy, N.Y., Apr. 29, 1960; s. Albert Pearson and Mabel (Williams) S. BArch, Syracuse U., 1983. Registered architect, N.Y. Assoc. Paris Architect, Latham, N.Y., 1983-86; from asst. to sr. architect State of N.Y., Albany, 1986—. Designer Tucker House, 1986, Capital Network Control Ctr., 1987, Gossett Youth Ctr., 1993, N.Y.S. Police Stas., 1999. Mem. AIA, Porsche Club (Albany). Home: 1827 Union St Schenectady NY 12309-6434

SCOTT, EDWARD WILLIAM, JR. computer software company executive; b. Panama City, Panama, May 25, 1938; s. Edward William and Janice Gertrude (Grimison) S.; m. Cheryl S. Gilliland, apr. 23, 1988; children: Edward William, Heather Yolanda Deirdre, Reece Donald. BA, Mich. State U., 1959, MA, 1963; BA, Oxford (Eng.) U., 1962. Personnel specialist Panama Canal Co., 1962-64, staff asst. to dir. personnel, 1964-66; personnel officer IRS, Detroit, 1966-68; staff personnel mgmt. specialist U.S. Dept. Justice, Washington, 1968-69, chief personnel systems and evaluation sect., 1970-72; dir. U.S. Dept. Justice (Office Mgmt. Programs), 1972-74; asso. dep. commr. planning and evaluation U.S. Dept. Justice (U.S. Immigration and Naturalization Service), 1974-75, dep. asst. atty. gen. adminstrn., 1972-75; asst. sec. for adminstrn. (Transp. Dept.), 1977-80; pres. Office Power, Inc., Washington, 1980-81; dir. mktg. Computer Consoles, Inc., 1981-84; v.p. mktg. Dest Systems, 1984-85; dir. govt. mktg. Sun Microsystems, Mountain View, Calif., 1985-88; exec. v.p. Pyramid Tech., 1988-95; founder, pres. BEA Sys., Inc., San Jose, Calif., 1995—. Founder Ctr. for Global Devel., Washington; founder, pres. escottVentures, Inc.; pres. U.S. Dept. Justice Fed. Credit Union, 1970-73. Recipient Presdl. Mgmt. Improvement certificate, 1971; Spl. Commendation award Dept. Justice, 1973; also Spl. Achievement award, 1976; William A. Jump Meml. award, 1974; presdl. sr. exec. service rank of Disting. Exec., 1980; Mich. State U. scholar, 1957-60. Mem.: Phi Kappa Phi, Phi Eta Sigma. Democrat. Office: BEA Sys Inc 2315 N 1st St San Jose CA 95131-1010 E-mail: ed@escottventures.com.

SCOTT, FRED DACON, surgeon; b. Folsom, Calif., Mar. 12, 1962; s. Winfield Morrill and LaRee (Taggart) S.; m. Deborah Lynn Weese, May 16, 1986; children: Emily Diane, Dacon Spencer, Andrew Tucker, Peter Allen. BS in Biology, Phillips U., Enid, Okla., 1986; DO, Okla. State U., Tulsa, 1990. Diplomate Nat. Bd. Osteo. Med. Examiners, Am. Osteo. Bd. Surgery; bd. cert. in gen. surgery. Intern Mt. Clemens (Mich.) Gen. Hosp., 1990-91, resident in gen. surgery, 1991-95, chief resident in gen. surgery, 1994; mem. gen. surgery staff Passavant Area Hosp., Jacksonville, Ill., 1995-99, chmn. continuing med. edn. com., 1996-2000; mem. gen. surgery Staff Crawford Meml. Hosp., 2000, chief surgery svc., 2000—02. Stake missionary LDS Ch., 1992-96, Sunday Sch. tchr., 1991-96, deacon, tchrs. quorums instr., 1986-89, elders quorum/1st counselor, sec., 1989-90, 92-95, 2d counselor to bishop Jacksonville ward, 1997-98, 98-99, Springfield (Ill.) stake Jacksonville Ward bishop, 1998-2000; mem. U.S. rifle team U.S. Olympic Com., 1980-81; asst. scoutmaster Walbash Valley coun. Boy Scouts Am., 2000-2002. Named to Outstanding Young Men of Am., 1988; named All-Am. Coll. Rifle, NRA, 1981. Mem. AMA, Am. Coll. Osteo. Surgeons, Am. Osteo. Assn., Ill. Med. Assn., Ill. Assn. Osteo. Physicians and Surgeons, Morgan Scott Counties Med. Soc. (pres.-elect 1997, pres. 1998), Crawford County Med. Soc., Atlas Frat. Republican. Avocations: gardening, bonsai, photography, camping. Home: 606 N Allen St Robinson IL 62454-1102 Office: 1000 North Allen St Robinson IL 62454

SCOTT, FREDERICK ISADORE, JR. editor, business executive; b. Balt., Oct. 27, 1927; s. Frederick Isadore and Rebecca Esther (Waller) S.; m. Viola Fowlkes, Feb. 4, 1949. B.E. in Chem. Engring, Johns Hopkins, 1950; MS in Mgmt. Engring, Newark Coll. Engring., 1956. Chem. process engr. in research and devel. RCA, Harrison, N.J., 1951-59; with Kearfott div. Gen. Precision Aerospace, Little Falls, 1960-62; asst. sales mgr. Isotopes, Inc., Westwood, 1964-66; mgr. capacitor sect. Wellington Electronics, Inc., Englewood, 1967-68; owner F.I. Scott & Assos. (med. equipment), Montclair, 1968-80; tech. product mktg. and editorial svcs. F.I. scott & Assocs., Check, Va., 1980-86; editor instrumentation publ. Am. Lab. and Internat. Lab., Fairfield, Conn., 1968-80, cons. editor, 1980—; pres. Group Tech., Ltd., 1979—; editor Am. Clin. Lab., 1990—. Served with AUS, 1946-47. Mem. Am. Chem. Soc. (sr.), AAAS, N.Y. Acad. Sci., IEEE (editor newsletter No. N.J. sect. 1957-58, chmn. publs. com. 1958-59), N.Y. Micros. Soc. Home and Office: 1 E Chase St Apt 410 Baltimore MD 21202-2597 E-mail: fiscott@ziplink.net. *Perhaps the most significant aspect of my life is a long-felt realization that each person is ultimately responsible for his or her condition in life. Application of this principle continually requires that the individual assess a failure in such a way as to determine how his or her actions might have avoided it or, if unavoidable, how its recurrence can be obviated. Accepting responsibility in this manner can, I believe, lead the way toward a society based on a federation of autonomous individuals delegating authority to units of government when appropriate but clearly retaining the capability to recall that delegated authority should it be abused.*

SCOTT, G. JUDSON, JR. lawyer; b. Phila., Nov. 16, 1945; s. Gerald Judson and Jean Louise (Evans) S.; m. Ildiko Kalman, Mar. 21, 1971; children: Nathan Emory, Lauren Jean. AA, Foothill Jr. Coll., Los Altos, Calif., 1965; BA, U. Calif., Santa Barbara, 1968; JD cum laude, U. Santa Clara, 1975. Bar: Calif. 1975, U.S. Dist. Ct. (no. dist.) Calif. 1975, U.S. Ct. Appeals (9th cir.) 1975, U.S. Supreme Ct. 1981. Assoc. Feldman, Waldman & Kline, San Francisco, 1975-76, Law Offices John Wynne Herron, San Francisco, 1976-80; of counsel firm Haines & Walker, Livermore, 1980; ptnr. Haines Walker & Scott, 1980-84; officer, dir., shareholder firm Smith, Etnire, Polson and Scott, Pleasanton, Calif., 1984-88; pvt. practice, 1988—. Judge pro tem Livermore-Pleasanton Mcpl. Ct., 1981-83; settlement commr. Alameda County Superior Ct., 1994—, judge pro tem, 2001—; lectr. Calif. Continuing Edn. of Bar. Contbg. author: Attorney's Guide to Restitution, 1976; editor: The Bottom Line, 1989-91. Pres. Walnut Creek Open Space Found., Calif., 1981-83. Rear adm. USNR, 1968-2001. Mem. ATLA (sustaining), Consumer Attys. Calif. (reviewer of pending Calif. legis.), Am. Coll. Barristers (sr. counsel), Ea. Alameda County Bar Assn. (v.p. 1981-82), Calif. State Bar (mem. standing com. on lawyer referral svcs. 1985-88, mem. exec. com. law practice mgmt. sec. 1988-93, chair 1992-93), Alameda County Bar Assn. (chmn. law office econs. com. 1986-87, mem. jud. nomination evaluation com. 1996-97, bd. dirs. 1997-98, v.p. 1999, pres.-elect 2000, pres. 2001, chair task force 1997), Alameda-Contra Costa County Trial Lawyers Assn., Livermore C. of C. (past chmn. growth study 1983), Pleasanton C. of C., Million Dollar Advs. Forum. Republican. Episcopalian. Office: 6140 Stoneridge Mall Rd Ste 125 Pleasanton CA 94588-3233

SCOTT, GARY LEROY, photographic manufacturing executive, photographer; b. Portland, Oreg., May 14, 1954; s. Glenn Howard and Esther Ruth (Robinson) S. Grad., USN Sch. Photography, Pensacola, Fla., 1974; BS, U. Oreg., 1979, MS, 1982. Photographer and filmmaker Scott Cinema and Visual, Inc., various locations, 1969—; computer traffic operator Burlington No. R.R., Portland, 1979-81; instr. U. Oreg., Eugene, 1981-82; S.E. dist. sales mgr. E. Leitz, Inc., 1984-87; mgr. profl. products Fla. divsn. Fuji Photo Film USA, Inc., Lake Mary, Fla., 1987-2000, mgr. profl. products Pacific N.W. divsn. Vancouver, Wash., 2000—. Media cons., advt. copywriter, TV and film script writer, 1984—; lectr. in field. Served with USN, 1972-76. U. Oreg. Sch. Journalism research grantee, 1981. Mem. Am. Soc. Media Photographers, Profl. Photographers of Am. Republican. Avocations: history, photography exhibitions, outdoor activities. Home and Office: 2219 NW 112th Cir Vancouver WA 98685

SCOTT, GARY THOMAS, historian; b. Wichita Falls, Tex., Mar. 9, 1944; s. Thomas Clifford, Jr. and Lillian (Hanks) Fecher. BA, Southwestern U., Georgetown, Tex., 1966; MA, U. N.C., Chapel Hill, 1969. History instr. Tusculum Coll., Greeneville, Tenn., 1969-70, Herringswell Manor Sch., Bury St. Edmunds, UK, 1970-71; asst. to clk. of the works Washington Nat. Cathedral, 1971-75; archtl. historian Nat. Park Svc., Washington, 1976-82, regional historian, 1982-95, historian Nat. Capital area, 1995—; chief historian Nat. Capital Region, 1996—. Lectr., tour leader Smithsonian Inst., Washington, 1981—; prin. N.Am. rep. in course on archtl. conservation hist. bldgs. Property Svcs. Agy. and English Heritage of Brit. Govt., West Dean Coll., Chichester, Sussex, Eng., 1982-90. Author: The Kappa Alpha Order-1865-1897, 1994, Aquia and Seneca Stone, White House History, 1998. Rep. Nat. Park Svc., D.C. Bicentennial, Washington, 1991—; mem. Committee of One Hundred, Washington, 1993—, U.S. Capitol Cornerstone Bicentennial, Washington, 1993, Washington Monument Cornerstone Centennial, 1998; active Hist. Soc. Washington, 1977—, So. Hist. Assn., 1980—; mem. Friends Attingham Summer Sch., N.Y.C., 1981—, Preservation Roundtable, Washington, 1989—; pres. Victorian Soc., Washington, 2002—. Recipient Disting. Pub. Svc. award, Kappa Alpha Order, 1988. Mem. Scottish Rite (33d degree), Masons (Master 1996), Cosmos Club Washington, Kappa Alpha Order (chief alumnus 1991-95). Episcopalian. Avocations: book and antique collector. Office: Nat Park Svc National Capital Region 1100 Ohio Dr SW Washington DC 20242-0001

SCOTT, GENEVA LEE SMITH, nursing educator; b. Codell, Kans., Nov. 2, 1943; d. Lester Lee and Lennicejean Leota (Lynch) Smith; m. Dennis G. Scott, Feb. 20, 1965; children: J.D., Shane, Deminy. BS, Fort Hays Kans. State Coll., 1965; BS in Nursing, Fort Hays State U., 1979; MS in Nursing, West Tex. State U., 1986. Charge nurse Hadley Regional Med. Ctr., Hays, Kans.; sch. nurse Borger (Tex.) Ind. Sch. Dist.; clin. and classroom instr. North Cen. Kans. Area Vocat. Tech. Sch., Hays; nursing instr. St. Philip's Coll., San Antonio; sch. nurse Bryan Ind. Sch. Dist., 1993-97; instr. nursing edn. Blinn Coll., Bryan, Tex., 1997-98, Weatherford (Tex.) Coll., 1998, vocat. nursing instr., 1998-2000, instr. associates degree in nursing program, 2000—. Scholarship grant, 1983. Mem. Am. Nurses Assn., Phi Delta Kappa, Beta Sigma Phi (membership chairperson, Girl of Yr. 1978). Home: 405 W Spring St Weatherford TX 76086 E-mail: scott@wc.edu.

SCOTT, GEORGE COLE, III, investment advisor; b. N.Y.C., July 9, 1937; s. George Cole Scott II and Anne Blair Clark Martindell; m. Leslie Jane Daniels, Apr. 12, 1969; children: Jane Leslie, Anne Blair, John Cole. BA, U. Wash., 1969. Advt. reporter Am. Weekly, London, 1966-68; stockbroker Anderson & Strudwick, Richmond, Va., 1969-73, Scott & Stringfellow, Richmond, 1973-78, Piper, Jaffray & Hopwood, Seattle, 1978-82, Wheat, First Securities, Inc., Richmond, 1982-87, Anderson & Strudwick, Richmond, 1988—. Pres. Closed-End Fund Advisors, Richmond, Va., 1996— ; dir.

Bergstrom Capital Corp., Seattle, 1976—. Co-author: Investing in Closed-End Funds: Finding Value and Building Wealth, 1991; pub., editor: The Scott Letter: Closed-End Fund Report, 1988--; contbr. to Closed-End Country Fund Report, Barron's and other publs.; contbr. articles to profl. jours. Founder Seattle-Christchurch, New Zealand Sister City Assn. With USCG, 1960-64. Recipient Disting. Citizen award State of Wash., 1981. Mem. Richmond Soc. Fin. Analysts (assoc.), Soc. Cincinnati, Country Club Va., Soc. Cin., Wash. Athletic Club (Seattle). Episcopalian. Avocations: freelance writing, travel. Home: 8659 Rio Grande Rd Richmond VA 23229-7822 Office: 707 E Main St Richmond VA 23219-2814 E-mail: closend@richmond.infi.net.

SCOTT, GEORGE GALLMANN, accountant; b. Hattiesburg, Miss., July 8, 1928; s. John Havers and Rebecca Evelyn (Gallmann) S.; m. Patsy T. Womack, June 27, 1953; 1 child, George Gallmann. BS, Millsaps Coll., 1949. Accredited bus. acct., tax advisor, 1992; accredited in acctg. and taxation Nat. Accreditation Coun. for Accountancy. Clk. Spanish Trail Transport, Mobile, Ala., 1949—50, asst. auditor, 1953—55; bookkeeper Met. Engraving & Electrotype Co., Richmond, Va., 1952—53; chief clk. Mobile (Ala.) office Ctrl. Truck Lines of Tampa, Fla., 1955—56; gen. auditor M.R.&R. Trucking Co., Crestview, 1956—66, sec.-treas., 1967—77; pub. acct. enrolled to represent taxpayers before IRS, 1979—. Mem. data processing adv. com. Okaloosa-Walton C.C., Niceville, Fla., 1965- 66, 72-73; mem. Okaloosa County Gen. Advisory Com. for Devel. Vocat. Edn., 1973, 79. Bd. dirs. Okaloosa Cmty. Concert Assn., 1982-87; chmn. Crestview Downtown Devel. Bd., 1988-89; bass-baritone soloist, 1953—, choir dir. Meth. Ch., 1966-83, chmn. ofcl. bd., 1971-73, chmn. fin. com., 1974-75, 79-81, audit com., 1977-86, mem. com. on lay personnel, 1979-87, chmn., 1983-87, 89-90, mem. com. on pastor-parish rels., 1980-86, coun. on ministries, 1985, trustee, 1985-87, treas., 1990-95; mem. Walton Co. C. of C. With U.S. Army, 1950-52. Mem. Nat. Assn. Accts., Nat. Assn. Enrolled Agts., Am. Trucking Assn. (nat. acctg. and fin. coun. 1956-77), Southeastern Acctg. and Fin. Coun. (bd. dirs. 1974-77), Fla. Assn. Enrolled Agts., Crestview Downtown Mchts. Assn. (bd. dirs. 1980-84, treas. 1980-84), Greater Crestview C. of C. (chmn. bus. ethics com. 1973-74, bd. dirs. 1981-83, treas. 1982-83), Fla. Accts. Assn. (bd. govs. 1979-80, pres. N.W. Fla. chpt. 1979-80), DeFuniak Springs Bus. and Profl. Assn., Kiwanis (past treas., past sec., past pres.), Pi Kappa Alpha. Home: 244 Seminole Trail Crestview FL 32536-2326

SCOTT, GERALD WESLEY, retired American diplomat; b. Oklahoma City, Aug. 7, 1940; s. Charles Wesley and Dorothy Bernadine (Heidlage) S.; m. Frances Helen Gardner-Brown, Aug. 9, 1975; children: Charles Alan, Michael Tacon. BS in Fgn. Svc., Georgetown U., 1962; MA, Johns Hopkins U., 1969, Naval War Coll., 2000. Commd. fgn. svc. officer, 1969; vice consul Am. Consulate Gen., Danang, Viet Nam, 1973-75; polit. officer Am. Embassy, Rome, 1980-83; advisor polit. and security affairs U.S. Mission to UN, N.Y.C., 1983-85; dep. chief of mission Am. Embassy, Mbabane, Swaziland, 1985-88, polit. counselor Kinshasa, Zaire, 1988-92, Nairobi, Kenya, 1992-93, dep. chief of mission Kinshasa, 1993-95; ambassador to The Gambia, Banjul, 1996-98; internat. affairs advisor Naval War Coll., Newport, R.I., 1998-2000; ret., 2000. Cons. internat. and security affairs, 2000—, sr. advisor U.S. delegation to U.N. Gen. Assembly, 2001-, mem. U.S. delegation to 58th session of U.N. Commn. on Human Rights, 2002. Lt. USNR, 1962-67. Decorated Air medal, Navy Commendation medal. Mem. Am. Fgn. Svc. Assn. (William R. Rivkin award 1992), SAR, Sons of the Revolution, Lotos Club (N.Y.C.), Army and Navy Club (Washington). Roman Catholic. Office: PO Box 430 Duncan OK 73534 E-mail: deskofgwscott@aol.com.

SCOTT, GREGORY ALAN, pharmacist, writer; b. Newport, Vt., June 10, 1954; s. S. Gerald Scott Sr. and Elizabeth A. Scott; m. Linda M. Scott, Apr. 21, 1996; children: Matthew Taccone, Ryan. BA in Chemistry, U. N.H., 1976, MS in Analytical Chemistry, 1979; PharmD, U. Pacific, 1981. Registered pharmacist. Clin./staff pharmacist Dartmouth-Hitchcock Med. Ctr., Hanover, NH, 1982—83; instr. in clin. pharmacology, dept. of medicine Dartmouth Med. Sch., 1982—93; clin. pharmacist for drug info. Dartmouth-Hitchcock Med. Ctr., 1982—89, asst. dir. clin. and informational pharmacy svcs., 1989—93; v.p. sci. affairs Clin. Comm. Inc., Greenwich, Conn., 1993—98; dir. continuing edn. Sci. Exch. Inc., 1993—2000; pres. and owner WriteHealth, LLC, Stamford, 2000—. Cons. to the therapeutic agts. and pharmacy rev. com. Veterans Adminstrn. Med. and Regional Office Ctr., White River Junction, Vt., 1986—90; reviewer pharmacotherapy Am. Coll. Clin. Pharmacy, Kansas City, Mo., 1989—98; surveyor Accreditation Coun. for Continuing Med. Edn., Chgo., 2000—. Contbg. author: book Clinical Pharmacology Basic Principles in Therapeutics, 3rd edit., 1992; contbr. articles to profl. jours. Mem. bd. of ch. devel. First Congl. Ch. Stamford, 2002; bd. of trustees First Congl. Ch. of Stamford, 1996—2001. Mem.: Am. Coll. Clin. Pharmacy (reviewer Pharmaco Therapy 1989—98), Am. Soc. Health-Sys. Pharmacists (reviewer Am. Jour. Hosp. Pharmacy 1989—98), Am. Soc. Clin. Pharmacology and Therapeutics, Am. Med. Writers Assn., Alliance for Continuing Med. Edn., Stamford C. of C. Avocations: carpentry, travel. Office: WriteHealth LLC 110 van Rensselaer Ave Stamford CT 06902 Office Fax: 203-325-9945. E-mail: gscott96@optonline.net.

SCOTT, HARLEY EARLE, publisher, historian; b. Buffalo, Oct. 17, 1934; s. Earle Marcus and Grayce Etta (Scheffler) S. BA, U. Buffalo, 1960; AM, Clark U., 1963; EdD, Ind. U., 1976. Tchr. geography Col. E. Brooke Lee Jr. High Sch., Kemp Hill, Md., 1965-66; instr. in geography Chgo. State U., 1966-71; asst. prof. geography SUNY, New Paltz, 1976-77; pres. Cayuga Creek Hist. Press, Lancaster, N.Y., 1981—; town historian Lancaster, 1982—. Author: Tales of the Muskoka Steamboats, 1969, More Tales of the Muskoka Steamboats, 1980, Tales of Old Lancaster, 1981, Steamboats Today, 1986, Steam Tugs and Supply Boats of Muskoka, 1987, Tales of West Main Street, 1998. Writer Lancaster Enterprize, 1982—; active Muskoka Sun, Ontario, 1969—. Clark U. scholar, 1961, 62. Mem. AAUP, Assn. Am. Geographers. Lutheran. Avocations: steamboat designing, crystal sets, steamboating. Home: 22 Brookfield Pl Lancaster NY 14086-2112 also: 381 NE 2d St Boca Raton FL 33432

SCOTT, HAROLD LEE, JR. retail executive; b. Joplin, Mo., Mar. 14, 1949; s. Harold Lee and Avis Viola (Parsons) S.; m. Linda Gale Aldridge, June 7, 1969; children: Eric Sean, Wyatt Parson. BBA, Pitts. State U., Kans., 1971. Br. mgr. Yellow Freight System, Springdale, Ark., 1972-78; mgr. Queen City Warehouse, Springfield, Mo., 1978-79; dir. transp. Wal-Mart Stores, Inc., Bentonville, Ark., 1979-83, v.p. distbn., 1983-2000, pres., CEO, 2000—. Bd. dirs. Pvt. Truck Council, Washington, 1985-86. Republican. Methodist. Avocations: reading, quail hunting. Office: Wal-Mart Stores Inc 702 SW 8th St Bentonville AR 72716-6299*

SCOTT, HOWARD WINFIELD, JR. temporary help services company executive; b. Greenwich, Conn., Feb. 24, 1935; s. Howard Winfield and Janet (Lewis) S.; m. Joan Ann MacDonald, Aug. 12, 1961; children: Howard Winfield III, Thomas MacDonald, Ann Elizabeth. BS, Northwestern U., 1957. With R.H. Donnelly Corp., Chgo., 1958-59; sales rep. Masonite Corp., Chgo. and Madison, Wis., 1959-61, Manpower Inc., Chgo., 1961-63, br. mgr. Kansas City, Mo., 1963-65, regional mgr. Salespower divsn. Phila., 1965-66; asst. advt. mgr. soups Campbell Soup Co., Camden, N.J., 1966-68; pres. PARTIME, Inc., Paoli, Pa., 1968-74; dir. mktg. Kelly Svcs., Inc., Southfield, Mich., 1974-78; pres. CDI Temporary Svcs., Inc., 1978-91, Dunhill Pers. Sys., Inc., Woodbury, N.Y., 1991-94; v.p. SOS Temporary Svcs., Salt Lake City, 1994; COO SOS Staffing Svcs., 1995-97, CEO, 1997; COO Empire Staffing Svcs., LLC, N.Y.C., Tempositions Group of Cos., N.Y.C., 2000. With AUS, 1957-58. Mem. Nat. Assn. Temporary Svcs. (sec. 1970-71, pres. 1971-73, bd. dirs. 1982-91), Kappa Sigma. Republican. Home: 400 E 84th St Apt 14C New York NY 10028-5609 also: 1204 Annapolis Sea Colony E Bethany Beach DE 19930 also: Tempositions Group of Cos 420 Lexington Ave New York NY 10170-0002 E-mail: hscott@tempositions.com.

SCOTT, HUGH PATRICK, physician, naval officer; b. Phila., Feb. 12, 1938; s. Hugh Patrick and Martha (Papiana) S.; m. Diane Marie Lopatzie, July 1, 1961; children: Karen, Brendan, Catherine. BA, LaSalle Coll., 1960; DO, Phila. Coll. Osteo. Medicine, 1964, LLD (hon.), 1991. Diplomate Am. Osteo. Bd. Ophthalmology and Otolaryngology. Intern Detroit Osteo. Hosp., Highland Park, Mich., 1964-65, resident otorhinolatyngology, 1965-68; lt. med. corps USNR, 1967, advanced through grades to rear adm., 1991; naval med. officer U.S. Naval Dispensary N.O.B., Norfolk, Va., 1968-70, Submarine Squadron 10, Groton, Conn.; Submarine Group 2; naval med. officer Naval Submarine Med. Ctr., New London, Conn., 1975-83; dir. undersea medicine and radiation health Naval Med. Command, Washington, 1983-86; comdg. officer Naval Hosp., Groton, 1986-88, Camp Lejeune, N.C., 1988-90; fleet surgeon Comdr. in Chief, U.S. Pacific Fleet, Pearl Harbor, Hawaii, 1990-91; asst. chief for operational medicine and fleet support Bur. Medicine and Surgery, Washington, 1991-92; dir. med. resources, plans and policy Office Chief of Naval Ops., 1992-94. Asst. clin. prof. medicine Mich. State U., Lansing, 1970—75; pvt. practice, Madison Heights, Mich., 1970—75; cons. Am. Coll. Undersea and Hyperbaric Medicine, Washington, 1985—86, 1994—96; sr. program mgr. Data Sys. & Svcs. divsn. Northrop Grumman Co., 1998—99; sr. med. officer Northrop Grumman Info. Tech.; sr. v.p. Geo-Ctrs. Inc., 2000—; mem. sr. exec. med. adv. com. for mil. medicine Johns Hopkins U. Applied Physics Lab.; mem. faculty U. So. Calf. Health Scis. Campus for Advanced Biotelecomms. and Bio Informatics; sr. med. adv. Northrop Grumman Info. Tech., 2001—. Decorated Legion of Merit, Gold Star (3). Fellow Osteo. Coll. Ophthalmology and Otolaryngology, Am. Acad. Otolaryngology and Head and Neck Surgery; mem. Am. Osteo. Coll. Otolaryngology--Head and Neck Surgery (past pres.), Assn. Mil. Osteopathic Physicians and Surgeons (2nd v.p.). Republican. Roman Catholic. Home: 3707 Merlin Way Annandale VA 22003-1326 Office: Northrop Grumman Info Tech 8110 Gatehouse Rd Falls Church VA 22042 E-mail: hscott@northropgrumman.com.

SCOTT, ISADORE MEYER, former energy company executive; b. Wilcoe, W.Va., Nov. 21, 1912; s. David and Libby (Roston) S.; m. Joan Rosenwald, Feb. 14, 1943; children: Betsy Scott Kleeblatt, Peggy, Jonathan D. AB, W.Va. U., 1934, MA, 1938; JD, Washington and Lee U., 1937; LLD, West Va. U., 1983. Bar: Va. 1937. Practiced law, Richmond, Va., 1937-38; v.p. Lee I. Robinson Hosiery Mills., Phila., 1938-42; with Winner Mfg. Co., Inc., Trenton, 1947-61, v.p., 1947-51, pres., 1951-61; chmn. bd. Tri-Instl. Facilities, Inc., Phila., 1962-78, TOSCO Corp., L.A., 1976—83, vice-chmn. bd., 1983—87, chmn. bd. Bd. dirs., chmn. Univ. City Assocs., Inc.; founder, mem. U.S. Adv. Bd. Brit.-Am. Project. Bd. dirs. S.E. Pa. chpt. ARC, Internat. Rescue Com., Univ. City Sci. Ctr., Phila.; mem. adv. com. Urban Affair Partnership; bd. dirs. emeritus, former mem. exec. com., vice-chmn. Phila. Mus. Art; former chmn. World Affairs Council Phila.; mem. Phila. Com. Fgn. Rels.; trustee emeritus Washington and Lee U.; emeritus trustee George C. Marshall Found.; former chmn. Christ Ch. Preservation Fund, Phila., Jefferson House Restoration, Phila. With inf. U.S. Army, 1942-46, NATOUSA, ETO. Decorated Legion of Merit, Silver Star, Purple Heart, Bronze Star (U.S.); Crown of Italy; medal of merit Czechoslovakia; Mentioned-in-dispatches, Eng.; fellow Mus. Am. Jewish History Mem. Va. State Bar, Phila. Club, Gulph Mills Golf, Anglers of Phila., Masons, Phi Beta Kappa, Omicron Delta Kappa, Order of Coif. (hon.). Clubs: Phila.; Gulph Mills Golf, Anglers of Phila. Lodges: Masons. Republican. Jewish.

SCOTT, IVAN CARL, historian, educator; b. Iowa City, Sept. 9, 1928; s. Wilbur Lloyd and Gladys Georgina Scott; m. Melvia Mary Atta, 1958 (div. June 1984); children: John, Thomas, David; m. Barbara Jean Kettlewell. BA, William and Mary Coll., 1959; MA, U. Pa., 1961, PhD, 1964. Asst. prof. Memphis State U., 1964-65, W.Va. State U., Morgantown, 1965-67; prof. U. Toledo, 1967-85, prof. emeritus, 1985—. Author: The Roman Question, 1969, The Rise of the Italian State, 1980, Upton Sinclair, 1997, Bromfield, The Forgotten Author, 1998, Jew vs. Arab, 2001. With U.S. Army, 1946—49. Fulbright scholar, U. Paris, 1962-63. Mem. Delta Tau Kappa. Avocations: fiction writing, citrus growing, Texas plantations. Home: 9143 10th St Fort Ripley MN 56449

SCOTT, JACQUELINE DELMAR PARKER, educational association administrator, business administrator, consultant, fundraiser, educator; b. L.A., May 18, 1947; d. Thomas Aubrey and Daisy Beatrice (Singleton) Parker (div.); children: Tres Mali, Olympia Ranee, Stephen Thomas. AA in Theatre Arts, L.A. City Coll., 1970; BA in Econs., Calif. State U., Dominguez Hills, Carson, 1973; MBA, Golden Gate U., 1979; EdD, Pepperdine U., 1999. Cert. parenting instr., 2000; holder various Microsoft certs. Sales clk. Newberry's Dept. Store, L.A., 1963-65; long distance operator Pacific Telephone Co., 1965-66; PBX operator Sears, Roebuck & Co., 1966-68; retail clk. Otey's Grocery Store, Nashville, 1968-69; collector N.Am. Credit, L.A., 1970-71; office mgr. Dr. S. Edward Tucker, 1972-74; staff coord. sch. edn. dept. Calif. State U., 1973-74; from bank auditor to corp. loan asst. Security Pacific Bank, L.A., 1974-77; from dist. credit analyst to asst. v.p. Crocker Nat. Bank, 1977-80; from capital planning adminstr. to project bus. mgr. TRW, Inc., Redondo Beach, Calif., 1980-87, lab. sr. bus. adminstr., 1984-86, project bus. mgr., 1986-87, div. sr. bus. adminstr., 1987-92; ptnr., co-author, co-facilitator, cons. Diversified Event Planners, Inc., L.A., 1990-93; asst. area devel. dir. United Negro Coll. Fund, 1993-96; cons. parenting edn., 1994—. Cmty. coll. instr.; cons. in field. Co-founder career growth awareness com. TRW Employees Bootstrap, Redondo Beach, Calif., 1980, pres., 1983-84; role model Inglewood High Sch., TRW Youth Motivation Task Force, Redondo Beach, 1981-83, Crozier Jr. High Sch., 1981-83, Monroe Jr. High Sch., Redondo Beach, 1981-83, Frank D. Parent Career Day, TRW Affirmative Action Com., Redondo Beach, 1987, St. Bernard's Career Day, 1991; chairperson community involvement com., 1981, chairperson disaster com., 1989-90; chairperson gen. and local welfare com. TRW Employees Charitable Orgn., 1989-90, disaster com. chair, 1988-89, bd. dirs. 1987-89; pres. Mgmt. Effectiveness Program Alumnae, L.A., 1982-83, TRW Employees Bootstrap Program Alumnae, 1983-84; group leader Jack & Jill of Am., Inc., South L.A., 1980-81, parliamentarian, 1986-87, v.p., 1981-82, chpt. pres., 1984-86, regional dir., 1987-89, nat. program dir., 1992-96, liaison to Young Black Scholars Program, 1986—; bd. dirs. Adolescent Pregnancy Child Watch, 1993—; nat. program dir., bd. dirs. Jack & Jill Am. Found., 1992-96; L.A. mem. Nat. Black Child Devel. Inst., 1994—; vol. ARC, 1994; parenting instr. Am. Red Cross, 1994-96; founder Jack & Jill of Am. Leadership Devel. Program, 1993. Recipient commendation NAACP, 1985, United Negro Coll. Fund, 1986, United Way, 1988, Austistic Children's Telephon, 1980, Inglewood Sch. Dist., 1981, Pres. award Harbor Area Chpt. Links, Inc., 1985, Women of Achievement award City of L.A., Black Pers. Assn., 1994. Mem. Black Women's Forum (sponsor), Phi Delta Kappa, Delta Sigma Theta. Avocations: reading, dancing. E-mail: jscott4@earthlink.net.

SCOTT, JAMES ARTHUR, radiologist, educator; b. Cleve., Aug. 23, 1950; s. Robert James and Margaret Emma (Hinz) S.; m. Phyllis Virginia Gauthier, Oct. 3, 1981. SB, MIT, 1972; MD, Boston U., 1976. Diplomate Am. Bd. Radiology, Am. Bd. Nuclear Medicine. Resident Harvard U. Med. Sch.-Mass. Gen. Hosp., Boston, 1976-80, fellow, 1980-81, instr., 1982-83, asst. prof., 1984-93, assoc. prof., 1994—. Mem. editl. adv. bd. Jour. Nuclear Medicine, Am. Jour. Roentgen. Recipient New Investigator Rsch. award NIH, 1984-87. Mem. Soc. Sci. Exploration, Sigma Xi, Am. Coll. Radiology, AAAS, Phi Lambda Upsilon, Theta Xi. Lutheran. Avocations: writing, golf, history of religions. Office: Div Nuclear Medicine Mass Gen Hosp Boston MA 02114 E-mail: scott@helix.mgh.harvard.edu.

SCOTT, JAMES HUNTER, JR. investment executive; b. Balt., Jan. 28, 1945; s. James Hunter and Marialice (Short) S.; m. Katheen Ann Bilderback, Sep. 1, 1973; children: Andrew James, Elizabeth Ann. BA, Rice U., 1967; MS, Carnegie Mellon U., 1970, PhD, 1975. Instr. Carnegie Mellon U., Pitts., 1969-71; rsch. fellow Fed. Res. Bank of Cleve., 1971-72; asst. prof. U. Wis., Milw., 1972-75; from asst. prof. to prof./divisional rep. fin. Columbia U., N.Y.C., 1975-87; mng. dir. Prudential Ins. Co., Newark, 1987-97; chmn. PTC Svcs., 1991—; CEO Prudential Diversified Investment Strategies, Short Hills, N.J., 1994-97; sr. mng. dir. Prudential Investments, 1997—. Vis. asst. prof. Stanford (Calif.) U., 1974-75, assoc. prof., 1979; adj. prof. grad. sch. bus. Columbia U., 1988—; dir. Inst. for Quantitative Rsch. in Fin., N.Y.C., 1995—; with Goldman, Sachs, Kinsey & Co., 1981-82; trustee adminstrv. com. Eastern Air Lines Pilots Investment Plan, Miami, 1985-91; dir. Prudential Trust Co., 1996—. Bd. editors Fin. Analysts Jour., 1998—; contbr. over 25 articles to profl. jours. Pres. bd. trustees Alpine (N.J.) Cmty. Ch., 1986-89, v.p., 1998—; v.p. bd. trustees Tenafly (N.J.) Bd. Edn., 1998—; mem. Grad. Sch. Indsl. Adminstrn. Coun. on Fin., Carnegie Mellon U. Mem. Am. Econ. Assn., Am. Fin. Assn. Methodist. Office: Quantitative Mgmt Prudential Investments 2 Gateway Ctr Fl 4 Newark NJ 07102-5003

SCOTT, JEFFREY LYLE, protective services official; b. Toledo; s. Mylous and Florastine S. Student, U. Toledo, 1977-80. Dist. mgr. DuBois Chems., Detroit, 1988-90; pres. F&S Chems., 1991-94; police officer City of Toledo (Ohio), 1994—. Candidate Toledo City Coun., 1993, Ohio State Senate, Toledo, 1994. With Civil Air Patrol, 1995-2001. Mem. Smithsonian Inst.

SCOTT, JOHN ROLAND, business law educator; b. Wichita Falls, Tex, May 13, 1937; s. John and Margaret S.; m. Joan Carol Redding, Sept. 5, 1959; 1 child, John Howard. Llb, Baylor Sch. Law, Waco, Tex., 1962. Bar: Tex. 1962, Alaska 1970, Tex., 1965, U.S. Dist. Ct. (we. dist.), U.S. Dist. Ct. Alaska 1975. Assoc. litigation sect. Lynch & Chappell, Midland, Tex., 1962-65; regional atty. Atlantic Richfield Co., 1965-79; sr. atty. Anchorage, 1969-77, Dallas, 1977-80; v.p., assoc. gen. counsel Mitchell Energy & Devel. Corp., Houston, 1980-82; asst. gen. counsel Hunt Oil Co., Dallas, 1982-84, v.p., chief counsel, 1984-91, sr. v.p. gen. counsel, 1994-2001; adj. prof. bus. law Dallas Bapt. U., 2001—. Bar examiner in Alaska, 1974-77 Mem. State Bar Tex. (lectr.), Dallas Bar Assn., ABA, Phi Alpha Delta. Republican. Office: 3801 Hanover Ave Dallas TX 75225-7471 E-mail: jorоscl3@aol.com.

SCOTT, JOHN BROOKS, research institute executive, retired; b. Morenci, Ariz., Aug. 8, 1931; s. Brooks and Lucile (Slagle) S.; m. Jo Ann Rohrbach, June 5, 1987; children from previous marriage: Janice, Steven, Sarah. BS, U. Ariz., 1957, MA, 1959. Asst. prof. systems engring. U. Ariz., Tucson, 1959-61; mgr. Bell Aerosystems Co., 1961-62; sr. v.p. IIT Research Inst., Annapolis, Md., 1962-90, pres. Chgo., 1990-97. Author papers on computer software, electromagnetic compatibility. Past pres. bd. dirs. Md. Hall for Creative Arts, Inc.; past chmn. Md. Hall Found.; past mem. bd. govs. IIT Rsch. Inst.; past trustee Ill. Inst. Tech. Mem. Greater Annapolis C. of C. (pres. 1987); mem. Phi Kappa Phi, Sigma Pi Sigma, Pi Mu Epsilon. Home: 2937 S Atlantic Ave Apt 605 Daytona Beach FL 32118-6045

SCOTT, JOHN CARLYLE, retired gynecologist, oncologist; b. Mpls., Sept. 24, 1933; s. Horace Golden and Grace (Melges) S.; m. Beth Krause, 1958 (div. 1977); m. Paola Maria Martini, Feb. 8, 1986; children: Jeff, David, Suzanne, Danielle. AB, Princeton U., 1956; BS, MD, U. Minn., 1961. Diplomate Am. Coll. Ob-gyn., Pan Am. Ob-gyn. Soc. Intern Sch. Medicine Marquette U., Milw., 1961-62, resident Sch. Medicine, 1962-66; resident Harvard Med. Sch., Boston, 1965; Am. Cancer fellow Marquette Med. Sch., Milw., 1966-67, instr. ob-gyn., 1966-67; clin. instr. ob-gyn. U. Wash. Med. Sch., Seattle, 1968-75, clin. asst. prof., 1975-85, clin. assoc. prof., 1985—, ret., 1998. Mem. faculty adv. com. dept. ob-gyn. U. Wash., Seattle, 1973-97; adj. prof. dept. ob-gyn. U. S.C., 1995—. Author: First Aid for N.W. Boaters, 1977; author Am. Jour. Ob-Gyn., 1970, 75, 77, 97, Jour. Neurologic and Orthopedic Surgery. Bd. dirs. Renton (Wash.) Handicapped Ctr., 1968-70, March of Dimes, 1974-79; bd. dirs. enabling sys. U. Hawaii, Honolulu, 1977-80. Capt. U.S. Army, 1950-52, Korea. Decorated U.S. Senate Medal of Freedom, Bronze and Silver Stars, Pres. Ronald Reagan's Task Force Medal of Merit and Eternal Flame of Freedom. Fellow Royal Soc. Medicine (gynecology and oncology sects.), Am. Coll. Ob-Gyn, Internat. Coll. Surgeons (v.p. 1997—, pres. 1999-2001, past pres. 2001—); mem. Seattle Gynecol. Soc. (pres. 1978), Baker Channing Soc., Sigma Xi. Avocations: photography, constrn., ornithology, sailing, skiing. Home: 726 16th Ave E Seattle WA 98112-3916

SCOTT, JOHN CONSTANTE, marketing company executive; b. Charleston, S.C., Jan. 31, 1941; s. John C. and Annabelle (Holmes) S.; m. Mary Frances Turner. BS in Psychology, St. Joseph's U., Phila., 1975; JD, Temple U., 1979. Commd. USAF, 1962, advanced through grades to lt. col.; served in Vietnam; resigned, 1972; personnel mgr. Campbell Soup Co., Camden, N.J., 1972-79, corp. mgr. employee relations, 1980-84; v.p. ops. Insilco Corp., Meriden, Conn., 1984-89; v.p. human resources Howmet Corp., Greenwich, 1989-92; pres. StarMedia, Inc., 1992—. Mem. pres.'s coun. St. Joseph's U., 1985-90. Mem. ABA, N.J. Bar Assn., Pa. Bar Assn., Res. Officers Assn. (life), Greater Meriden C. of C. (bd. dirs. 1986-89). Roman Catholic. Avocations: mountain hiking, flying. Office: 15 E Putnam Ave Ste 320 Greenwich CT 06830-5424 E-mail: starmedia@compuserve.com. *Peace: The product of justice; politics: the major subset of religion; law (human) rules that institutionalize political power (often as not related to justice).*

SCOTT, JOHN EDWARD SMITH, lawyer; b. St. Louis, Aug. 6, 1936; s. Gordon Hatler and Luella Margarite (Smith) S.; m. Beverly Joan Phillips, Dec. 17, 1960; 1 dau., Pamela Anne. AB, Albion Coll., 1958; JD, Wayne State U., 1961. Bar: Mich. 1961, U.S. Dist. Ct. (ea. dist.) Mich. 1962, U.S. Dist. Ct. (we. dist.) Mich. 1970, U.S. Tax. Ct. 1979, U.S. Ct. Appeals (6th cir.) 1964, U.S. Supreme Ct. 1966. Law clk. Supreme Ct. Mich., Lansing, 1961-62; assoc. Dickinson, Wright, Moon, Van Dusen & Freeman, Detroit, 1962-69, ptnr., 1970—. Adj. prof. U. Detroit Law Sch., 1967-71. Supreme Ct. appointee State Bar Rep. Assembly, Detroit, 1972-77; mayor City of Pleasant Ridge, Mich., 1973-81; commr. Mich. Appellate Defender Commn., Detroit, 1979—, chmn., 1992—; hearing referee Mich. Civil Rights Commn., Detroit, 1974-80; chmn. Detroit Legal Aid & Defender Commn., 1972-77; chmn. case flow mgmt. com. Mich. Supreme Ct., 1989-90. Fellow Am. Coll. Trial Lawyers, Internat. Soc. Barristers, Internat. Acad. Trial Lawyers; mem. ABA (chmn. trial evidence com. sect. litigation 1988-91), Am. Bd. Advs., Am. Bar Found., Internat. Assn. Def. Counsel, Mich. Bar Found., Detroit Golf Club, Order of Coif (hon.). Office: Dickinson Wright PLLC 500 Woodward Ave Ste 4000 Detroit MI 48226-3416

SCOTT, JOHN MCGREGOR, oil & gas industry executive, real estate investor; b. Brighton, Sussex, Eng. came to U.S., Sept. 1994; s. Edward McGregor Scott and Margret Joan Goldrich; m. Candida Jane Scott, Apr. 11, 1977 (div. Sept. 1988); m. Trude Koby, June 24, 1996; 1 child, Asia Koby. BSc in civil engring., Leicester U., Eng., 1977; MBA, London Bus. Sch., 1990. Chartered engr. Assoc. dir. Global Engring., London, 1982-88; mgr. R&D Texaco, 1988-90, mgr. prospects, 1990-92, mgr. properties Aberdeen, Eng., 1992-94, gen. mgr. L.Am. Coral Gables, Fla., 1994-96, gen. mgr. Venezuela Houston, 1996-98, gen. mgr. Brazil, 1999—. Lectr. Inst. Project Mgrs., London, 1990-92. Dir. Jr. Achievment, Houston, 1999—, Houston Symphony, 1999—. Buddhist. Avocations: travel, motorsports, history. Office: 1111 Bagby St # 3533 Houston TX 77002-2551

SCOTT, JOHN PAUL, medical educator; b. Kamunting, Malaysia, June 26, 1956; came to U.S., 1991; s. Joseph and Agnes (Beldon) S.; m. Lesley Carol Poole, Dec. 5, 1981; children: Christopher Michael, Elizabeth Mary, David Matthew. MB ChB, Otago U., Dunedin, New Zealand, 1979, MD, 1990; MS, Cambridge U., England, 1992; MS in Econs., U. London, 1999; LLB (hon.), U. Wolverhampton, 2000; LLM, U. Glamorgan, 2002, U. Glasgow, 2002. Resident Otago U., Dunedin, New Zealand, 1979-83; assoc. prof. transplantation Mayo Clinic, Rochester, Minn., 1991-96, prof., 1996—. Internat. advisor, 2000—. Contbr. articles to profl. jours. Fellow dept. pulmonary medicine Otago U., 1984-85, Cambridge U., 1985-88, sr. fellow, 1988-91. Fellow Royal Coll. Physicians (internat. advisor 2000—), Royal Australian Coll. Physicians, Am. Coll. Physicians, Royal Statis. Soc.; mem. Am. Thoracic Soc. (Minn. rep. 1993-96), Royal Soc. New Zealand, Internat. Soc. Philosophical Enquiry, Mayo Thoracic Soc. (pres. 1996-99). Avocations: philosophy, economics, chess, climbing, travel. Office: Mayo Clinic 200 1st St SW Rochester MN 55905-0002

SCOTT, JOHN TROY, economics educator; b. Honolulu, Sept. 4, 1947; AB in Econs., English, U. N.C., 1969; PhD in Econs., Harvard U., 1976. Asst. prof. Dartmouth Coll., Hanover, N.H., 1977-83, assoc. prof., 1983-89, prof. econs., 1989—. Economist, bd. govs. Fed. Res. System, 1976-77; economist, line of bus. program, FTC, 1980-81, cons., 1981-86; cons., Dept. Justice, 1982. Assoc. editor Jour. Indsl. Econs., 1984-89; mem. editorial bd. Rev. of Indsl. Orgn., 1988—; contbr. articles to profl. jours. 1st lt. U.S. Army, 1969-72. Mem. Phi Beta Kappa, Delta Phi Alpha. Office: Dartmouth Coll Dept Econs Hanover NH 03755

SCOTT, JOHN WALTER, chemical engineer, research management executive; b. Berkeley, Calif., May 27, 1919; s. John Walter and Cora Viola (Wampfler) S.; m. Jane Ellen Newman, June 27, 1942; children— Nancy, Barbara, Charles, James, Richard BS in Chemistry, U. Calif.-Berkeley, 1941, MS in Chem. Engring., 1951. Registered profl. chem. engr., Calif. Process and catalyst research and devel. Chevron Research, Richmond, Calif., 1946-67, v.p., 1967-84, cons., 1985—. Contbr. articles to profl. jours.; patentee in field Trustee U. Calif.-Berkeley Found., 1985-91; adv. coun. Lawrence Hall of Sci.,

1990-97; mem. coun. Town of Ross, Calif., 1992-96. Capt. U.S. Army, 1941-46. Fellow Am. Inst. Chem. Engrs. (awards com. 1979-84, award 1978), AAAS; mem. Nat. Acad. Engring., Am. Chem. Soc., Am. Petroleum Inst. (chmn. research data info. services 1971-73, 77-80, cert. of appreciation 1983) Avocations: history; travel. Home: PO Box 1466 Sonoma CA 95476-1466

SCOTT, JOYCE ALAINE, university official; b. Long Beach, Calif., May 21, 1943; d. Emmett Emery Scott and Grace (Evans) Wedum BA, U. Conn., 1964; MA, U. Va., 1966; PhD, Duke U., 1973. From instr. to assoc. prof. U. Wyo., Laramie, 1971-74, asst. dean, 1974-78, asst. v.p. acad. affairs, 1976-81, assoc. v.p. acad. affairs, 1981-84; provost, v.p. SUNY-Potsdam, 1984-86; exec. v.p. Wichita State U., Kans., 1986-90, v.p. on spl. assignment, 1990-91; sr. cons. Am. Assn. State Colls. and Univs., 1991-92, v.p. acad. and internat. programs, 1992-97; deputy commr. Mont. U. System, Helena, 1998—. Mem. Commn. on Ednl. Credit and Credentials of Am. Council on Edn., Washington, 1982-87; cons. faculty Am. Open U., Lincoln, Nebr., 1981-82. Contbr. articles to profl. jours. Trustee Jones Internat. U. Mem. MLA, AAHE, Am. Assn. Tchrs. French, Phi Beta Kappa, Phi Sigma Iota. Republican. Presbyterian. Office: Office Commr Higher Edn Box 59620-3101 Helena MT 59620-3101 E-mail: jscott@oche.montana.edu.

SCOTT, JOYCE M. C. academic administrator; b. N. Plainfield, N.J., Feb. 17, 1924; d. Charles Chester Sr. and Martha England Murphey Yost; m. William Scott, Jan. 8, 1952; children: Elizabeth V. K. Hartzell, Terry L., Jyothi J., Shanti J. BA in Bibl. Edn., Columbia Internat. U., 1946; MA in Missions cum laude, Ea. Bapt. Theol. Sem., Phila., 1972; LittD (hon.), London Inst. Applied Rsch., 1993; DD (hon.), Internat. Inst. Ch. Mgmt., Madras, India, 1991. Ordained Am. Bapt. Ch., 1990. Tchr. pub. schs., 1946—49; dir. religious edn. Presbyn. Ch., 1949—50; clin. lab. supr. Christian Hosp., Karimnagar, India, 1961-66; corr., treas. Mission Mid. Sch., Tchr. Tng. Sch., Andhra, India, 1966-75; supr. Clin. Lab. Clough Meml. Hosp., Ongole, India, 1966-75; supr., treas. dept. youth Christian Edn., 1972-75; corr., mgr. Edn. and Rehab. Handicapped Children, 1972-75; corr., bursar New Life Ctr. Children, Narasaraopet, India, 1972-75; bursar, advisor adult literacy program Samavesham Telugu Bapt. Chs., India, 1967—77; exec. asst. India Bible Lit., 1975-86; dir. World Home Bible League, 1980-83; dir., founder-dir. all India adult literacy program Literacy India Trust, 1984—. Assoc. gen. dir. India Bible Lit., 1973—. Author: Happiness - An Illustrated Flip Chart, 1979, Guide to Happiness Study, 1973, Discovering Bible Truths, 1983, Beyond Doubt, 1994; contbg. author: World Literacy: Teaching to Read in the 21st Century, 2002; contbr. articles to profl. jours. Chmn. adult edn. com. Andhra Pradesh State Christian Coun., 1967—77; mem. Assocs. of World Mission of Am. Bapt. Ch., 1996—. Recipient Mother Edn. award Tharigoppula Welfare Soc., 1989; named Disting. Alumnus Columbia Internat. U., 1995. Republican. Avocations: music, reading, pets. Home: 116 Fairview Ave Dover PA 17315-1316 Office: Scipture Ministries India 22 S Main St Dover PA 17315-1506

SCOTT, JUDITH MYERS, elementary education educator; b. Loredo, Mo., Dec. 29, 1940; d. Wilbur Charles and Dora Emma (Frazier) Myers; m. David Ronald Scott, Dec. 18, 1965; children: Russell Myers, Geoffrey Douglas. BA in Edn., Ariz. State U., 1962, MA in edn., 1970. Cert. tchr., Ariz. Tchr. 2d grade Scottsdale (Ariz.) Elem. Dist., 1962-64; tchr. 1st grade Cahuilla Sch., Palm Springs, Calif., 1965, Palm Crest Sch., La Canada, 1968-69; tchr. Ak Chin Community Sch., Maricopa, Ariz., 1969-70; grad. asst. Ariz. State U., Tempe, 1970-71; pvt. tutor, 1970-77; tchr. Dayspring Presch., 1978-83; tchr. 3d grade Waggoner Elem. Sch., Kyrene, Ariz., 1984-86; reading specialist Tempe Elem. Sch. Dist., 1986-90, tchr., trainer collaborative literacy intervention project, 1990—. Exec. dir. Beauty for All Seasons, Tempe, 1982-86; presenter in field. Coord. New Zealand Tchr. Exch., Tempe Sister Cities, 1992—. Mem. NEA, ASCD, IRA, ARA, Ariz. Sch. Admisntrs., Ariz. Edn. Assn. Methodist. Avocations: Painting, reading, hiking. Home: 1940 E Calle De Caballos Tempe AZ 85284-2507 Office: Tempe Elem Sch Dist 3205 S Rural Rd Tempe AZ 85282-3853

SCOTT, JULIA KIM, school nurse; b. Vancouver, Wash., July 12, 1955; d. Irving Ferdinand and Virginia Mae (DuNann) Weisenborn; m. Curtis Alan Scott, Aug. 18, 1979. BSN, Pacific Luth. U., 1977; MS, U. Portland, Oreg., 1988. RN, Wash.; cert. CPR instr.-trainer. Staff nurse surg. unit S.W. Wash. Hosps., Vancouver, charge nurse labor/delivery unit; sch. nurse Vancouver Sch. Dist., Battle Ground (Wash.) Sch. Dist. Maj. USAFR, 1985—. Mem. ANA (cert., mem. test devel. com., sch. nursing cert. exam), NEA, Wash. State Nurses Assn., Nat. Assn. Sch. Nurses, Sch. Nurse Orgn. of Wash., Wash. Edn. Assn., Res. Officers Assn., Sigma Theta Tau. E-mail: scott.julia@bgsd.k12.wa.us.

SCOTT, JUSTINE FORD, counselor, educator; b. Newton, N.C., Nov. 3, 1942; d. Laddie Henry, Sr. and Vera Burton Ford; m. Jerry Scott, June 24, 1972; children: David, Alicia. BS, N.C. A&T State U., 1970; MEd, DePaul U., 1999. Cert. tchr., Ill. Customer svc., sales asst. GE, Oak Brook, Ill., 1979-92; tchr.'s aid Sch. Dist. 60, Zion, 1992-94; 6th grade tchr. Sch. Dist. 187, North Chicago, 1994-99; SEP counselor Coll. of Lake County, Grayslake, 1999—. Mentor, Sisters Taking Care, Chgo.; mem. chancel choir, 2d Bapt. Ch., Evanston, Ill. Mem. Am. Counseling Assn., Ill. Counseling Assn., Chgo. Counseling Assn. E-mail: jfordscott@msn.com.

SCOTT, KATHRYN FENDERSON, lawyer; b. Augusta, Ga., June 6, 1970; d. Robert Thomas Fenderson and Christine (Cunningham) Cormier; m. Charles Dean Scott. BA, Eckerd Coll., St. Petersburg, Fla., 1992; JD, Stetson U., St. Petersburg, 1995. Bar: Fla. 1995, U.S. Dist. Ct. (mid. dist.) Fla. 1995, U.S. Ct. Appeals (11th cir.) 1997. Assoc. Govan, Burns & Jones, St. Petersburg, 1995-97; ptnr. Scott & Fenderson, 1997—. Editl. bd. Paraclete, St. Petersburg Bar Assn., 1996-99; mentor program Stetson U. Coll. Law, St. Petersburg, 1996—. Recipient Am. Jurisprudence award Lawyer's Coop. Pub., 1992. Mem. ABA, Assn. Trial Lawyers Am., Assn. Fla. Trial Lawyers, St. Petersburg Bar Assn., Clearwater Bar Assn. Office: Scott and Fenderson 4554 Central Ave Ste L Saint Petersburg FL 33711-1046 Fax: 727-321-4499. E-mail: fenderlaw@aol.com.

SCOTT, KATHY LYNN, peri-operative nurse; b. Waukegan, Ill., Apr. 22, 1962; d. Howard E. and Roberta L. (Richman) S. ASN, Coll. of Lake County, Grayslake, Ill., 1984, AS in Mid. Mgmt., 1985; student, No. Ill. U., 1980-82; computer cert., Winter Pk. Tech. Sch., 2002; Comp. TIA A+ cert., Winter Park Tech. Sch., 2002. RN, Fla. Staff nurse oncology unit Humana Hosp. of Lucerne, Orlando, Fla., Winter Park (Fla.) Meml. Hosp.; staff devel. coord. Manor Care, Orlando; asst. dir. of nursing Regents Park Nursing Home, Winter Park; oper. rm. staff nurse Fla. Hosp., Orlando; pvt. pilot rating Air Orlando, Fla., 1999. Mem. Assn. Oper. Rm. Nurses, Phi Theta Kappa. mem. AOPA Home: 2424 Tree Ridge Ln Orlando FL 32817-2725

SCOTT, KENNETH ELSNER, mechanical engineering educator; b. Webster, Mass., May 18, 1926; s. Henry Anderson and Amanda (Elsner) S.; m. Elizabeth Ann Oldham, June 21, 1952; children— Kenneth Elsner, Cynthia Lynne, Jeffrey Alan, Donald Leighton. BSMechE, Worcester Poly. Inst., 1948, MS, 1954. Faculty Worcester Poly. Inst., 1948-91, prof. mech. engring., 1966-91, prof. emeritus, 1991—, George I. Alden prof. engring., 1971-75, inst. dir. audio-visual devel., 1971-74, dir. instructional TV, 1974-90, dir. CAD Lab., 1981-93, acting head dept. mech. engring., 1988-89. Active Bd. Health, Holden, Mass., 1963-70. With AUS, 1944-46. Recipient Trustees' award for Outstanding Tchr. of Year, 1971, Western Electric Fund award for excellence in instrn. New Eng. sect. Am. Soc. Engring. Edn., 1972, Tchg. Excellence and Campus Leadership award Sears-Roebuck Found., 1990-91, William R. Grogan award in recognition of support for Mission of Worcester Poly. Inst., 1998. Fellow ASME (exec. com. Worcester sect. 1952-57, sec.-treas. 1955-56, chmn. 1956-57, region I chmn. profl. divns. com. 1957-59, chmn. agenda, audit, budget and nominating com. Worcester 1957-58, chmn. symposium lubrication Worcester sect. 1957-58, chmn. Adm. Earle award com. 1958-59, chmn. devel. com. 1960-61); mem. Am. Soc. Engring. Edn. (sec.-treas. New Eng.), Sigma Xi, Pi Tau Sigma, Tau Beta Pi. Home: 9750 Cypress Lake Dr Fort Myers FL 33919-6064

SCOTT, KENNETH EUGENE, lawyer, educator; b. Western Springs, Ill., Nov. 21, 1928; s. Kenneth L. and Bernice (Albright) S.; m. Viviane H. May, Sept. 22, 1956 (dec. Feb. 1982); children: Clifton, Jeffrey, Linda; m. Priscilla Gay, July 30, 1989; children: Ashley, Shaler. BA in Econs., Coll. William and Mary, 1949; MA in Polit. Sci., Princeton U., 1953; LLB, Stanford U., 1956. Bar: N.Y. 1957, Calif. 1957, D.C. 1967. Assoc. Sullivan & Cromwell, N.Y.C., 1956-59, Musick, Peeler & Garrett, L.A., 1959-61; chief dep. savs. and loan commr. State of Calif., 1961-63; gen. counsel Fed. Home Loan Bank Bd., Washington, 1963-67; Parsons prof. law and bus. Stanford (Calif.) Law Sch., 1968-95, emeritus, 1995—; sr. rsch. fellow Hoover Instn., 1978-95, emeritus, 1995—; fellow Am. Acad. Berlin, 2001. Mem. Shadow Fin. Regulatory Com., 1986—, Fin. Economists Roundtable, 1991—; bd. dirs. Am. Century Mut. Funds, Mountain View, Calif. Author: (with others) Retail Banking in the Electronic Age, 1977; co-editor: The Economics of Corporation Law and Securities Regulation, 1980. Mem. ABA, Calif. Bar Assn., Phi Beta Kappa, Order of Coif, Pi Kappa Alpha, Omicron Delta Kappa. Home: 610 Gerona Rd Stanford CA 94305-8453 Office: Stanford Law Sch Stanford CA 94305-8610 E-mail: kenscott@stanford.edu.

SCOTT, KERRIGAN DAVIS, private investor, philanthropist; b. Magdalene, Fla., Sept. 26, 1941; s. Thurman Thomas and Jacqueline (Glenister) S.; children: Katherine, Stephanie, Jennifer. N.D. U. Va., 1964. Pvt. investor, Hilton Head Island, S.C., 1965—. Aide-de-camp to gov. of Tenn. with rank of col. Recipient Presdl. Legion Merit, Shield of Valor medal, White House Letter Commendation. Author: Aristocracy and Royalty of the World, 1983, Hereditary Baron in the Nobility of France. Mem. bd. regents Liberty U., Lynchburg, Va.; bd. dirs. Aid to Hospitalized Vets.; assoc. Library of Congress; pres. The Cittanova Found. Recognized as His Royal Highness, Prince of Cittanova by Govts. of Albania and San Marino (Italy). Episcopalian. Club: Shipyard Plantation Racquet. Home: Windmill Harbour Plantation 5 Yacht Club Dr Hilton Head Island SC 29926-1242

SCOTT, LEAMON EDWARD, JR. social worker, educator, writer; b. L.A., Nov. 19, 1950; s. Leamon Edward Scott, Alice Bolden Cato. BFA/African-Am. Studies, Calif. State U. Dominguez Hills, 1974. Sr. social worker Adult Protective Svcs. L.A. County, L.A., 1974—. Instr. Corrective Behavior Inst., L.A., 1998—. Author: Beyond the Bayou, 2002; performer (poetic dialogue): Welcome to Wordmusik, 1999. Named Musician of Yr., David Star Jordan H.S., 1966, 1967; scholar Bank of Am. Scholarship, 1968, Omega Psi Phi S;cholarship, 1968—69. Democrat. Avocations: theater , reading, jazz, jogging, art. Home: 640 W 4th St Unit 402 Long Beach CA 90802

SCOTT, LEE HANSEN, retired holding company executive; b. Atlanta, Sept. 25, 1926; s. Elbert Lee and Auguste Lillian (Hansen) S.; m. Margaret Lee Smith, July 20, 1951; children: Bradley Hansen, Randall Lee. B.E.E., U. Fla., 1949. With Fla. Power Corp., St. Petersburg, 1949-94, dir. constrn., maintenance and operating, 1968-71, v.p. customer ops., 1971-77, sr. v.p. ops., 1977-83, pres., 1983-88, chmn. bd., 1988-90, also bd. dirs., Fla. Progress Corp.; ret., 1994. Bd. dirs. Sun Banks; cons. in field. Pres. St. Petersburg chpt. ARC, 1977, Pinellas Com. of 100, 1980, Community Services Council, 1970, St. Petersburg Progress, 1983, Bus. and Industry Employment Devel. Council, 1983; chmn. bd. United Way. Served with USAF, 1944-46. Named Mr. Sun of St. Petersburg, 1990. Mem. Fla. Engring. Soc., IEEE, Elec. Council Fla. (pres. 1979), St. Petersburg C. of C. (v.p. 1980), Fla. C. of C. (pres. 1987-88), Pinellas Suncoast C. of C. (past chmn., chmn. bd. trustees). Presbyterian. Home: 601 Apalachee Dr NE Saint Petersburg FL 33702-2766

SCOTT, LINDA BYRNE, artist; b. San Francisco, Apr. 14, 1947; d. Daniel Thomas and Ellen Almeda (Flesher) Byrne; m. Darrell Scott, July 16, 1972 (div. 1982); children: Sarah Byrne, Tina Corrine; m. Edward Joseph Baldus, May 2, 1983. AA, City Coll. San Francisco, 1968; BA, Calif. State U. Sonoma, 1970; MFA, U. Idaho, 1995. Artist Taylor Agy., San Rafael, Calif., 1970-71, Holiday Magic, San Rafael, 1971-72; tchr. art Sch. Dist. 1, Lewiston, Idaho, 1982—. Co-owner, treas. Holbrook Gallery, Lewiston, 1987-91; artist Diversified Art and Design, Lewiston, 1987—. Exhibited in solo and group shows in Idaho and Wash., Calif., Oreg., Ariz., Ill. and Can. Mem. Nat. Watercolor Soc., Northwest Watercolor Soc., Women's Caucus for Art (v.p. Idaho chpt. 1996). Democrat. Avocation: travel. Home: 1926 6th St Lewiston ID 83501-3884 E-mail: scottbaldus@cableone.net.

SCOTT, LOLITA JEAN, social worker; b. Owensboro, Ky., Apr. 21, 1957; d. James Thomas Jr. and Jewell Dean (Walls) Howard; m. Lindsey Scott, Aug. 15, 1980 (div. 2001); 1 child, Latavia Seneca Scott. AA, Ea. Ky. U., 1980, BSW, 1993; MA in Marriage and Family Therapist, Louisville Theol. Sem., 1999. With child protective svcs. Ky. Dept. Social Svcs., Richmond, 1993, 94-95; social worker sr. placement Richmond Family Resource Ctr., 1993; asst. tchg. parent Spring Meadows, Louisville, 1994; sr. case mgr. Seven Counties Svcs., 1995—2001; with Family & Children's Counseling Ctrs., 2001—. Clin. therapist assoc. Ctr. for Family Ministries, Archdiocese of Louisville, 1996—; mem. adoption-foster care rev. bd., 1998-99. Singer Ea. Ky. Ensemble, 1975-78, Tommy Jones workshop Cmty. Choir, 1995-96; vol. tutor Ky. Dept. Adult Edn. and Literacy, Richmond, 1993; vol. Women's Abuse Ctr., Owensboro, Ky., 1989, Telford Cmty. Ctr., Richmond, 1991. Mem. Am. Assn. Christian Counselors; Am. Assn. Marriage and Family Therapy, Ky. Assn. Marriage and Family Therapy, Omega Psi Phi Pearl. Democrat. Baptist. Avocations: bicycling, volleyball, movies, reading, dancing. Home: Apt 18 5508 Delmaria Way Louisville KY 40291-4906 Office: Family & Childrens Counseling Ctrs 731 S 31st St Louisville KY 40211 E-mail: arose4aqueen@aol.com.

SCOTT, LOUIS EDWARD, advertising agency executive; b. Waterbury, Conn., June 17, 1923; s. Louis Arthur and Ellen (Eckert) S.; m. Phyllis Corrine Denker, Jan. 27, 1942; children: Susan Louise, Eric Richard, Jane Lynn. BS, U. Calif., Berkeley, 1944. Sr. account exec. McCarty Co., L.A., 1946-50; from mem. staff to dir. Foote, Cone & Belding, 1950—61; dir. Foote, Cone & Belding/Honig, 1961—98. Bd. dirs. Smart and Final Corp., Casino Internat., True North Comm.. Chmn. publicity com. Los Angeles Community Chest, 1960; patron mem. Los Angeles YMCA; mem. Freedoms Found.; chmn. So. Calif. advisory bd. Advt. Council; mem. exec. advisory bd. Art Center Coll. Design. Served with U.S. Maritime Service, also USNR, World War II. Named Western Advt. Man of Year, 1972 Mem. Am. Assn. Advt. Agys. (dir., past chmn. Western region), Coronado Cays Yacht Club, Rio Verde Country Club, Seattle Yacht Club, Cruising Club Am. Home: 19119 E Tonto Trail Rio Verde AZ 85263 also: PO 182247 Coronado CA 92178 E-mail: scottlouphyl@aol.com.

SCOTT, MARGARET SIMON, retired mortgage broker; b. Boston, May 12, 1934; d. Frank A. and Margaret Alice (Gotham) Simon; m. Walter Neil Scott, Nov. 21, 1959 (div. June 1997); 1 child, Walter David Kimbley. BA in Physics, Wellesley Coll., 1956; MA in Polit. Sci., Boston U., 1965; MS in Human Resources Mgmt., U. Utah, 1974. Ordained elder 2000. Rsch. asst. Bell Tel. Labs., Whippany, N.J., 1956-58; rsch. asst. med. sch. U. Louisville, 1959-60, Harvard U., Boston, 1960-64; instr. polit. sci. Trinity U., San Antonio, 1966-67; cons. info. systems U.S. Dept. Labor, Washington, 1968; dir. manpower planning N.Y.C. Human Resources Adminstrn., 1968-71; asst. v.p. First Nat. City Bank, N.Y.C., 1972-77; v.p. Citibank, N.A., 1978-86, AMEV Asset Mgmt., Inc., N.Y.C., 1986-88; pres. Mortgage Adv. Svcs., Inc., 1988-99. Vol. Jr. League, Louisville, 1957; bd. mgr. N.Y. Jr. League, N.Y.C., 1970—74; sec. 1095 Park Ave Corp., 1977—86; bd. mgrs. McBurney YMCA, 1995—2000, chmn., 1998—2000; trustee United Adult Ministries, 1998—, mem. exec. com., 1999—, chair, fin. com., 1999—; trustee First Presbyn. Ch. in the City N.Y., 1995—98, pres., 1997—98; trustee N.Y. City Presbytery, 1996—98, treas., 1998—2002, ruling elder, 2000—; mem. steering com. Presbyn. Welcome, 1999—; co-moderator N.Y. City Presbytery, 2001—; bd. trustees Presbyn. Synod of Northeast, 2002—; bd. dirs. YWCA, N.Y.C., 1980—85, chair, 1983—85. Mem.: Wellesley Club. Democrat. Home: 441 W 24th St New York NY 10011-1253 E-mail: margaretnyc@hotmail.com.

SCOTT, MARIANNE FLORENCE, retired librarian, educator; b. Toronto, Dec. 4, 1928; d. Merle Redvers and Florence Ethel (Hutton) S. BA, McGill U., Montreal, Que., Can., 1949, BLS, 1952; LLD (hon.), York U., 1985, Dalhousie U., 1989; DLitt (hon.), Laurentian U., 1990. Asst. librarian Bank of Montreal, 1952-55; law librarian McGill U., 1955-73, law area librarian, 1973-75, dir. libraries, 1975-84, lectr. legal bibliography faculty of law, 1964-75; nat. librarian Nat. Library of Can., Ottawa, Ont., 1984-99, ret., 1999. Co-founder, editor: Index to Can. Legal Periodical Lit, 1963—; contbr. articles to profl. jours. Decorated officer Order of Can., 1995; recipient IFLA medal, 1996. Mem. Internat. Assn. Law Libraries (dir. 1974-77), Am. Assn. Law Libraries, Can. Assn. Law Libraries (pres. 1963-69, exec. bd. 1973-75, honored mem. 1980—), Can. Library Assn. (council and dir. 1980-82, 1st v.p. 1980-81, pres. 1981-82), Corp. Profl. Librarians of Que. (v.p. 1975-76), Can. Assn. Research Libraries (pres. 1978-79, past pres. 1979-80, exec. com. 1980-81, sec.-treas. 1983-84), Ctr. for Research Libraries (dir. 1980-83), Internat. Fedn. Library Assns. (honor com. for 1982 conf. 1979-82, chair com. on copyright and other legal matters 1998—), Conf. of Dirs. of Nat. Libraries (chmn. 1988-92). Home: 119 Dorothea Dr Ottawa ON Canada K1V 7C6 E-mail: mfscott@rogers.com.

SCOTT, MARK ALDEN, hospital network executive; b. Chattanooga, Dec. 4, 1959; s. Dewey Alden and Rowena (Lowery) S.; m. Donna Ruth Kibble, Sept. 11, 1982; children: Matthew, Jacob. Student, Tenn. Tech. U., Cookeville, 1978-80, Chattanooga State U., 1981, 93—. Cert. network engr. Programmer Jerry Bell Constrn., Chattanooga, 1986-88; PC specialist Siskin Steel & Supply, 1988-89; support and network mgr. Tiger Data Systems, 1989-90, programmer, 1990; system cons. Data Concepts, 1990—; microcomputer specialist Meml. Hosp., 1991-93, network mgr., 1993-96, mgr. network svcs., 1996—, PACS sys. mgr., 1997—. Mem. Netware Users Internat., Chattanooga Area Netware Users Group (pres.). Republican. Baptist. Avocations: photography, volleyball, computers, music. Home: 8411 Forest Breeze Dr Harrison TN 37341-6952 Office: Memorial Hospital 2525 Desales Ave Chattanooga TN 37404-1102 E-mail: pacsman@bellsouth.net., mark_scott@memorial.org.

SCOTT, MARY CELINE, pharmacologist; b. Los Angeles, July 14, 1957; d. Walter Edward and Shirley Jean (Elvin) S. BS in Biol. Sci., U. Calif., Irvine, 1978; MS in Biology, Calif. State U., Long Beach, 1980; PhD in Pharmacology, Purdue U., 1985; MBA in Pharm.-Chem. Studies, Fairleigh Dickinson U., 1995. Teaching asst. Calif. State U., Long Beach, 1979-80, Purdue U., West Lafayette, Ind., 1980-82, grad. instr., 1982-83, rsch. fellow, 1983-85, 1988-89, Mayo Found., Rochester, Minn., 1985-87; sr. scientist Schering-Plough, Bloomfield, N.J., 1989-92, assoc. prin. scientist Kenilworth, 1993-98, prin. scientist, 1998-2000; mgr. U.S. Regulatory Affairs, 2000—02, Worldwide Regulatory Affairs , 2002—. Contbr. articles to profl. jours. Mem. at large bd. dirs. Washington Rock coun. Girl Scouts U.S.A. Mem.: AAAS, Soc. Neurosci., Internat. Soc. for Study Xenobiotics, Am. Soc. Pharm. and Exptl. Therapeutics, Am. Chem. Soc. Democrat. Office: Schering-Plough Rsch Inst Worldwide Reg Affairs 2000 Galloping Hill Rd Kenilworth NJ 07033-1310 E-mail: mary.scott@spcorp.com.

SCOTT, MELLOUISE JACQUELINE, educational media specialist; b. Sanford, Fla., Mar. 1, 1943; d. Herbert and Mattye (Williams) Cherry; m. Robert Edward Scott, Jr., July 1, 1972; 1 child, Nolan Edward. BA, Talladega Coll., 1965; MLS, Rutgers U., 1974, EdM, 1976, EdS, 1982. Media specialist Seminole County Bd. Edn., Sanford, 1965-72, Edison (N.J.), 1972-98; ret. Edison (N.J.) Bd. Edn., 1999. Mem. ALA, N.J. Ret. Educators Assn., NEA. Baptist. Home: PO Box 1771 Sanford FL 32772-1771

SCOTT, MICHAEL COLEMAN, philosophy educator; b. Orange, Calif., Sept. 24, 1945; s. Clarence Coleman and Wilma Coetta (Neel) S.; div. Mar. 1981. BA, Calif. State U., Long Beach, 1974, MA, 1976. Cert. tchr., Calif. Instr. ESL, Coastline Coll., Fountain Valley, Calif., 1976, Santa Ana (Calif.) Coll., 1976-79; instr. philosophy Saddleback Coll. North, Irvine, Calif., 1979-80; part-time instr. philosophy Orange Coast Coll., Costa Mesa, 1980-85, instr. philosophy, 1985—. Cons. Orange County Mental Health, Santa Ana, 1975-76. Author poetry. With USN, 1962-63. Mem. People for Ethical Treatment of Animals, Rat Fan Club. Socialist. Avocations: music, ethology, science.

SCOTT, MICHAEL DENNIS, lawyer; b. Mpls., Nov. 6, 1945; s. Frank Walton and Donna Julia (Howard) S.; m. Blanca Josefina Palacios, Dec. 12, 1981; children: Michael Dennis, Cindal Marie, Derek Walton. BS, MIT, 1967; JD, UCLA, 1974. Bar: Calif. 1974, U.S. Dist. Ct. (no., so. and cen. dists.) Calif. 1974, U.S. Patent Office 1974, U.S. Ct. Appeals (9th cir.) 1974, U.S. Supreme Ct. 1978, U.S. Ct. Appeals (fed. cir.) 1989. Systems programmer NASA Electronics Research Lab., Cambridge, Mass., 1967-69, Computer Sciences Corp., El Segundo, Calif., 1969-71, Univac, Valencia, 1971; from assoc. to ptnr. Smaltz & Neelley, Los Angeles, 1974-81; exec. dir. Ctr. for Computer/Law, 1977-94; pvt. practice, 1981-86, 88-89; pres. Law and Tech. Press, 1981-94; ptnr. Scott & Roxborough, Los Angeles, 1986-88, Graham & James, 1989-93; v.p., gen. counsel Sanctuary Woods Multimedia, Inc., San Mateo, Calif., 1993-94; of counsel Steinhart & Falconer, San Francisco, 1995-97; ptnr. Hosie Wes Sacks & Brelsford, Menlo Park, Calif., 1997-98, Perkins Coie LLP, 1998—. Adj. assoc. prof. law Southwestern U., L.A., 1975-80, 2001—, Loyola U., L.A., 1997-99, 2002--, Pepperdine U., L.A., 2001—; chmn. World Computer Law Congress, L.A., 1991, 93. Author: (with David S. Yen) Computer Law Bibliography, 1979, The Scott Report, 1981-86, Computer Law, 1984, Scott on Computer Law, 1991, Multimedia: Law and Practice, 1993, Scott on Multimedia Law, 1996, (with Warren S. Reid) Year 2000 Computer Crisis: Law Business Technology, 1998, Internet and Technology Law Desk Reference, 1999—, Intellectual Property and Licensing Law Desk Reference, 2001, Telecommunications Law Desk Reference, 2002—; editor in chief: Computer/Law Jour., 1978-94, Software Protection, 1982-92, Software Law Jour., 1985-94, Internat. Computer Law Adviser, 1986-92, Cyberspace Lawyer, 1996—, E-Commerce Law Report, 1998—. Mem. Computer Law Assn. (bd. dirs. 1994-99), Calif. State Bar Assn. Office: 1620 26th St Santa Monica CA 90404-4013

SCOTT, MIMI KOBLENZ, psychotherapist, actress, publicist, journalist, playwright; b. Albany, N.Y., Dec. 15, 1940; d. Edmund Akiba and Tillie (Paul) Koblenz; m. Barry Stuart Scott, Aug. 13, 1961 (dec. Nov. 1991); children: Karen Scott Zantay, Jeffrey B. BA in Speech, English Edn., Russell Sage Coll., 1962; MA in Speech Edn., SUNY, Albany, 1968; M in Social Welfare, SUNY, 1985; PhD in Psychology, Pacific Western U., Encino, Calif., 1985. Cert. tchr., social worker. Tchr. English, speech Albany Pub. Schs., 1961-63; hostess, producer talkshow Sta. WAST-TV 13, Albany, 1973-75; freelance actress N.Y.C., 1975-77; producer, actress Four Seasons Dinner Theater, Albany, 1978-82; instr. of theatre Albany Jr. Coll., 1981-83; pvt. practice psychotherapy Albany, N.Y., 1985-92; exec. producer City of Albany Park Playhouse, 1989-92; actor self-employed N.Y.C., 1992—; actor Off Broadway show Grandma Sylvia's Funeral, 1996-98. Guest psychotherapist Sally Jessy Raphael Show, 1992, 93, Jane Whitney Show, 1994, A Current Affair, 1995, News Talk TV, 1995; founder Manhattan Playwrights Inc., 2001. Scriptwriter, dir., actress TV movie, 1985; feature writer Backstage, 1995-96; featured in ind. film Mr. Vincent, Sundance '97; book and lyricist (musical) Dressing Room, Soho Playhouse, N.Y.C., 2000. Event organizer AmFar, 1985; co-chmn. March of Dimes Telethon, 1985-86; fundraiser Leukemia Found., 1987, Aids Benefit, N. Miami Beach, Fla., 1988; elected to SUNY Albany U. Found., 1990. Recipient FDR Nat. Achievement award March of Dimes, 1985, Recognition Cert. Capital Dist. Psychiat. Ctr., 1983, 84, 85; named Woman of Yr. YWCA, 1986, Commr. Albany Tricentennial Celebration, 1986; Mimi Scott Day proclaimed by Mayor of Albany, 1989. Mem. AEA, SAG, AFTRA, NASW. Jewish. Avocations: horseback riding, boating, golf, tennis. Home and Office: 211 W 71st St Apt 6A New York NY 10023-3767

SCOTT, MURIEL ANNE, social services administrator; b. Bklyn., Jan. 11, 1938; d. Malcolm Joseph and Muriel Blandine (Whitney) Griffin; m. Llewellyn Earl Tracy, Apr. 6, 1956 (div. 1972); m. Carl Edward Scott, Feb. 21, 1974; children: Mark Alan Tracy, Scott Anthony Tracy. BS, U. So. Maine, 1976, MEd, 1978. Middle sch. tchr. Cape Elizabeth (Maine) Middle Sch., 1974-76; supr. Foster Grandparents, Pownal, Maine, 1976-77, Salvation Army Meals, Portland, 1977-78; dir. RSVP Ctrl. Sr. Citizens, Augusta, 1978-79, dir. nutrition, 1979-80, asst. dir., 1980-85; exec. dir. Sr. Spectrum, 1985—. Cons. Nat. Assn of AAAs, Washington, 1979-80, Bur. Maine Elderly, Augusta, 1980; del. White House Conf. on Aging, 1995. Bd. dirs. Sr. Legis. Advocacy Coalition, Augusta, 1992—. Mem. Maine Assn. Area Agys. (chair 1989-92), Nat. Assn. AAAs (bd. dirs. 1994—), Nat. Inst. Sr. Ctrs. (bd. dirs. 1989-94), Home Resources of Maine (bd. dirs. 1994—). Avocations: sailing, gardening, painting. Home: PO Box 425 Boothbay ME 04537-0425 Office: Sr Spectrum 320 Water St Augusta ME 04330-4644

SCOTT, NANCY ELLEN, psychologist; b. El Paso, Tex., Nov. 1, 1960; d. Robert Churchill and Annie Jo (Schmidt) S. BS, U. Tex., El Paso, 1982; MS, Springfield Coll., 1985; MA, Columbia U., 1987, EdM, 1989; PhD, Fordham U., 1996. Cert. tchr., Tex., cert. clin. hypnotherapy; lic. psychologist, N.Y. Assoc. Occupl. Health Consulting Inc., West Nyack, N.Y., 1985-88; psychiat. rehab. counselor Met. Hosp., N.Y.C., 1988-91; psychotherapist Met. Ctr. for

Mental Health, 1991-96; psychology intern Albert Einstein Coll. of Medicine, Bronx, N.Y., 1991-92; psychologist Albert Einstein Coll. Medicine, 1992-94, Bronx Psychiat. Ctr., Bronx, 1994-95; assessor Assessment Sys., Inc., N.Y.C., 1995; pvt. practice, 1995—; neuropsychologist Burke Med. Rsch. Inst., White Plains, NY, 1996-99, dir. neuropsychol. assessment program, 1999—2001. Contbr. articles to profl. jours. Mem. APA. Office: 168 Fifth Ave Ste 2N New York NY 10010 Fax: 212-304-9758. E-mail: Nscottphd5ave@cs.com.

SCOTT, NATHAN ALEXANDER, JR. minister, literary critic, religious educator; b. Cleve., Apr. 24, 1925; s. Nathan Alexander and Maggie (Martin) S.; m. Charlotte Hanley, Dec. 21, 1946; children: Nathan Alexander III, Leslie K. AB, U. Mich., 1944; BD, Union Theol. Sem., 1946; PhD, Columbia U., 1949; LittD, Ripon Coll., 1965, St. Mary's Coll., Notre Dame, Ind., 1969, Denison U., 1976, Brown U., 1981, Northwestern U., 1982, Elizabethtown Coll., 1989; LHD, Wittenberg U., 1965; DD, Phila. Div. Sch., 1967; STD, Gen. Theol. Sem., 1968; LHD, U. D.C., 1976; DD, The Protestant Episcopal Theological Seminary in Va., 1985; HumD, U. Mich., 1988; LHD, Wesleyan U., 1989, Bates Coll., 1990; STD, Univ of the South, 1992; DD, Kenyon Coll., 1993, Wabash Coll., 1996; Ordained priest Episcopal Ch., 1960; canon theologian Cathedral St. James, Chgo., 1967-76. dean of chapel, Va. Union U., 1946-47; instr. humanities, Howard U., 1948-51, asst. prof., 1951-53, assoc. prof., 1953-55; asst. prof. theology and literature, U. Chgo., 1955-58, assoc. prof., 1958-64, prof., 1964-72, Shailer Mathews prof. of theology and lit., 1972-76, prof. English, 1967-76; Commonwealth prof. religious studies, U. Va., 1976-81, William R. Kenan prof. religious studies, 1981-90, prof. English, 1976-90, prof. emeritus, 1990—. Author: Rehearsals of Discomposure: Alienation and Reconciliation in Modern Literature, 1952, The Tragic Vision and the Christian Faith, 1957, Modern Literature and the Religious Frontier, 1958, Albert Camus, 1962, Reinhold Niebuhr, 1963, The New Orpheus: Essays toward a Christian Poetic, 1964, The Climate of Faith in Modern Literature, 1965, The Broken Center: Studies in the Theological Horizon of Modern Literature, 1966, Ernest Hemingway, 1966, The Modern Vision of Death, 1967, Adversity and Grace: Studies in Recent American Literature, 1968, Negative Capability: Studies in the New Literature and the Religious Situation, 1969, The Unquiet Vision: Mirrors of Man in Existentialism, 1969, The Wild Prayer of Longing: Poetry and the Sacred, 1971, Nathanael West, 1971, Three American Moralists: Mailer, Bellow, Trilling, 1973, The Poetry of Civic Virtue: Eliot, Malraux, Auden, 1976, Mirrors of Man in Existentialism, 1978, The Poetics of Belief: Studies in Coleridge, Arnold, Pater, Santayana, Stevens and Heidegger, 1985, Visions of Presence in Modern American Poetry, 1993; co-editor Jour. Religion, 1963-77, (with Ronald Sharp) Reading George Steiner, 1994; adv. editor Religion and Lit., Literature and Theology, Callaloo. Fellow Am. Acad. of Arts and Scis.; mem. Soc. Arts, Religion and Contemporary Culture, Soc. for Values in Higher Edn. (Kent fellow), MLA., Am. Acad. Religion (pres. 1986), Century Assn. (N.Y.C.), Quadrangle Club, Arts Club (Chgo.), Greencroft Club (Charlottesville, Va.). Office: U Va Dept Religious Studies Charlottesville VA 22903

SCOTT, NORMAN LAURENCE, engineering consultant; b. Meadow Grove, Nebr., Oct. 17, 1931; s. Laurence Ray Scott and Ruth Louise Braun; m. Joan Culbertson, Jan. 21, 1956; 1 child, Douglas Jay. BS in Civil Engring., U. Nebr., 1954. Registered profl. engr., Ill., Fla., Md., Minn., Va., Tex.; registered structural engr., Ill. Sales engr. R.H. Wright & Son, Ft. Lauderdale, Fla., 1956-58; mgr. Wright of Palm Beach, West Palm Beach, 1958-59; exec. sec. Prestressed Concrete Inst., Chgo., 1959-63; gen. mgr. Wiss, Janney, Elstner & Assoc., Northbrook, Ill., 1963-66; pres., chmn. The Consulting Engrs. Group Inc., Mt. Prospect, 1966—. 1st lt. USAF, 1954-56. Mem. ASCE (life), Am. Concrete Inst. (hon., pres. 1983-84, Henry C. Turner medal 1993), Ill. Soc. Profl. Engrs. (pres. North Shore chpt. 1962). Republican. Home: 701 Chatham Dr Glenview IL 60025-4403 Office: The Consulting Engrs Group 55 E Euclid Ave Mount Prospect IL 60056-1283

SCOTT, NORMAN ROSS, electrical engineering educator; b. N.Y.C., May 15, 1918; s. George Norman and Lillias B.H. (Ogg) S.; m. Marjorie M. Fear, Apr. 6, 1950; children: Mari, George, Ian, Charles. BS, MS, MIT, 1941; PhD, U. Ill., 1950. Asst. prof. elec. engring. U. Ill., Urbana, 1946-50; asst. prof. to prof. elec. engring. U. Mich., Ann Arbor, 1951-87, assoc dean Coll. Engring., 1965-68, dean Dearborn Campus, 1968-71, prof. emeritus of elec. engring. and computer sci., 1987—. Cons. Nat. Cash Register Co., Dayton, 1956-65; mem. math. and computer sci. rsch. adv. com. AEC, Washington, 1961-63. Editor-in-chief IEEE Trans. on Computers, N.Y.C., 1961-65; author: Analog and Digital Computer Technology, 1959, Electronic Computer Technology, 1970, Computer Number Systems and Arithmetic, 1985. Maj. U.S. Army, 1941-46. Fellow IEEE. Home: 2260 Gale Rd Ann Arbor MI 48105-9512 Office: U Mich EECS Dept Ann Arbor MI 48109

SCOTT, NORMAN ROY, academic administrator, agricultural engineering educator; b. Spokane, Wash., Sept. 6, 1936; s. Roy Samuel and Agnes Sarafia (Lilljegren) S.; m. Sharon R. Cogley, June 17, 1961; children: Robin, Nanette, Shirlene. BS in Agrl. Engring., Wash. State U., 1958; PhD, Cornell U., 1962. Mem. faculty agrl. engring dept. Cornell U., Ithaca, N.Y., 1962—, chmn. agrl. engring. dept., 1978-84, dir. office for rsch. agrl. experimentation sta., 1984-89, v.p. rsch. and advanced studies, 1989-98. Mem. bd. on agriculture NRC, Nat. Acad. Scis., 1993-96. Contbr. articles to profl. jours.; patentee in field. Recipient Alumni Achievement award Wash. State U., 1995. Fellow ASHRAE, Am. Inst. for Med. and Biol. Engring. (founding 1991), Am. Soc. Agrl. Engrs. (tech. v.p. 1989-92, pres. elect 1992-93, pres. 1993-94, Henry Glese award 1989, McCormick-Case Gold Medal award 2002); mem. AAAS, N.Y. Acad. Scis., Nat. Acad. Engring., Am. Soc. for Engring. Edn., Instrument Soc. Am. (sr.). Democrat. Methodist. Avocations: sailing, golf. Home: 1662 Taughannock Blvd Trumansburg NY 14886-9120 Office: Cornell U 216 Riley Robb Hall Ithaca NY 14853-5701 E-mail: nrs5@cornell.edu.

SCOTT, OLOF HENDERSON, JR. priest; b. Phila., May 13, 1942; s. Olof Henderson and Julia Irene (Rutroff) S.; m. Eva Jakowenko, Sept. 13, 1969; children: Lisa Ann, Christopher Olof, Timothy Nicholas. BA in Physics, Franklin and Marshall Coll., 1964; MS in Nuclear Engring., Pa. State U., 1966; postgrad., St. Vladimir's Orthodox Theol. Sem., 1975-76. Ordained deacon Antiochian Orthodox Christian Ch., 1975, priest, 1976, archpriest, 1988. Ops. engr. S3G ops. Knolls Atomic Power Lab., GE Co., Schenectady, N.Y., 1966-68, project engr. S3G ops., 1968-69; lead nuclear engr. Seabrook Nuclear project Pub. Svc. Co. of N.H., Manchester, 1969-70; project engr. VEPCO projects Nuclear Energy Sys. divsn. Westinghouse Elec. Co., Monroeville, Pa., 1970-72, project mgr. VEPCO projects Nuclear Energy Sys. divsn., 1972-74, regional sales mgr. mktg., 1974-75; pastor St. George Orthodox Ch., Charleston, W.Va., 1976—; dean of clergy Appalachian-Ohio Valley Deanery, 1976—. Spiritual advisor NAC-SOYO of Archdiocese, 1977-82, vice-chmn. inter-orthodox and inter-faith rels., 1987—; mem. exec. bd. W.Va. Coun. Chs., 1977—; bd. govs. Nat. Coun. Chs., 1977—, mem. nominating com., 1979-81, exec. com., 1985-96, membership com., 1988-91, unity and rels., 1989-92, ch. world svc., 1997—; mem. West Va. Ecumenical Coalition on Infant Mortality, 1992-96. Contbr. articles to profl. jours. Bd. dirs. Religious Coalition for Cmty. Renewal in Charleston, 1987-95, Charleston Ch. Recreation Assn., 1998—, Kanawha Home for Children, 1986-89, pres., 1989; long-range planning com. W.Va. State Rep. Exec. Com., 1985-87; adv. bd. Nat. Ctr. for Human Rels., 1997-98; del. 8th Assembly of WCC, Harare, Zimbabwe, 1998. Mem. Acad. Parish Clergy (pres. W.Va. chpt. 1983-85), Am. Nuclear Soc., St. Vladimir's Theol. Found., Charleston Ministerial Assn., Order of St. John of Jerusalem-Knights Hospitellers (chaplain 1985—), Order of St. Ignatius of Antioch, Soc. for Preservation and Encouragement Barbershop Quartet Singing in Am. Inc. (v.p. 1984-85), Pa. State Club W.Va. (pres. 1984-88), Alden Kindred of Am., Sigma Pi Sigma, Delta Sigma Phi. Avocations: camping, barbershop quartet, motorcycling. Home: 4409 Staunton Ave SE Charleston WV 25304-1743 Office: St George Orthodox Ch PO Box 2044 Charleston WV 25327-2044 *My thoughts on life are but mere recitations of the Holy Scripture and my feeble attempts at making Those words and Thoughts my own.*

SCOTT, OTTO, writer; b. N.Y.C., May 26, 1918; s. Otto Felix and Katherine (McGivney) S.; m. Rose Massing (div. 1952); 1 child, Katherine; m. Nellie Mouradian (div. 1963); children: Mary, Philipa; m. Anna Barney Scott, Apr. 29, 1963; 1 child, Ann Elizabeth. MA in Polit. Sci., Valley Christian U., Fresno, Calif., 1985. Mem. staff United Features Syndicate, N.Y.C., 1939-40; v.p. Globaltronix de Venezuela, Caracas, 1954-56, Mohr Assocs., N.Y.C., 1957-59, Becker, Scott & Assocs., N.Y.C., 1960-63; editor Bill Bros., 1964-67; asst. to chmn. Ashland (Ky.) Oil, Inc., 1968, 69; edn. writer, reviewer San Diego Union Tribune, 1970; sr. writer Chalcedon Found., Vallecito, Calif., 1982-94. Cons. Ashland Oil, Inc., 1972—; editor, pub. Otto Scott's Compass, Seattle, 1990—. Author: History Ashland Oil (The Exception) 1968, Robespierre: Voice of Virtue (History French Revolution), 1974, The Professional: Biography of J.B. Saunders, 1976, The Creative Ordeal: History of Raytheon Corporation, 1976, James I: The Fool as King, 1976, 86, Other End of the Lifeboat (History of South Africa), 1985, Buried Treasure: The Story of Arch Mineral, 1987, The Secret Six: The Fool as Martyr, 1987, The Great Christian Revolution, 1991, The Powered Hand, History of Black and Decker, 1994. With U.S. Merchant Marine, 1941-47. Mem. Author's Guild, Overseas Press Club, Com. for Nat. Policy, Com. for Monetary Rsch. and Edn. Presbyterian. Office: Otto Scotts Compass Uncommon Books 175 W High St Somersworth NH 03878-1525

SCOTT, OWEN MYERS, JR. nuclear engineer; b. Birmingham, Ala., Oct. 15, 1952; s. Owen Myers and Sarah (Watson) S.; m. Eleanor Eason, July 15, 1978; 1 child, Owen Myers III. BCE, Auburn U., 1977; MBA, U. Ala., Birmingham, 1981; MS Nuclear Engring., Ga. Inst. Tech., 1986. Registered profl. engr., Ala., Fla., Ga., Miss. Physics lab. instr. Auburn (Ala.) U., 1977; civil/structural design engr. So. Co. Svcs., Inc., Birmingham, 1977-84, nuclear analysis engr., 1984-90; sr. nuclear analysis engr. So. Nuclear Co., 1991—. Pres. So. Investors, Birmingham, 1994—. Co-author (computer program) radiol. shielding analysis, 1986. Instr., advisor Jr. Achievement/Project Bus., Birmingham, 1982. Recipient Tech. award Electric Power Rsch. Inst., 1995. Mem. Am. Nuclear Soc., ASCE, Nat. Mgmt. Assn., Omicron Delta Epsilon. Methodist. Avocations: golf, music, computer programming, clockmaking, woodworking. Home: 3876 Timberline Way Birmingham AL 35243-2452 Office: So Nuclear Co 40 Inverness Center Pkwy PO Box 1295 Birmingham AL 35201-1295

SCOTT, PAMELA MOYERS, physician assistant; b. Clarksburg, W.Va., Jan. 5, 1961; d. James Edward and Norma Lee (Holbert) Moyers; m. Troy Allen Scott, July 19, 1986. BS summa cum laude, Alderson-Broaddus Coll., 1983; M Physician Asst. Studies, U. Nebr., 1999. Cert. physician asst. Physician asst. Weston (W.Va.) State Hosp., 1983-84, Rainelle (W.Va.) Med. Ctr., 1984-2000, Brierwood Med. Ctr., 2000—01; self employed locum tenens Med. lecturing, med. writing, cons., 2001—. Support faculty physician asst. program Coll. W.Va., 1994-99, mem. physician asst. adv. coun. 1993-94, physician asst. program admission selection com., 1994-99; keynote spkr. Alderson-Broaddus Coll. Ann. Physician Assn. Banquet, 1992, 2001, 1st Physician Asst. Convocation Ceremony, 1998; presenter civa. Task Force on Adolescent Pregnancy and Parenting State Meeting, Charleston, 1992, Cannan Valley, 1998, W.Va. Primary Care Assn. Ann. Conf., Beckley, W.Va., 1994, W.Va. State Rural Health Conf., Morgantown, 1992, Chinese Med. Soc., Beijing, 1992; guest Lifetime TV med. program Physician Jour. Update, 1993; adv. coun. W.Va. Rural Health Networking, 1994-95, W.Va. Rural Networking Managed Care Policy Group, 1996, W.Va. Coalition for Managed Care Options, 1997; participant Ann. Cont. Med. Edn. Meeting Ill. Acad. Physician Assts., Chgo., 1999; spkr., presenter in field. Mem. editl. bd. Jour. Am. Acad. Physician Assts., 1995-98, dept. editor Procedures in Family Practice Dept., 1996—; contbr. articles to profl. jours., chpts. to textbook. Mem. W.Va. State Task Force on Adolescent Pregnancy and Parenting, 1992-2000, sec., 1996-98; mem. W.Va. Rural Networking Managed Care Study Group, 1995, W.Va. Rural Networking Managed Care Policy Group, 1996; mem. adv. com. W.Va. State Bur. Pub. Health Family Planning, 1997-2000; mem. Greenbrier County P.A.T.C.H. Spkr.'s Bur., 1996—; mem. Meadow Bridge Cmty. Adv. Group, 1997-2000, Meadow Bridge Domestic Violence Prevention Task Force, 1998-2000. Named Young Career Woman of Yr. Rainelle chpt. and Dist. V of W. Va., Citation of Honor at State Level of Competition, Bus. and Profl. Women's Club, 1986, Nominee for W. Va. Women's Commn. Celebrate Women award, 1996, 97, 98; recipient W.Va. Gov.'s award for Outstanding Rural Health Practitioner, 1997, Alderson Broaddus Coll.'s Alumni Achievement award, 1995, Harry Bennington Meml. award, 2001. Fellow: Fellowship of Christian Physicians Assts., Assn. Family Practice physician Assts. (newsletter editor 2001—), W.Va. Assn. Physician Assts. (chmn. membership com. 1989—91, nominations and elections com. 1990—91, pres. 1991—94, presenter Continued Med. Edn. Conf. 1993, immediate past pres. 1994—95, presenter Continued Med. Edn. Conf. 1996, chair ann. med. Jeopardy tournament 1997—2001, student activities com. 1999—2000, chmn. mentoring program 1999—2000, presenter Continued Med. Edn. Conf. 2000), Am. Acad. Physician Assts. (mem. rural health caucus 1991—98, del. to People's Rep. China 1992, W.Va. chief del. Ho. of Dels. Nat. Conv. 1992, W.Va. del. 1992—98, mem. pub. edn. com. 1992—98, W.Va. chief del. Ho. of Dels. Nat. Conv. 1994, presenter ann. CME conf. San Antonio 1994, presenter ann. CME conf. Las Vegas 1995, W.Va. chief del. Ho. of Dels. Nat. Conv. 1996, chair pub. edn. com. 1996—98, W.Va. chief del. Ho. of Dels. Nat. Conv. 1997, presenter ann. CME conf. Mpls. 1997, W.Va. chief del. Ho. of Dels. Nat. Conv. 1998, bd. advisor elections com. 1998—99, dir.-at-large 1998—2002, bd. on fin. 1998—, alt. del. 1999—2000, chair bd. commn. on external affairs 1999—2001, bd. advisor pub. rels. com. 2000—01, presenter ann. CME conf. Anaheim 2001, chair bd. commn. internal affairs 2001—02, bd. advisor clin. affairs coun. 2001—02, pres.-elect 2002—, bd. on budget 2002—, bd. on appts. chair 2002—, bd. advisor leadership adv. com. 2002—, bd. advisor to constituent rels. com. 2002—, Outstanding Physician Asst. of Yr. 1991). Republican. Baptist. Avocations: reading, handicrafts, shopping. Home and Office: PO Box 43 Williamsburg WV 24991-0043 E-mail: pamscottpa@citlink.net.

SCOTT, PAUL BRUNSON, engineer; b. Flint, Mich., Sept. 8, 1937; s. Walter Wood and Alice Grace (Brunson) S.; m. Janet Lee Absher, Aug. 30, 1968 (div. 1975); 1 child, Cyrena. SB, SM, MIT, 1959, ScD, 1965. Asst. prof. MIT, Cambridge, Mass., 1965-67, U. So. Calif., L.A., 1967=73; prin. scientist Xonics, Inc., Van Nuys, Calif., 1972-79; cons. Touchstone Technology, Northridge, 1979-87, 1990—; pres. MammoCare, U.S.A., Simi Valley, 1987-90. Bd. dirs. Calif. Hydrogen Bus. Coun., 2000. Mem. Am. Solar Energy Soc., AAAS, Nat. Hydrogen Assn. (bd. dirs. 2000-02). Achievements include patents in UF6 Separation, Solar Energy, X-Ray Imaging, Laser Design. Home: 11248 Chimineas Ave Northridge CA 91326-2509

SCOTT, PETER BRYAN, lawyer; b. St. Louis, Nov. 11, 1947; s. gilbert Franklin and Besse Jean (Fudge) S.; children: Lindsay W., Sarah W., Peter B. Jr. AB, Drury Coll., 1969; JD, Washington U., St. Louis, 1972, LLM, 1980. Bar: Mo. 1972, Colo. 1980; diplomate Ct. Practice Inst.; accredited estate planner, advanced wealth specialist planner. Pvt. practice, St. Louis, 1972-80; assoc. McKie and Assocs., Denver, 1980-81; ptnr. Scott and Chesteen, P.C., 1981-84, Veto & Scott, Denver, 1984-92; pvt. practice, 1992—. Tchr. Denver Paralegal Inst., Red Rocks C.C. Mem. Evergreen Christian Ch., Disciples of Christ. Capt. USAR, 1971-79. Mem. ABA, Mo. Bar Assn., Colo. Bar Assn., 1st Jud. Dist. Bar Assn. Republican. Home: 6305 W 6th Ave Unit C18 Lakewood CO 80214-2359 Office: Ste 2-103 777 S Wadsworth Blvd Lakewood CO 80226

SCOTT, PETER DALE, writer, retired English language educator; b. Montreal, Jan. 11, 1929; s. Francis Reginald and Marian Mildred (Dale) S.; m. Mary Elizabeth Marshall, June 16, 1956; children: Catherine Dale, Thomas, John Daniel; m. Ronna Kabatznick, July 14, 1993. BA, McGill U., Montreal, Que., Can., 1949, PhD, 1955; postgrad, Inst. d'Etudes Politiques, Paris, 1950, Univ. Coll., Oxford, Eng., 1950-52. Fgn. service officer Canadian Dept. External Affairs, Ottawa, Ont., 1957-61; asst. prof. speech U. Calif., Berkeley, 1961-66, from asst. prof. to assoc. prof. English, 1966-80, prof., 1980-94; ret., 1994. Author: The War Conspiracy, 1972, Crime and Cover-Up, 1977, Coming to Jakarta, 1988, Listening to the Candle, 1992, Deep Politics and the Death of JFK, 1993, Crossing Borders, 1994, Deep Politics Two, 1995, Drugs, Contras, and the CIA, 2000, Minding the Darkness, 2000; co-author: The Assassinations, 1976, The Iran-Contra Connection, 1987, Cocaine Politics, 1991. Fellow Internat. Ctr. Devel. Policy (Freedom award 1987). Mem. Assn. for Responsible Dissent (bd. dirs. 1988). Avocation: birdwatching. Office: U Calif Dept English Berkeley CA 94720-0001 E-mail: pdscottweb@hotmail.com.

SCOTT, RALPH C. physician, educator; b. Bethel, Ohio, June 7, 1921; s. John Carey and Leona (Laycock) S.; m. Rosemary Ann Schultz, June 26, 1945; children: Susan Ann, Barbara Lynne, Marianne Elizabeth. BS, U. Cin., 1943, MD, 1945. Diplomate: Am. Bd. Internal Medicine (subspecialty cardiovascular disease). InternUniv. Hosps. U. Iowa, 1945-46; resident, asst. dept. pathology Coll. Medicine U. Cin., 1948-49, fellow internal medicine Coll. Medicine, 1949-53, fellow cardiology Coll. Medicine, 1953-57, mem. faculty Coll. Medicine, 1950—, prof. medicine Coll. Medicine, 1968—; staff clinics Cin. Gen. Hosp., 1950-75, clinician in internal medicine, 1952-75, dir. cardiac clinics, 1965-75, attending physician med. service, 1958—. Staff VA Hosp., Cin. 1954-86, 1992—, cons., 1961-86, 92—; attending physician Med. Svc., Christian R. Holmes Hosp., Cin., 1957-86; attending staff USAF Hosp., Wright Patterson AFB, 1960—; staff Good Samaritan Hosp., Cin., 1961—, cons., 1967—; staff Jewish Hosp., Cin., 1957—, cons., 1968—; cons. Children's Hosp., Cin., 1968—; attending physician Providence Hosp., Cin., 1971—, dir. cardiology, 1971-94. Contbr. articles to med. jours.; editorial bd. Am. Heart Jour, 1967-79, Jour. Electrocardiology, 1967—; editor: Electro-Cardiographic-Pathologic Conf., Jour. Electrocardiology, 1967—, Clin. Cardiology and Diabetes, 5 vols, 1981. Capt. AUS, 1946-48. Nat. Heart Inst. grantee, 1964-68, 67-74, 76-82, 1985-90. Fellow ACP, Am. Coll. Cardiology, Am. Coll. Chest Physicians, Coun. Clin. Cardiology, Coun. Clin. Epidemiology and Prevention; mem. Ohio State Med. Assn., Cin. Acad. Medicine, Cen. Soc. Clin. Rsch., Am. Heart Assn., Cin. Soc. Internal Medicine, Heart Assn. Southwestern Ohio, Am. Fedn. for Clin. Rsch., Internat. Cardiovascular Soc., Am. Soc. Preventive Cardiology, Sigma Xi, Alpha Omega Alpha, Phi Eta Sigma, Phi Chi. Home: 2955 Alpine Ter Cincinnati OH 45208-3407 Office: U Cin Med Ctr Divsn Cardiology PO Box 670542 Cincinnati OH 45267-0001

SCOTT, RALPH GORDON, retired engineer, association editor; b. Scranton, Pa., May 28, 1916; s. William Edward and Blanche Mae (Linker) S.; m. Virginia Elaine Wolfe, Sept. 30, 1948 (dec. Aug. 1999); 1 child, Patricia Caroline. Grad., Wilmington (Del.) H.S., 1934. Advt. rep. News Jour. Co., Wilmington, 1935-59, plant engr., 1959-79. Sr. warden, lay reader Episcopal Ch., Del., 1953-88; sec. Civic Assn., New Castle, 1985-95. Master sgt. USAAC, 1941-46, ETO. Mem.: VFW, Air Force Assn., Am. Inst. Plant Engrs. (pres. Wilmington chpt., dir. Ea. divsn. 1959—82, svc. life mem., cert.), Bad 2 Assn. (sec. 1989—, newsletter editor 1980—), Am. Legion. Republican. Anglican Catholic. Avocation: portrait painting. E-mail: ScottyRose@juno.com.

SCOTT, RALPH MASON, physician, radiation oncology educator; b. Leemont, Va., Nov. 23, 1921; s. Benjamin Thomas and Marion Hazel (Mason) S.; m. Alice Latine Francisco, Dec. 21, 1946; children: Susan Taylor, Ralph Mason, John Thomas. BA, U. Va., 1947; MD, Med. Coll. Va., 1950. Diplomate Am. Bd. Radiology (trustee 1965-76, treas. 1969-70, v.p. 1970-72, pres. 1972-74). Intern Robert Packer Hosp., Sayre, Pa., 1953-54, resident, 1954-57, dir. radiation therapy and nuclear medicine sect., 1957-59; with Christie Hosp. and Holt Radium Inst., Manchester, England, 1956-57; asst. prof. radiology U. Chgo. Med. Sch., 1959-60; assoc. prof. radiology, dir. radiation therapy and radioisotopes U. Louisville Med. Sch., 1960-64, prof., dir. radiation therapy, 1964-77; prof. and chmn. dept. rad. and oncology U Louisville, 1974-77; prof. radiation therapy U. Louisville Med. Sch., 1981-82; prof. emeritus U. Louisville, 1995; dir. J. Graham Brown Regional Cancer Ctr., Health Scis. Ctr. U. Louisville Med. Sch., 1981-82; dir. dept. radiation medicine Christ Hosp., Cin., 1982-93; ret. Clin. prof. radiology U. Cin. Coll. Medicine, 1982-93; prof., chmn. dept. therapeutic radiology U. Md. Sch. Med., 1977-80; dir. radiation therapy program div. cancer rsch. resources and ctrs., Nat. Cancer Inst. (on leave from U. Louisville), 1976-77. Pres. Ky. divsn. Am. Cancer Soc., 1972-73; bd. dirs. Living Arrangements for the Developmentally Disabled, 1993-95, No. Ky. Assn. for the Retarded, 1993-95, Day Spring Inc., 1993-95, United Health Care, 1994-95, Seven Counties Svcs., Inc., 1997—, J. Graham Brown Regional Cancer Ctr. Corp., 1997—. Lt. (j.g.) USNR, 1943-45. Fellow Christie Hosp. and Holt Radium Inst., Manchester, Eng., 1956-57. Mem. Am. Roentgen-Ray Soc. (exec. coun. 1968—, chmn. exec. coun. 1972-73), AMA, Am. Coll. Radiology (vice chmn. commn. on cancer 1968-69), Am. Radium Soc., Am. Soc. Therapeutic Radiologists, Assn. U. Radiologists, Radiol. Soc. N.Am., Pi Kappa Alpha, Phi Chi. Home: 5516 Tecumseh Cir Louisville KY 40207-1692

SCOTT, RAYMOND PETER WILLIAM, chemistry research educator, writer; b. Erith, Eng., June 20, 1924; came to U.S., 1969; s. Ronald and Annie (Hoadley) S.; m. Barbara Winifred Doreen Strange, Apr. 20, 1946; children: Kerry Raymond, Kevin Francis. B.Sc., U. London, 1946, D.Sc., 1958. Lab. leader Burroughs Welcome, Dartford, Eng., 1946-48; chief chemist APCM, 1948-52; research mgr. Benzole Producers, Watford, Eng., 1952-60; divisional mgr. Unilever, Sharnbrook and Bedfordshire, Eng., 1960-69; dir. phys. chemistry Hoffamn La Roche, Nutley, N.J., 1969-80; dir. applied rsch. Perkin-Elmer, Norwalk, Conn., 1980-86; sometime rsch. prof. dept. chemistry Georgetown U., Washington, 1986-2000; writer, cons., 2001—. Rsch. prof. dept. chemistry Birkbeck Coll., London. Author: Liquid Chromatography Detectors, 1977, 3d edit., 1987, Contemporary Liquid Chromatography, 1976, Liquid Chromatography Column Theory, 1991, Silica Gel and Bonded Phases, 1993, Liquid Chromatography for the Analyst, 1994, Chromatography Techniques, 1995, Chromatography Detectors, 1996, Tandem Techniques, 1996, Introduction to Analytical Gas Chromatography, 1997, Chiral Chromatography, 1998, Quantitative Chromatographer Analysis, 2000, Chromatography Theory, 2002; editor: Gas Chromatography, 1960, Small Bore Columns in Liquid Chromatography, 1983. Recipient Tswett medal Am. Internat. Symposia on Chromatography, 1978; recipient Tswett award USSR Tech. Inst. Moscow, 1978, Martin medal in chromatography Chromatography Group Gt. Britain, 1982 Fellow Royal Soc. Chemistry (chartered, Analysis and Instrumentation award 1988), Am. Inst. Chemists (cert.), Am. Chem. Soc. (Chromatography award 1977). Home: Great Sanders House Hurst Ln London TN33 0PE England Office: Sci Dirs Ltd 7 Beaumont Business Ctr Banbury OX16 7TN England

SCOTT, REGINA See LUNDGREN, REGINA ELLEN

SCOTT, RICHARD ELTON, health facility administrator; b. St. Louis, Oct. 3, 1939; s. Earl Ray and Celeste (Roark) Scott; m. Carol Jenkins, Sept. 3, 1960; children: Suzanne Scott Abbe, Richard E. Jr. BA, Baylor U., 1971; MS, Trinity U., 1978. Various positions Hillcrest Bapt. Med. Ctr., Waco, Tex., 1961-78, asst. adminstr., 1973-78, v.p., 1978-90, exec. v.p., 1990-92, pres., CEO, 1992—; adminstrv. resident Scott & White Clinic, Temple, 1973-78. Chmn. VHA S.W., Inc., Dallas, 1997—98; ores. Bapt. Hosp. Assn., 1999—; co-founder, bd. dirs. Cmty. Health Action Ptnrs.; bd. dirs. Waco Family Practice Found. Pres. exec. com., bd. Dr. Pepper Mus., Waco, 1996; chmn. Waco Bus. League, 1989; chmn. bd. United Way, Waco, 1989, Greater Waco C. of C., 1991; chmn. bd. trustees First Bapt. Ch., Waco, 2000. Named Leonard A. Duce award, Trinity U. Healthcare Alumni Assn., San Antonio, 1997, Vol. or Yr., United Way, Waco, 1991. Mem.: Vol. Hosps. Am. Southwest, Tex. Hosp. Assn., Rotary. Office: Hillcrest Health Sys 3000 Herring Ave Waco TX 76708-3239 Fax: 254-202-9420.

SCOTT, RICHARD THOMAS THOMAS, JR. reproductive endocrinologist; b. Selma, Ala., Nov. 28, 1958; s. Richard Thomas and Cynthia Marvin (Coleman) S.; m. Blair MacKerer, June 16, 1979; children: Whitney Blair, Katherine Leigh, Richard Thomas III. BS in Chemistry, Randolph Macon Coll., 1979; MD, U. Va., Charlottesville, 1983. Diplomate Nat. Bd. Med. Examiners, Am. Bd. Ob-Gyn., reproductive endocrinology divsn; bd. cert. high complexity lab dir. embryology, andrology, endocrinology, Am. Bd. Bioanalysts. Commd. 2nd lt. USAF, 1979, advanced through grades to lt. col., 1993; intern Wilford Hall USAF Med. Ctr., San Antonio, 1983-84, resident, 1984-87, chief reproductive endocrinology Lackland AFB, Tex., 1989-93; fellow Jones Inst. for Reproductive Medicine, Ea. Va. Med. Sch., Norfolk, 1987-89; chief reproductive endocrinology Uniformed Svcs. U. Health Scis., Bethesda, Md., 1993—, asst. prof., 1990—, assoc. prof., 1993—. Adj. scientist S.W. Found. Biomed. Rsch., 1990—, dir. Assisted Reproductive Technology, Reproductive Medicine Assocs. of N.J., Morristown, N.J. Ad hoc reviewer Fertility and Sterility, Jour. Clin. Endocrinology and Metabolism, Ob-Gyn., Am. Jour. Ob-Gyn., Contraception, Maturitas, Jour. Pediatric and Adolescent Gynecology, Internat. Jour. Infertility, Jour. In Vitro Fertilization and Embryo Transfer; contbr. articles to profl. jours. Lt Col USAF, 1993—95, Uniformed Services University of the Health Sciences. Grantee Surgeon Gen., Wyeth

Rsch., Solvay Pharm. Rsch., Hitachi of Am., Tap Pharms. Fellow Am. Coll. Obstetricians and Gynecologists (chmns. award Armed Forces dist. meeting 1988, Searle award 1989, Prof. of Yr. 1991); mem. Am. Fertility Soc. (Best Poster award 1988), N.Am. Menopausal Soc., Soc. Air Force Clin. Surgeons, Endocrine Soc., Soc. Reproductive Endocrinologists, Phi Beta Kappa, Chi Beta Phi, Omicron Delta Kappa. Office: RMA of NJ 111 Madison Ave Ste 100 Morristown NJ 07960-6083

SCOTT, ROBERT ALLYN, academic administrator; b. Englewood, N.J., Apr. 16, 1939; s. William D. and Ann F. (Waterman) S.; children: Ryan Keith, Kira Elizabeth. BA, Bucknell U., 1961; PhD, Cornell U., 1975; LLD, Ramapo Coll., 2000. Mgmt. trainee Procter & Gamble Co., Phila., 1961-63; asst. dir. admissions Bucknell U., Lewisburg, Pa., 1965-67; asst. dean Coll. Arts and Scis. Cornell U., Ithaca, 1967-69, assoc. dean, 1969-79, anthropology faculty, 1978-79; dir. acad. affairs Ind. Commn. for Higher Edn., Indpls., 1979-84, asst. commr., 1984-85; pres. Ramapo (N.J.) Coll., 1985-2000, Adelphi U., 2000—. Cons. Sta. WSKG Pub. TV and Radio, 1977-79, also to various colls. and univs., pubs., 1966—; mem. curriculum adv. com. Ind. Bd. Edn., 1984-87, Lilly Endowment Think Tank, 1984-86; mem. nat. adv. panel Ind. 21st Century Schooling Project, 1990-92; U.S. rep. to creation of U. Mobility Asian-Pacific, 1993—; U.S. rep. to meetings of Coun. European Rectors, 1991—; sr. advisor to U.S. State Dept. on Higher Edn. in Unesco European Region, 1997—; U.S. del. to UNESCO N.Am. and World Confs. on Higher Edn., 1998; sr. cons., chair N.J. Higher Edn. Restructuring Team, 1994; bd. dirs. iRV. Author books and monographs; editorial bd. Cornell Rev., 1976-79; book rev. editor Coll. and Univ., 1974-78; cons. editor Change mag., 1979—; cons. editor Jour. Higher Edn., 1985—; exec. editor Saturday Evening Post book div. Curtis Pub. Co., 1982-85; contbr. articles to sociols., ednl. and popular publs. Trustee Bucknell U., 1976-78, First Unitarian Ch., Ithaca, 1970-73, 78-79, chmn., 1971-73, Unitarian Universalist Ch. of Indpls., 1980-85. With USNR, 1963-65. Spencer Found. rsch. grantee, 1977; recipient Sagamore of the Wabash award, 1986, Prudential Found. Leader of Yr. award, 1987, Disting. Svc. award West Bergen Mental Health Ctr., 1991, NYU Presdl. medal, 1994, Sci. and Edn. award Boy Scouts Am., 1993, Raoul Wallenberg Humanitarian Leadership award, 2000. Fellow Am. Anthrop. Assn.; mem. Am. Sociol. Assn., Am. Assn. Higher Edn., Coun. on Liberal Arts and Scis. (chair 1990-93), Am. Coun. on Edn. Commn. On Internat. Edn. (chair 1991-93), LI Assn., Global Kids, Inc., Higher Edn. Colloquium (chmn. 1982-84, 96-98), N.J. Assn. of Coll. and Univs. (chair 1991-92), Bucknell U. Alumni Assn. (bd. dirs. 1971-80, pres. 1976-78, Outstanding Achievement 1991), Indian Trail Club, Century Assn., Phi Kappa Psi, Phi Kappa Phi. Office: Adelphi U Garden City NY 11530

SCOTT, ROBERT CORTEZ, congressman, lawyer; b. Washington, Apr. 30, 1947; s. Charles Waldo and Mae (Hamlin) S. BA, Harvard U., 1969; JD, Boston U., 1973; LLD (hon.), Commonwealth Coll., Hampton, Va., 1988. Pvt. practice, Newport News, 1973—91; del. Va. Ho. Dels., Richmond, 1978—83, senator, 1983—93; mem. U.S. Congress from 3rd Va. dist., Washington, 1993—; mem. edn. and workforce com., judiciary com. Br. pres. NAACP, Newport News, 1974-80; pres. bd. Peninsula Legal Aid Ctr., Hampton, 1977-81; mem. state exec. bd. March of Dimes, Va., 1987—; chmn. 1st dist. Dem. Party Va., 1980-85; bd. dirs. Hampton Roads March of Dimes; adv. com. Peninsula Boy Scouts Am. Recipient Brotherhood Citation award Nat. Conf. Christians & Jews, 1985, Child Adv. award Va. Acad. Pediatrics, 1987, Disting. Svc. award Va. State Fraternal Order Police, 1987, Outstanding Legislator award So. Health Assn., 1989. Mem. Peninsula C. of C., Alpha Phi Alpha, Sigma Pi Phi. Democrat. Office: US House of Reps 2464 Rayburn Ho Office Bldg Washington DC 20515-4603*

SCOTT, ROBERT ELLIS See ROBERTS, MARK

SCOTT, ROBERT GENE, lawyer; b. Montague, Mass., Aug. 29, 1951; s. Edwin Ray and Barbara Agnes (Painchaud) S.; m. Laura Beth Williams, May 27, 1978; children: Jason Robert, Amanda Marie, Leah Beth. BS, U. Notre Dame, 1973, MS, 1975; postgrad., U. Tex., 1975-76; JD, U. Notre Dame, 1980. Bar: Ind. 1980, U.S. Dist. Ct. (no. dist.) Ind. 1980, U.S. Patent Office 1980, Mo. 1981, U.S. Dist. Ct. (we. dist.) Mo. 1981, U.S. Ct. Appeals (11th cir.) 1986, U.S. Ct. Appeals (8th cir.) 1987, U.S. Ct. Appeals (10th cir.) 1987, Kans. 1989, U.S. Dist. Ct. Kans. 1989, U.S. Supreme Ct. 1999. Asst. women's basketball coach U. Notre Dame, Ind., 1977-80; assoc. atty. Oltsch, Knoblock & Hall, South Bend, 1980-81; atty. Swanson, Midgley et al, Kansas City, Mo., 1981-82; exec. adminstr. Coun. of Fleet Specialists, Shawnee Mission, Kans., 1982-83; atty. Levy and Craig, Kansas City, Mo., 1983-89, Turner, Vader & Koch, Chartered, 1989-93; pvt. practice, 1993-95, 98; atty. Neill, Scott, Terrill & Embree, LLC, Lenexa, Kans., 1996-98; pvt. practice, 1998—. Mem. Equilaw panel arbitrators Panel Arbitrators, U.S. Dist. Ct. (we. dist.) Mo. Precinct committeeman Johnson County Rep. Party, Kans., 1983-84. Mem. ABA, Ind. Bar Assn., Mo. Bar Assn., Kansas City Bar Assn., Kansas City Lawyers Assn., Kans. Bar Assn., Wyandotte County Bar Assn., Johnson County Bar Assn., Am. Arbitration Assn. (mem. panel of arbitrators, constrn. arbitrator adv. bd.), Nat. Assn. Security Dealers (panel arbitrators, complex litigation panel), Nat. Arbitration Forum (panel of arbitrators), Notre Dame Club of Kansas City (pres. 1985-86), S.W. United Soccer Club of Kans. (pres. 1994-96), Heartland Soccer Assn. (v.p. 1997—). Republican. Roman Catholic. Office: 303 E Poplar Olathe KS 66061 E-mail: bob@rscottlaw.com.

SCOTT, ROBERT HAYWOOD, JR. lawyer; b. Hazelton, Pa., Mar. 27, 1941; s. Robert Haywood and Marjorie Jane (Briggs) S.; m. Sandra Lou Carroll, June 6, 1966; children: Paige Carroll, Robert Haywood. AB magna cum laude, Kenyon Coll., 1963; JD with distinction, Duke U., 1966. Bar: Mo. 1969, Kans. 1966, Ohio 1972. Assoc. Hoskins King Springer McGannon and Hahn, Kansas City, Mo., 1970-72; operating v.p., sr. counsel Federated Dept. Stores, Cin., 1972-83; ptnr. Roberts Fleischaker & Scott, Joplin, Mo., 1983-88; chief exec. officer W&S Mfg., Inc., 1988-92, also chmn. bd. dirs.; CEO Robert Scott Investment Banking, 1988—. Chmn. Deep Sea Archaeology Rsch. Coun., 1994—. Contbr. articles to profl. jours. Served to capt. USAF, 1966-70. Mem. Mo. Bar Assn., Order of the Coif, Phi Beta Kappa. Republican. Episcopalian. Home: 1330 Valle Dr Joplin MO 64801-1074

SCOTT, ROBERT LANE, chemist, educator; b. Santa Rosa, Calif., Mar. 20, 1922; s. Horace Albert and Maurine (Lane) S.; m. Elizabeth Sewall Hunter, May 27, 1944; children: Joanna Ingersoll, Jonathan Armat, David St. Clair, Janet Hamilton. S.B., Harvard U., 1942; MA, Princeton U., 1944, PhD, 1945. Sci. staff Los Alamos Lab., 1945-46; Frank B. Jewett fellow U. Calif., Berkeley, 1946-48; faculty UCLA, 1948—, prof. chemistry, 1960-92, prof. emeritus, 1993—, chmn. dept., 1970-75. Author: (with J.H. Hildebrand) Solubility of Nonelectrolytes, 3d edit, 1950, rev., 1964, Regular Solutions, 1962, Regular and Related Solutions, 1970; Contbr. articles to profl. jours. Guggenheim fellow, 1955; NSF sr. fellow, 1961-62; Fulbright lectr., 1968-69 Fellow AAAS, Am. Phys. Soc.; mem. Am. Chem. Soc. (Joel Henry Hildebrand award 1984), Royal Soc. Chemistry (London), Sigma Xi. Home: 11128 Montana Ave Los Angeles CA 90049-3509 E-mail: scott@chem.ucla.edu.

SCOTT, ROBERT LEE, speech educator; b. Fairbury, Nebr., Apr. 19, 1928; s. Walter Everett and Ann Maria (Jensen) S.; m. Betty Rose Foust, Sept. 13, 1947; children— Mark Allen, Janet Lee, Paul Matthew. BA, U. No. Colo., 1950; MA, U. Nebr., 1951; PhD, U. Ill., 1955. Asst. prof. speech U. Houston, 1953-57; asst. prof. U. Minn., 1957-59, assoc. prof., 1959-63, prof., 1963-2000, prof. emeritus, 2000—, chair dept. speech communication, 1971-89, chair dept. Spanish and Portuguese, 1992-94, dir. Sch. Journalism and Mass Comm., 1995-97. Author: Rhetoric of Black Power, 1969, Moments in the Rhetoric of the Cold War, 1970; contbr. articles to profl. jours. Recipient Teaching award Coll. of Liberal Arts, U. Minn., 1981. Mem. Nat. Comm. Assn. (editor Quar. Jour. Speech 1971-74, Winans-Wichelns Rsch. award 1970, Charles H. Woolbert Rsch. award, 1981, Douglas-Ehninger Disting. Scholar award 1989, Disting. Scholar of Assn. 1992), Ctrl. States Speech Assn., Internat. Soc. for Study of Rhetoric. Office: U Minn Dept Comm Studies Minneapolis MN 55455-0194 E-mail: scott033@umn.edu.

SCOTT, ROBERT MONTGOMERY, museum executive, lawyer; b. Bryn Mawr, Pa., May 22, 1929; s. Edgar and Helen Hope (Montgomery) S.; m. H. Gay Elliot, June 30, 1951 (div. 1997); children: Hope Tyler Scott Rogers, Janny Scott Ritter, Elliot Montgomery. AB, Harvard U., 1951; LLB, U. Pa., 1954; DHL (hon.), Thomas Jefferson U., 1996. Ptnr. Montgomery McCracken Walker & Rhoads, Phila., 1961-82, of counsel, 1982-88; spl. asst. to U.S. Amb. to Ct. of St. James, London, 1969-73; hon. Brit. consul Phila., 1979-83; pres., chief exec. officer Phila. Mus. Art, 1982-96, hon. chmn., 1997—. Pres. Acad. Music of Phila., 1973-80; mem. adv. bd. First Union Bank Atlantic. Trustee Phila. Mus. Art, 1965—, Royal Oak Found., 1978-86, Inst. Cancer Rsch., Fox Chase Cancer Ctr., 1960-86, Lankenau Hosp., 1959-86, U. Pa., 1975-80, William Penn Found., 1986-91; pres. Mary Louise Curtis Book Fedn., 1989—, Curtis Inst. of Music, 1994—; bd. dirs. Glyndebourne Assn. Am., Inc. Recipient Superior Honor award Dept. State, 1973, Gov. of Pa. award for Leadership in the Arts, 1996, Citizen of Yr. awad Penjerdel Coun., 1996, Hospitality City U.S.A. Grand award Greater Phila. Hotel Assn., 1996. Fellow Am. Bar Found.; mem. Am. Assn. Mus., Greater Phila. Cultural Alliance, Phila. Club (pres. 1997—), Knickerbocker Club, White's Club. Republican. Home: Ardrossan 807 Newtown Rd Villanova PA 19085-1031

SCOTT, ROBERT WILLIAM, mediator, lawyer, educator, consultant; b. Washington, June 29, 1952; s. Robert Vernon and Louise Wentz S.; m. Deborah Lynn French, June 4, 1977; children: Zachary D., Travis M. BS, Drexel U., 1974; JD, U. Balt., 1980; MS in Conflict Mgmt., George Mason U., 1990. Bar: Va. 1980, D.C. 1981, U.S. Dist. Ct. (ea. dist.) Va. 1982, U.S. Ct. Appeals (4th cir.) 1982; cert. gen. and family mediator. Analyst Planning Rsch. Corp. U.S. Dept. Justice, Washington, 1980-82, analyst Koba Assocs., Inc., 1982-85; pvt. practice Springfield, Va., 1985-93; mediator No. Va. Mediation Svc., Fairfax, 1990—, mediation coord., 1993-94; exec. dir. No. Va. Mediation Svc. Inst. Conflict Analysis and Resolution Svc., George Mason U., 1994—. Panelist U.S. Dept. Justice Americans with Disabilities Act, A Mediation Program, 1998; fair housing conciliation panelist Va. Fair Housing Office, 1995; task force appointment Fairfax County Legal Assistance Task Force, 1995-97, Va. Commonwealth U., 1997-98; chair employee adv. com. Drug Enforcement Adminstrn./NADDIS contract employees, Washington, 1981-85; mediator evaluator Mediator Cert. Program Md. Com. on Dispute Resolution, 1996; marriage celebrant Fairfax County Cir. Ct., 1992-94. Mem. crisis intervention Alexandria (Va.) Hotline, 1989-91; bd.dirs. Newington Forest Cmty. Assn., Springfield, 1989-90. Named to Leadership Fairfax Class of 1999, 1998. Mem. D.C. Bar Assn., Va. State Bar (apptd. mem. pub. rels. subcom. Va. State Bar/Va. Bar Assn. joint com. alt. dispute resolution 1997, apptd. mem. cmty. mediation subcom. Va. State Bar/Va. Bar Assn. joint com. alt. dispute resolution 1998), Assn. for Conflict Resolution. Office: No Va Mediation Svc Inst Conflict Analysis Resolution George Mason U 4D3 4260 Chain Bridge Rd Ste A2 Fairfax VA 22030-4297

SCOTT, RONALD, lawyer; b. Lexington, Mich., Aug. 31, 1947; BA, Baylor U., 1969; JD, U. Tex., 1975. Bar: Tex. 1975. Mem. Bracewell & Patterson, Houston. Mem. State Bar Tex., Tex. Bar Found., Houston Bar Found., Houston Bar Assn., Order of Barristers, Phi Delta Phi. Office: Bracewell & Patterson South Tower Pennzoil Pl 711 Louisiana St Ste 2900 Houston TX 77002-2781 E-mail: RScott@Bracepatt.com.

SCOTT, RUTH LOIS, dental hygiene educator; b. Chanute, Kans., Aug. 28, 1934; d. Walter Roy and Ruth Lois (Cunningham) Harder; m. Charles Calvin Scott, July 3, 1956 (div. July 1963); children: Valerie Elizabeth, Matthew Stuart, David Bruce. BA in Psychology and Theatre with honors, U. Kans., 1958; Cert. in Dental Hygiene, U. Mo.-Kansas City, 1954, MS in Dental Hygiene Edn., 1972. Asst. prof. U. Iowa Coll. Dentistry, 1972—73, instr. to clin. instr. dept. dental hygiene, 1969—71, asst. prof. dept. preventive dentistry, asst. prof. comprehensive dentistry for adults, 1973—77, asst. prof. div. dental hygiene, 1977—81, assoc. prof., 1981—97; prof. emerita U. Mo.-Kansas City Sch. Dentistry, 1998—; pvt. practice dentistry Kans., Mo., 1954—. Small animal vet. cons., 1998—. Contbr. articles to profl. jours. Charter mem. Kansas City chpt. Parents Without Ptnrs. Recipient Dental Hygiene Alumni Svc. award U. Mo.-Kansas City, 1992; named Student Coun. Instr. of Yr., 1992. Mem. Am. Dental Hygienists Assn., Mo. Dental Hygienists Assn., Greater Kansas City Dental Hygiene Component Soc., U. Mo.-Kansas City Dental Hygiene Alumni Assn., U. Mo.-Kansas City Alumni Assn., Kansas U. Alumni Assn., Center State Tai Chi ChuanPhi Beta Kappa, Sigma Phi Alpha (exec. sec. 1990-96), Phi Psi, Phi Kappa Phi. Unitarian-Universalist. E-mail: scott_lois@hotmail.com.

SCOTT, SAMUEL JOSEPH, art educator, artist; b. Seattle, July 22, 1952; s. William Francis Scott, Mary Ann Scott; m. B. Dianne Swain; children: Jeremiah, Hannah, Jacob. A, Shoreline CC, 1972; BFA, U. Wash., 1975. Assoc. prof. art Everett (Wash.) CC, 1975—98, Shoreline CC, Seattle, 1999—. Assoc. prof. art U. Wash., Seattle, 1977; workshop presenter various colls. and univs., 1978—2001. Reviewer, exhibitions include 10-40 Invitational Show, Bellevue Art Mus., 1986, one-man shows include Edmonds Arts Festival Mus., 1987, reviewer, exhibitions include Teapot Invitational, Janet Huston Gallery, Wash.., 1990, The Hekinan Collection, Japan, 1991; juror Arts of the Terrace, Mountlake Terrace, Wash., 1992;exhibitions include Northwest Artists Show, Smithsonian Inst., 1993; juror Edmonds At Festival, Wash., 1996, 2001; contbr. articles. Recipient Purchase award, Edmonds (Wash.) Arts Festival, 1977, 1st. pl. in 3D art, Arts of Terrace, Mountlake, Wash., 1996, 1st pl. in craftswork, Shoreline Arts Festival, Shoreline, Wash.; scholar Alumni Meml. scholar, U. Wash., 1974—75. Mem.: Wash. Potters Assn. (member 1989—2002), Northwest Designer Craftsmen (member 1982—2002), Phi Beta Kappa (member 1975—2002). Roman Catholic. Avocations: Am. art pottery, Am. and European paintings, Northwest crafts. Office: Shoreline Cmty Coll 16101 Greenwood Ave N Seattle WA 98133 Personal E-mail: cheerspots@yahoo.com.

SCOTT, SANDRA LYNN (SANDY SCOTT), artist, sculptor, printmaker; b. Dubuque, Iowa, July 24, 1943; d. Jim and Dolly (Dillon) S. Student, Kansas City (Kans.) Art Inst., 1962-63. Animation background artist Calvin Motion Pictures, 1963-65; freelance portrait artist, illustrator Kona Coast, Hawaii, 1969, San Francisco, 1969; instr. Scottsdale Artists Sch., Ariz., 1987, Loveland Acad. Fine Art, 1992, The Fechin Inst., Taos, N.Mex., 1995. One woman shows include: Nat. Cowboy Hall Fame, 1978, Pen & Brush, N.Y., 1988; group shows include: Cheyenne Frontier Days Governor's Invitational Western Art Show, 1992, 93, 94, 95, Loveland Rotary's Colo. Invitational Art Show, 1992, 93, 94, 95, Nat. Wildlife Mus. Art Show, 1992, 93, 94, 95, Nat. Acad. Western Art, 1993, 94, Am. Women Artist Art Show, 1993, The West Show Tucson Mus. Art, 1993, Artist of Am. Denver Rotary Show, 1993, 94, 95, Nat. Cowboy Hall Fame, 1995, Western Art Exhibit, China; private collections include: Nat. Cowboy Hall Fame, Trammell Crow Corp., Mus. Arts and Crafts, Opryland Hotel, Miramichi Salmon Mus., Sebastiani Vineyards Collection, El Pasco Zoo, Vickers Oil Corp., Mustang Oil Corp., Ritz Carlton Hotel, Hillsdale Coll., Nat. Wildlife Mus., City Fort Collins, Brookgreen Gardens. Recipient Ann Huntington Sculpture award Catherine Lorillard Wolfe Art Club, 1982, Merit Sculpture award Northwest Rendezvous Group, 1987, 88, Hubbard Art Excellence award, 1991, Sculpture award Am. Profl. Artists League, 1991; recipient Sculpture prize Allied Artists, 1983, Catherine Lorillard Wolfe Art Club, 1983, Salmagundi Club, 1983, Am. Artists Profl. League, 1982, 83, Pen and Brush, 1984, Knickerbocker Artists, 1984, Ellen P. Speyer prize Nat. Acad. Design, 1988; recipient Gold medal for Sculpture Nat. Acad. Western Art, 1992.. Mem. Soc. Animal Artists, Am. Artist Profl. League, Pen & Brush, Northwest Rendezvous Group, Catherine Lorillard Wolfe Art Club. Home: 200 Gregory Rd Fort Collins CO 80524-1502

SCOTT, SHELLY SILVAN, nutrition therapist, consultant; b. Chgo., Dec. 26, 1965; d. Albert Rudy and Doris (Keiffer) Silvan; m. Anthony Ernest Scott, Dec. 1, 1991; children: Anthony Ernest Scott II, Boston Nealand, Alana Brigette. BS in Dietetics, La. State U., 1990. Registered dietitian Com. on Dietetics Registration, Chgo., 1991, lic. nutritionist La. Bd. Cert. Nutritionist, Baton Rouge, 1991, cert. diabetes educator Am. Assn. Diabetes Educators, 1999. Nutrition coord. Earl K. Long Med. Ctr., Baton Rouge, 1991-92, registered dietitian specialist, 1992-96; clin. dietitian Lane Meml. Hosp., Zachary, La., 1996-98; clin. dietitian cons. Greenwell Springs (La.) Hosp., 1998—. Cons. long term care and home health Profl. Nutrition and Consulting Svcs., La., 1992—; seed initiative cons., 2001—; cons. dietitian Baton Rouge HTN and Kidney Ctr., 2001—; cons. Matria Diabetes Ctr., 2000—; staff Speakers Bur. Roche Pharmaceutical, 2002—. Mem.: Baton Rouge Dietetic Assn., Am. Diabetic Assn. Edn., Am. Dietetic Assn. Avocation: Avocations: aerobics, race walking, reading, self improvement. Office: Profl Nutrition & Cons Svcs PO Box 661 Baton Rouge LA 70821-0661 E-mail: shelly_scott@hotmail.com.

SCOTT, SIDNEY BUFORD, financial services company executive; b. Richmond, Va., Mar. 3, 1933; s. Buford and Mary (Nixon) S.; m. Susan Elder Bailey, Sept. l9, 1959; children: Sidney Buford Jr., Elizabeth Scott Cech, George Reily Bailey. Student, Yale U., 1951-53; BA, U. Va., l955; LLD (hon.), St. Paul's Coll., 1982. Chmn. Scott & Stringfellow Inc., Richmond, 1974—. Bd. dirs. Ethyl Corp.; mem. regional firms adv. com. N.Y. Stock Exch., 1982-85; chmn. bd. trustees Securities Industry Found. for Econ. Edn., 1976-86; trustee Va. Retirement Sys., 1984-94; dir. Nat. Coun. Econ. Edn. Bd. dirs. Atlantic Rural Expn., Hollywood Cemetery, Police Benevolent Assn., Richmond Renaissance, Va.; trustee, chmn. Elk Hill Farm, Inc.; bd. visitors U. Va., 1987-94; former vice rector, bd. visitors Va. Commonwealth U.; past chmn. United Way Greater Richmond; vestryman, past sr. warden St. Paul's Episcopal Ch.; bd. dirs., past pres. Sheltering Arms Hosp; past bd. dirs., v.p. Big Bros. Am.; past bd. dirs., chmn. Big Bros. Richmond, Met. Found., also others. Sgt. U.S. Army, 1956-58. Recipient Outstanding Young Man of Yr. award Richmond Jr. C. of C., 1964, outstanding svc. award Va. Coun. on Econ. Edn., 1976, 80, Brotherhood award NCCJ, l981, George P. Baker medal Joint Coun. on Econ. Edn., 1986, Bd. Mem. of Yr. award Va. Assn. Children's Homes, 1987. Mem. Securities Industry Assn. (governing coun. 1976-78), Raven Soc., Beta Gamma Sigma. Democrat. Home: 4919 Lockgreen Cir Richmond VA 23226-1748 Office: PO Box 1575 Richmond VA 23218-1575

SCOTT, STANLEY DEFOREST, real estate executive, former lithography company executive; b. Hudson County, N.J., Nov. 2, 1926; s. Stanley DeForest and Anne Marie (Volk) S.; m. Mary Elizabeth Hazard, Dec. 30, 1953. BA, U. So. Calif., 1950. Gen. mgr. Alfred Scott Pubs., N.Y.C., 1951-56; chmn., pres. S.D. Scott Printing Co., Inc., 1956-92; gen. ptnr. 145 Hudson St. Assocs.; co-chmn. mus. and art com. Fraunces Tavern Mus., 1973-87, chmn., 1998-99. Assoc. J. Carter Brown Libr.; former mem. Mayor's Industry Adv. Com.; former bd. dirs., Bus. Relocation Com. With USNR, 1944-46. Frick Collection fellow. Mem. Soc. Mayflower Descs., Soc. Colonial Wars, Pilgrims U.S., S.R. (bd. mgrs. 1969—, treas. 1972-73, 3d v.p. 1975-77, 2d v.p. 1977-79, 92-94, 96-98, 2000-02), Am. Numismatic Soc., English-Speaking Union U.S. (patron), Royal Oak Found., Am. Assocs. Royal Acad. Arts (patron), Am. Friends English Heritage, St. George's Soc., Am. Friends of the Brit. Mus. (patron), Sir John Soane's Mus. Found. (patron), Am. Friends of Hermitage Mus., Met. Mus. Art, Mus. Modern Art, Morgan Libr., Am. Mus. in Brit. (coun. 1986—), N.Y. Hist. Soc., Mt. Vernon Ladies Assn. (adv. com), Grolier Club, Knickerbocker Club, Union Club, The Church Club of N.Y., Merchants Club (v.p. 1985-94). Republican. Episcopalian. Home: One Sutton Pl South New York NY 10022-2471 Office: 145 Hudson St New York NY 10013-2103 E-mail: ScttHUDSON@aol.com.

SCOTT, STEPHEN BRINSLEY, theater producer; b. Pitts., Aug. 27, 1950; s. Robert Crawford and Lucille (Hendrickson) S. BS in Edn., U. Kans., 1972; MA, U. Denver, 1973. Artistic dir. Creede (Colo.) Repertory Theatre, 1976-78; chair dept. theatre Baker U., Baldwin, Kans., 1978-80; dir. edn. and cmty. svcs. Goodman Theatre, Chgo., 1980-84, dir. arts in edn., 1986-88, artistic assoc., 1988-94, assoc. producer, 1994—; dir. ednl. programs Chgo. Internat. Theatre Festival, 1985-86. Spl. instr. Loyola U. Chgo., 1987-95; instr. Columbia Coll., Chgo., 1981-85, 92-97, Latin Sch. Chgo., 1984-86, Roosevelt U., 1997—; mem. arts in edn. panel Nat. Endowment for Arts, Washington, 1990-91. Mem. adv. panels Ill. Arts Coun., Chgo., 1984-87; mem. com. League Chgo. Theatres, 1990—; cmty. rep. local sch. coun. Franklin Sch., Chgo., 1990-94. pres. Chgo. Coalition for Arts in Edn., 1983-85. Named Outstanding Lectr. Chgo. Cultural Ctr., 1981, 84, Outstanding Dir. Joseph Jefferson Citation Nominations, 1987, 97, award for outstanding ensemble Joseph Jefferson Award Com., 1999, After Dark award for outstanding dir., 2001. Mem. Ill. Theatre Assn. (exec. com. 1987-97), Soc. Stage Dirs. and Choreographers Ill. Alliance for Arts in Edn., Ill. Arts Alliance, Phi Beta Kappa. Democrat. Home: 124 W Polk St Apt 207 Chicago IL 60605-1766 Office: Goodman Theatre 170 N Dearborn St Chicago IL 60601 E-mail: stevescott@goodman-theatre.org.

SCOTT, STEPHEN CARLOS, academic administrator; b. Greenville, S.C., Sept. 20, 1949; s. Carlos O'Dell and Christina (Nikitas) S.; m. Patsy Jordan, Apr. 13, 1968; children: Stephanie Christina, Lance Stephen. BA, Clemson (S.C.) U., 1971, MEd, 1975, EdD, 1987. Owner, mgr. Scotty's Inc., restaurant, Clemson, 1967-71; tchr. math. Pickens (S.C.) Sr. High Sch., 1972-74; instr. bus. Tri-County Tech. Coll., Pendleton, S.C., 1974-76, head dept., 1976-78, dir. br. campus Easley, 1978-80; dean bus. Greenville Tech. Coll., 1980-85, assoc. v.p., 1985-88; pres. Southeastern C.C., Whiteville, N.C., 1988-99; exec. v.p. N.C. C.C. Sys., 1999—2002; pres. Lenoir CC, 2002—. Cons. P.C.E. Fed. Credit Union, Liberty, S.C., 1975-88, Jacobs Mfg. Co., Clemson, 1979-80, Flat Rock Shelter Ctr., Easley, 1980-85; bd. mem. N.C. Rural Ctr. Contbr. articles to profl. jours. and mags. Pres. So. Shelter Ctr., Greenville, 1986-88, Good Shepherd Found., Whiteville, 1990-92; bd. dirs. Good Shepherd, 1988-91; chmn. Columbus County Sch. Bond Dr., 1989, Am. Heart Fund Drive Columbus County, 1992; co-chmn. Columbus County Long Range Planning Com., 1989-91; vice chmn. Pvt. Industry Coun. Region O, 1992—; founding dir. Habitat for Humanity Columbus County, 1992; pres. bd. dirs. Columbus County Rural Health Ctr., 1994; bd. dirs. N.C. Rural Ctr., 2000—. Recipient award for patriotism U.S. Savs. Bonds Program, 1987. Mem. Am. Assn. Community and Jr. Colls. (Pres.'s Acad.), Rotary (bd. dirs. Whiteville 1990-92, pres. 1992-93). Presbyterian. Avocations: running, chess, numismatics, reading. Home: 104 Hibiscus Dr Clayton NC 27520-8714 E-mail: scs320@lenoircc.edu.

SCOTT, STEVEN JAMES, purchasing engineer; b. Iowa Falls, Iowa, July 28, 1955; s. James Harold and Ann (Hauberg) S.; m. Pamela Jane, Apr. 7, 1984; children: William Steven, Rachel Elizabeth. BSME, U. Ill., Champaign, 1977; MBA, U. Iowa, 1984. Registered profl. engr., Ill.; cert. purchasing mgr., Ill. Coop. engr. Deere & Co., Moline, Ill., 1975-77, engr., 1977-84, sr. engr., 1984-88, mgr., 1988—. Home: 1413 13th St Moline IL 61265 Office: Deere & Co 1 John Deere Pl Moline IL 61265-8010 E-mail: scottstevenj@johndeere.com.

SCOTT, STUART L. real estate company executive; b. Montreal; s. David George and Jean (Lothian) S.; m. Anne O'Laughlin, Nov. 26, 1982; children: Alexis L., Sarah Scott Tornes, Charity A., Christina A., Fiona L., Christopher G., Phoebe B. BA in Enlish Lit., Hamilton Coll., 1961; JD, Northwestern U., 1964. Atty. SEC, 1964-66; sr. v.p., asst. to chmn., bd. dirs. Arthur Rubloff & Co., 1966-73; pres. Equity Assocs., Inc. div. LaSalle Ptnrs., Inc., Chgo., 1973-75; from pres. to chmn., CEO LaSalle Ptnrs., Inc., 1975—99; chmn. Jones Lang LaSalle Inc., 2002—. Bd. dirs. Hartmarx Corp., LaSalle Hotel Properties. Bd. dirs. Rehab. Inst. Chgo., chmn. 8 yrs.; charter trustee Hamilton Coll., Clinton, N.Y.; trustee Lyric Opera Chgo. Named Real Estate Exec. of Yr. 1998, Comml. Property World. Mem. Chgo. Club, Econ. Club Chgo., Comml. Club Chgo., Old Elm Club. Office: Jones Lang LaSalle Inc 200 E Randolph Dr Chicago IL 60601

SCOTT, SUSAN SHATTUCK, secondary education educator; b. Cambridge, Mass., Sept. 12, 1945; d. Kenneth Elton and Phyllis Shattuck; m. Robert Allen Scott, Dec. 27, 1968 (div. 1973); 1 child, Kenneth Charles. BS in Edn., Boston State Coll., 1967; M in Math., Worcester Poly. Inst., 1990. Cert. secondary math. tchr., Mass. Tchr. South Jr. H.S., Weymouth, Mass., 1967-73; editor Houghton-Mifflin Co., Boston, 1973-74; tchr. Ctrl. Jr. H.S., Weymouth, 1974-81, South H.S., Weymouth, 1981-90, Weymouth H.S./Vocat. Tech. H.S., 1990—. Freelance editor Houghton Mifflin, Boston, 1974-75. Treas. Singles' Group, Duxbury Bapt. Ch., 1976-78, Stone Village Condo. Assn., Wareham, Mass., 1993-96. Mem. Nat. Coun. Tchrs. Math. Avocations: walking, swimming, reading, gardening, cooking. Home: 234 Rand Hill Rd Alton Bay NH 03810 Office: Weymouth HS/Vocat Tech HS 1051 Commercial St Weymouth MA 02189-1636

SCOTT, SYLVIA JANE, small business owner; b. Charleston, Jan. 31, 1945; d. John Mitchell and Christabelle Lillian Johnson; m. Nathanial Myers, 1960 (dec. Mar. 9, 1998); children: Tia Johnson, Nathanial Myers, Norma Griffin, Tralane Mason, Sonia Melton, Troi Mack, Myer Micheal. Student, Trident Tech. Coll., 1975; cosmetology cert., 1987. Cert. Cosmetology. Owner Shear Beauty, Charleston, SC, 1988—, Rental Units, Charleston, 1997—, Scott Supply, Charleston, 1999—. Author: The Bookdweller, 2002. Recipient cert., Carolina Monority Supplier Council , Inc. Roman Catholic. Achievements include patents for multi-page doll bookmarks; scheduling board.

SCOTT, T. GORDON, chemistry and math educator, writer; b. Laconia, N.H., Nov. 27, 1941; s. William Stafford and Jeanne Richardson Scott; m. Elizabeth Mary Winterberg, Mar. 11, 1995. AB, U. Pa., 1963; BA with honours, Cambridge (Eng.) U., England, 1965, MA, 1970; PhD, U. Ill., 1969. Profl. tchg. cert., Pa.; postgrad. tchg. lic., Va. Tchg. asst. U. Ill., Champaign-Urbana, 1965-66; asst. prof. chemistry Oberlin (Ohio) Coll., 1969-70; lectr. biochemistry U. Calif., Santa Barbara, 1971; cons. Sci-Math Cons., Uniontown, Pa., 1972-75; supr. secondary studies Westminster Acad., Carmichaels, 1975-79; asst. prof. chemistry Alderson-Broaddus Coll., Philippi, W.Va., 1981-84; assoc. prof. chemistry Bryan Coll., Dayton, Tenn., 1984-86, Knoxville (Tenn.) Coll., 1987-89, Union Coll., Barbourville, Ky., 1989-91, Jarvis Christian Coll., Hawkins, Tex., 1992-98; with Chem. Edn. Cons. USA, 1998-2000; instr. math. Winona (Tex.) Ind. Sch. Dist., 1998-99; instr. math, chemistry and astronomy Pittsylvania County (Va.) Schs., 2000—; tchr. Dan River H.S., Ringgold, Va., 1999—; adj. prof. chemistry and pharmacology Danville (Va.) C.C., 1999—, Nat. Coll., Danville, 1999—. Rsch. assoc. DuPont Chem. Co., Inc., Phila., 1963, EPA, Phila., 1988, Edgewood-Aberdeen Rsch. U.S. Army, Aberdeen Proving Ground, Md., 1993; vis. prof. La. Coll., Pineville, 1992; cons. with Transition State Assocs., Danville, Va.; adj. assoc. prof. biology Danville C.C., Va., 1999—; adj. instr. pharm. Nat. Coll., 2001-. Author: (with others) Synthetic Procedures in Nucleic Acid Chemistry, 1968, Spectroscopic Model Studies of NAD, 1969; contbr. articles to Jour. Am. Chem., Soc., 1967, 1970, 1972. Musician with Danville Recorder Consort, Danville Area Choral Arts Soc. Thouron fellow John R.H. Thouron Found., 1963-65; grantee NSF, 1996-97, Army Rsch. Orgn., 1993-95, Robert A. Welch Found., 1996-98. Mem. Am. Chem. Soc., Cambridge U. Chem. Soc., Am. Sci. Affiliation (dir. 1998), Rotary Internat. (chmn. internat. edn. com. 1977-81). Avocations: kayaking, exploring ideas, swimming competitively, Renaissance music (treble and tenor blockflute), astronomy. Office: Dan River HS Dept Sci Pittsylvania Co Schs 100 Dan River Wildcat Dr Ringgold VA 24586 E-mail: ps8411@adelphia.net.

SCOTT, TERRY LEE, communications company executive; b. Rockford, Ill., Oct. 21, 1950; s. Wilson C. and Marie G. (Bunger) S.; divorced; 1 child, Andrea; m. Jenny Scarborough, Aug. 1, 1981; children: Brady, Tiffany. BS in Acctg. magna cum laude, Bradley U., 1972. CPA, Ill., Tex. Audit prin. Arthur Young and Co., Dallas, 1972-82; v.p. fin. and adminstrn., treas. Paging Network Inc., 1982-90; sr. v.p. Paging Network, Inc., 1990-92, pres., CEO, bd. dirs., 1993-95, Terion Inc., 1995-97, chmn., CEO, 1997-99, dir., 1999—; chmn., CEO Terry Scott Enterprises, Plano, Tex., 1997—. Bd. dirs. XY Point Corp., Terion, Inc., Locate Networks, Inc., MobileStar Inc., Peoples Choice TV Corp. Mem. AICPA, Tex. Soc. CPAs, Phi Kappa Phi, Zeta Pi. Methodist. Office: Terry Scott Enterprises 1704 Riviera Dr Plano TX 75093-2910 E-mail: tscott1704@aol.com.

SCOTT, THEODORE R. lawyer; b. Mount Vernon, Ill., Dec. 7, 1924; s. Theodore R. and Beulah (Flannigan) S.; children: Anne Laurence, Sarah Buckland, Daniel, Barbara Gomon. AB, U. Ill., 1947, JD, 1949. Bar: Ill. 1950. Law clk. to judge U.S. Ct. Appeals, 1949-51; pvt. practice Chgo., 1950—; assoc. Spaulding Glass, 1951-53, Loftus, Lucas & Hammand, 1953-58, Ooms, McDougall, Williams & Hersh, 1958-60; ptnr. McDougall, Hersh & Scott, Chgo., 1960-87; of counsel Jones, Day, Reavis & Pogue, 1987-97, Rockey, Milnamow & Katz, 1998—. 2nd lt. USAAF, 1943-45. Decorated Air medal. Fellow Am. Coll. Trial Lawyers; mem. ABA, Ill. Bar Assn., Chgo. Bar Assn., 7th Cir. Bar Assn. (past pres.), Legal Club Chgo., Law Club Chgo., Patent Law Assn. Chgo. (past pres.), Union League Club, Exmoor Country Club (Highland Park, Ill.), Phi Beta Kappa. E-mail: tsb24nav2aol.com. Home: 1569 Woodvale Ave Deerfield IL 60015-2350

SCOTT, THOMAS JEFFERSON, JR. lawyer, electrical engineer; b. Montgomery, Ala., Dec. 30, 1943; s. Thomas Jefferson Sr. and Irene (Feagin) S.; m. Betsy Sue Mackta, Apr. 25, 1981; children: Elspeth Watts, Marguerita Taylor, Thomas Jefferson III. BEE, Yale U., 1966, BA in Econs., 1967; JD, Vanderbilt U., 1974. Bar: Va. 1974, D.C. 1975, N.Y. 1980, U.S. Dist. Ct. D.C. 1986, U.S. Dist. Ct. (ea. dist.) Va. 1993, U.S. Tax Ct. 1981, U.S. Ct. Fed. Claims, 1982, U.S. Ct. Appeals (fed. cir.) 1982, U.S. Ct. Appeals (4th cir.) 1993, U.S. Supreme Ct. 1984. Trial atty. civil div. U.S. Dept. of Justice, Washington, 1974-78; assoc. Cooper & Dunham, N.Y.C., 1978-80, sr. trial counsel civil div., 1980-85; ptnr. Pennie & Edmonds, Washington, 1985-90, Howrey & Simon, Washington, 1990-97, Hunton & Williams, Washington, 1997—. Capt. USNR, 1966-71. Decorated D.F.C. Mem. ABA, Am. Intellectual Property Law Assn. Office: Hunton & Williams 1900 K St NW Washington DC 20006-1110 E-mail: tscott@hunton.com.

SCOTT, VICKI SUE, school system administrator; b. Pine Bluff, Ark., Feb. 16, 1946; d. John Wesley and Ruby Gray (Whitehead) and Hannah (Lewis) S. BA, Hendrix Coll., 1968; MS in Edn., U. Cen. Ark., 1978, postgrad., 1979-84, U. Ark., 1983-85, Ark. State U., 1993-94. Cert. adminstrn., secondary sch. prin., middle sch., secondary health and phys. edn. Tchr., coach Brinkley (Ark.) Pub. Schs., 1968-76, Lonoke (Ark.) Jr. and Sr. High Schs., 1976-77, S.E. Jr. High Sch., Pine Bluff, 1978-92, asst. prin., 1992-2000, dir. summer sch., 1991, 92; prin. White Hall (Ark.) Jr. H.S., White Hall, Arkansas, 2000—. AIDS educator Arkansas River Edn. Svc. Coop., Pine Bluff, 1989-92. Active Leadership Pine Bluff, 1993-94. Scholar Assn. Women Ednl. Suprs., 1985; named Outstanding Young Women of Am., 1974. Mem.: DAR, ASCD, NMSA, AAMLA, Ark. Leadership Acad., Nat. Assn. Sch. Secondary Prins., Ark. Activities Assn., Ark. Assn. Ednl. Adminstrs., Order Ea. Star, Phi Delta Kappa, Delta Kappa Gamma (Epsilon chpt. pres., scholar 1994). Baptist. Avocations: tennis, reading, hiking, travel, golf. Home: 3215 S Cherry St Pine Bluff AR 71603-5983 Office: White Hall Jr HS 8106 Dollarway Rd White Hall AR 71602-6999 E-mail: scottv@whjr.arsc.k12.ar.us., vscott@seark.net.

SCOTT, WALTER, JR. business consultant; b. Balt., July 24, 1925; s. Walter and Margaret Catherine (Pfeiffer) S.; m. Barbara Main, July 6, 1946 (dec. 1964); children: Stephen Walter, Susan Marjorie, Cynthia Margaret, Christopher Main; m. Mary Joan Braun, Aug. 5, 1966 (dec. 1986); m. Helene Lyda Burke, May 1, 1987. AB, Duke U., 1945; MBA with distinction, Harvard U., 1949. Advtg. mgr. The Quaker Oats Co., Chgo., 1950-57; v.p. mktg. J.H. Filbert, Inc., Balt., 1957-67, pres., 1968-77; div. gen. mgr. Cen. Soya Co., Ft. Wayne, Ind., 1972-77; exec. v.p. Fairmont Foods Co., Des Plaines, Ill., 1978-81; pres. McKeon, Scott, Woolf & Assocs., Palo Alto, Calif., 1982-84; chmn. bd. Integral Cons. Group, Mill Valley, 1986-87, Scott, Woolf & Assocs., Palo Alto, 1984—2001, Mulford Moreland & Assocs., San Jose, Calif., 1986-89. Chmn., speaker pres. courses, Am. Mgmt. Assn., N.Y.C., 1970-90; trustee Calif. Inst. Integral Studies, San Francisco, 1983-89. With USNR, 1943-46, PTO. Mem. Phi Beta Kappa. Home and Office: 1450 Redford Dr Palm Springs CA 92264

SCOTT, WALTER COKE, retired sugar company executive, lawyer; b. Norfolk, Va., July 20, 1919; s. Walter Coke and Rosemary (White) S.; m. Virginia Kemper Millard, May 14, 1949; children: Mary Lyman (Mrs. K. Logan Jackson), Roberta (Mrs. Frederick Warth), Alexander McRae, Buford Coke. BS, Hampden-Sydney Coll., 1939; JD, U. Va., 1948. Bar: Va. 1947, Ga. 1954. Atty. U.S. Dept. Justice, Jacksonville, Fla., 1948; commerce atty. S.A.L. Ry., Norfolk, 1948-54; commerce counsel, gen. solicitor Central of Ga. Ry., Savannah, 1954-60; v.p. Cen. of Ga. Ry., (Norfolk Southern), 1960-62, dir., 1960-88; ptnr. law firm Hitch, Miller & Beckmann, Savannah, 1956-60; sr. v.p., sec. Savannah Foods & Industries, Inc. (formerly Savannah Sugar Refining Corp.), 1962-72, exec. v.p., mem. exec. com., 1972-87, also dir. Exec. v.p., sec. mem. exec. com., dir. Everglades Sugar Refinery, Inc., Clewiston, Fla., 1964-87; sec., mem. exec. com., dir. The Jim Dandy Co., Birmingham, Ala., 1968-81; bd. dirs. 1st Union Nat. Bank Savannah, Atlanta, 1975-91. Pres., chmn. exec. com. Historic Savannah Found., 1963-64; bd. dirs. United Community Services, 1965-68, pres., 1967; gen. chmn. United Community Appeal, 1966; mem. Chatham-Savannah Met. Planning Commn., 1963-68; trustee, chmn. finance com. Telfair Acad. Arts and Scis., 1964-67; trustee, vice chmn. Savannah Country Day Sch., 1967-69, chmn., 1970-72; Bd. dirs., chmn. finance com. Savannah Speech and Hearing Center, 1967-70; bd. dirs. Savannah Symphony Soc., Inc. Mem. Va. State Bar, Ga. State Bar, St. Andrews Soc., Savannah Benevolent Assn. (pres. 1990-92), Patrick Henry Soc., Thomas Jefferson Soc., Lile Law Soc., Kappa Sigma, Omicron Delta Kappa, Phi Alpha Delta, Chi Beta Phi, Pi Delta Epsilon. Clubs: Chatham, Oglethorpe, Savannah Golf. Episcopalian. Home: 3710 Abercorn St Savannah GA 31405-3303

SCOTT, WALTER DILL, management educator; b. Chgo., Oct. 27, 1931; s. John Marcy and Mary Louise (Gent) S.; m. Barbara Ann Stein, Sept. 9, 1961; children: Timothy Walter, David Frederick, Gordon Charles. Student, Williams Coll., 1949-51; BS, Northwestern U., 1953; MS, Columbia U., 1958. Cons. Booz, Allen & Hamilton, NYC, 1956—58; assoc. Glore, Forgan & Co., 1958—63, ptnr. Chgo., 1963-65; pntr. Lehman Bros, 1965-72, sr. ptnr., 1972-73, also bd. dirs.; assoc. dir. econs. and govt. Office Mgmt. and Budget, Washington, 1973-75; sr. v.p. internat. and fin. Pillsbury Co., Mpls., 1975-78, exec. v.p., 1978-80, also bd. dirs.; pres., CEO, Investors Diversified Svcs., Inc., 1980-84; group mng. dir. Grand Met. PLC, 1984-86, also bd. dirs.; chmn. Grand Met USA, 1984-86; prof., sr. Austin fellow Kellogg Sch. Mgmt., Northwestern U., Evanston, Ill., 1988—. Bd. dirs., vice chmn. Intermatic, Inc. Bd. dirs. Chgo. Cmtys. in Schs., Ctr. for Exec. Women, Leadership for Quality Edn. Lt. (j.g.) USN, 1953-56. Home: 55 Meadowview Dr Northfield IL 60093-3547 Office: Northwestern U Kellog Sch Mgmt 2001 Sheridan Rd Evanston IL 60208-0814 E-mail: wds@kellogg.northwestern.edu.

SCOTT, WALTER NEIL, physiologist, educator; b. Evansville, Ind., Mar. 2, 1935; s. Paul Kruger and Pauline Virginia (Kimbley) S.; children: Walter David Kimbley, Benjamin Bray. BS, Western Ky. State Coll., 1956; MD, U. Louisville, 1960. Intern New Eng. Ctr. Hosp., Boston, 1960-61, resident, 1961-62; NIH fellow medicine Mass. Meml. Hosps., Boston, 1962-63; USPHS fellow biophys. lab. Harvard Med. Sch., Brookline, Mass., 1963-65; spl. NIH fellow biochemistry MIT, Cambridge, 1965-66; biochemist Sch. Aerospace Medicine, San Antonio, 1966-68, acting chief biochem. pharmacology div., 1967-68; asst. prof. Mt. Sinai Grad. Sch., N.Y.C., 1968-71; mem. grad. faculty CUNY, 1968-82; asst. prof. ophthalmology Mt. Sinai Med. Sch., 1971-74, assoc. prof. ophthalmology, 1974-79, research prof. ophthalmology, 1979-82, asst. dean research, 1976-81, assoc. dean, 1981-82; chmn. dept. biology NYU, N.Y.C., 1982-87, prof., 1982—. Lancaster vis. prof. Western Ky. U., 1980; mem. cornea task force Nat. Eye Inst., 1972, vision rsch. program com., 1975—79; cons. metabolic biology program NSF, 1976—91; cons. VA Hosp. Dept. Medicine, 1998—2000; attending physician divsn. endocrinology Beth Israel Med. Ctr., 2001—. Contbr. articles to sci. publs. Trustee Inst. Applied Biology, 1986—. Served to capt. USAF, 1966-68 Fellow N.Y. Acad. Scis. (gov. 1978-82, pres. 1983, chmn. conf. organizing com. 1980-81, 87-88); mem. Am. Physiol. Soc., Am. Soc. Biol. Chemists, Biophys. Soc., Soc. Exptl. Biology and Medicine (editorial bd. procs.), Am. Heart Assn., AAAS, Am. Chem. Soc., Am. Soc. Nephrology, N.Y. Acad. Medicine (com. pub. health 1986—), Endocrine Soc., Soc. Cell Biology, Sigma Xi, Alpha Omega Alpha. Office: NYU Dept Biology 1009 Main Bldg Washington Sq E New York NY 10003 E-mail: walter.scott@nyu.edu.

SCOTT, WILLIAM CLEMENT, III, private investor; b. N.Y.C., Apr. 25, 1934; s. William Clement and Susan L. (Cameron) S.; m. Cindy L. Taylor, Dec. 5, 1981; children by previous marriage: Katherine Louise, David Campbell. AB, Coll. William and Mary, Williamsburg, Va., 1956. Self-employed, 1956-64; v.p. Booz-Allen & Hamilton, N.Y.C., 1964-69; group v.p. Cordura Corp., Los Angeles, 1969-72; exec. v.p. Western Pacific Industries, N.Y.C., 1972-76, pres., chief operating officer, 1976-87; pvt. investor N.Y.C., 1987-88; chmn., CEO Panavision Inc., 1988-98. Bd. dirs. Edison Control Corp., Vari-Lite, Inc., Audio Visual Svcs. Corp. Bd. dirs. Opera Orch. of N.Y., pres., 1988-97; bd. dirs., pres. Met. Opera Club N.Y.C. Mem. Met. Opera Club N.Y.C., Racquet and Tennis Club, Hay Harbor Club, Fishers Island Country Club, Coral Beach Club (Bermuda), Royal Bermuda Yacht Club. Republican. Episcopalian. Office: 885 3rd Ave Ste 3020 New York NY 10022-4834 E-mail: wcscott@att.net.

SCOTT, WILLIAM CORYELL, medical executive; b. Sterling, Colo., Nov. 22, 1920; s. James Franklin and Edna Ann (Schillig) S.; m. Jean Marie English, Dec. 23, 1944 (div. 1975); children: Kathryn, James, Margaret; m. Carolyn Florence Hill, June 21, 1975; children: Scott, Amy Jo, Robert. AB, Dartmouth Coll., 1942; MD, U. Colo., 1944, MS in OB/GYN, 1951. Cert. Am. Bd. Ob-Gyn., 1956, 79, Am. Bd. Med. Mgmt., 1991. Intern USN Hosp., Great Lakes, Ill., 1945-46, Denver Gen. Hosp., 1946-47; resident Ob-Gyn St. Joseph's Hosp., Colo. Gen. Hosp., Denver, 1946-51; practice medicine specializing in Ob-Gyn Tucson, 1951-71; assoc. prof. emeritus U. Ariz. Med. Sch., 1971—; v.p. med. affairs U. Med. Ctr., 1984-94. Contbr. articles to med. jours. and chpt. to book. Pres. United Way, Tucson, 1979-80, HSA of Southeastern Ariz., Tucson, 1985-87; chmn. Ariz. Health Facilities Authority, Phoenix, 1974-83. Served to capt. USNR, 1956-58. Recipient Man of Yr. award, Tucson, 1975. Fellow ACS, Am. Coll. Ob-Gyn, Pacific Coast Ob-Gyn Soc., Ctrl. Assn. of Ob-Gyn; mem. AMA (coun. on sci. affairs 1984-93, chmn. 1989-91), Am. Coll. Physician Execs., Ariz. Med. Assn. Republican. Roman Catholic. Avocations: golf, gardening, photography. Address: HC 1 Box 923 Sonoita AZ 85637-9705 E-mail: cbarc3@netscape.net.

SCOTT, WILLIAM FLOYD, accountant; b. Woodland, Miss., Feb. 26, 1936; s. Robert Fulton and Sarah Etta (Watson) S.; m. Carolyn Marie Pierce, Dec. 12, 1958; children: David, Ricky, Stephen, Julie. BS in Bus. Adminstrn., Delta State U., Cleveland, Miss., 1957. Staff acct. Reynolds Elec. & Engring., Las Vegas, Nev., 1957-62, sr. auditor, 1962-65, dir. internal auditing, 1965-70; sr. staff acct. Davis & Mosher, CPAs, Pasadena, Tex., 1970-72; owner Scott & Co., CPAs, 1972—2001; mng. dir. Scott, Forrest & Co., PLLC, 2002—. Chmn. fin. com. Meml. Bapt. Ch., Pasadena, 1974-80, treas., 1974—. Mem. AICPA, Tex. Soc. CPAs, Pasadena Noon Optimist Club (treas. 1973-75). Avocations: reading, gardening, sports. Office: Scott Foreest & Co PLLC CPAs 4620 Fairmont Pky Ste 200 Pasadena TX 77504-3328 E-mail: nmfscott@swbell.net.

SCOTT, WILLIAM PAUL, lawyer; b. Staples, Minn., Nov. 8, 1928; m. Elsie Elaine Anderson, Feb. 7, 1968; children: Jason Lee, William P., Mark D., Brian D., Scott; stepchildren: Thomas J. (dec.), Terri L. Weeding-Berg. ALA, U. Minn., 1949; BSL, St. Paul Coll. Law, 1952, JD, 1954. Bar: Minn. 1954. Atty., right of way divsn. Minn. Hwy Dept., 1945-52, civil engr., traffic and safety divsn., 1953-55; practice law Arlington, Minn., 1955-61, Gaylord, 1963-67; sr. ptnr. Scott Law Offices and predecessors, Pipestone, 1967—. Probate, juvenile judge Sibley County, Minn., 1956-61; Minn. pub. examiner, 1961-63; county atty. Sibley County, 1963-68, city atty., Pipestone, 1979-2002. Sibley County Rep. chmn., 1961. Served with USMCR, 1946-50, from 2d lt. to lt. col. USAF Res., 1950-88, ret. Recipient George Washington Honor medal Freedoms Found., 1970, 72. Mem. TROA, VFW, DAV, Minn. Bar Assn., Mensa, Am. Legion, Res. Officers Assn. Home: PO Box 689 Pipestone MN 56164-0689 Office: Park Plz Offices Pipestone MN 56164 E-mail: scottlaw@rconnect.com.

SCOTT, WILLIAM PROCTOR, III, lawyer; b. Berkeley, Calif., Dec. 1, 1946; s. William Proctor Jr. and Marcia (Wood) S.; children: William Proctor IV, Jennifer Anne. BS, MIT, 1968; JD cum laude, U. Pa., 1975. Assoc. Ballard Spahr Andrews & Ingersoll LLP, Phila., 1975-82, ptnr., 1982-2000, Nixon Peabody LLP, Albany, N.Y., 2000—. Regional chmn. MIT Ednl. Coun., 1988-2000. Bd. dirs. Cathedral Village, 1998—. Lt. (j.g.) USNR, 1969-72. Office: Nixon Peabody LLP Omni Plz 30 S Pearl St Albany NY 12207-3425 E-mail: wscott@nixonpeabody.com.

SCOTT, W(ILLIAM) RICHARD, sociology educator; b. Parsons, Kan., Dec. 18, 1932; s. Charles Hogue and Hildegarde (Hewit) S.; m. Joy Lee Whitney, Aug. 14, 1955; children: Jennifer Ann, Elliot Whitney, Sydney Brooke. AA, Parsons Jr. Coll., 1952; AB, U. Kans., 1954, MA, 1955; PhD, U. Chgo., 1961; PhD in Econs. (hon.) , Copenhagen Sch. Bus., 2000, Helsinki Sch. Econs., 2001. From asst. prof. to assoc. prof. sociology Stanford (Calif.) U., 1960-69, prof., 1969-99, prof. emeritus, 1999—, chair dept. sociology, 1972-75. Courtesy prof. Sch. Medicine, Stanford U., 1972—, Sch. Edn., Grad. Sch. Bus., 1977—; fellow Ctr. for Advanced Study in Behavioral Scis., 1989-90; dir. Orgns. Rsch. Tng. Program, Stanford U., 1972-89, Ctr. for Orgns. Rsch., 1988-96; mem. adv. panel Sociology Program NSF, Washington, 1982-84; mem. epidemiol. and svc. rsch. rev. panel NIMH, Washington, 1984-88; mem. Commn. on Behavioral and Social Scis. and Edn., NAS, 1990-96; vis. prof. Kellogg Grad. Sch. Mgmt., Northwestern U., winter 1997, Hong Kong U. Sci. and Tech., fall 2000. Author: (with O.D. Duncan et al) Metropolis and Region, 1960; (with P.M. Blau) Formal Organizations, 1962, Social Processes and Social Structures, 1970; (with S.M. Dornbusch) Evaluation and the Exercise of Authority, 1975, Organizations: Rational, Natural and Open Systems, 1981, rev. edit., 2003; (with J.W. Meyer) Organizational Environments: Ritual and Rationality, 1983, edit., 1992; (with A.B. Flood) Hospital Structure and Performance, 1987; (with J.W. Meyer), Institutional Environments and Organizations: Structural Complexity and Individualism, 1994, Institutions and Organizations, 1995, rev. edit., 2001; (with S. Christinsen) The Institutional Construction of Organization, 1995; (with M. Ruef et al) Institutional Change and Healthcare Organizations: From Professional Dominance to Managed Care, 2000; editor Ann. Rev. of Sociology, 1986-91; (with R. Cole) The Quality Movement and Organization Theory, 1999. Fellow Woodrow Wilson, 1954-55; mem. Nat. Commn. Nursing, 1980-83; chair Consortium Orgns. Rsch. Ctrs., 1989-91; elder First Presby. Ch., Palo Alto, Calif., 1977-80, 83-86. Social Sci. Rsch. Coun. fellow, U. Chgo., 1959; named Edmund P. Learned Disting. Prof., Sch. Bus. Adminstrn., U. Kans, 1970-71; recipient Cardinal Citation for Disting. Svc. Labette C.C., Parsons, 1981, Disting. Scholar award Mgmt. and Orgn. Theory divsn. Acad. Mgmt., 1988, Richard D. Irwin award for scholarly contbns. to mgmt. Acad. Mgmt., 1996. Mem. Inst. Medicine, Am. Sociol. Assn. (chmn. sect. on orgns. 1970-71, mem. coun. 1989-92), Acad. Mgmt., Sociol. Rsch. Assn., Macro-Organizational Behavior Soc., Phi Beta Kappa. Democrat. Presbyterian. Home: 940 Lathrop Pl Stanford CA 94305-1060 Office: Stanford U Dept Sociology Bldg 120 Stanford CA 94305 E-mail: scottwr@stanford.edu.

SCOTT, WINSTON E. academic administrator; BMus, Fla. State U., 1972; M.Aero. Engring., U.S. Naval Postgrad. Sch., 1980. Commd USN, 1972, advanced through grades; with Helicopter Anti-Submarine Squadron Light Thirty Three, North Island, Calif., 1974—78, Fighter Squadron Eighty Four, NAS Oceana, Va., 1978—86; aero. engring. duty officer, prodn. test pilot Naval Aviation Depot, Jacksonville, Fla., 1986; dir. product support dept. USN; dep. dir. tactical aircraft systems dept. Naval Air Devel. Ctr., Warminster, Pa.; with NASA/Johnson Space Ctr., 1992—97, mission specialist, 1996—97; v.p. student affairs Fla. State U., Tallahassee. Mem. Aeronautics and Space Engring. Bd., Nat. Acads.; assoc. instr. elec. engring. Fla. A&M U., Fla. C., Jacksonville. Office: Florida State Univ 313 Westcott Blvd Tallahassee FL 32306*

SCOTT-BATTLE, GLADYS NATALIE, retired social worker; b. Cambridge, Mass., Sept. 16, 1933; d. Dudley Fairfax and Bessie Mae (Mitchell) Scott; m. James Henry Battle, Jr., Oct. 18, 1953 (div. 1975); children: Gregory, James, Jameel. BA, Fordham U., 1975; MSW, Columbia U., 1978. Lic. clin. social worker; cert. social worker, tchr., N.Y. Program dir. Cmty. Svc. Soc., N.Y.C., 1978-79; corp. liaison cities and schs., 1979-80; psychotherapist Harlem Interfaith Counseling, 1980-81; psychiat. social worker Met. Hosp., 1981-83, N.Y.C. Bd. Edn., 1983—; ret. Cons. N.Y. State Disability Determinations, 1982—, N.Y.C. Family Ct., 1987, family and criminal ct.-selected cases. V.p. Women Who Help Other People, N.Y.C., 1985; bd. dirs. Morningside Gardens Coop., N.Y.C., 1986; vol. Met. Mus. Art. Mem. NASW, Nat. Assn. Black Social Workers, United Fedn. Tchrs., Internat. Assn. Social Workers, Bus. and Profl. Women's Club. Democrat. Avocations: visiting museums and art galleries, painting, theatre, travel. Home: 510 W 123rd St Apt 5 New York NY 10027-5004

SCOTT-BUCZAK, ALMA, human relations executive; b. Phila., May 29, 1952; d. Thomas Harrison Scott and Georgia Belle Neal; m. William Myron Buczak, July 2, 1983; 1 child, Derrick. AB in Econs., Lafayette Coll., 1974; MA in Human Resources Mgmt., New Sch. U., 1987. Rsch. analyst Pfizer, N.Y.C., 1974-75, mgr. human rels., 1981-89, dir. human rels., 1989—; ops. analyst Fed. Res. Bank of N.Y., 1975-76, mgmt. recruiter, 1976-78, supr. compensation and benefits, 1978-81. Mem. adv. panel to bd. trustees Lafayette Coll., Easton, Pa.; bd. advisors New Sch., N.Y.C.; v.p. bd. dirs. Coun. on Adoptable Children, N.Y.C.; dir. religious edn. Victory Tabernacle FBH Ch., Teaneck, N.J. Named Nlack Achievers in Industry, Harlem YMCA, 1989; Lubin scholar New Sch., 1987. Mem. NAFE. Republican. Avocations: family activities, working with youth, reading. Office: Pfizer Inc 235 E 42nd St New York NY 10017-5755 Fax: 201-886-8073. E-mail: almascottbuczak@aol.com., scotta@pfizer.com.

SCOTT-CARTER, HELEN CHRISTINA, retired educator; b. Washington, Oct. 30, 1936; d. Henry Cartis and Rubie Louise (McKnight) Scott; m. Manford Carter; children: Orthlyn M. Allen-Holt, Michael E. Carter, Donna Carter-Scott, Christopher Carter. BS, D.C. Tchrs. Coll., 1959; MA, St. John's Coll., 1970; postgrad., Va. Tech., 1980; PhD, Logos Christian Coll., 1996. Tchr. English, history, Egyptology, humanities1985 Langley Jr. High Sch., Washington, 1960, asst. prin., 1985-91; ret. Author: Zion's History Parts I & II, 1994, Zion Explains The Apostles' Creed, 1996, The Jesus G.A.N.G., 1997, With What We Have (Stewardship), 1997, Show Them, 1998, Good Fruit A.M.E. Churcy, 2000, The Best Gift Yet, 2000, Gifts Money Can't Buy, 2001, God's Spa, 2001, Zion Says Happiness Is Using Good Manners, 2001, Zion Explains Holy Communion, 2002. Dist. dir. Christian edn. AME Zion Ch., 1985-97, dir. Children's Ministry, 1994—; regional v.p. Assembly of Christian Educators; pres. S.C.O.T.T. Connection Inc. Cmty. Devel. Corp. Mem. D.C. Reading Coun., D.C. Tchrs. English, Phi Delta Kappa, Alpha Kappa Alpha. Democrat. Avocations: designing, sewing, reading, traveling, writing children's books. Home: 1303 Quid Ct Capitol Heights MD 20743-5243

SCOTT-FINAN, NANCY ISABELLA, government administrator; b. Canton, Ohio, June 13, 1949; d. Milton Kenneth and Gertrude (Baker) Scott; m. Robert James Finan II, Aug. 23, 1986. Student, Malone Coll., 1970-73; BA magna cum laude, postgrad., U. Akron, 1976, Kent State U., 1977; MA in Internat. Transactions, George Mason U., 1995. Legal sec. Krugliak, Wilkins, Griffiths & Dougherty, Canton, 1969, Amerman, Burt & Jones, Canton, 1970-77; legal sec., paralegal Black, McCuskey, Souers & Arbaugh, Ohio, 1977-81; administrv. staff mem. com. on judiciary U.S. Senate, Washington, 1981-86; adminstrv. asst. to counsel to Pres., The White House, 1986-89; adminstrv. asst. to former counsel to pres. O'Melveny & Myers, 1989; asst. dir. congl. rels. Office Legis. Affairs U.S. Dept. Justice, 1989-91; spl. asst. to asst. atty. gen. U.S. Dept. of Justice, 1991—. Substitute tchr. North Canton City Sch. System, 1979-80; residential tutor Canton City Sch. System, 1980-81, Fairfax (Va.) County Sch. System, 1983; instr. dance and exercise Siffrin Home for Developmentally Disabled, Canton, 1980. East coast regional v.p. for spl. projects Childhelp U.S.A., Washington, 1988-90; mem. Rep. Women of Capitol Hill, Washington, 1984-95; bd. mem. Have a Heart Homes for Abused Children, Washington, 1990-91. Mem. AAUW, Women of Washington, Corcoran Gallery Art, Nat. Mus. Women Arts. Presbyterian. Office: US Dept Justice 950 Pennsylvania Ave NW Washington DC 20530-0001

SCOTT-FLANTON, VERNITA LYNN, consultant; b. Gary, Ind., Oct. 22, 1958; d. Rochelle Ophelia (Williams) Greene; 1 child, Sean Miles Scott. Chief exec. officer Jade, Inc., Palmdale, Calif., 2000—. Mem.: Women in Mgmt., Greater L.A. World Trade Ctr. Assn., Andrews U. Alumni Assn., Mizpah Alumni Assn. Democrat. Adventist. Avocations: racquetball, horseback riding, skiing, hiking. E-mail: jade7inc@yahoo.com.

SCOTTI, ANTHONY JOHN, JR. historian, educator; b. Mineola, N.Y., May 5, 1965; s. Anthony John and Lynda Joyce S.; m. Laura Lee, June 14, 1997. BA, Greensboro Coll., N.C., 1987; MA, Wake Forest U., 1991; PhD, U. S.C., Columbia, 1995. History instr. Greensboro Coll., N.C., 1994-95, Midlands Tech. Coll., S.C., 1996—; history series editor Bruccoli Clark Layman, Columbia, 1996—. Author: Brutal Virtue: The Myth and Reality of Banastre Tarleton, 2002; editor: American Eras, 1998, History in Dispute, 2003—, World Eras, 2003. Recipient scholarships, Greensboro Coll., 1983-87, Wake Forest U., 1987-88. Avocations: jogging, hiking, mil. minatures. Office: Bruccoli Clark Layman 2006 Sumter St Columbia SC 29201-2157 E-mail: tscotti@bcl-manly.com.

SCOTTI, DENNIS JOSEPH, educator, researcher, consultant; b. N.Y.C., Apr. 20, 1952; s. Joseph Charles and Theresa (Giancola) S. BS, Stony Brook U., 1974; MBA, Adelphi U., 1977; MS, Temple U., 1980, PhD, 1982. Bd. cert. in healthcare mgmt.; cert. healthcare fin. profl., managed care profl.; diplomate Am. Coll. Healthcare Execs. Dep. chief adminstr. Dept. Mental Health Devel. Ctr., Suffolk, N.Y., 1975-77; asst. prof. Rutgers U., N.J., 1980-83; assoc. prof. Fairleigh Dickinson U., 1983-88, prof., 1989—. Exec. v.p. Presscott Assocs., Ltd., Avon, Conn., 1989—; mem. Regents Adv. Coun. Author: Strategic Management in the Health Care Sector, 1988; contbr. articles to profl. jours. Mem. Regents Adv. Coun. N.J. Recipient Tchg. Excellence award Exec. Master of Bus. Adminstrn., 1997. Fellow Healthcare Fin. Mgmt. Assn.; mem.

Assn. for Health Svcs. Rsch., Med. Group Mgmt. Assn., Health Planning and Mktg. Soc., Acad. Mgmt., Peoples Med. Soc., Health Decisions Assembly, Phi Theta Kappa, Delta Mu Delta. Office: Fairleigh Dickinson U 1000 River Rd Teaneck NJ 07666-1996

SCOTTI, MICHAEL JOHN, JR. medical association executive; b. N.Y.C., Oct. 30, 1938; s. Michael John and Florence (Ellis) S.; m. Susan Faye Suit, Aug. 25, 1961; children: Michael John III, Pamela Anne, Jennifer Beth. BS, Fordham Coll., 1960; MD, Georgetown U., 1965; postgrad., Indsl. Coll., Washington, 1982-83. Diplomate Am. Bd. Internal Medicine, Am. Bd. Family Practice; CAQ Geriat. Commd. 2d lt. U.S. Army, 1963, advanced through grades to maj. gen., 1990; dir. residency program Dept. Family Practice, Ft. Gordon, Ga., 1976-79; family practice cons. Surgeon Gen., Washington, 1979-80; dir. Grad. Med. Edn. U.S. Army, 1980-82; comdr. army hosp. Ft. Polk, La., 1983-86; dir. quality assurance Army Med. Dept., Washington, 1986-88, dir. profl. svcs., 1988-90; comdg. gen. European 7th Med. Comd, Heidelberg, Fed. Republic Germany, 1990-95; ret. maj. gen., 1995; v.p. AMA, Chgo., 1996—. Assoc. prof. Georgetown U. Sch. Medicine, 1986; chmn. Def. Med. Standardization, Ft. Detrick, Md., 1988-90; prof. Uniformed Svcs. U., Bethesda, Md., 1990. Health cons. Nat. PTA, Chgo., 1976-79. Named Person of Yr. Phi Delta Kappa, 1976. Fellow: ACP, Am. Acad. Family Physicians (vice spkr. 1988—90, apkr., bd. dirs. 1990—92); mem.: AMA (v.p. med. edn. 1995—2000, sr. v.p. profl. stds. 2000—). Office: AMA 515 N State St Chicago IL 60610-4325 E-mail: michael_scotti@ama-assn.org.

SCOTTO, RENATA, soprano; b. Savona, Italy, Feb. 24, 1935; m. Lorenzo Anselmi. Studied under, Ghirardini, Merlino and Mercedes Llopart, Accademia Musicale Savonese, Conservatory Giuseppe Verdi, Milan. Opera singer Robert Lombardo Assocs., 1979—. Presenter master classes Juilliard Sch., N.Y.C., Curtis Inst., Phila., Yale U., Russian Opera Ctr., Moscow, Tokyo U., young argist program La Scale, Milan, N.Y. Met. Opera; dir. young artist program Verdi Festival, Parma, Italy, 2000; dir. Tosca, Grand Opera Miami, 2001 Roles include Feldmarschallin in Der Rosenkavalier (Franco Abiati and Frankfurter Allgemeine awards), 1992, Kundry in Parsifal, German Schweing Fewtival, 1995, La Voix Humaine, Maggio Musicale Fiorentino, also in Barcelona, Spain, Amsterdam, The Netherlands, Klytemnestra in Elektra, Balt., 2000; performes with leading orchs. of world, giving concerts and master classes; ; performs Les Nuits d'Ete (Berlioz), Strauss and Mahler songs, Erwartung (Schoenberg), Santa Cecilia Acad. Orch., Rome, 1994. Bd. dirs. Santa Cecilia Acad., Rome; opened Renata Scotto Opera Acad., Albisola Marina, Italy, 1997—; staged Il Parata (Bellini), Festival Belliniano, Catania, Italy, 1993, staged new prodn. La Sonnambula, 1994; dir. new prodn. La Traviata, N.Y.C. Opera, 1995. Recipient Emmy award for Best Live Mus. Event in TV for Live from Lincoln Ctr., 1995. Office: 5 Stone Hollow Way Armonk NY 10504 Also: care Theatre of La Scala via Filodrammatici 2 Milan Italy

SCOTT-WILLIAMS, WENDY LEE, information technology specialist; b. Buffalo, Jan. 22; d. Arthur Raymond and June Amelia Schutt; m. Nigel Simon Scott-Williams, Feb. 29, 1980. BA cum laude, SUNY, Buffalo, 1975; MA with honors, Cambridge U., 1979; MLIS with honors, CUNY-Queens Coll., 1987. Applications rep. Barrister, N.Y.C., 1982-83; coord. computer systems Stroock & Stroock & Lavan, 1983-87; tech. svcs. mgr. Batten, Barton, Durstein & Osborn (BBDO) Worldwide, 1987-92; adminstr., mgr. info. resources Fairchild Publs., 1992-96; info. resource mgr. March of Dimes Birth Defects Found., White Plains, N.Y., 1996—. Active N.Y. Zool. Soc. Mem. Spl. Librs. Assn., Cambridge Union Soc., Oxford-Cambridge Soc., Nature Conservancy, Greenpeace. Presbyterian. Avocations: travel, gardening. Office: March of Dimes Birth Defects Found Nat Hdqs 1275 Mamaroneck Ave White Plains NY 10605-5298

SCOULAR, ROBERT FRANK, lawyer; b. Del Norte, Colo., July 9, 1942; s. Duane William and Marie Josephine (Moloney) S.; m. Donna V. Scoular, June 3, 1967; children— Bryan T., Sean D., Bradley R. BS in Aero. Engring., St. Louis U., 1964, JD, 1968. Bar: Mo. 1968, Colo. 1968, N.D. 1968, U.S. Supreme Ct. 1972, Calif. 1979. Law clk. to chief judge U.S. Ct. Appeals (8th cir.), 1968-69; ptnr. Bryan, Cave, McPheeters & McRoberts, St. Louis, 1969-89, mng. ptnr. Los Angeles, 1979-84, exec. com., 1984-85, sect. leader tech., computer and intellectual property law, 1985-89; ptnr. Sonnenschein, Nath, Rosenthal, Chgo., 1990—, mng. ptnr. L.A., 1990—, mem. policy and planning com., 1995—. Co-leader intellectual property practice, 1990-98; dir. Mo. Lawyers Credit Union, 1978-79. Contbr. articles to profl. jours. Bd. dirs. St. Louis Bar Found., 1975-76, 79; bd. dirs., vice chmn., gen. counsel L.A. Area Coun. Boy Scouts Am.; league commr. Am. Youth Soccer Orgn.; mem. alumni coun. St. Louis U., 1979-82, dean's coun. Sch. Law, 2000—; hon. dean Dubourg Soc. Recipient Nat. Disting. Eagle Scout award. Mem. ABA (nat. dir. young lawyers div. 1977-78), Bar Assn. Met. St. Louis (v.p. 1978-79, sec. 1979, chmn. young lawyers sect. 1975-76), Los Angeles County Bar Assn., Assn. Bus. Trial Lawyers, Calif. Bar. Assn., Mo. Bar (chmn. young lawyers sect. 1976-77, disting. svc. award), Computer Law Assn., Fed. Bar Assn. Home: 1505 Lower Paseo La Cresta Palos Verdes Peninsula CA 90274-2066 Office: Sonnenschein Nath & Rosenthal 601 S Figueroa St Ste 1500 Los Angeles CA 90017-5720

SCOUT, TERRENCE HOUSER, business educator; b. Bellefonte, Pa., Aug. 19, 1946; s. Charles George and Margaret Helen (Houser) S.; m. Jacqueline Ann Miller, June 8, 1968; children: Justin Bartholomew, Matthew Kyle, Joy Elizabeth, Joshua Michael. BS in Edn., Shippensburg U., 1968; MA in Sociology, U. Calif., Riverside, 1972, PhD in Sociology, 1976; MBA, U. N.C., Charlotte, 1983. Secondary tchr. Big Spring Sch. Dist., Newville, Pa., 1969-70; rsch. assoc. U. Calif., Riverside, 1972-74; asst. prof. U. N.C., Charlotte, 1974-84; assoc. prof., chmn. Washington Coll., Chestertown, Md., 1984—. Mem. editl. bd. Jour. Mgmt. Sys., 1988—. Vice chmn. Kent County Bd. Edn., Chestertown, 1987-98; pres. Md. Assn. Bds. Edn., Annapolis, 1993-94. Mem. Kent County C. of C. (pres. 1995). Republican. Methodist. Home: 301 Washington Ave Chestertown MD 21620-1416 Office: Washington Coll 300 Washington Ave Chestertown MD 21620-1438

SCOVEL, MARY ALICE, retired music therapy educator; b. Grand Rapids, Mich., Jan. 28, 1936; d. Carl Edward and Alice Bertha (Bieri) Sennema; m. Ward Norman Scovel, July 7, 1956; children: Marcia, Katherine. MusB, Western Mich. U., 1969; MusM, Mich. State U., 1975. Registered music therapist; bd. cert. Asst. prof. music Grand Valley State U., Allendale, Mich., 1969-75; instr. U. Dayton (Ohio), 1975-78, Muskegon (Mich.) Community Coll., 1978-80; intern dir. Battle Creek (Mich.) Adventist Hosp., 1980-84; prof. music therapy Western Mich. U., Kalamazoo, 1984-95; ret., 1995; owner, pvt. practice Health Harmonics, Honolulu, 1997-98; ret., 1998. Cons. Pre-sch. Physically Handicapped, Wyo., Mich., 1974, Doris Klausen Devel. Ctr., Battle Creek, 1985-86; music therapist, sound practitioner and trainer, Tahlequah, Okla., 1995-97; pvt. practice health harmonics, 1997—; chmn. Multi-clinic, Kalamazoo, 1988-89. Author: Music Therapy in Treatment of Adults, 1990; co-editor Music Therapy Perspectives; cited in The Mozart Effect by Don Campbell, 1997; contbr. articles to profl. jours. Lay del. United Meth. Ch., Albion, Mich., 1991. Mem. Am. Music Therapy Assn. (del.), Nat. Assn. Mental Illness, Great Lakes Region Music Therapy (past pres.), Mich. Music Therapists, AAUW, Pi Delta Alpha, Pi Kappa Lambda. Avocations: quilting, reading, cross country skiing, singing, swimming. Home: 77 Port Tack Hilton Head Island SC 29928 E-mail: mwscovel@aol.com.

SCOVIL, ROGER MORRIS, international business consultant; b. Greenville, S.C., Apr. 23, 1929; s. Roger Peniston and Sophia Rose (Herbert) S.; m. Mary Earle Nock; children: Randolph, Frances, Elizabeth. Student, Davidson Coll., 1946-48; BS in Civil Engring., N.C. State U., 1951. Registered profl. engr., Ga., S.C., P.R. Project mgr. McKoy-Helgerson Co., Greenville, 1953-63; v.p., maintenance div. mgr. Daniel Constrn. Co., 1963-66; v.p., Caribbean div. mgr. Daniel Internat. Corp., San Juan, P.R., 1966-74, v.p. Europe and Middle East Brussels and Jeddah, Saudi Arabia, 1974-79; v.p. internat. mkgt. Daniel Constrn. Co., Greenville, 1980; pres. Polysius Corp., Atlanta, 1981-88; sr. v.p., dir. Lockwood Greene Systems Corp., 1988-97. Sr. v.p., dir. Lockwood Greene Internat., Atlanta, 1991-95, pres., 1995-97; mem. operating bd. Lockwood Greene Engrs., Inc., 1995-97, bd. dirs., chmn. exec. com. World Trade Ctr., Atlanta, 1995—. Author: Get Ahead: Scovil's 7 Rules for Success in Management. Mem. Atlanta Dist. Export coun., 1996—; bus. adv. bd. So. Ctr. for Internat. Studies, 2000—; bd. dirs. N.C. State Engring. Found., 1998-2001, Ga. tech. chpt. AIESEC, 1996—. Capt. U.S. Army, 1951-53. Mem. Atlanta World trade Ctr. (bd. dirs.), Internat. Club Atlanta, Brazilian Am. C. of C. Ga. (bd. dirs. 1997—, pres. 1997-99, chmn. emeritus, 1999—), Tau Beta Pi, Chi Epsilon, Sigma Phi Epsilon. Episcopalian. Home: 6025 Riverwood Dr NW Atlanta GA 30328-3732

SCOVILL, CURTIS NEAL, physician; b. Cleve., Jan. 4, 1941; s. Warner E. and Grace Virginia (Curtis) S; m. Susan D. Talbott, July 27, 1991. AB, Oberlin Coll., 1963; MD, Tufts U., 1967. Diplomate Am. Bd. Internal Medicine, 1972, Nat. Bd. Med. Examiners, 1968. Intern Rochester (N.Y.) Gen. Hosp., 1967-68, resident, 1968-70; physician pvt. practice, Newton Square, Pa., 1973-75, Paoli, 1975—. Lt. comdr. USNR, 1971-73. Endocrinology fellow NYU, N.Y.C., 1970-71 Mem. Am. Diabetes Assn., Phila. Endocrine Soc., Thyroid Soc. Phila. Office: 202 Paoli Meml Med Bldg Paoli PA 19301

SCOVILLE, JAMES GRIFFIN, economics educator; b. Amarillo, Tex., Mar. 19, 1940; s. Orlin James and Carol Howe (Griffin) S.; m. Judith Ann Nelson, June 11, 1962; 1 child, Nathan James. BA, Oberlin Coll., 1961; MA, Harvard U., 1963, PhD, 1965. Economist ILO, Geneva, 1965-66; instr. econs. Harvard U., Cambridge, Mass., 1964-65, asst. prof., 1966-69; assoc. prof. econs. and labor and indsl. relations U. Ill.-Urbana, 1969-75, prof., 1975-80; prof. indsl. rels. Indsl. Rels. Ctr., U. Minn., Mpls., 1979—, dir., 1979-82, dir. grad. studies, 1990-97. Cons. ILO, World Bank, U.S. Dept. Labor, Orgn. for Econ. Cooperation and Devel., AID; labor-mgmt. arbitrator. Author: The Job Content of the US Economy, 1940-70, 1969, Perspectives on Poverty and Income Distribution, 1971, Manpower and Occupational Analysis: Concepts and Measurements, 1972, (with A. Sturmthal) The International Labor Movement in Transition, 1973, Status Influences in 3rd World Labor Markets, 1991. Mem. Am. Econ. Assn., Indsl. Rels. Rsch. Assn. (v.p. internat. sect. 1998, pres. 1999), Internat. Indsl. Rels. Assn. Office: U Minn Ind Rels Ctr 3-289 CSOM Minneapolis MN 55455 E-mail: jscoville@csom.umn.edu.

SCOVILLE, JOSEPH G. federal magistrate, judge; b. 1949; BA with high honors, Mich. State U., 1971; JD magna cum laude, U. Mich., 1974. Bar: Ill. 1974, U.S. Dist. Ct. (no. dist.) Ill. 1974, Mich. 1976, U.S. Dist. Ct. (we. dist.) Mich. 1976, U.S. Supreme Ct. 1981. Assoc. McDermott, Will & Emery, Chgo., 1974-76; ptnr. Warner, Norcross & Judd, Grand Rapids, Mich., 1976-88; magistrate judge U.S. Dist. Ct. (we. dist.) Mich., 1988—. Mem. Fed. Bar Assn., Mich. State Bar, Grand Rapids Bar Assn. Office: US Dist Ct We Dist Mich 602 Fed Bldg 110 Michigan St NW Grand Rapids MI 49503-2313 Fax: (616) 456-2074. E-mail: scoville@miwd.uscourts.gov.

SCOVILLE, LYNDA SUE, special education educator, writer; b. Pampa, Tex., Jan. 5, 1945; d. Kenneth E. and Opal Myrle (Turner) Scoville; m. Bruce C. Ward, Oct. 1, 1976 (div. Nov. 1997); children: J. Wade Bainum, Jennifer L. Manzoor. BS in Edn., Emporia (Kans.) State U., 1967; MS in Edn., U. Kans., 1973; AS, Wichita (Kans.) State U., 1997. Cert. learning disabled, educable mentally handicapped, psychology, composition and lit., Ariz., Calif., Kans., Tex. Tchr. educable mentally handicapped and learning disabled Shawnee Mission (Kans.) Pub. Schs., 1967-69; tchr. headstart program Hutchinson Pub. Schs., 1968; tchr. educable mentally handicapped Chanute High Sch., Iola, Kans., 1974-76; tchr. learning and behavior disabled Sedgwick County Area Spl. Edn. Svcs. Coop., Goddard, 1979-80; tchr. learning disabled Butler County Sch. Bd. Coun. Spl. Edn. Coop., El Dorado, 1986-87, tchr. educable mentally handicapped Augusta Mid. Sch., 1999-2000; tchr. learning disabled Wichita Pub. Schs., 1987-89; writer, rschr. Andover, Kans., 1989-91; legal adminstrv. asst., 1992-94; tchr. learning and behavior disabled So. Tex. Ind. Sch. Dist., Mercedes, 1995-96; paralegal Legal Temps, 1999-2000; tchr. resource specialist program Alvord Pub. Schs., Riverside, Calif., 2000—01; tchr. cross categorical bilingual Wakefield Mid. Sch., Tucson, 2002—. Tucson Unified Sch. Dist., 2002—03. Author: A Scoville Branch in America: A Genealogy and Story (1660-1990). U. Kans. grant. Mem. AAUW, ASCD, NAFE, DAR (Eunice Sterling chpt. registrar), Nat. Fedn. Paralegal Assns., Coun. for Exceptional Children, Kans. Paralegal Assn., Psi Chi. Home: Apt 15203 10700 N La Reserve Drive Oro Valley AZ 85737-8776 E-mail: dgsville@swbell.net.

SCOWCROFT, BRENT, retired air force officer, government official; b. Ogden, Utah, Mar. 19, 1925; s. James and Lucile (Ballantyne) S.; m. Marian Horner, Sept. 17, 1951 (dec. 1995); 1 dau., Karen. BS, U.S. Mil. Acad., 1947; MA, Columbia U., 1953, PhD, 1967; postgrad., Georgetown U., 1958. Commd. 2d lt. USAF, 1947, advanced through grades to lt. gen., 1974; asst. prof. dept. social sci. U.S. Mil. Acad., 1953-57; asst. air attache Am. Embassy, Belgrade, Yugoslavia, 1959-61; assoc. prof. dept. polit. sci. U.S. Air Force Acad., Colo., 1962-63, prof., head dept., 1963-64; mem. staff long range planning div. Office Dep. Chief Staff Plans and Ops., Washington, 1964-67; assigned Nat. War Coll., 1967-68; staff asst. Western Hemisphere region Office Asst. Sec. Def. Internat. Security Affairs, Washington, 1968-69; dep. asst. dir. plans for nat. security matters office Dep. Chief Staff Plans and Ops., 1969-70; spl. asst. to dir. Joint Staff, Joint Chiefs of Staff, 1970-71; mil. asst. to Pres., 1972-73; dep. asst. to Pres. for nat. security affairs, 1973-75; asst. to Pres. for nat. security affairs, 1975-77; mem. Pres.'s Gen. Adv. Com. on Arms Control, 1977-80; vice chmn. Kissinger Assocs., Inc., 1982-89; asst. to Pres. Nat. Security Coun., Washington, 1989-93; pres. Forum for Internat. Policy, 1993—. Bd. dirs. Nat. Bank Washington, Pennzoil-Quaker State and Quallcomm, Inc., Qualcomm, Inc., Pennzoil Quaker State Co., Am. Coun. on Germany; chmn. Pres.'s Commn. on Strategic Forces; mem. Pres.'s Commn. on Def. Mgmt., Pres. Spl. Rev. Bd. on Iran/Contra Affair; pres. The Scowcroft Group, 1994—. Bd. dirs. Atlantic Council U.S.; Bd. visitors U.S. Air Force Air U., 1977-79; mem. adv. bd. Georgetown Center for Strategic and Internat. Studies. Decorated D.S.M. with two oak leaf clusters, Legion of Merit with oak leaf cluster, Air Force Commendation medal, D.S.M. Dept. Def., Nat. Security medal; recipient Medal of Freedom, 1991; named Hon. Knight Brit. Empire, 1993. Mem. Council Fgn. Relations (bd. dirs.), UN Assn. U.S. (vice chmn.), Am. Polit. Sci. Assn., Acad. Polit. Sci. Mem. Ch. Jesus Christ of Latter-day Saints. Office: # 500 900 17th St NW Ste 500 Washington DC 20006-2507

SCOWN, MICHAEL JOHN, lawyer; b. Glen Ellyn, Ill., Apr. 19, 1959; s. William Floyd and June Althea Scown; m. Catherine Maria Sevilla, Oct. 10, 1992. AB in Polit. Sci., U. Calif., Berkeley, 1981; JD, U. San Francisco, 1985. Bar: Calif. 1985, U.S. Dist. Ct. (no. dist.) Calif. 1985, U.S. Ct. Appeals (9th cir.) 1985. Fgn. svc. officer U.S. Dept. State, 1985-88; assoc. Russin & Vecchi, San Francisco, 1988-92, ptnr., 1993-98; regional counsel Intel Capital, Hong Kong, 1999—. Contbr. articles to profl. jours.; editor: U. San Francisco Law Rev., 1984-85. Chmn. bd. govs. Am. C. of C., Ho Chi Minh City, Vietnam, 1995-96, bd. govs., 1994-98. Mem. ABA, Olympic Club. Office: Intel Semiconductor Ltd 32/F 2 Pac Pl 88 Queensway Hong Kong Hong Kong E-mail: michael.j.scown@intel.com.

SCOZZARI, ALBERT, portfolio manager, inventor; b. Chgo. BA, Northeastern Ill. U., 1973; MPA, Ill. Inst. Tech., 1974; PhD, Columbia Pacific U., 1986. Cons. World Bank Group, 1987-99. Adj. prof. bus. studies. Ill. Inst. Tech., 1975, Columbia Pacific U., 1986; artist-in-residence Ariz. Coun. Fine Arts, 1999. Author: Mass Communications in Politics, 1978, Managing for Effectiveness, 1986, Management in the 90s, 1990, Vietnam Faces, 1995, Field Cross, 1996, The Mountain, 1997, The Trail, 1997, A Collection of Verses and Poems, 1997. Pres. Homeowners Assn., Phoenix, 1992-96, Scozzari Meml. Scholarship Fund, 1991—. With USNR, 1961-66, ret. ANG, 1979-87. Mem. Am. Fedn. Musicians (life), Assn. Stage and Film Actors (life), Am. Poets and Writers Guild (life), Am. Mensa Assn. (life), Vietnam Vets. Am. (life), Adventurers Club. (life). Home: PMB 1004 110 Rainbow Dr Livingston TX 77399-1010 E-mail: alsmondousa@yahoo.com.

SCRABECK, JON GILMEN, dental educator; b. Rochester, Minn., Dec. 6, 1938; s. Clarence and Nancy Alma (Brown) S.; m. DeAnn Louise Jacks, June 16, 1962; children: Joan Louise, Erik Jon. Student, Contra Costa Coll., San Pablo, Calif., 1964-66, U. Calif., Berkeley, 1966-67; DDS, UCLA, 1971; MA in Edn., U. Colo., 1985. Pvt. practice, Santa Rosa, Calif., 1971-78; sr. instr. U. Colo. Sch. Dentistry, Denver, 1978-79, asst. prof., 1980-86, dir. patient care, 1979-80, acting dir. clin. affairs, 1980-81, acting assoc. dean, acting div. chmn., 1984-85; dept. chmn. Marquette U. Sch. Dentistry, Milw., 1986-90, assoc. prof., 1986—, assoc. prof. tenure, 1989, curricular head, 1990—. Cons. Dental Student mag.,1983-86, Colo. Bd. Dentistry, Denver, 1985-86, Dentist mag., 1986-90, VA, Milw., 1987-90. Editor Jour. Colo. Dental Assn., 1980-86; contbr. articles and abstracts to dental jours. Mem. vol. staff Morey Dental Clinic, Denver, 1982-85, Health Fair, Denver, 1983-85; ofcl. judge S.E. Wis. Sci. Fair, Milw., 1988—. Fellow Internat. Coll. Dentists, Acad. Dental Materials, Am. Coll. Dentists, Pierre Fauchard Acad.; mem. ADA (coun. on journalism 1984-86, coun. on dental rsch. 1986-88, manuscript reviewer 1988—), Acad. Operative Dentistry, Wis. Dental Assn. (assoc. editor Jour. 1987—), Omicron Kappa Upsilon, Alpha Gamma Sigma. Roman Catholic. Avocations: foreign and domestic travel, photography, boating, fishing, water skiing. Home: W349s10140 Bittersweet Ct Eagle WI 53119-1851 Office: Marquette U Sch Dentistry 604 N 16th St Milwaukee WI 53233-2117

SCRAGG, THOMAS WILLIAM, librarian, historical researcher, solicitor; b. Wirral, Cheshire, Eng., Sept. 19, 1940; s. Joseph and Norah Scragg; m. Isabel Mary Thomas, Apr. 3, 1972; children: Maximian Rhys Joseph, Halcyon Rosemary Louise, Sophia Isabel Hannah, Mortimer Henry Thomas. BA with honours, Sch. Slavonic and E. European Studies, U. London; B.Phil., U. Liverpool; MA, Manchester Poly., Eng.; postgrad., King's Coll., U. London, U. Wales, Aberystwyth; Dipl.Lib., F.L.A., Manchester Libr. Sch. Solicitor Supreme Ct., 1968—; music adviser, hist. rschr., program annotator Chester Festival, 1967, 1986—88, Festival in Gt. Irish Houses, 1970—81, Queen's Festival, U. Belfast, 1971, 1972, Newcastle-upon-Tyne Festival, 1972—75, Portsmouth Festival, 1977—78, Dublin Festival, Royal Dublin Soc., 1979, Alfred Beit Found., 1979—81, Leeds Castle Festival, 1987, Music Assn. Ireland, others. Photographic cons., cataloguer Sir Compton MacKenzie's Jethou Record Collection, 1973—75; music libr. cons. Granada TV Ltd., 1973—75; libr., archivist Knowsley Libr., 1974—91. Author: articles, festival program material, Claudio Arrau Discography, 1978, 2d edit., 1982; author: (joint) Library Association Standards for Local Studies Provision in Public Libraries, 1989. Fellow: Libr. Assn. (Charles Nowell Meml. prize 1992), Soc. Antiquaries of Scotland, Royal Soc Arts, Royal Geog. Soc.; mem.: E.S.U., Anglo-Polish Music Circle Gt. Britain (hon. v.p. 1970), Polish Inst. Arts and Scis. Am. (assoc.), Soc. Genealogists, Royal Mus. Assn., Soc. Archivists, Law Soc., Internat. Assn. Religious Freedom. Avocations: travel, history of public concerts, historical discography. Home: The Woodcroft Barnston Wirral CH6 11BU England

SCRAMUZZO, EILEEN J. b. Detroit, Sept. 7, 1924; d. Walter and Kathryn (Vicmanic) Joyce; m. James Mignogna, Nov. 10, 1947 (dec. July 14, 1970); 1 child James ; m. Carl Scramuzzo, Nov. 19, 1984. Student , Dobbins Vocat. Sch. (U.S. Army related), 1942, MacCormack Coll., 1957, CNA, 1985. Inspector U.S. Army Odnance, Phila., 1942—44; clk. Sears, Altoona, 1944—52; key punch operator Western Elec., Chgo., 1952—57, Burlington Northern RR, Chgo., 1957—73; store owner Roger Park Stationers, 1975—78; computer operator St. Francis Hosp., 1978—80, Western Electric, Chgo., 1981—86. Staff mem. CNA Home Care, Chgo., 1986—94. Author: (short stories) D Day, 1967 (Marshall Field monetary award $5000, 1996). Mem.: Am. Legion, Irish Am. Heritage Ctr., Ramada Swimming Club. Democrat. Roman Catholic. Avocations: dancing, singing, swimming, writing. Home: 5103 N St Louis Ave Chicago IL 60625

SCRENOCK, PAUL STEVEN, lawyer; b. Summerville, N.J., Mar. 29, 1952; s. Joseph John and Elsie (Neuman) S.; m. Angie Screnock, June 3, 1997; children: Brent, Matthew, David, Rebecca & Ryan. BA, U. Wis., 1974; JD, John Marshall Sch. Law, 1977. Bar: Wis. 1977, Ill. 1978, U.S. Dist. Ct. (we. dist.) Ill. 1978. Assoc. Screnock Law Office, Baraboo, Wis., 1977-79; pvt. practice Friendship and Westfield, 1979—, Adams, 1979—. Incorporator Damon A. Renner Scholarship Fund Inc., 1987; chartered sec. Adams County United Way Inc., 1988—; sec., bd. dirs. adv. bd. Villa Pines, Friendship, 1982—. Mem. ABA, Wis. Bar Assn., Tri-County Bar Assn., Adams County Jaycees (chartered pres. 1979). Office: 333 N Main St Adams WI 53910-9658 Fax: 608-339-7787.

SCREPETIS, DENNIS, retired nuclear engineer, consultant; b. Hoboken, N.J., Feb. 12, 1930; s. George and Athanasia (Stasinos) S.; m. Betty Pravasilis, Sept. 17, 1960. Student, Stevens Inst. Tech., Bklyn. Poly. Inst., Cooper Union, Rutgers U. Registered profl. engr., N.J., N.Y. Nuc. engr. Vitro Corp. Am., N.Y.C., 1957-60; project engr. Gen. Cable Corp., Bayonne, N.J., 1960-63; project mgr. AMF Atomics, York, Pa., 1963-65; sr. staff engr. nuc. divsn. Combustion Engring. Corp., Windsor, Conn., 1965-66; corp. engr. Std. Packaging Corp., N.Y.C., 1966-68; v.p. engring. Ea. Schokbeton, Bound Brook, N.J., 1968-74; cons. engr. Ft. Lee, 1974-99; ret., 1999. Mem. Am. Biog. Inst. Rsch. Assn. (bd. dirs.), Internat. Biog. Ctr. (bd. dirs.). Greek Orthodox. Achievements include patentee in nuclear science. Home and Office: 2200 N Central Rd Fort Lee NJ 07024-7557

SCRIBNER, CHARLES, III, publisher, art historian, lecturer; b. Washington, May 24, 1951; s. Charles and Joan (Sunderland) S.; m. Ritchie Harrison Markoe, Aug. 4, 1979; children: Charles IV, Christopher Markoe. AB, Princeton U., 1973, MFA, 1975, PhD, 1977. Editor Charles Scribner's Sons, N.Y.C., 1975—, dir. subs. rights, 1978-82, pub. paperback div., 1982-83, exec. v.p., 1983-84; v.p. Macmillan Pub. Co., 1984-94. Instr. dept. art and archaeology Princeton U., 1976-77; mem. adv. coun. Princeton U. Library, 1981-90, 98—; mem. adv. coun. dept. art and archaeology Princeton U., 1983-91, 99—; trustee Princeton U. Press, 1984-90, Homeland Found., 1987—; bd. advisors Wethersfield Inst., 1985—; bd. dirs. Met. Opera Guild, 1990-92. Author: The Triumph of the Eucharist - Tapestries by Rubens, 1982, Rubens, 1989, Bernini, 1991. Trustee St. Paul's Sch., Concord, N.H., 1994—. Mem. Assn. Princeton U. Press. Clubs: Racquet and Tennis (N.Y.C.); Ivy (Princeton); Piping Rock (N.Y.). Roman Catholic. Avocations: music, art, opera. Office: Charles Scribners Sons 12th Fl 1230 Avenue of the Americas New York NY 10020 E-mail: scribner@alumni.princeton.edu.

SCRIBNER, JOHN E. lawyer; Office: Clifford Chance Rogers & Wells 2001 K St NW Washington DC 20006

SCRIBNER, MARGARET ELLEN, school evaluator, senior consultant; b. Pana, Ill., Oct. 20, 1948; d. William M. and Beatrice Faye (Springman) S.; m. John E. McNeal, Aug. 15, 1977 (div. Oct. 1981); m. Leonard P. Basak Jr., Mar. 13, 1986; children: L. Phillip III, Cassandra. BS in Social Work, Spalding U., 1970. Coord. Gov.'s Inaugural Com., Springfield, Ill., 1972; sr. cons. Ill. State Bd. Edn., Chgo., 1970—, acting divsn. supr., 2001—. Dir. on bd. and corp. sec. Ventura 21, Inc., Roselle, Ill., 1984-87; mem. Ill. Common Performance Mgmt. Project Team, 1996—. Mem. Uptown Cmty. Orgn., Chgo., 1978-80; charter mem., organizer Margate-Ainslie Block Club, Chgo., 1979-80. Recipient cert. of recognition Ill. State Bd. Edn., Springfield, 1975, 77, 78. Mem. Nat. Assn. State Adminstrs. and Suprs. Pvt. Schs. (sec. 1999-2002), Bus. and Profl. Women Chgo. (historian 1978-79), Internat. Leadership Tng. Inst. (cert. 1974), Ill. Athletic Club (Chgo.), Brookwood Country Club (Wood Dale, Ill.). Republican. Roman Catholic. Avocations: golf, clarinet, wave colors, writing. Office: Ill State Bd of Edn 100 W Randolph St Ste 14-300 Chicago IL 60601-3283

SCRIBNER, SHERLIE ANN, educator; b. Mobile, Ala., Aug. 24, 1945; d. Murl and Eva Coggin Scribner; children: Michael Svestka, Lauren Svestska, Christopher Svestka. BA in English and Philosophy, Baylor U., 1966; MEd, U. Va., 1976; MA, EdD in Ednl. Adminstrn., Columbia U., 1980; diploma, Nat. Def. U., 1984. Classroom tchr. Virginia Beach (Va.) Pub. Schs., 1966-69, Internat. Sch., Bangkok, 1969-70; reading resource tchr. Fairfax (Va.) County Pub. Schs., 1973-76; sr. evaluator U.S. Gen. Acctg. Office, Washington, 1980-97; CEO Children's Fund, 1997—; devel. officer Washington Episcopal Sch., Bethesda, Md., 1999-2000; program dir., tchr. profl. studies U. Va. Sch. Continuing and Profl. Studies, 2000-2001; ESL tchr. Fairfax (Va.) County Pub. Sch., 2001—. Contbr. articles to profl. jours., reports to U.S. Congress. Trustee Episcopal Ctr. for Children; bd. dirs. Tiny Findings Daycare Ctr., Washington; founder Children's Fund, Children's Resource Network, Ctr. for Children's Studies, Child Survival Fund, Children's Hunger Relief Network, Free the Children Fund, Children's Edn. and Enrichment Fund, Children's Spl. Needs Fund, Christian Children's Relief Fund, all Washington. Mem. World Orgn. Presch. Edn. Baptist. Address: Children's Fund PO Box 7936 Mc Lean VA 22106-7936 E-mail: SherlieScribner@aol.com.

SCRICCO, FRANCIS M. electronics company executive; BS, Worcester Poly. Inst.; MS in Bus., Columbia U. With The Boston Cons. Group; various mgmt. positions GE Corp.; pres. Whirlpool, Can.; group pres. Fisher Sci.

Internat.; exec. v.p., COO Arrow Electronics Inc., Melville, N.Y., 1997-99, pres., COO, 1999-2001, pres., CEO, 2001—; also bd. dirs. Office: Arrow Electronics Inc 25 Hub Dr Melville NY 11747-3509*

SCRIGGINS, LARRY PALMER, lawyer, director; b. Englewood, N.J., Nov. 27, 1936; s. Thomas Dalby and M. Patricia (Fowler) S.; m. Victoria Jackola, Feb. 17, 1979; children: Elizabeth J., Thomas P. AB, Middlebury Coll., 1958; JD, U. Chgo., 1961. Bar: Md. 1962. Law clk. to chief judge Md. Ct. Appeals, 1962; assoc. Piper & Marbury, L.L.P., Balt., 1962-69, ptnr., 1969-98, vice chmn., 1988-93, mem. exec. com., CFO, 1993-98; sr. counsel Piper Marbury Rudnick & Wolfe LLP, 1999-2001, ptnr. emeritus, 2001—. Mem. legal adv. com. N.Y. Stock Exch., 1992-96; bd. dirs. USF & G Corp., 1979-98, Center Stage Assocs., 1979-89, Balt. Choral Arts Soc., 1979-96, Balt. Conv. Bur., 1982-95, YMCA of Greater Balt., 1987-94, Fund for Ednl. Excellence, 1990-98, chmn. bd. trustees, 1993-98; bd. dirs. Nat. Aquarium in Balt., bd. govs. 1987-93; bd. dirs. Balt. Symphony Orchestra, 1996-2001. Contbr. articles to profl. jours. Fellow: Am. Bar Found.; mem.: ABA (sect. on bus. law coun. 1972—76, chair 1991—92, vice chair and editor-in-chief The Bus. Lawyer 1989—90, chmn. law and acctg. com. 1985—88, chmn. com. corp. laws 1996—2000, chmn. ad hoc com. on ethics 2000 1999—), AICPA (planning com. 1989—92), Fin. Acctg. Stds. Bd., Task Force in Fin. Instruments, Am. Law Inst., Am. Judicature Soc., Md. Bar Assn. (coun. 1976—78, chmn. 1977—78, mem. com. on corp. laws 1981—84). Home: 13663 E Columbine Dr Scottsdale AZ 85259-3752 Office: Piper Rudnick & Wolfe LLP 6225 Smith Ave Baltimore MD 21209-3600 E-mail: larry.scriggins@piperrudnick.com.

SCRIMGEOUR, GARY JAMES, writer, educator; b. Auckland, New Zealand, Jan. 15, 1934; came to U.S., 1957; s. Colin Graham and Caroline Lenna (Hardie) S. BA with honors, U. Sydney, Australia, 1954; MA in English, Wash. U., 1959; PhD, Princeton U., 1968. Asst. personnel officer Dexion Ltd., London, 1956-57; mem. faculty dept. English Fla. U., Gainesville, 1959-61, Rutgers U., New Brunswick, N.J., 1963-64, Ind. U., Bloomington, 1964-69; editor, writer Benjamin Blom, Inc., N.Y.C., 1969-70; chief of social systems div. and head editorial office Sch. of Pub. and Environ. Affairs, Ind. U., 1970-74; dir. Profl. Studies Assocs., Bloomington, 1973—; editor Coll. Engring. U. Nev.-Reno, 1992-94, sr. editor Coll. Bus. Adminstrn., 1994—. Cons. for research in alcoholism, ct. systems, hwy. safety and design of seminars to various govt. agys., schs. and social orgns., 1970—. Author: A Woman of Her Times, 1982, The Garden Inspector, 1993; contbr. numerous manuals on ct. systems and alcohol safety to profl. publs. and articles on lit. criticism to lit. jours. Jane E. Procter fellow Princeton U., 1968. Office: 369 Bret Harte Ave Reno NV 89509 E-mail: gscrim@unr.nevada.edu.

SCRIMSHAW, NEVIN STEWART, physician, nutrition and health educator; b. Jan. 20, 1918; m. Mary Ware Goodrich, 1941; 5 children. BA with honors, Ohio Wesleyan U., 1938; MA in Biology, Harvard U., 1939, PhD in Physiology, 1941, MPH, 1959; MD with honors, U. Rochester, 1945. Intern Gorgas Hosp., 1945-46; Rockefeller postdoctoral fellow U. Rochester, NY, 1946—47, Merck NRC fellow, 1947—49; asst. resident in ob-gyn. Strong Meml. Hosp., Genesee Hosp., 1948—49; dir. Inst. Nutrition C.Am. and Panama, Guatemala, 1949—61, cons. dir. Guatemala, 1961—65, cons. Guatemala, 1965—. Cons. nutrition Pan-Am. San Bur. WHO, 1948—49, regional advisor on nutrition, 1949—53; dir. Clin. Rsch. Ctr. MIT, 1962—66, 1979—83, dir. internat. food and nutrition program, 1976—88, prof. human nutrition, 1961—76, head dept. nutrition and food sci., 1961—79, inst. prof., 1976—87, emeritus, 1988—; vis. prof. Columbia U., N.Y.C., 1976—88, vis. lectr., 1961—66, Harvard U., 1968—85; adj. prof. Tufts U.; mem. gov. adv. com. NIH; chmn. internat. com. NRC; dir. devel. studies divsn. UN U., 1985—86, food nutrition program, 1975—97, sr. advisor, 1998—; mem. adv. com. WHO, Nutrition Found., others. Editor (with others): Amino Acid Fortification of Protein Foods, 1971, Nutrition, National Development and Planning, 1973, The Economics, Marketing and Technology of Fish Protein Concentrate, 1974, Development: Significance and Potential for the Tropics, 1976, Single-Cell Protein: Safety for Animal and Human Feeding, 1979, Nutrition Policy Implementation: Issues and Experience, 1983, Diarrhea and Malnutrition: Interactions, Mechanisms and Interventions, 1983, Chronic Energy Deficiency, 1987, Acceptability of Milk and Milk Products in Populations with Lactose Intolerance, 1988, Nutrition in the Elderly, 1989, Activity, Energy Expenditure and Energy Requirements of Infants and Children, 1990, RAP: Rapid Assessment Procedures: Qualitative Methodologies for Planning and Evaluation of Health Related Programs, 1992, Protein-energy Interactions, 1992, Community-based Longitudinal Nutrition and Health Studies: Classical Examples from Guatemala, Haiti, and Mexico, 1995, The Effects of Improved Nutrition in Early Childhood: The Institute of Nutrition of Central American and Panama Follow-up Study, 1995, The Nutrition and Health Transition of Democratic Costa Rica, 1995, Energy and Protein Requirements, 1996, Causes and Consequences of Intrauterine Growth Retardation, 2000; contbr. articles to profl. jours. Trustee Rockefeller Found., 1971—83, Pan-Am. Health and Edn. Found., 1986—92; pres. Internat. Nutrition Found. for Developing Countries, 1982—. Recipient Osborne and Mendal award, 1960, Internat. award, Inst. Food Technologists, 1969, medal of honor, Fundacion F. Cuenca Villoro, Spain, 1978, Bristol-Myers prize, 1988, Alan Shawn Feinstein award, 1991, World Food prize, 1991, Kellogg award in internat. nutrition, 2002, others. Fellow: APHA (v.p. 1978, award of excellence in promoting and protecting health of people 1974), AAAS, Am. Soc. Clin. Nutrition, Royal Soc. Health, Am. Soc. Nutritional Scis.; mem.: NAS (chair applied biol. sect. 1973—76, 1988—91), others, Internat. Epidemiol. Assn., Internat. Union Nutritional Scis. (pres. 1978—81), Am. Epidemiol. Soc., Am. Physiol. Soc., Mass. Med. Soc., New Eng. Pub. Health Assn., Mass. Pub. Health Assn., Am. Bd. Nutrition, Am. Coll. Preventive Medicine, Am. Acad. Arts and Scis., Inst. Medicine NAS, Am. Coll. Nutrition. Home and Office: Sandwich Mountain Farm PO Box 330 Campton NH 03223-0330 Fax: 603-726-4614. E-mail: nevin@cyberportal.net.

SCRIPPS, DOUGLAS JERRY, music educator, conductor, director; b. Grand Rapids, Mich., Aug. 25, 1942; s. Kenneth Witvoet and Marguerite F. (Rottier) S.; m. Betty Ann Broersma Porter, July 24, 1963 (div. Aug. 1974); children: Elisabeth Ann Scripps Blue, Theodore Jon; m. Merilee Elaine Collins, Apr. 5, 1975; children: Daniel Collins, Taylor Douglas, Adam Rottier. Student, Eastman Sch. Music, 1961, 62; BA, Calvin Coll., 1965; student, U. Music and Dramatic Art, Vienna, 1965—66; MM, U. Mich., 1970. Prin. trumpet player Grand Rapids Symphony Orch., 1961-65, assoc. conductor, 1976-85; dir. music Grand Rapids City Coll., 1967-78; conductor Lake St. Clair Symphony, Detroit, 1970-72, Alma (Mich.) Symphony Orch., 1985—; music dir. Grand Rapids Ballet, 1979-99; asst. prof. music Ctrl. Mich. U., Mt. Pleasant, 1981-84; prof. music, dept. chair Alma Coll., 1985—. Guest condr. Interlochen Ctr. Arts, Joffrey Ballet, Bay View Music Festival, Blue Lake Fine Arts Camp; vis. prof. Grand Valley State U., Calvin Coll., 1977-81; adjudicator various midwest comps., 1968-95. Am. Heritage Assn. study abroad lectr., Vienna, 1999. Mem. Am. Symphony Orch. League, Internat. Soc. Verdi Studies, Nat. Assn. Schs. Music. Avocations: reading, travel, sailing. Office: Alma Coll 614 W Superior St Alma MI 48801-1511

SCRIVEN, WAYNE MARCUS, lawyer; b. Sumter, S.C., Aug. 31, 1953; s. Philip Roosevelt and Sarah Ella (Pringle) S. BA in History Edn. cum laude, Va. Union U., 1975; JD, Golden Gate U. Sch. of Law, 1979. Bar: Va. 1980, U.S. Dist. Ct. (ea. dist.) Va. 1980, U.S. Ct. Appeals (4th cir.) 1980, S.C. 1982, U.S. Dist. Ct. S.C. 1982, U.S. Supreme Ct. 1984, Calif. 1987, U.S. Dist. Ct. (no. dist.) Calif. 1986, U.S. Ct. Appeals (9th cir.) 1986, D.C. 1993, U.S. Dist. Ct. D.C. 1994, U.S. Dist. Ct. Md. 1994, U.S. Ct. Appeals (fed. cir.) 1994, D.C. Directing atty. Petersburg (Va.) Legal Aid Soc., 1980-81; staff atty. Carolina Regional Legal Svcs. Corp., Florence, S.C., 1981-82; solo practice atty., 1982-85, Richmond, Va., 1985-86, San Francisco, 1986-93, Washington, 1993—. Contract atty. Neighborhood Legal Asst. Program, Marion, S.C., 1982-83, pro bonocontract atty., 1983-85, Carolina Regional Legal Svcs. Corp., Florence, 1983-85, Bar Assn. of San Francisco, 1987-93; notary public, S.C., 1981-91, Va., 1986-91. Bd. dirs. Young Men's Christian Assn., Florence, 1982-83, Pee Dee Crisis Ctr., Florence, 1983-84, San Francisco Neighborhood Legal Asst. Program, 1992-93. Named one of Outstanding Young Men of Am., U.S. Jaycees, 1982; recipient Outstanding Lawyer in Pub. Svc., Bar Assn. San Francisco, 1988-91. Mem. ABA, Washington Bar Assn., Assn. Trial Lawyers of Am., U.S. Supreme Ct. Hist. Soc. Baptist. Avocations: fishing, guitar playing, nature trail walking. Office: Scriven & Assocs 7900 Sudley Rd Ste 420 Manassas VA 20109 also: Scriven & Assocs 1225 Eye St NW Ste 500 Washington DC 20005-3914 Fax: (703) 369-7158. E-mail: Wayne-Marcus-Scriven@abanet.org.

SCRIVER, CHARLES ROBERT, medical scientist, human geneticist; b. Montreal, Que., Can., Nov. 7, 1930; s. Walter deM. and Jessie (Boyd) S.; m. E.K. Peirce, Sept. 8, 1956; children: Dorothy, Peter, Julie, Paul. BA cum laude, McGill U., Montreal, 1951, MDC.M. cum laude, 1955; DSc (hon.), U. Man., 1992, U. Glasgow, 1993, U. Montreal, 1993, Utrecht U., 1999. Intern Royal Victoria Hosp., Montreal, 1955-56; resident Royal Victoria and Montreal Children's hosps., 1956-57, Children's Med. Center, Boston, 1957-58; McLaughlin travelling fellow Univ. Coll., London, 1958-60; chief resident pediatrics Montreal Children's Hosp., 1960-61; asst. prof. pediatrics McGill U., 1961, prof. biology Faculty of Sci., prof. pediatrics Faculty of Medicine, 1969—; Alva prof. human genetics, 1994—. Mem. med. adv. bd. Howard Hughes Med. Inst., 1981-88; dir. Med. Rsch. Coun. Group in Genetics, 1972-94; assoc. dir. Can. Genetic Diseases Network, 1989-98. Co-author: Amino Acid Metabolism and Its Disorders, 1973, Garrod's Inborn Factors in Disease, 1989; sr. editor Metabolic and Molecular Bases Inherited Disease, 1986—; contbr. more than 550 rsch. publs. in field. Decorated Order of Can. Que., Mont.; named Royal Coll. lectr., 1992, Disting. Scientist, Med. Rsch. Coun., 1995—; named to Can. Med. Hall of Fame, 2001, Can. Sci. Engring. Hall of Fame, 2001; recipient Wood Gold medal, McGill U., 1955, Gairdner Internat. award, Gairdner Found., 1979, Prix Michel-Sarrazi, Club de Rech Clir du Que., 1988, Ross award, Can. Pediatric Soc., 1990, Award of Excellence, Genet Soc. Can., 1992, Prix d'Excellence, Inst. Rsch. Clin. de Montreal, 1993, Prix du Quebec, Wilder Penfield, 1995, Medal of Merit, Can. Med. Assn., 1996, Lifetime Achievement award, March of Dimes Birth Defects Found., 1997, Querci Found. prize, Italy, 2001; grantee Markle scholar, 1962—67. Fellow: AAAS, Royal Soc. London (Can. Rutherford lectr. 1983), Royal Soc. Can. (McLaughlin medal 1981), Royal Coll. Physicians of Ireland (hon.), Am. Coll. Med. Genetics (hon.); mem.: Am. Acad. Pediat. (Mead Johnson award for rsch. in pediat. 1968), Soc. Francaise de Pediat., Brit. Pediat. Assn. (50th Anniversary lectr. 1978), Assn. Am. Physicians, Am. Soc. Clin. Investigation, Am. Pediat. Soc. (pres. 1994—95), Am. Soc. Human Genetics (dir. 1971—74, pres. 1986—87, William Allan award 1978, Award of Excellence in Human Genetics Edn. 2001), Soc. Pediat. Rsch. (pres. 1975—76), Can. Soc. Clin. Investigation (pres. 1974—75, G. Malcolm Brown Meml. award 1979, Henry Friesen award 2001). Office: McGill Univ-Montreal Childrens Hosp Rsch Inst 2300 Tupper St Montreal QC Canada H3H 1P3 E-mail: mc77@musica.mcgill.ca.

SCRIVNER, THOMAS WILLIAM, lawyer; b. Madison, Wis., Sept. 10, 1948; s. William H. and Jane (Gehrz) S.; m. Meredith Burke, Aug. 16, 1980; children: Allison, David. AB, Duke U., 1970, MAT, 1972; JD, U. Wis., 1977. Assoc. Michael, Best & Friedrich LLP, Milw., 1978-85, ptnr., 1985—. Mem. ABA, Wis. Bar Assn., Milw. Bar Assn. (labor sect.), Corp. Practice Inst. (pres. 1989-92). Episcopalian. Home: 4626 N Cramer St Milwaukee WI 53211-1203 Office: Michael Best & Friedrich LLP 100 E Wisconsin Ave Ste 3300 Milwaukee WI 53202-4108

SCROGGIE, WAYNE LEE, trade and computing consultant; b. July 19, 1949; s. James Heburn and Edith (Harrington) S. BA, Eastern Wash. State Coll., 1975; MBA, U. Wash., 1977. Indsl. engr. Boeing Comml. Airplane Co., Everett, Wash., 1978; fin. planner Boeing Marine Systems, Seattle, 1978-81; cost and schedules engr. ASW/SOW program Boeing Aerospace Co., Kent, Wash., 1981-84; cost and schedules engr. Boeing Comml. Airplane Co., Renton, 1984-87; systems analyst Boeing Computer Svcs., 1987-94; bus. owner Northeast Rim, Seattle, 1994-2001; programmer Danzas AEI, 2001—. With USAF, 1968-72. Mem. Latin Trade Com., World Trade Club (bd. advisers 1983-88), Asia Soc., Asian Mgmt. Bus. Assn., Assn. Internat. Students in Econs. and Commerce, U. Wash. MBA Alumni Assn., Assn. MBAs, China Club of Seattle (pres. 1992-94, bd. dirs. 1995—), World Affairs Coun. Home: 2740 47th Ave SW Seattle WA 98116-2904

SCROGGS, E. JANE, social worker, educator; b. Blanchard, Okla., Apr. 11, 1937; d. Charles Elmer and Gertrude (Moore) Lowry; m. James Edward Scroggs, Dec. 22, 1979; 5 children. BA in Social Work, U. Okla., 1973, MSW, 1975, PhD, 1984. Cert. social worker, Ark. Vis. asst. prof. social work U. Ark., Fayetteville, 1986-90; ret. Lectr. Hiroshima Joguakquim, 1969-70, Cuttingham U. Coll., Liberia, 1981. Bd. dirs. League Women Voters, NWAR Food Bank, Fayetteville Open Channel. Mem. AAUW, NASW (exec. dir. Okla. chpt. 1977-79), LWV (bd. dirs. 1985-87). Democrat. Presbyterian (elder). Avocations: camping, horseback riding, gardening, watercolor painting.

SCROGGS, LARRY KENNETH, lawyer, state legislator; b. Beebe, Ark., Oct. 8, 1941; s. Kenneth Chalmers and Mildred Lorene (McDonald) S.; m. Mary Patricia Rushing, Aug. 25, 1967; children: Larry Kenneth Jr., James Kevin, Michael Kyle. BA, Harding U., 1963; JD, Vanderbilt U., 1971. Bar: Tenn. 1971, U.S. Dist. Ct. (we. dist.) Tenn. 1971, U.S. Ct. Appeals (8th cir.) 1982, U.S. Ct. Appeals (6th cir.) 1989, U.S. Supreme Ct. 1981. Assoc. Law Firm of Leo Bearman, Memphis, 1971-72, Holt, Batchelor, Spicer, Memphis, 1972-76, ptnr., 1976-80, Less & Scroggs, Memphis, 1980-92; pvt. practice, Germantown, Tenn., 1992-96; ptnr. Scroggs & Rogers, Collierville, 1997—; mem. Tenn. Ho. of Reps., Nashville, 1997—. Mcpl. ct. judge City of Germantown, 1980-86; atty. for County Trustee, Shelby County, Memphis, 1990—. Mem. campaign steering com. George Bush for Pres., Memphis, 1987-92; vol. Ed Bryant for Congress campaign, Memphis, 1994, Don Sundquist for Gov. campaign, Memphis, 1994. Lt. U.S. Navy, 1964-67, Vietnam. Mem. ABA, Tenn. Bar Assn., Memphis Bar Assn. (bd. dirs. 1990-91). Republican. Mem. Ch. of Christ. Avocations: photography, boating, tennis. Office: Scroggs & Rogers 110 E Mulberry St Ste 200 Collierville TN 38017-2675

SCROGGS, ROBIN JEROME, theology educator; b. Raleigh, N.C., Oct. 14, 1930; s. James Wade Scroggs and Lucille Dowd; m. Leah Margaret Self Bennett, June 29, 1954 (div.); 1 child, Mark Wade; m. Marilee Ruth Munger, May 29, 1971; 1 child, Jonathan Paul. AB, U. N.C., 1951, B in Music, 1952; BDiv, Duke U., 1955; PhD, Princeton U., 1962. From instr. to assoc. prof. and chmn. dept. religion Dartmouth Coll., Hanover, N.H., 1959-69; assoc. prof., then prof. Chgo. Theolog. Sem., 1969-86, acting dean, 1974-75; Edward Robinson prof. Biblical theology Union Theolog. Sem., N.Y.C., 1986-97, prof. emeritus, 1997—. Lectr. numerous coll., univs. and chs. throughout U.S., Can. and Germany. Author: The Last Adam, 1967, Paul for a New Day, 1977, the New Testamentand Homosexuality, 1983, Christology in Paul and John, 1988, The Text and the Times, 1993; translator: Glory and the Way of the Cross: The Gospel of Mark, 1972; contbr. numerous articles to jours. Mem. Soc. Biblical Lit., Studiorum Novi testamenti Societas,chgo. Soc. bibllical Rsch. (pres. 1979-80), Cath. Biblical Assn. Avocations: music, keyboarding, choral conductor. Home: 10 Van Dyk Pl Pompton Plains NJ 07444-1654 E-mail: rscroggs@msn.com.

SCRONCE, GARY WAYNE, engineer; b. Greensburg, Kans., Apr. 15, 1961; s. Cecil Pearlie Scronce and Arlene Lucille Scronse; m. Wendy Matherne, Oct. 14, 1995; children: Laura Marie, Grant David. BS in Nuclear Engring., Kans. State U., 1984, MS in Nuclear Engring., 1987. Engr.-in-tng. La. Design system engr. Gulf States Utilities Co., St. Francisville, La., 1986-88, nuclear fuels engr., 1988-91, sr. nuclear fuels engr., 1991-94; fuel fabrication coord. Entergy Opers., Inc., 1994-98; risk analyst/task leader Innovative Emergency Mgmt., Baton Rouge, 1998-2001, project mgr., 2001—. Basketball coach West Feliciana Biddy Basketball, St. Francisville, 1988-92; softball coach Maringouin Lions Club, Twin Rivers League, Maringouin, La., 1993-94; soccer coach Pointe Coupee Youth Soccer, New Roads, La., 1996; mem. Iberville Parish Local Emergency Planning Com., 2001. Mem. La. Nuclear Soc. (chmn. 1986-2000, mem. exec. com. 2001), Am. Nuclear Soc., La. Emergency Preparedness Assn. Home: 10660 Center St Maringouin LA 70757-3123 Office: Innovative Emerg Mgmt Inc 8555 United Plaza Blvd Ste 100 Baton Rouge LA 70809-2258 E-mail: gary.scronce@iem inc.com.

SCRUGGS, CATHERINE LYNN, financial manager; b. 1966; BS in Fin. & Acctg., Miami U., 1988. CPA. Global bus. unit fin. mgr. N.Am. paper products Procter & Gamble, Cin., 1988—, Fine Arts Fund campaign chair, 2000. Campaign cabinet United Way, Cin., 1996, spl. promotions chair, 1996; mem. acctg. adv. bd. Miami U., 1998-2002. Mem. Miami U. Alumni Assn. (pres. Cin. chpt. 1993-95). Office: Procter & Gamble PO Box 599 Cincinnati OH 45201-0599

SCRUGGS, EARL EUGENE, entertainer; b. Cleveland County, N.C., Jan. 6, 1924; s. George Elam and Georgia Lula (Ruppe) S.; m. Anne Louise Certain, Apr. 18, 1948; children: Gary Eugene, Randy Lynn, Steven Earl. HHD in Folk Music (hon.), Gardner-Webb Coll., 1986. Banjo player, 1945—; formed Earl Scruggs Revue, 1969—; major performances include Carnegie Hall, N.Y.C., Wembley Festival, London, Washington Moratorium for Peace, 1969, also rock festivals, coll. concerts; TV appearances include NET-TV Spl. Earl Scruggs: His Family and Friends, 1971, Midnight Spl., NBC-Harper Valley U.S.A. Spl., NBC Country Music Awards Show, Phil Donahue Show, Mike Douglas Show, Austin City Limits, 1977, The Grand Ole Opry's 60th Anniversary Show, 1985, The Nashville Network spl. The American Music Shop, 1990, The Grand Ole Opry's 65th Anniversary Show, 1991, Country Music Assn. Awards Show, 1991, Country Music Assn. Hall of Fame 25th Anniversary TV show, 1992, The Legend of The Beverly Hillbillies, CBS-TV, 1993, Folk Sound USA-Revlon Revue, The Tonight Show, Les Crane Show, Mac Davis Special, The Johnny Cash Show, The Hootenanny Show, Frank McGee's Here and Now, Ernie Ford Show, Jimmy Dean Show, The Anatomy of Pop, Kraft's American Profile, The Roots of Country, CBS-TV, 1994, Red Hot and Country, TNN-TV, 1995, A Night at the Ryman, TNN-TV, 1995, An Evening of Country Greats, 1998, TNN-TV, CMA 40th Anniversary Celebration, CBS-TV, 1998; rec. artist: Columbia Records, 1950—; albums include: Nashvilles Rock, Dueling Banjos, Kansas State, I Saw the Light, Earl Scruggs Revue, Rockin' Cross the Country, Family Portrait, Top of the World, Anniversary Special Vol. I and Vol. II, Live! At Austin City Limits, Earl Scruggs: His Family and Friends Soundtrack, Today and Forever, Bold and New, American-Made, World-Played, others; recorded theme song for TV series The Beverly Hillbillies, 1962, also made guest appearances; composer (with others) movie score Where The Lilies Bloom, 1973, also Earl Scruggs Revue rec. music soundtrack for movie; composer instrumental Foggy Mountain Breakdown (used in movie Bonnie and Clyde, Grammy award 1968, Grammyy award 2001, Broadcast Music, Inc. award 1969); star: (movie) Banjo Man, 1975; guest appearance (TV movie) Return of the Beverly Hillbillies, 1981; author: (book) Earl Scruggs and the 5-String Banjo, 1968. Apptd. hon. mem. Lt. Gov.'s Staff, State of Tenn., 1987. Named Artist of Yr. Hi-Fi Inst., 1975, Best Country and Bluegrass Banjoist, Frets mag., 1980; recipient Country Music award best instrumental group Billboard Mag., 1975, Cert. of Merit Internat. Bluegrass Music Assn., 1988, Order of the Long Leaf Pine award Gov. State of N.C., 1988, cert. appreciation Tenn. Gov. Ned McWherter, 1990, Spl. Citation of achievement recognition of nat. popularity over 1 million broadcasts of Foggy Mountain Breakdown, Broadcast Music, Inc., 1993, N.C. Folk Heritage award, N.C. Arts Coun. Dept Cultural Resources, others; inducted into Gibson Hall of Fame, 1981, Country Music Assn. Hall of Fame, 1985, Internat. Bluegrass Music Assn. Hall of Honor, 1991, Starwalk-Nat. Acad. Recording Arts & Scis., 1997; Nat. Heritage fellow NEA, 1989; Nat. Medal of Arts presented by Pres. George Bush at White House, 1992; recipient N.C. Heritage award N.C. Arts Coun. Dept. Cultural Resources, 1996, 11 Grammy's nominations including Grammy award vocal collaboration Same Old Train, 1998; inducted into N.C. Hall of Fame on Grand Ole Opry, 1999, lifetime achievement award Gibson Guitar Corp., 2002, Achievements include developer Scruggs style of banjo playing; inventor Scruggs Tuning Pegs.

SCRUGGS, ELAINE M. mayor; m. Larry Scruggs; 1 child, Jennifer. Former mgmt. specialist; elected mem. Glendale (Ariz.) City Coun., 1990-93; mayor City of Glendale, 1994, re-elected, 1996, 98, 2000. Past chmn. Maricopa (Ariz.) Assn. Govts., chair youth policy adv., chmn. Regional Pub. Transp. Authority, chmn. Ariz. Mcpl. Water Users Assn., chair Maricopa Assn. Govt. Regional Aviation Systems policy com.; chair Ariz. Mcpl. Tax Code Commn. Dir. Glendale Leadership Program, 1984-89; mem. Ariz. Coalition for Tomorrow, Ariz. Women in Mcpl. Govt.; mem. youth adv. commn., Mayor's Alliance Against Drugs and Gangs. Mem. Glendale C. of C. Office: Office Mayor 5850 W Glendale Ave Glendale AZ 85301-2563*

SCRUGGS, MICHANGELO DARREN, podiatrist, writer; b. St. Louis, Apr. 18, 1974; s. Michael Warren and Daisy Jenkins Scruggs. BA in Biology, Fisk U., 1996; D of Podiatric Medicine, Ohio Coll. Podiatric Medicine, 2002. Coord. HIV prevention edn. BABAA, St. Louis, 1996—97; tchr. St. Louis Pub. Schs., 1997—98; author, CEO, pub. Footprint Media, Cleve., 2001—. Author: (novel) The Men's Room, 1999, Blood Thicker Than Water, 2001. Mem.: Am. Podiatric Med. Student Assn., Student Nat. Podiatric Med. Assn. Avocations: writing, cooking, singing, shopping, movies. E-mail: footprint@aol.com.

SCRUGGS-LEFTWICH, YVONNE, association executive; BA in Polit. Sci. cum laude, N.C. Ctrl. U.; postgrad., Freie U., Berlin, Deutsche Hoch Schule Politics, Johns Hopkins U.; MA in Pub. Adminstrn., U. Minn.; PhD in City and Regional Planning, U. Pa. Housing rsch. technician City Phila. Evaluation Project; coord. rsch. and planning, exec. dir. The Wharton Ctr.-North Phila. Settlement House; cmty. renewal specialist Phila. Cmty. Renewal Program; assoc. dir. Phila. Coun. for Cmty. Advancement Ford Founds. Gray Areas Project, dep. dir. planning, 1962-65; fed. liaison officer U.S. Dept. HUD, 1965-69; coord. field svcs., human resources ctr. U. Pa. Wharton Sch., 1970-75; chairperson, assoc. prof. grad. dept. city/regional planning Howard U., 1974-77; prof. city and regional planning Howard U. Sch. Arch. and Planning, 1979-81; head U.S. del. to OECD and ECE U.S. Dept. HUD, 1977-79, dep. asst. sec. cmty. planning and devel., exec. dir. Pres. Carter's Urban/Regl. Policy Group, 1977-79; regional dir. DHCR, Buffalo, 1981-82; commr. N.Y. State Divsn. Housing and Cmty. Renewal, 1982-85; dep. mayor City Phila., 1985-87; bd. chair, COO Y.E.L. Corp., Bklyn. & Harlem, 1987-91; dir. Urban Pol. Inst., Nat. Pol. Inst., Exec. Leadership Seminar, Joint Ctr. for Pol. and Econ. Studies, 1991—. Lectr. grad. dept. city and regional planning U. Pa., Phila., 1970-76, vis. lectr. urban affairs program, 1978-80, vis. prof. grad. dept. city and regional planning, 1985-87, vis. prof. Fels Ctr. Govt., 1985, vis. prof. grad. program dynamics of orgn., 1987; sr. cons. Jeffalyn Johnson and Assocs., Falls Church, Va., 1980-81; adj. prof. planning SUNY, Buffalo, 1981-82; vis. prof. polit. power and urban diversity Grad. Sch. Polit. Mgmt., George Washington U., 1990-2000; vis. prof. U.S. Info. Agy., Kenya, Ethiopia, South Africa, Nigeria, Ghana; vis. expert West German Office Fgn. Rels. Bd. dirs. Crime Prevention Assn., 1964-69, Mid City YMCA, 1964-71, Gaudenzia House, 1969-72; pres. Phila. Assn. Intergroup Rels. Ofcls., 1967; trustee SUNY, Buffalo, 1982-86; pres. Geneva B. Scruggs Cmty. Health Ctr., 1982-85; bd. dirs. State N.Y. Mortgage Agy., 1983-85, Housing Fin. Agy. N.Y. State, 1983-85, N.Y. State Mortgage Loan Enforcement Corp., 1983-85, N.Y. State Project Fin. Agy.; co-chair Gov.'s Task Force on the Homeless, 1983-85; chair Gov.'s Housing Policy Task Force, 1983-85; exec. com. Women in Govt., 1984, 85; v.p., trustee Milton S. Eisenhower Found., 1991—; bd. mem. Washington Planning Workshop; v.p. Pa. Housing Fin. Agy., 1983-85, Commonwealth Pa.; commr. Mobile Home Stds. Commn., Commonwealth Pa.; bd. dirs. Phila. Coun. for Cmty. Advancement; bd. dirs., membership com. World Affairs Coun.; others. Fulbright fellow, Berlin; study scholar Johns Hopkins U.; Ford Found. grantee, 1979-81. Mem. ASPA, Am. Planning Assn., Nat. Assn. Planners (bd. mem., Diana Donald award), Nat. Coun. Negro Women, Nat. Polit. Congress Black Women, Greater Washington Urban League, Alpha Kappa Alpha (Alpha Chi chpt.), Pi Gamma Nu. Office: Black Leadership Forum Inc 1090 Vermont Ave NW Ste 1290 Washington DC 20005-4963

SCRUSHY, RICHARD M. health facility executive; Grad., U. Ala., Birmingham, 1974; Doctorate (hon.) , Troy State U. Tchr. U. Ala. Sch. Health Related Professions, Birmingham; v.p. Lifemark Corp.; founder, CEO HealthSouth Corp., Birmingham, 1984—2002, chmn. Ala., 1984—. Bd. dirs. Scandipharm, Inc., Bus. Coun. Ala., Capstone Capital Corp., MedPartners, Inc., U. Ala. Birmingham Pres. Coun. Advisor, head Workers' Compensation Form Task Force; mem. Ala. Cert. of Need Rev. Bd. Ala. State Health Planning and Devel. Agy.-So. Coll.'s Bd. Trustees. Named Man of the Yr., Birmingham Bus. Jour., 1996, Nat. Hon. Chmn. for Class of 1996, Nat. Multiple Sclerosis Soc.; recipient Humanitarian of Yr. award, Arthritis Found., 1994. Office: HealthSouth Corp One HealthSouth Pkwy Birmingham AL 35243*

SCUDDER, EDWARD WALLACE, JR. newspaper and broadcasting executive; b. Newark, Dec. 8, 1911; s. Edward Wallace and Katherine (Hollifield) Scudder; m. Louise Bagby Fry, Jan. 19, 1945; children: Katherine Allison Tiballi, Mary Gale Doe, Edward, Robert. AB, Princeton, 1935. Pres. Newark Evening News, 1950-70, Newark Broadcasting, Newark, to 1978. Trustee Paper Mill Playhouse, Millburn, N.J., Newark Mus., Lake Placid (N.Y.) Edn. Found. Lt. (j.g.) to lt. comdr. USNR Air Force, 1942-46. Mem. Short Hills Club, Gulfstream Golf Club, Gulfstream Bath and Tennis Club. Home: Birchate PO Box 1222 Lake Placid NY 12946-5222 also: 401 Linton Blvd Delray Beach FL 33444-8157

SCUDDER, THAYER, anthropologist, educator; b. New Haven, Aug. 4, 1930; s. Townsend III and Virginia (Boody) S.; m. Mary Eliza Drinker, Aug. 26, 1950; children: Mary Eliza, Alice Thayer. Grad., Phillips Exeter Acad., 1948; AB, Harvard U., 1952, PhD, 1960; postgrad., Yale U., 1953-54, London Sch. Econs., 1960-61. Rsch. officer Rhodes-Livingstone Inst., No. Rhodesia, 1956-57, sr. rsch. officer No. Rhodesia, 1962-63; asst. prof. Am. U., Cairo, 1961-62; rsch. fellow Ctr. Middle East Studies, Harvard U., 1963-64; asst. prof. Calif. Inst. Tech., Pasadena, 1964-66, assoc. prof., 1966-69, prof. anthropology, 1969-2000, prof. emeritus, 2000—; dir. Inst. for Devel. Anthropology, Binghamton, N.Y., 1976—; commr. World Commn. on Dams, 1998-2000. Cons. UN Devel. Program, FAO, IBRD, WHO, Ford Found., Navajo Tribal Coun., AID, World Conservation Union, Lesotho Highlands Devel. Authority, South China Electric Power Joint Venture Corp., U.S. Nat. Rsch. Coun., Que.-Hydro, Environ. Def. Fund, Ministry of Industry and Handicrafts, Lao People's Dem. Republic. Author: The Ecology of the Gwembe Tonga, 1962; co-author: Long-Term Field Research in Social Anthropology, 1979, Secondary Education and the Formation of an Elite: The Impact of Education on Gwembe District, Zambia, 1980, No Place to Go: The Impacts of Forced Relocation on Navajos, 1982, For Prayer and Profit: The Ritual, Economic and Social Importance of Beer in Gwembe District, Zambia, 1950-1982, 1988, The IUCN Review of the So. Okavango Integrated Water Development Project, 1993. John Simon Guggenheim Meml. fellow, 1975; recipient Lucy Mair medal for applied anthropology Royal Anthropol. Inst., 1998. Mem. Am. Anthrop. Assn. (1st recipient Solon T. Kimball award for pub. and applied anthropology 1984, Edward J. Lehman award 1991), Soc. Applied Anthropology (Bronislaw Malinowski award 1999), Am. Alpine Club. Office: Calif Inst Tech # 228 77 Pasadena CA 91125-0001 E-mail: tzs@hss.caltech.edu.

SCULCO, THOMAS PETER, surgeon; b. N.Y.C., Feb. 20, 1944; s. Alfred Francis and Mary Jacqueline Sculco; m. Cynthia Davis, June 4, 1966; children: Sarah Jane, Peter. AB in Classics, Brown U., 1965; MD, Columbia U., 1969. Intern in gen. surgery Roosevelt Hosp., N.Y.C., 1969-70, resident in orthopedic surgery, 1970-71, Hosp. for Spl. Surgery, 1971-74, asst. attending orthopedic surgery, 1977-83, N.Y. Hosp., 1977-83, Meml. Hosp., N.Y.C., 1977-83; assoc. attending orthopedic surgery Hosp. for Spl. Surgery, 1983-91, attending surgeon in orthopedics, 1991—, N.Y. Hosp., 1991—; cons. orthopedic surgeon Mary Manning Walsh Nursing Home, 1978—, Meml. Hosp., 1983—, Bronx Vets. Adminstrn. Hosp., 1987—; from asst. to assoc. prof. clin. surgery Cornell U., 1977-91, prof. clin. surgery in orthopedics, 1991—. Chief surg. arthritis svc. Hosp. for Spl. Surgery, 1993—, dir. orthopedic surgery, 1993—; sr. scientist Hosp. for Spl. Surgery, 1996—. Mem. editl. bd. Surg. Blood Mgmt. Forum, 1997. Trustee N.Y. chpt. Arthritis Found., 1997—; mem. Carnegie Hill Assn., St. Bernard's Sch.; bd. dirs. Westerley (R.I.) Cmty. Chorus, 190-96; sponsor Westerley Pub. Libr., 1996; patron Met. Opera, Carnegie Hall. Recipient Clint Compere award Twentieth Century Orthopedic Assn., 1997, Lifetime Achievement award Arthritis Found., 1999; recipient numerous grants. Mem. AMA, N.Y. County Med. Soc., Am. Acad. Orthopedic Surgeons (com. on data svcs. chmn. 1981-85, com. musculoskeletal specialty socs. 1986-90, coord. com. on health policy 1986-89, task force on data chmn. 1987, com. on clin. policies 1991—, patent edn. com. 1999—, liaison to bd. trustees Arthritis Found. 1999—, bd. dirs. 1999-2001), N.Y. Acad. Medicine, N.Y. State Orthopedic Soc., Eastern Orthopedic Soc., Am. Orthopedic Soc., Interurban Orthopedic Assn., Am. Rheumatism Assn., Orthopedic Rsch. and Edn. Found., Knee Soc. (founding mem. 1983, exec. com. 1983-84, program chmn. 1986, membership com. 1986-93, chmn. 1992-93, edn. com. 1990-94, chmn. 1993-94), Assn. VA Orthopedic Surgeons (founder 1986, sec.-treas. 1986-88), Assn. for Arthritis Hip and Knee Surgery, Acad. Orthopedic Soc., Physicians Sci. Soc., Med. Strollers, Internat. Soc. Tech. in Arthroplasty, Am. Austrian Found. (bd. dirs. 2000—), Hip Soc. (membership com. 2000—, Otto Aufranc Rsch. award 1991, Charnley Rsch. award 1995). Office: The Hosp for Spl Surgery 535 E 70th St New York NY 10021

SCULL, CHRISTINA, writer; b. Bristol, Eng., Mar. 6, 1942; came to U.S., 1995; d. Robert Stanley and Eileen Hannah (Abbott) S.; m. Wayne Gordon Hammond, Dec. 12, 1994. BA, U. London, 1971. Librarian Sir John Soane's Mus., London, 1971-95. Author: The Soane Hogarths, 1991; co-author: J.R.R. Tolkien: Artist and Illustrator, 1995 (Mythopoeic scholar 1996); co-editor Roverandom (J.R.R. Tolkien), 1998, Farmer Giles of Ham (J.R.R. Tolkien), 1999. Avocations: book-collecting, art, music. Home: 30 Talcott Rd Williamstown MA 01267-2418

SCULLEY, PATRICK DAVID, army officer; b. Jamestown, N.Y., Sept. 12, 1947; s. Claude Francis and Hildegarde Ruth (Anderson) S.; m. Peggy Ann Carroll, Aug. 26, 1967; children: Patricia, Paul, Perry, Peter. BA, Washington and Jefferson Coll., 1969; DDS, SUNY, Buffalo, 1973; MA in Health Svcs. Mgmt., Webster U., 1994. Diplomate Fed. Svcs. Bd. Gen. Dentistry, Am. Bd. Oral Medicine, Am. Bd. Gen. Dentistry, Am. Coll. Health Care Execs. Commd. U.S. Army, advanced through grades to maj. gen., 1999; gen. practice resident Kimbrough Army Hosp., Ft. Meade, Md., 1973-74; gen. dentist U.S. Army MEDDAC, White Sands Missile Range, N.Mex., 1974-76; gen. dentistry resident U.S. Army DENTAC, Ft. Knox, Ky., 1977-79, clinic chief Ft. Riley, Kans., 1979-81; comdr. 576th Med. Detachment, Bad Kreuznach, West Germany, 1982-85; staff officer U.S. Army Health Svcs. Command, Ft. Sam Houston, Tex., 1985-86, asst. inspector gen., 1986-88; dental cons. Dept. Army Surgeon Gen.'s Office, Washington, 1988-90; student U.S. Army War Coll., Carlisle Barracks, Pa., 1990-91; comdr. U.S. Army Dental Activity, Ft. Bragg, N.C., 1991-92; dir. dental svcs. Health Svcs. Command U.S. Army, 1992-93, comdr. Dental Command, 1993-95, asst. surgeon gen. pers., 1996, commdg. gen. U.S. Army Ctr. Health Promotion and Preventive Medicine, 1996-99, acting dep. surgeon gen., 1998-99, dep. surg. gen./chief Army Dental Corps, chief of staff U.S. Army Med. Command, 1999—2002, ret., 2002; exec. dir. Sigma Xi, 2002—. Instr. oral medicine gen. practice residency, Ft. Riley, 1980-81; mem. bd. examiners Fed. Svcs. Bd. Gen. Dentistry, Washington, 1986-90; mem. bd. examiners Am. Bd. of Gen. Dentistry, 1991-95 Asst. high sch. football coach Bad Kreuznach Am. High Sch., 1982-83; basketball coach Vienna (Va.) Youth Inc., 1988-89, Cath. Youth Orgn., San Antonio, 1985-86; softball coach Girls Recreation Softball League, Manhattan, Kans., 1981. Fellow Am. Coll. Dentists; mem. ADA (alt. del. Ho. of Dels. 1999-2000), Am. Coll. Health Care Execs., Internat. Coll. Dentists, Am. Acad. Oral Medicine, Am. Assn. Endodontists, Am. Dental Edn. Assn., Acad. Gen. Dentistry (chmn. self-assessment com. 1988-91, mem. examination coun. 1988-92, pres. Army chpt. 1988-91, chmn. reference com. on adminstrn. communications and constrn. and bylaws, 1990, ho. of dels. 1988-91, long range planning coun. 1997-98, chmn. long range planning coun. 1998-99, chmn. strategic advancement com. 1999-2002, Disting. Svc. award 1999), Am. Bd. of Gen. Dentistry, Assn. Mil. Surgeons U.S. (federal healthcare adminstr. of yr. 2001), Pierre Fouchard Acad., Omicron Kappa Upsilon. Republican. Roman Catholic. Avocation: coaching athletics. Office: Sigma Xi 99 Alexander Dr Research Triangle Park NC 27709

SCULLIN, FREDERICK JAMES, JR. federal judge; b. Syracuse, N.Y., Nov. 5, 1939; s. Frederick James and Cleora M. (Fellows) S.; m. Veronica Terek Sauro, Aug. 31, 1984; children: Mary Margaret, Kathleen Susan, Kellie Anne, Rebecca Rose; 1 stepchild, Angel Jenette Sauro. BS in Econs., Niagara U., 1961; LL.B., Syracuse U., 1964. Bar: N.Y. 1964, Fla. 1976, U.S. Dist. Ct. (no. dist.) N.Y. 1967, U.S. Supreme Ct. 1971. Assoc. Germain & Germain, Syracuse, 1967-68; asst. dist. atty. Onondaga County, 1968-71; asst. atty. gen. N.Y. State Organized Crime Task Force, 1971-78, dir. regional office, 1974-78; chief prosecutor, dir. Gov.'s Council on Organized Crime State of Fla., Tallahassee, 1978—; sole practice Syracuse, 1979-82; U.S. atty. for No. Dist. N.Y., 1982-92; judge U.S. Dist. Ct. (no. dist.) N.Y., 1992—, chief judge. With U.S. Army, 1964-67, Vietnam; col. USAR. Decorated Air medal, Bronze Star; Cross of Gallantry (Vietnam); recipient Meritorious Svc. Cross, UN svc. medal, UN Campaign medal, 5 stars; Nat. Def. medal, N.Y. State Dist Svc. medal, various others. Mem. Am. Judicature Soc., Fla. Bar Assn., Fed. Bar Assn., Fed. Bar Coun., Onon City Bar Assn., Jud. Conf. U.S. Office: US Dist Ct US Courthouse 100 S Clinton St Syracuse NY 13261-6100 E-mail: fscullin@nynd.uscourts.gov.

SCULLION, KEVIN PETER, lawyer; b. Chgo., June 9, 1952; s. Peter and Annette (Murphy) S. Student, Purdue U., 1970-72; BA, Northwestern U., 1974; postgrad., Tulane U. Law Sch., Grenoble, France, 1976; JD, DePaul U., 1977, LLM in Taxation, 1986; MBA, U. Chgo., 1979; student, U. Edinburgh, Scotland, 1979. Bar: Ill. 1977, U.S. Dist. Ct. (no. dist.) Ill. 1977, Ind. 1978, Fla. 1978, U.S. Dist. Ct. (so. dist.) Ind. 1978, D.C. 1980, U.S. Dist. Ct. (ea. dist.) Mich. 1991, U.S. Dist. Ct. Ariz. 1992; CPA, Ill.; series 65 lic. NASD. In-house counsel Fin. Fed. Savs. & Loan Assn., Olympia Fields, Ill., 1977-79; assoc. firm Quinn, Jacobs & Barry, Chgo., 1979-83; tax mgr. Price Waterhouse, 1983-86; sr. v.p. Graves Reich & Co., Inc., Northfield, Ill., 1986-91; ltd. ptnr. Graver, Bokhof & Goodwin, Chgo., 1991-2000; mng. dir., co-founder Aberdeen Wealth Mgmt. LLC, 2000—. Mem. ABA, AICPA, Chgo. Bar Assn., Ill. State Bar Assn., Ind. State Bar Assn., Ill. CPA Soc., Internat. Assn. Fin. Planners. Roman Catholic. Avocations: running, reading, travel. Home: 386 Muskegon Ave Calumet City IL 60409-2347

SCULLION, ROSEMARIE, literature educator; Co-editor: Celine and the Politics of Difference, 1995, Studies in Twentieth Century Literature, South Central Rev. Substance; contbr. articles. Mem.: Modern Lang. Assn. Am. (exec. coun. 2000—). Office: Univ Iowa 716 Jefferson Bldg 467 Phillips Hall Iowa City IA 52242 E-mail: rosemarie-scullion@uiowa.edu.

SCULLION, TSUGIKO YAMAGAMI, non-profit organization executive; b. China, June 30, 1946; d. Hajime and Akemi (Murazumi) Yamagami; m. William James Scullion, Nov. 26, 1971; 1 child, James. BA, Baldwin-Wallace Coll., 1970; MA, Sch. Internat. Tng., 1971. Area cons. Conn. AFS Internat./Intercultural Programs, N.Y.C., 1972-73, regional mgr. for Asia and Pacific, 1973-78, dir. internat. ops., 1978-81, v.p. Europe, Africa, Middle East, 1981-83, v.p. program svcs., 1083-85, exec. v.p., 1985-87, U.S. Com. UNICEF, N.Y.C., 1988-95; mgmt. cons. strategic planning, mktg. and fund-raising, 1995-96; chief oper. officer Synergos Inst., 1996-98; spl. advisor for exec. dir. Japan Commn. for UNICEF, 1998—. Bd. dirs. Oberlin Shansi Meml. Assn., Whitby Sch., AFS Japan. Avocations: golf, classical music, ballet. Home: Breeze Place A 4-7-9 Minami Azabu Minato-ku Tokyo 106-0047 Japan

SCULLY, BONNIE DIANE, financial planner; b. Anchorage, June 11, 1948; d. Oakley Walter and Patricia Alberta (Campbell) Baron; m. J. Robert Scully, Aug. 28, 1971; children: Amanda Rose, John Robert Jr. BA in English, Spring Hill Coll., 1970; CFP, Coll. for Fin Planning, Denver, CO, 1986. CFP. Flight attendant Delta Airlines, Atlanta, 1970; bank teller Ctrl. Nat. Bank, Richmond, Va., 1971; educator St. Elizabeth Sch., 1972-74; dept. chmn. airline and travel career program Nat. Coll. Bus., Rapid City, S.D., 1976-77; tax preparer H&R Block, Iowa City, 1978-80; bus. mgr. Dr. J. Robert Scully, Asheville, N.C., 1980-83; fin. planner Parsec Fin. Mgmt., 1983-88; fin. counselor Cath. Social Svcs., 1995—. Author: The Scully Files - Organizing Your Finances, The Scully Files - A Young Couple's Blueprint for Managing Money. Mem. Leadership Asheville, 1983; bd. dirs. Jr. Achievement, Asheville, 1984-86, Children's Home Soc., Asheville, 1987-89; bd. dirs., allocation com. United Way, Asheville, 1986-88; treas., bd. dirs. St. Joan of ARC Parish Coun., 1986-88; pres. PTA, Asheville Cath. Sch., 1996-97; chmn. spl. event com. St. Joseph Hosp., 1996-97; bd. dirs. Belechere Entertainment Com., bd. dirs. Jesuit House of Prayer, 1995-98; vol. ABCCM (Asheville Buncombe Community Christian Ministry), 1995-98. Mem. ADA, (regional treas. 1997-98), Buncombe County Dental Aux. (treas. 1995-98). Roman Catholic. Avocations: writing, yoga, travel, reading, sewing. Home and Office: 450 N Griffing Blvd Asheville NC 28804-2814

SCULLY, ERIK VINCENT, lawyer, accountant; b. Pitts., Mar. 24, 1957; s. Vincent C.A. and Gloria Dolores (Peterson) S.; m. Margaret Mary Scully, Sept. 10, 1982; children: Erik John, Ryan Frederick, Meghan Marie. BA, Syracuse U., 1979; JD, St. Louis U., 1982; postgrad., Duquesne U., Pitts., 1986. Bar: Pa. 1982, U.S. Tax Ct. 1983; CPA, Pa. Asst. bank officer Mark Twain Bankshares, Inc., St. Louis, 1980; law clk. Thomas, Mottaz & Eastman, Alton, Ill., 1981-82; with Mercer, Mercer, Carlin and Scully, Pitts., 1982-91; ptnr. Scully & Scully, 1992-94, Scully & Scully, L.L.P., Pitts., 1995—. Mem. Pitts. Ctr. for the Arts, Soc. Sculptors of Pitts. Mem. Pa. Bar Assn., Allegheny County Bar Assn. (taxation sect.), Pa. Inst. CPAs (taxation sect., com. on govt. rels.). Home: 10550 Grubbs Rd Wexford PA 15090-9424 Office: Scully & Scully LLP 2220 Koppers Bldg Pittsburgh PA 15219

SCULLY, GERALD WILLIAM, economics educator; b. N.Y.C., June 13, 1941; s. Francis Joseph Scully and Helen Zimmerman; divorced; children: Deirdre K., Audra L. BA, Fairleigh Dickinson U., Teaneck, N.J., 1962; MA, The New Sch., N.Y.C., 1965; PhD, Rutgers U., 1968. Asst. prof. econs. Ohio U., Athens, 1966-69; assoc. prof. So. Ill. U., Carbondale, 1969-72; prof. So. Meth. U., Dallas, 1972-85, U. Tex., Dallas, 1985—; dean Sch. Mgmt., U. Tex., 1987-88. Vis. prof. Harvard Coll., Cambridge, Mass., 1975-76; sr. fellow Nat. Ctr. for Policy Analysis, Dallas, 1980—; cons. World Bank, Washington, 1985—. Author: Business of Major League Baseball, 1989; Constitutional Environments and Economic Growth, 1992; contbr. articles on econs. to profl. jours. NIH grantee Bethesda, Md., 1971-72; Earhart Found. fellow, Ann Arbor, Mich., 1989, 90; Bradley scholar Heritage Found., Washington, 1990—. Mem. Am. Econ. Assn., Pub. Choice Soc., Mont Pelerin Soc., Dallas C. of C. Avocation: sailing. Home: PO Box 88 San Cristobal NM 87564-0088

SCULLY, JOHN CARROLL, life insurance marketing research company executive; b. Springfield, Mass., Mar. 16, 1932; s. James and Frances (Carroll) S.; m. Barbara A. Fougere, Sept. 7, 1953; children: Kathleen, Margaret, John, James, Patricia, Mary Ellen, Susan. BA, Holy Cross Coll., 1953; C.L.U., Boston U., 1963; postgrad., Dartmouth Inst., 1977. With John Hancock Mut. Life Ins. Co., 1953-92, gen. agent, 1966-75, sr. v.p. agency dept. Boston, 1975-80, pres. retail sector, 1980-92; pres. emeritus Life. Ins. Mktg. Rsch. Assoc., Windsor, Conn., 1992-97. Bd. dirs. Greater Boston YMCA, 1975-91; chmn. Mass. campaign Holocaust Meml. Mus., 1985—; div. chmn. United Way, 1985—; bd. dirs. Cath. Charities, 1986—; trustee Springfield Coll., 1986, Suffolk U., 1986—. With U.S. Army, 1954-56. Mem. Am. Coll. Life Underwriters, Nat. Assn. Life Underwriters (v.p. Ind. 1973-75), Life Ins. Mktg. and Rsch. Assn. (past chmn.), Gen. Agts. and Mgrs. Assn. (past pres. Indpls. Nat. Mgmt. award 1973-75), Life Underwriter Tng. Coun. (past chmn.), Greater Boston C. of C. (bd. dirs. 1985—), Wellesley Club, Executives Club (past pres.), Algonquin Club (bd. dirs.), KC. Roman Catholic. Home: Unit 414 4800 N AIA Vero Beach FL 32963 Office: Limra Internat PO Box 208 Hartford CT 06141-0208 E-mail: jscully@limra.com.

SCULLY, JOHN EDWARD, JR. banker; b. Chgo., Jan. 18, 1943; s. John Edward and Ann Berenice (Allenbrand) S.; m. Mary Julia Purvin, June 11, 1966; children: Melissa, Julie, John Edward III. BA, U. Notre Dame, 1964; MA, DePaul U., 1966. Supr., No. Trust Co., Chgo., 1968-69, with personnel dept., 1969-74, personnel officer, 1974-77, bond investment officer, 1977-80; asst. v.p. First Nat. Bank of Chgo., 1980-82, v.p., 1982-87; first v.p. Exch. Nat. Bank, 1987-90; sr. v.p. ABN AMRO, 1990—; mem. mgmt. com. LaSalle Bank, Chgo. Bd. dirs. Chgo. Heart Assn., 1987—. Maj. gen. USAR, 1964-96. Mem. Am. Soc. Pers. Adminstrs., Employment Mgrs. Assn., Res. Officers Assn., Mil. Order World Wars, Assn. U.S. Army, Am. Legion, VFW, USO of Ill., Riverside Swim Club, Union League Chgo. (dir. 1993-96, 2d v.p., pres. 1999-2000). Roman Catholic. Home: 258 Lawton Rd Riverside IL 60546-2337 Office: LaSalle Nat Corp Chicago IL 60603

SCULLY, JOHN THOMAS, obstetrician, gynecologist, educator; b. N.Y.C., Mar. 11, 1931; s. John Thomas and Mildred Frances (Dunstrop) S.; children: John, Helen Mary, Thomas, Nora, James, Sara, Megan, Devin. BS, Georgetown U., 1952; MD, U. Mex., 1959. Diplomate Am. Bd. Ob-Gyn. Intern, Nassau Hosp., 1959-60, resident, 1960-63; practice medicine specializing in ob-gyn, 1963—; sr. attending dept. ob-gyn St. Peter's Med. Center, Robert Wood Johnson U. Hosp.; clin. prof. ob-gyn Rutgers U. Med. Sch., 1971—. Fellow ACS, Am. Coll. Ob-Gyn; mem. N.J. Med. Soc., Middlesex County Med. Soc., N.J. Ob-Gyn Soc., N.J. Right to Life (charter) Republican. Roman Catholic. Office: 23 Duke St New Brunswick NJ 08901-1738

SCULLY, KEVIN SLEAN, orthopaedist, surgeon; b. Pitts. s. Joseph Edwin and Josephine Alice S. BA, U. Va., 1974, MD, 1978. Diplomate Am. Acad. Orthopaedic Surgery. Intern Mary Hitchcock Hosp., 1978-79; resident in orthopaedics U. Va., 1979-83; fellow in arthroscopy Washington Adventist Hosp., 1983-84; v.p. Atlantic Orthopedics, Wilmington, NC. Vol. Spl. Olympics. Fellow Am. Acad. Orthopaedic Surgery. Roman Cath. Avocations: shooting sports, golf, fishing, aerial combat simulation. Home: 327 Seabreeze Blvd Wilmington NC 28409 Office: Coastal Orthopaedics PA 1616 Medical Center Dr Wilmington NC 28401-7521 Fax: 910-762-5927.

SCULLY, MARTHA SEEBACH, speech and language pathologist; b. S.I., Nov. 1, 1951; d. Henry F. and Rose Anne (Callahan) Seebach; m. Roger Tehan Scully, Dec. 29, 1979; 1 child, Roger Tehan. BA, Trinity Coll., 1972; MS, George Washington U., 1974; postgrad., Syracuse (N.Y.) U., 1976-79. Lic. speech-lang. pathologist, Md. Clin. supr. Syracuse U., 1976-79; speech-lang. pathologist Fairfax (Va.) County Pub. Schs., 1979—. Bd. dirs. Trinity Coll., Washington, Nat. Children's Choir, 1987-91; trustee Davis Meml. Goodwill Industries, 1994-96, bd. dirs. Goodwill Guild, 1990—, chair ball; docent Folger Shakespearean Libr.; chmn. Nat. Challenge Com. of Disabled, 1985; mem. Ear Ball, 1988, 89; mem. Internat. Children's Festival, 1990, 91; co-chmn. Jr. League of Washington Capital Collection, 1990; chmn. Salvation Army Garden Party, 1992, Washington Embassy Tour, 1993; mem. bd. edn. Holy Cross Sch., Garrett Park, Md., 2001. Recipient First Order Affiliation Order of Franciscans mirror, 1985; named Outstanding Woman in Am., 1987, 88. Mem. Am. Biog. Inst., Am. Speech-Lang.-Hearing Assn., Coun. for Exceptional Children, Montgomery County Assn. for Hearing Impaired Children, Benevolent and Protective Order Elks (mem. Washinton-Rockville lodge, lecturing knight 1999, esteemed loyal knight 2000). Home: 10923 Wickshire Way Rockville MD 20852-3220

SCULLY, STEPHEN J. plastic surgeon; b. Lawrence, Mass., Jan. 29, 1937; s. Joseph A. and Frances M. (Hart) S.; m. Diane Loretta Lizotte, Apr. 22, 1967; children: Stephen, Christopher, Caroline, Jacqueline. AB summa cum laude, Merrimack Coll., 1958; MD cum laude, Georgetown U., 1962. Surg. resident Tufts New Eng. Med. Ctr., Boston, 1962-67; plastic surg. resident NYU, N.Y.C., 1969-72. Trustee Holy Family Hosp., Methuen, Mass., 1993, Merrimack Coll., North Andover, Mass., 1993. Lt. comdr. USNR, 1967-69. Fellow ACS; mem. Am. Soc. Plastic Surgeons, Am. Soc. Aesthetic Plastic Surgery. Roman Catholic. Avocations: photography, skiing. Office: Plastic Cosmetic Reconstr Surgery Inc 451 Andover St North Andover MA 01845-5044

SCULLY, THOMAS A. federal agency administrator; Bachelor's Degree, U. Va.; JD, Cath. U. Staff asst. Fed. Election Commn., 1979—81, U.S. Senator Slade Gorton, 1981—85; atty. Akin, Gump, Strauss, Hauer & Feld, LLP, 1986—88; comm. staff Bush-Quayle Campaign, 1988, dep. dir. congl. affairs; assoc. dir. human resources, vets. and labor Office Mgmt. and Budget, 1989—92, counselor to the dir., 1992—93; pres., CEO Fedn. Am. Hosps., 1995—2001; ptnr. Patton Boggs, LLP, Washington; dep. asst. to the pres. White House; CEO, adminstr. Ctrs. for Medicare and Medicaid Svcs. Dept. HHS, Washington. Office: Dept HHS Ctrs for Medicare and Medicaid Svcs 200 Independence Ave SW Washington DC 20201*

SCULLY-POWER, PAUL D. astronaut; b. Sydney, Australia, May 28, 1944; , naturalized, 1982; married; 6 children. BS in Applied Math., U. Sydney, 1966, postgrad. diploma of edn. Scientific officer, 1st permanent head oceanographic group Royal Australian Navy, 1967—72; Australian Navy Exch. Scientist USN, 1972—74, USN Underwater Systems Ctr., New London, Conn., 1972—74, Office Naval Rsch., Washington, 1972—74; invited to assist Earth Observations team, Skylab Project USN, 1972—74; planner, dir. joint Australia, New Zealand, U.S. project ANZUS EDDY, 1974—75; apptd. fgn. prin. investigator, Heat Capacity Mapping Mission NASA, 1976; sr. scientist, tech. specialist, staff of Assoc. Tech. Dir. Rsch. and Tech. Naval Underwater Systems Ctr., 1977—; astronaut crew NASA STS-41G Challenger, 1984. Contbr. articles to profl. sci. jours. Mem.: AAAS, Australian Marine Scis. Assn., U.S. Naval Inst., Am. Meteorol. Soc., Acoustical Soc. Am., Am. Geophys. Union. Office: Astronaut Office/CB NASA Johnson Space Ctr Houston TX 77058-*

SCULT, MEL, Judaic studies educator, researcher; b. Paterson, N.J., May 28, 1934; s. Morris and Bertie (Lifshutz) S.; m. Ruth Bermant, Aug. 11, 1959 (div. May 1979); children: Rachel Ilana, Joshua Raphael; m. Barbara R. Gish, Mar. 22, 1987. BA, NYU, 1955; BHL, Jewish Theol. Sem., N.Y.C., 1956, DHL (hon.), 1987; AM in Tchg., Harvard U., 1959; PhD, Brandeis U., 1967; DHL (hon.), Rabbinical Coll., 1999. Tchr. history Concord (Mass.) Acad., 1959-67, Akiba Hebrew Acad., Phila., 1967-69; tchg. fellow Brandeis U., Waltham, Mass., 1963-67; prof. religion Vassar Coll., Poughkeepsie, N.Y., 1969-75; mem. faculty New Sch., N.Y.C., 1979; prof. Judaic studies Bklyn. Coll., CUNY, 1975—, dir. religion program, 1980—. Mem. Jewish studies adv. bd. CUNY, 1987. Author: Converting the Jews, 1978, Dynamic Judaism, 1985, The American Judaism of Mordecai Kaplan, 1990, Judaism Faces the 20th Century: A Biography of Mordecai Kaplan, 1993, Schechter's Seminary, 1997, Journals of M.M. Kaplan, 2001; mem. editl. bd. Reconstructionist Jour., 1984—. Grantee Nat. Found. for Jewish Culture, 1968, 99, rsch. grantee Vassar Coll., 1973, travel grantee Am. Coun. Learned Socs., 1973, grantee Littauer Found., 1990, 2000. Mem. Am. Jewish Hist. Soc. (acad. coun. 1989—), Assn. for Jewish Studies (bd. dirs. 1991-95), Jewish Coalition for Higher Edn. Avocation: computers. Office: CUNY Bklyn Coll Dept Judaic Studies Brooklyn NY 11210 E-mail: motke@prodigy.net.

SCURLOCK, ARCH CHILTON, chemical engineer; b. Beaumont, Tex., Jan. 29, 1920; s. Marvin and Mary (Chilton) S.; m. Maurine Spurbeck, Nov. 27, 1945 (div.); children: Arch, Susan, Marvin Curtis; m. Nancy Morrison Yonick, Nov. 16, 1962; children: Mary, Nancy, Margaret Ann. BS in Chem. Engring, AB in Physics, U. Tex., 1941; MS, Mass. Inst. Tech., 1943, Sc.D., 1948; spl. course meteorology, U. Chgo., 1944. Research asso. chem. engring. dept. Mass. Inst. Tech., 1946-48; asst. dir. chemistry Engring. Research Assocs., 1948-49; pres. Atlantic Research Corp., Alexandria, Va., 1949-62, chmn. bd., 1962-65; pres., dir. Research Industries Inc., Alexandria, 1968—. Chmn. TransTechnology Corp., 1969-92, Halifax Corp. Served to lt. (s.g.) USNR, 1943-46. Mem. AAAS, AIAA, Am. Inst. Chem. Engrs., Am. Chem. Soc., Am. Phys. Soc., Am. Meteorol. Soc., Am. Def. Preparedness Assn., Combustion Inst., Univ. Club (Washington), Belle Haven (Va.) Country Club, Army Navy Country Club (Va.), Mid-Ocean Club (Tuckers Town, Bermuda), Phi Beta Kappa, Sigma Xi, Tau Beta Pi. Home: 1753 Army Navy Dr Arlington VA 22202-1633 Office: 123 N Pitt St Alexandria VA 22314-3133

SCUSERIA, GUSTAVO ENRIQUE, theoretical chemist; b. San Fernando, Buenos Aires, Argentina, July 30, 1956; came to U.S., 1985; naturalized U.S. citizen; s. Eraldo L. and Alicia (Capitanelli) S.; m. Ana Inés Ilvento, Apr. 17, 1982; children: Ignacio, Tomás. BS, MS, U. Buenos Aires, 1979, PhD in Physics, 1983. Grad. asst. U. Buenos Aires, 1979-83, asst. prof., 1983-85; rsch. assoc. U. Calif., Berkeley, 1985-87; sr. rsch. assoc. U. Ga., Athens, 1987-89; asst. prof. Rice U., Houston, 1989-93, assoc. prof., 1993-95, prof., 1995-2000, Robert A. Welch prof. chemistry, 2000—. Camille and Henry Dreyfus Teacher scholar Camille and Henry Dreyfus Found., 1992, IBM Partnership award IBM Corp., 1998-99. Fellow AAAS; mem. Am. Chem. Soc., Am. Phys. Soc., Materials Rsch. Soc. Office: Rice U Dept Chemistry PO Box 1892 Houston TX 77251-1892 E-mail: guscus@rice.edu.

SCUTT, CHERYL LYNN, marketing communications executive; b. Columbus, Ind., Dec. 7, 1948; d. Russell O. and Hazel Jeannette (Gordon) S. BA in Journalism, Ind. U., 1971. Freelance writer various nat. orgns. various orgns., Bloomington, Ind., 1971—; feature writer, columnist The Herald-Telephone, 1971-80, asst. lifestyles editor, 1980-83; comm. assoc. United Way of Mid. Tenn., Nashville, 1983-85, asst. comm. dir., 1985-88, v.p. comm., 1988-94; pres. Scutt Comm. Svcs., Antioch, Tenn., 1994—. Instr. Ind. U. H.S. Journalism Inst., Bloomington, 1981, 82; presenter in field United Way Am., 1988-93. Mem. Nat. Profl. Adv. Mktg. Com./United Way of Am., 1990-92; comm. coun. mem. Nashville Area C. of C., 1993-94; pub. rels. and devel. comm. cons. Adolescent Pregnancy and Prevention Coun., Nashville, 1992-93; pub. rels. com. ARC, Nashville, 1994—; pub. rels. com. League for Hearing Impaired, 1995-96. Recipient Gold award United Way Am., 1984, Silver award, 1984, 85, 87, Spl. Recognition award, 1985, Second Century Initiative award, 1988, 90, 90, 91, 1st Pl. award UPI, 1975, 1st Pl. award Women's Press Club Ind., 1976, 77, 78, 79, 83, Edn. award Am. Lupus Soc.,

1981, Diamond award Nashville Advt. Fedn., 1984, 86, 87, 88, 89, Merit award, 1984, 87, 88, 1st Pl. award 7th Dist. Advt. Fedn., 1984, Merit award Nashville chpt. Pub. Rels. Soc. Am., 1988, numerous others. Mem. ASCAP, Soc. Profl. Journalists, N.Am. Assn. Ventriloquists, Sierra Club, The Wildernes Soc. Avocations: songwriting, boating, reading, ventriloquism, guitar.

SCUTT, ROBERT CARL, lawyer; b. Newark, Dec. 24, 1950; s. Charles E. and Lois L. (Armstrong) S. BA, Union Coll., 1973; JD, Duke U., 1976. Bar: N.Y. 1977, U.S. Dist. Ct. (we. dist.) N.Y. 1977, U.S. Tax Ct. 1978. Assoc. Harris, Beach & Wilcox, Rochester, N.Y., 1976-83, ptnr., 1984—. Mem. N.Y. State Bar Assn., Am. Health Lawyers Assn. Office: Harris Beach LLP 99 Garnsey Rd Pittsford NY 14534

SCWARZ, MAGGIE, writer; b. New York, Ny, Apr. 28, 1954; d. Joseph and Barbara Goldsmith Schwarz. BA, U. Colo., Boulder, CO, 1972—76; MA, NYU, New York, NY, 1976—78. Vp, copy supr. J. Walter Thompson Healthcare, Nyc, NY, 1987—93; freelance writer New York, 1994—96; copy supr. NCI Advt., 1997—97, Lewis Grace Bozell, Ft. Lee, NJ, 1998—98; freelance writer New York, NY, 1999—. Vol. Lenox Hill Hosp., New York, NY, NY Cycle Club, New York, 2002—02. Mem.: Am. Med. Writers Assn. Avocations: windsurfing, distance running, cycling, cycling, cycling. Home: 31 Union Sq W Apt 3B New York NY 10003-3212 Personal E-mail: mschwarzny@aol.com.

SCZUDLO, WALTER JOSEPH, lawyer; b. Fairbanks, Alaska; s. Walter and Dolores J. Sczudlo; children: Lauren Hall, Elizabeth Fairbanks, Walter Christopher; m. Rebecca Grey Tucker. AB, Middlebury Coll., 1975; JD, Golden Gate U., 1979; LLM, Georgetown U., 1987; postgrad., U. Calif., Santa Barbara, 1972, Tulane U., 1971-72, Vt. Law Sch., 1976-77. Bar: Alaska 1979, Calif. 1980, D.C. 1986, U.S. Ct. Appeals (9th cir.) 1980, U.S. Ct. Appeals (D.C. cir.) 1986, U.S. Dist. Cts. (no., cen., ea. and so. dists.) Calif., U.S. Dist. Ct. Alaska, U.S. Ct. Claims, U.S. Tax Ct. Law clk. to presiding justice Alaska Supreme Ct., 1978-79; assoc. atty. Merdes, Schaible, Staley and Delisio, Anchorage, 1979-82; legis. dir., gen. counsel U.S. Senator Murkowski, Washington, 1982-84; sr. tax assoc. Schramm and Raddue, Santa Barbara, Calif., 1984-85; dir. congl. rels., counsel Natural Gas Supply Assn., Washington, 1985-88; Washington counsel Shell Oil Co., 1988-96; v.p., Washington counsel Intercontinental Energy Corp., 1996-99; gen. counsel, vice pres. pub. affairs and comms. Assn. Fundraising Profls., Washington, 1999—; prin. ptnr. WEBK Broadcasting 105.3 FM, Killington, Vt., 1985—. Dir. Sun's Edge, Inc., Santa Barbara, 1987—, Natural Gas Roundtable, Washington, 1987—. Author: (with other) Washington Legal Foundation, 1988. Com. chmn. Steve Cowper for Gov., Anchorage, 1982. Recipient Am. Jurisprudence award Bancroft-Whitney Pub. Co., 1978. Roman Catholic. Avocations: mountaineering, cross-country skiing, tennis. Home: 6700 Loring Ct Bethesda MD 20817-3148 Office: AFP 1101 King St Ste 700 Alexandria VA 22314-2944 E-mail: wsczudlo@AFPNET.org.

SEA, SHERRY LYNN, poet; b. Winchester, Ky., Sept. 23, 1966; d. Wallace Glen and Brenda Shirley (Huff) Hatton; m. Everett Sea, Aug. 16, 1986; children: Reva Diane, Krystal Roxanne. Grad. h.s., Irvine, Ky. Contbr. poetry to A Treasury of Famous Poems, Okla. City. Mus., Nature's Echoes. Recipient Golden Poet award World of Poetry, 1988, Diamond Homer award Famous Poets Soc., 1996, 98, Letter of Honor Oklahoma City Cmty. Found., 1997, Outstanding Achievement in Poetry award Famous Poets Soc., 1998. Avocations: camping, hunting, fishing, discovering new places, nature. Home: PO Box 183 Lancaster KY 40444-0183

SEAB, CHARLES GREGORY, astrophysicist, educator; b. Ft. Benning, Ga., May 26, 1950; s. James A. and Ruby (Jones) S.; m. Peggy R. McConnell, May 9, 1979; 1 child, Jenna R. McConnell-Seab. BS in Physics, La. State U., 1971, MS in Physics, 1974; PhD in Astrophysics, U. Colo., 1982. Engring. analyst, programmer Mid. South Svcs., New Orleans, 1974-77; NRC rsch. assoc. NASA Ames Rsch. Ctr., Mountain View, Calif., 1983-85; rsch. scientist U. Calif., Berkeley, 1985, Va. Inst. Theoretical Astronomy, Charlottesville, 1985-87; vis. asst. prof. U. New Orleans, 1987-89, asst. prof., 1989-91, assoc. prof. astrophysics, 1991-96, prof., 1996—. Bd. dirs. Freeport McMoran Obs., New Orleans; tchg. fellow, chmn. physics dept. D. leyda U., 2002—. Author: Astronomy, 1994, Study Guide for Universe, 1997; contbr. articles to profl. jours., chpts. to books. Capt. USAR, 1971-80. Nat. Merit scholar, 1967-71. Mem. Am. Assn. Physics Tchrs., Am. Astron. Soc., Astron. Soc. Pacific, Pontchartrain Astronomy Soc., Planetary Soc., Phi Kappa Phi, Sigma Pi Sigma. Avocations: amateur astronomy, tennis. Office: U New Orleans Physics Dept Lakefront Fmt New Orleans LA 70148-0001

SEABOLT, RICHARD L. lawyer; b. Chgo., Aug. 28, 1949; *Wife, Kathleen Hallissy, also graduated with a Juris Doctor from Hastings College of Law, University of California, in 1975, and was a deputy district attorney from 1975 to 1993. Sons Jack and Will Seabolt are 14 and 12, and students in the Piedmont, California schools. Father, Lee Seabolt, before retirement was President and Chairman of Selz Seabolt Associates, a Chicago-based public relations firm.* BGS with distinction, U. Mich., 1971; JD, U. Calif., Hastings, 1975. Bar: Calif. 1975. With Hancock, Rothert & Bunshoft, San Francisco, 1975—, ptnr., 1981—. *Hancock, Robert & Bunshoft has offices in San Francisco, Los Angeles, Tahoe City, and London, England and focuses its practice on complex business and insurance litigation. Lead defense lawyer, representing certain Underwriters' at Lloyd's of London in an environmental insurance coverage trial between Aerojet-General Corporation and 54 insurers. After a ten month trial, the jury rendered a verdict for the defendants. The defense verdict in that case was featured in 1992 articles in California Law Business and the National Law Journal as among the largest cases tried to a defense verdict in California and in the United States for that year. In 1997 California Supreme Court Affirmed that verdict.* Frequent speaker and author profl. jours., Large Complex Case Panel-Constrn., Am. Arbitration Assn. Mem. ABA, Am. Arbitration Assn. (large complex case panel), State Bar Calif. (exec. com. litigation sect., jury instr. subcom.), Bar Assn. San Francisco. Office: Hancock Rothert & Bunshoft LLP Four Embarcadero Ctr San Francisco CA 94111-4106 E-mail: rlseabolt@HRBLaw.com.

SEABORG, DAVID MICHAEL, evolutionary biologist; b. Berkeley, Calif., Apr. 22, 1949; s. Glenn Theodore and Helen Lucille (Griggs) S.; m. Adele Fong Yee, June 17, 1990. BS, U. Calif., Davis, 1972; MA, U. Calif., Berkeley, 1974. Biology tchr. U. Calif., Berkeley, 1972-73; biol. rschr., photographer Trans Time Labs, 1978; pvt. practice, 1974—; hypnosis and self-hypnosis tchr. Open Edn. Exchange, Oakland, Calif., 19788-81; biol. tchr. Oakland Mus., 1983-87; rsch. biologist, dept. ecology and evolutionary biology U. Calif., Irvine, 1987; pres. dir. rsch Found. for Biol. Conservation and Rsch., Lafayette, 1983—; radio talk show host Sta. KPFA, Berkeley, 1996; biology and life sci tchr. Phillip and Sala Burton Acad. H.S., San Francisco, 1996-97; lab. chem. Biodynamics U. Calif., Berkeley, 1975; comedian, 1969—. Vol. asst. to curator Smithsonian Instn. 1966-67; lectr. sci, philos., environ. issues, 1974—; contbr. articles to profl. jours., Inventor game, Sum-It, 1981; originator, theory of evolution based on organisms as integrated systems; chmn. Com. for Arts and Lectures, U. Calif., Berkeley, 1974-75; chmn. master of ceremonies, Bastille Day, Lafayette (Calif.)-Langeac Soc., 1982-86, 98-2000. Environ. organizer, founder U Turn Soc. to make U Turn from destruction of to preservation of earth, Glenn Seaborg Fund for Open Space to save Bay Area hillsides, World Rainforest Fund to save world's rain forests. Recipient Meritorius Svc. award Smithsonian Inst., 1967, Animal Photograph award Soc. Photographic Scientists and Engrs., 1967; award winning poet, 1997, 99. Mem.: Lafayette Gen. Plan Adv. Com., Calif. Aggie Alumni Assn., Calif. Alumni Assn., Nat. Resources Def. Coun., Earth Island Inst., World Wildlife Fund, Zero Population Growth, Greenpeace, Desert Tortise Preserve Com., Nature Conservancy, Save the Bay Assn., Rainforest Action Network, Sierra Club, Club of Rome USA (v.p. 1998—2001, bd. dirs. 1995—). Democrat. Address: 1888 Pomar Way Walnut Creek CA 94598-1424 E-mail: davidseaborg@juno.com.

SEABORNE, LINDA LEE, real estate broker; b. Durand, Mich., June 2, 1948; d. Ira R. and Betty Jean (Ray) Merrill; m. Arthur Roy Seaborne, July 15, 1978. Degree in real estate, U. Mich., 1982. Supr. several state agys., Mich., 1968-78; broker, owner Re/Max Properties Inc., Petoskey, 1978-83; broker Exec. Real Estate Service Inc., Sarasota, Fla., 1984-87, Schlott Realtors inc., Sarasota, 1987—. Mem. Realtor's Nat. Mktg. Inst. (cert.), Nat. Assn. Realtors, Sarasota Bd. Realtors, Women's Council Realtors (chair 1986, pres. Emmet County chpt. 1982-83, Million Dollar Club 1986-87), Am. Bus. Women's Assn. (chair 1985-87, Woman of Yr. 1987), Women's Owners Network (pres. elect 1987), Grad. Realtors Inst. (cert.), Bus. and Profl. Women (pres. 1982-84). Clubs: Women's Resource Ctr. Republican. Roman Catholic. Avocations: dancing, traveling. Home: 1768 Pine Harrier Cir Sarasota FL 34231-3355

SEABROOK, JOHN MARTIN, retired food products executive, chemical engineer; b. Seabrook, N.J., Apr. 16, 1917; s. Charles Franklin and Norma Dale (Ivins) S.; m. Anne Schlaudecker, Apr. 5, 1939 (div. 1951); children: Carol Ormsby (Mrs. Jacques P. Boulanger), Elizabeth Anne; m. Elizabeth Toomey, 1956; children: John Martin, Bruce Cameron. BS in Chem. Engring, Princeton, 1939; LL.D. (hon.), Gettysburg Coll., 1974. Registered profl. engr., N.J., Del. Engr. Deerfield Packing Corp., 1939-41; v.p. Seabrook Farms Co., 1941-50, exec. v.p., 1950-54, dir., 1941-59, pres., 1954-59, chief exec. officer, 1955-59; dir. Pa. Reading & Seashore Line, 1950-63, N.Y. Ctrl. R.R., 1964-69, Penn Ctrl. R.R., 1968-71; cons. IU Internat. Corp., Wilmington, Del., 1959, v.p., 1960-65, dir., 1963-87, pres., 1965-73, 74-78, chief exec., 1967-80, chmn. bd., 1969-82, chmn. exec. com., 1982-87. Pres., bd. dirs. Cumberland Automobile & Truck Co., 1954-59, Cumberland Warehouse Corp., 1954-59, Salem Farms Corp, N.J., 1948—; chmn. bd. dirs. Frick Co., Waynesboro, Pa., 1959-68; chmn., bd. dirs. S.W. Fabricating & Welding Co., Inc., Houston, 1964-68; chmn. Divcon, Inc., Houston, 1967-69; pres. bd. dirs. Internat. Utilities Overseas Capital Corp., Wilmington, 1966-82, chmn., 1970-80; v.p. Gen. Waterworks Corp., Phila., 1959-66, pres., 1966-68, chmn., 1968-71; chmn. bd. dirs. GWC Inc., Phila., 1971-73; pres. Brown Bros. Contractors, Inc., Phila., 1960, chmn. bd. dirs., 1965-67; pres. Am. Portable Irrigation Co., Eugene, Oreg., 1961, chmn. bd. dirs., 1966-68; chmn. bd. dirs. Gotaas-Larsen Shipping Corp., 1963, chmn., 1979, pres., CEO, 1982-88; chmn. bd. dirs. Amvit Corp., Cleve., 1964-68; bd. dirs. Echo Bay Mines Ltd., South Jersey Gas Co., Folsom, N.J., South Jersey Industries, Inc., Folsom, Bell Atlantic Corp.; dir. emeritus Bell Atlantic-N.J., Inc. Mem. N.J. Migrant Labor Bd., 1945-67, chmn., 1955-67; mem. N.J. Bd. Higher Edn., 1967-70, Pres.' Air Quality Adv. Bd., 1968-70; bd. dirs. Brandywine Conservancy, Inc., 1972-95, pres., 1992-93, hon. dir., 1997—; trustee Eisenhower Exch. Fellowships, 1974-85; trustee Hitchcock Found., 1991-96, chmn., 1993-96. Mem.: Coaching Club (N.Y.C. and U.K.), Wilmington (Del.) Club, Phila. Club, Knickerbocker Club (N.Y.C.), Racquet and Tennis Club (N.Y.C.), Phi Beta Kappa. Home and Office: 55 Nimrod Rd Salem NJ 08079-4323 E-mail: jmsdrives@snip.net.

SEACHRIST, DENISE, music educator; b. Youngstown, Ohio, Feb. 2, 1960; d. Glen Wilbert and Eloise Rapp Seachrist. MusB, Heidelberg Coll., 1982; MusM, Youngstown State U., 1985; PhD, Kent State U., 1993. Assoc. prof. Kent State U., Warren, Ohio, 1994—. Dir. Kent Trumbull Choir, Warren, 1996—; bd. mem. Warren Philharm., 1998—; guest dir. Symphony Women's Chorus, Youngstown, 1998; spkr. in field. Contbr. chapters to books, entries to dictionaries; author: Musical World of Halim El-Dabh. Mem.: Soc. for Ethnomusicology (sec. Niagara chpt. 1997—98), Am. Musicological Soc., Soc. for Am. Music, Coll. Music Soc., Internat. Alliance for Women in Music. Democrat. Mem. United Church of Christ. Avocations: reading, swimming, music, golf, photography. Home: 1443 Stafford Ave NE Warren OH 44483-4339 Office: Kent State Univ 4314 Mahoning Ave NW Warren OH 44483-1998 E-mail: dseachri@kent.edu.

SEACORD, ROBERT CHARLES, computer scientist; b. Yonkers, N.Y., June 5, 1963; married. BS in Computer Sci., Rensselaer Poly. Inst, 1983. Mem. tech. staff X Consortium, Cambridge, Mass., 1995—96; sr. mem. tech. staff Software Engring. Inst., Carnegie Mellon U., Pa., 1996—. Author: (book) Building Systems from Commercial Components, 2001, Modernizing Legacy Systems, 2002. Office: Carnegie Mellon U Software Engring Inst Pittsburgh PA 15213 Office Fax: 412-268-5758. Business E-Mail: rcs@sei.cmu.edu.

SEADEN, GEORGE, civil engineer; b. Cracow, May 26, 1936; s. Simon and Mary (Guttman) S.; m. Linda Helen Mutch, Mar. 18, 1978; children: Amy Elisabeth, Maia Claire. BE, McGill U., Montreal, Que., Can., 1958; MS, Harvard U., 1968; postgrad., Northwestern U., 1992. Engr. Gatineau Power, Hull, Que., 1958-59, Ent. Fougerolle, Paris, 1960-62; mgr. Warnock Hersey Ltd., Montreal, 1959-60; assoc. Cartier, Coté, Piette, 1962-67; sr. advisor Ministry Urban Affairs, Ottawa, Ont., Can., 1969-71; pres. Archer, Seaden & Assoc., Inc., Montreal, 1971-84; dir. gen. Inst. Rsch. in Constrn. Nat. Rsch. Coun., Ottawa, 1985-97, chief Constrn. Tech. Group, 1995-97; exec.-in-residence Faculty Adminstrn. U. Ottawa, 1997—. Vis. prof. U. Ottawa, 1968-73; mem. Can. Constrn. Rsch. Bd., 1985-91, Constrn. Industry Devel., Can., 1988-93, Civil Engring. Rsch. Found., 1993—, Rsch. Bd. Am. Pub. Works Assn., 1994-97; dir. Continental Automated Bldg. Assn., 1995-97, Can. Rsch. Mgrs. Assn., CERIU; pres. Conseil Internat. du Batiment, Rotterdam, The Netherlands, 1989-92; vice chair Constrn. for Sustainable Devel. in the Twenty First Century Conf., Washington, 1996; chair INFRA 2000, Montreal; mem. jury to select best Can. Constrn. projects and engring. design; lectr. numerous univs. and rsch. ctrs. Co-editor: Trends in Building Construction Worldwide, 1989, Innovation in Construction, 2001; mem. editl. bd. Bldg. Rsch. and Practice, Constrn. Bldg. Rev., 1991—; contbr. numerous articles to profl. publs. Chmn. bd. dirs. St. Andrew's Sch., Westmount, Que., 1975-82. Fellow Am. Soc. Civil Engrs.

SEADER, JUNIOR DEVERE (BOB SEADER), chemical engineering educator; b. San Francisco, Aug. 16, 1927; s. George Joseph and Eva (Burbank) S.; m. Joyce Kocher, Aug. 12, 1950 (div. 1960); m. Sylvia Bowen, Aug. 11, 1961; children: Steven Frederick, Clayton Mitchell, Gregory Randolph, Donald Jeffrey, Suzanne Marie, Robert Clark, Kathleen Michelle, Jennifer Anne. BS, U. Calif., Berkeley, 1949, MS, 1950; PhD, U. Wis., 1952. Instr. chem. engring. U. Wis., Madison, 1951-52; group supr. chem. process design Chevron Rsch. Corp., Richmond, Calif., 1952-57, group supr. engring. rsch., 1957-59; prin. scientist heat transfer and fluid dynamics rsch. Rocketdyne div. N.Am. Aviation, Canoga Park, Calif., 1959-65, sr. tech. specialist, summer 1967; prof. chem. engring. U. Idaho, 1965-66, U. Utah, Salt Lake City, 1966—, chmn. dept. chem. engring., 1975-78; tech. cons. Trustee CACHE Corp., Austin, Tex.; inst. lectr. Am. Inst. Chem. Engrs., 1983, also dir., 1983-85. Author 8 books; assoc. editor IEC Rsch. jour., 1986-99; co-author widely used vapor-liquid equilibrium correlation. Served with USNR, 1945—46. Recipient Disting. Teaching award U. Utah, 1975, Donald L. Katz lectureship, 1990, Dean's Tchg. award U. Utah, 1998. Fellow Am. Inst. Chem. Engrs. (Computing in Chem. Engring. award 1988); mem. ACS, Sigma Xi, Phi Lambda Upsilon. Heat transfer rsch. connected with the devel. of rocket engines associated with the Apollo and Space Shuttle projects, 1960-65; rsch. on tar sands, process synthesis, catalyst effective factors, bifurcation analysis. Home: 13696 Vestry Rd Draper UT 84020-7521 Office: U Utah Dept Chem Engring Rm 3290 50 S Central Campus Dr Salt Lake City UT 84112-9203 E-mail: j.seader@m.cc.utah.edu.

SEADLER, STEPHEN EDWARD, social scientist; b. N.Y.C., 1926; s. Silas Frank and Doris Amy Seadler; children: Einar Austin, Anna Carin. AB in Physics, postgrad. in atomic and nuclear physics, Columbia U., 1947; postgrad. with George Gamow in relativity, cosmology, and quantum mechanics, George Washington U., 1948-50. Electronic engr. Cushing & Nevell, Warner Inc., N.Y.C., 1951-54; seminar leader, leader trainer world politics Am. Found. for Continuing Edn., 1955-57; exec. dir. Medimetric Inst., 1957-59; mem. long range planning com., chmn. corporate forcasting com., mktg. rsch. dir. W.A. Sheaffer Pen Co., Ft. Madison, Iowa, 1959-65; founder Internat. Dynamics Corp., Ft. Madison and N.Y.C., 1965, pres., 1965-70; originator DELTA program for prevention and treatment of violence, 1970; founder, pres. ID Ctr., Ft. Madison, now N.Y.C., 1968—. Mgmt. cons. in human resources devel. and conflict reduction, N.Y.C., 1970-73; pres. UNICONSULT computer-based mgmt. and computer scis., N.Y.C., 1973-76; speaker on decision support systems, internat. affairs and ideological arms control; author/speaker (presentation) Holocaust, History and Arms Control; originator social sci. of ideologics and ideotopology; spl. works collection accessible via On-line Computer Lib. Ctr. Instr. polit. sci. Ia. State Penitentiary, 1959-62; guest speaker on radio and television. Author: Principai Idiologica: A Treatise on Combatting Human Malignance, 1999, Ending the Bronze Age, 2001, (online monograph) Terror War and Peace at terror1.com, 2001; contbr. , , articles. Served with AUS, 1944-46. Recipient 20th Century Achievement Award medal Internat. Biographical Ctr., U.K., 1995; named to The Wisdom Hall of Fame by The Wisdom Soc., 1997. Mem.: UN Assn.-USA, Forum on Physics and Soc., Fgn. Policy Assn., Am. Mgmt. Assn. (lectr. 1963—68), Am. Sociol. Assn., N.Y. Acad. Scis., Acad. Polit. Sci., Am. Statis. Assn., Am. Phys. Soc., IEEE, Union of Concerned Scientists, Friends of West Point, Masons. Office: ID Ctr PO Box 824 Dover NJ 07802-0824 E-mail: ses146@columbia.edu. *In retrospect, a single, predominant thread has woven through my entire life since childhood, sometimes as a primary track, sometimes as parallel, but always as relentless destiny: to gain such learning and skills as to enable me to revolutionize mankind's thinking, slay the dragons of racism, religionism, ethnicism and other ideologies of malevolence, oppression and war, and bring true peace for the first time. To accomplish that mission requires development of a single comprehensive framework, which has become the new field of ideologics, and a single comprehensive, revolutionary work employing that framework, to appear at the foothills of the new millennium. That work is the book Principia Ideologica.*

SEAGER, DAUNA GAYLE OLSON-STOKES, speech therapist; b. Logan, Utah, Sept. 22, 1925; d. Helmar Alexander and La Rena Barnes (Jones) Olson; m. Arch Jr. Stokes, Aug. 5, 1943 (dec. Apr.il 1970); children: Jeffrey David, John Phillip, Jeannette; m. Floyd W. Seager, July 7, 1973 (dec. Oct. 1996). AS, Weber State U., 1964; BS, MS in Audiology Speech Pathology, Utah State U., 1969. X-ray ech., physician asst. Robins X-Ray, Ogden, Utah, 1946-52; asst. to supt. Lyman (Wyo.) Pub. Schs., 1952-60; clinic supr. Utah State U., Logan, 1965-69; speech, language, hearing therapist Weber/Davis Sch. District, Ogden, Farmington, Utah, 1969-73, various, 1970-90; co-founder, coord. Clinic at O.R.M., Ogden, 1988—. Bd. dirs. Weber County DUP Mus., Ogden. Author: Pioneer Settlers, 1990; contbr. articles to profl. jours. Co-founder Seager Indigent Clinic, Ogden Mission, Utah, 1988—; organized Stroke Club for Families of CVA Support Group, Ogden, 1972-74, Stroke Unit St. Benedict's Hosp., Ogden, 1972-74, Parent Child Tchr. Group, Ogden, 1970-73; mem. Ogden Sesquicentennial Com., OgSesqui, 2000—, Weber County Sesquicentennial, 2000; co-chair Ogden Mayor's Cemetery Enhancement Commn; mem. cmty. rels. com. McKay Dee Hosp., 2000—. Fellow Utah State U., Logan, 1967-68, 68-69. Mem.: DAR, Mus. Action Team, Fedn. Ogden Bus. Profl. Women Internat., Weber County Women's Legis. Coun. and Rep. Women, Weber Far South Ctr. Co., Utah Mus. Assn. (bd. dirs.), Ogden Mayors Project (cemetery com., sesquicentennial com.), Altrusa Internat., Daus. of Utah Pioneers, Aglaia Club. Mem. Lds Ch. Avocations: historian/lecturer, writer, golfer, bridge, swimmer, ballroom dance instr. Home and Office: 4046 South 895 East Ogden UT 84403-2416

SEAGER, STEVEN ALBERT, small business owner, accountant; b. Phelps, N.Y., Oct. 17, 1958; s. Harold John and Eleanor Ruth (Vogel) S.; m. Linda Ann Lee, Oct. 11, 1980 (div. Nov. 1991); children: Anna M., Ashley I., Amy E.; m. Nataliya Aslanyan, Oct. 14, 1994; children: Stephanie E., Geniya A. AA in Acctg., C.C. of Finger Lakes, 1978; postgrad., SUNY, Geneseo, 1978, 89. Bookkeeper Exxon Co. USA, Clifton Springs, NY, 1977-79; acct. MXR Innovations, Inc., Rochester, N.Y., 1980-81, credit mgr., 1981-83, asst. controller, 1983-84; mgr.-cost and gen. acctg. Nat. Brands Beverage, 1984-87; owner/propr. Reader's Rendezvous Bookstore, Phelps, 1987-90; acctg. mgr. Almor Corp., Warsaw, 1990-92, mgr. fin., 1992-94; owner, operator La Mancha Prodns., 1993—; ptnr. A A A Store Signage, Geneseo, N.Y., 1993-95; registered rep. MetLife, Rochester, 1995—. Author: Songs From the Heart, 1988 (Golden Poet award 1989, 90), Thirteenth at Love's Table, 1992 (Poet of Merit award 1992), Diamonds in The Rough, 1993 (Poetry Acad. award, 1993). Mem. Phelps-Clifton Springs Sch. Bd., Clifton Springs, 1989-90, Phelps Hist. Dist. Com., 1990, Phelps Comty. Theater, 1978-87, Geneseo Comty. Theatre, 1993—. Recipient Rep. Senatorial Medal of Freedom, 1993, Rep. Legion of Merit medal, 1993, Rep. Merit medal, 1997, Rep. Majority medal, 1997. Roman Catholic. Avocations: poetry, chess, reading, theatre. Office: MetLife 200 Canal View Blvd Ste 220 Rochester NY 14623-2809

SEAGLE, EDGAR FRANKLIN, environmental engineer, consultant; b. Lincolnton, N.C., June 27, 1924; s. Franklin Craig and Lillie Mae (James) S.; m. Doris Elaine Long, Mar. 23, 1958; children: Rebecca Jane, Mary Elaine, James Craig, William Franklin. AB in Chemistry, U. N.C., 1949, MS in Pub. Health, 1954; BCE, U. Fla., 1961; DPH, U. Tex., 1974. Registered profl. engr., Ala. Sr. sanitarian Health Dept., City of Charlotte, N.C., 1950-52, chief indsl. hygiene sect., 1956-59; sanitation cons. N.C. State Bd. Health, Raleigh, 1954-56; engr. dir. USPHS, Rockville, Md., 1961-78; asst. dir. Fellowship Office Nat. Acad. Scis., Washington, 1978-83; pub. health engr. Dept. of Environ., State of Md., Balt., 1985-88; ind. engring. cons. Rockville, 1984-85, 88—. Contbr. articles to profl. publs. With USN, 1943-46, PTO. Mem. ASCE, APHA, Am. Acad. Environ. Engrs. (diplomate). Methodist. Home and Office: 14108 Heathfield Ct Rockville MD 20853-2760 E-mail: efseagle@mindspring.com.

SEAGLE, J. HAROLD, lawyer; b. Marion, N.C., May 9, 1947; s. Rufus James and Alma Rhoda (McMahan) S.; m. Linda Jean Cranford, June 3, 1967; 1 child, James Mark. BA, U. N.C., 1973, JD, 1977. Bar: N.C. 1977; U.S. Dist. Ct. (ea., middle, we. dists.) N.C. 1977, 88, 92; U.S. Ct Appeals (4th cir.) 1982; U.S. Supreme Ct. 1982. Assoc. atty. Rountree & Newton, Wilmington, N.C., 1977-79; ptnr. Rountree & Seagle, L.L.P., 1979—. Past pres. Fifth Jud. Dist. Bar. Bd. trustees and bd. deacons Winter Park Baptist Ch.; past moderator Wilmington Baptist Assn.; bd. dirs. Rescue Mission of Cape Fear; past adv. Bd. Coastal Bioethics Network; past chmn. annual fund drive Am. Cancer Soc.; past sect. chmn. Cape Fear United Way. Mem.: N.C. Bar Coun. of Pres. Wilmington Inns of Ct. (exec. com., master), Maritime Law Assn. of U.S. (proctor), Southeastern Admiralty Law Inst. (chmn.), N.C. Coll. of Advocacy, N.C. Acad. Trial Lawyers, N.C. State Bar, N.C. Bar Assn., New Hanover County Bar Assn. (co-chair grievance com.). Avocations: acoustic guitar, motorcycle racing. Office: Rountree & Seagle LLP 2419 Market St Wilmington NC 28403-1135 E-mail: hseagle@rountreeseagle.com.

SEAGO, DIANA MARIE, college administrator; b. Kansas City, July 30, 1949; d. Gordon Eugene and Rita Marie (Ohmes) S. BA, Mt. St. Scholastica Coll., 1971. Joined Order of St. Benedict. Tchr. St. Joseph Grade Sch., Shawnee, Kans., 1971-72; asst. dir. admissions Donnelly Coll., Kansas City, 1972-73; dir. residence hall Benedictine Coll., Atchison, 1973-78; assoc. dir. campus ministry Washburn Cath. Campus Ctr., Topeka, 1978-80; dir. RCIA St. Mary Ch., Tulsa, 1980-91; comm. svc. Williams Telecom., 1991-92; dir. gift planning, then assoc. v.p. devel. Benedictine Coll., 1992—. Cons. in field. Author of poems. Recipient Sertoma Club Kans Citizens award, 1967. Mem. HTML Writers Guild, Scriptorium, Coun. for Advancement and Support of Edn. Democrat. Roman Catholic. Avocations: fishing, guitar, harmonica, needlework, Internet. Office: Benedictine Coll 1020 N 2nd St Atchison KS 66002-1402

SEAGREN, ALICE, state legislator; b. 1947; m. Fred Seagren; 2 children. BS, SE Mo. State U. Mem. Minn. Ho. of Reps., 1993—. Active Bloomington (Minn.) Sch. Bd., 1989-92. Mem. Bloomington C. of C. (bd. dirs. 1990-92), Phi Gamma Nu, Alpha Chi Omega. Republican. Home: 9730 Palmer Cir Bloomington MN 55437-2017 Office: Minn Ho of Reps State Capital Building Saint Paul MN 55155-0001 E-mail: rep.alice.seagren@house.leg.state.mn.us.

SEAGREN, STEPHEN LINNER, oncologist; b. Mpls., Mar. 13, 1941; s. Morley Raymond and Carol Christine (Linner) S.; m. Jill Garrie; 1 child, Sean Garrie. AB, Harvard U., 1963; MD, Northwestern U., 1967. Diplomate Am. Bd. Internal Medicine, Am. Bd. Med. Oncology, Am. Bd. Radiology. From asst. prof. to assoc. prof. radiology and medicine U. Calif., San Diego, 1977-88, prof., 1988—, chief divsn. radiation oncology. Contbr. over 80 articles to profl. jours. Bd. dirs. Wellness Cmty., San Diego, 1988—, chair profl. adv. com., 1988—; chair radiol. oncology com. Cancer and Acute Leukemia Group, Chgo., 1986-98; assoc. dir. U. Calif. San Diego Cancer Ctr., 1998-2000. Lt. comdr. USNR, 1971-73. Fellow ACP. Avocations: physical fitness, bridge, skiing, golf, tennis. Office: U Calif San Diego Med Ctr 200 W Arbor Dr San Diego CA 92103-9000 E-mail: sseagren@ucsd.edu.

SEAGULL, HELEN ANN, paralegal, educator, public relations consultant; b. Milw. 1 child, Keith Allen. Student, U. Wis., 1979, Cambridge (Eng.) U., 1981; BA magna cum laude, U. So. Calif., 1981; postgrad., Calif. State U., Fullerton, 1984, 88, Calif. State U., San Bernardino, 1990-91, Calif. State U., Dominguez Hill, 1991, Coll. Osteo. Medicine, Pomona, Calif., 1992-94; PhD in Edn., Pacific Western U., 1991. Cert. tchr., Calif., med. asst./instr., Calif. Price index compiler Bur. Labor Statistics, Milw., 1972-74; reporter, feature writer Post Newspaper, 1972-78; advt. writer, proofreader Bruce Barry & Gleysteen, 1975-78; med. asst. Drs. Jack Klieger and John Massart, 1976-78; editorial asst. KFWB News Radio, L.A., 1979; asst. program coord. talk show People Tonight, CNN TV, 1980; instr. St. Boniface Parochial Sch., Anaheim, Calif., 1986; tutor/instr. Reading Game, Upland; instr., curriculum developer Pegasus U. Calif., Irvine, 1986; instr. Calif. State U., Fullerton, 1984-85; office mgr., resume writer Profl. Resume Co., Ontario, Calif., 1987; instr., dir., curriculum developer med. assisting program Sawyer Bus. Coll., Pomona, 1987-92; dir., instr., curriculum developer med. assisting program Pacific Coast Coll., Santa Ana, 1989-90. Pub. rels. cons., bus. instr. Sawyer Bus. Coll., Pomona, 1988-92; English tutor, Seoul, South Korea, 1985; med. instr. Westech Coll., Pomona, 1992-97; hearing rep., paralegal Law Offices of Keith A. Seagull, Pomona, 1995—. Author: (mystery trilogy) Devil's Horn, 1981; (poems) Potpourri, 1980; co.-dir., producer children's TV show Library Playhouse, 1974. Co-pres. St. Vincent DePaul Soc., Fullerton, 1984-86; bd. trustees Platt Coll., Ontario, Calif., 2001-; chmn. L.A. County Forum for Legal Secs., 2002-. Hearst Co. scholar. Mem. Internat. Women's Writing Guild, Am. Assn. Med. Assts., Calif. Physician Assts., Soc. Profl. Journalists, Pomona Valley Citrus Legal Sec.'s Assn. (pres. 2000—), Foothill Valley Bus. Women's Club, Ontario C. of C., Pomona C. of C., Chino C. of C., Phi Beta Kappa. Roman Catholic. Avocations: skydiving, sailplaning, sailing, composing, skiing. Home: 3254 Summer Island Ct Ontario CA 91761-0412 E-mail: haseagull@earthlink.net.

SEAGULL, KEITH ALLEN, lawyer; b. Milw., Apr. 19, 1957; s. Louis and Helen Ann S.; m. Asma Parveen, Nov. 20, 1994; 1 stepchild, Samia; 1 child, Sasha Y. BS, U. Wis., Milw., 1977; JD, Southwestern U., L.A., 1981; cert. atendance, Cambridge U., 1981. Bar: Calif. 1990; cert. specialist workers' compensation State Bar Calif. Bd. Legal Specialization. Law clerk Law Offices Steven M. Hanna, Fullerton, Calif., 1981-85; asst. office mgr. Joe Kay Design & Constrn., 1985-89; adjuster Wausau Ins., Pasadena, 1989-90; atty., adjuster Springfield Ins., Covina, 1990-91; atty. Law Offices Rose, Klein & Marias, L.A., 1991, Stephen G. Krutzsch & Assocs., ITT Hartford Ins., Brea, Calif., 1991-94, Law Office James Max Stewart, Temecula, 1994-95; prin. Law Offices Keith A. Seagull, Pomona, 1995—. Mem. ABA, Calif. Applicants' Attys. Assn., Eastern Bar Assn. L.A. County, Masons. Avocations: sailing, world religions, walking, music, politics.

SEAL, JOHN S., JR. manufacturing company executive; b. Phila., May 20, 1944; s. John S. Sr. and Gertrude Eva (Abbott) S.; m. LoriAnn LaBonte; children: Kathryn, Ashley and Kristen (twins), Heather, Stephen, Spencer, Mackenzie, Riley. BS in Econs., Drexel U., 1967; MBA, Dartmouth Coll., 1971. CPA, N.Y. Asst. to exec. v.p. fin. Gould Inc., Chgo., 1971, dir. electronics group fin. planning Newton Upper Falls, Mass., 1972-73; pres., treas., CEO Nat. Comms. Industries Co., Greenwich, Conn., 1973-76, chmn., 1973-79; exec. v.p. Boyerton (Pa.) Burial Casket Co., 1976-77; v.p., gen. mgr. comms. products divsn. FSC Corp., Pitts., 1977-79; sr. v.p. Butcher and Singer Inc. subs. Butcher and Co. Inc., Phila., 1979-85; pres. Sovereign Group Inc. subs. Butcher and Co. Inc., 1983-85, Seal Devel. Co., Phila., 1985-88; mng. dir. Essex Fin. Group, 1988-97; CFO telecoms. Spiraduct, Inc., Montgomeryville, Pa., 1997-00. Bd. dirs. RTG Svcs., Inc., 1992—, Rittenhouse Sq. Fitness Club, Phila., 1983-89. Trustee Please Touch Mus., Phila., 1987-90; bd. dirs. alumni bd. Drexel U., Phila., 1983-92. With U.S. Army, 1967-68. Mem. AICPA, N.Y. Soc. CPAs, Conn. Soc. CPAs. Republican. Mem. Ch. of Christ. Club: Union League (Phila.). Avocations: helicopter pilot, boating, traveling. Home: 18210 SE Ridgeview Dr Tequesta FL 33469-8124 Office: Spiroduct Inc 170 Keystone Dr Montgomeryville PA 18936-9637 Fax: (561) 741-7875.

SEALANDER, JOHN ARTHUR, writer, educator; b. Urbana, Ill., June 19, 1948; s. John A. and Lucille (Rehm) S. BA in Art and BArch, U. Ark., 1972. Copywriter Cole & Weber, Seattle, 1973-74; copy supr. Kraft Smith Advt., 1974-76; writer, producer The Richards Group, Dallas, 1978-79; sr. writer The Bloom Agy., 1980-81; assoc. creative dir. Popejoy & Fischel, 1981-82; sr. writer Bozell & Jacobs, 1982-83; assoc. creative dir. Cunningham & Walsh, 1983-84; sr. writer Tracy-Locke, 1977-78, 84-85, Stern/Monroe Advt. Inc., Dallas, 1985-87, Puskar, Gibbon, Chapin Inc., Dallas, 1987-90, Sealander & Co., Dallas, 1990—. Bd. dirs. New Sch. of Art and Design, Dallas; instr. So. Meth. U., Dallas, 1979-83; photographer True Redd & Assocs., Dallas, 1980; producer, dir. PBS, Moscow, Idaho, 1972-73. Dir. (film) When I Grow Up, I'm Going To Be Old, 1972; songwriter: All The Good Men Are Taken, 1985, Child of the '80s, 1985. Mem. Art Dirs. Club (v.p. Seattle chpt. 1975-76). Avocations: photography, songwriting, web page design, music. Office: Sealander & Co 611 N Buckner Blvd Dallas TX 75218-2708 E-mail: john@sealander.com.

SEALE, JAMES LAWRENCE, JR. agricultural economics educator, international trade researcher; b. Memphis, Mar. 12, 1949; s. James Lawrence and Mary Helen (Keefe) S.; divorced. BA, U. Miss., 1972; postgrad., U. Chgo., 1978-79; PhD, Mich. State U., 1985. Agrl. vol. Peace Corps, Tondo, Zaire, 1973-75; agrl. advisor Harvard Inst. for Internat. Devel., Abyei, Sudan, 1978; specialist Mich. State U., Fayoum, Arab Republic of Egypt, 1980-83; asst. prof. agrl. econs. U. Fla., Gainesville, 1985-90, assoc. prof. agrl. econs., 1990-95, prof. agrl. econs., 1995—. Vis. prof. U. Leicester (Eng.), 1992, 94, hon. vis. fellow, 1995. Author: (with H. Theil and C.F. Chung) International Evidence on Consumption Patterns, 1989; editor: Journal of Agricultural and Applied Economics, 1998-2001; contbr. articles to profl. jours. Vol. Farmer to Farmer, UOCA, Namibia, 1994, Farmer to Farmer, Wenrock Internat., 1994; vol. agrl. bus. svcs. Wenrock Internat., Far Eastern Russia, 1998. NIMH scholar U. Chgo., 1978-79; traveling scholar U. Mich., 1979; rsch. fellow Cairo U., 1980-83; McKethan-Matherly rsch. fellow, 1986-88, McKethan-Matherly sr. rsch. fellow, 1991-94. Mem. Am. Econs. Assn., Am. Agrl. Econs. Assn., Internat. Assn. Agrl. Economists, Econometrics Soc., Caribbean Agro-Econ. Soc., Internat. Agrl. Trade Rsch. Consortium, Gamma Sigma Delta. Episcopalian. Avocation: scuba diving, karate. Home: 530 NW 50th Blvd Gainesville FL 32607 Office: U Fla Dept Food and Resource 2111 McCarty PO Box 110240 Gainesville FL 32611-0240

SEALE, JAMES MILLARD, retired religious organization administrator, clergyman; b. Middlesboro, Ky., Oct. 4, 1930; s. Albert Tyler and Edith Josephine (Buchanan) S.; m. Mary Dudley Harrod; children: William Alan, Ann Lynn Seale Hazelrigg. BA, Transylvania U., 1952; BD, Lexington Theol. Sem., 1955, MDiv, 1963, D Ministry, 1981. Ordained to ministry Christian Ch. (Disciples of Christ), 1951. Student pastor various Christian Chs., Ky., 1949-54; pastor 1st Christian Ch., Pikeville, 1954-58, Erlanger (Ky.) Christian Ch., 1958-61; sr. minister 1st Christian Ch., Mt. Sterling, Ky., 1961-70, Paris, 1978-82; stewardship sec. Gen. Office Christian Ch., Indpls., 1970-74; adminstr. Christian Ch. Home of Louisville, 1974-78; dir. devel. Christian Ch. Homes Ky., Louisville, 1978; pres. Disciples of Christ Hist. Soc., Nashville, 1983-95, pres. emeritus, 1995. Author: A Century of Faith and Caring, 1983, Forward From The Past, 1991; editor jour. Discipliana, 1983-92. Pres. Kiwanis Club, Pikeville, 1957, Mt. Sterling, 1963, lt. gov., Ctrl. Ky., 1965. Avocations: writing, photography, golf, fishing.

SEALE, JOHN CLEMENT, director, cinematographer; b. Warwick, Queensland, Australia, Oct. 5, 1942; s. Eric Clement and Marjorie Lyndon (Pool) S.; m. Louise Lee Mutton, Sept. 23, 1967; children: Derin Anthony, Brianna Lee. Grad. high sch., Sydney, Australia; PhD (hon.) , Griffith U., 1997. Camera asst. film dept. Australian Broadcasting Com., 1962-68; freelance technician, camera operator various films, series, commls., 1968-76. Dir. feature film, Till There Was You, 1989-90. Dir. photography: Goodbye Paradise (Golden Tripod 1982), Careful, He Might Hear You (Best Cinematography 1983), Witness, 1984 (Golden Tripod 1984, Oscar nomination 1986, Brit. Acad. award nomination 1986), The Hitcher, 1985, Children of a Lesser God, 1985 (Golden Tripod 1985), The Mosquito Coast, 1986, Stakeout, 1987, Gorillas in the Mist (Brit. Acad. award nomination 1989, Premier Mag. Cinematographer of the Yr. 1989), Rainman, 1988 (Acad. award nomination 1988, Artistic Achievement award 1989), Dead Poets Society, 1989, The Doctor, 1991, Lorenzo's Oil, 1992, The Firm, 1993, The Paper, 1993, Beyond Rangoon, 1994, The American President, 1995, The English Patient, 1995-96 (Best Cinematography award L.A. Film Critics Assn., Acad. award Cinematography, 1996, Brit. Acad. award 1996, Best Cinematography award Am. Soc. Cinematographers 1996, European Best Cinematography award 1997, Chgo. Film Critics award, Fla. Film Critics award), Ghosts of Mississippi, 1996, City of Angels, 1997, At First Sight, 1998, The Talented Mr. Ripley, 1998, The Perfect Storm, 1999, Harry Potter, 2000, Dreamcatcher, 2002, Cold Mountain, 2002. Recipient Film Critics Cir. Australia 1990 Tribute; named European Cinematographer of Yr., 1997. Mem. Australian Cinematographers Soc. (named Cinematographer of Yr. 1982, 84, Inaugural mem. Hall of Fame 1997), Am. Soc. Cinematographers, Order of Australia. Avocations: building boats, sailing.

SEALE, ROBERT L. former state treasurer, political organization chairman; b. Inglewood, Calif., Oct. 4, 1941; m. Judy Seale (dec.). BSA, Calif. Poly. U. Former contr. and sr. fin. officer Rockwell Internat.; sr. accountant Ernst & Ernst, L.A.; mng. ptnr. Pangborn & Co., Ltd. CPA's, 1985-88; former state treas. State of Nev.; chair. Nev. Rep. Party, 2000—. Former treas. Nev. Rep. Com. Mem. Nat. Assn. State Treas. (past pres.). Address: 8625 W Sahara Ave Las Vegas NV 89117 Office: 528 S Decatur Blvd Las Vegas NV 89107-3931*

SEALE, ROBERT MCMILLAN, office services company executive; b. Feb. 1, 1938; s. Robert McMillan and Margaret Sutherland (Miller) S. BA, Emory U., 1959. With N.Y. Life Ins. Co., San Francisco, 1960-67, Dictaphone Office Svcs. divsn. Dictaphone Corp., San Francisco, 1967-69; pres. Am. Profl. Svc., Inc., Dictation West Miss Jones' Word Processing, various locations, 1969-93; pres. Environments West, 1980-86, Los Arcos Properties, 1980—. Founder Seale Orgn., 1993; lectr. in field. Contbr. articles in field to profl. jours. Bd. dirs. The Rose Resnic Ctr. for Blind and Handicapped, Computer Based Patient Record Inst.; med. word processing cons. to hosps., health care insts., office equipment mfrs.; chmn. San Francisco Mayor's Com. for Employment of Handicapped, 1971-73; mem. Calif. Gov.'s Planning and Adv. Com. for Vocat. Rehab. Planning, 1968-69; pres. Calif. League for Handicapped, 1968-70, bd. dirs., 1966-73, 84-89, adv. coun., 1973-77; v.p. Stebbins Found., 1980-89; pres. Stebbins Housing Corp., 1980-89; assoc. St. Francis Hosp. Found., 1990—; sec., founder Palm Springs Coalition of Neighborhoods. Recipient Spoke and Spark award U.S. Jr. C. of C., 1967, KABL Outstanding Citizen's award, 1965, 71. Mem. Am. Health Info Mgmt. Assn., Adminstrv. Mgmt. Soc., Sales and Mktg. Execs. Assn., Am. Assn. Med. Transcription (Disting. Svc. award 1985), Med. Transcription Industry Alliance, Emory U. Alumni Assn., Emory Lamplighters Soc., U.S. C. of C., Las Palmas Alliance (chmn.), Delta Tau Delta. Office: 280 W Camino Sur Palm Springs CA 92262-4303

SEALL, STEPHEN ALBERT, lawyer; b. South Bend, Ind., Oct. 24, 1940; s. Stephen Henry and Mildred Rita (MacDonald) S.; m. Barbara Ann Halloran, June 25, 1966; children: John Paul, Edward Andrew, Ann Marie. BA, Purdue U., 1963; postgrad., Cornell U. Grad. Sch. Bus. Adminstrn., 1963; LLB, U. Notre Dame, 1966. Bar: Ind. 1966, U.S. Claims Ct. 1973, U.S. Tax Ct. 1968, U.S. Ct. Appeals (6th cir.) 1980, U.S. Ct. Appeals (7th cir.) 1969, U.S. Supreme Ct. 1973. Assoc. Thornburg, McGill, Deahl, Harman, Carey & Murray, South Bend, 1966-71; ptnr. Barnes & Thornburg and predecessor firm Thornburg, McGill, Deahl, Harman, Carey & Murray, 1972—, vice chmn. and mgmt. com., mng. ptnr. South Bend office, 1985—2001. Spkr. in field. (Mem. editl. bd.) Notre Dame Law Rev., 1964—66. Mem. Mayor's Com. on Downtown Devel., South Bend, 1975-77, Mayor's Com. on Utilization of Downtown Bldgs., South Bend, 1988-96; trustee Project Future, South Bend, 1986-2002; exec. com. Meml. Hosp. South Bend, Inc., 1999—; dir. Meml. Health Found., 1992-98, Meml. Health Sys., 1997—, United Way of St. Joseph County, Inc., 1992-98, Conv. and Tourism Industry Coun., 1994-2000. Fellow Am. Coll. Tax Counsel, Am. Bar Found., Ind. Bar Found.; mem. ABA (taxation sect.), Ind. State Bar Assn. (chmn. taxation sect. 1977-78), Summit Club (chmn. 1976-77), Morris Park Country Club (bd. dirs., sec. 1998-2001). Democrat. Roman Catholic. Avocations: golf, softball, weightlifting. Home: 17705 Waxwing Ln South Bend IN 46635-1328 Office: Barnes & Thornburg 600 1st Source Bank Ctr 100 N Michigan St Ste 600 South Bend IN 46601-1632

SEALS, MARGARET LOUISE, newspaper editor; b. Buckhannon, W.Va., Oct. 27, 1944; d. James Richard and Helen Margaret (Brown) Crumrine; m. Harry Eugene Seals, Jan. 10, 1975. BS in journalism, W. Va. U., 1966; MS in mass. comm., Va. Commonwealth U., 1983. Reporter, copy editor Democrat & Chronicle, Rochester, N.Y., 1966-67, Dayton (Ohio) Daily News, 1967-68; copy editor Richmond (Va.) Times-Dispatch, 1968-75, copy desk slot editor, 1975-81, exec. news editor, 1981, asst. mng. editor, 1982-92, dep. mng. editor, 1992-93, mng. editor, 1994—. Mem. Leadership Metro Richmond, 1986, mem. adv. bd. sch. mass. comm. Va. Commonwealth U., 1988-93; mem. vis. com. Sch. Journalism, W.Va. U., 1999—. Named Outstanding Woman in Comms. YWCA Met. Richmond, 1989; recipient Perley Isaac Reed award W.Va. U. Journalism Sch. Alumni Assn., 1996. Mem.: Richmond Assn. Black Journalists, Nat. Assn. Black Journalists, Va. Press Assn. (dir. 2001—), AP Mng. Editors (dir. 1993—95, 1998—2001, editor APME News 1993—94, treas. 1996—97), Va. Press Women (pres. 1990—92, 2d v.p. 1988—90, treas. 1986—88, Press Woman of Yr. 1986, Communicator of Achievement award 1997), Soc. Profl. Journalists (pres. Va. profl. chpt. 2000—02, bd. dirs. Va. profl. chpt. 1998—), Nat. Fedn. Press Women (bd. dirs. 1990—92, Communicator of Achievement award 1997), Phi Kappa Phi. Avocations: history, historical fiction, jazz, walking. Office: Richmond-Times Dispatch PO Box 85333 Richmond VA 23293-5333 E-mail: lseals@timesdispatch.com.

SEALS, RYAN BROWN, electronics engineer; b. Coleman, Tex., July 23, 1920; s. William Harrison and Ocia Mae (Brown_ S.; m. Mary Jo Taylor, Aug. 31, 1941 (div. Feb. 1942); m. doris Jo Brown, Mar. 29, 1942 (div. Nov. 1961); 1 child, Sandra Jean Seals Harmes; m. Jeanette Ceil Meadows, July 28, 1967. BA, Tex. A&M U., 1941; BS in Physics and Math., Daniel Baker Coll., 1952; postgrad., So. Meth. U., Tex. Christian U, U. So. Miss., 1953-78; PhD in Elec. Engring., Shelbourne U., 1987; PhD, 20th Century U., 2000. Cert. flight instr. Asst. chief engr. Sta. KNET Radio, 1941-42; asst. head electronics tng. Kelly Field, San Antonio, 1942-44; chief engr. Sta. KSTA Radio, Coleman, 1947-52; design engr. through project dir. Collins Radio Co., Dallas, 1952-71. Cons. electronics, Dallas, Austin (Tex.), Los Angeles, 1972; systems engr., program mgr. Litton Data Systems divsn., Pascagoula, Miss., 1972-81, sr. staff engr., 1981-87, cons., 1987-92; chief engr. Svc. Industries, 1992—; instr. Jackson County Jr. Coll., Gautier, Miss., 1972-80. Adviser, Elec. Ectronics Sch., Jackson County Jr. Coll., 1972-86; chief check pilot CAP Squadron Group 3 Miss., 1973-79. With USN, 1944-46. Mem. IEEE (sr.), Aircraft Owners and Pilots Assn., Exptl. Aircraft Assn. (chpt. founder, pres. 1980-83, 91, tech. counselor, flight advisor), Internat. Aerobatics Club (chpt. founder, pres. 1979-85, profl. air show pilot, bd. dirs.). Presbyterian. Home and Office: Air Park Estates 6320 Lockheed St Plano TX 75093-6511 E-mail: rseals@flash.net.

SEALS, THEODORE HOLLIS, public relations executive; b. Chgo., Oct. 26, 1950; s. Jack H. and Costello C. Seals. BA, Yale U., 1973. Reporter, rewriteman Chgo. Sun Times, 1974—78; corp. sec., sr. editor C-BREM Comm. Corp., 1983—. Home: 7228 S Rhodes Ave Chicago IL 60619

SEALS, WANDA RIVERS, county official, writer; b. Mobile, Ala., Feb. 6, 1961; d. Charles and Lucinda (Frost) Rivers; m. James Seals III, Jan. 22, 1982; children: Shanthalitta, James. AS in Applied Arts, Bishop State Jr. Coll., 1985. Presch. tchr. Toulminville Warren United Meth. Ch., Mobile, Ala., 1992—99; asst. program coord. Prichard Housing Authority, 1999—. Pres. Twice As Strong Prodns., Mobile, 1999—2002. Author: Pinby and the Choo Choo, 1998, Expressions Through Experiences, 1998, Every Soul has a Story, 2002. Chmn. Religion & Race, Mobile, 2000—02; sec. Kuumba Assn. of the Arts, 1998—2002. Pvt. Nat. Guard U.S. Army, 1979—81. Recipient Certificate of Appreciation, Camp Marlin Youth Leadership Acad., 2000, Dedication & Svc. plaque, Harlem Area Wood & Seed, 2001. Mem.: Prichard Area C. of C. Democrat. Methodist. Avocation: arts & crafts. Home: 649 New Jersey St Apt 10 Mobile AL 36603 Office: Richard Housing Authority 226 Bernard St Mobile AL 36610

SEALY, VERNOL ST. CLAIR, scientist; came to U.S., 1962; m. Josephine Doreen Nanton, May 8, 1965; children: Vernetta, Vernol Jr. Gen. cert. edn., U. London, 1962; LLB, La Salle Ext. U., Chgo., 1967; BS in Zoology, Howard U., 1968, Med. Tech. cert., 1969, MS in Microbiology, 1971; MPH, U. Mich., 1974; PhD in Religion summa cum laude, Trinity Theol. Sem., Newburgh, Ind., 1988; Cultural Doctorate in Sacred Philosophy, World U., Tucson, 1984. Ordained to ministry Seventh-day Adventist Ch. as elder, 1978; registered microbiologist. Elder Seventh-day Adventist Ch., mem. adminstrv. bd. Mich., 1975-81, Ypsilanti, 1981-84, dir. personal ministries, 1981-82; mem. adminstrv. bd. Oakwood Seven-day Adventist Ch., Melvindale, Mich., 1986—; med. technologist D.C. Gen. Hosp., 1970-73; clin. lab. hematologist St. Joseph Mercy Hosp., 1973—. With nursing, neuro-psychiatry unit Freedmen's Hosp., Howard U., Washington; conducted M.S. rsch. NIH, 1970-71. Past mem. Boy's Scout Assn.; commandant Brit. Red Cross Soc. Fellow Royal Soc. Health; mem. Adventist Theol. Soc., Am. Soc. Clin. Pathologists (cert. med. technologist, hematologist), N.Y. Acad. Scis., Internat. Biog. Assn. (life patron), Am. Biog. Inst. and Rsch. Assn. (rsch. bd. advisors, dep. gov. 1988—). Home: 3667 Helen St Ypsilanti MI 48197-3760 *To know the Creator-Redeemer God and to be like Him, is man's highest destiny. To reveal His presence through a constant exhibition of His love, is to know Him, and to be like Him: For God is Love.*

SEAMAN, ALFRED JARVIS, retired advertising agency executive; b. Hempstead, L.I., N.Y., Sept. 17, 1912; s. Alfred J. and Ellen (Delaney) S.; m. Mary M. Schill, Sept. 26, 1937 (dec. June 1975); children: Marilyn Hollingsworth, Susan, Barry, Deborah; m. Honor S. Mellor, July 16, 1977. BS, Columbia U., 1935; LittD, L.I. U., 1987. Account exec. Fuller & Smith & Ross, Inc., N.Y.C., 1937-41; partner Knight & Gilbert. Inc., Boston, 1941-43; with Compton Advt., Inc., N.Y.C., 1946-59, exec. v.p., creative dir., dir., 1954-59; vice chmn. bd., chmn. exec. com. SSC & B, Inc., 1959-60, pres., chief exec. officer, 1960-79, chmn., chief exec. officer, 1979-81. Dir., mem. exec. com. Interpublic Group of Cos., Inc. Hon. bd. dirs., adv. council, founding chmn. Advt. Ednl. Found.; bd. dirs., hon. dir. com. Advt. Council.; chmn. planning bd., 1962—, mayor Village Upper Brookville, 1966-98; chmn. emeritus Samuel Waxman Cancer Research Found. Lt. USNR, 1943-46. Named to Advt. Hall of Fame, 1983 Mem.: U.S. Sr. Golf Assn., Creek (Locust Valley, L.I.) (pres.), Piping Rock (Locust Valley, L.I.), Racquet and Tennis (N.Y.C.), Jupiter Island (Fla.), Nat. Golf Links Am. (Southampton, N.Y.), Seminole (Fla.), Hobe Sound Yacht (Fla.). Home: Wolver Hollow Rd Upper Brookville Oyster Bay NY 11771 also: Jupiter Island 126 Gomez Rd Hobe Sound FL 33455-2424 Office: 220 E 42nd St New York NY 10017-5806

SEAMAN, ARLENE ANNA, retired musician, educator; b. Pontiac, Mich., Jan. 21, 1918; d. Roy Russell and Mabel Louise (Heffron) S. BS, life cert., Ea. Mich. U., 1939; MMus, Wayne State U., 1951; postgrad., Colo. Coll., 1951-52, Acad. Music, Zermatt Switzerland, 1954, 58, U. Mich. Guest conductor Shepherds and Angels, Symphonie Concertante, 1951; asst. conductor Detroit Women's Symphony, 1960-68; adjudicator Mich. State Band and Orch. Festivals, Solo and Ensemble Festivals, 1950-70, Detroit Fiddler's Band Auditions, 1948-52, Mich. Fedn. Music Clubs, 1948-55; tchr. Ea. Mich. U., 1939-42, Hartland Sch. Music, 1939-42, Pontiac (Mich.) Pub. Schs., 1942-45, Detroit Pub. Schs., 1945-73, pvt. studio, 1973-90. Performer cello South Oakland Symphony, 1958-65, Detroit Women's Symphony, 1951-68, Riviera Theatre Orch., 1959, 60, Masonic Auditorium Opera, Ballet Seasons, 1959-65, Toledo Ohio Symphony, 1963-70, others; performer trumpet Detroit Brass Quartet, 1974-78; piano accompanist various auditions, recitals, solo and ensemble festivals; composer: Let There Be Music, 1949, Fantasy for French Horn and Symphonic Band, 1951. Mem. Quota Internat., Delta Omicron. Home: 6231 N Montebella Rd #347 Tucson AZ 85704

SEAMAN, BARBARA (ANN ROSNER), author; b. N.Y.C., Sept. 11, 1935; d. Henry Jerome and Sophie Blanche (Kimels) Rosner; m. Gideon Seaman, Jan. 13, 1957 (div.); children: Noah Samuel, Elana Felicia, Shira Jean. BA (Ford Found. scholar), Oberlin Coll., 1956, LHD (hon.), 1978; cert. in advanced sci. writing (Sloan-Rockefeller fellow), Columbia U., 1968. Columnist Brides Mag., N.Y.C., 1964-68; columnist, contbg. editor Ladies' Home Jour., 1965-69; editor child care and edn. Family Circle, 1970-73; contbg. editor Omni mag., 1978; cons. FYI, ABC-TV, 1979-80; v.p. for devel. David Brooks Prodns., 1990-94; contbg. editor MS Mag., 1993—; columnist Hadassah Mag., 2000—. Cons. U.S. Senate subcom. on monopoly: Nelson pill hearings, 1970; presented testimony to Senate and Congl. coms., 1970—; lectr. in field; participant TV discussion shows; tchr. Coll. New Rochelle, 1975, Sagaris Inst., 1975, CUNY, 1993; founding mem. N.Y. Women's Forum, 1973-99; co-founder Nat. Women's Health Network, 1975—, Comm. Consultants for Choice, 1985-86, Nat. Task Force Sexual Malpractice, 1985-86, Families Against Sexually Abusive Therapists and Other Profls., 1992—; v.p. Women's Med. Ctr., N.Y.C., 1971-73; mem. ERA Emergency Task Force, 1979; adv. coun. Feminist Press, Old Westbury, N.Y., 1975; adv. bd. Feminist Ctr. for Human Growth and Devel., 1979, Women's History Libr., Berkeley, Calif., 1973-75; steering com. Women's Forum, 1974; adv. bd. NOW, N.Y., 1973, Women's Guide to Books, 1974, Jewish Women for Affirmative Action, Evanston, Ill., 1973—, Jour. Women and Health, 1975, Jewish Feminist Orgn., N.Y.C., 1975; chair com. domestic violence Nat. Coun. Women's Health, 1993-98; judge for various journalism awards. Author: The Doctors' Case Against the Pill, 1969, rev. edit., 1980, 25th anniversary edit., 1995, Free and Female, 1972; (with G. Seaman) Women and the Crisis in Sex Hormones, 1977, Lovely Me: The Life of Jacqueline Susann, 1987, anniversary edit., 1996; (with Gary Null) For Women Only: Your Guide to Health Empowerment, 2000; contbg. author: foreword to Lunaception, 1975; The Bisexuals, 1974, Career and Motherhood, 1979, The Menopause Industry, 1994; author (play) I Am a Woman, 1972; (movie) Scandalous Me: The Jackie Susann Story, 1998; contbr. (anthologies) Rooms with No View, 1974, Women and Men, 1975, Seizing Our Bodies, 1978, Women's Health Care: A Guide to Alternatives, 1984; Encyclopaedia of Childbirth, 1992, Lawyers Manual on Domestic Violence: Representing the Victim, 1995, The Conversation Begins, 1996, Real Majority Media Minority, 1997, The Reader's Companion to U.S. Women's History, 1997, Jewish Women in America: An Historical Encyclopedia, 1997, Textbook of Women's Health, 1997, Women's Health, 1999, Routledge International Encyclopedia of Women, 2001, Hands On! 33 More Things Every Girl Should Know, 2001; cons. (film) The Pill, 1999; narrator (film) Taking Our Bodies Back, 1974; contbr. articles to newspapers, popular mags.; books and articles translated into Spanish, German, Dutch, Turkish, Japanese, Hebrew, French, Italian. Alumni cons. women's studies program Oberlin Coll., 1975; motivation com. Am. Cancer Soc., 1973; adv. com. Older Women's Health Project, NYU Med. Ctr., 1980; bd. dirs. Safe Transp. of People, N.Y.C., 1975, Women's Health Newsletter, 1983; adv. bd. DES Action, 1977, 7 Stones Press, 1997-; cons. Nat. Task Force on DES, 1978; contraceptive rsch. br. HEW, 1980; v.p., bd. dirs. ARM (Abortion Rights Moblzn.), 1981—; hon. bd. dirs. Carcinogen Info. Program, St. Louis, 1981, Am. Friends of Rabin Med. Ctr., 1998—; ; trustee Nat. Coun. on Women in Medicine, 1990—; chmn. adv. bd. Coalition for Family Justice, 1991—; co-chair Domestic Violence com. N.Y. Women's Agenda, 1992-93, del. Can.-USA Women's Health Forum, 1996; host com. Womens Health Day, Beijing, Plus-Five UN Reunion, 2000; cons. FDA Patient Labels on Oral Contraceptives, 2000-01; nat. judge Project Censored Award, 1997-. Recipient citation for books as first to raise issue of sexism in health care as world-wide issue Libr. of Congress, 1973, citation as author responsible for patient package inserts on prescriptions HEW, 1970, Matrix award, 1978, Pioneer Woman award Resources Divsn. of Am. Assn. Retired Persons, 1986, Athena award Nat. Coun. Women's Health, 1992, Health Advocacy award Health Policy Adv. Ctr., APHA, 1994, Project Censored award, 1996, Postal Service Women's Rights Movement stamp, 2000; inviting com. Am. Writers Congress. Mem. PEN, Authors Guild, Nat. Assn. Sci. Writers. Address: 110 W End Ave Apt 5D New York NY 10023-6348

SEAMAN, DARYL KENNETH, oil company executive; b. Rouleau, Sask., Can., Apr. 28, 1922; BSME, U. Sask., 1948, LLD (hon.), 1982, U. Calgary, 1993. Cert. mech. engr. CEO Bow Valley Industries Ltd., Calgary, Alta., Can., 1962-70, 85-91, chmn., chief exec. officer Can., 1970-82; chmn. Box Valley Industries Ltd., Can., 1982-85; pres. Bow Valley Industries Ltd., Can., 1985-87, chmn., 1991-92. Bd. dir. Far West Mining Ltd., Pure Techs. Ltd., E-tronics, Inc., Bow Valley Energy Ltd.; co-owner Calgary Flames Hockey Club, bd. dir.; chmn. Dox Investments, Inc., pres.; hon. regent Athol Murray Coll. of Notre Dame, 2001—. Mem. Royal Commn. Econ. Union and Devel. Prospects for Can., 1982-85; active numerous coms. for fundraising U. Sask.; hon. chmn. The Western Heritage Centre Soc.; chmn. nat. adv. com. Banff Sch. Mgmt. Served with RCAF, 1941-45, North Africa, Italy. There is no repetition since it is indicated as an award you received and as a membership. Mem. Assn. Profl. Engrs., Geologists and Geophysicists (hon. life, Frank Spragins award, 1985, McGill Mgmt. Achievement award, 1979), Order of Canada 1993, Western Heritage Centre Soc., Ranchmen's Club, RAF Club, Earl Grey Golf Club, Calgary Petroleum Club, Calgary Golf and Country Club, U.

Calgary Chancellor's Club. Progressive Conservative. Mem. United Ch. Can. Avocations: ranching, golf, hunting, skiing. Home and Office: Dox Investments Inc 500 333 5th Ave SW Calgary AB Canada T2P 3B6

SEAMAN, DUNCAN CAMPBELL, civil engineer; b. Norfolk, Va., Sept. 17, 1957; s. Harold Duncan and Catherine Claire (Munsee) S.; m. Tammy Jean Quattlebaum, Dec. 19, 1981; children: Duncan Russell, Katharine Jeanne. BSCE, The Citadel, 1980; MSCE, Clemson U., 1986. Registered profl. engr., S.C. Commd. 2d lt. U.S. Army Corps Engrs., 1980, advanced through grades to maj., co. comdr. Mo., 1983-84, civil engr. St. Louis, 1986-87, dep. resident engr., 1987-89, resigned, 1989; project mgr. Rust Constrn. Co., Birmingham, Ala., 1989—97; program mgr. BMW Project, Greenville, S.C.; constrn. mgr. Lockwood Greene, Spartanburg, 1997—99; dept. mgr. plant engring. BMW Mfg. Corp., 1999—. Campaign vol. United Way, Birmingham, 1990; fund raiser Boy Scouts Am., Birmingham, 1990. Mem. ASCE, Am. Assn. Cost Engrs., Project Mgmt. Inst., Soc. Am. Mil. Engrs., Chi Epsilon. Republican. Home: 329 Parkside Dr Simpsonville SC 29681-5241

SEAMAN, IRVING, JR. banker; b. Milw., July 14, 1923; s. Irving and Anne (Douglas) S.; m. June Carry, June 24, 1950; children: Peter Stewart, Marion Carry, Irving Osborne, Anne Douglas (dec.); m. Barbara R. Gardner, May 22, 2002. BA, Yale U., 1944. With Continental Ill. Nat. Bank & Trust Co., Chgo., 1947-61, v.p., 1959-61; pres., chief exec. officer, dir. Nat. Boulevard Bank, Chgo., 1961-65, chmn. exec. com., chief exec. officer, dir., 1966-76; vice chmn. bd., dir. Sears Bank and Trust Co., Chgo., 1976-77, pres., chief operating officer, dir., 1977-82; sr. cons. Burson-Marsteller, Chgo., 1982-94. Chmn. bd. Associated Bank Chgo., 1985—. Mem. Northwestern U. Assn.; life mem. bd. dirs. Lake Forest Hosp.; bd. dirs. United Way of Chgo., 1975-89, pres., 1979; bd. dirs. United Way/Crusade of Mercy, 1980-89, 94-95, vice chmn., 1980-81; trustee Chgo. Symphony Orch., 1987—. Lt. (j.g.) USNR, WWII. Mem. Commonwealth Club, Econ. Club, Chgo. Club, Comml. Club, Racquet Club, Onwentsia Club, Winter Club, Old Elm Club (Highland Park, Ill.), Shoreacres Club (Lake Bluff, Ill.), Augusta Nat. Golf Club (Ga.), Marsh Landing Club (Fla.), Sawgrass (Fla.) Country Club. Home: 946 Elmtree Rd Lake Forest IL 60045-1410 Office: Assoc Bank Chgo 200 E Randolph St Chicago IL 60601-6436

SEAMAN, JEROME FRANCIS, actuary; b. Oak Park, Ill., Nov. 4, 1942; s. William Francis and Bernice Florence (Haughey) S.; m. Jacquelyn Ann Robinson, Aug. 22, 1970; children: Carolyn, John. BA, U. Notre Dame, 1964; MA, Northwestern U., 1991. Asst. actuary Combined Ins. Co. of Am., Chgo., 1966-73; v.p., actuary United Equitable Life Ins. Co., Skokie, 1975-77; mgr. Peat Marwick Mitchell & Co., Chgo., 1973-75, 77-78; nat. dir. actuarial svcs. Arthur Young & Co., 1978-83; pres., cons. actuary Jerome F. Seaman & Assocs., Evanston, 1983—. Dir. Polysystems, Inc., Chgo., 1987-91. Contbr. articles to profl. jours. Recipient Commendation for Svc. Pres. Ronald Reagan, 1982. Fellow Soc. of Actuaries, Conf. of Cons. Actuaries; mem. Am. Acad. Actuaries (task force on risk based capital health orgns. 1993-95). Democrat. Unitarian Universalist. Avocations: running, hiking, classical music, opera, baseball. Home: 2107A Sherman Ave Evanston IL 60201-6116 Office: Jerome F Seaman & Assocs 2107 A Sherman Ave Evanston IL 60201-6116 E-mail: jfseaman@hotmail.com.

SEAMAN, JOHN, artist; b. Providence, June 28, 1936; s. Robert Gordineer and Bertha May Lewis Seaman. BA, Swarthmore Coll., Pa, 1956. Sci. editor The Columbia Press, New York, NY, 1959—60; owner Art Photography, 1989—; sci. writer The Am. Institute of Physics, 1966—67; assoc. editor The Data Comm. User Mag., Valley Stream, 1974—75, Electronic Products Mag., Garden City, 1975—77; computing practices editor Assn. for Computing Machinery, New York, 1979—80; owner Art Photography, 1989—2002; assoc. editor The Data Comm. User Mag., Valley Stream, 1974—75, Electronic Products Mag., Garden City, 1975—77; computing practices editor Assn. for computing Machinery, New York, 1979—80. Organizer & leader Eleotheria Salon, New York, NY, 1989—, Morningside Garden's Computer Group Colloquia, New York, NY, 1995—; organizer and leader Morningside Gardens Life Sketch Group, New York, NY, 1998—. Prin. works include My Own Oevre of Classic Art Nude Photos. Recipient 8 Awards for Nude Photography, Met. Camera Club Coun.; scholar Westinghouse Sci. Rsch. Scholarship, Westinghouse Corp., 1952. Mem.: Art Students League (life). Avocations: skydiving, naturism, classical concerts. Home: 501 West 123rd Street #13E New York NY 10027-5006 Personal E-mail: johnseaman2b@juno.com.

SEAMAN, ROBERT E., III, lawyer; b. Chgo., Apr. 2, 1947; s. Robert E. II and Rae June (Blair) S.; children: Kimberly Desiree, Charissa Alaine, Robert E. IV, Jason Robert. BA in Polit. Sci., The Citadel, 1969; JD, U. Va., 1972; postdoctoral, N.Y. Inst. Fin., 1975-77, Harvard U., 1979. Bar: N.Y. 1975, S.C. 1978, U.S. Dist. Ct. (so. dist.) N.Y. 1975, U.S. Tax Ct. 1980, U.S. Ct. Appeals (2nd cir.) 1975, U.S. Ct. Appeals (4th cir.) 1979, U.S. Supreme Ct. 1979, U.S. Ct. Mil. Appeals 1980. Assoc. Breed, Abbott & Morgan, N.Y.C., 1972-74; v.p.-legal, asst. sec. Paine, Webber, Jackson & Curtis Inc. and subs., 1974-77, asst. to chmn. bd. PaineWebber Inc., 1974-77; assoc. gen. counsel Col. Life and Accident Ins. Co., Columbia, S.C., 1977-80; sole practice, 1980—. Gen. counsel Jacom Computer Services, Inc., Northvale, N.J., 1977—; chmn. The dorchester Group, 1987—; bd. dirs., gen. counsel Internat. Chem. Cons., Ltd., 1983-88; pres. Titan Trading Co., Inc., Columbia, 1984-86, Comptel Data Sys., 1984—; chief exec. officer, pub. Up2Date Market Adv. Service, Columbia, 1985-87; chmn. bd., CEO Race Mktg. Assocs. Inc.; lectr. various ednl. instns. Co-author: How to Use the Relative Strength Index to Increase Trading Profits, 1986, Legal Issues in the Leasing Process, 1991; editor in chief: The Reading Guide and Virginia Law School Outline Series, 1971-72; sr. editor Va. Law Weekly, 1970-72; contbr. articles to profl. jours. Student senator S.C. Legislature, 1968-69; mem. coll. presdl. adv. com., state dir. Collegiate Counsel of UN, 1968-69; trustee Faith United Meth. Ch.; coord. phon-a-thon campaign Midlands S.C. youth div. YMCA, 1980-82; class chmn. Citadel Devel. Found., 1980; chpt. chmn., campaign adv. com. chmn., vice chmn. exec. com. Midlands chpt. March of Dimes, 1978-81; mem. task force Greater Columbia C. of C.; vice chmn. bd. KIDS North Jersey, 1990-94; founder, chmn. The Millennium Found., 1992—. Served capt. M.I., inf. U.S. Army, 1972 -77, Res., 1977-83. Robert R. McCormick scholar McCormick Found., and Chgo. Tribune, 1965-69, DuPont scholar U. Va., 1969-72; winner Estate Planning contest 1st Nat. Bank Chgo., 1971; recipient Leadership award Citadel Devel. Found., 1979-80, named Young Man of Yr., S.C. Greater Met. Area Jaycees, 1980; recipient Recognition award Nat. March of Dimes, 1981; named Knight Comdr., Grand Cross, Min. Fin. and Advocar Gen., Order St. John Knights of Malta. Mem. Assn. of Bar of City of N.Y., ABA (state regulation of securities com., subcom. on oil and gas, subcom. on regulation of equipment leasing, securities industry assn. compliance divsn. 1974-77), Am. Assn. Equipment Lessors, Info. Tech. Resellers Assn., NYSE, AMEX, Nat. Assn. Securities Dealers (registered rep.), Commodities Futures Trading Commn. (registered prin.), N.Y. Bar Assn., S.C. Bar Assn., Citadel Brigadier Club (bd. dirs.), Ill. Citadel Club (pres.), Knights of Malta (Knighted and designated Knight Comdr., Grand Cross, Minister of Fin. and Avocar Gen. Order of St. John), Pi Sigma Alpha; Clubs: Yale Club N.Y.C., Rockland Country Club, Com. of 100 Club, Met. Bus. Club, Palmetto Soc., Toastmasters (pres. Lexington chpt., ann. impromptu speech contest champion, Toastmaster of Yr. 1979). Office: 560 Route 303 Orangeburg NY 10962-1314

SEAMAN, RONALD LEON, educator; b. Seaman, Ohio, Feb. 10, 1947; s. Thomas Allen and Pauline Albertine (Black) S.; m. Patricia Ann Plata, July 8, 1977 (div. Feb. 1994); children: Matthew Ticannes, Emma Marie, Christopher Thomas. BSEE, U. Cin., 1970; PhD in Biomed. Engring., Duke U., 1975; MS in Mgmt., Ga. Inst. Tech., 1987. Instr. U. Tex. Health Sci. Ctr., Dallas, 1976-79; rsch. engr. II Ga. Inst. Tech., Atlanta, 1979-82, sr. rsch. engr., 1982-86; assoc. prof. La. Tech. U., Ruston, 1986—. Mem. NRC transp. rsch. bd. com. Transp. for Transp. Disadvantaged, Washington, 1988-91; speaker and presenter in field. Contbr. articles to profl. jours. Judge Regional Sci. Fairs, Tex., La., 1978, 89, 90, 92-94. Recipient numerous rsch. fellows, grants and awards in field. Mem. IEEE (sr. mem., engring. mgmt. soc., AdCom mem., 2d v.p. publications, chpts. com. chmn., Atlanta sect. chmn., vice chmn., sec. treas.), AAAS, Am. Soc. Engring. Edn., N.Y. Acad. Scis., Soc. Neurosci., Bioelectromagnetics Soc., Eta Kappa Nu, Tau Beta Pi. Office: La Tech U Dept Biomed Engring PO Box 3185 Ruston LA 71272-0001

SEAMAN, ROUAL DUANE, data processing company executive; b. East Chicago, Ind., Apr. 25, 1930; s. Elmer Earl and Roxanna Isabelle (Bennett) S.; m. Sadako Itabashi, July 29, 1957; 1 child, Victor Shayne. Student, U. Mo., 1950-51, Jochi Daigaku, Tokyo, 1956, U. Houston, 1966-69. Mgmt. trainee GE Corp., Atomic Energy Commn., Richland, Wash., 1951-52; project mgr. Dynalectron Corp., Ft. Worth, 1952-63; project supr. Apollo Test Facility N.Am. Rockwell Project Apollo, NASA, Houston, 1964-69; mktg. mgr. Gen. Space Corp., 1969-70; pres. AIM Fin. Systems Group, Inc., 1970—98. Bd. dirs. Am. Credit Control; ptnr. Automated Info. Mgmt., 1984—; ptnr. CA$SH Enterprises, 1989—. Author software. Pres. Tex. Intercity Football, Inc., Harris/Galveston County, 1971, League City (Tex.) Little League, 1972; mem. S.W. Football Ofcls. Assn., 1976; mem. Better Bus. Bur., Houston, 1982—; mem. KC Sch. Governance Task Force. With USAF, 1947-50. Recipient Recognition award Greater Houston Partnership, 1990. Mem. Am. Guild of Patient Mgmt., Houston C. of C., Nat. Fedn. Ind. Businesses, Nat. Assn. Pvt. Enterprise, Tex. Hosp. Assn., Tex. Hosp. Info. Systems Soc., Healthcare Fin. Mgrs. Assn., 100 Club of Houston, Smithsonian Instn., Am. Mus. Natural History, N.E. Alumni Assn. (res.), KC Optimist Club (bd. dir.). Republican. Christian/Bhuddist. Avocations: golf, baseball, football, gardening, travel.

SEAMAN, WILLIAM BERNARD, physician, radiology educator; b. Chgo., Jan. 5, 1917; s. Benjamin and Dorothy E. S.; m. Veryl Swick, February 26, 1944; children: Marvin Gene, Cheryl Dorothy, William David. Student, U. Mich., 1934-37; MD, Harvard U., 1941. Diplomate Am. Bd. Radiology. Intern Billings Hosp., U. Chgo., 1941-42; asst. radiology Yale U. Sch. Medicine, 1947-48, instr., 1948-49; instr. radiology Washington U. Sch. Medicine, St. Louis, 1949-51, assoc. prof., 1951-55, prof., 1955-56; prof. radiology, chmn. dept. Coll. Phys. and Surg., Columbia U., 1956-82; James Picker prof. emeritus Columbia U., 1982—. Dir. radiology service, trustee Presbyn. Hosp., N.Y.C. Served as maj. USAAF, 1942-46; flight surgeon. Recipient W.B. Cannon medal Soc. Gastro-intestinal Radiologists, 1979, Gold medal Am. Coll. Radiology, 1983 Mem. Radiol. Soc. N.A., Am. Roentgen Ray Soc. (pres. 1973-74, gold medal 1988), Am. Coll. Radiology (pres. 1980-81), Assn. U. Radiologists (pres. 1955-56, Gold medal 1979), N.Y. Roentgen Soc. (pres. 1961-62), N.Y. Gastroent. Soc. (pres. 1965-66), Soc. Chmn. Academic Radiology Depts. (pres. 1967-68), Eastern Radiol. Soc. (pres. 1985-86). Presbyterian. Home: 2108 Devonshire Way Palm Beach Gardens FL 33418-6873

SEAMANS, ANDREW CHARLES, editorial and public relations consultant, columnist, author; b. Hillside, N.J., Sept. 10, 1937; s. Thomas Randall and Marie Josephine (Mazur) S.; m. Marion Gloria Lufbery, Aug. 25, 1956 (div. June 1986); children: Andrew Charles, Darryl Wayne, Marion Gloria Seamans Raynor, Dawn Louise Wheeler. AS cum laude, No. Va. Community Coll., Annandale, 1989. Lic. real estate salesman, Va. Editorial writer U.S. Press Assn., McLean, Va., 1968-70; pub. rels. asst. Nat. Right to Work Com., Washington, 1970; assoc. editor Human Events, 1970-81; mng. editor Heritage Features Syndicate, 1981-91; syndicated columnist The Answer Man Creators Syndicate, L.A., 1985—; chief copy editor The Hill Newspaper, Washington, 1996—. Bd. dirs., pub. rels. cons. Marine Learning Inst., St. Louis, 1980—. Author: Who, What, When, Where, Why In the World of American History, 1991, Who, What, When, Where, Why In the World of World History, 1991, Who, What, When, Where, Why In the World of Nature, 1992; co-author: Whose FBI?, 1974. Bd. dirs. McLean Little League Baseball, Inc., 1975-83, pres., 1982-83; pres. Rahway (N.J.) Young Rep. Club, 1964-66; chmn. platform com. Union County Young Reps., N.J. Young Reps., various other Rep. orgns. Recipient cert. of appreciation McLean Little League Baseball, 1978, named to Hall of Fame, 1985. Mem. Pub. Rels. Soc. Am., Soc. Profl. Journalists (bd. dirs. D.C. chpt. 1986-87, membership dir. 1986-87, 89-90, dir. pub. info. 1988), No. Va. Assn. Historians, Va. Hist. Soc., Internat. Platform Assn., Nat. Press Club. Episcopalian. Home and Office: Horizon House 603 1300 Army Navy Dr Arlington VA 22202-2054

SEAMANS, ROBERT CHANNING, JR. astronautical engineering educator; b. Salem, Mass., Oct. 30, 1918; s. Robert Channing and Pauline (Bosson) S.; m. Eugenia Merrill, June 13, 1942; children: Katherine (Mrs. Louis Padulo), Robert Channing III, Joseph, May (Seamans Baldwin), Daniel M. BS, Harvard U., 1939; MS, MIT, 1942, ScD, 1951; grad. exec. program bus. adminstrn., Columbia U., 1959; DSc, Rollins Coll., 1962, NYU, 1967; DEng, Norwich Acad., 1971, Notre Dame U., 1974, Rensselaer Poly. Inst., 1974, U. Wyo., 1975, George Washington U., 1975, Lehigh U., 1976, Thomas Coll., 1980, Curry Coll., 1982. Successively instr. dept. aero. engring., staff engr. instrumentation lab., asst. prof., project leader instrumentation lab., asso. prof. Mass. Inst. Tech., 1941-55; chief engr. Project Meteor, 1950-53, dir. flight control lab., 1953-55; mgr. airborne systems lab., chief systems engr. airborne systems dept. RCA, 1955-58, chief engr. missile electronics and controls div., 1958-60; asso. adminstr. NASA, 1960-68, dep. adminstr., 1965-68, cons., 1968-69; vis. prof. MIT, 1968, Hunsaker prof., 1968-69; sec. air force, 1969-73; pres. Nat. Acad. Engring., 1973-74; adminstr. ERDA, Washington, 1974-77; Henry R. Luce prof. environment and pub. policy MIT, 1977-84, sr. lectr. dept. aeros. and astronautics, 1984-96, dean Sch. Engring., 1978-81. Mem. sci. adv. bd. USAF, 1957-62, assoc. adviser, 1963-67. Bd. overseers Harvard U., 1968—74; trustee emeritus Mus. Sci. , Boston, Sea Edn. Assn., Nat. Geog. Soc., Carnegie Inst., Washington, Woods Hole Oceanographic Inst. Recipient naval ordnance devel. award 1945, Godfrey L. Cabot award Aero Club New Eng., 1965, disting. svc. medal NASA, 1965, 69, Robert H. Goddard meml. trophy, 1968, disting. pub. svc. medal Dept. Def., 1973, exceptional civilian svc. award Dept. Air Force, 1973, Gen. Thomas D. White U.S. Air Force Space Trophy, 1973, Ralph Coats Roe medal ASME, 1977; achievement award Nat. Soc. Profl. Engrs., Thomas D. White Nat. Def. award, 1980, exceptional svc. award Dept. Air Force, 1985. Fellow Am. Acad. Arts and Scis., Am. Astron. Soc., IEEE, AIAA (hon., Lawrence Sperry award 1951); mem. Internat. Acad. Astronautics, Am. Soc. Pub. Adminstrn., Nat. Acad. Engring. (Arthur M. Bueche Award, 1994, Daniel Guggenheim award 1996), AAAS, Air Force Acad. Found., Fgn. Policy Assn., Coun. on Fgn. Rels., Sigma Xi. Clubs: Harvard (Boston); Manchester Yacht (Mass.); Essex County (Mass.); Chevy Chase, Metropolitan (Washington); Cruising of Am. (Boston Sta.).

SEAMANS, WILLIAM, writer, commentator, former television and radio journalist; b. Providence, July 8, 1925; s. William and Mary Seamans; m. Jane Kingsbury, Sept. 15, 1951; children: Laurie, Jonathan, Adam. AB, Brown U., 1949; MS, Columbia U., 1952. Freelance journalist, 1952-53; journalist CBS News, 1953-63; producer evening news ABC News, 1963-65, European producer, 1965-70, field producer N.Y.C., 1970-72, corr., bur. chief Tel Aviv, 1972-92; commentator Vt. Pub. Radio, lectr., freelance writer, 1992—. Producer Nightline in Israel Week (including Palestinian-Israeli town meeting) (Emmy award, Dupont award). Served with inf. AUS, 1942-45. Decorated Bronze Star medal; CBS Murrow News fellow Columbia U., 1961-62. Mem. Writers Guild Am., Nat. Acad. TV Arts and Scis. (Emmy award 1961, 89), Overseas Press Club Am. (award for best radio reporting invasion of Cyprus 1974, award for best fgn. affairs documentary Yitzhak Rabin biography 1975), Nat. Press Club (Washington), Fgn. Corrs. Assn. in Israel. E-mail: bseamans@monad.net.

SEAMON, KATINA WRIGHT, educational consultant;

SEAPKER, JANET KAY, museum and architectural history consultant; b. Pitts., Nov. 2, 1947; d. Charles Henry and Kathryn Elizabeth (Dany) S.; m. Edward F. Turberg, May 24, 1975. BA, U. Pitts., 1969; MA, SUNY, Cooperstown, 1975. Park ranger Nat. Park Svc., summers 1967-69; archtl. historian N.C. Archives and History, Raleigh, 1971-76, hist. preservation adminstr., 1976-77, grant-in-aid adminstr., 1977-78; dir. Cape Fear Mus. (formerly New Hanover County Mus.), Wilmington, N.C., 1978-2000; ret.; archtl. historian-preservation/mus. cons. Bd. dirs. Bellamy Mansion Found., Wilmington, 1986-89, 91-97, Lower Cape Fear Hist. Soc., Wilmington, 1985-88; N.C. rep. S.E. Mus. Conf., 1986-90; bd. dirs. Cape Fear Coast Conv. and Vis. Bur., 1997-2001, sec., 2001; field reviewer Inst. Mus. Svcs., 1982-2001. Contbr. articles to profl. jours. Bd. dirs. Downtown Area Revitalization Effort, Wilmington, 1979-81, Thalian Hall Ctr. for Performing Arts, 1996-98; bd. dirs. Hist. Wilmington Found., 1979-84, pres., 1980-81; mem. Cmty. Appearance Commn., Wilmington, 1984-88, 250th Anniversary Commn., Wilmington, 1986-90. Grad. program fellow SUNY, Cooperstown, 1969-70; recipient Profl. Svc. award N.C. Mus. Coun., 1982, Woman of Achievement award YWCA, 1994. Mem. Am. Assn. Mus. (accreditation vis. com. 1983-2001, reviewer mus. assessment program 1982-2002), Nat. Trust Hist. Preservation, Southeastern Mus. Conf. (N.C. state rep. 1986-90), N.C. Mus. Coun. (sec.-treas. 1978-84, pres. 1984-86), Hist. Preservation Found N.C. (sec. 1976-78). Presbyterian. Home and Office: 307 N 15th St Wilmington NC 28401-3813 E-mail: jseapker@aol.com.

SEAQUIST, ERNEST RAYMOND, astronomy educator; b. Vancouver, B.C., Can., Nov. 19, 1938; s. Egron Emanuel and Sigrid Alice (Back) S.; m. Gloria Stewart Jenkins, June 11, 1966; children: Jonathan William, Carolyn Suzanne. BASc, U. B.C., Vancouver, 1961; MA, U. Toronto, Ont., Can., 1962, PhD, 1966. Lectr. astronomy U. Toronto, 1965-66, asst. prof., 1966-72, assoc. prof., 1972-78, prof., 1978—, assoc. chmn. dept., 1974-88, chmn., 1988-99, dir. David Dunlap Obs. Ont., 1988-99. Contbr. author: Classical Novae, 1989; also over 150 articles. Rsch. grantee Natural Scis. and Engring. Rsch. Coun. Can., 1967—. Mem. Internat. Astron. Union, Am. Astron. Soc., Can. Astron. Soc. (pres. 1986-88). Avocations: painting and sketching, collecting antiques. Office: U Toronto Dept Astronomy 60 St George St Toronto ON Canada M5S 1A7 E-mail: seaquist@astro.utoronto.ca.

SEARBY, RICHARD HENRY, lawyer; b. July 23, 1931; s. Henry and Mary Searby; m. Caroline McAdam, 1962; 3 sons. MA (hons.), U. Oxford. Bar: London 1956, Victoria, Australia 1957. Assoc. to Chief Justice of Australia Rt. Hon. Sir Owen Dixon, 1956-59; ind. lectr. law relating to executors and trustees U. Melbourne, 1961-72; bd. dirs. News Corp. Ltd., Australia, 1977-92, chmn. Australia, 1981-91; bd. dirs. News Internat. plc, U.K., 1981-92, dep. chmn. U.K., 1987-92. Dep. chmn. Times Newspapers Holdings Ltd., 1981-89; bd. dirs., chmn. S. China Morning Post, 1987-92, Equity Trustees Executors and Agy. Co. Ltd., 1975-2000; bd. dirs. Amrad Corp. Ltd., 1992—, Tandem Australian Ltd., 1992—, BRL Hardy Ltd., Woodside Petroleum Ltd., 1998—. Chmn. Geelong Grammar Sch., 1983-89; mem. coun. Nat. Libr. Australia, 1992—, Mus. of Victoria, 1993-97 Decorated QC (Australia) 1971. Mem.: Melbourne, Australian (Melbourne). Avocations: reading, music, tennis, fishing. Office: 23A Hampden Armadale 3143 Victoria Australia also: 1 Spring St Melbourne 2010 Victoria Australia

SEARCY, ASHBURN PIDCOCK, SR. anesthesiologist; b. Thomasville, Ga., Oct. 23, 1937; s. Floyd Hartsfield and Anna Ashburn (Pidcock) S.; m. Nancy Rieves Ford, July 6, 1963; children: Ann Maxwell, Ashburn Pidcock Jr. BA in Humanities, Emory U., 1959; MD, Med. Coll. Ga., 1965. Fellow pathology Med. Coll. Ga., Augusta, 1962-63, resident anesthesiology, 1966-68; rotating intern U. Hosp., 1965-66; staff St. Joseph's Hosp., 1968-76, Univ. Hosp., Augusta, 1968-76, Ga. Bapt. Med. Ctr., Atlanta, 1976-77, Northside Hosp., Atlanta, 1977-78, Kennestone Hosp., Marietta, 1978—2000, emeritus staff, 2000—; staff Columbia Marietta Surg. Ctr., 1989—, Emory-Adventist Hosp., Smyrna, Ga., 1991-2001, Wellstar Paulding Hosp., Dallas, 1998—, Mountainside Med. Ctr., Jasper, 1999—2001; chief anesthesiology Mid. Ga. Hosp., Macon, 2001—. Mem. staff Coffee Reg. Med. Ctr., Douglas, Ga., 1999—, Archbold Meml. Hosp., Thomasville, Ga., 2000—, Colquitt Reg. Med. Ctr., Moultrie, Ga., So. Surgery Ctr., La Grange, Ga., 2000—, Appling County Health Sys., Baxley, Ga., 2000—, Chestatee Reg. Med. Ctr., Dahlonega, Ga., 2000—, Tanner Med. Ctr., Villa Rica, Ga., 2000—2001, So. Crescent Anesthesia, Newman Hosp.,Newman, Ga., 2000—; bd. dirs. Citizens Bank, Cairo, Ga., 1979-95, adv. dir., 1995—. Mem. AMA, Am. Soc. Anesthesiologists, Ga. Soc. Anesthesiologists, Med. Assn. Ga., Cobb County Med. Soc. Bahá'í.

SEARCY, DOROTHY JAMES, missionary; b. Yalaha, Fla., Oct. 8, 1924; d. Roland and Irma Kathryn (Bayan) James; married, Mar. 29, 1942 (widowed 1999); children: Gloria Rolanda Searcy Baird, Paul Raphael, Martha Loraine Searcy Bullard. Student, Lee Coll. (now Lee U.), Cleveland, Tenn., 1959-60. Missionary, Ch. of God, Nigeria, 1956-59, Panama and Canal Zone, 1960-66; editor-in-chief Ch. of God newsletters, various chs., various cities and countries, 1966—. Republican. Avocations: writing, songwriting, crafts, Scrabble, nature walks. Home: 27440 Lime Ave Yalaha FL 34797-3204

SEARCY, JANE BERRY, retired educational administrator, counselor; b. Birmingham, Ala., Dec. 21, 1951; d. Francis Clifford and Mary Jacqueline (Meeks) Berry; m. Joseph Alexander Searcy III, July 3, 1982; children: Margaret Alice, Joseph Alexander IV. BA in Elem. Edn., Birmingham So. Coll., 1973; MA in Spl. Edn., U. Ala., 1975, EdS in Spl. Edn., 1977, EdD in Spl. Edn., 1982. Cert. elem. and spl. edn. tchr., Ala. Tchr. spl. edn. Tuscaloosa (Ala.) County Schs., 1974-75, Montgomery (Ala.) County Schs., 1975-77, Tuscaloosa City Schs., 1977-79, curriculum assoc., 1979-86, dir. spl. edn., 1986-99; counselor K-12 Tuscaloosa Acad., 1999—. Instr. W. Ala. U. Coll. Edn., 1985-87, adj. prof., 1988—; cons. L.E.A.D. Acad., Montgomery, 1989-90; agy. rep. Child Protection Team, Tuscaloosa, 1986—, Tuscaloosa Autism Coun., 1988—; mem. Ala. Legis. Task Force, West Ala. Early Intervention Coun., Tuscaloosa, 1982—. Mem. adv. bd. Rural Infant Stimulation Environment, U. Ala., Tuscaloosa, 1988—; bd. dirs. Tuscaloosa Assn. for Retarded Citizens, 1987-94, 2000—, Child Protection Team, 1982—, Miracle Riders of West Ala., 1994—, RISE program, U. Ala, 1980—, Sheriff's Kids Act Program; bd. dirs. Children's Ctr. of Tuscaloosa, 1998-2000, pres. 1998-2000; sec. bd. dirs. Ala. Choir Sch., 1996—; bd. dirs. Tombigbee coun. Girl Scouts U.S., 1994-97, disabilities coord., fin. com., 1993—, coun. trainer, 1997—, tri-state chair tng. for trainers, 2001; assoc. chair, 1997-2001; active Women Committed to Excellence, 1998; mem. Forerunners Edn. Com., 1996—. Recipient Profl. of the Yr. award Tuscaloosa Assn. for Retarded Citizens, 1994. Mem. ASCD, Coun. Exceptional Children, Ala. Coun. Exceptional Children (Outstanding SPE Coord. in Ala. 1995), Tuscaloosa Coun. Exceptional Children, Ala. Coun. Sch. Adminstrn. and Supervision (bd. dirs. 1994-97), Ala. ASCD, Nat. Coun. Adminstrs. in Spl. Edn. (nat. bd. dirs.), Ala. Counseling Assn., Ala. Coun. Adminstrs. in Spl. Edn. (state pres. 1992-94, CASE del. to Sino-Am. conf. on exceptionality, Beijing, China 1995, Southeastern area CASE conf. chair 1996), Leadership Tuscaloosa (bd. dirs. 1996—), Alpha Delta Kappa (v.p. Epsilon chpt. 1984-86, pres. 1986-88, State Leadership Appreciation award 1988), Phi Delta Kappa, Alpha Omicron Pi (chpt. rels. adv. 1983-85, 2000—), Kappa Delta Pi. Home: 505 Rice Valley Rd NE Tuscaloosa AL 35406-2704

SEARCY, LEON, JR. football player; b. Washington, Dec. 21, 1969; m. Sonya; children: Malika-Maya, Kenya Imani; stepchild, Willie. Degree in Sociology, Miami. Offensive tackle Pittsburgh Steelers, 1992-95; football player Super Bowl, 1995; offensive tackle Jacksonville Jaguars, 1996—2001; guard Miami Dolphins, 2002—. Active Searcy Found., Jacksonville, Orlando, Fla., Jacksonville's Lee Boys and Girls Club; supporter numerous holiday efforts to feed homeless and assist elderly; supporter coll. scholarships to deserving H.S. students; spokesperson Kidney Found., 1999, Jacksonville Bone Marrow Donor Registry. Named All-Pro team Sports Illustrated, 1995, second-team All-Pro, AP, Pro Football Newsweekly, 1999, Best Right Tackle in NFL, The Sporting News, 1999; named to Pro Bowl, 1999. Office: Miami Dolph 7500 SW 30th St Fort Lauderdale FL 33314*

SEARLE, ANDREW BARTON, fund raising consultant; b. Washington, Aug. 30, 1962; s. Harvey Russell and Louise Morgan (Cowles) S. BA, Haverford Coll., 1984. Asst. to exec. dir. Springfield (Mass.) Ctr. Bus. Dist., Inc., 1984-86; asst. dir., regional capital campaign Smith Coll., Northampton, Mass., 1986-88; assoc. dir. devel. Watkinson Sch., Hartford, Conn., 1988-91; dir. devel. Wilmington (Del.) Friends Sch., 1991-93, Lawrence Acad., Groton, Mass., 1993-96; prin. Andrew Searle Fund Raising Counsel, 1996—. Trustee Alumni Program Coun., 1992-2000, v.p., 1999-2000, spkr./panelist various confs., 1989-00; spkr./panelist various confs. Coun. for Advancement and Support of Edn., 1991-98; spkr. Nat. Assn. of Ind. Schs., 2000. Contbr. articles to profl. publs.; columnist Funding Private Schools, Boston, 1996—. Trustee Summer Theatre at Mount Holyoke Coll., South Hadley, Mass., 1994—2001, pres., 1997—98; trustee Svc. Providers, Inc., Springfield, 1988—91, Groton (Mass.) Pub. Libr., 1998—; corporator StageWest, Springfield, 1988—91; bd. dirs. Gay & Lesbian Advs. and Defenders, Boston, 2001—. Avocation: genealogical research. Home and Office: PO Box 1016 Groton MA 01450-3016 E-mail: absearle@cs.com.

SEARLE, PETER J. lawyer; b. Summit, N.J., Nov. 6, 1959; s. Richard L. and Joan M. S.; m. Melissa A., Aug. 8, 1992; children: Keenan, Kevin, Kathryn, Kaitlyn. BA, Calif. State U., Fullerton, 1982; JD, Southwestern U. Sch. Law, 1986. Atty. Chase, Rotchford, Drukker & Bogust, L.A., 1986-96; v.p., claims mgr. CNA Comml. Ins., Brea, Calif., 1997—2000; full time mediator Mediation Settlement Corp., Anaheim Hills, 2001—. Mem. ABA, L.A. Co. Bar Assn., Orange Co. Bar Assn., Riverside Co. Bar Assn., So. Calif. Mediation Assn., Am. Def. Inst., Calif. Constrn. Defect Claims Mgrs. Assn. (chair 1997—). Office: Mediation Settlement Corp Judicate W 751 S Weir Canyon Rd #157-663 Anaheim CA 92808-

SEARLE, PHILIP FORD, banker; b. Kansas City, Mo., July 23, 1924; s. Albert Addison and Edith (Thompson) S.; m. Jean Adair Hanneman, Nov. 22, 1950 (dec. Nov. 1990); 1 child, Charles Randolph; m. Jean Walker, Oct. 4, 1992 (dec. oct. 1993); m. Elizabeth Gordon, Nov. 4, 1994. AB, Cornell U., 1949; grad. in banking, Rutgers U., 1957, 64. With Geneva (Ohio) Savs. & Trust Co., 1949-60, pres., 1959-60; pres., sr. trust officer Northeastern Ohio Nat. Bank, Ashtabula, 1960-69; pres., CEO BancOhio Corp., Columbus, 1969-75; chmn., CEO Flagship Banks, Inc., Miami, 1975-84; chmn. bd. Sun Banks, Inc., Orlando, 1984-85, cons., 1986-94. Mem. faculty Sch. Banking, Ohio U., 1959-70, Nat. Trust Sch., Northwestern U., Evanston, Ill., 1965-68; corp. adv. com. Nat. Assn. Securities Dealers, 1981-83; v.p., fed. adv. coun. to bd. govs. FRS, 1983-85; chmn. Nat. Adv. Bd. to Oversight Bd. for Resolution Trust Corp., 1991-92. Co-author: The Management of a Trust Department, 1967. Past chmn. bd. regents Stonier Grad. Sch. Banking, Rutgers U., 1974-76, past mem. faculty; trustee Fin. Acctg. Found., Norwalk, Conn., 1989-93. Capt. AUS, 1943-46, 51-52, ETO. Decorated Bronze Star; named outstanding citizen in Ashtabula County, 1967. Mem. Am. Bankers Assn. (bd. dirs. 1972-74, governing coun.), Bank Adminstrn. Inst. (nat. chmn. 1987-88, bd. dirs. Chgo. 1985-89), Fla. Bankers Assn. (bd. dirs. 1979-81, coun. 1981), Ohio Bankers Assn. (pres. 1970-71), Assn. Bank Holding Cos. (pres. 1979-81), Fla. C. of C. (bd. dirs. 1978-82), Royal Poinciana Golf Club (Naples, Fla.), Naples Yacht Club, Catawba Island Club (Port Clinton, Ohio), Phi Kappa Tau.

SEARLE, ROBERT FERGUSON, minister; b. Auburn, N.Y., July 13, 1951; s. Loren Rawson and Esther Lucille (Ferguson) S. BS, Cornell U., 1973; MDiv, Princeton Theol. Sem., 1977; cert. pastoral care, Gordon D. Hoople Inst., Syracuse, N.Y., 1981; DMin, Asbury Theol. Sem., 1997. Ordained deacon United Meth. Ch., 1978, ordained elder, 1980. Clin. pastoral edn. Ancora Psychiat. Hosp., Hammonton, NJ, 1977, Bethany Med. Ctr., Kansas City, Kans., 1977-78; pastor of Blodgett Mills Freetown and McGraw (N.Y.) United Meth. Ch., 1978-84; pastor Pennsylvania Ave. United Meth. Ch., Pine City, N.Y., 1984-98; chaplain resident Duke U. Med. Ctr., 1998-99; chaplain U.S. Army Res., 1991—; pastor Clyde United Meth. Ch., 1999—; adj. prof. spiritual formation Northeastern Sem., Rochester, NY, 2000—; contract chaplain Canadaique and Syracuse VA Hosp., 2000—. Mem. dist. bd. Ordained Ministry, Syracuse, N.Y., 1980-84, mem. conf. bd., 1980-85, dist. youth dir., Syracuse, 1981-84; mem. Cortland County Youth Bur., 1980-81; mem. hosp. com. Cortland County Coun. of Chs., 1980-84. Mem. McGraw Bd. Edn., 1981-84; bd. dirs. Meals on Wheels, Elmira, 1985-88; bd. dirs. CPC, Elmira, 1985-93; mem. edn. and rsch. instl. rev. bd. Arnot Ogden Hosp., Elmira, 1995-98; mem. cmty. bd. Southport Correctional Facility, 1987-98; spiritual dir. Spiritual Exercises, High Acres, Geneva, N.Y., 1986-98, 99—, spiritual dir. Walk to Emmaus, Rome, N.Y., 1993; mem. design team Ctrl. Lakes Dist. Acad. Spiritual Devel. Mem.: Charles Wesley Soc., Am. Assn. Christian Counselors, Knights Templar (St. Omers Commandery # 19), Royal and Select Masters (So. Tier coun. # 16), Royal Arch Mason (Elmira chpt. # 42), Marathon Lodge # 438. Republican. Avocations: reading, exercise, travel, music. Home: 5905 Draper St Wolcott NY 14590-1148 Office: 72 Sodus St Clyde NY 14433 E-mail: roo27@aol.com.

SEARLE, RODNEY NEWELL, state legislator, farmer, insurance agent; b. Camden, N.J., July 17, 1920; s. William Albert and Ruby Marie (Barrus) S.; m. Janette Elizabeth Christie, May 17, 1941 (dec.); children: R. Newell Jr., Linda Jennison Grant, Alan John; m. Ruth Anne Bartlett, May 6, 2001. BA, Mankato State U., 1960; DHL, Winona State U., 2001. Prodn. coordinator Johnson & Johnson, New Brunswick, N.J., 1940-47; farmer Waseca, Minn., 1947—; spl. agt. John Hancock Mut. Ins. Co., 1961-84; mem. Minn. Ho. of Reps., St. Paul, 1957-80, speaker, 1979—. Author: Minnesota Standoff—The Politics of Deadlock, 1990. Lay reader St. John's Episcopal Ch., 1952—; chmn. Upper Mississippi River Basin Commn., 1981-82; pres. Minn. State U. Bd., 1981-92; chmn. Minn. Higher Edn. Bd., 1991-92; bd. dirs. Minn. Wellsprings, 1984-90; emeritus mem. adv. bd. Hubert H. Humphrey Inst.; emeritus mem. coun. Minn. Hist. Soc.; bd. dirs. Minn. Agrl. Interpretive Ctr., 1983—; mem. Waseca County Hist. Bd., 1995—. Named Minn. State Tree Farmer of Yr., 1978 Mem. Am. Tree Farm System, Nat. Conf. State Legislators, Minn. Forestry Assn. (bd. dirs. 1991-2001), Masons, Rotary (pres. club 1968). Republican.

SEARLE, WILLIAM ROSS, academic administrator, artist, educator; b. Oak Bluffs, Mass., Sept. 25, 1936; s. George Raymond and Margaret Anderson Searle; m. Diane Lois McCarty; children: Gregory, Jennifer. MFA, RISD, 1961—63; BFA, Mass. Coll. Art, 1957—61. Chmn. art dept. Lawrence Acad., Groton, Mass., 1963—70, St. Margarets-McTernan Sch., Waterbury, Conn., 1974—77, Thayer Acad., Braintree, Mass., 1977—2000. Dir. art gallery Lawrence Acad., Groton, 1968—70, St. Margarets-McTernan Sch., Waterbury, 1974—77; dir. Thayer Gallery Thayer Acad., Braintree, 1977—2000. Ltd. edit. prints Historic Martha's Vineyard, 1993, mural 350th Anniversary, Braintree, Mass., 1990; Represented in permanent collections West Point Mus., Eastern Bank, Sports Mus. New Eng., King Ctr., Atlanta, Cape Mus. Fine Arts. SP3 United States Army, 1954—57, United States and Eniwetok. Home: 59 Shields Rd Mashpee MA 02649 Personal E-mail: wrsearle@aol.com.

SEARLES, ANNA MAE HOWARD, educator, civic worker; b. Osage Nation Indian Terr., Okla., Nov. 22, 1906; d. Frank David and Clara (Bowman) Howard; A.A., Odessa (Tex.) Coll., 1961; BA, U. Ark., 1964; M.Ed., 1970; postgrad. (Herman L. Donovan fellow), U. Ky., 1972—; m. Isaac Adams Searles, May 26, 1933; 1 dau., Mary Ann Rogers (Mrs. Herman Lloyd Hoppe). Compiler news, broadcaster sta. KJBC, 1950-60; corr. Tulsa Daily World, 1961-64; tchr. Rogers (Ark.) H.S., 1964-72; tchr. adult class rapid reading, 1965, 80; tchr. adult edn. Learning Center Benton County (Ark.), Bentonville, 1973-77, supr. adult edn., 1977-79; tchr. North Ark. C.C., Rogers, 1979-90, CETA, Bentonville, 1979-82; tchr. Joint Tng. Partnership Act, 1984-85; coordinator adult edn. Rogers C. of C. and Rogers Sch. System, 1984—. Sec. Tulsa Safety Council, 1935-37; leader, bd. dirs. Girl Scouts U.S.A., Kilgore, Tex., 1941-44, leader, Midland, Tex., 1944-52, counselor, 1950-61; exec. sec. Midland Community Chest, 1955-60; gray lady Midland A.R.C., 1958-59; organizer Midland YMCA, Salvation Army; dir. women's div. Savings Bond Program, Midland; mem. citizens com. Rogers Hough Meml. Library, women's aux. Rogers Meml. Hosp.; vol. tutor Laubach literacy orgn., 1973—; tutor Laubach Lit. Orgn., 1973-96; sec. Beaver Lake Literacy Council, Rogers, 1973-83, Little Flock Planning Commn., 1975-77, Benton County Hist. Soc., 1981—; pub. relations chmn. South Central region Nat. Affiliation for Literacy Advance, 1977-79; bd. dirs. Globe Theatre, Odessa, Tex., Midland Community Theatre, Tri-County Foster Home, Guadalupe, Midland youth centers, DeZavala Day Nursery, PTA, Adult Devel. Center, Rogers CETA, 1979-81; vol. recorder Ark. Hist. Preservation Program, 1984—; docent Rogers Hist. Mus., 1988—, vol. tutor; with Ptnrs. in Edn., 1995-96. Recipient 21 yr. pendant Benton Hist. Soc., Nice People award Rogers C. of C., 1987, Thanks badge Midland Girl Scout Assn., 1948, Appreciation Plaque award Ark. Natural Heritage Commn., 1988; Cert. of recognition, Rogers Pub. Schs., 1986, Cert. of Recognition, Beaver Lake Literacy Coun., 1993; Instr. of Yr. award North Ark. Community Coll. West Campus, Conservation award Woodmen of the World Life Ins. Soc., 1991, Vol. of Yr. award Rogers Hist. Mus., 1993, 95. Mem. NEA (del. conv. 1965), Ark. Assn. Public Continuing and Adult Edn. (pres. 1979-80), South Central Assn. for Lifelong Learning (sec. 1980-84), PTA (life), Future Homemakers Am. (life; sec. 1980—), Benton County Hist. Soc. (life, pub. rels. chmn. 1990-96, recording sec. 1990-96), Delta Kappa Gamma (Disting. Acheivement award Beta Pi chpt. 1992). Episcopalian. Clubs: Altrusa (pres. 1979—), Apple Spur Community (Rogers), Garden Club Rogers (publicity chmn. 1994-95, garden therapy 1994-96). Home: 2808 N Dixieland Rd Rogers AR 72756-2146

SEARLES, EDNA LOWE, artist, illustrator, composer; b. Minden, La., Sept. 10, 1936; d. Prentiss W. Lowe; m. Thomas D. Searles; children: Dan, Laura, Carol, Prentiss. AA, Mont. Coll., 1975; BA in Edn., La. Poly., 1958. Tchr. pub. sch., La. & Ga., 1958-65. Guest curator Delaphine Visual Art Ctr., Frederick, Md., 1995, East Meets West. Illustrator Soy for the 21st Century, 1984, ABC Coloring Book, 1994, Mind Children, 1995, Mind Travel, 1998, About You, 1998, Choose Life, 2002;one-woman shows include Arnot Art Mus., Elmira, N.Y., 1988, Va. Tech State U., 1989, Gwinnett Coun. of the Arts Gallery, Ga., 1990, VA Honorarium, 1990, Other: Affiliation and Exhibits, Janice Aldridge Gallery, Georgetown, Washington, 1996, Sculpture on the Ground, Md., 1994, 1999, The Artist's Gallery, Frederick, Md., 1997—2002, The Garden Gallery, Carlisle, Pa., 1999—, Nancy Stamm's Galleria, 1999—, Gallery of New Masters, Sandy Spring, Md., 2000—01, Millinneum Exhibit Music for the Eyes, 1999—2000, Musicians and All that Jazz, Frederick, Md., 2000, Gallery of New Masters, Olney, Md., 2000—01, Boarman Art Ctr., Martinsburg, W.Va., 2001. Past pres. Clarksburg (Md.) Comty. Assn. Recipient Juror's award for painting Montgomery County Art, 1993, Internat. Gold medal for painting Accademia Italia, 1973; named Wilson Wims Citizen of Yr. Clarksburg Comm. Assn., 1974. Mem.: DAR (vice regent 2001—02, Pleasant Plains of Damascus chpt.), Nat. League of Am. Pen Women (pres. Chevy Chase chpt. 1980—82, br. pres. 2002—). Methodist. Achievements include invention of music system for the deaf to "see" music as art. Avocations: hammered dulcimer, composing music, folk singer, harp, piano.

SEARLES, LYNN MARIE, nurse; b. Cherryvale, Kans., Oct. 29, 1949; d. Darrell Eugene and Beva Caroline (Waller) Stringer; m. Martin Dale Searles, Aug. 23, 1970; children: Jeremy Dale, Michelle Le Anne. Assoc. in Fine Arts, Labette Cmty. Jr. Coll., Parsons, Kans., 1969, ADN, 1970. RN, Kans., Calif. Evening med.-surg. charge nurse Coffeyville (Kans.) Meml. Hosp., 1970-72, med.-surg. head nurse, 1972-73, relief evening house supr. and emergency rm. nurse, 1974, head nurse recovery rm., 1974-81; head nurse recovery rm., ambulatory care unit Coffeyville Meml. Med. Ctr., 1981-83, head nurse recovery rm., ambulatory care unit and surgery, 1983-84; dir. family planning, rural home health aide and multi phasic screening clinics, AIDS edn. and counseling Jefferson County Health Dept., Oskaloosa, Kansas, 1984-87; nurse III, health facility surveyor Lawrence dist. Kans. Dept. Health and Environ., Lawrence, Kans., 1988—. Mem. Nazarene Healthcare Fellowship, Kans. Pub. Health Assn., Am. Soc. Post Anesthesia Nurses (charter mem.). Republican. Nazarene Ch. Avocations: needlecraft, gardening, interior decorating. Office: Kans Dept Health and Environment 808 W 24th St Lawrence KS 66046-4417

SEARLES, THOMAS DANIEL, society administrator; b. New Orleans, Aug. 6, 1937; s. Eugene Harve and Mary Louise (Swan) S.; m. Edna Winifred Lowe, Mar. 10, 1956; children: Thomas Daniel II, Laura Louise, Carol Gay, Prentiss Eugene. BS, La. Tech. U., 1960; postgrad., Montgomery Coll. Field rep. So. Pine Inspection Bur., Pensacola, Fla., 1960-65, Am. Lumber Std. Com., Germantown, Md., 1965-70, pres., 1970—. U.S. rep. to lumber com., UN ECE, Geneva, 1974-82; appointee to Industry Sectory Adv. Com., Sec. Commerce, Washington, 1986—, Industry Functional Adv. Com., Sec. Commerce, Washington, 1986—. Vice pres. Clarksburg (Md.) Community Assn., 1988. Mem. Am. Soc. Assn. Execs., Standard Engrng. Soc., Greater Washington Soc. Assn. Execs. Republican. Methodist. Office: Am Lumber Standard Com PO Box 210 Germantown MD 20875-0210

SEARLS, EILEEN HAUGHEY, retired lawyer, librarian, educator; b. Madison, Wis., Apr. 27, 1925; d. Edward M. and Anna Mary (Haughey) S. BA, U. Wis., 1948, JD, 1950, MS in LS, 1951. Bar: Wis. 1950. Cataloger Yale U., 1951-52; instr. law St. Louis U., 1952-53, asst. prof., 1953-56, assoc. prof., 1956-64, prof., 1964-2000, law libr., 1952-2000. Chmn. Coun. Law Libr. Consortia, 1984-90; sec. Bd. of Conciliaton and Arbitration, Archdiocese of St. Louis, 1986-98. Named Woman of Yr. Women's Commn., St. Louis U., 1986. Mem. ABA, ALA, Wis. Bar Assn., Bar Assn. Met. St. Louis, Am. Assn. Law Librs. (Marian Gould Gallagher Disting. Svc. award 1999), Mid Am. Assn. Law Librs. (pres. 1984-86), Mid Am. Law Sch. Libr. Consortium (chmn. 1980-84), Southwestern Assn. Law Librs., Altrusa Club. Office: 3700 Lindell Blvd Saint Louis MO 63108-3412

SEARS, ALAN EDWARD, lawyer; b. Chattanooga, Oct. 31, 1951; s. Edward Lee and Anna Maria (Shepperd) S.; m. Paula Scott Lebeau, Nov. 11, 1988; children: Kelley, Shelby, Anna Marie, Rebecca, Isaiah, Isabella. BA, U. Ky., 1974; JD, U. Louisville, 1977. Bar: Ky. 1977, U.S. Supreme Ct. 1980, Ariz. 1987, D.C. 1989, Calif. 1990, U.S. Dist. Ct. (we. and ea. dists.) Ky., U.S. Dist. Ct. Ariz., U.S. Dist. Ct. D.C., U.S. Ct. Appeals (D.C., 4th, 5th, 6th, 7th, 9th, 11th and D.C. cirs.), U.S. Tax Ct., U.S. Dist. Ct. (ctrl. & so. dists.) Calif. Asst. corp. counsel City of Ashland, Ky., 1977-78; assoc. Johnson, Dunnagan & Martin, Ashland, 1977-79, Amshoff & Amshoff, Louisville, 1979-81; chief criminal div., asst. U.S. atty. U.S. Dept. Justice, 1981-85, exec. dir. atty. gens. commn. on pornography Washington, 1985-86; assoc. solicitor U.S. Dept. Interior, 1986-87; exec. dir. Children's Legal Found., Phoenix, 1987-90; assoc. Snell & Wilmer, 1990; exec. dir., gen. counsel Nat. Family Legal Found., 1990-91; asst. U.S. atty. U.S. Dept. Justice, 1991-93; pres., gen. counsel Alliance Def. Fund, 1993—. Cons. and pub. speaker to numerous organizations. Co-author: Time, Place & Manner Regulation, 1989, Prosecution & Trial of Obscenity Case, 1988; contbr. chpts. to books. Bd. dirs. Ariz. Family Rsch. Inst. Phoenix, 1988-92, Lincoln Caucus Ednl. Corp., Phoenix, 1990—, Nat. Family Legal Found., Phoenix, 1991—; precinct capt. Rep. Party, 1979-81, legis. dist. chmn., 1980-81; mem. campaign staff Gov. Louie Nunn, 1979, and Senator Cook for U.S. Senate, 1974, other party activities. Mem. ABA, Ariz. Lawyers Div. Federalist Soc. (dir. 1988—), Calif. Bar Assn., Ariz. Bar Assn., Ky. Bar Assn., D.C. Bar Assn. Office: Ste 165 15333 N Pima Rd Scottsdale AZ 85260-2781

SEARS, DAVID ALAN, medical educator; b. Portland, Oreg., Oct. 20, 1931; s. Harry J. and Huldah M. (Meyer) S.; m. Yvonne D. Bowles, June 22, 1958; children: Geoffrey B., Cameron J., Andrea Y. Sears Andrews. BS, Yale U., 1953; MS, U. Oreg., 1958, MD, 1959. Cert. in internal medicine and hematology. Intern, resident in internal medicine U. Rochester (N.Y.) Sch. Medicine and Dentistry, 1959-62, fellow in hematology, 1962-63; rsch. hematologist Walter Reed Army Inst. Rsch., Washington, 1963-66; asst. prof. hematology U. Rochester Sch. Medicine and Dentistry, 1966-69; from assoc. prof. to prof. medicine U. Tex. Health Scis. Ctr., San Antonio, 1969-80; prof. medicine Baylor Coll. Medicine, Houston, 1980—2002, prof. emeritus, 2002—. Local, state and nat. bd. dirs., various other offices Am. Cancer Soc., 1971—. Contbr. chpts. to books, articles to profl. jours. Elder Presbyn. Ch. Capt. U.S. Army, 1963-66. Recipient St. George medal Am. Cancer Soc., Anne Norris Humanitarian award Sickle Cell Assn. Mem. ACP, Am. Soc. Hematology, Am. Fedn. Med. Rsch., Internat. Soc. Hematology, Alpha Omega Alpha. Office: Baylor Coll Medicine 1 Baylor Plz Houston TX 77030-3411

SEARS, DAVID O'KEEFE, psychology educator; b. Urbana, Ill., June 24, 1935; s. Robert R. and Pauline (Snedden) S.; divorced; children: Juliet, Olivia, Meredith. BA in History, Stanford U., 1957; PhD in Psychology, Yale U., 1962. Asst. prof. to prof. psychology and polit. sci. UCLA, 1961—, dean social scis., 1983-92. Dir. Inst. for Social Sci. Rsch., 1993—. Author: Public Opinion, 1964, Politics of Violence, 1973, Tax Revolt, 1985, Political Cognition, 1986, Social Psychology, 2000, Racialized Politics, 2000. Fellow Am. Acad. Arts and Scis.; mem. Soc. for Advancement Socio-Econs. (pres. 1991-92), Internat. Soc. Polit. Psychology (pres. 1994-95). Office: UCLA Psychology Dept Los Angeles CA 90095-0001 E-mail: sears@psych.ucla.edu.

SEARS, DONNA MAE, designer, illustrator; b. St. Paul, Oct. 23, 1951; d. Raymond and Shirley Marie (Dupre) Waldoch; m. Mark D. Sears, Sept. 4, 1993. BA in Art and Edn., Cardinal Stritch Coll., Milw., 1969-73; postgrad., Rock Valley Coll., Rockford, Ill., 1985, 87, 89-90, So. Ill. U., 1983; cert. of tng., Computervision Tech. Ctr., Itasca, Ill., 1986, 88. Electronic assembler Warner Electric Co., Marengo, Ill., 1973-75, machine hand, 1976-78, quality assurance lead insp., 1978-80, draftswoman, 1980-86, CAD-sr. draftswoman, l986-87; tchr. art Stephen Mack Sch. Dist., Rockford, 1975, Harrison Sch. Dist., Wonder Lake, Ill., 1975-76; CAD specialist Greenlee Textron Inc., Rockford, 1988-89; asst. buyer Ingersoll Milling, 1989-90; asst. office mgr. and sign maker Shake-A-Leg Signs, 1990-92; tech. writer and illustrator Mathews Co., Crystal Lake, Ill., 1992; engrng. CAD illustrator Clinton Electronics, Loves Park, 1993-2000; engrng. adminstrn., mfg. engrng. Pacific Bearing Co., Roscoe, 2000—. Author: (with others) Treasured Poems of America, 1990, Poetic Voices of America, spring 1992, Anthology of American Poetry, fall 1991 (awards of Poetic Excellence 1992), Distinguished Poets of America, spring 1993, The Sound of Poetry, spring 1993. Vol. Boone County Conservation Dist., 1990-92; mem. choir St. James Ch., Belvidere, Ill., 1985-93; assoc. mem. Spl. Olympics. Recipient Leadership award YWCA, Rockford, 1988. Mem. Am. Bus. Women's Assn., Macktown Living History Edn. Ctr. (bd. dirs., sec. 1999-2002). Roman Catholic. Avocations: bicycling, art, gardening, fishing. Office: Pacific Bearing Co 6402 Rockton Rd Roscoe IL 61073 E-mail: donnase@pacific-bearing.com.

SEARS, DOUGLAS WARREN, lawyer; b. Newton, Mass., June 11, 1947; s. Douglas Hubbard and Anne (Thomas) S.; m. A. Suzanne Tuggle, Oct. 3, 1976; children: Rebecca Anne, Douglas Warren Jr. BA, Harvard Coll., 1969, MDiv, 1976; MEd, Boston State Coll., 1980; JD, Suffolk U., 1986. Bar: Mass. 1987, U.S. Dist. Ct. Mass., 1987, U.S. Ct. Appeals (1st cir.) 1987, U.S. Supreme Ct. 1996. Secondary sch. tchr. various schs., 1969-87; assoc. Peckham, Lobel, Casey, Prince & Tye, Boston, 1987-89, Allen Rodman, P.C., Malden, Mass., 1989-91; dep. dir. divsn. dispute resolution Dept. Indsl. Accidents, Boston, 1991—; of counsel Law Office of Raymond J. Paczkowski. Co-min. Christ's Ch. Longwood, Brookline, Mass., 1986—; chmn. Rep. Town Com., Tewksbury, 1992—; mem. Tewksbury Hist. Commn., 1992—; sec. bd. trustees Tewksbury (Mass.) Hosp., 1993—; spl. asst. atty. gen., 1994—; mem. Tewksbury Sch. Com., 1995—, mem. bd. sel., 2002; mem. Govs. Adv. Com. on Chaplains in State Instns., Boston, 1996—; assoc. mem. Rep. State Com., Boston, 1996— Mem. Tewksbury/Wilmington Elks (justice 1995—). Unitarian-Universalist. Avocation: gardening. Office: Dept Indsl Accidents 600 Washington St Boston MA 02111-1704

SEARS, EDWARD L. English language educator, real estate investor; b. Pratt, Kans., Jan. 27, 1954; s. Melvin Leroy and Deloris Fay (Owens) S. BA in English, West Tex. State U., 1990; MA in English, Tex. Tech. U., 1993. Firefighter Dodge City (Kans.) Fire Dept., 1981-83, Amarillo (Tex.) Fire Dept., 1983-86; tutor Writing Ctr. West Tex. State U., Canyon, 1987-90, Tex. Tech. U., Lubbock, 1990-92, tchg. asst., 1990-92; writing lab. super. South Plains Coll., Levelland, Tex., 1992—, asst. prof. English, 1993—. Ssgt. USAF, 1977-81. Democrat. Roman Catholic. Office: South Plains Coll Reece Ctr 528 Gilbert Dr Lubbock TX 79416

SEARS, EDWARD MILNER, JR. newspaper editor; b. Bluefield, W.Va., Dec. 28, 1944; s. Edward Milner and Helene (Stras) S.; m. Jo Ann Langworthy, May 15, 1971; 1 child, Helene Mateer. BS in Journalism, U. Fla., 1967. Makeup editor Atlanta Constn., 1970, news editor, 1971-73, feature editor, 1974, city editor, 1975-76, asst. mng. editor, 1977, mng. editor, 1978-80, Atlanta Jour., 1980-82, Atlanta Jour. and Atlanta Constn., 1982-85; editor Palm Beach Post, 1985—. Served with U.S. Army, 1968-69. Mem. Fla. Soc. Newspaper Editors, Am. Soc. Newspaper Editors, Sigma Delta Chi. Home: 230 Dyer Rd West Palm Beach FL 33405-1218 Office: Palm Beach Post 2751 S Dixie Hwy West Palm Beach FL 33405-1233 E-mail: esears@pbpost.com.

SEARS, JOANN MARIE, school librarian; b. Lafayette, Ind., Aug. 3, 1974; d. Robert E. and Teresa A. Sears. BS, Purdue U., 1996; MLS, Ind. U., 1998. Sci. and tech. reference libr. Auburn U. Libr., Ala., 1998—. Contbr. articles. Mem.: Spl. Libraries Assn., Phi Beta Kappa. Office: Auburn Univ Libr 231 Mell St Auburn AL 36849 Business E-Mail: searsjo@auburn.edu.

SEARS, JOHN PATRICK, lawyer; b. Syracuse, N.Y., July 3, 1940; s. James Louis and Helen Mary (Fitzgerald) S.; m. Carol Jean Osborne, Aug. 25, 1962; children: James Louis, Ellen Margaret, Amy Elizabeth. BS, Notre Dame U., 1960; LL.B., JD, Georgetown U., 1963. Bar: N.Y. bar 1963. Clk. N.Y. Ct. Appeals, 1963-65; asso. firm Nixon, Mudge, Rose, Guthrie, Alexander & Mitchell, 1965-66; mem. staff Richard M. Nixon, 1966-69; dep. counsel to Pres. Nixon, 1969-70; ptnr. Gadsby & Hannah, Washington, 1970-75, Baskin & Sears, Washington, 1977-84; pvt. practice, 1984—. Mgr. Ronald Regan's Presdl. Campaign, 1975-76, 79-80; polit. analyst NBC Today Show, 1984-89; mem. Wall Street Jour. bd. of polit. experts, 1984—; columnist LA Times, Newsday, 1992—. Sr. advisor Jack Kemp for V.P. Campaign, 1996. Fellow Kennedy Inst. Politics, Harvard, 1970 Home: 2801 New Mexico Ave NW Washington DC 20007-3921 Office: 2021 K St NW Washington DC 20006-1003

SEARS, JOHN WINTHROP, lawyer; b. Boston, Dec. 18, 1930; s. Richard Dudley and Frederica Fulton (Leser) S.; m. Catherine Coolidge, 1965 (div. 1970). AB magna cum laude, Harvard U., 1952, JD, 1959; MLitt, Oxford U., 1957. Bar: Mass. 1959, U.S. Dist. Ct. Mass. 1982. Rep. Brown Bros. Harriman, N.Y.C., 1959-63, Boston, 1963-66; mem. Mass. Ho. Reps., 1965-68; sheriff Suffolk County, Mass., 1968-69; chmn. Boston Fin. Commn., 1969-70, Met. Dist. Commn., 1970-75; councilor-at-large Boston City Coun., 1980-82; trustee Sears Office, Boston, 1975—. Contbr. articles to profl. jours. Apptd. bd. dirs. Fulbright Scholarship, 1991-93; trustee Christ's Ch., Longwood, Brookline, Mass., 1965—, Sears Trusts, Boston, 1975—; hon. trustee J. F. Kennedy Libr., 1991—; bd. dirs. Am. Mus. Textile Heritage, 1987-97, Shirley-Eustis Assoc., Environ. League, Mass., 1994-97; Rep. candidate Sec. State, Mass., 1978, Gov. of Mass., 1982; vice chmn. Ward 5 Rep. Com., 1965-69, 75-85; chmn. Rep. State Com., 1975-76, mem., 1980-85; del. Rep. Nat. Conv., 1968, 76, State Conv., 1966-92; mem. U.S. Electoral Coll., 1984; bd. dirs. United South End Settlements, 1966—, chmn., 1977-78. Lt. comdr. USNR, 1952-54, 61-62. Recipient Outstanding Pub. Servant award Mass. Legis. Assn., 1975; Rhodes scholar, 1955 Mem. Mass. Bar Assn., New Eng. Hist. and Geneal. Soc. (bd. dirs., councillor 1977-82), Mass. Hist. Soc., Handel and Haydn Soc. (gov. 1982-87), Signet Soc., Boston Atheneum, Tennis and Racquet Club, Somerset Club, The Country Club (Brookline), St. Botolph Club, Wednesday Evening Club of 1777, Thursday Evening Club of 1846 (pres. 1999), Spee Club (Cambridge chpt., pres., trustee), Phi Beta Kappa. Republican. Home: 7 Acorn St Boston MA 02108-3501 *As the working years come to an end, some of us look for ways to teach, to help neighbors, especially those in need, to build up the beauty and excellence we may have encountered in our own lives, and do our best to pass them on to others.*

SEARS, LEAH J. state supreme court justice; b. June 13, 1955; d. Thomas E. and Onnye J. Sears; married; children: Addison, Brennan. BA, Cornell U.; JD, Emory U.; M in Apellate Jud. Process, U. Va.; JD (hon.), Morehouse Coll., 1993. Judge City Ct. Atlanta; atty. Alston & Bird, Atlanta; trial judge Superior Ct. Fulton County; justice Supreme Ct. Ga., Atlanta, 1992—. Contbr. articles to profl. jours. Bd. dirs. Sadie G. Mays Nursing Home, Ga. chpt. Nat. Coun. Christians & Jews; mem. adv. bd. United Way Drug Abuse Action Ctr., Outdoor Activity Nature Ctr.; mem. Cornell U. Women's Coun.; mem. steering com. Ga. Women's History Month, Children's Def. Fund Black Cmty. Crusade Children; founder Battered Women's Project, Columbus, Ga. Recipient Outstanding Young Alumna award Emory U., One of 100 Most Influential Georgians Ga. Trend mag., Excellence in Pub. Svc. award Ga. Coalition Black Women, 1992, Outstanding Woman of Achievement YWCA Greater Atlanta, One of Under Forty & On the Fast Track, 1993. Mem. ABA (chair bd. elections), Nat. Assn. Women Judges, Ga. Bar Assn., Women's Forum Ga., Gate City Bar Assn., Atlanta Bar Assn. (past chair jud. sect.), Ga. Assn. Black Women Attys. (founder, pres.), Fourth Tuesday Group, Jack & Jill Am. (Atlanta chpt.), Links Inc. (Atlanta chpt.), Alpha Kappa Alpha. Office: Ga Supreme Ct 244 Washington Street Atlanta GA 30334-9007*

SEARS, MARY HELEN, lawyer; b. Syracuse, N.Y. d. James Louis and Helen Mary (Fitzgerald) Sears. AB, Cornell U., 1950; JD with honors, George Washington U., 1960. Bar: Va. 1960, D.C. 1961, U.S. Supreme Ct. 1963. Chemist Allied Chem. and Dye Corp., Syracuse, 1950-52, Hercules Powder Co., Wilmington, Del., 1952-55; patent examiner U.S. Patent Office, Washington, 1955-60; pvt. practice, 1960-61; assoc. Irons, Birch, Swindler & McKie, 1961-69; mem. firm Irons and Sears, 1969-84; chmn. trade regulation practice dept. Memel, Jacobs, Pierno, Gersh & Ellsworth, 1984-87; ptnr., chmn. intellectual property and unfair competition practice dept. Ginsburg, Feldman & Bress, 1987-91; ptnr., chmn. intellectual property and telecomm. practice group Reid & Priest, 1991-94; founder, chmn. M. H. Sears Law Firm, 1994—. Mem. adv. bd. Boardroom Reports, Inc., N.Y.C., 1980-85; mem. Cornell U. Coun., 1981-87, 89-93, life mem., 1995—, mem. adminstrv. bd., 1984-86. Contbr. articles to various publs. Recipient Outstanding Performance award U.S. Dept. Commerce, 1957; named to Guide to the World's Leading Patent Law Experts Euromoney Publs., PLC, 1995, 97. Mem.: ABA (co-chmn. appellate practice com., litigation sect. 1989—92), D.C. Bar Assn., Va. State Bar Assn., Internat. Trademark Assn., Licensing Execs. Soc., Am. Soc. Internat. Law, Am. Intellectual Property Law Assn., George Washington U.

Law Alumnae Assn. (bd. dirs. 1995—2001), Am. Chem. Soc., Order of Coif, Phi Alpha Delta. Republican. Office: MH Sears Law Firm Chartered 910 17th St NW Ste 800 Washington DC 20006-2606 E-mail: Mhsears@mhsears.com.

SEARS, ROBERT STEPHEN, finance educator, university dean; b. Odessa, Tex., May 27, 1950; s. William Bethel and Leola Vernon (Little) S.; Reva Dana Flournoy, Aug. 17, 1973; children: Matthew Stephen, Elizabeth Rea. AAS, Odessa Jr. Coll., 1970; BA summa cum laude, Tex. Tech. U., 1973, MS, 1976; PhD, U. N.C., 1980. Supr. Bethel Enterprises, Odessa, Tex., 1973-74; tchg. asst. Tex. Tech U., Lubbock, 1974-76, dir. Inst. Banking and Fin. Studies, 1988-98; tchg. asst. U. N.C., Chapel Hill, 1976-79; asst. prof. U. Ill., Champaign, 1979-85, assoc. prof., 1985-88; rsch. prof. Bur. Econ. and Bus., 1984; tchg. asst. Lubbock Bankers Assn., 1990—; chmn. dept. fin. Tex. Tech U., 1997-2001, interim dean Coll. Bus., 2000, sr. exec. assoc. dean, Coll. Bus, 2001—. Cons. Cameron Brown Mortgage Co., Raleigh, N.C., 1978-80, Howard Savs. Bank, Livingston, N.J., 1980; asset mgr., trustee, pvt. investors, 1984—. Author: Investment Management, 1993, (chpt), Modern Real Estate, 1980, 84; assoc. editor Rev. of Bus. Studies, 1989-95, Jour. Fin. Rsch., 1990-96, Internat. Chmn. fin. com. Temple Bapt. Ch., Champaign, Ill., 1982, bd. deacons, 1982-88, chmn. deacons, lay leader, 1983; Sunday sch. tchr. Carrboro (N.C.) Bapt. Ch., 1977-79; bd. deacons Ind. Ave. Bapt. Ch., Lubbock, 1989-96, Sunday sch. tchr., 1991-92, master design com., 1993-96; trustee All Saints Episcopal Sch., 1995—, treas., 2000; bd. deacons Southcrest Bapt. Ch., Lubbock, 1998—. Rsch. grantee Cameron Brown Mortgage Co., Raleigh, N.C., 1978-80, U. Ill, Champaign, 1980-84, 86-87, Investors in Bus. Edn., Champaign, 1980-81, 84; recipient Excellence in Undergrad. Tchg. award U. Ill. Champaign, 1984-85, Award for Outstanding Coll. Educator Champaign-Urbana, Ill. Jaycees, 1983-84, Coll. of Commerce Alumni Assn. Undergrad. Excellence in Tchg. award U. Ill., 1981-82; Mortar Bd., Omicron Delta Kappa Leadership scholarship and Svc. award Tex. Tech U., 1997-98, Pres.'s Excellence in Tchg. award Tex. Tech U., 1993-94, Acad. Achievement award Tex. Tech U., 1994-95. Mem. Am. Fin. Assn., Southwestern Fin. Assn. (pres. 1989-90, v.p., program chmn. 1988-89, sec., treas. 1986-88, bd. dirs. 1984-86, mem. program com. 1985-86, 89—), Fin. Mgmt. Assn. (mem. program com. 1986, 89-94, 97, 99-2001), So. Fin. Assn. (mem. program com. 1986), Western Fin. Assn. (mem. program com. 1986), Ea. Fin. Assn., Lake Ridge Country Club. Republican. Baptist. Avocations: golf, walking, participating in sports with my children. Office: Tex Tech U COBA Lubbock TX 79409-2101

SEARS, SANDRA LEE, computer consultant; b. Rochester, N.Y., Apr. 25, 1952; AB with distinction, Cornell U., 1974; MA, U. Conn., 1976, postgrad., 1976-81. Cert. in data processing. Tng. cons. Ins. Crime Prevention Inst., Westport, Conn., 1977-78; systems analyst Data Directions, Bloomfield, 1978-79; prin. S. S. Prindle Consulting, Manchester, 1979-81; dir. info. svcs. Conn. Attys. Title Ins., Rocky Hill, 1981-85; mgr., systems, programming Community Health Care Plan, Inc., Wallingford, 1985-87; assoc. dir. Mass. Mutual Life Ins., Springfield, Mass., 1987-91; cons. mgr. Coopers & Lybrand Cons., East Hartford, Conn., 1991-96; dir. info. architecture and data warehousing CIGNA Healthcare, Bloomfield, 1996-97; divsn. dir. advanced devel. solutions divsn. Advanced Computing Techniques, Glastonbury, 1997-98; practice dir. data warehousing and knowledge mgmt. PRT Group, Inc., Windsor, 1998-99; sr. mgr. KPMG Cons., Hartford, 1999-2001; prin. The Preceptor Group, Manchester, Conn., 2001—. Adj. faculty U. New Haven, West Haven, Conn., 1976-77, Eastern Conn. State U., Willimantic, 1986-2001, Manchester C.C., 1989—; participant Tex. Instruments' Case Satellite Seminar, 1989. Mentor Career Beginnings, Hartford, 1991-95. Presdl. scholar Nat. Merit Program, 1970, William Stout scholar Cornell U., 1973, AAUW fellow U. Conn., 1981. Mem. Cornell Club of Greater Hartford (mem. admissons vol. programs alumni adv. com., exec. bd., book award chair 1987—), Cornell Alumni Admissions Amb. Network (chair 1983-86), Mortar Board, Phi Kappa Phi, Pi Mu Epsilon. Office: The Preceptor Group 10 Gardner St Manchester CT 06040-5625 E-mail: slsears@preceptorgroup.com.

SEARS, STEVEN LEE, screenwriter, consultant; b. Ft. Gordon, Ga., Dec. 23, 1957; s. Richard Bruce Sr. and Marian (Dean) S. AA, U. Fla., 1976; BA in Theater cum laude, Fla. State U., 1980. Writer Stephen J. Cannell Prodns., Hollywood, Calif., 1984-88, story editor, 1987-88, VIACOM/Hargrove/Silverman Prodns., 1988; writer A. Shane Prodns., Superboy Prodns., 1989; exec. story cons. Highwayman Glen Larson/New West Prodns., Universal City, Calif., 1988; writer TV pilots Columbia Pictures TV, 1990. Writer (TV shows) Riptide, 1984-86, Hadcastle & McCormick, 1985, The A-Team, 1986-87, Stingray, 1987, Jesse Hawkes, 1989, Superboy, 1989, Grand Slam, 1989, Hardball, 1989, Who Gets Harry?, 1989, Robin's Hoods, 1994, Walker, Texas Ranger, 1994, (TV pilots) Harry O'Fell-Detective from Hell, 1990, The Inquisitor, 1990, (screenplay) Endangered Species, (interactive movie) Dreadnought, 1995, (TV show) Itsy Bitsy Spider, 1995; story editor TV shows J.J. Starbuck, 1987-88, The Father Dowling Mysteries, 1988; co-producer (TV show) Swamp Thing, 1991; producer (TV show) Raven, 1992-93; supervising prodr. (TV show) Xena Warrior Princess, 1995-97, co-exec. prodr., 1997—; exec. prodr. (feature) The Last Perfect Wave, 1995, (TV pilot) Sheena, 1999, (series) Sheena, 2000-01. Mem. AFTRA, SAG, Writers Guild Am. Democrat. Avocations: traveling, computers, karate.

SEARY, LAWRENCE ANTHONY, cinematographer, news assignment editor, field operations manager; b. N.Y.C., June 13, 1951; m. Phyllis Cole, Oct. 2, 1976; children: Tara Ann, Paul Anthony. BFA, NYU, 1973. News cameraman, assignment desk supr., prodr. NBC, N.Y.C., 1974—. Recipient N.Y. State Broadcast award UPI, 1987. Mem. NATAS (bd. govs. 1996-2000, Emmy award nominations 1978, 82, 94, 95, Emmy award 1978, mem. awards com.), N.Y. Press Photographers Assn., Mensa, N.Y. Press Club (2d v.p., bd. trustees, Feature Video award 1994). Democrat. Roman Catholic. Office: NBC 30 Rockefeller Plz Rm 728E New York NY 10112-0002 E-mail: larry.seary@nbc.com.

SEASE, GENE ELWOOD, public relations company executive; b. Portage, Pa., June 28, 1931; s. Grover Chauncey and Clara Mae (Over) S.; m. Joanne D. Cherry, July 20, 1952; children: David Gene, Daniel Elwood, Cheryl Joanne. AB, Juniata Coll., 1952; B.D., Pitts. Theol. Sem., 1956, Th.M., 1959; PhD, U. Pitts., 1965, M.Ed., 1958; LL.D., U. Evansville, 1972, Butler U., 1972; Litt.D., Ind. State U., 1974; DD, U. Indpls., 1989. Ordained to ministry United Methodist Ch., 1956; pastor Grace United Meth. Ch., Wilkinsburg, Pitts., 1952-63; conf. dir., supt. Western Pa. Conf. United Meth. Ch., Pitts., 1963-68; lectr. grad. faculty U. Pitts., 1965-68; mem. staff U. Indpls., 1968-89, asst. to pres., 1968-69, pres., 1970-88, chancellor, 1988-89, pres. emeritus, 1989—; chmn. Sease, Gerig & Assocs., Indpls., 1989—. Bd. dirs. Indpls. Life Ins. Co., Bankers Life Ins. Co. of N.Y. Author: Christian Word Book, 1968; also numerous articles. Pres. Greater Indpls. Progress Com., 1972-75, Marion County Sheriff's Merit Bd.; mem. Ind. Scholarship Commn.; cons. Time Warner; bd. dirs. Indpls. Conv. Bur., Ind. Law Enforcement Tng. Acad., 500 Festival, Crossroads coun. Boy Scouts Am., Community Hosp. Indpls., St. Francis Hosp.; chmn. Ind. State Fair Commn. Mem. Internat. Platform Assn., English Speaking Union, Japan-Am. Soc. Ind., Ind. C. of C. (bd. dirs.), Indpls. C. of C. (bd. dirs.), Ind. Schoolmen's Club, Ind. State Fair Commn., Econ. Club of Indpls. (bd. dirs.), Skyline Club (bd. dirs.), Phi Delta Kappa, Alpha Phi Omega, Alpha Psi Omega. Clubs: Mason (Indpls.) (33 deg., Shriner), Kiwanian. (Indpls.), Columbia (Indpls.).

SEASE, SUSAN G. social worker; b. Columbia, S.C., Sept. 8, 1955; d. David Lloyd and Betty Lou Gore; m. George Andrew Sease Jr., Apr. 28, 1978; children: Ruth Auria, Mary Lebannon. AD, Florence Darlington Tech Coll., Florence, S.C., 1977; BA, Coker Coll., Hartsville, S.C., 1978. Lic. social worker; cert. criminal justice specialist. Rsch. and planning technician Florence Police Dept., 1978-79; juvenile police officer Darlington Police Dept., 1979-80; cmty. specialist Dept. Juvenile Justice, Marion, S.C., 1980-88; social worker, svc. coord. Continuum of Care for Emotionally Disturbed Children, Florence, 1989—2001; tchr. autistic resource Lester Elem. Sch., 2001—. Sec. Pee Dee Criminal Intelligence Coun., Florence, 1978-80; resource person Gov.'s Subcom. on Mentally Retarded Offender, Columbia, S.C., 1981. Bd. dirs. Big Sisters of S.C. Florence, 1984-87; chair St. Jude Bike a Thon, Quinby, S.C., 1983, 84, 88. Mem. N.Am. Assn. Christians in Social Work, Nat. Assn. Forensic Councelors, United Meth. Women (v.p. Florence dist. 1994-98, chair social concerns 1999—), Order Eastern Star. Republican. Methodist. Avocations: directing chldren and youth choir at church, writing poetry, reading. Home: 259 Quinby Cir Quinby SC 29506-7220 Office: Lester Elementary School East Palmetto St Florence SC 29506

SEASHORE, MARGRETTA REED, physician; b. Red Bank, N.J., June 20, 1939; d. Robert Clark Reed and Lillie Ann (Heaviland) R.; m. John Seashore, Dec. 26, 1964; children: Robert H., Carl J., Carolyn L. BA, Swarthmore Coll., 1961; MD, Yale U., 1965. Diplomate Am. Bd. Pediatrics, Am. Bd. Med. Genetics, Nat. Bd. Med. Examiners. Intern in pediatrics Yale U. Sch. Medicine, Haven, Conn., 1965-66, asst. resident in pediatrics, 1966-68, postdoctoral fellow in genetics and metabolism, depts. of pediatrics and medicine, 1968-70; clin. asst. prof. pediatrics U. Fla. Coll. Medicine, Gainesville, 1970-71; attending physician Hope Haven Children's Hosp., Jacksonville, Fla., 1970-73; asst. prof. pediatrics Duval Med. Ctr., 1970-71; attending physician Duvall Med. Ctr. U. Hosp. Jacksonville, 1970-73; asst. prof. pediatrics U. Fla. Coll. Medicine, 1971-73; attending physician Shands Teaching Hosp., Gainesville, Fla., 1971-73; asst. clin. prof. human genetics and pediatrics Yale U. Sch. Medicine, 1974-78; attending physician Yale-New Haven Hosp., 1974—; cons. physician Bridgeport (Conn.) Hosp., 1974—; attending physician Danbury (Conn.) Hosp., 1977—; dir. Genetic Consultation Svc. Yale-New Haven Hosp., 1977-86; from asst. prof. to assoc. prof. human genetics and pediatrics Yale U. Sch. Medicine, 1978-90; cons. physician Lawrence and Meml. Hosp., New London, Conn., 1979—, Norwalk (Conn.) Hosp., 1981—; dir. Genetic Consultation Svc. Yale-New Haven Hosp., 1989—; prof. genetics and pediatrics Yale U. Sch. Medicine, 1990—. Contbr. chpts. to books. Fellow Am. Acad. Pediatrics (chair com. on genetics 1990-94, mem. screening com. Conn. chpt. 1977—, mem. genetics com. 1989-94), Am. Coll. Med. Genetics (founder, mem. screening subcom. 1993—); mem. AMA, AAAS, Am. Soc. Human Genetics (mem. genetic svcs. com. 1986-91), Soc. Inherited Metabolic Disorders (bd. dirs. 1989—, sec. 1991-96, pres. 1997), Soc. for Study of Inborn Errors of Metabolism, New Eng. Genetics Group (co-dir. 1992-95, chmn. outreach com. 1979-89, chmn. screening com. 1989-93, mem. steering com. 1979-98). Avocations: music, gardening, sewing, computers. Office: Yale U Sch Med Dept Genetics 333 Cedar St New Haven CT 06510-3289 E-mail: margretta.seashore@yale.edu.

SEATON, ALBERTA JONES, biologist, educator, consultant; b. Houston, Dec. 31, 1924; d. Charles Alexander and Elizabeth (Polk) Jones; m. Earle Edward Seaton, Dec. 24, 1947 (dec. Aug. 1992); children: Elizabeth Wamboi, Dudley Charles. BS in Zoology and Chemistry, Howard U., 1946, MS in Zoology, 1947; ScD in Zoology, U. Brussels, 1949. Asst. prof. Spelman Coll., Atlanta, 1953-54; assoc. prof. biology Tex. So. U., Houston, 1954-60, prof. biology, 1960-72, 91-95; adminstr. Ministry Edn., Bermuda, 1973-76; lectr. biology Bermuda Coll., Devonshire, 1976-78; prof. anatomy Sch. Allied Health U. Tex. Health Ctr., Houston, 1979-80; cons. sci. sect. Nat. Inst. Pedagogy Ministry of Edn. Sci., Victoria, Seychelles, 1980-89. Head dept. biology Wiley Coll., Marshall, Tex., 1950-51; dir. NSF Summer Sci. Inst. Tex. So. U., 1957-59, gen. studies program, 1970-72, undergrad. and grad. rsch. in biology, 1954-72; mem. Univ. Honors Program Com., Tex. So. U., 1960-70; chair self-study com., Tex. So. U., 1969-71, ednl. policies com., 1968-72; lectr. biology U. Md., USN Air Sta., Bermuda, 1972-78; supr. adminstrn. and budget Office of the Minister Ministry Edn., Bermuda, 1973-76; lectr. in field. Author, editor: Conserving the Environment, Part 1, 1984; editor: Reprints of Agrinews, 1982; co-author, co-editor: Conserving the Environment, Part 2, The Seychelles, 1986, Conserving the Environment, Part 3, Focus on Aldabra, 1991; contbr. articles to profl. jours. Evaluator grant proposals NSF, 1957-72; active regional meetings Com. on Undergrad. Edn. in Biol. Sci., 1967-72, AAC-AAUP confs. on curriculum improvement, 1970-72; chair nurses licensing bd., Hamilton, Bermuda, 1973-75; mem. Endangered Species Com., Hamilton, 1974-77. Postdoctoral fellow Calif. Inst. Tech., Pasadena, 1959-60, NSF postdoctoral fellow Roscoe B. Jackson Lab., Bar Harbor, Maine, 1959, U. Brussels, 1965-66. Mem. AAAS, AAUP (apptd. to ad hoc coms. 1968-71, sec.-treas. Tex. State Conf. 1968-70), AAUW, Am. Assn. Zoologists, Assn. des Anatomistes, Assn. Women in Sci., Tex. Acad. Sci., Beta Kappa Chi, Beta Beta Beta. Episcopalian. Home and Office: 3821 Gertin St Houston TX 77004-6503 E-mail: seatonstar@aol.com.

SEATON, CAROLLE CARTER, educator, writer; b. Oklahoma City, Sept. 18, 1939; d. Robert Henry and Claire (Haggard) Carter; m. James Cagney Seaton, Oct. 24, 1959 (dec.); children: Jene, James II, Ernest. B degree, U. West Fla., 1975, M degree, 1980, cert. edn. specialist, 1990. Kindergarten tchr. Santa Rosa Schs., Gulf Breeze, Fla., 1975-83, head gifted programs, 1983-85, staffing specialist Milton, 1985-95, program facilitator, 1995—. Editor: One Kid at a Time; author poetry. Chairperson Interagy. Coun., Milton, 1995-96. Mem. Fla. Assn. for the Gifted (regional rep. 1985-95), NEA. Avocations: diving, photography, charter boat captain, biking. Home: 907 Aquamarine Dr Gulf Breeze FL 32563-3001 Office: Santa Rosa Sch Dist 305 Berryhill St Milton FL 32570-4824

SEATON, EDWARD LEE, newspaper editor and publisher; b. Manhattan, Kans., Feb. 5, 1943; s. Richard Melvin and Mary (Holton) S.; m. Karen Mathisen, Sept. 4, 1965; children: Edward Merrill, John David. AB cum laude, Harvard U., 1965; postgrad., U. Cen., Quito, Ecuador, 1965-66, U. Mo., 1966-67. Staff writer Courier-Jour., Louisville, 1968-69; editor-in-chief, pub. Manhattan Mercury, 1969—. Bd. dirs., officer 8 other newspaper and broadcasting affiliates; mem. adv. com. Knight Internat. Press Fellowship Program; mem. Pulitzer Prize bd., 1992-01, chmn., 2001; mem. Columbia U., Cabot Awards Bd. Contbr. articles to profl. jours. Chmn. Alfred M. Landon lecture patrons Kans. State U.; chmn. Latin Am. Scholarship Program Am. Univs., Cambridge, Mass., 1986-87. Decorated comendador Order of Christopher Columbus (Dominican Republic); Fulbright scholar, 1965; recipient Cabot prize Columbia U., 1993. Mem. Am. Soc. Newspaper Editors (pres. 1998-99), Inter-Am. Press Assn. (pres. 1989-90), Internat. Ctr. Journalists (bd. dirs. 1990-2001), Internat. Press Inst., Kans. C. of C. and Industry (pres. 1987), Fly Club (Harvard U.). Avocations: tennis, cooking. Office: 318 N 5th St Manhattan KS 66502-5910

SEATON, ROBERT FINLAYSON, retired finance company executive; b. Hancock, Mich., Nov. 28, 1930; s. Donald W. and Mary Lucille (Finlayson) S.; m. Helen Jean Roberts, Apr. 18, 1954; children: Scott, Sandy. BS, Mich. Technol. U., 1952; MBA, Stanford, 1956; postgrad., Ind. U., 1966, U. So. Calif., 1973. Asst. sec. Palo Alto (Calif.) Mut. Savs. and Loan Assn., 1956-60; asst. v.p. Am. Savs. and Loan Assn. No. Calif., 1960-63; v.p. 1st Western Savs. and Loan Assn., Las Vegas, 1963-67; v.p., sec. Fed. Home Loan Bank, Cin., 1967-72; pres., chief exec. officer 2d Fed. Savs. and Loan Assn., Cleve., 1973, Cardinal Fed. Savs. Bank, Cleve., 1973-87, chmn., 1987-88; sr. v.p. Planned Giving Systems, Inc., 1989-90, pres., 1990-94. Trustee The Orange Schs. Found.; v.p. Luth. Housing Corp.; trustee, treas. N.E. Ohio Coun. Higher Edn.; hon. trustee Parkworks. Lt. USNR, 1952—54. Republican. Methodist. Home: 16 Pepper Creek Dr Cleveland OH 44124-5248

SEATON, SHIRLEY SMITH, academic administrator, consultant; b. Cleve. d. Kibble Smith and Cecil Wright; m. J. Lawrence Seaton, Oct. 2, 1965; 1 child, Eric Dean. BA, MA in History, Howard U., 1949; MEd, Case Western Res., 1956; EdD, U. Akron, 1981; cert. in Chinese history and culture, Beijing Normal U. Tchr. Cleve. Dist., 1950-59, dir. social studies, 1976-87; prin. Lafayette Dike, Cleve., 1959-63, 65-76; with Stas. WEWS-TV, WVIZ-TV, 1963-67; adj. prof. Cleve. State U., 1988-90; adminstr. John Carroll U., University Heights, Ohio, 1990—. Program dir. Office Econ. Opportunities, Cleve., 1965; peer rev. Ohio Profiency Test, 1986—; cons. Basics and Beyond, Cleve., 1990—. Coord. Ctr. Civic Edn., 11th Congress Dist., 1987—; peer interview chair Fulbright tchr. exch. U.S. Dept. State, 1994-99, 2001-2002; trustee Western Res. Hist. Soc., Cleve., 1996—, Ret. Vol. Program, Cleve., 1997—; commr. City of Cleveland Heights, Ohio, 1997—. Recipient Ohio Humanitarian award Govt. of Ohio, 1992; Fulbright grantee USIA, 1959, 82. Mem. Fulbright Assn., Nat. Alliance Black Edn., Coalition 100 Black Women, Phi Delta Kappa, Alpha Kappa Alpha. Episcopalian. Avocation: bridge. Home: 3680 Bendemeer Rd Cleveland Heights OH 44118 Office: John Carroll U 20700 North Blvd University Heights OH 44118

SEATON, VAUGHN ALLEN, retired veterinary pathology educator; b. Abilene, Kans., Oct. 11, 1928; m. Clara I. Bertelrud; children: Gregory S., Jeffrey T. BS, DVM, Kans. State U., 1954; MS, Iowa State U., 1957. Pvt. practice, Janesville, Wis., 1954; instr. pathology Vet. Diagnostic Lab. Iowa State U., Ames, 1954-57, from asst. to assoc. prof. pathology Vet. Disgnostic Lab., 1957-64, prof., head Vet. Diagnostic Lab., 1964-94. Lab. coord. regional emergency animal disease eradication orgn. Animal and Plant Health Inspection Svc. USDA, 1974—; mem. rsch. com. Iowa Beef Industry Coun., 1972-85; mem. adv. bd. Iowa State Water Resources Rsch. Inst., 1973-80; cons. several orgns. Co-author: (monographs) Feasibility Study of College of Veterinary Medicine, 1972, Veterinary Diagnostic Laboratory Facilities-State of New York, 1970; bd. dirs. Iowa State U. Press, 1985-88, mem. manuscript com., 1982-85; contbr. articles to profl. jours. Trustee Ames Pub. Libr., 1979-85; mem. Iowa State Bd. Health, 1971-77, v.p., 1976-77; bd. dirs. Masonic Edn. Found., 1985-88. Mem. AVMA, Am. Assn. Vet. Lab. Diagnosticians (bd. govs. 1973-88, pres. 1968, E.P. Pope award 1980), Am. Coll. Vet. Toxicologists, U.S. Animal Health Assn., Iowa Vet. Med. Assn. (pres. 1971), North Ctrl. Assn. Vet. Lab. Diagnosticians, Western Vet. Conf. (exec. bd. 1986-90, v.p. 1994, pres.-elect 1995, pres. 1996), World Assn. Vet. Lab. Diagnosticians (pres. 1980-86), Ames C. of C. (bd. dirs. 1970-73), Phi Kappa Phi, Phi Zeta (pres. 1964), Alpha Zeta, Gamma Sigma Delta. Office: Iowa State U Coll Vet Medicine Vet Diagnostic Lab Ames IA 50011-0001

SEATOR, LYNETTE HUBBARD, freelance writer; b. Chgo., Mar. 23, 1929; d. Alvin Glen and Thelma May (Mulnix) Hubbard; m. Gordon Douglas Seator, June 8, 1949 (dec. 1988); children: Pamela, Penelope, Patricia, Glen. BS, Western Ill. U., 1963; MA, U. Ill., 1965, PhD, 1972. Teaching asst. U. Ill., Champaign-Urbana, 1963-66; instr. Western Ill. U., Macomb, 1966-67; prof. Spanish, Ill. Coll., Jacksonville, 1967-89, Dunbaugh disting. prof., 1976, Pixley prof. humanities, 1988, prof. emeritus, 1989—; columnist Jacksonville Jour.-Courier, 1991-96. Symposium dir. New Understandings of Experience of Women, Moscow, 1991, Jacksonville, 1992, Ill. Coll., 1998; dir. poetry workshop Jacksonville (Ill.) Correctional Facility, 1993-2000. Editor, pub. (poems) Hear Me Out: Poems from Prison, 1996, Speaking Through the Bars: Poems by Women, 1999; author: (poetry) After the Light, 1992, Behind the Wall Poems, 1999; editor: Changing Lives of Russian Women: Conversations and Contentions, 1999; also articles to profl. jours. and newspaper. Pub. rels. dir. Habitat for Humanity, Jacksonville, 1992-96; translator Amnesty Internat., Jacksonville, 1992; bd. dirs. West Ctrl. Ill. Coun. on Fgn. Affairs; pres. Ill. Humanities Coun., Ctrl. Ill. Regional Planning Com., 1999—. Recipient Sears-Roebuck faculty award Ill. Coll., 1988. Mem. MLA, Poets and Writers, Ill. Writers (bd. dirs. 1983-87, 92-95), Midwest L.Am. Studies Assn., Feministas Unidas, Midwest Concerns, Phi Kappa Phi. Democrat. Avocations: travel, swimming, biking, gardening, canoeing. Home: 1609 Mound Ave Jacksonville IL 62650-2257 also: Apt 1906 1000 N Lake Shore Dr Chicago IL 60611 Office: Ill Coll Jacksonville IL 62650 E-mail: lseator@csj.net.

SEATS, PEGGY CHISOLM, marketing executive; b. Lisman, Ala., Oct. 12, 1951; d. William H. and Bernice (Berry) Chisolm; m. Melvin Seats (div.). BA in Communications cum laude, Lewis U., 1974; grad. cert. in event mgmt., George Washington U., 1995; MA in Pub. Comm., Am. U., 1997; grad. cert. in intercultural comm., Vaxjo (Sweden) U., 1997. Account exec. Globe Broadcasting, Chgo., 1976-78, Merrill Lynch, Chgo., 1978-79, Transp. Displays, Inc., Chgo., 1979-81; with Reverie, Inc., 1981—; nat. accounts mgr. Soft Sheen Products Co., Chgo., 1981-83; mktg. cons. Reverie, Inc., 1983-85; pub. rels., mktg. mgr. Proctor & Gardner Advt., 1985-86; dir. pub. rels., mktg. Morris Brown Coll., Atlanta, 1986-87; mgr. mktg. Howard U. Press, Washington, 1989-90; cons. White House Initiative on Historically Black Colls., Univs., 1990-92. State advisor U.S. Congl. Adv. Bd., Ill., 1982. Contbr. numerous articles to newspapers and mags. Founder Benjamin Banneker Meml. Fund, Washington, 1996; mem. Com. 100; organizer S.W. Waterfront Initiative, 2000—; bd. dir. Congl. Award Found. Recipient Kizzie award Black Women Hall of Fame, Chgo., 1981, Svc. award Nat. Assn. Women in Media, Chgo., 1982. Mem. Internat. Platform Assn., Internat. Assn. Bus. Communicators, Internat. Spl. Events Soc., Pub. Rels. Soc. Am., Black Pub. Rels. Soc. (founder Atlanta chpt.), Nat. Assn. Market Developers, World Affairs Coun., Lewis U. Alumni Assn. (bd. dirs. Ill. 1979), Washington Interdependence Coun. (founder, exec. dir. 1996). Unitarian Universalist. Avocations: music, art collecting, reading. Home: 2020 Pennsylvania Ave NW Washington DC 20006-1811 E-mail: pcseats@aol.com.

SEAU, JUNIOR (TIANA SEAU JR.), professional football player; b. Samoa, Jan. 19, 1969; Student, U. So. Calif. Linebacker San Diego Chargers, 1990—. Player Super Bowl XXVIV, 1994. Named to Sporting News Coll. All-Am. Team, 1989, to Pro Bowl Team, 1991-93, 96, to Sporting News NFL All Pro Team, 1992, 93. Office: San Diego Chargers PO Box 609609 San Diego CA 92160-9609*

SEAVE, AVA, media specialist; b. Phila., Apr. 30, 1955; d. Edwin and Shirley Seave; m. Bruce C. Greenwald, May 3, 1987; 1 child, Diana. AB, Brown U., 1977; MBA, Harvard U., 1982. Photo, art editor House Plants and Porch Gardens and Gardening Mag., Villanova, Pa., 1977-80; mgr. market research Dell Publishing, N.Y.C., 1982-85, dir. book sales, 1985-87; dir. market planning TVSM, 1987-89; gen. mgr. TV Times, 1989-91; circulation dir. Village Voice, N.Y.C., 1991-93, gen. mgr., 1993-96, Scholastic, Inc., N.Y.C., 1996-98; prin. Quantum Media Assocs., 1998—; pres., CEO AskShirley.com, Inc., 1999-2000. Bd. dirs. Poets in Pub. Service, N.Y.C., 1985-95. Contbr. articles to Phila. Inquirer; contbg. editor The Am. Poetry Rev., 1977—. County com. woman Dem. Ctrl. Com., N.Y.C., 1983-84; bd. dirs. Pembroke Ctr. for Study and Teaching of Women, 1992—, Brown Alumni Monthly, 1995-97; founder Harvard Bus. Sch. Network for Women Alumni Mktg. to Kids Spl. Interest Group, 1998-99. Mem. Harvard Bus. Sch. Club (v.p. mem. com. 1986-89, bd. dirs. 1988-89, program com. 2001-). Jewish. E-mail: seave@quantummedia.net.

SEAVER, ROBERT LESLIE, retired law educator; b. Brockton, Mass., June 13, 1937; s. Russell Bradford and Lois (Marchant) S.; m. Marjorie V. Rote, Aug. 21, 1960 (div. 1974); children: Kimberly, Eric, Kristen; m. Elizabeth A. Horwitz, May 22, 1984. AB cum laude, Tufts U., Medford, Mass., 1958; JD, U. Chgo., 1964. Bar: Ohio 1964, U.S. Ct. Appeals (6th cir.) 1964, U.S. Dist. Ct. (so. dist.) Ohio 1965. Assoc. Taft, Stettinius and Hollister, Cin., 1964-66; v.p., sec., gen. counsel IDI Mgmt. Inc., 1966-74; pvt. practice, 1974-75; prof. law emeritus No. Ky. U. Salmon P. Chase Coll. Law, Highland Heights, 1975—; of counsel Cors & Bassett, Cin., 1993-99; ret., 1999. Cons. in field, 1975—. Author/editor: Ohio Corporation Law, 1988; contbr. chpts. to books. Advisor subcom. on pvt. corps of Ky. Commn. on Constl. Rev., 1987. With USMC, 1958-61. Recipient Justice Robert O. Lukowsky award of Excellence Chase Law Sch. Student Bar Assn., 1986. Republican. Unitarian Universalist. Avocations: duplicate bridge (life master), history. Home: 826 Woodscene Ct Cincinnati OH 45230-4334 E-mail: rseaver@cinci.rr.com.

SEAVEY, CHRISTOPHER GORDON, psychotherapist, addiction counselor; b. Syracuse, N.Y., Dec. 4, 1942; s. Gordon Crowell and Shirley Edith Seavey; m. Eudene Sawyer, Aug. 8, 1965 (div. Mar. 1983); children: Sandra, Sherry, Gordon; m. Nancy Bowen, 1983. BA in Human Svcs., U. Mass., Boston, 1986; MA in Rehab. Counseling, U. South Fla., Ft. Myers, 1991; PhD in Psychotherapy, Internat. U. Grad. Studies, 2001. Sr. counselor Project Turnabout, Hingham, Mass., 1982-86; counselor Coastal Cmty. Counseling, Braintree, 1986-87, South Shore Coun. on Alcoholism, Quincy, 1987; chem. dependency counselor II David Lawrence Ctr., Naples, Fla., 1989-90; vocat. rehab cons. Intracorp, 1990-96; acting dir. Addiction Recovery Ctr., Ft. Myers, Fla., 1993-98; clin. dir. Assisted Addiction Recovery, Naples, 1995—. Bd. dirs. AAR Counseling, Naples, Human Svc. Inc., Ft. Myers, 1995-97; mem. adv. bd. Naples Rehab. Inc., 1994-97. Mem. adj. bd. Project Help, Naples, 1996—; chmn. Collier County Depression Coalition, Naples, 1997. Recipient Book award U. Mass., Boston, 1986; U. Calif. San Francisco fellow, 1986; Tobacco Coalition grantee, 1998. Mem. NADAAC, Fla. Rehab. Assn. (pres. S.W. Fla. chpt. 1994—, Svc. award 1999), S.W. Fla. Marriage and Family Counseling Assn., Fla. Mental Health Counselors (treas.), Phi Kappa Phi. Office: AAR Counseling 1061 Collier Centerway Ste 6 Naples FL 34110-1603 E-mail: aaa@aarservices.com.

SEAVEY, WILLIAM ARTHUR, lawyer, vintner; b. Los Angeles, Aug. 28, 1930; s. Arthur Jones and Dorothy (Keyes) S.; m. Mary van Beuren, June 25, 1955; children: Dorothy K., Arthur V.B., William G., Frederic A., Charles K. AB, Princeton U., 1952; LLB, Harvard U., 1955; grad. Inst. Internat. Studies, U. Geneva, Switzerland, 1956, D in Polit. Sci., 1970. Bar: Calif. 1957, U.S. Dist. Ct. (so. and no. dist.) Calif. 1957, U.S. Ct. Appeals (9th cir.) 1957. Assoc.

Luce, Forward, Kunzel & Scripps, San Diego, 1956-57; asst. U.S. atty. U.S. Dist. Ct. (so. dist.) Calif., 1957-59; with Noon & Seavey, San Diego, 1959-65; lectr. in internat. law and econ., asst. to pres. Mills Coll., Oakland, Calif., 1968-74; ptnr. Richards & Seavey, San Francisco, 1974-76, Davis, Stafford, Kellman & Fenwick, San Francisco, 1976-78; of counsel Friedman, Olive, McCubbin, Spalding, Bilter, Roosevelt etal, 1987—. Proprietor Seavey Vineyard, Napa County, 1981—. Author: Dumping Since the War: The Gatt and National Laws, 1970. Councilman City of Coronado, Calif., 1960-62, mayor 1962-64; trustee French-Am. Internat. Sch., San Francisco, 1968-96; pres. English Speaking Union, San Francisco, 1982-85, Alliance Francaise, San Francisco, 1979-81; chair Javits Fellowship Bd., Washington, 1989-92; mem. Columbus Fellowship Found. Bd., Washington, 1993-99; dir. San Francisco Com. on Fgn. Rels., 1995-98, chmn., 1998—. Mem. ABA, Calif. Bar Assn., San Francisco Bar Assn., Am. Soc. Internat. Law. Clubs: Pacific Union, Cercle de l'Union, World Trade (San Francisco), The Met. (Washington). Republican. Avocation: skiing, jazz piano. Home: 90 Hazel Ln Piedmont CA 94611-4033 Office: 425 California St Fl 22 San Francisco CA 94104-2102 also: 1310 Conn Valley Rd Saint Helena CA 94574-9624 E-mail: waseavey@pacbell.net., info@seaveyvineyard.com.

SEAWELL, DONALD RAY, lawyer, publisher, arts center executive, producer; b. Jonesboro, N.C., Aug. 1, 1912; s. A.A.F. and Bertha (Smith) S.; m. Eugenia Rawls, Apr. 5, 1941; children: Brook Ashley, Donald Brockman. AB, U. N.C., 1933, JD, 1936, DLitt, 1980; LHD, U. No. Colo., 1978. Bar: N.C. 1936, N.Y. 1947. With SEC, 1939-41, 45-47, Dept. Justice, 1942-43; chmn. bd., dir., pub., pres. Denver Post, 1966-81; chmn. bd., dir. Gravure West, L.A., 1966-81; dir. Swan Prodns., London; of counsel firm Bernstein, Seawell, Kove & Maltin, N.Y.C., 1979—; chmn. bd., chief exec. officer Denver Ctr. for Performing Arts, 1972—. Ptnr. Bonfils-Seawell Enterprises, N.Y.C.; bd. vis. U. N.C. Chmn. bd. ANTA, 1965—; mem. theatre panel Nat. Coun. Arts, 1970-74; bd. govs. Royal Shakespeare Theatre, Eng.; trustee Am. Acad. Dramatic Arts, 1967—, Hofstra U., 1968-69, Cen. City Opera Assn., Denver Symphony; bd. dirs., Air Force Acad. Found., Nat. Ints. Outdoor Drama, Walter Hampden Meml. Library, Hammond Mus.; pres. Helen G. Bonfils Found., 1972-97, pres. emeritus, 1997—, chmn. fin. com., 1997—, Denver Opera Found.; Population Crisis Com., 1982-91; bd. dirs. Family Health Internat., Found. for Internat. Family Health; bd. visitors N.C. Sch. Arts, 1992-98; pres. Frederick G. Bonfils Found., 1972-92; chmn. Civilian Mil. Inst. Recipient Am. Acad. Achievement award, 1980, Tony award for producing On Your Toes, 1983, Voice Rsch. and Awareness award Voice Found., 1983, Arts and Entertainment Cable Network award, 1987, Third Millenium Leadership award Am. Diabetes Assn., 1996, Colo. Tourism Hall of Fame award, 1999, Thomas Degaetani award U.S. Inst. for Theatre Tech., 2000, Benjamin F. Stapleton, Jr. award, 2000, Mayor's Millennium award, 2000, Downtown Denver award for Tantalus, 2001, Disting. Svc. award U. Colo., 2000, AWARE Honoree award, 2001. Mem. Bucks Club (London), Dutch Treat Club (N.Y.C.), Denver Country Club, Denver Club, Cherry Hills Country Club, Mile High Club (Denver), Garden of Gods Club (Colorado Springs, Colo.). Office: Denver Ctr for Performing Arts 1050 13th St Denver CO 80204-2157 E-mail: geary@dcpa.org.

SEAWELL, THOMAS ROBERT, artist, retired educator; b. Balt., Mar. 17, 1936; s. Robert James and Cynthia Edith (Bass) S.; m. Barbara Louise Frey, Nov. 30, 1985; children: James Bradford, Lee Thomas, Gustin Charles, Jay Turner Frey. B.F.A., Washington U., 1958; M.F.A., Tex. Christian U., 1960. Mem. faculty dept. art SUNY-Oswego, 1963-91, prof., 1973-91; vis. artist Ox Bow Print Symposium, 1985, Ann. Matrix Artist, U. Dallas, 1989, Midwestern State U., 1993, East Tenn. State U., 1997, Henderson State U., 1997. Juror 50th Cooperstown Nat., 1985, Nat. Print Exhbn., Minot State U., N.D., 1985., Rochester Print Club Annual, Meml. Art Gallery U. Rochester, 1988. One-man exhbns. include retrospective U. Md., Baltimore County, 1983, Retrospective Tyler Art Gallery, SUNY, Oswego, 1991, Univ. Gallery, Tex. A&M U., Commerce, 1995, Brazos Gallery, Dallas, 1997; group exhbns. include Contemporary Am. Prints in Leningrad, USSR, 1983-84, The Collagraph, U. Mont., 1987; traveling exhbn. So. Arts Fedn. Traveling Exhbn. "A Sense of Place," 1986—, Columbia Coll., 1996-97, Art in the Metroplex, J.M. Moody Gallery, Ft. Worth, Tex., 1997, Contemporary Tex. Clay, Dallas Visual Arts Ctr., 1997, To Have and to Hold, Irving (Tex.) Arts Ctr. Main Gallery, 1998, Kennedy-Douglass Ctr. for the Arts Nat. Ceramic Competition, 1999, Woodmere Art Mus., 1999, San Angelo Mus. Fine Arts, 2000, Ark. State U., 2000, U. Wis., Parkside, 2000, Oxford Gallery, Rochester, N.Y., 2000; represented in permanent collections Bklyn. Mus., DeCordova Mus. Art, Rochester Meml. Art Gallery, Pushkin Mus., USSR, Brit. Mus., Munson-Williams-Proctor Inst., Library of Congress, Portland Art Mus.; commd. print editions: Geldermann Securities Ltd., 1985-92. Recipient Joseph A. Cain Meml. Purchase award for sculpture Del Mar Coll., 1999. Mem. Boston Printmakers, Phila. Water Color Soc., Soc. Am. Graphic Artists. Home: 1513 Park St Commerce TX 75428-3071 E-mail: tseawell@9plus.net.

SEAWELL, WILLIAM THOMAS, former airline executive; b. Pine Bluff, Ark., Jan. 27, 1918; s. George Marion and Harriet (Aldridge) S.; m. Judith Alexander, June 12, 1941; children: Alexander Brooke, Anne Seawell Robinson. BS, U.S. Mil. Acad., 1941; JD, Harvard U., 1949. Commd. 2d lt. U.S. Army, 1941; advanced through grades to brig. gen. USAF, 1959; comdr. 401st Bombardment Group, ETO, World War II, 11th Bomb Wing SAC, 1953-54; dep. comdr. 7th Air Div., 1954-55; mil. asst. to sec. USAF, 1958-59, to dep. sec. def., 1959-61; comdt. cadets U.S. Air Force Acad., 1961-63; ret., 1963; v.p. operations and engring. Air Transport Assn. Am., Washington, 1963-65; sr. v.p. ops. Am. Airlines, N.Y.C., 1965-68; pres. Rolls Royce Aero Engines Inc. U.S. subsidiary Rolls Royce, Ltd., 1968-71; pres., chief operating officer Pan Am. World Airways Inc., N.Y.C., 1971-72, chmn. bd., 1972-81. Decorated Silver Star, D.F.C. with three oak leaf clusters, Air medal with three oak leaf clusters; Croix de Guerre with palm France). Mem.: Wings (N.Y.C.), Pine Bluff Country. Home: 21 Westridge Dr Pine Bluff AR 71603-7149

SEAWORTH, MARY ELLEN, lawyer; b. Bismarck, N.D., Oct. 28, 1947; d. George H. and Margaret M. (Fortune) S.; m. Henry H. Howe, Dec. 4, 1976; children: Oren, Deborah, Tavia, Christopher. Student, Coll. St. Teresa, 1965-68; BA in Speech and Theatre, U. N.D., 1971, BS in Edn., 1973, JD, 1983. Bar: Minn. 1983, N.D. 1984, U.S. Dist. Ct. N.D. 1984. Ptnr. Howe and Seaworth, Grand Forks, N.D., 1983—. Instr. (part time) legal assistance program Northland Community Coll., Thief River Falls, Minn., 1988, 89. Editorial staff N.D. Law Review, 1982-83. Trustee Grand Forks Symphony, 1984-94; bd. dirs. Greater Grand Forks Community Theatre, 1983—, LWV, 1991—; mem. com. Gov.'s Commn. Children Adolescents at Risk, 1985-86; commr. for Commn. Uniform State Laws, 1985-95; Dem. com. person. Recipient Women Who Care award U. N.D. Women's Ctr., 1986; named one of Outstanding Young Women Am., 1984.. Mem. N.D. Bar Assn. (chmn. family law sect. 1988, 96, Minn. Bar Assn., Trial Lawyers Nat. & State, ABA (family law sect.), Am. Acad. Matrimonial Lawyers. Office: Howe and Seaworth Law Offices 421 Demers Ave Grand Forks ND 58201-4507 E-mail: seaworthm@hotmail.com.

SEAWRIGHT, JAMES L., JR. sculptor, educator; b. Jackson, Miss., May 22, 1936; s. James L. and Josephine (Power) S.; m. Mabelle M. Garrard, June 22, 1960; 1 child, James Andrew. Student, U. of South, 1953-54, Delta State Coll., 1954-55; BA in English, U. Miss., 1957; postgrad., Art Students League of N.Y., 1961-62. Tech. supr. Columbia-Princeton Electronic Music Center, N.Y.C., 1963-69; tchr. Sch. Visual Arts, 1967-69; dir. visual arts program Princeton U., 1972-2001, prof. coun. of humanities and visual arts, 1992—. Asst. to choreographer, Henry St. Playhouse, N.Y.C., 1962-63, spl. effects, tech. cons., Mimi Garrard Dance Co., N.Y.C., 1964— ; sculptor represented in permanent collections, Mus. Modern Art, N.Y.C., Whitney Mus., N.Y.C., N.J. State Mus., Trenton, Guggenheim Mus., N.Y.C., Wadsworth Atheneum, Hartford, Conn., others; pub. commns. for SEA-TAC Internat. Airport, Seattle, Logan Internat. Airport, Boston; also pvt. collections. Served with USN, 1957-61. Recipient Theodoron award Guggenheim Mus., 1969, Am. Acad. Arts and Letters Art award, 1997; Graham Found. Advanced Study in Arts fellow, 1970. Mem. Am. Abstract Artists, Phi Delta Theta. Democrat. Episcopalian. Office: 185 Nassau St Princeton NJ 08544-2003 E-mail: jims@princeton.edu., james@seawright.net.

SEAY, AMY JO, interior designer; b. Menomonee Falls, Wis., Sept. 12, 1965; d. Donald Arthur and Dorothy Patricia (Krutz) Nienow. BS, U. Wis., Stevens Point, 1987. Interior designer Forrer Bus. Interiors, Milw., 1987—. Vol. Sojourner Truth House, Milw., 1994—. Mem. Am. Soc. Interior Designers. Methodist. Avocations: photography, traveling, sports. Home: W249n7198 Hillside Rd Sussex WI 53089-2526

SEAY, JOHN DAVID, gynecologist; b. Fairfield, Ala., May 28, 1942; MD, U. Ala. Sch. Medicine, 1969. Diplomate Am. Bd. Ob-Gyn. Intern St. Vincent's Hosp., Birmingham, 1969-70; resident in ob-gyn. U. South Ala., Mobile, 1972-75; staff Gilmore Meml. Hosp., Armory, Miss. Fellow Am. Coll. Ob-Gyn.; mem. AMA, Am. Assn. Gynecol. Laparascopy. Office: Phys & Surgeons Clinic 900 Earl Frye Blvd Ste A Amory MS 38821-5507

SEAY, SUZANNE, financial planner, educator; b. Tulsa, May 3, 1942; d. James Paul and Ann (Maxey) S. BS, Hardin-Simmons U., 1964; MA, Ariz. State U., 1966. Cert. fin. planner; registered investment advisor. Tchr. Baker (Oreg.) Pub. Schs., 1964-65, Govt. of Guam, Agana, 1966-68, Hollister, Calif., 1968-74, Tehran (Iran) Am. Sch., 1974-75, Am. Sch. Isfahan, Iran, 1975-78; internat. pubs. rep. World Editions, Hollister, 1978-87; fin. planner, investment adviser Clock Tower Fin. (name now Royal Alliance), Monterey, Calif., 1984—; tchr. fin. planning Gavilan Coll., Gilroy, 1988-95, Monterey Peninsula Coll., 1988-94, Hartnell Coll., Salinas, Calif., 1989-94. Spkr. Monterey County Women's Fair, Salinas, Calif., 1988, Bay Area Profl. Women's Conf., 1989, S.E. Asia Tchrs. and Counselors Conf., 1987, RVing Women Nat. Conf., 1998, 99, 2000, 01. Fin. columnist RVing Women mag., 1995—; talk show host Fin. Planning for Peace of Mind, Phoenix, 2002. Mem. Am. Field Svc., Hollister, 1987-96; treas. San Benito Hospice, Hollister, 1987-91; bd. dirs. St. Bonaventure Indian Mission and Sch., 2000—; speaker in field. Mem.: Fin. Planning Assn., Assn. for Advancement of RVing (bd. dirs. 2000—02). Democrat. Avocations: motorhome, traveling, reading. Home: 2571 N Avenida San Valle Tucson AZ 85715-3404 E-mail: suzyseay@aol.com., suzanne@suzanneseay.com.

SEBALLOS, RAUL JOHN, internist, medical educator; b. Manila, Feb. 11, 1961; came to U.S., 1968; s. Raul Hernandez and Rosalinda Seballos; m. Sandra Kay Seballos, Apr. 27, 1991; children: Spencer, Evan, Anna. BA, Case Western Res. U., 1983; MD, Med. Coll. of Ohio, 1988. Diplomate Am. Bd. Internal Medicine. Staff physician Outreach Profls. Inc., Cleve., 1995-97, The Cleve. Clinic Found., 1997—; asst. prof. clin. medicine dept. internal medicine Ohio State U. Sch. of Medicine, Columbus, 1999—. Med. dir. Cleve. Clinic's Nurse on Call Program, 1998—, Hamlet Manor Nursing Home, Chagrin Falls, Ohio, 1998-99. Contbr. articles to profl. jours., chpt. to book. Basketball referee The City Mission, Cleve., 1991—, 9th grade proficiency exam math. tutor, 1995—. Fellow ACP (judge, abstract reviewer, assocs. com.); mem. Assn. Philippine Physicians of Ohio. Avocations: basketball, mountain biking. Office: The Cleve Clinic Found 9500 Euclid Ave Desk A-11 Cleveland OH 44195 Fax: 216-445-6494.

SEBASTIAN, JAMES ALBERT, obstetrician, gynecologist, educator; b. Milw., Feb. 20, 1945; s. Milton Arthur and Bernice Marian (Friske) S.; m. Jacqulin Victoria Johnson, June l4, l969; children: Mila, Joel, Jon, Marnie. BS, U. Wis., 1966, MD, l969. Diplomate Am. Bd. Ob-Gyn. Commd. officer USN, l965, advanced through grades to lt. comdr., 1972; intern U.S. Naval Hosp., St. Albans, N.Y., 1969-70; resident in ob-gyn. Naval Regional Med. Ctr., Portsmouth, Va., l970-72, mem. staff, 1976-77, Naval Hosp., Taipei, Taiwan, l972-76; resigned, l977; pvt. practice, Duluth, Minn., l977—. Assoc. clin. prof. ob-gyn U. Minn. Med. Sch., Duluth, 1977—; pres. clin. faculty dept. ob-gyn. U. Minn., Mpls., 1999-02. Fellow Am. Coll. Ob-Gyn. (bd. dirs. Minn. sect. 1996-99, best rsch. paper award Armed Forces dist. 1976); mem. Am. Fertility Soc., Minn. Perinatal Assn. (bd. dirs. 1978-87, pres. 1985-86), Kiwanis (pres. 1989-90). Office: Duluth Ob-Gyn Assocs 1000 E 1st St Ste 204 Duluth MN 55805-2297

SEBASTIAN, PETER, international affairs consultant, former ambassador; b. June 19, 1926; m. Harvel Huddleston, Dec. 11, 1951; 1 child, Christopher BA, U. Chgo., 1950; postgrad., U. d'Aix-Marseille, Nice, France, 1949, New Sch. for Social Research, N.Y.C., 1950, Nat. War Coll., 1969-70. Dir., owner cons. co., N.Y.C., 1950-57; U.S. Fgn. Service officer Dept. State, Washington, 1957-76, dep. exec. sec., 1976-77, sr. seminar, 1977-78; U.S. consul gen. Casablanca, Morocco, 1978-80; minister, counselor Am. embassy, Rabat, Morocco, 1980-82; dir. for North Africa Dept. State, Washington, 1982-84; ambassador to Tunisia Tunis, 1984-87; ambassador-in-residence Ctr. for Strategic Internat. Studies, Georgetown U., Washington, 1987-88; cons in fgn. affairs to the public and pvt. sector, lectr., 1988—. Mem. V.P. Bush's task force on border control, 1988—89. Contbr. poems to Osmose, 1949; author studies for the pvt. sector U.S. Dept. State and other U.S agys. Served to sgt. AUS, 1944-46 Decorated Ouissam Alaouite (Morocco), numerous U.S. mil. decorations; recipient Presdl. Meritorious Service award, 1985. Mem. Am. Fgn. Svc. Assn., Nat. Geog. Soc., Mid. East Inst. Episcopalian. Avocations: painting, drawing, photography. E-mail: Batuta@aol.com.

SEBASTIAN, PHYLIS SUE, real estate broker, art appraiser; b. Childersburg, Ala., Jan. 24, 1945; d. Albert Freeman and Era Mae (McGowin) Ingram; m. Robert Emmett Martin, March 31, 1965 (div. Sept. 1976); children: Connie, Michael, Toni, Robert; m. Thomas Haskell Sebastian III, June 26, 1985; stepchildren: Shellie, Tabitha, Cherie, Thomas IV. Ordained minister Progressive Universal Life Ch., 2002; lic. real estate broker. Owner, broker Phylis Sebastian Real Estate, Farmington, Mo, 1989-97, U.S. Auto Sales, Park Hills, 1993-96; owner Bus. Legal Svs., Mo., 1997; part owner La Femme Fine Antique Auction Svc., Ironton. Author: Marriages in Madison County Missouri 1848-1868, 1998, 1910 Census for Madison County Missouri, 1998; contbr. articles to newspapers; author numerous poems; hostess radio show, St. Louis, 1970s. Co-founder Astrological Assn., St. Louis, 1976-77, Mo. Mental Health Consumer Network, 1989-93, Mineral Area chpt. 1989-93. Mem. Nat. Gardening Club, Libr. Congress, Smithsonian, Nat. Hist. soc., Geneal. Assn. Madison County, Mo. (founder, sec., treas.). Mem. Lds Ch. Avocations: genealogy, astrology, reading, walking, gardening. Home: 5231 West 72 Highway Fredericktown MO 63645 Office: Arcadia Valley Auction Company Inc and Real Estate 315A W Russell St Ironton MO 63650-1316 E-mail: phylis@phylissebastian.com.

SEBASTIAN, SANDRA MARY THOMPSON, clinical counselor, social worker; b. Moncton, Can., June 14, 1943; came to U.S., 1965; d. Alan G. E. Thompson and Jean Glenn Hyde Thompson Hart; m. John Francis Sebastian, Jr., Aug. 12, 1967; children: Byron David, Colin Alan. Diploma, Queen Elizabeth's Coll., Surrey, Eng., 1962, Morley Coll, London, 1965; BA in Sociology, Miami U., 1986; MS in Mental Health Counseling, Wright State U., 1995. Lic. profl. clin. counselor. Rsch. sec. St. Thomas' Hosp. Med. Sch., London, 1962-65; prodn. editor Ency. Britannica, Chgo., 1966-67; sec. Miami U., Oxford, Ohio, 1980-86; social worker Butler CY.CSB, Hamilton, 1987-95, Family Preservation, 1992-95; mental health counselor, child/adolescent, adult therapist Hamilton Counseling Ctr., 1995—. Spkr. in field. Apptd. commr. on volunteerism State Ohio, 1986-87; mem. Conflict Resolution Svcs., 1991—, Oxford Citizens for Peace & Justice, 1988—, Butler County AIDS Task Force, 1990; v.p. McGuffey Sch. PTA, Oxford, 1978. Mem. ACA, Am. Mental Health Counselors Assn., Internat. Assn. Play Therapy, NAACP (Oxford chpt.), UN Assn. USA, Miami U. Women's Club (v.p. 1980), Sigma Chi Iota. Democrat. Unitarian Universalist. Avocations: traveling, classical music, reading, writing. Home: 220 Mckee Ave Oxford OH 45056-9060 Office: Hamilton Counseling Ctr 111 Buckeye St Hamilton OH 45011-1645

SEBASTIAN, SUZIE, producer, stunt woman; b. Redding, Calif., Aug. 2, 1962; d. Richard Werner and Hildegard (Goettel) Guenther; m. Ted Sebastian, June 6, 1984 (div. July 1990). AA, Shasta Coll., 1985. Freelance tv prodr., prodn. mgr. comml.s., 1985-91; freelance underwater model, stunt woman; expedition leader, hostess Adventures on Scuba Dive Travel, Santa Barbara, Calif., 1991—; documentary TV prodr. Discovery Channel, 1998-2000. Asst. instr. Filming Sharks in the Wild, Nassau, Bahamas, 1996—. Prodr.: documentaries, ednl. videos; (picture editor, underwater model): Tom Campbell's Film and Video Prodns., 1991—; prodr.: Navy Seals: In Harms Way, How to Survive Hellweek. Mem. Divers Alert Network, Internat. Documentary Assn.. Avocations: snow skiing. Home: 919 Veronica Springs Rd Santa Barbara CA 93105-4500 Office: Adventures on Scuba 238 Las Alturas Rd Santa Barbara CA 93103-2170 E-mail: suziesebastian@hotmail.com.

SEBASTIANELLI, CARL THOMAS, clinical psychologist; b. Jessup, Pa. s. Carlo and Antonia (Antonelli) S. BS in Psychology magna cum laude, U. Scranton, 1965; MA in Psychology, Temple U., 1967; postgrad. in clin. psychology, L.I. U., 1968-70; PhD in Psychopathology/Psychotherapy, Clayton U., 1983. Lic. psychologist, Pa. Psychologist Farview State Hosp., Waymart, Pa., 1967-68; clin. psychology doctoral intern N. Dauphin Mental Health/Mental Retardation Ctr., 1970-71; clin. psychology doctoral intern family therapy ctr. Harrisburg (Pa.) State Hosp., 1970-71, clin. psychologist, 1971-77, chmn. psychology forum, 1974-76, clin. psychologist Psychiat. Treatment Ctr., 1977-79; pvt. practice clin. psychology Comprehensive Health Svcs. Ctr., Dunmore, Pa., 1979-90, ind. pvt. practice clin. psychology, 1990—. Mem. adj. faculty U. Scranton, 1979-86, Pa. State U., 1973-86; mem. state bd. Pa. Social Services Union, 1974-75; media commentator psychopathology topics, 1979—. Contbr. articles to profl. jours., UPI; interviewed for articles in newspapers and nat. mags.; featured in Pa. Dept. Welfare publ. on subject of family therapy tng. Pa. Profl. Edn. Program scholar L.I. U.; recipient award N.E. Pa. chpt. Am. Diabetes Assn., 1980. Mem. APA, Internat. Acad. Behavioral Medicine Counselling and Psychotherapy, Anxiety Disorders Assn. Am., Nat. Register Health Svc. Providers in Psychology. Home: 1224 Monroe Ave Scranton PA 18509-2808

SEBASTIANELLI, MARIO JOSEPH, internist, nephrologist, health services administrator; b. Jessup, Pa., Sept. 14, 1935; s. Carlo and Antonia (Antonelli) S.; m. Alena Marie Drazdauskas, June 26, 1993; children: Mario, Alexa, Marco. BS in Biology, U. Scranton, 1958; MD, Jefferson Med. Coll., 1962. Diplomate Am. Bd. Internal Medicine. From sr. instr. to assoc. prof. medicine Hahnemann U., Phila., 1969-87; pvt. practice Scranton, Pa., 1971—; chief nephrology, founding dir. hemodialysis Moses Taylor Hosp., 1972-76; founding med. dir. Pa. Regional Tissue Bank, 1983-91; dir. inpatient hemodialysis svcs. Comty. Med. Ctr., 1996—; founding med. dir. Fresenius Med. Care Dialysis Svcs. Dunmore, 2001—. Mem. senateconfirmed gov. apptd. Govs. Renal Disease Adv. Com., Harrisburg, Pa., 1973-76; creator, owner Comprehensive Health Svcs. Ctr., Dunmore, Pa., 1979—; founding med. dir. Diagnostic Lab., Dunmore, 1981-95. Contbr. articles to profl. jours. Bd. dirs. Scranton Lackawanna Human Devel. Agy., Scranton, 1977-82. Lt. USNR, 1963-65. Fellow ACP; mem. AMA, Am. Soc. Internal Medicine, Am. Soc. Nephrology, Internat. Soc. Nephrology, Renal Physicians Assn., KC (4th degree), Alpha Omega Alpha. Republican. Roman Catholic. Avocations: fishing, swimming, travel, sports cars, reading. Office: Comprehensive Health Svcs Ctr 1416 Monroe Ave Ste 206 Dunmore PA 18509-2477

SEBASTIANI, PAOLA, statistician, educator; b. Brescia, Italy, Jan. 16, 1964; d. Vincenzo Sebastiani and Giuseppina Canavesi; life ptnr. Marco F. Ramoni. BSc in Math., U. of Perugia, Italy, 1987; MSc, U. Coll., London, Eng., 1990; PhD in Stats., U. of Rome, Italy, 1992. Ricercatore U. of Perugia, Perugia, Italy, 1990—95; lectr. City U., London, 1995—98, The Open U., Milton Keynes, England, 1998—2000, Imperial Coll., London, 2000; asst. prof. U. of Mass., Amherst, Mass., 2000—. Contbr. articles to profl. jours. Mem.: Am. Statis. Assn. Personal E-mail: sebas@math.umass.edu.

SEBE;JAIS, MELANIE, federal agency administrator; m. Bob Sabelhaus; 2 children. With IBM; founder Exclusive Interim Properties Ltd. (now Bridgestreet Accomodations), Balt., 1986—97; v.p. global sales Bridgestreet Accomodations (formerly Exvlusive Interim Properties Ltd.), 1997—98; deputy adminstr. Small bus. Adminstrn., Washington, 2002—. Bd. dirs. United Way, Alzheimer's Assn. Ctrl. Md.; co-chair Nat. Summit Women in Philanthropy. Recipient Outstanding Vol. Fundraiser of Yr. award, Assn. Fundraising Profls., Md., 2002. Office: Small Bus Adminstrn 409 3d St SW Washington DC 20416*

SEBERT, STEPHEN L. physician; b. Richwood, W.Va., Aug. 16, 1951; s. Lowell E. and Thelma (Dorsey) S.; m. Janet Westfall, May 19, 1973; children: Paul, Jennifer. BA in Chemistry, W.Va. Wesleyan Coll., Buckhannon, 1973; MD, W.Va. U., 1977. Diplomate Am. Bd. Family Practice. Pvt. practice, Lewisburg, W.Va., 1980-89; practicing physician W.Va. U. Med. Corp., Morgantown, 1989-98, Cheat Lake Physicians, 1989-2001; assoc. prof. family medicine W.Va. U. Sch. Medicine, Morgantown, 1989-98; county health officer Monongalia County, 1994-98; practicing physician Cheat Lake Urgent Care and Family Practice, 2001—. Med. dir. Monongalia County Hospice, Morgantown, 1994-98, Monongalia County Health Dept., 1994-98. Contbr. articles to profl. jours. Mem. task force Health Care Planning Commn., W.Va. State Govt., Charleston, 1992. Mem. AMA, W.Va. State Med. Assn. (exec. com. 1997), Am. Acad. Family Physicians (sec. bd. dirs. W.Va. chpt., chair 2000, pres. W.Va. chpt. 1999), Cheat Lake Rotary Club (bd. dirs. 1997-98). Republican. Methodist. Avocations: camping, fishing, hunting, skiing. Home: 148 Lamplighter Dr Morgantown WV 26508-8649 Office: Cheat Lake Urgent Care and Family Practice 710 Venture Dr Morgantown WV 26508

SEBOLD, RUSSELL PERRY , III, Romance languages educator, writer; b. Dayton, Ohio, Aug. 20, 1928; s. Russell Perry and Mary (Kiger) S.; m. Jane Norvell Hale, Nov. 24, 1955; children: Mary Norvell, Alice Hale. Student, U. Chgo., 1945-47; BA, Ind. U., 1949; MA (Woodrow Wilson fellow), Princeton U., 1951, PhD, 1953; D.Phil. and Letters (hon.), U. Alicante, Spain, 1984. Instr. Spanish, Duke U., 1955-56; instr. Spanish, U. Wis., 1956-58, asst. prof., 1958-62, assoc. prof., 1962-66; prof. Spanish, chmn. dept. fgn. langs. and lits. U. Md., 1966-68; prof. Spanish, U. Pa., 1968-88, chmn. dept. Romance langs., 1968-78, Edwin B. and Leonore R. Williams prof. Romance langs., 1988—. Mem. adv. com. Soc. Ibero-Am. Enlightenment, 1968—, treas., 1969—; steering com. Am. Soc. Eighteenth Century Studies, 1970—; corresponding academician Royal Spanish Acad., 1993—, Royal Acad. Humane Letters of Barcelona, 1993—. Author: Tomás de Iriarte: poeta de rapto racional, 1961, El rapto de la mente, 1970, 2nd edit., 1989, Colonel Don José Cadalso, 1970, Cadalso: el primer romántico europeo de España, 1974, Novela y autobiografía en la Vida de Torres Villarroel, 1975, Trayectoria del romanticismo español, 1983, Descubrimiento y fronteras del neoclasicismo español, 1985, Bécquer en sus narraciones fantásticas, 1989, De Ilustrados y románticos, 1992, La novela romantica en España, 2000, La perduración de la modalidad clásica, 2001; author, editor: Fray Gerundio de Campazas (José Francisco de Isla), 4 vols, 1960-64, 2d edit., 1992, Visiones y visitas de Torres con don Francisco de Quevedo por la Corte (Diego de Torres Villarroel), 1966, 2d edit., 1991, Numancia destruida (Ignacio López de Ayala), 1971, Poética (Ignacio de Luzán), 1977, Comedias (Tomás de Iriarte), 1978, 2d edit., 1986; Gustavo Adolfo Bécquer (antología crítica), 1985, Vida (Diego de Torres Villarroel), 1985, Rimas (Gustavo Adolfo Bécquer), 1991, (with David T. Gies) Ilustración y neoclasicismo, 1992, Noches lúgubres (José de Cadalso), 1993, (with Jesus Perez Magallon) El hombre practico (Conde de Fernán Nuñez), 1996, Cartas marruecas, Noches lúgubres (Jose de Cadalso), 1999, 2d edit., 2002; gen. editor: Hispanic Rev., 1968-97; adv. editor Eighteenth Century Studies, 1983—, Cuadernos para Investigación de la Literatura Hispánica, 1987—, Discurso Literario, 1987—, El Gnomo, 1992—, Dieciocho, 1994—, Siglo XIX, 1995—, Salina, 1999—; columnist ABC newspaper, Madrid, 1985—; contbr. articles to profl. jours. Served with AUS, 1953-55. Guggenheim fellow, 1962-63; Am. Philos. Soc. grantee, 1971, 76, 82; Am. Council Learned Socs. fellow, 1979-80; recipient Elio Antonio de Nebrija Internat. prize U. Salamanca, 2001. Mem. Am. Assn. Tchrs. Spanish and Portuguese, Am. Assn. Tchrs. French, Ctr. 18th Century Studies (Oviedo, Spain), Sociedad de Literatura Española del Siglo XIX, Hispanic Soc. Am. (corr. mem.), Phi Beta Kappa, Phi Gamma Delta, Sigma Delta Pi. Episcopalian. Home: 16 Flintshire Rd Malvern PA 19355-1108 Office: U Pa Dept Romance Langs Philadelphia PA 19104-6305 E-mail: rpsebold@earthlink.net.

SEBOROVSKI, CAROLE, artist; b. San Diego, June 16, 1960; d. Stanley and Eleanor Ononsko S. BFA, Calif. Coll. Arts and Crafts, 1982; MFA, Hunter Coll., 1987. Artist: solo exhibitions include: Damon Brandt Gallery, N.Y.C., 1986, Hunter Coll. Art Gallery, N.Y.C., 1986, Lorence-Monk Gallery, N.Y.C., 1988, 89, Galerie Karsten Greve, Paris, 1991, 94, Cologne, 1992, Milan, 1995, Angles Gallery, Santa Monica, Calif., 1991, 92, 93, 96, Betsy Senior Contemporary Prints, N.Y.C., 1993, John Weber Gallery, N.Y.C., 1993, 95, John Berggruen Gallery, San Francisco, 1994, Locks Gallery, Phila., 1997, Karsten Greve, Koln, 1997, Galerie Karsten Greve, Milan, Italy, 1997, 2001, John Weber Gallery, N.Y.C., 1998, Cheryl Haines Gallery , San Francisco, 2000, 2002, Mitchell-Innes and Nash Gallery, N.Y.C., Miller Block Gallery, Boston, 2001; group exhbns. at: Willard Gallery, N.Y.C., 1984, Nora Haime Gallery, N.Y.C, 1985, 86, 93, 95, Manhattan Arts Ctr., N.Y.C., 1985, Hillwood

Art Gallery L.I. Univ., Brookville, N.Y., 1985, Damon Brandt Gallery, 1985, 86 (2), 87, Mus. de Arte, La Tertuila, Columbia, 1986, Weatherspoon Gallery, Greensboro, N.C., 1986, Barbara Krakow Gallery, Boston, 1986, 88, 90 (travels to John C. Stoller & Co., Mpls.), Anne Plumb Gallery, N.Y.C., 1987, Am. Acad. and Inst. Arts and Letters, 1987, Bklyn. Mus., 1987, Lorence-Monk Gallery, 1987, 89 (3), 90, 91 (2), Carnegie Mellon U. Art Gallery, Pitts., 1988, Reynolds/ Minor Gallery, Richmond, Va., 1988, John Good Gallery, N.Y.C., 1988, 92, Pamela Auchincloss Gallery, N.Y.C., 1988, Dart Gallery, Chgo., 1988, Angles Gallery, 1989, Persons & Lindell Gallery, Helsinki, Finland, 1989, Anderson Gallery Va. Commonwealth U., Richmond, 1989, Baxter Gallery, Richmond, 1989, Hillwood Art Gallery, Brookville (travels through 1991 to Blum Helman Gallery, N.Y.C., Richard F. Brush Gallery, Canton, N.Y., Contemporary Mus. Art, Caracas, Venezuela), Cheryl Haines Gallery, San Francisco, 1989, 94, 96, Security Pacific Corp. Gallery, Santa Monica, 1990, Meml. Art Gallery U. Rochester, N.Y., 1990, Hood Mus. Art Dartmouth Coll., Hanover, N.H., 1990, San Francisco Mus. of Art, 1991, Pfizer, Inc. (Mus. Modern Art, N.Y. Collection), 1991, John Berggruen Gallery, 1991, travelling exhbn. to Anthony Ralph Gallery at Earl McGrath, L.A., Mars Gallery, Tokyo, Katonah Mus. Art, N.Y., Ind. U. Fine Arts Gallery, Kerr Gallery, Alberta Coll. of Art, Can., Huntsville Mus. Art, Ala., Worcester Art Mus., Mass., Lamont Gallery N.H., San Diego State U. Gallery, 1992, Barbara Mathes Gallery, N.Y.C., 1993, Transamerica Pyramid Lobby, San Francisco, 1993, travelling exhbn. to The Drawing Ctr., N.Y., Corcoran Gallery Art, Washington, Santa Monica Mus., L.A., The Forum, St. Louis, Am. Ctr., Paris, 1993, Addison Gallery, Andover, Mass., 1994, John Weber Gallery, 1994, 96, Huntington Gallery Mass. Coll. Art, Boston, 1995, Rice U. Art Gallery, Houston, 1995, The Altered Stages, N.Y., 1995, Brooke Alexander Gallery, N.Y.C., 1995, Thread Waxing Space, N.Y., 1996, Duchess County C.C., N.Y., 1996, Gallery 7, Hong Kong, 1996, Century Club, N.Y.C., 1996, Dutchess Coll., N.Y., 1997, Vassar Coll., Poughkeepsie, N.Y., 1997, Mus. Cantonale d'Arte, Lugano, Switzerland, 1997, Kunst-Mus., Ahlen, Germany, 1998, Kunstmus., Winterhur, Switzerland, 1998, Acad. der Kunste, Berlin, 1999, Mitchell-Innes and Nash, N.Y.C., Nohra Haime Gallery, N.Y.C., Margaret Thatcher Projects, N.Y.C., 1999, San Francisco Mus. Modern Art, Calif., 2000, Block Mus., Chgo., 2000, Contemporary Mus., Honolulu, 2000, Fogg Art Mus., 2000, Neuberger Mus. Art, Purchase, NY, 2000, Lyman Allyn Mus, Conn., 2000, Yale Art Galley, 2002, Nohra Haine Gallery, N.Y.C., 2002, others; represented in permanent collections including Whitney Mus. Art, N.Y., Paine Webber, N.Y., Weatherspoon Art Gallery, Greensboro, N.C., J. Walter Thompson, N.Y., Refco Collection, Chgo., Panza Collection, Italy, San Francisco Mus. Modern Art, Mus. Modern Art, N.Y., Mus. Cantonale d'Arte, Lugano, Switzerland, Met. Mus. Art, N.Y., Merril Lynch Inc., N.Y., MIT Visual Ctr., Hood Mus. Art, Hanover, N.H., Fogg Art Mus., Harvard U., Cambridge, Mass., Cleve. Ctr. Contemporary Art, Chase Manhattan Bank, N.Y., Carnegie Mus. Art, Pitts., Bklyn. Mus., Balt. Mus., Anderson Collection, Calif., Addison Gallery, Phillips Acad., Andover, Mass., Bklyn. Mus. Grantee Pollock-Krausner Found., 1986, NEA, 1991, Art Devel. Com., 1997; named Artist in Residence, Villa Monalvo, Saratoga, Calif., 1989, Djerassi Found., Calif., 1990; Agnes Bourne fellow in visual arts, 1990. Achievements include works in permanent collections of: Weatherspoon Art Gallery, Greensboro, N.C., Whitney Mus. of Art, N.Y.C., Refco Collection, Chgo., Met. Mus. of Art, MIT Visual Ctr., Fogg Art Mus., Harvard U., Cleve. Ctr. for Contemporary Art, Carnegie Mus. of Art, Pitts., Bklyn. Mus., Balt. Mus., Addison Gallery, Phillips Acad., Andover, Mass. Home: 225 W 12th St Apt 51 New York NY 10011-7764

SEBREN, LUCILLE GRIGGS, retired educator; b. Chesterfield, S.C., May 21, 1922; d. Manley Oscar and Clara Blanche (Rivers) Griggs; m. Herbert Lee Sebren, Dec. 19, 1943; children: Herbert Lee Jr., George Hall, Samuel Robert Franklin. BA, Flora Macdonald Coll., Red Springs, N.C., 1942; MEd, Coll. of William and Mary, 1966. Cert. tchr., Va., N.C., S.C. Tchr. Cheraw (S.C.) Elem. Sch., 1942-44; tchr. kindergarten Larchmont Meth. Ch., Norfolk, Va., 1951-53; tchr. Norfolk Acad., 1953-89, supr., cons., adminstr. primary dept., 1970-89, master tchr., cons. elem. grades, 1970-89, asst. to dir. of admissions, 1987—. Contbr. articles to profl. jours. Mem. Va. Symphony and Symphony Aux., Norfolk, 1946—, Norfolk Soc. Arts, 1970—, Chrysler Mus., Norfolk, 1965—, Va. Opera Assn., Norfolk, 1974—, Norfolk Forum, 1980—, U.S. Capitol Hist. Assn., 1983—, Smithsonian Instn., Met. Opera Guild, Nat. Trust Historic Preservation, Hermitage Mus. Found. Aux.; pres. Philanthropic Ednl. Orgn., 1993-96, v.p., 2001—; bicentennial mem. Libr. Congress. Recipient Disting. Svc. award Norfolk Acad., 1991. Mem. AAUW (sec. exec. bd. 1974-76), Joie de Vivre (treas. 1994—), Old Dominion U. Faculty Wives Club (pres. 1958-60), Town-N-Gown (bd. dirs. 1992—, chaplain 1993-96, v.p. 1995-96, pres.-elect 1996-97, pres. 1997—), Old Dominion U. Town-N-Gown (pres.-elect 1998-99, pres. 1999—), bd. dirs.Old Dominion U. Town-N-Gown, 1992—, parliamentarian, 2001—, Nat. Cathedral Assn., Nat. Trust for Historic Preservation, Nat. M.I. Hummel Club, Hon. Order Ky. Cols., Internat. Assn. Torch Clubs, Inc., Alpha Delta Kappa Internat. (pres., past state, provincial, nat. pres. 1995—, pres. Va. 1978-80, S.E. region 1981-83, internat. grand chaplain 1983-85, internat. grand pres.-elect 1985-87, internat. grand pres. 1987-89, internat. exec. bd. 1985-91, pres.-elect internat. past state pres. 1993-95, pres. 1995—), Kappa Delta Pi. Republican. Baptist. Avocations: reading, travel, collecting antique glassware and Hummels, music. Office: Norfolk Acad 1585 Wesleyan Dr Norfolk VA 23502-5591

SEBRING, MARJORIE MARIE ALLISON, former home furnishings company executive; b. Burnsville, N.C., 1926; d. James William and Mary Will (Ramsey) Allison Shockey; 1 child, Patricia Louise Banner Krohn. Student, Mars Hill Coll., 1943, Home Decorators Sch. Design, N.Y.C., 1948, Wayne State U., 1953; cert. home furnishings rep., U. Va., 1982. Dir. decorating divsn. Robinson Furniture, Detroit, 1949-57; head buyer Tyner Hi-Way House, Ypsilanti, Mich., 1957-63, Town and Country, Dearborn, 1963-66; instr. Nat. Carpet Inst., 1963-71; owner Adams House, Inc., Plymouth, Mich., 1966-72; exec. v.p. mktg. and sales, regional sales and mktg. mgr. Triangle Industries, L.A., 1972-89; co-owner Markham-Sebring, Inc., St. Petersburg, Fla., 1983-89. Dir. contract divsn. Kane Furniture, 1984-85; co-owner Accessories, Etc., 1985-89; chmn. bd. Heritage Lakes, U.S. Home; co-owner, dir. Talamanca Pipeline Ltd., Costa Rica. Vol. coord. Pasco County Clk. Ct., Suncoast Theatre; adv. bd. Webster Coll.; charter mem. Presdl. Task Force; pres. Presbyn. Ch. Seven Springs; bd. dirs. Fla. Health and Human Svc., Fla. Presbyn. Homes, Gills Trinity YMCA, 2001—; chmn. bd. dirs. Two Westminster Condominium Assn.; mem. Tampa Bay Presbytery Rev. and Evaluation; bd. dirs. James P. Gills Suncoast YMCA, 2001—; citizens adv. com. Pasco County, 2001-. Recipient recognition for work with youth and aged; named to Fla. Finest List, Gov. of Fla., 1994. Mem. Internat. Home Furnishings Assn., Fla. Home Furnishings Rep. Assn. (officer), Am. Security Coun. (coun.), Williamsburg Found., USCG Aux., Nat. Audubon Soc., Internat. Platform Assn., Pasco County Planning Com., Bd. Dir., Heritage Lake Assn. Republican. Achievements include contbr. creative display to Better Homes & Gardens, 1957-64. Home: 4902 Cathedral Ct New Port Richey FL 34655-1486 Fax: 727 375-7702. E-mail: sebring5@earthlink.net.

SEBRING, PENNY BENDER, education educator, researcher; b. Nevada City, Calif., Oct. 22, 1942; d. Carl S. and Eunice Goforth Bender; m. Robert Sebring, 1964 (div. 1982); 1 child Lisa Sebring Carreras ; m. Charles A. Lewis, June 9, 1984; children: Peter C. Lewis, Kathryn C. Lewis. BA, Grinnell Coll., Iowa, 1964; MEd, Pa. State U., 1978; PhD, Northwestern U., Evanston, Ill., 1984. Vol. Peace Corps, Venezuela, 1964—66, instr., 1966; social studies tchr. Bellefonte Area H.S., Pa., 1967—71; Upward Bound tchr. Pa. State U., State College, 1969, rsch. asst. Coll. of Edn., 1976—77, staff specialist, 1979—80; survey dir. NORC U. Chgo., 1984—87, sr. survey dir., 1987—90, sr. rsch. assoc., 1990—. Author: School Leadership and the Bottom Line, 2000; co-author: School-Based Management in the United States, 1999, Charting Chicago School Reform, 1998. Vice chmn. bd. trustees Grinnell Coll., 1993—, McGaw YMCA, Evanston, Ill., 1993—; vis. com. divsn. social scis. U. Chgo., 2001—. Fellow Univ. fellow, Northwestern U., 1981—83. Mem.: Am. Evaluation Assn., Am. Ednl. Rsch. Assn., Phi Delta Kappa (Rsch. award 1985). Office: Consortium on Chicago Sch Rsch 1313 E 60th St Chicago IL 60637

SEBRIS, ROBERT, JR. lawyer; b. N.Y.C., May 20, 1950; s. Robert and Ruth (Kagis) S.; m. S. Lawson Hollweg, Sept. 8, 1973; children: Jared Matthew, Bryan Taylor. BS in Indsl. Labor Rels., Cornell U., 1972; JD, George Washington U., 1978. Bar: D.C. 1978, Wash. 1980. Labor rels. specialist Onondaya County Office labor rels., Syracuse, N.Y., 1973-74, U.S. Dept. Labor, Washington, 1972-75; labor rels. mgr. U.S. Treasury Dept., 1975-78; employee rels. mgr., 1978-80; assoc. Davis, Wright, Todd, Riese & Jones, Seattle, 1980-84; ptnr. Davis, Wright, Tremain, Bellevue, Wash., 1985-92, Sebris Busto, P.S., Bellvue, 1992—. Expert witness T.E.A.M. Act Amendments NLRA U.S. Senate hearing, 1997. Co-Author: Employer's Guide to Strike Planning, 1985; contbr. articles to profl. jours. Mem. Bellevue C.C. Found., 1988-95, pres., 1995-96; chair employment law cert. program U. Wash. Law Sch., 1996-97. Mem. ABA (health law forum, labor and employment law sect., com. on employee rights), Wash. Bar Assn., D.C. Bar Assn., Seattle/King County Bar Assn. (chmn. labor law sect. 1991-92), Pacific Coast Labor Law Conf. (planning com. 1980-93, chmn. 1991-92), Am. Health Lawyers Assn., Soc. Human Resource Mgmt. Avocations: golf, soccer, coaching youth sports. Home: 16301 Mink Rd NE Woodinville WA 98072-9463 Office: Sebris Busto PS Ste 325 14205 SE 36th St Bellevue WA 98006 E-mail: rsebris@sebrisbusto.com.

SECHREST, LARRY J. economist, educator; b. Detroit, Oct. 12, 1946; s. Howard J. and Frances C. Sechrest; m. Donna R., May 6, 1971; children: J. Kyle, R. Tara. BA in History, U. Tex., Arlington, 1968, MA in Econs., 1985, PhD in Econs., 1990. Instr. U. Tex., Arlington, 1985-90; prof. econs. Sul Ross State U., Alpine, Tex., 1990—. Adj. scholar Ludwig von Mises Ins., Auburn, Ala., 1996—; found. scholar Found. Advancement of Monetary Edn., 1996—; mem. editl. bd. Quar. Jour. Austrian Econs., 1996—; mem. bd. advisors Jour. Ayn Rand Studies, 1999—. Author: Free Banking, 1993; co-editor: Capital and Production, 2000; contbr. chpt. to book, articles to profl. jours.; co-editor (with Jorg Guido Hulsmann): Capital and Production, 2000. Fellow Inst. Humane Studies, Fairfax, Va., 1987-88; listed Guide to Pub. Policy Experts, Heritage Found., Washington, 2000. Mem. Nat. Assn. Scholars, Am. Statis. Assn., The Hist. Soc., Soc. Devel. Austrian Econs., Internat. Maritime Econ. History Assn., So. Econ. Assn., N.Y. Acad. Scis. Libertarian. Avocations: maritime history, yacht design, firearms, marine art, golf. Office: Sul Ross State U 400 N Harrison St Alpine TX 79832-8300 E-mail: larrys@sulross.edu.

SECHRIST, CHALMERS FRANKLIN, JR. electrical engineering educator; b. Glen Rock, Pa., Aug. 23, 1930; s. Chalmers F. and Lottie V. (Smith) S.; m. Lillian Beatrice Myers, June 29, 1957; children: Jonathan A., Jennifer N. BE in Elec. Engring., Johns Hopkins U., 1952; MS, Pa. State U., 1954, PhD in Elect. Engring., 1959. Sr. engr. Bendix Corp., summers 1952, 53, 54; instr. elec. engring. Pa. State U., 1954-55; staff engr. HRB-Singer, Inc., State College, Pa., 1959-65; from asst. prof. to prof. elec. engring. U. Ill., Urbana, 1965-96, assoc. head instructional programs dept. elec. and computer engring., 1984-86, asst. dean engring., 1986-96, prof. Emeritus, 1996—; program dir. divsn. undergrad. edn. NSF, Washington, 1992-96; adj. prof. engring. Fla. Gulf Coast U., 1998—. Acting sci. sec. Sci. Com. on Solar-Terrestrial Physics, 1981; chmn. publs. com. Middle Atmosphere Program, 1980-86, editor handbook, 1981-86; mem. adv. com. on tech. edn. Fla. Dept Edn., 2001-. Editor: Proc. Aeronomy Confs, 1965, 69, 72; contbr. articles to profl. jours. NSF grantee. Fellow: IEEE (edn. activities bd. 1990, 1992—93, 1997, 1998, 1999, tech. activities bd. 1991—92, chmn. com. on pre-coll. edn. Ednl. Activieites Bd. 1997—99, mem. oversight subcom. Virutal Mus. 2000—, mem. awards and recognition com. edn. activities bd. 2000—01, precoll. edn. coord. com. edn. activities bd. 2000—, Millennium medal 2000); mem.: Am. Soc. Engring. Edn., Am. Meteorol. Soc., Am. Geophys. Union, Edn. Soc. of IEEE (v.p. 1989—90, pres. 1991—92, Achievement award 1993). Home: 14315-C Harbour Links Ct Fort Myers FL 33908-7952 Home Fax: 239-454-3383. E-mail: csechrist@comcast.net.

SECK, MAMADOU MANSOUR, ambassador, career officer; b. Dakar, Senegal, July 3, 1935; children: Ndeye, Safi, Makura, Astou Dior, Sonia Penda. Attended, St. Cyr Milit. Acad., France, Salon Air Force Acad., French Air War Coll., Institut des Hautes Etudes de la Def. Nat. Commanding officer 1st Senegalese Air Force Squad, 1966; comdr. 1st Senegalese Air Force, 1972; dep. chief gen. staff, 1980-84; spl. chief of staff to Pres. of Republic of Senegal, chief of staff of Sene-Gambia Confedn., 1984; gen. chief of staff, gen. chief Confedn., 1988; chmn. Joint Chiefs of Staff of Senegal, 1988-93; amb. to U.S. Govt. of Republic of Senegal, 1993—; amb. to Mex., Argentina, Jamaica, Haiti, Trinidad and Tobago, Barbados, 1993—. Decorated Senegal, France, Gabon, Hollan, Luxembourg. Office: Embassy of Republic of Senegal 2112 Wyoming Ave NW Washington DC 20008-3926

SECKAR, JOEL ANDREAS, toxicologist, chemist; b. Phila., Feb. 2, 1946; s. Valentine Joseph and Elizabeth Arlene Seckar; m. Donna Joyce Pruden, June 22, 1968; children: Christina Seckar-Agnew, Janna Lynn. BA, Gettysburg Coll., 1968; PhD, U. Cin., 1973; MS, U. San Francisco, 1984. Diplomate Am. Bd. Toxicology. From sr. rsch. chemist to toxicologist Pennwalt Corp., King of Prussia, Pa., 1973—90; sr. project mgr. Roy F. Weston, West Chester, 1990-93; master toxicologist R.J. Reynolds Tobacco Co., Winston-Salem, NC, 1993—2002, prin. toxicologist, 2002—. Contbr. articles to profl. jours. Capt. U.S. Army, 1973. Mem. Soc. Toxicology, Am. Chem. Soc., Soc. Environ. Toxicology and Chemistry, Am. Coll. Toxicology. Presbyterian. Avocations: model railroading, photography. Home: 1720 Curraghmore Rd Clemmons NC 27012 Office: RJ Reynolds Tobacco Co PO Box 1487 Winston Salem NC 27102 Fax: 336-741-0815. E-mail: jseckar@triad.rr.com.

SECOLA, JOSEPH PAUL, lawyer; b. Hartford, Conn., May 18, 1959; s. Pasquale Anthony and Anna Maria; m. Mary Alice Ipavich, June 20, 1982; children: Peter, Sharon, Mary Joy, Timothy, Paul, Andrew. BA in History, Fairfield U., 1981; JD, Oral Robert U., 1984. Bar: Conn. 1984, N.Y. 1985, U.S. Dist. Ct. Conn. 1985, Va. 1986, U.S. Dist. Ct. (so. dist.) N.Y. 1988, U.S. Ct. Appeals (2d cir.) 1989, U.S. Supreme Ct. 1990, U.S. Dist. Ct. (we. dist.) N.Y. 1996. Pvt. practice, Brookfield, Conn., 1984—; judge of probate Dist. of Brookfield, 2001—. Mem. bd. edn. City of Milford, Conn., 1989-90, Greater Danbury (Conn.) Cath. Elem. Schs., 1992-96 Mem. Nat. Employment Lawyers Assn., Am. Trial Lawyers Assn., Conn. Trial Lawyers Assn., Conn. Bar Assn., Conn. Employment Lawyers Assn., Litchfield County Bar Assn., Greater Danbury Bar Assn. Republican. Roman Catholic. Avocations: sports, N.Y. Yankees. Office: Ste 500 67 Federal Rd Bldg A Brookfield CT 06804-2538 Fax: (203) 740-2355. E-mail: jpsecolalaw@aol.com.

SECOMANDI, NICOLA, research scientist; b. Pordenone, Italy, Jan. 17, 1969; came to U.S., 1993; s. Achille Secomandi and Mariangela Modolo; m. Carla Como, Jan. 5, 1996; 1 child, Matteo Nicholas. Laurea, U. Venice, Italy, 1992; MS, U. Houston, 1993, PhD, 1998. Assoc. scientist Pros Revenue Mgmt. (formerly Pros Strategic Solutions), Houston, 1998-99, scientist, 1999-2000, sr. scientist, 2000—; rsch. assoc. Cornell U., Ithaca, 2001; mgr. El Paso Merchant Energy, Houston, 2001—. Mem. Inst. for Ops. Rsch. and Mgmt. Scis. (pres. 2000—), Nat. Energy Svcs. Assn., U. Houston Alumni Assn., Beta Gamma Sigma. Avocations: golf, skiing, mathematics. Home: Unit 142 2222 Maroneal St Houston TX 77030-3238 Office: El Paso Merchant Energy 1001 Louisana St Houston TX 77002 E-mail: nsecomandi@hotmail.com.

SECOR, DONALD TERRY, JR. geologist, educator; b. Oil City, Pa., Nov. 22, 1934; s. Donald Terry and Mary Elizabeth (LaRue) S.; m. Dorothy Eisenhart, June 15, 1959; children: Beth Ann, Jane Marie, Carol Lynn. BS, Cornell U., 1957, MS, 1959; PhD, Stanford U., 1963. Asst. prof. geology U. S.C., Columbia, 1962-66, assoc. prof., 1966-79, prof., 1979-99, chmn. dept., 1966-68, 77-81, disting. prof. emeritus, 1999—. Am. Assn. Petroleum Geologists Disting. lectr., 1978-79; recipient U. S.C. Ednl. Found. award, 1991; NSF grantee, 1966-70, 76-94, U.S. Geol. Survey grantee, 1979-82. Fellow Geol. Soc. Am.; mem. Am. Geophys. Union, AAAS E-mial. Office: U SC Dept Geol Scis Columbia SC 29208-0001 E-mail: secor@geol.sc.edu.

SECOR, HAROLD EDWIN, retired obstetrician/gynecologist; b. Towanda, Pa., Mar. 21, 1925; Student, The Citadel, 1943-44, U. Mo., 1945; MD, Baylor U., 1949. Diplomate Am. Bd. Ob-Gyn. Intern Robert Packer Hosp., Sayre, Pa., 1949-50; resident Meth. Hosp., Houston, 1952-54; pvt. practice Bellaire, Tex., 1954-61; fellow Precept-Gulf Coast Med. Ctr., Wharton, 1961-63; obstetrician, gynecologist Rugley and Blasiogome Clin., 1963-89, ret., 1989. Mem. hon. staff Gulf Coast Med. Ctr., Wharton, 1994. Capt. Med. Svc. Corps. U.S. Army, 1950-52, Korea. Mem. ACOG, Tex. Assn. Ob-Gyns.

SECOR, WILLIAM ROBERT, writer; b. Indpls., Nov. 8, 1937; m. Mary Lou Mohler, Apr. 5, 1980; children: Patricia A., Michael P. BA in History, Ind. U., 1978, MS in Edn., 1979. Tchr. Denver Pub. Schs. Author: Who Knows?, 1999. Home: 15241 W Domingo Ln Sun City West AZ 85375-2946 also: 2677 S Xanadu Way Unit A Aurora CO 80014-2223 E-mail: secor70s@aol.com.

SECORD, LLOYD DOUGLAS, healthcare administrator; b. Lachine, Que., Can., Nov. 22, 1946; s. George William and Gladys Mable (Wilson) S.; m. Louise Margaret Morrison, Dec. 21, 1966; children: Steven Lloyd, Gordon Arthur, Mary Elizabeth. BS in Chemistry, U. New Brunswick, 1968; M of Adminstrn., U. Toronto, Ont., Can., 1970. Cert. accreditation surveyor Can. Coun. on Health Facilities, 1990-92. Adminstrv. resident Toronto East Gen. and Orthopaedic Hosp., 1969-70; adminstrv. asst. Moncton Hosp., summer 1968, asst. adminstr., 1970-75; exec. dir. Kiwanis Nursing Home Inc., 1975—; facility adminstr. Region 2 Hosp. Corp., Sussex, N.B., Can., 1992-98; sec. Sussex Health Ctr. Svcs. Inc., Bryant Dr. Holdings Inc., 1975—, CEO, adminstr. hosp., 1975-98; region dir. capital projects Atlantic Health Scis. Corp., 1998—. Chmn. adv. com. Min. Health; mem. Fundy Linen Svcs. Inc., 1976-92; mem. regional hosp. planning com. Health Region II, 1974-76; commr. of oaths, 1975—. Bd. dirs. Atlantic Bapt. Sr. Citizen's Home Inc., 1973-79, original bldg. com., 1971-74, rec. sec., 1971-74, chmn. bldg. com.; founding chmn. Comty. Based Svcs. Coord. Com. for Sussex, 1981; founding pres. Sussex Sr. Housing Inc., 1981, 82; established Sussex Health Ctr. Svcs. Inc., 1991, Bryant Dr. Holdings Inc., 1992-93; founding sec. Kings County Wellness Ctr., 1997; bd. trustees, bd. deacons Sussex United Bapt. Ch.; dir. Sussex br. Order of St. John, 1976-78, 90-92; trombonist Sussex Comty. Adult Band, 1989—; sec. Kings County Wellness Ctr., 1997—. Lord Beaverbrook scholar, Leonard Found. scholar. Fellow Can. Coll. Health Svc. Execs., Soc. Mgmt. Accountants Can., Am. Coll. Health Care Execs. (affiliate, regent for Atlantic provinces and Quebec 1992-2001, membership oral examiner 1984, 85, 86, 88, 93, 95, 96, mem. ethics com. 1985-88), Can. Coll. Health Svc. Execs. (various provincial coms., nat. bd. dirs. 1997-2000), Soc. Mgmt. Accts. Can. (cert., mem. provincial coun. 1977-88, provincial sec.-treas. 1982, provincial chmn. 1987, nat. edn. svcs. com. 1985, 86, nat. bd. dirs. 1986, 87, nat. strategic planning com. 1986); mem. New Brunswick Hosp. Assn. (numerous provincial coms.), New Brunswick Assn. Nursing Homes (numerous provincial coms.), Northeastern Can./Am. Health Coun. (Can. co-chmn. 1991-94, co-chair internat. mini conf. on rural health care New London, N.H. 1988, chair bi-ann. conf. Montreal 1991), Provincial Ambulance Operators Assn. (exec. com. 1990-96), Sussex and Dist. C. of C. (pres. 1985), Kiwanis Club Sussex Inc. (pres. 1985, 99). Avocations: band, golf, gardening, painting, education. Office: Sussex Health Ctr 75 Leonard Dr Sussex NB Canada E4E 2P7

SECREST, JAMES SEATON, SR. lawyer; b. Middletown, Ky., Dec. 9, 1930; s. Elmer S. and Linney (Witherbee)S.; m. Mary Sue Corum, Sept. 2, 1950; children: James Seaton, Lynne Suzanne. JD, U. Louisville, 1954. Bar: Ky. 1954. Ptnr. Goad & Secrest, Scottsville, Ky., 1955-62; solo practice, 1962-77; ptnr. Secrest & Secrest, 1977—. City judge pro tem Scottsville, 1955-58; judge Allen County, 1958-61; city atty. Scottsville, 1962-66; atty. Allen County, 1966-89, dep. judge-exec., 1990-99; bd. dirs. Barren River Area Devel. Dist., 1970, mem. regional bd. ethics; mem. adv. bd. dirs. Starbank, Scottsville, 1998; bd. dirs. Commonwealth Health Corp. Mem. Scottsville C. of C. (pres. 1962), Ky. County Attorneys Assn. (pres. 1973), Ky. Assn. Counties (bd. dirs. 1985-86), ABA, Ky. Bar Assn. Clubs: Rotary (pres. 1960). Republican. Methodist. Home: 714 Secrest Ln Scottsville KY 42164 Office: Secrest & Secrest PO Box 35 210 W Main St Scottsville KY 42164-1123 E-mail: jsecrest@nctc.com.

SECULAR, SIDNEY, writer, weather forecaster, actor, model, voiceover specialist, fundraiser, small business and mailorder marketing consultant; b. N.Y.C., Dec. 20, 1940; s. Benjamin and Mollie (Stern) Secular; m. Mildred Vance Vance, Nov. 1, 1969. BA, SUNY, Stony Brook, 1962. Cert. HS tchr. Contract asst. U.S. Army, Bklyn., 1962-66; contract specialist USN, Washington, 1966-67, FDA, Washington, 1967-68; contracting officer Dept. Justice, 1968-81; conf./expo organizer, counselor to small bus. SBA, 1986-97; govt. mktg. cons. to small bus. Silver Spring, Md., 1997—. Mem. consumer bd. Giant Food corp., WSSC Water Utility; freelance writer, Silver Spring, Md., 1985—; weather broadcaster Washington Weatherline, Bethesda, Md., 1982—91, Comprehensive Weather Svcs., 1982—85, Verizon Comm., 1991—; total quality mgmt. cons., 1995—. Activist Citizens to Preserve Old Silver Spring, 1981—, East Sliver Spring Citizens Assn., 1981—; chief election judge Montgomery County, 2000—. With U.S. Army, 1963—69. Recipient Performance and Suggestion awards, U.S. DEA and SBA. Mem.: ASPA, Area Small and Disadvantaged Bus. Coun., Am. Meteorol. Soc., Nat. Contract Mgmt. Assn., Ctr. Hiking Club (trails dir. 1975), Masons. Avocations: investments, immigration reform, entreprenuel activities, American history, environmental improvement. Home: 740 Silver Spring Ave Silver Spring MD 20910-4661 Office Fax: 301-588-7668. E-mail: sidsecular1@aol.com.

SECUNDA, EUGENE, marketing professional, educator; b. Bklyn., June 15, 1934; s. Sholom and Betty (Almer) Secunda; m. Shirley Carol Frummer, Sept. 23, 1961; children: Ruthanne, Andrew. Comml. degree, N.Y. Inst. Photography, 1955; BS, NYU Sch. Bus., 1956; MS, Boston U., 1962; PhD, NYU, 1988. News editor Sta.-WBMS, Boston, 1956-57; reporter New London (Conn.) Daily Day, 1958-59; publicist various Broadway shows, 1959-62; sr. publicist 20th Century Fox Film Corp., N.Y.C., 1962-65; with J. Walter Thompson Co., 1965-73, dir. corp. and pub. affairs, 1974-78, sr. v.p., dir. entertainment group, 1974-80, dir. entertainment div., 1978-80; sr. v.p., dir. comm. svcs. N.W. Ayer Internat., 1980-82; pres. Barnum/Secunda Assocs., 1982-85, Secunda Mktg. Comm., N.Y.C., 1985—. Adj. prof. advt. NYU, N.Y.C., 1972—85, prof. mktg. and advt. Grad. Sch. Bus., 1985—88, prof. mktg., 1993—96, adj. prof. mktg. and media studies, 1996—; prof. mktg. and advt. Baruch Coll. CUNY, 1988—93; prof. mktg. Adelphi U., Garden City, NY, 1993—96; guest lectr. FBI Acad., Columbia U., UCLA. Contbr. articles to profl. jours. Mem. Greenwicy Village Trust. With USAR, 1957—63. Mem.: NATAS, Am. Mktg. Assn., Mcpl. Arts Soc., Am. Acad. Advt., Internat. Advt. Assn., Internat. Comm. Assn. Address: 30 5th Ave New York NY 10011-8859

SECUNDA, JOHN, writer; Author: (short stories) Coming Home, 1999. Sect. chmn. Amnesty Internat., Miami, Fla., 1988—91. Home: 9392 SW 77 Ave Miami FL 33156

SEDACCA, ANGELO ANTHONY, police officer, educator, notary; b. Bronx, N.Y., Mar. 14, 1971; s. Joseph and Marie Ann (Rella) S; m. Diane Bockino (div.); children: Christopher Michael, Nicholas Anthony. BA in French Studies, BA in Italian Studies, Fordham U., 1993; MA in French Lang. and Civilization, NYU, 1995; postgrad. Inst. Religious Studies, St. Joseph's Sem. Professed mem. Secular Franciscan Order; notary pub., N.Y., 1996—. Asst. Tae Kwon Do instr. U.S.A. Martial Arts Ctr., 1991-94; vol. translator Franciscans Internat., N.Y.C, 1995—; tchr. theology and Italian, Salesian H.S., New Rochelle, N.Y., 1995-96; fin. officer premium financing A.I. Credit Corp., N.Y.C., 1996-97; bartender Pelham Country Club, New Rochelle, N.Y., 1997-98; police officer NYPD, 1998—, 40th Precinct, 1999—. Vol. translator Ops. Unit, 1999—; cert. expert Marijuana/Hashish Field Testing, 2000—, cert. RADAR Enforcement, 2001—; adj. prof. French, Fordham U., 2001—; investigator Internat Affairs Bus., 2002—. Eucharistic min. and lector, 1990—. Recipient Internat. Sash of Academia, Internat. Cultural Diploma of Honor, Man of Yr. medals, 1998-99. Mem. Cath. League, KC (4th degree), N.Y./N.J Bartenders' Assn., Nat. Notary Assn., Fraternal Order Police, Internat. Police Assn., London Diplomatic Acad. (founder counsellor 2000), Knights of Pythias, Order of Malta Aux., Noble Order Internat. Ambassadors, Fordham Club, Alpha Mu Gamma, Gamma Kappa Alpha. Roman Catholic. Avocations: martial arts, philosophy, civil and canon law, country music, theater. Home: 2066 Yates Ave Bronx NY 10461-1709

SEDDON, JOHANNA MARGARET, ophthalmologist, epidemiologist; b. Pitts. BS, U. Pitts., 1970, MD, 1974; MS in Epidemiology, Harvard U., 1976. Intern Framingham (Mass.) Union Hosp., 1974-75; resident Tufts New Eng. Med. Ctr., Boston, 1976-80; fellow ophthalmic pathology Mass. Eye and Ear Infirmary, 1980-81, clin. fellow vitreoretinal Retina Svc., 1981-82; instr. clin. ophthalmology Harvard Med. Sch., 1982-84, asst. prof., asst. surgeon ophthalmolgy, 1984, assoc. prof., 1989—; assoc. surgeon, dir. ultrasound svc. Mass. Eye and Ear Infirmary, 1989—, orgn. epidemiology rsch. unit, 1984-85, dir. epidemiology unit, 1985—, surgeon in ophthalmology, 1992—; assoc. prof. faculty dept. epidemiology Harvard Sch. Pub. Health, 1992—. Mem. com. vision Commn. Behavioral and Social Scis. and Edn., NRC, NAS, Washington, 1984; mem. divsn. rsch. grants NIH, 1987-89, 94—; mem. sci. adv. bd. Found for Fighting Blindness, 1994—, Macular Degeneration Internat., 1994—. Author books and articles in field, especially in field of ocular tumors and macular degeneration; mem. editl. staff ophthalmic jours. Recipient NIH Nat. Svc. Rsch. awards, 1975, 80-81, Lewis R. Wasserman merit award Rsch. to Prevent Blindness for contbns. to ophthalmic rsch., 1996; grantee, prin. investigator Nat. Eye Inst., 1984—, Nat. Cancer Inst., 1986; med. sch. scholar, 1970-74, Henry H. Clark Med. Edn. Found. scholar, 1973. Mem. AMA, APHA, Am. Acad. Ophthalmology (Honor award 1990), Am. Med. Women's Assn., Assn. Rsch. in Vision and Ophthalmology (elected, chair epidemiology sect. 1990, trustee clin. vision epidemiology sect. 1992-97. v.p. 1996-97), Soc. Epidemiologic Rsch., New Eng. Ophthal. Soc., Am. Coll. Epidemiology, Retina Soc., Macula Soc., Mass. Soc. Eye Physicians and Surgeons (v.p. 2000-2002). Home: 4 Louisburg Sq Boston MA 02108-1203 E-mail: jseddon@earthlink.net.

SEDDON, PRISCILLA TINGEY, painter; b. Boston, Apr. 1, 1938; d. Richard Hume and Mildred Gurina (Lundgren) Tingey; m. James Alexander Seddon, Jr., Nov. 28, 1959; children: Amy, Sarah, Carroll, Alice. BFA, Tufts U., 1989; Cert., Sch. of the Mus. of Fine Arts, Boston, 1990, Postgrad. 5th Yr., 1991. Associated with Imagining Angels: World AIDS Day Show, Howard Yezersky Gallery, Boston, 1995, others. Exhbns. include: U. Bridgeport, Conn., 1997, Gallery 84, N.Y.C., 1996, Erector Square Gallery, New Haven, Conn., 1996, Harvard U., Cambridge, Mass., 1996, ArtsWorcester Gallery, Worcester, Mass., 1995, Wellesley Coll., Mass., 1994, Grove Street Gallery, Worcester, 1993, Carvajal Sculpture Gallery, Boston, 1992; works include metal work, paintings and sculptures. Grantee MIT Coun. for Arts, Cambridge, 1988, Firstnight, Inc., Boston, 1991, Hingham Edn. Found., Mass., 1993. Mem. Womens Caucus for Art, Visual AIDS. Avocation: watercolour.

SEDEI RODDEN, PAMELA JEAN, therapist; b. Johnstown, Pa., Jan. 31, 1956; d. Joseph and Betty Ruth (Watkins) Sedei; m. William Eugene Rodden, Dec. 4, 1982; 1 child Gretchen Jean Rodden. BA, Southwestern Coll., Winfield, Kans., 1977; MS, Pittsburg (Kans.) State U., 1979; PhD, Western Colo. U., 1983. Lic. profl. counselor Colo., diplomate in psychotherapy, cert. cognitive behavior therapist, nat. cert. counselor, domestic violence counselor, criminal justice specialist. Staff psychologist Autumn Manors Inc., Florence, Kans., 1982-83; clin. psychologist Richmond (Tex.) State Hosp., 1984-86; unit psychologist Wheat Ridge (Colo.) Regional Ctr., 1986-89, acting unit dir., 1989; dir. behavioral svcs. Colo. State Divsn. Devel. Disabilities, Denver, 1989-97; dir. Forensic Mental Health Svcs., Boulder, 1997—2001, Pamela JS Rodden & Assocs., Fort Collins, 2001—. Dir. Rodden Consultants, Longmont, Colo., 1986—90, Rodden Assocs., 2001—02. Co-author: A Model For Interdisciplinary On Site Evaluation of People Who Have Dual Diagnosis, 1991. Fellow: Am. Coll. Forensic Examiners; mem.: ACA, Assn. Treatment of Sexual Abusers (clin. mem.), Nat. Assn. Dual Diagnosis (bd. dirs., pres. Columbine chpt.). Republican. Roman Catholic. also: 315 W Oak St Ste 204 Fort Collins CO 80521-2724 E-mail: pjsrodden@aol.com.

SEDELMAIER, J. J. filmmaker; b. Chgo., Mar. 11, 1956; s. John Josef and Marie S.; m. Patrice Estella Masters, Nov. 4, 1981. Student, Millikin U., 1974-75; BS in Art, U. Wis., 1979. Asst. animator Perpetual Motion Pictures, N.Y.C., 1981-82; asst. animator, animator Buzzco Prodns., 1982-84, The Ink Tank Corp., N.Y.C., 1984-85, producer, 1985-86, exec. producer, 1986-88, assoc. dir., dir., exec. producer, rep., 1989-91; pres., producer, dir. J. J. Sedelmaier Prodns., White Plains, N.Y., 1991—. Launched Beavis and Butthead for MTV-(Art Dirs. Club gold medal, BDA awards, Comm. awards, Hatch awards; subject of retrospectives: Ottawa Animation Festival, 1997, Cinematique Quebecoise, 1997; acclaimed series of cartoons for "Saturday Night Live", animated peacocks for NBC, Captain Linger series for Cartoon Network; co-creator Ambiguously Gay Duo, X-Presidents, Fun with Real Audio; prodr. (3 episodes) Schoolhouse Rock; prodr., dir. Harvey Birdman Attorney@Law; vis. artist Sch. Visual Arts. Prodr., dir. Saturday TV Funhouse, Captain Linger, Harvey Birdman-Attorney at Law. Recipient Annecy Film Festival, France, N.Y. Festivals, Annie award, Mobius award, medal Multiple N.Y. Festivals, Multiple Worldfest. Mem. Am. Inst. Graphic Artists, Assn. Internat. Film Animation, Art Dirs. Club (2 Gold medals), Shore Line Interurban Hist. Soc., Chgo. Transit Posters. Avocations: collecting illustrations, animation art, animation film cons. Office: 199 Main St White Plains NY 10601-3200 E-mail: sedelmaier@aol.com.

SEDELMAIER, JOHN JOSEF, filmmaker; b. Orrville, Ohio, May 31, 1933; s. Josef Heinrich and Anne Isabel (Baughman) S.; m. Barbara Jean Frank, June 6, 1965; children: John Josef, Nancy Rachel, Adam Frederich. BFA, Art Inst. Chgo. at U. Chgo., 1955. Dir. art Young and Rubicam, Chgo., 1955-61; dir. art, assoc. creative dir. Clinton E. Frank, 1961-64; dir. art, producer J. Walter Thompson, 1964-67; pres. Sedelmaier Film Prodns., 1967—. Spkr. British Design & Art Direction Pres. Lectr. SEries, London, 1998. Retrospective exhibits Mus. Broadcast Communications, Chgo., 1988, Mus. Broadcasting, L.A., 1991, Mus. TV and Radio, N.Y.C., 1992. Recipient Golden Ducat award for short film MROFNOC Mannheim Film Festival, 1968, Golden Gate award for short film Because That's Why, San Francisco Film Festival, 1969, 82 Clio awards, 1968-92, numerous Gold, Silver and Bronze Lion awards Cannes Film Festival, 1972-90, Gold Hugo award Chgo. Film Festival, 1976, 91, 2d Ann. IDC Creative award, Chgo., 1980, Internat. Broadcasting award for world's best TV comml., 1980, 86, Clio award for dir. of yr., 1981, London Internat. Advt. awards, 1986-88, numerous awards Internat. Festival of N.Y., 1984-93, Ann. Achievement award Assn. Ind. Comml. Producers, 1988; named Advt. Person of Yr., Chgo. Advt. Club, 1984, Jewish Communicator of Yr., 1985; named one of 50 Pioneers & Visionaries Who Made TV America's Medium, Advt. Age Mag., 1995; profiled in Communication Arts mag., Mar. 1976, Print mag., Jan. 1982, Fortune mag., June 1983, Newsweek mag., Nov. 1986, numerous others; featured on 60 Minutes, 48 Hours; subject of cover story Esquire mag., Aug. 1983; included in Arts & Entertainment's Top 10 Greatest Commls. of All Time, 1999; inducted The Art Dirs. Hall Fame, 2000. Office: Sedelmaier Film Prodns Inc 858 W Armitage Ave # 267 Chicago IL 60614-4329

SEDEÑO, EUGENE RAYMOND, electronics engineer, consultant; b. Honolulu, Aug. 31, 1952; s. Josephine Marie Sedeño Rosa; m. Theresa Ann Contreras, Dec. 28, 1980; children: Roxanne Guadelupe, Raymond Contreras. ASET, Heald Engring. Coll., 1974; BSEE, Coll. Allied Sci., 1980; MBA, Calif. Coast U., 2002. Field svc. engr. Bausch & Lomb, San Leandro, Calif., 1974—81; project mgr. Tylan Corp., Carson, 1981—85; field svc. supr. Sci. Atlanta, Santa Fe Springs, 1985—86; facilities and systems engr. Refractory Composities, Inc., Whittier, 1986—90, cons., 1985—91; supr. test and integration Thermco Systems, Orange, 1989—90; field engring. So. Calif. Edison, 1990—. With U.S. Army, 1970—76. Mem. Am. Mgmt. Assn., Mensa. Democrat. Roman Catholic. Avocations: kenpo karate, kobudo, kajukenbo, photography, collecting antique books. Home: 16137 Minnetonka St Victorville CA 92392-9146 Office: So Calif Edison 12353 Hesperia Rd Victorville CA 92392-4797 Fax: (760) 951-3115. E-mail: Eugene.Sedeno@sce.com.

SEDER, JEFFREY A. entrepreneur; b. Phila., Sept. 1, 1948; m. Nina L.S. Burnaford, Aug. 29, 1998; 1 child, Meriwether Jessica. AB magna cum laude, Harvard U., 1970, JD, MBA, 1976. Bar: Pa. 1976. CEO EOB, Inc., Chester County, Pa., 1977—99, Craftex Mills, Inc., Blue Bell, 1984-99, Boston Stores, L.A., 1991-93; exec. prodr. feature films of Big Picture Alliance, Phila., 1994—. Contbr. articles to profl. jours. Bd. dirs. Buck and Doe Trust, Unionville, Pa., 1984—. John Harvard scholar Harvard U., 1968, 69, 72. Mem. Phila. Bar Assn., Phi Beta Kappa. Avocations: dancing, motorcycle roadracing. Home: Houyhnhnm Farm 1055 Doe Run Rd Coatesville PA 19320 Office: EQB Inc 501 Hicks Rd West Grove PA 19390

SEDERBAUM, ARTHUR DAVID, lawyer; b. N.Y.C., Sept. 14, 1944; s. William and Harriet (Warschauer) Sederbaum; m. Francine Haba, Dec. 30, 1967 (div. Aug. 1982); children: Rebecca, David; m. Phyllis Padow, Jan. 18, 1988 (div. Aug. 2002); 1 child Elizabeth. AB cum laude, Columbia U., 1965, JD, 1968; LLM, NYU, 1972. BAr: N.Y. 1968, Fla. 1980, U.S. Dist. Ct. (so. and ea. dists.) N.Y. 1972. Assoc. Zissu Nelper & Martin, N.Y.C., 1968-70, Berlack, Israels & Liberman, N.Y.C., 1970-72, Rubin Baum Levin Constant & Friedman, N.Y.C., 1972-76; ptnr. Certilman, Haft, Balin, Buckley, Kremer & Hyman, 1976-88, Olshan, Grundman, Frome, Rosenzweig & Orens, N.Y.C., 1988-92, Patterson, Belknap, Webb & Tyler, L.L.P., N.Y.C., 1992—. Mem. adv. bd. Bur. Nat. Affairs Estates, Gifts and Trusts Jour.; mem. adv. bd. NYU Inst. Fed. Taxation, CCH Fin. and Estate Planning. Author: Setting Up and Executing Trusts, 1988; contbr. articles to Tax Mgmt. Estates, Gifts and Trusts Jour. Recipient J.K. Lasser Tax prize NYU Inst. Fed. Taxation, 1968. Fellow Am. Coll. Trusts and Estates Coun.; mem. ABA, N.Y. State Bar Assn. (vice chmn. com. on estate planning trustes and estates law sect.), Assn. Bar City N.Y. (com. surrogates cts.), Practicing Law Inst. (chmn. income taxatin of estates and trusts program). Office: Patterson Belknap Webb & Tyler LLP Ste 1405 1133 Avenue Of The Americas New York NY 10036-6710 Home: 91 High St Armonk NY 10504-1226 E-mail: adsederbaum@pbwt.com.

SEDERBAUM, WILLIAM, marketing executive; b. N.Y.C., Dec. 22, 1914; s. Harry and Sarah (Steingart) S.; m. Harriet Warschauer, Aug. 29, 1940; children: Arthur David, Caroline Joan. BS, NYU, 1936, MA, 1943, PhD. Assoc. Sigmund Pines Co., Pub. Accts., 1935-38; tchr. N.Y.C. pub. schs., 1935-39; restaurant propr., 1939-41; v.p. Schenley Distillers Co., N.Y.C., 1941-61; pres. Distbrs. New Eng., 1956-61, Melrose Distillers Co., 1959-60, Park & Tilford Distillers Co., 1959-61; exec. v.p. Meade & Co., 1961-62; v.p., mktg. dir. J. T. S. Brown Distillers Co., 1962-65; mktg. cons., 1965-67; exec. v.p., gen. mgr. Fulton Distbg. Co., 1967-77; asst. gen. mgr., dir. spl. projects Am. Distbrs. Fla., 1977—. Instr. acctg. Fla. Jr. Coll., 1984-89 Mem. Eleanor Roosevelt Cancer Com.; mem. U.S. Olympic Games Com.; exec. com. Fedn. Jewish Charities, March of Dimes; bd. dirs. Jacksonville Urban League, 1975-87; mem. Com. of 100; bus. cons. Jr. Achievement Project, Jacksonville; chmn. bd. trustees, pres. men's club Reform Cong. of Merrick, L.I. Recipient Arch award NYU; named Chevalier, Confrerie de la Chaine des Rotisseurs, Bailliage de Jacksonville, Fla. Mem. Jacksonville Wholesale Liquor Assn. (pres. 1970-76), Jacksonville Symphony Assn., Jacksonville Civic Music Assn., Jacksonville C. of C. (econ. edn. com., airline svc. com., hon. adm. of flag ship Am. Airlines), Kappa Phi Kappa. Clubs: River, Carriage (N.Y.C.); NYU, Playboy, Key. Home: 4305 Plaza Gate Ln Apt 201 Jacksonville FL 32217-4439 Office: Am Distbrs Fla 6867 Stuart Ln S Jacksonville FL 32254-3438 *Live life the way it should be-not the way it is.*

SEDGWICK, ALEXANDER, historian, educator; b. Boston, June 8, 1930; s. William Ellery and Sarah (Cabot) S.; m. Charlene Mary Maute, June 24, 1961; children— Catherine Maria, Alexander Cameron BA, Harvard U., 1952, PhD in History, 1963. Asst. prof. history Dartmouth Coll., 1962-63; assoc. prof. U. Va., Charlottesville, 1963-66, 1966-74, prof., 1974—, chmn. history dept., 1979-85, dean Coll. Arts and Scis., 1985-90, dean grad. studies, 1990-95, univ. prof., 1995-97, univ. prof. emeritus, 1997—. Mem. adv. com. in history Sr. Fulbright Awards Council for Internat. Exchange of Scholars. Author: The Ralliment in French Politics 1890-98, 1965, The Third French Republic, 1870-1914, 1968, Jansenism in Seventeenth Century France, Voices in the Wilderness, 1977, The Travails of Conscience. The Arnauld Family and the Ancien Regime, 1998; co-author: Church, State and Society Under the Bourbon Kings of France, 1982, For Want of a Horse, 1985, That Gentle Strength, 1980, Les Discour sur les Révolutions, 1991, History Today, 1991, Chroniques de Port-Royal, 1993, 95. Served with U.S. Army, 1952-54. Fulbright fellow, 1960-62; recipient Am. Coun. Learned Socs. grant-in-aid, 1967-68, Am. Philos. Soc. grant-in-aid, 1971. Mem. AAUP (nat. council 1976-79), Soc. French Hist. Studies (sec. 1979-83, pres. 1983-84), Am. Hist. Assn., Century Assn. Home: 1409 Rugby Rd Charlottesville VA 22903-1240 E-mail: as6d@virginia.edu.

SEDGWICK, LEVONNE, retired school program administrator; b. Seattle, Feb. 22, 1928; d. Albert Mark and Cecil Irene (Whitley) Nachtwey; m. Robert Ellwood Campbell (div. 1972); children: Caron Candace, Mindy Sue; m. Edward Thomas Sedgwick, Oct. 2, 1976. MS in Edn., Portland State U., 1970. Tchr. Our Lady of Assumption Elem. Sch., Atlanta, 1960-62, Our Lady of Providence Child Ctr., Portland, Oreg., 1963-68, Estacada (Oreg.) Union High Sch., 1969-70, Psychiat. Day Treatment Ctr./U. Oreg. Med. Sch./Portland State U., 1970-73; coord. Coleytown Developmental Ctr., Westport, Conn., 1973-77; dir. spl. programs Yamhill County Intermediate Edn. Dist., McMinnville, Oreg., 1977-78; dir. student svcs. Centennial Sch. Dist., Portland, 1978-93; pvt. practice as mediator, cons. and facilitator, contract spl. edn. investigations, 1993—. Pres. Oreg. Assn. Sch. Suprs., 1980-81, Adminstrv. Consultation and Tng. Bd. dirs. Am. Plaza Condominium Assn., Portland, 1990-96, 99—. Mem. Coun. Adminstrs. Spl. Edn., Coun. Exceptional Children (pres. Oreg. fedn. 1987-88, gov. 1989-92), Phi Delta Kappa. Avocations: travel, photography, cooking. Home: 2309 SW 1st Ave Apt 843 Portland OR 97201-5008

SEDLACEK, RICHARD LEO, retired surgeon; b. Iowa City, Apr. 13, 1924; MD, U. Iowa Coll. Medicine, 1948. Cert. surgery. Intern Letterman Gen. Hosp., San Francisco, 1948-49, resident in surgery, 1949-52; with St. Luke's Hosp. and Mercy Hosp., Cedar Rapids, Iowa, 1956-89; retired, 1989. Mem. AMA, Iowa State Med. Assn., LoCMS.

SEDLAK, JAMES WILLIAM, organization administrator; b. Tarrytown, N.Y., Nov. 17, 1943; s. Jacob Frank and Catherine Eva (Sedlak) S.; m. G. Michaeleen Bizub, June 17, 1967; children: Frank George, Jeanette Michele Sedlak Veltri, Terri Lynn Rose Sedlak Ferrara. BS in Physics, Manhattan Coll., 1967; MS in Indsl. Adminstrn., Union Coll., Schenectady, 1975. Customer engr. IBM, N.Y.C., 1963-67, semicondr. engr. East Fishkill, N.Y., 1967-80, sr. engr. Harrison, 1980-92; co-founder, nat. dir. Stop Planned Parenthood, La Grangeville, 1986-93; pres., writer, editor The Ryan Report, STOPP (Stop Planned Parenthood) Internat., 1994-98; v.p. pub. policy and edn. Am. Life League, Inc., Stafford, Va., 1998—. Former guest lectr. med. ethics Mt. St. Mary's Coll., Newburgh, N.Y.; guest lectr. ethics Vassar Coll., Poughkeepsie, N.Y., 1986-92. Author: Quarterly Dividends, 1975, Parent Power!!, 1990, Deadly Deception, 1996; co-author: Title X: The Six Billion Dollar Scam, 1997; contbr. to pro-life publs. Past pres. PTO; mem. bd. advisors Am. Life League, Inc.; former mem. faculty Apostles of Life Leadership Acad., Human Life Internat.; cons. to nat. and internat. pro-life groups; speaker numerous state-wide pro-life convs. and events, U.S., Can., Mex., Italy, Australia, No. Ireland, Eng. and New Zealand; workshop presenter nat. convs. Concerned Women for Am., Human Life Internat., Am. Life League; numerous appearances on radio and TV. Recipient Dutchess County Right to Life Pro-Lifer of Yr. award, 1984, Expectant Mother Care N.Y. Pro-Life Champion award, 1987, family life award Parent's Roundtable, 1987, Unsung Hero award Am. Life League, 1988, Disting. Svc. to Life award Grand Haven (Mich.) Pro-Lifers, 1993, also others. Mem. KC (3d degree). Roman Catholic. Office: Am Life League Inc PO Box 1350 Stafford VA 22555-1350 E-mail: jwsedlak@aol.com.

SEDLAK, RICHARD, naturopath, physical therapist; b. Berwyn, Ill., July 7, 1944; s. Richard and Alice H. (Tejcek) S. D in Naprapathy, Nat. Coll. Naprapathy, Chgo., 1966; postgrad., Lincoln Coll. Naturopathy, 1967; D in Chiropractic Medicine, Palmer Coll. Chiropractic Medicine, 1970; BS in Phys. Therapy, Wheatfield Coll., 1975, MS in Phys. Therapy, 1978, PhD, 1979; D in Nutrimedicine, John F. Kennedy Ctr. Acad., 1989; PhD in Psychology and Clin. Nutrition, Notre Dame De Lafayette U., 1989; postgrad., Mazinic Ctr., Berwyn, Ill., 1993-94. Diplomate Nat. Bd. Chiropractic and Phys. Therapy, Am. Bd. Phys. Therapy Examiners; cert. naprapath, myotherapist. Phys. therapist West Suburban Hosp., Oak Park, Ill., 1964-66; pvt. practice naturopath, phys. therapist Berwyn, 1970—; cons. phys. therapist Pershing Convalescent Home, Stickney, 1985-87. Assoc. dean Nat. Coll. Naprapathy, 1966-69, prof. endocrinology and diagnosis, 1968-71, prof. naprapathy, 1973; founder United Health Assn., 1976; counselor holistic health Bernadine U., 1989. Spl. police officer City of Cicero, 1968-90. Recipient Cert. of Merit, Am. Massage Therapy Assn., 1969, Cert. of Achievement Palmer Coll. of Chiropractic Medicine, 1970, Cert. Achievement AMA, 1980. Fellow Soc. for Nutrition and Preventive Medicine, Ill. Naprapathic Assn., Am. Back Soc.; mem. Acad. Holistic Practitioners, Am. Assn. Nutritional Cons., Interant. Assn. Counselors and Therapists. Democrat. Presbyterian. Avocations: collects statues of the saints. Home: 5537 W 24th Pl Cicero IL 60804-2733 Office: 3223 Harlem Ave Berwyn IL 60402-2807 *Personal philosophy: Words to live by: Honor thy Mother and Father. Always love and cherish your Mother, you have her once in your life.*

SEDLAK, S(HIRLEY) A(GNES), freelance writer, novelist; b. Chgo., Sept. 06; d. Frederick Jesse and Agnes (Baum) Machacek; m. Harold Otto Sedlak; 1 child, Linda Carol. Student, Morton Jr. Coll., Cicero, Ill. Editor children's books Benefic Press subs. Harcourt Brace Jovanovich, Westchester, Ill., 1973-75; publicity and pub. rels. The Nat. League of Am. Pen Women, Inc., Chgo. br., 1987-89. Author: (internet) Bury Her Gently, 2001. Home: 2226 S 9th Ave North Riverside IL 60546

SEDLAK, VALERIE FRANCES, English language educator, university administrator; b. Balt., Mar. 11, 1934; d. Julian Joseph and Eleanor Eva (Pilot) Sedlak; 1 child, Barry. AB in English, Coll. Notre Dame of Md., 1955; MA, U. Hawaii, 1962; PhD, U. Pa., 1992. Grad. teaching fellow East-West Cultural Ctr. U. Hawaii, 1959-60; adminstrv. asst. Korean Consul Gen., 1959-60; tchr. Boyertown (Pa.) Sr. High Sch., 1961-63; asst. prof. English U. Balt., 1963-69; assoc. prof. Morgan State U., Balt., 1970-2000, assoc. prof. English emerita, 2001—, asst. dean Coll. Liberal Arts, 1995-2000, sec. to faculty, 1981-83, faculty research scholar, 1982-83, 92-93, communications officer, 1989-90, dir. writing for TV program, 1990-97; exec. dir. Renaissance Inst. Coll. of Notre Dame of Md., 2000—. Cons. scholar Md. Humanities Coun., 1992—. Author poetry and lit. criticism; exec. assoc. editor Middle Atlantic Writer's Assn. Rev., 1989-2000; assoc. editor Md. English Jour., 1994-2000, Morgan Jour. Undergrad. Rsch., 1995-2000; editor Liberal Arts Rev., 1996-2000. Coord. Young Reps., Berks County, Pa., 1962-63; chmn. Md. Young Reps., 1964; election judge Baltimore County, Md., 1964-66; regional capt. Am. Cancer Soc., 1978-79; mem. adv. bd. Md. Our Md. Anniversary, 1984, The Living Constitution: Bicentennial of the Fed. Constitution, 1987 Morgan-Penn Faculty fellow, 1977-79, Nat. Endowment Humanities, 1984; named Outstanding Teaching Prof., U. Balt. Coll. Liberal Arts, 1965, Outstanding Teaching Prof. English, Morgan State U., 1987. Mem. MLA, South Atlantic MLA, Coll. Lang. Assn., Coll. English Assn. (Mid-Atlantic Group v.p. 1987-90, pres. 1990-92, exec. bd. 1992—, nat. bd. dirs. 2001—, liaison officer 1993—), Women's Caucus for Modern Langs., Md. Coun. Tchrs. English, Md. Poetry and Lit. Soc., Md. Assn. Depts. English (bd. dirs. 1992—), Mid. Atlantic Writers' Assn. (founding 1981, exec. assoc. editor Mid. Atlantic Writers' Assn. Rev. 1989-2000), Delta Epsilon Sigma (v.p. 1992-94, pres. 1994-96), Pi Kappa Delta. Roman Catholic. Home: 17049 Keeney Mill Rd New Freedom PA 17349 Office: Coll of Notre Dame of Maryland Renaissance Inst 4701 N Charles St Baltimore MD 21210-2404 E-mail: vsedlak@ndm.edu.

SEDLER, ROBERT ALLEN, law educator; b. Pitts., Sept. 11, 1935; s. Jerome and Esther (Rosenberg) S.; m. Rozanne Friedlander, Jan. 24, 1960; children: Eric, Beth. BA, U. Pitts., 1956, JD, 1959. Bar: D.C. 1959, Ky. 1968, Mich. 1979; U.S. Supreme Ct. 1969. Asst. prof., assoc. prof. law St. Louis U., 1961-65; assoc. prof. law, asst. dean Addis Ababa U., Ethiopia, 1963-66; assoc. prof. to prof. law U. Ky., Lexington, 1966-77; prof. law Wayne State U., Detroit, 1977—, disting. prof. law, Gibbs chair civil rights & civil liberty, 2000—. Author: American Constitutional Law, 2000, Across State Lines, 1989: Applying the Conflict of Law to Your Practice, 1989 (with R. Cramton) The Sum and Substance of Conflict of Laws, 1987, Ethiopian Civil Procedure, 1968; contbr. articles to profl. jours. Gen. counsel ACLU Ky., 1971-76. Gershenson Disting. Faculty fellow, Wayne State Univ., 1985-87. Mem. ABA, AAUP, Phi Beta Kappa, Order of the Coif. Democrat. Jewish. Home: 18851 Capitol Dr Southfield MI 48075-2680 Office: Wayne State U 468 Ferry Mall Detroit MI 48202-3620 E-mail: rsedler@aol.com., rsedler@wayne.edu.

SEDLER, ROZANNE FRIEDLANDER, social worker, educator; b. Greensburg, Pa., June 16, 1938; d. Ernest and Belle (Marchel) Friedlander; m. Robert Allen Sedler, Jan. 24, 1960; children: Eric Mark, Beth Ellen. BA, U. Pitts., 1960; MSW, St. Louis U., 1962. Social worker Family & Children's Svc., St. Louis, 1962-63; lectr. Sch. of Social Work Haile Selassie U., Addis Ababa, Ethiopia, 1963-66; social worker U. Ky. Med. Ctr., Lexington, 1966-68, Renaissance Home Health Care, Detroit, 1984-86; geriatric social worker Jewish Family Svc., Southfield, Mich., 1986—. Chair Jewish Family Svc.-Am. Fedn. of State, County, Mcpl. Employees Local 1640; mem. exec. bd. AFSCME Local 1640; chair Oakland County bd. dirs. ACLU. Mem. Am. Fedn. State, County and Mcpl. Employees (pres. Local 1640, chair Jewish Famil Svc. Bargaining Unbit, bd. dirs.). Democrat. Jewish. Home: 18851 Capitol Dr Southfield MI 48075-2680 Office: Jewish Family Svc 24123 Greenfield Rd Southfield MI 48075-3116 E-mail: rozsedler@aol.com.

SEDLIN, ELIAS DAVID, physician, orthopedic researcher, educator; b. N.Y.C., Jan. 21, 1932; s. Arnold Boris and Sonia Lipschitz Sedlin; m. Barbara Sue Zidell, July 9, 1960; children: Faith Avril, Adrian. BS in Biology, U. Ala., 1951; MD, Tulane U., 1955; D.Med. Sci., U. Gothenburg, Sweden, 1966. Diplomate: Am. Bd. Orthopedic Surgery. Intern Mobile (Ala.) Gen. Hosp., 1955-56; resident Charity Hosp., New Orleans, 1956-57; chief resident Bronx (N.Y.). Mcpl. Hosp., 1959-60; sr. resident Henry Ford Hosp., Detroit, 1960-61, rsch. assoc., emergency room lectr., 1961-63, NIH fellow, 1963-64; jr. attending physician Detroit Receiving Hosp., 1962-63; spl. NIH fellow dept. orthopedic surgery Sahlgrenska Sjukhuset, Gothenburg, 1964-66; asst. prof. dept. orthopaedic surgery Albert Einstein Coll. Medicine, 1966-69, assoc. prof., 1969-75, prof., 1975—, dir. orthopaedic surgery, 1969-79; prof. orthopaedic surgery Mt. Sinai Sch. Medicine, 1980—. Contbr. to multiple symposia, profl. meetings, also articles to profl. jours. Served to capt. AUS, 1957-59. Fulbright scholar, 1962; NSF postdoctoral fellow, 1964; recipient P.D. McGehee award Mobile Gen. Hosp., 1956; Ludvic Hektoen gold medal AMA, 1963; Nicholas Andry award Assn. Bone and Joint Surgeons, 1964 Fellow ACS, AAAS, Am. Acad. Orthopaedic Surgeons; mem. Orthopaedic Rsch. Soc., Phi Beta Kappa. Office: 133 E 73d St New York NY 10021

SEDLOCK, JOY, psychiatric social worker; b. Memphis, Jan. 23, 1958; d. George Rudolph Sedlock and Mary Robson; m. Thomas Robert Jones, Aug. 8, 1983. AA, Ventura (Calif.) Jr. Coll., 1978; BS in Psychology, Calif. Luth. U., 1980; MS in Counseling and Psychology, U. LaVerne, 1983; MSW, Calif. State U., Sacramento, 1986. LCSW. Research asst. Camarillo (Calif.) State Hosp., 1981, tchr.'s aide, 1982; sub. tchr. asst. Vertura County Sch. Dist., 1981; teaching asst. Ventura Jr. Coll., 1980-82, tchr. adult edn., 1980-84; psychiatric social worker Yolo County Day Treatment Ctr., Broderick, Calif., 1986, Napa (Calif.) State Hosp., 1986—. Bd. dirs. Napa County Humane Soc., Wildlife Rescue Ctr. of Napa Co. Home: PO Box 1095 Yountville CA 94599-1095

SEDOR, FRANK A. chemist; b. E. Chgo., Ind., Nov. 21, 1944; s. Stephen and Julia S.; m. Judith Anne Sedor; children: Julia, Christine. BA, Wabash Coll., 1966; PhD, U. Fla., 1971. Diplomate Am. Bd. Clin. Chemistry. Asst. dir. clin. chemistry Duke U. Med. Ctr., Durham, NC, 1978-82, dir. outpatient labs., 1982-92, dir. clin. chemistry, 1992—. Contbr. articles to profl. jours. Mem. Am. Assn. Clin. Chemistry (pres. 2000—); fellow Nat. Acad. Clin. Biochemistry (bd. dirs. 1993-98). Avocations: gardening, books. Office: Duke U Med Ctr PO Box 3015 Durham NC 27710-0001

SEDRA, ADEL SHAFEEK, electrical engineering educator, academic administrator; b. Assouut, Egypt, Nov. 2, 1943; arrived in Can., 1966; s. Chafik and Hélène (Monsour) S.; m. Doris M. Barker, May 5, 1973; children: Paul Douglas, Mark Andrew. BSEE, Cairo U., 1964; MASc in Elec. Engring., U. Toronto, Ont., Can., 1968, PhDEE, 1969. Registered profl. engr., Ont. Instr. Cairo U., 1964-66; asst. prof. elec. engring. U. Toronto, 1969-72, assoc. prof., 1972-78, prof., 1978—, chmn. dept., 1986-93, v.p., provost, chief acad. officer, 1993—. Pres. Elec. Engring. Consociates Ltd., Toronto, 1979-81; bd. dirs. Info. Tech. Rsch. Ctr., Toronto, 1988-93; mem. rsch. coun. Can. Inst. for Advanced Rsch., 1994—; bd. dirs. Can. Inst. for Telecomms. Rsch.; del. Oxford U. Press, 1995—. Co-author: Filter Theory and Design, 1978, Microelectronic Circuits, 1982, 4th edit., 1998 (also Spanish, Korean, Greek, Italian, Portuguese, Chinese, Persian, and Hebrew transls.), SPICE, 1997; contbr. over 120 articles to sci. jours. Operating grantee Nat. Scis. and Engring. Rsch. Coun. Can., 1970—; Ryerson Poly. Inst. fellow, 1988. Fellow IEEE (Darlington best paper award 1984, Edn. medal 1996, Cir. and Sys. Soc. Edn. award 1994, Guillemin Cauer Best Paper award 1987, Golden Jubilee medal 2000, 3d Millennium medal 2000), Can. Acad. Engrs.; mem. Am. Soc. Engring. Edn. (Terman award 1988), Info. Tech. Assn. Can. (Tech. Achievement award 1993), Assn. Profl. Engrs. Ont. Home: 18 High Park Blvd Toronto ON Canada M6R 1M4 Office: U Toronto Off VP & Prov 27 Kings College Cir Simcoe Hall Toronto ON Canada M5S 1A1

SEDWAY, LYNN MASSEL, real estate economist; b. Washington, Nov. 26, 1941; d. Mark S. and Jean M. (Magnus) Massel; m. Paul H. Sedway, June 12, 1966; children: Mark, Carolyn, Jan. BA in Econs., U. Mich., 1963; MBA, U. Calif., Berkeley, 1976. Economist San Rafael (Calif.) Redevel. Agy., 1976-78; prin. Sedway & Assocs., San Francisco, 1978—. Instr. Appraisal Bus. Sch. U. Calif., Berkeley; bd. dirs. San Francisco Devel. Fund; corporate bd. mem. AMB Properties, Alexander, Baldwin and Matson, Bridge Housing, The Swig Company. Mem. Berkeley Bus. Sch. Fund Council, 1984-86; chmn San Rafael Downtown Retail Com., 1985; bd. dirs. San Francisco Devel. Fund, 1985—; CAC mem. Dominican Coll., San Rafael, 1983-87, mem. Fisher Center Policy Advisory Bd. of the Haas School, Public and Real Estate Council Mem. Urban Land Inst. (chair. retail comml. coun.), former chair, San Francisco District Council, Internat. Coun. of Shopping Ctrs., Housing Devel. Fin. Corp. (bd. dirs. Marin, Calif. chpt. 1984—), San Francisco Chamber of Commerce (former bd. of dirs.), City Club Intl. House, Marin C. of C. (bd. dirs. 1984-87), San Rafael C. of C., Lambda Alpha (past pres., bd. dirs.), Internat. Land Econs. Soc., San Francisco Municipal Fiscal Advisory Com. Avocation: tennis. Home: 2449 Pacific Ave San Francisco CA 94115-1237

SEE, CAROLYN, English language educator, novelist, book critic; b. Pasadena, Calif., Jan. 13, 1934; d. George Newton Laws and Kate Louise (Sullivan) Daly; m. Richard Edward See, Feb. 18, 1955 (div. June 1959); 1 child, Lisa Lenine; m. Tom Sturak, June 11, 1959; 1 child, Clara Elizabeth Marya. BA, Calif. State U., L.A., 1958; PhD, UCLA, 1963. Prof. English, Loyola Marymount Coll., L.A., 1970-85, UCLA, L.A., 1985—; book critic L.A. Times, 1981-93, Washington Post, 1993—. Author: Rhine Maidens, 1980, Golden Days, 1986, Making History, 1991, Dreaming: Hard Luck and Good Times In America, 1995, The Handyman, 1999, Making a Literary Life, 2002. Bd. dirs. Calif. Arts Coun., L.A., 1987-91, Day Break, for homeless, Santa Monica, Calif., 1989—, Friends of English, UCLA, 1990—; buddy for life AIDS Project Los Angeles, AIDS relief, L.A., 1990—. Recipient award Sidney Hillman Found., 1972, Robert Kirsch award L.A. Times, 1994; PEN Ctr. USA West Lifetime Achievement award 1998; grantee Nat. Endowment for Arts, 1980, Guggenheim fellow, 1990-91. Mem. Writers Guild Am., Libr. Found. Calif., PEN Ctr. USA West (pres. 1990-91), Nat. Book Critics Cir. (bd. dirs. 1986-90). Democrat. Avocations: gardening, sailing, dancing, brush clearing. Home: 17339 Tramonto Dr Pacific Palisades CA 90272-3124 Office: UCLA Dept English 405 Hilgard Ave Los Angeles CA 90095-9000

SEE, EDMUND M. lawyer; b. Marietta, Ohio, Oct. 9, 1943; s. Edgar Thorpe and Katherine M. (Merriam) S.; m. Ellen Engler, June 5, 1976; children: Kevin, Gregory, Tyler. BA, Wesleyan U., Middletown, Conn., 1965; JD, Harvard U., 1971. Bar: Conn. 1971. Assoc. Day, Berry & Howard, Hartford, Conn., 1971-77, ptnr., 1978—. Chmn. Mcpl. Fin. Practice Group. Vol. Peace Corps, Gabon, 1965-67, Vista, 1968-69; pres. bd. dirs. Legal Aid Soc., 1977-85, Hartford Arch. Conservancy, 1983-86; trustee St. Joseph Coll., 1991—; dir. Conn. Bar Found., 1994—; corporator Hartford Sem., 1994—. Mem. ABA, Conn. Bar Assn., Hartford County Bar Assn., Nat. Assn. Bond Lawyers, Conn. Govtl. Fin. Officers Assn., U.S. Govtl. Fin. Officers Assn., Phi Beta Kappa. Office: Day Berry & Howard LLP Cityplace 25th Fl Hartford CT 06103-3499 E-mail: emsee@dbh.com.

SEE, SAW-TEEN, structural engineer; b. Georgetown, Penang, Malaysia, Mar. 23, 1954; came to U.S., 1974; d. Hock-Eng and Ewe-See (Lim) S.; m. Leslie Earl Robertson, Aug. 11, 1982; 1 child, Karla Mei. BSCE, Cornell U., 1977, MCE, 1978. Registered profl. engr., N.Y., Calif., Conn., Fla., Mass., Md., N.J., Ohio, Pa., Wash., Ark., Ill., Tex. Design engr. Leslie E. Robertson Assocs., R.L.L.P., N.Y.C., 1978-81, assoc., 1981-85, ptnr., 1986—, mng. ptnr., 1990—. Cons. M of Engrng. class Cornell U., 1994-95, mem. adv. coun. Sch. Civil and Environ. Engrng., 1999—; project dir., project mgr. Miho Mus., Kyoto, Japan, West Side H.S., N.Y.C., Jr. H.S. 234, Bklyn., Jewelry Trade Ctr., Bangkok, Bilboa (Spain) Emblematic bldgs., Internat. Trade Ctr., Barcelona, Spain, Seattle Art Mus., San Jose (Calif.) Convention Ctr., San Jose Arena; project dir. Hong Kong Sta. South West & North East Tower Structural Audit, Balt. Conv. Ctr., Rock 'N Roll Hall of Fame and Mus., Cleve., Pontiac Marina Hotel and Retail, Singapore, acad. bldgs. and greenhouse, SUNY, Binghamton, N.Y.; project mgr. Coll. of Law bldg. U. Iowa, Iowa City, Neiman-Marcus store, San Francisco, AT&T Exhbn. bldg., N.Y.C., Bank of China Tower, Hong Kong, AIG Tower, Hong Kong, Bellevue Hosp., N.Y.C., W.J. Clinton Presdl. Ctr., Little Rock, Ark., Shanghai World Fin. Ctr., PPG Hdqs., Pitts., AT&T Corp. Hdqs., N.Y.C.; ptnr.-in-charge Nat. Constn. Ctr., Phila. Contbr. articles to profl. jours. Named to Those Who Made Marks in the Constrn. Industry in 1988, Engrng. News Record, N.Y.C., 1989, Spl. Recognition award Profl. Women in Constrn., 2002. Fellow ASCE (performance study team World Trade Ctr. with FEMA), Archtl. League, Coun. on Tall Bldgs. and Urban Habitat (past chairperson com. on gravity loads and temperature effects 1982-85), Architects, Designers, Planners for Social Responsiblity, N.Y. Assn. Cons. Engrs. (dir. 1989-93, structural codes com. 1991—). Avocations: sailing, skiing, reading, photography. Home: 45 E 89th St Apt 25C New York NY 10128-1230 Office: Leslie E Robertson Assocs RLLP 30 Broad St Fl 47 New York NY 10004-2304 E-mail: sts@lera.com.

SEEBACH, LYDIA MARIE, physician; b. Red Wing, Minn., Nov. 9, 1920; d. John Henry and Marie (Gleusen) S.; m. Keith Edward Wentz, Oct. 16, 1959; children: Brooke Marie, Scott. BS, U. Minn., 1942, MB, 1943, MD, 1944, MS in Medicine, 1951. Diplomate Am. Bd. Internal Medicine. Intern Kings County Hosp., Bklyn., 1944; fellow Mayo Found., Rochester, Minn., 1945-51; pvt. practice Oakland, Calif., 1952-60, San Francisco, 1961—. Asst. clin. prof. U. Calif., San Francisco, 1981—; mem., vice chmn. Arthritis Clinic, Presbyn. Hosp., San Francisco, 1961-88, pharmacy com., 1963-78; chief St. Mary's Hosp. Arthritis Clinic, San Francisco, 1968-72; exec. bd. Pacific Med. Ctr., San Francisco, 1974-76. Contbr. articles to med. jours. Fellow ACP; mem. AMA, Am. Med. Womens Assn. (pres. Calif. chpt. 1968-70), Am. Rheumatism Assn., Am. Soc. Internal Medicine, Pan Am. Med. Womens Assn. (treas.), Calif. Acad. Medicine, Calif. Soc. Internal Medicine, Calif. Med. Assn., San Francisco Med. Soc., San Francisco Med. Assn., San Francisco Soc. Internal Medicine, No. Calif. Rheumatism Assn., Internat. Med. Women's Assn., Mayo Alumni (bd. dirs. 1983-89), Iota Sigma Pi. Republican. Lutheran. Avocations: music, cooking, gardening, needlepoint. Office: 490 Post St Ste 939 San Francisco CA 94102-1414

SEEBERT, KATHLEEN ANNE, international sales and marketing executive; d. Harold Earl and Marie Anne (Lowery) S. MM, MA, Northwestern U., 1983. Dir. mktg. MidAm. Commodity Exch., 1982-85; internat. trade cons. to Govt. of Ont. Can., 1985-90; dir. mktg. and program devel. Internat. Orientation Resources, 1990-94; v.p. Am. Internat. Group, 1995-97; dir. KPMG Peat Marwick LLP, 1997-98; cons. Watson Wyatt & Co., 1999—. Guest lectr. U. Dayton, U. Notre Dame, Northwestern U., Kellogg Alumni Chgo., French-Am. C. of C., Internat. Employee Relocation Coun., Soc. Intercultural Educators, Trainers and Rschrs., ASTD, Ill. CPA Soc., SBA, KPMG Peat Marwick, Pricewaterhousecoopers, Ernst & Young, Nat. Fgn. Trade Coun., William M. Mercer, Inc., Minn. Employee Relocation Coun., MRA, CRC, Chgo. Relocation Coun., Ky. Relocation Coun., Chgo.-Midwest Credit Mgmt. Assn. Nat. bd. dirs. U. Dayton. Mem. Futures Industry Assn. Am. (treas.), Greater Cin. C. of C., Notre Dame Club Chgo., Kellogg Mgmt. Club Chgo. Republican. Roman Catholic. Office: 303 W Madison St Ste 2400 Chicago IL 60606-3395

SEED, BRIAN BRUCE, music educator; b. Anchorage, Jan. 4, 1966; s. Gerald Bruce and Marilyn Marie Seed; m. Stephanie Louise Brown, June 24, 1995; children: James, Mark. Grad., Armed Forces Sch. of Music, Norfolk, Va., 1984—85; BMus Edn., Willamette U., 1990, MA Tchg., 1991. Cert. tchr. Oreg., 1994. Radio announcer KSJJ - KPRB Radio , Redmond, Oreg., 1987—88; radio announcer/news reporter KBND-KLRR Radio, Bend, 1989—91; youth program dir. Holland Am. Cruise Line, Seattle, 1992—95; advt./tech. cons. The Mattress Factory, Inc., Bend, 1997—; band dir. Molalla H.S./Molalla River Sch. Dist., 1991—2001, Summit H.S./Bend-LaPine Sch. Dist., Bend, 2001—. Chair North Lancaster Neighborhood Assn., Salem, Oreg., 1994—98; founder, pres. Molalla River Cmty. Concert Assn., 1998—2001. Specialist 4 U.S. Army, 1984—87, Ft. Hood, Tex. Recipient Army Commendation Medal, U.S. Army, 1987, Army Achievement Medal, 1986—87, Good Conduct Medal, 1987. Mem.: Oreg. Edn. Assn., Oreg. Music Educators Assn., Music Educators Nat. Conf., Arthritis Found., Am. Legion. Conservative. Mem. Christian Ch. (Disciples Of Christ). Avocation: music, computers, movies, history, travel. Home: 2446 NE 6th St Bend OR 97701 Office: Summit HS 2855 NW Clearwater Dr Bend OR 97701 Personal E-mail: seedb@bendnet.com.

SEEDER, RICHARD OWEN, infosystems specialist; b. Chgo., May 4, 1947; s. Edward Otto and Betty Jane (Reamer) S. BA, Trinity U., 1969; M in Mgmt., Northwestern U., 1979; MS, DePaul U., 1993. Programmer, analyst R.R. Donnelley & Sons Co., Chgo., 1972-76, project mgr., 1977-80; mgr. systems devel. Joint Commn. Accreditation of Healthcare Orgns., 1980-84, dir. mgmt. info. systems, 1985-89; dir. info. svcs., 1989-92; v.p. AApex Info. Systems., Skokie, Ill., 1992—. Cons. Internat. Printworks, Newton, Mass., 1981-82. Served to 1st lt. U.S. Army, 1969-71, Korea. Mem. Assn. MBA Execs., Healthcare Info. and Mgmt. Systems Soc., Am. Mgmt. Assn., Mensa. Clubs: Northwestern U. Mgmt. Avocations: sports, gardening. Home: 2224 Maple Ave Northbrook IL 60062-5208 Office: AApex Info Systems 9230 Lotus Ave Skokie IL 60077-1150

SEEDLOCK, ROBERT FRANCIS, engineering and construction company executive; b. Newark, Feb. 6, 1913; s. Frank Andrew and Mary Elizabeth (Prosner) S.; m. Hortense Orcutt Norton, Sept. 1, 1937 (dec. Aug. 2000); children: Robert Francis, Elizabeth Munsell Seedlock Morrissette, Walter Norton, Mary Marion. Grad., Armed Forces Staff Coll., 1948, Nat. War Coll., 1958. Registered profl. engr., D.C., Pa. Commd. 2d lt. U.S. Army, 1937, advanced through grades to maj. gen., 1963; asst. to dist. engr. Pitts., 1937-39, Tulsa Aircraft Assembly Plant, 1941; regtl. exec. bn. comdr. Engr. Unit Tng. Ctr., Camp Claiborne, La., 1942; asst. theatre engr. CBI; also comdr. Burma Road Engrs.; also chief engr. Shanghai Base Command, 1943-45; mem. Gen. Marshall's Mediation Mission, Peking, 1946-47; mem. gen. staff U.S. Army; mem. Am. del. Far Ea. Commn., 1948-49; aide to chief staff U.S. Army, 1949-54; mem. U.S. del. NATO Ministerial Conf., 1952-53, dep. divsn. engr. Mediterranean divsn., 1954-57, mil. asst. to asst. sec. def. for pub. affairs, 1958-62. Div. engr. Missouri River, Omaha, 1962-63; sr. mem. UN Mil. Armistice Commn., Korea, 1963-64; dir. mil. personnel Office dep. chief of staff for personnel Dept. Army, 1964-66; dir. mil. constrn. Office Chief of Engrs., 1966; commdg. gen. U.S. Army Engr. Ctr. and Ft. Belvoir, Va. and comdt. U.S. Army Engr. Sch., Ft. Belvoir, 1966-68, ret., 1968; pres. Yuba Industries, 1968-69, v.p. Standards Prudential Corp. (merged with Yuba Industries), 1969-70; vice pres., dir. Petro-Chem. Devel. Co., Inc., N.Y.C., 1968-70, Petchem. Constrn. Co., N.Y.C., 1968-70, Petrochem Isoflow Furnaces, Ltd. (Can.), 1968-70; dir. constrn. and devel. Port Authority of Allegheny County, Pitts., 1970-73; assoc. Parsons, Brinckerhoff-Tudor-Bechtel, Atlanta, 1973-77; prog. dir. Ralph M. Parsons Co., Pasadena, Calif., Phila. and Washington, 1977-83; cons. 1983-97; dir. T.Y. Lin Internat., 1985-89; chief liaison, cons. Chinese Acad. Sci. for Beijing Inst. Mgmt., 1985-89; U.S. rep. to Permanent Tech. Com. Number 1 of Permanent Internat. Assn. of Navigation Congresses, 1984-93; pres. First Am. chapt. Burma Star Assn., 1984-98; chmn. Sino-Am. Ventures Inc., 1987—; cons. The Knowledge Co., 1989-92, Dove & Assocs., 1990. Contbr. to mil. and engring. jours. Bd. dirs. Army and Air Force Exch. and Motion Picture Svc., 1964; mem. Miss. River Commn., 1962-63, Bd. Engrs. Rivers and Harbor, 1962-63, Def. Adv. Commn. Edn., 1964; chmn. Mo. Basin Inter-Agy. Com., 1962-63; fed. rep., chmn. Big Blue River Compact Commn., 1962-63; mem. U.S. Com. on Large Dams, 1962-82; exec. bd. Nat. Capital Area coun. Boy Scouts Am., 1967-68, Atlanta area coun., 1975-77. Decorated DSM, Legion of Merit with oak leaf cluster; chevalier Legion of Honor (France); 1st class grade A medal Army, Navy, Air Force, also spl. breast order Yun Hui (China); named Engr. of Yr., Met. Atlanta Engrng. Soc., 1976, Ga. Engr. of Yr. in Govt., Ga. Soc. profl. Engrs., 1976; recipient Silver Beaver award Boy Scouts Am., 1977, Case Alumni Assn. Golf medal, 1985. Fellow Soc. Am. Mil. Engrs. (nat. dir., Cathedral Latin Alumni Assn. Man of the Yr. award 1992); mem. ASCE (hon., aerospace divsn. program com. 1980-82, sec. exec. com. 1982-83, chmn. 1984-85, editor Jour. Aerospace Engrng. 1986-93), Assn. U.S. Army, West Point Soc. N.Y. (life), West Point Soc. Atlanta (pres. 1976), Burma Star Assn. (pres. 1st Am. chpt. 1982-98), Army-Navy Country Club (sec., chmn. bd. govs. 1952-54, 61-62), Met. Club (N.Y.C.), Oglethorpe Club (Savannah, Ga.), Ansley Golf Club (Atlanta). Roman Catholic. Home and Office: 1824 The Jefferson 900 N Taylor St Arlington VA 22203 E-mail: rfseedlock@juno.com.

SEEGAL, JOHN FRANKLIN, lawyer; b. Newton, Mass., May 21, 1946; s. Samuel Melbourne and Martha (Lewenberg) S.; m. Barbara Ellen Wayne, Apr. 2, 1982; children: Sarah Rachel, Laura Rose. BA, Harvard U., MBA, JD, Harvard U., 1973. Assoc. Orrick, Herrington & Sutcliffe, LLP, San Francisco, 1973-78, ptnr., 1979—. Co-chmn. Inst. on Securities Regulation, 2001—. Mem. ABA, Calif. Bar Assn. Republican. Jewish. Office: Orrick Herrington & Sutcliffe LLP 400 Sansome St San Francisco CA 94111-3143

SEEGER, JAMES M. vascular surgeon; BS, MIT, 1969; MD, Med. Coll. Ga., 1973. Resident in gen. surgery U. Utah, 1980; fellow in vascular surgery Eastern Va. Med. Sch., 1981; asst. prof. dept. surgery U. Fla. Coll. Medicine, Gainesville, 1992-96, assoc. prof., 1986-93, prof., 1993—, chief sect. vascular surgery, 1989—; chief vascular surgery svc. VA Med. Ctr., 1982—98, assoc. chmn. dept. surgery, 2000—. Adj. prof., dept. materials sci. and engring., 1992—. Mem. editl. bd. 3 jours.; contbr. over 100 articles to profl. jours.; editor/co-editor 3 books in field; 3 patents in field. Home: 3415 NW 31st St Gainesville FL 32605-2166 Office: U Fla Coll Medicine Surgery Dept PO Box 100286 Gainesville FL 32610-0286 E-mail: seeger@surgery.ufl.edu.

SEEGER, MELINDA WAYNE, realtor; m. Robert Charles Seeger; 1 child, Jeffrey Wayne. Chief occupl. therapy Rehab. Inst. Oreg., Portland, 1964-66; supr. phys. disabilities and gen. medicine and surgery occupl. therapy Mpls. VA Hosp., 1966-68; supr. phys. disabilities occupl. therapy Nat. Naval Med. Ctr., Bethesda, Md., 1968-71; assoc. chief rehab. svcs., dir. occupl. therapy UCLA Med. Ctr., 1974-85, cons., prin. investigator rheumatology divsn. dept. medicine, 1985-86; realtor Merrill Lynch Realty, L.A., 1987-95, Re/Max Estate Properties, Beverly Hills, Calif., 1995-96, Nelson Shelton & Assocs., Beverly Hills, 1996—. Author, editor articles in field. Mem. utilization rev. com. Vis. Nurse Assn. L.A., 1975-85, mem. profl. adv. com., 1979-80; mem. exec. com. Allied Health Professions sect. Arthritis Found., 1980-85, chmn. edn. com., 1982-85, mem. profl. edn. com.; bd. dirs. Calif. Occupl. Therapy Found., 1984-85, Westwood-Holmby Hills Homeowners Assn.; mem. adv. bd. Save Westswood Village L.A. Recipient Spl. Achievement award Nat. Naval Med. Ctr., 1971, Outstanding Performance award, 1971, Spl. Performance award UCLA, 1980, 84, Addie Thomas Svc. award for outstanding svc. to rheumatology cmty. Arthritis Found., 1986, Cert. of Appreciation award, 1989; mem. Million Dollar Club. Mem. Am. Occupl. Therapy Assn., Occupl. Therapy Assn. Calif., Allied Health Professions Assn. (chmn. edn. com. 1982—), L.A. Bd. Realtors, San Fernando Valley Bd. Realtors, West L.A. C. of C., Million Dollar Club, Blue Diamond Club. Office: 355 N Canon Dr Beverly Hills CA 90210-4704

SEEGMILLER, JARVIS EDWIN, biochemist, educator; b. St. George, Utah, June 22, 1920; m. Roberta Eads, 1950 (dec. 1992); children: Dale S. Maudlin, Robert E., Lisa S. Taylor, Richard L.; m. Barbara A. Ellertson, 1995. AB, U. Utah, 1942; MD, U. Chgo., 1948. Asst. U.S. Bur. Mines, Utah, 1941; asst. nat. def. rsch. com. Northwestern Tech. Inst., 1942-44; asst. medicine U. Chgo., 1947-48; intern Johns Hopkins Hosp., 1948-49; biochemist Nat. Inst. Arthritis and Metabolic Diseases, 1949-51; rsch. assoc. Thorndike Meml. Lab. Harvard Med. Sch., 1952-53; vis. investigator Pub. Health Rsch. Inst., N.Y.C., 1953-54; chief sect. human biochemical, genetics, asst. sci. dir. Nat. Inst. Arthritis and Metabolic Diseases, 1954-69; prof. dept. medicine, dir. divsn. rheumatology U. Calif., San Diego, 1969-90, founding dir. Stein Inst. Rsch. Aging, 1983-90, prof. emeritus medicine, assoc. dir. Stein Inst. Rsch. Aging, 1990—. Vis. scientist U. Coll. Hosp. Sch. Medicine, London, 1964-65; Harvey Soc. lectr., 1970. Contbr. numerous articles to profl. jours. Macy scholar Basel Inst. Immunology; Guggenheim fellow Swiss Inst. Exptl. Cancer Rsch., Lausanne, 1982-83, John Simon Guggenheim Meml. Found. fellow, 1982, Fogarty Internat. fellow Oxford U., 1989. Mem. Nat. Acad. Sci., Harvey Soc. (hon.), Am. Soc. Biol. Chemists, Am. Rheumatism Assn., Am. Fedn. Clin. Rsch., Am. Soc. Human Genetics, Am. Soc. Clin. Investigation, AAAS, Assn. Am. Physicians, Am. Acad. Arts and Sci. Office: U Calif San Diego 9500 Gilman Dr La Jolla CA 92093-0664 E-mail: jseegmiller@ucsd.edu.

SEEHAUSEN, RICHARD FERDINAND, architect; b. Indpls., Mar. 17, 1925; s. Paul Ferdinand and Melusina Dorothea (Nordmeyer) S.; m. Phyllis Jean Gates, Dec. 22, 1948; children: Lyn, Dirk. Student, DePauw U., 1943-44, Wabash Coll., 1944, State U. Iowa, 1944; BArch, U. Ill., 1949. Registered profl. arch. Ptnr. Johnson, Kile, Seehausen & Assocs., Inc. archs., engrs., Rockford, Ill., 1955-82, pres., 1974-82, Richard F. Seehausen-Arch., Inc., Rockford, 1983—. Mem. com. jail planning and constrn. stds. Bur. Detention Facilities, Ill. Dept. Corrections, 1970-73; analyst Dept. Def., 1962-66; analyst Fed. Fall-Out Shelter, 1962—. Prin. works include No. Ill. U. Ctr., Harrison Hall, Lorado Taft, Oreg., also Health Svc. Bldg., Winnebago County Courthouse, Rockford, St. Mark Luth. Ch., Christ Meth. Ch., 1st Presbyn. Ch., Rochelle, Ill., Forest Hills Free Ch., Rockford, Messiah Luth. Ch., Rock Falls, Ill., Ch. of the Nazarene, Freeport, Ill., McHenry County Ct. House, Woodstock, Ill., Stephenson County Courthouse, Freeport, Ogle County Pub. Safety Bldg., Oreg., DeKalb H.S., Page Park Spl. Edn. Sch., Rockford, Oak Crest Retirement Ctr., Sycamore/DeKalb, Ill., Social Security bldgs., Racine, Sheboygan, Oshkosh and Janesville, Wis., Freeport YWCA Bldgs., renovation Carroll County Ct. House, DeKalb Area Retirement Ctr., Old Winnebago County Courthouse, Rockford, Rockford Mut. Ins. Home Office Bldg., Court Street Meth. Ch., Rockford, Willows Personal Care Ctr., others. Bd. dirs. Rockford Boys Club, Lincoln Pk. Boys Club, past dir.; trustee Emmanuel Luth. Ch., Rockford, 1989-92; mem. Nat. Trust Hist. Preservation, 2000—. Served with USN, 1943-45, USNR, 1945-47, lt. USAF, 1949-55. Mem. AIA (dir. No. Ill. chpg. 1966-68, 75-77, pres. chpt. 1978-79), Ill. Coun. of Am. Inst. Archs., U. Ill. Alumni Assn., Mason (Shriner), Kiwanian, Forest Hills Country Club (gov. 1970-72), Saddle Brooke Country Club, Lamdba Chi Alpha. Lutheran. Office: Richard F Seehausen Arch Inc 65297 E Emerald Ridge Dr Tucson AZ 85739-1434 E-mail: dicknjean@worldnet.att.net.

SEEHRA, MOHINDAR SINGH, physics educator, researcher; b. Panjab, Pakistan, Feb. 14, 1940; came to U.S., 1963; s. Bakhshish Singh and Rattan (Kaur) S.; m. Harbhajan Kaur, May 12, 1963; children: Jasmeet, Parveen. BS, Panjab U., 1959; MS, Aligarh (India) U., 1962; PhD, U. Rochester, 1969. Instr. chemistry Arya Coll., Nawanshahr, India, 1959-60; lectr. physics Jain Coll., Ambala City, India, 1962-63; asst. prof. physics W.Va. U., Morgantown, 1969-73, assoc. prof., 1973-77, prof., 1977-91, Eberly disting. prof. physics, 1992—. Contbr. more than 180 articles to profl. jours. Rsch. fellow A.P. Sloan Found., 1973-75, ORAU Summer fellow, 1976, 77, 84, 85; recipient Outstanding Rsch. award Coll. Arts and Scis., U. W.Va., 1985. Fellow Am. Phys. Soc., , Inst. Physics (Eng.). Office: WVa State U Dept Physics PO Box 6315 Morgantown WV 26506-6315 E-mail: mseehra@wvu.edu.

SEEK, JASON B. music educator; b. Memphis, May 25, 1971; s. Gregory W. and Kay R. Seek. MusB Edn., Ouachita Bapt. U., 1993. Cert. K-12 instruminstrumental music tchr. Tenn. Dir. of bands Arlington, Barret's Chapel, and Jeter Elem. Schs., Arlington, Tenn., 1994—96, Collierville (Tenn.) Mid. Sch., 1996—. Consulting for bands Shelby County Schools, Memphis, 1999. Composer: (clarinet music) Festival Clarinet Duets and Trios, 2002. Mem.: Music Educators Nat. Conf. Lutheran. Avocation: travel. Home: 4299 Cedar Hills Bartlett TN 38135 Office: Collierville Middle Sch 146 College St Collierville TN 38017 Office Fax: 901-853-3327. Personal E-mail: jasbris@aol.com.

SEELENFREUND, ALAN, retired pharmaceutical company executive; b. N.Y.C., Oct. 22, 1936; s. Max and Gertrude (Roth) S.; m. Ellyn Bolt; 1 child, Eric. BME, Cornell U., 1959, M. in Indsl. Engring., 1960; PhD in Mgmt. Sci., Stanford U., 1967. Asst. prof. bus. adminstrn. Grad. Sch. Bus. Stanford U., Palo Alto, Calif., 1966-71; mgmt. cons. Strong, Wishart and Assocs., San Francisco, 1971-75; various mgmt. positions McKesson Corp., 1975-84, v.p., chief fin. officer, 1984-86, exec. v.p., chief fin. officer, 1986-89, chmn., CEO, 1989-97, chmn., 1997-99, also bd. dirs., chmn., 1997—2002; ret., 2002. Mem. Nature Conservancy, World Wildlife Fund, St. Francis Yacht Club, Villa Taverna Club, Pacific Union Club. Avocations: sailing, skiing, hiking. Office: McKesson Corp 1 Post St Ste 3275 San Francisco CA 94104-5296

SEELER, RUTH ANDREA, pediatrician, educator; b. N.Y.C., June 13, 1936; d. Thomas and Olivia (Patten) S. BA cum laude, U. Vt., 1959, MD, 1962. Diplomate Am. Bd. Pediatrics, Am. Bd. Pediatric Hematology/Oncology. Intern Bronx (N.Y.) Mcpl. Hosp., 1962—65; pediats. hematology/oncology fellow U. Ill., 1965—67; dir. pediatric hematology/oncology Cook County Hosp., 1967—84; prof. pediatrics and pediatric edn. Coll. Medicine U. Ill., Chgo., 1984—; assoc. chief pediatrics Michael Reese Hosp., 1990—97, acting chief pediatrics, 1997—99; pediatrician St. Anthony's Hosp./U. Ill. Coll. Medicine, 1999—2001. Course coord. pediatrics Nat. Coll. Advanced Med. Edn., Chgo., 1987-96; mem. subboard Pediatric Hematology/Oncology, Chapel Hill, 1990-95. Mem. editl. bd. Am. Jour. Pediatric Hematology/Oncology, 1985-95. Founder camp for hemophiliacs Hemophilia Found., Ill., 1973—2000, med. dir., pres., 1981—85; jr. and sr. warden, treas. Ch. Our Saviour, Chgo., 1970—92, 2002—. Mem.: Phi Beta Kappa, Gamma Phi Beta Found. (trustee 1994—2000, 2002—). Avocations: triathalons, biking, swimming. Office: U Ill Coll Medicine Pediats M/C 856 840 S Wood St Chicago IL 60612-7317

SEELEY, DAVID STEVENS, education educator; b. N.Y.C., Apr. 23, 1931; s. Nathaniel Stevens and Louise (Talbot) S.; m. Anna Mae Menapace, July 4, 1955; children: Nathaniel, Sarah, Anne, Mary, Louise. BA, Yale U., 1953, JD, 1956; EdD, Harvard U., 1970. Bar: Conn. Atty. HEW, Washington, 1956-59; dir. Harvard-Nigeria Peace Corps tchr. tng. Harvard U., Ibadan, Nigeria, 1961-62; spl. asst. to commr. U.S. Office of Edn., Washington, 1963-65, asst. commr. edn., 1965-67; dir., office of edn. liaison N.Y.C. Mayor's Office, 1967-68; sr. assoc. Met. Applied Rsch. Ctr., 1968-69; dir. Pub. Edn. Assn., N.Y.C., 1969-80; adj. prof. Coll. of S.I./CUNY, 1980-86, prof. edn., coord. ednl. adminstrn. program, 1987—; prof. edn. Grad. Ctr. CUNY, 1991—. Author: Education Through Partnership, 1981; contbr. articles to profl. jours. Mem. N.Y. State Curriculum and Assessment Coun., Albany, 1992-94; co-chair S.I. 2000, 1992-95; trustee Pub. Edn. Assn., 1980-97. Home: 66 Harvard Ave Staten Island NY 10301-1311 Office: CUNY College of Staten Island 2800 Victory Blvd Staten Island NY 10314-6609

SEELEY, JOHN GEORGE, horticulture educator; b. North Bergen, N.J., Dec. 21, 1915; s. Howard Wilson and Lillian (Fiedler) S.; m. Catherine L. Cook, May 28, 1938 (dec. Feb. 1999); children: Catherine Ann, David John (dec. 1995), Daniel Henry, George Bingham, Thomas Dyer. BS, Rutgers U., 1937, MS, 1940; PhD, Cornell U., 1948. Research asst. N.J. Agrl. Exptl. Sta., 1937-40, foreman ornamental gardens, 1940-41; instr. floricultural sci. Cornell U., Ithaca, N.Y., 1941-43, 45-48, asst. prof., 1948-49, prof. floricultural sci., 1956-83, prof. emeritus, 1983—, head dept. floriculture, 1956-70; prof. floriculture Pa. State U., 1949-56; D.C. Kiplinger chair floriculture, prof. horticulture Ohio State U., 1984-85. Asst. agronomist Bur. Plant Industry Dept. Agr., 1943-44; chemist Wright Aero. Corp., Paterson, N.J., 1944-45. Trustee Kenneth Post Found., 1956-84, Fred. C. Gloeckner Found., 1970—, pres., 1993—. Recipient Best Sr. award in Agriculture, Rutgers U., 1937, S.A.F. Found. for Floriculture Rsch. & Edn. award, 1965, Cornell Edgerton Career Teaching award, 1983. Fellow AAAS, Am. Soc. Hort. Sci. (pres. 1982-83, chmn. bd. 1983-84, Leonard H. Vaughan rsch. award 1950, Bittner Extension award 1982); mem. Internat. Soc. for Hort. Sci. (hon. mem award, 1992), mem. Am. Acad. Floriculture (hon.), Am. Hort. Soc. (Liberty Hyde Bailey award 1998), Soc. Am. Florists (Hall of Fame 1979), Mass. Hort. Soc. (Silver medal 1980), Am. Carnation Soc., Ohio Florists' Assn. (hon.), N.Y. Flower Growers Assn., Pa. Flower Growers Assn., Sigma Xi, Phi Kappa Phi, Alpha Zeta (chancellor 1936-37), Pi Alpha Xi (pres. 1951-53), Epsilon Sigma Phi, Phi Epsilon Phi. Lodges: Rotary Internat. (dist. gov. 1973-74). Presbyterian. Home: 403 Savage Farm Dr Ithaca NY 14850-6506

SEELEY, MARK, agronomist; b. Gary, Ind., May 3, 1942; s. Clayton Barron and Margaret Louise (Cook) S. BS, Purdue U., 1967; MA in Edn., Austin Peay State U., 1971. Staff asst. Purdue U., 1962; tchr. sci. Lake Ctrl. Sch. Corp., St. John, Ind., 1967-68, Gary, 1972-73; mgr. agronomic crops R.L. Schultz Farms, Hobart, Ind., 1973-94, dir. Lupin introduction and devel., 1980-94. Bd. dirs. On Line Electric Inc., mem. exec. steering com. corp. svcs. Mem. Lake Area United Way Vol. Svc., Lake County Health Fair, 1974; sci. and engring. judge 26th and 27th Calumet Regional Sci. Airs. Mem. AAAS, NSPE, Am. Inst. Biol. Scis., Am. Soc. Hort Sci. (food quality and nutrition working group), Am. Soc. Agrl. Engrs. (pres.'s club 1980-94), Ind. Soc. Profl. Engrs.

(scholarship com. Calumet chpt. 1982-83, co-chmn. 1984-85), Am. Soc. Agronomy, Am. Soc. Plant Physiologists, Coun. Agrl. Sci. and Tech. (mem. Century Club 1983), Crop Sci. Soc. Am., Fedn. Am. Scientists, Internat. Soc. Hort. Sci., Soil Sci. Soc. Am., Lake Michigan Flyers Assn., U.S. Hang Gliding Assn., Am. Soc. Quality. Address: 6126 Colorado Street Hobart IN 46342

SEELIG, GERARD LEO, management consultant; b. Schluchtern, Germany, June 15, 1926; came to U.S., 1934, naturalized, 1943; s. Herman and Bella (Bach) S.; m. Lorraine Peters, June 28, 1953; children: Tina Lynn, Robert Mark and Carol Ann (twins). BEE, Ohio State U., 1948; MS in Indsl. Mgmt, N.Y. U., 1954. Registered profl. engr., Ohio. Electronics engr. Martin Corp., Balt., 1948-50; sr. engr. Fairchild Aircraft Co., Farmingdale, N.Y., 1950-54; program mgr. RCA, Moorestown, N.J., 1954-59, Van Nuys, Calif., 1959-61; div. mgr. Missile & Space Co. div. Lockheed Aircraft Corp., 1961-63; v.p., gen. mgr. Lockheed Aircraft Corp. (Lockheed Electronics div.), Los Angeles, 1963-68; exec. v.p. Lockheed Electronics Co., Inc., Plainfield, N.J., 1968-69, pres., 1969-71; group exec., exec. asst. to office of pres. ITT, N.Y.C., 1971-72, corp. v.p., 1972-79, sr. v.p., 1979-81, exec. v.p., 1981-83; pres. indsl. and tech. sector Allied Corp., exec. v.p. N.J., 1983-87. Disting. exec. lectr. Rutgers Grad. Sch. Mgmt.; exec.-in-residence, vis. prof. Columbia U. Grad. Sch. Bus.; bd. dirs. 5 corps.; cons. various investment firms. Served with AUS, 1944-46. Recipient Disting. Alumnus award Ohio State U., 1987. Fellow AIAA (assoc.); mem. IEEE (sr.).

SEELIGSON, MOLLY FULTON, professional life coach, education consultant; b. Dallas, Sept. 4, 1942; d. Bernard L. and Helen (Smith) Fulton; m. John M. Seeligson, Nov. 26, 1965; 1 child, Michael Bernard. BS, So. Meth. U., 1964. Cert. tchr., Tex.; cert. Hearth Math coach. Pvt. tutor, Dallas, 1957-71; co-founder, bd. dirs., administr. Clear Spring Sch., Eureka Springs, Ark., 1974-93, exec. dir., 1993-95. Bd. dirs. Eureka Springs Child Devel. Ctr., 1975-78, Legacy, Inc., Dallas, First Arvest Bank, 1994—, Fulton Acad., Org. for Atma Yidya Ednl. Found.; founding bd. The Wellness Ctr., 1994; designer La Poynor Ednl. Project, La Rue, Tex.; life and bus. coach; cons. in field. Author, pub. Sidereal Almanac, 1987-98. V.p. Hist. Dist. Mchts. Assn., Eureka Springs, 1972-73. Avocations: calligraphy, Indian culture, scrapbooking, jewelry making, gardening.

SEELY, ELLEN WELLS, endocrinologist; b. N.Y.C., Sept. 25, 1955; d. Robert Daniel and Marcia (Wells) S.; m. Jonathan David Strongin, June 11, 1983; children: Jessica, Matthew. BA magna cum laude, Brown U., 1977; MD, Columbia U., 1981. Diplomate Am. Bd. Internal Medicine, Endocrinology and Metabolism. Residency internal medicine Brigham & Women Hosp., Boston, 1981-84, fellow in endocrinology, 1984-87; rsch. fellow medicine Harvard U., 1984-87; dir. clin. rsch. endocrine hypertension divsn. Brigham & Women's Hosp., 1987—; asst. prof. medicine Harvard Med. Sch., 1991—2001, assoc. prof. medicine, 2001—; assoc. physician Brigham & Women's Hosp., 1987-95; assoc. prof. medicine Harvard Medical Sch., Boston, 2001; physician Brigham & Women's Hosp., 1996—. Med. internship selection com. Brigham and Women's Hosp., 1983—94, co-dir. endocrinology fellowship tng. program, 1993—95; dir. Pregnancy-Related Endocrine and Hypertensive Disorders Clinic, 1988—; co-dir. Diabetes and Pregnancy Clinic, 1988—2002; mem. admissions com. Harvard Med. Sch., 2001—. Contbr. articles to profl. jours. Capps scholar in diabetes Harvard Med. Sch., 1994-96, Harvard Med. Sch. scholar in medicine, 1998-99. Fellow: Coun. for High Blood Pressure Rsch.; mem.: ADA, Internat. Soc. Study of Hypertension in Pregnancy, Endocrine Soc., Sigma Xi. Office: Brigham & Women's Hosp 221 Longwood Ave Boston MA 02115-5804

SEELY, JAMES MICHAEL, defense consultant, retired naval officer, small business owner; b. Los Angeles, Oct. 15, 1932; s. Louis K. and Mary Edith (Gleason) S.; m. Gail Margaret Deverman, July 13, 1957; children: Ted Andrew, Nina Marie. BS, UCLA, 1955; MS, George Washington U., 1976. Commd. ensign USN, 1955, advanced through grades to rear adm.; student pilot, 1955-56; attack pilot, 1957-75; comdg. officer Attack Squadron 165, Naval Air Sta. Whidbey Island, Wash., 1972-73; comdr. Carrier Air Wing 9, Naval Air Sta. Lemoore, Calif., 1974-75; comdg. officer U.S. Naval Air Sta., Whidbey Island, 1977-79; dep. dir. DCNO (Air Warfare, OP-50), Pentagon, Washington, 1979-82; dir. Joint Analysis Directorate, Office Joint Chiefs Staff, Washington, 1982-84; comdr. Medium Attack Tactical Electronic Warfare Wing, Pacific Fleet, Naval Air Sta. Whidbey Island, 1984-86; dir. DCNO (Air Warfare, OP-50), Pentagon, 1986-88; dep. comptr. of Navy, 1988-89; ret., 1989; with RRP Def. Cons. Assocs., Arlington, Va., 1989—. Vietnam combat duty with Attack Squadrons 93, 152, 165 flying from aircraft carriers USS Enterprise, Hancock, Bon Homme Richard, Shangri-La and Constellation; 447 combat missions. Decorated Defense Superior Service, Legion of Merit (3), D.F.C. (4), Bronze Star, Air Medal (43), Navy Commendation medal with combat v (7). Mem. Naval Inst., Tailhook Assn., Assn. Naval Aviation, Marine Corps Aviation Assn., Red River Valley Fighter Pilots Assn., Navy League, Assn. Old Crows, Golden Eagles, Sigma Pi. Republican. Roman Catholic. Avocations: sports, automobiles. Home: 5730 Shropshire Ct Alexandria VA 22315-4027 E-mail: jimseely@ix.netcom.com.

SEELY, JOHN FRANCIS, physicist, researcher; b. Raleigh, N.C., July 16, 1946; s. John Frank and Lucille Joyner Seely; children: Laurel, Adrienne. PhD, U. Tenn., 1973. Physicist Naval Rsch. Lab., Washington, 1977—. Contbr. articles to profl. jours. Fellow, Optical Soc. Am.

SEELY, ROBERT DANIEL, physician, medical educator; b. Woodmere, N.Y., Nov. 4, 1923; s. Harry and Ethel (Weil) S.; m. Marcia Ann Wells, June 19, 1953; children: Ellen Wells, Anne Wells. BS, NYU, 1943; MD, Columbia U., 1946. Intern Mt. Sinai Hosp., N.Y.C., 1946-47, asst. resident in medicine, 1950-51, resident in pathology, 1951-52, chief resident in medicine, 1952-53; Sara Welt fellow in cardiovascular research Presbyn. Hosp., 1953-54; instr. dept. physiology, cardiovascular research Western Res. U., Cleve., 1947-48; chief rheumatic heart disease clinic Mt. Sinai Hosp., N.Y.C., 1961-70, attending physician medicine and cardiology, 1978—, chief of service dept. medicine, 1979—, clin. prof. medicine, cardiology Sch. Medicine, 1970—; practice medicine specializing in cardiovascular disease, 1953—. Contbr. articles to profl. jours. Served to capt. M.C. AUS, 1948-50. Recipient Solomon Berson Meml. award Mt. Sinai Hosp., 1977 Fellow Am. Coll. Cardiology, ACP; mem. N.Y. Heart Assn., AMA, N.Y. County Med. Soc., Soc. Cert. Internists N.Y., Phi Beta Kappa, Alpha Omega Alpha, Beta Lambda Sigma Office: 49 E 96th St # 11D New York NY 10128-0782 E-mail: billybobseedy@cs.com.

SEELY, ROBERT EUGENE, management consultant; b. Bangor, Mich., Oct. 23, 1941; s. Leroy W. and Ruth A. Seely. Cert., A&M U., 1961; BBA, West Mich. U., 1969. Officer Am. Nat. Bank, Kalamazoo, 1969-74; v.p. mktg. and fin., gen. mgr. Portage Rapid Cut, 1974-78; chief exec. officer Sutliff & Case, Inc., Peoria, Ill., 1978-81; chief oper. officer Allied Material Handling Co., 1981-83; pres. S.E.R., Inc., Kalamazoo, 1983-86; bus./mgmt. cons. Seely & Assocs., L.L.C., 1986—. Mem. adv. com. C & S Plastic Climax, Mich., 1996—88; advisor to bd. dirs. Simpson Enterprises, 1990—2001; bd. dirs. Maro, Inc., Venureprise, Inc., Kalamazoo, Portage Rapid Cut, Allied Material Handling, New World Condo Assn., Champion Furnace Pipe, Wonder Makers, Inc., Exhibit House, Portage Dist. Libr. Contbr. articles to profl. pubis. First chmn. Kalamazoo Valley Quality Coun., 1993-95; bd. dirs. Portage Dist. Libr.; mem. City of Portage Devel. Authority. With U.S. Army, 1966-68, Vietnam. Recipient Cert. of Appreciation Gov. of Mich., Cert. South Mich. Water Quality Commn., 1978, Cert. of Achievement Entrepreneurship Inst., 1983. Mem. Soc. Plastics Engrs., Nat. Assn. Corp. Dirs., Portage Small Bus. Assn. (bd. dirs.), Austin Lake Riparian (pres. 1991-93, bd. dirs.), C. of C. (chmn. small bus. week 1990, chmn. small bus. coun. 1991-92, organizer and 1st chmn. mfg. coun. 1992-96, Portage dir. Kalamazoo county)), Kal Valley Cmty. Quality Coun. (1st chmn. 1993, 94), Kal County C. of C. (bd. dirs. 1996-99). Avocations: golf, racquetball, skiing. Home: 9930 E Shore Dr Portage MI 49002-5879 Office: PO Box 924 Portage MI 49081-0924

SEEM, EVELYN ASHCRAFT, music educator; b. Sedgwick, Kans., July 10, 1915; d. Frank T. and Esther Hege Ashcraft; m. Herbert A. Seem, June 19, 1938 (dec. Mar. 1994); children: Herbert A. Jr., Quinda Marie Seem-Hatfield. Diploma, Sherwood Music Sch., 1936; B in Piano, Phillips U., 1936, postgrad. Tchr. Phillips U., Enid, Okla., 1960—80; pvt. piano tchr. Mem. Nat. Music Tchrs. Assn., Okla. Music Tchrs. Assn. Presbyterian. Home: 722 W Illinois Ave Enid OK 73701-7302

SEEMAN, ISADORE, human services administrator, consultant; b. Balt., Aug. 15, 1916; s. Morris and Sophia (Kostman) S.; m. Shirley Cohen; children: David, Jonathan, Philip. BS, Columbia U., 1943; MPH, U. Mich., 1947. Tchr. Balt. City Pub. Schs., 1938-40; adminstrv. asst. Balt. City Health Dept., 1942-44, dir. vital records, 1944-47, dir. health info., 1947-49; exec. sec. health sect. United Cmty. Svcs., Washington, 1949-52, asst. exec. dir., 1952-54, exec. dir., 1954-57, Health & Welfare Coun. of the Nat. Capital Area, Washington, 1957-72; chief health br. budget office U.S. Dept. Health, Edn. and Welfare, 1972-73; dir. divsn. of evaluation U.S. Dept. Health and Human Svcs., 1973-76, acting dep. asst. sec. health planning & evaluation, 1976-77, dir. long-range planning Office of Asst. Sec., 1977-78, dir. divsn. of evaluation Nat. Ctr. for Health Svc. Rsch. Hyattsville, Md., 1978-82, project mgr. Nat. Mortality Followback Survey, 1982-86; cons. health statistics Silver Spring, Md., 1986—. Bd. dirs. Kaiser Permanente Mid-Atlantic, 1994—, mem. adv. coun., 1993—; pres. Metro Washington Pub. Health Assn., 1987-89; chair policy and mgmt. com. Met. Washington Pub. Health Assessment Ctr., 1999—. Author: National Mortality Follow-Back Survey, 1986 Summary, 1993; contbr. articles to profl. jours. Mem. APHA. Jewish. Avocations: playwriting, acting, writing poetry.

SEEMAN, JULIUS, psychologist; b. Balt., Apr. 17, 1915; s. Morris and Sophia (Kostman) S.; m. Esther Millon, July 2, 1944; children: Larry, Bradley. PhD, U. minn., 1948. Lic. psychologist. Counselor U. Minn. Counseling Bur., Mpls., 1945-47; asst. prof. U. Chgo., 1947-53; prof. and clin. dir. Peabody/Vanderbilt Univs., Nashville, 1953-85, prof. emeritus, 1985—. Chmn. Tenn. Licensing Bd., 1957. Contbr. articles to profl. jours., books. Disting. Sr. Contbr., Am. Psychol. Assn., 1986. Fellow Am. Forensic Assn.; mem. Tenn. Psychol. Assn. (pres. 1956, Outstanding Sr. Psychologist award 1992), Am. Psychol. Assn. (com. chair 1956-57). Avocations: music, walking. Home: 4008 Iroquois Ave Nashville TN 37205-3828 E-mail: jules.seeman@vanderbilt.edu.

SEEMAN, MELVIN, sociologist, educator; b. Balt., Feb. 5, 1918; s. Morris and Sophie (Kostman) S.; m. Alice Ruth Zerbola, June 30, 1944; children—Teresa E., Paul D. BA, Johns Hopkins U., 1944; PhD, Ohio State U., 1947. Asst. prof. sociology Ohio State U., 1947-52, assoc. prof., 1953-59; prof. UCLA, 1959-88, prof. emeritus, 1988—. Mem. Am. Sociol. Assn. Home: 21532 Paseo Serra St Malibu CA 90265-5112 Office: UCLA Dept Sociology 405 Hilgard Ave Los Angeles CA 90095-9000 E-mail: mseeman@conet.ucla.edu.

SEEMANN, ROSALIE MARY, international business and foreign policy association executive; b. St. Louis, July 30, 1942; d. Ulysses Sylvester and Helen Maire (Hootselle) Simon; m. Richard Vaughn, Jan. 20, 1968 (dec.); 1 child, Heather Elizabeth. Student, Lindenwood Colls., St. Charles, Mo., 1973-76, Harris Tchrs. Coll., St. Louis, 1961, U. Fla., Gainesville, 1964. Vol. U.S. Peace Corps, Brazil, 1964-66; tech. analyst, group leader Conductron-Mo., St. Charles, 1966-71, bus. mgr., 1971-77; maintenance engr. McDonnell Douglas Astronautics, St. Louis, 1977-78; mgr. supply support Northrop Def. Systems Divsn., Rolling Meadows, Ill., 1978-80; logistics mgmt. cons. Logistic Support Svcs., Spring Grove, 1980-85; mgr. reliability, maintanability, integrated logistic Recon/Optical, Inc., Barrington, 1985-90; v.p., exec. dir. Mid-Am. Com. Internat. Bus. & Govt. Coop., Chgo., 1991-97; exec. dir. World Affairs Coun., St. Louis, 1997-99; founder, pres. Mid-West Inst. Internat. Exch., 1999—; v.p. global initiatives World Trade Ctr., St. Louis, 1999—2001. Bd. dirs. Libr. Internat. Rels., Chgo.-Kent Coll. Law, Prime Med. Products. Bd. dirs. U. Mo.-St. Louis Chancellor's Coun., internat. affairs com.; bd. dirs. World Affairs Coun. Am.; mem. women's bd. Goodman Theatre, Chgo.; active Girl Scouts U.S.A. Recipient commendation Conductron-Mo., 1967, pres. award Recon-Optical, 1989. Mem. Am. Soc. Assn. Execs. (internat. sect. coun. 1996—), Nat. Coun. Internat. Visitors, Am. Women Internat. Understanding, Soc. Logistics Engrs. (Mem. of Yr. award, sr. mem.), English Speaking Union, Japan Am. Soc., Chgo. Coun. Fgn. Rels. (Chgo. com.), Assn. Old Crows, Coun. Women Leaders, Execs. Club Chgo., Arts & Edn. Coun. Greater St. Louis, Internat. Trade Assn., Senate Constantine Prophyrogenetus Internat. Assn. (Greece, hon. pres.), Inst. Mid. East Studies Al-Mamun. Fax: (636) 745-2352.

SEETHARAMAN, MYSORE LAKSHMINARAYANA, internist; b. Mysore, Karnataka, India, Apr. 4, 1953; came to U.S., 1995; s. Seethalakshmi and Lakshminarayana S.; m. Uma, April 18, 1984; children: Raghunandan, Abhay. MBBS, Mysore Med. Coll., 1978. Diplomate Am. Bd. Internal Medicine, Nat. Bd. Examinations in Respiratory Diseases, India. Med. officer Primary Health Ctr., Pondicherry, India, 1979-80, Jipmer, Tuberculosis & Chest Diseases, Pondicherry, India, 1980-87, asst. prof. India, 1987-92, assoc. prof. India, 1992-95; chief resident Coney Island Hosp., N.Y.C., 1997-98; asst. attending physician Ida G. Israel Cmty. Health Ctr., Bklyn., 1998—2001, assoc. attending physician, 2001—. Commonwealth Med. fellow Commonwealth Fellowships Commn., London, Eng., 1990-91. Fellow Am. Coll. Chest Physicians; mem. AMA, ACP, Indian Med. Assn., Indian Chest Soc. Mem. Ramkrishna Mission Ch. Avocations: classical music, biographies and autobiographies of famous people. Home: 9 Nixon Ct Apt 6D Brooklyn NY 11223-6507 Office: Ida G Israel Cmty Health Ctr 2201 Neptune Ave Brooklyn NY 11224-2311 E-mail: mseetha@pol.net.

SEETHARAMAN, PERUVEMBA B. marketing educator; b. Bombay, June 19, 1970; s. Peruvemba S. and Chandra Balasubramaniam; m. Gayathri Muthuswamy, Dec. 9, 1998. B in Tech., Indian Inst. Tech., Madras, India, 1991; MS, U. Utah, 1993; PhD, Cornell U., 1998. Asst. prof. Washington U., St. Louis, 1998—. Mem. Am. Mktg. Assn., Inst. Ops. Rsch. and Mgmt. Scis., Am. Statis. Assn. Hindu. Avocations: travel, movies, tamil music. Home: 1112 Jade Wind Dr Ballwin MO 63011 Office: PO Box 1133 Saint Louis MO 63188-1133 E-mail: seethu@olin.wustl.edu.

SEFF, RICHARD, actor, writer; b. N.Y.C., Sept. 23, 1927; s. Chester and Henrietta (Levy) Siff. BA, NYU, 1947. Agt. MCA, Inc., N.Y.C., 1954-62; sec., treas. Hesseltine, Bookman & Seff, 1962-69; v.p. Creative Mgmt. Assn., 1969-74. Staff writer Theater Week Magazine, N.Y.C, 1988—. Author: (musical book) Shine!, 2001; (plays) Paris Is Out, 1969-70, The Whole Ninth Floor starring Alan Alda, 1966; appeared on Broadway in Darkness At Noon, 1950-52, Herzl, 1976, The Seagull, 1982, End of the World, 1984, Musical Comedy Murders of 1940, 1987; off-Broadway in Modigliani, 1979-80, Childe Byron, 1981, Richard II, 1982, Angels Fall, 1984, Only You, 1987, Summer and Smoke, 1988, Established Price, 1990, Countess Mitzi, 1991, Lend Me a Tenor, 1991, The Cocktail Hour, 1992, The Truth Teller, 1995, The Countess, 1999-2000; appeared in films The Onion Field, 1979, Being There, 1979, Where The Buffalo Roam, 1980, A Stranger is Watching, 1982, Quiz Show, 1994, The Hours, 2002. Recipient Carbonell award for best featured actor in play Angels Fall, Carbonell (Fla.) Com., 1984. Avocations: financial planning, theatrical investment, travel.

SEFFRIN, JOHN REESE, health science association administrator, educator; b. Hagerstown, Ind., May 19, 1944; s. Theodore H. and Mary Ellen (Reese) Seffrin; m. Carole Sue Washburn, Apr. 16, 1966; 1 child Mary. BS in Edn., Ball State U., 1966, DSc (hon.) , 1994; MS, U. Ill., 1967; PhD in Health Edn., Purdue U., 1970. Asst. prof. health edn. Purdue U., West Lafayette, Ind., 1970—76, assoc. prof., 1976—79; prof., chmn. dept. applied health sci. Ind. U., Bloomington, 1979—92; CEO Am. Cancer Soc., Atlanta, 1992—. Trustee Am. Cancer Soc. Found., 1992—; guest lectr. various pub. health orgns. and schs., 1970—; bd. dirs. Healthcare Inc. Nat. bd. dirs. Am. Lung Assn., 1980—90; treas. Partnership for Prevention of Premature Death, Disease and Disability, 1991—; mem. Pres.'s Commn. on Improving Econ. Opportunity in Cmtys. Dependent on Tobacco Prodn. While Protecting Pub. Health, 2000—; pres. State Welfare Bd. Ind. Dept. Pub. Welfare, 1979—80, 1982—84; treas. Midwest Nuc. Bd., 1973—75; chmn. cmty. edn. com. Am. Lung Assn., 1981—83, v.p., 1980, pres., 1982; chmn. bd. dirs. Nat. Health Coun., 1998—2000; bd. dirs. Nat. Ctr. for Tobacco-Free Kids, 1996—; bd. trustees The Scripps Rsch. Inst., 1999—; bd. advisors Discovery Health Media, 2000—; bd. dirs. Wabash Ctr. for the Mentally Retarded, 1970—73. Named commr.-at-large, Nat. Commn. Health Edn. Credentialing, 1995—2000, Sagamore of Wabash, State of Ind., 1980, 1988; recipient cert. appreciation, Surgeon Gen. of Pub. Health Svc., 1992, Outstanding Alumn us award, Ball State U., 1982. Fellow: Am. Sch. Health Assn. (mem. governing coun. 1979—81, 1982—89, pres. 1987—88, Howe award 1991); mem.: NAS (Nat. Cancer Policy Bd. 1997—), AMA, Am. Acad. Family Physicians (pub. adv. bd. 1999—), Rsch. Am. (bd. dirs. 1996—), Independent Sector (bd. dirs. 1997—, 1997—), Nat. Interagy. Coun. on Smoking and Health (bd. dirs. 1979—), Internat. Union Against Cancer (pres. 2000—, ex-officiio mem. U.S. nat. com. 2000—), Ind. Assn. for Health, Phys. Edn. and Recreation (pres. 1976, Cert. of Appreciation 1977, Honor award 1982), Am. Cancer Soc. (dir. Ind. Divsn. 1977—90, chmn. Ind. Divsn. 1982—85, dir.-at-large to nat. bd. dirs., chmn. nat. pub. edn. com. 1984—87, nat. v.p. 1986—87, chmn. nat. bd. dirs. 1989—91), Ind. Thoracic Soc. (mem. governing coun. 1977—84), Ind. Family Health Coun. (dir. 1979—81, v.p. 1980—81, pres. 1981), Ind. Assn. Health Educators (pres. 1975—76), Assn. for Advancement Health Edn. (bd. dirs. 1989—92), Nat. Assn. State Bds. of Edn. (commn. on sch. cmty. role in improving adolescent health 1989—90), Eta Sigma Gamma, Phi Delta Kappa. Roman Catholic. Office: Am Cancer Soc 1599 Clifton Rd NE Atlanta GA 30329-4250*

SEFTEL, DONNA SELENE, architect; b. N.Y.C., Apr. 26, 1956; d. Lawrence and Roslyn (Kaufman) S.; 1 child, Morgan Luc. Student, 1st Berlin Summer Acad., 1977, Royal Danish Acad. Fine Arts, 1978, Columbia U., 1978; BArch, Cornell U., 1980; postgrad., New Sch. for Social Rsch, N.Y.C., 1997. Registered arch., N.Y., N.J. Arch. Steven Holl Archs., N.Y.C., 1985-86; prin. Donna Selene Seftel Archs., 1986—; artist-in-residence Mott Hall, 1987—88; lectr. Archtl. League N.Y., 1987, Acad. Art and Design, Linz, Austria, 1988, Cooper-Hewit Nat. Mus. Design, 1988, CCNY, 1990, 1992, RISD, 1993, Pa. State U., 1994, Columbia U., 1995, Queensland U., RMIT, Australia, 1999; critic Royal Swedish Inst. Tech., Stockholm, 1991, Cornell U., 1991, Columbia U., 1992, 1995, Parsons Sch. Design, 1992—95. Artist-in-residence Mott Hall, N.Y.C., 1987—88; lectr. Archtl. League N.Y., 1987, Acd. Art and Design, Linz, Austria, 1988, Cooper-Hewit Nat. Mus. Design, 1988, CCNY, 1990, 92, Cornell U., 1991, Pa. State U., 1994, Columbia U., 1992, 95. Projects include Rapid Indsl. Plastics, 1985, Vacant Lots, 1987, Calif. Life Guard Tower, 1988, Theatricus Formicus, Gordon Lighting and Lightscreen, 1989, Recycling Industry, 1990, Nara Convention Ctr. Competition, 1991, Lego: Gate of Gates, Culebra House, P.R., 1992, Kulturzeile, Vienna, Austria, 1993, Interactive Playhouse, Greene Loft, N.Y.C., 1996, S-network offices, 1994-97, Wild Pitch Records, Filiberti House, 1994, Tribeca Loft, 1995; prodn. designer ind. feature film Burn, 1997; one-woman show Atelier Lorenz Mandl Gasse, Vienna, Austria, 1993; exhibited in group shows, including Urban Ctr., N.Y.C., Archtl. League N.Y., 1987, Kirsten Kiser Gallery for Arch., L.A., 1988, Grand Cen. Sta., 1989, Downtown Whitney Mus., N.Y.C., Gallery 91, N.Y.C., 1989, Storefront for Art & Arch., Nat. Inst. Archtl. Edn., N.Y.C., Cooper-Hewitt Nat. Mus. Design, N.Y.C., 1990, Moderna Museet, Kulturhuset, Stockholm, 1991, Deutsches Architektur Mus., Frankfurt am Main, 1992, Gammel Dok Ctr. for Danish Architecture, Copenhagen, Kasteel d'Erp, Baarlo, Belgium, Kunsthal, Rotterdam, Cornell U., Ithaca, N.Y., 1993, City Art Ctr., Edinburgh, Mus. Finnish Architecture, Helsinki, Mus. fur Gestaltung, Zurich, Katonah Mus. of Art, Haus der Arch., Graz, 1994, Grande Arche in La Defense, Paris, Norton Mus. Art, Palm Beach, 1995, Mus. Decorative Arts, Lausanne, 1996, Gemeente Mus., Helmond, The Netherlands, Mus. de Civilisation, Quebec City, Arch. Ctr., Berlin, 1997; pub. in various publs. including N.Y. Times, DOMUS, Metropolis, Architecture Record, AIA N.Y. Architecture, World Architecture, Shelter & Dreams-Katonah Mus. Catalogue, Unpvt. House-MOMA Catalogue, Mama 27, Gate of The Present-LEGO Catalogue, Ideas for New Social Bldgs., Vacant Lots, New Schs. for N.Y., Showrooms, Front 3, Archtl. Edn. for Children at Mott Hall-Dist. 6, N.Y.C., etc. Recipient award Young Archs. Forum 6, Archtl. League N.Y., 1987, project award N.Y. chpt. AIA, 1989; architecture fellow N.Y. Found. for Arts, 1988; Pritzger fellow Djerassi Resident Artists Program, Woodside, Calif., 1995, in collections of Lego, Denmark and Yamagiwa, Japan. Democrat. Jewish. Address: 95 Drake Ln Manhasset NY 11030-1227 E-mail: dseftel@earthlink.net.

SEFTON, MILDRED MCDONALD, retired educator; b. E. Liverpool, Ohio, June 21, 1942; d. David Eugene and Hannah Susannah (McElhaney) McD.; m. Melvin Dale Sefton, July 10, 1965 (div. Sept. 1972). BS in Edn., Ind. U. of Pa., 1964; MS in Edn., Carnegie Mellon U., 1970. Home econs. tchr. Ctr. Area Sch. Dist., Monaca, Pa., 1964-66, Ambridge (Pa.) Area Sch. Dist., 1966-95, dept. chair, 1972-95; tchr. Wheeler Sch. of Bus., Pitts., 1980-82; dir. Artcraft Concepts, Balston Spa, N.Y., 1977-82; co-owner Winner Trade, Beaver, Pa., 1995—. Bd. dirs. Beaver Area Heritage Found. Dir. accessions Beaver Area Hist. Mus., 1997—; mem., exec. sec. bd. dirs. Beaver Area Heritage Found, 1998—; mem. Beaver County Bicentennial Com., 1999-2000. Mem. NEA, Pa. Edn. Assn., Pa. Assn. Family and Consumer Scis., Nat. Assn. Family and Consumer Scis. Republican. Presbyterian. Home: 1360 River Rd Beaver PA 15009-2523 Office: Winner Trade 1360 River Rd Beaver PA 15009-2523

SEGA, RONAD M. federal agency administrator; BS in Math. and Physics, USAF Acad., 1974; MS in Physics, Ohio State U., 1975; grad., Squadron Officers Sch., 1979; PhD in Elec. Engring., U. Colo., 1982; grad., Air Command and Staff Coll., 1985, Air War Coll., 1991; doctorate (hon.) , Clarkson U., 1993; grad. Mgmt. Inst., Harvard U., 1997; doctorate (hon.) , Bridgewater State Coll., 1998; exec. program in global security, Harvard U., 2001. Dir. def., rsch. and engring. Dept Def., Washington, 2001—; commd. 2d lt. USAF, 1974, advanced through grades to maj. gen., 2001; dean Coll. Engring. and Applied Sci. U. Colo., Colorado Springs; astronaut Space Shuttle Discovery, 1990; dir. ops. NASA, Russia, 1994—95; payload comdr. 3d Shuttle/Mir docking mission Atlantis , 1996. Contbr. articles to tech. publs. Decorated Legion of Merit, Def. Meritorious Svc. medal, Meritorious Svc. medal with oak leaf cluster; recipient inductee, Ohio Vets. Hall of Fame, 1994; fellow Air Force rsch. fellow, Air Force Office Sci. Acad., 1980. Fellow: AIAA (assoc. Achievement award 1996), Inst. for Advancement of Engring.; mem.: IEEE (sr.), Aerospace Edn. Found. (trustee 2000). Office: Dept Def Dir Def Rsch and Engring 3030 Defense Pentagon Washington DC 20301-3030

SEGAL, BERNARD LOUIS, physician, educator; b. Montreal, Que., Can., Feb. 13, 1929; came to U.S., 1961, naturalized, 1966; s. Irving and Fay (Schecter) S.; m. Idajane Fischman, Feb. 17, 1963; 1 dau., Jody Segal. BSc cum laude, McGill U., 1950, postgrad., 1950-51, MD, C.M. high standing, 1955. Diplomate Am. Bd. Internal Medicine. Intern Jewish Gen Hosp., Montreal, 1955-56; resident Balt. City Hosp., 1956-57, Beth Israel Hosp., Boston, 1957-58, Georgetown Med. Ctr., Washington, 1958-59, St. George's Hosp., London, Eng., 1959-61; pvt. practice internal medicine and cardiology Phila., 1961—; prof. medicine Med. Coll. Pa., Hahnemann U., 1996—; prof. medicine, sr. attending physician Jefferson Med. Coll./Thomas Jefferson U., 1998—. Dir. cardiology Thomas Jefferson U., 1998. Author: Auscultation of the Heart, 1965; Editor: Theory and Practice of Auscultation, 1964, Engineering in the Practice of Medicine, 1966, Your Heart, 1972, Arteriosclerosis and Coronary Heart Disease, 1972; mem. editl. bd. Am. Jour. Cardiology, 1970—, Clin. Echocardiography, 1978; contbr. articles to profl. jours. Fellow ACP, Am. Coll. Cardiology (chmn. scholar-trainee com., trustee 1969-71), Am. Coll. Chest Physicians; mem. N.Y. Acad. Scis., Alpha Omega Alpha. Home: 1156 Red Rose Ln Villanova PA 19085-2121 Office: Thomas Jefferson Hosp Gibbon Bldg 111 S 11th St Ste 6215 Philadelphia PA 19107-4824 also: 401 E City Line Ave Ste 525 Bala Cynwyd PA 19004-1125

SEGAL, CORIN, engineering educator, researcher; b. Bucharest, Romania, Feb. 15, 1952; came to U.S., 1987; s. Sami and Eva Segal. BS, Poly. Inst. Bucharest, 1975; PhD, U. Va., 1991. Engr. Aeronaves Enterprise, Brashov, Romania, 1975-80; chief tech. bur. Miromit, Ltd., Ashkelon, Israel, 1980-81; sr. engr. Israel Aircraft Industries, Tel Aviv, 1981-87; asst. prof. engring. U. Fla., Gainesville, 1991-98, assoc. prof., 1998—. Mem. AIAA (sr.), The Combustion Inst.

SEGAL, DAVID ROBERT, sociology educator; b. N.Y.C., June 22, 1941; s. Harry and Daisy Rose Segal; m. Mady Wechsler, Dec. 25, 1976; 1 child, Eden Heather. BA, Harpur Coll., 1962; MA, U. Chgo., 1963, PhD, 1967; DHL (hon.), Towson U., 1991. From asst. prof. to assoc. prof. U. Mich., Ann Arbor, 1966-75; tech. area chief U.S. Army Rsch. Inst., Arlington, Va., 1973-75; prof. U. Md., Coll. Pk., 1975—; dir. Ctr. Rsch. Mil. Orgn., 1995—. Vis. rsch. fellow U. Bonn, Germany, 1971; guest scholar Brookings Inst., Washington, 1981-84; disting. vis. prof. U.S. Mil. Acad., W. Point, N.Y., 1988-89; mem. bd. visitors U.S. Army War Coll., Carlisle, Pa., 1997-01. Co-author: The All-Volunteer Force, 1977, Recruiting for Uncle Sam, 1989, Peace Keepers and Their Wives,

1993, The Postmodern Military, 2000. Spl. asst. peace ops. Chief Staff U.S. Army, Washington, 1993-95; mem. task force Def. Sci. Bd., Washington, 1998-00. Fellow Inter-Univ. Sem. Armed Forces and Soc. (pres. 1995—); mem. Am. Sociol. Assn. (chair sect. peace and war 1991-92), D.C. Sociol. Soc. (pres. 1994-95, Morris Rosenberg award 1997). Avocations: tennis, astronomy. Office: U Md Dept Sociology College Park MD 20742-1315 E-mail: dsegal@socy.umd.edu.

SEGAL, FREDERICK LESLIE, lawyer; b. N.Y.C., Oct. 7, 1947; children: Sabrina Meredith, Elysia Meghan. BS, U. Pitts., 1970; JD, Hofstra U., 1973; LLM, NYU, 1979. Bar: Pa. 1979, N.Y. 1974, U.S. Patent and Trademark Office 1975, U.S. Supreme Ct. 1978, U.S. Ct. Appeals (2d cir.) 1974, U.S. Dist. Ct. (we. dist.) Pa. 1979, U.S. Dist. Ct. (ea. and so. dists.) N.Y. 1974, U.S. Ct. Customs and Patent Appeals 1976, U.S. Ct. Claims 1976, U.S. Ct. Appeals D.. 1982, U.S. Customs Ct. 1976, U.S. Tax Ct. 1976. Clk. U.S. Dist. Ct. (ea. dist.) N.Y., Bklyn., 1973—74; assoc. Mendes & Mount, N.Y.C., 1974—78, Hart & Hume, N.Y.C., 1978—79, Rosenberg & Kirschner, Pitts., 1979—81, Berger Kapetan, Malakoff & Meyers, Pitts., 1981—82; sole practice, 1982—. Patent agt., atty. U.S. Patent and Trademark Office, Washington, 1982—; arbitrator Am. Arbitration Assn., 1983—, Ct. Common Pleas Allegheny County, Pitts., 1981—. With N.G. U.S. Army, 1970—72. Scholar, N.Y. State scholar, 1971—73. Mem.: ATLA, ABA, Pa. Trial Lawyers Assn., Allegheny County Bar Assn., Pa. Bar Assn., U. Pitts. Golden Panther Alumni Assn. (bd. dirs. 1983—), Men of Achievement. Democrat. Jewish. Home: 1740 Beechwood Blvd Pittsburgh PA 15217-1714 Office: Manor Complex 564 Forbes Ave Ste 1004 Pittsburgh PA 15219-2903

SEGAL, GARY L. lawyer; b. Miami Beach, Fla., Dec. 30, 1954; m. Cathy A. Segal, May 29, 1977; children: Kenneth, Paula. BS, Boston U., 1972-76; JD, Cath. U., 1976-79. Bar: Md. 1979, D.C. 1981, U.S. Dist. Ct. D.C., U.S. Dist. Ct. Md., U.S. Ct. Appeals (4th cir.), U.S. Supreme Ct. Staff atty. Office Fed. Register, Washington, 1979-81; ptnr. Galfond & Segal, Rockville, Md., 1981-92; pvt. practice, 1992—. Mem. Md. Bar Assn., D.C. Bar Assn., Montgomery County Bar Assn., Md. Trial Lawyers Assn. Office: 600 Jefferson Plz Ste 308 Rockville MD 20850 E-mail: garysegal@his.com.

SEGAL, GARY STEPHEN, investment and venture capital company executive; b. Vancouver, B.C., Can., Sept. 18, 1952; s. Joseph and Rosalie (Wosk) S.; m. Nanci Ann Golick, Aug. 30, 1979; 4 children. BA, U. B.C., 1974; LLB, U. We. Ont., London, 1979. Bar: B.C. Articled student Freeman & Co., Vancouver, 1979-80, assoc. lawyer, 1980-85; v.p. Kingswood Capital Corp., 1985—; pres. Kingswood Venture Capital Corp., 1990—. Bd. dirs. E-Z-Rect Mfg. Inc., North Vancouver, StorkCraft Mfg. Inc., Richmond, B.C., Sterling Shoes Inc., Richmond, Arteif Furniture Mfg. Inc., Edmonton, Alta. Mem. Can. Bar Assn., Vancouver Bd. Trade, Vancouver Lawn Tennis and Badminton Club, Richmond Golf and Country Club, Simon Fraser U. Pres.'s Club. Avocations: tennis, basketball, piano, languages. Office: Kingswood Capital Corp 701 W Georgia St Ste 520 Vancouver BC Canada V7Y 1A1

SEGAL, GERALDINE ROSENBAUM, sociologist; b. Aug. 26, 1908; d. Harry and Mena (Hamburg) Rosenbaum; m. Bernard Gerard Segal, Oct. 22, 1933; children: Loretta Joan Cohen, Richard Murry. BS in Edn., U. Pa., 1930, MA in Human Rels., 1963, PhD in Sociology, 1978; MS in Libr. Sci., Drexel U., 1968; LittD (hon.), Franklin & Marshall Coll., 1990. Social worker County Relief Bd., Phila., 1931-35; sociologist, 1935—. Cons. and lectr. in field. Author: In Any Fight Some Fall, 1975, Blacks in the Law, 1983. Bd. dirs. NCCJ, 1937-47, 82—. sec., 1983-91; bd. overseers U. Pa. Sch. Social Work, 1983-97; bd. dirs. Juvenile Law Ctr., 1984-98; chair Phila. Tutorial Project, 1966-68; 1st v.p. U. Pa. Alumnae Assn., 1967-70. Co-recipient Nat. Neighbors Disting. Leadership in Civil Rights award, 1988; recipient Drum Major award for Human Rights, Phila. Martin Luther King, Jr. Assn. for Nonviolence, 1990, Brotherhood Sisterhood award NCCJ, 1994. Democrat. Jewish. Home: 2401 Pennsylvania Ave Apt 19c44 Philadelphia PA 19130-3003

SEGAL, HARVEY MORDECAI, physician; b. Ulm, Germany, Nov. 9, 1948; came to U.S., 1951; s. Izak and Celia Segal; m. Nelly Segal, July 25, 1987; 1 child, Frederique. MD, Case Western Res. U., 1982. Diplomate in internal medicine and hematology Am. Bd. Internal Medicine. Resident in internal medicine U. Minn. Hosps., Mpls., 1982-85, fellow in hematology, 1985-87; hematologist/oncologist Cancer Care of Maine, Bangor, 1987—. Jewish. Office: Cancer Care of Maine 417 State St Ste 20 Bangor ME 04401-6617

SEGAL, HOWARD PAUL, history educator; b. Phila., July 15, 1948; s. Alexander David and Irene Sylvia (Goldsmith) S.; m. Deborah D. Rogers, Nov. 26, 1988; children: Richard William Rogers, Raechel Maya Rogers. AB, Franklin and Marshall Coll., Lancaster, Pa., 1970; MA, Princeton U., 1972, PhD, 1975. Lectr. and Taft postdoctoral fellow in history U. Cin., 1975-76; lectr. and Killam postdoctoral fellow in history Dalhousie U., Halifax, N.S., Can., 1976-78; asst. prof. history U. Mich., Ann Arbor, 1978-83; lectr. in history of sci. Harvard U., Cambridge, Mass., 1984-86; asst. prof. history U. Maine, Orono, 1986-88, assoc. prof. history, 1988-92, prof. of history, 1992-96, Bird and Bird prof. history, 1996—. Author: Technological Utopianism in American Culture, 1985, (with A. Marcus) Technology in America: A Brief History, 1989, 2d edit. 1999, Future Imperfect, 1994; co-editor: Technology, Pessimism and Post-Modernism, 1994. Am. Philos. Soc. rsch. grantee, 1979; Andrew Mellon faculty fellow, 1984-85. Mem. Am. Hist. Assn., Orgn. Am. Historians, Am. Studies Assn., Soc. for History of Tech., Am. Soc. Engring. Edn., Phi Beta Kappa, Phi Alpha Theta. Democrat. Jewish. Office: Univ of Maine Dept of History 5774 Stevens Hall Orono ME 04469-5774

SEGAL, IRVING RANDALL, lawyer; b. Allentown, Pa., Oct. 15, 1914; s. Samuel I. and Rose (Kantor) S.; m. Eleanor F. Smolens, Dec. 26, 1943; children: Betsy A. Segal Carter, Kathy J., Robert J. BA, U. Pa., 1935; LLB, 1938. Bar: Pa. 1938. Instr. polit. sci. U. Pa., 1938-42; law clk. Ct. Common Pleas No. 4, Phila. County, Pa., 1938-39; assoc. Schnader, Harrison, Segal & Lewis, Phila., 1939-49, ptnr., 1949-92, sr. counsel, 1993—. Permanent mem. Jud. Conf. 3d Circuit U.S. Ct. Appeals; regional rationing atty. OPA, 1942 Author: May It Please the Court, 1998. V.p. Nat. Kidney Disease Found., 1954-59, hon. life del., 1959-64; pres. Nephrosis Found., Phila., 1953-56; bd. mgrs. Woman's Hosp. Phila., 1957-64, v.p., 1962-63; bd. Jewish Edn., Phila., 1948-72; trustee YMHA, YWHA, 1954-58. Served to capt. Judge Adv. Gen. Dept. AUS, 1942-46. Decorated Mil. Commendation medal. Fellow Am. Coll. Trial Lawyers (regent 1976-79, sec. 1979-80); mem. ABA (corrections com. 1980-87, jud. selection tenure and compensation com. 1988-93, com. on legal problems of the elderly 1997-99), Pa. Bar Assn., Phila. Bar Assn. (chmn. sr. lawyers 1996-99), Am. Law Inst., Am. Bar Found. (50-yr. award 1999), Am. Judicature Soc., World Peace Through Law, Am. Acad. Polit. and Social Sci., Order of Coif, Phi Beta Kappa, Pi Gamma Mu (pres., 1934-35), Delta Sigma Rho. Jewish (dir., v.p. temple). Clubs: Phila. Lawyers, Art Alliance, Locust, Army and Navy of Washington Home: 210 W Rittenhouse Sq Apt 2306 Philadelphia PA 19103-5776

SEGAL, JACK, mathematics educator; b. Phila., May 9, 1934; s. Morris and Rose (Novin) S.; m. Arlene Stern, Dec. 18, 1955; children: Gregory, Sharon. BS, U. Miami, 1955, MS, 1957; PhD, U. Ga., 1960. Instr. math. U. Wash., Seattle, 1960-61, asst. prof., 1961-65, assoc. prof., 1965-70, prof., 1970-1999, chmn. dept., 1975-78, prof. emeritus, 2000—. Author: Lecture Notes in Mathematics, 1978, Shape Theory, 1982. NSF postdoctoral fellow Inst. Advanced Study, Princeton, N.J., 1963-64; Fulbright fellow U. Zagreb, Croatia, 1969-70, U. Coll. London hon. rsch. fellow, 1988; Nat. Acad. Sci. exch. prof. U. Zagreb, Croatia, 1979-80. Mem. Am. Math. Soc. Home: 8711 25th Pl NE Seattle WA 98115-3416 Office: U Washington Dept Mathematics Seattle WA 98195-0001 E-mail: segal@math.washington.edu.

SEGAL, JEFFREY A. political scientist, educator; b. Bklyn., Oct. 3, 1956; s. Eli Segal, Irene Isabella Hills, Phyllis L. Harmin; m. Christine R. Ripa; children: Michelle, Paul. PhD, Michigan State University, East Lansing, MI, 1980—83, MA, 1978—80; BA, University at Albany, Albany, NY, 1974—78. Professor State University of New York at Stony Brook, Stony Brook, NY, 1982—. Author: (book) The Supreme Court and the Attitudinal Model Revisited, 2002, Majority Rule or Minority Will, 1999 (C. Herman Pritchett Award, 2000), The Supreme Court Compendium, 1994 (Outstanding Academic Books, Political Science, 1993-1997, Choice, 1998), Suprme Court Compendium, 1994 (Best Research Books Award, Lingua Franca, 1995), (Book) The Supreme Court and the Attitudinal Model, 1993, Senate Elections, 1992, (Journal Article) Law and Society Review, 2002, Judicature, 2001, American Journal of Political Science, 2001, American Political Science Review, 2000, Political Research Quarterly, 2000, American Journal of Political Science, 2000, Journal of Politics, 1998, American Political Science Review, 1997, Journal of Politics, 1996, American Political Science Review, 1996, American Journal of Political Science, 1996, Journal of Politics, 1995, American Journal of Political Science, 1994, American Political Science Review, 1994, American Journal of Political Science, 1992, American Political Science Review, 1990, Western Political Quarterly, 1990, Judicature, 1990, Women and Politics, 1990, Legislative Studies Quarterly, 1990, American Political Science Review, 1989, Western Political Quarterly, 1988, Journal of Politics, 1987, 1986, Judicature, 1986, American Journal of Political Science, 1985, American Political Science Review, 1984, Harvard Journal on Legislation, 2002. Trustee Mount Sinai Board of Education, Mount Sinai, NY, 2002. Mem.: Midwest Political Science Association (Chair, Program Committee 2001—02), Law and Courts Section, American Political Science Association (Secretary-Treasurer 1990—93), Southern Political Science Association, American Political Science Association; : Midwest Political Science Association (Executive Council 1995—97). Jewish. Avocation: basketball. Home: 41 Hawthorne St. Mount Sinai NY 11766 Office: SUNY Stony Brook Department of Political Science Stony Brook NY 11794

SEGAL, JONATHAN BRUCE, editor; b. N.Y.C., May 12, 1946; s. Clement and Florence Lillian (Miller) S.; m. Haidi Kuhn, June 30, 1974. BA, Washington Coll., 1966. Writer, editor N.Y. Times, N.Y.C., 1966-73; editor Quadrangle/N.Y. Times Book Co., 1974-76; sr. editor Simon & Schuster, 1976-81; exec. editor, editor-in-chief, editorial dir., v.p. Times Books, 1981-89; editor-at-large Random House, 1985-89; v.p., sr. editor Alfred A. Knopf, 1989—. Contbr. articles to popular jours. Democrat. Jewish. Home: 115 E 9th St Apt 12E New York NY 10003-5420 Office: Alfred A Knopf 299 Park Ave New York NY 10171 E-mail: jsegal@randomhouse.com.

SEGAL, LINDA GALE, insurance executive; b. Panama City, Fla., Dec. 14, 1947; d. Homer Ford Jr. and Mary Virginia (Phillmon) F. m. Howard Arthur Segal, Dec. 29, 1970; 1 child, David Samuel. Student, Orlando (Fla.) Jr. Coll., 1966-69, Rollins Coll., 1972. Sales asst. Sta. WESH-TV, Orlando, Fla., 1973-76; mktg. coordinator Sta. WFBC-TV, Grenneville, S.C., 1976-77; traffic mgr. STa. WRDW-TV, Augusta, Ga., 1978-80; field underwriter Liberty Life Ins. Co., Greenville, 1980-81; agt. benefits dept. J. Rolfe Davis Ins. Agy., Orlando, 1981-84; sr. market sales rep. Humana, Inc., 1984-86; dir. mktg. Nat. Med. Mgmt., 1986-87; sr. account exec. Physicians Health Plan Fla., Inc., Tampa, 1987-88, N.E. Fin. Services, Orlando, 1988-89; mktg. mgr. Ins. Mgmt. Svcs., Inc., Greenville, S.C., 1989-90; regional mktg. dir. Horizons Internat. Inc., St. Augustine, Fla., 1991-92; dir. bus. devel. ResCare Home Health, Inc., Jacksonville, 1992—. Pvt. practice ins. cons., Tampa and Orlando, Fla., 1986-89. Mem. Am. Bus. Women's Assn., Nat. Assn. Profl. Saleswomen, Nat. Assn. Health Underwriters, Assn. Life Underwriters, Women Life Underwriters Confedn., Nat. Assn. Securities Dealers (registered rep.). Republican. Office: 4329 Falling Leaf Ct Jacksonville FL 32258-4535 E-mail: lgs@itilink.com.

SEGAL, LORE, writer; b. Vienna, Austria, Mar. 8, 1928; came to U.S., 1951, naturalized, 1956; d. Ignatz and Franzi (Stern) Groszmann; m. David I. Segal, Nov. 3, 1960 (dec.); children: Beatrice Ann, Jacob Paul. BA in English, Bedford Coll., U. London, Eng., 1948. Prof. writing div. Sch. Arts, Columbia U., also Princeton U., Sarah Lawrence Coll., Bennington Coll.; prof. English U. Ill., Chgo., 1978-92, Ohio State U., 1992-97. Author: Other People's Houses, 1964; Lucinella, 1976, Her First American, 1985; (children's book) Tell Me A Mitzi, 1970, All the Way Home, 1973, Tell Me a Trudy, 1977; The Story of Mrs. Brubeck and How She Looked for Trouble and Where She Found Him, 1981, The Story of Mrs. Lovewright and Purrless Her Cat, 1985, Morris the Artist, 1999; translator: (with W.D. Snodgrass) Gallows Songs, 1968, The Juniper Tree and Other Tales from Grimm, 1973, The Book of Adam to Moses, 1987, The Story of King Saul and King David, 1991; contbr. short stories, articles to N.Y. Times Book Rev., Partisan Rev., New Republic, The New Yorker, others. Guggenheim fellow, 1965-66; Council Arts and Humanities grantee, 1968-69; Artists Public Service grantee, 1970-71; CAPS grantee, 1975; Nat. Endowment Arts grantee, spring 1982, 1987; NEH grantee, 1983; Acad. Arts and Letters award, 1986. Address: 280 Riverside Dr New York NY 10025-9010 E-mail: lsegal70@aol.com.

SEGAL, MARTIN ELI, retired actuarial and consulting company executive; b. Vitebsk, Russia, Aug. 15, 1916; came to U.S., 1921, naturalized, 1928; s. Isidor and Anna (Title) S.; m. Edith Levy, June 17, 1937; children: Susan Segal Rai, Paul. LHD (hon.), Pratt Inst., 1976; MusD (hon.), Mannes Coll. Music, 1976; LHD (hon.), Grad. Ctr. CUNY, 1979, L.I. U., 1986, NYU, 1988; D in Music (hon.), Manhattan Sch. Music, 1999. Various positions ins. industry, 1935-39; founder The Segal Co., consultants and actuaries, N.Y.C., 1939, pres., CEO, 1939-67, chmn. bd., 1967-91, chmn. emeritus, 1991—. Pres. Wertheim Asset Mgmt. Svcs., Inc., N.Y.C., 1972-75, chmn., bd., 1975-82; ptnr. Wertheim & Co., investment bankers, N.Y.C., 1967-82. Founding chmn. The N.Y. Internat. Festival of the Arts, Inc., 1985-2002; chmn. bd. Lincoln Ctr. Performing Arts, Inc., 1981-86, chmn. emeritus, 1986—; organizing co-chmn. Internat. Conf. on Future of Arts Edn., 1999; bd. dirs. Pub. Radio Internat., 1981-94, dir. emeritus, 1994-98; counselor at large, 1998—; co-chmn. Conf. on Intellectual Property The Arts and Tech., 1994; chmn. arts and culture com., N.Y. 92, N.Y. 93, N.Y. 94, N.Y. 95; mem., bd. dirs. Nat. Bldg. Mus., 1983-91; founding mem., bd. advisers Libr. of Am., 1984—; trustee Am.-Scandinavian Found., 1986-91, adv. trustee, 1991—; bd. visitors Grad. Sch. and Univ. Ctr., CUNY, 1983-96; bd. dirs. The Grad. Ctr. Found., Inc., 1996—, ASCAP Found., 1997—; mem. adv. com. arts Harvard and Radcliffe, 1993-99, mem. office for the arts coun., 1999—; bd. trustees, chmn. exhibitions com. Mus. Modern Art, 1978-81; trustee Inst. for Advanced Study, Princeton, N.J., 1972-91, trustee emeritus, 1991—; trustee City Ctr. Music and Drama, 1971—, pres. Cultural Assistance Ctr., Inc., 1977-82, chmn., 1982-84; founding pres. Film Soc. of Lincoln Ctr., 1968-78, pres. emeritus, 1978—; mem. adv. com. Tony voter Am. Theater Wing, 2000—; mem. adv. coun. Theatre Devel. Fund, 1992—; mem. Nat. Bd. of Young Audiences, Inc., 1979—; mem. adv. bd. Concert Artists Guild, 1983-2000; founding mem. publs. com. The Pub. Interest, 1965—; mem. vis. com. Harvard U. Sch. Pub. Health, 1979-92, dean's coun. Sch. Pub. Health, 1990—; bd. dirs. Helena Rubinstein Foundn., 1972-95; chmn. mayor's Com. on Cultural Policy, 1974; founding chmn. Commn. for Cultural Affairs City of N.Y., 1975; chmn. pub. svc. awards com. Fund for City of N.Y., 1978, 79, bd. dirs., 1978-87; co-chair China cultural exchange mission, Ctr. US-China Arts Exchange, 1979; founder Film Guild N.Y., 1940-41. Decorated Royal Swedish Order of Polar Star, 1984; officer of Arts and Letters, Ministry of Culture of French Govt., 1984; recipient cert. of merit Mcpl. Art Soc., 1974; spl. award Internat. Film Importers and Distbrs. Am., 1973; N.Y.C. Mayor's award of honor for arts and culture, 1982; Ann. award of distinction Mus. City of N.Y., 1982; Concert Artists Guild award, 1983; Disting. Am. of Fgn. Birth award Internat. Ctr. N.Y.C., 1985; John H. Finley medal Alumni Assn. CCNY, 1985; Town Hall Friend of the Arts award, 1987; Dirs. Emeriti award Lincoln Ctr. for Performing Arts, Inc., 1987; N.Y. State Gov's. Arts award, 1989; Pres.'s award Grad. Sch. and Univ. Ctr. of City Univ. of N.Y., 1990; City of N.Y. Edn. Fund award LWV, 1984; award for svc. to music Third Street Music Sch. Settlement, 1981; Annual Arts Leadership award Alumni and Friends of LaGuardia H.S., 1985; Songwriters' Hall of Fame Patron of the Arts award, 1988; Nat. Fedn. Music Clubs Presdl. Citation award, 1989; Creative Arts Rehab. Ctr. Pub. Spirit award, 1989; Honor medal The Nat. Arts Club, 1992; Lincoln Ctr. Laureate, 1997; Our Town Treasure award Mus. City of N.Y., 1998; Civic Leadership award Citizens Union, 1998; Arts Roundtable award of honor, 1998; Martin E. Segal Theatre Ctr., CUNY Graduate Ctr, 2000; Acting Co. Joan Warburg Humanitarian award, 2001; S.L.E. Found (lupus) award, 2001 Fellow: Royal Soc. (London); mem.: Players Club, The Pilgrims of the U.S., Century Assn. Democrat. Jewish. Office: 375 Park Ave Ste 2602 New York NY 10152-2699

SEGAL, PHYLLIS NICHAMOFF, lawyer, federal agency administrator; b. Apr. 18, 1945; d. Sidney and Theresa Helen (Uroff) Nichamoff; m. Eli J. Segal, June 13, 1965; children: Jonathan, Mora. Student, Brandeis U., 1962-65; BA, U. Mich., 1966; JD, Georgetown U., 1973. Bar: N.Y. 1974, U.S. Dist. Ct. (so. and ea. dists.) N.Y. 1975, Mass. 1983, U.S. Supreme Ct. 1979. Assoc. Weil, Gotshal and Manges, N.Y.C., 1973-77; legal dir. NOW Legal Def. and Edn. Fund., 1977-82, gen. counsel, 1986—. Chmn. Fed. Labor Rels. Auth., Washington, 1994—; gen. counsel Exec. office Transp. and Constrn., Commonwealth of Mass., 1984-86; past dep. Atty. Gen. State of Mass., Boston; adj. asst. prof. law NYU, 1980-82; fellow Bunting Inst. Radcliffe Coll., 1982-83; cons. U.S. Commn. Civil Rights. Contbr. articles to profl. jours. Mem. Commn. on Party Reform Nat. Dem. Party, 1972-73, mem. Compliance Rev. Commn., 1974-76; mem. adv. bd. Mass. Commn. Against Discrimination, 1983—. Mem. ABA, Fedn. Women Lawyers Jud. Screening Panel, Mass. Bar Assn. Home: 314 Dartmouth St Ph Boston MA 02116-1809 Office: Fed Labor Rels Auth 607 14th St NW Washington DC 20005-2000*

SEGAL, RICHARD ARTHUR, JR. advertising agency executive; b. Hamilton, Ohio, Mar. 16, 1957; s. Richard Arthur and Frances Margaret (Clem) S.; m. Miriam Barnes, Dec. 8, 1978 (div. Feb. 1982); 1 child, Cameron Reid; m. Adrien Kim Stacy, July 30, 1983; children: Marshall Elliott, Noah Alexander. Grad. high sch., Hamilton. Adminstrv. asst. Cuyahoga County Rep. Cen. and Exec. Com., Cleve., 1975-76; dir. scheduling and advance '76 Taft for Senate Com., Cin., 1976-77; dispatcher Butler county Sheriff's Office, Hamilton, 1977-78; campaign mgr. Atkins for Congress, Cin., 1978; exec. asst. to chmn. Ohio Rep. Party, Columbus, 1978-80; dir. pub. rels. Ohio Ho. Reps., 1980; v.p. Alpha Tech. Svcs., Hamilton, 1980-81; CEO HSR Bus. to Bus. Inc., Cin., 1981—. Mem. opinion rsch. panel Wall St. Jour., 1995. Contbr. articles to profl. jours. Mem. city coun. City of Hamilton, 1982—84; sr. advisor Forbes for Pres., Washington, 2000; mem. Butler County Rep. Cen. and Exec. Com., 1976—90; elder Evang. Free Ch.; mem. gen. com. 2002 Cin. Billy Graham Mission; bd. dirs. Fitton Ctr. Creative Arts, 1999. His company named Agy. of the Yr., Advt. Age. Bus. Mktg., 1994, 97, 2001, eCommerce champion, B to B Mag., 2000. Mem. Bus. Mktg. Assn., Greter Cin. C. of C. Avocations: reading, sporting clays, Civil War history, fitness, canoeing. Office: HSR Bus to Bus Inc 300 E-Business Way Ste 500 Cincinnati OH 45241 E-mail: rsegal@hsr.com.

SEGAL, ROBERT MARTIN, lawyer; b. Atlantic City, Apr. 7, 1935; s. Nathan Albert and Edna (Dutkin) S.; m. Rhoda Sue Luber, June 8, 1958; children— Deborah Ann, William Nathan, Elizabeth Ann Student, Cornell U., 1953-54; BS in Econs., U. Pa., 1957; LLB cum laude, Harvard Law Sch., 1960. Bar: Pa. 1961. Assoc. Wolf, Block, Schorr & Solis-Cohen LLP, Phila., 1960-69, ptnr., 1969—, chmn., exec. com., 1978-79, 82-83, 86-87, 89-98. Hon. pres. Jewish Employment and Vocat. Svc. Contbr. articles to profl. jours. and mags. Constable of elections Lower Merion Twp., Pa., 1970-72; bd. dirs. Jewish Family and Children's Agy., Am. Jewish Com., Feinstein Ctr. for Am. Jewish History at Temple U., Greater Phila. Urban Affairs Coalition; bd. govs. Rep. Jewish Coalition; former trustee Hahnemann U., Fedn. Jewish Agys., Phila. Rehab. Plan, Inc., Rosenbach Mus. and Libr. Mem. ABA, Pa. Bar Assn., Phila. Bar Assn., Internat. Coun. Shopping Ctrs., Urban Land Inst. (assoc.), Am. Coll. Real Estate Lawyers, Phila. Bar Found. (trustee 1981-87), Am. Law Inst., Harvard Law Sch. Assn. Phila., The Federalist Soc. (bd. advisors Phila. chpt.), Wharton Club, Chaine des Rotisseurs, L'Ordre Mondial, Sunday Breakfast Club, La Coquille Club, Harvard Club, Beta Gamma Sigma. Avocations: golf, swimming. Office: Wolf Block Schorr & Solis-Cohen LLP 1650 Arch St Fl 22 Philadelphia PA 19103-2097 E-mail: rsegal@wolfblock.com.

SEGAL, ROBERT S. retail executive; b. New Haven, Nov. 4, 1954; s. Leonard and Barbara Segal; m. Mariquita A.K. Segal, Aug. 7, 1977; 1 child, James Q. AB, Ripon Coll., 1975; MA, NYU, 1977; postgrad., U. Ill., 1981. Buyer Hecht Co., Arlington, Va., 1981-87; mktg. mgr. Lechmere, Woburn, Mass., 1987-89; v.p. merchandising Rickel Home Ctr., Plainfield, N.J., 1989-90; dir. merchandising Best Products, Richmond, Va., 1990-93; sr. v.p. merchandising Fresh Fields, Rockville, Md., 1993-94; v.p. merchandising Shopko, Green Bay, Wis., 1995—. Mem. adv. bd. Internat. Housewares Show, Chgo., 1998—. Contbr. articles to profl. jours.. Bd. dirs. Autism Soc. of Am. Found., 2000-2001, Orgn.for Autism Rsch., 2002—. Mem. Phi Beta Kappa.

SEGAL, SCOTT, interventional radiologist; b. Bklyn., May 3, 1968; s. Lenoard and Susan S.; m. Lisa, Mar. 27, 1999. BS, Union Coll., 1989; MD, Albert Einstein Coll. Medicine, N.Y.C., 1993. Diplomate Am. Bd. Radiology, cert. added qualification in vascular & interventional radiology 01. Resident in radiology Montefiore Med. Ctr., Bronx, N.Y., 1994-98, fellow in interventional radiology, 1998-99. Office: Berkshire Med Ctr 725 North St Pittsfield MA 01201

SEGAL, SIMON, real estate executive, finance company executive; b. Havana, Cuba, Apr. 16, 1941; brought to U.S., 1955, naturalized, 1970; s. Govsey and Julia (Getzug) S.; B.C.E., Cornell U., 1965; MS in Mgmt., Fla. Internat. U., 1982; MS in Fin., Fla., Internat. U., 1987, MBA, 1999. Owner, Simon Segal Constrn. Co., Miami Beach, 1971-75; pres. Investex Realty Corp., Miami, Fla., 1973-75, S.S. Investments, Inc., Miami, 1975-85, Siber, Inc., Miami, 1984-2001, Fla. Real Estate of Miami Corp., 2001-. Recipient Key to City of Miami, 1974, Key to City of South Miami, 1975; registered profl. engr., Fla.; registered real estate and mortgage broker, Fla. Mem. Fla. Engring. Soc., Nat. Soc. Profl. Engrs., ASCE (sec. 1970), Cornell Soc. Engrs., Greater Miami, Cuban Am. (founder, pres. 1971), Internat. (senator) Jr. C.'s of C., Soc. Am. Mil. Engrs., Cornell U., Peekskill Mil. Acad., Fla. Internat. U. alumni assns., Beta Gamma Sigma. Home: 8777 Collins Ave Ph 3 Surfside FL 33154-3406 Office: Fla Real Estate of Miami Corp 2740 NW 112 Ave Miami FL 33172

SEGAL, URIEL, music director; b. Jerusalem, 1944; Asst. condr. N.Y. Philharm.; condr. laureate Century Orch., Osaka, Japan; music dir. Chautauqua Symphony, N.Y., Louisville Orch. Rec. for London-Decca, EMI; condr. European tour Stuttgart Radio Symphony, 1972, now prin. guest condr. Condr. English Chamber Orch., Israel Philharm., Berlin Philharm., royal Concertgebouw, London Symphony, Orch. Paris; condr. orchs. in Houston, Chgo., Dallas, St. Paul, Colo., Milw., Cin. Recipient 1st prize Internat. Mitropolous Conducting Competition, 1969. Office: Louisville Orch 300 W Main St Ste 100 Louisville KY 40202-2930*

SEGAL, VLADIMIR M. metallurgist, researcher; b. Barashi, USSR, Oct. 3, 1936; came to U.S., 1989; s. Miron S. and Rahei N. (Volfovich) S.; m. Galina M. Freidlina, Feb. 20, 1962; children: Svetlana, Leonid. MSME, Tech. U., 1959, Phd in Metallurgy, 1965; ScD in Metallurgy, Acad. Scis., 1974. Devel. engr. Minsk Tractor Plant, Minsk, Buelorussia, 1959-65; sr. scientist Acad. Scis., Buelorussia, 1965-86; prof. Engring. Inst., Lygansk, Ukraine, 1986-89; design engr. Interstate Forging Industry, Navasota, Tex., 1990-92; rsch. engr. Texas A&M U., College Station, 1992-95; principal rsch. scientist Honeywell Electronics, Spokane, Wash., 1996—. Author: 8 books in Russian, 1966-95. Achievements include invention of new metalworking techniques for materials processing for properties; over 50 patents in field. Home: 1906 S Sonora Dr Veradale WA 99037-8011 Office: Honeywell Electronics 15128 E Euclid Ave Spokane WA 99216-1801 E-mail: vladimir.segal@honeywell.com.

SEGALAS, HERCULES ANTHONY, investment banker; b. N.Y.C., Mar. 21, 1935; s. Anthony Spiros and Katherine A. (Michas) S.; m. Margaret Wharton, Sept. 18, 1956; children: Donnell Anthony, Stephen Wharton, Katherine Lacy Devlin. BS, Yale U., 1956. Various engring. and mfg. positions Procter & Gamble Co., Cin., 1956-65; pres. for Latin Am., mgr. Internat. Flavors and Fragrances, N.Y.C., 1965-68; exec. v.p. William D. Witter Inc., 1969-76; sr. v.p. Drexel Burnham Lambert Inc., 1976-87, mng. dir., 1987-88, also bd. dirs., 1976-88; mng. dir. head consumer products investment banking group PaineWebber Inc. Investment Banking Group, 1988-99, also bd. dirs.; mng. dir., chmn. global consumer products Investment Banking Group, Schroder & Co., Inc., 1999-2000; mng. dir., chmn. consumer products investment group Solomon Smith Barney, 2000—01; ptnr. Sawaya, Segalas & Co., 2001—. Bd. dirs. Nantucket Land Coun., Mass., 1982-85; mem. corp. Nantucket Cottage Hosp., 1984-85. Mem. Morristown Field Club, Nantucket Yacht Club (bd. govs. 1987-93, mem. exec. com. 1988-93), The Windsor Club. Republican. Avocations: tennis, sailing, languages, woodworking, golf. Home: 10625 Wittington Ave Vero Beach FL 32963-4734 Office: Sawaya Segalas & Co 1633 Broadway 3d Fl New York NY 10019 E-mail: hsegalas@aol.com.

SEGALL, HAROLD ABRAHAM, lawyer; b. N.Y.C., May 22, 1918; s. Morris and Mildred (Borkan) S.; m. Edith S. Besser, Jan. 27, 1952; children— Mark E., Grant D., Bruce K. BA with distinction, Cornell U., 1938; LLB cum laude, Yale U., 1941. Bar: N.Y. 1941. Practiced in, N.Y.C., 1946—; assoc. mem. firm Gilbert, Segall and Young, 1946-49, ptnr., 1949-93, sr. counsel, 1994-2001, Holland & Knight LLP, N.Y.C., 2001—. Vis. lectr. Yale U. Law Sch., 1974-75, Yale U. Sch. Orgn. and Mgmt., 1983-85, Fordham Law Sch., 2001. Author: (with R.B. Kelley) Estate Planning for the Corporate Executive, 1971, Representing the Seller of a Closely-Held Business, 1973, reprint, 1976; (with J.A. Arouh) How to Prepare Legal Opinions-Boldness and Caution, 1979, reprint, 1990; (with M.S. Sirkin) Providing for Withdrawal from a Joint Venture, 1982, Seventeen Suggestions for Improving Communications with Clients and Colleagues, 1994, reprint, 1995, How to Keep Improving a Highly Successful Law Firm, 1994, An Executive's Lesson in the Law from a Typical Business Encounter, 1996, Then and Now: The Commercial Practice of Law for Over Fifty Years, 1997; contbr. articles to profl. jours.; editor Yale Law Jour., 1939-41. Mem. council State U. N.Y. at Purchase, 1974-79; Counsel United Republican Finance Com., N.Y. State, 1955-61, Rep. City Com., N.Y.C., 1961, Nat. Rep. Citizens Com., 1962, Keating for Senator Com., 1964, Eisenhower 75th Birthday Com., 1965, Friends of the Gov. Wilson Team, 1974, Gov.'s Club, N.Y., 1965-75; trustee, v.p., treas. Philip D. Reed Found. Inc., 1989-96; bd. dirs. Oneita Knitting Mills, 1973-83. Served to maj. AUS, World War II, ETO and PTO. Recipient Edgar M. Cullen prize, 1939 Mem. ABA, Bar City N.Y. (com. on trademark and unfair competition 1967-69, chmn. subcom. legislation 1968-69), Jewish Community Center, Elmwood Country Club (gov. 1966-70, 73-75), Order of Coif, Phi Beta Kappa, Phi Kappa Phi, Phi Sigma Delta. Home: 60 Woodlands Rd Harrison NY 10528-1419 Office: 195 Broadway New York NY 10007-3505 E-mail: hasegall@hklaw.com.

SEGALL, JAMES ARNOLD, lawyer; b. Columbus, Ohio, Aug. 19, 1956; s. Arthur and Greta Helene (Cohen) S.; m. Janice Faye Wiesen, Mar. 14, 1981; children: Gayle Helene, Aryn Michelle, Craig Lawrence. BA, Coll. of William and Mary, 1978; JD, Washington and Lee U., 1981. Bar: Va. 1981, U.S. Dist. Ct. (ea. dist.) Va. 1981. Assoc. Phelps & King P.C., Newport News, Va., 1981-84, Buxton & Lasris P.C., Yorktown, 1984-85; sole practice Newport News, 1985-89; pres. James A. Segall & Assocs., 1990-91, James A. Segall & Assocs., P.C., 1991-92, Segall & Moody, Newport News, 1992-98; ptnr. Krinick, Segall, Moody & Lewis, Va., 1998-2000, Krinick, Segall, Moody, Lewis & Allen, Newport News, 2001—. Lectr. Hampton Roads Regional Acad. Criminal Justice, 1986-89. Bd. dirs. ct.-apptd. Spl. Adv. Program, Newport News, 1986-87, Hamton-Newport News Cmty. Svcs. Bd., 1993-2002, treas., 1995-96, 99-2002, vice-chair, 1996-97, chair 1997-99; participant coop. office edn. program Newport News Pub. Schs., 1987-90; lectr. vol. programs 7th Dist. Ct. Svc. Unit, 1986-89; active City Newport News Cable TV Adv. Commn., 1990-93, Newport News Dem. City Com., 1990-91; bd. dirs. Rodef Sholom Temple, 1992-94, United Jewish Comty., the Va. Peninsula, Inc., 1990—, chmn. spl. activities and fundraising com., 1990-91, chmn. bylaws com., 1992-93, 95—, campaign coun., 1995—, cmty. rels. coun., 1995-98, v.p. human svcs., 1998-2000, v.p. fin. and adminstrn., 2002—; Sunday school teacher, Rodef Sholom Temple, 2001—. Mem. Newport News Bar Assn., Va. Trial Lawyers Assn., Va. Coll. Criminal Def., B'nai B'rith (pres. 1989-91), Ruritan (sec. 1985-87), Moose. Avocations: computers, history, philosophy. Home: 306 Dogwood Dr Newport News VA 23606-3728 Office: Krinick Segall Moody Lewis & Allen 525 Oyster Point Rd Newport News VA 23602-6014

SEGARRA, TYRONE MARCUS, pharmacist, medicinal chemist; b. N.Y.C., Oct. 6, 1959; s. Saris Enrique and Delia Esther (Medina) S. BS in Pharmacy, U. P.R., 1982; MS in Medicinal Chemistry, U. Iowa, 1984, PhD in Medicinal Chemistry, 1988; MBA in Health Care Mgmt. and Mktg., SUNY, Buffalo, 1994. Registered pharmacist, N.Y., Md., Iowa. Staff relief pharmacist Ross Rexall Pharmacy, Belle Plaine, Iowa, 1983-87; postdoctoral rsch. assoc. SUNY, Buffalo, 1987-88; staff pharmacist Rite Aid Corp., 1988-89, Cy's Elma (N.Y.) Pharmacy, 1989-90, Fay's Drugs (now Eckerd's Drugs), Buffalo, 1990—; apptd. to cooperation spkr.'s bur. Eckerd's Drugs, 1998. Part-time asst. prof. in chemistry Erie C.C., SUNY, 1994—; nominee N.Y. Bd. Pharmacy, 2000; clin. instr. U. Bufffalo Pharmacy Preceptorship Program, 2001—. Vol. City Mission, Buffalo, 1993. Mem. Am. Chem. Soc. (mem. organic divsn., medicinal chemistry, chemistry and th e law, mktg. and bus. econs.), Internat. Platform Assn. Democrat. Roman Catholic. Avocations: guitarist, editl. writing, reading, baseball, photography. Office: Eckerd's Drugs No 5822 5917 S Transit Rd Lockport NY 14094-2904

SEGE, ROBERT DAVID, pediatrician; b. San Jose, Calif., June 4, 1958; s. George and Carol Sege; m. Karen E. Victor, Aug. 14, 1983; children: Adam, Rachel, Aaron. BS, Yale Coll., 1980; PhD, MIT, 1986; MD, Harvard U., 1988. Diplomate Am. Bd. Pediatrics. Intern Children's Hosp., Boston, 1988-89, resident, 1989-91; attending physician The Floating Hosp. for Children, 1991—, assoc. chief, divsn. of gen. pediatrics, 1998—; assoc. prof. Tufts U. Sch. Medicine, 1991—. Mem. core faculty Harvard Injury Control Rsch. Ctr., Boston, 1997—. Contbr. articles to profl. jours. Pres. The Children's Ctr. of Brookline, 1999; bd. dirs. Citizens for Safety, Boston, 1996-98. Generalist physician faculty scholar Robert Wood Johnson Found., 1993. Fellow Am. Acad. of Pediatrics; mem. Ambulatory Pediatrics Assn. (regional chair 1999—), Mass. Med. Soc. (com. chair 1999—). Office: New England Med Ctr 750 Washington St Box 351 Boston MA 02111

SEGEL, J. NORMAN, garment manufacturing company executive; b. Toledo, Aug. 1, 1939; BBA, Western Res. U., 1961; MBA, Adelphi U., 1980. Accountant Bobbie Brooks, Cleve., 1961-62; contr. Stacy Ames, Long Island City, N.Y., 1962-65, dir. finance, 1965-66, sec.-treas., 1966-70, exec. asst. to pres., 1968-70; v.p. Fairfield-Noble, Inc., 1970-77; treas. Levin & Hecht Inc., N.Y.C., 1977-79; v.p. fin. Parsons Place Apparel Co. Ltd., 1979-89, dir., 1982-86; v.p. fin. DLH Apparel Co. dba Diana Hartman, 1989-91; contr. Hiram Cohen & Son, Inc., 1991—. Treas. Stephanie Queller Ltd., 1982-86; pres. Jupiter Internat. Inc., 1994-96; sec., treas. JZNS Assoc., 1985-2000, pres., 2000—. Home: 3447 5th St Oceanside NY 11572-5133 Office: 486 Willis Ave Williston Park NY 11596-1737

SEGEL, KAREN LYNN JOSEPH, lawyer, taxation specialist; b. Youngstown, Ohio, Jan. 15, 1947; d. Samuel Dennis and Helen Anita Joseph; m. Alvin Gerald Segel, June 9, 1968 (div. Sept. 1976); 1 child, Adam James. BA in Soviet and East European Studies, Boston U., 1968; JD, Southwestern U., 1975. Bar: Calif., 1996, U.S. Tax Ct., 1996, U.S. Dist. Ct. (cen. dist.) Calif., 1996, U.S. Ct. Appeals (9th cir.), 1997. Adminstrv. asst. Olds Brunel & Co., N.Y.C., 1968-69, U.S. Banknote Corp., N.Y.C., 1969-70; tax acct. S.N. Chilkov & Co. CPA's, Beverly Hills, Calif., 1971-74; intern Calif. Corps. Commr., 1975; tax. sr. Oppenheim Appel & Dixon CPA's, L.A., 1978, Fox, Westheimer & Co. CPA's, L.A., 1978, Zebrak, Levine & Mepos CPA's, L.A., 1979; ind. cons. acctg., taxation specialist Beverly Hills, 1980—. Settlement officer L.A. County Superior Ct., 2000; law student mentor Southwestern U., 1996-2002, tax moot ct. judge, 1997. Editorial adv. bd. Am. Biog. Inst. High sch. amb. to Europe People-to-People Orgn., 1963. Mem. Calif. State Bar, Women's Inner Circle of Achievement, Complex Litig. Inns of Ct., L.A. County Bar Assn, Beverly Hills Tinseltown Rose Soc. Avocations: collecting seashells, lhasa apso dog breeding, art, travel, music. E-mail: kjslaw@earthlink.net.

SEGEL, MARK CALVIN, diagnostic radiologist; b. Detroit, Apr. 13, 1956; s. Louis and Sara Lee (Eichler) S.; m. Carol Ruth Graff, July 15, 1990; children: Alec, Blake. BS, U. Mich., 1977; MD, U. Tex., Dallas, 1981. Diplomate Am. Bd. Radiology. Intern in pathology St. Paul Hosp., Dallas, 1981-82; resident in radiology U. Pitts., 1982-85; fellow in breast imaging M.D. Anderson Cancer Inst. U. Tex., Houston, 1985-86; chief breast imaging Karmanos Cancer Inst. Wayne State Med. Sch., Detroit, 1986—. Named one of Best Drs. of Midwest, 1996, Best Drs. of Am., 1998. Mem. Am. Roentgen Ray Soc., Radiol. Soc. N.Am. Avocations: biking, jogging. Office: Dept Radiology Harper Hosp 3990 John R St Detroit MI 48201-2018 E-mail: segelm@karmanos.org.

SEGEL, SALLY Y. gynecologist, educator; b. San Francisco, Nov. 25, 1967; d. Nathan and Esme Marian Segel; m. Howard K. Song, Apr. 9, 1994; 1 child Derek Robert Song. BA, U. Pa., 1989; MD, Stanford U., 1994. Asst. prof. Emory U. Sch. Medicine, Atlanta, 2001—. Mem.: Am. Coll. Ob-gyn. (jr. fellow), Soc. Maternal Fetal Medicine (assoc.). Office: Emory U Sch Medicine 4th Fl 69 Jesse Hill Sr Dr Atlanta GA 30303

SEGELMAN, ALLYN EVAN, dentist, researcher, insurance executive; b. Boston, July 25, 1947; s. Edward David John and Harriett Sylvia (Shuman) S.; m. Sandra Ruth Steiman, June 17, 1973 (div. Aug. 1995); children: Tovah Chanah, Rayna Devorah. AB in Biology, Boston U., 1969; DMD, Tufts U., 1973; SM in Epidemiology, Harvard U., 1997. Diplomate Am. Bd. Oral and Maxillofacial Surgery, Am. Bd. Oral Medicine. Intern Tufts-New Eng. Med. Ctr., 1973-74, fellow in oral cancer, 1974-75; resident Boston City Hosp., 1975-77, chief resident, 1976-77; pvt. practice oral and maxillofacial surgery Mass., 1977-95; asst. clin. prof. oral and maxillofacial surgery Tufts U. Sch. of Dental Medicine, Boston, 1980—; rsch. fellow in dental care adminstrn. Harvard Sch. of Dental Medicine, Harvard Sch. Pub. Health, 1996-97; dental ops. and policy dir. Blue Cross Blue Shield, N. Quincy, Mass., 1997—. Dir. dental consultative svcs. New Eng. Area Comprehensive Hemophilia Care Ctr., Worcester, Mass., 1977-78; cons. managed care benefit sys. Blue Cross Blue Shield of Mass., Boston, 1984-97; cons. Ctrl. Mass. Healthcare Inc., Worcester, 1992, Mass. Pro Inc. and Nat. Quality Health Coun., Waltham, 1995. Editor: Procedural Terminology for Oral and Maxillofacial Surgery, 1985, Procedural Terminology with Glossary, 1985; contbr. articles to profl. jours. Gov.'s appointee Legis. Spl. Commn. on Sch. Bus Safety, Boston, 1985-88; bd. registration in dentistry appointee Mass. Dept. Pub. Health Prescription Monitoring Program, Boston, 1994—; chmn. sch. com. Congregation Mishkan Tefila, Newton, Mass., 1993-95, bd. trustees, 1983-95. Recipient Brotherhood award Mass. Com. of Catholics, Protestants and Jews, 1965. Fellow Am. Acad. Oral Medicine (pres. 1996-97), Am. Assn. Oral and Maxillofacial Surgeons (chmn. spl. com. coding and nomenclature 1991-94), Mass. Dental Soc. Anesthesiology (pres. 1987-88); mem. Tufts U. Dental Alumni Assn. (exec. coun., pres. 1985-86), Omicron Kappa Upsilon. Democrat. Jewish. Avocations: photography, theology, nosology. Home: 243 Independence Dr Chestnut Hill MA 02467-3628 Office: Blue Cross Blue Shield Mass Dental Ops and Policy 100 Hancock St Ste 3 North Quincy MA 02171-1752 E-mail: spock8762@aol.com.

SEGELMAN, ALVIN BURTON, pharmaceutical executive, researcher, scientist, consultant; b. Boston, Sept. 27, 1931; s. Joseph Theodore and Anna (Klein) Segelman; m. Florence Hannah Pettler, Apr. 27, 1972 (dec. Jan. 7, 1994); children: Lauren Beth, Sheera Toba. BS, Mass. Coll. Pharmacy, 1954, MS, 1967; PhD, U. Pitts., 1971. Registered pharmacist Mass., cert. nutritional specialist Am. Coll. Nutrition. Chief pharmacist Kenmore Pharmacy, Boston, 1954—61; pres. Bell Pharmacy, Somerville, 1961—67; instr. pharmacognosy and microbiology pharmacognosy dept. U. Pitts., 1967—71; asst. prof. pharmacognosy dept. Rutgers U., Piscataway, NJ, 1971—74, assoc. prof., chmn. pharmacognosy dept., 1974—90; v.p. R&D health scis. Nature's Sunshine Products, INc., Provo, Utah, 1990—2000; CEO Pharmacognosy Rsch. Inst., Orem, 2001—. Sci. cons. numerous pharm. cos., 1972—90; prin. investigator rsch. Rutgers Biomed. Rsch. Grants, New Brunswick, 1972—85, U.S. Pub. Health Svc. Grant, Washington, 1973; co-prin. investigator rsch. Am. Cancer Soc., Washington, 1987—88; expert med. cons. U.S. Congress Select Com. on Aging, Washington, 1981—83; vis. prof. Jagellonian U., Cracow, Poland, 1989, Patrice Lamumbe U., Moscow, 1999. Co-author: Antibiotics in Historical Perspective, 1981; contbr. articles to profl. jours.; sci. reviewer: various profl. and sci. jours. Mem. various coms. Acad. Pharm. Scis., Washington, 1976—89; mem. med. adv. com. Planned Parenthood Middlesex County, New Brunswick, NJ, 1979—90. 2nd lt. U.S. Army, 1957—59. Fellow: Linnean Soc. Avocations: small arms pistol competition, ethnopharmacognosy research and writing, mountain climbing. Home: 54 West 680 South Orem UT 84058 Office: Pharmacognosy Rsch Inst 54 West 680 South Orem UT 84058

SEGER, LINDA SUE, script consultant, lecturer, writer; b. Peshtigo, Wisc., Aug. 27, 1945; d. Linus Vauld and Agnes Katherine Seger; m. Theodore Newton Youngblood, Jr., Aug. 28, 1968 (div. Jan. 1970); m. Peter Hazen LeVar, April 12, 1987. BA in English, Colo. Coll., Colorado Springs, 1967; MA in theatre arts, Northwestern U., Evanston, 1968; MA in religion and arts, Pacific Sch. of Religion, Berkeley, 1973; ThD in drama and theology, Graduate Theological U., Berkeley, 1976; MA in Feminist Spirituality, Immaculate Heart Coll. Ctr., L.A., 2000. Instr. drama Grand Canyon Coll., Phoenix, 1969-71; instr. drama and theology McPherson (Kans.) Coll., 1976-77; instr. drama and humanities LaVerne (Calif.) U., 1977-79; asst. Provisional Theatre, L.A., 1979-80, Tandem/TAT, L.A., 1980-81; story analyst EMI Films, 1982-83; pvt. practice script cons., 1981—; pvt. practice lectr., author, 1984—. Author: Making a Good Script Great , 1988, Creating Unforgettable Characters, 1990, The Art of Adaptation, 1992, When Women Call the Shots, 1996, Making a Good Writer Great, 1999, WEBTHINKING: Connecting Not Competing for Success, 2002; co-author: From Script to Screen, 1994. Mem. NOW, Women in Film. Democrat. Mem. Soc. Of Friends. Avocations: horseback riding, piano, travel. Home and Office: 4705 Hagerman Ave Cascade CO 80809 E-mail: lsseger@aol.com.

SEGERHAMMAR, SHARON K. special education administrator; b. Marysville, Kans., June 25, 1947; d. Wayne P. and Laura O. Baker; m. Carl R. Segerhammar; children: Todd R., Kyle W. (dec.). BS in Elem. Edn., Emporia State U., 1969, MS in Curriculum and Instrn., 1974; EdS in Edn. Leadership, U. Ala., 1996, EdD in Edn. Leadership, 2000. Tchr. elem. edn. USD 244, Burlington, Kans., Saudi Arabia Internat. Sch., Riyadh; tchr. spl. edn. Learning Coop. N. Ctrl. Kans., Concordia, Calhoun County Schs., Anniston, Ala., Rome (Ga.) City Schs.; spl. edn. adminstr. Cobb County Schs., Marietta, Ga. Mem. ASCD, Profl. Orgn. Ga. Educators, Coun. Exceptional Children. Avocations: reading, counted cross stitch, knitting, bridge. Office: Cobb County Schs 514 Glover St Marietta GA 30060 E-mail: skseg@msn.com.

SEGERSTEN, ROBERT HAGY, lawyer, investment banker; b. Boston, June 24, 1941; s. Wendell C. and Claire H. S.; m. Marie E. Makinen, Feb. 13, 1965; children: Amanda Beth, Vanessa Bryce. AB, Bates Coll., 1963; JD, Boston U., 1970. Bar: Mass. 1970. Assoc. Nessen & Csaplar, Boston, 1970-75; v.p. March Co., 1975-77; pres. March-Eton Corp., Concord, Mass., 1977-82; ptnr. Nessen, Goodwin & Segersten, 1977-82, Kane & Segersten, Dedham, Mass., 1983-85; pres. Woodbine Optical Corp., Easton, 1990—. Adj. prof. Sch. Am. Studies, Boston U.; adj. prof. real estate law Bentley Coll. Officer, bd. dirs. Friends of The Jimmy Fund, Boston. Served to lt. USN, 1963-67. Mem. ACLU, Mass. Bar Assn. Democrat. Episcopalian. Home: 64 Folsom Ave Hyannis MA 02601-4823 Office: 14 Norfolk Ave Easton MA 07375

SEGESVÁRY, VICTOR GYÖZÖ, retired diplomat; b. Miskolc, Hungary, Feb. 20, 1929; came to U.S., 1984; s. Viktor and Margit (Kovács) S.; m. Andrea Bárczay, Jan. 20, 1955 (div. Nov. 1957); 1 child, Gábor; m. Monika Schwarz, Dec. 28, 1968. PhD in Polit. Sci., Grad. Inst. Internat. Studies, Switzerland, 1968; DD, U. Geneva, 1973. Asst., libr. Reformed Theol. Acad., Budapest, Hungary, 1953-56; sec. gen. African Inst., Geneva, 1961-63; asst. editor, market rsch. officer Bus. Internat. S.A., 1963-66; market rsch. officer SESAF S.A., 1967-68; chief rsch. dept. Henry Dunant Inst. Internat. Red Cross, 1968-71; cons. Internat. Trade Ctr., UNCTAD/GATT, 1969-71; tech. advisor market rsch.-market study Internat. Trade Ctr., Algiers, Algeria, 1971-72; sr. trade promotion advisor, project mgr. UNCTAD/GATT/ITC, 1973-74, chief advisor in internat. econ. rels., project mgr. Kabul, Afghanistan, 1975-79, Bamako, Mali, 1979-83; sr. advisor, cons. UN Devel. Programme, African countries, 1984-93. Sr. advisor, cons. dept. for tech. cooperation for devel. UN, N.Y.C., 1985-88. Author: Le réalisme khrouchtchévien: Politique soviètique au Proche-Orient, 1968, La Rèforme et l'Islam, 1500-1550, 1973, reprinted with English preface and summary, 1998, A Ràday Könyvtár 18. századi története, 1992, Inter-Civilizational Relations and the Destiny of the West: Dialogue or Confrontation?, 1998, 2d edit., 2000, From Illusion to Delusion: Globalization and the Contradictions of Late Modernity, 1999, 2d edit., 2001, Existence and Transcendence: An Anti-Faustian Essay in Philosophical Anthropology, 1999, 2d edit., 2002, Dialogue of Civilizations: An Introduction to Civilizational Analysis, 2000. Sec.-gen. Internat. Fedn. Students in Polit. Sci., Geneva, 1958-59. Home: 330 E 39th St Apt 21 New York NY 10016-2187 E-mail: segesvary@un.org.

SEGGER, MARTIN JOSEPH, museum director, art history educator; b. Felixtowe, Eng., Nov. 22, 1946; s. Gerald Joseph and Lillian Joan (Barker-Emery) S.; m. Angele Cordonier, Oct. 4, 1968; children: Cara Michelle, Marie-Claire, Margaret Ellen. BA, U. Victoria, B.C. Can., 1969, diploma in edn., 1970; MPhil, U. London, 1973. Prof. art history U. Victoria, 1970-74; museologist Royal B.C. Mus., Victoria, 1974-77; dir. Maltwood Art Mus., prof. art history U. Victoria, 1977—, dir. cmty. rels., 2001—. Cons. Nat. Mus. Corp., Ottawa, 1977, UNESCO, O.E.A., Cairo, 1983. Author: exhbn. catalogue House Beautiful, 1975, Arts of the Forgotten Pioneers, 1971, Victoria: An Architectural History, 1979, (commendation Am. Assn. State and Local History 1980), This Old House, 1975, This Old Town, 1979, British Columbia Parliament Buildings, 1979, The Heritage of Canada, 1981, Samuel Maclure: In Search of Appropriate Form, 1986 (Hallmark award 1987, 98), (a guide) St. Andrew's Cathedral, 1990, The Development of Gordon Head Campus, 1988, An Introduction to Museum Studies, 1989, An Introduction to Heritage Conservation, 1990, Botswana Live, 1994, Exploring Victoria's Architecture, 1996; contbr., cons. British Columbia Encyclopedia, 2000. Bd. govs. Heritage Can. Found., 1979-83; chmn. City of Victoria Heritage Adv. Com., 1975-79; bd. dirs. Heritage Trust, 1977-86, B.C. Touring Coun., Sta. CFUV Radio, B.C. Govt. House Found., 1987-93, Royal B.C. Mus., 1996-99; co-chair Brit. Columbia Arts Festival; mem. B.C. Heritage Adv. Bd., 1973-83; councillor City of Victoria, 1987-93; vice-chair Provincial Capital Commn., 1991-2001; pres. Assn. Vancouver Island Municipalities, 1993-94; chmn. B.C. Festival of the Arts, 1999; bd. dirs. Internat. Coun. Mus.-Can., 1999, Victoria Coll. Art, 2001—, Victoria Harbour Authority, 2002--; mem. heritage policy rev. com. Govt. of Can., 2001--, mem. cultural diversity experts com., 2002--. Decorated knight Equestrian Order of Holy Sepulchre of Jerusalem; recipient award Heritage Can. Communications, 1976, Heritage Conservation award Lt. Gov. B.C., 1989, Harley J. McKee award Assn. Preservation Technology, 1994; named Hon. Citizen City of Victoria, 2000, named Arts Citizen of Yr., 2001. Fellow Royal Soc. Arts, Can. Mus. Assn. (counsellor 1975-77); mem. Internat. Coun. Mus. (chair internat. com. for tng. of pers. 1995-98), Internat. Coun. Monuments and Sites (bd. dirs. 1980-82), Soc. Study Architecture Can. (bd. dirs. 1979-81), Authors Club (London), Can Mus. Dirs. Orgn., Carnavon Club, Union Club (Victoria). Roman Catholic. Avocations: travel, motor mechanics, water color painting. Home: 1035 Sutlej St Victoria BC Canada V8V 3P2 E-mail: msegger@uvic.ca.

SEGGERMAN, ANNE CRELLIN, foundation executive; b. Los Angeles, May 13, 1931; d. Curtis Vergil and Yvonne (LaGrave) Crellin; m. Harry G.A. Seggerman, Apr. 14, 1951; children: Patricia, Henry, Marianne, Yvonne, Suzanne, John. Studies with Albert Levesque, Paris, 1948-50; Student, Sch. Decorative Arts, Paris, 1950, Sch. of the Louvre, 1950, Albertus Magnus Coll., 1951; D.H.L. (hon.), Sacred Heart U., 1980. French tchr., Beverly Hills, Calif., 1958-60; translator World Affairs Council, Los Angeles, 1958-60; staff mem. West Side Sch. Gifted Children, Beverly Hills, 1958-60; pres. Huxley Inst. for Bio-Social Research, Fairfield, Conn., 1972—, 4th World Found. Interfaith Media Action, Fairfield, 1977—, Steiner Prodns., Fairfield, 1981—; founder The Com. for Guadalupe Research, 1982—. Bd. dirs. Anuk, Inc. Co-founder Christian/Jewish Ctr. Understanding Sacred Heart U., Fairfield, Conn.; active Pres. Reagan's Health Task Force Resources Com. on Health Adv. Couns. of U.S. Dept. Health and Human Svcs.; mem. Pres.'s Com. Mental Retardation, 1981-86, Com. Housing Handicapped Families, 1989; mem. Nat. Coun. on Disability, 1992-95; bd. dirs. Easter Seal Rehab. Ctr., Fairfield, Internat. Coll. Applied Nutrition, World Health Med. Group, Cath. League for Religion and Civil Rights. Recipient Am. Assn. Sovereign Mil. Order of Malta, 1991, Cmdr. of Equestrian Order of Holy Sepulchre of Jerusalem, 1991. Mem. Nat. Health Fedn., The Inst. for Study of Human Knowledge, Am. Holistic Med. Inst., Internat. Acad. Preventive Medicine, Calif. Orthomolecular Soc., Am. Phys. Rsch., Fairfield County Organic Gardeners.

SEGGEV, JORAM SIMON, allergist, clinical immunologist; b. Tel-Aviv, Israel, Apr. 7, 1944; came to U.S., 1986; s. Rudolf and Elizabeth (Staub) Landsberg; m. Varda Alexandri, Oct. 3, 1968; children: Guy, Michal, Itai. MD, Hebrew U., Jerusalem, 1970. Internal Medicine, Allergy and Clin. Immunology. Dir. pulmonary function lab., attending physician Truman Meml. Va. Hosp., Columbia, Mo., 1986-90; asst. prof., dir. adult allergy clinic, attending physician U. Mo., Columbia Sch. Medicine, 1986-90; dir. adult allergy clinic, attending physician, 1986-90; asst. prof. medicine Med. Coll. Wis., Milw., 1990-91; staff physician allergy and clin. immunology sect. Clement J. Zablocki VA Med. Ctr., 1990-91; assoc. prof. U. Nev. Sch. Medicine, Las Vegas, 1991-96; pvt. practice allergy and immunology, 1996—; clin. prof. medicine dept. internal medicine U. Nev. Sch. Medicine, 1996—, chief divsn. allergy, clin. immunology, 1993-98. Presenter in field of asthma and allergic disease; sec., treas. Mo. State Allergy Soc., 1989-90; mem. sub. committee on Rehab. in Asthma, Acad. Allergy and Immunology, 1992; mem. com. quality care in asthma Am. Acad. Allergy, 1993; mem. courtesy staff Children's Hosp. Wis., Milw., 1990-91; mem. assoc. provisional staff dept. internal medicine Valley Hosp. Med. Ctr., Las Vegas, 1992-94, courtesy staff, 1994—; mem. courtesy staff Humana-Sunrise Hosp., Las Vegas, 1994—, Columbia-Sunrise Mountain View Hosp., Las Vegas, 1994—; mem. courtesy staff dept. internal medicine, pediats. Columbia-Sunrise Hosp., Las Vegas, 1996—, Lake Mead Hosp., Las Vegas, 1996—; active staff dept. internal medicine Summerlin Hosp. Med. Ctr., Las Vegas, 1997-99, cons. staff, 1999; active staff Univ. Med. Ctr., Las Vegas, 1992-98, assoc. staff, 1999—. Author 2 chpts. in Pulmonary Diseases, 1988. Lectr. Better Breathers Club, Columbia, Mo., 1988; participant Children's Miracle Telethon, Las Vegas, 1991. Recipient grant Winthrop Pharm., U. Nev. Sch. Medicine, 1991-93, Merit review award Dept. VA, Columbia, Mo. and Milw., 1988-91 Fellow ACP, Am. Acad. Allergy, Asthma and Immunology (mem. commn. on rsch. 1989-91), Am. Coll. Allergy, Asthma and Immunology (mem. commn. on asthma 1989-2000, mem. workshop on geriatrics 2000—, mem. subcom. on workshops 1998-99); mem. Am. Thoracic Soc., Am. Assn. Immunologists, N.Y. Acad. Scis., Western Soc. Allergy and Immunology, Clark County Med. Soc. Office: 3196 S Maryland Pkwy Ste 409 Las Vegas NV 89109-2315 Address: C9-292 7500 N Lake Mead Blvd Las Vegas NV 89128-0448 Fax: 702-360-0666. E-mail: seggevj@jsmd.salu.net.

SEGGEV, MEIR, radiologist, educator; b. Burgas, Bulgaria, Jan. 23, 1939; came to U.S., 1969, naturalized, 1976; s. Bouco and Helen (Bejerano) S.; m. Ruth Lerner, Dec. 30, 1964 (div. Apr. 1978); 1 child, Yael.; m. Sandra Lee Slarsky, Apr. 7, 1979. MD, Hebrew U. Hadassah, Jerusalem, 1969. Diplomate Am. Bd. Radiology. Resident in radiology Harvard Med. Sch., Beth Israel Hosp., Boston, 1970-73; radiologist Peter Bent Brigham Hosp., 1973-74, Hale Hosp., Haverhill, Mass., 1974—; assoc. radiologist Beth Israel Hosp., Boston, 1974—; clin. instr. radiology Harvard Med. Sch., 1973—. Mem. AMA, Am. Inst. Ultrasound in Medicine, Am. Roentgen Ray Soc., Radiol. Soc. N.Am., Am. Coll. Radiology, Mass. Med. Soc., Harvard Club. Home and Office: 236 Fairview Rd Palm Beach FL 33480-3320

SEGLIN, JEFFREY L. columnist, educator; b. Plattsburgh, N.Y., Dec. 26, 1956; s. Lester L. and Beverly K. Seglin; m. Nancy L. Long, Jan. 18, 1986; children: Edward Coleman, Bethany Whitemyer. BA, Bethany Coll., 1978; cert., Radcliffe Pub. Course, Cambridge, Mass., 1978; MTS, Harvard U., 1981. Exec. editor Inc. Mag., Boston, 1989—98; asst. prof. Emerson Coll., 1999—; bus. ethics columnist Sunday New York Times, N.Y.C., 1998—. Author: (novels) The Good, the Bad and Your Business, 2000. Fellow fellow, Ctr. for the Study of Values in Pub. Life at Harvard U., 1998-1999, Poynter Ethics fellow, Poynter Inst. for Media Studies, 2001. Office: Emerson Coll 120 Boylston St Boston MA 02116 Personal E-mail: jseglin@post.harvard.edu. Business E-mail: jseglin@post.harvard.edu.

SEGLUND, BRUCE RICHARD, lawyer; b. Lansing, Mich., June 3, 1950; s. Richard Oswald and Josephine Ann (Kraus) S.; m. Connie Sue Roberts, June 19, 1970; children: Jennifer Lynne, Nicole Marie. BS, Mich. State U., 1973; JD, Thomas M. Cooley Law Sch., 1979. Bar: Mich. 1981, U.S. DIst. Ct. (ea. dist.) Mich. 1981. Assoc. Michael W. Reeds, P.C., Walled Lake, Mich., 1981-82; sole practice, 1982-85; ptnr. Mick and Seglund, 1985-89, Connelly, Crowley, Groth and Seglund, Walled Lake, 1989—. Mem. Mich. Bar Assn. (mem. character and fitness com. dist. J 1988-2000), Oakland County Bar Assn. (lectr. 1984), Mich. Jaycees (pres. Walled Lake 1982-83, execllence award 1982-83, pres. of yr. 1982-83), Walled Lake C. of C. (bd. dirs. scholarship fund 1985-88). Lodges: KC (adv. 1982-94). Roman Catholic. Home: 8618 Buffalo Dr Commerce Township MI 48382-3408 Office: Connelly Crowley Groth & Seglund 2410 S Commerce Rd Walled Lake MI 48390-2129 E-mail: ccgs@ismi.net.

SEGNER, EDMUND PETER, III, natural gas company executive; b. Dallas, Oct. 23, 1953; s. Edmund Peter Jr. and Martha Fairfax (Smith) S.; m. Kathryn Louise Daily, July 10, 1976; children: Peter Michael, Christian James. BSCE, Rice U., 1976; MA in Econs., U. Houston, 1980. CPA, Tex. Acct. Touche Ross & Co., Houston, 1976-78; asst. v.p. planning United Gas Pipe Line Co., 1978-86; asst. v.p. rsch. Drexel Burnham Lambert, N.Y.C., 1986-88; v.p. pub. and investor rels. Enron Corp., Houston, 1988-90; sr. v.p. pub. and gov. rels., investor Enron Corp, 1990-92, exec. v.p., chief staff, 1992-98; vice-chmn., chief of staff Enron Oil & Gas Co., 1997-99; pres., chief of staff EOG Resources, Inc., 1999—. Lectr. civil engring. Rice U., Houston, 1982-84, 97—. Bd. dirs. Zool. Soc. Houston, 1992-95, Greater Houston Partnership for Ednl. Excellence, 1991-93, Sam Houston Area coun. Boy Scouts Am.; treas. Tex. Nature Conservancy, 1992—, vice-chmn., 1999-2001, chmn., 2001; chmn. Cmty. Ptnrs., 1993-95; trustee Houston Mus. Natural Sci., 1999—. Mem. Houston Soc. Fin. Analysts, Houston City Club, Briar Club, Lochinvar Golf Club, Coronado Club, Catamount Club. Republican. Lutheran. Home: 4130 Tennyson St Houston TX 77005-2750 Office: EOG Resources Inc 333 Clay St Ste 4200 Houston TX 77002-4501

SEGNER, EDMUND PETER, JR. civil engineer, educator; b. Mar. 28, 1928; s. Edmund Peter and Elsie E. (Grenwelge) S.; married, Nov., 1952; children: Eddie, John, Nancy, Sandra, Sharon. BSCE, U. Tex., Austin, 1949; MSCE, U. Tex., 1952; PhD, Tex. A&M U., 1962. Assoc. v.p. for rsch. Memphis State U., 1976-90; chmn. dept. civil and environ. engring. U. Ala., Birmingham, 1990-95, prof. emeritus, 1996—. Home: 1554 Fairway View Dr Birmingham AL 35244-1314 Office: Dept Civil and Environ Engring U Ala At Birmingham Birmingham AL 35294-0001

SEGO, RONALD M. astronaut, retired military officer; b. Cleve., Dec. 4, 1952; BS in Math. and Physics, USAF Acad., 1974; MS in Physics, Ohio State U., 1975; PhD in Elec. Engring., U. Colo., 1982; DSc (hon.) , Clarkson U., 1993. Commd. 2d lt. USAF, 1974; advanced through grades to Col. USAFR; resigned USAF, student pilot, 1975—76; instr. pilot USAFB, Fort Williams AFB, Ariz., 1976—78; mem. faculty USAF Acad. , Colo. Springs, Colo., 1979—82; asst. prof. dept. elec. and computer engring. U. Colo. , 1982—85, assoc. prof., 1985—90, prof., 1990; astronaut NASA Johnson Space Ctr., Houston, 1991—96; dean coll. engring. and applied sci. U. Colo., Colo. Springs, 1996—. Tech. dir. Lasers and Aerospace Mechanics Directorate USAF Acad. , Colo. Springs, Colo., 1987—88; rsch. assoc. prof. Physics U. Houston / Space Vacuum Epitaxy Ctr., 1989—90; adj. prof. Physics U. Houston, 1998—. Decorated 2 Space Flight medals NASA; named Disting. Grad., USAF Acad/, 1974, Reserve Officer of Yr., IMA Air Force Space Command, 1988; named to Acad. Hall of Fame, Macedonia (Ohio) HS, 1988; recipient Superior Achievement award, NASA Dir. Ops., Russia, 1995. Fellow: AIAA (assoc.), Inst. for Advancement of Engring.; mem.: IEEE, Soc. Photo-Optical Instrumentation Engrs., Am. Phys. Soc., Assn. Space Explorers, Air Force Reserve Officers Assn., Eta Kappa Nu. Office: Astronaut Office/CB Johnson Space Ctr Houston TX 77058

SEGREST, SHARON LARISA, management educator; b. Raleigh, N.C., Nov. 11, 1967; d. Alden M. Segrest and Priscilla Martin. BS in Bus. Adminstrn., U. N.C., 1989; MBA, Meredith Coll., 1994; PhD in Mgmt., Fla. State U., 1999. Sales rep. Pillsbury Co., Raleigh, NC, 1989—92, Sandoz Nutrition, Raleigh, 1992—93; asst. prof. mgmt. Calif. State U., Fullerton. Acad. coord. Fullerton Extended Edn. Calif. State U., 2001—02; spkr. numerous internat. and nat. confs. Contbr. articles to profl. jours. Recipient Best Paper award, Nat. Acad. Mgmt., 1998; grantee, Calif. State U., 1999—2001. Mem.: Internat. Fedn. Scholary Assns. Mgmt. (presenter Gold-coast, Australia 2002), Western Acad. Mgmt. (new faculty consortium participant 2002, nomination Best Paper award 2002), Acad. Mgmt. Avocations: travel, running, reading, scuba diving. Office: Calif State U Coll Bus and Econs Fullerton CA 92834-6848 Office Fax: 714-278-2438.

SEGUIN, DAVID GERARD, community college official; b. Fulton, N.Y., Apr. 17, 1943; s. Leonell Joseph and Jasmine (Dumany) S.; m. Katherine Shiely (div. Oct. 1977); m. Brenda G. Eastman, Sept. 17, 1983; 1 child, Shivani. AA, Onondaga Community Coll., Syracuse, N.Y., 1964; BA in Psychology, Trinity U., 1967, MS in Psychology, 1970; PhD in Psychology, U. Toledo, 1985. Instr., prof. Jamestown (N.Y.) C.C., 1970-86, ad hoc assoc. dean, 1986-88, assoc. dean, 1988—, dir. instnl. rsch., 1991—, chmn. div. behavioral scis., 1975-77. Bd. dirs. Rsch. & Planning Human Svcs. Chautauqua County. Contbr. articles to profl. jours. Bd. dirs. Chautauqua County (N.Y.) Tchrs. Resource Ctr., 1987-88, Rsch. & Planning Human Svcs. Chautauqua County, 1996-2000. Mem. Am. Psychol. Soc. (charter), Assn. Instl. Rsch., North Ea. Assn. Instl. Rsch., SUNY Assn. Instl. Rschrs. and Planning Officers (past pres.). Democrat. Roman Catholic. Avocations: jazz, golf. Office: Jamestown Community Coll 515 Falconer St Jamestown NY 14701-1920

SEGUR, WINTHROP HUBBARD, JR. management and businees educator; b. Hartford, Conn., May 21, 1936; s. Winthrop Hubbard and Althea (Rosen) S. BS in Math., Trinity Coll., Hartford, Conn., 1958; MA in Math., Bowdoin Coll., 1965; PhD in Agrl. Econs., U. Calif., Davis, 1980. Instr. math. Thacher Sch., Ojai, Calif., 1961-68; cmty. organizer United Farm Workers, Delano, 1968-73; asst. prof. econs. U. of the Pacific, Stockton, 1979-85; lectr. econs. and bus. Calif. State U., Chico, 1985-87; staff economist United Farm Workers, Keene, Calif., 1987-89; prof. bus. and mgmt. U. Redlands, 1989—, chair dept., 1989-95. Mem. agrl. adv. com. Calif. State Assembly, Stockton, 1983-85; mem. com. on long range planing Calif. State Senate, Stockton, 1985-87; mem. Farm Labor Estimation project U.S. Dept. Labor, Washington, 1988-91; bd. dirs. Calif. Inst. for Rural Studies, Davis, 1992—. Contbr. articles to profl. jours. Chair rural econs. alternatives project com. Am. Friends Svc. Com., Stockton, 1983-85. Mem. AAUP, 1996—, Indsl. Rels. Rsch. Assn. (chpt. pres. 1994, 97), S.W. Labor Studies Assn. (conf. cir. 1992), Am. Agrl. Econs. Assn., Am. Econ. Assn. Avocations: spring training, Shelby Am., Calif. Hwy 99, Brautigan, Bauer. Office: U Redlands Mgmt Bus ANWC E Colton Ave Redlands CA 92373

SEGURA, JOSEPH WESTON, urologist, educator; b. Little Rock, Mar. 12, 1940; s. H. Weston and Jane Ann (Nadeau) S.; m. Marianne Gilchrist, Sept. 25, 1965; children: Alison, Sarah, Cynthia, Leal, Suzanne. AB, Princeton U., 1961; MD, Northwestern U., Chgo., 1965. Diplomate Am. Bd. Urology. Staff physician Peace Corps, Santiago, Chile, 1966-68; intern Charity Hosp., New Orleans, 1965-66; resident in urology Mayo Clinic, Rochester, Minn., 1968-72, cons., 1972—, instr. urology, 1973-74, asst. prof., 1974-78, assoc. prof., 1978-84, prof., 1983—, Carl Rosen prof., 1984—. Co-editor: Transurethral Surgery, 1979. Fellow ACS; mem. Am. Urol. Assn., Am. Assn. Genitourinary Surgeons, Endourology Soc., Can. Urol. Assn., North Ctrl. Sect. Am. Urol. Assn. Home: 810 60th Ave SW Rochester MN 55902-8726 Office: Mayo Clinic 200 1st St SW Rochester MN 55905-0002

SEHILI, MAHMOUD, artist; b. Tunis, July 27, 1931; m. Gabriele Buth, Apr. 11, 1959; children: Thouraya, Lilia, Raouf. Student, Fine Arts Sch., Tunis; diploma supérieur des arts plastiques, Ecole des Beaux-Arts, Paris. Tchr. Inst. Technol. d'Art, d'Arch. et d'Urbanisme, Tunis; dir. Irtissem Art Gallery, 1977—. Recipient Golden medal Cagnes sur Mer, 1st prize Town of Tunis, 1963, others. Avocations: music, playing the luth, composition of Arabic music, fishing. Home: 4 Rue Victor Hugo Carthage Tunisia

SEHORN, JASON, football player; b. Sacramento, Apr. 15, 1971; m. Angie Harmon. Student in Comm., U. S.C. Football player minor leagues Chgo. Clubs Orgn.; profl. football player N.Y. Giants, 1994—. Established Sehorn's Ctr. to assist single-parent families; supporter Homes for the Holidays programs, other programs , Newark. Recipient MVP honors. Office: NY Football Giants Giants Stadium East Rutherford NJ 07073*

SEHRING, ADOLF, artist, sculptor; b. Urupinsk, Russia, June 8, 1930; came to the U.S., 1949; s. George Henry M. and Clair (Burstin) S.; married, 1992; children: Nina, Marc. Student, Acad. Fine Arts, Germany, 1946-49. Pres. A. Sehring Studio Inc., Orange, Va., 1970—, Am. Artist Portfolio Inc., Orange, 1987—. Lectr. in field. One man shows include Grand Palais, Paris, 1980, Bayley Mus., Va., 1983, Va. Mus., 1984, World Bank, Washington, 1985, Yokohama, Japan, 1989, Newport Beach, Calif., 1993, Palm Desert, Calif., 1994; commd. by the Vatican to paint the ofcl. portrait of Pope John Paul II, Hearst Castle, Calif., to sculpt Pocahontas bronze, Town of Gloucester, Va., bronze in collection of Pres. Bush; represented in permanent collections Chrysler Mus., Am. Embassy, Stockholm, Bayly Mus., Victoria and Albert Mus.; represented in 10 galleries. With U.S. Army, 1951-53, Korea. Decorated 14 combat medals; recipient Stalin medal for art, 1937, Rias award, 1946. Avocations: antiques, gardening, birds. Home: Tetley Plantation Tetley Dr Somerset VA 22972 Office: A Sehring Studio Tetley Plantation Somerset VA 22972 E-mail: lsregina@aol.com.

SEHY, STEPHEN M. systems support specialist; BS, U. Ill.; MBA, U. Chgo. CPA Ill. Product mgr. Omron Systems, Schaumburg, 1988—94; mgr. external devel. Nat. Edn. Tng. Group, Naperville, 1994—2001; software/tng. exec., 2001—. Avocations: reading, bicycling.

SEI, IBRAHIM, process engineer; b. Freetown, Sierra Leone, Mar. 23, 1969; s. Juma Mohamed and Ayeshat S.; m. Aminata Bailoh-Jalloh, July 10, 1999; children: Juma, Kenya. BS, U. Md., 1995, PhD, 2000. Process engr. IBM, Endicott, N.Y., 1996-99; sr. process engr. Intel Corp., Rio Rancho, N.Mex., 2000—. Mem. AIChE, Am. Electroplaters and Surface Finishers Soc., Inc., Am. Chem. Soc., Nat. Soc. Black Engrs. Home: Apt 1413 201 Country Club Dr SE Rio Rancho NM 87124 Office: Intel Corp 4100 Sara Rd Rio Rancho NM 87124 E-mail: ibrahim.sei@intel.com.

SEIB, BILLIE MCGHEE RUSHING, nursing administrator, consultant; b. Brookport , Ill., Mar. 04; d. Frank and ILA (Paris) McGhee; m. Alfred Rushing, Jan. 2, 1958 (dec.); children: Lisa, Libbi; m. Bob Seib, Mar. 21, 1986. Diploma, DePaul Sch. Nursing, St. Louis, 1947; postgrad. in oper. rm. nursing, Washington U., St. Louis, 1950; BS, U. St. Francis, Joliet, 2002. Cert. geriat. nurse, ANCC. Dir. oper. rm. Jennie Stuart Med. Ctr., Hopkinsville, Ky.; clin. mgr. oper. rm. Meml. Med. Ctr., Savannah, Ga.; mgr. oper. rm. Meth. Med. Ctr., Oak Ridge, Tenn.; coord. oper. rm. Parkwest Hosp., Knoxville; mem. oper. rm. pool Ft. Sanders Park West Hosp., 1992-93; geriat. supr. Briarcliff Health Care Ctr., Oak Ridge, Tenn., 1993-96, Windwood Health Care Ctr. (now Beverly Health & Rehab. Ctr.), Clinton, 1996—, asst. DON, 1997—2001. Cons. Washington, Fla., Ky., Nev.; mgr., owner N.Y. Fashio Her Way, Oak Ridge, Tenn., 1997—. Mem. Assn. Oper. Rm. Nurses (cert., bd. dirs., past pres. East Tenn. chpt.), Am. Gerontol. Nursing Assn. Home: 133 Lakeview Hills Ln Clinton TN 37716-5957 E-mail: bjs@icx.net.

SEIB, KENNETH ALLEN, English educator; b. Shelby, Ohio, Mar. 27, 1938; s. Frank Seib and Grace Wanamaker; m. Lorna Jane Maddocks, July 1966 (div. 1986). BA in English, Ashland U., 1960; MA in English, Columbia U., 1961; PhD in English, U. Pitts., 1966. Prof. English, chair Calif. State U., Fresno, 1972-89, founding faculty English San Marcos, 1989-90, Heartland C.C., Bloomington, Ill., 1992-95; vis. prof. English U. Ill., Urbana, 1990-91; dean arts and scis. Truckee Meadows C.C., Reno, 1995-96, lectr. in English and humanities, 1996—. Author: James Agee: Promise and Fulfillment, 1968; contbr. over 20 articles to profl. jours. Fellow Woodrow Wilson Found., 1960-61, Andrew Mellon Found., 1962-63; Fulbright-Hays tchg. grantee, 1970-71, NEH grantee, 1979-81. Avocations: sports, classical music. Home: 10082 Zeolite Dr Reno NV 89506-1600 E-mail: kenseib@aol.com.

SEIBEL, KLAUSPETER, conductor; b. Offenbach, Germany; Assoc. music dir. Freiburg, Lubeck, Kassel, Frankfurt operas, 1963-75; music dir. Freiburg Opera and Philharmonic; assoc. music dir. Hamburg Opera; prof. conducting Hamburg Conservatory; music dir. Nuremberg Symphony, 1980, Kiel Opera and Philharmonic, 1987, La. Philharmonic Orch., 1995—. Permanent guest condr. Hamburg and Dresden operas; guest condr. symphony orchs. Berlin, Hamburg, Frankfurt, Bratislava, Copenhagen, Reykjavik; guest condr. Am. Opera of Julliard Sch. in N.Y., San Diego Symphony, New Orleans Opera, Spokane Symphony. Recipient Prize Nicolai Malko and Dimitri Mitropoulos competitions. Office: La Philharmonic Orch 305 Baronne St Ste 600 New Orleans LA 70112-1619 E-mail: KPSeibel@aol.com.*

SEIBER, RICHARD ALLAN, retired minister; b. L.A., Nov. 15, 1932; s. Edward Maurice and Dorothy Mildred (Ball) S.; m. Wilma Ellen Shook, Sept. 24, 1955; children: Bruce Wayne, Roger Kent, Dale Eugene, Michael Allan. BA in History, U. Puget Sound, 1958; MDiv, Garrett Biblical Inst., 1960; grad., Air Command & Staff Coll., Maxwell AFB, 1962, Air War Coll., 1970. Ordained elder United Meth. Ch., 1960. Enlisted USAF, 1950, advanced through grades to lt. col., chaplain, 1960-76; student pastor Meth. Ch., Algona-Pacific, Wash., 1955-57, Sciota-Friendship, Ill., 1957-60; pastor United Meth. Ch., Spanaway, Wash., 1976-83, Epworth-LeSourd United Meth. Ch., Tacoma, 1983-97; ret. United Meth. Ch., 1997. Mem. editl. bd. Meth. History United Meth. Ch., Madison, NJ, 1982—86, mem. gen. conf. archives and history, NJ, 1980—88, mem. jurisdictional conf. archives and history, NJ, 1980—, pres. jurisdictional conf. archives and history, NJ, 1980—84; chmn. com. on chaplains Pacific N.W. Conf., 1977—88. Editor: Memoirs of Puget Sound: David Blaine, 1978, Methodist History Index: Oct. 1962-July 1982, 1984, Jour. Henry Bridgeman Brewer, 1839-48, 1986; contbr. Sprague, Lamont, Edwarl, WA, 1881-1981, 1982, Religious Heritage of Washington State, 1988, Illustrated History of Methodism, 1999. Mem. Tacoma Mayor's Task Force on Vets. Affairs, 1986-91; chmn. Ministry with Service People—Co-NeXion, Tillicum, Wash., 1976-79, 87-90; mem. Wesley Homes Corp., Des Moines, Wash., 1984—; v.p. exploring, exec. com. Mount Rainier Coun., Boy Scouts Am., 1976-81, v.p. rels., 1981-92, mem. nat. coun., rep. Pacific Harbors, 1999—. Recipient Silver Beaver award Boy Scouts Am., 1977, God and Svc. recognition award Boy Scouts Am., 1988, James E. West fellow, 1997. Mem. SAR (chpt. pres. 1989-91), Air Force Assn. (state pres. 1994-98, Exceptional Svc. award 1999), Mil. Chaplain's Assn. (Puget Sound chpt. pres. 1985-93), Nat. Eagle Scout Assn., Scouting Heritage Assn. (life, charter), Air Force Hist. Found., Retired Officers' Assn. (life), Air War Coll. Alumni Assn. (life). Avocations: stained glass, genealogy, clocks, early Northwest church history, collecting Royal Doulton. Home: 5323 97th Avenue Ct W University Place WA 98467

SEIBERLICH, CARL JOSEPH, retired naval officer; b. Jenkintown, Pa., July 4, 1921; s. Charles A. and Helen (Dolan) S.; m. Trudy Germi, May 29, 1952; children: Eric P., Heidi M., Curt A. BS, U.S. Mcht. Marine Acad., 1943; grad., Armed Forces Staff Coll., 1959. Commd. ensign U.S. Navy, 1943, advanced through grades to rear adm., 1971; designated naval aviator, 1947; comdg. officer Airship ZPM-1, 1949, Air Anti-Submarine Squadron 26, 1961, U.S.S. Salamonie, 1967, U.S.S. Hornet, 1969; dir. recovery astronauts Apollo 11 and 12 lunar missions, 1969; comdr. anti-submarine warfare group 3 Flagship U.S.S. Ticonderoga, 1971; comdr. task force 74 Viet Nam Ops., 1972; asst. dep. chief naval ops. for air warfare Navy Dept., 1975-77; dep. chief naval personnel, 1977-78; comdr. Naval Mil. Personnel Command, 1978-80; with VSE Corp., 1980-82; pres. U.S. Maritime Resource Ctr.; dir. mil. program Am. Pres. Lines, 1983-95, TranSystems Corp., Reston, Va., 1996—. Co-chmn. intermodal task force Nat. Rsch. Coun., Transp. Bd.; mem. NAFTA Info. Exch. & Automation working group. Vice pres. Naval Aviation Mus. Found.; active Boy Scouts Am. Decorated Legion of Merit (6), Air medal; recipient Harmon Internat. trophy for devel. 1st variable depth towed sonar, 1951; Vincent T. Hirsch Maritime award Navy League, 1995. Mem. VFW, AIAA, Am. Soc. Naval Engrs., Soc. Naval Architects and Marine Engrs., Am. Helicopter Soc., U.S. Naval Inst., U.S. Naval Sailing Assn. (commodore 1979), Am. Angus Assn., Tailhook Assn., Navy Helicopter Assn., Naval Airship Assn., Early and Pioneer Naval Aviators Assn., Nat. Def. Transp. Assn., Navy League U.S. (maritime affairs com.), Propeller Club, Order of Daedalians, U.S. Mcht. Marine Acad. Alumni Assn., Assn. Naval Aviation, Am. Legion, N.Y. Yacht Club, Nat. Space Club, Delta Sigma Pi. Clubs: N.Y. Yacht, Nat. Space. Home: Seagate Farm 1510 Loudoun Dr Haymarket VA 20169-1120 Office: TranSystems Corp 2100 Reston Pkwy Ste 202 Reston VA 20191-1200 *Maintain a clear set of moral values, prepare yourself professionally, maintain physical fitness, persevere as you move toward your goal. Value personal relationships. Never give less than your best; never accept less than the best. Don't trade on the accomplishments of yesterday. Have fun and at times pause and admire the flowers.*

SEIBERLING, JOHN FREDERICK, former congressman, law educator, lawyer; b. Akron, Ohio, Sept. 8, 1918; s. J. Frederick and Henrietta (Buckler) S.; m. Elizabeth Pope Behr, June 4, 1949; children— John B., David P., Stephen M. AB, Harvard U., 1941; LLB, Columbia U., 1949. Bar: N.Y. 1950, Ohio 1955. Assoc. mem. firm Donovan, Leisure, Newton, Lumbard & Irvine, N.Y.C., 1949-53; atty. Goodyear Tire & Rubber Co., Akron, 1954-71; mem. 92d-99th Congresses from 14th Ohio Dist.; mem. com. on judiciary, com. on interior and insular affairs, chmn. subcom. on public lands; vis. prof. law U. Akron, 1987, 90, dir. Ctr. for Peace Studies, 1991-96; ptnr. Goldman, Seiberling, Davis & Tsarnas, Akron, 1988-89. Served to maj. AUS, 1942-46. Mem. United Ch. of Christ. Home: 154 Tecumseh Ln Akron OH 44321-2753

SEIBERT, ALBERT FRANK, chemical engineer; b. Houston, Oct. 29, 1958; s. Albert Frank and Cecilia Ruth (Williams) S. BSChemE, U. Houston, 1982; MSChemE, U. Tex., Austin, 1984, PhD in Engring., 1986. Rsch. assoc. Separations Rsch. Program, Austin, 1986-92, rsch. engr., 1993, tech. mgr., 1993—. Cons. J.L. Humphrey & Assocs., Austin, 1987—. Author: Fluid Mixture Separation Technologies for Cost Reduction and Process Improvement, 1986; contbr. articles to profl. jours. Getty Oil scholar, 1981-82; recipient Excellence award ARCO, 1982. Mem. AIChE, N.Am. Membrae Soc. Achievements include applied research in liquid and supercritical extraction, distillation packings and trays; discovery use of high pressure carbon dioxide for cleaning oily water in a column contactor; contributed to the development of the membrane extractor and high capacity co-flo distillation tray. Office: U Tex CES Bldg 133 10100 Burnet Rd Austin TX 78758-4445

SEIBERT, EARL HENRY, JR. (SI SEIBERT), diversified financial services company executive; b. Evansville, Ind., July 10, 1952; s. Earl H., Sr. and Elaine D. S.; m. Dawn Duenke, Jan. 2, 1987; children: Heather Lea, Megan Natalie. BS in Advt./ Mktg., Ind. U., 1974. Sales rep. Geo. A. Hormel & Co., Chgo., 1974-79, nat. product mgr. Austin, Minn., 1979-82, dist. sales mgr. St. Louis, Detroit, 1982-85; dir. mktg. Habbersett Sausage, Media, Pa., 1985-88; divsnl. v.p. Charles Givens Orgn., Orlando, Fla., 1988-91; pres. Seibert Group, Inc., Town & Country, Mo., 1988—, Strategic Asset Mgmt., Creve Coeur, 1991—. Recipient Mr. Jr. Achievement award, 1970. Mem. Internat. Assn. Reg. Fin. Cons., Internat. Assn. Fin. Planners, Charles J. Givens Orgn.-Delta Group (pres. 1986-88). Office: Strategic Asset Mgmt 2200 W Pont Plaza Dr # 206 Saint Louis MO 63146

SEIBERT, MARY LEE, college official; b. Evansville, Ind., Jan. 30, 1942; d. Ernest Hensley and Lillian (Schmadel) S. BS, Ind. U., 1963, MS, 1973, EdD, 1979. Cert. med. technologist, med. asst. Lab. supr. Wishard Meml. Hosp., Indpls., 1964-67; chmn. life scis. div. Ind. Tech. Coll., 1967-73; assoc. prof., program dir. Ind. U. Sch. Medicine, 1973-79; assoc. project coordinator Am. Assn. State Colls. and Univs., Washington, 1979-81; dean coll. allied health professions Temple U., Phila., 1981-90; assoc. provost, dean grad. studies Ithaca (N.Y.) Coll., 1990-99, acting provost, 1996-98; v.p. acad. affairs, dean faculty Utica (N.Y.) Coll. of Syracuse U., 1999—. Vis. prof. U. Tex. Med. Br., Galveston, 1985. Assoc. editor Jour. Med. Tech., 1985-86; mem. edit. bd. Jour. Allied Health. Fellow Am. Soc. Allied Health Profls. (hon., chmn. forum on allied health data, rsch. com. 1983-89, bd. dirs. 1990-92, Outstanding Mem. award 1986); mem. Am. Soc. Clin. Lab. Sci. (profl. affairs com. 1986-89), Am. Assn. Med. Assts. (hon.), Nat. Coun. on Health Professions Edn., Nat. Acad. Scis. (bd. health care svcs. inst. of medicine 1993-99), Phi Delta Kappa, Pi Lambda Theta, Pi Kappa Phi. Republican. Avocations: reading, walking, sailing. Home: 16 Bean Hill Ln Ithaca NY 14850-8537 E-mail: mseibert@utica.edu.

SEIBERT, RUSSELL JACOB, botanist, research associate; b. Shiloh Valley, Ill., Aug. 14, 1914; s. Erwin W. and Helen A. (Renner) S.; m. Isabelle L. Pring, Dec. 26, 1942; children: Michael, Donna, Lisa. AB, Washington U., St. Louis, 1937, MS, 1938, PhD, 1947. With U.S. Dept. Agr., 1940-50, botanist-geneticist rubber plant investigations Haiti, 1941-42, botanist-geneticist Peru, 1943-46, Costa Rica, 1947-49; dir. Los Angeles State and County Arboretum, Arcadia, Calif., 1950-55, Longwood Gardens, Kennett Square, Pa., 1955-79; adj. curator tropical horticulture Marie Selby Bot. Garden, Sarasota, Fla., 1979-96. Adj. prof. dept. hort. U. Del., 1960-79; head dept. arboreta and bot. gardens, Los Angeles County, 1952-55; Am. del. Internat. Soc. Hort. Sci., 1960-70; chmn. Am. Hort. Council-U.S.A. (hort. exhbn.), 1960; (floriade), Rotterdam, Holland; v.p. XVII Internat. Hort. Congress, 1966; chmn. Am. Hort. Film Festival, 1964-69 Recipient Frank N. Meyer Meml. medal Am. Genetic Soc., 1966, Arthur Hoyt Scott Garden and Horticulture medal Swarthmore Coll., 1975, Disting. Svc. awrd Hort. Soc. N.Y., 1969, award of merit Am. Assn. Bot. Gardens and Arboreta, 1982. Mem. AAAS, Am. Hort. Soc. (pres. 1964-65, Liberty Hyde Bailey medal 1975), Am. Inst. Biol. Scis., Rotary, Sigma Xi, Phi Sigma, Gamma Sigma Delta. Home: 1613 Caribbean Dr Sarasota FL 34231-5305

SEIBOLD, JAMES RICHARD, physician, researcher; b. Washington, Apr. 5, 1950; s. Herman Rudolph and Clara Bond (Taylor) S.; m. Margaret Frances Bennett, Jan. 20, 1968; children: Jon Drew, Zachary Bennett. BS, La. State U., 1972; MD, SUNY, Stony Brook, 1975. Diplomate Am. Bd. Internal Medicine, Am. Bd. Rheumatology. Intern in medicine L.I. Jewish Hosp., New Hyde Park, N.Y., 1975-76, resident in medicine, 1976-78; fellow in rheumatology U. Pitts., 1978-80; asst. prof. medicine Robert Wood Johnson Med. Sch. U. Medicine and Dentistry N.J., New Brunswick, 1980-86, assoc. prof., 1986-92, prof., 1992—, chief rheumatology, 1986-91, dir. clin. rsch. ctr., 1989-95. Mem. adv. bd. Ctr. for Advanced Biotech. and Medicine, Piscataway, N.J., 1989-95, dir. Scleroderma program 1995—; W.H. Conzen chair clin. pharmacology Schering-Plough Found., 1989. Author: (chpt.) Rheumatology, 1988, 91, 94, 95, 99, 2001; contbr. over 300 articles to profl. jours. Bd. dirs. Scleroderma Found. Fellow ACP, Am. Coll. Rheumatology (regional coun. 1985), Scleroderma Clin. Trials Consortium (founder 1994). Mem. Soc. Of Friends. Home: 16 Durham Rd Skillman NJ 08558-1805 Office: U Medicine and Dentistry NJ Robert Wood Johnson Med Sch 1 RW Johnson Pl MEB 556 New Brunswick NJ 08903-0019 E-mail: seiboljr@umdnj.edu.

SEIDE, PAUL, civil engineering educator; b. N.Y.C., July 22, 1926; s. Julius David and Sylvia (Eiler) S.; m. Joan Cecilia Matalka, Jan. 7, 1951; children: Richard Laurence, Wendy Jane Seide Kielsmeier. B.C.E., CCNY, 1946; M. Aero. Engring, U. Va., 1952; PhD, Stanford U., 1954. Aero. research scientist Nat. Adv. Commn. for Aeros., Langley AFB, Va., 1946-52; research asst. Stanford Calif. U., 1952-53; research engr. Northrop Aircraft Co., Hawthorne, Calif., 1953-55; head methods and theory sect. TRW Inc., Los Angeles, 1955-60; head methods and research sect. Aerospace Corp., El Segundo, Calif., 1960-65; prof. civil engring. U. So. Calif., L.A., 1965-91, prof. emeritus, 1991—, assoc. chmn. dept. civil engring., 1971-73, 81-83; Albert Alberman vis. prof. Technion-Israel Inst. Tech., Haifa, 1975; vis. prof. U. Sydney, Australia, 1986, U. Canterbury, N.Z., 1986. Cons. Northrop Inc., 1972-77, Aerospace Corp., 1966-68, Rockwell Inc., El Segundo, 1982-85 Author: Small Elastic Deformations of Thin Shells, 1975; contbr. numerous articles to profl. jours. NSF fellow, 1964-65 Fellow ASME, Am. Acad. Mechanics; mem. ASCE (life), Tau Beta Pi, Sigma Xi. Democrat. Jewish. Home: 300 Via Alcance Palos Verdes Peninsula CA 90274-1105

SEIDEL, CARL WILLIAM, business executive, consultant; b. Hempstead, N.Y., Aug. 18, 1938; s. Charles Francis and Wilma Marie Seidel; m. Suzanne Winslow Dana; children: Lisa Marie, Michael Dana, Rebecca Suzanne, Elaine Marie. BS in Chemistry, U. Wis., 1959; MS in Chemistry, U. Notre Dame, 1962. Chemist, mktg. mgr. Nuclear Sci. and Engring., Pitts., 1962-69; product mgr. New England Nuclear, Billerica, Mass., 1969-73, asst. divsn. mgr., 1973-79, gen. mgr. new products, 1979-81; various positions, mfg. mgr. pharm. divsn. DuPont, 1981-91; assoc. dir. DuPont Merck, 1991-97; pres., CEO Internat. Isotopes, Denton, Tex., 1997-99; pres. Carl W. Seidel & Assocs., Cons., 1999—. Cons. Dept. of Energy, Washington, 1990-2001; tech. advisor U.S. Pharmocpiea, Bethesda, 1995-2000; com. mem. Am. Nat. Stds. Inst., Gaithersburg, 1975. Co-editor Mössbauer Effect Methodology, Vol. 8, 1973, Vol. 9, 1974, Vol. 10, 1976; editor: The Mössbauer Effect and Its Application in Chemistry, 1967. Town rep., Chelmsford, Mass., 1980-97. Mem. Internat. Isotope Soc., Am. Coll. Nuclear Physicians, Legatus, Soc. of Nuclear Medicine (sec.-treas. therapy coun.), Am. Chem. Soc., European Soc. of Nuclear Medicine, Russell Mill Swim and Tennis (pres. 1972-75), C. of C. Republican. Roman Catholic. Avocations: tennis, travel. Home and Office: 208 Royal Oaks Pl Denton TX 76210-5580

SEIDEL, FREDERICK LEWIS, poet; b. St. Louis, Feb. 19, 1936; s. Jerome Jay and Thelma (Cartun) S.; children: Felicity, Samuel. AB, Harvard U., 1957. Occasional lectr., Rutgers U., New Brunswick, 1964—; Paris editor, Paris Review, 1961, advisory editor, 1962. Author: (poetry) Final Solutions, 1963, Sunrise, 1979 (Lamont Poetry prize Acad. Am. Poets 1980, Am. Poetry Rev.

prize 1980, Nat. Book Critics Circle award for poetry 1981), Men and Woman: New and Selected Poems, 1984, Poems 1959-1979, 1989, These Days, 1989, My Tokyo, 1993, Going Fast, 1998, The Cosmos Poems, 2000, Life on Earth, 2001. Guggenheim Fellow, 1993.

SEIDEL, GEORGE ELIAS, JR. animal scientist, educator; b. Reading, Pa., July 13, 1943; s. George E. Sr. and Grace Esther (Heinly) S.; m. Sarah Beth Moore, May 28, 1970; 1 child, Andrew. BS, Pa. State U., 1965; MS, Cornell U., 1968, PhD, 1970; postgrad., Harvard U. Med. Sch., Boston, 1970-71. Asst. prof. physiology Colo. State U., Ft. Collins, 1971-75, assoc. prof., 1975-83, prof., 1983-93, univ. disting. prof., 1993—. Vis. scientist Yale U., 1978-79, MIT, 1986-87; mem. bd. on agr. NRC. Co-editor: New Technologies in Animal Breeding, 1981; contbr. articles to profl. jours. Recipient Alexander Von Humboldt award, N.Y.C., 1983, Animal Breeding Research award Nat. Assn. Animal Breeders, Columbia, Mo., 1983, Clark award Colo. State U., 1982, Upjohn Physiology award, 1986; Gov's. award for Sci. and Tech., Colo., 1986. Mem. AAAS, NAS, Am. Dairy Sci. Assn., Am. Soc. Animal Sci. (Young Animal Scientist award 1983), Soc. for Study of Reprodn., Internat. Embryo Transfer Soc. (pres. 1979, disting. svc. award 2001). Home: 3101 Arrowhead Rd Laporte CO 80535-9374 Office: Colo State U Animal Repro Biotech Lab Fort Collins CO 80523-0001

SEIDEL, JOAN BROUDE, stockbroker, investment advisor; b. Chgo., Aug. 16, 1933; d. Ned and Betty (Treiger) Broude; m. Arnold Seidel, Aug. 18, 1957; children: David, Craig. BA, UCLA, 1954; postgrad., N.Y. Inst. Fin. Registered prin., investment advisor Morton Seidel & Co. Inc., L.A., 1970-74, v.p., 1974-93; pres., 1993—; also bd. dirs. Morton Seidel & Co. Inc., L.A. Instr. UCLA Extension, 1979-84. Treas. City of Beverly Hills, Calif., 1990-2001, chmn. rent adjustment bd., 1989-90, mem., 1983-89; mem. investment com. YWCA, L.A., 1987—, treas. Greater L.A., 1992-95; bd. dirs. Discovery Fund for Eye Rsch., L.A., 1987—, treas., 1999—; corp. dir. Queen's Care. Named Citizen of Yr. Beverly Hills C. of C., 1993. Fellow Assn. for Investment Mgmt. and Rsch.; mem. Am. Technion Soc. (v.p. 1998-2002, pres. 2002—), Nat. Assn. Security Dealers (dist. bus. conduct com. 2S 1993-95, 98-2000, small firm adv. bd. 1998-2000, chair dist. 2 1999-2000), L.A. Soc. Fin. Analysts, Orgn. Women Execs., Bond Club, Rotary, Phi Sigma Alpha. Avocations: reading, travel. Home: 809 N Bedford Dr Beverly Hills CA 90210-3023 Office: Morton Seidel & Co Inc 8730 Wilshire Blvd Ste 530 Beverly Hills CA 90211-2792 E-mail: seidel350@aol.com.

SEIDEL, LIZBETH J. pianist, educator; b. Reading, Pa., May 8, 1953; d. Robert E. and Elizabeth J. Seleski; m. John A. Seidel, July 7, 1979; children: Jonathan, Christine. B in Music, Ithaca Coll., 1975; M in Music, Temple U., 1979; ArtsD in Music, Ball State U., 2001. Cert. nat. music tchr. Instr. U. Wis., Superior, 1993—94, Ball State U., Muncie, Ind., 1998—2001. Grantee humanities initiative, Ball State U., 2000. Mem.: Music Tchrs. Nat. Assn. (grantee tchr. enrichment), Ind. Music Tchrs. Assn. (bd. dirs.). Home: 300 S Shady Ln Muncie IN 47304-4351

SEIDEL, MARTIN, lawyer; b. Beuthen, Poland, Oct. 4, 1932; s. Martin and Anna Seidel; m. Ingelore Roggemann; children: Carola, Ronald. Law degree, U. Cologne, Germany, 1956, D Utrius Juris, 1960; great law degree, State North Rhine-Westphalia, Germany, 1961; Prof. (hon.), U. Münster, Germany, 1989. Legal advisor dept. European integration Fed. Ministry Econs., Bonn, Germany, 1962-97. Permanent rep. of Germany to Ct. Justice of European Cmty., 1972-89; mem. German del., legal advisor Conf. European Union on Econ. and Monetary Union, 1989-91; lectr. European law univs. Münster, Saarbrücken, Bonn, Germany, Danube U., Austria, 2 Norwegian univs., 1982-2000; mem. directorate Inst. on European Integration, Berlin. Author: Constitutional and Legal Aspects of Economic and Monetary Union, 2000; contbr. numerous articles on European law, econs and monetary union, and integration policy issues to profl. jours. Decorated officier Ordre Arts et Lettres (France). Mem. German Soc. on European Law (bd. dirs.). Avocation: piano playing. Home: Hobsweg 73 D-53125 Bonn Germany

SEIDEL, ROBERT WAYNE, science historian, educator, institute administrator; b. Kansas City, Mo., June 9, 1945; s. Wayne Herman and Harriet Anita (Day) S.; m. Alison Publicover, Aug. 26, 1972 (div. 1989); 1 child, Mary Ruth; m. Christine Ruth Stack, July 1, 1993. BA, Westmar Coll., 1967; MA, U. Calif., Berkeley, 1968, PhD, 1978. Exhibit designer Lawrence Hall Sci., Berkeley, 1970-72; specialist Poland 4-city tour USIA, Warsaw, 1971-72; grad. rsch. and teaching asst. U. Calif., 1972-78; asst. prof. Tex. Tech U., Lubbock, 1978-83, dir. rsch. history of engring. program, 1979-83; rsch. historian U. Calif., Berkeley, 1980-82, Laser History Project, Albany, Calif., 1983-85; adminstr. Bradbury Sci. Mus., Los Alamos, N.Mex., 1985-90, overview project leader, 1990-92; sr. staff mem. Ctr. Nat. Security Studies, 1992-94; dir. Charles Babbage Inst., U. Minn., Mpls., 1994-99; ERA Land Grant prof. History of Tech. U. Minn., 1994-99, prof. chem. engring., 1999—. Author: Lawrence and His Laboratory: A History of the Lawrence Berkeley Laboratory, 1989, Los Alamos and the Making of the Atomic Bomb, 1995. Mem. N.Mex. Sci. Ctr. Commn., 1989-92; bd. dirs. The Bakken Mus., 1994—. Woodrow Wilson fellow, 1967, U. Calif. Regent's fellow, 1968, German Marshall Fund fellow, Grenoble, France, 1975, Sr. fellow Dibner Inst., MIT, 2001; recipient Bicentennial Essay prize Nat. Sci. Tchrs. Assn., 1976. Mem. AAUP, History Sci. Soc., Soc. for History Tech. Democrat. Avocation: computer simulations. Home: 5625 Woodlawn Blvd Minneapolis MN 55417-2667 Office: 151 Amundson Hall/U Minn Minneapolis MN 55455 E-mail: rws@tc.umn.edu.

SEIDEL, SAMUEL LEARNED RICHARD CARTUN, governmental researcher; b. N.Y.C., Sept. 10, 1966; s. Frederick and Phyllis (Ferguson) Seidel; m. Ann L.M. Smith, June 30, 2001. BA, U. Calif., Berkeley, 1988; postgrad., Georgetown U., 1997-99, Harvard U., 1999-2001. Exec. asst. to Eunice Kennedy Shriver The Joseph F. Kennedy, Jr. Found., Washington, 1994; rsch. asst. Office of Technology Assessment U.S. Congress, 1994-95, Office of Sci. and Technology Policy The White House, Washington, 1995-96; rsch. assoc. Nat. Rsch. Coun., 1997; ind. environ. cons./planner. Home and Office: 34 Gorham St Cambridge MA 02138-1905

SEIDEL, SELVYN, lawyer, educator; b. Long Branch, N.J., Nov. 6, 1942; s. Abraham and Anita (Stoller) S.; m. Deborah Lew, June 21, 1970; 1 child, Emily. BA, U. Chgo., 1964; JD, U. Calif., Berkeley, 1967; diploma in law, Oxford U., 1968. Bar: N.Y. 1970, D.C. Ct. Appeals 1982. Ptnr. Latham & Watkins, N.Y.C., 1984—. Adj. prof. Sch. Law, NYU, 1974-85; instr. Practicing Law Inst., 1980-81, 84. Contbr. articles to profl. jours. Bd. dirs. Citizen Scholarship Fund Am., 1995-2000. Mem. ABA, N.Y. County Bar Assn., N.Y.C. Bar Assn. (mem. fed. cts. com. 1982-85, internat. law com. 1989-92, 95-96, art law com. 1997-2000), Boalt Hall Alumni Assn. (bd. dirs. 1980-82). Office: Latham & Watkins 885 3rd Ave New York NY 10022-4802 E-mail: selvyn.seidel@lw.com.

SEIDEL, TAMMY SUE, secondary education educator; b. Roswell, N.Mex., Feb. 19, 1959; d. Harold C. and Nina Sarah (Nelson) Miller; m. David J. Seidel, Apr. 18, 1987; 1 child, Sarah Brianna. BBA, Ea. N.Mex. U., 1981; MA in Tng. and Learning Tech., U. N.Mex., 1992. Customer svc. rep. First Interstate Bank, Hobbs, N.Mex., 1983; sys. sales cons. Moore Bus. Forms, 1983-85; mktg. tchr. Los Alamos (N.Mex.) H.S., 1985—. Finalist Golden Apple Found. award 1996, KOAT TV Top Tchrs. award, 1997; nominee Los Alamos Tchr. of Yr. award, 1998. Mem. Am. Vocat. Assn., Mktg. Edn. Assn., N.Mex. DECA (chmn. bd. govs. 1994-96, mem. bd. govs. 1996-2002, state officer/advisor 1996-97), N.Mex. Mktg. Edn. Assn. (treas. 2000-2002, 15-Yr. award 2000), Los Alamos Schs. Credit Union (bd. dirs. 1992-96), , Phi Kappa Phi. Avocations: swimming, reading, walking. Office: Los Alamos High Sch 1300 Diamond Dr Los Alamos NM 87544-2280

SEIDEN, HENRY (HANK SEIDEN), advertising executive; b. Bklyn., Sept. 6, 1928; s. Jack S. and Shirley (Berkowitz) S.; m. Helena Ruth Zaldin, Sept. 10, 1949; children: Laurie Ann, Matthew Ian. BA, Bklyn. Coll., 1949; MBA, CCNY, 1954. Trainee Ben Sackheim Advt. Agy., 1949-51; nat. promotion mgr. N.Y. Post Corp., 1951-53; promotion mgr. Crowell-Collier Pub. Co., Inc., 1953-54; copy group head Batten, Barton, Durstine & Osborn, Inc., 1954-60; v.p., creative dir. Keyes, Madden & Jones, 1960-61; sr. v.p., assoc. creative dir. McCann-Marschalk, Inc., 1961-65, chmn. plans bd., 1964-65; creative dir., dir., prin. Hicks & Greist, Inc., N.Y.C., 1965—, sr. v.p., 1965-74, exec. v.p., 1974-83, COO, 1983—, pres., 1986—; CEO Ketchum/Hicks & Greist Inc., 1987-89; chmn., CEO Ketchum Advt., 1989-91; exec. v.p. Ketchum Comm. Inc., also bd. dirs.; vice chmn. Jordan, McGrath, Case & Taylor, Inc., 1992—; chmn., CEO The Seiden Group, Inc. Bd. dirs. Ketchum Internat. Inc.; guest lectr. Bernard M. Baruch Sch. Bus. and Pub. Adminstrn., CCNY, 1962—, Baruch Coll., 1969—, New Sch. Social Scis., 1968, 72,73, Sch. Visual Arts, 1979, 80—, Lehman Coll., CCNY, 1980—, Ohio U., 1981, Newhouse Grad. Sch., Syracuse U., 1981, NYU, 1983; cons. pub. rels. and comm. to mayor City of New Rochelle, N.Y., 1959—; cons. mktg. dept. Ohio State U.; cons. to pres. N.Y.C. City Coun., 1972-73; cons. Postmaster Gen. U.S., 1972-74; comm. advisor to commr. N.Y.C. Police Dept., 1973—, hon. dept. commr., 1991—, spl. cons. to commr., 1992—. Author: Advertising Pure and Simple, 1976, Advertising Pure and Simple: The New Edition, 1990; contbg. editor: Madison Ave. mag, 1966— , Advt. Age, Mag. Age; guest columnist: N.Y. Times, 1972. Vice commr. Little League of New Rochelle; bd. dirs. Police Res. Assn. N.Y.C., 1973—, pres. exec. com.; bd. dirs. Cancer Rsch. and Treatment Fund, Inc., pres., 1992—; bd. dirs. Am. Heart Assn., Transmedia Network, Inc.; bd. dirs., chmn. New York's Finest Found., 1975—, pres., 1996; bd. dirs., sr. v.p. Drug Enforcement Agy. Found., 1995—. Recipient award Four Freedoms Found., 1959, award Printers Ink, 1960, promotion award Editor and Pub., 1955, Am. TV Commls. Festival award, 1963-69, Effie award Am. Mktg. Assn., 1969, 70, award Art Dirs. Club N.Y., 1963-70, award Am. Inst. Graphic Arts, 1963, Starch award, 1969, spl. award graphic art lodge B'nai B'rith Greater N.Y., 1971, 87, award of highest honor FBI Nat. Acad., 1994. Mem. NATAS, Am. Inst. Mgmt. (assoc.), Drug Enforcement Agts. Found. (sr. v.p. 1995), Advt. Club N.Y. (exec. judge Andy awards, award 1963-65), Advt. Writers Assn. N.Y. (Gold Key award for best newspaper and mag. advts. 1962-640, Copy Club (co-chmn. awards com., Gold Key award for best TV comml. 1969), Alpha Phi Omega. Home: 1056 5th Ave New York NY 10028-0112 Office: The Seiden Group 708 3rd Ave New York NY 10017-4201 E-mail: hankruthseiden@aol.com., handseiden@theseidengroupadr.com. *Be yourself but don't take yourself too seriously.*

SEIDEN, LEWIS S. neuroscientist; b. Chgo., Aug. 1, 1934; s. Alex and Dorothy Fein Seiden; m. Anne Elizabeth Maxwell, Dec. 27, 1962; children: Alex, Effie Seiden Ivey, Sam. BA, U. Chgo., 1955, BS, 1958, PhD, 1962; MD (hon.) , U. Göteborg, Sweden, 1999. Neuroscientist Dept. pharmacology and physiol. sci. U. Chgo., Chgo. Home: 5544 S Woodlawn Ave Chicago IL 60637 E-mail: lseiden@midway.uchicago.edu.

SEIDEN, PAUL, insurance agent, consultant; b. Rzeszow, Poland, Nov. 16, 1920; came to US., 1939, naturalized, 1943; s. Simon and Amalia Grauer S.; m. Ida Perlin, Nov. 27, 1943 (div. 1961); children: Mark D., Henry A.; m. Judith Ellen Barkalow, Jan. 19, 1962; children: Lewis J., Eve M. Student, CUNY, 1939-41; MS in Mgmt., MS in Fin. Svcs., Am. Coll., 1985. Real estate broker Simon J. Boss Realty Co., Bklyn., 1948-51; life ins. agt. Phoenix Mutual Life Ins. Co., N.Y.C., 1952-56; asst. gen. agr. Aetna Life Ins. Co., Miami, 1956-61; gen. agt. Nat. Life Vt., Beverly Hills, Calif., 1962-90, agt. Encino, 1991—. Cons. mktg., pres. Income Devel. Corp., Encino, 1968—. 1st Lt. U.S. Army, WWII ETO, 1942-46. Mem. Nat. Assn. Life Underwriters, U.S. Army Ret. Officers Assn., West Dade Masonic Lodge # 388, Am. Legion, Kosciuszko Found., Simon Wiesnthal Ctr. Jewish. Avocations: trap and skeet shooting, dancing, swimming, history studies, teaching. Home: 24671 Cordillera Dr Calabasas CA 91302-2512 Office: Income Devel Corp 5729 Ostrom Ave Encino CA 91316-1407

SEIDEN, STEVEN ARNOLD, executive search consultant; b. N.Y.C., Feb. 18, 1936; s. Leon and Eleanor (Troy) S.; m. Katherine Cohen, June 8, 1965; children: Lisa Brooke, Hilary Anne. AB, Yale U., 1958. Pres. Seiden Krieger Assocs., 1984—. Mem. N.Y. Stock Exchange Regulatory Adv. Com., 1981-83, policy com. Am. Council for Capital Formation, 1982-87. *Steven Seiden is known for his expertise in recruiting top executives for corporations in transition. Among his clients are many of America's most publicized acquisitive entrepreneurs who seek out undermanaged companies needing new chief executives as well as operational, financial, and marketing talent. These incluce conglomerates, international holding companies, merchant banks, LBO organizations, and venture capitalists. Additionally he finds new management and directors for companies emeging from bankruptcy, or involved in proxy contests.* Mem. adv. bd. Registered Rep. Mag., 1982-84. Served with U.S. Army, 1961—62. Mem.: U.S. C. of C. (small bus. coun. 1985—89), Internat. Assn. Corp. and Profl. Recruiters (editl. bd. 1993—95), N.Y. Biotech. Assn., Turnaround Mgmt. Assn. (program co-chair N.Y. chpt. 1991—92), N.Y. Soc. Security Analysts, Securities Industry Assn. (bd. dirs. 1981—83), Assn. Corp. Growth (bd. dirs., asst. v.p. 1987—88), Wall St. Tax Assn. (bd. dirs. 1981—83), Bond Club, Century Country Club. Republican. Office: Seiden Krieger Assocs 375 Park Ave New York NY 10152-0002

SEIDEN, STEVEN JAY, lawyer; b. N.Y.C., June 21, 1960; s. Martin S. and Rita (Glazer) S.; m. Kathryn LaRussa, Sept. 30, 1984; children: Robert B., Daniel M., Michael J. BA, SUNY, Oneonta, 1981; JD, Hofstra U., 1984. Bar: N.Y. 1985, U.S. Dist. Ct. (ea. and so. dists.) N.Y. 1985, U.S. Supreme Ct. 1995, U.S. Ct. Appeals (fed. cir.) 1995, U.S. Ct. Fed. Claims 1995, U.S. Ct. Appeals for the Armed Forces, 1995. Assoc. Shapiro, Baines,Saasto & Shainwald, Mineola, N.Y., 1984-88; ptnr. Seiden & Kaufman, Carle Place, 1988-93, 95—, Seiden, Kaufman, & Bosek, Carle Place, 1993-95. Mem. ABA, N.Y. State Bar Assn., N.Y. State Trial Lawyers Assn., Assn. Trial Lawyers Am., Nassau County Bar Assn., L.I. Trial Lawyers Assn. (bd. dirs.), Civil Justice Found. (founding sponsor). Jewish. Office: Seiden & Kaufman 1 Old Country Rd Ste 114 Carle Place NY 11514-1821

SEIDEN, STEVEN SAMUEL SUTTON, university educator; b. Pensacola, Fla., July 13, 1967; s. Steven Samuel Sutton Seiden and Carol Anne Kleemann; m. Tracey Ann Rovello, July 7, 1996. PhD, U. Calif., Irvine, 1997. Postdoc. rschr. Tech. U., Graz, Austria, 1997—98; postdoc. fellow Max-Planck-Inst., Saarbruecken, Germany, 1998—99; asst. prof. La. State U., Baton Rouge. Contbr. articles to profl. jours. Mem.: EATCS, ACM. Office: La State U 298 Coates Hall Baton Rouge LA 70803

SEIDENBERG, IVAN G. telecommunications company executive; b. N.Y.C., Dec. 10, 1946; s. Howard and Kitty (Zaretsky) S.; m. Phyllis A. Maisel, Dec. 13, 1969; children: Douglas, Lisa. BS in Math., CUNY, 1972; MBA in Mktg. Mgmt., Pace U., 1980. Various engring. positions N.Y. Tel., 1966-74; dist. mgr. transmission design AT&T, Basking Ridge, NJ, 1974-76, dist. mgr. tech. planning, 1976-78, div. mgr. fed. regulatory N.Y.C., 1978-81, asst. v.p. mktg., 1981-83; v.p. fed. relations Nynex Corp., Washington, 1983-86, former v.p. external affairs, former pres. and vice chmn., chmn., CEO, 1995-98, Bell Atlantic Corp, N.Y.C., 1999-2000; CEO Verizon Comm. (formerly Bell Atlantic Corp.). Bd. dirs. Boston Properties Inc., CVS Corp., Honeywell, Wyeth. Bd. dirs. N.Y. Hall Sci., Nat. Urban League., Pace U., Mus. TV and Radio, Verison Found. Sgt. U.S. Army, 1966—68, Vietnam. Mem. U.S. Telephone Assn. (bd. dirs. 1985—), Rockland Bus. Council (trustee 1987). Office: Verizon Communications Ste 200b 1095 Avenue Of The Americas New York NY 10036-6704*

SEIDENBERG, RITA NAGLER, education educator; b. N.Y.C., Mar. 24, 1928; d. Jack and Anna (Weiss) Nagler; m. Irving Seidenberg, Apr. 10, 1949; children: Jack, Melissa Kolodkin. BA, Hunter Coll., 1948; MS, CCNY, 1968; PhD, Fordham U., 1985. Cert. reading tchr., specialist, N.Y. Reading tchr. East Ramapo (N.Y.) Sch. Dist., 1967-68, clinician reading ctr., 1968-83, reading diagnostician, 1983-85, student support specialist, 1985-94. Instr. N.Y. State Dept. Edn., 1978; presenter Northeastern Rsch. Assn., 1978, 85, N.Y. State Reading Assn., 1986-94, 96, 97, Parents and Reading: IRA, 2000; adj. asst. prof. Fordham U. Grad. Sch. Edn., 1986-89, adj. assoc. prof., 1989—. Mem. Internat. Reading Assn., N.Y. State Reading Assn. (presenter 1997, 2000), Phi Delta Kappa, Kappa Delta Pi. Avocations: reading, art mus., opera, travel. Office: Fordham U Grad Sch Edn 113 W 60th St New York NY 10023-7484

SEIDENSTICKER, EDWARD GEORGE, Japanese language and literature educator; b. Castle Rock, Colo., Feb. 11, 1921; s. Edward George and Mary Elizabeth (Dillon) S. BA, U. Colo., 1942; MA, Columbia U., 1947; postgrad., Harvard U., 1947-48; LittD (hon.), U. Md., 1991. With U.S. Fgn. Service, Dept. State, Japan, 1947-50; mem. faculty Stanford U., 1962-66, prof., 1964-66; prof. dept. Far Eastern langs. and lit. U. Mich., Ann Arbor, 1966-77; prof. Japanese Columbia U., 1977-85, prof. emeritus, 1986—. Author: Kafu the Scribbler, 1965, Japan, 1961, Low City, High City, 1983, Tokyo Rising, 1990, Very Few People Come This Way, 1994; transl.: (by Murasaki Shikibu) The Tale of Genji, 1976. Served with USMCR, 1942-46. Decorated Order of Rising Sun Japan; recipient Nat. Book award, 1970; citation Japanese Ministry Edn., 1971; Kikuchi Kan prize, 1977; Goto Miyoko prize, 1982; Japan Found. prize, 1984; Tokyo Cultural award, 1985; Yamagata Banto prize, 1992. Home: 1350 Ala Moana Blvd Apt 3103 Honolulu HI 96814-4229 *"Make yourself a routine and stick to it," said my childhood piano teacher when I went off to college. I have never had, as some people seem to have, great plans for my future; but if a person has a serious routine and sticks resolutely with it, something is bound to get accomplished.*

SEIDERMAN, ARTHUR STANLEY, optometrist, consultant, author; b. Phila., Nov. 28, 1936; s. Morris and Anne (Roseman) S.; children: David, Leeann, Scott. Student, U. Vienna (Austria) Med. Sch., 1965; OD, Pa. Coll. of Optometry, 1963; AB, W.Va. Wesleyan Coll., 1959; MA, Fairleigh Dickinson U., 1973. Pvt. practice, Elkins Park, Pa., 1971-94, Plymouth Meeting, 1994-99. Vision cons. U.S. Olympic Teams, Phila. Flyers Hockey Team. Co-author: The Athletic Eye, 1983, 20/20 Is Not Enough, 1990; mem. editoral adv. bd. Jour. of Learning Disabilities, 1979—. Vice pres. Jewish Nat. Fund, Phila., 1988—. Capt. U.S. Army, 1963-68. Fellow Am. Acad. Optometry, Coll. of Optometrists in Vision Devel.; mem. Multidisciplinary Acad. of Clin. Edn. (pres.), Internat. Reading Assn. (pres. disabled group 1987-89). Home: 427 Springview Ln Phoenixville PA 19460

SEIDL, DANIEL ROBERT, music educator; b. Chilton, Wis., Nov. 12, 1965; s. Robert Walter and LouAnn Seidl. BA, U Wis., Green Bay, 1989. Cert. music edn. H.s. vocal tchr. Campbellsport (Wis.) Sch. Dist., 1989—. Music bd. mem. Hope Luth. Ch., Fond du Lac, Wis., 1994—98. Mem.: Music Educators Nat. Conf. Lutheran. Avocations: travel, reading, variety band. Home: Apt 237 597 W Arndt St Fond Du Lac WI 54935 Office: Campbellsport School Dist 114 West Sheboygan St Campbellsport WI 53010 Personal E-mail: danseidl@charter.net. E-mail: dseidl@csd.k12.wi.us.

SEIDL, JAMES C. librarian; b. Luxemburg, Wis., Sept. 13, 1947; s. Cletus B. and Alice Seidl; m. Kathleen Rae, May 1, 1976; children: David, Susan. BS, U. Wis., Oshkosh, 1970; MLS, George Peabody Coll., 1975. Head extension dept. Decatur (Ill.) Pub. Libr., 1975-80, head home reading dept., 1980-82, supr. adult svcs., 1982-85, asst. city librarian, 1985-86, city librarian, 1986-92; dir. Woodlands Libr. Coop., Albion, Mich., 1992—. Bd. dirs. United Way, Decatur, 1987-88; mem. Ill. State Libr. Adv. Com., Springfield, 1990-92; mem. Mich. Libr. Consortium, Lansing, 1993-96. Mem. ALA, Mich. Libr. Assn., Mich. Coop. Dirs. Assn. (chmn. 1996-2000), Rotary (bd. dirs. 1989-92, 95-96, v.p. 1996-98, pres.-elect 1999, pres. 1999-00). Avocations: woodworking. Office: Woodlands Libr Coop 415 S Superior St Ste A Albion MI 49224-2174 E-mail: jseidl@monroe.lib.mi.us.

SEIDLER, B(ERNARD) ALAN, lawyer; b. N.Y.C., Nov. 26, 1946; s. Aaron H. and Ethel T. (Berkowitz) S.; m. Lynne Aubrey, Jan. 21, 1978; children: Jacob A., Morgan H., Lily R. BA, Colgate U., 1968; JD, Seton Hall U., 1972. Bar: N.Y. 1973, U.S. Dist. Ct. (ea., no. and so. dists.) N.Y. 1975, U.S. Ct. Appeals (2d cir.) 1976, U.S. Ct Appeals (3d cir.) 1984, U.S. Supreme Ct. 1977. Staff atty. N.Y. Legal Aid Soc., N.Y.C., 1972-75; sole practitioner N.Y.C. and Nyack, N.Y., 1975—. Mem. Snedens Landing Tennis Assn. (Palisades, N.Y.), Palisades Swim Club (pres.). Office: 127 S Broadway Nyack NY 10960-4433

SEIDLER, DORIS, artist; b. London, Nov. 26, 1912; m. Bernard Seidler, Sept. 5, 1935; 1 son, David. Group exhbns. include Bklyn. Mus. Bi-Ann., Vancouver Internat., Honolulu Acad. Arts, Pa. Acad. Fine Arts, Phila., Soc. Am. Graphic Artists, Assoc. Am. Artists Gallery, Jewish Mus., N.Y.C., Albright-Knox, 1994, Brit. Mus. Recent Acquisitions, 1997; represented in permanent collections Libr. of Congress, Smithsonian Instn., Washington, Phila. Mus. Art, Bklyn. Mus., Seattle Mus. Art, Whitney Mus., Nat. Gallery Art, Nassau County (N.Y.) Mus. Fine Arts, Brit. Mus., London, Victorial and Albert Mus. London, Pallant House Coll., Eng., Portland Mus. Art, Oreg., Birmingham Mus., Eng., 1999. Address: 14 Stoner Ave Great Neck NY 11021-2101

SEIDMAN, ALAN, educational administrator; b. Orono, Maine, Dec. 28, 1949; m. Barbara Tors, Aug. 16, 1986; 1 stepchild, Jason Tors. BA, Glassboro State Coll., 1971, MA, 1974; EdD, Syracuse U., 1990. Cert. elem tchr., prin., cert. supervision, N.J. Tchr. Glassboro (N.J.) Pub. Schs., 1971-75; dir. admissions Cayuga County C.C., Auburn, N.Y., 1975-78, Westchester C.C., Valhalla, 1978-94; assoc. v.p. for student svcs. Parkland Coll., Champaign, Ill., 1994-95; sr. assoc. Collegeways Assocs., Concord, N.H., 1995-98; asst. v.p. for enrollment svcs. West Chester U., 1998-99; dean student affairs New Eng. Coll. Optometry, Boston, 2000—. Presenter in field. Editor Jour. Coll. Student Retention: Rsch. Theory and Practice; contbr. articles to profl. jours. Recipient Chancellor's award for excellence in profl. svc. SUNY, 1992. Mem. Am. Assn. Collegiate Registrars and Admissions Officers, Nat. Assn. Student Pers. Adminstrs. Home: 30 Windsong Cir Bedford NH 03110-4644

SEIDMAN, CHRISTINE E. medical educator; BA, Harvard U.; MD, George Washington U., 1978. Resident in internal medicine Johns Hopkins U., Balt.; resident in cardiology Mass. Gen. Hosp., Boston; staff Brigham and Women's Hosp. Harvard U., 1987, dir. cardiovasc. genetics svc., prof.; assoc. investigator Howard Hughes Med. Inst. Mem.: Inst. Medicine. Office: Harvard U Siedman Lab Alpert Bldg., 5th Fl Boston MA 02115-5701*

SEIDMAN, DAVID N(ATHANIEL), materials science and engineering educator; b. N.Y.C., July 5, 1938; s. Charles and Jeanette (Cohen) S.; m. Shoshanah Cohen-Sabban, Oct. 21, 1973; children: Elie, Ariel, Eytan. BS, NYU, 1960, MS, 1962; PhD, U. Ill., Urbana, 1965. Postdoc. assoc. Cornell U., Ithaca, N.Y., 1964-66, asst. prof. materials sci. and engring., 1966-70, assoc. prof. materials sci. and engring., 1970-76, prof. materials sci. and engring., 1976-85, Northwestern U., Evanston, Ill., 1985-96, Walter P. Murphy prof. materials sci. and engring., 1996—. Vis. prof. Technion, Haifa, 1969, Tel-Aviv U., Ramat-Aviv, 1972; Lady Davis vis. prof. Hebrew U., Jerusalem, 1978, 80-81, prof. materials sci., 1983-85; vis. scientist C.E. de Grenoble, 1981, C.N.E.T.-Meylan, 1981, C.E. de Scalay, 1989, U. Goettingen, 1989, 92; sci. cons. Argonne (Ill.) Nat. labs., 1985-94. Mem. editl. bd., editor spl. issues (jour.) Interface Sci., 1993—2001, editor-in-chief, 2002—, mem. editl. bd. Materials Sci. Forum , 1996—; contbr. numerous articles to profl. jours. Recipient Max Planck Rsch. prize Max-Planck-Gesellschaft and the A. von Humboldt-Stiftung, 1993; Guggenheim fellow, 1972-73, 80-81, Humboldt fellow, 1989, 92; named chair for phys. metallurgy Gordon Conf., 1982. Fellow Am. Phys. Soc., The Materials Soc. (mem. fellows award com. 2002--, Hardy Gold medal 1967); mem. AAAS, Am. Soc. Metals Internat., Am. Ceramic Soc., Materials Rsch. Soc., Microscopy Soc. Am., A. von Humboldt Soc. Am., Internat. Field-Emission Soc. (mem. steering com. 1997—2002, pres. 2000—02), Böhmische Phys. Soc. Democrat. Jewish. Achievements include research in microstructural evolution, internal interfaces, atomic-scale imperfections in metals and semiconductors, atom-probe microscopy and electron microscopy. Avocations: reading, history, travel. Home: 9056 Tamaroa Ter Skokie IL 60076-1928 Office: Northwestern U MS&E Dept MLSB Evanston IL 60208-3108 E-mail: d-seidman@northwestern.edu.

SEIDMAN, ELLEN SHAPIRO, lawyer, government official; b. N.Y.C., Mar. 12, 1948; d. Benjamin Harry Shapiro and Edna (Eysen) Stern; m. Walter Becker Slocombe, June 14, 1981; 1 child, Benjamin William. AB, Radcliffe Coll., 1969; JD, Georgetown U., 1974; MBA, George Washington U., 1988. Bar: D.C., 1975. Law clk. U.S. Ct. of Claims, Washington, 1974-75; assoc. Caplin & Drysdale, 1975-78; atty., advisor U.S. Dept. of Transportation, 1978-79, dep. asst. gen. counsel, 1979-81; assoc. gen. counsel Chrysler Corp Loan Guaranty Bd., 1981-84; atty., advisor U.S. Dept. of Treasury, 1981-86, spl. asst. to the Under Sec. Fin., 1986-87; dir. strategic planning Fed. Nat. Mortgage Assn., 1987-88, v.p., asst. to chmn., 1988-91, sr. v.p. regulation rsch. and econs., 1991-93; spl. asst. to the pres. for econ. policy The White House, 1993-97; dir. Office Thrift Supervision U.S. Dept. Treasury, 1997—2001; sr. counsel, Minority Staff, fin. svcs. com. U.S. Ho. of Reps., 2002—. E-mail: ellen.seidman@mail.house.gov., esseidman@aol.com.

SEIDMAN, GLENN ELLIOTT, sales and marketing professional; b. June 18, 1953; m. Charlene Goldberg, 1988; children: Brooke, Michelle. BA, CUNY, 1975; MA, NYU, 1977. Asst. dir. student activities Columbia U.,

N.Y.C., 1978-83; assoc. dean students Poly. U., Bklyn., 1983-88; territory mgr. Quality Products & Svcs., Reading, Pa., 1988—. Mem. Queens Coll. Alumni Assn. (pres. 1987-89). Home: 5 Yates Ave Jericho NY 11753-1418

SEIDMAN, L(EWIS) WILLIAM, television commentator, publisher; b. Grand Rapids, Mich., Apr. 29, 1921; s. Frank E. and Esther (Lubetsky) S.; m. Sarah Berry, Mar. 3, 1944; children: Thomas, Tracy, Sarah, Carrie, Meg, Robin. AB, Dartmouth Coll., 1943; LL.B., Harvard U., 1948; MBA, U. Mich., 1949. Bar: Mich. 1949, D.C. 1977. Spl. asst. fin. affairs to gov. of Mich., 1963-66; nat. mng. partner Seidman & Seidman C.P.A.s, N.Y.C., 1969-74; asst. for econ. affairs to Pres. Gerald R. Ford, 1974-77; dir., chief fin. officer Phelps Dodge Corp., N.Y.C., 1977-82, vice chmn., 1980-82; dean Coll. Bus. Adminstrn. Ariz. State U., Tempe, 1982-85; chmn. RTC FDIC, Washington, 1989-91; chief commentator Sta. CNBC-TV, 1991; pub.-bd. Bank Dir. Mag., 1992. Chmn. Detroit Fed. Res. Bank Chgo., 1970, RTC, 1989-91; co-chair White House Conf. on Productivity, 1983-84. Lt. USNR, 1942-46. Decorated Bronze Star. Mem. D.C. Bar Assn., Chevy Chase Club (Md.), Univ. Club (N.Y.C.), Crystal Downs Club (Mich.), Nantucket Yacht Club (MA). Home: 825 Audubon Dr Bradenton FL 34209-7304 Office: CNBC 8th Flr 1025 Connecticut Ave NW Washington DC 20036-5405 E-mail: lws1025@aol.com.

SEIDMAN, MARIAN TAYLOR, adult education educator; b. Montclair, N.J., Oct. 25, 1954; d. John Albert and Virginia Anne (Cooney) Taylor; m. Stephen Michael Seidman, Aug. 17, 1979; 1 child, Julie Anne. BS in Elem. Edn., U. Hartford, West Hartford, Conn., 1976; MEd, West Chester (Pa.) U., 1990. Cert. reading specialist, elem. edn. tchr. Tchr. Our Lady of Mt. Carmel Sch., Boonton, N.J., 1977-79, Catawba County Schs., Hickory, N.C., 1980-82, St. Joseph Sch., Big Bend, Wis., 1982-87; tchr., evaluator Del. County Lit. Coun., Chester, Pa., 1991—. Author: Study Guide for the Pennsylvania Driver's Manual, 1996, 2000. Mem. Internat. Reading Assn., Del. Valley Reading Assn., Keystone State Reading Assn., Pa. Assn. for Adult Continuing Edn., Laubach Lit. Action. Avocations: gardening, crafts, baking, reading. Office: Del County Lit Coun Chester PA 19013

SEIDMAN, MICHAEL DAVID, surgeon, educator; b. Detroit, Oct. 14, 1960; s. Melvin and Rita Seidman; m. Lynn Ann Gaberman; children: Jake, Marlee, Kevin. BS in Human Nutrition, U. Mich., 1981, MD, 1986. Resident in Otolaryngology, Head and Neck Surgery Henry Ford Hosp., Detroit, 1986-91, attending physician, surgeon, 1992—, regional coord. Oto-HNS West Bloomfield, Mich., 1996-00, dir. divsn. oto/neuroto, 2000—; fellow in Otology, Neurotology, Skull Base Surgery Ear Rsch. Found., Sarasota, Fla., 1991-92; staff physician Sarasota Mem. Hosp., 1991-92; assoc. staff physician Doctors Hosp., Sarasota, 1991-92; asst. clin. prof. Wayne State U., Detroit, 1993—. Med. advisor Self Help Hard of Hearing People Inc., Bethesda, 1988—, mem. healthcare com., 1990-93; bd. dirs. Ear Rsch. Found., 1992—. Contbr. chpts. to books including Common Problems of the Ear, 1996, others; contbr. articles to profl. jours.; mem. editl. bd. Oto-HNS Jour., Hearing Rsch. Recipient Clin. Investigator Devel. award NIH, 1994-99, Fowler award Best Scientific Thesis, 2000. Fellow ACS; mem. AAAS, Am. Neurotology Soc., Am. Tinnitus Assn., Assn. Rsch. Otolaryngology (edn. com. 1992—), Sir Charles Bell Soc., Am. Acad. Oto-HNS. Avocations: downhill and water skiing, tennis, exercising. Achievements include patents in therapeutic treatment for mitochondrial function, health scan-nutritional survey and in a supplement that improves age-related hearing loss. Office: Henry Ford Health Systems 6777 W Maple Rd West Bloomfield MI 48322-3013

SEIDMAN, SAMUEL NATHAN, investment banker, economist; b. N.Y.C., Mar. 31, 1934; s. Hyman and Pauline (Seidman) S.; m. Herta Lande, Sept. 4, 1964 (dec.); m. Evelyn Patricia Dooley. BA, Bklyn. Coll., 1955; PhD, NYU, 1964. Instr. Douglass Coll., Rutgers U., New Brunswick, N.J., 1960-62; v.p. Lehman Bros. Internat., N.Y.C., 1962-70; pres. Seidman & Co. Inc., 1970—; pres., founder Productivity Techs. Corp., 1971—. Dir. Amrep Corp., N.Y.C., Harken Oil Corp., Dallas; dir., chmn. Victoria Station Corp., San Francisco, 1985-87. Trustee Mental Health Assn. N.Y., N.Y.C. 1980— . Served to pfc. U.S. Army, 1954-56 Univ. fellow Inst. Labor Relations, NYU, N.Y.C., 1957-58; Fulbright scholar U. Philippines, 1959-60 Mem. Am. Econ. Assn., Univ. Club (N.Y.C.), Lake Waramug Country Club (Conn.). Avocations: music; history of Asia. Office: Seidman & Co Inc 509 Madison Ave New York NY 10022-5501

SEIDMAN, STEPHEN BENJAMIN, computer science educator; b. N.Y.C., Apr. 13, 1944; s. Sylvan and Anne (Levine) S.; m. Barbara Heidemarie Koppe, Aug. 24, 1969; children: Miriam, Naomi. BS, CCNY, 1964; AM, U. Mich., 1965, PhD, 1969. Asst. prof. math. NYU, 1969-72, George Mason U., Fairfax, Va., 1972-76, assoc. prof. math., 1976-84, prof. computer sci., 1984-90; prof., dept. head computer sci., engring. Auburn (Ala.) U., 1990-96; prof., chair dept. computer sci. Colo. State U., Ft. Collins, 1996—. Author: Assembly Language programming in Compass, 1987. Mem. IEEE Computer Soc., Assn. for Computing Machinery.

SEIDMON, E. JAMES, urologist; b. N.Y.C., Apr. 26, 1947; s. Edward Edgar and Dorothy (Solomon) S.; m. Nancy F. Friedman, Nov. 11, 1979; children: Eric Matthew, Emily Ann. BS, Hobart Coll., 1969; MA, SUNY, Buffalo, 1971; MD, U. Guadalajara, Mex., 1975. Diplomate Am. Bd. Urology. Intern Rochester (N.Y.) Gen. Hosp., 1976-77; resident in surgery Beth Israel Med. Ctr., N.Y.C., 1977-78; resident in urology Albany (N.Y.) Med. Ctr., 1978-80, Montifiore Med. Ctr., Bronx, N.Y., 1980-82; fellow in urologic oncology Roswell Park Meml. Inst., Buffalo, 1982-83; asst. prof. Temple U. Hosp., Phila., 1983-88, assoc. prof., 1988-95, prof. of urology, 1995—. Mem. editl. bd. Current Urologic Therapy, 3rd edit., 1994; contbr. articles to profl. jours. Fellow ACS; mem. Am. Urol. Assn., Mid Atlantic Urol. Assn., Soc. Univ. Urologists, Radiation Therapy Oncoloyg Group, So. Coop. Oncology Group, Soc. Urologic Oncology. Achievements include development of antegrade stent, ureteral safety wire guide, corporal balloon dilator. Office: Temple U Hosp Dept Urology Broad and Ontario St Philadelphia PA 19140

SEIERSEN, NICHOLAS STEEN, management consultant; b. Geneva, Switzerland, June 23, 1955; s. Ove Steen and Kamini Shoshiela (Bhandari) S.; m. Sylvie Jacqueline Fenouillet, Nov. 7, 1981. BSc with honors, U. Sussex, 1976; MBA, Pacific State U., L.A., 1987. Project chief Metra Proudfoot Internat. Mgmt. Cons., Brussels, 1977-81; unit mgr. Auchan Hypermarkets, Paris, 1981-83; internat. controller Pain Jacquet Group, 1983-85; sr. cons. A.T. Kearney Mgmt. Cons., 1985-88; European mktg. mgr. Digital Equip. Corp., 1988-95; dir. sales, mktg., logistics and distbn. European Mfg. Expertise Ctr., Digital Equipment Corp., 1995-96; prin. KPMG Mgmt. Consulting LP Consumer and Indsl. Markets, Toronto, Canada, 1996—99, cons., 1999—. Scientific bd. Logistique & Mgmt. Jour. (in French); adv. bd. Petrah Knowledge Solutions; editl. com. Global Supply Chain Forum mgmt. jour., Ligostics Quarterly. Editl. adv. bd.: Logistics Quar. Jour., 2001—; contbr. articles. Mem. U.S. Bus. Logistics Assn. (coun. logistics mgmt., v.p. 1998-2000, pres. Toronto Roundtable) 2000-2002, Can. Assn. for Logistics Mgmt., French Assn. Logistics Mgmt. (bd. dirs. 1994-96). Office: KPMG Cons LP 20 Bay St Ste 1100 Toronto ON Canada M5J 2X9 E-mail: nseiersen@kpmg.ca.

SEIFEL, MARY WILLIAMS, family nurse practitioner; b. Northampton, Mass., Jan. 8, 1967; d. Gordon Oliver and Mary Louise (Belden) Williams; m. Scott Alan Seifel, Nov. 1, 1997. BSN, Boston Coll., 1989; MSN, U. Mass., 1994. RN, Mass.; cert. nurse practitioner. Staff nurse Children's Hosp., Boston, 1989-91; oper. rm. nurse/recovery Boston Eye Surgery and Laser Ctr., 1991-92; home health nurse, pediatrics Olsten Pediatrics, Springfield, Mass., 1993-94; family nurse practitioner Dr. Gary Jeznach, Sturbridge, 1994-2000, Dr. David McKay, Springfield, 2001—. Author: (resource manual) Asthma Management in Schools, 1994. Mem. Mass. Coalition Nurse Practitioners. Avocations: skiing, biking, hiking. Home: 34 Wright St Palmer MA 01069-1118 Office: Dr David McKay 2 Medical Center Dr Ste 301 Springfield MA 01107

SEIFER, ARNOLD DAVID, systems engineer; b. Newark, Apr. 22, 1940; s. Abe W. and Bessie R. (Coopersmith) Seifer. BS in Math., Rensselaer Poly. Ins., 1962, MS, 1964, PhD, 1968. Rsch. specialist Gen. Dynamics Corp., Groton, Conn., 1967—73; sr. staff mathematician Applied Physics Lab., Laurel, Md., 1973—76; sr. staff engr. Emerson Elec. Co., St. Louis, 1976—80; prin. engr. Raytheon Co., Wayland, Mass., 1980—92; sr. prin. systems engr. BAE Systems, Nashua, NH, 1992—. Contbr. articles to profl. jours. Mem.: IEEE (sr.), Soc. Indsl. and Applied Math., Sigma Xi. Home: 16 Ledgewood Hills Dr Apt 303 Nashua NH 03062-4452 Office: BAE Systems PO Box 868 Nashua NH 03061-0868

SEIFER, MARC JEFFREY, psychology educator; b. Far Rockaway, N.Y., Feb. 17, 1948; s. Stanley Cyclone and Thelma (Imber) S. BA, U. R.I., 1970; postgrad., New Sch. for Social Rsch., 1970-72, Sch. Visual Arts, 1971; MA, U. Chgo., 1974; PhD, Saybrook Inst., 1986. Cert. handwriting expert. Investigator neurol. study hand writing of schizophrenics Billings Hosp., Chgo., 1972-73; coll. instr. Providence Coll. Sch. of Continuing Edn., 1975-90, U. R.I. Extension, Providence, 1975-80, Bristol C.C., Fall River, Mass., 1980—, C.C. of R.I., Warwick, 1988—; expert handwriting neurol. investigation epileptic split brain writers UCLA, 1986; handwriting expert U. R.I. Crime Lab, Kingston, 1974-75; assoc. editor Jour. of Occult Studies, Providence, 1977-79; editor MetaScience, Kingston, 1979—, Jour. Am. Soc. Profl. Graphologists, Bethesda, Md., 1989—; instr. Roger Williams U., Bristol, R.I., 2000—. Dir. MetaSci. Found., Kingston, 1979—; handwriting expert Dept. Social Svcs. and R.I. Atty. Gen.'s Office, Providence, 1990—; lectr. on Tesla U.S. Mil. Acad., West Point, NY, 1982, Colo. Coll., Colorado Springs, 1984, CCNY, 1984, Zagreb, Yugoslavia, 86, Colorado Springs, 92, Colorado Springs, 96, UN, 1997, L.A., 99, Mesa, Ariz., 2000, Indsl. Light and Magic, San Rafael, Calif., 2001; lectr. on graphology, Jerusalem, 1985, U. Vancouver, B.C., Canada, 1986, Oxford (Eng.) U., 1987, Santa Fe, 91, Cambridge (Eng.) U., 1992, Ann Arbor, Mich., 94, N.Y.C., 97, N.Y.C., 2000, Brandeis U., 2000, Honolulu, 01; lectr. on consciousness U. Ariz., Tucson, 1996; cons. Inventors Series Discover Channel and Koch TV, 1994, The American Experience, PBS and Elevator Pictures, 1995, BBC, 1995, Biography A&E, 1998, Good Morning America, 2000, The History Channel, 2001, Uri Geller Internet Radio Show, 2001. Author: Startez Encounter, 1988, The Man Who Harnessed Niagara Falls, 1991, Polish transl., 2001, Handwriting and Brainwriting, 1992, Hail to the Chief, 1991, Mr. Rhode Island: The Stephen Rosati Story, 1994, Wizard: The Life and Times of Nikola Tesla, 1996 (designated as a book of unusual interest and merit, Publishers Weekly, 1996, designated as serious piece of scholarship, Sci. Am., 1997, high recommendation AAAS, 1997), (screenplay) Tesla: The Lost Wizard (performed at Producer's Club Theater, 1996, video docudrama 1997), 1992, video, 1984; contbr. chapters to books; contbg. editor: Extraordinary Science, 1996, 2000, The Tesla Journal, 1997, Wired, 1998; co-editor: Jour. Conscientology, 1999; contbg. editor: Civilization, 2000; contbr. articles to profl. jours. and publs. including N.Y. Times, Psychiatric Clinics N.Am., The Economist, R.I. Monthly, Civilization. Fellow Am. Coll. Forensic Examiners (bd. dirs. 1992-93); mem. APA, Am. Soc. Profl. Graphologists (bd. dirs. 1989—), Tesla Soc., Nat. Bur. Document Examiners, Nat. Soc. for Graphology. Avocations: snorkeling, bridge. Home: PO Box 32 Kingston RI 02881-0032 E-mail: mseifer@netsense.net.

SEIFER, RONALD LESLIE, psychologist; b. Liberty, N.Y., Oct. 23, 1942; s. Leon and Pearl (Treibitz) S.; m. Gail Sandra Eagerman, May 29, 1967; children: David Marc, Robert Eric. BA, Queens Coll., 1964; MA, Northeastern U., 1967; PhD, U. Maine, 1971. Lic. psychologist, Fla., N.Y. Intern psychologist Albert Einstein Coll. Medicine, Bronx, N.Y., 1968-69; psychologist St. Vincent's Hosp., Harrison, N.y., 1969-71; supervising psychologist Saratoga County Mental Health Ctr., Saratoga Springs, N.Y., 1971-76; psychologist Brevard County Mental Health Ctr., Melbourne, Fla., 1976-79; pvt. practice clin. psychology Melbourne and Palm Bay, 1978—; med. staff Holmes Regional Med. Ctr., Melbourne, 1979—. Coord. TOP Soccer, Fla. Youth Soccer Assn., 1990-95; chair, psychology dept., psychiatry dept., Holmes Regional Med. Ctr., Melbourne, 2000—. Rsch. fellow Northeastern U., 1964-66. Mem.: APA, Brevard County Psychol. Assn. (founding pres. 1979—80), Fla. Soc. Clin. Hypnosis (treas. 1985—88), Fla. Psychol. Assn. (founding pres. child/adolescent/family divsn. 1997—98). Avocations: gardening, fishing, parenting. Office: 2123 Franklin Dr NE Palm Bay FL 32905

SEIFERLE, REBECCA ANN, poet, editor, publisher; b. Denver; d. Arthur Mase and Mary Kathryn S.; m. Phillip Joseph Valencia, Aug. 11, 1978; children: Ann Seiferle-Valencia, Maria Seiferle-Valencia, Jacob Seiferle-Valencia. BA in English and History, U. State N.Y., 1984; MFA, Warren Wilson Coll., 1989. Poet Tumblewords: N.Mex. Arts Program, Santa Fe, 1986—; creative writing instr. San Juan Coll., Farmington, N.Mex., 1990-2001. Editor, pub. (online mag.) The Drunken Boat, 2000—. Author: (poetry collections) The Ripped Out Seam, 1994 (Bogin award Poetry Soc. Am. 1991), The Music We Dance To, 1999 (Cecil Hemley award Poetry Soc. Am. 1998), Bitters, 2001 We. States Book award, Pushcart prize 2002); contbr. (anthology) New Mexico Poetry Renaissance, 1994, Saludos: Poemas de Nuevo Mexico, 1995, Best American Poetry 2000, The Poet's Child, 2002, The Extraordinary Tide: New Poetry by American Women, 2001; translator Spanish of Cesar Vallejo, Trilce, 1992, Spanish of Alfonso d'Aquino and ernest Lumbrenas, Reversible Monuments, 2002. Active letter writing campaigns Amnesty Internat., 1984-2001. Recipient prize Nat. Writer's Union, 1986, award Embers Poetry Contest, 1985. Mem. PenWest, Poets and Writers (Writers Exch. award 1990). Home: 5602 Tarry Terr Farmington NM 87402 E-mail: editor@thedrunkenboat.com.

SEIFERT, GEORGE, retired professional football coach; b. San Francisco, Jan. 22, 1940; m. Linda Seifert; children: Eve, Jason. Grad., U. Ufah, 1963. Asst. football coach U. Utah, 1964; head coach Westminster Coll., 1965; asst. coach U. Iowa, 1966, U. Oreg., 1966-71; secondary coach Stanford U., 1972-74; head coach Cornell U., 1975-76; from secondary coach to defensive coord. San Francisco 49ers, 1980-89, head coach, 1989-96, Carolina Panthers, Charlotte, 1999—2001. With AUS, 1963. Named NFL Coach of Yr. The Sporting News, 1990, 94.*

SEIFERT, LUKE MICHAEL, lawyer; b. Smyrna, Tenn., Apr. 8, 1957; s. Donald R. and Joan (Clemas) S.; m. Kathleen Louise Schaffer, Aug. 1, 1980; children: Joseph, Nicholas, Peter, Rachel. BA, Creighton U., 1979; JD, William Mitchell Sch. of Law, St. Paul, 1983. Bar: U.S. Dist. Ct. Minn., Minn. Page Minn. Ho. of Reps., St. Paul, 1980, com. adminstr., 1981-82; assoc. Holmen Law Office, St. Cloud, 1983-87; pvt. practice, 1987-98; assoc. Quinlivan Law Firm, 1998—2001, ptnr., 2001—. Mem. ABA, Minn. Bar Assn., Minn. Trial Lawyers Assn., Minn. Def. Lawyers Assn., Stearns Benton Bar Assn. (sec., treas. 1986-87, v.p. 1987-88, pres. 1988-89), K.C. (guard 1986-87, advocate 1987-90), Delta Theta Phi. Home: 1305 W Oakes Dr Saint Cloud MN 56303-0741 Office: Quinlivan Hughes Law Firm PO Box 1008 600 Wells Fargo Ctr Saint Cloud MN 56302 E-mail: lseifert@quinlivan.com.

SEIFERT, PATRICIA CLARK, cardiac surgery nurse, educator, consultant; b. Springfield, Mass., Apr. 4, 1945; d. Thomas W. and Kathleen E. (O'Malley) Clark; m. Gary F. Seifert, Sept. 10, 1966; children: Kristina S. Glenn, Philip A. BA in History, Trinity Coll., 1967; ADN, No. Va. Community Coll., 1976; MS in Nursing, Cath. U. Am., 1988. RN, Va., D.C.; cert. oper. rm. nurse, first asst. nurse. Head nurse cardiac surgery Fairfax Hosp., Falls Church, Va., 1976-88; adminstrv. dir. Washington Hosp. Ctr., 1988-89; oper. room coord. cardiac surgery Arlington (Va.) Hosp., 1989-97, Alexandria (Va.) Hosp., 1995—97; mgr. open heart surgery Halifax Med. Ctr., Daytona Beach, Fla., 1997—98; coord. cardiovasc. svcs. Arlington (Va.) Hosp., 2000—02; innovations liaison Sandel Med. Industries, Chatsworth, Calif., 2002—. Mem. adv. bd. AORN Surg. Knowledgebase, Surg. Info. Sys., Ethicon Endo-surgery Nursing; lead coord. Nursing Orgn. Alliance, 2001-02; lectr./cons. in field. Author: (books) Clinical Assessment Tools for Use with Nursing Diagnosis, 1989, Cardiac Surgery, 1994, 2002; contbr. chpts. in Alexander's Care of the Patient in Surgery, 12th rev. edit., 2002, Cardiovascular Nursing, 7th rev. edit., 1991, Perioperative Care Planning, 2d rev. edit., 1996, The RN First Assistant: An Expanded Perioperative Role, 3d rev. edit., 1999, Core Curriculum for the RN First Assistant, 3d rev. edit., 1999, CNOR Study Guide, rev. edit., 1999; contbr. numerous articles to profl. jours. Fellow: Am. Acad. Nursing; mem.: Va. Nurses's Assn. (dist. 8 bd. dirs. 1987—91, Nurse of Year award 1984), Assn. Perioperative RN's (nat. nominating com. 1991—93, pres. No. Va. chpt. 1994—95, nat. bd. dir. 1994—98, nat. pres.-elect 1998—99, nat. pres. 1999—2000, RN 1st asst.), Am. Heart Assn. (coun. on cardiovasc. nursing), Assn. Perioperative RN's Found. (sec. 1999—2001), Am. Assn. for History of Nursing, Sigma Theta Tau (pres. Eta Alpha chpt. 1990—92, Virginia Henderson fellow). Home: 6502 Overbrook St Falls Church VA 22043-1942 Fax: 703-237-1259. E-mail: seifertpc@aol.com.

SEIFERT, STEPHEN WAYNE, lawyer, performing arts executive; b. Washington, May 25, 1957; s. Arthur John and Frances E. (Smith) S. BA summa cum laude, Yale U., 1979; JD, Stanford U., 1982. Bar: Colo. 1982, U.S. Dist. Ct. Colo. 1982, U.S. Ct. Appeals (10th cir.) 1982, U.S. Ct. Appeals (5th cir.) 1987, U.S. Supreme Ct. 1988. Ptnr.. Fairfield and Woods P.C., Denver, 1982-98; mng. dir. Fairfield & Woods P.C., 1990-92, 95-96; chmn. bd. dirs. Opera Colo., 1989-92, pres., exec. dir., 1997-2001; exec. dir. Newman Ctr. for Performing Arts U. Denver, 2002—. Author: Colorado Creditors' Remedies--Debtors' Relief, 1990; contbg. author: Colorado Methods of Practice; contbr. articles to profl. jours. Trustee Denver Metro C. of C., Denver Pub. Libr. Friends Found., Yale-Harvard Regatta Com., Allied Arts Inc., Rocky Mt. Region Inst. Internat. Edn.; mem. adv. bd. program in health care ethics, humanities and law U. Colo. Health Scis. Ctr.; mem. chancellor's scholars and leaders coun. U. Colo., Denver. Mem. Law Club Denver (v.p. 1992-93, pres. 1993-94), Univ. Club, Phi Beta Kappa.

SEIFERT, THOMAS LLOYD, lawyer; b. Boston, June 6, 1940; s. Ralph Frederick and Hazel Bell (Harrington) S.; m. Ann Cecelia Berg, June 19, 1965. BS cum laude, Ind. U., 1962, JD cum laude, 1965. Bar: Ill. 1965, Ind. 1965, N.Y. 1979. Assoc. law firm Keck, Mahin & Cate, Chgo., 1965-67; atty. Essex Group, Inc., Ft. Wayne, Ind., 1967-70, Amoco Corp., Chgo., 1970-73; assoc. gen. counsel, asst. sec. Canteen Corp., 1973-75; sec., gen. counsel The Marmon Group, Inc. (and predecessor cos.), 1975-78; v.p., gen. counsel, sec. Hanson Industries, Inc., N.Y.C., 1978-82; sr. v.p. law, chief fin. officer Petrie Stores Corp., 1982-83; mem. Finley, Kumble, Wagner, Heine, Underberg, Manley, Myerson & Casey, 1983-87, Paul, Weiss, Rifkind, Wharton & Garrison, N.Y.C., 1987-91; gen. counsel, chief legal officer Sterling Grace Capital Mgmt., L.P. and affiliated cos., 1991—. Note editor Ind. Law Jour., 1964-65. Named to Ind. Track and Cross Country Hall of Fame, 1993. Mem. ABA, N.Y. State Bar Assn., Order of Coif, The Creek, Beta Gamma Sigma. Home: Museum Tower 15 W 53d St Apt 31 E New York NY 10019-5401 Office: Sterling Grace Capital Mgmt 405 Park Ave New York NY 10022 E-mail: rumpole800@aol.com., tlseifertpc@aol.com.

SEIFF, ERIC A. lawyer; b. Mt. Vernon, N.Y., Apr. 25, 1933; s. Arthur N. and Mathilde (Cohen) S.; m. Sari Ginsburg, June 26, 1960 (div. Oct. 1983); children: Judith C., E. Kenneth, Dean A.; m. Meredith Feinman, Jan. 15, 1984; children: Abigail, Sarah. BA, Yale U., 1955; LLB, Columbia U., 1958. Bar: N.Y. 1958, U.S. Dist. Ct. (so. dist.) N.Y. 1960, U.S. Dist. Ct. (ea. dist.) N.Y. 1981, U.S. Ct. Appeals (2d cir.) 1965, U.S. Supreme Ct. 1967. Assoc. Bower and O'Connor, N.Y.C., 1959-60, Yellin, Kramer & Levy, N.Y.C., 1961; asst. dist. atty. N.Y.C. Dist. Atty.'s Office, 1962-67; asst. counsel Agy. for Internat. Devel., Washington, 1967-70, counsel Rio de Janeiro, 1970-72; gen. counsel N.Y. State Divsn. Criminal Justice Svcs., 1972-74; dep. chief atty. Legal Aid Soc. Criminal Def., N.Y.C., 1974-75; first dep. commr. N.Y. State Investigation Commn., 1975-77, chmn., 1977-79; ptnr. Seiff, Kretz & Maffeo (formerly Scoppetta & Seiff), 1981—; spl. dist. atty. Bronx County, 1986-89. Spl. asst. atty. gen. State of N.Y., Gov.'s Task Force Investigating Conduct of Attica Prosecutions, 1975. Bd. dirs. Legal Aid Soc., N.Y.C., 1994-2000; Prisoners' Legal Svcs., N.Y.C., 1989—, Lawyers Fund for Client Protection, N.Y., 1980—. Recipient Frank S. Hogan Meml. award Frank S. Hogan Assn., 1994. Mem. N.Y. Criminal Bar Assn. (bd. dirs. 1980—, past pres.), Bar Assn. City N.Y. (chmn. project on the homeless 1999—). Office: Seiff Kretz & Maffeo 645 Madison Ave New York NY 10022-1010

SEIFF, STEPHEN S. ophthalmologist; b. L.A., Sept. 30, 1925; s. Max and Minnie F. (Feldman) S.; m. Gloria Louise Holtzman, Apr. 16, 1950; children: Stuart R., Sherri Seiff Sloane, Karen Seiff Sacks. AA, UCLA, 1945; AB, U. Calif., Berkeley, 1946; MD, U. Calif., San Francisco, 1949. Diplomate Am. Bd. Ophthalmology. Intern County Gen. Hosp., L.A., 1949-50; fellow in anesthesiology Lahey Clinic, Boston, 1950-51; resident in ophthalmology U. Calif., San Francisco, 1952-55; clin. prof. dept. ophthalmology UCLA, 1956—; pvt. practice Beverly Hills, Calif., 1955—; clin. chief divsn. ophthalmology Cedars/Sinai Med. Ctr., L.A., 1957—; attending ophthalmologist Children's Hosp., 1956-94. Lectr. in field; assoc. examiner Am. Bd. Ophthalmology. Collaborating author: Clinical Anticoagulant Therapy, 1965; contbr. articles to profl. jours. Bd. dirs. That Man May See Inc., San Francisco; former exec. com. mem. UCLA Hosp. Lt. M.C. USNR, 1950-52. Recipient Sr. Honor award UCLA Dept. Ophthalmology, 1994. Fellow ACS, Am. Acad. Ophthalmology; mem. L.A. Soc. Ophthalmology (past pres.), Frederick Cordes Eye Soc. (past nat. pres.), Am. Soc. Cataract and Refractive Surgery (founding mem.). Avocation: sailing. Office: 435 N Roxbury Dr Ste 107 Beverly Hills CA 90210-5003 E-mail: sseiff@aol.com.

SEIFFER, NEIL MARK, photographer; b. Bklyn., July 18, 1960; s. Martin Henry and Eileen S. AAS in Bus. Adminstrn., County Coll. Morris, 1980; BS, Montclair State Coll., 1984. Spl. projects photographer Billboard Pubs., 1987-95; beauty-event photographer Lancome, Elizabeth Arden, Christian Dior, Chanel, 1988-91; celebrity/entertainment photographer, West Paterson, N.J., 1984—, N.Y.C., 1995—. Official photographer 1st annual Touchstone Awards for Women in Music, 1997; founder Thought for Food OnScreen Menu Selection. Author: Photographic Guidelines for Performing and Recording Artists, 1987, Model's Guide/What You Need to Know About a Modeling Career, 1994, Neil Seiffer's Photographic Guidelines for the Performing Artist, 1995, Neil Seiffer's Photo Tips for Actors, 1996; photographer spl. project include Billboard Publs., 1987-95, Lancome, Elizabeth Arden, Chanel, and Christian Dior, 1988-91, Dunn & Bradstreet, 1995; inventor photo adjustable-platform to increase productivity for still-life comml. photographers. Achievements include invention of photo adjustable platform to increase productivity for commercial still-life photographers; creator ultimate digital press kit for recording and performing artists. Home: 147 Overmount Ave Apt A West Paterson NJ 07424-3221 E-mail: photoaccess@netzero.net.

SEIFOULLAEV, ROUSTAM KAFAR, mathematician, programmer; b. Baku, Azerbaijan, Mar. 30, 1953; s. Kafar Suleiman and Alexandra Konstantin (Sen) S.; m. Alia Anatoly Guseinova, Nov. 28, 1981 (div. Oct. 1994); 1 child, Anar; m. Zemfira Djafar Ismail-zade, Nov. 24, 1997; chldren: Zaour, Anar. MS, Baku State U., 1975, PhD, 1979; DSc, Inst. Math. and Mechs., Baku, 1994. Prof. Baku State U., 1979-97, Western U., Baku, 1995-97, head dept. fgn. rels., 1995-97; sr. rsch. fellow Inst. Math. and Mechanics, 1992-97; prof. Univ. extension U. Tex., Austin, 1998—, prof., rsch. fellow Inst. for Geophysics, 1998—. Sys. cons. DHV Cons. BV, Amersfort, Netherlands; expert Higher Attestation Commn., Baku, 1996-97. Mem. editl. bd. Singular Integral Operators, 1983-97. Internat. Sci. Found. grantee, 1993; Brit. Coun. scholar, 1983-84. Mem. N.Y. Acad. Sci., Azerbaijan Math. Soc. (treas. 1981-90, editor Procs. 1994-97), U. Tex. Club. Avocations: music, chess, swimming. Office: U Tex Inst for Geophysics Bldg 600 Rm 135 4412 Spicewood Springs Rd Austin TX 78759-8500 E-mail: roustam@utig.ig.utexas.edu.

SEIGARS, BRIAN A. air traffic controller; b. San Antonio, June 29, 1962; s. James Arthur and Gypsy Rose Seigars; m. Wanda Marie Hamel, July 5, 1980 (div. Aug. 1997); children: Jason A., Jennifer A., Jessica A., Jaymes A. A in Airways Sci., C.C. Air Force, Enid, Okla., 1995; AAS, No. Okla. Coll., 1997. ATC radar approach and final contr. 1877 Comm. Squadron, Holloman AFB, N.Mex., 1980—83; ATC radar watch supr. 2182 Comm. Squadron, Lorwe AFB, Maine, 1983—87; ATC radar sr. watch supr. 1916 Comm. Squadron, Pease AFB, NH, 1987—90; ATC radar watch supr. 71st Ops. Support Squadron, Vance AFB, Okla., 1990—93, ATC radar team chief, 1994—2000; ATC radar sr. watch supr. 8th Ops. Support Squadron, Kinsan Air Base, Republic of Korea, 1993—94; ATC radar watch supr. 80th Ops. Support Squadron, Sheppard AFB, 2001—. Author: A Tiger's Tale, 2000, short stories. Coach, mgr., player Loring Northstars, Loring AFB, 1984—87, Vance Talons, Vance AFB, 1994—99. Decorated USAF Achievement medal with three oak leaf clusters, USAF Commendation medal with 4 oak leaf clusters. Mem.: Internat. Poet Laureate Lit. Guild. Republican. Baptist. Avocations: writing, poetry, softball. Home: 307 Ellis Burkburnett TX 76354 Office: 80th Ops Support Squadron Sheppard AFB TX

SEIGEL, ANDREW MARK, music educator, consultant; b. Phillipsburg, Nj, Apr. 11, 1965; m. Felicia Seigel; children: Yes. Bachelor of Sciene in Music Edn., West Chester U., West Chester, PA, 1983—87; Masters of Sci. in Curriculum Devel. and Supervision, Rowan U., Glassboro, NJ, 1989—93. Music Teacher k-12 PA Dept. of Edn., 1987, NJ Dept. of Edn., 1988, Supervisor of Education & Curriculum Development Specialist NJ Dept. of

Edn., 1993, Orff Level I Am. Orff Schulwerk Assn., 1987, Elementary Teacher NJ Dept. of Edn., 1994. Music tchr., band, choral, instrumental lessons, percussion ensemble, and gen. music Hamilton Twp Pub. Schools, Mays Landing, NJ, 1988—; percussion instr./arranger Delsea H.S. Marching Band, Franklinville, 1993—; black belt martial arts instr. Modern Bujustu / Olympic Karate Ctr., Vineland, 2002—; artist percussionist Regional Musicals, Southern New Jersey region, 1988—. Pres. South Jersey Choral Directors Assn., Turnersville, NJ, 1999—; exec. bd. of directors NJ Music Educators Assn., NJ, 1998—; consulting mem. Atlantic County Profl. Devel. Bd., Mays Landing, NJ, 2001—; chmn. Governor's Tchr. Recognition Program, Hamilton Twp Schools Mays Landing, NJ, 1994—; ava coord. Wm. Davies Mid. Sch., Mays Landing, NJ, 2001—; mentor Hamiltown Twp. Pub. Schools, Mays Landing, NJ, 1993—94; coop. tchr. / student tchr. advisor Hamilton Twp. Pub. Schools, Mays Landing, NJ, 2002—; summer enrichment instr. Hamilton Twp. PTA, Mays Landing, NJ, 1996—; gifted & talented project advisor Hamilton Twp Pub. Schools, Mays Landing, NJ, 1996—. Author: (article in tempo state music magazine) Your Guide to Professional Development for Music Educators; musician: (numerous cd recordings) VQR Digital and AMP Pro recordings; olympicconference concert band conductor (conduct top region junior high band), region elementary chorus conductor (south jersey regional chorus), all south jersey concert band conductor (conductor of top junior high region band). Recipient Summa Cum Laude Grad., West Chester U., 1987, Kappa Delta Pi Honor Soc. in Edn., 1987, West Chester U. Symphony Student Condr., 1987, Who's Who Among America's Teachers, Who's Who, 2000; grantee Variable amounts for classroom music tech., Hamilton Twp. Edn. Assn., 1993-1995, Over $15,000 For Music Tech. And Music Bus. Edn., Hamilton Twp. Bd. of Edn., 1995-2002. Mem.: Assn. for Supervision & Curriculum Devel., United Martial Arts Referee's Assn., Percussive Arts Soc., Am. Choral Directors Assn., Nat. Band Assn., NJ Music Educators Assn., Music Educators Nat. Conf., Hamilton Twp. Edn. Assn., South Jersey Choral Directors' Assn., South Jersey Band Directors Assn., NJ Edn. Assn., NEA. Achievements include Numerous Music Educational Curricula Written; Workshop Clincian for New Jersey State Music Convention; development of Seminar Provider for Regional Education Roundtables; design of Region III SJCDA Webmaster; first to Founder of the Easton High School Percussion Ensemble. Office: Davies Middle School 1876 Dennis Foreman Drive Mays Landing NJ 08330 Personal E-mail: sjcda@hotmail.com.

SEIGEL, JAN KEARNEY, lawyer; b. Bayonne, N.J., Feb. 7, 1947; s. Max and Margaret (Kearney) S.; m. Judy L. Mascuch, Aug. 29, 1971; children: Margaret, Emily, Jonas, Luke. BSBA, Georgetown U., 1968, JD, 1971; LLM in Taxation, NYU, 1974. Bar: N.J. 1971, D.C. 1972, Ga. 1972, U.S. Ct. Appeals (3d cir.) 1979, U.S. Supreme Ct. 1979. Law sec. to Hon. Theodore Rosenberg Superior Ct. of N.J., Paterson, 1971-72; asst. prosecutor Passaic County Pros.'s Office, 1972-76; pvt. practice Ridgewood, 1976-98; sr. ptnr. Seigel & Mongiardo, P.C., N.J., 1990—. Mem. faculty William Paterson Coll., 1974-79; lectr. N.J. Inst. for Continuing Edn., 1981—, N.J. State Bar and various county bar assns. Recipient Police Hon. Legion award Police Chiefs Assn. of N.J., 1980. Mem. ABA (rep. of N.J. young lawyers divsn. 1980-82), N.J. State Bar Assn. (Young Lawyer of Yr. award 1983, bd. trustees 1978-79), Passaic County Bar Assn. (bd. trustees 1973-81), Bergen County Bar Assn. Office: Seigel & Mongiardo 505 Goffle Rd Ridgewood NJ 07450-4027

SEIGEL, JERROLD EDWARD, historian, writer; b. St. Louis, June 9, 1936; s. William and Katherine (Ginsberg) S.; m. Jayn Rosenfeld, Aug. 28, 1966; children: Micol, Jessica. AB, Harvard U., 1958; PhD, Princeton U., 1963. Instr. Princeton (N.J.) U., 1962-65, asst. prof., 1965-68, assoc. prof., 1968-78, prof. history, 1978-88, NYU, N.Y.C., 1988—; Kenan prof., 1994—. Vis. prof. history Maitre d'Etudes, Ecoles des hautes études, Paris, 1988-94; finalist Nat. Book Critics Cir., 1987. Author: Rhetoric and Philosophy, 1968, Marx's Fate, 1978, Bohemian Paris, 1986, Private Worlds of Marcel Duchamp, 1995. Fulbright fellow Inst. Internat. Edn., 1961-62; NEH fellow, 1979-80, 87-88; res. Am. Acad. Rome, 2000. Mem. N.Y. Inst. for Humanities, Phi Beta Kappa. Home: 48 Horatio St New York NY 10014-1614 Office: NYU History Dept 53 Washington Sq S New York NY 10012-1098 E-mail: jes3@nyu.edu.

SEIGEL, STUART EVAN, lawyer; b. N.Y.C., Mar. 25, 1933; s. Philip Herman and Betty Sarah (Leventhal) S.; m. Joyce Roberta Meyers (div.); children: Charles Meyers, Lee Bennett, Suzanne Marcie; m. Sherry Diane Jackson,Sept. 24, 1989. BS, N.Y. U., 1953, LLB, 1957; LLM in Taxation, Georgetown U., 1960. Bar: N.Y. 1958, D.C. 1958. Atty. Office Chief Counsel, IRS, Washington, 1957-65, Office Tax Legis. Counsel, Dept. Treasury, Washington, 1965-69, assoc. tax legis. counsel, 1968-69; ptnr. firm Cohen and Uretz, Washington, 1969-77; chief counsel IRS, 1977-79; ptnr. firm Williams and Connolly, 1979-89, Arnold and Porter, N.Y.C., 1989—. Lectr. George Washington U. Sch. Law, 1970-73; adj. prof. law Antioch Sch. Law, 1973-76, Georgetown U. Sch. Law, 1981. Mem. ABA, Am. Law Inst., Am. Coll. Tax Counsel, N.Y. State Bar Assn. Clubs: Metropolitan (Washington). E-mail: stuart. Office: Arnold and Porter 399 Park Ave New York NY 10022-4690 E-mail: seigel@aporter.com.

SEIGENTHALER, JOHN LAWRENCE, retired newspaper executive; b. Nashville, July 27, 1927; s. John and Mary (Brew) S.; m. Dolores Watson, Jan. 3, 1955; 1 son, John Jr. Student, Peabody Coll.; Nieman fellow, Harvard. Staff corr. Nashville Tennessean, 1949-60, editor, 1962-72, pub., 1973-82, pres., 1979-82, chmn., 1982-92; editorial dir. USA Today, 1982-92, ret., 1992; anchor NBC, N.Y.C. Chmn. freedom forum First Amendment Ctr., Vanderbilt U., Nashville, 1992—; adminstrv. asst. to atty. gen. U.S., 1961; dir. Tennessean Newspapers, Inc., German-Marshall Fund, 1978—. Mem. U.S. Adv. Commn. Information, 1962-64, Pres.'s Jud. Nominating Commn., 1978-79. Mem. Am. Soc. Newspaper Editors (dir., pres.), Sigma Delta Chi.

SEIGFREID, JAMES THOMAS, lawyer; b. Kansas City, Mo., Nov. 5, 1931; s. Ira Jerome and Irene A. (Welling) S.; m. Donna Lee Olsen, Aug. 20, 1955; children: James T. Jr., Mark W., Stephen L., Susan Seigfreid Crowe. BA, U. Mo., 1953, JD, 1955. Bar: Mo. 1955, U.S. Dist. Ct. (we. dist.) Mo. 1957, U.S. Ct. Appeals (8th cir.) 1958, U.S. Ct. Appeals (10th cir.) 1972, U.S. Tax Ct. 1989. Atty. Dietrich Davis Burrell Dicus & Rowlands, Kansas City, 1957-74; atty., chmn. Seigfreid Bingham Levy Selzer & Gee P.C., 1974—2001. Former sec., bd. dirs. Hunt Midwest Real Estate Devel., Kansas City, Hunt Midwest Enterprises; sec. Kansas City Chiefs Football Club Inc., Chiefs' Children's Fund. 1st lt. JAGC, USAF, 1955-57. Recipient St. Thomas More award, 1968, Skill Integrity & Responsibility award Associated Gen. Contractors, Jefferson City, Mo., 1991. Mem. ABA, Mo. Bar Assn., Metro. Bar Assn., Mission Hills Country Club, Bear's Paw Country Club. Roman Catholic. Avocations: golf, travel, reading. Office: Seigfreid Bingham Levy Selzer & Gee PC 911 Main St Ste 2800 Kansas City MO 64105-5301 E-mail: jseigfreid@sblsg.com.

SEIGLER, DAVID STANLEY, botanist, chemist, educator; b. Wichita Falls, Tex., Sept. 11, 1940; s. Kenneth R. and Floy M. (Wilkinson) S.; m. Janice Kay Cline, Jan. 20, 1961; children: Dava, Rebecca. BS in Chemistry, Southwestern (Okla.) State Coll., 1961; PhD in Organic Chemistry, U. Okla., 1967. Postdoctoral assoc. USDA No. Regional Lab., Peoria, Ill., 1967-68; postdoctoral fellow dept. botany U. Tex., Austin, 1968-70; asst. prof. botany U. Ill., Urbana, 1970-76, assoc. prof., 1976-79, prof. botany, 1979—, head dept. plant biology, 1988-93. Curator U. Ill. Herbarium, 1993—. Author: Plant Secondary Metabolism, 1999; editor: Crop Resources, 1977, Phytochemistry and Angiosperm Phylogeny, 1981; contbr. numerous articles to profl. jours. Recipient Fulbright Hays Lecturer award Fulbright Commn., Argentina, 1976, (alternate) Germany, 1995-96, study award Deutsche Akademischer Austauschdienst, Germany, 1995, Rupert Barneby award N.Y. Bot. Garden, 1997. Mem. Phytochem. Soc. N.Am. (pres. 1988-89), Bot. Soc. Am., Am. Chem. Soc., Am. Soc. Plant Taxonomists, Internat. Soc. Chem. Ecology (pres. 1990-91). Mem. Assembly of God Ch. Avocation: genealogy. Home: 510 W Vermont Ave Urbana IL 61801-4931 Office: U Ill Dept Plant Biology 265 Morrill Hall 505 S Goodwin Ave Urbana IL 61801-3707 E-mail: d-seigler@uiuc.edu.

SEIGLER, ELIZABETH MIDDLETON, retired counselor; b. Athens, Ga., Aug. 18, 1928; d. Robert Meriwether and Marie (Davis) Middleton; m. Charles Judson, Aug. 24, 1955; children: Mary Seigler Peacock, Charles Middleton. BSEd, U. Ga., 1949, MEd, 1955; EdS, Ga. State U., 1976. Tchr., coach Talbot County H.S., Talbotton, Ga., 1949-50; tchr. Atlanta Public Schs., 1950-60, counselor, 1960-85. Mem. S.C. Geneal. Soc. (Old Edgefield dist. archives chpt., Anderson County chpt.), The Meriwether Soc., Inc., Ga. Ret. Educators Assn., Atlanta Ret. Tchrs. Assn., Am. Assn. Ret. Persons, Delta Kappa Gamma, Alpha Lambda Delta, Kappa Delta Pi. Baptist. Avocations: gardening, genealogy.

SEIGLER, MICHAEL EDWARD, lawyer, librarian; b. Tallahassee, Oct. 14, 1948; s. Claude Milo and Roberta Bradford (Whitfield) S.; m. Janet Cummings, Feb. 19, 1971; children: Kelly Elizabeth, Megan Whitfield. AA, Lake Sumter C.C., 1968; BS, Fla. State Univ., 1970; MS, 1974; JD, Atlanta Law Sch., 1980. Bar: Ga. 1980, U.S. Ct. Appelas (5th cir.) 1980, U.S. Ct. Appeals (11th cir.) 1980, U.S. tax Ct. 1985, U.S. Supreme Ct. 1985, Cert. tchr. Libr. tchr. Sumter Correctional Inst., Bushnell, Fla., 1970-73; asst. libr. dir. Leesburg Pub. Libr. (Fla.), 1974-75, libr. dir., 1975-77, Atlanta Law Sch., 1979-81; atty. Brooks & Brock, Marietta, Ga., 1981-83; libr. Port Charlotte Pub. Libr., 1983-84; assoc. Brooks & Brock, Marietta, Ga., 1985, Brock & Barr, Marietta, 1985-86, Brock & Clay, 1987; judge pro hoc vice State Ct. of Cobb County, 1986; pvt. practice, 1986—. Asst. dir. Pine Mountain Regional Libr., 1988-95; libr. dir. Smyrna Pub. Libr.; design judge Ben Franklin Awards, 2001. Columnist Smyrna Vinings Living, 2000—; contbr. articles to jours. Vol. worker ACLU, Atlanta, 1979; mem. Fla. State U. Libr. Com., Tallahassee, 1974, Children's Program Com., Port Charlotte, 1983, Port Charlotte Cultural Ctr. Adv. Com., 1984, Pine Mountain Arts Coun., past bd. dirs.; mem. Cobb County Dem. Exec. Com., 1986-87; exec. com. Cobb Christmas, 1986-87; com. mem. Smyrna Cmty. Culture, 2000—; mem., sec. program com. WRFG. Named Tchr. of Yr., Sumter Correctional Inst., 1973. Mem. Nat. Libr. Assn. (com. chmn. 1975-76), Fla. Libr. Assn. (caucus chmn. 1976-77), Ga. Libr. Assn. (mem. com. chmn. 1992—, sec. 1993-94, parliamentarian 1997, 1st v.p. 1999, pres. 2000), Metro Atlanta Libr. Assn. (v.p. 1997, pres. 1998), Southeastern Libr. Assn. (mem. com. 1988—, convention chair 2000, com. chair 2001—), ALA (con. spkr.), Atlanta Law Sch. Alumni Assn. (treas. 1986-90), Fla. State U. Alumni Assn. (life), Ga. Libr. Video Assn. (pres. 1991-92), Mensa (sec. 1987, 89, pres. Ga. chpt. 1988, mediator Ga. chpt. 2000—, trustee Mensa Edn. and Rsch. Found. (v.p. 1993), Ga. Coun. Media Orgn. (chair steering com. 2000), Leadership Meriwether (pres. 1993). Home: 3023 Bay Berry Dr SW Marietta GA 30008-5674 Office: 100 Village Green Cir SE Smyrna GA 30080-3478

SEIGLIE, CARLOS, finance educator; b. Remedios, Cuba, Jan. 5, 1957; s. Carlos Manuel Seiglie, Haydee Seiglie. PhD, U. Chgo., 1991. Asst. prof. Rutgers U., Newark, 1991—94, assoc. prof., 1994—. Contbr. articles. Mem.: numerous orgns., Phi Beta Kappa. Office: Rutgers Univ Dept Econ 360 King Blvd Newark NJ 07102 Personal E-mail: seiglie@andromeda.rutgers.edu.

SEIGMAN, DEBORAH WERST, literature educator; b. Philadelphia, Pa., July 25, 1936; d. Weston Homer Werst and Jennie Veronica Marmora; m. James Edward Seigman. BS biology, Chestnut Hill Coll., Philadelphia, PA, 1958. Chemistry and biology educator Moravian Acad., Bethlehem, Pa., 1959—59; secondary english and latin educator Tompton, 1960—61; educator Bethlehem, Bethlehem, 1961—62, Dept. of Def. Dependents Sch., Kagnew Station, Ethiopia, 1962—66, St. Joseph Elem. Sch., Killeen, Tex., 1975—76, Killeen H.S., Killeen, 1976—84; english dept. chairperson Yokota H.S., Yokota, Japan, 1984—89; educator Killeen H.S., Killeen, Tex., 1989—. R-Consevative. Roman Catholic. Avocations: reading, gardening, writing, singing, travel. Office: Killeen High School 500 North 38th Street Killeen TX 76543 Office Fax: 254-680-2424. E-mail: jseigman@tenet.edu.

SEIKEL, GEORGE R. engineer; b. Akron, Ohio, Nov. 30, 1933; s. George R. and Lucile (Riley) S.; m. Alice Hudak, Mar. 2, 1957 (dec. Dec. 25, 1999); children: Linda Ann Seikel Slife, Mary Elizabeth Seikel Crummer, George R. BS magna cum laude, U. Notre Dame, 1955, MS in Engring. Mechanics, 1957. With NASA, 1956-81, chief plasma physics br., 1966-78, mgr. MHD Systems and MHD Project office, 1978-81; founder, pres. SeiTec, Inc., Cleve., 1982—. Organizer, chmn. sessions for various nat., internat. meetings; lectr. in field; faculty U. Notre Dame, 1955-57. Contbr. articles to profl. jours. Active Boy Scouts Am., Rocky River, Ohio, 1975-79, Eagle Scout; pres. St. Christophers PTA, Rocky River, 1973-74; prin., tchr. religion program St. Christopher H.S., 1965-70. Recipient NASA Outstanding Achievement and Group Achievement awards; U. Notre Dame teaching fellow, 1955-57; ASME Grad. Study award, 1955; U. Notre Dame scholar, K.C. Ednl. Trust Fund, 1950-55. Mem. AIAA (chmn. plasmadynamics and lasers tech. com. 1980-83), Sigma Xi, Notre Dame Alumni Club. Roman Catholic. Office: PO Box 81264 Cleveland OH 44181-0264

SEIL, RICHARD DAVID, music educator, musician; b. Fairview, Ohio, Sept. 20, 1967; s. Ludwig and Arlene Seil. Bachelor of Musical Arts, Baldwin-Wallace Coll., 1989; MusM, Ind. U., 1993; postgrad., U. Cin., 1994—. Assoc. instr. Sch. Music Ind. U. , Bloomington, 1991—92, music dir. chamber opera Sch. Music, 1991—92; pvt. piano tchr. Cin., 1994—96; piano tchr. Cin. Music Acad., 1997—99; music dir. theater Ashland C.C., Ky., 2000—01, asst. prof. music, 2000—01; vis. instr. piano and music theory Albion Coll., Mich., 2001—. Musician: (piano concerto) Beethoven Piano Concerto #5 in E-Flat Major, Op. 73Emperor", 1998. Mem.: Music Educators Nat. Conf., Coll. Music Soc. Avocations: football, jogging, violin. Office: Albion Coll Sch Music 611 East Porter Albion MI 49224 Personal E-mail: klavier2@hotmail.com. Business E-mail: rseil@albion.edu.

SEILER, CHARLOTTE WOODY, retired English language educator; b. Thorntown, Ind., Jan. 20, 1915; d. Clark and Lois Merle (Long) Woody; m. Wallace Urban Seiler, Oct. 10, 1942 (wid. Aug. 2002); children: Patricia Anne Seiler Bootzin, Janet Alice Seiler Sawyer. AA, Ind. State U., 1933; AB, U. Mich., 1941; MA, Ctrl. Mich. U., 1968. Tchr. elem. schs., Whitestown, Ind., 1933-34, Thorntown, 1934-37, Kokomo, 1937-40, Ann Arbor, Mich., 1941-44, Willow Run, 1944-46; instr. English divsn. Delta Coll., University Center, 1964-69, asst. prof., 1969-77, ret., 1977. Organizer, dir. Delta Coll. Puppeteers, 1972-77. Mem. Friends of Grace A. Dow Meml. Libr., 1974—, treas., 1974-75, 77-79, corr. sec., 1975-77; mem. Midland Art Assn.; adv. bd. Salvation Army, 1980-91, sec., 1984-87; leader Sr. Ctr. Humanities program Midland Sr. Ctr., 1977—. Mem. AAUW (fellow 1979), Mich. Libr. Assn., Midland Symphony League, Tuesday Rev. Club (pres. 1979-80), Seed and Sod Garden Club (v.p. 1986-87, pres. 1987-88), Pi Lambda Theta, Chi Omega. Presbyterian. Home: 652 Blackburn Blvd North Port FL 34287

SEILER, FRITZ ARNOLD, physicist; b. Basel, Switzerland, Dec. 20, 1931; came to U.S., 1980; s. Friedrich and Marie (Maibach) S.; m. Mary Catherine Coster, Dec. 22, 1964; children: Monica, Simone, Daniel. BA in Econs., Basel Sch. of Econs., 1951; PhD in Physics, U. Basel, 1962. Rsch. assoc. U. Wis., Madison, 1962-63; scientific assoc. U. Basel, 1963-69, privat dozent, 1969-75, dozent, 1975-80; sr. scientist Lovelace Inhalation Toxicology Inst., Albuquerque, 1980-90; sr. tech. assoc. IT Corp., 1990-92, disting. tech. assoc., 1992-96; v.p. Inst. Regulatory Sci., 1996-97; prin. Sigma Five Cons., Los Lunas, N.Mex., 1997—. Cons. Swiss Dept. Def., 1968-74; vis. scientist Lawrence Berkeley Labs., 1974-75. Contbr. numerous articles to profl. jours. With Swiss Army staff, 1964-75. Fellow Am. Phys. Soc., Health Physics Soc., Soc. for Risk Analysis, Fachverband fuer Strahlenschutz, Am. Nat. Stds. Inst. (mgmt. coun. 1987—, com. N14 1986—). Office: Sigma Five Consulting PO Box 1709 Los Lunas NM 87031-5193 Fax: 505-866-5197. E-mail: faseiler@nmia.com.

SEILER, JAMES ELMER, judge; b. LaCrosse, Wis., Sept. 2, 1946; s. Elmer Bernard and Margaret Theresa (Mader) S.; m. Sonia Gonzales, Feb. 9, 1968; children: Rebecca, Cristina. BA, U. Wis., LaCrosse, 1968; JD, U. Wis., 1973. Bar: Wis. 1973, Minn. 1981, U.S. Supreme Ct. 1985, Mo. 1986. Pvt. practice, Balsam Lake, Wis., 1973-81; in-house counsel Farm Credit Banks, St. Paul, 1981-85; corp. counsel Hussmann Corp., St. Louis, 1985-94; adminstrv. law judge Social Security, Evansville, Ind., 1994-95, Office of Hearings and Appeals, Creve Coeur, Mo., 1995—; chief adminstrv. law judge Hearing Office, 1997—. Candidate Dist. Atty., Polk County, Wis., 1980. With U.S. Army, 1969-71. Avocations: soccer coach, swimming, water skiing, running. Home: 18 Harbor Point Ct Lake Saint Louis MO 63367-1336 Office: 11475 Olde Cabin Rd Saint Louis MO 63141-7130

SEILER, KAREN PEAKE, organizational psychologist; b. Seattle, Jan. 31, 1952; d. Louis Joseph and Donna Mae (Waters) Tomaso; m. Arthur J. Seiler; children from previous marriage: Jeremy S. Peake, Anthony K. Peake. BA/BSW magna cum laude, Carroll Coll., 1987; postgrad., MIT, 1994. Cert. strategic planning Pacific Inst.; cert. orgnl. cons. Covey Learning Ctr., 1993. Admissions counselor Shodair Children's Hosp., Helena, Mont., 1984-86; asst. dir., counselor Career Tng. Inst., 1986-90; pres. Corp. Cons., 1990—. Apptd. amb. Mont. Ambs., 1990—; active Gov.'s Task Force on Econ. Devel., 1991-94; chairperson Mont. Dist. Export Coun./U.S. Dept. Commerce, 1992-96; exec. com. mem. Mont. World Trade Ctr., Missoula, 1995—, chmn. 1996—; pres. Coun. Carroll Coll., 1997—. Mem. YWCA, 1986-90, pres., 1989; mem. Bus. and Profl. Women's Orgn., 1987-93, sec., 1990; pres. Helena Area Econ. Devel. Coun., 1989-92; exec. com. Leadership Helena, 1990-91; monitoring chair Concentrated Employment Program Pvt. Industry Coun., Mont., 1990—; bd. dirs., exec. com. Mont. Women's Capital Fund, 1990-95; exec. com. Mont. Race for the Cure, 1994—. Mem. NAFE, Partnership for Employment and Tng., Delta Epsilon Sigma (Outstanding Citizen award). Roman Catholic. Avocations: sailing, world travel. Home and Office: 315 N Park Ave Helena MT 59601-5060

SEILER, WALLACE URBAN, chemical engineer, deceased; b. Evansville, Ind., Aug. 31, 1914; s. Samuel Alfred and Anna Beatrice (Grossman) S.; m. Charlotte Woody, Oct. 10, 1942; children: Patricia Anne, Janet Alice. Student, U. Evansville, 1932-34; BS, Purdue U., 1937; postgrad., U. Mich., 1945-46. Engr. Dow Chem. Co., Midland, Mich., 1937-39, cons. rsch. engr. Ann Arbor, 1939-49, tech. sve. engr. Midland, 1950-55, mgr. solvents field svc., 1955-64, contract R & D specialist, 1964-80. Chemical engineer; b. Evansville, Ind., Aug. 31, 1914; s. Samuel Alfred and Anna Beatrice (Grossman) S.; student U. Evansville, 1932-34; BS, Purdue U., 1937; postgrad. U. Mich., 1945-46; m. Charlotte Woody, Oct. 10, 1942; children: Patricia Anne, Janet Alice. With Dow Chem. Co., 1937-80, engr., Midland, Mich., 1937-39, cons. rsch. engr., Ann Arbor, Mich., 1939-49, tech. svc. engr., Midland, 1950-55, mgr. solvents field svc., 1955-64, contract R & D specialist, 1964-80. Mem. AAAS, Am. Chem. Soc., Am. Inst. Chemists, Sigma Xi, Tau Beta Pi, Phi Lambda Upsilon. Mem. AAAS, Am. Chem. Soc., Am. Inst. Chemists, Sigma Xi, Tau Beta Pi, Phi Lambda Upsilon. Home: North Port, Fla. Died Aug. 28, 2002.

SEILING, SHARON LEE, family economics educator; b. Okmulgee, Okla., Aug. 25, 1946; d. Dent and Ruth Burgess; m. John Seiling; 1 child, Clark. BS, Okla. State U., 1968, MS, 1971; PhD, Cornell U., 1980. Tchr. Pauls Valley (Okla.) H.S., 1968-71; grad. asst. Okla. State U., Stillwater, 1971-73; lectr. Calif. Polytechnic State U., San Luis Obispo, 1973-75; grad. asst. Cornell U., Ithaca, N.Y., 1975-78; asst. prof. Fla. State U., Tallahassee, 1978-85, Ohio State U., Columbus, 1985-91, assoc. prof., 1991—. Grad. faculty lectr. Ohio State U., 1995. Assoc. editor Family and Consumer Scis. Rsch. Jour., 1996—2002; contbr. articles to profl. jours. Bd. govs. Ohio Coun. Against Health Fraud, 1989-93; mem. Gov.'s Task Force on Housing and Cmty. Devel., Tallahassee, 1979; mem. housing adv. com. Columbus Urban League, 1994-95; bd. dirs. Creative Play Ctr., 1998-99. Grantee Hewlett Found., 1994, USDA, 1998. Mem. LWV (pres. 1983-84), Am. Assn. Housing Educators (v.p. 1988-89), Am. Assn. Family and Consumer Scis. (sec.-treas. family econs./resource mgmt. divsn. 1996-98), Ohio Assn. Family and Consumer Scis. (chmn. N. Ctrl. Regional Rsch. Team, 2001-). Democrat. Methodist. Office: 265 Campbell Hall 1787 Neil Ave Columbus OH 43210-1295

SEILS, WILLIAM GEORGE, lawyer; b. Chgo., Aug. 9, 1935; s. Harry H. and Hazel C. (Sullivan) S.; m. Evelyn E. Oliver, Sept. 8, 1956; children: Elizabeth Ann, Ellen Carol, Eileen Alison. AB, JD, U. Mich., 1959. Bar: Ill. bar 1959. Since practiced in, Chgo.; ptnr. Arvey, Hodes & Costello & Burman, 1968-87; gen. counsel, sec., sr. v.p. Richardson Electronics, Ltd., LaFox, Ill., 1986—. Contbr. articles to profl. jours.; asst. editor: Mich. Law Rev, 1958-59. Mem. Ill. Bar Assn., Order of Coif. Office: Richardson Electronics Ltd PO Box 393 40w267 Keslinger Rd Lafox IL 60147-0393 E-mail: wgs@rell.com.

SEIM, ANDREW, investment company executive, venture capitalist; b. Bremen, Germany, Apr. 8, 1969; came to U.S., 1995; s. Roland and Friedel (Fischer) S.; m. Peggy Grabow, Apr. 8, 1994; 1 child, Ashley-Vivian. MBA, Handelsschule Anckelmann, Hamburg, Germany, 1989. V.p. IASM, Hamburg, Germany, 1989-91, ABA Enterprises, Inc., Bad Harzburg, Germany, 1995; pres. Taurus Investment, Bradenton, Fla., 1995—; v.p. Stamford (N.Y.) Fin., 1996—. Bd. dirs. BG Banking Equipment, Bowling Green, Ky., Apollo House, Berlin. Contbr. articles to profl. jours. Bd. dirs. Stamford (N.Y.) Theatrical Fund, 1996—; sponsor Police Athletic League, Bradenton, Fla., 1997. Mem. Stamford Inst. (prof. emeritus). Avocations: golf, sailing, reading, fishing. Office: Taurus Investment 1401 Manatee Ave W Ste 905 Bradenton FL 34205-6702

SEINFELD, JERRY, comedian; b. Bklyn., Apr. 29, 1955; s. Kal and Betty S. Grad. with degree in theatre communications, Queens (N.Y.) Coll., 1976. Former salesman. Stand-up comedian, 1976—; joke-writer (TV series) Benson, ABC, 1980; actor, co-writer, prod. (TV series) Seinfeld, NBC-TV, 1989-97 (Emmy award Outstanding Comedy Series, 1993, Emmy nomination, Lead Actor - Comedy Series, 1994), (TV movie) The Ratings Game, 1984, The Tommy Chong Roast, 1986, The Seinfeld Chronicles, 1990, I'm Telling You for the Last Time, 1999; (film) Comedian, 2002; writer Jerry Seinfeld-Stand-Up Confidential, 1987; author: Sein Language, 1993.; guest appearances The Larry Sanders Show, 1992, News Radio, 1995. Recipient Am. Comedy award funniest male comedy stand-up, 1988, funniest actor in a TV series, 1992. Jewish. Avocations: Zen, yoga.*

SEINFELD, JOHN HERSH, chemical engineering educator; b. Elmira, N.Y., Aug. 3, 1942; s. Ben B. and Minna (Johnson) S. BS, U. Rochester, 1964; PhD, Princeton U., 1967; DSc honoris causa, U. Patras, Greece, 2002, Carnegie Mellon U., 2002. Asst. prof. chem. engring. Calif. Inst. Tech., Pasadena, 1967-70, assoc. prof., 1970-74, prof., 1974—. Louis E. Nohl prof., 1980—, exec. officer for chem. engring., 1973-90, chmn. engring. and applied sci. div., 1990-2000. Allan P. Colburn meml. lectr. U. Del., 1976; Camille and Henry Dreyfus Found. lectr. MIT, 1979; mem. coun. Gordon Rsch. Confs., 1980-83; Donald L. Katz lectr. U. Mich., 1981; Reilly lectr. U. Notre Dame, 1983; Dean's Disting. lectr. U. Rochester, 1985; Katz lectr. CUNY, 1985; McCabe lectr. N.C. State U., 1986; Lewis lectr. MIT, 1986; Union Carbide lectr. SUNY, Buffalo; Van Winkle lectr. U. Tex., 1988; Bicentennial lectr. La. State U., 1988; Ida Beam lectr. U. Iowa, 1989, David Mason lectr. Stanford U., 1989; Julian Smith lectr. Cornell U., 1990; Merck lectr. Rutgers U., 1991; Henske Disting. lectr. Yale U., 1991; lectr. AIChE, 1980; Centennial lectr. U. Pa., 1993; Miles Disting. lectr. U. Pitts., 1994; Kelly lectr. Purdue U., 1996; Disting. rsch. lectr. Carnegie Mellon U., 1998; Berkeley lectr. U. Calif., Berkeley, 1998; Sigma Xi lectr., 1998—, Merck Sharp & Dohme lectr. U. P.R., 1998; Hess lectr. U. Va., 1998; inaugural disting. lectr. U. Toledo, 1999; Priestley lectr. Commonwealth Scientific and Indsl. Rsch. Orgn., 2000; Amundson lectr. U. Houston, 2002. Author: Numerical Solution of Ordinary Differential Equations, 1971, Mathematical Methods in Chemical Engineering, Vol. III, Process Modeling, Estimation and Identification, 1974, Air Pollution: Physical and Chemical Fundamentals, 1975, Lectures in Atmospheric Chemistry, 1980, Atmospheric Chemistry and Physics of Air Pollution, 1986, Fundamentals of Air Pollution Engineering, 1988, Distributed Parameter Systems--Theory and Applications, 1989, Atmospheric Chemistry and Physics, 1998; assoc. editor Environ. Sci., Tech., 1981-97; mem. editorial bd. Computers, Chem. Engring, 1974-96, Jour. Colloid and Interface Sci, 1978-95, Advances in Chem. Engring, 1980—, Revs. in Chem. Engring, 1980—, Aerosol Sci. and Tech., 1981-93; assoc. editor: Atmospheric Environment, 1976—. Recipient Donald P. Eckman award Am. Automatic Control Coun., 1970, Pub. Svc. medal NASA, 1980, Disting. Alumnus award U. Rochester, 1989; Camille and Henry Dreyfus Found. Tchr. Scholar grantee, 1972. Fellow Japan Soc. Promotion Sci., AIChE (bd. dirs. 1988-91, mem. editl. bd. jours. 1985—, Allan P. Colburn award 1976, William H. Walker award 1986, Warren K. Lewis award 2000), NAE, Am. Assn. Adv. Sci.; mem. Am. Soc. Engring. Edn. (Curtis W. McGraw Rsch. award 1976, George Westinghouse award 1987), Assn. Aerosol Rsch. (bd. dirs. 1983—, v.p. 1988-90, pres. 1990-92), Am. Acad. Arts and Scis., Am. Chem. Soc. (Svc. through Chemistry award 1988, Creative Advances in Environ. Sci. and Tech. award 1993), Internat. Aerosol Rsch. Assembly (Fuchs award 1998, Nev. medal 2001), Sigma Xi, Tau Beta Pi. Home: 525 S Catalina Ave Pasadena CA 91106-3306 Office: Calif Inst Tech Divsn Engring Applied Sci Pasadena CA 91125-0001 E-mail: seinfeld@caltech.edu.

SEIPEL, JOHN HOWARD, lawyer, neurologist, consultant, medical executive; b. Pitts., Nov. 9, 1925; s. John Howard and Marie Elizabeth (Schaser) S.; m. Janice Lois Duffney, July 4, 1959; children: Janice Marie, John Howard III, Tabitha Ann, William Joseph. BS in Chemistry, Carnegie-Mellon U., 1946, MS in Chemistry, 1947; PhD in Chemistry, Northwestern U., 1958; MD, Harvard U., 1954; JD, George Mason U., 1990. Diplomate in neurology, aviation, aerospace medicine, penologic medicine and clin. pharmacology Am. Bd. Forensic Examiners, Am. Bd. Forensic Medicine. Rotating intern Pa. Hosp., 1954-55, surg. resident, 1955-56; residency program in neurology Georgetown U. Med. Ctr., Washington, 1958-61, asst. resident, then chief resident Med. Ctr., 1959; chief resident D.C. Gen. Hosp., 1960; rsch. fellow in neurology Georgetown U., Washington, 1960-61, chief neurology lab. Georgetown Clin. Rsch. Inst., 1961-66, clin. instr. dept. neurology Georgetown Hosp., 1959-78, asst. prof. dept. neurology, 1978-79; chief electrodiagnostic sect. U.S. VA Hosp., 1967-69; dir. neurol. rsch. Md. Psychiat. Rsch. Ctr., Balt., 1969-78; chief med. officer D.C. Dept. Corrections, Lorton, Va., 1979—; sr. cons. in neurology Aviation Med. Svc., FAA, Washington, 1972—. Cons. various orgns. in field, 1961—. Author: (monograph) The Biophysical Basis and Clinical Applications of Rheoencephalography, 1966 (S. Wier Mitchell award 1966); also book chpts., articles. Master Hunter Edn. instr. Va. Dept. Game and Wildlife, Richmond, 1976—. Capt. USPHS, 1956-58, maj. Res., 1965-81. Greenwalt fellow NYU, 1961. Fellow Brit. Royal Soc. Medicine, Am. Coll. Legal Medicine, Am. Coll. Clin. Pharmacology, Am. Coll. Forensic Examiners (life, bd. advisors for profl. stds. 1995); mem. So. Med. Assn., Va. State Bar Assn., D.C. Bar Assn., Izaac Walton League Am. (chpt. pres., state 1st v.p., other offices 1972—), Sigma Xi (sr.), Phi Lambda Upsilon, Phi Delta Phi. Avocations: hunting, fishing, antique glass and automobiles, collecting firearms. Home: 5335 Summit Dr Fairfax VA 22030-6523 Office: Central Facility PO Box 25 Lorton VA 22199-0025

SEIREG, ALI A(BDEL) (ALI ABDEL HAY SEIREG), mechanical engineer; b. Arab Republic of Egypt, Oct. 26, 1927; came to U.S., 1951, naturalized, 1960; s. Abdel Hay and Aisha Seireg; m. Shirley Marachowsky, Dec. 24, 1954; children: Mirette Elizabeth LaFollette, Pamela Aisha Terry. BSME, U. Cairo, 1948; PhD, U. Wis., 1954. Lectr. Cairo U., 1954-56; staff adv. engr. Falk Corp., Milw., 1956-59; assoc. prof. theoretical and applied mechanics Marquette U., 1959-64, prof., 1964-65; prof. emeritus (Kaiser chair) mech. engring. U. Wis., Madison, 1965—; Ebaugh Prof. U. Fla., Gainesville, 1986—. Cons. in field.; chmn. U.S. council Internat. Fedn. Theory of Machines, 1974-94; co-chmn. 5th World Congress of Theory of Machines, 1979, 1st USSR-USA Conf. on Composite Materials, 1989. Author: Mechanical Systems Analysis, 1969, Biomedical Analysis of Musculoskeletal Structure for Medicine and Sports, 1989, Optimized Motion Planning, 1994, The Kinematic Geometry of Gearing, 1995, Optimizing the Shape of Mechanical Elements, 1997, Friction and Lubrication in Mechanical Design, 1998; editor: Computers in Mechanical Engring.; editor in chief SOMA, Engineering for the Human Body, 1986-90; contbr. articles to profl. jours. Recipient Kuwait prize for sci., 1987. Fellow ASME (Richards Meml. award 1973, Machine Design award 1978, Design Automation award 1990, chmn. div. design engring. 1977-78, chmn. computer tech. 1978-81, policy bd. comm. 1978-80, policy bd. gen. engring. 1979-80, chmn. Century II Internat. Computer Tech. Conf. 1980, founding chmn. computer engring. div. 1980-81, v.p. systems and design 1981-85, sr. v.p., chmn. council on engring. 1985-90, pres. Gen. Rsch. Inst. 1984—), Am. Soc. Engring. Edn. (George Westinghouse award 1970), Soc. Exptl. Stress Analysis, Am. Inst. Med. and Biol. Engring. (founding fellow), Am. Gear Mfg. Assn. (E. P. Connell award 1974), Automation Research Council; mem. Chinese Mech. Engring. Soc. (hon.), USSR Acad. Sci. (fgn.), Russian Acad. Sci. (fgn.), Yugoslav Acad. Engring. (fgn.). Office: 1513 University Ave Madison WI 53706-1539 E-mail: aaseireg@facstaff.wisc.edu. *I have always tried my best to look beyond what I hear, to think beyond what I see, to give more than I receive, and to do good as its own reward.*

SEITEL, FRASER PAUL, public relations executive; b. Jersey City, June 6, 1946; s. Robert and Helen (Barmad) S.; m. Rosemary Kierstein, Dec. 20, 1969; children: Raina, David. BJ, U. Mo., 1964; MA, U. N.D., 1970; MBA, NYU, 1977. Pub. rels. officer Chase Manhattan Bank, N.Y.C., 1970-73, v.p., 1974-85, sr. v.p., dir. pub. affairs, 1985-92; mng. ptnr. Emerald Ptnrs., Ft. Lee, N.J., 1992—; sr. counselor Burson Marsteller, N.Y.C., 1992—; sr. counselor investor rels. and mktg. communications Greater N.Y. Savs. Bank, 1994-97. Pub. rels. con. Hill and Knowlton, N.Y.C., 1973; instr. Profl. Devel. Inst., N.Y.C., Ragan Comms., Chgo., Estes Park Inst., Colo.; columnist U.S. Banker, 1989—94, Odwyerpr.com, 2001—, Profit Mag., 1993—95. Author: The Practice of Public Relations, 8th edit., 2000; co-author: Idea Wise, 2002; pub., editor: The Public Relations Strategist, 1995—2001, columns editor: PRSA Tactics mag., 1994—95, columnist: odwyerpr.com, 2001—; contbr. CNN, MSNBC, Fox News Channel, CNBC. Col. USAR, 1969-76. Named among Top 100 Pub. Rels. Profls. of 20th century PR Week. Mem. Pub. Rels. Soc. Am., Bank Mktg. Assn. Avocations: baseball, football, basketball, tai chi, rugby. Office: 177 Main St Ste 215 Fort Lee NJ 07024-6936 E-mail: yusake@aol.com.

SEITELMAN, MARK ELIAS, lawyer; b. N.Y.C., Apr. 14, 1955; s. Leo Henry and Pearl (Elias) S. BA, Bklyn. Coll., 1976; JD, Bklyn. Law Sch., 1979. Bar: N.Y. 1980, U.S. Dist. Ct. (ea., so., and we. dists.) N.Y. 1980, U.S. Supreme Ct. 1995, U.S. Ct. Mil. Appeals, 1995. Law asst. Criminal Ct., Bklyn., 1979; law clk. to Hon. Justice Aaron D. Bernstein N.Y. Supreme Ct., 1980; assoc. Lester, Schwab, Katz & Dwyer, N.Y.C., 1981-87, Weg and Myers, 1987-88, Kroll & Tract, 1988-90; pvt. practice N.Y.C., 1990—. Appeared on WABC TV Eyewitness News; interviewed by N.Y. Daily News, N.Y. Newsday, N.Y. Law Jour., Crain's NY Bus. Mem. ABA, ATLA (sustaining mem. motor vehicle and small practice sect.), N.Y. State Bar Assn., N.Y. County Bar Assn. (ins. and supreme ct. coms.), N.Y. State Trial Lawyers Assn. (sustaining mem., bd. dirs., mem. spkrs. bur., conv. com., legis. com., contbg. editor Trial Lawyers Quar.), N.Y. State Trial Lawyers Inst. (CLE program chmn., lectr.), Bklyn. Bar Assn. (legis. com., employment law com.). Office: 111 Broadway 9th Fl New York NY 10006

SEITMAN, DAVID TODD, anesthesiologist; b. Bklyn., Oct. 21, 1952; m. Kathryn Nemiroff (dec.), Nov. 20, 1983; 1 child, Matthew. MSBME, Case Western Res. U., 1977; MSME, Case We. Res. U., 1977, MD, 1981. Diplomate Am. Bd. Anesthesiology. Intern Presbyn. U. of Pa. Med. Ctr., 1981-82; resident U. Pa., 1982-84; asst. prof. Allegheny Univ. Hosps., Center City, 1989-95; assoc. prof. Hahnemann Hosp., Phila., 1995-96, Robert Wood Johnson Med. Sch., New Brunswick, N.J., 1996-2000; staff anesthesiologist Virtua Meml. Hosp., Mt. Holly, 2000—. Asst. prof. Pa. Coll. Podiatric Medicine, Phila., 1989-97. Contbr. chpts. in books and articles to profl. jours. Mem. AMA, IEEE, Am. Soc. Anesthesiologists, Soc. Tech. in Anesthesia (pres. 2002-), Soc. Obstetrical Anesthesiologists and Perinatologists, Am. Soc. Regional Anesthesia. Avocations: computers, model railroading. Home: 3 Highland Ct Linwood NJ 08221 Office: Advanced Anesthesia Assoc PC 1 E New York Ave Somers Point NJ 08224

SEITMAN, JOHN MICHAEL, lawyer, arbitrator, mediator; b. Bloomington, Ill., Feb. 9, 1942; BS, U. Ill., 1964, JD, 1966. Bar: Calif., U.S. Dist. Ct. (so., cen., no. and ea. dists.) Calif., U.S. Ct. Appeals (9th cir.). Prin. Lindley, Lazar & Scales, San Diego, 1966-97; full-time neutral JAMS, 1997—. Lectr. in continuing legal edn. Bd. dirs. San Diego County Bar Found., 1983-89, treas., 1983-84, pres., 1988-89; del. to 9th Cir. Jud. Conf., 1986, 88. Fellow Am. Bar Found.; mem. ABA, State Bar Calif. (pres. 1991-92), San Diego County Bar Assn. (pres. 1986). Office: PO Box 2156 Del Mar CA 92014-1456

SEITZ, FREDERICK, former university administrator; b. San Francisco, July 4, 1911; s. Frederick and Emily Charlotte (Hofman) S.; m. Elizabeth K. Marshall, May 18, 1935. AB, Leland Stanford Jr. U., 1932; PhD, Princeton U., 1934; Doctorate Hon. Causa, U. Ghent, 1957; DSc (hon.), U. Reading, 1960, Rensselaer Poly. Inst., 1961, Marquette U., 1963, Carnegie Inst. Tech., 1963, Case Inst. Tech., 1964, Princeton U., 1964, Northwestern U., 1965, U. Del., 1966, Poly. Inst. Bklyn., 1967, U. Mich., 1967, U. Utah, 1968, Brown U., 1968, Duquesne U., 1968, St. Louis U., 1969, Nebr. Wesleyan U., 1970, U. Ill., 1972, Rockefeller U., 1981; LLD (hon.), Lehigh U., 1966, U. Notre Dame, 1962, Mich. State U., 1965, Ill. Inst. Tech., 1968, N.Y. U., 1969; LHD (hon.), Davis and Elkins Coll., 1970, Rockefeller U., 1981, U. Pa., 1985, U. Miami, 1989. Instr. physics U. Rochester, 1935-36, asst. prof., 1936-37; physicist research labs. Gen. Electric Co., 1937-39; asst. prof. Randal Morgan Lab. Physics, U. Pa., 1939-41, assoc. prof., 1941-42; prof. physics, head dept. Carnegie Inst. Tech., Pitts., 1942-49; prof. physics U. Ill., 1949-57, head dept., 1957-64, dir. control systems lab., 1951-52, dean Grad. Coll., v.p. research, 1964-65; exec. pres. Nat. Acad. Scis., 1962-69; pres. Rockefeller U., N.Y.C., 1968-78; dir. Richard Lounsbery Found., 1980—, pres., 1995—2002, U. Miami (Fla.), 1989. Trustee Ogden Corp., 1977—; dir. tng. program Clinton Labs., Oak Ridge, 1946-47; chmn. Naval Rsch. Adv. Com., 1960-62; vice chmn. Def. Sci. Bd., 1961-62, chmn., 1964-68; sci. adviser NATO, 1959-60; mem. nat. adv. com. Marine Biomed. Inst. U. Tex., Galveston, 1975-77; mem. adv. group White House Conf. Anticipated Advances in Sci. and Tech., 1975-76; mem. adv. bd. Desert Rsch. Inst., 1975-79, Ctr. Strategic and Internat. Studies, 1975-81; mem. Nat. Cancer Adv. Bd., 1976-82; dir. Akzona Inc. Author: Modern Theory of Solids, 1940, The Physics of Metals, 1943, Solid State Physics, 1955, The Science Matrix, 1992, On the Frontier: My Life in Science, 1994, Stalin's Captive: Nikolaus Riehl and the Soviet Race for the Bomb, 1995, Electronic Genie: The Tangled History of Silicon. Trustee Rockefeller Found., 1964-77, Princeton U., 1968-72, Lehigh U., 1970-81, Rsch. Corp., 1966-82, Inst. Internat. Edn., 1971-78, Woodrow Wilson Nat. Fellowship Found., 1972-82, Univ. Corp. Atmospheric Rsch., Am. Mus. Natural History, 1975—; trustee John Simon Guggenheim Meml. Found., 1973-83, chmn. bd., 1976-83; mem. Belgian Am. Edn. Found.; bd. dirs. Richard Lounsbery Found., 1980—. Decorated Order of the Brilliant Star (Republic of China); recipient Franklin medal Franklin Inst. Phila., 1965, Hoover medal Stanford U., 1968, Nat. Medal Sci., 1973, James Madison award Princeton U., 1978, Edward R. Loveland Meml. award ACP, 1983, Vannevar Bush award Nat. Sci. Bd., 1983, J. Herbert Holloman award Acta Metallurgica, 1993, Von Hippel award Materials Rsch. Soc., 1993, Joseph Henry medal Smithsonian Instn., 1997. Fellow Am. Phys. Soc. (pres. 1961); mem. NAS, Am. Acad. Arts and Scis., AIME, Am. Philos. Soc., Am. Inst. Physics (chmn. governing bd. 1954-59), Inst. for Def. Analysis, Finnish Acad. Sci. and Letters (fgn. mem.), Phi Beta Kappa Assos. Address: Rockefeller U 1230 York Ave New York NY 10021-6307

SEITZ, JAMES EUGENE, retired college president, freelance writer; b. Columbia, Pa., July 27, 1927; s. Joseph Stoner and Minnie (Frey) S.; m. Florence Arlene Dutcher, Apr. 5, 1950; children: Diane Louise, Ellen Kay, Linda Marie, Karl Steven. BS, Millersville State Coll., 1950; MEd, Pa. State U., 1952; PhD, So. Ill. U., 1971. Tchr. pub. schs., Pa., 1950-56; lectr. Temple U., Phila., 1956-62; asst. prof. engr. tech. Kans. State U., Pitts., 1962-65; dean Mineral Area Coll., Flat River, Mo., 1965-69, Coll. of Lake County, Gravslake, Ill., 1969-73; founding pres. Edison State Community Coll., Piqua, Ohio, 1973-85; freelance writer Sidney, 1985—. Founding sec./treas. Ohio Tech. and C.C. Assn., Columbus, 1976; speaker at nat. confs. of educators, 1960-85. Author: Woodcarving: A Designer's Notebook, 1989, Country Creations, 1991, Selling What You Make, 1992, Effective Board Participation, 1993, Substance for the Soul, 1999; contbr. articles to profl. jours. Founding pres. Exch. Club Grayslake, 1970; pres. Epicurian Soc., Sidney, Ohio, 1978-79; mediator Mcpl. Ct., Sidney, 1992—; sr. citizens' steering com. Arbor Day Found.; founding pres. Sr. Ctr. of Sidney-Shelby Co., 1996—, mem. choir, 2001—, named Outstanding Sr. Citizen, 2001. Recipient Leadership and Svc. award Pa. State U. Alumni Soc., 1990; named Oustanding Sr., Sr. Ctr. of Sidney-Shelby County, 2001. Mem. Am. Assn. Ret. Persons (founding chpt. pres. 1990-91), Assn. for Career & Tech. Edn., VFW (charter Post 8757), Am. Legion (scholarship com. and judge Post 217 1996-97, exec. com. 1997-2001, publicity dir. 1998-2000), Sidney Singing Soldiers, 1996— (pres., 1998), Shelby Woodcarvers Guild (founding pres. 1999), Iota Lambda Sigma. Avocations: woodworking, lecturing. Home: 55 Brown Rd Sidney OH 45365-8949 E-mail: jseitz@voyager.net.

SEITZ, KARL RAYMOND, editor; b. Corpus Christi, Tex., Sept. 26, 1943; s. Kerlin McCullough and Martha Elisabeth (Tillman) S.; m. Patricia Jean Floyd, June 13, 1970; 1 child, Lee Kerlin. BA, Birmingham So. Coll., 1970. Copy editor Birmingham (Ala.) Post-Herald, 1967-70, asst. news editor, 1970-73, chief editorial writer, 1973-78, editor editorial page, 1978—. Dir. Birmingham Post-Birmingham Typographical Union Pension Plan, 1983-90, chmn., 1986-90; dir. Goodfellow Fund, Inc., Birmingham, 1983—, v.p., 1986—. Active exec. in residence Birmingham So. Coll., 1987, Leadership Birmingham, 1986—, mem. mem.'s coun., 1998—2001. With USN, 1961—64. Mem. Am. Acad. Polit. and Social Sci., Nat. Conf. Editorial Writers, Acad. Polit. Sci. Home: 1212 30th Street S Birmingham AL 35205-1910 Office: Birmingham Post Herald PO Box 2553 Birmingham AL 35202-2553 E-mail: kseitz@postherald.com.

SEITZ, MARY LEE, mathematics educator; BS in Edn. summa cum laude, SUNY, Buffalo, 1977, MS in Edn., 1982. Cert. secondary tchr., N.Y. Prof. math. Erie C.C.-City Campus, Buffalo, 1982—. Reviewer profl. jours. and coll. textbooks. Reviewer profl. jours. Mem. N.Y. Maths. Assn. Two Yr. Colls., Assn. Maths. Tchrs. N.Y., N.Y. Assn. Two Yr. Colls., Inc., Internat. Platform Assn., Pi Mu Epsilon. Avocations: gardening, photography, bird watching. Office: Erie C C-City Campus 121 Ellicott St Buffalo NY 14203-2601 *Consider the words of Peter Marshall, U.S. Senate chaplain, who said, "Give to us clear vision that we may know where to stand and what to stand for—because unless we stand for something, we shall fall for anything.".*

SEITZ, NICHOLAS JOSEPH, magazine editor; b. Topeka, Jan. 30, 1939; s. Frank Joseph and Lydia Natalie (Clerico) S.; m. Velma Jean Pfannenstiel, Sept. 12, 1959; children: Bradley Joseph, Gregory Joseph. BA, U. Okla., 1966. Sports editor Manhattan (Kans.) Mercury, 1960-62, Norman (Okla.) Transcript, 1962-64, Okla. Jour., Oklahoma City, 1964-67; staff Golf Digest mag., Norwalk, Conn., 1967—, editor, 1973-82; editorial dir. Golf Digest and Tennis, 1982-90; editorial dir. Sports/Leisure divsn. N.Y. Times Co. Mag. Group, 1991-92, sr. v.p., editor in chief, 1992-98, editor at large, 1999—. Syndicated golf instrn. and commentary CBS Radio Network; commentary ESPN TV Network. Author: Superstars of Golf, 1978; (with Dave Hill) Teed Off, 1977; (with Tom Watson) Getting Up and Down, 1983, Getting Back to Basics, 1991, Tom Watson's Strategic Golf, 1993; contbr. articles to profl. jours.; anthologized in: Best Sports Stories. Named Okla. Sports Writer of Year Nat. Sportswriters and Sportscasters Assn., 1965; winner contests Nat. Basketball Writers Assn.; winner contests Golf Writers Assn.; recipient Lincoln A. Werden award for outstanding contbn. to golf journalism, 1993, Meml. Tournament Golf Journalism award, 2000, PGA Lifetime Achievement in Journalism award, 2002. Home: 36 Hunt St Norwalk CT 06853-1015 Office: 5520 Park Ave Trumbull CT 06611-3426 E-mail: nseitz@optonline.net.

SEITZ, VICTORIA ANN, marketing educator; b. Rio de Janeiro, Aug. 7, 1956; (parents Am. citizens); d. Richard Joseph and Betty Jean (Merrill) S.; m. James Milton Smallwood, Jan. 5, 1985 (div. Aug. 1987); m. Stephen P. Wilson, Aug. 29, 1992 (div. Nov. 2000). BS in Apparel Design, Kans. State U., 1978; MS in Apparel Merchandising, Okla. State U., 1984, PhD in Apparel Merchandising, 1987. Fashion coord. Burdines Dept. Stores, Miami, Fla., 1978-80; asst. dept. mgr. Saks Fifth Avenue, Ariz., 1980-81, dept. mgr., 1981-82; grad. teaching asst. clothing, textiles and mdse. dept. Okla. State U., Stillwater, 1983-85, grad. teaching and rsch. assoc., 1986-87; asst. prof. U. North Tex. Sch. Human Resource Mgmt., Denton, 1988-91; prof. dept. mktg. Calif. State U., San Bernardino, 1991—. Asst. fashion designer, cons. Fred Baggs Inc., Miami, 1978-85; panel moderator, participant, presenter numerous confs. and convs.; cons. on image direct mktg., advt., pub. rels. and merchandising, various cos. Author: Power Dressing, 1991, Your Executive Image, 1992, 2000; syndicated fashion columnist, 1985-89; columnist Beauty-Walk.com, 2001--; contbr. articles to profl. jours. Recipient numerous grants and awards; fellow Eleanor Radell Sole Acad.; scholar Fulbright, Romania, 2002—. Mem.: Direct Selling Edn. Found. (bd. dirs. 1999—2002), Inland Empire Ad Club (pres., bd. dirs.), Direct Mktg. Assn. North Tex. (bd. dirs. 1988—91). Republican. Roman Catholic. Avocations: travel, exercise. Office: Calif State U Dept Mktg 5500 University Pkwy San Bernardino CA 92407-2318

SEITZ, WALTER STANLEY, cardiovascular research consultant; b. L.A., May 10, 1937; s. Walter and Frances Janette (Schleef) S. BS in Physics and Math., U. Calif., Berkeley, 1959; PhD in Biophysics, U. Vienna, 1981, MD, 1982. Health physicist U. Calif. Radiation Lab., 1959-61; rsch. assoc. NIH at Pacific Union Coll., 1961-63; physicist Lockheed Rsch. Labs., Palo Alto, Calif., 1961-63; staff scientist Xerox Corp., Pasadena, 1963-66; sr. scientist Applied Physics Cons., Palo Alto, 1966-75; instr. clin. sci. U. Ill Coll. Medicine, Urbana, 1983-84; cons. cardiology Cardiovascular Rsch. Inst. U. Calif. Sch. Medicine, San Francisco, 1987—; sr. scientist Inst. Med. Analysis and Rsch., Berkeley, 1987—. Contbr. articles to profl. jours. Postdoctoral Rsch. fellow, U. Calif. San Francisco, 1984. Fellow Am. Coll. Angiography; mem. AAAS, Royal Soc. Medicine London, N.Y. Acad. Scis., Physicians for Social Responsibility. Avocations: reading, music, hiking. Office: IMAR Cons Inc 38 Panoramic Way Berkeley CA 94704-1828

SEITZ, WILLIAM HENRY, JR. orthopedic surgeon; b. N.Y.C., Jan. 12, 1950; s. William Henry and Catherine (Kehoe) S.; m. Susan Andrea Versenyi, June 4, 1972; children: David William, Eric Alexander, William Henry III, Elizabeth Andrea. BS, Fairfield U., 1971; grad. cert. phys. therapy, Columbia U., 1972, MD, 1979. Diplomate Am. Bd. Med. Examiners. Resident in gen. surgery St. Vincent's Med. Ctr., N.Y.C., 1979-81; resident in orthopaedic surgery Columbia Presbyn. Med. Ctr., 1981-83, chief resident, 1983-84, Annie C. Kane fellow in hand surgery, 1984-85; clin. instr. Case Western Res. U., Cleve., 1985-87, asst. clin. prof., 1987-94, assoc. clin. prof., 1995—. Chmn. dept. orthop. surgery Orthop. Inst. , Cleve., 1997—99, Mt. Sinai Med. Ctr., Cleve., 1997—99; dir. Cleve. Orthop. & Spine Hosp./Luth. Med. Ctr., Cleve., 1999—, Cleve. Clin. Health Sys., 1999—; head of hand and upper extremity surgery, orthop. rehab. Mt. Sinai Med. Ctr., Clevel., 1985—99; cons. Nisonger Ctr. for Child Devel., Columbus, Ohio, 1985—, Cuyahoga County Md. Mental Retardation, Cleve., 1986—; spkr., presenter in field; dept. staff Orthop. Surgery Cleve. Clin. Found., 2000—. Editor Current Opinion in Orthops.-Hand and Wrist, 1994-99; mem. editl. bd. Jour. Hand Surgery, 1994-99; reviewer JBJS, 1993—; contbr. articles to profl. jours. Fellow Am. Acad. Orthopedic Surgeons; mem. Am. Soc. for Surgery of Hand (internat. traveling fellow 1992-93, Sterling Bunnell fellow 1992, Summer L. Koch award 1990), Am. Orthopedic Assn., Am. Shoulder and Elbow Surgeons Soc., Orthopedic Rsch. Soc., Orthopedic Trauma Assn. Roman Catholic. Home: 3398 Kenmore Rd Shaker Heights OH 44122-3462 Office: Cleve Orthop & Spine Hosp Luth Med Ctrdic Surgery West 25th St Cleveland OH 44113 E-mail: seitz@core.com.

SEIWALD, ROBERT J. retired inventor; b. Ft. Morgan, Colo., Mar. 26, 1925; BS in Chemistry, U. San Francisco; PhD in Organic Chemistry, St. Louis U., 1954. Prof. organic chemistry U. San Francisco, 1957-89; ret., 1989. Inducted Nat. Inventors Hall of Fame, 1995. Office: Nat Inventors Hall of Fame 221 S Broadway St Akron OH 44308-1505*

SEJNOWSKI, TERRENCE JOSEPH, science educator; b. Cleve., Aug. 13, 1947; s. Joseph Francis and Theresa (Cudnik) S.; m. Beatrice Alexandra Golomb, Mar. 24, 1990. BS, Case Western Res. U., 1968; PhD, Princeton U., 1978. Rsch. fellow Harvard Med. Sch., Boston, 1979-82; prof. biophysics Johns Hopkins U., Balt., 1982-90; prof. U. Calif. San Diego, Salk Inst., La Jolla, 1988—. Investigator Howard Hughes Med. Inst., 1991—; bd. dirs. San Diego McDonnell-Pew Ctr. for Cognitive Neurosci., 1990-98, Inst. for Neural Computation, U. Calif. San Diego., 1990—. Editor-in-chief Neural Computation, 1989—; co-inventor: (with others) the Boltzmann machine and NET talk; mem. editl. bd. Sci. Mag., 1990—. Pres. Neural Info. Processing Sys. Found. Recipient Presdl. Young Investigator award NSF, 1984, Wright prize Harvey Mudd Coll., 1996; Sherman Fairchild Disting. scholar Calif. Inst. Tech., 1993. Fellow IEEE (Neural Network Pioneer award 2002; mem. Soc. for Neurosci., Am. Phys. Soc., Internat. Neural Network Soc. (governing bd. 1988-92, Hebb prize 1999), Am. Math. Soc., Assn. Rsch. in Vision and Ophthalmology, Am. Assn. Artificial Intelligence, Biophys. Soc., Optical Soc. Am., Am. Psychol. Soc., Am. Psychol. Assn., N.Y. Acad. Scis., Fedn. Am. Soc. Exptl. Biophysics, Soc. Neuroscience, Internat. Soc. Neuroethology, Soc. Math. Biology. Achievements include co-invention of the Boltzmann machine, of NETtalk, a neural network for text-to-speech. Office: Salk Inst PO Box 85800 San Diego CA 92186-5800 E-mail: terry@salk.edu.

SEKANINA, ZDENEK, astronomer; b. Mlada Boleslav, Czechoslovakia, June 12, 1936; came to U.S., 1969; s. Frantisek Sekanina and Hedvika Sekaninova; m. Jana Soukupova, Apr. 1, 1966; 1 child, Jason. Diploma, Charles U., Prague, Czechoslovakia, 1959, PhD in Astronomy, 1963. Astronomer Stefanik Obs., Prague, 1959-66, Ctr. for Numerical Math., Charles U., Prague, 1967-68; vis. scientist Inst. d'Astrophysique, Univ. de Liege, Cointe-Ougree, Belgium, 1968-69; physicist Smithsonian Astrophys. Obs., Cambridge, Mass., 1969-80; mem. tech. staff Jet Propulsion Lab., Pasadena, Calif., 1980-81, rsch. scientist, 1981-84, sr. rsch. scientist, 1984—. Assoc. Harvard Coll. Obs., Cambridge, 1969-80; mem. NASA Comet Sci. Working Group, 1977-80; cons. Jet Propulsion Lab., 1977-80; prin. U.S. co-investigator Particulate Impact Analyzer Experiment, Dust Impact Detector Sys. Experiment, European Space Agy.'s Giotto Mission to Comet Halley, 1980-89; mem. NASA-European Spacy Agy. Comet Halley Environ. Working Group, 1980-89; discipline specialist Near Nucleus Studies Network, Internat. Halley Watch, 1982-90; mem. imaging sci. subsys. team Comet Rendezvous Asteroid Flyby Mission, 1986-92; mem. sci. definition team ESA/NASA Comet Nucleus Sample Return Mission, 1988—; co-investigator STARDUST Discovery Mission, 1994—. Editor Comet Halley Archive, 1982-91; mem. editorial bd. Kosmicke Rozhledy, 1963-69. Recipient Exceptional Sci. Achievement medal NASA, 1985; minor planet named Sekanina, 1976. Mem. Internat. Astron. Union (mem. commns. 15, 20, 22, mem. organizing commn. 22 1976-82, organizing commn. 15 1979-85, mem. working group on comets 1988—, assoc. dir. Ctrl. Bur. for Astron. Telegrams 1970-80), COSPAR (working group 3, panel C, exec. mem. 1980-82), Learned Soc of Czech Republic (hon. 1996—), Czech Astron. Soc. (hon. 2001-). Roman Catholic. Office: Jet Propulsion Lab 4800 Oak Grove Dr Pasadena CA 91109-8001 E-mail: zs@sek.jpl.nasa.gov.

SEKELY, MARY ANN, librarian; b. Pitts., Sept. 25, 1950; BS, Pa. State U., 1973; MLS, U. Pitts., 1980. Info. specialist Info. and Vol. Svcs., Pitts., 1980-81; adminstrv. asst. The Bank Ctr., 1982-84; indexer H.W. Wilson Co., Bronx, N.Y., 1984-87; asst. editor Pub. Affairs Info. Svc., N.Y.C., 1987-95, editl., mktg. and systems assoc., 1995-98; libr. Bklyn. Pub. Libr., 1998—. Adult literacy tutor Ctrl. Learning Ctr., Bklyn. Pub. Libr., 1998—. Asst. editor (index) Pub. Affairs Info. Svc. Internat. Interviewer Mayor's Vol. Action Ctr., N.Y.C., 1992-95. Mem. ALA, Spl. Libr. Assn.

SEKERKA, ROBERT FLOYD, physics educator, scientist; b. Wilkinsburg, Pa., Nov. 27, 1937; s. John Jacob and Vivian Mae (Smith) S.; m. Dianne Thompson, Apr. 30, 1960 (div. Apr. 1981); children: Lee Ann, Robert Thompson; m. 2d Carolyn Lee Confer, May 24, 1981. BS in Physics, U. Pitts., 1960; AM, Harvard U., 1961, PhD, 1965; PhD (hon.), U. Timisora, Romania, 1996. Engr. Westinghouse Rsch. Labs., Pitts., 1965-68, mgr. materials growth and properties dept., 1968-69; lectr. Carnegie-Mellon U., 1967-69, assoc. prof., 1969-72, prof. metallurgy and materials sci., 1972-82, dept. head, 1976-82, prof. physics and math., dean Mellon Coll. Sci., 1982-91, Univ. Prof., 1991—. Mem. space studies bd. NRC, 1989-91. Assoc. editor Jour. Crystal Growth, 1971-94; Metallurgical Trans., 1970-76; editorial bd. Applied Microgravity Tech., 1987-90. Past bd. dirs. Forbes Health Sys., Pitts., Pitts. Regional Ctr. for Sci. Tchrs.; past vice chmn. bd. dirs. NMR Inst.; past mem. rsch. com. Allegheny Singer Rsch. Inst., Pitts. Recipient A.G. Worthing award U. Pitts., 1959, Philip M. McKenna Meml. award, 1980, Bruce Chalmers award TMS, 1998; Woodrow Wilson fellow, 1960, NSF fellow, 1962-65. Fellow: Am. Phys. Soc., Am. Soc. Metals, Japanese Soc. for Promotion of Sci.; mem.: Internat. Assn. Crystal Growth (pres. 2001, Frank prize 1992), Am. Assn. Crystal Growth (mem. exec. com.), Minerals Metals Materials Soc., Edgewood Country Club, Sigma Xi, Phi Beta Kappa, Omicron Delta Kappa. Home: 307 S Dithridge St Atrium 911 Pittsburgh PA 15213-3514 Office: Carnegie Mellon U Dept Physics 6416 Wean Hall Pittsburgh PA 15213-3890 E-mail: sekerka@cmu.edu.

SEKINE, DEBORAH KEIKO, systems analyst, programmer; b. Honolulu, Dec. 1, 1952; d. Yoshiteru and Yaeko (Matsuda) Isa; m. Andrew K. Sekine, May 8, 1993. BA in Math. with distinction, BEd with distinction, U. Hawaii, 1974, MS in Computer Sci., 1976, MBA, 1987. Data analyst, engr. in-charge Kentron, Honolulu, 1977-81; sys. analyst Am. Savs., 1981-82; analyst, programmer City and County of Honolulu, 1982—. Cons. Am. Savs., Honolulu, 1982. Contbr. articles to profl. jours. Vol. Hawaii Dem. Conv., Honolulu, 1984, Mayoral campaign, 1988, 92; com. co-chair Hui Makaala,

Honolulu, 1989—; caregiver Makiki Christian Ch., Honolulu, 1991—. Mem. IEEE, Assn. for Computing Machinery, Am. Fedn. State County Mcpl. Employees, U. Hawaii MBA Alumni Assn., Phi Kappa Phi. Mem. United Ch. of Christ. Avocations: jogging, reading, writing, tennis, listening to gospel music. Home: 3322 George St Honolulu HI 96815-4319

SEKIYA, GERALD YOSHINORI, lawyer; b. Honolulu, Aug. 28, 1942; s. Shoji and Yachiyo (Baba) S.; m. Fay Naomi Shioji, Aug. 7, 1965; children: Jan, Gregory, Derek. BSEE, U. Ill., 1965; JD, U. Calif., San Francisco, 1968. Bar: Calif. 1968, Hawaii 1969, U.S. Dist. Ct. Hawaii, U.S. Dist. Ct. (no. dist.) Calif. 1968, U.S. Ct. Appeals (9th cir.) 1968, U.S. Supreme Ct. 1987. Law clk. U.S. Dist. Ct. (no. dist.), San Francisco, 1968-70; assoc., ptnr. Pratt, Moore, Bortz & Case, Honolulu, 1970-73; ptnr. Cronin, Fried, Sekiya, Kekina & Fairbanks, 1973—. Reader Calif. State Bar Exam Com., San Francisco, 1970; mem. Hawaii Supreme Ct. Civil Rules Com., Honolulu, 1984—; mem. Hawaii Supreme Ct. Family Ct. Rules Com., 1989—; commr. Hawaii Jud. Arbitration Com., 1985—, Jud. Conduct Com., 1993—, chmn., 1994—. Coach Hawaii Kai Community Activities, 1978-80; mgr. Manoa Youth League. Mem. Am. Bd. Trial Advocates (pres. 1996—), Am. Inns of Ct. IV, Hawaii Bar Assn. (dir. 1980-81, 85-86), Hawaii Trial lawyers Assn. (pres. 1979), Hawaii Acad. Plaintiff Attys. (pres. 1985), Am. Coll. Trial Lawyers, Order of Coif. Office: Cronin Fried Sekiya Kekina & Fairbanks 841 Bishop St Ste 1900 Honolulu HI 96813-3962

SEKLER-KATZ, RUDOLFINE, internist, psychiatrist; b. Cernowitz, Romania, Aug. 11, 1924; came to U.S., 1967; d. Aron and Anna Sekler; widowed. MD, U. West Timisoara, Romania, 1950. Resident St. John's Hosp., Queens, N.Y., Mt. Sinai Hosp./Elmhurst Divsn.; attending physician in internal medicine, psychiat. cons. N.Y.C., 1971—. Office: 96-08 70th Ave Forest Hills NY 11375-5823

SEKOWSKI, CYNTHIA JEAN, corporate executive, contact lens specialist; b. Chgo., Feb. 14, 1953; d. John L. and Celia L. (Matusiak) S. PhD in Health Svcs. Adminstrn., PhD in Health Scis., Columbia Pacific U., 1984; grad., Realtor Inst., 1998. Chief contact lens dept. Lieberman & Kraff, Chgo., 1974-87; pres., CEO Seko Eye Care, Inc., 1988—; realtor Country Club Realty Group, Naples, Fla., 1995—2002, John R. Wood, Inc. Realtors, 2002—. Rschr., technologist U. Ill., Chgo., 1976-78. Mem. Chgo. Zool. Soc., 1984—, Little City Inner Circle, 1991—; sponsor Save the Children Orgn., 1983—; asst. to campaign mgr. Rep. state senatorial candidate, Chgo., 1972; pres. Compass Point Condo Assn., Naples, Fla., 1996-99; budget com. Windstar Country Club Master Homeowner's Assn., Naples, 1996-99. Fellow: Contact Lens Soc. Am.; mem.: Women's Coun. Realtors, Naples Area Bd. Realtors, Nat. Assn. Realtors, Fla. Assn. Realtors, Nat. Contact Lens Examiners, Better Vision Inst., Opticians Assn. Am., Ill. Soc. Opticianry, Soc. of the Little Flower, Nat. Wildlife Fedn., Columbia Pacific U. Alumnae Assn., U.S. Golf Assn., Nat. Geog. Soc., S.W. Fla. Conservancy, The Phoenix Soc. (med. profl.), Vanderbilt Country Club (residents adv. bd. 1999—2001, vice-chmn. adminstrn. com. 2001—). Roman Catholic. Avocations: gardening, reading, photography, writing poetry, golf. Office: John R Wood Inc Realtors 3255 Tamiami Trl N Naples FL 34103 E-mail: luvfla@mindspring.com.

SEKULER, ROBERT WILLIAM, psychology educator, scientist; b. Elizabeth, N.J., May 7, 1939; s. Sidney and Mary (Siegel) S.; m. Susan Pamela Nemser, June 25, 1961; children: Stacia, Allison, Erica. AB, Brandeis U., 1960; ScM, Brown U., 1963, PhD, 1964; postgrad. (NIH postdoctoral fellow), MIT, 1964-65. Prof. psychology Northwestern U., Evanston, Ill., 1973-89, chmn. dept., 1975-79, prof. ophthalmology Med. Sch., 1978-89, prof. neurobiology and physiology, 1982-89, assoc. dean Coll. Arts and Scis., 1985-89, John Evans prof. neurosci., 1986-89; v.p. Optronix, Inc., 1980-82; provost, dean of faculty Brandeis U., Waltham, Mass., 1989-91, Louis and Frances Salvage prof. psychology, 1989—; mem. Ctr. for Complex Systems, 1990—. Rsch. prof. biomed. engrng. Boston U., 1992—, adj. prof. cognitive and neural sys., 1994—; dir. program in cognitive scis. Brandeis U., 1998—; vis. prof. psychology U. Toronto, 2000; cons. NWSF, NIH, AAAS, USAF, U. Calif., APA; chmn. vision com. NRC-N AS; chmn. working group on visual function and aging NRC, chmn. working group on aging workers and visual impairment; scientist Rotman Inst. Baycrest Geriatric Ctr., 2000. Author: (with D. Kline and K. Dismukes) Aging and Human Visual Function, 1981, (with R. Blake) Perception, 1985, Hungarian edit., 2000, 4th edit., 2001, Star Trek on the Brain, 1998, paperback edit., 1999, Japanese edit., 2000; editor: Perception & Psychophysics, 1971-86, Jour. Exptl. Psychology, 1973-74, Vision Rsch. Jour., 1974-79, 80-92, Optics Letters, 1977-79, Am. Jour. Psychology, Ophthalmic and Physiol. Optics, 1986-99, Intelligent Systems, 1986-92, Psychology and Aging, 1987-92; contbr. Oxford Textbook of Geriatric Medicine, 1992, 99, Ency. of Psychology, 1999; contbr. articles to profl. jours. Grantee Nat. Inst. Neurol. Diseases and Stroke, USAF, NSF, Nat. Eye Inst., Nat. Inst. Aging, USN, James McDonnell Found., Alzheimer's Found. Fellow: AAAS, Am. Psychol. Soc., Optical Soc. Am.; mem.: Knowles Inst. for Hearing Rsch. (bd. dirs. 1988—90), Psychonomic Soc., Neurosci. Soc., Assn. Rsch. in Vision and Ophthalmology, Sigma Xi. Home: 64 Strawberry Hill Rd Concord MA 01742-5502 Office: Brandeis U Ctr for Complex Systems Waltham MA 02454

SEKULOVICH, MALDEN See MALDEN, KARL

SELAND, JOHN JOSEPH, priest, educator; b. Scranton, Pa., May 2, 1938; arrived in Japan, 1976; s. John Andrew and Laura (Stalheber) S. BA, SUNY, Albany, 1963, Divine Word Sem., Ill., 1968; MA, Loyola U., Chgo., 1970; PhD, U. Calif., Riverside, 1976. ordained, Bordentown, N.J., 1968. Prof. Nanzan U., Nagoya, Japan, 1979—. Author: (textbook) An Essential History of English Literature, 1991, Reflections on the Daily Gospels, 1993, Fighting It Out, 1999. Mem. Rural Asia Solidarity Assn. (leader, guide Japanese students exposure programs 1981—). Home: Logos Ctr 104 Yagumo-cho Showa-ku Nagoya 466 Japan Office: Nanzan U Yamazato-cho 18, Showa-ku Nagoya 466 Japan E-mail: seland@ps.nanzan-u.ac.jp.

SELANDIA, ELIZABETH, acupuncturist, Oriental medicine physician; b. Santa Barbara, Calif., Apr. 3, 1945; d. Fredrick Bunnell and Anna LaVerne (Welch) Pulling Jr.; m. William Kent Selandia, July 1966 (div. July 1977); 1 child, Karina Vanessa; m. Carsten Hennier, Feb. 4, 1981 (div. June 1986). Student, Sch. Holography, Emeryville, Calif., 1978; AA in French/Behavioral Sci./Humanities, Coll. of Marin, Kentfield, Calif., 1992; BA in Native Am. Studies and Linguistics, U. Calif., Berkeley, 1994; MA in Mus. Studies, San Francisco State U., 2000; postgrad. in art history, Calif. State U., Chico, 2001—. Diplomate NCCR; lic. acupuncturist, Calif. Astrology tchr. De Kosmos, Amsterdam, 1971-72; importer Langebortistan, Copenhagen, 1972-77; self-employed editor/writer, 1981—; acupuncturist Larkspur, Calif., 1987—; editl./adminstrv. asst. Unix/World Mag., Mountain View, 1985-91. Test writer Acupuncture Exam Com., Sacramento, Calif., 1996, 2000. Author, multimedia designer, photographer: The Paradigms of Museum Architecture Trends: Neoclassical and Modern, 1800-2000, 2001; editor/author: Gently Whispered: Oral Teachings of V.V. Kalu Rinpoche, 1994, 1999 Dead Heat--A Pictorial: The Importation of Arabian Horses from the Middle East to San Simeon Stables, 1999; author/artist: Tiger Inside, Dragon Outside, 1996; artist cloth art in crocheted wool; exhbn. of textile collection Sophienholm Musée, Lyngby, Denmark, 1976, Smithsonian Mus., Washington, 1983. Art show coord. United Astrologers Congress, Monterey, Calif., 1995. Recipient highest honors in Native Am. Studies, U. Calif., Berkeley, 1994 (only person to have done so), Huang Di award 7th Internat. Congress Chinese Medicine, 1998. Mem. Nat. Mus. Am. Indian (charter), No. Calif. Film Inst., Asian Arts Mus. (charter), Mensa, Young Scandinavians Club, Alpha Gamma Sigma. Democrat. Buddhist. Avocations: knitting, reading, swimming, dancing, foreign travel. Home and Office: PO Box 777 Middletown CA 95461

SELANNE, TEEMU, professional hockey player; b. Helsinki, Finland, July 3, 1970; Hockey player Winnipeg Jets, 1992—95, Phoenix Coyotes, 1995—97, Anaheim Mighty Ducks, 1997—2001, San Jose Sharks, 2001—. Played in All-Star Game, 1996, 94, 93. Named Rookie of Yr. Sporting News, 1992-93, All Rookie team, 1992-93; Recipient Calder Meml. Trophy, 1992-93. Office: San Jose Sharks HP Pavilion 525 West Santa Clara Street San Jose CA 95113*

SELBO, RAY GORDON, consultant and seminar speaker; b. Jamestown, N.D., Mar. 23, 1940; s. Arthur Gordon Selbo (dec.) and Helen E. (Peterson) Selbo Johnson (dec.); m. Joy Marget Bostrom, May 29, 1964; children: Jon Gordon, James Everett. Student, U. Minn., 1958-59. Various positions to dir. sales edn. Am. Hardware Mutual Ins. Co., Minn., Calif., 1959-77; prin., pub. spkr., cons. RGS Assocs., 1973-2000; with Collateral Control Corp., St. Paul, Chgo., 1977-79, v.p. sales and ops., 1978-79; cons. Universal Tng. Systems Corp., Chgo., 1980-81; internat. dir. tng. Schwan's Sales Enterprises Inc., Marshall, Minn., 1981-96; founder, pres. R.G. Selbo, Inc., 2000—. Bd. dirs. United Way, Marshall, Minn., 1981-95, bd. pres., 1985-87; bd. dirs. Pioneer Pub. TV, 1991-96, bd. 1st v.p., 1996. Served with U.S. Army, Vietnam, 1963-65. Avocations: crossword puzzles, reading. Office: 4015 Lancaster Ln N Apt 1 Plymouth MN 55441-1739 Fax: (612) 593-1355. E-mail: rgselbo@qwest.net.

SELBY, CECILY CANNAN, dean, educator, scientist; b. London, Feb. 4, 1927; d. Keith and Catherine Anne Cannan; m. Henry M. Selby, Aug. 11, 1951 (div. 1978); children: Norman, William, Russell; m. James Stacy Coles, Feb. 21, 1981. AB cum laude, Radcliffe Coll., 1946; PhD in Phys. Biology, MIT, 1950. Teaching asst. in biology MIT, 1948-49; adminstrv. head virus study sect. Sloan-Kettering Inst., N.Y.C., 1949-50, asst. mem. instr., 1950-55; instr. microscopic anatomy Cornell U. Med. Coll., 1955-57; tchr. sci. Lenox Sch., N.Y.C., 1957-58, headmistress, 1959-72; nat. exec. dir. Girl Scouts U.S.A., N.Y.C., 1972-75; adv. com. Simmons Coll. Grad. Mgmt. Program, 1977-78; mem. Com. Corp. Support of Pvt. Univs., 1977-83; spl. asst. acad. planning N.C. Sch. Sci. and Math., 1979-80, dean acad. affairs, 1980-81, chmn. bd. advisors, 1981-84. Cons. U.S. Dept. Commerce, 1976-77; dir. Avon Products Inc., RCA, NBC, Loehmanns Inc., Nat. Edn. Corp. pres. Am. Energy Ind., 1976; co-chmn. commn. pre-coll. math. and sci. Nat. Sci. Bd., 1982-83; adj. prof. NYU, 1984-86, prof. sci. edn., 1986-94; mem. policy steering com. Gov. Cuomo's Conf. on Sci. and Engrng., 1989-90; affil. scholar Radcliffe Pub. Policy Ctr. of Harvard U., 2000-2001. Contbr. articles to profl. jours., chpt. to book. Founder, chmn. N.Y. Ind. Schs. Opportunity Project, 1968-72; mem. invitational workshops Aspen Inst., 1973, 75, 77, 79; trustee MIT, Bklyn. Law Sch., Radcliffe Coll., Woods Hole Oceanographic Instn., Women's Forum N.Y., N.Y. Hall of Sci., 1982—, vice chmn., 1989—, trustee Girls Inc., 1992—, Nat. Coun. Women in Medicine, 1990-94; mem. Yale U. Peabody Mus. Adv. Coun., 1981-89; co-chair program in sci., soc. and gender Radcliffe Inst. of Harvard U., 1999-2001. Named affiliated scholar, Harvard U., 2001; recipient Woman Scientist of Yr. award, N.Y. chpt. Am. Women in Sci., 1992, Alumnae Achievement award, Radcliffe Coll., 2001. Fellow Am. Women Sci., N.Y. Acad Scis.; mem. Century Assn. Club, Woods Hole Golf Club, Cosmopolitan Club, The Explorers Club, Sigma Xi, Phi Delta Kappa. Home and Office: 1 E 66th St New York NY 10021-5854 also: 100 Ransom Rd Falmouth MA 02540-1652 E-mail: selbyc@aol.com.

SELBY, DIANE RAY MILLER, fraternal organization administrator; b. Lorain, Ohio, Oct. 11, 1940; d. Dale Edward and Mildred (Ray) Miller; m. David Baxter Selby, Apr. 14, 1962; children: Elizabeth, Susan, Sarah. BS in Edn., Ohio State U., 1962. Sec. Kappa Kappa Gamma Frat., Columbus, Ohio, 1962-63, editor, 1972-86; tchr. Hilliard (Ohio) High Sch., 1963-65; exec. dir. Mortar Bd., Inc. Nat. Office, Columbus, Ohio, 1986—. Editor The Key of Kappa Kappa Gamma Frat. 1972-86 (Student Life award, 1983, 84, 85). Founding officer Community Coordinating Bd., Worthington, Ohio, 1983; pres. PTA Coun., Worthington, 1984, Worthington Band Boosters, 1985; sec., treas. Sports and Recreation Facilities Bd., Worthington, 1986—; mem. sustaining com. Jr. League Columbus, 1991-93, docent Kelton House, 1979—. Mem. Mortar Bd., Inc., Twig 53 Children's Hosp. (assoc.), Assn. Coll. Honor Soc. (mem. exec. com. 1999-2001, chmn. bylaws com.), Ladybugs and Buckeyes, Kappa Kappa Gamma (House Bd. vp. 1997-2000). Republican. Lutheran. E-mila. Home: 6750 Merwin Pl Columbus OH 43235-2838 Office: Mortar Bd Inc 1200 Chambers Rd Ste 201 Columbus OH 43212-1754 E-mail: selby.1@osu.edu.

SELBY, FREDERICK PETER, investment banker; b. Mannheim, Germany, Mar. 31, 1938; s. Ernest and Margaret (Lassman) S.; m. Lillian E. Howard, Sept. 18, 1960; children: Christopher, Andrea, Stephanie. BS in Econ., U. Pa. Various positions Weyerhaeuser Timber Co., 1960—62; football coach William Penn Charter Sch., Phila., 1960—62; mktg. cons. Barrington Assocs., NYC, 1962—64; adviser Nepal Indsl. Devel. Corp. (U.S. Dept. State and AID), Kathmandu , 1962—. Mgmt. cons., 1963-65; v.p., dir. Reeves Broadcasting Corp., N.Y.C. 1965-67; dir., CEO Previews, Inc., 1966-67; mng. ptnr. Graham Loving & Co., mems. N.Y. Stock Exchange, N.Y.C., 1968-69; v.p. corp. fin. Burnham & Co., N.Y.C., 1969-70; dir. corp. fin. Wood, Walker & Co., N.Y.C., 1971-74; cons. corp. devel. Penn-Dixie Industries, N.Y.C.; cons. corp. fin. Bankers Trust Co. cons. to chmn. G & W Natural Resources Co., N.Y.C., 1974-79; pres., CEO H.C. Sleigh N.A., Inc. subs. H.C. Sleigh Ltd., Australia, 1980-84; sr. v.p., dir. corp. fin. Banque Arabe Internationale D'Investissement, N.Y.C., 1984-85; chmn., CEO Randy Internat. Air Freight, N.Y.C., 1986-87; chmn., mng. dir. Selby Capital Ptnrs., N.Y.C., 1987-99; bd. dirs. Gristede's Foods, Inc. (formerly Designcraft Corp.), 1987—, fin. advisor to chmn.; ltd. ptnr., mng. dir., Chart Group, N.Y.C., 2000-01. Co-author: Why, When and How to Go Public, Corporate Earnings, Cash or Cosmetics, Foreign Investment in the USA; contbr. articles to travel publs. Mem. N.Y. Soc. Security Analysts, Am. Alpine Club, Explorers' Club (lectr., fin. com., specialist on Nepal and Himalayas), Kappa Sigma. Home: 300 E 74th St Apt 33F New York NY 10021-3746

SELBY, HUBERT, JR. writer; b. N.Y.C., July 23, 1928; s. Hubert and Adalin (Layne) S.; m. Inez Taylor, Apr. 23, 1955 (div. 1960); children: Claudia, Kyle; Suzanne Schwartzman, Dec. 26, 1969; children: Rachel, William. Student public schs., Bklyn. Author: Last Exit to Brooklyn, 1964, The Room, 1971, The Demon, 1976, Requiem for a Dream, 1978, Song of the Silent Snow, 1986, The Willow Tree, 1998, Waiting Period, 2002; screenwriter: Day and Night, 1986, Remember the Sabath Day, 1974, Love Your Buddy Week, 1978, Solder of Fortune, 1990, Requiem for a Dream, 1998, Fear the X, 2000. Served with U.S. Mcht. Marine, 1944-46. Mem. Writers Guild Am. (West chpt.), Authors Guild.

SELBY, JEROME M. mayor; b. Wheatland, Wyo., Sept. 4, 1948; s. John Franklin and Claudia Meredith (Hudson) S.; m. Gloria Jean Nelson, June 14, 1969; children: Tyan, Cameronn, Kalen. BS in Math., Coll. Idaho, 1969, MA in Ednl. Adminstrn., 1974; MPA, Boise State U., 1978. Assoc. engr. Boeing Co., Seattle, 1969-71; dir. evaluation WICHE Mountain States Regional Med. Program, Boise, 1971-74; dir. rsch., evaluation Mountain States Health Corp., 1974-76, with health policy analysis and accountability, 1976-78; dir. health Kodiak (Alaska) Area Native Assn., 1978-83; mgr. Kodiak Island Borough, 1984-85, mayor, 1985-98, bus., mcpl. and fisheries cons., 1998—; regional dir. planning and devel. Providence Health System, 1998—. Proprietor Kodiak Tax Svc., 1978—, Registered Guide, Kodiak, 1987—; cons. Nat. Cancer Inst., Washington, 1973-78, others. Contbr. articles to profl. jours. Treas. ARC, Kodiak, 1978-93, bd. dirs., 1978-95, chmn., 1989-90, mem. western ops. hdqrs. adv. bd., 1986-92, mem. group IV and V nat. adv. coj., 1986-89, nat. bd. govs., 1989-95, chmn. chpt. rels. com., 1994-95; pres. S.W. Alaska Mcpl. Conf., Anchorage, 1988-89, v.p., 1986-87, treas., 1996-98, bd. dirs., 1986-98; pres. Alaska Mcpl. League Investment Pool, Inc., 1992-98; v.p. Alaska Mcpl. League, 1988-90, pres., 1990-91, bd. dirs., 1988-98; bd. dirs. Alaska Mcpl. League Jt. Ins. Assn. Bd., 1995—, v.p., 1996-98, pres., 1998-2000; mem. Alaska Resource Devel. Coun., 1987-2001, exec. com., 1989-2000; bd. dirs. Alaska State C. of C., 2000—; mem. policy com. of outer continental shelf adv. bd. U.S. Dept. Interior, 1990—, vice chair, 1996-98, chair, 1998-2000; chmn. Natural Gas Subcom., 2000-01; co-chair Alaska Task Force, 1995—; mem. Com. on Oil Pollution Act, 1995; mem. Nat. Assn. Counties, Cmty. and Econ. Devel. Steering Com., 1990-98, Alaska govtl. roles task force, 1991-92; mem. Alaska state/local govt. task force, 1996-98; chmn. Kodiak Island Exxon Valdez Restoration Com., 1991-95; dir. Kodiak Health Care Found., 1992—, v.p. 1992—; co-chmn. Arctic Power, 1993—; bd. dirs. Western Interstate Region Nat. Assn. of Counties, 1993-98; bd. dirs. Alaska Oceans, Seas, Fisheries Rsch. Found., 1998—, pres., 1998—; mem. environment, energy and land use steering com. Nat. Assn. Counties, 1997-98; mem. grad. med. edn. com. Alaska Family Practice Residency, 2000-01; mem. Koniag Edn. Found., 2002—; mem. Oiled Regions of Alaska, 2001—, pres., 2002—. Paul Harris fellow, 1987, 88, 91, 92, 96; recipient Outstanding Contbn. award Alaska Mcpl. League, 1994, Disting. Alumni award Albertson Coll. of Idaho, 1997, Lifetime Achievement award Alaska Mcpl. League, 1998. Mem. Alaska Conf. Mayors, Nat. Soc. Tax Profls., Acad. Polit. Sci., Alaska Mcpl. Mgrs. Assn., Kodiak C. of C. (dir. 1983-99), Rotary (bd. dirs. 1989-97, treas. 1989-93, v.p. 1993-94, pres.-elect 1994-95, pres. 1995-96). Office: Providence Health Systems PO Box 196604 3200 Providence Dr Anchorage AK 99519-6604

SELBY, JOHN HORACE, surgeon; b. Springfield, Mass., Nov. 11, 1919; s. Howard Williams and Ethel (Wagg) S.; children by previous marriage: John H., Susan, Sherrill, Lucinda; m. Carolyn Symes, Feb. 14, 1970. AB, Dartmouth Coll., 1941; MD, Boston U., 1944; postgrad., U. Pa., 1948. Diplomate Am. Bd. Thoracic Surgery, Am. Bd. Surgery. Intern Mary Hitchcock Meml. Hosp., Hanover, N.H., 1944-45; resident New Eng. Deaconess Hosp., Boston, 1945-46, Portsmouth Naval Hosp., Boston, Mass. Meml. Hosp., Boston, 1949-50, Boston City Hosp., 1950-51; thoracic surgeon Lubbock, Tex., 1952—; chief surgery Meth. Hosp., 1954-56, 64-65, chief thoracic surgery, 1964-73, 77-79; chief of staff St. Marys Hosp., 1973; chief surgery, 1970, U. Hosp., 1973. Active staff Meth. Hosp., St. Marys, Health Scis. Ctr.; dir. med. staff affairs Highland Hosp., 1986-92; hon. staff West Tex. Hosp.; cons. staff South Park Hosp., Meml. Hosp., Seminole Hosp., Mercy Hosp., Slaton Hosp., Cook Meml. Hosp., Levelland Hosp.; med. dir. HMI, Inc., 1986-93; clin. prof. surgery Tex. Tech. Med. Sch., 1975—. Regional med. dir. Tex. Med. Found. Peer Rev. Orgn., 1986-94; med. care adv. com. Tex. Dept. Human Svcs., 1990-94, chmn. physician payment adv. com., 1991-94; chmn. bd. South Plains Health Sys., 1975-81; active Statewide Health Coord. Coun., 1977-85, exec. com., 1979; adv. com. Lubbock County Hosp. Dist. Bd., 1979; trustee, med. dir. All Am. Security Life Ins. Co., 1954-55; bd. dirs. Tex. Tb Assn., Pres., 1967-68; bd. dirs. Lubbock Cmty. Planning Coun., 1954-56, Inst. for Internat. R & D, Lubbock Area Found., 1983—, treas., 1985; chmn. adv. bd. Salvation Army, 1956-57 Fellow ACS, Am. Coll. Chest Physicians, Internat. Coll. Surgeons, Internat. Acad. Medicine, Southwetern Surg. Coll.; mem. AMA, So. Thoracic Surgery Assn., S.W. Surg. Conf., Am. Thoracic Soc., Tex. Trudeau Soc. (pres. 1959-60), Lubbock-Crosby-Garza County Med. Soc. (pres. 1984), Panhandle S-Plains Med. Soc., Tex. Med. Assn. (ho. of dels. 1979—), com. on health planning 1979-83, coun. on socioecons. 1983-90, chmn. 1985-90), Am. Cancer Soc. (dir. Tex. divsn. 1961-63), South Plains Heart Assn. (pres. 1957), Lubbock County Tb Assn. (pres. 1959-60, pres. South Plains Kidney Found. 1989—), Sigma Chi (Order Constantine 1994—), Rotary Internat. (pres. Lubbock 1980-81, dist. govs. rep. 1981-82, gov. nominee 1982-83, gov. 1983-84, inter. nat. assembly 1985). Home: Ste 1216 1500 Broadway Lubbock TX 79401 Office: 1500 Broadway Ste 1207 Lubbock TX 79401-3107 E-mail: jselbymd@cs.com.

SELBY, LELAND CLAY, lawyer; b. Granite City, Ill., July 4, 1944; s. William Edward and Agnes (Newell) S.; m. Diane Schryver, Aug. 20, 1966; children: Leland Clay, Timothy Schryver, Amanda Elizabeth. BA, U. Richmond, 1966; LLB, U. Va., 1969. Bar: Conn. 1969, N.Y. 1989. Assoc. Hirschberg, Pettengill & Strong, Greenwich, Conn., 1969-74; ptnr. Hirschberg, Pettengill, Strong & Nagle, 1974-78, Whitman & Ransom, Greenwich, 1978-93, Whitman Breed Abbott & Morgan, Greenwich, 1993-95; mem. Fogarty Cohen Selby & Nemiroff LLC, 1995—. Bd. dirs., v.p. Stamford (Conn.) Ctr. for Arts, 1989—; chmn. bd. govs. Greenwich Found. for Cmty. Gifts, 1980-90; pres. United Way of Greenwich, 1978-80; bd. dirs. Retirement Sys., Town of Greenwich, 1993-2001, Greenwich Symphony Orch., 1986-95; co-pres. Greenwich chpt. English-Speaking Union; bd. dirs. English-Speaking Union U.S. Named Greenwich Young Man of Yr., Greenwich Jaycees, 1974. Fellow Am. Coll. Trust and Estate Counsel; mem. ABA, Conn. Bar Assn., N.Y. State Bar Assn., Greenwich Bar Assn., Preston Mountain Club (sec. 1999—), Riverside Yacht Club, Va. Club of N.Y.C., Harpoon Club of Greenwich. Episcopalian. Avocations: fly fishing, sporting clays, hiking, reading, travel. Home: One Pinecrest Rd Riverside CT 06878 Office: Fogarty Cohen Selby & Nemiroff 88 Field Point Rd Greenwich CT 06836-2508

SELBY, NAOMI ARDEAN, women's health nurse, medical/surgical nurse; b. Duncan, Okla., Jan. 17, 1946; d. Orbie J.N. Sr. and Dorothy Naomi (Foster) S. BSN, Tex. Woman's U., 1969. Staff nurse, head nurse labor and delivery Meth. Med. Ctr., Dallas; cons., staff nurse ob-gyn. Southeastern Meth. Hosp., staff nurse, operating room; head nurse ob-gyn. Yukon Delta Regional Hosp./USPHS/Indian Health Svc., Bethel, Alaska; nurse mgr. cen. supply rm./oper. rm. Yukon Kuskokwim Delta Regional Hosp./USPHS Indian Health Svc. Mem. Assn. Operating Room Nurses. Home: Box 2830 Bethel AK 99559-2830

SELBY, ROBERT IRWIN, architect, educator; b. Evanston, Ill., Jan. 26, 1943; s. William Martin and Alice (Irwin) S.; m. Barbara Jean Kenaga, June 19, 1965; 1 child, Michael Scott. BArch, U. Ill., 1967, MArch, 1985. Registered architect, Ill. V.p. The Hawkweed Group Ltd., Chgo., Soldiers Grove and Osseo, Wis., 1971-84; prin. Robert I. Selby, Architect, Champaign, Ill., 1984—; asst. prof. architecture U. Ill., 1984-88, assoc. prof., 1988—, chmn. design divsn., 1988-93, coord. China program, 1988-91. Cons. housing rsch. and devel. program U. Ill., Urbana, 1985—; bd. editors U. Ill. Sch. Architecture jour., 1986-89, 96-97; chair exec. com. East St. Louis action rsch. project, 1995-96, 99-2001, sec. 1997-98, treas. 1998-99, dir., 2001-2002; presenter papers at internat. confs. on rebuilding cities and creating affordable housing. Author: (with others) The Hawkweed Passive Solar House Book, 1980; editor: (monograph) Urban Synergy: Process, Projects and Projections, 1993; contbr. chpt. to book and articles to profl. jours.; exhbn. of work (with E.N. Bacon) New Visions for Phila., 1993; featured soloist on trumpet and flugelhorn Parkland Big Band, 1998—. Served with USAFR, 1966-72. Mem. AIA (sec. Champaign-Urbana sect. 1985, pres. 1987, v.p., pres.-elect Ctrl. Ill. chpt. 1989, pres. 1990, pres.-elect AIA of Ill. 2001, bd. dirs. 1998—), Environ. Design Rsch. Assn. (chmn. 21st ann. internat. conf., co-editor conf. procs. 1988-90), Gargoyle Honor Soc., Alpha Rho Chi, Delta Upsilon (bd. dirs. U. Ill. 1991). Avocations: music, photography. Home: 909 W Union St Champaign IL 61821-3323 Office: U Ill Sch of Architecture 611 Taft Dr Champaign IL 61820 E-mail: r-selby@uiuc.edu.

SELBY, RONALD JAY, electrical engineer; b. Huntington, Ind., Nov. 9, 1952; s. Jerrod and Avonelle (Scott) S.; m. Janet Ann Hollis, Sept. 25, 1982; 1 child, Laura Elizabeth. BSEE, Purdue U. of Indpls., 1985; MSEE, Rochester Inst. Tech., 1991. ngr.-in-tng., Ind. Apprentice/journeyman electrician Internat. Brotherhood Elec. Workers, Indpls., 1976-84; devel. engr. mfg. R&D orgn. Eastman Kodak, Rochester, N.Y., 1985-92; project engr. Prologix Sys. Integration, Indpls., 1992-96; sr. engr. Ind. Automation, Noblesville, 1996, SELCO Engrng., Indpls., 1996—2001, Made2Manage Sys., Indianapolis, 2001—. Em. IEEE, Instrument Soc. Am., Ctrl. Ind. Bycycling Assn., Purdue U. at Indpls. Engrng. Sch. Alumni Assn. (bd. dirs. 1995). Avocations: bicycling, hiking, gardening. Home: 10901 Marquette Rd Zionsville IN 46077-9489 Office: Made2Manage Sys 9002 Purdue Rd Indianapolis IN 46268 E-mail: rjselby@iquest.net.

SELCHER, WAYNE A. political science educator; BA in Spanish magna cum laude, Lebanon Valley Coll., 1964; MA in L.Am. Studies, U. Fla., 1965, PhD in Polit. Sci., 1970. Tchr. Elizabethtown (Pa.) Coll., 1969—, chair dept. polit. sci., 1970-96, prof. internat. studies, 1984—, dir. internat. studies, 1983-98. Scholar-analyst U.S. Dept. State, 1981-86; exec. com. mem. Pa.-Bahia Brazil Com., Ptnrs. of the Ams., 1990-97; vis. rsch. prof. grad. program Sch. Adminstrn., Fed. U. Bahia, Salvador, Brazil, 1996. Author: The Afro-Asian Dimension of Brazilian Foreign Policy, 1956-72, 1974, Brazil's Multilateral Relations: Between First and Third Worlds, 1978; editor, contbr.: Brazil in the International System: The Rise of a Middle Power, 1981, Political Liberalization in Brazil: Dynamics, Dilemmas, and Future Prospects, 1986; contbr. chpts. to books and articles to profl. jours. Fulbright-Hays dissertation grantee, 1968, Howard Heinz Endowment grantee, 1984, Fulbright Lecturing grantee Coun. for the Internat. Exch. Scholars, 1989, Fulbright faculty rsch. abroad grantee, 1979, 90. Mem. Internat. Studies Assn., L.Am. Studies Assn., MIddle Atlantic Coun. L.Am. Studies, Brazilian Studies Assn. (exec. com. 1997-98). Office: Dept Polit Sci Elizabethtown Coll Elizabethtown PA 17022 E-mail: selchewa@etown.edu.

SELCHICK, JEFFREY MARK, arbitrator, judge; b. N.Y.C., July 22, 1951; s. Bernard and Irene Selchick; m. Cathy Lynn Persans, Jan. 26, 1974; children: Lauren Anne, Brian Bernard, Karen Ruth, Alyson Hope. BA, SUNY, Plattsburgh, 1971; JD, Union U., Albany, N.Y., 1975. Bar: N.Y. 1976, U.S. Dist. Ct. (no. dist.) N.Y. 1976, U.S. Supreme Ct. 1979. Asst. counsel SUNY, Albany,

1975-76, N.Y. State Gov.'s Office of Employee Rels., Albany, 1976-78, dep. counsel, dir. litigation, 1978-82; arbitrator, 1982—. Adj. prof. law Union U., Albany, 1989-92; instr. Cornell U., Ithaca, N.Y., 1982-85; cons. N.Y. State Labor-Mgmt. Inst., Albany, 1985—; judge Village of Menands, N.Y., 1986—. Mem. Am. Arbitration Assn., Nat. Acad. Arbitrators, N.Y. State Magistrate's Assn., N.Y. State Bar Assn. Avocations: jogging, competitive pistol shooting, writing. Home and Office: PO Box 11-280 Albany NY 12211-0280 E-mail: selchick@nycap.rr.com.

SELDEN, MARGERY JULIET STOMNE, music educator; b. Chgo., Sept. 05; d. Edwin and Nellie Juliet (Sorlie) Stomne; m. Paul Hubert Selden Jr., Dec. 30, 1950 (dec. July 28, 1973); children: Paul H. III, Margery Selden Johnson, Harold Frederick II, Charles B. II; m. Clem C. Williams Jr., July 22, 1989 (dec. Nov. 9, 1992). AB, Vassar Coll., 1946; MA, Yale U., 1948, PhD, 1951. Cert. vis. health aide, N.J.; lic. water safety instr. ARC. From instr. to asst. prof. to assoc. prof. Wayne State U., Detroit, 1950-65; assoc. prof. North Cen. Coll., Naperville, Ill., 1964-68; from assoc. prof. to prof. Coll. of St. Elizabeth, Convent Station, N.J., 1968-79; adj. prof. Passaic County Coll., Paterson, 1980-89, Kalamazoo Valley Coll., 1994—. Composer anthems; contbr. numerous articles to profl. publs. Vol. Upjohn Nursing Home. Winner Patriotic Song Contest, Mil. Order of World Wars, 1976; recipient Cert. of Merit, Hoboken, N.J., 1981, Composer award Fisher Found., 1996. Mem.: Am. Guild Organists, Am. Musicol. Soc., Nat. Assn. Composers USA, Nat. Guild Piano Tchrs., Music Tchrs. Nat. Assn., Sons of Norway (lodge pianist), Phi Beta Kappa, Sigma Alpha Iota. Republican. Lutheran. Avocations: swimming, square dancing. Home: 6710 Evergreen St Portage MI 49024-3220

SELDEN, ROBERT WENTWORTH, physicist, science advisor; b. Phoenix, Aug. 11, 1936; s. Edward English and Mary Priscilla (Calder) S.; m. Mary Tania Hudd, June 1958 (div. 1976); 1 child, Ian Scott; m. Marjorie Anne Harmon, Feb. 20, 1977; children: Brock, Thane, Shawna, Kirsten. BA in Physics cum laude, Pomona Coll., 1958; MS in Physics, U. Wis., 1960, PhD in Physics, 1964. Rsch. assoc. Lawrence Livermore (Calif.) Nat. Lab., 1965-67, staff mem., 1967-73, group leader, 1973-78, asst. assoc. dir., 1978-80; div. leader applied theoretical physics Los Alamos (N.Mex.) Nat. Lab., 1980-83, dep. assoc. dir. strategic def. rsch., 1983-84, assoc. dir. theoretical and computational physics, 1984-86, dir. Ctr. for Nat. Securities Studies, 1986-88, assoc. dir. for lab. devel., 1991-94; chief scientist USAF, Washington, 1988-91, panel chmn. sci. adv. bd., 1984-88, 91-96, chmn. sci. adv. bd., 1999—; cons. Los Alamos, 1994—. Chmn. study group on reactor materials and nuclear explosives U.S. Dept. Energy, 1976-78; mem. ballistic missile def. techs. adv. panel U.S. Congress Office Tech. Assessment, 1984-85, The Pres.'s Defensive Tech. Study Team, Washington, 1983; strategic adv. group U.S. Strategic Command, 1996—; jt. adv. com. Sec. Def., Sec. Energy, 1996—. Editor Rsch. Jour. Lawrence Livermore Nat. Lab., 1976-77; contbr. sci. and tech. papers to profl. jours. Pres. Livermore Cultural Arts Coun., 1969-72; chmn. Livermore Sister City Orgn., 1973, Planning Commn. City of Livermore, 1971-76; bd. dirs. Orch. of Santa Fe, 1986-88. Capt. U.S. Army, 1964-67. Grad. fellow Edward John Noble Found., 1958-62; recipient Theodore von Karman award for outstanding contbn. to def. sci., 1989, medal for outstanding pub. svc. U.S. Sec. Def., 1996; decorated for exceptional civilian svc. USAF, 1988, 91, 96. Mem. AAAS, Am. Phys. Soc., N.Y. Acad. Sci., Air Force Assn. Avocations: tennis, hiking, music. Office: 624 La Bajada Los Alamos NM 87544-3805 E-mail: selden@cybermesa.com.

SELDES, MARIAN, actress; b. N.Y.C. d. Gilbert and Alice (Hall) S.; m. Julian Claman, Nov. 3, 1953 (div.); 1 child, Katharine; m. Garson Kanin, June 19, 1990 (dec. Mar. 1999). Grad., The Dalton Sch., N.Y.C., 1945, Neighborhood Playhouse, 1947; DHL, Emerson Coll., 1979. Faculty drama and dance divsn. Juilliard Sch. Lincoln Center, N.Y.C., 1969-91. Bd. dirs. The Acting Co. Appeared with Cambridge (Mass.) Summer Theatre, 1945, Boston Summer Theatre, 1946, St. Michael's Playhouse, Winooski, Vt., 1947-48, Bermudiana Theatre, Hamilton, Bermuda, 1951, Elitch Gardens Theatre, Denver, 1953, The Cretan Woman, Lysistrata, 1955 (actress/artist-in residence Stanford U.); Broadway appearances include Medea, 1947, Crime and Punishment, 1948, That Lady, 1949, Tower Beyond Tragedy, 1950, The High Ground, 1951, Come of Age, 1952, Ondine, 1954, The Chalk Garden, 1955, The Wall, 1960, A Gift of Time, 1962, The Milk Train Doesn't Stop Here Any More, 1964, Tiny Alice, 1965, A Delicate Balance, 1967 (Tony award for best supporting actress), Before You Go, 1968, Father's Day, 1971 (Drama Desk award), Mendicants of Evening (Martha Graham Co.), 1973, Equus, 1974-77, The Merchant, 1977, Deathtrap, 1978, Ivanov (Drama Desk nomination), 1997, Ring Around the Moon, 1999, 45 Seconds from Broadway, 2001; off-Broadway appearances include Diff'rent, 1961, The Ginger Man, 1963 (Obie award), All Women Are One, 1964, Juana LaLoca, 1965, Three Sisters, 1969, Am. Shakespeare Festival, Stratford, Conn., Mercy Street at Am. Place Theater, N.Y.C., 1969, Isadora Duncan, 1976 (Obie award), Painting Churches, 1983, 84 (Outer Critics Circle award 1984), Other People, Berkshire Theatre Festival, 1969, The Celebration, Hedgerow Theater, Pa., 1971, Richard III, N.Y. Shakespeare Festival, 1983, Remember Me, Lakewood Theatre, Skowhegan, Maine, Gertrude Stein and a Companion, White Barn Theatre, Westport, Conn., 1985, Lucile Lortel Theatre, N.Y.C., 1986, Richard II, N.Y. Shakespeare Festival, 1987, The Milk Train Doesn't Stop Here Anymore, WPA Theatre, N.Y.C., 1987, Happy Ending, Bristol (Pa.) Riverside Theatre, 1988, Annie 2 John F. Kennedy Ctr., Washington, 1989-90, Goodspeed Opera House, Chester, Conn., 1990, A Bright Room Called Day, N.Y. Shakespeare Festival, 1991, Three Tall Women, River Arts, Woodstock, N.Y., 1994, Another Time, Am. Jewish Theatre, 1993, Breaking the Code, Berkshire Theatre Festival, 1993, Three Tall Women, Vineyard Theatre, N.Y.C., 1994, Promenade Theatre, 1994-95, nat. tour, 1995-96, Boys From Syracuse, City Ctr., N.Y.C., 1997, Dead End: Williamstown, 1997, Dear Liar, Irish Repertory Theater, 1999, The Matchmaker: Williamstown, 1998, Tongue of a Bird, Mark Taper Forum, 1998, Sail Away, Carnegie Hall, 1999, Mad About The Boy, Carnegie Hall, 1999, The Torch-Bearers, 2000, Ancestral Voices, 2000, The Skin at our Teeth, 2000, Williamstown, The Play About the Baby, Alley Theatre, Houston, 2000; engaged in nat. tour Medea, 1947; The Butterfly Collection, Playwrights Horizon, NY, 2000, The MAY About the Baby, NY, 2001, Play Yourself, 2002; U.S. entry Berlin Festival, 1951, nat. tour Three Tall Women, 1995-96; film appearances include The Greatest Story Ever Told, Gertrude Stein and a Companion, 1988, In a Pig's Eye, 1988, The Gun in Betty Lou's Handbag, 1992, Tom and Huck, 1995, Digging to China, 1997, Home Alone 3, 1997, Affliction, 1997, Celebrity, 1998, The Haunting, 1999, Town and Country, 1999, Duets, 1999, Hollywood Ending, 2002; (TV series) Good and Evil, 1991, Murphy Brown, 1992, Truman, 1995, Cosby, 1996, 98, Trinity, 1998, The Others, 2000; (miniseries) If These Walls Could Talk 2, 2000, Nero Wolfe, 2001 (A&E), The Education of Max Bickford, 2002; also appeared on CBS Radio Mystery Theater, 1976-81, Theatre Guild on The Air, One Life to Live, 1998, Remember WENN, 1999; author: The Bright Lights, 1978, Time Together, 1981. Bd. dirs. Neighborhood Playhouse, The Acting Co., Nat. Repertory Theatre, Theatre Hall of Fame, 1996. Winner Ovation award Theater L.A. for Three Tall Women, 1996, Conn. Critics award for Three Tall Women, 1996; recipient Madge Kennedy/Sidney Kingsley award Dramatists Guild Fund, 2000, Obie award for sustained achievement. Mem. Players Club, Century Assn. Home: 210 Central Park S Apt 19D New York NY 10019-1426

SELDNER, BETTY JANE, environmental engineer, consultant, aerospace company executive; b. Balt., Dec. 11, 1923; d. David D. and Miriam M. (Mendes) Miller; m. Warren E. Gray, June 20, 1945 (div. 1965); children: Patricia, Deborah; m. Alvin Seldner, Nov. 15, 1965; children: Jack, Barbara. BA in Journalism, Calif. State U., Northridge, 1975, MA in Communications, 1977. Dir. pub. info. United Way, Van Nuys, Calif., 1958-63, dir. edn. Los Angeles, 1963-68; dir. pub. relations, fin. San Fernando Valley Girl Scout Council, Reseda, Calif., 1968-73; asst. dir. pub. info. Calif. State U., Northridge, 1973-75; dir. environ. mgmt. HR Textron Corp., Valencia, Calif., 1975-87; environ. engr. Northrop Aircraft, Hawthorne, 1987-88, EMCON Assocs., Burbank, 1988-92, Atkins Environ., 1992-93, Seldner Environ., Valencia, Calif., 1993—; pres. Seldner Environ. Svcs., 1993—. Author non-fiction. Named Woman of Yr., Santa City C. of C. and vol. orgns., 2000. Mem. Santa Clarita Valley Environ. Mgrs. Soc. (chmn. bd. dirs. 1984), San Fernando Valley Round Table (pres. 1971-72), Hazardous Materials Mgrs.' Assn., Zonta Internat., Valencia Indsl. Assn. (environ. chair). Republican. Jewish. Avocation: sailing. E-mail: Betty13ix@attbi.com.

SELES, MONICA, professional tennis player; b. Novi Sad, Yugoslavia, Dec. 2, 1973; came to U.S., 1986; d. Karolj and Esther Seles. Profl. tennis player, 1989—. Winner Houston, 1989, 91, 92, Oakland, 1990, 92, L.A., 1990, 91, Tampa, 1990, 91, U.S. Hardcourts, 1990, Lipton, 1990, 91, Roland Garros, 1990, 91, 92, Italian Open, 1990, German Open, 1990, French Open, 1990, 91, 92, Va. Slims, 1990, 91, 92, Phila., 1991, Milan, 1991, Tokyo Nichirie, 1991, 92, U.S. Open, 1991, 92, Australian Open, 1991, 92, 93, 96, Italian Open Doubles (with Kelesi) 1990, (with Capriati) 1991, (with Sukova), 1992, Essen, 1992, Indian Wells, 1992, Barcelona, 1992, Chgo., 1993, Can. Open, 1995, 96, Amelia Island, 1999; finalist Dallas, 1989, Brighton, 1989, Palm Springs, 1991, U.S. Hardcourts, 1991, Hamburg, 1991, Italian Open, 1991, San Diego, 1991, Oakland, 1991, Wimbledon, 1992, Italian Open, 1992, L.A., 1992, Can. Open, 1992, Paris indoors, 1993, U.S. Open, 1995, Can. Open, 1999, Tokyo Cup, 1999; singles semifinalist , New Orleans, 1988, Roland Garros, Washington, 1989, European indoors, 1989, Washington, 1990, Australian Open, 1999, French Open, 1999, New Haven Open, 1999; doubles semifinalist (with A. Smith) Australian Open, 1991, (with Nagelsen), Chgo., 1993; named Yugoslavia's sportwoman of yr., 1985, World #1 ranked player, 1991, 92, #3 players in terms of career titles as a teenager, 1993; ranked 9th, 1999; recipient 1990 Rado Topspin award, Ted Tinling Diamond award Va. Slims, 1990, Grand Slam Title, 1996; named Tennis Mag./Rolex Watch Female Rookie of Yr., 1989, World Champion, 1991, 92, Comeback Player of Yr. Tennis mag., 1995, Profl. Female Athlete by Yr., 1995. Achievements include 3rd player in the Open-era to capture the Australian and Roland Garros in same calendar year; named youngest #1 ranked player in tennis history for women and men at 17 years, 3 months, 9 days; has won a total of 44 Singles events throughout professional tennis career. Office: care Internat Mgmt Group 1 Erieview Plz Cleveland OH 44114-1715*

SELESKY, DONALD BRYANT, software developer; b. Englewood, N.J., Jan. 7, 1948; s. Harold Francis and Bernice Evelyn (Deacon) S.; m. Janet Borna (div.); m. Sandy Lynn Berke, Sept. 11, 1983. BA in Econ., Cornell U., 1970; MBA in Mktg., Columbia U., 1977; MS in Computer Sci., Boston U., 1990. Sr. Arthur Andersen & Co., N.Y.C., 1971-75; bus. sys. analyst Nabisco Inc., East Hanover, N.J., 1975-77; cons., 1977-81, 82-83; mgr. data processing Kings Dept. Stores, Watertown, Mass., 1981-82; sys. analyst The Analytical Scis. Corp., Reading, 1983-84; prin. software engr. Lotus Devel. Corp., Cambridge, 1984-86; prin. Ksoft, Westford, 1986—. Sr. software engr. Kurzweil Applied Intelligence, Waltham, Mass., 1995-98, product mgr., 1997-98; patentee in field. Author (software) @BASE, 1987; co-author (software) Look and Link, 1988, Monarch, 1991, Monarch for Windows, 1994; patentee in field. Mem. Nashoba Valley Photo Club, Appalachian Mountain Club. Avocations: backpacking, photography, kayaking, shooting, biking. Home and Office: Ksoft 15 Bradley Ln Westford MA 01886-2544

SELESNICK, SAMUEL HYMAN, otolaryngologist; b. Flemington, N.J. MD, NYU, 1985. Diplomate Am. Bd. Otolaryngology. Intern St. Vincent's Hosp., N.Y.C., 1985-86, resident in surgery, 1986-87; resident in otolaryngology Manhattan EET Hosp., 1987-90; fellow in neurotology U. Calif., San Francisco, 1990-91; chief neurotology Manhattan EET Hosp., 1991—; mem. staff Lenox Hill Hosp., N.Y.C., Meml. Sloan-Kettering Cancer Ctr., N.Y.C.; prof. otorhinolaryngology Cornell U., vice chmn. dept. otorhinolaryngology Weill Coll. Medicine. Fellow ACS; mem. AMA, Am. Acad. Otolaryngology/Head and Neck Surgery, Am. Otological Soc., Med. Soc. State N.Y., Triological Soc., Am. Neurotology Soc. Office: Starr 541 Dept Oto 525 E 68th St New York NY 10021-4870

SELETZ, JULES MORTIMOR, surgeon; b. Chgo., 1930; BA in Biology, Va. Mil. Inst., 1953; MD, U. Health Scis., Chgo., 1958. Diplomate Am. Bd. Surgery, FACS. Intern, then resident in gen. surgery Boston City Hosp., 1958-63, mem. staff, 1963-74; mem. faculty Sch. Medicine Tufts U., 1963-82; mem. staff Newton Weslesley Hosp., 1963-82; mil. surgeon U.S. Army, 1982-94; mem. staff Keller Army Cmty. Hosp., West Point, N.Y., 1990-94; physician surveyor Joint Com. Accreditation Healthcare Orng., 1994-01. Author mystery/med. thriller novels and hist. fiction. Home: PO Box 1087 Lincoln NH 03251-1087 E-mail: jseletz@earthlink.net.

SELF, DIANNE LOGAN, communications company executive; b. Chattanooga, June 18, 1949; d. James N. and Kathryn (Bartlett) Logan; m. Mark E. Self, May 9, 1980; children: Patricia Bartlett, Marcile Christine. Student, U. Tenn., Nashville, 1969-70. Br. mgr. Internat. Tel. & Tel., Beaumont, Tex., 1978-83; cons., officer Self & Assocs., Inc., Euless, 1985—; pres. Hicom, Inc., Colleyville, 1993—, S&A Equip., Euless, 1992—. Vol. Freedom Ride Found., 1987—; supporter Christian Children's Fund. Mem. NAFE, Nat. Small Bus. United, Nat. Fedn. Ind. Bus., Dallas C. of C. Avocations: water painting, writing, reading, horseback riding. Home: 1805 Arthur Dr Hurst TX 76054 Office: Hicom Inc 1114 S Airport Cir Ste 130 Euless TX 76040-6842 E-mail: sna7900@aol.com, dianne@snaequipment.com

SELF, MADISON ALLEN, finance company executive; b. Ozawkie, Kans., June 30, 1921; s. Benjamin B. and Margaret E. (Allen) S.; m. Lila M. Reetz, Sept. 1, 1943; 1 son, Murray A. BS in Chem. Engring, U. Kans., 1943. Engr. York Corp., 1943-44; salesman and researcher Sharples Chems., Inc., 1944-47; with Bee Chem. Co., Lansing, Ill., 1947-84, chmn. bd., chief exec. officer, until 1984; pres. Allen Fin., Inc., 1984—; chmn. bd. dirs. Tioga Internat., Inc., 1989-99. Life trustee Ill. Inst. Tech. Mem. Chief Exec. Orgn., World Pres.'s Orgn., Hinsdale Golf Club. Office: Allen Fin Inc 907 N Elm St Ste 302 Hinsdale IL 60521-3645 E-mail: maself@voyager.net.

SELF, MARK EDWARD, communications consultant; b. Tyler, Tex., Dec. 6, 1955; s. Edward and Ruby (Rogers) S.; m. Dianne Logan; children: Patricia Bartlett, Marcile Christine. Student, Tenn. Tech. Sch., 1973-76. Gen. mgr. Gulf Telephone Inc., Beaumont, Tex., 1980-82; gen. sales mgr. CSC Telephone Inc., Tyler, 1982-83; v.p. sales Teleci Inc., Irving, Tex., 1983-85; cons. Self & Assocs., Inc., Grapevine, Tex., 1985—; pres. S&A Equipment Co., 1990—; v.p. mktg. Hicom, Inc., Euless, Tex., 1994—. Fundraiser Freedom Ride Found., Dallas, 1987. Named Outstanding Young Men of Am., 1985. Mem. Am. Hotel and Motel Assn., Nat. Office Machine Dealer Assn., Nat. Fedn. Ind. Bus., Dallas C. of C., Masons. Avocations: fishing, hunting, woodworking. Home: 3442 Spring Willow Dr Grapevine TX 76051-6516 Office: Self & Assocs 1114 S Airport Cir Ste 130 Euless TX 76040-6842 E-mail: sna7900@aol.com.

SELFE, EDWARD MILTON, lawyer; b. St. Paul, Sept. 26, 1921; s. Edward Milton and Eleanor (Moen) S.; m. Rena Hill McMurry, July 10, 1950 (div. Oct. 1979); children: Murry, Edward, James; m. Jane Comer Bowron, Dec. 31, 1979. BA, Presbyn. Coll., Clinton, S.C., 1943; LLB, U. Va., 1950. Bar: N.Y., Va., Ala. Asst. prof. law Law Sch., U. Va., Charlottesville, 1950-51; assoc. Shearman & Sterling, N.Y.C., 1951-52, Bradley Arant Rose White, Birmingham, Ala., 1952-57, ptnr., 1957-2000, of counsel, 2000—; vice chmn. Secor Bank, 1988-91, gen. counsel, 1991-93. Chmn. Birmingham-Jefferson County Transit Authority, 1972-82. Served to capt., inf. U.S. Army, 1943-47, ETO. Decorated Silver Star, Bronze Star (V), Purple Heart. Fellow Am. Coll. Tax Counsel; mem. ABA, Ala. Bar Assn., Birmingham Bar Assn. Democrat. Avocation: tennis (ranked 4th nationally in men's singles-age 80, 2002). Home: 84 Arlington Crest 2600 Arlington Ave S Birmingham AL 35205-4167 Office: Bradley Arant Rose & White One Federal Pl 1819 Fifth Ave N Birmingham AL 35203-2104

SELFRIDGE, CALVIN, lawyer; b. Winnetka, Ill., Dec. 20, 1933; s. Calvin Frederick and Violet Luella (Bradley) S. BA, Northwestern U., 1956; JD, U. Chgo., 1960. Bar: Ill. 1961. Trust officer Continental Ill. Nat. Bank & Trust Co., Chgo., 1961-71; pvt. practice, 1972-76 and from 79; mem. Howington, Elworth, Osswald & Hough, 1976-79; pres., dir. Northwest Newspapers Corp., from 1977, Des Plaines (Ill.) Pub. Co., 1977-90. Pres., bd. dirs. Scholarship Fund Found., 1965-99; trustee, pres. Lawrence Hall Youth Svcs., 1982—; trustee, vice-chmn. Ill. Soc. Colonial Wars. With AUS, 1959. Mem. Chgo., Am., Ill. Bar Assn., Law Club Chgo., Legal Club Chgo., Chi Psi, Phi Delta Phi, Attic Club (gov., past pres.), Univ. Club, Racquet Club (Chgo.), Balboa Club (Mazatlan, Mex.), Indian Hill Country Club (Winnetka, Ill.), Mid Day Club (Chgo.). Republican. Congregationalist. Home: Chicago, Ill. Died May 29, 2000.

SELFRIDGE, GEORGE DEVER, retired dentist, retired naval officer; b. Pitman, N.J., Sept. 24, 1924; s. William John and Edith (Gorman) S.; m. Ruth Motisher, 1948; children: Pamela Ruth, Kimberly Dawn, Cheryl Beth. Student, Gettysburg Coll., 1942-43, Muhlenburg Coll., 1943-45; DDS, U. Buffalo, 1947; MA, George Washington U., 1974. Commd. lt. (j.g.) USN, 1948, advanced through grades to rear adm., 1973; intern Naval Dental Sch., Bethesda, Md., 1948-49, Naval Hosp., St. Albans, N.Y., 1949-50; asst. dental officer U.S.S. Midway, 1949-51; with USN, 1951-64; sr. dental officer U.S.S. Randolph, 1958-60, U.S.S. Cadmus, 1964-65, U.S.S. Vulcan, 1965-66, Svc. Force, 1964-66, Submarine Force, Atlantic Fleet, 1967-69; from asst. dir. grad. edn. to comdg. officer Navy Grad. Dental Sch., Bethesda, 1969-76; exec. officer Norfolk (Va.) Navy Dental Clinic, 1972-73; ret. USN, 1976; dean Dental Sch., Washington U., St. Louis, 1976-86; dir. dental services Barnes Hosp., 1976-87, Children's Hosp., St. Louis, 1976-87; exec. dir. Am. Bd. Orthodontics, 1986-97; ret., 1998. Adv. bd. VA Hosp., St. Louis, 1977-79; mem. exec. coun. Cen. Region Testing Svc., 1976-86; adv. com. St. Louis Jr. Coll. Dist., 1976-86. Contbr. articles to med. jours. Decorated Legion of Merit; recipient commendation medals, Greater St. Louis Gold Medallion award, 1995, Spl. Recognition award Am. Bd. Orthopedics, 1996. Mem. ADA, Am. Coll. Dentists, Internat. Coll. Coll. Dentists (dep. registrar, sec. U.S. sect.), Assn. Mil. Surgeons U.S., Omicron Kappa Upsilon. Republican. Home: 14545 Foxham Ct Chesterfield MO 63017-5620

SELIG, KARL-LUDWIG, language and literature educator; b. Wiesbaden, Germany, Aug. 14, 1926; naturalized, 1948; s. Lucian and Erna (Reiss) S. *Karl-Luding Selig came to the USA during WWII and had to learn English. He was given two Horatio Alger Books, Benjamin Franklin's Poor Richard's Almanac and two dictionaries. In this spirit and to express his gratitude for all the hospitality he received and the opportunities made possible, he is now involved in a new enterprise and "hobby." He gives dictionaries to highly motivated immigrants from many countries and a global background; language is pivotal to hold and bind our country.* BA, Ohio State U., 1946, MA, 1947; postgrad., U. Rome, Italy, 1949-50; PhD, U. Tex., 1955. Asst. prof. Romance langs. and lit. Johns Hopkins U., Balt., 1954-58; assoc. prof. U. N.C., Chapel Hill, 1958-61, U. Minn., Mpls., 1961-63; vis. prof. U. Tex., Austin, 1963-64, prof. Romance langs. and lit., 1964-65; Hinchliff prof. Spanish lit. Cornell U., Ithaca, N.Y., 1965-69, dir. grad. studies in Romance lit., 1966-69; prof. Spanish lit. Columbia U., N.Y.C., 1969—. Brown Found. fellow, vis. prof. Spanish and comparative lit. U. of the South, Sewanee, Tenn., 1990; vis. prof. U. Munich, 1963-64, U. Berlin, 1967; vis. prof. U. Greifswald, Germany, 1991-96, hon. prof., 1996—; cons. prof. Ohio State U., Columbus, 1967-69; vis. lectr. U. Zulia, Maracaibo, Venezuela, 1968; dir. summer seminar NEH, 1975, cons., 1975-77; vis. scholar Ga. U. Sys., 1977; vis. rsch. scholar Fondation Hardt, Vandoeuvres, Switzerland, 1959, Herzog August Bibliothek Wolfenbüttel, Fed. Repubic Germany, 1979—; mem. com. grants-in-aid Am. Coun. Learned Soc., 1969-73; chmn. Comparative Lit. Program and Colloquia, Columbia Coll., 1976-88. *Karl- Ludwig Selig earned a varsity "O" letter from Ohio State in 1946. A scull was named after him by Columbia College Crew. Columbia College students established a scholarship in his name.* Author: The Library of Vincencio Juan de Lastanosa, Patron of Gracián, Geneva, 1960, Studies on Alciato in Spain, 1990, Studies on Cervantes, 1993; also numerous articles, revs.; editor: (Thomas Blundeville) of Councils and Counselors, 1963, (with A. G. Hatcher) Studia Philologica et Litteraria in Honorem L. Spitzer, 1958, (with J. E. Keller) Essays in Honor of N. B. Adams, 1966, (with R. Brinkmann) Theatrum Europaeum. Festschrift E. M. Szarota, 1982, (with S. Neumeister) Theatrum Mundi Hispanicum, 1986, (with R. Somerville) Florilegium Columbianum: Essays in Honor of Paul Oskar Kristeller, 1987, (with E. Sears) The Verbal and the Visual: Essays in Honor of William Sebastian Heckscher, 1990, Polyanthea Essays on Art and Literature in Honor of William Sebastian Heckscher, 1993, Mira de Amescua, La hija de Carlos Quinto, 2002; assoc. editor Modern Lang. Notes, 1955-58; mng. editor Romance Notes, 1959-61; editor: U. N.C. Studies in Comparative Lit, 1959-61, Bull. Comediantes, 1959-64, assoc. editor 1964-68, mem. editl. bd., 1979-88; co-editor Yearbook of Comparative Lit., Vol. IX, 1960; editorial bd. Colección Támesis, London, 1962-79, Romanic Rev., 1969-89, Teaching Lang. Through Lit, 1978-88; assoc. editor Hispania, 1969-74, Ky. Romance Quar, 1973-85; gen. editor Revista Hispánica Moderna, 1971-86; mem. nat. adv. bd. MLA Internat. Bibliography, 1978-88; editorial bd. Yale Italian Studies, 1976-80. Recipient Mark Van Doren award Columbia, 1974, spl. citation Columbia Coll. Alumni Assn., 1991, Festschrift, Über Texte, 1997; fellow Fulbright Found., Rome, 1949-50, Newberry Libr., 1958, Folger Shakespeare Libr., 1959, 63, Belgian Am. Ednl. Found., 1961, 62; sr. fellow Mediaeval and Renaissance Inst. Duke U., 1978; Fulbright rsch. scholar Utrecht, The Netherlands, 1958-59; DAAD rsch. grantee, 1979; Karl-Ludwig Selig scholarship named in his honor, Columbia Coll., 2001. Mem. MLA (sec., then chmn. Romance sect. 1965-66, chmn. comparative lit. 1973, James Russell Lowell prize com. 1989-90, chmn. 1990), Internat. Assn. Hispanists, Am. Comparative Lit. Assn., Coll. Art Assn., Acad. Lit. Studies, Am. Friends Herzog August Bibliothek (bd. dirs. 1996—), Phi Beta Kappa (hon.). Home: 30 E 37th St Apt 8J New York NY 10016-3054

SELIG, MARTHA KEISER, social work consultant; b. N.Y.C., Dec. 25, 1912; D. Jacob H. and Sadie (Hammer) Keiser; B.A., Hunter Coll., N.Y.C., 1932; M.S., CCNY, 1933; postgrad. Columbia U., 1933-38; diploma N.Y. Sch. Social Work, 1939; m. Kalman Selig, Mar. 23, 1935; children— Judith Selig Rubenstein, Elaine Selig Gould. Clin. psychologist Edn. Clinic, CCNY, 1932-44; exec. dir. Jewish Community Services L.I., 1944-46; exec. dir. community services Fedn. Jewish Philanthropies N.Y., 1946-74; dir. redevel.-Jewish Bd. Family Svcs., ret.; vis. prof. Adelphia U., Garden City, N.Y., also Jewish Theol. Sem., N.Y.C., 1974—; guest lectr. Columbia U., Wurzweiler Sch. Social Work, Hunter Coll. Sch. Social Work, 1974-79; cons. health and welfare agys. and founds., 1974—; bd. dirs. Martha K. Selig Ednl. Inst. Jewish Bd. Family & Children's Svcs.; exec. bd. Am. Jewish Com.; bd. dirs. Council Vol. Child Care Agys. N.Y.C., Hebrew Arts Sch., Nat. Found. for Jewish Culture; mem. Mayor's Commn. on Child Care, N.Y. State Adv. Commn. on Welfare, N.Y. State Gov.'s Commn. on Alcohol and Drug Abuse N.Y.C. Commn. on Mental Health. Recipient Naomi Lehman Meml. award, 1960, Samuel W. and Rose Hurowitz award Fedn. Jewish Philanthropies N.Y., 1975; named to Hunter Coll. Hall of Fame, 1976; also ednl. assn. CCNY. Mem. Nat. Assn. Social Workers, Acad. Cert. Social Workers, Nat. Conf. Jewish Communal Service (past pres.). Author papers in field. Home: 22 E 88th St New York NY 10128-0502

SELIG, MICHAEL EMIL, communications educator; b. Galveston, Tex., Nov. 5, 1954; s. Oury Levy and Miraim Claire (Pozmantier) S.; m. Michelle Graham, May 28, 1989. BS, U. Tex., 1977, MA, 1980; PhD, Northwestern U., 1983. Visiting asst. prof. U. Vt., Burlington, 1983-86; asst. prof. Emerson Coll., Boston, 1986-91, assoc. prof., 1991—; dir. film program, 1992-93, 94—. Editor (acad. jour.) Jour. Film and video, 1987-92, book rev. editor, 1992-94; assoc. editor Mass. Jour. Comms., 1992—; contbr. articles to comms. publs. Mem. Soc. for Cinema Studies, Univ. Film and Video Assn. (bd. dirs. 1987-92). Office: Emerson Coll 120 Boylston St Boston MA 02116-4624

SELIG, OURY LEVY, port financial consultant; b. Galveston, Tex., Sept. 24, 1924; s. Andrew Lionel and Freda (Schreiber) S.; m. Miriam Claire Pozmantier, Aug. 22, 1948; children: Michael, Debra, Madeline, James. BBA, U. Tex., 1949, postgrad., 1950, U. Houston, 1953-56. Asst. bus. adminstr. of hosp. U. Tex. Med. Br., Galveston, 1952-54; acct. Port of Galveston, 1954-57, asst. auditor, 1957-64, asst. to gen. mgr., 1964-69, dir. fin. and adminstrn., 1966-74, dep. exec. dir., 1974-88; lectr. in marine transp. Tex. A&M U., Galveston, 1998-2000. Author: (with E. Kalketenidou) Public Port Financing in the United States, 1994, An Analysis of U.S. Public Port Profitability and Self-Sufficiency 1985-1994, 1997. Life mem. Bay Area coun. Boy Scouts Am., Galveston, 1963—; v.p. Galveston County Jewish Welfare Assn., 1982-84; trustee Galveston Wharves, 1994-97. Sgt. USAF, 1943-46. Recipient Nehemiah Gitelson award, Alpha Epsilon Pi, 1948, Silver Beaver award Boy Scouts Am., 1968, Shofar award, Boy Scouts Am., 1968, Disting. Service award, Galveston Jaycees, 1968. Mem. Am. Assn. Port Auths. (hon. life, chmn. fin. com. 1972-76, chmn. risk mgmt. com. 1981-85, vice chmn. task force on tax reform 1985-86, Important Svc. award 1987), Tex. Water Conservation Assn. (life, pres. 1979-80), Galveston Hist. Found., Friars Club. Democrat. Avocations: gardening, reading. Home and Office: 11 Colony Park Cir Galveston TX 77551-1737 E-mail: olselig@wt.net.

SELIG, PHYLLIS SIMS, retired architect; b. Topeka, Nov. 16, 1931; d. Willis Nolan and Victoria Clarinda (Oakley) Sims; m. James Richard Selig, Mar. 31, 1957; children: Lin Ann, Susan Nan, Sarah Jo. BS in Architecture, U. Kans., 1956. Realtor Assoc. Realty, Lawrence, Kans., 1965-70; v.p. finance and housing Alpha Phi Internat. Fraternity, Inc., Evanston, Ill., 1968-74, chief exec. officer, internat. pres., 1974-78, trustee, 1978-80; sr. engr. tech. Nebr. Pub. Power, Columbus, 1980-86, staff architect, 1986-89, archtl. supr., 1989-96; retired, 1996. Republican. Lutheran. Avocations: wood working, painting.

SELIG, TODD IRVING, municipal official; b. Springfield, Mass., June 7, 1969; s. Steven David and Margaret Ann S. AB, Syracuse U., 1991; MPA, U. N.H., Durham, 1994. Intern/asst. town mgr. Town of Raymond, N.H., 1993-94; asst. to city mgr. City of Laconia, 1994; town adminstr. Town of New Boston, N.H., 1994-98; bus. adminstr. Hopkinton (N.H.) Sch. Dist., 1998-2001; town adminstr. Town of Durham, N.H., 2001—. Mem. Internat. City/County Mgmt. Assn., N.H. Mcpl. Mgmt. Assn., Phi Beta Kappa. Avocation, stock market. Home: 44 Oshea Ln Laconia NH 03246-3022 Office: Town of Durham 15 Newmarket Rd Durham NH 03824

SELIG, WILLIAM GEORGE, university official; b. Prince Rupert, B.C., Can., Sept. 25, 1938; s. George Oliver Selig and Minerva Junuetta (Brand) Goodale; m. Judith Margaret Sprague, June 20, 1964; children: Cheryl, Cynthia. BA, Cen. Washington State Coll., 1961, MA, 1968; CAGS, U. Mass., 1972, EdD, 1973. Tchr. Sharon (Mass.) High Sch., 1963-64, Hydaburg (Alaska) Grade Sch., 1964-65, W. Puyallup (Wash.) Jr. High Sch., 1966-69; dir. spl. edn. Northampton (Mass.) Schs., 1969-73, 1974-76; asst. prof. Westfield (Mass.) State Coll., 1973; dir. pupil svcs. Longmeadow (Mass.) Pub. Schs., 1976-80; prof. Regent U., Virginia Beach, Va., 1980-83, dean, prof., 1984-89, provost, 1989-2000; Disting. prof. ednl. leadership, 2000—. Bd. dirs. Set Net, Virginia Beach; pres. Motivational Teaching Systems, Inc.; spl. edn. adv. bd. dirs. Virginia Beach Pub. Schs.; bd. trustees Klingberg Family Ctrs., New Britain, Conn., 1991—. Author: Training for Triumph, 1984, Loving Our Differences, 1989, Handbook of Individualized Strategies for Classroom Discipline, 1995. Episcopalian. Avocations: skiing, tennis. Office: Regent University 1000 Regent University Dr Virginia Beach VA 23464-9800 E-mail: georsel@regent.edu.

SELIG, ZACHARY JAY, artist, writer; b. Seguin, Tex., Nov. 24, 1949; s. Marvin Arthur Selig; children: N/A N/A, N/A N/A. Student, U. of the Ams., Mexico City, Mexico, 1967, Transylvania Coll., 1968, U. Houston, 1969, The Art Students League N.Y., 1969—73, Parsons Sch. Design, 1970—71, Painting Studio of Bridget Bates Tichernor, Mexico City, Mexico, 1970—74, L'Ecole Des Beux Arts, Paris, 1991—92. Cert. interior design/fashion design. Pres. ZJS Interiors, N.Y.C., 1970—75; pres. fashion design ZJS Studios, Zihuatenejo, Mexico, 1974—79, pres. Santa Monica, Calif., 1981—93. Book.

SELIGER, MARK ALAN, photographer; b. Amarillo, Tex., May 23, 1959; s. Maurice and Carol Lee (Singer) S. BS, East Tex. State U., 1981. Contbg. photographer Rolling Stone Mag., N.Y.C., 1989-93; chief photographer GQ mag., 1993—; contbg. photographer Vanity Fair. Recipient Excellence in Journalism award Page One, 1988, Excellence awards Comm. Arts, 1988, 89, 90, 91, 92, 93, Creativity certs. Distinction Art Direction Mag., 1989, 93, Merit award Art Dirs. Club, 1991, Distinctive Merit award 1991, 92, Excellence certs. Am. Photography, 1991, 92, Distinctive Merit awards Soc. Pub. Designers, 1992, Distinguished Alumni award East Tex. State U., 1993; Mark Seliger Photography Scholarship named in his honor East Tex. State U., 1994, Alfred Eisenstuedt Photography award Single Image, 1999. Mem. Am. Soc. Mag. Photographers. Office: Rolling Stone Mag 1290 Avenue Of The Americas Fl 2 New York NY 10104-0295

SELIGMAN, DANIEL, editor; b. N.Y.C., Sept. 25, 1924; s. Irving and Clare (O'Brien) S.; m. Mary Gale Sherburn, May 23, 1953; children: Nora, William Paul. Student, Rutgers U., 1941-42; AB, NYU, 1946. Editl. asst. New Leader, 1946; asst. editor Am. Mercury, 1946-50; assoc. editor Fortune, 1950-59, editl. bd., 1959-66, asst. mng. editor, 1966-69, exec. editor, 1970-77, assoc. mng. editor, 1977-87, contbg. editor, 1988-97, Forbes, 1997—. Sr. staff editor all Time, Inc. (publs.), 1969-70. Author: A Question of Intelligence: The IQ Debate in America, 1992. Home: 190 E 72nd St New York NY 10021-4370 E-mail: ad453@aol.com.

SELIGMAN, DELICE, lawyer; b. Worcester, Mass. m. Frederick Seligman. AB, MA, Clark U.; JD, NYU, 1971. Bar: N.Y. 1972, U.S. Dist. Ct. (so. and ea. dists.) N.Y. 1973, U.S. Supreme Ct. 1979. Assoc. Legal Aid Soc. Nassau County, Mineola, N.Y., 1972-76; ptnr. Seligman, Stein & Abromowitz, Garden City, 1976-86, Seligman & Seligman, N.Y.C., N.Y., 1986—. Legal counsel Contemporary Sculptors, Roslyn, N.Y., 1987-90, Artists Network Great Neck, N.Y., 1987-90, Woodstock Animal Rights Movement, Legal Action for Animals, Stop Graffiti Now, Inc.; pres. Wildlife Legal Action, Inc. Bd. dirs. For Our Children and Us, Hicksville, N.Y., 1985—; pres. Vol. Lawyers for Animal Rights, 2001—, Animal Advocates, Inc., 1999—. Mem. N.Y. State Bar Assn., Nassau Women's Bar Assn. (pres. 1982-83), Bar Assn. Nassau County (chair arts com. 1984-85), Phi Alpha Delta. Home: Runge Rd Shokan NY 12481 Office: 26 Broadway New York NY 10004-1703 also: Seligman & Seligman 70 Main St Kingston NY 12401-3802

SELIGMAN, FREDERICK, lawyer; b. Bklyn. s. Martin and Florence (Alperin) S.; m. Delice Felice. AB, Clark U., 1957; JD, N.Y. Law Sch., 1972. Bar: N.Y. 1973, U.S. Dist. Ct. (so. and ea. dists.) N.Y. 1974, U.S. Tax Ct. 1974, U.S. Ct. Appeals (2d cir.) 1975, U.S. Supreme Ct. 1979. Atty. N.Y.C. (N.Y.) Police Dept., 1972-73; asst. dist. atty. N.Y. County, N.Y.C., 1973-79; pvt. practice, 1980-85; ptnr. Seligman & Seligman, 1986—. Mem. N.Y. Criminal Bar Assn., N.Y. State Defenders Assn. Home: Runge Rd Shokan NY 12481 Office: Seligman & Seligman 26 Broadway New York NY 10004-1703

SELIGMAN, GEORGE BENHAM, mathematics educator; b. Attica, N.Y., Apr. 30, 1927; s. George Frederick and Florence Rose (Benham) S.; m. Irene Alice Schwieder, July 3l, l959; children: Barbara, Karen. AB, U. Rochester, l950; MA, Yale U., l95l, PhD, 1954. Instr. math. Princeton (N.J.) U., l954-56, Yale U., New Haven, l956-57, asst. prof., l957-60, assoc. prof., l960-65, prof., l965-82, James E. English prof., 1982-97, prof. emeritus, 1997—. Author: Modular Lie Algebras, 1967, Rational Methods, 1976, Constructions of Lie Algebras and Their Modules, 1988; mem. editorial bd. Am. Scientist, 1980-90. With USNR, l945-46. Mem. Am. Math. Soc. (com. mem.), Math. Assn. Am. Democrat. Avocation: gardening. Home: 143 Woodlawn St Hamden CT 06517-1341 Office: Yale U Dept Math PO Box 208283 New Haven CT 06520-8283 E-mail: selig@math.yale.edu.

SELIGMAN, JOEL, dean; b. N.Y.C., Jan. 11, 1950; s. Selig Jacob and Muriel (Bienstock) S.; m. Friederike Felber, July 30, 1981; children: Andrea, Peter. AB magna cum laude, UCLA, 1971; JD, Harvard U., 1974. Bar: Calif. 1975. Atty., writer Corp. Accountability Rsch. Group, Washington, 1974-77; prof. law Northeastern U. Law Sch., 1977-83, George Washington U., 1983-86, U. Mich., Ann Arbor, 1986-95; dean law U. Ariz., Tucson, 1995-99; dean sch. law Washington U., St. Louis, 1999—. Cons. Fed. Trade Commn., 1979-82, Dept. Transp., 1983, Office Tech. Assessment, 1988-89; chair adv. com. on mkt. info. SEC, 2000-2001; reporter Nat. Conf. of Commrs. on Uniform State Laws, Uniform Securities Act, 2001. Author (with others) Constitutionalizing the Corporation: The Case for the Federal Chartering of Giant Corporations, 1976, The High Citadel: The Influence of Harvard Law School, 1978, The Transformation of Wall Street: A History of the Securities and Exchange Commission and Modern Corporate Finance, 1982, The SEC and the Future of Finance, 1985, (multi-volume) Securities Regulation; contbr. articles to profl. jours. Mem. State Bar Calif., Am. Law Inst. (adv. com., advisor corp. governance project), AICPAs (profl. ethics exec. com. 2000—). Office: Wash U Sch Law CB 1120 1 Brookings Dr Saint Louis MO 63130-4862

SELIGMAN, LYNN, literary agent; b. N.Y.C., Feb. 25, 1947; d. Siegbert and Kay Reis Seligman; div. Apr. 6, 1996; children: Samuel Patterson, Emma Patterson. BA, Goucher Coll., 1967; MA, Columbia U., 1970. ESL tchr. N.Y.C. Schs., 1976-77; asst. sub. rights Thomas Y. Crowell, N.Y.C., 1977-79; mgr. serial rights Doubleday & Co. (now BDD), 1979-81; assoc. dir. sub. rights Simon & Schuster, 1979-81; ind. lit. agt. Julian Bach Lit. Agy., Inc. (now Internat. Mgmt. Group), 1981-85, Upper Montclair, N.J., 1985—. Woodrow Wilson scholar, Woodrow Wilson Found., 1968. Mem. Women's Media Group, Other Agt.'s Group, Phi Beta Kappa. Democrat. Jewish. Avocations: reading, ballet, cooking, Scrabble. Home and Office: 400 Highland Ave Montclair NJ 07043-1102

SELIGMAN, THOMAS KNOWLES, museum administrator; b. Santa Barbara, Calif., Jan. 1, 1944; s. Joseph L. and Peggy (Van Horne) S.; children: Christopher, Timothy, Dylan. BA, Stanford U., 1965; BFA with honors, San Francisco Acad. Art, 1967; MFA, Sch. Visual Art, N.Y.C., 1968. Tchr., mus. dir. Peace Corps, Liberia, 1968-70; curator dept. Africa, Oceania and Ams. Fine Arts Museums, San Francisco, 1971-88, dep. dir. edn. and exhbns., 1972-88, dep. dir. ops. and planning, 1988-91; dir. Stanford (Calif.) U. Cantor Arts Ctr., 1991—. Mem. cultural property adv. com. USIA, 1988-92, Nat. Endowment for Art Indemnity Panel, 1992-95. Author mus. catalogues, articles in field. Trustee Internat. Coun. Mus./Am. Assn. Mus., 1990-94, Am. Fedn. Arts, The Christensen Fund, 2000, Assn. Art Mus. Dirs.; adv. coun. Acad. Art Coll. Grad. Program. Fellow Nat. Endowment Arts, 1974-75, 87. Mem. Assn. Art Mus. Dirs.(trustee 2002-04), Am. Assn. Mus., Leaky Found. Address: Cantor Ctr for Visual Arts Stanford U Lomita Dr & Museum Way Stanford CA 94305-5060

SELIGMANN, WILLIAM ROBERT, lawyer, author; b. Davenport, Iowa, Oct. 10, 1956; s. William Albert and Barbara Joyce (Carmichael) S.; m. Carole Lee Francis; children: D Anna, Matthew. BA, U. Calif., Santa Barbara, 1979; JD, Santa Clara U., 1982. Bar: Calif. 1983, U.S. Dist. Ct. (no. dist.) Calif. 1983. Assoc. Office of J.R. Dempster, Cupertino, Calif., 1983-85; city atty. City of Campbell, 1985—; ptnr. Dempster, Seligmann & Raineri, Los Gatos, 1985—2001, pvt. practice, 2001—. Judge pro tem, Santa Clara County, 1992—. Bd. dirs. Los Gatos C. of C. Mem. Santa Clara County Bar Assn. (civil practice com., judiciary com., exec. bd. pub. law sect.), State Bar of Calif. (exec. bd. pub. law section, 2001—). Avocations; cross country skiing, scuba diving, swimming, writing, Aikido. Office: 333 Church St Santa Cruz CA 95060 also: Ste 206 236 N Santa Cruz Ave Los Gatos CA 95030 E-mail: bill@southbaylaw.com.

SELIGSON, CARL H. business executive; b. N.Y.C., Feb. 25, 1935; s. Harold P. and Lilian (Yohalem) S.; m. Joan Escott, May 19, 1957 (div. Nov. 1969); children: Susan S. Pattenaude, Barbara S. Zweig, Nina Priven, Eric M. Drath; m. Bonnie Laskin, Mar. 6, 1983. AB, Brown U., 1956; postgrad., NYU Grd. Sch. Bus. Adminstrn., 1961-63. Textile salesman Cohn, Hall, Marx Co., Montreal, Can., 1958-61; security analyst Burnham & Co., N.Y.C., 1961-67, Kuhn, Loeb & Co, N.Y.C., 1967-71; mng. dir. Merrill Lynch, 1971-87, Kidder, Peabody & Co., N.Y.C., 1987-90; sr. exec. cons. regulated industries Deloitte & Touche, 1990-92; mng. dir. Prudential Securities, 1992-95; sr. advisor Andersen Consulting, 1996-2000; sr. v.p. energyLeader.com, 2000; sr. advisor Prospect Street Ventures, 2001—, K Road Mgmt., 2002—. Contbr. articles to profl. jours. including Pub. Utilities Fortnightly, Telephony, Fin. Exec., The Southern Banker, Coal Monthly and Energy News. Bd. dirs. Nuclear Energy Inst., Washington, 1988-95. With U.S. Army Counter Intelligence Corps. Fellow Fin. Analysts Fedn.; mem. Univ. Club. Avocations: water sports, travel, theatre. Office: K Road Mgmt 330 Madison Ave New York NY 10017

SELIGSON, GARY MARC, musician; b. West Orange, N.Y., Sept. 14, 1960; s. Kurt and Lore Seligson; m. Lucy Gentry Vance, July 1, 2000. MusB cum laude, U. Hartford, 1983; studied with Alexander Lepak; studied with Gary Chester, N.Y.C., 1984-85. Endorser, clinician, tchr. various instruments. Drummer, percussionist: (Broadway shows) The King and I, Disney Radio City Music Hall, Christmas, N.Y.C., 1983-84, On Your Toes, Dreamgirls, N.Y.C. and nat./internat. tours, 1985-87, Cats, Les Miserables, Miss Saigon, nat. and internat. tours, 1988-97; Broadway and studio drummer NBC-TV, ABC-TV, PBS-TV, Disney: Lion King, Chicago, Rent, N.Y.C., 1999; drummer, house contractor, arranger: (Broadway show) Aida, N.Y.C., 1999— (Tony award 2000, Grammy award 2000); drummer, arranger: (Broadway workshop) Souls, 1999, (Broadway show) Gershwin's Fascinating Rhythm, 1999, Original Bank Ejectrode, 1998—; musician, arranger: Broadway Cares Equity Fights AIDS, 1997—, various other AIDS orgns., U.S., 1986—; TV appearances include NBC Today Show, 1999, ABC Good Morning America, 2000, ABC The View, 2000; percussionist: (rec.) Compassion, 1999; featured in Modern Drummer Mag. Mem. Am. Fedn. Musicians. Avocations: swimming, running, ethnic and jazz music. Home: Apt 8B 340 W 72d St New York NY 10023

SELIGSON, JUDITH, artist; b. Phila., July 8, 1950; d. David and Harriet Tutelman Seligson; m. Allan M. Greenberg, Sept. 7, 1938; 1 child, Hannah Leah. BA cum laude, Harvard U., 1973. One-woman shows include Jane Haslem Gallery, Washington, 1992, Anita Friedman Fine Art, N.Y.C., 1997, Schlesinger Libr., Radcliffe Coll., Cambridge, Mass., 1997, exhibited in group shows at Gary Snyder Fine Art, N.Y.C., 1998, 2002, Signal 66, Washington, 2001, Exit Art, N.Y.C., 2002, ; contbr. articles.

SELIGSON, MITCHELL A. Latin American studies educator; b. Hempstead, N.Y., Nov. 12, 1945; s. Morris and Ethel (Finkel) S.; m. Susan Berk, June 18, 1967; 1 child, Amber Lara. BA cum laude, Bklyn. Coll., 1967; MA, U. Fla., 1968; PhD, U. Pitts., 1974. Vol. U.S. Peace Corps, Costa Rica, 1968-70; asst. prof./assoc. prof. U. Ariz., Tucson, 1974-85; prof. U. Pitts., 1986-93, Daniel H. Wallace prof. polit. sci., 1994—, dir. Latin Am. studies, 1986-92, rsch. prof., 1992—. Cons. to U.S. AID, Guatemala, Honduras, Nicaragua, Costa Rica, Ecuador, Jamaica, Panama, El Salvador, Peru, Bolivia, Paraguay, 1980—. Author, editor: Peasants of Costa Rica and the Development of Agrarian Capitalism, 1980, The Gap Between Rich and Poor, 1984, Authoritarians and Democrats, 1987, Elections and Democracy in Central America, 1989, rev. edit. 1995, Development and Underdevelopment, 1993, The Political Economy of Global Inequality, 1998. Fulbright fellow, Costa Rica, 1986, Rockefeller Found. fellow, 1985-86; grantee Social Sci. Rsch. Coun., Ford Found., NSF, Mellon Found., Heinz Endowment. Mem. Am. Polit. Sci. Assn., Latin Am. Studies Assn. (chmn. fin. com. 1991). E-mial. Office: U Pitts Dept Polit Sci Pittsburgh PA 15260 E-mail: seligson@pitt.edu.

SELIGSON, THEODORE H. architect, interior designer, art consultant; b. Kansas City, Mo., Nov. 10, 1930; s. Harry and Rose (Haith) S.; m. Jacqueline Rose, Dec. 27, 1964 (div. 1976). BArch, Washington U., St. Louis, 1953. Registered architect, Mo., Kans. Intern Marshall & Brown, Kansas City, Mo., 1949-54; designer, head design Kivett & Myers, 1954-62; prin. Design Assocs., 1955—, Atelier Seligson, Kansas City, Mo., 1962-64; pres. Seligson, Eggen, Inc., 1964-73, Seligson Assocs., Inc., Architects Planners, Kansas City, 1973-97, Seligson Assocs., Inc., Archs. Planners, Kansas City, 1973-97; prin. Foss, Seligson, Lafferty, 1997—. Vis. lectr. adult edn. U. Mo.-Kansas City, 1958-61, vis. prof. arch., 1989—; tchr., critic Kansas City Art Inst., Mo., 1961-64, 71-72, adj. prof., 1986, 89, 91, 92; adj. prof. Kansas State U., 1991-92, 97; vis. prof. Washington U., St. Louis, 1975, 77, 78, 81, 86, 91, U. Kans., Lawrence, 1978, 79, 80, 91, 92; art cons. Design Assocs., Kansas City, Mo., 1955—. Projects pub. in archtl. jours. V.p. Friends of Art Nelson-Atkins Mus. Art, Kansas City, bd. dirs. 1963-67, chmn. selections com., 1981, vis. curator, 1972, 87; chmn. Capitol Fine Arts Commn. Mo., 1983-90, Kansas City Worlds Fair goals and themes subcom., 1985-90; bd. dirs. Westport Tomorrow, Kansas City, 1980-87, Hist. Kansas City Found., 1984-90; pres. Native Sons of Kansas City, 1989, bd. dirs. 1978-94, Westport Cmty. Coun., 1973-75; bd. govs. Truman Med. Ctr., Kansas City, 1998—; mem. Kansas City Key to City Commn., 2001—. Recipient Urban Design award Kansas City Mcpl. Art Commn., 1968, 74, 78; Nat. Archtl. award Am. Inst. Steel Constrn., 1970; Nat. award ASID/DuPont Corian, 1989. Fellow AIA (Kansas City chpt. pres. 1983, bd. dirs. 1979-84, Design Excellence award 1966, 68, 70, 74, Ctrl. States Regional award 1974, 78, Honor award for outstanding svc. to chpt. and profession 1982-83); mem. Mo. Coun. Archs., Am. Soc. Interior Designers, Nat. Coun. Archtl. Registration Bds. (task analysis adv. com. 1988-90), Soc. Archtl. Historians (pres. 1973-75, bd. dirs. 1994-97). Jewish. Office: Foss Seligson Lafferty 106 W 14th St Kansas City MO 64105-1914

SELIN, IVAN, entrepreneur; b. N.Y.C., Mar. 11, 1937; s. Saul and Freda (Kuhlman) Selin; m. Nina Kallet, June 8, 1957; children: Douglas, Jessica. BE, Yale U., 1957, ME, 1958, PhD, 1960; DSc, U. Paris, 1962. Rsch. engr. Rand Corp., Santa Monica, Calif., 1960-65; sys. analyst Dept. Def., Washington, 1965-67, dep. asst. sec. def., 1967-69, acting asst. sec. for systems analysis, 1969-70; founder, chmn. bd. Am. Mgmt. Systems, Inc., Arlington, Va., 1970-89; undersec. state Dept. State, Washington, 1989-91; chmn. NRC, 1991-95; chmn., CEO Phoenix Internat., 1995—. Lectr. UCLA, 1961-63; chmn. mil. econ. adv. panel to CIA, 1978-89; chmn. e-Numerate Solutions, Inc., BZL Biologics. Author: Detection Theory, 1964; contbr. articles to profl. jours. Pres. Corp. Against Drug Abuse, 1988-95; bd. dirs., gov. UN Assn. U.S., 1979-89; exec. com. Greater Washington Research Ctr., Fed. City Council; trustee Asia Soc., 1996-98; chmn., bd. dirs. Smithsonian Nat. Mus. of Am. History, 1996—. Recipient Disting. Civilian Svc. medal, 1970, Disting. Svc. medal Sec. of State, 1991; Fulbright scholar, 1959-61; Ford Found. grantee, 1952-54. Mem. IEEE (editor Trans. on Info. Theory 1960-65), Coun. Fgn. Rels., Yale Club, Sigma Xi, Tau Beta Pi. Home: 1455 Ocean Dr # 1602 Miami Beach FL 33139 Office: Phoenix Internat Inc PO Box 58277 Washington DC 20037-5503

SELIN, NINA EVVIE, philanthropist; b. N.Y.C., Dec. 16, 1935; d. Louis Harry and Ida Cantor; m. Ivan Selin, June 8, 1957; children: Douglas Scott, Jessica Beth. BS, Boston U., 1957. Cert. elem. tchr., Conn. Tchr. West Haven (Conn.) Sch. Dist., 1957-60; dir. Nat. Consumers League, Washington, 1968-75; propr. Relax-Relocation Cons., 1975-80; vice chmn. Phoenix Internat. Power Plant Co., 1995-98; chmn. Nat. Aquarium, 1986—. Bd. dirs. Am. Cancer Soc., 1972-87, Nat. Geog. Soc., 1995—, Mt. Sinai Hosp. Found., Miami Beach, Fla., 1998—, Rep. Nat. Com., 1991—; chmn. Selin Family Found., Del., 1995; judge Nathan Davis award AMA, Washington, 2001. Recipient Disting. Svc. award Am. Cancer Soc., 1987, Mt. Sinai Found., 1999. Mem. Internat. Club III, Welcome to Washington Internat. Club. Avocations: exotic travel, scuba diving, reading, public service. Home: 1455 Ocean Dr Apt 1602 Miami FL 33139 Office: Phoenix Internat 1050 17th St NW Washington DC 20036 E-mail: nselin@phnx-intl.com.

SELINER, BARBARA ANN, elementary education educator; b. Salem, Oreg., July 4, 1950; d. Elmer Sylvester and Charlotte Marie (McKee) Meade; m. Donald Joseph Seliner, Aug. 11, 1985; children: Kayla Marie, Brandon Joseph. Bachelor's degree, Oreg. Coll. Edn., 1973, Master's degree, 1977. Cert. learning specialist, tchr. Elem. tchr. Tillamook (Oreg.) Sch. Dist., 1973-76; diagnostician Diagnostic Ctr., Oreg. Coll. Edn., Monmouth, 1977; specialist, tchr., devel. severely learning disabled program David Douglas Sch. Dist., Portland, Oreg., 1977-86, tchr. 5th and 3d grade, 1986-90, tchr. severe emotionally disturbed, 1991-92, tchr. 3d grade, 1992-93, tchr. 5th grade, 1993-97, tchr. 3d grade, 1997, tchr. 4th grade, 1998—. Mem. Insvc. State Cadre Team Pub. Law 94-142, Oreg., 1978-81; chmn. supts. com. staff devel. David Douglas Sch. Dist., Portland, 1981-83; sch. store coord. Gilbert Park Elem., David Douglas Sch. Dist., Portland, 1994-95, 96-97, safety patrol coord., 1995-96. Co-developer web page for Gilbert Park Elem. Sch., 1996-97; contbr. articles to profl. publs. Avocations: tole painting, growing dahlias, woodworking, going to the beach, spending time with family. Office: Gilbert Park Elem Sch 13132 SE Ramona St Portland OR 97236-4113 E-mail: barbara_seliner@ddouglas.k12.or.us.

SELIS, STUART L. financial consultant, underwriter; b. Washington, Feb. 1, 1951; s. Sidney M. Selis and Betty (Pollock) Kuhne; m. Pamela Naftolin, Oct. 27, 1977 (div. Mar. 1989); children: Michael J., Lisa K.; m. Cherie Sternberg, June 20, 1990. BA, Mich. State U., 1973. CLU, chartered fin. con. Account mgr. Sagemark Consulting of Lincoln Nat. Corp., Southfield, Mich., 1980—. Pres. Farmington Green West Homeowners Assn., Farmington Hills, Mich., 1984-85; mem. Farmington Hills Parks and Recreation Commn., 1987-97; mem. Mich. regional adv. bd. Anti-Defamation League of B'nai B'rith, 1991-96; bd. dirs. Young Israel West Bloomfield, 1995—. Mem. Nat. Assn. Life Underwriters, Am. Soc. CLU's. Republican. Jewish. Home: 6436 Summer Ct West Bloomfield MI 48322-2234 Office: Sagemark Consulting Inc 26555 Evergreen Rd Ste 1600 Southfield MI 48076-4206

SELK, ELEANOR HUTTON, artist; b. Duboise, Nebr., Oct. 21, 1918; d. Anderson Henry and Florence (Young) Hutton; m. Harold Fr3ederick Selk, Aug. 3, 1940; children: Honey Lou, Katherine Florence. RN, St. Elizabeth Hosp., Lincoln, Nebr., 1938. Nurse, Lincoln, 1938-40, Denver, 1940-50; with Colo. Bd. Realtors, 1956-66; owner, mgr. The Pen Point, graphic art studio, Colorado Springs, 1974-94; instr. history and oil painting, 1994—. One-woman shows Colo. Coll., 1970, 72, Nazarene Bible Coll., 1973, 1st Med. Ch., 1971 (all Colorado Springs); exhibited in group shows U. So. Colo., 1969, 70, 71, 72, Colorado Springs Art Guild, 1969-72, Pike's Peak Artists Assn., 1969-73, Mozart Art Festival, Pueblo, Colo., 1969-74, numerous others; represented in permanent collection U.S. Postal Svc., Pen-Arts Bldg., Washington, Medic Alert Found. Internat. Hdqrs., Turlock, Calif., Colorado Springs Music Co. Piano Gallery. Contbr. med. articles, short stories, poetry to newspapers. Rec. sec. Colo. chpt. Medic Alert Found. Internat., 1980-90, chairperson El Paso County and Colorado Springs chpt., 1980-90, Colo. bd. dirs., 1980-89, rec. sec., 1980-89. Recipient 3d pl. award Nat. Tb and Respiratory Disease and Christmas Seal Art Competition, 1969, finalist award Benedictine Art competition Hanover Trust Bank, N.Y.C., 1970, numerous awards and certs. for pub. svcs. and art, award Music of the Baroque, 1991, Editors Choice award Nat. Libr. Poetry, 1993. Mem. Nat. League Am. Pen Women (rec. sec. 1972-74, travelling art slide collection 1974—, designer jewelry, awards for book cover art, numerous Gold Bangle awards). Home: 518 Warren Ave Colorado Springs CO 80906-2343

SELKE, OSCAR O., JR. physiatrist, educator; b. Houston, Mar. 13, 1917; s. Oscar Otto and Orile Mollie (Medlenka) S.; m. Edith Hicks Hardey, July 10, 1943; children: Charles Richard, Carolyn Selke Brophy, Barbara Selke-Kern, Bruce Hardey. BA, U. Tex., 1938; MD, U. Tex., Galveston, 1941; postgrad., U. Pa., 1945-46. Diplomate Am. Bd. Phys. Medicine and Rehab. Intern, resident Hermann Hosp., Houston, chief phys. medicine and rehab., 1946-76, chief emeritus, 1977—, med. dir. sch. phys. therapy, 1947-65; mem. clin. faculty phys. medicine and rehab. Baylor U. Coll. of Medicine, 1950—, emeritus, 1985—. Chief phys. medicine and rehab. Methodist Hosp., 1952-60, St. Luke's Hosp., 1953-63, Tex. Children's Hosp., 1953-63, Ctr. Pavilion Hosp., 1966-77, Park Plaza Hosp., 1975—; mem. clin. faculty phys. medicine and rehab. U. Tex. Post-grad. Sch. of Medicine, 1952-63, U. Tex. Med. Sch., Houston, 1972—; area cons. VA in Phys. Medicine and Rehab., 1950-66; med. adv. bd. United Cerebral Palsy of Tex., 1959-73, bd. dirs., 1967-70, Gulf Coast, 1971-74; bd. dirs. Harris County Cerebral Palsy Treatment Ctr., 1947-50, 68-71, pres., 1952, med. adv. bd., 1947-70; bd. dirs. Muscular Dystrophy Assn. Gulf Coast, pres., 1953; med. adv. bd. Muscular Dystropy Assn. Am., 1972-76; bd. dirs. Child Guidance Ctr. of Houston, 1949-55, Soc. Crippled Children and Adults, Houston, 1958-62; med. adv. bd. Harris County Muscular Dystrophy Assn., 1950-76, Harris County Multiple Sclerosis Soc., 1958-60, Am. Rehab. Found., 1961-66; mem. bd. Am. Registry of Phys. Therapists, 1957-71. Mem. editorial bd. Archives of Phys. Medicine and Rehab., 1957-72. Capt. USAF, 1942-45. Mem. AMA (residency rev. com. phys. medicine and rehab. 1970-75, past chmn. phys. medicine and rehab sect., Cert. of Appreciation 1975), Am. Assn. Electrodiagnostic Medicine, Am. Acad. Phys. Medicine and Rehab., Am. Congress Rehab. Medicine, Tex. Phys. Medicine and Rehab. Soc. (past pres.), Tex. State Med. Assn., Harris County Med. Assn., Houston Phys. Medicine and Rehab. Soc. (past pres.). Presbyterian. Avocations: writing, growing orchids. Home: Apt 402 3209 Village Green Dr Waco TX 76710-1469

SELKIRK, ALEXANDER MACDONALD, JR. lawyer; b. Jamaica, N.Y., Oct. 2, 1943; s. Alexander MacDonald and Anne (Roth) S.; m. Joanne Patrician Diskant, July 21, 1974; children: Marianne C., Victoria L. BA in Polit. Sci., St. Johns U., Jamaica, 1965; JD, N.Y. Law Sch., 1970; LLM in Trade Regulation, NYU, 1973. Bar: N.Y. 1971, U.S. Dist. Ct. (so. and ea. dists.) N.Y. 1972, U.S. Ct. Appeals (2d cir.) 1972, U.S. Supreme Ct. 1976, Fla. 1991. Sr. staff atty. Hartford Ins. Co., N.Y.C., 1971-74; assoc. Richard C. Mooney, Esq., Hempstead, N.Y., 1974-77; sr. trial atty. Home Ins. Co., Huntington Sta., 1978-80; asst, county atty. Suffolk County, Hauppauge, 1980-88; assoc. Garcia & Stallone Esqs., Melville, 1988-90, CIGNA Ins. Co., Woodbury, 1990-95; trial counsel Martin Fallon Mulle, Huntington, 1995—. Arbitrator Suffolk County Dist. Ct. 10th Jud. Dist., 1982-88; instr. N.Y. State JAG's Sch., 1997—. Feature writer Ronkonkoma Rev., 1986-90; contbr. articles to legal publs. Committeeman Suffolk County Rep. Com., Ronkonkoma, N.Y., 1977-92; del. 10th Jud. Dist. Conv. Suffolk County, 1981-84; v.p. Holbrook Rep. Club, 1979-81, pres., 1981-83; bd. dirs. Holbrook Youth Devel. Corp., 1985-91; pilot legal officer Nassau sr. squadron CAP, 1978-84; counsel. Com. for A Drug Free Holbrook, 1988-90. Maj. JACG, N.Y. Army N.G., 1983—. Mem. Am. Arbitration Assn. (comml.

arbitrator), N.Y. State Bar Assn., Internat. Platform Assn., Suffolk Country Bar Assn., NYU Alumni Assn., Holbrook C. of C. (bd. dirs. 1981—, v.p. 1987-89, pres. 1984-91, 92-93), Gt. Neck (N.Y.) Sportsman's Club, KC (adv. 1981-84, 87—, trustee 1984-87), Lions (bd. dirs. 1985-86, v.p. 1986-87, pres. 1987-88). Roman Catholic. Home: 12 Glen Summer Rd Holbrook NY 11741-5006 Office: Martin Fallon Mulle 100 E Carver St Huntington NY 11743-3593

SELKIRK, JAMES KIRKWOOD, biochemist, researcher; b. N.Y.C., Dec. 3, 1938; s. James Kirkwood and Doris (Schuler) S.; m. Carole Ann Bozzone, Sept. 16, 1961; children: James Kirkwood, David Edward. BS, Coll. Environ. Sci. and Forestry, Syracuse (N.Y.) U., 1964; PhD, Syracue U. Upstate Med. Ctr., Syracuse, 1969. Postdoctoral fellow McArdle Lab. Cancer Rsch., U. Wis., Madison, 1969-72; staff fellow Nat. Cancer Inst., NIH, Bethesda, Md., 1972-74, sr. staff fellow, 1974-75; sr. staff scientist unit leader chem. carcinogenesis biology divsn. Oak Ridge (Tenn.) Nat. Lab., 1975-85; chief carcinogenesis and toxicology evaluation br. nat. toxicology program Nat. Inst. Environ. Health Scis., 1985-89, assoc. dir. divsn. toxicology rsch. and testing, 1989-92, chmn. carcinogen mechanism group Lab. Molecular Carcinogenesis, 1992—; adj. prof. Oak Ridge Biomed. Grad. Sch., U. Tenn., 1975-85; spl. asst. to sci. dir. for technology devel. Nat. Inst. Evniron. Health Scis., 1997-2000; mem. breast cancer task force NIH, 1979-82; mem. com. on pyrenes and analogs NAS, 1981-83; chmn. Interagy. Testing Commn., 1986-90; deputy dir. Nat. Ctr. Toxicogenomics, 2000—. Author rsch. articles, chpts. in books; mem. editl. bd. Carcinogenesis Jour., 1984-87, 91-93, Cancer Rsch., 1981-86, Environ. Perspectives, 1993-98. Mem. Orange County Planning Bd., 1997—; chmn. Weaver Dairy Precinct, Dem. Party Orange County, 1996-99. With AUS, 1959-61. Recipient U.S. Interagy. Testing Com. Exemplary Svc. award, 1992. Mem. Am. Cancer Soc. (carcinogenesis study sect. 1975-78, 92-96). Home: 30119 Settle Dr Chapel Hill NC 27517 Office: Nat Inst Environ Health Scis PO Box 12233 Research Triangle Park NC 27709 E-mail: selkirk@niehs.nih.gov.

SELKOE, DENNIS JESSE, neurologist, researcher, educator; b. N.Y.C., Sept. 25, 1943; s. Herbert E. and Mary P. (Lille) S.; m. Polly Ann Strasser, Jan 24, 1967; children: Gregory, Kimberly. BA, Columbia U., 1965; MD, U. Va., 1969. Diplomate Am. Bd. Psychiatry and Neurology, Nat. Bd. Med. Examiners. Intern in medicine Hosp. U. Pa., Phila., 1969-70; rsch. assoc. NIH, Bethesda, Md., 1970-72; resident in neurology Peter Bent Brigham/Children's Hosp., Boston, 1972-74, chief resident in neurology, 1974-75; rsch. assoc. Harvard Med. Sch., 1975-78, asst. prof. neurology, 1978-82, assoc. prof., 1982-85, assoc. prof. neurology and neurosci., 1985-90, faculty mem. div. on aging, 1980—, prof. neurology and neurosci., 1990—, Vincent and Stella Coates prof. neurol. diseases, 2001—; co-dir. Ctr. Neurologic Diseases Brigham and Women's Hosp., 1985—. Mem. sci. adv. bd. Alzheimer's Disease Assn., Chgo., 1983-89; mem. Gov.'s Commn. on Alzheimer's Disease, Mass., 1985-87; neurosci. adv. com. Howard Hughes Med. Inst., 1996—. Author over 200 articles, book chpts. on biochemistry and molecular biology of Alzheimer's Disease. Asst. surgeon USPHS, 1970-72. Recipient Wood-Kalb Found. prize Alzheimers Disease Assn., 1984, Med. Rsch. award Met. Life Found., 1986, LEAD award Nat. Inst. on Aging, 1988, NIH Merit award, 1991—, Arthur Cherkin award UCLA, 1995, Mathilde Solowey award in neurosci. Found. for Advanced Edn. in Scis., NIH, 1998, Rita Hayworth award Alzheimer's Assn., 1995, Boerhaave medal U. Leiden, 1998, Pioneer award Alzheimer's Assn., 1999; grantee Bristol-Myers Squibb Neurosci., 1990. Fellow Am. Acad. Neurology (Potamkin prize 1989, Dr. A.H. Heineken prize for Medicine 2002); mem. Am. Neurol. Assn., Soc. for Neurosci., Am. Assn. Neuropathologists, World Fedn. Neurologists, AAAS. Office: Harvard Med Sch Brigham & Womens Hosp 77 Avenue Louis Pasteur Boston MA 02115-5727

SELKOWITZ, ARTHUR, advertising agency executive; b. N.Y.C., May 26, 1943; s. Harry and Anne (Lichten) S.; m. Betsey Wattenberg, Apr. 15, 1967; children: Adam, Jed. AB, Syracuse (N.Y.) U., 1965. Account exec. Dancer Fitzgerald Sample, 1969-71; with Benton & Bowles, Inc., N.Y.C., 1971-82, v.p., account supr., 1972-75, sr. v.p., mgmt. supr., 1975-81, sr. v.p., account dir., 1981-82; founder, pres. Penchina, Selkowitz Inc., N.Y.C., 1982-90; exec. v.p. internat. D'Arcy, Masius, Benton & Bowles, 1990-94, pres. Asia and Pacific, 1995-96, pres. N.Am., 1996-97, chmn., CEO, 1997-2000; vice chmn., chief client officer BCom3 Group, Inc., 2001—. Dancer Fitzgerald Sample, N.Y.C., 1966-71. Office: BCom3 Group Inc 825 8th Ave New York NY 10019 E-mail: arthur.selkowitz@bcom3group.com.

SELKOWITZ, LARRY BRYAN, lawyer; b. Pitts., Feb. 27, 1947; s. Harry and Rose (Steiner) S.; m. Sharon Eileen Selkowitz, Feb. 15, 1975; children: Adrian A., Jonathan E. BS, Pa. State U., 1969; JD, Dickinson Sch. Law, 1972. Bar: Pa. 1972. Dep. atty. gen. Pa. Dept. Justice, Harrisburg, 1972-75; sr. asst. consumer advocate Office of Consumer Advocate, 1976-79; prin. Reager, Selkowitz & Adler, P.C., 1979-94; chmn. appellate rev. panel Pa. Dept. Edn., 1992-94; asst. U.S. atty. health care fraud coord. U.S. Atty.'s Office Mid. Dist. Pa., 1994—. Pres., bd. dirs. Outreach, Inc., Harrisburg, 1990-92; chmn. bd. dirs. Harrisburg chpt. ARC, 1989-91, state chmn., 1992-93; chmn. Paxtang Boro Recreation Com., 1992-94. Recipient Dirs. award for Affirmative Civil Enforcement, Dept. Justice, 1997, Dirs. award for Superior Performance, Dept. Justice, 2000. Mem. Pa. Bar Assn. (chmn. com. on handicapped rights 1987-89, vice chmn. com. on rights of exceptional children 1989-91). Avocation: coaching youth soccer. Office: US Attys Office 228 Walnut St Harrisburg PA 17101-1714 E-mail: Larry.Selkowtiz@usdoj.gov.

SELKOWITZ, LUCY ANN, security officer; b. Pitts., Oct. 15, 1956; d. Thomas Francis and Matilda Margaret (Carlini) Donato; m. Jeremiah Anthony Barry, Jan. 10, 1976 (div. July 1979); 1 child, Jeremiah; m. Stanley Irwin Selkowitz, Aug. 19, 1987; children: Lori, Lee, Mattie. Grad., William Boyd, 1974. Cert. EMT, Pa. Owner, buyer Tillie's Antiques, Pitts., 1972-86; legal aide Selkowitz & Assoc., 1986-94; armed security officer Wackenhut Corp., 1994—. Dance performer Shade Sisters, 1992—. Counselor troubled youths, Clairton, Pa., 1986—; active PTA, chair 1995—. Mrs. Am. Finalist, 1990-91. Avocations: jet skiing, camping, animal care, on-stage dance performer. Home: 100 Farm Ln Clairton PA 15025-3362 Office: Wackenhut Inc Rt 88 Castle Shannon PA 15234

SELL, GEORGE R. mathematician, educator; s. George P. and Alice Sell; m. Geraldine M. Sell, June 14, 1958; children: George, Mark, Marie, Paula, Thomas, Eric. BS, Marquette U., 1957, MS, 1958; PhD, U. Mich., 1962; Doctorate (hon.) , St. Petersburg U. (also known as Leningrad State U.), Russia, 1990. B Pierce instr. math Harvard U., Cambridge, Mass., 1962—64; asst. prof. math. U. Minn., Mpls., 1964—67; assoc. prof. math. U. So. Calif., L.A., 1967—68, U. Minn., Mpls., 1967—73, prof. math., 1973—; program dir. NSF, Washington, 1977—78. Dir. Army High Performance Computing Rsch. Ctr., 1989; lectr. in field. Co-author: (book) Linear Operator Theory in Engineering and Science, 1971; author: Dynamics of Evolutionary Equations, 2002. Grantee for the IMA at U. Minn., NSF, 1982—87, for the AHPCRC at U. Minn., US Army Rsch. Ctr., 1989—94. Office: U Minn Sch Math 206 Church St SE Minneapolis MN 55455

SELL, JOAN ISOBEL, mobile home company owner; b. Johnson City, Tenn., May 5, 1936; d. Earl Walter and Jeanne Mason (Lyle) S.; m. Dale L. Moss, Jan. 15, 1956 (div. Nov. 1977); children: Carol Anne, John D. BS, East Tenn. State U., Johnson City, 1961. Cert. tchr., Tenn., Ga. Tchr. Asbury Sch., Johnson City, 1961-62, Richard Arnold High Sch., Savannah, Ga., 1964-66, Windsor Forest High Sch., Savannah, 1966-67, Boones Creek High Sch., Jonesborough, Tenn., 1967-77; co-owner Moss-Sell Mobile Homes, Johnson City, 1978-88, Biddix Budget Homes, Inc. (formerly Budget Mobile Homes), Johnson City, 1978-87, v.p., sec., 1987—; pres., treas. Budget Homes, Inc. (formerly Biddix Budget Homes), 1988-92; owner McKinley Park, 1970—; sec. Piedmont Fin. Svcs. Inc., 1999—2001; pres. Sell Properties, Inc., Johnson City, 1997—. Pres. Sell Properties, Inc., 1997—. Bd. dirs. Ashley Acad., Johnson City, 1997-2000. Mem. Tenn. Manufactured Housing Assn. (state bd. dirs. 1993-95), N.E. Tenn. Manufactured Housing Assn. (pres.), DAR, UDC, Order Ea. Star. Mem. Brethren Ch. Home: 3 Caitlin Ct Johnson City TN 37604-1147 Office: PO Box 5189 Johnson City TN 37602-5189

SELL, ROBERT EMERSON, electrical engineer; b. Apr. 23, 1929; s. Cecil Leroy and Ona Arletta (Stevens) S.; m. Ora Lucile Colton, Nov. 7, 1970. BS, U. Nebr., 1962. Registered profl. engr., Nebr., Mo., Ill., Ind., Ohio, W.Va., Ky., Ark., Tex., Oreg., Wash., Calif. Chief draftsman Dempster Mill Mfg. Co., Beatrice, Nebr., 1949-53; designer-engr. U. Nebr., Lincoln, 1955-65; elec. design engr. Kirkham, Michael & Assocs., Omaha, 1965-67, Leo A. Daly Co., Omaha and St. Louis, 1967-69; mech. design engr. Hellmuth, Obata, Kassabaum, St. Louis, 1969-70; chief elec. engr. Biagi-Hannan & Assocs., Inc., Evansville, Ind., 1971-74; elec. project engr. H.L. Yoh Co. under contract to Monsanto Co., Creve Coeur, Mo., 1974-77, Dhillon Engrs., Inc., Portland, Oreg., 1978-85; project coord. Brown-Zammit-Enyeart Engring., Inc., San Diego, 1985-88; elec. engr. Morgen Design, Inc., 1988; lead elec. engr. Popov Engrs., Inc., 1988-89; mech. and elec. specialist Am. Engring. Labs., Inc. divsn. Profl. Svc. Industries, Inc., 1990—. Instr. Basic Inst. Tech., St. Louis, 1971. Mem. ASHRAE, IEEE. Home and Office: PO Box 261578 San Diego CA 92196-1578

SELL, WILLIAM EDWARD, legal educator; b. Hanover, Pa., Jan. 1, 1923; s. Henry A. and Blanche M. (Newman) S.; m. Cordelia I. Fulton, Aug. 20, 1949 (dec.); 1 son, Jeffrey Edward. AB, Washington and Jefferson Coll., 1944, LHD, 1973; JD, Yale U., 1947; LLD, Dickinson Sch. Law, 1968. Bar: D.C. 1951, Pa. 1952. Instr. law U. Pitts., 1947-49, asst. prof. law, 1949-51, assoc. prof. law, 1953-54, prof. law, 1954-77, assoc. dean, 1957-63, dean, 1966-77, disting. svc. prof. law, 1977-94; emeritus dean, disting. svc. prof. law, 1994—; sr. counsel firm Meyer, Unkovic & Scott, Pitts., 1977-94. Vis. prof. U. Mich. Law Sch., 1957; past pres. Pa. Bar Inst.; bd. dirs. St. Clair Health Corp., Exec. Svc. Corp., Little Lake Theatre; sec. Little Lake Manor Corp.; cons. jud. edn. Supreme Ct. Pa., 1998-2002. Author: Fundamentals of Accounting Lawyers, 1960, Pennsylvania Business Corporations, 3 vols., 1969, revised, 1991, Sell on Agency, 1975, also articles; editor: Pennsylvania Keystone Lawyers Desk Library. Past pres., bd. dirs. St. Clair Meml. Hosp., St. Clair Hosp. Found.; past chmn. St. Clair's Health Corp. With USAAF, WWII; bd. dirs. Exec. Svc. Corps. Fellow Am. Bar Found. (life); mem. ABA, Pa. Bar Assn., Allegheny County Bar Assn., Assn. Am. Law Schs., Am. Law Inst. (life), Univ. Club, Phi Beta Kappa, Order of Coif, Pi Delta Epsilon, Phi Gamma Delta, Phi Delta Phi, Omicron Delta Kappa. Presbyterian (elder, deacon). Home: 106 Seneca Dr Pittsburgh PA 15228-1029 Office: U Pitts Sch Law 531 Law Bldg Pittsburgh PA 15260 Fax: (412) 531-9203. E-mail: sell@law.pitt.edu.

SELLARS, ARLENE JUDY, gerontology nurse; b. Monticello, Iowa, May 14, 1943; d. Elwill John Louis and Elfrieda Behrends; m. LeRoy G. Khorll, 1965 (div. 1973); children: Angela Elizabeth, Lois Ailene; m. Daniel Wilbur Osterkamp, Apr. 19, 1975 (div. Jan. 1991); 1 child, Tanya Lou; m. Kenneth LaVerne Sellars, Nov. 22, 1995. Student, Washington U., St. Louis, 1963, St. Louis U., 1964; diploma in nursing, St. Louis City Hosp., 1965; student, Kirkwood Area Tech. Coll., Cedar Rapids, Iowa, 1970—. RN, Mo., Iowa; cert. in CPR-First Aid; cert. in hearing conservation; cert. in indsl. nursing/hazardous materials. Head nurse in orthopedics, asst. to o.r. supr.; staff nurse Sr. Home Inc.-Health Care Iowa, Monticello; charge nurse Beverly Enterprises, Cedar Rapids; staff nurse Willow Gardens Nursing Home, Marion, Iowa, Crestview Acres Care Ctr., Marion; indsl. plant nurse Pork Industry IBP, Inc., Columbus Junction, Iowa, 1991—. Cons. Mary Kay Cosmetics. Maj. Operation Desert Shield USAR, 1990—2002. Mem. Nat. League for Nursing, Iowa Nurses Assn., Mo. Nurses Assn. Home: 633 Park St Ainsworth IA 52201-9470

SELLECK, TOM, actor; b. Detroit, Jan. 29, 1945; s. Robert D. and Martha S.; m. Jacquelyn Ray, 1970 (div. 1982); 1 stepson, Kevin; m. Jillie Joan Mack, Aug. 7, 1987; 1 child, Hannah Margaret. Student, U. So. Calif. TV appearances include The Rockford Files, Friends, 1996, 2000; star TV series Magnum P.I. 1980-88, The Closer, CBS series, 1998—; films include Midway, 1976, Coma, 1982, High Road to China, 1983, Lassiter, 1984, Runaway, 1985, Three Men and a Baby, 1987, Her Alibi, 1989, An Innocent Man, 1989, Quigley Down Under, 1990, Three Men and a Little Lady, 1990, Folks!, 1992, Mr. Baseball, 1992, In and Out, 1997, The Love Letter, 1999; TV films include The Sacketts, 1979, Divorce Wars, 1982, Louis L'Amour's "The Shadow Riders", 1982, Broken Trust, 1995, Ruby Jean and Joe, 1996, Last Stand at Saher River, 1998, Louis l'Amour's Crossfire Trail, 2000; exec. prodr. (series) B.L. Stryker, 1989-90, (TV movie) Revealing Evidence, 1990. Office: care Esme Chandlee 2967 Hollyridge Dr Los Angeles CA 90068-1949

SELLER, GREGORY EROL, marketing executive, writer, consultant; b. Denver, Oct. 4, 1953; s. Otto Gustave and Dolores Louise (Crawford) S. BBA, U. Colo., 1975. Account exec. Gt.-West Life, L.A., 1975-79, asst. v.p. group devel. Denver, 1980-84; v.p. govt. mkts. and nat. accts. Great-West Life, L.A., 1988—; pres., chief exec. officer Benefits Communication Corp., Denver, 1985-87, sr. v.p. govt. mkts., 1991—. Bd. dirs. Benefits Communication Co. Editor newsletter Focus on 457, 1988—. Mem. vestry, treas. St. Thomas Episc. Ch., Hollywood, Calif., 1989-93. Mem. Delta Upsilon. Democrat. Home: 26 Pienza Laguna Niguel CA 92677-8623 Office: Great West Life Ste 560 18111 Von Karman Ave Irvine CA 92612-7131

SELLER, ROBERT HERMAN, cardiologist, family physician; b. Phila., Mar. 21, 1931; s. David and Elsie (Straussman) S.; m. Maxine Schwartz, June 3, 1956; children: Michael, Douglas, Stuart. AB, U. Pa., 1952, MD, 1956. Intern. Grad. Hosp. of U. Pa., Phila., 1956-57; research asst. dept. pharmacology U. Pa., 1953-55; resident in cardiology, research fellow Am. Heart Assn., Phila. Gen. Hosp., 1957-58; resident in internal medicine Albert Einstein Med. Ctr., Phila., 1958-59, chief resident, 1959-60; instr. medicine Hahnemann Med. Coll. and Hosp., Phila., 1960-64, asst. prof., 1964-69, assoc. prof., 1969-72, dir. Service F, 1962-67, asst. coordinator mil. edn. for nat. def., 1961-64, dir. div. family medicine, 1967-72, acting chmn. dept. family medicine and community health, 1972-74, prof. medicine, family medicine and community health, 1973-74; practice medicine, specializing in cardiology Buffalo, 1974—; prof., chmn. dept. family medicine, prof. medicine SUNY-Buffalo, Deaconess Hosp., 1974-82, chmn. dept. family practice and dir. family practice residency program, 1974-82; prof. medicine and family medicine SUNY-Buffalo, 1974-2000; emeritus prof. medicine and family medicine, 2000—. Author: Differential Diagnosis of Common Complaints, 1986, 4th edit., 2000; contbr. articles to profl. jours. NIH grantee, 1972-75; Deaconess Hosp. family practice resident tng. grantee, 1975— ; health professions spl. projects grantee, 1975— Fellow ACP, Am. Coll. Cardiology, Am. Acad. Family Physicians, Phila. Coll. Physicians; mem. AMA, N.Y. Med. Soc., Erie County Med. Soc., Am. Fedn. Clin. Research, Am. Heart Assn., Soc. of Tchrs. of Family Medicine, N.Y. Acad. Sci., N.Y. Acad. Family Physicians. Home: 125 Crestwood Ln Buffalo NY 14221-1462 Office: 1542 Maple Rd Buffalo NY 14221-3625

SELLER, STEVEN MARK, pharmacist; b. Buffalo, June 2, 1952; s. Marvin Philip Seller and Molly (Kramer) Lettman. BS in Natural Sci., Niagara U., 1974; BS in Pharmacy, Mass. Coll. Pharmacy, 1976. Cert. geriatric practitioner. Clin. rotation Beth Israel Hosp., Boston, 1976; pharmacist CVS Pharmacy, Braintree, 1977-78; pharmacy mgr. Mall Drugs, Boston, 1978; store and pharmacy mgr. Wagner Leader Drugs, Buffalo, 1978-80; pharmacy mgr. James Super Drug, 1980-83; pharmacist Buffalo RX Ctr., 1983-85; clin. instr. Sch. Pharmacy SUNY, Buffalo, 1984-87, 2001—; pharmacist Health Care Plan, 1985-94; clin. pharmacy dir. Brookside Park Pharmacy, East Aurora, N.Y., 1994-97; asst. mgr. Benwood LTC Pharmacy, Tonawanda, 1997-98; mgr. pharmacy svcs. Sheehan Meml. Hosp., Buffalo, 1998—2001; site supr. pharmacy svcs. Kaleida Health, 2001—. Cons. pharmacist to nursing homes, pharm. cos. and PBM's, 1983—. Bd. rev. Jour. Cons. Pharmacist, 1990-93. Mem. Mason, Albright-Knox Art Gallery. Fellow: Am. Soc. Cons. Pharmacists (upstate dir. N.Y. state chpt. 1985—95, orgnl. affairs coun. 1990—91, 1997—2001); mem.: Nat. Alumni Assn. Niagara U., Alumni Assn. Mass. Coll. Pharmacy. Democrat. Jewish. Avocations: golf, sailing, softball, traveling, raquetball. E=mail. Home: 75 Groton Dr # B Buffalo NY 14228-2538 Office: Kaleida Health 3 Gates Cir Buffalo NY 14209 E-mail: sseller@kaleidahealth.org.

SELLER, WENDY, artist; b. N.Y.C., Mar. 24, 1949; d. Arthur Norman and Suzanne (Hulse) Seller; m. William E. Howcroft, May 26, 2001. BA in Art Edn., R.I. Sch. Design, 1975; MFA, U. Ill., 1977. Adj. faculty R.I. Sch. Design, Providence, 1988—; asst. prof. Simmons Coll., Boston, 1991—. Adj. faculty R.I. Coll., Providence, 1990-92; vis. instr. Mass. Coll. Art, Boston, 1994, 97-99; instr. Art Inst. Boston, 1980-82; lectr. bus. strategies for the artist Ky. Found. for Women and Louisville Visual Artists Assn., 1997, Women's Caucus for Art Nat. Conv., Boston, 1996, Mass. Coll. of Art, 1996. (one-woman shows) Lenore Gray Gallery , Providence , 2001, Belenky Gallery , N.Y.C., 1998, 00, De Ville Galleries, L.A., 1997, 1998, Pepper Gallery , Boston, 1995, Va. Lynch Gallery, Tiverton, R.I., 1994, 1999, www.guild.com, 1999—2000, Clark Whitney Gallery , Lenox, Mass., 1993, Trustman Art Gallery , Boston, 1990, Bannister Gallery, Providence, 1990, (group shows) Attleboro Mus., 2000, The R.I. Found., 2000, The Norman Rockwell Mus. , Stockbridge, Mass., 1999, Mus. of Art, R.I. Sch. Design, 1990, 1992, 1995, 1997, 1999, 2001, R.I. Sch. Design traveling exhbn. , 1997—98, Woods Gerry Gallery , Providence, R.I. , 1999, Artcetera, Boston, 1998, 2000, Bristol Art Mus. , R.I., 1998, De Cordova Mus., Lincoln, Mass., 1998, Howard Yezerski Gallery, Boston, 1992—97, Wood Meml. Libr., 1997, Craighead-Green Gallery, Dallas, 1997, Schloss Moskgkan, Dessau, Germany, 1997, Canyon Crossing Gallery, Brattleboro, Vt., 1997, Agora Gallery , N.Y.C., 1997, Erector Square Gallery, New Haven, Conn., 1996, The New Art Ctr. , Newton, Mass., 1991, 1995, Elaine Horwitch Galleries , Scottsdale, Ariz. , 1994, (permanent collections) Fidelity, Boston, Hasbro Children's Hosp. , Providence, Simandl and Geer Law Firm, Livingston, N.J., R.I. Hosp. , Providence, Belenky Gallery, N.Y.C. , DeCordova Mus., Lincoln, Clements/Howcroft, Boston, DeVille Galleries, L.A. , Colville Pub. , Santa Monica, Calif. , Art Inc., Dessau, Germany, Simons Coll., Boston Sch. Mus. Fine Arts, Boston , (featured in publs.) New Am. Paintings, 1993, 1996, 1999, The Potters Profl. Handbook , 1999, CEDCOs Women Artists Calendar , 1996—97, 1999, Women Artists Datebook , 1996—99, In Praise of the Muse: Women Artists Datebook, 1998. Artist-in-residence grantee Cultural Edn. Collaborative, Boston, 1984, TryArts Project Mass. Coun. on Arts, 1977-78; recipient Bronze medal Multi-Image Film Festival, 1983; winner talent competition Arts Spectrum Mag., 1996; grantee RISD, 2000, Newton (Mass.) Cultural Coun., 2000. Studio: Claflin Sch Studios 449 Lowell Ave Apt 1 Newtonville MA 02460-2115 E-mail: wseller@attbi.com.

SELLERS, BARBARA JACKSON, federal judge; b. Richmond, Va., Oct. 3, 1940; m. Richard F. Sellers; children: Elizabeth M., Anne W., Catherine A. Attended, Baldwin-Wallace Coll., 1958-60; BA cum laude, Ohio State U., 1962; JD magna cum laude, Capital U. Law Sch., Columbus, Ohio, 1979. Bar: Ohio 1979, U.S. Dist. Ct. (so. dist.) Ohio 1981, U.S. Ct. Appeals (6th cir.), 1986. Jud. law clk. Hon. Robert J. Sidman, U.S. Bankruptcy Judge, Columbus, Ohio, 1979-81; assoc. Lasky & Semons, 1981-82; jud. law clk. to Hon. Thomas M. Herbert, U.S. Bankruptcy Ct., 1982-84; assoc. Baker & Hostetler, 1984-86; U.S. bankruptcy judge So. Dist. Ohio, 1986—. Lectr. on bankruptcy univs., insts., assns. Recipient Am. Jurisprudence prize contracts and criminal law, 1975-76, evidence and property, 1976-77, Corpus Juris Secundum awards, 1975-76, 76-77. Mem. Columbus Bar Assn., Am. Bankruptcy Inst., Nat. Conf. Bankruptcy Judges, Order of Curia, Phi Beta Kappa. Office: US Bankruptcy Ct 170 N High St Columbus OH 43215-2403 E-mail: barbara_sellers@ohsb.uscourts.gov.

SELLERS, FRED EVANS, accounting educator; b. Lexington, Mo., Feb. 28, 1941; s. James MacBrayer and Rebekah Hall (Evans) S.; m. Katherine Ann Griggs, May 3, 1969; children: Mark Griggs, Rebekah Field. BA in History, Yale U., 1965; MBA, U. Kans., 1976, PhD in Bus., 1984. CPA, Tex. Reporter Kansas City (Mo.) Star, 1965-66, copy editor, 1966-70, Washington Star, 1970-72, asst. nat. editor, 1972-73; asst. prof. U. Tulsa, 1979-87; assoc. prof. Southwestern U., Georgetown, Tex., 1987—, chair dept. econs. and bus., 1994—. Sec., treas. planning com. U. Tulsa Conf. Accts., 1980-87. Contbr. articles to profl. jours. Trustee Wentworth Mil. Acad., Lexington, Mo., 1986—, pres., 1990-92; trustee Williamson County (Tex.) Literacy Coun., 1989-91; treas., bd. dirs. St. John's Presch., Tulsa, 1984-87; conv. del. Episc. Diocese Okla., 1984, 85; audit com. St. John's Episc. Ch., Tulsa, 1983-87; bishop's com. Grace Episc. Ch., 1989, jr. warden, 1989, bishop's warden, 1990; alt. Tex. State Rep. Conv., 1988; treas. Georgetown Area United Way, 1993-99. Mem. Inst. Mgmt. Accts. (dir. manuscripts Austin chpt. 1988-96), Am. Acctg. Assn. (membership com. 1980-81), AICPA, Tex. Soc. CPAs (ednl. instns. com. Austin chpt.), Rotary. Avocations: bridge, piano, singing, jogging. Home: 1610 E 15th St Georgetown TX 78626-7206 Office: Southwestern U Dept Econs and Bus Adminstrn Georgetown TX 78627-0770

SELLERS, FRED WILSON, accountant; b. Alexander City, Ala., Apr. 29, 1942; s. Fred Wilson and Helen (Hagan) Sellers); m. Nancy Wilbanks, July 11, 1964; children: Fredrick Hagan, Robert Wilbanks. BS, U. Ala., 1964; MBA, L.I. U., 1966; postgrad., U. Wis., Madison, 1974. CPA, N.C., Ala.; cert. fraud examiner; cert. fin. svcs. auditor. Staff acct. Ernst & Young, Winston-Salem, N.C., 1966-69; comptr. Citibanc Group, Inc., Andalusia, Ala., 1969-73; various positions, then sr. v.p., gen. auditor AmSouth Bank, Birmingham, 1973-98. Bd. dirs. Better Bus. Bur., Mobile, Ala., 1984-86. Mem. budget com. United Way, Birmingham, 1982-83. Mem. AICPA, N.C. Assn. CPAs, Ala. Assn. CPAs, Ala. United States Air Force Acad. Parents Club (pres. 1993-94, 94-95), Vestavia Country Club, The Club, Univ. Club (Tuscaloosa). Avocations: travel, photography. Home and Office: 2112 Viking Cir Birmingham AL 35216-3325

SELLERS, GREGORY JUDE, physicist; b. Far Rockaway, N.Y., June 20, 1947; s. Douglas L. and Rita R. (Dieringer) S.; m. Lucia S. Kim, Nov. 26, 1983; 1 child, Kristin Kim. AB in Physics, Cornell U., 1968; MS, U. Ill., 1970, PhD, 1975. Sr. scientist B-K Dynamics, Inc., Rockville, Md., 1974-76; with Allied-Signal Corp., Morristown, N.J., 1976-88, applications physicist, 1977-88; product supr. Amphenol Fiber Optic Products, Naperville, Ill., 1985-88; mgr. Cinch Connectors, Elk Grove, 1988-91; pres. Forss, Inc., Naperville, 1991-96, Fotron, Inc., Naperville, 1995—. Bd. dirs. Thermo-Tek, Inc., N.J., Fotron. Mem. AAAS, IEEE, Am. Phys. Soc. Achievements include development and commercialization of electronic connectors and fiber optic products; development of applications for polymeric materials and glassy metals in the electrical and electronics arena. Co-inventor adhesive bonding metallic glass, electromagnetic shielding, testing of thermal insulation, amorphous antipilferage marker, amorphous spring-shield, multiple fiber positioner for optical fiber connection, raised rib waveguide ribbon for precision optical interconnects. Home and Office: Fotron Inc 7S 515 Oak Trails Dr Naperville IL 60540

SELLERS, JIMMIE, construction executive; b. Florence, S.C., Aug. 4, 1951; s. Kisar and Evell Sellers; m. Lorraine Conley Sellers, Aug. 25, 1996; children: Jimmy, Nikita Reneel stepchild Teran Correia. Advanced welding cert., Coosa Valley Vocat.-Tech. Sch., 1971; small bus. mgmt. course, Floyd Jr. Coll., 1974. Cardiac care provider Am. Heart Assn., Rome, 1997; medic 1st aid EMP Am. , Catersville, 2002. Author: (poetry) America at the Millennium, 2000. Min. Pentecostal Assembly of the World. Sgt. 1st class U.S. Army, 1988. Mem.: Handyman Club Am., VA Assn. Pentecostal. Avocations: drawing, wood carving, playing guitar, writing, building. Home: 109 Battey Dr Rome GA 30165

SELLERS, MARJORIE STEVENSON, retired principal; b. New Orleans, July 10, 1931; d. Samuel Sr. and Lillie Neldare Brown; m. Melvin Stevenson, Feb. 27, 1950 (dec.); children: Melvin Jr. (dec.), Carl F. Anthony (dec.).; m. Lloyd Sellers, Jan. 27, 1974 (dec.). BA in Elem. Edn., Southern U., 1964, MEd in Elem. Edn., 1967; MS in Adminstrn. and Supervision, Alcorn State U., 1982; postgrad., Grambling State U. Dir., tchr. daycare and kindergarten Immaculate Conception Ch., Baton Rouge, 1964-66; tchr. grade 2nd, 6th Carver Elem., De Ridder, 1966-68; tchr. math, social studies, reading grades 6,7,8 Walker (La.) Jr. High Sch., 1968-69; acting corr. title I Dept. Corrections, Baton Rouge, 1969-72; instr. reading Alcorn State U., Lorman, Miss., 1972-95; coord. tutor program E.B.R. Recreation/Parks, Baton Rouge, 1995-98; program dir. summer camp, 1995-96; prevention counselor, 1997-98; prin. St. Francis Xavier Sch., Baton Rouge, 1998—; substitute tchr./counselor East Baton Rouge Parish. Adj. faculty U. So. Miss., Natchez, 1975, Sch. Nursing Alcorn State U., Natchez, 1981-82, 90. Stay-In-School challenge grantee Entergy Corp., 1996, Drug Prevention/Edn. program grantee Baton Rouge Found., 1997; Am. coll. scholar U.S. Achieve Acad., 1990. Mem. AARP, AAUW, Nat. Assn. Devel. Edn., Internat. Reading Assn., La. Recreation/Parks, Phi Delta Kappa (sec., pres. 1980). Democrat. Roman Catholic. Avocations: reading, sewing, church activities, ball games, shopping.

SELLERS, PATRICIA ANN, home health nurse; b. Salamanca, N.Y., May 22, 1946; d. Elmer Ellsworth Long and Elizabeth June (Anderson) Eckman; m. William Russell Sellers, Apr. 21, 1967; children: Donna Sue, Joanne Marie. Diploma, Oil City Sch. Nursing, 1967; stroke nurse, West Pa. Reg. Med. Program, 1971. RN, Pa. Staff nurse Oil City Hosp., Oil City, Pa., 1967-68, Butler County Meml. Hosp., Butler, 1968-70; asst. head nurse Grove City

Hosp., Grove City, 1970-81; clin. coord. United Community Hosp., 1981-82, asst. head nurse in surg. unit, 1982-90, nurse mgr. in surg. unit, 1990-93, staff nurse in home health svc., 1993—. Chmn. audit com. United Community Hosp., 1975-80, chmn. patient edn. com., 1980-81. Mem. Order of Ea. Star. Democrat. Presbyterian. Avocations: coin collecting, crocheting. Home: 3325 Oneida Valley Rd Emlenton PA 16373-2111 Office: United Community Hosp 631 N Broad Street Ext Grove City PA 16127-4603

SELLERS, PETER HOADLEY, mathematician, educator; b. Phila., Sept. 12, 1930; s. Lester Hoadley and Therese (Tyler) S.; m. Lucy Bell Newlin, June 21, 1958; children: Mortimer, Therese, Mary, Lucy Bell BA, U. Pa., 1953, MA, 1958, PhD, 1965. Math. tchr. Kangaru Sch., Embu, Kenya, 1961-63; programmer U. Pa., Phila., 1958-61; mem. faculty Rockefeller U., N.Y.C., 1966—. Johnson Found. postdoctoral fellow, 1963-65 Mem. editl. bd. Genomics, 1986-97; author: Combinatorial Complexes, 1979; contbr. articles to profl. jours. Trustee Coll. of the Atlantic, Bar Harbor, Maine, 1985-96; curator Rockefeller Hist. Instrument Collection, 1997—. Lt (j.g.) USNR, 1953-55 Mem. Am. Math. Soc., Math. Assn. Am., Soc. Indsl. and Applied Math. Democrat. Episcopalian. Avocation: boat building. Home: 413 W Stafford St Philadelphia PA 19144-4407 Office: Rockefeller Univ 1230 York Ave New York NY 10021-6399 E-mail: sellers@rockefeller.edu.

SELLERS, PIERS J. astronaut; b. Crowborough, Sussex, Apr. 11, 1955; married; 2 children. BS in Ecol. Sci., U. Edinburgh, Scotland, 1976; PhD in Biometeorology, Leeds U., Eng., 1981. Astronaut, mission specialist NASA, Johnson Space Ctr., Houston, 1996—. Recipient Arthur Fleming award, 1995. Fellow: Am. Geophys. Union; mem.: Am. Meteorology Soc. (Houghton award 1997). Achievements include research in how the earth's biosphere and atmosphere interact, computer modeling of climate system, satellite remote sensing studies and field work. Office: Astronaut Office/CB NASA Johnson Space Ctr Houston TX 77058

SELLERS, WAYNE CHADICK, newspaper publisher, editor, retired; b. Brady, Tex., Mar. 10, 1916; s. Marcellus Stephenson Sellers and Martha Jane Chadick; m. Camilla Ann Browning, June 29, 1946 (dec. June 1996). BA, Tex. Tech U., 1938; postgrad., U. Tex., 1940-41. Statistician Ft. Worth Star-Telegram, 1943-50; prodn. mgr. San Francisco News, 1951-52; bus. mgr. Sherman (Tex.) Democrat, 1953-59; pub. Rock Hill (S.C.) Herald, 1959-66; editor, pub. Palestine (Tex.) Herald-Press, 1966-80. Mem. bd. mgrs. Tex. State R.R., 1969-73; mem. adv. coun. U. Tex. Coll. communication, Austin, 1979—. Chmn. Palestine United Way, 1968, Northeast Tex. Lib. Sys. Adv. Coun., Garland, 1986—, Palestine Pub. Libr. Bd., 1979—; vol. lobbyist Tex. Libr. Assn., 1983; chmn. Reporter Bd., United Meth. Ch., Dallas, 1980-82. Named to Hall of Fame Tex. Tech U. Sch. Mass Comm., Lubbock, 1979; named Trustee of Yr. Tex. Libr. Assn., Houston, 1981, Nat. Advocacy Honor Roll Mem., Am. Libr. Assn., chgo., 2000, Builder of Palestine, Palestine C. of c., 1982, Mr. Books, Tex. State Libr. and Archives Commn., Austin, 1983. Democrat. Methodist. Avocations: amateur radio, travel, collecting books. Home: 215 Stephanie Dr Palestine TX 75803-8505

SELLES, ROBERT HENDRIKUS, actuary, consultant; b. Amsterdam, Nov. 8, 1938; came to U.S., 1969; s. Albertus Hendrikus and Jansje Suzanna (Cordes) S.; m. Manuela Ioana Cazaban Sava-Goiu Comnene, Aug. 26, 1966 (div. Mar. 1978); 1 child, Melina Joanna. B of Commerce with honors, U. Manitoba, 1961. Actuarial asst. Can. Premier Life Ins. Co., Winnipeg, Manitoba, Canada, 1961-62; asst. actuary Sun Life Assurance Co. Can., Montreal, 1962-69; sr. v.p. Hay/Huggins Co., Inc., Phila., 1969-75, 77-79, 1991—, Boston, 1975-77, San Francisco, 1979-84, 87-91, N.Y.C., 1984-87. Fellow Soc. Actuaries; mem. Conf. Cons. Actuaries, Am. Acad. Actuaries, Internat. Benefits Found., Western Pension and Benefits Conf., Actuaries Club San Francisco, Netherlands Soc. Phila. (pres. 1993-96, 99-2000, bd. dirs. 1991—, Netherlands Am. Assn. Delaware Valley (bd. dirs. 1993-96), Gavel Soc., Rainbow River Inc. (pres. 1995—). Home: 1420 Locust St Apt 34-A Philadelphia PA 19102-4220 E-mail: rselles@aol.com.

SELLEY, MICHAEL L. pharmaceutical company executive; b. Woking, Surrey, U.K., Jan. 20, 1948; s. Stanley John and Rosina Lillian Selley; m. Angela Grace Charlton, July 30, 1966 (div. Sept. 1976); m. Pamela Kay Foulser, Oct. 29, 1977; 1 child, Timothy Michael. BSc, U. London, 1968; MSc, U. Alta., Edmonton, 1971; PhD, U. Sydney, 1975. Sr. rsch. scientist Sandoz Pharma Ltd., Basle, Switzerland, 1975-84; sr. rsch. fellow John Curtin Sch. Med. Rsch. Inst. Advanced Studies, Australian Nat. U., Canberra, 1985-95; chief of staff Office of the Min. for Sci. Tech., 1996-97; chmn. and mng. dir. Pan Australia Labs Pty. Ltd., Symondstown, 1997-98; pres., CEO Angiogen Pharms. Pty. Ltd., Weston Creek, 1999—. Cons. Asia/Pacific region Panlabs Inc., Seattle, 1988-95. Contbr. articles to profl. jours. Anutech Canberra Tech. Partnership grantee, 1991-93. Fellow Royal Australian Chem. Inst., Commonwealth Club. Achievements include research on the role of free radicals in neurodegenerative disease; the development of new anti-angiogenesis drugs. Avocations: horseback riding, golf, classical music, wine. Home: 19 Holmes St Turramurra NWS 2074 Australia Office: Angiogen Pharms Pty Ltd 512 Pacific Hwy Turramurra NSW 2074 Australia E-mail: mllselley@angiogen.com.au.

SELLI, CESARE, urologist, researcher; b. Perugia, Italy, Feb. 27, 1950; s. Mario Selli and Giuseppina Pascoletti. MD, Pisa U. Med. Sch., Italy, 1974. Fellow in urology SUNY, 1976-77; rsch. fellow Florence U., 1977-81, 82-87; fellow in urologic surgery Duke U., Durham, N.C., 1981-82; assoc. prof. urology Rome U., 1987-91; assoc. prof. Florence U., 1991-96; chmn. urology Udine U., 1996-2000; prof., chmn. urology Pisa U., 2000—. Referee European Urology, 1995, Urology, 1995, Jour. Urology, 2000. Mem. ACS, Am. Urolog. Assn., European Urolog. Assn., Soc. Internat. Urology. Roman Catholic. Avocations: skiing, fishing. E-mail: c.selli@dc.med.unipi.it.

SELLICK, KATHLEEN A. hospital administrator; b. Phoenix; m. Phil Sellick; 1 child Grace. BS, Ariz. State U.; MBA, U. Chgo. Grad. Sch. Bus. With Am. Med. Internat., Beverly Hills, Calif., Westgate Med. Ctr., Denton, Tex., Mayo Clinic, Rochester, Minn.; v.p. adminstrn. and dir. outreach devel. Hoag Meml. Hosp. Presbyn., Newport Beach, Calif.; exec. v.p. and COO St. Joseph Hosp., Orange; assoc. exec. dir. and COO U. Wash. Med. Ctr., Seattle, 1999—2001, exec. dir., 2001—. Office: U Wash Med Ctr 1959 NE Pacific St Box 356151 Seattle WA 98195-6151*

SELLIN, ERIC, linguist, poet, educator; b. Phila., Nov. 7, 1933; s. Thorsten and Amy (Anderson) S.; m. Birgitta Sjöberg, Jan. 25, 1958; children: Frederick, Christopher. BA, U. Pa., 1955, MA, 1958, PhD, 1965. Asst. instr. French U. Pa., Phila., 1955-56, 1957-58, 1959-60; lectr. Am. lit. U. Bordeaux, France, 1956-57; instr. French Clark U., Worcester, Mass., 1958-59; lectr. creative writing U. Pa., 1960-62; instr. French Temple U., Phila., 1962-65, asst. prof., 1965-67, assoc. prof., 1967-70, prof., 1970-91, chmn. dept. French and Italian, 1970-73, founder, dir. Center for Study of Francophone Lit. of North Africa, 1981—2001; prof. French Tulane U., New Orleans, 1991-2001, chmn. dept. French and Italian, 1995-97, prof. emeritus, 2001—. USIS lectr., Africa and Near East, 1981-83, 85, 88-91, manuscript reader, cons. in field; sr. Fulbright-Hays lectr., Algiers, Algeria, 1968-69, Dakar, Senegal, 1978-79. Author: The Dramatic Concepts of Antonin Artaud, 1968, The Inner Game of Soccer, 1976, Soccer Basics, 1977, Reflections on the Aesthetics of Futurism, Dadaism and Surrealism-a Prosody Beyond Words, 1993, (poetry) Night Voyage, 1964, Trees at First Light, 1973, Tanker Poems, 1973, Borne Kilométrique, 1973, Marginalia, 1979, Crépuscule prolongé à El Biar, 1982, Nightfall over Lubumbashi, 1982, Night Foundering, 1985, Dead of Noon, 1992; editor: Africana Jour., 1983-87, CELFAN Edit. Monographs, 1987-2001, CELFAN Rev., 1981-2001; contbr. numerous articles to profl. jours. Recipient faculty prize in Romance langs. U. Pa., 1955; Am. Philos. Soc. fellow, 1970, 82, NEH sr. fellow, 1973-74; Temple U. rsch. grantee, 1970, 82; sr. Fulbright-Hays Rsch. scholar Francophone Lit., Rabat, Morocco, 1989. Mem. Modern Langs. Assn., Phi Beta Kappa.

SELLIN, THEODORE, foreign service officer, consultant; b. Phila., June 17, 1928; s. Thorsten and Amy (Anderson) S.; m. Taru Jarvi, July 10, 1965; 1 child, Derek. Student, U. Uppsala, Sweden, 1946-48; BA, U. Pa., 1951, MA, 1952. Joined Fgn. Svc., Dept. State, 1952; vice consul Copenhagen, 1952-56; rsch. analyst Dept. State, Washington, 1956-58; program officer Office Internat. Confs., 1965-67; acad. tng. staff U. Ind., 1958-59; 2d sec. Am. Embassy, Helsinki, Finland, 1959-64, 1st sec., polit. officer, 1971-73, 1st sec., labor-polit. officer Oslo, 1967-71; polar affairs officer Dept. State, 1975; consul gen. Goteborg, Sweden, 1978-80; fgn. rels. cons. Dept. State, Washington, 1980—. Office: Dept State A/RPS/IPS/CR/IR Washington DC 20520

SELLS, BOAKE ANTHONY, private investor; b. Ft. Dodge, Iowa, June 24, 1937; s. Lyle M. and Louise (Gadd) S.; m. Marian S. Stephenson, June 20, 1959; children: Damian, Brian, Jean Ann. BSC, U. Iowa, 1959; MBA, Harvard U., 1969. Bus. office mgr. Northwestern Bell Tel., Des Moines, 1959-63; salesman Hydraulic Cos., Ft. Dodge, 1964-67; pres. Cole Nat. Corp., Cleve., 1969-83; vice chmn. Dayton Hudson Corp., Mpls., 1983-84, pres., 1984-87; chmn., pres., chief exec. officer Revco D.S., Inc., Twinsburg, Ohio, 1987-92. Bd. dirs. Promus Cos. (name changed to Harrah's Entertainment, Inc.), NCS Healthcare. Trustee Cleve. Ctr. for Contemporary Art, Cleve. Play House.

SELLS, BRUCE HOWARD, biomedical sciences educator; b. Ottawa, Ont., Can., Aug. 15, 1930; s. Charles Henry and Nell (Worth) S.; m. Bernice May Romain, Sept. 19, 1953; children: Jennifer, Monica, David, Lisa. BS, Carleton U., 1952; MA, Queen's U., 1954; PhD, McGill U., 1957. Demonstrator McGill U., Montreal, Ont., Can., 1954-57; rsch. assoc. Columbia U., N.Y.C., 1961-62; asst. prof. St. Jude Children's Hosp.-U. Tenn., Memphis, 1962-68; assoc. prof. St. Jude Children's Hosp., 1964-72, mem., 1968-72; prof., dir. molecular biology Meml. U. Nfld., St. John's, Can., 1972-83, assoc. dean Can., 1979-83; prof. molecular biology U. Guelph, Ont., Can., 1983-96, dean biol. sci. Can., 1983-95, univ. prof. emeritus, 1997—; exec. dir. Can. Fed. Biol. Socs., 1999—. Adv. com. Ont. Health Rsch. Coun., 1992. Contbr. articles to profl. jours. Rsch. fellow Damon Runyon Meml. Fund, Brussels, 1957-59, Copenhagen, 1959-60; Killam Sr. Rsch. fellow U. Paris, 1978-79; grantee NIH, 1963-72, NSF, 1965-69, Med. Rsch. Coun. Can., 1972-93, Damon Runyon Meml. Fund for Cancer Rsch., 1962-76, Nat. Found.-March of Dimes, 1974-78, Muscular Dystrophy Assn. Can., 1974-78, Nat. Cancer Inst. Can., 1979-83, Nat. Scis. and Engring. Rsch. Coun., 1990-2001, Vis. Prof. award Institut Pasteur, Paris, 1989; Exch. fellow Natural Scis. and Engring. Rsch. Coun. of Can., 1994. Fellow Royal Soc. Can. (rapporteur microbiology and biochemistry divsn. 1985-87, convenor 1987-89); mem. Acad. Sci. of Royal Soc. Can. (life scis. divsn. fellowship rev. com. 1990-92), Am. Soc. Microbiologists, Am. Soc. Biol. Chemists, Am. Soc. Cell Biology, Can. Biochemistry Soc. (pres. 1981-82, Ayerst award selection com. 1990), Med. Rsch. Coun. (Centennial fellowships com., chmn. com. on biotech. devel. grants 1983-85, standing com. for Can. Genetic Disease Network 1991-92, chmn., 1992-97), Nat. Rsch. Coun. Can. (biol. phenomena subcom. 1983-86, chmn. steering group, sci. criteria for environ. quality com. 1986, E.W.R. Steacie Prize com. 1986-88), Assn. Can. Deans of Sci. (co-founder 1989). Home: 227 Coutts Bay Rd RR # 5 Perth ON Canada K7H 3C7 Office: U Guelph 305-1750 Courtwood Crescent Ottawa ON Canada K2C 2B5 E-mail: bsells@CFBS.org., Bruce.Sells@sympatico.ca.

SELLS, COLIN DAVID, meteorologist; b. Nuremberg, Germany; s. Jack David Sells and Ursula Daltrop; m. Mary Alice Loedding, July 18, 1981; 1 child, James Walter Sells. BA in Polit. Sci., U. South Fla., 1974; AS in Meteorology, C.C. USAF, Washington, 1985. Agrl. technician, climatologist Fla. Inst. Food and Agrl. Scis., Ruskin, Fla., 1988-90; meteorol. technician Nat. Weather Svc., St. Paul Island, Alaska, 1990-91, meteorologist Anchorage, 1991—. Guest lectr. U. dept. geography U. Alaska, Anchorage, 1994-01; mem. Baseline Proficiency Standards team Nat. Weather Svc., 1999-2001. Contbr. articles to profl. jours. Judge Alaska State Sci. Fair, Anchorage, 1993, 97, 99; union steward Nat. Weather Svc. Employees Orgn., Anchorage, 1994—; spokesman local TV Christmas children's spl., Anchorage, 1996-99. Served with USAF, 1977-87. Mem. Am. Meteorol. Soc., Am. Geophys. Union. Avocations: tournament chess (class A rating), martial arts (Black Belt Tae Kwon Do). Home: 1600 Turpin St Anchorage AK 99504-2559 Office: Nat Weather Svc Ctr Weather Svc Unit 700 N Boniface Ave Anchorage AK 99506-1612 E-mail: Colin.Sells@NOAA.GOV.

SELLS, KEVIN DWAYNE, marine engineer; b. Bridgeport, Conn., Sept. 20, 1958; m. Ketruthai Houngsatjakul, July 14, 1986; children: Corey A., David H. III. Vidhya Sarah. AS in Quality Assurance, Ft. Steilacoom C.C., Tacoma, 1984; BS in Marine Engring., Pierce Coll., 1987. Nuc. shipfitter elec. boat divsn. Gen. Dynamics, Groton, Conn., 1976-79; quality assurance surveyor Tacoma Boatbuilding Co., 1979-81, marine constrn. planner, 1981-84; sr. logistics engr. F.E. Basil, Washington, 1984-86; ship repair engr. C. Long Assocs., Bangkok, Thailand, 1987-89, sr. logistics analyst Tucson, 1989—. Mem. Soc. Naval Architects, Am. Archeology Soc., Smithsonian Inst., Libr. Congress. Achievements include research and implementation of modular shipbuilding techniques; revamped Saudi Arabian naval supply system. Avocations: auto mechanics, photography, hiking, archeology. Office: 425 W Calle Margarita Tucson AZ 85706-5317

SELM, ROBERT PRICKETT, engineer, consultant; b. Cin., Aug. 9, 1923; s. Frederick Oscar and Margery Marie (Prickett) S.; m. Rowena Imogene Brown, Nov. 25, 1945 (div. Jan. 1975); children: Rosalie C. Selm Pace, Linda R. Selm Partridge, Robert F., Michael E.; m. Janis Claire Broman, June 24, 1977. BSChemE, U. Cin., 1949. Registered profl. engr. Enlisted U.S. Army, 1943, advanced through grades to sgt. CBI Marianas, 1943-46, commd. capt., 1949, resigned, 1954; design engr. Wilson & Co., Salina, Kans., 1954-67, gen. ptnr., 1967-81, sr. ptnr., 1981-89; ptnr. in charge Wilson Labs., 1956-88, chmn. bd. dirs.; dir. Upper Eagle Valley Water Authority, Avon, Colo., 1994—; ind. investor Salina, Kans., 1989—. Contbr. articles to profl. jours.; patentee in field. Mem. Gov.'s Adv. Commn. on Health and Environ. Named Engr. of Yr. Kans. Engring. Soc., Topeka, 1986. Fellow AIChE; mem. NSPE (state chmn. environ. resource com., nat. legis. and govt. affairs com. 1988-91), Am. Chem. Soc., Am. Water Works Assn., Water Pollution Control Fedn., Am. Acad. Environ. Engrs. (diplomate), Petroleum Club, Salina Country Club (pres. 1986), Elks, Shriners. Republican. Episcopalian. Avocations: golf, lapidary arts. Office: Wilson & Co 1700 E Iron Ave Salina KS 67401-3403 Home: 2160 Sherwood Ln Salina KS 67401-6979

SELMAN, JAN COLLINS, artist; b. Boston, Apr. 4, 1945; d. James George and Dorothy Margarite (Euscher) Collins; m. Edwin Selman, Dec. 16, 1965 (div. June 1979); children: Jodie Michelle Selman, Stacey Elaine Kean. Student, Sch. of Mus. Fine Arts, 1962-64; AS, Cape Code C.C., 1981. Fine artist, owner Selman Studio, Avon, Mass., 1966-78, Falmouth, 1978—; owner Jan Collins Selman Fine Art, 1997—. Cons. Emerson House Womans Program, Falmouth, 1980. One-woman shows include Cape Mus. Fine Arts, Dennis, Mass., 2002; contbr. (paintings) Am. Artist Mag., 1991, Nantucket Jour., 1991, Cap Cod Life Mag., 1992-93; permanent collections include Duxbury Mus. Complex, Cape Mus. of Fine Arts, Provincetown Art Mus.; contbg. artist (film) Where are the Children, 1983. Juror awards for h.s. students Congrl. Arts Competition, Duxbury, 1990. Recipient 3rd Prize internat. competition Corel Systems Corp., 1991, 92. Mem. The Pastel Soc. of Am., Copley Soc. of Boston. Provinceton Art Assn., Cape Code Art Assn. Baptist. Avocations: filming documentaries on contemporary Cape Cod artists to donate to local museums, writing childrens short stories, printing iris type prints of original paintings by means of computer hardware and software. Office: Selman Studio 79 Pinecrest Beach Dr East Falmouth MA 02536-4725

SELMANOFF, MICHAEL KIDD, neuroendocrinologist, research scientist, educator; b. Mpls., July 18, 1949; AB in Biology, Earlham Coll., 1970; PhD in Neurobiology, U. Conn., 1974. Postdoctoral fellow in reproductive neuroendocrinology U. Calif. Sch. Medicine, San Francisco, 1974-77; asst. prof. physiology U. Md. Sch. Medicine, Balt., 1977-82, assoc. prof. with tenure, 1982-91, prof., 1991—. Reviewer grants NSF, 1977—; lectr. in field. Co-author: (with Booth) Population Press Book, 1970, (with others) Comportamiento y Violencia, 1976, Cell Biology of Hypothalamic Neurosecretion, 1978, A Multidisciplinary Approach to Aggression Research, 1981, Prolactin. Basic and Clinical Correlates, 1985; reviewer: (manuscripts) numerous profl. jours. 1976—; mem. editl. bd. Endocrinology, 1989—, Biology of Reprodn., 2000–; contbr. articles to profl. publs.and encys. Recipient Rsch. Career Devel. award Nat. Inst. Neurological and Communicative Diseases and Stroke, NIH, 1982-87; grantee numerous NIH, 1981—; summer fellow Inst. Study of Health and Soc., Washington, 1970, predoctoral fellow U. Conn., Storrs, 1970-71, NDEA 1971-74; acad. scholar Earlham Coll., Richmond, Ind., 1966-67. Mem. AAAS, Internat. Brain Rsch. Orng.-World Fedn. Neuroscientists, Endocrine Soc., Soc. for Neurosci., Am. Physiological Soc., Soc. Study Reproduction. Office: U Md Sch Medicine Dept Physiology 655 W Baltimore St Baltimore MD 21201-1509

SELMI, WILLIAM, JR. lawyer; b. Phila., June 18, 1937; s. William and Eleanor (Mishler) S.; m. Joan H. Silver, Dec. 4, 1966 (div. 1976); children: William III, Richard Kern; m. Karen Ladd Wheeler, Sept. 19, 1998. AB, U. Miami, Coral Gables, Fla., 1969, JD, 1972. Bar: Fla. 1972, U.S. Dist. Ct. (so. dist.) Fla. 1973, U.S. Supreme Ct., 1976. Ptnr. Peer & Selmi, Jensen Beach, Fla., 1972-79; pvt. practice law Okeechobee, 1979—. Pres. Kiwanis Club, Jensen Beach, 1978; bd. dirs. Jensen Beach C. of C., 1977-78, Martin County Dem. Com., Stuart, Fla., 1977, Okeechobee br. ARC, 1990-95, Okeechobee United Way, 1993-97. Avocations: military history, fishing. Home: 136 SW 85th Ave Okeechobee FL 34974-1554 Office: 306 NW 5th St Okeechobee FL 34972-2565

SELOVER, WILLIAM CHARLTON, corporate communications and governmental affairs executive; b. Long Beach, Calif., Dec. 12, 1938; s. John Jesse and Myrtis Charlton (Holmes) S.; m. Mary-Louise Hutchins, Jan. 5, 1963 (div. 1985); children: Victoria, Edward. BA, Principia Coll., 1960, MA, U. Va., 1962. Editl. staff Christian Sci. Monitor, from congl. corr. to diplomatic corr., 1964-71; spl. asst. to sec. of the navy USN, 1971; mem. White House Coun. on Internat. Econ. Policy, Washington, 1971-72; history and archives divsn. chief Cost of Living Coun., Exec. Office of the Pres., 1973-74; asst. to adminstr. U.S. EPA, 1974-75, 77-78; from staff mem. White House Domestic Coun. to asst. to V.P. Nelson Rockefeller White House, 1975-76; speechwriter Pres. Gerald R. Ford, 1976; pub. affairs exec. Ford Motor Co., Detroit, 1978-88, pub. affairs mgr. diversified products ops., regional pub. affairs mgr., 1988-91; v.p. corp. comms. and govtl. affairs USL Capital Corp. (subs. Ford Fin. Svcs. Group), 1991-96; prin. The Chaparral Working Group, San Francisco, 1997—. Speechwriter for chmn. and CEO of Ford Motor Co., Henry Ford II; editor autobiography former Pres. Richard M. Nixon, 1977. Helen Dwight Reid Found. fellow, Carnegie Found./Maxwell Grad. Overseas fellow, 1962. Mem. Conference Bd. (coun. corp. comm. execs.), Nat. Press Club, Press Club Detroit, Press Club L.A., Motor Press Guild, Internat. Motor Press Assn., Leadership Detroit Alumni Assn., Am. Polit. Sci. Assn. Address: 1257 Union St San Francisco CA 94109-1922

SELTSER, RAYMOND, epidemiologist, educator; b. Boston, Dec. 17, 1923; s. Israel and Hannah (Littman) S.; m. Charlotte Frances Gale, Nov. 16, 1946; children: Barry Jay, Andrew David. MD, Boston U., 1947; MPH, Johns Hopkins U., 1957. Diplomate Am. Bd. Preventive Medicine (trustee, sec.-treas. 1974-77), Am. Bd. Med. Specialties (mem. exec. com. 1976-77). Asst. chief med. info. and intelligence br. U.S. Dept. Army, 1953-56; epidemiologist divsn. internal health USPHS, 1956-57; from asst. prof. to prof. epidemiology Johns Hopkins U. Sch. Hygiene and Pub. Health, Balt., 1957-81, assoc. dean, 1967-77, dep. dir. Oncology Ctr., 1977-81; dean U. Pitts. Grad. Sch. Pub. Health, 1981-87, prof. epidemiology, 1981-88, emeritus dean, prof. epidemiology, 1988—; assoc. dir. USPHS Ctrs. for Disease Control, Rockville, Md., 1988-90; assoc. dir. Ctr. for Gen. Health Svcs. Extramural Rsch. Agy. for Health Care Policy and Rsch., 1990-95, sr. advisor spl. population rsch. Ctr. Primary Care Rsch., 1995-98; med. and healthcare advisor Dept. Va Office Inspector Gen. Office Health Care Inspections, Chevy Chase, Md., 1997—. Cons. NIMH, 1958-70, also various govtl. health agys., 1958-79; expert cons. Pres.'s Commn. on Three Mile Island, 1979-80; mem. Three Mile Island Adv. Panel Health, Nat. Cancer Inst. Cancer Control Grant Rev. Com., Pa. Dept. Health Preventive Health Service Block Grant Adv. Task Force, Gov.'s VietNam Herbicide Info. Commn. Pa.; chmn. Toxic/Health Effects Adv. Com., 1985-87. Trustee, mem. exec. com., chmn. profl. adv. com. Harmarville Rehab. Ctr., Pitts., 1982-87; bd. dirs. Health Edn. Ctr., Media Info. Service. Served to capt. AUS, 1951-53, Korea. Decorated Bronze Star; recipient Centennial Alumni citation Boston U. Sch. Medicine, 1973; elected to Johns Hopkins Soc. of Scholars, 1986. Fellow AAAS, APHA (mem. governing coun. 1975-77, chmn. EPI sect. coun. 1979-80), Pa. Pub. Health Assn. (bd. dirs. 1985-88, pres.-elect 1986-88), Am. Coll. Preventive Medicine, Am. Heart Assn.; mem. Am. Epidemiol. Assn., Internat. Epidemiol. Assn., Am. Soc. Preventive Oncology, Am. Cancer Soc. (bd. dirs. Pa. divsn. 1985-87, mem. exec. com. 1986-87), Assn. Schs. Pub. Health (sec. 1969-71, mem. exec. com., chmn. edn. com. 1983-87), Soc. Med. Cons. Armed Forces, Soc. Epidemiologic Rsch., Nat. Coun. Radiation Protection and Measurements (consociate), Johns Hopkins Alumni Coun. (mem. exec. com. 1994-97), Sigma Xi, Delta Omega. E-mail: rseltser@msn.com.

SELTZER, BARRY S. federal judge; b. 1954; BA magna cum laude, Hamilton Coll., 1976; MBA, JD, NYU, 1980, LLM in Taxation, 1984. Atty. Trenam, Simmons, Kemker, Scharf, Barkin, Frye & O'Neill, Tampa, Fla., 1980-82; asst. U.S. atty. So. Dist. Fla., 1984-88; judge Broward County Ct., 1988-91; magistrate judge U.S. Dist. Ct. (so. dist.) Fla., Ft. Lauderdale, 1991—. Comment editor NYU Law Rev. of Law and Social Change. Recipient Spl. Achievement award Dept. Justice, commendations Drug Enforcement Agy., U.S. Secret Svc., Bur. of Alcohol, Tobacco and Firearms, Postal Inspection Svc., U.S. Customs Svc., USDA. Mem. ABA, Fed. Bar Assn., Fla. Bar, Broward County Bar Assn., Fed. Magistrate Judges Assn., Stephen Booner Inn of Ct. (past pres.), B'nai B'rith Justice Unit, Beta Gamma Sigma. Office: 109 US Courthouse 299 E Broward Blvd Fort Lauderdale FL 33301-1944

SELTZER, BOB, public relations executive; Grad., Syracuse U. Journalist Gannett Pubs.; mem. corp. pub. rels. dept. GAF Corp.; gen. mgr., pres. Porter Novelli, N.Y.C.; chmn., CEO Ogilvy Pub. Rels. Worldwide. Office: Ogilvy Public Relations Worldwide 909 3rd Ave New York NY 10022-4731

SELTZER, JEFFREY LLOYD, diversified financial services company executive; b. Bklyn., July 27, 1956; s. Bernard and Sue (Harris) S.; m. Ana Isabel Sifre, Sept. 2, 1985; children: Ian Alexander, Pamela Allison. BS in Econs. cum laude, U. Pa., 1978; JD, Georgetown U., 1981. Bar: N.Y. 1982. Assoc. Austrian, Lance & Stewart, N.Y.C., 1981-85; assoc. gen. counsel, asst. v.p. Shearson Lehman Bros., 1986; mng. dir. Lehman Bros., 1986-94; dep. chmn., mng. dir. CIBC Oppenheimer Corp., 1994-99; exec. v.p., COO Adirondack Trading Ptnrs., 1999—; assoc. Merrill Lynch Ctr. for Study of Internat. Fin. Mkts. and Svcs., Zarb Sch. Bus., Hofstra U. , 2001—. Spl. prof. law Hofstra U., 1999, faculty assoc. Merrill Lynch Ctr. Study Internat. Fin. Svcs. and Mkts. Zarb Sch. Bus. Author: The U.S. Greeting Card Market, 1977, Starting and Organizing a Business, 1984, Swap Risk Management: A Primer, 1988, A View for the Top: The Role of the Board of Directors and Senior Management in the Derivatives Business, 1995, Financial Strategy Roundtable: Derivatives, 1995. Mem. Nat. Policy Forum, 1994—97; mem. U.S. Trade Adv. Com. on Svc. Industries, Washington, 1990—94; mem. local adv. bd. County of Nassau, 1997—99; mem. adv. bd. Huntsman Program in Internat. Studies and Bus. U. Pa., Phila., 1997—; mem. securities industry coalition Bush-Quayle campaign, 1992; mem. small bus. adv. coun. Rep. Nat. Com., Washington, 1984—90; mem. nat. adv. coun. U.S. SBA; policy analyst Reagan-Bush Com., Arlington, Va., 1980; advisor Friends of Giuliani, N.Y.C., 1989, New Yorkers for Lew Lehrman, N.Y.C., 1981—82; dir. Nassau County Sports Commn., 1997—, mem. exec. com.; vice chmn., trustee Inst. Internat. Bankers, 1998—99; chmn. Class of 1978 fundraising U. Pa., 1997—. Recipient Disting. Alumnus award W. C. Mepham H.S., 1994. Mem. ABA, Re. Nat. Lawyers Assn., Federalist Soc., Ctr. for Study of Presidency, Securities Industry Assn. (chmn. swap and derivative products com. 1990-94). Home: 3 Yates Ln Jericho NY 11753-1418 Office: 120 W 45th St New York NY 10036-

SELTZER, JOANNE, poet; b. Detroit, Nov. 21, 1929; d. Samuel Zellman (dec.) and Ethel Goldstein (dec.); m. Stanley Seltzer, Feb. 10, 1951; children: Laura Lees, Ellen Hoffmann, Andrew Seltzer, Cynthia Seltzer. BA, U. Mich., 1951; MA, The Coll. of St. Rose, 1978. Freelance writer, 1973—. Mem. nat. steering com., dir. polit. action Feminist Writers' Guild, 1983-85. Author (chapbook) Adirondack Lake Poems, 1985, Suburban Landscape, 1988, Inside Invisible Walls, 1989. Recipient poetry awards, World Order of Narrative and Formalist Poets, 1986—2000, Tucumcari Lit. Rev., 1989, Amelia Islander mag., 1999, Sudden Opportunity Stipend, N.Y. Found. for the Arts, 1991. Mem. The Internat. Women's Writing Guild, Am. Lit. Transl. Assn., Associated Writing Programs, The Poetry Soc. Am., Poets & Writers, Hudson Valley Writers Guild. Jewish. Avocations: recreational walking, elderhostels, vegetarian cooking, serving a cat. Home: 2481 McGovern Dr Schenectady NY 12309

SELTZER, LEO, documentary filmmaker, educator, lecturer; b. Montreal, Que., Can., Mar. 13, 1910; came to U.S., 1916; s. Boris and Atalia (Gerowitz) S.; m. Elaine Basil, Apr. 15, 1941 (div. 1950); children: Janzie, John; m. Dicky Ransohoff, 1951 (div. 1963). BA, U. Mass., 1979. Faculty CCNY, 1949-54, New Sch. Social Rsch., 1949-51; pres. Leo Seltzer Assocs., Inc., N.Y.C., 1950-90; faculty Columbia U., 1954-60, Phila. Coll. Art, 1955-56, NYU, N.Y.C., 1966-67; dir. audio-visual therapy program pediatrics ward Univ. Hosp., 1970-76; instr. film prodn. workshop Sch. Visual Arts, 1969-84; adj. prof. performing and creative arts Coll. S.I., N.Y., 1977-78; prof. film Bklyn. Coll., 1978-83, prof. emeritus film, 1983—. Lectr. in U.S. and abroad, including Mus. Modern Art, N.Y.C., Marymount Coll., Ghent U., Belgium, Libr. Congress, others. Prodr., dir. over 60 social documentaries and TV films in 35 countries, including First Steps, UN Divsn. Social Affairs, 1946 (Acad. award for best documentary 1947), Fate of a Child, UN Divsn. Tech. Assistance, 1949, For the Living, City of N.Y., 1952, (with Walter Cronkite) Conquest of Aging, 1958, All the Years, 1959, Jacqueline Kennedy's Asian Journey, 1962, Progress Through Freedom (pres. Kennedy's visit to Mex.), 1962, (with Edward R. Murrow) The American Commitment, USIA, 1963, Report on Acupuncture, 1977, (with John Huston) Let There Be Light; prodr., dir.: Nat. Film Bd. Can., 1941; chief cons. visual aids City of N.Y., 1941-42; prodr.: N.Y.C. Mcpl. Film and TV Unit Sta. WNYC, 1949-50; film biographer to White House for Pres. Kennedy, 1962; exec. prodr. Quadrant Comms., Inc., 1973-75 (7 citations Cannes and Edinburgh Film Festivals 1948-63); films are in U.S. Nat. Archives, Libr. of Congress, in collection and distributed by Mus. Modern Art; photographs are in Houston Mus. Fine Arts collection, Nat. Gallery Can., Visual Studies Workshop, Rochester, N.Y., N.Y.C. 5th Ave. Libr.; reconstructed 6 Am. social documentary films of 1930's in 1978 for Mus. Modern Art Film Archives, 1976-77; subject of TV program by Bill Moyers, A Walk Through the Twentieth Century, Blackside Prodns., CBC, BBC TV; contbr. film footage to Nat. Geographic, History Channel, others. 1st lt. Signal Corps. U.S. Army; directed tng. and information films for U.S. Army and public; officer in charge of Film and Equipment Depot, ETO, 1947. Recipient Acad. award for best documentary, 1948, Silver medals Venice Film Festival, 1949, Freedom's Found. award, 1953, Golden Reel award Scholastic Mag., 1955, Robert Flaherty award CCNY, 1956, Silver medal Atlanta Internat. Film Festival, 1977; honored in tribute Mus. Modern Art, 1990; oral history N.Y. Fifth Ave. Libr. Archives. Mem. Dirs. Guild Am. (charter). Achievements include research on Early American social documentary films. Home and Office: 368 E 69th St New York NY 10021-5706

SELTZER, MITCHELL SHERMAN, hotel executive; b. Abington, Pa., June 10, 1948; s. Larry and Mary Ellen (Gallagher) S.; m. Laura Ann Hayhurst Seltzer; 1 child, M. Babe. BA, Pa. State U., 1971. Chef Valley Forge Hilton Hotel, King of Prussia, Pa., 1974-77, Cutillo's Restaurant, Pottstown, 1977-79; gen. mgr. Unisys Edn. Ctr., Malvern, 1984-88; gen. mgr. Dave Thomas Ctr. Duke U., Durham, N.C., 1988-90; gen. mgr. Am. Coll. Marriott Corp., Bryn Mawr, Pa., 1990-92; gen. mgr. Certain-teed Corp. World Hdqr. Marriott Corp., 1992-94; gen. mgr., operating ptnr. First Noah's Corp., 1994-97, Hospitality Staff Phila., 1997-98; gen. mgr. Profl. Edn. and Conf. Ctr., Kent State U., 1999—. Avocations: skiing, golf. Home: 2219 Applegrove St NW North Canton OH 44720-6252 E-mail: mseltzer@stark.kent.edu.

SELTZER, RICHARD C. lawyer; b. N.Y.C., Sept. 3, 1943; s. Edward and Beatrice (Fishman) S.; m. Carol Reische, Aug. 31, 1969; children: Wendy, Mark. BA, Harvard U., 1965; JD, Columbia U., 1968. Bar: N.Y. 1969, U.S. Dist. Ct. (so. and ea. dists.) N.Y. 1969, U.S. Ct. Appeals (5th cir.) 1978, U.S. Ct. Appeals (2nd cir.) 1987, U.S. Supreme Ct. 1995. Ptnr. Kaye Scholer LLP, N.Y.C., 1969—. Mem. ABA, Assn. of Bar of City of N.Y. Office: Kaye Scholer 425 Park Ave New York NY 10022-3506

SELTZER, RICHARD WARREN, JR. writer, editor, consultant; b. Clarksville, Tenn., Feb. 23, 1946; s. Richard Warren and Helen Isabella (Estes) S.; m. Barbara Ann Hartley, July 28, 1973; children: Robert, Heather, Michael, Timothy. BA, Yale U., 1969; MA in Comparative Lit., U. Mass., 1972. Editor Benwill Pub., Boston, 1973-79; sr. communications cons., Internet cons. Digital Equip. Corp., Maynard, Mass., 1979-98; ind. internet cons. and writer, 1998—. Pub. B&R Samizdat Express, Boston, 1974—. Author: Name of Hero, 1981, Lizard of Oz, 1974, Now and Then, 1976; editor: Internet-on-a-Disk, 1994—, Please Copy This Disk, 1993—, The Alta Vista Search Revolution, 1997, Shop Online the Lazy Way, 1999, Ethiopia Through Russian Eyes, 2000, Take Charge of Your Website, 2001, Web Business Boot Camp, 2001, My Internet: A Personal View of Internet Business Opportunities; author short stories. With USAR, 1969-75. Mem. Internat. Assn. Bus. Communicators, U.S. Chess Fedn. Avocations: chess, Internet, Russian translation. Home: PO Box 161 West Roxbury MA 02132-0002 E-mail: seltzer@samizdat.com.

SELTZER, VICKI LYNN, obstetrician, gynecologist; b. June 2, 1949; d. Herbert Melvin and Marian Elaine (Willinger) S.; m. Richard Stephen Brach, Sept. 2, 1973; children: Jessica Lillian, Eric Robert. BS, Rensselaer Poly. Inst., 1969; MD, NYU, 1973. Diplomate Am. Bd. Ob-Gyn. Intern Bellevue Hosp., N.Y.C., 1973-74, resident in ob-gyn., 1974-77; fellow gynecol. cancer Am. Cancer Soc., 1977-78, Meml. Sloan Kettering Cancer Ctr., N.Y.C., 1978-79; assoc. dir. gynecol. cancer Albert Einstein Coll. Medicine, 1979-83; assoc. prof. ob-gyn. SUNY, Stony Brook, 1983-89; prof. ob-gyn. Albert Einstein Coll. Medicine, 1989—. V.p. women's health svcs. North Shore-L.I. Jewish Health Sys., 199—; chair ob-gyn. North Shore Univ. Hosp., 1999—, chair med. bd., 2001—; chair ob-gyn. L.I. Jewish Med. Ctr., 1993—; dir. ob-gyn. Queens Hosp. Ctr., Jamaica, N.Y., 1983-93, pres. med. bd., 1986-89. Author: Every Woman's Guide to Breast Cancer, 1987; editor-in-chief: Primary Care Update for the Ob-Gyn, 1993—; editor: Women's Primary Health Care, 1995, 2d edit., 2000; mem. editl. bd. Women's Life mag., 1980-82, Jour. of the Jacobs Inst. Women's Health, 1990-95; contbr. numerous articles to profl. jours.; host Weekly Ob-Gyn. TV Program, Lifetime Med. TV. Chair health com. Nat. Coun. Women, N.Y.C., 1979-84; mem. Mayor Beame's Task Force on Rape, N.Y.C., 1974-76; bd. govs. Nat. Coun. Women's Health, 1985-94; chair Coun. on Resident Edn. in Ob-Gyn., 1987-93. Recipient citation Am. Med. Women's Assn., 1973, Nat. Safety Coun., 1978, Achiever award L.I. Ctr. Bus. and Profl. Women, 1987; Galloway Fund fellow, 1975. Fellow N.Y. Obstet. Soc. (pres. 1999-2000), Am. Coll. Ob-Gyn. (v.p. 1993-94, pres.-elect 1996-97, pres. 1997-98, gynecol. practice com. 1981, examiner Am. Bd. Ob-Gyn. 1988—); mem. Women's Med. Assn. (v.p. N.Y. 1974-79, editl. bd. jour. 1985—, resident rev. com. for ob-gyn. 1993-98), Am. Med. Women's Assn. (com. chair 1975-79, editl. bd. jour. 1986—), N.Y. Cancer Soc., NYU Sch. Med. Alumni Assn. (bd. govs. 1979—, v.p. 1987-91, pres. 1992-93), Alpha Omega Alpha. Office: LI Jewish Med Ctr New Hyde Park NY 11040

SELTZER, VIVIAN CENTER, clinical psychologist, educator; b. Mpls., May 27, 1931; d. Aaron M. and Hannah (Chazanow) Center; m. William Seltzer; children: Jonathan, Francesca S. Rothseid, Aeryn S. Fenton. BA summa cum laude, U. Minn., 1951; MSW, U. Pa., 1953; PhD, Bryn Mawr Coll., 1976. Lic. psychologist; cert. sch. psychologist; lic. social worker, Pa.; cert. marriage and family therapist. Family counselor, Phila. and Miami, Fla., 1953-60; pvt. practice Phila., 1965—; prof. human devel. and behavior U. Pa., 1976—. Exch. prof. U. Edinburgh, 1979-80; vis. prof. Hebrew U., Jerusalem, 1984-85; chair internat. com. U. Pa., various other coms., chair faculty senate. Author: Adolescent Social Development: Dynamic Functional Interaction, 1982, The Psychosocial Worlds of the Adolescent, 1989; contbr. articles to profl. jours. Mem. bd. regents Gratz Coll., Phila., 1965—, v.p., 1989-97, chair acad. affairs com., 1980—. Mem. APA, Pa. Psychol. Assn., Phila. Soc. Clin. Psychologists (bd. dirs. 1975-86, 99—, program chair 1980-86, 2001—), Internat. Coun. Psychologists, Phi Beta Kappa. Fax: 215-573-2099. E-mail: seltzer@ssw.upenn.edu.

SELTZER, WILLIAM, statistician, social researcher, former international organization director; b. N.Y.C., Sept. 22, 1934; s. William B. Seltzer and Edith S. (Goldman) Alt.; m. Jane E. Berger, Nov. 20, 1970; children: Benjamin, Ezra. BA, U. Chgo., 1956. Rsch. asst. Health Info. Found., N.Y.C., 1957-60; statistician U.S. Bur. Census, Suitland, Md., 1960-64; advisor Pakistan Inst. Devel., Econs. and Cen. Statis. Office, Karachi, 1964-68; staff assoc. Population Coun., N.Y.C., 1968-74; br. chief UN Statis. Office, 1974-86, dir., 1986-94; sr. advisor to under-sec.-gen. Dept. Econ. and Social Info. and Policy Analysis, 1993-94; sr. rsch. schlar Fordham U., 1995—. Mem. com. on population and demography, chair panel on data collection NAS, Washington, 1977-82, mem. Roundtable on the Demography of Forced Migration, 2001--; cons. UN Population Fund, 1995, Internat. Criminal Tribunal for Rwanda, 1996, UN Stats. Divsn., 1996-98, Internat. Labor Office, 1997, World Bank, 1997-98. Author: Poems, 1960, Politics and Statistics, 1994; co-author: Population Growth Estimation, 1973; also various UN documents, jour. articles, reports. Fellow Am. Statis. Assn. (chair social stats. sect. 1983-84, chair com. on internat. rels. 1986-87, chair com. on profl. ethics 2000—), Royal Statis. Soc. (hon.;); mem. Population Assn. Am., Internat. Statis. Inst., Internat. Assn. Ofcl. Statisticians. Mem. Soc. Of Friends. Office: Fordham U Dept Sociology and Anthropology 441 E Fordham Rd Bronx NY 10458-5149 E-mail: seltzer@fordham.edu.

SELVADURAI, ANTONY PATRICK SINNAPPA, civil engineering educator, applied mathematician, consultant; b. Matara, Sri-Lanka, Sept. 23, 1942; arrived in Can., 1975; s. Kanapathiyar Sinnappa and W. Mary Adeline (Fernando) S.; m. Sally Joyce; children: Emily, Paul, Mark, Elizabeth. Diploma in Engring., Brighton Poly., U.K., 1964; Diploma, Imperial Coll./London U., 1965; MS, Stanford U., 1967; PhD in Theoretical Mechanics, U. Nottingham, 1971; DSc, U. Nottingham, Eng., 1986. Registered profl. engr., Can.; chartered mathematician, U.K. Staff rsch. engr. Woodward Clyde Assocs., Oakland, Calif., 1966-67; rsch. assoc. dept. theoretical mechanics U. Nottingham, 1969-70; lectr. dept. civil engring. U. Aston, Birmingham, Eng., 1971-75; asst. prof. civil engring. Carleton U., Ottawa, Ont., Can., 1975-76, assoc. prof. Can., 1976-81, prof. Can., 1982-93, chmn. dept. Can., 1982-90, Davidson Dunton Rsch. lectr. Can., 1987; prof., chmn. dept. civil engring./applied mechanics McGill U., Montreal, 1993-96. Vis. rsch. scientist Bechtel Group, Inc., San Francisco, 1981-82; vis. prof. U. Nottingham, 1986, Inst. de Mécanique de Grenoble, France, 1990; cons. Atomic Energy of Can. Ltd., Pinawa, Man., 1983-96—, Ministry of Transp. Ont., Toronto, 1984-97, Fleet Tech., Ottawa, 1988—, Atomic Energy Control Bd., 1987—. Author: Elastic Analysis of Soil Foundation Interaction, 1979, (with R.O. Davis) Elasticity and Geomechanics, 1996m Plasticity and Geomechanics; editor: Mechanics of Structured Media, 1981, (with G.Z. Voyiadjis) Mechanics of Material Interfaces, 1986, Developments of Mechanics, 1987, (with M.J. Boulon) Mechanics of Geomaterial Interfaces, 1995, Mechanics of Poroelastic Media, 1996, Partial Differential Equations in Mechanics, Vol. 1. Fundamentals, Laplace's Equation, Diffusion Equation, Wave Equation, 2000, Vol. 2, The Biharmonic Equation, Poisson's Equation, 2000. Recipient Rsch. award Alexander von Humboldt Found., 1997; King George VI Meml. fellow English Speaking Union of Commonwealth, 1965, rsch. fellow SRC, U.K., 1969, Erskine fellow U. Canterbury, New Zealand, 1992, 98, Killam rsch. fellow Can. Coun. for Arts, 2000-02. Fellow Am. Acad. Mechanics, Can. Soc. Civil Engring. (Leipholz medal 1991), Assoc. Prof. Engrs. of Ont. (Engring. medal for rsch. 1993), Engring. Inst. Can., Inst. Math. and Its Applications; mem. Internat. Assn. for Computer Methods and Advances in Geomechanics (award for significant paper in the category theory computational analytical 1994, paper prize computational and analytical theory category 1997, John Booker medal 2001). Roman Catholic. Office: McGill U Dept Civil Engring Montreal QC QC Canada H3A 2K6 E-mail: patrick.selvaduria@mcgill.ca.

SELVAGGI, SUZANNE MARIE, pathologist, educator; b. Amityville, N.Y., Apr. 6, 1952; d. Gerald Anthony and Gilda Mary Selvaggi; m. Robert Bruce Washabaugh, June 10, 1978; 1 child, Sarah Jane Washabaugh. BA in Biology, Case Western Res. U., 1974; MD, Albert Einstein Med. Coll., 1978; pathologist, NYU Med. Ctr., 1983. Asst. prof. pathology Cornell Med. Ctr., N.Y.C., 1983-85, Wayne State U., Detroit, 1987-90; assoc. prof. pathology U. Mich., Ann Arbor, 1990-97, Loyola U. Med. Ctr., Maywood, Ill., 1997—2001; prof. U. Wis., Madison, 2001—. Author: (book) Fine Needle Aspiration of Pelvic Organs, 1997; mem. editl. rev. bd. Diagnostic Cytopathology, 1995—, Cancer Pathology, 1997—; sect. editor Diagnostic Cytopathology, 1999—; contbr. articles to med. jours. Mem. Am. Soc. Clin. Pathologists, Am. Soc. Cytopathology, Am. Soc. Gynecologic Pathologists, Papanicolaou Soc. Cytopathology. Home: 2940 Ivanhoe Glen Fitchburg WI 53711 Office: U Wis Hosp and Clinics 600 Highland Ave Madison WI 63792 E-mail: sselvaggi@facstaff.wisc.edu.

SELVAIS, PHILIPPE LEON, endocrinologist; b. Tournai, Belgium, Jan. 25, 1965; s. Michel and Renee (Boudailliez) S. MD, U. Louvain, 1989, PhD, 1997, BPhil, 1998. Resident in internal medicine U. Louvain, 1989-91, rsch. fellow, 1991-93; rsch. asst. Belgian Fund for Scientific Rsch., Brussels, 1993-94; adj. scientist NIH, Bethesda, Md., 1994-95; resident internal medicine U. Louvain, 1996-99; chief endocrine unit Hornu Med. Ctr., Brussels, 2000—. Sr. cons. U. Hosp. Erasme, Brussels, 2000—. Contbr. articles to profl. jours. Recipient Rsch. prize NATO, 1994. Mem. European Soc. for Clin. Investigation, Belgian Soc. for Internal Medicine, Belgian Diabetes Assn., Belgian Hypertension Com., Belgian Endocine Soc., Belgian Thyroid Club. Roman Catholic. Avocations: Western philosophy, collecting Sherlock Holmes memorabilia. Office: UCL/DIAB 5474 Hornu Med Ctr Rt de ppocrate B-7301 Hornu Belgium

SELVER, PAUL DARRYL, lawyer; b. N.Y.C., May 28, 1947; s. Rene T. Selver and Marilyn (Steiner) Pomerance; m. Ellen J. Roller, Jan. 22, 1984; children: Adam, Max, Katelyn. BA magna cum laude, Harvard U., 1969, JD, 1972. Bar: N.Y. 1973. Assoc. Hale Russell & Gray, N.Y.C., 1972-74; ptnr. Brown and Wood (formerly Tufo and Zuccotti), 1974-94, Battle Fowler, N.Y.C., 1994-2000, Paul Hastings Janofsky & Walker, N.Y.C., 2000—. Lectr. of law Columbia U. Law Sch., 1994-97; assoc. adj. prof. Sch. Architecture, Planning and Preservation Columbia U., N.Y.C., 1986-88. Author: (N.Y. practice guide book) Real Estate: Land Use Regulations, 1986; edit. bd. Metroplis Mag., 1983-86. Mem. Manhattan Cmty. Bd. #6, N.Y.C., 1974-76, Westside Transit Com., N.Y.C., 1987; bd. dirs. Manhattan Bower Corp., N.Y.C., 1983-97; mem. Sch. Facilities Planning Commn., Mountain Lakes, N.J., 1996-97. Mem.: ABA, Assn. of Bar of City of N.Y. Office: Paul Hastings Janofsky & Walker LLP 75 E 55th St New York NY 10022-3205

SELVIG, JETTIE PIERCE, lawyer; b. Bee Branch, Ark., Dec. 16, 1932; d. Jefferson Davis Pierce and Ruba Ann Bivens; m. Rolf S. Selvig Sr., Jan. 27, 1962; children: Rolf S. Jr., Erik K., John L. LLB, U. Ark., 1954. Bar: Ark. 1953, Calif. 1961, U.S. Supreme Ct. 1969. Pvt. practice, 1961—. Bd. dirs. San Francisco Neighborhood Legal Assistance Found., 1975. Recipient Cert. of Honor, Bd. Suprs. of City and County of San Francisco, 1969, Countess of Pulaski Proclamation, Quorum Ct. of Pulaski County, 1969, Silver Bowl of Appreciation, Girl Scouts Am.; named Hidden Heroine, San Francisco Bay Girl Scout Coun., 1976. Mem. Nat. Assn. Women Lawyers (state del., assembly del., bus. mgr., treas., v.p., pres.-elect, pres. 1969-70, chairperson, mem. women in pub. svc. com. 1971-75), Calif. State Bar (disciplinary com. 1972-74), Calif. Applicants' Attys. Assn. (dir. No. Calif. chpt. 1974, v.p. 1975, pres. 1976, 77, sec. and pres.-elect statewide assn., pres. statewide assn. 1981-82, life mem.), Queen's Bench (life, asst. sec.-treas., dir. 1972, treas. 1973, mem. Law Day com., chmn. publicity com., v.p. 1974, pres. 1975, Lifetime Achievement award 1995, found. pres. 1974-76), Women's Equity Action League (treas. Calif. divsn. 1970-72, pres. Calif. divsn. 1973), Legal Aid Soc. San Francisco (bd. dirs. 1976), Lawyer's Club San Francisco (life), del. to state bar conv.) Democrat. Home and Office: 469 Molino Ave Mill Valley CA 94941-3380 Fax: 415-383-6605. E-mail: jettiecoleen@msn.com.

SELVIN, BEATRICE, retired anesthesiologist; b. Hartford, Conn., Oct. 13, 1922; BA, U. Mich., 1942; MD, N.Y. Med. Coll., 1945. Diplomate Am. Bd. Anesthesiology. Intern Queens (N.Y.) Gen. Hosp., 1945-46; resident U. Chgo. clinics, 1946-47, Columbia-Presbyn. Med. Ctr., N.Y.C., 1947-48, mem. staff, 1948-54, Meml. Ctr. for Cancer, N.Y.C., 1945-63, U. Md. Hosp., Balt., 1964-86, ret., 1986. Prof. U. Md. Sch. Medicine, Balt., 1964-86. Bd. dirs. Sanctuary Project Life, 1995—. Mem. AMA, Am. Soc. Anesthesiologists, Md. State Med. Soc. (mem. com. addictions 1986—). Home: 251 Longpoint Rd Crownsville MD 21032-1853

SELVIN, DAVID F. retired editor, journalist; b. Tooele, Utah, Mar. 12, 1913; s. Sol. J. and Fania Selvin; m. Susan Small, Jan. 31, 1939 (dec. Apr. 2000); children: Steve, Michael, Joel. BS, U. Calif., Berkeley, 1933, MA, 1935; LLD (hon.), San Francisco State U., 2000. Labor editor various local, state and nat. publs., 1943-89. Cons., pub. rels. profl. various local, regional and nat. unions, 1943-85. Author: Sky Full of Storm, 1966, 75, The Other San Francisco, 1969, A Place in the Sun, 1981, A Terrible Anger, 1996. Chair adv. bd. Labor Archives and Rsch. Ctr., San Francisco State U., 1986—. Staff sgt. AUS, 1944-46. Sr. Fulbright scholar, 1961-62. Avocation: photography. Home: 63 Fairlawn Dr Berkeley CA 94708

SELWOOD, PIERCE TAYLOR, lawyer; b. Evanston, Ill., July 31, 1939; s. Pierce Wilson and Alice (Taylor) S.; m. Alexis Fuerbringer, June 8, 1964; children: Allison, Jonathan. AB, Princeton U., 1961; JD, Harvard U., 1964. Bar: Calif. 1965, U.S. Dist. Ct. (cen. dist.) Calif. 1965, U.S. Dist. Ct. (no. dist.) Calif. 1966, US. Dist. Ct. (ea. dist.) Calif. 1989, U.S. Ct. Appeals (9th cir.) 1970. Assoc. Sheppard, Mullin, Richter & Hampton, L.A., 1964-70, ptnr., 1971—, chmn. litigation dept., 1986-91. Lectr. Calif. Continuing Edn. Bar, Berkley, 1970-84, Practicing Law Inst., N.Y.C., 1980s, ABA Nat. Inst., Chgo., 1986. Mem. ABA (chmn. various subcoms. 1984-89), Calif. Bar Assn., L.A. County Bar Assn., Assn. Bus. Trial Lawyers (bd. gov.s 1977-79), Jonathan Club (L.A.), Princeton Club So. Calif. (pres. 1970-72). Republican. Episcopalian. Avocations: tennis, hiking, camping, travel. Office: Sheppard Mullin Richter & Hampton 333 S Hope St Fl 48 Los Angeles CA 90071-1406

SELWYN, DONALD, engineering administrator, researcher, inventor, educator; b. N.Y.C., Jan. 31, 1936; s. Gerald Selwyn and Ethel (Waxman) Selwyn) Moss; m. Delia Nemec, Mar. 11, 1956 (div. Mar. 1983); children: Laurie, Gerald, Marcia; m. Myra Rowman Markoff, Mar. 17, 1986 BA, Thomas A. Edison Coll. N.J., 1977. Svc. engr. Bendix Aviation, Teterboro, N.J., 1956-59; svc. mgr. Bogue Electric Mfg. Co., Paterson, 1959; proposal engr. advanced design group Curtiss-Wright Corp., East Paterson, 1960-64; ind. bioengr., rehab. engring. cons. N.Y.C., 1964-67; pres. bd. trustees, exec. tech. and tng. dir. Nat. Inst. for Rehab. Engring., Hewitt, N.J., 1967—. Cons. N.Y. State Office Vocat. Rehab., 1964—, Pres.'s Com. on Employment of Handicapped, 1966—, bus. and industry and for Am. with Disabilities Act compliance, also numerous state rehab. agys., health depts., vol. groups, agys. for handicapped in fgn. countries; cons., trainer computer applications. Contbr. articles on amateur radio, rehab. of severely and totally disabled to profl., gen. mags. Trustee Nat. Inst. for Rehab. Engring., Rehab. Research Center Trust. Decorated Knight of Malta; recipient Humanitarian award U.S. Ho. of Reps., 1972, Bicentennial Pub. Service award, 1975. Mem. Am. Acad. Consultants, I.E.E.E. (sr.), Soc. Tech. Writers and Pubs. (sr.), Nat. Rehab. Assn., N.Y. Acad. Scis., Mensa. Achievements include being the developer or co-developer field-expander glasses for hemianopsia, tunnel and monocular vision, electronic speech clarifiers, electronically guided wheelchairs, off-road vehicles and cars for quadriplegics, others; patentee indsl., mil. and handicapped rehab. inventions; expert, cons. on handicapped employment, handicapped product safety including design, manufacture, labelling and user instrnl. material, 1990—. Office: Nat Inst Rehab Engring PO Box T Hewitt NJ 07421-1020 E-mail: dons@TheOffice.net. *As I travel the road of life, it becomes more and more evident to me that people matter most, and technology is useful and good only so long as it serves man, and man is not made to serve technology. From technician I have evolved to humanist, using technology only as a tool. Always think positive. Don't waste your time or emotional energy on people who do not appreciate your good will. Think only about those who do, and you'll achieve more and enjoy life.*

SELYA, BRUCE MARSHALL, federal judge; b. Providence, May 27, 1934; s. Herman C. and Betty (Brier) S.; children: Dawn Meredith Selya Sherman, Lori Ann BA magna cum laude, Harvard U., 1955, JD magna cum laude, 1958. Bar: D.C. 1958, R.I. 1960. Law clk. U.S. Dist. Ct. R.I., Providence, 1958-60; assoc. Gunning & LaFazia, 1960-62; ptnr. Gunning, LaFazia, Gnys & Selya, 1963-74, Selya & Iannuccillo, Providence, 1974-82; judge U.S. Dist. Ct. R.I., 1982-86, U.S. Ct. Appeals (1st cir.), Providence, 1986—. Judge Lincoln Probate Ct., R.I., 1965-72; mem. R.I. Jud. Council, 1964-72, sec., 1965-70, chmn., 1971-72; mem. Gov.'s Commn. on Crime and Adminstrn. Justice, 1967-69; del. Nat. Conf. on Revisions to Fed. Appellate Practice, 1968-82; mem. various spl. govtl. commns. and adv. groups Chmn. bd. trustees Bryant Coll., Smithfield, R.I., 1986-92; bd. dirs. Lifespan Health Sys., chmn. bd. dirs., 1994—, mem. bd. trustees R.I. Hosp. subs. Recipient Louis Dembitz Brandeis medal for disting. legal svc. Brandeis U., 1988, Neil Houston award Justice Assistance of Am., 1992. Mem. ABA, FBA, Fed. Judges Assn., R.I. Bar Assn. (chmn. various coms.), R.I. Bar Found., U.S. Jud. Conf. (mem. com. on jud. br.), Am. Arbitration Assn., Am. Judicature Soc. (bd. dirs.). Jewish. Home: 224 George St Providence RI 02906-3115 Office: US Ct Appeals US Courthouse 1 Exchange Terr Rm 316 Providence RI 02903*

SELYEM, BRUCE JADE, freelance/self-employed photographer; b. Cleve., Aug. 24, 1953; s. Edwin Joseph and Ursula Anna (Neustadt) S.; m. Leslie Ann Smith Shaw, Aug. 25, 1975 (div. Mar. 1982). m. Barbara Jean Krupp, 1998. BS in Photography, Mont. State U. Color photo lab. technician Mont. State U., Bozeman, 1986-88, plant pathology lab. asst., 1987-88, tchg. asst., 1989, staff photographer Mus. of the Rockies, 1989—2002. Trail crew leader Chugach Nat. Forest, Seward, Alaska, 1989; mem. Historic Preservation Bd. Gallatin County, Bozeman, 1992-98, chmn., 1995-98; founder, pres. Country Grain Elevator Hist. Soc., Bozeman, 1996—. Photog. contbr.: Glacier Country, Montana's Indians, Montana Almanac, Digging Up Tyrannosaurus Rex, Tyrannosaurus Rex, also numerous other books, mags., reports, catalogs and profl. jours. Asst. fire chief East Glacier Park (Mont.) Vol. Fire Dept., 1979-83. Recipient Program Spkr. award Mont. Com. for the Humanities, 1996—. Avocations: hiking, backpacking, cross country skiing, canoeing, traveling. Home: 155 Prospector Trl Bozeman MT 59718-7988 E-mail: bselyem@grainelevatorphotos.com.

SELZ, PETER HOWARD, art historian, educator; b. Munich, Germany, Mar. 27, 1919; came to U.S., 1936, naturalized, 1942; s. Eugene and Edith S.; m. Thalia Cheronis, June 10, 1948 (div. 1965); children: Tanya Nicole Eugenia, Diana Gabrielle Hamlin; m. Carole Schemmerling, Dec. 18, 1983 Student, Columbia U., U. Paris; MA, U. Chgo., 1949, PhD, 1954; DFA, Calif. Coll. Arts and Crafts, 1967. Instr. U. Chgo., 1951-56; asst. prof. art history, head art edn. dept. Inst. Design, Ill. Inst. Tech., Chgo., 1949-55; chmn. art dept., dir. art gallery Pomona Coll., 1955-58; curator dept. painting and sculpture exhbns. Mus. Modern Art, 1958-65; dir. univ. art mus. U. Calif., Berkeley, 1965-73, prof. history of art. 1965—; Zaks prof. Hebrew U., Jerusalem, 1976. Vis. prof. CUNY, 1987; mem. pres.'s council on art and architecture Yale U., 1971-76. Author: German Expressionist Painting, 1957, New Images of Man, 1959, Art Nouveau, 1960, Mark Rothko, 1961, Fifteen Polish Painters, 1961, The Art of Jean Dubuffet, 1962, Emil Nolde, 1963, Max Beckmann, 1964, Alberto Giacometti, 1965, Directions in Kinetic Sculpture, 1966, Funk, 1967, Harold Paris, 1972, Ferdinand Holder, 1972, Sam Francis, 1975, The American Presidency in Political Cartoons, 1976, Art in Our Times, 1981, Art in a Turbulent Era, 1985, Chillida, 1986, Twelve Artists from the GDR, 1989, Max Beckmann: The Self Portraits, 1992, William Congdon, 1992, Beckmann, 1996, Gottfried Helnwein, 1997, Beyond the Mainstream, 1997; co-author: Theories and Documents of Contemporary Art, 1996, Beyond the Mainstream, 1998, Barbara Chase-Riboud, 1999, Nathan Oliveira, 2001; editor: Art in Am., 1967—, Art Quar., 1969-75, Arts, 1981-92, Cross-Currents in Modern Art, 2000, Nathan Oliveira, 2001; contbr. articles to art publs. Trustee Am. Crafts Coun., 1985—89, Marin Mus. Assn., 1993—; mem.adv. coun. archives Am. Art, 1971—; mem. acquisitions com. Fine Arts Mus., San Francisco, 1993; pres. Berkeley Art Project, 1988—93; project dir. Christo's Running Fence, 1973—76; commr. Alameda County Art Commn., 1990—95; bd. dirs. Richmond Art Ctr., 1998—; chair Berkeley Art Festival, 1997—2000; trustee Neue Galerie, New York, 2001—. Decorated Order of Merit Fed. Republic Germany; Fulbright grantee Paris, 1949-50; fellow Belgian-Am. Ednl. Found.; sr. fellow NEH, 1972; resident Rockefeller Found. Study Ctr., Bellagio, 1994. Mem. Coll. Art Assn. Am. (dir. 1959-64, 67-71), AAUP, Internat. Art Critics Assn. Office: U Calif Dept Art History Berkeley CA 94720-0001

SELZ, THALIA CHERONIS, writer, educator; b. Chgo., Oct. 15, 1925; d. Nicholas Dimitrios and Irene (Hamlin) Cheronis; m. Peter Howard Selz, June 10, 1948 (div. Aug. 1965); children: Tanya Nicole Eugenia Selz, Gabrielle Hamlin Selz Mync. BA, Oberlin Coll., 1947; MA, U. Chgo., 1951. Instr. English Pomona Coll., Claremont, Calif., 1955-57; lectr. dept. writing Columbia U., N.Y.C., 1966-67; instr. English Queens Coll., Flushing, N.Y., 1967-68, 70-71, Northeastern Ill. U., Chgo., 1976-79; vis. fiction writer U. Mo.,

Columbia, Mo., 1979-81; writer-in-residence Trinity Coll., Hartford, Conn., 1981-98, writer-in-residence grad. studies, 1996-98. Cons. N.Y. Coun. on Arts, N.Y.C., 1969-70; founder, editor Story Quar., Highland Park, Ill., 1974-78; judge lit. competitions, U.S., Can., 1979—. Contbr. (book) Best American Short Stories, 1962, Prize Stories-O. Henry Awards, 1963, American Fiction #3, 1992. Recipient O. Henry award, 1963, Ill. Arts Coun. award for fiction, 1978, 81; NEA Creative Writing fellow, 1981-82; winner Writers' Workshop Memoirs Contest, 1997; grantee Conn. Commn. on Arts, 1990-91, Papanikolas Charitable Trust, 1991-92. Fellow MacDowell Colony Fellows, Yaddo Fellows; mem. Assn. Writing Programs, Greek-Am. Women's Network, Modern Greek Studies Assn., Poets & Writers Inc. Democrat.

SELZER, KENNETH A. neurologist, editor; b. N.Y.C., Mar. 2, 1954; s. Milton C. and Sylvia (Bennett) S.; m. Lynn Dunbar, Mar. 2, 1955; 1 child, Jenna Nicole. BA in Chemistry, SUNY, 1977; MD, UCLA, 1982; postgrad., Harvard Bus. Sch., 1987-90. Diplomate Am. Bd. Neurology and Psychiatry. Internship St. Mary's Hosp., Long Beach, Calif., 1982-83; med. dir. Mercy Carepoint Family Med. Group, San Diego, 1983-88; pres., CEO Integrated Healthcare Svcs., Inc., 1983-88; gen. ptnr. La Jolla Cons. Group, 1989-90; editor-in-chief Neuropractice, 1993—; CEO INC Rsch., 1996—. Prin. investigator TPA trial for acute treatment Ischemic Strokes Vanderbilt U., 1992; biomed. rsch. asst. SUNY, Binghamton, 1974-76. N.Y. State Regents scholar, 1972-76. Home: 7175 Eagle Heights Dr Mattawan MI 49071 Office: Pharmacia 700 Portage Rd Kalamazoo MI 49001

SEMAAN, SALAAM J. healthcare researcher; b. Apr. 12, 1959; BS in Biology and Chemistry, Am. U. Beirut, Labanon, 1980; MPH in Epidemiology and Biostatistics, Am. U. Beirut, Lebanon, 1982; DPH in Health Svcs., Evaluation, and Policy Rsch., John Hopkins U., 1990. Survey rschr. and analyst Office Profl. Stds. and Sys. Analysis Ministry Health, Manama, Bahrain, 1981-82; primary health care officer dept. health care programs Save the Children Found., Beirut, 1982-85; rsch. assoc. Sch. Nursing U. Pa., Phila., 1990-91; dir. rsch. dept. orthopedic surgery Albert Einstein Med. Ctr., 1992; sr. rsch. assoc. divsn. rsch. and evaluation Phila. Health Mgmt. Corp., 1993—96; behavioral scientist divsn. HIV/AIDS Prevention Ctrs. Disease Control and Prevention, Atlanta, 1996-2001, dep. assoc. dir. for sci. divsn. STD prevention, 2001—. Reviewer Women and Health, 1997—; contbr. articles to profl. jours. Mem. APHA, CDC Behavioral and Social Scis. Working Group. Home: 3292 Clairmont North NE Atlanta GA 30329 Office: 1600 Clifton Rd NE # E02 Atlanta GA 30329-4018

SEMAK, MICHAEL WILLIAM, photographer, educator; b. Welland, Ont., Can., Jan. 9, 1934; s. John and Lena (Roketsky) S.; m. Annette Antoniuk, Jan. 30, 1960; children: James, Arlene. Student archtl. tech., Ryerson Poly. Inst., 1956-58. Freelance photographer Toronto-Pickering, 1961—; mem. faculty York U., Toronto, 1971—, assoc. prof. photography, 1977—. Exhibitor one-man shows, Image Gallery, N.Y.C., 1972, Il Diaframma Canon Gallery, Milan, Italy, 1976, Enjay Gallery, Boston, 1977, Ukraina Soc., Kiev, U.S.S.R., 1980, 81, group shows, Ont. Art Gallery, 1967, Expo '67 Internat. Exhbn., Montreal, 1967, Neikrug Gallery, N.Y.C., 1971; represented in permanent collections, Nat. Film Bd. Can., Ottawa, Nat. Gallery Can., Ottawa, Mus. Modern Art, N.Y.C., UN, Geneva. Recipient Photo Excellence Gold medal Nat. Film Bd., 1969; recipient Excellence award Pravda newspaper, Moscow, 1970, 71, Excellence diploma Fedn. Intenationale de l'art Photographique, Switzerland, 1972 Home: 1796 Spruce Hill Rd Pickering ON Canada L1V 1S4 Office: Dept Photography York U 4700 Keeles St Toronto ON Canada M3J 1P3 *I see many contradictions around us, social realities which I believe rob us of our self-esteem and individuality. Must we continually accept and succumb to the never-ending hot baths for the mind society offers us? I wish my photography and words to disturb the complacent and the sleeper. I offer you cold showers for the mind.*

SEMAN, CHARLES JACOB, research meteorologist; b. Ripon, Wis., May 5, 1960; s. Leon Charles and Loretta Marie (Soda) S. BS in Meteorology, U. Wis., 1982, MS in Meteorology, 1985, PhD in Meteorology, 1991. Vis. scientist Nat. Meteorol. Ctr., Washington, 1991-93; rsch. assoc. Geophys. Fluid Dynamics Lab., Princeton, N.J., 1993—. Mem. Am. Meteorol. Soc. (Howard T. Orville award 1982), N.Y. Acad. Scis., Geophys. Fluid Dynamics Lab. Employees Assn. (sec. 1994-95, treas. 1995-96), Phi Beta Kappa. Avocations: music, reading. Home: 2-08 Fox Run Dr Plainsboro NJ 08536 Office: Geophys Fluid Dynamics Lab Forrestal Campus Rt 1 S Box 308 Princeton NJ 08542-0308 E-mail: cjs@gfdl.noaa.gov.

SEMAN, IRENE SALLY, interior designer; b. Bklyn., 1943; cert. interior design N.Y. Sch. Interior Design, 1961; postgrad. Miami Dade Coll., Nova U., Broward Community. Owner, pres. Seman & Graham, 1978-82, Irene Seman Interiors, Ft. Lauderdale, Fla., 1964—; cons. interior design, 1979—. Selected to design rooms for Open Design Houses. Talk show guest. Contbr. articles to newspapers. Bd. dirs. Friends for Life, U. Miami Med. Sch. Aux., 1979—; mem. Friends Ft. Lauderdale Mus., 1976—; mem. Miami Art Ctr., Lowe Mus., Brandeis U., City of Hope, Common Cause, Humane Soc. Mem. Nat. Home Fashions League, Nat. Small Bus. Assn., Nat. Assn. Women Bus. Owners, Ctr. for Group Counseling of Orgn. for Rehab. Through Tng., Am. Contract Bridge League, Phi Sigma Sigma Alumni. Democrat. Clubs: Country of Am., Inverrary Country. Avocations: travel, bridge, art collecting, theatre, music, philosophy. Home and Office: 3301 Spanish Moss Ter Fort Lauderdale FL 33319-5004

SEMANIK, ANTHONY JAMES, instructional technology coordinator; b. Cleve., Mar. 2, 1942; s. Anthony Joseph and Angela Theresa (Peters) S.; m. Elaine Maria Christian, Apr. 20, 1968. BS in Edn., Kent State U., 1965, MEd, 1969. TV coord. Kent (Ohio) State U., 1967-71; TV producer/dir. High/Scope Ednl. Rsch. Found., Ypsilanti, Mich., 1971-72; dir. learning resource ctr. Mercy Coll. of Detroit, 1972-78; ind. media designer/cons. Detroit, 1972—; pub. affairs specialist Detroit bn. recruiting command U.S. Army, 1980-84, pub. affairs specialist tank-automotive command Mich., 1984-85; dir. learning resource ctr. U. Detroit Mercy, 1985-96; dir. media svcs. Wayne State U., 1996-97; supr. learning techs. Ctr. Advanced Tech., Focus: Hope, Detroit, 1997—. Chair Detroit Ednl. Cable Consortium, 1992-97; pres. Southeast Mich. TV Edn. Consortium, 1999-2000, pres., 2001—. Producer, designer, dir., editor instructional-educational multimedia and video programs-series for univ. and cable TV, 1985—; editor: (video programs) Elders in the New Japan, 1987, China and its Elders, 1989. Chmn. Detroit Ednl. Cable Consortium, 1992-97. With U.S. Army, 1965-67. Mem. Consortium of Coll. and Univ. Media Ctrs., Assn. for Ednl. Comms. and Tech., U.S. Distance Learning Assn., Mich. Assn. Media in Edn., Detroit Tech. Coalition (steering com.), Phi Delta Kappa. Avocations: photography, videography, music, reading, computers. Home: 7176 Green Farm Rd West Bloomfield MI 48322-2824 Office: Focus Hope Ctr Advanced Tech 1400 Oakman Blvd Detroit MI 48238-2848 E-mail: semanit@focushope.edu., semanika@sprynet.com.

SEMAYA, FRANCINE LEVITT, lawyer; b. N.Y.C., Mar. 26, 1951; d. Julie and Ann (Tannenbaum) Levitt; m. Richard Semaya, Aug. 3, 1975; children: Stefanie Rachel, David Steven, Scott Brian. BA magna cum laude, Bklyn. Coll., 1973, MS magna cum laude, 1975; JD cum laude, N.Y. Law Sch., 1982. Bar: N.Y. 1983, U.S. Dist. Ct. (ea. and so. dists.) N.Y. 1983, U.S. Supreme Ct. 2000. Sr. legal analyst, atty. Am. Internat. Group, Inc., N.Y.C., 1977-83; assoc. counsel, asst. v.p. Beneficial Ins. Group, Inc. (formerly Benico, Inc.), Peapack, N.J., 1983-87; v.p., counsel Am. Centennial Ins. Co., 1985-87; legal/reins. cons., 1987; counsel reins. Integrity Ins. Co. in Liquidation, Paramus, N.J., 1988-91; ptnr. Werner & Kennedy, N.Y.C., 1991-99; sr. ptnr. Cozen O'Connor, 1999—. Spkr. in field. Author: Insurance Insolvency--A New Generation, 2001, Insurance Insolvencies 2002-2003: Is the Industry Prepared?; editor: Law and Practice of Insurance Insolvency Revisited, 1999, State of Insurance Regulation: Today and Tomorrow, 1991; contbg. editor: Reference Handbook Ins. Co. Insolvency, 4th edit., 1999; contbr. articles to profl. jours. Mem. ABA (sect. del. to ho. dels. 1998—, tort and ins. practice sect. coun. 1994-97, chmn. task force on ins. insolvency 1995-2000, chmn. professionalism com. 1997-98, chmn. pub. regulation of ins. law com. 1990-91, chair pub. rels. com. 1993-94, co-editor State Regulation Ins. 1991), Internat. Assn. Ins. Receivers, N.Y. State Bar Assn., Practicing Law Inst. (ins. law adv. com. 1995—), Assn. Bar City N.Y. (ins. law com.), Fedn. Regulatory Counsel, Phi Beta Kappa. Avocations: reading, travel. Office: Cozen O'Connor 16 Fl 45 Broadway Atrium New York NY 10006-3007 E-mail: fsemaya@cozen.com.

SEMERARO, MICHAEL ARCHANGEL, JR. civil engineer; b. Paterson, N.J., Dec. 15, 1956; s. Michael Archangel and Ann Ruth (Windish) S.; m. Diane Cathleen Hartley, Oct. 12, 1986; children: Michael Archangel III, Laura Nicole, Chelsea Brooke, Julia Megan. BCE, Lehigh U., 1979; MCE, MIT, 1982; MBA, Rutgers U., 1989. Registered profl. engr., N.J., N.Y., Pa., Conn., Va., Mass., Mich., Ohio, Calif.; registered profl. planner, N.J. Engr. DeGrace and Assocs., Wayne, N.J., 1978; prin., v.p. Langan Engrng. and Environ. Svcs., Elmwood Park, 1979—. Presenter in field. Pres. Passaic County (N.J.) 4-H Assn., 1992-94; chmn. exploring com. Passaic County/No. N.J. Boy Scouts Am., 1986-89, mem. exec. bd., 1986—, com. chmn., 2001—; leader Preakness Aggies 4-H Club, Wayne, 1977—; founding chmn. Passaic County Fair, 1988. Recipient Corp. Ethics award Paterson Fedn. of K.C., 1998. Mem. ASCE, AAAS, N.Am. MOSS Users Group (founding pres. 1989-91), GDS Nat. Users Group (chmn. civil engrng. spl. interest group 1990-93, dir. 1995-99), MIT Club No. N.J. (bd. govs. 1984—, pres. 1992-94 edn. counselor 1996—), Chi Epsilon. Roman Catholic. Home: 2 Warner Way Wayne NJ 07470-4161 Office: Langan Engrng Environ Svcs River Drive Ctr Ste I Elmwood Park NJ 07407 E-mail: msemeraro@langan.com.

SEMIATIN, CHARLES PAUL, computer science consultant; b. Balt., Apr. 21, 1948; s. David and Yetta (Dobkin) S. BA in Physics, U. Md. at Balt. County, 1974, MS in Applied Math., 1985. Abstract impressionist artist, Mass., Md., 1968—; composer, pianist, 1968—; rschr. in applied Math. U. Md. at Baltimore County, Catonsville, 1986-96; cons. computer scientist various orgns., 1971—. Contbr. articles to profl. jours. Achievements include rsch. in applications of chaos theory to math.-psychology; discoverer of Rip Theory of Elementary Particles, first theory to use mirror topology for "string" particles. Home and Office: 6636 Eberle Dr Apt 203 Baltimore MD 21215-8223

SEMLYEN, ADAM, electrical engineering educator; b. Gherla, Romania, Jan. 10, 1923; came to Can., 1969; naturalized, 1974; s. Aurel and Anna (Gyorgy) S.; m. Mary Semlyen; 1 child Georgeta. Diploma in engring., Poly. Inst. Timisoara, Romania, 1949; PhD, Poly. Inst. Iasi, Romania. Engr. Regional Power Auth., Timisoara, 1949-51; mem. faculty Poly. Inst. Timisoara, 1949-69, prof., 1968-69; prof. dept. elec. engring. U. Toronto, Ont., 1969-88, prof. emeritus, 1988—. Fellow IEEE (life). Home: 65 High Park Ave # 2203 Toronto ON Canada M6P 2R7 Office: U Toronto Dept Elec & Computer Engring 10 King's College Rd Toronto ON Canada M5S 3G4 E-mail: adam.semlyen@utoronto.ca.

SEMMENS, JOHN HOWARD, economist; b. Oswego, N.Y., Oct. 28, 1945; s. Charles Alfred Semmens and Mildred Catherine (Schnably) Giordano; m. Dainne Kresich, Apr. 16, 1990; children: Harold Alfred, Ayn Lucile, Jefferson Henry. BA, Montclair State Coll., 1967; cert. bus. mgmt., U. Calif., Riverside, 1975; MBA, Ariz. State U., 1980. Teaching asst. Ariz. State U., Tempe, 1967-69; asst. mgr. Circle K, 1971-72; mgmt. analyst Ariz. Bank, Phoenix, 1972-75; research analyst Ariz. Dept. Transp., 1976-77, economist, 1977-82, sr. policy analyst, 1982-88, sr. mktg. analyst, 1988-90, special asst. to dir. of plannign, 1990—. Instr. econs. Phoenix Coll., 1983—; research assoc. Heartland Inst., Chgo., 1987—; economist Laissez Faire Inst., 1987—. Author numerous Ariz. Dept. Transp. publs. and conbtr. articles to profl. jours. and newspapers. Served to ensign USNR, 1969-71. Research fellow Goldwater Inst., Phoenix, 1988—. Libertarian. Home: 828 N Poplar Ct Chandler AZ 85226-1836 Office: Ariz Dept Transp 206 S 17th Ave Rm 310B Phoenix AZ 85007-3213

SEMMENS, RAYMOND THOMAS, health care educator, consultant; b. Cornwall, Eng., Apr. 30, 1946; came to U.S., 1951, naturalized, 1965; s. James Thomas and Mary (Rawlings) S.; m. Christina Ann Peabody, Apr. 27, 1974 (div. Mar. 1984); 1 child, James Bennett. AA, Northwood Inst., Midland, Mich., 1968, BBA, 1970; postgrad. U. Evansville, 1977-83. Dir. admissions Northwood Inst., Cedar Hill, Tex., 1970-71, dean of students, West Baden, Ind., 1971-77; edn. coordinator St. Mary's Med. Ctr., Evansville, Ind., 1977-81; corp. dir. tng. Medco Ctrs., Inc., Evansville, 1981-83; dir. edn. wellness Baton Rouge Gen. Med. Ctr., 1983-86; exec. dir. La. Cancer and Cardiovascular Insts., 1986—; bd. dirs. Am. Cancer Soc., Baton Rouge, Citizens CPR, Baton Rouge. Staff exec. dir. Mich. Young Ams. for Freedom, 1966-68, nat. bd. dirs., Washington, 1968-70; chmn. Young Rep. Northwood Inst., 1967-68. Recipient Gold award Am. Heart Assn., 1980; named Hon. Citizen, City of Indpls., 1972, named Hon. Ky. Col. Mem. Am. Soc. Tng. and Devel. (sec. 1983-84), Am. Soc. Health Care Edn. and Tng., Capital Areas Soc. Health Care Edn. and Tng., La. Soc. Health Care Edn. and Tng., Phi Sigma Beta. Methodist. Avocations: politics, travel, golfing, biking. Office: Baton Rouge Gen Med Ctr 3600 Florida Blvd Baton Rouge LA 70806-3842

SEMMES, SALLY PETERSON, choreographer, dancer; b. Rockford, Ill., Nov. 17; d. Edwin Carl and Eva Victoria (Sjuneson) Peterson; m. David Hamilton Semmes, Jan. 8, 1955; children: Melissa Kay Semmes-Thorne, Laurie Ruth. BS in Edn., U. Wis., 1953, postgrad., 1957-58, 61-62, San Diego State U., London campus, 1976, Northwestern U., 1977. Cert. English, speech/theater tchr., Wis. Tchr. English and speech Oshkosh (Wis.) H.S., 1953-54, Madison (Wis.) East H.S., 1955; instr. Patricia Stevens Finishing Sch., 1956; pvt. tchr. dance Phillips, Wis., 1957-60; project asst. Wis. Idea Theatre U. Wis, Madison, 1963-66; test adminstr. Manitowoc (Wis.) Counseling Ctr., 1967; tchr. English and speech Valders (Wis.) H.S., 1978-81; pub. info. U. Wis., Manitowoc, 1970-72, instr. dance, 1972-78, instr. pub. speaking, 1983—, instr. remedial Coll. English, 1992, freelance instr. dance, 1982-95, tchr. Hatrack Kids classes reading motivation, 1982—; owner Sally Semmes Ednl. Workshops, 1983—; staff Next Act Theatre, 2000. Narrator Green Bay (Wis.) Symphony Childrens Concerts, 1977-81, Manitowoc Symphony Orch., 1992; founder, pres., treas. The Hatrack Storytellers, Inc., 1967—. Choreographer (musicals) Anything Goes, Mame, Guys and Dolls, The Fantasticks, Broadway Bound, Joseph and the Amazing Technicolor Dreamcoat, (mus. revues including) 7 Showtime Shows, Manitowoc; dir.: (plays) Anything Goes, The Male Animal, The Boor, The Ugly Duckling, Our Town, The Sandbox, The Staring Match, The Imaginary Invalid; performer: (numerous productions) Daytrips, Trip to Bountiful, Tuck Everlasting, Love Letters, Dancing at Lughnasa, Lovers, Rules of the Game, The Resounding Tinkle, Baby with the Bathwater, The Man Who Came to Dinner, Blithe Spirit, The Glass Managerie, The White House, The Royal Family, See How They Rum, Talking With, Marvin's Room, Eleemosynary, (groups) Milw. Repertory Theater, First Stage Milw., Kohler Arts Ctr., Next Act Theatre, Renaissance Theatreworks. Pub. svc. videos City of West Allis Am. Cancer Soc. assisted living, 1998—; lay reader St. James Episcopal Ch., Manitowoc, 1984—97; dir. Miss Manitowoc pageant, 1972—75, Miss Calumet County pageant, New Hosltein, Wis., 1974; guest artist Creative Arts Week Minn. Episcopal Cathedral, Mpls., 1997; editor's asst. Wis. Mag. of History of Wis. State Hist. Soc., 1958. Recipient Cultural Achievement award Manitowoc and Two Rivers C. of C., 1984, Cert. of Appreciation Manitowoc Pub. Libr., 1987; named Sec. Yr. Manitowoc Manpower. Mem.: AARP, NAACP, Nature Conservancy, LWV, Environ. Defense, Arthritis Found., Wis Alliance for Arts Edn., World Wildlife Fedn., PEO Sisterhood, Sierra Club, Phi Beta. Avocations: baking, travel, reading, film. Home and Office: 8501 Old South Rd #305 Middleton WI 53562

SEMON, WARREN LLOYD, retired computer sciences educator; b. Boise, Ida., Jan. 17, 1921; s. August and Viola Lorreta (Eastman) S.; m. Ruth Valerie Swift, Dec. 1, 1945; children— Warren Lloyd, Nolan David, Jonathan Richard, Sue Anne. Student, Hobart Coll., 1940-43; S.B., U. Chgo., 1944; MA, Harvard, 1949, PhD, 1954. Instr. math. Hobart Coll., 1946-47; lectr. applied math. Harvard U., Cambridge, Mass., 1956-61, asst. dir. computation lab., 1954-61; head applied math. dept. Sperry Rand Research Ctr., Sudbury, 1961-64; mgr. computation and analysis lab. Burroughs Research Ctr., Paoli, Pa., 1964-67; prof. computer sci. Syracuse (N.Y.) U., 1967-84, prof. emeritus, 1984—, dir. system and information sci., 1968-76, dean Sch. Computer and Info. Sci., 1976-84. Cons. USAF, 1957, NSA, 1957, Lockheed Electronics Corp., 1967, Monsanto Co., 1972. Contbr. profl. jours. Served to 1st lt. USAAF, 1943-46, MTO. Fellow IEEE; mem. Assn. Computing Machinery, Math. Assn. Am., IEEE Computer Soc. (chmn. publs. com. 1972-74, bd. govs. 1973-74, editor-in-chief 1975-76), Sigma Xi. Address: PMB F54807 3590 Round Bottom Rd Cincinnati OH 45244-3026

SEMOS, WILLIAM, management consultant, educator, air transportation executive; b. Manchester, N.H., May 16, 1940; s. Harry J. and Helen Semos; m. Constance Ione Kalogeras, Oct. 13, 1974; children: Mark H., Stephen P. AB, Dartmouth Coll., 1962; MBA, U. Chgo., 1967. Mktg. analyst, sr. mktg. analyst United Air Lines, Chgo. and San Francisco, 1967-73; assoc. Golightly & Co., Mgmt. Cons., N.Y.C., 1973-75; staff v.p. mktg. Marriott Corp., Washington, 1976-79; counsel, senate aviation subcom. U.S. Govt., 1979-81; exec. asst. to chmn. Civil Aero. Bd., 1982; v.p. corp. comms. Western Airlines, L.A., 1983-87; v.p. corp. affairs worldwide Mattel Inc., 1988-91; adj. prof. Loyola Marymount U., 1991—; mgmt. cons., v.p.-N.Am., Lufthansa Consulting, Encino, Calif., 1999—. Adv. dir. Wicat Corp., Orem, Utah, 1988-90; exec.-in-residence U. Wash., Seattle, 1987; mem. mktg. adv. coun. Calif. Tourism Corp., Sacramento, 1985-87. Corp. outreach Rep. Presdl. Campaign, L.A., 1988. 1st lt. U.S. Army, 1962-65. Greek Orthodox. Avocations: fishing, wine collecting, reading. Office: Lufthansa Consulting 16133 Ventura Blvd Ste 1245 Encino CA 91436-2425

SEMOUCHKINA, ELENA, physicist, researcher; b. Tomsk, Russia, May 1, 1956; arrived in US, 1997; m. George Semouchkin, Apr. 26, 1985; children: Alex Semouchkin, Vassilissa Semouchkin. A in German, Tomsk State U., 1974, A in Modern Dance, MS in Engring. with highest distinction, Tomsk State U., 1978, PhD in Physics and Math., 1986; PhD in Materials, Pa. State U., 2000. Rsch. asst. Physics-Tech. Inst., Tomsk, 1979-83, sr. rschr., 1984-92; sci. cons. NEOS Co., St. Petersburg, Russia, 1992-94; sr. rschr. State Tech. U., 1994-97; rsch. asst. Pa. State U., University Park, 1997-2000, rsch. assoc., 2001—. Contbr. articles to sci jours. Recipient Young Siberian Scientist award, 1985, Xerox Rsch. award, Pa. State U., 2001; scholar Lenin, Tomsk State U., 1974—78. Russian Orthodox. Avocations: downhill skiing, dancing, reading, drawing, painting. Home: 544 Easterly Pkwy State College PA 16801-6403 Office: Pa State U Materials Rsch Lab University Park PA 16802 E-mail: eas203@psu.edu.

SEMOWICH, CHARLES JOHN, art historian, art dealer and appraiser, curator, artist, musician; b. Binghamton, N.Y. s. Zeekie and Alice (Osgood) S. BA, SUNY, Binghamton, 1971; MFA, Cath. U., 1972; PhD, Internat. Coll., L.A., 1981. Owner, operator Semowich Fine Arts, Albany, 1982—; dir. music Riverside Universalist Cong., 1997—. Adj. prof. Empire State Coll., Albany, Saratoga Springs, N.Y., 1987—; cons. LePetit Musèe, 1994—, Van Stedman Fine Arts, 1995—; curator Print Club of Albany, 1999—; instr. Chautauqua (N.Y.) Instn., 1988-90; curator Susquehanna County Hist. Soc., Montrose, Pa., 1976; guest curator SUNY, Albany, 1991; chmn. 19th nat. print exhbn. Print Club of Albany, 1995, 20th nat. print exhbn., 1998; spkr. N.Y. State Coun. on the Humanities, 1996-2000; artist-in-residence Fulton St. Gallery, Troy, N.Y., 2001.. Exhibiting (mural) artist Rensselaer River Park; author: Am. Furniture, 1984; co-editor : Dorothy Lathrop-A Centenary Celebration, 1991, William Buttre: Furniture History, 1993; composer: original music published in Albany Carillon Book and Fenwick Parva Press; nationwide performances; contbr. articles Dictionary of Art and profl. jours; performer in Albany Carillon, others. V.p. Rensselaer City Arts Coun., 1995-98; chair art com. Empire State Aeroscis. Mus., Schenectady, N.Y., 1991-93; mem. Chenango Town Bicentennial Commn., Chenango Bridge, N.Y., 1976, Mayor's Task Force for Arts, Albany, 1990; mem. visual arts com. Albany-Tula Alliance, 1992—; chmn. composition competition Ea. N.Y. Organist Guild, 1996, Albany Carillon 70th Anniversary Com., 1996; Rep. committeeman Rensselaer, N.Y., 1996--7, chmn., 1998-2000; juror Kingston N.Y. Area Children's Art Exhibit, 1996; bd. dirs. Eastern N.Y. Am. Guild Organists, 1996-99; mem. Rensselaer City Centennial Com., 1996-97; candidate for city clk. City of Rensselaer, 1997; mem. bicentennary com. City of Albany, 1997; bd. dirs., sec. Rensselaer City Rep. Com., 1998, chmn. 1998-2000; chmn. 70th anniversary com. Albany City Carillon, 1998; pres., founder Friends of Albany City Carillon, 1998—. Recipient 1st pl. award Regina Bell Ringers, 1987, 2nd and 3rd art prizes N.Y. State Fair, 1970, hon. mention Rensselaer Movement Exhbn., 1997. Mem. Am. Guild Organists (historian Ea. N.Y. chpt. 1986—), Soc. Am. Graphic Artists (mem. adv. coun. 1993—), Pub. Employees Fedn. (steward 1991-95, chair membership com. 1992-93), Guild Carollonneurs N.Am. (assoc.), Nat. Coalition Ind. Scholars, N.Y. State Archaeol. Assn. (officer Triple Cities chpt. 1977-81), Artist Action Group (co-chair 1975-76), Print Club Albany (pres. 1989-2000, Cogswell award 2000, Disting. Mem. award 2001), Capital Area Archivists (sec. 1993-94, bd. dirs. 1994), Mus. Prints and Printmaking (pres. 1990-98), Broome County Landmark Soc. (pres. 1975-76), Masons (Most Wise Master Rose Croix chpt. 1995, Master Wadsworth lodge 1998-99, Sovereign Prince 1999-2000, cmty. svc. award 2000), Shriners (organist 1992-97). Avocations: organist, airplane pilot, motorcycling, archaeology. Home: 242 Broadway Rensselaer NY 12144-2705 E-mail: semowich@bigfoot.com.

SEMPLE, CECIL SNOWDON, retired manufacturing company executive; b. Assam, India, Aug. 12, 1917; came to U.S., 1927, naturalized, 1948; s. Fordyce B. and Anne (Munro) S. BA, Colgate U., 1939. Buyer R.H. Macy & Co., 1939-42, 46-48; buyer, div. supt. Montgomery Ward, 1948-50; v.p. Nachman Corp., Chgo., 1950-55; sales mgr. radio receiver dept. Gen. Elec. Co., Bridgeport, Conn., 1955-60, mktg. cons. merchandising N.Y.C., 1966-67, gen. mgr. audio products dept., 1967-68, dep. div. gen. mgr. housewares div., 1968-69, gen. mgr. housewares div., 1969, v.p., 1969-71, v.p. corp. customer relations, 1971-85; v.p. Rich's Inc., Atlanta, 1960-62, sr. v.p., dir., 1962-66. Trustee Peoples Bank., Bridgeport, 1975-89, trustee emeritus. Bd. dirs. Nat. Jr. Achievement Inc., 1974-86, Bridgeport Area Found., 1970-91, dir. emeritus, 1991—; bd. dirs. Bridgeport Hosp., 1970-93, chmn., 1983-89, dir. emeritus, 1993—; bd. trustees Colgate U., 1970-84, vice chmn. 1978-84; trustee emeritus, past pres., bd. dirs. Alumni Corp.; chmn. So. Conn. Health Svc. Inc., 1990-93. Served to maj. USAAF, 1942-46. Mem. St. Andrews Soc. State N.Y. (chmn. bd. mgrs. 1968-70), Delta Kappa Epsilon Clubs: Brooklawn Country (Fairfield, Conn.), Fairfield Country. Home: 25 Cartright St Bridgeport CT 06604-2047

SEMPLE, DONITA C. nurse; b. Meriden, Conn., Jan. 29, 1940; d. Donald James and Elizabeth Anderson; m. Stuart William Semple, Dec. 9, 1961; children: Stuart Scott, Craig William, Jill Lynn, Kim Jayne, Steven Cameron. Advanced nursing program, Ctrl. Conn. State U.; BS in Bus. Mgmt., Teikyo U., 1999. RN, Conn.; cert. emergency nurse; cert. in profl. healthcare quality. Asst. head nurse emergency svcs. Waterbury (Conn.) Hosp., 1968-93, quality mgmt. analyst/coord., 1993—. Mem. Nat. Assn. Health Care Quality, Conn. Assn. Health Care Quality. Office: Waterbury Hosp 64 Robbins St Waterbury CT 06708-2600

SEMPLE, JAMES WILLIAM, lawyer; b. Phila., Nov. 18, 1943; s. Calvin James and Marie (Robinson) S.; m. Ellen Burns, Nov. 26, 1966; children: Megan Semple Greenberg, Luke Robinson. AB, St. Joseph's U., Phila., 1965; JD, Villanova U., 1974. Bar: Del. 1974, U.S. Dist. Ct. Del. 1974, D.C. 1975, U.S. Ct. Appeals (3d cir.) 1982, U.S. Tax Ct. 1996. Ptnr. Morris, James, Hitchens & Williams, Wilmington, 1983—. Lectr. numerous seminars; mediator Superior Ct. Voluntary Mediation Program. Mem.: ABA, Am. Judicature Soc., Fedn. Defense and Corp. Counsel, Am. Bd. Trial Advs. Office: Morris James Hitchens & Williams, LLP PO Box 2306 Wilmington DE 19899-2306 E-mail: jsemple@morrisjames.com.

SEMPLE, LLOYD ASHBY, lawyer; b. St. Louis, June 7, 1939; s. Robert B. and Isabelle A. S.; m. Cynthia T. Semple, Aug. 26, 1961; children: Whitney, Sarah, Lloyd Jr., Terrell. BA, Yale U., 1961; JD, U. Mich, 1964. Bar: Mich. 1964. Assoc. Dykema Gossett, Detroit, 1964-70, ptnr., 1971—; chmn., 1994—. Councilman, mayor pro tem City of Grosse Pointe Farms, Mich, 1975-83; chmn. bd. trustees Detroit Med. Ctr. Corp.; chmn. bd. dirs. Detroit Zool. Soc.; dir., trustee, sec. Karmanos Cancer Inst. Mem. ABA, Mich. Bar Assn., Detroit Bar Assn., Country Club Detroit, Yondotega Club, Detroit Athletic Club, Yale Club (N.Y.C.), Bohemian Club (San Francisco). Episcopalian. Home: 57 Cambridge Rd Grosse Pointe Farms MI 48236-3004 Office: Dykema Gossett 400 Renaissance Ctr Ste 3500 Detroit MI 48243-1602 E-mail: lsemple@dykema.com.

SEMPLINER, JOHN ALEXANDER, artist; b. Grosse Pointe, Mich., Jan. 4, 1953; s. Arthur William and Elaine Marie (Wood) S.; m. Lorraine Ann Fraser, May 24, 1986. BA, George Washington U., 1974; MFA, Pratt Inst., 1976. Lectr. Am. Coll. in London, 1985—, Archtl. Assn., 1989-97. One-man shows Ward-Nasse Gallery, N.Y.C., 1976, Bucknell U. Gallery, Lewisburg, Pa., 1978,

Olshonsky Gallery, Washington, 1981, Crucial Gallery, London, 1988, 89, Grosvenor Gallery, London, 1993, Philharmonic Ctr. for Arts, Naples, Fla., 1995, Consell Comarcal, La Seu d'Urgell, Spain, 1999. Mem. Savile Club, Chelsea Arts Club, Royal Automobile Club, Queens Club, St. Hubert Club, Marylebone Cricket Club, Bucks Club, Sigma Chi (pres. Epsilon chpt. 1973-74, sec. N.Y.C. alumni chpt. 1976-77). Libertarian. Mem. Ch. of England. Avocations: real tennis, rackets, fishing, shooting, stalking. Home: 134 Westbourne Terrace Mews London W2 England Studio: Britannia Works Dace Rd London E3 England

SEMROD, T. JOSEPH, banker; b. Oklahoma City, Dec. 13, 1936; s. L.J. and Theda Jo (Hummel) S.; m. Janice Lee Wood, June 1, 1968 (div. 1988); children: Ronald, Catherine, Christopher, Elizabeth; m. Jaye Patricia Hewitt, May 27, 1989; 1 child, Kelsey. BA in Polit. Sci., U. Okla., 1958, LLB, 1963. Bar: Okla. 1963. With Liberty Nat. Bank, Oklahoma City, 1963-81, v.p., 1967-69, sr. v.p., 1969-71, exec. v.p., 1971-73, pres., 1973-81, Liberty Nat. Corp., Oklahoma City, 1976-81; chmn. bd., pres., CEO United Jersey Banks (now UJB Fin. Corp.), Princeton, N.J., 1981-96; chmn., CEO Summit Bancorp. (merged with UJB Fin. Corp.), 1996—; chmn., bd. dirs., CEO Summit Bank, N.J., 1981—; vice chmn. Fleet Boston Fin., 2001—; chmn. Fleet Bank, N.J., 2001—. Bd. dirs Fed. Res. Bank N.Y., Internat. Fin. Conf., chmn., 1994. Trustee, mem. exec. com. Nat. Urban League, 1963-95; mem. bd. advisors Outward Bound, Inc., 1984-2000, Ind. Coll. Fund N.J., 1986-90; commr. Citizens Commn. on Aids, 1988-90; chmn. bd. regents Stonier Grad. Sch. Banking, Rutgers U., 1983; mem. N.J. Transp. Trust Fund Authority, 1985-87; chmn. The Partnership for N.J., 1989-2001, trustee; mem. N.J. Com.-U.S. Savings Bonds com.; chmn. banking industry U.S. Savs. Bonds campaign, 1992-93. 1st lt. U.S. Army, 1958-60. Mem. Am. Bankers Assn., N.J. Bankers Assn., N.J. Bar Assn., Okla. Bar Assn., Bankers Roundtable (bd. dirs. 1995-97), Regional Plan Assn. (bd. dirs. 1989-91), Youn Pres. Orgn., Am. Running and Fitness Assn. (bd. dirs. 1983-86), N.J. C. of C. (bd. dirs., vice chmn. 1998-99, co-chair prosperity N.J. 1998-2000, chmn. 1999-2000), Drumthwacket Found. (chmn. 1990-94), Bedens Brook Club (Skillman, N.J.), River Club (N.Y.C.), Jasna Polana TPC (Princeton), Coral Beach Club (Bermuda), Nassau Club, Tournament Players Club, Adirondack League Club (Old Forge, N.Y.), The Port Royal Club (Naples, Fla.). Democrat. Roman Catholic. Office: FleetBoston Fin 301 Carnegie Ctr Princeton NJ 08540

SEMSEKWA, AMIR A.M.T. JUMA, management executive; b. Dar-Es-Salaam, Tanzania, 1942; s. Juma J.M.S. Semsekima and Aisha Ibrahim; m. Said Kivugo; 4 children. Grad., U. Calif. Sch. Internat. Law, 1989; cert., Columbia Pacific U., San Rafael, Calif., 1989. Investor Avington Internat., The Netherlands, 1991-96; agt. Elsevier Sci. Tech., London, 1996-97, BDI Germany Supplies, Mindelheim, 1996—, Thomas Register, N.Y.C., 1997, MRI Catalogue Scis., Oxford, Eng., 1997, Lab. Safety Supply, Wis., 1996-97. Agent Export Directory, U.S., 1988, Internat. Tech., U.S., 1990—, NRI, United Kingdom, 1990—; asst. mgr. Pharm/Chem., Tanzania, 1990—. Author: Statistical Methods, 1992, 2d edit., 1997, Practical Methods for Design, 1995, Statistical Analysis, 1987, Analyzing Statistical Science, 1992; contbr. articles to profl. jours. Mem. CCM, Tanzania, 1972—, Tafori, Tanzania, 1992, CRDB 1996; limited membership of bd. dirs. AS Membership Share, Tanzania. Mem. N.Y. Acad. Scis. Moslem. Avocation: sports.

SEMYONOV, OLEG G. political scientist; b. Abakan, Siberia, Russia, Jan. 3, 1944; arrived in U.S., 1997; s. Gabriel P. and Anna G. Semyonov; m. Eugenia V. Khorochilova, Oct. 5, 1971; children: Xenia, Nick. MS, Moscow State U., 1967; PhD, Lebedev Inst. Physics, Moscow, 1981. Rsch. scientist VNIIEF, Arzamas, Russia, 1967—70, Inst. Atomic Energy, Moscow, 1970—71; sr. scientist Lebedev Inst. Physics, 1971—97; sr. rsch. engr. Applied Laser and Fusion Tech., Hull, Canada, 1999—2001, SUNY, Stony Brook, 2001—. Cons. ALFT, Inc., Hull, 2001; tech. transl. KAHOT, Inc., Bklyn., 1998. Contbr. Russian Orthodox. Achievements include patents for 4 patents in field of x-ray sources and their application; discovery of effect of polarization of x-ray lines of highly ionized atoms in a high-current discharge and suggested a theoretical model to explain it; microrelief and internal structure modification of solid films irradiated by pulsed x-rays. Avocations: tennis, guitar. Office: SUNY Stony Brook 212 Old Chemistry Bldg Stony Brook NY 11794 E-mail: osemyon@aol.com.

SEN, ASHA, English educator; b. Calcutta, India, Dec. 2, 1963; came to U.S., 1987; d. Pradip Chandra and Aloka Sen. MA, Bangalore (India) U., 1986, Purdue U., 1989, PhD, 1996. Media asst. Media Ctr., Bangalore, 1985-86; lectr. in English Jyoti Nivas, 1986-87, 89-90; tchg. asst. in English Purdue U., West Lafayette, Ind., 1987-89, 90-96; asst. prof. U. Wis., Eau Claire, 1996—. Contbr. articles, essays to profl. publs. Rsch. grantee Purdue U., 1995, U. Wis.-Madison, 1998, U. Wis.-Eau Claire, 1998-99. Mem. MLA, Midwest MLA. Avocations: reading, writing, film, music, animals. Office: U Wis Eau Claire Dept English Eau Claire WI 54701 E-mail: sena@uwec.edu.

SEN, ASHISH KUMAR, government administrator, urban planner, educator, statistician; b. Delhi, India, June 8, 1942; came to U.S., 1967, naturalized, 1985; s. Ashoka Kumar and Arati Sen; m. Colleen Taylor. BS with honors, Calcutta U., 1962; MA, U. Toronto, Ont., Can., 1964, PhD, 1971. Research assoc., lectr. dept. geography Transp. Center, Northwestern U., 1967-69; mem. faculty Center Urban Studies, U. Ill., Chgo., 1969—, prof., 1978—, dir. Sch. Urban Planning, 1991; dean Center Urban Studies, U. Ill. (Sch. Urban Scis.), 1977-78, acting dir., 1992; pres. Ashish Sen. and Assocs., Chgo., 1977-98; dir. Urban Transp. Ctr., 1997-98; dir. Bur. Transp. Stats. U.S. Dept. Transp., 1998—. Author: Regression Analysis: Theory, Methods and Applications, 1990, Gravity Models of Spatial Interaction Behavior, 1995; also articles. Mem. Chgo. Bd. Edn., 1990-95; chmn. budget com. 1992-94; bd. trustees Asian Inst., 1993-95. Fellow Royal Statis. Soc., Am. Statis. Assn.; mem. Regional Sci. Assn., Transp. Rsch. Bd., Cliffdwellers. Hindu. Home: 2557 W Farwell Ave Chicago IL 60645-4617

SEN, ASOK C. research scientist; b. Calcutta, India, Jan. 1, 1950; came to U.S., 1982; s. Kiran C. and Mira S.; m. Sragdhara Sen; children: Arka, Santara. PhD in Chemistry, Calcutta U., India, 1981. Post doctoral fellow U. Ill., Chgo., 1982-83, U. Fla., Gainesville, 1984-88; sci. assoc. Schepens Eye Inst. Harvard Med. Sch., Boston, 1988-91; rsch. scientist ImmunoGen, Inc., Cambridge, Mass., 1991-94; sr. scientist Avant Immunotherapeutics, Needham, 1995-99, Stryker Biotech, Hopkinton, 1999—. Contrbr. over 31 articles to profl. jours. including J. Biol. Chemistry, Jour. Chem. Soc., Jour. Pharm. Pharmacology, others. Mem. Protein Soc. Home: 114B Olde Derby Rd Norwood MA 02062 Office: Stryker Biotech 35 South St Hopkinton MA 01748-2218 E-mail: sen.asok@strybio.com.

SEN, PABITRA N. physicist, researcher; b. Calcutta, India, Sept. 5, 1944; came to U.S., 1968; s. Bibudh N. and Uma (Sen) S.; m. Susan Shu, Feb. 18, 1984; children: Indra, Maya. MS, Calcutta U., 1966; PhD, U. Chgo., 1972. Mem. profl. staff Xerox, Palo Alto, Calif., 1973-76; sr. scientist Xonics, Santa Monica, 1976-78; sci. adv. Schlumberger, Ridgefield, Conn., 1978—. Vis. prof. U. de Provence, Marseille, France, 1985, Hong Kong U. Sci. & Tech., 1997; guest rsch. fellow Royal Soc., Eng., 1988-89; vis. scientist MIT, 1999—. Fellow Am. Phys. Soc., Inst. Physics. Achievements include explanation of laws of conduction and diffusion in porous media, explanation of huge dielectric constants in rocks and tissues, introduction of elastic and continuum percolation theories, new methods of probing porous media by nuclear magnetic resonance. Home: 52 Woodlawn Dr Ridgefield CT 06877-5120 Office: Schlumberger Doll Rsch-Lib Old Quarry Rd Ridgefield CT 06877

SEN, RAJAN, civil engineer, educator; b. Cambridge, Eng., Oct. 11, 1945; s. Srichandra and Pratibha Sen; children: Vikram, Rohan. BTech, Indian Inst. Tech., India, 1968; MA Sc., U. B.C., Vancouver, 1970; PhD, SUNY, Buffalo, 1984. Registered profl. engr., Fla. Engr. HECB Dept. Transport, London, 1974-79, engr. BES, 1979-83; with Freeman Fox & Ptnrs., Londond, summer 1980; from asst. to assoc. prof. civil and environ. engring. U. South Fla., Tampa, 1984-93, prof., 1993-97, Samuel and Julia Flom chair and prof., 1997—. Adj. prof. sch. architecture U. South Fla., Tampa, 1986—; with Fla. Masonry Handbook Com., 1991-93; adv. panel Nat. Sci. Found., Washington, 1993-94, panel reviewer, 1995, 99, U.S. del., 1995, 97; mem. Internat. Sci. Com. SRRS2, Calif. Co-editor Advanced Composite Materials in Civil Engineering; contbr. chpts. to books. Judge Best Masonry Structure contest Masonry Contractors' Assn; sci. advisor Disasterville; advisor suspension bridge project Fla. Coll. Recipient cert. merit Am. Inst. Architects, 1992. Fellow Am. Soc. Civil Engrs. (subcom. advanced composites 1989-91, mem. editl. bd.); mem. ACI (bd. dirs. Fla chpt. 1988-89, coms. 440, 444), Soutea. Coalition for Composites in Infrastructures. Office: U South Fla Dept Civil & Environ Engr Fowler Ave Tampa FL 33620 E-mail: sen@eng.usf.edu.

SENA, DAVID ANDREW, neuropsychologist; b. Easthampton, Mass., Mar. 23, 1932; s. Andrew Charles and Christine Zapka Sena; m. Carol Anne Sena, May 12, 1956 (dec. Nov. 1988); children: David II, Heather, Kimberley, Caryn; m. Glenda Kay Sena, Sept. 30, 1995; children: Crysta, Jared. BS, U. Mass., 1952; EdM, Harvard U., 1963; PhD, U. Denver, 1980. Lic. psychologist, Colo. Asoc. prof. air sci. MIT, Cambridge, 1960-63; dir. cadet counseling USAF Acad., Colo., 1966-71; dir. social actions Air Forces, Osan AFB, Korea, 1971-72; dir. alcohol svcs. divsn. Pikes Peak Mental Health Ctr., Colorado Springs, Colo., 1973-77; founder, dir. Colorado Springs Neuropsychology Lab., P.C., 1978—. Adj. assoc. prof. Chapman Coll., Colorado Springs, 1977-86; mem. adv. bd. Colo. Head Injury Found., Denver, 1980-90; program com. divsn. of clin. neuropsychology APA, Washington, 1989-92; pres. El Paso County Psychol. Soc., Colorado Springs, 1974-75, Colo. Neuropsychology Soc., Denver, 1993-95. Contbr. articles to profl. jours. Mem. adv. bd. Goodwill Industries, Colorado Springs, 1984-89; adv. com. Salvation Army Adult Rehab. Ctr., Colorado Springs, 1976-92; bd. dirs. Pine Cone Acres Homeowners Assn., Black Forest, Colo., 1997—. Lt. col. USAF, 1952-72. Fellow Nat. Acad. Neuropsychology; mem. Internat. Neuropsychology Soc., Am. Owners and Breeders of Peruvian Paso Horses, Colo. Neuropsychology Soc. (pres. 1993-95), Peruvian Paso Horse Registry of N.Am., Centennial State Peruvian Horse Club. Avocation: Peruvian Paso horses. Home: The Lazy S 9160 Pine Cone Rd Colorado Springs CO 80908-2214 Office: Colorado Springs Neuropsychology Lab and Brain Tng Clin PC 3715 Parkmoor Village Dr Colorado Springs CO 80917-5200

SENDA, JUN-ICHI, economics educator; b. Okayama, Japan, Jan. 30, 1937; BA, Kobe U., 1959, MA, 1961; PhD, Nagoya (Japan) U., 1971. Assoc. prof. Nagoya Gakuin Univ., Seto, Japan, 1964-67, Nagoya U., 1968-71, asst. prof., 1971-83, prof., 1983—. Author: Contemporary Monetary Policy, 1974, The Theory of Interest, 1982, Banks and Securities Firms at the Crossroads, 1986, Japan's Financial System, 1997. Office: Nagoya U Dept Econs Furo-cho Chikusa-ku/Nagoya Nagoya 464-01 Japan

SENDAX, VICTOR IRVEN, dentist, educator, dental implant researcher; b. N.Y.C., Sept. 14, 1930; s. Maurice and Molly R. S.; m. Deborah deLand Cobb, Dec. 17, 1969 (div. June 1976); 1 child, Jennifer Reiland; m. Marcia Ayer Pearson, Dec. 13, 1986; children: Anneliese Chase, Cordelia Ayer. Grad., Tanglewood Music Ctr., 1953; BA, NYU, 1951, DDS, 1955; postgrad., Harvard U. Sch. Dental Medicine, 1969-72. Diplomate Am. Bd. Oral Implantology/Implant Dentistry (pres. 1996, dir.). Commr. N.Y. State Dental Svc. Corp., 1969-73; pres., dir. BioDental Rsch. Found., Inc., N.Y.C., 1975—; pres. Victor I. Sendax, D.D.S., P.C., 1972—, Sendax Mini Dental Implant Ctrs. Mgmt., Inc., 1985—; assoc. attending implantologist St. Lukes-Roosevelt Hosp. Dental Implant Ctr., N.Y.C., 1979—; vol. attending implantologist Beth Israel Hosp., 1991—, Beth Israel North Hosp., N.Y.C., 1991—. Adj. assoc. prof. implant prosthodontics Columbia U. Sch. Dental and Oral Surgery, N.Y.C., 1974-92; vis. lectr. dept. implant dentistry NYU Coll. Dentistry; faculty 1st Dist. Dental Soc. Sch. for Continuing Dental Edn.; mem. dental implant rsch. programs adv. com. Nat. Inst. Dental Rsch., HHS; cons. Julliard Sch. Voice and Drama, N.Y.C., 1972—, Vocal Dynamics Lab. Dept. Otolaryngology, Lenox Hill Hosp., N.Y.C., 1970-90; founder Sendax Seminars; 1st dir. implant prosthodontics resident program Columbia U. Sch. Dental and Oral Surgery and Columbia Presbyn. Hosp. Editor: Dental Clinics of North America: HA-Coated Dental Implants, 1992; mem. editl. bd. Oral Implantology, 1979—; patentee in mini-implants, oral implant magnetics, implant abutments and sinus graft implant stabilizers. Bd. dirs. City Ctr. Music and Drama, Inc. divsn. Lincoln Ctr. Performing Arts, N.Y.C., 1966-75; mem. adv. bd. Amagansett (N.Y.) Hist. Assn., 1969-89; trustee Leukemia Soc. Am., N.Y.C., 1967; bd. dirs. Schola Cantorum, 1980-90, Soc. Asian Music, 1965-76. Capt. Dental Corps USAF, 1955-57. Recipient Cert. of Honor, Brit. Dental Implant Assn., 1988., Aaron Gershkoff Meml. award for Outstanding Contbns. and Dedication to Oral Implantology Am. Acad. of Implant Dentistry, 1996. Fellow: Royal Soc. Medicine Gt. Britain, Am. Acad. Implant Dentistry (nat. pres. 1981), Internat. Coll. Dentists, Am. Coll. Dentists; mem.: ADA (ho. of dels. 1969), Japan Soc., N.Y. Acad. Scis., Internat. Assn. Dental Rsch., Am. Assn. Dental Rsch. (implant group), Fedn. Dentaire Internat., Am. Analgesia Soc., Acad. of Osseointegration, Am. Assn. Dental Schs. (chmn. spl. interest group on dental implant edn.), Century Assn., Sigma Epsilon Delta. Home: 70 E 77th St Apt 6A New York NY 10021-1811 Office: Mini Dental Implant Ctr 30 Central Park S Rm 14B New York NY 10019-1628 E-mail: vis@sendax-minidentimpl.com. *I stand in awe of mankinds' eternal need to innovate and push back the frontiers of knowledge, while tempering the harsher realities of existence with a perspective born of our cultural heritage.*

SENDERLING, JON TOWNSEND, journalist, public affairs specialist; b. Phila. s. John Chester and Elizabeth (Nogle) S.; m. Elizabeth Marie Broadbent, Mar. 27, 1965; children: Jon, Tracy. Student, Ursinus Coll., 1960, Temple U., 1961-64; student (fellow), Stanford U., 1970. Reporter Bucks County Courier Times, Levittown, Pa., 1966-68, Wilmington (Del.) News-Jour., 1968-70; reporter, mag. writer, columnist, spl. projects editor Trenton (N.J.) Times, 1970-76; gen. assignments editor, state editor, nat.-fgn. editor Dallas Times Herald, 1976-80, editorial page dir., 1981-86; dep. fgn. editor Newsday, Melville, L.I., N.Y., 1987-89; pub. affairs mgr. EDS Corp., Dallas, 1989-97, mgr. corp. message strategy, 1997-99; pub. affairs mgr. LandSafe, Plano, Tex., 2000-01; exec. dir. news and info. U. Tex. at Dallas, Richardson, 2001—. Author: play The Trashman, 1970. Recipient disting. service award for editorial writing Sigma Delta Chi, 1982, also 16 awards state press assns. Office: 5400 Legacy Dr Plano TX 75024-3105

SENDO, TAKESHI, mechanical engineering educator, researcher, author; b. Ena City, Japan, Aug. 5, 1917; s. Shigeyoshi and Michie (Yamamoto) S.; m. Hide Okamoto, Apr. 16, 1945; children: Mitsuyoshi, Sachiko, Kazuyasu. B of Engring., Tokyo U., 1941. Prof. mech. engring. Meijo U., Nagoya City, Japan, 1959-90, hon. prof. Japan, 1990—. Curator libr. Meijo U., Nagoya City, 1975-80. Author: Treatise of High Speed Deformation of Metal, 1993, 2nd edit., 1994, Experiment: Behavior of Al Column by Drop Hammer Test, 1959-90; contbr. over 60 articles to profl. jours. Mem. cmty. activity com. Local Self-Governing Orgn., Moriyama City, Japan, 1990, 91. Served to lt. comdr. Japanese Navy, 1941-45. Fellow Japan Soc. Mech. Engring., Japan Soc. Precision Engring. Avocations: composing Haiku and Tanka, trying essay, jogging. Home: 21-8 Choei Moriyama-ku Nagoya 463 Japan

SENDROW, JERROLD B. financial services executive; b. N.Y.C., Oct. 1, 1944; s. Harry and Sylvia (Greenberg) S.; m. Silvia Escalante, Sept. 30, 1989 (div. Sept. 1995); children: Eric, Lisa. BBA, Baruch Coll., 1970. CFP. Treas. Thomas Cook Travel, Inc., N.Y.C., 1974-84, Don Travel, Inc., N.Y.C., 1984-86; contr. Pisa Bros., Inc., 1987-93; v.p. fin. MSW Columbia Travel Group, 1993-94; v.p., CFO, bd. dirs. 800 Travel Sys., Inc., Tampa, Fla., 1994-99; prin., owner e*Travelmart.com, 1999—; prin. J.B. Sendrow & Assocs., N.Y.C., 1987—. Bd. dirs. 321 Apts. Corp., N.Y.C. Bd. dirs. Carrollwood Key Homeowners Assn., Tampa. With U.S. Army, 1965-67. Republican. Avocations: sailing, travel, chess, computers. Home: 5546 Carrollwood Key Dr Tampa FL 33624-5732 E-mail: sendrow@att.net.

SENECAL, CONNIE MONTOYA, special education educator; b. Iloilo, Panay, Philippines, Oct. 23, 1945; came to U.S., 1968; d. Pedro Altaya Montoya and Esperanza Canoy Tupino; m. William S. Goodyear Jr., Oct. 26, 1968 (div. Nov. 1981); children: Stacy, Katie; m. John Joseph Senecal, Dec. 31, 1982; 1 child, Amy (died 3/29/98). BA, U. Guam, Agana, 1967; MA, U. No. Colo., 1970. Cert. tchr., Colo., Tex. Med. social worker Dept. Pub. Health and Welfare, Agana, 1967-68; tchr. emotionally disturbed-behavior disordered students Boulder (Colo.) Valley Pub. Schs., 1970-83, Dept. of Def. Dependents Schs., Mannheim, Germany, 1989, cons., behavior mgmt. specialist Heidelberg, Germany, 1986-89; resource tchr. Ft. Campbell (Ky.) Schs., 1983-86; tchr. Northside Ind. Schs., San Antonio, 1990-95, N.E. Ind. Sch., San Antonio, 1995—. Presenter workshops. Recording sec. Panay/Negros Filipino Assn., Agana, 1967; sec. AAUW, Agana, 1968. Tchr. of Year, Stahl Elem., NEISD, 1997-98. Mem. NEA, Coun. Exceptional Children. Democrat. Roman Catholic. Avocations: collecting Russian lacquer boxes, fairy tale plates, German tins. Office: Stahl Elem Sch 5222 Stahl Rd San Antonio TX 78247-1798

SENECHAL, ALICE R. judge, lawyer; b. Rugby, N.D., June 25, 1955; d. Marvin William and Dora Emma (Erdman) S. BS, N.D. State U., 1977; JD, U. Minn., 1984. Bar: Minn. 1984, U.S. Dist. Ct. Minn. 1984, N.D. 1986, U.S. Ct. Appeals (8th cir.) 1987. Law clk. U.S. Dist. Judge Bruce M. Van Sickle, Bismarck, N.D., 1984-86; with Robert Vogel Law Office, Grand Forks, 1986—. U.S. magistrate judge, 1990—. Office: Robert Vogel Law Office 106 N 3rd St Ste 202 Grand Forks ND 58203-3703

SENEFF, SMILEY HOWARD, business owner; b. Odon, Ind., June 28, 1925; s. Smiley and Ada Fern (Howard) S.; m. Barbara Jean Daum, July 17, 1950 (div. 1966); children: Nancy Kay Secrest, Cheryl Evans; m. Mary Ann Beeler, Mar. 12, 1966; children: Jill Midtbo, Judy Hiland, Jacalyn Harness, Jennifer Peverill, Donald. Student, Duke U., 1945; BS, Ind. U., 1950. Mem. acctg. staff Armour and Co., Indpls., 1950-52, Chevrolet Comml. Body Co., Indpls., 1952-54; owner, mgr. Seneff Hardware and Appliance, Plainfield, Ind., 1955-66, Catalina Motel, Indpls., 1966-73, Smiley's Pancake and Steak, Indpls., 1972—, Smiley's Car Wash, Indpls., 1972—. Mem. County Zoning Bd., 1959-63; Rep. precinct committeeman, del. to state Rep. conv., 1959-63. Mem. Elks, Rotary (pres.), Masons, Scottish Rite, Shriners. Avocations: golf, swimming, walking. Home: 1115 Woodridge Brownsburg IN 46112 Office: Seneff Inns Inc 1307 S High School Rd Indianapolis IN 46241-3128

SENER, JOSEPH WARD, JR. securities company executive; b. Balt., June 30, 1926; s. Joseph Ward and Clara (Hodshon) S.; m. Ann Clark TenEyck, May 3, 1952 (dec. Oct. 1967); children: J. TenEyck, Beverley T., Joseph Ward III; m. Jean Eisenbrandt-Johnston, Feb. 6, 1971. AB, Haverford (Pa.) Coll., 1950; diploma, Inst. Investment Banking, U. Pa., 1954. With John C. Legg & Co., Balt., 1950-70, gen. partner, 1961-70; exec. v.p., dir. Legg, Mason & Co., Inc., Balt., 1970-72; vice chmn. bd. dirs., chief adminstrv. officer Legg Mason Wood Walker, Inc., 1976-80; dir. Legg Mason, Inc., 1982-96. Bd. dirs. Chesapeake Bank and Trust, Chestertown, Md., 1986-96, chmn., 1992-96. Trustee emeritus Boys' Latin Sch., Balt., pres. bd. trustees, 1980-82; chmn. emeritus bd. govs. Chesapeake Bay Maritime Mus. Served with USAAF, 1944-46. Mem. Nat. Assn. Securities Dealers (past dist. chmn.), Balt. Security Analysts Soc. (past pres.), Md. Club (Balt.). Republican. Episcopalian.

SENERCHIA, DOROTHY SYLVIA, author, urban planner; b. Warwick, R.I. d. Vincenzo Ralph and Theresa Felicia (Petrarca) S. BA, Pembroke Coll., Brown U., 1955; Cert., U. Florence, Italy, 1956. Cert. urban planner, N.Y.C. Tchr. Berlitz Sch. Langs., Florence, 1955-56; adminstrv. asst. Sheraton Corp. Am., N.Y.C., 1956-57, Inter-Am. Coun., N.Y.C., 1958-59, Roger Stevens Devel. Corp., N.Y.C., 1960-61; urban planner N.Y.C. Dept. City Planning, 1962-96. Author: Silent Menace, 1990; co-producer, co-star film The Funeral, 1980; solo concert violinist, 1945-62; co-founder singing group The Chattertocks of Brown U., 1952. One of the pioneers in cmty organization in the urban planning process, N.Y.C., 1962-68; one of the early pioneers in women's movement, N.Y.C., 1969; mem. planning com. 1970 Women's March, N.Y.C., 1970; counselor Big Sisters Orgn., N.Y.C., 1969-82. Mem.: Vet. Feminists Am. (co-founder, adv. bd.), Life- Affirming Group (founder), The East River Round Table (founder). Avocations: foreign languages, music, travel, floral design.

SENESE, DONALD JOSEPH, former government official, research administrator; b. Chgo., Apr. 6, 1942; s. Leo Carl and Joan (Schaffer) S.; m. Linda Faye Wall, Dec. 29, 1973; 1 dau., Denise Nicole. BS in History, Loyola U., 1964, MA, 1966; PhD, U. S.C., 1970; postgrad., Sophia U., Tokyo, 1970, Nat. Chengchi U., Taipei, Taiwan, 1971; cert. in adminstrv. procedures, U.S. Dept. Agr. Grad. Sch., 1976. Assoc. prof. history Radford (Va.) U., 1969-72; legis. asst. Senator from Va., 1973; legis. dir. to Rep. from Tex., 1973-76; sr. research assoc. House Republican Study Com., U.S. Ho. of Reps., Washington, 1976-81; asst. sec. for ednl. research and improvement U.S. Dept. Edn., 1981-85; pres. Senese Edn. Enterprises, Inc., 1985-96; dep. asst. sec. to asst. sec. Office Territorial and Internat. Affairs, Dept. Interior, Washington, 1989-93; writer, cons. SEE, Inc., Alexandria, Va.; instr. U.S.Dept. of Agrl. Grad. Sch., 1995—2001. Mem. child care liability task force study, Dept. Labor, 1989; v.p., dir. rsch. The 60 Plus Assn., Rosslyn, Va., 1997—. Author: Indexing the Inflationary Impact of Taxes, 1978, Modernizing the Chinese Dragon, 1980, Asianomics: Challenge and Change in Northeast Asia, 1981; editor: Ideas Confront Reality, 1981, Sweet and Sour Capitalism, 1985, Democracy in Mainland China, 1986; co-author: Can The Two Chinas Become One?, 1989; editor: George Mason and The Legacy of Constitutional Liberty, 1989. Vice chmn. Alexandria (Va.) Rep. Com., 1976-78, staff Rep. Nat. Com., 1987-89; mem. Alexandria Hist. Records Commn., 1979-84; mem. Fairfax County History Commn., 1985—, chmn., 1990-91; Fairfax County Bicentennial of U.S. Constn. Com., 1986-91; dir. Nat. Ctr. for Presdl. Rsch., 1987—; dir. opposition rsch. Rep. Nat. Com., 1995-96; dir. of rsch Co-Chairman Rep. Nat. Com., 1996. Recipient William P. Lyons Master Essay award, 1967; Freedoms Found. award, 1981, 85, 90; named Outstanding Man of Yr. Jaycees, 1976, 78, Sec. Labor Exceptional Achievement award, 1990; inducted St. Rita H.S. (Chgo.) Hall of Fame, 1984. Mem. Univ. Profs. for Acad. Order, No. Va. Assn. History, Order Sons of Italy, Pi Gamma Mu, Phi Alpha Theta, Delta Sigma Rho-Tau Kappa Alpha Roman Catholic. Office: PO Box 6886 Alexandria VA 22306-0886 *It has been important to have a philosophy of government which emphasizes honesty, integrity, a Ciceronian concept of duty, cost-effective public service, and a committment to the American heritage and traditions. These views have been reinforced by the support of family, friends, and a spiritual faith.*

SENF, MARY, secretary, artist, writer, poet; b. Elwood, N.J., Oct. 12, 1931; d. Sylvester and Mary (Esposito) Barone; m. Frederick W. Senf Jr. (div. 1977); 1 child, Nancy McGillicuddy. Grad. high sch., Hammonton, N.J.; cert., Washington Sch. of Art, 1965. Sec. Radio Corp. Am., Cherry Hill, N.J., 1951-71, Catalytic Co., Phila., 1973-74, United Engrs., Phila., 1976-82, Phila. Nat. Bank, 1986-92. Author: Amethyst Sunset, 2000. Leader Girl Scouts U.S., Elwood, 1951; pres. Yoga Soc., Hammonton, 1971. Elected to Championship Basketball Hall of Fame Hammonton H.S., 1994. Mem. South Jersey Poetry Soc. Home: 80 Broadway Apt 20 Hammonton NJ 08037-1184

SENFT, MASON GEORGE, musician; b. Bklyn., Nov. 1, 1942; s. Arthur and Ann (Nagel) S. BA cum laude, Adelphi U., 1964. Pvt. practice accompanist/vocal coach, Roslyn Heights, N.Y., 1964—. Tchr. Adelphi U., Garden City, N.Y., 1964-73; dir. Nat. Scholastic Aptitude Tng. Inst., Garden City, 1966-69; musical dir. Tibbits Opera House, Coldwater, Mich., 1972-73, Canal Fulton (Ohio) Playhouse, 1974-84, Island Lyric Opera, Garden City, 1980—, A Small Co. in America, Glen Cove, N.Y., 1984—; cons. Island Chamber Symphony Orch., Glen Head, N.Y., 1985—, Nat. Grand Opera, Tilles Ctr., Greenvale, N.Y., 1988—, PBS TV spl. Christmas with Flicka, 1988, Dark Summer debut by Christine Berl, Lincoln Ctr. Chamber Soc., Alice Tully Hall, N.Y., 1989, Glimmerglass Opera, 1992—; accompanist to Frederica von Stade 350th Convocation Celebration, Harvard U., Cambridge, Mass., 1986; accompanist ARC benefit concert In Concert, Carnegie Hall, 1989, Met. Opera Gala, N.Y.C., 1994; music coach The Aspern Papers, Dallas Opera, debut 1988; cons. N.Y. Virtuoso Chamber Symphony, 1989—; music coach DiCapo Opera Co., 1975—; accompanist concert in honor of Queen Margrethe II of Sweden, The White House, 1991, hist. gala concert at Steinway Hall, N.Y., 1991, gala concert for Met. Opera Four Seasons Hotel, 1993. Author: Chimera, 1997, Elusive Thought, 1998, Windows, 1998; (orchestrator): (films) Liberty Heights, 1998; prodr.: (CD) A Memorial Tribute-To the Fallen Heroes of September 11, 2001. Apptd. to the Rep. Presdl. Task Force, 2001. Recipient citation for lifetime achievement N.Y. State Assembly, 1994. Mem. Musicians Union Local 802, L.I. Singers Soc. (accompanist 1985-96), Mensa. Avocations: travel, writing, metaphysics. Home: 300 Edwards St Roslyn Heights NY 11577-1140 E-mail: msenft@optonline.net.

SENG, JEFFREY FRAZIER, artist, poet; b. Omaha, Apr. 6, 1953; s. Hubert Leonard and Elizabeth Nan (Davis) S.; m. Patricia Ann Morello, July 8, 1978. BFA magna cum laude, U. Nebr., Omaha, 1976. One-man show Sheldon Meml. Art Gallery, Lincoln, 1979; group exhibits Yellowstone Art Ctr., Billings, Mont., 1980, Nebr. Wesleyan U., Lincoln, 1980, Sheldon Meml. Art

Gallery, 1982, Mus. Nebr. Art, Kearney, 1989, 92, 93, others; represented in permanent collections of Virtuosity: The Juried Exhbn. CD ROM, 1995, Sheldon Meml. Gallery, Lincoln, Nebr., M.O.N.A. Kearney, Inc. Mem. Phi Kappa Phi. Avocations: reading, music, cinema, art exhibitions. Home: 11306 Jones St Omaha NE 68154-3365

SENGERS, JOHANNA M. H. LEVELT, thermophysicist; b. Amsterdam, The Netherlands, Mar. 4, 1929; married, 1963; 4 children. Drs, U. Amsterdam, 1954, PhD in Physics, 1958; PhD (hon.), Delft U. Tech., 1992. Rsch. assoc. U. Amsterdam, Van der Waals Lab, 1954-58, 59-63, U. Wis., Inst. Theoretical Chemistry, Madison, 1958-59; physicist heat divsn. Inst. Basic Stds., Nat. Bur. Stds., Gaithersburg, Md., 1963-78; group leader thermophysics divsn. Nat. Engring. Lab., 1978-87; sr. fellow thermophysics divsn. Nat. Inst. Standards and Tech., 1983-95, fellow emeritus, 1995—. Lectr Cath. U., Louvain, Belgium, 1971; rsch. assoc. Inst. Theoretical Physics, U. Amsterdam, 1974-75; regent's prof. chemistry U. Calif., L.A., 1982. Chair working group A Internat. Assn. Properties Steam, 1985-90; pres. Internat. Assn. Properties Water and Steam, 1991-92. Recipient Silver medal U.S. Dept. Commerce, 1972, Gold medal, 1978, Wise award Interagy. Com. Women in Sci. and Engring., 1985, Alexander von Humboldt Rsch. award Alexander von Humboldt-Stiftung, Bonn, Germany, 1991. Fellow: AAAS, Am. Phys. Soc., Internat. Assn. Properties Water and Steam (hon.); mem.: ASME, AIChE, Dutch Soc. Scis., European Physics Soc., Netherlands Royal Acad. Sci. (corr.), Nat. Acad. Engring., Nat. Acad. Sci. Office: Phys & Chem Properties Div Nat Inst Stds & Tech 100 Bureau Dr Stop 8380 Gaithersburg MD 20899-8380 E-mail: johanna.sengers@nist.gov.

SENGPIEHL, PAUL MARVIN, lawyer, former state official; b. Stuart, Nebr., Oct. 10, 1937; s. Arthur Paul and Anne Marie (Andersen) S.; B.A., Wheaton (Ill.) Coll., 1959; M.A. in Pub. Adminstrn., Mich. State U., 1961; J.D., Ill. Inst. Tech.-Chgo. Kent Coll. Law, 1970; m. June S. Cline, June 29, 1963; children— Jeffrey D., Chrystal M. Bar: Ill. 1971, U.S. Supreme Ct. 1982. Adminstrv. asst. Chgo. Dept. Urban Renewal, 1962-65; supr. Ill. Municipal Retirement Fund, Chgo., 1966-71; mgmt. officer Ill. Dept. Local Govt. Affairs, Springfield, 1971-72, legal counsel, Chgo., 1972-73; spl. asst. atty. gen. Ill. Dept. Labor, Chgo., 1973-76; asst. atty. gen. Ct. of Claims div. Atty. Gen. of Ill., 1976-83; hearing referee Bd. Rev., Ill. Dept. Labor, 1983-84; local govt. law columnist Chgo. Daily Law Bull., 1975-84; instr. polit. sci. Judson Coll., Elgin, Ill., 1963. Republican candidate for Cook County Recorder of Deeds, 1984; dep. committeeman Oak Park Twp Rep. Orgn.; elected alt. del., served del. Rep. Nat. Conv., 1992; People's Choice candidate pres. Oak Park Village, 1993; elected Rep. committeeman Oak Park Twp., 1994-98; elected del. Rep. Nat. Convention, 1996; co-chmn. Cook County Jail Ministry Bd. Mem. Ill. Bar Assn. (local govt. law sect. council 1973-79, vice chmn. 1976-77, co-editor local govt. newsletter 1976-77, chmn. 1977-78, editor newsletter 1977-78, state tax sect. council 1979-82, 84-85), Chgo. Bar Assn. (local govt. com., chmn. legis. subcom. 1978-79, sec. 1979-80, vice chmn. 1980-81, chmn. 1981-82, state and mcpl. tax com.), John Ericsson Rep. League Ill. (state sec. 1983-85, 95—, sec. Cook County 1982-97, pres. 1997—), Oak Park-River Forest C. of C. (sm. bus. coun., 1991—). Baptist (vice chmn. deacons 1973-76, 79-80, moderator 1983-86, supt. Sunday sch. 1986-93). Home: 727 N Ridgeland Ave Oak Park IL 60302-1735

SENGUPTA, ABHIJIT, engineer, consultant; b. Silchar, Assam, India, Sept. 27, 1964; s. Gouranga Prasad and Bharati Sengupta; m. Aporna Kali Sengupta; children: Aniket. PhD Engring., Wayne State U., Detroit, Michigan, 1993, MS Engring., 1991, Indian Inst. of Tech., Kanpur, India, 1988; BS Engring., Jadavpur U., Calcutta, India, 1986. Cert. CQE, CRE, CQA, Am. Soc. for Quality, 2000. Product design engr. Ford Motor Co., Dearborn, Mich., 2001—, quality engr., 1999—2001, Ovonic Battery, Troy, 1997—99; process engr. Gen. Motors-Ovonic, 1995—97; materials engr. Veltec Laboratories, Taylor, 1994—95; quality engr. Quigley Industries, Southfield, 1994; rsch. assoc. Wayne State U., Detroit, 1993—94. Assoc. v.p. Am. Soc. for Quality, Detroit, 1998—. Mem.: Am. Soc. for Materials, Soc. for Reliability Engineers, Am. Soc. for Quality. Avocations: photography, astronomy, tennis, golf, fishing. Home: PO Box 10293 Detroit MI 48210 Office: Ford Motor Company Dearborn MI 48120 E-mail: senguptaa@hotmail.com.

SEN GUPTA, BARUN KUMAR, geology educator, researcher; b. Jamshedpur, Bihar, India, July 31, 1931; s. Tarapada and Sulata (Das Gupta) Sen Gupta; m. Mandira Gupta, May 12, 1956; children: Sangaree, Upai. BS with honors, Calcutta U., 1951, MS, 1954, Cornell U., 1961; PhD, Indian Inst. Technology, Kharagpur, India, 1963. Apprentice geologist Dalmia Cement Ltd., Calcutta, India, 1955; from asst. lectr. to lectr. Indian Inst. Tech., Kharagpur, 1955-66; postdoct. fellow, rsch. scientist Bedford Inst. Oceanography, Dartmouth, N.S., Can., 1966-68; from asst. prof. to prof. U. Ga., Athens, 1969-79; prof. geology La. State U., Baton Rouge, 1979—2001, H.V. Howe prof. geology, 2001—. Vis.prof. U. Rio Grande do Sul, Porto Alegre, Brazil, 1974, U. Bordeaux, France, 1985—86; vis. scientist Petrobras , Rio de Janeiro, 1999. Editor: (Book) Modern Foraminifera, 1999; contbr. articles to profl. jours. and chpts. to books. Fellow, pres. Cushman Found. Foraminiferal Rsch., 1987-88. Fulbright sr. fellow U. Utrecht (The Netherlands), 1992-93; rsch. grantee NSF, 1969-72, 75-79, 82-90, NATO, 1986-92, Mineral Mgmt. Svc., 1995—. Fellow Geol. Soc. Am. (W.S. Cole award 1995); mem. AAAS, AAUP, Paleontol. Soc. Office: La State U Dept Geology & Geophysics Baton Rouge LA 70803-4101

SENGUPTA, DEBASIS, research scientist; b. Sanctoria, West Bengal, India, July 30, 1963; arrived in U.S., 1997; s. Nityananda Sengupta, Pusparani Sengupta; m. Sumathy Raman, June 18, 1995. BS in Science, M in Science and Phys. Chemistry, U. Burdwan, India; PhD, Indian Inst. Sci., Bangalore, India, 1994. Postdoctoral fellow U. Leuven, Belgium, 1994—97; faculty rsch. assoc. Ariz. State U., Tempe, 1997—2000; rsch. scientist CFD Rsch. Corp., Huntsville, Ala., 2000—. Contbr. articles to profl. jours. Achievements include invention of catalytic conversion of NOx.

SENGUPTA, JATI KUMAR, economics educator; b. Rampurhat, Bengal, India, Jan. 4, 1934; came to U.S., 1976; s. Kshudiram and Anima (Choudhury) S.; m. Krishna Majumder, June 5, 1965; children: Rimita, Ajeen. MA, Calcutta (India) U., Bengal, 1955; PhD, Iowa State U., 1962. Prof. econs. and stats. Iowa State U., Ames, 1962-66; prof. econs. and ops. rsch. Indian Inst. Mgmt., Calcutta, 1967-72, dir., 1972-76; mem. faculty U. Calif., Santa Barbara. Cons. U.S. AID (Agy. for Internat. Devel.), 1962-63, Ford Found., 1969, The World Bank, Washington, 1975-77. Author: Stochastic Optimization and Economic Models, 1986, Applied Mathematics for Economics, 1987, Efficiency Analysis by Production Frontiers, 1989, New Growth Theory, 1998, Dynamic and Stochastic Efficiency Analysis, 2000; mem. editorial bd. Jour. Econs., Internat. Jour. Systems Sci. Fulbright scholar U.S. Ednl. Found. in India, 1960, Centennial scholar Iowa State U., 1962. Mem. Econometric Soc., Inst. Mgmt. Scis. Office: Univ Calif North Hall Santa Barbara CA 93111 E-mail: sengupta@econ.ucsb.edu.

SENGUPTA, MRITUNJOY, mining engineer, educator; b. Cuttack, Orissa, India, Oct. 24, 1941; came to U.S., 1968; s. Chandi P. and Bani S.; m. Nupur Bagchi, Jan. 15, 1981; children: Shyam S. ME, Columbia U., 1971, MS, 1972; PhD, Colo. Sch. of Mines, 1983. Mining engr. Continental Oil Co., Denver, 1977-78, United Nuclear Corp., Albuquerque, 1978-80, Morrison-Knudson Co., Boise, Idaho, 1975-77, 80-82; assoc. prof. U. Alaska, Fairbanks, 1983-88, prof., 1989-95. Cons. UN Devel. Program, 1987. Author: Mine Environmental Engineering, vols. I and II, 1989, Environmental Impacts of Mining, 1992, Bioremediation Engineering for Mining and Mineral Processing Wastes, 1997, Mineral Industry of India: Planning, Development and Foreign Investment Opportunities, 2001; contbr. articles to profl. publs. Recipient Gold medal Mining Metall. Inst. of India, 1976, Nat. Merit scholarship Govt. of India, 1959-63. Mem. NSPE, So. Mining Engrs. Achievements include development of new concepts for mine design in Colo. Home: PO Box 13713 Mill Creek WA 98082-1713 E-mail: msengupta@msn.com.

SENHAUSER, DONALD A(LBERT), pathologist, educator; b. Dover, Ohio, Jan. 30, 1927; s. Albert Carl and Maude Anne (Snyder) S.; m. Helen Brown, July 22, 1961; children: William, Norman. Student, U. Chgo., 1944-45; BS, Columbia U., 1948, MD, 1951; grad. with honors, U.S. Naval Sch. Aviation Medicine, 1953. Diplomate Am. Bd. Pathology. Intern Roosevelt Hosp., N.Y.C., 1951-52; resident Columbia-Presbyn. Hosp., 1955-56, Cleve. Clinic, 1956-60; instr. in pathology Columbia U., 1955-56; fellow in immunopathology Middlesex Hosp. Med. Sch., London, 1960-61; mem. dept. pathology Cleve. Clinic Found., 1961-63; assoc. prof. pathology U. Mo., 1963-65; prof., asst. dean Sch. Medicine U. Mo., 1969-70, dir. teaching labs., 1968-70, prof., vice-chmn. dept. pathology, 1965-75; prof., chmn. dept. pathology Coll. Medicine Ohio State U., 1975-92, chair emeritus, 1992, prof. Sch. Allied Med. Professions, 1975-95; prof. emeritus, 1995—. Dir. labs. Ohio State U. Hosps., 1975-92; pres. Univ. Reference Lab., Inc., 1984-86, CEO, 1986-92; bd. dirs. Columbus area chpt. ARC, 1978-82; cons. in field; WHO-AMA Vietnam med. edn. project mem. U. Saigon Med. Sch., 1967-72; vis. scientist HEW, 1972-73; acting dir. Ctrl. Ohio Regional Blood Ctr., 1976-79. Mem. editorial bd. Am. Jour. Clin. Pathology, 1965-76. With USN, 1945-46; lt. M.C. USNR, Korea, China; now capt. USNR ret. Served with USN, 1945-46; served as lt. M.C. USNR, Korea, China; now capt. USNR, Ret. Recipient Lower award Bunts Ednl. Found., 1960-61 Mem. AAAS, Coll. Am. Pathologists (bd. govs. 1980-86, v.p. 1989-90, pres.-elect 1990-91, pres. 1991-93, immediate past pres. 1993—, Pathologist of Yr. 1994, Hartman award 1998), Am. Soc. Clin. Pathologists, Assn. Pathology Chmn., Am. Assn. Pathology, Internat. Acad. Pathology, Assn. Am. Med. Colls., Am. Assn. Blood Banks, Ohio Soc. Pathologists (gov. 1979, pres. 1987-89), Ohio Hist. Soc., Masons, Sigma Xi. Lutheran. Home: 1256 Clubview Blvd N Columbus OH 43235-1226 Office: 333 W 10th Ave Columbus OH 43210-1239 E-mail: donaldsenhauser@cs.com.

SENHOLZI, GREGORY BRUCE, secondary school educator; b. Amityville, N.Y., Apr. 16, 1952; s. Joseph Bruce and Beverly Ann (Sullivan) S.; m. Rochelle Ann Birnbaum, Nov. 20, 1976; children: David, Vicki. BA, Iona Coll., 1974; MLS, SUNY, Stony Brook, 1976. Salesman, printer R.H. Macy's, Huntington, N.Y., 1967-74; math. and computer tchr. Sachem Sch. Dist., Lake Ronkonkoma, 1974—; math. chair Seneca Jr. H.S., NY, 2001—. Computer specialist Tex. Instruments, N.Y., 1982-84; audio video specialist Dart Audio Video, Centereach, N.Y., 1984-88; consulate, curriculum specialist Sachem Sch. Dist., 1978-2001. Deacon local Roman Cath. ch., Wading River, N.Y., 1989—, spiritual dir. 2001—. Mem. Adoptive Parents Com. (bd. dirs., workshop leader 1984—), K.C. (treas. 1988—). Avocations: swimming, acting, skiing, singing, travel. Home: 129 Gregory Way Calverton NY 11933-1138 Office: Sachem Sch Dist Main St Holbrook NY 11742 E-mail: gsenholz@optonline.net.

SENIE, HARRIET F. art historian; b. N.Y.C., Sept. 23, 1943; d. Ernest Freitag and Gerda Goetz; m. Stephen R. Senie, 1965 (div. 1972); 1 child, Laura. BA, Brandeis U., 1964; MA, Hunter Coll., 1971; PhD, Inst. Fine Arts, 1981. Gallery dir. SUNY, Old Westbury, 1979-82; assoc. dir. The Art Mus. Princeton (N.J.) U., 1982-85; dir. mus. studies, prof. art history The City Coll. CUNY, 1985—, doctoral faculty The Grad. Sch. and Univ. Ctr., 1997—. Vis. disting. prof. Carnegie Mellon U., 2000. Author: Contemporary Public Sculpture, 1992, The Tilted Arc Controversy: Dangerous Precedent?, 2001; co-editor, contbr. Critical Issues in Public Art, 1992, 98, Complex Identities: Jewish Consciousness and Modern Art, 2000, Memory and Oblivion: Acts of the XXIXth International Congress of the History of Art, 1996; contbr. articles to jours. Mem. Am. Assn. Mus., Am. Studies Assn., Coll. Art Assn. Home: 215 Sackett St Brooklyn NY 11231-3621 Office: The City Coll CCNY Art Dept Convent Ave & 138th St New York NY 10031 E-mail: hfsenie@rcn.com.

SENIOR, BRENT ANTHONY, otolaryngologist, educator; b. Detroit, June 7, 1964; s. Gerald William and Juanita Ann (Brondell) S.; m. Dana Lynn Dystant, Sept. 8, 1990; children: Rebecca, Benjamin, Grace, Anna. BS summa cum laude, Wheaton Coll., 1986; MD, U. Mich., 1990. Diplomate Am. Bd. Otolaryngology. Intern Boston U., 1990-91; resident Boston U.-Tufts U., 1991-95; fellow U. Pa., Phila., 1995-96; sr. staff Henry Ford Hosp., Detroit, 1996-99; assoc. prof. otolaryngology, head and neck surgery U. N.C., 1999—. Contbr. articles to profl. jours. Fellow ACS; mem. Am. Acad. Otolaryngology (mem. continuing edn. faculty 1997—), Am. Acad. Otolaryngology Head and Neck Surgery, Am. Rhinology Soc. (cons. to bd. dirs.), Soc. Univ. Otolaryngologist Head & Neck Surgeons, Am. Acad. Sleep Medicine, Christian Med. and Dental Soc., Newton Fisher Soc., Walter Work Soc. Office: UNC Otolaryngology Head & Neck Surgery 610 Burnett Womack Clb # 7070 Chapel Hill NC 27599-0001 Address: 106 Brannon Ct Chapel Hill NC 27516-8099 E-mail: Brent_senior@med.unc.edu.

SENIOR, JOHN ROBERT, internist, gastroenterologist, consultant; b. Phila., July 17, 1927; s. John Henry and Catherine (Cumming) S.; m. Sara Elizabeth Spedden, Dec. 27, 1952; children: John Ormond, Laura Bruns Council, Lisa Ann Bonetti. BS in Physics, Pa. State U., 1950; MD, U. Pa., 1954. Diplomate Am. Bd. Internal Medicine, Am. Bd. Gastroenterology. Intern Hosp. U. Pa., Phila., 1954-55, resident in medicine, 1955-57, clin. fellow in gastroenterology, 1957-59; rsch. fellow in gastroenterology Mass. Gen. Hosp.-Harvard U., Boston, 1959-62; rsch. fellow Harvard U., Cambridge, 1959-62; dir. gastrointestinal rsch. lab. Phila. Gen. Hosp.-U. Pa., 1962-70; clin. prof. of medicine U. Pa., 1970-79, adj. prof. medicine, 1980—; dir. regulatory affairs E.R. Squibb & Sons, Princeton, N.J., 1979-81; v.p. clin. affairs Sterling-Winthrop Rsch. Inst.-Sterling Drug Corp. Worldwide, N.Y.C. and Rensselear, N.Y., 1981-84; pres. pers. cons. corp. Merion, Pa., 1984-95; prin. med. cons. for internat. pharm. R&D G. H. Besselaar Assocs., Princeton, N.J., 1986-93, Therakos, Inc., West Chester, Pa., 1994-95; reviewing med. officer for gastrointestinal drugs FDA, Rockville, Md., 1995—99, sr. scientific advisor to dir. Office of Drug Safety, 2000—. Mem. gastrointestinal rsch. staff (without compensation) VA Med. Ctr., Phila., 1991—; mem. adv. coun. Nat. Inst. Diabetes and Kidney and Digestive Diseases, Bethesda, Md., 1981-85; senatorial liaison Nat. Commn. Digestive Diseases, Washington, 1978-80. Author: Towards Evaluation of Competence in Medicine, 1976; author, editor: Medium Chain Triglycerides, 1968; contbr. articles to profl. jours. With USNR MC, 1945-84; rear adm. 1977-84. Fellow: ACP; mem.: Am. Gastroenterol. Soc., Am. Soc. Clin. Investigation, Am. Assn. Study of Liver Diseases (pres. 1973—74), Cosmos Club (Washington), Alpha Omega Alpha, Phi Beta Kappa, Phi Kappa Phi, Sigma Pi Sigma. Republican. Episcopalian. Achievements include first publication of mechanisms of intracellular metabolism and absorption of dietary fats; first hospital screening of donor blood for hepatitis B and of unifying hypothesis with in vitro and in vivo validation for mechanism and kinetics of cholesterol gallstone dissolution by bile acids; first U.S. studies of ursodeoxycholic acid for treatment of chronic cholestatic liver diseases. Home: 54 Merbrook Ln Merion Station PA 19066-1618 Office: 15B-33 Parklawn HFD-400 5600 Fishers Ln Rockville MD 20857-0001 E-mail: SeniorJ@cder.fda.gov.

SENIOR, RICHARD JOHN LANE, textile rental service executive; b. Datchet, Eng., July 6, 1940; arrived in U.S., 1972, naturalized, 1977; s. Harold Dennis Senior and Jane Lane Dorothy (Chadwick) Senior Rigg; m. Diana Morgan, Dec. 19, 1966; children: Alden, Alicia, Amanda. MA, Oxford U., 1962; MIA, Yale U., 1964. Mgmt. cons. McKinsey & Co., Inc., London, Chgo., 1967-74; pres., CEO Morgan Svcs., Inc., Chgo., 1974—. Bd. dirs. Northwestern Meml. Healthcare, 1992-2001, Northwestern U. Assocs., Northwestern Meml. Found., Ball Hort. Co., Near South Planning Bd.; regional adv. bd. Kemper Ins. Cos., 1994-96. Pres. bd. trustees Latin Sch., Chgo., 1979-83; bd. dirs. Chgo. Crime Commn., 1994-99. Hon. scholar Oxford U. Mem. Uniform and Textile Svc. Assn. (bd. dirs. 1996-99, exec. com. 2001—, chair 2002—), Textile Rental Svcs. Assn. Am. (pres. 1983-85, dir., mem. exec. com. 1978-86), Racquet Club (mem. bd. govs. 1983-91), Chgo. Club, Glen View Club, Casino (mem. bd. govs. 1991-96, treas. 1993-94), Econ. Club, Yale Club Chgo. (bd. dirs. 1991-95, AYA del. 1992-95). Home: 1500 N Lake Shore Dr Chicago IL 60610-6657 Office: Morgan Svcs Inc 323 N Michigan Ave Chicago IL 60601-3798 E-mail: senior@morganservices.com.

SENIOR, THOMAS BRYAN A. electrical engineering educator, researcher, consultant; b. Menston, Yorkshire, Eng., June 26, 1928; came to U.S., 1957; s. Thomas Harold and Emily Dorothy (Matthews) S.; m. Heather Margaret Golby, May 4, 1957; children— Margaret, David, Hazel, Peter. B.Sc., Manchester U., 1949, M.Sc., 1950; PhD, Cambridge U., 1954. Sr. sci. officer Royal Radar Establishment, Malvern, Eng., 1952-57; rsch. scientist U. Mich., Ann Arbor, 1957-69, prof. elec. engring., 1969-84, prof. elec. and computer sci., 1984-98, Arthur F. Thurnau prof., 1990-98, prof. emeritus, 1998—, dir. radiation lab., 1975-87, assoc. chmn. elect. engring. & computer sci. dept., 1984-90, acting chmn., 1987-88, assoc. chmn. acad. affairs, 1991-98. Cons. in field. Author: (with Bowman and Uslenghi) Electromagnetic and Acoustical Scattering by Simple Shapes, 1969; Mathematical Methods in Electrical Engineering, 1986; (with Volakis) Approximate Boundary Conditions in Electromagnetics, 1995; contbr. articles to profl. jours. Fellow IEEE (3d Millennium medal, AP-S Disting. Achievement award 2000); mem. Internat. Sci. Radio Union (chmn. U.S. nat. com. 1982-84, vice chmn. Com. B. 1985-87, chmn. 1988-90, pres. 1996-99, Van der Pol Gold medal 1993). Home: 1919 Ivywood Dr Ann Arbor MI 48103-4527 Office: U Mich Dept Elec Engring Comp S Ann Arbor MI 48109 E-mail: senior@eecs.umich.edu.

SENKARIK, MIKKI, oil painter; b. Oak Ridge, Tenn., Dec. 2, 1954; d. GEorge and Cleta (VanMarter) S. BFA, U. South Fla., 1976; MS in Med. Illustration, Med. Coll. Ga., 1979. Freelance med. illustrator, San Antonio and Corsicana, Tex., 1979-90. Mem. adv. bd. LOOPS Internat., Odessa, Tex., 1990—; bd. dirs. Flying Horse Ltd., Virginia Beach, Va. Guest Contbr. Equine Images, Ft. Dodge, Iowa, 1990—, Equus, Gaithersburg, Md., 1991—; one-woman shows include Lyon Gallery, Scottsdale, Ariz., Forms Gallery, Del Ray Beach, Fla., Pitzer's of Carmel (Calif.); represented by Alexandra Stevens Gallery. Fundraiser/voter registration Rep. Women's Party, 1976—; fin. contbr. Shelter of Abused Women, Galveston, Tex., 1994—. Recipient award of excellence Assn. Med. Illustrators, 1983, 85, 87, 88, 91. Avocations: travel, writing. Office: 301 E 5th Ave Corsicana TX 75110-5342

SENKAYI, ABU LWANGA, environmental scientist; b. Mpigi, Uganda, Oct. 16, 1943; came to U.S., 1973; s. Alamanzane Buza and Manjeri (Nalwoga) Abalyawo; m. Sunajeh Nansamba, Dec. 27, 1969; children: Ali K., Sala N. BS, Makerere U., Kampala, Uganda, 1971, MS, 1973; PhD, U. Calif., Davis, 1977. Rsch. scientist Tex. A&M U., College Station, 1977-87; sr. soil chemist Ebasco Environ. Svcs., Dallas, 1987-90; soil chemist PRC Environ. Mgmt., Inc., 1990-96; sr. soil scientist Railroad Commn. of Tex. (Surface Mining/Reclamation Divsn.), Austin, Tex., 1996-97; environ. scientist U.S. EPA, Dallas, 1997—. Tech. cons. U.S. EPA Region 6. Author 7 book chpts.; contbr. articles to Soil Sci. Soc. Am. Jour., Soil Sci. Jour., Clays and Clay Minerals Jour. Recipient PRC-EMI Exceptional Performance award, 1991, Fed. Ingeragy. Recognition award, 2000. Mem. Soil Sci. Soc. Am., Clay Mineral Soc., Mineral. Soc. Gt. Britain, Sigma Xi. Achievements include research on the chemistry and mineralogy of lignite, mineralogical weathering processes in soils, and problems associated with reclamation of surface-mined lands. Home: 1122 De Havilland Ave Duncanville TX 75137-4742 Office: US EPA Region 6 Compliance Assurance and Enforcement Divsn Dallas TX 75202-2733

SENN, PETER RICHARD, economist, consultant; b. Milw., Nov. 22, 1923; s. Paul and Dorothie (Severens) S.; m. Mary Stone, Aug. 28, 1947; children: Martha, Paul. Student, Oreg. State Coll., 1941-43; cert. in elec. engring., Syracuse U., 1944; MA in Econs., U. Chgo., 1947; Docteur en droit with honors, U. Paris, 1951. Asst. prof. econs. Pa. State U., 1950-52; assoc. prof. econs. and social sci. Wright Jr. Coll., Chgo., 1953-64; prof. econs. and social sci. Chgo. City Coll., 1964-84; cons., researcher, author, prof. emeritus various orgns., Chgo., 1985—. Asst. dir. ethical and moral standards project Nat. Inst. Labor Edn., 1960-62; TV coord. Chgo. Bd. Edn., 1962; bd. dirs. Law in Am. Soc. Found.; trustee Ill. Coun. Econ. Edn., 1984-87; bd. dirs. Pivan Engring. Co., 1955-75, Rentronics Corp., 1973-75; keynote speaker state legis. conf. Ill. coun. NASW, 1974.. Author: Social Science and Its Methods, 1971, (with others) The World of Economics, 1988. Project dir. Chgo. Area Plan for Workers' Mental Health Roosevelt U., Chgo., 1963-64' co-dir. cooperative project for 2-yr. colls. NSF, 1971; active Nat. Task Force on Test of Econ. Literacy Joint Coun. Econ. Edn., 1976-79. Tech. sgt. U.S. Army, 1942-46. Decorated Philippine Liberation medal with bronze star. Mem. Am. Econs. Assn., Am. Ednl. Rsch. Assn., Am. Evaluation Assn., Apple, IBM, Microsoft Programmers and Developers Assn. (cert.), Ill. Consumer Edn. Assn. (founder, parliamentarian 1973-80), Social Sci. Edn. Consortium (founder), Social Sci. History Assn., Ill. Econs. Assn. (pres. 1975). Avocations: wilderness camping, fishing, canoeing. Home: 1121 Hinman Ave Evanston IL 60202-1310

SENN, RICHARD ALLAN, environmental safety professional; b. LaCrosse, Wis., Dec. 20, 1946; s. Hugo and Evelyn Ruth (Winters) S.; m. Denise Marie Corriveau, May 6, 1989; 1 stepchild, Danelle Marie Wiersma. BS in Chemistry and Bus., U. Wis., 1970, BS in Environ. Scis., 1975; MBA in Mgmt., U. Wis., Whitewater, 1980. Cert. hazardous materials mgr., 1990, chem. hygiene officer, 1998. Analytical chemist Warf Inst., Madison, Wis., 1970-75, scientist, 1975-77; scientist II Raltech Scientific Svcs., 1977-78, herbicide sect. leader, 1978-82; environ. chemist III U. Wis., 1982-84; pres. 4 Lakes Volleyball Assn., 1981-83; owner Sports Mgmt. Svcs., 1981-83; lab/safety mgr. Agracetus, 1984-86, environ. health safety mgr. Middleton, Wis., 1984-97; pres. 4 Lakes Enterprises (formerly 4 Lakes Recreation Inc.), Verona, 1984-98. Instr. U. Wis. Ext. Engring., 1993—; co-owner Howling at the Moon, 1997—. Author: (with others) Waste Minimization in Research and Academic Institutions, 1995; mem. editl. adv. bd. Lab. Safety and Environ. newsletter, 1998-2000; assoc. editor Desk Reference on Hazardous Materials Mgmt. Vol. WHA-Pub. TV, Madison, 1991—; grad. asst. Dale Carnegie. Mem. Fedn. Environ. Techs. (Madison chpt. program chmn. 1986—, pres., founder 1990-92), Acad. Cert. Hazardous Materials Mgrs. (bd. dirs. Greater Wis. chpt. 1993—, pres. 1996, nat. bd. dirs. 1998-2000), U. Wis. Madison Volleyball Booster Club (bd. dirs. 1987-95). Avocations: photography, camping, travel, volleyball, investments. Home: 6066 Whalen Rd Verona WI 53593-9274 Office: Agracetus Campus Monsanto Co 8520 University Grn Middleton WI 53562-2508 E-mail: fourlakent@aol.com.

SENNEMA, DAVID CARL, museum and arts administration consultant; b. Grand Rapids, Mich., July 6, 1934; s. Carl Edward and Alice Bertha (Bieri) S.; m. Martha Amanda Dixon, Feb. 22, 1958; children: Daniel Ross, Julia Kathryn, Alice Dixon. BA, Albion Coll., 1956. Mgr. Columbia Music Festival Assn., 1964-67; exec. dir. S.C. Arts Commn., Columbia, 1967-70; assoc. dir. Fed.-State Partnership and Spl. Projects program Nat. Endowment for the Arts, Washington, 1971-73; prof. arts adminstrn., dir. cmty. arts mgmt. program Sangamon State U., Springfield, Ill., 1973-76; dir. S.C. Mus. Commn., Columbia, 1976-85; bus. mgr. Palmetto Mastersingers, 1986-96. Cons. in field. Co-author: Columbia, S.C. A Postcard History, 1997. Mem. adv. panel Nat. Endowment for the Arts Music, 1968-70; chmn. Springfield Arts Commn., 1975-76. Served with U.S. Army, 1957-58. Mem. Rotary. E-mail: dsennema@sc.rr.com.

SENSABAUGH, MARY ELIZABETH, financial consultant; b. Eastland, Tex., Aug. 15, 1939; d. Johnnie and L.G. (Tucker) Roberts; m. Dwight Lee Sensabaugh, Dec. 22, 1956; children: Robert Lee, Mark Jay. Student, Odessa Jr. Coll., 1959-63, U. North Tex., 1963-67. Sr. acct. Braniff Internat. Airlines, Dallas, 1967-68; acct. Computer Bus. Services, 1968-72; sec.-treas. Robert D. Carpenter, Inc., 1972-76; controller Broadway Warehouses, 1976-78; asst. controller S.W. Offset, 1978-79; sec.-treas., cons. Carpenter, Carruth & Hover, Inc., 1979-92; sec.-treas. Roberts, Taylor and Sensabaugh, Inc., Hurst, Tex., 1992-95; pvt. practice Irving, 1995—. Mem. Nat. Assn. Women in Constrn. (bd. dirs. Dallas chpt. 1983-84), Internat. Platform Assn., Beta Sigma (pres. Irving, Tex. chpt. 1973-74), NAFE. Avocations: playing organ and piano, reading, handcrafts. Home and Office: 702 Hughes Dr Irving TX 75062-5601

SENSENBRENNER, F(RANK) JAMES, JR. congressman; b. Chgo., June 14, 1943; s. F. James and Margaret (Luedke) S.; m. Cheryl Warren, Mar. 26, 1977; children: F. James III, Robert Alan. AB, Stanford U., 1965; JD, U. Wis., 1968. Bar: Wis. 1968, U.S. Supreme Ct. 1972. State rep. Wis. Assembly, Madison, 1969-75; state sen. Wis. Senate, 1975-79; asst. minority leader, 1976-79; mem. U.S Ho. of Reps., Washington, 1979—, chmn. jud. com., 2001—, chmn. sci. com., 1997-2001. Mem. Friends of Milw. Mus., Riverside Nature Ctr. Republican. Episcopalian. Mem. Am. Philatelic Soc., Chenequa Country Club, Capitol Hill Club. Home: PO Box 186 Menomonee Falls WI 53052-0186 Office: 2332 Rayburn House Office Bldg Washington DC 20515-4909

SENSENICH, ILA JEANNE, judge; b. Pitts., Mar. 6, 1939; d. Louis E. and Evelyn Margaret S. BA, Westminster Coll., 1961; JD, Dickinson Sch. Law, 1964, JD (hon.), 1994. Bar: Pa. 1964. Assoc. Stewart, Belden, Sensenich and Harrington, Greensburg, Pa., 1964-70; asst. pub. defender Westmoreland (Pa.) County, 1970-71; U.S. magistrate judge We. Dist. Pa., Pitts., 1971—. Adj. prof. law Duquesne U., 1982-87. Author: Compendium of the Law of Prisoner's Rights, 1979; contbr. articles to profl. jour. Trustee emeritus Dickinson Sch. Law. Vis. fellow Daniel & Florence Guggenheim program in criminal justice Yale Law Sch., 1976-77. Mem. ABA, Fed. Magistrate Judges

Assn. (sec. 1979-81, 88-89, treas. 1989-90, 2d v.p. 1990-91, pres.-elect 1992-93, pres. 1993-94), Pa. Bar Assn. (comn. on women in the profession 1998—), Allegheny County Bar Assn. (fed. .ct. sect.), Nat. Assn. Women Judges, Westmoreland County Bar Assn., Allegheny County Bar Assn. (fed. sect., com. women in law), Womens Bar Assn. We. Pa., Am. Judicature Soc. Democrat. Presbyterian. Avocations: skiing, sailing, bicycling, classical music, cooking. Office: 518B US PO And Courthouse Pittsburgh PA 15219

SENSIPER, SAMUEL, consulting electrical engineer; b. Elmira, N.Y., Apr. 26, 1919; s. Louis and Molly (Pedolsky) S.; m. Elaine Marie Zwick, Sept. 10, 1950; children— Martin, Sylvia, David. BSEE, MIT, 1939, ScD, 1951; EE, Stanford U., 1941. Asst. project engr. to sr. project engr., cons. Sperry Gyroscope, Garden City, Great Neck, N.Y., 1941-51; sect. head and sr. staff cons. Hughes Aircraft, Culver City, Malibu, Calif., 1951-60. Lab. div. mgr. Space Gen. Corp., Glendale, Azusa, Los Angeles, 1960-67; lab. mgr. TRW, Redondo Beach, Calif., 1967-70; cons. elec. engr., Los Angeles, 1970-73; dir. engring. Transco Products, Venice, Calif., 1973-75; cons. elec. engr. in pvt. practice, Los Angeles, 1975—95, cons. 1995—; faculty U. So. Calif., Los Angeles, 1955-56, 79-80 Contbr. articles to profl. jours.; patentee in field. Recipient Cert. of Commendation U.S. Navy, 1946; indsl. electronics fellow M.I.T., 1947-48 Fellow IEEE, AAAS; mem. Calif. Soc. Profl. Engrs., MIT Alumni Assn., Stanford Alumni Assn., Electromagnetics Acad., Sigma Xi, Eta Kappa Nu. Home and Office: 3775 Modoc Rd #109 Santa Barbara CA 93105-4465 E-mail: sensiper1@ieee.org.

SENSOR, MARY DELORES, hospital official, consultant; b. Erie, Pa., July 20, 1930; d. Sergie Pavl Malinowski and Leocadia Mary Francis (Machalinski) Harner; m. Robert Louis Charles Sensor, Apr. 21, 1945; children: Robert Louis Paul, Stephen Maxmillian Augustus, Therese Blaze, Kathryn Anne. MS in Health Care Adminstrn., Gannon U., 1986, MS in Health Svc. Adminstrn., 1988; BS in Hosp. Adminstrn., Daemon Coll., 1972. Intern in hosp. adminstrn. Harvard U., Boston, 1972; dir. med. records St. Mary Hosp., Langhorne, Pa., 1972-74, Moses Taylor Hosp., Scranton, 1975-77, Erie County Geriatric Ctr., Fairview, 1988-92; dir. utilization rev. Millcreek Cmty. Hosp., Erie, 1983—. Cons. prof. in hosp. adminstrn. and med. records U. Pitts., 1972-74, Temple U., 1972-74; contbr. paper 6th World Congress Automated Med. Data, Washington; presenter paper Computer Adaptation of SNOMed to DRG Assignment, to 12th Ann. Symposium on Computer Application in Med. Care, Washington. Bd. dirs. St. John Kanty Prep. Sch., Erie, 1970-71, pres. Ladies Aux., 1970-71; mem. Siebenburger Singing Soc. Mem. Am. Med. Record Assn., Pa. Med. Record Assn., N.W. Pa. Med. Record Assn. (2d treas. 1982-84), Nat. Assn. Quality Assurance Profls., Pa. Assn. Quality Assurance Profls. Roman Catholic. Avocations: professional classical dancing, researcher early man's migration patterns, gourmet cooking, collecting jazz. Home: 3203 Regis Dr Erie PA 16510-2612

SENT, ESTHER-MIRJAM, economist; b. Doesburg, Gelderland, Netherlands, Mar. 9, 1967; d. Arno Sent and Alie Mulder-Kerkhof; m. Greg Kucich. PhD, Stanford U., 1994. Asst. prof. U. Notre Dame, Ind., assoc. prof., 1994—. Author: (book) The Evolving Rationality of Rational Expectations, 1998 (Gunnar Myrdal Book prize, 1999); editor: Science Bought and Sold, 2002. Bd. dirs., Webmaster Pet Refuge, Mishawaka, 1999. Mem.: European Soc. for History of Econ. Thought, Assn. for Evolutionary Econs., Philosophy of Sci. Assn., Soc. for Social Studies of Scis., History of Sci. Soc., European Assn. for Evolutionary Polit. Economy (rsch. area coord. 1998), Internat. Network for Econ. Methodology (bd. dirs. 2001), History of Econs. Soc. (elec. comms. 1996—97), Am. Econ. Assn. Avocations: ballet, piano, reading, dogs. Office: U Notre Dame Dept Econs Notre Dame IN 46556 Office Fax: 219-631-8809. Business E-Mail: sent.2@nd.edu.

SENTELLE, DAVID BRYAN, federal judge; b. Canton, N.C., Feb. 12, 1943; s. Horace Richard Jr. and Maude (Ray) Sentelle; m. Jane LaRue Oldham, June 19, 1965; children: Sharon Lewis, Regan Herman, Rebecca Acheson. AB, U. N.C., 1965, JD with honors, 1968. Bar: N.C. 1968, N.C. (U.S. Dist. Ct. (we. dist.)) 1969, (U.S. Ct. Appeals (4th cir.)) 1970. Assoc. Uzzell & Dumont, Asheville, NC, 1968—70; asst. U.S. atty. City of Charlotte, 1970—74, dist. judge, 1974—77; ptnr. Tucker, Hicks, Sentelle, Moore & Hodge, P.A., Charlotte, 1977—85; judge U.S. Dist. Ct. (we. dist.) N.C., 1985—87, U.S. Ct. Appeals D.C., 1987—. Adj. prof. Fla. State U. Coll. Law; presiding judge Spl. Divsn. for Appointment of Ind. Counsels, 1992—. Contbr. articles. Chmn. Mecklenburg County Rep. Com., 1978—80, N.C. State Rep. Conv., 1979—80. Fellow, Dameron Found., 1967. Mem.: Mecklenburg County Bar Assn., Shriners, Masons (Scottish Rite), Am. Inn of Ct. Found., Edward Bennett Williams Inn of Ct. (pres.). Baptist. Office: US Court of Appeals 333 Constitution Ave NW Washington DC 20001-2866

SENTER, KAROLYN ELIZABETH, protective services officer; b. St. Louis, Feb. 28, 1959; d. Harold Ewing and Ola Mae (Watkins) S.; m. Mark Stephen Travis, Sep. 14, 1985 (div. July 1987). BA in Adminstrn. of Justice, U. Mo., Kansas City, 1982; MEd in Counseling with honors, U. Mo., St. Louis, 1994. Investigator State of Mo., St. Louis, 1984-85; patient educator Planned Parenthood of Greater Dallas, 1985-86; counselor First Offender Program Dallas Police Dept., 1986-89; agent Mo. Divn. of Child Support Enforcement, St. Louis, 1989-90; dep. juvenile officer Family Ct. 22d Judd. Circuit of Mo., 1991-94, asst. mgr. probation dept. Family Ct., 1994—. Cmty. spkr. juvenile divn. Family ct. spkr's. bur., St. Louis, 1992—. Co-host A Different Point of View, weekly cmty. edn. radio program on WGNU Radio, St. Louis, 1996—. Active Mo. Juvenile Justice Assn., 1995—. Mem. ACA, Am. Coll. Couns. Assn., Delta Sigma Theta. Avocations: oil painting, playing piano, reading, writing, traveling, computers. Office: Family Ct Juvenile Divn 920 N Vandeventer Ave Saint Louis MO 63108-3530 Address: 8618 Brookshire Ln Apt B Saint Louis MO 63132-4722

SENTER, LYONEL THOMAS, JR. federal judge; b. Fulton, Miss., July 30, 1933; s. L. T. and Eva Lee (Jetton) S. BS, U. So. Miss., 1956; LL.B., U. Miss., 1959. Bar: Miss. 1959. County pros. atty., 1960-64; U.S. commr., 1966-68; judge Miss. Circuit Ct., Circuit 1, 1968-80, U.S. Dist. Ct. (no. dist.) Miss., 1980-82, chief judge, 1982-98, sr. judge, 1998—. Mem. Miss. State Bar Office: US Dist Ct Ste 229 725 Dr Martin Luther King Jr Blvd Biloxi MS 39530

SENTER, MERILYN P(ATRICIA), former state legislator and freelance reporter; b. Haverhill, Mass., Mar. 17, 1935; d. Paul Barton and Mary Etta (Herrin) Staples; m. Donald Neil Senter, Apr. 23, 1960; children: Karen Anne Hussey, Brian Neil. Grad., McIntosh Bus. Coll., 1955. Sec. F.S. Hamlin Ins. Agy., Haverhill, Mass., 1955-60; free lance reporter Plaistow-Hampstead News, Rockingham county newspapers, Exeter and Stratham, N.H., 1970-89; mem. N.H. Gen. Ct., 1988-96. Chmn. Hwy. Safety Com., Plaistow, N.H., 1976—; sec., bd. dirs. Region 10 Commn. Support Svcs. Inc., Atkinson, N.H., 1982-88; chmn. Plaistow Area Transit Adv. Com., 1990-93; active Devel. Disabilities Coun., 1993-99; mem. Plaistow Bd. Selectmen, 1996—; mem. Rockingham Planning Commn., 1994—; chmn., 2000-2001; bd. dirs. Gr. Salem/Gr. Derry Regional Transp. Coun., 2000—. Named Woman of Yr., N.H. Bus. and Profl. Women, 1983, Nat. Grange Citizen of Yr., 1992. Republican. Avocations: nature, grandchildren, handicapped issues. Home and Office: 11 Maple Ave Plaistow NH 03865-2221 E-mail: mse1056673@aol.com.

SENTHIL NATHAN, SELVARAJ, internist, geriatrician; b. Madras, India, July 11, 1957; s. Selvaraj and Duraichi Chellappa. MBBS, Madras U., 1981, MD, 1984, DM, 1989. Diplomate Am. Bd. Internal Medicine, Am. Bd. Geriatrics., Am. Bd. Hospice and Palliative Medicine; cert. med. rev. officer; bd. cert. in hospice and palliative medicine. Resident in internal medicine Stanley Med. Coll., Madras, 1981-84; fellow in pathology Madras Med. Coll., 1985-87; fellow in oncology Cancer Inst., Madras, 1987-89; resident in internal medicine Eng., Ireland, 1990-93; resident in inteneral medicine U. Medicine and Dentistry of N.J., 1993-95; fellow in internal medicine/geriatrics U. Tex. Med. Br., Galveston, 1995-96; physician internal medicine and geriatrics Cmty. Action Orgn. of Lawrence County, 1996-97; med. dir. Holzer Sr. Care Ctr., Bidwell, Ohio, 1997—. Cons. internal medicine and geriat. Holzer Med. Ctr., Gallipolis, Ohio; clin. asst. prof. dept. family and cmty. health Marshall U. Sch. Medicine, Huntington, W.V. Fellow Acad. Medicine of N.J.; mem. ACP. Avocations: internet, surfing, computers, alternative medicine research. Home: 25 E South St Jackson OH 45640-1638 Office: 90 Jackson Pike Gallipolis OH 45631-1560

SENYARD, CORLEY PRICE, JR. engineering executive, consultant; b. Baton Rouge, Feb. 6, 1956; s. Corley P. Sr. and Suzanne (Jackson) S.; m. Kathleen Finley, June 11, 1977; children: Brandy Adelle, Kristen Sheena. BS in Computer Sci., La. State U., 1977; postgrad., Fla. Inst. Tech., 1979-80. Sr. engr. Boeing Aerospace, Wichita, Kans., 1977-79, Harris Corp., Melbourne, Fla., 1979-81; staff prodn. engr. Amoco Prodn. Co., Lafayette, La., 1981-84; sr. staff engr. Quad-S Cons., Inc., League City, Tex., 1984-87, assoc. engr., 1987-89; v.p., engr. Quad-S Consultants, Inc., 1987-94; nat. mfg. cons. CSC, Chgo., 1994-96, ptnr., 1999—2001; prin. e-commerce CSC Cons., Chgo., 1996—2001; mgmt. cons. Sencom Cons., 2001—. Bd. dirs. Quad-S Cons., Inc., League City; co-owner CBT, Ltd., Baton Rouge, 1986-93; dir. ops. Computer Scis. Corp., Hanover, Md., 1994; speaker profl. confs. Contbr. articles to profl. jours.; patentee in field. Mem. APICS, INFORMS, IEEE, Computer Soc. of IEEE, ACM-Siggraph, Assn. for Computing Machinery, Am. Soc. Quality Control. Republican. Office: PO Box 44 Nicholson MS 39463-0044

SENZEL, ALAN JOSEPH, analytical chemistry consultant, music critic; b. L.A., May 26, 1945; s. Bernard and Esther Mildred (Shykin) s.; m. Phyllis Sharon Abt, June 22, 1969; children: Richard Steven, Lisa Beth. BS in Chemistry, Calif. State U., Long Beach, 1967; MS, UCLA, 1969, PhD, 1970. Assoc. editor Am. Chem. Soc., Washington, 1970-74; methods editor Assn. Ofcl. Analytical Chemists, 1974-78; info. dir. Chemistry Industry Inst. Toxicology, Research Triangle Park, NC, 1978-79; pvt. cons. Raleigh, 1978—. Cons. Engring.-Sci., Cary, N.C. and Fairfax, Va., 1978-81, Corning Glass Works, Raleigh, 1979-85, Research Triangle Inst., Research Triangle Park, 1983-87, Combustion Engring., Chapel Hill, N.C., 1984-89, Kilkelly Environ. Assocs., Raleigh, 1985-87, Integrated Lab. Sys., Durham, 1987-88, Tech. Resources, Inc., Rockville, Md., 1987, Am. Petroleum Inst., Washington, 1990-91, Sanford Cohen & Assocs., Inc., McLean, Va., 1993—, Glaxo Pharms., 1993-98, Stewart Pesticide Registration Assocs., Inc., 1993-95, Spray Drift Task Force, 1993-94, Am. Agrl. Svcs., Inc., Cary, N.C., 1994-96, Entropy, Inc., 1995-96, Enthalpy Analytical Lab., Inc., 1996-97, Advanced Concepts Bus. Comms., Inc., 1997-98, Kultech, Inc., 1997—, Quin Inc., 1998-99, Bayer Pharms., 1998-99, TPS Inc., 1998-99; publs. mgr. IUPAC Secretariat, 1999-2002; music critic Raleigh News and Observer, 1982-90, Spectator Mag., 1990-94; dep. mgr. Environ. Sys. Group, Environ. Resources Mgmt. Inc., Exton, pa., 1988; project scientist Agrl. divsn. Residu Chem. dept. CIBA-GEIGY Corp., Greensboro, N.C., 1989-93. Editor: Instrumentation in Analytical Chemistry, 1973, Newburger's Manual of Cosmetic Analysis, 1977 (FDA award 1978), Safety in the Laboratory, 1984 (STC award 1985); assoc. editor: Official Methods of Analysis, 1975; editor Inclusions Quar., 1993-94; publs. mgr. Internat. Union Pure and Applied Chemistry, 1999-2002. Pres. Congregation Sha'arei Israel, 1981-83, Raleigh Chamber Music Guild, 1997-99. Mem. Soc. Tech. Comm. (treas. 1983-85, v.p. 1985-87, achievement award 1985), Am. Chem. Soc., Assn. Ofcl. Analytical Chemists, Bridge Club (Raleigh), Capitol Club, Vanderbilt Club, B'nai B'rith. Republican. Jewish. Avocations: music, tennis, basketball, bridge. Home and Office: 7704 Audubon Dr Raleigh NC 27615-3403 E-mail: asenzel@yahoo.com.

SENZEL, MARTIN LEE, lawyer; b. Rochester, N.Y., June 21, 1944; s. Albert Benjamin and Besse (Lipson) S.; m. Dagni Maren Belgum, Feb. 17, 1979; 1 child, Whitney. BA, Yale U., 1966, LLB, 1969. Bar: N.Y. 1971, U.S. Dist. Ct. (so. dist.) N.Y., U.S. Ct. Appeals (2nd cir.) 1973. Assoc. Cravath, Swaine & Moore, N.Y.C., 1969-77, ptnr., 1977—2000. Mem. ABA, N.Y. State Bar Assn., Assn. Bar City N.Y. Home: 101 Central Park W New York NY 10023-4204 Office: Cravath Swaine & Moore Worldwide Plaza 825 8th Ave Fl 38 New York NY 10019-7475 E-mail: msenzel@cravath.com.

SEPKO, KAREN LUCIA, chemical engineer, consultant, business owner; b. Moses Lake, Wash., Apr. 9, 1962; BS in Chem. Engring., U. Ariz., 1987; MBA, U. Toledo, 1998. Project engr. Manville Sales Corp., Corona, Calif., 1987-90; plant engr. NCR Corp., Brea, 1990-91; process engr. Martin Marietta Magnesia Specialties, Woodville, Ohio, 1994-97; new product devel. project mgr. Owens-Ill., Perrysburg, 1997—; bus. owner Sepko & Assocs. Global Health & Wellness. Environ. cons., Fontana, Calif., 1991. Author: (book) Paint Tng. Manual, 1985. Avocations: stained glass, golf, real estate investor. Home and Office: 8945 Rolling Hill Rd Holland OH 43528-9267

SEPPALA, JUHA ILMARI, economist, educator; b. Mpraeso, Ghana, Oct. 21, 1966; s. Yrjo Ilmari Seppala, Hilkka Marjatta Seppala; m. Silve Katariina Parviainen. PhD, U. Chgo., 2000; M in Social Scis., U. Helsinki, 1992. Asst. prof. U. Ill., Champaign, 2000—; lectr. U. Chgo., 1998—2000; rsch. asst. Hoover Instn., Stanford, Calif., 1994—97; programmer analyst Union Bank of Finland, Espoo, Finland, 1988—93. Summer intern Bank of Finland, Helsinki, 1993, fin. economist, 1994—95; tchg. asst. U. Chgo., 1997; summer assoc. J.P. Morgan Securities Inc., N.Y.C., 1998; vis. scholar Bank of Finland, Helsinki, 1999. Contbr. Grantee rsch. grant, U. Ill., 2001; scholar scholarship, Yrjo Jahnsson Found., 1992—93, 1995—98. Mem.: Am. Fin. Assn., Econometric Soc., Am. Econ. Assn. Independent. Avocation: Avocations: reading, exercise, travel, opera. Office: University of Illinois 1206 S Sixth St Champaign IL 61820 Office Fax: (217) 244-6678. Business E-Mail: seppala@uiuc.edu.

SEPPALA, KATHERINE SEAMAN (MRS. LESLIE W. SEPPALA), retail company executive; b. Detroit, Aug. 22, 1919; d. Willard D. and Elizabeth (Miller) Seaman; B.A., Wayne State U., 1941; m. Leslie W. Seppala, Aug. 15, 1941; children: Sandra Kay, William Leslie. Mgr. women's bldg. and student activities adviser Wayne State U., 1941-43; pres. Harper Sports Shops, Inc., 1947-85, chmn. bd., treas., sec., v.p. 1985—; ptnr. Seppala Bldg. Co., 1971—. Mich. service chmn. women grads. Wayne State U., 1962—, 1st v.p., fund bd., Girl and Cub Scouts; citizen's adv. com. on sch. needs Detroit Bd. Edn., 1957—, mem. high sch. study com., 1966—; chair, loan fund bd. Denby H.S. Parents Scholarship; bd. dirs., v.p. Wayne State U. Fund; precinct del. Rep. Party, 14th dist., 1956—, del. convs.; mem. com. Myasthenia Gravis Support Assn. Recipient Ann. Women's Svc. award Wayne State U., 1963. Recipient Disting. Alumni award Wayne State U., 1971. Mem. Intercollegiate Assn. Women Students (regional rep. 1941-45), Women Wayne State U. Alumni (past pres.), Wayne State U. Alumni Assn. (dir., past v.p.), AAUW (dir. past officer), Council Women as Public Policy Makers (editor High lights) Denby Community Ednl. Orgn. (sec.), Met. Detroit Program Planning Inst. (pres.), Internat. Platform Assn., Detroit Met. Book and Author Soc. (treas.), Mortar Bd. (past pres.), Karyatides (past pres.), Anthony Wayne Soc., Alpha Chi Alpha, Alpha Kappa Delta, Delta Gamma Chi, Kappa Delta (chmn. chpt. alumnae adv. bd.). Baptist. Clubs: Zonta (v.p., dir.); Les Cheneaux. Home: Grosse Pointe, Mich. *Being successful has made it possible for me to help so many others along the way.* Died Mar. 4, 2002.

SEPULVADO, JOSEPH MICHAEL, computer information scientist; b. Cheyenne, Wyo., Aug. 16, 1952; s. Joseph Martin and Ann Mildred (Shipp) S.; m. Cynthia Marie Howell, July 31, 1982 (div. Aug. 1987); m. Shirley Rae Benham; children: Julie Ann, Angela Dyan. BS, U. Okla., 1972. Cert. data processor, data educator, computer programmer. Sr. systems analyst Pub. Svc. Co. of Okla., Tulsa, 1978-80; application supr. Cotton Petroleum Corp., 1980-81; cons. Forte Info. Svcs., 1981-82; instr. Tulsa Jr. Coll., 1982-84; sr. systems analyst Citgo Petroleum Corp., Tulsa, 1984; cons. Computer Horizons, inc., Jacksonville, Fla., 1984-85, Computer Assistance, Inc., Dallas, 1985-87, IMI Systems, Inc., Dallas, 1987-97; ind. contractor, 1997—. With USAF, 1981. Roman Catholic. Avocations: reading, fishing. Home: 1701 Windmire Dr Mesquite TX 75181-1555 E-mail: jmsepulvado@attbi.com.

SEQUEIRA, MANUEL ALEXANDRE, JR. lawyer; b. Oct. 31, 1931; came to U.S., 1946, naturalized, 1954; s. Manuel Alexandre and Cecilia Maria (Xavier) S.; m. Angela Maria Lopes, Feb. 15, 1958; children: Joseph, Michael, Peter, Robert. BA, U. Notre Dame, 1955, JD, 1956. Bar: N.Y. 1957, U.S. Dist. Ct. (so. and ea. dists.) N.Y. 1958, U.S. Ct. Appeals (2d cir.) 1967, U.S. Supreme Ct. 1971. Assoc. atty. Hill, Rivkins, Carey, Loesberg, O'Brien & Mulroy, N.Y.C., 1956-67; litigation house counsel Am. Internat. Group (Sequeira, Rienzo & Gillies), 1967-82; pvt. practice Mahopac, N.Y., 1983—. Mem. Christian Legal Soc., Westchester Bar Assn. Roman Catholic. Office: PO Box 563 Mahopac NY 10541-0563 E-mail: doubledomer@rcn.com.

SEQUEIRA, RAFAEL FRANCIS, cardiologist, medical educator; b. Nairobi, Kenya, Apr. 10, 1939; came to U.S., 1979; m. Kathleen Patricia Sequeira, Apr. 20, 1975; children: Raphael, Anthony, John. MA, U. Coll. Dublin, 1964. Diplomate Am. Bd. Cardiology. Intern Mater Hosp. Univ. Coll. Dublin (Ireland), 1969-70; resident Stobhill Hosp. Univ. Glasgow (Scotland), 1970-73; fellow in cardiology Univ. Bristol (Eng.) Royal Infirmary, 1974-77; prof. medicine U. Miami, Fla.; prin. investigator divsn. cardiology U. Miami Sch. Medicine. Contbr. articles to profl. jours. Fellow Am. Coll. Cardiology, Royal Coll. Physcians U.K. Office: U Miami Divsn Cardiology PO Box 16960 Miami FL 33101-6960

SÉQUIN, CARLO H. computer science educator; b. Winterthur, Switzerland, Oct. 30, 1941; came to U.S., 1970; s. Carl R. and Margrit (Schaeppi) S.; m. Margareta Frey, Oct. 5, 1968; children: Eveline, Andre. BS, U. Basel, Switzerland, 1965, PhD, 1969. Mem. tech. staff Bell Labs., Murray Hill, N.J., 1970-76; vis. Mackay lectr. U. Calif.-Berkeley, 1976-77, prof. elec. engring. computer scis., 1977—, assoc. chmn. computer sci., 1980-83, assoc. dean capital projects, 2001—. Contbr. 200 articles to profl. jours.; author first book on charge-coupled devices; patentee integrated circuits. Fellow IEEE, Assn. Computing Machinery, Swiss Acad. Engring. Scis. Office: U Calif Dept EECS Computer Scis Divsn Soda Hall Berkeley CA 94720-1776

SERAFIN, DONALD, plastic surgeon, educator; b. N.Y.C., Jan. 18, 1938; s. Stephen Michael and Julia (Sopko) S.; m. Patricia Serafin; children: Allison Elizabeth, Christina Julia, Donald Stephen, Lara Leigh. AB, Duke U., 1960, MD, 1964. Diplomate Am. Bd. Surgery, Am. Bd. Plastic Surgery. Surg. intern Grady Meml. Hosp., Atlanta, 1964-65; resident in surgery Emory U. Hosp., 1965-69; asst. resident in plastic and reconstructive surgery Duke U. Med. Ctr., Durham, N.C., 1971-73, chief resident, 1973-74; Christine Kleinert fellow in hand surgery U. Louisville Hosp., 1972-73; practice medicine specializing in plastic surgery, Durham. Mem. staff Durham County Gen. Hosp.; asst. prof. plastic, reconstructive and maxillofacial surgery Duke U., 1974-77, assoc. prof., 1977-81, prof., 1981-2000, prof. emeritus, 2000—, chief divsn. plastic reconstructive and maxillofacial and oral surgery, 1985-95, chmn. Plastic Surgery Rsch. Coun., 1983. Assoc. editor Jour. Reconstructive Microsurgery; contbr. articles to profl. jours. Served to maj. M.C., USAF, 1969-71, to col. M.C., USAR. Decorated Air Force Commendation medal, Army Commendation medal. Fellow ACS; mem. AMA, Internat. Soc. Reconstructive Microsurgery, Am. Soc. Plastic Surgeons, Am. Assn. Plastic Surgeons, Am. Soc. Aesthetic Plastic Surgery, Am. Soc. Surgery Hand, Am. Assn. Hand Surgery, Am. Burn Assn., Plastic Surgery Rshc. Coun., N.C. Soc. Plastic, Maxillofacial and Reconstructive Surgeons, Southeastern Soc. Plastic and Reconstructive Surgeons. Office: NC Specialties Hosp 1110 N Main St Durham NC 27701

SERAFIN, JOHN ALFRED, art educator; b. Washington, Nov. 3, 1942; s. John Bernard and Elizabeth (Pichette) S.; m. Josephine Azzarello, Apr. 12, 1969 (div. 1990); children: John Calvin, Michael Joseph, Mary Elizabeth. Student, Syracuse U., 1967-69, MS, 1974; BFA, U. Utah, 1971. Cert. tchr., N.Y. Graphic artist Sears, Roebuck and Co., Syracuse, 1967-68; dir. advt. Around the Town mag., 1969; tchr. art Blodgett Jr. High Sch., 1971-76, Roberts Elem. Sch., Syracuse, 1986-87, Fowler High Sch., Syracuse, 1976—. Yearbook adviser Blodgett Jr. High Sch., 1971-75, coach track, 1971-74, coach cross-country, 1972-74; jr. class adviser Fowler High Sch., 1977-78. Artist mag. cover design U. Utah Pharmacy Mag., 1970, Fine Art Index Internat., 1995 edit., Chgo.; group exhbns. include Syracuse Stage, 1989-92, N.Y. State Fair, 1977, 89, 90, Everson Mus., Syracuse, 1985, Cooperstown (N.Y.) Nat. Show, 1991, Westmoreland Nat. Art Show, Latrobe, Pa., 1995, Nat. Design Congress of Art & Design Exhbn. Art Reach '95, Salt Lake City, Tex. Nat. Show, Stephen Austin State U., 1996, Stad Diksmuide World Show, Brussels, 1996; represented by Montserrat Art Gallery, N.Y.C., Limner Gallery, N.Y.C., Agora Gallery, N.Y.C.; painting included in Mut. of N.Y. M.O.N.Y. Art Collection, N.Y.C. Recipient award of Excellence, Manhattan Arts Mag., N.Y.C. Mem. N.Y. State United Tchrs., Syracuse Tchrs. Assn. (rep. 1972-75), Associated Artists Galleries, Allied Artists of N.Y., Nat. Art Educators Assn., Syracuse U. Orange Pack and Alumni Assn., Crimson Club U. Utah Alumni Assn., N.Y. State Art Tchrs. Assn., Cooperstown Art Assn., Elks, Moose. Democrat. Avocations: Syracuse University sports, brewing, blues music, working out, travel. Office: Fowler H S 227 Magnolia St Syracuse NY 13204-2796 Home: 113 Euclid Dr Fayetteville NY 13066-1919 *The artist can turn the not yet into reality.*

SERAFIN, THOMAS JOSEPH, photographer, writer; b. Buffalo, July 28, 1952; s. Joseph Thomas and Mary Helen Serafin; 1 child Christine. Photographer Modernage, L.A., 1984—. Author: (book) Relics-The Forgotten Sacramental, 1999, The Simony Report, 1999. Founder Internat. Crusade Holy Relics, L.A., 1996—2002; dep. mem. assembly Internat. Parliament Safety & Peace, Palermo, Italy, 2001—. With USAR, 1970—76. Decorated knight Order Immaculate Conception Vila Vicosa, Duke Braganca, 36th Titular King of Portugal. Mem.: Apostolate Holy Relics (pres., CEO 2002). Roman Catholic. Office: Ichrusa/Apostolate Holy Relics PO Box 21301 Los Angeles CA 90021 Personal E-mail: info@ICHRusa.com. Business E-Mail: info@ICHRusa.com.

SERAFYN, ALEXANDER JAROSLAV, retired automotive executive; b. Stare Selo, Ukraine, Mar. 27, 1930; came to U.S., 1949; s. Leon and Ahaphia (Peretiatko) S.; m. Zenia Maria Sylvestruk, July 5, 1958; children: Lesia, Lidia, Myron, Roman. BA, Wayne State U., 1954, MBA, 1960; PhD, Kensington U., 1983. Mgr. fin. analysis Ford (France) S.A., Paris, 1964-66; budget analysis mgr. Ford Motor/Indsl. and Chem. Div., Southfield, Mich., 1967; asst. ops. controller Ford Motor/Paint and Vinyl Ops., Mt. Clemens, 1968, ops. controller, 1969-71; controller Ford South Africa, Port Elizabeth, 1972-73; asst. div. controller Ford Motor/Metal Stamping Div., Dearborn, Mich., 1974-80, Ford Motor/Body and Assembly Ops., Dearborn, 1981-82; bus. plans and adminstrv. mgr. Ford Motor/Mfg. Ops., 1983-84; program mgr. Mazda Ford Motor/Body and Assembly Ops., 1985-90. Bd. dirs. Selfreliance Fed. Credit Union, Warren, Mich. Contbr. articles to profl. jours. Adviser Ukrainian Nat. Assn., 1994-98, auditor 1998—, pres. Detroit dist., 1989—, exec. v.p., 1987-89; treas. Shevchenko Sci. Soc., Detroit, 1989—, v.p., 1997—. Named Ukrainian of Yr., Ukrainian Grads. of Detroit and Windsor, 1980, Disting. Alumnus, Wayne State U. Sch. Bus., 1995. Mem. Acad. Engring. Scis. Ukraine, Ukrainian Engrs. Soc. Am. (sr. mem., bd. dirs. 1991-97), Ukrainian Engring. Soc. (pres. Detroit br. 1978-79), Ukrainian Nat. Assn. (Fraternalist of Yr. award 1991), World Found. Ukrainian Med. Assns. (bd. dirs. 1996—), also others. Republican. Ukrainian Catholic. Avocations: golf, skiing, travel, writing, reading. Home: 2565 Timberwyck Trail Dr Troy MI 48098-4103

SERATT, RODGER CALVIN, manufacturing executive; b. Poplar Bluff, Mo., Feb. 5, 1950; s. Calvin Eulas Seratt and Evelyn Berneice Mitchell. BS, U. Ark., 1971. Lic. Real Estate Broker Ark. V.p. rsch., editor newsletter Energy Independence Techs. Corp., Fayetteville, Ark., 1976-80; pres., CEO Ozark River Farms, Inc., Fairdealing, Mo., 1980—, Colombian Leather Co., Inc., Fairdealing, 1999—; owner, mfr. Cole Manufactured Housing, 2001—. Instr. Escuelas Aeronauticas, Naylor, Mo., 1998—. Author: Future Trends in Personnel Management, 1970, The Alcohol Fuel Book, 1981, Fly Safe and Easy, 1998, Vuelo Facil Y Seguro, 2000; editor: The Alcohol Fuel Rev., 1978. Deacon Order of Grand Masons, Fayetteville, 1971-74; active Jaycees, chmn. Lake Wilson project, Fayetteville, 1974-76; mem. pub. rels. com. C. of C., Fayetteville, 1976-78; mem. broker adv. com. Ark. Bd. Realtors, Fayetteville, 1974-76; elected Constable 5th Dist., Fayetteville, 1979-81. 1st lt. inf. U.S. Army, 1971-74. Recipient Athletic scholarship U. Ark., 1970, 71, scholarship award Men's Interhouse Congress U. Ark., 1969. Mem. Aircraft Owners and Pilots Assn., Experimental Aircraft Assn., Nat. Arbor Day Found., Nat. Audubon Soc. Avocations: swimming, flying, playing guitar, building cars. Home: RR 1 Box 2000 Naylor MO 63953 Office: Ozark River Farms Inc RR 1 Box 2001 Naylor MO 63953 Fax: 573-857-2034. E-mail: rodger@semo.net., sales@coleleather.com.

SERBAROLI, FRANCIS J. lawyer, educator, writer; b. N.Y.C., Feb. 8, 1952; AB, Fordham U., 1973, JD, 1977. Bar: N.Y. 1978, U.S. Dist. Ct. (ea. and so. dists.) N.Y. 1978, U.S. Ct. Appeals (2d and D.C. cirs.) 1979, U.S. Supreme Ct. 1983. Asst. atty. gen. N.Y. State Dept. Law, 1978-80; ptnr. Cadwalader Wickersham & Taft, N.Y.C., 1995—. Vice chmn. N.Y. State Pub. Health Coun., 1995—; health law columnist The N.Y. Law Jour. Author: The Corporate Practice of Medicine Prohibition in the Modern Era of Health Care,

1999. Trustee Loyola Sch., N.Y.C., chmn. Fellow N.Y. Acad. Medicine; mem. Am. Health Lawyers' Assn., N.Y. State Bar Assn., Assn. Bar City N.Y. Office: Cadwalader Wickersham Taft 100 Maiden Ln New York NY 10038-4818

SERBER, WILLIAM, radiation oncologist, educator; b. Phila., Oct. 26, 1912; s. David and Rose Jean (Frankel) S.; m. Jane Greenberg, June 16, 1938; children: John, Ellen. BA, Yale U., 1934; MD, U. Pa., 1938. Bd. cert. in radiology and nuclear medicine; lic. physician, Pa. Intern. Phila. Gen. Hosp., 1938-40, resident in radiology, 1940-42; assoc. in radiology Hahnemann Med. Coll., 1951-52, asst. prof., 1952-60; instr. in radiology U. Pa., 1947-52, vis. lectr., 1952-61, clin. asst. prof., 1961-66, asst. prof. clin. radiology, 1966-77; from assoc. prof. to prof. clin. radiation oncology Hahnemann U., Phila., 1977-91, prof. therapeutic radiology, 1991-95; prof. radiation oncology and nuclear medicine Med. Coll. Pa. and Hahnemann U., 1995-97; staff Hahnemann U. Hosp., 1977-97. Assoc. dir. dept. radiology Albert Einstein Med. Ctr., Phila., 1950-60; staff radiation oncology Sacred Heart Hosp., Norristown, Pa., 1978-94, mem. cancer com., 1978-94; staff radiation oncology Montgomery Hosp., Norristown, 1978-97, Suburban Gen. Hosp., Norristown, 1988-97; contbr. articles to profl. jours. Maj. U.S. Army, 1942-46. Recipient award for outstanding leadership Brady Cancer Rsch. Inst., 1994. Fellow Am. Coll. Radiology; mem. Am. Radium Soc., Am. Soc. for Therapeutic Radiology and Oncology, Phila. County Med. Soc. Home: Apt 231 5555 Paradise Dr # 231 Corte Madera CA 94925-1851

SERBIN, GUY, research scientist; b. Phila., Jan. 17, 1972; s. Richard A. Serbin and Hadassah Ben Dor, Susan I. Serbin (Stepmother); m. Sheera Esther Kuslansky. BSc, Ben Gurion U.of the Negev, Beer Sheva, Israel, 1996; MSc, Ben Gurion U. of the Negev, Beer Sheva, Israel, 2001. Grad. tchg. asst. dept. geology Ben Gurion U., Beer Sheva, 1996—99; vis. rsch. scientist dept. PS&B Utah State U., Logan, 1998—99; network adminisstr. 2001 Computing Svcs., Jerusalem, 1999—2000; grad. rsch. asst. dept. PS&B Utah State U., Logan, 2000—02. Sgt. Israeli Def. Forces, 1990—93. Mem.: IEEE, Am. Geophys. Union. Jewish. Avocations: photography, computer gaming, travel, hiking, bicycling. Office: Utah State U Dept Plants Soils and Biomet Logan UT 84322-4820 Office Fax: 435-797-2117. Personal E-mail: gserbin@mendel.usu.edu. Business E-Mail: gserbin@mendel.usu.edu.

SERBIN, RICHARD MARTIN, lawyer; b. Pitts., Dec. 21, 1947; s. Bernard Serbin and Ella (Stone) Kublanov; m. Francie M. Buncher, June 2, 1974; children: Lawrence B., Haley E., Joshua H. BA, U. Pitts., 1970; JD, Duquesne U., 1974. Bar: Pa. 1974, N.C. 1996, U.S. Dist. Ct. (mid. dist.) Pa. 1974, U.S. Dist. Ct. (we. dist.) Pa. 1980, U.S. Ct. Appeals (3d cir.) 1981, U.S. Supreme Ct. 1985; cert. Nat. Bd. Trial Advocacy (civil). Assoc. Barron & Zimmerman, Lewistown, Pa., 1974-77; ptnr. Mullen, Casanave, Carpenter & Serbin, Altoona, 1977-81, Levine, Reese & Serbin, Altoona, 1982-97, Reese, Serbin, Kovacs & Nypaver, Altoona, 1997—. Asst. dist. atty. Juniata County, Mifflintown, Pa., 1976-77; instr. Pa. State U., Altoona, 1979-83, 89; adj. settlement judge for Western Dist. Ct., Pa. Bd. dirs. Jewish Fedn., Altoona, 1980-89, Temple Beth Israel, Altoona, 1983-86, Pleasant Valley Community Living, 1982-86, Big Brothers/Sisters of Blair County, 1987-95; mem. Big Brothers and Friends of Boys, 1978-80. Mem. ABA, ATLA, Pa. Trial Lawyers Assn. (bd. govs. 1988-90), Blair County Bar Assn., Million Dollar Advocates Forum. Democrat. Jewish. Avocations: tennis, skiing. Office: Reese Serbin Kovacs & Nypaver 85 Logan Blvd Altoona PA 16602-3123

SERCHUK, IVAN, lawyer; b. N.Y.C., Oct. 13, 1935; s. Israel and Freda (Davis) S.; children: Camille, Bruce Mead, Vance Foster. BA, Columbia U., 1957, LLB, 1960. Bar: N.Y. 1961, U.S. Dist. Ct. (so. dist.) N.Y. 1963, U.S. Ct. Appeals (2d cir.) 1964, U.S. Tax Ct. 1966. Law clk. to judge U.S. Dist. Ct. (so. dist.) N.Y., N.Y., 1961-63; assoc. Kaye, Scholer, Fierman, Hays & Handler, 1963-68; dep. supt., counsel N.Y. State Banking Dept., N.Y.C., Albany, 1968-71; mem. Berle & Berle, 1972-73; spl. counsel N.Y. State Senate Banks Com., 1972; mem. Serchuk & Zelermyer LLP, White Plains, N.Y., 1976—. Lectr. Practising Law Inst., 1968-71. Mem. N.Y. State Bar Assn., Assn. of Bar of City of N.Y. Home: Mead St Waccabuc NY 10597 Office: Serchuk & Zelermyer LLP 81 Main St White Plains NY 10601-1711 E-mail: iserchuk@s-zlaw.com.

SERCOMBE, WILLIAM JOHN, geologist; b. Strathroy, Ont., Mar. 26, 1955; came to U.S., 1981; s. Raymond S.; 1 child, Daniel. BASc in Applied Sci., U. Toronto, 1978. Profl. engr. Geologist Amoco, various locations, 1978—. Contbr. numerous articles to sci. jours. Active Boy Scouts Am. Achievements include first to interpret Himalayas and Carpathians correctly. Home: PO Box 4381 Houston TX 77210-4381

SEREBRIER, JOSÉ, musician, conductor, composer; b. Montevideo, Uruguay, Dec. 3, 1938; came to U.S., 1956; s. David and Frida (Wasser) S.; m. Carole Farley, Mar. 29, 1969; 1 child, Lara Adriana Francesca. Diploma, Nat. Conservatory, Montevideo, 1956, Curtis Inst. Music, 1958; BA, U. Minn., 1960; studied with Aaron Copland, Anatal Dorati, Pierre Monteux. Ind. composer, condr., 1955—. Apprentice condr. Minn. Orch., 1958-60; assoc. condr. Am. Symphony Orch., N.Y.C., 1962-66; music dir. Am. Shakespeare Festival, 1966; composer-in-residence Cleve. Orch., 1968-71; artistic dir. Internat. Festival of Ams., Miami, 1984—, Festival Miami, 1985—; guest condr. numerous orchs. including London Symphony, London Philharm., Paris Radio, Cleve. Symphony Orch., Phila. Symphony Orch., Pitts. Symphony Orch.; founder, artistic dir. Festival Miami (internat. arts festival), 1984. Composer: (for orch.) Variations on a Theme from Childhood, (for chamber) Symphony for Percussion, Concerto for Violin and Orch. (recorded by Royal Phila. Orch. on ASV), (concerto for harp and orch.) Colores Magicos, 1970, also works for chorus, voice, keyboard; recs. for RCA, CRI, ASV, KEM, Disc, Trax Classique, EMI, Tioch, Chandos, Varese-Sarabande Decca, IMG, Pickwick, BMG, Bis Records, Vox, Dinemec, Conifer Classics, with various orchs.; condr. for many recs. including Sibelius Symphony No. 1, Holst's The Planets, Carmen, Poulenc's opera La Voix Humaine, Shostakovich Film Suites vol. 1, 2 and 3(Deutsche Schallplatten award 1988), Carole Farley Sings French Songs (Deutsche Schallplaten award 1988), (home video) Kultur, Prokoviev's Alexander Nevsky, Beethoven's Eroica and Tchaikovsky Symphony No. 1 with Sydney and Melbourne Symphony Orch., Mendelssohn Symphonies, Beethoven Symphonies, Bloch's Violin Concerto and Serebrier's Poema Elegiaco CD, 1992, Le Orchestral Music of Tchaikovsky (several vols.), Laserdisc of Operas The Telephone by Menotti and La Voix Humaine by Poulenc with Scottish Chamber Orch., 1992, Royal Philharm. Orch., 1992, Dvörak Symphonies with Czech State Philharm. for Conifer/BMG, Music of Janacek and Chadwick (4 CDs) for R.R., Hindemith CD with Philharmonia Orch. for ASV; (first complete recording) Partita; (world-premiere recordings) Winterreise, Fantasia; solo-violin sonata with London Philharm. Orch.; Gershwin CD with Royal Scottish Nat. Orch. for Dinemec; Delius songs and orch. works, Grieg songs, London Philharmonic Orch. recording for Dinemic. Recipient Ford Found. Condr.'s award, Alice M. Ditson award, 1976, commn. award Nat. Endowment Arts, 1978, Deutsche Schall Platten Critics award, Music Retailers Assn. award for Best Symphony Rec., 1991; Guggenheim fellow, 1958-60; Rockefeller Found. grantee, 1968-70. Mem. Am. Symphony Orch. League, Am. Music Ctr., Am. Fedn. Musicians. Home: 270 Riverside Dr New York NY 10025-5209 E-mail: caspi123@aol.com. *A composer has the duty to communicate with his audience. The academic-intellectual composer of the 50's has become obsolete. Writing just for one's colleagues has fortunately been proven a dead-end.*

SEREBRYANY, ANDREY NINELOVICH, physical oceanographer, researcher; b. Severomorsk, USSR, Apr. 5, 1953; s. Ninel Semenovich and Irina Il'inichna (Shishkina) S.; m. Nataliya Nickolaevna Deeva, Apr. 27, 1991 (div. June 1995). MSc in Engring and Physics, Moscow Inst. Electronic Equip., 1977; PhD in Phys. and Math. Scis., Marine Hydrophys. Inst., Sevastopol, USSR, 1988; DSc in Phys. Oceanography and Acoustics, N.N. Andreyev Acoustics Inst., Moscow, 2000. Engr. N.N. Andreyev Acoustics Inst., Moscow, 1977-84, jr. rschr., 1984-88, rsch. scientist, 1988-92, sr. rsch. scientist, 1992—2002, leading rsch. scientist, 2002—. Guest scientist U. NSW, Canberra, Australia, 1994; mem. acad. coun. N.N. Andreyev Acoustics Inst., 1998—; participant in 21 marine and oceanic rsch. cruises worldwide, 1971—; vis. acad. U. NSW Canberra, Australia, 2000; vis. scientist Cath. U. Am., Washington, 2001; vis. scientist NASA Goddard Space Flight Ctr., Greenbelt, MD, 2001. Contbr. 40 articles to profl. jours., 22 papers to internat. confs.; inventor in field in oceanographic instrumentation. Grantee Internat. Sci. Found., 1993, Russian Found. Basic Rsch., 1998-99, 2002-, U.S. Civilian Rsch. and Devel. Found. Ind. States of Former Soviet Union, 2000-2002; recipient Inventor of USSR badge State Com. of Inventions, Moscow, 1990. Mem. Am. Geophys. Union, Nat. Geographic Sc., Russian Acoustical Soc., Chinese Am. Oceanic Atmospheric Assn. Avocation: alpine skiing. Home: Akademik Pavlov Str 30 Apt 55 121 552 Moscow Russia Office: N N Andreyev Acoustics Inst Shvernik Str 4 117036 Moscow Russia E-mail: serebryany@akin.ru.

SEREDA, GRIGORIY ALEKSANDROVICH, research scientist, chemistry educator; b. Moscow, May 19, 1966; s. Alexander T. and Rita A. S.; m. Marina S., Jan. 30, 1999; 1 child, Timothy. MS in Chemistry (hon.), Moscow State U., 1988; PhD in Chemistry, 1992. Asst. prof. Moscow State U., 1996-99; rsch. assoc. U. Wis., Madison, 1999—2002; asst. prof. U. S., 2002—. Contbr. articles to profl. jours.; inventor in field. Grantee Russian Found. Basic Rsch., 1996-98; recipient Young Talents of Russia award Russian Acad. Scis., 1997. Mem. ACS. Office: U Wis 1101 University Ave Madison WI 53706 E-mail: grigori@chem.wisc.edu.

SERENBETZ, ROBERT, retired manufacturing executive; b. Rockville Centre, N.Y., Apr. 18, 1944; s. Raymond Robert Serenbetz and Mildred (Egner) Clapp; m. Karen Jeanne Jackson, Dec. 30, 1967; children: Todd, Gregg, Kathryn. AB, Dartmouth Coll., 1966; MBA, Harvard U., 1968. Mktg. staff asst. to group product mgr. Colgate-Palmolive Co., N.Y.C., 1968-75; dir. mktg. Colgate-Palmolive Colombia, Cali, Colombia, 1975-77; v.p. mktg. Colgate-Palmolive Canada, Toronto, Ont., Can., 1977-81; v.p. mktg. western hemisphere Warner-Lambert Co., Morris Plains, N.J., 1981; pres. Warner-Lambert Can., Toronto, 1981-85; pres. Latin Am., Asia, Australia Warner-Lambert Co., Morris Plains, 1986-89; pres. Am. Chicle, 1989-91; pres., COO DNA Plant Tech. Corp., Cinnaminson, N.J., 1991-92, pres., CEO Oakland, Calif., 1992-94, chmn., CEO, 1994-96; COO DNAP Holding Corp., Calif., 1996-98. Mem. adv. bd. Coun. Ams., N.Y.C., 1987-89; mem. steering com. Pharm. Mfrs. Assn., Washington, 1987-89; bd. dirs. Caribbean/Cen. Am. Com., Washington, 1989; mem. adv. bd. Coun. for Internat. Unity, N.Y.C., 1987-89. Bd. dirs. Notch Brook Resort Gen. Ptnrs. Condominium Assn., Stowe, Vt., 1988-94; pres. bd. dirs. Seaside Homeowners Assn., Isle of Palms, S.C., 1997—; active U.S. Postal Svc. Mktg. Adv. Bd., 1990—, vice chmn., 1998—. Mem. Nat. Candy Wholesalers Assn. (bd. dirs. 1989-91), Morris County C. of C. (bd. dirs. 1989-91), Leadership Inc. (bd. dirs. Phila. br. 1993-94), Union League (Phila.), Wild Dunes Club (Isle of Palms, S.C.), Lookaway Golf Club (Buckingham, Pa.). Republican. Episcopalian. Avocations: golf, stamp collecting, photography, tennis. E-mail: bobserenbetz@prodigy.net.

SERENE, HARRY E. surgeon; b. Pitts., June 4, 1943; s. Michael Francis and Clara Louisa (Huff) S.; m. Linda Jean Hootman, Feb. 28, 1970; children: Amy, Scott. BA, California U. Pa, 1965; MD, Creighton U., 1969. Diplomate Am. Bd. Surgery. Intern Harrisburg (Pa.) Hosp., 1969-70; resident Western Pa. Hosp., Pitts., 1970-74; pvt. practice. Mem. staff St. Clair Meml. Hosp., Pitts. Mem. ACS, AMA, Pa. Med. Soc., Masons. Republican. Presbyterian. Office: Serene Surgery Assocs Ltd 1050 Bower Hill Rd Ste 205 Pittsburgh PA 15243-1868

SERGENT, JOHN S. hospital administrator, medical educator; m. Carole Sergent; children: Ellen, Katie. MD, Vanderbilt U., 1966. Pvt. practice; chair dept. medicine St. Thomas Hosp., Nashville, 1988—95; mem. faculty Vanderbilt U., 1975—88, prof. medicine, 1988—; chief med. officer Vanderbilt U. Hosp. and Clinic, 1995—. Mem.: Am. Coll. Rheumatology (pres. 1992—). Office: Vanderbilt U 111 21st Ave S D-3300 MCN Nashville TN 37232-2104*

SERGEY, JOHN MICHAEL, JR. distribution company executive; b. Chgo., Nov. 17, 1942; s. John Michael and Helen Ann (Bruchan) S.; m. Sharon Lee Ourada (div. 1982); children: John Michael III, Elisabeth Ann, Mark William, Tanya Ruth; m. Pamela Lynne Murphy, Aug. 8, 1987; children: Brian M., Sarah L. BA in Bus., Northwestern U., 1968; MBA, U. Chgo., 1976. Mgr. rolled products A. M. Castle, Chgo., 1959-74; v.p. Dietzgen Corp., 1974-78; dir. sales and mktg. Avery Label, Azusa, Calif., 1978-80; v.p., gen. mgr. Fasson Roll div. Avery, Painesville, Ohio, 1980-84; group v.p. Soabar Products Group div. Avery, Phila., 1984-87, Materials Group div. Avery, Painesville, 1987-89; pres., CEO GAF Materials Corp., Wayne, N.J., 1989-96; CEO Strategic Distbn., Inc., Bensalem, Pa., 1997—. Office: Strategic Distbn Inc 3220 Tillman Dr Ste 200 Bensalem PA 19020-2028

SERI, ISTVAN, physician, researcher; b. Szombathely, Hungary, Apr. 15, 1951; came to U.S., 1986; s. Istvan and Katalin (Orszagh) S.; m. Eva Novoszel, Oct. 11, 1975; children: David, I. Adam. MD, Semmelweis Med. Sch., Budapest, 1976; PhD, Hungarian Acad. Scis., Budapest, 1985. Resident in pediat. Semmelweis Med. Sch., Budapest, 1976—79, instr. in pediat., 1979—84, asst. prof. in pediat., 1984—91; rsch. fellow Karolinska Inst., Stockholm, 1984—86; rsch. fellow in nephrology Harvard Med. Sch., Boston, 1986—88, fellow in neonatology, 1988—91, instr. in pediat., 1991—94; asst. prof. in pediat. U. Pa., Phila., 1994—2000, assoc. prof., 2000—01; clin. dir. neonatal svcs. Children's Hosp. Phila., U. Pa., 1994—2001; prof. pediat. Children's Hosp., L.A., Calif., 2001—, med. dir. fetal diagnosis and therapy ctr., 2001—; head divsn. neonatology U. So. Calif., 2001—. Clin. dir. neonatal svcs. Children's Hosp. Phila., U. Pa., 1994-2001. Editor Perinatal and Neonatal Medicine, 2000—; contbr. over 50 articles to profl. jours. Recipient Janeway award Children's Hosp. Boston, 1991-92, CHRC award NIH, Washington, 1991-92, Clin. Investigator award NIH, 1992-94, Blockley-Osler tchg. award U. Pa., 2000, Faculty Tchr. of Yr. Children's Hosp. of Phila., 1999-2000; established Istvan Seri Faculty Tchg. award Children's Hosp. Phila. and U. Pa., 2001. Fellow Am. Acad. Pediatrics; mem. AAAS, Am. Heart Assn., Hungarian Med. Assn., Soc. Pediat. Rsch., European Soc. Pediat. Rsch. Avocations: soccer, tennis, bridge. Office: 4650 Sunset Blvd Los Angeles CA 90027 E-mail: seri51@attglobal.net., iseri@chla.usc.edu.

SERIO, JOHN N. language educator; b. Buffalo, Oct. 8, 1943; s. Nicola and Amelia (Zona) S.; m. Faye Ann Walters, Aug. 19, 1972; children: Alisa, Alexis, Andrew. BS, SUNY, Buffalo, 1965; MA, Northwestern U., 1966; PhD, U. Notre Dame, 1974. Instr. English Valparaiso (Ind.) U., 1966-70; tchg. asst. U. Notre Dame, Ind., 1971-73; asst. prof., assoc. prof. Clarkson U., Potsdam, N.Y., 1974-89, prof., 1989—. Pres. Wallace Stevens Soc., Potsdam, 1983—, jour. editor, 1983—; sec.-treas. Coun. Editors of Learned Jours., Gainesville, Fla., 1990-95. Author: Annotated Bib of W. Stevens, 1994, Teaching W. Stevens, 1994; contbr. articles to profl. jours. Recipient Fulbright award to Greece Coun. Internat. Exch. Scholars, 1993, Belgium, 1998; grantee NEH, 1976, 84, 91, Phoenix award for significant editl. achievement, Coun. Editors Learned Jours., 1990, Outstanding Tech. Article award Tech. Comm., 1989. Office: Clarkson Univ 8 Clarkson Ave Potsdam NY 13676-1403 E-mail: serio@clarkson.edu.

SERLIN, DAVID H. history educator; b. Thousand Oaks, Calif., Nov. 10, 1967; s. Emanuel King and Renee (Levine) S. BA, Temple U., 1990; MA, U. Mich., 1992; PhD, NYU, 1999. Lectr. history NYU, N.Y.C., 1994-98; lectr. Am. Studies CUNY, Staten Island, N.Y., 1996-98; lectr. history Pratt Inst., Bklyn., 1997-98; lectr. lit. Bennington (Vt.) Coll., 1994-97; rsch. historian Nat. Libr. Medicine, NIH, Bethesda, Md., 1999-2001; asst. prof. history and Am. studies Albright Coll., Reading, Pa., 2001—. Rsch. asst. Margaret Sanger Papers, N.Y.C., 1992-94; vis. prof. history U. Md., 2000-2001; vis. prof. urban studies Parsons Sch. of Design, 2001; hist. cons. Nat. Libr. Medicine, 2001-. Co-editor: Policing Public Sex, 1996, Artificial Parts & Practical Lives, 2002; editor Index Mag., Stockholm, 1996-98, Merge mag., Stockholm, 1997-99; editor, columnist Cabinet mag., 2000—; contbr. articles/essays to books. Mellon rsch. fellow Am. Philos. Soc., 1997-98, Smithsonian fellow Nat. Mus. Am. History, 1998-99; Louis Lerner fellow, 1993-94; Wood fellow Coll. Physicians Phila., 1999-2000; inaugural recipient Career Devel. award in 20th century history of sci. or medicine Jack D. Pressman-Burroughs Wellcome, 2000; Hackman rsch. residency N.Y. State Archives, 2001-2002. Mem. AAAS, Am. Studies Assn., Soc. for History of Tech., History of Sci. Soc., Soc. for Social Studies of Sci., Orgn. of Am. Historians, Com. for Lesbian and Gay History. Avocations: composing music for piano, guitar and saxophone, photography, record collecting, travel. Home: 168 DeGraw St Apt 2 Brooklyn NY 11231-3030 Office: Dept History Albright Coll PO Box 15234 Reading PA 19612-5234 Business E-Mail: dserlin@alb.edu.

SERNA, PATRICIO, state supreme court chief justice; b. Reserve, N.Mex., Aug. 26, 1939; m. Eloise Serna; children: Elena Patricia, Anna Alicial stepchild John Herrera. BSBA with honors, U. Albuquerque, 1962; JD, U. Denver, 1970; LLM, Harvard U., 1971; postgrad., Nat. Jud. Coll., 1985, postgrad., 1990, postgrad., 1992, postgrad., 1994. Bar: N.Mex. 1970, Colo. 1971, U.S. Dist. Ct. N.Mex. 1970. Probation and parole officer State of N.Mex., Santa Fe, Las Cruces, 1966—67; spl. asst. to commn. mem. Equal Opportunity Commn., Washington, 1971—75; asst. atty. gen. State of N.Mex., Santa Fe, 1975—79; pvt. practice, 1979—85; dist. judge First Jud. Dist., 1985—96; supreme ct. justice N.Mex. Supreme Ct., 1996—2001, chief justice, 2001—. Adj. prof. law Georgetown U., Washington, 1973, Cath. U., Washington, 1974—75; faculty advisor Nat. Jud. Coll., Reno, 1987. Exhibitions include N.Mex. Mus. Fine Arts, Gov.'s Gallery, Santa Fe. Active Citizens Organized for Real Edn., Santa Fe, No. N.Mex. Martin Luther King Jr. State Holiday Commn., Santa Fe; past bd. dirs. Santa Fe Group Homes Inc. With U.S. Army, 1963—65. Mem.: Santa Fe Bar Assn., No. N.Mex. Am. Inns of Ct., Nat. Coun. Juvenile and Family Ct. Judges, Nat. Hispanic Bar Assn., N.Mex. Hispanic Bar Assn., N.Mex. Bar Assn., Fraternal Order of Police, Fraternal Order of Eagles, Elks, Phi Alpha Delta. Avocations: hiking, fishing, Ping Pong, chess, painting. Office: NMex Supreme Ct PO Box 848 Santa Fe NM 87504-0848

SERNETT, RICHARD PATRICK, lawyer, consultant; b. Mason City, Iowa, Sept. 8, 1938; s. Edward Frank and Loretta M. (Cavanaugh) S.; m. Janet Ellen Ward, Apr. 20, 1963; children: Susan Ellen, Thomas Ward, Stephen Edward, Katherine Anne. BBA, U. Iowa, 1960, JD, 1963. Bar: Iowa 1963, Ill. 1965, U.S. Dist. Ct. (no. dist.) Ill. 1965, U.S. Supreme Ct. 1971. House counsel, asst. sec. Scott, Foresman & Co., Glenview, Ill., 1963-70, sec., legal officer, 1970-80; v.p., law sec. SFN Cos., Inc., 1980-83, sr. v.p., sec., gen. counsel, 1983-85, exec. v.p., gen. counsel, 1985-87; pvt. practice Northbrook, Ill., 1988-90; v.p., sec., gen. counsel Macmillan/McGraw-Hill Sch. Pub. Co., 1990-92; v.p. Bert Early Assoc., Chgo., 1992-93; ptnr. Sernett & Blake, Northfield, Ill., 1993-95; ret., 1995. Mem. U.S. Dept. State Adv. Panel on Internat. Copyright, 1972-75. Chmn. bd. dirs. Iowa State U., Broadcasting Co., 1987-94. Mem. ABA (chmn. copyright div. 1972-73, com. on copyright legis. 1967-68, 69-70, com. on copyright office affairs 1966-67, 79-81, com. on program for revision copyright law 1971-72), Am. Intellectual Property Law Assn., Am. Soc. Corp. Secs., Ill. Bar Assn. (chmn. copyright com. 1971-72), Chgo. Bar Assn., Patent Law Assn. Chgo. (bbd. mgrs. 1979-82, chmn. copyright law com. 1972-73, 77-78), Copyright Soc. U.S.A. (trustee 1972-75, 77-80), North Shore Country Club (Glenview, Ill.), Wyndemere Country Club (Naples, Fla.). Home: 2579 Fairford Ln Northbrook IL 60062-8101

SERNYAK, MICHAEL JOSEPH, psychiatrist, educator; b. Upper Darby, Pa., Dec. 6, 1961; s. Michael Joseph and Patricia Anne Sernyak; m. Ismene Leonida Petrakis, May 18, 1991; children: Alexander, Zoe. BA, Amherst Coll., 1983; MD, Jefferson Med. Coll., 1987. Diplomate Am. Bd. Psychiatry and Neurology. Intern Greenwich Hosp., 1987-88; resident dept. psychiatry Yale U., 1988-91; unit chief Conn. Med. Health Ctr., New Haven, 1991-96; asst. prof. Yale U., 1992-98, assoc. prof., 1998—. Dir. schizophrenia program VA Conn. Healthcare Sys., West Haven, 1996-2000, chief psychiatry svc., 2000. Office: VA Conn Med Heatlh Ctr Psychiatry Svc 116A 950 Campbell Ave West Haven CT 06516 E-mail: Michael.Sernyak@yale.edu.

SERÔDIO, ILIDIO DE AYALA, civil engineer; b. Pangim, India, Nov. 21, 1945; s. Francisco António and Maria Francisca Diniz (de Ayala) S.; m. Anna Eva Peggy Lundström, June 19, 1970 (div. 1979); m. Maria João Saraiva de Menezes, June 26, 1993; children: Vanessa, Ines, Bernardo. Degree civil engring., Inst. Superior Tech., Portugal, 1969; MS in Civil Engring., Purdue U., 1971; MBA, U. Geneve, 1979. Traffic engr. Junta Autónoma de Estradas, Lisbon, Portugal, 1969-72, head divsn. Luanda, Angola, 1972-75; asst. prof. U. Luanda, 1972-75; pres. Consulplano SA, Lisbon, 1975—; dir. Parkman Cons., U.K., 1982-86, Profabril AsiaConsult, Macau, 1982-98; gen. mgr. Asia Cons. Pacific Ltd., Hong Kong, 1990—, Global Infocentre Hong Kong Ltd., 1991-94; engring. pres. Profabril SA, Lisbon, 1993—; group pres. PCG Profabril Consulplano Group, 1996—; dir. PCG Engring., U.S., 1997—; dir., pres. Proman, Lisbon, 1998—; dir. Cobrapi Engring., Profabril Engring., Brazil, 1998—, China Corp. Ltd., Hong Kong, 2000—. Mem. adv. bd. Nat. Computer Ctr. Luanda, 1972-75, Banco Privado Portugues, 1996-99; chmn. AsiaConsult Straits, Malaysia, 1996-97. V.p. Portuguese-Chinese C. C. and Industry, Lisbon, 1996—. Lt. Portuguese Mil., 1972. Recipient O'Farril Hwy. Outstanding award Internat. Rd. Fedn., Washington, 1971. Mem. ASCE, Inst. Transp. Engrs. Am. Club Lisbon, Profl. Engrs. Assn. (bd. dirs.), AIP Portuguese Industry Assn. (bd. dirs. 1997—), Proforum Assn. for Engring. Devel., Lisbon (bd. dirs. 1995—). Avocations: skiing, tennis, golf. Office: Profabril SA P Alvalade 6 P-1700-076 Lisbon Portugal E-mail: ayala@profabril.pt.

SEROKA, JAMES HENRY, social sciences educator, university administrator; b. Detroit, Mar. 5, 1950; s. Henry S. and Mary (Wyoral) S.; m. Carolyn Marie White, June 27, 1970; children: Mihail, Maritsa. BA, U. Mich., 1970; MA, Mich. State U., 1972, PhD, 1976. Labor mkt. analyst U.S. Dept. of Labor, Washington, 1970-71; asst. prof. U. N.C., Greensboro, 1976-77, Appalachian State U., Boone, N.C., 1977-79, So. Ill. U., Carbondale, 1979-81, assoc. prof., 1981-87, prof., dir., 1987-88; prof., head div. humanities and social scis. Pa. State U., Erie, 1988-90; prof. U. North Fla., Jacksonville, 1990-98; dir. Ctr. for Pub. Leadership, 1991-98; vis. prof. internat. security studies U.S. Air War Coll., Maxwell AFB, Ala., 1997-98; prof. Auburn (Ala.) U., 1998—; dir. Ctr. for Govtl. Svcs., Auburn. Dir. Master of Pub. Affairs Program Soc. Ill. U., 1987-88, Rural and Small Town Adminstrn. Project, 1980-85; asst. dir. Appalachian Regional Bur. Govts., Boone, N.C., 1977-79; manpower planning analyst U.S. Dept. Labor, Washington, 1970-71; exchange prof. Fakultet Politickih Nauka, Univerzitet u Beogradu, Yugoslavia, 1986; vis. prof. Air War Coll., Montgomery, Ala.; sr. researcher Coun. for the Internat. Exchange Scholars Yugoslavia, 1980; mem. state adv. com. Gov.'s Rural Affairs Coun. for State of Ill., 1988; dir. Ctr. Govt. Svcs., Auburn, 1998—. Co-author: Political Organizations in Social Yugoslavia, 1986 (Choice award 1987); editor Rural Public Adminstration, 1986; co-editor: Developed Socialism, 1982, Comparative Political Systems, 1990, Yugoslavia: The Failure of Democratic Transformation, 1992; contbr. numerous articles to profl. jours. Recipient Akademischer Austausch Dienst Lang. scholar Fed. Republic of Germany, 1988 and numerous other grants, traveling fellows. Mem. Am. Soc. Pub. Adminstrn. (so Ill. chpt. 1982-83), Nat. Civic League, Am. Polit. Sci. Assn., Internat. Polit. Sci. Assn., Midwest Polit. Sci. Assn., So. Polit. Sci. Assn., Southwestern Polit. Sci. Assn., Western Polit. Sci. Assn., Policy Studies Orgn., Acad. Polit. Sci., Rural Sociol. Assn., Internat. Studies Assn., Am. Assn. Advancement of Slavic Studies, Western Social Sci. Assn., Cmty. Devel. Soc., Rotary Internat. (Paul Harris fellow). Office: Auburn U Ctr Govtl Svcs 2236 Hayden Ctr Auburn AL 36849

SEROTA, SCOTT, medical association administrator; Creator, leader Physicians Preferred Health Inc., Mo.; v.p. health care mgmt. PruCare, St. Louis, 1980; v.p. group ops., v.p. health care mgmt. Prudential Ins. Co., Chgo.; pres., CEO Rush Prudential Health Plans , 1993—96; overseer Blue Tech. Evaluation Ctr. Blue Cross and Blue Shield Assn., COO, sr. officer, exec. v.p. sys. devel., pres., CEO, 2000—. Office: Horizon Healthcare NJ PO Box 820 Newark NJ 07101*

SEROTA, SUSAN PERLSTADT, lawyer, educator; b. Chgo., Sept. 10, 1945; d. Sidney Morris and Mildred (Penn) Perlstadt; m. James Ian Serota, May 7, 1972; children: Daniel Louis, Jonathan Mark. AB, U. Mich., 1967; JD, NYU, 1971. Bar: Ill. 1971, D.C. 1972, N.Y. 1981, U.S. Dist. Ct. (no. dist.) Ill. 1971, U.S. Dist. Ct. (so. dist.) N.Y. 1981, U.S. Dist. Ct. (ea. dist.) N.Y. 1985, U.S. Ct. Claims 1972, U.S. Tax Ct. 1972, U.S. Ct. Appeals (D.C. cir.) 1972. Ptnr. Pillsbury Winthrop LLP, N.Y.C., 1982—. Adj. prof. Sch. Law, Georgetown U., Washington, 1974-75; mem. faculty Practicing Law Inst., N.Y.C., 1983—. Editor: ERISA Fiduciary Law, 1995, Supplement, 2000; assoc. editor Exec. Compensation Jour., 1973—75, dep. editor Tax Mgmt., Estate and Gift Taxation and Exec. Compensation, 1973—75, mem. editl. adv. bd. Benefits Law Jour., 1973—, Tax Mgmt. Compensation Jour., 1993—, mem. bd. editors ERISA and Benefits Law Jour., 1992—, contbr. articles to profl. jours., —. Fellow: Am. Coll. of Employee Benefits Counsel (dir., charter fellow), Am. Coll. Tax Counsel; mem.: ABA (chmn. joint com. employee benefits 1987—88, chmn. com. employee benefits, taxation sect. 1991—92, vice-chair taxation sect. 1999—2001), Am. Bar Retirement Assn. (dir. 1994—, pres. 1999—2000), N.Y. State Bar Assn. (exec. com. tax sect. 1988—92), Internat. Pension and Employee Benefit Lawyers Assn. (co-chair 1993—95). Democrat. Office: Pillsbury Winthrop LLP One Battery Park Pla New York NY 10004-1490 E-mail: sserota@pillsburywinthrop.com.

SEROW, WILLIAM JOHN, economics educator; b. N.Y.C., Apr. 8, 1946; s. William John and Dorothea (Goyette) S.; m. Elizabeth Goetz, Aug. 24, 1968; 1 child, Erika. BA, Boston Coll., 1967; MA, Duke U., 1970, PhD, 1972. Rsch. dir. Univ. Va., Charlottesville, 1970-81; prof., dir. Fla. State U., Tallahassee, 1981—. Editor: Handbook of International Migration, 1990; author: Population Aging in the United States, 1990. Capt. U.S. Army, 1967-73. Grantee Fla. Health Care Cost Containment Bd., 1988-90, Nat. Instn. Aging, 1983-89, NIMH, 1984-86, Govt. of Indonesia, 1992-98, TVA, 1997-98, 99-00. Mem. Internat. Union for Scientific Study of Population, Population Assn. Am., Am. and Western Econ. Assns., So. Demographic Assn. (pres. 1986-87), So. Regional Sci. Assn. (pres. 1982-83), Gerontol. Soc. Am. Avocations: railroads, Sherlock Holmes, baseball rsch. Office: Fla State U Ctr for Study of Population Tallahassee FL 32306-2240

SERPEDIN, ERCHIN, electrical engineering educator, researcher; b. Constanta, Romania, Sept. 13, 1967; came to U.S., 1995; s. Risan and Neni Serpedin. BSEE, Poly. Inst. Bucharest, Romania, 1991; specialization degree in transmission/processing information, Higher Sch. Electricity, Paris, 1992; MSEE, Ga. Inst. Tech., 1992; PhD in Elec. Engring., U. Va., 1999. Rsch. asst. Poly. Inst. Bucharest, 1989-91, instr., 1993-95; rsch. asst. Higher Sch. Electricity, 1992; tchg. asst. U. Va., Charlottesville, 1995-96, rsch. asst., 1995-99, lectr. elec. engring. dept., 1999; asst. prof. elec. engring. Tex. A&M U., College Station, 1999—. Contbr. articles to sci. jours., including IEEE Trans. on Signal Processing. Fellow U. Va., 1995; grantee NSF, 2000. Mem. IEEE, Am. Soc. for Engring. Edn., Math. Assn. Am. Avocations: literature, music, jogging. Home: Tex A&M U Dept Elec Engring College Station TX 77843-3128 E-mail: serpedin@ee.tamu.edu.

SERPE-SCHROEDER, PATRICIA L. elementary education educator; b. La Porte, Ind., Feb. 1, 1949; d. Fred J. and Priscilla (Nowak) Serpe; children: Matthew Aaron, Scott Allan. BA, Purdue U., 1971, MS in Edn., 1976, PhD in Ednl. Adminstrn., 1999. Cert. tchr., administr., Ind. Tchr., grades 1-2 Westville (Ind.) Sch.; tchr., grade 2 Lincoln Sch., Highland, Ind.; tchr. grades 1, 2, 4 Iddings Sch., Merrillville, 1985-92; prin. Hudson Lake Elem. Sch., New Carlisle, 1992-94; title I coord. New Prairie Sch. Corp., 1994-98; prin. Morgan Twp. Elem. Sch., Valparaiso, Ind., 1998—; dir. day svc. program Dungarvin Ind. Inc., LaPorte; dir. edn. Midwest Ctr. for Youth and Families, Kouts. Mem. drug-free, sci. textbook, elem. computer coms. New Prairie United Sch. Corp.; presenter in field; com. of practitioners for title I Ind. State Dept. of Edn. Recipient Ind. State grant. Mem. NEA, ASCD, Ind. Tchrs. Assn., Merrillville Tchrs. Assn. (sec., membership chmn., mem. computer and tech. coms. for sch. corp., bldg. adv. com.), Nat. Assn. Sch. Prins., Ind. Assn. Sch. Prins., Ind. Prins. Leadership Acad., New Prarie Classroom Tchrs. Assn. (sec.), Kappa Delta Pi, Delta Kappa Gamma, Pi Delta Phi, Phi Kappa Phi. Home: 804 Pennsylvania Ave La Porte IN 46350-2957

SERPICK, ARTHUR ALLEN, health facility administrator, physician; b. Balt., Feb. 21, 1935; s. Jacob and Dorothy (Tapper) S.; married, Sept. 13, 1979. BS, Univ. Md., 1957, MD, 1959. Staff assoc. Nat. Cancer Inst., Bethesda, Md., 1963-65; head med. svc. Balt. Cancer Soc., Balt., 1965-70; head oncology Md. Gen. Hosp., 1970-87; head dept. medicine St. Joseph Med. Ctr., Towson, 1983—2002, v.p. med. affairs, 2002—. Medicare Carrier adv. com. for Md. Active Am. Cancer Soc., 1968-76. Fellow Am. Coll. Physicians, Internal Soc. Hemtology; mem. Am. Coll. Physicians Execs., Am. Soc. Clinical Oncology, Am. Soc. Hematology. Office: St Joseph Med Ctr 7601 Osler Dr Towson MD 21204-7508

SERRA, PATRICIA JANET, social services administrator; b. St. Louis, Aug. 9, 1933; d. Lewis John and Constance Loyola (Egan) Protheroe; m. Mauricio Tadeo, Sept. 3, 1960; children: Mauricio Antonio, Patricia Suzanne, Mark Lewis. BS, St. Louis U., 1955; MSW, San Jose (Calif.) State U., 1974. Social worker Associated Catholic Charities, New Orleans, 1956-61; med. social worker Charity Hosp., 1961-63; counselor City of New Orleans, 1963-64; child welfare worker City of San Francisco, 1964-66; social worker Cath. Social Svc., San Francisco, 1970-74; counselor Golden Gate Regional Ctr., 1974-76; case mgr. San Andreas Regional Ctr., San Jose, 1976-84; program mgr. United Cerebral Palsy Assn. Santa Clara, Mountain View, Calif., 1984—. Faculty field instr., San Jose State U., San Jose, 1985—. Mem. Santa Clara County Commn. for Persons with Disabilities. Recipient awards of recognition United Cerebral Palsy Assn. Santa Clara, San Mateo Counties, 1989, Bd. Suprs. County San Mateo, Calif., 1989, Spl. Tech. Ctr., Mountain View, Calif., 1991. Mem. Nat. Assn. Social Workers, Acad. Cert. Social Workers; lic. clin. Soc. Worker (LCSW). Republican. Roman Catholic. Avocations: travel, skiing, theater, reading. Home: 4556 Bald Eagle Way San Jose CA 95118-2019 Office: 480 San Antonio Rd Ste 215 Mountain View CA 94040-1218 E-mail: patlito@ixnetcom.com., pat@ucpscsm.org.

SERRAGLIO, MARIO, architect; b. Bassano, Veneto, Italy, Apr. 13, 1965; came to U.S., 1972; s. Luciano G. and Maria P. (Bellon) S. BS in Architecture, Ohio State U., 1988. Real estate agent Four Star Realty, Columbus, Ohio, 1984—; treas. Columbus Masonry, Inc., 1985-86; v.p. Serraglio Masonry, Inc., Columbus, 1986-87; pres. Serraglio Constrn., 1987—; residential designer Gary A. Bruck, SGR, Inc., 1988-89, Sullivan Gray Ptnrs., Columbus, 1989-92; project mgr. John Regan Archs., 1992-93; prin. Architettura Serraglio, Inc., Reynoldsburg, Ohio, 1995—. Mem. AIA, Nat. Assn. Realtors. Office: Architettura Serraglio 7404 E Main St 2d Fl Reynoldsburg OH 43068-2166 Fax: (614) 759-6986. E-mail: mario@iwaynet.net.

SERRANO, JOSE E. congressman; b. Mayaguez, P.R., Oct. 24, 1943; s. Jose E. and Hipolita (Soto) S.; m. Mary Serrano; children: Lisa Marie, Jose Marco, Justine, Jonathan, Benjamin. With Mfrs. Hanover Trust Co., 1961-69; mem. Bd. Edn. N.Y., 1969-74; former N.Y. State Assemblyman Albany, from 1975; mem. 102nd-106th Congress from 18th (now 16th) N. Y. dist.N.Y., Washington, 1991—; chmn. Congl. Hispanic Caucus, 1993-94; mem. 107th Congress appropriations com., 1996—. Ranking Dem. transp. com. Ranking mem. subcom., legis. br., mem. 4 subcom. agrl. Rural Devel., Food & Drug Adminstrn. and related agys. Roman Catholic. Office: 2342 Rayburn Hob Washington DC 20515-0001 also: 890 Grand Concourse Bronx NY 10451-2828*

SERRANO, ODEAN, environmentalist, researcher; b. L.A. d. Olmedo E. and Alice (Odean) S.; life ptnr.: Christopher Mark Atkinson. BS in Math., U. South Fla., 1989; MS in Environ. Sci. and Policy (hon.), Johns Hopkins U., Balt., 1999; postgrad., George Mason U., Fairfax, Va., 1999—. Shuttle ops. engr. NASA Kennedy Space Ctr., Cape Canaveral, Fla., 1989-92, payloads ops. engr., 1992-94; hdqrs. environ. program mgr. Environ. Mgmt. divsn. NASA, Washington, 1994—. NASA rep. to Internat. Coral Reef Initiative, ICRI, Australia, 2000—. Mem. IMAGE, St. Louis, 2000—. Mem. AAAS, Soc. Women Engrs. Democrat. Avocations: triatholons, swimming, snow skiing, water skiing, travel. Office: NASA 300 E St SW Washington DC 20546-0001 Office Fax: (202) 358-2861. E-mail: oserrano@hq.nasa.gov.

SERRE, JEAN-PIERRE, mathematician, scholar; b. Bages, France, Sept. 15, 1926; s. Jean and Adèle (Diet) S.; m. Josiane Heulot, Aug. 10, 1948; 1 child, Claudine. Baccalauréat, Lycée de Nîmes, France, 1944; agrégation, Ecole Normale Supérieure, France, 1948; Phd, U. Paris, 1951; Dr. (hon.) , Cambridge (Eng.) U., 1978, U. Stockholm, 1980, U. Glasgow, Scotland, 1983, U. Athens, 1996, Harvard U., 1998, Durham U., 2000, London U., 2001. Prof. Coll. de France, Paris, 1956—, prof. emeritus. Author: Groupes algébriques et corps de classes, 1959, Corps Locaux, 1962, Lie Algebras and Lie Groups, 1965, Représentations linéaires des groupes finis, 1968, Cours d'arithmétique, 1970, Trees, 1980, Collected Papers, 1986, 2000. Recipient Fields Medal award Amsterdam, 1954, Prix Balzan, 1985, Leroy P. Steele prize Am. Math. Soc., 1995, Wolf prize, Israel, 2000. Mem. Acad. Sci. Paris, Royal Soc. London (hon. fellow), London Math. Soc. (hon.), Nat. Acad. Sci. U.S. (fgn.), Nederland Acad. Sci. (fgn.), Acad. Sci. Stockholm (fgn.). Home: 6 Ave de Montespan 75116 Paris France Office: Coll de France 3 rue d'Ulm 75005 Paris France E-mail: serre@dmi.ens.fr.

SERRIE, GRETCHEN IHDE, retired symphony executive director; b. Chgo., Sept. 3, 1937; d. Aaron John and Olive Jane (Tipler) Ihde; m. Hendrick Serrie, Sept. 3, 1959; children: Karim Jonathan, Keir Ethan. BA, U. Wis., 1959. Violinist Fla. Orch., Tampa, 1974-78, Fla. West Coast Symphony, Sarasota, 1972-86, dir. youth programs, 1974-77, exec. dir., 1977—2001. Recipient Partnership award Sarasota Ballet Fla., 1994; named Best Administered Musical Orgn., State Fla. Cultural Instns. Program, Tallahassee, 1997—. Mem. Sarasota County Arts Coun. (Arts Leadership award 1993). Republican. Avocations: traveling, reading. Home: 636 Mecca Dr Sarasota FL 34234 Office: 709 N Tamiami Trail Sarasota FL 34236-4047

SERRIE, HENDRICK, anthropology and international business educator; b. Jersey City, July 2, 1937; s. Hendrick and Elois (Edge) S.; m. Gretchen Tipler Ihde, Sept. 3, 1959; children: Karim Jonathan, Keir Ethan. BA with honors, U. Wis., 1960; MA, Cornell U., 1964; PhD with distinction, Northwestern U., 1976. Dir. Solar Energy Field Project, Oaxaca, Mex., 1961-62; instr. U. Aleppo, Syria, 1963-64; asst. prof. Beloit (Wis.) Coll., 1964-69, Calif. State U., Northridge, 1969-70, Purdue U., West Lafayette, Ind., 1970-72, New Coll./U. South Fla., Sarasota, 1972-77; tchr. Pine View Sch., 1978; prof. anthropology, internat. bus. Eckerd Coll., St. Petersburg, Fla., 1978—, dir. internat. bus. overseas programs, 1981—. Sr. rsch. assoc., Human Resources Inst., St. Petersburg, 1988—. Author, editor: Family, Kinship, and Ethnic Identity Among the Overseas Chinese, 1985, Anthropology and International Business, 1986, What Can Multinationals Do for Peasants, 1994, The Overseas Chinese: Ethnicity in National Context, 1998; writer, dir. films: Technological Innovation, 1962, Something New Under the Sun, 1963; contbr. articles to Wall Street Jour. and Wall Street Jour. Europe. Tchr. Sunday sch., North United Methodist Ch., Sarasota, 1977—. Exxon scholar, So. Ctr. for Internat. Issues, Atlanta, 1980-81; Presdl. fellow Am. Grad. Sch. Internat. Mgmt., 1991; recipient Leavy award, Freedoms Found., Valley Forge, Pa., 1989. Fellow Am. Anthropol. Assn., Soc. Applied Anthropology; mem. So. Ctr. Internat. Issues, Acad. Internat. Bus., Tampa Bay Internat. Trade Coun., Internat. Soc. Intercultural Edn., Tng. and Rsch. Republican. Avocations: singing, drawing, beach walking, cycling, sailing. Home: 636 Mecca Dr Sarasota FL 34234-2713 Office: Eckerd Coll Dept Internat Bus Saint Petersburg FL 33733 E-mail: serrieh@eckerd.edu.

SERRIN, JAMES BURTON, mathematics educator; b. Chgo., Nov. 1, 1926; s. James B. and Helen Elizabeth (Wingate) S.; m. Barbara West, Sept. 6, 1952; children: Martha Helen Stack, Elizabeth Ruth, Janet Louise Sucha. Student, Northwestern U., 1944-46; BA, Western Mich. U., 1947; MA, Ind. U., PhD, 1951; DSc, U. Sussex, 1972; DSc in Engring., U. Ferrara, Italy, 1992; DSc in Math., U. Padova, Italy, 1992. With MIT, Cambridge, 1952-54; mem. faculty U. Minn., Mpls., 1955—, prof. math., 1959-95, Regents prof., 1968—, head Sch. Math., 1964-65; emeritus, 1995. Vis. prof. U. Chgo., 1964, 75, Johns Hopkins U., 1966, U. Sussex, 1967-68, 72, 76, U. Naples, 1979, U. Modena, 1988, Ga. Inst. Tech., 1990. Author: Mathematical Principles of Classical Fluid Mechanics, 1957. Mem. Met. Airport Sound Abatement Council, Mpls., 1969— . Recipient Disting. Alumni award Ind. U., 1979 Fellow AAAS; mem. NAS, Am. Math. Soc. (G.D. Birkhoff prize 1973), Math. Assn. Am., Soc. for Natural Philosophy (pres. 1969-70), Finnish Acad. Sci. and Letters. Home: 4422 Dupont Ave S Minneapolis MN 55409-1739

SERRITELLA, JAMES ANTHONY, lawyer; b. Chgo., July 8, 1942; s. Anthony and Angela (Deleonardis) S.; m. Ruby Ann Amoroso, Oct. 3, 1981. LLD, North Park U., 1996; BA, SUNY-S.I., 1965, Pontifical Gregorian U., Rome, 1966; postgrad., DePaul U., 1966-67; MA, U. Chgo., 1968, JD, 1971. Bar: Ill. 1971, U.S. Dist. Ct. (no. and ea. dist.) Ill. 1971, U.S. Supreme Ct. 1976, U.S. Tax Ct. 1985, U.S. Ct. Appeals (fifth cir.) 1995, U.S. Ct. Appeals (sixth cir.) 1992, U.S. Ct. Appeals (seventh cir.) 1993, U.S. Ct. Appeals (ninth cir.) 1996. Ptnr. Kirkland & Ellis, Chgo., 1978; ptnr. Reuben & Proctor, 1978-86, Mayer, Brown & Platt, Chgo., 1986-97, Burke, Warren, MacKay & Serritella, PC, Chgo., 1997—. Lectr. in field. Contbr. articles to profl. jours. Exec. bd. govt. rels. com. United Way of Chgo., 1979-84; bd. dirs. Child Care Assn. Ill., 1975-79, Lyric Opera Guild, 1979-84; v.p. Comprehensive Community Svcs. of Met. Chgo., 1976-81; chmn. adv. bd. DePaul U. Coll. Law Ctr. Ch./State Studies, 1982—, dean's vis. com., 1982—; trustee Mundelein Coll., 1982-86, St. Xavier Coll., St. Mary of the Lake Sem., 1982-83, Sta. WTTW Chgo. Pub. TV, 1978-81, Loretto Hosp., 1989-91; mem. geriatrics/gerontology steering com. McGaw Med. Ctr. Northwestern U., 1981-82; adv. bd. N.Am. Coll., 1990-92; mem. Bus. Execs. for Econ. Justice, 1988-94, State wide citizens com. on Child Abuse and Neglect, 1988-94; bd. advisors Alzheimer's Ctr. Rush-Presbyn.-St. Luke's Med. Ctr., 1990—; cons. Union of Bulgarian Founds., 1992, Internat. Acad. for Freedom of Religion and Belief, Budapest, Hungary, 1992. Recipient St. Joseph Sem. Rerum Novarum award, 1999. Fellow Am. Bar Found.; mem. ABA, FBA, NCCJ (adv. com. on ch., state and taxation), Am. Assn. homes for Aging, Nat. Health Lawyers Assn., Ill. State Bar Assn. (bd. govs., spl. com. on jud. redistricting), Ill. Bar Found. (charter), Chgo. Bar Assn. (com. on evaluation of jud. candidates), Cath. Lawyers Guild (bd. govs.), Canon Law Soc. Am. (active mem.), Diocesan Attys. Assn. (exec. com.), Nat. Cath. Cemetery Conf., Cath. Health Assn., The Chgo. Club, Econ. Club, Tavern Club. Office: Burke Warren MacKay & Serritella PC IBM Plaza 22nd Fl 330 N Wabash Ave Chicago IL 60611-3603 E-mail: jserritella@burkelaw.com.

SERRITELLA, WILLIAM DAVID, lawyer; b. Chgo., May 16, 1946; s. William V. and Josephine Dolores (Scalise) S. JD, U. Ill., Champaign, 1971. Bar: Ill. 1971, U.S. Dist. Ct. (no. and cen. dists.) Ill. 1972, U.S. Dist. Ct. (ea. and we. dists.) Wis. 1995, U.S. Ct. Appeals (7th cir.) 1974, U.S. Supreme Ct. 1979, U.S. Dist. Ct. (so. dist.) Ind. 1997. Law clk. U.S. Dist. Ct., Danville, Ill., 1971-72; ptnr. Ross & Hardies, Chgo., 1972—. Arbitrator Am. Arbitration Assn. Mem. ABA, Ill. Bar Assn., Chgo. Bar Assn., Nat. Assn. R.R. Trial Counsel (Ill.), Soc. Trial Lawyers, Defense Rsch. Inst., Legal Club, Trial Lawyers Club (Chgo.). Office: Ross & Hardies 150 N Michigan Ave Ste 2500 Chicago IL 60601-7567 E-mail: williamserritella@rosshardies.com.

SERSEN, HOWARD HARRY, interior designer, cabinetry consultant; b. Chgo., Apr. 20, 1929; s. Harry S. and Bertha A. Sersen; m. Judith Ann Nelson, Sept. 22, 1956; children: Mark Howard, Diane Lynn Krause, Karen Judith Skadow, Amy Louise Gibbons. BFA, Sch. Art Inst. Chgo., 1956. Cert. kitchen designer. Engaged in store planning, mdse. display, furniture design Paul MacAlister and Assocs., Lake Bluff, Ill., 1952-55, Silvestry Art, Chgo., 1955-56, Montgomery Ward & Co., Chgo., 1956-60, Riebold Co., Chgo., 1960-61, Sears, Roebuck & Co., Chgo., 1961-68; custom cabinet and kitchen design Reynolds Enterprises, Inc., River Grove, Ill., 1967-76; prin. Howard Sersen design, Park Ridge, 1976—. Design and planning cons. for kitchens and related storage cabinetry for homes and offices; mfr., distbr. to showrooms; visual merchandising display cons. to small retail stores. Kitchen editor Qualified Remodeler mag.; contbr. articles to display, home improvement and kitchen mags.; feature in several books and in Chgo. Tribune. Art dir. park Ridge Party, 1964; mem. Park Ridge Heritage com., 1992—; v.p. Park Ridge Hist. Soc., 1996-97, bd. dirs., 1995, v.p., 1996-97, pres., 1998-99. Served with U.S. Army, 1952-54. Recipient 1st Place award Bicentennial Kitchen Design Contest, Wood-Mode Cabinets, 1974, Design award Wood Office Furniture Inst. Design Competition, 1952, award Design in Hardwoods Competition, 1958, Showroom Design award Nat. Kitchen and Bath Assn., 1st Place award for kitchen design/21st Century Elkay Mfg. Co., 1996, others. Mem. Soc. Cert. Kitchen Designers (sec. Chgo.-Midwest chpt. 1974-75, bd. councillors 1977-81, gov. 1978-82, designer emeritus 1998, Kitchen Design award 1972), Park Ridge Jaycees, Park Ridge C. of C., park Ridge Univ. Club, Park Ridge Rotary (bd. dirs., bull. editor), Masons, Order de Molay (chevalier). Home and Office: 1608 Courtland Ave Park Ridge IL 60068-5335

SERSTOCK, DORIS SHAY, retired microbiologist, educator, civic worker; b. Mitchell, S.D., June 13, 1926; d. Elmer Howard and Hattie (Christopher) Shay; m. Ellsworth I. Serstock, Aug. 30, 1952; children: Barbara Anne, Robert Ellsworth, Mark Douglas. BA, Augustana Coll., 1947; postgrad., U. Minn., 1966-67, Duke U., summer 1969, Communicable Disease Ctr., Atlanta, 1972. Bacteriologist Civil Svc., S.D., Colo., Mo., 1947-52; rsch. bacteriologist U. Minn., 1952-53; clin. bacteriologist Dr. Lufkin's Lab., 1954-55; chief technologist St. Paul Blood Bank of ARC, 1959-65; microbiologist in charge mycology lab. VA Hosp., Mpls., 1968-93. Instr. Coll. Med. Scis., U. Minn., 1970-79, asst. prof. Coll. Lab. Medicine and Pathology, 1979-93. Contbr. articles to profl. jours. Mem. Richfield Planning Commn., 1965-71, sec., 1968-71; extended ministries commn. Wood Lake Luth. Ch., Richfield, 1993-94; rep. religious coun. Mall Am., Bloomington, Minn., 1993-94; chief nursery caregiver Christ the King Luth. Ch., Bloomington, 1994-99; mem. Rep. Presdl. Task Force, Nat. Rep. Senatorial Com., 1997. Fellow Augusta Coll.; named to Exec. and Profl. Hall of Fame; recipient Alumni Achievement award Augustana Coll., 1977, Superior Performance award VA Hosp., 1978, 82, Cert. of Recognition, 1988, Golden Spore awards Mycology Observer, 1985, 87; name engraved on founders' wall Ronald Reagan Rep. Ctr., 2000. Mem. Richfield Women's Garden Club (pres. 1959), Wild Flower Garden (chmn. 1961). Republican. Home: 7201 Portland Ave Minneapolis MN 55423-3218 E-mail: dsv9@juno.com.

SERTICH, KELLI ANN, land use planner; b. Riverside, Calif., Nov. 9, 1959; d. Robert Sr. and Lillian Patricia (Hale) S. AAS in Constrn. Drafting, Glendale C.C., 1981; BS in Design Urban Planning, Ariz. State U., 1983. Draftsman, facilities planner Washington Elem. Sch. Dist., Phoenix, 1980-83; planner various pvt. sector planning & archtl. firms, 1983-88; dir. planning & econ. devel. Town of Buckeye (Ariz.), 1988-93; dir. tourism & econ. devel. City of Williams (Ariz.), 1993-95; dir. cmty. devel., interim city mgr. City of Bisbee (Ariz.), 1995-98; sr. planner Cmty. Scis. Corp., Phoenix, 1998; sr. planner policy analyst Maricopa County Dept. Transp., 1998-2000; planning project mgt. Flood Control Dist. Maricopa County, 2000—. Pres. Bisbee Christmas in April, 1997; chmn. Ariz. Cmty. Found. Cochise Project Team, Bisbee, 1997; chmn. Buckeye Clean and Beautiful, 1989-93. Mem. Am. Planning Assn., Ariz. Planning Assn. (dir.-at-large 2000-01, sec. 1994-99). Roman Catholic. Avocations: sewing, horseback riding, travel, gardening. Office: Maricopa County Flood Control 2801 W Durango St Phoenix AZ 85009-6357

SERTNER, ROBERT MARK, producer; b. Phila., Oct. 7, 1955; s. Morton I. Sertner and Laurie (Hymes) Blicker BBA, U. Tex., 1977. Ptnr. von Zerneck/Sertner Films, Los Angeles, 1985—. Prodr.: (TV films) Inside the Osmonds, The Doris Duke Story, Hostage Flight, Too Young to Die? (INH Best Movie award), The Courtmartial of Jackie Robinson, Combat High, To Heal A Nation, 1987 (Best Picture Internat. TV Movie awards), Trouble in City of Angels, Celebration Family, Proud Men, Gore Vidal's Billy the Kid (winner Houston Film Festival), Man Against the Mob, Maybe Baby, Robin Cook's Mortal Fear, Take Me Home Again, The Big One: The Great Los Angeles Earthquake, Queenie, Jackie Collins' Lady Boss, The West Side Waltz, Living in Oblivion, 1994 (Best Picture award Sundance Film Festival, 1994), God's Lonely Man (Sundance Film Festival nomination, 1986), Joyce Carol Oates' We Were the Mulvaneys, Within These Walls; (TV miniseries) Outbreak, Geronimo (TNT Native American miniseries), The Broken Chain (TNT Native American miniseries), Lakota Woman (TNT Native American miniseries), Crazy Horse (TNT Native American miniseries). Mem. Acad. TV Arts and Scis., Hollywood Radio and TV Soc., Nat. Acad. Cable Programming, Mus. of Broadcasting Creative Coun., Caucus for Producers, Writers and Dirs. Office: von Zerneck/Sertner Films Ste 301 13425 Ventura Blvd Sherman Oaks CA 91423-3999

SERUYA, JOSEPH, manufacturing company official; b. Bklyn., Oct. 3, 1950; s. Sam and Sarah (Gateno) S.; m. Janet C. Freedland, Oct. 27, 1974; 1 child, Samuel Leon. Student, CUNY, 1972-73; BEd, Herzliah Inst., N.Y.C., 1973. Mgr. accounts receivable Golden Health Care Apparel Co., Bklyn., 1974-76; collections mgr. Import Assocs. N.Y., N.Y.C., 1977-78; credit analyst Staff Builders, 1978-80; asst. credit mgr. Gelmart Industries, Queens, N.Y., 1980-84; mgr. corp. credit Commodore Mfg. Corp., Bklyn., 1984—. Contbr. articles to bus. publs. and Hebrew lang. periodicals. Cantor; tchr. religious studies. Scholar Herzliah Inst., Israel, 1971-72. Mem. Toy Mfrs. Am., Noel Christmas Mfrs. Assn. (credit advisor). Jewish. Avocations: travel, collecting music of Middle East, Hebrew and Arabic languages. Home: 1305 Avenue P Brooklyn NY 11229-1105

SERVAAS, BEURT RICHARD, corporate executive; b. Indpls., May 7, 1919; s. Beurt Hans and Lela Etta (Neff) S.; m. Cory Jane Synhorst, Jan. 7, 1950; children: Eric, Kristin, Joan, Paul, Amy. Student, U. Mex., Mexico City, 1938-39; AB, Ind. U., 1940, MD, 1970; postgrad., Purdue U., 1941; D Bus. Mgmt., Ind. Inst. Tech.; LHD (hon.), Butler U. Agt. CIA, China, 1946; v.p. constrn. Vestar Corp., N.Y.C., 1948; founder, chief exec. officer, chmn. bd. No. Vernon Forge, Inc. Rev. Pub. Co., SerVaas Labs., Indpls., 1949—. Chmn. bd. SerVaas, Inc., Indpls. and affiliated cos. Curtis Pub. Co., Forge Mexicana, Edgerton Tool, Dependable Engring., SerVaas Mgmt., SerVaas Rubber, Premier, Indpls. Rubber Co., Bridgeport Brass Co.; bd. dirs. Bank One Ind. Pres. City-County Coun., Indpls.; chmn. Ind. State Commn. Higher Edn., Kirksville Coll. Osteo. Medicine; bd. dirs. Coll. Univ. Corp., Ind. Pub. Health Found., Robert Schuller Ministries; past chmn. bd. dirs. Ind. State Bd. Health, Nat. Fgn. Rels. Commn. With USNR, 1941—45. Decorated Bronze Star, Army Commendation medal; recipient Horatio Alger award, 1980. Mem. NAM, Am. Acad. Achievement (Golden Plate award 1973), Assn. Am. Med. Colls., Ind. C. of C., Indpls. C. of C., Marion County Hist. Soc., Ind. Hist. Soc., Newcomen Soc. N.Am., U.S. Naval Res. Assn., World Future Soc., Am. Legion, Columbia Club, Econ. Club, Indpls. Athletic Club, Indpls. Press Club, Meridian Hills Country Club, Phi Delta Kappa. Presbyterian. Home: 2525 W 44th St Indianapolis IN 46228-3249 Office: Office of the City County Coun 241 City-County Bldg 200 E Washington St Indianapolis IN 46204-3307 also: SerVaas Inc 1000 Waterway Blvd Indianapolis IN 46202-2155

SERVIDIO, BARBARA J. science educator, mathematician, educator; b. Cleve., Apr. 10, 1950; d. Anthony G. and Angela B. Laurenzi; m. Carmine F. Servidio, July 1, 1978 (dec. May 1998); children: Carmine R., John A. BA in Math. and Physics, Kent State U., 1972; MS in Physics, Fairleigh Dickinson U., 1975. Math tchr. Caldwell (NJ) Bd. Edn., 1972—79; math and sci. tchr. Stuart Country Day Sch., Princeton, 1988—90, Montgomery Bd. Edn., Skillman, 1990—. Trainer assessors for nat. bd. cert. of tchrs. Ednl. Testing Svc., Princeton, 1995—. Mem.: NEA, Assn. Math. Tchrs. NJ, NJ Edn. Assn., Delta Kappa Gamma (treas. 1996—).

SERVIES, RICHARD L. secondary education educator; b. Crawfordsville, Ind., Aug. 22, 1939; s. Edward and Ruth (Kahle) S.; m. M. Carol Smith, Aug. 7, 1965; children: Scott Christopher, Tammy Elizabeth. BS, Ind. State U., 1963, MS, 1969. Cert. secondary math. educator. Tchr. math., coach East Chgo. (Ind.) Washington High Sch., 1963-68, Florence (Ariz.) Union High Sch., 1968-72; vol. U.S. Peace Corps, Ghana, West Africa, 1972-74; tchr. math. Jacksonville (Ind.) High Sch., Ill., 1974-76, Gary (Ind.) Pub. Schs., 1976-80, Lowell (Ind.) High Sch., 1980-94; math. tchr. Garden City (Kans.) High Sch., 1995-96, Andrean H.S., Merrillville, Ind., 1996—. Tchr. in Space participant NASA, 1985-86. Named to Curriculum Devel. NSF, 1970-71; recipient Superior Achievement award Ariz. Interscholastic Assn. Coach Football Class B Champions, 1969. Home: 106 Johnson Dr Crawfordsville IN 47933-1019

SERVINSKI, SARAH JANE (SARAH JEROUE), language arts educator; b. Detroit, Sept. 13, 1944; d. Edward Lawrence and Frances Elizabeth (Henne) Jeroue; m. Leonard Charles Servinski, July 31, 1965; children: Charles, Mary Servinski-Draves, Michael, Katherine, Andrew. BA, Mich. State U., 1965, MA, 1978; EdS, Cen. Mich. U., 1990. Cert. tchr., adminstr., Mich. Tchr. elem. and secondary schs., Mich., 1965-80; assoc. prof. lang. arts Northwood U., Midland, 1980-90; field placement coord. Saginaw Valley State Univ./Coll. of Edn., University Center, 1991-95; owner Maple Hill Farm, Midland, 1990—. Adj. prof. English Saginaw Valley State U., 1996-98; communications cons.; co-founder Maple Hill Nursery and Flowers, Midland, 1977, Maple Hill Equip. Sales and Svc., Midland, 1987; founder Maple Hill Children's Shop, Midland, 1983; adj. prof. lang. arts Delta Coll., University Center, Mich., 1990–; ednl. devel. counselor, UAW-GM EDC Program, U. Mich., 1998-2000; asst. dir. profl. edn. Ctrl. Mich. U., Mt. Pleasant, 2000-02. Mem. Dow Corning Citizens Community Adv. Panel, Midland, Mich, 1991-92. Republican. Roman Catholic. Home: 2674 N Eastman Rd Midland MI 48642-7850 E-mail: sjser@aol.com.

SERVIS, WILLIAM GEORGE, lawyer; b. Rochester, N.Y., July 1, 1922; s. Harry Hall and Lois Ellen Servis; m. Valentine Agnes Reynouard, June 24, 1947; children: Ronald, Terry, Kim Powell. LLD, N.Y. Law Sch., 1957. Bar: N.Y., U.S. Dist. Ct. N.Y. Counsel Hon. John J. Conway, Rochester, 1958-60; asst. dist. atty. Dist. Atty.'s Office, 1960-71; pvt. practice, 1971—. Lectr. Police and Fire Acad., Rochester, 1960-71, Monroe County Magistrates Assn., 1966-70; counsel Western Monroe Hist. Soc., Brockport, N.Y., 1960-70,

Clarkson Town, 1965-75, Spencerport Vol. Ambulance, Spencerport, N.Y., 1965-97. With USN, 1942—46. Mem. ABA, N.Y. State Bar Assn., Monroe County Bar Assn. Republican. Mem. United Ch. Of Christ. Avocations: sailing, swimming. Home: 60 Laurelcrest Dr Spencerport NY 14559-2304 Office: 1379 Long Pond Rd Rochester NY 14626

SERVODIDIO, PAT ANTHONY, broadcast executive; b. Yonkers, N.Y., Nov. 9, 1937; s. Pasquale and Catherine (Verdisco) S.; children: Christian, Alexa. BS, Fordham U., 1959; postgrad., St. John's U., N.Y.C., 1960-63. Asst. to bus. mgr. Sta. WCBS-TV, N.Y.C., 1960-64; account exec. Sta. WTNH-TV, New Haven, 1964-66; account exec., N.Y. sales mgr. RKO TV Reps., N.Y.C., 1967-74; v.p., N.Y. sales mgr. Sta. WOR-TV, 1974-79, v.p., gen. sales mgr., 1979-81; v.p., gen. mgr. Sta. WNAC-TV, Boston, 1981-82; pres. RKO TV, N.Y.C., 1982-87, RKO Gen., Inc., N.Y.C., 1987-91, also bd. dirs.; v.p., gen. mgr. Sta. WKYC-TV, Cleve., 1991-92; pres. Multimedia Broadcasting Co., Cin., 1992-94; broadcast cons., 1995—. Bd. regents St. Peter's Coll., 1983-99; mem. com. future financing Rutgers U., New Brunswick, N.J., 1983-85; dir. TV bur. Advt. Bd., 1993-94; bd. dirs. Internat. Radio and TV Found., 1983-93, Assn. for Maximum Svc. TV, Inc., 1993-95. With U.S. Army, 1959-62. Office: 380 Lexington Ave Ste 1700 New York NY 10168-0002

SERWATKA, WALTER DENNIS, publishing executive; b. Irvington, N.J., July 19, 1937; s. Walter F. and Grace R. (Sheehan) S.; m. Beverly M. Farrell, Aug. 10, 1963 (div. Feb. 1988); children: David, Nora, Nancy; m. Constance L. Holcomb, May 10, 1991. BBA in Acctg., Upsala U., 1959; MBA in Fin., Fairleigh Dickinson U., 1966; postgrad., Harvard U., 1978, Columbia U., 1979, Stanford U., 1985. With treas.'s dept. WESTVACO, N.Y.C., 1964-68; dir. fin. analysis Random House Co., 1968-72; with McGraw-Hill Info. Systems Co., 1972-83; from contr. Sweet's divsn. to asst. contr. McGraw-Hill, Inc., N.Y.C., 1972-76, sr. v.p., contr., 1976-79, group v.p. real estate info. svcs., 1979-83, sr. v.p. group mfg. and circulation svcs., 1985, exec. v.p., CFO, 1985-88, exec. v.p. ops., 1989—92; exec. v.p. fin. and svcs. McGraw-Hill Publs. Co., 1983-84; pres. McGraw-Hill Info. Svcs., 1988-89. Trustee Upsala Coll., East Orange, N.J. Served with U.S. Army, 1959-62. Mem. Fin. Exec. Inst., Mag. Pubs. Assn., Am. Inst. Accts., Planning Execs. Inst., Pvt. Sector Council.

SERWER, ALAN MICHAEL, lawyer; b. Detroit, Aug. 31, 1944; s. Bernard Jacob and Marian (Borin) S.; m. Laurel Kathryn Robbert, June 6, 1968; children: David Matthew, Karen Anne. BA in Econs., U. Mich., 1966; JD, Northwestern U., 1969. Bar: Ill. 1969, D.C. 1980, U.S. Dist. Ct. (no. dist.) Ill. 1970, U.S. Ct. Appeals (7th cir.) 1979, U.S. Supreme Ct. 1979, U.S. Ct. Appeals (6th cir.) 1982, U.S. Ct. Appeals (5th cir.) 1983, U.S. Ct. Appeals (11th cir.) 1984, U.S. Ct. Appeals (9th cir.) 1986. Trial atty. U.S. Dept. Labor, Chgo., 1969-78, counsel safety and health, 1978-79; assoc. Haley, Bader & Potts, 1979-82, ptnr., 1983-87; mem. Bell, Boyd & Lloyd, 1987—. Mem. Ill. Bar Assn., Chgo. Bar Assn., Assn. Trial Lawyers Am. Home: 233 Woodland Rd Highland Park IL 60035-5052 Office: Bell Boyd & Lloyd 70 W Madison St Ste 3200 Chicago IL 60602-4244

SERWER, GERALD ARTHUR, medical educator; b. Oklahoma City, June 24, 1946; m. Milton J. and Ora L. S.; m. Sheryl Smith, Dec. 13, 1981; children: Bradley, Valerie, Kathleen, James, Laura. BA, Rice U., 1968; MD, Duke U., 1972. Diplomate Am. Bd. Pediatrics, Am. Bd. Pediatric Cardiology. Asst. prof. Duke U., Durham, N.C., 1975-82, assoc. prof., 1982-86, U. Mich., Ann Arbor, 1986-92, prof., 1992—. Author: Echo in Ped Heart Disease, 1990, 2nd edit., 1997; contbr. articles to profl. jours. Fellow Am. Acad. Pediatrics (Young Investigator's award 1979), Am. Coll. Cardiology, N. Am. Soc. Pacing and Electrophysiology; mem. Am. Heart Assn. (Achievement award 1978), Soc. Pediatric Rsch. Office: U Mich Box 0204 1500 E Medical Center Dr Ann Arbor MI 48109-0005 E-mail: gserwer@umich.edu.

SERWY, ROBERT ANTHONY, accountant; b. Chgo., Mar. 26, 1950; s. Anthony J. and Bernice (Zubek) S.; m. Margaret A. Smejkal, Aug. 12, 1972; children: Karen, Steven. BS in Engring., U. Ill., 1972; MBA, Northwestern U., 1974. Mgr. cons. Arthur Andersen & Co., Chgo., 1974-83; dir. fin. planning Teepak, Inc., Oak Brook, Ill., 1983-85; sr. mgr. cons. Peat Marwick & Mitchell, Chgo., 1985-86; dir. cons. Warady & Davis, Deerfield, Ill., 1986—. F.C. Austin scholar, 1972. Mem. AICPA, Ill. CPA Soc. Roman Catholic. Avocations: amateur radio, microcomputers, football. Home: 203 Buckingham Ct Grayslake IL 60030-3479 Office: Warady & Davis 108 Wilmot Rd Ste 500 Deerfield IL 60015-5108

SESHAN, SURYA VENKATA, pathologist; b. Rajahmundry, India, Sept. 3, 1952; came to U.S., 1976; d. Lakshminarayana Sastry and Ramana Venkata (Hota) Lanka; m. Thirumoorthi Venkata Seshan, Feb. 23, 1975; children: Karthik Siva, Nandini Lakshmi. Grad., Govt. Med. Coll., 1969, B of Medicine and Surgery, 1974. Intern Med. Coll. Affiliated Hosps., Mysore, India, 1974-75, K.R. Hosp., Mysore, India, 1975; physician Johnston-Willis Hosp., Richmond, Va., 1977-78; resident pathology N.Y. Hosp. Coll., Met. Hosp. Ctr., N.Y.C., 1978-82, chief resident anatomic pathology, 1979-80, chief resident clin. pathology, 1981; assoc. clin. prof. Mt. Sinai Sch. Medicine; clin. prof., dir. labs. U. Medicine and Dentistry N.J., Paterson, N.J. Guest lectr. and cons. in field. Chief editor: Classification of Tubulo-interstitial Diseases, 1999; editor: The Kidney in Collagen-Vascular Diseases, 1993; mem. writing com. Classification of Glomerular Diseases, 2d edit., 1994; contbr. articles to profl. jours. Rsch. fellow Renal Pathology fellow Barnert Hosp., 1982-84, Vis. fellow Mt. Sinai Hosp., 1982-84. Fellow Am. Soc. Clin. Pathology, Coll. Am. Pathologists; mem. AMA, Am. Soc. Nephrology, Renal Pathology Soc., Nat. Kidney Found., Internat. Acad. Pathology, Women in Nephrology, N.J. Soc. Pathology. Avocations: Indian classical music, lang. analysis, reading, table tennis. Office: Barnert Hosp Dept Pathology 680 Broadway Paterson NJ 07514-1422

SESLAR, PATRICK GEORGE, writer, artist; b. Ft. Wayne, Ind., Sept. 20, 1947; s. Dale Milton and Alice Georgiana (Lincoln) S.; m. Lin L. Coleman, Sept. 20, 1968. BS in Psychology, Purdue U., 1969. Contbg. editor The Artist's Mag., Cin., 1985—; columnist Trailer Life Mag., Agoura, Calif., 1988-90. Author: Painting Seascapes in Sharp Focus, 1987, Wildlife Painting Step by Step, 1995, Painting From Photographs, 1999, The One Hour Watercolorist, 2001; co-author: Painting Nature's Peaceful Places, 1993; exhibiting artist Art Sales and Rental Gallery, Phila., 1996—, Phila. Mus. Art, 1996—. Recipient Award of Merit, Winter Pk. Art Festival, 1995, 3d pl. (painting) Coconut Grove Arts Festival, 1996, Juror's award (painting) Cherry Creek Arts Festival, 1997. Mem. Nat. Assn. Ind. Artists. Avocations: backpacking, mountain biking, hiking. Home and Office: 5580 La Jolla Blvd # 334 La Jolla CA 92037-7651

SESONSKE, ALEXANDER, nuclear and chemical engineer; b. Gloversville, N.Y., June 20, 1921; s. Abraham and Esther (Kreitzer) S.; m. Marjorie Ann Mach, Apr. 17, 1952 (dec. Jan. 1995); children: Michael Jan, Jana Louise. B.Chem. Engring., Rensselaer Poly. Inst., 1942; MS, U. Rochester, 1947; PhD, U. Del., 1950. Engr. Chem. Constrn. Corp., N.Y.C., 1942; chem. engr. Manhattan Project, 1943-45, Columbia-So. Chem. Corp., 1945-46; staff Los Alamos Sci. Lab., 1950-54, 60-61, cons., 1961-63; faculty Purdue U., Lafayette, Ind., 1954, prof. nuclear and chem. engring., 1959-86, prof. emeritus, 1986—, asst. chmn. dept. nuclear engring., 1966-73. Cons. Oak Ridge Nat. Lab., 1963-67, Electric Power Research Inst., 1974; mem. rev. com. Argonne (Ill.) Nat. Lab., 1965-67, 75-81; ind. cons. 1986—. Author: (with Samuel Glasstone) Nuclear Reactor Engineering, 1963, 4th edit., 1994, Nuclear Power Plant Design Analysis, 1973; mem. editorial bd. Advances in Nuclear Sci. and Tech., 1972—; contbr. numerous articles to profl. jours. Recipient Wall of Fame award U. Del., 1988. Fellow Am. Nuclear Soc. (Arthur H. Compton award 1987); mem. Am. Inst. Chem. Engrs., Am. Soc. Engring. Edn., Sigma Xi, Omega Chi Epsilon. Achievements include research on nuclear fuel mgmt., liquid metal heat transfer and nuclear reactor engring. Home and Office: 24441 Calle Sonora Apt 331 Laguna Beach CA 92653-7707 E-mail: alses1@cs.com.

SESSIONS, BETTYE JEAN, humanities educator; b. Jacksonville, FL, Jan. 29, 1934; d. John Henry and Willene Porter Hayes; m. Malcolm G.A. Sessions, July 7, 1956; children: Sabrina F., Malcolm G.A. II, Byron Craig. BA, Fla. A&M U., 1956; MAT, Jacksonville U., 1967. Tchr. English, humanities Duval County Pub. Schs., Jacksonville, Fla., 1957—72; prof. humanities Fla. C.C., 1972—90; news corr. Fla. Times - Jacksonville Jour., 1981—86; profl. writer, author and poet Jean-Aubrey Ideas, Inc., Jacksonville, 1985—2001.

SESSIONS, GEORGE PURD, physician; b. Dawson, Ga., July 9, 1931; s. George Purdee and Jessie Louise (Ferguson) S.; m. Martha Ann Hernandez, June 30, 1960; children: William Dean, Neal Bradley, Annette Elaine. BS, U. Ga., 1952; MD, Med. Coll. of Ga., 1955. Diplomate Am. Bd. Anesthesiology. Intern Macon (Ga.) Hosp., 1955-56; sr. asst. surgeon USPHS, New London, Conn., 1956-58; resident Charity Hosp., New Orleans, 1958-60; instr. in anesthesia Emory U., Atlanta, 1960-61; chief dept. anesthesiology DeKalb Gen. Hosp., Decatur, Ga., 1961-81, Scottish Rite Hosp., Decatur, 1965-74, Decatur Hosp., 1972-82; pres. DeKalb Anesthesia Assocs., P.A., 1970-95. With USPHS, 1956-58. Mem. AMA, Med. Assn. of Ga., So. Med. Assn., Am. Soc. Anesthesiology, Ga. Soc. Anesthesiology (pres. 1972-73). Avocations: piano, gardening, genealogy. Home: 1658 Mason Mill Rd NE Atlanta GA 30329-4133 E-mail: G.Sessions@mindspring.com.

SESSIONS, JEFFERSON BEAUREGARD, III, senator; b. Hybart, Ala., Dec. 24, 1946; s. Jefferson Beauregard and Abbie (Powe) S.; m. Mary Montgomery Blackshear, Aug. 9, 1969; children: Mary Abigail, Ruth Blackshear, Samuel Turner BA, Huntingdon Coll., Montgomery, Ala., 1969; JD, U. Ala., 1973. Bar: Ala. 1973. Assoc. Guin, Bouldin & Porch, Russellville, Ala., 1973-75; asst. U.S. atty. U.S. Dept. Justice, Mobile, 1975-77, U.S. atty., 1981-93; assoc., ptnr. Stockman & Bedsole Attys., 1977-81; ptnr. Stockman, Bedsole & Sessions, 1993-94; atty. gen. State of Ala., 1996; U.S. senator from Ala., 1997—. Mem. U.S. atty. gen's. adv. com., 1987-89, vice-chmn. 1989; mem. judiciary, health, edn., labor & pensions armed svcs. coms. Presdl. elector State of Ala., 1972; trustee, mem. exec. com. Mobile Bay Area Partnership for Youth, 1981-95; chmn. adminstrv. bd. Ashland Pl. United Meth. Ch., Mobile, 1982; 1st v.p. Mobile Lions Club, 1993-94. Capt. USAR, 1975-85 Recipient U.S. Atty. Gen's. award for significant achievements in the war against drug trafficking U.S. Atty. Gen. William P. Barr, 1992. Mem. ABA, Ala. Bar Assn., Mobile Bar Assn. Home: 1119 Hillcrest Xing E Mobile AL 36695-4505 Office: 493 Senate Russell Office Bldg Washington DC 20510-0001 E-mail: senator@sessions.senate.gov.*

SESSIONS, JUDITH ANN, librarian, university library dean; b. Lubbock, Tex., Dec. 16, 1947; d. Earl Alva and Anna (Mayer) S. BA cum laude, Cen. Fla. U., 1970; MLS, Fla. State U., 1971; postgrad., Am. U., 1980, George Washington U., 1983. Head libr. U. S.C., Salkehatchie, 1974-77; dir. Libr. and Learing Resources Ctr. Mt. Vernon Coll., Washington, 1977-82; planning and systems libr. George Washington U., 1981-82, asst. univ. libr. for adminstrn. svcs., acting head tech. svcs., 1982-84; univ. libr. Calif. State U., Chico, 1984-88; univ. libr., dean of libr. Miami U., Oxford, Ohio, 1988—. Cons. Space Planning, SC, 1976, DataPhase Implementation, Bowling Green U., 1982, TV News Study Ctr., George Washington U., 1981; asst. prof. dept. child devel. Mt. Vernon Coll., 1978—81; mem., lectr. U.S.-China Libr. Exch. Del., 1986, 91; lectr., presenter in field; mem. coord. com. OhioLink Adv. Coun., 1995—2001, v.p., 1996—97, chair, 1998—2000; mem. gov. bd. OhioLink, exec. com., 1998—2001; mem. OCLC Users Coun., 1998—2001; convenor Pub. Acad. Libr. Group, 1999—2000. Contbr. articles, book revs. to profl. jours. Trustee Christ Hosp., Cin., 1990-94, Deaconness Gamble Rsch. Ctr., Cin., 1990-94, OhioNet, 1990-94, treas. 1993; bd. dirs. Hamilton (Ohio) YWCA, 1994-98, pres., 1995-96, v.p., 1996-97, 97-98; mem. OCLC user's coun., 1998—. Recipient award for outstanding contbn. D.C. Libr. Assn., 1979; rsch. grantee Mt. Vernon Coll., 1980; recipient Fulbright-Hayes Summer Travel fellowship to Czechoslovakia, 1991. Mem. ALA (Olofson award 1978, councillor-at-large policy making group 1981-94, coun. com. on coms. 1983-84, intellectual freedom com. 1984-88, directions and program rev. com. 1989-91, fin. and audit subcom. 1989-90, mem. exec. bd. 1989-94, mem. del. to Zimbabwe Internat. Book Fair 1997), Assn. Coll. and Rsch. Librs. (editorial bd. Coll. and Rsch. Librs. jour. 1979-84, nominations and appointments com. 1983-85, faculty status com. 1984-86), Libr. and Info. Tech. Assn. (chair legis. and regulation com. 1980-81), Libr. Adminstrn. and Mgmt. Assn. (bd. dirs. libr. orgn. and mgmt. sect. 1985-87), Calif. Inst. Librs. (v.p., pres. elect 1987-88), Mid-Atlantic Regional Libr. Fedn. (mem. exec. bd. 1982-84), Jr. Mems. Round Table (pres. 1981-82), Intellectual Freedom Round Table (sec. 1984-85), Freedom to Read Found. (trustee 1984-88, v.p. 1985-86, treas. 1986-87, pres. 1987-88), Rotary, Beta Phi Mu. Home: 45 Waters Way Hamilton OH 45013-6324 Office: Miami U Edgar W King Oxford OH 45056

SESSIONS, PETE, congressman; b. Mar. 22, 1955; m. Juanita; children: Bill, Alex. Grad., Southwestern U., 1978. With Southwestern Bell Telephone Co., Southwestern Com. Rsch.; v.p. pub. policy Nat. Ctr. Policy Analysis; mem. U.S. Congress from 5th Tex. dist., 1997—; mem. rules com. Bd. mem. YMCA; active United Meth. Ch. Mem. Rotary Club. Avocations: hiking, mountain climbing, running.*

SESSIONS, ROY BRUMBY, otolaryngologist, educator; b. Houston, July 28, 1937; s. Roy Brumby and Elizabeth (Compton) S.; m. Mary Cousart, Aug. 28, 1976; children: Kate, Elizabeth, Abigail, Matthew. BS, La. State U., Baton Rouge, 1958; MD, La. State U., New Orleans, 1962. Resident gen. surgery and otolaryngology Washington U. Sch. Medicine, St. Louis, 1965-69; asst. prof. Baylor Coll. Medicine, Houston, 1969-73, assoc. prof., 1973-83; prof. head and neck surgery Meml. Sloan Kettering Cancer Ctr., N.Y.C., 1983-89; prof., chmn. dept. otolaryngology, head and neck surgery Med. Sch. Georgetown U., Washington, 1989-97; chmn. dept. otolaryngology, head and neck surgery Beth Israel Med. Ctr., N.Y.C., 1998—, assoc. dir. Cancer Ctr., co-dir. Inst. Head and Neck Surgery, 1998—. Contbr. articles to profl. jours., chpts. to books; author one textbook. Lt. comdr. USN, 1962-65. Roman Catholic. Home: 411 Forest St Rye NY 10580 Office: Beth Israel Med Ctr 10 Union Sq E Ste 4J New York NY 10003-3314

SESSIONS, WILLIAM LAD, philosophy educator, administrator; b. Somerville, N.J., Dec. 3, 1943; s. William George and Alice Edna (Billhardt) Sessions; m. Vicki Darlene Thompson, Aug. 28, 1965; children: Allistair Lee, Laura Anne. BA magna cum laude, U. Colo., 1965; MA in Comparative Study of Religion, Union Theol. Sem., N.Y.C., 1967; postgrad., Oxford (Eng.) U., 1967-68; PhD, Yale U., 1971; postdoctoral studies, Stanford U., 1976, Harvard U., 1977-78. Tchg. fellow Yale U., 1969; instr. U. Conn., Waterbury, 1970-71; asst. prof. philosophy Washington and Lee U., 1971-77, assoc. prof., 1977-83, prof., 1983—, Ballengee 250th Anniversary prof., 1999—. Instr. So. Sem., 1972; vis. prof. St. Olaf Coll., 1985—86; assoc. dean Coll. Washington and Lee U., 1992—95, acting dean, 1995—96, 2001—02, head philosophy dept., 1996—. Author: The Concept of Faith, 1984, Reading Hume's Dialogues , 2002; contbr. Ruling elder Lexington (Va.) Presbyn. Ch., 1983—89, tchr. Sunday sch., 1984—, ruling elder, 2002. Grantee Glenn grantee, Washington and Lee U., 1975—, Babcock Found., 1976, NEH, 1977, 1983, 1986, Mellon Found., 1978—79, Mellon East Asian Studies, 1990. Mem.: Soc. Christian Philosophers (steering com. ea. region 1986—90, 1992—95, 1997—98, exec. com. 1987—90), Soc. for Philosophy of Religion (exec. coun. 1988—94, v.p. 1991, pres. 1992), Va. Philos. Assn., Am. Philos. Assn., Phi Beta Kappa (exec. com. W&L chpt. 1986—95, 1998—2000, v.p. 1989—91, pres. 1991—93). Office: Washington & Lee U Dept of Philosophy Lexington VA 24450 E-mail: sessionsl@wlu.edu.

SESSIONS, WILLIAM STEELE, former government official, lawyer; b. Ft. Smith, Ark., May 27, 1930; s. Will Anderson and Edith A. (Steele) S.; m. Alice Lewis, Oct. 5, 1952; children: William Lewis, Mark Gregory, Peter Anderson, Sara Anne. BA, Baylor U., 1956, LLB, 1958; hon. degree, John C. Marshall Law Sch., St. Mary's U., 1989; LLD (hon.), Dickinson Coll., 1988, Flagler Coll., 1990, Davis & Elkins Coll., 1992, McMurry U., 1997. Bar: Tex. 1959; U.S. Dist Ct. (Western Dist.) Tex.; Ct. Appeals (5th Cir.). Ptnr. McGregor & Sessions, Waco, Tex., 1959-61; assoc. Tirey, McLaughlin, Gorin & Tirey, 1961-63; ptnr. Haley, Fulbright, Winniford, Sessions & Bice, 1963-69; sect. chief, govt. ops sect. criminal divsn. U.S. Dept. Justice, Washington, 1969-71; U.S. atty. U.S. Dept Justice, U.S. Dist. Ct., (we. dist), San Antonio, 1971-74; dist. judge U.S. Dist. Ct. (we. dist.) Tex., 1974-87, chief judge, 1980-87; dir. FBI, Washington, 1987-93; ptnr. Sessions & Sessions, San Antonio and Washington, 1995-2000, Holland & Knight, LLP, San Antonio and Washington, 2000—. Bd. dirs., chmn. book com. Fed. Jud. Ctr., Washington, 1981—; mem. Tex. Commn. on Judicial Efficiency, 1995, Tex. Commn. on a Representative Student Body, 1998, Gov.'s Task Force on Homeland Security, Gov.'s Anti-Crime Commn., Tex., 2002. Contbr. articles to profl. jours. Active Dr. Martin Luther King Jr. Fed. Holiday Commn., 1991-96, hon. bd. dirs., 1993-94; bd. trustees Nat. Environ. Edn. & Tng. Found., Inc., 2001—. Lt. USAF, 1951-55; capt. USAFR, Recipient Rosewood Gavel award St. Mary's U. Sch. Law, San Antonio, 1982, Disting. Alumni award Baylor U., Golden Plate award Am. Acad. Achievement, 1988, Law Enforcement Leadership award Assn. Fed. Investigators, 1989, medal of honor DAR, 1989, Disting. Eagle Scout award Boy Scouts Am., 1990, Person of Yr. award Am. Soc. for Indsl. Security, 1990, Magna Charta award Baronial Order of Magna Charta, 1990, Price Daniel Disting. Pub. Svc. award Baylor U., 2002; named Lawyer of Yr., Baylor Law Sch., 1988, Father of Yr., Nat. Fathers Day Com., 1988, Ellis Island Congl. Medal of Honor, 1992; inducted into Eagle Scout Hall of Fame, 1998. Fellow ABA (chmn. spl. com. on judicial independence 1997—, Nat. Law Day chmn. 2000-02); mem. Jud. Conf. U.S. (com. on ct. adminstrn., chmn. jud. improvements subcom. 1983-85, ad hoc com. on automation to subcom. 1984-87, mem. ad hoc ct. reporter com. 1984-87), San Antonio Bar Assn. (bd. dirs. 1973-74), Fed. Bar Assn. (pres. San Antonio sect. 1974), Am. Judicature Soc. (exec. com. 1982-84), Dist. Judges Assn. of 5th Cir. (pres. 1982-83), State Bar of Tex. (chmn. com. to develop procedures for cert. state law questions to Supreme Ct. by Fed. Cts. 1983-85), Waco McLennan County Bar Assn. (pres. 1968), San Antonio Inns of Ct. (pres. 1986), William S. Sessions Inns of Ct. Republican. Methodist. Avocations: hiking, climbing, canoeing. Office: Holland & Knight LLP Ste 100 2099 Pennsylvania Ave NW Washington DC 20006 Fax: (202) 955-5564. E-mail: wsession@hklaw.com.

SESSLER, ANDREW MARIENHOFF, physicist; b. Bklyn., Dec. 11, 1928; s. David and Mary (Baron) S.; m. Gladys Lerner, Sept. 23, 1951 (div. Dec. 1994); children: Daniel Ira, Jonathan Lawrence, Ruth. BA in Math. cum laude, Harvard U., 1949; MA in Theoretical Physics, Columbia U., 1951, PhD in Theoretical Physics, 1953. NSF fellow Cornell U., N.Y., 1953-54; asst. prof. Ohio State U., Columbus, 1954, assoc. prof., 1960; on leave Midwestern Univs. Research, 1955-56; vis. physicist Lawrence Radiation Lab., 1959-60, Niels Bohr Inst., Copenhagen, summer 1961; rschr. theoretical physics U. Calif. Lawrence Berkeley Lab., Berkeley, 1961-73, rschr. energy and environment, 1971-73, dir., 1973-80, sr. scientist plasma physics, 1980-94, disting. sr. staff scientist, 1994—. U.S. advisor Panjab U. Physics Inst., Chandigarh, India; mem. U.S.-India Coop. Program for Improvement Sci. Edn. in India, 1966, high energy physics adv. panel to U.S. AEC, 1969-72, adv. com. Lawrence Hall Sci., 1974-78; chmn. Stanford Synchrotron Radiation Project Sci. Policy Bd., 1974-77, EPRI Advanced Fuels Adv. Com., 1978-81, BNL External Adv. Com. on Isabelle, 1980-82; mem. sci. pol. bd. Stanford Synchrotron Radiation Lab., 1991-92; L.J. Haworth dist. scientist Brookhaven Nat. Lab., 1991-92. Mem. editl. bd. Nuclear Instruments and Methods, 1969—; correspondent Comments on Modern Physics, 1969-71; contbr. articles in field to profl. jours. Mem. hon. adv. bd. Inst. Advanced Physics Studies, LaJolla Internat. Sch. Physics, 1991—; mem. Superconducting Super Collider Sci. Policy Com., 1991—93. Recipient E.O. Lawrence award U.S. Atomic Energy Commn., 1970, U.S. Particle Accelerator Sch. prize, 1988; fellow Japan Soc. for Promotion Sci. at KEK, 1985. Fellow AAAS (nominating com. 1984-87), Am. Phys. Soc. (chmn. com. internat. freedom scientist 1982, study of directed energy weapons panel 1985-87, chmn. panel pub. affairs 1988, chmn. divsn. physics of beams 1990, chmn. com. applications of physics 1993, councilor for divsn. physics of beams 1994-97, pres.-elect 1997, pres. 1998, past pres. 1999, Nicholson medal 1994, Robert R. Wilson prize 1997); mem. NAS, IEEE, Fedn. Am. Scientists Coun. (vice chmn. 1987-88, chmn. 1988-92), N.Y. Acad. Sci., Assoc. Univ. Inc. (bd. dirs. 1991-94). Office: U Calif Lawrence Berkeley Lab 1 Cyclotron Rd MS 71 259 Berkeley CA 94720-0001 E-mail: AMSessler@lbl.gov.

SESSLER, DONNA JEAN HOTZ, secondary education educator; b. Iowa City, May 3, 1954; d. Raymond Louis and Marie Frances (Klouda) Hotz; m. Allen Henry Sessler, Aug. 8, 1992. BA in Psychology, U. Iowa, 1975; MA in Spl. Edn., U. No. Iowa, 1981. Multicategorial resource tchr. grades 6-12 Beaman-Conrad-Liscomb Community Schs., Conrad, Iowa, 1978-84; multicategorical resource tchr. grades 6-8 Iowa Falls (Iowa) Community Sch., 1984—. Mem. NEA, Iowa Pollettes (sec. 1995-97), Iowa Falls Edn. Assn. (negotiations team 1988-90), Iowa Edn. Assn., Coun. for Exceptional Children. Roman Catholic. Avocations: painting, writing, walking. Office: Riverbend Mid Sch 1124 Union St Iowa Falls IA 50126-1435

SESSOMS, ALLEN LEE, academic administrator, former diplomat, physicist; b. N.Y.C., Nov. 17, 1946; s. Albert Earl and Lottie Beatrice (Leff) Sessoms; children from previous marriage: Manon Elizabeth, Stephanie Csilla. BS, Union Coll., Schenectady, N.Y., 1968; PhD, Yale U., 1972; DSc (hon.), Union Coll., 1998; PhD (hon.), Soka U., Japan, 2000. Sci. assoc. CERN, Geneva, 1973-78; asst. prof. physics Harvard U., Cambridge, Mass., 1974-81; sr. tech. advisor OES, State Dept., Washington, 1980-82; dir. Office Nuclear Tech. & Safeguards, State Dept., 1982-87; counselor for sci. and tech. U.S. Embassy, Paris, 1987-89, polit. minister, counselor Mexico City, 1989-91, dep. chief of mission, 1991-93; exec. v.p., v.p. for acad. affairs U. Mass. Sys., Boston, 1993-95; pres. CUNY Queens Coll., Flushing, N.Y., 1995-2000; lectr., fellow Belfer Ctr. for Sci. and Internat. Affairs, JFK Sch. Govt., Harvard U., Cambridge, Mass., 2000—. Mem. adv. com. U.S. Sec. Energy; mem. NCAA Pres. Coun., 1996-2000. Contbr. articles to profl. jours. Adv. com. mem. U.S. Sec. of Energy; bd. dirs. Milestone Fund, Drawing Ctr., Big Apple Circus; mem. adv. coun. Toda Internat. Ford Found. travel/study grantee, 1973-74; Alfred P. Sloan Found. fellow, 1977-81; recipient Wilbur Cross medal Yale Grad. Sch. Alumni, 1999, Medal of Highest Honor, Soka U., 1999; officer dans l'Order des Palmes Académiques, 1999. Mem. AAAS, Am. Phys. Soc., N.Y. Acad. Sci., Cosmos Club. E-mail: vonSessoms@aol.com., allen_sessoms@KSG.Harvard.edu.

SESSOMS, SANDRA LEA, hospital administrator; m. Frank E. Sessoms, June 18, 1988. Diploma in Nursing, St. John's Hosp. Sch. Nursing, Pitts., 1978; BS in Nursing, LaRoche Coll., Pitts., 1988; M in Pub. Mgmt., Carnegie Mellon U., Pitts., 1990. RN, cert. profl. healthcare quality; cert. case mgmt. adminstr. Cons., supr. Options HCCC, Pitts., 1985-89; nurse ICU Shadyside Hosp., 1982-90, utilization rev./quality improvement coord., 1990-92; asst. v.p., quality assurance/case mgmt. nursing Suburban Gen. Hosp., 1992—98, dir. care, quality and regulatory mgmt., 1998—2000; dir. system compliance West Penn Allegheny Health Sys., 2000—. Cons. McKenna & Assocs., Charleston, W.Va., 1997, Charleston, 2000—. Mem. Nat. Assn. Healthcare Quality, Western Pa. Assn. Healthcare Quality (sec., bd. mem. 1992-94, pres. elect 1995, pres. 1996, past pres. 1997). Avocation: antiquing. Office: West Penn Allegheny Health Sys 2 Allegheny Ctr Pittsburgh PA 15212 Business E-Mail: ssessoms@wpahs.org.

SESTANOVICH, MOLLY BROWN, writer; b. Denver, Nov. 30, 1921; d. Ben Miller and Mary (McCord) Brown; m. Stephen Nicholas Sestanovich, July 9, 1949; children: Stephen, Mary, Robert Benjamin. Student, Fairmont Jr. Coll., 1939-41. Radio comml. writer Young & Rubicam Advt., N.Y.C. and Hollywood, Calif., 1941-47; radio scriptwriter Korean Broadcasting Co., Seoul, 1947-48; substitute tchr. County Sch. Bd., Montgomery County, Md., 1956-58; syndicated polit. columnist Lesher Newspapers, various locations, 1971-91; freelance polit. writer Moraga, Calif., 1991—. Active internat. women's orgns., Italy, Thailand, Singapore, Finland, Venezuela, 1949-70. Writer LWV, Diablo Valley, Calif., 1970, 91. Recipient prize for contbn. to cause of peace and justice Mt. Diablo Peace Ctr., 1989. Mem. Am. Fgn. Svc. Assn., Lamorinda Dem. Club (program chmn. 1985). Unitarian Universalist. Avocations: genealogy, gardening. Home: 15 Idlewood Ct Moraga CA 94556-1107 E-mail: mollysteve@cs.com.

SESTINA, JOHN E. financial planner; b. Mar. 17, 1942; s. John J. and Regina Sestina; m. Mary Barbara Jezek, Dec. 20, 1970; 1 child, Alison. BS, U. Dayton, 1965; MS in Fin. Svc., Am. Coll., 1982. Cert. fin. planner, chartered fin. cons. With John E. Sestina and Co., Columbus, Ohio, 1967—. Author: Complete Guide to Professional Incorporation, 1970, Managing To Be Wealthy, 1988, 2d edit. 2000, Fee-Only Financial Planning, How to Make It Work For You, 1991, 2d edit. 2000; (video tape series) Managing To Be Wealthy (4 series), 1987; contbr. articles to profl. jours.; contbr. weekly fin. planning segment AM Columbus, WOSU-AM, 1979—. Named one of Nation's 200 Best Fin. Advisors of 1996-98, Worth Mag. Mem. Soc. Ind. Fin.

Advisers (past pres., Fin. Planner of Yr. award 1982), Internat. Assn. Fin. Planners, Nat. Assn. Personal Fin. Advisors (founder, pres.), Inst. Cert. Fin. Planners, Fin. Planning Clubs Internat. (founder). Office: 1161 Bethel Rd Ste 201 Columbus OH 43220-2606

SESTINI, VIRGIL ANDREW, retired biology educator; b. Las Vegas, Nov. 24, 1936; s. Santi and Merceda Francesca (Borla) S. BS in Edn., U. Nev., 1959; postgrad., Oreg. State U., 1963-64; MNS, U. Idaho, 1995; postgrad., Ariz. State U., 1967, No. Ariz. U., 1969. Cert. tchr., Nev. Tchr. biology Rancho H.S., 1960-76; sci. chmn., tchr. biology Bonanza H.S., Las Vegas, 1976-90, ret., 1990. Co-founder, curator exhibits Meadows Mus. Nat. History, 1993-94; part-time tchr., sci. chmn. Meadows Sch., 1987-94; ret., 1994; edn. specialist, cell biologist SAGE Rsch., Las Vegas, 1993, ret., 1998; founder Da Vinci Enterprises, Las Vegas, 1995. Author: Lab Investigations for High School Honors Biology, 1992, Laboratory Investigations in Microbiology, 1992, Genetics Problems for High School Biology, 1995, Science Laboratory Report Data Book, 1995, Field and Museum Techniques for the Classroom Teacher, 1995, Selected Lab Investigations and Projects for Honors and AP Biology, Vol. I Microbiology, 1995, Telecommunications: A Simulation for Biology Using the Internet, 1995; co-author: A Biology Lab Manual for Cooperative Learning, 1989, Metrics and Science Methods: A Manual of Lab Experiments for Home Schoolers, 1990, Experimental Designs in Biology I: Botany and Zoology, 1993, Designs in Biology: A Lab Manual, 1993, Integrated Science Lab Manual, 1994, Supplemental Experiments and Field Studies for AP Biology, 1998; contbr. articles to profl. jours. including The Sci. Tchr., Am. Biology Tchr., Fine Scale Models, Ships in Scale, IPMS Jour. With USAR, 1959-65. Reciepient Rotary Internat. Honor Tchr. award, 1965, Region VIII Outstanding Biology Tchr. award, 1970, Nev. Outstanding Biology Tchr. award Nat. Assn. Biology Tchrs., 1970, Nat. Assn. Sci. Tchrs., Am. Gas Assn. Sci. Tchg. Achievement Recognition award, 1976, 80, Gustov Ohaus award, 1980, Presdl. Honor Sci. Tchr. award, 1983; Presdl. award excellence in math. and sci. tchg., 1984, Celebration of Excellence award Nev. Com. on Excellence in Edn., 1986, Hall of Fame award Clark County Sch. Dist., 1988, Excellence in Edn. award, 1987, 88, Spl. Edn. award 1988, NSEA Mini-grants, 1988, 89, 92, World Decoration of Excellence medallion World Inst. Achievement, 1989, Cert. Spl. Congrl. Recognition, 1989, Senatorial Recognition, 1989, mini-grant Jr. League Las Vegas, 1989, Excellence in Edn. award Clark Country Sch. Dist., 1989; named Nev. Educator of Yr., Milken Family Found./Nev. State Dept. Edn., 1989; grantee Nev. State Bd. Edn., 1988, 89, Nev. State Edn. Assn., 1988-89. Mem. AAAS, NEA, Nat. Assn. Taxidermists, Nat. Sci. Tchrs. Assn. (life, Nev. state membership chmn. 1968-70), Nat. Assn. Biology Tchrs. (life, OBTA dir. Nev. state 1991-93), Am. Soc. Microbiology, Coun. for Exceptional Children, Am. Biographic Inst. (rsch. bd. advisors 1988), Nat. Audubon Assn., Nat. Sci. Suprs. Assn., Am. Inst. Biol. Scis., Nautical Rsch. Guild, Internat. Plastic Modelers Soc., So. Nev. Scale Modelers (Las Vegas coord., Modeloberfest, 1995), Silver State Scale Modelers Guild. Avocations: scale models, military figures, scale models circus, photography. E-mail: v.sestini@lvcm.com.

SESTOFT, LEIF, endocrinologist, researcher, educator; b. Hellerup, Copenhagen, Denmark; s. Leif Thorkil and Ingeborg (Laursen) S.; m. Gerda Lippert (div. June 1970); children: Dorte Maria, Morten Leif; m. Liselotte Heslet, Sept. 22, 1973; 1 children: Jacob. MD, Copenhagen U., 1965; D Med. Sci., Odense (Denmark) U., 1975. Intern Kalundborg Hosp., Denmark, 1965-67, Bispebjerg Hosp., Copenhagen, 1967-69; rsch. fellow Inst. Biochemistry, 1969-74; cons. Herlev (Denmark) U. Hosp., 1975-77; head hosp. Hvidćre, Gentofte, Denmark, 1977-82; sr. cons. Herlev Hosp., 1982-85, Rigshosp., Copenhagen, 1986-87, Gentofte U. Hosp., 1987-91; pvt. practice endocrinology Copenhagen, 1984—; censor med. biochemistry U. Copenhagen, 1976—. Co-author: Short Term Regulation of Liver Metabolism, 1981; translator comments: on Franz Kafka Bibliotek for Laeger, 1981; inventor Novo pen system. Bd. dirs. Ctr. for Alcohol Rsch., Copenhagen, 1990; chmn. Danish Assn. for Study of Obesity, Copenhagen, 1987-89. Avocations: golf, sailing. Home and Office: Oster Sogade 32 DK 1357 Copenhagen Denmark

SESTRIC, ANTHONY JAMES, lawyer; b. St. Louis, June 27, 1940; s. Anton and Marie (Gasparovic) S.; m. Carol F. Bowman, Nov. 24, 1966; children: Laura Antonette, Holly Nicole, Michael Anthony. Student, Georgetown U., 1958-62; JD, Mo. U., 1965. Bar: Mo. 1965, Minn. 1996, U.S. Ct. Appeals (8th cir.) 1965, U.S. Ct. Appeals (7th cir.) 1984, U.S. Dist. Ct. Mo. 1966, U.S. Dist. Ct. (no dist.) Tex. 1985, U.S. Dist. Ct. Ill. 1994, U.S. Tax Ct. 1969, U.S. Supreme Ct. 1970, U.S. Claims Ct. 1986. Law clk. U.S. Dist. Ct., St. Louis, 1965-66; ptnr. Sestric, McGhee & Miller, 1966-77, Fordyce and Mayne, 1977-78, Sestric & Garvey, 1978-96, Sestric Law Firm, St. Louis, 1996—. Spl. asst. to Mo. atty. gen., St. Louis, 1968, spl. asst. circuit atty., 2001—; mem. Fed. Jud. Selection Commn., 1993, U.S. Jud. Selection Commn., 1993-94; gen. chmn. 22nd jud. cir. bar com., 1995, mem. Region XI disciplinary com., 2001—. Contbr. articles to profl. jours. Hearing officer St. Louis Met. Police Dept.; active St. Louis Air Pollution Bd. Appeals and Varience Rev., 1966-73, chmn., 1968-73; active St. Louis Airport Commn., 1975-76; dist. vice-chmn. Boy Scouts Am., 1970-76; bd. dirs. Full Achievement, Inc., 1970-77, Legal Aid Soc. St. Louis, 1976-77, Law Libr. Assn. St. Louis, 1976-78, Thomas Dunn Memls., 1995-98, Marquette Learning Ctr., 1995-98; v.p. bd. St. Elizabeth Acad., 1985-86 Mem. ABA (state chmn. judiciary com. 1973-75, cir. chmn. con. condemnation, zoning and property use 1975-77, standing com. bar activities 1982-88), Nat. Conf. Bar Pres.'s (exec. coun. 1987-90), Mo. Bar Assn. (vice-chmn. young lawyers sect. 1973-76, bd. govs. 1974-77, chmn. law practice mgmt. com. 1997-99), Bar Assn. Met. St. Louis (chmn. young lawyers sect. 1974-75, exec. com. 1974-83, 94-95, pres. 1981-82, bd. govs. 1995-98, chmn. survey com. 1999). Home: 3967 Holly Hills Blvd Saint Louis MO 63116-3135 E-mail: ajsestric@juno.com.

SETCHELL, JOHN STANFORD, JR. color systems engineer; b. Bklyn., Dec. 4, 1942; s. John Stanford and Elisa (Muenzfeld) S.; m. Cynthia Florence Andreasen, Feb. 27, 1965; 1 child, Anitra Lesa. BS in Physics, Rensselaer Polytech Inst., 1963; MS in Physics, U. Ill., 1969. Rsch. physicist Mfg. Tech. Kodak Apparatus Div., Rochester, N.Y., 1969-82; supr. project engr. Copy Products Eastman Kodak Co., 1982-84; supr. engr. Electronic Photography Div. Eastman Kodak Co., 1985-88; product planning dir. Printer Products Div. Eastman Kodak Co., 1989-90; color systems engr. Digital & Applied Imaging group Systems Products Div. Eastman Kodak Co., 1991—. Lectr. in field. Contbr. articles to profl. jours. Advisor Sea Exploring Ship 303, Webster, N.Y., 1980—; leader Pioneer Club, Rochester, 1990-92; worship leader Covenant Presbyn. Ch., Rochester, 1987—; singer Cathedral Choir Sch., Rochester, 1991—. Lt. USN, 1963. Mem. Am. Soc. Testing and Materials (chmn. com. B-4 1981-82), Am. Scientific Affiliation, Assn. Old Crows, Chi Gamma Iota. Republican. Achievements include research includes color image processing in desktop computers, digital color printing, environmental effects on electronic materials. Home: 376 English Rd Rochester NY 14616-2425 Office: Eastman Kodak 1700 Dewey Ave Rochester NY 14650-0001

SETH, KAMAL KISHORE, physicist, researcher; b. Lucknow, India, Mar. 10, 1933; arrived in U.S., 1954; s. Raj Kishore and Jawahar Devi Seth; m. Frances May Phllips; children: Raj, Camilla, Kim. BSc, Lucknow U., 1951, BSc with honors, 1953, MSc, 1954; PhD, U. Pitts., 1957. Jr. rsch. assoc. Brookhaven Nat. Lab., Upton, NY, 1956—57; rsch. assoc. Duke U., Durham, NC, 1957—61; asst. prof. Northwestern U., Evanston , Ill., 1961—64, assoc. prof., 1964—73, prof., 1973—. Prof. Japan Soc. Promotion of Sci., Tokyo, 1971; VIP prof. Nat. Inst. Nuclear Physics U. Turin, Italy, 1991; Humbold Prizetager A.V. Humboldt Stiftung, Munich, 1997—2001. Contbr. more than 200 articles to profl. jours. Named Outstanding New Citizen of Yr., Chgo. Met. Coun., 1967. Fellow: Am. PHys. Soc. Achievements include research in neutron physics, nuclear reaction mechanisms, pion physics, exotic nuclei; charmonium spectroscopy, antiproton physics, exotic radrons. Avocations: painting, music. Home: 2323 Central Park Ave Evanston IL 60201 Office: Northwestern U Physics Dept Evanston IL 60208 Fax: 847-491-4050. E-mail: kseth@northwestern.edu.

SETHI, A.S. (JIM SETHI), finance educator; b. Nirali, Pakistan, Jan. 24, 1935; s. Tarlok S. and Raj K. Sethi; m. Minocha Sundershan, Jan. 2, 2002; 1 child Sandeep. MS, U. Wis., 1962; cert. in health adminstrn., Cornell U., 1969; PhD, U. Manchester, England, 1974. Prof. health adminstrn. U. Ottawa, Canada, 1974—98; prof. bus. Cariboo Coll. B.C., Kamloops, Canada, 1998—99, U. Mont., Dillon, 1999—. Chief cons. STC Cons., Ottawa, 1998—; mem. adv. bd. McGraw-Hill Ann. Editions-Internet and Bus., Guilford, Conn., 2000—. Co-author: Strategic Management of Technostress in an Information Society; chief editor: Jour. Comparative Sociology and Ethics, 2002; author: Human Resource Management in the Health Care Sector: A Guide for Administrators and Professionals, Advanced Studies in Collective Bargaining in Canada, U.K. and USA, Strategic Team Leadership for Transforming Workplace Stress into Organizational Excellence, Developing Leadership Skills for the 21st Century. Founder Inst. for Leadership Excellence, Ottawa, 1998—, Indsl. Rels. Inst., Ottawa, 1996—99. Scholar, Fulbright Found., 1960—61, Rotary Found., 1990—91. Mem.: Inst. Internat. Mktg. (pres. 1998—99). Office: U. Mont Western 710 S Atlantic St Dillon MT 59725 E-mail: J_Sethi@wmc.edu.

SETHI, DEEPAK, leadership development/marketing executive; b. Jhelum, India, July 1, 1945; s. Siriram and Prakash (Kathuria) S.; m. Anita Johar, May 15, 1973; children: Ripka, Reeti. BSME, MS U., Baroda, India, 1968; MBA in Mktg., Pa. State U., 1977. Sales engr. Indian Oil Corp., Bombay, 1968-73; mktg. rep. Control Data Corp., N.Y.C., 1977-79; mem. staff domestic and internat. mktg. AT&T, Basking Ridge, N.J., 1979-88, v.p. exec. edn. Somerset, 1979-99; v.p. exec. and leadership devel. The Thomson Corp., Stamford, Conn., 1999—. Spkr. mgmt. devel. confs. Co-editor: (co. publ.) Marketing Spectrum, The Leader of the Future, 1996, The Organization of the Future, 1997; quoted in Bus. Week, Wall St. Jour. and N.Y. Times; contbg. author: Learning Journeys, 2000; contbr. articles to Coaching for Leadership, Leader to Leader, jours., books. Fellow Rotary Found., 1973. Mem. ASTD, Mgmt. Devel. Forum, Inst. Mgmt. Studies, N.Y. Human Resource Planning Soc. (pres., bd. dirs.), Am. Mktg. Assn., Peter Drucker Found. Leadership Coun. Home: 92 Beaufort Ave Livingston NJ 07039-1703 E-mail: dicksethi@hotmail.com.

SETHI, SANDEEP, environmental engineer; b. New Delhi, India, Jan. 27, 1969; came to U.S., 1991; s. Satish Kumar and Champa (Bhasin) S. BS in Civil Engring. with honors, Birla Inst. Tech. & Sci., Pilani, India, 1991; MS in Environ. Engring., Rice U., 1994, PhD in Environ. Engring., 1997. Registered profl. engr., Calif. Engr. Nat. Informatics Ctr., New Delhi, 1991; rsch. asst. Rice U., Houston, 1991-97; sr. engr. Metcalf & Eddy, Inc., Atlanta, 1997-99; project and rsch. engr. Carollo Engrs., Santa Ana, Calif., 1999—. Chair, invited spkr. membrane technology sessions ASCE 1999 Conf.; lectr. Calif. State U., Long Beach, 2000. Contbr. articles to internat. and profl. jours.; reviewer: Jour. Environ. Engring., Jour. Am. Water Works Assn. Mem. Water Environment Fedn., Am. Water Works Assn. (invited spkr. 1999 conf.), N.Am. Membrane Soc., Santa Ana River Basin Sect. Calif. Water Environment Assn. (rsch. achievement award com. 1999). Avocations: music, computer programming, literature, photography, traveling. Achievements include: development of unified model for performance of membrane filtration processes, incorporating multiple transport mechanisms, which can predict the observed minimum in permeate flux with particle size; first researcher to simulate comparison of constant pressure and constant flux modes of operation in ultrafiltration and microfiltration based on detailed mathematical modeling; developer of cost model for membrane processes incorporating separate correlations for major system components and a changing economy of scale with the design mix; optimization of hollow-fiber membrane design; optimization of membrane system operation; optimization of single and integrated nanofiltration systems; developer of computer software package for membrane systems for the U.S. EPA; rsch. contributions in numerical simulation, sensitivity analysis, and optimization of non-linearly constrained systems and application of advanced computational techniques to solve complex research engineering problems. Office: Carollo Engrs 3100 S Harbor Blvd Ste 200 Santa Ana CA 92704-6810

SETHI, SHYAM SUNDER, management consultant; b. Rawalpindi, Pakistan, July 11, 1942; s. Balraj and Shakuntala (Sawhney) S.; m. Kiran Nair, Oct. 17, 1972; children: Seema, Shana. B.E. in Mech. Engring., Birla Inst. Tech., Ranchi, India, 1964; MSI.E., U. Wis., 1970. Cert. mgmt. cons. V.p. Drake Sheahan/Stewart Dougall, N.Y.C., 1970-80; pres., ptnr. Distbn. Mgmt. Assocs., Inc., Princeton, N.J., 1980-96; exec. dir. Dechert-Hampe & Co./DMA, 1996-2000; pres. Distbn. Mgmt. Assocs., Inc., 2001—. Cons. in supply chain, logistics, inventory mgmt., ops. for maj. consumer goods, indsl. and retail cos., Europe, S.Am. and U.S.; spkr. internat. logistics conf. Contbr. articles to profl. jours. Pres. N.J. chpt. Coun. Logistics Mgmt., 1987-88, N.J. chpt. Inst. Mgmt. Consultants, 1987-88. Mem. Yacht Assn. India. Hindu. Avocations: tennis, sailing. Home: 4 Haelig Ct Bridgewater NJ 08807-2377 Office: DMA Inc PO Box 6843 Bridgewater NJ 08807-0843 E-mail: sethinj@optonline.net.

SETHI, SURESH PAL, management educator, researcher; b. Ladnun, Rajashtan, India, July 8, 1945; came to the U.S., 1967; s. Gulab Chand and Manak Bai Sethi; m. Andrea Sethi, May 25, 1988; children: Chantal Angelina, Anjuli Sulochana. BTech in Mech. Engring. with honors, Indian Inst. Tech., Bombay, 1967; MBA, Wash. State U., 1969; MS in Indsl. Adminstrn., Carnegie Mellon U., 1971, PhD, 1972. Instr. fin. Carnegie Mellon U., Pitts., 1969-70; asst. prof. mgmt. sci. Rice U., Houston, 1972-73; from asst. prof. to assoc. prof. U. Toronto, Ont., Can., 1973-77, prof. ops. mgmt. Can., 1978-92, prof., dir. lab. mfg. Can., 1992-97; Ashbel Smith prof. U. Tex. Dallas, Richardson, 1997—. Vis. assoc. prof. Carnegie Mellon U., Pitts., 1977-78. Author: Optimal Control Theory, 1981, 2d edit., 2000, Hierarchical Decision Making in Stochastic Manufacturing Systems, 1994, Optimal Consumption and Investment with Bankruptcy, 1997; assoc. editor Inst. Ops. Rsch. and Mgmt. Scis., 1994-96, Jour. Math. Analysis and Applications, 2000—; sr. editor M&SOM, 2001--; adv. editor POMS, 1990--. Founder Gulab Chand Sethi Charitable Trust, Ladnun, India, 1980; dist. sci. fair judge Plano (Tex.) Ind. Sch. Dist., 1999--. Fellow IC2 Inst., Royal Soc. Can., N.Y. Acad. Scis.; mem. AAAS, Inst. Ops. Rsch. and Mgmt. Scis., Can. Operational Rsch. Soc. (Award of Merit 1996), Can. Acad. Scis. and Humanities. Avocations: photography, jogging, travel, art. Home: 4428 Longfellow Dr Plano TX 75093-3217 Office: U Tex Dallas 2601 N Floyd Rd Richardson TX 75080-1407 Fax: 972-883-2089. E-mail: sethi@utdallas.edu.

SETHNA, BEHERUZ NARIMAN, university president, marketing, management educator; b. Bombay, July 31, 1948; came to U.S., 1973; s. Nariman Dhanjishaw and Mithu Nariman (Mistry) S.; m. Madhavi Kaji, May 25, 1974; children: Anita B., Shaun B. B in Tech. with honors, Indian Inst. Tech., Bombay, 1971; MBA, Indian Inst. Mgmt., Ahmedabad, 1973; MPhil, Columbia U., 1975, PhD in Bus., 1976; student, Ind. U., 1986, Harvard U., 1991. Cert. computing profl. Inst. for Cert. Computing Profls. Engring. and mgmt. trainee various corps., Bombay, 1968-69, 70-72; case writer, trainee Clarion Advt., 1973; project mgr., cons. Lever Bros. Co., N.Y.C., 1974-76; prof., chair mktg. and mgmt. info. systems Clarkson U., Potsdam, N.Y., 1976-89, dir. grad. programs, 1978-80; mktg., rsch. and strategic planning mgr. Procter & Gamble (India)/Richardson Hindustan (Vicks), Bombay and Westport, Conn., 1980-81; interim exec. v.p. acad. and student affairs; dean Coll. of Bus., chief acad. officer Lamar (Tex.) U., 1989-94, Gulf States Utilities prof. bus., 1991-94; pres. State U. W. Ga., Carrollton, 1994—; interim sr. vice chancellor Univ. Sys. Ga., 1999—; pres. Ga. Assn. Colls., 2000-2001. Mem. adv. coun. SUNY-Canton (N.Y.) Coll., 1975-89; cons. in field. Author: Research Methods in Marketing, 1984; contbr. articles to profl. jours. Scoutmaster Boy Scouts Am., Potsdam, 1987-89, pack com. chair, den leader, 1987-89, mem. dist. bd., 1991-94, mem. exec. bd. Atlanta Area coun., 1997—, Pres.'s Scout Gold Cord, 1966; leader Girl Scouts U.S., Beaumont, 1989-94. Recipient Instrl. Innovation award Decision Scis. Inst., 1984, 85, 86, 87, 88, 89, Minority Achiever's award Role Model award, 1991, Dean's Leadership award Acad. Bus. Adminstrn., 1993, Nat. Svc. award, 1996, Alumnus award (hon.), 1999, Carroll County Citizen of Yr., 1999; Fulbright scholar U.S. Info. Agy., 1986-87; U.S. Dept. Energy grantee, 1980, IBM Corp. grantee, 1984, AT&T grantee, 1985; Paul Harris fellow Rotary Internat., 1997. Mem. Rotary (polio plus edn. chair). Avocations: family, scouting. Home: 107 Windsong Ct Carrollton GA 30117-8978 Office: State U W Ga Office Pres Carrollton GA 30118-0001 E-mail: bsethna@westga.edu.

SETLIFFE, CHARLES DAVID, hospital administrator; b. Aug. 11, 1931; s. David Bert and Willie Mae (Fussell) S.; m. Eva Gertrude Holladay, Nov. 17, 1951; children: Charles Vaden, David Scott, Susan Lynn. BS, U. Chattanooga, 1956; MHA, Washington U., St. Louis, 1965. Sales rep. Chemetron Corp., Chattanooga, 1956—59; hosp. purchasing agt. Meml. Hosp., 1960-63; asst. adminstr. Ft. Sanders Presbyn. Hosp., Knoxville, 1964-67, Sts. Mary and Elizabeth Hosp., Louisville, 1968-81, adminstr., 1975-81; pres., CEO Wilson Meml. Hosp., N.C., 1981-91, pres. emeritus, 1992—; bd. dir. Centura Bank, Wilson, NC. Health care cons., 1992—; cons. United Emergency Svcs., Inc., 1999—; mem. found. bd. dirs. Meml. Hosp., Chattanooga, 1996—, chmn., 1999—2001; adminstr. Univ. Surg. Assocs., Inc., Chattanooga, 1995; dir. Statewide Health Coord. Coun., Ky., 1982—83, Ky. Health Sys. Agy.-West, Louisville, 1978—81. Bd. dirs. Health Edn. Found. Ea. N.C., 1981-91, treas., 1982-91, exec. com., 1985-91, chmn. bldg. study com., 1984-85, N.C. Constituent of Nat. League Nursing, 1986-91, chmn. fin. com., 1987, Wilson Concerts, Inc., 1982-85, Hospice of Wilson, Inc., 1983-91, Wilson ARC; sec., treas. Hosp. Adminstrs. Ea. N.C., 1983, vice chmn., chmn., 1984; bd. dirs. United Way Wilson County, 1982-86, 88-91, Centura Bank, Wilcon, N.C., 1989-91; mem. adv. com. Wilson County Tech. Coll., Blue Cross-Blue Shield N.C. Sgt. USAF, 1951—55. Recipient Cross Mil. Svc., John W. Dunham chpt. United Daus. Confederacy, 1989; named Ky. Col., 1977. Mem. Ky. Hosp. Assn. (life, bd. dirs. 1976-81), N.C. Hosp. Assn. (life, mem. coun. fin.), Tenn. Hosp. Assn., Wilson County C. of C. (bd. dirs. 1984-86, chmn. accreditations com. 1986, health care cost containment com. 1983-91), Am. Legion. Republican. Presbyterian. Avocations: tennis, traveling. Home: 35 Oliver Ct Signal Mountain TN 37377-2456 Office: Wilson Meml Hosp 1705 Tarboro St SW Wilson NC 27893-3437

SETLIN, ALAN JOHN, entrepreneur; b. N.Y.C., Oct. 27, 1933; s. Samuel and Alyce (Inginito) S.; children: Susan Marie, Peggy Ann, Gina Marie, Alycia Ruth, Alana Jean; m. Deborah Ann Kozlowski, Oct. 14, 1986. Student, U. Miami. CLU. V.p. Figurette, Ltd., Miami, Fla., 1956-60; ptnr. Robins & Clarke, N.Y.C., 1960-63; leading agt. Equitable Life Ins. Co., 1963; gen. agt. Madison Life Ins. Co., 1963-66, Beneficial Nat. Life Ins. Co., N.Y.C., 1967-72; pres., chief exec. officer Alliance Assoc., Inc., Beverly Hills, Calif., 1972—; ptnr. McMutry & Bell, Inc., 1982—; chief exec. officer Emergency Help, Inc., 1989-91; COO, dir. Clinica Medica Familiar, L.A., 1993-96; COB, CEO Futurenet On-Line, Inc., Valencia, Calif., 1996—. Bd. dirs. Six Million Dollar Forum, 1979-80. Mem. Rep. Senatorial Inner Circle, 1988-90. Sgt. AUS, 1952-54. Mem. Nat. Assn. Life Underwriters (fed. legis. chmn. Western States div. 1980-81, pres. L.A. chpt. 1979-80), CLU Assn. (pres. county chpt. 1979-80), Million Dollar Round Table (life), Golden Key (nat. com.). Roman Catholic. Avocations: weightlifting, boxing, skiing, white water rafting, motorcycling. Office: Futurenet On-Line Inc 12711 Ventura Blvd Ste 480 Studio City CA 91604-2456

SETLOW, JANE KELLOCK, biophysicist; b. N.Y.C., Dec. 17, 1919; d. Harold A. and Alberta (Thompson) Kellock; m. Richard Setlow, June 6, 1941; children— Peter, Michael, Katherine, Charles. BA, Swarthmore Coll., 1940; PhD in Biophysics, Yale U., 1959. With dept. radiology Yale U., 1959-60; with biology div. Oak Ridge Nat. Lab., 1960-74; biophysicist Brookhaven Nat. Lab., Upton, N.Y., 1974—. Mem. recombinant DNA molecule program adv. com. NIH, chmn., 1978-80 Author articles; mem. editorial bd. jours. Predoctoral fellow USPHS, 1957-59; postdoctoral fellow, 1960-62 Mem. Biophys. Soc. (pres. 1977-78), Am. Soc. Microbiology. Democrat. Home: 57 Valentine Rd Shoreham NY 11786-1243 Office: Biology Dept Brookhaven Nat Lab Upton NY 11973

SETLOW, RICHARD BURTON, biophysicist, researcher; b. N.Y.C., Jan. 19, 1921; s. Charles Meyer and Elsie (Hurwitz) S.; children: Peter, Michael, Katherine, Charles; m. Neva Delihas, Mar. 3, 1989. AB, Swarthmore Coll., 1941; PhD, Yale U., 1947; DSc, U. Toronto, 1985; MD, U. Essen, 1993. Assoc. prof. Yale U., 1956-61; biophysicist Oak Ridge (Tenn.) Nat. Lab., 1961-74, sci. dir. biophysics and cell physiology, 1969-74; dir. U. Tenn.-Oak Ridge Grad. Sch. Biomed. Scis., 1972-74; sr. biophysicist Brookhaven Nat. Lab., Upton, N.Y., 1974—, chmn. biology dept., 1979-87, assoc. dir. life scis., 1985-98, assoc. lab. dir., 1998. Prof. biomed. scis. U. Tenn., 1967-74; adj. prof. biochemistry SUNY, Stony Brook, 1975—. Author: (with E.C. Pollard) Molecular Biophysics, 1962; editor: (with P.C. Hanawalt) Molecular Mechanisms for Repair of DNA, 1975. Recipient Finsen medal Internat. Assn. Photobiology, 1980, Enrico Fermi award U.S. Dept. Energy, 1988. Mem. NAS, Am. Acad. Arts and Scis., Biophys. Soc. (pres. 1969-70), Internat. Com. Photobiology (pres. 1972-76), Radiation Rsch. Soc., Am. Soc. Photobiology, Am. Soc. Biochemistry and Molecular Biology, Am. Soc. Cancer Rsch., Environ. Mutagen Soc. (award 2002), 11th Internat. Congress on Photobiology (hon. pres. 1992), Phi Beta Kappa. Home: 4 Beachland Ave East Quogue NY 11942-4941 Office: Brookhaven Nat Lab Dept Biology Upton NY 11973 E-mail: setlow@bnl.gov., setlow@hamptons.com.

SETO, MICHAEL C. music educator, minister; s. Haruo Emerson and Daisy Hara Seto; m. Leokadia (Lucky) V. Lobay, Aug. 18, 1973; children: Christopher, Sumi, Robyn. BA in Music, Calif. State U., Sacramento, 1974; M in Ministry, North Am. Bapt. Sem., Sioux Falls, S.D., 1977. Ordained to minister Bapt. Ch., 1977; cert. tchr. Calif. Traveling music tchr. Sacramento Unified Sch. Dist., 1979—93; pastor First Japanese Bapt. Ch., 1980—93; pastor English lang. ministries Cmty. Bapt. Ch., San Mateo, 1993—98; music tchr. San Mateo (Calif.)/Foster City Sch. Dist., 1998—2000, Natomas Unified Sch. Dist., Sacramento, 2000—. Mem.: Calif. Music Educators Assn. Avocations: soccer referee, arranging music, gardening, collecting stuffed plush teddy bears and raccoons. Office: Natomas HS 3301 Rosin Blvd Sacramento CA 95834 Personal E-mail: mcseto@aol.com. E-mail: mseto@natomas.k12.ca.us.

SETO, WILLIAM RODERICK, public accounting company executive; b. N.Y.C., July 2, 1954; s. James and Dorothy (Tsang) S. BS, U. Pa., 1976; JD, Cornell Law Sch., 1979. Bar: N.Y. 1980; CPA. Ptnr. Ernst & Young, Atlanta; S.E. area dir. internat. tax, 1986—. Mem. bd. advisors Fgn. Sales Corp./Domestic Internat. Sales Corp. Tax Assn., 1994-95; lectr. in field. Mem. editl. bd. Atlanta Internat. Mag., 1992-94. Mem. Leadership Atlanta. Named one of Top Tax Advisors in U.S., Internat. Tax Rev. mag., 1995. Mem. ABA, AICPA, N.Y. Bar Assn., Internat. Fiscal Assn. Office: Ernst & Young 2800 Nations Bank Plz 600 Peachtree St NE Ste 2800 Atlanta GA 30308-2215

SETON, FENMORE ROGER, manufacturing company executive, civic worker; b. Bridgeport, Conn., Nov. 27, 1917; m. Phyllis Winifred Zimmerman, Apr. 5, 1942; 1 child, Diana Seton Adams Wakerley. BA in English, Yale U., 1938; EdM, So. Conn. State Coll./Yale U., 1956; LLD (hon.), U. New Haven, 1990; DHL (hon.), Albertus Magnus Coll., 1994. Asst. prof. air sci. and tactics Yale U., New Haven, 1952-56; pres., chief exec. officer Seton Name Plate Corp., 1956-81. Pres. Nat. Assn. Metal Etchers, Washington, 1968-69, Internat. Mktg. Device Assn., Chgo., 1973-74, mfrs. div. New Haven C. of C., 1974-79; chmn. Am. Nat. Standards Com. A13, N.Y.C., 1972-82. Apptd. Pres.'s Com. on Employment of People With Disabilities, Washington, 1973—; world pres. Rehab. Internat., World Secretariat in N.Y.C., 1988-92; bd. govs. U. New Haven, 1979—; treas. Save the Children Fedn., Westport, Conn., 1984-88; assoc. fellow Calhoun Coll. Yale U., 1976—; bd. dirs. Gaylord Hosp., 1995—; trustee Albert B. Sabin Vaccine Found., 1994—. Recipient Citation of Honor Sec. HEW, Washington, 1976, Preminger medallion People-To-People program Com. for Handicapped, Washington, 1988, Elm and Ivy award Yale U., 1985, Pub. Svc. award Social Security Adminstrn., 1992, Yale medal Pres. Yale U. on behalf of Bd. Govs. Assn. Yale Alumni, 1992, Disting. Svc. award Pres. of U.S., 1992, Seal of City of New Haven, Conn., 1999; named. Nat. Vol. of Yr., Easter Seal Soc., 1997. Fellow Inst. Dirs. (U.K.); mem. Cercle de l'Union Interallié (Paris), Explorers Club (N.Y.C.), Circumnavigators Club (N.Y.C.), Elizabethan Club (New Haven), Mory's Assn. (New Haven), New Haven Country Club. Republican. Home: 121 Old Farm Rd Hamden CT 06517 E-mail: seton@cshore.com.

SETRAKIAN, BERGE, lawyer; b. Beirut, Lebanon, Apr. 14, 1949; came to U.S. 1976; s. Hemayak and Arminee S.; m. Vera L. Nazarian, Nov. 22, 1975; children: Ani, Lara. Diplome d'Etudes de Doctorat, U. Lyons, France, 1973; Diplome d'Etudes de Doctorat Droit Compare, F.I.E.D.C., Strasbourg, France, 1974; Licence en Droit Francais, Licence en Droit Libanais, U. St. Joseph, Beirut, 1972. Bar: Beirut 1972, N.Y. 1983. Assoc. Tyan & Setrakian, Beirut, 1972-76; ptnr. Whitman & Ransom, N.Y.C., 1976-93, Whitman, Breed, Abbott & Morgan, N.Y.C., 1993-2000, Winston & Strawn, N.Y.C., 2000—. Bd. dirs. Cedars Bank, Calif., 1987—, Bank Audi, U.S.A., 1991; fgn. law cons., N.Y., 1978. Bd. dirs., v.p., sec. Armenian Gen. Benevolent Union, N.Y.C., 1977-2002, pres., 2002-; pres. Worldwide Youth orgns., 1978—; bd. dirs. Armenian Assy. of Am., Washington, 1978-87; bd. dirs. Am. Task Force for Lebanon,

1988—; bd. dirs. Am. U. Armenia, 1992—. Mem. ABA, N.Y. Bar Assn., Beirut Bar Assn., U.K. Law Soc., Am. Fgn. Law Assn., Englewood Field Club. Office: Winston & Strawn 200 Park Ave New York NY 10166-0005 E-mail: bsetraki@winston.com.

SETRIGHT, MILDRED ALBERTA, educator; b. Milw., Apr. 10, 1919; d. Edward Peter and Adelheid M. (Schultz) S. BS, Milw. State Tchrs. Coll., 1941. Tchr. Bd. of Edn., Elcho, Wis., 1941-43, Waukesha, 1943-44, Appleton, 1944-45, Milw., 1944-46, 60-87, Downers Grove, Ill., 1947-48, Cath. Bd. of Edn., Milw., 1958-60, Bd. Edn., Milw., 1960-87. Mem. Emily's List, Washington, 1995—; treas. Shorewood Sr. Ctr., Milw., 1988-91, sec. 1992-94, vice chmn. 1995, chmn. 1995-97, governing bd. 1995-97; pres. Christian Women's Assn., 1995-2000; mem. SS Peter and Paul Ch., Milw. Mem. AAUW, Milw. Retired Tchrs. Assn., Wis. Retired Tchrs. Assn., U. Wis.-Milw. Guild for Learning in Ret., Florentine Opera Club, Whitefish Bay Woman's Club. Avocations: music, painting, traveling, reading, needlework. Home: 2631 N Murray Ave Milwaukee WI 53211-3624

SETSER, DONALD WAYNE, chemistry educator; b. Great Bend, Kans., Jan. 2, 1935; s. Leo Wayne and Velma Irene (Hewitt) S.; m. Carole Sue Schulze, June 2, 1969; children: Bradley Wayne, Kirk Wesley, Brett Donald. BS, Kans. State U., 1956, MS, 1958; PhD, U. Wash., 1961. Asst. prof. Kans. State U., Manhattan, 1963-66, assoc. prof., 1966-68, prof. chemistry, 1968-2000, Alumni Disting. prof. chemistry, 1984-2000, prof. emeritus, 2000—. Vis. prof. U. Grenoble, France, 1981, 84, 87, 91; fisitor Bogazici U., Turkey, 2000. Editor Reactive Intermediates, 1976; contbr. more than 300 articles to profl. jours. Recipient Rank prize electro-optics divsn., 1992. Fellow Am. Phys. Soc.; mem. Am. Chem. Soc. (Midwest award St. Louis sect. 1984). Home: 414 Wickham Rd Manhattan KS 66502-3751 Office: Kans State U Dept Of Chemistry Manhattan KS 66506 E-mail: setserdw@ksu.edu.

SETTERHOLM, JEFFREY MILES, systems engineer; b. Rochester, N.Y., May 8, 1946; s. Vernon Miles and Grace Lorraine (Bogema) S.; m. Donna Jean Stollenwerk, July 6, 1974; children: Gregory Todd, Vincent Michael. BS in Engring., Applied Sci. cum laude, Yale U., 1968; MS in Sys. Sci. and Math., Washington U., 1976. Electronic engr. McDonnell Douglas Aircraft Divsn., St. Louis, 1974, sr. engr. flight simulation, 1976-78; prin. devel. engr. mil. avionics divsn. Honeywell Inc., Mpls., 1978-84; prin. engr. aerospace divsn. Rosemount, Inc., Burnsville, Minn., 1984-92; ind. software tech. cons. Lakeville, 1992-94; geodetic scientist Geospan Corp., Mpls., 1994—. Author: The Philosophy Works Manual, 1993. Capt. USAF, 1969-73. Decorated DFC. Mem. AIAA, Soc. Automotive Engrs. Lutheran. Achievements include patents in field; origination of the computer configurable six-axis hand controller concept; invention of surveying from non-coplanar images; research in virtual cockpit concepts. Home: 8095 230th St E Lakeville MN 55044-8287 Office: Geospan Corp 10900 73d Ave N Ste 136 Maple Grove MN 55369 E-mail: jeff@setterholm.com.

SETTERS, PAULA LOUISE HENDERSON, physics educator; b. Kay Jay, Ky., July 18, 1949; d. Louis and Lora (Bruce) H.; m. Charles Mullikin Setters; children: Philip Bennett, Lora Elizabeth. BS in Physics, Western Ky. U., 1970, postgrad., 1992; MA in Sci. Edn., U. Ala., 1974. Cert. secondary tchr. Tchr. Warren Ctrl. H.S., Bowling Green, Ky., 1970-71, Homewood (Ala.) H.S., 1971-75, LaRue County H.S., Hodgenville, Ky., 1976-99, ret., 1999; adj. prof. Campbellsville U., 1998—. Profl. devel. presenter AEL, Charleston, W.Va., 1995-98, Ky. Instrnl. Tech. Leaders, Frankfort, Ky., 1994-98; rsch. asst. Dept. of Energy TRAC at Los Alamos (N.Mex.) Nat. Lab., 1991; strategic planning com. LaRue County Bd. Edn., 1992-99; site-based coun. LaRue County H.S., 1996-99. Chair spl. programs United Meth. Women, Hodgenville, 1990; pres. Hodgenville Elem. PTO, 1980-81; chair LaRue County Relay for Life, 2000-01. Mem. Nat. Sci. Tchrs. Assn., Am. Assn. Physics Tchrs., Ky. Sci. Tchrs. Assn., Ky. Assn. Physics Tchrs., Elizabethtown Hardin LaRue Ret. Tchrs. Assn. Republican. Methodist. E-mail: psetters@campbellsvil.edu.

SETTIS, SALVATORE, archaeologist, art historian; b. Rosarno, Italy, June 11, 1941; s. Rocco and Carmela (Megna) S.; m. Chiara Frugoni, Dec. 9, 1965 (div. 1982); children: Silvano, Andrea, Marta; m. Maria Michela Sassi, Jan. 4, 1984; children: Bruno, Nicola. Grad., U. Pisa, Italy, 1963; PhD, Scuola Normale Superiore, Pisa, 1965. Asst. prof. U. Pisa, 1965—69, lectr., 1969—75, prof., 1976—84, dean Faculty Letters and Philosophy, 1978—81; prof. Scuola Normale Superiore, Pisa, 1984—, dean Faculty Letters and Philosophy, 1986—91; dir. Getty Rsch. Inst. for History Art and Humanities, Santa Monica, Calif., 1994—99, Scuola Normale Superiore, Pisa, 1999—. Author: La Tempesta Interpretata, 1978, La Colonna Traiana, 1988, I Greci, 5 vols., 1996—2001, Laocoonte Fama e Stile, 1999. Office: Scuola Normale Superiore Piazza dei Cavalieri 7 56100 Pisa Italy E-mail: direttore@sns.it.

SETTLE, ERIC LAWRENCE, lawyer; b. N.Y.C., July 28, 1961; s. Elliott Titus and Thelma (Radzvill) S.; m. Robin Marks, Aug. 23, 1986; children: Adam Harrison, Alexander Howard. AB cum laude, Colgate U., 1983; JD with honors, George Washington U., 1986. Bar: Pa. 1986, U.S. Dist. Ct. (ea. dist.) Pa. 1987, U.S. Dist. Ct. (mid. dist.) Pa. 1995, U.S. Ct. Appeals (3d cir.) 1992, U.S. Supreme Ct. 1995. Assoc. Wolf, Block, Schorr & Solis-Cohen, Phila., 1986-90, Fox, Rothschild, O'Brien & Frankel, Phila., 1990-95; dep. gen. counsel to gov. Commonwealth of Pa., 1995-97; regional gen. counsel Aetna (now Aetna Inc.), Blue Bell, Pa., 1997—2002; sr. v.p., gen. counsel Americhoice Health Svcs. Inc., Vienna, 2001—. Trustee Colgate U., Hamilton, N.Y., 1983-86, Bryn Mawr Rehab. Hosp., 1993-94; pres. Riverview Condominium Assn., Phila., 1991-93; counsel Craig Snyder for U.S. Congress, Phila., 1992. George Cobb fellow Colgate U., 1981, 82. Mem. ABA (young lawyers divsn., career issues com. 1992-93), Pa. Bar Assn. (exec. com. young lawyers divsn. 1992-93), Phila. Bar Assn. (young lawyers sect. exec. com. 1990-92, dir. bar edn. ctr. 1993-95, trustee Phila. Bar Found., 1994), Phi Alpha Delta (marshal 1984-85). Home: 1148 N Woodbine Ave Narberth PA 19072-1245 Office: Americhoice Corp 8045 Leesburg Pike Ste 650 Vienna VA 22182 E-mail: esettle@americhoice.com.

SETTLER, EUGENE BRIAN, record company executive; b. Balt., Apr. 24, 1936; s. Myer Martin and Esther (Levinson) S.; m. Phyllis Goldfinger, June 10, 1956 (div. Oct. 1975); m. Sharon O'Brasky, May 27, 1976 (div. July 1988); children: Richard Dean, Michael Scott, Robert Marc; m. Margery Shulman, June 1, 1991; children: Gabrielle Shulman, Whitney Shulman. BS in Bus., Loyola Coll., Balt., 1957. V.p. Edge Ltd., Washington, 1954-65; dir. mktg. Epic Records, N.Y.C., 1965-71; exec. v.p. Music West/Music 2, 1971-73; exec. v.p. mktg. RCA Records, 1971-73; pres. Rimiro Corp., 1971-73; exec. v.p. Transcontinental Music Corp., Los Angeles, 1973-76; pres. Request Records, Hollywood, Fla., 1976-82; exec. v.p. Kid Stuff div. IJE, Inc., Plantation, 1982-87; pres. Internat. Mgmt. and Mktg. Sales Co., 1987-88; pres., COO The Singing Machine Co., Inc., Boca Raton, 1988-96; COO, dir. Golden Entertainment Corp., 1996—. Cons. in field; bd. dirs. LCS Entertainment, Inc., Music West/Music 2, The Singing Machine Co. Inc., Parker Highland East Corp., Monad Records, Inc.; pres. Setco, Inc., Oldies But Goodies, Inc., USA Oldies.com, Music Oldies.com. Music arranger: (film) Raiders of the Lost Ark, 1981, (album) Hooked on Exercise, 1983. Dir., treas. Ft. Lauderdale Film Festival, 1986-88. Mem. Nat. Assn. Rec. Arts and Scis., Friars Club. Lodges: Masons, B'nai Brith. Home and Office: 4605 S Ocean Blvd Apt 4C Highland Beach FL 33487-5339 E-mail: esett@aol.com.

SETTLES, ALEXANDER, university researcher; b. Wilmington, DE; m. Elena Shainyan. Master Public Administration, University of Delaware, Newark, Delaware, 1994—96. Assistant Policy Scientist University of Delaware, Newark, 1996—2002. Mem.: American Planning Association (Chapter Executive Board Memeber 1998—2002), American Society for Public Administration (Chapter President 2000—02). Office: University of Delaware 180 Graham Hall Newark DE 19716

SETTLES, F. STAN, JR. engineering educator, manufacturing executive; b. Denver, Oct. 3, 1938; s. Frank S. and Dorothy Marie (Johnson) S.; m. Evelyn Brown, June 10, 1961; children: Frank S. III, Richard, Charles, Michael. BS in Prodn. Tech., Indsl. Engring., LeTourneau Coll., Longview, Tex., 1962; MS in Indsl. Engring., Ariz. State U., 1967, PhD in Indsl. Engring., 1969. Sr. systems analyst AiResearch Mfg. Co., Phoenix, 1968-70, project mgr., 1970-74, mgr. operational planning, 1974-80; mgr. indsl. engrs. Garrett Pneumatic Systems, 1980-83; mgr. indsl. mfg. engring. Garrett Turbine Engring. Co., 1983-85; v.p. mfg. ops. AiResearch Mfg. Co., Torrance, Calif., 1985-87; dir. indusl. mfg. engring. The Garrett Corp., Phoenix, 1987-88; dir. planning Garrett Engine Div., 1988-92; asst. dir. White House Office of Sci. and Tech. Policy, 1992-93; program dir. NSF, 1992-94; prof., chmn. indsl. and systems engring. dept. U. So. Calif., L.A., 1994—. Faculty assoc. Ariz. State U., Tempe, 1974-85, 90-92, rsch. prof., 1992-94. Mem. sch. bd. Tempe Elem. Sch. Dist., 1976-80; mem. YMCA Indian Guides, nat. chief, 1978-79. Fellow Inst. Indsl. Engrs. (pres. 1987-88, Ops. Rsch. award 1980); mem. Nat. Acad. Engrs., Soc. Mfg. Engrs. (sr.), Inst. Ops. Rsch. and Mgmt. Sci. (sr.), Am. Soc. Quality Control, Am. Soc. Engring. Edn. Republican. Presbyterian. Home: 1310 E Ocean Blvd Unit 1602 Long Beach CA 90802-6917 Office: U So Calif Dept Indsl Sys Engring Los Angeles CA 90089-0001

SETTLES, WILLIAM FREDERICK, secondary and university educator, administrator; b. Aurora, Ill., Sept. 24, 1937; s. Arnold Joseph and Cleo Dorothy (Frazier) S.; m. June Ardith Cooper, Dec. 22, 1967; children: Sandi, Jim, Amanda, Caryn. BS, No. Ill. U., 1959, MS, 1961. Educator Aurora East Schs., 1959-62, Anaheim (Calif.) Union H.S. Dist., 1962-63, Joliet (Ill.) H.S. Dist., 1963-67; dean Sandburg H.S., Orland Park, Ill., 1967-68; asst. prin. St. Charles (Ill.) Pub. H.S., 1968-70; asst. prof. Western Ill. U., Macomb, 1970-72; tchr. social scis. Glenbard H.S. Dist., Glen Ellyn, Ill., 1972-96. Author: Life Under Communism, 1982; weekly newspaper columnist Ill. Copley Newspapers, Aurora, 1965-67; contbr. articles to profl. jours. Avocations: world travel, writing, photography. Home: PO Box 1121 Aurora IL 60507-1121

SETZER, HERBERT JOHN, chemical engineer; b. N.Y.C., Oct. 23, 1928; s. Leo and Barbara (Hafner) S. m. Elizabeth Bernadette Curran, May 30, 1957; children: Stephen Lawrence, Robert Drew, John Herbert, Brian Edmund. BChemE, CUNY, 1951; MChemE, NYU, 1958. Engr. U.S. Army Ordnance Corps Redstone Arsenal, Huntsville, Ala., 1955-57; rsch. asst. NYU, 1958-61; rsch. engr. Internat. Fuel Cells (joint venture United Techs. Corp., Hartford, Conn. and Toshiba Corp., Tokyo), 1962-92; vis. lectr. Am. Internat. Coll., Conn., from 1993. Holder 21 U.S. patents chem. processing and hydrogen generation, other patents in Can., Europe, Africa, Asia, Australia; contbr. tech. papers in field to pubis. Chmn. troop com. Long Rivers coun. Boy Scouts Am., 1971-81, com. mem., 1973-81. With U.S. Army, 1951-56. Recipient Mason award, NYU, 1962, Spl. award United Techs. Corp., 1980. Mem. Catalyst Soc. New Eng., Sigma Xi, Elks. Roman Catholic. Died Mar. 11, 2000.

SETZLER, EDWARD ALLAN, lawyer; b. Kansas City, Mo., Nov. 3, 1933; s. Edward A. and Margaret (Parshall) S.; m. Helga E. Friedemann, May 20, 1972; children: Christina, Ingrid, Kirstin. BA, U. Kans., 1955; JD, U. Wis., 1962. Bar: Mo. 1962, U.S. Tax Ct. 1962. Assoc. Spencer, Fane, Britt & Browne, Kansas City, 1962-67, ptnr., 1968-2000, mng. ptnr., 1974-77, 78-82, chmn. trust and estate sect., 1974-2000; ptnr. Husch & Eppenberger, LLC, 2000—. Lectr. CLE programs U. Mo. and Kansas City Sch. Law, 1983-95; mem. Jackson County Probate Manual Com., 1988; Mo. rep. to joint editl. bd. Uniform Probate Code, 1989-99. Co-author: Missouri Estate Administration, 1984, supplements, 1987—2001; contbg. editor, co-editor: Understanding Living Trusts, 1990; ; co-author, co-editor, reviewer: Missouri Estate Planning, 1986; contbg. editor: A Will is Not the Way--The Living Trust Alternative, 1988; bd. editors: Wis. Law Rev., 1961—62. Amb., bd. govs., bd. dirs., chmn. found. com. Am. Royal, 1982—; mem. planning giving com., bus. coun. Nelson Atkins Mus. Art, 1984—; mem. deferred giving com. Children's Mercy Hosp., 1991—; mem. Kansas City Estate Planning Symposium Com., 1984-92, chmn., 1991; mem. adv. com. Greater Kansas City Cmty. Found., 2000—. Fellow Am. Coll. Trust and Estate Counsel (state chmn. 1992-97, mem. state membership com. 1986-2001); mem. ABA, Mo. Bar Assn. (lectr., vice chmn. probate and estate planning com. 1994-97), Kansas City Met. Bar Assn. (lectr., chmn. probate and trust 1979, 92, vice chmn. 1983-85, 91, legis. rev. com. 1991-95), Estate Planning Soc. Kansas City (co-founder 1965, pres. 1983-84, dir. 1984-85, mem. social com. 1968—), Order of Coif, Sigma Chi, Phi Delta Phi. Office: 1200 Main St Ste 1700 Kansas City MO 64105-2100 Fax: 816-421-0596. E-mail: edward.setzler@husch.com.

SETZLER, WILLIAM EDWARD, chemical company executive; b. Bklyn., Dec. 20, 1926; s. William Edward and Gertrude A. (Seyer) S.; m. Dorothy C. Kress, Dec. 2, 1950 (dec. Mar. 1987); children: William John, Heather A.; m. Lenore Kelly, July 13, 1991. B of Chem. Engring., Cooper Union, 1950; MS in Liberal Studies, Columbia U., 1993. V.p. ops. Argus Chem. Corp., N.Y.C., 1950-66; v.p. engring., then group v.p. Witco Chem. Corp. (now Crompton Corp.), 1966-75, exec. v.p., 1975-90, ret., 1990, also bd. dirs.; chmn. and CEO Faimount Chem. Inc., 1993-97. Author and patentee in field. Served with USAAF, 1945-46. Mem. Am. Inst. Chem. Engrs., Soap and Detergent Assn. (bd. dirs.), The Dorothy Setzler Fund (pres. 1991—). Home: 3921 Lincoln St Seaford NY 11783-2115 E-mail: billchair@att.net.

SEUBERT, CHRISTOPH NIKOLAUS, anesthesiologist, educator, researcher; b. Munich, Aug. 13, 1963; came to U.S., 1994; s. Klaus Konrad and Elisabeth Theresa Seubert; m. Charlotte Scheuerpflug, Nov. 24, 1989; children: Philipp, Sebastian. MD, Albert Ludwigs U., Freiburg, Germany, 1991; PhD, Ludwig Maximilian U., Wuerzburg, Germany, 1992. Diplomate Am. Bd. Anesthesiology. Fellow in cardiovascular anesthesia dept. anesthesiology U. Fla., Gainesville, 1998-2000, asst. prof. dept. anesthesiology, 2000—. Recipient T.W. Andersen award U. Fla. Anesthesia Alumni Assn., 1997, Rsch. fellowship Am. Heart Assn., 1998-2000. Office: Univ Fla Dept Anesthesiology 1600 SW Archer Rd Rm M509 Gainesville FL 32610-0254

SEUNG, THOMAS KAEHAO, philosophy educator; b. Jungju, Korea, Sept. 20, 1930; m. Kwihwan Hahn, May 29, 1965; children: Hyunjune Sebastian, Kwonjune Justin, Haesue Florence. BA, Yale U., 1958, MA, 1961, PhD, 1965. Instr. Yale U., 1963-65; asst. prof. Fordham U., 1965-66; mem. faculty dept. philosophy U. Tex., Austin, 1966—, prof. in philosophy, 1972—, prof. in govt., 1985—, prof. in law, 1993—, Jesse H. Jones prof. liberal arts, 1987—. Author: The Fragile Leaves of the Sybil, 1962, Kant's Transcendental Logic, 1969, Cultural Thematics, 1976, Structuralism and Hermeneutics, 1982, Semiotics and Thematics, 1982, Intuition and Construction, 1993, Kant's Platonic Revolution, 1994, Plato Rediscovered, 1996. Served as officer Korean Army, 1950-53. Recipient Wilbur Lucius Cross medal Yale Grad. Sch. Alumni Assn., 1988; Soc. Religion in Higher Edn. fellow, 1969-70; Am. Council Learned Soc. fellow, 1970-71; NEH fellow, 1977-78 Office: U Tex Dept Philosophy Austin TX 78712 Mailing: PO Box 28055 Austin TX 78755 E-mail: t.k.seung@mail.utexas.edu.

SEVCENKO, IHOR, history and literature educator; b. Radosc, Poland, Feb. 10, 1922; came to U.S., 1949, naturalized, 1957; s. Ivan and Maria (Cherniatynska) S.; m. Oksana Draj-Xmara, Apr., 1945 (div. 1953); m. Margaret M. Bentley, July 16, 1953 (div. 1966); m. Nancy Patterson, June 18, 1966 (div. 1995); children: Catherine, Elisabeth. Dr.Phil., Charles U., Prague, Czechoslovakia, 1945; Doct. en Phil. et Lettres, U. Louvain, Belgium, 1949; PhD (hon.), U. Cologne, Germany, 1994. Fellow in Byzantinology Dumbarton Oaks, 1949-50, dir. studies, 1966, prof. Byzantine history and lit., 1965-75, sr. research assoc., 1975—; lectr. Byzantine and ancient history U. Calif., Berkeley, 1950-51; fellow Byzantinology and Slavic lit., research program USSR, 1951-52; instr., then asst. prof. Slavic langs. and lit. U. Mich., 1953-57; mem. faculty Columbia U., 1957-72, prof., 1962-65, adj. prof., 1965-72; vis. prof. Harvard U., 1973-74, prof., 1974-92, emeritus, 1992. Vis. fellow All Souls Coll., Oxford U., 1979-80, Wolfson Coll., Oxford U., 1987, 93; vis. mem. Princeton Inst. for Advanced Study, 1956; vis. prof. Munich U., 1959, Coll. de France, spring 1985, Cologne U., fall 1992, 96, Ctrl. European U., Budapest, spring and fall 1995, spring 1997; treas., acting treas., bd. dirs. Am. Rsch. Inst. in Turkey, 1964-66, 67, 75—; assoc. dir. Harvard Ukrainian Rsch. Inst., 1973-89, acting dir., 1977, 85-86; chmn. Nat. Com. Byzantine Studies, 1966-77; mem. Internat. Com. for Greek Paleography, 1983—; guest of the rector Collegium Budapest, spring 1998. Author: Etudes sur la polémique entre Théodore Métochite et Nicéphore Choumnos, 1962, Society and Intellectual Life in Late Byzantium, 1981, Ideology, Letters and Culture in the Byzantine World, 1982, Byzantium and the Slavs in Letters and Culture, 1991, Ukraine Between East and West, 1996; co-author: Der Serbische Psalter, 1978, Life of St. Nicholas of Sion, 1984; contbr. articles to profl. jours. Guggenheim fellow, 1963, Humboldt-Forschungspreistraeger, 1985, Hruševs'kyj medal Sci. Sevčenko Soc., 1996. Fellow Mediaeval Acad. Am., Brit. Acad. (corr.); mem. Am. Philos. Soc., Am. Acad. Arts and Scis., Ukrainian Acad. Arts and Scis., Sci. Sevcenko Soc., Société des Bollandistes Belgium (adj.), Accademia di Palermo (fgn.), Internat. Assn. Byzantine Studies (v.p. 1976-86, pres. 1986-96, hon. pres. 1996—), Christian Archeological Soc. of Athens (hon.), Austrian Acad. Sci. (corr.), Accademia Pontaniana of Naples (fgn.), Nat. Acad. of Ukraine Sci. (fgn.), Acad. Humanities Rsch. (Moscow), Cosmos Club (Washington), Harvard Club (N.Y.C.), Phi Beta Kappa (hon.). Office: Harvard Univ 204 Boylston Hall Cambridge MA 02138

SEVELY, MARIA, architect; b. Ankara, Turkey, Sept. 28, 1957; d. Marvin and Josephine (Lowndes) S. BArch, Tulane U., 1978. Designer with August Perez & Assocs., New Orleans, 1977, Curtis & Davis/Daniel Mann Johnson & Mendenhall, New Orleans, 1978-80; with Richard Meier & Ptnrs., N.Y.C., 1981-82, Bruner/Cott & Assocs., Cambridge, Mass., 1985; project designer Sasaki Assocs., Boston, 1985—91; project designer, assoc. Akira Yamashita & Assocs., 1992-95; sr. architect, designer Pei Cobb Freed & Ptnrs., N.Y.C., 1996-98; project architect Philip Johnson/Alan Ritchie Archs., 1999—. Archtl. projects include Piazza d'Italia, New Orleans, 1977, One Magazine Square (AIA Honor award 1979), New Orleans, La Regie Renault, Paris, 1981, Windsor Place, Boston, 1985, Holyoke (Mass.) C.C., 1985, Sage Labs., Natick, Mass., 1986, Corp. Ctr., Boston, 1986, Resort at Ocean Edge (AIA/Boston Soc. Archs. PRISM Gold award 1987, Builders' Choice award 1987), Cape Cod, Dartmouth Park housing, Marborough, Mass., 1987, U.S. Holocaust Meml. Mus., Washington, Cathedral of Hope, Dallas. Scholar vis. scholar, Harvard U., 1980—82, Wellesley Coll., R.I. Sch. Design. Mem. AIA (assoc., N.Y. chpt. dialogue com. 1996—, vice chair 2000—), The Copley Soc. (fresh paint artists 1993, 94). Home: 5 Tudor City Pl New York NY 10017-6853 Office: Philip Johnson/Alan Ritchie Archs 375 Park Ave New York NY 10152-0002 E-mail: msevely@ureach.com.

SEVER, JOHN LOUIS, medical researcher and educator; b. Chgo., Apr. 11, 1932; s. John Louis and Harriet (Link) Sever; m. Gerane Werle, Mar. 3, 1956; children: Kimberly, Beverly, Valerie. BA, U. Chgo., 1952; MD, BS, MS, PhD, Northwestern U., 1957. Head sect. infectious diseases NINDS, NIH, Bethesda, Md., 1960—71, chief infectious diseases, 1971—88; chmn. pediatrics Children's Nat. Med. Ctr., Washington, 1988—90, prof. pediatrics, ob-gyn., immunology, microbiology and tropical medicine, 1988—. Cons. NIH, Bethesda, 1988—, Rotary Internat., Evanston, Ill., 1989—, WHO, Geneva, 1991—. Editor: 11 med. books; contbr. Capt., 1960—88. Recipient Kimbel award, Am. Soc. for Microbiology, 1979, Wellcome Diagnostics award, Pan Am. Med. Virology, 1989, Meritorious Alumni award, Northwestern U., 1989, Pasteur award, Microbiology Soc., 1987, Abbott award, 1996, Soc. for Biomolecular Screening award, 2001. Mem.: Pan Am. Soc. Rapid Viral Diseases, Assn. Med. Lab. Immunologists (pres. 1994—95, Erwin Witer award 1997), Teratology Soc. (pres. 1976—77), Assn. Med. Clin. and Lab. Immunologists (pres. 1992—94), Infectious Disease Soc. of Ob-Gyn. (pres. 1994—96, Ortho-McNeill award 1998), Country Glen Club, Potomac Rotary Club. Avocation: gardening.

SEVERDIA, ANTHONY GEORGE, chemistry researcher; b. Sharon, Pa., Sept. 20, 1946; s. George Anthony and Angela Mary (Tomich) S. BS, Pa. State U., 1968; MS, Case Western Reserve U., 1971, PhD, 1974. Rsch., teaching assoc. Rensselaer Poly. Inst., Troy, N.Y., 1975-77; chemist N.Y. U., 1977-79, 82-83, Columbia U., N.Y.C., 1979-82; analytical chemist Mallinckrodt Group, Terre Haute, Ind., 1983-92; sr. chemist analytical sci. Sanofi-Synthelabo Rsch., Gt. Valley, Pa., 1992—. Contbr. articles to profl. jours.; presenter in field. Recipient Summer fellowship NSF, Cleve., 1971. Mem. Am. Chem. Soc. (exec. com., treas. Terre Haute sect. 1991-92), Soc. Applied Spectroscopy, The Internat. Soc. for Optical Engring. Home: 301 Pritchard Ln Wallingford PA 19086-6104 E-mail: aseverdia@comcast.net.

SEVERE, SALVATORE FRANCIS, school psychologist; b. Batavia, N.Y., Dec. 10, 1947; s. Anthony Wayne and Mary (Calarco) S.; m. Dianne M. Heckman; children: Anthony, Leah, Alyssa, Dominic. BA, Canisius Coll., Buffalo, 1969; MS, Buffalo State U., 1973; PhD, Ariz. State U., 1981. Cert. sch. psychologist. Tchr. Connors Children's Ctr., Buffalo, 1970-76; sch. psychologist Cartwright Sch. Dist., Phoenix, 1976—. Author: How to Behave So Your Children Will Too!, 1996. With N.Y. State Air N.G., 1964-75. Recipient Golden Achievement award Nat. Sch. Pub. Rels. Assn., 1989. Mem. Ariz. Assn. Sch. Psychologists (pres. 1997—). Home: 1951 E Velvet Dr Tempe AZ 85284-4702

SEVERIN, SCOTT ROBERT, veterinarian, army officer; b. Aurora, Colo., May 30, 1954; s. Glenn Arden and Joan Ward (Herrick) S.; m. Carrie Lynne Edgar, Aug. 20, 1977; children: Shaunna Kaye, Kayle Dawn. BS, Colo. State U., 1976, DVM, 1979, MS, 1990. Diplomate Am. Coll. Vet. Preventive Medicine. Capt. U.S. Army, 1979; advanced through grades to col., 2000; comdr. Mid-Atlantic Dist. Vet. Command U.S. Army, 1994—97; veterinarian Def. Logistics Agy., Ft. Belvoir, Va., 1997-99; chief food safety and pub. health Office Surgeon Gen., Falls Church, 1999-2000; dep. dir. vet. svc. activity Dept. Def., 2000—. Mem. AVMA, Am. Assn. Food Hygiene Veterinarians, Am. Assn. Pub. Health Veterinarians, Am. Assn. Wildlife Veterinarians, Wildlife Disease Assn. Office: DODVSA/OTSG 5109 Leesburg Pike Ste 667 Falls Church VA 22041-3208 Home: 10060 Belvoir Dr Fort Belvoir VA 22060-2115

SEVERIN-HANSEN, JEANNE ANNE, poet; b. Delhi, N.Y., Aug. 29, 1948; d. Frank Rivers and Margaret Rosellen MacGowan; married; 1 child Margaret Eum Sil. AA, Suffolk C.C., Selden, N.Y., 1975; BA, SUNY Empire State, Old Westbury, 1994. With State Farm Ins., Melville, NY. Author: poems; editor: column. Mem.: Hunting Sch. Ballet Guild. Office: State Farm Ins 1305 Old Walt Whitman Rd Melville NY 11747

SEVERINO, ELIZABETH FORREST, consulting company executive, advanced spiritual healer and animal communicator; b. Bryn Mawr, Pa., Dec. 29, 1945; d. John Joseph and Elizabeth (Patton) Girard-diCarlo; m. Joseph Domenic Severino, Oct. 20, 1973 (div. Oct. 1983); 1 child, Nicole Marie. AB, Vassar Coll., 1967; MS in Computer Sci., Syracuse U., 1969; DD, Universal Life Ch., 1977; D of Religious Studies, U. Global Religious Studies, 2000. Ordained spiritual healer. Systems programmer IBM Corp., Poughkeepsie, N.Y., 1967-71, competitive analyst Phila., 1977-79; systems analyst Fidelity Bank, 1971-72; mng. editor Auerbach Pubs., 1972-77; v.p. editorial and technology McGraw-Hill Pubs., Delran, N.J., 1979-81; v.p. Symcro Systems, Pennsauken, 1981-82; pres. The PC Group, Inc., Cherry Hill, 1982—, also bd. dirs.; pres. The Healing Connection, 1996—. Bd. dirs. Tech E-Writers, Cherry Hill, Simple Solutions, Inc., Cherry Hill. Author: Guide to International Computer Systems Architecture, 1976, Do-It-Yourself Vibrant Mind/Body/Spirit Health, 1995, Reiki: The Healer's Touch, 1995, Diet to Raise Your Spiritual Level, 1996, The Animals' Viewpoint on Dying, Death, and Euthanasia, 2001; (poetry) Garden of Life, 1995, 100 Breaths, 1998; contbr. over 125 articles to profl. jours.; choreographer Faust, Der Vampyr, Sound of Music. Vol. exec. dir. Nat. Reiki Assn., 1995—. Recipient Editors Choice award Nat. Libr. Poetry, 1995. Mem. Assn. Personal Computers Cons. (bd. dirs. Phila. chpt., pres. 1987-90), NAFE, Phila. Area Computer Soc., Inst. Noetic Scis., U.S. Amateur Ballroom Dancers Assn. (Phila. chpt. bd. dirs.), South Jersey Holistic Health Assn. (treas.). Republican. Episcopalian. Avocations: skiing, golf, competitive ballroom dancer. E-mail: spirit1@beyond1.com.

SEVERINO, ROBERTO, foreign language educator, academic administration executive; b. Catania, Italy, July 19, 1940; s. Giuseppe and Alba (Scroppo) S. Student, State U. Catania, Italy, 1960-62; BA, Columbia Union Coll., 1967; MA, U. Ill., 1969, PhD, 1973. Head acct., pers. dir. Industria Nazionale Apparecchiature Scientifiche, Milan, 1961-63; teaching asst., lang. lab. supv. Columbia Union Coll., Takoma Park, Md., 1965-67; grad. teaching asst. U. Ill., Urbana, 1967-70, coord. Corr. Sch., 1970-71; instr. dept. French and Italian U. Mass., Amherst, 1971-73; prof. dept. Italian Georgetown U., Washington, 1973—, acting chmn., 1987, chmn. dept., 1988—; pres., co-founder Nat. Inst. Contemporary Italian Studies, 1986—; co-founder Associazione Internazionale del Diritto e dell'Arte, 1994—; pres. emeritus Am. U. of Rome, 1990-93, chair. Lit. dir. Georgetown U. Elec. Text Repository, Italian Archive, 1988-91, Ultramarina, 1992-96; mem. adv. bd. Nat. Italian Am. Found. Nat. Christopher Columbus 1992 Celebration; mem. U.S. delegation to 1st Conf. on Italian lang. and culture in U.S., 1987; lectr., speaker in field; founder Georgetown Poetry Series; pres. Coun. Promotion of Italian Lang. in Am. Schs., 1999—; hon. pres. U.S. Assn. Internat. Antonietta Labisi, 2000—. Author: Le soluzioni immaginarie, 1985, The Signs and Sounds of Italian,

1985, A carte scoperte, 1990, Presente imperfetto ed altri tempi, 1992, The Battle for Humanism, 1994, A Dumas: Mariano Stabile Sindaco di Palermo, 1994; co-author: Periscopio, 1986, International Nuclear Agreements Multi-lingual Glossary, 1988, United Nations Organization Multilingual Glossary, 1988, Regularizing the Irregular Italian Verb, 1990, Preserving and Promoting Italian language and Culture in North America, 1997, Napoleon: One Image, Ten Mirrors, 2002; translator; The Next 6000 Days by Saverio Avveduto, 1987; editor: (serials) Segni, 1985-88, Hispano-Italic Studies, 1976, 79; mem. editorial bd. Educazione Comparata, 1993—; contbr. articles to profl. jours.; translator: Angelo Scandurra: The Hot-Tempered Musician and Other Poems, 1996, M. Rotelli's E. Sanguineti, If, For Me, You Write a Poem, 1999, Francesco Battiato: Amnesia of the Blue, 2000; editor: Giuseppe Severino: Ricordi di Castelnuovo primi '900. Scene di vita paesana, 1992; co-founder, U.S. editor: Colophon, An Internat. Jour. Arts and Letters, 1997—. Trustee Joel Nafuma Refugee Ctr., Rome, 1993—; chmn. Strega Lit. Prize, Washington D.C. Jury, 1997-2001; mem. jury Prima Parete in Concerto, Lion's Internat. Art Prize, Catania, 1998—, Spoleto Poetry Prize, 1999—. Rsch. grantee Interuniversity Ctr. European Studies, 1977; recipient Accademia Internazionale di Lettere, Scienze, Arti medal, 1983, Internat. Poetry prize, 1986, Gold Cross Cavaliere dell'Ordine al Merito della Repubblica Italiana, 1983, Gold medal Italian Ministries of Univs. and Sci. Rsch., 1988, Marranzano d'Argento prize, 1989, Gold Commander class Cross al Merito della Repubblica Italiana, 1990, Georgetown U. Vicennial Disting. Svc. medal, 1994, Telamone prize, 1995, Top Sprint: Siciliani nel Mondo award, 2000. Mem. MLA, So. Atlantic Modern Lang. Assn., Nat. Assn. Secondary Sch. Prins. (mem. sch. partnerships internat. Italian adv. coun. 1988—), Italian Am. Cultural Found., Italian Cultural Soc. (pres. 1979-81, 83-85, Outstanding Svc. award 1983, chmn. acad. policy com. 1981—), Assn. Internationale Critiques Literaires and Associazione Italiana Critici Letterari, Greater Washington Assn. Tchrs. Fgn. Langs. (mem. award selection com. 1983-85), Manuscript Soc., Renaissance Soc. Am., Circolo Culturale Italiano (hon.), Am. Club (Rome), Touring Club Italiano (hon.), Gamma Kappa Alpha (v.p. 1990—, sec.-treas. and chpt. advisor 1985-90), World Jurist Assn. Ctr. Assocs. (U.S. pres. 1993—, chmn. program devel. and fin. com. 2000—), Associazione Internazionale del Diritto e dell'Arte (v.p. 1994—), Nat. Italian Am. Found. Coun. of 1,000, Napoleonic Soc. Am., Soc. di Studi Valdesi, Istituto Internazionale di Epistemologia la Magna Grecia, Unione Nazionale per la lotta contro l'Analfabetismo, Sons of Italy. Home: 4949 Quebec St NW Washington DC 20016-3230 Office: Georgetown U Dept Italian 37th And O Sts NW ICC 307 Washington DC 20057-0001 E-mail: Severiro@gunet.georgetown.edu.

SEVERO, RICHARD, writer; b. Newburgh, N.Y., Nov. 22, 1932; s. Thomas and Mary Theresa (Farina) S.; m. Emöke Edith de Papp, Apr. 7, 1961. BA, Colgate U., 1954; postgrad., NYU Inst. Fine Arts, 1955-56, Columbia U. Sch. Architecture and Urban Planning, 1964-65. News asst. CBS, N.Y.C., 1954-55; reporter Poughkeepsie (N.Y.) New Yorker, 1956-57, A.P., Newark, 1957-61, N.Y. Herald Tribune, 1961-63; writer TV news CBS, N.Y.C., 1963-66; reporter Washington Post, 1966-68; reporter, correspondant, feature writer N.Y. Times, N.Y.C., 1968—, investigative and environ. reporter, 1973-77, sci. and environ. reporter, 1979—. Assoc. Seminar on the City, Columbia U., 1966-69; vis. lectr. Am. culture Vassar Coll., 1985-99; bd. dirs. Hudson Valley Philharm., 1998-99, Colgate U. Alumni Corp., 1988-92. Author: Lisa H., 1985; (with Lewis Milford) The Wages of War, 1989 (Am. Legion Nat. Comdr.'s award 1990); contbr. articles to mags. Poynter fellow-in-residence Vassar Coll., 1974 75; CBS News fellow, 1964-65; Recipient Front Page award Washington-Balt. Newspaper Guild, 1967; Journalistic award H.A-.V.E.N., 1969; Schaeffer Gold Typewriter award N.Y. Newspaper Reporters Assn., 1969; Page One award Newspaper Guild of N.Y., 1970; hon. mention Mike Berger award Columbia U., 1970; Leone di San Marco award Italian Heritage and Culture Com., 1982; George Polk Meml. award L.I. U. Sch. Journalism, 1975; Hudson River Fisherman's Assn. award, 1976; Mike Berger award Columbia U., 1976; James Wright Brown award Deadline Club, Sigma Delta Chi, N.Y.C., 1976; Feature award N.Y. Press Club, 1977; Page One award Newspaper Guild N.Y., 1977, 82; Media award Am. Cancer Soc., 1977; hon. mention Heywood Broun Meml. award Am. Newspaper Guild, 1977; Penney-Mo. Newspaper award U. Mo. Sch. Journalism, 1978; Media award Agt. Orange Victims Internat., 1982; Page One award N.Y. Newspaper Guild, 1982; Gift of Life award N.Y. Blood Ctr., 1991, Spl. Writing award Soc. of the Silurians, 1992. Home: 83 Balmville Rd Newburgh NY 12550-1917 E-mail: riseve@nytimes.com.

SEVERS, WALTER BRUCE, pharmacology educator, researcher; b. Pitts., June 10, 1938; s. Walter Bruce and Pauline Marie (Sever) S.; m. Anne Elizabeth Daniels, Apr. 25, 1970; children: Mary, Jane, Steven, William, Katherine. BS, U. Pitts., 1960, MS, 1963, PhD, 1965. Postdoctoral fellow NIH, Bethesda, Md., 1966-68; asst. prof. pharmacology Coll. Medicine, Pa. State U., Hershey, 1968-71, assoc. prof., 1971-77, prof., 1977-99, prof. emeritus, 1999—. Cons. pharmacology/toxicology, 1999—; v.p. for sci. affairs Ednl. Horizons, Inc., Lemoyne, Pa., 1998—; ad hoc grant cons. NIH, U.S. Army, NSF. Mem. editl. Bd. Am. Jour. Physiology, 1978-98; assoc. editor Pharmacology, 1998-2000; contbr. numerous articles, chpts., revs. to profl. publs. Recipient Disting. Alumnus award U. Pitts., 1978, I.M. Setchenov medal Acad. Med. Sci. USSR, 1983, Blue medal for sci. Acad. Med. Sci., Bulgaria, medal for sci. U. Belgrade; NASA grantee, 1976-98. Fellow Am. Coll. Clin. Pharmacology; mem. Am. Physiol. Soc., Am. Soc. Pharmacology and Exptl. Therapeutics, Soc. for Neurosci., Soc. for Exptl. Biology and Medicine, Sigma Xi (pres. Pa. State U. chpt. 1981-82), Kiwanis (pres. Hershey area 1980, bd. dirs.). Republican. Roman Catholic. Avocations: reading, camping, hiking. Home: 1011 Grubb Rd Palmyra PA 17078-3510 Office: Pa State U Coll Medicine Dept Pharm Mail Code H78 500 University Dr Hershey PA 17033-2360 E-mail: wbs2@psu.edu.

SEVERS, WILLIAM FLOYD, actor; b. Britton, Okla., Jan. 8, 1932; s. Harry Lysander Fletcher and Katherine Lucinda (McAuliffe) S.; m. Mary Anne Proctor, Jan. 18, 1964 (div. 1971); 1 child, Pilar; m. Barbara Alice Schonger, Sept. 9, 1978; children: Katherine Meghan, Erin Christine. AA, Pasadena Playhouse Coll., 1956. Appeared on Broadway in Cut of the Axe, 1959-60, The Moon Is Blue, 1962, On Borrowed Time, 1991-92, nat. tour Look Homeward, Angel, 1960; co-star nat. tour Spoon River, 1964; actor Secret Storm, All My Children, One Life to Live, Guiding Light, Texas, Search for Tomorrow, Another World, Loving, 1963-93; other TV appearances include Armstrong Circle Theatre, 1963, The Defenders, 1964, World War II, A GI Diary, 1978, Nurse, 1980, Muggable Mary, 1986, Law and Order, recurring role as Hon. Henry Fillmore, 1990-99, Hallmark Hall of Fame, Grace and Glorie, 1998, Law and Order: Criminal Intent, 2000; appeared in films including Funny Farm, 1988, Regarding Henry, 1991, Meet the Parents, 2000, Revolution #9, 2000, 13 Conversations About 1 Thing, 2001; actor European tour West Side Story, 1990-91, 94, Asian tour West Side Story, 1999; actor, voice artist numerous commls., 1964—. Staff sgt. USAF, 1946-53. Mem. SAG, AFTRA, Actors Equity Assn., Pasadena Playhouse Alumni Assn. Democrat. Avocations: reading, golf. Home: 10 Waterside Plz Apt 6F New York NY 10010-2610 Office: Michael Hartig Agency Ltd 156 5th Ave New York NY 10010-7002

SEVERSON, GLEN ARTHUR, circuit court judge; b. Sioux Falls, S.D., Mar. 9, 1949; s. Arthur and Muriel S.; m. Mary K. Schweitzer, May 24, 1975; children: Thomas, Kathryn. BS, U. S.D., 1972, JD, 1975. Bar: S.D. 1975, U.S. Dist. Ct. S.D., 1976, U.S. Ct. Appeals (8th cir.) 1989, Minn. 1990. Dep. states atty. Beadle County, Huron, S.D., 1975-76; ptnr. Benson, Wehde, Martin & Severson, 1976-82, Fingerson, Severson & Nelson, Huron, 1982-93; cir. ct. judge Sioux Falls, 1993—. City atty. City of Huron, 1977-92; pres. S.D. Mcpl. Attys. Assn., Pierre, 1985. Bd. dirs. S.D. Bd. Water and Natural Resources, Pierre, 1986-92, Huron Area C. of C., 1983-86. Name one of Oustanding Young Men of Am., 1977. Mem. ABA, S.D. Bar Assn., Minn. Bar Assn., S.D. Judges Assn. (pres. 2000-2001). Roman Catholic. Avocations: flying, fishing, hunting, reading. Office: 425 N Dakota Ave Sioux Falls SD 57104-2400

SEVERSON, ROGER ALLAN, bank executive; b. Thief River Falls, Minn., Sept. 2, 1932; s. Alfred Gerhard and Esther Olga (Landro) S.; m. Beverly Diane Hays, Aug. 30, 1953; children: Eric Hays, Holle Diane. BS, U. Minn., 1954. Group v.p. First Nat. Bank, Mpls., 1952-73; pres. FBS Fin., Inc., 1974-77; exec. v.p. F&M Savs. Bank, 1977-82; sr. v.p. First Nat. Bank, St. Paul, 1983-85; exec. v.p. Shelard Nat. Bank, Mpls., 1985-86, TCF Bank Savs., Mpls., 1986-92; ret., 1992. Mem. Robert Morris Assocs., 1980-92; trustee Heitman Mortgage Investors, Chgo., 1970-71, Mass. Mut. Mortgage Realty Investors, Springfield, 1972-85. Vice chmn. bd. of trustees The Am. Luth. Ch., Mpls., 1976-81; trustee Children's Health Ctr., Mpls., 1971-72; bd. dirs. Goodwill Industries, Mpls., 1967-70. Fellow Versterheim Mus.; mem. Ethics in Pub. Policy Ctr., Ctr. for Am. Experiment, Sons of Norway. Home: 8321 Essex Rd Chanhassen MN 55317-8705

SEVERY, LAWRENCE JAMES, psychologist, educator; b. Detroit, Mar. 30, 1943; m. Linda Andrea Anstensen, Aug. 20, 1966; children: Beth Andrea, Lisa Ellen. BS in Psychology, Wayne State U., 1965; MA in Psychology, PhD in Psychology, U. Colo., 1970. Rsch. asst. Inst. Behavioral Sci., U. Colo., Denver, 1968-69; predoctoral trainee Inst. Genetics and Behavior for Psychologists, U. Colo., 1969; asst. prof. psychology, sr. rsch. scientist Ark. Rehab. Rsch. and Tng. Ctr., U. Ark., 1970-71; various positions to prof., dept. psychology U. Fla., Gainesville, 1971—, R. David Thomas Endowed Legis. prof. psychology, 1988—, assoc. dean for student affairs Coll. Liberal Arts and Scis., 1990-98. Rsch. fellow Inst. Population Studies, U. Exeter, Devon, Eng., 1982, sr. rsch. assoc. Behavioral Rsch. Inst., 1976-77, postdoctoral trainee, U. N.C. Population Ctr.'s summer inst., 1973 and others; scholar-in-residence Family Health Internat., Research Triangle Park, N.C., 1998-99, tech. advisor for behavioral rsch., 2000-02, dir. divsn. of behavioral and social scis., 2002—; cons. in field. Author: A Contemporary Introduction to Social Psychology, 1976, Advances in Population: Psychosocial Perspectives, Vol. 1 1993, Vol. 2, 1994, Vol. 3, 1999; contbr. articles, book chpts. and monographs to profl. publs. Recipient numerous grants in population and health fields. Fellow APA (numerous coms. divsn. population and environ., pres. 2002—); mem. APHA, Population Assn. Am. (psycho-social workshop program chmn. 1982, 92), Assn. Consumer Rsch., Internat. Assn. Applied Psychology. Home: 10127 SW 48th Pl Gainesville FL 32608-7174 Office: U Fla Coll Liberal Arts and Scis Dept Psychology PO Box 112250 Gainesville FL 32611-2250

SEVERY, LINDA ANDREA, social worker; b. N.Y.C., June 15, 1945; d. Frithjof Ole and Gudrun (Eriksen) Anstensen; m. Lawrence James Severy, Aug. 20, 1966; children: Beth Andrea, Lisa Ellen. Diploma, Henry Ford Hosp. Sch. Nursing, Detroit, 1966; AA, Santa Fe Community Coll., Gainesville, Fla., 1978; BS in Journalism with high honors, U. Fla., 1982. RN, Mich., Colo. Nurse Henry Ford Hosp., 1966, Boulder (Colo.) Meml. Hosp., 1967-70; sec. specialist U. Fla. Coll. Dentistry, Gainesville, 1986-87; sec., aide coord. Alachua County Older Ams. Coun., 1983-85, 88-89, case mgr., 1989-90, aide supr., 1990; project dir. Area Agy. on Aging, 1990-91, Santa Fe HomeCare, Gainesville, 1991; in charge social svcs. Alachua Nursing Ctr., 1991-92; aging resource specialist Mid-Fla. Area Agy. on Aging, 1992-97; regional coord. dept. elder affairs SHINE Program, 1997-99. Mem. health adv. com. Alachua County Sch. Bd., 1982-85; sec. spl. projects Interagy. Coun. for Elderly, Gainesville, 1989-92; v.p. Upjohn Homehealth Care Adv. Coun., 1990-91; mem. RSVP Adv. Coun., 1995-99. Mem. Gold Key. Democrat. Presbyterian. Avocation: Gator fan. Home: 10127 SW 48 Pl Gainesville FL 32608

SEVIER, ERNEST YOULE, lawyer; b. Sacramento, June 20, 1932; s. Ernest and Helen Faye (McDonald) S.; m. Constance McKenna, Apr. 12, 1969; children: Carolyn Stewart, Katherine Danielle. AB, Stanford U., 1954, JD, 1956. Bar: Calif. 1956, U.S. Supreme Ct. 1965. Asso. mem. firm Sedgwick, Detert, Moran & Arnold, San Francisco, 1958-62; mem. firm Severson & Werson, 1962-99. Served with USAF, 1956-57. Fellow Am. Bar Found.; mem. ABA (chmn. tort and ins. practice sect. 1982-83, exec. coun. 1976-84, chmn. standing com. on assoc. comms. 1988-90, chmn. coord. com. on Outreach to Pub. 1989-90, chmn. standing com. on lawyers responsibility for client protection 1991-94, commn. on non-lawyer practice 1992-95), Calif. Bar Assn. Office: Severson & Werson 1 Embarcadero Ctr Fl 26 San Francisco CA 94111-3715

SEVIER, JACOB THOMAS, music educator; b. Honolulu, May 29, 1976; s. Sammy Lynn and Marcia Tarbell Sevier. MusB Edn., S.E. Mo. State U., 2000. Cert. tchr. music edn. K-12. Asst. band dir. Sullivan C-2 Schs., Mo., 2000—02. Co-coord. marching band festival Sullivan Band, 2000—02. Scholar Music scholar, S.E. Mo. State U., 1995. Mem.: MSTA, Phi Mu Alpha Sinfonia. Conservative. Avocations: juggling, travel, bicycling. Home: 99 Deer Run Dr Warrenton MO 63383 Personal E-mail: jacobsevier@yahoo.com.

SEVIK, MAURICE, acoustical engineer, researcher; b. Istanbul, Turkey, Mar. 19, 1923; s. Benjamin and Esther (Barzilai) S.; m. Jacqueline Delannoy, June 2, 1953; children: Michele, Martine. DIC, Imperial Coll. Sci. Tech., London, 1946; PhD, Pa. State U., 1963. Registered profl. engr., Ont. With Bristol Aircraft Corp., U.K., 1946-51; sr. structures engr. Avro Aircraft Ltd., Can., 1952-59; prof. aerospace engring., dir. Garfield Thomas Water Tunnel, Pa. State U., University Park, 1959-72; mem. assoc. tech. dir. ship signatures directorate David Taylor Rsch. Ctr., Bethesda, Md., 1972-96, sr. rsch. scientist, 1996-99; ret., 1999. Vis. prof. Cambridge (Eng.) U., 1970; cons. USAF Office Sci. Rsch. 1965; cons. applied physics lab. U. Wash., Seattle, 1999—. Contbr. articles to profl. jours. Overseas fellow Churchill Coll., Cambridge U., 1970; recipient Gold Medal award The Am. Soc. of Naval Engrs., 1990, Disting. Alumni award Central Pa. chpt. Acoustical Soc. of Am., Charles B. Martell Tech. Excellence award Nat. Security Indsl. Assn., 1992, Robert Dexter Conrad award Office Naval Rsch., 1996, French decoration Ordre Nat du Mérite, 1997; Dr. M. M. Sevik Acoustic Data Analysis Ctr. Bldg. named in his honor. Fellow ASME (Rayleigh lectr. 1995, Per Bruel Gold medal for noise control and acoustics 1996), Acoustical Soc. Am., Sigma Xi; mem. Nat. Acad. Engring. Home: 2 Spruce Ct Hilton Head Island SC 29928 Office: David Taylor Model Basin 9500 Macarthur Blvd West Bethesda MD 20817-5700 E-mail: msevik@aol.com.

SEVILLA, ENID N. production company executive; b. Davao City, The Philippines, June 12, 1953; d. Victor J. and Emerita N. Sevilla. Student, U. Santo Tomas, Manila, 1973, Sisters Formation Inst., Quezon City, The Philippines, 1981. Cert. legal sec., cert. notary pub., Calif. Comm. rschr., writer Nat. Office Mass Media, Manila, 1973-76; fin. officer, tchr. Religious of the Assumption, 1977-85; sec. Craig Printing, L.A., 1986-88; legal sec. S. Roger Rombro, ALC, 1988-93; gen. mgr., fin. officer Paulist Prodns., Inc., 1995—. Office: Paulist Prodns Inc 17575 Pacific Coast Hwy Pacific Palisades CA 90272-4148

SEVILLA, STANLEY, lawyer; b. Cin., Apr. 3, 1920; s. Isadore and Dienna (Levy) S.; m. Lois A. Howell, July 25, 1948; children: Stanley, Susan, Donald, Carol, Elizabeth. BA in Econs. with high honors, U. Cin., 1942; JD, Harvard U., 1948. Bar: Calif. 1949. Since practiced in, Los Angeles; assoc. Williamson, Hoge & Curry, 1948-50; mem. firm Axelrod, Sevilla and Ross, 1950-75, Stanley Sevilla (P.C.), 1975—. Gen. counsel La.-Pacific Resources, Inc., 1970-90. Bd. dirs. Caesars World, Inc., 1989-95. With USAAF, 1942-46. Mem. Beverly Hills Bar Assn., Phi Beta Kappa, Tau Kappa Alpha. Home: 16606 Merrivale Ln Pacific Palisades CA 90272-2236 Office: PO Box 308 Pacific Palisades CA 90272-0308

SEVIN-RODGERS, IMOGENE, occupational and environmental health sciences consultant; b. Rochester, Pa., Nov. 13, 1945; d. Irvin Edward and Hester Pearl (Barto) Sevin; m. John W. Horm (div. 1974); m. James Earl Rodgers, July 4, 1982 (div. July 1997); 1 child, Kimberly. BS, U. Pitts., 1967; PhD, Duquesne U., 1975; MS in Bus., Johns Hopkins U., 1994. Rsch. asst. U. Pitts., 1968-71; assoc. Allegheny Gen. Hosp., Pitts., 1975-76; chemist dept. health human svcs. Nat. Inst. Occupl. Safety and Health, Rockville, Md., 1976-80; health scientist U.S. Dept. Labor/OSHA, Washington, 1980-89; sci. coord. EPA, 1989-93; cons. occupl. and environ. health scis., 1993—; sr. chemistry mgr. Tech. Resources Internat., Inc., Rockville, 1997—. Guest lectr. OSHA Tng. Inst., Chgo., 1989; small bus. cons., 1996-98. Author: (with others) Handbook of Radiation Measurement and Protection, 1979, Alpha-2u-Globulin: Association with Chemically Induced Renal Toxicity and Neoplasia in the Male Rat, 1991; contbr. articles to profl. jours. Animal rights activist, 1995-96. Mem. APHA, NAFE, Soc. for Risk Analysis, Rho Chi. Achievements include research on occupational and environmental hazard assessment, on occupational exposure to formaldehyde, and on cancer risk assessment. Office: 6500 Rock Spring Dr Ste 650 Bethesda MD 20817-1197 E-mail: jsevin@tech-res.com., IRodg49751@aol.com.

SEWARD, GEORGE CHESTER, lawyer; b. Omaha, Aug. 4, 1910; s. George Francis and Ada Leona (Rugh) S.; m. Carroll Frances McKay, Dec. 12, 1936 (dec. 1991); children: Gordon Day, Patricia McKay (Mrs. Dryden G. Liddle), James Pickett, Deborah Carroll (Mrs. R. Thomas Coleman). BA, U. Va., 1933, LLB, 1936. Bar: Va. 1935, N.Y., Ky., D.C., U.S. Supreme Ct. With Shearman & Sterling, N.Y.C., 1936-53, Seward & Kissel LLP, N.Y.C., 1953—. Dir. Witherbee Sherman Corp., 1952-66, pres. 1964-66, Howmet Corp., 1955-75, Chas. P. Young Co., 1965-72, Howmedica Inc., 1970-72, Benson Mines, Inc., 1980-85; trustee Benson Iron Ore Trust, 1969-80. Author: Basic Corporate Practice, 1977, Seward and Related Families, 1994; co-author: Model Business Corporation Act Annotated, 1960, We Remember Carroll, 1992. Trustee Arts and Scis. Coun. U. Va., 1983-93, pres., 1991-93; trustee Edwin Gould Found. for Children, 1955-96, Nature Conservancy of Ea. L.I., 1969-80, N.Y. Geneal. and Biog. Soc. Named to Louisville Male H.S. Alumni Assn. Hall of Fame, 1991; commd. Ky. Col., 1993. Fellow Am. Bar Found. (chmn. model corp. acts com. 1956-65), N.Y. State Bar Found.; mem. Internat. Bar Assn. (hon. life pres., hon. pres., founder sect. on bus. law, lectr. series named in his honor, New Delhi 1988, Lisbon 1992, Budapest 1993, Geneva 1994), ABA (chmn. bus. law sect. 1958-59, chmn. sect. com. corp. laws 1952-58, chmn. sect. banking com. 1960-61, mem. ho. of dels. 1959-60, 63-74, mem. joint com. with Am. Law Inst. on continuing legal edn. 1965-74), Athenaeum Lit. Assn. (Louisville), Downtown Assn. (N.Y.C.), Knickerbocker Club, N.Y. Yacht Club, Univ. Club (Chgo.), Met. Club (Washington), Bohemian Club (San Francisco), Gardiner's Bay Country Club (Shelter Island, N.Y.), Greencroft Club (Charlottesville, Va.), Cum Laude Soc., Raven Soc., Order of Coif, Phi Beta Kappa Fellows (pres. 1969-75), Phi Beta Kappa, Theta Chi, Delta Sigma Rho. Home: 48 Greenacres Ave Scarsdale NY 10583-1436 Office: Seward & Kissel LLP One Battery Park Plz New York NY 10004 also: Internat Bar Assn 271 Regent St London W1R 7PA England

SEWARD, GRACE EVANGELINE, retired librarian; b. L.A., Feb. 2, 1914; d. William Henry and Maud Leuty (Elphingstone) S. BA, Calif. State, L.A., 1959; MLS, U. So. Calif., L.A., 1961. Cert. tchr., Calif. Page L.A. County Pub. Library, San Gabriel, Calif., 1927-37, asst. branch librarian, 1938-40; various clerical positions Zoss Const./Consolidated, San Diego, 1941-42; time keeper Cal Ship Constrn., Wilmington, Calif., 1942-45; turkey ranch mgr. Bagnard Turkey Ranch, Baldwin Park, 1945-47; filing clerk Union Hardware, L.A., 1947-49; library asst. Rosemead (Calif.) H.S., 1949-60; librarian Anaheim (Calif.) Union H.S., 1960-61; catalog head librarian Pasadena (Calif.) City Coll., 1961-79; library classifier Pasadena City Coll., 1979-81. Author: (bibliographies) Man and Environment, 1970, Black America, 1978, (index) American Rose Mag., 1989—90; editor: Bull. Rose Soc. Rose Parade, 1974—87, Bull. Rancho de Quarte Garden Club, Daisy Chain, 1996—. Mem. Am. Rose Soc. (life, life judge, cons. 1978—, elected dist. dir. Pacific S.W. 1985-88, Pacific S.W. Dist. Silver Honor medal 1991, Outstanding Dist. Judge award 1995), L.A. Rose Soc. (life, Bronze Honor medal 1994), Pacific Rose Soc. (life), Royal Nat. Rose Soc. (life), Calif. Garden Clubs (life, pres. Rancho De Duarte 1991-96), Calif. Libr. Assn., Beta Phi Mu (hon.). Avocations: rosarian, gardener, book collector. Home: 2397 Morslay Rd Altadena CA 91001-2715

SEWARD, JAMES PICKETT, internist, educator; b. N.Y.C., Oct. 14, 1949; s. George C. and Carroll Frances (McKay) S. AB, Harvard U., 1971; M of Pub. Policy, U. Calif., Berkeley, 1977; MD, U. Calif., San Francisco, 1977. Diplomate Am. Bd. Internal Medicine, Am. Bd. Occupational Medicine, Am. Bd. Med. Mgmt. Resident U. Calif. Hosps., San Francisco, 1977-80; Robert Woods Johnson postdoctoral fellow U. Calif., 1980-82; med. dir. health svcs. Lawrence Livermore Nat. Lab., 1994—; dir. preventive medicine residency U. Calif., Berkeley, 1991-95, assoc. clin. prof. San Francisco, 1983—, assoc. clin. prof. Sch. Pub. Health Berkeley, 1986—. Fulbright scholar, 1972-73. Fellow Am. Coll. Preventive Medicine, Am. Coll. Occupl. and Environ. Medicine, Am. Coll. Physicians Execs., Calif. Acad. Preventive Medicine (pres.), We. Occupl. and Environ. Med. Assn. (bd. dirs.), Calif. Med. Assn. Office: HSD L723 LLNL PO Box 808 Livermore CA 94551-0808

SEWARD, JEFFREY JAMES, lawyer, protective services official, educator, administrator; b. Rochester, Pa., Aug. 21, 1953; s. Kelson Charles and Virginia Emma (McConnell) S. BA, Ohio No. U., 1975, JD, 1986; MS, U. Nebr., 1979. Bar: Iowa 1990, Mich. 1998. Security cons. North Hills Passavant Hosp., Pitts., 1975-77; state trooper Nebr. State Patrol, Omaha, 1977-84; pvt. practice law Omaha and Council Bluffs, 1986—. Cons. Overland Corp., 1988-89, Fire Photo Corp., Omaha, 1980-91; instr. law enforcement State Nebr., 1979; instr. environ. law and hazardous materials Nebr. State Patrol, 1979-92, technician hazardous material, 1979-84, investigator accidents, 1978-84; adj. faculty U. Nebr., Omaha, Lincoln, Southwestern Community Coll., Iowa, Lakeland Coll., West Allis, Wis.; corp. counsel Farmers Telephone Co., 1990-93, S&M Oil Co., 1990—, Environ. Protection Instrn. Cons. Corp., 1991-2000, GSI-Environ. Cons. Corp., 1991-2000, Environ. Assessment Group, 1990-2000, Firstier Bank, 1990-92, Bank One Trust Co., 1992-95, Merrill Lynch Trust Co., 1995-96, Comerica Bank, 1996-2001, So. Mich. Bank & Trust, 2001--. Law Enforcement Assistance Adminstrn. scholar, 1978-79; recipient Life Saving award Am. Heart Assn., 1982, Am. Jurisprudence award Bancroft-Whitney Co., 1986, 87. Mem ABA, ATLA, Nat. Assn. Chiefs of Police, State Troopers Assn. Nebr., Peace Officers Assn. Nebr., Mich. State Bar Assn., Kalamazoo County Bar Assn., Environ. Assessment Assn., Am. Bankers Assn., Iowa State Bar Assn., Omaha Bar Assn., Delta Theta Phi. Republican. Lutheran. Avocation: car collecting. Home and Office: 7480 Saint George Cir Portage MI 49024-7832

SEWARD, JOHN EDWARD, JR. insurance company executive; b. Kirksville, Mo., June 12, 1943; s. John Edward and Ruth Carol (Connell) S.; children: Mitch, Justina. BS in Fin., St. Joseph's Coll., 1968. CLU, CPCU, cert. profl. ins. agt. Mgr. acctg. svcs. Guarantee Res. Life Ins. Co., Hammond, Ind., 1965-69; asst. contr. Gambles Ins. Group, Mpls., 1969-71, N.Am. Cos., Chgo., 1971-73; v.p., treas. Home & Auto Ins. Co., 1973-75, bd. dirs., 1974-83; pres., chief exec. officer, dir. Universal Fire & Casualty Ins. Co., 1983-88, acting chmn. bd., pres., chief exec. officer, 1988, chmn. bd., pres., chief exec. officer, 1989-92; co-founder, pres., CEO J&J Underwriting Svcs., Inc., 1992-93, chmn., CEO, 1994; v.p. Concord Gen., 1993—; pres. Classictire & Marine Ins. Co., 1994; pres., CEO Bus. Risk Svcs., 1995—. Bd. dirs., v.p., treas., v.p. fin. Calumet Coun. Boy Scouts Am., 1981-85; mem. Shriners Hosp.-Teddy Bear Club, 1980; mem. exec. com. Chgo. Baseball Cancer Charities, 1981—; co-chmn. Ron Kittle's Ind. Sports Charities, 1989. Named to Wall of Fame, T.F. South High Sch., 1993. Fellow Life Mgmt. Inst.; mem. Am. Biog. Inst. (dep. gov.). Home: 1124 Lisa Ln Schererville IN 46375-1183 Office: Bus Risk Svcs 1124 Lisa Ln Schererville IN 46375-1183

SEWARD, NANCY H. retired band director, composer; b. Henryetta, Okla., Aug. 9, 1930; d. Albert Louis and Grace Wood Heitmann; m. Raymond Kenneth Seward, Aug. 21, 1952 (dec. Dec. 1980); children: Steven Kenneth, Lynn Annette Seward Fryer. B Music Edn. cum laude, Ctrl. Meth. Coll., 1952; postgrad., U. Mich., 1952, U. Mo., Columbia, 1964, U. Mo., Kansas City, 1973-74. Band dir. Leavenworth (Kans.) pub. schs., 1952-54, Excelsior Springs (Mo.) pub. schs., 1954-58, Ruskin H.S., Hickman Mills, Mo., 1958-64, Ctrl. Meth. Coll., Fayette, 1964-66, Richmond (Mo.) pub. schs., 1967-81, Stet Pub. Schs., 1967-73, Polo (Mo.) pub. schs., 1982-90; ret., 1990. Dir. band in Tournament of Roses Parade, Pasadena, Calif., 1960, several televised half-time shows for Kansas City Chiefs football games, also Kansas City Royals and St. Louis Cardinals; adjudicator, clinician at festivals and contests in Midwest and Can., 1964—. Composer, arranger numerous works for concert bands. Recipient 2d pl. award Richmond Band, Internat. Youth and Music Festival, Vienna, Austria, 1981, disting. alumni award Ctrl. Meth. Coll., 1978; named to Mo. Bandmasters Hall of Fame, 1993. Mem. World Assn. for Symphonic Bands and Ensembles, Nat. Band Assn., Women Band Dirs. Internat., Mo. Bandmasters' Assn., Tex. Bandmasters' Assn., Music Educators Nat. Conf., Mo. Music Educators Assn., Phi Beta Mu. Avocations: reading, genealogy. Home: 206 E Main St Richmond MO 64085-1812

SEWARD, RICHARD BEVIN, lawyer; b. Bartlesville, Okla., May 27, 1932; s. Fredrick W. and Kittie Lea (Hudson) S.; m. Loydell E. Nash, Aug. 1, 1954; children: Ann M., Elizabeth, Amy M. BS, Okla. State U., 1954; postgrad., Tulsa U., 1959-62; JD, So. Methodist U., 1971. Bar: Tex. 1968. Personnel mgr. Unit Rig and Equipment Co., Tulsa, 1958-62, Gifford-Hill Cos., Dallas, 1962-66; labor cons., 1966-68; partner firm Stanfield & Seward, 1978-83; sole practice law Farmersville, Tex., 1983—. Served with AUS, 1955-57. Mem. Order of Coif. Home and Office: 14340 County Road 550 Farmersville TX 75442-7034 E-mail: sewfolly@aol.com.

SEWARD, TROILEN GAINEY, retired psychologist; b. Petersburg, Va., Nov. 26, 1941; d. Troy L. and Mary (Nester) Gainey; m. William E. Seward III, June 29, 1963; children: Susan Blair, William E. IV. BA, Coll. William and Mary, 1963, MEd, EdS, Coll. William and Mary, 1980; MEd, Va. Commonwealth U., 1977. Elem. tchr., Petersburg, 1963-67; secondary tchr. Surry (Va.) Acad., 1967-76, guidance counselor, 1976-77; headmistress Tidewater Acad., Wakefield, Va., 1977-79; psychologist Peninsula Child Devel. Clinic, Newport News, 1980-82; sch. psychologist Dinwiddie (Va.) Pub. Sch., 1982-89, dir. pupil pers. svcs., spl. edn., 1990-93, dir. student svcs., 1993-95, supt. Va., 1996—2001; ret., 2002. Mem. human rights com. Southside Tng. Ctr., Petersburg, 1986—. Trustee Ritchie Meml. ch., Claremont, Va., 1971—; mem. Town Coun., Claremont, 1984-90, mem. fin. com., 1984-90. Mem. Nat. Assn. Sch. Psychologists (del. 1992-94), Va. Assn. Sch. Psychologists (chair cert. and licensure com. 1985-87, legis. chair 1987—, pres. 1989-91), Delta Kappa Gamma, Phi Kappa Phi. Episcopalian. Home: PO Box 266 Claremont VA 23899-0266

SEWARD, WILLIAM W(ARD), JR. writer, retired educator; b. Surry, Va., Feb. 2, 1913; s. William Ward and Elizabeth (Gwaltney) S.; m. Virginia Leigh Widgeon, Dec. 27, 1941; children: Virginia R. Godwin, Leigh W. Huston. AB, U. Richmond, 1934, MA, 1935; grad. fellow, Duke U., 1938-39, 40-41. English tchr. pub. schs., 1935-38; instr. U. Richmond, 1939-40, summer 1944; head English dept. Greenbrier Mil. Sch., 1941-42; prof., head English dept. Tift Coll., 1942-45; faculty Old Dominion U., Norfolk, Va., 1945, 47—, prof., 1957-77, prof. emeritus, 1977—, head dept. English, 1947-61. Lectr. U. Va. extension div., 1952-54 Author: The Quarrels of Alexander Pope, 1935; editor: The Longer Thou Livest the More Fool Thou Art (W. Wager), 1939, Literature and War, 1943, Skirts of The Dead Night, 1950, Foreword to Descent of the White Bird (Barbara Whitney), 1955, Contrasts in Modern Writers, 1963, My Friend Ernest Hemingway: An Affectionate Reminiscence, 1969; contbr. to book: The True Gen: An Intimate Portrait of Hemingway by those Who Knew Him (Denis Brian), 1988, Remembering Ernest Hemingway (interviews by James Plath and Frank Simons), 1999; mem. editl. bd.: Lyric Virginia Today, 1956; contbr. articles to profl. jours. Recipient Charles T. Norman medal for best grad. in English U. Richmond, 1934 Mem. Poetry Soc. Va. (pres. 1952-55), Hemingway Soc., Internat. Mark Twain Soc. (hon.), Va. Writers Club (emeritus), Princess Anne Country Club, Virginia Beach Sports Club, Phi Beta Kappa, Kappa Alpha, Pi Delta Epsilon. Methodist. Home: 701 Cavalier Dr Virginia Beach VA 23451-3837

SEWELL, ANDREW, music director; m. Mary Anne Sewell; children: Anna, Lydia, Alistair. MMus, U. Mich.; studied with Gustav Meier. Past asst. condr. Memphis Symphony; past resident condr. Toledo Symphony Orch.; music dir. Mansfield (Ohio) Symphony, Wis. Chamber Orch., Madison; music dir., condr. Wichita (Kans.) Symphony Orch., 2000—. Guest condr. orchs. Detroit, Japan, Mex., Can., New Zealand. Recipient Young Achiever's award Australian Guarantee Corp., Star award New Zealand Aotea Performing Arts Trust, 1997. Office: Wichita Symphony Orch 225 W Douglas Ave Ste 207 Wichita KS 67202-3181*

SEWELL, CHARLES HASLETT, banker; b. Buford, Ga., Jan. 16, 1928; s. Grover C. and Jennie G. (Haslett) S.; m. Margaret Gillespie, Sept. 9, 1985; children: Anna E., William H., John L. BA, Emory U., 1951. Econs., mgmt. cons. Rsch. and Cons. Corp., Atlanta, 1952-72; sr. v.p. Deposit Guaranty Nat. Bank, Jackson, Miss., 1972-74, exec. v.p., 1974—; chmn., CEO Deposit Guaranty Mortgage Co., 1976-91; acting dean Millsaps Coll. Grad. Sch. Mgmt., 1994. Cons. in field; chmn. Miss. Econ. Council, 1983—; chmn. Sml. Bus. Devel. Ctr. U. Miss, Oxford, 1979— Contbr. articles to profl. jours. Trustee Miss. State Libr. Commn., 1983—; chmn. Miss. Com. for Humanities, 1983—; pres. Miss. Symphony Orch., 1988-89; chmn. Miss. internat. adv. bd. Emory U. Coll. Arts and Scis., 1992—; exec.-in-residence Else Sch. Mgmt., Millsaps Coll. Mem. University Club (Jackson). Republican. Presbyterian. Home: 25 Village Green Cir Jackson MS 39211-2927 Office: Millsaps Coll Grad Sch Mgmt Jackson MS 39210

SEWELL, CHARLES ROBERTSON, geologist, exploration company executive, investor; b. Malvern, Ark., Feb. 7, 1927; s. Charles Louis and Elizabeth (Robertson) S.; m. Margaret Helen Wilson, Dec. 26, 1953 (dec. July 1985); children: Michael Stuart, Charles Wilson, Marion Elizabeth; m. Louise T. Worthington, Nov. 29, 1985; 1 child, Ginger B. BS, U. Ark., Fayetteville, 1950; MA, U. Tex., Austin, 1955; postgrad., U. Tex., 1961—64. Registered geologist, Ariz. Well logging engr. Baroid, Houston, 1950; ast. metallurgist Magcobar, Malvern, Ark., 1951; geologist Socony-Mobil Petroleum Co., Roswell, N.Mex., 1955; sr. geologist Dow Chem. Co., Freeport, Tex., 1956-61; spl. instr. U. Tex., Austin, 1962-65; pvt. practice, 1962-65; dist. geologist, mgr. Callahan Mining Corp., Tucson, 1965-68; owner, cons. geologist Sewell Mineral Exploration, Worldwide, 1968—. Extensive work USSR-CIS, 1988—. Contbr. articles to profl. jours. Elder Presbyn. Ch., Tucson, 1973—. With USN, 1944-46, 51-53. NSF grantee, 1962-64. Mem. AIME, Ariz. Geol. Soc., Mining Found. Southwest (bd. govs. 1982-86, 90—, pres. 1984, Hall Fame com. 1998—), Masons. Republican. Achievements include discovery/co-discovery of numerous metallic and non-metallic ore deposits in Ctrl. Am., Nigeria, Greece, Tajikistan, others; extensive work on gold/silver systems in western U.S., Mexico, Costa Rica and Kazakhstan. Home and Office: 5825 S Old Spanish Trl Tucson AZ 85747-9487 E-mail: rockpickone@aol.com. *Personal Philosophy: To win you must, at sometime in life, move out into harms way.*

SEWELL, ELIZABETH PERRY, investor, real estate broker; b. Odessa, Tex., Jan. 4, 1957; d. Charles Robert and Nancy Joanna (White) Perry; m. Richard William Sewell, Aug. 6, 1977; 1 child, Lauren Diane. B.B.A., Tex. A&M U., 1979, M.B.A., 1980. Teaching asst. fin. dept. Tex. A&M U., College Station, 1979-80; gas contract analyst United Tex. Transmission, subs. United Energy Resources, Houston, 1980-82; sr. fin. analyst United Energy Resources, Houston, 1982-84; chmn. bd. Ventura Realty, Inc., Houston, 1984— . Mem. Nat. Assn. Female Execs., Am. Mgmt. Assn. Presbyterian. Avocations: snow skiing; car racing. Office: Ventura Realty Inc 20 Gage Ct Houston TX 77024-4409

SEWELL, GLORIANA, piano teacher; b. Huntington, N.Y., June 6, 1948; d. Reavis Staggs and Evelyn (Vilches) Kurlowich; m. C. Eugene Sewell, Aug. 8, 1969; children: Keren Ligowski, Daniel Sewell. BA in Piano, Bob Jones U., 1970. Piano tchr. in pvt. practice, Santa Barbara, Calif., 1970-71, Sodus, N.Y., 1971-78; Suzuki piano tchr. in pvt. practice Quakertown, Pa., 1979-86, Milford Square, 1986—; Kindermusik tchr. Milford Square Music Studio, 1996—. Piano accompanist ch. choir Assembly of the Word, Milford Square, 1993—. Recipient Tchr. award for 1st Pl. Winner, Baldwin Jr. Keyboard Competition, 1985, 1992, 2000, Tchr. of Yr. award, 1989, award, Music Tchrs. Nat. Assn. Student Composition Competition, 1993, 1994, 2001. Mem.: Dalcroze Soc. Am., Nat. Guild Piano Tchrs., Am. Orff-Schulwerk Assn., Kindermusik Educations Assn., Suzuki Assn. of Ams., Pa. Music Tchrs. Assn. (v.p. 1999—2001, pres. 2001—, pres. Lehigh Valley chpt. 1991—92, co-dir. spring music festival 1997), Music Tchrs. Nat. Assn. Avocation: gardening. Home and Office: Milford Square Music Studio PO Box 199 2244 Milford Square Pike Milford Square PA 18935

SEWELL, JOHN WILLIAMSON, research association executive; b. Cleve., Dec. 19, 1935; s. William and Hilda F. (Gaunt) S.; m. Maryann Strauss, July 19, 1958; children: Gregory J., Michael P. BA, U. Rochester, 1957; MA, NYU, 1967. Fgn. service officer Dept. State, 1961-68; asst. to dir. Bur. Intelligence Research, Dept. State, Washington, 1968-70; asst. to pres. Brookings Inst., 1970-71; v.p. Overseas Devel. Council, 1971-77, exec. v.p., 1977-79, pres., 1980-2000; sr. scholar Woodrow Wilson Internat. Ctr., 2001—. Mem. Bretton Woods Com., North-South Roundtable; vice chair Internat. Ctr. for Rsch. on Women; mem. Internat. Adv. Group for 1995 World Summit for Social Devel.; spl. advisor to the adminstrn. UNDP, 1988-99; chair Working Group on Devel. of Role of Internat. Monetary Fund; global advisor World Resources Inst. Author: U.S. Foreign Policy and the Third World Agenda, 1985-86; Growth, Exports, & Jobs in a Changing World Economy: Agenda 1988; co-editor: United States Budget for a New World Order, FY, 1992, Challenges and Priorities in the 1990s: An Alternative U.S. International Affairs Budget, FY, 1993; contbr. articles to jours. Pres. Nat. Choral Found., 1969-75. With U.S. Army, 1958-60. Mem. Coun. on Fgn. Rels., Cosmos Club. Home: 7614 Morningside Dr NW Washington DC 20012-1557 E-mail: jwsewell@stapower.net.

SEWELL, MARSHA JUDITH, interior designer, product designer; b. Cleve., June 16, 1945. Student Kent State U., 1963-65; B.F.A., Royale Academiedes Beaux Arts, Brussels, 1966; postgrad. Cleve. State U., 1966-67. Cert. Nat. Council for Interior Design Qualification. Residential designer Teetzel Co., Grosse Pointe, Mich., 1971-74, various design firms, San Diego, 1974-77; owner Marsha Sewell and Assocs., San Diego, 1977— ; pres. AEMESCO, Inc., San Diego, 1977— . Comml. renovations include: San Diego Civic Theatre (AIA/Am. Soc. Interior Designers Orchid award of Excellence 1980), Temple Emanu-El, San Diego, La Jolla Village Inn and Terrarium Restaurant, Sea Coast Inn, San Diego, Signatures de Paris retail store, La Jolla, Glorietta Bay Inn, Coronado, Calif., McBride Agy., La Jolla, Mt. La Jolla Community Ctr., exec. offices Titan Corp.; new constrn. projects include condominiums, real estate and med. offices, furniture showroom. Contbr. numerous articles to design, interior decorating and gen. interest mags. Recipient Merit award for Forecast 80's, AIA, 1982; Design for Better Living award for Forecast 80's, Am. Wood Council, 1982; Appreciation award Youth Employment Program San Diego City Schs., 1980; named one of 85 San Diegans to Watch in '85, San Diego Mag. Mem. Am. Soc. Interior Designers (Presdl. citation for disting. service 1980, 81, bd. dirs. San Diego 1979-81, active various coms.), San Diego Hist. Soc. (designer for Showcase Ho. 1979-84). Address: 629 5th Ave San Diego CA 92101-6915

SEWELL, PHYLLIS SHAPIRO, retail chain executive; b. Cin., Dec. 26, 1930; d. Louis and Mollye (Mark) Shapiro; m. Martin Sewell, Apr. 5, 1959; 1 child, Charles Steven. BS in Econs. with honors, Wellesley Coll., 1952. With Federated Dept. Stores, Inc., Cin., 1952-88, research dir. store ops., 1961-65, sr. research dir., 1965-70, operating v.p., research, 1970-75, corp. v.p., 1975-79, sr. v.p., research and planning, 1979-88. Bd. dirs. Lee Enterprises, Inc., Davenport, Iowa, Pitney Bowes, Inc., SYSCO Corp. Bd. dirs. Nat. Cystic Fibrosis Found., Cin., 1963—; chmn. divsn. United Appeals, Cin., 1982; mem. bus. adv. coun. Sch. Bus. Adminstrn., Miami U., Oxford, Ohio, 1982-84; trustee Cin. Cmty. Chest, 1984-94, Jewish Fedn., 1990-92, Jewish Hosp., 1990—; mem. bus. leadership coun. Wellesley Coll., 1990—, Fordham U. Grad. Sch. Bus., 1988-89. Recipient Alumnae Achievement award Wellesley Coll., 1979, Disting. Cin. Bus. and Profl. Woman award, 1981, Directors' Choice award Nat. Women's Econ. Alliance, 1995; named one of 100 Top Corp. Women Bus. Week mag., 1976, Career Woman of Achievement YWCA, 1983, to Ohio Women's Hall of Fame, 1982.

SEWELL, RALPH BYRON, investment broker, financial planner, manager; b. Oklahoma City, May 24, 1940; s. Ralph Llewellyn and Amy (Taylor) S.; m. Beverly Jean Bainbridge, Jan. 23, 1962; children: Michael Timothy, Pamela Jean. BS in Engring. Physics, U. Okla., 1963; MS in Fin. Planning, Coll. for Fin. Planning, 1994. Cert. fin. planner. Project engr. Kerr McGee Corp., Oklahoma City, 1969; sr. engr. Consumers Power Co., Charlevoix, Mich., 1969-70, nuclear licensing adminstr. Jackson, 1970-77; ops. mgr. Plateau Resources Ltd., Grand Junction, Colo., 1977-80; investment broker Boettcher & Co., 1980-83, spl. ptnr., 1983-87; v.p. investments A.G. Edwards & Sons, Inc., 1987-90, assoc. v.p., 1990-94, v.p., 1994—. Lt. USN, 1963-68. Recipient Appreciation award Bus. Partnership Program Bd. Edn. Sch. Dist. #51, 1989, 90. Mem. Inst. of Cert. Fin. Planners, Lions. Republican. Avocations: tennis, fishing, cross country skiing. Office: AG Edwards & Sons Inc 501 Main St Grand Junction CO 81501-2607 Home: 884 Quail Run Dr Grand Junction CO 81505-8608

SEWELL, RICHARD HERBERT, historian, educator; b. Ann Arbor, Mich., Apr. 11, 1931; s. Herbert Mathieu and Anna Louise (Broene) Sewell; m. Natalie Paperno, Jan. 13, 1971; 1 child Rebecca Elizabeth. AB, U. Mich., 1953; MA, Harvard U., 1954, PhD, 1962. Asst. prof. No. Ill. U., DeKalb, 1962-64, U. Wis., Madison, 1965-67, assoc. prof., 1967-74, prof, 1974-95, prof. emeritus, 1995—. Vis. lectr. U. Mich., Ann Arbor, 1964—65; adv. bd. Lincoln and Soldiers Inst. Gettysburg Coll., Pa., 1990—. Author: (book) John P. Hale and the Politics of Abolition, 1965, Ballots for Freedom, 1976, A House Divided, 1988; contbr. articles to profl. jours. Lt. (j.g.) USNR, 1954—57. Mem.: Hist. Soc. Wis., So. Hist. Assn., Soc. Civil War Historians, Phi Beta Kappa, Phi Kappa Phi. Avocation: white-water rafting. Home: 2206 Van Hise Ave Madison WI 53726 E-mail: rhsewell@wisc.edu.

SEWELL, ROBERT GEORGE, librarian; b. Stillwater, Okla., Aug. 28, 1942; s. William Hamilton and Elizabeth Sewell; m. Barbara Judy Love, Jan. 27, 1963; 1 child, Jamin Robert. BS in Asian Studies, U. Wis., 1964; MA in Japanese Lit., Columbia U., 1967; PhD in Comparative Lit., U. Ill., 1976, MLS, 1982. Japanese bibliographer Asian libr. U. Ill., Urbana-Champaign, 1970-80, reader's svcs. coord., 1978-80, asst. to dir. libr. collections, 1983-86; asst. dir. for collection mgmt. and devel. SUNY, Stony Brook, 1986-89; assoc. univ. libr. for collection devel. and mgmt. Rutgers U. N.J., 1989—. Contbr. articles to profl. jours. Home: 29 Coan Pl Metuchen NJ 08840-2523 Office: Rutgers U 169 College Ave New Brunswick NJ 08901-1163 E-mail: rgsewell@rci.rutgers.edu.

SEWELL, RODNEY MILTON, biologist; b. Frederick, Md., July 5, 1946; BS in Psychobiology, Hood Coll., 1974. Operating room tech. USN, 1967-70; biologist NIMH/LBEB, 1974-79; systems integrator LAMDA, 1983—. Mem. IEEE Computer Soc., N.Y. Acad. Scis., AAAS, Am. Chem. Soc., Am. Psychol. Soc. Achievements include research in developmental and comparative aspects of neurobiology and behavior, computer-assisted learning devices. Office: Lab Med Devices PO Box 30634 Bethesda MD 20824-0634

SEWELL, WILLIAM GEORGE, III, electronics engineer; b. Roanoke, Va., Dec. 14, 1950; s. William George Jr. and Elizabeth Marie (Morrison) S.; m. Verna Landry, Aug. 25, 1970 (div. 1974); children: Ronald Allen, Bryan Joseph; m. Colleen Rose Gaynor, May 15, 1981. BS in Engring., U. Ill., Chgo., 1980; PhD, Calif. U., Modesto, 1983. Electronic technician 928 Airlift Group, Chgo., 1972-74; with FAA, 1974-85, staff engr. Wheeling, Ill., 1980-82, regional nav. and landing systems engr. Chgo., 1982-85; with Jerry Thompson & Assocs., Kensington, Md., 1987-88; v.p. Navcom Systems, Inc., 1988-89, B2 Software, Inc., 1988-89; v.p., CEO The Thinkk Corp., 1988-89; founder, CEO Software Coalition, 1989—; v.p. Holmes & Narver, Inc., 2000-01, DMJM Holmes & Narver, Inc., 2001—. Dir. comm. and info. systems group SEMA, Inc., 1990—93; dir. comm. solutions Jacobs Facilities, Inc., 1993—2000; Sverdrup fellow, 1998; v.p. DMJM Holmes & Narver, 2000—, AECOM Techs., 2000—; pres. GEOLINC, 2002—; cons. engr. W.G. Sewell & Assocs., Internat., Niles, Ill., 1981—88; chair TIA Indsl. Telecoms Standards Body, 1999—2001. Contbr. articles to tech. publs. Mem. Chgo. Coun. Fgn. Rels., 1976-80. Served with USAF, 1970-72, Vietnam. Recipient 1st prize Am. Soc. Electro-Surgery, 1982. Mem. IEEE (chair telecomm. industry assoc. indsl. stds. group), Soc. Automotive Engrs., Aircraft Owners and Pilots Assn. Achievements include invention of high speed turn control for land vehicles, 1980; co-inventor child's hidden identification and location device, 1990. Office: 1300 Wilson Blvd Ste 1100 Arlington VA 22209-2307 E-mail: bill.sewell@dmjmhn.com.

SEXSON, RICHMOND LOCKWOOD, baseball player; b. Portland, Oreg., Dec. 29, 1974; m. Kerry Sexson. 1st baseman Milw. Brewers, 2000—. Achievements include third in Brewers franchise history to hit 40 home runs in a season. Office: Milw Brewers 1 Brewers Way Milwaukee WI 53214*

SEXSON, STEPHEN BRUCE, education writer, educator; b. Silver City, N.Mex., May 29, 1948; s. Ralph Dale and Wanda Claudean (McMahan) S.; m. Barbara Jane Davis, May 24, 1968; children: David Paul, Linda Carol. BA in Rhetoric and Pub. Address, Pepperdine U., 1969, MA in Pub. Comm., 1975; PhD in Higher Edn., Okla. State U., 1990. Asst. to supt. Morongo Unified Sch. Dist., 29 Palms, Calif., 1973-77; corp. trainer Merrill Lynch Realty, Dallas, 1979-81; sch. psychologist Texhoma (Tex.) Sch. Dist., 1982-83; assoc. prof., dir. Christian Student Ctr. Okla. Panhandle State U., Goodwell, 1982-84; rsch. resident Okla. State U., Stillwater, 1984-87; mem. spl. programs staff L.A. Unified Sch. Dist., 1987-93; dir. Edwest Edn. Rsch., Burbank, Calif., 1991—; lectr. Chapman U., 1998—. Guest lectr. edn. Okla. State U., Stillwater, 1993-94, U. Tulsa, 1993-94; conv. spkr. Merrill Lynch Realty-Relo, Atlanta, 1979; prof. Chapman U., 1998—; lectr. Verbal Comm. Inst., Palm Desert, Calif., 2001—. Author: The Magic Classroom, 1995, The Values Rich Teacher, 1996; contbr. articles to profl. jours. Mem. ASCD, Am. Assn. Sch. Adminstrs., Nat. Assn. of Sch. Psychologists, Lions Club, Phi Delta Kappa. Avocations: computing, travel, theatre. Home: PO Box 1853 Twentynine Palms CA 92277-1250 Office: Chapman U Coachella Valley Campus 42-600 Cook St Ste 134 Palm Desert CA 92211 E-mail: SteveSexson@aol.com.

SEXTON, CHARLINE, secondary education educator; b. Kennett, Mo., Dec. 01; d. Charles Jerome and Dora Myrtle (Wilburn) Lemonds; m. Marcus L. Sexton, Mar. 3, 1939; children: Charolyn Linch, Dan Sexton, Marc Sexton, Elizabeth Morrison. BA with honors, U. Tex Arlington, 1969, MA, 1976. Tchr. English Ft. Worth I.S.D., 1969-83. Author: (mag.) Arlington Review, 1966. Lectr. various churches, Tex., Ark., Tenn., 1963-98. Mem. Ex Libris Book Review Club. Avocation: reading.

SEXTON, DAVID FARRINGTON, lawyer, investment banking executive; b. Montclair, N.J., Aug. 20, 1943; s. Dorrance and Marjorie (McComb) S.; m. Ann Hemelright, Feb. 27, 1971; children: James, Ashley, Christopher. AB cum laude, Princeton U., 1966; JD cum laude, U. Pa., 1972. Bar: N.Y. 1972. Assoc. Sullivan & Cromwell, N.Y.C., 1972-77; with First Boston Corp., 1977-90, v.p., gen. counsel, 1980-83, mng. dir., gen. counsel, 1983-86; mng. dir., pres. First Boston Internat. Ltd., 1986-90; sr. exec. v.p., dir. Yamaichi Internat. (America), Inc., N.Y.C., 1990-95, vice-chmn., 1995-98; pres., CEO The Farrington Group, LLC, 1998—. Bd. dirs. Access Wellness Diagnostic Tech., Inc., ExcelAire Svcs., Inc.; adj. prof. law Fordham U., 1985—86; mem. U.S.-Japan Friendship Commn., Washington, 1990—94. Lt. USNR, 1966-69. Mem. Assn. Bar City N.Y., Racquet and Tennis Club, N.Y. Yacht Club, Ivy Club, Bucks Harbor Yacht Club (bd. govs. 1991—), The Nat. Assn. of Japan Am. Socs. (bd. dirs. 1998—). Republican. Presbyterian.

SEXTON, DIANA ELIZABETH, communications company executive; b. Hartford, Conn., Jan. 24, 1953; d. Donald E. and Johanna D. Sexton. BA, Smith Coll., 1974. Sales rep. The Archer Group, N.Y.C., 1974-81, sales mgr., 1981-86, v.p. mktg., 1986-92, The Arrow Group, Torrington, Conn., 1992-96, exec. v.p., 1996—. Mem. AAUW, Assn. for Profl. Women (v.p. 1996—), Women in the Arts, Mus. of Contemporary Arts, Wadsworth Atheneum. Avocations: watercolors, dance. Office: PO Box 2137 Torrington CT 06790-8137

SEXTON, DONALD LEE, retired business administration educator; b. New Boston, Ohio, June 14, 1932; s. Benjamin Franklin and Virgie Marie (Jordan) S.; m. Levonne Bradley, June, 1954 (div. June 1964); 1 child, Rhonda Jane; m. Carol Ann Schwaller, Dec. 18, 1965; children: David Lee, Douglas Edward. BS in Math. and Physics, Wilmington Coll., 1959; MBA, Ohio State U., 1966, PhD in Mgmt., 1972. Indsl. engr. Detroit Steel Corp., Portsmouth, Ohio, 1959-61; sr. rsch. engr. Rockwell Internat., Columbus, 1961-68; v.p. merchandising R.G. Barry Corp., 1968-74; v.p., gen. mgr. Henri Fayette, Inc., Chgo., 1976; gen. mgr. M.H. Mfg. Co., Jackson, Miss., 1976-77; assoc. prof. Sangamon State U., Springfield, Ill., 1977-79; Caruth prof. entrepreneurship Baylor U., Waco, Tex., 1979-86; Davis prof. free enterprise Ohio State U., Columbus, 1986-94, prof. emeritus, 1994—; dir. Nat. Ctr. for Entrepreneurial Rsch. Kauffman Found., Kansas City, Mo., 1994-97, scholar-in-residence, 1997-2000. Adj. faculty Nova Southeastern U., Ft. Lauderdale, Fla., 1997-99; mem. adv. bd. SBA, Columbus, 1986-94; rsch. adv. bd. U. So. Calif., L.A., 1986-90. Co-author: Entrepreneurship Education, 1981, Experiences in Small Business, 1982, Starting A Business in Texas, 1983; co-editor: Encyclopedia of Entrepreneurship, 1981, Art and Science of Entrepreneurship, 1986, Women Owned Business, 1989, Entrepreneurship: Creativity and Growth, 1990, The State of the Art of Entrepreneurship, 1991, Leadership and Entrepreneurship, 1996, Entrepreneurship: 2000, 1996, The Handbook of Entrepreneurship, 1999, Strategic Entrepreneurship, 2002. Served to staff sgt. USAF, 1951-55. Recipient Leavy Free Enterprise award Freedoms Found. Valley Forge, 1985, Cert. Appreciation SBA, Washington, 1984, 85, Outstanding Contbn. to Entrepreneurship Edn. award Assn. Coll. Entrepreneurs, 1991, Disting. Alumni award Wilmington Coll., 1993, Entrepreneurship Adv. of the Yr., 1997; named Adv. of Yr.-Innovation SBA, Dallas, 1982, 83, 84. Mem. Internat. Coun. for Small Bus. (sr. v.p. 1986), U.S. Assn. for Small Bus. (v.p. pub. rels. 1987), Acad. Mgmt. (chmn. entrepreneurship com. 1981, mem. adv. bd. 1984-85), Masons, Shriners, Eagles, Am. Legion, Alpha Tau Omega. Republican. Baptist. Avocation: golf. Home: 196 Bellerive Ln Summerville SC 29483-5032 E-mail: dlsexton@aol.com.

SEXTON, JEAN ELIZABETH, librarian; b. Boone, N.C., June 24, 1959; d. Warren G. and Carol Jean (Smith) S. AA, Chowan Coll., Murfreesboro, N.C., 1979; AB, U. N.C., 1981, MLS, 1983. Cataloging libr. U. N.C. (formerly Pembroke State U.), 1983-89, coord. tech. svcs., 1989-92, asst. dir., coord. tech. svcs., 1992—. Cons. Whitaker Libr. Chowan Coll., 1989-2001. Editor Libr. Lines, 1992, 1998-; contbr. articles to profl. jours. Order of Silver Feather. Mem. N.C. Libr. Assn., Southeastern Libr. Assn., Am. Henerocallis Soc., N.C. Zool. Soc., N.C. Aquarium Soc., Nat. Trust for Historic Preservation. Democrat. Baptist. Avocations: growing/breeding daylilies, collecting estate jewelry, needlework. Home: 8662 NC Highway 211 W Red Springs NC 28377-6036 Office: U NC Pembroke Sampson-Livermore Libr Pembroke NC 28372

SEXTON, JERRY LEE, multimedia company executive, consultant; b. Malden, Mo., Aug. 4, 1954; s. Jack and Ann (Yater) S.; m. Pamela Sue Mischler, May 20, 1984; children: Christopher James, Jennifer Nicole. BS in Mass. Comm., Fla. State U., 1976; MS in Pub. Rels., Am. U., 1984; postgrad., Air Command and Staff Coll., Maxwell AFB, Ala., 1990. Commd. 2d lt. USAF, 1976, advanced through grades to lt. col., 1991, comdr. Det. 13 1369 audiovisual squadron, 1980-81, mem. pub. rels. staff Office Sec. Def. Washington, 1981-84, dep. dir. ops. 1352 audiovisual squadron San Bernardino, Calif., 1984-87, dir. ops. 1363 audiovisual squadron Honolulu, 1987-90, comdr. Def. Visual Info. Sch. Denver, 1991-95; dir. ops. Media Lab Inc., Louisville, 1995-96; CEO Digital Metropolis Inc., Denver, 1996—. Instr. Leeward C.C., Honolulu, 1988-90; mem. faculty Denver U., 1995—; mem. adv. coun. Fed. Imaging Expositions, Washington, 1993-95, U. Colo., Denver, 1996—. Prodr. (multimedia CD) Hewlett-Packard HPVEE, 1997, (motion picture) Internment of the Unknown Soldier, 1985 (award 1985), (videotape) Armed Forces Day Nat. TV Spots, 1984, (multimedia prodn.) Mil. Airlift Command Briefing, 1987. Mem. Colo. Film and Video Assn., Nat. Press Photographers Assn. (conv. com. 1993-95), Denver Advt. Fedn., Air Force Assn., South Metro Denver C. of C. Republican. Baptist. Avocations: hiking, soccer, biking, computers, photography. Office: Digital Metropolis Inc 2000 Arapahoe St Apt 101 Denver CO 80205-2538

SEXTON, JOEL STEVEN, pathologist, forensic pathologist; b. Spartanburg, S.C., May 1, 1936; s. Charles Frank and Nuel (McAmis) Sexton; m. Lu Lynn Galt, Apr. 9, 1960; children: Sibyl Lynn Sexton Wessler, Steven Lawrence, Susan Lucinda, Shiela Louise. BA, U. Va., 1958; MS in Chemistry, Med. Coll. S.C., 1964; MD, Med. U. S.C., 1968. Diplomate in anat., clin. and forensic pathology Am. Bd. Pathology. From instr. chemistry to assoc. prof. Med. Coll. S.C., Charleston, 1961—79; assoc. prof. pathology Med. U. S.C., 1979-83; dir. pathology Newberry County Meml. Hosp., Newberry, SC, 1983—. County med. examiner Charleston County, 1973-83; cons. forensic pathologist Newberry Pathology ASsocs., 1983—. Lt. USN, 1959-61. Named Nat. Pistol Shooting Coach of Yr., U.S. Olympic Com., 1998. Fellow Am. Acad. Forensic Sci., Coll. Am. Pathologists (insp.); mem. AMA, Nat. Assn. Med. Examiners, Am. & Can. Acad. Pathology, S.C. Soc. Pathologists, Internat. Assn. for Indentification. Methodist. Avocations: pistol shooting and coaching college team, fishing, hunting. Office: Newberry County Memorial Hosp PO Box 839 Newberry SC 29108-0839

SEXTON, JOHN EDWARD, lawyer, dean, law educator; b. Bklyn., Sept. 29, 1942; s. John Edward and Catherine (Humann) S.; m. Lisa Ellen Goldberg; children: Jed, Katherine. BA, Fordham U., 1963, PhD, 1978; JD, Harvard U., 1979. Bar: N.Y. 1981, U.S. Supreme Ct. 1984. Prof. religion St. Francis Coll., Bklyn., 1965-75; law clk. U.S. Ct. Appeals, Washington, 1979, 80, U.S. Supreme Ct., Washingtont, 1980-81; prof. law NYU, N.Y.C., 1981—, dean law sch., 1988—2002, pres., 2002—. Dir. Washington Sq. Legal Services, N.Y.C., 1983—, Pub. Interest Law Found., N.Y.C., 1983-85. Author: A Managerial Model of the Supreme Court, 1985, Federal Jury Instructions-Civil, 1985, How Free Are We? A Study of the Constitution, 1985, Cases and

Materials in Civil Procedure, 1988. Dir. Root-Tilden Scholarship Program, 1984-88. Mem. Assn. of Am. Law Schs. (pres. 1997-98). Home: 29 Washington Sq W New York NY 10011-9180 Office: NYU 70 Washington Sq S New York NY 10012-1099*

SEXTON, JOHN JOSEPH, oral and maxillofacial surgeon, educator; b. Boston, Dec. 4, 1947; s. Bernard Thomas and Margaret Theresa (Carrigg) S.; m. Judith Whelden, Aug. 21, 1971; 1 child, Benjamin. BS, Boston Coll., 19770; DMD, Tufts U., 1975; MScD, Boston U., 1978, CAGS, 1979. Diplomate Am. Bd. Oral and Maxillofacial Surgery. Orthognathic fellow Boston U. Inst. for Correction of Facial Deformities, 1976-77; intern, jr. resident, chief resident Boston U./Tufts U., 1975-79; asst. prof. Goldman Sch. Dental Medicine, Boston U., 1979-81; chief oral and maxillofacial surgery Beth Israel Hosp., Boston, 1981—, dir. maxillofacial trauma svc., 1990—, dir. mucosal disorders unit, 1990—. Cons. dermatology Beth Israel Hosp.; asst. prof. oral and maxillofacial surgery Harvard Med. Sch., Boston. Contbr. numerous articles to profl. jours. Avocations: philosophy, physics, history, travel. Office: Beth Israel Hosp 372 Washington St Wellesley MA 02481 also: Beth Israel Deaconess and Oral Maxillofacial Surgery 372 Washington St Ste 2500 Wellesley MA 02481-6202

SEXTON, KAREN KAY, piano teacher, singer, actress; b. Knoxville, Iowa, Jan. 28, 1943; d. Eugene Hufford and Stella Arloise (Smith) Dodds; m. Loren Lee Splittgerber, June 10, 1962 (div. July 1970); 1 child, Brek Loren; m. Charles Benny Sexton, Sept. 6, 1970. Student, U. Oreg., Eugene, 1960-61, U. Colo., 1961-62. Cert. Master's Tchr., 1975. Singer Houston Pops Orch., 1980-82; actress, Dallas, 1988—; ind. piano tchr. Sexton Piano Studio, Mission Viejo, Calif., 1972-77, Houston, 1977-82, Plano, Tex., 1982—. Adjudicator in numerous states, 1979—; singer Dallas Symphony Chorus, 1995—; speaker and panel mem. numerous local, regional and state confs. Author articles; appeared in comml. and indsl. films. Vol. Rep. Party, Mission Viejo, 1974, Am. Heart Assn., Plano, 1995—. Mem. Nat. Guild Piano Tchrs. (adjudicator), Houston Piano Tchrs. Forum (pres. 1978-82), Houston Music Tchrs. Assn., Music Tchrs. Nat. Assn. Tex. Music Tchrs. Assn. (dist. chmn.), Dallas Music Tchrs. Assn. (pres. 1990-92). Republican. Baptist. Avocations: tennis, handiwork, reading. Home and Office: 6800 Honey Creek Ln Plano TX 75023-2045

SEXTON, MARY ANN, information systems professional, music educator, pastoral musician; b. Omaha, Sept. 15, 1951; d. Walter Dudley and Josephine Mary Hoffmann James; m. Michael Herman Sexton, Dec. 30, 1978; children: Paul Michael, Bridget Marie, Stephanie Josephine. B in Music Edn., U. Nebr., 1973; MA in Pastoral Studies, U. St. Thomas, 1999. Tchr. Holy Name H.S., Omaha, 1973-74, Duschene Acad., Omaha, 1974-76; computer programmer Burroughs Corp., St. Paul, 1976-81; computer tchr. Dakota County Tech. Coll., Rosemount, 1983-93; database adminstr. Minn. Citizens Concerned for Life, Mpls., 1993—. Accompanist St. Joseph Cath. Ch., Rosemount, 1979-98; pvt. piano tchr., Apple Valley, Eagen, Minn., 1984—; music dir. St. Michael's Cath. Ch., West St. Paul, 1998—; historic interpreter Minn. Hist. Soc., Mpls., 1985-93. State del. Dem. Party, Minn., 1978, 80, Rep. Party, Minn., 1996, 98, 2002; mem. Health and Human Svcs. Adv. Com., Dakota County, 1981-88; singer Dakota Valley Civic Chorus, 1992-97, 2001-. Mem. Minn. Music Tchrs. Assn. Roman Catholic. Avocations: sewing, knitting.

SEXTON, OWEN JAMES, vertebrate ecology educator, conservationist; b. Phila., July 11, 1926; s. Gordon and Elizabeth May (Evans) S.; m. Mildred Lewis Bloomsburg, Apr. 5, 1952; children: Kenneth, Jean, Ann, Carolyn. Student, Sampson Coll., 1947-48; BA, Oberlin Coll., 1951; MA, U. Mich., 1953, PhD, 1956. Sr. teaching fellow Washington U., St. Louis, 1955-56, instr., 1956-57, asst. prof., 1957-62, assoc. prof., 1962-68, prof. vertebrate ecology, 1968-97, dir. Tyson Rsch. Ctr., 1996-99, prof. emeritus, 1998—, dir. emeritus, 2001—. Vis. prof. U. Mich. Biol. Sta., Pellston, 1975-83; cons. UNESCO, 1974-75; adj. curator St. Louis Sci. Ctr., 1986-88. Pres., bd. dirs. Mo. Prairie Found., Columbia, 1968-99; pres. Wild Canid Survival and Research Ctr., St. Louis, 1971-73; sec. Contemporary Art Soc., 1972-73; bd. dirs. Creve Coeur Figure Skating Club, 1982-89; mem. membership com. U.S. Figure Skating Assn., 1987-90. NSF fellow, 1966-67; vis. research fellow U. New Eng., 1984. Fellow Herpetologists League; mem. Am. Soc. Icthyologists and Herpetologists, Ecol. Soc. Am., Soc. Study of Amphibians and Reptiles, Orgn. Tropical Studies (bd. dir. 1976-85). Democrat. Home: 13154 Greenbough Dr Saint Louis MO 63146-3622 Office: Tyson Rsch Ctr PO Box 258 Eureka MO 63025 E-mail: sexton@biology.wustl.edu.

SEXTON, ROBERT FENIMORE, educational organization executive; b. Cin., Jan. 13, 1942; s. Claude Fenimore and Jane (Wisenall) S.; m. Pam Peyton Papka, Sept. 15, 1985; children: Rebecca, Robert B., Ouita Papka, Paige Papka, Perry Papka. BA, Yale U., 1964; MA in History, U. Wash., Seattle, 1968, PhD in History, 1970; DHL (hon.), Berea Coll., 1990, Georgetown Coll., Ky., 1993, Eastern Ky. U., 2000. Asst. prof. history Murray (Ky.) State U., 1968-70; dir. Office Acad. Programs, Commonwealth of Ky., Frankfort, 1970-73; assoc. dean, exec. dir. Office Exptl. Edn. U. Ky., Lexington, 1973-80; dep. exec. dir. Ky. Coun. Higher Edn., Frankfort, 1980-83; exec. dir. Prichard Com. for Acad. Excellence, Lexington, 1983—; founder, pres. Ky. Ctr. Pub. Issues, 1988—. Vis. scholar Harvard U., Cambridge, Mass., 1992, 94; chair Nat. Ctr. for Internships, Washington, 1973-80, Coalition for Alternatives in Post-Secondary Edn., Washington, 1977-80; bd. dirs. Editl. Projects in Edn., Consortium Policy Rsch. in Edn., Ky. Long Term Policy Rsch. Ctr., Edn. Commn. of the States; adv. bd. Consortium for Prodn. in Schs., 1992-94. Pub. The Ky. Jour., 1988-2001; editor book series: Public Papers of Governors of Kentucky, 1973-86; contbr. articles to profl. jours. Co-chmn. Carnegie Ctr. for Literacy, Lexington, 1990-93; mem. Gov.'s Task Force on Health Care, Frankfort, 1992—; bd. dirs. Ky. Inst. Edn. Rsch. Fund for Improvement in Postsecondary Edn., 1993-2000; chair Bluegrass Edn. Work Coun., Lexington, 1978-80; founder, steering com. Gov.'s Scholars Program, Frankfort, 1983-85. Recipient Charles A. Dana award for pioneering achievement, 1994. Mem. Am. Assn. Higher Edn. (bd. dirs. 1979-83). Democrat. Avocations: fishing, travel. Office: Prichard Com Acad Excell 167 W Main St Ste 310 Lexington KY 40507-1702

SEXTON, WENDELL PHILLIP JAMES, elementary school educator; b. Kansas City, Mo., Mar. 28, 1928; BA, Ctrl. State U., Wilberforce, Ohio, 1954; postgrad. studies in Elem. Edn., Ind. U., Gary, 1962, U. Mo., Kansas City, 1964. Cert. tchr. Colo, Tex. Substitute tchr. Gary (Ind.) Pub. Schs.; tchr. Warren Beatty Me. Hosp., Westfield, Ind., Chgo. Pub. Schs.; writer Gary (Ind.)Crusader; tchr. Denver Pub. Sch.; interviewer Tex. Employment Office, Houston. Writer- in-residence Tex. Commn. on Arts, Palestine, 1974—75; writer, mem. Tex. Commn. on the Arts, Austin, 1975—2001. Author: (book) Why Should I Love the White Man, 1970, Poet's Corner, 1975. V. p. Turner Elementary Sch. Coun., Houston, 1991. Mem.: NAACP, Buffalo Soldiers, Kappa Alpha Phi. Avocations: boxing, dancing, genealogy, mathematics. Home: 4303 Rosebud Dr Houston TX 77053 E-mail: KappaDad@aol.com.

SEXTON ATKINS, JANNAH, artist, educator; b. Frankfurt, Germany, Sept. 10, 1951; d. Thomas Logan Sexton and Wanda Jean (Spurlock) Ingram; m. Charles E. Atkins, Apr. 13, 1985. AA, Kauai C.C., Hawaii, 1975; studied sculptural clay with Toshiko Takaezu, 1975; cert., Windtree Sch. Drawing and Illustration, 1990; studied with David Passalacqua, studied monoprints with Rodney Konopaki, 1990, studied with David Passalacqua; BFA cum laude, U. Alaska, Anchorage, 1990, BA cum laude, 1992. Art educator various Alaskan arts orgns., Alaska, 1990—; art dir. ARCA Murals, 1993-94; dir. and owner Earthwind Studio, Anchorage, 1994—; curator of exhibits Alaska Pacific U., 1995—; curator Alaska Contemporary Art Bank Alaska State Coun. on Arts, 1997—. Leader various art workshops, 1991-94; bd. dirs. Visual Arts Ctr. Alaska, 1992-94, exhbn. coord., 1992; vol. juror asst. Anchorage Mus. History and Art, 1993; exhbn. coord. Grandview Gardens Cultural Ctr., Alaska, 1994; art juror reflections program Nat. PTA, 1995; display asst. Nordstroms, 1995-96; scenic artist Anchorage Opera, 1995-96; mural asst. Blaines Art Supply, 1996, 97, 98; adj. prof. art history Alaska Pacific U., Anchorage, 1996—. Exhibitions include Callanetics Studio, Anchorage, 1995, Stonington Gallery, Anchorage, 1995, Pratt Mus., Homer, 1996, Alaska Pacific U., Anchorage, 1996, Fireweed Gallery, Homer, 1996, Blaines Art and Frame, Homer, 1996, Toast Gallery, Anchorage, 1997, Bunnell St. Gallery, Homer, Alaska, 1997; represented in permanent collections Pratt Mus.; represented in pvt. collections. Pol. advocacy advisor People First, Anchorage, 1993-95; rep. arts adv. commn. Municipality of Anchorage, 1994—. Recipient Ceramic award Kauai C.C. Arts Festival, 1975, Hon. Mention U. Alaska, Anchorage, 1988, 1989, Best Graphic Design/Illustration, 1990, hon. mention Am. Coll. Theatre Festival and Northwest Drama Competition, 1989, XXIV all Alaska juried, 1992; Alaska Found. scholar, 1984, 85, 86, 87; Chancellor's scholar, 1986, 87; Saradell Ard scholar, 1989, 90. Avocations: art, skiing, mountain biking. Home and Office: 1747 Talkeetna St Anchorage AK 99508-3244

SEYB, LESLIE PHILIP, chemist, researcher; b. Franklin, Iowa, May 11, 1915; s. Hugo Philip and Clara Magdalena (Wahres) Seyb; m. Helen Standiford, Nov. 18, 1939 (dec. Sept. 1998); children: Stefan Michael, Stanford Philip; m. Lucille Harnden, Aug. 15, 1999. BA, Coe Coll., 1935; MS, U. Iowa, 1937, PhD, 1939. Patent atty. asst. Phillips Petroleum Co., Bartlesville, Okla., 1939—42; chem. group leader Diamond Alkali Co., Painesville, Ohio, 1942—50, mgr. rsch., 1950—56, assoc. dir. rsch., 1956—63; sr. scientist Pacific NW Water Lab., Corvallis, Oreg., 1964—70; assoc. dir. rsch. U.S. Environ. Lab., 1970—75; sr. scientist U.S. EPA, 1975—78. Co-author: (novels) Seyb Genealogy, 1952; patentee in field. Chmn. troop com. Boy Scouts, Painesville, 1962—64; chmn. Phi Lambda Upsilon, Iowa City, 1938—39. Mem.: Am. Chem. Soc. (chmn. 1960—61), Sigma Xi. Avocations: hiking, reading, gardening, bridge, fishing. Home: 2960 NW Jackson Ave Corvallis OR 97330-5106

SEYBERT, JANET ROSE, lawyer, military officer; b. Cin., Feb. 7, 1944; d. Peter Robert and Helen Rose (Young) S. BA in Classics, BS in Edn., U. Cin., 1966; MA in Classics, U. Iowa, 1968; JD, Chase Coll. Law, 1975; ML, Army JAG Sch., 1984. Bar: Ohio 1975, U.S. Ct. Mil. Appeals 1975, Colo. 1981, U.S. Ct. Claims 1985; cert. mortgage investor; cert. profl. clown. Instr. Latin, ancient history Salem Coll., Winston-Salem, N.C., 1968-70; instr. N.C. Gov.'s Sch., 1969; instr. phys. edn., Latin Kemper Hall, Kenosha, Wis., 1970-71; instr. in Latin Carthage Coll., 1970-71; commd. 2d lt. USMC, 1972; completed interservice transfer to USAF, 1978, advanced through grades to maj., 1982, lawyer USAF Acad. Colo., 1978-81; chief civil law Sheppard AFB, Tex., 1981-84; dep. staff judge adv., chief mil. justice Homestead AFB, Fla., 1984-88; chief civil law Lowry AFB, Colo., 1988-91; pvt. practice, 1991—; owner, pres. The Seybert Funding Cos., 1991—. Atty. The Seybert Funding Cos.; legal advisor Armed Forces Disciplinary Control Bd., Child and Family Advocacy Coun. USAF, Homestead AFB, 1984-88; designer handicapped accessible houses. Vol. Muscular Dystrophy Assn., Colorado Springs, 1978-81; contbr. Ellis Island Resoration Program, Homestead AFB, 1985-88; active Nat. Mus. Women in Arts, Nat. Air and Space Mus.; officer in charge Lowry Silver and Blue Choir; charter mem. Women in Military Svc. to Am. Meml. Mem. ABA, Judge Adv. Assn., Edn. Profl. Assn., Ohio Bar Assn., Fed. Bar Assn., Colo. Bar Assn., Colo. Women's Bar Assn., Am. Bus. Women's Assn. (chmn. audit com. Homestead charter chpt., hist. com. 1987, pres. Visions charter chpt. 1990-91, 91-92, Top 10 Bus. Women 1987, Woman of Yr. 1987), Am. Legion, Ret. Officers Assn., Colo. Clowns, Phi Beta Kappa, Kappa Delta Pi. Avocations: photography, woodcarving, knitting, drawing, crocheting. Home: 1175 S Lima St Aurora CO 80012-4111

SEYBERT, JOANNA, federal judge; b. Bklyn., Sept. 18, 1946; BA, U. Cin., 1967; JD, St. John's U., 1971. Bar: N.Y. 1972, U.S. Dist. Ct. (ea. and so. dists.) N.Y. 1973. Trial staff atty. Legal Aid Soc., N.Y.C., 1971-73, sr. staff atty. Mineola, N.Y., 1976-80; sr. trial atty. Fed. Defender Svc., Bklyn., 1973-75; bur. chief Nassau County Atty's Office, Mineola, 1980-87; judge Nassau County Dist. Ct., Hempstead, N.Y., 1987-92, Nassau County Ct., Mineola, 1992-94, U.S. Dist. Ct. (ea. dist.) N.Y., Uniondale, 1994—. Mem.: Nassau Lawyers Assn. (past pres.), Fed. Judges Assn. (v.p.), Theodore Roosevelt A. Inns of Ct. (past pres.), Bar Assn. Nassau County, Internat. Assn. Judges (del.). Office: 1034 Federal Plz Central Islip NY 11722-4443

SEYBOLDT, CAROLINE, interior decorator, artist; b. Lincoln, Nebr., Mar. 28, 1931; d. Arthur John and Erna (Lohrmann) Doege; children: Charles, David, Ann Duffy, Steven. BA in Polit. Sci., Valparaiso U., 1953. Cert. ICD. Dir. TransDesigns, Ft. Wayne, Ind. Cons. interior decoration, Ft. Wayne. Artist: permanent display Concordia Sem., Ft. Wayne. Recipient Bus. Excellence awards, 1987, '89. Home: 115 Bent Creek Blvd Lake Lure NC 28746-9700

SEYDEL, JOHN, university educator; PhD, Texas A&M U., 1990. Asst. prof. U. Miss., Oxford, 1990—95; assoc. prof., dept. chair Ark. State U., Jonesboro, 1995—. Gen. mgr. Seydel Design & Consulting, Jonesboro, 1972—2002. Commr. McCall Planning & Zoning Commn. 1st lt. U.S. Army, 1971—72. Mem.: Soc. Mfg. Engrs. (chpt. chmn. 1994—95, Disting. Svc. award 1993). Office: Ark State Univ PO Box 239 State University AR 72467

SEYDEL, ROBERT EMORY, mathematician, educator; b. Davenport, Iowa, Aug. 29, 1942; s. Robert Emory and Mildred Faye (Gauley) Seydel; m. Wanda Jean Bontrager; children: Robert Emory, Matthew Raymond, Joy Elena Maria. BS, Iowa Wesleyan Coll., 1965; MS, Colo. State U., 1968, Ga. Inst., 1980; PhD, U. Iowa, 1973. Cert. tchr. Ill., Mo., Ill. Assoc. prof. math. No. State U., Aberdeen, SD, 1977—78; engr. Kockheed Missile Space, Sunnyvale, Calif., 1980—83, Kaiser Aerospace Co., San Jose, 1983—85, McDonnell Douglas Co., St. Louis, 1986—88; assoc. prof. math. Quincy (Ill.) U., 1988—90; physics tchr. Duchesne H.S., St. Charles, Mo., 2000—01; math. tchr. Southeastern H.S., Augusta, Ill., 2001—. Substitute tchr. St. Charles County schs., 1990—2000; adj. prof. math. San Jose State U., 1983, U. Mo., St. Louis, 1988; jr. coll. tchr. Evergreen Vocat. C.C., Cabrillo Coll., 1981—92. Fellow, U. Tex., 1965. Mem.: NEA, Soc. Indsl. and Applied Math., Math. Assn. Am., Am. Math. Soc. Republican. Mem. United Ch. Of Christ. Avocations: hiking, camping. Home: 2427 Spring St Quincy IL 62301 Office: Southeastern HS PO Box 155 Augusta IL 62311 E-mail: DoctorBob59@hotmail.

SEYDNEJAD, SAEID REZA, engineering educator, consultant; b. Tehran, Iran, Sept. 1, 1965; s. Mehdi and Mehrangiz (Niknafs Kermani) S. BSc, Sistan & Baluchestan U., Zahedan, Iran, 1988; MSc, Sharif U. Tech., Tehran, Iran, 1991; PhD, Imperial Coll., London, 1998. Elec. engring.; biomed. engring. Lectr. Sistan & Baluchestan U., Zahedan, Iran, 1991-94; lectr. Azad U., Iran, 1992-93; sr. engr. Electroteb Co., Iran, 1992-94; DSP engr. GE Power Control Sys., Toronto, Ont., Can., 1997-2000; DSP design engr. optical networks Nortel Networks, Ottawa, Can., 2000—; sr. elec. engr. Royal Old Brompton Hosp., London, 1998. Cons. engr. Zahedan (Iran) Med. U., 1992-93. Contbr. articles to profl. jours. Mem. IEEE, Iranian Inst. Elec. Engrs. Avocations: camping, sports, music, travel. Office: Nortel Networks 1341 Baseline Ave Ottawa Canada K2C 0A7 E-mail: saeid_seyd@yahoo.com.

SEYDOUX, GERALDINE, molecular biologist; BS, U. Maine, 1986; PhD in Molecular Genetics, Princeton U., 1991. Postdoctoral trainee Carnegie Instn. Washington, Balt., 1991—95; asst. prof. molecular biology and genetics Sch. Medicine Johns Hopkins U., 1995—. Recipient Jr. Faculty Rsch. award, Am. Cancer Soc., 1996, Searle Scholars award, 1997, Presdl. Early Career award for scientists and engrs., NIH, 1999; fellow, Packard Found., 1996; scholar Basil O'Connor Starter scholar, March of Dimes, 1996. Office: Johns Hopkins U Sch Medicine 725 N Wolfe St 1515 PCTB Baltimore MD 21205*

SEYFERT, WAYNE GEORGE, secondary education educator, anatomy educator; b. Roslyn Park, N.Y., Nov. 23, 1947; s. George William Seyfert and Helen Francis (Weiss) Marks; m. Kathleen A. Kearns, May 23, 1970 (div. 1980); children: Sean Francis, Kerry Noelle, Adam Wayne. BS in Biology, SUNY, Cortland, 1969; MS in Biology, L.I. U. at C.W. Post, 1973; profl. diploma in sch. adminstrn., CUNY at Queen's Coll., N.Y.C., 1988. Cert. biology and secondary sci. tchr., N.Y.; cert. sch. adminstr. and supr., N.Y.; cert. sch. dist. adminstr., N.Y. Jr. h.s. sci. tchr. Port Washington (N.Y.) Schs., 1969-70; sci. tchr. Lawrence (N.Y.) Pub. Schs., 1970—; instr. North Shore Sci. Mus., Plandome, N.Y., 1973-75; adj. prof. human anatomy and physiology Nassau C.C., Garden City, 1975—, N.Y. Inst. Tech., 1994—. Summer program dir. Sci. Mus. L.I., Plandome, 1976-85; environ. cons. Town of Brookhaven, L.I., 1978-80. Contbr. articles to profl. publs. Membership chmn. Boy Scouts Am., Sunrise dist., N.Y., 1978-79; mem. conservation adv. coun. Town of Brookhaven, 1977-79; mem. L.I. Sci. Congress exec. bd., 1985-98. Recipient Ednl. Leadership award Lawrence Ednl. Found., 1998, named L.I. Educator of Month, Hofstra U./TV Channel 12, L.I., 1995, Person of the Yr., Nassau Herald, 1998, STANYS Nassau County H.S. Sci. tchr. of yr., 1998. Mem. AAAS, Am. Fedn. Tchrs., Adj. Faculty Assn., Nat. Sci. Tchrs. Assn., Nat. Biology Tchr. Assn., Am. Philatelic Soc., Am. 1st Day Cover Soc., Am. Revenue Assn., Am. Perfin Soc., Am. Precanceled Stamp Soc., United Postal Stationary Soc., Meter Stamp Soc., State Revenue Assn., Am. Airmail Soc., Earlygomme Soc., Christmas Seal and Charity Seal Soc., N.Y. Acad. Scis., N.Y. State United Tchrs., Sci. Tchrs. Assn. N.Y. State, L.I. Cover Soc., Lawrence Tchrs. Assn. (1st v.p. 1984-2001), MACUB Soc. for Neutobiology. Achievements include writing first history of America's first prairie and performance of first environmental study to trace an area's environmental change since first European encroachment. Home: PO Box 116 Woodmere NY 11598-0116 Office: Lawrence HS 2 Reilly Rd Cedarhurst NY 11516-1002

SEYFERTH, DIETMAR, chemist, educator; b. Chemnitz, Germany, Jan. 11, 1929; came to U.S., 1933; s. Herbert C. and Elisabeth (Schuchardt) S.; m. Helena A. McCoy, Aug. 25, 1956; children— Eric Steven, Karl Dietmar, Elisabeth Mary. BA summa cum laude, U. Buffalo, 1951, MA, 1953; PhD, Harvard, 1955; Dr. honoris causa, U. Aix-Marseille, 1979, Paul Sabatier Univ., Toulouse, France, 1992. Fulbright scholar Tech. Hochschule, Munich, Germany, 1954-55; postdoctoral fellow Harvard U., 1956-57; faculty MIT, 1957—, prof. chemistry, 1965-2000, prof. emeritus, 2000—, Robert T. Haslam and Bradley Dewey prof., 1983-99. Cons. to industry, 1957—; prof. emeritus, 2000—. Author: Annual Surveys of Organometallic Chemistry, 3 vols, 1965, 66, 67; regional editor: Jour. Organometallic Chemistry, 1963-81; coordinating editor revs. and survey sects., 1964-81; editor: Organometallics, 1981— ; contbr. research papers to profl. lit. Recipient Disting. Alumnus award U. Buffalo, 1964, Alexander von Humboldt Found. sr. award, 1984, Clifford C. Furnas Meml. award SUNY-Buffalo, 1987; Guggenheim fellow, 1968. Fellow AAAS, Am. Inst. Chemists, Inst. Materials, Am. Acad. Arts and Scis.; mem. NAS, Am. Chem. Soc. (Frederic Stanley Kipping award in organosilicon chemistry 1972, disting. svc. award advancement inorganic chemistry 1981, award in organometallic chemistry, 1996, Arthur C. Cope Sr. Scholar award 2003), Materials Rsch. Soc., Am. Ceramic Soc., Royal Soc. Chemistry, Gesellschaft Deutscher Chemiker, German Acad. Scientists-Leopoldina, Phi Beta Kappa, Sigma Xi. Office: MIT 77 Massachusetts Ave Rm 4-382 Cambridge MA 02139-4307 E-mail: seyferth@mit.edu.

SEYFERTH, VIRGINIA M. public relations executive; b. Detroit; BA, Grand Valley State U., Allendale, Mich. With pub. rels. dept. St. Jude Children's Rsch. Hosp., 1977-79, AMOCO Oil Co., 1979-81, Amway Corp., 1981-84; pres. Seyferth & Assocs., Inc., Grand Rapids, Mich., 1984—. Office: Seyferth & Assocs Inc Ste 202 40 Monroe Ctr. NW Grand Rapids MI 49503*

SEYHOUN, HOUSHANG, architect; b. Tehran, Iran, Aug. 22, 1920; s. Zia and Moloud S.; m. Nouchine Massoumeh, May 11, 1953; children: Maryam, Nader. Grad., Faculty Fine Arts, U. Tehran, 1944; D d'état, Nat. Superior Sch. Fine Arts, Paris, 1948. Asst. Faculty Fine Arts, U. Tehran, 1949-53; prof. U. Tehran, 1953; dean of faculty Faculty Fine Arts, U. Tehran, 1962-70; mem. coun. Tehran City Hall, 1967-71. Lectr. on architecture, art; interviewee in field; lectr. tour of N.E. U.S., 1986, including presentations at the Smithsonian Inst., Washington, Harvard U., Columbia U. and others. Mem. editing com. Architecture Francaise; prin. works include monuments in memory of Avicenna at Hamadan, Khayam at Neychabour, Nader Shah at Machhad, Sepah Bank of Tehran; exhibits include religious art of mankind Musee hors du Temps, Nice, France, 1981 (hon. French citizenship), U. So. Calif., L.A., 1989 (spl. presentation from mayor and dean Sch. Architecture), World Bank, Washington, Ferry Bldg., 1989, Wests Vancouver Libr., 1984-85, also others; author: Regards Sur Liran, 1974, Half a Century of Artistic Activities in the World of Art and Architecture, 1998. Mem. Mcpl. Coun. City Tehran, Coun. Urbanization Iran; v.p. I.C.O.M.O.S.; mem. Higher Coun. U. Iran, Coun. Urban Devel. in Iran. Mem. Iranian Architects Soc. (pres.). Home: 2066 Marine Dr West Vancouver BC Canada V7V 1J9 Fax: 604-926-6519.

SEYMORE, PEARL, interior design consultant; b. Bklyn., Aug. 15, 1927; d. Joe and Tania Bard; student Bklyn. Coll., 1945-47, Pratt Inst., 1952-56, New Sch. Social Research, N.Y. U.; m. Lutzker Seymore, Mar. 2, 1947 (div. July 1960); children— Rochelle Diane Lewis, Amy Sharon Gottlieb. Salesperson, Charles S. Nathan, Inc., N.Y.C., 1956-60, dir. design, 1960-65, v.p. in charge design and sales coordination, 1965-69; dir. design Brenner Desk & Design Co., Newark, 1969-75; design, sales coordinator Gen. Office Equipment Co., Saddlebrook, N.J., 1975-79; owner Pearl Seymore Design Assocs., Inc., Hackensack, N.J., 1979— . Work pub. in profl. publs. Recipient Design awards Mcpl. Bldg., City Long Beach, N.Y., 1964, Berlitz Sch. Lang, Rockefeller Center, N.Y., 1965, Internat. Flavors and Fragrances, N.Y.C., 1967. Mem. Am. Soc. Interior Designers, Inst. Bus. Designers, Designers Lighting Forum, Nat. Trust for Historic Preservation, Meadowlands C. of C., N.J. Soc. Architects, Commerce and Industry Assn. No. N.J. Office: 479 Main St Hackensack NJ 07601-5932

SEYMOUR, BARBARA LAVERNE, lawyer; b. Columbia, S.C., July 9, 1953; d. Leroy Semon and Barbara Lucile (Youngblood) Seymour. BS, S.C. State Coll., 1975; JD, Georgetown U., 1979; MBA, Harvard U., 1985. Bar: S.C. 1979, Tex. 1984, U.S. Dist. Ct. (ea. dist.) Tex. 1983, U.S. Dist. Ct. (so. dist.) Tex. 1985, U.S. Tax Ct. 1986, U.S. Claims Ct. 1991. Tax atty. Texaco Inc., White Plains, N.Y., 1979-80, Houston, 1980-98; exec. asst. Office of the CFO-Gen. Counsel, Equilon Enterprises LLC, 1998-99, asst. sec., counsel, 1999—. Mem. IRS Commr.'s Adv. Group, 1995-97; mem. Simplified Tax and Wage Reporting Sys. Working Group, 1994-97; loaned exec. for task force to audit Tex. Employment Commn. by Gov. of Tex., 1987-88. Troop leader Girl Scouts U.S., White Plains, 1979-80, asst. troop leader, Houston, 1981-82; bd. dirs. Sickle Cell Assn. of the Tex. Gulf Coast, Houston, 1986-92, treas., 1986-88, pres., 1988-90, chair 25th ann. gala, 1996; vol. allocation panel United Way of the Tex. Gulf Coast; bd. dirs. Found. for Main St., The Assistance Fund, Sandra Organ Dance Co., v.p., 2000—; mem. Black Exec. Exch. program Nat. Urban League 1980-; bd. dirs., exec. com. Houston Area Urban League, 1995-2001, 3d v.p., 1998-2000, 2001—, treas. 2002—, 1st v.p., 2000-2001, chair 1997 Equal Opportunity Day Dinner, co-chair Host Com., Nat. Urban League Conf., 99; bd. dirs., asst. treas. Sheila Jackson Lee for Congress, 1995-97. Named one of 50 Outstanding Young Leaders of the Future, Ebony Mag., 1983; recipient Disting. Bus. Alumnus award S.C. State Coll., 1991, Eagle award Nat. Eagle Leadership Inst., 1995; selected for Leadership Houston, Leadership Am., 1990; finalist Five Outstanding Young Houstonians award Jaycees, 1988, one of 10 Foremost Fashionables in Houston, Alpha Kappa Alpha, 1994; named 2001's ABC channel 13 Woman of Distinction. Mem. ABA (environ. tax com., employment tax com.), Houston Black Women Lawyers Assn. (sec. 1981-82, treas. 1982-83), Houston Bus. Forum (bd. dirs. 1983, 87-90, treas. 1988-89, sec. 1989-90), Nat. Bar Assn. (com. chmn. 1982-83), S.C. Bar Assn., Tex. Bar Assn., Harvard U. Bus. Sch. Black Alumni Assn. (historian 1985-86), Black Law Alumni Coun. of Georgetown U. Law Ctr., W.J. Durham Soc., The Links, Inc. (v.p. Houston chpt. 1996-2000, pres. 2000—, chair 1995 Cotillion), Alpha Kappa Alpha. Democrat. Roman Catholic. Office: Equilon Enterprises LLC 1100 Louisiana St Ste 1066 Houston TX 77002-5220 E-mail: blseymour@equilon.com.

SEYMOUR, DOROTHY Z. See MILLS, DOROTHY

SEYMOUR, EVERETT HEDDEN, JR. lawyer; b. Tuxedo Park, N.Y., Apr. 16, 1958; s. Everett Hedden and Deborah (Robinson) S. BA, Yale U., 1980; JD, U. Va., 1986. Bar: N.Y. 1988, U.S. Dist. Ct. (so. and ea. dists.) N.Y. 1988, Conn. 1988, U.S. Dist. Ct. Conn. 1988. Law clk. to justice U.S. Dist. Ct., New Haven, 1986-87; assoc. Davis Polk & Wardwell, N.Y.C., 1987-97; v.p., asst. gen. counsel J.P. Morgan Chase & Co., 1997—. Articles rev. editor U. Va. Law Rev., 1984-86. Office: JP Morgan Chase & Co 270 Park Ave 39th Fl New York NY 10017-2014

SEYMOUR, FREDERICK PRESCOTT, JR. industrial engineer, consultant; b. Oak Park, Ill., June 19, 1924; s. Frederick Prescott and Ivy Louise (Horder) S.; m. Janet Mary Stocking, Oct. 15, 1960; children: Robert Prescott, Bruce Stocking, Mary Janet. BS, Cornell U., 1948; MS in Commerce, U. Ill., 1951; MBA, U. Chgo., 1957. Indsl. engr., dir. planning, exec. salesman R.R. Donnelley and Sons Co./Lakeside Press, Chgo., 1951-72; regional dir. U.S. Postal Svc., 1972-76; dir. advt. Spiegel, Inc., 1976-80; pres. Frederick P. Seymour and Assocs., Inc., Winnetka, Ill., 1980—. Pres. Cornell Univ. Club. Chgo., 1960-61, Exec. Program Club, Chgo., 1972-73; mem. Postmaster Gen.'s adv. com., Washington, 1973—. Contbg. editor: Gravure mag., 1982—; contbr. articles to profl. jours. Precinct capt. New Trier Rep. Orgn., Winnetka,

1970-72. With USN, 1944-46, PTO. Mem. ASME (life), Cornell Soc. Engrs., Graphic Communications Assn. (Innovator award 1988), Gravure Assn. Am., Graphic Arts Industry Rsch. and Engring. Coun. (exec. com.), Econ. Club Chgo.

SEYMOUR, JAMES CRAIG, theater educator, actor, director; b. Millburn, N.J., Dec. 5, 1948; s. Ralph devillers Seymour and Francis Mary Craig Seymour-Brown; m. Libby McNeill, Sept. 19, 1983 (div. June 1989); 1 child, Alexandra McNeill; m. Larissa Plaxa, June 28, 1996; 1 stepchild, Vadim. BA, Boston U., 1971; MA, MPhil, CUNY, 1995, PhD, 1997. Tchr. Colo. Coll., 1978, U. N.C., Chapel Hill, 1999-2000, Queens Coll. CUNY, 1998—, Baruch Coll., CUNY, 1989-90, Marymount Manhattan Coll., 1991-97, Franklin Pierce Coll., Queens Coll., CUNY, Baruch Coll., CUNY, Franklin Pierce Coll., 1998, Colo. Coll. Appeared in off-Broadway prodns.: Moonchildren, Small Craft Warnings, Broadway prodn. I Love My Wife, also regional theater prodns. at Manhattan Theatre Club, Playwrights Horizons, Cir. Repertory Co., Long Wharf Theatre, Trinity Repertory Co., Buffalo Studio Arena, Portland Stage Co., Signature Theatre Co.; dir. prodns. at Ensemble Studio Theatre, Birmingham Theatre, Detroit, Marymount Manhattan Theatre, Franklin Pierce Coll., Peterborough Players, UNC. Mem. AFTRA, SAG, Actors Equity Assn. Avocations: swimming, tennis, biking, piano, guitar. Home: 159 Kings Hwy Orangeburg NY 10962-1906 E-mail: jimbo125@aol.com.

SEYMOUR, JANE, actress; b. Hillingdon, Middlesex, Eng., Feb. 15, 1951; came to U.S., 1976; d. John Benjamin and Mieke Frankenberg; m. David Flynn, July 18, 1981 (div. 1991); 2 children; m. James Keach, May 15, 1993; 2 children (twins). Student, Arts Ednl. Sch., London. Appeared in films Oh What A Lovely War, 1968, The Only Way, 1968, Young Winston, 1969, Live and Let Die, 1971, Sinbad and the Eye of the Tiger, 1973, Somewhere in Time, 1979, Oh Heavenly Dog, 1979, Lassiter, 1984, Head Office, Scarlet Pimpernel, Haunting Passion, Dark Mirror, Obsessed with a Married Woman, Killer on Board, The Tunnel, 1988, The French Revolution, Tochiny Wild Horses, 2002; TV films include Frankenstein, The True Story, 1972, Captains and The Kings, 1976 (Emmy nomination), 7th Avenue, 1976, The Awakening Land, 1977, The Four Feathers, 1977, Battlestar Galactica, Dallas Cowboy Cheerleaders, 1979, Our Mutual Friend, PBS, Eng., 1975, Jamaica Inn, 1982, Sun Also Rises, 1984, Crossings, 1986, Keys to Freedom, Angel of Death, 1990, Praying Mantis, 1993; A Passion for Justice: The Hazel Brannon Smith Story, 1994; Broadway appearances include Amadeus, 1980-81, I Remember You, 1992, Matters of the Heart, 1991, Sunstroke, 1992, Praying Mantis, 1993, Heidi, 1993; TV mini-series include East of Eden, 1980, The Richest Man in the World, 1988 (Emmy award), The Woman He Loved, 1988, Jack the Ripper, 1988, War and Remembrance, 1988, 89; host PBS documentary, Japan, 1988; TV series: Dr. Quinn: Medicine Woman, 1993-98 (Emmy nomination, Lead Actress - Drama, 1994, 98, Golden Globe award 1996), A Marriage of Convenience, CBS, 1998, A Memory in My Heart, CBS, 1999, Murder in the Mirror, CBS, 2000, Enslavement: The True Life Story of Fanny Kemble, Showtime, 2000, Blackout, CBS, 2000, Yesterday's Children, CBS, Dr. Quinn Winters Heart, 2001, Heart of a Stranger, 2002; author: Jane Seymour's Guide to Romantic Living, 1986, Two at a Time, 2001; co-author: Yum, Splat, 1998, Boing, 1999. Decorated Order Brit. Empire; recipient OBE award, 2000; named Hon. Citizen of Ill., Gov. Thompson, 1977. Mem. Screen Actors Guild, AFTRA, Actors Equity, Brit. Equity. Office: Guttman Assocs 118 S Beverly Dr Ste 201 Beverly Hills CA 90212-3016

SEYMOUR, JEFFREY ALAN, governmental relations consultant; b. L.A., Aug. 31, 1950; s. Daniel and Evelyn (Schwartz) S.; m. Valerie Joan Parker, Dec. 2, 1973; 1 child, Jessica Lynn. AA in Social Sci., Santa Monica Coll., 1971; BA in Polit. Sci., UCLA, 1973; MPA, 1977. Councilman aide L.A. City Coun., 1972-74; county supr.'s sr. dep. L.A. Bd. Suprs., 1974-82; v.p. Bank of L.A., 1982-83; prin. Jeffrey Seymour & Assocs., L.A., 1983-84; ptnr. Morey/Seymour & Assocs., 1984—. Mem. comml. panel Am. Arbitration Assn., 19845. Chmn. West Hollywood Parking Adv. Com., L.A., 1983-84; chmn. social action com. Temple Emanuel of Beverly Hills, 1986-89, bd. dirs. 1988-93, v.p. 1990-93; v.p. Congregation N'Vay Shalom, 1994-95; mem. Pan Pacific Park Citizens Adv. Com., L.A., 1982-85; bd. dirs. William O'Douglas Outdoor Classroom, L.A., 1981-88; mem. bd. regents U. Calif., 2001-02; pres. Alumni Assns. U. Calif., 2001-02; chair UCLA Fund, 2002--. Recipient plaques for svcs. rendered Beverlywood Cheviot Hills Dem. Club, L.A., 1981, Jewish Fedn. Coun. Greater L.A., 1983, certs. of appreciation, L.A. Olympic Organizing Com., 1984, County of L.A., 1984, City of L.A., 1987, Santa Monica Mountains Conservancy, 1999, UCLA Alumni Assn., 2002, others; commendatory resolutions, rules com. Calif. State Senate, 1987, Calif. State Assembly, 1987, 96, County of L.A., 1987, City of L.A., 1987, Regents of UCLA, 2002. Mem. Am. Soc. Pub. Adminstrn., UCLA Alumni Assn. (mem. govtl. steering com. 1983-97, bd. dirs. 1995—, chair govtl. rels. steering com. 1995-97, chair bd. dirs. 1995-97, pres. 1998-2000); exec. sect. Calif. Fedn. Young Dems., 1971; mem. Calif. Dem. Cen. Com., 1979-82; pres. Beverlywood-Cheviot Hills Dem. Club, L.A., 1978-81; co-chmn. Westside Chancellor's Assocs. UCLA, 1986-88; mem. L.A. Olympic Citizens Adv. Com.; mem. liaison adv. commn. with city and county govt. for 1984 Olympics, 1984; v.p. comty. rels. metro region, Jewish Fedn. Coun. of L.A., 1985-87, co-chmn. urban affairs commn., 1987-89, vice chmn., 1989-90, subcom. chmn. local govt. law and legislation commn., 1990, chmn. campus outreach task force, 1994; mem. adv. bd. Nat. Jewish Ctr. for Immunology & Respiratory Medicine, 1991-93; bd. dirs. Hillel Coun. of L.A., 1991; mem. platform on world peace and internat. rels. Calif. Dems., 1983; pres. 43d Assembly Dist. Dem. Coun., 1975-79; arbitrator BBB, 1984; trustee UCLA Found., 1989-97; pres. UCLA Jewish Alumni, 1992-95; mem. Santa Monica Mountains Conservancy adv. com., 1996-99; mem. cabinet Jewish Cmty. Rels. Com. Greater L.A., 1994, chair campus outreach task force, 1994-95, govtl. rels. commn., 1995-96, v. chair Jewish Cmty. Rels. com. Jewish Fedn. Coun. Greater L.A., 1998; mem. bd. dirs., Century City C of C, 1998, adv. bd. L.A. Peace Now. Office: Morey Seymour Assocs Ste 604 5757 W Century Blvd Los Angeles CA 90045

SEYMOUR, LESLEY JANE, magazine editor-in-chief; b. San Juan, P.R. BA, Duke U., 1978. Reporter Women's Wear Daily, 1978, N.Y. Daily News Tonight, 1981-82; writer, sr. editor Vogue Mag., 1982-91; beauty dir. Glamour Mag., 1994-97; editor-in-chief YM/Young & Modern, N.Y.C., 1997-98, Redbook, 1998—2001, Marie Claire mag., N.Y.C., 2001—. Office: Marie Claire 1790 Broadway New York NY 10019

SEYMOUR, MARY FRANCES, lawyer; b. Durand, Wis., Oct. 20, 1948; d. Marshall Willard and Alice Roberta (Smith) Thompson; m. Marshall Warren Seymour, June 6, 1970; 1 foster child, Nghia Pham. BS, U. Wis., LaCrosse, 1970; JD, William Mitchell Coll., 1979. Bar: Minn. 1979, U.S. Dist. Ct. Minn. 1979, U.S. Ct. Appeals (8th cir.) 1979, U.S. Supreme Ct. 1986. With Cochrane and Bresnahan, P.A., St. Paul, 1979-94, Loper & Seymour, P.A., 1994—. Mem.: ABA, Ramsey County Bar Assn., Minn. Bar Assn. Office: Loper & Seymour PA 24 4th St E Saint Paul MN 55101-1002 E-mail: mseymour@loperseymour.com.

SEYMOUR, MCNEIL VERNAM, lawyer; b. St. Paul, Dec. 21, 1934; s. McNeil Vernam and Katherine Grace (Klein) S.; children: Margaret, McNeil Vernam, James, Benjamin; m. Mary Katherine Velner, May 15, 1993. AB, Princeton U., 1957; JD, U. Chgo., 1960. Bar: Minn. 1960, U.S. Dist. Ct. Minn. 1960. Mem. Seymour & Seymour, St. Paul, 1960-71; mem. firm Briggs & Morgan, 1971—, ptnr., 1976—. Chmn., bd. trustees Thomas Irvine Dodge Nature Ctr.; sec., bd. dirs. Ramsey County Law Libr., 1972—76; pres., treas. White Bear Unitarian Ch., 1964—65; trustee, treas. Oakland Cemetery Assn. With U.S. Army, 1960—62. Mem. Minn. Bar Assn., Ramsey County Bar Assn., Somerset Country Club. Republican. Unitarian Universalist. Home: 886 S Highview Cir Mendota Heights MN 55118-3686 Office: Briggs & Morgan W-2200 1st Nat Bank Bldg Saint Paul MN 55101 E-mail: MSeymour@Briggs.com.

SEYMOUR, PETER SIMPSON, retired publishing executive, writer; b. N.Y.C., Jan. 4, 1933; s. John Davenport and Frances Simpson Seymour; m. Carole Ann Horner, Mar. 1, 1953 (div. Dec. 1960); children: Steve, Bill, Kathy Jenkins; m. Salene Walsh, Mar. 25, 1965 (div. Jan. 1999); 1 child Paisley Leeds. BA, Yale U., 1955. Writer, editl. dir. Hallmark Cards, Kansas City, Mo., 1955—63, editl. and design dir., 1972—78; copywriter, account exec. Fuller & Smith & Ross, L.A., 1964—65; freelance writer, 1966—71, 1979—88; v.p. Intervisual Books, Inc., Santa Monica, 1989—95; ret.; freelance writer. Creative cons. Gibson Greeting Cards, Cin., 1981—86; spkr. in field. Author numerous children's books, (plays) Price of a New Soul, 1967, (musical) Greetings, 1984; contbr. articles to profl. jours.; , author poetry and book revs. Civil rights activist, 1961—70; organizer Bradley for Mayor, L.A., 1970—72. Democrat. Buddhist. Avocations: painting, golf, tennis.

SEYMOUR, RICHARD BURT, health educator; b. San Francisco, Aug. 1, 1937; s. Arnold Burt-Oakley and Florence Marguerite (Burt) S.; m. Michelle Driscoll, Sept. 15, 1963 (div. 1972); children: Brian Geoffrey, Kyra Daleth; m. Sharon Harkless, Jan. 5, 1973. BA, Sonoma State U., 1969, MA, 1970. Freelance writer, Sausalito, Calif., 1960—; coord., adminstr. Coll. of Mendocino, Boonville, 1971-73; bus. mgr. Haight Ashbury Free Clinics, San Francisco, 1973-77; exec. adminstr., dir. tng. and edn. projects Height Ashbury Free Clinics, 1977-87; instr. John F. Kennedy U., Orinda, Calif., 1986—; asst. prof. Sonoma State U., Rohnert Park, 1985—; pres., chief exec. officer Westwind Assocs., Sausalito, 1988—. Cons. Haight Ashbury Free Clinics, San Francisco, 1987—, treas., bd. dirs.; chmn. World Drug Abuse Treatment Network, San Francisco, 1988—; coord. Calif. Collaborative Ctr. for Substance Abuse Policy Rsch., 1997—; bd. dirs. Slide Ranch. Author: Physician's Guide to Psychoactive Drugs, 1987, Drug Free, 1987, The New Drugs, 1989, The Psychedelic Resurgence, 1993, Compost College, 1997, Clinicians' Guide to Substance Abuse, 2001; editor-in-chief Internat. Addictions Infoline, 1995; mng. editor Jour. of Psychoactive Drugs, 1996; exec. editor: Alcohol MD.com, 1999—; contbr. articles to profl. jours. Mem. Calif. Health Profls. for New Health Policy, Washington, 1976-80; chmn. Marin Drug Abuse Adv. Bd., San Rafael, Calif., 1979-81, CalDrug Abuse Svcs. Assn., Sacramento, 1975-79; mem. Alcohol and Drug Counselors Edn. Project, 1985—, San Francisco Delinquency Prevention Commn., 1981—, Calif. Primary Prevention Network, 1980—. Grantee NIMH, 1974—, Nat. Inst. on Drug Abuse, 1974—. Mem. Internat. Platform Assn., Commonwealth Club of Calif., Internat. Soc. Addiction Jour. Editors (bd. dirs., treas. 2000—). Democrat. Episcopalian. Avocations: travel, writing, landscape painting, camping. Office: Westwind Assocs 90 Harrison Ave Apt C Sausalito CA 94965-2240 E-mail: hapjpd@hafreeclinics.org.

SEYMOUR, RICHARD DEMING, technology educator; b. Shelby, Ohio, Oct. 3, 1955; s. G. Deming and Elizabeth (Peterson) S.; m. Vicki Stebleton; 1 child, Ryan. BS in Edn., Ohio State U., 1978; MA, Ball State U., 1982; EdD, W.Va. U., 1990. Tchr. Crestview Sr. High Sch., Ashland, Ohio, 1978-81; from instr. to assoc. prof. Ball State U., Muncie, Ind., 1982—. Vis. instr. W.Va. U., Morgantown, 1985, Oreg. State U., 1990-91. Co-author: Exploring Communications, 1987, rev. edit., 2000; co-editor: Manufacturing in Technology Education, 1993. Advisor 4-H Clubs, Richland County, Ohio, 1978-81; dir. tech. in-svc. workshops Ind. Dept. Edn., Indpls., 1988-2000. Named technology tchr. educator of yr. Coun. on Technology Tchr. Edn., 1998. Mem.: Tech. Edn. Collegiate Assn. (internat. advisor 1990—92, nat. contest coord. 1992—), Am. Soc. Engring. Edn., Tech. Educators Ind. (pres. 1995—96), Ind. Math., Sci., Tech. Alliance (bd. dirs. 1994—), Coun. on Tech. Tchr. Edn., Soc. Mfg. Engrs., Internat. Tech. Edn. Assn. (bd. dirs. 1992—94, chmn. internat. conf. 1999, award of distinction 1999), Phi Delta Kappa, Epsilon Pi Tau. Methodist. Avocations: model railroads, sports, travel. Office: Ball State U Dept Industry Tech Muncie IN 47306-0255 E-mail: rseymour@bsu.edu.

SEYMOUR, STEPHANIE KULP, federal judge; b. Battle Creek, Mich., Oct. 16, 1940; d. Francis Bruce and Frances Cecelia (Bria) Kulp; m. R. Thomas Seymour, June 10, 1972; children: Bart, Bria, Sara, Anna. BA magna cum laude, Smith Coll., 1962; JD, Harvard U., 1965. Bar: Okla. 1965. Practice, Boston, 1965—66; opractice Tulsa, 1966—67; practice Houston, 1968—69; assoc. Doerner, Stuart, Saunders, Daniel & Anderson, Tulsa, 1971—75, ptnr., 1975—79; judge U.S. Ct. Appeals (10th cir.) Okla., 1979—94, 2000—, chief judge, 1994—2000. Mem. U.S. Jud. Conf., 1994—, com. defender svcs., 1985—90, chmn., 1987—90, com. to review cir. council conduct and disability, 1996—; joint fed. tribal rels. com. 9th and 10th cirs., 1993—; mem. Okla. State Fed. Tribal Judicial Coun., 1993—94. Task force Tulsa Human Rights Commn., 1972—76; legal adv. panel Tulsa Task Force Battered Women, 1971—77; trustee Tulsa County Law Libr., 1977—78. Mem.: ABA, Am. Inns of Ct. (Council Oak chpt.), Nat. Assn. Women Judges, Fed. Judges Assn., Tulsa County Bar Assn., Okla. Bar Assn. (assoc. bar examiner 1973—79), Phi Beta Kappa. Office: US Courthouse 333 W 4th St Ste 4-562 Tulsa OK 74103-3819

SEYMOUR, THADDEUS, English educator; b. N.Y.C., June 29, 1928; s. Whitney North and Lola Virginia (Vickers) S.; m. Polly Gnagy, Nov. 20, 1948; children— Elizabeth Halsey, Thaddeus, Samuel Whitney, Mary Duffie, Abigail Comfort AB, U. Calif., 1950; MA, U. N.C., 1951, PhD, 1955; D.H.L. (hon.), Wilkes Coll., 1968; LL.D. (hon.), Butler U., 1971, Ind. State U., 1976; LLD (hon.), Wabash Coll., 1984, U. Cen. Fla., 1990, Stetson U., 1990; DHL (hon.), Rollins Coll., 1990. Mem. faculty Dartmouth Coll., 1954-69, prof. English, dean coll., 1959-69; pres. Wabash Coll., Crawfordsville, Ind., 1969-78, Rollins Coll., Winter Park, Fla., 1978-90, prof. English, 1978—. Pres. Ind. Conf. Higher Edn., 1977; v.p. Assoc. Colls. Ind., 1978; vice-chmn. Fla. Ind. Colls. Fund Past mem. Ind. Bicentennial Commn.; trustee Park-Tudor Sch., 1970-78, Bach Festival Soc., Winter Park Pub. Libr., 1998—; chmn. Fla. selection com. Rhodes Scholarship Trust, 1983-88; chmn. Habitat for Humanity of Winter Park, 1994—; sec.-treas. Winter Park Health Found., 1998—. Mem. Cmty. Found. Ctrl. Fla. (bd. dirs.), Ring 219 (charter), Internat. Brotherhood Magicians, Century Assn., Rotary, Omicron Delta Kappa. Home: 1350 College Pt Winter Park FL 32789-5700 E-mail: tseymour@rollins.edu.

SFEKAS, STEPHEN JAMES, lawyer, educator; b. Balt., Feb. 12, 1947; s. James Stephen and Lee (Mesologites) S.; m. Joanne Lorraine Murphy, May 27, 1973; children: James Stephen, Andrew Edward Stephen, Christina Marie; m. Elizabeth Ruff, Nov. 1, 1997. BS in Fgn. Svc., Georgetown U., 1968, JD, 1973; MA, Yale U., 1972. Bar: Md. 1973, U.S. Dist. Ct. Md. 1974, U.S. Ct. Appeals (4th cir.) 1974. Law clk. U.S. Dist. Ct., Balt., 1973-74; assoc. firm Frank, Bernstein, Conaway & Goldman, 1974-75; asst. atty. gen. State of Md., 1975-81; assoc. firm Tydings & Rosenberg, 1981-82, ptnr., 1983-86; with firm Miles & Stockbridge, 1986-90; ptnr. Weinberg & Green, 1991-98, Saul, Ewing, LLP, Balt., 1998—2001; counsel Cook & Di Franco, LLC, 2001—. Instr. legal writing C.C. Balt., 1976-79; instr. legal ethics Goucher Coll., Balt., 1979; adj. prof. adminstrv. law U. Md., Balt., 1981-93, health, 1993—, law sch. U. Balt., 1993—. Editor Georgetown Law Jour., 1972-73; contbr. articles to legal publs. Bd. dirs. Md. region NCCJ, 1981-89, co-chmn. Md. region, 1986-89, Orthodox Christian Laity, 1990—98, Ctrl. Md. Ecumenical Coun., 1991—93, Balt. Assn. for Retarded Citizens Vol. for Med. Engring., 2001-; mem. Piraeus Sister City Com., City of Balt., 1983-89; mem. parish coun. Greek Orthodox Cathedral of Annunciation, Balt., 1981-84; mem. internat. com. Balt. region ARC, 1984-85; mem. adv. com. on bread for the world Dept. Ch. and Soc., Greek Orthodox Archdiocese North and S.Am., 1984—; pres. Greek Orthodox Counseling and Social Svcs. of Balt., 1984-88; ; mem. bylaw com. Girl Scouts Ctrl. Md., 1989-91, Md. Leadership Program, 1997; mem. pres.'s adv. coun. U. Md., Baltimore County. Danforth fellow, Woodrow Wilson fellow, WHO fellow, London, 1979. Fellow: Md. Bar Found., Soc. for Values in Higher Edn. (bd. dir. 2002—); mem.: ABA (forum com. on health law, Grant Morris fellow 1979), Am. Health Lawyers Assn., Bar Assn. Balt. City, Md. Bar Assn. Democrat. Office: Cook & Di Franco LLC Ste 1810 120 E Baltimore St Baltimore MD 21202 E-mail: ssfikas@saul.com.

SFERRAZZA, ANTHONY CARL, historian; b. N.Y.C., June 13, 1959; s. Carl Richard and Marie Jane (Martirano) Sferrazza. BA in History, George Washington U., 1983. Writer Presdl. Inaugural Book Com., Washington, 1980—81, 1984—85, 1988—89, Exec. Office of Pres., Washington, 1981—82, White House Preservation Fund, Washington, 1983—84; speechwriter Office of First Lady Nancy Reagan, 1985—86; instr. George Washington U., 1994; contbg. editor George Mag., N.Y.C., 1997—99; bibliographer, bd. dirs. Nat. First Ladies Libr, Canton, Ohio, 1996—. Freelance hist. writer Style sect. Washington Post, Washington, 1985—98; hist. cons. Nat. Mus. Am. History, Smithsonian Instn., Washington, 1990—92; hist. source Office of First Lady Hillary Clinton, Washington, 1993—2001. Author: First Ladies: The Saga of the Presidents' Wives and Their Power, 1789,1990, 2 vols., 1990—91, As We Remember Her: Jacqueline Kennedy Onassis in the Words of Her Friends and Family, 1997, Florence Harding: The First Lady, The Jazz Age and the Death of America's Most Scandalous President, 1998, The Kennedy White House: Family Life and Pictures, 1961-1963, 2001. Named Bicentennial Honoree, U. Louisville, 1997; recipient Spl. Book Collections, Brandeis U. Libr., 2001. Episcopalian. Avocations: hiking, boxing.

SFIKAS, PETER MICHAEL, lawyer, educator; b. Gary, Ind., Aug. 9, 1937; s. Michael E. and Helen (Thureanos) S.; m. Freida Platon, Apr. 24, 1966; children— Ellen M., Pamela C., Sandra N. BS, Ind. U., 1959; JD, Northwestern U., 1962. Bar: Ill. 1962, U.S. Dist. Ct. (no. dist.) Ill. 1963, U.S. Ct. Appeals (7th cir.) 1963, U.S. Supreme Ct. 1970, U.S. Ct. Appeals (9th cir.) 1976, U.S. Ct. Appeals (3d cir.) 1981, U.S. Ct. Appeals (D.C. cir.) 1984, U.S. Dist. Ct. (cen. dist.) Ill. 1988. Atty. Legal Aid Bur., United Charities Chgo., 1962-63; sr. ptnr. Peterson & Ross, Chgo., 1970-95; chief counsel, assoc. exec. dir. div. legal affairs ADA, 1995—; sr. ptnr. Bell, Boyd & Lloyd, 1996—. Prosecutor Village of LaGrange Park, Ill., 1969-74; mem. rules com. Ill. Supreme Ct., 1975-95, mem. spl. joint com. on discovery rules, 1995; arbitrator Nat. Panel Arbitrators, 1972—; adj. prof. Loyola U. Sch. Law, 1978—; guest lectr. U. Ill. Coll. Dentistry, 1988-95; lectr. corp. counsel inst. Northwestern U. Sch. Law, 1984, lectr. Ray Garret Jr. Corp. and Securities Law Inst., 1996. Co-author: Antitrust and Unfair Competition Practice Handbook, 1996; contbr. articles to profl. jours. Mem. Ill. steering com. Ct. Watching Project, LWV, 1975-77; pres. Holy Apostles Greek Orthodox Ch. Parish Coun., 1987-89; co-pres. Oak Sch. PTO, 1989-90; mem. to select sch. supr., dist. 86, DuPage County, Ill., 1993-94. Recipient Maurice Weigle award, Chgo. Bar Found., 1973, Fones award and hon. membership, Conn. Dental Assn., 1998. Fellow Am. Bar Found., Am. Coll. Trial Lawyers, Chgo. Bar Found. (life); mem. ABA (editor in chief Forum Law Jour. sect. ins., negligence and compensation law 1972-76), Ill. Bar Found. (bd. dirs.), Northwestern U. Law Alumni Assn. (1st v.p. 1985-86, pres. 1986-87, Svc. award 1990), Ill. State Bar Assn. (bd. govs. 1970-76, chmn. antitrust law sect. coun. 1986-87), Chgo. Bar Assn. (editl. bd. Chgo. Bar Record 1973-84), Bar Assn. 7th Fed. Cir., Ill. Inst. Continuing Legal Edn. (chmn. profl. antitrust problems program 1976, author program on counseling corps., antitrust and trade regulation), Legal Club Chgo. (sec.-treas. 1984-86, v.p. 1989-90, pres. 1990-91). Office: Bell Boyd & Lloyd 70 W Madison St Ste 3300 Chicago IL 60602-4284 E-mail: P.Sfikas@BellBoyd.com.

SFIRRI, MARK STEPHEN, artist, educator; b. Chester, Pa., Aug. 1, 1952; s. George Louis and Rose Agatha Sfirri; married Aug. 18, 1979; 1 child, Samuel. BFA, R.I. Sch. Design, 1974, MFA, 1978. Prof. art Bucks County C.C., Newton, Pa., 1980—. Lectr. in field. Exhibited in group shows at Am. Craft Mus., N.Y.C., 1977, 88, Port of History Mus., Phila., 1983, 88, 91, Workbench Gallery, N.Y.C., 1986, Ft. Wayne (Ind.) Mus. Art, 1989, Sansar Gallery, Washington, 1989, 93, Arrowmont Sch. Arts and Crafts, Gatlinburg, Tenn., 1990, Pa. Acad. Fine Arts, Phila., 199, Parsons Sch. Design, N.Y.C., 1992, Hagley Mus., Wilmington, Del., 1993, R.I. Sch. Design Mus., Providence, 1993, Renwick Gallery, Washington, 1996, Berman Mus. Art, Collegeville, Pa., 1997, James A. Michener Art Mus., Doylestown, Pa., 1998, Yale U. Art Gallery, New Haven, Conn., 1999, Ark. Craft Ctr., Little Rock, 2000, Mint Mus. Craft and Design, Charlotte, N.C., 2000, Mpls. Inst. Art, 2001; represented in numerous pvt. and profl. collections. Recipient fellowship Pa. Coun. Arts, 1987, winner Beckett Sports Publs., 1996. Fax: 215-794-2510. E-mail: sfirri@comcat.com.

SGANGA, JOHN B. furniture holding company executive; b. Bronx, N.Y., Nov. 21, 1931; s. Charles and Marie (Crusco) S.; m. Evelyn Joan Battilana, Jan. 19, 1957; children: Mark, John B. Jr., Matthew. BS in Acctg. cum laude, Bklyn. Coll., 1961; postgrad., Bernard Baruch Coll. Systems analyst DIVCO, Wayne, N.Y., 1965-67; mgr. mgmt. cons. svcs. Coopers & Lybrand, CPAs, N.Y.C., 1967-74; sr. v.p. fin. and adminstrn. Aurora Products Co. subs. RJR Nabisco, West Hempstead, N.Y., 1974-79; contr. Gt. Lakes Carbon Corp., N.Y.C., 1979-80, v.p., 1980-81, sr. v.p. fin., CFO, 1981-86; v.p. Cunard Line, Ltd., 1988; exec. v.p. CFO Consolitated Furniture Corp. (formerly Mohasco Corp.), 1989—, also bd. dirs. Contbr. articles to profl. jours.; editl. adv. to Financial Management mag. Served with USNR, 1950-54. Mem. Inst. Cert. Mgmt. Cons. (a founder), Inst. Mgmt. Accts., Fin. Execs. Internat. (past chmn. com. M.I.S.), Treas.'s Club. Home: 21312 Tarraco Mission Viejo CA 92692-5921 Office: Consolidated Furniture Corp 445 Park Ave at 57th St Ste 905 New York NY 10022-2606

SGARAMELLA, PETER, chemical products executive, technical consultant; b. Molfetta, Bari, Italy, Jan. 6, 1928; came to U.S., 1954; s. Riccardo and Maria (Masta) S.; m. Mary Caputi, Aug. 3, 1953; children: Richard, Robert, Maria. PhD, U. Bari, Italy, 1951. Chief chemist Aerosol Techniques, Bridgeport, Conn., 1955-61; lab. mgr. Beecham Products, Clifton, N.J., 1961-67; dir. rsch. Shulton/Am.-Cyanamid, 1967-93; tech. dir. Fluid Packaging, Lakewood, 1993-98, ret., 1998. Spkr. seminars and tech. presentations in U.S. and internat. Contbr. articles to profl. jours.; prin. author several patents Leader Boy Scouts Am., 1964-70; mem. com. Knights of Columbus, 1984-90; chmn., moderator several trade assn. ann. meetings. Mem. ICA Fellowship Soc. (adminstrn.), FMA Native Town Fedn. (trustee), Soc. Cosmetic Chemists, Kiwanis. Roman Catholic. Avocations: travel, reading, photography. Home: Shadow Lake Village 36 Claremont Ct Red Bank NJ 07701-5418

SGRO, BEVERLY HUSTON, day school administrator, educator, state official; b. Ft. Worth, Jan. 12, 1941; d. James Carl and Dorothy Louise (Foster) Huston; m. Joseph Anthony Sgro, Feb. 1, 1964; children: Anthony, Jennifer. BS, Tex. Woman's U., 1963; MS, Va. Poly. Inst. and State U., 1974, PhD, 1990. Cert. tennis teaching profl. Instr. of deaf Midland (Tex.) Ind. Sch. System, 1963-64; speech pathologist Arlington (Tex.) Pub. Sch. System, 1964; rsch. asst. Tex. Christian U., 1964-65; tennis profl. Blacksburg (Va.) Country Club, 1977-81; from coord. for Greek affairs to exec. asst. to v.p. student affairs Va. Poly. Inst. and State U., Blacksburg, 1981-89, dean of students, 1989-93; sec. of edn. Commonwealth of Va., Richmond, 1994-98; interim head Collegiate Sch., 1998-99; head Carolina Day Sch., Asheville, N.C., 1999—. Adj. faculty Coll. Edn., Va. Poly. Inst. and State U.; lectr., presented papers at numerous symposia and convs., 1983—. Trustee Foxcroft Sch., Middleburg, Va., 1989-98, pres. bd. trustees, 1993-96; bd. dirs. Habitat Humanity. Mem. AACD, Nat. Assn. Student Pers. Adminstrs., Am. Coll. Pers. Assn. (sec., com. mem. 1986-88), Omicron Delta Kappa, Phi Kappa Phi, Phi Upsilon Omicron, Pi Lambda Theta, Sigma Alpha Eta, Zeta Phi Eta. Avocations: reading, travel, theatre. Home: 22 Hilltop Rd Asheville NC 28803-3030 Office: Carolina Day Sch 1345 Hendersonville Rd Asheville NC 28803-1923 E-mail: bsgor@cdschool.org.

SGRO, JOSEPH ANTHONY, retired psychologist, educator; b. New Haven, Nov. 22, 1937; s. Fred and Tullia (Francesconi) S.; m. Beverly Ann Huston, Feb. 1, 1964; children: Anthony, Jennifer. BA, Trinity Coll., 1959; MS, Lehigh U., 1961; PhD, Tex. Christian U., 1966. Asst. prof. Old Dominion U., Norfolk, Va., 1965-67, Va. Poly. Inst. & State U., Blacksburg, 1967-71, assoc. prof., 1971-79, prof., 1979-99; prof. emeritus, 1999—; dept. head psychology Va. Poly. Inst. & State U., Blacksburg, 1982-96, mem. exec. bd., sec.-treas. coun. grad. dept. psychology, 1990-92, chmn., 1992-93. Adj. prof. Warren Wilson Coll., 2000; vice-chmn. Va. Bd. Psychologists Examiners, Richmond, 1970-75. Editor: Virginia Tech Symposium on Applied Behavioral Science, 1980. Mem. Am. Psychol. Assn., Southeastern Psychol. Assn. (chmn. assn. heads depts. psychology 1987-89), Ea. Psychol. Assn., Va. Psychol. Assn. (pres. 1974-76), Omicron Delta Kappa, Psi Chi, Sigma Xi. Avocations: golf, cooking. Home: 22 Hilltop Rd Asheville NC 28803-3030 E-mail: jsgro@charter.net.

SGROI, DONALD ANGELO, obstetrician, gynecologist; b. Newark, Aug. 20, 1943; s. Joseph and Mary (Desimone) S.; m. Phyllis Ann Intorelli, Nov. 19, 1967; children: Donna, Felisa, Chela, Gabriela, Alexandria. BS, Fairleigh Dickinson U., 1970; MD, Autonomous U. Guadalajara, Mex., 1974. Diplomate Am. Bd. Ob-Gyn. Sr. tech. aide Bell Labs., Berkley Heights, N.J., 1967-70; intern St. Michael's Med. Ctr., Newark, 1974-76; resident in ob-gyn. St. Joseph's Med. Ctr., Paterson, N.J., 1976-78, chief resident, 1978-79; assoc. attending physician Wayne (N.J.) Gen. Hosp., 1980-84, co-chmn. dept. ob-gyn., 1980-84, attending physician, 1984-2000, chmn. tissue rev. com., 1984-88, mem. tissue rev. com., 1988-94, chmn. dept. ob-gyn., 1998-2000, co-chmn. dept. ob-gyn., 2000—. Sec., treas. med. exec. com., 1988-91, mem. peer assessment com., 1988-91, quality assurance com., 1988-2000, credentials com., 1988--; mem. Peer Rev. Orgn. of N.J., 1991-2000. Fellow Am. Coll. Ob-Gyn., Am. Fertility Soc. (jr.); mem. Internat. Assn. Gynelogic Laparoscopist, Internat. Corr. Soc. Obstetricians and Gynecolgists. Roman Catholic. Home: 27 Shinnecock Trl Franklin Lakes NJ 07417-1033 Office: 401 Hamburg Tpke Ste 104 Wayne NJ 07470-2139

SHA, RICHARD T. computer company executive; b. Kiangsu, China, Jan. 12, 1934; came to U.S., 1958, naturalized, 1972; s. Chin-Fung and Yu-Nei S.; m. Marjorie Y., Sept. 15, 1962; children: Richard C., Elaine E. BSEE, Taipei Inst. Tech., Taiwan, 1956; MSEE, U. Idaho, 1959; PhD in Computer EE, U. Pitts., 1968. Rsch. engr. Perkin-Elmer Corp., Norwalk, Conn., 1960-61; devel. engr. Hewlett-Packard Co., Rockwell, N.J., 1961-62; project engr. Western Union Telegraph Co., N.Y.C., 1962; mem. rsch. staff T.J. Watson Rsch. Ctr., IBM, 1968-74; corp. staff on info. system tech. IBM, White Plains, N.Y., 1974-84; assoc. dir. comprehensive math. and sci. program Columbia U., N.Y.C., 1979-80; pres. Internat. Sysware Corp., Bedford, N.Y., 1984—. Patentee in field; contbr. tech. papers to publs. Mem. IEEE (sr. mem.; chpt. chmn. Comms. Soc. N.Y. 1979-80, 87-88, chmn. Computer Soc. N.Y. chpt. 1982-84, session chmn. NTC 1981, session co-organizer INFOCOM 1983, seminar chmn. 1979-84, Certs. of Appreciation 1974-79, 81-83, Region I awards 1983, 85, Computer Soc. Outstanding Svc. award 1984), AAAS, N.Y. Acad. Scis., Sigma Xi. Democrat. Baptist. Home: 46 White Birch Rd Pound Ridge NY 10576-2326 Office: PO Box 913 Bedford NY 10506-0913 E-mail: rsha11234@aol.com.

SHAAR, H. ERIK, academic administrator; V.p. acad. affairs Shippensburg U. of Pa., until 1986; pres. Lake Superior State U., Sault Sainte Marie, Mich., 1986-92, Minot (N.D.) State U., 1992—. Office: Minot State U Office of Pres 500 University Ave W Minot ND 58707-0002

SHABACK, JEAN ANN, management consultant; b. N.Y.C., July 14, 1952; d. Nicholas Shaback. B.S., Coll. Environ. Sci. and Forestry, SUNY-Syracuse, 1974; M.S., Rensselaer Poly. Inst., 1979. Research assoc. Eastman Dental Ctr., Rochester, N.Y., 1974-79; documentation analyst Xerox Corp., Webster, N.Y., 1979-81, sr. documentation analyst, 1981-82, tech. publ. planner, 1982-83; mgr. AT&T Info. Systems, Morristown, N.J., 1983-85; mem. tech. staff, 1985; mgmt. cons. Bell Communications, Piscataway, N.J., 1985-87; sr. mgmt. cons. Technidoc Assocs., Princeton, N.J., 1987—; founder, dir. Princeton Grand Prix Cir. tennis, 1985—. League dir. advanced Women's Winter Tennis League, Princeton, N.J., 1985— . Mem. Am. Soc. Tng. and Devel. (newsletter editor Rochester chpt. 1979-83). Avocations: tennis, horseback riding, sailing, travel.

SHABANOWITZ, HARRY, electronics engineer, educator; b. Brooklyn, Ny, Nov. 11, 1918; s. Abraham and Ida Shabanowitz; m. Sophie Mackoff Shabanowitz, May 8, 1943; children: Judith, Robert B. BS, Coll. City NY, New York, NY, 1949; MA, Columbia U., New York, NY, 1950; PhD, Syracuse U., Syracuse, NY, 1974. Sr. design and devel. engr. Westinghouse Elec. Corp., Elmira, NY, 1951—65, GE, Syracuse, 1965—66; prof. math. Elmira Coll., Elmira, 1966—85, prof. emeritus, math., 1985—. Tech. mgr. NASA. Contbr. articles to profl. jours. Maj. U.S. Army, Various. Fellow Coll. Math. Inst., NSF, 1967, Inst. on the History and Philosophy of Sci. and Math., 1968. Mem.: Am. Assn. U. Professors (chpt. pres. 1966—85), The NY Acad. Sciences, Alpha Sigma Lambda, Beta Tau Chpt. Achievements include patents for Photoconductive surface, electronic storage tube, 1966; Administration (NASA) Apollo lunar television camera for electronic transmission of man's first excursion on the surface of the moon, 1969. Home: 205 Scenic Drive Horseheads NY 14845

SHABAZ, JOHN C. judge; b. West Allis, Wis., June 25, 1931; s. Cyrus D. and Harriet T. Shabaz; children: Scott J., Jeffrey J., Emily D., John D. BS in Polit. Sci., U. Wis., 1999; LLB, Marquette U., 1957. Comd. 2d. lt. U.S. Army, 1954, resigned as capt., 1964; pvt. practice law West Allis, Wis., 1957—81; mem. Wis. Assembly, 1965—81; judge U.S. Dist. Ct. (we. dist.) Wis., 1981—96, chief judge, 1996—2001. Office: US Dist Ct PO Box 591 Madison WI 53701-0591

SHABICA, CHARLES WRIGHT, geologist, earth science educator; b. Elizabeth, N.J., Jan. 2, 1943; s. Anthony Charles and Eleanor (Wright) S.; m. Susan Ewing, Dec. 30, 1967; children: Jonathan, Andrew, Dana. BA in Geology, Brown U., 1965; PhD, U. Chgo., 1971. Prof. earth sci. Northeastern Ill. U., Chgo., 1971—; disting. prof., 1991; pres. Shabica & Assocs. Coastal Cons., Inc., Northfield, Ill., 1985—. Chmn. bd. dirs. Aesti Corp., 1991-96; rsch. collaborator Nat. Park Svc., 1978-82, 89—; adj. prof. Coll. V.I., St. Thomas, 1980, adj. prof. environ. sci. Northwestern U., Evanston, 1999—; Kellogg fellow Northeastern Ill. U., 1979—; chmn. Task Force on Lake Michigan, Chgo., 1986-89; mem. Chgo. Shoreline Protection Commn., 1987-88; cons. Shedd Aquarium, Chgo., 1991; mem. Ft. Sheridan Commn., 1989-90; bd. dirs. Winnetka (Ill.) Hist. Soc. Editor: (with Andrew A. Hay) Richardson's Guide to the Fossil Fauna of Mazon Creek, 1997. Commr., packmaster Boy Scouts Am., Winnetka, Ill., 1984-88. Coop. Inst. for Limnology and Ecosystems Rsch. Lab. fellow. Mem. Internat. Assn. for Great Lakes Rsch., Am. Shore and Beach Preservation Assn. (bd. dirs., pres. Great Lakes chpt.), Sigma Xi. Home: 326 Ridge Ave Winnetka IL 60093-3842 Office: 550 W Frontage Rd Ste 3400 Northfield IL 60093-1246

SHACK, R. BRUCE, plastic surgeon; b. Vernon, Tex., Oct. 7, 1947; s. Nathan Lee and Patsy Lee (Holliday) S.; m. Sharon Summers Frazier, Aug. 16, 1969 (div. 1982); children: Robert David, Nathan Andrew; m. Wanda Kaye, Nov. 11, 1984; children: Jerion Elizabeth, Austin Ryan. BS, Midwestern U., 1969; MD, U. Tex., 1973. Diplomate Am. Bd. Plastic Surgery, cert. added qualification in hand surgery. Resident in gen. surgery Vanderbilt U. Med. Ctr., Nashville, 1973-78, resident in plastic surgery, 1978-80; asst. prof. surgery Johns Hopkins Med. Sch., Balt., 1980-82; from asst. prof. to prof., chmn. plastic surgery Vanderbilt U. Med. Ctr., 1982—. Fellow Am. Coll. Surgeons, So. Surg. Assn.; mem. AMA, Am. Assn. Plastic Surgeons, Am. Soc. Maxillofacial Surgeons, Am. Soc. Plastic Surgeons, Am. Soc. Reconstructive Microsurgery, Am. Soc. Aesthetic Plastic Surgery, H. William Scott, Jr. Soc., John B. Lynch Soc., John Staige Davis Soc. Plastic Surgeons Md., Nashville Acad. Medicine, Nashville Surg. Soc., Southeastern Soc. Plastic and Reconstructive Surgeons, So. Med. Assn., Tenn. Soc. Plastic Surgeons. Republican. Methodist. Avocations: golf, travel, shooting. Office: Vanderbilt U Med Ctr 2100 Pierce Ave Ste 230 Nashville TN 37212-3156 E-mail: bruce.shack@mcmail.vanderbilt-edu.

SHACKELFORD, JAMES FLOYD, materials science educator, researcher; b. Springfield, Mo., Sept. 1, 1944; s. Amos Franklin and Opal Leona Shackelford; m. Penelope Lea Openshaw, Dec. 11, 1971; 1 child Scott. BS, U. Wash., Seattle, 1966, MS, 1967; PhD, U. Calif., Berkeley, 1971. Postdoctoral fellow U. Calif., Berkeley, 1971, McMaster U., Hamilton, Canada, 1972—73; asst. prof. U. Calif., Davis, 1973—79, assoc. prof., 1979—84, prof., 1984—, assoc. dean, 1984—2001, dir. integrated studies, 2001—. Author: (book) Introduction to Materials Science for Engineers, 1984, Introduction to Materials Science for Engineers, 2nd Edition, 1988, Introduction to Materials Science for Engineers, 3rd Edition, 1992, Introduction to Materials Science for Engineers, 4th Edition, 1996, Introduction to Materials Science for Engineers, 5th Edition, 2000; editor: CRC Handbook of Materials Science and Engineering, 1992, CRC Practical Handbook of Materials Selection, 1995, CRC Materials Science and Engineering Handbook, 2nd Edition, 1994, CRC Handbook of Materials Science and Engineering, 3rd Edition, 2001; author: Bioceramics, 1999; editor: Bioceramics - Applications of Ceramic and Glass Materials in Medicine, 1999. Fellow: Am. Ceramic Soc. (Outstanding Educator 1996); mem.: ASM Internat. Office: U Calif Dept Chem Engring and Materials Sci Davis CA 95616 Office Fax: 530-752-9554. Business E-Mail: jfshackelford@ucdavis.edu.

SHACKELFORD, MARTIN ROBERT, social worker; b. Boonville, Mo., May 22, 1947; s. Hugh and Carol Lois (Schoene) S. BA in History, U. Mich., 1969. Driver Yellow Cab, Saginaw, Mich., 1969-70; sales clk. Waldenbooks, 1972; eligibility worker Saginaw County Dept. Social Svcs., 1972-73, employment worker, 1973-77, delinquency svcs. worker, 1977—2002. Charter mem. social work adv. com. Saginaw Valley State U., 1981—. Contbr. articles on JFK assassination to profl. jours. Bd. dirs. Valley Film Soc., Saginaw, 1978-97, ACLU, 1978—, Ctrl. Mich. Br., 1978—, Lone Tree Coun., 1978-, Temple Theatre Film Bd., 1999-2000. Avocations: film, photography, reading, writing, creative experimentation. Home: 216 N Webster St # 2 Saginaw MI 48602-4243 E-mail: mshack@concentric.net.

SHACKELFORD, PATRICIA ANN, lawyer; b. Wilmington, Ohio, Sept. 27, 1953; d. Edward E. and Natalie (McIntire) S.; m. John S. Wood, Aug. 14, 1993; 1 stepchild, John W. II. BA cum laude, Trinity U., 1974; JD cum laude, Baylor U., 1993. Bar: Tex., U.S. Dist. Ct. (ea. dist.) Tex. 1997, U.S. Dist. Ct. (we. dist.) Tex. 1997, U.S. Dist. Ct. (so. dist.) Tex. 1997, U.S. Dist. Ct. (no. dist.) Tex. 1997, U.S. Ct. Appeals (5th cir.) 1997, U.S. Supreme Ct. 1997, U.S. Ct. Appeals (10th cir.) 1998. Paralegal David L. Perry & Assocs., Corpus Christi, Tex., 1983-91; atty. Ct. Appeals for 13th Jud. Dist., 1993-95; assoc. Matthews & Branscomb, 1995, Perry & Haas, Corpus Christi, 1996, ptnr., 1997-98, 99—, Edwards, Perry & Haas, Corpus Christi, 1998-99. Mem. ABA, ATLA, Am. Health Lawyers Assn., Tex. Trial Lawyers Assn., State Bar Assn. Tex., Corpus Christi Bar Assn. (treas. 1998—). E-mial. Office: Perry & Haas Ste 2300 802 N Carancahua St Corpus Christi TX 78470-0002 E-mail: pshackelford@perryhaas.com.

SHACKELFORD, SCOTT ADDISON, air force officer, chemist; b. Long Beach, Calif., Aug. 11, 1944; s. Richard Walter and Phyllis Marian (Pearson) S.; m. Alpha Marilyn Coon, Aug. 23, 1969; children: Laura DeAnna, Vicki LeAnna. Student Colo. State U., 1962-64; BA, Simpson Coll., 1964-66; MA, No. Ariz. U., 1968; PhD, Ariz. State U., 1973. Second lt. U.S. Air Force, 1972, advanced through grades to major, 1990; rsch. chemist F.J. Seiler Rsch. Lab., U.S. Air Force Acad., Colo., 1972-74, rsch. group chief, 1974-77,instr., asst. prof. dept. chemistry and biol. scis., 1977-78; lang. student Nat. Def. Lang. Inst., Monterey, Calif., 1978; exchange scientist DFVLR-Institut fuer Chemische Antriebe und Verfahrenstechnik, Hardthausen A.K., Fed. Republic Germany, 1978-80; rsch. sect. chief Air Force Rocket Propulsion Lab., Edwards AFB, Calif., 1980-84; rsch. liaison officer European Office Aerospace Rsch. and Devel., London, 1984-87; dir. Aerospace Rsch. Liaison, 1986-88; sr. scientist F.J. Seiler Rsch. Lab. USAF Acad., Colo., 1987—; chief Energetics and Properties Chemistry Rsch., 1988—; sec. Tri-Svcs. Joint Tech. Coordinating Group/Munitions Devel./Working Party for Explosives, Washington, 1975-77; lab. rsch. task mgr. to Air Force Office Sci. Research, Washington, 1981-84, 88—; nat. propellant survey cons., 1981-82; mem. sci. adv. com. Simpson Coll., Indianola, Iowa, 1983-87; chmn.-elect Jannaf combustion sub-com. panel Chem. Combustion Kinetics, 1988—; lectr. in field. Contbr. articles to profl. publs. Patentee in field. Co-mgr. Tee Ball Youth Baseball Team, Fort Collins, Colo., 1964; asst. coach Am. Legion Summer Baseball Team, Pacifica, Calif., 1967, 68; Sunday school tchr. Village Christian Ch., Colorado Springs, Colo., 1975-77; adult class leader Base Protestant Chapel, Edwards, Calif., 1984, chmn. community christian ch. permanent relocation com, 1989—. Recipient Research and Devel. award U.S. Air Force Chief-of-Staff, 1982, Alumni Achievement award Simpson Coll. Alumni Assn., 1985. Mem. Am. Chemical Soc. (fluorine div.). Mem. Disciples of Christ. Ch. Current work: In-situ mechanistic studies of thermochemical decomposition and combustion processes with deuterium isotope effects, polynitroalphatic synthesis, selective organic fluorination with xenon difluoride. Subspecialties: Organic chemistry; Condensed Phase Reaction Mechanisms. Home: 1913 Carlton Ave Colorado Springs CO 80909-2169

SHACKLEFORD, WILLIAM ALTON, SR. minister; b. Red Springs, N.C., Aug. 5, 1947; s. Purcell and Pearl (Walton) S.; m. Rebecca Belsches, Dec. 2, 1972; children: Kristal Lynn, William Alton Jr. Student, Hampton U., 1965-67, U. Richmond, 1969, 70; DD (hon.), Va. Sem. and Coll., 1990. Ordained to ministry Unity Bapt. Mins.' Conf., 1977. Pastor Cedar Grove Bapt. Ch., Charles City, Va., 1979-82, St. Paul High Street Bapt. Ch., Martinsville, 1986—. Past pres. Bapt. Sunday sch. and Bapt. Tng. Union Congress of Va., chmn. exec. bd., 1997—; past pres. Sunday sch. Union of Hampton and Adjoining Cities, Unity Bapt. Min.'s Conf., Newport News, Va.; corr. sec. Va. Bapt. State Conv., 1986-96; sr. technician tech. svc. Badishe Corp., Williamsburg, Va., 1967-81, asst. supr. corp. office svcs., 1981-86. Author: Replacing the Fallen Angels, 2000; contbr. articles to Martinsville Bull. Apptd. supt. Schs. Adv. Coun.; mem. Child Abuse and Neglect Multidiscipline Team; exec. bd. Martinsville Voter's League, 1987—; mem. overall econ. devel. com., ad hoc drug and alcohol abuse com., past mem. adminstrv. bd. Martinsville Dept. Social Svcs.; adv. coun. Good News Jail and Prison Ministries; past chmn. bd. dirs., adv. com., mem. editl. bd. Patrick Henry Drug and Alcohol Coun.; mem. Martinsville City Sch. Bd., 1991-2000, chmn. 1998-2000; past chmn. bd. trustees Va. Sem. and Coll., Lynchburg, Va., 1992-96; v.p. Va. One Ch. One Child, 1992—; mem. edn. com. Va. Mcpl. League, 1993-95. Named Outstanding Min. Nat. Hairston Clan, 1988; recipient Dedicated Svc. award Va.'s One Ch. One Child Program, 1989, others. Mem. NAACP, Smith River Bapt. Assn. (moderator 2000—), Martinsville and Henry County Ministerial Alliance (com.). Home: 405 3rd St PO Box 5223 Martinsville VA 24115-5223 Office: St Paul High Street Bapt Ch PO Box 1003 401 Fayette St Martinsville VA 24112-2514 E-mail: pastorwmshackleford@peoplepc.com. *I live with the assurance that the invisible hand of God works to bless and exalt those who commit the totality of their existence to serve God and benefit humanity.*

SHACKLETON, JOHN DOUGLAS, music educator, consultant; b. Poughkeepsie, Ny, Aug. 22, 1945; s. Robert Douglas and Constance Mary Shackleton; m. Nancy Elyse Gates; children: Samuel Robert, Katy Clark. BA Music Ed., Ithaca Coll., Ithaca, NY, 1963—67. Cert. Educator State of NY. Music educator Waterloo Ctrl. Sch., Waterloo, NY, 1967—69, Wappingers Falls Ctrl. Sch., Wappingers Falls, 1969—73, Rhinebeck Ctrl. Sch. Dist., Rhinebeck, 1973—. Spring musical maestro Rhinebeck Ctrl. Sch., Rhinebeck, NY, 1973—, dir. meml. day marching band, NY, 1973—, dir. of steel drum band, NY, 1997—. Dir. sr. citizen drop-in ctr. Christ Episcopal Ch., Poughkeepsie, NY, 1983—85, summer camp dir., 1991; ombudsman Office of the Aging, Poughkeepsie, 1996. Recipient Outstanding Young Educator, NY State Jaycees, 1978, Outstanding Contbn., Devereaux Cmty. & Family Partnership, 1999. Episcopalian. Home: 10 Ferris Lane Poughkeepsie NY 12601

SHACKLETON, MARY JANE, small business owner; b. Colorado Springs, Colo., Oct. 20, 1934; d. James Emrie and Thelma Isabella (Vittetoe) Mc Carty; m. William H. Shackleton, Apr. 25, 1953; children: Denise, Dennis, Danette, Donna, Donald. Grad. high sch., Montebello, Calif. Owner Chi Town/Radio Shack, Oscoda, Mich., 1978—, East Tawas, 1983-97. Bd. dirs. Oscoda Downtown Devel. Authority. Named Woman of Distinction Mitten Bay Girl Scout Coun., 1999. Mem. Toastmasters (competent, sec. Lake Huron chpt. 1988-89, sec.-treas. 1991-92), Oscoda C. of C. (bd. dirs. 1985-90), Oscoda Mchts. Assn. (sec.-treas.), Quota Club Iosco (bd. dirs. 1990-91). Republican. Roman Catholic. Avocation: biking, golf. Home: 3852 N Huron Rd Oscoda MI 48750-8806

SHACKLETON, RICHARD JAMES, lawyer, director; b. Orange, N.J., May 24, 1933; s. S. Paul and Mildred W. (Welsh) S.; m. Katharine L. Richards, June 16, 1956; children: Katharine Margaret, Julia Anne, Forrest Maxwell. Student, Kalamazoo Coll., 1957; JD, Rutgers U., 1961. Bar: N.J. 1961, U.S. Dist. Ct. N.J. 1967, U.S. Dist. Ct. (ea. dist.) N.Y. 1987, U.S. Dist. Ct. (so. dist.) N.Y. 1986, U.S. Dist. Ct. (we. and no. dists.) N.Y. 1997, U.S. Ct. Appeals (3rd cir.) 1983, U.S. Ct. Appeals (4th cir.) 1986 , U.S. Supreme Ct. 1969, Fed. Bar Coun. N.J. 1988. Ltd. atty. Berry Whitson & Berry, 1961; practice Ship Bottom, N.J., 1961—; sr. ptnr. Shackleton, Hazeltine & Dasti, 1965-84, Shackleton, Hazeltine & Bishop, Ship Bottom, 1984—. Pres. Beach Haven Inlet Taxpayers Assn., 1958—68, Ocean County Vis. Homemakers Assn., 1966—72, Brodhead Watershed Assn., 1997—98; mem. U.S. Dist. Ct. N.J. Hist. Soc.; bd. dirs., v.p. Brodhead Protective Assn. Mem. ABA (litigation sect., product liability com.), Am. Judicature Soc., Fed. Bar Coun. N.Y., N.J. Bar Assn., N.Y. Bar Assn., Ocean County Bar Assn., Def. Rsch. Inst. (mem. med. device and products sect.), Ocean County Lawyers Club, Henryville Conservation Club (chmn. bd.), Henryville Flyfishers Club (pres.), The Anglers' Club Phila., Phila. Gun Club, Sandy Island Gun Club (life), NRA (life), Gun Owners Am. (life), Brodhead Protective Assn. (bd. dirs.), Brodhead Watershed Assn. (bd. dirs., pres. 1997-98, 2001-02), Ancient Inc. Order of the Beefeater. Home: 5614 West Ave Beach Haven NJ 08008-1059 Office: 22d St at Long Beach Blvd Ship Bottom NJ 08008 E-mail: shblaw@aol.com.

SHACKMAN, BEVERLY ANNE, lawyer; b. Winnipeg, Man., Can., Apr. 24, 1945; came to U.S., 1966; d. Louis and Fannie (Packer) Sisskind; m. Carl Shackman, June 26, 1966 (div. Apr. 1989); children: Megan, Dina; m. Lawrence J. Cohn, Jan. 4, 1992. BA, Bklyn. Coll., 1971; JD, Rutgers U., 1981; LLM in Taxation, NYU, 1987. Bar: N.J., 1981, N.Y. 1982. Law clk. Organized Crime Strike Force U.S. Dept. Justice, Newark, 1980-81; law clk. to Hon. Michael A. Andrew, Jr. Tax Ct. N.J., New Brunswick, 1981-82; assoc. Paul, Weiss, Rifkind, Wharton & Garrison, N.Y.C., 1982-85, Kronish, Lieb, Weiner & Hellman, N.Y.C., 1985-89, Leboeuf, Lamb, Leiby & MacRae, N.Y.C., 1989-93; pvt. practice, 1993—. Of counsel Stein, Bliablias, McGuire, Pantages & Gigl, Livingston, N.J., 1996-98; staff reporter Women's Rights Rutgers Newark Law Sch., 1980-81. Mem. ABA (real property and probate sect.), N.Y. Bar Assn. (trusts and estates sect.), Assn. Bar City N.Y. Avocations: reading, writing poetry, cooking, music, film. also: 251 Westfield Ave Clark NJ 07066

SHACKMAN, DANIEL ROBERT, psychiatrist; b. N.Y.C., Nov. 15, 1941; s. Nathan H. and Dorothy K. Shackman. BA, Columbia U., 1962, MD, 1966. Diplomate Am. Bd. Psychiatry and Neurology. Intern Mount Sinai Hosp., N.Y.C., 1966-67, resident, chief resident, fellow, 1967-70; psychiatrist USAF, Spokane, Wash., 1970-72; clin. and adminstrv. staff Brentwood VA Hosp., L.A., 1972-79; pvt. practice psychiatry, 1975-87, Santa Barbara, Calif., 1984—. Asst. clin. prof. UCLA Sch. Medicine, L.A., 1975—87; psychiat. cons. CAlif. Dept. Rehab., L.A., 1975—87; cons. psychiatrist Sanctuary Psychiat. Ctrs., Santa Barbara, 1984—2001; chmn. dept. psychiatry Santa Barbara Cottage Hosp., 1990—92. Bd. dirs. Family Counseling Svc., Spokane, 1971-72. Maj. USAF, 1970-72. Mem. Am. Psychiat. Assn., Am. Acad. Child/Adolescent Psychiatry, So. Calif. Psychiat. Soc. (dist. councillor 1989-92), Am. Soc. Clin. Psychopharmacology. Avocations: music appreciation and performance, computer science. Office: 924 Anacapa St Santa Barbara CA 93101-2115 Mailing: PO Box 15699 San Francisco CA 94115

SHACTER, DAVID MERVYN, lawyer; b. Toronto, Ont., Can., Jan. 17, 1941; s. Nathan and Tillie Anne (Schwartz) S. BA, U. Toronto, 1963; JD, Southwestern U., 1967. Bar: Calif. 1968, U.S. Ct. Appeals (9th cir.) 1969, U.S. Supreme Ct. 1982. Law clk., staff atty. Legal Aid Found., Long Beach, Calif., 1967-70; asst. city atty. City of Beverly Hills, 1970; ptnr. Shacter & Berg, Beverly Hills, 1971-83, Selwyn, Capalbo, Lowenthal & Shacter Profl. Law Corp., 1984-99; pvt. practice, 1999—. Del. State Bar Conf. Dels., 1976—; lectr. Calif. Continuing Edn. of Bar, 1977, 82, 83, 86; judge pro tem L.A. and Beverly Hills mcpl. cts.; arbitrator L.A. Superior Ct., 1983—, also judge pro tem; disciplinary examiner Calif. State Bar, 1986. Bd. dirs. and pres. Los Angeles Soc. Prevention Cruelty to Animals, 1979-89. Mem.: City of Hope Med. Ctr. Aux., Am. Arbitration Assn. (nat. panel arbitrators, neutral arbitrator, panel chmn.), Beverly Hills Bar Found. (pres. 1995—, bd. govs. 1998—2001), Beverly Hills Bar Assn. (bd. govs. 1985—, sec. 1987—88, treas. 1988—89, v.p. 1989—90, pres.-elect 1990—91, pres. 1991—92, editor-in-chief jour.), Nat. Assn. Securities Dealers (arbitrator 1998—), West Los Angeles C. of C., Wilshire C. of C. (bd. dir. 1985—87, gen. counsel 1985—87). Office: 2566 Overland Ave Ste 550 Los Angeles CA 90064-3371 E-mail: david@shacter.org.

SHACTER, JAMES DETMERS, editor, writer; b. Chgo., Apr. 14, 1926; s. Joseph Andrew and Helen Seidman Shacter; m. Nancy Louise Blankenberg, Dec. 30, 1997; m. Ruth Evelyn Bjorn, Aug. 1, 1958 (dec. Sept. 5, 1994); 1 child Joseph Edwin. BS, U. Ill., 1948. Copy editor UP, Milw., Chgo., Detroit, Washington, N.Y.C., 1947—55; chief copy editor World Book Ency., Chgo., 1955—81; freelance editor, writer, 1981—. Author: Piano Man, 1975, Loose Shoes, 1994, Jazz Party, 2000. Yeoman 3d class USN, 1944—46. Avocation: traditional jazz.

SHADARAM, MEHDI, electrical engineering educator; b. Tehran, Iran, Apr. 19, 1954; came to U.S., 1976; s. Ali and Masoumeh (Bayram) S.; m. Luz Elena Inungaray, Mar. 24, 1990; 1 child, Jacob Benjamin. BSEE, U. Sci. and Tech., Tehran, 1976; MSEE, U. Okla., 1981, PhD, 1984. Registered profl. engr., Tex. Lab. asst. elec. engring. dept. U. Okla., Norman, 1979-81, lab. instr. elec. engring. dept., 1982-84; project engr. Ra Nav Lab., Oklahoma City, 1981-82; asst. prof. elec. engring. dept. U. Tex., El Paso, 1984-90, assoc. prof. elec. engring dept., 1990-97, prof. elec. engring dept., 1997—, Schellenger prof., chmn. elec. engring. dept., 1999—. Chmn. elec. engring. dept. U. Tex., El Paso, 1999-2000. Contbr. articles to profl. jours. Recipient Faculty Fellowship award Assoc. Western U., 1990, 1991, Advising the Best Thesis award U. Tex. El Paso, 1990, ASEE Faculty fellow, 1995-96. Mem. IEEE (sr. mem., chmn. 1988-90, treas. 1987), Optical Soc. Am., Soc. Photo Optical and Instrumentation Engrs., Eta Kappa Nu. Home: 6518 Jim De Groat Dr El Paso TX 79912-7319 Office: U Tex at El Paso Elec Engring Dept El Paso TX 79968-0001 E-mail: shadaram@utep.edu.

SHADDINGER, DAWN ELIZABETH, medical researcher; b. Doylestown, Pa. Diploma in nursing, Allentown (Pa.) Hosp., 1983; BSN, Gwynedd (Pa.)-Mercy Coll., 1989; MSN, LaSalle U., 1994. Cert. ACLS, BLS. Staff nurse Doylestown Hosp., 1983-97, nursing and adminstrv. coord., 1987-90, nursing clin. coord. critical care, 1990-97, nursing rsch. coord., 1994-99, dir. clin. rsch., 1999-2001; adminstrv. dir. Ctr. of Cardiac & Vascular Rsch. Washington Adventist Hosp. , 2001—. Contbr. articles to profl. jours. Mem. AACN (cert., S.E. chpt.), Am. Coll. Cardiovascular Nursing-ACCN (lipid nurse task force), Am. Assn. Neurosci. Nurses, Am. Heart Assn., Assn. Clin. Rsch. Profls., Sigma Theta Tau. Office: 7600 Carroll Ave Silver Spring MD 20912 E-mail: dshaddin@ahm.com.

SHADDOCK, CARROLL SIDNEY, lawyer; b. Beaumont, Tex., July 7, 1940; s. Carroll Bitting Jr. and Hulda Martha (Gaertner) S.; m. Dorothea Schulze, Nov. 30, 1963; children: Carroll Christian, Peter Eric, Matthew Nolan. BA, Rice U., 1962; JD, Yale U., 1965. Ptnr. Locke Liddell & Sapp LLP, Houston, 1967—. Chmn. Scenic Am., Washington, 1985-92, Scenic Tex., 1992—, Trees for Houston, 1982—, Billboards Limited, Houston, 1982-92. Republican. Lutheran. Avocations: church music, golf, travel. Home: 1715 South Blvd Houston TX 77098-5419 Office: Locke Liddell & Sapp LLP JP Morgan Chase Tower 600 Travis St Ste 3200 Houston TX 77002-2910 E-mail: cshaddock@lockeliddell.com.

SHADDOCK, PAUL FRANKLIN, SR. human resources director; b. Buffalo, Apr. 7, 1950; s. William Edmund and Rhea (Riester) Shaddock; children: Paul Jr., Jessica. BS, State U. Coll. N.Y., Buffalo, 1973; MBA, SUNY, Binghamton, 1975. Warehouse mgr. Ralston Purina Co., Denver, 1976-77; prodn. supr. Samsonite Corp., 1978-79, labor rels. rep., 1979-83; dir. human resources NBI, Inc., 1984-89, United Techs. Corp., Colorado Springs, Colo., 1990-95, Rockwell Semiconductor Sys., Newport Beach, Calif., 1995-96; v.p. human resources CSG, Systems, Inc., Denver, 1996—. Mem. Colo. Alliance of Bus., Denver, 1983-85, 90—, exec. com. U. Colo., Colorado Springs, 1990—. Mem. Assn. of Quality Participation, Am. Personnel Assn., Colo. Human Resource Assn., Human Resource Electroncis Group, Mountain States Employers Coun., S. Metro C. of C. Republican. Roman Catholic. Avocations: swimming, tennis, skiing. Home: 4900 S Ulster St 4-110 Denver CO 80237

SHADDOCK, WILLIAM EDWARD, JR. lawyer; b. Lake Charles, La., Jan. 18, 1938; s. William Edward Shaddock and Edith (Burton) Plauche; m. Winifred Craig Gorham, Aug. 2, 1958; children: Stephen Gorham, Mary Craig, Nancy Edith. BS, La. State U., 1960, JD, 1963. Bar: La. 1963, U.S. Dist. Ct. (we. dist.) La. 1964, U.S. Supreme Ct. 1968, U.S. Ct. Appeals (5th cir.) 1981; cert. specialist in estate planning and adminstrn. La. Bd. Legal Specialization. Assoc. Plauche & Stockwell, Lake Charles, La., 1963-66; ptnr. Stockwell, Sievert, Viccellio, Clements & Shaddock, L.L.P., 1966—. Fellow Am. Coll. Trusts and Estates Counsel. Republican. Methodist. Avocations: fishing, hunting, photography. Office: Stockwell Sievert Viccellio Clements & Shaddock LLP PO Box 2900 One Lakeside Plz 4th Fl Lake Charles LA 70602 E-mail: weshaddock@ssvcs.com.

SHADDUCK, PHILLIP PRICE, surgeon; b. Long Beach, Calif., May 24, 1961; s. Jack P. and Helen L. (Luebkert) S.; m. Debra L. Browning, Feb. 16, 1991; chil dren: Michael P., Grant M. BS in Biomed. Scis. magna cum laude, U. Calif., Riverside, 1983; MD, UCLA, 1986. Diplomate Am. Bd. Surgery, Nat. Bd. Med. Examiners; cert. ATLS instr. Intern in surgery Duke U. Med. Ctr., Durham, N.C., 1986-87, jr. asst. resident in surgery, 1987-88, postdoctoral fellow, 1988-90, sr. asst. resident in surgery, 1990-92, chief resident in surgery, 1992-93, asst. cons. prof. surgery, 1993—; pvt. practice; attending surgeon Durham VA Med. Ctr., 1993—, Durham Regional Hosp., 1993—, mem. med. coun., 1997—, chief gen. surgery, 2000—. Vice chmn. credentialing N.C. Preferred Providers, Inc., 1995-99; bd. dirs. Piedmont Physicians Alliance, IPA, treas., 1996-99, chmn. fin. com., 1996-99; vis. cons. surgeon King Faisal Specialist Hosp. and Rsch. Ctr., Riyadh, Saudi Arabia, 1993, vis. prof., 1993-95; mem. med. staff adv. coun. Durham Ambulatory Surg. Ctr.,

1999—. Contbr. articles to med. jours., chpts. to books. Deacon, mem. various coms. Cole Mill Road Ch. of Christ, Durham; med. and surg. missionary Clinica Medica Saint and outreadh clinics, Tegucigalpa, Honduras, 1997-2001. Recipient Nat. Rsch. Svc. award NIH, 1988-90. Fellow ACS; mem. Am. Hernia Soc., Soc. Am. Gastrointestinal Endoscopic Surgeons, Soc. Laparoscopic Surgeons, Soc. for Surgery Alimentary Tract, Sabiston Surg. Soc., Phi Beta Kappa. Avocations: music, travel, water sports, basketball. Office: Regional Surg Assocs PO Box 15698 4301 Ben Franklin Blvd Durham NC 27704-2145

SHADDY, ROBERT E. pediatric cardiologist; b. Ft. Riley, Kans., Oct. 25, 1954; s. Raymond W. and Marjorie C. (Reith) S.; m. Jamee J. Roberts, June 9, 1984; children: Aaron James, Tyler John. BS in Psychology, Boston Coll., 1976; MD, Creighton U., 1980. Diplomate in pediatrics and pediatric cardiology Am. Bd. Pediatrics. Resident in pediatrics U. Iowa, Iowa City, 1980-83; fellow in pediatric cardiology U. Calif., San Francisco, 1983-86; practice pediatric cardiology, 1986—; med. dir. heart transplant program Primary Children's Med. Ctr., Salt Lake City, 1990—; assoc. dir. pediatric cardiology U. Utah, 1995—. Contbr. articles to profl. jours. Pres. Utah affiliate Am. Heart Assn., Salt Lake City, 1994-95. Recipient Golden Anniversary prize for disting. clin. investigation U. Utah Sch. Medicine Alumni Assn., 1997. Fellow Am. Acad. Pediatrics, Am. Coll. Cardiology; mem. Internat. Soc. for Heart and Lung Transplantation, Phi Beta Kappa. Office: U Utah/PCMC 100 N Medical Dr Ste 1500 Salt Lake City UT 84113-1103

SHADE, DEBRA L. biomedical researcher; b. Quincy, Ill., Aug. 12, 1961; d. Elvin D. and Virginia L. Starman. BS, Quincy Coll., 1983; PhD, U. North Tex., Ft. Worth, 2000. Rsch. technician Washington U., St. Louis, 1984-86; rsch. asst. U. Tex. Southwestern Med. Sch., Dallas, 1986-89; assoc. scientist Alcon Labs., Ft. Worth, 1989-90, scientist I, 1990-93, scientist II, 1993-97, sr. scientist I, 1998—2000, sr. scientist II, 2002—. Patentee in field of retinal neuroprotection. Mem.: Soc. for Exptl. Biology and Medicine. Achievements include patent in field. Office: Alcon Rsch Ltd Glaucoma Rsch R3-24 6201 South Fwy Fort Worth TX 76134-2001 E-mail: debra.shade@alconlabs.com.

SHADEGG, JOHN B. congressman; b. Phoenix, Oct. 22, 1950; s. Stephen and Eugenia Shadegg; m. Shirley Shadegg; children: Courtney, Stephen. BA, U. Ariz., 1972, JD, 1975. Advisor U.S. Sentencing Commn.; spl. asst. atty. gen. State of Ariz., 1983-90; spl. counsel Ariz. State Ho. Rep. Caucus, 1991-92; pvt. practice; mem. U.S. Congress from 4th Ariz. dist., 1995—; mem. commerce com., fin. svcs. com.; asst. whip U.S. Ho. Reps. Mem. Victims Bill of Rights Task Force, 1989-90; mem. Fiscal Accountability and Reform Efforts Com., 1991-92; counsel Arizonian's for Wildlife Conservation, 1992; chmn. Proposition 108-Two-Thirds Tax Limitation Initiative, 1992. Rep. Party Ballot Security chmn., 1982; active Corbin for Atty. Gen., 1982-86; Rep. Precinct committeeman; chmn. Ariz. Rep. Caucus, 1985-87; chmn. Ariz. Lawyers for Bush-Quayle, 1988; mem. steering com., surrogate spkr. Jon Kyl for Congress, 1988-92; former pres. Crime Victim Found.; founding dir. Goldwater Inst. Pub. Policy; chmn. Ariz. Juvenile Justice Adv. Coun.; mem. adv. bd. Salvation Army; mem. vestry Christ Ch. of Ascension, 1989-91; mem. class II Valley Leadership; bd. dirs. Ariz. State U. Law Soc. Office: US House Reps 432 Cannon Ho Office Bldg Washington DC 20515-0001*

SHADEL, WILLIAM GUSTAV, psychologist, educator; b. Washington, Jan. 22, 1968; s. William Gustav Shadel, Sandra Jean Shadel; m. Nicole A. DaCosta, Oct. 3, 1998; children: Mila, Gustav. BA, Temple U., 1990; MA, U. Ill., Chgo., 1992, PhD, 1995. Lic. psychology 1996. Asst. prof. psychiatry and human behavior Brown Med. Sch., Providence, 1997—2001; asst. prof. psychology U. Pitts., 2001—. Grantee, Nat. Cancer Inst., 1999—, Nat. Inst. Drug Abuse, 1999—2001. Mem.: APA, Am. Psychol. Soc., Soc. Behavioral Medicine, Soc. Rsch. Nicotine and Tobacco. Office: Univ Pitts 130 N Bellefield Ave Ste 510 Pittsburgh PA 15260

SHADER, RICHARD IRWIN, psychiatrist, pharmacologist, educator; b. Mt. Vernon, N.Y., May 27, 1935; s. Myer and Beatrice (Epstein) S.; m. Aline Brown, Sept. 21, 1958 (dec. Aug. 2002); children: Laurel Beth, Jennifer Robin, Robert Andrew. Student, Harvard U., 1952-56; MD, NYU, 1960; grad., Boston Psychoanalytic Inst., 1970. Diplomate Am. Bd. Psychiatry and Neurology (dir. 1977-84, treas. 1982-83, pres. 1984). Intern Greenwich Hosp., Conn., 1960-61; resident in psychiatry Mass. Mental Health Ctr., Boston, 1961-62, 64-65, NIMH, Bethesda, Md., 1962-64; asso. prof. psychiatry Harvard Med. Sch., 1970-79; prof. dept. psychiatry Tufts U. Med. Sch., Boston, 1979—, chmn. dept., 1979-91; psychiatrist in chief New Eng. Med. Ctr. Hosp., 1979-91; prof. pharmacology Tufts U. Med. Sch., 1989—, chmn. dept. pharmacology and exptl. therapeutics, 1991-93. Author: (with A. DiMascio) Psychotropic Drug Side Effects, 1970, (with D.J. Greenblatt) Benzodiazepines in Clinical Practice, 1974, Manual of Psychiatric Therapeutics, 1975, 2d edit., 1994; editor: Psychiatric Complications of Medical Drugs, 1972, (with A. DiMascio) Clinical Handbook of Psychopharmacology, 1970, (with D.J. Greenblatt) Pharmacokinetics in Clinical Practice, 1985, (with A. DiMascio) Butyrophenones in Psychiatry, 1972; MAOI Therapy, 1988, (with J.P. Tupin and D.S. Harnett) Handbook of Clinical Psychopharmacology, 1988, (with others) Drug Interactions in Psychiatry, 1989, 2d edit., 1995, Clinical Manual of Chemical Dependence, 1991; editor-in-chief Jour. Clin. Psychopharmacology, 1980—. Bd. dirs. Med. Found., Inc., 1980-87. Served with USPHS, 1962-64. Joseph J. Michaels merit scholar, 1968-69; fellow Ctr. for Advanced Study in Behavioral Scis., Stanford, Calif., 1990-91; recipient Seymour Vestermark award Am. Psychiat. Assn., 1988, 90. Mem. AMA, Mass. Med. Soc., Am. coll. Neuropsychopharmacology (v.p. 1984, pres. 1990), Am. Soc. Clin. Pharmacology & Therapeutics, Am. Soc. Pharmacology and Exptl. Therapeutics. Democrat. Jewish. Office: Tufts U Sch Medicine 136 Harrison Ave Boston MA 02111-1817

SHADEROWFSKY, EVA MARIA, photographer, writer, computer communications specialist; b. Prague, Czechoslovakia, May 20, 1938; came to U.S., 1940; d. Felix Resek and Gertrude (Telatko) Frank; children: Tom, Paul. Student, Oberlin Coll., 1955-56; BA, Barnard Coll., 1960. One-woman shows include Esta Robinson Gallery, 1982, Fairleigh Dickinson U., 1983, Donnell Libr., N.Y.C., 1985, Piermont (N.Y.) Libr., 1987, The Turning Point, Piermont, N.Y., 1988, Hopper House, Nyack, N.Y., 1989, Puchong Gallery, N.Y., 1991, Rockland Ctr. for Arts, 1992, exhibited in group shows at Soho Photo Gallery, N.Y., 1974, Fashion Inst. Tech., N.Y.C., 1975, Portland (Maine) Mus. Art, 1977, Maine Photog. Workshop, Rockport, 1978, Marcuse Pfeifer, N.Y., 1977, 1978, Foto, 1982, Barnard Coll., N.Y.C., 1983, Rockland Ctr. for Arts, 1978, 1987, 1989, 1996, Print Club, Phila., 1988; represented in collections at Bklyn. Mus., Portland (Maine) Mus. Art, Met. Mus. Art, N.Y.C., Chrysler Mus. Art, Va., Ilford Collection, N.J.; author, photographer: Suburban Portraits, 1977; photographer Women in Transition, 1975, Earth Tones, 1993, The Womansource Catalog and Review: Tools for Connecting the Community of Women, 1996, poetry critic/essayist Contact II, 1980—93, contbr. story to anthology, 1980—93, Moondance Mag., 1999, Touching Fire, 1989, Sexual Harassment: Women Speak Out, 1992, Lovers, 1992, The Time of Our Lives, 1993, photography to Camera 35 mag., Shots mag., Shutterbug. Recipient Photography award Rockland Ctr. for Arts, 1978, Gt. Am. Photo Contest, 1981, Demarais Press, 1982, Harrison Art Coun., SUNY-Purchase, 1982, The Cape Codder, 1976, 79-82. Home and Office: 265 Maple Rd Valley Cottage NY 10989-1426 E-mail: evas@aol.com.

SHADISH, WILLIAM RAYMOND, retired plastic surgeon; b. Bridgeville, Pa., May 16, 1924; s. Jacob and Elizabeth (Straus) S.; m. Karen Leigh Phillips, Oct. 25, 1972. MD, L.I. Coll. Medicine, 1949. Asst. chief plastic surgery svcs. Walter Reed Gen. Hosp., Washington, 1959-62; chief plastic surgery svcs. Letterman Gen. Hosp., San Francisco, 1962-66; pvt. practice Redding (Calif.) Hosps., 1966-92; ret., 1992. Mem. adv. bd. Dept. Vets. Affairs, Washington, 1989-2000. Lt. col. U.S. Army, 1949-66. Mem. VFW, DAV, No. Calif. Emergency Care Coun., Korean War Vets., Am. Ex-POW. Republican. Roman Catholic. Avocations: fossils, travel, gardening. Home: 845 Redbud Dr Redding CA 96001-0142 E-mail: wshadish@chw.edu.

SHADLEY, ROBERT D. retired army officer; b. Circleville, Ohio, Aug. 5, 1942; BS in Indsl. Engring., MS in Indsl. Engring., Purdue U.; M of Mil. Arts and Scis., Army Command/Gen. Staff Coll. Commd. 2d lt. U.S. Army, 1965, advanced through grades to maj. gen., 1997; served in Vietnam and Desert Shield/Desert Storm; exec.officer to the comdg. gen. U.S. Army Materiel Command, 1992-94; dir. for logistics U.S. Atlantic Command, 1994-95; chief of ordnance, comdg. gen. U.S. Army Ordnance Ctrs. and Schs., 1995-97; dep. comdg. gen. for ordnance U.S. Army Combined Arms Support Command, Aberdeen Proving Ground, Md., 1995, 97; dep. chief of staff for logistics Hdqrs. U.S. Army Forces Command, Ft. McPherson, Ga., 1997-2000. Decorated Disting. Svc. medal, Legion of Merit with 2 oak leaf clusters, Bronze Star medal with oak leaf cluster, others. Address: Alliant Techsystems MN11-2020 5050 Lincoln Dr Edina MN 55436-1097

SHADOAN, WILLIAM LEWIS, judge; b. Galesburg, Ill., July 12, 1931; s. William Parker and Hortense (Lewis) S.; m. Katherine E. Thomson, 1961; children: Ann-Wayne Harlan, Kate, Tom. BS, U. Ky., 1955; JD, U. Louisville, 1961. Bar: Ky. 1961, U.S. Dist. Ct. (we. dist.) Ky. 1961. City atty., Wickliffe, Ky., 1963; county atty. Ballard County, 1963-76; chief regional judge 1st cir. Wickliffe, 1983—. Chmn. Ballard County Dem. Party, 1963; trustee Meth. Ch., Wickliffe, 1961-84; advisor Selective Svc., Peducah, Ky., 1968; chmn. Wickliffe C. of C., 1967-71; mem. exec. com. Ky. Hist. Soc., Frankfort; vice chmn. Ky. Cert. of Need and Lic. Bd., 1973-84; named assoc. justice Ky. Surpeme Ct., 1984. Capt. U.S. Army, 1955-59. Mem. ABA, Ky. Health Systems Assn. (vice chmn. 1976-82), Ky. Bar Assn. (Outstanding Judge 1997), Assn. Trial Lawyers Am., Ky. County Ofcls. Bd. (chmn. 1976-80), Miss. River Commn. (chmn. 1976-83), Ky. County Attys. Assn. (pres. 1966-77), First Dist. Bar Assn. (pres.), Masons (Wickliffe, 32 degree), Shriners (Madisonville, Ky.), Orer Ea Star, Elks. Home: RR 2 Wickliffe KY 42087-9804 Office: Ballard Courthouse 4th St Wickliffe KY 42087

SHADRACH, JEAN HAWKINS (MARTHA SHADRACH), artist; b. La Junta, Colo., Nov. 7, 1926; d. Lloyd Marion Hawkins and Martha May (Hawkins) Sudan; widowed, 1987; children: John M., Karolyn Sue Shadrach Green. BA, U. Colo., 1948. Owner Artique, Ltd. Gallery, Anchorage, 1971-87. Instr. Foothills Art Ctr., Golden, 1988-89, Prince William Sound C.C., Cordova, Alaska, 1993, Kachemak Bay C.C., Homer, Alaska, 1994, 97, UAA, 1996, 97, 98, 99; facilitator mktg. art seminars; guest lectr. Cunard Cruise Lines, 1988-90, 95, 97. Bd. dirs. Bird Treatment and Learning Ctr., Anchorage, 1994, 97, Anchorage Art Selection Com., 1984. Recipient gov.'s award for excellence in art, Anchorage, 1970, drawing award All Alaska Juried Show, 1970, 1st prize Fairbanks Watercolor Soc., 1987; Paul Schwartz Meml. award Sumi-e Soc. Am., 1993. Mem. Alaska Watercolor Soc. (v.p. 1994-95, award 1988). Home: 3530 Fordham Dr Anchorage AK 99508-4558 E-mail: jeanshadrach@gci.net.

SHADRICK, DOROTHY JO, management consultant; b. Denver, Nov. 3, 1951; d. Herbert Eugene and Marian Rose (Walsh) Forbis; 1 child, Dawn Michele. BBA, U. Denver, 1985; MBA, U. Phoenix, 2000. Cert. exhbn. mgr., Colo. Asst. dir. meetings Assn. Operating Rm. Nurses, Denver, 1978-87; v.p. Price & Assocs., 1987; pres. Assn. Conf. and Exhbn. Mgmt., Aurora, Colo., 1987—. Contbr. articles to profl. jours. Recipient Spl. Recognition award U. Denver, 1985. Mem. Colo. Soc. Assn. Execs. (bd. dirs., Pres.'s award 1995), Am. Soc. Assn. Execs., Nat. Assn. Exhbn. Mgrs. (v.p. 1981, pres. 1982, Pres.'s award 1982). Office: Assn Confs and Exhbns Mgmt 6000 E Evans Ave Ste 3-205 Denver CO 80222-5423

SHADWICK, GERALD, management educator; b. Emporia, Kans. m. Jeannine Wedell, June 5, 1954; children: Jeffrey, Monte, Jay, Nancy. BS with honors, Kans. State U., 1954; JD with honors, George Washington U., 1967. Bar: Va. 1967, U.S. Supreme Ct., 1991. Legis. asst. Congressman Graham Purcell, Washington, 1963-66; adminstrv. asst. Senator Frank Carlson, 1967-68; pres. First Nat. Bank, Salina, Kans., 1969-86; chmn., pres., CEO Bank One, Greeley, Colo., 1986-96; Monfort exec. prof. mgmt. U. No. Colo., 1996—. Adv. bd. GE Johnson Constrn. Inc., Colorado Springs, Colo., 1984—; bd. dirs. Jaymark Oil and Gas LLC, Denver. Bd. dirs. Cmty. Found., Greeley, 1995-2000; treas. Greeley Philharm. Orch., 1995-1999; trustee Aims C.C., Greeley, 1996-99. Capt. USAF, 1954-58. Mem. Rotary Club (pres. 1999-2000). Home: 1720 37th Ave Greeley CO 80634-2804 Office: U No Colo Monfort Coll Business 17th St At 8th Ave Greeley CO 80639-0001 E-mail: gerald.shadwick@unco.edu.

SHADWICK, VIRGINIAANN GREER, librarian; b. Danville, Ky., Oct. 10, 1942; d. William Frederick and Helen Louise (Smith) Greer; m. Gordon Leon Shadwick, Dec. 31, 1979 (dec.); 1 child, Laila Jenan Uthman (dec.). BA, Mich. State U., 1964; MSLS, U. Ky., 1967; postgrad., U. Calif., Berkeley, 1983-86. Libr. San Francisco State U., 1968—. Mem. pers. commn. Laguna Salada Union Sch. Dist., Pacifica, Calif., 1979-91. Mem. Am. Birding Assn., Calif. Tchrs. Assn. (bd. dirs. 1995—, state higher edn. WHO 1995), Calif. Faculty Assn. (pres. 1985-89), Nat. Edn. Assn. Nat. Coun. Higher Edn. (pres. 1989-95, James M. Davenport Meml. award 1998). Democrat. Buddhist. Avocation: bird watching. Home: 483 Andover Dr Pacifica CA 94044-1717 Office: San Francisco State U Libr 1630 Holloway Ave San Francisco CA 94132-1722 E-mail: shadwick@sfsu.edu.

SHADZI, BAHRAM, engineering executive; b. Esfahan, Iran, Dec. 22, 1948; came to U.S., 1967; s. Javad and Robab (Emadolsadati) S.; m. Judith I. Shadzi, Sept. 18, 1971; children: Javad, Taraneh, Peymon. BSChemE, U. Minn., 1972, MSChemE, 1976. Chem. process engr. 3M Co., St. Paul, 1973-76; supt. pulp mill Iran Wood & Paper Ind., Gilan, Iran, 1976-81; prin. scientist Control Data Corp., Mpls., 1981-84, process devel. mgr., 1984-86, mgr. advanced media devel. Omaha, 1986-89; process engring. mgr. Seagate Tech. Corp., 1989-92; engring. mgr. HMT Tech. Corp., Fremont, Calif., 1992—2000; dir. mfg. process engring. Illumnia, Inc., San Diego, 2002—. Pres. mgmt. club Seagate Tech. Corp., 1987-89. Contbr. articles to profl. jours. Mem. AIChE. Achievements include patents (with others) for the development and innovation related to magnetic computer disks and the application of spin coating technology for manufacture of computer disks. Home: 10187 Byrne Ave Cupertino CA 95014-2845

SHAEFFER, CHARLES WAYNE, investment counselor; b. Bridgeton, Pa., Dec. 12, 1910; s. Bartram Augustus and Carolyn I. (Morton) S.; m. Ruth S. Smyser, Oct. 2, 1937; children— Charles Wayne, Ann B. (Mrs. Clark F. MacKenzie), Julia P. BA, Pa. State U., 1933; MBA, Harvard, 1935; LL.D., Loyola Coll., 1974. Investment counselor Mackubin Legg & Co., Balt., 1935-37; with T. Rowe Price Assos., Inc. (formerly T. Rowe Price & Assos., Inc.), 1938—, chmn. bd., 1966-76, pres., 1963-74, cons., 1976—; pres. T. Rowe Price Growth Stock Fund, Inc., 1968-74, chmn. bd., 1974-76, Rowe Price New Income Fund, 1973—. Dir. Rowe Price New Horizons Fund, Inc., 1966— , Rowe Price New Era Fund, Inc., Rowe Price Prime Res. Fund; trustee Monumental Properties Trust; lectr. investment mgmt. Balt. Coll. Commerce, 1938-70, Johns Hopkins, 1960-72 Trustee Pa. State U., Franklin Sq. Hosp.; bd. mgrs. Bryn Mawr Sch., U. Balt.; bd. dirs. Md. chpt. Nature Conservancy; chmn. bd. dirs. Md. Shock-Trauma Found. Recipient Distinguished Alumni award Pa. State U. Coll. Bus. Adminstrn., 1971-72 Mem. Investment Counsel Assn. Am. (pres. 1970-73, gov. 1965—), No-Load Mut. Fund Assn. (pres. 1972-75), Investment Co. Inst. (gov. 1968— , chmn. 1975-76), Alpha Sigma Phi, Pi Gamma Mu, Delta Sigma Pi. Clubs: Maryland (Balt.), L'Hirondelle (Balt.), Merchants (Balt.), Center (Balt.), Elkridge (Balt.); Green Spring Valley Hunt (Garrison, Md.); Laurel Fish and Game Assn. (York, Pa.), Lafayette (York, Pa.); Seaview Country (Absecon, N.J.); Farmington Country (Charlottesville, Va.). Episcopalian. Home: 603 Brightwood Club Dr Lutherville Timonium MD 21093-3632 Office: 100 E Pratt St Baltimore MD 21202-1009

SHAEFFER, CHARLIE WILLARD, JR. cardiologist; b. Phila., Feb. 8, 1938; s. Charlie Willard and Lucy Virginia (Chambliss) S.; m. Claire Brightwell, Feb. 24, 1959; children: Charlie Willard III, James Robert. BS, Fla. State U., 1960; MD, Washington U., St. Louis, 1964. Diplomate Am. Bd. Internal Medicine, Am. Bd. Cardiovascular Disease, Am. Bd. Critical Care Medicine. Rotating intern Naval Hosp., Bethesda, Md., 1964-65, resident in internal medicine Oakland, Calif., 1965-68, fellow cardiology Bethesda, 1968-70, staff cardiology Portsmouth, Va., 1970-71, chief, cardiology, 1971-74; cardiologist, corp. sec. Desert Cardiology Cons., Inc., Rancho Mirage, Calif., 1974—. Cons. Naval Hosp., San Diego, 1974-75; head cardiology Eisenhower Med. Ctr., Rancho Mirage, Calif., 1976-78, pres., med. staff, 1982-83; instr. Advanced Cadiopulmonary Life Support, Am. Heart Assn., Dallas, 1983—. Contbr. articles to profl. jours. Pres. Riverside (Calif.) County Heart Assn., 1978—79; Calif. affiliate Am. Heart Assn., Burlingame, Calif., 1984—85, Desert divsn. Palm Desert, 1989—90, chmn. S.W. Region, 1989—90, 1992—93, chmn. pub. policy subcom., 1996—99, chair tobacco issues subcom., 1998—; bd. dirs. Eisenhower Med. Ctr., Rancho Mirage, 1990—93, Eisenhower Meml. Hosp., Rancho Mirage, 1990—93. Recipient Bronze Svc. award Calif. affiliate Am. Heart Assn., 1982, Silver Svc. award 1983, 85, 87, Gold Svc. award 1988, named Physician Vol. of Yr., 1996; honoree Eisenhower Med. Ctr. Aux., 1999; recipient Sol Azteca award La Prensa Hispansa, 2000. Fellow ACP, Clin. Cardiology Am. Heart Assn., Am. Coll. Cardiology, Am. Coll. Chest Physicians. Avocations: jogging, music, reading, travel. Office: Desert Cardiology Cons 39000 Bob Hope Dr Rancho Mirage CA 92270-3221 E-mail: cshaeffer@emc.org.

SHAEFFER, RUTH GILBERT, retired nonprofit corporation executive; b. Cleve., Apr. 10, 1923; d. Homer Elsworth and Eleanor Jane (Irwin) G.; m. Robert Edwin Shaeffer, Dec. 26, 1949 (dec. 1969); children: George, Susan Ulanowsky, Mary Carol Fogg, Barbara Schmitt. BA, Coll. Wooster, 1943; PhD, MIT, 1946. Sr. cons. McMurry Co., Chgo., N.Y.C., 1946-60; exec. dir. Permanent Adminstrv. Com., N.Y.C., 1960-63; assoc. rsch. dir. Nowland and Co., Greenwich, Conn., 1963-65; mgr. adult learning systems edn. div. Xerox Corp., N.Y.C., 1965-68; sr. rsch. assoc. human resources Conf. Bd., 1968-88; human resources cons., 1988-90. Pres. Living and Learning Inst., 1996-98; pres. Kendal at Oberlin Residents Assn., 1998-99; bd. dirs., Kendal at Oberlin, 2002—. Author: Nondiscrimination in Employment, 3 vols., 1973, 75, 80, Developing Strategic Leadership, 1985, Building Global Teamwork for Growth and Survival, 1989, also others; editor: Tested Techniques of Personnel Selection, 1955; contbr. articles to profl. jours. Pres. Roosevelt Island Coun. of Orgns., Inc., 1990-95; v.p. Roosevelt Island Residents Assn., N.Y.C., 1981-89, sec., 1976-81. Mem. Human Resource Planning Soc., Mgmt. Devel. Forum (v.p. 1969-75), Phi Beta Kappa. Democrat. Home: 14 Kendal Dr Oberlin OH 44074-1901

SHAEFFER, THELMA JEAN, primary school educator; b. Ft. Collins, Colo., Feb. 1, 1949; d. Harold H. and Gladys June (Ruff) Pfeif; m. Charles F. Shaeffer, June 12, 1971; 1 child, Shannon Emily. BA, U. No. Colo., 1970, MA, 1972. Cert. profl. tchr., type B, Colo. Primary tchr. Adams County Dist 12 Five Star Schs., Northglenn, Colo., 1970-84, title I (lang. arts) tchr., 1984-97, title I, read succeed tchr., 1992-97; tchr. McElwain Elem. Sch., Denver, 1999—. Mem. policy coun. Adams County Dist. # 12 Five Star Schs., Northglenn, 1975-79, dist. sch. improvement team, 1987-89; presenter Nat. Coun. Tchrs. of English, 1990; assessor Nat. Bd. Tchrs., 2000. Vol. 1992 election, Denver, alumni advisor for Career Connections U. No. Colo., 1993-97; mem. supervisory bd. Sch. Dist. 12 Credit Union. Mem. Colo. Tchrs. Assn. (del. 1992), Dist. Tchrs. Edn. Assn. (exec. bd. mem. 1991-93), Internat. Reading Assn. (pres. Colo. coun. 1988), Internat. Order of Job's Daus. (coun.), Order Ea. Star, Delta Omicron. Episcopalian. Home: 2575 Urban St Lakewood CO 80215 Office: McElwain Elem Sch 1020 Dawson Dr Denver CO 80229-4909

SHAEVSKY, MARK, lawyer; b. Harbin, Manchuria, China, Dec. 2, 1935; came to U.S., 1938, naturalized, 1944; s. Tolio and Rae (Weinstein) S.; m. Lois Ann Levi, Aug. 2, 1964; children: Thomas Lyle, Lawrence Keith. Student, Wayne State U., 1952-53; BA with highest distinction, U. Mich., 1956, JD with highest distinction, 1959. Bar: Mich. 1959. Law clerk to presiding judge U.S. Dist. Ct., Detroit, 1960-61; assoc. Honigman Miller Schwartz & Cohn, 1961-64; ptnr. Honigman, Miller, Schwartz & Cohn, 1965-69, sr. ptnr., 1969—2001, of counsel, 2001—. Instr. law Wayne State U. Law Sch., Detroit, 1961-64; comml. arbitrator Am. Arbitration Assn., Detroit; bd. dirs. Charter One Fin. Inc., Charter One Bank. Contbr. Wayne State U. Law Rev., U. Mich. Law Rev., 1957-59, asst. editor, 1958-59. Dir. Detroit Mens Orgn. of Rehab. through Tng., 1969-79; mem. exec. bd. Am. Jewish Com., Detroit, 1965-74; trustee Jewish Vocat. Svcs., Detroit, 1973-76; sec., dir. Am. Friends Hebrew Univ., Detroit, 1976-84; mem. capital needs com. Jewish Welfare Fedn., Detroit, 1986-97; trustee William Beaumont Hosp., 1997—, bd. dirs., 2002—; trustee Beaumont Found., 1997—; bd. dirs. Shaevsky Family Found., 2000—. With U.S. Army, 1959-60. Burton Abstract fellow, 1959. Mem. ABA, Mich. Bar Assn., Franklin Hills Country Club, Detroit Athletic Club, Order of the Coif, Phi Beta Kappa. Home: The Hills of Lone Pine 4750 N Chipping Gln Bloomfield Hills MI 48302-2390 Office: Honigman Miller Schwartz & Cohn 2290 First National Bldg Detroit MI 48226 E-mail: mzs@honigman.com.

SHAFER, CAROL LARSEN, retired book reviewer; b. Spencer, Iowa, Sept. 20, 1907; d. John Adolph and Emma Louise (Cook) Larsen; m. Boyd Carlisle Shafer, June 6, 1932 (dec. Feb. 1992); children: Kirstin A. Moritz, Anders C. Shafer. BA, Morningside Coll., 1930; MA, U. Iowa, 1931. Social worker United Charities, Chgo., 1931-32; supr. social work Dunn County, Menomonie, Wis., 1933-35; book reviewer Mpls. Tribune and Mpls. Star, 1964-73, Tucson, 1975-86. Author: Filter of Time, 1996; co-author: Life, Liberty and the Pursuit of Bread, 1940; contbr. articles to profl. jours. Mem. AAUW. Home: 1923 E Joyce Blvd # HC Fayetteville AR 72703-5398

SHAFER, ERIC CHRISTOPHER, minister; b. Hanover, Pa., Apr. 10, 1950; s. B. Henry and Doris M. (Von Bergen) S.; m. Kristi L. Owens, Nov. 24, 1973. BA, Muhlenberg Coll., 1972; MDiv, Hamma Sch. Theology, 1976. Ordained to ministry Luth. Ch. Am., 1976. Pastor Holy Trinity Meml. Luth. Ch., Catasauqua, Pa., 1976-83; asst. to Bishop Northeastern Pa. Synod, Wescosville, 1983-92; staff commn. for fin. support Evang. Luth. Ch. in Am., Chgo., 1988-92, asst. dir. dept. for comm., 1992-93, dir. dept. for comm., 1993—. Contbg. editor The Lutheran mag., 1989-92. Trustee Muhlenberg Coll., Allentown, Pa., 1972-83; chmn. Luth. Film Assn., 1995—; chmn. Comm. Commn., Nat. Coun. Chs. in USA, 1996—, mem. exec. bd., 1996—. Democrat. Avocations: running, computers, photography, travel. Office: Evang Luth Ch in Am 8765 W Higgins Rd Chicago IL 60631-4178 E-mail: eshafer@elca.org.

SHAFER, JAMES ALBERT, health care administrator; b. Chgo., Aug. 26, 1924; s. James Earl and Kathleen (Sutterland) S.; m. Irene Jeanne Yurcega, June 20, 1948; children: Kathleen Mary, Patricia Ann. Technician Zenith Radio Corp., Chgo., 1946-47; owner, operator Eastgate Electronics, 1947-61; applications engr. Perfection Mica Co., Bensenville, Ill., 1961-71; pres. Electronics Unltd., Northbrook, 1972-73, Ariz. Geriatric Enterprises Inc., Safford, 1974-86; sec.-treas. Saguaro Care Inc., 1988—. Republican. Roman Catholic. Avocations: computers, photography. Home: PO Drawer H 10729 W Cottonwood Wash Rd Pima AZ 85543-0630 Office: Saguaro Care Inc PO Drawer H Pima AZ 85543 E-mail: JSHAFER@EAZNET.COM.

SHAFER, JEANNINE, music teacher, retired elementary school educator; b. Denver, Dec. 10, 1929; d. Clifford John and Agnes Amelia (Pearson) Bronelle; m. James Roy Shafer, June 22, 1952; children: Timothy Lee, Stephanie Ann Shafer Adams. B in Music Edn., U. Denver, 1951. Cert. tchr., Colo. Organist Highlands Luth. Ch., Denver, 1948-62; elem. tchr. Denver Pub. Sch., 1951-56, 60-61; elem. music tchr. Adams County Dist. # 50, Westminster, Colo., 1962-85; organist Luth. Ch. of Hope, Broomfield, 1970-82; pvt. piano tchr., 1985—; salesperson Allison's Pl., Boulder, 1987-89; coord. music Luth. Ch. of Hope, Broomfield, 1998—. Pres. Broomfield Coun. on the Arts and Humanities, 1994-97; scheduler, attendant Broomfield Emergency Ambulance Svcs., Broomfield, 1970-75; mem. task force Task Force to City Coun., Broomfield, 1977-2000. Mem. Broomfield Music Tchrs. Assn. (chmn. piano festival 1994-96), Order of Eastern Star (organist, past matron), Sigma Alpha Iota (past pres., 50th Yr. mem.). Republican. Avocations: reading, knitting, embroidery, traveling. Home: 720 W 1st Ave Broomfield CO 80020-2261

SHAFER, JOHN MILTON, hydrologist, consultant, software developer; b. Findlay, Ohio, Mar. 18, 1951; s. Paul Eugene and Mary Ethel (Schwyn) S.; m. Elise Ann Dunne, Apr. 11, 1980; children: Paul Emery, Jessica Elise, Elise Ann. BS in Earth Sci., Pa. State U., 1973; MS in Resource Devel., Mich. State U., 1975; PhD in Civil Engring., Colo. State U., 1979. Cert. hydrologist #218. Asst. rsch. prof. Colo. State U., Fort Collins, 1979-80; rsch. engr. Battelle Meml. Inst., Richland, Wash., 1980-83, sr. rsch. engr., 1983-84; hydrologist Ill. State Water Survey, Champaign, 1984-85, asst. head ground water sect., 1985-90, prin. hydrologist, 1988-91, head hydrology div., 1990-92; assoc. dir., rsch. prof. Earth Scis. and Resources Inst., U. S.C., Columbia, 1992-95, dir., 1995—. Cons. pvt. cos., 1984—; owner GWPATH, Columbia, S.C., 1992; v.p. Environ. and Archtl. Signage, Findlay, Ohio; prin. hydrologist, co-owner Applied Hydrogeologic Rsch., Inc., Seattle, 1995-00. Developer software, 1987; contbr. articles to profl. jours. Recipient John C. Frye Meml. award in geology, 1991, Ill. Groundwater Sci. Achievement award, 1993. Mem. Intergovt. Coord. Com. Groundwater, Am. Geophys. Union, Am. Inst. Hydrology (pres. Ill. sect. 1985-92), Nat. Ground Water Assn., Ill. Groundwater Assn., Sigma Xi. Presbyterian. Avocations: tennis, handball, woodworking, model building. Home: 321 Lake Front Dr Columbia SC 29212-2426 Office: Earth Scis Resouces Inst U SC 901 Sumter St Columbia SC 29201-3961 E-mail: jshafer@sc.rr.com.

SHAFER, RAYMOND PHILIP, lawyer, business executive; b. New Castle, Pa., Mar. 5, 1917; s. David Philip and Mina Belle (Miller) S.; m. Jane Harris Davies, July 5, 1941; children: Diane Elizabeth, Raymond Philip, Jane Ellen. AB cum laude, Allegheny Coll., 1938, LLD, 1963; LLB, Yale, 1941; hon. LLD degrees. Bar: N.Y., Pa. Assoc. Winthrop, Stimson, Putnam & Roberts, N.Y.C.; pvt. practice Meadville, Pa., 1945-63; counsel Shafer, Swick, Bailey, Irwin and Stack; dist. atty. Crawford County, 1948-56; mem. Pa. Senate from 50th Dist., 1959-63; lt. gov. Pa., 1963-67; gov. Commonwealth Pa., 1967-71; vis. prof. U. Pa., 1973—; counselor to v.p. of U.S., 1975-77; ptnr., sr. counselor Coopers & Lybrand, 1977-88. Past pres., chmn. bd. trustees Allegheny Coll., Meadville, Pa. Chmn. Nat. Commn. on Marijuana and Drug Abuse; chmn. Nat. Com. U.S.-China Rels.; chmn. Nat. Coun. on Pub. Svc.; world bd. govs. USO; mem. adv. bd. Am. Enterprise Inst.; active charitable, cmty. drives; bd. dirs., vice chmn. Atlantic Coun. U.S., Am.-China Soc.; trustee Cleve. Clinic Found., Freedoms Found; vice chmn. Nat. Legal Ctr. Pub. Interest. With USNR, 1942-45, PTO. Recipient Gold medal Soc. Family of Man, 1972, numerous humanitarian and civic awards. Mem. ABA, Pa. Bar Assn., Crawford County Bar Assn. (pres. 1961-63), Council Fgn. Relations, Masons (33d degree), Phi Beta Kappa, Phi Kappa Psi. Republican. Office: Shafer Swick Bailey Irwin Stack & Millin 360 Chestnut St Meadville PA 16335 *One makes a living by what one gets. One makes a life by what one gives.*

SHAFER, ROBERT TINSLEY, JR. judge; b. Cin., Sept. 11, 1929; s. Robert Tinsley and Grace Elizabeth (Welsh) S.; m. Barbara Jean Hough, Dec. 27, 1950; children: Richard Hough, Janet Lee Shafer Davis, Charles Welsh. BA, Coll. of Wooster, 1951; JD, U. Cin., 1956. Bar: Fla. 1956, U.S. Ct. Appeals (5th cir.) 1963, U.S. Dist. Ct. (so. dist.) Fla. 1961, U.S. Supreme Ct. 1965. Asst. trust officer 1st Nat. Bank, Ft. Myers, Fla., 1956-57; ptnr. Henderson, Franklin, Starnes & Holt, P.A., 1957-77; cir. judge 20th Jud. Cir. State of Fla., 1977-92, chief cir. judge, 1985-89, sr. judge, 1992—. Mem. com. for ret. and sr. judges Nat. Conf. State Trial Judges. Contbr. article to Corp. Law, 1955-56 (Goldsmith Corp. Law prize, 1956). Elder Covenant Presbyn. Ch., 1982-85; mem. jud. commn. Fla. Presbyn. Synod, 1960-63; chmn. Lee County chpt. Red Cross, Ft. Myers, 1963; chair Permanent Judicial Commn., Peace River Presbytery, Presbyn. Ch. U.S.A. 2nd lt. USMCR, 1951-53, PTO, Korea. Mem. ABA, Fla. Conf. Cir. Judges (exec. com. 1986-88), Fla. Bar Assn. (bd. govs. Jr. Bar sect. 1961-64), Lee County Bar Assn. (pres. 1968), Am. Judges Assn., Am. Judicature Soc., Nat. Conf. Met. Cts. Calusa Inn of Ct. Republican. Avocations: bicycling, travel, reading, walking. Home: 2704 Shriver Dr Fort Myers FL 33901-5931

SHAFER, ROBERTA W. CROW (ROBBIE SHAFER), human resources executive, career marketing and executive outplacement consultant, venture capital consultant; b. Long View, Tex., Oct. 31, 1950; d. George Clifford and Marie (Mitchell) C.; m. Gary Stuart Shafer, July 23, 1988. Student, U. Ala., 1968-70; AFA in Fine Arts-Drama, Music, Am. Musical & Dramatic Acad., N.Y.C., 1972. Cert. pers. cons., Nat. Assn. Pers. Cons. Exec. trainee/retail merchandising and mgmt. Bergdorf-Goodman, N.Y.C.; account exec., cons. Lawrence Agy., 1974-77; dist. sales mgr. Career House, Bensalem, Pa., N.Y.C., 1977-82; dir. rsch. and recruiting Retail Recruiters, Internat., N.Y.C., 1982-83; dir. exec. search/retail and mfg. Lloyd Cons., Inc., N.Y.C. and Chgo., 1983-85; dir. human resources R.P. McCoy Apparel, Ltd. dba Labels for Less, N.Y.C., 1985-87. Pvt. practice venture capital and human resources consulting, N.Y.C., 1987—89; ind. cons. Donaldson, Lufkin & Jenrette, N.Y.C., 1987—88; guest lectr. Lab. Inst. Tech., St. John's U., Dowling Coll., N.Y.C., 1985—95; v.p. Ann H. Tanners Co., NYC, 1988—90; pres. Crow-Shafer Assocs., N.Y.C., 1990—95, CareerCrafters, 1991—95, Career Crafters Ala., Huntsville, 1995—, Career Crafters Internat., Huntsville, 2001—. Charter mem., bd. dirs. New Bus. Network, 1996—98. Mem.: Women's Econ. Devel. Coun. (bd. dirs. Scholarship Fund 1998—2000), Nat. Assn. Pers. Cons. Democrat. Episcopalian. Avocations: attending theatre and concerts, international traveling, studying foreign cultures and languages, collecting antiques, vintage collectibles. Home and Office: 8341 White Flagg Ln SE Apt 2010 Huntsville AL 35802-4606 E-mail: robbieCCA@aol.com., success@career-crafters.com.

SHAFER, STEPHEN QUENTIN, physician; b. Barrytown, N.Y., Dec. 18, 1944; s. Frederick Quentin and Margaret (Creal) S.; m. Elizabeth Jay Shafer, July 2, 1966; children: Theodora, David, Miranda. BA, Harvard U., 1966; MD, Columbia U., 1970, MPH, 1978. Diplomate Am. Bd. Internal Medicine, Am. Bd. Neurology and Psychiatry. Intern Harlem Hosp., N.Y.C., resident, Presbyn. Hosp., N.Y.C.; assoc. clin. prof. Coll. Physicians and Surgeons Columbia U., 1988-2000, clin. prof. Coll. Physicians and Surgeons, 2000—; attending neurologist Harlem Hosp. Ctr., 1988—. Home: 285 Riverside Dr New York NY 10025-5276 Office: Harlem Hosp Ctr 506 Lenox Ave New York NY 10037-1802 E-mail: sqs1@columbia.edu.

SHAFER, SUSAN WRIGHT, retired elementary school educator; b. Ft. Wayne, Dec. 6, 1941; d. George Wesley and Bernece (Spray) Wright; 1 child, Michael R. BS, St. Francis Coll., Ft. Wayne, 1967, MS in Edn., 1969. Tchr. Ft. Wayne Community Schs., 1967-69, Amphitheatre Pub. Schs., Tucson, 1970-96; ret., 1996. Odyssey of the Mind coord. Prince Elem. Sch., Tucson, 1989-91, Future Problem Solving, 1991-95. Tchr. Green Valley (Ariz.) Cmty. Ch., Vacation Bible Sch., 1987-89, dir. vacation bible sch., 1989-93. Mem.: PEO (pres. chpt. 2001—02), AAUW, NEA (life), Phi Delta Kappa, Alpha Delta Kappa (historian Epsilon chpt. 1990—), Delta Kappa Gamma (pres. Alpha Rho chpt.). Republican. Methodist. Avocations: reading, traveling, walking. Home: 603 W Placita Nueva Green Valley AZ 85614-2827

SHAFER, THOMAS W. real estate executive; b. Wenatchee, Wash., Dec. 3, 1941; 1 child, Katrina M. Broughton. BS, Wash. State U., 1965; MS, San Diego State U., 1972. Cons. Mex. Devel., 1972-80; devel. mgr. Am. Diversified, Encino, Calif., 1976-82; v.p. Pilchers Ltd., London, 1982-90, MGM Fin., San Diego, 1997—; mng. dir. M&T Investment Bankers, 1990-97; CEO Broadway Fin., 2000—. Author: Real Estate and Economics, 1976, Urban Growth and Economics, 1978. With USN, 1965-70, Vietnam. Office: Broadway Financial Plaza A # 176 501 W Broadway San Diego CA 92101-3536 E-mail: tws120341@cox.net.

SHAFER-KENNEY, JOLIE E. writer, columnist; b. Roswell, N.Mex., Oct. 26, 1953; d. Jack Ernest and Betty Marie (Halstead) Shafer; m. David A. Kenney (div.); children: Matthew Alan, Jack Andrew. Grad., Parks Sch. Bus., 1972; student, Colo. State U., 1971, 74, U. Pitts., 1995-96. Dept. mgr. Joslins Dept. Store, Aurora, Colo., 1972-73; flight attendent United Airlines, 1974-84, publicity rep. com., 1980-84; v.p. Surg. Assocs., Inc., Latrobe, Pa., 1991-98; asst. Women and Talent Gifted Women Forum, Am. Online, 1997-98; ind. contractor AOL, Inc., 1997-99; staff Online Psychol. Svcs., Inc. AOL, 1995-97, seminar host, 1995-97; with prodn. staff AOL's Comty. Matters, 1997-98, AOL's Alt. Health and Healing, 1997-98. Editl. dir. CelebrityStores-.com., 1999—; editor-in-chief Winetree Pub. and The Wine Mag., 1999-2000. Feature/content writer Entertainment Asylum, 1997-99, Electra, 1997-98; editl. dir. Celebritystores.com, 1999—; editor-in-chief Winetree Pub., 1999-2000, www.thewineadvisor.com, www.thewinemagazine.com, www.winetree-publishing.com, 1999-2000; featured columnist ShoutingOut.com; contracted feature writer Gaiam, Inc., 2000—; nat. content writer digitalcity.com, 2000—; author: ASK JES, 1999 (pub. in Chicken Soup for the Soul 1999); contbr. 6th Bowl of Chicken Soup for the Soul, 1999; journalist: AOL's Internat. News, 1997-98, AOL TW's Digital City, Inc. (www.digitalcity.com, cbsswitchboard.com, AOL KW: Pitts.), 1999—; lic. syndicated columnist, ASK JES tm and TEENS ASK JESm; content provider: iSyndicate.com, 1999—; mng. editor: Feedbackforthought.com, 2001—; contbr. articles to online jours. and newspapers; patent pending in field. Mem. AAUW, Nat. Mus. of Women in Arts, Inst. Noetic Scis., Sea Shepherd Conservation Soc., Ctr. for Marine Conservation, Sierra Club, MADD. Avocations: French language and culture, philosophy, gun control, patient's rights, spirituality. E-mail: jes@askjes.com.

SHAFF, BEVERLY GERARD, education administrator; b. Oak Park, Ill., Aug. 16, 1925; d. Carl Tanner and Mary Frances (Gerard) Wilson; m. Maurice A. Shaff, Jr., Dec. 20, 1951 (dec. June 1967); children: Carol Maureen, David Gerrard, Mark Albert. MA, U. Ill., 1951; postgrad., Colo. Coll., 1966, 73, Lewis and Clark Coll., 1982, Portland State U., 1975-82. Tchr. Haley Sch., Berwyn, Ill., 1948-51; assoc. prof. English, Huntingdon Coll., Montgomery, Ala., 1961-62; tchr. English, William Palmer High Sch., Colorado Springs, Colo., 1964-67, 72-76, dir., 1967-72; tchr. English, Burns (Oreg.) High Sch., 1976-78; tchr. English as 2d lang. Multnomah County Ednl. Svc. Dist., Portland, Oreg., 1979-85; coord. gen. studies Portland Jewish Acad., 1984-90; with Indian Edn. Prog./Student Tng. Edn. Prog. (STEP) Portland Pub. Schs., 1990-92, 95—; tchr. St. Thomas More Sch., Portland, 1992-95; tchr. Indian Edn. Act Program Portland Pub. Schs., 1995—. Del. Colorado Springs Dem. Com., 1968, 72; active Rainbow Coalition, Portland; ct. apptd. spl. adv. CASA; mem. Lake Oswego Libr. Bd., Citizens Rev. Bd. Mem. Nat. Assn. Admnstrs., Nat. Assn. Schs. and Colls., Nat. Coun. Tchrs. Math., Nat. Coun. Tchrs. English. Home: 430 NE 16th Ave Apt 201 Portland OR 97232-2886

SHAFFAR, SCOTT WILLIAM, engineer; b. Ill., Dec. 1, 1962; s. Robert Shaffar and Lorraine Shaffar Olson; m. Renee Shaffar, June 29, 1991. BS in Aerospace Engring., Calif. Poly., 1984; MS in Engring., U. Calif., Irvine, 1993, PhD in Mech. and Aerospace Engring., 1997. Engr. Northrop, Pico Rivera, Calif., 1984-86, engr. II, 1986-88, engr. sr., 1988-92; engr. specialist Northrop-Grumman, 1992—96, sr. tech. specialist, 1996—98, project mgr., 1999—. Coun. mem. The Conf. Bd. Learning and Knowledge Mgmt. Coun. Northrop Grumman fellow., 1993-97. Mem. AIAA (sr. mem.), ASME. Republican. Achievements include patent for lean burn injector, testing engineer on B-2 (Steath Bomber) Program. Home: 40 Straw Flower Irvine CA 92620-1250 Office: Northrop Grumman Corp 1 Hornet Way El Segundo CA 90245-2804

SHAFFER, ALFRED GARFIELD (TERRY SHAFFER), service organization executive; b. Sunbury, Pa., Jan. 5, 1939; s. Alfred G. and Betty Marjorie (Vogel) Shaffer; m. Nancy Jane Dawson, Aug. 29, 1976. BS, Susquehanna U., 1961. Cert. tchr., Pa. Tchr. Danville (Pa.) Sch. Dist., 1962-69; mgr. club svc. Kiwanis Internat., Chgo., 1969-74, dir. program devel., 1974-81, dir. program svcs. Indpls., 1982-85, dir. spl. svcs., 1985-87, asst. sec. spl. svcs., 1987-88, asst. to internat. sec., 1988-94, exec. dir., 1994—; corp. affairs cons. Nat. Easter Seal Soc., Chgo., 1981-82; adminstr. Circle K Internat., 1982; mem. Pres.'s Com. on Employment of Handicapped, 1983-86. Chmn. adv. coun. 70001 Ltd., Indpls., 1984-86; mem. adv. bd. Salvation Army, Indpls., 1996—; bd. govs. Children's Miracle Network, 2001—. Recipient Gold Key of Svc., Pa. Dist. Key Clubs, 1964, Tablet of Honor Kiwanis Internat. Found., award of gold Indiana Kiwanis. Mem. Am. Soc. Assn. Execs., ACLU, Ind. Civil Liberties Union, Indps. Athletic Club, 500 Festival Assocs., USAC Winners' Cir., Travelers Protective Assn., Kiwanis (pres. Selinsgrove, Pa. 1964, lt. gov. Pa. 1966-67, pres. Chgo. 1970-72, pres. Northwest Indpls. 1991-92, Outstanding Svc. award 1981, Kiwanian of Yr. 1966, 85). Lutheran. Home: 5688 N Broadway St Indianapolis IN 46220-3073 Office: Kiwanis International 3636 Woodview Trce Indianapolis IN 46268-3196 E-mail: agtshaffer@kiwanis.org.

SHAFFER, ANITA MOHRLAND, counselor, educator; b. Racine, Wis., Apr. 5, 1939; d. Milton Arthur and Gudrun Amanda Stoffel. BS magna cum laude, U. Wis., 1961; MEd, U. Wash., 1966; postgrad., Ariz. State U., 1971-76. Cert. in elem. edn., social sci. secondary edn., spl. edn., Tex., Ariz.; lic. profl. counselor, Tex.; diplomate Internat. Acad. Behavioral Medicine, Counseling and Psychotherapy. Tchr. Racine Unified Dist. 1, 1961-63, Edmonds Sch. Dist. 15, Lynnwood, Wash., 1963-70, Ariz. Dept. Corrections, Phoenix, 1971-77; tchr. spl. edn. Pasadena (Tex.) Ind. Sch. Dist., 1977-78, spl. edn. counselor, 1978-90, elem. counselor, 1990-98; univ. supr. U. Houston, 1998—. Ednl. cons., 1998—. Mem. ACA, NAFE, Internat. Platform Assn., Mus. Fine Arts Houston (patron), Beta Sigma Phi, Pi Lambda Theta. Home: 5905 Woodway Place Court Houston TX 77057-2005

SHAFFER, AUDREY JEANNE, health information administrator, educator; b. Hutchinson, Minn., Nov. 24, 1929; d. Floyd R. and Edna C. (Seppman) Kleiman; m. Frank L. Shaffer, July 15, 1948; 1 child Cynthia Lou Shaffer Wilkinson. BS, Loma Linda U., 1973; MA, Ctrl. Mich. U., 1982. Registered health info. adminstr. Med. records clk. San Bernardino County Hosp., Calif., 1948-50; radiology receptionist White Meml. Med. Ctr., L.A., 1950-52; med. records clk. Portland (Oreg.) Adventist Hosp., 1952-53; mgr. med. records Tempe (Ariz.) Cmty. Hosp., 1953-54; mem. faculty Loma Linda (Calif.) U., 1975-96, 99—. Dir. med. info svcs. Corona Cmty. Hosp., Corona, Calif., 1973—89; cons. med. records Calif., Utah, Fla., and Philippines, 1981—93, China, 1993—; pilot and med. asst. Liga Internat., Mexico, 1964—68; chmn. Corona Blood Bank, 1957—68. Chmn. vols. Corona Cmty. Hosp. Aux., 1965—68; supr. archeology Caesarea Expdn. Am. Sch. Oriental Rsch., Israel, 1974—. Recipient Vol. Svc. award, Corona Cmty. Hosp., 1968, Congeniality award, Caesarea Archeol. Exhbn., 1975, Alumna of Yr. award Sch. Allied Health Professions, Loma Linda U., 1992. Mem.: Inland Quality Assurance Network (pres. 1988), Nat. Assn. Healthcare Quality, Inland Area Health Info Assn. (pres. 1992—93), Calif. Health Info. Assn. (quality assurance com. 1980—81, pub. rels. com. 1988—91), Am. Health Info. Mgmt. Assn., Loma Linda U. Med. Rec. Alumni (pres. 1979—81), Archeol. Inst. Am., Corona Flying Club (sec. 1960—68), Women's Improvement Club (program chmn. 1960—61). Home and Office: 880 Encanto St Corona CA 92881-3501

SHAFFER, BERNARD WILLIAM, mechanical and aerospace engineering educator; b. N.Y.C., Aug. 7, 1924; s. Abraham and Eva (Ellinsky) S.; m. Florence Solow, Feb. 23, 1947 (dec. Oct. 29, 1986); children: Janet Ilene, Roberta Franceen. BME, CCNY, 1944; MSME, Case Inst. Tech., 1947; PhD, Brown U., 1951. Registered profl. engr., N.Y., R.I. Aero. rsch. scientist flight propulsion rsch. lab. NACA (now NASA), Cleve., 1944-47; spl. lectr. applied mechanics Case Inst. Tech., 1946-47; rsch. assoc., grad. div. applied math. and engring., instr. Brown U., Providence, 1947-50; asst. prof. mech. engring. NYU, N.Y.C., 1950-53, assoc. prof., 1953-58, prof., project dir. rsch. divsn., 1958-73; prof. dept. mech. and aerospace engring. Poly. U., Bklyn. and Farmingdale, N.Y., 1973-93, prof. emeritus, 1993—. Cons. in field; mem. adv. coun. Coll. Aeros., N.Y.C., 1982—; vis. rsch. prof. mech. engring. Fla. Atlantic U., Boca Raton, 1992, Disting. vis. rsch. prof., 1993-95, 97—. Contbr. articles to profl. jours. Bd. dirs. Harbor Hills Civic Assn., Great Neck, N.Y., 1968-71. With USAAF, 1944-47. Recipient various govt. grants. Fellow ASME (Richards Meml. award 1968); mem. AIAA (assoc. fellow), Sigma Xi, Tau Beta Pi, Pi Tau Sigma. Avocations: golf, swimming.

SHAFFER, DAVID JAMES, lawyer; b. Springfield, Ohio, July 30, 1958; s. Frank James Shaffer and Martha Isabelle (Hardman) Matthews; children: Brynn Danielle, Jedediah Clay. BA, Wittenberg U., 1980; JD, Stanford U., 1983. Bar: Calif. 1984, U.S. Dist. Ct. (no. and ea. dists.) Calif. 1984, U.S. Ct. Appeals (9th cir.) 1984, U.S. Dist. Ct. (so. dist.) Calif. 1985, U.S. Dist. Ct. (we. dist.) Wash. 1986, D.C. 1988, U.S. Dist. Ct. D.C. 1988, U.S. Ct. Appeals (D.C. cir.) 1988, U.S. Dist. Ct. (no. dist.) Tex. 1991, U.S. Supreme Ct. 1993, Md. 1994, U.S. Dist. Ct. Md. 1997. Supr. field ops. U.S. Census Bur., Columbus, Ohio, 1980; legal intern Natural Resources Def. Coun., Inc., San Francisco, 1982-83; assoc. Gibson, Dunn & Crutcher, San Jose, Calif., 1983; law clk. to Judge Betty B. Fletcher, U.S. Ct. Appeals for 9th Cir., Seattle, 1983-84; assoc. Gibson, Dunn & Crutcher, San Jose, 1984-87, Arnold & Porter, Washington, 1987-92; ptnr. Semmes, Bowen & Semmes, 1992-94, Arter & Hadden, Washington, 1995-99, Thelen Reid & Priest LLP, Washington, 1999—. Contbr. articles to profl. and legal jours. Campaign mgr. Clark County Dem. Party, Springfield, 1978-80; organizer Citizens for Sensible County Planning, Fairfax, Va., 1989-94. Alumni scholar Wittenberg U., 1976. Mem. ABA, FBA (chmn. EEO com. 1992-94, individual rights and responsibilities 1994-95, co-chmn. alt. dispute resolution 1995-96, mem. governing bd. labor law and labor rels. sect., editor newsletter Labouring Oar, Outstanding Svc. award 1992), D.C. Bar Assn., Calif. Bar Assn., Order of Coif. Avocations: music, hiking, nature study. Office: Thelen Reid & Priest LLP 701 Pennsylvania Ave NW Washington DC 20004-2608 E-mail: dshaffer@thelenreid.com.

SHAFFER, DONALD, lawyer; b. Cleve., Oct. 6, 1928; s. Nathan and Ruth (Glaser) S.; m. Doris Freed, June 10, 1949; children: Nathan, Robert, David. BA, Bklyn. Coll., 1949; JD, NYU, 1991. Bar: N.Y. 1992, U.S. Dist. Ct. (so. dist.) N.Y. 1992. Cooperating atty. ACLU, N.Y.C., 1992—. Legal dir. Nassau Civil Liberties Union, Mineola, N.Y., 1995—. Co-chair New Politics Club of L.I., 1999—; mem. state com. Working Families Party, State of N.Y., 1998—. Office: ACLU 125 Broad St Fl 17 New York NY 10004-2400

SHAFFER, DOROTHY BROWNE, retired mathematician, educator; b. Feb. 12, 1923; arrived U.S., 1940; d. Hermann and Steffy (Hermann) Browne; m. Lloyd Hamilton Shaffer, July 25, 1943 (dec. 1978); children: Deborah Lee, Diana Louise, Dorothy Leslie. AB, Bryn Mawr Coll., 1943; MA, Harvard U., 1945, PhD, 1962. Mathematician MIT, Cambridge, 1947-48; assoc. mathematician Cornell Aero. Lab., Buffalo, 1952-56; mathematician Dunlap & Assocs., Stamford, Conn., 1958-60; lectr. grad. engring. U. Conn., 1962; prof. math. Fairfield (Conn.) U., 1963-92, prof. emeritus, 1992—. Vis. prof. Imperial Coll. Sci. and Tech., London, fall 1978, U. Md., College Park, spring 1981; vis. prof. U. Calif.-San Diego, summer 1981; vis. scholar, 1986; NSF faculty fellow IBM-T.J. Watson Research Center, Yorktown Heights, N.Y., 1979. Contbr. numerous papers in math. analysis. Mem. Am. Math. Soc., Math. Assn. Am., Assn. Women in Math., London Math. Soc. Achievements include patent in Viscosity Stabilized Solar Pond. Home: 156 Intervale Rd Stamford CT 06905-1311 Office: Fairfield U Dept Math & Computer Sci Fairfield CT 06430 E-mail: dbshaffer@fair1.fairfield.edu.

SHAFFER, DOUGLAS D. lawyer; b. Cin., Oct. 16, 1957; s. Harold and Ruth (Noble) S.; m. Leslie, June 8, 1992; children: William, Samuel. BS, Ohio State U., 1980; JD magna cum laude, Pepperdine Sch. Law, 1984. Atty. Luce, Forward, Hamilton & Scripps, San Diego, 1984-87, O'Melvery & Myers, L.A., 1988-90, Sanford Gage, esq., Beverly Hills, Calif., 1990-93, Michael Piuze, Esq., L.A., 1993-97, Law Offices of Douglas Shaffer, Santa Monica, Calif., 1997—. Expert witness. Scholar Pepperdine Sch. Law, 1982-84. Democrat. Avocations: triathlons, road races. Office: Law Office of Douglas Shaffer 1299 Ocean Ave Ste 900 Santa Monica CA 90401-1042 E-mail: DSHAFLAW@AOL.COM.

SHAFFER, FRANCES, real estate broker; b. Washington, Nov. 18, 1923; d. John George and Lucie Marie (Quinn) Lesch; m. Elroy James Shaffer, Aug. 13, 1942 (div. Apr. 1973); 1 child, Vernon James. Student, Colo. U., 1975. Lic. real estate broker. Seller new homes Shaffer Constrn., Englewood, Colo., 1956-73; pres. Par-Mac Realty, 1969-78; real estate broker Shaffer Realty Metro Brokers, 1978-2001; ret. Mem. Bd. Adjustments and Appeals, City of Englewood, 1987-92, mem. Housing Task Force, 1989-90; dir. youth camps Calvary Temple, Denver, 1969-79. Recipient Multi List award South Suburban Bd. Realtors, Littleton, Colo., 1975, named Realtor of Yr., 1997. Mem. Nat. Assn. Realtors, Colo. Assn. Realtors (bd. dirs. 1978-80), Metro Brokers Inc. (sec. 1981-84).

SHAFFER, HARRY GEORGE, economics educator; b. Vienna, Austria, Aug. 28, 1919; came to U.S., 1940; s. Max Schaffer and Teofilia (Infeld) Schaffer Weissman; m. Betty Rosenzweig, June 7, 1987; children by previous marriages: Bernard Charles, Ronald Eric, Len Joseph, Tanya Elaine. BS, NYU, 1947, MA, 1948, Ph.D, 1958. Instr. Concord Coll., Athens, W.Va., 1948-50; instr. U. Ala., Tuscaloosa, 1950-56; from asst. prof. to prof. U. Kans., Lawrence, 1956-69, prof. econs. and Soviet and East European studies, 1969-90, emeritus, 1990—. Vis. prof. Portland State Coll., Oreg., summer 1963, U. Calif.-Davis, 1973-74 Author: English-Language Periodic Publications on Communism, 1971, Periodicals on the Socialist Countries and on Marxism, 1977, Women in the Two Germanies, 1981; author booklet: The U.S. Conquers the West, 1974; also numerous papers, articles; editor: The Soviet Economy, 1963, rev. edit., 1969, The Soviet System in Theory and Practice, 1965, 2d edit., 1984, The Communist World: Marxist and Non-Marxist Views, 1967, (with Jan Prybyla) From Under-Development to Affluence: Western, Soviet and Chinese Views, 1968; editor, contbg. author: The Soviet Treatment of Jews, 1974, Soviet Agriculture, 1977, American Capitalism and the Changing Role of Government, 1999 Served with M.I., U.S. Army, 1943-44 Mem. Am. Econ. Assn., Assn. Comparative Econ. Studies, AAUP, Ams. for Democratic Action, Common Cause, NAACP, Unity Ch., Beta Gamma Sigma Democrat. Jewish. Home: 2510 Jasu Dr Lawrence KS 66046-4537 Office: U Kans Dept Econs 226A Summerfield Hall Lawrence KS 66045-7522

SHAFFER, JEROME ARTHUR, philosophy educator; b. N.Y.C., Apr. 2, 1929; s. Joseph and Beatrice (Leibowitz) S.; m. Olivia Anne Connery, Sept. 3, 1960 (div. 1985); children: Diana, David; m. Eliana Bar-shalom, Aug. 7, 1994. BA, Cornell U., 1950; PhD, Princeton U., 1952; MA in Marital and Family Therapy, U. Conn., 1996. Prof. philosophy Swarthmore (Pa.) Coll., 1955-67; prof. U. Conn., Storrs, 1967-94, prof. emeritus, 1994—, head dept. philosophy, 1976-94; individual, marital, and family therapist, 1995—. Exec. sec. Council Philos. Studies, 1965-72. Author: The Philosophy of Mind, 1968, Violence, 1970, Reality, Knowledge, and Value, 1971; contbr. articles to profl. jours. Served with U.S. Army, 1953-55. Fulbright fellow, 1952-53, fellow Ctr. for Advanced Study Behavioral Scis., 1963-64, NEH sr. fellow, 1973-74, Cambridge Clare Hall vis. fellow, 1987. Mem. Am. Philos. Assn., Phi Beta Kappa, Phi Kappa Phi. Home: 36 Clear View Dr Mansfield Center CT 06250-1608 Office: U Conn Dept Philosophy # U-54 Storrs Mansfield CT 06268 E-mail: jshaffer@uconn.edu.

SHAFFER, JILL, clinical psychologist; b. Columbus, Ohio, May 18, 1958; d. Melvin Warren and Emily (White) S.; m. Robert K. Yost, Jan. 9, 1991; children: Melanie Jill Yost, Robison Kimber Yost. BS in Psychology with honors, Wright State U., 1984, PsyD, 1988. Lic. psychologist, Ohio. Psychology talk show producer/participant Sta. WHIO-AM, Dayton, Ohio, 1981-83; psychology asst. and organizer Terrap S.W. Ohio, 1981-83; psychology trainee Oakwood Forensic Ctr., Lima, Ohio, 1984-85, Wright State U., Dayton, 1984-87; predoctoral resident South Community Mental Health Ctr., 1987-88; postdoctoral trainee Fulero and Assoc., 1988-89; pvt. practice, 1989—. Supervising psychologist GERI-Tech of Dayton, 1990-92; cons. psychologist disability evaluations for worker's compensation, 1989—; state examiner Indsl. Commn. of Ohio, 1989—; owner, pres. Rent Right Inc. Property Mgmt. Software. Author: (article) Strategic Intervention with Transvestism, 1989. Recipient scholarship Sch. of Profl. Psychology, 1985. Mem. APA, NOW, Ohio Psychol. Assn., Dayton Area Psychol. Assn. Avocations: home improvement, gardening, camping, sailing, biking. Office: PO Box 790 Dayton OH 45402-0790

SHAFFER, JUDY ANN, educator, data processing professional; b. Dec. 24, 1942; d. Vernon Sherwood and Josephine (Bean) Peterson; m. James Nelson Shaffer Jr., Feb. 28, 1970. BS, Morningside Coll., 1965; MS, Iowa State U., 1969; postgrad., NC State U. Tchr. math. Plaza Jr. H.S., Virginia Beach, Va., 1971; instr. Ivy Ind. Vocat. Tech. Coll., Ft. Wayne, Ind., 1973—74, Ind. Purdue U., Ft. Wayne, 1974—76; programmer Bowmar, 1976—77; programmer analyst GTE Data Svc., 1979—87, 1990; instr. dept. math. scis. Ind. Purdue U., 1987—89; edn. specialist Misys Health Care Sys., 1993—2002; ret., 2002. Instr. Star II Purdue U., Lafayette, Ind.; mem. assoc. faculty Ind. Purdue U., Ft. Wayne, 1984—85. Charter mem. Ft. Wayne Area Cmty. Band, 1979—90; mem. Raleigh Concert Band, 1990—2002, Kingdom of the San Cmty. Band, 2002—. Mem.: PEO, Kappa Mu Epsilon. Avocations: music, model railroading, golf.

SHAFFER, LEMUEL JOSEPH, obstetrician, educator; b. Chgo., Sept. 27, 1953; s. Edward and Laurel Shaffer; children: Lemuel H., Derrick Umphlett, John Umphlett. BS, DePaul U., 1975; MD, Chgo. Med. Sch., 1983. Resident ob/gyn Cook County Hosp., Chgo., 1988; attending physician Mt. Sinai Hosp., 1998—. Asst. prof. Chgo. Med. Sch., 1998—. Lt. col. USAF, 1986—. Fellow: ACOG; mem.: Am. Coll. Physician Executives. Avocation: Avocations: running, golf. Home: Apt 10125 4800 S Chicago Beach Dr Chicago IL 60615-7032

SHAFFER, MARGARET MINOR, retired library director; b. New Orleans, Sept. 20, 1940; d. Milhado Lee and Margaret Minor (Krumbhaar) S. BS, Nicholls State U., Thibodaux, La., 1962; MLS, La. State U., 1965. Asst. dir. Terrebonne Parish Pub. Libr., Houma, La., 1965-72, dir., 1973-95; ret., 1995. Named Woman of Yr., Houma Bus. and Profl. Women's Club, 1981. Mem. ALA, La. Libr. Assn. (chmn. pub. libr. com. 1986-87), Southeastern Libr. Assn. Democrat. Episcopalian. Avocations: crafts, travel. Home: 2678 Highway 311 Schriever LA 70395-3240

SHAFFER, MARY LOUISE, art educator; b. Blufton, Ind., Nov. 23, 1927; d. Gail H. and Mary J. (Graves) S. AB, Northwest Nazerene U., 1950; MA, Ball State U., 1955; EdD, MS, Ind. U., 1964. Art and music tchr. Kuna (Idaho) H.S., 1950-55; asst. prof. art Northwest Nazerene U., Nampa, Idaho, 1955-56, head art dept., 1971-98, dir. Friesen Art Galleries, 1997-2000, faculty emeritus, 1998; asst. prof. art Pasadena (Calif.) U., 1956-61; prof. art Olivet Nazarene U., Kankakee, Ill., 1964-71. Dir. music Kankakee Congl. Ch., 1964-71, Nampa Christian Ch., 1971-76, Nampa Meth. Ch., 1976-81; juror Nampa Art Guild Painting Show, 1994; head art policy coun. Northwest Nazarene U.; spkr. in field. One-woman show Friesen Art Galleries, 1999; participant European Images Art Show, 1989; cover artist Nazarene Internat. Mag., 1989; painting retrospective, 1999. Dir. music Van Nuys (Calif.) Nazarene Ch., 1957-60. E.I. Lilly grantee, 1961-62; women's singles tennis champion Kankakee, Ill., 1966, 67, 68, Boise (Idaho) Racquet and Swim Club, 1973, Idaho Sr. Tennis champion Sun Valley, 1984; watercolor Sun Valley Mountain selected to go to moon on Endeavour Space Shuttle, 1992. Mem. NAFE, Nat. Art Edn. Assn., Idaho Arts Edn. Assn., Nat. Assn. Univ. Women, Nat. Mus. Women in the Arts, Boise Racquet Swim Club, Boise Art Mus. Avocations: travel, music, renovating buildings, watercolor painting, tennis. Home: Shaffer Studios 4755 E Victory Rd Meridian ID 83642-7011

SHAFFER, PAUL E. retired banker; b. Rockford, Ohio, Aug. 3, 1926; s. Randall J. and Zelah V. (Alspaugh) S.; m. Dorothy L. Schumm, June 26, 1951; children: Paula Kay, Patti Lee. Grad., U. Wis. Sch. Banking, 1954; cert., Am. Inst. Banking; DHL (hon.), Purdue U., 1985. With Rockford Nat. Bank, 1945-48; asst. nat. bank examiner Treasury Dept., 1948-52; with Ft. Wayne (Ind.) Nat. Bank, 1952-65, from exec. v.p. to chmn., CEO, 1965-70, chmn., CEO, 1970-92, chmn. emeritus, 1993-95, ret., 1995, 1996. Bd. dirs. Old First Nat. Bank, Bluffton, Ind. Pres. Downtown Fort Wayne Assn., 1965, Credit Bur., Fort Wayne, 1962, Jr. Achievement, 1967-69; treas. Fort Wayne Better Bus. Bur., 1968, Ind.-Purdue Devel. Fund; mem. regional adv. com. Comptroller Currency, 1968-70; commr. Ft. Wayne Conv. and Tourism Authority.; past bd. dirs. Fort Wayne Conv. Bur., Fort Wayne Philharmonic Orch., Parkview Meml. Hosp.; bd. dirs. Caylor-Nickel Hosp., Ft. Wayne campus Ind. U., Ind.-Purdue Found., Taxpayers Research Assn.; past bd. dirs. United Community Services, chmn. drive, 1970-71; past bd. dirs. Fort Wayne YMCA, v.p., 1964-67; bd. adviser Ind. U.-Purdue U., Ft. Wayne; mem. fin. adv. bd. Luth. Social Services; bd. govs. Assn. Colls. Ind.; chmn. vol. com. U.S. Savs. Bonds, Allen County, Ind., numerous other civic activities. Served with USAAF, 1945. Mem. Am. Inst. Banking (past pres. Ft. Wayne chpt.), Am. Bankers Assn. (governing coun. 1978-79), Ind. Bankers Assn. (past pres., bd. dirs.), Ft. Wayne C. of C. (past v.p., bd. dirs.), Ind. C. of C. (state dir.), Execs. Club (past pres.), Ft. Wayne Country Club, Summit Club, Quest Club, Ft. Wayne Press Club, Mad Anthonys Club, Sycamore Hills Country Club, Masons (33rd degree), Shriners, Bonita Bay (Fla.) Golf Club. Home: 11132 Carnoustie Ln Fort Wayne IN 46814-9014

SHAFFER, PETER (SIR PETER SHAFFER), playwright; b. Liverpool, Eng., May 15, 1926; s. Jack and Reka (Fredman) S. BA, Cambridge U., Eng., 1950. Conscript coal mines, Eng., 1944-47; with N.Y. Pub. Libr., N.Y.C., 1951-54, Boosey & Hawkes, London, 1954-55; lit. critic Truth, 1956-57; music critic Time and Tide, 1961-62; freelance playwrite, 1957—. Vis. prof. contemporary drama Oxford (Eng.) U., 1994-95. Author: (plays) Five Finger Exercise, 1958 (Evening Standard Drama award 1958, N.Y. Drama Critics Cir. award 1960), The Private Ear, 1962, The Public Eye, 1962, It's About Cinderella, 1963, The Royal Hunt of the Sun, 1964, Black Comedy, 1965, The White Liars, 1967, The Battle of Shrivings, 1970, Equus, 1973 (Best Play Tony award 1975, Outer Critics Cir. Best Play award 1975), Amadeus, 1979 (Evening Standard Drama award 1979, London Drama Critics award 1979, Best Play Tony award 1980, Plays and Players Best Play award 1980), Yonadab, 1985, Lettice and Lovage, 1987 (Evening Standard Drama award 1988), The Gift of the Gorgon, 1992, Whom Do I Have the Honor of Addressing?, Chichester Festival Theatre, 1996, (screenplays) Follow Me!, 1971, Equus, 1977 (Acad. award nomination for best screenplay adaptation 1977), Amadeus, 1984 (Acad. award for best screenplay adaptation 1984), (TV plays) The Salt Land, 1955, Balance of Terror, 1957, (radio plays) The Prodigal Father, 1955, Whom Do I Have the Honor of Addressing?, 1989, (novels, with Anthony Shaffer) The Woman in the Wardrobe, 1951, How Doth the Little Crocodile?, 1952, Withered Murder, 1955. Created knight, 2001; decorated comdr. Order Brit. Empire; recipient Hamburg Shakespeare prize, 1987, William Inge award for disting. achievement in Am. theatre, 1992. Fellow Royal Soc. Lt. (London chpt.). Address: The Lantz Office 200 W 57th St Ste 503 New York NY 10019-3211

SHAFFER, RICHARD, communications executive; BA in Philosophy, U. Okla. Prin., founder, pub. Technologic Ptnrs., 1984—. Past sci. and tech. editor Wall Street Jour.; past columnist Forbes; columnist Fortune; editl. dir. Fortune Tech. Guides, Wall St. Jour. Tech. Summits, Wall St. Jour. Healthcare Summits. Mem. vestry St. Bartholomew's Episcopal Ch., N.Y.C. Office: Technologic Pntrs 120 Wooster St New York NY 10012-5200

SHAFFER, RICHARD JAMES, lawyer, former manufacturing company executive; b. Pe Ell, Wash., Jan. 26, 1931; s. Richard Humphrys and Laura Rose (Faas) S.; m. Donna M. Smith, May 13, 1956; children: Leslie Lauren Shaffer Litsinger, Stephanie Jane Athenton. BA, U. Wash.; LL.B., Southwestern U. Bar: Calif. Vice pres., gen. counsel, sec. NI, Inc., Long Beach, Calif., 1974-89; gen. counsel Masco Bldg. Products Corp., 1985-89; pvt. practice, Huntington Beach, Calif., 1989—. Mem. ltd. liability co. drafting com. and task force Calif. State Bar, 1992-94; lectr. on ltd. liability cos. Trustee Ocean View Sch. Dist., 1965-73, pres., 1966, 73; mem. fin. adv. com. Orange Coast Coll., 1966; mem. Long Beach Local Devel. Corp., 1978-89, Calif. Senate Commn. on Corp. Governance, Shareholders' Rights and Securities Transactions, 1986-97, chmn. drafting com. ltd. liability co. act for senate com., 1991-93; mem. City of Huntington Beach Pers. Commn., 1996-98; bd. dirs. Huntington Beach Libr. Patrons, 1996-98. Mem. ABA, Nat. Assn. Securities Dealers (bd. arbitrators), Calif. Bar Assn. (exec. com. corp. law dept. com. bus. sect. 1981-88), Orange County Bar Assn., Huntington Harbour Yacht Club, Wanderlust Skiers of Huntington Harbour (pres.).

SHAFFER, RICHARD PAUL, business owner, retired career military officer; b. Ft. Worth, Oct. 12, 1949; s. Clinton Ollis and Sylvia (Katz) S. AA in Bus., Coll. of the Mainland, 1975; BBA in Bus., Sam Houston State U., Huntsville, Tex., 1975, MBA in Bus., 1976. Pers. technician U.S. Govt., Houston, 1968-75; pers. recruiter M.D. Anderson Cancer Hosp., 1976-79; acctg. auditor State of Tex., Galveston, 1979-82; owner, fin. planner Co. Benefits, 1982—; owner Shaffer & Assocs. Real Estate, 1982—. Mem. Rep. Party. Master sgt. USAFR, 1967-87. Mem.: Modern Woodmen of Am., N.G. Assn. of Tex. Methodist. Avocations: pilot, swimming, fishing, dancing, reading. Home: 743 Marlin Bayou Vista Hitchcock TX 77563-2611 Office: Co Benefits 743 Marlin St Hitchcock TX 77563-2611

SHAFFER, SHEILA WEEKES, mathematics educator; b. Syracuse, N.Y., Oct. 20, 1957; d. Carroll Watson and Reina Lou (Yonker) Judd; m. Jason Craig Shaffer, June 4, 1983 (div. Sept. 1994). BA, SUNY, Albany, 1979, MS, 1982. Cert. tchr. English/Math., N.Y.; cert. advanced prof. in English and Math, Md. English tchr. Cortland (N.Y.) HS, 1979-81, Prince George's County, Upper Marlboro, Md., 1984-86, math. tchr., 1986-87, math. tchr./coord., 1990-95, 96-99; math./English tchr. Camden HS, St. Mary's, Ga., 1988-90; math tchr. Frederick County, Va., 1995-96, Kingston City (N.Y.) Schs., 1999—. Mem. SAT com. The Coll. Bd., N.Y.C., 1993-96. Mem. Nat. Coun. Tchrs. Math. Avocations: reading, hiking, gardening. Office: Kingston City Schools 61 Crown St Kingston NY 12401-3833

SHAFFER, SHERRILL LYNN, economist; b. Tyler, Tex., Aug. 1, 1952; s. Douglas Marsene and Ethel Elizabeth (Green) S.; m. Margaret Jane Ahrens, Jun 20, 1987; 1 child, David Carsten. BA, Rice U., 1974; MA, Stanford U., 1978, PhD, 1981. Rsch. asst. Stanford (Calif.) U., 1976-79, instr., 1979-80; from economist to chief Fed. Res. Bank N.Y., N.Y.C., 1980-88; from rsch. officer, economist to asst. v.p./discount officer Fed. Res. Bank Phila., 1988-97; John A. Guthrie disting. prof. banking and fin. svcs. U. Wyo., Laramie, 1997—. Chmn. tenure & promotion com., mem. grad. coun., 2000—, mem. MBA adv. com., grad. admissions com., 1999-2000, mem. grad. program rev. com., 2000—; violinist solo and with orchs., Calif., N.Y., 1976-88; cons. asst. Rosse & Olszewski, Palo Alto, Calif., 1978-80. Assoc. editor to editor Jour. Econs. and Bus., 1993—; contbr. articles to profl. jours. Sec. bd. dirs. N.Y. Arts Group, N.Y.C., 1982—83; mem. program com. So. Fin. Assn., 1996; exec. adv. coun. mem. dept. fin. Temple U., 1996—97; bd. advisors cultural programs series U. Wyo., 1999—; mem. fin. com. St. Matthew's Cathedral, Laramie, Wyo., 1998—, mem. vestry, 1999—2002; bd. dirs. artist selection com. Tri-County Concerts Assn., 1996—. Recipient Messier cert. Astronomical League, 1993. Mem. AAAS, Am. Econ. Assn., Am. Math. Soc., Math. Assn. Am., N.Am. Econs. and Fin. Assn., Indsl. Orgn. Soc., N.Y. Acad. Scis., Fin. Mgmt. Assn. (program com. 1991, 2001, nat. awards com. 2000, 2001), So. Fin. Assn. (program com. 1996), Delaware Valley Amateur Astronomers (observing chmn. 1993, publicity chmn. 1994-96), Chamber Music Am, editl. bd., Jour. Regulatory Econs., 2002-. Episcopalian. Avocations: hiking, astronomy, computer programming, theology, number theory, cycling. Home: 30 Silver Spur Rd Laramie WY 82072-9563 Office: U Wyo Dept Econs and Fin PO Box 3985 Laramie WY 82071-3985 E-mail: shaffer@uwyo.edu.

SHAFFER, SUSAN E. nutrition specialist; b. Nashville, Apr. 14, 1947; d. James G. and Esther W. Shaffer. B.A. in English, Elmhurst (Ill.) Coll., 1969; MS in Nutrition, Rutgers U., 1992. Mem. claim dept. Allstate Ins. Co., 1971-76, unit mgr., Springfield, Pa., 1976-77, regional life claim mgr., Basking Ridge, N.J., 1977-79, dist. claim mgr., Latham, N.Y., 1979-87; rsch. asst. food sensory lab. Rutgers U., New Brunswick, N.J., 1991-94, asst. to dir. mktg. Rescar Inc., Downers Grove, Ill, 1994—. Mem. Ins. Inst. Am. (assoc. in mgmt.). Office: Millennium Rail Inc 3 Westbrook Corporate Ctr Westchester IL 60154

SHAFFER, TERRY GEORGE, pastor; b. Meadville, Pa., Oct. 22, 1953; s. George William and Arlene (Robinson) S.; m. Sondra Lee Knight, July 21, 1973 (div. Mar. 1994); m. Beverly LoElen Buckner, July 1, 1994. BA in Sociology, Edinboro (Pa.) U., 1975; MDiv, Wesley Theol., Washington, 1978. Assoc. pastor Sharpsville (Pa.) United Meth. Ch., 1978-79; pastor Tenth St. United Meth. Ch., Erie, Pa., 1979-85, Marchand (Pa.) Charge Ch., 1985-90, Laketon Heights United Meth. Ch., Pitts., 1990-94, Albright United Meth. Ch., Pitts., 1994—. Assoc. dean Western Pa. Sch. of Mission, Pitts., 1995-96, dean, 1996-98; pres. Zoarhome, Pitts., 1995-98; vice chair chaplains, U. Pitts., 1997-98; mission amb. for African Ch. in western Pa., 1994-95. Vice pres. Zoar Home, 1998-2001. Recipient Cmty. Spirit award Jewish Assn. of Aging for Alleghany County, 1999. Mem. Kiwanis (lt. gov. Pitts. divsn. 1998-2000, chair human spiritual values Pa. dist. 2000-2002, host convention 2002-), United Methodist Ch. (mission support chmn. conf. western Pa. 2002). Avocations: model railroading, travel, camping. Home and Office: Albright United Meth 486 S Graham St Pittsburgh PA 15232-1267 E-mail: TGshaffer@aol.com.

SHAFFER, THOMAS LINDSAY, lawyer, educator; b. Billings, Mont., Apr. 4, 1934; s. Cecil Burdette and Margaret Jeanne (Parker) S.; m. Nancy Jane Lehr, Mar. 19, 1954; children: Thomas, Francis, Joseph, Daniel, Brian, Mary, Andrew, Edward. BA, U. Albuquerque, 1958; JD, U. Notre Dame, 1961; LL.D., St. Mary's U., 1983. Bar: Ind. 1961. Assoc. Barnes, Hickam, Pantzer, & Boyd, Indpls., 1961-63; prof. law U. Notre Dame, Ind., 1963-80, assoc. dean, 1969-71, dean, 1971-75, Robert and Marion Short prof., 1988-97; Robert and Marion Short prof. emeritus, 1997—; supervising atty. Notre Dame Legal Aid Clinic, 1991—; prof. law Washington and Lee U., 1980-87, Robert E.R. Huntley prof. law, 1987-88. Vis. prof. UCLA, 1970-71, U. Va., 1975-76, U. Maine, 1982, 87, 98, Boston Coll., 1992; mem. Ind. Constl. Revision Commn., 1969-70, Ind. Trust Code Study Commn., 1968-71; reporter Ind. Jud. Conf., 1963, 67. Author: Death, Property, and Lawyers, 1970, The Planning and Drafting of Wills and Trusts, 1972, 4th edit., 2001, Legal Interviewing and Counseling, 1976, 3rd edit., 1998, On Being a Christian and a Lawyer, 1981, American Legal Ethics, 1985, Faith and the Professions, 1987, ; co-author: Lawyers, Law Students, and People, 1977, Cases in Legal Interviewing and Counseling, 1980, American Lawyers and Their Communities, 1991, Property Cases, Materials and Problems, 1992, 2nd edit., 1998, Lawyers, Clients, and Moral Responsibility, 1994; co-editor: The Mentally Retarded Citizen and the Law, 1976; contbr. articles to legal jours. Served with USAF, 1953-57. Frances Lewis scholar Washington and Lee U., 1979; recipient Emil Brown Found. Preventive Law prize, 1966, Presdl. citation U. Notre Dame, 1975, St. Thomas More award St. Mary's U., 1983, Law medal Gonzaga U., 1991, Jour. Law and Religion award, 1993. Mem. Ind. State Bar Assn., Jewish Law Assn., Nat. Lawyers Assn. Roman Catholic. Home: 1865 Champlain Dr Niles MI 49120-8935 Office: Notre Dame Legal Aid Clinic 725 Howard St South Bend IN 46617-1529

SHAFFERT, KURT, retired lawyer, chemical engineer; b. Vienna, July 20, 1929; s. Rudolph nee Schafranik and Irma (Altar) S.; m. Judith Pytel, June 12, 1955; children: Elona Ruth, Robin Laurette. BChemE, CCNY, 1951; LLB cum laude, NYU, 1963. Bar: N.Y. 1963, D.C. 1965, U.S. Supreme Ct. 1967, U.S. Patent and Trademark Office 1964. Chem. engr. Diamond Alkali Co., Newark, 1951-54; process devel. engr. Am. Cyanamid Co., Stamford, Conn., 1957-59; patent liaison engr. Uniroyal Inc., 1959-63; assoc. Arthur, Dry & Kalish, N.Y.C., 1963-66, Office of Robert F. Conrad, Washington, 1966-69; sr. ptnr. Shaffert, Miller & Browne, 1970-74; sr. trial atty. intellectual property sect. Antitrust divsn. Dept. of Justice, 1974-85, professions and intellectual property sect., 1985-94, intellectual property guidelines task force, 1994, civil task force, 1994-2000; ret., 2000. Mem. Bethesda-Chevy Chase Jewish Comm. Group, 1965, pres., 1973-74, v.p. 1972-73, treas. 1971-72; mem. Jewish Comm. Ctr. of Greater Wash., 1970-78, bd. dirs., 1973-78; provided tape recorded Holocaust recollections for Stephen Spielberg Holocaust Archive Survivors of the Shoa Visual History Found., 1998. With U.S. Army, 1955-56. Mem. ABA (antitrust sect., patent, trademark and copyright sect.), Profl. Assn. Antitrust Divsn. Dept. of Justice (pres. 1978-79), Bar Assn. D.C. (council del. 1972-74), D.C. Bar Assn.

SHAFFNER, PATRICK NOEL, retired architectural engineering executive; b. Burlington, N.C., Nov. 1, 1939; s. Samuel Hubert and Martha Jane (Noel) Shaffner; m. Patricia Anne Anders, June 12, 1961; children: Scott Anders, Kimberly Page, Melissa Hope. BS, Va. Poly. and State U., 1961. Registered profl. engr., Va. and others. Structural engr. Hayes, Seay, Mattern & Mattern, Roanoke, Va., 1963-68; sr. structural engr. Sherertz & Franklin, 1968-72; ptnr. Sherertz, Franklin, Crawford, Shaffner, 1972-87; chmn., CEO Sherertz, Franklin, Crawford, Shaffner, Inc., 1988-98. Bd. dirs. Va. Tech. Coll. Engring. Com. 100; CHIP, v.p. Roanoke Found. for Downtown, Inc. Capt. Corps. Engrs., U.S. Arm, 1961-63. Paul Harris fellow. Fellow ASCE; mem. AIA (assoc.), Roanoke Regional C. of C. (Small Bus. Person of Yr. 1991), Rotary (pres. Roanoke club 1986). Lodges: Rotary (Roanoke) (pres. 1986). Republican. Baptist. Home: 2635 Turnberry Rd Salem VA 24153-7483 Office: SFCS, Inc 305 S Jefferson St Roanoke VA 24011-2003 E-mail: shaffner@adelphia.net.

SHAFFNER, RANDOLPH PRESTON, shop owner, educator, writer, publisher; b. Winston-Salem, N.C., Jan. 17, 1940; s. Emil Nathaniel and Anna Jackson (Preston) S.; m. Margaret Farmer Rhodes; children: Eric Randolph, Edward David, Joseph Andrew, Thomas Matthew, Jackson Rhodes. Student, Davidson Coll., 1958-60; BA in English with honors in writing, U. N.C., 1962, MA in Comparative Lit., 1969, PhD, 1973. Surveyor's lineman Joyce Mapping Co., Winston-Salem, 1955-58, 62; counselor, scoutmaster Camp Sequoyah, Weaverville, N.C., 1959; track repairman Alaska R.R., Anchorage, 1960; case handler Emard Packing Co., 1960, AYR Canneries, Seldovia, Alaska, 1961; tchr. U.S. Peace Corps., Chiengrai, Thailand, 1963-65, St. Christopher's Sch., Richmond, Va., 1969-71; instr. U. N.C., 1968-69, 71-73; asst. prof. Fairfield U., Conn., 1973-78, Western Carolina U., 1984, 87, Continuing Edn. program World Materpieces, Highlands, N.C., 1987-89; moderator Highlands lecture series Western Carolina U., 1989-92. Editor John F. Blair Pub., Winston-Salem, 1966-68; bookseller, owner Cyrano's Bookshop, Highlands, N.C., 1978—; founder, pub. Faraway Pub., 2001; asst. to dean Sch. Libr. Scis. U. N.C., Chapel Hill, 1973-74; literary mag. adv., mem. various subcoms. Dept. Eng. Fairfield Univ., 1973-78. Author: Apprenticeship Novel, 1984, Tree Ordinance for Town of Highlands, 1987, Good Reading Material, Mostly Bound and New: The Hudson Library 1884-1994, 1994, Heart of the Blue Ridge: Highlands, North Carolina, 2001; (with others) Nineteenth Century Literature Criticism, Vol. 21, 1989; contbr. poetry to N.C. Poetry Soc. anthology Here's to the Land, 1992; contbr. short stories to mags; contbr. Heritage of Macon Co., N.C., Vol. 2, 1999. Lectr. with Alexander, String Quartet, Words & Music, 1989, 92, 94, for Western Carolina U., Highlands lectr. series, 1991, 92, 93, 2000; instr. Ctr. for Life Enrichment, 2001; chmn. ARC Disaster Svcs., Fairfield, 1974-78, Zoning Bd. of Adjustment, Highlands, 1981-83, 85-90; pres., bd. trustees Hudson Libr., Inc., Highlands, 1987-90, 99-2001, chmn. libr. com., 1995-99; trustee Hudson Libr. Bascom-Louise Art Gallery, 1987-90, 95-99, Highlands Land Trust, Inc., 1995-96; bd. dirs. Highlands Cultural Art Ctr., 1987; fundraisingcom. Highlands Permanent Endowment Scholarships, 1987-89; Town of Highlands Millennium Com., 1999; historian Highlands Hist. Soc., Inc., 1999—; vice chmn. bd. missions Greenfield Hill Congl. Ch., Fairfield, Conn., 1977, chmn. scholarship co., 1975-77; bd. dirs. ARC, Fairfield, 1974-78; chaperon Am. Inst. for Fgn. Study, Grenoble, France, 1970. Recipient God and Country award, 1955, Outstanding Pres. and Trustee award Hudson Libr. and Bascom-Louise Gallery, 1990; Goethe Inst. scholar German Embassy, Munich, Fed. Rep. Germany, 1965, Univ. Besançon, France, 1965. Mem.: Highlands Biol. Found. (exec. com. 1986—, bd. trustees 1981—, environ. protection com. 1986, fund raising com. 1986, treas. 1990—, adv. com. on Nature Ctr. 1992—), Highlands Mchts. Assn. (chmn. fin. com., treas. 1984—87, chmn. tree com. and beautification com. 1984—89), Southeastern Booksellers Assn., Am. Booksellers Assn., Am. Acad. Poets, N.C. Poetry Soc., Writers' Workshop, Am. Comparative Lit. Assn., Internat. Comparative Lit. Assn., Nat. Peace Corps Assn., Clan Morrison Soc., Highlands Hist. Soc., Highlands C. of C., Trail Hikers Am., Rotary (Outstanding Vol. award 1989), Lambda Iota Tau (founder, faculty moderator Delta Omicon Ch. 1975—80). Democrat. Moravian. Avocations: construction, reading, travel, hiking, camping. Home: 608 Hickory St Highlands NC 28741-0765 Office: Cyrano's Bookshop 390 Main St Highlands NC 28741 E-mail: cyranos@earthlink.net.

SHAFII, BAHMAN, statistician, researcher; b. Tehran, Iran, Dec. 12, 1954; s. Mahmood and Akhtar Shafii; m. Sima Safaei; children: Sara Azar. BS with hon., Rezaeyeh U.., Rezaeyeh, Iran , 1977; MS, U. Idaho, 1980, MS, 1982, PhD, 1988. Lectr. Wash. State U., Pullman, Wash., 1984—88; dir. statis. programs U. of Idaho, Moscow, 1988—. Contbr. articles over 70 to profl. jours. Recipient Paul Howe Shepard award, Am. Pomological Soc., 1998. Mem.: NCR-170 Rsch. Advances Agrl. Statistics (Secretary 1995—2001), Am. Statis. Assn. (President 1995—96), Internat. Biometric Soc., Sigma Xi. Avocations: travel, music, poetry. Office: Statistical Programs University of Idaho PO Box 442337 Moscow ID 83844-2337 Fax: 208-885-6654. Business E-Mail: bshafii@uidaho.edu.

SHAFIR, MICHAIL KLEYNER, medical educator, educator; b. Shanghai, China, July 16, 1943; came to U.S., 1974; s. George and Isabella (Kleyner) S.; m. Adela Fruhling, May 6, 1967; children: Alan, Daniela. MD, U. Chile, 1967. Resident Gustave Roussy Cancer Inst., Villejuif, France, 1967-70; surgeon Lopez Perez Cancer Inst., Santiago, Chile, 1970-74; resident Mt. Sinai Hosp., N.Y.C., 1974-79, attending surgeon, 1979—; prof. surgery, neoplastic diseases Mt. Sinai Sch. Medicine, 1985-89, assoc. clin. prof., 1989-97, clin. prof. surgery, 1997—. Cons. in field. Jr. Faculty fellow Am. Cancer Soc., N.Y.C., 1982. Fellow Am. Coll. Surgeons; mem. Am. Soc. Clin. Oncology, N.Y. Surg. Soc., Soc. Surg. Oncology. Jewish. Office: 1021 Park Ave New York NY 10028-0959 E-mail: michail.shafir@msnyuhealth.org.

SHAFRAN, HANK, public relations executive; b. Boston, Nov. 13, 1945; s. Milton and Pauline (Hoffman) S.; m. Jane D. Shafran, Aug. 11, 1969 (div. Apr. 1982); children: Michael, Debra; m. Antoinette M. Delisi, July 26, 1987. BS, Boston U., 1968. Account exec. Burson-Marsteller, N.Y.C., 1968-71; exec. asst. to dir. Gov.'s Com. on Criminal Justice, Boston, 1971-77; dir. communications Computer Libr. Systems Inc., Newton, 1977-78; dir. pub. rels. Arnold & Co., Boston, 1979-83; dep. commr. Mass. Dept. Commerce, 1983-84; exec. v.p., ptnr. Cone Comms., 1984-91; crisis/litigation comms. cons., 1991—; dir. comms. Bingham Dana LLP, Boston, 1995—. V.p. Ronald McDonald House, Brookline, Mass., 1979—. Mem. Counselors Acad. Pub. Rels. Soc. Am., New England Broadcasting Assn., Advt. Club of Greater Boston, Publicity Club New England. Democrat. Jewish. Avocation: music. E-mail: hshafran@bingham.com.

SHAFRITZ, DAVID ANDREW, physician, research scientist; b. Phila., Oct. 5, 1940; s. Saul and Ethel (Kohn) S.; m. Sharon C. Klemow, Aug. 16, 1964; children: Gregory S., Adam B., Keith M. AB in Chemistry with honors, U. Pa., 1962, MD, 1966. Diplomate Nat. Bd. Med. Examiners, Am. Bd. Internal Medicine. Intern, then asst. resident U. Md. Hosp., Balt., 1966-68; rsch. assoc. NIH, Bethesda, Md., 1968-71; clin. and rsch. fellow Mass. Gen. Hosp., Boston, 1971-73; instr. Harvard Med. Sch., 1971-73, asst. prof. medicine, 1973; asst. prof. medicine and cell biology Albert Einstein Coll. Medicine, Yeshiva U., Bronx, N.Y., 1973-76, assoc. prof., 1976-81, prof. medicine and cell biology, 1981—, dir. Marion Bessin Liver Rsch. Ctr., 1985—, Herman Lapota prof. liver disease rsch. (endowed chair), 1992—. Cons. integrated Genetics, Inc., Framingham, Mass., 1981-86, Immuno, Vienna, Austria, 1986-91, Innovir, Inc., N.Y.C., 1991-98, Eugenetech Internat., Inc., Ramsey, N.J., 1991-93, Ctrs. for Med. Innovation, 1997-2001; temp. advisor WHO, Geneva, 1983; mem. Nat. Com. for Clin. Lab. Stds., Villanova Pa., 1983—, Renaissance Techs., 1996—, Affymetrix, Inc., 1997—; sci. adv. bd. com. liver cancer program Inst. for Cancer Rsch., Fox Chase and Phila., 1987—, mem. rev. panel C. study sect. Nat. Inst. Diabetes and Digestive and Kidney Diseases, 1988-92, chmn., 1991-92; mem. cen. coord. com. Liver Tissue Procurement and Distbn. Sys., 1986-95, Nat. Inst. Health Metabolic Pathology Study sect., 1995-99; mem. Nat. Bd. Med. Examiners and U.S. Med. Exam. Com., 1996-98. Co-author: The Liver: Biology and Pathobiology, 1982, 4th edit., 2001, Hepatobiliary Diseases, 1991; assoc. editor Hepatology, 1981-86; mem. editl. bd. Jour. Med. Virology, 1982-93, Hepatology, 1990-96, Jour. Virology, 1992-98; contbr. numerous rsch. articles and revs. to profl. pubs.; contbr. chpts. to books; patentee in field. Trustee Westchester Jewish Ctr., Mamaroneck, N.Y., 1980-86. Lt. comdr. USPHS, 1968-71. Recipient Merck award U. Pa., 1962, Morton McCutcheon Meml. Rsch. prize Sch. Medicine, 1966, Career Scientist award Irma T. Hirschl Trust, N.Y.C., 1974-79, NIH Merit award, 1994, Disting. Rsch. Achievement award Am. Liver Found., 2000; European Molecular Biology Orgn. fellow, 1978; recipient Rsch. Career Devel. award NIH, 1975-80, spl. rsch. fellow, 1971-73, rsch. grantee, 1974—. Mem. Am. Assn. for Study of Liver Diseases, Internat. Assn. for Study of Liver, Am. Gastroenterol. Assn., Am. Soc. Biochemistry and Molecular Biology, Am. Soc. Investigative Pathology, Am. Soc. Clin. Investigation, Assn. Am. Physicians, N.Y. Acad. Scis., Harvey Soc., Interurban Clin. Club (sec./treas. 1996-99, pres. 1999-2000). Democrat. Jewish. Avocations: jogging, tennis. Home: 4 Pheasant Run Larchmont NY 10538-3423 Office: Yeshiva U Albert Einstein Coll Med Marion Bessin Liver Rsch Ctr 1300 Morris Park Ave Bronx NY 10461-1926 E-mail: shafritz@aecom.yu.edu.

SHAFTON, FRANCINE ARIES, social worker; b. Chgo., May 18, 1927; d. Philip Lazarus and Anne (Zimmerman) Aries; m. Morton Jack Shafton, Dec. 18, 1949; children: Judith, Janet Shafton Bronitsky, Phyllis Shafton Katz. BA, U. Wis., 1948; MA in Social Work, U. Chgo., 1950. Social worker Tucson Child Guidance Ctr., 1967-81, Tucson Unified Sch. Dist., 1983-94. Mem. NASW (qualified clin. social worker 1985-93, diplomate 1988), NEA, Acad. Cert. Social Workers, Democrat. Jewish. Avocations: reading, traveling. Home: 5921 E Rosewood St Tucson AZ 85711-1534

SHAGAM, MARVIN HÜCKEL-BERRI, private school educator; b. Monongalia, W.Va. s. Lewis and Clara (Shagam) S. AB magna cum laude, Washington and Jefferson Coll., 1947; postgrad., Harvard Law Sch., 1947-48, Oxford (Eng.) U., 1948-51. Tchr. Mount House Sch., Tavistock, Eng., 1951-53, Williston Jr. Sch., Easthampton, Mass., 1953-55, Westtown (Pa.) Sch., 1955-58, The Thacher Sch., Ojai, Calif., 1958—; English dept. head Kurasini Internat. Edn. Centre, Dar-es-Salaam, Tanzania, 1966-67; dept. head Nkumbi Internat. Coll., Kabwe, Zambia, 1967-68. Vol. visitor Prisons in Calif., 1980-95, Calif. Youth Authority, 1983-93; sr. youth crisis counsellor InterFace, 1984-94. With U.S. Army, 1942-46, 1st lt. M.I. res.,1946-57. Danforth Found. fellow, 1942; Coun. for the Humanities fellow, Tufts U., 1983. Mem. Western Assn. Schs. and Colls. (accreditation com.), Great Teaching (Cooke chair 1977—), Phi Beta Kappa, Delta Sigma Rho, Cum Laude Soc. Republican. Avocations: hiking, camping, travel. Home: 5025 Thacher Rd Ojai CA 93023-8304 Office: The Thacher Sch 5025 Thacher Rd Ojai CA 93023-9001 Fax: 808-646-9490. E-mail: mshagam@thacher.org.

SHAGAN, BERNARD PELLMAN, endocrinologist, educator; b. Bklyn., Sept. 29, 1935; s. Samuel David and Pearl (Pellman) S.; m. Maureen Helen Oshever Amster, June 24, 1957 (div. 1970); children: Ellen Ruth Basch, Brian Ross; m. Phoebe Orange, Aug. 24, 1972; 1 child, Adam Irwin. AB, Harvard U., 1956; MD, NYU, 1960. Diplomate Am. Bd. Internal Medicine; bd. cert. endocrinology and metabolism. Chief sect. endocrinology Coney Island Hosp., Bklyn., 1968-79; chief sect. endocrinology, assoc. prof. medicine East Tenn. State U. Quillen Dishner Coll. Medicine, Johnson City, 1979-84; assoc. chmn., then acting chmn. dept. medicine Nassau County Med. Ctr., East Meadow, N.Y., 1984-87; assoc. prof. clin. medicine SUNY, Stony Brook, 1985-87; chmn., program dir. dept. medicine Monmouth Med. Ctr., Long Branch, N.J., 1987-96; prof. clin. medicine Hahnemann U., Med. Coll. Pa., Phila., 1988—; pvt. practice in endocrinology and metabolism Shrewsbury, N.Y., 1997-98, West Long Branch, NJ, 1998—2002; pvt. practice of endocrinology Long Branch, 2002—; dir., diabetes teaching center Monmouth Medical Center, 2002—. Contbr. articles to med. jours. Capt. M.C., U.S. Army, 1966-68. Fellow ACP (gov. N.J. 1996-2000), Am. Coll. Endocrinologists; mem. Am. Assn. Clin. Endocrinologists, Am. Diabetes Assn., Endocrine Soc. Jewish. Avocations: music, singing, piano. Office: 107 Monmouth Rd Ste 205 West Long Branch NJ 07764-1000 E-mail: bshagan@monmouth.com.

SHAGAN, STEVE, screenwriter, novelist, film producer; b. N.Y.C., Oct. 25, 1927; Film technician Consol. Film, Inc., N.Y.C., 1952-56, RCA, Cape Canaveral, Fla., 1956-59; asst. to publicity dir. Paramount Pictures, Hollywood, Calif., 1962-63. Prodr.: (TV series) Tarzan, 1966); prodr., writer movies for TV, Universal and CBS, Hollywood, Calif., 1968-70; writer original screenplay: Save the Tiger, 1972 (Writers Guild award, Acad. award nominee 1973); prodr. film, author screenplay: City of Angels (produced as movie Hustle), 1975, novel, screenplay The Formula, 1979, screenplay Voyage of the Damned, 1976 (Acad. award nominee); writer, prodr. film The Formula, 1980; author: (novels) Save the Tiger, 1972, City of Angels, 1975, The Formula, 1979, The Circle, 1982, The Discovery, 1985, Vendetta, 1986, Pillars of Fire, 1989, A Cast of Thousands, 1993, (screenplays) Primal Fear, 1996, Gotti, 1996 (Emmy nominee Best Screenplay). Served with USCG, 1944-46. Mem. Writers Guild Am. (bd. dirs. West chpt. 1978-82).

SHAGHOIAN, CYNTHIA LYNNE, accountant; b. Niagara Falls, N.Y., Apr. 23, 1962; d. Ralph and Joanne Lynne (Ishman) S. AAS in Acctg. with merit, Niagara County C.C., Sanborn, N.Y., 1982; BBA in Acctg. magna cum laude, Niagara U., 1984. CPA, N.Y. Staff acct. Salada Wynne Kling and Co. CPAs, Niagara Falls, 1985-88; fin. analyst Lockport (N.Y.) Meml. Hosp., 1988-90; acctg. mgr. Brown & Co. CPAs, Niagara Falls, 1990-96; pvt. practice, 1996-97; acctg. mgr. Brown & Co. LLP CPAs, 1997-98, ptnr., 1999—. Fundraising com. Lockport Meml. Hosp., 1990. Vol. United Way of Niagara, 1991, Arthritis Found., Tonawanda, N.Y., 1992—; membership subcom. Niagara Falls Area C. of C., 1994-97; mem. Campaign Com. to Elect Greg Danoian to Niagara Falls City Coun., 1994. Mem. AICPA, N.Y. State Soc. CPAs. Democrat. Avocations: softball, basketball, reading, writing, continuing edn. Home: 504 22nd St Niagara Falls NY 14301-2320

SHAGOURY, CHARLES JOSEPH, retired radiologist; b. Boston, Aug. 31, 1918; AB cum laude, Harvard U., 1940; MD, Boston U., 1943. Intern Boston City Hosp., 1944, resident in radiology, 1951-54; retired, 1994. Fellow Am. Coll. Radiology; mem. AMA, Am. Roetgen Ray Soc., Radiol. Soc. N.Am., New England Roetgen Ray Soc. E-mail: doc2@metrocast.net.

SHAH, AASHIT K. neurologist; b. Baroda, India, Feb. 19, 1964; m. Jigna Shah; children: Aashka, Ananya. MBBS, N.H.L. Mcpl. Med. Coll., Gujarat, India, 1987. Diplomate Am. Bd. Neurology. Intern Interfaith Med. Ctr., Bklyn., 1988-89; res. Wayne State U. Detroit Med. Ctr., 1989-92, fellowship, 1992-93; staff neurologist Hutzel Hosp., Detroit, 1993, Harper Hosp., Detroit, 1993, Detroit Rec. Hops., 1993. Assoc. prof. Wayne State U., 1993. Office: 8A-UHC/Dept Neur 4201 Saint Antoine St Detroit MI 48201-2153 E-mail: ashah@med.wayne.edu.

SHAH, GIRISH POPATLAL, information technology consultant; b. Junagadh, India, Apr. 11, 1942; came to U.S., 1963; s. Popatlal Gulabchand and Lalitaben Popatlas (Kamdar) S.; m. Devmani Manilal Jhaveri, June 18, 1968; children: Nivisha, Munjal, Bhavin. B in Tech., Indian Inst. Tech., Bombay, 1963; MS, U. Calif., Berkeley, 1965. Project analyst IBM Corp., Palo Alto, Calif., 1965-67; v.p. Optimun Systems, Inc., 1967-72; pres. Banking Systems Internat. Corp., Jakarta, Indonesia and Campbell, Calif., 1972-76; dir. software services Tymshare Transactions Services, San Francisco, 1980-83; sr. scientist McDonnell Douglas Corp., Fremont, 1984-86; dir. corp. devel. Sysorex Internat., Inc., Cupertino, 1986-87, v.p. Mountain View, 1987-96; sr. v.p. Sysorex Info. Systems Inc., 1987-91; exec. cons. IBM Corp., Mountain View , 1996—. Mem. adv. bd. Goodwill Industries, San Francisco, 1980—82; bd. dirs. Gujarate Cultural Assn., 1982; city gov. Fedn. Indo-Am. Assns., Fremont, Calif., 1991—95; mem. pres.'s coun. Fedn. Jain Assocs. N.Am., 1995—, v.p., 1999—2001, treas., 2001—; exec. com. Jain Ctr. No. Calif. , 1999—; bd. dirs. Jain Ctr. No. Calif., 1996—; chmn. temple bd. dirs. Jain Ctr., 1990—94; co-chmn. Jaina Conv., 1991—94; mem. Jaina Charitable Trust, 1995—. J.N. Tata Trust nat. scholar, 1963. Mem. Assn. Indians in Am. (v.p. 1980). Democrat. Home: 4048 Twyla Ln Campbell CA 95008-3721 Office: IBM Corp 5600 Cottle Rd San Jose CA 95193-0001 *Personal philosophy: Be truthful in personal and professional life while maintaining integrity and personal ethics. Reverance for all life, compassion, non-possessiveness, non-violence and vegetarianism.*

SHAH, HARESH CHANDULAL, civil engineering educator; b. Godhra, Gujarat, India, Aug. 7, 1937; s. Chandulal M. and Rama Shah; m. Mary-Joan Dersjant, Dec. 27, 1965; children: Hemant, Mihir. BEngring., U. Poona, 1959; MSCE, Stanford U., 1960, PhD, 1963. From instr. to assoc. prof. U. Pa., Phila., 1962-68; assoc. prof. civil engring. Stanford (Calif.) U., 1968-73, prof., 1973—, chmn. dept. civil engring., 1985-94, John A. Blume prof. engring., 1988-91, Obayashi prof. engring., 1991-97, dir. Stanford Ctr. for Risk Analysis, 1987-94, Obayashi prof. engring. emeritus, 1998—. Trustee Geohazards Internat.; bd. dir. OYO-RMS, Inc., Japan, ERS, R.M. Software Ltd., India, Risk Mgmt. Solutions, Inc., World Seismic Safety Initiative, Buildfolio, Inc.; cons. in field; pres. World Seismic Safety Initiative, 1994—. Author 1 book; contbr. over 250 articles to profl. jours. Mem. ASCE, Am. Concrete Inst., Earthquake Engring. Rsch. Inst., Seismol. Soc. Am., Sigma Xi, Tau Beta Pi. Avocations: hiking, climbing, travel. Office: Risk Mgmt Solutions Inc 149 Commonwealth Dr Menlo Park CA 94025-1133 E-mail: shah@cive.stanford.edu., hareshs@riskinc.com.

SHAH, HASH N. plastics technologist, researcher; b. Radhanpur, Gujarat, India, Mar. 25, 1934; came to U.S., 1973; s. Navinchandra M. and Taraben Shah; m. Hansa Shah, Dec. 25, 1959; children: Saumil, Viral. BS with honors, U. Bombay, 1955, BS in Tech., 1957, MS in Tech., 1960; degree, S. German Plastic Centre, Würtzburg, Germany, 1970. Notary pub. Rsch. engr. Info-Chem, Fairfield, N.J., 1975-79, Becton Dickinson, Fairfield, 1980-83; tech. dir. Shah Plasti-coats and Prints, Bombay, 1983-85; cons., engr. Johnson & Johnson, Warren, N.J., 1989-90; rsch. scientist, engr. Convatec, Bristol Myers & Squibb, Skillman, 1990—. Sr. editor Bombay Technologist Centennial, 1960. Rep. freeholder, New Brunswick, N.J., 1986; mem. cultural commn. City of Piscataway, N.J., mem. citizen police acad.; mem. solid waste mgmt. Middlesex County, N.J. Indian Govt. scholar 1958-60; German Govt. scholar, 1968-70; recipient award Materials of Engring. mag., 1976. Mem.: AAAS, Chem. Engring., Soc. Plastics Engrs. (sr.; bd. dirs. 1979—80), Indo-Am. Sr. Citizens Assn. (Piscataway, N.J., hon. gen. sec., sec.). Democrat. Mem. Jainistic Temple. Achievements include patent for disposable cassette for continuous drug delivery system by infusion pump; patents for surgical sharp disposable kit, heat sinker pannels, packaging for heat sensitive sterile single use clinical thermometers. Home: 1906 Mindy Ln Piscataway NJ 08854-5990 Office: Convatec Bristol Meyers & Squibb Co 200 Headquarters Park Dr Skillman NJ 08558-2624 E-mail: hashshah@hotmail.com.

SHAH, INDRAVADAN SOMALAL, physician; b. Sankheda, India, Dec. 23, 1944; m. Arvinda Shah. Pre-Med. Diploma, M.S. U., Baroda, India, 1964; MD, Baroda Med. Coll., 1970; Diploma in Dermatology/Venereology, S.S.G. Hosp./Baroda Med. Coll., 1972. Intern Cook County Hosp., Chgo., 1972-73, resident in internal medicine, 1973-75; physician with staff privileges Trinity Hosp., Dodge City, Kans., 1975-76, Humana Hosp., Dodge City, 1977, Palm Harbor Gen. Hosp., Garden Grove, Calif., 1978, St. Joseph Hosp., Orange, 1978, Santa Ana (Calif.) Tustin Cmty. Hosp., 1978, Santa Teresita Hosp., Duarte, Calif., 1978—; internal medicine physician Meth. Hosp., Arcadida, 1979—; physician with staff privileges Foothill Presbyn. Hosp., Glendora, 1991-93. Investigator participant studies Ciba Geigy Pharm. Co., 1986, Parke Davis Pharms. Co., 1992, Upjohn Pharm. Co., 1993, others; cons. in field. Fellow ACP, Am. Coll. Internat. Physicians; mem. Calif. Soc. Internal Medicine, Am. Soc. Internal Medicine, Physicians From India, Am. Diabetic Assn., Am. Soc. Hypertension, Indian Med. Assn. of Greater L.A. (life), others.

SHAH, JAMES M. actuary; b. Amadhara, India, Feb. 4, 1943; came to U.S., 1980; s. Manekchand Keshrichand and Kamuben Manekchand Shah; m. Urmila Jashwantlal Shah, May 16, 1966; children: Meeta, Keena, Jatin. BS, Gujarat U., India, 1965; MS, Gujarat U., 1969; MA, Georgetown U., 1983; MS, U. Nebr., 1986. Sr. rsch. asst. Nat. Inst. Rural Devel., Hyderabad, India, 1972-74; rsch. officer Population Ctr. World Bank Population Project, Bangalore, India, 1974-77; actuarial analyst Shelby (Ohio) Ins. Co., 1987-90; actuary ins. dept. State of N.D., Bismarck, 1990-91; pres. A S D Consulting Svcs., Mansfield, Ohio, 1991-2000; asst. actuary Blue Cross Blue Shield Utica, Utica, N.Y., 2000. Contbr. articles to profl. jours. UN fellow Ministry of Fgn. Affairs, 1978; recipient Outstanding Young Person award Garden City Jaycees, 1977, 7th Summer Seminar award U. Hawaii, 1976. Mem. Internat. Actuarial Assn. (cert. 1996), Internat. Union for Sci. Study of Population, Soc. Actuaries (cert. 1994), Am. Acad. Actuaries (cert. 1994). Avocations: travel, reading, table tennis. Home: 91 S Ireland Blvd Mansfield OH 44906-2220 Office: ASD Cons Svcs 91 S Ireland Blvd Mansfield OH 44906 E-mail: shahjim@hotmail.com.

SHAH, JAMI J. mechanical engineering educator, researcher; b. Karachi, Pakistan, July 11, 1950; came to U.S., 1975; s. Maqsood A. and Nasim K. Shah. BSME, NED Engring. Coll., Karachi, 1973; MSMetE, U. Pitts., 1976; PhDME, Ohio State U., 1984. Engr. Pakistan Steel, Karachi, 1973-75; prodn. engr. Pakistan Oxygen, 1976-80; assoc. prof. Ariz. State U., Tempe, 1984—. Cons. rsch. area in application of artificial intelligence techniques to engring. design and mfg. automation; tchr. creativity techniques in engring. & bus. Author: 2 books; contbr. more than 120 rsch. papers to profl. jours.; founding editor: ASME Transactions, founding editor: Jour. Computing and Info. Sci. Fellow: ASME. Avocations: hiking, climbing, desert plants. Office: Ariz State U Dept Mech Engring Tempe AZ 85287

SHAH, JAYPRAKASH BALVANTRAI, civil engineer; b. Jamshedpur, India, Nov. 2, 1946; came to U.S., 1969; s. Balvantrai Talakchand and Mangala Shah; m. Bharti Shah, Nov. 29, 1972; children: Bejal, Rupal. MS, Wayne State U., 1970; MBA, U. Detroit, 1981. Profl. engrs., Mich. Construction engr. George Jerome and Co., Detroit, 1970-71; ops. engr. Oakland County DPW, Pontiac, 1971-79; chmn., pres. Spalding, Dedecker and Assoc., Inc., Rochester Hills, 1979—. Pres. Am. Coun. Engring. Cos. of Mich., 2001—02. Contbr. articles to profl. jours. Planning commr. Waterford Twp., Mich., 1987—2002; dir. Oakland County Econ. Devel. Corp., Pontiac, 1982—, chmn. 1994; mem. Water Twp. Zoning Bd., 1989-94; chmn. Waterford Twp. Planning Commn. Recipient Best Design award Walchand Coll. Bd., 1968. Fellow ASCE (chmn. Mich.-Ohio Dist. Coun. 1984-85, chmn. engring. mgmt. divsn. 1990-91, pres. Mich. sect. 1980-81, Outstanding Engr. of Yr. 1993), Am. Soc. Engrs. from India (life, pres. 1982, Outstanding Engr. of Yr. award). also: Spalding Dedecker 905 South Blvd E Rochester Hills MI 48307-5358

SHAH, MANOJ RAMESHCHANDRA, psychiatrist; b. Ahmedabad, India, Sept. 5, 1945; came to U.S., 1970; s. Rameshchandra Sankalchand and Kusum Rameshchandra (Kapadia) S.; m. Prerna Dave, July 13, 1972; children: Sejal Manoj, Malav Manoj. Student, St. Xavier's Coll., 1962-64; med. student, B.J. Med. Coll., 1964-68. Diplomate Am. Bd. Psychiatry, Am. Bd. Child Psychiatry. Rotating intern New Civil Hosp., Ahmedabad, 1968-69; resident M.P. Shah Cancer Hosp., 1969-70; rotating intern Flushing (N.Y.) Hosp., 1970-71, from resident to chief resident gen. psychiatry, 1971-74; from resident to chief resident child psychiatry Mt. Sinai Hosp., Elmhurst, N.Y., 1974-76; dir. hosp. svcs., sr. psychiatrist B.M. Inst. Mental Health, Ahmedabad, 1976-78; child psychiatrist Angel Guardian Home, Bklyn., 1978-88; rsch. psychiatrist child behavior disorders clinic Schneider Children's Hosp., New Hyde Park, N.Y., 1988-91, med. dir. child & adolescent behavior ctr., 1992-2000; coord. crisis intervention program Schneider Children's Hosp. of Long Island Jewish Med. ctr., New Hyde Park, N.Y., 1988-98; med. dir. Rap Clinic, 2000—; asst. prof. psychiatry SUNYAl, Stony Brook, 1980-89, Albert Einstein Coll. Medicine, Bronx, N.Y., 1989—. Staff child psychiatrist L.I. Jewish Hillside Med. Ctr., N.Y., 1978-81; physician-in-charge ambulatory svcs. divsn. child and adolescent psychiatry Schneider Children's Hosp., 1997-98; cons. psychiatrist East Plains Mental Health Ctr., Hicksville, N.Y., 1981-83, Commack (N.Y.) Consultation Ctr., 1983-84; med. dir. Help-Aid-Directions, Hicksville, 1983-84, Outreach Consultation Ctr., Wantagh, N.Y., 1983-84; pvt. practice, Westbury, N.Y., 1978-88; coord. crisis intervention program Schneider Children's Hosp., 1988-98; bd. visitors, mem. Pilgrim Psychiat. Ctr.; cons. psychiatrist Massapequa Gen. Hosp., Seaford, N.Y., 1981-83 Bd. dirs. Mercy Haven, Inc., West Babylon, N.Y., 1980—; vol. attending physician South Oaks Hosp., Amityville, N.Y., 1981-83, L.I. Jewish Hillside Med. Ctr., New Hyde Park, 1978—. Recipient spl. award Cultural Festival of India, 1991, Cmty. Svc. award New Hyde Park Found., 2000. Fellow APA (com. poverty, homelessness and psychiat. disorders 1998—, Astra-Zeneca minority fellowship selection com. 1996—), Royal Coll. Psychiatrists (U.K.); mem. AMA, Med. Soc. State of N.Y., N.Y. Coun. Child & Adolescent Psychiatry, Am. Acad. Child & Adolescent Psychiatry, Ahmedabad Med. Assn., Indian Med. Soc., Nassau County Psychiat. Soc. (health care reform com. 1994-95, pres. 1994-96), Queens County Psychiat. Soc. (chair CME com. 1996—, pres.-elect 1996-97, pres. 1997-98. dep. rep. APA 1999-2000), Indo-Am. Psychiat. Assn. (newsletter editor 1980-84, sec. 1989-92, pres.-elect 1992-94, pres. 1994-96, chair bd. trustees 2000—), Am. Assn. Child & Adolescent Psychiatry (ethnic and cultural issues com. 1991-94), Fedn. Indian Assns. (chair med. & dental svcs. 1991). Office: Schneider Childrens Hosp LI Med Ctr 26901 76th Ave Rm 135 New Hyde Park NY 11040-1434

SHAH, NANDLAL CHIMANLAL, physiatrist; b. Sadra, Gujarat, India, July 3, 1933; came to U.S., 1969; s. Chimanial D. and Dahiben C. (Shah) Shah; m. Indira N. Shah, May 15, 1960; children: Sandip N., Tushar N. Student, M.G. Sci. Inst., Ahmedabad, India, 1952; MB, BS, B.J. Med. Coll., Ahmedabad, India, 1957. Diplomate Am. Bd. Phys. Medicine and Rehab., Am. Bd. Quality Assurance and Utilization Review Physicians. Intern Yonkers (N.Y.) Gen. Hosp., 1970; resident in internal medicine St. Barnabas Hosp., Bronx, N.Y., 1971; resident in phys. medicine and rehab. Albert Einstein Coll. Medicine, 1971-74; staff physiatrist, dir. med. svcs. Inst. Phys. Medicine and Rehab., Peoria, Ill., 1974-79; med. dir. Thomas Rehab. Hosp., Asheville, N.C., 1979-81; staff physiatrist phys. medicine and rehab. Charlotte (N.C.) Inst. Rehab. (formerly Charlotte Rehab. Hosp.), 1981; pvt. practice Carolina Rehab. Clinic, Charlotte, 1981-99, ret., 2000. Mem. Masons. Hindu. Avocations: Indian classical music, social, cultural and religious programs.

SHAH, NATWARLAL BHOGILAL, physician; b. Halol, Gujarat, India, Nov. 2, 1937; came to U.S., 1966; s. Bhogilal Chunilal Shah; m. Pushpa Chimanlal, Feb. 27, 1959; children: Paresh, Pragnesh, Smita. MB, BS, Gujarat U., 1964. Diplomate Am. Bd. Pediat. Intern Freedmont Hosp, Washington, 1966-67; resident in pediats. Howard U, 1966-69; fellow in adolescent medicine Children's Hosp., 1969-71; pvt. practice Gambriles, Md., 1975-93, Crofton (Md.) Ctr., 1975—. Fellow Am. Acad. Pediat. (Md. chpt.); mem. Am. Assn. Physicians India, State of Md. Med. Soc. Office: 1667 Crofton Ctr Crofton MD 21114-1303 Fax: (410) 721-8874.

SHAH, NAYAN, internist; b. Botad, India, July 21, 1956; came to U.S., 1978; s. Rasiklal Shah; m. Jayu Shah; children: Suketu, Shalin. MD, Bombay U., 1979. Diplomate Am. Bd. Internal Medicine, Am. Bd. Gastroenterology. Pvt. practice, Hollywood, Md., 1984—. Dir. Tri-County Endoscopy Ctr., Hollywood, 1989. Fellow Am. Coll. Gastroenterology; mem. Am. Soc. Gastrointestinal Endoscopy. Office: 24035 Three Notch Rd Hollywood MD 20636

SHAH, NEETA MINAL, internist; b. Bombay, India, Dec. 15, 1963; came to U.S., 1987; d. Harshadray Ambalal and Leena (Harshadray) Shah; m. Minal Jasvant Shah, Feb. 7, 1987; children: Neil, Devan, Karishma. MD, J.N. Med. Coll., Belgaum, India, 1987. Diplomate Am. Bd. Internal Medicine. Resident in internal medicine Flushing (N.Y.) Hosp. Med. Ctr., 1988-91, emergency rm. physician, 1991, clin. instr., 1994—, asst. program dir., 1996-99, program dir. internal medicine, 1999-2000; pvt. practice Lewis County Gen. Hosp., Lowville, N.Y., 1992-93; program dir. internal medicine North Shore Univ. Hosp., Forest Hills, 2000—. Mem. AMA, ACP, Assn. of Program Dirs. in Internal Medicine. Office: North Shore U Hosp 102-01 66th Rd Forest Hills NY 11375 E-mail: nmshah@pol.net.

SHAH, RASESH HARSHADRAY, engineer; b. Bombay, Nov. 24, 1954; came to U.S., 1973; s. Harshadray Chimanlal and Nirmala Harshidrary (Shah) S.; m. Shilpa Rasesh, Nov. 2, 1979; children: Rishi, Suril. BSME, U. Toledo, 1977, MS in Indsl. Engring., 1982, MBA in Fin., 1986. Project engr. Sargent & Lundy Engrs., Chgo., 1977-78; with The Andersons, Maumee, Ohio, 1978—, mgr. maintenance and adminstrv. svcs., 1982-88, dir. engring. and maintenance, 1988—. Pres. India Assn. of Toledo, 1986; bd. dirs. Planned Parenthood N.W. Ohio, Toledo, 1987; mem. bd. of trustees Hindu Temple of Toledo, 1989—. Mem. Am. Soc. Indsl. Engrs. (sr.), Orgn. Energy Engrs., Rotary (scholarship 1974-77), Tau Beta Pi, Pi Tau Sigma. Republican. Avocations: reading, crossword puzzles, tennis, volleyball. Home: 8929 Sand Ridge Dr Holland OH 43528-9223 Office: The Andersons 507 Illinois Ave Maumee OH 43537-1708

SHAH, SAMEER NAREN, financial advisor, management consultant; b. Cleve., Aug. 21, 1964; s. Naren C. and Neena N. Shah. BA, Amherst (Mass.) Coll., 1986; MBA, Stanford (Calif.) U., 1991. CFA; CFP. Bus. analyst McKinsey & Co., N.Y.C., 1986-88, assoc., 1991-93, mgr., 1993-95, assoc. Madrid, 1988-89; mgr. Mitchell Madison Group, 1996-97; mng. dir. Shah & Assocs., Tampa, Fla., 1997—. Mem. Nat. Assn. Personal Fin. Advisors, Assn. Investment Mgmt. and Rsch., Fin. Planning Assn. Republican. Home: 659 Loggerhead Island Dr Satellite Beach FL 32937 Office: Shah & Assocs 7028 Bonaventure Dr Tampa FL 33607 E-mail: sameers1@aol.com.

SHAH, SANDY, physician; b. Baroda, India, Oct. 10, 1967; BS, Rutgers U., 1989; DO, N.Y. Coll. Osteo. Medicine, Old Westbury, 1994; postgrad., U. Miami, 2002—. Diplomate Am. Bd. Internal Medicine, cert. pulmonary technician. Rsch. technician, hematology dept. Thomas Jefferson U. Hosp., Phila., 1989—90; pulmonary/critical care U. Pa., 1989—90; osteo. rotating intern Long Beach (N.Y.) Meml. Hosp., 1994-95; resident in internal medicine Cooper Hosp./Univ. Med. Ctr., Camden, N.J., 1995-98; fellow in cardiology UMDNJ/Robert Wood Johnson U. Hosp., New Brunswick, NJ, 1998—2001; clin. dir. Merck Cardiovasc., Phila., 2000—; staff Vets. Affairs Health Care Sys., E. Orange, N.J., 2000—. Disting. Scholars Program scholar, 1985-89, Garden State scholar, 1985-89. Mem. AMA, ACP, Am. Coll. Cardiology, Am. Osteo. Assn., Am. Coll. Osteo. Physicians and Surgeons, N.J. Assn. Osteo. Physicians and Surgeons, Am. Heart Assn., Doctors of World. Avocations: music, tennis, art, travel, theater. Home: Timbercreek Unit 209 1801 Laurel Rd Lindenwold NJ 08021

SHAH, SANJAY G. internist, cardiologist; b. Ahmedabad, Gujarat, India; m. Manisha S. Shah; children: Ashmi, Jay. MBBS, N.H.L. Muni Med. Coll., Ahmedabad, 1985. Diplomate Am. Bd. Internal Medicine with subspecialty in cardiovascular disease. Resident in internal medicine SUNY, Bklyn., 1988-91, attending physician, 1991-92, fellow in cardiology, 1992-95; pvt. practice Cardiology Specialist Ltd., Virginia Beach, Va., 1995—. Fellow Am. Coll. Cardiology. Avocations: music, travel, reading, cricket and other sports. Office: 1016 Independence Blvd Virginia Beach VA 23455-5503

SHAH, SHIRISH ANANTLAL, pharmacist; b. Bombay, India, Apr. 26, 1938; s. Anantlal T. and Lilavati A. (Choksi) S.; m. Portia Rose Dahling, Apr. 30, 1966; children: Sanjay, Kishan, Kinnari. BS in Pharmacy, U. Bombay, 1961; MS, U. Conn., 1964; PhD, U. Iowa, 1975. Scientist product devel. Armour Pharm. Co., Kankakee, Ill., 1963-69; head pharm. product devel. sect. Pennwalt Corp., Rochester, N.Y., 1969-72; sr. pharm. scientist USV Pharm. Corp., Tuckahoe, 1975-76; asst. mgr. pharm. research Johnson & Johnson Baby Products Co., Piscataway, N.J., 1976-79; dir. research and tech. services Zenith Labs., Inc., Northvale, 1979-85; v.p. devel. and tech. affairs Lemmon Co., Sellersville, Pa., 1985-87; dir. product devel. Ciba Consumer Pharm., Edison, N.J., 1988-89; mgr. R&D DuPont Pharm., Garden City, N.Y., 1990-91; mgr. new product devel. Perrigo Co., Allegan, Mich., 1992—2001; v.p. sci. affairs Paddock Labs, Inc., Mpls., 2002—. Mem. Am. Assn. Pharm. Scientists, Am. Pharm. Assn., Drug Info. Assn., Am. Chem. Soc., Rho Chi, Phi Lamda Upsilon. Lodges: Masons. Hindu. Home: 607 Springwood Dr Kalamazoo MI 49009-9390 E-mail: s.shah@paddocklabs.com.

SHAH, SHIRISH KALYANBHAI, computer science, chemistry and environmental science educator; b. Ahmedabad, India, May 24, 1942; came to U.S., 1962, naturalized, 1974; s. Kayyanbhai T. and Sushilaben K. S.; m. Kathleen Long, June 28, 1973; 1 son, Lawrence. BS in Chemistry and Physics, St. Xavier's Coll. Gujarat U., 1962; PhD in Phys. Chemistry, U. Del., 1968; cert. in bus. mgmt., U. Va., 1986; PhD in Cultural Edn. (hon.), World U. West, 1986. Asst. prof. Washington Coll., Chestertown, Md., 1967-68; dir. quality control Vita Foods, 1968-72; asst. prof., assoc. prof. sci., adminstr. food, marine sci. and vocat. programs Chesapeake Coll., Wye Mills, 1968-76; assoc. prof., prof. sci., chmn. dept. tech. studies C.C. of Balt., 1976-91; assoc. prof. chemistry Coll. Notre Dame of Md., 1991—2002, Towson U., Towson, Md., 2002—. Chmn. computer sys. and engring. techs., 1982-89, project facilitator telecom. curriculum and lab., 1985-89, coord. tech. studies, 1989-91; adj. prof. Phys. Sci. Coppin State Coll., 1996-98; mem. Balt. City Adult Edn. Adv. Com., 1982-89, Distance Learning Task Force, 1996-97; chmn. Coll. wide computer user com., 1985-91; coun. mem. Faculty R&D, 1994-97; adj. prof. chemistry Townson U., 1998—, Morgan State U., 1999—; lectr./prof. chemistry Villa Julie Coll., 2002—; cons. joint apprentice com. Baltimore City Govt., 1980-91. Contbr. articles to profl. jours. Permanent mem. Rep. Senatorial Com.; charter mem. Rep. Presdl. Task Force; mem. Congl. Adv. Com., 1983—; adviser Young Reps., 1992-2002. Recipient Phoenix award Am. Chem. Soc., 1996, 97, Pub. Rels. award, 1996, Sci. Policy award, 2000. Fellow Am. Inst. Chemists (co-chair internat. com. 2002); mem. IEEE, APHA, NSTA, Am. Lung Assn. (com. 1971-80, bd. dirs. 1971-80), Am. Lung Assn. Md. (bd. dirs. 1971-80), Am. Chem. Soc. (chmn.-elect Md. Sect. 1995-96, chmn. 1996-98, chair kids and chemistry program of Md. sect. 1996-99, bd. dirs. 1971-80, sec. Mid-Atlantic regional conf.), Assn. Indsl. Hygiene (chmn. com. govt. rels. Md. sect. 1998—, chair pub. rels. com. 2000--, pres.-elect Chesapeake sect. 2002-2003), Data Processing Mgmt. Assn., Nat. Environ. Tng. Assn., Nat. Assn. Indsl. Tech. (dir. local region, bd. accreditors 1989-95), Am. Vocat. Assn., Am. Tech. Edn. Assn., Am. Fedn. Tchrs., Md. State Tchrs. Assn., Md. Assn. Cmty. and Jr. Colls. (v.p. 1977-78, pres. 1978-97), Sigma Xi, Epsilon Pi Tau, Iota Lambda Sigma Nu. Roman Catholic. Home: 5605 Purlington Way Baltimore MD 21212-2950 Office: Chemistry Dept Towson University Towson MD 21252- E-mail: sshah@towson.edu., dr.shah@juno.com.

SHAH, SURENDRA POONAMCHAND, engineering educator, researcher; b. Bombay, Aug. 30, 1936; s. Poonamchand C. and Maniben (Modi) S.; m. Dorothie Crispell, June 9, 1962; children: Daniel S., Byron C. BE, B.V.M. Coll. Engring., India, 1959; MS, Lehigh U., 1960; PhD, Cornell U., 1965. Asst. prof. U. Ill., Chgo., 1966-69, assoc. prof., 1969-73, prof., 1973-81; prof. civil engring Northwestern U., Evanston, Ill., 1981—, dir. Ctr. for Concrete and Geomaterials, 1987—, prof. civil engring., 1989—, Walter P. Murphy prof. of engring., 1992—. Cons. govt. agys. and industry, U.S.A., UN, France, Switzerland, People's Republic China, Denmark, The Netherlands; vis. prof. MIT, 1969, Delft U., The Netherlands, 1976, Denmark Tech. U., 1984, LCPC, Paris, 1986, U. Sidney, Australia, 1987; NATO vis. sci. Turkey, 1992; disting. vis. prof. Nat. Singapore U., 1999. Co-author: Fiber Reinforced Cement Composites, 1992, High Performance Concrete and Applications, 1994, Fracture Mechanics of Concrete, 1995; contbr. more than 400 articles to profl. jours.; editor 12 books; mem. editorial bds. 4 internat. jours.; editor-in-chief Jour. Concrete Sci. and Engring. Recipient Thompson award ASTM, Phila., 1983, Disting. U.S. Vis. Scientist awrd Alexander von Humboldt Found., 1989, Swedish Concrete award, Stockholm, 1993, Engring. News Record award of Newsmaker, 1995, Charles Perkow award, 1997. Fellow Am. Concrete Inst. (chmn. tech. com., Anderson award 1989, 99, Henry Crown award 2000), Internat. Union Testing and Rsch. Labs. Materials and Structures (chmn. tech. com. 1989—, mgmt. adv. bd. 1996—, Gold medal 1980); mem.

ASCE (past chmn. tech. com., mem. exec. com., mem. adv. bd. 1998—, Richard J. Caroll Meml. Lectr. 2001, vis. chair prof.). Home: 921 Isabella St Evanston IL 60201-1773 Office: Northwestern U Tech Inst Rm A130 2145 Sheridan Rd Evanston IL 60208-0834

SHAH, SYED-WAQAR, science educator; m. Ulfat Zahara Bukhari; children: Syed Hassan Waqar, Syed Ahsan Bilal, Syed Annis Waqar, Mansoora Marriam Bukhari, Shala Sharif Bukhari. Faculty of Sci., Govt. Coll., Lahore, Pakistan, 1970; BSc Biology, Govt. Saadiq Egerton Coll., Bahawalpur, Pakistan, 1973; B.Ed. in Sci. Edn., B. Zakariya U., Multan, Pakistan, 1977; M.Ed. in Secondary Edn., U. Punjab, Lahore, 1980; M.Ed. in Ednl. Leadership, Wayne State U., 1996. Tchr. sci., botany, zoology and gen. sci. Govt. H.S., M.Ghar, Pakistan, 1977-79; tchr. sci., math. and social studies U. Lab. Sch. IER, Lahore, Pakistan, 1980-83; assoc. prof. U. Punjab, 1984-99; tchr. Wayne County RESA, Mich., 1990-91; substitute tchr. Dearborn and Hamtramck Pub. Schs., 1995-96; faculty. U. Punjab Inst. Edn. and Rsch., Lahore, 1999—. Chmn. acad. affairs com. U. Punjab, Lahore, 1997-99, mem. acad. staff assn., 1983-99, chmn. estate and maintenance com., 1993-94, mem. budget and purchase com., 1994-94. sec. student affairs com., 1986-88. Scholar Sch. Bd. Edn., Multan, Pakistan, 1965. Mem. Wayne State Alumni Assn. Home: PO Box 4244 Falls Church VA 22044 E-mail: waqara@yahoo.com.

SHAH, VINOD PURUSHOTTAM, research scientist; b. Baroda, Gujarat, India, Sept. 2, 1939; came to U.S., 1960; s. Purushottam and Taraben Shah.; m. Manjula Shah, Feb. 18, 1965; children: Manish, Sujata. B in Pharmacy, U. Madras, 1959; PhD in Pharm. Chemistry, U. Calif., San Francisco, 1964. Pharm. R & D chemist Sarabhai Chems., Baroda, India, 1964-69; postdoctoral rsch. fellow U. Calif., San Francisco, 1969-75; sr. rsch. chemist, tech. coord. FDA, Washington, 1975-81, pharmaconkinetic reviewer Rockville, Md., 1981-84, br. chief, 1984-88, asst. dir., 1988-90, assoc. dir., 1990-94, sr. rsch. scientist, 1994—. Expert mem. Bd. of Pharmacology Sci., Internat. Fedn. of Pharmacology. Editor: Integration of Pharmocokinetics, Pharmacodynamics and Toxicokinetics in Rational Drug Development, 1993, Topical Drug Bioavailability, Bioequivalence and Penetration, 1993; contbr. articles to profl. jours.; adv. bd. Skin Pharmacology Jour., 1987-92. Recipient Gold medal U. Madras, 1959. Fellow Am. Assn. Pharm. Scientists (co-chair sci. workshops 1986—), Am. Assn. Pharm. Scientists. Achievements include development of invitro release/dissolution methodology for topical, transdermal and water insoluble drug dosage forms for use as a quality control test, guidelines for industry for (1) dissolution studies, (2) bioavailability/bioequivalence studies for oral and topical dermatological drug products, (3) bioanalytical methods validation, (4) scale-up and post approval changes. Home: 11309 Dunleith Pl North Potomac MD 20878-2566 Office: FDA 1451 Rockville Pike Rockville MD 20852-1420 E-mail: shahvi@cder.fda.gov.

SHAHABUDDIN, SYED, management information science educator; b. Swat, Pakistan, Mar. 2, 1939; came to U.S., 1967, naturalized, 1985. s. Badshah and Sherin S.; m. Razia Shahabuddin, Sept. 16, 1967; children: Khalid, Rohena. BA, Peshawar (Pakistan) U., Pakistan, 1962; MBA, Karachi (Pakistan) U., 1965, Kent State U., 1968; PhD, U. Mo., 1976. Assoc. prof. mgmt. info. sci., acting chmn. dept. Talladega (Ala.) Coll., 1969-75; asst. prof. mgmt. info. sci. U. Notre Dame (Ind.), 1975-80; assoc. prof. mgmt. info. sci. Cen. Mich. U., Mt. Pleasant, 1980-84, prof. mgmt. info. sci., 1984—, chmn. dept., 1984-86. Contbr. articles to prof. jours. Mem. Am. Statis. Assn., Am. Decision Scis. Assn., Am. Computing Machinery Assn., Data Processing Mgmt. Assn., Mgmt. Sci. Inst. Home: PO Box 57 Midland MI 48640-0057

SHAHAN, SHERRY JEAN, writer, educator; b. Long Beach, Calif., Aug. 14, 1949; d. Frank Rowe Webb and Sylvia Jean (Brunner) Benedict; m. Edgar Harold Shahan, Oct. 23, 1982; children: Kristina Michelle Beal, Kyle Shannon Beal. BS in Social Scis., Calif. Poly. State U., San Luis Obispo, 1978. Lectr. Saddleback Coll. Writers Conf., Orange County, Calif., 1992, Cuesta Community Coll., San Luis Obispo, 1988—, Calif. Reading Assn., 1998—, Nat. Coun. Tchrs. English, 1999—. Author: (books) Dashing Through the Snow: The Story of the Jr. Iditarod (a photo essay, 1997), (mid. grade novel) Frozen Stiff, 1998, (photoessay) The Little Butterfly, 1998, (photoessay) Fifth Grade Crush, 1986, Barnacles Eat With Their Feet: Delicious Facts About the Tide Pool Chain, (2 photo essay), 1996, (photograph only), The Sunflower Family, 1996, Telephone Tag, 1996, Wait Until Dark: Seven Scary Sleep-Over Stories, 1996, (photo essay) Feeding Time at the Zoo, 2000, (picture book) A Jazzy Alphabet, 2002, (collection of romantic short stories), True Love, 1996, Working Dogs, 1999; contbr. articles, photographs numerous regional and nat. newspapers and mags. Mem. Authors Guild, Soc. Am. Travel Writers, So. Calif. Children's Booksellers, Soc. Children's Book Writers, Pi Gamma Mu. Home and Office: 2603 Richard Ave Cayucos CA 93430 E-mail: Kidbooks@thegrid.net.

SHAHEEN, C. JEANNE, governor; b. St. Charles, Mo., Jan. 28, 1947; m. William H. Shaheen; 3 children. BA, Shippensburg U., 1969; M of Social Sci. in Polit. Sci., U. Miss., 1973. Mem. N.H. Senate, 1991-96; gov N.H., 1997—. Democrat. Protestant. Office: Office of Governor State House 107 N Main St Rm 208 Concord NH 03301-4951*

SHAHIDEHPOUR, MOHAMMAD, dean, academic administrator, engineering educator; b. Tehran, Iran, July 27, 1955; came to U.S., 1977; m. Jamie Winkler, Sept. 8, 1989; children: Dustin, Ryan, Andrew. BS, Sharif U., Tehran, 1977; MS, U. Mo., 1978, PhD, 1981. Prof. Ill. Inst. Tech., Chgo., 1983—, dean, 1994—, assoc. v.p. rsch., 1999—. Author: Power Systems, 1999; contbr. articles to profl. jours. Named Oustanding Rschr. Edison Electric Inst. Mem. IEEE (editor 1999—), HKN (pres. 2000—), Sigma Xi, Tau Beta Pi. Achievements include 2 patents. Office: Ill Inst Tech 3300 S Federal St Chicago IL 60616-3793

SHAHID-GARCIA, MARIA DE LOURDES, foreign language educator; b. Lagos de Mareno, Jalisco, Mex., May 10, 1960; d. Jose Isabel García and Marcelina García-Diaz; m. Shahid Iqbal, Oct. 9, 1990; children: Mussarat Iqbal, Maira Iqbal. M in Internat. Pub. Comm., Calif. State U., Chico, 1988, M in Internat. Pub. Comm., 1994. Spanish prof. Butte Coll., Oroville, Pa., 1989—, Calif. State U., Chico, 1989—. Author: Tips for Successful Spanish, 1994, Say it in Spanish, 1998; editor, prodr. (T.V. program) Sabias Que?, 1992—. Chmn. Sch. Evangelization, Chico, 2001. Recipient First prize San Francisco Poetry Contest, 1986. Mem. Calif. Tchrs. Assn., Hispanic C. of C. (pres. 1999—). Roman Catholic. Home: 4 Roberto Ct Chico CA 95928

SHAHIED, IKE I. science educator; BA, Eastern Nazarene Coll., 1959; MS, U. Tenn., 1964; PhD, Colo. State U., 1973. Sr. rsch. chemist Aerospace Med. Rsch. Lab. USAF, Dayton, 1973—74; prof., dept. chmn. St. George's Med. Coll., Grenada, 1977—86; prof. Cleveland Coll., Kansas City, Mo., 1986—89; prof., head biochemist Life U., Marietta, Ga., 1989—94; prof. St. Matthew's Med. Coll., Belize, 1997—98, Ctrl. Bapt. Coll., Conway, Ark., 2001—. Mem.: AAAS, N.Y. Acad. Scis., Truman Libr. Inst. Avocations: writing, swimming. Office: Ctrl Capt Coll Conway AR 72034

SHAH-JAHAN, M. M. economist; b. Dhaka, Bangladesh, June 30, 1943; came to U.S., 1975; s. M.M. Serajul Hoq and Ayesha A. Khaton; m. Mahmuda Khatun, Aug. 15, 1972; children: Al M., Nydia. BA in Bus., Dacca U., 1963, MA in Bus., 1964; MA in Econs., Georgetown U., 1982; PhD in Econs., Georgetown-PW U., 1987. Asst. prof. edn. dept. Dacca Coll., 1965-75, sec. gen. prof. staff coun., 1971-75; audit supr. Marriott Corp., Arlington, Va., 1975-81; economist Potomac Electric Power Co., Washington, 1981—. Cons. economist World Bank, Washington, 1988-89; economist and currency trader NBI, Md., 1997-98, Potomac Futures, Va., 1997-98. Author: (with M.R. Khan) Principles of Income Tax, 1970, Principles of Banking, 1974, An Econometric Forecasting Model, 1987, Jordan: A Macroeconomic Projection, 1988, U.S. Macroeconomic Outlook, 1989, The Open Economy Macro Model for Policy and Planning in the Developing Economies, 1993, Twenty-Five Year Macroeconomic Outlook for Bangladesh, 1994, Unemployment, Inflation and Monetary Policy, 1997, Currency Trading Strategy: A Floor Traders Model, 1998. Govt. of Pakistan scholar, 1964. Mem. Am. Econ. Assn., Soc. Govt. Economies, Nat. Economists Club, Swimming Club. Democrat. Moslem. Avocations: tennis, swimming, movies, travel, photography. Home: 1223 S Buchanan St Arlington VA 22204-3407 Office: Potomac Electric Power Co 1900 Pennsylvania Ave NW Washington DC 20068-0002

SHAHJAHAN, MUNIR, medical researcher; b. Dhaka, Bangladesh, July 23, 1962; s. Muhammad Shahjahan and Monika Jahan; m. Sabrina Sultana, Feb. 16, 1990; children: Mashroor Jahan, Monika Jahan. MBBS, MD, Dhaka Med. Coll., 1990; MPH, U. Tex., Houston, 1996. House physician Dhaka Med. Coll. Hosp., 1991-93; lectr., med. officer Med. Coll. Women, Dhaka, 1993-94; rsch. asst. Sch. Pub. Health U. Tex., Houston, 1994-97; sr. rsch. asst., data mgr., clin. rsch. protocol coord., sr. data analyst M.D. Anderson Cancer Ctr., U. Tex., 1998—; rsch. asst. Sch. Pub. Health AIDS Ednl. and Tng. Ctr. for Tex. and Okla., 1997-98. Project coord. Healthmetrica, Dhaka, 1992-93. Contbr. articles to profl. jours. Founder v.p. Rotaract Club of Dhaka Med. Coll., 1986-87. Recipient Scholarship award for acad. excellence Govt. of Bangladesh, 1983-90. Mem. APHA, Am. Soc. Blood and Marrow Transplantation. Mem., Am. Soc. Clin. Oncology, Mem, Assoc. Clin. Rsch. Profls. Avocations: reading, music, sports. Office: MD Anderson Cancer Ctr 1515 Holcombe Blvd # 423 Houston TX 77030-4009

SHAHMIRI, ANIS AHMAD, internist; b. Srinagar, India, Nov. 1, 1963; came to U.S., 1995; s. Javid Ahmad and Ismet Shahmiri; m. Shireen Shahmiri, Feb. 1995. MB BS, Govt. Med. Coll., Srinagar, 1986; postgrad., Inst. Med. Scis., Srinagar, 1990-91. Diplomate Am. Bd. Internal Medicine. Gen. practice medicine Dept. Health and Med. Svcs., Dubai, United Arab Emirates, 1991-95; resident in medicine Nassau County Med. Ctr., East Meadow, N.Y., 1995-98; internist Ctrl. Fla. Heart Ctr., Ocala, 1998—. Attending physician Munroe Regional Med. Ctr., Ocala, 1998—, Ocala Regional Med. Ctr., 1998—. Moslem. Avocations: photography, cricket, golf, philately, computers. Home: 2614 SE 25th Ct Ocala FL 34471-0700 Office: Ctrl Fla Heart Ctr 17820 SE 109th Ave Ste 111 Summerfield FL 34491-8968 E-mail: aashahmiri@aol.com.

SHAHSHAHANI, AHMAD, economics educator; b. Tehran, Iran, Sept. 14, 1947; came to U.S., 1971; s. Housein Shahshahani and Zahra (Heshmat) Zommorodian; m. Shahla Mohtasham; 1 child, Ramina. Cert. in English, U. Cambridge, 1968; BS, U. Tehran, 1969; MA, U. Colo., 1973, PhD, 1976. Asst. prof. econs. Tehran U., 1976-80; research fellow Hoover Instn., Stanford, Calif., 1980-82; fin. analyst Unity in Diversity Council, L.A., 1983-84; asst. prof. Calif. State U., 1984-91, Northridge, 1985-87; economist U.S. Dept. Treasury, Glendale, Calif., 1991-93; economist, mgr. U.S. Dept. Treasury, IRS, L.A., 1993—. Mem. corp. fin. team Baraban Securities, Culver City, Calif., 1983-87; fellow Internat. Rsch. Ctr. Energy and Econ. Devel., Boulder, 1976-87; fin. advisor Tissurama-Knitex Industries, L.A., 1987-91. Author: Economics for Students, 1972, 2d edit., 1977, An Introduction to the Theory of Employment, 1974, 2d edit., 1977, An Econometric Model of Iran, And Its Application, 1978, Economist Report Writing Guide, 2001, Economist Program website, 1999—; editor Econ. Issues, 1995-2000; also articles to profl. jours. Fellow Tehran U., 1974-76, scholar U. Colo., Boulder, 1973-74. Mem. Nat. Assn. Securities Dealers (series 7 lic.), Omicron Delta Epsilon. Avocations: tennis, jogging, travelling. Home: 11939 Gorham Ave Apt 101 Los Angeles CA 90049-5362 Office: US Dept of Treasury IRS 225 W Broadway Glendale CA 91204-1331

SHAIK, FATIMA, college official, writer; b. New Orleans, Oct. 24, 1952; d. Mohamed and Lily Shaik; m. James Little; children: Celeste, Sophia. Student, Xavier U., New Orleans, 1970-72; BS, Boston U., 1974; MA, NYU, 1978. Reporter New Orleans Times-Picayune, 1973, 75; various editl. positions McGraw-Hill, N.Y.C., 1976-88; asst. prof. journalism So. U. New Orleans, 1989-90; dir. comm. St. Peter's Coll., Jersey City, 1990—. Author: The Mayor of New Orleans: Just Talking Jazz, 1987, 89, Melitte, 1997, 2000 (Am. Book Assn. Pick of Lists 1997), The Jazz of Our Street, 1998 (Parent Choice award), Mardi Gras Day, 1999 (Best Books of '99 Bank St.); also contbr. essays and stories to books. Fellow NEH, 1981; rsch. and writing grantee Kittredge Fund, 1997; lit. residency New Orleans Pub. Schs., 2000. Mem. Nat. Writers Union, Writers Room (bd. dirs. 1990-98), Third World Writers (contbr. newsletter 1982-83). Office: St Peter's Coll Comm Program 121 Glenwood Ave Jersey City NJ 07306 E-mail: shaik_f@spc.edu.

SHAIKH, FAROOK A. addictions physician; b. Oct. 1, 1958; MB BS, U. Bombay, India, 1983. Pvt. practice, Falls Church, Va., 1988—; intern, resident Our Lady of Mercy Med. Ctr., 1984—87; addictionologist Arlington (Va.) Hosp., 1988—. Address: 6305 Castle Pl Ste 3C Falls Church VA 22044-1905

SHAIKH, MUHAMMAD A. physician; b. Karachi, Pakistan, Nov. 20, 1959; MB BS, U. Karachi, 1985. Diplomate Am. Bd. Internal Medicine, Am. Bd. Infectious Diseases. Intern Bronx-Lebanon Hosp. Ctr., N.Y., 1991-92, resident, 1992-94; fellow in infectious diseases Mt. Sinai Med. Ctr., N.Y.C., 1994-96. Office: Ste 208 425 Holderrieth Blvd Tomball TX 77375 E-mail: mashaikh@yahoo.com.

SHAIKH, MUZAFFAR ABID, management science educator; b. Bombay, Jan. 5, 1946; came to U.S., 1966; s. Shaikh A. Razzaque and Khudaija R. Shaikh; m. Farhat Anjum, Dec. 29, 1968; children: Mahjabeen, Shahbaaz, Shoaib. BS, U. Bombay, 1966; MS, Kans. State U., 1968; PhD, U. Ill., 1983. Mgmt. sci. rsch. analyst Caterpillar Inc., Peoria, Ill., 1968-85; sr. staff engr. Harris Corp., Melbourne, Fla., 1985-87; assoc. prof. Fla. Inst. Tech., 1987-92, prof. mgmt. sci., 1992—, assoc. dean Sch. Bus., 1992—97, dir. engring. mgmt., Coll. Engring., 1999—. Cons. Harris Corp., Melbourne, 1987-92, Grumman Corp., Melbourne, 1987-92. Assoc. editor Trans. of Simulation, 1989-96, INCOSE Sys. Engring. Jour., 1998-; N.Am. editor Bus. Process Mgmt. Jour., 2002-; contbr. over 1000 articles to profl. jours. Fellow Sigma Xi; sr. mem. Ops. Rsch. Soc. Am., Inst. Mgmt. Sci., Inst. Indsl. Engrs. Home: 409 Crystal Lake Dr Melbourne FL 32940-1934 Office: Fla Inst Tech 150 W University Blvd Melbourne FL 32901-6975

SHAIKH, NAZRUL ISLAM, industrial engineer, researcher; s. Nisar Ahmed and Deeba Shaikh. B in Chem. Engring. , India Inst. Tech., Bombay, 2000; MSEE, MS in Indsl. Engring., postgrad., Pa. State U., 2002—. Intern Nat. Chem. Labs, Pune, India, 1997—99; grad. lectr. Pa. State U., State College, 2001, tchg. asst., 2001, rsch. asst. indsl. engring., 2000—. Contbr. articles. Scholar Nat. Merit scholar, Govt. of India, Jit Paul scholar, Apeejay Edn. Soc. Mem.: IIE, INFORMS, Interact Club (dir.), Tau Beta Pi. Home: 445 Waupelani Dr Apt D-17 State College PA 16801 Office: Dept Indsl Engring 310 Leonhard Bldg State College PA 16802 E-mail: nis109@psu.edu.

SHAIKH, SAAD, physician; b. Reading, Pa., Aug. 23, 1973; s. Mohammed Ainuddin and Shahnaz (Qureshi) S.; m. Naazli Mohsin, June 19, 1998. BS summa cum laude in Biochemistry, UCLA, 1993; MD, U. Calif., Davis, 1997. Medical intern Univ. Calif., Irvine, Calif., 1997-98; resident ophthalmologist Stanford Univ. Medical Ctr., Stanford, 1998-2001; vitreoretinal fellow William Beaumont Hosp., Royal Oak, Mich., 2001—. Contbr. articles to profl. jours. Recipient Dunn prize in biochemistry, 1992, Merck award for excellence in chemistry, 1993, Ron Michels Found. award, 2001; fellow Heed Ophthalmic Found. fellow, 2001, Knapp Found., 2002. Mem.: Phi Beta Kappa. Avocations: basketball, literature, rollerblading.

SHAIKH, ZAHIR AHMAD, toxicologist, educator; b. Jullundur, India, Mar. 31, 1945; came to U.S., 1972; naturalized U.S. citizen, 1994; s. Zafer Ahmad and Mehmooda Begum (Chohan) S.; m. Mary Butterfield, Aug. 23, 1975; children: Faraz, Kashan, Summur. BSc, U. Karachi, Pakistan, 1965, MSc, 1967; PhD, Dalhousie U., 1972. Rsch. assoc. environ. health U. Okla., Oklahoma City, 1972-73; sr. postdoctoral fellow toxicology U. Rochester, N.Y., 1973-75, asst. prof., 1975-81, assoc. prof., 1981-82; assoc. prof. pharmacology and toxicology U. R.I., Kingston, 1982-86, prof., 1986. Chmn. dept. pharmacology and toxicology U. R.I., Kingston, 1985-96, chmn. dept. biomed. scis., 1996—, mem. toxicology study sect., 1985-89. Contbr. articles to profl. jours. NIH fellow, 1973-75; NIH grantee, 1975—. Fellow Pakistan Acad. Med. Scis.; mem. Am. Soc. Pharmacology and Exptl. Therapeutics, Soc. Toxicology (past pres. metal sect.). Achievements include research in heavy metal metabolism and toxicology, in the role of metallothionein in metal toxicology, in metal transport, in detoxification processes, in biological indicators of metal exposure, in toxicology (medicine) and environmental toxicology. Office: Dept Biomed Scis Coll Pharm Univ Rhode Island Kingston RI 02881 E-mail: zshaikh@uri.edu.

SHAIKUN, MICHAEL GARY, lawyer; b. Ky., Mar. 17, 1942; s. Leon J. and Cleo (Taub) S.; m. Phyllis Miriam Cohen, Aug. 21, 1964; children: Benjamin, Stephanie, Alissa. BS in Econs. with highest honors, U. Pa., 1963; JD, Harvard U., 1966. Bar: Ky. 1966, U.S. Dist. Ct. (we. dist.) Ky. 1966. Assoc. Greenebaum Doll & McDonald PLLC, Louisville, 1966-69, mem., 1970—. Contbr. articles to profl. jours. Bd. dirs. Jewish Cmty. Fedn. Louisville, 1971—, past pres.; past chmn. Found. for Planned Giving, Jewish Cmty. Fedn., Louisville; bd. dirs., chmn. fin. devel. YMCA Safe Place Svcs., 1995—. Mem. ABA, Ky. Bar Assn., Louisville Bar Assn. Democrat. Jewish. Avocation: computers. Home: 5907 Burlington Ave Louisville KY 40222-6118 Office: Greenebaum Doll & McDonald PLLC 3300 National City Tower Louisville KY 40202 E-mail: MGS@gdm.com.

SHAIN, IRVING, retired chemical company executive and university chancellor; b. Seattle, Jan. 2, 1926; s. Samuel and Selma (Blockoff) S.; m. Mildred Ruth Udell, Aug. 31, 1947; children: Kathryn A., Steven T., John R., Paul S. BS in Chemistry, U. Wash., 1949, PhD in Chemistry, 1952. From instr. to prof. U. Wis., Madison, 1952-75, vice chancellor, 1970-75, chancellor, 1977-86; provost, v.p. acad. affairs U. Wash., Seattle, 1975-77; v.p. Olin Corp., Stamford, Conn., 1987-92, ret., 1992, also bd. dirs. Mem. tech. adv. bd. Johnson Controls, Inc., Milw., 1980—; trustee Univ. Rsch. Park, Inc., Madison, pres., 1984-86, v.p., 1987—; mem. Nat. Commn. on Superconductivity, 1989-90; mem. CEO bd. advisors Kamahameha Schs., Hawaii, 2002--. Contbr. articles on electroanalytical chemistry to profl. jours. Bd. dirs. Madison Gen. Hosp., 1972-75; v.p. Madison Cmty. Found., 1984-86; mem. CEO adv. bd. Kamehameha Schs./Bishop Estates, 2002-. With U.S. Army, 1943-46, PTO. Fellow AAAS, Wis. Acad. Scis., Arts and Letters; mem. Am. Chem. Soc., Electrochem. Soc., Conn. Acad. Sci. and Engring., Phi Beta Kappa, Sigma Xi, Phi Kappa Phi. Home: 2820 Marshall Ct # 8 Madison WI 53705-2270 E-mail: ishain@facstaff.wisc.edu., i.shain@worldnet.att.net.

SHAIN, KENNETH STEPHEN, software company executive, author, industrialist; b. Bridgeport, Conn., Sept. 24, 1952; s. Albert Benjamin and Gladys Ann (Lustig) S.; m. Nancie Ann Taylor, Apr. 23, 1983; children: Ian Alexander, Kevin Mitchell, Andrew Thomas. BA, U. Mass., 1978. Prin. Shain Assocs., Atlanta, 1982-87, 93—; chmn., pres. Geovision, Inc., Norcross, 1985-93, cons.; pres. Cyco Internat., Inc., Atlanta, 1995-98; CEO MENSI, Inc., 1999-2001; pres. XOBOX Corp., 2001—; v.p. sales and mktg. SYNAPS, Inc., Atlanta, 2002—. Chmn. mech. engring. curriculum com. Gov.'s High-Tech Adv. Coun., State of Ga., 1984. Recipient Cert. Appreciation Gov.'s Office of Ga., 1985; named Entrepreneur of Yr. finalist, 1987, 89. Mem. Soc. Mfg. Engrs. (sr., chmn. 1983-84), Computer and Automated Systems Assn. (sr.), Nat. Info. Standards Orgn., Southeastern Software Assn., ACM Siggraph. E-mail: kenshain@attbi.com.

SHAIN-ALVARO, JUDITH CAROL, physician assistant; b. Bronx, N.Y., Aug. 13, 1953; d. Frank and Pearl (Crausman) Shain; m. Virgilio S. Alvaro, May 13, 1990; 1 child, Jessica Blaire. BS in Biology, Fairleigh Dickinson U., 1975; BS, Physician Asst. Cert., Baylor Coll. Medicine, Houston, 1978. Lic. physician asst., N.Y., N.J.; BLS, ACLS, Am. Heart Assn. Postgrad. surg. residency program for physician assts. Montefiore Med. Ctr. and Albert Einstein Coll. Medicine, Bronx, NY, 1979—81; physician asst. dept. cardiothoracic surgery North Shore U. Hosp., Manhasset, N.Y., 1981-84; lic. med. officer Passenger Cruise Ships, Miami, Fla., 1984-88; med. cons. The Floating Hosp., Bankers Trust Co., N.Y.C., 1988-89; sr. physician asst. pers. health svcs. St. Vincent's Hosp. and Med. Ctr., 1990—93; sr. physician asst. N.J. Med. Sch. Nat. Tuberculosis Ctr., 1993—2001. Faculty N.J. Aids Edn. Tng. Ctr., physician asst. rep. to N.J. AIDS Edn. Tng. Ctr., 1995—; mem. Nat. Physician Asst. Working Group to Nat. AIDS Edn. Tng. Ctr., 1995—; lectr. in field. Trustee Sisterhood Congregation B'nai Israel, Congregation B'nai Israel; mayoral appointee Fair Lawn Boro Coun. Planning Bd. Adv. Com. Broadway Redevel., 1999-2001 Fellow Am. Acad. Physician Assts., N.J. State Soc. Physician Assts., N.Y. State Soc. Physician Assts.; mem. Filipino Am. Assn. Fair Lawn. Jewish. Avocations: travel, theater, reading. Home: 0-80 27th St Fair Lawn NJ 07410

SHAINE, FREDERICK MORDECAI, newspaper executive, consultant; b. Cambridge, Mass., Feb. 5, 1916; s. Joseph and Mollie (Prescott) S.; m. Sylvia Pollack, Mar. 21, 1944; 1 child, Frederick Mordecai Jr. (Rick). Student, U. Vt., 1934-35; BA, Columbia U., 1970. From copy boy to advt. sales rep. Boston Herald, 1933, 36-41; advt. rep. O'Mara & Ormsbee, N.Y.C., 1946-58; advt. dir. Book Rev. N.Y. Herald Tribune, 1958-63; bus. mgr. Book Week Nat. Sun newspaper supplement, 1963-66; bus. mgr. Book World, Sun. book rev. Washington Post/Chgo. Tribune, N.Y.C., 1966-72; dir. N.Y. ops. European Stars and Stripes, 1972-95. Cons. to Armed Forces Info Svcs., Dept. Def., 1996-97; transl. from Italian: And No Quarter, 1972; reviewer and translator various publs. Mem. adv. coun. Casa Italiana, Columbia U., 1967-70. With USCG, 1941-45. Mem. Soc. for Italian Hist. Studies, Columbia Club. Avocations: reading, travel, translating, bridge. Home: 930 5th Ave Apt 12F New York NY 10021-2651 also: PO Box 473 Shelter Island Heights NY 11965-0473

SHAINMAN, IRWIN, music educator, musician; b. N.Y.C., June 27, 1921; s. Samuel and Gussie (Pollack) S.; m. Bernice Cohen, Aug. 29, 1948; children—Joan, Jack. BA, Pomona Coll., 1943; MA, Columbia, 1948; Premier Prix, Conservatoire Nat. de Musique de Paris, France, 1950. Prof. music, curator Paul Whiteman collection Williams Coll., Williamstown, Mass., 1948-91, prof. emeritus, 1991—; chmn. music dept., 1971-77; dean faculty, 1972-73; coordinator performing arts, 1973-76; Class of 1955 prof. music, 1980-91. Tchr. ext. U. Mass., 1952-55, Mass. State Coll., North Adams, 1957, also Bennington Coll. Composer's Conf. and Chamber Music Ctr.; cons. advanced placement program Coll. Entrance Exam. Bd., 1969-75; mem. edn. com. Saratoga Performing Arts Ctr., 1967-68; pres. Williamstown Theatre Found., 1972-77, South Mountain Concert Assn., 1980-96. Condr., Berkshire Symphony, 1950-65, also Williams Coll. band, brass ensemble and woodwind ensemble, 1st trumpet, Albany (N.Y.) Symphony Orch., 1960-65, Vt. Symphony Orch., 1954-58; contbr. articles to profl. jours.; columnist: Berkshire Eagle; author: Avoiding Cultural Default and Other Essays, 1991. Mem. merit aid panel Mass. Arts Council, 1984. Served with AUS, 1942-45. Decorated Purple Heart, Combat Inf. badge.; N.Y. Philharmonic scholar, 1934-35; Recipient Danforth Found. Tchrs. award, 1957-58 Mem. Am. Musicological Soc., Coll. Music Assn., Music Critics Assn. Home: 88 Baxter Rd Williamstown MA 01267-2111

SHAIR, DAVID IRA, human resources executive; b. N.Y.C., May 1, 1921; s. Henry and Jessie (Brinn) S.; m. Hortense Spitz, Oct. 18, 1947. BA, CUNY, 1940; MBA, NYU, 1950. Assoc. Benj. Werne Assocs., N.Y.C., 1952-70; dir. labor relations London Records, Inc., 1970-80; v.p. personnel Carl Fischer, Inc., 1980-92; mgmt. cons., freelance writer, 1993—. Author various articles on personnel and labor relations. Arbitration panel, Better Bus. Bureau, 1999—. Served with inf. U.S. Army, 1942-45, ETO. Decorated Purple Heart. Mem. Soc. Adminstrv. Mgmt. (v.p. 1986-87, exec. v.p. 1987-90), Human Resources Assn. N.Y. (bd. dirs. 1996-2000, treas. 1994-95, editor Newsletter 1995-98, strategic planning com. 1999—, chair pub. rels. com. 1999—, sr. advisor 2001--, Dirs. Forum, Breiger award 1996-97). Jewish. Avocation: photography. Home: 6 Peter Cooper Rd Apt 10A New York NY 10010-6709 also: 7 Rosemaries Ln PO Box 3099 East Hampton NY 11937-0396 E-mail: D1s521@aol.com.

SHAKELY, JOHN BOWER (JACK SHAKELY), foundation executive; b. Hays, Kans., Jan. 9, 1940; s. John B. and Martha Jean (Gaston) S.; 1 child, Benton. BA, U. Okla., 1962. Vol. Peace Corps., Costa Rica, 1963-64; editor publs. Dept. Def., 1967-68; dir. devel. U. Okla., 1968-70, Resthaven Mental Health Ctr., L.A., 1970-74; pres. Jack Shakely Assocs., 1974-75; sr. adv. Grantsmanship Ctr., 1975-79, Coun. on Founds., Washington, 1979; pres. Calif. Community Found., L.A., 1980—. Lectr. in field. Bd. dirs. Emergency Loan and Assistance Fund, 1985—, chair bd. dirs., 1988-93; mem., vice chair L.A. Am. Indian Commn.; bd. dirs. So. Calif. Assn. Philanthropy, 1980—, Comic Relief, 1987—; chmn. bd. dirs. Nonprofit Channel. Served to 1st lt. U.S. Army, 1965-68. Decorated Army Commendation medal; named Nat. Philanthropy Day Outstanding Exec., L.A. Com. Nat. Philanthropy Day, 1989. Office: 445 S Figueroa St Ste 3400 Los Angeles CA 90071-1638

SHAKER, REZA, gastroenterologist, educator; b. Tehran, Iran, Mar. 21, 1949; came to U.S., 1982; s. Borhan and Ashraghie (Mohager) S.; children: Anisa, Faran. MD, Tehran U., 1975. Lic. physician, Wis., N.Y, Fla., Wash. Gen. med. practice, Khoy, Iran, 1975-77; resident surgery Sinai U. Hosp., Tehran, 1977-80, London Hosp., 1980-81; resident internal medicine Kingsbrook Jewish Med. Ctr., Bklyn., 1982-85, chief med. resident, 1984-85; fellow gastroenterology Med. Coll. Wis., Milw., 1985-88, dir. MCW Dysphagia Inst., 1990—, chief divsn. gastroenterology and hepatology, 1996—, dir. Digestive Disease Ctr., 1996—; mem. attending staff Froedtert Meml. Luth. Hosp., 1988—, Zablocki VA Med. Ctr., Milw., 1988—. Asst. prof. medicine Med. Coll. Wis., Milw., 1988-93, asst. prof. surgery, 1993-95, assoc. prof. medicine, 1993-96, assoc. prof. radiology, 1993-97, assoc. prof. surgery, 1995-97, prof. medicine, gastroenterology, 1996—, prof. radiology, 1997—, prof. surgery, otolaryngology and human comm., 1997—; co-founder Med. Coll. Wis. Dysphagia Inst., 1990; moderator Am. Gastroenterol. Assn. Rsch. Forum, Digestive Disease Week, New Orleans, 1991, Boston, 1993, San Diego, 1995, San Francisco, 1996, Washington, 1997; mem. expert panel for assessment of evaluation and mgmt. of swallowing dysfunction Am. Acad. Neurology, 1993; mem. Gastroenterology Leadership Coun. Curriculum Task Force on Motility, Diverticular Disease and Functional Illnesses, 1994; mem. radioactive drug rsch. com. Milwaukee County Med. Complex, 1995; moderator XV Internat. Symposium on Gastrointestinal Motility, Session on Pharyngo-Esophageal Motor Function, Rome, 1995; co-moderator plenary session IV Dysphagia Rsch. Soc., 4th Ann. Meeting, 1995; lectr. Dodds-Donner Annual Lecture, Dysphagia Rsch. Soc., McLean, Va., 1994; lectr. orgns., workshops, univs.; program dir. 1st and 2d Internat. Symposium on Supraesophageal Complications of Reflux Disease, 1996, 98. Guest editor Dysphagia Jour., 1993, 94, Am. Jour. Medicine Supplement, 1997; reviewer Am. Jour. Physiology, Jour. Applied Physiology, Gastroenterology, Can. Jour. Physiology and Pharmacology, Gastrointestinal Endoscopy, Digestive Diseases and Sci.; mem. editl. bd. Dysphagia jour., 1992; mem. AGA abstract rev. com., 1992-93, 96, 97; contbr. articles to profl. jours., chpts. to books. Grantee Dept. Vets. Affairs, 1989-90, 90-96, Janssen Rsch. Found., 1988-91, 94-95, Glaxo Inc. Rsch. Inst., 1993-94, NIH, 1989—. Mem. Am. Motililty Soc. (mem. tng. and edn. subcom. 1994), Am. Soc. Gastrointestinal Endoscopy (Endoscopic Career Devel. award 1990-92), Milw. Acad. Medicine, Dysphagia Rsch. Soc. (founder, pres. 1992-93, mem. at large governing bd. 1996), Midwest Gut Club, Am. Fedn. Clin. Rsch., Am. Coll. Gastroenterology, Am. Physiol. Soc., Assn. Subspecialty Profs., Am. Coll. Gastroenterology. Mem. Baha'i Faith. Achievements include discoverer of four new airway protective mechanisms: esophagoglottal closure reflex, pharyngo-upper esophageal sphincter contractile reflex, pharyngo-glottal closure reflex laryngo-ues reflex; creator of shaker exercise for treating dysphagia; development of transnasal unsedated esophagogastroduodenoscopy; avocations: swimming, tennis. Office: Froedtert Meml Luth Hosp Med Coll Wis 9200 W Wisconsin Ave Milwaukee WI 53226-3522

SHAKER, WILLIAM HAYGOOD, marketing professional, public policy reformer; b. Downey, Calif., Apr. 22, 1938; s. Elmer S. and Marylee Shaker; m. Joanna Drummond, Jan. 28, 1966; children: Catherine Patricia, Marylee, Marcus, Matthew. *Children include: Catherine Patricia (Shaker) Scanlon (SA, NVCC), Marylee (Shaker) Verdi (BA, GMU; BSN, Gerogetown University), twin sons, Marcus Shaker (BS, JMU; MD, University of Virginia) and Matthew Shaker (BS, JMU; MS George Washington University). Biographies of William's great-grandfather, Bishop Atticus Haygood (b. 1839), great-aunt, Laura Haygood (b. 1845), and wife, Joanna's great-great-great-grandfather, George Taylor, are published in Marquis' Who Was Who in America.* BS in Engring., U. So. Calif., 1964; MS in Engring., U. Mich., 1969. Registered profl. engr., Calif. Exec. Dow Chem. Co., Midland, Mich., 1966-78; v.p. Nat. Legal Ctr. for the Pub. Interest, Washington, 1979; exec. v.p. Nat. Tax Limitation Com., 1980-86; pres. Am. Coun. for Health Care Reform, Arlington, Va., 1982—, Heart to Heart Found., Arlington, 1982—; CEO Washington Mktg. Group, 1987—; pres. Health PAC, 1994—. Pres. RepublicanPac.com, 2000—, Rule of Law Com., 2001—. Author: Health Care Reform, 1994, also legis. and govt. publs.; editor: Electric Power Reform, 1979; editor, pub. millennium edit. The Man of Galilee, 2001; contbr. articles to profl. jours. Founder, chmn. Taxpayers United, Mich., 1972-84. Mem. Govtl. Rsch. Assn. (most effective presentation of govtl. rsch. award 1973), Direct Mktg. Assn. (echo awards 1982-97, maxi awards 1987-2001), Pub. Rels. Soc. (silver anvil 1979), Am. Conservative Union (health care reform award 1995). Republican. Lutheran. Office: Washington Mktg Group 2507 N Harrison St Arlington VA 22207 E-mail: william.shaker@twmg.com.

SHAKESPEARE, EASTON GEOFFREY, insurance broker, consultant; b. Mar. 20, 1946; s. Easton Gladstone George and Leonie (Phillips) S.; m. Maria Adina Prescott, Apr. 20, 1968; children: Christpher Geoffrey, Collin Maurice. Group rep. The Guardian Life Ins. Co., N.Y.C., 1979-87; ins. cons. Easton Shakespeare & Assocs. Ins. Agy., Matawan, NJ, 1987—; real estate assoc. Century 21 Iavarone Realty and Era Teitel/Reich Realtors, 1990—, ERA Tietel/Reich Realtors, Matawan, 1990-91, Prudential N.J. Realty, Matawan, 1991; dir., treas. F.F. & G. Assocs., Newark, 1991-93. Cons. Met. Life Ins. Co., 1991, vol. programs Winston Fin. Svcs., Bay Head, N.J.; pres. Capital Employee Benefit Svcs., Inc., 1993; gen. agt. U.S. Life Ins. Co.; dir., instr. Fin. Supermarket Ins. Sch., Matawan, N.J.; mem. ins. faculty Fairleigh Dickinson U., Madison, N.J.; mng. gen. agt. Old Line Life, 1995—; pres. EMCC Marketing Corp., 1997. Mem.: NAACP, Nat. Assn. Life Underwriters, Soc. Fin. Svcs. Profls. (Atlanta chpt.). Home and Office: PO Box 55 Lithonia GA 30058-0055

SHAKESPEARE, EDWARD ORAM, III, retired secondary school educator; b. Villanova, Pa., May 29, 1924; s. Edward Oram and Henrietta MacDonald (Wilson) S.; m. Sarah Harrison Lowry, June 12, 1947 (dec. Mar. 1983); children: Edward O. IV (dec.), John L., David A.; m. Shirley Winter, Apr. 13, 1985. AB, Haverford Coll., 1949; MA, Cornell U., 1950. English and sci. tchr. Park Sch., Balt., 1950-52, Haverford (Pa.) Sch., 1952-56; copy editor W. B. Saunders Co., Phila., 1956-58; English tchr. William Penn Charter Sch., 1958-61, 66-71, English dept. chmn., 1961-66, dir. curriculum, 1968-71; English dept. chmn. Friends' Ctrl. Sch., Overbrook, Pa., 1971-75; English tchr. Baldwin Sch., Bryn Mawr, 1975-81, Shipley Sch., Bryn Mawr, 1981-87; ret., 1987. Chmn. English com. Nat. Assn. Ind. Schs., Boston, 1969-76, Ind. Sch. Tchr. Assn. Greater Phila., 1969-71. Author: Drama: From Print to Performance, 1973; prin. editor: Understanding the Essay, 1966, 3d edit., 1991, A Teacher's Notebook: English, 5-9, Vol. I, 1975, Vol. II, 1977. Bd. mgrs. Haverford Coll., 1975-80, mem. corp., 1981—; bd. trustees Green Tree Sch., Phila., 1972-84, 85—; bd. dirs. Del. Valley Friends Sch., Paoli, 1990-99; chmn. bd. trustees First Unitarian Ch. Phila., 1971-72; mem. Dem. Com. Radnor Township, Wayne, Pa., 1964-84, chmn. 1976-78; mem. Dem. Com. Lower Merion, Haverford, 1986-94. With U.S. Army, 1943-45, ETO. Braitmayer fellow Nat. Assn. Ind. Schs., 1967. Mem. Franklin Inn Club. Democrat. Avocations: acting and directing in dramatics, writing fiction and poetry, oil painting. Home: 600 E Cathedral Rd Philadelphia PA 19128-1933

SHAKESPEARE, FRANK, ambassador; b. N.Y.C., Apr. 9, 1925; s. Francis Joseph and Frances (Hughes) S.; m. Deborah Anne Spaeth, Oct. 9, 1954; children: Mark, Andrea, Fredricka. BS, Holy Cross Coll., 1945; D.Eng. (hon.), Colo. Sch. Mines, 1975; DCS (hon.), Pace U., 1979; LLD (hon.), Del. Law Sch., 1980, Sacred Heart U., 1985, U. Dallas, 1987, Pepperdine U., 1990, Nichols Coll., 1991, Marquette U., 1993; D of Pub. Svc. (hon.), Hillsdale Coll., 1996. Formerly pres. CBS-TV Services; exec. v.p. CBS-TV Stas.; dir. USIA, 1969-73; exec. v.p. Westinghouse Electric Corp., 1973-75; pres. RKO Gen. Inc., N.Y.C., 1975-85, vice chmn., 1983-85; U.S. ambassador to Portugal Lisbon, 1985-87; U.S. ambassador to The Holy See Vatican City, 1987-89. Chmn. Heritage Found., 1975-85, dir., 1989—; chmn. Radio Free Europe/Radio Liberty, Inc., 1976-85; dir. Bradley Founhd., 1989—. Served to lt. (j.g.) USNR, 1945-46. Mem.: Union League. Home: 303 Coast Blvd La Jolla CA 92037-4630

SHAKHMUNDES, LEV, mathematician; b. Leningrad, USSR, Dec. 29, 1933; came to Can., 1975; s. Yudel and Alexandra (Voitsekhovskaya) S.; children: Nadia, Daniel. MS, Leningrad U., 1957; PhD, Leningrad Poly. Inst., 1965. Engr., rsch. assoc., cons. various instns., Leningrad, 1957-74; rsch. asst. U. Toronto, 1976-78; sr. cons. analyst Union Gas Ltd., Chatham, Ont., Can., 1978-98, cons. Can., 1998—. Author: A Better Organization: Facing Challenges to Mankind and Civility, 2001, We Are Different, So What, 1999, A Better Organization: Facing Challenges to Mankind and Civility, 2001; co-author: Economic Efficiency of Capital Expenditures (in Russian), 1969; contbr. articles to Soviet and U.S. acad. periodicals; patentee Ministry Sci. and Tech. USSR. Mem. Assn. Profl. Engrs. Ont., Can. Econs. Assn. Avocations: sports. Home: PO Box 383 Chatham ON Canada N7M 5K5 E-mail: lev@WeAreDif.net.

SHAKIBANASAB, LAUREN VORWERK, music director, educator; b. Chattanooga, Nov. 17, 1959; d. Norman Thomas and E. Charlsie Vorwerk; m. Reza Shakibanasab, Nov., 15, 1961; children: David Reza, Joseph Reza, Alexander Reza, Samuel Reza. MusB, Converse Coll., 1981; postgrad., Coll. Charleston, 1981-83; MusM, So. Ill. U., 1995; pvt. piano study, Paris, 1984. Piano tchr. Shakibanasab Studio, Summerville, S.C., 1985—; music dir. Knightsville United Meth. Ch., 1995-98, Midland Park United Meth. Ch., North Charleston, S.C., 1999-2001. Accompanist St. Luke's Children's Ctr., Summerville, 1999—; freelance accompanist; spl. events coord. Piccolo Spoleto, 1990, 91; performer, 1982; real estate investor; coord. Serenade Summerville Concert Series, 2001—. Music dir.: Rejoice, The Lord King, 1998, Prime Time Christmas, 1999, Shepherds, Stars and a Savior, 1999, Walk In The Light, 1999. Mem. Music Tchrs. Nat. Assn., Am. Guuild Organist, S.C. Piano Festival Assn. Episcopalian. Avocations: gardening, swimming. Home: 215 W Carolina Ave Summerville SC 29483-4356

SHAKNO, ROBERT JULIAN, hospital administrator; b. Amsterdam, Holland, Aug. 15, 1937; came to U.S., 1939, naturalized, 1944; s. Rudy C. and Gertrude (Loeb) S.; m. Elka Linda Baum, June 10, 1962; children: Steven Lee, Deborah Sue. BBA (scholar 1955), So. Methodist U., 1959; M.H.A., Washington U., St. Louis, 1961. Adminstrv. asst. Mt. Sinai Hosp., Chgo., 1961—63; asso. adminstr. Tex. Inst. Rehab. and Research, Houston, 1963—65; asst. adminstr. Michael Reese Hosp., Chgo., 1965—70, v.p., hosp. dir., 1970—73; asso. exec. dir. Cook County Hosp., Chgo., 1973—75; pres. Hackensack Med. Center, NJ, 1975—85, Mt. Sinai Med. Ctr., Cleve., 1985—96; dir. nat. strategy practice KPMG Peat Marwick, 1996-98; v.p. med. affairs, vice dean sch. of medicine Case Western Res. U., 1998—. Bd. dirs. Ohio Hosp. Inc. Co.; pres. & CEO Jewish FAmile Svc. Cleve., 2000—. Mem. editorial bd. Mgmt. Series, Am. Coll. Healthcare Execs. Mem. Leadership Cleve.; bd. dirs. Premier Hosp. Alliance, chmn., 1994-96; bd. dirs. The New Cleve. Inc., Univ. Circle Inc., Cleve., Cleve. Sight Ctr.; trustee Hope Lodge, Cleve. chpt. Am. Cancer Soc.; chmn. elect, bd. dirs. Jewish Family Svcs.; chmn. social svcs. divsn. United Jewish Appeal, Cleve., 1987-88, chmn. health cabinet, 1990, gen. co-chmn., 1990—; chmn. Hosp. Pacesetter campaign United Way, chmn. health svcs. portfolio, 1988-89, oversight commn., 1992-93. Served to 1st lt. USAR, 1960-66. Named Young Adminstr. of Yr., Washington U., 1968 Fellow Am. Coll. Hosp. Adminstrs.; mem. Am. Hosp. Assn. (coun. urban hosps., del. coun. on met. hosps., rep. regional policy bd.), Washington U. Alumni Assn. (past pres.), Greater Cleve. Hosp. Assn. (bd. dirs.), Ohio Hosp. Assn. (bd. dirs.), Cleve. Sight Ctr. (trustee, bd. dirs.), Sigma Alpha Mu (past pres.). Home: 32050 Meadow Lark Way Pepper Pike OH 44124-5508 Office: Case Western Res U Sch Medicine 10900 Euclid Ave Rm T-101 Cleveland OH 44106-1712

SHAKOW, ALEXANDER, economist, government official; b. Apr. 12, 1937; s. David and Sophie (Harap) S.; m. Patricia Connell, Dec. 26, 1967; children: John, Peter, Thomas. BA with honors, Swarthmore Coll., 1958; PhD in Internat. Rels./Econ. Devel., London Sch. Econs., 1962. Assoc., dep., then dir. Indonesia program U.S. Peace Corps, Washington and Jakarta, Indonesia, 1963-65, asst., dep. then dir. Office Vol. Tng. Washington, 1965-67; dir. Office Indonesia Affairs-Office Asia Devel. Planning, US AID, 1968-74, dep. asst. adminstr., then asst. adminstr. program-policy, 1974-81; spl. policy advisor, chief policy unit, sr. advisor internat. econ. affairs World Bank, 1981-85, chief internat. econ. affairs, 1985-87, dir. strategic planning and rev., dir. external affairs, 1987-94, exec. sec. World Bank/IMF devel. com., 1995—2002; dep. sec. World Bank group World Bank/IMF, 1997—2002, acting v.p., sec., 2001—. Chmn. bd. sci. and tech. for internat. devel. NAS, Washington, 1989-95. Bd. govs. Inst. Devel. Studies, Sussex, Eng., 1991—. Recipient William A. Jump Meritorious award for outstanding pub. svc. William A. Jump Meml. Found., 1967. Mem. Am. Friends London Sch. Econs. (founding). Avocations: carpentry, gardening, reading. Fax: 301-993-3218. E-mail: ashakow@worldbank.org.

SHALALA, DONNA EDNA, university administrator, former federal official, political scientist, educator; b. Cleve., Feb. 14, 1941; d. James Abraham and Edna (Smith) S. AB, Western Coll., 1962; MSSC, Syracuse U., 1968, PhD, 1970; 39 hon. degrees, 1981-91. Vol. Peace Corps, Iran, 1962-64; asst. prof. polit. sci. CUNY, 1970-72; assoc. prof. politics and edn. Tchrs. Coll. Columbia U., 1972-79; asst. sec. for policy devel. and research HUD, Washington, 1977-80; prof. polit. sci., pres. Hunter Coll., CUNY, 1980-87; prof. polit. sci., chancellor U. Wis., Madison, 1987-93; sec. Dept. HHS, Washington, 1993-2001; pres. U. Miami, 2001—. Author: Neighborhood Governance, 1971, The City and the Constitution, 1972, The Property Tax and the Voters, 1973, The Decentralization Approach, 1974. Mem. Trilateral Commn., 1988—92, Knight Commn. on Intercollegiate Sports, 1989—91; bd. govs. Am. Stock Exch., 1981—87; trustee TIAA, 1985—89, Com. Econ. Devel., 1982—92; bd. dirs. Inst. Internat. Econs., 1981—92; bd. dirs. Children's Def. Fund, 1980—93, Am. Ditchley Found., 1981—93, Spencer Found., 1988—92, M&I Bank of Madison, 1991—92, NCAA Found., 1991; trustee Brookings Inst., 1989—92. Ohio Newspaper Women's scholar, 1958, Western Coll. Trustee scholar, 1958-62; Carnegie fellow, 1966-68; Guggenheim fellow, 1975-76; recipient Disting. Svc. medal Columbia U. Tchrs. Coll., 1989. Mem. ASPA, Am. Polit. Sci. Assn., Nat. Acad. Arts and Scis., Nat. Acad. Pub. Adminstrn., Coun. Fgn. Rels., Nat. Acad. Edn. (Spencer fellow 1972-73). Office: U Miami Office of Pres 230 Ashe Bldg Coral Gables FL 33146

SHALAM, JOHN JOSEPH, car stereo and cellular telephone company executive; b. Alexandria, Egypt, Dec. 10, 1933; came to U.S., 1948, naturalized, 1973; s. Murad Joseph and Vicky (Harari) S.; m. Jane Bishop, Mar. 9, 1970; children— Ari M., David M., Marc J. Student, pvt. schs. From exec. trainee to trader U.K. dept. Continental Grain Co., N.Y.C., 1955-58; v.p. Lynn Supply Co., 1958-61; pres. Custom Imports, Inc., 1961-63, Audiovox Corp., Hauppauge, N.Y., 1963—, now also Chmmn. & CEO. Mem. JP Morgan-Chase Met. Adv. Bd. Mem. bd. advisors SUNY Coll. at Old Westbury. Mem. Consumer Electronic Industry Assn. (bd. govs.), Ben Franklin Soc., U. Pa. Alumnae Assn., Penn Club N.Y., Old Westbury Horsemen's Found. (past pres.), Wharton Sch. Club L.I. and N.Y., Glen Oaks Country Club (bd. govs.), Confrerie de la Chaine des Rotisseurs. Republican. Jewish. Office: Audiovox Corp 150 Marcus Blvd Hauppauge NY 11788-3794 Business E-Mail: jshalam@audiovox.com.

SHALEK, JAMES ARTHUR, JR. insurance agent, financial consultant; b. Chgo., May 3, 1947; s. James Arthur and Evelyn Pearl (Kubitz) S.; m. Susan Ellen Keto, Feb. 12, 1977; 1 child, Stephanie Catherine. BA, Hope Coll., Holland, Mich., 1969. CLU, ChFC. Instr. 7th and 8th grade math. Big Hollow Grade Sch., Ingleside, Ill., 1970-73; agt. Penn Mut. Life Ins. Co., Oak Brook, 1973-75; sr. agt. The Prin. Fin. Group, Oak Brook Terrace, 1975—. Fin. sec. First Congl. Ch. United Ch. of Christ, Geneva, Ill., 1991-94; pres. Midwest Epilepsy Ctr., Lombard, Ill., 1982-83. Mem. Soc. Fin. Svc. Profls., Nat. Assn. Ins. and Fin. Advisors (Nat. Quality award 14 yrs., nat. Sales Achievement award 15 yrs.) Ill. Life Underwriters Assn. (nominating com. 1992), Ill. Assn. Ins. and Fin. Advisors (bd. dirs. 2002-), DuPage Area Assn. Ins. and Fin. Advisors (nat. com. 1992-95, pres. 1990-91, bd. dirs. 1980-95, Mem. of Yr. 1998), Million Dollar Round Table. Republican. Avocations: skiing, swimming, golf, weight training. Home: 556 Red Tail Ln Yorkville IL 60560 Office: The Prin Fin Group 3001 Butterfield Rd Ste 150 Oak Brook IL 60523-1107 E-mail: shalek.james@principal.com.

SHALHOUP, JUDY LYNN, marketing communications executive; b. Charleston, W.Va., Oct. 25, 1940; d. George Ferris and Mary Margaret (Moses) Shalhoup; m. William Mainella. BA, Morris Harvey Coll., Charleston, 1967; MS, W.Va. U., 1970. With Union Carbide Corp., 1960-92, publicity mgr. plastics, 1971-73, coatings materials div. advt. mgr., 1973-82, mgr. mktg. comm. splty. chems. div., 1982-85, mgr. mktg. comm., solvents and coatings materials div., 1982-92; chmn. GMJC Assocs., 1992—. V.p., gen. mgr. Fruit Bowl, Charleston, 1975-78. Recipient Best Teller award Bus. Profl. Advt. Assn., 1978-84, 86-87, Pro-Com award 1991, Excellence in Bus.-to-Bus. Advt. award, 1989, Objectives and Results Advt. award Am. Bus. Press, 1978, Clio Advt. Recognition award, 1978-86, Clio award, 1984, Andy award, 1983, 84, Nutmegger award, 1985. Mem. Telefood Assn., Internat. Platform Assn., Assn. Nat. Advt., Inc., SSPC, AAAS, Nat. Paint and Coatings Assn. (comm. com.), Fedn. Socs. Coatings Tech., Bus. Profl. Advt. Assn. (Star awards for excellence 1989-90, Procom award 1990).

SHALIKASHVILI, JOHN MALCHASE, retired military career officer; b. Warsaw, Poland, June 27, 1936; s. Dimitri and Maria (Ruediger) S.; m. Gunhild Bartsch, Apr. 18, 1963 (dec. Aug. 1965); m. Joan E. Zimpelman, Dec. 27, 1966; 1 child, Brant. BSME, Bradley U., 1958; attended, Naval War Coll., 1969-70, U.S. Army War Coll., 1977-78; MA in Internat. Affairs, George Washington U., 1970; LLD (hon.), U. Md., 1993, Bradley U., 1994. Joined U.S. Army, 1958, advanced through grades to gen., 1992—, various troop and staff assignments Alaska, U.S., Fed. Republic of Germany, Vietnam, Korea, 1959-75, commdr. 1st bn. 84th field arty. Wash., 1975-77; dep. chief of staff ops. So. European Task Froce U.S. Army, Vicenza, Italy, 1978-79; comdr. div. arty., 1st Armored Div. U.S. Army, Nuernberg, Fed. Republic of Germany, 1979-81, chief., politico-mil div., later dep. dir. ODCSOPS Washington, 1981-84, asst. div. comdr. 1st. Armored div. Nuernberg, Fed. Republic of Germany, 1984-86, dir. strategy, plans, policy ODCSOPS Washington, 1986-87; comdg. gen. 9th inf. div. Ft. Lewis, Wash., 1987-89; dep. comdr.-in-chief Hdqrs. USAREUR and 7th Army, Heidelberg, Fed. Republic of Germany, 1989-91; asst. to chmn. Joint Chiefs of Staff, Washington, 1991-92; Supreme Allied Comdr. Europe, Comdr.-in-Chief U.S. Forces Europe, 1992-93; chmn. Joint Chiefs of Staff, 1993-97. Bd. trustees Bradley U.; mem. Buffalo Soldier Meml. Hon. Com. Decorated Def. D.S.M. with 3 oak leaf clusters, D.S.M. (Army) with oak leaf cluster), D.S.M. (Navy), D.S.M. (Air Force), D.S.M. (Dept. Trans.), Legion of Merit with 2 oak leaf clusters, Bronze Star medal with V device, Meritorious Svc. medal with 3 oak leaf clusters, Air medal, Joint Svc. Commendation medal, Army Commendation medal, Nat. Def. Svc. medal with bronze svc. star, Armed Forced Expeditionary medal, Republic of Vietnam Svc. medal with silver service star, S.W. Asia Svc. medal with bronze svc. star, Humanitarian Svc. medal, Army Svc. Ribbon, Overseas Svc. Ribbon with bronze Arabic numeral 5, Inter-Am. Def. Bd. medal, Kuwait Liberation medal, Order of Combat Infantryman badge, Parachutist badge, Joint Chiefs of Staff Identification badge, Army Staff Identification badge, Brazilian Order of Mil. Merit with 1st and 2d award, French Grand Officer of Nat. Merit, Belgian Grand Cordon of Order of Leopold, German Order of Merit with star and sash, Japanese Order of Rising Sun, Argentine Order of May in Grade of Gt. Cross for Mil. Merit, Korean Order of Nat. Security Merit, Tong-IL medal, Bintang Yudha Dharama Utama Hon. Decoration (Indonesia), Kuwait Def. medal, Grand Cross of Royal Norwegian Order of Merit, Grand Cross of Mil. Merit medal of Portuguese Republic, Republic of Vietnam Gallantry Cross with 2 silver and 1 bronze star, Republic of Vietnam Armed Forces Honor medal 1st class, Republic of Vietnam Armed Forces Honor medal 1st class, Republic of Vietnam Campaign medal, Republic of Vietnam Chung My medal 2d class, Tng. Svc. medal 1st class, Netherlands Comdr. Order Orange Nassau with swords, Mexican U.S. Mil. Merit 1st class, Great Cross Repub. Poland; recipient Chilean Bernardo Higgins award, Dwight D. Eisenhower Dist. Svc. award Vets. Fgn. Wars, Dist. Alumni Achievement award George Washington U. Mem. Assn. U.S. Army, Field Arty. Assn., Armed Forces Benefit Assn., Ret. Officers Assn., SHAPE Officers' Assn., Coun. Fgn. Rels., Am. Acad. Achievement, Mil. Order of Carabao, Army and Air Force Benefit Assn.

SHALINSKY, JOSEPH GEORGE, pharmacist, pharmaceutical executive; b. Kansas City, Kans., July 6, 1916; s. Herman and Freda (Iskowitz) S.; m. Charlotte Louise Zolotor, Jan. 18, 1953; children: Robert Alan, Lee Bryan, Jonathan Neil. BS in Pharmacy, U. Mo., Kansas City, 1939. Registered pharmacist, Kans., Mo. Pres. Shalinsky Drug Co. Inc., Kansas City and Overland Park, Kans., 1953—. Mem. adv. coun. U. Kans. Sch. of Pharmacy, 1967—; mem. Kans. Drug Abuse Adv. Coun., 1974, Gov.'s Conf. on Eradication of Marijuana, 1969; procurement chmn. Wyandotte County "Sabin on Sunday" Cmty. Polio Immunization Program; chmn. Johnson County Pharmacy Theft Prevention Program, 1978; bd. dirs. Salvation Army, 1953—; mem. exec. com. Crosslines Retirement Ctr., 1953—. Recipient Alumni Achievement award U. Mo. Kansas City, 1974, Disting. Svc. award U. Kansas City Alumni Assn., 1961, 50-Yr. Pharmacist award Kans. Bd. Pharmacy, Mo. Bd. Pharmacy. Fellow Am. Coll. Apothecaries; mem. VFW, Am. Pharm. Assn. (pres. Greater Kansas City chpt. 1947), Nat. Assn. Bds. of Pharmacy (chmn. com. on continuing edn. 1967, blue ribbon com. on exams. 1967, exec. bd. 1975-76, treas. 1977, 2d v.p. 1977, pres. 1980, chmn. bd. dirs. 1981), Nat. Assn. Retail Druggists, Am. Assn. Colls. of Pharmacy, Kans. Pharmacists Assn. (exec. com. 1967-84, dist. dir. Wyandotte/Johnson County 1947, Bowl of Hygeia award 1989, Pharmacist of Yr. award 1981), Mo. Pharm. Assn., Kans. Pharmacy Tripartite Com., Greater Kansas City Pharmacists Assn., U. Mo. Kansas City Pharmacy Alumni Assn. (pres. 1960-61), U. Mo. Kansas City Pharmacy Found. (pres. 1963-64, bd. dirs. 1964-75, chmn. bd. dirs. 1975—, Joseph G. Shalinsky Scholarship Fund established in his honor 1996), Am. Legion, Fleet Res. Assn., Ret. Officers Assn., Optimist, Kansas City C. of C., Argentine Activities Assn. (pres. 1972-74, Cmty. Svc. award 1988), B'nai B'rith. Home: 9201 Fontana St Shawnee Mission KS 66207-2632

SHALIT, HANOCH, imaging scientist, executive; b. Tel-Aviv, July 1, 1953; came to U.S., 1982; s. Mordechai and Yael (Bryskier) S.; m. Cleri Machlouzarides, May 17, 1992; children: Antonia, Alexander. BSc with honors, Poly. of Cen. London, 1978; PhD in Physics, London U., 1981. Asst. photographic scientist John Hadland Ltd., Bovingdon, Eng., 1977-78; demonstrator London U., 1978-81; asst. prof. Rochester (N.Y.) Inst. of Tech., 1981-82; sr. photographic scientist Chemco Photo Products, Glen Cove, N.Y., 1982-83, sr. rsch. project mgr., 1984-87; dir. of photographic sci. Fonar Corp., Melville, 1987-88; pres. IMATEC Ltd., N.Y.C., 1988-2000. Mem. stds. com. Digital Image Comm. in Medicine. Contbr. articles to profl. jours; patentee in field. With M.C. Israeli Army, 1971-74. Recipient scholarship, London U., 1978-81. Mem. Soc. for Imaging Sci. and Tech., Brit. Assn. for Crystal Growth, Soc. Motion Picture and TV Engrs. (voting mem., subcom. on med. imaging), Am. Coll. of Radiology, Nat. Elec. Mfg. Assn., Internat. Soc. Optical Engring. Home: 245 E 63rd St Apt 34B New York NY 10021-7400

SHALITA, ALAN REMI, dermatologist; b. Bklyn., Mar. 22, 1936; s. Harry and Celia; m. Simone Lea Baum, Sept. 4, 1960; children: Deborah (dec.) and Judith (twins). AB, Brown U., 1957; BS, U. Brussels, 1960; MD, Bowman Gray Sch. Medicine, 1964; DSc (hon.), L.I. U., 1990. Intern Beth Israel Hosp., N.Y.C., 1964-65; resident dept. dermatology NYU Med. Ctr., 1967-68, NIH tng. grant fellow dept. dermatology, 1968-70, instr. dermatology, 1970-71; asst. prof. NYU, 1971-73, Columbia U., 1973-75; assoc. prof. medicine, head divsn. dermatology SUNY Downstate Med. Ctr., Bklyn., 1975-79, prof., 1979—, head divsn. dermatology, 1979-80, chmn. dept. dermatology, 1980—, asst. dean, 1977-83, acting dean Queens campus, 1983-84; assoc. dean clin. affairs SUNY Health Sci. Ctr., Bklyn., 1989-92, assoc. provost for clin. affairs, 1992-93, assoc. v.p. clin. affairs, 1993—. Disting. tchg. prof. SUNY Health Sci. Ctr., Bklyn., 1996—; asst. attending in dermatology Univ. Hosp., N.Y.C., 1970-73, Bellevue Hosp. Ctr., 1970-73, Manhattan VA Hosp., 1971-73, Presbyn. Hosp., 1973-75; mem. med. bd. Kings County Hosp. Ctr.; cons. dermatology Bklyn. VA Hosp., 1975—; chief dermatology Brookdale Med. Ctr., 1977-90; chief dermatology Univ. Hosp. of Bklyn., 1975—; chief dermatology Kings County Hosp. Ctr., Bklyn., 1975—, acting med. dir., 1989-92; med. dir. Univ. Hosp. Bklyn., 1992-96. Pres. Temple Shaaray Tefila, N.Y.C., 1982-86, chmn. bd. trustees, 1987-95. Lt. M.C. USNR, 1965-67. Recipient Torch of Liberty award Anti-Defamation League, 1987, Surg. and Pediatric awards Beth Israel Hosp., N.Y.C., 1965, Leah Dickstein Man of Good Conscience award, Women's Med. Assn. of N.Y;, 1999, Leadership in Urban Med. Edn. award Arthur Ashe Inst. for Urban Health, 1999; spl. fellow NIH, 1970-73. Mem.: AAAS, AMA, Venezuelan Dermatology Soc., Argentina Dermatology Soc., Brit. Assn. Dermatologists, N.Y. Dermatol. Soc. (pres. 1989—90), Dermatol. Soc. Greater N.Y. (pres. 1980—81), N.Y. State Dermatol. Soc., N.Y. Acad. Medicine, N.Y. State Med. Soc., N.Y. Acad. Scis., Internat. Soc. Dermatology, Assn. Profs. Dermatology (sec.-treas. 1988—94, pres. 1996—98), Soc. Cosmetic Chemists, Am. Soc. Dermatol. Surgery (past bd. dirs.), Am. Dermatol. Assn. (sec.-treas. 1996—2001, pres. 2001—02), Dermatology Found. (trustee), Soc. Investigative Dermatology, Am. Acad. Dermatology (bd. dirs. 1983—87, v.p. 1995—96), Polish Dermatology Soc. (hon.), Soc. Francaise de Dermatology (hon.), Alpha Omega Alpha. Republican. Home: 70 E 77th St New York NY 10021-1811 Office: 450 Clarkson Ave Brooklyn NY 11203-2056 E-mail: ashalita@downstate.edu. *Treat others with compassion, dignity and respect, add a little humor to everyone's life. Speak up for what you truly believe, be charitable.*

SHALKOP, ROBERT LEROY, retired museum director; b. Milford, Conn., July 30, 1922; s. Bertram Leroy and Dorothy Jane (Boardman) S.; m. Antoinette Joan Benkowsky, Dec. 7, 1963; 1 son, Andrew Goforth. Student, Maryville (Tenn.) Coll., 1940-42; MA, U. Chgo., 1949; postgrad., Sorbonne, 1951-52. Dir. Rahr Civic Center, Manitowoc, Wis., 1953-56, Everhart Mus., Scranton, Pa., 1956-62, Brooks Meml. Art Gallery, Memphis, 1962-64; assoc. dir. Colorado Springs (Colo.) Fine Arts Center, also curator Taylor Mus., 1964-71; dir. Anchorage Mus. History and Art, 1972-87; pvt. practice mus. cons. Salisbury, N.C., 1987-94; archaeologist Smithsonian Instn., 1948, 50, Am. Found. Study Man, 1951, U. Wash., 1953, State U. Idaho, 1960. Author: Wooden Saints, the Santos of New Mexico, 1967, A Comparative View of Spanish Colonial Sculpture, 1968, Arroyo Hondo, the Folk Art of a New Mexican Village, 1969, A Comparative View of Spanish Colonial Painting, 1970, A Show of Color: 100 Years of Painting in the Pike's Peak Region, 1971, Russian Orthodox Art in Alaska, 1973, Sydney Laurence, an Alaskan Impressionist, 1975, Eustace Ziegler, 1977, Contemporary Native Art of Alaska, 1979, Henry Wood Elliott, 1982; Editor: An Introduction to the Native Art of Alaska, 1972; assoc. editor: Exploration in Alaska, 1980. Served with USAAF, 1942-45. Mem. Am. Assn. Museums. Home and Office: 309 W Marsh St Salisbury NC 28144-5345

SHALLCROSS, DEANNE, investment company executive; Exec. v.p. mktg. TIAA-CREF, N.Y.C., 1996—. Office: TIAA-CREF 730 3d Ave New York NY 10017 E-mail: dshallcross@tiaa-cref.org.

SHALLCROSS, DORIS JANE, creative behavioral educator; b. Cranford, N.J., Feb. 28, 1933; d. John William and Ethel Belle (Ruth) S. BA, Montclair State Coll., 1955; MA, Wesleyan U., Middletown, Conn., 1962; EdD, U. Mass., 1973. Tchr. Hunterdon Cen. High Sch., Flemington, N.J., 1955-61, Roosevelt Jr. High Sch., Cleveland Heights, Ohio, 1961-65, Cleveland Heights H.S., 1965-67; adminstr. Cleveland Heights Pub. Schs., 1967-69; dir. humanistic edn. Montague (Mass.) Pub. Schs., 1972-75; program devel. specialist Tchr. Corps., SUNY, Oneonta, N.Y., 1976-78; asst. prof. edn. divsn. home econs. U. Mass., Amherst, 1978-82, prof., dir. grad. studies in creativity, 1982-95; pres. Shallcross Creativity Inst., Haydenville, Mass., 1995—. Pres. bd. trustees Creative Edn. Found., Buffalo, 1989-94; co-dir. Global Odyssey, 1992—; bd. dirs. Ctr. for Critical and Creative Thinking, Hartford, Conn., 1989-92, 95—; prof. internat. grad. program in creativity U. Santiago, Santiage de Compostela, Spain, 1999. Author: Teaching Creative Behavior, 1981; co-author: The Growing Person, 1985, Leadership: Making Things Happen, 1987, Intuition: An Inner Way of Knowing, 1989; cons. editor Jour. Creative Behavior, 1967—; contbr. articles to profl. jours. Mem. Planning Bd., Town of Williamsburg, 1981-89; v.p. bd. dirs. Pioneer Valley Performing Arts H.S., 1995-98, pres., 1998—; chair edn. com. Arts in Edn. Ctr., pres. 2002-; bd. dirs. Mass. Charter Schs. Assn., 2001—. Recipient Disting. Leader award, Creative Edn. Found., 1986; grantee, NSF, 1987-89, U. Mass., 1987-89. Mem. NEA, Mass. Soc. of Profs., Inst. for Noetic Scis., Am. Creativity Assn. (bd. dirs. 1990-93). Avocations: music, golf, reading, gardening. Home and Office: 26 S Main St Haydenville MA 01039-9735

SHALLER, RUSSELL R. manufacturing executive; b. Cin., June 5, 1963; s. George and Joanne Shaller; m. Mary Kelly, Oct. 4, 1986; children: Joseph children: John, Thomas. MBA, U. Del., 1998. Gen. mgr. W. L. Gore & Assocs., Elkton, Md., 1995—, product mgr. Newark. Home: 3 Beechwood Dr Landenberg PA 19350 Office: WL Gore & Assocs 402 Vieves Way Elkton MD 21921-3936 Personal E-mail: whatever38@msn.com.

SHALOM, LILIANE WINN, investment company executive, consultant; b. Casablanca, Morocco, May 28, 1940; d. Joseph and Madeleine Levy; 1 child Dominique Winn. Brevet Etudes Premier Cycle, Alliance Israelite, Casablanca, 1956; cert. proficiency in English, U. Mich., 1960. English tchr. U.S. Info. Agy., Casablanca, 1959-61; multilingual guide, interpreter for VIPs, heads of state UN, N.Y.C., 1962-65; designer-ptnr., v.p. I.Q. Originals, Inc., 1977-82; pres. EON Holdings, Inc., 1981—, L.S. Cons., 1991—; cons. Applied Energy Svcs., Alexandria, Va., 1992—95, Airbus Industrie, Toulouse, France, 1999—2000. Editor, pub., contbr. The Sephardi World quar. mag., 1975-82. Fin. com. Carter for Pres., N.Y.C., 1975-76, Moynihan for Senate, N.Y.C., 1976, Dukakis for Pres., N.Y.C., 1987-88; chmn. fundraising Congl. Fgn. Rels. Com., N.Y.C., 1986. Recipient Louise Waterman Wise award Am. Jewish Congress, 1984, Stanley Isaacs Human Rels. award Am. Jewish Com., N.Y., 1986; named Comdr. of Ouissam Alaouite, King of Morocco, 1987. Mem. Am. Sephardi Fedn. (pres. 1975-82), World Zionist Congress (presidium 1971—), Moroccan Jewish Orgn. (founder, chmn. 1978), United Jewish Appeal (bd. dirs.), Hebrew Immigration Aid Soc. (v.p. 1990—), World Jewish Congress (econ. and social commn.). Democrat. Office: 645 5th Ave Ste 710 New York NY 10022-5910

SHALOWITZ, ERWIN EMMANUEL, civil engineer; b. Washington, Feb. 13, 1924; s. Aaron Louis and Pearl (Myer) S.; m. Elaine Mildred Langerman, June 29, 1952; children: Ann Janet, Aliza Beth, Jonathan Avram. Student, U. Pa., U. Notre Dame, 1944-45; BCE, George Washington U., 1947, postgrad., 1948-49; grad. soil mechanics, Cath. U., 1951; MA in Pub. Adminstrn. (fellow U.S. Civil Service Commn.), Am. U., 1954. Registered profl. engr., Washington. Engr. Klemitt Engring. Co., N.Y.C., 1947; with cons. firm Whitman, Requardt & Assos., Balt., 1947-48; chief structural research engr., head def. research sect., project officer and tech. adviser for atomic tests Bur. Yards and Docks, Dept. Navy, Washington, 1948-59; supervisory gen. engr. spl. asst. for protective constrn. programs, project mgr. for bldg. systems, chief research br., chief mgmt. information, chief contracting procedures and support, chief contract evaluation and analysis, Pub. Bldgs. Service, Gen. Services Adminstrn., 1959—98; acquisition/procurement exec., also team leader/project mgr. Electronic Acquisition Sy. Pub. Bldgs. Svc., Gen. Svcs. Adminstrn., 1998; now mgr. ednl. svc. for individual improvement, Bethesda, Md., 1998—. Chmn. fed. exec. tng. program U.S. Civil Service Commn., 1950; fallout shelter analyst Dept. Def.; chmn. GSA Fire Safety Com., GSA Fallout Protection Com., GSA Bldg. Evaluation Com.; mem. Interagy Com. on Housing Rsch. and Bldg. Tech.; mem. Nat. Evaluation Bd. Architect-Engr. Selections; mem. standing com. on procurement policy Nat. Acad. Sci. Bldg. Research Adv. Bd. and Interagency Com. on Procurement Curriculum Rev.; coordinator pub. bldgs. design and constrn. Small Bus. Program and Minority Enterprise and Minority Subcontracting Programs. Contbr. articles profl. jours. Served to engring. officer USNR, 1944-46. Recipient Commendable Svc. award GSA, 1968, Outstanding Performance recognition, 1976, 77, 79, 83, 87, 93-96, Superior Accomplishment award, 1995, others; Engr. Alumni Achievement award George Washington U., 1985. Fellow ASCE, Am. Biog. Inst.; mem. Soc. Advancement Mgmt., Am. Biog. Inst. (nat. bd. advisors), Soc. Am. Mil. Engrs., Sigma Tau, Pi Sigma Alpha. Jewish. Home: 5603 Huntington Pkwy Bethesda MD 20814-1132 E-mail: eshalowitz@aol.com. *PRINCIPLES: Look beyond the material for lasting values and meaning, optimize managerial effectiveness by creating an objective and challenging climate in an organization, delve into the underlying causes of problem areas for meaningful solutions, and persevere in spite of obstacles. IDEAS: Cultural pluralism; the intrinsic potential of each individual; and love, appreciation, and support of one's family as indispensable for real accomplishment. GOALS: To attain the highest level of professional accomplishment within my capabilities and to continue to have a rich, happy, and fulfilling family life. STANDARDS OF CONDUCT: To be fair, consistent, and straightforward; and to avoid over-reacting.*

SHALOWITZ, HOWARD A. lawyer; b. Chgo., June 23, 1961; s. Mervin and Aileen (Goldstein) S. BA, U. Pa., 1983; JD, Washington U., 1987. Bar: Mo. 1987, Ill. 1988, U.S. Dist. Ct. (ea. dist.) Mo. 1988, U.S. Ct. Appeals (8th cir.) 1991, U.S. Ct. Appeals (7th cir.) 1993, U.S. Supreme Ct. 1994. Pvt. practice, St. Louis, 1987—. Legis. asst. Office of U.S. Senator Howard Metzenbaum, Washington, 1987; rsch. analyst Ill. Law Enforcement Commn., Chgo., 1981; mem. faculty Ctrl. Agy. for Jewish Edn., 1989-98; Dem. candidate Mo. state senate 24th dist., 1998. Lead tenor Gilbert and Sullivan operettas, 1979-84. Cantor; pres. St. Louis Circle Jewish Music, 1993-96, bd. dirs., 1987—. Bessie Bodek Miller scholar U. Pa., Phila., 1981-82; Glendy Burke Oratory medal Tulane U., New Orleans, 1981. Mem. ABA, Mo. Bar, Bar Assn. Met. St. Louis (chmn. lawyer referral and info. svc. com., pres.-elect, mem. exec. bd. govs., chmn. ambassador com.), Cantors Assembly. Office: 7108 Northmoor Dr Saint Louis MO 63105-2108 E-mail: howard@shalowitz.org.

SHAM, LU JEU, physics educator; b. Hong Kong, Apr. 28, 1938; s. T.S. and Cecilia Maria (Siu) Shen; m. Georgina Bien, Apr. 25, 1965; children: Kevin Shen, Alisa Shen. GCE, Portsmouth Coll., Eng., 1957; BS, Imperial Coll., London U., Eng., 1960; PhD in Physics, Cambridge U., Eng., 1963. Asst. rsch. physicist U. Calif. at San Diego, La Jolla, 1963-66, assoc. prof., 1968-75, prof., 1975—, chair dept. physics, 1995-98, dean div. natural scis., 1985-89; asst. prof. physics U. Calif. at Irvine, 1966-67; rsch. physicist IBM Corp., Yorktown Heights, N.Y., 1974-75. Reader Queen Mary Coll., U. London, 1967-68. Assoc. editor Physics Letters A., 1992—; contbr. sci. papers to profl. jours. Recipient Churchill Coll. studentship, Eng., 1960-63, Sr. U.S. Scientist award Humboldt Found., Stuttgart, Germany, 1978, Faculty Rsch. lectr. award, 2000; fellow Guggenheim Found., 1984, Chancellor Assocs. award for Excellence in Rsch., 1995. Fellow Am. Phys. Soc.; mem. AAAS, NAS, Acad. Sinica Republic of China, Optical Soc. Am. Democrat. Avocation: tennis, folk dancing. Office: U Calif San Diego Dept Physics 0319 La Jolla CA 92093-0319 E-mail: lsham@ucsd.edu.

SHAMASH, YACOV, dean, electrical engineering educator; b. Iraq, Jan. 12, 1950; BSEE, Imperial Coll., London, 1970; PhD in Control Systems, Imperial Coll., 1973. Postdoctoral fellowin elec. engring. Tel-Aviv U., 1973-75, from lectr. elec. engring. to sr. lectr. elec. engring., 1975-78; prof. elec. engring. Fla. Atlantic U., Boca Raton, 1977-85; prof., chair dept. elec. engring. dept. Wash. State U., Pullman, 1985-92; dean engring. SUNY, Stony Brook, 1992—. Bd. dirs. KeyTronics, Spokane, Wash., 1990—; vis. asst. prof. U. Pa., Phila., 1976-77. Contbr. over 100 articles to profl. jours., book chpts. Fellow IEEE (sr.). Office: SUNY Coll Engring & Applied Sci Stony Brook NY 11790-2200

SHAMBAUGH, CATHERINE ANNE, elementary education educator; b. Urbana, Ohio, Dec. 5, 1958; d. Richard Parke and Elizabeth Anne (Hubbard) S. BA, Wittenberg U., Springfield, Ohio, 1981; MEd, Kent State U., 1988. Cert. elem. tchr., math. clinician, Ohio. Tchr. Strongsville (Ohio) City Schs., 1981—. Bd. dirs. Caesar's Forum Theatre Co., 1999—. Martha Holden Jennings Found. grantee, 1985, Strongsville Assn. for Gifted and Talented grantee, 1989. Mem. Nat. Coun. Tchrs. Math., Ohio Coun. Tchrs. Math. (v.p. elem. 1995-98, Outstanding Math. Classroom Tchr. award 1994), Greater Cleve. Tchrs. Math. (Outstanding Math. Classroom Tchr. award 1991), Strongsville Edn. Assn. (v.p. 1989-92, 2001-02), Nat. Tchr. Tng. Inst. (master tchr.), Phi Delta Kappa, Delta Kappa Gamma (rec. sec. 2000-02). Episcopalian. Avocations: horseback riding, reading, crafts, bird watching. Home: 741 Walwick Ct Berea OH 44017-2760 Office: Edith Whitney Elem Sch 13548 Whitney Rd Strongsville OH 44136-1951

SHAMBAUGH, IRVIN CALVIN, JR. aptitude test firm executive; b. Harrisburg, Pa., June 7, 1943; s. Irvin Calvin and Viola Mary (Diebler) S.; m. Amy Willcox, Jan. 3, 1975. BS in Geol. Sci., Pa. State U., 1964; postgrad. MIT, 1964-65, Tex. Christian U., Ft. Worth, 1974-76, East. Tex. State U., 1976-77. Research coord. Johnson O'Connor Research Found., Ft. Worth, 1965-76; pres., chief scientist Aptitude Inventory Measurement Service, Dallas, 1976—; centennial fellow Coll. Earth and Min. Scis. Penn. State U., 1996. Author: The Test-Taker's Guide to Career Literature, 1982, Test Manual for Selected AIMS Worksamples, 1986, Books About Careers, 1986, Career Facts: Where to Find Them and How to Use Them, 1992, The AIMS Guide to Career Facts, 1997; co-author: AIMS Information About Aptitudes, 1979, The Aptitude Handbook: A Guide to the AIMS Program, 1996, 2d edit., 1998; co-author, editor: You and Your Aptitudes, 1983; developer Activity Preference Questionnaire, 1994, psychometric instrument III Interest Inventory, 1996; contbr. numerous reports and research bulls. to profl. pubis.; developer AIMS test battery, 1976—. Served with USMC, 1966-68. Mem. Am. Counseling Assn., Assn. Assessment in Counseling, Am. Psychol. Assn. (assoc.), Am. Psychol. Soc., Nat. Coun. Measurement in Edn., AAAS, Am. Statis Assn., Nat. Assn. Coll. Admissions Counselors, Nat. Assn. Test Dirs. Home: 934 Westbrook Dr Garland TX 75043-5243 Office: Aptitude Inventory Measurement Svc 12160 Abrams Rd Ste 314 Dallas TX 75243-4525

SHAMBAUGH, STEPHEN WARD, lawyer; b. South Bend, Ind., Aug. 4, 1920; s. Marion Clyde and Anna Violet (Stephens) S.; m. Marilyn Louise Pyle (dec. 1993); children: Susan Wynne Shambaugh Hinkle (dec. 1998), Kathleen Louise Shambaugh Thompson. Student, San Jose State Tchrs. Coll., 1938-40, U. Ark., 1951; LLB, U. Tulsa, 1954. Bar: Okla. 1954, Colo. 1964. Mem. staff Reading & Bates, Inc., Tulsa, 1951-54; v.p., gen. mgr., legal counsel Reading & Bates Drilling Co. Ltd., Calgary, Alta., Can., 1954-61; sr. ptnr. Bowman, Shambaugh, Geissinger & Wright, Denver, 1964-81; sole practice, 1981-97; now ret. Dir., fin. counsel various corps. Col. USAF ret. Mem. Colo. Bar Assn., Okla. Bar Assn., P-51 Mustang Pilots Assn., Masons, Elks, Phi Alpha Delta.

SHAMBUREK, ROLAND HOWARD, physician; b. Adell, Wis., June 7, 1928; s. William and Catherine (Illig) Shamburek; m. Gladys Irene Gibbons, June 21, 1952; children: Steven J., Robert D., Daniel J. BS, U. Wis., 1950, MD, 1953; MPH, Harvard U., 1960; grad., U.S. Army War Coll., Carlisle Barracks, Pa., 1972. Diplomate Am. Bd. Preventive Medicine. Commd. 1st lt. M.C., U.S. Army, 1953, advanced through grades to col., 1968, with Surgeon Gen.'s Office, 1966-70, 72-75; intern St. Joseph's Hosp., Marshfield, Wis., 1953-54; grad. U.S. Naval Sch. of Aviation Medicine, Pensacola, Fla., 1957; resident in preventive (aerospace) medicine USAF Sch. Aerospace Medicine, Brooks AFB, 1960-63; service in Europe, 1955-56, 63-66, Office of Army Surgeon Gen., Washington, 1966—70, 1972—75; comdr. 67th EVAC Hosp., Vietnam, 1970-71, U.S. Army Med. Pers. Support Agy., 1975-77; ret. U.S. Army, 1977; exec. v.p. Aerospace Med. Assn., 1977-79; clin. practice Pentagon Health Clinic, Washington, 1981-85; med. researcher Office of Army Surgeon Gen., 1985-87. Med. monitor Canary Island Tracking Sta. for Gemini missions NASA, 1965—66. Contbr. scientific papers. Decorated Legion of Merit with oak leaf cluster. Mem.: AMA (del. 1978), Internat. Acad. Aviation and Space Medicine, Soc. NASA Flight Surgeons, U.S. Army Flight Surgeons, Soc. Med. Cons. Armed Forces, Aerospace Med. Assn. (v.p. 1968—69), Am. Coll. Preventive Medicine (v.p. 1968—69), Assn. Mil. Surgeons (John Shaw Billings award 1968). Address: 3700 Moss Dr Annandale VA 22003-1915

SHAMES, HENRY JOSEPH, lawyer; b. Milw., Jan. 20, 1921; s. Aron and Jennie (Greenberg) S.; m. Beverly Cleveland Van Wert, June 9, 1972; children: Stephen H., Suzanne Shames Sattelmeyer, Sarah Shames Phillips, Diana Shames Strandberg. AB, U. Chgo., 1942; JD, Harvard U., 1948. Bar: Ill. 1949, Calif. 1962. Mem. firm Arvey, Hodes & Mantynband, Chgo., 1949-61; partner Pacht, Ross, Warne, Bernhard & Sears, Los Angeles, 1962-75, Grossman & Shames, Los Angeles, 1975-83, Rosenfeld, Parnell & Shames Inc., Los Angeles, 1984-86; counsel Patterson, Belknap, Webb and Tyler, 1986-87. Chmn. bd. Switzer Center, Los Angeles, 1966-73 Served with USNR, 1943-46. Mem. Assn. Bus. Trial Lawyers (bd. govs. 1973-76, v.p. 1973-76), Calif. State Bar Assn., So. Calif. Def. Counsel, Los Angeles County Bar Assn., Phi Beta Kappa. Home: 4906 La Ramada Dr Santa Barbara CA 93111-1518 E-mail: henry.beverly@verizon.net.

SHAMES, JORDAN NELSON, health care executive, consultant health services; b. Malden, Mass., June 27, 1949; s. Abraham and Annette (Harris) S.; m. Joni Schechter, Apr. 15, 1984; children: Robert Zachary, Rebecca Naomi. BS in Polit. Sci., Allegheny Coll., 1971; postgrad., U. Ky., 1973-74, New Sch. for Social Rsch., N.Y.C., 1983-85. Real estate and nursing home property mgr. H.R.F. Co., Triplex Ltd., Bethpage, N.Y., 1974-77; L.I., N.Y.C. area mgr. Quality Care, Rockville Centre, 1977-80; exec. dir. Health Force, East Meadow, 1980-82; adminstr. Med. Personnel Pool, White Plains, 1982-83; exec. dir. Continental Health Affiliates, 1983-85, Community Home Care, Bronx, N.Y., 1985-88; pres., CEO Neighbors Home Care, 1989—. Mem. profl. adv. bd. Beth Abraham Hosp. Home Health Agy., Bronx, NY, 1986—; bd. dir. Home Health Mgmt., Inc.; chmn. bd. Bronx Cmty. Home Care, Inc., 1989—; interviewee Nat. Pub. Radio, 1989; bd. dir. Bedford Park Multi-Svc. Ctr., Bronx, 1991—, vice chmn. bd., 1997—, chmn. devel. com., 1994—; bd. dir. St. Marys Children and Family Svcs., bd. dir. fin. com., 1997—; chmn. bd. trustees NY State Health Care Providers, pub. policy com., 2001—; chmn. bd. trustees Self Ins. Trust for DBL, 1995—99; sec. bd. Health Care Providers, 2001—. Co-author: Home Health Services Quarterly, 1985, Caring Mag., 1987, 89; presenter in field. Bd. dirs. Bedford Park Multi-Svc. Ctr., Bronx, 1991—; mem. lobby renovation com. Gerard Owners Corp. Coop., Forest Hills, 1986-87, chmn. fin. com., 1991-92; mem. community affairs com. Forest Hills Jewish Ctr., 1990-95; bd. trustees NYS Health Care Providers Self Ins. Trust for Workers Compensation, 1999—; treas., chmn. Investment and Fin. Com., 2000—. Recipient Army Commendation medal, 1974, Cert. Appreciation, Am. Heart Assn., 1976. Mem.: NYC Chpt. NYS Assn. Health Care Providers (chmn. 1997—98, healthcare worker of yr. com. 1997—2000, ann. jour. chmn. 1997—2000, chmn. dept. health liaison com. 1997—, bd. dir. 1997—, treas. 1997—99, v.p. 1999—2001, pres. 2001—), NY State Home Care Assn. (ann. meeting com. 1990, presenter ann. meeting 1990, 1991, svcs. com. 1991, nominating com. 1992), Nat. Assn. Home Care (presenter ann. meeting 1985, 1989), Rotary Internat. (Paul Harris fellow 1992), Masons. Republican. Jewish. Avocations: biking, swimming, fine dining. Office: Neighbors Home Care 2532 Boston Rd Bronx NY 10467-9004 E-mail: jshames@neighborshomecare.com.

SHAMIM, MAH TALAT, chemist; b. Karachi, Pakistan, Sept. 7, 1952; came to U.S., 1976; d. Syed Hasan and Askaribi (Nuzhat) Akhtar; m. A. Najm Shamim, Dec. 20, 1975. BS in Chemistry, Karachi U., 1972, MS in Chemistry, 1973, Howard U., 1981, PhD in Chemistry, 1983. Postdoctoral fellow NIH, Bethesda, Md., 1983-89, sr. staff fellow, 1989-91; chemist EPA, Washington, 1991-93, sect. chief environ. fate and effects divsn., 1993-97, chief environ. risk br. environ fate and effects divsn., 1997—. Panelist U.S. Merit Sys. Protection Adv. Bd., Washington, 1996—; mem. internat. environ. fate workgroups. Co-author: Rejection Rate Analysis: Environmental Fate Guidelines, 1995; contbr. articles to profl. jours. Mem. Am. Chem. Soc., Assn. Asian-Pacific Ams. Avocations: gardening, writing poetry, writing short stories, oil painting, sewing. Achievements include development of highly selective adenosine receptor antagonists which are used as effective probes in studying the nature of this class of receptors; designed and developed a wide range of heterocycles which show cardiac stimulant, behavioral stimulant and tracheal stimulant activities; contributed significantly in the development and harmonization of OECD environmental fate guidelines for environmental fate studies for pesticides which are required by international regulatory agencies for the registration of pesticides. Office: Environ Protection Agy 401 M St SW Washington DC 20024-2610 E-mail: shamim.mah@epa.gov.

SHAMIS, EDWARD ANTHONY, JR. lawyer; b. Pensacola, Fla., Dec. 12, 1949; s. Edward Anthony Sr. and Mona Kathryn (McLaughlin) S.; m. Elizabeth Handley, Jan. 24, 1971; children: Ashley Vera, Edward Anthony III. BS, La. State U., 1972, JD, 1974. Bar: La. 1974, U.S. Dist. Ct. (ea. dist.) La. 1975, U.S. Tax Ct. 1981, U.S. Ct. Appeals (5th cir.) 1982, U.S. Supreme Ct. 1983. Pvt. practice, Slidell, La., 1974—. Spl. counsel to Slidell City Coun., 1984—. Bd. dirs. Pope John H.S., Slidell, 1988-90, Children's Wish Endowment Fund, Inc. (formerly Northshore Children's Endowment Fund) 1991—; mem., pres. St. Tammany Assn. for Children with Learning Disabilities, Slidell, 1976-81; chmn. Slidell Bd. Zoning Adjustments, 1976-81; past mem. Boys Club; past mem. and chmn. St. Tammany Parish Ethics Commn. Mem. ATLA, La. Bar Assn. (hos. of dels. 1985-86, 88-89, 89-90, 94-97), Slicell Bar Assn. (pres. 1978-79), La. Trial Lawyers Assn. (pres.'s adv. coun. 1980-81, 84-85, 89-90, 95-96). Republican. Avocations: hunting, fishing, computers. Office: 486 Brownswitch Rd Slidell LA 70458-1102 E-mail: EShamisjr@aol.com.

SHAMMAS, NAZIH KHEIRALLAH, environmental engineering educator, consultant; b. Homs, Syria, Feb. 18, 1939; came to U.S., 1991; s. Kheirallah Hanna and Nazha Murad (Hamwi) S.; m. Norma Massouh, July 28, 1968; children: Sarmed Erick, Samer Sam. Engring. degree with distinction, Am. U., Beirut, Lebanon, 1962; MS in Sanitary Engring., U. N.C., 1965; PhD in Civil Engring., U. Mich., 1971. Instr. civil engring. Am. U., Beirut, Lebanon, 1965-68, asst. prof. civil engring., 1972-76; tchg. fellow U. Mich., Ann Arbor, 1968-71; asst. prof. civil engring. King Saud U., Riyadh, Saudi Arabia, 1976-78, assoc. prof., 1978-91; prof. environ. engring. Lenox (Mass.) Inst. Water Tech., 1991-2001, dean edn., 1992-93; sr. prof. Sr. U., 1994—. Adj. prof. environ. sci., Berkshire C.C., 1995—; cons., ptnr. Cons. and Rsch. Engrs., Beirut, 1973-76; advisor, cons. Riyadh Water and Sanitary Drainage Authority, 1979-83; Ar-Riyadh Devel. Authority, 1977-93, Assoc. Cons. Engring. Team, 1994-99; assoc. cons. Vakakis Internat., 1995—; planning assoc. Berkshire Regional Planning Commn., 1999—. Co-author: Environmental Sanitation, 1988, Wastewater Engineering, 1988; contbr. over 30 articles to profl. jours. and confs. Recipient block grant U. Mich., 1968-70, Excellence in Tchg. award King Saud U., 1981, 84. Mem. ASCE, Water Environ. Fedn., Am. Water Works Assn., New Eng. Water Environ. Assn., New Eng. Water Works Assn., Internat. Water Assn., Assn. Environ. Engring. and Sci. Profs. Achievements include research on biological and physicochemical remediation processes, math. modeling of nitrification process, water and wastewater mgmt. in developing countries, water conservation, wastewater treatment and reuse, appropriate tech. for developing countries, multidisciplinary studies in environmental management and planning. Home: 35 Flintstone Dr Pittsfield MA 01201 E-mail: nshammas@localnet.com.

SHAMMAS, NICOLAS WAHIB, internist, cardiologist; b. Amyoun, El-Koura, Lebanon, Jan. 31, 1963; arrived in U.S., 1988; s. Wahib Nicolas and Vera Yousuf (El-Helou) Shammas; m. Gail Ann Hanson, Feb. 22, 1991; children: Waheeb John, Andrew Nicholas, Anna Elizabeth. BSc with distinction, Am. U. Beirut, Lebanon, 1983, MD, MSc in Physiology, Am. U. Beirut, Lebanon, 1987, Diploma in Computer Programming, 1985. Diplomate Am. Bd. Internal Medicine, Am. Bd. Cardiology and Interventional Cardiology. Postdoctoral rsch. fellow Am. U. Beirut, 1987-88; resident in internal medicine U. Iowa Hosps., Iowa City, 1988-91; instr. medicine, clin. fellow cardiology U. Rochester (N.Y.) Med. Ctr., 1991-94; fellow assoc. in cardiology U. Iowa Hosps., Iowa City, 1994—95; mem. staff Genesis Med. Ctr., Davenport, 1995—; clin. asst. prof. U. Iowa. Founder Mastermind Pub., Phenix Realty Co., 1997, Midwest Cardiovasc. Rsch. Found. Author (with others): Flavors of Lebanon, 1995; contbr. articles to profl. jours. Am. U. Beirut Univ. Rsch. Bd. awardee, 1986-87, John C. Sable Meml. Heart award J.C. Sable Fund, 1993, Trainee Investigator award for clin. rsch. meeting, Balt., 1994. Fellow: ACP, Soc. Cardiac Angiography and Interventions, Am. Coll. Cardiology, Coll. Chest Physicians; mem.: AMA, Am. Soc. Nuclear Cardiology, Iowa Med. Soc., Am. Soc. Internal Medicine, Am. Fedn. Clin. Rsch. Achievements include research in basic cardiology: prostacyclin and transmembrane calcium movements; adrenergic binding sites in hypertrophied rat hearts induced by renovascular hypertension; myocardial viability in hybernating myocardium; coronary flow reserve; principal investigator at Genesis Medical Center for several large multicenter national and international clinical trials, including SYMPHONY, BEST, LIMIT-AMI, ATLAS; SPORT, ASSENT.2, SLIDE, SUPORT, NOET, Xanadu, MiniCrown Registry, others. Office: Cardiovasc Medicine PC 1236 E Rusholme St Ste 300 Davenport IA 52803-2400

SHAMOO, ADIL ELIAS, biochemist, biophysicist, educator; b. Baghdad, Iraq, Aug. 1, 1941; came to U.S., 1964, naturalized, 1973; s. Elias M. and Mariam T. (Mansour) S.; m. Joan Hutchison, Dec. 16, 1967 (div. Dec. 1997); children: Abraheem, Zachary, Jessica. B.Sc. in Physics, U. Baghdad, 1962; MS in Physics (grad. fellow), U. Louisville, 1966; PhD in Biophysics, CUNY, 1970. Instr. engring. physics Speed Sch., U. Louisville, 1965-68; asst. prof. physiology City U. N.Y., 1971-73; guest worker Lab. Biophysics and Neurochemistry, NIH, Bethesda, Md., 1972-73; asst. prof. radiation biology and biophysics U. Rochester, 1973-75; guest prof. Max-Planck Inst. Biophysics, Frankfurt, West Germany, 1977-78; assoc. prof. radiation biology and biophysics U. Rochester, 1975-79; prof., chmn. dept. biol. chemistry U. Md., Balt., 1979-82, head membrane biochemistry research lab., 1982-90, prof. dept. biochemistry and molecular biology, 1982—. Cons. div. biol. scis. Kodak Co., Rochester, 1976-77; NIH tng. fellow U. Louisville, 1967; investigator Am. Heart Assn., 1976-79; Neurosci. Rsch. Program fellow, Boulder, Colo., summer 1977; pres. Sci. Profls. Inc., 1985-95; chmn. symposia, various cons. in field; mem. organizing coms. workshops in field; adj. prof. dept. physics East Carolina U., Greenville, N.C., 1996-2000; bd. dirs. Friends Rsch. Inst., 1994-2001. Editor (with M.W. Miller) Membrane Toxicity, 1977, Carriers and Channels in Biological Systems, 1975, Carriers and Channels in Biological Systems-Transport Proteins, 1980, Regulation of Calcium Transport Across Muscle Membranes, 1985, Principles of Research Data Audit, (with R. Verna) Biotechnology Today, 1995, Ethics in Neurobiological Research with Human Subjects, 1997; editor in chief Membrane Biochemistry, 1977-93, Accountability in Research: Policies and Quality Assurance, 1988—; mem. editl. bd. Molecular and Cellular Biochemistry, 1987-94, Quality Assurance: Good Practice Regulation and Law, 1991—; contbr. articles and abstracts to profl.

jours., chpts. to books. Bd. dirs. Alliance for Mentally Ill of Md., 1990-93, Friends Rsch. Inst. Inc., 1994—; mem. rsch. monitoring com. Nat. Alliance for Mentally Ill, bd. dirs. 1994-97; pres. faculty senate U. Md., Balt., 1993-94; mem. coun. univ. systems U. Md., 1994-97; mem. adv. com. Vantage Pl., 1995-97; bd. dirs. Howard County Mental Health Authority, 1997-00, pres., 1997-2000; bd. dirs. Citizens for Responsible Care and Rsch., 1998—, v.p., 1998—; mem. Nat. Human Rsch. Protections Adv. Com., 2000—. Recipient Advocacy award Mental Health Assn. Md., 1994, Disting. Svc. award Alliance for Mentally Ill of Md., 1994, Howard County Mental Health Auth., 1999. Mem. AAAS, AAUP (chpt. sec. 1971-72), Basic Sci. Council of Am. Heart Assn., Am. Soc. Biol. Chemists and Mol. Biol., Am. Coll. Sports Medicine, Am. Assn. Physics Tchrs., Am. Soc. Bioethics and Human Values, Am. Physiol. Soc., Biophys. Soc. (Cole Membrane Award Com. 1983-84, chmn. biophysics subgroup 1982-83, council 1986-89), Membrane Biophys. Group (chmn. 1982-83, sec.-treas. 1983-85, co-chmn. U.S. bioenergetics group 1979-80), Md. Acad. Scis. (chmn. com. programs and exhbns. 1986-87, sci. council 1985-89), N.Y. Acad. Scis., Coun. of Biology (editor 1989—), Soc. Quality Assurance. Achievements include patents for liquid scintillators. Office: 108 N Greene St Baltimore MD 21201-1503 E-mail: ashamoo@umaryland.edu.

SHAMOS, MORRIS HERBERT, physicist educator; b. Cleve., Sept. 1, 1917; s. Max and Lillian (Wasser) S.; m. Marion Jean Cahn, Nov. 26, 1942; 1 son, Michael Ian. AB, NYU, 1941, MS, 1943, PhD, 1948; postgrad., MIT, 1941-42. Faculty NYU, 1942—, prof. physics, 1959-83, prof. emeritus, from 1983; chmn. dept. Washington Sq. Coll., 1957-70; sr. v.p. research and devel. Technicon Corp., 1970-75, chief sci. officer, 1975-83, also dir., prin. sci. cons., 1983-92; pres. M.H. Shamos & Assocs., 1983—; chmn. Protein Databases, Inc., 1985-90, Sci. Imaging Corp., 1985-88; Med. Mktg. Internat., 1992-94; dir. Anagen Ltd., 1989-92, Nat. Assn for Sci., Tech. & Soc., 1990-91, Anagen Holdings, Ltd., 1992-97, Xsirius, Inc., 1993-96; chmn. Med. Mktg. Internat., 1992-94. Cons. pvt. industry; cons. Armament Center, USAF, 1955-57, Tung-Sol Electric, Inc., 1949-65, Office Pub. Information, UN, 1958, NBC, 1957-67, AEC, 1957-70, N.Y. Eye and Ear Infirmary, 1961-64, 79— , L.I. Jewish Hosp., 1962— , N.Y.C. Health Dept., 1961-70, Technicon Instruments Corp., 1964-70, U.S. Office Edn., 1964-72. Author: Great Experiments in Physics, 1959, The Myth of Scientific Literacy, 1995 (Ness award 1995); co-editor: Recent Advances in Science, 1956, Industrial and Safety Problems of Nuclear Technology, 1950; cons. editor Addison-Wesley Pub. Co., 1965-69; adv. bd. Jour. Coll. Sci. Teaching, 1971-80, Clin Lab. Guide Am. Chem. Soc., 1972-76. Dir. tng., N.Y.C. Office Civil Def., 1950-54; subscribing mem. N.Y. Philharmonic Soc.; mem. adv. council Pace U., 1971— , N.Y. Poly. Inst., 1980— ; trustee Hackley Sch., 1971-80, Westchester Arts Council. Poly. U. fellow Fellow N.Y. Acad. Scis. (past chmn. phys. sci., bd. govs. 1977-83, rec. sec. 1978-80, v.p. 1980-81, pres. 1982), AAAS; mem. IEEE, AAUP, AFTRA, NSTA (pres. 1967), Am. Chem. Soc., Nat. Assn. Ednl. Broadcasters, Am. Phys. Soc., Assn. Physics Tchrs. Britain, Chemist's Club, Am. Assn. Clin. Chemists, Cosmos Club, Phi Beta Kappa, Sigma Xi, Pi Mu Epsilon, Sigma Pi Sigma. Clubs: Cosmos, Chemists. Achievements include spl. research atomic and nuclear physics, biophysics. Home: Bronx, NY. Died May 2002.

SHAMY, CAROLYN GRAHAM, foundation educator; b. Moreland, Ark., July 24, 1939; d. Jack and Ruth (Teague) Graham; m. James Edward Shamy, Aug. 24, 1958; children: Linli, Stephen, Susanna. AS, Ark. Tech. U., 1959; BA, Thomas Edison Coll., 1977; postgrad., Rutgers U. Phys. edn. tchr. East Brunswick (N.J.) Pub. Sch., 1962-65; nursing asst. med. edn. program Carrier Found., Belle Mead, N.J., 1977-81, devel. specialist, 1981—. Cons. Women Aware, Middlesex County, N.J., 1976-77. Mem. Princeton Holistic Soc. Democrat. Avocations: reading, travel, drama, piano. Home: 757A Liverpool Cir Lakehurst NJ 08759-5212 Office: Carrier Found Rte 601 Belle Mead NJ 08502

SHANAHAN, BRENDAN FREDERICK, professional hockey player; b. Mimico, Ont., Canada, Jan. 23, 1969; Formerly with St. Louis Blues; with Hartford Whalers, 1995-97; forward Detroit Red Wings, Detroit, 1997-. Played in NHL All-Star Game, 1994, 96; named to NHL All-Star First Team, 1993-94; mem. Stanley Cup Champions Detroit Red Wings, 1997, 1998, 2002; mem. Canadian Olympic Hockey team 2002 (Gold medal) Office: care Detroit Red Wings 600 Civic Center Dr Detroit MI 48226-4408*

SHANAHAN, EILEEN FRANCES, secondary education educator; b. Bethlehem, Pa., Sept. 10, 1949; d. Edward Vincent and Geraldine Mary (Gilligan) S. BA, Moravian Coll., 1971. Cert. secondary tchr. in Spanish, English, N.J. Tchr. Kingsway Regional High Sch. Dist., Swedesboro, N.J., 1971—. Mem. NEA, N.J. Edn. Assn., Gloucester County Edn. Assn., Fgn. Lang. Educators N.J., Kingsway Edn. Assn. (sec. membership), Archaeol. Soc. N.J., Hellertown Hist. Soc., Gloucester County Hist. Soc. Democrat. Roman Catholic. Avocations: archaeology, historical research, genealogy.

SHANAHAN, ELIZABETH ANNE, art educator; b. High Point, N.C., Apr. 5, 1950; d. Joe Thomas and Nancy Elizabeth (Moran) Gibson; m. Robert James Shanahan, Aug. 31, 1969 (div. Mar. 1987); children: Kimberly Marie Shanahan Conlon, Brigette Susanne Shanahan Foshee. Student, Forsyth Tech. Coll., 1974-83, Tri-County Tech. Coll., 1989, Inst. of Children's Lit., 1989. Owner cleaning bus., Winston-Salem, N.C., 1985-86, 87; instr. Anderson (S.C.) Arts Coun., 1987—, Tri-County Tech. Coll., Pendleton, S.C., 1987-98. Artist Wild Geese, 1985 (Best in Show). Active Libr. of Congress, 1994. Mem. Anderson Art Assn. (con. 1987—), Met. Arts Coun. (Upstate Visual Arts divsn.), Triad Art Assn. (pres. Kernersville, N.C. chpt. 1984-85), Nat. Mus. Women in Arts (charter), Libr. of Congress (charter). Avocations: writing, sewing, traveling, decorating. Home: 2519 Mountain View Church Rd King NC 27021-7645

SHANAHAN, MICHAEL FRANCIS, manufacturing executive, former hockey team executive; b. St. Louis, Oct. 29, 1939; m. Mary Ann Barrett; children: Megan Elizabeth, Michael Francis Jr., Maureen Patricia. BS in Commerce, St. Louis U.; postgrad., Wash. U., St. Louis; LHD (hon.), St. Louis Rabbinical Coll., 1987. With McDonnell Douglas Automation Co., St. Louis, 1962-73, sales mgr., 1969-71, br. mgr., 1971-72, mktg. dir. cen. region, 1972-73; mktg. v.p. Numerical Control Inc., 1973-74, pres., 1974-79; v.p. Cleve. Pneumatic Co. (formerly Numerical Control Inc.), 1979-82; chmn., chief exec. officer Engineered Air Systems Inc., 1982—; former chmn., ceo St. Louis Blues Hockey Team. Bd. dirs. Engineered Air Systems Inc. (chmn.), St. Louis Blues Hockey Inc. (chmn.); adv. com. Nat. Hockey League; mem. U.S. Senatorial Bus. Adv. Bd.; bd. dirs. Capital Bank and Trust of Clayton, The Graphic Arts Ctr. Inc., Kilo Rsch. Found. (vice chmn.). Bd. dirs. Am. Heart Assn., St. Louis Ambassadors, Catholic Charities of St. Louis, Galway Sister City Com., The Backstoppers, Christmas in St. Louis Found.; nat. bd. dirs. Boys Hope; bd. trustees, pres. coun. St. Louis U.; adv. bd. Safe Kids; hon. bd. Paraquad; hon. chmn. Small Bus. Week in St. Louis, 1989; hon. co-chmn. Veteran's Day Observance and Parade, 1989; co-chairperson AMC Cancer Rsch. Ctr. Community Svc. award. Named St. Louis Ambassador of Yr., 1986, Olivette Businessman of Yr., 1987, St. Louis Bus. Leader of Yr. Coll. Bus. Adminstrn., So. Ill. U. at Carbondale, 1987,Outstanding Philanthropist St. Louis chpt., Nat. Soc. Fund Raising Execs., 1987; recipient Spirit of Life award City of Hope Labor Mgmt., 1987, St. Louis U. Alumni Merit award, 1987, Meritorious Svc. to Sports award MS Soc., 1987, Presdl. Sports award Maryville Coll., 1987, Sales Exec. of Yr. award Sales and Mktg. Execs. of Met. St. Louis, 1988, St. Louis Port Coun.'s Mgmt. Man of the Yr. award Greater St. Louis Area and Vicinity Port Council, Maritime Trades Dept., AFL-CIO, , 1989. Mem. Alzeimer's Disease and Related Disorders Assn. (hon.), St. Louis Counts, Hawthorn Found., St. Louis Club, Mo. Athletic Club, Old Warson Country Club, Boone Valley Country Club. Office: Engineered Support Systems Inc 1270 N Price Rd Saint Louis MO 63132-2316

SHANAHAN, MIKE, professional football coach; b. Oak Park, Ill., Aug. 24, 1952; m. Peggy, children: Kyle, Krystal. BS Phys. Edn., Eastern Illinois U., Charleston, Ill., 1974; MS Phys. Edn., 1975. Student coach Eastern Illinois U.; asst. coach U. Oklahoma, 1975-76; offensive coord., No. Ariz. U., 1976-77, Ea. Ill. U., 1977-78, U. Minn., 1979-80; offensive coord., U. Fla., 1980-84, asst. head coach, 1983-84; receivers coach Denver Broncos, 1984-87; head coach Los Angeles Raiders, 1988-89; asst. coach Denver Broncos, NFL, 1989-91; offensive coordinator San Francisco 49ers, 1992-94; head coach Denver Broncos, 1995—. Avocations: golf, travel. Office: Denver Broncos 13655 Broncos Pkwy Englewood CO 80112-4150*

SHANAHAN, ROBERT B. bank executive; b. Buffalo, Jan. 8, 1928; s. Bart J. and Florence (Dietrich) Shanahan; m. Janet I. Mulholland, Feb. 6, 1954; children: Maureen Shanahan DeRose, Timothy, Karin Halpern, Molly Healy, Colleen Collins, Mark, Ellen Becker. BS in Econs., U. Pa., 1951. New bus. rep. Assocs. Discount Corp., Buffalo, 1951-55; pres. Universal Time Plan, Inc., 1956-67; v.p. Norstar Bank, 1967-69, sr. v.p., 1969-72, exec. v.p., dir., 1972-91. Bd. dirs. Eastern States Bankcard Assn. Contbg. author: book The Bankers Handbook, 1978, mem. adv. coun.: Banking Mag., 1978—84; contbr. articles to profl. jours. Chmn. Cath. Charities Buffalo, 1986—87, 1989—90; pres. Multiple Sclerosis Assn. Western N.Y., 1982—86; trustee Theodore Roosevelt Inaugural Site, Inc., 1983—; pres. Buffalo Coun. World Affairs, 1984—86. With U.S. Army, 1944—46. Decorated Knight Holy Sepulchre Order, Knight Comdr., Knight Comdr. with star, Knight Grand Cross; recipient Past Pres.'s award, Multiple Sclerosis Assn., 1985. Mem.: N.Y. State Bankers Assn. (mem. exec. com. consumer divsn. 1988—90), Am. Bankers Assn. (bd. dirs. 1977—84, chmn. installment lending divsn. 1978—79, edn., policy and devel. coun. 1983—84, Eagle award 1978), Buffalo Area C. of C., Cherry Hill Club (Ridgeway, Ont., Can.) (pres. 1992—93), Buffalo Club, U. Pa. Club Western N.Y. (bd. dirs.). Republican. Roman Catholic. Home: 109 Half Moon Cir Apt A3 Lantana FL 33462-5455

SHANAHAN, SHEILA ANN, pediatrician, educator; m. Justin Laurence Cashman Jr., Sept. 14, 1968; children: Justin III, Gillis. BA, Trinity Coll., 1963; MD cum laude, Med. Coll. Pa., 1969. Diplomate Nat. Bd. Med. Examiners, Am. Bd. Pediats. Intern Presbyn. Hosp., N.Y.C., 1969-70, resident in pediats., 1970-72, asst. in clin. pediats., 1972-75, assoc. clin. pediats., 1975-78; pvt. practice specializing in pediats. Greenwich, Conn., 1972-78; asst. attending Greenwich Hosp., 1972-73, assoc. attending, 1973-78; from instr. to assoc. Columbia Coll. Physicians and Surgeons, N.Y.C., 1972-78; asst. prof. pediats. George Washington U. Sch. Medicine, Washington, 1980—, Georgetown U. Sch. Medicine, Washington, 1984—; pvt. practice specializing in pediats., 1984—. Attending dept. ambulatory medicine Children's Hosp. Nat. Med. Ctr., Washington, 1980-84; courtesy staff Georgetown U. Hosp., Washington, 1984—, George Washington U. Hosp., 1984—, Sibley Meml. Hosp., Washington, 1984—, Columbia Hosp. for Women, 1984—, Children's Hosp. Nat. Med. Ctr., 1984—. Fellow Am. Acad. Pediats.; mem. Am. Women's Med. Assn. Office: 4900 Massachusetts Ave NW Washington DC 20016-4358

SHANAHAN, THOMAS M. judge; b. Omaha, May 5, 1934; m. Jane Estelle Lodge, Aug. 4, 1956; children: Catherine Shanahan Trofholz, Thomas M. II, Mary Elizabeth, Timothy F. AB magna cum laude, U. Notre Dame, 1956; JD, Georgetown U., 1959. Bar: Nebr., Wyo. Mem. McGinley, Lane, Mueller, Shanahan, O'Donnell & Merritt, Ogallala, Nebr.; assoc. justice Nebr. Supreme Ct., Lincoln, 1983-93; judge U.S. Dist. Ct. Nebr., Omaha, 1993—. Office: US Dist Ct 111 S 18th Plz Ste 3141 Omaha NE 68102

SHANAMAN, FRED CHARLES, JR. business consultant; b. Tacoma, June 21, 1933; s. Fred Charles and Marjorie Blanch (Jeffries) S.; m. Jane Francis Aram, July 7, 1962; children: Fred C. III, Mara Shanaman Burke. BA, Dartmouth Coll., 1957; postgrad., U. B.C., Vancouver, 1958. Sales rep. Air Reduction Co., San Francisco, 1958-62; pres. Bulk Distbrs., Tacoma, 1962-75, Pyrodyne Corp., Tacoma, 1964-75, Toys Galore, Tacoma, 1964-75, Youth Entrepreneurship Corp., Tacoma, 1978-86; pres., owner Rainier Mgmt. Corp., 1970—. Bd. dirs. Puget Sound Bancorp., Tacoma, Bellingham (Wash.) Nat. Key Bank of Wash., Tacoma Rockets Hockey Club, Puget Sound Hockey Ctrs.; presdl. appt. to commerce sec. Elliot Richardson's Regional Rep. in N.W., 1975-77; sec. of commerce spokesman and prin. liaison, 1975-77; mem. Commerce Dept. rep. Fed. Regional Coun. and Pacific N.W. River Basins Commn., 1975-77. Author: 101 Money Making Ideas for Young Adults 10 to 18 Year of Age, 1980, The First Official Moneymaking Book for Kids of All Ages, 1983, The Best is Yet to Come: Retirement A Second Career, 1984. Chmn. NCAA Womens Final Four, Tacoma, 1988-89; commr. Ice Hockey Goodwill Games, Seattle, 1990; past bd. dirs. Annie Wright Sch., Faith Home, United Way, Tacoma Symphony, Bellarmine Preparatory Sch., Greater Lakes Mental Health Clinic, Tacoma Actors Guild, Assn. of Washington Bus., Mary Bridge Hosp., Tacoma Leukemia Soc., Vt. Acad., and others. Mem. Tacoma Country Club, Canterwood Country Club, Elks, Lakes Club, Gyro Club, Le Mirador (Switzerland). Republican. Episcopalian. Avocations: fishing, skiing, antique collecting, Christmas decoration collection.

SHANAS, ETHEL, sociology educator; b. Chgo., Sept. 6, 1914; d. Alex and Rebecca (Rich) S.; m. Lester J. Perlman, May 17, 1940; 1 child, Michael Stephen AB, U. Chgo., 1935, AM, 1937, PhD, 1949; LHD (hon.), Hunter Coll., N.Y.C., 1985. Instr. human devel. U. Chgo., 1947-52, rsch. assoc. prof., 1961-65; sr. rsch. analyst City of Chgo., 1952-53; sr. study dir. Nat. Opinion Rsch. Ctr., Chgo., 1956-61; prof. sociology U. Ill., 1965-82, prof. emerita, 1982—. Vice chmn. expert com. on aging UN, 1974; mem. com. on aging NRC, Washington, 1978-82, panel on statistics for an aging population, 1984-86; mem. U.S. Com. on Vital and Health Stats., Washington, 1976-79. Author: The Health of Older People, 1962; (with others) Old People in Three Industrial Societies, 1968; editor: (with others) Handbook of Aging and the Social Sciences, 1976, 2d edit., 1985 Bd. govs. Chgo. Heart Assn., 1972-80; mem. adv. council on aging City of Chgo., 1972-78 Keston lectr. U. So. Calif., 1975; recipient Burgess award Nat. Council on Family Relations, 1978; Disting. Chgo. Gerontologist award Assn. for Gerontology in Higher Edn., 1988. Fellow Gerontol. Soc. Am. (pres. 1974-75, Kleemeier award 1977, Brookdale award 1981), Am. Sociol. Assn. (chmn. sect. on aging 1985-86 Disting. Scholar award, 1987); mem. Midwest Sociol. Soc. (pres. 1980-81), Inst. Medicine of Nat. Acad. Scis. (elected mem.) Home: 222 Main St Evanston IL 60202-2488

SHANBACKER, FRANK MORSE, III, television news producer; b. Bryn Mawr, Pa., Oct. 2, 1946; s. Frank M. Jr. and Adele (Sislian) S. BA in English, U. Pa., 1968; MA in English, NYU, 1970. Page NBC, N.Y.C., 1970, awards writer, 1970-72, researcher news spl. broadcasts, 1972-73, writer news spl. broadcasts, 1973-79, producer Nightly News, 1979-90, producer Expose, 1990-91, ops. producer Dateline NBC, 1992, sr. producer news spl. programs, 1990. Profiled in: Anchors--Brokaw, Jennings, Rather, 1990. Treas. Midtown North Precinct Community Coun., N.Y.C., 1991-92. Emmy nominee TV Acad. Arts and Scis., 1989. Avocations: reading, traveling, swimming, cinema, theatre. Office: NBC News 30 Rockefeller Plz Rm 408 New York NY 10112-0002 E-mail: frank.shanbacker@nbc.com.

SHANDS, HENRY LEE, plant geneticist, administrator; b. Madison, Wis., Aug. 30, 1935; s. Ruebush George and Elizabeth (Henry) S.; m. Catherine Miller, Nov. 20, 1962; children: Deborah A., Jeanne A., James L. BS, U. Wis., 1957; MS, Purdue U., 1961, PhD, 1963. NSF fellow Swedish Seed Assn., Svalov, 1962-63; asst. prof. Purdue U., West Lafayette, Ind., 1963-66, asst. prof. botany and plant pathology, 1965-66; rsch. agronomist, leader ea. wheat project Dekalb Hybrid Wheat, Inc., Lafayette, 1966-79; rsch. agronomist, dir. sunflower rsch. Dekalb Genetics and predecessor firms, Glyndon, Minn., 1979-86; nat. program leader for plant germplasm USDA Agrl. Rsch. Svc., Beltsville, Md., 1986-92, assoc. dep. adminstr. for genetic resources, 1992-97, asst. adminstr. genetic resources, 1997-2000; dir. Nat. Ctr. for Genetic Resources Preservation, Fort Collins, Colo., 2000—. Mem. AID Project, Minas Gerais, Brazil, 1963-65. 1st lt. U.S. Army, 1957-59. Recipient 1st Victor M. Bendelow Meml. Lectr. award U. Man., 1992. Fellow AAAS, Am. Soc. Agronomy, Crop Sci. Soc. Am. (Frank N. Meyer medal for plant genetic resources 1992); Am. Genetic Assn., Genetics Soc. Can., Am. Phytopath. Soc. Office: USDA-ARS 1111 S Mason St Fort Collins CO 80521-4500

SHANDS, WILBOURN COUPERY, surgeon; s. Harley Roseborough and Bessie Nugent Shands; m. Janet Kuilk; children: Susan Shands Jones, Nancy Shands Staddard, Janet, Elizabeth Coupery Shands Henningen. BS magna cum laude, MD magna cum laude, Vanderbilt U.; MS Surgery. Gen. surgeon, 1948—78; med. officer, 1979—99; emeritus clin. prof. surgery VA; fellow in surgery; fellow in oncologic surgery. Home: 144 Glenway Dr Jackson MS 39216-4101

SHANDS, WILLIAM RIDLEY, JR. lawyer; b. Richmond, Va., Nov. 23, 1929; s. William Ridley and Josephine (Winston) S.; m. Lynneth Williams, May 31, 1958; children: William Tyler, Laura Sawyer. BA, Hampden-Sydney Coll., 1952; LLB, U. Va., 1958. Bar: Va. 1958. Atty., assoc. Christian, Barton, Epps, Brent & Chappell, Richmond, 1958-61; counsel The Life Ins. Co. of Va., 1961-66, asst. gen. counsel, 1966-68, assoc. gen. counsel, 1968-71, gen. counsel, 1971-73, v.p., gen. counsel, 1973-78, sr. v.p., gen. counsel, 1978-79; sr. v.p. law and public affairs Continental Fin. Services Co., Richmond, 1980-85; sr. v.p., sec. Life Ins. Co. Va., 1985-88; sr. counsel Sands, Anderson, Marks & Miller, 1988-98; ret., 1998. Chmn. Eastern Appeal Bd. Selective Svc. System, 1969; pres., chmn. bd. dirs. Trinity Episcopal High Sch., 1971-72; bd. dirs. Richmond Area Heart Assn., 1965-71, Southampton Cotillion, 1970-72; vestryman St. Michael's Episc. Ch., 1965-68, sr. warden, 1968. Served with AUS, 1952-55, Philippines. Mem. Va. Bar Assn., Richmond Bar Assn., Assn. Life Ins. Counsel (pres. 1987-88), Am. Coun. Life Ins. (chmn. legal sect. 1982-83), Commonwealth Club, Country Club Va. Home: 3811 Darby Dr Midlothian VA 23113-1318

SHANE, CHARLES WILLIAM, communication company executive, marketing consultant; b. Johnstown, Pa., Feb. 6, 1938; Student, Pa. State U., 1958-61. Newspaper advt. salesperson Voice of North Hills, Pitts., 1962-63; advt. mgr. Suburban Newspapers, Inc., 1963-65; dir. pub. rels. Pitts. History and Landmarks Found., 1965-70; founder, pres. advt. and pub. rels. Shane & Assocs. Inc., 1970-82; founder, editor, pub. Exec. Report Mag., 1981-86; pub. Managing Mag. Katz Sch. Bus. U. Pitts., 1986-87; founder, pres. Shane Communications, Inc., 1986—; pub., editor Builder/Architect Mag., 1988—; dir. mktg. St. Francis Health Sys., 1998—. Pub.: A History of the Pittsburgh Builders Exchange, 1886-1986, 1986; pub., editor Pa. Soc. Profl. Engrs. mag., 1965-71, Charette Mag., 1964-72; pub. St. Francis Jour. Medicine, 1996; photography exhbn. 3 Rivers Arts Festival, Pitts., North Hills Arts League. Trustee Mt. Lebanon Libr., Pitts., 1991-92; bd. dirs. St. Francis Health Found., Pitts., 1986—. With USN, 1956-62. Named Media Adv. of Yr. for Pa., SBA, 1986. Mem. AIA (assoc.), Am. Soc. Interior Design (assoc.), Builders Assn. Met. Pitts., North Suburban Builders Assn., Remodelers Coun. Pitts. (dir. 1992—), Wash. County Builders Assn., Westmoreland County Builders Assn. Avocations: fly fishing, antique automobiles. Home: 110 Atlanta Pl Pittsburgh PA 15228-1306

SHANE, DONEA LYNNE, retired nursing educator; b. Jefferson, Iowa, Mar. 5, 1939; m. William D. Shane, Jr., Dec. 30, 1962; children: Craig Lloyd, Lynnea Lee. Diploma, Iowa Meth. Sch. Nursing, 1960; BSN, Calif. State U., Long Beach, 1984; MS in Health Edn., U. N.Mex., 1973, PhD in Ednl. Adminstrn., 1986. RN, N.Mex. Insvc. instr., supr. Bernalillo County Med. Ctr., Albuquerque, 1969-71; dir. health edn. group N.Mex. Regional Med. Program, 1972-75; coord. RN-BSN nursing students U. N.Mex., 1975-82, assoc. dean baccalaureate program Coll. Nursing, 1987-96, dean, 1996-97; ret., 1997; exec. dir. N.Mex. Consortium for Nursing Workforce Devel., 1999—. Author: Returning to School: A Guide for Nurses; contbr. articles to profl. publs. Mem. ANA, N.Mex. Nurses Assn. (state pres. 1978-80), Nat. League for Nursing (state pres. 1998-00), Sigma Theta Tau.

SHANE, DORIS JEAN, respiratory therapist, administrator; b. Granite City, Ill., June 30, 1949; d. Elbert Paul and Arline Marie (Zitt) S. AS with clin. honors in respiratory therapy, Presbyn.-St. Luke's Hosp., Chgo., 1973. Registered respiratory therapist. Chief therapist Michael Reese Med. Ctr., Chgo., 1973-78; dir. respiratory therapy Edgewater Hosp., 1978-81; dir. respiratory care svcs. Mt. Sinai Med. Ctr., Miami Beach, Fla., 1981-87; chmn. adv. coun. Respiratory Therapy Miami-Dade Cmty., 1984-87. Healthcare cons. Shane and Assoc., 1987—; coord. rep. Care-Green Briar Nursing Ctr., South Miami Hosp., 1987-88; adminstrv. program dir. of vent and TBI programs West Gables Rehab. Hosp., 1988-89, v.p. health care planning & devel. Intergrated Health Svcs., 1989-97; pres. Shane Assocs., 1997-98; dir. profl. svcs. Home Med. of Am., Inc., 1997-2000; v.p. Profl. Bus. Svcs.: Life Care Solutions, 2000—. Bd. dirs. Sunny Shores Sea Camp, Miami, 1983-87, Frank M. Rodde Cmty. Ctr., Chgo., 1980; chmn. credit com. Mt. Sinai Fed. Credit Union, 1986. Mem. NAFE, Dade-Monroe Am. Lung Assn. (bd. dirs. 1982-90), Fla. Soc. Respiratory Therapy (v.p. 1984-85), Am. Assn. Respiratory Therapy, Internat. Assn. Quality Circles, Am. for Respiratory Care Adminstrs., Am. Bus. Women Assn., Fla. Coun. Aging. Democrat. Avocations: tennis, biking. Home and Office: 1085 Scarlet Oak St Hollywood FL 33019-4810

SHANE, JEFFREY NEIL, lawyer; b. N.Y.C., Mar. 27, 1941; s. Albert and Ann (Semanoff) S.; m. D. Jean Wu, June 27, 1992. AB, Princeton U., N.J., 1962; LL.B., Columbia U., N.Y.C., 1965. Bar: D.C. 1966. Trial atty. FPC, Washington, 1966-68, Dept. Transp., Washington, 1968-70, spl. asst. to gen. counsel, 1970-72; traveled in Africa, Europe, 1972-73; researcher Environ. Law Inst., Washington, 1974-75; mem. UN Task Force on Human Environ., Bangkok, 1975-77; atty., cons. environ. law in developing countries, Washington, 1978-79; asst. gen. counsel internat. law Dept. Transp., Washington, 1979-83, dep. asst. sec. policy and internat. affairs, 1983-85, asst. sec. policy and internat. affairs, 1989-93; dep. asst. sec. transp. affairs Dept. of State, 1985-89; counsel Wilmer, Cutler & Pickering, 1993-96, ptnr., 1997-2000, Hogan & Hartson, Washington, 2000—. Adj. prof. law Georgetown U., Washington, 1985-89 ; cons. and lectr. transp. law and policy; mem. Archl. and Transp. Barriers Compliance Bd., 1989-93, vice-chmn., 1992-93; vice chmn. Adv. Com. on Confs. in Ocean Shipping, 1990-91; chmn. commn. on air transport Internat. C. of C., Paris, 1994—; chmn. mil. airlift com. Nat. Defense Transp. Assn., 1994—. Co-author: Developing Economies and the Environment, 1978; co-author-editor: NEPA in Action: The Impact of the National Environmental Policy Act on Federal Decision-Making, 1975, Environmental and Natural Resource Management in Developing Countries, 1979. Recipient Sec.'s award for meritorious achievement Dept. Transp., 1971, Sr. Exec. Service Disting. Performance award Dept. State, 1987, Presdl. Meritorious Rank award, 1988. Mem.: ABA (chmn. forum on air and space law 2001—), Columbia Country Club, Wings Club (N.Y.C. bd. govs. 1995—98), Internat. Aviation Club (Washington chpt. pres. 1999—2000), Aero Club (Washington bd. govs. 1984—86), Cosmos Club. Home: 5015 Rockwood Pkwy NW Washington DC 20016-1913 Office: Hogan & Hartson 555 13th St NW Washington DC 20004-1109 E-mail: JNShane@hhlaw.com.

SHANE, JOHN MARDER, endocrinologist; b. Kansas City, Mo., Oct. 5, 1942; s. Henry Kamsler and Ruth (Marder) S.; m. Eileen Goodart, June 18, 1967; children: Robert M., Edward G. BS, U. Okla., 1964, MD, 1967. Diplomate Am. Bd. Ob-Gyn., Am. Bd. Reproductive Endocrinology; cert. master gardener. Resident Harvard Med. Sch., Boston, 1970-73, fellowship, 1973-75, instr., 1970-75, asst. prof., 1975-78; pvt. practice Tulsa, 1978-99. Lectr., cons. Tutorial Svcs. Internat., England, 1984—; bd. dirs. St. Francies G.I.F.T. Lab., Tulsa; cons. to preimplantation genetics project Chapman Genetics Inst., Children's Med. Ctr., Tulsa. Author: CIBA Symposium Infertility: Diagnosis and Treatment; contbr. articles to profl. jours. and publs. Active Tulsa Garden Ctr., 1988—; bd. dirs. Temple Israel, Tulsa, 1985-86, Up With Trees Found., 2000—, Tulsa, master gardener. Capt. USAF, 1967-69. Recipient Annual award Boston Obstet. Soc., 1977; named one of Best Doctor's in Am., Tulsa's Best Doctors, Tulsa People Mag. Mem. ACS, Tulsa Gynecol. Soc. (past pres. 1986-87), Soc. Reproductive Endocrinologists, Tulsa bonsai Soc. (bd. dirs. 1988—), Am. Coll. Ob-Gyn. (v.p. 1971-92, pres. New England Jr. divsn. 1972-73), Am. Bonsai Soc. (nat. bd. dirs.), Chanie des Rotisseurs (l'Ordre Mondial, Tulsa v.p., Bronze Star 2001), Southside Rotary of Tulsa (bd. dirs., pres. 1997—98, Nat. Arboretum Bonsai Pavillion (nat. bd. dirs.). Republican. Jewish. Avocations: gardening, bonsai, collector oriental arts, woodturning.

SHANE, RITA, opera singer, educator; b. N.Y.C. d. Julius J. and Rebekah (Milner) S.; m. Daniel F. Tritter, June 22, 1958; 1 child, Michael Shane. BA, Barnard Coll., 1958; postgrad., Santa Fe Opera Apprentice Program, 1962-63, Hunter Opera Assn., 1962-64; pvt. study with, Beverly Peck Johnson, Elizabeth Schwartzkopf, Bliss Hebert. Adj. prof. voice Manhattan Sch. of Music, 1993-95. Prof. voice Eastman Sch. Music Rochester U., 1989—, Aspen Music Sch., 1999, Hamamatsu, Japan, 2000—02; pvt. tchr., N.Y.C., 1978—; judge Richard Tucker Music Found., Met. Opera Regional Auditions. Performer with numerous opera cos., including profl. debut, Chattanooga Opera, 1964, Met. Opera, San Francisco Opera, N.Y.C. Opera, Chgo. Lyric Opera, San Diego Opera, Santa Fe Opera, Teatro alla Scala, Milan, Italy,

Bavarian State Opera, Netherlands Nat. Opera, Geneva Opera, Vienna State Opera, Phila., New Orleans, Balt. Opera, Opera du Rhin, Strasbourg, Scottish Opera, Teatro Reggio, Turin, Opera Metropolitana, Caracas, Portland Opera, Minn. Opera, also others; world premiere Miss Havisham's Fire, Argento; Am. premieres include Reimann-Lear, Schat-Houdini, Henze-Elegy for Young Lovers; participant festivals, including Mozart Festival, Lincoln Center, N.Y.C., Munich Festival, Aspen Festival, Handel Soc., Vienna Festival, Salzburg Festival, Munich Festival, Perugia Festival, Festival Canada, Glyndebourne Festival, performed with orchs. including Santa Cecilia, Rome, Austrian Radio, London Philharmn., Louisville, Cin., Cleve., Phila., RAI, Naples, Denver, Milw., Israel Philharm., rec. artist, RCA, Columbia, Louisville, Turnabout, Myto labels, also radio and TV. Recipient Martha Baird Rockefeller award, William Matheus Sullivan award. Mem. Am. Guild Mus. Artists, Screen Actors Guild, Nat. Assn. Tchrs. Singing. Office: care Daniel F Tritter 330 W 42nd St New York NY 10036-6902

SHANE, SANDRA KULI, postal service administrator; b. Akron, Ohio, Dec. 12, 1939; d. Amiel M. and Margaret E. (Brady) Kuli; m. Fred Shane, May 30, 1962 (div. 1972); 1 child, Mark Richard; m. Byrl William Campbell, Apr. 26, 1981 (dec. 1984). BA, U. Akron, 1987, postgrad., 1988-90. Scheduler motor vehicle bur. Akron Police Dept., 1959-62; flight and ops. control staff Escort Air, Inc., Akron and Cleve., 1972-78; asst. traffic mgr. Keen Transport, Inc., Hudson, Ohio, 1978-83; mem. ops. and mktg. staff Shawnee Airways and Essco, Akron, 1983-86; in distbn. U.S. Postal Svc., 1986—. Rec. sec. Affirmative Action Coun., Akron, 1988-90. Asst. art tchr. Akron Art Mus., 1979; counselor Support, Inc., Akron, 1983-84; com. chmn. Explorer post Boy Scouts Am., Akron, 1984-85. Mem. Bus. and Profl. Women's Assn. (pres.), Delta Nu Alpha. Democrat. Roman Catholic. Avocations: painting, sculpting, fabric design. Home: 455 E Bath Rd Cuyahoga Falls OH 44223-2511

SHANE, WILLIAM WHITNEY, astronomer; b. Berkeley, Calif., June 3, 1928; s. Charles Donald and Mary Lea (Heger) S.; BA, U. Calif., Berkeley, 1951, postgrad., 1953-58; ScD, Leiden (The Netherlands) U., 1971; m. Clasina van der Molen, Apr. 22, 1964; children: Johan Jacob, Charles Donald. rsch. assoc. Leiden U., 1961-71, sr. scientist, 1971-79; prof. astronomy, dir. Astron. Inst., Cath. U. Nijmegen, The Netherlands, 1979-88; guest prof. astronomy Leiden U., 1988-93; C.H. Adams fellow Monterey (Calif.) Inst. Rsch. Astronomy, 1994—. With USN, 1951-53. Fellow AAAS; mem. Internat. Astron. Union (commns. 33, 34), Am. Astron. Soc., Astron. Soc. Netherlands, Astron. Soc. of the Pacific, Phi Beta Kappa. Achievements include research on structure and dynamics of galaxies, observational astronomy. Home: 9095 Coker Rd Prunedale CA 93907-1401 Office: Monterey Inst Rsch Astronomy 200 8th St Marina CA 93933-6002

SHANEFIELD, DANIEL JAY, ceramics engineering educator; b. Orange, N.J., Apr. 29, 1930; s. Benjamin and Nan (Leichter) S.; m. Elizabeth Davis, June 28, 1964; children: Alison, Douglas. BS in Chemistry, Yale U., 1952; PhD in Chemistry, Rutgers U., 1962. Sr. project engr. ITT Group, Nutley, N.J., 1962-67; sr. mem. tech. staff AT&T Bell Labs., Princeton, 1967-86; disting. prof. Rutgers U., New Brunswick, 1986—. Adv. panel NSF, 1990—; course dir. Ctr. for Profl. Advancement, U.S. and The Netherlands, 1993—; cons. in field; presenter at profl. confs. *Dr. Shanefield developed a new ceramic insulator via the "tape casting" process. Over 200 million of these have been made, and there is one in almost every telephone line in the United States. He also invented a method for electroplating less gold than usual on contacts, which resulted in cost reductions for AT&T of eleven million dollars per year. Bell Labs advertised this resource-saving advancement in The New Yorker, the Scientific American, etc. Dr. Shanefield also developed the double-blind audio test for hi-fi components and wrote four cover stories for Stereo Review, etc.* Author: Organic Additives and Ceramic Processing, 1996; co-author: Defects in Gold Plating, 1981, Industrial Electronics for Engineers, Chemists and Technicians, 2000; contbr. 4 chpts. to tech. books, articles to profl. jours.; co-inventor 17 patents; assoc. editor Jour. Am. Ceramic Soc., 1987-99. With U.S. Army, 1952-54, Korea. Fellow Am. Inst. Chemists, Am. Ceramic Soc. (Best Paper award); mem. IEEE (life; chmn. stds. com. 1984-99), Am. Chem. Soc., Ceramic Assn. of N.J. (Man of Yr. award 1996). Republican. Avocations: modifying sports cars, writing audio, stereo articles. Office: Rutgers U Ceramics Engring Dept 607 Taylor Rd Piscataway NJ 08854-8065 Fax: 732-445-3258.

SHANER, BRONWYN MARIAN, elementary education educator; b. Buffalo, Aug. 12, 1937; d. Warren Eugene and Myfanwy Rosetta (Murray) Boone; m. Byrns William Long, Mar. 4, 1961 (dec. Sept. 1983); 1 child, Karen Anne Long Clark; m. Richard Leroy Shaner, Mar. 30, 1991. BS in Edn., SUNY, Buffalo, 1960, MS in Edn., 1989. Cert. tchr., N.Y. Tchr. art Brittonkill Ctrl., Troy, N.Y., 1960-61; tchr. spl. and elem. edn. Buffalo Pub. Schs., 1961-66, tchr. elem., from 1990; ret., 1999. Dir. advt. Cayuga Mfg. Corp., Blasdell, N.Y., 1981-83. Actress, costume designer, stage hand East Aurora Children's Theater, 1971-74. Bd. dirs. LWV, Kenmore, East Aurora and Clarence, N.Y., 1967-90; bd. deacons 1st Presbyn. Ch., Clarence, 1991-93. Mem. DAR, NEA. Republican. Avocations: reading, cooking, sailing. Home: Clarence, NY. Died Aug. 10, 2001.

SHANG, ER-CHANG, physicist; b. Sheng Yain, Liaonin, China, Feb. 5, 1932; came to U.S., 1986. BS in Theoretical Physics, Peking U., Beijing, China, 1958; PhD equivalent, Inst. Acoustics, Acad. Sinica, Beijing, 1982. Asst. prof. Inst. of Acoustics, Beijing, 1958-62, assoc. prof., 1962-75, prof., 1975-82, dep. dir., 1982-86; sr. rsch. assoc. AOML/NOAA, Miami, Fla., 1983-84, Wave Propagation Lab./NOAA, Boulder, Colo., 1987-88, NRC postdoctoral advisor, 1991—; rsch. assoc. CIRES/U. Colo./NOAA, Boulder, 1988-91, rsch. prof., supervisor, 1991—. Vis. scientist Scripps Inst. Oceanography, U. Calif. San Diego, La Jolla, 1982-83; vis. prof. U. Wis., Madison, 1983, Yale U., New Haven, 1986-87. Author: Underwater Acoustics, 1981; editor-in-chief Jour. Computational Acoustics. Recipient Nat. award for sci. Nat. Com. of Sci, Beijing, 1982, 89. Fellow Acoustical Soc. Am. Achievements include new method of source localization in ocean waveguides--matched mode processing; modal ocean acoustic tomography and applied for El Nino monitoring; impact of mode-coupling on modal travel time in ocean waveguide; modal theory in shallow water acoustics. Office: ETL/NOAA 325 Broadway St Boulder CO 80305-3337

SHANG, XUHONG, art educator, artist; b. Shanghai, May 11, 1960; came to U.S., 1986; s. Siwu and Jian (Xu) Shang; m. Ruiju Shen, Sept. 6, 1986; children: Joan, Ray. BA, Shanghai Tchrs. U., 1984; MA, Ill. State U., 1989; MFA, Temple U., 1992. Asst. prof. Shanghai Tchrs. U., 1984-86; instr. Warren County C.C., Washington, 1992-93; prof. painting Savannah (Ga.) Coll. Art and Design, 1993-99; assoc. prof. art Kans. State U., Manhattan, Kans., 1999—. Regional Visual Arts fellow Nat. Endowment for the Arts, 1995, Art Matter Inc. fellow, 1993. Avocations: swimming, jogging. Fax: (785) 532-0334. E-mail: xuhong@ksu.edu.

SHANG, YI, computer scientist, educator; b. Taiyuan, Shanxi, China, Sept. 25, 1967; came to U.S., 1991; s. Zhixiang Shang; m. Lei Zhu, July 3, 1970. PhD, U. Ill., 1997. Rsch. asst. U. Ill., Champaign-Urbana, 1991-97; asst. prof. U. Mo., Columbia, 1997; rsch. scientist Xerox Palo Alto (Calif.) Rsch. Ctr., 2000—02, Palo Alto (Calif.) Rsch. Ctr., 2002—. Rsch. grantee U. Mo., 1998-2000; rsch.grantee NSF, 1998-2001, DARPA, 2001—. Mem. IEEE, ASEE, AAAI. Office: Palo Alto Rsch Ctr 3333 Coyote Hill Rd Palo Alto CA 94304 E-mail: yshang@parc.com.

SHANGGUAN, DONGKAI, mechanical engineer; b. Henan, China, Dec. 12, 1963; arrived in U.S., 1989; BSME, Tsinghua Univ., 1984; DPhil, U. Oxford, 1989. Postdoctoral vis. fellow U. Cambridge, Cambridge, England, 1989; postdoctoral rsch. fellow U. Ala., Tuscaloosa, Ala., 1989—91; supr., sr. tech. specialist advanced mfg. Ford Motor Co./Visteon Corp., Dearborn, Mich., 1991—2001; mgr. corp. R&D Flextonics Internat., San Jose, Calif., 2001—. Mem. transactions rev. com. Soc. Automotive Engrs., 1997—2001; bd. adv. Soc. Mfg. Engrs., Dearborn, 1998—2001; bd. rev. Metallurgical & Materials Transactions, 1998—2001; spkr. in field. Author: Cellular Growth of Crystals, 1991; contbr. articles to profl. jours. Recipient Outstanding Young Mfg. Engr. award, Soc. Mfg. Engrs., 1998, Human Rels. award, City of Livonia, 2000. Achievements include patents for 14 in U.S. and internat.

SHANI, HEZEKIAH GYUNDA PYUZA, thoracic and cardiovascular surgery; BS, Gustavus Adolphus Coll., St. Peter, Minn., 1965; MB, ChB, Makerere Med. Sch., Kampala, Uganda, 1970. Intern medicine, pediat. and surgery Mulago Cons. Hosp., Kampala, Uganda, 1970-71; practice gen. medicine, surgery, pediat., and ob-gyn. Tanzania, 1971-76; resident in gen. surgery N.C. Bapt. Hosp., Bowman Gray Sch. Medicine, Wake Forest U., N.C., 1976-77, New Britain Gen. Hosp., U. Conn., 1977-78; resident in gen. surgery to chief resident gen. surgery Jewish Hosp., Cin., 1978-82; fellow in cardiovasc. surgery Jewish and Christ Hosps., 1982-83; fellow/chief fellow in thoracic and cardiovasc. surgery Univ. Med. Ctr., 1983-85; pvt. practice thoracic and cardiovascular surgery, 1986—. Fellow ACS, Am. Coll. Chest Physicians, Am. Heart Assn.; mem. AMA, Soc. Thoracic Surgeons, Internat. Soc. Endovascular Specialists, Acad. Medicine Cin., Ohio State Med. Assn., Cin. Surg. Soc., Soc. Critical Care Medicine. Office: 3120 Burnett Ave 401 Cincinnati OH 45229 E-mail: drhgpshani@fuse.net.

SHANK, GLENNA KAYE, medical and surgical nurse, nursing educator; b. Fulton County, Ill., Feb. 10, 1956; d. Glenn R. and Dorothy M. (Mosher) Post; m. Stephen G. Shank, July 1998; children: Troy David, Valerie Renee. Diploma, Lakeview Sch. Nursing, Danville, Ill., 1978; BSN, Bradley U., 1985; postgrad., U. Ill., Peoria. CNA; cert. in CPR, rehab., Alzheimer's care. Clin. instr. Spoon River Coll., Canton, Ill., nursing asst. instr.; staff nurse Lakeview Med. Ctr., Danville, St. Francis Med. Ctr., Peoria, also chairperson for patient edn., 1989-90; clin. educator med.-surg. St. Francis Hosp., 1992—, clin. educator for oncology and cmty. clinic, 1995—. Address: 13279 N Central School Ln Lewistown IL 61542-9157

SHANK, JOHN G. legislative staff member; b. Seattle, Mar. 27, 1955; s. John F. and Marilyn E. Shank; m. Andrea R. Gatta, July 1, 1995; children: Joseph, Michael. BS, Wilamette U., 1977; postgrad., U. Chgo., 1978—79. Legis. asst. Congressman Al Ullman, Washington, 1979—80; cons. Ullman Assocs., Inc., 1981—82; profl. staff Sentate Appropriations Com., 1982—95, House Appropriations Com., Washington, 1995—. Republican. Roman Catholic. Avocations: Avocations: reading, cooking. Office: House Appropriations Com US Capitol Washington DC 20515

SHANK, MAURICE EDWIN, aerospace engineering executive, consultant; b. N.Y.C., Apr. 22, 1921; s. Edwin A. and Viola (Lewis) S.; m. Virginia Lee King, Sept. 25, 1948; children: Christopher K., Hilary L. Shank-Kuhl, Diana L. Shank. BS in Mech. Engring., Carnegie-Mellon U., 1942; D.Sc., MIT, 1949. Registered profl. engr., Mass. Assoc. prof. mech. engring. MIT, Cambridge, 1949-60; dir. advanced materials R&D Pratt & Whitney, East Hartford, Conn., 1960-70; mgr. materials engring. and rsch., 1971-72; dir. engring. tech., 1972-80; dir. engine design and structures engring. Pratt & Whitney, East Hartford, Conn., 1980-81, dir. engring. tech., 1981-85, dir. engring. tech. assessment, 1985-86; v.p. Pratt Whitney of China, Inc., 1986-87; pvt. exec. cons. to industry and govt., 1987—. Cons. editor McGraw-Hill Book Co., N.Y.C., 1960-80; adv. com. to mechanics div. Nat. Bur. Standards, Washington, 1964-69; vis. com. dept. mech. engring. Carnegie-Mellon U., Pitts., 1968-78; corp. vis. coms. depts. materials sci. and engring., dept. aeros. and astronautics MIT, 1968-74, 79-92; mem. rsch. and tech. adv. coun. com. on aero. propulsion NASA, Washington, 1973-77, mem. aero. adv. com., 1978-86; mem. aero. and space engring. bd. NRC, 1989-92; lectr. in field. Contbr. articles to profl. jours. Served to maj. U.S. Army Corps. of Engrs., Ordnance Corps, 1942-46, Middle East/North Africa. Fellow AIAA, ASME, AIME, Am. Soc. Metals; mem. Nat. Acad. Engring., Conn. Acad. Sci. and Engring. Clubs: Cosmos. Episcopalian. Avocations: boating; fishing.

SHANK, RUSSELL, librarian, educator; b. Spokane, Wash., Sept. 2, 1925; s. Harry and Sadie S.; m. Doris Louise Hempfer, Nov. 9, 1951 (div.); children: Susan Marie, Peter Michael, Judith Louise. BS, U. Wash., 1946, BA, 1949; MBA, U. Wis., 1952; DrLS, Columbia U., 1966. Reference libr. U. Wash., Seattle, 1949; asst. engring. libr. U. Wis.-Madison, 1949-52; chief pers. Milw. Pub. Libr., 1952; engring.-phys. scis. libr. Columbia U., N.Y.C., 1953-59, sr. lectr., 1964-66, assoc. prof., 1966-67; asst. univ. libr. U. Calif.-Berkeley, 1959-64; dir. sci. libr. N.Y. Met. Reference and Rsch., 1966-68; dir. librs. Smithsonian Instn., Washington, 1967-77; univ. libr. prof. UCLA, 1977-89, asst. vice chancellor for libr. and info. svcs. planning, 1989-91, univ. libr., prof. emeritus, 1991—. Cons. Indonesian Inst. Sci., 1970; bd. cons. Pahlavi Nat. Library, Iran, 1975-76; pres. U.S. Book Exchange, 1975; bd. trustees Freedom to Read Found., 1989—. Trustee OCLC, Inc., 1978-84, 87, chmn., 1984; mem. library del. People's Republic of China, 1979; bd. dirs. Am. Council on Edn., 1980-81. Served with USNR, 1943-46. Recipient Disting. Alumnus award U. Wash. Sch. Librarianship, 1968, Role of Honor award Freedom to Read Found., 1990, Disting. Alumnus award Columbia U. Sch. Libr. Sci., 1992; fellow Coun. on Libr. Resources, 1973-74. Fellow AAAS; mem. ALA (pres. 1978-79, coun. 1961-65, 74-82, exec. bd. 1975-80, chmn. internat. rels. com. 1980-83, pres. info. sci. and automation div. 1968-69), Assn. Coll. and Rsch. Librs. (pres. 1972-73, Hugh Atkinson award 1990), Assn. Rsch. Librs. (bd. dirs. 1974-77), Beta Phi Mu. Home: 12919 Montana Ave Apt 101 Los Angeles CA 90049-4843 E-mail: RShank@ucla.edu. *Intellectual freedom is the paramount human right. It is the American's premier heritage. Without it the claim to democracy is a sham. Should the principles of our society fade or perish, the survival of this freedom alone would justify the nation's experience. The freedom to think, to read, and to speak will be our enduring monument. Their diffusion throughout the world must be our unending crusade.*

SHANK, THOM LEWIS, real estate executive, entertainment consultant, author; b. Butler, Pa., Apr. 23, 1953; s. Berdyne Delmont and Florence Elizabeth (Glasser) S. BA in Sociology, U. Pa., 1974; MBA, Pepperdine U., 1981. Negotiator Worldmark Travel, N.Y.C. and Phila., 1971-76; retail ops. mgr. Just Plants, Inc., Roxborough, Pa., 1973-79; founder, mgr. The Best-direct mail sales, Edgemoor, Del., 1974-79; property mgr. Moss and Co., Westwood, Calif., 1977-82; talent mgr. Thom Shank Assocs., Brentwood, 1979-84; pres., founder The Great Am. Amusement Co., Palm Desert, 1979-84; sales exec. Fred Sands Realtors, Brentwood, 1981-85; sales and mktg. dir. Coldwell Banker, Newport Beach, Calif., 1985-86, Great Western Ranches, Burbank, 1988-95; dist. and regional mgr. E.R.A. Real Estate, Pasadena, 1986; owner Century 21 Realtors, Tarzana, 1987-89; resorts dir. Prudential Jon Douglas Co., Beverly Hills, 1996—. Lutheran. Avocations: tennis, flying, reading, film, photography. Office: 301 N Canon Dr Beverly Hills CA 90210-4722

SHANK, WILLIAM O. lawyer; b. Hamilton, Ohio, Jan. 11, 1924; s. Horace Cooper and Bonnie (Winn) S.; m. Shirleen Allison, June 25, 1949; children—Allison Kay, Kristin Elizabeth. BA, Miami U., Oxford, O., 1947; JD, Yale, 1950. Bar: Ohio, Ill., U.S. Supreme Ct. Pvt. practice, Hamilton, Ohio, 1951-55, Chgo., 1955—; mem. firm Shank, Briede & Spoerl, Hamilton, Ohio, 1951-55; assoc. Lord, Bissell & Brook, Chgo., 1955-58; atty. Chemetron Corp., 1958-60, sr. atty., 1960-61, gen. atty., asst. sec., 1961-71, sec., gen. counsel, 1971-78; v.p., gen. counsel, sec. Walgreen Co., Deerfield, Ill., 1978-89; ptnr. Burditt & Radzius, Chartered, Chgo., 1989-98; exec. v.p. Internat. Bus. Resources, Inc., 1993—; ptnr. Williams Montgomery & John Ltd., 1998—. Mem. bus. adv. coun. Miami U., Oxford, Ohio, 1975—; arbitrator 19th Jud. Cir., Ill., 1995—; adv. bd. eLawForum, Washington, 1999—. Bd. dirs. Coun. for Cmty. Svcs. Met. Chgo., 1973-77; trustee Libr. Internat. Rels., 1971-78; bd. dirs. Chgo. Civic Fedn., 1984-89, Walgreen Drug Stores Hist. Found., 1990—; mem. Chgo. Crime Commn., 1985-89. 1st lt., pilot 8th Air Force, USAAF, World War II, ETO. Fellow Am. Bar Found. (life); mem. ABA (com. corp. gen. counsel), Ill. State Bar Assn., Chgo. Bar Assn. (chmn. com. on corp. law depts. 1971-72, 89-90), Am. Soc. Corp. Secs. (pres. Chgo. regional group 1983-84, nat. bd. dirs. 1984-87), Yale U. Law Sch. Assn. (past pres. Ill. Alumni, exec. com. New Haven), Walgreen Alumni Assn. (pres. 1992-94), Legal Club (pres. 1979-80), Law Club, Lawyers Club (Chgo.), Univ. Club, Econ. Club, Yale Club of Chgo., Omicron Delta Kappa, Phi Delta Phi, Sigma Chi. Home: 755 S Shore Dr Crystal Lake IL 60014-5530 Office: Williams Montgomery & John Ltd 20 N Wacker Dr Ste 2100 Chicago IL 60606 E-mail: wos@willmont.com.

SHANKAR, GAUTHAM, associate, financial services & sales trader; b. Mumbai, Maharashtra, India, Sept. 6, 1974; s. A.G. Shankar, Lalitha Shankar. Bachelor of Pharmacy (Honors), Birla Institute of Technology & Science, Pilani, Pilani, Rajasthan, India 333031, 1992—96; Master of Business Administration, Pennsylvania State University, Smeal College of Business, State College, PA, 1996—98. Consultant i2 Technologies Inc., Dallas, 1998—2000; Associate Goldman, Sachs & Co., New York, NY, 2000—02. Author: (Publication) Impact of GATT on Indian Pharmaceutical Markets, 1996. Mem.: Penn State Alumni Association (Member 1998—2002).

SHANKAR, RAVI, musician, sitar player, composer; b. Apr. 7, 1920; m. Sukanya Rajan; children: Shubho, Geetali, Anoushka. Studied under, Ustad Allauddin Khan of Maihar; trained in Guru-Shishya tradition, pupil of Ustad Allauddin Khan, 1938. Solo sitar player; former dir. music All India Radio, also founder Nat. Orch.; founder, dir. Kinnara Sch. Music, Bombay, 1962, Kinnara Sch. Music, L.A., 1967; many recordings of traditional and exptl. variety in India, U.K., U.S., including Tana Mana, 1987; concert tours in Europe, U.S., The East; vis. lectr. U. Calif., 1965; appeared in film Raga, 1974; fellow Sangeet Natak Akademi, 1976; responsible for music and choreography for ASIAD, 1982; film scores: Pather Panchali, The Flute and the Arrow, Nava Rasa Ranga, Charly, Gandhi, and many musical compositions including Concerto for Sitar No. 1, 1971, No. 2, 1981, Ghanashyam, 1989, and numerous ragas and talas; author: My Music, My Life, 1969, Rag Anurag (Bengali), (autobiography) Raga Mala, 1997. Recipient Deshikottam award, 1982; Silver Bear of Berlin; award of Indian Nat. Acad. Music, Dance and Drama, 1962; award of Padma Bhushan, 1967, Padma Vibushan, 1981, Internat. Music Coun. UNESCO award, 1975; elected to the Rajya Sabha, India, 1986; recipient 16 hon. doctorates around the world; recipient Grand prize Fukuoka Asian Cultural Prizes, Japan, 1991, Ramon Magsaysay award, The Philippines, 1992, Bharatiya Vidya Bhavan Mahatma Gandhi award, 1992, U.K. Ho. of Commons Shield, 1995, Crystal award, Switzerland, 1995, Premium Imperial Arts award, Japan, 1997, Light of Asia award, U.S., 1997, Juliet Hollister award, U.S., 1998, The Polar Music prize, Sweden, 1998, Bharat Ratna, India, 1999; named Commdr. of Legion of Honour, France, 2000. Address: care Sullivan Sweetland 28 Albion St London W2 2AX England

SHANKARAN, SEETHA, physician, educator, researcher, administrator; b. Wellington, Madras, India, May 4, 1945; came to U.S., 1971; m. M. K. Aravind; children: Santosh Aravind, Vinod Aravind, Maya Aravind. Degree, Queen Mary's Coll., Madras, India, 1962; MD, Madras Med. Coll., 1968. Diplomate Am. Bd. Pediatrics, Am. Bd. Neonatal Perinatal Medicine. Instr. pediatric Wayne State U., Detroit, 1975-77, from asst. prof. to assoc. prof., 1977-90, prof., dir. neotnatal-perinatal, 1990—. Dir. neonatal-perinatal medicine Children's Hosp., Detroit, 1987—, chair. CHM bioethics com., 1997—; dir. regional neonatal programs Detroit Med. Ctr., 1990—; mem. PI Nat. Inst. of Health Neonatal Rsch. Network, 1991—. Contbr. articles to profl. jours. Chair adv. bd. neonatology Cutting Edge, 1994—; mem. initial rev. group Nat. Inst. Child Health and Human Devel., Washington, 1997—. Named Caroline Duncan Disting. Women Medicine La. State U., 1995. Office: Children's Hosp Mich 3901 Beaubien St Detroit MI 48201-2119 E-mail: s_shankaran@wayne.edu.

SHANKEL, DELBERT MERRILL, microbiology and biology educator; b. Plainview, Nebr., Aug. 4, 1927; s. Cecil Wilfred and Gladys Dalton (Dodd) S.; m. Carol Jo Mulford, Sept. 10, 1962; children: Merrill, Jill, Kelley. BA, Walla Walla Coll., 1950; PhD, U. Tex., 1959. Tchr. Walla Walla Coll. Acad., College Place, Wash., 1950-51; instr. San Antonio Coll., 1954-55; asst. prof., assoc. prof. microbiology and biology U. Kans., Lawrence, 1959-68, prof., 1968—, asst. dean, assoc. dean arts and sci., 1966-72, acting dean, 1973, exec. vice chancellor, 1974-80, 86, 90-92, acting chancellor, 1980-81, chancellor, 1994-95, prof. and chancellor emeritus, 1996. Cons., evaluator North Ctrl. Assn. Colls. and Schs., Chgo., 1969-96, commr., 1991-95. Editor: (conf. procs.) Antimutagenesis and Anticarcinogenesis: Mechanisms, Vols. 1-3, 1986, 89, 93; assoc. editor Mutation Rsch., 1992-95. Active numerous civic orgns. With U.S. Army, 1952-54. Named Outstanding Educator award Mortar Bd., U. Kans., 1982, 85, 90, Disting. Alumnus of Yr., Walla Walla Coll., 1989; recipient numerous grants for sci. rsch. Fellow Am. Acad. Microbiology; mem. Am. Soc. for Microbiology (past chmn. edn. com., mem., chmn. numerous coms.), Environ. Mutagen Soc. (chmn. pub. policy com. 1991-93, nat. coun. 1994-97, mem., chmn. numerous coms.), Genetics Soc. Am., Soc. Gen. Microbiology (Gt. Britain), Radiation Rsch. Soc., Sigma Xi (pres. U. Kans. chpt. 1967). Republican. Unitarian Universalist. Avocations: sports, music, theater, reading. Office: U Kans 1002 Haworth Hl Lawrence KS 66045-0001 E-mail: shankel@ku.edu.

SHANKLIN, KENNETH DALE, plastic and reconstructive surgeon; b. Toluca, Ill., Dec. 21, 1931; s. Walter Arthur and Elsie Ida Josephine (Holz) S.; m. Doris Gay Minton, July 24, 1955 (div. Jan. 21, 1971); 1 child, Steven Dale; m. Colleen Jean Wheeler, July 30, 1978. BS, U. Ill., 1954; MD, U. Utah, 1967. Diplomate Am. Bd. Med. Specialists in gen. surgery, plastic surgery; lic. Calif. Commd. 2d lt. USAF, 1955, advanced through grades to lt. col., ret., 1977; intern Wilford Hall USAF Med. Ctr., San Antonio, 1967-68, resident in plastic surgery, 1972-74, resident in gen. surgery Travis AFB, Calif., 1968-72; assoc. clin. prof. plastic surgery U. Tex., San Antonio, 1974-77; asst. clin prof. plastic surgery U. Calif., Davis, 1977-84; pvt. practice plastic surgery Fresno, Calif., 1977-93; assoc. clin. prof. plastic surgery U. Calif., San Francisco, 1984—; acting chief med. officer Mil. Entrance Processing Sta., Sacramento, 1994—. Bd. dirs., pres. Valley Children's Hosp. Med. Staff, Fresno; bd. dirs. Liga Flying Physicians, Fresno, 1995-98. Producer, dir. films for sci. meetings (Outstanding award 1976). Mem. Am. Soc. Plastic Surgeons, Internat. Congress of Plastic and Reconstructive Surgeons (bd. dirs. 1983-91), Am. Med. Soc. Vienna, Mil. Order of the World Wars (dept. N. Calif. cmmdr. 1996-97, region 14 cmmdr. 1998-99, Disting. Chpt. Cmmdr. 1997, Silver Patrick Henry Patriotism award, 1997), Am. Legion (dist. vice cmmdr. 1998-99, dist. comdr. 1999-2000, vice cmmdr. Calif. 2001-02), Rotarian. Avocations: tchg., flying. E-mail: shanklinken@aol.com.

SHANKMAN, GARY CHARLES, art educator; b. Washington, Sept. 30, 1950; s. Bernard and Barbara Emeline (Robertson) S. BFA, Boston U., 1972; MFA, Am. U., 1975; postgrad., Koninklijke Academie, Antwerp, 1975-76, Skowhegan Sch. Painting and Sculpture, Maine, 1978. Instr. No. Va. Community Coll., Woodbridge, Va., 1978-85; instr. continuing edn. dept. U. D.C., Washington, 1978-86, Md. Coll. Art and Design, Silver Spring, 1981-86, Smithsonian Instn., Washington, 1978—; prof. Sage Coll. of Albany, NY, 1986—. Judge Ea. N.Y. State regional scholastic art exhbn. N.Y. State Mus., Albany, 1987—, Marblehead (Mass.) Festival of Arts, 1997; artist-in-residence, City of Rockville, Md., 1977, State of Okla., 1980, Byrdcliffe Art Colony, 1997. One-man shows include Seta House, Antwerp, Belgium, 1976, H.C. Dickens, London, 1982, Mickelson Gallery, Washington, 1981, 85, 88, 92, 96, Shelnutt Gallery, RPI, Troy, N.Y., 1989, Yates Gallery, Siena Coll., Loudonville, N.Y., 1999, Canterbury Gallery, Albany, N.Y., 1997, The Canajoharie (N.Y.) Libr. and Art Gallery, 2001; 2 person show at Oakroom Artists Gallery, Schenectady, N.Y., 2000; group exhbns. include Miller Gallery, Cin., 1992, The Nisk-Art Gallery, Niskayuna, N.Y., 1993, Rathbone Gallery, Sage JCA, Albany, N.Y., Dietel Gallery, Troy, 1993, Broadway Gallery, Albany, 1994, 95, Mickelson Gallery, 1978-99, Cert. Framing and Gallery, Loudonville, N.Y., 1995, The Artworks Gallery 21, Glens Falls, N.Y., 1995, Fulton St. Gallery, Troy, N.Y., 1997, Stage Gallery, Merrick, N.Y., 2000, 01, Colonil Nat. Morningside Gallery, Latham, N.Y., 1999, 2000, Carrie Haddad Gallery, Hudson, N.Y., 2000, Trudy Labelle Fine Art, Naples, Fla., 2001, Parker GAllery, Washington, 2002, Fine Arts Bldg. Gallery, Chgo., 2002, others; represented in permanent collections Mabee-Gerrer Mus. of Shawnee, Okla., Superior Ct. Art Trust, Washington. Internat. Telephone and Telegraph fellow to Belgium, 1975. Home: 86 Lawnridge Ave Albany NY 12208-3118 Office: Sage Jr Coll 140 New Scotland Ave Albany NY 12208-3425 E-mail: shankg@sage.edu.

SHANKS, ANN ZANE, filmmaker, producer/director, photographer, writer; b. N.Y.C. d. Louis and Sadye (Rosenthal) Kushner; m. Ira Zane (dec.); children— Jennifer, Anthony; m. Robert Horton Shanks, Sept. 25, 1959; 1 child, John. Student, Carnegie-Mellon U., Columbia U., 1949. Tchr., moderator spl. symposiums Mus. Modern Art, N.Y.C.; tchr. New Sch. U. Photographer, writer for numerous mags. and newspapers; producer, dir.: (movie shorts) Central Park, 1969 (U.S. entry Edinburgh Film Festival, Cine Golden Eagle award, Cambodia Film Festival award), Denmark... A Loving Embrace (Cine Golden Eagle award 1973), Tivoli, 1972-79 (San Francisco Film Festival award, Am. Film Festival award), (TV series) American Life Style (Silver award, 5 Gold medal awards Internat. TV and Film Festival N.Y., 2

Cine Golden Eagle awards), He's Fired, She's Hired; producer CBS TV Drop-Out Mother; producer, dir., writer (TV short) Mousie Baby; dir. (TV movie) Friendships, Secrets and Lies, NBC; producer: (TV movie) Drop-out Father, CBS, (video spl.) The Avant-Garde in Russia 1910-1930, Arts and Entertainment channel, ABC Morning Show, Good Afternoon Detroit; producer, dir. (TV spl.) A Day in the Country, PBS, (Emmy award nomination); producer, dir. (Off Broadway play) S.J. Perelman in Person; producer Broadway play, Lillian; exec. producer Gore Vidal's Am. Pres. Channel Four, London, Discovery channel, U.S.; exhibited photographs Mus. Modern Art, Mus. City N.Y., Transit Mus., Brooklyn Heights, N.Y., Met. Mus. Art, Jewish Mus., Howard Greenburg Gallery, N.Y.C., 1999; one woman show Ann Shanks total work, N.Y. Hist. Soc., N.Y.C., June 2003-Sept.2003; author: (photographs and text) The Name's the Game, New Jewish Ency; author, photographer, writer: Old Is What You Get, Busted Lives...Dialogues with Kids in Jail, 1983; writer, photographer Garbage and Stuff; photography in collections of Merv Griffin, N.Y. Pub. Libr., Mus. of City of N.Y., Met. Mus., N.Y., others; represented in permanent collections N.Y. Pub. Libr. Recipient awards from internat. photography competitions. Mem. Am. Soc. Mag. Photographers (bd. govs.), Overseas Press Club Am., Women in Film (v.p.), Dirs. Guild Am. *I guess I have "adolescent enthusiasm" for most of my work. It gives me infinite pleasure to be alive and have the chance to take an idea and see it through to its final form on the screen, or on the television set...savoring all the headaches, joys and the working together— step-by-step. I seek responsibility for my work , my family, and those I love.*

SHANKS, EUGENE RAYLIS, JR. banker; BA, Vanderbilt U., 1969; MA, PhD, Stanford U., 1974. With Bankers Trust Co., N.Y.C., 1973—78, pres., dir., 1992-95; pres. NetRisk, Inc., Greenwich, Conn., 1996—; with Bankers Trust Co., N.Y.C., 1980—92. Treas. Tenn. Valley Bancorp, 1978—80, Commerce Union Bank, 1978—80. Trustee Vanderbilt U.; bd. dirs. Posse Found. Office: NetRisk Inc One E Weaver St Greenwich CT 06831

SHANKS, GERALD ROBERT, retired insurance company executive; b. Knox, Ind., Dec. 12, 1942; s. Robert William and Beatrice (Lane) S.; m. Carol Sue Turner, Aug. 14, 1965. AB, Ind. U., 1965. CPCU. Claims adjuster Fireman's Fund, Indpls., 1965-70, claims supr. Chgo., 1970-76, claims mgr. Pitts., 1977-79; in human resources CNA, Chgo., 1978-82; recruiter Don Howard Pers., 1982-83; asst. claims mgr. Fireman's Fund, Boston, 1983-84, claims mgr. Detroit, 1984-85; v.p. claims, bd. dirs. Interstate Nat. Corp. subs. Fireman's Fund, Chgo., 1985-92, sr. v.p., sr. claims officer, 1992-97; ret., 1997. Bd. dirs. Geo. F. Brown and Sons, Chgo., Interstate Nat. Corp., Chgo. Ins. Co. and Interstate Indemnity Co., Interstate Fire and Casualty Co., ret. 1997. Mem. Soc. CPCU, Union League Club of Chgo., Ky. Col. Republican. Meth. Avocations: golf, cattle. Home: 1600 Wheeler Rd Fountain Run KY 42133-9404 E-mail: shanks@scrtc.com.

SHANKS, HERSHEL, editor, writer; b. Sharon, Pa., Mar. 8, 1930; s. Martin and Mildred (Freedman) S.; m. Judith Alexander Weil, Feb. 20, 1966; children: Elizabeth Jean, Julia Emily. BA, Haverford (Pa.) Coll., 1952; MA, Columbia, 1953; LLB, Harvard, 1956. Bar: D.C. 1956. Trial atty. Dept. Justice, 1956-59; pvt. practice Washington, 1959-88; ptnr. Glassie, Pewett, Beebe & Shanks, 1964-88; editor Bibl. Archaeology Rev., Washington, 1975—. Pres. Bibl. Archaeology Soc., 1974—, Jewish Ednl. Ventures Inc., 1987—. Author: The Art and Craft of Judging, 1968, The City of David, 1973, Judaism in Stone, 1979, Jerusalem--An Archaeological Biography, 1995, The Mystery and Meaning of the Dead Sea Scolls, 1998, also articles; co-editor: Recent Archaeology in the Land of Israel, 1984; editor: Ancient Israel, A Short History, 1988, revised edit., 1999, Christianity and Rabbinic Judaism, 1992, Understanding the Dead Sea Scrolls, 1992; editor Bible Rev., 1985—, Moment mag., 1987—, Archaeology Odyssey, 1998—. Mem. ABA, D.C. Bar Assn., Am. Schs. Oriental Rsch., Cosmos Club, Phi Beta Kappa. Home: 5208 38th St NW Washington DC 20015-1812 Office: Bibl Archaeology Soc 4710 41st St NW Washington DC 20016-1706 E-mail: hshanks@bib-arch.org. *I try to take time to identify what is important in my life, to focus on that and ignore the rest when it conflicts. It takes conscious effort not to dissipate energy on activities and attitudes that don't matter in the big picture of my priorities. Free to concentrate on what I value most, I try to accomplish something each day in a regular, habitual way.*

SHANKS, JUDITH WEIL, editor; b. Montgomery, Ala., Nov. 2, 1941; d. Roman Lee and Charlotte (Alexander) Weil; m. Hershel Shanks, Feb. 20, 1966; children: Elizabeth Shanks Alexander, Julia Emily. BA in Econs., Wellesley Coll., 1963; MBA, Trinity Coll., 1980. Econs. asst. Export-Import Bank, Washington, 1963-68; cons. econs. and social sci., 1968-76; researcher Time-Life Books, Alexandria, Va., 1976-80, prin. researcher, 1980-83, illustrations editor, 1983, adminstrv. editor, 1984-95, dir. editl. adminstrn., 1996; assoc. curator S.C. Jewish Heritage Exhibit, Coll. Charleston, 1998—. Vol. Mentors, Inc. Recipient Sr. Rsch. award Hadassah Internat. Rsch. Inst. on Jewish Women at Brandeis U. Democrat. Jewish. Avocations: dancing, scuba diving, hiking, gardening, research on women. Home: Box 42456 Washington DC 20015

SHANKS, KATHRYN MARY, health care administrator; b. Glens Falls, N.Y., Aug. 4, 1950; d. John Anthony and Lenia (Combs) S. BS summa cum laude, Spring Hill Coll., 1972; MPA, Auburn U., 1976. Program evaluator Mobile (Ala.) Mental Health, 1972-73; dir. spl. projects Ala. Dept. Mental Health, Montgomery, 1973-76; dir. adminstrn. S.W. Ala. Mental Health/Mental Retardation, Andalusia, 1976-78; adminstr. Mobile County Health Dept., 1978-82; exec. dir. Coastal Family Health Ctr., Biloxi, Miss., 1982-95; cons. med. group practice, 1995—; ptnr. Shanks & Allen, Mobile, 1979—; healthcare consulting pvt. practice, 1995—; practice dir. USA Health Svcs. Found., 1999—2001; practice mgr. Humana Mil. Healthcare Svcs., 2002—. Cons. S.W. Health Agy., Tylertown, Miss., 1984-86; instr., mgr. dept. pediats. U. South Ala., 1997-99; preceptor Sch. Nursing, U. So. Miss., Hattiesburg, 1983, 84; advisor Headstart Program, Gulfport, Miss., 1984-95; LPN Program, Gulf Coast C.C., 1984-95; lectr. Auburn U., Montgomery, 1977-78. Bd. dirs. Mobile Cmty. Action Agy., 1979-81, Moore Cmty. House; mem. S.W. Ala. Regional Goals Forum, Mobile, 1971-72, Cardiac Rehab. Study Com., Biloxi, Miss., 1983-84, Mothers and Babies Coalition, Jackson, Miss., 1983-95, Gulf Coast Coalition Human Svcs., Biloxi, 1983-95; exec. dir. Year for Miss., 1993-94. Spring Hill Coll. Pres.'s scholar, 1972. Mem. ACLU, Miss. Primary Health Care Assn. (pres.), Med. Group Mgmt. Assn., Soc. for Advancement of Ambulatory Care, Spring Hills Alumni Assn. Avocations: tennis, home restoration, golf.

SHANMAN, JAMES ALAN, lawyer; b. Cin., Aug. 1, 1942; s. Jerome D. and Mildred Louise (Bloch) S.; m. Marilyn Louise Glassman, June 11, 1972; 1 child, Ellen Joan. BS, U. Pa., 1963; JD, Yale U., 1966. Bar: N.Y. 1967, U.S. Ct. Mil. Appeals 1971, U.S. Supreme Ct. 1971, U.S. Ct. Appeals (2d cir.) 1972, U.S. Dist. Ct. (so. and ea. dists.) N.Y. 1972, U.S. Ct. Internat. Trade 1976, U.S. Ct. Appeals (fed. cir.) 1987, U.S. Dist. Ct. (ea. dist.) Mich. 1989, U.S. Ct. Appeals (7th cir.) 1999. Assoc. Cahill Gordon & Reindel, N.Y.C., 1971-74, Freeman, Meade, Wasserman, Sharfman & Schneider, N.Y.C., 1974-76; mem. firm Sharfman, Shanman, Poret & Siviglia, P.C., 1976-95; ptnr. Camhy Karlinsky & Stein LLP, 1995-96; mem. firm Sharfman, Siviglia, Poret, Kook, Ross & Shanman, P.C., 1996-98; ptnr. Edwards & Angell, LLP, 1998—. Speaker on reins. law topics. Capt. USAF, 1966-71. Mem.: ABA, ARIAS.US (cert. arbitrator), Bailliage de Conn., Confrérie de la Chaine des Rôtisseurs, Am. Arbitration Assn. (comml. panel arbitrators 1980—), Assn. of Bar of City of N.Y. (com. ins. law 1985—88, 1990—92, 1998—2001, com. profl. liability ins. 1988—92, com. on assn. ins. plans 1989—), N.Y. State Bar Assn. Office: Edwards & Angell LLP 750 Lexington Ave New York NY 10022-1253 E-mail: jshanman@ealaw.com.

SHANMUGAM, GANAPATHY, geologist, researcher; b. Sirkali, Tamilnadu, India, Apr. 23, 1944; came to U.S., 1970; s. Ganapathy Mudaliar and Sambooranam; m. Jean Marie Barham, Aug. 21, 1976. BSc in Geology and Chemistry, Annamalai U., South India, 1965; MSc in Applied Geology, Indian Inst. Tech., Bombay, 1968; MS in geology, Ohio U., 1972; PhD in Geology, U. Tenn., 1978. Rsch. geologist Mobil Exploration & Product Tech. Ctr., Dallas, 1978-82, sr. rsch. geologist, 1982-84, assoc., 1984-85, rsch. assoc., 1985-89, sr. rsch. assoc., 1989-93, assoc. geol. rsch. advisor, 1993-96, geol. scientist, 1996-2000; adj. prof. geology U. Tex., Arlington, 2000—. Conf. chmn. Geol. Soc. London, 1996; debate panelist Am. Assn. Petroleum Geologists, Dallas, 1997. Author: Dimensions and Geometries of Deep-Water Systems, 1998; contbr. over 100 articles to profl. jours. Geology adv. bd. U. Tenn., Knoxville, 1985-89. Recipient Silver medal Indian Inst. Tech., 1968; Penrose grantee Geol. Soc. Am., 1976-78; recipient best Paper award Nigerian Assn. Petroleum Explorationists, 1995. Mem. Soc. Sedimentary Geology (nominating com. 1993), Nat. Geog. Soc., Sigma Gamma Epsilon (v.p. 1976-77). Achievements include questioning of the deep-water turbidite paradigm and advocation of sandy debris flows in forming deep-water petroleum reservoirs. Avocation: photography. Office: U Tex Arlington Dept Geology PO Box 19049 Arlington TX 76019-0001 E-mail: shanshanmugam@aol.com.

SHANMUGAM, KANNON KUMAR, lawyer; b. Lawrence, Kans., Nov. 15, 1972; s. Sam and Radha Shanmugam. AB, Harvard U., 1993, JD, 1998; MLitt, Oxford U., 1995. Intern to Hon. Deanell Reece Tacha U.S. Ct. Appeals 10th Cir., Lawrence, 1990; intern to Hon. Robert Dole U.S. Senate, Washington, 1991; intern The Kansas City (Mo.) Star, 1992-93; summer assoc. Sidley & Austin, Chgo., 1996, Cravath Swaine & Moore, N.Y.C., 1997; law clk. to Hon. J. Michael Luttig U.S. Ct. Appeals 4th Cir., Alexandria, Va., 1998-99; law clk. to Hon. Antonin Scalia U.S. Supreme Ct., Washington, 1999-2000; assoc. Kirkland & Ellis, 2000—. Editor-in-chief Harvard Independent, Cambridge, Mass., 1991-92; mem. staff Harvard Jour. Law & Technology, Cambridge, 1995-96; asst. mng. editor Harvard International Law Jour., Cambridge, 1995-96; exec. editor Harvard Law Rev., Cambridge, 1996-98. Contbr. articles to profl. jours. Presdl. scholar, 1989, Marshall scholar, 1993. Office: Kirkland & Ellis 655 15th St NW Washington DC 20005

SHANNAHAN, WILLIAM PAUL, lawyer; b. Detroit, Nov. 21, 1934; s. William and Jean (Boyle) S.; m. Saracia L. Price, Sept. 24, 1983; children: MeglynAnne, Michael-Padraic. AB, U. Detroit, 1956; JD, Georgetown U., 1958. Bar: D.C. 1958, Mich. 1958, Calif. 1962. Ptnr. Higgs, Fletcher & Mack, La Jolla, Calif., 1967-81, Aylward, Kintz, et al, La Jolla, 1981-87, pvt. practice, La Jolla, 1987—. With U.S. Army, 1959-60. Democrat. Roman Catholic. Office: 1200 Prospect St Ste 425 La Jolla CA 92037-3660

SHANNON, CAROLYN JEAN, interior designer; b. Vincennes, Ind., Nov. 22, 1943; d. Melvin Eugene and Melita Harriet (Bair) Powell; children: Timothy Carl, Heather Caroline. BA in Telecomms. and Interior Design, Ind. U., 1985. Interior designer Buchanan & Sons Furniture, also Kitchen and Bath Ctr., Bloomington, Ind., 1975-81; also freelance, 1975-81; sales mgr. Kittle's Ethan Allen, Bloomington and Indpls., 1981-82; owner, cons. The Profl. Woman, career enhancement seminars, Bloomington, 1982-84; interior designer Interiors, 1984-87; owner Carolyn Shannon Interiors, Bloomington and Chgo., 1987—. Dir. Atlas Galleries, Chgo., 1991-94; exec. dir. Inner Circle Edn., 2000—. Rep. Local Coun. of Women, owners Bloomington Hosp., 1985—. Mem. NAFE, Am. Soc. Interior Designers, Golden Key, Phi Beta Kappa, Psi Iota Xi, Phi Delta Kappa (scholarship 1984). Methodist. Avocations: bridge, travel, tennis, antique collecting and dealing. Home: 10471 W Grandview Dr Columbus IN 47201-8699 E-mail: tbcs@iquest.net.

SHANNON, CYNTHIA JEAN, biology educator; b. Phila., Feb. 19, 1961; d. Foster Lloyd and Nancy Ellen (Chapman) Shannon. AA, Fullerton (Calif.) Coll., 1981; BA in Psychology, Calif. State U., Fullerton, 1986; BS in Zoology, Calif. Poly. State U., 1985, MS in Biology, 1991; postgrad. in ecology and evolution, Riverside. Biology instr. Calif. State Poly. U., Pomona, Calif., 1986-91, Mt. San Antonio Coll., Walnut, 1986—, chair biology dept., 1996-97. Mem. AAAS, Ornithological Soc. N.Am., So. Assn. Naturalists, Golden Key, Phi Kappa Phi. Democrat. Avocations: bird watching, hiking, dogs, food and wine, reading. Office: Mt San Antonio Coll 1100 N Grand Ave Walnut CA 91789-1341 E-mail: cshannon@mtsac.edu.

SHANNON, DONALD HAWKINS, retired editor; b. Auburn, Wash., Feb. 1, 1923; s. Ernest Victor and Fern (McConville) S.; m. Sally van Deurs, June 13, 1952; children— John McConville, Susanna Shepard. BA, Stanford, 1944; postgrad., Law Sch., 1946-47. Reporter Brazil Herald, Rio de Janeiro, 1947-48; Reporter UPI, London, 1949-51, Western Reporters, Washington, 1951-53; mem. staff L.A. Times, 1954-92, bur. chief, 1962-65, bur. chief for Africa, 1965-66, bur. chief, 1966-71, UN, N.Y.C., 1971-75, UN (Washington bur.), 1975-92; sr. editor Georgetown and Country, Washington, 1996-99. Served with AUS, 1944-46, PTO. Mem. Nat. Press Club, Fed. City Club, City Tavern Club, Overseas Press Club (N.Y.C.), Phi Gamma Delta. Address: 1068 30th St NW Washington DC 20007-3822

SHANNON, ELIZABETH JOANNA, writer, literary agent; b. Belfast, Co. Down, Great Britain and Northern Ireland, Feb. 2, 1961; , naturalized, U.S., 2002; d. James Ernest Blythe, Maureen Blythe; m. Neil Stuart Shannon. Degree in Dramatic Arts and Lit., London Theatre Sch., 1986. Consulting editor Ricia Mainhardt Agy., N.Y.C., 1997—; agt. Pacific NW Lit. Assocs., Portland, Oreg., 1999—. Kay Snow contest coord. Willamette Writers, Portland, 1999—. Author: (Adaptation of book into stageplay) Anne of Green Gables, 1991, (screenplays) Belfast's Fair City, 2001, Tempest Raised, 2000; actor: (plays) MacBeth, 1984; (films) Vision of the Fool, 1986; (plays) Relatively Speaking, 1990, (British tour) Cavalcade Theatre Co., 1987, Footprints Theatre Co, 1988. Personal E-mail: lizzyshannon@yahoo.com.

SHANNON, IRIS REED, health consultant; b. Chgo. d. Ira Paul and Iola Sophia (Williams) Reed; m. Robert Alwood Shannon, Aug. 21, 1853. BS in Nursing, Fisk U.-Meharry Med. Coll., 1948; MA, U. Chgo., 1954; PhD, U. Ill., Chgo., 1987; D in Pub. Svc. (hon.), Elmhurst Coll., 1993. Staff nurse Chgo. Bd. Health, 1948-50; instr. pub. health nursing Meharry Med. Coll., Nashville, 1951-56; tchr.-nurse, health coordinator child devel. Head Start, Chgo. Bd. Edn., 1957-66; dir. community nursing Mile Sq. Neighborhood Health Center, Presbyn.-St. Luke's Hosp., Chgo., 1966-69; co-dir. nurse assoc. programs Rush Presbyn.-St. Luke's Hosp., 1971-76; chairperson community nursing Rush U., Chgo., 1972-77, acting chairperson, 1988-90; asst. prof. pub. health nursing U. Ill., 1971-74; assoc. prof. cmty. nursing Rush U., 1974-97, health sys. mgr., 1988—, health cons., 1974-78. Adj. faculty Sch. Pub. Health, U. N.C., 1977—85; mem. profl. adv. bd. Vis. Nurse Assn. Chgo., 1973—75; cons. Video Nursing, Inc.; mem. profl. adv. com. Mile Sq. Home Health Unit, Chgo., 1975—77; mem. nat. adv. coun. on nurse tng. HEW, 1978—81; mem. Nat. Task Force on Credentialing in Nursing, 1979—82; mem. Chgo. regional com. Ill. White House Conf. on Children, 1979—80; v.p. Chgo. Bd. Health, 1989—. Recipient award of merit, Ill. Pub. Health Assn., 1979, 1989—2000, Outstanding Achievement award, YWCA of Met. Chgo., 1988, Disting. Svc. award, Chego. chpt. Meharry Alumni, 1989, Lowenberg Chair of Excellence in Nursing, Memphis State U., 1993, Bd. Trustees' Svc. medal, Rush-Presby. St. Luke's Med. Ctr., 1996. Fellow: APHA (chmn. pub. health nursing sect. 1977—79, governing coun. 1980—82, exec. bd. 1985—87, pres. 1988—89, governing coun. 1989—99), Am. Acad. Nursing, Royal Soc. Health (hon. 1989); mem.: ANA (Pearl McIver Pub. Health Nurse award 1998), Inst. of Medicine of NAS, Delta Sigma Theta, Sigma Theta Tau. Home: 3100 S King Dr Chicago IL 60616-3634 E-mail: irisshannon@aol.com.

SHANNON, JAMES PATRICK, foundation consultant, retired food company executive; b. South St. Paul, Minn., Feb. 16, 1921; s. Patrick Joseph and Mary Alice (McAuliffe) S.; m. Ruth Church Wilkinson, Aug. 2, 1969. BA in Classics, Coll. St. Thomas, St. Paul, 1941; MA in English, U. Minn., 1951; PhD, Yale U., 1955; JD, U. N.Mex., 1973; LL.D., U. Notre Dame, 1964, Macalester Coll., 1964; LLD, Lora Coll., 1964, DePaul U., 1965, St. Mary's Coll., 1965, Carleton Coll., 1965; LL.D., Creighton U., 1966; LLD, Northland Coll., Ashland, Wis., 1979, William Mitchell Coll. Law, 1980; LittD, Seton Hall, 1965, Coe Coll., Cedar Rapids, Iowa, 1966, U. Minn., 1966; JUD, Lawrence U., 1969. Ordained priest Roman Catholic Ch., 1946; asst. prof. history Coll. St. Thomas, 1954-56, pres., 1956-66; aux. bishop Archdiocese of St. Paul, 1965-68; pastor St. Helna Parish, Mpls., 1966-68; tutor Greek St. John's Coll., Santa Fe, 1969-70, v.p., 1969-70; columnist, writer, found. cons., 1970-79, 88-90; mem. firm Sutin, Thayer & Browne, Albuquerque, Santa Fe, 1973-74; exec. dir. Mpls. Found., 1974-78; v.p. Gen. Mills, Inc., 1980-88; sr. cons. Nat. Coun. on Founds., Washington, 1988—. Dir. Midwest Importers, Inc., 1988-96. Author: Catholic Colonization on the Western Frontier, 1957, Reluctant Dissenter, 1998. Bd. dirs. James H. Hill Libr., St. Paul, 1985-94, Inst. Ecumenical and Cultural Rsch., Collegeville, Minn., 1985—, chmn., 1990-94; bd. dirs. Ind. Sector, Washington, 1988-94, N.Mex. Cmty. Found., 1991-95, Gen. Svc. Found., 1991-94; coun. Conf. Bd., 1982-88; chmn. Rhodes Scholarship Selection Com. for Upper Midwest Selection Com., 1976-86; chmn. coun. founds., Washington, 1984-85; vice chmn. Found. Ctr., N.Y.C.; sr. cons. Coun. on Founds. Mem. D.C. Bar Assn., N.Mex. Bar Assn., Minn. Bar Assn., Mpls. Club (bd. govs. 1989-96, pres. 1994-95). Democrat. Address: PO Box 112 Wayzata MN 55391-0112

SHANNON, JIMMIE L. accountant; b. Lincoln, Ark., Feb. 8, 1943; s. Lacy T. and Pearl M. Shannon; m. Gloria A. Shannon, Mar. 2, 1963; children: Christopher G., Joshua L. BSBA, U. Ark., 1968. CPA. Various BKD, LLP, Ft. Smith, Ark., 1967-74, ptnr., 1974—. Pres. Ark. State Bd. Pub. Acctg., Little Rock, 1994-99. Mem. Ark. Soc. CPAs (pres. 2002), Optimist Club (Optimist of the Yr. 1981), Ft. Smith Noon Exch. Club. Republican. Baptist. Avocations: tennis, hunting. Office: BKD CPAs 5000 Rogers Ave Ste 700 Fort Smith AR 72903 E-mail: JShannon@bkd.com.

SHANNON, JOE, JR. lawyer; b. Nov. 9, 1940; s. Joe and Juanita Elizabeth (Milliorn) S.; children: Kelley Jane, Joseph Patrick, Shelley Carol. BA, U. Tex., 1962, LLB, 1963. Bar: Tex. 1963, U.S. Supreme Ct. 1977, U.S. Dist. Ct. (no. dist.) Tex. 1970, U.S. Ct. Appeals (5th cir.) 1977, U.S. Dist. Ct. (we. dist.) 1998; cert. family law Tex. Bd. Legal Specialization, matrimonial arbitrator. Ptnr. Shannon & Shannon, Ft. Worth, 1963-72; adminstrv. asst. to spkr. Tex. Ho. of Reps., Austin, 1970; chief criminal div. Tarrant County Dist. Atty., Ft. Worth, 1972-78; pvt. practice, 1978-99; ptnr. Snakard & Gambill, 1986-90; chief econ. crimes Tarrant County Dist. Atty., 1999—. Adj. prof. Tex. Weslyan Sch. Law. Mem. Tex. Ho. of Reps., 1964-70. Fellow Tex. Bar Found., Am. Acad. Matrimonial Lawyers (cert.); mem. ABA, State Bar of Tex. (adv. com. family law, state bd. legal specialization 1985-99, dist. grievance com. 1973-76, chmn. 1975-76, 95—, sec. 2d ct. appeals adv. com. 1995—), N. Tex. Family Law Specialists, Tarrant County Family Law Bar Assn. (pres. 1998), Tarrant County Bar Assn. (dir. 1999-2001, sec. treas. 2002), Phi Alpha Delta, Masons, Shriners. Office: 1701 River Run Fort Worth TX 76107-6579 E-mail: jshannon@tarrantcounty.com. *Notable cases include: State vs. Cullen Davis, 1977, richest man to be tried for murder; State vs. Mutscher, bribery conspiracy trial of Tex. House Speaker and assocs.*

SHANNON, JOHN SANFORD, lawyer, retired railway executive; b. Tampa, Fla., Feb. 8, 1931; s. George Thomas and Ruth Evangeline (Garrett) S.; m. Elizabeth Howe, Sept. 22, 1962; children: Scott Howe, Elizabeth Garrett, Sandra Denison. AB, Roanoke Coll., 1952; JD, U. Va., 1955. Bar: Va. 1955. Assoc. Hunton Williams Gay Powell & Gibson, Richmond, Va., 1955-56; solicitor Norfolk & Western Ry., Roanoke, 1956-60, asst. gen. solicitor, 1960-64, gen. atty., 1964-65, gen. solicitor, 1965-68, gen. counsel, 1968-69, v.p. law, 1969-80, sr. v.p. law, 1980-82; exec. v.p. law Norfolk (Va.) So. Corp., 1982-96, ret., 1996. Bd. dirs. Norfolk So. Ry. Co., Pocahontas Land Corp., Va. Holding Corp., Norfolk and Western Ry. Co. Editor-in-chief: Va. Law Rev, 1954-55. Chancellor Episcopal Diocese Southwestern Va., 1974-82; pres. bd. trustees North Cross Sch., Roanoke, 1973-82; trustee, past chmn. exec. com. Roanoke Coll., Salem, Va.; bd. dirs. Legal Aid Soc., Roanoke Valley, 1969-80, pres., 1970-79; trustee Chrysler Mus., Norfolk, 1982-94, Norfolk Acad., 1987-99. Mem. Va. Bar Assn., Norfolk and Portsmouth Bar Assn., Shenandoah Club, Roanoke Country Club, Norfolk Yacht and Country Club, Harbor Club, Order of Coif, Sigma Xi, Omicron Delta Kappa, Phi Delta Phi. Home: 7633 Argyle Ave Norfolk VA 23505-1701

SHANNON, KYLE, Internet company executive; Founder Urban Desires, World Wide Web Artists Consortium; co-founder Agency.com, 1995, chief creative officer, 1995-2000, chief people officer. Office: Agency.com 20 Exchange Pl New York NY 10005-3201

SHANNON, LARRY REDDING, public relations professional; b. St. Joseph, Mo., Apr. 5, 1949; s. Charles R. Jr. and Dorothy May (Dunham) Redding. Student, U. Tex., Arlington, 1967-69. Announcer Sta. KVIL, Dallas, 1968, Sta. KFJZ, Ft. Worth and Dallas, 1968-78; pvt. practice pub. rels. and advt., Ft. Worth, 1978-85; pvt. practice pub. rels., advt. and mgmt., N.Y.C., 1985-86; adminstrv. asst. to former spkr. Jim Wright, U.S. Ho. of Reps., Ft. Worth, 1986-97; dir. investor comm. Arch Petroleum Inc., 1998—. Pres. First Strategy Corp. Democrat. Avocations: reading, travel. Office: PO Box 17563 Fort Worth TX 76102-0563

SHANNON, LYLE WILLIAM, sociology educator; b. Storm Lake, Iowa, Sept. 19, 1920; s. Bert Book and Amy Irene (Sivits) S.; m. Magdaline W. Shannon, Feb. 27, 1943; children: Mary Shannon Will, Robert William, John Thomas, Susan Michelle. BA, Cornell Coll., Mount Vernon, Iowa, 1942; MA, U. Wash., 1947, PhD, 1951. Acting instr. U. Wash., 1950-52; mem. faculty dept. sociology U. Wis., Madison, 1952-62, assoc. prof., 1958-62; prof. sociology U. Iowa, Iowa City, 1962—, chmn. dept. sociology and anthropology, 1962-70, dir. Iowa Urban Community Research Ctr., 1970-91; dir. emeritus, 1991—; prof. emeritus U. Iowa, Iowa City, 1991—. Vis. prof. Portland State U., Wayne State U., U. Wyo., U. Colo. Author: Underdeveloped Areas, 1957, Minority Migrants in the Urban Community, 1973, Criminal Career Continuity: Its Social Context, 1988, Changing Patterns of Delinquency and Crime: A Longitudinal Study in Racine, 1991, Developing Areas, 1995, Socks and Cretin: Two Democats Helping Bill with the Presidency, 1995, Alcohol and Drugs, Delinquency and Crime, 1998; editor: Social Ecology of the Community series, 1974-76. With USNR, 1942-46. Mem. AAAS, Am. Sociol. Assn., Midwest Sociol. Soc., Population Assn. Am., Soc. Applied Anthropology, Am. Soc. Criminology, Phi Beta Kappa. Lodges: Kiwanis. Democrat. Home: River Heights Iowa City IA 52240-9147 Office: Univ Iowa W504 Seashore Hall Iowa City IA 52242-1407

SHANNON, MALCOLM LLOYD, JR. lawyer, educator; b. Phila., Jan. 27, 1946; m. Jeanne Marie Halle, Dec. 28, 1974; children: Travis Alan, Kate Meredith. BBA, U. N.Mex., 1968, JD, 1971. Bar: N.Mex. 1971, U.S. Supreme Ct. 1976, Tex. 1981, Colo. 1984, Calif. 1986. Counsel Gen. Atomics, 1991—. Lectr. mining and pub. land law U. N.Mex. Adv. com. solar energy application Tech. Vocat. Inst. of Albuquerque Pub. Schs., 1976; judge N.Mex. State Sci. Fair 1978-80; mem. ednl. accountability com. Cherry Creek Sch. Dist., 1984-86; bd. dirs. Denver U./Pioneer Jr. Hockey Assn., 1991-94. Author publs. in field. Mem. ABA, Am. Corp. Counsel Assn. Republican. Roman Catholic. Home: 6199 S Jamaica Ct Englewood CO 80111-5714 Office: 7800 E Dorado Pl Ste 200 Englewood CO 80111

SHANNON, MARGARET ANNE, lawyer; b. Detroit, July 6, 1945; d. Johannes Jacob and Vera Marie (Spade) Van De Graaf; m. Robert Selby Shannon, Feb. 4, 1967. Student, Brown U., 1963-65; BA in History, Wayne State U., 1966, JD, 1973. Bar: Mich. 1973. Housing aide City of Detroit, 1967-68; employment supr. Sinai Hosp., Detroit, 1968-69; assoc. gen. counsel regulatory affairs Blue Cross Blue Shield Mich., 1969-80; ptnr. Honigman Miller Schwartz and Cohn, 1980-95, of counsel, 1996—. Nat. Merit scholar, 1963-66. Mem. ABA (vice-chmn. pub. regulation of ins. law com. 1981-82), Mich. State Bar (chmn. health care com. 1991, 92, co-chmn. payor subcom. health law sect.), Nat. Health Lawyers Assn., U. Liggett Sch. Alumni (bd. govs.). Home: 629 Rosa Ct West Palm Beach FL 33410- Office: Honigman Miller Schwartz and Cohn 2290 First National Bldg Detroit MI 48226-3583 E-mail: mshannon@honigman.com.

SHANNON, MARY LOU, adult health nursing educator; b. Memphis, Apr. 4, 1938; d. Sidney Richmond Shannon and Lucille (Gwaltney) Cloud. BSN, U. Tenn., 1959; MA, Columbia U., 1963, MEd, 1964, EdD, 1972. Staff nurse City of Memphis Hosps., 1959—60, instr. Sch. Nursing, 1960—62; asst. prof. U. Tenn., 1964—70, assoc. prof., 1970—73, prof., 1973—89; prof., chair adult health dept. Sch. Nursing U. Tex., Galveston, 1989—98, prof., 1989—2000, prof. emeritus, 2000—. Bd. dirs. Nat. Pressure Ulcer Adv. Panel, Buffalo, 1987-96; vis. prof. U. Alta., Edmonton, Can., 1982, Union U., Memphis, 2001; mem. project adv. bd. RAND, Santa Monica, Calif., 1994. Contbr. chpts. to books in field and to periodicals; mem. editl. bd. Advances in Wound Care, 1987-2000. Trustee Nurses Edn. Funds, N.Y.C., 1972-86. Mem. AAAS, ANA, Nat. League Nursing (bd. of rev. 1983-86), Orthopedic Nurses Assn., So. Nursing Rsch. Soc., Am. Assn. for History of Nursing, Sigma Xi, Sigma Theta Tau, Phi Kappa Phi. Avocations: travel, reading.

SHANNON, PETER MICHAEL, JR. lawyer; b. Chgo., Oct. 13, 1928; s. Peter Michael Sr. and Marian (Burke) S.; m. Anne M. Mueller, April 3, 1969; children: Peter III, Stephen, Heather, Eamon. BA, St. Mary of the Lake, Mundelein, Ill., 1949, MA, 1952, STL, 1953; JCL, Gregorian U., Rome, 1958; JD, U. Calif., Berkeley, 1971. Bar: Calif. 1972, D.C. 1972, Ill. 1988, U.S. Dist.

Ct. Md. 1972, U.S. Dist. Ct. D.C. 1972, U.S. Dist. Ct. (no. dist.) Ill. 1988, U.S. Ct. Appeals (1st, 2d, 3d, 4th, 5th, 6th, 7th, 8th, 9th, 10th and D.C. cirs.) 1972-75, U.S. Supreme Ct. 1975. Supervisory atty. litigation U.S. Dept. of Justice, Washington, 1971-75; sr. appellate atty. ICC, 1975-77, dir. enforcement, 1977-80; ptnr. Shannon, et al, 1980-82, Keck, Mahin & Cate, Chgo., 1982-96, Arnstein & Lehr, Chgo., 1996—2001; pvt. practice Peter M. Shannon, Jr., P.C., We. Springs, Fla., 2001—. Author: Energy and Transportation Implications of Ratemaking Policy Concerning Sources of Energy, 1980, Disposition of Real Estate by Religious Institutions, 1987, The Dual Approach of Civil Law Courts to Ecclestical Related Disputes, 1988. Mem. ABA (chmn. transp. com., adminstrv. law and regulatory practice sect. 1984-87, coun. mem. 1988-91), Ill. Bar Assn., Chgo. Bar Assn., Am. Acad. Hosp. Attys., Assn. Transp. Law, Logistics and Policy, Canon Law Soc. (pres. 1965-66), Ctr. for Disability and Elder Law (pres. 1997-99). Office: 4546 Wolf Road Western Springs IL 60558-1562

SHANNON, RICHARD STOLL, III, financial executive; b. N.Y.C., Mar. 22, 1943; s. Richard Stoll Jr. and Margaret (Cather) S.; m. Ann Wright Schmidt, June 14, 1965; children: Clea Cather, Kathryne Baltzelle, Arianna Wright. BA, Stanford U., 1966, MA, 1969; PhD, Harvard U., 1973. Asst. prof. U. Mich., Ann Arbor, 1973-78; mgr., trustee, gen. ptnr. various family trusts, partnerships and corps. Englewood, Colo., 1978-84; pres. Shannon Mgmt. Corp., 1985—. Author: The Arms of Achilles, 1975; editor (with others) Oral Literature and The Formula, 1976. Bd. dirs. Cherryvale Sanitation Dist., Englewood, 1984—, pres., 1986-93; regional chmn. Stanford Ann. Fund/Keystone Project, 1985-98; mem. Rackham Advancement Coun., U. Mich., 1992-97. Teaching fellow Harvard U., 1970-73. Mem. Am. Philol. Assn., Denver C. of C., Cherry Creek Commerce Assn., Cherry Hills Country Club, Denver Petroleum Club, Phi Beta Kappa. Avocations: golf, fishing, reading, research. Office: Shannon Mgmt Corp # 112 3609 South Wadsworth Blvd Lakewood CO 80235

SHANNON, ROBERT RENNIE, optical sciences center administrator, educator; b. Mt. Vernon, N.Y., Oct. 3, 1932; s. Howard A. and Harriebell Shannon; m. Helen Lang, Feb. 13, 1954; children: Elizabeth, Barbara, Jennifer, Amy, John, Robert. BS, U. Rochester, 1954, MA, 1957. Dir. Optics Lab. ITEK Corp., Lexington, Mass., 1959-69; prof. Optical Scis. Ctr., U. Ariz., Tucson, 1969—, dir., 1983-92; prof. emeritus Optical Scis. Ctr., U. Ariz., 1992—. Cons. Lawrence Livermore Lab., 1980-90; trustee Aerospace Corp., 1985-94, 96—; mem. Air Force Sci. Adv. Bd., 1986-90; mem. NRC Commn. on Next Generation currency, 1992-94, NRC Commn. on Optical Sci. and Engring., 1996-97; mem. com. on def. space tech. Air Force Studies Bd., 1989-93, Hubble Telescope Recovery Panel, 1990; mem. tech. adv. bd. Nat. Reconnaissance Office; bd. dirs. Precision Optics Corp., 1999-2001. Editor: Applied Optics and Optical Engineering, Vol. 7, 1980, Vol. 8, 1981, Vol. 9, 1983, Vol. 10, 1987, Vol. 11, 1992, Art and Science of Optical Design, 1997; editor Engring. and Lab. Notes, 1995-98. Fellow Optical Soc. Am. (pres. 1985, mem. engring. coun. 1989-91), Soc. Photo-Optical Instrumentation Engrs. (pres. 1979-80, mem. SPIE/OSA jt. task force 1998, Goddard award 1982, Gold medal 1996), treas. internat. commn. for optics, 1993-99; mem. NAE, Tucson Soaring Club (past pres.), Sigma Xi. Home: 7040 E Taos Pl Tucson AZ 85715-3344 Office: U Ariz Optical Scis Ctr Tucson AZ 85721-0001 E-mail: rshannon@u.arizona.edu.

SHANNON, STEPHEN CURTIS, dean, occupational health physician; b. Frederick, Md., Dec. 9, 1948; s. James Lee and Mary Catherine (Fry) S.; m. Barbara Jean Winterson, Jul. 31, 1971; children: Joyce Megan Shannon-Winterson, Sally Catherine Shannon-Winterson. BA in hist., U. Md., 1971, MA in Am. hist., 1975; DO, U. New Eng. Coll. Osteopathic Medicine, 1986; MPH, Harvard U., 1990. Diplomate Am. Bd. Preventive Medicine and Family Practice. Program mgr. WESM-FM Radio, Prince Frederick, Md., 1971-73; instr. Am. hist. U. Md., College Park, 1973-79; congl. rels. analyst U.S. Dept. Energy, Washington, 1979-80; family practice resident Brighton Medical Ctr., Portland, Maine, 1986-88; preventive medicine resident U. Mass. Medical Ctr., Worcester, Mass., 1988-90; medical epidemiologist Mass. Dept. Pub. Health, Boston, 1990-92; asst. prof. U. New Eng. Coll. Osteopathic Medicine, Biddeford, Maine, 1990-95; medical dir. Ctr. Health Promotion Brighton Medical Ctr., 1991-95; dir. occupational health Maine Bureau of Health, Augusta, 1990-95; acting dean U. New Eng. Coll. Osteo. Medicine, 1995—. Med. epidemiologist cons. Maine Bur. Health, 1990-91; chair occupational health sect. Brighton Med. Ctr., 1994—. Editor: The Maryland Historian, 1976-78; contbr. articles to profl. jours. Exec. com. York County Health Svcs. Bd., Saco, Maine; bd. dirs. Maine Inst. Occupational Health Edn., Waterville, Maine, 1993—, Brighton Consortium, 1991—. Recipient New Eng. Found. Osteopathic Medicine award, 1986, U.S. Sec. Health & Human Svcs. award for Health Promotion, 1984, Ciby-Geigy award for Outstanding Comm. Svc., 1984, fellow William Randolph Hearst, U. Md., 1979. Mem. Am. Pub. Health Assn., Maine Pub. Health Assn. (bd. dirs. 1993—), Am. Osteopathic Assn., Maine Osteopathic, Physicians for Nat. Health Program, Am. Coll. Occupational & Environ. Medicine. Democrat. Avocations: canoeing, hiking, camping, writing, reading. Office: U New Eng 11 Hills Beach Rd Biddeford ME 04005-9599*

SHANNON, THOMAS ALFRED, retired educational association administrator emeritus; b. Milw., Jan. 2, 1932; s. John Elwood and Eleanor Ann (Mitchell) S.; m. Barbara Ann Weidner, June 26, 1954; children: Thomas Alfred, Paul J., Suzanne L., Terrence D. BS, U. Wis, 1954; JD, U. Minn., 1961. Bar: Minn. 1961, Calif. 1963, U.S. Supreme Ct. 1965, D.C. 1977, Va. 1984; Life cert. as sch. adminstr., Calif.; cert. assoc. exec. Am. Soc. Assn. Execs. Pvt. practice law, Mpls., 1961-62; schs. atty. San Diego City Schs., 1962-73; dept. supt., gen. counsel, 1973-77; exec. dir. Nat. Sch. Bds. Assn., Washington, 1977-97, ret., 1997. Adj. prof. law and edn. U. San Diego; vis. prof. edn. U. Va.; adv. mem. Edn. Commn. of States; prof. Nat. Acad. Sch. Execs., 1971—; legal counsel Am. Assn. Sch. Adminstrs., 1973-77; adj. prof. edn. adminstrn. George Washington U., 1996-97. Exec. pub. The Am. Sch. Bd. Jour., 1977-96, Exec. Educator, 1978-96, Sch. Bd. News, 1981-96. Chmn. San Diego County Juvenile Justice Commn., 1973-74; mem. nat. coun. Boy Scouts Am., 1979-97; bd. dirs. Found. for Teaching Econ., San Francisco, 1993—. With USN, 1954-59. Mem. VFW (life), Am. Bar Assn. (chmn. com. public edn. 1978-82), Nat. Orgn. on Legal Problems of Edn. (pres. 1973), Nat. Sch. Bds. Assn. (chmn. council sch. attys. 1967-69) Home: 3811 26th St N Arlington VA 22207-5241 E-mail: tombar2@juno.com.

SHANNON, WILLIAM NORMAN, III, marketing and international business educator, food service executive; b. Chgo., Nov. 20, 1937; s. William Norman Jr. and Lee (Lewis) S.; m. Bernice Urbanowicz, July 14, 1962; children: Kathleen Kelly, Colleen Patricia, Kerrie Ann. BS in Indsl. Mgmt., Carnegie Inst. Tech., 1959; MBA in Mktg. Mgmt., U. Toledo, 1963. Sales engr. Westinghouse Electric Co., Detroit, 1959-64; regional mgr. Toledo Scale, Chgo., 1964-70; v.p. J. Lloyd Johnson Assoc., Northbrook, Ill., 1970-72; mgr. spl. projects Hobart Mfg., Troy, Ohio, 1972-74; corp. v.p. mktg. Berkel, Inc., La Porte, Ind., 1974-79; gen. mgr. Berkel Products, Ltd., Toronto, Can., 1975-78; chmn. Avant Industries, Inc., Wheeling, Ill., 1979-81; chmn., pres. Hacienda Mexican Restaurants, South Bend, Ind., 1978—; chmn. Ziker Shannon Corp., 1982-88, Hacienda Franchising Group, Inc., South Bend, Ind., 1987—. Assoc. prof. mktg. and internat. bus. St. Mary's Coll., Notre Dame, Ind., 1982—; chmn. Hacienda Franchise Group, Inc., 1987-96, Hacienda Mex. Restaurants Mgmt., Inc., 1994-96; sr. chmn. Hacienda Mex. Restaurants, 1996—; mem. London program faculty, 1986, 89, 92, 94, coord. internat. bus. curriculum, 1989—, mktg. curriculum, 1983, 88, 95—; advisor Coun. Internat. Bus. Devel., Notre Dame, 1991—; mng. dir. Alden & Torch Lake Railway, 1995—. Co-author: Laboratory Computers, 1971; columnist small bus. Bus. Digest mag., 1988—; bd. editors Jour. Bus. and Indsl. Mktg., 1986—; mem. bd. editorial advisors South Bend Tribune Business Weekly, 1990—; contbr. articles to profl. jours. V.p. mktg. Jr. Achievement, South Bend, Ind., 1987-90; pres. Small Bus. Devel. Coun., South Bend., 1987-90; bd. dirs. Ind. Small Bus. Coun., Indpls., 1986—, Mental Health Assn., South Bend, 1987-90, Michiana World Trade Orgn., Internat. Bus. Edn., 1989-91; Entrepreneurs Alliance Ind., 1988-92, Nat. Small Bus. United, Washington, 1989-92, Women's Bus. Initiative, 1986-90, dir. ednl. confs., 1986-90; chmn. bd. trustees, Holy Cross Coll., Notre Dame, Ind., 1987—, chmn. edn. com., 1993—; chmn. St. Joseph County Higher Edn. Coun., 1988-91, Nat. Coun. Small Bus., Washington, 1988—; Midwest region adv. coun. U.S. SBA, 1988-91; at-large mem. U.S. Govt. Adv. Coun. on Small Bus., Washington, 1988-90, 1994—, chmn. Bus. and Econ. Devel. Com., 1988-90, 1994—; vice chmn. Internat. Trade Com., 1994—; mem. nat. adv. coun. Women's Network for Entrepreneur Tng., 1991—; mem., vice chmn. State of Ind. Enterprise Zone Bd., 1991—; elected del. White House Conf. Small Bus., Washington, 1986; bd. dirs. Ind. Small Bus. Devel. Ctrs. Adv. Bd. Named Small Bus. Person of the Yr., City of South Bend, 1987, Small Bus. Advocate of the Yr., State of Ind., 1987, Ind. Entrepreneur Advocate of the Yr., 1988. Mem. Am. Mktg. Assn. (chmn. Mich./Ind. chpt., pres. 1985-86), U.S. Assn. Small Bus. and Entrepreneurship (nat. v.p. for entrepreneurship edn. 1991-92, nat. v.p. entrepreneurship devel. 1992—), Ind. Inst. New Bus. Ventures (mktg. faculty 1987-91), Michiana Investment Network (vice chmn. 1988-91), SBA (adminstrn. adv. coun. 1988—, contbg. editor Our Town Michiana mag. 1988-91), U.S. C. of C., Nat. Coun. Small Bus. (Washington), South Bend C. of C. (bd. dirs. 1987—, vice chmn. membership 1993—), Assn. for Bus. Communications (co-chmn. Internat. Conf. 1986), Univ. Club Notre Dame (vice chmn.), Shamrock Club Notre Dame (exec. dir., trustee 1993—), Rotary. Roman Catholic. Home: 2920 S Twyckenham Dr South Bend IN 46614-2116 Office: Saint Mary's Coll Dept Bus Adminstrn Eco Notre Dame IN 46556 *Enjoy good fortune resulting from LUCK, an acronym for (L) Learning how to (U)Use your talents with genuine (C) Concern on how your (K) Knowlege can benefit others.*

SHANNON-HALLAM, ISABELLE LOUISE, education director; b. Newton, Mass., Sept. 5, 1934; d. Clarence Edward and Evelyn Florence (Peters) Overlock; m. Albert M. Shannon, Dec. 20, 1970 (div. 1982); children: Clare Louise Lord, William Christopher Lord; m. O. Keith Hallam, July 18, 1998. BA in French, Wheaton (Ill.) Coll., 1956; MA in French Lit., Boston U., 1970; PhD in Comparative and Internat. Edn., Mich. State U., East Lansing, 1977. Cert. French tchr., instrnl. supr., Va., French tchr., Mass. Tchr. French Belmont (Mass.) High Sch., 1966-70, East Lansing Pub. Schs., 1973-77; outreach dir. Can. Studies Ctr. Duke U., Durham, N.C., 1977-79; prof., dir. secondary edn. Va. Wesleyan Coll., Norfolk, 1979-98, coord. edn. dept., 1997-98, prof. emeritus, 1998—. Presenter in field; reviewer Longman Pubs., N.Y.C., 1987—; evaluator, tchr. edn. programs Va. Dept. Edn., 1985-87. Host, program cons. Options in Edn., WHRV-FM, Norfolk, 1991-95; contbr. articles to profl. jours. Mem. adminstrv. bd. Cmty. United Meth. Ch., Virginia Beach, Va., 1985-92, chair, 1988, chair staff parish com., 1995-97, mem. bldg. com., 1999—; mem. Va. Symphony League, Norfolk, 1986-89; bd. dirs. Norfolk Sister Cities, 1987-92. Mem. ASCD, Assn. Tchr. Educators, Va. Assn. Colls. Tchr. Edn. (exec. bd. 1985-86, 90-94, pres.-elect 1992-94), Am. Assn. Coll. Tchr. Edn. (chief instl. rep. 1992-98), Assn. Ind. Liberal Arts Colls. Tchr. Edn. Avocations: reading, genealogy, bridge, art, travel. E-mail: ihallam@cox.net.

SHANNY, RAMY, physicist; b. Jerusalem, Israel, Nov. 6, 1935; s. Meir and Batia Shanny, Batia Shanny; m. Laura Eileen Hamilton; children: Emily, 0000 0000; m. Shula Dafny (div. Dec. 0, 1976); children: Ronnit, Micky. PhD, Princeton U. Rsch. physicist GE, Valley Forge, Pa., 1968—69, Naval Rsch. Lab., Washington, 1969—70, br. head, 1970—71; exec. v.p. Inesco Inc., La Jolla, Calif., 1972—82; pres. Advanced Power Technologies, Inc., Washington, 1986—. Exec. v.p. Inesco Inc., La Jolla, Calif., 1972—82. Recipient Exec. Svc. award, Naval Rsch. Lab., 1974. Fellow: Am.Phys. Soc.; mem.: IEE, N.Y. Acad. Sci. Home: 1412 21st St Nw Washington DC 20036 Office: Advanced Power Technologies, Inc. 1250 24th St Nw 3d Fl Washington DC 20037 Home Fax: 202-223-1377; Office Fax: 202-223-1377. Personal E-mail: shanny@apti.com. Business E-Mail: shanny@apti.com.

SHANSBY, JOHN GARY, investor; b. Seattle, Aug. 25, 1937; s. John Jay and Jule E. (Boyer) S.; m. Joyce Ann Dunsmore, June 21, 1959 (div.); children: Sheri Lee, Kimberly Ann, Jay Thomas; m. Barbara Anderson De Meo, Jan. 1, 1983 (div.); m. Jane Robinson Dettner, May 1, 1990. BA, U. Wash., 1959. Mktg. exec. Colgate-Palmolive Co., N.Y.C., 1959-67; subs. pres. Am. Home Products Corp., 1968-71; v.p. Clorox Co., Oakland, Calif., 1972-73; ptnr. Booz, Allen & Hamilton, San Francisco, 1974-75; chmn. bd., chief exec. officer, dir. Shaklee Corp., 1975-86; mng. gen. ptnr. The Shansby Group, 1986—. Former chmn. Calif. State Commn. for Rev. of Master Plan Higher Edn.; founder J. Gary Shansby chair mktg. strtegy U. Calif., Berkeley; trustee Calif. State U. Mem. San Francisco C. of C. (past pres.), Villa Traverna Club, Pennask Lake Fishing Club (B.C.), Sky Club of N.Y.C., Sigma Nu. Republican. Office: The Shansby Group 250 Montgomery St San Francisco CA 94104-3406

SHAO, DALEI, molecular biologist, researcher; b. Hangzhou, Zhejiang province, China, Jan. 27, 1970; d. Deyu Shao and Liquan Wu; m. Yihe Wang. PhD, Hahnemann U., 1996. Sr. scientist Wyeth Ayerst Rsch., Collegeville, Pa., 1999—; postdoctoral fellow U. Pa., Phila., 1996—99. Recipient Nat. Rsch. Svc. award, NIH, 1998—99. Mem.: N.Y. Acad. Sci. Achievements include research in modulating nuclear receptor function. Office: Wyeth Ayerst Rsch 500 Arcola Rd Collegeville PA 19426

SHAO COLLINS, JEANNINE, magazine publisher; married; 1 child. BA in Econs., U. Rochester. Various advt. sales mgmt. positions Woman's Day, N.Y.C., Prevention mag.; N.Y. advt. mgr. Ladies' Home Jour., Meredith Corp., N.Y.C., 1993-95, advt. dir. Better Homes and Gardens, Des Moines, 1995-98, assoc. pub., 1998-99, pub., 1999—, v.p., 2000—. Office: Better Homes and Gardens 1716 Locust Street Des Moines IA 50309-3023*

SHAPAZIAN, ROBERT MICHAEL, publishing executive; b. Fresno, Calif. s. Ara Michael and Margaret (Azhderian) S. BA, U. Calif., 1964; AM, Harvard U., 1965, PhD in Renaissance English and Fine Arts, 1970. Design assoc. Arthur Elrod Assocs., L.A., 1971-73; v.p. El Mar Corp, Fresno, Calif., 1973-87; dir., art dir. The Lapis Press, Venice, 1987—. Mem. photographic forum San Francisco Mus. Art, 1982-85, Mus. Modern Art, N.Y.C., 1985; mem. photographic com. Met. Mus. Art, N.Y.C., 1994; dir. Gagosian Gallery, L.A. Author: Metaphorics of Artificiality, 1970, Maurice Tabard, 1985; editor: Surrealists Look at Art, 1991 (AIGA award 1991, N.Y. Art Dirs. award 1991), A Witch, 1992 (AIGA award 1992, N.Y. Art Dirs. award 1992, L.A. Art Dirs. award 1992), Pacific Wall (AIGA award 1993), Albucius (We. Art Dirs. award 1993, N.Y. Art Dirs. award 1994), Sam Francis: Saturated Blue, Writings from the Notebooks, 1996. Bd. dirs. Big Brothers/Big Sisters, Fresno, Calif., 1980-82, Film Forum, L.A., 1984-86, Grunwald Ctr. for Graphic Arts, UCLA, 1996—. Recipient Individual Achievement award Lit. Market Pl., N.Y.C., 1992, 23 awards for art direction and design; named Chevalier in Order of Arts and Letters, Govt. of France. Mem. Harvard Club (N.Y.C.). Avocations: twentieth century art, illustrated books, experimental photography.

SHAPER, CHRISTOPHER THORNE, sales executive; b. Columbus, Ohio, Sept. 6, 1955; s. Charles R. and M. Caroline (Garringer) S. BA, Wake Forest U., 1977; MA in Mgmt., Coll. of Notre Dame, 1992. Sales rep. Intex Products Inc., Winston-Salem, N.C., 1978; tech. sales rep. Am. Can Co., Oak Brook, Ill., 1979-81, J.T. Baker Chem. Co., Atlanta, 1981-83; corp. accts. rep. Erachem Comilog, Inc., Balt., 1983-84, industry sales mgr., 1984-92, dir. mktg. and sales, 1992–. Mem. Am. Chem. Soc., Am. Feed Industries Assn. Republican. Roman Catholic. Avocations: sports, reading. Office: Erachem Comilog 610 Pittman Rd Baltimore MD 21226-1792 E-mail: CShaper@Erachem-Comilog.com.

SHAPERE, DUDLEY, philosophy educator; b. Harlingen, Tex., May 27, 1928; s. Dudley and Corinne (Pupkin) S.; m. Hannah Hardgrave; children—Hannah Elizabeth, Christine Ann; children by previous marriage: Alfred Dudley, Catherine Lucretia. BA, Harvard U., 1949, MA, 1955, PhD, 1957. Instr. philosophy Ohio State U., 1957-60; asst. prof. U. Chgo., 1960-65, asso. prof., 1965-67, prof., 1967-72, mem. com. on evolutionary biology, 1969-72, chmn. undergrad. program in history and philosophy of sci., 1966-72, chmn. com. on conceptual founds. sci., 1970-72; prof. U. Ill., Urbana, 1972-75, chmn. program in history and philosophy of sci., 1972-75; prof. U. Md., College Park, 1975-84; Z. Smith Reynolds prof. philosophy and history of sci. Wake Forest U., 1984—2002; ret., 2002. Mem. com. on history and philosophy of sci. U. Md., 1975-84; chmn. program in history and philosophy of sci. U. Md., 1983-84.; vis. prof. Rockefeller U., 1965-66, Harvard U., 1968; mem. Inst. Advanced Study, Princeton, N.J., 1978-79, 81, 89, Otto Neugebaur fellow, 2001; spl. cons. (program dir.) program in history and philosophy of sci. NSF, 1966-75; Sigma Xi nat. bicentennial lectr., 1974-77. Author: Philosophical Problems of Natural Science, 1965, Galileo: A Philosophical Study, 1974, Reason and the Search for Knowledge, 1984; editorial bd.: Philosophy of Sci., Studies in History and Philosophy of Sci.; rev. bd.: Philosophy Research Archives; contbr. articles to profl. jours. Served with AUS, 1950-52. Recipient Quantrell award for excellence in undergrad. teaching U. Chgo., 1968; Disting. Scholar-Tchr. award U. Md., 1979-80 Fellow AAAS (sec. sec. 1972); mem. APA, Philosophy of Sci. Assn., History of Sci. Soc., Am. Philos. Assn., Acad. Internat. de Philosophie des Scis. Home: 3125 Turkey Hill Ct Winston Salem NC 27106-4951 E-mail: shapere@wfu.edu.

SHAPERO, HARRIS JOEL, pediatrician; b. Winona, Minn., Nov. 22, 1930; s. Charles and Minnie Sara Shapero; m. Byong Soon Yu, Nov. 6, 1983; children by previous marriage: Laura, Bradley, James, Charles. AA, UCLA, 1953; BS, Northwestern U., 1954, MD, 1957. Diplomate in occup. medicine Am. Bd. Preventive Medicine; qualified med. evaluator Indsl. Med. Coun.; ind. med. examiner, Calif.; cert. aviation medicine FAA. Intern Los Angeles County-Harbor Gen. Hosp., 1957-58, resident in pediatrics, 1958-60, staff physician, 1960-64; attending physician Perceptually Handicapped Children's Clinic, 1960-63; disease control officer for Tb Los Angeles County Health Dept., 1962-64; pvt. practice medicine specializing in pediatrics and occup. medicine, Cypress, Calif., 1965-86; pediatric cons. L.A. Health Dept., 1983-85, disease control officer sexually transmitted diseases, 1968-78; emergency rm. dir. AMI, Anaheim, Calif., 1968-85; mem. med. staff Anaheim Gen. Hosp., Beach Cmty. Hosp., Norwalk Cmty. Hosp.; courtesy staff Palm Harbor Gen. Hosp., Bellflower City Hosp.; pediatric staff Hosp. de General, Ensenada, Mex., 1978—; primary care clinician Sacramento County Health, 1987-88; practice medico-legal evaluation, 1986-92. Founder Calif. Legal Evaluation Med. Group; apptd. med. examiner in preventive and occup. medicine State of Calif. Dept. Indsl. Rels., 1989; health care provider, advisor City of Anaheim, City of Buena Park, City of Cypress, City of Garden Grove, Cypress Sch. Dist., Magnolia Sch. Dist., Savanna Sch. Dist., Anaheim Unified Shc. Dist., Orange County Dept. Edn.; pediatric and Tv cons. numerous other orgns.; FAA med. examiner; founder Pan Am. Childrens Mission. Author: The Silent Epidemic, 1979. Named Headliner in Medicine, Orange County Press Club, 1978. Fellow Am. Coll. Preventive Medicine; mem. Los Angeles County Med. Assn., Los angeles County Indsl. Med. Asns., Am. Pub. Health Assn., Mex.-Am. Border Health Assn. Republican. Jewish. Avocations: antique books and manuscripts, photography, graphics, beekeeping. Home: PO Box 228 Wilton CA 95693-0228 Office: 5411 Madison Ave Ste 1 Sacramento CA 95841-3151 E-mail: hjswilton2000@yahoo.com.

SHAPIRO, ADAM MARC, otolaryngologist; b. N.Y.C., 1960; s. Stanley and Dee S.; m. Pamela Beth Berkowsky. BA, Cornell U., 1982; MD, George Washington U., 1986. Diplomate Am. Bd. Otolaryngology, Nat. Bd. Med. Examiners. Assoc. Maliner & Clark, Hollywood, Fla., 1992-93, Assocs. Otolaryngology, Reston, Va., 1993—2002, V.I. Ear, Nose and Throat, St. Thomas, 2002—. Clin. asst. prof. otolaryngology George Washington U. Hosp., Washington. Contbr. articles to profl. jours. Fellow ACS, Am. Acad. Otolaryngology, Am. Rhinologic Soc.; mem. Am. Acad. Otolaryngic Allergy, AMA, Am. Acad. Facial Plastic and Reconstructive Surgery. Avocations: comml. pilot, scuba diving, marine aquarist, skiing, bicycling. Office: VI Ear Nose & Throat VI Med Found Bldg Ste 111 9150 Estate Thomas Saint Thomas VI 00802

SHAPIRO, ALAN MEYER, meteorology educator, researcher; b. Seattle, Sept. 28, 1962; s. Bernard and Isabel Jane (Gallagher) S.; m. Sandra Jean Diez-Luckie, Aug. 12, 1991. BS, Cornell U., 1983; MA, Johns Hopkins U., 1985, PhD, 1987. Postdoctoral scientist Nat. Meteorol. Ctr., Camp Springs, Md., 1987-89, Ctr. for Analysis and Prediction of Storms, Norman, Okla., 1990, rsch. scientist, 1991-92, sr. rsch. scientist, 1993-95; asst. prof. meteorology U. Okla., 1996-2001, assoc. prof., 2001—. Contbr. articles to profl. jours. Mem. AAAS, Am. Meteorol. Soc., Am. Math. Soc., Am. Geophys. Union, Soc. for Indsl. and Applied Math. Avocations: origami, hiking, sailing. Home: 2821 Astor Dr Norman OK 73072-2262 Office: U Okla 100 E Boyd St Rm 1310 Norman OK 73019-1015

SHAPIRO, ALEENA RIEGER, lawyer; b. Jaslo, Poland; m. Richard A. Shapiro; children: Randi, Deborah. JD, NYU, 1981, LLM in Taxation, 1985. Bar: N.Y. 1982, U.S. Dist. Ct. (so. and ea. dists.) N.Y. 1982, U.S. Tax Ct. 1982. Ptnr. Shapiro and Wender, L.L.P., 1997—; prin. Aleena R. Shapiro, Atty., N.Y.C., 1989-97; assoc. Willkie Farr & Gallagher, 1981-84, Battle Fowler, N.Y.C., 1984-87, Patterson, Belknap Webb & Tyler, N.Y.C., 1987-89. Mem. ABA (tax sect.), N.Y. State Bar Assn. (tax sect.), Assn. of Bar of City of N.Y. E-mial. Office: 230 Park Ave Fl 26 New York NY 10169-2699

SHAPIRO, ALLAN DAVID, plant biology educator; b. Cleve., Oct. 27, 1965; s. Paul Y. and Susan T. Shapiro; m. Gina Beth Dyen-Shapiro, Aug. 1, 1993; children: Danielle Amanda, Andrew Scott. BS, MIT, 1988; PhD, Stanford U., 1994. Post-doctoral fellow U. Calif., Berkeley, 1994-97; asst. prof. dept. plant and soil scis. U. Del., Newark, 1997—, asst. prof. dept. biol. scis., 1999—. Office: Univ Del Del Biotech Inst 15 Innovation Way Newark DE 19711 E-mail: ashapiro@udel.edu.

SHAPIRO, ANNA, microbiologist, researcher; b. N.Y.C., Jan. 11, 1910; d. Samuel and Esther (Cohen) Lewis; m. Joseph Shapiro, Feb. 7, 1933 (dec. 1985); children: Joan Elisabeth Brandston (dec.), Joel Elias. BS in Biology and Chemistry, NYU, 1931, MS in Bacteriology, 1934, PhD in Microbiology, 1971. Lab. asst. Bellevue Med. Sch., NYU, 1931-33, instr., 1933-36; lectr. Hofstra U., L.I., 1963, Queensborough U., CUNY, Queens, 1964; rsch. asst. Haskins Lab. of Pace Univ., N.Y.C., 1971-80, rsch. assoc., 1980-83. Author: Methods of Enzymology, 1980, The In Vitro Cultivation of Pathogens of Tropical Diseases, 1980; contbr. articles to profl. jours. Mem. AAAS, N.Y. Acad. Sci. (Disting. Svc. award 1992), Sigma Xi. Achievements include rsch. in the conversion of Nitrobacter agilis from a strict autotroph to a heterotroph by using replica plating techniques which can be considered an adaptive mutation; blockade of respiratory systems of parasites by using iron chelators--this work led to research in pathogenic African trypanosomes. Home: 2 Fifth Ave Apt 9J New York NY 10011

SHAPIRO, ASCHER HERMAN, mechanical engineer, educator, consultant; b. Bklyn., May 20, 1916; s. Bernard and Jennie (Kaplan) S.; m. Sylvia Charm, Dec. 24, 1939 (div. 1959); children: Peter Mark, Martha Ann, Bernett Mary; m. Regina Julia Lee, June 4, 1961 (div. 1972); m. Kathleen Larke Crawford, Sept. 6, 1985. Student, CCNY, 1932-35; SB, MIT, 1938, ScD, 1946; DSc (hon.), Salford U., Eng., 1978, Technion-Israel Inst. Tech., 1985. Asst. mech. engring. MIT, 1938-40, faculty, 1940—, prof. mech. engring., 1952—, prof. charge fluid mechanics divsn., mech. engring. dept., 1954-65, Ford prof. engring., 1962-75, chmn. faculty, 1964-65, head dept. mech. engring., 1965-74, inst. prof., 1975-86, inst. prof. emeritus, sr. lectr., 1986—; vis. prof. applied thermodynamics U. Cambridge, Eng., 1955-56; Akroyd Stuart Meml. lectr. Nottingham (Eng.) U., 1956; editor Acad. Press, Inc., 1962-65. Cons. United Aircraft Corp., M.W. Kellogg Co., Arthur D. Little, Inc., Hardie-Tynes Mfg. Co., Carbon & Carbide Chems. Corp., Oak Ridge, Rohm & Haas Co., Ultrasonic Corp., Jackson & Moreland (Engrs.), Stone & Webster, Bendix Aviation, Oak Ridge Nat. Lab., Acushnet Processing Co., Kennecott Copper Co., Welch Sci., Sargent-Welch, Bird Machine Co., Organogenesis, Inc., CARR Separations, Inc., others; served on sub-coms. on turbines, internal flow, compressors and turbines NACA; mem. Lexington Project to study and report on nuclear powered flight to AEC, summer 1948; dir. Project Dynamo to study and report to AEC on technol. and econs. nuclear power for civilian use, 1953, Lamp Wick study Office Naval Research, 1955; mem. tech. adv. panel aeronautics Dept. Def.; cons. ops. evaluation group Navy Dept.; sci. adv. bd. USAF, 1964-66; founder, mem. Nat. Com. for Fluid Mechanics Films, 1962— , chmn., 1962-65, 71— ; chmn. com. on ednl. films Commn. on Engring. Edn., 1962-65; dir. lab. for devel. power plants for use in torpedoes Navy Dept., 1943-45; mem. ad hoc med. devices com. FDA, HEW, 1970-72; mem. com. Nat. Council for Research and Devel., Israel, 1971— ; mem. com. sci. and pub. policy Nat. Acad. Scis., 1970-74 Author: The Dynamics and Thermodynamics of Compressible Fluid Flow, vol. 1, 1953, vol. 2, 1954 (with Chinese translation), Shape and Flow, 1961 (Japanese, Italian, German and Spanish translations); also 3 ednl. films, 39 videotape lecture series: Fluid Dynamics, 1984; contbr. over 130 articles to sci. jours.; mem. editl. bd. Applied Mechanics, 1955-56; mem. editl. com. Ann. Rev. Fluid Mechanics, 1967-71; mem. editl. bd. MIT Press, 1977-87, chmn., 1982-87; patentee fluid metering equipment, combustion chamber, propulsion apparatus, gas turbine aux., magnetic disc, magnetic disc storage device, vacuum pump (2), low-density wind tunnel, recipe calculator, decanter. Mem. Town Meeting

Arlington, Mass.; chmn. 1st Mass. chpt. Atlantic Union Com., 1951-52, mem. council, 1954—; bd. govs. Technion, Israel Inst. Tech., 1968-89. Recipient Naval Ordnance Devel. award, 1945; joint certificate outstanding contbn. War and Navy depts., 1947; Richards Meml. award ASME, 1960; Worcester Reed Warner medal, 1965; Fluids Engring. award, 1981; Townsend Harris medal Coll. City N.Y., 1978 Fellow AIAA, ASME (hon., Richards Meml. award 1960, Worcester Reed Warner medal 1965, Fluids Engring. award 1981, Daniel C. Drucker medal 1999), Am. Acad. Arts and Scis. (councillor 1967-71); mem. AAAS, NAS (sci. and pub. policy com. 1973-77), Am. Sci. Films Assn., Nat. Acad. Engring. (adv. com. on edn. 1985-89), Am. Inst. Med. and Biol. Engring. (founding fellow), Biomed. Engring. Soc. (charter mem. 1968), Am. Soc. Engring. Edn. (Lamme medal 1977), MIT Faculty Club, Cavendish Club (Brookline, Mass.), Sigma Xi, Tau Beta Pi, Pi Tau Sigma. Home: 111 Perkins St Apt 86 Jamaica Plain MA 02130-4320

SHAPIRO, BRAHM, nuclear medicine physician, endocrinologist; b. Johannesburg, South Africa, Feb. 2, 1949; came to U.S., 1979; s. Norman and Claudia (Botha) S.; m. Lorraine Marilyn Fig, January 26, 1975; children: Jonathan Daniel, Bernard Joel. MB BChir, U. Cape Town, South Africa, 1973, PhD, 1978; student, Hammersmith Hosp., London, 1975; MSc in Nuc. Medicine, U. London, 1979. Diplomate Am. Bd. Nuc. Medicine. Intern Groote Schuur Hosp., Cape Town, 1974, resident, 1974-76-78; fellow in endocrinology U. Cape Town, 1976-78; registrar in nuc. medicine St. Bartholomew's Hosp., London, 1978-79; fellow in endocrinology U. Mich., Ann Arbor, 1979-81, from asst. prof. to prof. internal medicine, 1981—, prof. radiology, 2000—; mem. staff VA Med. Ctr., 1992—. Editor Internal Medicine; Clin. Exptl., 1992—, Thyroidology; Clin. Lab., 1993—; mem. editl. bd. Nuc. Medicine Comm. 1996—, Jour. Nuc. Medicine, 1999; contbr. over 90 chpts. to books, over 225 articles to profl. jours. Fellow Am. Coll. Endocrinology; mem. NRA, Am. Thyroid Assn., Soc. Nuc. Medicine, Endocrine Soc., European Assn. Nuc. Medicine, Jews Preservation Firearms Ownership, Alpha Omega Alpha (hon.). Avocations: medical history, marksmanship, metal working. Home: 1484 Green Rd Ann Arbor MI 48105-2808 Office: U Mich Med Ctr 1500 East Med Ctr Dr Ann Arbor MI 48109 E-mail: brshapir@umich.edu.

SHAPIRO, BURTON LEONARD, oral pathologist, geneticist, educator; b. N.Y.C., Mar. 29, 1934; s. Nat Lazarus and Fay Rebecca (Gartenhouse) S.; m. Eileen Roman, Aug. 11, 1958; children— Norah Leah, Anne Rachael, Carla Faye. Student, Tufts U., 1951-54; D.D.S., NYU, 1958; MS, U. Minn., 1962, PhD, 1966. Faculty U. Minn. Sch. Dentistry, Mpls., 1962—, assoc. prof. div. oral pathology, 1966-70, prof., chmn. div. oral biology, 1970-79, prof., chmn. dept. oral biology, 1979-88, prof. dept. oral pathology and genetics, 1979-88, dir. grad. studies, mem. grad. faculty genetics, 1966—, prof. dept. oral sci., 1988—, mem. grad. faculty pathobiology, 1979; prof. dept. lab. medicine and pathology U. Minn. Sch. Medicine, 1985—, mem. Human Genetics Inst., 1988—, univ. senator, 1968-72, 88-93; also mem. med. staff U. Minn. Health Scis. Center; exec. com. Grad. Sch. U. Minn., chmn. health scis. policy rev. council, chmn. univ. faculty consultative com., 1988-92; chmn. univ. fin. and planning com. Grad. Sch. U. Minn., 1988. Hon. research fellow Galton Lab. dept. human genetics Univ. Coll., London, 1974; spl. vis. prof. Japanese Ministry Edn., Sci. and Culture, 1983 Mem. adv. editorial bd.: Jour. Dental Research, 1971— ; Contbr. articles to profl. jours. Served to lt. USNR, 1958-60. Am. Cancer Soc. postdoctoral fellow, 1960-62; advanced fellow, 1965-68; named Century Club Prof. of Yr., 1988. Fellow Am. Acad. Oral Pathology, AAAS; mem. Internat. Assn. Dental Research (councilor 1969), Am. Soc. Human Genetics, Craniofacial Biology Soc. (pres. 1972), Sigma Xi, Omicron Kappa Upsilon. Home: 148 Nina St # 2 Saint Paul MN 55102-2160 Office: U Minn Sch Dentistry Dept Oral Sci Minneapolis MN 55455 E-mail: burt@umn.edu.

SHAPIRO, DAVID, artist, art historian; b. N.Y.C., Aug. 28, 1916; s. Jacob and Ida (Katz) S.; m. Cecile Peyser, June 18, 1944; children: Deborah Jane, Anna Roberta. Student, Ednl. Alliance Art Sch., 1933-35, Am. Artists Sch., 1936-39. Instr. Smith Coll., 1946-47, Bklyn. Coll., summer, 1947; asst. prof. art U. B.C., 1947-49; mem. faculty dept. art New Coll., Hofstra U., 1961—63; prof. fine art New Coll., Hofstra U., 1972—81, prof. emeritus, 1981—; prof. fine art, artist-in-residence U. Belgrade, Yugoslavia, 1981. Vis. critic Vt. Studio Ctr., Johnson, Vt., 1990. Author: Social Realism: Art as a Weapon, 1973, Abstract Expressionism: A Critical Record, 1989; one-man shows include Ganso Gallery, N.Y.C., 1955, Milch Gallery, N.Y.C., 1958, 61, 63, Galleria Dell'Orso, Milan, 1971, U. Belgrade Gallery, 1981; 50 yr. retrospective T.W. Wood Art Gallery, Vt. Coll. Arts Ctr., 1987; represented in permanent collections Bklyn. Mus., Met. Mus., Libr. Congress, Nat. Mus., Smithsonian Instn., Phila. Mus. Art. Fulbright grantee, 1951-52, 52-53; MacDowell fellow, 1976; Tamarind fellow, 1976; Nat. Endowment Arts, grantee, 1978; Fulbright grantee, 1980-81. Mem. Soc. Am. Graphic Artists (pres. 1968-70), L.A. Printmakers, Coll. Art Assn. Home: 453 Atkinson Rd Cavendish VT 05142-9602 Home (Winter): 926 Ave Majorca Apt O Laguna Woods CA 92653 *My work and my family are the main interests in my life. Both make it very worthwhile.*

SHAPIRO, DAVID BENJAMIN, researcher; b. Chgo., Apr. 7, 1954; s. Leopold Julius and Virginia Lucille Shapiro. BA, Reed Coll., 1982; MA, Northwestern U., Evanston, Ill., 1986, U. Chgo., 1988; postgrad., U. Ill.-Chgo., 1995—. Computer operator Joslyn Mfg., Chgo., 1974—75; rschr. Survey Ctr., 1982—83; rsch. analyst AMA, 1988—89, United Way, Chgo., 1990—92; rschr. Inst. on Disability and Human Devel., U. Ill., 1993—95. Mem.: Am. Polit. Sci. Assn. Avocations: reading, parrots.

SHAPIRO, DAVID L. lawyer; b. Corsicana, Tex., May 19, 1936; s. Harry and Alice (Laibovitz) S. BA, U. Tex., 1967; JD, St. Mary's U., 1970. Bar: Tex. 1970, U.S. Dist. Ct. (we. dist.) Tex. 1972, U.S. Supreme Ct. 1975, U.S. Ct. Appeals (5th cir.) 1981. Assoc. Law Office Jim S. Phelps, Houston, 1971; pvt. practice, Austin, 1972—. Spl. counsel com. human resources Tex. Ho. Reps., Austin, 1973-74; counsel subcom. health svcs. Tex. Senate, Austin, 1983-87. With U.S. Army, 1959-61. Mem.: Travis County Bar Assn., Austin Criminal Def. Lawyers Assn., Coll. of State Bar of Tex., Travis County Bar Assn. (sec.-treas. 1977—78, dir. 1979, pres. family law sect. 1980—81), State Bar Tex. (chmn. lawyer referral svc. com. 1980—82, adminstrn. of justice com. 1990—93, jury svc. com. 1998—2001, contbr. Media Law Handbook supplement 1986). Democrat. Avocations: automobiles, reading. Office: 1200 San Antonio St Austin TX 78701-1834

SHAPIRO, EDWARD MURAY, dermatologist; b. Denver, Oct. 6, 1924; s. Isador Benjamin and Sara (Berezin) S.; student U. Colo., 1941-43; m. Ruth Young, Oct. 14, 1944; children: Adrian Michael, Stefanie Ann; m. Dorothy Rosmarin, July 22, 1990. AB with honors, U. Tex., 1948, MD, 1952. Intern, Jefferson Coll. Medicine Hosp., Phila., 1952-53; resident in dermatology U. Tex. Med. Br., Galveston, 1953-55; resident in dermatology Henry Ford Hosp., Detroit, 1955-56, asso. in dermatology div. dermatology, 1956-57; clin. instr. dermatology Baylor U. Coll. Medicine, Houston, 1957-68, assoc. clin. prof., 1968—; staff Ben Taub Gen. Hosp., Houston, 1958—; active staff Columbia Bayshore Hosp., 1962—, Meml. Hosp., Pasadena, 1958—. Served with USAAF, 1943-46. Henry J. N. Taub research grantee, 1958-60; diplomate Am. Bd. Dermatology. Fellow Am. Acad. Dermatology; mem. AMA, Tex. Med. Assn., Tex. Dermatol. Soc. (pres.-elect 1988, pres. 1989-90), South Cen. Dermatol. Assn. (bd. dirs. 1987-88), Harris County Med. Assn. (pres. S.E. br. 1968-69), Houston Dermatology Assn., Houston Art League, Gulf Coast Art Soc., Am. Physicians Art Assn. (v.p. 1993). Jewish. Clubs: B'nai B'rith, Rotary Internat. (Paul Harris fellow 1995, 97). Contbr. articles in field to med. jours. Office: 1020 Pasadena Blvd Pasadena TX 77506-4700

SHAPIRO, EDWARD ROBERT, psychiatrist, administrator educator psychoanalyst; b. Boston, Sept. 13, 1941; s. Jacob and Ruth (Yankelovich) S.; m. Donna Elmendorf; 1 child, Joshua Jackson; 1 child from previous marriage, Jacob Matthew; 1 stepchild, Zachary Andrew Robbins. BA magna cum laude, Yale U., 1962; MA in Anthropology, Stanford U., 1966; MD, Harvard U., 1968. Diplomate Am. Bd. Psychiatry and Neurology. Intern in medicine Beth Israel Hosp., Boston, 1968-69; resident in psychiatry Mass. Mental Health Ctr., 1969-72, chief resident in psychiatry, 1971-72; clin. assoc. NIMH, Bethesda, Md., 1972-74; dir. Adolescent and Family Treatment and Study Ctr. McLean Hosp., Belmont, Mass., 1974-89, dir. Psychosocial Tng. and Consultation, 1989-91; bd. dirs. Ctr. for Study of Groups and Social Systems, Boston, 1983-90, A.K. Rice Inst., Washington, 1983-90, dir. Nat. Group Rels. Conf., 1989-91; faculty mem. Boston Psychoanalytic Inst., 1978—; assoc. clin. prof. psychiatry Harvard Med. Sch., Boston, 1982—; med. dir., CEO The Austen Riggs Ctr., Stockbridge, Mass., 1991—. Dir. The Erik H. Erikson Inst. for Edn. and Rsch., 1994-2000. Co-author: (with A.W. Carr) Lost in Familiar Places: Creating New Connections Between the Individual and Society, 1991; editor: The Inner World in the Outer World: Psychoanalytic Perspectives, 1997; mem. editorial bd. Jour. Adolescence, 1977-82, Psychiatry, 1988—; assoc. editor Jour. Adolescence, 1982-84; contbr. articles to profl. jours. Mem. Yale Russian Chorus. With USPHS, 1972-74. Recipient Isenberg Teaching award McLean Hosp., 1980, Rsch. prize Soc. for Family Therapy and Rsch., 1984, Felix and Helen Deutsch Sci. prize Boston Psychoanalytic Inst., 1980. Fellow Am. Psychiat. Assn., Am. Coll. Psychoanalysis, A.K. Rice Inst.; mem. Am. Psychoanalytic Assn., Am. Family Therapy Assn. Avocation: music. Office: The Austen Riggs Ctr PO Box 962 25 Main St Stockbridge MA 01262-0962

SHAPIRO, EDWIN STANLEY, lawyer, judge; b. Bklyn., Jan. 14, 1931; s. Harry I. and Ann (Safanie) S.; m. Sandra I. Bernstein, Sept. 15, 1957; children: James A., Sarah E. BA, Trinity Coll., Hartford, Conn., 1952; LLB, JD, Harvard Law Sch., 1955. Bar: N.Y. 1956, U.S. Dist. Ct. (so. and ea. dist.) N.Y. 1956, U.S. Ct. Appeals 1957. Atty. Levin & Weintraub, N.Y.C., 1956-57; pvt. practice, 1957-59; ptnr. Smith, Shapiro & Scheier, 1959-62, Basch, Seits & Shapiro, N.Y.C., 1970-74, Seits & Shapiro, N.Y.C., 1974-81; town justice Ossining, N.Y., 1980—; pvt. practice N.Y.C., 1981-95, Briarcliff Manor, N.Y., 1996—. Lawyer Staten Island Open Lands Found., 1965-67. Mem. Assn. of Bar of City of N.Y. (com. on state cts. 1982-83, environ. law com. 1970-73, corrections com. 1996-98). E-mail: shaplaw@bestweb.net.

SHAPIRO, ELI, business consultant, educator, economist; b. Bklyn., June 13, 1916; s. Samuel and Pauline (Kushel) S.; m. Beatrice Ferbend, Jan. 18, 1946 (dec. July 1999); 1 child, Laura J. AB, Bklyn. Coll., 1936; A.M., Columbia U., 1937, PhD, 1939. Instr. Bklyn. Coll., 1936-41; rsch. assoc. Nat. Bur. Econ. Rsch., 1938-39; cons. Nat. Bur. Econ. Research, 1939-42; mem. rsch. staff Nat. Bur. Econ. Rsch., 1955-62; asst. prof. fin. U. Chgo., 1946-47, asso. prof., 1948-52, prof., 1952; prof. fin. Mass. Inst. Tech., 1952-61; assoc. dean Mass. Inst. Tech. (Sch. Indsl. Mgmt.), 1954-58, Alfred P. Sloan prof. mgmt., 1976-84, Alfred P. Sloan prof. emeritus, 1984—; prof. fin. Harvard Bus. Sch., 1962-72, Sylvan C. Coleman prof. fin. mgmt., 1968-72; chmn. fin. com., dir. Travelers Ins. Cos., Hartford, Conn., 1971-78, vice chmn. bd., dir., 1976-78; chmn. bd. Mass. Co., 1971-72; pres. Nat. Bur. Econ. Research, 1982-84. Chmn. bd. Fed. Home Loan Bank Boston, 1970-89; econ. analyst div. monetary rsch. U.S. Dept. Treasury, 1941-42; economist rsch. div. OPA, 1941-42; staff cons. Com. Econ. Devel., 1950-51, mem. rsch. adv. com., 1961-64, 69—, project dir., 1966-69; cons. to sec. treasury; mem. enforcement commn. WSB, 1952-53; cons. Inst. Def. Analyses; dep. dir. Rsch. Com. on Money and Credit, 1959-61. Author: (with others) Personal Finance Industry and Its Credit Standards, 1939, (with Steiner) Money and Banking, 1941, Development of Wisconsin Credit Union Movement, 1947, Money and Banking, 1953, (with others), 1958, (with D. Meiselman) Measurement of Corporate Sources and Uses of Funds, 1964, (with others) Money and Banking, 1969, (with Wolf) The Role of Private Placement in Corporate Finance, 1972; Editor: (with W.L. White) Capital for Productivity and Growth, 1977. Served from ensign to lt. USNR, 1942-46. Recipient Econ. Dept. award Bklyn. Coll., 1936, Honors Day award for distinguished alumni, 1949 Fellow Am. Acad. Arts and Scis.; mem. Nat. Bur. Econ. Research (pres.), Am. Econ. Assn., Council Fgn. Relations, Am. Fin. Assn. Home and Office: 180 Beacon St Boston MA 02116-1408

SHAPIRO, ELLEN GOLDBERG, music educator; b. Oil City, Pa., Nov. 19, 1942; d. Harry Gene and Dorothy (Gordon) Goldberg; m. Samuel Shapiro, Aug. 8, 1971; children: Jeremy Aaron, Jessica Leigh. Student, Eastman Sch. Music, 1960-61; BA, Northwestern U., 1965; M of Music, Boston U., 1970. Tchr. music Scituate (Mass.). Pub. Schs., 1970-71; tchr. piano South Shore Conservatory Music, Hingham, Mass., 1970-75; tchr. music Willingboro (N.J.) Pub. Schs., 1977-79, Cinnaminson (N.J.) Pub. Schs., 1979-81; dir., tchr. Shapiro Sch. Music, Marlton, N.J., 1981—; music tchr. Evesham Township Pub. Schs., NJ, Westhampton (N.J.) Pub. Schs. Lectr. Phila. Music Tchrs. Assn., 1987, 2002. Contbr. articles to profl. mags. and jours. Chmn. publicity com. PTA, Marlton, 1986; mem. adv. com. Womens Am. Orgn. for Rehab. through Tng., Marlton and Medford, N.J., 1983-85; active Hadassah, Natick, Mass., bull. editor, 1973-75; chair Sylvia Denbo Meml. Scholarship. Mem. Nat. Guild Piano Tchrs. (faculty, adjudicator 1985—, chmn. 1981, Nat. Hall Fame), South Jersey Music Tchrs. Assn. (pres.), Music Tchrs. Nat. Assn. (sec. Eastern div. 1990-91), Phila. Music Tchrs. Assn., Federated Music Clubs Am. Avocation: writing. Home: 136 Five Crown Royale Marlton NJ 08053-2805 E-mail: mough71@aol.com.

SHAPIRO, FRED DAVID, lawyer; b. Cleve., Nov. 10, 1926; s. Isadore R. and Lottie (Turetsky) S.; m. Helen Solomon, Sept. 5, 1948; children— Gary N., Ira R., Diane S. BA cum laude, Ohio State U., 1949; LL.B., Harvard U., 1954. Bar: Ohio 1954. Since practiced in, Cleve.; sr. atnr. Shapiro and Lodwick, Co., L.P.A, 1994—. Served with USNR, 1945-46. Mem. Ohio Bar Assn., Greater Cleve. Bar Assn., Cuyahoga County Bar Assn., The Rowfant Club, Phi Beta Kappa. Jewish. Home: 29226 S Woodland Rd Cleveland OH 44124-5737

SHAPIRO, FRED LOUIS, physician, educator; b. Mpls., Aug. 18, 1934; s. Ralph Samuel and Dora (Cullen) S.; m. Merle Sandra Rosenzweig, June 23, 1957; children: Wendy Judith, Richard Scott. BA magna cum laude, U. Minn., 1958, BS, MD, U. Minn., 1961. Intern Hennepin County Med. Ctr., Mpls., 1961-62, resident in internal medicine, 1962-65, instr., 1965-68, chief nephrology, 1965-84; med. dir. Regional Kidney Disease Program, 1966-84; asst. prof. U. Minn., Mpls., 1968-71, assoc. prof., 1971-75, prof., 1975—. Pres. Hennepin Faculty Assocs., 1983-95. Contbr. articles to profl. jours. With USNR, 1953-55. Mem. Phi Beta Kappa, Sigma Xi, Alpha Omega Alpha. Home: 3490 Fairway Ln Minnetonka MN 55305-4451

SHAPIRO, GARY EVAN, newspaper journalist; b. Lewiston, Maine, Feb. 5, 1964; s. Sherman George and Charlotte (Cominsky) S. AB, Harvard U., 1986; JD, Columbia U., 1993. Assoc. Skadden Arps Slate Meagher & Flom, N.Y.C., 1993-94; writer, event prodr., 1994-99; journalist Forward newspaper, 1999—. Contbg. editor Am. Scholar, 2000—; note editor Columbia Jour. Environ. Law, 1993; contbr. numerous articles to profl. jours.; prodr. numerous programs on diplomacy, history, arch., bus., arts and lit., politics and econs., sci., edn., philosophy. Recipient Charles William Eliot medal for Citizenship, 1986, Cox Medal, Phillips Exeter, 1982; John Finley Traveling fellow, 1986. Mem. Overseas Press Club, Nat. Arts Club (lit. com. 1997—), Harvard Club (program com. 1995-2000). Avocation: book collecting. Home: 27 W 44th St # 50 New York NY 10036-6613 Office: Forward Newspaper 45 E 33rd St New York NY 10016-5336

SHAPIRO, GARY JOHN, lawyer; b. San Francisco, Oct. 4, 1941; s. Herbert H. and Raye (Wall) S.; m. Dana Bloom, July 5, 1964; children: Karen Hillary, Anne S. Mulvaney. BS, U. Calif.-Berkeley, 1963, JD, 1966. Bar: Calif. 1966, U.S. Dist. Ct. 1967, U.S. Ct. Appeals 1967. Law clk. Oliver D. Hamlin, U.S. Ct. Appeals, 9th Cir., 1966-67; assoc. Dinkelspiel & Dinkelspiel, San Francisco, 1967-69; ptnr. firm Buchman, Kass & Shapiro, Profl. Corp., Oakland, 1970-75; of counsel Steefel, Levitt & Weiss, 1985—2002. Judge pro tem Alameda County Mcpl. Ct., San Leandro-Hayward Jud. Dist., 1972; ptnr. Shapiro Assocs., Mill Valley; mem. faculty San Francisco Law Sch., 1968-71; mem. faculty John F. Kennedy U. Sch. Law, Sch. Bus. Adminstrn., 1977-79, Am. Coll., Bryn Mawr, Pa., 1977-79, Golden Gate U. Grad. Sch. Banking, Fin. and Real Estate, 1979-81; lectr. various tax and real estate seminars. Contbr. articles to legal jours. Pres. Estate Planning Coun. of East Bay, San Francisco, 1980; trustee, sec. Jacques and Esther Reutlinger Found.; trustee Hetzel Family Found.; trustee, chair, chair fin. com. Pacific Grad. Sch. Psychology; trustee, chair investment com. St. Francis Hosp. Found.; trustee, pres., chair fin. com. Judah L. Magnes Mus.; bd. dirs. Temple Emanu El, San Francisco, 1989—95; bd. dirs. Am. Friends Ben Gurium U.; Bd. dirs., pres. Endowment Found. of Jewish Welfare Fedn., 1985—87; Jewish Nat. Fund; bd. dirs., treas. Jewish Family Svc. Agy, Alameda County, Am. Friends Shaare Zedak Hosp.; Jewish Fedn. Greater East Bay. Mem.: ABA, Bar Assn. San Francisco, Hebrew Free Loan Assn. (bd. dirs.), Am. Israel Pub. Affairs Com. of No. Calif. (bd. dirs., vice chmn., nat. exec. com.), Troon Club, Lake Merced Club, Concordia Argonaut Club, Order of Coif. Republican. Jewish. Office: One Embacadero Center 29th Floor San Francisco CA 94111 E-mail: shapirog@alumni.haas.org.

SHAPIRO, GEORGE HOWARD, retired lawyer; b. St. Louis, Nov. 10, 1936; s. Isadore T. and Alice (Schucart) S.; m. Mary Kenney Leonard, 1977 (div. 1994); m. Ray Ann Kremer, 1999; 1 child, Ellen. BA, Harvard U., 1958, LLB, 1961; postgrad., London Sch. Econs., 1961-62. Bar: Ga. 1960, D.C. 1963. Atty. U.S. Dept. Labor, Washington, 1962-63; assoc. Arent Fox Kintner Plotkin & Kahn, 1963-69, ptnr., 1970-99; ret., 2000. Co-author: 'Cable Speech' The Case for First Amendment Protection, 1983; editor: New Program Opportunities in the Electronic Media, 1983, Current Developments in CATV, 1981. With USAR, 1962-68. Frank Knox Meml. fellow Harvard U., 1961-62. Mem. D.C. Bar Assn., Fed. Communications Bar Assn. Democrat. Jewish. Avocation: skiing. Home: Apt 906 3180 Mathieson Dr NE Atlanta GA 30305-1871 E-mail: GHSinATL@aol.com.

SHAPIRO, GILBERT, retired history and sociology educator; b. N.Y.C., July 1, 1926; children: Laura Jane, Amy Ruth. BA, Cornell U., 1947, PhD, 1954. From instr. to asst. prof. dept. sociology and anthropology Oberlin (Ohio) Coll., 1955-59; asst. prof. dept. sociology and anthropology Wayne State U., Detroit, 1959-61; assoc. prof. dept. sociology and anthropology Washington U., St. Louis, 1961-65, dir. Social Sci. Inst., 1963-64; rsch. assoc. prof., Inst. Human Scis. Boston Coll., 1965-68; prof. sociology and history U. Pitts., 1968-88, prof. emeritus sociology and history, 1988—. Dir. d'Etudes Ctr. Hist. Rsch., Ecole Pratique des Hautes Etudes, Paris, 1973; vis. rsch. scholar Max Planck Inst. for History, Göttingen, Germany, 1978; vis. prof. dept. history Carnegie-Mellon U., Pitts., 1988-91 Author: (book) Revolutionary Demands: A Content Analysis of the Cahiers de Doléances of 1789, 1998 (Soc. for French Hist. Studes David Pinkney prize 1999); contbr.: (book) Text Analysis for the Social Sciences: Methods for Drawing Statistical Inferences from Texts and Transcripts, 1997, Sociological Methodology 1975, 1975, The Dimensions of Quantitative Research in History, 1972; contbr. articles to profl. jours. Sgt. U.S. Army, 1945-47. Home: Apt 503 4625 5th Ave Pittsburgh PA 15213 E-mail: gns@vms.cis.pitt.edu.

SHAPIRO, GILBERT LAWRENCE, orthopedist; b. Lewiston, Maine, June 14, 1931; s. Samuel and Freda (Meyer) S.; m. Frima Lee Goldman, Aug. 28, 1955; children: Beth S. Lewyckyi, Karen S. Goldaber, Ruth A. BA, Dartmouth Coll., 1953; MD, Tufts U., 1957. Diplomate Am. Bd. Orthopaedic Surgery. Pvt. practice orthopaedic surgery, New Bedford, Mass., 1963—. Mem. Orthopaedic Overseas Bd., 1997—, treas., 2000—. Bd. dirs. Cmty. Found. of Southeastern Mass., 1997—; trustee St. Luke's Hosp., New Bedford, 1989-96; pres. bd. trustees. Pilgrim Healthcare (HMO), Norwell, Md., 1991-95, Old Dartmouth Hist. Soc. (whaling mus.), New Bedford, 1991-95; trustee Southcoast Health Sys., 1996—; co-pres. bd. Harvard-Pilgrim Health Care, 1996, chair fin. com., 1996-98, bd. dirs., 1997—; pres. bd. com. Found. of Southeastern Mass., 2001—. Mem. ACS, Am. Acad. Orthopaedic Surgeons, New England Orthopaedic Soc. (pres. 1988-90), Ea. Orthopaedic Soc. Office: 84 Grape St New Bedford MA 02740-2143

SHAPIRO, GREGG, writer; b. Chgo., June 2, 1959; s. Jerry and Shirel Shapiro; life ptnr. Rick Karlin. BFA, Emerson Coll., Boston, 1983. Music and cinema editor Lambda Pubs. (Windy City Times), Chgo., 1995—; music editor Next Mag., N.Y.C., 1999—. Named to Gay and Lesbian Hall of Fame, Adv. Coun. on Gay and Lesbian Issues, Chgo., 1999. Personal E-mail: Gregg1959@aol.com.

SHAPIRO, HAROLD DAVID, lawyer, educator; b. Chgo., Apr. 15, 1927; s. Charles B. and Celia (Nierenberg) S.; m. Beatrice Cahn, June 6, 1950; children: Matthew D., Michael Ann, Nicholas J. BS, Northwestern U., Chgo., 1949, JD, 1952. Adminstrv. asst. State of Ill. Dept. Fin., Springfield, 1952; assoc. Sonnenschein Nath & Rosenthal, Chgo., 1953-59, ptnr., 1959—; Edward A. Harriman adj. prof. law Northwestern U., Chgo., 1970—. Sec., bd. dirs. West Side Affordable Housing, Inc., West Side Village, Inc. Trustee, mem. exec. com., sec. Jr. Achievement of Chgo.; bd. dirs. Schwab Rehab. Ctr., Chgo.; pres. Homan & Arthington Found., 1995—96, The Ringer Found., 2000—, Northwestern U. Law Sch. Alumni Assn., Chgo., 1984—85, chmn. dean's adv. coun., 1997—99. Served with Seabees USNR, 1945—50, PTO. Recipient Merit award Northwestern U., 1988. Mem. Ill. Bar Assn., ABA, Chgo. Bar Assn., Chgo. Council Lawyers, Legal Club of Chgo. (pres.), Law Club of Chgo., Order of Coif, Wigmore Key, Standard Club, Met. Club, Cliff Dwellers, Chicago Club, Lake Shore Country Club. Democrat. Jewish. Home: 34 Linden Ave Wilmette IL 60091-2837 Office: Sonnenschein Nath & Rosenthal 8000 Sears Tower 233 S Wacker Dr Ste 8000 Chicago IL 60606-6491

SHAPIRO, HAROLD TAFLER, academic administrator, economist; b. Montreal, Que., Can., June 8, 1935; s. Maxwell and Mary (Tafler) S.; m. Vivian Bernice Rapoport, May 19, 1957; children: Anne, Marilyn, Janet, Karen. BComm, McGill U., Montreal, 1956; PhD in Econs. (Harold Helm fellow, Harold Dodds sr. fellow), Princeton U., 1964. Asst. prof. econs. U. Mich., 1964-67, assoc. prof., 1967-70, prof., 1970-76, chmn. dept. econs., 1974-77, prof. econs. and pub. affairs, from 1977, v.p. acad. affairs, 1977-79, pres., 1980-87; research adv. Bank Can., 1965-72; pres. Princeton U., 1988-2001; pres. emeritus, prof. econ. and pub. affairs Woodrow Wilson Sch., Princeton U., 2001—. Bd. dirs. Dow Chem., DeVry Inst., Hastings Ctr., HCA; trustee Univs. Rsch. Assn., 1988—; mem. exec. com. Assn. Am. Univs., 1985-89, N.J. Commn. on Sci. and Tech., 1988-91; mem. Pres.'s Coun. Advisors on Sci. and Tech., 1990-92; chmn. com. on employer-based health benefits Inst. Medicine, 1991; bd. overseers Robert Wood Johnson Med. Sch., 2000—. Editor: (with William G. Bowen) Universities and Their Leadership, 1998. Trustee Alfred P. Sloan Found., 1980—, Interlochen Ctr. for Arts, 1988-95, U. Pa. Med. Ctr., 1992—, Ednl. Testing Svc., 1994—; dir. Am. Coun. Edn., 1989-92; chmn. Spl. Presdl. Com., The Rsch. Librs. Group, 1980-91; mem. Gov.'s High Tech. Task Force, Mich., 1980-87; mem. Gov.'s Commn. on Jobs and Econ. Devel. (Mich.), 1983-87; mem. Carnegie Commn. on Coll. Retirement, 1984-86; mem. Pres. Bush Coun. Advisors on Sci. and Tech., 1990-92; chair Nat. Bioethics Adv. Commn., 1996—; chair Inst. Medicine's Com. on Employer-Based Health Benefits; trustee Univ. Corp. for Advanced Internet Devel., 2000—; mem. Ednl. Testing Svc., 1994-2000. Recipient Lt. Gov.'s medal in commerce McGill U., 1956 Fellow Am. Acad. Arts and Scis., Mich. Soc. Fellows (sr.); mem. Inst. Medicine of NAS, Am. Philos. Soc., Nat. Bur. Econ. Rsch. (bd. dirs.). Office: Princeton U Woodrow Wilson School 355 Wallace Hall Princeton NJ 08544-1013*

SHAPIRO, HARRY DEAN, lawyer; b. Louisville, June 21, 1940; s. Herman Shapiro and Toby (Spector) Levy; m. Linda Siegel, Dec. 19, 1970; 1 child, Deborah Anne. BS, U. Louisville, 1962, JD, 1964. Bar: Ky. 1964, D.C. 1968, Md. 1970. Trial and appellate atty. U.S. Dept. Justice, Washington, 1964-70; assoc. Venable, Baetjer & Howard, Balt., 1970-74, ptnr., 1975-87; sr. ptnr., head of tax practice Weinberg & Green, 1987—98, chmn. corp. dept., 1993-95; transaction group coord., 1995-98; head tax practice Saul Ewing LLP, 1998-99; chmn. tax dept. Saul, Ewing, Remick & Saul LLP, 1999—. Author: Federal Tax Liens, 1981; contbr. articles to profl. jours. Mem. Md. State Bd. Edn., 1990-97; v.p. Assoc. Jewish Charities of Balt., Inc. 1991-94; vice chmn. The Assoc. Jewish Cmty. Fedn. Balt. 1987-89, asst. treas., 1989-91, mem. exec. com., 1993-97; trustee Sinai Hosp., Balt., 1987-90; counsel Balt. Mus. Art, 1984-97, trustee, 1984-96, sec., 1985-92, v.p., sec., 1992-94, v.p., 1994-96; dir., 1989-96; chmn. Joint Budgeting Coun., 1993-96, Coun. Jewish Fedns.; trustee Acad. Art Mus., Easton, 1998—. Capt. USAR, 1967-70. Recipient Disting. Alumni award Brandeis Sch. of Law, 1996, Chmn.'s award Balt. Mus. Art, 1996. Mem. ABA (tax sect.), Md. State Bar Assn., Ky. Bar Assn., D.C. Bar Assn., Md. Club, Center Club. Home: 7903 7 Mile Ln Baltimore MD 21208-4306 Office: Saul Ewing LLP 100 S Charles St Ste 1500 Baltimore MD 21201-2771 E-mail: hshapiro@saul.com. *Our country is at a crossroads in its history, and it is becoming clear that a sea change is necessary. Basic reforms must occur in our governmental and educational structures. The question is whether we have the intelligence to reject the cries for bigger government and more taxes to solve these problems when fundamental action is required.*

SHAPIRO, HARVEY, poet; b. Chgo., Jan. 27, 1924; s. Jacob J. and Dorothy (Cohen) S.; m. Edna Lewis Kaufman, July 23, 1953 (div.); children— Saul, Dan. BA, Yale U., 1947; MA, Columbia U., 1948. Instr. English Cornell U., 1949-50, 51-52; creative writing fellow Bard Coll., 1950-51; mem. editl. staff Commentary, New Yorker, 1955-57, N.Y. Times Mag., N.Y.C., 1957, asst. editor, 1964-75; editor N.Y. Times Book Rev., 1975-83; dep. editor N.Y. Times Mag., 1983-96, consulting editor, 1996—2002. Author: The Eye, 1953, The Book and Other Poems, 1955, Mountain, Fire, Thornbush, 1961, Battle Report, 1966, This World, 1971, Lauds, 1975, Nightsounds, 1978, The Light Holds, 1984, National Cold Storage Company, 1988, A Day's Portion, 1994, Selected Poems, 1997, How Charlie Shavers Died and Other Poems, 2001. Served with USAAF, World War II. Decorated D.F.C., Air medal with 3 oak leaf clusters.; Rockefeller Found. grantee in poetry, 1967 Club: Elizabethan (New Haven), Century (N.Y.). Office: NY Times 229 W 43rd St New York NY 10036-3913

SHAPIRO, HARVEY DEAN, writer; b. Duluth, Minn., Oct. 5, 1944; s. Myer and Florence (Titch) S.; m. Paula M., Oct. 5, 1969; children: Samantha Meinetz., Andrew Jason Meinetz. BA with honors, Univ. Wis., 1966; Master of Pub. Affairs, Princeton U., 1968; MA, Univ. Chgo., 1970. Freelance writer, 1969—. Cons. Ford Found., Rand Corp., Pres.'s Commn. on Income Maintenance Programs, Cabinet Com. on Cable Communications, Russell Sage Found., N.Y.C. Planning Dept., U.S. SBA, Urban Inst.; polit. speech writer for various candidates for pub. office. Contbr. numerous articles to L.A. Times, N.Y. Times, others. Active in The Tamiment Soc., N.Y. Walter Bagehot Fellow Columbia U. 1976; recipient Overseas Press Club Award 1979. Mem. Nat. Book Critics Circle, Phi Beta Kappa. Jewish.

SHAPIRO, IAN, political science educator; b. Johannesburg, South Africa, Sept. 29, 1956; came to U.S., 1978; s. Hillel Abbe Shapiro and Sonia Machanick; m. Judith Watkins, Sept. 18, 1982; children: Xan Alexander, Yani Alexandra. BSc with honors, U. Bristol, Eng., 1978; PhD in Polit. Sci., Yale U., 1983, JD, 1987. Asst. prof. polit. sci. Yale U., New Haven, 1984-88, assoc. prof., 1988-92, prof., 1992—, dir. program in ethics, politics and econs., 1992-98, William R. Kenan, Jr., prof. polit. sci., 2000—, chair polit. sci. dept., 1999—. Author: The Evolution of Rights in Liberal Theory, 1986, Political Criticism, 1990, Pathologies of Rational Choice, 1994, (with D. Green) Democracy's Place, 1996, Democratic Justice, 1999; editor Nomos, 1990—. Fellow Guggenheim Found., 1988-89, Ctr. for Advanced Study, 1998-99, Carnegie Corp. N.Y., 2000-02, Am. Acad. Arts and Scis., 2000. Mem. Am. Soc. Polit. and Legal Philosophy (mem. coun. 1990-2000), Am. Polit. Sci. Assn. (mem. coun. 1996-98), Leo Strauss prize 1984. Avocations: skiing, horseback riding, jogging, gym. Office: Yale U Dept Polit Sci PO Box 208301 New Haven CT 06520-8301 E-mail: ian.shapiro@yale.edu.

SHAPIRO, IRWIN IRA, physicist, educator; b. N.Y.C., N.Y., Oct. 10, 1929; s. Samuel and Esther (Feinberg) S.; m. Marian Helen Kaplun, Dec. 20, 1959; children: Steven, Nancy. AB, Cornell U., 1950; A.M., Harvard U., 1951, PhD, 1955. Mem. staff Lincoln Lab. MIT, Lexington, 1954-70; Sherman Fairchild Distinguished scholar Calif. Inst. Tech., 1974; Morris Loeb lectr. physics Harvard, 1975; prof. geophysics and physics MIT, 1967-80, Schlumberger prof., 1980-84; Paine prof. practical astronomy, prof. physics Harvard U., 1982-97; sr. scientist Smithsonian Astrophys. Obs., 1982—; dir. Harvard-Smithsonian Ctr. for Astrophysics, 1983—; prof. Harvard U./Timken, 1997—. Cons. NSF, NASA. Contbr. articles to profl. jours. Recipient Albert A. Michelson medal Franklin Inst., 1975, award in phys. and math. scis. N.Y. Acad. Scis., 1982, Einstein medal Einstein Soc. Bern, 1994; Guggenheim fellow, 1982. Fellow AAAS, Am. Geophys. Union (Charles A. Whitten medal 1991, William Bowie medal 1993), Am. Phys. Soc.; mem. AAAS, NAS (Benjamin Apthorp Gould prize 1979), Am. Astron. Soc. (Dannie Heineman award 1983, Dirk Brouwer award 1987, Gerard Kuiper award 1997), Am. Philos. Soc., Internat. Astron. Union, Phi Beta Kappa, Sigma Xi, Phi Kappa Phi. Home: 17 Lantern Ln Lexington MA 02421-6029 Office: Harvard-Smithsonian Ctr Astrophysics 60 Garden St Cambridge MA 02138-1516 E-mail: ishapiro@cfa.harvard.edu.

SHAPIRO, ISAAC, lawyer; b. Tokyo, Jan. 5, 1931; s. Constantine and Lydia (Chernetzky) S.; m. Jacqueline M. Weiss, Sept. 16, 1956; children: Tobias, Alexandra, Natasha. AB, Columbia U., 1954, LLB, 1956; postgrad., U. Paris, 1956-57. Bar: N.Y. 1957, U.S. Supreme Ct. 1971, Paris 1991. Assoc. Milbank, Tweed, Hadley & McCloy, N.Y.C., 1956-65, ptnr., 1966-86, resident ptnr. Tokyo, 1977-79; ptnr. Skadden Arps Slate Meagher & Flom LLP, N.Y.C., 1986—2001; resident ptnr. Skadden Arps Slate Meagher & Flom, Hong Kong, 1989-90, Paris, 1990—; of counsel Skadden Arps Slate Meagher & Flom LLP, N.Y.C., 2001—; tchg. fellow comparative law NYU, 1959-61. Lectr. Soviet law, 1961-67; adj. asst. prof. NYU, 1967-69, adj. assoc. prof., 1969-71, 74-75; adj. prof. and dir. Russian Legal Studies, Columbia Law School, 1999-2000; bd. dirs. Bank of Tokyo Mitsubishi Trust Co., N.Y.C., 1975-77, 80-2001, Enherent, Inc., Dallas, Tex., 81-. Author: (with Hazard and Maggs) The Soviet Legal System, 1969; author: Japan: The Risen Sun (in Japanese), 1982; editor: The Middle East Crisis-Prospects for Peace, 1969; contbr. articles to profl. jours. Mem. Joint Com. U.S.-Japan Cultural and Ednl. Cooperation, Washington, 1972-78; mem. Japan-U.S. Friendship Commn., 1975-78; mem. svcs. policy adv. com. to U.S. Trade Rep., 1981-91; trustee Nat. Humanities Ctr., Triangle Park, N.C., 1976-89, Bank of Tokyo Mitsubishi Found., 1996-2001; trustee, v.p. Chamber Music Soc. Lincoln Ctr., 1980-86, Isamu Noguchi Zaidan, Japan, 1999—; trustee, pres. Isamu Noguchi Found., N.Y., 1985—; trustee, chmn. Ise Cultural Found., 1984-90; bd. dirs. Bus. Coun. for Internat. Understanding, 1989-95, Nat. Com. for U.S.-China Rels., 1989-95, Asian Cultural Coun., 1980—; bd. adv. Trust for Mutual Understanding, N.Y.C., N.Y., 1985-. With U.S. Army, 1950-52. Fulbright scholar, 1956-57. Mem.: ABA, Barristers Chambers London, N.Y. State Bar Assn., Coun. Fgn. Rels., Japan Soc. Office: Skadden Arps Slate Meagher & Flom LLP 4 Times Sq New York NY 10036-6522

SHAPIRO, JACOB, physicist, educator; b. N.Y.C., Sept. 4, 1925; s. Isaac and Bella (Baseman) S.; m. Shirley Prusky; children: Robert, Jean. BS, CCNY, 1944; MS, Brown U., 1948; PhD, U. Rochester, 1954. Diplomate Am. Bd. Health Physics. Physics instr. U. R.I., 1946-47; physicist Atomic Energy Commn., N.Y.C., 1944-46; rsch. assoc. U. Rochester, N.Y., 1953-55; supr. radiation analysis Gen. Dynamics Corp., Groton, Conn., 1955-60; lectr. biophysics Harvard U. Sch. Pub. Health, Cambridge, 1961—; sr. scientist environ. health and safety Harvard U., 1996-97. Lectr. in nuclear engring. U. Conn., Groton, 1958-60; radiation protection officer Harvard U., 1961-96. Author: Radiation Protection, 1972, 2nd edit., 1981, 4th edit., 2002; contbr. article to profl. jour. Cons. Concord (Mass.) Bd. Pub. Health, 1981-96, Tech. Edn. Rsch. Ctr., Cambridge, Mass., 1988, sci. by mail Boston Mus. Sci., 1990-99. With USN, 1944-46. Fellow Health Physics Soc. Avocations: reading, playing piano, hiking.

SHAPIRO, JAMES EDWARD, judge; b. Chgo., May 28, 1930; BS, U. Wis., 1951; JD, Harvard U., 1954. Bar: Wis. 1956, U.S. Dist. Ct. (ea. dist.) Wis. 1956, U.S. Ct. Appeals (7th cir.) 1962, U.S. Supreme Ct. 1971. Sole practice, Milw., 1956-57; resident house counsel Nat. Presto Industries, Eau Claire, Wis., 1957-60; ptnr. Bratt & Shapiro, Milw., 1960-64; sole practice, 1964-74; ptnr. Frank, Hiller & Shapiro, 1974-82; judge U.S. Bankruptcy Ct., 1982—, chief judge, 1996-2000. Mem. Bayside Bd. Appeals, Wis., 1969-77; Milw. county ct. commr., 1969-78; dir. Milw. Legal Aid Soc., 1969-77. Served to 1st lt. U.S. Army, 1954-56. Jewish. Office: US Courthouse 140 Fed Bldg 517 E Wisconsin Ave Milwaukee WI 53202-4500 E-mail: james_e_shapiro@wieb.uscourts.gov.

SHAPIRO, JOAN ISABELLE, laboratory administrator, nurse; b. Aug. 26, 1943; d. Macy James and Frieda Lockhart; m. Ivan Lee Shapiro, Dec. 28, 1968; children: Audrey, Michael. RN Nurse Grant Hosp., Columbus, Ohio, 1975-76, Cardiac Thoracic and Vascular Surgeons Ltd., Geneva, 1977—; mgr. non-invasive lab., 1979—. Owner operator Shapiro's Mastiff's 1976-82; sec.-treas. Sounds Svcs., 1976—, Mainstream Sounds Inc., 1980-84; co-founder Cardio-Phone Inc., 1982—, Edgewater Vascular Inst., 1987-89, Associated Profls., 1989-92; v.p., bd. dir. Computer Specialists Inc., 1986-89; founder, pres. Vein Ctr., Edema Ctr. Ltd. Mem. Soc. Non-invasive Technologists, Soc. Peripheral Vascular Nursing (cmty. awareness com. 1984—), Oncology Nursing Soc., Internat. Soc. Lymphology, Kane County Med. Soc. Aux. (pres. 1983-84, adviser, 1984-85). Lutheran. Home: Cardiac Thoracic/Vas Surg PO Box 325 Fort Fairfield ME 04742-0325

SHAPIRO, JOEL ELIAS, artist; b. N.Y.C., Sept. 27, 1941; s. Joseph and Anna (Lewis) S.; m. Ellen Phelan; 1 dau., Ivy Bess. BA, NYU, 1964, MA, 1969. One-person shows include Paula Cooper Gallery, N.Y.C., 14 shows 1970-90, The Clocktower Gall., Inst. Art and Urban Resources, NYC, 1973, Mus. Contemporary Art, Chgo., 1976, Albright-Knox Art Gallery, Buffalo, 1977, Gallery M. Bochum, W. Ger., 1978, Galerie Mukai, Tokyo, 1980, 81, 88, 91, Asher/Faure, L.A., 1980, 89, 91, Whitechapel Gallery, London, 1980, Haus Lange, Krefeld, W. Ger., 1980, Moderna Museet, Stockholm, 1980, Brown U., 1980, Ackland Art Mus., Chapel Hill, N.C., 1981, Contemporary Arts Ctr., Cin., 1981, Israel Mus., Jerusalem, 1981, Portland Ctr. Visual Arts, Oreg., 1982, Whitney Mus. Am. Art, N.Y.C., 1982, Galerie Aronowitsch, Stockholm, 1984, Delahunty Gallery, Dallas, 1980, Donald Young Gallery, Chgo., 1987, Stedelijk Mus., Amsterdam, 1985, Kunstmuseum, Dusseldorf, 1985, Staatliche Kunsthalle, Baden-Baden, 1986, Seattle Art Mus., 1986, Galerie Daniel Templon, Paris, 1986, 88, The John and Mable Ringling Mus., Sarasota, 1986, John Berggruen Gallery, San Francisco, 1987, Hirshhorn Mus. and Sculpture Garden, Washington, 1987, Hans Strelow, Dusseldorf, Germany, 1988, Toledo Mus. Art, 1989, Waddington Gallery, London, 1989, Museet I Varberg, Sweden, 1990, Balt. Art Mus., 1990, Des Moines Art Ctr., 1990, Ctr. for Fine Arts, Miami, 1991, IVAM Centre Julio Gonazlez, Valencia, Spain, 1990, John Berggruen Gallery, San Francisco, 1991, Pace Gallery, 1993, Galerie Karsten Greve, Cologne, Germany, 1993, Gallery Seomi, Seoul, 1994, 96, Galerie Aronowitsch, Stockholm, 1995, Karsten Greve, Paris, 1995, Pace Wildenstein Gallery, N.Y., 1995, Walker Art Ctr./Mpls. Sculpture Garden, 1995, Nelson-Atkins Mus. Art/Kansas City Sculpture Park, 1996, Pace Wildenstein Gallery, N.Y., 1996, Galerie Biedermann, Munich, Germany, 1997; Addison Gallery, Andover, Mass., 1997, Haus der Kunst, Munich, 1997, solo exhbt., Barlach Halle K, Hamburg, 1998, Pace Wildenstein, N.Y., 1998; Galerie Jamileh Weber, Zurich, Switzerland, 1997, Pace Wildenstein, Los Angeles, 1999, Amer. Acad. in Rome, 1999, Boston Mus. of Fine Arts, 1999, New Art Ctr., Salisbury, England, 1999, Yorkshire Sculpture Park, Wakefield, England, 1999-2000, Nat. Gallery of Canada, 1999-2000, John Berggruen Gallery, San Francisco, 2000, timothy Taylor Gallery, London, 2000, Spoleto Festival USA, Charleston, S.C., 2000, McNay Art Mus., San Antonio, Tex., 2000-01, Denver Art Mus., 2001, Galerie Daniel Templon, Paris, 2001, PaceWildenstein, N.Y., 2001, The Metropolitan Mus. Art, N.Y., 2001, Gerald B. Cantor Rooftop Galleries, N.Y., 2001; numerous group exhibits; permanent collections and commns. include Mus. Modern Art, N.Y.C., Whitney Mus. Art, N.Y.C., Walker Art Center, Mpls., Met. Mus. Art, N.Y.C., Albright Knox Art Gallery, Buffalo, Detroit Inst. Art, Stedelijk Mus., Amsterdam, Moderna Museet, Stockholm, Dallas Mus. Art, Centre Pompidou, Paris, Nat. Gallery Art, Washington, Brit. Mus., London, Bklyn. Mus., Cocoran Gallery, Washington, Fogg Art Mus. at Harvard U., Cambridge, Mass., High Mus. Art, Atlanta, Hirshhorn Mus. and Sculpture Garden at Smithsonian Instn., Washington, Israel Mus., Jerusalem, Kunsthaus Zürich, Switzerland, Mus. Contemporary Art, L.A., Mus. Fine Arts, Boston, Mus. Modern Art, Friuli, Italy, Parrish Art Mus., Southampton, N.Y., Phila. Mus. Art, Tate Gallery, London, commissions include Cigna Corp., Phila., 1983-84, Fukuoka (Japan) Sogo Bank, 1988, Creative Artists Agy., L.A., 1988-89, Kawamura Meml. Mus. Art, Chiba, Japan, 1988-89, Govt. Svc. Adminstrn., L.A., 1988-90, Hood Mus. Art at Dartmouth Coll., Hanover, N.H., 1989-90, U.S. Holocaust Meml. Mus., Washington, 1993, Sony Music Entertainment, N.Y.C., 1994-95, Friedrichstadt Passagen, Berlin, 1994-95, Kansas City (Mo.) Internat. Airport, 1995-96, Addison Gall. of Amer. Art, Mass.; represented by Pace Wildenstein Gallery, N.Y.C., Cleve. Mus. Art, N.C. Mus. Art, Raleigh, Des Moines Art Ctr., Pace Gallery, N.Y.C., Embassy of U.S.A., Ottawa, Can. Recipient Nat. Endowment for Arts award, 1975, Brandeis award, 1984, Skowhegan medal, 1986. Mem. Am. Acad. and Inst. Arts and Letters (Merit award 1990), Am. Acad. Arts & Letters, Swedish Royal Acad. Art. Office: care Pace Idenstein 32 E 57th St New York NY 10022-2513

SHAPIRO, JUDITH, social worker; b. Cedarhurst, N.Y., Dec. 9, 1932; d. Morris Abraham and Ruth (Zwiren) Stock; m. Herbert Shapiro, Feb. 3, 1957; children: Mark, Nina. BA, U. Cin., 1970; MSW, Ohio State U., 1972; post-grad., Xavier U., 1984-85. Lic. ind. social worker, Ohio; cert. sch. social worker. Social worker Jewish Community Ctr., Cin., 1972-73, Cin. Ctr. Devel. Disorders, 1975-78; asst. prof. of social work Sch. of Social Work, Univ. Cincinnati, 1978-80; coord. Legal Aid Soc. Cin., 1981-82; exec. dir. Clermont County Assn. for Retarded Citizens, Batavia, Ohio, 1982-86; coord. social svcs. Lincoln Heights Health Ctr., Cin., 1988-90. Co-founder Coop. Nursery Sch., Atlanta, 1964-66; bd. mgrs. Wesley Child Care Ctr., Cin., 1973. Mem. exec. bd. NAACP, Rochester, 1960-61; v.p. North Avondale Sch. PTA, 1969-75; bd. dirs. Woman's City Club Greater Cin., 1973-75; co-founder Concerned Citizens for Quality Edn., Cin., 1974; mem. nat. bd. Women's Internat. League for Peace and Freedom, 1979-92, pres. Midwest region, 1991-92; participant observer Mind/Body Med. Inst., Deaconess Hosp., Harvard Med. Sch., 1990. Glanzberg scholar, 1970-72. Mem. NASW, Am. Assn. Mental Deficiency. Home: 3990 Beechwood Ave Cincinnati OH 45229-1408

SHAPIRO, JUDITH R. academic administrator, anthropology educator; b. N.Y.C., Jan. 24, 1942; Student, Ecole des Haute Etudes Inst. d'Etudes Politiques, Paris, 1961—62; BA, Brandeis U., 1963; PhD, Columbia U., 1972. Asst. prof. U. Chgo., 1970—75; fellow U. Calif. , Berkeley, 1974—75; Rosalyn R. Schwartz lectr., asst. prof. anthropology Bryn Mawr Coll., Pa., 1975—78, assoc. prof., 1978—85, prof., 1985—94; pres. Barnard Coll., 1994—. Chmn. dept. Bryn Mawr Coll., 1982—85, acting dean undergrad coll., 1985—86, provost, 1986—94. Contbr. articles to profl. jours. Nat. adv. com. Woodrow Wilson Nat. Fellowship Found.; chair bd. dirs. Consortium on Financing Higher Edn.; bd. dirs. Fund for the City of N.Y.; chair bd. dirs. Women's Coll. Coalition. Fellow, Woodrow Wilson Found., 1963—64, Columbia U., 1964—65, Younger Humanist fellow, NEH, 1974—75, Am. Coun. Learned Socs., 1981—82, Ctr. for Advanced Study in the Behavioral Scis., 1989; grantee Summer Field Tng. grant, NSF, 1965, Ford Found., 1966, NIMH, 1974—75, Social Sci. Rsch. Coun., 1974—75. Mem.: Social Sci. Rsch. Coun. (com. social sci personnel 1977—80), Am. Anthrop. Assn. (ethics com. 1976—79, bd. dirs. 1984—86, exec. com. 1985—86), Am. Ethnol. Soc. (nominations com. 1983—84, pres. elect 1984—85, pres. 1985—86), Phila. Anthrop. Soc. (pres. 1983), Women's Forum, Sigma Xi, Phi Beta Kappa. Office: Barnard Coll Office of the Pres 3009 Broadway New York NY 10027-6501

SHAPIRO, JULIA CLARE, laboratory manager; b. Donetsk, Ukraine, U.S.S.R., July 21, 1937; d. Vladimir and Gita (DerBandiner) Aronin; m. Mark Abraham Shapiro, Aug. 23, 1960; 1 child, Elaine Valerie. MS in Chemistry, Kishinev U., 1959; PhD, Acad. Sci., 1970. Sr. technician Acad. Sci., Kishinev, U.S.S.R., 1960-70; sr. scientist Inst. Microwires, 1970-74; sr. sci. Rsch. Wine Inst., 1974-78; chemist Scott Specialty Gases, Troy, Mich., 1980-84, lab. mgr., 1984—. Prof. in chemistry Kishinev U., 1970-74. Contbr. articles to profl. jours. Mem. Am. Chem. Soc. Avocations: reading, music. Home: 16890 NW Waterford Way Portland OR 97229-1876 Office: Scott Specialty Gases 1290 Combermere Dr Troy MI 48083-2733

SHAPIRO, LARRY J. pediatrician, scientist, educator; b. July 6, 1946; s. Philip and Phyllis Shapiro; m. Carol-Ann Uetake; children: Jennifer, Jessica, Brian. AB, Washington U., St. Louis, 1968, MD, 1971. Diplomate Am. Bd. Pediat., Am. Bd. Med. Examiners, Am. Bd. Med. Genetics. Intern St. Louis Children's Hosp., 1971—72, resident, 1971—73; rsch. assoc. NIH, Bethesda, Md., 1973—75; asst. prof. Sch. Medicine UCLA, 1975—79, assoc. prof., 1979—83, prof. pediat. and biol. chemistry, 1983—91; investigator Howard Hughes Med. Inst., 1987—91, W.H. and Marie Wattis Disting. Prof.; prof., chmn. dept. pediat. U. Calif.-San Francisco Sch. Medicine, 1991—; chief pediat. svcs. U. Calif.-San Francisco Med. Ctr., 1991—. Contbr. numerous articles to profl. publs. Served to. lt. comdr. USPHS, 1973—75. Fellow: AAAS, Am. Acad. Pediat. (E. Mead Johnson award in rsch. 1982); mem.: Am. Acad. Arts and Scis., Am. Pediatric Soc. (coun. mem. 1999—2001, pres.-elect 2001—02), Am. Soc. Clin. Investigation, Am. Soc. Human Genetics (coun. 1985—88, pres.-elect 1995, pres. 1997), Assn. Am. Physicians, Soc. for Inherited Metabolic Disease (coun. 1983—88, pres. 1986—87), Western Soc. for Pediatric Rsch. (coun. 1983—87, pres. 1989—90, Ross award in rsch. 1981), Soc. Pediatric Rsch. (coun. 1984—87, pres. 1991—92), Inst. Medicine of NAS. Office: U Calif Dept Pediat 505 Parnassus Ave San Francisco CA 94143-0001

SHAPIRO, LEO J. social researcher; b. N.Y.C., July 8, 1921; m. Virginia L. Johnson, Feb. 9, 1952; children: David, Erik, Owen, Amy. BA, U. Chgo., 1942, PhD, 1952. Survey specialist Fed. Govt. Agy., Washington, 1941-45, Sci. Rsch. Assn., Chgo., 1948-52; prin., founder Leo J. Shapiro and Assocs., 1952-91; pres. Greenhouse, Inc., 1991—2001, SAGE LLC Survival & Growth Enterprise, Chgo., 2002—. Bd. dirs. Field of Flowers, Brand Name Ednl. Found. Fellow U. Chgo., 1949. Fellow Social Sci. Research Council; mem. Am. Sociol. Assn., Phi Beta Kappa.

SHAPIRO, LUCILLE, molecular biology educator; b. N.Y.C., July 16, 1940; d. Philip and Yetta (Stein) Cohen; m. Roy Shapiro, Jan. 23, 1960 (div. 1977); 1 child, Peter; m. Harley H. McAdams, July 28, 1978; stepchildren: Paul, Heather. BA, Bklyn. Coll., 1962; PhD, Albert Einstein Coll. Medicine, 1966. Asst. prof. Albert Einstein Coll. Medicine, N.Y.C., 1967-72, assoc. prof., 1972-77, Kramer prof., chmn. dept. molecular biology, 1977-86, dir. biol. scis. div., 1981-86; Eugene Higgins prof., chmn. dept. microbiology, Coll. Physicians and Surgeons Columbia U., 1986-89; Joseph D. Grant prof. devel. biology Stanford U. Sch. Medicine, 1989-97, chmn. dept. devel. biology, 1989-97, Virginia and D.K. Ludwig prof. of cancer rsch. dept. devel. biology, 1998—; dir. Beckman Ctr. Molecular & Genetic Medicine Stanford U., 2001—. Mem. bd. sci. counselors NIH, Washington, 1980—84; mem. bd. sci. advisors G.D. Searle Co., Skokie, Ill., 1984—86; mem. sci. adv. bd. Smith-Kline Beecham, 1993—2000, past bd. dirs., 1996—2000; mem. sci. adv. bd. GlaxoSmithKline, 2001—, bd. dirs., 2001—; mem. sci. adv. bd. PathoGenesis, 1995—2000, Ludwig Found., 2000—; trustee Scientists Inst. for Pub. Info., 1990—94; lectr. Harvey Soc., 1993; DeWitt Stetten disting. lectr., 89, 2002; John M. Lewis lectr. Rockefeller U., 1998; Marker lectr. Pa. State U., 1999; Lundberg lectr. Gothenburg U., Sweden, 1999; honors lectr. NYU, 1998; disting. scientist lectr. NAS, 1999; Crawford lectr. U. Iowa, 1999; Oshman lectr. Baylor U., 2000; Adam Neville lectr. U. Dundee, Scotland, 2001; Genome lectr. Harvard U., 2001; Jessup lectr. Columbia U., 2002; past bd. dirs. Silicon Graphics, Inc., 1993—2000. Editor: Microbiol. Devel., 1984; mem. editorial bd. Jour. Bacteriology, 1978-86, Trends in Genetics, 1987—, Genes and Development, 1987-91, Cell Regulation, 1990-92, Molecular Biology of the Cell, 1992—, Molecular Microbiology, 1991-96, Current Opinion on Genetics and Devel., 1991—; contbr. articles to profl. jours. Mem. sci. bd. Helen Hay Witney Found., N.Y.C., 1986-94, Biozentrum, Basel, 1999—, Hutchinson Cancer Ctr., Seattle, 1999; mem. grants adv. bd. Beckman Found., 1999—; co-chmn. adv. bd. NSF Biology Directorate, 1988-89; vis. com., bd. overseers Harvard U., Cambridge, Mass., 1987-90; mem. sci. bd. Whitehead Inst., MIT, Boston, 1988-93; mem. sci. rev. bd. Howard Hughes Med. Inst., 1990-94, Cancer Ctr. of Mass. Gen. Hosp., Boston, 1994; mem. Presidio Coun. City of San Francisco, 1991-94; mem. pres. coun. U. Calif., 1991-97. Recipient Hirschl Career Scientist award, 1976, Spirit of Achievement award, 1978, Alumna award of honor Bklyn. Coll., 1983, Excellence in Sci. award Fedn. Am. Soc. Exptl. Biology, 1994; Jane Coffin Child fellow, 1966; resident scholar Rockefeller Found., Bellagio, Italy, 1996. Fellow AAAS, Am. Acad. Arts and Scis., Am. Acad. Microbiology; mem. Nat. Acad. Sci., Inst. Medicine of Nat. Acad. Sci., Am. Soc. Biochemistry and Molecular Biology (nominating com. 1982, 87, coun. 1990-93), Am. Heart Assn. (sci. adv. bd. 1984-87). Avocation: watercolor painting. Office: Stanford U Sch Medicine Beckman Ctr Dept Devel Biology Stanford CA 94305

SHAPIRO, MARCIA HASKEL, speech and language pathologist; b. N.Y.C., Nov. 6, 1949; d. Ben and Edna Haskel; m. Louis Shapiro, Aug. 1, 1981. BA, Hunter Coll., 1982; MA, NYU, 1983; MA in Speech Pathology, U. Ctrl. Fla., 1991; PhD, Barrington U., 2001. Cert. deaf educator, Fla. Tchr. deaf Pub. Sch. 47, N.Y.C., 1983-84; speech pathologist St. Francis Sch. for the Deaf, Bklyn., 1984-86, Seminole County Schs., 1986-87, Lake County Schs., 1987-89, Orange County Schs., Orlando, Fla., 1989-91, West Volusia Meml. Hosp., Deland, 1991-93, Orlando Regional Med. Ctr., 1993, Sand Lake Hosp., 1993-98; staff head swallowing dept. Leesburg Regional Med. Ctr., 1994; dir. speech pathology Fla. Hosp., Waterman, 1995—, rsch. assoc. dysphasia study. Mem. AFTRA, EQUITY, Am. Speech and Hearing Assn., Annals of Deaf, Coun. Am. Instrs. of the Deaf, Alexander Graham Bell Assn. for Deaf. E-mail: marcy6116@aol.com.

SHAPIRO, MARIAN KAPLUN, psychologist; b. N.Y., July 13, 1939; d. David and Bertha (Pearlman) Kaplun; m. Irwin Ira Shapiro, Dec. 20, 1959; children: Steven, Nancy. BA, Queens Coll., 1959; MA in Tchg., Harvard U., 1961, EdD, 1978. Cert. psychologist. Tchr. North Quincy (Mass.) HS, 1962-64; instr. Carnegie Inst., Boston, 1968-74; staff psychologist South Shore Counselling Assn., Hanover, 1978-80; pvt. practice Lexington, 1980—. Adj. instr. Mass. Sch. Profl. Psychology, Dedham, 1985—. Author: (book) 2nd Childhood: Hypnoplay Therapy with Age--Regressed Adults, 1989; contbr. articles to profl. jours., poetry to lit. jours. Fellow: Am. Orthopsychiatric Assn.; mem.: APA, New Eng. Soc. Clin. Hypnosis, Internat. Soc. Study Dissociation, New Eng. Soc. Treatment Trauma and Dissociation, Am. Soc. Clin. Hypnosis (cert. cons.), Am. Soc. Group Psychotherapy (clin.), N.E. Soc. Group Psychotherapy, Mass. Psychol. Assn., Pi Lambda Theta, Sigma Alpha. Jewish Quaker. Avocations: music, singing, piano, violin, writing poetry. Home and Office: 17 Lantern Ln Lexington MA 02421-6029 E-mail: mkshapiro@rcn.com.

SHAPIRO, MARK, advertising executive; b. St. Louis, June 7, 1951; s. Harvey and Florley (Schimmel) S.; m. Patricia Suzanne Moore, Nov. 26, 1975; children: Andrew Phillip, Max Manlin. BA in English, Wash. U., 1973; MA in Journalism, U. Mo., 1975. Writer Maritz Inc., St. Louis, 1975-77, assoc. creative dir., 1977-78; creative dir. The Hanley Partnership, 1979-81, sr. v.p., 1981-84; mng. ptnr. The Hermann Group, 1984-86, pres., 1986—, Louis London (formerly The Hermann Group), St. Louis, 1988-90; CEO Louis London, 1990-99; chmn. & CEO Momentum N. Am., St. Louis MO, 1999—. Recipient N.Y. Art Dirs. award, 1982, Print ICA award, 1981-82. Mem. St. Louis Advt. Club, St. Louis Advt. Fed. (Flair award 1982-86, Addys award 1987), NIJADC-St. Louis, Phi Beta Kappa. Office: Momentum 6665 Delmar Blvd Ste 300 Saint Louis MO 63130-4525*

SHAPIRO, MARK HOWARD, physicist, educator, academic dean, consultant; b. Boston, Apr. 18, 1940; s. Louis and Sara Ann (Diamond) S.; m. Anita Rae Lavine, June 8, 1961; children: David Gregory, Diane Elaine, Lisa Michelle. AB with honors, U. Calif., Berkeley, 1962; MS (NSF coop. fellow), U. Pa., 1963, PhD, 1966. Research fellow Kellogg Radiation Lab., Calif. Inst. Tech., Pasadena, 1966-68; vis. assoc. divsn. math., physics and astronomy Calif. Inst. Tech., 1976—; research assoc. Nuclear Structure Research Lab. U. Rochester (N.Y.), 1968-70; mem. faculty Calif. State U., Fullerton, 1970—, prof. physics, 1978—, acting assoc. dean Sch. Math., Sci. and Engring., 1985-86, acting dir. Office Faculty Research and Devel., 1986-87, chmn. physics dept., 1989-96, 98-01; dir. tchr. enhancement program NSF, Washington, 1987-88. Tour speaker Am. Chem. Soc., 1983-85 Editor, publisher: The Irascible Professor, 1999; contbr. over 125 articles to profl. jours. Pres. Pasadena Young Democrats, 1967-68; mem. pub. info. and edn. com. Calif. Task Force on Earthquake Preparedness, 1981-85; bd. dirs. Calif. State U. Fullerton Found., 1982-85. Grantee Research Corp., 1971-74, Calif. Inst. Tech., 1977-78, U.S. Geol. Survey, 1978-85, Digital Equipment Corp., 1982, NSF, 1985-87, 90—. Mem. AAAS, Am. Phys. Soc., Am. Assn. Physics Tchrs. (profl. concerns com. 1990-93, chmn. 1991-93), Am. Geophys. Union, N.Y. Acad. Scis., Materials Rsch. Soc., Coun. on Undergrad. Rsch. (physics/astronomy councillor 1993—). Achievements include research in experimental nuclear physics, experimental nuclear astrophysics, geophysics and atomic collisions in solids. Office: Calif State Univ Physics Dept Fullerton CA 92834-6866 E-mail: mshapiro@fullerton.edu.

SHAPIRO, MARSHA N. social worker; b. Phila., July 19, 1954; MSW, U. Pa., 1981. LCSW N.J., bd. cert. diplomate EMDR traind clinician. Clin. social worker Jewish Family Svc., Harrisburg, Pa., 1981-83, Asbury Park, N.J., 1984-90, Advanced Psychol. Assessments, Freehold, NJ, 1990—94; pvt. practice clin. social work Dayton and Toms River, 1994—. Avocations: dancing, hiking, tennis, photography, guitar. Office: 214 Washington St Toms River NJ 08753

SHAPIRO, MARTIN FREDERICK, internist, educator; b. Montreal, Que., Can., June 17, 1948; came to U.S., 1976; s. Myer and Tillie (Abramovitch) S.; m. Barbara Vickrey, July 14, 1990; children: Matthew Loren, Daniel Vickrey. MD, McGill U., 1969; MPH, UCLA, 1978, PhD, 1983. Asst. prof. medicine UCLA, 1980-86, assoc. prof., 1986-92, prof. medicine, 1992—, chief divsn. of gen. internal medicine, health svcs. rsch., 1992—; cons. The Rand Corp., Santa Monica, Calif., 1988—. Mem. Assn. of Am. Physicians, Am. Soc. for Clin. Investigation. Office: U Calif 911 Broxton Ave Divsn of Gen Internal Med Los Angeles CA 90095-1736

SHAPIRO, MARVIN LINCOLN, communications company executive; b. Erie, Pa., Feb. 12, 1923; s. Hyman and Flora (Burstein) S.; m. B. Gertrude Berkman, Oct. 25, 1946; children: Susan Jo, Barbara Ann, Jonathan David. BS, Syracuse U., 1948; postgrad., Williams Coll., 1966, Columbia U., 1975. Account exec. WSYR, Syracuse, 1948-50; account exec. sta. WCAU-TV, Phila., 1950-55, nat. sales mgr., 1956-58; account exec. CBS TV Spot Sales, Chgo., 1955-56, N.Y.C., 1958-60; with TV Advt. Reps., Inc., 1961-66, exec. v.p., 1965-66, pres., 1968-69, dir., vice chmn., 1969-77, chmn., 1978; pres. Radio Advt. Reps., Inc., N.Y.C., 1966-68, dir., vice chmn., 1969-77; exec. v.p., COO, pres. sta. group Westinghouse Broadcasting Co., Inc., N.Y.C., 1969-77, sr. v.p., 1978-83, also dir., 1969-83; pres., dir. Foxwood Comm. Inc., N.Y.C., 1983—; mng. dir. Veronis, Suhler & Assocs., 1983—; pres., dir. Farragut Comm., Inc., 1992-99, Columbia Empire Broadcasting Corp., Yakima, Wash., 1992-96. Bd. dirs. Broadcasting Ptnrs. Holdings, L.P., 1996-2000, VS&A Spectrum, Inc., 1997-2000; chmn. bd. Micro-Relay, Inc., 1974-83; chmn. bd. dirs., pres. CATV Enterprises, Inc., 1970-83. Boxing official Pa. Athletic Commn., 1952-55; Bd. dirs. TV Bur. Advt., 1974-81, chmn., 1977-79; bd. dirs. Radio Advt. Bur., 1970-77; With USAAF, 1942-45. Decorated Air medal with 9 oak leaf clusters.; recipient Communications Alumni award Syracuse U., 1960 Mem. Internat. Radio and TV Soc., DAV, Alpha Epsilon Rho (hon.). Clubs: Long Ridge (Stamford). Home: 26 Foxwood Rd Stamford CT 06903-2207 Office: Foxwood Communications Inc 866 United Nations Plz New York NY 10017-1822

SHAPIRO, MARVIN SEYMOUR, lawyer; b. N.Y.C., Oct. 26, 1936; s. Benjamin and Sally (Book) S.; m. Natalie Kover, July 12, 1959; children: Donna, Meryl. AB, Columbia U., 1957, LLB, 1959. Bar: D.C. 1959, Calif. 1962. Atty. appellate sect. Civil Div. U.S. Dept. Justice, Washington, 1959-61; ptnr. Irell & Manella, L.A., 1962-99, mng. ptnr., 1992-97. Lectr. U. So. Calif. Tax Inst., Calif. Continuing Edn. of the Bar, Practising Law Inst. Articles editor Columbia Law Rev., 1958-59. V.p., bd. dirs. Jewish Fedn. Coun., L.A., 1985-95; treas. Alan Cranston Campaign, 1974, 80, 86; chmn. credentials com. Dem. Nat. Com., 1972-76; bd. dirs. L.A. Opera Co., 1997—. Mem. Beverly Hills Barristers (pres. 1970). Avocations: travel, golf. Home: 432 N Cliffwood Ave Los Angeles CA 90049-2620

SHAPIRO, MATHIEU JODE, lawyer; b. Phila., Feb. 17, 1969; s. Irving Lawrence and Sharon (Gertner) Shapiro; m. Jessica Sarah Singai, Aug. 18, 1996; children: Jacob Singai, Alexandra Haya. BA, Amherst Coll., 1991; JD, Boston Coll., 1995. Bar: Pa. 1995, N.J. 1995, U. S. Dist. (ea. dist.) Pa. 1996, U.S. Dist. Ct. N.JJ. 1996, U.S. Ct. Appeals (3d cir.) 1997. Assoc. Obermayer, Rebmann, Maxwell & Hippel, Phila., 1995—. Bd. dirs. Friends Select Alumni Bd., Phila., 1996—. Mem. ABA, Pa. Bar Assn., Phila. Bar Assn. Office: Obermayer Robmann Maxwell & Hippel 1617 J F K Blvd Ste 1900 Philadelphia PA 19103 E-mail: Mathieu.shapiro@obermayer.com.

SHAPIRO, MATTHEW DAVID, economist, educator; b. Mpls., Apr. 11, 1958; s. Irving and Janet (Reinstein) S.; m. Susan L. Garetz, Oct. 21, 1989; children: Benjamin Avigdor, Molly Kendall. BA summa cum laude, MA, Yale U., 1979; PhD, MIT, 1984. Jr. staff economist Coun. Econ. Advisers, Washington, 1979-80, sr. economist, 1993-94; asst. prof. Yale U., New Haven, 1984-89; assoc. prof. U. Mich., Ann Arbor, 1989-95, prof., 1995—, sr. rsch. scientist, 2000—. Rschr. Nat. Bur. Econ. Rsch., Cambridge, Mass., 1986—; mem. acad. adv. coun. Fed. Res. Bank Chgo., 1995-; mem. com. on nat. stats. NAS, 1999-; mem. Fed. Econ. Stats. Adv. Com., 2000-. Bd. editors Am. Econ. Rev., 1993-96, 00—, co-editor, 1997-00; contbr. articles to profl. jours. Recipient Paul A. Samuelson Cert. of Excellence, TIAA-CREF, 1997; Olin fellow Nat. Bur. Econ. Rsch., Cambridge, 1986-87, Alfred P. Sloan fellow Sloan Found., 1991-93. Mem. Am. Econ. Assn., Econometric Soc., Phi Beta Kappa. Office: U Mich Dept Econs 611 Tappan Ave Ann Arbor MI 48109-1220

SHAPIRO, MAURICE MANDEL, astrophysicist; b. Jerusalem, Israel, Nov. 13, 1915; came to U.S., 1921; s. Asher and Miriam R. (Grunbaum) S.; m. Inez Weinfield, Feb. 8, 1942 (dec. Oct. 1964); children: Joel Nevin, Elana Shapiro Ashley Naktin, Raquel Tamar Shapiro Kislinger. BS, U. Chgo., 1936, MS, 1940, PhD, 1942. Instr. physics and math. Chgo. City Colls., 1937-41; chmn. dept. phys. and biol. scis. Austin Coll., 1938-41; instr. math. Gary Coll., 1942; physicist Dept. Navy, 1942-44; lectr. physics and math. George Washington U., 1943-44; group leader, mem. coordinating council of lab. Los Alamos Sci. Lab., U. Calif., 1944-46; sr. physicist, lectr. Oak Ridge Nat. Lab., Union Carbon and Carbide Corp., 1946-49. Cons. div. nuc. energy for propulsion aircraft Fairchild Engine & Aircraft Corp., 1948-49; head cosmic ray br. nucleonics div. U.S. Naval Research Lab., Washington, 1949-65, supt. nucleonics div., 1953-65, founder, chief scientist Lab for Cosmic Physics, 1949-82, apptd. to chair of cosmic ray physics, 1966-82, chief scientist emeritus, 1982—; lectr. U. Md., 1949-50, 1952—, assoc. prof., 1950-51, vis. prof. physics and astronomy, 1986—; vis. prof. physics and astronomy U. Iowa, 1981-84; vis. prof. astrophysics U. Bonn, 1982-84; vis. scientist Max Planck Inst. für Astrophysik, W. Ger., 1984-85; cons. Argonne Nat. Lab., 1949; cons. panel on cosmic rays U.S. nat. com. IGY; lectr. physics and engring. Nuclear Products-Erco div. ACF Industries, Inc., 1956-58; lectr. E. Fermi Internat. Sch. Physics, Varenna, Italy, 1962; vis. prof. Weizmann Inst. Sci., Rehovoth, Israel, 1962-63, Inst. Math. Scis., Madras, India, 1971; Inst. Astronomy and Geophysics Nat. U. Mex., 1976; vis. prof. physics and astronomy Northwestern U., Evanston, Ill., 1978, exec. dir. Astrophysics Assocs.(non profit corp.) 1995—; cons. space rsch. in astronomy Space Sci. Bd., Nat. Acad. Scis., 1965; cons. Office Space Scis., NASA, 1965-66, 89; prin. investigator Gemini S-9 Cosmic Ray Expts., NASA, 1964-69, Skylab, 1967-76, Long Duration Exposure Facility, 1977—; mem. Groupe de Travail de Biologie Spatiale, Council of Europe, 1970—; mem. steering com. DUMAND Consortium, 1976—, mem. exec. com., 1979-82, mem. sci. adv. com., 1982—; lectr. Summer Space Inst., Deutsche Physikalische Gesellschaft, 1972; dir. Internat. Sch. Cosmic-Ray Astrophysics, Ettore Majorana Centre Sci. Culture, Erice, Italy, 1977—; chmn. U.S. IGY com on interdisciplinary research, mem. nuclear emulsion panel space sci. bd.; Nat. Acad. Scis., 1959— ; chief U.S. rep., steering com. Internat. Coop. Emulsion Flights for Cosmic Ray Research; cons. CREI Atomics, 1959—; vis. com. Bartol Research Found., Franklin Inst., 1967-74; mem. U.S. organizing com. 13th and 19th Internat. Confs. on Cosmic Rays; mem. sci. adv. com. Internat. Confs. on Nuclear Photography and Solid State Detectors, 1966—; mem. Com. of Honor for Einstein Centennial, Acad. Naz. Lincei, 1977; mem. Internat. Organizing com. Tex. Symposia on Relativistic Astrophysics, 1976—; Regents lectr. U. Calif. Riverside, 1985; Edison lectr. Naval Rsch. Lab award, 1990. Mem. editorial bd. Astrophysics and Space Sci., 1968-75; assoc. editor: Phys. Rev. Letters, 1977-84; editor (NATO) ASI Series on Cosmic-Ray Astrophysics; contbr. to Am. Inst. Handbook of Physics, various encys. Mem. exec. bd. Cong. Beth Chai, Washington, 1987—; trustee Nat. Capital Astronomers, Washington, 1989—; mem. internat. panel Chernobyl World Lab., 1988. Recipient Disting. Civilian Svc. award Dept. Navy, 1967, medal of honor Soc. for Encouragement au Progrés, 1978, Sr. U.S. Scientist award Alexander von Humboldt Found., 1982, Profl. Achievement citation U. Chgo., 1992; Guggenheim fellow, 1962-63. Fellow Am. Phys. Soc. (chmn. organizing com. div. cosmic physics, chmn. 1971-72, com. on publs. 1977-79), AAAS, Washington Acad. Scis. (past com. chmn., Disting. Career in Scis. award, 1993); mem. Am. Astron. Soc. (exec. com. div. high-energy astrophysics 1978—, chmn., 1982), Philos. Soc. Washington (past pres.), Am. Technion Soc. (Washington bd.), Alexander von Humboldt Assn. of Am. (pres. Washington area chpt. 2000—), Assn. Los Alamos Scientists (past chmn.), Assn. Oak Ridge Engrs. and Scientists (past chmn.), Fedn. Am. Scientists (past mem. exec. com., nat. council), Internat. Astron. Union (organizing com. commn. on high-energy astrophysics), Internat. Conf. on Cosmic Rays (Victor Hess Meml. lectr., Rome, 1995), Phi Beta Kappa, Sigma Xi (Edison lectr. 1990). Clubs: Cosmos (Washington). Achievements include patents in field; discovery of first definitive evidence for production of cosmic ray secondaries in the interstellar medium; first determination of the source composition of cosmic rays; research in cosmic radiation, composition, origin, propagation, and nuclear transformations; in high-energy astrophysics; in particles and fields; in nuclear physics, neutron physics and fission reactors; in hydrodynamics and gamma-ray and neutrino astronomy. Office: 205 S Yoakum Pkwy Apt 1514 Alexandria VA 22304-3838 *In scientific achievement, good judgement (e.g., in choice of research problems)is sometimes more important than brilliance.*

SHAPIRO, MEL, playwright, director, drama educator; b. Bklyn., Dec. 16, 1935; s. Benjamin Shapiro and Lillian (Lazarus) Bestul; m. Jeanne Elizabeth Shapiro, Feb. 23, 1963; children: Joshua, Benjamin. BFA, MFA, Carnegie-Mellon U., 1961. Resident dir. Arena Stage, Washington, 1963-65; producing dir. Tyrone Guthrie Theater, Mpls., 1968-70; master tchr. drama NYU, N.Y.C., 1970-80; guest dir. Lincoln Ctr. Repertory, 1970; dir. N.Y. Shakespeare Festival, 1971-77; prof. Carnegie Mellon U., Pitts., 1980-90, head. dept., 1980-87. Head acting UCLA Sch. Theater, Film and TV, 1990—. Dir. N.Y.C. prodns. The House of Blue Leaves, 1970, Bosoms and Neglect, 1978, Marco Polo Sings a Solo, 1998, Taming of the Shrew, 1999; co-adaptor mus. Two Gentlemen of Verona, 1971 (Tony award); author: (plays) The Price of Admissions, 1984 (Drama-Logue mag. award), The Lay of the Land (Joseph Kesselring award 1990), A Life of Crime, 1993; (books) An Actor Performs, 1996, The Director's Companion, 1998. With U.S. Army, 1955-57. Recipient N.Y. Drama Critics award, 1971, 72, Obie award Village Voice, 1972, Drama Desk award, 1973, Drama-logue award, 1993. Mem. Soc. Stage Dirs. and Choreographers (founder, editor The Jour. 1978). Office: UCLA Sch Theatre Film & TV 405 Hilgard Ave Los Angeles CA 90095-9000 E-mail: mshapiro@ucla.edu.

SHAPIRO, MICHAEL BRUCE, lawyer; b. Akron, Ohio, 1947; BBA summa cum laude, Kent State U., 1969; JD magna cum laude, U. Mich., 1972. Bar: Mich. 1972. Ptnr. Honigman Miller Schwartz & Cohn, LLP, Detroit. Mem. Nat. Assn. of Real Estate Investment Trusts subcom. on state and local taxes, citizens property tax commn. Mich. Senate, 1986-87. Mem. ABA, Am. Property Tax Counsel, State Bar of Mich., Inst. Property Taxation, Order of the Coif, Beta Alpha Psi, Pi Sigma Alpha, Beta Gamma Sigma. Office: Honigman Miller Schwartz & Cohn 2290 1st Nat Bldg Detroit MI 48226 E-mail: mbs@honigman.com.

SHAPIRO, MICHAEL EDWARD, museum director; b. N.Y.C., Nov. 15, 1949; s. Edward Aaron and Sylvia (Fishman) S.; m. Elizabeth Harvey, 1977; 2 children. BA, Hamilton Coll., 1972; MA, Williams Coll., 1976, Harvard U., 1978, PhD, 1980. Asst. prof. dept. art history Duke U., Durham, N.C., 1980-84; curator 19th-20th century art St. Louis Art Mus., 1984-92, chief curator, 1987-92; dir. Los Angeles County Mus. Art, 1992-93; dir. mus. programs, chief curator High Mus. Art, Atlanta, 1994-95, dep. dir., chief curator, 1996-99, dir., 2000—. Mng. curator Impressionism: Paintings Collected by European Mus., 1999. Author: Bronze Casting and American Sculpture, 1985; contbg. author: Frederic Remington: The Masterworks, 1988, George Caleb Bingham, 1990; mng. curator, editor Rings: Five Passions in World Art, 1996; co-curator Impressionism: Paintings Collected by European Museums, 1998.

SHAPIRO, MICHAEL HENRY, government executive; b. Bayonne, N.J., Sept. 23, 1948; s. William and Sophie (Slotkin) S. BS, Lehigh U., 1970; MS, Harvard U., 1972, PhD, 1976. Assoc. prof. Harvard U., Cambridge, Mass., 1976-82, analyst, 1980-81, br. chief, 1981-83, dir. econs. and tech. divsn., 1983-89; dep. asst. adminstr., air and radiation U.S. EPA, Washington, 1989-93, dir. office of solid waste, 1993-99, dep. asst. adminstr., solid waste and emergency response, 1999—. Office: EPA # 5101 1200 Pennsylvania Ave NW Washington DC 20460-0002

SHAPIRO, NELLA IRENE, surgeon; b. N.Y.C., Nov. 13, 1947; d. Eugene and Ethel (Pearl) S.; m. Jack Schwartz, Oct. 16, 1977; children: Max, Molly. BA, Barnard Coll., 1968; MD, Albert Einstein Coll., 1972. Resident in gen. surgery Montefiore Hosp., N.Y.C., 1972-76; mem. staff North Cen. Hosp., Bronx, N.Y., 1976-77, Bronx Mcpl. Hosp., 1977-87; chief gen. surgery Bronx Mcpl. Hosp. Ctr., 1983-87; mem. staff in gen. surgery Albert Einstein Coll. Hosp., Bronx, 1977-93, chief gen. surgery, 1991-93; atty. Lear Surg. Assocs., 1993-94; pvt. solo practice Bronx, 1994—. Asst. prof. surgery Albert Einstein Coll., Bronx, 1980—; assoc. dir. gen. surgery Weller Hosp., Bronx, 1991-93; co-founder Whaecom Breast Ctr., Bronx, 1991—. Fellow Am. Coll. Surgeons. Avocations: travel, skiing. Office: 1515 Jarrett Pl Bronx NY 10461-2606

SHAPIRO, NELSON HIRSH, lawyer; b. Feb. 3, 1928; s. Arthur and Anna (Zenitz) S.; m. Helen Lenora Sykes, June 27, 1948; children: Ronald Evan, Mitchell Wayne, Jeffrey Mark, Julie Beth. BEE, Johns Hopkins U., 1948; JD, George Washington U., 1952. Bar: D.C. 1952, Va. 1981. Patent examiner U.S. Patent Office, 1948-50; patent advisor U.S. Signal Corps, 1950-52; mem. Shapiro & Shapiro, Arlington, Va., 1952-98, Vorys, Sater, Seymour and Pease LLP, Washington, 1998-2001, Miles & Stockbridge, McLean, Va., 2001—. Patentee; contbr. articles to legal publs. and Ency. of Patent Practice and Invention Mgmt., 1964. Mem. ABA, Am. Patent Law Assn., Bar Assn. D.C., Order of Coif, Tau Beta Pi. Home: 7001 Old Cabin Ln Rockville MD 20852-4531 Office: 1751 Pinnacle Dr Ste 500 Mc Lean VA 22102-3833 E-mail: nshapiro@milesstockbridge.com.

SHAPIRO, NICHOLAS JOHN, real estate executive; b. Highland Park, Ill., Sept. 30, 1963; s. Harold David and Beatrice Cahn Shapiro; m. Elizabeth Hemke, Sept. 16, 1990; children: Daniel Frederick, Martin David. AB, Harvard U., 1985; M in Urban Planning and Policy, U. Ill., Chgo., 1996. Fin. analyst LaSalle Ptnrs. Inc., Chgo., 1985-88; v.p. Chgo. Equity Fund, 1989—, Ill. Equity Fund, Chgo., 1997—; pres. Cmty. Reinvestment Fund, 1997—. Cellist Columbia (Mo.) Civic Orch. Bd. mem. Airport Adv. Bd., Columbia, Mo., 1999—. Mem. Lambda Alpha. Democrat. Home: 4013 Newport Ct Columbia MO 65203-5859 Office: Cmty Reinvestment Fund 1 E Superior St Ste 604 Chicago IL 60611-2597

SHAPIRO, NINA LISBETH, pediatric otolaryngologist; b. N.Y.C., June 19, 1965; d. Stanley and Dee Shapiro. AB, Cornell U., 1987; MD, Harvard U., 1991. Diplomate Am Bd. Med. Examiners, Am. Bd. Otolaryngology-Head and Neck Surgery. Clin. fellow in otology and otolaryngology Harvard Med. Sch., Boston, 1992-96; fellow in pediatric otolaryngology Great Ormond St. Hosp., London, 1996, Children's Hosp. of San Diego, 1997; asst. prof. pediatric otolaryngology UCLA Sch. Medicine, 1997—. Cons. Rand Corp., Santa Monica, Calif., 1998—. Contbr. articles to profl. jours. Recipient Certificat d'Honneur, Concours Nat. de Francais, 1979, 80, Charles Ferguson awrd for clin. rsch. Am. Soc. for Pediatric Otolaryngology, 1998; Kellogg Found. rsch. grantee, 1986-87. Fellow AAAS, Am. Acad. Pediatrics; mem. Am. Acad. Otolaryngology-Head and Neck Surgery, Soc. for Ear, Nose and Throat Advances in Children, Soc. Univ. Otolaryngologists, Am. Cleft Palate-Craniofacial Assn., L.A. Soc. Otolaryngology-Head and Neck Surgery, Phi Beta Kappa. Avocations: flute, piccolo, running, bicycling. Office: UCLA Div Head and Neck Surgery 62-158 CHS 10833 Leconte Ave Los Angeles CA 90095-0001 E-mail: nshapiro@ucla.edu.

SHAPIRO, NORMAN RICHARD, Romance languages and literatures educator; b. Boston, Nov. 1, 1930; s. Harry Alexander and Eva (Goldberg) S. BA, Harvard U., 1951, MA, 1952, PhD, 1958; Diplôme de Langue et Lettres Françaises, Université d'Aix-Marseille, 1956, MA (hon.), 1972. Instr. French Amherst Coll., 1958-60; asst. prof. romance langs. and lits. Wesleyan U., 1960-65, assoc. prof., 1965-71, prof., 1971—. Editor: Echos, 1965, Palabres, 1973; translator, editor: Négritude, 1971; translator: Four Farces by Georges Feydeau, 1970, Comedy of Eros, 1971, Kamouraska by Anne Hébert, 1973, Virginie, or the Dawning of the World by Joseph Majault, 1974, The Camp of The Saints by Jean Raspail, 1975, Feydeau, First to Last, 1982, Fables from Old French: Aesop's Beasts and Bumpkins, 1983, A Fitting Confusion by Georges Feydeau, 1985, The Pregnant Pause, or Love's Labor Lost, by Georges Feydeau, 1987, The Brazilian by Henry Meilhac and Ludovic Halévy, 1987, A Slap in the Farce by Eugène Labiche, 1988, A Matter of Wife and Death by Eugène Labiche, 1988, Fifty Fables of La Fontaine, 1988, The Fabulists French: Verse Fables of Nine Centuries, 1992, La Fontaine's Bawdy: Of Libertines, Louts and Lechers, 1992, A Flea in Her Rear, or Ants in Her Pants, and Other Vintage French Farces, 1994, Fifty More Fables of La Fontaine, 1998, Selected Poems from Les Fleurs du Mal, 1998, One Hundred and One Poems of Paul Verlaine, 1999 (MLA Scaglione award 2000), All Gall: Malicious Monologues and Ruthless Recitations, 1999, Once Again, La Fontaine, 2001, Take Her, She's Yours, or Till Divorce Do Them Part, 2001, The Jew of Seville, by Victor Sejour, 2002, The Fortune Teller, by Victor Sejour, 2002, Lyrics of the French Renaissance: Maror, De Bellay and Ronsard, 2002; composer: Three Songs, 1961; mem. editl. bd. Tex. Rev.; contbr. articles, transls. and revs. to profl. jours. Mem. African Studies Assn., Am. Assn. Tchrs. French, Universala Esperanto-Asocio, Esperanto League N.Am., Judezmo Soc., Am. Lit. Transl. Assn. (Disting. Translation award 1992), Am. Translators Assn., Dramatists Guild, Beast Fable Soc. (editorial bd. Bestia), Poetry Soc. of Am., Acad. of Am. Poets, Signet Soc. of Harvard, Delta Kappa Epsilon. Jewish. E-mial. Office: Wesleyan U Dept Romance Langs & Lit 300 High St Middletown CT 06459-3233 E-mail: nshapiro@wesleyan.edu.

SHAPIRO, PAUL ARNOLD, museum director; b. Framingham, Mass., Oct. 30, 1946; s. Morris and Ann Helen S.; m. Stephanie Boiangiu, Aug. 15, 1975 (div. Dec. 1994); children: Eve Ilana, Daniel Isaac. BA, Harvard U., 1968; M of Internat. Affairs, Columbia U., 1970, MPhil in History, 1980. Assoc. editor U.S. Info. Agy., Washington, 1976-80, program officer, 1980-81, exec. asst. to assoc. dir., 1981-89, dir. cmty. rels., 1989-97; exec. asst. to dir. U.S. Holocaust Meml. Mus., 1997-99, dir. ctr. advanced holocaust studies, 2000—. Editor Jour. Internat. Affairs, 1969-70; assoc. editor Problems of Communism, 1976-80; contbr. articles to profl. jours. Bd. dirs. Temple Rodef Shalom, 1986-88. Fulbright Hays fellow, 1973-76, Internat. Rsch. & Exch. fellow, 1973-76, Josephine de Karman fellow, San Diego, 1980-81, George Washington U. fellow, 1980-81. Avocations: singing, piano. Office: US Holocaust Mus 100 Raoul Wallenberg Pl Washington DC 20024

SHAPIRO, PAUL SAUVEUR, chemical engineer, researcher; b. Pitts., Dec. 4, 1942; s. Carl Lynwood and Lillian Ruth (Simon) S.; m. Melissa Friedland, Jan. 19, 1986 (div. 1997); 1 child, Felix Benjamin. SB in Chem. Engring., MIT, 1963, SM in Chem. Engring., 1965, postgrad., 1967-71; EdM in Ednl. Planning, Harvard U., 1966. Expert cons. HEW and Action, Washington, 1972-76; sr. staff officer NRC, 1976-77; cons. Office Sci. and Tech. Adviser World Bank, 1977-80; cons. on nat. and internat. sci. and tech. AID, NSF and other agys., 1980-81; cons. Office Toxic Substances EPA, 1981-82, environ. engr. Office of Solid Waste, 1983-84, program mgr. Office R&D, 1985-94, CSI coord. Office R&D, 1994—. Vis. sr. rschr. Tel Aviv (Israel) U., 1979. Contbr. over 20 articles to profl. publs. Vol., advisor Vols. in Tech. Assistance, Arlington, Va., 1978-81; chmn. career edn. adv. coun. Washington Pub. Schs.; vice chmn. Early Environs., Inc. Fellow NDEA, NDFL, 1967, 70. Mem. AIChE (program coord.), Fed. Water Quality Assn. (sec.), Air and Waste Mgmt. Assn. (work group leader), MIT Club of Washington (pres.), MIT Luncheon Club (pres.), Sigma Xi, Phi Delta Kappa. Democrat. Jewish. Achievements include development of mitigation research programs for radon, indoor air pollution, stratospheric ozone protection, global climate change, and mixed hazardous and radioactive wastes; development of pollution prevention research programs with metal finishing and electronics industries; development with SBA and DOC of cooperative technical assistance programs for small business; co-development and implementation of EPA's highest priority program, The Common Sense Initiative including development of the first national sectoral environmental R&D plan; project officer environmental research grants. Avocations: mysteries, swimming, singing, computers. Home: 1312 4th St SW Washington DC 20024-2202 Office: EPA Office R&D (8722R) 401 M St SW Washington DC 20024-2610

SHAPIRO, PAULA, retired maternal/women's health nurse; b. Pitts., Nov. 16, 1927; d. Ben and Esther (Halpert) Cohn; m. Bernard Shapiro, July 17, 1982; children: Eugene Hershorin, Gary Hershorin, Marc Hershorin, Jay Hershorin, Ellen Fenerty, Kenneth, Fred, Stacy Pierce. RN, Montefiore Hosp. Sch. Nursing, 1948; BS, Phila. U., 1987. RN, Pa. Nursing care coord. Thomas Jefferson U. Hosp., Phila.; asst. supr. operating rm. Wakefield (R.I.) Gen. Hosp.; staff RN operating rm. Jefferson Hosp., Phila., ret., 1993. Contbr. articles to profl. jours. Vol. Thomas Jefferson U. Hosp. Home: 1500 Locust St Apt 2216 Philadelphia PA 19102-4317 E-mail: bpshap@aol.com.

SHAPIRO, PHILIP ALAN, lawyer; b. Chgo., May 14, 1940; s. Joe and Nettie (Costin) Shapiro; m. Joyce Barbara Chapnick, May 29, 1966; children: David Ian, Russell Scott, Mindi Jennifer. AA, Wilson Coll., 1960; BS in Fin., So. Ill. U., 1965; MBA, Nat. Univ., San Diego, Calif., 1975; MBA in Mktg. with distinction, San Diego State U., San Diego, 1977; JD, JD, Western State U., 1985. Bar: Calif. 1988. Spl. agt. U.S. Secret Svc., Washington, 1965-67, Chgo., 1967-77; mgr. divsn. sales Roche Labs. divsn. Hoffman-La Roche, Inc.; account exec. Cellular Comm., Inc., San Diego, 1985; with Complete Comm., 1983—; assoc. Law Office Jeffrey S. Schwartz, 1988-91; pvt. practice, 1991—. Chair gen. and solo practice sect. State Bar of Calif. Editor (law rev.): We. State U. Coll. Law. Mem. adv. bd. Spreckes Elem. Sch., San Diego, 1976—77; mem. Univ. City Town Coun., 1977; pres. Congregation Beth El, La Jolla, 1976—79. With USMC, 1958—60. Recipient Merit award, U.S. Treasury Dept., 1965, Israel Solidarity award, 1977, U. Of Judaism award, 1978. Mem.: ABA (vice chmn. gen. practice sect.), San Diego Bus. Referrals (pres. 1998—99), San Diego County Bar Assn., State Bar Calif. (Wiley W. Manuel award 1990, 1991, exec. com. gen. practice sect.), Calif. Trial Lawyers Assn., Thomas Jefferson Sch. of Law Alumni Assn. (bd. dirs.). Office: PO Box 178475 San Diego CA 92177-8475 Fax: 858-483-4639. E-mail: pshaplaw@san.rr.com.

SHAPIRO, RAQUEL, school psychologist, educator, counselor; b. Havana, Cuba; came to U.S., 1941; d. Morris and Ida (Antosvilsky) Rebe; m. Nathan Shapiro, Jan. 11, 1948; 1 child, Ronald. BS, R.I. Coll., 1960, MEd, 1966, CAGS, 1972; EdD, Boston U., 1985. Cert. sch. counselor, sch. psychologist, tchr., R.I. Prin., psychologist, counselor, tchr. Providence (R.I.) Sch. Dept., 1960-73; psychologist, counselor, prof. R.I. Coll., Providence, 1973—. Mem. Nat. Assn. Sch. Psychologists, Nat. Assn. Lab. Schs., Ea. Psychol. Assn., R.I. Sch. Psychologists. Assn., Pi Lamdba Theta, Delta Kappa Gamma (pres. 1990). Avocations: photography, music, theater. Office: Rhode Island Coll Henry Barnard Sch 600 Mount Pleasant Ave Providence RI 02908-1924 E-mail: rshapiro@ric.edu.

SHAPIRO, RAYMOND L. lawyer; b. N.Y.C., Aug. 1, 1934; s. Alexander and Sadye (Morrison) S.; m. Judith Manis, Dec. 23, 1956; children: Joel, Todd, Lisa. BS, Temple U., 1956, LLB, 1959. Ptnr. Wexler, Weisman, Forman & Shapiro, Phila., 1959-84, Blank, Rome, Comisky & McCauley, Phila., 1984—. Author: Dunlap-Hanna Pa. Forms, 1963-83, Pa. Civil Practice Handbook, 1973-83; contbg.-author: Business Workouts Manual. Trustee Phila. Fedn. Jewish Agys., 1979—, treas., 1984-87, v.p., 1987-90; pres. Jewish Pub. Group, 1992-95. Fellow Am. Coll. Bankruptcy (v.p., chmn. bd. dirs. 1997-2001); mem. ABA, Nat. Bankruptcy Conf., Pa. Bar Assn., Phila. Bar Assn. Office: Blank Rome Comisky & McCauley LLP One Logan Sq Philadelphia PA 19103-6998

SHAPIRO, RICHARD ALAN, surgeon; b. Chgo., 1927; MD, Loyola U., Maywood, Ill., 1949. Diplomate Am. Bd. Surgery, Am. Bd. Hospice and Palliative Medicine. Intern Michael Reese Hosp., Chgo., 1949—50, resident in surgery, 1950—51, 1953—66, sr. attending surgeon; clin. prof. U. Ill.; physician Chgo. ctrl. program Vitas Hospice, Ill.; pvt. practice, 1956—95. Mem.: ACS. Office: 700 N Sacramento Blvd Ste 201 Chicago IL 60612 E-mail: RichardShapiro@vitas.com.

SHAPIRO, RICHARD ALLEN, lawyer; b. Phila., Feb. 27, 1958; s. A. Morton and Sandra Shapiro; m. Judith L. Dickert, May 30, 1982; children: Sara, Sharon. BA in Politics, Brandeis U., 1980; JD, Rutgers U., 1983. Bar: N.J. 1983, Pa. 1983, U.S. Dist. Ct. N.J. 1983, U.S. Dist. Ct. (ea. dist.) Pa., 1984, U.S. Ct. Appeals (3rd cir.) 1985. Prin. Shapiro & Shapiro, P.C., Cherry Hill, N.J., 1983—; solicitor Camden County Coll., Blackwood, 1987—. Mem. Camden County Workforce Investment Bd., 1995—; del. Dem. Nat. Conv., N.Y.C., 1992; chmn. Cherry Hill Dem. Party, 1991—; vice chmn. Camden County Dem. Party, 1997—2000; bd. dirs. Jewish Nat. Fund So. N.J. Region, Cherry Hill, 1996—. Office: Shapiro and Shapiro PC 1415 Route 70 E Ste 508 Cherry Hill NJ 08034-2238

SHAPIRO, RICHARD CHARLES, publishing sales and marketing executive; b. Bklyn., May 28, 1936; s. Isidore and Sylvia (Rappaport) S.; m. Marilyn Joyce Bialy, Feb. 17, 1957 (div. 1974); children: Joseph, Scott; m. Francine L.

Shaw, Sept. 19, 1975. BS in Edn., Golden State U., 1978, MBA, 1981; PhD in Bus. Adminstrn., Honolulu U., 1987. Lic. real estate broker, Ill. Sales mgr. Coca Cola Bottling Co. of N.Y., 1955-62; affiliate Effective Motivation Assocs./Success Motivation inst., Bethpage, N.Y., 1965-68; v.p. sales, dir. Field Enterprises, Chgo., 1962-78; pres., CEO Snack-In, Inc., Detroit, 1978-82; sr. ptnr. Directions Growth and Strategy Cons., Chgo., 1982-95; v.p. domestic & internat. mktg. & sales Ency., oper. officer Ency. Brit.-Compton's Learning Co., 1991-93, specialist network mktg. & relationship mktg., CEO, pres., bd. dirs.; CEO Am.'s Home Detailing Corp., 1995—, CEO, chmn. bd., 2001—; pres., COO Am.'s Deep Clean Divsn., Deerfield, Ill., 1995—; CEO and chmn. emeritus Am.'s Home Detailing Corp.; instr. grad. studies mktg. mgmt., instr. human resources mgmt. Robert Morris Coll., Chgo., 2001—. Instr. planning Life Underwriter Tng. Coun., L.I., 1965-66; assoc. editor Media Technics Pub. Assn., Lake Forest, 1988; bd. dirs. Master Deep Clean Co., Nat. Video Libr.; spkr. on mktg., sales and leadership; cons. in field; liaison with Chgo. Daily News, Chgo. Sun Times, WFLD-TV; founder Discovery Toy Divsn. Pub.: Real Estate Property Marketing News; author various self-improvement cassettes; writer storyarts; contbr. articles to profl. jours.; author bus. writings, 1993-95. Active Explorers, high schs., youth clubs, 1965-74; founder, pres. Abundance and Goodwill Soc., 1968—. Served with USAF, 1957-60. Recipient Leadership award Am. Sales Masters, 1968, 1999-2000, POPAI-OMA Best Industry Point of Purchase Display and Mktg. award, 1992; named Sales/Mktg. Execs. Leadership Recruiter/Trainer of Decade award. Mem. Salesmen With a Purpose, Chgo. Computer Soc., Effective Motivation Assocs., Deercreek Tennis Club (tchr.). Avocations: wild-water rafting, white-water canoeing, camping, tennis, writing. E-mail: ahd10@yahoo.com.

SHAPIRO, RICHARD GERALD, retired department store executive, consultant; b. N.Y.C., Apr. 24, 1924; s. David and Sophie (Hayflich) S.; m. Lila Eig, July 27, 1951; children— Judith, Amy, Donald. BA, U. Mich., 1946; MBA, Harvard, 1948. With Lord & Taylor, N.Y.C., 1948-64, v.p., 1959-63, sr. v.p., 1963-64; also mem. adv. bd.; pres. Wm. Filene's Sons Co., Boston, 1965-68, chief exec. officer, chmn. bd., 1968-73; pres. Gimbel Bros. Corp., N.Y.C., 1973-76; v.p. W.R. Grace & Co., pres. sporting goods div., 1977-79, pres. splty. store div., 1979-84; pres. Richard Shapiro Assocs., 1979—; sr. v.p. Montgomery Ward, Inc., 1986-88. Bd. dirs. Assoc. Merchandising Corp., Nitrotec Corp., Capital Market Fund; retail chmn. Greater N.Y. Fund, 1963; chmn. merc. div. Mass. Bay United Fund, 1967 Mem. corp. Simmons Coll., Boston Mus. Fine Arts (permanent); bd. dirs. Mass. Mchts.; bd. dirs Family Counseling and Guidance Centers, 1969-72, v.p., 1970; trustee Brandeis U. Served with AUS, 1942-46. Mem. Harvard Bus. Sch. Assn. (gov.) Home: 10019 Gable Manor Ct Potomac MD 20854-5000 E-mail: rgsle@webtv.net.

SHAPIRO, ROBERT, lawyer; b. Plainfield, N.J., Sept. 2, 1942; BS in Fin., UCLA, 1965; JD, Loyola U., L.A., 1968. Bar: Calif. 1969, U.S. Ct. Appeals (9th cir.) 1972, U.S. Dist. Ct. (cen., no. & so. dists.) Calif. 1982. Dep. dist. atty. Office of Dist. Atty., L.A., 1969-72; sole practice, 1972-87, 88—; of counsel Bushkin, Gaims, Gaines, Jonas, 1987-88; Christensen, Miller, Fink & Jacobs, 1988-95; ptnr. Christensen, Miller, Fink, Jacobs, Glaser, Weil & Shapiro, 1995—. Author: Search for Justice, 1996, Misconception, 2001. Recipient Am. Jurisprudence award Bancroft Whitney, 1969. Mem. Nat. Assn. Criminal Def. Lawyers, Calif. Attys. for Criminal Justice, Trial Lawyers for Pub. Justice (founder 1982), Century City Bar Assn. (Best Criminal Def. Atty. 1993). Office: 2121 Avenue Of The Stars Fl 19 Los Angeles CA 90067-5010

SHAPIRO, ROBERT DONALD, management advisor, venture catalyst; b. Milw., Sept. 11, 1942; BS with honors, U. Wis., 1964. Cons. actuary Milliman & Robertson, Inc., Milw., 1965-80; dir. Life Ins. Cons. TPF&C, 1980-85; mng. dir. Merrill Lynch Capital Markets, 1986-87; pres. The Shapiro Network, Inc., 1987—. Home: 4923 N Oakland Ave Milwaukee WI 53217-6052 Office: 312 E Wisconsin Ave Ste 700 Milwaukee WI 53202-4305

SHAPIRO, ROBERT FRANK, investment banking company executive; b. St. Louis, Dec. 19, 1934; s. Eugene J. and Clara (Katz) S.; m. Anna Marie Susman, Dec. 21, 1960; children: Albert Andrew, Robert Jr., Jeanne Savitt. Grad., St. Louis Country Day Sch., 1952; BA, Yale U., 1956. Assoc. Lehman Bros., N.Y.C., 1956-67, ptnr., 1967-73, dir., sr. mng. dir., 1970-73; ptnr. Wertheim & Co., 1974; exec. v.p. Wertheim & Co., Inc., N.Y.C., 1974-75, pres., 1975-86; co-chmn. Wertheim Schroder & Co., Inc., 1986-87; chmn. RFS and Assocs., Inc., N.Y.C., 1988—, New Street Capital Corp., 1992-94; vice-chmn. Klingenstein, Fields & Co., L.P., N.Y.C., 1997—. Bd. dirs. TJX Cos., Inc., Genaera Corp., The Burnham Fund, chmn. nominating com. N.Y. Stock Exch., 1980, mem. regulatory adv. com., 1988—, surveillance com., 1989—; bd. govs. Am. Stock Exch., 1970-76. Trustee Lenox Hill Hosp., Skowhegan; mem. gov. bd. Yale U. Art Gallery, New Haven, 1993—; trustee Louis Comfort Tiffany Found. Mem. Securities Industry Assn. (chmn. 1985, Bond Club N.Y. (pres. 1987-88, Yale Club, Century Country Club, Knickerbocker Club. Office: Klingenstein Fields & Co LLC 787 7th Ave New York NY 10019-6018

SHAPIRO, RON, surgeon; b. L.A., July 13, 1954; MD, Stanford U., 1980. Diplomate Am. Bd. Surgery. Resident in surgery Mt. Sinai Hosp., N.Y.C., 1980-86; fellow in transplantation surgery U. Pitts., 1986-88, from instr. to asst. prof. surgery, 1989-94, assoc. prof., 1994-2000, dir. renal transplantation, 1997—; mem. staff Presbyn.-Univ Children's Hosp.; prof., 2000—. Fellow ACS; mem. Assn. Acad. Surgeons, Am. Soc. Transplant Surgeons, Am. Soc. Transplant Physicians, Am. Surg. Assn., Transplantation Soc., Ctrl. Surg. Assn., Cell Transplant Soc., Internat. Pancreas and Islet Transplantation Assn., Soc. Univ. Surgeons, Internat. Pediatric Transplant Soc. Office: U Pittsburgh 4 Falk Clin 3601 5th Ave Pittsburgh PA 15213-3403 E-mail: shapiror@msx.upmc.edu.

SHAPIRO, RONALD GARY, psychologist; b. Providence, Oct. 10, 1953; s. Nathan and Raquel (Rebe) S. BA, U. Rochester, 1975; MA, Ohio State U., 1977, PhD, 1981. Cert. human factors profl. Teaching, rsch. assoc. Ohio State U., Columbus, 1975-81; asst. prof. Denison U., Granville, Ohio, 1981-82; prin. assoc. Dunlap and Assocs. Inc., Norwalk, Conn., 1982-85; sr. engring. mgr. IBM, Poughkeepsie, N.Y., 1985-96, consulting human resources profl., 1996—. Evening faculty U. Conn., Stamford, 1983-85, Dutchess C.C., Poughkeepsie, 1986—. Contbr. articles to Psychol. Rev., Jour. Exptl. Psychology and other profl. jours. Recipient Grad. Sch. Leadership award Ohio State U., 1979; recipient Sr. Engring. Mgr. promotion IBM, 1993. Mem. APA, Soc. Indsl. Orgnl. Psychologists, Soc. Psychologists in Mgmt., Human Factors and Ergonomics Soc. (nat. program com. 1994—), SHARE, Inc. (IBM rep. 1987-91), Sigma Xi, Phi Kappa Phi. Achievements include design of computer products for easy use by people ; tng. and edn. of future profls. in human factors; presentation to assist students in career decisions and communication human factors principles to non-human factors profls., skills assessment and development processes and systems. Home: 96 Fox Run Poughkeepsie NY 12603-3517 Office: IBM MS P384 522 South Rd Poughkeepsie NY 12601-5400

SHAPIRO, SANDER S. endocrinologist, educator, obstetrician, educator, gynecologist, educator; b. Beacon, NY, Sept. 9, 1937; AB, U. Mich., 1958, MD, 1963. Diplomate Am. Bd. Ob-Gyn. (subspecialty bd. in reproductive endocrinology). Instr. spl. forces US Army Med. Corps, Ft. Bragg, NC, 1965—67; instr. ob-gyn. Harvard Med. Sch., Boston, 1971—72, U. Colo., Denver, 1973—74; asst. prof. ob-gyn. U. Wis., Madison, 1974—79, assoc. prof., 1979—89, dir. reproductive endocrinology, 1982—2000, prof. ob-gyn., 1989—. Capt. U.S. Army, 1965—67. Home: 3902 Priscilla Ln Madison WI 53705 Office: U Wis Dept Ob-Gyn-CSC 600 Highland Ave Madison WI 53792-6188

SHAPIRO, SANDER WOLF, retired lawyer; b. St. Louis, Sept. 24, 1929; s. Robert and Bess (Fisher) S.; m. Lottie F. Frankel, Aug. 14, 1955; children: Julie A. Shapiro Schechter, Susan B. Shapiro Schmitz. BA, Rice U., 1951; postgrad., Columbia U., 1951-52; JD, U. Tex., 1954. Atty. tax div. Dept. Justice, Washington, 1955-57; atty. advisor U.S. Tax Ct., 1957-58; ptnr. Clark, Thomas, Winters & Shapiro, Austin, Tex., 1958-84; sr. ptnr. Shapiro, Edens & Cook, 1984-91; of counsel Jenkens & Gilchrist, P.C., 1991-2000; ret. Adj. prof. law U. Tex., 1975-2000; lectr. in tax field. Author, editor Tex. Franchise Earned Surplus and Tax, 1985—, Family Solutions to Family Concerns, 1991—, A Walk Through Form 706, 1991—; co-editor Tex. Tax Svc., 1986-94. Bd. dirs. Austin Symphony Orch. Soc., 1974-97, dir. emeritus, 1997—, fin. v.p., 1980-95; bd. dirs. U. Tex. Coll. Fine Arts Adv. Coun., 1987-95, pres., 1991-94; bd. dirs. Capital of Tex. Pub. Telecomm. Coun., 1988-97, pres., 1994-95; bd. dirs. Ronald McDonald House of Ctrl. Tex., Austin, 1990-98, pres., 1994-95, adv. dir., 1998—; bd. dirs. Capital Met. Transit Authority, 1988-91, chair, 1990; bd. dirs. Austin Cmty. Found., 1985-92, pres., 1991; adv. coun. U. Tex. Press, 1998—, vice chmn. 1999, chmn. 2000. Sander W. Shapiro Presdl. Scholarship in Law at U. Tex. endowed in his honor by Jenkens & Gilchrist, 1992; recipient Disting. Lawyer award Travis County, 1999. Fellow Am. Bar Found. (life), Am. Coll. Tax Counsel, Tex. Bar Found. (sustaining life); mem. ABA, State Bar of Tex., Am. Law Inst., Nat. Assn. State Bar Tax Sects. (bd. dirs., chair 1997), Tex. Law Rev. Assn. (pres. 1992-93). Avocations: reading, music, golf. Office: Jenkens & Gilchrist PC 600 Congress Ave Ste 2200 Austin TX 78701-2977 E-mail: sws@austin.rr.com.

SHAPIRO, SANDOR SOLOMON, hematologist; b. Bklyn., July 26, 1933; BA, Harvard U., 1954, MD, 1957. Intern Harvard med. svc. Boston City Hosp., 1957-58, asst. resident, 1960-61; asst. surgeon divsn. biol. std. NIH, USPHS, 1958-60; NIH spl. fellow MIT, 1961-64; from instr. to assoc. prof. Cardeza Found. Jefferson Med. Coll., Phila., 1964-72, prof. medicine, 1972—, assoc. dir., 1978-85, dir., 1985-2000. Mem. hematology study sect. NIH, 1972-76, 78-79; mem. med. adv. coun. Nat. Hemophilia Found., 1973-75; chmn. Pa. State Hemophilia Adv. Com., 1974-76. Mem. Am. Soc. Clin. Investigation, Am. Soc. Hematology, Am. Assn. Immunologists, Assn. Am. Physicians, Internat. Soc. Thrombosis and Hemostasis. Achievements include research in hemostasis and thrombosis, prothrombin metabolism, hemophilia, lupus anticoagulants, endothelial cells. Office: Thomas Jefferson U Cardeza Found Hematologic Rsch 1015 Walnut St Philadelphia PA 19107-5005

SHAPIRO, SANDRA, lawyer; b. Providence, Oct. 17, 1944; d. Emil and Sarah (Cohen) S. AB magna cum laude, Bryn Mawr Coll., Pa., 1966; LLB magna cum laude, U. Pa., 1969. Bar: Mass. 1970, U.S. Dist. Ct. Mass. 1971, U.S. Ct. Appeals (1st cir.) 1972, U.S. Supreme Ct. 1980. Law clk. U.S. Ct. Appeals (1st cir.), Boston, 1969-70; assoc. Foley, Hoag & Eliot LLP, 1970-75, ptnr., 1976—. Mem. bd. bar overseers Mass. Supreme Judicial Ct., 1988-92, mem. gender bias study com., 1986-89. Contbr. articles to profl. jours. Bd. dirs. Patriots' Trail coun. Girl Scouts U.S., 1994-97; mem. bd. overseers Boston Lyric Opera, 1993-99, New England Conservatory of Music, 1995-2001, Celebrity Series of Boston, 1997—. Woodrow Wilson fellow, 1966. Mem.: ABA (ethics, profl. and pub. edn. com. 1994—), U. Pa. Law Sch. Alumni Assn. (bd. mgrs. 1990—94), Boston Bar Assn. (mem. coun.), Mass. Bar Assn. (chmn. real property sect. coun., com. on profl. ethics), Nat. Women's Law Ctr. Network, New Eng. Women in Real Estate, Women's Bar Assn. Mass. (pres. 1985—86), Boston Club, Order of Coif. Office: Foley Hoag LLP 155 Seaport Blvd Boston MA 02210-2600 E-mail: sshapiro@foleyhoag.com.

SHAPIRO, STANLEY K. lawyer; b. Bklyn., Feb. 7, 1956; s. Solomon K. and Rebecca Shapiro; m. Ann Hirsch, Aug. 4, 1985; children: Zachary Solomon, Eliezer Kahane, Rose Mariasha Hirsch, Carrie Daniela Hirsch. BA magna cum laude, SUNY, Albany, 1977; JD cum laude, U. Mich., 1980. Bar: N.Y. 1981, U.S. Dist. Ct. (so. and ea. dists.) N.Y. 1981, U.S. Ct. Appeals (2d cir.) 1988. Assoc. Cahill Gordon & Reindel, N.Y.C., 1980-85; pvt. practice, 1985—. Spl. asst. dist. atty. Dist. Atty.'s Office, N.Y. County, N.Y.C., 1982-83. Treas. Not Just Blacks & Jews in Conversation. Mem. N.Y. County Lawyers Assn. Office: 111 John St Ste 800 New York NY 10038

SHAPIRO, STEPHEN MICHAEL, lawyer; b. Chgo., May 3, 1946; s. Samuel H. and Dorothy A. (D'Andrea) S.; m. Joan H. Gately, Oct. 30, 1982; children: Dorothy Henderson, Michael Clifford. BA magna cum laude, Yale U., 1968, JD, 1971. Bar: Ill. 1971, Calif. 1972, D.C. 1991, U.S. Dist. Ct. (no. dist. trial bar) Ill. 1992, U.S. Ct. Appeals (all cirs.), U.S. Supreme Ct. 1975. Law clk. U.S. Ct. Appeals (9th cir.), San Francisco, 1971-72; ptnr., sr. mem. appellate practice Mayer, Brown & Platt, Chgo., 1972-78, 83—; asst. to solicitor gen. U.S. Dept. Justice, Washington, 1978-80, dep. solicitor gen., 1981-82. Trustee Product Liability Adv. Found. Co-author: Supreme Court Practice, 2002; contbr. articles to profl. jours. Mem. ABA, Am. Law Inst., Am. Acad. Appellate Lawyers, Supreme Ct. Hist. Soc., Phi Beta Kappa. Republican. Jewish. Office: Mayer Brown Rowe & Maw 190 S La Salle St Ste 3100 Chicago IL 60603-3441

SHAPIRO, STEPHEN ROBERT, cardiologist; b. Framingham, Mass., Sept. 17, 1942; s. Morris and Ann (Kartiganer) S.; m. Harriet Ruth Roberts, Aug. 4, 1963; children: Jonathan Alan, Caryn Beth, David Philip. BS, Tufts Coll., 1963; MD, NYU, 1967. Resident in pediatrics Boston City Hosp., 1967-69; pediatric cardiology fellowship Cardiovascular Rsch. Inst., U. Calif., San Francisco, 1971-73; pediatric cardiologist Children's Hosp., Washington, 1973-84, Child Cardiology Assocs., Fairfax, Va., 1984—. Lt. comdr. USN, 1969-71. Fellow Am. Coll. Cardiology, Am. Acad. Pediatrics; mem. Am. Heart Assn. Democrat. Jewish. Avocations: art, wine, classical music. Office: Child Cardiology Assocs 8318 Arlington Blvd Ste 250 Fairfax VA 22031-5218 E-mail: s_shapiro@childcardiology.com.

SHAPIRO, STUART CHARLES, computer scientist, educator; b. N.Y.C., Dec. 30, 1944; s. Louis M. and Bertha (Rubinstein) S.; m. Caren Dee Knight, July 16, 1972. BS, MIT, 1966; MS, U. Wis., 1968, PhD, 1971. Lectr. computer scis. dept. U. Wis., Madison, 1971; vis. asst. prof. Ind. U., Bloomington, 1971-72, asst. prof., 1972-77, assoc. prof., 1977-78; asst. prof. SUNY, Buffalo, 1977-78, assoc. prof., 1978-83, prof., 1983—, chmn., 1984-90, 96-99. Pres. Principles of Knowledge Representation and Reasoning, Inc., 1998-2000; rsch. scientist Nat. Ctr. for Geographic Info. and Analysis, 1989—. Author: Techniques of Artificial Intelligence, 1979, LISP: An Interactive Approach, 1986, Common Lisp: An Interactive Approach, 1992; editor: Encyclopedia of Artificial Intelligence, 1987, paperback edit., 1990, 2d edit., 1992, (with Lucja Iwanska) Language for Knowledge and Knowledge for Language, 2000; contbr. articles to profl. jours. Grantee NSF, 1971—; recipient numerous grants for computer sci. research, 1971—. Fellow Am. Assn. Artificial Intelligence; mem. IEEE (sr.), Assn. Computing Machinery (chmn. spl. interest group on artificial intelligence 1991-95), Assn. Computational Linguistics, Cognitive Sci. Soc., Sigma Xi. Home: 142 Viscount Dr Buffalo NY 14221-1770 Office: Univ at Buffalo Dept of Comp Sci & Engring 201 Bell Hall Buffalo NY 14260-2000 Personal E-mail: shapiro@adelphia.net . Business E-Mail: shapiro@cse.buffalo.edu.

SHAPIRO, SUMNER, retired naval officer, business executive; b. Nashua, N.H., Jan. 13, 1926; s. Maurice David and Hannah (Goodman) S.; m. Eleanor S. Hymen, June 14, 1949; children: Martha, Steven, Susan. BS, U.S. Naval Acad., 1949; MS, George Washington U., 1966; postgrad., Naval War Coll., 1966, U.S. Army Inst. Advanced Soviet and Eastern European Studies, 1961. Commd. ensign U.S. Navy, 1949; advanced through grades to rear adm.; asst. naval attache U.S. Navy (Am. embassy), Moscow, 1963-65; dep. asst. chief of staff for intelligence U.S. Naval Forces Europe, London, 1967-69; comdg. officer Naval Intelligence Processing System Support Activity, Washington, 1969-72; asst. chief staff for intelligence U.S. Atlantic Command and U.S. Atlantic Fleet, Norfolk, Va., 1972-76; dep. dir. naval intelligence, 1976-77; comdr. Naval Intelligence Command, Washington, 1977-78; dir. naval intelligence, 1978-82; ret., 1982; v.p. for advanced planning BDM Internat., 1983-89; pres. The Sumner Group Inc., 1989—. Pres. Naval Intelligence Found. Decorated D.S.M., Legion of Merit and others., Nat. Intelligence D.S.M., Netherlands Order Orange-Nassau, Brazil Order Naval Merit, French Nat. Order Merit, others Mem. Naval Intelligence Found. (pres.), Naval Intelligence Profls. (bd. dirs.), U.S. Naval Inst., Assn. Former Intelligence Officers, Nat. Mil. Intelligence Assn., Nat. Security Industries Assn., U.S. Naval Acad. Alumni Assn., Naval Submarine League.

SHAPIRO, SYLVIA, psychotherapist; b. Bklyn., Aug. 16, 1938; d. Benjamin B. and Rose (Friedman) Bluming; m. Jay Citron, Oct. 25, 1962 (div. May 1976); children: Doni, Yosi, Eli, Yoav, Ilana. DSW, Yeshiva U., 1988. Cert. social worker; lic. social worker, N.Y.; cert. marriage and family therapist. Pvt. practice psychotherapy, Hackensack, N.J., 1989—. Home and Office: 240 Prospect Ave Apt 694 Hackensack NJ 07601-7700 E-mail: sdiyya@aol.com.

SHAPIRO, THEODORE, psychiatrist, educator; b. N.Y.C., Feb. 26, 1932; s. Herman Alexander and Nettie (Rosenblatt) S.; m. Joan May Itkin, June 26, 1955; children: Susan, Alexander Herman. BA, Wesleyan U., 1953; MD, Cornell U., 1957. Diplomate Am. Bd. Psychiatry and Neurology, Am. Bd. Child Psychiatry, Am. Psychoanalytic Assn. Intern Montefiore Hosp., N.Y.C., 1957—58; resident in psychiatry NYU-Bellevue Hosp., 1958—61, rsch. assoc. child psychiatry, 1961—65; instr. to prof. NYU Sch. Medicine, 1960—76; prof. psychiatry and pediatrics Cornell U. Med. Coll., N.Y.C, 1976—2002, emeritus prof., 2002—; vice chair for child and adolescent psychiatry, 1995—; asst. lectr. N.Y. Psychoanalytic Inst., N.Y.C., 1970—86, tng. and supervising analyst, 1986—. Cons. Alcohol, Drug Abuse and Mental Health Adminstrn., WHO, Washington, Geneva, Copenhagen, 1980-82, Am. Acad. Child and Adolescent Psychiatry, Washington; chair com. on stewardship Task Force Future, 1980-82, acad. sec., 1981-83, chair work group on sci. issues, 1988-89, chair com. editorship and stewardship of jour., 1984-86, 90-92; participant in APA bilateral exch. in Ea. Europe, 1992; mem. reviewer child psychopathology and treatment rev. com. NIMH, 1994-98. Author: Clinical Psycholinguistics, 1979; co-editor: Infant Psychiatry, 1976; editor: Psychoanalysis and Contemporary Science, 1976, Structure in Psychoanalysis, 1991, Affect: Psychoanalytic Perspectives, 1992; co-author: Manual of Panic-Focused Psychodynamic Psychotherapy, 1996; editor Jour. Am. Psychoanalytic Assn., 1984-93; book rev. editor Internat. Jour. Psychoanalysis, 1993—; co-editor Research in Psychoanalysis, 1995; contbr. articles to profl. jours. Recipient Sandor Rado lectureship Columbia Psychoanalytic Clinic, 1991, Prager lectureship George Washington U. Sch. Medicine, Exie Welsch lectureship N.Y. Coun. on Child and Adolescent Psychiatry, 1995; NIMH residency tng. grantee, 1976-86; recipient Wilfred C. Hulse N.Y. Coun. Child Psychiatry, 1982, Harry Bakwin Meml. NYU, 1982, Maurice Laufer lectureship E.P. Bradley Hosp., 1982, Lauretta Bender Ann. Lectureship, 1997, Brill lectureship N.Y. Psychoanalytic Inst., 1999. Fellow Am. Acad. Child Psychiatry (sec. 1981-83), Am. Psychiat. Assn.; mem. Soc. Profs. Child Psychiatry (chmn. com. on edn. 1982-90, keynote spkr. 1999), Group for Advancement of Psychiatry (chmn. com. on child psychiatry 1985-90), Am. Bd. Psychiatry & Neurology (com. on child and adolescent psychiatry 1987-93, chmn. 1992-93), N.Y. Psychoanalytic Soc. Jewish. Office: Weill Med Coll Cornell U Payne Whitney Clinic PO Box 140 New York NY 10021-0012 E-mail: tshapiro@med.cornell.edu.

SHAPIRO, WALTER ELLIOT, political columnist; b. N.Y.C., Feb. 16, 1947; s. Salem Seeley and Edith Geraldine (Herwitz) S.; m. Meryl Gordon, Aug. 24, 1980. BA, U. Mich., 1970, postgrad., 1970-71. Reporter Congl. Quarterly, Washington, 1969-70; editor Washington Monthly, 1972-76; spl. asst. U.S. Sec. Labor, Washington, 1977-78; Presdl. speechwriter The White House, 1979; reporter Washington Post, 1979-83; gen. editor Newsweek, N.Y.C., 1983-87; sr. writer Time Mag., 1987-93; White House corr. Esquire mag., 1993-97; polit. columnist USA Today, 1995—. Contbg. editor Washington Monthly, 1976—. Leadership fellow Japan Soc., U.S.-Japan, 1991. Mem. Judson Welliver Soc. Jewish. Avocations: standup comedy, rotisserie baseball. Home: 201 W 86th St Apt 1105 New York NY 10024-3351 Office: 3133 Connecticut Ave NW Apt 315 Washington DC 20008-5105

SHAPIRO, WILLIAM, automobile company executive; b. N.Y.C., July 31, 1948; s. Jerome and Anne S.; m. Marsha F. Shapiro, Mar. 24, 1974; 1 child, JacLynn A. BChemE, CCNY, 1970; MChemE, NYU, 1972; MBA, Pace U., 1976. Registered profl. engr., N.Y., N.J. Program mgr. N.Y.C. Dept. Air Resources, 1971-75; engr. dept. emissions EPA, N.Y.C., 1975-76; engr. dept. safety and emissions Volvo Cars N.Am., Rockleigh, N.J., 1976-86, mgr. regulations and compliance, 1986-96, dir. regulatory and environ. affairs, 1996—. Mem. adv. bd. EPA, Washington, 1992—, Dept. Transp., Washington, 1983-88; spkr. in field. Mem. sci. fair edn. forum, River Vale, N.J., 1992. Recipient award Ford Motor Co. 2000 Heroes for the Planet. Mem. Soc. Automotive Engrs. (svc. award 1990). Democrat. Jewish. Avocations: golf, running, reading, travel. Home: 245 Thayer St River Vale NJ 07675-6255 Office: Volvo Cars NAm A R-C-E Rockleigh NJ 07647 E-mail: jsmsws@aol.com.

SHAPIRO, WILLIAM MAURICE, emergency medicine physician, administrator, researcher; b. Phila. m. Jane Catherine Fitzgerald, Sept. 26, 1992; 1 child, Erin Rose. BA, Temple U., 1972; MD, Hahnemann U., 1976. Diplomate Am. Bd. Internal Medicine, Am. Bd. Emergency Medicine. Dir. emergency dept. Herrick Meml. Hosp., Tecumseh, Mich., 1986-87, Villa View Cmty. Hosp., San Diego, 1989-90; physician Scripps Clinic and Rsch. Found., La Jolla, Calif., 1991—; dir. San Diego divsn. Staticon Internat., 1990-99; prin. investigator n Touch Rsch. San Diego, 2000—. Dir. EMT course Raisin Twp. Fire Dept., Tecumseh, 1985-86; dir. ACLS courses Harborview Med. Ctr., San Diego, 1990-93; expert reviewer Med. Bd. Calif. Recipient commendation Tecumseh City Coun., 1985. Fellow ACP, Am. Coll. Emergency Physicians, Am. Acad. Emergency Medicine. Avocations: music, skiing, windsurfing. Office: Scripps Clinic Divsn Urgent Care/EM MS 218 10666 N Torrey Pines Rd La Jolla CA 92037-1092

SHAPIRO, YANINA, psychology educator; b. Moscow, Russia, Aug. 2, 1948; came to the U.S., 1975; p. Boris Yakoulevich and Irina Dmitrievna (Churikova) S. BS, MS in Mech. Engring., Moscow Bauman U.; EdM in Human Devel., Harvard U., 1986, EdD in Human Devel. and Psychology, 1991; BA in English, Coll. Fgn. Langs., Moscow; Cert. of German Studies, Vienna U., postgrad., 1981-82. Editor Inst. Info., Moscow, 1975, Gulf Pub. Co., Houston, 1975-76; engr. Ford Motor Co., Dearborn, Mich., 1976-79, Dowland Bach Co., Anchorage, 1979; tech. cons. Exxon Rsch. and Engring., N.Y.C., 1980-81; engring. instr. dept. engring. Tufts U., Mass., 1982-83; engr. Dept. Transp., Cambridge, 1983-87; asst. prof. psychology St. Francis Coll., Loretto, Pa., 1992-93, Ea. Oreg. State Coll., La Grande, 1993-94, rschr., writer, 1994-96; psychologist Fairview Tng. Ctr., Salem, Oreg., 1996-97; CEO, sr. scientist Corp. Psychology and Mental Fitness, Portland, 1997—. Contbr. articles to profl. jours. Mem. AAAS, APA, Am. Psychol. Soc., Soc. for Neurosci., Internat. Soc. for Theoretical Psychology, Internat. Soc. for Applied Psychology. Democrat. Avocations: teaching, film, music, travel, hiking.

SHAPIRO, ZALMAN MORDECAI, chemist, consultant; b. Canton, Ohio, May 12, 1920; s. Abraham and Minnie (Pinck) S.; m. Evelyn Greenberg, June 24, 1945; children: Joshua, Ezra David, Deborah Esther. BA, Johns Hopkins U., 1942, MA, 1945, PhD, 1948. Rsch. assoc. Johns Hopkins for Nat. Rsch. Coun., Balt., 1942-45; instr. chemistry Johns Hopkins U., 1946-48; sr. engr. Westinghouse Electric Corp., Pitts., 1948; mgr. phys. chemistry, mgr. chem. metallurgy AEC Bettis Naval Nuc. Power Lab., Westinghouse, West Mifflin, Pa., 1949-56, asst. divsn. mgr. pressurized water reactor divsn., 1956-57; pres., chmn. bd. Nuc. Materials and Equipment Corp., Apollo, Pa., 1957-70; pres., chmn. of bd. Numec Instruments and Controls Corp., 1960-70, Numec Decontamination Corp., Apollo, 1961-70, Isotope & Radiation Enterprises, Israel, 1964-70; pres. Assoc. Tech. and Bus. Consultants, Pitts., 1970—. V.p. Arco Chem. Co., Phila., 1967-70. Contbr. 2 chpts. to books; patentee in field. Mem. Govs. Sci. and Tech. Coun., Harrisburg, 1963-64; cons. Pa. Subcom. on Atomic Energy, Harrisburg, 1970-71; founder, vice-chmn., Ams. for Energy Independence, Washington, 1975—; organizer Project Pacesetter, Allegheny County, 1976. Named hon. fellow Technion Israel Inst. Tech., Haifa, 1988. Fellow Am. Nuc. Soc. (citation of merit); mem. AAAS, Am. Soc. Metals, Am. Chem. Soc., Phi Beta Kappa, Sigma Xi. Avocations: sailing, wood working. Home: 1045 Lyndhurst Dr Pittsburgh PA 15206-4535 Office: ASTECH 6334 Forbes Ave Pittsburgh PA 15217-1717 E-mail: zalmanms@aol.com.

SHAPO, MARSHALL SCHAMBELAN, lawyer, educator; b. Phila., Oct. 1, 1936; s. Mitchell and Norma (Schambelan) S.; m. Helene Shirley Seidner, June 21, 1959; children: Benjamin, Nathaniel. AB summa cum laude, U. Miami, 1958, JD magna cum laude, 1964; AM, Harvard U., 1961, SJD, 1974. Bar: Fla. 1964, Va. 1977, Ill. 1993. Copy editor, writer Miami (Fla.) News, 1958-59; instr. history U. Miami, 1960-61; asst. prof. law U. Tex., 1965-67, asso. prof., 1967-69, prof., 1969-70; prof. law U. Va., 1970-78, Joseph M. Hartfield prof., 1976-78; Frederic P. Vose prof. Northwestern U. Sch. Law, Chgo., 1978—; of counsel Sonnenschein, Nath & Rosenthal, 1991-2001. Vis. prof. Juristisches Seminar U. Gottingen (Fed. Republic Germany), 1976; cons. on med. malpractice and tort law reform U.S. Dept. Justice, 1978-79; mem. panel on food safety Inst. Medicine, NAS, 1978-79; vis. fellow Centre for Socio-legal Studies, Wolfson Coll., Oxford, vis. fellow of Coll., 1975, Wolfson Coll., Cambridge, 1992, 2001; mem. Ctr. for Advanced Studies, U. Va., 1976-77; cons. Pres.'s Commn. for Study of Ethical Problems in Medicine and Biomed. and Behavioral Rsch., 1980-81; reporter Spl. Com. on Tort Liability System Am. Bar Assn., 1980-84; del. leader People to People Citizen Amb.

program delegation to East Asia Tort and Ins. Law, 1986; lectr. appellate judges' seminars ABA, 1977, 83, 90; reporter symposium on legal and sci. perspectives on causation, 1990; advisor Restatement of the Law, Third, Torts: Products Liability, 1992-97. Author: Towards a Jurisprudence of Injury, 1984, Tort and Compensation Law, 1976, The Duty to Act: Tort Law, Power and Public Policy, 1978, A Nation of Guinea Pigs, 1979, Products Liability, 1980, Public Regulation of Dangerous Products, 1980, The Law of Products Liability, 1987, Tort and Injury Law, 1990, 2d edit., 2000, The Law of Products Liability, 2 vols., 2d edit., 1990, 4th edit., 2001, supplements, 1991, 92, 93, 95, 96, 97, 98, 99, Products Liability and the Search for Justice, 1993, (with Helene Shapo) Law School Without Fear, 1996, 2d edit., 2002, Basic Principles of Tort Law, 1999; (with Page Keeton) Products and the Consumer: Deceptive Practices, 1972, Products and the Consumer: Defective and Dangerous Products, 1970, (with D. Jacobson & A.N. Weber) International e-Commerce: Business & Legal Issues, 2001, (with G. Hernandez & others) eBusiness & Insurance, 2001; mem. editl. bd. Jour. Consumer Policy, 1980-88, Products Liability Law Jour.; author: A Representational Theory of Consumer Protection: Doctrine, Function and Legal Liability for Product Disappointment, 1975; mem. adv. bd. Loyola Consumer Law Reporter; contbr. articles to legal and med. jours. NEH sr. fellow, 1974-75 Mem. Am. Law Inst., Am. Assn. Law Schs. (chmn. torts compensation systems sect. 1983-84, torts round table coun. 1970). Home: 1910 Orrington Ave Evanston IL 60201-2910 Office: Northwestern U Sch Law 357 E Chicago Ave Chicago IL 60611-3059

SHAPOSHNIKOV, YAKOV DAVID, gastroenterologist; b. USSR, July 4, 1944; came to U.S., 1987; s. David Solomon and Dvora Bruchas (Chapovetsky) S.; m. Lilian Tandeitnik, Aug. 30, 1974; 1 child, Rimma. MD, Pavlov Med. Sch., 1967; PhD, Petrov Inst. Oncology, 1971. Diplomate Am. Bd. Internal Medicine. Intern Millard Fillmore Clinic, Buffalo, 1989-90; resident SUNY-Buffalo Hosp., 1990-92; fellow in gastroenterology U. Buffalo, 1992-95; attending physician Millard Fillmore Hosp., Buffalo, 1995-97, Kenmore Mercy Hosp., Buffalo, 1996-97, Buffalo Gen. Hosp., 1996-97; pvt. practice Las Vegas, 1997—. Clin. instr. SUNY, Buffalo. Contbr. over 100 articles to profl. jours. Fellow ACP; mem. Am. Coll. Gastroenterology. Jewish. Address: 1612 Hidden Springs Dr Las Vegas NV 89117-5427 Office: 2020 Goldring Ave #906 Las Vegas NV 89106

SHAPPIRIO, DAVID GORDON, biologist, educator; b. Washington, June 18, 1930; s. Sol and Rebecca (Porton) S.; m. Elvera M. Bamber, July 8, 1953; children: Susan, Mark. BS with distinction in Chemistry, U. Mich., 1951; A.M., Harvard U., 1953, PhD in Biology, 1955. NSF postdoctoral fellow in biochemistry Cambridge U., Eng., 1955-56; rsch. fellow in physiology Am. Cancer Soc.-NRC, U. Louvain, Belgium, 1956-57; mem. faculty U. Mich., Ann Arbor, 1957—, prof. zool. and biology, 1967-99, Arthur F. Thurnau prof., 1989-94, prof. emeritus, 1999—, assoc. chair div. biol. scis., 1976-83, acting chair, 1978, 79, 80, 82, coord. NSF undergrad. sci. edn. program, 1962-67, dir. honors program Coll. Lit. Sci. and Arts, 1983-91. Vis. lectr. Am. Inst. Biol. Scis., 1966-68; reviewer, cons. to pubs. on textbook devel.; reviewer rsch. and ednl. tng. grant proposals NSF, NIH, mem. program site visit teams. Author rsch. on biochemistry and physiology growth, devel., dormancy; invited spkr., rsch. symposia of nat. and internat. orgns. in field. Recipient Disting. Teaching award U. Mich., 1967, Excellence in Edn. award, 1991, Bausch & Lomb Sci. award, 1974; Lalor Found fellow, 1953-55; Danforth Found. assoc. Fellow AAAS; mem. Am. Inst. Biol. Scis. (vis. lectr. 1966-68), Am. Soc. Cell Biology, Biochem. Soc., Soc. Exptl. Biology, Assn. Biol. Lab. Edn., Xerces Soc., Phi Beta Kappa (v.p. U. Mich. chpt. 1995-97, pres. 1997—). Office: U Mich Dept Biology 2014 Natural Sci Bldg Ann Arbor MI 48109-1048

SHAR, ALBERT OSCAR, academic program director, consultant, mathematics educator; b. Bklyn., Mar. 11, 1944; s. Hillard Bernard and Rose (Podolsky) S.; m. Cynthia Mallin; children: Jonathan, Daniel. BA in Math., Brandeis U., 1965; MA in Math., Fordham U., 1966; PhD in Math., U. Pa., 1970. Vis. asst. prof. U. Colo., 1970-71; prof. U. N.H., Durham, 1971-87, faculty fellow, 1979-81, prof., exec. dir. computer svcs., 1981-87; exec. dir. Office of Info. Tech. U. Pa. Sch. Medicine, Phila., 1987—, adj. assoc. prof., 1988—. Vis. prof. Forschungsinstitut fur Math., E.T.H., Zurich, Switzerland, 1977-78; cons. Nursing Home Infirmary Project, Phila., 1988, Health Scis. Libr. Consortium, Phila., 1987, The Works Fitness Club, Dover, N.H., 1984, Lowy Inc., N.Y.C., 1983, KDJ Assocs., Reading, Mass., 1981, others. Contbr. articles to profl. jours.

SHARAFELDIN, IBNOMER MOHAMED, science educator, consultant; b. Debkar, Kurd Fan, Sudan, Jan. 1, 1954; s. Mohamed Sharafeldin Osman and Kheria Mohamed Abuullah. PHD, Claremonthraduate Sch., Claremont, 1972—75; LLB, U. Khartoum, Khartoum, Sudan, 1976—80; Masters Pub. Admin, U. So. Calif., Los Angeles, 1981—81. Bar: Sudanese Bar Assn. 2002. Tchr. Ministery Edn., Sudan, Sudan, 1978—78; assoc. judge Sudan Judiciary, Omdurman, Sudan, 1979—79; rschr. Internat. Instn. IT, Herndun, Va., 1981—81; field faculty adviser Vermount Coll. N.H., Washington, 1982—82; academic adviser Saudi Ednl. Mission, 1983—83; coll. instrector Coppin State Coll., Baltimore, Md., 1984—84; adminstrv. chaplain Md. Correctional J.C., Hagerstown, 1992—. Author: (dissertation) Human Resource Management, (articles to professional journals) American Journal M.S.S., Int. Political Science Abstracts. Trustee Consumer Driven Svc., Hanerstown, Md., 1993—95. Mem.: Admin Istration, Am. Assn. Muslim Social Soc., Am. Soc. Pub. Achievements include Dissertation Catalog (University Microfilms International). Avocations: soccer, travel, swimming, reading, movies. Home: PO Box 555 Hagerstown MD 21741

SHARBAUGH, W(ILLIAM) JAMES, plastics engineer, consultant; b. Pitts., Apr. 13, 1914; s. Oliver Michael and Sarah Marie (Wingenroth) S.; m. Eileen Carey, May 14, 1938; children: William James Jr., Eileen Sharbaugh Pinkerton, Susan Sharbaugh Coté. BS in Engring., Carnegie Inst. Tech., 1935. Project engr. MSA Corp., Pitts., 1935-46; founder, gen. mgr. ENPRO, Inc., St. Louis, 1947-62; mgr. plastics div. Vulcan Rubber and Plastic, Morrisville, Pa., 1962-67; v.p. engring. and mfg. FESCO div. Celanese, Pitts., 1967-72; exec. v.p. plastics div. Lenox, Inc., St. Louis, 1970-72; div. mgr. Crown Zellerbach, Inc., San Francisco, 1972-77; pres. Plastics Assocs., Cons., Newport Beach, Calif., 1977—; founder ISOBET USA, Inc. Dir. devel. and tech. Crown Zellerbach, Inc.; pres. Western Plastics Pioneers; cons. nat. and internat. plastics cos.; pres. Plastics Assics., Inc., 1996—; founder Advanced Bldg. Tech., 1995; industry orofl. witness on forensics of plastic product failures. Author tech. papers, reports. Named to, Plastics Hall of Fame. Mem. Soc. Plastics Engrs. (first pres. Pitts. sect.), Soc. Plastics Industry. Republican. Roman Catholic. Achievements include patents for military products, consumer items and the development of ISOBET construction materials. Office: Plastics Assocs Inc 37 Morena Irvine CA 92612-1719 Fax: (949) 651-6460. E-mail: j.sharbaugh@att.net.

SHARBEL, JOSEPH MICHAEL, priest; b. Kansas City, Mo., July 16, 1955; s. George Michael Sharbel and Mary Elizabeth Gauss. BA, Rockhurst Coll., 1977; MDiv, U. Toronto, Toronto, Ont., Canada, 1984; MA, U. Notre Dame, 1998. Assoc. pastor St. Mary's Cath., Winnipeg, Canada, 1985—88; dir. liturgy Archdiocese of Winnipeg, Canada, 1987—88; pastor Our Lady of Victory Ch., Canada, 1988—91, John XXIII Parish, Winnipeg, Canada, 1991—97, St. Dominic's Parish, Neepawa, Canada, 1997—98, St. Peter's Parish, Kansas City, Mo., 1999—. Vice chair Western Liturgy Conf., Edmonton, Canada, 1994—97. Contbr. articles to profl. jours. Active Environ. and Art Commn., Kansas City, 1999—, Southtown Coun., Kansas City, 1999—. Mem.: Liturgy Network. Avocations: cooking, travel, theatre. Office: St Peters Parish 6415 Holmes Kansas City MO 64131-1198 Office Fax: 816-363-8157. E-mail: jshabel1@aol.com.

SHARBONEAU, LORNA ROSINA, artist, educator, author, poet, illustrator; b. Spokane, Wash., Apr. 5, 1935; d. Stephen Charles Martin and Midgie Montana (Hartzel) Barton; m. Thomas Edward Sharboneau, Jan. 22, 1970; children: Curtis, Carmen, Chet, Cra, Joseph. AA in Arts, Delta Coll., 1986; studies with Steve Lesnick, Las Vegas, Nev.; studies with Bette Myers/Zimmerman, Phoenix and Bonners Ferry, Idaho. Prin. Sharboneau's Art Gallery, Spokane, 1977-80; tchr. art Michell's Art Gallery, 1978-79; art therapist Vellencino Sch. Dist., Calif., 1981-83; ind. artist Lind, Wash., 1948—. Dir., producer, stage designer Ch. of Jesus Christ of LDS, San Jose, Sonora, Modesto, Calif., 1978 (1st. place road show San Jose); dir. Sharboneau's Art Show, Spokane, 1979, Hands On-Yr. of the Child; platform spkr., poet, fundraiser, libr., 1984-87; asst., apprentice to Prof. Rowland Cheney, Delta Coll., Stockton, Calif., 1985, 86, 87; demonstrated drip oil technique, Bonners Ferry, Idaho, Spokane, Wash., Stockton, Calif., Delta Coll. Author, illustrator: Through the Eyes of the Turtle Tree, The One-Armed Christmas Tree, The Price of Freedom, 1994, William Will, Bill Can, Song of the Turtle Tree, Chet's Ottle-Bottle: The Unbreakable Bottle, One Drop of Water and a Grain of Sand, The Price of Freedom; poet; prolific artist completed over 4000 paintings and drawings, displayed works in galleries through western states; featured in Magnolia News, Seattle, Delta Coll. Impact, Stockton, Calif., Stockton Record, Union Democrat, Sonora, Calif., Lincoln Center Chronicle, Stockton, Calif., Spokesman Rev., Spokane, Wash., Modesto (Calif) Bee, Angels Camp, Calif., Union Democrat, Sonora, Calif., New-Letter, Ch. of Jesus Christ of L.D.S 1st ward, Sonora; artist mixed media, oil, drip oil works, sculptures, pastel, watercolor; illustrations pen and ink, acrylic; sculptor bronze, lost wax method, ceramic art, soap stone, egg-tempra, original techniques, collage, variation on a theme. Dir., programmer, fundraiser Shelter Their Sorrows, Sonora, Calif., 1989-92, vol. Cmty. Action Agy. and Homeless Shelter; fundraiser for Homeless Flood Victims of No. Calif., 1997. Recipient Golden Rule award J.C. penny, 1991, Recognition award Pres. George Bush, cert. Spl. Congl. Recognition Congressman Richard H. Lehman, 3rd Pl. Best Show East Valley ARtists/Pala Show, 1973, 74, 75, 3d Pl. Artist of Yr., 1974, Valley Fair, Santa Clara, Calif., 1974, 1st and 2d Pl. Spokane County Fair, 1978, 3 honorable mentions, 4 premiums, 1979, 3 1st Pl., 3 2d Pl., 2 3rd Pl., honorable mention Calaveras County Fair/Angels Camp, Calif., 1983, 1st and 3rd Pl. Unitarian Art Festival, Stockton, Calif., 1984, 2d Pl., 1985, 3d Pl., 1986, 1st Pl. Lodi Art Ann., 1985, 3rd Pl., 1986, 1st Pl. 1987, 1st Pl., 1988, honorable mental SJCAC Junque Art Show, Stockton, 1985, 1st Pl Ctrl. Calif. Art League, Modesto, 1986, 88, 2d Pl. 1995; 3d Pl. Camilla Art Show, San Jose, Calif., 1974, and numerous others; 1st, 2d, and 3d Pl., Spokane County Fair, 1978; 4 honorable mentions, Sonora, Calif., 1993, 2nd Pl. Ctrl. Calif. Art Show, 1996. Mem. Ctrl. Sierra Arts Coun., Mother Lode Artists Assn., Sacramento Fine Arts Ctr., Inc., Internat. Platform Assn. (Judges Choice conv. arts competition 1993), The Planetary Soc., The Nat. Mus. of Women of Arts. Mem. Ch. of Jesus Christ of LDS. Achievements include: homeless shelter kitchen named in her honor, Sonora. Avocations: mathematics, astronomy, baseball, archeology. Office: PO Box 5015 Sonora CA 95370-2015

SHARE, RICHARD HUDSON, lawyer; b. Mpls., Sept. 6, 1938; s. Jerome and Millicent S.; m. Carolee Martin, 1970; children: Mark Lowell, Gregory Martin, Jennifer Hillary, Ashley. BS, UCLA, 1960; JD, U. So. Calif., 1963. Bar: Calif. Sup. Ct. 1964, U.S. Dist. Ct. (cen. and so. dists.) Calif., U.S. Supreme Ct. 1974. Field agt. IRS, 1960-63; mem. law divsn., asst. sec. Avco Fin. Svcs., 1963-72; founder Frandzel and Share, A Law Corp., L.A., 1972-99, Richard Hudson Share & Assocs., 1999—. Lectr. Nat. Bus. Inst., Creditor's Rights; adj. prof. Loloya Law Sch., 1999. Pub. N.Mex. Bus. Jour., 2001. Mem. Calif. Bankers Assn. Office: PO Box 1003 Pacific Palisades CA 90272-1003 also: 150 N Santa Anita Ave Ste 530 Arcadia CA 91006-3127 E-mail: sharelaw@aol.com.

SHARER, JOHN DANIEL, lawyer; b. Bklyn., Sept. 19, 1950; s. Albert Robert and Alda Loretta (Tapiro) S.; m. Kathleen Gail Donaldson, Feb. 14, 1981; 1 child, Stephanie Erin. AB, Dartmouth Coll., Hanover, N.H., 1972; JD, U. Pa., 1975. Bar: Pa. 1975, N.J. 1975, D.C. 1976, N.Y. 1989, Va. 1994. Law clk. Superior Ct. Pa., Hon. Edmund B. Spaeth, Jr., Phila., 1975-76; assoc. Sutherland, Asbill & Brennan, Washington, 1976-82, ptnr., 1982-94; counsel Christian & Barton, L.L.P., Richmond, Va., 1994-95, ptnr., 1996-99; sr. counsel Dominion Resources Svcs. Inc., 1999-2001; mng. counsel electric delivery and telecom., 2001—. Mem. faculty Va. State Bar Professionaism Course, 2001—. Bd. dirs. Wakefield Sch., Marshall, Va., 1990-94; pres. Dartmouth Club of Cen. Va. Mem. Phi Beta Kappa. Republican. Avocations: classical music, judicial biographies, computers, dogs. Home: 12317 North-lake Ct Richmond VA 23233-6635 Office: 120 Tredegar St PO Box 26532 Richmond VA 23261-6532 E-mail: john_d_sharer@dom.com.

SHARER, KEVIN W. healthcare products company executive; b. Clinton, Iowa, Mar. 2, 1948; m. Fay M. Sharer; children: Heather, Keith. BS in Aero. Engring, U.S. Naval Acad., 1970; MS in Aero. Engring., U.S. Naval Postgrad. Sch., 1971; MBA, U. Pitts., 1982. Commd. lt. USN, 1970, advanced through grades to lt. comdr., resigned, 1978; with AT&T, 1978-82; cons. McKinsey & Co., 1982-84; pres., chief exec. officer GE Am. Communications, Princeton, N.J., 1984-89; exec. v.p. MCI Telecommunications Corp., Washington, 1989-92; pres., COO Amgen Inc., Thousand Oaks, Calif., 1992-2000, CEO, 2000—, chmn., bd. dirs. Office: Amgen Inc 1 Amgen Ctr Dr Thousand Oaks CA 91320-1799*

SHARER, TIMOTHY JOSEPH, music educator; b. Wayne, Nebr., Oct. 18, 1952; s. Cletus Joseph and Vona Lou Sharer; m. Beth Ann Bergt, Dec. 21, 1974; children: Corbin. PhD, U. Nebr., Lincoln, 1994. Cert. tchr. Nebr., 1975. Chair dept. of music Lincoln SE H.S., 1982—95; assoc. prof. music Wayne (Nebr.) State Coll., 1995—. Sec. Wayne Pub. Schs. Found., 1997. Recipient NE Nebr. Tchr. Acad. Coord. award, Wayne State Coll. and Nebr. Dept. of Edn., 2000—. Mem.: Nebr. Music Educators Assn. (bd. dirs., dir. NE Music Mentor Program 1996—2002). Republican. Evangelical Christian. Avocations: music, Bible study. Office: Wayne State Coll 1111 Main St Wayne NE 68787

SHARETT, ALAN RICHARD, lawyer, environmental and disability litigator, mediator and arbitrator, law educator; b. Hammond, Ind., Apr. 15, 1943; children: Lauren Ruth, Charles Daniel; m. Cherie Ann Vick, Oct. 15, 1993. Student, Ind. U., 1962-65; JD, DePaul U., 1968; advanced postgrad. legal edn., U. Mich. and U. Chgo., 1970-71; postgrad., Fla. Internat. U., 1999-2000; cert. mediator, Am. Arbitration Assn., 1994; cert. tng. and human resource devel., Fla. Internat. U., 2000. Bar: Ind. 1969, N.Y. 1975, U. S. Ct. Appeals (2d cir.) 1975, U.S. Ct. Appeals (7th cir.) 1974, U.S. Supreme Ct. 1973. Assoc. World Peace Through Law Ctr., Washington, 1967-68, Call, Call, Borns and Theodoros, Gary, Ind., 1969-71; judge protem Gary City Ct., 1970-71; environ. dist. atty. 31st Jud. Cir., Lake County, Ind., 1971-75; counsel Dunes Nat. Lakeshore Group, 1971-75; mem. Cohan, Cohan and Smulevitz, 1971-75; town atty. Independence Hill, Ind., 1974-75; judge pro tem Superior Ct., Lake County, 1971-75; pvt. practice Flushing, N.Y., 1980-82, Miami Beach, Fla., 1988—; lead trial counsel, chmn. lawyers panel No. Ind. ACLU, 1969-71; liaison trial counsel Lake County and Ind. State Health Depts., and Atty. Gen., 1971-75. Professorial dir. NYU Pub. Liability Inst., N.Y.C., 1975-76; speaker, guest lectr., adj. faculty ATLA, Ind. U., Purdue U., NYU, Ind. U., De Paul U., Valparaiso U., St. Joseph Coll., U. Miami; coll. paralegal instr., 1970-89; adj. faculty prof. constl. law Union Inst., Miami, Cin., 1990-92; adj. prof. environ. litigation and alternative dispute resolution Ward Stone Coll., Miami, 1994; guest prof. internat. environ. law Dept. Internat. and Comparative Law, hemispheric Interam., U. Miami, 1992—; mem. adv. panel, seminar speaker on internat. environ. law Interam. Dialogue on Water Mgmt., 1993; speaker on environ. transactions and litigation, North Dade county Fla. Bar Assn., 1995—; seminar speaker on environ. politics, U. Miami Dept. Environ. Sci., 1995—; mem. Nat. Dist. Attys. Assn., 1972-75, mem. environ. protection com.; pres. ESI Group, Nat. Environ. Responsibility Cons. Inc. Editor-in-chief DePaul U. The Summons, 1967-68; mem. staff DePaul Law Rev., 1968; contbr. articles to profl. jours. Gen. counsel Marjory Stoneman Douglas Friends of Everglades, 1992-93; asst. atty. gen., chair fed. and constnl. practice litigation group N.Y. State, N.Y.C., 1976-78; mem. Coalition Fla. Save Our Everglades Program; diplomate, vice chancellor Law-Sci. Acad. Am., 1967. Recipient Honors award in forensic litigation Law-Sci. Acad. Am., 1967. Mem. ABA (nat. article editor law student divsn. 1967-68, nat. com. environ. litigation, com. fed. procedures, com. toxic torts, hazardous substances and environ. law, com. energy resources law, com. internat. environ. law, com. internat. litigation, environ. interest group, sect. natural resources, energy and environ. law, judge negotiation competition championship round, law student divsn., midyr. meeting 1995, sect. sci. and tech., biotech. com., environ. law and pub. health com., standing com. sci. evidence, spl. com. legal edn., nat. toxic and hazardous substances and environ. law com., sect. tort and ins. practice, corp. gen. counsel com., non-profit orgns. com., media law and defamation torts com., tort and hazardous substances and environ. law com., govt. and pub. sector lawyers divsn.), AAAS, Judicature Soc., Nat. Orgn. Social Security Claimants Reps. (sustaining), Am. Arbitration Assn. (cert. program in mediation 1993), ASTD, Soc. Human Resource Mgmt., Assn. Bar City N.Y., N.Y. County Lawyers Assn. (com. on fed. cts. 1977-82), ATLA (nat. coms. toxic, environ. and pharm. torts, environ. litigation), Environ. Law Inst., Am. Immigration Lawyers Assn., Ill. State Bar Assn. (staff editor 1967-68), N.Y. State Bar Assn. (environ. law sect., family law sect.), Ind. State Bar Assn. (environ. law sect., internat. law sect., trial practice sect.), Fla. Assn. Environ. Profls., Greater Miami C. of C. (trustee 1993-94, com. environ. awareness, environ. econs., biomed. exch., planning and growth mgmt., internat. econ. devel., bus. and industry econs. devel., govtl. affairs, ins., internat. banking, Europe/Pacific), N.Y. Acad. Sci., The Planetary Soc., Astron. Soc. of Pacific, Am. Acad. Poets, Soc. Cross Astron. Soc., The Planetary Soc., Astron. Soc. Office: ESI Group Nat Environ Responsibility Cons Inc 14630 Bull Run Rd Ste 213 Miami Lakes FL 33014-2017 E-mail: arsharett@mindspring.com.

SHARF, STEPHAN, automotive company executive; b. Berlin, Dec. 30, 1920; came to U.S., 1947; s. Wilhelm and Martha (Schwartz) S.; m. Rita Schantzer, June 17, 1951. Degree in Mech. Engring., Tech. U., Berlin, Fed. Republic Germany, 1947. Tool and die maker Buerk Tool & Die Co., Buffalo, 1947-50; foreman Ford Motor Co., 1950-53, gen. foreman, 1953-58; with Chrysler Corp., Detroit, 1958-86, master mechanic Twinsburg stamping plant, 1958-63, mfg. engring. mgr., 1963-66, mfg. prodn. Twinsburg stamping plant, 1966-68, plant mgr. Warren stamping plant, 1968-70, plant mgr. Sterling stamping plant, 1970-72, gen. plants mgr. stamping, 1972-78, v.p. Engine and Casting div., 1978-80, v.p. Power Train div., 1980-81, exec. v.p., mfg., dir., 1981-85, exec. v.p. internat., 1985-86, also bd. dirs.; pres. SICA Corp., Troy, Mich., 1986—. Bd. dirs. Integral Vision Inc. Columnist Ward's Auto World Common Sense mag., 1987—. Bd. dirs. Jr. Achievement, Detroit council Boy Scouts Am.; trustee, v.p. Oakland U. Mem. Soc. Auto Engrs., Detroit Engring. Soc. Clubs: Wabeek Country. Home: 966 Adams Castle Dr Bloomfield Hills MI 48304-3713 Office: SICA Corp PO Box 623 Troy MI 48099-0623 Office Fax: 248-433-3937. E-mail: SICA@concentric.net.

SHARICK, MERLE DAYTON, JR. retired insurance executive, auctioneer, broker; b. Bloomington, Ill, May 5, 1946; s. Merle Dayton and Joyce Madeline (Reed) S.; m. Cheryl Jean Easterday, Dec. 28, 1966; children: Amber Dawn, Cami Nicole. BA, Southwestern Coll., Winfield, Kans., 1968; MS in Edn., U. Kans., 1970. Tchr., coach Kans. High Schs., Lawrence, Hutchinson, 1968-73, asst. prin., prin. Buhler, Inman, Leoti, 1973-77; auctioneer, real estate salesman R.E.I.B., Inc., Hutchinson, Kans., 1977-78; acct. exec. Mortgage Guaranty Ins. Co., 1978-81, regional sales mgr. Shawnee Mission, Kans., 1981-83, Houston, 1983-86, divsn. risk mgr. Atlanta, 1986-90, regional dir. Charlotte, N.C., 1990-93; v.p., mgr. risk mgmt. Republic Mortgage Ins. Co., Winston-Salem, 1993-99; mgr. S.E. divsn. Sheldon Good & Co. Auctions, Charlotte, 1999-2001; sr. v.p. Infinity Info. Solutions and Gen. Info. Svcs., Chapin, SC, 2001—. Sports editor Winfield (Kans.) Daily Couier, 1966-68; grad. asst. U. Kans., Lawrence, 1968-70; owner, operator Riverside Home Style Laundry, South Hutchinson, Kans., 1975-79, founder, owner, The Sport Shack, Hutchinson, Kans., 1977-79; mem. Fredde Mac UNBOG Adv. Group, 1995—; spkr. in field. Active in Rep. support groups, Houston, Atlanta, 1983—. Fellow Inst. for Devel. Ednl. Adminstrs.; mem. Nat. Assn. Rev. Appraisers and Mortgage Underwriters (bd. dirs. 1989-93, Ark. Traveler award 1995), Mortgage Bankers Am., Ga. Mortgage Bankers, Mortgage Bankers Carolinas, N.C. Bankers Assn., N.C. Alliance Cmty. Fin. Instns., S.C. League Savs. Instns., Fla. Mortgage Bankers, Tex. Mortgage Bankers, Charlotte Mortgage Bankers, The Housing Roundtable, Nat. Assn. Realtors, Nat. Auctioneers Assn., N.C. Auctioneers Assn., S.C. Auctioneers Assn., Charlotte Region Comml. Bd. Realtors, Tower Club (Charlotte), Charlotte Touchdown Club. Baptist. E-mail: auctionmerle@aol.com., msharick@infinitylinks.com.

SHARIF, ADEL A. science educator; b. Ardebil, Azerbaijan, Jan. 1, 1970; PhD, U. Calif., Irvine. Prof. U. Mich., Flint.

SHARIF, KHALID, educational association administrator; b. Lahore, Pakistan, May 2, 1936; m. Farhat, Sept. 20, 1970; 3 children. Diploma, Inst. Affaires Internat., Paris, Academia Argentina Diplomacia, Mem. Caricom, Carribbean States; PhD (hon.), Addison State U., World Acad. Assn. Masters Univ, Monchengladbach, Germany, Australian Inst. Coord. Rsch., Victoria; LLD, London Inst. Applied Rsch., Third World Coll. Internat., Paris. Sec. Pakistan Students Fedn., London, 1956-58; gov. Lewisham Inst. Adult Edn., 1987-90; sch. gov. Waverley Girls high Sch., Peckham Rye Sch., 1987-90; mem. Amnesty Internat., 1992-98; Lord of Rock Island County Rosecommon, Ireland, 1997—. Lord Manor Gt. Pollicott, 1999, Manor Gt. Linton, 2000. Cmty. devel. worker Wandsworth Anglo-Indian Welfare Assn., London, 1970-72; mem. mgmt. com. Southwark Coun. Cmty. Rels., London, 1972-75, treas., 1985-86, Southwark Coun. Vol. Svc., London, 1975-78, King's/Southwark Cmty. Health Coun., London, 1983-85, three boroughs project Commn. Racial Equality, London, 1988-91; cmty. rep. Southwark Police Consultative Group, London, 1981-84, Bromley Cmty. Police Consultative Group, 1988-92, Lewisham Police Consultative Group, London, 1994-95; mem. help on arrest scheme juveniles, lay vis. Southwark Police Stas., London, 1981-84; gen. sec. Southwark Asian Cmty. Orgn., London, 1981-84; trustee Camberwell Consokidated Charities, London, 1983-85; vice chmn. race subcom. Southwark Borough Coun., London, 1984-86; chmn. sch. gov. body Ivydale Primary Sch., London, 1983-86, Robert Browning Primary Sch., London, 1983-85; ind. chmn. tenancy agreements Southwark Arbitration Tribunals, London, 1984-86; mem. bd. vis. HM Prison, Wandsworth, London, 1984-92; mem. S.E. London Valuation Cmty. Charge Tribunals, London, 1984-92; chmn. Bromley Asian Cmty. Orgn., London, 1988-92, Lewisham Asian Cmty. Orgn., London, 1992-95; founder, chmn. Day Ctr., Lunches Club Sr. Citizens, Bromley, Kent, Eng., 1988-91; gov. Brockley Sch., Lewisham Edn. Authority, London, 1994-95, Kilmorie Sch., 1994-95, mem. edn. appeals tribunal, 1995—; mem. edn. appeals tribunal Southwark Edn. Authroity, London, 1995—; senator Coun. States Protection Life, Palermo, Italy, 1995—. Named Lord of Camster, Baron, Royal Order Bohemian Crown, Count, Order of San Ciriaco, Knight Commdr., Lofsensic Urninius Order, Knight, Grand Prior Templar Order, Order of Holy Grail, Circulo Nobilario Los Caballeros Universals, Capt., Order Eagle of Sea, Knight of Yr., Internat. Assn. Writers Artists, 1995; grantee Coat of Arms, 2001. Fellow Australian Inst. Coord. Rsch.; mem. Brit. Constnl. Monarchy Assn., Inst. Heraldic Genealogical Studies, Royal Soc. St. George, Meml. Soc. Great Britain, Royal Humane Soc. (gov.), Maison Internat. Intellectuals, Monarchist League. 786.Freeserve-.CO.uk. Address: 11 High St London SE20 7HJ England E-mail: Dr.Khalid@Sharif.

SHARIF, M. ALAN, interventional cardiologist; b. Damascus, Syria, June 24, 1967; came to U.S., 1990; Aleppo Med. Sch., 1990. Bd. cert. internal medicine, cardiology and interventional cardiology. Intern, then resident Sinai Hosp., Wayne State U., Detroit, 1992-95; chief resident Sinai Hosp., 1995-96; fellow in cardiology Brown U., Providence, 1996-99; interventional cardiology fellow Brown U., Miriam Hosp., 1999-2000; chmn. divsn. cardiology Ingham Regional Med. Ctr., Lansing, Mich. Asst. prof. Mich. State U. Fellow Am. Coll. Cardiology; mem. ACP-Am. Soc. Internal Medicine. Office: Thoracic Cardiovasc Inst 405 W Greenlawn Ste 220 Lansing MI 48910 E-mail: msharif@tciheart.com.

SHARIF, ORZALA, research scientist; b. Kabul, Afghanistan, Oct. 26, 1974; arrived in U.S., 1980; d. Ghulam Farouq and Sima Sharif; m. Joseph Khalid Shalizi, July 10, 1998. BS Biochemistry, U. Calif., San Diego, 1997. Rsch. assoc. Immune Response Corp., Carlsbad, Calif., 1997—98; rsch. scientist DNA Scis. Labs., LaJolla, 1998—. Mem.: Afghan-Am. Youth Orgn. (edn. coord.). Home: 14870 Fox Hunt Ln San Diego CA 92128-3730

SHARIFF, ASGHAR J. geologist; b. Haft Kel, Iran, July 28, 1941; came to U.S., 1964, naturalized, 1978; s. Abdulwahab and Sakineh (Kamiab) S.; m. Kay L. Schoenwald, Aug. 9, 1969; 1 child, Shaun. BS, Calif. State U., Northridge, 1971, MS, 1983. Cert. prof. geologist Why. Petroleum geologist Iranian Oil Exploration and Producing Co., Ahwaz, 1971-74; geol. cons. D.R.L., Inc., Bakersfield, Calif., 1974-76, Strata-log, Inc., Bakersfield, 1976-79, Energy Log, Inc., Sacramento, 1979-80; geologist U.S. Dept. Energy, Washington, 1980-81, Bur. Land Mgmt. Dept. Interior, Washington, 1981-89, asst. dist. mgr. Rawlins, Wyo., 1989-93, chief reservoir mgmt. group Casper, 1993—. Contbr. articles to profl. jous. Mem. Am. Assn. Petroleum Geologists, Soc. Petroleum Engrs. E-mail: asghar_shariff@blm.gov.

SHARIFF, ISMAIL, economics educator; b. Mysore, Karnataka, India, Dec. 5, 1937; came to U.S., 1961; s. Mahmood and Begum (Bee) S.; m. Sajida Begum, Oct. 16, 1960; children: Mansoor, Mazkoor. BA with honors, U. Mysore, 1958, MA in Econs., 1960; PhD in Econ. Policy and Devel., U. Wis., 1965. Sr. statis. asst. State Govt. Mysore, 1960-61; rsch. assoc. ERS/USDA, Wis., 1965-66; asst. prof. U. Wis., Madison, 1967-69, Green Bay, 1969-72, assoc. prof., 1972-75, prof. regional analysis, chmn. econs. dept., 1978—. Econ. adviser to Nigeria, UN, 1975-77; cons. World Bank, Washington, 1990—. Office: U Wis Dept Regional Analysis 2420 Nicolet Dr Green Bay WI 54311-7003

SHARIFY, NASSER, educator, author, librarian; b. Tehran, Iran, Sept. 23, 1925; came to U.S., 1953, naturalized, 1972; s. Ebrahim and Eshrat (Saghafy) S.; m. Homayoun Taslimy, June 14, 1950 (div. 1978); children: Sharareh, Shahab. Licencie es Lettres, U. Tehran, 1947; MS, Columbia U., 1954, Dr. L.S., 1958. Editorial staff Teheran jours. Rah-e Now, Jahan-e Now, Saba, Jonb va Jush, 1943-51; translator, announcer All India Radio, 1948-49; librarian, dep. dir. Library of Parliament Iran, Tehran, 1949-53; cataloger Library of Congress, 1954-55; program asst. libraries devel. sect. UNESCO, Paris, 1959-61; acting chief servicing sect. Dept. Edn., 1962-63; dir. gen. Ministry Edn., Tehran, 1961-62; asst. prof. library and info. scis. and internat. edn. U. Pitts., 1963-66; founder, dir. Internat. Library Info. Center, 1964-66; vis. lectr. SUNY Albany Sch. Library Sci., summer, 1966; dir. internat. librarianship and documentation, internat studies and world affairs SUNY, Oyster Bay, 1966-68; dean, prof. grad. sch. library and info sci. Pratt Inst., Bklyn., 1968-87, chmn. inst. research council, 1971-89, disting. prof., dean emeritus sch. computer, info. and library scis., 1987—; pres. B.E.L.T., Inc., internat. planning cons., 1981—. Dir. Grad. Library Tng. Program, UNESCO Mission, Nat. Tchrs. Coll., Tehran, 1960; Iran's Ofcl. del. to UNESCO Conf. Ednl. Pubs., Geneva, 1961, SE Asia Edn. Secs. Conf., Murree, Pakistan, 1961, Internation Conf., on Cataloging Prins., Paris, 1961, CENTO Libr. Devel. Conf., Ankara, Turkey, 1962; chmn. standing com. for preparation reading materials for new literates UNESCO, Tehran, 1961-62; mem. U.S. AID Mission, Turkey, Iran, Pakistan, 1966; dir. Conf. on Internat. Responsibility Coll. and Univ. Librarians, Oyster Bay, 1967; U.S. del. 33d Conf. and Internat. Congress on Documentation, Tokyo, 1967; ALA del. UN Conf. on Non-Govtl. Orgn., 1969; cons. U.S. AID, Conf. on Book Devel., 1967; mem. adv. bd. Ency. Libr. and Info. Scis., 1969—; chmn. Pre-Am. Library Assn. Conf. Inst. on Internat. Libr. Manpower, Edn. and Placement in N.Am., Detroit, 1970; mem. Am. del. Internat. Fedn. Libr. Assn. Conf., Liverpool, Eng., 1971, Budapest, 1972, Grenoble, France, 1973, Washington, 1974, Brussels, 1977, Montreal, 1982, Chgo., 1985, Barcelona, 1992; organzier USAID sponsored Global Info. Village Conf., Rabat, Morocco, Bklyn., N.Y., 1997, spkr., 1997; bldg. cons. Learning Resources Center, Nat. Tchrs. Coll., Iran, 1972-73, cons. campus planning, 1972-73; UNESCO cons. missions to plan and evaluate Nat. Sch. Info. Sci., Morocco, 1973-74, 79-81, 89; cons. U.S. Info. Agy., Morocco, 1991, 92, 95; chmn. Conf. on Orgn. and Control of Info for Islamic Research, 1982; chmn. bd. cons. to Nat. U. Iran, 1974-75, Pahlavi Nat. Library of Iran, 1975-77; speaker Symposium Internat. sur l' information Economique, Casablanca, Morocco, 1990; inaugural speaker Ctr. Documentation et D'Information Multimedia, Rabat, Morocco, 1995. Author: cataloging of Persian works Including Rules for Transliteration Entry and Description, 1959, Book Production, Importation and Distribution in Iran, Pakistan and Turkey, 1966; Beyond the National Frontiers: The International Dimension of Changing Library Education for a Changing World, 1973; The Pahlavi National Library of the Future, 17 vols., 1976, other books; contbr. to Ency. of Library and Info. Sci., 1969, ALA World Ency. Library and Info. Services, 1980, 86, library jours., 1973—, Bookmark, 1972, Library Education in the Middle East, 1991, Remembering Rangathan: A Sentimental Reflection, 1992; contbr. poetry to various jours. and anthologies, 1947-51, 67, 91-93 lyrics to Iranian motion pictures and recs., 1948-52; works on display at Archieves of Hoover Inst. on War Revolution and Peace, Stanford U.; Contbr. to: film script for motion picture Morad, 1951-52. Trustee Bklyn. Public Library, 1970-82; pres. Maurice F. Tauber Found., 1981— . Recipient Taj (crown) medal and citation for disting. svc. Mohammad Reza Shah Pahlavi, Shah of Iran, 1978, Kaula Gold medal and citation for disting. svc. to internat. librarianship, 1985; named for Annual Nasser Sharify Lecture Series, Sch. of Computer Info. and Libr. Scis., Pratt Inst., 1988—; writings by and about Nasser Sharify are preserved at Archives of Hoover Instn. on wars, revolutions and peace., Stanford U., Stanford, Calif. Mem. ALA (chmn. com. equivalencies and reciprocity 1966-71, mem. UNESCO panel, mem. nominating com. 1970-71, chmn. Pakistan, Iran, Turkey, Morocco, and Middle East Resource panels, internat. library edn. com. 1973—, mem. com. internat. library schs. div. library edn. 1968-72, coordinator country resources panels, internat. library edn. com. library edn. div. 1973-78), N.Y. Library Assn. (dir. library edn. sect. 1969-72), Pub. Library Assn. (task force on internat. relations 1981-86), Am. Assn. Library Schs. (chmn. govtl. relations com., 1984-88), Am. Soc. Info. for Sci., Spl. Librarian Assn., Internat. Fedn. Library Assns. (adv. group library edn. 1971-73, v.p. library schs. sect. 1973-77). Home: 252 Jericho Tpke Westbury NY 11590-1213 Office: Pratt Inst Sch Info and Libr Sci 200 Willoughby Ave # 4 Brooklyn NY 11205-3899 E-mail: nsharify@aol.com. *If I am asked to wash a car, I try to make it spotless. If I am to write a book, I try to make it faultless. But it seems that I always find spots on the shining surface of the car, and faults in many well-written pages of the book. This gives me another reason to live for another day.*

SHARK, WILLIAM MARK, physician; b. San Diego, Mar. 15, 1948; s. Leonard Lee and Marcia R. (Kaner) S.; m. Lorelei Shark, Aug. 25, 1989. BA summa cum laude, U. Calif., San Diego, 1970; MD, U. Calif., Davis, 1977. Cert. Am. Bd. Internal Medicine. Internal medicine residency Cedars Sinai Med. Ctr., 1970-80, cardiology fellow, 1980-83, consulting physician, 1982—. Instr. advanced cardiac life support AHA. Co-author: Cardiac Disease and Rehabilitation, 1982; contbr. articles to profl. jours. Jewish. Avocations: painting, fine arts.

SHARKEY, JONATHAN, muncipal official; b. Boston, July 18, 1949; s. Victor B. and Lillian C. Sharkey; m. Beverly Merrill Kelley; 1 child, Nathaniel W. BA, U. Mass., 1971. Cert. mediation Ventura Coll. Law. Mem. city coun. City of Port Hueneme, Calif. Dir. Ventura (Calif.) Regional Sanitation Dist., 1995—, Beach Erosion Authority, 1995—. Democrat. Office: City of Port Hueneme 250 N Ventura Rd Port Hueneme CA 93041 E-mail: cityhall@isle.net.

SHARKEY, LEONARD ARTHUR, automobile company executive; b. Detroit, May 21, 1946; s. Percy and Lillian (Peros) S.; m. Irene Johnson, Aug. 9, 1969 (div. Nov. 1991); children: Michelle, Wesley Tucker (step-son). Cert. pvt. pilot. Tool and diemaker Ford Motor Co., Dearborn, Mich., 1965-85; indsl. hazardous substance educator Ford Motor co., 1985-86, indsl. health, safety and energy control educator, 1987-88, tool and diemaker leader, 1989—; non-fiction author Individual Initiative, Brighton, 1989—. Author: Journey Into Fear (reprinted title Split Decision, 1997), 1995, Hidden Shadows - An Opening to the Windows of the Mind, 1996. Mem. Mich. Rep. Party. Mem. Nat. Geog. Soc., Nat. Rifle Assn., Boat U.S., Drummond Island Sportsman's Club, Mich. United Conservation Clubs. Avocations: boating, shooting sports, political awareness studies, Biblical prophetic studies, theater.

SHARKEY, RICHARD DAVID, architectural artisan, inventor, musician; b. Columbus, Ohio, May 8, 1957; s. John David and Beatrice Diane (Ziesler) S.; m. Melissa Duke Smith, Dec. 21, 1980 (div. 1995); children: Flax Allistair Linden, Ambrosia Rose Ashley; m. Ann Marie Strong, May 1, 1999 (div. Nov. 2000). Student, U. No. Colo., 1975-77, Emporia State U., 1977-78, U. Denver, 1978-81. Music tchr., pvt. studio, piano, cello, composition theory, Evergreen, Colo., 1978-82; pvt. bus., period residential restoration Sharkey and Assocs., Evergreen and Denver, 1978-86; stair apprentice Denver Stair Co., 1985-86; stair master Heidelberg Stair Co., Evergreen, 1986; pvt. bus., designer period staircases, millwork O'Searcaigh, Ltd., Evergreen and Denver, 1986-90; with Archtl. Artworks, Englewood, Colo., 1993-95, Form & Structure Ltd., Denver, 1995-96; prin. Adobe Homes, 1996—, Archtl. Artisans, Questa, N.Mex., 1997—. Cons. archtl. product design and devel. Heidelberg Stair, Evergreen, Frank's Woodworking, Lyons, Colo., ICS, Boulder, Pierce Segerberg & Spaeh Architects, Vail, Colo., Charles Cunnifree & Assoc., Apsen, Colo., numerous manufacturers, contractor, architecture, design firms, 1987—; cons. archtl. design period features. Composer numerous piano and cello compositions, 1972—; designer, inventor numerous archtl. products, machines, tools and accessories. Mem. LATIR vol. fire dept., 1999—. Recipient scholarship Outward Bound Colo., Optimist Club of Evergreen, 1973, music grant, U. No. Colo., Greeley, 1975-76, Emporia (Kans.) U., 1977; scholar U. No. Colo., 1976. Mem. Internat. Soc. Archtl. Artisans (pres., founder 1988—), Denver Cherry Creek Club (charter mem.), Rotary. Mem. Christian Science Ch. Avocations: art history, architecture history, collecting and designing of architectural products, musician, ballroom dancing. Home and Office: HC 81 Box 7002 Questa NM 87556-9710

SHARKEY, THOMAS DAVID, educator, botanist; b. Detroit, Jan. 28, 1953; s. Robert Hugh and Patricia June (Elliott) S.; m. Paulette Marie Bochnig June 21, 1974; 1 child, Jessa Sung. BS in Biology, Mich. State U., 1974, PhD in Botany and Plant Pathology, 1980. Postdoctoral fellow Australian Nat. U., Canberra, 1980-82; assoc. rsch. prof. Desert Rsch. Inst., Reno, 1982-87; asst. prof. U. Wis., Madison, 1987-88, assoc. prof., 1988-91, prof., 1991—. Assoc. dir. Biolog. Scis. Ctr., Reno, Nev., 1983-87; chmn. dept. botany U. Wis., Madison, 1992-94; dir. Biotron, U. Wis., Madison, 1993—. Editor: Trace Gas Emissions from Plants, 1991, Photosynthesis: Physiology and Metabolism, 2000; contbr. more than 100 articles to profl. peer-reviewed jours. Mem.: AAAS, Internat. Soc. Photosynthesis Rsch., Am. Soc. Plant Biologists. Home: 5901 S Highlands Ave Madison WI 53705-1108 Office: Univ Wis Dept Botany 430 Lincoln Dr Madison WI 53706-1313 E-mail: tsharkey@wisc.edu.

SHARKEY, VINCENT JOSEPH, lawyer; b. Newport, R.I., May 25, 1944; s. Vincent Joseph and Dorothy (Auvil) S.; m. Joyce Toomey, Dec. 27, 1969; children: Alison, Christina, John, Julia. BA in Econs., Yale U., 1966; JD, U. Va., 197l. Bar: N.J. 1971, U.S. Ct. Appeals (3d cir.) 1985. Asst. prosecutor Bergen County Prosecutor's Office, Hackensack, N.J., 1971-72; pvt. practice, Bergen County, 1972-75; ptnr. Riker, Danzig, Scherer, Hyland & Perretti, Morristown, N.J., 1979—. Lt. U.S. Army, 1966-68. Mem. ABA, N.J. Bar Assn., Bergen County Bar Assn., Yale U. Alumni Assn. (pres. Bergen County chpt. 1986-88). Office: 1 Speedwell Ave Morristown NJ 07960-6838 E-mail: vsharkey@riker.com.

SHARLACH, JEFFREY, public relations executive; b. Conn., June 11, 1953; BA, Northwestern U., 1974; JD, NYU, 1977. V.p., client svc. mgr. Burson-Marsteller, N.Y.C., 1982-85; v.p., dir. creative svcs. Carl Byoir & Assocs., 1986-88; exec. v.p. internat. ops. Rowland Worldwide, 1988-93; pres., CEO Jeffrey Group, Miami Beach, Fla., 1993—. Mem. Pub. Rels. Soc. Am. Office: Jeffrey Group 1111 Lincoln Rd Ste 800 Miami Beach FL 33139-2451

SHARMA, ARJUN DUTTA, cardiologist; b. Bombay, June 2, 1953; came to U.S., 1981; s. Hari D. and Gudrun (Axelsson) S.; m. Carolyn D. Burleigh, May 9, 1981; chldren: Allira, Eric, Harrison. BSc, U. Waterloo, Ont., Can., 1972; MD, U. Toronto, Ont., 1976. Intern Toronto Gen. Hosp., 1976-77, resident in medicine, 1978-80, St. Michael's Hosp., Toronto, 1980-81; residency medicine Toronto Gen. Hosp., 1977-78; Rsch. assoc. Washington U., St. Louis, 1981-83; asst. prof. pharmacy and toxicology U. Western Ont., London, 1985-89, asst. prof. medicine, 1983-89, assoc. prof. medicine, 1989-90; dir. interventional electrophysiology Sutter Meml. Hosp., Sacramento, 1990-95. Abstract reviewer, faculty of ann. sci. sessions N.Am. Soc. for Pacing and Electrophysiology, 1993-97; assoc. clin. prof. U. Calif., Davis, 1990-96, clin. prof. medicine, 1997—; cons. Medtronic Inc., Mpls., 1985-2000, Telectronics Pacing Sys., Inc., 1990-94, Ela Med., 2000—, Guidant, 2000—; mem. rsch. com. Sutter Inst. Med. Rsch., 1991-97; mem. exec. com. Sutter Heart Inst., 1992; program dir. Update in Tachyarhythmia Mgmt., Palm Springs, 1996, Pacing Defibrillation and Electrophysiology, Squaw Valley, 1997; mem. atrial fibrillation adv. bd. Guidant Inc. Reviewer profl. jours., including Circulation, Am. Jour. Cardiology; contbr. articles to profl. publs. Mem. coun. for basic sci. Am. Heart Assn., chmn. ann. sci. session, 1989. Recipient John Melady award, 1972, Dr. C.S. Wainwright award, 1973-75, Rsch. prize Toronto Gen. Hosp., 1979, 80, Ont. Career Scientist award Ont. Ministry of Health, 1983-89; Med. Rsch. Coun. Can. fellow, 1981-83. Fellow ACP, Am. Coll. Cardiology; mem. Am. Fedn. Clin. Rsch., Canadian Cardiovasc. Soc., N.Y. Acad. Scis., Sacramento Eldorado Med. Soc. Avocations: skiing, tennis, philately. Office: 3941 J St Ste 260 Sacramento CA 95819-3633 E-mail: skeedud1@aol.com.

SHARMA, BHAVENDER PAUL, biotechnologist; b. Patiala, Punjab, India, Oct. 22, 1949; s. Tribhawan Nath and Parkash Wati Sharma; m. Kathryn Ann Bilinski, Aug. 15, 1973; children: Anjana, Nealinder. BSc in chem. engring., Punjab U., India, 1969; MPhil, Rutgers U., 1974, PhD, 1977; MBA, Syracuse U., 1985. Instr. Rutgers U., New Brunswick, N.J., 1975-76; sr. project engr. Corning (N.Y.) Inc., 1976-83; dir. tech. and strategic planning Genencor Internat., Inc., South San Francisco, Calif., 1983-91; pres. InterSpex Products, Inc., Foster City, 1991-94; exec. dir. CV Therapeutics, Inc., Palo Alto, 1994—2001; sr. dir. Telik, Inc., San Francisco, 2001—. Editor newsletter and web site INSAF, West Orange, N.J., 1996—. Mem. AIChE, Am. Assn. Pharm. Scientists, Parenteral Drug Assn., Am. Chem. Soc. Office: Telik Inc 750 Gateway Blvd South San Francisco CA 94080 Fax: 650-570-5215. E-mail: BPSharma@Telik.com.

SHARMA, HARISH CHANDRA, real estate broker; b. Madras, Tamilnad, India, Nov. 3, 1948; came to U.S., 1976; d. Dharam Jit and Dropadi (Devi) Jigyasu; m. Anuradha H. Sharma, June 13, 1974; children: Nivedita, Rahul. BS, Annamalai U., Nagar, India, 1970; MS, Calif. Coast U., Santa Ana, 1984; MBA, Amber U., 1985. Chem. engr. Kothari Ltd., Madras, 1971-73, Lone Star Gas Co., Pyote, Tex., 1978-79; sr. sales engr. Mirch Mirex Ltd., Madras, 1973-76; agent Artha Garza, Dallas, 1980-83; broker USA Realty, Plano, Tex., 1983-84; owner, broker Century 21 Northeast, 1984-86; broker Century 21 Accent I, Allen, Tex., 1986—. Cons. Sharma Real Estate, Plano, 1985—. Recipient Dir.'s award Nat. Dean's List, 1984-85. Mem. Collin County Bd. Realtors, Dallas County Bd. Realtors, Nat. Assn. Realtors, Am. Inst. Chem. Engrs., Am. Chem. Soc. Democrat. Hindu. Avocations: reading, yoga. Office: US Mil Acad MAEN-EV West Point NY 10996

SHARMA, MANOJ, health educator, research physician; b. New Delhi, Nov. 24, 1963; came to U.S., 1992; s. Basant L. and Shakuntala Sharma; m. Sulekha Sharma, Feb. 3, 1991; children: Ankita Anna, Malvika Molly. MB BChir, U. Delhi, New Delhi, 1987; MS, Minn. State U., 1994; PhD, Ohio State U., 1997. Lic. Med. Coun. India; cert. in health and family welfare mgmt., health edn. specialist; diploma in tng. and devel. Resident in internal medicine Safdarjang Hosp., New Delhi, 1987-88; program officer cmty. health Vol. Health Assn. India, 1988-92; rsch. asst. health sci. Minn. State U., Mankato, 1992-94; rsch. & tchg. assoc. health edn. Ohio State U., Columbus, 1994-95; health promotion supr. Columbus Health Dept., 1995-97; asst. prof. cmty. health edn. U. Nebr., Omaha, 1997—2000, assoc. prof. cmty. health edn., 2001—. Cons. health and medicine Plan Internat., New Delhi, 1989-92; expert tech. resource devel. consortium NIH Family Welfare Mgmt., New Delhi, 1991-92; guest lectr. population demographic St. Mary's Coll., St. Paul, 1992-93; cons. evaluation Assn. Italiana Amici di Raoul Follerea, Bologna, Italy, 1997—. Author: (book) Practical Stress Management, 1995; contbr. rsch. articles to profl. jours. Mem. adv. bd. Am. Cancer Soc., Omaha, 1998—, World Gym Fitness Ctrs., Columbus, 1995-97; mem. membership com. Indian Soc. for Tng. and Devel., New Delhi, 1989-92. Health Promotion grantee Ctrs. for Disease Control and Prevention, 1995-97, Weight Control Program grantee Omaha Tribe, 1997-98, Evaluation of Smoking Cessation Programs in Nebr. grantee Nebr. Health & Human Svcs., 1999-2000, Asthma Prevention grantee EPA, 1999-2001; Lead Prevention grantee EPA, 1999—. Fellow Am. Inst. Stress, Soc. Pub. Health Educators (Best Dissertation 1997); mem. APHA, Am. Sch. Health Assn. (life, Best Dissertation 1997), Indian Sci. Congress Assn. (life), Indian Assn. Preventive and Social Medicine (life), Eta Sigma Gamma (life). Hindu. Avocations: yoga, meditation, stamp and coin collection, traveling. E-mail: manoj. Office: U Nebr at Omaha 6001 Dodge St Omaha NE 68182-0001 E-mail: sharma@unomaha.edu.

SHARMA, PREM S. novelist, retired dean; b. Mandalay, Burma, June 22, 1932; came to U.S., 1961; s. Devi Lal and Laj Sharma; m. Anita Sharma, May 24, 1958; children: Leena, Maddie. LDS, Royal Coll. Surgeons, Edinburg, 1956; MS, Marquette U., 1961, DDS, 1974. Head of dentistry clin. Marquette U., Milw., 1965-68, dept. chair, 1968-72, asst. dean acad. affairs, 1972-82, assoc. dean acad. affairs, prof. dentistry, 1982-94; author, novelist, 1994—. Curriculum cons. ADA, Chgo., 1986-92. Author: Mandalay's Child, 1999. Pres. Milw. Ethnic Coun., 1996—; chmn. Gov.'s Adv. Coun. on Asian Affairs, Wis., 1992-99, Gov.'s Adv. Coun. on Ethnic Affairs, 2000—; mem. Presdl. Adv. Coun. on HIV/AIDS. Recipient Disting. Alumnus award Marquette U., 1995, Nat. Merit award, 2001. Mem. Am. Coll. Dentists (past pres., assoc. editor jour. 1986-92), Am. Soc. Dentistry for Children (past pres., award of Excellence 1992). Avocations: golf, tennis, travel, photography. Home: 1900 W Woodbury Ln Glendale WI 53209

SHARMA, SANTOSH DEVRAJ, obstetrician/gynecologist, educator; b. Kenya, Feb. 24, 1934; came to U.S., Jan. 1972; d. Devraj Chananram and Lakshmi (Devi) S. BS, MB, B.J. Medical Sch., Pune, India, 1960. House surgeon Sasson Hosp., Poona, India, 1960-61; resident in ob-gyn. various hospitals, England, 1961-67; house officer Maelor Gen. Hosp., Wrexham, U.K., 1961-62; asst. prof. ob-gyn. Howard U. Med. Sch., Washington, 1972-74; assoc. prof. John A. Burns Sch. Med., Honolulu, 1974-78, prof., 1978 --. Fellow Royal Coll. Ob-Gyn., Am. Coll. Ob-Gyn. Avocations: travel, photography, environmental protection. Office: 1319 Punahou St Rm 824 Honolulu HI 96826-1032

SHARMAN, DIANE LEE, secondary school educator; b. Harvey, Ill., May 12, 1948; d. Eric Melvin and Josephine A. (Kut) Van Patten; m. Richard Lee Sharman, Nov. 3, 1973; children: Daria Lee, Deedra Lee. BS, Purdue U., 1970; MBA, U. Chgo., 1973. Cert. secondary sch. math. tchr., Tex. Computers sales rep. GE, Chgo., 1970-73; mgr. sold equipment Xerox Corp., Rochester, N.Y., 1973-81, mgr. fin. ops. analysis worldwide Stamford, 1981-84; math. tchr. Conroe (Tex.) Ind. Sch. Dist., 1993—. Mem. DAR, Nat. Coun. Tchrs. of Math., Assn., Tex. Profl. Educators, Purdue Alumni Assn. (life), Nat. Charity League, U. Chgo. Alumni Assn. Avocations: golf, horseback riding. Home: 26 Fernglen Dr The Woodlands TX 77380-3955 Office: Knox HS 12104 Sawmill Rd The Woodlands TX 77380-2133 E-mail: rshar45854@aol.com., dsharman@comoe.isd.tenet.edu.

SHARMAN, RICHARD LEE, telecommunications executive, consultant; b. Warren, Pa., Oct. 23, 1932; s. Scott Albert Sr. and Viola Lena Marie (Kittner) S.; m. Diane Lee Van Patten, Nov. 3, 1973; children: Daria Lee, Deedra Lee; children by previous marriage: Suzanne Annette, Cynthia Lee. BS in Engring. Physics, U. Toledo, 1959; MSEE, Cornell U., 1961. Project engr. advanced electronics ctr. GE, Syracuse, N.Y., 1965-68, mgr. infrared and optics, electronics lab., 1965-68, mgr. info. networks, info. sys. divsn. Bethesda, Md., 1968-73; mgr. comml. analysis Xerox Corp., Rochester, N.Y., 1973-78, mgr. mktg. sys., 1978-80; v.p. bus. sector GTE Corp., Stamford, Conn., 1980-84; v.p. mktg. GTE Mobilnet Inc., Houston, 1984-87, gen. mgr. Tex. region, 1987-90; v.p. ops. GTE Mobilnet Inc. Hdqrs., 1990-92; pres., owner Mgmt. Consulting Svcs. Co., The Woodlands, 1993—. Adj. faculty Montgomery Coll., 1997—; bd. dirs. Cellular Comms. Corp., Irvine, Calif., 1985-87; mem. Svc. Corps of Ret. Execs., 1998—. Contbr. articles profl. jours. With USCG, 1951-54. Mem. Am. Mktg. Assn. (exec.), Cornell Alumni Assn. (admissions amb.), Tau Beta Pi. Republican. Episcopalian. Avocation: photography. Home and Office: 26 Fernglen Dr The Woodlands TX 77380-3955

SHARMAN, WILLIAM, professional basketball team executive; b. Abilene, Tex., May 25, 1926; m. Joyce Sharman; children from previous marriage: Jerry, Nancy, Janice, Tom. Student, U. So. Calif. Basketball player Washington Capitols, 1950-51, Boston Celtics, 1951-61; coach L.A./Utah Stars, 1968-71, L.A. Lakers, 1971-76, gen. mgr., 1976-82, pres., 1982-88, spl. cons., 1991—. Author: Sharman on Basketball Shooting, 1965. Named to All Star 1st Team, NBA, 1956-59, 2nd Team, 1953, 55 (game MVP), 60, All League Team, 7 times, named Coach of Yr., 1972, One of Top Players in NBA History, league 50th anniversary, 1997, league leader free-throw percentage, 7 times; named to Basketball Hall of Fame, 1975, Naismith Basketball Hall of Fame, 1976; named All-Am., twice; inductee U. So. Calif. Hall of Fame, 1994; Porterville H.S. gymnasium renamed in his honor, 1997. Home: 7510 W 81st St Playa Del Rey CA 90293-8807 Office: LA Lakers 555 N Nash St El Segundo CA 90245-2818

SHAROFF, JERROLD LIONEL, obstetrician-gynecologist; b. N.Y.C., Aug. 3, 1927; s. Nathan and Dorothy (Gordon) S.; m. Helene Pincus, Sept. 14, 1952; childreen, Nancy, Aileen. BA, Syracuse U., 1949; MA, U. Mo., Columbia, 1950; MD, U. Health Scis./Chgo. Med. Sch, 1954. Diplomate Am. Bd. Ob-Gyn. Intern Beth Israel Hosp., N.Y.C., 1954-55; resident in ob-gyn. Morrisania City Hosp., 1955-58; pvt. practice, 1958-90; chief ob/gyn clinic Queens Hosp. Ctr., 1990-95; asst. chief gynecol. clinic Westchester County Med. Ctr., 1995—; ptnr. Comp. Ctr. Health Practices, N.Y.C., 1995—. Fellow ACS, ACOG; mem. AMA, Westchester Ob/Gyn Soc. E-mail: wasabipop@aol.com.

SHARON, MARK WILLIAM, family practice physician; b. Antigo, Wis., Mar. 23, 1953; s. Robert William and Joyce Elizabeth Sharon; m. Maureen Ann Healy, June 9, 1979 (div. July 1991); children: Alexander, Phillip; m. Barbara Ann Nigh, Dec. 30, 1992. BS, Marquette U., 1975; MD, Med. Coll. Wis., 1979. Diplomate Am. Bd. Family Practice. Resident in family medicine U. Ill., Rockford, 1979-82; family practice physician Plymouth (Wis.) Clinic, 1982—; chief of staff Valley View Med. Ctr., Plymouth, 1990-92. Med. advisor Rocky Knoll Health, Plymouth, 1982-2000, Plymouth Sch. Dist., 1986—, North Kettle Moraine Nordic Cki Club, Greenbush, Wis., 1996—. Pres. Sheboygan County Med. Soc., Sheboygan, Wis., 1991-93. Mem. AMA (Physician Recognition award 1982—), Am. Acad. Family Physicians, Wis. Acad. Family Physicians, Wis. Soc. Ob-Gyn. Roman Catholic. Avocations: Nordic skiing, tennis, golf, bicycling, running. Office: Sheboygan Clinic 2636 Eastern Ave Plymouth WI 53073

SHARON, NATHAN, biochemist; b. Brisk, Poland, Nov. 4, 1925; arrived in Israel, 1934; m. Rachel Itzikson, 1948; children: Esther, Osnat. MS, Hebrew U., Jerusalem, 1950, PhD, 1953; Dr. (hon.), U. Rene Descartes, Paris, 1990. Rsch. asst. Agrl. Rsch. Sta., Rehovot, Israel, 1949-53; rsch. asst. dept. biophysics Weizmann Inst. Sci., Israel, 1954-57, rsch. assoc. dept. biophysics Israel, 1957-60, sr. scientist dept. biophysics Israel, 1960-65, assoc. prof. dept. biophysics Israel, 1965-68, prof. dept. biophysics Israel, 1968-90, prof. emeritus Israel, 1991—. Vis. scientist numerous univs. and colls. Author: Complex Carbohydrates: Their Chemistry, Biosynthesis and Functions, 1975; co-editor: Biotechnological Applications of Proteins and Enzymes, 1977, The Lectins: Properties, Functions and Applications in Biology and Medicine, 1986; co-author: Lectins, 1989; contbr. over 400 articles to profl. jours. Recipient Laundau prize Mifal Hapyis, Israel, 1973, Weizmann prize in exact scis. City of Tel Aviv, 1977, Olitzki prize Israel Soc. Microbiology, 1989, Datta lectureship award Fedn. European Biochem. Socs., 1987, Bijvoet medal Utrecht U., 1989, Israel prize in Biomed. and Med. Rsch., 1994. Mem. Am. Chem. Soc., Biochem. Soc. Eng., Am. Soc. Biol. Chemists (hon.), European Molecular Biology Orgn., Israel Acad. Scis. and Humanities, Academia Europaea, Polish Acad. Sci. (fgn. mem.), Am. Soc. Microbiology (hon.), , Internat. Sci. Writers Assn., Israel Biochem. Soc. (pres. 1969-70), Soc. for Complex Carbohydrates, Fedn. European Biochem. Socs. (chmn. 1980-81), Internat. Glycoconjugate Orgn. (pres. 1989-91), Am. Soc. Microbiology (hon.). Avocation: swimming. Home: 77 Mishmeret Afeka Tel Aviv 69012 Israel Office: Weizmann Inst Sci Biol Chemistry Rehovot 76100 Israel E-mail: nathan.sharon@weizmann.ac.il.

SHARON, TIMOTHY MICHAEL, physicist; b. Portsmouth, Va., Aug. 21, 1948; s. Lester Clark and Ruth May (Banister) Sharon; m. Carla Deon Colley, Dec. 17, 1977. Student, Santa Ana Coll., 1966—68; BA, U. Calif., Irvine, 1970, MA, 1972, PhD, 1976. Jr. specialist solid state theory U. Calif., Irvine, 1976; rsch. asst. radiation physics Med. Ctr. and Sch. Medicine, 1976—77; cons. to attending staff Rsch. and Edn. Found., 1976—77; mktg. physicist Varian Assoc., Irvine, 1977—78; prin. engr., program mgr. Spectra Rsch. Sys., Newport Beach, Calif., 1977—82; v.p. Brewer-Sharon Corp., 1981—86, Micor Instruments, Inc., Irvine, 1983—86; pres., CEO Medelec Instruments Co., Inc., Newport Beach, 1986—88; pres. Pacific Crest Enterprises, El Toro, 1988—91; pres., CEO Novus Group NA, 1991—96; pres. Instafil, Lake Forest, 1995—. Adj. faculty physics and engring. Columbia Pacific U., San Rafael, Calif., 1981—87; dean Sch. Engring., Newport U., Newport Beach, Calif., 1983—87; mem. adv. panel on pub. Am. Inst. Physics, 1974—75. Editor (assoc.): (jour.) Future Oncology, 2000—01; contbr. articles to profl. jours. Fellow: Brit. Interplanetary Soc. (assoc.); mem.: Nat. Hist. Soc., Am. Film Inst., Assn. Advancement Med. Instrumentation, IEEE, Am. Assn.

Physicists in Medicine, Am. Phys. Soc., AAAS, Club 33, Smithsonian Instn., Nat. Geographic Soc., Intertel, Mensa, Acad. Magical Arts, Festival of Arts Laguna Beach, Alpha Gamma Sigma, Phi Theta Kappa, Sigma Pi Sigma.

SHARON, YITZHAK YAAKOV, physicist, educator; b. Tel Aviv, Feb. 29, 1936; came to U.S., 1948; s. Abraham Sharon-Schwadron and Dina Freidenberg; m. Sandra Brook, Jan. 13, 1991; 1 child, Dina Avrahama. AB with highest honors, Columbia U., 1958; MA in Physics, Princeton U., 1960, PhD in Physics, 1966. Asst. Inst. for Advanced Study, Princeton, N.J., 1965-66; asst. prof. Northeastern U., Boston, 1966-72; assoc. prof. Richard Stockton Coll., Pomona, N.J., 1972-75, prof. physics, 1975—, trustee fellow in scis., 2000-01. Cons. Ednl. Svcs., Inc. Phys. Sci. Study Commn., 1962-63; vis. prof. Temple U., Phila., 1970-71, U. Montreal, 1970; vis. fellow Princeton U., 1980-82, 91-92; summer physicist Nat. Bur. Standards, Washington, 1971, Oak Ridge (Tenn.) Nat. Lab., 1969, Lawrence Radiation Lab., Berkeley, Calif., 1968; visitor Rutgers U., 1995—. Contbr. articles to profl. jours. Grantee NSF, N.J. Dept. Higher Edn., Ctr. for Theology and Natural Scis. Mem. Am. Phys. Soc., Am. Assn. Physics Tchrs., Sigma Xi, Phi Beta Kappa. Jewish. Home: 19 James Ave Kendall Park NJ 08824-1620 Office: Richard Stockton Coll NJ Dept Physics Pomona NJ 08240 E-mail: sharon@physics.rutgers.edu.

SHARP, ALFRED JAY, retired personnel relations executive; b. Elmira, N.Y., Oct. 18, 1929; s. Albert Jay Sharp and Berneita May (Doughty) Purdy; m. Alberta Marie Rohring, Dec. 27, 1948 (div.); children: Dannie Neil, Sharon Eileen. Machine operator Eastman Kodak Co., Rochester, N.Y., 1951-71, technician, 1971-82; staff asst. Mfg. Materials Mgmt., 1982-86; systems analyst Corp. Relations, 1986; ret., 1986. Dir. Teen Session Youth Group, Rochester, 1973-78; pres. 36 West Avenue Inc., Fairport, N.Y., 1979-87. Master sgt. USAF, 1947-49, USAFR, 1952-89. Mem. Am. Mgmt. Assn., Assn. Bus. Mgmt. (instr. scholarship chmn. 1986-2002), Air Force Sgts. Assn. (Divsn. 1 pres. 1974-81, cons. 1981-87, treas. 1981-90, conv. mgr. 1984-91, numerous awards 1981, 82, 87, 90, 91, 94, Rep. Senatorial Medal of Freedom), Am. Legion, Moose. Republican. Avocations: reading, writing, fishing, music. Home: 54 Red Bud Rd Rochester NY 14624-4718 Office: 343 State St Rochester NY 14650-0001

SHARP, ALLEN, federal judge; b. Washington, Feb. 11, 1932; s. Robert Lee and Frances Louise (Williams) S.; children: Crystal Catholyn, Scarlet Frances. Student, Ind. State U., 1950-53; AB, George Washington U., 1954; JD, Ind. U., 1957; MA, Butler U., 1986. Bar: Ind. 1957. Practiced in, Williamsport, 1957-68; judge Ct. of Appeals Ind., 1969-73, U.S. Dist. Ct. (no. dist.) Ind., South Bend, 1973—. Served to JAG USAF, Res. Mem. Ind. Judges Assn., Blue Key, Phi Delta Kappa, Pi Gamma Mu, Tau Kappa Alpha. Republican. Mem. Christian Ch. Club: Mason. Office: US Dist Ct 124 Fed Bldg 204 S Main St South Bend IN 46601-2122

SHARP, ANNE CATHERINE, artist, educator; b. Red Bank, N.J., Nov. 1, 1943; d. Elmer Eugene and Ethel Violet (Hunter) S. BFA, Pratt Inst., 1965; MFA, Bklyn. Coll., 1973. Tchr. art Sch. Visual Arts, 1978-89, NYU, 1978, SUNY, Purchase, 1983, Pratt Manhattan Ctr., N.Y.C., 1982-84, Parsons Sch. Design, N.Y.C., 1984-90, Visual Arts Ctr. of Alaska, Anchorage, 1991, Anchorage Mus. Hist. and Art, 1991, 93, 94, 95, U. Alaska, Anchorage, 1994-96, Fashion Inst. Tech., SUNY, 1997-98; lectr. AAAS, The 46th Arctic Divsn. Sci. Conf., U. Alaska, Fairbanks, 1995. One-person shows Pace Editions, N.Y.C., Ten/Downtown, N.Y.C., Katonah (N.Y.) Gallery, 1974, Contemporary Gallery, Dallas, 1975, Art in a Public Space, N.Y.C., 1979, Eatontown Hist. Mus., N.J., 1980, N.Y. Pub. Library Epiphany Br., 1988, Books and Co., N.Y., 1989, The Kendall Gallery, N.Y.C., 1990, Alaska Pacific U., Carr-Gottstein Gallery, Anchorage, 1993, Internat. Gallery Contemporary Art, Anchorage, 1993, Art Think Tank Gallery, N.Y.C., 1994, U.S. Geol. Survey, Reston, Va., 1994, Stonington Gallery, Anchorage, 1994, on TV Ltd. Benefit, N.Y.C., 1998-2000; group shows include Arnot Art Mus., Elmira, N.Y., 1975, Bronx Mus., 1975, Mus. Modern Art, N.Y.C., 1975-76, Nat. Arts Club, N.Y.C., 1979, Calif. Mus. Photography, Riverside, 1983-92, Jack Tilton Gallery, N.Y.C., 1983, Lincoln Ctr., N.Y.C., 1983, Cabo Frio Print Biennale, Brazil, 1983, Pratt Graphic Ctr., N.Y.C., 1984, State Mus. N.Y., Albany, 1984, Kenkeleba Gallery, N.Y.C., 1985, Hempstead Harbor Art Assn., Glen Cove, N.Y., 1985, Mus. Mod. Art, Weddel, Fed. Republic of Germany, 1985, Kenkeleba Gallery, N.Y.C., 1985, Paper Art Exhbn. Internat. Mus. Contemporary Art, Bahia, Brazil, 1986, Mus. Salon-de-Provence, France, 1987, Mus. Contemporary Art, Sao Paulo, Brazil, 1985-86, Salon de Provence, France, 1987, Adirondack Lakes Ctr. for Arts, Blue Mountain Lake, N.Y., 1987, Kendall Gallery, N.Y.C., 1988, Exhibition Ctr. Parsons Sch. Design, N.Y.C., 1989, F.M.K. Gallery, Budapest, Hungary, 1989, Galerie des Kulturbundes Schwarzenberg, German Dem. Republic, Q Sen Do Gallery, Kobe, Japan, 1989, Anchorage Mus. History and Art, 1990-91, 94, U. Alaska, Anchorage, 1990, 91, Coos Art Mus., Coos Bay, Oreg., 1990, Spaceship Earth, Mus. Internat. de Neu Art, Vancouver, Can., 1990, Councourse Gallery, Emily Carr Coll. Art and Design, 1990, Nat. Mus. Women in the Arts, Washington, 1991, Visual Arts Ctr. Alaska, 1991, 92, Nomad Mus., Lisbon, Portugal, 1991, Mus. Ostdeutsche Gallery, Regensberg, Germany, 1991, Mcpl. Mus. Cesley Krumlov (So. Bohemia) CSFK, Czechoslovakia, 1991, Böltmiche Dörter Exhbn. Hochstrass 8, Munich, 1992, BBC-TV, Great Britain, U.K., Sta. WXXI-TV, Rochester, N.Y., 1992-93, Site 250 Gallery Contemporary Art., Fairbanks, 1993, Santa Barbara (Calif.) Mus. Art, 1993, The Rochester (N.Y.) Mus. and Sci. Ctr., 1990-94, Space Arc: The Archives of Mankind, Time Capsule in Earth Orbit, Hughes Comm., Divec TV Satellite Launch, 1994, Stonington Gallery, Anchorage, 1994, 95, UAA Art Galley U. Alaska, 1995, Arctic Trading Post, Nome, Alaska, 1995, Allan P. Kikbuarts Ctr. Gallery at the Lawrenceville (N.J.) Sch., 1996, Blue Mountain Gallery, N.Y., 1998, The Book Room, Jersey City, 2000, 2001, A.I.R. Gallery, 2002; represented in permanent collections Smithsonian Instn., Nat. Air and Space Mus., Washington, Albright Knox Gallery, Buffalo, St. Vincent's Hosp, N.Y.C., N.Y. Pub. Libr., N.Y.C., U.S. Geol. Survey, Reston, Va., White House (Reagan, Bush adminstrns.), Site 250 Gallery Contemporary Art, Fairbanks, Alaska, Anchorage Mus. History and Art, others; Moon Shot series to commemorate moon landing, 1970-76, Cloud Structures of the Universe Painting series, 1980-86, Am. Landscape series, 1987-89, Thoughtlines, fall 1986, Swimming in the Mainstream with Her, U. Va., Charlottesville; author: Artist's Book - Travel Dreams U.S.A., 1989, Artworld-Welt Der Kunst, Synchronicity, 1989—, Art Think Tank: Projects in Art and Ecology, 1990—, The Alaska Series, 1990—, Potraits in the Wilderness, 1990—; columnist: Anchorage Press, 1995—. Sponsor Iditorod Trail Com., Libby Riddles. Tchg. fellow Bklyn. Coll., 1972; Artist-in-residence grantee Va. Center for Creative Arts, 1974, Artpark, Lewiston, N.Y., 1980, Vt. Studio Colony, 1989; recipient Pippin award Our Town, N.Y.C., 1984, certificate of Appreciation Art in Embassy program U.S. Dept. State, 1996. Mem. Mus. Women in Arts, Pratt Inst. Alumni Assn., The Planetary Soc., Internat. Assn. Near-Death Studies, Art and Sci. Collaborations. Address: Murray Hill Station PO Box 1776 New York NY 10156-1776 also: Decker Morris Gallery 621 W 6th Ave Anchorage AK 99501-2200 also: Fine Art Gallery Site 250 Custaman St Ste 2A Fairbanks AK 99701 also: On Television Ltd 388 Broadway New York NY 10013-3542 *As an active painter I explore the mysteries of the 20th century space adventure in my American landscapes, painted directly from nature and in planetary landscapes, fantastic pictures of the cosmos. I believe it is in the reconciliation between inner and outer experience, through a personal sense of humor and use of universal symbols that a mystical or cosmic harmony can be expressed in art.*

SHARP, CELESTE ELAINE, civic worker; b. Tulsa, Feb. 7, 1966; d. Charles Earl and Gwen Rowaina (Knowles) Halstead; m. Jarrett Minton Sharp, Apr. 13, 1985; children: Catherine Elisia, Shelby Elizabeth, Weston Marshall. CAD/CAM programmer La Follette Machine & Tool Co., Inc., 1989—. Mem. choir LaFollette (Tenn.) Meth. Ch., 1987-89, tchr. elem. and jr. high sch. Sunday sch., 1988-97, co-dir. Vacation Bible Sch., 1988, crafts organizer Vacation Bible Sch., 1989; mem. 1st Bapt. Holiday Orch., 1998, 99, bell choir, 1988-97, 99—. Mem. Christian Women's Club (nursery chmn. 1988-89), United Meth. Women. Republican. Avocations: antiques, decorating, music, walking, reading. Home: 1420 Sharps Ridge Ln La Follette TN 37766-2870

SHARP, DANIEL ASHER, foundation executive; b. San Francisco, Mar. 29, 1932; s. Joseph C. and Miriam (Asher) S.; m. Jacqueline Borda, 1967 (div. 1975); 1 son, Benjamin Daniel; m. Revelle Pergament Allen, 1989. BA, U. Calif.-Berkeley, 1954; JD, Harvard U., 1959. Bar: Calif. 1959. Dep. atty. gen. State of Calif., San Francisco, 1959-61; asst. dir. internat. programs U.S. Peace Corps, Washington, 1961-62, assoc. dir. Cuzco, Peru, 1962-64; acting dir. Peace Corps, La Paz, Bolivia, 1964; creator, dir. Staff Tng. Ctr. Peace Corps, Washington, 1965-68; dir. div. edn. resources U.S. Peace Corps, 1966, 1988—; dir. edn. and Latin Am. programs, asst. dir. Adlai Stevenson Inst. Internat. Affairs, U. Chgo., 1968-70; dir. tng. ITT, Latin Am., 1970-72; mgr. mgmt. devel. ITT World Hdqrs., N.Y.C., 1973; from dir. human resources devel. to dir. inter-Am. affairs Xerox Corp. (Xerox LatinAm. group), 1973—79; from dir. internat. affairs to internat. cons. Xerox Corp. Hdqrs., 1979—97, sr. internat. advisor InterMatrix Group, 1990—; pres., CEO Columbia U. Am. Assembly, 1987—2002, Royal Instn. World Sci. Assembly, 2002—. Adj. prof. internat. and pub. affairs Columbia U., 1991—; sr. moderator, faculty Aspen Inst., 1995—; chmn.'s coun. Eisenhower Exch. Fellowships, 2000—; U.S. del. UN Econ. and Social Coun., Geneva, 1961, OAS, San Juan, 1986; negotiated 6 treaties U.S. Govt.; U.S. rep. Internat. Conf. on Vol. Programs, The Hague, Netherlands, 1961; outside bd. adv. coun. Macmillan Ltd. (U.K.), 1982; rep. U.S. bus. cmty. nat. task force on Europe Bus. and Industry Adv. Com., regional trade blocs, Paris, 1989; cons. in field. Editor: United States Foreign Policy and Peru, 1972, Los Estados Unidos y La Revolucion Peruaña, 1972, U.S. editor European Business Journal, 1988-95; contbr. articles to N.Y. Times, Wall St. Jour., Internat. Herald Tribune, and chapters in several books. Chmn. adv. bd. Coun. of Ams., 1978-85; bd. dirs. Overseas Devel. Coun., 1980-96, Internat. Ctr. of N.Y., 1980-88, Fund for Multinat. Mgmt. Edn., 1979-85, Accion, 1980-88, World Press Inst., 1986-89, Forum for World Affairs, 1987-95, Stamford Symphony, 1987-91; bd. advs. Landegger Program in Internat. Bus. Diplomacy, Sch. Fgn. Svc., Georgetown U., 1981-92, Econ. Growth Ctr., Yale U., 1987, Consortium on Competitiveness and Coop., U. Calif., 1987-90, Fletcher Sch. Law and Diplomacy, 1984-89; bd. vis. Duke U. Inst. of Policy Scis. and Pub. Affairs, 1988-91; active U.S./Mex. Bus. Coun., 1981-87; gen. coord. polit. coms., Spain, 2001; adv. sec. gen. Club of Madrid. With U.S. Army, 1954-55; capt. Res. Recipient Medalla de Oro y Diploma de Honor del Consejo Provincial del Cuzco, 1963, Manchester Leadership award, 1992; Woodrow Wilson fellow Princeton, N.J., 1981-85. Mem. State Bar Calif., Coun. on Fgn. Rels., Century Assn., Mid-Atlantic Club (bd. dirs.), Nat. Com. on U.S.-China Rels. Home and Office: 94 Campbell Dr Stamford CT 06903-4032 *Changing careers frequently keeps life exciting, as one must constantly learn new roles and ideas and organizations. Public service and the not-for-profit sector are ultimately more satisfying, but the management skills learned in the private sector are practically indispensable.*

SHARP, DAVID HOWLAND, physicist; b. Buffalo, Oct. 14, 1938; s. Russel Howland and Margaret (Dorries) E.; m. Gloria Evanitsky, Jan. 9, 1982; children: Lisa E., Michelle L.; stepchildren: Brian P. Riepe, Michael A. Riepe. AB, Princeton U., 1960; PhD, Calif. Inst. Tech., 1964. Mem. staff Los Alamos (N.Mex.) Nat. Lab., 1974—84, fellow, 1984—, group leader complex systems group, theoretical divsn., 2002—, sci. advisor applied physics divsn., 2002—. Fellow AAAS, Am. Phys. Soc. Home: 174 Laguna St Los Alamos NM 87544-2603 E-mail: dhs@lanl.gov., dglsharp@earthlink.net.

SHARP, DONALD EUGENE, bank consultant; b. Chgo., Nov. 4, 1929; s. Arthur Eugene and Alma (Melchior) S.; m. Phyllis Stevens, Sept. 11, 1954; 1 child, John Stevens. BA in Polit. Sci., Denison U., 1952; MA in History, Columbia U., 1959. Cert. econ. developer. With Chem. Bank, 1962-86, v.p. regular credit com., 1976-86; v.p. N.Y. Job Devel. Authority, 1986-91; lending cons. Community Mutual Savings Bank, 1992-96, The Merchants Bank of N.Y. (divsn. of Valley Nat. Bank), 1996-2001. Contbr. articles to profl. jours. Trustee Village of Bronxville, N.Y., 1989-91. Sgt. U.S. Army, 1952-54, Korea. Mem. Am. Econ. Devel. Coun., Northeastern Econ. Devel. Assn., Acad. Polit. Sci., Shenorock Shore Club, Skytop Club, Rotary, Omicron Delta Kappa. Democrat. Episcopalian. Home: 66 Avon Rd Bronxville NY 10708-1721

SHARP, DOUGLAS ANDREW, secondary school educator, educator; b. Austin, Tex., July 19, 1945; s. Jack Weston and Jean Ernestine (Beeman) S.; m. Marylin Gene Martin, Jan. 20, 1977. BA in Math., Tex. A&M U., 1967, MS in Math., 1970, postgrad., 1969-71; EdD, La Salle U., Mandville, La., 1993. Teaching fellow dept. math. Tex. A&M U., College Station, 1967-71; chmn. math. dept., asst. coach/coach athletics dept. Southfield Sch., Shreveport, La., 1972-73; coach athletics dept. St. John's Sch., Houston, 1975, chmn. math. dept., 1981-93, master teaching chair math., 1987-89; disting. vis. lectr. U. Houston, 1989-90, adj. prof., 1990. Contbr. articles to profl. jours. Recipient Excellence in Teaching award Fin. Dept. U. Houston, 1993, Outstanding Tchr. award Tandy Technol. Scholars, 1993-94. Mem. Am. Math. Soc., Am. Soc. Composer, Authors and Pubs., Am. Statistical Assn., Math. Assn. Am. (Edyth May Stiffe award 1991, 97), Calculus and Elem. Analysis Tchrs. Houston, Nat. Coun. Tchrs. Math., Cum Laude Soc. Office: St John's Sch 2401 Claremont Ln Houston TX 77019-5897

SHARP, ISADORE, hotel facility executive; b. Toronto, Ont., Can., Oct. 8, 1931; m. Rosalie Wise; children: Jordan, Gregory, Anthony, Christopher (dec.). Degree in architecture, Ryerson Inst. Tech., 1952; LLD (hon.), U. Guelph, 1992, U. Toronto, 1994. Founder Four Seasons Hotels and Resorts, Toronto, 1960—, chmn., CEO, 1961—. Dir. Bank Nova Scotia, Clairvest Group, Inc.; mem. adv. bd. Fin. Post; mem. Premier's adv. com. on exec. resources Province Ont. Active Can. Cancer Soc.; dir. Terry Fox Humanitarian Award Program, Nat. Terry Fox Run, Coun. Can. Unity; founder Terry Fox Run Program; co-chmn. United Jewish Appeal, 1985; mem. bd. govs. Mt. Sinai Hosp., Toronto; mem. govs. coun. N. York Gen. Hosp. Recipient Ruth Hartman Frankel Humanitarian award Can. Cancer Soc., Disting. Svc. award N.Y.-based World Rehab. Fund, 1989, Ryerson Alumni Award of Distinction, 1998; named Corp. Hotelier of World, Hotels and Restaurants Internat. Mag., 1988, Officer de la Confrerie des Amis de L'hotellerier Internat., Internat. Hotel Assn., 1988, NEGEV Dinner Honoree, Jewish Nat. Fund. Can., 1989, Man of Yr., Foodsvc. and Hospitality mag., 1989, CEO of Yr., Fin. Post Mag., 1992, Officer of Order of Can., Gov. Gen. Can., 1993; named to Can. Bus. Hall of Fame, 1998; Ryerson U. fellow, 1983. Office: Four Seasons Hotels 1165 Leslie St Toronto Ontario Canada M3C 2K8 E-mail: nicola.blazier@fourseasons.com.

SHARP, J(AMES) FRANKLIN, finance educator, investment portfolio manager; b. Johnson County, Ill., Sept. 29, 1938; s. James Albert and Edna Mae (Slack) S. BS in Indsl. Engring., U. Ill., 1960; MS, Purdue U., 1962, PhD, 1966, cert. mgmt. acctg., 1979. Chartered fin. analyst, 1980; cert. in fin. mgmt., 1997. Asst. prof. engring., econs. Rutgers U., New Brunswick, N.J., 1966-70; assoc. prof. NYU Grad. Sch. Bus., N.Y.C., 1970-74; supr. bus. research AT&T, 1974-77, dist. mgr. corp. planning, 1977-81, dist. mgr. fin. mgmt. and planning, 1981-85; prof. fin. Grad. Sch. Bus. Pace U., 1975-91; chmn. Sharp CFA Rev. & Inst. for Investment Edn., 1987-96, Sharp Seminars, 1996—. Speaker, moderator meetings, 1965—; cons. Sharp Investment Mgmt., 1967—. Contbr. numerous articles to profl. publs.; corr.: Interfaces, 1975-78; fin. editor: Planning Rev., 1975-78. Mem. N.Am. Soc. Corp. Planning (treas. 1976-77, bd. dirs. at large 1977-78), Inst. Mgmt. Sci. (chpt. v.p. acad. 1972-74, chpt. v.p. program 1974-75, chpt. v.p. membership 1975-76, chpt. pres. 1976-77), Internat. Affiliation Planning Socs. (coun. 1978-84), N.Y. Soc. Security Analysts (CFA Rev. 1985-87), Ops. Rsch. Soc. Am. (pres. corp. planning group 1976-82), AAUP (v.p. Pace U. chpt. 1988-90), Theta Xi. Republican. Office: 315 E 86th St Apt 7H New York NY 10028-4740

SHARP, KATHERINE STREET, artist, business owner; b. Chattanooga, Oct. 1, 1924; d. Thomas Grinter and Louise Hunt Street; m. Alfred Dandridge Sharp, Jr., Sept. 6, 1947 (dec. Nov. 10, 1984); children: Alfred III, Thomas, Louise Sharp Reagan. BA cum laude, Sweet Briar Coll., 1947. Pres., treas. The Uncommon Market, Nashville, 1979-85, Custommat, Nashville, 1985—. Mem.-at-large Jr. League Nashville, 1960-62; pres. St. Luke's Cmty. House, Nashville, 1970-72, Episcopal Women of Diocese of Tenn., Nashville, 1975-77; co-founder, mgr. This-n-That Thrift Shop, Nashville, 1971-72. Mem. Centennial Club. Avocations: volunteering, gardening, bridge, writing. Home and Office: 9180 Hester Beasley Rd Nashville TN 37221 Fax: 615-646-1017. E-mail: katherine.sharp@worldnet.att.net.

SHARP, LEWIS I. museum director; Dir. Denver Art Mus. Office: Denver Art Mus 100 W 14th Avenue Pkwy Denver CO 80204-2749*

SHARP, LINDA, professional basketball coach; Profl. basketball coach U. S.C., 1977—89, L.A. Sparks of WBNA, 1997; head coach Concordia U. , 2000; profl. basketball coach Phoenix Mercury, 2002—. Color commentator Fox TV. Named WCAA Coach of Yr., Sporting News Coach of Yr. ; named to Women's Hall of Fame, 2001. Office: 201 E Jefferson St Phoenix AZ 85004 Office Fax: 602-514-8303.*

SHARP, MITCHELL WILLIAM, advisor to prime minister; b. Winnipeg, Man., Can., May 11, 1911; s. Thomas and Elizabeth (Little) S.; m. Daisy Boyd, Apr. 23, 1938 (dec.); 1 son, Noel; m. Jeannette Dugal, Apr. 14, 1976 (dec.); m. Jeanne d'Arc Labrecque, Sept. 1, 2000. BA, U. Man., 1934, LL.D. (hon.), 1965; postgrad., London Sch. Econs., 1937-38; hon. Dr. Social Sci., U. Ottawa, 1970; LLD (hon.), U. Western Ont., 1977, Carleton U., 1994, McMaster U., 1995. Statistician Sanford Evans Statis. Service, 1926-36; economist James Richardson & Sons, Ltd., 1936-42; officer Canadian Dept. Fin., Ottawa, 1942-51, dir. econ. policy div., 1947-51; assoc. dep. minister Canadian Dept. Trade and Commerce, 1951-57, dep. minister, 1957-58; v.p. Brazilian Traction, Toronto, Can., 1958-62; mem. Can. Ho. of Commons, from 1963; minister trade and commerce, 1963-65; minister fin., 1965-68; sec. state external affairs, 1968-74; pres. Privy Council, house leader, 1974-76; resigned, 1978. Commr. No. Pipeline Agy., 1978-88. Decorated companion Order of Can. Fellow Royal Conservatory Music (hon.). Address: 2-140 Rideau Terr Ottawa ON Canada K1M 0Z2 Office: Langevin Block Ottawa ON K1A 0A2 Canada

SHARP, PAMELA ANN, quality assurance engineer; b. Pullman, Wash., Dec. 20, 1950; d. Robert Melvin and Vivian Lois (Steele) Olson; m. David William Sharp, June 16, 1973; children: Jaime David, Erik Scott. Student, Big Bend C.C., Moses Lake, Wash., 1969-70; BS in Zoology, Wash. State U., 1973; postgrad., Portland State U., 1976. Lab. technician The Carter Mining Co., Gillette, Wyo., 1977-79, lab. supr., 1979-80, quality control supr., 1980-81, engring. analyst, 1982-88, engr. quality control, 1988-89; owner Sharp Consulting, 1989—, Landscape Design, 1993—; leader auditor tng. ISO 9000; owner Prairie Skullpture. Obedience dog tng. instr., 1990—. Supt. Campbell County Fair, Gillette, 1985-87. Recipient Friend of Edn. award, Campbell County Sch. Dist., Wyo., 1998. Mem. AIME, ASTM (proximate analysis chmn. 1985-95, chmn. on-line analysis com., apptd. U.S.A. expert on on-line analysis to ISO), Am. Water Ski Assn. (regular judge 1974-91, ea. regional water ski trick record 1975, 3d nat. trick title 1962, state champion in tricks Wash., Idaho, Mont. 1961-73, 2d 1987 Western region women's III tricks). Republican. Presbyterian. Avocations: handball, photography, water skiing, watercolors.

SHARP, PAUL DAVID, institute administrator; b. Youngstown, Ohio, Nov. 3, 1940; s. Robert Henderson and Kathryn (Tadsen)S.; m. Carole G. Graff, Sept. 16, 1967; children: David Allen, Kathryn Sharp Snyder. BA cum laude, Kenyon Coll., Gambier, Ohio, 1962; MPA, Auburn U., 1974. Commd. 2d lt. USAF, 1962, advanced through grades to col., 1983, intelligence officer, 1962-80, comdr. Detachment 1, 7450th Intelligence Squadron Germany, 1980-83, comdr. 480th Reconnaissance Tech. Group Langley AFB, Va., 1983-85, dir. intelligence systems HQ Tactical Air Command, 1985-86, dep. chief intelligence Tactical Air Command, 1986-88; mgr. operational intelligence group Battelle Meml. Inst., Columbus, Ohio, 1988-89, mgr. fgn. tech. assessment group, 1989-91, mgr. intelligence projects/programs, 1991-92, v.p. bus. devel. fgn. sci. and tech., 1992-95, dir. fgn. sci. and tech. programs, 1995-98; dir. Air Force spl. programs Batelle Meml. Inst., 1998-99, mgr. spl. programs office, 1999-2000; mgr. Internat. Tech. Assessments Product Line, 2000—. Student career coun. Kenyon Coll., Columbus, 1992—. Trustee Brandywine Assn., Yorktown, Va., 1987, Chase Assn., Powell, Ohio, 1991. Decorated Legion of Merit. Mem. Nat. Mil. Intelligence Assn., Armed Forces Communications and Electronics Assn., Air Force Assn., Retired Officers Assn., Sigma Pi (pres. Lambda chpt. 1961-62). Republican. Episcopalian. Avocations: golf, woodworking, photography, music. Office: Battelle Meml Inst 505 King Ave Columbus OH 43201-2681

SHARP, PAUL FREDERICK, former university president, education consultant; b. Kirksville, Mo., Jan. 19, 1918; s. Frederick J. and L. Blanche (Phares) S.; m. Rosella Ann Anderson, June 19, 1939; children: William, Kathryn, Paul Trevor. AB, Phillips U., 1939; PhD, U. Minn., 1947; LLD (hon.), Tex. Christian U., 1961, Austin Coll., 1978, Drake U., 1980; LHD (hon.), Buena Vista Coll., 1967, U. Nev., Towson State U., 1980, Oklahoma City U., 1996, U. Okla., 1997; LittD (hon.), Limestone Coll., 1971; HHD, Okla. Christian U. Sci. & Arts, 1992. Instr. U. Minn., 1942, 46-47, vis. lectr., 1948; asso. prof. Am. history Iowa State U., 1947-54; prof. Am. history, chmn. Am. Instns. program U. Wis., 1954-57, vis. lectr., 1953, San Francisco State Coll., 1950, U. Oreg., 1955; Fulbright lectr. Am. Instns., univs. Melbourne, Sydney, 1952; pres. Hiram Coll., 1957-64; chancellor U. N.C., Chapel Hill, 1964-66; pres. Drake U., Des Moines, 1966-71, U. Okla., Norman, 1971-78, pres. emeritus, Regents' prof., 1978-88, pres. emeritus, Regents' prof. emeritus, 1988—; disting. prof. history U. Sci. and Arts, Okla., 1990—96. Dir. Am. Coun. on Edn. Insts. for Coll. and Univ. Presidents, 1977-79; vis. lectr. Harvard U. Bus. Sch. summer session, 1970-72. Author: Agrarian Revolt in Western Canada, 1948, Old Orchard Farm, Story of an Iowa Boyhood, 1952, Whoop-Up Country, Canadian American West, 1955; cons. author: Heritage of Midwest, 1958; editor: Documents of Freedom, 1957; contbr. articles to profl. jours. Pres. Norman Cmty. Found., 1995-97, Okla. State Coun. Aging, 1997-99. USN liaison officer His Majesty's Australian Ship, Hobart, 1943-46. With USNR, 1943-47. Recipient Iowa State U. Alumni Fund award, 1952, award of merit Am. Assn. State and Local History, 1955, Silver Spur award Western Writers Am., 1955, Fulbright award to Australia, 1952; named to Okla. Higher Edn. Hall of Fame, 1995; Minn. Hist. Soc. grantee, 1947, 48, Social Sci. Rsch. Coun. grantee, 1949, 51; Ford Faculty fellow, 1954, Guggenheim fellow, 1957. Mem. Phi Beta Kappa, Phi Kappa Phi, Phi Delta Kappa, Pi Gamma Mu, Phi Alpha Theta. Mem. Christian Ch. (Disciples Of Christ). Home: 701 Mockingbird Ln Norman OK 73071-4829 Office: U Okla 630 Parrington Oval Rm 105 Norman OK 73019-4037

SHARP, PHILLIP ALLEN, biologist, educator; b. Ky., June 6, 1944; s. Joseph Walter and Katherin (Colvin) S.; m. Ann Christine Holcombe, Aug. 29, 1964; children: Christine Alynn, Sarah Katherin, Helena Holcombe. BA, Union Coll., Barbourville, Ky., 1966, LHD (hon.), 1991; PhD, U. Ill., 1969; DSc (hon.) , U. Ky., 1994, Bowdoin Coll., 1995, U. Tel Aviv, Israel, 1996, Albright Coll., 1996; hon. degree (hon.) , U. Glasgow, 1998, U. Uppsala, 1999, Thomas Moore Coll., 1999, U. Buenos Aires, 1999, No. Ky. U., 1999, PhD (hon.) , 2001. NIH postdoctoral fellow Calif. Inst. Tech., 1969—71; sr. research investigator Cold Spring Harbor (N.Y.) Lab., 1972—74; assoc. prof. MIT, Cambridge, 1974—79, prof. biology, 1979—99, Inst. prof., 1999—, head dept. biology, 1991—99, dir. Ctr. Cancer Rsch., 1985—91. Dir. The McGovern Inst. Brain Rsch., 2000—; co-founder, mem. sci. bd., dir. BIOGEN, 1978—, chmn. sci. bd., 1987—; mem. Pres.'s Adv. Coun. on Sci. and Tech., 1991—97; mem. presdl. appt. Nat.Cancer Adv. Bd. NIH, 1996; chmn. GM Cancer Rshc. Found. Awards Assembly, 1994—; mem. sci. bd. Ludwig Inst., 1998—; mem. bd. scientific govs. Scripps Rsch. Inst., 1999—; bd. trustees MGH, 2002—; co-founder, chair of sci. bd. and mem. of bd. dirs. Alnylan Pharm. Inc., 2002—. Mem. editl. bd.: Cell, 1974—95, Mem. editl. bd.: Jour. Virology, 1974—86, Mem. editl. bd.: Molecular and Cellular Biology, 1974—85, Mem. editl. bd.: RNA, 1995—. Trustee Alfred P. Sloan Found., 1995—. Co-recipient Nobel Prize in Physiology of Medicine, 1993; named Class of '41 chair, 1986—87, John D. MacArthur chair, 1987—92, Salvador E. Luria chair, 1992—99; recipient awards, Am. Cancer Soc., 1974—79, Eli Lilly, 1980, Nat. Acad.Sci./U.S. Steel Found., 1980, Howard Ricketts award, U.Chgo., 1985, Alfred P. Sloan Jr. prize, Gen. Motors Rsch. Found., 1986, award, Gairdner Found. Internat., 1986, N.Y. Acad.Scis., 1986, Louisa Horwitz prize, 1988, Albert Lasker Basic Med. Rsch. award, 1988, Dickson prize, U. Pitts., 1990. Fellow: AAAS, Royal Soc. Edinburgh (hon.); mem.: Inst. of Medicine of NAS (elected mem.), Am. Philos. Soc. (elected mem.), Am. Soc. Biochemistry and Molecular Biology (elected mem. coun.), European Molecular Biology Orgn. (assoc.), Am. Acad. Arts and Scis., Am. Soc. Microbiology, NAS (councilor 1986). Home: 36 Fairmont Ave Newton MA 02458-2506 Office: MIT Ctr for Cancer Rsch 40 Ames St Rm E17529B Cambridge MA 02139-4307 E-mail: sharppa@mit.edu.

SHARP, REX ARTHUR, lawyer; b. Liberal, Kans., Jan. 1, 1960; s. Gene Hugh and Jo Ann (King) S.; m. Lori Renee Lewis, May 23, 1987; children: Lori Alexandra, Lewis Arthur, William Hugh. Student, U. Okla., 1978-79; AB in Econs. with honors & distinction, Stanford U., 1982; JD cum laude, U. Mich., 1985. Bar: Tex. 1985, Kans. 1985, Okla. 1986, Colo. 1988, Mo. 2000, U.S. Dist. Ct. (so. and no. dists.) Tex., U.S. Dist Ct. (we. and no. dists.) Okla., U.S. Dist. Ct. Kans., U.S. Dist Ct. (we. dist.) Mo. , U.S. Ct. Appeals (10th cir.), U.S. Supreme Ct.; civil trial cert. N.B.T.A. Litigation assoc. Fulbright & Jaworski, Houston, 1985-87; assoc. Neubauer, Sharp, McQueen, Dreiling & Morain, Liberal, 1987-89; ptnr. McKinley, Sharp, McQueen, Dreiling, Morain & Tate, P.A., 1989-97, Husch & Eppenberger, Kansas City, Mo., 1997-2000, Sharp Law LLC, Prairie Village, Kans., 2000; stockholder Gunderson, Sharp, & Rhein, P.C., 2000—. Asst. city atty. City of Liberal, 1988-93, city atty., 1993-97. Avocation: golf. Office: Gunderson Sharp Trout & Rhein PC 4121 W 83d St Ste 256 Prairie Village KS 66208 Fax: 913-901-0419. E-mail: rexsharp@birch.net.

SHARP, RICHARD L. retail company executive; b. Washington, Apr. 12, 1947; Student, U. Va., 1965-66, Coll. of William and Mary, 1968-70. Programmer Group Health Inc., Washington, 1970-75; founder, pres. Applied Systems Corp., 1975-81; with Circuit City Stores, Inc., Richmond, Va., 1982—, exec. v.p., 1982-84, pres., 1984-86, pres., CEO, 1986-94, chmn., pres., CEO, 1994-97, chmn., CEO, 1997-2000, chmn., 1997—. Bd. dirs. Flextronics Internat. With USAF, 1967-70.

SHARP, RONALD ALAN, English literature educator, author; b. Cleve., Oct. 19, 1945; s. Jack Trier and Florence (Tenenbaum) S.; m. Inese Brutans, June 22, 1968; children: Andrew Janis, James Michael. BA, Kalamazoo Coll., 1967; MA, U. Mich., 1968; PhD, U. Va., 1974. Instr. in English Western Mich. U., Kalamazoo, 1968-70; from instr. to acting pres. Kenyon Coll., Gambier, Ohio, 1970—2002, acting pres., 2002—. Dir. Keats Bicentennial Conf., Harvard U., 1995. Author: Keats, Skepticism and the Religion of Beauty, 1979, Friendship and Literature: Spirit and Form. 1986; translator: Teatro Breve (Garcia Lorca), 1979, editor (with Eudora Welty) The Norton Book of Friendship, 1991, (with Nathan Scott) Reading George Steiner, 1994, (with Robert Ryan) The Persistence of Poetry: Bicentennial Essays on John Keats, 1998, Selected forms of Michael Harper, 2002; co-editor Kenyon Rev., 78-82; contbr. articles to profl. jours. Recipient award for editl. excellence Ohioana Assn., 1980; fellow Nat. Humanities Ctr., 1981, 86, NEH, 1981, 84-87, 93, 94, 96, 98, Ford Found., 1971, Mellon Found., 1980, Danforth Found., 1971, English Speaking Union, 1973, Am. Coun. Learned Socs., 1986. Mem. MLA, NEH (chmn's. adv. group humanities edn. 1987), Wordsworth-Coleridge Assn., Keats-Shelley Assn. Jewish. Home: 11671 Kenyon Rd Mount Vernon OH 43050-8633 Office: Kenyon Coll Office of President Gambier OH 43022

SHARP, RONALD ARVELL, sociology educator; b. Vivian, La., Sept. 29, 1941; s. Walter Arvell and Virginia (Refield-King) S.; m. Imelda Idalia Pena, Sept. 16, 1967; children: Ronald Arvell II, Donald Allen. BS in Edn., Cameron U., 1976; BA in Sociology, SUNY, Albany, 1977; MEd in Counseling Psychology, U. Okla., 1978; PhD in Sociology, Clayton U., 1985. Ret. U.S. Army, 1960-82; radiologic technologist VA Hosp., Temple, Tex., 1983-84; vets. counselor Vets. Outreach Program, San Antonio, 1982-83; dir. personnel & mktg. Heran Pharms., 1988-91; prof. sociology Ctrl. Tech. Coll., Killeen, 1991-95; instr. sociology Tex. State Tech. Coll., Waco, 1995-96, Academia Assocs., 1996—. Part-time instr. Ctrl. Tex. Coll., 1980-82, City Coll. Chgo., 1981, Big Bend C.C., Mannheim, Germany, 1981-82; instr. Acad. Health Scis., 1977-79. Contbr. articles to profl. jours. Coach Youth Soccer Orgns., San Antonio and Mannheim, 1976-82. Nat. Coll. Radiology Technologists fellow, 1968. Mem. AAUP, DAV (past comdr.), VFW (past comdr.), Am. Sociol. Assn., Soc. Applied Sociology, Nat. Assn. Medics and Corpsmen (PNC), Am. Mil. Ret. Assn. (PNVP), Combat Medics Assn. (nat. dir.), La. Archeol. Soc., Choctaw Nation of Okla., Okla. Anthrop. Soc., La. Archeol. Conservancy, Caddoan Hist. Soc., Okla. Anthropol. Survey, Order of Alhambra, KC, Masons, Soc. for the Study of Social Problems, Four Winds Intertribal Soc., Hokshichankiya Soc., Psi Beta (chpt. sponsor), Alpha Kappa Delta, Psi Chi, Sigma Eta Sigma (nat. dir.). Roman Catholic. Avocations: soccer, golf, paleo-historic anthropology. Home: 9310 Oak Hills Dr Temple TX 76502-5272 Office: Academia Assocs Waco TX 76705 Office Fax: 254-870-3444.

SHARP, STEFANIE TERESA, lawyer; b. Reno, June 16, 1966; d. F. De Armond and Joyce Sharp. BA, U. Calif., San Diego, 1988; JD cum laude, U. San Francisco, 1992. Bar: Calif. 1993. Assoc. St. Claire, McFetridge, Griffen & Legernes, San Francisco, 1993-96, Wright, Robinson, Osthimer & Tatum, San Francisco, 1996-00, ptnr., 2001—. Mem. ABA, Calif. State Bar Assn., San Francisco Bar Assn. Republican. Avocations: running, mountain bike riding, scuba diving, horseback, riding. Office: Wright Robinson Osthimer & Tatum 44 Montgomery St Fl 18 San Francisco CA 94104-4602 E-mail: ssharp@wrightrobinson.com.

SHARP, SUSAN F. sociologist, educator; b. Lubock, Tex., Jan. 28, 1951; d. Richard Glover Sharp, Alice Bostick Haas; children: Jared Miles, Rachel Shada, Amy Bowles. B ., Tex. Tech U., 1980. M ., 1982; PhD, U. Tex., 1996. Assoc. prof. U. Okla., Norman, 1996—. Rschr. and site dir. Capital Jury Project. Editor: The Incarcerated Woman, 2002, (newsletter) DivisioNews, 2000—01; contbr. articles. Chair Okla. Coalition to Abolish the Death Penalty, Inc., Oklahoma City, 2001—02. Mem.: Soc. Applied Sociology, Midsouth Sociol. Assn., Acad. Criminal Justice Sci., Am. Soc. Criminology (exec. counselor divsn. women & crime 2001). Office: Univ Okla Dept Sociology 780 Van Vleet Oval KH 331 Norman OK 73019 Office Fax: 405-325-7825. Personal E-mail: ssharp2@cox.net. Business E-Mail: ssharp@ou.edu.

SHARP, THOMAS B. state legislator; b. Wilmington, Del., Mar. 8, 1940; m. Judy Sharp; children: Sharon, Thomas, Robert. Student, Tech. Sch. Mem. dist. 9 Del. Senate, Dover, 1974—, majority leader, 1978—96, chmn. com. to combat drug abuse, ins. and elec. com., chmn. jud. com., mem. adult and juvenile corrections, mem. ethics, exec. hwys. and transp. com., mem. labor and indsl. rels. com., mem. legis. coun. and pub. safety coms., pres., Pro Tempore, 1997—. Mem. New Castle County Bd. Bldg. Stds., New Castle County Vo-Tech Sch. Dist.; v.p., pres. Pinecrest Civic Assn.; past pres. Heritage Elem. PTA. Office: Del Senate PO Box 1401 Dover DE 19903-1401 also: Carvel Office Bldg 820 N. French St. Wilmington DE 19801*

SHARP, WILLIAM ROBERT, JR. shipbuilding company executive; b. Ft. Lewis, Wash., Aug. 17, 1942; s. William Robert and Martha Reese (Allen) S.; m. Rachel Ann Roark, Apr. 30, 1966; children: Charles Robert, Grant Harrison. BS Nuclear Engring., N.C. State U., 1964; M of Engring. Adminstrn., George Washington U., 1983; cert. in nuclear emergency planning, Harvard U., 2000. Nuclear engr. Newport News (Va.) Shipbuilding, 1965-66, mech. test engr., 1966-68, shift test engr., 1968-73, engring. supr., 1973-83, engring. mgr., 1983-85, mgr. submarine overhaul project, 1985-88, mgr. supplier quality, 1988-90, mgr. nuclear quality, 1990-99, dir. radiol. control, 1999—. Author weekly newsletter Head of Naval Reactors in Pentagon, 1983-90. Exec. bd. dirs. Colonial Va. Coun. Boy Scouts Am., 1995—; mem. adv. bd. Republican Nat. Com., 1993-97. Recipient Leadership award Tenneco Inc., 1995, Presdl. award for productivity improvement Cost Improvement Program, 1985. Mem. Soc. Naval Archs. and Marine Engrs., Am. Soc. Nondestructive Testing (dir. local sect. 1991-95), Engrs. Club Va. Peninsula (dir. 1975-80, past pres.), Propeller Club Port of Newport News, Nautilus Soc. (assoc.), Warwick Rotary (past bd. mem., treas. 1975-78), Tau Beta Pi, Phi Kappa Phi, Theta Tau (Rho chpt.). Presbyterian. Achievements include development of Improvements in the reactor plant overhausl process, of innovative valve repair technique, of new Navy-wide quality control procedure; built and made operational a 25 million dollar radiological support facility; patents in field. Home: 41 Garland Dr Newport News VA 23606-2260 E-mail: wsharp1@home.com.

SHARP, WILLIAM WHEELER, geologist; b. Shreveport, La., Oct. 9, 1923; s. William Wheeler and Jennie V. (Benson) S.; m. Rubylin Slaughter, 1958; children: Staci Lynn, Kimberly Cecile; 1 child from previous marriage, John E. BS in Geology, U. Tex., Austin, 1950, MA, 1951. Lic. pvt. pilot. Geol. Socony-Vacuum, Caracas, Venezuela, 1951-53, surface geol. chief Creole Venezuela, 1953-57; dist. devel. geologist, supr. exploration, devel. unitization of 132 multi-pay oil and gas fields, expert geol. witness, coll. recruiter, rsch. assoc. ARCO, 1957-85. Discovered oil and gas at Bayou Boullion, Bayou Sale, Jeanerette, La., Chandeleon Sound and Beaunegaurd Parish, La.; petroleum exploration in Alaska, Aus., Can., U.S. and S.A. Contbr. articles to profl. jours.; included in From Acorn to Oakbourne—History of Oakbourne Country Club, 1998.; contbr. artifacts/photos to Nimitz Mus., Fredricksburg, Tex., Tex. Meml. Mus., Benson Latin Am. Libr., U. Tex., Austin. Past dir. and chmn. U.S. Tennis Assn. Tournaments; pres. Lafayette Tennis Adv. Com., 1972; pres. Oakbourne Tennis Assn.; past dir. Jr. Achievement and United Fund Programs; contbr. to various mus. With USAF, 1943-46, PTO. Winner and finalist more than 75 amateur tennis tournaments including Conferate Oil Invitational, Gulf Coast Oilmen's Tournament, So. Oilmen's Tournament, Tex.-Ark.-La. Oilmen's Tournament; named Hon. Citizen of New Orleans, 1971, recipient Key to New Orleans. Mem. Dallas Geol. Soc., Lafayette Geol. Soc. (bd. dirs. 1973-74), Am. Assn. Petroleum Geologists (co-author Best of SEG conv. 1982), Tex. Astron. Soc., VFW, Am. Legion, Appaloosa Horse Club, Oakbourne Country Club Tennis Assn. (pres. 1976, organizer nat. boys tennis tournament 1976). Republican. Methodist. Achievements include drilled more than 30 successful wells at Bayou Boullion Field. Avocations: sports, music, history. Home: 7312 Mimosa Ln Dallas TX 75230-5446

SHARPE, CALVIN WILLIAM, law educator, arbitrator; b. Greensboro, N.C., Feb. 22, 1945; s. Ralph David and Mildred (Johnson) S.; m. Maya Annette Hall, Jan. 25, 1970 (div. Oct. 1975); 1 child, Kabral; m. Janice M. Jones, Apr. 13, 1978; children: Melanie, Stevie. BA, Clark Coll., 1967; postgrad., Oberlin Coll., 1968; MA, Chgo. Theol. Sem., 1996; JD, Northwestern U., Chgo., 1974. Bar: Ill. 1974. Tchr. elem. sch. N.Y. Sch. System, Bklyn., 1968-69; dir. homework study ctr. Ocean Hill Brownsville, 1969; investigator Ill. Gov.'s Task Force on Cook County Property Tax, Chgo., 1972-73; law clk. to judge Hubert L. Will U.S. Dist. Ct. (no. dist.) Ill., 1974-76; assoc. Cotton, Watt, Jones, King & Bowlus, 1976-77; trial atty. NLRB, Winston-Salem, N.C., 1977-81; asst. prof. U. Va., 1981-84; assoc. prof. Case Western Res. U., Cleve., 1984-88, prof., 1988—, John Deaver Drinko-Baker & Hostetler prof. law, 1999—, acad. dean, 1991-92. Exec. bd. Pub. Sector Labor Rels. Assn., Ohio, 1986—; chmn. evidence sect. Assn. Am. Law Schs., 1987-88; mem. Am. Labor Law Project to Soviet Union and Western Europe-People to People, 1988; mem. Youth Svcs. Adv. Bd. of the Cuyahoga County Juvenile Ct., 1989-91; cons. So. African Commn. on Concilation, Mediation and Arbitration, 1998—. Co-author: Understanding Labor Law, 1999. Bd. trustees Cleve. Hearing and Speech Ctr., 1985-88; bd. dirs. Garrett-Evang. Theol. Sem., 1999—, Cleve. Pub. Radio, 1993-94. Mem. Soc. Profls. in Dispute Resolution, Internat. Soc. Labor Law and Social Security, Indsl. Rels. Rsch. Assn. (convener and first chair labor and employment law sect. 1995-97), Labor Law Group Trust, Nat. Acad. Arbitrators (bd. govs. 2001—), Soc. of Benchers. Office: Case Western Res U Law Sch 11075 East Blvd Cleveland OH 44106-5409

SHARPE, DONALD CHARLES, service manager; b. Durham, N.C., July 28, 1956; s. Lawrence Albright and Virginia Ann (Pacofsky) S. Electrician, ICS Corr. Schs., Scranton, Pa., 1983. Cert. chlorofluorocarbons, motor vehicle air conditioning, pool and spa operator, notary pub., N.C., 1997; lic. real estate agt., N.C. Electrician USN, 1974-88; maintenance engr. Holiday Inn Exec. Ctr., Virginia Beach, Va., 1988-94; ind. contractor, 1994-95; maintenance asst. Sterling Forest Apts. Grubb Mgmt., Raleigh, N.C., 1995, svc. supr. Sterling Brook Apts. Carrboro, 1995-98; svc. mgr. Four Seasons Apartments, Raleigh, 1998-2000, Summit Properties, Durham, 2000—. Republican. Christian. Avocations: rare collectibles and books, archaeology, biblical research, history.

SHARPE, HENRY DEXTER, JR. retired manufacturing company executive; b. Providence, May 5, 1923; s. Henry Dexter and Mary Elizabeth (Evans) S.; m. Peggy Plumer Boyd, Aug. 1, 1953; children: Henry Dexter, Douglas, Sarah. Grad., Brown U., Providence, 1945. With Brown & Sharpe Mfg. Co., Providence, 1946-96, v.p., 1950-51, pres., 1951-76, chmn., chief exec. officer, 1976-80, chmn., 1980-96, ret., 1996. Vice chancellor Brown U., 1986-87. Bd. dirs. R.I. Pub. Expenditure Coun.; trustee, fellow Brown U., 1954-99; trustee Coll. of the Atlantic, 1992—. Lt. (j.g.) USNR, 1943-46. Mem. Nat. Machine Tool Builders Assn. (pres. 1969-70), Machinery and Allied Products Inst. (ret. mem. exec. com.) Office: Pojac Point Rd North Kingstown RI 02852-1031

SHARPE, JAMES SHELBY, lawyer; b. Ft. Worth, Sept. 11, 1940; s. James Henry and Wanzel (Vanderbilt) S.; m. Martha Moudy Holland, June 9, 1962; children: Marthanne Freeman, Caren Sharp, Stephen. BA, U. Tex., 1962, JD, 1965. Bar: Tex. 1965, U.S. Dist. Ct. (no. dist.) Tex. 1966, U.S. Dist. Ct. (ea. dist.) Tex. 1993, U.S. Ct. Appeals (5th and 6th cirs.) 1982, U.S. Ct. Appeals (fed. cir.) 1983, U.S. Ct. Appeals (10th cir.) 1992, U.S. Supreme Ct. 1972. Briefing atty. for chief justice Supreme Ct. of Tex., Austin, 1965-66; ptnr. Brown, Herman, Scott, Dean & Miles, Ft. Worth, 1966-84, Gandy Michener Swindle Whitaker & Pratt, Ft. Worth, 1984-87; shareholder Sharpe & Tillman, 1988—. Adj. prof. polit. sci. Tex. Christian U., Ft. Worth, 1969-79, Dallas Bapt. U., 1987, 1992-94; gen. counsel U.S.A. Radio Network, Internat. Christian Media, Denton Pub. Co. Pres. Ft. Worth-Tarrant County Jr. Bar, 1969-70, bd. dirs., 1968, sec., 1968, v.p., 1968-69; head marshal USA-USSR Track and Field Championships, Ft. Worth, USA-USSR Jr. Track and Field Championships, Austin, Tex., Relays, Austin, 1963—, NCAA Nat. Track and Field Championships, 1976, 80, 85, 92, 95, S.W. Conf. Indoor Track and Field Championships, 1987-96, Olympic Festival, San Antonio, 1993, Colorado Springs, 1995; 12 time head marshal S.W. Conf. Track and Field Championships, Big 12 Outdoor Conf. Track and Field Championship, 1997, 98, 99, 2001, head marshall 2000 Olympic Trials in Track and Field. USA/Mobil Track Championship, 1994, 95; USA Nat. Jr. Track Championship, 1994, 95, 98, 99, USA Track and Field Track Championship, 1997, 2001, 02, Master's Nat. Track and Field Nat. Championship, 1996, 98, 2002. Mem. ABA, State Bar of Tex. (dist. 7-A grievance com. 1983-85, com. adminstrn. of justice 1985-92, com. on ct. rules 1992—, chmn. 1992-93, 93-94). Baptist. Office: Sharpe & Tillman 6100 Western Pl Ste 901 Fort Worth TX 76107-4679 E-mail: utlawman@aol.com.

SHARPE, KATHRYN MOYE, psychologist; b. Barnesville, Ga., Nov. 27, 1922; d. Herbert Johnston and Henri Lucile (Winter) Moye; m. William Herschel Sharpe, Mar. 2, 1946; children: William Herschel Jr., Mark Stephens. AB, Piedmont Coll., Demorest, Ga., 1942; MA, U. N.C., 1947; PhD, U. S.C., 1975. Tchr., guidance counselor Charleston (S.C.) Pub. Schs., 1947-66; prof. sociology, chmn. dept. Bapt. Coll. at Charleston, 1966-88, prof. emeritus, 1988—; pvt. practice psychology, Charleston, 1975—. Named One of Twelve Outstanding Women in Greater Charleston by The Ctr. for Women; Kathryn Moye Sharpe scholarship given in her honor Bapt. Coll. at Charleston, 1988. Fellow Am. Assn. for Marriage and Family Therapy (approved supr., pres. S.C. div. 1975-77, disting. svc. award S.C. chpt. 1999). Congregationalist. Home and Office: 6 Cavalier Ave Charleston SC 29407-7702 E-mail: kmsharpe@comcast.com.

SHARPE, KATHRYN PECK, artist; b. Chgo., Nov. 21, 1942; d. Charles John and Kathryn (Assman) Peck; m. Richard Lammerding, Sept. 10, 1966 (div. Jan. 1976); children: Erik Wesley, Kiersten Lea; m. William Forsyth Sharpe, Apr. 5, 1986. Student, Colo. Woman's Coll., 1962; degree in design, N.Y. Sch. Interior Design, 1964. Interior designer Morton Textile, Chgo., 1964, Richardson's, Menlo Park, Calif., 1964-65; office mgr. Cutler-Hammer, 1977-79; faculty sec./adminstr. Stanford (Calif.) U., 1979-86; v.p., adminstr. William F. Sharpe Assocs., Los Altos, Calif., 1986-93; profl. fine artist, 1993—. Dir. Filoli-Arts Program, Woodside, Calif., 1998—, Norton Studio, 1996-98; bd. dirs. Open Studios of Santa Clara County. Mem. Oil Painters of Am., Santa Clara Valley Watercolor Soc., Calif. Watercolor Soc., Pacific Art League (cmty. site dir. 1996-98), Calif. Art Club. Democrat. Home and Office: 25 Doud Dr Los Altos CA 94022-2323 E-mail: kathy@kathysharpe.com.

SHARPE, KEITH YOUNT, retired lawyer; b. Hiddenite, N.C., July 11, 1930; s. Ruel Yount and Eileen Lois (Lackey) S.; m. Margaret Joyce Land, Aug. 27, 1955 (div.); children: Jonathan, Matthew, Leonora, Felicia. AB, Duke U., 1952; JD, Wake Forest U., 1957, MBA, 1982. Bar: N.C. 1957. Practiced law, Winston-Salem, N.C., 1957-62, 82-94; asst. solicitor Mcpl. Ct. of Winston-Salem, 1958-60; with Pilot Freight Carriers Inc., Winston-Salem, 1962-82, sr. v.p., 1967-76, v.p., 1976-82; also dir.; v.p., dir. Comml. Automotive Co., 1967-76, Terminal Warehouse Corp., 1967-82. Bd. govs. So. Motor Carriers Rate Conf., 1977-81 Served with inf. U.S. Army, 1952-54. Mem. Assn. Transp. Practitioners, Phi Alpha Delta, Theta Chi. Democrat. Episcopalian. Home: PO Box 19633 Asheville NC 28815-1633

SHARPE, ROBERT FRANCIS, equipment manufacturing company executive; b. Buffalo, Mar. 29, 1921; s. Bertram Francis and Agnes (Coppinger) S.; m. Audrey Rembe, July 10, 1943; 1 son, Robert Francis. BS in Chem. Engring, Rensselaer Poly. Inst., 1942. With Duriron Co., 1946—, mgr. pump sales, 1955-58, dir. research, devel., 1958-63, v.p. plastics ops., 1963-65, exec. v.p., 1967-68, pres., chief operating officer, 1968-69, pres., 1969-76, chief exec. officer, 1969-79, chmn. bd., 1978-83. Served with USAAF, 1943-46. Mem. Am. Inst. Chem. Engrs., Hydraulic Inst. Home: 15520 Whitney Ln Naples FL 34110-7611

SHARPE, ROBERT KENT, writer, director, producer, photographer; b. Chgo., Nov. 17, 1930; s. Byron C. and Helen Lee S.; m. Mary Kahn, 1955 (div. 1971); children: Steven W., Sharon E., Jonathan K., Julia A.; m. T. Tina Ditta, Apr. 26, 1980. BA in English, Brown U., 1953. Writer, dir. Ford Found., N.Y.C., 1956-57, CBS, N.Y.C., 1957-58, NBC Spl. Projects Dept., N.Y.C., 1959-61, free-lance dir., 1962-63; pres. Robert K. Sharpe Prodns., Inc., Ardsley, N.Y., 1965—, Hastings on Hudson, 1965—, RKS Devel. Corp., Ardsley, 1963-75. Producer, writer, dir.: (documentary) Before the Mountain Was Moved, 1969 (awards 1969-70); writer, dir.: (shorts) Night in a Pet Ship, 1959 (awards 1959-60), producer, writer, dir. (shorts) Pancho, 1966-67 (awards 1966-67), Joe, 1965 (awards 1965), Face of Excellence, 1962, The Forgotten, 1958 (awards 1958-59); screenwriter: (films) WFAT, 1982, The Long Night, 1962, Barbero, 1983, A Dead Issue, 1963, Computer, 1965, A Letter Home, 1965, Squaw Gap Speaking, 1976; dir.: (television) The Twentieth Century Series, 1962-63, Keep It Cool, Rhodes Scholar, The Jazz of Dave Brubeck, The Songs of Harold Arlen, Fire Brand on Ice - Stan Mikita, Here is New York, Buildings for Business and Government, Call it Courage, Equestrianism, others; staff writer, dir.: (television) Wisdom Series, 1959-61, The Ordeal of Woodrow Wilson as Told by President Herbert Hoover, The Seven Lively Arts Series, Omibus Series, 1956-57; producer, dir. (films) The Great Debate, 1963; writer, dir. (films) Light as You Like It, 1958; photographic series Assisi, 1953, Spanish Patterns, 1990, Interplay, 1998, The Unseen, 1999. Mem. Am. Soc. Media Photographers, Dirs. Guild Am., Photographic Adminstrs., Inc., Phi Beta Kappa. Democrat. Jewish. Avocations: amateur radio, HI-FI & electronics, wood working. Home and Office: 765 N Broadway Apt 15E Hastings On Hudson NY 10706 E-mail: rsharpe@earthlink.net.

SHARPE, ROLAND LEONARD, engineering company executive, earthquake and structural engineering consultant; b. Shakopee, Minn., Dec. 18, 1923; s. Alfred Leonard and Ruth Helen (Carter) S.; m. Jane Esther Steele, Dec. 28, 1946; children: Douglas Rolfe, Deborah Lynn, sheryl Anne. BSCE, U. Mich., 1947, MSE, 1949. Registered civil engr. and structural engr., Calif. Designer Cummins & Barnard, Inc., Ann Arbor, Mich., 1947-48; instr. engring. U. Mich., 1948-50; exec. v.p. John A. Blume & Assocs., engrs., San Francisco, 1950-73; chmn., founder Engring. Decision Analysis Co., Inc., Cupertino, Calif., 1974-87; cons. earthquake engr., 1987—. Mng. dir. EDAC, GmbH, Frankfurt, Germany, 1974-82; dir. EDAC; pres. Calif. Devel. & Engring. Co., Inc., Las Vegas, Nev., 1973-81; mem. nat. earthquake hazard reduction program adv. com. overviewing Fed. Emergency Mgmt. Agy., U.S. Geol. Survey, NSF and Nat. Inst. Stds. and Tech., 1990-93. Author: (with J. Blume, E.G. Kost) Earthquake Engineering for Nuclear Facilities, 1971; author, co-author over 200 engring. papers and reports; author of 3 chpts.: DOE Seismic Safety Manual, 1996. Mem. Planning Commn., Palo Alto, 1955-60; mng. dir. Applied Tech. Coun., Palo Alto, 1973-83; dir. Earthquake Engring. Rsch. Inst., 1972-75, now mem.; project dir., editor Tentative Provision for Devel. of Seismic Regulations for Buildings, 1978; tech. mgr., contbr., editor Data Processing Facilities: Guidelines for Earthquake Hazard Mitigation, 1987. Served with USMC, 1942-46. Recipient citation for contbn. to constrn. industry Engring. news Record, 1978-79, 86-87; chmn. U.S. Joint Com. on Earthquake Engring., 1982-88. Fellow ASCE (hon. mem. 1994, chmn. dynamic effects com. 1978-80, exec. com. structural div. 1980-84, 89-93, chmn. 1983, mgmt. group B 1989-93, Earnest E. Howard award 1994); mem. Japan Structural Cons. Assn. (hon. mem. 1992), Structural Engrs. Assn. Calif. (dir. 1971-73, chmn. seismology com. 1972-74), Structural Engrs. No. Calif. (dir. 1969-71, life mem.), Am. Concrete Inst. (life), Structural Engrs. World Congress (pres. 1995—, chair 1998). Home: 10320 Rolly Rd Los Altos CA 94024-6568 Office: Sharpe Struct Engrs 10320 Rolly Rd Ste 1 Los Altos CA 94024-6568 E-mail: rsharpe3@mindspring.com. *Personal philosophy: One's conduct should be beyond reproach both morally and ethically and I should serve each of my clients to the best of my ability.*

SHARPE, SHARON SUE, library media services administrator; b. San Antonio, May 8, 1950; d. Leonard William and Aline Isabel (Williamson) Boehme; m. Leland George Sharpe, June 1, 1978. BS in Curriculum/Instrn., Tex. A&M U., 1972, MEd in Ednl. Psychology, 1976; postgrad., Kans. State U., 1986-92. Tchr. Title I Snook (Tex.) Ind. Sch. Dist., 1975-76; migrant program tchr. Regional Svc. Ctr. VI, Huntsville, Tex., 1976-77; ednl. diagnostician Burleson/Milam Coop., Rockdale, 1977-78; tchr. 5th grade Geary County Unified Schs., Junction City, Kans., 1973-75, 78-80, bldg. libr. media specialist, 1980-86, coord. libr. media svcs., 1986—. Chmn. adv. bd. Geary County Cmty. Hosp., Junction City, 1993—; state chair Kans. William Allen White Children's Book award. Mem. ALA, ASCD, Kans. Sch. Librs. Assn., Kans. Assn. Supervision and Curriculum, Assn. Ednl. Comms. and Tech., Kans. Assn. Ednl. Commns. and Tech., Phi Delta Kappa, Delta Kappa Gamma. Methodist. Avocations: reading, genealogy, collecting. Office: Geary County Unified Schs 123 N Eisenhower Dr Junction City KS 66441-2054

SHARPE, TERRY LYNN, dermatologist; b. Chgo., Jan. 5, 1954; d. William and Mary S.; 1 child, Malia. BA, Stanford U., 1974; MD, U. Calif., San Francisco, 1979. Diplomate Am. Bd. Dermatology. Intern Boston City Hosp., 1979-80; resident Emory U., Atlanta, 1980-85, asst. prof. dermatology, 1985—. Clin. prof. dermatology Morehouse Sch. Medicine, Atlanta, 1987—. Mem. Nat. Med. Assn., Am. Acad. Dermatology, Am. Acad. Dermatol. Surgery, Ga. Derm. Soc., Atlanta Derm. Soc. Roman Catholic. Office: 1215 Eagles Landing Pkwy Ste 210 Stockbridge GA 30281-7280

SHARPE, WILLIAM FORSYTH, economics educator; b. Cambridge, Mass., June 16, 1934; s. Russell Thornley Sharpe and Evelyn Forsyth (Jillson) Maloy; m. Roberta Ruth Branton, July 2, 1954 (div. Feb. 1986); children: Deborah Ann, Jonathan Forsyth; m. Kathryn Dorothy Peck, Apr. 5, 1986. AB, UCLA, 1955, MA, 1956, PhD, 1961; DHL (hon.) , DePaul U., 1997. Economist Rand Corp., 1957—61; asst. prof. econs. U. Wash., 1961—63, assoc. prof., 1963—67, prof., 1967—68, U. Calif., Irvine, 1968—70; Timken prof. fin. Stanford U., 1970—89, Timken prof. emeritus, 1989—92; prin. William F. Sharpe Assocs., 1986—92; prof.fin. Stanford U., 1993—95, STANCO 25 prof. fin., 1995—99, emeritus, 1999—; chmn. Financial Engines, Inc., 1996—. Author: The Economics of Computers, 1969, Portfolio Theory and Capital Markets, 1970; co-author: Fundamentals of Investments, 1989, Fundamentals of Investments, 2d edit., 1993, Fundamentals of Investments, 3d edit., 2000, Investments, 6th edit., 1999. With U.S. Army, 1956—57. Recipient Graham and Dodd award, Fin. Analysts' Fedn., 1972, 1973, 1986—88, Nicholas Molodovsky award, 1989, Nobel prize in econ. scis., 1990, UCLA medal, 1998. Mem.: Am. Econ. Assn., Ea. Fin. Assn. (Disting. Scholar award 1991), Western Fin. Assn. (Enduring Contbn. award 1989), Am. Fin. Assn. (v.p. 1979, pres. 1980), Phi Beta Kappa.

SHARPE-ARRANT, KATHLEEN DIANE, accountant, small business owner; b. Suffern, N.Y., Sept. 29, 1955; d. Robert C. and Shirley A. (Oakley) Conklin (dec.); m. Leland J. Sharpe Jr., Sept. 26, 1986 (div. Apr. 1993); children: Angela D. Causey, Leland J. III; m. Laurence P. Arrant, Sept. 23, 2000. Asst. to project dir. S.C. Gov.'s Office, Columbia, 1982-83; asst. to exec. dir. S.C. Sentencing Guidelines Com., 1983-86; probation/parole officer S.C. Probation, Parole and Pardon Svcs., 1986-88; staff acct. Levitan & Yegidis, CPA's, Middletown, N.Y., 1988-91; mng. dir. Periwinkle Nat. Theatre, Monticello, 1991-94; owner, operator AAA Books & Tax, Bloomingburg, 1990—, Country Steppin' Prodns., Inc., Bloomingburg, 1993—. Owner, operator New To You Consignment Boutique, Montgomery, N.Y., 1999—. Founding dir. Gowns to Girls Program, 2000. With Signal Corps U.S. Army, 1975—77, USACC, Ft. Jackson, S.C. Mem. Nat. Tchrs. Assn., Nat. Soc. Accts. Republican. Lutheran. Avocations: singing, country dance instruction and choreography. Home: 7 Ivy Ln Bloomingburg NY 12721-4506 Office: 110 Clinton St Montgomery NY 12549 E-mail: Kathy_Sharpe@compuserve.com.

SHARPEE, RHODA ANDERSON, social worker; b. Cleve., May 11, 1938; d. Elmer F. and Ruth M. (Swanson) Anderson; m. Dale F. Sharpee, Sept. 5, 1964; children: Marc K., Sara L. BA, U. Dubuque, 1963; MSW, George Williams Coll., 1977; student, Sch. Social WorkDist. 79. Lic. clin. social worker, Ill. Sch. social worker Sch. Dist. 15, Palatine, Ill.; police social worker Hanover Twp. Youth Commn., Bartlett; case worker Fla. State Welfare, Miami; social worker Mendota State Hosp., Madison, Wis. Mem. NASW, Am. Humanistic Pscyh., Ill. Sch. Social Workers Assn., Inst. of Noetic Scis. Home: 448 N Stark Dr Palatine IL 60074-3825 E-mail: rhodale@newnorth.net.

SHARPELLETTI, DARRELL JOSEPH, lawyer; b. Southampton, N.Y., Dec. 2, 1956; s. Joseph Ralph and Harriet (Jones) S.; m. Stacey Jean Smith, May 10, 1997. BA, Southampton Coll., 1980; JD, Hofstra U., Hempstead, N.Y., 1983. Bar: N.Y. 1983, U.S. Ct. Mil. Appeals 1988, U.S. Supreme Ct. 1988. Assoc. Anthony J. Leanza, Riverhead, N.Y., 1983-85; pvt. practice, 1985—. Southampton Coll. scholar, 1975, U.S. Govt. Presdl. scholar, 1975, N.Y. State Regents scholar, 1975, Bulova Watch Co. scholar, 1975. Office: PO Box 1183 Westhampton Beach NY 11978

SHARPLES, D. KENT, college administrator; b. Swanton, Ohio, May 26, 1943; s. Morrill and Doris Elizabeth (Saeger) S.; m. Linda Mancini Sharples; children: Dawn, Steven. BS, Bowling Green State U., 1965, MEd, 1966; PhD in Edn]. Adminstrn., Ohio U., 1973. Tchr. Maumee (Ohio) Jr. H.S., 1966-67; instr. dept. engring. graphics Coll. Engring. and Tech., Athens, Ohio, 1967-73; project dir. S.C. State Bd. for Tech. and Comprehensive Edn., West Columbia, 1973-76; v.p. for edn., dean of instrn. Tri-County Tech. Coll., Pendleton, S.C., 1976-80; pres. Horry-Georgetown Tech. Coll., Conway, 1980-99, Daytona Beach (Fla.) C.C., 1999—. Mem. Am. Assn. Community and Jr. Colls. (chair small/rural coll. commn. 1983-87, bd. dirs. 1987), Assn. Community Colls Trustees, So. Assn. of Colls. and Schs., Council for Occupational Edn., Am. Tech. Edn. Assn., Myrtle Beach C. of C. Lodges: Rotary. Episcopalian. Office: Daytona Beach CC PO Box 2811 Daytona Beach FL 32120-2811

SHARPLES, RUTH LISSAK, public relations specialist, video producer; b. N.Y.C., Feb. 3, 1952; d. Saul and Nettie (Field) Lissak; m. Winston Sharples, June 26, 1981; stepchildren: Hadley, John, Gillian. BA, CUNY, 1973; MFA, Columbia U., 1975. Rschr. Am. Film Inst./Motion Picture Divsn. of Libr. of Congress, Washington, 1977-79; mgr. audio-visual programs Am. Soc. Microbiology, 1979-82; mgr. video tech. Am. Gas Assn., Arlington, Va., 1982-96; dir. comm. Am. Gas Cooling Ctr., 1996—. V.p., corp. sec. Cantab Motors, Ltd., Purcellville, Va., 1988—; corp. sec. Am. Gas Cooling Ctr., Arlington, 1996—. Editor Cool Times Newsletter, 1996-98. Mem. Nat. Trust Historic Preservation, Nature Conservancy, Mass. Audubon soc., English Heritage, Nat. Trust, Internat. TV Assn. Avocations: hiking, archaeology. Office: Am Gas Cooling Ctr 420 N Capitol St NW Washington DC 20001-1504

SHARPLES, WINSTON SINGLETON, automobile importer and distributor; b. Springfield, Mass., Oct. 24, 1932; s. Winston Singleton and Carmela (Parrino) S.; m. Jeanette Williams, July 1961 (div. Apr. 1981); children: John, Hadley, Gillian; m. Ruth Emily Lissak, June 26, 1981. BA, Harvard Coll., 1953; postgrad. drama, Yale U., 1956-57; MFA, Carnegie Mellon U., 1959; postgrad., Univ. Md., 1978-80. Freelance writer, 1959—; producer, dir. Mon. Valley Playhouse, Charleroi, Pa., 1959, Robin Hood Theater, Arden, Del., 1960-61; pres., film and music editor Synchro-Sound Inc., N.Y.C., 1961-71; prof. CUNY, 1969-74, Temple Univ., Phila., 1974-76, U. Md., College Park, 1978-79; adminstr. film preservation and documentation Am. Film Inst., Washington, 1976-78; prof. Howard Univ., 1978-80; pres. Cantab Motors, Ltd., Puncellville, Va., 1984—. Author: (with others) A Primer for Film-Making, 1971—; supr. Am. Film Inst. Catalog of Feature Films, 1960-69, 77; editor, music editor films and cartoons; contbr. articles to profl. jours. and mags. With U.S. Army, 1953-56. Nat. Endowment for the Humanities grantee, 1977. Mem. ASCAP, Archeol. Soc. Va., Am. Studies Assn., Univ. Film Assn. (v.p. 1975-76), Soc. for Cinema Studies, Soc. Automotive Engrs., Washington Automotive Press Assn., Morgan Car Club, Land Rover Owners Assn. Va., British Automobile Mfrs. Assn., Harvard Club (N.Y.C.). Democrat. Avocations: forestry, archeology. Home: 16657 Tree Crops Ln Round Hill VA 20141-2236 Office: Cantab Motors Ltd Valley Indsl Park 37251 E Richardson Ln Purcellville VA 20132-3505

SHARPLESS, JOSEPH BENJAMIN, former county official; b. Takoma Park, Md., Feb. 4, 1933; s. William Raiford and Julia Maude (Rouse) S.; m. Nancy Kathleen Steffen, July 28, 1962 (dec. Feb. 1988); 1 child, Carole Marie. BA, Earlham Coll., 1955; MS, Pa. State U., 1960. Instr. recreation Montgomery County Recreation Dept., Rockville, Md., 1957-58; from program supr. to dir. Recreation and Parks Dept., Livingston, N.J., 1959-70; chief recreation svc. Md.-Nat. Capital Park and Planning Commn. Prince George's County, Riverdale, Md., 1970-77, parks and recreation div. chief, 1977-95; ret., 1995—. Contbr. articles to profl. jours. V.p. Montpelier Cmty. Assn., South Laurel, Md., 1983-84, pres., 1985; mem. Md. Sports Adv. Com., 1988-92; Md. State Games Commr., 1986-91; bd. regents, instr. Sch. Sports Mgmt., N.C. State U., 1989-92; nat. volleyball chmn. AAU, 1966-69, 72, volleyball chmn. N.J. assn. 1961-70, volleyball chmn. Potomac Valley assn., 1971-73; U.S.A. volleyball nat. commr., 1976-81; mem. volleyball games staff 1996 Olympic Games, Atlanta; staff World Volleyball Congress, Atlanta, 1996; dir. volleyball Spl. Olympics Inc., 1994—, tech. del. Spl. Olympic World Summer Games, 1995, 99, 2003; trustee U.S. Volleyball Edn. Found., 1976—, sec., 1996—; pres. NJAAU, 1968-70. Recipient Pioneer award AAU, 1998. Fellow Nat. Recreation Parks Assn. (Berman Profl. Citation award Mid-Atlantic Regional Coun. 1995, Disting. Svc. award 1995); mem. U.S. Volleyball Assn. (bd. dirs. 1973—, mem. exec. com. 1976-80, 85-89, 92-96, v.p. 1973-90, 96—, regional commr. 1965-78, nat. ofcl. 1967-96, exec. cons. 1989-91, corp. sec. 1992-96, mng. editor pubs. 1994-98, regional commr. emeritus 2000, numerous awards), Nat. Intercollegiate Soccer Ofcls. Assn. (sec. 1966-68, treas. 1968-70), Am. Park and Recreation Soc. (bd. dirs 1977-80, nat. coun., coun. affiliate pres.), N.J. Recreation and Pks. Assn. (sec. 1965, v.p. 1966, pres. 1967), Md. Recreation and Pk. Assn. (v.p. 1975-77, pres. 1977-78, Mem. of Yr. 1975, Citation 1985), Ret. Life Profl. (Disting. Fellow award 1996), Sch. and College Soccer Officials Assn. (sec., treas. 1965-70), N.J. Soccer Ofcls. Assn. (sec./treas. 1966-70), Nat. Capitol Area Bd. Volleyball Ofcls. (sec. 1985-89). Republican. Mem. Soc. Of Friends. Home: 26205 S Cedarcrest Dr Sun Lakes AZ 85248-7206 E-mail: jsharp4usv@aol.com.

SHARPLESS, K. BARRY, chemist, educator; b. Phila., Apr. 28, 1941; m. Jan Dueser, Apr. 28, 1965; children: Hannah, William, Isaac. BA, Dartmouth Coll., 1963, hon. doctorate, 1995; PhD, Stanford U., 1968; hon. doctorate, Swedish Royal Inst. Tech., 1995, Tech. U. Munich, 1995, Cath. U. Louvain, Belgium, 1996. Postdoctoral assoc. Harvard U., Stanford U., to 1970, faculty dept. chemistry, 1977-80; faculty MIT, Cambridge, 1970-77, 1980-90; W. M. Keck prof. chemistry Scripps Rsch. Inst. and Skaggs Inst. of Chem. Biology, La Jolla, Calif., 1990—. Recipient Pual Janssen prize for Creativity in Organic Synthesis, Chem. Pioneer award, Am. Inst. Chemists, 1988, Prelog medal, Swiss Fed. Inst. Tech., Zurich, 1988, Scheele medal and prize, Swedish Acad. Pharm. Scis., Tetrahedron prize for Creativity in Organic Chemistry, 1993, King Faisal Internat. prize for sci., 1995, Microbial medal, Kitasato Inst., Tokyo, 1997, Harvey medal, Technion-Israel Inst. Tech., 1998, Benjarmin Franklin medal in chemistry, 2001, Wolf prize in chemistry, 2001, Nobel prize in Chemistry, 2001; fellow A. P. Sloan, 1987—88, Guggenheim, 1987—88; scholar Camille and Henry Dreyfus Tchr. . Fellow: AAAS, Am. Acad. Arts and Scis., Royal Soc. Chemistry (hon.); mem.: NAS (Award in Chemical Sciences 2000), Am. Chem. Soc. (Creative Work in Synthetic Organic Chemistry award 1983, Harrison Howe award Rochester chpt. 1987, Remsen award Md. sect. 1989, Arthur C. Cope award 1992, Roger Adams award 1997, Richards medal Northeastern sect. 1998, Top 75 Contbrs. to Chem. Enterprise 1998). Office: Scripps Rsch Inst BCC 315 10550 N Torrey Pines Rd La Jolla CA 92037-1000

SHARPSTEIN, RICHARD ALAN, lawyer; b. Boston, Oct. 20, 1950; s. Sidney Joseph and Marilyn (Weitzman) S.; m. Janice Burton, Oct. 20, 1979; children: Jessica Ashley, Katherine Erin, Michael Burton. BA, Tulane U., 1972, JD, 1975. Bar: U.S. Supreme Ct. 1976, Fla. 1976, U.S. Dist. Ct. (no. dist., so. dist., mid. dist.) Fla. 1976, U.S. Ct. Appeals (5th cir.) 1976, U.S. Ct. Appeals (11th cir.) 1980, U.S. Ct. Appeals (3d cir.) 1982, U.S. Ct. Appeals (4th cir.) 1983. Atty. Fla. Bar Assn., Miami, 1976—. Asst. state atty. Dade County, Miami, 1976-79; ptnr., pres. Sharpstein & Sharpstein, P.A., Miami, 1982—; of counsel Kluger Peretz Kaplan & Berlin, P.A., Miami. Mem. bd. editors Money Laundering Alert. Fellow Am. Bd. of Criminal Lawyers; mem. ABA, Acad. Fla. Trial Lawyers, Fla. Criminal Def. Attys. Assn. (v.p. 1985-86, pres. 1986-87, bd. dirs. 1986-92), Am. Inns of Covrt, Omicron Delta Kappa. Home: 1435 W 27th St Miami Beach FL 33140-4208 Office: Jorden Burt LLP 777 Brickell Ave Ste 5000 Miami FL 33131-4329

SHARPTON, THOMAS, physician; b. Augusta, Ga., July 15, 1949; s. Thomas and Elizabeth (Dozier) S. BA, Northwestern U., 1971; MS, Stanford U., 1973, MD, 1977. Intern Martinez (Calif.) VAMC, 1977-78, resident, 1978-80; mem. staff Kaiser Permanente Med. Group, Oakland, Calif., 1980—; asst. clin. prof. medicine U. Calif., San Francisco, 1994—. Cons. Berkeley (Calif.) Free Clinic, 1977—; chmn. peer review Kaiser Permanente Med. Group, Oakland, 1985-86; clin. mem. faculty U. Calif., San Francisco, 1992, asst. clin. prof., 1994; chair AIDS therapeutics com. No. Calif. Kaiser Hosps., 1996-2000. Mem. Alameda County Profl. Adv. Com., Oakland, 1984-88, Alameda County AIDS Task Force, Oakland, 1985-88. Fellow ACP; mem. Calif. Med. Assn., Alameda-Contra Costa Med. Assn., Am. Soc. Microbiology, Mensa, Sigma Pi Sigma, Phi Beta Kappa. Clubs: Phi Beta Kappa of No. Calif. Republican. Avocations: classical piano. Office: Kaiser PMG 280 W Macarthur Blvd Oakland CA 94611-5642 Business E-Mail: Thomas.Sharpton@kp.org.

SHARROCK-JACKSON, LINDA B. social worker; b. N.Y.C., Feb. 16, 1956; d. Willie Chelsea Jackson, Fannie Mae Jackson; m. Leon Sharrock, Feb. 27, 1995; children: Athena Johnson, Alethea Jackson, Althea Jackson, Walter Jackson. BSW, Mercy Coll., 1986; FDC tng., Cornell U., 2002. Social worker Peekskill City Sch. Dist., Peekskill, NY, 1987—. Author: Poetry From the Soul; author: (poetry) Titanic, 2001 (Pres.'s award). Avocation: writing. Home: 218 N James St Apt 4 Peekskill NY 10566-2848

SHARROW, LEONARD, musician, educator; b. N.Y.C., Aug. 4, 1915; s. Saul and Sonia (Berson) S.; m. Emily M. Kass, Oct. 22, 1942; 1 son, Neil Jason. Grad., Juilliard Sch. Music, 1935. Prin. bassoonist Nat. Symphony Orch., Washington, 1935-37; bassoonist NBC Symphony, N.Y.C., 1937-41, prin. bassoonist, 1947-51, Detroit Symphony, 1946-47, Chgo. Symphony Orch., 1951-64, Pitts. Symphony Orch., 1977-87; mem. faculty Juilliard Sch. Music, 1949-51; mem. faculty, performer Gunnison Music Camp, Western State Coll., Colo., 1962-63; pvt. teaching, 1946—; tchr. bassoon Ind. U. Sch. Music, Bloomington, Ind., part-time 1963-64, prof. music (bassoon), 1964-77; assoc. prof. Indiana U. of Pa., 1979-80; part-time faculty Pa. State U., 1979-80, 80-81; adj. prof. Sch. of Music, Carnegie Mellon U., 1981-86. Bassoon faculty New Eng. Conservatory Music, Boston, 1986-89; faculty, performer New Coll. Summer Music Festival, 1976-77, 79-86, Aspen Music Festival, 1967—, Waterloo Music Festival, 1979-80, 83, 86, Banff Ctr. for Arts, Can., 1982, Johannesen Internat. Sch. Arts Summer Festival, Victoria, B.C., Can., 1984, Nagano Aspen Music Festival, Japan, 1990-94; solo bassoonist World Philharm. Orch., Stockholm, 1985; Alan R. Rose fellow, guest artist, lectr., performer Victorian Coll. Arts, Melbourne, Canberra, Sydney, Australia, 1989; faculty Marrowstone Music Festival, Port Townsend, Wash., 1995-96. Mem. Am. Woodwind Quintet, 1964-77; Editor: major works for bassoon; performances chamber music groups, Washington, N.Y.C., Chgo. others; participant, Pablo Casals Festival, Prades, France, 1953, soloist, NBC Symphony, Chgo. Symphony Orch., Pitts. Symphony, Aspen Festival Orch.; TV concerts, Chgo. and Pitts. symphonies; solo recs.: Mozart Bassoon Concerto in B flat Major, with Arturo Toscanini and NBC Symphony, Vivaldi Concerti for Bassoon with Max Goberman and N.Y. Symphonietta, Leonard Sharrow Plays Bassoon Solos, with piano, Concerto da Camera for Bassoon and Orch. (Dan Welcher), Concerto for bassoon and orch. (Ray Luke); assisting artist: A Baroque Trumpet recital with Gerard Schwarz. Served with AUS, 1941-45. Recipient award Toscanini Collection Assn., 1985. Mem. AAUP, Pi Kappa Lambda. Office: 2005 Evergreen Ridge Dr Cincinnati OH 45215-5710

SHARROW, MARILYN JANE, library administrator; b. Oakland, Calif. d. Charles L. and H.Evelyn Sharrow; m. Larry J. Davis. BS in Design, U. Mich., 1967, MALS, 1969. Libr. Detroit Pub. Libr., 1968-70; head fine arts dept. Syracuse (N.Y.) U. Librs., 1970-73; dir. libr. Roseville (Mich.) Pub. Libr., 1973-75; asst. dir. librs. U. Wash., Seattle, 1975-77, assoc. dir. librs., 1978-79; dir. librs. U. Man., Winnipeg, Can., 1979-82; chief libr. U. Toronto, Can., 1982-85; libr. U. Calif., Davis, 1985—. Chair bd. North Regional Libr. Facility, 1999—2001. Recipient Woman of Yr. in Mgmt. award Winnipeg YWCA, 1982; named Woman of Distinction, U. Calif. Faculty Women's Rsch. Group, 1985. Mem. ALA, Assn. Rsch. Librs. (bd. dirs., v.p., pres.-elect 1989-90, pres. 1990-91, chair sci. tech. work group 1994-98, rsch. collections com. 1993-95, 2000-2002, preservation com. 1997-99), OCLC-Rsch. Librs. Adv. Com. (vice-chair 1992-93, chair 1993-94), Calif. State Network Resources Libr. Com., Can. Assn. Rsch. Libr. (pres. 1984-85). Office: U Calif Shields Libr 100 NW Quad Davis CA 95616-5292 E-mail: mjsharrow@ucdavis.edu.

SHARTLE, STANLEY MUSGRAVE, consulting engineer, land surveyor; b. Brazil, Ind., Sept. 27, 1922; s. Arthur Tinder and Mildred C. (Musgrave) S.; m. Anna Lee Mantle, Apr. 7, 1948; 1 child: Randy. Student, Purdue U., 1947-50. Registered profl. engr., land surveyor. Ind. chief dep. surveyor Hendricks County (Ind.), 1941-42; asst. hydrographer Fourteenth Naval Dist., Pearl Harbor, Hawaii, 1942-44; dep. county surveyor Hendricks County (Ind.), Danville, 1944-50, county engr., surveyor, 1950-54, county hwy. engr., 1975-77; staff engr. Ind. Toll Rd. Commn., Indpls., 1954-61; chief right of way engring. Ind. State Hwy. Commn., 1961-75; owner, civil engr. Shartle Engring., 1977-89; prin. Parsons Cunningham & Shartle Engrs., Inc., 1990—. Right of way engring. cons. Gannett Fleming Transp. Engrs., Inc., Indpls., 1983-88; part-time lectr. Purdue U. for Ind. State Hwy. Commn., 1965-67. Prin. works include residential subdiv., 1989 (named Indiana's Most Successful Ind. Bus. Jour., 1989); author: Right of Way Engineering Manual, 1975, Musgrave Family History, 1961, 95, Shartle Genealogy, 1955, (romance novel) Her Word of Honor, 2001; contbr. articles to tech. and sci. jours. Ex-officio mem., charter mem. exec. sec. Hendricks County (Ind.) Plan Commn., 1951-54; mem. citizen adv. com. Hendricks County Subdivision Control Ordinance, 1988—; citizens adv. com. transp. Indpls. Met. Planning Area. Recipient Outstanding Contbn. award Hendricks County Soil and Water Conservation Dist., 1976; Stanley Shartle Day proclaimed by Hendricks County, Ind., 1997. Mem. Am. Congress Surveying and Mapping (life), Nat. Soc. Profl. Surveyors, Ind. Soc. Profl. Land Surveyors (charter, life, bd. dirs. 1979), Nat. Geneal. Soc. (Quarter Century club), Ind. Toll Road Employees Assn. (pres. 1959-60), Internat. Right of Way Assn. (charter, founder chpt. 10), Geog. and Land Info. Soc. Avocations: astronomy, genealogy, geodesy. Home and Office: 6575 Kings Ct Avon IN 46123-9075

SHASHIDHARAN, KALATHIL KUNGATTY, emergency physician, internist; b. Cannanore, Kerala, India, Dec. 10, 1945; came to U.S., 1971; Student, St. Joseph's Coll., Calicut, India, 1963-64; MD, Jawaharlal Inst. PG Medicine, Pondicherry, 1970. Intern Providence Hosp., Washington, 1972; resident internal medicine Howard U., 1973-75; ER attending physician Church Hosp., Balt., 1975-88, St. Agnes Hosp., Balt., 1988-92, Sinai Hosp., Balt., 1992-93, Good Samaritan Hosp., Balt., 1993—. Mem. AMA, Am. Coll. Emergency Physicians.

SHASHIKANTH, BANAVARA N, mathematician, educator; b. Hyderabad, Andhra Pradesh, India, Mar. 5, 1968; s. Banavara Narayana and Leela Murthy. PhD, U. So. Calif., 1997. Rsch. scientist Nat. Aerospace Labs., Bangalore, India, 1991—93; postdoctoral scholar Calif. Inst. of Tech., Pasadena, 1998—2000. Contbr. articles to profl. jours. Fellow John Stauffer Grad. Sch. Fellowship, U. of So. Calif., 1997. Mem.: Am. Geophys. Union, Am. Math. Soc., Soc. of Indsl. and Applied Math. Business E-Mail: shashi@nm.nmsu.edu.

SHASHY, PAUL MOSES, urologist; b. Ocala, Fla., Nov. 25, 1925; m. Nancy Scott (dec. Nov. 1990); children: Paul Jr., William, Peter, Ann, James, Hugh. MD, U. Ala., Birmingham, 1949. Cert. Am. Bd. Urology. Intern St. Louis City Hosp., 1949-50; resident Grady Meml. Hosp., Emory U., Atlanta, 1950-53; fellow Ochsner Clinic, New Orleans, 1954-57. Clin. assoc. prof. urology U. Ala. Sch. Medicine, Birmingham. Office: Drs Shashy and Shashy PA 1722 Pine St Ste 204 Montgomery AL 36106-1158

SHASTEEN, DONALD EUGENE, government official; b. Englewood, Colo., Dec. 3, 1928; s. George Donald and Frances True (Meyers) S.; m. Shirley Mae Johnson, Aug. 8, 1954; children: Jon Randolph, Ron Winston, Sherilyn Sue. BA in Journalism, U. Colo., 1950. Reporter Omaha World-Herald, Des Moines, 1954-58, Lincoln, Nebr., 1958-66; exec. asst. to Senator Carl T. Curtis of Nebr., Washington, 1966-73, adminstrv. asst., 1973-78, to Sen. Gordon J. Humphrey, 1979-80; with transition group Senate Republican Conf., 1980; dep. under sec. for legislation and intergovtl. affairs Dept. Labor, 1981-83, dep. asst. sec. for vets. employment, 1983-85, asst. sec. for vets. employment and tng., 1985-89. Pres. Shasteen Assocs. Rep. nominee for U.S. Senate Nebr., 1978. Served with U.S. Army, 1951-52. Mem. Am. Legion, VFW, Am. Vets., Disabled Am. Vets., Phi Delta Theta. Republican. Lutheran. E-mail: shasteens@juno.com., shasteen@msn.com.

SHASTID, JON BARTON, wine company executive; b. Hannibal, Mo., Nov. 21, 1914; s. Jon Shepherd and Mary (Barton) S.; m. Natalie Kiliani, Dec. 16, 1944; children— Lucinda, Jon G.H., Victoria A., Thomas Bartwyn. Bar: Calif. bar 1959; C.P.A., Calif., Kans. Pub. accountant, Dodge City, Kans., 1938-42; v.p. finance Johnson Bronze Co., New Castle, Pa., 1946-54; exec. v.p., treas. E. & J. Gallo Winery, Modesto, Calif., 1954-88; pres. Gallo Wine Co. of La. at New Orleans, 1960-89. City councilman, Modesto, 1961-69. Served to capt. USAAF, 1942-46. Mem. State Bar of Calif., Am. Bar Assn., Calif. Soc. C.P.A.'s. Home and Office: 1700 Tice Blvd #444 Walnut Creek CA 94595

SHASTRY, SHAMBHU KADHAMBINY, scientist, engineering executive, consultant; b. Kerala, India, Aug. 29, 1954; came to U.S., 1978; s. Mahalinga K. and Parameshwari (Laxmi) S.; m. Suma S. Shastry, Dec. 30, 1984; children: Disha Laxmi, Divya Gowri. MS, Rensselaer Poly. Inst., 1980, PhD, 1982. Leader Microwave Semiconductor Corp., Somerset, N.J., 1982-85; sr. mem. tech. staff GTE Labs., Waltham, Mass., 1985-88; mgr. advanced tech. Kopin Corp., Taunton, 1988-91; dir. III-V Products, 1991-95; tech. and bus. devel. cons. Franklin, 1995—; pres. The Idea Co., 1995—. Reviewer: Pre-publication Review of S.K. Ghandhi's Book on VLSI Fabrication Principles; contbr. articles to profl. jours.; referee Applied Physics Letters, Jour. Applied Physics, 1985—. Vol. New Eng. Hindu Temple, Inc., Ashland, Mass., 1984—, IDRF, Inc., Washington, 1996—. Mem. IEEE, Am. Phys. Soc., Electrochem. Soc., Sigma Xi. Achievements include patents on hetereopitaxy of dissimilar materials, such as gallium arsenide on silicon, novel fabrication processes for manufacturing light emitting diodes and high technology business development. Office: 6 Oak Tree Ln Franklin MA 02038-4231

SHATALOV, MAXIM S. electrical engineer, researcher; b. St. Petersburg, Russia, Feb. 19, 1971; arrived in U.S., 1999; s. Sergey M. Shatalov, Nina F. Shatalova; m. Victoria A. Shatalova, Feb. 19, 1991; 1 child Nikita 1 child Alexander. MSEE, Electrotech. U., St. Petersburg, 1994; PhD in Physics and Math., A.F. Ioffe Inst., St. Petersburg, 1999. Rsch. scientist A.F. Ioffe Inst., St. Petersburg, 1994—99; rsch. assoc. U. S.C., Columbia, 1999—2001, rsch. asst. prof., 2001—. Vis. rsch. assoc. U. Coll. London, 1998. Contbr. , articles to profl. jours. Mem.: IEEE, Lasers and Electro Optics Soc. Office: Univ SC Dept Elec Engring 301 Main St Columbia SC 29208 Business E-Mail: shatalov@engr.sc.edu.

SHATIN, JUDITH, music composing educator; b. Boston, Nov. 11, 1949; d. Leo and Harriet Evelyn (Sommer) S.; m. Michael Kubovy, June 28, 1992. AB, Douglass, Coll., 1971; MM, Julliard Sch., 1974; PhD, Princeton U., 1979. Asst. prof. U. Va., Charlottesville, 1979-85, assoc. prof., 1985-92, prof., 1992—, chmn. McIntire dept. music, 1995—, William R. Kenan, Jr. prof., 1999—. Dir. Va. Ctr. Computer Music, 1988—. Composer: (orch.) Aura, 1981, (piano concerto) Passion of St. Cecilia, 1985, (flute concerto) Ruah, 1985, (piano trio) View from Mt. Nebo (commd. by Garth Newel Chamber Players), 1985, (piano trio) Ignoto Numine (commd. Monticello Trio), 1986, (flute, clarinet, violin, cello) Secret Ground (commd. by Roxbury Chamber Players), 1990, (soprano and tape) Three Summers Heat, 1989 (Barlow Found. Commn.), (orch.) Piping the Earth (commd. by Women's Philharm.), 1990, (flute and piano) Gabriel's Wing (commd. by Julia Bogorad and the Upper Midwest Flute Assn.), 1990, (flute and electronics) Kairos (Commd. Va. Commn. for the Arts), 1991, (chorus, brass quintet, tympani) We Hold These Truths (commd. U. Va., for Thomas Jefferson's 250th birthday), 1992, (string orch.) Stringing the Bow (commd. Va. Chamber Orch.), 1992, COAL (commd. as part of 2-yr. retrospective of work, sponsored by Lila Wallace- Readers Digest Arts Ptnrs. Program), 1994, (piano and percussion) 1492 (commd. Arioso Ensemble), 1992, (piano) Chai Variations on Eliahu HaNavi, 1995, (flute and guitar) Dreamtigers (commd. Ekko!), 1996, (chorus) Adonai Roi, 1995, (string quartet) Janus Quartet (commd. for the Arcata Quartet), 1994, (string quartet and electronic playback) Elijah's Chariot (commd. Kronos Quartet), 1995, (amplified clarinet with PVC extensions effects processor, foot pedals and playback sys.) Sea of Reeds (commd. F. Gerard Errante), 1997, (chorus and piano) Songs of War and Peace, 1998, (brass quintet) Fantasia sobre el Flamenco, 1998, (piano, cello, percussion) Houdini: Memories of a Conjurer, 1999 (commd. Core Ensemble), (wind quintet and piano) Ockeghem Variations (commd. Hexagon Ensemble), 2000, Run (piano quintet) (commd. Currants) 2001. Nat. Endowment for Arts Composer fellow, 1980, 85, 89, 92; recipient award Va. Commn. for the Arts, 1989. Mem. Am. Music Ctr., Am. Women Composers (pres. 1989-93), Am. Composers Alliance (bd. dirs. 1993-98), Internat. Alliance for Women in Music (chair nominating com. 1996-98, adv. bd. 1999—). Avocations: yoga.

SHATKIN, AARON JEFFREY, biochemistry educator; b. Providence, July 18, 1934; s. Morris and Doris S.; m. Joan A. Lynch, Nov. 30, 1957; 1 son, Gregory Martin. AB, Bowdoin Coll., 1956, DSc (hon.), 1979; PhD, Rockefeller Inst., 1961. Sr. asst. scientist NIH, Bethesda, Md., 1961-63, rsch. chemist, 1963-68; vis. scientist Salk Inst., La Jolla, Calif., 1968-69; assoc. mem. dept. cell biology Roche Inst. Molecular Biology, Nutley, N.J., 1968-73, full mem., 1973-77, head molecular virology lab., 1977-86, head dept. cell biology, 1983-86; dir. N.J. Ctr. Advanced Biotech. Medicine, 1986—; prof. molecular genetics UMDNJ, 1986—; univ. prof. molecular biology Rutgers U., New Brunswick, N.J., 1986—. Adj. prof. cell biology Rockefeller U.; vis. prof. molecular biology Princeton U. Mem. editl. bd. Jour. Virology, 1969-82, Archives of Biochemistry and Biophysics, 1972-82, Virology, 1973-76, Comprehensive Virology, 1974-82, Jour. Biol. Chemistry, 1977-83, 94-99, RNA Jour., 1995-96, Procs. of NAS, 1997—; editor Advances in Virus Rsch., 1983—, Jour. Virology, 1973-77; editor-in-chief Molecular and Cellular Biology, 1980-90. Served with USPHS, 1961-63. Recipient U.S. Steel Found. prize in molecular biology, 1977, N.J. Sci. and Tech. Pride award, 1989, Thomas Edison Sci. award State of N.J., 1991; Rockefeller fellow, 1956-61 Fellow AAAS, Am. Acad. Arts and Scis., Am. Acad. Microbiology, N.Y. Acad. Scis.; mem. NAS, Am. Soc. Microbiology, Am. Soc. Biol. Chemists, Am. Soc. Virology, Am. Chem. Soc., Am. Soc. Cell Biology, Harvey Soc. Home: 1381 Rahway Rd Scotch Plains NJ 07076-3452 Office: Ctr Advanced Biotech and Medicine 679 Hoes Ln Piscataway NJ 08854-5627 E-mail: shatkin@cabm.rutgers.edu.

SHATNER, WILLIAM, actor; b. Montreal, Que., Can., Mar. 22, 1931; s. Joseph and Anne S.; m. Gloria Rand, Aug. 12, 1956 (div. Mar. 1969); three children; m. Marcy Lafferty, Oct. 20, 1973 (div. 1996); m. Nerine Kidd, Nov. 15, 1997 (dec. Aug. 1999); m. Elizabeth Martin, Feb. 2001. BA, McGill U., 1952. Stage debut, 1952; appeared Montreal Playhouse, summers 1952, 53; played juvenile roles Canadian Repertory Theatre, Ottawa, 1952-53, 53-54; appeared Stratford Shakespeare Festival, Ont., 1954-56; Broadway appearances include Tamburlaine the Great, 1956, The World of Suzie Wong, 1958, A Shot in the Dark, 1961; films include The Brothers Karamazov, 1958, The Explosive Generation, 1961, Judgement at Nuremburg, 1961, The Intruder, 1962, The Outrage, 1964, Dead of Night, 1974, The Devil's Rain, 1975, Star Trek, 1979, The Kidnapping of the President, 1979, Star Trek: The Wrath of Khan, 1982, Star Trek III: The Search for Spock, 1984, Star Trek IV: The Voyage Home, 1986, (director) Star Trek V: The Final Frontier, 1989, Star Trek VI: The Undiscovered Country, 1991, National Lampoon's Loaded Weapon, 1992, Star Trek: Generations, 1994, Trekkies, 1997, Free Enterprise, 1998, Shoot or be Shot, 2000, Grown Lake, 2000, Miss Congeniality, 2000, American Psycho II, 2001; also TV movies and appearances on The Andersonville Trial, The Bastard, 1978, Disaster on the Coastliner, 1979, Secrets of a Married Man, 1984, North Beach and Rawhide, 1985, Columbo, 1993; star of TV show Star Trek, 1966-69, animated series, 1973-75; TV series Barbary Coast, 1975-76, The Babysitter, 1979, T.J. Hooker; host (TV series)

Rescue 911, CBS, 1989—, 3rd Rock From the SUn, 1996; dir. TV movie TekWar; author: (novels) TekWar, 1989, TekLords, 1991, TekLab, 1991, Tek Vengeance, 1992, Tek Secret, 1993, (memoirs) Star Trek Memories, 1993, Star Trek Movie Memories, 1994, Tek Power, 1994, Tek Money, 1995, The Ashes of Eden, 1995, Man O' War, 1996, Tek Kill, 1996, The Return, 1996, Avenger, 1997, Delta Search: Quest for Tomorrow, 1997, Delta Search: In Alien Hands, 1998, Delta Search: Step Into Chaos, 1999. Recipient Tyrone Guthrie award, 1956, Theatre World award, 1958. Mem. Actors Equity Assn., AFTRA, Screen Actors Guild, Dirs. Guild. Address: care of Melis Prodns 760 N La Cienega Blvd Los Angeles CA 90069-5204

SHATNEY, CLAYTON HENRY, surgeon; b. Bangor, Maine, Nov. 4, 1943; s. Clayton Lewis and Regina (Cossette) S.; m. Consuelo Perez Santibañez; children: Tony, Andy, Joel. BA, Bowdoin Coll., 1965; MD, Tufts U., 1969. Asst. prof. surgery U. Md. Hosp., Balt., 1979-82; assoc. prof. U. Fla. Sch. Medicine, 1982-87; clin. assoc. prof. Stanford (Calif.) U. Sch. Medicine, 1987—. Dir. traumatology Md. Inst. Emergency Med. Svcs., Balt., 1979-82; dir. trauma U. Hosp., Jacksonville, 1982-85; assoc. dir. trauma Santa Clara Valley Med. Ctr., 1992—; cons. VA Coop. Studies Program, Washington, 1980-90. Mem. editl. bd. Circulatory Shock, 1989-94, Panam Jour. Trauma, 1995-2000, Jour. Investigative Surgery, 2001--. Maj. U.S. Army, 1977-79. State of Maine scholar Bowdoin Coll., 1961-65. Fellow ACS, Southeastern Surg. Congress, Southwestern Surg. Congress, Soc. Surg. Alimentary Tract, Am. Assn. Surg. Trauma, Soc. Internat. de Chirurgie, Western Surg. Assn., Pacific Coast Surg. Assn., Phi Kappa Phi. Home: 900 Larsen Rd Aptos CA 95003-2640 Office: Valley Med Ctr Dept Surgery 751 S Bascom Ave San Jose CA 95128-2604 E-mail: cshatney@yahoo.com.

SHATTO, JOHN FREDERICK, court administrator; b. Frederick, Md., July 5, 1957; s. Paul Frederick and Dell (Napier) S.; m. Elizabeth Vandiver Scott, Aug. 16, 1980; children: Julia Reed, Scott Napier. BS in Psychology, Armstrong State Coll., 1985; MS in Adminstrn., Cen. Mich. U., 1988. Dep. ct. adminstr. County of Chatham, Savannah, Ga., 1986-91; ct. adminstr. Howard County Cir. Ct., Ellicott City, Md., 1991—. Fellow Inst. Ct. Mgmt.; mem. Nat. Assn. for Ct. Mgmt., Sigma Iota Epsilon. Episcopalian. Avocations: tennis, reading. Home: 9796 Chestnut Oak Ct Frederick MD 21701-6724 Office: Howard County Cir Ct 8360 Court Ave Ellicott City MD 21043-4550

SHATTUCK, CATHIE ANN, lawyer, former government official; b. Salt Lake City, July 18, 1945; d. Robert Ashley S. and Lillian Culp (Shattuck). BA, U. Nebr., 1967, JD, 1970. Bar: Nebr. 1970, U.S. Dist. Ct. Nebr. 1970, Colo. 1971, U.S. Dist. Ct. Colo. 1971, U.S. Supreme Ct. 1974, U.S. Ct. Appeals (10th cir.) 1977, U.S. Dist. Ct. D.C. 1984, U.S. Ct. Appeals (D.C. cir.) 1984. V.p., gen. mgr. Shattuck Farms, Hastings, Nebr., 1967-70; asst. project dir. atty. Colo. Civil Rights Commn., Denver, 1970-72; trial atty. Equal Employment Opportunity Commn., 1973-77, vice chmn. Washington, 1982-84; pvt. practice law Denver, 1977-81; mem. Fgn. Svc. Bd., Washington, 1982-84, Presdl. Personnel Task Force, Washington, 1982-84; ptnr. Epstein, Becker & Green, L.A. and Washington, 1984—. Lectr. Colo. Continuing Legal Edn. Author: Employer's Guide to Controlling Sexual Harrassment, 1992; mem. editorial bd. The Practical Litigator, 1988—. Bd. dirs. KGNU Pub. Radio, Boulder, Colo., 1979, Denver Exchange, 1980-81, YWCA Met. Denver, 1979-81. Recipient Nebr. Young Career Woman Bus. and Profl. Women, 1967; recipient Outstanding Nebraskan Daily Nebraskan, Lincoln, 1967 Fellow Am. Coll. of Labor and Employment Lawyers; mem. ABA (mgmt. chair labor and employment law sect. com. on immigration law 1988-90, mgmt. chair com. on legis. devels. 1990-93), Nebr. Bar Assn., Colo. Bar Assn., Colo. Women's Bar Assn., D.C. Bar Assn., Nat. Women's Coalition, Delta Sigma Rho, Tau Kappa Alpha, Pi Sigma Alpha, Alpha Xi Delta, Denver Club.

SHATTUCK, GARY G. lawyer; b. Nashua, N.H., 1950; m. Katherine H. Catlin, 1972. BA, U. Colo., 1972; JD magna cum laude, Vt. Law Sch., 1987. Bar: Vt. 1987, U.S. Dist. Ct. Vt. 1987, U.S. Ct. Appeals (2d cir.) 1992. Dep. sheriff Boulder County Sheriff's Dept., Boulder, Colo., 1973-75; patrol comdr. Vt. State Police, Waterbury, 1975-87; litigation assoc. Reiber, Kenlan, Schweibert & Hall, P.C., Rutland, Vt., 1987-89; asst. atty. gen. Office of Atty. Gen., Montpelier, 1989-91; suprvising atty. Vt. Drug Task Force, 1989-91; asst. U.S. atty. Organized Crime Drug Enforcement Task Force, U.S. Dept. Justice, Burlington, Vt., 1991—. Adj. prof. Castleton (Vt.) State Coll., 1997-98; U.S. Dept. Justice legal advisor to UN Mission in Kosovo, Pristina, 2000, Sarajevo, Bosnia-Herzegovina, 2001; anti-terrorism coord. Dist. Vt., 2002—. Bd. dirs. Rutland Mental Health, 1991; citizen's adv. com. Rutland Solid Waste Dist., 1987; del. Nat. Assn. Asst. U.S. Attys., 1994-99; bd. dirs. Vt. Archeol. Soc., 1998-99. Recipient Atty. Gen. Janet Reno Spl. Achievement award, 1993, award Dept. Justice for svc. in Kosovo. Mem. Lake Champlain Maritime Mus., Nat. Trust Historic Preservation, New Eng. Narcotic Enforcement Officers Assn. Office: Office of US Atty PO Box 570 Burlington VT 05402-0570 E-mail: garyshattuck@hotmail.com.

SHATTUCK, GEORGE CLEMENT, retired lawyer; b. Syracuse, N.Y., Sept. 2, 1927; s. Frank M. and Geneveive Mary (Hannon) S.; m. Sheila Eagan, Sept. 21, 1957 (div. 1985); children: Edward, George, Frank, Mark, Patrick; m. Carla A. Amussen, June 16, 1987; 1 child, Morgan. BS in Mgmt., Syracuse U., 1950, JD, 1953. Bar: N.Y. 1954, U.S. Supreme Ct. 1973. Retired ptnr., estate planning splty. practice group Bond, Schoeneck & King Law Firm, Syracuse, 1954-97. Author: Oneida Land Claims, 1991, Estate Planning for the Small Business Owner, 1993. Mem. Syracuse Bd. Edn., 1968-75. Roman Catholic. Avocations: writing, reading history and philosophy, fishing. Home: 5158 W Lake Rd Cazenovia NY 13035-9616

SHATTUCK, JOHN, diplomat, civil rights lawyer, educator; b. Pasedena, Calif., Sept. 22, 1943; s. H. Francis Jr. and Ruth (Murphy) S.; m. Petra Tölle, May 17, 1970 (dec. Mar. 1988); m. Ellen Hume, Feb. 14, 1991; children: Jessica, Rebecca, Peter, Susannah. BA magna cum laude, Yale U., 1965, JD, 1970; MA with 1st class hon. in internat. law, Cambridge U., Eng., 1967; doctorate (hon.), CUNY, 1995, Kenyon Coll., 2001; doctorate (hon.), U. R.I., 2002. Law clk. to Hon. Edward Weinfeld U.S. Dist. Ct. (so. dist.) N.Y., 1970-71; nat. counsel ACLU, 1971-77, dir. Washington office, 1977-84; v.p. govt., community and pub. affairs Harvard U., 1984-93, sr. assoc. sci. tech. and pub. policy program John F. Kennedy sch. govt., 1984-93; asst. sec. of state bur. democracy, human rights and labor Dept. of State, Washington, 1993-98; U.S. amb. Czech Republic, 1998-2000; CEO John F. Kennedy Presdl. Libr. Found., 2001—. Editor Yale U. Law Jour.; contbr. articles to profl. jours. Bd. dir. The Petra Fedn., Am. Friends of Czech Republic, ABA Ctrl. & E. Law Inst. Recipient UN Assn. Human Rights award1998, Am. Bar Assn. Ambassador award 2000, H.L. Mencken award Free Press Assn. 1985, Pub. Svc. award Yale U. Law Sch. 1988, Roger Baldwin medal 1984. Office: John F Kennedy Presdl Libr and Found/Columbia Point Boston MA 02125

SHATTUCK, LAWRENCE WILLIAM, admissions director; b. Nashua, N.H., Aug. 24, 1951; s. Fred and Shirley (Lundeen) S. AS, Middlesex C.C., Mass., 1975; MEd, Cambridge (Mass.) Coll., 1990. Admissions officer Tufts U. Sch. Dental Medicine, Boston, 1976-90; dir. admissions New Eng. Coll. Optometry, 1990—. Mem. Nat. Assn. Grad. Admissions Profls. (mem. membership com.), Nat. Assn. Advisors for the Health Professions, N.E. Assn. Advisors to the Health Professions. Home: 278 Manning St Unit 904 Hudson MA 01749-1046 Office: New Eng Coll Optometry 424 Beacon St Boston MA 02115-1129

SHATTUCK, MAYO ADAMS, III, integrated utility executive; b. Boston, Oct. 7, 1954; s. Mayo Adams Jr. and Jane (Bergwall) S.; m. Molly Anne George, Sept. 29, 1997; children: Mayo Adams IV, Kathleen Elizabeth, Spencer George, Wyatt Augustus. BA, Williams Coll., 1976; MBA, Stanford U., 1980. Analyst Morgan Guaranty Trust Co., N.Y.C., 1976-78; mgr. Bain & Co., Menlo Park, Calif., 1980-83; v.p. to mng. dir. and head of corp. fin. Alex Brown & Sons, San Francisco, 1985-91, pres. and COO Balt., 1991-97; co-chmn., CEO BT Alex Brown Inc., from 1997; vice chmn. Bankers Trust N.Y., from 1997; co-chmn., co-CEO, Deutsche Banc Alex Brown Inc., Balt., 1999—2001; pres., CEO, chmn. bd. Constellation Energy Group, 2001—02, chmn., pres., CEO, 2002—. Bd. dirs. Constellation Energy, Gap Inc., Deutsche Bank's U.S. Bank Bds./Bankers Trust Corp. and Bankers Trust Co. Trustee Noble & Greenough Sch.; adv. dir. U. Md., Balt., 1992—, U. Md. Balt. County. Mem. Young Pres. Orgn. Avocations: tennis, golf. Fax: 410-783-2889. E-mail: Mayo.Shattuck@constellation.com.

SHATTUCK, ROGER WHITNEY, author, educator; b. N.Y.C., Aug. 20, 1923; s. Howard Francis and Elizabeth (Colt) S.; m. Nora Ewing White, Aug. 20, 1949; children— Tari Elizabeth, Marc Ewing, Patricia Colt, Eileen Shepard. Grad., St. Paul's Sch., Concord, N.H., 1941; BA, Yale, 1947; D (honoris causa), U. Orléans, France, 1990. Information officer UNESCO, Paris, France, 1947-48; asst. editor Harcourt, Brace & Co., 1949-50; mem. Soc. Fellows, Harvard, 1950-53, instr. French, 1953-56; faculty U. Tex., Austin, 1956-71, prof. English, French, 1968-71, chmn. dept. French and Italian, 1968-71; Commonwealth prof. French U. Va., Charlottesville, 1974-88; univ. prof., prof. modern fgn. langs. Boston U., 1988-97. Mem. adv. bd. Nat. Translation Center, 1964-69, chmn., 1966-69; provediteur gen. Coll. de Pataphysique, Paris, 1961—; Fulbright prof. U. Dakar, Senegal, 1984-85. Author: The Banquet Years, 1958; poems Half Tame, 1964, Proust's Binoculars, 1963, Marcel Proust, 1974 (Nat. Book award 1975), The Forbidden Experiment, 1980, The Innocent Eye, 1984, Forbidden Knowledge, 1996, Candor and Perversion, 1999, Proust's Way, 2000; editor or co-editor: Selected Writings of Guillaume Apollinaire, 1950, Mount Analogue, (René Daumal), 1959, The Craft and Context of Translation (with William Arrowsmith), 1961, Selected works of Alfred Jarry, 1965, Occasions by Paul Valèry, 1970; mem. editl. bd. PMLA, 1977-78. Capt. USAAF, 1942-45. Decorated Ordre Palmes Academiques (France).; Guggenheim fellow, 1958-59; Fulbright research fellow, 1958-59; Am. Council Learned Socs. research fellow, 1969-70. Fellow AAAS; mem. Assn. Literary Scholars and Critics (pres. 1995-96).

SHATZ, CARLA J. biology educator; b. N.Y.C. BA in Chemistry, Radcliffe Coll., 1969; MPhil, Univ. Coll., London, 1971; PhD, Harvard U., 1976, postdoc., 1976—78. Assoc. prof. neurobiology Sch. Medicine Stanford U., Palo Alto, Calif., 1985—89, prof. neurobiology, 1989—92; investigator Howard Hughes Med. Inst., 1994—2000; Class of 1943 prof. neurobiology U. Calif., Berkeley, 1992—2000; prof., chair dept. neurobiology Harvard Med. Sch., Boston, 2000—. Mem. commn. on life scis. NRC, 1990—96; nat. adv. NIH, 1996—99; mem. coun. NAS, 1998—2001. Fellow: Inst. Medicine, Am. Philos. Soc., NAS, AAAS. Office: Harvard Med Sch Dept Neurobiology 220 Longwood Ave Boston MA 02115-5701

SHATZ, MARK ALLEN, psychologist, educator; b. Chgo., Apr. 7, 1955; s. Michael and Serna S.; m. Amanda L., June 26, 1999. BS, Ea. Ill. U., 1976, MA, 1977; PhD, U. Fla., 1983. Instr. Ea. Ill. U., Charleston, 1978-80; prof. psychology Ohio U., Zanesville, 1983—. Trainer, cons. Hospice Sout Ea. Ohio, Zanesville, 1988—; ethics com. Genesis Hosp., Zanesville, 1996—; crisis team Zanesville City Schs., 1996—. Author: Kissing Golf: The Keep it Simple (Stupid) Instructional Method, 1997; contbr. articles to profl. jours. Mem. Assn. Death Edn. Counseling (cert.), Am. Psychol. Soc. Avocations: cycling, golfing, hiking. Office: Ohio U Zanesville 1425 Newark Rd Zanesville OH 43701 E-mail: shatz@ohiou.edu.

SHATZ, PHILLIP, lawyer, banker, insurance executive; b. White Plains, N.Y., Sept. 1, 1926; s. Hyman and Ruth (Futoran) S.; m. Bettie Dorsey, Oct. 18, 1957 (dec.); children: Phillip Dorsey, Sallie Dean; m. Natalie Marshall, May 27, 1988. BS, Syracuse U., 1948; LLB, Columbia U., 1954. Bar: N.Y. 1954, U.S. Dist. Ct. (so. dist.) N.Y. 1955, U.S. Supreme Ct. 1960. Pres., chmn. bd. Rich, Shatz and Duncan, Inc., Mahopac, N.Y., 1948-75; v.p. Putnam County Fed. Savs. and Loan Assn., 1953-63, pres., chmn. bd., 1933-78; sole practice Mahopac, 1954-70; ptnr. Shatz & Braatz, 1970-74, Shatz & Thomsen, Mahopac, 1974-77, Shatz, Thomsen & Mace, Mahopac, 1977-80; sr. ptnr. McCabe & Mack, Poughkeepsie, NY, 1980—2000, of counsel, 2000—. Spl. prosecutor Putnam County; dir. Mid-Hudson Legal Svcs. Chmn. Putnam County Young Republicans. With USNR, 1943-46. Mem. ABA, N.Y. State Bar Assn., Dutchess County Bar Assn., Assn. Bar City of N.Y., Univ. Club (N.Y.C.). Home: 157 Skidmore Rd Pleasant Valley NY 12569-5001 Office: McCabe & Mack Esqs 63 Washington St Poughkeepsie NY 12601-2313 E-mail: pshatz@mccm.com.

SHATZ, STEPHEN SIDNEY, mathematician, educator; b. Bklyn., Apr. 27, 1937; s. Nathan and Agusta S.; children: Geoffrey, Adria. AB, Harvard U., 1957, A.M., 1958, PhD, 1962; A.M. (hon.), U. Pa., 1971. Instr. Stanford U., 1962-63, acting asst. prof., 1963-64; asst. prof. U. Pa., Phila., 1964-67, assoc. prof., 1967-69, prof. math., 1969—, chmn. dept. math., 1983-86. Vis. prof. U. Pisa, 1966-67; mem. Math. Scis. Rsch. Inst., 1986-87, Inst. Advanced Study, 1997. Author: Profinite Groups, Arithmetic and Geometry, 1972; contbr. articles to profl. jours. Mem. Am. Math. Soc. (editor Trans. 1975-78, coun. 1975-80, exec. com. coun. 1979-80). Office: U Pa Dept Math Philadelphia PA 19104-6395

SHAUB, MARVIN HOWARD, management consultant; b. N.Y.C., Aug. 15, 1940; s. Harry and Edith (Shulman) S.; m. Susan Jayne Deborah Colbert, July 2, 1962 (div. Oct. 1991); children: Lisa Ellen, Eric Steven, Joshua Evan Colbert Finley; m. Yuko Kumazawa, Dec. 24, 1991; 1 child, Nicole Hiromi. BA, Cornell U., 1962; MBA, Harvard U., 1964. Assoc. McKinsey & Co., N.Y.C., 1969-71; v.p. Franklin Mint Corp., Phila., 1971-85; pres., COO A. J. Wood Corp., 1985-86; founder, chmn. Lombardo & Shaub, 1987-96; pres., CEO Teletienda, Inc., Princeton, N.J., 1990—. 1st lt. USAF, 1964-67. Mem. Harvard Bus. Sch. Club (past pres., dir.). Republican. Jewish. Avocations: skiing, travel. Home: 385 Sayre Dr Princeton NJ 08540-5860 Office: Teletienda Inc 385 Sayre Dr Princeton NJ 08540-5860 E-mail: mhshaub@aol.com.

SHAUERS, MARGARET ANN, author; b. Hoisington, Kans., Nov. 20, 1943; d. John Felix and Leona Anna (Stegman) Krmela; m. Gerald D. Crotinger, Apr. 14, 1959 (div. Oct. 1961); 1 child, James Allen; m. Delbert M. Shauers, Dec. 27, 1962 (dec. Sept. 1995); children: Rochelle, Debra. Student, Barton County C.C., Great Bend, Kans., Ft. Hays U. Author: (novels) Girl of the Prairie, 1975, Dark Knight, 1976, (play and activity) Birth and Childhood of Jesus, 1997, File Folder Games for the Christian Classroom, 1998, puzzle book, 2000; contbr. more than 1,000 short stories, articles to jours. Vol. Crisis Mgmt. Team, Great Bend. Vol. Crisis Ctr., Great Bend, Kans., 1997. Mem. Authors Guild, Great Plains Writers Assn. (v.p. 1996-98), Kans. Authors Club (past dist. pres., Outstanding Journalistic Achievement award 1984). Presbyterian. Avocations: reading, grandchildren. E-mail: mshauers@kscable.com.

SHAUGHNESSY, EDWARD LOUIS, Chinese language educator; b. Sewickley, Pa., July 29, 1952; s. James Francis and Marie Rosalie (Kraus) S.; m. Gina Lynn Look, May 15, 1976 (div. Sept. 1992); m. Elena Valussi, Sept. 6, 1997. BA, U. Notre Dame, 1974; MA, Stanford U., 1980, PhD, 1983. Asst. prof. U. Chgo., 1985-90, assoc. prof., 1990-96, prof., 1996—, Lorraine J. and Herrlee G. Creel prof. of early China. Assoc. editor: Early China, 1985-88, editor, 1988-96; editor: New Sources of Early Chinese History: An Introduction to the Reading of Inscriptions and Manuscripts, 1997, (with Michael Loewe) The Cambridge History of Ancient China: From the Origins of Civilization to 221 R.C., 1999, China Empire and Civilization, 2000; author: Sources of Western Zhou History: Inscribed Bronze Vessels, 1991, I Ching, The Classic of Changes: The First English Translation of the Newly Discovered Second-Century B.C. Mawangdui Manuscripts, 1996, Before Confucius: Studies in the Creation of the Chinese Classics, 1997, (with Robert Poor and Harrie A. Vanderstappen) Ritual and Reverence: Chinese Art at the University of Chicago, 1989, (with Cai Fangpei and James F. Shaughnessy) A Concordance of the Xiaotun Nandi Oracle-Bone Inscriptions, 1988; contbr. essays to books. Andrew W. Mellon fellow for Chinese studies, 1984-85, divsn. of humanities jr. faculty fellow U. Chgo., 1986 Home: 711 S Dearborn St Apt 506 Chicago IL 60605-3819 Office: U Chgo East Asian Langs/Civilizat 1050 E 59th St Chicago IL 60637-1559 E-mail: e-shaughnessy@uchicago.edu.

SHAUGHNESSY, MARIE KANEKO, artist, business executive; b. Detroit, Sept. 14, 1924; d. Eishiro and Kiyo (Yoshida) Kaneko; m. John Thomas Shaughnessy, Sept. 23, 1959. *Grandfather, Rokusaburo Kaneko, was a textile dealer and immigrated to the United States from Japan in 1905. They established the "Oriental Art Goods" Store on Washington Blvd. in downtown Detroit opposite the J.L. Hudson Company Bldg. Having no offspring, they adopted Kiyo Yoshida, a niece of Masa Yoshida Kaneko, and brought her to Detroit in 1919. Kiyo Yoshida is the biographer's mother. Rokusaburo and Masako Kaneko brought Eishiro Kaneko, a nephew of Rokusaburo, to the States. They married and bore five children all born in Detroit. Eishiro felt he faced certain imprisonment as a Japanese in the months prior to World War II and was very concerned about being separated from his children and their immediate safety. Addendum: Biographer's grandfather, Rokusaburo Kaneko, is listed in the congressional record in the Library of Congresss as a pioneer in Detroit.* Assocs. in Liberal Arts, Keisen Women's Coll., Tokyo, 1944. Ops. mgr. Webco Alaska, Inc., Anchorage, 1970-88; ptnr. Webco Partnership, 1983-98, also bd. dirs. Faculty Art League Sch., Alexandria, Va. *Operation Manager of Webo Alaska, Inc, which business was serving as broker, distributor and warehousing product for U.S. corporations whose focus was to provide consumer products to the residents of the great State of Alaska. These products included exclusive distributorships for Duracell Batteries, L'eggs Pantyhose, S.C. Johnson Wax Co. Swift & Company (Military Only), T.J. Lipton Tea Company (Military Only), Lever Bros. (now Unilever), Kimberly Clark, Quaker Oats, Anchor Hocking Glassware, Ragu Specialty Foods, Chesebrough —Ponds (now Unilever), Maybelline Sales Corp, Dr. Scholl & Company, Wrigley Gum, among others.* Paintings, (Purchase award, 1986). Bd. dirs. Alaska Artists Guild, 1971—87; commr. Mcpl. Anchorage Fine Arts Commn., 1983—87; organizing com. Japanese Soc. Alaska, 1987. Recipient Art Affiliate award, Anchorage C. of C., 1975, 1978, 1984, Univ. Artists award, Alaska Pacific U., 1986, Am. Juror's Choice award, Sumi-E Soc. Am., 1994, Ikebana Internat. award, 1994, Dorothy Klein Meml. award, 1995, Yasutomo Calligraphy award, 1997, 1998, Oriental Calligraphy award, 1997, 1998, Sarasota Chpt Painting award, 1999, Paul Schwartz Meml. award, 2001, Sm. Works Exhibit 1st Pl. award, Wash. Watercolor Assn., 2001. Mem.: Nat. League Am. Penwomen (Grumbacher Gold medal award excellence 1993), Vienna Art Soc. (bd. dirs. 1995—96), Sumi-E Soc. Am. (past pres. 1992—94, bd. dirs., Nat. Capital Area chpt. past pres. awards 1990, Nat. Capital Area chpt. award 1990—92, 1994, Purchase award 1993), Va. Watercolor Soc. (pres. 1993, co-chmn. 2004 All State Juried Show), Potomac Valley Watercolorists (exhibits chair 1989—93, bd. dirs. 1989—99, newsletter editor 1993—96, v.p., workshop chair 1996—2001, awards 1989, 1991, Spl. award 1995), Alaska Watercolor Soc. (life; charter, Grumbacher Silver medal 1989), McLean Arts Club (1st pl. award 1991). Republican. Roman Catholic. E-mail: markaneko@aol.com.

SHAUGHNESSY, THOMAS WILLIAM, librarian, consultant; b. Pitts., May 3, 1938; s. Martin T. and LaVerne (O'Brien) S.; m. Marlene D. Reuben, Aug. 11, 1968; 1 child, Mark Andrew. AB, St. Vincent Coll., 1961; MLS, U. Pitts., 1964; PhD, Rutgers U., 1970. Asst. dean Rutgers U., New Brunswick, N.J., 1969-71; libr. dir. Rutgers-Newark, 1971-74; assoc. dean U. So. Calif., L.A., 1974-78; asst. libr. dir. U. Houston, 1978-82; libr. dir. U. Mo.-Columbia, 1982-89; univ. libr. and dir. U. Minn., Mpls.-St. Paul, 1989—2002. Rsch. dir. Chgo. Pub. Libr. Survey, 1968-69; cons. U. Tulsa Libr., 1982-83; mem. faculty exch. U.S. Info. Agy., Poland, 1998; bd. trustees O.C.L.C., 1997—. Author: (with Lowell A. Martin) Library Response to Urban Change, 1969, Developing Leadership Skills: A Source Book for Librarians, 1990. U.S. Office Edn. grantee Rutgers U., 1971; fellow Coun. Libr. Resources, 1973, sr. fellow, 1985; recipient Hugh C. Atkinson Meml. award, 1996, Pres.'s award for Outstanding Svc. U. Minn., 2002. Mem. ALA, Assn. Coll. and Rsch. Librs., Assn. Rsch. Librs. (cons. tng. fellow 1981, bd. dirs. 1989-92), Minn. Libr. Assn. Home: 5705 Wycliffe Rd Minneapolis MN 55436-2264 E-mail: tws@umn.edu.

SHAUL, ROGER LOUIS, JR. health care consultant, software executive, researcher; b. Hartford, Conn., Jan. 12, 1948; s. Roger Louis Shaul Sr. and Margot (Bradley) Vinson; m. Michele Marie Morland, Dec. 21, 1974; children: Lisa Marie, John Benjamin, Robert Louis. AA, Palm Beach Jr. Coll., Lake Worth, Fla., 1968; BS, U. Fla., 1970, MBA, 1974; cert., Yale U., 1981, U. N.C., 1984, Harvard U., 1996. Adminstrv. resident Univ. Hosp. of Jacksonville, Fla., 1974-79; dir. rev. svcs. Capital Health Sys. Agy., Durham, N.C., 1979; dir. Sun Alliance, Charlotte, 1979-83; v.p. Sun Health, Inc., 1983-87; pres. Preferred Med. Mktg. Corp., 1987—. Adj. faculty, lectr. Duke U., Durham, 1974-78, U. N.C., Chapel Hill, 1974-78; cons. in field. Contbr. articles to profl. jours. Com. mem. Mecklenburg County chpt. ARC, Charlotte, 1985, bd. dirs. Durham County chpt., 1976-79, chmn. fin. com., 1979; mem. missions com. Myers Pk. United Meth. Ch., Charlotte, 1989-95. Mem.: Healthcare Fin. Mgmt. Assn., Am. Coll. Healthcare Execs., Am. Hosp. Assn., Mecklenburg Entrepreneurial Coun., Civitan (pres., v.p., sec. Durham chpt. 1976—79). Republican. Methodist. Avocations: boating, skiing. Office: Preferred Med Mktg Corp Ste 240 7400 Carmel Executive Park Dr 240 Charlotte NC 28226-8415

SHAUL, WILLIAM ROBERT, secondary school educator, coach; b. Amsterdam, N.Y., Feb. 21, 1947; s. Robert Edson Shaul and Clara Louise (Bell) Bronk. BA in Math., Syracuse U., 1969, MS in Edn., 1991, microcomputer certification, 1997. Cert. tchr., N.Y. Math. tchr., basketball coach Cherry Valley-Springfield Ctrl. Sch., N.Y., 1969—. Named on Wall of Fame, Nat. Tchrs. Hall of Fame. Mem. Am. Math. Soc., Assn. Math. Tchrs. State N.Y. (county chmn., dist. rep. 1969—), Nat. Coun. Tchrs. Math., Basketball Coaches Assn. N.Y. State, Nat. Assn. Basketball Coaches, Nat. H.S. Athletic Coaches Assn., Nat. Fedn. Interscholastic Coaches Assn., Nat. Strength and Conditioning Assn., Phi Delta Kappa. Home: 140 Maple Ave Canajoharie NY 13317-1528 Office: Cherry Valley-Springfield Valley Sch Cherry Valley NY 13320

SHAUNNESSY, GEORGE DANIEL, medical company executive; b. Joliet, Ill., Apr. 15, 1948; s. Daniel Joseph and Florence Elizabeth (Dunfee) S.; divorced; children: Katherine Erin, Daniel Joseph, Ellen Frances. BS in Indsl. Adminstrn., St. Louis U., 1970; MHA, Xavier U., Cin., 1973. With Hosp. Affiliates Internat., Inc., Nashville, 1973-80, regional dir., Miami, 1977-78, v.p. subs. Hosp. Affiliates Mgmt. Corp., 1978-79, v.p. hosp. ops. Southeast Group, Atlanta, 1979-80; v.p. hosp. ops. Charter Med. Corp., Macon, Ga., 1980-86; sr. v.p. hosp. ops., 1986-87; pres. Foster Med. Corp., Phila., 1987-88; pres. Nat. Healthcare Inc., Atlanta, 1988-91; pres., CEO Affiliated Healthcare Systems, Inc., Atlanta, 1991-94, also bd. dirs.; pres., CEO Housecall Med. Resources, Inc., Atlanta, 1994-97; mng. ptnr., CEO Affiliated Mgmt. Svcs., Inc., 1997—; dir. Hosp. Corp., Assisted Living Corp.; trustee, officer, dir. numerous hosps. Home: 130 Grogans Lake Dr Atlanta GA 30350-3114

SHAUT, ROBERT WILLIAM, music educator, composer; b. Albany, Ny, Dec. 10, 1950; s. Adelbert Elmer Shaut and Dorothy Grace Demarest; m. Linda Jean Woscio, Mar. 30, 1974; children: Daniel, Andrea, Gina, David. Bachelor's of Music, SUNY, Fredonia, NY, 1973. Elem. music tchr. Poughkeepsie City Schools, Poughkeepsie, NY, 1974—79, instrumental music tchr., 1979—86; saxophone instr. Vassar Coll., 1985—96; instrumental music tchr. grades 6-8 Kingston City Schools, Kingston, 1986—; jazz ensemble instr. Kingston H.S., 1997—. Mem.: AFL, Cio Musicians' Union Locals 238 215, Music Educators Nat. Conf., Internat. Assn. of Jazz Edn. Achievements include Several musical compositions performed by universities, high school, middle school ensembles; Guest conductor for several all-county bands / jazz ensembles. Avocations: little league coach, girls' softball coach. Home: 35 Genesee Avenue Lake Katrine NY 12449 Personal E-mail: liboshaut@aol.com.

SHAVELSON, MELVILLE, writer, theatrical producer and director; b. N.Y.C., Apr. 1, 1917; s. Joseph and Hilda (Shalson) S.; m. Lucille T. Myers, Nov. 2, 1938; children: Richard, Carol-Lynne. AB, Cornell U., 1937. Mem. faculty sch. profl. writing U. So. Calif., 1998—2002. Author: How to Make a Jewish Movie, 1970, Lualda, 1975, The Great Houdinis, 1976, The Eleventh Commandment, 1977, Ike, 1979, Don't Shoot, It's Only Me, 1990; writer Bob Hope Pepsodent Show, NBC radio, 1938-43; screenwriter The Princess and the Pirate, 1944, Wonder Man, 1944, Room for One More, 1951, I'll See You in My Dreams, 1952; screenwriter, dir. The Seven Little Foys, 1954, Beau James, 1956, Houseboat, 1957, The Five Pennies, 1958, It Started in Naples, 1959, On the Double, 1960, Yours, Mine and Ours, 1968, The War Between Men and Women, 1972, The Legend of Valentino, 1975, Deceptions, 1985; screenwriter, dir., producer The Pigeon That Took Rome, 1962, A New Kind of Love, 1963, Cast a Giant Shadow, 1966, Mixed Company, 1974, The Great Houdinis, 1976, Ike, 1979; dir. The Other Woman, 1983; creator TV shows including Danny Thomas Show, ABC-TV, 1953, My World— and Welcome To It, NBC-TV, 1969; author Broadway mus. Jimmy, 1969. Recipient Screen Writers Guild award, 1959, Christopher award, 1959, Sylvania TV award, 1953, Acad. Award nominations (screenplay), 1955, 58, Screen Writers Ann. award nominations (screenplay), 1952 (2), 58, 59, 62, 68, 72, 75, Screen Writers award (best written Am. mus.), 1959, Award of Merit United Jewish Appeal, 1966. Mem. Dirs. Guild Am., Writers Guild Am. (exec. bd. dirs 1960-75, 78, pres. screen writers br. 1967, pres. found. 1975-96, pres. emeritus

1997—, v.p. 1996—), Acad. Motion Picture Arts and Scis. (mem. bd. govs.), Writer Guild Am. West (pres. 1969-70, 79-81, 85-87, Valentine Davies award 1979, Laurel award 1984, Morgan Cox award 1998), Sigma Delta Chi. Home and Office: 11947 Sunshine Ter Studio City CA 91604-3708

SHAVER, JAMES PORTER, education educator, university dean; b. Wadena, Minn., Oct. 19, 1933; BA magna cum laude, U. Wash., Seattle, 1955; MA in Teaching, Harvard U., 1957, EdD, 1961. Instr. Grad. Sch. Edn., Harvard U., 1961-62; assoc. prof., dir. Social Studies Curriculum Ctr., Ohio State U., Columbus, 1964-65; mem. faculty Utah State U. Coll. Edn., Logan, 1962-64, prof., 1965—, chmn. Bur. Rsch. Svcs., 1965-93, assoc. dean rsch., 1978-93, acting dean Sch. Grad. Studies, 1990-91, 92-93, dean, 1993-99, prof. emeritus secondary edn., 1999—. Mem. Commn. Youth Edn. for Citizenship, ABA, 1975-81; mem. edn. task force Am. Hist. Assn.-Am. Polit. Sci. Assn. Project '87, 1981-84; tech. advisor Nat. Ctr. on Effective Secondary Schs., 1988-91; mem. adv. bd. program in civic and moral edn. Inst. for Philosophy and Pub. Policy, U. Md., 1992—; mem. steering com. Nat. Assessment Ednl. Progress Civics Consensus Project, 1995-96. Co-author: Teaching Public Issues in the High School, 1966, 2d edit., 1974, Facing Value Decisions: Rationale-building For Teachers, 1976, 2d edit., 1982; editor: Building Rationales for Citizenship Education, 1977, Handbook of Research on Social Studies Teaching and Learning, 1991; co-editor: Democracy, Pluralism, and the Social Studies, 1968; also others. Recipient Outstanding Svc. and Tchg. award Utah Coun. for the Social Studies, 1975, 78, Lifetime Achievement award, 1998. Mem. AAAS, AAUP, Nat. Coun. Social Studies (pres. 1976, Exemplary Rsch. award 1977, Exemplary Rsch. Editor award 1991), Am. Ednl. Rsch. Assn., Phi Beta Kappa, Phi Kappa Phi. Home: PO Box 176 Hyrum UT 84319-0176 Office: Utah State U 2815 Old Main Hill Logan UT 84322-2815 E-mail: shaver@cc.usu.edu.

SHAVER, JOAN LOUISE FOWLER, adult education educator; BS in Nursing, U. Alberta, Can., 1966; M in Nursing, U. Wash., 1968-70, PhD in Physiology and Biophysics, 1976. Nursing instr. chair med. surgical prog. Holy Cross Hosp. Sch. Nursing, Calgary, Can., 1966-68; staff nurse Virginia Mason Hosp., Seattle, 1970-71; asst. prof. Sch. Nursing U. Ariz., Tucson, 1976-77; assoc. prof. U. Calgary, Can., 1977-80; asst. prof. Dept. Physiological Nursing U. Wash., Seattle, 1980-85, rsch. affil. Regl. Primate Rsch. Ctr., 1983-86, assoc. prof., 1985-89, chair Dept. Physiological Nusring, 1988-95, prof., 1989-95, prof., chair Dept. Biobehavioral Nursing & Health Systems, 1995-96, co-dir. Ctr. Women's Health Rsch., 1989-96; prof., dean Coll. Nursing U. Ill., Chgo., 1996—, co-dir. Rsch. Core Nat. Ctr. Excellence in Women's Health, 1997—. Mem. editl. bd. Health Care for Women Internat., 1984—, Heart and Lung: The Jour. of Critical Care, 1988-90, Jour. of Applied Nursing Rsch., 1988-91, IMAGE: Jour. Nursing Scholarship, editl. adv. bd. Nursing Rsch., 1997—, Biol. Rsch. for Nursing, 1999—, Jour. Nursing Scholarship, 2000—; contbr. artilces to profl. jours. Abe Miller Meml. scholar Alberta Assn. Registered Nurses, 1968-69; Kathryn McLaggen Meml. fellow Can. Nurses Found., fellow Am. Acad. Nursing Am. Nurses Assn., 1988—. Office: U Ill Coll Nursing 845 S Damen Ave # Mc802 Chicago IL 60612-7350*

SHAVER, JUDSON RAYFORD, academic administrator; b. Riverside, Calif., July 29, 1949; s. John Robert and Carol Jean Shaver; m. Deborah Page Boyer, Aug. 27, 1988; children: Nathan Robert, Sarah Margaret. BA, So. Calif. Coll., 1975; MA, U. Notre Dame, 1979, PhD, 1984. Asst. prof. Wheeling (W.Va.) Jesuit Coll., 1980-85; assoc. prof. Seattle U., 1985-90; dean, assoc. prof. Regis U., Denver, 1990-95; provost, v.p. acad. affairs, prof. Iona Coll., New Rochelle, N.Y., 1995-2001; pres. Marymount Manhattan Coll., N.Y.C., 2001—. Author: Torah and the Chronicler's History Work, 1989; contbr. author: Ezra and Nehemiah: On the Theological Significance of Making Them Contemporaries, 1992, Passover Legislation and the Identity of the Chronicler's Law Book, 1990; co-author: Understanding the Sunday Readings, 1980. Still fellow, 1983, Fulbright fellow, 1988, Danforth fellow, 1979, NEH, 1985. Mem. Am. Acad. Religion, Soc. Bibl. Lit., Soc. Values in Higher Edn., Larchmont Shore Club. Roman Catholic. Avocations: golf, theatre. Office: Marymount Manhattan Coll 221 E 71st St New York NY 10021 E-mail: jshaver@iona.edu.

SHAVER, KAREN, performing company executive, educator, design educator; b. Louisville; Student in piano, U. Louisville; degree in design, Louisville Collegiate Sch., Auburn U. Pvt. practice in adv., 1975—90, 1984—90; ptnr., vice chmn., CFO Sheehy, Knopf, and Shaver, 1990; ret., 1993; CEO Louisville Ballet, 2001—. Tchr. effective bus. practices to fgn. countries; pvt. con. Romania, Bucharest; guest lectr. mktg., adv., bus. Ky. colls.; tchr. sr. level graphic design classes U. Louisville; designer costumes several small theatres, Atlanta; graphic artist, creative dir. adv. industry. 1st woman chmn. bd. trustees Spalding U.; vice chmn. Louisville Area C. of C.; chmn. Louie Creative Competition; mem. bd. dirs. Louisville Orch. Bd. Dirs.; mem. bd. dirs. Leadership Louisville, Jr. Achievement, Mary Anderson Ctr. for Arts, U. Louisville Bus. Sch. Adv. Coun., Friends U. Louisville Music Sch., Louisville Collegiate Sch. Mem.: Adv. Club Louisville (pres., chmn.). Office: 315 E Main St Louisville KY 40202-1215*

SHAVER, TIMOTHY RODDY, surgeon; b. Chattanooga, Jan. 12, 1956; s. Dean Marion and Doris Jane (Sharp) S.; m. Karen Schaal, 1994. BS in Biology, Ea. Tenn. State U., Johnson City, 1978; MD, U. Tenn., 1982. Commd. 2d lt. U.S. Army, 1982, advanced through grades to lt. col., 1994; surg. intern Tripler Army Med. Ctr., Honolulu, 1982-83, surg. resident, 1983-84; transplantation fellow U. Pitts., 1987-88; chief transplantation svcs. Walter Reed Army Med. Ctr., 1988-95; dir. abdominal transplation svcs. Fairfax Hosp., Falls Church, Va., 1995-2000; pvt. practice surgery, 2000—. Med. dir. Washington Regional Transplant Consortium, 1990-94. Fellow ACS, Am. Soc. Transplant Surgeons; mem. AMA, Nat. Kidney Found. Lutheran. Avocations: woodworking, basketball, softball, theater, golf. Office: 360 Maple Ave W Ste E Vienna VA 22180

SHAVER, WILLIAM ADAM, forester; b. Salisbury, NC, Apr. 17, 1948; s. Walter Clifford and Algie (Bame) Shaver; m. Rebecca Kay Meeks, Mar. 29, 1969; children: Deana Michelle Shaver Loflin, Kelly Evonne. BS in Forestry, NC State U., Raleigh, 1971; BS in Conservation, NC State U, Raleigh, 1971. Cert. forester NC State Bd. Registration for Foresters. Forester H.W. Culp Lumber Co., New London, NC, 1995—. Tree farm insp. Am. Tree Farm System, Washington, 2001—. Deacon East Corinth Baptist Ch., Gold Hill, NC. Mem.: Soc. Am. Foresters, N.C. Forestry Assn. Republican. Baptist. Avocations: songwriting, playing the guitar. Home: 1190 Shaver Rd Richfield NC 28137-8736

SHAW, ALAN, lawyer, corporate executive; b. Long Branch, N.J., July 23, 1930; m. Margaret Knight, Oct. 15, 1959; children: Andrew Macbeth, Adriane Macbeth. AB, U. Mich., 1952; LLB, Harvard U., 1955. Bar: Mass. 1955, N.Y. 1958. Atty. Skadden, Arps, Slate, Meagher & Flom, N.Y.C., 1958-65; v.p., gen. counsel, sec. Athlone Industries Inc., Parsippany, N.J., 1966-93, also bd. dirs. Adj. prof. of Law, Fordham U., 1996—; arbitrator Am. Arbitration Assn., Nat. Assn. of Securities Dealers Regulation, Inc., N.Y. Stock Exch. Mem. membership com. Jefferson Soc. Morristown Meml. Hosp.; panelist Contract Dispute Resolution Bd., City of N.Y. With U.S. Army, 1955-57. Mem. ABA (sect. on corps., alt. dispute resolution sect.), N.J. Gen. Counsel Group, Assn. Bar City N.Y., Soc. Profls. in Dispute Resolution, Morristown (N.J.) Club, Washington Assn. (Morristown), Morris County Golf Club (Convent Station, N.J.), Harvard Club (N.Y.C.). Home: 490 S Maple Ave Basking Ridge NJ 07920-1327 Office: 1812 Front St Scotch Plains NJ 07076

SHAW, ALAN BOSWORTH, geologist, paleontologist; b. Englewood, N.J., Mar. 28, 1922; s. Carroll Harper and Natalie Frederique (Howe) S.; m. Helen Louise Wilson, Nov. 2, 1945 (div. Apr. 1952); m. Marian Tavenner Stoll, Mar. 11, 1954 (dec. Apr. 1981); children: Nancy Jeanne, Sally Ann; m. Mary Elizabeth Merrem, Sept. 3, 1982. AB magna cum laude, Harvard Coll., 1946; AM, PhD, Harvard U., 1949. Asst. prof. geology U. Wyo., Laramie, 1949-55; paleontologist Shell Oil Co., Denver, 1955-60; owner Nat. Elec. Svc., N.Y.C., 1960-61; consulting geologist Denver, 1961; supr. Pan Am. Rsch. currently BPAmoco, Tulsa, Okla., 1961-68; various positions Pan Am. Petroleum, Denver, 1968-76; chief paleontologist Amoco Prodn., Chgo., 1976-77, chief geologist, 1977-81; geol. rsch. cons. Amoco Rsch., Tulsa, 1981-85; ret., 1985. Oil industry rep. NRC Com. on Paleontology, Washington, 1963-69; mem. Com. on Paleontology and Stratigraphy Deep Sea Drilling Program, 1973-75. Author: Time in Stratigraphy, 1964; contbr. numerous articles to profl. jours. Served to 1st lt., USAAF, 1943-45. Recipient Moore Paleontology medal Soc. Sedimentary Geology, 1996. Mem. Paleontol. Soc. (pres. 1968). Achievements include invention of graphic correlation system for use of fossils in making time correlations of sedimentary rocks. Home: 1315 Kamira Kerrville TX 78028-8867 E-mail: shaw99@ktc.com.

SHAW, ALAN ROGER, financial executive, educator; b. Bklyn., July 7, 1938; s. Sewall S. and Vera (Dimmick) S.; children: Stephen S., Todd J., Bradley C.; m. Mary Elizabeth Hogg, May 30, 1987. Student, Susquehanna U., 1957, Adelphi U., 1963-66; LLD (hon.), Susquehanna U., 1999. Analyst Harris Upham & Co., N.Y.C., 1958-71, asst. v.p., 1971-73, v.p., 1973-75; 1st v.p. Smith, Barney, Harris, Upham & Co., 1975-80; sr. v.p. Smith Barney, 1980—. Tchr. N.Y. Inst. Fin., 1966— Mem. Market Technicians Assn. (pres. 1974), N.Y. Soc. Security Analysts, Securities Industry Assn. Inst. (trustee 1986-92), Southward Ho Country Club, Unqua Corinthian Yacht Club (commodore 1988-90). Home: 87 Wagstaff Ln West Islip NY 11795-5206 Office: Salomon Smith Barney Inc 388 Greenwich St New York NY 10013-2339

SHAW, ANDREW R. performing arts association administrator; MBA, U. Toronto. Cert. mgmt. cons. Pres., CEO Frederick Harris Music Co., Ltd., 1987—2002, Toronto Symphony Orch., Canada, 2002—. Gen. mgr. Kitchener-Waterloo Symphony Orch., Can. Chamber Ensemble, Chamber Music Inst. and Festival Concerts; adj. prof. Schulich Sch. Bus., adv. coun. Musician (cello): Royal Winnipeg Ballet Orch. Active Bd. Music Toronto. Office: Toronto Symphony Orch 212 King St W Toronto M5H 1K5 Canada

SHAW, ANN, social worker, educator; b. Columbus, Ohio, Nov. 21, 1921; d. Pearl Daniel and Sarah Frank (Roberts) White; m. Leslie Nelson Shaw (dec.); children: Valerie Lynne, Leslie Jr., Rebecca. AB, U. Redlands, 1943; MA, Ohio State U., 1944; MSW, U. So. Calif., L.A., 1968; DHL (hon.), U. Redlands, 1971. Cert. tchr. with specialization in secondary edn. and jr. coll., Calif. Instr. Va. Union U., Richmond, 1944-46; asst. prof. Cen. State Coll., Wilberforce, Ohio, 1946-48; adminstrv. asst. Job Corps Ctr. for Women, L.A., 1963-65; instr. UCLA ext., 1968-70; with L.A. Neighborhood Initiative. Chmn. bd. founders Savs. & Loan Assn., L.A., 1986-87; bd. dirs. Lloyds Bank Calif., L.A., 1978-86, Calif. Med. Ctr. Found., 1986—, U. So. Calif. Sch. Social Work, 1989-99; mem. Calif. Commn. Jud. Performance, 1976-80, Calif. Cmty. Found., L.A., 1986-95, Citizens Rev. Panel Selection of Chiefs of Police, 1992, Cathedral Ctr. Corp. of Episcopal Diocese of L.A., 1986-96, L.A. Neighborhood Initiative Bd., 1994-97, Calif. Legis. Joint State Task Force on Family, 1988-91; mem. nat. bd. YWCA L.A., 1963; corp. bd. dirs., met. bd. United Way, 1983-92; v.p., bd. dirs. L.A. Urban League, 1980-86; bd. counselors U. So. Calif. Sch. Social Work, 1987-99; mem. Black Women of Achievement, NAACP Legal Def. and Ednl. Fund, 1986-90; mem. Mayor's Task Force on Econ. Devel. for South Cen. L.A., 1989-92. Recipient Vol. of Yr. award NASW, 1975, Woman of Yr. award Calif. State Legis., 1987, Mayor's Cert. of Appreciation, 1987, award Calif. Welfare Archives, 1996. Episcopalian.

SHAW, ANTHONY, physician, pediatric surgeon; b. Shanghai, China, Oct. 31, 1929; s. Bruno and Regina (Hyman) S.; m. Iris Violet Azian, Mar. 12, 1955; children: Brian Anthony, Diana Shaw Clark, Daniel Aram. BA cum laude, Harvard Coll., 1950; MD, NYU, 1954. Diplomate Am. Bd. Surgery; cert. spl. competence pediat. surgery. Intern and resident in surgery Columbia-Presbyn. Med. Ctr., N.Y.C., 1954-56, 58-62; resident in pediat. surgery Babies Hosp., 1962; asst. prof. surgery Columbia U. Coll. Physicians and Surgeons, 1965-70; chief pediat. surgery St. Vincent's Hosp., 1963-70, Harlem Hosp. Ctr., N.Y.C., 1965-70; prof. surgery U. Va., Charlottesville, 1970-81, chief pediat. surgery Med. Ctr., 1970-81; prof. surgery UCLA, 1981-2001, emeritus prof. surgery, 2001—; chief pediat. surgery Olive View-UCLA Med. Ctr., Sylmar, 1986-2001. Expert witness on child abuse L.A. Superior Ct., 1986—; chmn. gov.'s adv. com. child abuse and neglect Commonwealth of Va., 1975-80; vis. prof. pediat. surgery People's Republic of China, 1985. Contbr. more than 220 articles to profl. jours. Mem. Gov.'s Task Force on Child Abuse Va., 1973-74. Capt. U.S. Army, 1956-58. Recipient Commrs. award Va. Dept. Social Svcs., 1980, award Gov.'s Adv. Bd., Cert. of Recognition HEW, 1978. Fellow Am. Pediat. Surg. Assn. (sec. 1982-85), ACS (v.p. 1987-89); mem. AMA, Pacific Coast Surg. Assn. (v.p. 1989-90), Am. Soc. Law, Medicine, and Ethics, Am. Profl. Soc. on Abuse of Children, Alpha Omega Alpha. Avocations: writing humor, grandchildren. Home and Office: One S Orange Grove Blvd # 9 Pasadena CA 91105 E-mail: shawpas@pacbell.net.

SHAW, ARTIE, musician, writer, lecturer; b. N.Y.C., May 23, 1910; s. Harry and Sarah Shaw; m. Margaret Allen; m. Lana Turner; m. Elizabeth Kern; 1 son, Steven Kern; m. Ava Gardner (div. Oct. 1946); m. Kathleen Winsor, Oct. 28, 1946; m. Doris Dowling (div.); 1 son, Jonathan; m. Evelyn Keyes, 1957 (div. June 1985). Extension work in lit., Columbia U.; MusD (hon.), U. Nebr., 1938, LittD (hon.); LHD (hon.), Calif. Luth. U., 1987; DFA (hon.), U. Ariz., 1995. Former owner firm Shooters Svc. and Dewey (gun mfrs.); pres. Artixo Prodns., Ltd. (film distbn. co.); lectr. colls. and univs.; ann. lectr. U. Calif., Santa Barbara, Oxnard Coll., Camarillo, Calif., Yale U., U. Pa., Memphis U. Orch. leader, 1936-54; appeared in motion pictures Dancing Coed, Second Chorus; also engaged in film, theatrical prodn.; producer Broadway mus. The Great Gatsby; recipient Downbeat award best Am. swing band, Esquire Mag. Poll award as favorite band of armed services, Hall of Fame award for rec. Begin the Beguine; Stardust, Nat. Acad. Rec. Arts and Scis. 1977); condr., composer numerous songs and orchestral works including Concerto for Clarinet; author: A Clarinet Method; The Trouble with Cinderella; I Love You, I Hate You, Drop Dead! Three Variations on a Theme; The Best of Intentions, and Other Stories, 1989. Former mem. exec. council, bd. Hollywood Ind. Citizens Com. Arts, Scis. and Professions. Served with USNR, 1942-44. Recipient Presdl. award Am. Soc. Mus. Arrangers, 1990. Achievements include being subject of film: Artie Shaw: Time is All You've Got (Academy Award for best feature-length documentary 1986).

SHAW, BARRY N. lawyer; b. Newark, July 31, 1940; s. Harry G. and Evelyn (Kruger) S.; m. Cheryl Lynn Rosen, Mar. 24, 1963; children: Jennifer B., Jonathan M. BS in Acctg., Rutgers U., 1962, LLB, 1965. Bar: Pa. 1966, N.J. 1974, U.S. Supreme Ct. 1988, Oreg. 1996; CPA, Pa. Tax supr. Coopers & Lybrand, Phila., 1965-68; corp. counsel Lincoln Bank, 1968-72, Waste Resources Corp., Phila., 1972-74; ptnr. Spivack, Dranoff & Shaw, 1974-75, Dranoff & Shaw, Phila., 1975-79, Jubanyik, Varbalow Tedesco Shaw & Shaffer, Cherry Hill, N.J., 1979-95, Dilworth, Paxson, Kalish & Kauffman (successor firm), Cherry Hill, 1995-97, Davis, Gilstrap, Hearn & Shaw PC, Ashland, Oreg., 1997-2000, Grantland, Blodgett & Shaw, LLP, Medford, 2000—. Lectr. in banking and real estate law. Author: Selected Decisions in Lender Liability Law, 1990, Environmental Lender Liability, 1992. Chmn. Shamong Twp. (N.J.) Planning Bd., 1990-93, Local Civic Assn.; active Shamong Twp. Com., 1993-97; mayor Shamong Twp., 1995; sec. Pinelands Mcpl. (Mayors') Coun., 1996-97. Mem. Oreg. State Bar, Jackson County Bar Assn., Rotary (pres. 2001-2002). Republican. Avocations: farming, writing. Office: Grantland Blodgett & Shaw LLP 1818 E McAndrew Rd Medford OR 97504 Fax: 541-770-1290. E-mail: bshaw@mighty.net.

SHAW, BRAD, information technology executive; b. Apr. 10, 1966; B in Journalism, Washington and Lee U. With Doremus Pub. Rels.; sr. account mgr. Ketchum Pub. Rels., N.Y.C.; dir. worldwide pub. rels. PepsiCo, Purchase; v.p. corp. comms. Gateway, Poway, Calif., 1999, now sr. v.p. corp. comms. Bd. dirs. San Diego Regional C. of C. Office: Gateway 14303 Gateway Pl Poway CA 92064 Office Fax: 858-848-3402.*

SHAW, BYERS WENDELL, surgeon, retired; b. Knox County, Ohio, Feb. 7, 1920; MD, Case Western Res. U., 1945. Diplomate Am. Bd. Surgery. Intern U. Hosps., Cleve., 1945-47, resident, 1947-50, now ret., 1989. Fellow ACS; mem. AMA.

SHAW, CAROLE, editor, publisher; b. Bklyn., Jan. 22, 1936; d. Sam and Betty (Neckin) Bergenthal; m. Ray Shaw, Dec. 27, 1957; children: Lori Eve Cohen, Victoria Shaw Locknar. BA, Hunter Coll., 1962. Singer Capitol Records, Hilton Records, Rama Records, Verve Records, 1952-65; TV appearances Ed Sullivan, Steve Allen, Jack Paar, George Gobel Show, 1957; owner The People's Choice, L.A., 1975-79; founder, editor-in-chief Big Beautiful Woman mag., Beverly Hills, Calif., 1979—. Creator Carole Shaw and BBW label clothing line for large-size women. Author: Come Out, Come Out Wherever You Are, 1982. Avocations: piano, painting, swimming, travel. Office: BBW Mag 6666 Brookmont Ter Apt 412 Nashville TN 37205-4622

SHAW, CHARLES ALDEN, engineering executive; b. Detroit, June 8, 1925; s. Fred Alden and Amy (Ellis) S.; m. Barbara Loveland, Mar. 9, 1963 (div. 1979); children: Amy Elizabeth, Polly Nicole; m. Jeanne Steves Partridge, Apr. 22, 1989. BS, Harvard U., 1945; MSEE, Syracuse U., 1958. Test and design engr. G.E., Syracuse-Schenectady, N.Y., 1947-51; chief engr. electronics divsn. Onondaga Pottery Co., Syracuse, 1951-60; mgr. semiconductor div. G.E., Syracuse-Schenectady, 1960-66; cons. to gen. dir. Bull-G.E., Paris, 1966-69; mgr. CAD sect. integrated cir. product dept. G.E., Syracuse, 1969-71, mgr. CAD ctr. solid state applied ops., 1971-78, mgr. computer support solid state applied ops., 1978-81; dir. CAD G.E. Intersil, Cupertino, Calif., 1981-88; cons. in field, 1988-89; mgr. tech. program Cadence Design Systems, Santa Clara, Calif., 1989—. Trustee Hidden Villa, Los Altos Hills, Calif., 1986—92; bd. dirs. Unitarian Universalist ch. , Livermore, 1999—2002. With USN, 1942—45, PTO. Mem. IEEE, Assn. Computing Machinery (chmn. spl. interest group SIGDA 1986-91), Design Automation Conf. (exec. bd. 1985-95), Harvard Club of Silicon Valley. Democrat. Unitarian Universalist. Avocations: skiing, scuba diving, music. Home: 4925 Monaco Dr Pleasanton CA 94566-7671 Office: 555 River Oaks Pkwy San Jose CA 95134-1917 E-mail: shawcha@attbi.com., shaw@cadence.com.

SHAW, CHARLES RAYMOND, journalist; b. Phila., Feb. 2, 1951; s. Charles Raymond Sr. and Dorothy Blanche (Buckman) S.; m. Francine Ruth Pennock, Jan. 14, 1983. BS in Journalism, Temple U., 1972; MS in Journalism, Columbia U., 1973. Staff writer Intelligencer Jour., Lancaster, Pa., 1973-83, asst. news editor, 1983-88, news editor, 1989-97, editor, 1997—. Mem. Pa. Soc. of Newspaper Editors, Am. Soc. Newspaper Editors, Pa. Assoc. Press (bd. dirs.). Office: Lancaster Newspapers Inc Intelligencer Jour 8 W King St Lancaster PA 17603-3824 E-mail: rshaw@lnpnews.com.

SHAW, CHARLES RUSANDA, government investigator; b. Detroit, Aug. 17, 1914; s. Leonard George and Harriet (Kratzer) S.; m. Sally Madeline Jock, May 3, 1947 (dec. June 1996); children: Patrick R., Sandra L. Keding (dec.), Janice L., Lisa Keding; stepchildren: Lillian Genna, Ruth Czenkus. Cert., Wicker Sch. of Fine Arts, 1936, Mich. Acad. Advt. Art, 1937; student, Intelligence Corps Sch., 1947. Freelance artist, Detroit, 1936-39; spl. agt. U.S. Army Counter Intelligence Corps, Washington, 1947-48, Office Spl. Investigations, USAF, Washington, 1948-66; pvt. investigator Charles Shaw Assocs., Mt. Clemens, Mich., 1966-84; contract investigator USAF & U.S. Customs Svc., Washington, 1984-94; entrepreneur-inventor neoteric products, patents pending C.R. Shaw Assocs., 1994—. Author: Immaculate Misconception, 1999. Master sgt. U.S. Army, 1939-45, PTO, ETO. Mem. Assn. Former OSI Spl. Agts. (chartered), Pearl Harbor Survivors Assn. Democrat. Roman Catholic. Avocations: fine arts, photography, gardening, home improvements. Home and Office: 59295 Bates Rd New Haven MI 48048-1728

SHAW, DANNY WAYNE, secondary education educator, consultant; b. Detroit, Jan. 18, 1947; s. George L. and Nina Margarete (Smith) S.; m. 2d Nancy Rivard Shaw, Feb. 29, 1980; 1 child, Christina Marie. BS, Wayne State U., 1973, MusM, 1975, EdS, 1979, PhD, 1982. Tchr. Dearborn (Mich.) Pub. Schs., 1973-74, Lincoln Park (Mich.) Schs., 1974-98. Pres. System Support Services, Lincoln Park, Trenton, Mich., 1982-98; rsch. asst. Wayne State U., 1980-81, adj. faculty, 1981-85; adj. faculty Marygrove Coll., Detroit, 1984. Mem. music adv. panel mich. Coun. Arts, 1976-84; mem. cultural commn. city of Trenton, 1997-98; mem. Leadership Beaufort Class 2000, pres. 2002—; bd. dirs. Beaufort Orch., 2001—. With USMC, 1965-68, Vietnam. Decorated Vietnam Svc. medal, Nat. Def. Svc. medal, Presdl. Unit citation, Campaign medal Rep. Vietnam; recipient cert. for outstanding acad. achievement Mich. Ho. Reps., 1975. Mem. VFW, Masons, Phi Delta Kappa. Home: 22 Brisbane Dr Beaufort SC 29902-5296

SHAW, DAVID ELLIOT, financial executive; b. Chgo., Mar. 29, 1951; s. Charles B. Jr. and Marilyn (Baron) S. BA, U. Calif., San Diego, 1972; MS, Stanford U., 1975, PhD, 1980. Pres. Stanford Systems Corp., Palo Alto, Calif., 1976-79; assoc. prof. Columbia U., N.Y.C., 1980-86; v.p. Morgan Stanley & Co., 1986-88; chmn. D.E. Shaw & Co., Inc. and Juno Online Svcs., Inc., 1988—. Schrödinger, Inc., N.Y.C., 1988—. Contbr. articles to profl. jours. Chmn. N.Y.C. Mayor's Panel on Tech. and Fin., 1987; mem. N.Y.C. Partnership Subcom. on Tech. and Fin., 1987; apptd. to Pres. Clinton's Com. of Advisors on Sci. and Tech., 1994; chmn. Pres. Clinton's Panel on Ednl. Tech., 1995. Mem. AAAS (bd. dirs. 1999), N.Y. Acad. Scis. (bd. govs. 1993-95), Coun. on Competitiveness (exec. com. 1998—). Democrat. Jewish.

SHAW, DAVID LYLE, journalist, writer; b. Dayton, Ohio, Jan. 4, 1943; s. Harry and Lillian (Walton) S.; m. Alice Louise Eck, Apr. 11, 1965 (div. Sept. 1974); m. Ellen Torgerson, July 17, 1979 (dec.); stepchildren: Christopher, Jordan; m. Lucy Stille, Apr. 14, 1988; 1 child, Lucas. BA in English, UCLA, 1965. Reporter Huntington Park Signal (Calif.), 1963-66, Long Beach Independent (Calif.), 1966-68, L.A. Times, 1968-74, media critic, 1974—. Author: WILT: Just Like Any Other 7-Foot, Black Millionare Who Lives Next Door, 1973, The Levy Caper, 1974, Journalism Today, 1977, Press Watch, 1984, The Pleasure Police, 1996; contbr. numerous articles to mags. including Gentlemen's Quar., Cigar Aficionado, Esquire, TV Guide, Bon Appetit, Food & Wine. Recipient Mellet Fund Nat. award, 1983, PEN West award, 1990, Calif. Bar Assn. Gold Medallion, 1990, Pulitzer Prize for disting. criticism, 1991, Soc. Profl. Journalists Non-Deadline Reporting award, 1999. Office: LA Times Times Mirror Sq Los Angeles CA 90012 E-mail: david.shaw@latimes.com.

SHAW, DAVID TAI-KO, electrical and computer engineering educator, university administrator; b. China, Mar. 13, 1938; came to U.S., 1960, naturalized, 1972; m. Katharine Lin-Yee Yang; children: Albert, Stanley. BSM.E., Nat. Taiwan U., Taipei, 1959; MS in Nuclear Engring., Purdue U., 1961, PhD, 1964. Asst. prof. div. interdisciplinary studies and research Sch. Engring., SUNY-Buffalo, 1964-67, assoc. prof. faculty engring. and applied scis., 1967-74, prof. elec. engring. and nuclear engring., aerospace and engring. sci., 1974-77, prof. elec. engring., 1974—, dir. lab. for power and environ. studies, 1978—. Exec. dir. State Inst. on Superconductivity, 1987-97; vis. prof. U. Paris, 1976-77; vis. scientist Centre d'Etudes Nucleairs de Fontenay-aux-Roses (France) Commissariat a L'Energie Atomique, 1976-77; vis. assoc. dept. environ. health engring. Calif. Inst. Tech., 1970-71; mem. U.S. del. French Commissariat a L'energie ATomique, 1974, U.S. del. Joint Nuclear Energy Agy. IAEA Internat. Liaison Group on Thermionic Elec. Power Generation, Paris, 1974; mem. U.S. vis. team USSR Acad. Scis. Editor: Fundamentals of Aerosol Science, 1978, Recent Developments in Aerosol Science, 1978, Assessment of Airborne Radioactivity, 1978; editor-in-chief: Jour. Aerosol Sci. and Tech., 1982-93; contbr. numerous articles to profl. publs. Mem. IEEE, ASME, AAAS, Am. Assn. Aerosol Rsch. (pres. 1982-85, Assn. award 1984, Internat. Aerosol Fellow award 1994), Sigma Xi, Sigma Pi Sigma. Office: SUNY-Buffalo Materials Rsch Lab/Ctr for Innovation Engring 330 Bonner Hall Buffalo NY 14260-1900 E-mail: dshaw@eng.buffalo.edu.

SHAW, DAVID WILLIAM, engineering educator; b. Whittier, Calif., Jan. 10, 1961; s. William Franklin and Mary Lou (LeMahieu) S.; m. Valerie Anne Arnold, Aug. 24, 1985; children: Kirsten, Rebecca, Evan, Adam. BSME, Geneva Coll., Beaver Falls, Pa., 1983; MSME, Ohio State U., 1986, PhD in Mech. Engring., 1988. Registered profl. engr., Pa. Grad. rsch. assoc. combustion lab. dept. mech. engring. Ohio State U., Columbus, 1983—88; mech. engr. process and reactor engring. br. Morgantown Energy Tech. Ctr., U.S. Dept. Energy, 1988-90; assoc. prof. mech. engring. Geneva Coll., Beaver Falls, 1996—2001, prof. mech. engring., 2001—. Mech. engr. high temp. reacting flows group Nat. Bur. Stds., summers, 1984, 85; summer faculty rschr. Oak Ridge Assoc. Univs., Pitts. Energy Tech. Ctr., summer 1992-95, 96, 99, Nat. Energy Tech. Lab., Pitts., 2000-2002. Contbr. articles to profl. jours. Dept. of Energy grad. trainee, 1985-86 Mem. ASME, Am. Soc. Engring. Edn. Republican. Presbyterian. Avocations: camping, music, canoeing. Office: Geneva College Dept Engring 3200 College Ave Dept Engring Beaver Falls PA 15010-3599

SHAW, DENIS MARTIN, university dean, former geology educator; b. St. Annes, Eng., Aug. 20, 1923; emigrated to Can., 1948; s. Norman Wade and Alice Jane Sylvia (Shackleton) S.; m. Pauline Mitchell, Apr. 6, 1946 (div.

1975); children— Geoffrey, Gillian, Peter; m. Susan L. Evans, Apr. 9, 1976. BA, Emmanuel Coll., Cambridge, Eng., 1943, MA, 1948; PhD, U. Chgo., 1951. Lectr. McMaster U., Hamilton, Ont., Can., 1949-51, asst. prof., 1951-55, asso. prof., 1955-60, prof. geology, 1960-89, prof. emeritus, 1989—, chmn. dept., 1953-59, 62-66, dean grad. studies, 1978-84. Assoc. prof. Ecole nationale supérieure de géologie appliquée, U. Nancy, France, 1959-60; invited prof. Inst. de Minéralogie, U. Genève, 1966-67 Exec. editor: Geochimica et Cosmochimica Acta, 1970-88; asso. editor: Handbook of Geochemistry, 1966—; Author: Masson Et Cie, 1964. Served with RAF, 1943-46. Fellow Royal Soc. Can. (W.G. Miller medal 1981); mem. Geol. Assn. Can., Geochem. Soc., Mineral. Assn. Can. (pres. 1964, Past Pres.' medal 1985), Am. Geophys. Union, AAAS, Geol. Soc. of Am. Address: McMaster U Sch Geography & Geology Hamilton ON Canada L8S 4M1

SHAW, DIANE D. retired elementary school educator, retired counseling administrator, volunteer; b. Fayetteville, Ark., Aug. 26, 1941; d. Robert Larry and Myra Fergus DeWese; m. Bobby G. Shaw, Dec. 27, 1961; children: Sherri Shaw Dillard, Brian Robert. BA, So. Meth. U., 1964; MEd, U. Ark., 1970. Elem. tchr. Springdale (Ark.) Pub. Schs., 1965—67, elem. counselor, 1978—88. Hon. chmn. Ozark Race for the Cure, Fayetteville, 2000; bd. dirs. Ozark Guidance Ctr., Springdale, 1992—, Single Parent Scholarship Fund, Springdale, 1993—, Arts Ctr. of the Ozarks, Springdale, 2000—. Mem.: Beta Sigma Phi. Methodist. Avocations: golf, gardening, snow skiing, hiking, travel.

SHAW, DIANNE ELIZABETH, school administrator; b. Greenville, Tex., Feb. 9, 1950; d. Charles V. Marshall and Margaret Virginia (Cowen) Johnson; m. Gary Allen Shaw, June 8, 1968; children: Daniel Phillip, Andrew Joseph. BA, East Tex. State U., 1978; MEd, Stephen F. Austin U., 1996. Cert. tchr., Tex.; cert. elem. edn. grades 1-8 and English; mid-mgmt. cert. Asst. ctr. supr. recreation dept. City of Arlington, Tex., 1968-73; substitute tchr. Quitman (Tex.) Ind. Sch. Dist., 1974-78; youth dir. 1st United Meth. Ch., Quitman, 1976-78; tchr. 1st grade Pine Tree Ind. Sch. Dist., Longview, Tex., 1978-81; kindergarten tchr. 1st Christian Ch., 1981-88; lead tchr., math. coord., environ. coord. K-12 Trinity Sch. of Tex., 1988-96; head of sch. St. Cyprian's Episcopal Sch., Lufkin, Tex., 1996-2001, Trinity Episcopal Sch., Marshall, 2001—. Elected to Diocese of Tex. Schs. Commn., 2000; pres. East Tex. Heads of Sch., 1999-2001. Leadership Lufkin grad., 1999; organizer comty. recycling project Trinity Sch. of Tex., Longview, 1994; mem. Angelina Beautiful Clean, C. of C., Lufkin, Tex., 1996-2001, mem. drug task force, 1996-2001; mem. Chamber Coalition for Better Cmty., 1999-2001; adv. com. Tex. State Tech. Coll., Marshall, 2002-; elected bd. dirs. Marshall Regional Arts Coun., 2001-. Presdl. scholar East Tex. State U., 1978; tech. grantee T.L.L. Temple Found., 1998, 99, 2000. Mem. ASCD, DAR, Nat. Assn. Episcopal Schs., Southwestern Assn. Episcopal Schs. (accrediting team 1995—, chair accrediting team 1998-99), Tex. Assn. Non-Pub. Schs. (regional dir. fall 1998—), So. Assn. Colls. and Schs. (Tex. state chair elem. and mid. schs. com. 2000—, exec. com. commn. on elem. and mid. schs. 2000—), SACS Commn. on Elem. and Middle Schs. (elected comn. mem. 1999—), Marshall C. of C. (edn. com. 2001—), Marshall Rotary Club, Phi Delta Kappa. Episcopalian. Avocations: reading, hiking, cross-country skiing. Office: Trinity Episcopal Sch 2905 Rosborough Springs Marshall TX 75672 E-mail: dshawtes@shreve.net.

SHAW, DONALD HARDY, lawyer; b. Oelwein, Iowa, June 1, 1922; s. John Hardy and Minnie (Brown) S.; m. Elizabeth Jean Orr, Aug. 16, 1946; children: Elizabeth Ann, Andrew Hardy, Anthony Orr. BS, Harvard U., 1942; JD, U. Iowa, 1948. Bar: Ill. 1949, Iowa 1948, cert. fin. planner 1983. With firm Sidley & Austin, Chgo., 1948-55; with Iowa-Ill. Gas & Electric Co., Davenport, Iowa, 1956-87, treas., 1960-72, v.p. finance, 1973-87, also dir.; of counsel Walton, Creen, Curry and Robertson, Davenport, Iowa, 1987-88, Newpor, Bell, Leon & Martinez, Davenport, 1989-98. Mem. Iowa State Bd. Regents, 1969-81, Iowa State TV-Radio Com., 1976-81; trustee St. Luke's Hosp., Davenport, 1966-91. Served to capt. USAAF, 1942-45. Recipient Philo Sherman Bennett award, 1942 Mem. Rock Island Arsenal Club, Outing Club, Harvard Club N.Y.C., Order of Coif, Duck Creek Tennis Club, Delta Theta Phi. Congregationalist. Home: 29 Hillcrest Ave Davenport IA 52803-3726

SHAW, DONALD LESLIE, Spanish language educator; b. Feb. 11, 1930; s. Stephen Leslie and Lily (Hughes) S.; m. Maria Concetta Cristini, June 30, 1958; children: Andrew Leslie, Sylvia Maria Pierina. BA, U. Manchester, Eng., 1952, MA, 1953; PhD, U. Dublin, Ireland, 1960. Asst. lectr. U. Dublin, 1955-57, U. Glasgow, Scotland, 1957-64, U. Edinburgh, Scotland, 1964-69, sr. lectr. Scotland, 1969-72, reader, prof. spanish Scotland, 1972-86; prof. spanish U. Va., Charlottesville, 1986—. Vis. prof. Brown U., Providence, 1967, U. Va., Charlottesville, 1983. Author: Historia de la Literatura Española, Siglo XIX, 1973, La Generación del 98, 1977, Nueva Narrativa Hispanoamericana, 1981, Alejo Carpentier, 1985, Borges' Narrative Strategies, 1992, Antonio Skármeta and the Post-Boom, 1994, The Post-Boom in Spanish American Fiction, 1998, A Companion to Spanish American Fiction, 2001. Served with RAF, 1953-55. Avocation: cycling. E-mail: dls6h@vriginia.edu. Home: 1800 Jefferson Park Ave Charlottesville VA 22903-3554 Office: U Va 115 Wilson Hall Charlottesville VA 22903-3238 Business E-Mail: dls@virginia.edu .

SHAW, DONALD RAY, lawyer; b. Hugo, Okla., Nov. 29, 1945; s. Jesse Vernon and Velma Lee (Atkinson) S.; m. Nelda Jan Finley, May 31, 1969; children: Britton, Taylor. BBA, U. Okla., 1968, JD, 1975. Bar: Okla. 1975, U.S. Dist. Ct. Okla. 1978, U.S. Ct. Appeals (10th cir.) 1980. Pvt. practice law, Idabel, Okla., 1975-77, 87—; dist. atty. Dist. 17, 1978-87. Sec., treas. McCurtain County Dem. Party, 1989-91. Lt. col. USAFR., 1969-95. Mem. ABA, Okla. Bar Assn., Okla. CPA's, Gideons (treas. 1980-86), Am. Legion (comdr. 1976-78, judge advocate 1978—), Res. Officers Assn. (life, v.p. Okla. chpt. 1989-91, pres. 1994-95), Lions (bd. dirs. 1985-86, 90-93). Lodges: Lions (bd. dirs. 1985-86), Elks. Democrat. Presbyterian. Home: 1312 E Madison Idabel OK 74745-5716 Office: 101 NE 3rd St PO Box 957 Idabel OK 74745-0957

SHAW, DORIS BEAUMAR, film and video producer, executive recruiter, management consultant; b. Pitts., July 13, 1934; d. Emerson C. and Doris Llorene (Rees) Beaumar; m. Robert Newton Shaw, July 6, 1957. BA summa cum laude, Lindenwood Coll., St. Charles, Mo., 1955. Writer, asst. to pres. Baker Prodns., Benton Harbor, Mich., 1955; asst. prodn. mgr. Condor Films, Inc., St. Louis, 1955-57; chief editor, asst. to v.p. Frederick F. Watson Inc., N.Y.C., 1957-58; v.p. Gen. Pictures Corp., Cleve., 1958-71; dir., editor, unit mgr. Cinecraft Inc., 1971-72; mgr. audio-visual dept. Am. Greetings Corp., 1972-73; proprietor Script to Screen Svcs., Chagrin Falls, Ohio, 1973-76; pres. D & B Shaw, Inc., Chardon, 1976-87, Hudson, 1987—, Execusearch, Inc., Hudson, 1987—, Infosearch Inc., Hudson, 1994—, Cybersearch, Inc., Hudson, 1995—. Film festival judge, tchr. Martha Holden Jennings Found./Hawken Sch., Gates Mills, Ohio, 1970-85; advisor teenage film contests, seminars Cleve. Bd. Edn., 1970-88; contest judge/film and video WVIZ-TV, Channel 25, Parma, Ohio, 1971—; guest lectr. Lindenwood Coll., 1973-80; adj. prof. U. Akron, 1990—; cons. to bus. and industry regarding sales, mktg., bus. mgmt., info. and rsch. svcs., computer multimedia prodn., web page design and devel. Writer, dir., editor, prodr. hundreds of film, video, multi-image, multi-media, audio/visual prodn., radio, TV commls. and programs; contbr. articles to profl. jours. Bd. trustees Ohio Boys Town, Cleve., 1957-68; mem. alumnae coun. Lindenwood Coll., 1973-77; publicity chmn. Geauga County Preservation Soc., 1984-91; active various charitable orgns. Named Outstanding Young Woman of Am., Fedn. of Women's Clubs, 1965, Alumna of Yr. Merit award Lindenwood Coll., 1971; recipient numerous awards and grants for film, video projects including Gold Camera Best Documentary award, 1979. Mem. Soc. Motion Picture and TV Engrs., Info. Film Prodrs. Am., Assn. for Multi Image (charter), Detroit Prodrs. Assn., Internat. TV and Video Assn. (charter), Internat. Comm. Industries Assn., Alpha Epsilon Rho. Republican. Avocations: science, travel, physical fitness, environmental issues, organic horticulture. Office: D & B Shaw Inc PO Box 335 Peninsula OH 44264-0335

SHAW, E. CLAY, JR. (CLAY SHAW), congressman; b. Miami, FL, Apr. 19, 1939; s. E. Clay and Rita (Walker) S.; m. Emilie Costar, Aug. 22, 1960; children: Emilie, Jennifer, E. Clay, John C. BS, Stetson U., 1961, JD, 1966; MBA, U. Ala., 1963. Bar: Fla. 1967; CPA, Fla. Asst. city atty. City of Ft. Lauderdale, 1968, chief city pros., 1968-69, assoc. mcpl. judge, 1969-71, city commr., 1971-73, vice mayor, 1973—75, mayor, 1975-80; mem. U.S. Congress from 22nd (formerly 15th) Fla. dist., 1981—; mem. ways and means com.; chmn. subcom. on human resources, 1995-98; chmn. social security subcom., 1999—. U.S. spl. ambassador to Papua New Guinea Independence; pres. U.S. Conf. Republican Mayors; mem. adv. and exec. bd. U.S. Conf. Mayors.; former chmn. mcpl. div. Ft. Lauderdale United Fund Campaign, 1971; former Young Rep. Club Broward County, Ft. Lauderdale Rep. Exec. Com.; past mem. exec. com. Rep. Nat. Com.; former mem. house select com. narcotics abuse and control; past bd. dirs. Broward County Traffic Assn.; mem judiciary com. Pub. Works and Transp. Bd. overseers Stetson Coll. Law. Home: 700 Coral Way Fort Lauderdale FL 33301-2532 Office: US Ho of Reps 2408 Rayburn Ho Office Bldg Washington DC 20515-0922*

SHAW, ELEANOR JANE, newspaper editor; b. Columbus, Ohio, Mar. 23, 1949; d. Joseph Cannon and Wanda Jane (Campbell) S. BA, U. Del., 1971. With News-Jour. newspapers, Wilmington, Del., 1970-82, editor HEW desk, asst. met. editor, 1977-80, bus. editor, 1980-82; topics editor USA Today, 1982-83; asst. city editor The Miami Herald, 1983-85; projects editor The Sacramento Bee, 1985-87, news editor, 1987-91, exec. bus. editor, 1991-93, editor capitol bur. news, 1993-95, state editor, 1995-99; mgr. employee comm. The McClatchy Co., Sacramento, 1999—. Bd. dirs. Del. 4-H Found., 1978-83. Mem. Calif. Soc. Newspaper Editors (bd. dirs. 1990-96), No. Calif. Wine Soc. (v.p. 1987-93, pres. 1993-2002). Office: The McClatchy Co PO Box 15779 Sacramento CA 95852-0779 E-mail: eshaw@mcclatchy.com.

SHAW, FRANKLIN PRAGUE, JR. retired army officer, government official; b. Covington, Ky., Aug. 7, 1920; s. Franklin Praque and Inez (Skees) S.; m. Martha Murphy Shaw, Aug. 18, 1946; children: Franklin III, William, Sandra, James. BS, U.S. Mil. Acad., 1943; MA, Yale U., 1950; grad., Army Command & Gen. Staff Coll., Ft. Leavenworth, 1958. Commd. 2d lt. U.S. Army, 1943; advanced through grades to lt. col. U.S.Army, 1959; various positions U.S. Army, 1943-64, ret., 1964; v.p. DMS Inc. (McGraw-Hill), Greenwich, Conn., 1965-70; dep. asst. sec. Dept. Def., Washington, 1973-78; dep. assoc. dir. Fed. Emergency Mgmt. Agy., 1980-82; def. intelligence officer Def. Intelligence Agy., 1984-86. Author, editor: Soviet Armored Vehicles and Antitank Weapons, 1954. Pres. La Mariposa Assn., Santa Fe, 1990-94, Santa Fe N.W. Adv. Con., 1993-97; chmn. Santa Fe N.W. Cmty. Plan Task Force, 1994-99. Decorated Bronze Star, Purple Heart. Mem. Assn. Grads. U.S. Mil. Acad., Assn. Yale Alumni, Santa Fe Coun. Internat. Rels., Army Navy Country Club, Santa Fe County Club. Democrat. Avocations: golf, photography. Office: 3232 Calle Celestial Santa Fe NM 87506

SHAW, GARY YALE, otolaryngologist; b. Detroit, Nov. 2, 1957; s. Bennett and Miriam Shaw; m. Kelly Marie Svenningsen, July 1, 1989 (div. July 1998); children: Hailey, Aaron; m. Amy Elizabeth Shaw, Aug. 25, 1998; children: Justin, Suzanna, Sarah, Jacob. BA in History and Chemistry, U. Mich., 1978; MD, McGill U., 1983. Diplomate Am. Bd. Otolaryngology, Am. Bd. Facial Plastic and Reconstructive Sugery. Resident in otolaryngology U. Chgo., 1983-89; fellow in reconstructive surgery La. State U., Shreveport, 1989-90, asst. prof., 1990-91, U. Kans., Kansas City, 1991-96, assoc. prof., 1996-98; dir. lab. U. Kans. Med. Ctr., 1991-98. Contbr. articles to profl. jours., chpts. to books; mem. editl. bd. Otolaryngol. Jour., 1996—. Recipient award So. Med. Assn., 1995; grantee PDT-Corp., 1996, Geriatrics, 1997. Fellow ACS. Avocations: tennis, skiing. Office: 6650 Troost Ave Ste 308 Kansas City MO 64131-1249

SHAW, GEORGE WILLIAM, lawyer; b. Rochester, N.Y., Dec. 19, 1924; s. Frank Clyde and Eleanor Louise (Watt) S.; m. Kathryn Foote, Oct. 30, 1945; children— G. William, Frank, Thomas, Brian. B.E. with honors, Yale U., 1945; LL.B., 1949. Bar: N.Y. 1950, U.S. Ct. Appeals (2d cir.) 1964, U.S. Supreme Ct. 1976. Assoc. Edward H. Cumpston, Rochester, 1949-56; ptnr. Cumpston & Shaw, Rochester, 1956-83; pres. Cumpston & Shaw, P.C., Rochester, 1983-92, of counsel, 1992—. Co-author: Some Thoughts on Trademarks for Gen. Practitioners. Mem. Penfield Zoning Bd. Appeals, N.Y., 1959-67; chmn. Penfield Planning Bd., 1967-72; mem. Penfield Historic Preservation Bd., 1975— . Mem. ABA, Monroe County Bar Assn., N.Y. State Bar Assn., Am. Intellectual Property Law Assn., Rochester Patent Law Assn. (pres. 1971-72), Tau Beta Pi, Phi Delta Phi. Republican. Episcopalian. Club: Hunt Hollow Ski (Naples, N.Y.). Lodge: Rotary. Office: Cumpston & Shaw 850 Crossroads Building Rochester NY 14614-1377

SHAW, GLORIA DORIS, art educator; b. Huntington, W.Va., Nov. 10, 1928; d. Charles Bert and Theodosia Doris (Shimer) Haley; m. Arthur Shaw, July 13, 1954 (dec. Aug. 1985); children: Deirdra Elizabeth, Stewart N. Student, SUNY, 1969-70, Art Students League, N.Y.C., 1969-70, 74; BA, SUNY, N.Y.C., 1980; postgrad., U. Tenn., 1982, Nat Kaz, Pietrasanta, Italy, 1992. Sculptor replicator Am. Mus. Natural History, N.Y.C., 1976-77; adj. prof. sculpture Fla. Keys C.C., Key West, 1983—. Prof. TV art history Fla. Keys C.C., 1989—; host moderator Channel 5 TV, Fla. Keys, 1982—; presenter Humanities Studies and Art History Channel 19 TV, 1995—, TV Jour. Channel 16, 1997—. Sculptor (portrait) Jimmy Carter, Carter Meml. Libr., 1976, Tennessee Williams, Tennessee Williams Fine Arts Ctr., 1982, UNICEF, 1978-79, (series) Fla. Panther and Audubon Wall Relief, 1985, (bust) AIDS Meml., 1990; one woman shows include Bank Street Coll., 1979, Hollywood Mus. of Art, 1985, Islander Gallery, 1983, Martello Mus., 1984, Greenpeace, 1987; exhibited in group shows at Montoya, West Palm Beach, Fla., 1989, N.Y.C. Bd. of Edn. Tour of Schs., 1979, Earthworks East, N.Y., 1987, Man and Sci., 1978, Cuban Club, Key West, Fla., 1991, Leda Bruce Gallery, Big Pine, 1992, Kaz, Pietrasanta, Italy, 1992, Fla. Keys C.C. Gallery, 1993, Tennessee Williams Fine Arts Ctr., Key West, 1993, Internat. Woman's Show, Fla. Keys, 1994, Joy Gallery, 1994, 95, 96, Baron Gallery, Girls of Mauritania to UNICEF, 1996; designer Windows at Greenpeace Bldg., Key West, 1985-88, Pieta at St. Paul's Key West, 1997, Ceramic bird murals, FKCC, 1997; curator Women's Art, Key West, 1999, murals, Tennessee Williams Fine Arts Ctr., 1999, relief nudes Fine Arts Bldg., 1999, St. Francis sculpture and seated figures Garden Club, 2001. Recipient Children and Other Endangered Species award Thomas Cultural Ctr., 1980, Purchase award Cuban C. of C., 1982, Sierra Club, 1983, Blue Ribbon, Martello Towers Art and Hist. Soc., 1985, Red Ribbon, South Fla. Sculptors, 1986, Endangered Species award Greenpeace, 1986. Mem. Nat. Sculpture Soc. of N.Y.C., Internat. Sculpture Ctr., Art Students League of N.Y.C. (life), Art and Hist. Soc. Democrat. Avocation: naturalist.

SHAW, GRACE GOODFRIEND (MRS. HERBERT FRANKLIN SHAW), publisher, editor; b. N.Y.C. d. Henry Bernheim and Jane Elizabeth (Stone) Goodfriend; m. Herbert Franklin Shaw (dec. 1992); 1 son, Brandon Hibbs. Student, Bennington Coll.; BA magna cum laude, Fordham U., 1976, MS, 1991. Reporter Port Chester (N.Y.) Daily Item; editorial coordinator World Scope Ency., N.Y.C.; assoc. editor Clarence L. Barnhart, Inc., Bronxville, N.Y.; freelance-writer for reference books; editing supr. World Pub. Co., mng. editor, sr. editor; mng. editor Peter H. Wyden Co., N.Y.C., 1969-70; assoc. editor Dial Press, 1971-72, sr. editor, 1972, David McKay Co., N.Y.C., 1972-75, Grosset & Dunlap, 1975-79; chief editor Today Press (Grosset), 1977-79; sr. editor, coll. dept. Bobbs-Merrill, N.Y.C., mng. editor, exec. editor trade div., 1979-80, pub., 1980-84; mng. editor Rawson Assocs. div. Macmillan Pub., 1985-91; pres. Grace Shaw Assocs., Scarsdale, N.Y., 1991-97; profl. respite provider Westchester Jewish Cmty. Svcs., 1997—. Home and Office: 85 Lee Rd Scarsdale NY 10583-5212

SHAW, GWEN ELLEN GROSE, psychiatric social worker; b. San Antonio, Dec. 31, 1936; d. Cecil Franklin and Ellen (Larkin) Grose; m. R. Preston Shaw, 1956; 1 child, Wendelin Shaw Weston. BA, MSSW, U. Tex., Austin, 1964. Lic. clin. social worker, Tex. Caseworker Family Svc. Assn., Midland, Tex., 1964-72, Mary Wood Ctr., Austin, 1972-76, Family Svc. Assn., Lubbock, Tex., 1978-83; pvt. practice psychotherapy, 1980—. Part-time psychotherapist Women's Protective Svcs., 1997—. Mem.: NASW (Mental Health Social Worker of Yr. - Lubbock 1999, 2000), Phi Beta Kappa. Home: 5325 20th St Lubbock TX 79407-2109 Office: 3515 22nd St Lubbock TX 79410-1307 E-mail: gwnshw@aol.com.

SHAW, HAROLD (FRANCIS HAROLD SHAW), retired performing arts administrator; b. Hebron, N.Y., June 11, 1923; Student, Ithaca Coll., 1942, Columbia, 1944, N.Y. U. Extension, 1948. Former assoc. Hurok Concerts, Inc., N.Y.C.; chmn., owner Shaw Concerts, Inc., 1969-99; ret., 1999; performing arts dir. Seattle World's Fair, 1961-62. Former concert mgr. Nathan Milstein, Vladimir Horowitz, Dame Janet Baker, Jessye Norman, Helen Donath, Jacqueline duPre, Wolfgang Holzmair, Jard van Nes, Mitsuko Uchida, Garrick Ohlsson, Shura Cherkassky, Horacio Gutiérrez, Julian Bream, John Williams, Elmar Oliveira, Kyoko Takezawa, Robert Shaw, Andrew Davis, and over 100 artists and attractions; exec. dir. President's Shakespeare Ann. Com., 1964. Dir. exec. staff, mem. performing arts com. Cultural Commn., N.Y.C., 1966; nat. chmn. Performing Arts Energy Commn., 1974; chmn. bd. trustees Am. Shakespeare Theatre, Stratford, Conn., 1974. With USAAF, 1942-43. Mem.: Am. Summer Stock Mgrs. Assn. (co-founder), Actors Equity Assn., Assn. Coll., Univ. and Cmty. Arts Adminstrs., Am. Symphony Orch. League, Internat. Performing Arts Adminstrs., Athletic Club, Phi Mu Alpha Sinfonia. E-mail: hshaw611@msn.com.

SHAW, HARRY EDMUND, English educator; b. Norristown, Pa., May 1, 1946; s. Robert W. and Harriet Kathryn Shaw; m. Judy M. Jensvold, Sept. 23, 1972; children: Christopher Wilson, Katharine Jensvold. AB, Harvard Coll., 1969; PhD, U. Calif., Berkeley, 1978. Asst. prof. Cornell U., Ithaca, NY, 1978-84, assoc. prof., 1984-90, dir. John S. Knight writing program, 1986-92, prof., 1990—, chair dept. English, 1999—2002. Author: (book) The Forms of Historical Fiction, 1983, Narrating Reality, 1999. Fellow Vis., Clare Hall, Cambridge, Eng., 1989—90. Home: 314 Turner Pl Ithaca NY 14850 Office: Dept English Goldwin Smith Hall Cornell U Ithaca NY 14853 E-mail: HES3@cornell.edu.

SHAW, HOWARD ANDREW, physician, university program director; b. Kansas City, Kans., Dec. 26, 1961; s. A Duane and Ola M.; m. Denise L., Oct. 4 1986 (div. 1997); children: Drew, James, Brandon, Robert; m. Julia A. Shaw. AS, Kansas City (Kans.) C.C., 1982; BGS, U. Kans., 1984, MD, 1988. Diplomate Am. Bd. Ob/Gyn, Am. Bd. Forensic Med. Assoc. prof. U. Okla., Tulsa, 1992-99, assoc. program dir., 1992-98, program dir., 1998—, assoc. prof., 1999—, vice chair, 1999—. Med. dir. sexual assault nurse exam, 1993—; bd. dirs. Domestic Violence Intervention, 1999—. Recipient Tchr. award Am. Acad. Family Practice, 1995, Faculty of Yr. Tching., Coun. on Resident Edn. in Ob-Gyn., 1999. Fellow Am Coll. Ob/Gyn (Best Oral Abstract 1997, chair Donald Richardson Price com. 1998, dist. VII health adv. com.); mem. AMA, Tulsa County Med. Soc. (chair). Office: U Okla 1145 S Utica Ave Ste 600 Tulsa OK 74104-4070 E-mail: howard-shaw@ouhsc.edu.

SHAW, JACK ALLEN, communications company executive; b. Auburn, Ind., Jan. 1, 1939; s. Marvin Dale and Vera Lucille (Harter) S.; m. Martha Sue Collins, Aug. 24, 1963; 1 child, Mark Allen. BSEE, Purdue U., 1962; DSc (hon.), Capitol Coll., 1994, DSc (hon.), 1995; D in Engring. (hon.), Purdue U., 1998. Project engr. Hughes Aircraft Co., El Segundo, Calif., 1962-69; dir. program mgmt. ITT Space Comms., Ramsey, N.J., 1969-74; v.p., corp. devel. Digital Comms. Corp., Gaithersburg, Md., 1974-78, exec. v.p., COO Germantown, 1978-81, pres., CEO, 1981-84, M/A-com Telecom divsn., Germantown, 1984-87; chmn., CEO Hughes Network Sys., Inc., 1988—, chmn., also bd. dirs., 1978—, Germantown, 1987-2000, corp. sr. exec. v.p. enterprise sector, 2000—; pres., CEO Hughes Elecs., 2001. Bd. dirs. Hughes Elec., DCC Ltd., Milton Keyes, Eng., Hughes Software Systems, Pvt. Ltd., New Delhi; XM Satellite Radio, Pan Am Sat; co-chmn. U.S.-India Comml. Alliance; exec. v.p. Hughes Electronics, 1999. Mem.: IEEE (sr.), Radio Club Am. (hon.). Republican.

SHAW, JAMES, computer systems analyst; b. Salt Lake City, June 26, 1944; s. James Irvin and Cleo Lea (Bell) S. Student, San Antonio Coll., 1962-64; BA in History, St. Mary's U., San Antonio, 1966. With VA Automation Ctr., Austin, Tex., 1967-99, sr. computer programmer analyst, 1984-87, supervisory computer programmer analyst, 1987-88, computer systems analyst, 1988-94, sr. computer systems analyst, 1994-99; sr. computer specialist VA Fin. Svcs. Ctr., 1999—. Conversion team manual to computerized acctg. VA, 1974-76; team leader conversion computerized acctg. sys. to database, 1984-88; team leader complete replacement of VA computerized acctg. sys., 1989-95, transfer NARA applications to VA Automation Ctr., 1997-98; sr. technician VA Electronic Healthcare Billing Project, 1999—. Active Smithsonian Institution, Planned Parenthood, Met. Mus. Art, Austin Mus. Art. Mem. Am. Assn. Individual Investors. Democrat. Home: 11603 Ladera Vista Dr # 12 Austin TX 78759-3998 Office: VA Fin Svcs Ctr 1615 Woodward St Austin TX 78772-0001

SHAW, JAMES T. school librarian; b. Colville, Wash., May 8, 1961; s. Jesse H. and Marydel A. Shaw. BA in History, Sonoma State U., 1983; MLS, U. N.C., 1985; MA in History, U. No. Iowa, 1987. Reference libr. U. No. Iowa, Cedar Falls, 1985—89; reference/govt. docs. libr. Calif. State U., Fullerton, 1989—92; govt. docs. libr. U. Nebr., Omaha, 1992—, faculty senate, 1998—2001. Trustee San. and Improvement Dist. 386, Douglas County, Nebr., 1999—. Grantee Margaret Ellen Kalp, U. N.C., 1983. Mem.: AAUP, Nebr. Libr. Assn. (treas. coll. and univ. sect. 1996—98, chair coll. and univ. sect. 1999—2000, Disting. Svc. award 2001), Assn. Coll. and Rsch. Librs. of ALA, Beta Phi Mu. Office: U Nebr Libr 6001 Dodge St Omaha NE 68182-0237 E-mail: jshaw@mail.unomaha.edu.

SHAW, JEANNE OSBORNE, editor, poet; b. Stone Mountain, Ga., June 1, 1920; d. Virgil Waite and Daisy Hampton (Scruggs) Osborne; m. Harry B. Shaw, Dec. 10, 1982; children: Robert Allan Gibbs, Marilyn Osborne Gibbs Barry. BA, Agnes Scott Coll., 1942. Editl. staff Atlanta Constitution, 1942; feature writer New London (Conn.) Day, 1943; book reviewer Atlanta Constitution, 1940-42, Atlanta Jour., 1945-48; poetry editor Banner Press, Emory U., 1957-59; book editor Georgia Mag., Decatur, 1957-73. Judge Nat. River of Words Poetry awards, 2002. Author: The Other Side of the Water, 1970 (author of yr. in poetry award Dixie Coun. Authors and Journalists), (chapbook) From Cowslip to Cobalt, 1971, Unravelling Yarn, 1979, Third Millennium Christmas, 2001; co-author: Noel: Poems of Christmas, 1979, They Continued Steadfastly, History of Druid Hills Baptist Church, 1987; author: Faithbuilders, 1982—84; contbr. poems, pen and ink sketches. Mem. nat. arts and humanities com. Learning for Life Boy Scouts Am., 2000—; Pres. Newton class Druid Hills Bapt. Ch., 1973—74, dir. ch. tng., 1978—79, ch. clk., 1995—2001. Recipient internat. narrative poem award Poets and Patrons, Inc., Chgo., 1992, Robert Martin, Burke, Otto, In Praise of Poetry awards N.Y. Poetry Forum, 1973, 79, 81, Westbrook award Ky. Poetry Soc., 1976, Ariz. award, 1981, Ind. State Fedn. of Poetry Clubs award, Ala. State Poetry Soc. award, 1990, Rev. Earl M. Smith meml. award, 1997, Joseph V. Hickey meml. award, 1998, Nat. Fedn. State Poetry Socs. Mem. Ga. Writers Assn. (lit. achievement award 1971), Poetry Soc. Ga. (John Clare prize, 1955, Katharine H. Strong prize 1975, Eunice Thomson prize 1976, 92, Jimmy Williamson prize 1977, Capt. Frank Spencer prize 1985, 88, Conrad Aiken prize 1987, 88, Sarah Cunningham prize 1989, 94, 97, Soc. prize 1989, 2001, Lucy McEntire prize 1990, 94, Grace Schley Knight prize 1991, 93, Gerald Chan Sieg prize 1991, 95, Harriet Ross Colquitt prize 1994, 95, Eva Tennyson Forbes meml. prize 1996, About Holes prize 1998, Monday prize 2001, Formal prize 2001), Atlanta Writers Club (pres. 1949-50, named Aurelia Austin Writer of Yr. in poetry 1971, Wyatt award 1986, 95, Light Verse award 1989, 90, 2001, Daniel Whitehead Hicky award 1991, 95, F. Levering Neely award 1991, Poet Laureate's award 1993, Ben Willingham award, Gerry Crocker award 1995, Villanelle award 1997, 98, Virginia Cole Veal award 1999), Ga. Poetry Soc. (traditional award 1984, 97, Cole and Ledford award 1986, Goreau award, 1987, 93, Melissa Henry award 1989, Charles and Virginia Dickson award 1990, Jo Ann Yeager Adkins award 1991, Poem About Atlanta award 1992, 14th Aniv. Free Verse award 1993, My Very Best Poem award 1995, Jabberwocky award 1997, Annette Peery award 1998, 99, 2001, Charles Bruehler award 2000, 22d Anniversary award 2002, artistic dir. 2000, judge Nat. River of Words Contest 2002), Phi Beta Kappa. Home: 809 Pinetree Dr Decatur GA 30030-2332

SHAW, JOHN FREDERICK, retired naval officer; b. Dallas, Oct. 14, 1938; s. John Frederick and Sarah E. (Crouch) S.; m. Janice Muren, July 14, 1962; children: Elizabeth Lee, Suzanne Michele. BS, U.S. Naval Acad., 1960; MS in Mgmt. with distinction, Naval Postgrad. Sch., Monterey, Calif., 1970; grad., Armed Forces Staff Coll., 1971. Commd. ensign USN, 1960, advanced through grades to rear adm., 1983; exec. officer USS Long Beach (CGN 9), 1978-79; comdg. officer USS Bainbridge (CGN 25), 1980-83; dir. guided missile destroyer 51, Arleigh Burke program Comdr. Naval Sea Systems Command, Washington, 1983-85, mgr. AEGIS shipbldg. program, 1985-87; comdr. Cruiser-Destroyer Group One, San Diego, 1987-88; dep. chief staff plans and policy Supreme Allied Comdr., Atlantic, Norfolk, Va., 1988-89, chief staff, 1989-91; ret., 1991; prof. joint mil. ops. Coll. Continuing Edn., Naval War Coll., San Diego, 1992-94. Bd. advisors United Svc. Benefit Assn., Kansas City, Kans., 1987-93; mem. cmty. bd. advisors Sam and Rose Stein Inst. for Rsch. on Aging, 1998—, membership chmn., 1999-2000, sec.-treas., 2000—; tax. cons. for elderly, AARP, 2000—. Trustee Coronado Libr., 1998—, exec. sec., 2001—. Decorated Def. D.S.M. , Legion of Merit with two gold stars, Meritorious Svc. medal with gold star, Navy Commendation medal with gold star, Meritorious Unit Commendation (civilian) USN . Mem. AARP, U.S. Naval Inst. (life), U.S. Naval Acad. Alumni Assn. (life, pres. Washington chpt. 1986, bd. govs. San Diego/Coronado chpt. 1996-99), Surface Navy Assn. (life), San Diego Navy League (dir. 1997—). Avocations: golf, reading, economics, travel. E-mail: jshaw14@aol.com.

SHAW, JOHN W. lawyer; b. Mo., 1951; BA, MA, U. Mo., 1973, JD, 1977. Bar: Mo. 1977. Ptnr. Bryan Cave, Kansas City, 1977-92, Lathrop & Norquist, 1983-92, Bryan Cave LLP, 1992-98, Berkowitz Feldmiller Stanton Brandt Williams and Shaw LLP, Kansas City, 1998—. Mem. ABA, Securities Industry Assn. (legal and compliance group), Mo. Bar, Def. Rsch. Inst. (chmn. firearms litigation subcom.), Order of Coif. Office: Berkowitz Feldmiller Stanton Brandt Williams and Shaw LLP Two Emmanuel Cleaver Blvd Ste 500 Kansas City MO 64112

SHAW, JOYCE M. librarian; b. Gulfport, Miss., Mar. 4, 1955; d. Philip Walker and Marion Joyce (Bendler) S.; 1 child, Oliver Shaw Kuttner. BA, U. New Orleans, 1978; MA, Roosevelt U., 1982; M Libr. and Info. Sci., Rosary Coll., River Forest, Ill., 1994. Libr. asst. Times Picayune Publs., New Orleans, 1976-78, Roosevelt U., Chgo., 1978-80, Field Mus. Natural History, Chgo., 1980-83; libr. Lincoln Park Zool. Gardens, 1983-94, Shaw/Walker Archs., Gulfport, Miss., 1994-95; head libr. Gulf Coast Rsch. Lab., Ocean Springs, 1995—. Mem. adv. bd. nature connections Chgo. Pub. Libr., 1984-86; mem. restoration adv. bd. Naval Constrn. Battalion Ctr., Gulfport, Miss., 1995—. Contbr. articles to profl. jours., including Spl. Librs., Jour. Miss. Acad. Scis., Ill. Librs. Conservation grantee Inst. Mus. Svc., 1986. Mem. Spl. Librs. Assn., Soc. for Conservation Biology, Internat. Assn. Marine Sci. Librs. and Info. Ctrs., Miss. Acad. Scis., Rotary Internat. Presbyterian. Avocation: reading. Office: Gulf Coast Rsch Lab 708 E Beach Blvd Ocean Springs MS 39564 E-mail: joyce.shaw@usm.edu.

SHAW, JULIE ANN, addiction counselor; b. Ridgewood, N.J., June 13, 1957; d. John Seymour and June (Langill) S. BS in Psychology, Ramapo Coll. of N.J., 1979; MA in Counseling, Montclair State Coll., 1983, postgrad., 1986—88, U. Bridgeport, 1988, 89, 90. Cert. alcohol and drug counselor, 1998. Income maintenance technician/worker Bergen County Bd. Social Svcs., Food Stamp div., Paramus, N.J., 1980-84; youth employment counselor Pvt. Industry Coun., Clifton and Passaic, 1985; youth svcs. dir. Borough of Tenafly (N.J.), Dept. Youth Svcs., 1986; substitute tchr. Bd. edn., Franklin Lakes, N.J., 1986-88, Ramapo/Indian Hills High Sch. Dist. Bd. Edn., Midland Park, Glen Rock, 1985; social worker Wellington Hall Nursing Home, Hackensack, 1987; mental health liaison counselor South Bergen Mental Health Ctr., Lyndhurst, 1988; alcoholism counselor alcohol recovery program Health Svcs. Dept., Bergen County, Hackensack, 1988-90, sr. alcoholism counselor, 1990—; social worker Wellington Hall Nursing Home, 1987. Parent workshop counselor Bergen County Parent Workshop Program, Chem. Awareness Program, Tenafly, 1986; counselor, cons. DWI Program, Hackensack, 1989—90, Easter Seals Program. Social svcs./music program coord. Jr. Womans Club UNICEF Program Chmn., Totowa Tng. Ctr. Devel. Disabled/Retarded Children, Wyckoff, N.J., 1981-85. Avocations: sailing, swimming, needlework, reading, playing piano. Office: Addiction Recovery Program 151 Hudson St Hackensack NJ 07601-6823

SHAW, KATHLEEN BENTLEY, violist; b. Richmond, Va., Nov. 10, 1962; d. Gilliam and Carolyn (Hargrave) Bentley; m. Roderick Kirkpatrick Shaw III, Jan. 11, 1992. Performer's cert., MusB, U. Fla., 1986; MusM, Fla. State U., 1989, MusD, 1994. Tchg. asst. Fla. State U., Tallahassee, 1988-94; co-chair region I Fla. Am. String Tchrs. Assn., Pensacola and Tallahassee, Fla., 1993-94, chair spl. projects, 1993-94; coord. chamber strings Fla. State U., Tallahassee, 1993; bus. adminstr. Dental office of Dr. Roderick K. Shaw, 1997—; music dir. Madison Presbyn. Ch., 1994-99; bus. adminstr. Dr. Roderick Shaw. Adminstr. Shelfer Emminent , scholar chair Fla. State U., Tallahassee, chairwoman seminar Playing Well Music Medicine Seminar for String Players, 1994; vis. artist U. N.C.-Greensboro, 1995. Violist Tallahassee Symphony Orch., 1988-94; author: The Sonata for Viola and Piano, 1994; performer over 50 concerts in Leon County Elem. Schs., Tallahassee, 1989-90; premiered 2 new suites for viola and piano Artists' Series of North Fla. C.C., 1999, Wardlaw-Goza-Smith Conf. Ctr., Madison, Fla. Dir. arts Madison Women's Club, 1995—96, dir. Arts Festival; choir dir. First United Meth. Ch., Madison, Fla., 2001—; bd. dirs. The Treasures of Madison County Mus., 1996—98. Travel grantee Fla. State U., Aspen, Colo., 1990, Carmel, Calif., 1994; nat. finalist Chamber Music Competition, Carmel, 1994. Mem. Am. String Tchrs. Assn. (bd. dirs. Fla. unit 1993-94). Methodist. Avocations: refinishing furniture, oil painting (portraits by commission). Home: 529 W Base St Madison FL 32340-2005

SHAW, KENDALL (GEORGE SHAW), artist, educator; b. New Orleans, Mar. 30, 1924; s. George Kendall and Florence Gladys (Worner) S.; m. Frances Glenn Fort, Oct. 31, 1955. Student, Ga. Inst. Tech., 1944-46; BS in Chemistry, Tulane U., 1949, M.F.A. in Painting, 1959; postgrad., La. State U., 1950. Instr. Columbia U., 1961-66, Hunter Coll., 1966-68, Parsons Sch. Design, N.Y.C., 1966-86, Lehman Coll., 1968-70, Bklyn. Mus. Art Sch., 1970-76; U.S. del. to UNESCO Conf., London, 1965. One-man shows include Orleans Gallery, New Orleans, 1959, 61, Columbia U., 1965, Bienville Gallery, New Orleans, 1968, Tibor de Nagy Gallery, N.Y.C., 1964, 65, 67, 68, Southampton Coll., 1969, John Bernard Myers Gallery, 1972, Alessandra Gallery, 1976, Lerner/Heller Gallery, N.Y.C., 1979, 81, 82, Bernice Steinbaum Gallery, N.Y.C., 1991, Artists Space, N.Y.C., 1992, The Gallery of South Orange, N.J., 1998, U. Richmond, Va., 1999, Tulane U., 2001; group shows include P.S.I., N.Y.C., 1977, Gladstone-Villani Gallery, N.Y.C., 1978, Galerie Habermann, Cologne, 1979, Modern Art Gallery, Vienna, 1980, Jacksonville Art Mus. (Fla.), 1983, Hudson Guild, N.Y.C., 1997, 2001, 2002, The Ogden Mus. So. Art, New Orleans, 2001, 2002, others; represented in permanent collections Sammlung Ludwig, Aachen, Bklyn. Mus., Albright-Knox Gallery, Buffalo, Mus. Contemporary Art, Nagaoka, Japan, Everson Mus., Syracuse, Chase Bank, N.Y.C., N.Y. U., N.Y.C., Polk Mus. Art, Lakeland, Fla., Orlando Mus. Art, Weatherspoon Art Gallery, Greensboro, N.C., Marsh Art Gallery, Richmond, Va., Tulane U., New Orleans, New Orleans Mus. of Art, Miss. Mus. Art, The Ogden Mus. So. Art, New Orleans. Albright-Knox Gallery, Buffalo. Served with USN, 1943-46. Recipient Disting. Alumnus award Tulane Coll., 2001. Mem. Coll. Art Assn., Artists Equity Assn. Democrat. Address: 916 President St Brooklyn NY 11215-1604

SHAW, KENDRICK MATTHEW, software engineer; b. Portland, Oreg. s. Donald and Kathey Irene S. BS in Computer Sci., MS in Computer Sci., Case Western Res. U., 1997. Software design engr. Microsoft Corp., Redmond, Wash., 1997—. Home: 9611 163rd Pl NE Redmond WA 98052-3134

SHAW, KENNETH ALAN, university president; b. Granite City, Ill., Jan. 31, 1939; s. Kenneth W. and Clara H. (Lange) Shaw; m. Mary Ann Byrne, Aug. 18, 1962; children: Kenneth William, Susan Lynn, Sara Ann. BS, Ill. State U., 1961, DHL, 1987; EdM, U. Ill., 1963; PhD, Purdue U., 1966, EdD (hon.) , 1990; DHL, Towson State, 1979, Ill. Coll., 1986. Tchr. history, counselor Rich Twp. High Sch., Park Forest, Ill., 1961-63; residence hall dir., instr. edn. Ill. State U., 1963-64; counselor Office Dean of Men, Purdue U., 1964-65, Office Dean of Men, Purdue U. (Office Student Loans), 1965-66; asst. to pres., lectr. sociology Ill. State U., 1966-69; v.p. acad. affair, dean Towson State U., Balt., 1969-76; pres. So. Ill. U., Edwardsville, 1977-79; chancellor So. Ill. U. System, 1979-86; pres. U. Wis. System, Madison, 1986-91; chancellor, pres. Syracuse U., 1991—. Bd. dirs. Unity Mutual Life Ins. Co., Key Bank of Ctrl. N.Y. Trustee CICU, Albany, NY, 1993—, Am. Coll. Testing, 1990—; bd. dirs. NCAA Pres. Commn., 1993—. Named Citizen of Yr., So. Ill. Inc., 1985; named to Ill. Basketball Hall of Fame, 1983; recipient Young Leader in Edn. award, 1980, Silver Anniversary award, NCAA, 1986, Coaches Silver Anniversary award, Nat. Assn. Basketball, 1986. Mem.: State Higher Edn. Exec. Officers Assn., Am. Higher Edn. Assn., Am. Social. Assn., Am. Coun. Edn. (com. on minorities in higher edn. 1987—91), Am. Assn. State Colls. and Univs. (external rels. com. 1986—88), Met. Devel. Assn. (bd. dirs. 1991—), Syracuse C. of C. (bd. dirs. 1991—), Pi Gamma Mu, Phi Delta Kappa. Office: Syracuse Univ Office of Chancellor 300 Tolley Admin Building Syracuse NY 13244-0001*

SHAW, L. EDWARD, JR. lawyer; b. Elmira, N.Y., July 30, 1944; s. L. Edward and Virginia Anne (O'Leary) S.; m. Irene Ryan; children: Christopher, Hope, Hillary, Julia, Rory BA in Econs., Georgetown U., Washington, 1966; JD, Yale U., New Haven, 1969. Bar: N.Y. 1969. Assoc. Milbank, Tweed, Hadley & McCloy, N.Y.C., 1969-77, ptnr., 1977-83; sr. v.p., gen. counsel Chase Manhattan Corp., 1983-85, exec. v.p., gen. counsel, 1985-96; vice chmn., gen. counsel Natwest Markets, 1996-97, pres., 1997-99; gen. counsel Aetna Inc., 1999—. Mem. Assn. Bar City N.Y., Winged Foot Golf Club, Phi Beta Kappa. Roman Catholic. Avocations: youth athletics, golf. Office: Aetna Inc RC4B 151 Farmington Ave Hartford CT 06156-3124 E-mail: ShawJL@aetna.com.

SHAW, LEANDER JERRY, JR. state supreme court justice; b. Salem, Va., Sept. 6, 1930; s. Leander J. and Margaret S. BA, W.Va. State Coll., 1952, LLD (hon.), 1986; JD, Howard U., 1957; PhD (hon.) in Pub. Affairs, Fla. Internat. U., 1990; LLD (hon.), Nova Law Sch., 1991, Washington & Lee Law Sch., 1991. Asst. prof. law Fla. A&M U., 1957-60; sole practice Jacksonville, Fla., 1960-69, 72-74; asst. pub. defender, 1965-69; asst. state's atty. Fla., 1969-72; judge Fla. Indsl. Relations Commn., 1974-79, Fla. Ct. Appeals (1st dist.), 1979-83; justice Fla. Supreme Ct., Tallahassee, 1983—, chief justice, 1990-92. Office: Fla Supreme Ct Supreme Ct Bldg 500 S Duval St Tallahassee FL 32399-6556 E-mail: SupremeCourt@FLCOURTS.ORG.

SHAW, LEON LINGANG, engineering educator, materials researcher; b. Fuzhou, Fujian, China; came to U.S., 1989; MEng, Fuzhou U., 1987; MS, PhD, U. Fla., 1992. Lectr. Fuzhou U., 1982-88; posdoctoral fellow U. Fla., Gainesville, 1992-93; rsch. scientist Systran Corp., Dayton, Ohio, 1993-94; asst. prof. U. Conn., Storrs, 1995-99, assoc. prof., 2000—. Vis. scientist Wright AFB Lab., Dayton, 1993-94; reviewer various jours., including Nanostructured Materials, Metallurgical and Materials Transactions, others, 1992—; hon. adv. prof. Harbin (China) Inst. Tech., 1999—; hon. guest prof. Fuzhou U., 1999—; organizer symposia, 1995—. Contbr. over 100 articles to sci. jours.; guest editor Metall. and Materials Transactions, 1998, Materials Sci. and Engring., 1998, 99; patents in field of high energy milling. Mem. AAUP, Am. Ceramic Soc., Am Soc. Metals Internat., Minerals, Metals and Materials Soc., Chinese Materials Rsch. Soc. Office: U Conn Dept Metallurgy and Materials Engring Storrs CT 06269 Fax: 860-486-4745. E-mail: lshaw@mail.ims.uconn.edu.

SHAW, LEONARD GLAZER, electrical engineering educator, consultant; b. Toledo, Aug. 15, 1934; s. A. Daniel and Mary (Glazer) S.; m. Susan Gail Weil, Dec. 24, 1961; children: Howard Benjamin, Mitchell Bruce, Jenny Louis. BSEE, U. Pa., 1956; MSEE, Stanford U., 1957, PhD, 1961. From asst. to assoc. prof. Polytech. U. N.Y., Bklyn., 1960-75, prof., 1975—, head dept. elec. engring. and computer sci., 1982-90, dean Sch. Elec. Engring. and Computer Sci., 1990-94, vice provost for undergrad. studies, 1995-96. Vis. prof. Tech. U., Eindhoven, Netherlands, 1970, Ecole Nationale Superieure de Mecanique, Nantes, France, 1977, U. Sussex, Brighton, Eng., 1998; cons. Sperry Systems Mgmt. Div., Great Neck, N.Y.; mem. grant rev. panels NSF, 1986—. Co-author: Signal Processing, 1975; contbr. articles to profl. jours. Rsch. grantee NSF, 1973, 81. Fellow: IEEE (mem. pub. bd. 1961—92, mem. various coms., editor-in-chief IEEE Press 1988—91, gen. chmn. Conf. of Decision and Control 1989, chmn. Tech. Field Award Coun. 1995—97), Control Sys. Soc. of IEEE (fin. v.p. 1992—93, 2000, pres.-elect 2001, pres. 2002); mem.: Am. Soc. Engring. Edn. Office: Polytech U 6 Metrotech Ctr Brooklyn NY 11201-3840 E-mail: lshaw@poly.edu.

SHAW, M. BEATRYCE, retired publishing executive, writer; b. Lexington, GA, Apr. 18, 1938; d. L.M. Edwards, Mardel Watkins; m. John W. Jones; children: Pecola A. Hill. Cert. John G. Hondros Acad. Real Estate 1988. Pub. Schooner Publs., Inc., Conway, SC, 1999—; owner/operator E. Keys, Inc., Cleve., 1977—88. Owner/operator Keys Sch. Svc., Cleve., 1980—82. Author: Mr. Browne's Roses, 2001. Vol. Project Friendship Big Sister Program, Cleve., 1978—88. Mem.: Exec. Womens' Golf Assn. Avocation: Avocations: public speaking, consulting, gardening, golf. Office: Schooner Publs Inc. 1610-D Church St PMB360 Conway SC 29526

SHAW, M. THOMAS, III, bishop; b. Battle Creek, Mich., Aug. 28, 1945; s. M.T. and Wilma Janes Shaw. BA, Alma (Mich.) Coll.; master's, Cath. U.; MDiv, Gen. Theol. Sem.; DD (hon.), Seabury We. Ordained priest Episcopal Ch., 1971. Mem. Co. of Mission Priests, Eng., 1970-72, Milw., 1972-74, Soc. St. John the Evangelist, Cambridge, Mass., 1974—; bishop Episcopal Diocese of Mass., 1994—. Office: 138 Tremont St Boston MA 02111-1318

SHAW, MARGERY WAYNE SCHLAMP, geneticist, physician, lawyer; b. Evansville, Ind., Feb. 15, 1923; d. Arthur George and Louise (Meyer) Schlamp; m. Charles Raymond Shaw, May 31, 1942 (div. Nov. 1972); 1 dau., Barbara Rae. Student, Hanover Coll., 1940-41; AB magna cum laude, U. Ala., 1945; MA, Columbia U., 1946; postgrad., Cornell U., 1947-48; MD cum laude, U. Mich., 1957; JD, U. Houston, 1973; DSc (hon.), U. Evansville, 1977, U. So. Ind., 1986. Intern St. Joseph Mercy Hosp., Ann Arbor, Mich., 1957-58; practice medicine specializing in human genetics, 1958-67; instr. dept. human genetics Med. Sch. U. Mich., 1958-61, asst. prof., 1961-66, assoc. prof., 1966-67; assoc. prof. dept. biology Grad. Sch. Biomed. Scis., U. Tex., Houston, 1967-69, prof., 1969-88, dir. Med. Genetics Ctr., 1971-83, acting dean, 1976-78, prof. emeritus, 1988—. Mem. genetics study sect. NIH, Bethesda, Md., 1966-70, genetics tng. com., 1970-74, adv. com. to dir., 1979-82; chromosome studies astronauts NASA, 1970-71; mem. med. adv. bd. Nat. Genetics Found., 1972-88; rsch. adv. bd. Planned Parenthood, Houston, 1972-79; vis. scholar Yale Law Sch., 1974; Andrew D. White prof.-at-large Cornell U., 1982-88; vis. prof. U. Utah, 1983; adj. prof. U. Houston Law Ctr., 1986-88. Mem. editl. bd. Am. Jour. Human Genetics, 1962-68, Am. Jour. Med. Genetics, 1977-87, Am. Jour. Law and Medicine, 1977-88; contbr. articles to profl. jours. First aid instr. ARC, 1962-67; unit chmn. United Fund, 1966. Recipient Billings Silver medal AMA, 1966, Achievement award AAUW, 1970-71. Mem. Am. Soc. Human Genetics (past sec., dir., pres. 1982), Genetics Soc. Am. (sec. 1971-73, pres. 1977-78, Wilhelmene Key award 1977), Tissue Culture Assn. (trustee 1970-72), Environ. Mutagen Soc. (coun.), Am. Soc. Cell Biology, Am. Soc. Law Medicine (trustee 1980-88), Phi Beta Kappa, Alpha Omega Alpha. Home: 2929 S Waterford Dr Apt 478 Spokane WA 99203-4404 E-mail: mwshaw23@juno.com.

SHAW, MARILYN MARGARET MITCHELL, artist, photographer; b. San Diego, Dec. 19, 1933; d. George Louis and Helen Frances (Wright) Mitchell; m. Robert Dale Shaw, Feb. 19, 1952; children: Austin Allen, Kenneth Duane, Frank Lloyd. BA in Fine Arts and Photography, Juniata Coll., 1989. Photographer The Daily News, Huntingdon, Pa., 1988-92; owner, tchr. Marilyn Shaw Studios, Tyrone, 1989—. Photographer The Jamesyouth, St. James. Luth. Ch., Huntingdon, 1987-92; photojournalist Easter Seals Telethon, 1991-92; art dir. Allegheny Riding Camp-The GrierSch., Tyrone, Pa., 1992; art instr. The Pa. House, Tyrone, 1995-97, Ben Franklin Crafts, Altoona, Pa., 1997—; art tchr. homeschooled students, 1994-97; art instr. Ctrl. Blair Recreation and Parks Commn., 2000-02. One-woman shows include Shoemaker Gallery, Huntingdon, 1989; group shows include Standing Stone Art League, Huntingdon, 1978-92, Washington St. Art Gallery, Huntingdon, 1991, 94, Cold Springs Med. Ctr., 1992; author, illustrator The Prize, 1989. Vol. The Huntingdon House, 1992—, Presbyn. Ch. House, Huntingdon, 1992-97, Tyrone Presbyn. Ch., 1995-98, Sinking Valley Presbyn. Ch., 1998-2001; mem. "visions" com. Ctrl. Pa. Festival Arts, 1997-99. Recipient numerous ribbons Huntingdon County Fair, 1978, 90, 91, Sinking Valley Farm Show, 1992, 94, 95, 96, 97, 98, 99, 2000, Huntingdon County Arts Coun., 1989, 90, 91, 2 Merit Certs. Photographers Forum, 1989, Vila Gardner Metzger art award, 1989, others. Mem. Women's League Juniata Coll., Nat. Mus. of Women in the Arts (charter mem.). Avocations: reading, fishing, needlecrafts, camping, travel. Home: 104 W 12th St Tyrone PA 16686-1634

SHAW, MARK HOWARD, lawyer, business owner, entrepreneur; b. Albuquerque, Aug. 26, 1944; s. Brad Oliver and Barbara Rae (Mencke) S.; m. Ann Marie Brookreson, June 29, 1968 (div. 1976); adopted children: Daniel Paul, Kathleen Ann, Brian Andrew; m. Roslyn Jane Ashton, Oct. 9, 1976; children: Rebecca Rae, Amanda Leith. BA, U. N.Mex., 1967, JD, 1969. Bar, N.Mex. 1969. Law clk. to presiding justice N.Mex. Supreme Ct., Santa Fe, 1969-70; ptnr. Gallagher & Ruud, Albuquerque, 1970-74, Schmidt & Shaw, Albuquerque, 1974-75; sr. mem. Shaw, Thompson & Sullivan P.A., 1975-82; chief exec. officer United Ch. Religious Sci. and Sci. Mind Publs., L.A., 1982-91; bus. owner, entrepreneur Santa Fe, 1991-94; mem. Coppler & Mannick, P.C., 1994-98; pvt. practice Santa Fe, Albuquerque, 1998—. Trustee 1st Ch. Religious Sci., Albuquerque, 1974-77, pres. 1977; trustee Sandia Ch. Religious Sci., Albuquerque, 1980-82, pres. 1981-82; trustee United Ch. Religious Sci., Los Angeles, 1981-82, chmn. 1982; trustee Long Beach (Calif.) Ch. Religious Sci., 1983-86, chmn. 1983-86; chmn. Bernalillo County Bd. Ethics, Albuquerque, 1979-82, trustee Santa Fe Rape Crisis Ctr., 1997-2000, pres., 1999-2000. Served as sgt. USMCR, 1961-69. Mem. N.Mex. Bar Assn. Avocation: sailing, fly fishing. Home: 13121 Nandina Ln SE Albuquerque NM 87123-4186 Office: 3733 Eubank Blvd NE Albuquerque NM 87111-3536

SHAW, MARTIN ANDREW, clinical and research psychologist; b. N.Y.C., Jan. 27, 1944; s. Aaron S. and Betty Shaw; m. Dorothy Korot, Nov. 7, 1971; 1 child, Anatole Bernard. BS, NYU, 1966; MA, Dalhousie U., 1972; PhD, U. Wis., 1977; postgrad. Advanced Inst. Analytic Psychotherapy, 1977-82. Art tchr. N.Y.C. Schs., 1966-69; art therapist Kingsbridge VA Hosp., Bronx, N.Y., 1969-71; grad. teaching asst. Dalhousie U., 1971-72, Killam Children's Hosp., Halifax Sch. for Blind, N.S., Can., 1971-72; psychometrician, cons. N.Y.C. Bd. Edn., 1977-80; staff therapist, staff psychologist Advanced Ctr. for Psychotherapy, Jamaica, N.Y., 1977-82; clin./child psychologist Health Ins. Plan, Mental Health Service, N.Y.C., 1980-84; pvt. practice clin. and clin. child psychology, N.Y.C., 1981-83, Gt. Neck, N.Y., 1981—; cons. psychologist Hearing and Speech Ctr. of L.I. Jewish-Hillside Med. Ctr., New Hyde Park, N.Y., 1986-87, Trinity-Pawling (N.Y.) Sch., 1986—; exec. dir. ORT Inst., Inc.; trustee Signal Hill Edn. Ctr., Inc., 1983-87; courtesy staff Four Winds Hosp., Katonah, N.Y.. Recipient Founders Day award, N.Y.U., 1966, VA commendation, 1970; lic. psychologist, N.Y. State. Fellow Soc. for Personality Assessment, Brit. Soc. for Projective Psychology (hon.); mem. APA, AAAS, N.Y. State Psychol. Assn., N.Y. Soc. Clin. Psychologists, Nassau County Psychol. Assn., N.Y. Acad. Scis., Internat. Rorschach Soc., Soc. Psychoanalytic Rsch., Internat. Platform Assn., N.AM. Adv. Com. to the World Court of the Environ., Pi Lambda Theta. Author: Object Relations Technique: Objectified Assessment/Basic Rationale, 1993; contbr. papers to profl. jours. and confs. Office: 333 E Shore Rd Ste 206 Manhasset NY 11030-2900

SHAW, MARY M. computer science educator; b. Washington, Sept. 30, 1943; d. Eldon Earl and Mary Lewis (Holman) Shaw; m. Roy R. Weil, Feb. 15, 1973. BA cum laude, Rice U., 1965; PhD, Carnegie Mellon U., Pitts., 1972. Asst. prof. to prof. computer sci. Carnegie Mellon U., Pitts., 1972—, assoc. dean computer sci. for profl. programs, 1992-99, Alan J. Perlis chair computer sci. Chief scientist Software Engring. Inst., Carnegie Mellon U., Pitts., 1984-88; mem. Computer Sci. and Telecommunications Bd., NRC, Washington, 1986-93. Author: (with W. Wulf, P. Hilfinger, L. Flon) Fundamental Structures of Computer Science, 1981, The Carnegie Mellon Curriculum for Undergraduate Computer Science, 1985, (with David Garlan) Software Architecture: Perspectives on an Emerging Discipline, 1996; contbr. articles to profl. jours. Recipient Warnier prize, 1993; named Woman of Achievement, YWCA of Greater Pitts., 1973. Fellow AAAS, IEEE (disting. lectr.), Assn. for Computing Machinery (SIGPLAN exec. com. 1979-83, Recognition of Svc. award 1985, 90); mem. Sigma Xi. Office: Carnegie Mellon U Dept Computer Sci Pittsburgh PA 15213

SHAW, MELVIN PHILLIP, physicist, engineering educator, psychologist; b. Bklyn., Aug. 16, 1936; s. Harry and Yetta (Stutsky) S.; m. Carol Joan Phillips, Sept. 5, 1959 (div. Feb. 1987); children: Adam, Evan; m. Bernetta Berger, May 16, 1987. BS, Bklyn. Coll., 1959; MS, Case Western Res. U., 1963, PhD, 1965; MA, Ctr. for Humanistic Studies, 1988. Research scientist United Techs. Research Labs., E. Hartford, Conn., 1964-68, scientist-in-charge, 1966-70; prof. Wayne State U., Detroit, 1970-96, prof. emeritus, 1997—; adminstrv. dir. Assocs. of Birmingham/Kingswood Hosp., 1991-93. Cons. Energy Conversion Devices, Troy, Mich., 1970-92. Co-author: The Gunn-Hilsum Effect, 1979, The Physics and Applications of Amorphous Semiconductors, 1988, The Physics of Instabilities in Solid State Electron Devices, 1992, Creativity and Affect, 1994. Fellow Am. Phys. Soc.; mem. IEEE (sr.), Am. Psychol. Assn. (assoc.). Avocations: cooking, walking, exercising, traveling.

SHAW, MELVIN ROBERT, lawyer; b. Bklyn., Nov. 23, 1948; s. Arthur and Pearl (Gutterman) S. BA in Polit. Sci., L.I. U., 1970; MPA, U. Ill., 1973; LLD (hon.), Roman Coll., Rome, 1974; BS in Law, Western State U., San Diego, 1984; JD, Thomas Jefferson Sch. of Law, 1984; MA in Human Behavior, Nat. U., 1985; MS in Mgmt., NYU, 1988; LLM in Health Law, DePaul U., 1989; postgrad., Golden Gate U., 1989; PhD in Pub. Health, NYU, 1993. Bar: Ind. 1985, U.S. Dist. Ct. (no. and so. dists.) Ind. 1985, U.S. Dist. Ct. (no. dist.) Calif. 1985, U.S. Dist. Ct. (ea. dist.) Wis. 1985, U.S. Dist. Ct. Hawaii 1985, U.S. Ct. Appeals (3d, 5th, 7th, 9th, D.C., fed. cirs.) 1985, U.S. Ct. Internat. Trade 1985, U.S. Ct. Mil. Appeals 1985, U.S. Ct. Fed. Claims 1985, U.S. Tax Ct. 1985, U.S. Supreme Ct. 1988, U.S. Dist. Ct. (no. dist.) Ill. 1989, U.S. Ct. Appeals for Vets. Claims 1990, U.S. Dist. Ct. (ea., so., and no. dists.) N.Y. 1992, USAF Ct. Criminal Appeals, 2001, USN/Marine Corp. Ct. Criminal Appeals, 2001. Exec. asst. N.Y. State Senate, Albany, 1969-71; polit. cons. Kirson & Shaw, Ltd., N.Y.C., 1972-76; pres. Master Pubs., Inc., Chgo., 1976-80; lectr. Inst. for Internat. Affairs, Washington, 1978—; sr. ptnr. Littlejohn & Shaw Assocs., N.Y.C., Chgo., San Diego, 1980-85; pvt. practice South Bend, Ind. and N.Y.C., South Bend, Ind., 1985-99; sr. ptnr. Shaw and Dessureau, NYC and South Bend, Ind., 1999—. Instr. law Calif. C.C.'s, 1985—; dir. Hudson Industries, San Diego, Master Commn., N.Y.C., Inst. for Internat. Affairs, 1979—. Editor Internat. Rels. Jour., 1982; contbr. articles to profl. jours. Active Am. Jewish Com., Dem. Nat. Com.; chmn., bd. govs. Mental Health and Criminal Justice Policy Inst. Am.; v.p. Shorefront Mental Health Bd. Mem. ABA, ACLU, FBA, ATLA, Ind. State Bar Assn., N.Y. State Bar Assn., Chgo. Bar Assn., Am. Soc. Internat. Law (chpt. pres. 1983-84), Am. Judicature Soc., Am. Arbitration Assn., Nat. Health Lawyers Assn., Am. Soc. Commns. and Media Execs., Am. Soc. Law, Medicine, and Ethics (active mem.), Nat. Assn. Mgmt. Execs., Amnesty Internat., Odd Fellows, Delta Theta Phi. Democrat. Jewish. Office: Shaw and Dessureau 82 Wall St Ste 1105 New York NY 10005-3600 E-mail: shawdessureau@lawyer.com.

SHAW, MICHAEL, biologist, educator; b. Barbados, W.I., Feb. 11, 1924; s. Anthony and Myra (Perkins) S.; m. Jean Norah Berkinshaw, Oct. 16, 1948; children— Christopher A., Rosemary E., Nicholas R., Andrew L. BSc, McGill U., 1946, MSc, 1947, PhD, 1949, DSc, 1975. Nat. Research Council Can. postdoctoral fellow Botany Sch., Cambridge U., 1949-50; Assoc. prof. biology U. Sask., 1950-54, prof., 1954-67, prof., head dept. biology, 1961-67; dean faculty agrl. scis. U. B.C., 1967-75, v.p. acad. devel., 1975-81, acad. v.p., provost, 1981-83, univ. prof., 1983-89, univ. prof. emeritus, 1989—. Mem. Sci. Council Can., 1976-82, Natural Scis. and Engring. Research Council Can., 1978-80 Contbr. articles to profl. jours. Recipient Queen's Silver Jubilee medal, 1977, gold medal Biol. Coun. Can., 1983. Fellow Royal Soc. Can. (Flavelle medal 1976), Can. Phytopath. Soc., Am. Phytopath. Soc., N.Y. Acad. Scis.; mem. AAAS, Can. Bot. Assn., Can. Soc. Plant Physiologists (gold medal 1971), Am. Soc. Plant Physiologists. Home: 1792 Western Pky Vancouver BC Canada V6T 1V3

SHAW, MICHAEL ALLAN, lawyer, mail order company executive; b. Evanston, Ill., July 14, 1940; s. Frank C. and Mabel I. (Peacock) S.; m. Genevieve Schrodt, Aug. 16, 1964; children: M. Ian, Trevor A. BA, Colo. State U., 1962; JD, U. Denver, 1965; MBA, DePaul U., 1969; postgrad., Columbia U., 1970. Bar: Ill. bar 1965. Practiced in, Chgo., 1965-83; asst. counsel, staff asst. to v.p. traffic Jewel Cos., Inc., Melrose Park, Ill., 1965-71; corp. sec., asst. treas., house counsel Wieboldt Stores, Inc., Chgo., 1972-83; pvt. practice law Naperville, Ill., 1983-89; pres. Kingston Korner, Inc., 1983—, Aztec Corp., Naperville, 1989—. Pres. Folk Era Prodns., producers folk music concert series, records, 1985—; editor Folk Music Editor, 1984; contbr. articles to legal jours. Mem. Village Planning Commn., Itasca, Ill., 1973-77; bd. dirs. Crimestoppers, Naperville, 1984—, chmn., 1988-94; session mem. Naperville Lumen Christi United Presbyn. Ch., 1984-85; chmn.

bldg. fin. com. Naperville Presbyn. Ch., 1989-93. Mem. Fox Valley Folklore Soc. (bd. dirs. 1991—). E-mails. Home: 6 S 230 Cohasset Rd Naperville IL 60540 Office: Aztec Corp 705 S Washington St Naperville IL 60540-6696 E-mail: allan@folkera.com.

SHAW, MICHAEL EVAN, librarian; b. N.Y.C., June 20, 1960; s. Lawrence Taylor and Noreen Mary Shaw. BA, Antioch Coll., Yellow Springs, Ohio, 1986; MLS, U. Pitts., 1993. Dir. libr. Ctr. Econ. Rsch. & Grad. Edn., Prague, Czech Republic, 1993; law libr. Affiliates, L.A., 1994-98; libr. L.A. Pub. Libr., 1994-98; br. mgr. Norfolk (Va.) Pub. Libr., 1998—. Internet trainer L.A. Pub. Libr., 1995. Mem. election com. Am. Fend. State, County & Mcpl. Employees, L.A., 1998. Mem. ALA, Va. Libr. Assn., Torch Club S. Hampton Rd. Avocations: fitness, bicycling, environment. Home: 4409 Newport Ave Norfolk VA 23508 Office: Norfolk Pub Libr 6525 Hampton Blvd Norfolk VA 23508 E-mail: michaels@npl.lib.va.us.

SHAW, MICHAEL J.P. business administration educator, researcher; b. Taipei, Taiwan, July 13, 1956; came to U.S., 1978; s. L.C. and C.C. (Hwang) S.; m. Crystal Shaw, Aug. 8, 1982. BS, Tsiug Hua U., Hsin-Chu, Taiwan, 1978; MS, SUNY, Buffalo, 1980; PhD, Purdue U., 1984. Asst. prof. U. Ill., Champaign, 1984-89, assoc. prof. bus. adminstrn., 1989—. Vis. assoc. prof. Robotics Inst., Carnegie Mellon U., Pitts., 1990; chair INFORMS, Coll. A.I., 1995—. Guest editor Inst. Indsl. Engring. Transactions, 1992, Decision Support Sys., 1993. Recipient Best paper award Tex. Instruments, 1987, 88, Internat. Bus. award Peat Marwick Found., 1989, 90. Mem. Internat. Chinese Info. Sys. Profls. Assn. Achievements include research in enterprise information technology, decision support systems, intelligent manufacturing. Office: U Ill Dept Bus Adminstrn MC-706 350 Commerce West Champaign IL 61820

SHAW, MILTON CLAYTON, mechanical engineering educator; b. Phila., May 27, 1915; s. Milton Fredic and Nellie Edith (Clayton) S.; m. Mary Jane Greeninger, Sept. 6, 1939; children: Barbara Jane, Milton Stanley. BSME, Drexel Inst. Tech., 1938; M of Engring. Sci., U. Cin., 1940, ScD, 1942; PhD (hon.), U. Louvain, Belgium, 1970; DEng (hon.), Drexel U., 1996. Rsch. engr. Cin. Milling Machine Co., 1938-42; chief materials br. NACA, 1942-46; with MIT, 1946-61, prof. mech. engring., 1953-61, head materials processing divsn., 1952-61; prof., head dept. mech. engring. Carnegie Inst. Tech., Pitts., 1961-75; univ. prof. (hon.) Carnegie-Mellon U., 1974-77; prof. engring. Ariz. State U., Tempe, 1977-86, emeritus prof. engring., 1986—. Cons., lectr. in field; pres. Shaw Smith & Assos., Inc., Mass., 1951-61; Lucas prof. Birmingham (Eng.) U., 1961; Springer prof. U. Calif., Berkeley, 1972; Distinguished guest prof. Ariz. State U., 1977; mem. Nat. Materials Adv. Bd., 1971-74; v.p. conf. com. Engring. Found., 1976-78. Recipient Outstanding Research award Ariz. State U., 1981, Am. Machinist award, 1972, Schlesinger award German Govt., 1997; P. McKenna award, 1975; Guggenheim fellow, 1956; Fulbright lectr. Aachen T.H., Germany, 1957; OECD fellow to Europe, 1964—. Fellow Am. Acad. Arts and Scis., ASME (Hersey award 1967, Thurston lectr. 1971, Outstanding Engring. award 1975, ann. meeting theme organizer 1977, Gold medal 1985, hon. 1980), Am. Soc. Lubrication Engrs. (hon., nat. award 1964), Am. Soc. Metals (Wilson award 1971, fellow 1981); mem. Internat. Soc. Prodn. Engring. Research (pres. 1960-61, hon. mem. 1975), Am. Soc. for Engring. Edn. (G. Westinghouse award 1956), Soc. Mfg. Engrs. (hon. mem. 1970, Gold medal 1958, Internat. Edn. award 1980, M.C. Shaw award 1999), Nat. Acad. Engring., Polish Acad. Sci., Am. Soc. Precision Engrs. (hon.), Japan Soc. Precision Engrs. (Internat. award 1999), Drexel 100. Home: Unit C119 2625 E Southern Ave Tempe AZ 85282-7633 Office: Ariz State U Engring Dept Tempe AZ 85287-6106 Fax: 480-965-1384.

SHAW, MILTON HERBERT, conglomerate executive; b. Phila., June 16, 1918; s. Milton Herbert and Ethel (Shane) S.; m. Rita P. Revins, Nov. 24, 1971. BS, U. Pa., 1949. cons. indsl. safety and workmen's compensation. Accountant Franklin Sugar Refinery, Phila., 1945-52; with Kaiser Metal Products, Inc., Bristol, Pa., 1952-61, mgr. ins. and taxes, 1955-61; with Kidde Consumer Durables Corp., Bala Cynwyd, Pa., 1961-88, asst. v.p., 1968-88, dir. corp. svcs. and risk mgmt., 1977-88; cons. Indsl. Safety-Workmans Compensation, 1988; cons. risk mgmt. Hanson Ind., 1989-98. Risk mgmt. and indsl. safety cons., 1988-99; owner Golden Grain Goldens; co-owner Potpourri Doll Promotions, Rita P. Shaw Porcelain Studio. Served with USNR, 1936-45. Mem. NRA, VFW (life), Escort Carriers Assn., Nat. Wildlife Fedn., Sigma Kappa Phi. Home and Office: 2209 Blackhorse Dr Warrington PA 18976-2118

SHAW, RANDY LEE, human services administrator; b. Revenna, Ohio, Oct. 18, 1945; s. Robert and Dorothy Mae (Turner) S.; m. Terri Marie Richardson, July 4, 1988; 1 child, Garrett Samuel. BTh, Ridgedale Sem., 1975, ThM, 1977. Cert. social worker, addictions counselor. Exec. dir. Boy's Recovery Home, Detroit, 1979; clin. dir. Boniface, 1979-83; unit dir. Problem Daily Living, 1983-84; clin. dir. Calvin Wells, 1984-86; exec. dir. Children Youth Equal Rights Adv. House, Pontiac, Mich., 1986-87, Touch of Hope, Hartford, 1988-89; program supr. New Ctr. Community Mental Health, Detroit, 1989-91. Exec. dir. Nat. Inst. Hypertension Studies, Detroit, 1979-88. Local rep., magician for Make-A-Wish Found.; exec. dir. Magicians Against Gangs, Ignorance, and Crime Intervention Program, M.A.G.I.C., 1991—. Mem. Soc. Am. Magicians (local pres. 1993-94), Magic Circle, Internat. Brotherhood of Magicians (local pres. 1993-94), Supreme Magic Club of U.K., Psychic Entertainers Assn. Home and Office: 5375 Antoinette Dr Grand Blanc MI 48439-4310 Fax: 760-281-7066. E-mail: majorshaw@yahoo.com.

SHAW, RICHARD DAVID, marketing and management educator; b. Pitts., Aug. 25, 1938; s. Richard Malburn and Jessie Ruth (Murray) S.; m. Adolphine Catherine Brungardt, Aug. 21, 1965; children: Richard David Jr., John Michael, Shannon Kathleen. BSBA, Rockhurst Coll., 1960; MS in Commerce, St. Louis U., 1964. Claims adjuster Kemper Ins. Group, Kansas City, Mo., 1961; tchr. acctg. Corpus Christi High Sch., Jennings, 1961-63; assoc. prof. econs. Fontbonne Coll., St. Louis, 1963-70, chmn. social behavioral sci. dept., 1968-70; mem. faculty, chmn. bus. div. Longview Community Coll., Lee's Summit, Mo., 1970-81, coord. mktg., 1979-81; workshop leader Rockhurst U., Kansas City, 1975—, prof. mktg., 1981—, chmn. mgmt. and mktg., 1983-85, co-chair MBA program, 1996—, co-chair Sch. of Mgmt. Undergrad. Programs, 1998—. Faculty moderator Jr. Execs. Assn., The Rock yearbook, Rockhurst U. Reps., Rockettes, co-chair undergrad. Sch. of Mgmt. programs, 1998—; pvt. cons., 1981—, chmn. freshman seminar com., 1994; instr. principles of mktg. on The Learning Channel on Cable TV for the PACE Program, 1994; chmn. sch. mgmt. curriculum com., 1993—; co-chair Task Force on Diversity, 1997. Author: Personal Finance, 1983, Principles of Marketing Study Guide, 1993, Contemporary Marketing Study Guide, 1994, Consumer Behavior Study Guide, 1997, Instructor's Manual for Michael Solomon's Consumer Behavior; co-author: Instructor's Resource Manual and Video Guide for Philip Kotler's Marketing Management, 9th edit.; cooperating author: Philip Kotler's Marketing Management. Mem. alumni bd. assessment task force Rockhurst U., 1971-73, 78-80, chmn. 30 yr. reunion com., 1990, 35 yr. reunion com., 1995, chmn. curriculum com., curriculum task force; chmn. Eastwood Hills Coun., Kansas City, 1974-76, bd. dirs., 1988-91, co-chmn. of Solid Rocks Faculty-Staff Fund Raising Campaign, 1994; lead couple Marriage Preparation Classes, Kansas City St. Joseph Dioceses, 1983—; co-chmn. Kansas City Vols. Against Hunger, 1975-80; campaign mgr. Larry Ferns for City Coun., Kansas City, 1975; bd. govs. Citizens Assn., 1976—. With USAR, 1960-64. Recipient Gov.'s Excellence in Teaching award, Mo., 1993, Harry B. Kies award Rockhurst U.; Hallmark fellow Rockhurst U., 1981-86; faculty devel. grantee Sch. Mgmt., Rockhurst U., 1984, 93, 95, 99. Mem. Am. Mktg. Assn., Soc. for Advancement of Mgmt., Mid-Am. Mktg. Assn., Alpha Sigma Nu, Kappa Delta Pi. Roman Catholic. Avocations: gardening, genealogy, photography. Home: 11014 Washington St Kansas City MO 64114-5177 Office: Rockhurst U 1100 Rockhurst Rd Kansas City MO 64110-2508 E-mail: dick.shaw@rockhurst.edu., shaw.manor@att.net.

SHAW, RICHARD EUGENE, cardiovascular researcher; b. Springfield, Ohio, Jan. 20, 1950; s. Eugene Russell and Marjorie Caroline Shaw; m. Nov. 26, 1976; 2 children. BA, Duquesne U., 1972; MA, U.S. Internat. U., San Diego, 1977; PhD, U. Calif., San Francisco, 1984. Cert. nuc. med. technologist. Nuclear Medicine Tech. Cert. Bd. Staff nuc. med. technologist Scripps Meml. Hosp., La Jolla, Calif., 1975-79; rsch. asst. U. Calif. San Francisco Sch. Medicine, 1980-85; mgr. rsch. programs San Francisco Heart Inst., Daly City, Calif., 1985-87, dir. rsch., 1988-90, dir. rsch. and ops., 1991—. Sr. advisor steering com. for databases Daus. of Charity Nat. Health Sys., St. Louis, 1993-96. Editor-in-chief Jour. Invasive Cardiology, 1989—; contbr. more than 200 articles and book chpts. to med. lit. Coach Am. Youth Soccer Orgn. and Youth Baseball Assn., bd. dirs., Burlingame, Calif., 1990-94; pres. Burlingame H.S. Athletic Boosters, 2000—. Fellow Am. Coll. Cardiology (nat. cardiac database com., outcomes assessment subcom. 1998—, NCOR task force 2001—, publs. subcom. 2001—), Am. Coll. Angiology; mem. Am. Heart Assn., Soc. for Clin. Trials, N.Y. Acad. Scis., Am. Statis. Assn., Am. Med. Informatics Assn., Soc. Behavioral Medicine. Avocation: music. Office: San Francisco Heart Inst Seton Med Ctr 1900 Sullivan Ave Daly City CA 94015-2200 E-mail: richardshaw@edochs.org.

SHAW, RICHARD GLENN, financial analyst; b. Queens, N.Y., Oct. 11, 1956; s. Martin and Patricia Ann Shaw; m. Karla N. Shaw; 1 child Michael Stone. BA, Jacksonville U., 1978. CFP, Registry of Certified Financial Planning Practitioners. Mgr. real estate devel. firm, 1980-84; owner mktg. corp., 1985-88; fin. advisor Lincoln Fin. Group, Overland Park, Kans., 1988—. Bd. dirs., trustee U. Mo.-Kansas City Conservatory Music. Mem. Internat. Assn. Fin. Planning, Estate Planning Soc. Kansas City, Internat. Baseball Fedn. Office: Lincoln Fin Group 10851 Mastin Ste 950 Overland Park KS 66210-2009

SHAW, RICHARD MELVIN, gemologist, gold company executive; b. L.A., Jan. 14, 1947; s. Melvin and Harriet Louise (Hammond) S.; m. Deanna Lee Revel, Mar. 9, 1968 (div. 1973); 1 child, Katharine Lillian; m. Janet Lynne Gribble, Dec. 31, 1981; 1 child: Jacquelyn Louise. Student, L.A. Valley Coll.-Van Nuys, 1965-67; grad., Gemological Inst. Am., 1976. Design coordinator Foxy Jon's Smokehouse Cabins, Inc., L.A., 1968-71; Pantera specialist, used car mgr. Bricker Lincoln-Mercury, 1971-74; designer Melvin Shaw & Assocs., Santa Monica, Calif., 1974-76; instr. Gemological Inst. Am., 1976-79, dir. rsch. and devel., 1979-82; ptnr., dir. sales and mktg. N.W. Gold Mktg., Woodland Hills, Calif., 1982-83; exec. v.p. Nat. Gold Distbr., Ltd., Canoga Park, 1983-86; pres., CEO Campbell Shaw, Inc., Woodland Hills, 1986—, founder AMPS divsn., 1993; founder, ptnr. Rick Shaw & Co., 1982—; lighting and sound contractor, dealer CSI Multimedia divsn. CSI, 1999—. Gemological cons., 1988. Developer, designer Diamond Pen instrument; developer of standardized microscope grading method. Mem. L.A. County Mus. Alliance, Mineral. Soc. So. Calif., Nat. Assn. Underwater Instrs., Instrument Soc. Am.

SHAW, ROBERT BURNS, poet, educator; b. Phila., July 16, 1947; s. Gordon Walter and Elizabeth Anne Shaw; m. Nancy Anne Olenchuk, June 21, 1969; children: Catherine Frances, Anthony Peter Gordon. BA, Harvard Coll., 1969; MPhil, Yale U., 1973, PhD, 1974. Briggs-Copeland lectr. English Harvard U., Cambridge, Mass., 1974-76; from asst. prof. to assoc. prof. English Yale U., New Haven, 1976-83; assoc. prof. English Mt. Holyoke Coll., South Hadley, Mass., 1983-91, prof. English, 1991—. Vis. prof. U. Fla., Gainesville, spring 1996 Author: (poetry collections) Comforting the Wilderness, 1977, The Wonder of Seeing Double, 1988, The Post Office Murals Restored, 1994, Below the Surface, 1999, Solving for X, 2002. Recipient James Boatwright prize for poetry, 1992, Hollis Summers prize, 2002; Creative Writing fellow NEA, 1987, fellow Ingram Merrill Found., 1990. Mem. Assn. Literary Scholars and Critics, Authors Guild, Poetry Soc. Am., Acad. Am. Poets. Democrat. Episcopalian. Avocations: walking, swimming, gardening. Office: Mt Holyoke Coll English Dept 50 College St South Hadley MA 01075 E-mail: rshaw@mtholyoke.edu.

SHAW, ROBERT GILBERT, state senator, restaurant executive; b. Erwin, N.C., Nov. 22, 1924; s. Robert Gilbert B. and Annie Elizabeth (Byrd) S.; m. Grace Lee Wilson, Jan. 29, 1951 (div. 1976); children: Ann Karlen, Barbara Jean; m. Linda Owens, May 27, 1982. AA, Campbell U., 1948; postgrad., U. N.C., 1948-50. Restaurateur, 1951—. County commr. County of Guilford, Greensboro, N.C., 1968-76; chair N.C. Rep. Party, Raleigh, 1975-77; minority leader N.C. Senate, Raleigh, 1984—; chair Guilford County Rep. Party, 1973-75; mem. Rep. Nat. Com., Washington, 1975-77. With USAAC, 1943-46. Named Legislator of Yr. Nat. Fedn. Wildlife, 1990. Mem. Elks (life, bd. govs. 1953—). Presbyterian. Avocations: fishing, hunting, politics. Home: 5105 Bennington Dr Greensboro NC 27410 Office: NC Senate 1129 Legislative Bldg Raleigh NC 27611 E-mail: RGB112224@aol.com.

SHAW, ROBERT WILLIAM, JR. management consultant, venture capitalist; b. Ithaca, N.Y., Aug. 10, 1941; s. Robert William and Charlotte G. (Throop) S.; m. Anne P. Meads, Aug. 29, 1964; children: Mark Andrew, Christopher Matthew. B of Engring. Physics, MSEE, Cornell U., 1964; PhD, Stanford U., 1968; MPA, Am. U., 1981. Postdoctoral fellow Cavendish Lab., Cambridge, Eng., 1968-69; mem. tech. staff Bell Tel. Labs., Murray Hill, N.J., 1969-72; with Booz Allen Hamilton, Bethesda, Md., 1972-83, sr. v.p. energy and environ. divsn., 1979-83, mem. oper. coun., 1981-83, also bd. dirs.; pres. Arete Ventures, Inc., 1983-97, Utech Venture Capital Corp., 1985—; gen. ptnr. Utech Venture Capital Corp. Fund I, 1985—2000, Utech Venture Capital Corp. Fund II, 1988—, Utech Venture Capital Corp. I Parallel Fund L.P., 1988—2001, Utech Venture Capital Corp. II Parallel Fund, L.P., 1991—, Utech Climate Challenge Fund, L.L.C., Bethesda, Md., 1995—; v.p. Can. Energy and Environment Ventures, Inc., 1993-95; pres. Arete Corp., Center Harbor, N.H., 1997—. Spl. ltd. ptnr. Nth Power Techs. Fund II; mem. investment com. Sustainable Asset Mgmt. Pvt. Equity Fund, Commons Capital LLC; mng. ptnr. Micro-Generation Tech. Fund, LLC, 1997—; mem. bd. energy and environ. sys. Nat. Rsch. Coun.; mem. energy com. Aspen Inst. Humanistic Studies, Investor's Cir.; bd. councillors China-U.S. Ctr. for Sustainable Devel.; chmn. bd. dirs. CellTech Power, Inc., Evergreen Solar, Inc., No. Power Sys., Inc., Proton Energy Sys., Inc.; bd. dirs. H2Gen Innovations, Inc. Contbr. articles to profl. jours. NASA trainee; Office Sci. rsch. fellow USAF, 1968-69. Mem. AAAS, Am. Phys. Soc. (mem. investment com.), Nat. Venture Capital Assn., Orgnl. Devel. Network, Assn. Humanistic Psychology, Inst. Noetic Scis., Internat. Transactional Analysis Assn., Sigma Xi, Tau Beta Pi, Phi Kappa Phi, Pi Alpha Alpha, Kappa Delta Rho. Home: PO Box 1664 Center Harbor NH 03226-1664 Office: PO Box 1299 Center Harbor NH 03226-1299 E-mail: aretecorp@cyberportal.net.

SHAW, RONALD AHREND, physician, educator; b. Toledo, July 20, 1946; s. Harold Michael and Eve Helen (Ganch) S.; m. Carol Ann Rapp, June 13, 1970; children: Robert, Benjamin, Daniel. BS, U. Toledo, 1968; MD, Washington U., 1972. Diplomate Am. Bd. Emergency Medicine. Intern, then resident in surgery St. Luke's Hosp., St. Louis, 1972-73, resident in surgery, 1973; mem. staff Bapt. Med. Ctr.-Montclair, Birmingham, Ala., 1976-81, chief emergency svc., 1979-81; assoc. dir. lifesaver flight ops. Caraway Meth. Med. Ctr., 1981-85; dir. emergency svc. sch. medicine U. Ala., 1985-89; asst. dir. emergency svc. R.I. Hosp., Providence, 1989-95; attending physician emergency dept. Bapt. Med. Ctr., Montgomery, Ala., 1996—; med. dir. emergency dept. Jackson Hosp., 2000—01; sec.-treas., med. staff Bapt. Med. Ctr., 2001—. Cons. U. Tex., Houston, 1986, Bell Helicopter, Ft. Worth, 1986, Mut. Assurance, Birmingham, 1986-89, NYU, 1988-89, R.I. State Med. Examiners Office, 1991-96, Fla. Dept. Health, EMS Office, 1991—, Joint Underwriters Assocs. of R.I., 1991-96; chmn. adv. bd. emergency svc. Ala. Dept. Pub. Health, 1986-89; med. dir. Emergency Med. Svcs. div. R.I. Dept. Health, 1990-95; med. dir. Health Care Rev., Inc., 1995-96. Bd. dirs. MADD, Ala., 1986, Univ. Emergency Medicine Found., 1995-96; mem. planning com. Youth Baseball, Vestavia Hills, ala., 1986, 87; mem. disaster com. City of Birmingham, 1984-89; mem. 911 Commn., State of R.I., 1991-96. Recipient Disting. Achievement award Birmingham Emergency Med. Svc., 1988. Fellow Am. Coll. Emergency Physicians (bd. dirs. Ala. chpt. 1984-89, steering com. EMS sect. 1991-94, sec.-treas. R.I. chpt. 1995-96); mem. AAAS, ACS (state com. on trauma R.I. chpt. 1990-96), N.Y. Acad. Sci., Med. Assn. Ala. (mem. coun. med. svc. 1985-86). Republican. Avocations: hunting, stamp collecting and computer programming.

SHAW, ROSLYN LEE, retired elementary education educator; b. Bklyn., Oct. 1, 1942; d. Benjamin Biltmore and Bessie (Banilower) Deretchin; m. Stephen Allan Shaw, Feb. 1, 1964; children: Laurence, Victoria, Michael. BA, Bklyn. Coll., 1964; MS, SUNY, New Paltz, 1977, cert. advanced study, 1987; cert. gifted edn., Coll. New Rochelle, 1986. Cert. sch. adminstr., supr., sch. dist. adminstr., reading tchr., tchr. N-6. Tchr. Hillel Hebrew Acad., Beverly Hills, Calif., 1965-66, P.S. 177, 77, Bklyn., 1964-65, 66-67, Middletown (N.Y.) Sch. Dist., 1974-77, reading specialist, 1977-99, compensatory edn. reading tchr., 1977-99, tchr. gifted children, 1984-87, asst. project coord. pre-K, 1988-89, instrnl. leader, 1989-93; ret., 1999. Adj. assoc. prof. SUNY, Coll. at New Paltz, 1997-98; newspaper in edn. coord. The Times Herald Record, 1999-2001, ednl. cons., 2001-. Pres. Middletown H.S. Parents' Club, 1983-86; bd. dirs. Mental Health Assn., Goshen, N.Y., 1980-81; mem. Middletown Interfaith Coun., 1983-85. Mem. Amy Bull Crist Reading Coun. (pres. 1989-91, 93-95, 2001), N.Y. State Reading Assn. (Coun. Svc. award 1990, regional dir. 1991-94, bd. dirs. 1991—, chair reading tchrs. spl. interest group 1993-94, pres.-elect 1999—, pres. 2000-01, past pres. 2001, regional dir. 2001, newsletter editor The Empire State Reading Scene), Internat. Reading Assn., Univ. Women's Club, Delta Kappa Gamma. Avocations: photography, walking, reading. Home: 21 Thatchwood Ct New Brunswick NJ 08902 Office: 21 Thatchwood Ct New Brunswick NJ 08902-1083 E-mail: iconsult@optonline.net.

SHAW, RUSSELL BURNHAM, author, journalist; b. Washington, May 19, 1935; s. Charles Burnham and Mary (Russell) S.; m. Carmen Hilda Carbon, July 19, 1958; children: Mary Hilda, Emily Anne, Janet, Charles, Elizabeth. BA, Georgetown U., 1956, MA, 1960. Staff writer Cath. Standard, Washington, 1956-57; reporter Nat. Cath. News Svc., 1957-66; dir. publs., pub. info. Nat. Cath. Ednl. Assn., 1966-69; dir. Nat. Cath. Office for Info., 1969-73; assoc. sec. for communication U.S. Cath. Conf., 1973-74, sec. for pub. affairs Nat. Conf. Cath. Bishops, 1975-87; dir. pub. info. KC, 1987-97; Washington corr. Our Sunday Visitor, 1997—; assoc. prof. Pontifical Univ. of the Holy Cross, 1996—; editor The Pope Speaks, 1998—. Consultor Pontifical Coun. for Social Comms., 1984—89, 2001—. Author: The Dark Disciple, 1961, Abortion on Trial, 1968, Church and State, 1979, Choosing Well, 1982, Why We Need Confession, 1986, Renewal, 1986, Signs of the Times, 1986, Does Suffering Make Sense?, 1987, To Hunt, To Shoot, To Entertain, 1993, Understanding Your Rights, 1994, Papal Primacy in the Third Millennium, 2000, Ministry or Apostolate—What Should the Catholic Laity Be Doing?, 2002; co-author: S.O.S. for Catholic Schools, 1970, Beyond the New Morality, 3d edit., 1988, Fulfillment in Christ, 1991, others; editor Ency. of Cath. Doctrine, 1997; columnist monthly mag. Washington Report, 1966—; columnist weekly newspaper Cath. Herald, 1999—. Mem. Equestrian Order of Holy Sepulchre of Jerusalem, Phi Beta Kappa. Roman Catholic. Home and Office: 2928 44th Pl NW Washington DC 20016-3555 E-mail: rshaw10290@aol.com.

SHAW, RUTH LEA, art educator; b. Newfield, NJ, June 7, 1916; d. Albert Lawrence and Ruby Beatrice (Kears) Miller; m. Kenneth Van Buren, July 3, 1937 (div. 1968); 1 child Ruth Hope ; m. Wilbert Shaw, June 12 (dec.). Tchr. fine arts dept. Indian River CC. Exhibitions include Orange Blossom Gallery. Home: 4860 River Oak Ln Fort Pierce FL 34981-4412

SHAW, SAMUEL ERVINE, II, retired insurance company executive, consultant; b. Independence, Kans., Apr. 10, 1933; s. Samuel Ervine and Jessie Elizabeth (Guernsey) S.; m. Dale Foster Dorman, June 19, 1954; children: Samuel Ervine III, Christopher Atwood, Elizabeth Foster. BA, Harvard U., 1954; JD, Boston Coll., 1965. Bar: Mass. 1965, U.S. Supreme Ct. 1971; enrolled actuary 1976-93; cons. actuary, 1987. With John Hancock Mut. Life Ins. Co., Boston, 1957-87, group pension and ins. actuary, 2d v.p., 1979-85, v.p., group ins. actuary, 1985-87; dir. Health Reins. Assn. Conn., Hartford, 1980-87; cons. Internat. Exec. Service Corps, Guayaquil, Ecuador, 1973, Jakarta, Indonesia, 1988, Perm, Russia, 1994, Pension Benefit Guaranty Corp., Washington, 1974-75, Nat. Hosp. Ins. Fund, Nairobi, Kenya, 1990. Mem. Brookline Hist. Commn. (Mass.), 1981-88, Brookline Retirement Bd., 1985-90; chmn. Brookline Com. on Town Orgn. and Structure, 1975-79. Served to maj. USAF, 1954-57. Fellow Soc. Actuaries; mem. Am. Acad. Actuaries, Internat. Actuarial Assn., ABA. Episcopalian. Home and Office: 131 Sewall Ave Brookline MA 02446-5314

SHAW, SEANA HIRSCHFELD, psychiatrist, educator; b. N.Y.C., Oct. 16, 1938; m. Jon Angus Shaw. MD, Med. Coll. Pa., 1962. Diplomate Am. Bd. Psychiatry and Neurology. Assoc. prof. clin. psychiatry U. Miami, Fla., 1989—. Fellow Am. Psychiat. Assn. Office: U Miami Dept Psychiatry 1400 NW 10th Ave Miami FL 33136-1000 E-mail: seanashaw@aol.com.

SHAW, STANLEY MINER, nuclear pharmacy scientist; b. Parkston, S.D., July 4, 1935; s. George Henry and Jensina (Thompson) S.; m. Excellda J. Watke, Aug. 13, 1961; children: Kimberly Kay, Renee Denise, Elena Aimee. BS, S.D. State U., 1957, MS, 1959; PhD, Purdue U., 1962. Instr. S.D. State U., 1960-62; asst. prof. bionucleonics Purdue U., West Lafayette, Ind., 1962-66, assoc. prof., 1966-71, prof. nuclear pharmacy, 1971—, head. divsn. nuclear pharmacy, 1990—; acting head Purdue U. Sch. Health Scis., 1990-93. Bd. pharm. spltys. Splty. Council Nuclear Pharmacy, 1978-82. Contbr. articles to profl. jours. Recipient Lederle Pharmacy faculty awards, 1962, 65, Parenteral Drug Assn. Rsch. award, 1970, Henry Heine Outstanding Tchr. award Sch. Pharmacy Purdue U., 1989, 93, 99, Disting. Alumnus award S.D. State U., 1991, Disting. Pharmacy Educator award AACP, 1994. Fellow Acad. Pharmacy Practice (chmn. sect. nuclear pharmacy 1979-80, historian 1981-85, mem.-at-large 1993-95, chmn.-elect 1995-96, chmn. 1996-97, Disting. Achievement award 1998), Am. Soc. Hosp. Pharmacy, Am. Pharm. Assn.; mem. Health Physics Soc., Am. Pharm. Assn. (ho. of dels. 1977, 79, 86, 92, Founder's award, Daniel B. Smith Practice Excellence award 2000), Sigma Xi, Phi Lambda Upsilon, Phi Lambda Sigma, Rho Chi. Home: 7208 W Greenview Dr Battle Ground IN 47920-9732 Office: Purdue U Sch Pharmacy West Lafayette IN 47907-1336

SHAW, STEPHEN RAGSDALE, trust investment executive; b. N.Y.C., Jan. 16, 1945; s. Harry Lee and Marie (Ragsdale) S.; m. Mary James Baskervill, June 9, 1969; children: Lee Berkeley, Stephen Stovall. BA in History, Coll. of William and Mary, 1969; postgrad., N.Y. Inst. of Fin., 1971; MBA in Fin., Loyola U., 1983. Sales rep. Lehigh Portland Cement Co., Allentown, Pa., 1969-71; account exec. W.E. Hutton & Co., Balt., 1971-74; asst. v.p. Union Trust Co., 1974-80; v.p. Mercantile Safe Deposit & Trust Co., 1980-83; v.p., sr. investment officer Wilmington Trust of Fla., N.A., Stuart, 1983-95; v.p. Wilmington Trust, FSB, 1995-99, No. Trust Bank, North Palm Beach, Fla., 1999—. Bd. dirs., treas. Second Sight Taping Studio, Inc., Jenson Beach, Fla., 1989-92. With USMCR, 1967-73. Fellow Assn. for Investment Mgmt. and Rsch. Republican. Episcopalian. Avocations: tennis, sailing, scuba diving. Home: 152 SE Harbor Point Dr Stuart FL 34996-1348 Office: Northern Trust Bank 11301 US Highway 1 North Palm Beach FL 33408-3040

SHAW, STEVEN JOHN, retired marketing educator, academic administrator; b. Hamilton, N.Y., Nov. 16, 1918; s. Constantine J. and Agnes (Tilicki) S.; m. Aracelis Goberna, June 8, 1952. BS, N.Y. State U., 1941; MS in Retailing, N.Y. U., 1946, PhD, 1955. Instr. mktg. U. Miami, Coral Gables, Fla., 1948-52; asst. prof. Tulane U., New Orleans, 1954-55, U. Fla., Gainesville, 1955-57; assoc. prof., then prof. U. S.C., Columbia, 1957-89, Disting. prof. emeritus, 1989—, dir. dept. mktg., 1968-72. Cons. Hoffman LaRoche, Nutley, N.J.; exec. dir. S.C.-Southwestern Colombia chpt. Ptnrs. of Ams., 1977-79, asst. exec. dir., 1987-91, also bd. dirs. Author: Salesmanship: Modern Viewpoints on Personal Communication, 1960, Marketing in Business Management, 1963, Cases in Marketing Management Strategy, 1971. Recipient N.Y. U. Founders Day award, 1956, Steven J. Shaw award for most scholarly article in Jour. Bus. Research. Mem. So. Marketing Assn. (pres. 1964), Beta Gamma Sigma (pres. 1965) Home and Office: 7600 Tryall Dr Hialeah FL 33015-2931

SHAW, TALBERT O. university president; BD, Andrews U., 1963; MA, U. Chgo., 1968, PhD, 1973. Dean of students Oakwood Coll., Huntsville, Ala., 1965-71; dean Howard U., Washington, 1971-76; dean Coll. Arts and Scis. Morgan State U., Balt., 1976-87; pres. Shaw U., Raleigh, N.C., 1987—. Office: Shaw U 118 E South St Raleigh NC 27601-2399

SHAW, TESHETESA S. pre-school educator; b. Harricountray, Tex., Dec. 17, 1978; d. Tom Henry and Thelio Maria Shaw. Tchr. Willow H.S., Houston, 1998—99, Acad. Learning Sta., Arcola, 1999—. Home: Rt 1, Box 444 3605 Kansas Fresno TX 77545

SHAW, TIMOTHY MILTON, political science educator; b. Frimley, Surrey, Eng., Jan. 27, 1945; came to Can., 1971; s. Arnold J. and Margaret E. (Milton) S.; m. Jane L. Parpart, Sept. 2, 1983; children: Laura, Lee Parpart; m. Susan M. Sturt, July 8, 1967 (div. 1980); children: Benjamin, Amanda. BA, Sussex U., Brighton, Eng., 1967; MA, E. Africa U., Kampala, Uganda, 1969, Princeton U., 1971, PhD, 1975. Prof. polit. sci. Dalhousie U., Halifax, N.S., Can., 1971-73, 74-78, Canada, 1980—2002; dir. Ctr. African Studies, 1983-

89, Ctr. for Fgn. Policy Studies, Halifax, 1993-2000, Internat. Devel. Studies Program, 1986-89; dir. BA and MA program, 1998-2000; dir. Pearson Inst., Halifax, 1985-87, Canadian Internat. Devel. Agy., 1994-95. Vis. faculty mem. Makerere U., Kampala, 1968-70, U. Zambia, Lusaka, 1973-74, Carleton U., Ottawa, Ont., Can., 1978-79, U. Ife, Nigeria, 1979-80, U. Zimbabwe, 1989, Rhodes U., South Africa, 1993, 2002, Warwick U., U.K., 1997, U. Western Cape & Stellenbosch U., South Africa, 1998—, Mbarara U. Sci. and Tech., 1998—, Aalborg U., 2000-01; cons. UN Econ. Commn. for Africa, Addis Ababa, Ethiopia, 1983-88 Editor: Palgrave Internat. Polit. Economy Series, London, 1984—; author: Reformism and Revisionism in Africa's Political Economy in the 1990s, 1993, (with Julius Ihonvbere) Illusions of Power: Nigeria in Transition, 1998; co-editor: (with Julius Nyangoro) Beyond Structural Adjustment in Africa, 1992, Corporatism in Africa, 1988, Political Economy of NICs, 1988, (with Larry A. Swatuk) The South at the End of the Twentieth Century, 1994, (with Julius E. Okolo) The Political Economy of Foreign Policy in ECOWAS, numerous others. Mem. New Dem. Party, Halifax, 1984—. Grantee, Social Sci. & Humanities Rsch. Coun. Can., Africa, 1981—, Ford Found., 1999—2001. Mem. Internat. Polit. Soc. Assn. (chair rsch. com. #40 on New World Orders), Can. Assn. Devel. Studies (pres. 1993-94), European Assn. Devel. Inst. (co-chmn. working group on new regulations), Can. Assn. African Studies (pres. 1984-85), Internat. Studies Assn. (pres. global devel. sect. 1995-96), Waegwoltic Club (Halifax). Avocations: jogging, cooking, building, travel. Home: 1143 Studley Ave Halifax NS Canada B3H 3R8 Office: Inst Commonwealth Studies U London 28 Russell Sq London WC1B 5DS England Fax: 0171-255-2160. E-mail: tim.shaw@sas.ac.uk.

SHAW, VIRGINIA RUTH, clinical psychologist; b. Salina, Kans., Dec. 10, 1952; d. Lawrence Eugene and Gladys S.; m. Joseph Eugene Scuro Jr., July 14, 1990. BA magna cum laude, Kans. Wesleyan U., 1973; MA, Wichita State U., 1975; PhD, U. Southern Miss., 1984. Diplomate Am. Bd. Med. Psychotherapists (fellow). Rsch. fellow Wichita (Kans.) State U., 1973-75; rsch. fellow, teaching fellow U. So. Miss., 1978-79, 80-81; staff psychologist Big Spring (Tex.) State Hosp., 1976-78; predoctoral clin. psychology intern U. Okla. Health Scis. Ctr., Oklahoma City, 1981-82; postdoctoral fellow in neuropsychology Neuropsychiat. Inst., UCLA, 1982-83; rsch. psychologist, neuropsychologist L.A. VA Med. Ctr. Wadsworth Div., 1983-84; clin. neuropsychologist Patton (Calif.) State Hosp., 1984-85; clin. neuropsychologist Brentwood div. LA VA Med. Ctr., 1985; clinical, neuropsychologist Timberlawn Psychiatric Hosp., Dallas, 1985-87, Dallas Rehab. Inst., 1987-93. Cons. clin. neuropsychology Dallas area hosps., Willowbrook Hosp., Waxahachie, Tex., Cedars Hosp., Waxahachie, 1988-96; br. chief, clin. psychologist Maui child and adolescent mental health team State of Hawaii Dept. Health, 1996—; presenter profl. meetings, 1975—. Contbr. articles to profl. jours. Mem. 500 Inc., Dallas, 1988—96, Maui Children's Coalition Coun., 1996—, Maui Spl. Edn. Adv. Coun., 1996—2000, Maui Cmty. Children's Coun., 1996—, So. Miss. Football, 1996—; mem. Dallas Mayor's com. Employment of the Disabled, 1987. Remiatte Meml. scholar Kans. Wesleyan U., 1970-73; recipient Nat. Disting. Svc. Registry award in rehab., 1989, Early Career Contbns. to Clin. Neuropsychology award candidate Nat. Acad. Neuropsychology, 1993, 94. Mem. AAUW (v.p. programs Maui chpt. 1996-98), APA Divsn. 35/Psychology of Women (student rsch. prize com. 1996), Internat. Neuropsychol. Soc., Nat. Head Injury Found., Assn. for Women in Psychology, Tex. Head Injury Found., Dallas Head Injury Found. (Vol. award, cert. appreciation 1991), Am. Congress Rehab. Medicine, Nat. Rehab. Assn., Nat. Acad. Neuropsychology (membership com. 1991-94, rsch. consortium 1991-96, co-chair poster program com. 1994, 95), Hawaii Psychology Assn. Avocations: coin collecting, skiing, gourmet cooking, travel, dancing. Office: 444 Hana Hwy Ste 202 Kahului HI 96732-2315 E-mail: vrshaw@camhmis.health.state.hi.us.

SHAW, WILLIAM FREDERICK, statistician; b. Bklyn., Feb. 24, 1920; s. Charles Peter and Josephine Veronica (Seusing) S.; m. Josephine Cannington Kerbey, Jan. 18, 1947; children— William Frederick, Teresa Anne. BBA, U. Miami, 1949; MA, George Washington U., 1953; postgrad. studies in econometrics, math. and computer scis., U.S. Dept. Agr. Grad. Sch., 1964-74; PhD (fellow), Walden U., 1977. Research asst. U. Miami, 1948-49; with Research and Stats. div. FHA, Washington, 1950-73, chief statistician, 1969—; chief statistician, dir. Advanced Statis. Analysis and Computer Applications Staff HUD, 1974-82, chief statistician, dir. housing stats. div., 1982-89, chief statistician, dir. info. systems div., 1990-91, chief statistician, dir. Office of Evaluation, 1991—. Pres. Kerbey-Shaw Assos. Served with F.A. AUS, 1943-45. Decorated Bronze Star medal valor in ground combat; recipient Superior Performance award HUD, 1977; named by Info. Resources Adminstrn. Coun. as Fed. Office Sys. Profl. of Yr., 1983. Mem. AAAS, Am. Statis. Assn., Am. Risk and Ins. Assn., Am. Real Estate and Urban Econ. Assn., Am. Econ. Assn., Am. Fin. Assn., N.Y. Acad. Scis., Nat. Assn. Rev. Appraisers and Mortgage Underwriters, Soc. Cost Estimating and Analysis, Res. Offcers Assn. U.S., 101st Airborne Divsn. Assn., Air Force Assn., Alpha Kappa Psi. Roman Catholic. Home: 6527 Byrnes Dr Mc Lean VA 22101-5227 Office: HUD 7th And D Sts SW Washington DC 20411-0001

SHAW, WILLIAM FREDERICK, investment company executive; b. Boston, July 26, 1960; s. Allen D. Shaw and Carol Lee (Mousley) Holbrook. BA, Suffolk U., 1982; MBA, Boston U., 1995. Lic. registered rep. MFS Investment Mgmt. Mkt. rsch. analyst John Hancock Advisers, Boston, 1985-87, mktg. cons., 1987-90; sales exec. John Hancock Advisors, 1990-93, dir. mktg., 1993-95; v.p. Fortis Pvt. Capital, N.Y.C., 1995-97; v.p. mktg. Scudder Investments, Boston, 1997-99; sr. v.p., dir. mktg. M.F.S. Investments, 1999—. Contbr. to Wall St. Jour., Kiplingers, Money Mag., Employee Benefit News, others. Fundraiser, campaign cons. Ted Kennedy election com., Boston; trustee Employee Benefit Rsch. Inst.; advisor Profit Sharing Coun. Am. U.S. Nat. Skating champion, Amateur Athletic Union, 1974-89. Mem. Internat. Assn. Bus. Communicators, South End Hist. Soc., Boston Algonquin Club. Avocations: skating, art collecting, antiques, travel. Home: The St Cloud Ste 30 567 Tremont St Boston MA 02118-3727 Office: 500 Boylston St Boston MA 02116-3740

SHAWCROSS, JOHN THOMAS, English educator; b. Hillside, N.J., Feb. 10, 1924; s. Ernest Edward and Lillian Anderson (Kuncken) S. AM, NYU, 1950, PhD, 1958; DLitt, Montclair State U., 1975, St. Bonaventure U., 1995. Prof. English Rutgers U., New Brunswick, N.J., 1963-67; prof. English U. Wis., Madison, 1967-70, CUNY, 1970-79, U. Ky., Lexington, 1979—. Author: John Milton: The Self and the World, 1992 (Milton Soc. award 1993), With Mortal Voice: The Creation of Paradise Lost, 1984, The Uncertain World of Samson Agonistes, 2001. Lt. (j.g.) U.S. Navy, 1942-46. Home: 4818 Hartland Pkwy Lexington KY 40515-1106 E-mail: jtshaw74@earthlink.net.

SHAWE, DANIEL REEVES, geologist; b. Gardnerville, Nev., May 24, 1925; s. Hamilton Bruce and Henrietta Frieda (Rhodes) S.; m. Helen Mae Cruikshank, Oct. 17, 1951; children: Jill J, Jennifer Sue, Scott Reeves. BS in Geology with great distinction, Stanford U., 1949, MS in Geology, 1950, PhD in Geology, 1953. Rsch. geologist U.S. Geol. Survey, Denver, 1951-53, 58-95, Grand Junction, Colo., 1953-58; chief Br. Rocky Mountain Mineral Resources, Denver, 1969-72; geologist emeritus U.S. Geol. Survey, 1995—. Author: Geology and Mineral Deposits of Thailand, 1984; editor, author: Geology and Resources of Fluorine, U.S., 1976, (series) Geology and Resources of Gold, U.S., 1988-92; contbr. over 150 reports to profl. publs. With USN, 1943-45. Recipient Meritorious Svc. award U.S. Dept. Interior, 1972. Fellow Geol. Soc. Am. (chmn. various coms. 1976-83); mem. Colo. Sci. Soc. (hon., pres. 1979), Soc. Econ. Geologists (com. chmn. 1969-88). Republican. Achievements include co-discovery of large bedded barite deposits in Nevada. Avocations: hunting, writing, Nevada archeology. Home: 8920 W 2d Ave Lakewood CO 80226 Office: US Geol Survey MS 973 PO Box 25046 Denver CO 80225-0046 E-mail: handdshawe@aol.com.

SHAWN, ERIC, author, artist; b. L.A., May 6, 1966; s. Jerome Edward Resnick and Bonnye Mae (Kennard) Ford. Graphic designer Kahtom Corp., L.A., 1986-87; pres., CEO, Shawn, Co., Simi Valley, Calif., 1987—. Computer programmer Scratch Pad, 1996. Inventor flat pack shaver; artist, designer www.ericshawn.com Computer Graphics World, 1993; screenwriter Palindrome, 1999. Instr. art Simi Cultural Arts Assn., 1995—. Libertarian. Avocations: philately, classical music, philosophy, physics, literature. Home and Office: 2860 Elizondo Ave Simi Valley CA 93065-4716

SHAWSTAD, RAYMOND VERNON, retired business owner, computer specialist; b. Brainerd, Minn., Mar. 17, 1931; s. Gerhard A. Shawstad and Ruth Catherine Hammond; stepson of Klaas Ostendorf. Student, Niederhauser Airways, 1947-51, San Bernardino Valley Coll., 1959-60, 65, West Coast U., 1960-62, UCLA Extension, 1966-81, Liberal Inst. Natural Sci. and Tech., 1973-83, Free Enterprise Inst., 1973-83, Kingsway Christian Coll., 1994-96, Marshalltown Jr. Coll., 1949. Salesman, Marshalltown, Iowa, 1952-53; asst. retail mgr. Gamble-Skogmo, Inc., Waverly, 1953-54, retail mgr. Iowa Falls, 1954-57; sr. programmer County of San Bernardino (Calif.), 1958-64; info. systems cons. Sunkist Growers, Inc., Van Nuys, Calif., 1965-75, sr. systems programmer, 1975-92. Univ. extension instr. UCLA, 1980-81; propr. artificial intelligence rschr. Lang. Products Co., 1980-97; propr., fin. educator Pennyseed Mgmt. Co., 1987-97; reader in geriatrics, propr., instr. econs. Liberal Pentagon, 1991-93, Liberal Propr., 1993-94; propr. Med. Investments, 1993-97; distbn. specialist, propr. Networking Group Co., 1992-97. Author numerous software programs; editor VM Notebook of GUIDE Internat. Corp., 1982-92; author: Seekers, Awake!, 1998; contbg. editor: Soldiers for the Truth, 1999. Vol. bedside music therapist VA Hosp., 1984-97; musician Project Caring, 1984-87; mentor The Caring Connection, 1993-94; vol. Meals-on-Wheels, 1993; rep. U.S. Senatorial Bus. Adv. Bd., Calif., 1988-92; mem. data processing adv. bd. City of Marshalltown, Iowa, 1993-97; vol. League of Mercy of Salvation Army; treas. Salvation Army, Marshalltown, 1997—, mem. Christian Reconstrn. Com., 2001—; patron DAV. With Iowa N.G., 1948-57; 1st lt. USAR, 1957-63. Mem. Am. Def. Preparedness Assn., Res. Officers Assn., Am. Legion, U.S. Naval Inst., Assn. U.S. Army, Toastmasters, Kiwanis. Home and Office: 303 Sunset Ln Marshalltown IA 50158-5146 *Personal philosophy: To search for knowledge for the survival of the human species without initiating force or fraud.*

SHAY, DAVID EUGENE, lawyer; b. Scranton, Pa., Nov. 9, 1962; s. Howard E. Jr. and Arlene (Pace) S.; m. Kimberly R. Grow, June 22, 1985; children: Daniel E., Andrew W., Matthew D. BS in Journalism, Kans. U., 1984, JD, 1988. Bar: Mo. 1988, U.S. Dist. Ct. (we. dist.) Mo. 1988, U.S. Ct. Appeals (5th and 8th cirs.) 1991, U.S. Dist. Ct. Kans. 2000. Reporter KDXE, Sulphur Springs, Tex., 1984, KTTR/KZNN, Inc., Rolla, Mo., 1984-85; shareholder Shughart, Thomson & Kilroy, P.C., Kansas City, 1988-99, Seigfreid, Bingham, Levy, Selzer & Gee, P.C., Kansas City, 1999—. Contbr. articles to profl. publs., chpt. to Mo. Bar Deskbook, 1991, 97. Mem. The Christian Ch. of Greater Kansas City, ministerial ethics com., 1999—; moderator Blue Valley Christian Ch. Mem. ABA, Mo. Bar Assn. (chair environ. and energy law com. 1995-97), Lawyers Assn. Kansas City (bd. dirs. 2000—, young lawyers sect. bd. dirs. 1991-97, young lawyers sect. officer 1993-97, young lawyers sect. pres. 1996-97), Kansas City Met. Bar Assn., Lawyers Encouraging Acad. Performance (dir. 1996-97), Order of Coif, Phi Kappa Phi. Republican. Mem. Christian Ch. (Disciples Of Christ). Office: Seigfreid Bingham et al 2800 Commerce Twr 911 Main St Ste 2800 Kansas City MO 64105-2069 E-mail: dshay@sblsg.com.

SHAY, MADELINE LEE BRUMMER, lawyer; b. N.Y.C., June 26, 1948; divorced. BA in Biology, Case Western Reserve U., 1970; MS in Med. Microbiology, Ohio State U., 1972; JD with honors, Ohio State U. Coll. Law, 1981. Bar: Ohio 1981, U.S. Dist. Ct. (so. dist.) Ohio 1981, Ct. of Internat. Trade. Bacteriologist Brown Labs., Columbus, Ohio, 1972; microbiologist St. Anthony Hosp., 1973-78; counsel The Procter & Gamble Co., Cin., 1981-90; asst. divsn. counsel North Atlantic divsn. U.S. Army Corps Engrs., N.Y.C., 1992—. Trustee Terr. Guild, Cin., 1989-92. Mem. ABA, Am. Soc. Microbiology, Nat. Registry of Microbiologists (specialist).). Home: 138A Poly Pl Apt 3B Brooklyn NY 11209-8486 Office: Ft Hamilton Mil Cmty 302 General Lee Ave Brooklyn NY 11209-8400

SHAY, ROSHANI CARI, political science educator; b. Milw., Oct. 5, 1942; d. Walter John and Dorothee May (Dahnke) O'Donnell; 1 child, Mark Sather. Student, Willamette U., 1960-63; BA, U. Oreg., 1968, MA, 1971, PhD, 1974. Adminstrv. asst. Dept. of Youth Svcs., Lubbock, Tex., 1963; tchg. asst., instr. U. Oreg., Eugene, 1969-72; vis. asst. prof. Oreg. State U., Corvallis, 1973-74, Willamette U., Salem, Oreg., 1973-79, Lewis and Clark Coll., Portland, 1976, 78; from asst. prof. to prof. Western Oreg. U., Monmouth, 1979—, chair history, polit. sci., pub. adminstrn. dept., 1991-94, chair social sci. divsn., 1994-2000. Author: (with others) The People of Rajneeshpuram, 1990, Annual Yearbook in the Sociology of Religion, 1995, (simulation) European Unity Project, 1982. Co-founder, v.p., sec.-treas Ind. Opportunities Unltd., Salem, 1986—; co-founder, sec. Inst. for Justice and Human Rights, San Francisco, 1988-94; bd. dirs. Oreg. UN Assn., Portland, 1982-2000, Salem UN Assn., 1982-91; v.p., pres., bd. dirs. Garten Svcs. Inc. for Disabled, Salem, 1989—; pres. Assn. Oreg. Faculties, 1989-91; mem. adv. bd. Connections Program for Disabled Deaf, Salem, 1989-2000; pres., bd. dirs. Model UN of the Far West, San Francisco, 1981-84, 86-88, 95-2000, 2002-; mem. Oreg. Women's Polit. Caucus. Danforth Found. fellow, 1968-74; named Woman of Achievement YWCA Tribute, Salem, 1990, Mem. of Yr., Oreg. Rehab. Assn., 1995. Mem. AAUW, Am. Fedn. Tchrs. (v.p., legis. officer local 2278 1982-88), Western Polit. Sci. Assn., Communal Studies Assn., Mental Health Assn. Oreg., Oreg. Acad. Sci., Soc. for Utopian Studies, Oreg. Hosp. Found., Oreg. Internat. Coun., Oreg. Mediation Assn., Phi Kappa Phi (pres., sec., treas.), Phi Alpha Delta Law Fraternity Internat. (Outstanding Faculty Advisor in USA, 2000). Democrat. Avocations: volunteer work with multiply disabled deaf, reading, meditation. Home: 348 S Main St Falls City OR 97344-9763 Office: Western Oreg U 345 Monmouth Ave N Monmouth OR 97361-1314 E-mail: shayr@wou.edu.

SHAY-BYRNE, OLIVIA, lawyer; b. Trenton, N.J., Aug. 14, 1957; d. Stewart and Elizabeth (Sherrill) B. Student, Vanderbilt U., 1975-76; BA, Bowdoin Coll., 1979; JD, U. Toledo, 1982; LLM in Taxation, Georgetown U., 1987. Bar: Tex. 1982, Ohio 1984, Md. 1985. Assoc. Whiteford, Taylor & Preston, Balt., 1984-87, Linowes & Blocher, Silver Spring, 1987-90; ptnr. Sutherland Asbill & Brenna LLP, Washington, 1996—2000, ReedSmith LLP, Washington, 2000—. Author: The At-Risk Rules Under the Tax Reform Act of 1986, The Door Closes on Tax Motivated Investments, IRS Issues New Guidelines for Management Contracts Used for Facilities Financed with Tax Exempt Bonds, 1993, RRA '93 Loosens Real Estate Rules for Exempt Organizations, 1993; contbr. articles to profl. jours. Mem. Tax Coun. for State of Md., Leadership Montgomery, 1996; bd. dirs. Bethesda Acad. Performing Arts, Inc.; chair GULC Nat. Tax Exempt Bond Conf., 1997. Mem. ABA (exempt orgn. com. taxation sect. 1991—), Md. Bar Assn. (coun. taxation sect.), Balt. City Bar Assn. (chmn. speakers bur. young lawyers sect.), Lawyers for Arts Washington, Comml. Real Estate Woman (bd. dirs., pres.), Profls. for Strathmore Hall (co-chmn.), D.C. Bowdoin Coll. Alumni Assn. (pres. 1992—), Howard County C. of C. (legis. com. 1989), Rotary. Home: 1083 Mill Field Ct Great Falls VA 22066 Office: Reed Smith LLP East Tower Fl 11 1301 K St NW Washington DC 20005

SHAYE, ROBERT KENNETH, cinema company executive; b. Detroit, Mar. 4, 1939; s. Max Mendle and Dorothy S.; m. Eva G. Lindsten, 1970; children: Katja, Juno. BBA, U. Mich., 1960; postgrad., Sorbonne, 1961; JD, Columbia U., 1964. Bar: N.Y. 1967. Chmn. of the bd., CEO New Line Cinema Corp., N.Y.C., 1967—. Trustee Neurosci. Inst., Am. Film Inst.; dir. Mind, Body Found. Bd. dirs. Legal Aid Soc., N.Y.C. Recipient 1st prize Rosenthal competition Soc. Cinematologists, 1964; recipient cert. of merit Inst. Copyrights and Patents, U. Stockholm, 1966; Recipient award ASCAP/Nathan Burkan Meml. competition, 1964; Fulbright scholar, 1964-66 Mem. Motion Picture Pioneers (bd. dirs.). Clubs: Friar's (N.Y.C.). Office: New Line Cinema 116 N Robertson Blvd West Hollywood CA 90048-3103 also: New Line Cinema Corp 888 7th Ave Fl 19 New York NY 10106-2599 *Life is a lot tougher than television watching in the '50's led me to believe.*

SHAYNE, LEONARD M(ARVIN), customs broker; b. N.Y., Sept. 29, 1920; s. Martin L. and Estelle (Greenberg) Shayne; m. Theresa Deerson, May 14, 1952; children: William Charles, Claudia Shayne Ferguson. BA, Columbia Univ., 1941. Clerk, bank examinations dept. Federal Reserve Bank N.Y., 1941; fighter group 8th Air Force U.S. Army Air Force, 1942-45; pres. Leading Forwarders Inc., N.Y., 1946-99. Dir. Am. Assn. Exporters & Importers, N.Y., 1949-99; bd. govs. N.Y. Forwarders & Brokers Assn., 1987-99; lectr. Baruch Sch. Bus. Adminstrn., 1948-60. Contbr. articles to profl. jours. Mem. Nat. Customs Brokers and Forwarders Assn. Am., Inc. (pres., dir., sr-counselor). Avocations: writing, tennis. Office: Leading Forwarders Inc 325 E 79th St New York NY 10021-0954 E-mail: leonard-shayne@att.net.

SHAYNER, JOHN ANTHONY, English language educator, university official; b. Ipswich, Suffolk, Eng., Aug. 27, 1945; came to U.S., 1950; s. Benny Anthony and Gladys Muriel (Pluckrose) S.; m. Katie Celesta Lenig, Aug. 13, 1983. BA in Latin, Columbia U., 1967; PhD in Classics, Stanford U., 1973. Instr. Raritan High Sch., Hazlet, NJ, 1973-74, Middlesex Coll., Edison, 1974-79; prof. English Centenary Coll., Hackettstown, 1979—, exec. asst. to pres., 1986-95, v.p. for adminstrn., 1995—, COO, 1997—. Co-author: (chpt.) Empowering Women, 1988; author, producer (video program) Origins of English, 1985, Triumph of English, 1986. Officer Panther Valley Ecumenical Ministry, Hackettstown, 1990—. N.J. Dept. Higher Edn. grantee, 1984, 85, 86, 87. Mem. Am. Philological Assn., Classic Assn. Atlantic States, Columbia Club of N.Y.C., Panther Valley Golf and Country Club. Episcopalian. Avocations: dogs, running, music, reading. Home: 13 Canada Goose Dr Hackettstown NJ 07840-3100 Office: Centenary Coll 400 Jefferson St Hackettstown NJ 07840-2184

SHAYO, STEPHEN MASHINDANO, accountant; b. Moshi, Tanzania, Sept. 1, 1954; s. Augustine Tamamu Shayo and Hyasinta Mkarawi Mangoti; m. Maria Elly Nyange, Aug. 9, 1986; children: Stephen, Deodatus, Angela, Amedeus, Consolata. Diploma, Inst. Purchasing and Supply, U.K., 1982. CPA; lic. tax cons. Tutor Dar-es-Salaam (Tanzania) Sch. Accountanty, 1979-82; tax and mgmt. cons. Massawe & Co., Tanzania, 1982-84; fin. cons. Internat. Fin. Adv. Svcs., Tanzania, 1984-85; mng. ptnr. Stephen Shayo & Co., Dar-es-Salaam, 1985—. Mng. dir. Fin. & Produrement Cons. Ltd., 1990—; bd. dirs. Afro Med. Supplies Ltd., Metro Agys. Councilor Christian Profls. of Tanzania, 1984, rep. affiliate Tanzania Episcopal Conf., 1987; chmn. Youth Devel. Fund, Tanzania, 1990. Fellow Nat. Bd. Accts. and Auditors, Tanzania Assn. Accts; mem. Tanzania Assn. Cons., Inst. Tng. and Devel. (assoc.). Roman Catholic. Avocations: music, poultry, horticulture, youth movements, health matters. Home: Plot 226 Blk F Mbezi Beach PO Box 5148 Dar es Salaam Tanzania Office: Stephen Shayo & Co Flr 1 Rm 105 Pamba House POB 5148 Dar es Salaam Tanzania E-mail: shayo@raha.com.

SHAYS, CHRISTOPHER, congressman; b. Bridgeport, Conn., Oct. 18, 1945; m. Betsi deRaismes, 1968; 1 child. BA, Principia Coll.; MBA, MPA, NYU. Vol. U.S. Peace Corps, 1968-70; state rep. State of Conn. (Dist. 147), Stamford, 1974-87; mem. U.S. Congress from 4th Conn. Dist., Washington, 1987—; fin. svcs. com., govt. reform com., sci. com. Republican. Office: House of Reps 1126 Longworth Ho Office Bldg Washington DC 20515-0704 also: 10 Middle Street, 11th Floor Washington DC 20515 also: Government Center 888 Washington Blvd. Bridgeport CT 06604*

SHAYS, RONA JOYCE, lawyer; b. N.Y.C., July 16, 1928; d. Samuel and Beatrice (Fleischer) Eskin; children: Douglas, Sharon; m. Henry C. Shays, Sept. 15, 1974. Student, U. Mich., 1944-47; LLB, Bklyn. Law Sch., 1950; MA, Columbia U., 1968. Bar: N.Y. 1950, U.S. Dist. Ct. (so. and ea. dists) N.Y. 1952. Law clk., assoc. Arthur Bardack, Esquire, Bklyn., 1947-51; assoc. Legal Aid Soc., Mineola, N.Y., 1951-52; legal asst. Mut. Life Ins. Co., N.Y.C., 1959-63; assoc. Hays, Sklar & Herzberg, 1963-68; from assoc. to ptnr. Mitchell Salem Fisher & Shays, 1968-76; ptnr. Sheresky, Kalman & Shays, 1976-77, Rosenthal & Shays, N.Y.C., 1977-95, Shays Kemper, N.Y.C., 1995-99, Shays, Rothman & Heisler, LLP, N.Y.C., 1999-2000, Shays, Heisler & Rosenthal, LLP, N.Y.C., 2000—. Named Matrimonial Law Arbitrator, Am. Acad. Matrimonial Lawyers, 1992. Fellow Am. Acad. Matrimonial Lawyers (sec. N.Y. state chpt. 1975-82, 90-91, v.p. N.Y. state chpt. 1984-85, 89-90, chair admissions com. N.Y. state chpt. 1986-91, counsel N.Y. state chpt. 1992-93, nat. co-chair interdisciplinary rels. com. 1990-94), Internat. Acad. Matrimonial Lawyers; mem. Assn. Bar City of N.Y. (matrimonial law com. 1982-85, 86-89, 92-95), Nat. Forum on Mental Health and Family Law (co-chair 1990-93), N.Y. State Interdisciplinary Forum on Mental Health and Family Law (co-chair 1986—). Office: Shays Heisler & Rosenthal LLP 276 5th Ave New York NY 10001-4509

SHAYWITZ, BENNETT ARTHUR, medical educator; MD, Yale U., 1963. Prof. pediats. and neurology Sch. Medicine Yale U., 1972—; co-founder, co-director National Inst. Child Health & Human Development-Yale Ctr. for the Study of Learning and Attention. Mem.: Inst. Medicine. Office: Yale New Haven Hosp LMP 3089 20 York St New Haven CT 06504-8900*

SHEA, ANN ELIZABETH WIEDEL, researcher, librarian; b. Los Angeles, Mar. 14, 1944; d. Arthur John and Helen Cecilia (Conaway) Wiedel; m. John Dennis Shea, Apr. 27, 1985. BA, Immaculate Heart Coll., Los Angeles, 1962-66; MS, U. So. Calif., 1966-67; MA, Calif. State U., Long Beach, 1975-80. Librarian WED Enterprises, Inc., Glendale, Calif., 1967-70, Security Pacific Nat. Bank, Los Angeles, 1970-80, head librarian, 1980-84, research officer, 1984—. Recipient Community Recognition award Ladera Lions Club, Inglewood, Calif., 1984. Mem. Spl. Libraries Assn. (pres. So. Calif. chpt. 1985-86), Centinela Bus. and Profl. Women. (pres. 1984-86), Conf. of Calif. Hist. Socs. (v.p. 1985-86, pres. 1986-87). Avocation: needlework. Home: 13613 Barlin Ave Downey CA 90242-5107

SHEA, BRENT MACK, social science educator; b. Oneida, N.Y., June 3, 1946; s. Mack Evered and Alice May (Meeker) Shea. BA, SUNY, Binghamton, 1968, MA, 1972, PhD, 1977. Vis. instr. Harpur Coll. SUNY, Binghamton, 1975-76, resident dir. Coll.-in-the-Woods, 1976-78, rsch. assoc., 1977-78; asst. prof. Sweet Briar (Va.) Coll., 1978-84, assoc. prof., 1984-92, prof., 1992—, chmn. dept. anthropology and sociology, 1986-90, 96-99; postdoctoral fellow Yale U., New Haven, 1985-86. Vis. fellow Yale U., New Haven, 1984-85; sci. collaborator Centro studi per l'Evoluzione Umana, Rome, Italy, 1990—; vis. scholar Summer Inst. for Survey Rsch. U. Mich., 1991; sec. of faculty Sweet Briar Coll., 1991-92; presenter, rschr. in field. Co-editor, contbg. author: Social Psychiatry across Cultures, 1995; co-editor Internat. Scope Rev., 2000-01; editor conf. procs. Work and Mental Health, 1996; editl. bd. Internat. Scope Rev., 1999—; contbr. articles to profl. jours., chpts. to books. Vis. fellow Yale U., New Haven, 1984-85, Sweet Briar faculty fellow Yale U., 1984-85, Centro studi per l'Evoluzione Umana Rome, 1992-93, NIMH postdoctoral rsch. fellow Instn. for Social and Policy Studies, Yale U., 1985-86; Regents scholar Harpur Coll. SUNY, 1964-68. Mem.: AAUP (chpt. pres. 1996—99, chair state com. on coll. and univ. governance 1998—2001, state exec. com. 1998—), Va. Sociol. Assn. (mem. exec. com. 1980—81, pres.), Ea. Ednl. Rsch. Assn. (dir. rsch. ethics 1979—83, bd. dirs. 1979—85, gen. sec. 1983—85), Ius Primi Viri Internat. Assn. Rome (v.p. bd. govs. 1994—), Internat. Sociol. Assn. (v.p. exec. bd. 1994—98, mental health and illness rsch. com.), Am. Sociol. Assn. (task force on internat. focus of Am. sociology 1999—2002), Soc. Automotive Historians. Avocations: classical piano, classic cars. Home: PO Box 1 Sweet Briar VA 24595-0001 Office: Sweet Briar Coll Dept Anthropology & Sociology Sweet Briar VA 24595

SHEA, CHRISTINA, mayor; Mayor City of Irvine, Calif., 1996—2000; pres. Christina Shea Consulting. Office: 302 Shadow Oaks Irvine CA 92618 E-mail: christina@christinashea.com.*

SHEA, DANIEL BARTHOLOMEW, JR. English language educator, actor; b. Mpls., Oct. 29, 1936; s. Daniel Bartholomew and Dorothea (Lonergan) S.; m. Kathleen Anne Williams, June 3, 1978; children: Timothy, Matthew, Catherine, Daniel, Emily. BA summa cum laude, Coll. St. Thomas, 1958; MA, Stanford U., 1962, PhD, 1966. Teaching asst. Stanford U., 1959-61; instr. to prof. English Washington U., St. Louis, 1962—, chmn. dept., 1978-84, 95-98; acting chair performing arts, prof. drama, 1995. Fulbright-Hays lectr. Univs. of Caen and Nice, France, 1968-69; vis. fellow Clare Hall, U. Cambridge, Eng., 1984-85 Author: Spiritual Autobiography in Early America, 1968, 2d edit., 1988; editorial bd.: Early Am. Lit, 1972-74; sect. editor: Columbia Literary History of the United States; contbr. chpts. to books. Woodrow Wilson fellow, 1958; NEH summer grantee, 1971 Mem. MLA (del. gen. assembly 1977-78), AFTRA, Equity. Home: 6138 Kingsbury Ave Saint Louis MO 63112-1102 Office: Washington Univ Dept of English Saint Louis MO 63130 E-mail: dbshea@artsci.wustl.edu.

SHEA, DAVID MICHAEL, state supreme court justice; b. Hartford, July 1, 1922; s. Michael Peter and Margaret (Agnes) S.; m. Rosemary Anne Sasseen, Apr. 28, 1956; children: Susan, Kathleen, Margaret, Rosemary, Christina,

Michael, Maura, Julie BA, Wesleyan U., 1944; LLB, Yale U., 1948. Bar: Conn. 1948. Assoc. Tunick & Ferris, Greenwich, Conn., 1948-49; assoc. Bailey & Wechsler, Hartford, 1949-57; ptnr. Bailey, Wechsler & Shea, 1957-65; judge Conn. Superior Ct., 1966-81; justice Conn. Supreme Ct., 1981-92, state judge referee, 1992—. Served with U.S. Army, 1943-46 Democrat. Roman Catholic. Office: Conn Superior Ct 95 Washington St Hartford CT 06106-4431

SHEA, DERMOT P. consumer advocate, lawyer; b. Springfield, Mass., Sept. 3, 1916; s. Michael Ignatius and Madeleine Helena (Mahoney) S. Student, U. Ottawa, 1934-36; JD, Boston Coll., 1939. Bar: D.C. 1950, U.S. Ct. Appeals (D.C. cir.) 1951, U.S. Supreme Ct. 1963. Law clk. Law Office of John D. O'Connor, Chicopee Falls, Mass., 1939-40; asst. to chief of press Fed. Pub. Housing Authority, Washington, 1941; pub. info. officer USIA, 1941; asst. to office of the chief Office of War Info., 1941-42; regional pub. rels. officer War Shipping Adminstrn., New London, Conn., 1942-46; claims atty. Aetna Casualty Ins. Co., Springfield, Mass., 1946-64; consumer advisor Spkr. of Mass. Ho. of Reps., Boston, 1972-85; pres. Mass. Consumers Assn., 1976-80; consumer advisor Mass. Consumers' Coalition, 1980—. Aide de camp Gov. Endicott Peabody, Boston, 1963-64. Exec. sec. Mass. Consumers Coun., Boston, 1964-72; bd. dirs. Consumer Fedn. of Am., Washington, 1989-98, Boston Concert Opera, 1979-84; town moderator Town Meeting, Granby, Mass., 1963-69; mem. Ward 5 Dem. Com., Boston, 1986—. Lt. U.S. Maritime Svc., 1942-46. Recipient Esther Peterson Consumer Svc. award, Consumer Fedn. Am., 2001. Democrat. Roman Catholic. Home: 1109 Boylston St Apt 1 Boston MA 02215 E-mail: terence_mcginty@ksg.harvard.edu.

SHEA, DION WARREN JOSEPH, university official, fund raiser; b. New London, Conn., June 10, 1937; s. Frank Steven and Violette Marie (Dion) S.; m. Elizabeth M. Siaba, Dec. 31, 1986; children from previous marriage: Dion Warren Joseph, Nancy Wallace. AB, ScB in Physics, Brown U., 1959; MA in Physics, Boston U., 1962; PhD in Physics, U. Colo., 1968. Mem. tech. staff RCA, 1959-62; asst. prof. physics Creighton U., 1967-68; NRC/Environ. Sci. Svcs. Adminstrn. fellow, rsch. assoc. Environ. Sci. Svcs. Adminstrn., Boulder, Colo., 1968-70; exec. dir. Soc. Physics Students, Am. Inst. Physics, 1970-87, mgr. edn. div., 1972-87; cons. ednl. and computer sytems, 1988—; dir. alumni affairs U.S. Merchant Marine Acad., Kings Point, NY, 1989-93; asst. dir. devel. CUNY Grad. Sch., 1993-99. Author sci. articles. Fellow AAAS; mem. Am. Phys. Soc., Am. Assn. Physics Tchrs., Assn. Coll. Honor Socs. (exec. com. 1984-86), Am. Soc. Assn. Execs., Assn. Fundraising Profls., Planned Giving Group Greater N.Y., Coun. Advancement and Support Edn., Sigma Xi, Sigma Pi Sigma, Sigma Chi, Huntington Bicycle Club (treas. 2000-01), Appalachian Mountain Club, Port Dive Club (treas. 1980-83). Home: 11821 Lionel Ln Golden CO 80403 Office: 11821 Lionel Ln Golden CO 80403 E-mail: Dion_Shea@yahoo.com.

SHEA, EDWARD EMMETT, lawyer, educator, author; b. Detroit, May 29, 1932; s. Edward Francis and Margaret Kathleen (Downey) S.; m. Ann Marie Conley, Aug. 28, 1957; children: Michael, Maura, Ellen. AB, U. Detroit, 1954; JD, U. Mich., 1957. Bar: Mich. 1957, Fla. 1959, N.Y. 1961. Assoc. Simpson Thacher & Bartlett, N.Y.C., 1960-63, Dykema, Wheat, Spencer, Detroit, 1963-69, Cadwalader Wickersham & Taft, N.Y.C., 1969-71; v.p., gen. counsel, chmn. Reichhold Chems., White Plains, N.Y., 1971-81; adj. prof. Pace U. Grad. Sch. Bus., N.Y.C., 1982—; counsel, ptnr. Windels, Marx, Davies & Ives, 1982-84; ptnr. Windels, Marx, Lane & Mittendorf, 1986—; sr. v.p., gen. counsel GAF Corp., 1984-86. Sec. Peridot Chems., 1988-97; lectr. N.Y. Inst. Fin., 1995—. Author: An Introduction to the U.S. Environmental Laws, 1995, The Lead Regulation Handbook, 1996, The McGraw-Hill Guidebook to Acquiring and Divesting Businesses, 1998; editor: The Acquisitions Yearbook, 1991-93; contbr. articles to profl. jours. Mem. adv. bd. N.Y. State Small Bus. Ctr. Program, 1988-93. 1st lt. JAGC, USAF, 1957-60. Mem. N.Y. Athletic Club. Office: Windels Marx Lane & Mittendorf 156 W 56th St Fl 23 New York NY 10019-3867 E-mail: eshea@windelsmarx.com.

SHEA, GEORGE WILLIAM, classicist, educator; b. Paterson, Nj, Oct. 7, 1934; s. George A. Shea and Helen Brueckmann (Shea); m. Shirley Ashton Shea; children: George Michael, Sarah Kathleen, Susan Elizabeth. BA, Fordham U., New York, NY, 1956; MA, Columbia U., New York, NY, 1960; PhD, Columbia U., New York, NY, 1966. Dean Fordham Coll., Lincoln Ctr., New York, NY, 1970—85; prof. classics Fordham U., 1967—. Author: (book) Spoiled Silk, Delia and Nemesis. 1st lt. USAR (INF). Mem.: The Columbia Club. Office: Fordham University 113 W 60th St 924 E New York NY 10023 Office Fax: 212-636-7153. E-mail: gshea@fordham.edu.

SHEA, GERALD PATRICK, engineering executive; b. N.Y.C., May 10, 1935; s. William James and Mary M. (Fitzmaurice) S.; m. Joan Elaine Bergener, Mar. 3, 1938; children: Jerry, Kevin, Kathleen O'Connell, William, Brian. BSCE, U. Notre Dame, 1956; MCE, NYU, 1963. Registered profl. engr., N.Y., N.J., Conn., Pa., Fla., Ark., S.C., Va. Bridge design engr. Parsons Brinckerhoff, N.Y.C., 1956-58; bridge engr. Bur. Pub. Roads, Richmond, Va., 1958-62; assoc. TAMS Consultants, N.Y.C., 1963-78; v.p. Louis Berger Internat. Inc., East Orange, N.J., 1978-97; corp. v.p. Louis Berger Group Inc., 1997-98; dir. gen., CEO Internat. Road Fedn., Washington, 1998-2001; sr. advisor to pres. Wilbur Smith Assocs., 2001—, also bd. dirs., 2001—. Bd. dirs., vice chmn. Internat. Road Fedn.; pres. Internat. Road Ednl. Found., hon. life dir. Contbr. numerous articles to profl. jours. Fellow Inst. Transp. Engrs.; mem. ASCE, Soc. Am. Mil. Engrs., MOLES. Roman Catholic. Avocations: golf, walking, travel, sailing. Home: 2 Otranto Ct Hilton Head Island SC 29928-6108 E-mail: gpshea@aol.com.

SHEA, GWYN, secretary of state; 2 children. Student, U. North Tex.; student , Dallas Baptist U.; grad., Dallas Baptist U. Police Acad. Served Ho. Ways and Means Com.; served Ho. Ins. Com.; pres. Nat. Coun. Ins. Legislators; served Tex. Ho. Reps. (R-Irving) , 1982—92; apptd. Tex. Worker's Compensation Ins. Facility , 1995; Sec. of State State of Tex., 2002—. Constable Dallas County Precint 2 Irving, Coppell, North Dallas, 1994, 96, 2000. Pres. Tex. Healthy Kids Corp. , 1997; former dir. Irving C. of C.; past pres. Women's Divsn. of C.; mem. adv. bd. Irving CARES; mem.a dv. bd. Profl. Secs. Internat.; mem. 1st Baptist Ch. , Irving; mem. adv. bds. Irving Infant Interventuion Ctr. Named to legis. commitment to people of Tex., Tex. Mun. League, Tex. Assn. Bus., Tex. Civil Justice League, Tex. Assn. Concerned Tax Payers ; recipient Legislative Leadership award, Tex. C. of C. Office: PO Box 12887 Austin TX 78711-2887*

SHEA, JAMES WILLIAM, lawyer; b. N.Y.C., July 10, 1936; s. William P. and Mildred E. (McCaffrey) S.; m. Ann Marie Byrne, June 6, 1964; children: James T., Kathleen A., Tracy A. BS, St. Peters Coll., 1957; JD, Fordham U., 1962; LLM in Taxation, NYU, 1965. Bar: N.Y. 1962, U.S. Dist. Ct. (so. and ea. dists.) N.Y. 1966, U.S. Supreme Ct. 1967. Revenue agent U.S. Treasury Dept., N.Y.C., 1961-63; tax atty. Kennecott Copper Corp., 1963-67; tax counsel CBS Inc., 1968-71; ptnr. Hunton & Williams and predecessor firm Conboy, Hewitt, O'Brien & Boardman, 1971—. Bd. dirs. Victory Van Lines Inc., N.Y.C. Rep. committeeman, Staten Island, N.Y., 1980; mem. adv. com. tax and fin. N.Y. State Charter Commn. City of S.I. Served to 1st lt. U.S. Army, 1957-61, to capt. USAR, 1962-72. Mem. N.Y. State Bar Assn., Richmond County Country Club S.I. (sec. 1993-96, v.p. 1996-98, pres. 1998-2000, bd. dirs. 1993—). Republican. Roman Catholic. E-mail: jshea.hunton.com. Home: 399 Tysens Ln Staten Island NY 10306-2844 Office: Hunton & Williams 200 Park Ave Rm 4300 New York NY 10166-0091

SHEA, JOHN DWANE, communications executive; b. Chgo., Sept. 28, 1939; s. John Stephen and Dorthy (Moryer) S.; m. Beverly M. Kehoe, July 22, 1993; children: Eric, April. MSMT, Trensumer Coll., Rome, 1960; BS in Electronic Tech., Phoenix Coll., 1961; MS of Strategic Intellegence, Def. Intelligenc Inst., 1978. V.p. Intergrated Circuit Engring. Corp., Scottsdale, Ariz., 1974-80; pres. Tech. Analysis Group, San Jose, 1980-84, Sierra Tech. Group, Lake Taho, Calif., 1984-86, Shea Tech. Group, Saratoga, 1986—. Author: Electrical Engineering Automatic Wafer FHB Manaufacturing, 1982, Electronic Intelligence, 1984, Japan Technology for Computing, 1985. Recipient Intelligence Achievement award Ministry of Def., 1989, Global Intelligence award, 1989. Fellow Assn. Former Intelligence Officers; mem. Armed Forces Communications and Electronics Assn., Assn. Old Crows, Am. Def. Preparedness Assn. Republican. Roman Catholic. Avocations: military history, flying jet fighters. Home: PO Box 3226 Saratoga CA 95070-1226 Office: Shea Tech Group Inc 51 E Campbell Ave Ste 1082 Campbell CA 95008-2047

SHEA, JOSEPH WILLIAM, III, lawyer; b. Cin., Jan. 3, 1947; s. Joseph W. Jr. and Gertrude Mary (Reardon) S.; m. Elaine N. Miller, May 29, 1971; children: J. Blane, Doyle Reardon, C. Lauer. BA, U. Cin., 1969; JD, No. Ky. U., 1974. Bar: Ohio 1974, Ky. 1990, U.S. Dist. Ct. Ohio 1974, U.S. Ct. Appeals (6th cir.) 1980, U.S. Supreme Ct. 1981; diplomate Nat. Bd. Trial Advocacy. Prin. Shea & Assocs., Cin., 1974—. Founder Lawriter Corp., Cin., 1983—; mem. Ohio Supreme Ct. Bd. Bar Examiners, 1983-90, chair 1988-89. Author: Shea's Forms for Ohio Trial Practice, 1983, Shea Civil Practice, 1985; contbg. author: Personal Injury in Ohio, CLE Inst., 1984, Civil Litigation in Ohio, 1991, 93, 95, 98, 2000, CLE Inst.; editor Ohio Verdict Reporter, vols. 1-310, 1976—; contbr. articles to profl. jours. Mem. Supreme Ct. Bd. Bar Examiners, 1982-89, chmn., 1988-89; diplomate Nat. Bd. Trial Advocacy, 1985—. Fellow Am. Coll. Trial Lawyers, Ohio Acad. Trial Lawyers (pres. 1981-82), Internat. Soc. Barristers; mem. Am. Bd. Trial Advocacy (adv. 1989—, nat. rep. 1990—), Ohio State Bar Assn., Ky. Bar Assn., Cin. Bar Assn., Nat. Bar Examiners (bd. examiners 1984-89, chmn.), Nat. Bd. Trial Advocacy (cert. trial specialist 1985—, nat. cert. bar examiner 1984-87, 91, 94, 2001). Roman Catholic. Avocations: sailing, snow skiing. Home: 510 Baum St Cincinnati OH 45202 Office: Shea & Assocs 600 Flatiron Bldg 401 E Court St Cincinnati OH 45202-1332

SHEA, KATHLEEN E. cultural resources specialist; b. Chgo., June 10, 1946; d. Leonard Edward and Margaret (O'Connor) S.; divorced; 1 child, Laura Lee. BS, NYU, 1971. Dir. conservation Washington U. Tech. Assn. Inc., St. Louis, 1983-88; commr. heritage and urban design City of St. Louis, 1988—. Fellow Leadership St. Louis Inc., 1994—. Office: City of St Louis 1015 Locust St Saint Louis MO 63101-1334

SHEA, MARTIN COYLE, physician; b. Memphis, Dec. 24, 1929; m. Trina M. Shea. BS, U. Tenn., Knoxville, 1952; MD, U. Tenn. Coll. Medicine, Memphis, 1952. Cert. Am. Bd. Otolaryngology, 1961; lic. Tenn. 1953. Assoc. clin. prof. U. Tenn. Ctr. for Health Scis., 1962—; MD Memphis Otologic Clinic, 1962-67, Shea, Hubbard & Futrell, Ear, Nose & Throat Group, Inc., 1967—. Contbr. numerous articles to profl. jours. Lt. comdr. Med. Corps USN, 1952-62. Mem. Memphis and Shelby County Med. Soc., Memphis and Shelby County Soc. Otolaryngology, AMA, Tenn. Med. Assn., Southern Med. Assn., Am. Acad. Ophthalmology and Otolaryngology, Am. Bd. Otolaryngology, Tenn. Acad. Ophthalmology and Otolaryngology, Pan Am. Med. Assn., Pan Am. Assn. Oto-Rhino-Laryngology & Broncheosophagology, Flying Physicisn's Assn., Soc. of Military Otolaryngologists, Am. Coun. Otolaryngology, Am. Laryngological, Rhinological & Otological Soc., Politzer Soc., Am. Coll. Surgeons. Home: 410 Colonial Rd Memphis TN 38117-4027 Office: Shea-Hubbard ENT Clinic 6027 Walnut Grove Rd Ste 41 Memphis TN 38120-2145

SHEA, PATRICK A. lawyer, educator; b. Salt Lake City, Feb. 28, 1948; s. Edward J. and Ramona (Kilpack) S.; m. Deborah Fae Kern, Sept. 1, 1980; children: Michael, Paul. BA, Stanford U., 1970; MA, Oxford U., Eng., 1972; JD, Harvard U., 1975. Bar: Utah 1976, D.C. 1979. Mem. profl. staff majority leader's office U.S. Senate, 1971, asst. staff dir. intelligence com., 1975—76; assoc. VanCott, Bagley, Salt Lake City, 1976—79, ptnr., 1980—85; counsel fgn. relations com. U.S. Senate, 1979—80; gen. counsel KUTV, Comm. Investment Corp., Std. Comm., 1985—91; dir. Bur. of Land Mgmt. Dept. of Interior, 1997-98; dep., asst. sec. interior Land & Minerals Mgmt., 1998-2000; of counsel Ballard, Spahr, Andrews & Ingersoll LLP, Salt Lake City, 2000—. Cons. judiciary com. U.S. Ho. of Reps., 1972-73; adj. prof. polit. sci. U. Utah, Salt Lake City, 1981-97. Chmn. Utah Democratic Party, Salt Lake City, 1983-85; v.p. Tomorrow-Today Found., Salt Lake City, 1982-84. Mem. Am. Rhodes Scholar Assn., Utah Bar Assn., D.C. Bar Assn., Stanford Alumni Assn. (pres.-elect 1983-84). Clubs: Alta. Roman Catholic. Office: Ballard Spahr Andrews & Ingersoll LLP One Utah Ctr Ste 600 201 S Main St Salt Lake City UT 84111-2221 Fax: 801-596-6802. E-mail: sheap@ballardspahr.com.

SHEA, STEPHEN MICHAEL, physician, educator; b. Galway, Ireland, Apr. 25, 1926; came to U.S., 1956, naturalized, 1966; s. Stephen and Margaret Mary (Cooke) S. BSc in Anatomy and Pathology, Univ. Coll., Galway Nat. U. Ireland, 1948; MB, BChir in Medicine, 1950, MSc in Pathology, 1951, MD, 1959. Diplomate: Am. Bd. Pathology. Intern St. Vincent's Hosp., Dublin, Ireland, 1950-51; Dr. Keenan traveling scholar, dept. physiology Univ. Coll., London, 1951-53, asst. lectr. pharmacology Dublin, 1953-56; resident in pathology Mallory Inst. Pathology, Boston City Hosp., 1956-59, chief resident, 1958-59; asst. prof. pathology U. Toronto, Ont., Can., 1959-61; from instr. to assoc. prof. Harvard U. Med. Sch., 1961-73; assoc. pathologist Mass. Gen. Hosp. and Shriners Burns Inst., Boston, 1972-73; prof. pathology Robert Wood Johnson Med. Sch., U.M.D.N.J., 1973—. Contbr. articles to profl. publs. Fellow Royal Coll. Pathologists (U.K.), Royal Coll. Physicians (Can.); mem. Am. Soc. Invest Pathologists, Internat. Acad. Pathology, Am. Soc. Cell Biology, Soc. Math. Biology, Microcirculatory Soc., Harvard Travellers Club, Harvard Club of Boston. Roman Catholic. Home: 1050 George St Apt 12L New Brunswick NJ 08901-1020 Office: UMDNJ-Robert Wood Johnson Med Sch Piscataway NJ 08854

SHEA, WILLIAM RENE, historian, science philosopher, educator; b. Gracefield, Que., Can., May 16, 1937; s. Herbert Clement and Jeanne (Lafreniere) S.; m. Evelyn Fischer, May 2, 1970; children: Herbert, Joan-Emma, Louisa, Cecilia, Michael. BA, U. Ottawa, 1958; LPh, Gregorian U., Rome, 1959; LTh, Gregorian U., 1963; PhD, Cambridge U., Eng., 1968. Assoc. prof. U. Ottawa, Ont., Can., 1968-73; fellow Harvard U., Cambridge, Mass., 1973-74; prof. history and philosophy of sci. McGill U., Montreal, 1974—; dir. d'etudes Ecole des Hautes Etudes, Paris, 1981-82. Sec.-gen. Internat. Union of History and Philosophy of Sci., 1981-89, pres., 1990-93; mem. gen. com. Internat. Coun. of Sci. Union, Paris, 1983-89; cons. Killam Found., Ottawa, Ont., 1983-85; mem. McGill Centre for Medicine, Ethics and Law, 1990-95; Hydro Que. prof. environ. ethics, 1992—; vis. prof. U. Rome, 1992; dir. Inst. History of Sci., U. Louis Pasteur, Strasbourg, 1995—. Author: Galileo Intellectual Revolution, 1972, The Magic of Numbers and Motion, 1991, Copernico, 2001; co-author: Galileo Florentine Residences, 1979; editor: Nature Mathematized, 1983, Otto Hahn and the Rise of Nuclear Physics, 1983, Revolutions in Science, 1988, Creativity in the Arts and Science, 1990, Persuading Science: The Art of Scientific Rhetoric, 1991, Interpreting the World, Science and Society, 1991, Energy Needs in the Year 2000: Ethical and Environmental Perspectives, 1994, Science and the Visual Image in the Enlightenment, 2000. Can. Coun. fellow, 1965-68, Can. Cultural Inst. fellow, Rome, 1973, Social Scis. and Humanities Rsch. Coun. Can., 1980-81, Inst. of Advanced Studies in Berlin fellow, 1988-89; recipient The Alexandre Koyre medal Internat. Acad. of History of Sci., 1993, Knight of the Order of Malta, 1993. Fellow Royal Soc. Can.; mem. Royal Swedish Acad. Scis. (fgn.), Academie D'Alsace, Academia Europaea, History of Sci. Soc. (coun. 1973-76), European Sci. Found. (standing com. for humanities 1989-95, chmn. 1999—), Can. Nat. Com. of History and Philosophy of Sci. (coun. 1982-93), Can. Philos. Assn., Internat. Acad. History of Sci. (pres. 1997-2001), Rotary. Home: 6 Rue Gottfried 67000 Strasbourg France Office: Inst d'Histoire des Scis 7 Rue de L'Universite 67000 Strasbourg France Fax: 0033 90 24 05 81.

SHEA-BISCHOFF, PATRICIA, secondary reading educator, education educator; BA in Secondary Edn., English, Fordham U., N.Y.C., 1968; MS in Secondary Edn., English, CUNY, 1971; MA in Reading, Kean Coll., Union, N.J., 1977. Tchr. lang. arts and reading Myra S. Barnes Intermediate Sch. #24, S.I. Recipient Maurice Wollin Tchr. of Yr. award, N.Y. State Reading Assn. Elementary and Secondary Sch. Tchr. of Yr. award, N.Y. Coalition for Pub. Schs. Tchr. of Yr. award, N.Y.C. and N.Y. State Literacy Advocate award; named Best Tchr., N.Y. Post. Mem. N.Y. Reading Assn. (past pres.), Internat. Reading Assn. (N.Y. state coord.). Home: 165 Kennington St Staten Island NY 10308-1641

SHEAD, WILLIAM C. lawyer; b. Sulphur Branch, Tex., Mar. 23, 1927; m. Thalia Smith, Dec. 19, 1950; children— Suzie, Sheri, Ginny, Libby, Katie. B.S., U. Houston, 1952, LL.M., 1954; J.D., South Tex. Coll. Law, 1959. Bar: Tex. 1960. Chief scout Mid-Continent div. Tidewater Oil Co.; lectr. Downtown Sch., U. Houston; asst. city atty. City of Houston; sole practice, Houston, 1960-86; assoc. judge, State of Tex., 1986— . Candidate Tex. Ho. Reps., 1962. Mem. ABA, Am. Judicature Soc., Assn. Trial Lawyers Am., Harris County Criminal Def. Lawyers Assn., Houston Bar Assn. (prison pre-release com., jud. qualifications com.), Nat. Assn. Criminal Def. Lawyers, Pasadena Bar Assn., Tex. Criminal Def. Lawyers Assn., Tex. Trial Lawyers Assn. Lodges: Masons, Lions. Office: 2927 Broadway St Houston TX 77017-1705

SHEAFFER, KAREN, county official, treasurer; b. Lewistown, Pa., Sept. 8, 1949; d. Clyde William and Betty Beatrice Krepps; m. James G. Sheaffer, Oct. 25, 1969; children: Jeremy James, Jarrod James. Adminstrv. asst. Kyburz Constrn., Edwards, Colo., 1982-86; bookkeeper Eagle (Colo.) County Treas., 1986-89, dep. treas., dep. pub. trustee, 1989-96, county treas., pub. trustee, 1996—. Bd. dirs. Colotrust. Mem.: Colo. County Pub. Trustees Assn., Colo. County Treas. Assn. (cert. county treas., Outstanding Treas. of Yr. 1998, 2000). Republican. Methodist. Office: Eagle County Govt 500 Broadway Eagle CO 81631

SHEAFFER, RICHARD ALLEN, electrical engineer; b. Bronxville, N.Y., May 30, 1950; s. Harold Aumond and Carol Lois (Henry) Sweet; children: Alan Michael Sheaffer, Russell Logan Sheaffer, Neil Andrew Sheaffer. BSEE, Pa. State U., 1972; MSEE, U. So. Calif., 1975; MBA, Pepperdine U., 1996. Registered profl. engr., Calif., Fla. Elec. engr. So. Calif. Edison Co., Rosemead, 1973-79, 80-90, Harris Controls div., Melbourne, Fla., 1979-80; cons. to elec. utility industry, 1990-91; sr. transmission planner San Diego Gas & Electric, 1991-2000; San Diego Gas & Electric rep. for decommissioning San Onofre Nuclear Generating Sta. Unit 1, 2000—. Project leader nomogram study for Pacific and S.W. transfer subcom. Western Systems Coordinating Coun., 1988, 91; project leader Ariz.-Calif. 7550 NW Path Rating, 1994-97. Author: 1984 West-of-the-River Operating Study, 1985, December 22, 1982 Disturbance Study, 1983. Mem. IEEE (Power Engring. Soc., Engring. Mgmt. Soc.), Am. Nuclear Soc., Phi Eta Sigma. Episcopalian. Avocations: running, bicycling, playing guitar, golf, fitness.

SHEAFFER, SUZANNE FRANCES, geriatrics nurse; b. Harrisburg, Pa., Feb. 8, 1963; d. Walter Richard and Catherine Frances (Mourawski) Markham; children: William Chester, Sarah Suzanne, Katye Iona; m. Paul L. Sheaffer Jr. LPN, Harrisburg Stelton Highs, Sch. Practical Nursing, 1984; ADN, Harrisburg (Pa.) Area C.C., 1984; BA in Long Term Care Adminstrn., St. Joseph Coll., 1994, postgrad., 1994—; BSN, York (Pa.) Coll., 1997. Lic. nursing home adminstr., Pa. Nurse ICU and critical care unit Meml. Hosp., York, Pa., 1987-88; staff nurse emergency dept. Polyclinic Med. Ctr., Harrisburg, 1988-91; assoc. prof. Nat. Edn. Ctr.-Jr. Coll., 1991; dir. nursing Camp Hill (Pa.) Care Ctr., 1991-92; resident assessment supr. Susquehanna Ctr., Harrisburg, 1992-94; dir. nursing Susquehanna Luth. Village, Millersburg, Pa., 1994-95; asst. adminstr. Dauphin Manor, Harrisburg, 1995—; mgr. clin. svcs. ea. divsn. HCR Manor Care; med. analyst Pa. Atty. Gen. Office. ACLS, CPR instr. Am. Heart Assn., Harrisburg, 1989—; BCLS, CPR instr. ARC, Harrisburg, 1992—; RN, paramedic Lebanon (Pa.) County First Aide and Safety Patrol, 1992—. Sec. Little People PTA, Harrisburg, 1991-92; pres. Student Human Resource Mgmt. Club, York (Pa.) Coll., 1992—; v.p. Prince of Peace PTO, 1997-98; cheerleading coach , Midget Footbal Assoc., 2002—. Recipient Nurse of Hope award Am. Cancer Soc., Dauphin County, Harrisburg, 1983-84. Mem. AACN, Pa. Nurses Assn., Pa. Dir. Nursing Assn. for Long Term Care, PANPHA (advocate), York Coll. Alumni Assn. (bd. dirs. Susquehanna Valley). Roman Catholic. Avocations: ceramics, ballet, flute.

SHEAFFER, WILLIAM JAY, lawyer; b. Carlisle, Pa., Jan. 18, 1948; s. Raymond Jay and Barbara Jean (Bell) S.; m. Carol Ann Madison, Jan. 5, 1974. BA cum laude, U. Cen. Fla., 1975; JD, Nova U., 1978. Bar: Fla. 1978, U.S. Dist. Ct. (mid. dist.) Fla. 1979, U.S. Dist. Ct. (so. and no. dists.) Fla. 1981, U.S. Ct. Appeals (5th and 11th cirs.) 1981, U.S. Supreme Ct. 1983. Atty. State of Fla., Orlando, 1978-79; pvt. practice, 1979—. Apptd. to merit selection panel to consider U.S. Magistrate Judge Applicants, 1995, 97, 99. Pres. City Coun. Edgewood, Fla., 2000-02; served to ensign class 4 USN, 1967-71. Mem.: ACLU, NACDL, ABA, Ctrl. Fla. Assn. Criminal Def. Attys., Nat. Bd. Trial Advocacy (bd. cert. criminal trial specialist), Am. Inns of Ct. (ctrl. Fla. master), Fed. Trial Lawyers Assn., Fla. Assn. Criminal Def. Lawyers Inc., Fed. Bar Assn., Orange County Bar Assn. (Guardian Ad Litem of Yr. 1994, award of excellence 1995), Fla. Bar Assn. (cert. criminal trial specialist, vice chmn. 9th jud. cir. grievance com. 1997, 1998), Tiger Bay Club. Democrat. Avocations: boating, running, skiing. Office: 609 E Central Blvd Orlando FL 32801-2916 Fax: 407-648-0683. E-mail: defenselaw@prodigy.net.

SHEAHAN, JOHN BERNARD, economist, educator; b. Toledo, Sept. 11, 1923; s. Bernard William and Florence (Sheahan) S.; m. Denise Eugénie Morlino, Nov. 29, 1946; children: Yvette Marie, Bernard Eugene. BA, Stanford U., 1948; PhD, Harvard U., 1954. Econ. analyst Office Spl. Rep. in Europe, ECA, Paris, France, 1951-54; mem. faculty Williams Coll., 1954-94, prof. econs. Mass., 1966-94, prof. emeritus. Mem. devel. adv. service Colombia adv. group Harvard, 1963-65; nat. research prof. Brookings Instn., 1959-60; vis. prof. El Colegio de México, Mexico City, 1970-71; Fulbright research scholar Institut de recherche économique et de planification, Université de Grenoble, France, 1974-75; vis. scholar Inst. Devel. Studies, U. Sussex, 1981-82; vis. fellow Ctr. for U.S.-Mexican Studies, U. Calif. at San Diego, 1991. Author: Promotion and Control of Industry in Postwar France, 1963, The Wage-Price Guideposts, 1967, An Introduction to the French Economy, 1969, Patterns of Development in Latin America, 1987, Conflict and Change in Mexican Economic Strategy, 1992, Searching for a Better Society: The Peruvian Economy from 1950, 1999. Mem. Presdl. Price Adv. Com., 1979-80. Mem. Latin Am. Studies Assn., New England Coun. Latin Am. Studies (pres. 1989-90), Phi Beta Kappa. Home: Syndicate Rd Williamstown MA 01267 Office: Williams Coll Dept Econs Williamstown MA 01267

SHEAHAN, ROBERT EMMETT, lawyer, consultant; b. Chgo., May 20, 1942; s. Robert Emmett and Lola Jean (Moore) S.; m. Pati Smith, Mar. 20, 1991. BA, Ill. Wesleyan U., 1964; JD, Duke U., 1967; MBA, U. Chgo., 1970. Bar: Ill. 1967, La. 1975, N.C. 1978. Vol. VISTA, N.Y.C., 1967-68; trial atty. NLRB, Milw., New Orleans, 1970-75; ptnr. Jones, Walker, Waechter, Poitevent, Carrere & Denegre, New Orleans, 1975-78; pvt. practice High Point, N.C., 1978—. Bd. dirs. Inst. for Effective Mgmt., Bus. Publs. Inst. Author: Employees and Drug Abuse: An Employer's Handbook, 1994, The Encyclopedia of Drugs in the Workplace, Labor and Employment Law in North Carolina, 1991, Personnel and Employment Law in North Carolina, 1992, Desk Book of Labor and Employment Law for Healthcare Employers' Desk Manual, 1995, North Carolina Lawyers' Desk Book; contbg. author: The Developing Labor Law, 1975—; editor: The World of Personnel; contbg. editor: Employee Testing and the Law; contbr. periodic supplements N.C. Gen. Practice Deskbook, 1992—. Bd. dirs. High Point United Way, 1979-83; mem. congl. action com. High Point C. of C., chmn., 1991—, bd. dirs., 1996—. Mem. ABA, N.C. Bar Assn., High Point Bar Assn., Ill. Bar Assn., La. Bar Assn., Sedgefield (N.C.) Country Club, String and Splinter Club, Island Club. Republican. Roman Catholic. Home: 8 Sabal Palm Ct Bald Head Island NC 28461 Office: Eastchester Office Ctr 603 Eastchester Dr Ste B High Point NC 27262-7647

SHEAN, TIMOTHY JOSEPH, manufacturing company executive; b. Norfolk, Va., Sept. 19, 1945; s. Hobart Philip S.; m. Adriana Bergo, July 12, 1970; children: Jonathan Michael, Arianne Marie. BSME, U. Notre Dame, 1967; postgrad., U. Va., 1991. Sales engr. Shean Equipment Co., Syracuse, N.Y., 1967-69; application engr. Gen. Electric Co., Schenectady, 1970-71, prodn. control supr., 1972-75, process devel. engr., 1975-78, project mgr., 1978-80, mgr. facilities and engring., 1980-83; plant mgr. Hughes Tool Co., Bristol, Va., 1983-85; mgr. mfg. Sandvik Rock Tools, Inc., 1985-89, gen. mgr., 1989-92, v.p., 1992-2000; pres. Sandvik Mineral Tools USA, 2000—, Sandvik CPD-MTD Prodn. Co., Bristol. Sr. patrolman Nat. Ski Patrol Sys., Wilminton, Vt., 1970-80; instr., trainer first aid ARC, Schenectady, 1975-78, vice-chmn. disaster svcs., 1976-77; mem. sch. bd. Schalmont Ctrl. Sch. Dist., Schenectady, 1979-82; cmty. involvement com. Bristol Sch. Dist., 1990; chmn. Literacy Acad. Bristol, 1991-92; chmn. fin. coun. St. Anne's Cath. Ch., 1992-96; mem. Va. Atty. Gens. Commn., 1995-96, Commn. on Future S.W. Va., 1995-97; bd. fellows Va. Intermont Coll., 1996-99; mem. pres.'s adv. bd. King Coll., 1997—; bd. dirs. Mfg. Tech. Ctr. S.W. Va., 1998—, Va. Mfg. Assn., 1999-2000, mem. The Conf. Bd., 1999-2002. Named one of Outstanding Young Men of Am., U.S. Jaycees, 1979. Mem. Soc. Mfg. Engrs., Nat.

Mining Assn. (chmn. resins group 1989-95, tech. com. 1990-96), Va. Coal Coun. (bd. dirs. 1993—), Bristol C. of C. (bd. dirs. 1994-2000, chmn. 1999-2000), Pres. Club. Roman Catholic. Avocation: skiing. Office: Sandvik Mineral Tools PO Box 639 Bristol VA 24203-0639

SHEAR, IONE MYLONAS, archaeologist; b. St. Louis, Feb. 19, 1936; d. George Emmanuel and Lella (Papazouglou) Mylonas; m. Theodore Leslie Shear, June 24, 1959; children: Julia Louise, Alexandra. BA, Wellesley Coll., 1958; MA, Bryn Mawr Coll., 1960, PhD, 1968. Rsch. asst. Inst. for Advanced Study, Princeton, N.J., 1963-65; mem. Agora Excavation, Athens, 1967, 72-94; lectr. art and archaeology Princeton U., 1983-84; lectr. Am. Sch. Classical Studies, Athens, summers 1989-98. Also excavator various other sites in Greece and Italy. Author: The Panagia Houses at Mycenae, 1987, Tales of Heroes: The Origins of the Homeric Texts, 2000; contbr. articles to profl. jours. Mem. Archaeol. Inst. Am., Greek Archaeol. Soc. (hon.). Address: 87 Library Pl Princeton NJ 08540-3015 also: Deinokratous 30 Athens 106-76 Greece

SHEAR, NATALIE PICKUS, public relations executive, management consultant; b. N.Y.C., Oct. 18, 1940; d. Sam and Mildred (Shulman) Pickus; m. Daniel H. Shear, Dec. 14, 1968 (dec. Apr. 1989); children: Adam Brian, Tamara Beth; m. Henry D. Lewis, Jan. 10, 1999. BA in Journalism, Fairleigh Dickinson U., 1962. Editorial asst. Show Bus. Newspaper, N.Y.C., 1962-64, The Jewish News, Newark, 1964-66; dir. Manhattan women's div., program asst. Am. Jewish Congress, N.Y.C., 1966-68; mng. editor The Jewish Week, Washington, 1968-71; dir. pub. rels. United Jewish Appeal, 1973-74; pub. affairs dir. Leadership Conf. on Civil Rights, 1977-83; pres. Natalie P. Shear Assocs., Inc., 1983—. Editor (newspaper) Books Alive, 1973-74; editor, pub. (newsletter) Trends, Inc., 1989-94. Vol. nat. bd. Ams. Dem. Action, 2001—; vol., bd. dirs. Nat. Jewish Dem. Coun., Washington, 1996—; bd. dirs. Urban Philharm. Soc., 1998-99; chairperson women's task force Am. Jewish Congress, Washington, 1984-86; v.p. Nat. Child Rsch. Ctr., Washington, 1974-76; pres. Ohr Kodesh Sisterhood, Chevy Chase, Md., 1980-82. Mem. Nat. Press Club. Avocations: needlework, crafts. Home: 4701 Willard Ave Chevy Chase MD 20815-4643 Office: 1629 K St NW Ste 802 Washington DC 20006-1637 E-mail: npshear@aol.com.

SHEAR, THEODORE LESLIE, JR. archaeologist, educator; b. Athens, Greece, May 1, 1938; s. Theodore Leslie and Josephine (Platner) S.; m. Ione Doris Mylonas, June 24, 1959; children: Julia Louise, Alexandra. AB summa cum laude, Princeton U., 1959, MA, 1963, PhD, 1966. Instr. Greek and Latin Bryn Mawr Coll., 1964-66, asst. prof., 1966-67; asst. prof. art and archaeology Princeton (N.J.) U., 1967-70, assoc. prof., 1970-79, chmn. program in classical archaeology, 1970-85, assoc. chmn. dept. art and archaeology, 1976-78, 82-83, prof. classical archaeology, 1979—; prof. archaeology Am. Sch. Classical Studies, Athens, 1988-94. Mem. mng. com. Am. Sch. Classical Studies, Athens, 1972—; mem. archaeol. expdns. to Greece and Italy, including Mycenae, 1953-54, 58, 62-63, 65-66, Eleusis, 1956, Perati, 1956, Corinth, 1960, Morgantina, Sicily, 1962; mem. Ancient Agora of Athens, 1955, 67, field dir., 1968-94; trustee William Alexander Procter Found., 1982-89, Princeton Jr. Sch., 1983—, pres., 1994—. Author: Kallias of Sphettos and the Revolt of Athens in 286 B.C., 1978; contbr. articles to profl. jours. White fellow Am. Sch. Classical Studies, 1959-60 Mem. Archaeol. Inst. Am., Am. Philol. Assn., Coll. Art Assn., Archaeol. Soc. Athens (hon.), Phi Beta Kappa. Clubs: Century Assn. (N.Y.C.); Nassau (Princeton); Princeton (N.Y.C.); Hellenic Yacht (Piraeus, Greece). Republican. Episcopalian. Home: 87 Library Pl Princeton NJ 08540-3015 also: 30 Deinokratous St Athens Greece

SHEARD, CHARLES, III, dermatologist; b. Toronto, Ontario, Can., Nov. 22, 1914; came to U.S., 1945; s. Charles Jr. and Alice Elizabeth (Ramsay) S.; m. Katherine Patricia Murphy, Nov. 19, 1937; children: Pamela Carol Sheard McGuiness, Wendy Alice Sheard Geyer. Sr. matriculation, Upper Can. Coll., Toronto, 1933; MD, U. Toronto, 1939. Diplomate Am. Bd. Dermatology. Intern Toronto Gen. Hosp., 1939-40; instr. physiology, anatomy U. Toronto Med. Faculty, 1940-41; surgical asst. resident Hosp. for Sick Children, Toronto, 1945; from resident to chief resident dermatologist Columbia Presbyn. Hosp., N.Y.C., 1945-49; assoc. prof. medicine Cornell U. Med. Coll., 1950-94, assoc. prof. emeritus, 1994—. Author: (textbook) Treatment in Dermatology, 1978; contbr. articles to profl. jours. Flight lt. RCAF, 1941-45. Fellow ACP, Royal Coll. Physicians (Can.); mem. Metro-Manhattan Dermatol. Soc. N.Y.C. (sec. 1970-80), Can. Club of N.Y., Royal Can. Yacht Club, Muskoka Lakes Golf and Country Club. Republican. Episcopalian. Avocations: sailing, fishing, golf.

SHEARER, DEREK NORCROSS, international studies educator, diplomat, administrator; b. L.A., Dec. 5, 1946; s. Lloyd and Marva (Peterson) S.; m. Ruth Y. Goldway, July 8, 1976; 1 child, Casey (dec.); stepchildren: Anthony, Julie. BA, Yale U., 1968; PhD, Union Grad. Sch., Yellow Springs, Ohio, 1977. Lectr. U. Calif., L.A., 1979-81; dir. internat. and pub. affairs ctr., prof. of pub. policy Occidental Coll., 1981-94, 98—; dep. under sec. U.S. Dept. Commerce, Washington, 1993; U.S. ambassador to Finland, U.S. Dept. State, 1994-97; prof. internat. affairs Occidental Coll., L.A., 1997—; internat. advisor Ziff Bros. Investments, 1998—. Fellow Econ. Strategy Inst., Washington, 1993; policy adv. to Presidential Candidate Bill Clinton, 1990-92; adv. on NATO peace keeping USN, 1997—; pub. policy fellow Woodrow Wilson Internat. Scholars Ctr., 1999-2000; dir. global affairs Occidental Coll., 2001—, Chevalier prof. diplomacy and world affairs, 2002--. Contbr. articles to profl. publs. Planning commr. City of Santa Monica (Calif.), 1984; bd. mem. Nat. Consumer Bank, Washington, 1991. Recipient Guggenheim Fellowship Guggenheim Found., 1984, U.S.-Japan Leadership fellow Japan Soc., 1991. Democrat. Avocations: basketball, tennis, travel, mysteries. Office: Global Affairs Occidental Coll Los Angeles CA 90041 E-mail: dshearer@oxy.edu.

SHEARER, PAUL SCOTT, government relations professional; b. Clinton, Ill., Feb. 27, 1948; s. Lloyd Jr. and Pauline Lucille (Glosser) S.; m. Barbara Boston, July 3, 1981; children: Jason J. Brunk, Carrie K. Premo. BS, U. Ill., 1970, MS, 1975. Asst. dir. cash mgmt. State Treas. Ill., Springfield, 1973-74, asst. CFO, 1974-77, chief fiscal officer, 1977-78; dir. vehicle svc. State of Ill., 1978-81; legis. asst. Senator Dixon U.S. Senate, Washington, 1981-84; exec. dir. Nat. Corn Growers Assn., St. Louis, 1984-90; dir. govt. rels. Halfpenny, Hahn, Roche & Marchese, 1990-93; dir. legis. affairs Zeneca Inc., Washington, 1993; dep. asst. sec. congl. rels. USDA, 1993-96; dir. nat. rels. Farmland Industries, Inc., Washington, 1996—. Mem. adv. com. Ill. Atty.'s Gen. Agr. Law, State of Ill., 1985-91; dean Coll. Agriculture, U. Ill., 1989-90, U. Ill. Dept. Agrl. Econs., 1986-89; mem. agrl. tech. com. for trade in animals and animal products USDA/U.S. Trade Rep., 1998—; U.S. del. to WTO Ministerial Conf., 1999; food security adv. com. USAID, 1998—. Del. Dem. Nat. Conv., 1978, Mo. Dem. State conv., 1988, Va. Dem. State Conv., 1992, 93, 94, 96, 97, 2000; mem. Police Bd. Commrs., Chesterfield, Mo., 1988-90; pres. Mo. River Dem. Club, 1987-89. Named to Hon. Order of Ky. Cols., 1990, Alpha Gamma Sigma nat. merit award, 1991; named to Villa Grove (Ill.) HS Alumni Hall of Fame. Mem. St. Louis Agr.-Bus. Club (sec.-treas. 1987-88, 2d v.p. 1988-89, v.p. 1989-90, pres. 1990), U. Ill. Alumni Assn., U. Ill. Coll. Agr. Alumni Assn. (dir. at large 1990), Ill. Group (chmn. 1993), Ill. State Soc. (bd. dirs. 1996—, pres. 2002—), Mo.-Kans. Forum (chmn. 1998-2000), Alpha Zeta (Honor Roll). Methodist. Home: 2744 Clarkes Landing Dr Oakton VA 22124-1120 Office: Farmland Industries Inc 1350 I St NW Ste 1240 Washington DC 20005 E-mail: psshearer@farmland.com.

SHEARER, ROBERT G. communications executive; b. Atlanta, Apr. 12, 1955; s. Vernon Hill and Elizabeth (Clarkson) S.; m. Cynthia Anchors, Aug. 27, 1977; children: Jonathan, Micah, Jeremy, Paul. AB, Davidson Coll., 1977; MA, ABD, PhD, Stanford U., 1979. Asst. prof. Va. Wesleyan Coll., Va. Beach, 1981-84; mktg. dir. Okla. Beverage Co., Bartlesville, 1984-86; sr. analyst CACI Internat., Fairfax, 1986-87; exec. v.p. Inforum, Inc., Nashville. V.p. Va. Soc. for Human Life, Norfolk, 1983, bd. dir. Tri County Pro-Life, Skiatouk, 1985. Mem. Fellow Fulbright Found.; mem. Am. Mktg. Assoc., Am. Soc. for Hosp. Mktg. Mennonite Brethren. Office: Inforum Inc 1130 8th Ave S Nashville TN 37203-4724

SHEARER, RONALD ALEXANDER, economics educator; b. Trail, C., Can., June 15, 1932; s. James Boyd and Mary Ann (Smith) S.; m. Renate Elizabeth Selig, Dec. 20, 1956 (dec.); children: Carl, Bruce. BA, U. B.C., 1954; MA, Ohio State U., 1955, PhD, 1959. Asst. prof. econs. U. Mich., 1958-62; economist Royal Commn. Banking and Finance, Toronto, 1962-63; mem. faculty U. B.C., Vancouver, 1963—, prof. econs., 1970-98, emeritus prof., 1998—, head dept., 1972-76. Co-author: Money and Banking, 1975, The Economics of the Canadian Financial System, 1994; editor: Trade Liberalization and a Regional Economy, 1971. Mem. Am., Canadian Econs. Assns. Office: U BC Dept Econs Vancouver BC Canada E-mail: rshearer@interchange.ubc.ca.

SHEARER, WALTER CHRISTIANS, scientific research administrator; b. Astoria, Oreg., Dec. 15, 1944; s. Aaron L. and Virginia Eleanor S. BS, Howard U., 1966; Doctorat d'Etat ès-Sciences, U. Paris, Orsay, France, 1973. Fgn. lectr. Tsukuba U., Sakura-mura, Ibaraki, Japan, 1975-78; sr. acad. officer UN U., N.Y.C., Tokyo, 1978—. Recipient Japan Soc. for Promotion of Sci. fellowship, 1973-75, Bourse Joliot-Curie, Commissariat à l'Energie Atomique, Paris, 1969-73. Mem. AAAS, Am. Geophys. Union, N.Y. Acad. Sci. Office: United Nations DC1-0872 One United Nations Plz New York NY 10017

SHEARER, WILLIAM THOMAS, pediatrician, educator; b. Detroit, Aug. 23, 1937; BS, U. Detroit, 1960; PhD, Wayne State U., 1966; MD, Washington U., St. Louis, 1970. Diplomate Am. Bd. Pediat., Am. Bd. Allergy and Immunology (chmn. 1994-95, dir. 1990-95, chair nominations com., clin. immunology soc.), Nat. Bd. Med. Examiners, cert. in diagnostic lab. immunology. Post-doctoral fellow in biochemistry dept. chem. Indiana U., Bloomington, 1966—67; intern in pediat. St. Louis Children's Hosp., 1970—71, resident in immunology in pediat., 1971—72, dir. divsn. allergy and immunology, 1974—78; fellow in immunology in pediat. Barnes Hosp., Washington U., St. Louis, 1972—74; spl. USPHA sci. rsch. fellow in medicine dept. medicine Washington U., 1972—74, assoc. prof., 1978, prof., 1978; prof. pediat., microbiology, immunology Baylor Coll. Medicine, Houston, 1989—, dir. AIDS rsch. ctr., 1991—; head sect. allergy & immunology Tex. Children's Hosp., 1978—. Mem. ACTU Cmty. Adv. Bd. Tex. Children's Hosp., Houston, 1991—; chmn. pediat. core com. pediat. AIDS clin. trial group Nat. Inst. Allergy and Infectious Diseases, NIH, Bethesda, Md., 1989—, ad hoc reviewer, Md., 1991, mem. therapeutics subcom. AIDS rsch. adv. com., Md., 1993—, chmn. pediat. AIDS clin. trial group immunology com., Md., 1994—, mem. pediat. AIDS clin. trials group exec. Com., Md., 1991—95, mem. spl. rev. com. persons affected by chronic granulomatous disease, Md., 1992; site visitor Gen. Clin. Rsch. Ctr. NIH, Bethesda, Md., 1993, vice chmn. pediat. AIDS clin. trials group exec. com., Md., 1996—; chmn. study populatoin/patient mgmt. com. Clin. Ctrs. for the Study of Pediat. Lung and Heart Complications of HIV Infection, Nat. Heart, Lung and Blood Inst., NIH, Bethesda, Md., 1989—, mem. AIDS ad hoc work group, Md., 1991; dir. Pediat. HIV/AIDS Clin. Rsch. Ctr., Houston, 1988—; chmn. exec. com. clin. trial intravenous gammaglobulin in HIV infected children Nat. Inst. Child Health and Human Devel., Bethesda, 1989—; dir. Am. Bd. Allergy and Immunology, 1990—95, chair, 1994—95; vice-chair exec. com. Pediat. AIDS Clin. Trials Group, 1996—. Editor: Pediatric Asthma, Allergy, and Immunology, 1989; editl. bd. Jour. Allergy and Clin. Immunology, 1993—, Clin. and Diagnostic Lab. Immunology, 1994—, editor Pediatric Allergy and Immunology, 1995—, Allergy and Immunology Tng. Program Dir., guest editor Seminar Pediatric Infectious Disease, 1990, contbr. intro. Allergy: Princples and Practice, 1992, contbr. articles to profl. jours. including New Eng. Jour. Medicine. AIDS cons. Houston Ind. Sch. Dist., 1986—; med. adv. Spring Br. Ind. Sch. Dist., Houston, 1987—; chmn. cmty. HIV/AIDS adv. group Tex. Med. Ctr., 1991—. Recipient faculty rsch. award, Am. Cancer Soc., 1977—79, Myrtle Wreath award, Hadassah, 1985, spl. recognition award, Am. Acad. Allergy and Immunology, 1994; grantee NIH, 1988—; scholar rsch., Cystic Fibrosis Found., 1974—77. Mem.: Clin. Immunology Soc. (chair Am. Bd. Allergy and Immunology nominations com. 1994—96, pres. 2001—02), Am. Acad. Allergy, Asthma and Immunology (assoc. chmn. for planning of 1997-98 internat. meetings, profl. ednl. coun.), Am. Acad. Allergy and Immunology (chmn. clin. and lab. immunology com. 1994—96, chmn. tng. program dirs. nat. issues subcom. 1994—96), Tex. Allergy and Immunology Soc. (chmn. nat. issues com. 1992—96, pres. 1994—96), Tex. Allergy Soc. (exec. com. 1990—), Am. Acad. Pediat. (exec. com. sect. allergy and immunology 1991—), Am. Soc. Clin. Investigation. Achievements include research in half-matched T-cell-depleted bone marrow transplants; membrane signal pathway of human B lymphcytes. Office: Baylor Coll of Med Allergy/Immun Clinic 6701 Fannin 9th Fl Houston TX 77030-2600

SHEARER, WILLIAM KENNEDY, lawyer, publisher; b. Marysville, Calif., Jan. 21, 1931; s. William and Eva (Kennedy) S.; m. Eileen Mary Knowland; Nov. 25, 1956; 1 child, Nancy Lorena; stepchildren: David, Douglas, Dianne. BA, San Diego State U., 1955; JD, Western State U., 1975. Bar: Calif. 1975, U.S. Dist. Ct. (so. dist.) Calif. 1975, U.S. Ct. Claims 1976, U.S. Supreme Ct. 1982, U.S. Ct. Appeals (fed. cir.) 1982, U.S. Ct. Appeals (9th cir.) 1983. Legis. asst. to Congressman James Utt, 1953, 55-56; exec. dir. San Diego County Rep. Cen. Com., 1956-58; pub. Oceanside-Carlsbad Banner, Oceanside, Calif., 1958-63; adminstrv. asst. Assemblyman E.R. Barnes, Sacramento, 1963-65; polit. campaign cons. Banner Advt., San Diego, Los Angeles, 1964-75; atty. Duke, Gerstel, Shearer LLP, San Diego, 1975—. Pub. newsletters Calif. Statesman, 1962—, Legis. Survey, 1963—, Fgn. Policy Rev., 1972—, Am. Ind., 1974—. Rep. nominee for State Assembly, San Diego County, 1956, 58; state chmn. Am. Ind. Party, Calif., 1967-70, nat. chmn. 1968-71, 73-77; nat. vice chmn. U.S. Taxpayers Party, 1992-96, chmn. 1996-99; Am. Ind. nominee for Gov., 1970; adv. com. Elections Com., Calif. Legislature, Sacramento, 1971-76; mem. Blue Ribbon Task Force on Calif.'s Home Constrn. Industry, 1996-97; bd. dirs. San Diego Gilbert & Sullivan Co., 1984-90, pres. 1986-88, v.p., 1985-86, 88-90. With U.S. Army, 1953-55. Mem. Calif. Bar Assn., San Diego County Bar Assn. Avocations: ancient Near Eastern history, gardening, music. Home: 8160 Palm St Lemon Grove CA 91945-3028 Office: Duke Gerstel Shearer LLP WKS 101 W Broadway Ste 1120 San Diego CA 92101-8296

SHEARES, BRADLEY T. pharmaceutical executive; BA in Chemistry, Fisk U., 1978; PhD in Biochemistry, Purdue U., 1982. Rsch. fellow dept. biochem. regulation Merck Inst. for Therapeutic Rsch., MRL, 1987—90; hosp. specialist internat. mktg. mgmt. MSD Internat., 1990; product mgr. AIDS/Devel. products Hosp. Products Mktg. Group, MSD, 1991; product mgr./sr. product mgr. Proscar, U.S. Human Health, 1991—92, dir. external bus. devel., 1992—93, sr. dir. hosp. bus. group, 1993—94, exec. dir. anti-infectives bus. group, 1995—96, v.p. anti-infectives bus. group, 1996—98, v.p. hosp. mktg. and sales, 1998—2001; pres. human health Merck & Co., Inc., Whitehouse Station, NJ, 2001—. Fellow NIH Postdoctoral, Ctr. for Cancer Rsch., MIT, 1983—85; scholar Lucille P. Markey, 1985—87. Mem.: AAAS, Am. Soc. for Microbiology, Am. Soc. Biol. Chemists (assoc.). Office: Merck and Co Inc One Merck Dr Whitehouse Station NJ 08889-0100*

SHEARIN, KATHRYN KAY, procurator, legal and humor writer; b. Norfolk, Va., Dec. 24, 1946; d. John Willis and Kathryn (Riecken) S.; m. James Charles Bray, June 1, 1969 (div. May 1973). BA, U. N.C., Greensboro, 1968; MA, Boston U., 1972; MS, N.C. State U., 1978; JD, Rutgers U., Newark, 1980; LLM in Taxation, Georgetown U., 1983. Bar: N.J. 1980, U.S. Dist. Ct. N.J. 1980, D.C. 1981, Md. 1982, U.S. Tax Ct. 1982, U.S. Supreme Ct. 1984, Del. 1986, U.S. Dist. Ct. Del. 1986, U.S. Cir. Ct. (3d cir.) 1987. Law clk. to magistrate U.S. Dist. Ct. N.J., Newark, 1978-79; prin. stat. State of N.J., Trenton, 1979-80; atty., adviser U.S. Dept. of Justice, Washington, 1982-83; editor tax law BNA Tax Mgmt., 1983-84; editor, pub. Common Law Revue CapriComp, Wilmington, Del., 1984-86; pvt. practice law, 1986-98; procurator, 1999—. Trust counsel, v.p., corp. sec. E.F. Hutton Trust Co., Wilmington, 1984-86; mng. atty. Hyatt Legal Svcs., 1986; lectr. in field. Author: (book) Diamond Dust, 1992; writer Del. Corp. Law Update, 1987—; contbr. poetry to anthologies. Libertarian candidate for atty. gen., Del., 1990; of counsel African Union 1st Colored Meth. Protestant Ch., 1991—; gen. counsel, trustee Project Gutenberg, 1999-2000. Mem. Profl. Orgn. Agts., Chtd. (founder, charter 1999). Libertarian. Home and Office: 1301 Maple Ave Elsmere DE 19805-5036 E-mail: ks24@georgetown.edu.

SHEARS, ROGER HAMMOND, investment company executive; b. June 27, 1949; , Cypress Coll., 19698, Calif. State U., 1971. Pres., CEO RHS Investment Corp., Lake Elsinore, Calif., 1986—; sr. v.p. Eagle Paper Co., N.Y.C., 1988-98; pres., CEO Eagle Dominion Energy Corp., Madisonville, Ky., 1997—. Office: 32940 Blackwell Blvd Lake Elsinore CA 92530-5949

SHEATS, JOHN EUGENE, chemistry educator; b. Atlanta, Dec. 20, 1939; s. Eugene Harold and Mildred Virginia (Pendergrass) S.; m. Margaret Joann Lee, May 27, 1972; 1 child, David S. BS in Chemistry, Duke U., 1961; PhD in Chemistry, MIT, 1966. Asst. prof. Bowdoin Coll., Brunswick, Maine, 1965-70; assoc. prof. chemistry Rider Coll. (name changed to Rider U. 1995), Lawrenceville, N.J., 1970-78, prof., 1978—. Presbyterian. Avocation: scuba diving. Office: Rider U 2083 Lawrenceville Rd Lawrenceville NJ 08648-3099

SHEATS, RACHEL GAY, computer and reading educator, videographer; b. Cassville, Mo., Feb. 15, 1964; d. R.G. Edmondson and Mary Louise Shultz; m. Charles Drew Sheats, Apr. 6, 1990; children: Zachariah, Joshua. AA in Country Music, Rogers State Coll., 1986; BS in Edn., Mo. So. State Coll., 1989; MEd in Ednl. Tech., U. Ark., 1996. Cert. tchr. 1-9 gen. edn. and reading specialist, Mo. Substitute tchr. Cassville Schs., Exeter (Mo.) Schs., Purdy (Mo.) Schs., 1989-90; reading specialist Cassville R-IV Schs., 1990—, computer literacy educator, 1998—. Tchg. intern U. Ark., 1994-95; prodn. cons. Jones TV Network, Springdale, Ark., 1995-96; curriculum cons. KOZK-TV, Springfield, Mo., 1994-96. Author: (ednl. workshops) The News and You!, 1991, The Book Report Alternative, 1992, Reading Buddies: A Community Effort, 1993, Reading Across the Curriculum with Style!, 1994, Internet Uses in Today's Classrooms, 1995, Teachers and Paraprofessionals: Building a Winning Team!, 1999, (video curriculum) Let's Start Cooking, 1995. Vol. Family Life Ctr., Cassville, 2000—. Recipient outstanding ednl. achievements award U. Mo. Ext. Ctr., 1992-93. Mem. Mo. Mid. Sch. Assn. (S.W. regional rep. 1999-2001). Home: Rt 4 Box 4188 Cassville MO 65625 Office: Cassville Mid Sch 1501 Main St Cassville MO 65625 Fax: (417) 847-3156. E-mail: rsheats@mo-net.com., rsheat@cassville.k12.mo.us.

SHEAVLY, ROBERT BRUCE, social worker; b. Detroit, Sept. 13, 1952; s. George Brown and Mary Jane (Hoover) S. BA, Georgetown U., 1974; MSW, U. Md., 1981. Lic. ind. clin. social worker; diplomate in clin. social work, Acad. Cert. Social Workers. Bookkeeper, accounts payable mgr. Capitol Area Ins. Assocs., Silver Spring, Md., 1974-77; asst. cons. The Wyatt Co., Washington, 1977-79; counselor Whitman-Walker Clinic, 1977-79; social worker Dept. Social Svcs. City Balt., 1980, Alcohol and Drug Abuse Program, U. Md. Sch. Medicine, Balt., 1980-81, instr., asst. dir. family violence unit, 1981-82; pvt. practice, 1982-83; social worker alcohol/drug abuse prevention/control program U.S. Army, Giessen (Germany) Cmty. Counseling Ctr., 1983-84; clin. supr. alcohol/drug abuse prevention/control program U.S. Army, Giessen Milcom, Cmty. Counseling Ctr., 1984-85; instr. drug and alcohol abuse divsn. 7th Army Tng. Ctr., Munich, Germany, 1985-91; dir. family program specialized treatment addiction recovery Walter Reed Army Med. Ctr., Washington, 1991-93, cons. dept. clin. pastoral edn., 1993-95; assoc. dir. Bill Austin Day Treatment Ctr. for Persons with AIDS Whitman-Walker Clinic, 1993-94; pvt. practice, 1994—. Presenter, guest lectr. in field. Ch. organist, dir. music Ch. of the Nativity, Washington, St. James Episcopal Ch., Washington, 1970-79; mem. diocesan commn. on liturgy and music Episcopal Diocese of Washington. Mem. NASW, Soc. Neuro-Linguistic Programming, Washington Soc. Jungian Psychology, Phi Kappa Phi. Episcopalian. Avocations: biking, scuba, sq. dancing, liturgics, ch. organist. Home: 2039 New Hampshire Ave NW Washington DC 20009-3479 Office: 1633 Q St NW Ste 200 Washington DC 20009-6351 E-mail: bob@dcpsychotherapy.com.

SHEBLE, GERALD B. engineering educator, consultant; b. St. Louis, Mar. 7, 1949; s. Walter W. and June M. (Schwalbe) S.; m. Mary Ann Best, Jan. 27, 1970 (div. Sept. 1993); children: Jason, Laura. BSEE, Purdue U., 1971, MSEE, 1975; PhD in Elect. Engring., Va. Tech., 1985. Methods engr. Commonwealth Edison, Chgo., 1971-73; engr. Systems Control, Inc., Palo Alto, Calif., 1975-76; cons. Control Data Corp., Mpls., 1976-80; sr. cons. Energy and Control Cons., 1980-86; assoc. prof. elect. engring. dept. Auburn (Ala.) U., 1986-90; prof. elect. and computer engring. dept. Iowa State U., Ames, 1990—. Tech. program subcom. Applications Neural Networks to Power Systems, Yokohama, Japan, 1993; power systems rep., curriculum com. Iowa State U., spring 1994, chmn. curriculum com., fall 1993, faculty search com., 1992—, disting. lectr. series chmn., 1992-93, profl. devel. com., 1991-93, grad. application review com., 1991-94, power area subcom., 1990—; engring. computer group Auburn U., 1989-90, elect. engring. computer users group chmn., 1986-90, power systems group, 1986-90; cons. and presenter in field. Contbr. articles to Electric Power Systems Rsch. Jour., Space Power Jour., Simulation. Grantee NSF, 1991-92, Rockwell Internat. Excellence, 1992, Electric Power Rsch. Ctr., 1991-95. Mem. IEEE (sr. mem., chmn. operating econ. working group 1986-93, adminstrv. subcom., system control subcom., system ops. subcom., system econ. subcom., power system engring. com.), Indsl. Applications Soc., Automatic Control Soc., Circuits & Systems Soc., Neural Networks Coun., Am. Soc. Engring. Educators, Congress Internat. Grands Reseaux Electric, Phi Kappa Phi, Eta Kappa Nu. Achievements include rsch. in brokerage optimization for multi-lateral electric power contracts and scheduling. Office: Iowa State Univ 107 Coover Hl Ames IA 50011-0001

SHECHTER, LAURA JUDITH, artist; b. Bklyn., Aug. 26, 1944; d. Philip and Jeannette (Newmark) Goldstein; m. Ben-Zion Shechter, Feb. 26, 1969; 1 son, Adam. BA with honors in Art, Bklyn. Coll., 1965. Case worker Dept. Social Service, N.Y.C., 1965-73; artist N.Y.C., 1965—; lectr., 1978—; curator Forum Gallery, N.Y.C., 1978; tchr. Parson Sch. Design, 1984, Nat. Acad. Design, N.Y.C., 1985-88, 94-98. Exhibited one-woman shows Forum Gallery, N.Y.C., 1976, 80, 83, Greenville County Mus. Art, 1982, Wustum Mus., Racine, Wis., 1982, Schoelkopf Gallery, N.Y.C., 1985, Staempfli Gallery, N.Y.C., 1987, 88, Rahr West Mus., Manitowoc, Wis., U. Richmond, 1991, Perlow Gallery, N.Y.C., 1992, 94, Pucker Gallery, Boston, 1984, 96, 99; group shows include Akron Art Inst., 1974, Minn. Mus. Art, St. Paul, 1981, Pa. Acad. Art, Phila., 1982, Boston Mus., 1982, Bklyn. Mus., 1980, 84, Nat. Mus. Am. Art, Washington, 1985, San Francisco Mus. Modern Art, 1985, Huntsville Mus., Ala., 1987, Butler Inst., Youngstown, Ohio, 1987, 88, Ind. U. Art Mus., Joplin, Mo., 1991, Ark. Art Ctr., 1992; represented in pub. collections including Boston Mus. Fine Art, Bklyn. Mus., Carnegie Inst., Indpls. Mus., Israel Mus., others. Recipient Creative Artist Pub. Service award N.Y. State, 1982 Mem. Artists Equity, Nat. Acad. Design. Home: 429 4th St Brooklyn NY 11215-2901 E-mail: laurart3@aol.com. *I believe that my work is always slowly changing through hard and consistent effort. There was a strong idea that initiated this work. Although that idea has been completely altered, it still exists.*

SHECHTMAN, HARRY, retired judge, law educator; b. Paris, Aug. 19, 1912; arrived in U.S., 1915; s. Solomon and Rose Shechtman; m. Betty Goodman, Nov. 20, 1940 (dec.). BS, L.I. U., 1933, LLD (hon.) , 1999; JD, Columbia U., 1938. Bar: N.Y. 1938. Pvt. practice, N.Y.C., 1938—78; adminstrv. law judge N.Y. State Health Dept., 1978—95. Adj. prof. Fla. Atlantic U., 1995—99; pres. Adminstrv. Law Judge Assn., N.Y.C., 1980—81. Pres. B'nai B'rith Met. Coun., N.Y.C., 1959—61; bd. trustees L.I. U., 1972—83. Mem.: B'nai B'rith, A.J.M. Schwartz Coll. Health Scis., Jewish Nat. Fund. Democrat. Jewish. Mailing: 44 Florida St Lido Beach NY 11561-1108

SHECHTMAN, RONALD H. lawyer; b. Hartford, Conn., Sept. 26, 1946; s. Allen A. and Jean (Bernstein) S.; m. Carolyn Meadow, Dec. 11, 1982; 1 child, Jonathan. BA, Amherst Coll., 1968; JD, NYU, 1972. Bar: U.S. Dist. Ct. (so. dist.) N.Y. 1973, N.Y. 1973, U.S. Ct. Appeals (2d cir.), U.S. Supreme Ct. Ptnr. Gordon & Shechtman PC, N.Y.C., 1972-85, Pryor, Cashman, Sherman & Flynn, N.Y.C., 1985—. Free speech com. ACLU, 1972, labor & employment com. N.Y.C. Bar Assn., 1988-91. Bd. advisors NYU Law Sch. Ctr. for Labor and Employment Law, 1997—; bd. dirs. The Creative Coalition, 1996—. Office: Pryor Cashman Sherman & Flynn 410 Park Ave Fl 10 New York NY 10022-4407

SHEDAKER, KATHLEEN EDITH, publishing executive; b. Boston, May 2, 1953; d. Richard Flave Shedaker and Jessica Mae Gould; m. Jon Patterson Speller Sr.; 1 child, Jon Patterson Speller Jr. AAS in Bus. Adminstrn., Monroe Coll., 2001. Rschr. Press Office Saudi Arabia, N.Y.C., 1986-96, Bosniac Nat. Coun. of Sanjak, N.Y.C., 1996, Backster Rsch. Found., San Diego, 1985; pub. Morning Star Chapel & Press, N.Y.C., 1986—. Dir. microgenepools.com, N.Y.C., 2000—. Author: (book) The American Dynasty, 1998, (rsch. monograph) Micro Gene Pools, 2000. Exec. dir. Anti-Communist Internat., N.Y.C., 1985—. Recipient Cold War Victory medal Anti-Communist Internat., 2000.

Mem.: N.Y. Geneal. and Biog. Soc., Morning Star Chapel (co-founder, Interfaith award 1996). Avocations: genealogy, music, art. Office: Anti-Communist Internat PO Box 1095 New York NY 10163-1095 E-mail: kathleenshedaker@lycos.com.

SHEDD, DONALD POMROY, surgeon; b. New Haven, Aug. 4, 1922; s. Gale and Marion (Young) S.; m. Charlotte Newsom, Mar. 17, 1946; children: Carolyn, David, Ann, Laura BS, Yale U., 1944, MD, 1946. Diplomate Am. Bd. Surgery. Intern Yale New Haven Hosp., 1946-47, asst. resident, resident, 1949-53; instr. surgery Yale U. Med Sch., New Haven, 1953-54, asst. prof., 1954-56, assoc. prof., 1956-67; chief dept. head and neck surgery Roswell Park Cancer Inst., Buffalo, 1967-96, prof. emeritus, 1996—; rsch. prof. emeritus SUNY at Buffalo, 1996—. Co-editor: Surgical and Prosthetic Speech Rehabilitation, 1980, Head and Neck Cancer, 1985; author: Historical Landmarks in Head and Neck Cancer Surgery, 2000; contbr. numerous articles to profl. jours. Founding bd. dirs. Hospice Buffalo, Inc., 1973-83. Served to capt. U.S. Army, 1947-49 Mem. Soc. Univ. Surgeons, Soc. Surg. Oncology, New Eng. Surg. Soc., Soc. Head and Neck Surgeons (pres. 1976-77). Avocations: sailing; windsurfing; tennis, history of medicine. Home: 671 Lafayette Ave Buffalo NY 14222-1435 Office: Roswell Park Cancer Inst Elm & Carlton Sts Buffalo NY 14263-0001 E-mail: donshedd@prodigy.net.

SHEDDEN, ARTHUR, pharmaceutical executive, consultant; b. 1954; m. Rebecca, 1989. BS, Westminster Coll., 1975; MD, Jefferson Med. Coll., 1980; MBA, U. Pa., 1998. Intern Wilmington (Del.) Med. Ctr., 1980-81; resident in ophthalmology U. Pitts., 1984; fellow in neuro-ophthalmology U. Miami, 1985; pvt. clin. practice Wilmington (Del.) Med. Ctr., Tulsa, Okla., 1986-88; assoc. dir. Merck & Co., Inc., West Point, Pa., 1988-91, dir., 1992-2000, Concept/Five Techs., Inc., Vienna, 2000—; ptnr. Shedden & Assocs. LLC, Blue Bell, Pa., 2001—. Mem. panel Streaming Media East, San Francisco, 1999., sr. med. dir. Pharmacia, Peapack, N.J., 2001—. Mem. planning com. New Ventures in Healthcare Wharton Sch. U. Pa., 1998. Fellow Am. Acad. Ophthalmology; mem. Alumni Assn. Jefferson Med. Coll. Home: 18 Cambridge Rd Bedminster NJ 07921-1610

SHEDLAWSKI, JOSEPH FERDINAND, materials manager, educator; b. Wilkes-Barre, Pa., Mar. 13, 1954; s. Joseph F. and Mary Catherine (Boinski) S. BS in Biology, Bucknell U., 1976; MBA in Fin. cum laude, Iona Coll., 1982. Cert. prodn. and inventory mgr., 1986. Chemist Lederle Labs, Pearl River, N.Y., 1976-77, 78-79, biologist, 1977-78, quality assurance, 1979-80, dist. planner, 1981-82, mfg. scheduler, 1982-83, material requirements planner, 1983-85, master scheduler, 1985-86, planning mgr., 1987-89, materials mgr., 1990-93, dir. ops. resource mgmt. NY, 1993—2001; dir., supply chain optimization Wyeth Consumer Healthcare, Madison, NJ, 2001—. Am. prodn. and inventory control cer. program instr. Bloomfield (N.J.) Coll., 1987—. Mem. Am. Prodn. and Inventory Control Soc. (editor 1988, program v.p. 1989, exec. v.p. 1990, pres. 1991, platinum award 1987, 88, 89, 90, 91, APICS region 2 dir. 1992-95, region 2 v.p. 1996, 97, Internat. Conf. speaker 1995, 96, v.p. membership and chpt. devel. 1998, chpt. Lifetime Svc. award 2001, region 2 v.p., 2002-03, spkr. Congress for Progress 2001-02). Republican. Roman Catholic. Avocations: antique cars, travel, wine. Home: 7 Dundee Ct Chestnut Ridge NY 10977-5915 Office: Wyeth Consumer Healthcare Supply Chain Opt Dept Madison NJ

SHEDLOCK, JAMES, library director, consultant; b. Detroit, Nov. 25, 1950; BA in English, U. Notre Dame, 1974; AM in LS, U. Mich., 1977. Reference and serials libr. St. Joseph Mercy Hosp., Pontiac, Mich., 1977-79; document delivery libr. Wayne State U. Med. Libr., Detroit, 1979-81; coord. online search svc. U. N.C. Health Scis. Libr., Chapel Hill, 1982-84; head pub. svcs. Med. Libr., Northwestern U., Chgo., 1985-88, assoc. dir., 1988-91, dir. Galter Health Scis. Libr., 1991—. Cons. U.N. High Commr. for Refugees, Cyprus, 1993-94, Med. Coll. Wis. Libr., 1996-97, La Porte (Ind.) Hosp., 1998. Mem. ALA, Med. Libr. Assn. (bd. dirs. 1997-99), Am. Med. Informatics Assn., Assn. Acad. Health Scis. Libr. Dirs. (rep.), Acad. Health Info. Profls. (disting.). Office: Northwestern U Galter Health Scis Libr 303 E Chicago Ave Chicago IL 60611-3093

SHEDLOCK, KATHLEEN JOAN PETROUSKIE, community health and research nurse; b. Victorville, Calif., Jan. 22, 1952; d. Frank A. and Joan O. (Bird) Petrouskie; m. Ronald Francis Shedlock, Dec. 1, 1973; children: Pamela, Alison. Diploma, York Hosp. Sch. Nursing, 1973; BSN, SUNY, Utica, 1978; MS in Cmty. Health Nursing, Syracuse U., 1991; MPA in Health Care, Maxwell Sch., 1991; postgrad., U. Rochester, 2000—. Cert. adult practitioner ANCC, cert. cmty. health clin. nurse specialist. Staff nurse, charge nurse emergency rm. Doctors' Hosp., Freeport, NY, 1973; staff nurse ICU SUNY Health Sci. Ctr., Syracuse, 1974—76; primary care nurse with pvt. practice ob.-gyn. physician Liverpool, NY, 1977—79; staff nurse post anesthesia care unit, diabetes educator Cmty. Gen. Hosp., Syracuse, 1978—87; trainer, supr. home health aides Upjohn Health Care Svcs., Liverpool, 1986; staff nurse, health educator Syracuse U. Health Svcs., 1986—88; mem. faculty Crouse Irving Meml. Hosp. Sch. Nursing, Syracuse, 1987—93; rsch. coord. breast cancer prevention trials Hematology-Oncology Assocs. Ctrl. N.Y., 1993—2000; oncology clin. specialist Amgen, Inc., 2000—02, AstraZeneca product devel. scientist, 2002—. Mem. adj. faculty Syracuse U., 1997-2000; mem. clin. trials nurse com. Nat. Surg. Adjuvant Breast and Bowel Project, 1996-2000; mem. psycho-oncology core com. cancer and leukemia group B, 1996-97; cons. planner Oneida (N.Y.) Nation Healthcare Program, 1990; reviewer Mosby Year Book Med. Pub., St. Louis, 1991; presenter at profl. confs. workshops; cons. Ctrl. N.Y. Coun. Occupl. Safety and Health, Syracuse, 1987-90; childbirth educator Childbirth Edn. Assn., Greater Syracuse, 1976-81, consumer rep., 1977; mem. protocol implementation rev. com. U. Rochester, 1998-2000. Bd. dirs. Onondaga County chpt. Am. Cancer Soc., 1993-2001, pres., 1997-2001. Mem. Oncology Nursing Soc. (health policy contact person 1994-96, ethics regional cons. 1994—, ethics, special interest group, coord.-elect, 2000-2001, coord. 2001—), N.Y. State Nurses Assn. (chair coun. on ethical practice 1990-94, coun. on continuing edn. 1997-99, dist. treas. 1990-94, chair nominating com. 1996-97, Excellence in Nursing award 1991, rsch. fellow 1999-2001), Eastern Rsch. Nursing Soc., Internat. Soc. Nurses in Genetics, Syracuse U. Nursing Alumni Assn. (pres. 1997-99), York Hosp. Sch. Nursing Alumni Assn., Sigma Theta Tau, Omicron, Iota Delta, Omicron Alpha (nominating com., steering com. 1995-97, rsch. com. 1997—). Avocations: running, swimming, biking.

SHEEDY, EVELYN MARDELLE, nonprofit corporation executive; b. Seattle, May 11, 1951; d. Charles Lloyd and Mardelle Thomas Cheetham; m. Robert Wilson Sheedy, Nov. 19, 1999. Student, internat. Tng. Massage Inst., Thailand, 1995. Lic. massage practitioner, Wash.; cert. svc. dog instr. Pvt. massage practitioner, Seattle, 1988-99; CEO Dog Ptnrs., Capistrano Beach, Calif., 2000—. Spkr., tchr. in field. Recipient appreciation award U. Ariz., 1999. Home and Office: 34701 Calle Rosita Capistrano Beach CA 92624 E-mail: dogpartner@cox.net.

SHEEDY, PATRICK THOMAS, judge; b. Green Bay, Wis., Oct. 31, 1921; s. Earl P. and Elsie L. (Brauel) S.; m. Margaret P. Mulvaney, Sept. 6, 1952; children: Michael, Mary, Kathleen, Patrick Thomas, Ann, Maureen. BS in Bus. Adminstrn., Marquette U., 1943, JD, 1948; LLM in Taxation, John Marshall Law Sch., 1972. Bar: Wis. 1948. Pvt. practice, Milw., 1948-80; judge Wis. Cir. Ct., 1980-90; chief judge 1st Jud. Dist., 1990-98. Past vice chmn. Archdiocesean Sch. Bd., Milw., chairperson, 1986—. Served to col. USAR, 1942-73. Decorated Legion of Merit. Mem. ABA (state del. 1983-85, 89-92, bd. govs. 1985-88), Wis. Bar Assn. (pres. 1974-75, bd. govs., exec. com.). Clubs: Exchange (pres.). Roman Catholic.

SHEEHAN, CHARLES VINCENT, investment banker; b. London, Dec. 19, 1930; came to U.S., 1931; s. Charles Vincent and Mary Margaret (Stokes) S.; m. Susan Ellen Rosar, May 5, 1962. BS, Georgetown U., 1952. Chief fin. officer Gen. Electric Co., Tokyo, Sydney, Australia and Sao Paulo, Brazil, 1962-64, 64-66, 67-71, staff exec. Fairfield, Conn., 1972-83, v.p. corp. exec. office, 1983-87; sr. v.p., chief fin. and adminstrn. officer Kidder, Peabody Group, Inc., N.Y.C., 1987-90. Bd. dirs. Fleet Trust Co. Chmn. Non-partisan Polit. Action Com. for Gen. Electric Co. employees, Fairfield, 1982-83. Served to lt. USN, 1952-54. Mem. Johns Island Club (Vero Beach, Fla.), Quail Valley Golf Club (Vero Beach, Fla.), Wildcat Cliffs Country Club (Highlands, N.C.) (pres. 1998-99). Republican. Roman Catholic. Avocations: golfing, surf fishing. Home (Summer): 560 Whiteside Mountain Rd Highlands NC 28741-7361 Home (Winter): 884 Indian Lane Vero Beach FL 32963

SHEEHAN, DONALD THOMAS, retired academic administrator; b. Winsted, Conn., Jan. 2, 1911; s. James J. and Louise (Coffey) S.; m. Betty Young, June 25, 1941; 1 son, Michael Terrence. Grad., Gilbert Sch., Winsted, 1931; BS in Edn, Syracuse U., 1935; student, Sch. Pub. Affairs, Am. U., 1936. Dir. health edn. D.C. Tb. Assn., 1937-39; dir. Washington office NCCJ, 1939-41; dir. Bur. Info. Nat. Cath. Welfare Conf., Washington, 194-42; spl. cons. to U.S. Commr. Edn., 1946; staff mem. John Price Jones Co., Inc. (pub. relations cons.), 1946-51; cons. civil def. edn. program, asst. adminstr. charge vol. manpower FCDA, 1951-54, cons. vol. manpower, 1954—; dir. pub. relations U. Pa., 1954-76, sec. corp., 1975-76, sec., v.p. emeritus, 1976—; spl. lectr. pub. relations Drexel U., 1957-72; cons. Nat. Bd. Med. Examiners, 1964—, Coll. Physicians Phila., 1973—, Citizens' Action Com. to Fight Inflation, 1974-75, Wistar Inst. Anatomy and Biology, 1979, Univ. Mus., U. Pa., 1982—, Inst. Environ. Medicine, 1983—. Mem. adv. com. Nat. Trust for Hist. Preservation; cons. Am. Philos. Soc., 1988—. Served from 1st lt. to lt. col. USAAF, 1942-46. Decorated Bronze Star medal. Fellow Coll. Physicians Phila. (hon. assoc.), ; mem. Public Relations Soc. Am., Pi Gamma Mu. Clubs: Nat. Press. Roman Catholic. Address: Cathedral Village A-410 600 E Cathedral Rd Philadelphia PA 19128

SHEEHAN, EDWARD JAMES, technical consultant, former government official; b. Johnstown, Pa., Dec. 31, 1935; s. Louis A. and Ethel F. (Schaefer) S.; m. Florence Ann Hartnett, June 17, 1958; children— Edward, James, John, William, Mary. BS in Physics, St. Francis Coll., 1959; MS (Sloan fellow), Mass. Inst. Tech., 1972. Project engr. Electronics Command, Dept. Army, 1959-61, project team leader electro-optic equipment for tanks, 1961-63, project team leader electro-optic equipment for infantry, 1963-65, tech. area dir. electro-optic night vision equipment, 1965-73, asso. lab. dir. for devel. engring., 1973-76; lab. dir. Night Vision Lab., Fort Belvoir, Va., 1976-79; founder, pres. Sheehan Assos. Inc., Alexandria, 1979-92; founder, CEO, chmn. Stardyne, Inc., Johnstown, 1990-96. Chmn. Nat. and Internat. Symposia for Electro-Optical Tech. and Applications. Recipient numerous awards including Meritorious Civilian Svc. award Dept. Army, Disting. Alumnus award in sci. St. Francis Coll., 1989; named Man of Yr., Combined Svc. Clubs, Johnstown, Pa., 1993. Home: 809 Luzerne St Johnstown PA 15905-2301

SHEEHAN, JAMES JOHN, historian, educator; b. San Francisco, May 31, 1937; s. James B. and Sally W. (Walsh) S.; m. 1960; 1 child, Michael L.; m. Margaret L. Anderson, Sept. 2, 1989. BA, Stanford U., 1958; MA, U. Calif., Berkeley, 1959, PhD, 1964. From asst. to assoc. prof. Northwestern U., Evanston, Ill., 1964-79; prof. Stanford (Calif.) U., 1979-86, chmn. dept., 1982-89, Dickason prof. in humanities, 1986—. Author: Lujo Brentano, 1966, German Liberalism, 1978, German History 1770-1866, 1989, Der Ausklang des alten Reiches, 1994, Museums in German Artworld, 2000; editor: The Boundaries of Humanity, 1991; contbr. articles to profl. jours. Decorated officer's cross Order of Merit; fellow Am. Council Learned Socs., 1981-82, NEH, 1985-86, Wissenschaftskolleg Berlin; Guggenheim fellow, 2000—. Fellow AAAS (Humboldt Rsch. prize 1995), Am. Acad. Berlin; mem. Royal Hist. Soc. (corr.), Am. Hist. Assn. (nominating com. 1979-81, chmn. conf. group on Ctrl. European history 1985-86), Am. Philos. Soc. Office: Stanford U Dept History Stanford CA 94305 E-mail: sheehan@stanford.edu.

SHEEHAN, JOHN PATRICK, endocrinologist, educator; b. Dublin, Mar. 12, 1952; came to U.S., 1982; s. John and Elizabeth Mary (McKimm) S.; m. Pauline Mary McDonnell, June 16, 1977; children: Ivan, Jason, Ciara. BSc, Trinity Coll., Dublin, 1973; MB, BChir, Trinity Coll., 1976. Diplomate Am. Bd. Internal Medicine. Diplomate Am. Bd. Endocrinology & Metabolism. Assoc. clin. prof. medicine Case Western Res. U., Cleve., 1985—; dir. diabetes mgmt. ctr. Univ. Hosps., 1985-92; dir. North Coast Inst. Diabetes & Endocrinology, Westlake, Ohio, 1992—. Fellow Am. Coll. Nutrition, Am. Coll. Endocrinology; mem. Am. Diabetes Assn., Diabetes Assn. of Greater Cleve. (trustee), Juvenile Diabetes Found. (med. adv. bd.), Endocrine Soc., Am. Assn. Clin. Endocrinologists, Internat. Soc. Clin. Densitometry. Office: 25101 Detroit Rd Ste 440 Westlake OH 44145-2545

SHEEHAN, KATHY RENEE, quality improvement administrator; b. Sept. 22, 1959; BSN, U. Akron, 1985. Legal nurse cons., Richmond, Va., 1999—; quality improvement mgr. So. Health Svcs., 1998—. Capt. USAR, 1985—. Mem. Res. Officers Assn. (life), Ctrl. Va. Healthcare Quality, Assn. Mil. Surgeons U.S. (life). E-mila. Home: 3520 Gregory Pond Rd Richmond VA 23236-1434 E-mail: ksheehan@cvty.com.

SHEEHAN, LARRY JOHN, lawyer; b. N.Y.C., Apr. 14, 1955; s. James Albert and Hortense Rose (Carlo) S.; m. Sylvia Margaret Poschman, Apr. 30, 1978; children: Nicole, Kelly, Daniel. BA, St. John's U., 1978; JD, N.Y. Law Sch., 1983. Bar: N.Y. 1984, U.S. Dist. Ct. (so. and ea. dists.) N.Y. 1984. Asst. dist. atty. Bronx Dist. Atty., N.Y.C., 1984-89; atty. in pvt. practice Scarsdale, N.Y., 1989—. Atty. N.Y.C. Assigned Counsel, N.Y.C., 1989—, Fed. Assigned Counsel Plan, So. Dist., N.Y., 1991—, Ea. Dist., N.Y., 1993—. Campaign mgr. Dem. Party, Yonkers, N.Y., 1989. Mem. N.Y. State Bar Assn., Bronx County Bar Assn., Westchester County Bar Assn., N.Y. State Criminal Trial Assn. Roman Catholic. Avocations: reading, brief writing, basketball, running. Home and Office: 111 Brook St Scarsdale NY 10583-5143

SHEEHAN, LAWRENCE JAMES, lawyer; b. San Francisco, July 23, 1932; AB, Stanford U., 1957, LLB, 1959. Bar: Calif. 1960. Law clk. to chief judge U.S. Ct. Appeals 2d Cir., N.Y.C., 1959-60; assoc. O'Melveny & Myers, L.A., 1960-68, ptnr., 1969-94, of counsel, 1995—. D. dirs. FPA Mut. Funds, Source Capital, Inc. Mem. ABA, Los Angeles County Bar Assn., Calif. Bar Assn., Order of Coif. Office: O Melveny & Myers 1999 Avenue Of The Stars Los Angeles CA 90067-6035 also: 400 S Hope St Los Angeles CA 90071-2801 E-mail: lsheehan@omm.com.

SHEEHAN, MICHAEL ANDREW, diplomat; b. Red Bank, N.J., Feb. 10, 1955; s. John M. and Janet M. (Purcell) S.; 1 child, Alexandra. BS, US Mil. Acad., 1977; MS in Fgn. Svc., Georgetown U., 1988. Commd. 2d lt. U.S. Army, 1977-97, advanced through grades to lt. col., ret., 1997; intelligence analyst White House Staff, Washington, 1989-91; dir. internat. programs Nat. Security Coun., 1992-93, dir. global issues, 1995-97; dir. POLMIL affairs U.S. Mission to UN, N.Y.C., 1993-95; dept. asst. sec. for internat. org. affairs U.S. Dept. State, Washington, 1997-98; coord. for counter terrorism Dept of State, 1998-2000; asst. sec. gen. Dept. Peacekeeping Ops., UN, N.Y.C., 2001—. Mem.: Coun. on Fgn. Rels., Spl. Forces Assn. Roman Catholic. Home: 2324 39th St NW Washington DC 20007-1722

SHEEHAN, MICHAEL GERARD, allergist; b. Syracuse, N.Y., Oct. 15, 1958; MD, SUNY, Syracuse, 1984. Diplomate Am. Bd. Allergy & Immunology. Resident in internal medicine Allegheny Genl. Hosp., Pitts., 1984-87; fellow in infectious diseases Presbyn. U. Hosp., 1987-88; with Group Practice Settings in Internal Medicine, 1988-91, Group Practice in Allergy and Clin. Immunology, 1994—; fellow in allergy & rheumatology Strong Meml. Hosp., Rochester, NY, 1991—94. Home: 7658 Linkside Dr Manlius NY 13104-2371 Office: 1200 E Genesee St Ste 103 Syracuse NY 13210-1936 E-mail: mgsheehan@msn.com.

SHEEHAN, MOLLY O'MEARA, think-tank associate, writer; b. Singapore, Dec. 9, 1970; d. James Thomas and Clare Lefebure O'Meara; m. Joseph Eugene Sheehan III, Jan. 15, 2000. BA in Biology and Asian Studies, Williams Coll., 1992; MS in Environ. Scis., Johns Hopkins U., 2000. Editor Urban Connections, Inc., Tokyo, 1992—93; rsch. asst. Carnegie Endowment for Internat. Peace, Washington, 1993—94; news asst. Asahi Shimbun, 1994—95; writer, rschr. Worldwatch Inst., 1996—. Spkr. in field. Author: City Limits: Putting the Brakes on Sprawl, 2001; contbr. chapters to books. Mem.: Nat. Press Club, N.Y. Acad. Scis. Avocations: running, biking, piano. Office: Worldwatch Inst 1776 Massachusetts Ave NW Washington DC 20036

SHEEHAN, NEIL, reporter, scholarly writer; b. Holyoke, Mass., Oct. 27, 1936; s. Cornelius Joseph and Mary (O'Shea) S.; m. Susan Margulies, Mar. 30, 1965; children— Maria Gregory, Catherine Fair. AB cum laude, Harvard, 1958; LittD (hon.) , Columbia Coll., Chgo., 1972; LHD (hon.) , Am. Internat. Coll., 1990, U. Lowell, 1991. Vietnam Bur. chief U.P.I., Saigon, 1962-64; reporter N.Y. Times, N.Y.C., Djakarta, Saigon, Washington, 1964-72. Author: The Arnheiter Affair, 1972, A Bright Shining Lie: John Paul Vann and America in Vietnam, 1988 (Nat. Book award 1988, Pulitzer Prize for gen. non-fiction 1989, Robert F. Kennedy book award 1989, Vetty award Vietnam Vets. Ensemble Theatre Co. 1989, Spl. Achievement award Vietnam Vets. Am. 1989, Outstanding Investigative Reporting award Investigative Reporters and Editors, Inc. of U. Mo. Sch. Journalism 1989, Amb. award English-Speaking Union 1989, John F. Kennedy award, Holyoke, Mass 1989), After the War Was Over: Hanoi and Saigon, 1992, also articles and book revs. for popular mags.; contbr. to The Pentagon Papers, 1971. Served with AUS, 1959-62. Recipient Louis M. Lyons award for conscience and integrity in journalism, 1964, Silver medal Poor Richard Club, Phila., 1964, certificate of appreciation for best article on Asia Overseas Press Club Am., 1967, 1st Ann. Drew Pearson prize for excellence in investigative reporting, 1971, Columbia Journalism awards, 1972, 89, Sidney Hillman Found. awards, 1972, 88, Page One award Newspaper Guild N.Y., 1972, Distinguished Service award and Bronze medallion Sigma Delta Chi, 1972, citation of excellence Overseas Press Club, 1972, Literary Lion award N.Y. Pub. Libr., 1992; Guggenheim fellow, 1973-74; Adlai Stevenson fellow, 1973-75; Lehrman Inst. fellow, 1975-76; Rockefeller Found. fellow in humanities, 1976-77; Woodrow Wilson Internat. Center for Scholars fellow, 1979-80 Mem. Soc. Am. Historians, Am. Acad. Achievement, Club: Lansdowne, London. Achievements include obtaining Pentagon Papers, 1971. Home: 4505 Klingle St NW Washington DC 20016-3580

SHEEHAN, ROBERT JAMES, II, management and market research consultant; b. Pitts., May 13, 1937; s. Regis James and Helen Lillian (O'Leary) S.; m. Marie Elizabeth Yoskovich, Apr. 24, 1964; children: Stephanie Ann, Robert James III. AB in Econs., U. Pitts., 1967, MA, 1970; postgrad., Am. U. Cert. mgmt. cons. Rsch. analyst Action Housing Inc., Pitts., 1960-63; from project rep. to dir. rehab. Urban Redevel. Authority Pitts., 1963-73; assoc. chief economist, dir. econ. rsch. Nat. Assn. Homebuilders, Washington, 1973-82, v.p econ. policy analysis, 1982-83; v.p. Regis J. Sheehan & Assocs., McLean, Va., 1983-96, pres., 1997—. Founding dir. Georgetown Cons., Inc., 1993—; vice-chmn. Fairfax County Housing and Redevel. Authority, 1988-92, chmn. 1993-95. cons. in field. Author: The Basics of Land Acquisition, 1985; co-pub., prin. contbr. Mgmt./Econs. & Constrn. Real Estate newsletters; contbr. articles to profl. jours. Pres. bd. dirs. Touchstone Theatre Co., 1984—; pres. Caths. for Housing, 1998—; founding mem. Superior Bus. Roundtable. Mem. ASTD, Nat. Economists Club, Inst. Mgmt. Cons. (pres. Washington chpt. 1989-96), Nat. Assn. Bus. Econs., KC. Roman Catholic. Avocations: walking, jogging, reading. Office: 2200 W Liberty Ave # 608 Pittsburgh PA 15226-1504

SHEEHAN, SUSAN, writer; b. Vienna, Austria, Aug. 24, 1937; came to U.S., 1941, naturalized, 1946; d. Charles and Kitty C. (Herrmann) Sachsel; m. Neil Sheehan, Mar. 30, 1965; children— Maria Gregory, Catherine Fair. BA (Durant scholar), Wellesley Coll., 1958; DHL (hon.), U. Lowell, 1991. Editorial researcher Esquire-Coronet, N.Y.C., 1959-60; free-lance writer, 1960-61; staff writer New Yorker mag., 1961—; contbg. writer Archtl. Digest, 1997—. Writer-in-residence, lectr. Georgetown U., 1999. Author: Ten Vietnamese, 1967, A Welfare Mother, 1976, A Prison and a Prisoner, 1978, Is There No Place on Earth for Me?, 1982, Kate Quinton's Days, 1984, A Missing Plane, 1986, Life For Me Ain't Been No Crystal Stair, 1993, The Banana Sculptor, the Purple Lady, and the All-Night Swimmer, 2002; contbr. articles to various mags., including N.Y. Times Sunday Mag., Washington Post Sunday Mag., Harper's, Atlantic, New Republic, McCall's, Holiday, Boston Globe Sunday Mag., Life. Judge Robert F. Kennedy Journalism awards, 1980, 84; mem. lit. panel D.C. Commn. on Arts and Humanities, 1979-84; mem. pub. info. and edn. com. Nat. Mental Health Assn., 1982-83; mem. adv. com. on employment and crime Vera Inst. Justice, 1978-86; chair Pulitzer Prize nominating jury in gen. non-fiction for 1988, 1994, mem., 1991. Recipient Sidney Hillman Found. award, 1976, Gavel award ABA, 1978, Individual Reporting award Nat. Mental Health Assn., 1981, Pulitzer prize for gen. non-fiction, 1983, Feature Writing award N.Y. Press Club, 1984, Alumnae Assn. Achievement award Wellesley Coll., 1984, Carroll Kowal Journalism award NASW, 1993, Disting. Grad. award Hunter Coll. H.S., 1995, Pub. Awareness award Nat. Alliance for Mentally Ill, 1995, Casey medal for meritorious journalism, 1997; fellow Guggenheim Found., 1975-76, Woodrow Wilson Internat. Ctr. for Scholars, 1981, Open Soc. Inst., 1998-99. Mem. Soc. Am. Historians, Phi Beta Kappa, Authors Guild, Landsdowne (London) Club. Home: 4505 Klingle St NW Washington DC 20016-3580 Office: New Yorker Mag 4 Times Sq New York NY 10036-7441

SHEEHAN, WILLIAM W. pathologist; b. Chgo., Feb. 25, 1939; s. John F. and Edith N. (Holden) S.; m. Carolyn F. Kreuz, June 1960 (div. 1979); children: Jonathan H., Jennifer L., Brian W.; m. Carol A. Bartlett, Jan. 28, 1980; 1 child, Craig A. AB, Harvard U., 1960; MD, Marquette U., 1964. Diplomate Am. Bd. Pathology, Am. Bd. Hematopathology. Resident in pathology Yale U., New Haven, 1964-66; USPHS trainee in pathology U. Chgo., 1966-69; asst. prof. U. So. Calif., L.A., 1971-75; assoc. prof., pres. clin. pathology U. Tex. Southwestern Med. Sch., Dallas, 1975-82; pathologist St. John Med. Ctr., Tulsa, 1982—. Asst. dir. hematology labs. Los Angeles County Hosp., L.A., 1971-75; chief lab. svc. Dallas VA Hosp., 1975-79; dir. hematology labs. Parkland Meml. Hosp., Dallas, 1975-82. Contbr. numerous articles to med. jours. Maj. M.C., U.S. Army, 1969-71. Fellow Am. Soc. Clin. Pathologists (Ward-Burdick award 1995), Coll. Am. Pathologists, Am. Soc. Hematology; mem. AMA. Achievements include research on malignant lymphomas. Office: St John Med Ctr 1923 S Utica Ave Tulsa OK 74104-6502

SHEEHAN-MILES, CHARLES EDWARD, writer; b. Atlanta, Feb. 12, 1971; s. Richard Edward and Rhonda Katrin Miles; m. Veronica Francis Sheehan, Apr. 1, 1994; children: Khalil, Amirah. Pres. Nat. Gulf War Resource Ctr., Inc., Washington, 2000—01, nat. sec., 2001—, also bd. dirs. Bd. dirs. Edn. Peace in Iraq Ctr. Author: (novels) Prayer at Rumayla, 2001. With U.S. Army, 1990—92. Personal E-mail: charles@sheehanmiles.com.

SHEEHE, BRIAN D. music educator; b. Elmira, N.Y., Feb. 1, 1972; s. Patrick D. and Georgianna Sheehe; m. Denise M. Archer, Nov. 17, 2002. MusB, Ohio No. U., 1994. Dir. of bands Montpelier (Ohio) Schs., 1994—97; band dir. Findlay City Schs., 1997—. Pres. Ohio No. U. Republicans, Ada, 1993—94. Mem.: Ohio Edn. Assn., Music Educators Nat. Conf., Kappa Kappa Psi. Home: 2801 S Main St Findlay OH 45840 Office: Findlay City Schs 301 Baldwin Ave Findlay OH 45840

SHEEHE, PAUL ROBERT, statistician, educator, biologist; b. Buffalo, Dec. 8, 1925; s. Robert Emmett and Mary Bernadette Sheehe; m. Genevieve Madelyn Richert; children: Nancy, Robert, Pauline, Mary Carapella, Richard. DSc, U. of Pitts., 1959. Biostatistician Roswell Pk. Meml. Inst., Buffalo, 1959—65; rsch. prof. neuroscience Upstate Med. U., Syracuse, 1965—. Cons. NIH, Washington, 1965—82. Contbr. articles to profl. jours. Lt. (jg) USN, 1944—46, U.S. Mem.: Am. Epidemiological Soc. Avocation: tennis. Office: Upstate Medical University 750 East Adams Street Syracuse NY 13210 Personal E-mail: sheehep@upstate.edu. Business E-Mail: sheehep@upstate.edu.

SHEEHY, BARRY MAURICE, management consultant; b. Nov. 17, 1951; came to the U.S., 1991; BA in History, Econs. cum laude, Loyola Coll., 1975; MA in History, McGill U., 1977; Comms. & Electronics and Engring., Can. Forces Sch. Comm. Electronic Engring. Officer Canadian Armed Forces, Savannah, Ga., 1975-80; quality mgr. City of Calgary, 1980-85; mgr. orgnl. efectiveness No. Telecom, 1985-87; pres. Achieve Internat., 1987-91, CPC Econometrics, Inc., 1991-94, CPC Econometrics Inc., Savannah, Ga., 1997—; ptnr. The Atlanta Cons. Group, 1994-96, Sentry Technology Group, 1996-97; pres. CPC Econometrics Inc., Savannah, Ga., 1998—. Mem. faculty Estes Pk.(Healthcare) Inst., Healthcare Governance Inst., Healthcare Forum; guest spkr. U.S. C. of C., Quality Coun. Can., Quality Coun. Mex., Microsoft Healthcare Forum, INC 500, Am. Express Bank Global Forum, others. Author: In Search of Quality: 4 Unique Perspectives, 43 Different Voices (Exec. Excellence 1995); (with others) Firing on All Cylinders, 1992, Economic Divide: Winners and Losers in an Age of Abundance, 1996, Winning the RAce, 1996; contbr. articles to profl. jours. Guest spkr. SCLC, Savannah Found. Officer Can. Armed Forces. Co-recipient Am. Soc. Indsl. Engrs. award, 1985. Office: CPC Econometrics Inc 38 Mulberry Bluff Dr Savannah GA 31406-3269

SHEEHY, JANICE ANN, education technology coordinator; b. Jersey City, Mar. 18, 1955; d. Thomas Patrick and Norma Grace (Hultman) Sheehy; m. L. Hillen, June 19, 1976 (div. 1982); 1 child, Adrienne Grace; m. I. Richard Feingold, May 17, 1987. BA, Jersey City State Coll., 1977; student, Fairleigh Dickinson U., 1978-80; EdM, Rutgers U., 1992; EdD, Nova Southeastern U., 1997. Cert. elem. tchr., supr. K-12, adminstr. K-12. Tchr. 2d grade Roosevelt Sch., Union City, N.J., 1977-88, tchr. math., 1988-98, chair sch. improvement team, 1994-98; tech. coord. Christopher Columbus Sch., 1999—. Mem. N.J. Math. Coalition, 1994—, N.J. Math. Curriculum Frameworks Dist. Leadership Team, Framework, 1994—. Com. woman Dem. Com., Hudson County, N.J., 1985-86. Mem. ASCD, AAUW, Nat. Coun. Tchrs. Math., Assn. Math. Tchrs. N.J., Kappa Delta Pi, Phi Delta Kappa. Avocations: travel, reading, computers. Home: 360 Roosevelt St Fairview NJ 07022-1716 Office: Christopher Columbus Mid Sch 1500 New York Ave Union City NJ 07087-4324

SHEEHY, JEROME JOSEPH, electrical engineer; b. Hartford, Conn., Dec. 3, 1935; s. Jeremiah and Anna (Foley) S.; m. Jean Ann Baldassari, Oct. 13, 1962; children: Caroline, Jerome, Daniel, Carlene. BSEE, U. Conn., 1962, MSEE, 1967. Electronic engr. USN Underwater Sound Lab., New London, Conn., 1962-69; mem. tech. staff Rockwell Internat., Anaheim, Calif., 1969-74; staff engr. Hughes Aircraft Co., Fullerton, 1974-83; systems engr. Norden Systems, Santa Ana, 1983-89; advanced engring. specialist Lockheed Martin Aircraft Svc., Ontario, 1990-97. Contbr. articles to Jour. Acoustical Soc. Am. With USAF, 1954-57. Mem. Acoustical Soc. Am., Tau Beta Pi, Eta Kappa Nu. Achievements include research in detection and estimation theory for non-gaussian noise, non-normal statistics. Home: 8 Sagitta Way Coto De Caza CA 92679-5102 E-mail: JandJSheehy@cox.net.

SHEEHY, JOHN PAUL, pediatrician; b. Jan. 19, 1949; AB, Bowdoin Coll., 1970; MD, N.Y. Med. Coll., 1975. Diplomate Am. Bd. Pediat., Am. Bd. Quality Assurance and Utilization Review Physicians. Intern N.Y. Med. Coll. Met. Hosp. Ctr., resident; chmn. quality assurance North Shore U. Hosp., Glen Cove, N.Y., 1988—, dir. dept. pediats., 1990—, chmn. med. bd. NY, 2000—. Contbr. articles to profl. jours. Office: 10 Medical Plz Glen Cove NY 11542-2193

SHEELEY, HARRIET SPIEGEL, social worker; b. Chgo., Oct. 5, 1949; d. Joseph and Rita (Weisdorf) Spiegel; children: Heather Leah Gornik, Brett Terrance Friedmann. BA, U. Ill., 1970; MSW, Loyola U., 1977. Lic. clin. social worker, Ill.; diplomate Am. Bd. Examiners in Clin. Social Work; type 73 sch. cert., Ill. Psychiat. social worker Infant Welfare Soc., Chgo., 1977-79; social worker maternity St. Francis Hosp., Evanston, Ill., 1981-85; dir. Evanston (Ill.) Shelter for Battered Women, 1985-86; social worker Sch. Dist. 21, Wheeling, 1987—. Field work instr. Sch. Social Work, Loyola U., Chgo. Contbr. poetry to anthologies. Area rep. Dist. 21 Ednl. Assn., Wheeling, Ill., 1992—97; mem. adv. bd. Family Focus, Evanston, 1984—85; mem. Padmasambhava Buddhist Ctr. Mem. NASW (clin. diplomate), NEA, Ill. Assn. Sch. Social Workers, Phi Beta Kappa (Chgo. chpt.), Phi Kappa Phi. Avocations: poetry, philosophy, traveling. Home: 8616 Hamlin Ave Skokie IL 60076-2210 Office: Sch Dist 21 999 W Dundee Rd Wheeling IL 60090-3986 E-mail: Faitlux@aol.com.

SHEELINE, PAUL CUSHING, hotel executive; b. Boston, June 6, 1921; s. Paul Daniel and Mary (Child) S.; m. Harriet White Moffat, May 23, 1948 (dec. 1962); children: Christopher White, William Emerson, Mary Child, Leonora Moffat; m. Sandra Dudley Wahl, July 24, 1965; 1 child, Abby Tucker. BS, Harvard U., 1943, JD, 1948. Bar: N.Y. 1949, D.C. 1986. Assoc. Sullivan & Cromwell, N.Y.C., 1948-54; with Lambert & Co., 1954-65, gen. ptnr., 1958-65; chief fin. officer Intercontinental Hotels Corp., 1966-71, pres., 1971-74, chief exec. officer, 1971-85, chmn. bd., 1972-87, cons., 1987-92; of counsel Verner, Liipfert, Bernhard, McPherson & Hand, Washington, 1986-93. Mem. Presdl. Bd. Advisors on Pvt. Sector Initiatives, Washington, 1987-89. Vice chmn. Community Service Soc. of N.Y., 1962-63; dir. Am. Assn. for UN, 1951-58; former mem. Harvard Overseers Com. to visit Center for Internat. Affairs and Dept. Romance Langs.; trustee East Woods Sch., Oyster Bay Cove, N.Y., 1959-68, Camargo Found., 1971—, St. Luke's/Roosevelt Hosp. Ctr., 1982-97; bd. dirs. Bus. Council for Internat. Understanding., 1975-88, Fgn. Policy Assn., 1981-90, Scientists' Inst. Pub. Info., 1984-91, Battle of Normandy Found., 1986-91; mem. bd. zoning appeals Village of Lloyd Harbor, N.Y., 1988—. Served to capt. USAAF, 1942-46. Decorated Silver Star medal, French Legion of Honor, Croix de Guerre with palm, Moroccan Ouissam Alaouite. Mem. Am.-Arab Assn. Commerce and Industry (chmn. bd. 1984-86), Phi Beta Kappa. Clubs: Cold Spring Harbor Beach; Harvard (N.Y.C.); North Haven Casino (Maine). E-mail: paul@sheeline.com.

SHEEM, SANG KEUN, fiber optics engineering professional; b. Seoul, Korea, Mar. 20, 1944; s. Eung-Taek and Ki-Jik (Oh) S.; m. Susan Kim, Mar. 22, 1970; children: Edward J., Shana J. MS in Engring., U. Calif., 1973, PhD in Engring., 1975. Rsch. physicist U.S. Naval Rsch. Lab., Washington, 1976-81; mgr. Rockwell Internat., Dallas, 1981-86; mgr. sensor program Lawrence Livermore (Calif.) Nat. Lab., 1986-99. Mem. corp. optical panel Rockwell Internat., Dallas, 1982-86; cons. Kaptron Fiber Optic Co., Palo Alto, Calif., 1987-88, Amaco Rsch. Ctr., Naperville, Ill., 1986-87; pres. Berkeley Optics Co., Livermore, 1994—. Contbr. articles, referee to profl. jours. Mem. IEEE, Optical Soc. Am., Korean Scientist and Engr. Assn. (pres. No. Calif. chpt. 1990-91), Internat. Platform Assn., Calif. Commonwealth Club. Achievements include 20 patents in fiber optics and integrated optics; major inventions include single-mode fiber couplers and self-biased optical fiber gyroscope. E-mail: ssheem@berkeley-optics.com.

SHEEN, PORTIA YUNN-LING, retired physician; b. Republic of China, Jan. 13, 1919; came to U.S., 1988; d. Y. C. and A. Y. (Chow) Sheen; m. Kuo, 1944 (dec. 1970); children: William, Ida, Alexander, David, Mimi. MD, Nat. Med. Coll. Shanghai, 1943. Intern, then resident Cen. Hosp., Chungking, Szechuan, China, 1943; with Hong Kong Govt. Med. and Health Dept., 1948-76; med. supt. Kowloon (Hong Kong) Hosp., 1948-63, Queen Elizabeth Hosp., Kowloon, 1963-73, Med. and Health Hdqrs. and Health Ctr., Kowloon, 1973-76, Yan Chai Hosp., New Territories, Hong Kong, 1976-87; ret., 1987. Fellow Hong Kong Coll. Family Physicians; mem. AAAS, British Med. Assn., Hong Kong Med. Assn., Hong Kong Pediatric Soc., N.Y. Acad. Sci. Methodist. Avocations: reading, music. Home: 1408 Golden Rain Rd Apt 7 Entry 1 Roosmoor Walnut Creek CA 94595-2442 E-mail: pylsheen@hotmail.com.

SHEERAN, MICHAEL JOHN LEO, priest, college administrator; b. N.Y.C., Jan. 24, 1940; s. Leon John and Glenna Marie (Wright) S. AB, St. Louis U., 1963, PhL, 1964, AM in Polit. Sci., 1967, AM in Theology, STL, St. Louis U., 1971; PhD, Princeton U., 1977. Joined Soc. of Jesus, 1957; ordained priest Roman Catholic Ch., 1970. Exec. editor Catholic Mind, N.Y.C., 1971-72; assoc. editor Am. Mag., 1971-72; assoc. chaplain Aquinas Inst., Princeton, N.J., 1972-75; asst. dean Regis Coll., Denver, 1975-77, dean of Coll., 1977-82, v.p. acad. affairs, 1982-92, acting pres., 1987-88, pres., 1993—. Retreat dir., cons. on governance for religious communities, 1970—. Author: Beyond Majority Rule, 1984; contbr. articles and editls. to publs. Trustee Rockhurst Coll., Kansas City, Mo., 1982-91, Creighton U., Omaha, 1985-95, U. San Francisco, 1985-94, 2001—, Loyola U., New Orleans, 1994-96, Rocky Mountain Coll. Art and Design, 1994-99, Regis Jesuit H.S., 1999—; chmn. Mile High United Way, 1999-2000. Ford Found. scholar, 1963. Democrat. Home: 3333 Regis Blvd Denver CO 80221-1099 Office: Regis U 3333 Regis Blvd Denver CO 80221-1099

SHEERAN, ROBERT T. academic administrator; b. Troy, N.Y. B in Classical Langs., Seton Hall U., 1967; postgrad., U.S. Sem., N.Am. Coll., Rome; theology licentiate degree, Gregorian U., Rome, 1971; MA in Theology, Princeton U.; D in Theology, Angelicum U., 1979; mgmt. devel. program, Harvard U., 1989. Ordained priest, 1970. Rector St. Andrew's Coll. Sem. Seton Hall U., 1980, asst. provost, 1987, assoc. provost, 1991, exec. vice chancellor, 1993-95, pres., 1995—. Participant Priests-in-Residence program Seton Hall U.; dir. advising program N.Am. Coll., Rome, 1974-79. Bd. dirs. Bergen Cath. H.S. Fellow Am. Coun. on Edn. (mem. Commn. on Women in Higher Edn.). Office: Seton Hall U 400 S Orange Ave South Orange NJ 07079-2697*

SHEETS, DOROTHY JANE, retired school librarian and educator; b. Grant, Ala., Jan. 17, 1933; d. Walker Samuel and Floria Mae (Parks) Campbell; m. Paul Beauford Sheets, Jan. 1, 1958 (div. July 1972); children: Wanda Kay, Jeffrey Lee, Sue Ann Sheets Cagle. AS, Snead Jr. Coll., 1953; BS, U. Ala., Tuscaloosa, 1956; MEd, Auburn U., 1968; grad., Writer's Digest Sch., Cin., 1996, Inst. Children's Lit., 1992; student, Nat. Radio Inst., Washington, 1997. Cert. tchr. and sch. libr., Ala. Children's libr. Cleve. Pub. Libr., 1956-58; tchr. reading Marshall County Bd. Edn., Guntersville, Ala., 1962-76, elem. libr., 1976-91. Pvt. tutor, Albertville, Ala., 1968—. Vol. tax preparer RSVP, Guntersville, 1992—. DAR scholar, 1955. Mem. NEA (life), Ala. Edn. Assn., Ala. Ret. Tchrs. Assn., Marshall County Ret. Tchrs. Assn., Am. Assn. Ret. Persons. Avocations: reading, storytelling, volunteering, gardening. Home: 407 Pecan Ave Albertville AL 35950-2733 E-mail: djsheets3@juno.com.

SHEETS, FREDRICK SIDNEY, career officer, retired, auditor; b. Greenville, S.C., Aug. 16, 1946; s. Sidney Wesley Sheets and Mabel Eve (Whitfield) Becht; m. Mary Cahterine White, July 14, 1973; children: Brenda Justine, Valerie Claire, Brian Arthur. BA, Ohio U., 1969; BBA, U. Tex., El Paso, 1986, M in Accountancy, 1988. CPA, Fla.; cert. acquisition profl. Dept. Def. Commd. 2d lt. U.S. Army, 1969, advanced through grades to lt. col., 1991, served in Korea, Germany, Vietnam, Md., Tex., Wash., to 1997; sr. auditor Def. Contract Audit Agy., Palm Bay, Fla., 1988—. Counselor, Vol. Income Tax Assistance, Melbourne, Fla., 1993—. Decorated Bronze Star. Mem. Inst. Mgmt. Accts., Am. Inst. CPA, Assn. Govt. Accts. (cert. govt. fin. mgr., pres-elect, sec.-treas., chpt. pres. 1989—, Mem. of Yr. 1994, 98, Superior Performance award 1995), Assn. Cert. Fraud Examiners, Brevard Fla. Inst. CPA (pvt. practice chair 1994—), Am. Volkssport Assn. (dir. S.E. region 1996—, Disting. Achievement award 1995), Fla. Volkssport Assn. (treas., pres. 1991—). Republican. Avocations: walking. Home: 800 Emerson Dr NE Palm Bay FL 32907-1460 Office: PO Box 61419 Palm Bay FL 32906-1419

SHEETS, HERMAN ERNEST, marine engineer; b. Dresden, Germany, Dec. 24, 1908; s. Arthur Chitz and Gertrude (Stern) S.; m. Norma Sams, Oct. 17, 1942 (dec. Dec. 1970); m. Paulann Hosler, May 29, 1982; children: Lawrence S., Michael R., Arne H., Diana E., Elizabeth J., Karn N. M.E., U. Dresden, 1934; Dr. Tech. Scis. in Applied Mechanics, U. Prague, Czechoslovakia, 1936. Engr. Prvni Brněnska Strojima, Brno, 1936-39; Chief engr. Chamberlin Research Corp., East Moline, Ill., 1939-42; mgr. research St. Paul Engring. & Mfg. Co., 1942- 44; project engr. Elliott Co., Jeannette, Pa., 1944-46; engring. mgr. Goodyear Aircraft Corp., Akron, Ohio, 1946-53; v.p. Electric Boat div. Gen. Dynamics Corp., Groton, Conn., 1953-69; v.p. engring, and research; prof. dept. ocean engring. U. R.I., Kingston, 1969-80, dept. chmn., 1971-79; dir. engring. Analysis and Tech., North Stonington, Conn., 1979-84; cons. engr. Groton, 1980—. Author numerous articles in field. Recipient citation sec. war. Fellow AIAA (asso.), ASME, AAAS; mem. N.Y. Acad. Scis., Nat. Acad. Engring., Soc. Naval Architects and Marine Engrs., Am. Soc. Naval Engrs., Marine Tech. Soc., Pi Tau Sigma. Home and Office: Mumford Cove 87 Neptune Dr Groton CT 06340-5421 Fax: 860-572-8266.

SHEETS, JOHN WESLEY, JR. research and development company executive; b. Jacksonville, Fla., Sept. 17, 1953; s. John Wesley and Alice Marie (Hagen) S.; m. Robin Adair Ritchie, June 27, 1987; children: Camille Barbara, Martha Elizabeth. BS in Zoology, U. Fla., 1975, MS in Materials Sci., 1978, PhD in Materials Sci., 1983; PMD, Harvard U., 1998. Grad. rsch. asst. U. Fla., Gainesville, 1976-78, grad. rsch. assoc., 1978-82; biomaterials engr. Intermedics Intraocular, Pasadena, Calif., 1982-84, mgr. biomaterials rsch., 1984-87; dir. rsch. Pharmacia Ophthalmics, 1987-88; dir. new product and process devel. IOLAB Corp. Johnson & Johnson, Claremont, Calif., 1988-94; v.p. surg. rsch. and devel. Alcon Labs., Ft. Worth, 1994—. Lectr. Calif. State Poly. U., Pomona, 1984; evaluator, chmn. subcom. Am. Nat. Standards Inst. Z80.7; U.S. Del. ISO; Accreditation Bd. for Engring. and Tech.; instr. U. North Tex. Health Sci. Ctr., 1996-2000. Contbr. articles to profl. jours. Mem. Soc. Biomaterials, Mensa, Sigma Xi, Tau Beta Pi, Alpha Sigma Mu. Avocations: weight training, cycling, cooking, backpacking. Home: 4001 Sarita Dr Fort Worth TX 76109-4740 Office: Alcon Labs 6201 South Fwy # R2-37 Fort Worth TX 76134-2099 *Personal philosophy: Build from basics: strength in discipline and personal integrity. Challenge the obvious and trivial solutions. Continuously seek improvements.*

SHEETS, MARTHA LOUISE, civic activist; b. Toledo, Mar. 25, 1923; d. Ira Elmo and Nellie Gertrude Merrill; m. Ted Charles Sheets, Dec. 21, 1946; children: Thomas Merrill, Susan Ruth, Laura Louise, Charles Ira. B in Edn., U. Toledo, 1945. Speaker in field. Charter mem., trustee, sec.-treas., v.p., pres. Citizens for Metroparks, Inc.; commr. Met. Park Dist. Bd., 1976; mem. Gov.'s Commn. Restoration of State Capitol Bldg., Nashville, 1986; historian designer show houses Chattanooga Symphony and Opera Guild, 1981-2000; appointee City Commn. to Greenway Adv. Bd., 1989, re-appointed, 1992-93; active numerous civic orgns. including garden clubs and ch. groups; active Save Outdoor Sculpture project Tenn. State Mus. and Smithsonian Inst., 1992-93; mem. com. Hamilton County (Tenn.) Bicentennial, 1996; Hamilton County appointee Scenic Cities Beautiful Commn., Chattanooga, 1999—. Mem. AAUW (chmn. 75th birthday luncheon 1982, grantee Ednl. Found prog.), ASME (chmn., pres. Northwest Ohio sect. women's aux.), Jr. Coterie Club (founding pres.), Zonta Internat. Svc. Club, Little Theatre Assocs. (past pres.), Murray Hills Garden Club (pres. 1991-92, 92-93), Tenn. Fedn. Garden Clubs (dist. hist. preservation chmn. 1981-85, state hist. preservation chmn. 1987-89, dist. III hist. preservation chmn. 1992-94, 2001-02, chmn. civic and roadside devel. Dist. III 1999-2000), Chattanooga Coun. Garden Clubs (awards chmn., hist. preservation chmn. 1992-94), Tenn. Fedn. Garden Clubs.

SHEETS, NELDA, artist; b. Roger Mills County, Okla., Oct. 31, 1931; d. Merril Ezra and Alice (Tucker) Johnson; m. Willis Davis Sheets, Nov. 12, 1949; children; Steve, Dana. Intr. Silva Method of Mind Devel., Laredo, Tex., 1967—; lectr., author Creativity Workshop, 1968—; artist Webb Gallery, Amarillo, 1980—. Trainer of instrs. Silva Method, 1971-85, conv. dir., 1973-80. Author: (book) Creative Study Skills, 1990, The Creativity Workshop, 1968; author, presenter workshop Creative Parenting. Pres. Area Arts Found., Amarillo, 1986; adv. com. Amarillo Coll. Adult Program, 1991. Democrat. Methodist.

SHEETZ, MICHAEL PATRICK, cell biology educator; b. Hershey, Pa., Dec. 11, 1946; s. David Patrick and Mary Patricia (Blumer) S.; m. Katherine Elliott, Jan. 25, 1968; children: Jonathan Patrick, Jennifer Mikaere, Courtney Elizabeth. BA, Albion Coll., 1968; PhD in Chemistry, Calif. Inst. Tech., 1972. Postdoctoral rsch. fellow U. Calif., San Diego, 1972-74; asst. prof. cell biology dept. physiology U. Conn. Health Ctr., Farmington, 1974-79, assoc. prof., 1980-85; prof. dept. cell biology and physiology Sch. Medicine, Washington U., St. Louis, 1985-90; prof., chmn. dept. cell biology Med. Sch., Duke U., Durham, N.C., 1990-00; prof. dept. biol. sci. Columbia U., N.Y.C., 2000—. Presenter profl. confs. Established investigator Am. Heart Assn., 1981-86. Javits Neurosci. grantee, 1986-93. Office: Columbia U Dept Biol Sci 1212 Amsterdam Ave New York NY 10027-7003 E-mail: ms2001@columbia.edu.

SHEFFEL, IRVING EUGENE, psychiatric institution executive; b. Chgo., July 5, 1916; s. Joseph and Jennie (Leibson) S.; m. Beth Silver, Aug. 2, 1942 (dec.); 1 child, Anita (dec.); m. Peggy Shelton, Apr. 6, 1996. AB, U. Chgo., 1939; M.P.A., Harvard U., 1946; LHD (hon.), Washburn U., 1987. Insp., wage and hour div. Dept. Labor, Chgo., 1940-41; mgmt. and budget analyst VA, Washington, 1946-48; budget analyst U.S. Bur. of Budget, 1948-49; controller, treas. Menninger Found., Topeka, 1949-73, v.p., 1973-93, v.p. emeritus, 1993—. Instr. Menninger Sch. Psychiatry. Bd. dirs. Washburn U. Art Center, 1969— , pres., 1971-73; treas. Karl Menninger lect. series, 1983—. Served to maj. U.S. Army, 1942-45. Fellow Assn. Mental Health Adminstrs. (charter); mem. Am. Soc. Public Adminstrn. (charter), Topeka Opera Soc. (treas. 1985—). Jewish. Home: 1215 SW 29th Ter Topeka KS 66611-2192 Office: PO Box 829 Topeka KS 66601-0829

SHEFFER, BRENT ALAN, lawyer; b. Canton, Ohio, Nov. 7, 1957; s. Dwight W. and JoAnne Sheffer; m. Hillary Ann Taylor, Sept. 2, 1995. BS in Fin. and Acctg., Ohio State U., 1979; JD, Capital U. Law Sch., 1990. Bar: Ohio 1990, U.S. Tax Ct. 1991, U.S. Dist. Ct. (so. dist.) Ohio 1992, U.S. Supreme Ct., 1995; CPA, Ohio. Contract specialist Ohio State U., Columbus, 1978-79; supr. auditing Coopers & Lybrand, CPA's, 1979-85; internal auditor Ctrl. Ohio Transit Authority, 1985-86, mgr. fin. planning and budget, 1986-89, mgr. fin., 1989-90; tax supr. Norman, Jones, Enlow & Co., Dublin, 1990-92; pvt. practice Columbus, 1992-97; assoc. Havens Willis, LLC, 1998—2001; sr. assoc. Saltz Shamis and Goldfarb, 2001—. Advisor Jr. Achievement, 1980-85, Hugh O'Brien Youth Leadership Seminars, 1985-91; ent. com. German Village Oktoberfest, 1986-96; bd. dirs. Ohio 4-H Found., 1975-77, mem. adv. com., 1988-90; bd. dirs. Columbus Jaycee Youth Found., 1985-91, 93-98; legal counsel Columbus Flight Watch, 1993-97, dir., 1997-99, pres. 1999-2001, dir. 2001—. Named one of Outstanding Young Men of Am., 1986; recipient Jr. Chamber Internat. Senatorship, 1997. Mem. ABA (tax com. 1990—), Ohio State Bar Assn., Columbus Bar Assn. (tax com. 1990—), AICPA, Inst. Mgt. Accts. (dir. 1985-88, 91-97, v.p. adminstrn. 1992-93, pres. 1993-94, editor program book 1995-97, bd. dirs. 1996-98), Ohio Soc. CPAs (Ohio accountancy bd. liaison 1991-93), Am. Assn. Atty.-CPAs, Columbus Jaycees (dir. 1985-88, 90-91, 93-99, Presdl. Achievement award 1986, Membership award 1987, newsletter editor 1993-94, pres. 1996-97, state pres. quarter award 1997, region Pres. of Yr. award 1997, bd. chmn. 1997-98), Sports Car Club Am. (chmn. membership 1982-83, regional exec. 1984-85, dir. Columbus 500 Rd. Race ops. 1987-88, Regional Exec. Worker award 1983, Regional Exec. award 1984, Regional Race Worker of Yr. award 1988, Jim Trueman Meml. Trophy 1988), Ohio State U. Sports Car Club (pres. 1978-80), Stuart Cameron McLeod Soc., 1996, Phi Delta Phi (charter com. 1988, treas. 1989-90, alumni chmn. 1990—). Avocations: sports car racing, rallying, bicycling, reading, skiing. Work. Home: 8050 Abbeyshire Ct Dublin OH 43016-8622 Office: Saltz Shamis and Goldfarb 1241 Dublin Rd Columbus OH 43215 also: 1241 Dublin Rd Columbus OH 43215-7048 Fax: 614-488-0095. E-mail: bsheffer@ssandg.com.

SHEFFIELD, CAROLE JEAN, political science educator; b. Norwich, Conn., Dec. 25, 1947; d. John Moore and Doris Edna Sheffield; m. David A. Orthmann, Aug. 10, 1985. BS, Eastern Conn. State coll., 1969; MA, Miami Ohio U., 1970, PhD, 1973. Prof. polit. sci. and women's studies William Paterson U., Wayne, N.J., 1973—. Author: Sexual Terrorism, 1994; contbr. articles to profl. jours. Named N.J. Prof. of Yr. The Carnegie Found., 1997, Outstanding Tchr. in Polit. Sci. Am. Polit Sci. Assn., Pi Sigma Alpha, 1998. Mem. Nat. Women's Studies Assn. Home: 56 Allison Ave Newfoundland NJ 07435 Office: William Paterson U 300 Pompton Rd Wayne NJ 07470-2152 E-mail: sheffieldc@wpunj.edu.

SHEFFIELD, FRANK ELWYN, lawyer; b. Tallahassee, Jan. 4, 1946; s. Byron Elmer and Essie Faustine (West) S.; m. Judith Elizabeth Powell, July 26, 1968 (div. July 1971); m. Janice Alicia Gentry, Feb. 22, 1975; stepchildren: Lorimer H. Blitch, Richard S. Noles; children: Brett Elwyn, Jennifer Alicia. BS in Mktg., Fla. State U., 1968, JD, 1972. Bar: Fla. 1972, U.S. Dist. Ct. (no. dist.) Fla. 1972, U.S. Ct. Appeals (5th cir.) 1975, U.S. Tax Ct. 1978, U.S. Ct. Appeals (11th cir.) 1982, U.S. Dist. Ct. (mid. dist.) Fla. 1983. Sole practice, Tallahassee, 1972, 73-78, 80—; assoc. Dye & Conner, 1973; ptnr. Michaels, Sheffield, Perkins & Collins, 1978-80; sole practice, 1980—. Mem. ABA, Fla. Bar Assn., Assn. Trial Lawyers Am., Acad. Fla. Trial Lawyers, Fla. Assn. Criminal Def. Lawyers, Delta Sigma Pi. Democrat. Mem. Assembly of God Ch. Avocations: woodworking, scuba diving, automobile restoration. Home: 4028 Old Bainbridge Rd Tallahassee FL 32303-2110 Office: 906 Thomasville Rd Tallahassee FL 32303-6220 E-mail: fesattrny@aol.com.

SHEFFIELD, NANCY, city agency administrator; b. Mpls. BA in Sociology and Psychology, U. Minn., 1969; postgrad., U. Wis., 1992. Participant City of Aurora (Colo.) Supervisory Cert. Series Program, 1988-90. Social worker LeSueur County Human Svcs. Cept., Le Centre, Minn., 1969-71; quality control reviewer Minn. Dept. Human Svcs., St. Paul, 1971-74, quality control supr., 1974-75; neighborhood planner City of Aurora, 1987, neighborhood support supr., 1987-94, acting mgr. Original Aurora Renewal, 1994-95, acting mgr. neighborhood support divsn., 1995, dir. neighborhood svcs., 1996—. Mem. PTO, vol. elem. sch. media ctr., 1980-86. E-mail. Office: City Aurora Dept Neighborhood Svcs 1470 S Havana St Aurora CO 80012-4090 E-mail: nsheffie@aurora.ci.co.us.

SHEFFIELD, SIMONE, business executive; m. Ronald Divincintio, Mar. 19, 1971 (dec. May 1979); children: Mary, Sharon, Samantha, Mark, Luke, Erica. Student, Ramapo Coll., 1973, So. Coll., 1974, St. Monica Coll., 1991. Asst. dist. mgr. United Artist Theatre Corp., N.Y.C., 1972-77; v.p. creative affairs Motown Records, Calif., 1977-81; CEO Canyon Entertainment, 1981—. Prodr. music videos, feature films and live prodns.; talent cons. Am. Music Awards, M.T.V. awards, Billboard awards, Grammy awards, Soul Train awards, Essence awards, Golden Globe awards, Peoples Choice awards, ESPN Sports awards, many others. Inventor tuck-a-way tissue. Democrat. Roman Catholic. Avocations: travel, rare coins, movie memorabilia, music. Office: Canyon Entertainment PO Box 256 Palm Springs CA 92263-0256

SHEFRIN, HAROLD MARVIN (HERSH SHEFRIN), economist, educator, consultant; b. July 27, 1948; came to U.S., 1974; s. Samuel and Clara Ida (Danzker) S.; m. Arna Patricia Saper, June 28, 1970. BSc with hons., U. Man., Winnipeg, 1970; M. of Math., U. Waterloo, Can., 1971; PhD, London Sch. Econs., 1974. Asst. prof. econs. U. Rochester, N.Y., 1974-79; asst. prof. U. Santa Clara, Calif., 1979-80, assoc. prof., 1981-86, chmn. econs., 1983-86, full prof., 1986—. Cons. Nuclear Regulatory Commn., U.S. Dept. Energy, Livermore, Calif., 1979-82, Syntex Corp., Palo Alto, Calif., 1983-90. Contbr. articles to profl. jours. Mem. Am. Econ. Assn., Econometric Soc., Western Econ. Assn., Western Fin. Assn., Fin. Mgmt. Assn., European Fin. Assn. Jewish. Achievements include co-developed economic theory of self control, behavioral finance, behavioral life cycle hypothesis, behavioral approach to financial market regulation; capital asset pricing and portfolios; contributor economic and Bayesian learning. Office: Santa Clara U Dept Econs Santa Clara CA 95053-0001

SHEFTEL, ROGER TERRY, merchant banker; b. Denver, Sept. 10, 1941; s. Edward and Dorothy (Barnett) S.; m. Phoebe A. Sherman, Sept. 7, 1968; children: Tisha B., Ryan B. BS in Econs., U. Pa., 1963. Comml. lending officer Provident Nat. Bank, Phila., 1963-65; asst. to pres. Continental Fin. Corp., Denver, 1965-68; v.p. Eastern Indsl. Leasing Corp., Phila., 1968-71, exec. v.p., dir., 1971-73, HBE Leasing Corp., Phila., 1971-73; dir. Kooly Kupp, Inc., Boyertown, Pa., 1974-77, pres., dir., 1977; prin. Trivest, Phila., 1973-77, pres., 1977-78, 1670 Corp., 1978-82, Am. Cons. Group, Inc., 1982-83; exec. v.p., dir. Argus Rsch. Labs., Inc., 1982-83; pres. Leasing Concepts, Inc., 1983-87, Brice Capital Corp., 1987-92, Rhodes Fin., Inc., 1992—. Dir. strategic planning Wharton Sch., U. Pa., 1999; pres. AttendByWeb, Inc., 1999—, AssignByWeb, Inc., 1999—; CEO, chmn. FlyOff, Inc., 1998—. Mem.: Friars Club. Home: 414 Barclay Rd Bryn Mawr PA 19010-1218 Office: Rhodes Fin Inc PO Box 7338 Saint Davids PA 19087-7338

SHEFTMAN, HOWARD STEPHEN, lawyer; b. Columbia, S.C., May 20, 1949; s. Nathan and Rena Mae (Kantor) S.; children from a previous marriage: Amanda Elaine, Emily Catherine; m. Karyn L. Jenkins. BS in Bus. Adminstrn., U. S.C., 1971, JD, 1974. Bar: S.C. 1974, U.S. Dist. Ct. 1975, U.S. Ct. Appeals (4th cir.) 1982. Assoc. Kirkland, Taylor & Wilson, West Columbia, S.C., 1974-75; ptnr. Sheftman, Oswald & Holland, 1975-77, Finkel & Altman, LLC, Columbia, 1977—. Mem. S.C. Bar Assn. (chmn. practice and procedure com. 1999-2001), S.C. Trial Lawyers Assn. (chmn. domestic rels. sect. 1982-83, bd. govs. 1987-93, 94-98), Richland Bar Assn., Met. Sertoma Club (pres. 1986-87). Jewish. Office: Finkel & Altman LLC PO Box 1799 Columbia SC 29202-1799 E-mail: hsheftman@finkellaw.com.

SHEHATA, SAID AHMED, surgeon, researcher; b. Alexandria, Egypt, Jan. 15, 1938; came to U.S., 1972; s. Ahmed Hassan and Nagia Aly (Abdeen) S.; m. Soraya Zakareya, Aug. 17, 1966; children: Samer, Deena, Sherene. MBChB cum laude, Alexandria U., 1962, M of Surgery, 1969. Diplomate Am. Bd. Surgery. Rotating intern Alexandria U. Hosp., 1962-63, surg. resident, 1963-66; surgeon Univ. Student Hosp.-Alexandria U. Sch. Medicine, 1968-70, lectr. surgery, 1969-70; sr. surg. registrar Whipps Cross Hosp., London, 1970-72; sr. chief surg. resident med. edn. program U. Ariz. Tucson Hosp., 1973-75; clin. assoc. prof. surgery Med. Coll. Ohio, Toledo, 1976—; pvt. practice Bowling Green, Ohio, 1975—. Dir. Vascular Lab. NW Ohio, Bowling Green, 1985—; cons. Ministry of Health, Saudi Arabia, 1981; vis. prof. State of Qatar, 1984, Alexandria U., 1986. Author: Cancer of Esophagus, 1969; contbr. articles to profl. jours. Maj. Egyptian Army, 1967-68. Fellow ACS, Royal Coll. Surgeons Edinburgh, Am. Coll. Abdominal Surgery; mem. Wood County Med. Soc. (pres. 1986-88). Republican. Moslem. Avocations: travel, tennis, fishing. Home: 284 Gould Ln Montecito CA 93108-2650

SHEHORN, HENRY WAYNE, real estate developer; b. Lawton, Okla., Jan. 22, 1935; s. Henry E. and Una Irene Shehorn; m. Gina Barclay, June 9, 1972; 1 child, Hollister Ann. BA in Bus., U. Nebr., 1969; MPA, U. Okla., 1973. Enlisted U.S. Army, 1960, advanced through grades to lt. col., 1984; pres. G & W Properties Corp., Leavenworth, Kans., 1978—; owner Fire Restoration Co., 1981—. Bd. dirs. Leavenworth Nat. Bank. Bd. dirs. Neighborhood House, Leavenworth; pres. Unified Sch. Dist. Bd., Leavenworth, 1989—. Mem. Assn. U.S. Army (pres. 1987-88), Leavenworth Rotary Club # 210, Leavenworth-Lansing Area C. of C. (pres. 1995, bd. dirs.). Republican. Avocations: golf, fishing, travel. Home: 215 Elm St Leavenworth KS 66048-3518 Office: G & W Properties Inc 779 Metropolitan St Leavenworth KS 66048-1469

SHEI, JULIANA CHIANG, international technology manager; b. Tokyo, Aug. 27, 1948; d. Wellington J. and Yoshiko (Araki) Chiang; m. Shen-Ann Shei; children: Irene, Ryan. BS, Nat. Cheng Kung U., Taiwan, 1971; MS, U. Mass., 1975; MBA, Rensselaer Poly. Inst., 1987. Tech. interpreter Shionogi Pharm. Co., Taiwan, 1971-73; gen. mgr. Enterpreneurial Pub. Co., Los Alamitos, Calif., 1975-77; asst. chemist Ames Lab. Iowa State U., 1977-81; rsch. scientist Tech. Ctr. U.S. Steel Corp., Monroeville, Pa., 1982-85; group coord. Sterling Drug Inc., Rensselaer, N.Y., 1986-91; internat. tech. mgr. GE Corp. R & D, Schenectady, 1991—. Contbr. to tech. publs.; patentee in field. Mem. NAFE, Assn. Women in Sci., Am. Chem. Soc. (sec.-treas. Pitts sect. 1983-84), Am. Mgmt. Assn., Profl. Women's Network (pres. Capital dist. N.Y. 1986—).

SHEIK, DUNCAN, musician, writer; b. Montclair, N.J. Recording artist. Musician: Duncan Sheik, 1996 (#1 position on billboard's Heatseekers and Alt. New Artist Albums, 1966, 30 weeks on Billboard 200, 1996), Humming, 1998; co-prodr.: Humming, 1998; musician: Phantom Moon, 2001. Office: c/o Atlantic Records Inc 1290 6th Ave Flr 28 New York NY 10104*

SHEIKH, ABDEL QADAR, engineering management executive; b. Silwad, Jordan, Jan. 13, 1948; came to U.S., 1967; s. Khalil Ayyad and Tamam Mohammad (Atra) Silwadi Sheik; m. Carmen Elsa Ortiz, June 7, 1973; children: Khalil, Samir, Farid, Samia. BSChE, U. P.R., Mayaguez, 1975; postgrad., Calif. State U., Turlock, 1983. Process engr., process supr. P.R. Olefins, Ponce, 1975-79; chief engr., ops. SWCC, Alkhobar, Saudi Arabia, 1979-80; field supt. Catalytic, Phila., 1980-81; project leader Aramco, Udhailyeh, Saudi Arabia, 1982-83; sr. process engr. Saudi Petrochem. Co., Sadaf/Sabic Jubail, Saudi Arabia, 1983-86; supt. Saudi Yanbu Petrochem. Co., Yanpet/Sabic, Yanbu, Saudi Arabia, 1986-91; utilities and off-sites mgr., engrng. constrn. cons. Arabian Indsl. Fibers Co., Ibn Rushd/Sabic, Yanbu/London, 1994-97. Cons. water treatment, Ponce, 1978. Mem. AIChE, Nat. Assn. Corrosion Engrs., Am. Chem. Soc. Home: PO Box 28476 Fresno CA 93729 E-mail: aqsk@yahoo.com.

SHEIKH, KEMAL A. lawyer; b. Aberdeen, Md., Jan. 14, 1956; s. Ramsey U. and Betty J. Nelson Sheikh. BA, Colby Coll., 1977; LLB magna cum laude, U. Edinburgh, Scotland, 1983; JD, U. Pa., 1985. Bar: N.Y. 1987. Assoc. Curtis, Mallet-Prevost Colt & Mosle, N.Y.C., 1985-97, spl. counsel, 1997—. Office: Curtis Mallet-Prevost Colt & Mosle 101 Park Ave Fl 34 New York NY 10178-0061

SHEIKH, SUNEEL ISMAIL, aerospace engineer, researcher; b. Bristol, Gloucester, Eng., Jan. 21, 1966; came to U.S., 1975, U.S. Citizen 1987; s. Hyder Ismail and Joan Mary (Duncan) S.; m. Kristen Louise Thul, May 23, 1998. BS in Aerospace Engring, Maths., U. Minn., 1988; MS in Aeronautics and Astronautics, Stanford U., 1990; postgrad., U. Md., 1999—. Lic. pvt. pilot, U.S.; cert. scuba diver Nat. Assn. Underwater Instrs. Student intern Honeywell, Inc., Mpls., 1989-90; assoc. engr. Martin Marietta Corp., Denver, 1990-91; sr. prin. rsch. scientist Honeywell, Inc., Mpls., 1991—. Cons., engr. Honeywell, Inc., Mpls., 1991. Recipient Honorable Mention award NSF, 1988. Mem. AIAA, Am. Astronautical Soc., Inst. Navigation, Planetary Soc., Nat. Space Soc., Aircraft Owners and Pilots Assn. Achievements include patents for attitude determination method and system and GPS multipath detection method and system. Home: 5005 Kenesaw St College Park MD 20740-1736 Office: Honeywell Inc 3660 Technology Dr Minneapolis MN 55418-1096 E-mail: sheikh@ssl.umd.edu.

SHEILS, DENIS FRANCIS, lawyer; b. Ridgewood, N.J., Apr. 7, 1961; s. Denis Francis and Anna Marie (Clifford) S.; m. Harriet A. Bonawitz, Sept. 17, 1988; 1 child, Denis F. BA, La Salle Coll., 1983; JD, Fordham U., 1986. Bar: N.Y. 1987, Pa. 1987, U.S. Dist. Ct. (ea. dist.) Pa. 1987, U.S. Ct. Appeals (3d cir.) 1987, U.S. Dist. Ct. (so. and ea. dists.) N.Y. 1992, U.S. Supreme Ct. 1994, U.S. Dist. Ct. (no. dist.) N.Y. 1997, U.S. Ct. Appeals (2d cir.) 1999. Assoc. Kohn, Swift & Graf, PC, Phila., 1987-97, shareholder, 1997—. Active Lower Makefield Twp. Cable TV Adv. Bd. Mem. AAAS, ABA, Phila. Bar Assn. Roman Catholic. Home: 2124 Ashley Rd Newtown PA 18940-3737 Office: Kohn Swift & Graf PC 21st Fl One South Broad St Philadelphia PA 19107 E-mail: dsheils@kohnswift.com.

SHEIMAN, RONALD LEE, lawyer; b. Bridgeport, Conn., Apr. 26, 1948; s. Samuel Charles and Rita Doris Sheiman; m. Deborah Joy Lovitky, Oct. 16, 1971; children: Jill, Laura. BA, U. Mich., 1970; JD, U. Conn., 1973; LLM in Taxation, NYU, 1974. Bar: Conn. 1973, U.S. Ct. Appeals (2d cir.) 1975, U.S. Supreme Ct. 1977, D.C. 1978, N.Y. 1981. Tax atty. Office of Regional Counsel IRS, Phila., 1974-78; pvt. practice Westport, Conn., 1978—. Mem. adv. bd. Early Childhood Resource and Info. Ctr., N.Y. Pub. Libr., N.Y.C. Mem.: ABA, Conn. Bar Assn., Fed. Bar Assn. Home: 128 Random Rd Fairfield CT 06432-1408 Office: 1804 Post Rd E Westport CT 06880-5607

SHEIN, JAY LESING, financial planner; b. Chgo., Jan. 27, 1951; s. Garrett Melchior and Evelyn (Blitt) Hamm; m. Val Margaret Rich, Dec. 14, 1984; children: Melissa Loree, Blair Charles, Christina Anne, Allison Marie, Lindsay Gayle. Student, Broward C.C., Davie, Fla., 1969-72, Cleve. Inst. Electronics, 1973-74; CFP, Coll. for Fin. Planning, Denver, 1990; MS in Taxation and Fin., PhD, LaSalle U., 1994; postgrad., U. Pa., 1998, NYU, 2002. Cert. investment mgr. analyst, investment strategist. Tech. technician Broward County Sch. Bd., Ft. Lauderdale, Fla., 1973-76; owner, mgr. Bus. and Tax Consulting Firm, 1976-83; dist. mgr. United Group and Group One, 1983-84; from account exec. to v.p. Compass Fin. Group, Inc., Lighthouse Point, Fla., 1984-90, pres., CEO, 1990—. Mem. adv. bd. devel. coun. Highlands Christian Acad., Pompano Beach, Fla., 1992—; mem. adj. faculty Rollins Coll., 1996; adj. prof. La Salle U., 1994—, Nova Southeastern U. Sch. Bus., 1995-2000, Fla. State U., 2000—, Fla. Gulf Coast U., 2001—, IMCA Cert. Investment Mgmt. Analyst Program, U. Pa. Wharton Sch., 1998— Author: Asset Allocation and Portfolio Structure, 1999; contbr. articles to newspapers and pubs. in field. Mem. Estate Planning Coun. of Broward County. Named One of Best 250 Fin. Advisers in Country, Worth mag., 2000, 2001; named one of Top 100 Fin. Planners, Mut. Fund mag., 2001. Mem. Investment Mgmt. Cons. Assn. (mem. editl. bd. Jour. Investment Consulting), Inst. CFP, Fin. Planning Assn., South Fla. Soc. of Inst. of CFPs (dir. ethics 1993-94, edn. chmn. 1994, pres. 1997, chmn. 1998), Fin. Planning Assn. South Fla. (chmn. edn. programs 1999—), Broward County Assn. Life Underwriters (v.p. 1992-94), Greater Ft. Lauderdale Tax Coun., Marine Industries of South Fla. Republican. Baptist. Avocations: volleyball, racquetball, travel. Office: Compass Fin Group Inc 3050 N Federal Hwy Ste 208 Lighthouse Point FL 33064-6866 E-mail: compassfinancial@hotmail.com.

SHEINART, KARA FAE, neurologist, educator; b. Queens, N.Y., July 11, 1963; d. Henry Jules and Toby (Kwitel) S.; m. Daniel Joseph Alpert, Mar. 4, 1990. BA, Johns Hopkins U., 1985; MD, SUNY Downstate, 1989. Diplomate Am. Bd. Psychiatry and Neurology, Nat. Bd. Med. Examiners. Intern, resident in neurology Mt. Sinai Med. Ctr., N.Y.C., 1989-93, fellow in cerebrovascular disease/stroke, 1993-95, clin. asst. prof. neurology, 1995—. Asst. attending physician Mt. Sinai Med. Ctr., 1995—. Fellow Am. Heart Assn. Stroke Coun.; mem. Am. Acad. Neurology. Office: Mt Sinai Med Ctr Dept Neur 1 Gustave L Levy Pl # 1137 New York NY 10029-6500 E-mail: sheink01@doc.mssm.edu.

SHEINBAUM, GILBERT HAROLD, international management consultant; b. N.Y.C., Apr. 20, 1929; s. Herman and Selma (Klimberg) S.; m. Inger Fredebo Thomsen, Aug. 28, 1971; children: Neil, Britt. AB in History, NYU, 1950; postgrad., CUNY, 1954-55, New Sch. for Social Rsch., 1955-56. Various fgn. svc. posts, Washington, Laos, France, Vietnam, Denmark, 1957-72; polit. officer U.S. Dept. of State, 1972-75; chargé d'affaires Am. Embassy, Antananarivo, Madagascar, 1975-77, dep. chief of mission Lilongwe, Malawi, 1977-79; Am. consul Cebu, Philippines, 1979-83; polit. counselor U.S. Mission to the UN, Geneva, 1983-86; dir. Colombo Plan (internat. orgn.), Colombo, Sri Lanka, 1986-91; cons. Nat. Security Edn. Program, Washington, 1992-95, Internat. Found. for Election Sys., Washington, 1995-96; sr. cons., advisor U.S. Dept. State, 1997—. Internat. observor Sri Lankan elections, 1993, 94. Author and editor articles on econ. devel. in Asia. Co-founder, trustee George Keyt Cultural Found., Colombo, 1987-91; bd. chmn. Overseas Children's Sch., Colombo, 1987-90; commr. Boy Scouts Am., Geneva, 1984-86; stage mgr., bd. dirs. Am. Light Opera Co., Washington, 1962-64. 1st lt. U.S. Army, 1951-53. Recipient Award of Recognition, Mindanao State U., Marawi, Philippines, 1983. Mem.: Assn. Diplomatic Studies, UN Assn. Asia, Diplomatic and Consular Officers Ret., Asia Soc., World Affairs Coun. of Washington DC, Am. Fgn. Svc. Assn., Soc. Internat. du Mèkong (founder, pres.). Avocations: tennis, running, touring, reading, public speaking. Home: 407 East St NE Vienna VA 22180-3577 E-mail: gsheinbaum@aol.com.

SHEINBAUM, STANLEY K. economist; b. N.Y.C., June 12, 1920; m. Betty Warner, May 29, 1964; 4 children. AB in Far East History summa cum laude, Stanford U., 1949, postgrad., 1949-53. Mem. faculty dept. econs. Stanford (Calif.) U., 1950-53, Mich. State U., East Lansing, 1955-60, U. Calif., Santa Barbara, 1963; pres. Bd. Police Commr., L.A., 1991-93. Pres. Fairtree Enterprises, 1980-90; cons. in econs. Ency. Brit., 1961-64, Calif. State Commn. Manpower and Tech., 1963-65; cons. fiscal policy Govt. South Vietnam, Saigon, 1957-59; cons. on Vietnam Spl. Ops. Rsch. Office Am. U., Washington, 1958-59; sr. fellow Ctr. for Study Dem. Instns., Santa Barbara, 1960-70; v.p. Warner Ranch, Inc., L.A., 1965-69. Cons. editor: Ramparts, 1965-73; mem. editorial bd. Democracy, 1981-84; pub. New Perspectives Quarterly, 1985—. Dec. candidate Congress, Santa Barbara and Ventura, 1966-68; del. Dem. Nat. Conv., 1968-72; So. Calif. fin. chmn. McGovern presdl. campaign, 1972; exec. dir. Com. to Improve Tchr. Edn., 1961-62; bd. dirs. , Com. for Pub. Justice, 1972-85, Bill of Rights Found., N.Y., 1973—, Ctr. for Law in Pub. Interest, L.A., 1976—, , People for Am. Way, Washington, 1980—; organizer, coord. legal def. team Pentagon Papers Trial, L.A., 1971-73; chmn. bd. dirs. ACLU Found., So. Calif., L.A., 1973-84; founder, bd. dirs. Energy Action Com., Washington, 1975-82; mem. Coun. on Fgn. Rels., 1990—; commr. Calif. Postsecondary Edn. Commn., 1978-80; bd. dirs. Presidio Savs. and Loan Assn. Santa Barbara, 1964-69; Music Ctr. Dance Assn., L.A., 1978-85, chmn. 1979-85, Helsinki Watch and Am. Watch, N.Y., L.A., 1981—; chmn. Human Rights Watch, Calif., 1987—; co-chmn., trustee Internat. Ctr. Peace in Mideast, Tel Aviv, 1982—; regent U. Calif., 1977-89, vice-chmn., 1983-84; founder Legal Def. Ctr., Santa Barbara, 1970—. Fulbright fellow, Paris, 1953-55, fellow Hoover Inst., Stanford U., 1955—. Mem. Phi Beta Kappa, Phi Eta Sigma. Home: 345 N Rockingham Ave Los Angeles CA 90049-2635

SHEINGOLD, DANIEL H. electrical engineer; b. Boston, Sept. 26, 1928; s. Louis S. and Elsie (Frank) S.; m. Ann Silverman, Aug. 2, 1953 (dec. Feb. 1995); children: Mark J., Laura S. Duffy. BSEE with distinction, Worcester Poly. Inst., 1948; MSEE, Columbia U., 1949. Engr. George A. Philbrick Rschs. Inc., Boston, 1949-55, application engring. mgr., 1957-63; v.p. George A. Philbrick Researches, Inc., Dedham, Mass., 1964-67; staff cons. Teledyne Philbrick, 1967-68; tech. mktg. mgr. Analog Devices, Inc., Norwood, Mass., 1969—. Editor: Analog-Digital Conversion Handbook, 1972, 3d edit., 1986, Nonlinear Circuits Handbook, 1974, Transducer Interfacing Handbook, 1980; editor Analog Dialogue jour., 1969—, others. With AUS, 1955-57. Fellow IEEE; mem. IEEE Instrumentation and Measurement Soc. (sec.-treas. 1976, v.p. 1977, pres. 1978), AAAS. Jewish. Avocations: music, walking, crosscountry skiing, reading. Office: Analog Devices Inc PO Box 9106 3 Technology Way Norwood MA 02062-9106 E-mail: dan.sheingold@analog.com.

SHEININ, ROSE, biochemist, educator; b. Toronto, Ont., May 18, 1930; d. Harry and Anne (Szyber) Shuber; m. Joseph Sheinin, July 15, 1951; children: David Matthew Khazanov, Lisa Basya Judith, Rachel Sarah Rebecca. BA, U. Toronto, 1951, MA (scholar), 1953, PhD in Biochemistry, 1956, LHD, 1985; DHL (hon.), Mt. St. Vincent U., 1985; DSc (hon.), Acadia U., 1987, U. Guelph, 1991. Demonstrator in biochemistry U. Toronto, Ont., Can., 1951-53, asst. prof. microbiology Can., 1964-75, asst. prof. med. biophysics Can., 1967-75, prof. microbiology Can., 1975-90, assoc. prof. med. biophysics Can., 1975-78, prof. med. biophysics Can., 1978-90, chmn. microbiology and parasitology Can., 1975-82, vice dean Sch. Grad. Studies Can., 1984-89; vice-rector acad. Concordia U., Montreal, Que., Can., 1989-94, prof. dept. biology Can., 1989-2000. Mem. Health Scis. Com.; vis. rsch. assoc. chem. microbiology Cambridge U., 1956-57, Nat. Inst. Med. Rsch., London, 1975-58; rsch. assoc. fellow divsn. biol. rsch. Ont. Caner Inst., 1958-67; sci. officer cancer grants panel Med. Rsch. Coun. Can.; mem. Can. Sci. Del. to People's Republic of China, 1973; mem. adv. com. Provincial Lottery Health Rsch. Awards; mem. adv. com. on biotech. NRC Can., 1984-87; mem. Sci. Coun. Can., 1984-87; adv. com. on sci. and tech. CBC, 1980-85; mem. bd. dirs. Can. Bacterial Disease Network, 1989-94; vis. prof. biochemistry U. Alta., 1971. Assoc. editor Can. Jour. Biochemistry, 1968-71, Virology, 1969-72, Intervirology, 1974-85; editl. bd. Microbiol. Revs., 1977-80; author, co-author various publs. Nat. Cancer Inst. Can. fellow, 1953-56, 58-61; Brit. Empire Cancer Campaign fellow, 1956-58; recipient Queen's Silver Jubilee medal, 1978, Woman of Distinction award Health and Edn., YWCA, 1988, Josiah Macy Jr. faculty scholar, 1981-82; fellow Ligue Contre le Cancer, France, 1981-82, Massey Coll., U. Toronto, 1981—, continuing sr. fellow, 1994—; hon. fellow Ryerson Polytech. U., 1993. Fellow Am. Acad. Microbiology, Royal Soc. Can. (chair women in scholarship com. 1990-93); mem. Can. Biochem. Soc. (pres. 1974-75), Can. Soc. Cell Biology (pres. 1975-76), Am. Soc. Virology, Am. Soc. Microbiologists, Can. Assn. Women in Sci., Internat. Assn. Women Bioscientists, Sigma Xi Rsch. Soc., Scitech. Soc. Complex Carbohydrates, Toronto Biochem. and Biophys. Soc. (pres. 1960-70, coun. 1970-74). E-mail: rose.sheinin@utoronto.ca.

SHEINKOPF, DAVID EPHRAIM, oral and maxillofacial surgeon; b. Bklyn., Mar. 27, 1947; s. Leo and Pearl S.; m. Shelley Nan Weiner, Aug. 31, 1975. BA, NYU, 1967; DDS, W.Va. U. Med. Ctr., 1972. Diplomate Am. Bd. Oral and Maxillofacial Surgery. Resident Sydenham Hosp., N.Y.C., 1972-74, Bronx-Mcpl. Hosp. Ctr., N.Y.C., 1974-77; pvt. practice oral surgery, 1977—. Fellow Am. Assn. Oral and Maxillofacial, Am. Dental Soc. Anesthesiology, Internat. Assn. Oral and Maxillofacial Surgeons, Am. Acad. Pain Mgmt., Acad. Osseointegration; mem. ADA, N.Y. County Dental Soc. (bd. dirs. 1990-94, 96-97). Office: 140 W 58th St Ste A New York NY 10019-2182

SHEINMAN, MORT, editor, consultant, writer, photographer; b. N.Y.C., Oct. 7, 1933; s. Irving and Molly (Feigenblatt) S.; m. Claire Rosenfeld, Aug. 27, 1967 (div.). BA in English, CCNY, 1954. Sports tabulator New York Daily News, 1956-58; reporter Women's Wear Daily, N.Y.C., 1960-69, news editor, 1970-71, mng. editor, 1971-2000, W Mag., N.Y.C., 1972-82, assoc. editor, 1982-2000; editl. dir. Publicis Dialog N.Y., 2000-01; journalism instr. Fashion Inst. Tech., 2001—. Cons., writer ATT Summer Olympics Exhibit, L.A., 1984, Pru Ctr. Obs., Boston, 1995. Contbr. articles and photographs to various publs. including Diverson mag., 1979—. With U.S. Army, 1954-56. Mem.: CCNY Comm. Alumni, Soc. of the Silurians, Nat. Arts Club. Home: 60 Gramercy Park N New York NY 10010-5423 E-mail: mortone@aol.com.

SHEKAR, SAM, health facility administrator; MD, MPH, U. Mich. Asst. surgeon gen., rear admiral USPHS Commd. Corps.; assoc. adminstr. HRSA, 1998, Bur. Primary Healthcare, HHS , 2002—. Devel. new campaign Kids Into Health Careers. Fellow: Am. Coll. Preventtive Medicine (bd. cert.). Office: US Dept Health and Human Svcs Health Resources and Svcs Adminstrn 5600 Fishers Ln Rm 14-45 Rockville MD 20857 Office Fax: 301-443-1989.*

SHEKER, WILLIAM CLYDE, dentist; b. Ft. Dodge, Iowa, Aug. 27, 1949; s. Clyde William and Carol LaVonne (Ekstrom) S.; m. Nancy Elizabeth Scheibe, Sept. 3, 1973; children: Carol Ann, Mary Katherine. BS, U. Iowa, 1971, DDS, 1974. Cert. in conscious sedation. Ptnr., dentist Midtown Dental Assoc., Wisconsin Rapids, Wis., 1977-91; pvt. practice, 1991—. Cons. in field. Capt. USAF, 1974-77. Fellow in conscious sedation, 1997. Fellow Acad. Gen. Dentistry; mem. ADA, Am. Acad. Implant Dentistry, Am. Soc. Dental Anesthesiology,, Wis. Dental Assn., Rotary. Republican. Lutheran. Avocations: tennis, trapshooting, fishing. Office: 420 3rd St S Wisconsin Rapids WI 54494-4350

SHEKHANI, SHAHID, medical oncologist, internist, researcher; b. Karachi, Sindh, Pakistan, June 1, 1965; , U.S., 1992; s. Yahya and Zarina Shekhani; m. Farah Moosajee. MB BChir, MD, U. Karachi, 1990. Med. resident Prince George's Hosp. Ctr., Cheverly, Md., 1996-99; hematology/oncology fellow Howard U. Hosp., Washington, 1999—2001; with Upper Peninsula Hematology Oncology Group, 2001—; med. attending Grand View Hosp., Ironwood, Mich., 2001—. Recipient Nat. Med. Assn. award, 2000, Roland Nickens award, 2000, 01. Mem. AMA, ACP, Am. Soc. Clin. Oncology, Am. Soc. Hematology. Moslem. Avocations: skiing, mountain biking, ice skating. Home: E4920 North Star Rd Ironwood MI 49938 Office: Grand View Clinic N10565 Grand View Ln Ironwood MI 49938 Office Fax: 906-932-5630. E-mail: SShekhani@gvhs.org., Shekhanis@hotmail.com.

SHEKHAR, STEPHEN S. obstetrician, gynecologist; b. New Delhi, Jan. 13, 1944; came to U.S., 1972; s. S.P. Jain and Shakuntala Mithal; m. Claudette Dorita, Jan. 6, 1978; children: Sasha, Stephen. MBBS, Punjabi U., Patiala, India, 1966. Surgeon Nat. Health Svc. U.K., 1966-72; intern Roosevelt Hosp.-Columbia Coll. Physicians and Surgeons, N.Y.C., 1972-73; resident in ob-gyn. St. Clare's Hosp., N.Y. Med. Coll., 1973-76, Harlem Hosp.-Columbia U., N.Y.C. and N.J., 1976-77; pvt. practice Studio City, Calif., 19777—. Mem. staff Los Angeles County-U. So. Calif. Med. Sch.; clin prof. ob-gyn. and family medicine U. So. Calif. Sch. Medicine. Fellow ACS, Am. Coll. Ob-Gyn., L.A. Soc. Ob-Gyn.; mem. AMA, Calif. Med. Assn., L.A. County Med. Assn. Home and Office: PO Box 1742 Medford OR 97501-0136

SHEKHARAN, RAJA A. engineer; b. Bangalore, Karnataka, India, May 22, 1966; s. Amala and Sarasa Sekharan; m. Radhika Raja, Feb. 20, 1998; 1 child, Archana. B Engring., Bangalore U., 1989, M Engring., 1991; PhD, U. Miss., 1996. Registered engr., Miss. Rsch. fellow, scientist B Ctrl. Rd. Rsch. Inst., New Delhi, 1991-92; grad. rsch. asst. U. Miss., Oxford, 1992-96; pavement engr. LAW PCS Divsn. Law Engring. and Environ. Scis., Beltsville, Md., 1997—. Contbr. articles to profl. jours. Fellow U. Miss., Oxford, 1993-96. Mem. Order Engrs., Chi Epsilon (treas. 1995-96). Avocations: aeromodeling, tennis, swimming. Home: 14800 4th St Laurel MD 20707-3764 Office: LAW PCS Divsn Engring & Environ Svcs 12104 Indian Creek Ct Ste A Beltsville MD 20705-1240 Fax: (301) 210-5032. E-mail: rshekhar@lawco.com.

SHELANSKI, MICHAEL L. cell biologist, educator; b. Phila., Oct. 5, 1941; s. Herman Alder and Bessie B.; m. Vivien Brodkin, June 9, 1963; children: Howard, Samuel, Noah. Student, Oberlin Coll., 1959-61; MD (Life Ins. Med. Research Fund fellow), U. Chgo., 1966, PhD, 1967. Intern in pathology Albert Einstein Coll. Medicine, N.Y.C., 1967-68, fellow in neuropathology, 1968-70, asst. prof. pathology, 1969-74; staff scientist NIH, Bethesda, Md., 1971-73; vis. scientist Inst. Pasteur, Paris, 1973-74; assoc. prof. neuropathology Harvard U., Cambridge, Mass., 1974-78; sr. research assoc., asst. neuropathologist Children's Hosp. Med. Center, Boston, 1974-78; prof., chmn. dept. pharmacology N.Y. U. Med. Center, N.Y.C., 1978-86; Delafield Prof., chmn. dept. pathology Coll. Physicians and Surgeons, Columbia U., 1987—; dir. pathology services Presbyn. Hosp., 1987—. Mem. Neurology A study sect. NIH, 1974-78; Pharmacological Scis. study sect., 1986-90; mem. sci. and med. adv. bd. Alzheimer's Disease and Related Disorders Assn., 1985-92, sec., 1987-92, mem. Zenith award panel, 1993-95; chmn. overhead powerline adv. panel State of N.Y., 1981-87; dir. Alzheimer's disease rsch. ctr. Columbia U., 1989—; mem. Am. Cancer Soc. IRG Panel, 1989-93, sci. adv. bd. Dystonia Assn., Amyotrophic Lateral Sclerosis Assn; elected mem., Inst. of Medicine, 1999. Mem. editl. bd. Jour. Neurochemistry, 1982-90, Jour. Neuropathology and Exptl. Neurology, 1983-85, Neuroscis., 1985—, Neurobiology of Aging, 1988-95, Lab. Investigation, 1989—, Brain Pathology, 1990-93. Served as sr. asst. surgeon USPHS, 1971-73. Guggenheim fellow, 1973-74 Mem. Am. Soc. Cell Biology, Am. Assn. Neuropathologists, Assn. Med. Coll. Pharmacologists, Am. Soc. Neurochemistry, Am. Assn. Physicians. Achievements include research on fibrous proteins of brain, aging of human brain, devel. neurobiology. Office: Columbia U Coll Physicians and Surgeons Dept Pathology 630 W 168th St New York NY 10032-3702*

SHELBURNE, JOHN DANIEL, pathologist; b. Washington, Aug. 27, 1943; s. Clarence Daniel and Edith (McDanel) S.; m. Katherine Howard Parrish, June 17, 1966; children: Mark, Kerri. BA, U. N.C., 1966; PhD, Duke U., 1971, MD, 1972. Intern, then resident Duke U. Med. Ctr., Durham, N.C., 1972-76; asst. prof. Duke U., 1973-78, assoc. prof., 1978-85, prof. pathology, 1985—; dir. electron microscopy lab. VA Med. Ctr., 1976-92, chief lab. svc., 1983-99, chief of staff, 1999—. Adv. WHO, Manila, 1990; panel mem. VA Program, Washington, 1987—; participant Nordrhein/Westfalen Exchange, Germany, 1988. Editor: Basic Methods in Biological X-Ray Microprobe, 1983; author, editor: Microprobe Analysis in Medicine, 1989, Biomedical Applications of Microprobe Analysis, 1999. Mem. Appalachian Trail Conf., Harpers Ferry, West, Va., 1970—; bd. dirs. Cen. Carolina Youth Soccer, Durham, 1987-90; founding mem. N.C. Soc. for Electron Microscopy and Microprobe, Research Triangle Park, N.C., 1980—. Recipient Morehead scholarship, 1961-66, AOA Med. Honorary Duke Med. Sch., 1970; named Med. Scientist Tng. Program participant NIH, 1966-72, Shelley Meml. lectr., 1985, Florey Meml. lectr., 1988. Fellow Coll. Am. Pathologists; mem. Am. Assn. Pathologists, Microscopy Soc. Am., Microbeam Analysis Soc. Democrat. Episcopalian. Home: 4302 Malvern Rd Durham NC 27707-5451 Office: Duke U Dept Pathology PO Box 3712 Durham NC 27710-3712 E-mail: john.shelburne@med.va.gov.

SHELBURNE, KELLY KAY, corporate communications specialist, web site designer; b. Houston, Aug. 2, 1970; d. Frank William Bauerschmidt and Linda Dianne Davis; m. Scott Alan Shelburne, June 3, 2000; children: Zoe Alexis, Olivia Grace. BA, Sam Houston State U., Huntsville, TX, 1998. Bus. analyst Hewitt Associates, Houston, 1995—98; sales mgr. Hoops & Links, Inc., 1999—99; comm. mgr. Compaq/Hewlett Packard, 1999—. Comm. cons. Gateway Bapt. Ch., Spring, Tex. Recipient Extra Miller Award, Compaq Computer Corp., 2001. Mem.: Pub. Rels. Soc. of Am. Baptist. Avocations: classical piano study, classical piano study, classical piano study, biking, church activities. Home: 19 Butterfly Branch Place The Woodlands TX 77382

SHELBY, BRYAN ROHRER, information systems consultant; b. Bryn Mawr, Pa., June 26, 1952; s. Albert Rohrer and Elizabeth Ellen (Griffinger) S.; m. Linda Yale Pole, Sept. 9, 1972; children: Caroline Belle, Christina Marie, Heather Lynn. AB in Math. cum laude, Harvard U., 1974. Programmer Litton Industries, Morris Plains, N.J., 1974-75; mgr. info. svcs. The Becker Co., East Orange, 1975-81; mgr. design and devel. Key Fin. Sys., Pine Brook, 1982-85; v.p., group project mgr. Bankers Trust Co., Jersey City, 1985-93; pres. Contek Sys., Inc., Madison, 1993—. Process reengring., project mgmt. and strategic tech. planning cons.; program mgmt. and life cycle methodology specialist; corp. expert in enterprise project mgmt. setup and adminstrn.; designer, project mgr., sys. integrator fin., portfolio mgmt., trust acctg., telecom., pub. Designer/project mgr./sys. integrator fin./portfolio mgmt./trust acctg./telecom./pub. Mem. IEEE, Am. Soc. Pension Actuaries. Democrat. Avocations: reading, building sandcastles. Office: Contek Systems Inc PO Box 292 Madison NJ 07940-0292 E-mail: bshelby@conteksystems.com.

SHELBY, CHARLES FRANCIS, priest, not-for-profit fundraiser; b. L.A., Feb. 18, 1941; s. Peter Paul and Ruth (Russell) S. Student, St. John's Sem. Coll., Camarillo, Calif., 1959-62; BA, St. Mary's Sem., Perryville, Mo., 1964; MDiv, De Andreis Sem., Lemont, Ill., 1984; MS, DePaul U., 1972. Ordained priest Roman Cath. Ch., 1968. Adminstr., mem. faculty St. Vincent's Sem., Montebello, Calif., 1971-73; mem. faculty St. Mary's Sem., Perryville, 1973-79; assoc. dir. Assn. Miraculous Medal, 1980-82, dir., pres., 1983—, internat. coord., 2002—. V.p. Nat. Cath. Devel. Conf., Hempstead, N.Y., 1992-96, pres., 1996-97, chair, 1997-98, past chair, 1998-2001; bd. trustees DePaul U., Chgo., 1998—. Mem. fin. com. Congregation of the Mission, St. Louis, 1980—; trustee Lazarist Trust, St. Louis, 1990—; treas. Ministerial Alliance, Perryville, 1975—. Mem. AAAS, Post Com, Perryville C. of C. Avocations: computer programming, photography, travel. Office: Assn of Miraculous Medal 1811 W Saint Joseph St Perryville MO 63775-1594 Business E-Mail: ammfather@amm.org.

SHELBY, JAMES STANFORD, cardiovascular surgeon; b. Ringgold, La., June 15, 1934; s. Jesse Audrey and Mable (Martin) S.; m. Susan Rainey, July 15, 1967; children: Bryan Christian, Christopher Linden. BS in Liberal Arts, La. Tech. U., 1956; MD, La. State U., 1958. Diplomate Am. Bd. Surgery, Am. Bd. Thoracic Surgery. Intern Charity Hosp. La., New Orleans, 1958-59, resident surgery and thoracic surgery, 1959-65; fellow cardiovascular surgery Baylor U. Coll. Medicine, Houston, 1965-66; practice medicine specializing in cardiovascular surgery Shreveport, La., 1967—. Mem. staff Schumpert Med. Ctr., Highland Hosp., Willis-Knighton Med. Ctr.; assoc. prof. surgery La. State U. Sch. Medicine, Shreveport, 1967—. With M.C., AUS, 1961-62. Recipient Woer of Medallion award La. Tech. U., 1982. Mem. AMA, Am. Coll. Cardiology, Soc. Thoracic Surgeons, Am. Heart Assn., Southeastern Surg. Congress, So. Thoracic Surg. Assn. Home: 6003 E Ridge Dr Shreveport LA 71106-2425 Office: 2751 Albert Bicknell Dr Ste 2G Shreveport LA 71103-3970 E-mail: jshelby@worldnet.att.net.

SHELBY, NINA CLAIRE, special education educator; b. Weatherford, Tex., Oct. 23, 1949; d. Bill Hudson and Roselle (Price) S.; m. Richard Dean Powell, May 29, 1971 (div. 1973); 1 child, Stoney Hudson. BA in English, Sul Ross State U., 1974, MEd, 1984; MA in English, U. Tex., 1995. Jr. high lang. arts educator Liberty Hill, Tex., 1974-75; H.S. resource educator Georgetown (Tex.) I. S. D., 1976-77; intermediate resource educator Raymondille (Tex.) I. S. D., 1977-81; educator of severe profound Napper Elem. Pharr (Tex.) San Juan Alamo Ind. Sch. Dist., 1981-90; H. S. life skills educator Pharr (Tex.) San Juan Alamo ISD North H.S., 1990-93; intermediate inclusion educator Carman Elem. Pharr (Tex.) San Juan Alamo Ind. Sch. Dist., 1993—2000, chair dept. spl. edn. Carman Elem., 1998—2000; primary resource/inclusion educator Elgin (Tex.) Primary Sch., 2000—. Coach asst. Tex. Spl. Olympics, Pharr, 1981—, sponsor vocat. adj. club, 1990-93, adaptive asst. device team, Edinburg, Tex., 1993-95; spl. edn. rep. to Elgin Primary Campus Performance Adv. Coun., 2000--. Asst. cub scout leader Boy Scouts Am., 1994-95, sec. parental com. bd. rev., 1997—; parent vol. boy's and girl's Club McAllen, 1992-96. Mem. DAR, Assn. of Tex. Profl. Educators, Alpha Delta Kappa. Democrat. Mem. Ch. of Christ. Avocations: reading, horticulture, piano, opera. Home: PO Box 426 Elgin TX 78621-0426 Office: Elgin Primary Sch Elgin ISD 1001 W 2d St Elgin TX 78621

SHELBY, RICHARD CRAIG, senator, former congressman; b. Birmingham, Ala., May 6, 1934; s. O.H. and Alice L. (Skinner) S.; m. Annette Nevin, June 11, 1960; children: Richard Craig, Claude Nevin. AB, U. Ala., 1957, LLB, 1963. Bar: Ala. 1961, D.C. 1979. Law clk. Supreme Ct. of Ala., 1961-62; practice law Tuscaloosa, Ala., 1963-79; prosecutor City of Tuscaloosa, 1964-70; spl. asst. atty. gen. State of Ala., 1969-70; U.S. magistrate No. Dist. of Ala., 1966-70; mem. Ala. State Senate, 1970-78, 96th-99th Congresses from 7th Ala. dist., 1979-87; mem. energy and commerce com.; mem. vets. affairs com.; U.S. senator from Ala., 1987—; mem. com. on appropriations, com. on banking, housing, and urban affairs, chmn. select com. on intelligence, spl. com. on aging. Active Boy Scouts Am.; pres. Tuscaloosa County Mental Health Assn., 1969-70; bd. govs. Nat. Legis. Conf., 1975-78. Mem. ABA, Ala. Bar Assn., Tuscaloosa County Bar Assn., D.C. Bar Assn., Exch. Club. Republican. Presbyterian. Home: 1414 High Forest Dr N Tuscaloosa AL 35406-2152 Office: US Senate 110 Hart Senate Bldg Washington DC 20510-0001*

SHELBY, RICHARD DAVID, trade association executive; b. Santa Maria, Calif., Apr. 29, 1946; s. Richard David and Grace Jane (Zahniser) S.; m. Susan Kay Buchanan, Aug. 25, 1972 (div. Aug. 1985); 1 child, Lisa Marie; m. Ellen Penman Sterling, Sept. 10, 1988; children: Lindsay Sterling, Allison McKee. BS, S.W. Okla. State U., 1970. From exec. dir. to state chmn. Okla. Rep. Party, Oklahoma City, 1971-79; dir. state opers. U.S. Senator Dewey F. Bartlett, 1975-76; exec. dir. Ford For President Commn., 1976; regional polit. dir. Reagan For President Commn., Washington, 1979-80, regional campaign dir., 1983-84; dep. dir. White House personnel U.S. Govt., 1981; nat. campaign dir. Rep. Nat. Commn., 1981-83; sr. v.p. Keefe Co., 1985-88; polit. dir. Nat. Rep. Senatorial Commn., 1989-91; pres. SKC & Assocs., 1991-92; sr. v.p. Health Ins. Assn Am., 1992-93, Odell, Simms & Assocs., McLean, Va., 1993-98; exec. v.p. Am. Gas Assn., 1998—. Bd. dirs. Free Enterprise Found., Norman, Okla., 1982—, U.S. English, Inc., Washington, 1994—, Strategic Perception, Inc., L.A., 1997—, Pub. Affairs Coun., Washington. Capt. USMC, 1972-75. Named Outstanding Young Man Am. Jaycees, 1975, Outstanding Alumnus. Southwestern Okla. State U. Mem. Student Loan Mktg. Assn. (bd. dirs. 1981-91), Capitol Hill Club, City Club. Avocations: running, travel. Home: 1119 Ingleside Ave Mc Lean VA 22101-2131 Office: Am Gas Assn 400 N Capitol St NW Ste 400 Washington DC 20001-1511

SHELBY, RONALD VAN DORN, information technology executive; b. Covington, Ind., Jan. 14, 1948; s. Richard Van Dorn and Edna Belle Shelby; m. Susan Gail Bamford, Dec. 28, 1984; 1 child Richard James Harold. BA, Wabash Coll., 1970; MAT, Ind. U., 1973; MBA, U. Toronto, 1984. Project leader Travelers Ins. Co., Toronto, Ont., 1976-79, mgr. data adminstrn., 1979-82; asst. dir. data processing div. Travelers Can., 1983-84; data adminstr. U.S. Dept. Interior, Washington, 1984-86; prin. Am. Mgmt. Sys., Arlington, Va., 1986-89; v.p. info. and tech. svcs. Conn. Mut. Life, Hartford, 1989-94; v.p. info. mgmt. divsn. USF & G Corp., Balt., 1994-96; v.p. tech. leader Am. Express Co., Phoenix, 1996-1998; chief tech. officer General Motors corp., Detroit, 1998-2000; CEO XML Solutions corp., McLean, Va., 2000—. Author: Selecting a DBMS, 1984, Project Manager's Guide to System Development, 1985, also chpts. to books; reviewing editor Data Resource Mgmt., 1989—. Mem. Data Adminstrn. Mgmt. Assn. (adv., bd. dirs., founder Washington chpt. 1988—, internat. pres. 1990). Episcopalian. Avocations: photography, baseball, jogging. Home: PO Box 2409 Vienna VA 22183 E-mail: ron@theshelbys.com.

SHELBY, TIM OTTO, secondary education educator; b. Longview, Wash., Mar. 23, 1965; s. William Richard and Ruth (Masser) S. BA in Edn., Eastern Wash. U., 1989. Cert. grades 4-12 English tchr., Wash., Calif. English tchr., head basketball and football coach Kahlotus (Wash.) H.S., 1989-90; tchr. various dists., 1990-92; English tchr., asst. basketball coach Kalama (Wash.) H.S., 1992-95; tchr. English, head basketball coach Frazier Mountain H.S., Lebec, Calif., 1995-97; English tchr., asst. basketball coach Shafter (Calif.) H.S., 1997-98; English tchr., asst. basketball coach, English dept. chmn. Mojave (Calif.) H.S., 1998—. Mem. ASCD, Nat. Coun. Tchrs. Eng., Calif. Edn. Assn. Roman Catholic. Avocations: travel, reading, coaching sports, theatre, movies. Home: 21330 Santa Barbara Dr Tehachapi CA 93561-8715 Office: Mojave Unified Sch Dist Mojave CA 93501

SHELDON, DEENA LYNN, television camera operator; b. Groveland, Mass., Mar. 10, 1962; d. Frederic J. and Penny Margolis. BS, Boston U., 1984. Co. mem. Body Lang. Dancers, 1986; mem. Michael Macchio's Jazz Co., 1980-85, Danny Sloan's Repertory, 1980-82, Celtic's Green Gang, 1980-82, Dean Brittenham's Shiley Elite Athletic Program. Camera operator Redsox and Bruins, Sta. WSBK-TV, Boston, 1985, Am.'s Cup, Major League Baseball and postseason play, Homerun Derby, Boston Marathon, Extreme Games, ESPN, 1986—; N.Y. Mets and N.Y. Islanders, Sportschannel, 1987-92; N.Y. Mets, Sta. WWOR-TV, 1987-92; Monday Night Football, Superbowl XXXIV, Ky. Derby, Triple Crown, Indy 500, Rose Bowl, Probowl, NFL Hall of Fame game, Superbowl XXIX halftime show, Dem. and Rep. convs., Presdl. inaugurations, 1993, 97, ABC, 1992—, Late Night with David Letterman, NFL, Triple Crown, Olympics, Phil Donahue Show, Macy's Day Parade, NBC, 1986—; Superbowl XXXV, NFL and championship games, Daytona 500, Joan Rivers Show, Major League Baseball and postseason play, CBS, 1987—; Superbowl, World Series, NFL, NHL, Fox Sports, 1994—; robotic camera operator Met. Life and Fuji blimps, NFL championship and playoff games, Daytona 500, Indy 500, 1989—. Youth counselor and instr. athleticism. Recipient Emmy awards for CBS's Postseason Major League Baseball, 1990, CBS's Daytona 500, 1993, ESPN's Extreme Games, 1995-98, N.Y. Emmy for N.Y. Mets, 1992-93, 93-94, Fox's Postseason Maj. League Baseball, 1999; Emmy nominee for ESPN's Am.'s Cup, 1995. Mem. NABET, Internat. Brotherhood Elec. Workers, Internat. Alliance Theatrical Stage Employees. Avocations: trail running, dancing, sunshine, instructing in athleticism. Home: 70445 Mottle Cir Rancho Mirage CA 92270 E-mail: deena.sheldon@verizon.net.

SHELDON, ELEANOR HARRIET BERNERT, sociologist, writer; b. Hartford, Conn., Mar. 19, 1920; d. M.G. and Fannie (Myers) Bernert; m. James Sheldon, Mar. 19, 1950 (div. 1960); children: James, John Anthony. AA, Colby Jr. Coll., 1940; AB, U. N.C., 1942; PhD, U. Chgo., 1949. Asst. demographer Office Population Rsch., Washington, 1942-43; social scientist USDA, 1943-45; assoc. dir. Chgo. Community Inventory, U. Chgo., 1947-50; social scientist Social Sci. Rsch. Coun., N.Y.C., 1950-51, rsch. grantee, 1953-55, pres., 1972-79; rsch. assoc. Bur. Applied Social Rsch. Columbia U., 1950-51, lectr. sociology, 1951-52, vis. prof., 1969-71; social scientist UN, N.Y.C., 1951-52; rsch. assoc., lectr. sociology UCLA, 1955-61; assoc. rsch. sociologist, lectr. Sch. Nursing U. Calif., 1957-61; sociologist, exec. assoc. Russell Sage Found., N.Y.C., 1961-72; vis. prof. U. Calif., Santa Barbara, 1971. Dir. H.J. Heinz Co., former dir. Mobil, Citicorp, Citibank, Equitable. Author: (with L. Wirth) Chicago Community Fact Book, 1949, America's Children, 1958, (with R.A. Glazier) Pupils and Schools in N.Y.C, 1965; editor: (with W.E. Moore) Indicators of Social Change, Concepts and Measurements, 1968, Family Economic Behavior, 1973; contbr. articles to profl. jours. Bd. dirs. Colby-Sawyer Coll., 1979-85, UN Rsch. Inst. for Social Devel., 1973-79; trustee Rockefeller Found., 1978-85, Nat. Opinion Rsch. Ctr., 1980-87, Inst. East-West Security Studies, 1984-88, Am. assembly, 1976-95. William Rainey Harper fellow U. Chgo., 1945-47 Fellow Am. Acad. Arts and Scis., Am. Sociol. Assn., Am. Statis. Assn.; mem. AAAS, U. Chgo. Alumni Assn. (Profl. Achievement award), Sociol. Rsch. Assn. (pres. 1971-72), Coun. on Fgn. Rels., Am. Assn. Pub. Opinion Rsch., Ea. Sociol. Soc., Internat. Sociol. Assn., Internat. Union Sci. Study of Population, Population Assn. Am. (2d v.p. 1970-71), Inst. of Medicine (chmn. program com. 1976-77), Cosmopolitan Club. Home and Office: 630 Park Ave New York NY 10021-6544

SHELDON, ELI HOWARD, minister; b. Monroe, Mich., May 25, 1937; s. Clarence O. and Orean Lavon (Longdon) S.; m. Freida Orene Townsend, Feb. 17, 1962; children: Stefanie Ann, Todd Howard. BA, Dallas Bapt. U., 1970; MDiv, Southwestern Bapt. Theol. Sem., 1973, D. Ministry, 1976. Ordained to ministry So. Bapt. Conv., 1971. Minister Plain View Bapt. Ch., Chalk Mountain, Tex., 1969-70, Eastside Bapt. Ch., Marietta, Okla., 1970-73, 1st Bapt. Ch., Roosevelt, 1974-77, Crown Heights Bapt. Ch., Oklahoma City, 1978—. Bd. dirs. Bapt. Gen. Convention Okla., Oklahoma City; adj. prof. Okla. Bapt. U., Shawnee, 1986—. Editor, writer, artist Crown Heights Comics; contbr. articles to newspapers and mags. Chaplain Lions Club, Roosevelt, 1974-77; chmn. Bi-Centennial Com., Roosevelt, 1975-76. Mem. Capital Bapt. Assn. (chmn. continuing edn. com. 1982—, mem. exec. bd. 1978—), Cowboy Hall of Fame (life). Home: 5732 NW 46th St Oklahoma City OK 73122-5101 Office: Crown Heights Bapt Ch 4802 N Western Ave Oklahoma City OK 73118-5295 *Every ministry can be improved if we use three phrases with genuine sincerity and concern. We love you, you're my friend, and we care about you.*

SHELDON, GEORGE FRANK, medical educator; b. Dec. 20, 1934; s. Richard Robert and Helen Irene (Zerzan) S.; m. Ruth Guy, Aug. 28, 1959; children: Anne Anderson, Elizabeth, Julia. BA, U. Kans., 1957, MD, 1961; postgrad., Mayo Clinic Grad. Sch., 1965. Intern Kans. U. Med. Ctr.; resident in surgery U. Calif., San Francisco, 1965-69; fellow in surg. biology Harvard Med. Sch. of Peter Bent Brigham Hosp., 1969-71; from asst. to prof. U. Calif., 1971-82; Dr. Zack D. Owens Disting. prof. surgery, dept. chmn. U. N.C., Chapel Hill, 1984—2001. Chmn. residency rev. com. accreditation Coun. for Grad. Med. Edn.; mem. Coun. Grad. Med. Edn. of Health and Human Svcs., 1986, chmn. 1998; mem. adminstrv. bd. Coun. Acad. Socs., chair, 1998-99; chmn. Merit Rev. Bd. for Surgery Va., AAMC, 2000, 01 Author: (with J.B. Runnell) Pictorial History of Kansas Medicine, 1961; (with Jill Ridky) Managing in Academics, 1993; editor: (with J.B. Davis) Clinical Surgery, 1995. With USPHS, 1962-64. Recipient Surgeon's award for Svc. to Safety, Nat. Safety Coun., 1993, Douglass Stubbs award Nat. Med. Assn., 1991, Disting. Faculty award Med. Alumni Assn. U. N.C., 2001; named Disting. Med. Alumnus, Kans. U., 2000. Hon. fellow Royal Coll. Surgeons of Edinburgh, Royal Coll. Surgeons Eng., European Surg. Assn., Assn. of Surgeons of Gt. Britain and Ireland, Phila. Acad. Surgeons (Hunterian Orator 2001); mem. ACS (sec. bd. govs., regent 1984-93, pres. 1998, Surgeon of Yr. 2001, Fitts Orator, 1987), Am. Bd. Surgery (chmn. 1989-90), Nat. Bd. Med. Examiners (test com. 1981-84), Am. Assn. Surgery of Trauma (pres. 1984, Fitts medal), Am. Surg. Assn. (sec. 1989-94, pres. 1994-95), Assn. Am. Med. Colls. (exec. com., chair elect 1999, chair 2000—), Soc. Surg. Chmn. (pres.), Coun. Acad. Socs. (chmn. 1998—, com. on gender equity and com. on health workforce), Inst. Medicine (sec. com. on employer based health ins. and tech. assessment edn. bds., Fluid Resuscitation com. on Nation's Physician Workforce 1996). Office: U NC at Chapel Hill Dept Surgery Campus Bx 7050 136 Burnett-Womack Bldg Chapel Hill NC 27599-7050 E-mail: gsheldon@med.unc.edu.

SHELDON, GILBERT IGNATIUS, clergyman; b. Cleve., Sept. 20, 1926; s. Ignatius Peter and Stephanie Josephine (Olszewski) S. Student, John Carroll U.; M.Div., St. Theol. Sem., 1970; D.Min., St. Mary Sem. and Ohio Consortium of Sems., 1974; HHD, Jesuit U. of Wheeling, 1993; STD, Franciscan U., Steubenville, 1994. Ordained priest Roman Cath. Ch., 1953, bishop, 1976. Assoc. pastor Cleve. Diocese, 1953-64, diocesan dir. propagation of faith, 1964-74; pastor, Episcopal vicar Lorain County, Ohio, 1974-76; aux. bishop Cleve., 1976—; vicar for Summit County, 1979-80, So. Region, 1980-92; bishop Steubenville, 1992—. Bd. dirs. Soc. Propagation of Faith, 1968-74, Diocesan Presbyteral Coun.; instr. theology St. John Coll.; clergy adv. bd. econ. edn. Akron U.; mem. Bishop's Com. Latin Am.; bd. trustees St. Mary Seminary, Diocesan Health Ins. Adv. Bd., Cath. Charities Corp.; former mem. bd. trustees Borromeo Coll.; mem. acad. bd. St, Mary Seminary; bd. dirs. Bishops' Com. Latin Am., adminstrv. com. Nat. Conf. Cath. Bishops/USCC, Nat. Adv. Coun., Bishops' Com. for Missions, Nat. Bd. Soc. for Propagation of Faith; bd. trustees Pontifical Coll. Josephinum. Goals for Greater Akron. Served with USAF, 1944—45. Mem. Nat. Conf. Cath. Bishops (adminstrv. bd. 1985—), Am. Legion, Cath. War Vets., Knights of Columbus, Order of Alhambra., Rotary Club Akron and Steubenville. Clubs: K.C. Lodges: Rotary (Akron). Avocations: golf, astronomy, photography, history, travel. Office: Diocese of Steubenville PO Box 969 Steubenville OH 43952-5969 E-mail: lnichols@diosteub.org.

SHELDON, INGRID KRISTINA, former mayor of Ann Arbor, bookkeeper; b. Ann Arbor, Mich., Jan. 30, 1945; d. Henry Ragnvald and Virginia Schmidt (Clark) Blom; m. Clifford George Sheldon, June 18, 1966; children: Amy Elizabeth, William David. BS, Eastern Mich. U., 1966; MA, U. Mich., 1970. Cert. tchr., Mich. Tchr. Livonia (Mich.) Pub. Schs., 1966-67, Ann Arbor Pub. Schs., 1967-68; bookkeeper Huron Valley Tennis Club, Ann Arbor, 1978—; acct. F.A. Black Co., 1984-88; coun. mem. Ward II City of Ann Arbor, 1988-92, mayor, 1993-2000. Cmn.r Housing Bd. Appeals, Ann Arbor, 1988-91; vice chmn. fin. and budget com. S.E. Mich. Coun. Govts. Treas. Huron Valley Child Guidance Clinic, Ann Arbor, 1984—, Ann Arbor Hist. Found., 1985—, Parks Adv. Commn., 1987-92, Ann Arbor Planning Commn., 1988-89; excellence com. Ann Arbor Pub. Schs. reorgn., 1985; treas. SOS Cmty. Crisis Ctr., Ypsilanti, Mich., 1987-93; precinct ward city vice chmn. Ann Arbor Rep. City Com., 1978—. Recipient Cmty. Svc. award Ann Arbor Jaycees, 1980, DAR Cmty. Svc. award, 1997; AAUW fellow, 1982. Mem. Mich. Mcpl. League (del. 1989-97, trustee, 1997—, pres. 1999-00), Ann Arbor Women's City Club (chair endowment com. 1989-90, fin. com. 1987-90, treas.), Rotary (former dir. Ann Arbor chpt.), Kappa Delta Pi, Alpha Omnicron Pi. Republican. Methodist. Avocation: musical theatre. Home: 1416 Folkstone Ct Ann Arbor MI 48105-2848 E-mail: aasheldon@aol.com.

SHELDON, J. MICHAEL, lawyer, educator; b. Mt. Carmel, Pa., Sept. 1, 1951; s. Lloyd Loomis and Helen Roberta (Sosnoski) S. AA, Harrisburg (Pa.) Community Coll., 1978; BS, Pa. State U., 1980; M in Journalism, Temple U., 1991; JD, Widener U. Sch. Law, 1996. News announcer Sta. WNUE-AM, Ft. Walton Beach, Fla., 1974-76, Sta. WFEC-AM, Harrisburg, 1977-78; announcer Sta. WCMB-AM, Wormleysburg, Pa., 1979-80; writer newspaper Pa. Beacon, Harrisburg, 1982-85; media specialist Commonwealth Media Svcs., 1982-86; dir. communications Pa. Poultry Fedn., 1986-89; news anchor Sta. WGAL-TV, Lancaster, Pa., 1989-90; dir. pub. rels. Profl. Ins. Agts. - Pa., Md., Del., Mechanicsburg, 1990-92; v.p. comm. and mktg. United Way of the Capital Region, Harrisburg, 1992-93, Widener U. Sch. of Law, 1994-96; pres. Open Mike Comm., Harrisburg, 1994—. Mem. adj. faculty dept. journalism Temple U., 1992; mem. faculty dept. humanities Pa. State U., 1995-97, 99—. Contbg. author: Pa. 12th Annual Civil Litigation Update, Spoliation of Evidence: Why You Can't Have Your Cake and Eat it Too, 1999; contbg. editor: A Practical Guidebook to Massachusetts Aviation Law, 1999; Contbr. articles to profl. jours. Pub. rels. advisor Cen. Pa. Leukemia Soc., Harrisburg, 1989-90; media advisor Polit. Campaign, Hershey, Pa., 1990. With USAF, 1969-73. Mem. U.S. Fed. Mid. Dist. Bar, Pa. Bar, Dauphin County Bar, VFW (life), Am. Legion, KC, Chi Gamma Iota, Delta Tau Kappa. Republican. Roman Catholic. Avocations: motorcycles, music, electronics, martial arts. Office: 6059 Allentown Blvd Harrisburg PA 17112-2672

SHELDON, JEFFREY ANDREW, social sciences researcher; b. Northampton, Mass., Sept. 1, 1959; s. Wallace J. and Marilyn M. S. BS, Springfield (Mass.) Coll., 1981; postgrad., U. Va., 1981-83; EdM in Adminstrn., Harvard U., 1990. Mem. sci. faculty, chmn. dept. The Forman Sch., Litchfield, Conn., 1984-89; fin. mgr. and adminstrn. The Clin.-Devel. Inst., Belmont, Mass., 1989-90; rsch. intern Ctr. for Law and Edn., Cambridge, 1989-90; owner, dir. Island Tutorials, Hilton Head Island, S.C., 1990-93; dir. instl. advancement Tech. Coll. of Lowcountry, Beaufort, 1993-97; dir. cmty. devel. project Ctr. Child and Family Studies, U. S.C., Columbia, 1999-2001, rsch. assoc. Inst. Families in Soc., 2001—. Mgmt. team Acad. C.C. Leadership Advancement Innovation & Modeling (ACCLAIM), 1995-97; resource devel. cons. in field; presenter in field. Bd. dirs. Beaufort Chamber Orch. Guild, 1994-96, 2d v.p.; mem. Leadership Hilton Head, 1994, Nat. Coun. for Resource Devel., Beaufort County Human Svcs. Coun., 1996; v.p. bd. dirs. Hilton Head Choral Soc., 1992-93, tenor, 1991-94; mem. core curriculum task force Beaufort 2000, 1992-93; candidate for Beaufort County Bd. Edn., Hilton Head, 1992, 94; bd. dirs. YMCA, Beaufort County, 1995, sec., 1996, 97; active ACCLAIM Project, Beaufort County, 1993-97; co-team leader Rural C.C. Initiative (Ford Found.). Klingenstein Summer Inst. fellow Columbia U., 1988. Mem. Paris Island Masters Swim Team, Greater Beaufort C. of C. (govt. rels. com., edn. com.), S.C. Local Masters Swim Clubs (bd. dirs. 2000—). Republican. Presbyterian. Avocations: swimming, cycling, triathlon, community service. Home: 302 Granby Crossing Cayce SC 29033-4349

SHELDON, Mrs. JOHN See GIBBONS, CELIA

SHELDON, LOIS ELIZABETH, social services administrator; b. Marion, Va., Oct. 20, 1942; d. Godfrey Hudson Coombs, Margaret Lillian Coombs; m. Jack Maurice Sheldon, Nov. 24, 1985. BS, San Diego State U., 1968; MPH, Loma Linda U., 1982; postgrad., Fuller Sem. Cert. med. technologist Calif. Med. technologist Sharp Hosp., San Diego, 1979—82; staff mem. Cmty. Health Agy., Romona, 1982—84, Health Sys. Agy., San Diego, 1984—86; dir. Christian Social Concerns, 1986—99; cons. Ministries Enterprises, 1999—. Author: The Rape of Ariel House, 1998; contbr. Recipient Leadership award, Channel 10, 1996, Brad Truax award, San Diego AIDS Assn., 1994. Mem.: APHA, Jr. League (Award 1992). Home: 6662 Del Cerro Blvd San Diego CA 92120

SHELDON, NANCY WAY, environmental management consultant; b. Bryn Mawr, Pa., Nov. 10, 1944; d. John Harold and Elizabeth Semple (Hoff) W.; m. Robert Charles Sheldon, June 15, 1968. BA, Wellesley Coll., 1966; MA, Columbia U., 1968, M in Philosophy, 1972. Cert. hazardous materials mgr., environ. auditor, Calif.; registered environ. profl., environ. assessor, Calif. Mgmt. cons. ABT Assocs., Cambridge, Mass., 1969-70; mgmt. cons. Harbridge House, Inc., 1970-79, L.A., 1977-79, v.p., 1977-79; mgmt. cons., pres. Resource Assessment, Inc., 1979—. Author: Social and Economic Benefits of Public Transit, 1973. Contbr. articles to profl. jours. Columbia U. fellow, 1966-68; recipient Nat. Achievement award Nat. Assn. Women Geographers, 1966. Mem. DAR, Nat. Environ. Health Assn., Nat. Ground Water Assn., Water Pollution Control Fedn., Water Environment Fedn., Fla. Pollution Control Assn., Grad. Faculties Alumni Assn. Columbia U. Office: Resource Assessment Inc 1192 Kittiwake Cir Sanibel FL 33957-3606

SHELDON, RICHARD ROBERT, Russian language and literature educator; b. July 12, 1932; s. Richard Robert and Helen Irene (Zerzan) S.; m. Karen Ryden Sears, Feb. 8, 1964; children: Katherine Palmer, John Ryden, Robert Charles, Rebecca Ann. BA, U. Kans., 1954; JD, U. Mich., 1960, MA, 1962; PhD, Mich. U., 1966. Chmn. Russian dept. Grinnell (Iowa) Coll., 1965-66; asst. prof. Dartmouth Coll., Hanover, N.H., 1966-70, assoc. prof., 1970-75, prof. Russian lang. and lit., 1975—, chmn. dept., 1970-81, 90-00, formerly dir. fgn. studies programs, chmn. com. on orgn. and policy, com. on admissions, com. on diversity, com. on off-campus study, dean of humanities, 1984-89, acad. dir. alumni coll., 1990. Vis. prof. U. Calif. Berkeley, 1968, Stanford (Calif.) U., 1974; cons. Coun. Internat. Ednl. Exchange, N.Y.C., 1967-83, Dept. Edn., Washington, 1979—, Cornell U. Press, Ithaca, N.Y., 1970—; sr. assoc. mem. St. Antony's Coll., Oxford, Eng., 1983-84. Translator, editor: (books by V. Shklovsky) A Sentimental Journey, 1970, Zoo or Letters Not About Love, 1971, Third Factory, 1977; compiler: Viktor Shklovsky: An International Bibliography of Works by and about Him, 1977; co-editor: Soviet Society and Culture, 1988; author articles, book revs., other transls. Chmn. bd. Norwich (Vt.) Day Care Ctr., 1980-81. Pfc. U.S. Army, 1955-57. Summerfield scholar, 1952-54; Nat. Def. Act fellow Dept. Edn., Washington, 1961-64, Alfred P. Lloyd fellow U. Mich., Ann Arbor, 1964-65, Ctr. Advanced Study fellow U. Ill., Urbana, 1969-70, Am. Coun. Learned Socs. fellow, 1970; Internat. Rsch. and Exchanges Bd. study grantee, USSR, 1964-65. Mem. Am. Assn. Advancement of Slavic Studies, Am. Assn. Tchrs. Slavic and East European Langs., Coun. of Mem. Instns. (exec. com., adv. com. to pres., vice chair 1995-97, subcom. priorities), Phi Beta Kappa, Phi Alpha Theta, Phi Delta Theta (pres. 1953), Delta Sigma Rho. Democrat. Episcopalian. Home: 86 S Main St Hanover NH 03755-2029 Office: Dartmouth Coll Russian Dept 44 N College St Hanover NH 03755-1801

SHELDON, ROBERT, composer; b. Chester, Pa., Feb. 3, 1954; s. Robert Sheldon and June Burnett; children: Marie. MusB in Edn., U. Miami, Coral Gables, Fla., 1975; MFA, U. Fla., 1980. Cert. tchr. secondary music Ill. Dir. instrumental music N. Shore H.S., W. Palm Beach, Fla., 1975—79; condr. Alachua County Youth Orch., Gainesville, 1979—83; dir. of bands P. K. Yonge Lab. Sch., 1980—83; dir. instrumental music S.E. H.S., Bradenton, 1983—89; asst. prof. music Fla. State U., Tallahassee, 1989—91; dir. of bands E. Peoria Cmty. H.S., Ill., 1991—. Composer C. L. Barnhouse Co., Oskaloosa, Iowa, 1980—; dir. marching chiefs Fla. State U., Tallahassee, 1989—91; composer Alfred Music, Van Nuys, Calif., 1997—. Author: (text book) The Complete Woodwind Instructor, 1996; composer: (concert band) Divertimento, 1976 (Am. Sch. Band Dirs. Assn. Volkwein Composition award, 1976), Fall River Overture, 1981, Intrada for Winds, 1983, A Bayside Portrait, 1984, Mark of Triumph, 1985, Manatee Lyruc Overture, 1986, Sandcastle Sketches, 1987, Southwest Saga, 1987, Bristol Bay Legend, 1988, Fanfare and Intermezzo, 1988, Crest of Nobility, 1989, Danse Celestiale, 1989, Ocean Ridge Rhapsody, 1989, Eagle Mountain Overture, 1990, Visions of Flight, 1990, The Corsair's Landing, 1991, Lindbergh Variations, 1991, Spirit Lake Overture, 1991, Silver Spring Soliloquy, 1992, A Symphonic Narrative, 1992, Willow Grove, 1992, Four Winds Overture, 1993, Pevensey Castle, 1993, West Highlands Sojourn, 1993, Images, 1994, Lost Colony, 1994, Red Rock Canyon, 1994, Appalachian Legacy, 1995, Voices from the Battlefield, 1995, Coldwater Creek, 1996, In the Shining of the Stars, 1996, Legend of Starved Rock, 1996, Prairiescape, 1996, Cape Fear Chonicles, 1997, Of Kindred Spirit, Century Point, 1998, A Lantern in the Window, 1998, A Longford Legend, 1998, Storybrook Mountain, Beyond the Higher Skies, 1999, The Crossings, 1999, Northwest Rising, 1999, (concert band-arrangement) Spoon River, 1999, (concert band) Chanteys, 2000, Let Evening Come, 2000, The Pioneer's Passage, 2000, Prelude on an Old English Hymn, 2000, Garden of the Black Rose, 2001, Gently Touch the Sky, 2001, Ghost Fleet, 2001, Hill Country Holiday, 2001; : Infinite Horizons, 2001, Ritmico, 2001; : A Simple Celebration, 2001, Winds of Morocco, 2001, Barrier Reef, 2002, Brule River Celebration, 2002, Chiaroscuro: Symphonic Dances in Shaded of Darkness and Light, 2002, (concert band arrangement) Christmastimes Three, 2002, (concert band) A Joyful Journey, 2002, Quixotic Episode, 2002, Rock Island Trail, 2002. Named Outstanding Internat. Bandmaster, Phi Beta Mu, 1990; recipient Stanbury award for the outstanding young band dir., Am. Sch. Band Dirs. Assn., 1985. Mem.: Am. Soc. Composers, Authors and Publishers (Std. Award of Excellence in Composition 1988—2002), Music Educators Nat. Conf., Phi

Mu Alpha Sinfonia. Avocations: travel, music, art. Office: East Peoria Community HS 1401 East Washington St East Peoria IL 61611 Office Fax: 309-694-8322. Personal E-mail: robertsheldon@hotmail.com. E-mail: robertsheldon@hotmail.com.

SHELDON, SIDNEY, author, producer; b. Chgo., Feb. 11, 1917; s. Otto and Natalie (Marcus) S.; m. Jorja Curtright, Mar. 28, 1951 (dec. 1985); 1 dau., Mary; m. Alexandra Kostoff, 1989. Ed., Northwestern U. Started as reader, Universal and 20th Century Fox Studios; author: novels The Naked Face, 1970, The Other Side of Midnight, 1975, A Stranger in the Mirror, 1976, Bloodline, 1977, Rage of Angels, 1980, Master of the Game, 1982, If Tomorrow Comes, 1985, Windmills of the Gods, 1987, The Sands of Time, 1988, Memories of Midnight, 1990, The Doomsday Conspiracy, 1991, The Stars Shine Down, 1992, Nothing Lasts Forever, 1994, Morning, Noon and Night, 1995, The Best Laid Plans, 1997. Tell Me Your Dreams, 1998; creator, writer, producer: Nancy, The Patty Duke Show, I Dream of Jeannie; created TV show Hart to Hart; author: plays including Roman Candle, Jackpot, Dream With Music, Alice in Arms, Redhead; writer: screenplays including Billy Rose's Jumbo, The Bachelor and the Bobby-Soxer, Easter Parade, Annie Get Your Gun; writer, dir.: screenplays including Dream Wife, Buster Keaton Story; writer: screenplays including Anything Goes, Never Too Young; recipient Acad. award for screenplay The Bachelor and the Bobby-Soxer 1947, Tony award for Redhead 1959, Writers Guild Am. Screen awards for Easter Parade, 1948, Annie Get Your Gun 1950, Edgar Allan Poe award Mystery Writers Am. for Naked Face, 1970. Served with USAAF, World War II. Inducted into the Guinness Book of Records as the Most Translated Author for 1997. Address: care William Morrow & Co Press Rels 1350 Ave of Americas New York NY 10019-4702

SHELDON, TED PRESTON, library dean; b. Oak Park, Ill., July 5, 1942; s. Preston and Marjorie Sheldon; m. Beverly Stebel; children: Kathy, Mark. BA, Elmhurst (Ill.) Coll., 1964; MA, Ind. U., 1965, PhD, 1976; MLS, U. Ill., 1977. Asst. archivist U. Ill., Urbana, 1976-77; reference librarian U. Kans., Lawrence, 1977-79, head collection devel., 1979-81; assoc. dir. libraries SUNY, Binghamton, 1981-83, U. Mo., Kansas City, 1983-85, dean libraries, 1985—. Pres. Mo. Libr. Network Corp., 1991-95. Author: Population Trends, 1976, Kans. Coll. Devel. Policy, 1978, History, Sources Social Science, 1985; co-author: ANSI/ISO/AES audio/video data preservation stds., 1997—. Mem. ALA, Am. Nat. Stds. Inst./Audio Engrng. Soc. (joint tech. commn. 1994—), Mus. Libr. Assn., Internat. Assn. Sound Archives, Assn. Recorded Sound Collection (mng. editor jour 1988-95, pub. jour. 1995—, pres. 1996-98, pub. 1996—). Office: U Mo Libraries 5100 Rockhill Rd Kansas City MO 64110-2481

SHELDON, TERRY EDWIN, lawyer, business consultant, advisor; b. Sacramento, June 22, 1945; s. Earl M. and Christine M. S.; m. Jan L. Winters, Aug. 26, 1966; children: Jeffrey, Tiffini, Melissa. BS magna cum laude, Abilene Christian U., 1967; JD, So. Meth. U., 1970. Bar: Calif. 1970. Assoc. Bronson, Bronson & McKinnon, San Francisco, 1970-74; gen. counsel, also dir. Consol. Capital Cos., Emeryville, Calif., 1974-83, exec. v.p., chief oper. officer, 1984-85, cons., advisor, 1986-87; pres., trustee Consol. Capital Spl. Trust, 1980-85; exec. v.p., trustee Consol. Capital Realty Investors, 1975-85, Consol. Capital Income Trust, 1978-85, Consol. Capital Income Opportunity Trust, 1983-85, Consol. Capital Income Opportunity Trust 2, 1985; chmn. Nat. Syndication Forum (a div. of RESSI), 1981-82; real estate securities specialist RESSI. V.p., prin. Alpha Venture Corp., Walnut Creek, Calif., 1987; bus. cons., 1988—. Chmn. bd. visitors adv. com. Coll. of Bus. Adminstrn. Abilene Christian U., 1990. Mem. ABA, Calif. Bar Assn., Nat. Assn. Securities Dealers (direct participation programs com., real estate com., standing adv. com. to bd. govs. 1980-83), Nat. Syndication Forum. Republican. Mem. Ch. of Christ.

SHELDON, THOMAS DONALD, educator, administrator; b. Canastota, N.Y., July 15, 1920; s. Harry Ellsworth and Sadie Joyce (McNulty) S.; m. Helen Elizabeth Kyser, Aug. 29, 1941; children: Thomas, Paul, Edward, Patricia, Curtis, Roberta, Kevin, Kelly. BS, Syracuse U., 1942, MS, 1949, Ed.D., 1958; grad., Air Command and Staff Coll., 1972. Tchr. sci., coach Split Rock (N.Y.) High Sch., 1942-43; tchr. sci., coach, vice prin., prin. Minoa (N.Y.) High Sch., 1946-59; prin., asso. supt. Hempstead (N.Y.) High Sch., 1959-63; supt. Hempstead Pub. Schs., 1963-68, Balt. City Schs., 1968-71; dep. commr. N.Y. State Edn. Dept., Albany, 1971-77; pres. Utica Coll. of Syracuse U., 1977-82; interim pres. Mohawk Valley Community Coll., 1983; then interim pres. Onondaga Community Coll., 1984, now hon. pres. emeritus; prof. ednl. adminstrn. Syracuse U., N.Y., 1984-85; supt. Sewanhaka Central High Sch. Dist., 1985-86; interim pres. Munson-Williams-Proctor Inst., 1990-91; exec. dir. Syracuse U. Relations, N.Y.C., 1987-93; chmn. Edn. Profls. Internat., 1977-9. *Dr. Tom Sheldon earned national recognition for scholastic and college teaching and administration. Central New York knew him for outstanding teaching and coaching. During fourteen years at Minoa, New York, his teams won twenty division, county and state sectional championships. Minoa six-man football teams won seventy-eight of eighty games played and were twice named mythical national champions. "Coach" is equally fond of his students' impressive records in state biology, chemistry and physics examinations. Dr. Sheldon became president of the New York coaches association and later as New York deputy commissioner occasioned restoration of state championship tournaments for girls and boys.* Co-author and editor various N.Y. State Regents publs., 1971-76. Served with U.S. Army, 1943-46; served to col. USAF, 1972-77, Berlin; to brig. gen. Air N.G. 1955-77. First recipient Outstanding Grad. award Syracuse U. Sch. Edn., 1977; recipient Outstanding Md. Educator award Md. State Council PTA's, 1969; Disting. Am. Educator award Freedoms Found., 1966; Conspicuous Service medal N.Y. State Gov., 1976; N.Y.C. PSAL medal, 1978; named to Balt. Afro-Am. Honor Roll, 1970 Mem. VFW (life), N.Y. State PTA (hon. life), N.Y. State Coaches Assn. (pres. 1957), Am. Legion, Phi Delta Kappa. Clubs: Lions (hon. life). Home: 437 Fox Rd Bridgeport NY 13030 Office: Edn Profls Internat 437 Fox Rd Bridgeport NY 13030

SHELDON EPSTEIN, VIVIAN, author, publisher; b. N.Y.C., June 21, 1941; d. Herman and Hilde (Breslau) Sheldon; m. Ted Epstein, Jr., June 13, 1962; Ted III (dec.), Elizabeth Darien Epstein. BA in History, Edn., U. Denver, 1962. Cert. tchr., Colo. Tchr. Denver Pub. Schs., 1962-67; author, publisher VSE Publ. Co. LLC, Denver, 1975—. Speaker, presenter to schs., univs., educator workshops, 1984—, extraordinary coun. on inter-racial books for children. Author: (books) History of Colorado for Children, 1975, The ABCs of What a Girl Can Be, 1980, History of Women for Children, 1984, History of Women Artists for Children, 1987 (CHOICES Best Books List 1987), History of Women in Science for Young People, 1994 (AAAS Best Sci. Books for children 1992-95), History of Colorado's Women for Young People, 1998. Mem. Nat. Mus. of Women in the Arts (sec. Denver chpt. 1987-93). Avocations: tennis, walking, riding tandem bike. Home and Office: VSE Publisher LLC 212 S Dexter St Denver CO 80246-1055 E-mail: vsepublisher@earthlink.net.

SHELDRICK, GEORGE MICHAEL, chemistry educator, crystallographer; b. Huddersfield, Great Britain, Nov. 17, 1942; s. George and Elizabeth S.; m. Katherine E. Herford, 1968; 4 children. Student, Huddersfield New Coll., Jesus Coll., Cambridge. Lectr. Cambridge U., Eng., 1966-78; prof. structural chemistry U. Göttingen, Germany, 1978—; with Inst. Anorg Chemie, Germany. Contbr. numerous articles to profl. jours. Recipient Meldola and Corday-Morgan medals, Royal Soc. Chemistry, Leibniz prize, Deutsche Forschungsgemeinschaft, A.L. Patterson award, Am. Crystallographic Assn., 1993, Carl-Hermann medal, Deutsche Gesellschaft fur Kristallographie, 1999. Fellow: Royal Soc. (London, Mineral Sheldrickite named in honor 2001). Achievements include authorship of widely used computer programs for crystal structure determination; mineral sheldrickite named in his honor. Office: Lehrstuhl Strukturchemie Tammannstrasse 4 D-37077 Göttingen Germany E-mail: gsheldr@shelx.uni-ac.gwdg.de.

SHELEF, LEORA AYA, healthcare educator, researcher; m. Mordecai Shelef; children: Roy M., Dori S. B.Sc. Chem. Eng./Food Eng., Israel Inst. of Tech.-Technion, Haifa, Israel, 1956, M.Sc. Eng. Mech., 1959, D.Sc. Food Eng./Biotech., 1963. Rsch. assoc. Wayne State Univ., Detroit, 1967—71, asst. prof., 1971—74, assoc. prof., 1974—79, prof., 1979—. Chair Wayne State Univ., Nutrition & Food Sci. Dept., Detroit, 1983—92; vis. prof. Israel Inst. of Tech., Haifa, Israel, 1998—; fulbright vis. scholar CIES, Washington, 1990—. Recipient Sci. Faculty Profl. Devel. Award, NSF, Wash., DC, 1978, Outstanding Grad. Mentor Award, Wayne State Univ., 1995. Fellow: Am. Acad. of Microbiology. Achievements include patents for Co-author, Calcium Fortification of Soymilk, 1989; co-author, Simple Sequence Repeats in Bacteria, 2001. Avocations: tennis, swimming, reading. Office: Wayne State Univ 410 W Warren Detroit MI 48202 Office Fax: 313-577-8616.

SHELEK-FURBEE, KATHERINE, social worker educator; b. Wheeling, W.Va., Nov. 7, 1953; d. Charles Edward and Mary Alice (Booth) Shelek. BA, Alderson-Broaddus Coll., 1975; MSW, W.Va. U., 1980. Lic. clin. social worker, Acad. Cert. Social Workers. From pers. coord. to nutrition dir. and statis. Family Svc. of the Upper Ohio Valley, Wheeling, 1975-84; asst. prof. Bethany (W.Va.) Coll., 1984-95, assoc. prof., 1995—2002, prof., 2002—. Vol. Easter Seal Rehab. Ctr., Wheeling, 1990—. Mem. NASW. Democrat. Roman Catholic. Avocations: reading, aerobics, cross stitching. Office: Bethany Coll 100D Steinman Hall Bethany WV 26032 E-mail: k.shelek-furbee@mail.bethany.wr.edu.

SHELGREN, RICHARD ERIC, JR. (SVEN SHELGREN), film and television producer; b. Buffalo, Aug. 11, 1951; s. Richard Eric Sr. and Mary Ann (Veigel) S.; m. Margaret Ballard, Feb. 10, 1973 (div. Jan. 1983); m. Kyra Fetch Shelgren, Oct. 5, 1985 (div. 1998); children: Cody Tyler, Roxanne Leigh. BA with honors, Haverford Coll., 1973; postgrad., Columbia U., 1976. Shop mgr., dispatcher Feature Systems, N.Y.C., 1978-79; freelance prodn. asst., 1979-80; prodn. mgr. Johnston Films, 1980-83, producer, exec. producer, 1983-84; exec. producer Stiefel & Co., 1984-88; producer, exec. producer Jon Francis Films, San Francisco, 1988-94; exec. producer RCR, Inc., L.A., 1994—; exec. prodr. Dektor Film, 1994—. Film researcher Cinematheque Francaise, Paris, 1973-74. Troop leader Boy Scouts Am., 1965-69. Recipient Gold and Silver Lions awards Cannes (France) Film Festival, 1991, 92, 93, Moma Best Commls. award AICP, 1992, 93, 94, Clio award, 1994, Andy award, 1993-94. Mem. Dirs. Guild Am. (unit prodn. mgr. 1992), Nat. Parks and Conservation Assn., World Wildlife Fund, Greenpeace, Sierra Club. Roman Catholic. Avocations: children, writing, reading, sports, camping. E-mail: Svenrcr@earthlink.net., sven5347@aol.com.

SHELL, BARBARA PAMPLIN, civic worker; b. Colonial Heights, Va., Sept. 3, 1928; d. Jennings Cornile and Blanche B. (Temple) Pamplin; B.S., Madison Coll., 1949; m. Louis Calvin Shell, Aug. 5, 1950; children— Pamela, Patricia. Tchr. chemistry, physics Chesterfield County Schs., 1949-51; chemist Brown and Williamson Tobacco Co., Petersburg, Va., 1951-52. Vice-mayor, Petersburg, 1976-78, mem. City Council, 1974-78; mem. Gov. Godwin's Local Govt. Adv. Council, 1977-78; legis. asst. to del. Va. Gen. Assembly, 1983— ; pres. PTA Council, Petersburg, 1967-68; sec. State Va., Student Council Assns. Adv. Bd., 1968-70; chmn. dist. adv. com. Petersburg Public Schs., Emergency Sch. Assistance Act, 1974-75; pres. Women's Soc. Christian Service, St. Mark's United Meth. Ch., 1969-71, mem. adminstrv. bd., 1969-71, 84— , treas. United Meth. Women, 1980-81, pres., 1984— ; mem. adv. bd. Salvation Army, 1972-75; mem. Va. Mcpl. League's Community Devel. Policy Com., 1975-78; mem. Nation's League of Cities Community Devel. Policy Com., 1976-78; mem. Interstate 95 Adv. Coms., 1974-82; mem. Crater Planning Dist. Commns. Legis. Com., 1976-78; mem. exec. bd. Va. Citizens Planning Assn., Inc., 1978-83, chmn. com. on regional work-shops for planning commrs., 1981-83; mem. state ethnic minority task force Va. ann. conf. United Meth. Ch., 1980— ; v.p. govt. affairs Petersburg C. of C., 1980-81, bd. dirs., 1980-82; co-chmn. public employees div. United Way of Southside Va., 1981-82. Recipient Hon. Life Membership award Va. Congress Parents and Tchrs., 1966; Life Membership Award Women's Soc. Christian Service, 1967; named Petersburg Woman of Yr., Beta Sigma Phi, 1975.

SHELL, KARL, economist; b. Paterson, N.J., May 10, 1938; s. Joseph J. and Grace (De Young) S.; m. Susan Witherow Schulze, Jan. 27, 1962; children: Stephanie Shell Read, Jason. AB in Math. with honors, Princeton U., 1960; PhD in Econs., Stanford U., 1965; MA (hon.), U. Pa., 1971. Asst. and assoc. prof. econ. MIT, Cambridge, 1964-68; assoc. prof. U. Pa., Phila., 1968-70, prof., 1970-87; prof. econs. Cornell U., Ithaca, NY, 1986—. Vis. prof. Stanford U., Calif., 1972-73, Autonomous U. Barcelona, 1989, Bocconi Inst. Mgmt., Milan, Italy, 1990, U. Calif., San Diego, 1992, Doshisha U., Kyoto, Japan, 1995, NYU, 2000; adj. prof. U. Paris, 1979-81, 91; rschr. CEPREMAP, Paris, 1977-78; dir. Ctr. for Analytic Rsch. in Econs. and the Social Scis., Phila., 1975-86; Ctr. for Analytic Econs., Ithaca, 1986-92; pvt. practice econ., Ithaca, 1964—. Co-author: Economic Theory of Price Indices, 1972, Economic Analysis of Production Price Indexes, 1998; editor: Optimal Economic Growth, 1967, Jour. Econ. Theory, 1968—; co-editor: Investment and Finance, 1972, Hamiltonians, 1976, Economic Complexity, 1989. Woodrow Wilson Found. fellow, 1960-61, 63-64; Ford Found. faculty rsch. fellow, 1967-68; Guggenheim fellow, 1977, Ctr. for Advanced Study in Behavioral Sci. fellow, 1984; Fulbright scholar, Barcelona, Spain, 1989, fellow Churchill Coll., Cambridge, England, 1996. Fellow Econometric Soc.; mem. Am. Econ. Assn., Econ. Study Soc., Soc. for Promotion of Econ. Theory, Princeton Club (N.Y.C.), Sigma Xi. Republican. Episcopalian. Home: 917 Wyckoff Rd Ithaca NY 14850-2130 Office: Cornell U Dept Econs 402 Uris Hall Ithaca NY 14853-7601

SHELL, OWEN G., JR. retired banker; b. Greenville, S.C., June 19, 1936; s. Owen and Katherine S.; m. Mary Ruth Trammell, Aug. 9, 1980; children: Katherine Sloan, Mary Carroll, Robert Owen, James Walker. BS, U. S.C., 1960; postgrad., Stonier Grad. Sch. Banking, 1971; grad., Advanced Mgmt. Program, Harvard U., 1979. Tech. supt. Deering-Milliken, Inc., 1962-63; v.p. Citizens & So. Nat. Bank S.C., Columbia, 1968-71, sr. v.p., 1971-74, exec. v.p., 1974-79; pres., dir., chief exec. officer First Am. Nat. Bank, Nashville, 1979-86; vice chmn. bd., dir. First Am. Corp., 1979-86; chmn., pres., chief exec. officer Sovran Bank/Tenn., Nashville, 1986-91; pres. Nations Bank of Tenn. (formerly Sovran Bank), 1992-96; pres. asset mgmt. group NationsBank Corp., St. Louis, 1997-99; pres. Asset Mgmt. Bank of Am., 1997—2002; ret., 2002. Bd. dirs. Nashville br. Fed. Res. Bank, Atlanta. Chmn. bd. INROADS/Nashville; chmn. Leadership Nashville, Tenn. Performing Arts Found., Mid. Tenn. coun. Boy Scouts Am., Vanderbilt U. Owen Grad. Sch. Mgmt.; trustee Met. Nashville Pub. Edn.; bd. dirs. Tenn. Bus. Roundtable, Tenn. Tomorrow. Mem.: Assn. Res. City Bankers, Old Sarson Country Club (St. Louis), Harvard Club N.Y.C., Belle Meade Country Club, Omicron Delta Kappa, Kappa Alpha. Presbyterian. Home: 4412 Chickering Ln Nashville TN 37215-4915

SHELL, ROBIN, vice president charity; Diploma in Estate Mgmt., Royal Agrl. Coll., 1962; diploma in Vocational Guidance Counsel, Kent Coll., 1970. Gen. farm worker, 1959-60; asst. farm mgr., 1963-65; travelling sect. U. & Coll. Christian Fellowship, North England, Scotland, 1965-69; career adv. schs. in Hampshire, U.K., 1970-74, Southhampton Inst. Higher Edn., U.K., 1974-77, Svc. Children's Edn. Authority, U.K., 1977-81; field dir. British Relief & Devel. Agency, Thailand, 1981-84; dist. career adv. Winchester, U.K., 1984-86; asst. to exec. v.p. Food for the Hungry Internat., Geneva, Switzerland, 1986-88; dep. dir., internat. ops. FHI, 1988-91, v.p., 1991-98; sr. v.p. Habitat for Humanity, 1998—.

SHELLEDY, JAMES EDWIN, III, newspaper editor; b. Spencer, Iowa, Nov. 11, 1942; s. James E. Jr. and Patricia L. (Cornwall) S.; m. Susan Emily Thomas, Mar. 7, 1986; 1 child, Ian Whittaker. BA, Gonzaga U., 1966. Reporter Spkesman-Rev., Spokane, Wash., 1963-66; tchr., coach Kootenai High Sch., Harrison, Idaho, 1967-71; reporter AP, Boise, 1971-72; reporter, editor Lewiston (Idaho) Morning Tribune, 1973-80; editor, pub. Moscow, 1981-91; editor The Salt Lake Tribune, Salt Lake City, 1991—; editor, pub. Daily News, Pullman, Wash., 1981—91. Juror Pulitzer Prize Com., Columbia U., 1987-88; dir. Investigative Reporters and Editors, 1978-82; bd. dirs. New Directions for News, 1989-96, Newspaper Agy. Corp., 1994-99; mem. AP audit com., N.Y.C., 1982-91. Dir. Idaho Parks Found., Boise, 1976-78, Idaho-Washington Symphony, Pullman, Wash., 1986-89; commr. Idaho Lottery Commn., Boise, 1989-91; adv. bd. Utah YWCA, 1992-97; bd. visitors La. State U. Sch. Comms., 1995—. Roman Catholic. Avocations: golf, sailing. Office: The Salt Lake Tribune 143 S Main St Ste 400 Salt Lake City UT 84111-1945

SHELLEMAN, JOYCE M. finance educator; b. Gettysburg, Pa., Jan. 7, 1954; d. George Franklin and Alice Shelleman; m. Jeffrey F. Shields, Oct. 8, 1988. BA in Psychology, Millersville (Pa.) U., 1979; MPA, Pa. State U., 1980; PhD in Bus. Adminstrn., U. Pitts., 1991. Lectr. in bus. adminstrn. U. Pitts., 1987—89; vis. asst. prof. mgmt., adj. prof. Hood Coll., Frederick, Md., 1993—96; assoc. grad. prof. MBA leadership program Franklin Pierce Coll., Portsmouth, NH, 1998—99; asst. prof. mgmt. Frostburg State U., Hagerstown, Md., 2000—. Adj. lectr. Johns Hopkins U., Balt., 1995; prin. e-advise.org, Portland, Maine, 2001—; cons. in field. Mentor Women's Network for Entrpreneurial Tng. U.S. Small Bus. Adminstrn., Balt., 1994—95; mem. steering com. Carroll 2000 C. of C., Carroll County, 1994—95; co-founder Writer's Exch., Westminster, 1992; mem. interdisciplinary health edn. com. Area Health Edn. Ctr., Cumberland, 1983—84. Mem.: U.S. Assn. for Small Bus. and Entrepreneurship, Acad. Mgmt., Pi Alpha Alpha (award for outstanding achievement in master's project 1981), Beta Gamma Sigma. Office: Frostburg State U Hagerstown Ctr 20 Public Sq Hagerstown MD 21740 Fax: 301-791-4025. E-mail: jshelleman@frostburg.edu.

SHELLEY, BERNARD FRANKLIN, pressure vessel consultant; b. Welch, W.Va., Aug. 21, 1946; s. Bernard and Angeline (Trapasso) S.; m. Mary Sarah Dunne, Nov. 27, 1973; children: David P., Lynnette M. BSME, W.Va. Inst. Tech., 1968; MMAE, U. Del., 1974. Profl. engr. W.Va. Engr. DuPont, Wilmington, Del., 1968-71; rsch. engr. Frlnklin Inst. Rsch. Labs., Phila., 1971-73; engr. Hercules, Inc., Wilmington, Del., 1973-75; mech. engring. assoc. ICI, Inc., 1975-92; design specialist Alstates/BE&K, 1992-95; cons. DuPont, 1995—. Treas./vice-chmn. Belltown Woods Civic Assn., Newark, 1987-90. Mem. ASME (sect. sec., treas., vice-chmn. 1968-71, mem. RTP-1 sect. X coms.), NSPE. Democrat. Roman Catholic. Avocations: model railroading, computers. Home: 102 Lakeside Dr Middletown DE 19709-1371 Office: DuPont PO Box 80840 Wilmington DE 19880-0840 E-mail: bernard.f.shelley@usa.dupont.com.

SHELLEY, CAROLE, actress; b. London, Aug. 16, 1939; came to U.S., 1964; d. Curtis and Deborah (Bloomstein) S.; m. Albert G. Woods, July 26, 1967 (dec.). Student, Arts Ednl. Sch., 1943-56, Prepatory Acad. Royal Acad. Dramatic Art, 1956-57. Studied with Iris Warren and Eileen Thorndike. Trustee Am. Shakespeare Theatre., 1974-82. Appeared in revues, films, West End comedies, including Mary Mary at the Globe Theatre; first appeared as Gwendolyn Pigeon in stage, film and TV versions of The Odd Couple, Absurd Person Singular; The Norman Conquests (L.A. Drama Critics Circle award 1975); appeared as Rosalind in As You Like It, as Regan in King Lear, as Neville in She Stoops to Conquer, Stratford, Ont., Can., 1972, as Mrs. Margery Pinchwife in The Country Wife, Am. Shakespeare Festival, Stratford, Conn., 1973, as Nora in A Doll's House, Goodman Theatre, Chgo., as Ann in Man and Superman, Shaw Fest., 1977, as Lena in Misalliance, Zita in Grand Hunt,1980, Stepping Out, 1986 (Tony nomination 1986), Broadway Bound, 1987-88; appeared in: The Play's the Thing, Bklyn. Acad. Music, 1978; played Eleanore in stage prodn. Lion in Winter, 1987; other stage appearances include Nat. Co. of The Royal Family (L.A. Drama Citics Circle award 1977), The Elephant Man (Outer Critics Circle award 1978-79 season, Tony award for best actress 1978-79 season), What the Butler Saw, 1989; appeared inaugural season, Robin Phillips Grand Theatre Co., London, Ont., Can., 1983-84, Broadway and Nat. Co. of Noises Off, 1985, Waltz of the Toreadors, 1986, Oh Coward, 1986-87; appeared as Kate Jerome in Broadway Bound by Neil Simon, The Nat. Co. and L.A. Premiere, 1987-88; played Lettice in Lettice and Lovage, Globe Theatre, London, 1989-90, Frosine in The Miser, 1990, Cabaret Verboten, 1991, The Destiny of Me, 1992-93, Later Life, 1993 (Outer Critics nominee), Richard II, 1994, London Suite (Neil Simon) 1995, Show Boat, 1995-96, 98, The Film Society, 1997, The Last Night of Ballyhoo, 1997-98, Cabaret, 1999; films include: The Boston Strangler, The Odd Couple, The Super, 1990, Devlin, 1991, Quiz Show, 1993, The Road to Wellville, 1993; created voice characters in Walt Disney films Robin Hood, The Aristocats, Hercules. Recipient Obie Award for Twelve Dreams N.Y. Shakespeare Festival, 1982 Jewish. Office: care Duva-Flack Assocs Inc 200 W 57th St New York NY 10019-3211

SHELLEY, CLYDE BURTON, artist; b. Murphy, Tex., Mar. 21, 1922; s. Jesse Dewey and Florrie Elizabeth (Eldridge) S.; m. Freddie Lavern Mitchell, Aug. 31, 1946 (dec. Aug. 1978); m. Grace Rosamond Muder, Dec. 24, 1979. Student, Ohio Weslayan U., 1944-45, Art Ctr. Sch., L.A., 1957-58. Artist Interstate Theatres, Inc., Dallas, 1941-42, Oakite Products, N.Y.C., 1946-47; cartoonist Reddy Kilowatt, Inc., 1947-50; freelance cartoonist, comml. artist, 1950-52, Dallas, 1952-55, L.A., 1955-56, Las Vegas, 1970-75; comml. artist Northrup Corp., Hawthorne, Calif., 1956-59; indsl. illustrator Douglas Aircraft Corp., Long Beac, El Segondo, 1959-62; comml. artist Nortronics, Palos Verdes, 1962-64; sr. illustrator Holmes & Narver, Inc., Honolulu, 1964-70, Las Vegas, 1964-70; sr. artist Houston Post Newspaper, 1975-87. One man shows at First City Nat. Bank, 1985, 87; exhibited in group shows at Clampitt Paper Co., Houston, 1985, Sportsman's Gallery, Galleria, Houston, 1986, Marriott Hotel, Houston, 1990, Lone Star Restaurant, Houston, 1991-92, CMR Gallery, Corpus Christi, Tex., 1994, 96; contbr. cartoons Am. Mag., Bluebook Mag., King Features Syndicate, AT&T, Las Vegas Sun, Las Vegas Rev./Jour., others; caricaturist Mem. Houston World Affairs Coun., 1996—. With U.S. Navy, 1942-46. Mem. Houston Mus. Fine Arts, Braeburn Valley West Civic Club, Am. Legion. Avocations: running, physical fitness, reading, politics, world affairs. Home and Office: 9443 Portal Dr Houston TX 77031-2212

SHELLEY, E. DORINDA, dermatologist; b. St. Louis, Oct. 28, 1940; d. Robert G. and Ellen (Shattuck) Loeffel; m. Walter B. Shelley, Jan. 25, 1980; children: Thomas, Katharine, William. BA, Mt. Holyoke Coll., 1962; MD, U. Mo., 1966. Intern St. Luke's Hosp., St. Louis, 1966-67; resident in dermatology U. Mo., Columbia, 1967-70; postdoctoral fellow Stanford U., Palo Alto, Calif., 1970-71, asst. prof. dermatology, 1971-74, U. Ill., Chgo., 1974-75, assoc. prof., 1975-78, prof., chmn. Peoria, 1978-83; prof., chief dermatology Med. Coll. Ohio, Toledo, 1983-97, clin. prof. dermatology, 1997—. Cons. FDA, Rockville, Md., 1974—82. Author (with W.B. Shelley): Advanced Dermatologic Therapy, 1986; author: Advanced Dermatologic Diagnosis, 1992, A Century of International Dermatological Congresses, 1992, Advanced Dermatologic Therapy II, 2001, Shelley's 77 Skins, 2002; co-editor: Adolescent Dermatology, 1978; contbr. over 200 articles to profl. jours. Mem.: Noah Worcester Dermatol. Soc. (bd. trustees 2002—), Royal Soc. Medicine, Am. Dermatol. Assn., Mich. Dermatol. Soc., Ohio Dermatol. Soc., Women's Dermatol. Soc. (bd. dirs. 1980, pres. 1980, historian 1996—), Am. Acad. Dermatology (chmn. evaluation com. on ann.program 1994—99), Cosmos Club (Washington). Home: 21171 W River Rd Grand Rapids OH 43522-9703 Office: Med Coll Ohio Ruppert Health Ctr 3120 Glendale Ave Toledo OH 43614-5811 E-mail: ancampbell@mco.edu.

SHELLEY, HERBERT CARL, lawyer; b. Stamford, Tex., Jan. 28, 1947; s. Carl B. and Lourena A. (Whitley) S.; m. Jerilyn S. Ray, Aug. 9, 1969; children: Megan, Caitlyn, Daniel. BA, Columbia Coll., 1969; JD, Vanderbilt U., 1972; LLM Internat. and Comparative Law magna cum laude, Vrije Universiteit Brussel, Brussels, Belgium, 1973. Bar: D.C. 1973, Md. 1985, U.S. Ct. Appeals (fed. cir.) 1981, U.S. Ct. Internat. Trade 1982, U.S. Supreme Ct. 1987. Atty./adv. U.S. Tariff Commn., Washington, 1973-74; Internat. trade specialist, asst. Office dir. Office Tariff Affairs U.S. Dept. Treasury, 1974-76; internat. trade negotiator Office Spl. Trade Reps., Geneva, Switzerland, 1976-79; ptnr. Plaia & Schaumberg, Washington, 1979-86, Howrey & Simon, Washington, 1986-99, Steptoe & Johnson LLP, Washington, 1999—. Mem. ABA, D.C. Bar Assn., Md. Bar Assn. Avocations: skiing, golf, cooking, travel. Office: 1330 Connecticut Ave NW Washington DC 20036-1704

SHELLEY, SALLY SWING, United Nations official, broadcaster; b. Kent, Eng., Aug. 3, 1924; (parents Am. citizen); d. Raymond Gram and Betty Gram Swing. BA, Smith Coll., Northampton, Mass., 1945; postgrad., U. Paris, 1946-48; MFA, Columbia U., N.Y.C., 1972. Fgn. corr. UPI, Paris, 1948-50; exec. dir. Am. Soc. Indsl. Designers, 1952-57; prin. pub. rels. firm, 1955; joined UN Secretriat, 1972, served as chief info. officer UNESCO, N.Y.C., 1968-72; chief info. Internat. Women's Yr., chief edn. info. programs UN, 1972-76, joined Secretariat, 1972, chief non-govtl. orgn. sect., 1984—86; dir. pub. affairs ASPCA, N.Y., 1986; pub. rels. cons. to Ctr. Against Apartheid UN, 1986-89, election supr. Namibia, 1989; UN radio corr. AP spl. assignment Deutsche Welle (Voice of Germany), Maryknoll Radio Network, N.Y.C., 1986—; spl. asst. to sec.-gen. World Meteorol. Orgn. for Pub. Awareness, 1964-95. Instr. polit. sci. and formation of pub. opinion Baruch Sch. Pub. Adminstrn., CCNY, 1961-62; pres. Books for a Better World, 1990. Author: Development Education, 1974, Women Helping Women, 1977; contbr. articles to profl. publs. Trustee William Allanson White Inst., Robert Flaherty Found. Internat. Film Seminars; initiated Tree Project, 1985, Internat. Fund Rural Women. Named One of Conn.'s Outstanding Women, Conn. Gov. Grasso, 1975; recipient Outstanding Svc. awards Asian Lions Club, N.Y., Rotary Club, Stamford, Conn., Rotary Club, Syracuse, N.Y., Eleanor Roosevelt 60th Anniv. Human Rights award League Bus. and Profl. Women, N.Y., 1980, World Peace prize Brahma Kumari World Spiritual U., Rajasthan, India, 1984. Mem. Coun. Fgn. Rels., Nat. Assn. Negro Bus. club (hon. life), Negro Bus. and Profl. Women's Club (hon. life), Smith Coll. Club N.Y. Home: 510 E 23d St Apt 11G New York NY 10010 Fax: 203-227-2365.

SHELLEY, WALTER BROWN, physician, educator; b. St. Paul, Feb. 6, 1917; s. Patrick K. and Alfaretta (Brown) S.; m. Marguerite H. Weber, 1942 (dec.); children: Peter B., Anne E. Kiselewich, Barbara A. (dec.); m. E. Dorinda Loeffel, 1980; children: Thomas R., Katharine D., William L. BS, U. Minn., 1940, PhD, 1941, MD, 1943; MA honoris causa, U. Pa., 1971; MD honoris causa, U. Uppsala, Sweden, 1977. Diplomate: Am. Bd. Dermatology (pres. 1968-69, dir. 1960-69). Instr. physiology U. Pa., Phila., 1946-47, asst. instr. dermatology and syphilology, 1947-49, asst. prof. dermatology, 1950-53, assoc. prof., 1953-57, prof., 1957-80, chmn. dept., 1965-80; prof. dermatology U. Ill. Peoria Sch. Medicine, 1980-83; prof. medicine (dermatology) Med. Coll. Ohio, 1983-97, emeritus prof. medicine, 1997—. Instr. dermatology Dartmouth Coll., 1949-50; Regional cons. dermatology VA, 1955-59; mem. com. on cutaneous system NRC, 1955-59, Commn. Cutaneous Diseases, Armed Forces Epidemiological Bd., 1958-61, dep. dir., 1959-61; cons. dermatology Surgeon Gen. USAF, 1958-61, U.S. Army, 1958-61; mem. NRC, 1961-64 Author (with Crissey): Classics in Clinical Dermatology, 1953; author: (with Pillsbury, Kligman) Dermatology, 1956; author: Cutaneous Medicine, 1961; author: (with Hurley) The Human Apocrine Sweat Gland in Health and Disease, 1960; author: (with Botelho and Brooks) The Endocrine Glands, 1969; author: Consultations in Dermatology with Walter B. Shelley, 1972, Consultations II, 1974; author: (with Shelley) Advanced Dermatologic Therapy, 1987; author: Advanced Dermatologic Diagnosis, 1992, A Century of International Dermatological Congresses, 1992, Advanced Dermatologic Therapy II, 2001, Shelley's 77 Skins, 2001; mem. editl. bd. Jour. Investigative Dermatology, 1961—64, Archives of Dermatology, 1961—62, Skin and Allergy News, 1970—93, Excerpta Medica Dermatologica, 1960—, Cutis, 1972—, Jour. Geriatric Dermatol, 1993; assoc. editor: Jour. Cutaneous Pathology, 1972—81; editl. cons. Medcom, 1972—. Served as capt. M.C. AUS, 1944-46. Recipient Spl. award Soc. Cosmetic Chemists, 1955, Hellerstrom medal, 1971, Am. Med. Writers Assn. Best Med. Book award, 1973, Dohi medal, 1981, Rothman medal Soc. for Investigative Dermatology, 1987, Rose Hirschler award, 1990. Master A.C.P.; fellow Assn. Am. Physicians, St. John's Dermatol. Soc. London (hon.); mem. AMA (chmn. residency rev. com. for dermatology 1963-67, chmn. sect. dermatology 1969-71), Assn. Profs. Dermatology (pres. 1972-73), Pacific Dermatol. Assn. (hon.), Am. Dermatol. Assn. (hon., dir., pres. 1975-76), Soc. Investigative Dermatology (hon. pres. 1961-62), Am., Phila. physiol. socs., Brit. Dermatol. Soc. (hon.), Phila. Dermatol. Soc. (pres. 1960-61), Mich. Dermatol. Soc., Ohio Dermatol. Soc. (hon.), Am. Acad. Dermatology (Gold medal 1992, hon. pres. 1971-72), Pa. Acad. Dermatology (pres. 1972-73), Am. Soc. for Dermatologic Surgery, North Am. Clin. Dermatol. Soc. (hon.), Noah Worcester Dermatological Soc., Royal Soc. Medicine; corr. mem. Nederlandse Vereniging Van Dermatologen, Israeli Dermatol. Assn., Finnish Soc. Dermatology, Swedish Dermatol. Soc., French Dermatologic Soc.; fgn. hon. mem. Danish Dermatol. Assn., Japanese Dermatol. Assn., Dermatol. Soc. S.Africa. Home: 21171 W River Rd Grand Rapids OH 43522-9703 Office: Med Coll Ohio 3120 Glendale Ave Toledo OH 43614-2595 Fax: 419-383-6285. E-mail: ancampbell@mco.edu.

SHELLHORN, RUTH PATRICIA, landscape architect; b. L.A., Sept. 21, 1909; d. Arthur Lemon and Lodema (Gould) S.; m. Harry Alexander Kueser, Nov. 21, 1940. Student dept. landscape architecture, Oreg. State Coll., 1927-30; landscape architecture program, Cornell U. Coll. Architecture, 1930—33. Pvt. practice landscape architecture, various cities, Calif., 1933—; exec. cons. landscape architect Bullocks Stores, 1945-78, Fashion Sqs. Shopping Ctrs., 1958-78, Marlborough Sch., L.A., 1968-93, El Camino Coll., Torrance, Calif., 1970-78, Harvard Sch., North Hollywood, 1974-90. Cons. landscape architect, site planner Disneyland, Anaheim, Calif., 1955, U. Calif., Riverside Campus, 1956-64, numerous others, also numerous gardens and estates; landscape architect Torrance (Calif.) City Goals Com., 1969-70; cons. landscape architect City of Rolling Hills (Calif.) Community Assn., 1973-93. Contbr. articles to garden and profl. publs.; subject of Oct. 1967 issue Landscape Design & Constrn. mag. Named Woman of Year, Los Angeles Times, 1955, Woman of Year, South Pasadena-San Marino (Calif.) Bus. Profl. Women, 1955; recipient Charles Goodwin Sands medal, 1930-33, Landscape Architecture award of merit Calif. State Garden Clubs, 1984, 86, Horticulturist of the Yr. award So. Calif. Hort. Inst., numerous nat., state, local awards for excellence. Fellow Am. Soc. Landscape Architects (past pres. So. Calif. chpt.), Phi Kappa Phi, Kappa Kappa Gamma (Alumni Achievement award 1960) Achievements include projects subject of Oct. 1967 issue of Landscape Design and Constrn. Mag. Home and Office: 362 Camino De Las Colinas Redondo Beach CA 90277-6435 *Integrity, honesty, dependability, sincerity, dedication, and a willingness to give more than is expected in service, are the basic principles which have guided my career. Never losing sight of the importance of the individual, I have tried to create total environments of harmony and beauty to which each individual can relate in a very personal and pleasureable way, and for a little while, can find a calm oasis in a busy and demanding world.*

SHELLOW, ROBERT, management service company executive, consultant; b. Milw., Sept. 22, 1929; s. Henry G. and Sadie (Myers) S.; m. Dorothea Laadt, Aug. 30, 1963; children: Sarah Katherine, Leslie Suzzane. BA, Reed Coll., 1951; MA, U. Mich., 1952, PhD, 1956. Commd. USPHS, Bethesda, Md., 1955; advanced through grades to commdr. Psychol. U.S. Bureau Prisons, 1955-58; asst. dep. dir. Nat. Adv. Commn. on Civil Disorders, 1967-68; dir. pilot programs D.C. Dept. Pub. Safety, 1968-70; prof. Carnegie-Mellon U., Pitts., 1970-76; pres. IMAR Corp., Washington, 1978—. Cons. in field; expert witness psychol. deterence, security negligence cases, state and fed. cts., 1978—. Author: Issues in Law Enforcement, 1976; contbr. numerous articles to profl. jours. USPHS fellow U. Mich., 1953. Fellow Am. Psychol. Assn.; mem. Nat. Bus. Aircraft Assn., Internat. Assn. Profl. Security Cons. (v.p. 1987-89, pres. 1989-91), Sigma Xi. Avocations: sailing, automobile and boat restoration. Office: IMAR Corp PO Box 34528 Bethesda MD 20827-0528 E-mail: imarcorp@mindspring.com.

SHELLY, ANN CONVERSE, education educator, administrator; b. Lansing, Mich., July 5, 1943; d. Marshall Hough and Adelaide Louise (Crowell) Converse; m. Robert Keith Shelly, Sept. 12, 1964; children: Marshall Keith, Elizabeth Louise. BA, Mich. State U., 1965, MA, 1970, PhD, 1973. Asst. prof. SUNY, Geneseo, 1974-77; coord. tchr. prep. W.Va. State Dept. Edn., Charleston, 1977—78; prof., dir. tchr. prep. Bethany (W.Va.) Coll., 1978—90; prof. chair curriculum and instrn. U. Ala., Birmingham, 1990—94; prof., dean Coll. Edn. Ga. So. U., Statesboro, 1994—96; chair, tchr. edn. Ashland U., Ohio, 1996—2000, prof., 1996—. Cons. in field. Contbg. author: Mainstreaming Preparation, 1989; contbr. articles to profl. jours. Sec., bd. dirs. Interfaith Hospitality House, Birmingham, 1991—; bd. dirs. A.G. Gaston Boys and Girls Club, Birmingham, 1992—. NSF grantee, 1992. Mem. ASCD (bd. dirs. 1987-91), Am. Assn. Colls. of Tchr. Edn. (inst. rep., bd. dirs. 1987-90), Assn. Tchr. Educators, Kappa Delta Epsilon, Kappa Delta Pi, Phi Delta Kappa, Phi Kappa Phi. Democrat. Episcopalian. Avocations: sewing, quilting. Office: Ashland U Coll Edn 319 Bixler Ashland OH 44805

SHELLY, THADDEUS RUBEZ, III, trust company executive; b. Memphis, Aug. 29, 1953; s. Thaddeus R. and Beverly Claire Agnew S.; m. Helen Totty Edwards, June 26, 1982; children: Charles Edwards, James Thaddeus, Robert Willis, Beverly Lee. BA in Econs., Hampden-Sydney Coll., 1975; MBA, Coll. William & Mary, 1984. Tchr. Amezia (Va.) Acad., 1975-77; coach Hampden-Sidney (Va.) Coll., 1977-78; coach, athletic dir. Carlyle Sch., Martinsville, Va., 1978-80; tchr., coach Norfolk (Va.) Acad., 1980-82; v.p. Goldman, Sachs & Co., Phila., 1984-92; v.p., dir. pvt. client svcs. Legg Mason, Inc., Balt., 1992-98; mng. dir., resident mgr. Bessemer Trust Co., Washington, 1998—. Youth league coach Severna Park (Mass.) Green Hornets, 1995—; past vice chmn. Md. chpt. U.S. Olympic Com., Balt., 1994-96. Recipient Alumni Svc. award, Coll. William & Mary, 1994. Republican. Presbyterian. Avocations: youth sports, boating, skiing. Home: 255 Oak Ct Severna Park MD 21146 Office: Bessemer Trust Co 1050 Connecticut Ave NW Washington DC 20036

SHELOV, STEVEN PATRICK, pediatrician, educator; b. Honolulu, Nov. 19, 1944; s. Sidney M. and Faith R. S.; m. Marsha Liberman, Aug. 30, 1968; children: Joshua, Danielle, Eric. BS, Yale, 1966; MD, Med. Coll. Wisc., 1971; MS in Med. Admin., U. Wisc., 1995. Diplomate Am. Bd. Pediatrics. Intern, then resident Montefiore Med. Ctr., Bronx, 1971-74, chief resident, 1974-75; asst. dir. amb. pediat. Albert Einstein Coll. Med., N.Y., 1977-79; dir. pediat. edn. Montefiore Med. Ctr., 1980—, prof. and vice chmn. pediat., 1989-97; chmn. pediat. Maimonides Med. Ctr., Brooklyn, 1997—; prof. pediat. SUNY, 1997—. Editor: Caring for Your Baby and Young Child: Birth to 5, 1991, 1996, Pediatrics, 1996, Guide to Your Child's Symptoms, 1997, The First Year of Life, 1998. Recipient Geo. Armstrong award Ambulatory Pediat. Assn., 1996. Office: Maimonides Med Ctr 4802 10th Ave Brooklyn NY 11219-2844 E-mail: sshelov@maimonidesmed.org.

SHELP, RONALD KENT, non-profit, business and trade association executive, author, lecturer, consultant; b. Cartersville, Ga., Sept. 29, 1941; s. Clarence Harrison Mulkey and Willie Marion (Puckett) Shelp; m. Anna June Mueller, Feb. 14, 1982 AB cum laude, U. Ga., 1964; MA, Johns Hopkins SAIS, Washington, 1966; postgrad., London Sch. Econs., 1981—. Asst. to U.S. Senator Richard Russell, Washington, 1964-66; exec. sec. Internat. Ins. Adv. Council, 1966-73; co-founder, exec. v.p. Art Enterprise Internat., 1970-72; asst. mgr. internat. divsn. U.S. C. of C., 1970-73; exec. sec. Assn. Am. C. of C. in Latin Am., 1969-73; v.p. Am. Internat. Group, N.Y.C., 1973-85; v.p., mem. pres.' operating com. Celanese Corp., 1985-87; v.p. Hoechst Celanese Corp., 1987; pres., CEO N.Y.C. Partnership, 1987-93, N.Y. C. of C. and Industry, 1987-93; exec. com. Burson-Marsteller, N.Y.C., 1994-96, vice-chmn., 1995-96; chmn., CEO Kent Global Strategies, 1996—; exec. com. Dieferbach, Elkins, N.Y., 1996-97; chmn., CEO Curatorial Art. Adv. Svc., N.Y.C., 1998—; pres., CEO B2Bstreet.com, 1999—2001; chmn. Anne McBride Co., 2001—. Bd. dirs. Advantage Internat., Inc., MIMS Corp.; cons. OECD, Paris, 1982, mem. U.S. Del., 1978-85; chmn. U.S. Govt.-Svcs. Ind. Adv. Com., Washington, 1980-85; adj. prof. internat. bus. and econs. NYU, 1982-84. Co-author: Reference Manual on Doing Business in Latin America, 1979, A New International Commodity Regime, 1979, Service Industries and Economic Development, 1984, Industrial Policy: Business and Politics in The United States and France, 1985, The U.S. Trade Deficit: Impact and Implications, 1985, Revitalizing the U.S. Economy, 1986, Services in Transition: The Impact of Information Technology on the Service Sector, 1986, The Insurance Industry in Economic Development, 1986, Entrepreneurship: The Key to Economic Growth, 1986, Managing Services: Marketing Operations and Human Resources, 1988; author: Beyond Industrialization, 1981, (3d edit. in Japanese) ; contbr. articles to Foreign Policy, Wall Street Jour., N.Y. Times, L.A. Times, Boston Globe, Forbes, Christian Science Monitor, Jour. Social Econ. Studies, Across the Board, Financier, Georgetown Law Jour., Policy Options, contbr. and coord. artwork (book) Wrestling With History, 1996; cons.: book Testimony: Vernacular Art of the African-American South, 2001. Dir. Pan Am. Devel. Found., Washington, 1981-87, Johns Hopkins SAIS, Washington, 1982-89, 90-95, Internat. Peace Acad., N.Y.C., 1983-89; trade and econ. advisor Presdl. Campaign of Sen. Gary Hart, Washington, 1983-84, 86-87; adv. bd. Overseas Devel. Council, Washington, 1983-91, N.Y.C. Coun. on Econ. Edn., 1988-95; bd. dirs. Citizens Budget Commn., N.Y.C., 1985-87, Fund for Modern Cts., N.Y.C. Indsl. Tech. Assistance Corp., 1987-89, Mus. American Folk Art, 1987-90, Corp. Fund for Dance, 1987-91, Econ. Devel. Corp., N.Y.C., 1988-93, Manhattan Theatre Club, 1992-2001, N.Y.C. Housing Partnership Devel. Co., vice chmn., 1992-94; chmn. World Environ. Ctr., 1987-88; mem. Mayor's Mgmt. Adv. Task Force, 1990-93, Mayor's Adv. Com. to Productivity, 1990-93, Mayor's Task Force on Telecommunications Network Reliability, 1990-93, N.Y. State Indsl. Cooperation Coun., 1989-93, N.Y. State Job Trng. Partnership Coun., 1989-94, N.Y. State Telecomm. Exchange, 1992-93, Mayor's Coun. of Econ. Advisors, 1992-93. With USAR, 1966-72. Crown Zellerbach fellow Johns Hopkins SAIS, 1964, Francis P. Bolton fellow, 1965. Mem. Coun. Fgn. Rels., Econ. Club N.Y., Phi Beta Kappa. Democrat. Avocations: collecting African Am. vernacular art of the South, tennis, skiing, exploration, fly fishing. Home: 5 E 16th St New York NY 10003-3112 Office: Anne McBride Co 630 3d Ave Fl 5 New York NY 10017 E-mail: Kentglobal@mindspring.com.

SHELTON, BESSIE ELIZABETH, school system administrator; b. Lynchburg, Va. d. Robert and Bessie Ann (Plenty) Shelton. BA (scholar), W.Va. State Coll., 1958; student, Northwestern U., 1953-55, Ind. U., 1956; MS, SUNY, 1960; diploma, Profl. Career Devel. Inst., 1993. Young adult libr. Bklyn. Pub. Libr., 1960-62; asst. head cen. ref. divsn. Queens Borough Pub. Libr., jamaica, N.Y., 1962-65; instrnl. media specialist Lynchburg Bd. Edn., 1966-74, ednl. rsch. specialist, 1974-77; ednl. media assoc. Allegany County Bd. Edn., Cumberland, Md., 1977—. Guest singer Sta. WLVA, 1966—, WLVA-TV Christmas concerts, 1966—;cons. music and market rsch. Mem. YWCA, Lynchburg, 1966—, Fine Arts Ctr., Lynchburg, 1966—; ednl. adv. bd., nat. research bd. Am. Biog. Inst.; mem. U.S. Congl. Adv. Bd., USN Nat. Adv. Coun.; amb. goodwill Lynchburg, Va., 1986. Named to Nat. Women's Hall of Fame. Mem. AAUW, NEA, NAFE, Md. Tchrs. Assn., Allegany County Tchrs. Assn., Va. Edn. Assn., State Dept. Sch. Librs., Internat. Entertainers Guild, Music City Songwriters Assn., Vocal Artists Am., Internat. Clover Poetry Assn., Internat. Platform Assn., Nat. Assn. Women Deans, Adminstrs. and Counselors, Intercontinental Biog. Assn., World Mail Dealers Assn., N.Am. Mailers Exch., Am. Assn. Creative Artists, Am. Biog. Inst. Rsch. Assn., Tri-State Cmty. Concert Assn., Pi Delta Phi, sigma Delta Pi, Nat. Travel Club, Gulf Travel Club. Democrat. Baptist. Home: PO Box 187 Cumberland MD 21501-0187

SHELTON, BETTY CLARE, organization executive; b. South Range, Mich., Mar. 8, 1940; d. Robert R. Salo and Rauha O. Liimatainen; m. Charles E. Shelton, Aug. 31, 1959 (div. May 1982); children: Kimberly, Taylor, Christine. BA, U. Ky., 1984. Sec. City of Garden City, Garden City, Mich., 1958-62, Ford Motor Co., Dearborn, 1962-67, Plymouth, 1970-71, Whirlpool Corp., Danville, Ky., 1975-77; coun. field dir. Girl Scout Coun. Tropical Fla., Miami, Fla., 1982-88, coun. adult devel. dir., 1988-94, dir. vol. svcs., 1994-99, asst. exec. dir. membership/mktg. tng., 1999—. Mem. faculty continuing edn. Fla. Internat. U., mem. alumni bd., 1989-95. Photograph exhibited by Photogroup of Miami, Inc., Coral Gables. Instr. Girl Scouts U.S. Miami, 1988—, hostess, coun. asst., co-dir. Girl Scouts Nat. Conv., Miami Beach, 1990; vol. first aid instr. ARC, Miami, 1989—; active Dirs. of Vols. in Agys., 1988-99, exec. bd., 1994-99, v.p., 1995-97, tri-county conf. com., 1996, treas., 1994-95, pres., 1998, chair nominating com., 1999; bd. dirs. Waters Edge Assn., 1994-96, v.p., 1994-95, pres., 1995-96, mem. Waters Edge Dock Com., 1997, chair disaster preparation com., 2000, budget com., 2000-01; com. mem. Nat. Vol. Week Com. of Dade County, 1998—; mem. steering com. Vol. Miami, 1998-99; mem. Dade Co. vol. orgns. active in disasters, 1994—. Mem. AAUW, Miami Woman's Club (2d v.p. 2000-02, 1st v.p. 2002—). Avocations: reading, sailing, photography, genealogy. Home: 100 Edgewater Dr Apt 310 Miami FL 33133-6939 Office: Girl Scout Coun Tropical 11347 SW 160th St Miami FL 33157-2703

SHELTON, BONNIE LEE, association executive; b. Waterloo, Iowa; d. Darrell Lee and Leona Shelton; children: Jeffrey David Blankenship, Daniel James Blankenship. BS in Comms. with high honors., U. Ill., 1971, MS in Journalism, 1974; CSS in Adminstrn. and Mgmt., Harvard U., 1989. Cert. Assn. Exec. (CAE), Am. Soc. of Assn. Execs. (ASAE), 1993. Staff writer, columnist The News-Gazette, Champaign, Ill., 1965-71; asst. to pres. Internat. Features Enterprises, Inc., Rome, 1971-75; dir. publs. News Bur., exec. editor Grad. Sch. Bus. Ind. U., Bloomington, 1975-78; dir. comms. and ednl. devel. Nat. Fedn. Bus. and Profl. Women, Washington, 1978-83; exec. dir. Unitarian Universalist Women's Fedn., Boston, 1983-88; communications cons., property mgr., 1988-90; exec. dir. Nat. Assn. Rehab. Profls. Pvt. Sector, Newton, 1990-95, Soc. for Mktg. Profl. Svcs., Alexandria, VA, 1995-99, N.Am. Assn. for Environ. Edn., Washington, 2000—01; v.p. Am. Coll. Health Care Profls. , 2001—02; pres. Exec. Strategies for Assn. Mgmt., 2002—. Presenter paper 1984 Congress Internat. Assn. Religious Freedom, Tokyo. Recipient Dudley McAllister Meml. award Excellence in Pub. Affairs reporting. Mem.: Greater Washington Assn. Execs., Am. Soc. Assn. Execs., Harvard Club, Kappa Tau Alpha.

SHELTON, DAVID HOWARD, economics educator; b. Winona, Miss., Nov. 30, 1928; s. Tuttle M. and Kate (Moss) S.; m. Margaret Murff, Feb. 4, 1951; children: David Keith, Sarah Katherine, Susan Esther. BA, Millsaps Coll., 1951; MA, Ohio State U., 1952, PhD, 1958. Instr. Ohio State U., 1958; asst. prof. U. Del., 1958-63, asso. prof., 1963-65; prof. U. N.C., Greensboro, 1965—, head dept. econs., bus. adminstrn., 1967-70, dean Sch. Bus. and Econs., 1970-83, head dept. econs., 1988-93, prof. emeritus, 1993—. Cons. Joint Council on Econ. Edn., 1969-72, N.C. Dept. Pub. Instrn., 1970-73 Trustee N.C. Council on Econ. Edn., 1971-96, chmn., 1971-75, pres., 1975-85. Served with USN, 1946-48. M.D. Lincoln fellow, 1956-57; H.L. and Grace Doherty fellow, 1957 Mem. Beta Gamma Sigma, Omicron Delta Kappa, Kappa Sigma. Episcopalian. Home: 3609 Dogwood Dr Greensboro NC 27403-1010 Office: UNC 462 Bryan Bldg Greensboro NC 27412-0001

SHELTON, DOROTHY DIEHL REES, lawyer; b. Manila, Sept. 16; came to U.S., 1945; d. William Walter John and Hedwig Diehl; m. Charles W. Rees, Jr., June 15, (div. 1971); children: Jane Rees Stebbins, John B., Anne Rees Slack, David C.,; m. Thomas C. Shelton, Mar. 4, 1977. BA in Music, Stanford Univ.; JD, Western State Univ. Coll. Law. Bar: Calif. U.S. Dist. Ct. (so. dist.) Calif. Pvt. practice, San Diego, 1977—. Mem. ABA, Calif. State Bar, San Diego County Bar Assn., Consumer Attys. San Diego, Stanford U. Alumni Assn., Jr. League San Diego, Gt. Pyrenees Club Am., Dachshund Club Am., Nu Beta Epsilon. Avocations: gardening, reading, Great Pyrenees dogs. Office: 110 W C St Ste 711 San Diego CA 92101-3906

SHELTON, ELIZABETH COLLEY, social worker; b. Atlanta, Mar. 26, 1920; d. John Edmonds and Bess (Hollowell) Colley; m. Charles Bascom Shelton Jr., Oct. 22, 1940 (dec. Febr. 1990); children: Charles III, Elizabeth Colley Case, Rosser Edmonds. Attended, Sweet Briar (Va.) Coll., 1937-40; BA in Sociology, U. Tenn., Chattanooga, 1963; postgrad., U. of the South, Sewanee, Tenn., 1990-98. Caseworker Hamilton County Family Svcs., Chattanooga, 1970-72; caseworker prin. Fulton County Dept. of Family and Children Svcs., Atlanta, 1973-97. Bd. dirs. Midtown Assistance Ctr., Atlanta, 1988-97. Sustainer Jr. League of Atlanta, 1946—. Mem. Ga. Conf. on Social Welfare (bd. dirs. 1993-96), Ga. County Welfare Assn., Daus. of the King, Svc. and Prayer Group, Soc. Companions of Holy Cross, Symphony and Alliance Theater. Republican. Episcopalian. Home: Apt 320 3750 Peachtree Rd NE Atlanta GA 30319-1322

SHELTON, HENRY H. federal agency administrator; b. Tarboro, N.C., Jan. 2, 1942; m. Carolyn L. Johnson; children: Jon, Jeff, Mark. BS, N.C. State U.; MS, Auburn U.; grad., Air Command and Staff Coll., Nat. War Coll. Commd. 2d lt. U.S. Army, 1963, advanced through grades to gen., 1996; with 5th Spl. Forces Group, Vietnam, 173d Airborn Brigade, Vietnam; comdr. 3d Bn., 60th Infantry, 9th Infantry Divsn., Ft. Lewis, asst. chief of staff for ops.; comdr. 1st Brigade, 82d Airborne Divsn., Ft. Bragg, N.C.; chief of staff 10th Mountain Divsn., Ft. Drum, N.Y.; with ops. directorate Joint Chiefs of Staff, Washington, 1987, asst. divsn. comdr. for ops. 101st Airborne Divsn., 1989-91; comdr. 82d Airborne Divsn., Ft. Bragg, N.C., XVIIIth Airborne Corps., 1993, Chief of U.S. Spl. Ops. Comman, 1996; chmn. Joint Chiefs of Staff, Washington, 1997—. Decorated Def. D.S.M. with two oak clusters, D.S.M., Bronze Star with V device with three oak clusters, Purple Heart, Legion of Merit with oak leaf cluster. Office: Dept of Def Joint Chiefs of Staff The Pentagon Washington DC 20318-0001 Fax: 908-771-8618.

SHELTON, JAMES D. hospital administrator; BA Polit. Sci., History , La. State U.; MS Bus., Pub. Adminstrn., U. Mo. Hosp. adminstr. La., Iowa, N.C., Ga., Ill., Mo.; exec. v.p., sr. v.p., regional v.p. Nat. Med. Enterprises (now called Tenet); chmn., pres., CEO Triad Hosps., 2000—. Chmn. Fedn. Am. Health Sys. , 1999; mem. bd. govs. ; chmn. Triad Bd. Dirs., Exec. Com. Office: Triad Hosps 13455 Noel Rd 20th Fl Dallas TX 75240 Office Fax: 972-663-3945.*

SHELTON, JAMES DOUGLAS, banker; b. Boynton Beach, Fla., Feb. 28, 1939; s. Clarence Wilton and Lou Anna (Ward) S.; m. Claudia Ellen Marshall, Oct. 20, 1973; children: Christopher John, Ryan Marshall. BA, Duke U., 1961; MDiv, Union Sem., 1965; STM, Boston U., 1966; SEP, Stanford U., 1975. Adj. prof. N.Y. Sem., N.Y.C., 1966-68; asst. treas. Bankers Trust Co., 1968-71; v.p. Chase Manhattan Bank, 1971-84; sr. v.p. Conn. Bank & Trust, Hartford, 1984-88; chmn., pres., chief exec. officer First Fed. Savs., East Hartford, Conn., 1988-2001. Bd. dirs. Conn. On-Line Computer Ctr., Avon, chmn., 1989-2001; bd. dirs. Community Bank League of New Eng., Boston, chmn., 1989-96; mem. Conn. Legislature Interstate Banking Task Force, Hartford, 1989-90. Bd. dirs. Jr. Achievement North Ctrl. Conn., Windsor, 1986-90, Sci. Ctr. Conn., West Hartford, 1988-94, Riverfront Recapture, Inc., Hartford, 1994-98; corporator Am. Sch. for the Deaf, West Hartford, 1986-2001. Mem. Am. Cmty. Bankers Assn. (bd. dirs. 1995-2001), New Eng. Automated Clearing House Assn. (bd. dirs. 1983-98), Rotary. Avocations: skiing, golf.

SHELTON, JAMES KEITH, journalism educator; b. Altus, Okla., Oct. 28, 1932; s. Willis Oscar and Theodosia Agnes (Rupert) S.; m. Deborah Kennedy Evans, Dec. 26, 1953; children: Leslie Lynn, Lawrence Evans. BA, Midwestern State U., 1954; MA, U. North Tex., 1972. Reporter Lawton (Okla.) Constn., 1954; wire editor Wichita Falls (Tex.) Record-News, 1956-59; city hall reporter, polit. writer Dallas Times Herald, 1959-65; mng. editor, exec. editor Denton (Tex.) Record-Chronicle, 1965-69, 79-88; faculty mem., dir. pub. info. U. North Tex., Denton, 1969-79, journalist-in-residence, 1988—. Author: What Journalists Should Know About Business, 1993. Mem. Supreme Ct. Task Force on Jud. Ethics, Austin, 1992-94. with U.S. Army, 1954-56. Mem. Soc. Profl. Journalists, Freedom on Info. Found. of Tex., Inc. (sec., bd. dirs.). Democrat. Methodist. Home: 621 Grove St Denton TX 76209-7323 Office: Univ North Tex PO Box 305280 Denton TX 76203-5280 E-mail: shelton@unt.edu.

SHELTON, JOANNA REED, economist; b. Orange, Tex., Mar. 16, 1951; d. John Alexander and Winifred Irene (Gormley) S.; m. Richard David Erb, Mar. 22, 1980. BA, Duke U., 1974; MA, Johns Hopkins U., 1977. Researcher, writer Congl. Quarterly, Inc., Washington, 1974-75; internat. economist offices of internat. trade policy, internat. monetary affairs, office of the secretary U.S. Dept. Treas., 1978-83; sr. advisor on Japan Motorola, Inc., 1984; profl. staff mem., economist U.S. Ho. of Reps. Com. on Ways and Means, 1984-92; dep. asst. sec. trade policy and programs U.S. Dept. State, 1992-95; dep. sec. gen. OECD, Paris, 1995—. Co-author: Subsidies in Internat. Trade, 1984; contbr. articles to profl. jours. Mem. adv. coun. Johns Hopkins U. Sch. of Advanced Internat. Studies, Washington, 1986-92; mem. adv. com. Fulbright Scholar selection for northeast Asia, Washington, 1989-91. Mem. Japan-Am. Soc. (trustee 1990-92), Cosmos Club of Washington. Avocations: tennis, horseback riding, flute. Office: Orgn for Econ Co-op & Devel 2 re Andre Pascal 75775 Paris Cedex 16 France

SHELTON, JODY, educational association administrator; b. Norton, Kans., Aug. 4, 1944; d. James Pratt and Rita Merle (Thompson) Shelton. BA, Ottawa U., 1967; MEd, Emporia State U., 1977; EdD, Kans. U., 1991. Tchr. Belvoir Elem. Sch., Topeka, 1967-68, Ctrl. Elem. Sch., Olathe, 1968-77; prin. Westview Elem. Sch., 1977-80, Tomahawk Elem. Sch., Olathe, 1980-88; asst. supt. human resources Olathe Dist. Schs., 1988-97, asst. supt., 1997—; exec. dir. Am. Assn. Sch. Pers. Adminstrs., 2002—. Cons. Master Tchr., Manhattan, Kans., 1981-86; adj. prof. Emporia (Kans.) State U., 1990—; chair North Ctrl. Edn. Team, 1984; mem. adv. coun. Sch. Edn., Kans. U., Lawrence, 1992—; mem. com. Five Yr. Tech. Plan, Olathe, 1991—. Contbr. articles to profl. jours. Bd. dirs. Temporary Lodging for Children. Recipient Outstanding Jayne award Jaycees, 1972, Outstanding Young Woman Kans., 1980. Mem. NAESP (Nat. Disting. Prin. award 1987-88), AASPA (affiliate), Kans. Career Devel. and Placement Assn., Kans. Assn. Elem. Sch. Prins. (pres., Nat. Disting. Prin. award 1987-88, Olathe C. of C., United Sch. Adminstrs. (bd. dirs.), Optimist. Avocations: theatre, reading, aerobics, bridge, dancing, traveling. Home: 11546 S Brentwood Dr Olathe KS 66061-9388 Office: Olathe Dist Schs 14160 S Black Bob Rd Olathe KS 66062-2024 E-mail: jodysks@comcast.net.

SHELTON, L. ROBERT, retired federal official; BS in Bus. Mgmt., U. Md., 1976; MBA, Am. U., 1978. Economist Office of Automotive Fuel Economy Stds. Nat. Hwy. Traffic Safety Adminstrn., 1977-81; mgmt. analyst Office of Info. and Regulatory Affairs/Office Mgmt. & Budget, 1981-82; auto industry analyst, Office of Dep. Asst. Sec. U.S. Dept. Commerce, 1982-83; program analyst Motor Vehicle Requirements Divsn. Nat. Hwy. Traffic Safety Adminstrn., 1983-85, chief Analysis Divsn., 1986-91, dir. Office of Regulatory Analysis, 1991-96, acting assoc. adminstr. for plans and policy, 1996, assoc. adminstr. safety performance stds., 1996-99, exec. dir. office of adminstr., 1999—2002; ret., 2002. Office: Office of Adminstr 400 7th St SW Rm 5220 Washington DC 20590-0001

SHELTON, OLGA-JEAN, school counselor; b. Omaha, Aug. 10, 1957; d. Howard Kenton and Doris Jean (Harkness) Zion. Student, U. Minn., 1975-77; BA, Adams State U., Alamosa, Colo., 1980; MS, Emporia (Kans.) State U., 1987. Cert. in counseling and lang. arts, Colo. Tchr. speech Upward Bound, Alamosa, 1980; tchr. English Wyandotte High Sch., Kansas City, Kans., 1980-81; tchr. English and speech Bishop Ward High Sch., 1984-86; grad. asst. Emporia State U., 1986-87; counselor Winfield (Kans.) High Sch., 1987-88, Perry (Kans.)-Lecompton High Sch., 1988-91, Clear Creek High Sch., Idaho Springs, Colo., 1991-93, Heritage High Sch., Littleton, 1993-96, Elbert (Colo.) Schs., 1996-98, Arvada Middle Sch., Jefferson County (Colo.) Schs., 1998—. Instr. psychology Highland (Kans.) Community Coll., 1989. Editor newsletter for Kans. Sch. Counselors Assn., 1988-91. Grantee in field. Mem. Am. Sch. Counselors Assn., Rocky Mountain Soc. Adlerian Psychology (pres. 1993), Kans. Assn. Counseling and Devel. (bd. dirs. 1990-91), Kans. Sch. Counselors Assn. (pub. rels. chmn. 1988-89, pres. 1990-91), Colo. Sch. Counselors Assn. (grants chmn. 1994-95), Jefferson County Counselor Assn. (middle sch. co-chair), Optimist Club (Arvada, pres. 2002—). Democrat. Avocations: collecting, reading, travel. Home: 11718 Elk Head Range Rd Littleton CO 80127-3706 E-mail: jshelto@jeffco.k12.co.us.

SHELTON, PETER ARTHUR, civil engineer; b. Buffalo, Aug. 28, 1930; s. Peter Stanley and Esther Kathleen (Kurtz) S.; m. Phong Thi Nguyen, Apr. 28, 1968; children: Nhu My, Joe Chau. Student, Kensington Bus. Coll., 1950; BSCE, U. Calif., Berkeley, 1954. Gen. supt. Morrison Knudsen, Boise, 1982-90; project mgr. Raymond Internat., N.Y.C., 1955-72; gen. supt. Santa Fe-Braun, Alhambra, Calif., 1972-82; dir., treas. Con Seacon, Inc., Buffalo, 1970—; project engr. West Valley (N.Y.) Nuclear Svc. Co., 1990—. Mem. ASCE, NSPE, NRA, Soc. Am. Mil. Engrs., Soaring Soc. Am., Niagara Soaring Club. Republican. Avocation: soaring. Home: 41 Pine Ridge Rd Buffalo NY 14211-2709 Office: West Valley Nuclear Svc 10282 Rock Springs Rd West Valley NY 14171-9702

SHELTON, PHILIP ANDERSON, criminal investigator, writer; b. Coeur d'Alene, Idaho, July 3, 1938; s. Philip Anderson and Mildred Evelyn (Wendt) S.; 1 child, Thane Kevit. Student, Chico (Calif.) State Coll., 1957, U. Calif., Davis, 1960-62, Sacramento State U., 1973-75; BS in Criminology, U. Ala., 1996; postgrad. in Writing, Norwich U., 1996—. Cert. criminal investigator, Calif.; lic. pvt. investigator, Calif. Fraud investigator Philip A. Shelton Profl. Investigations, Sacramento, 1960-64, owner, operator, 1964-77; chief investigator Yolo County Conflict Def., Woodland, Calif., 1966-69; investigator Fed. Pub. Defender, Sacramento, 1975, chief investigator Fresno, 1977-78, Santa Barbara (Calif.) County Pub. Defender, 1978-96; dir. Calif. Death Penalty Rev. and Re-investigation, Santa Barbara, 1996—. Author short stories and novella. Bd. dirs. Santa Barbara Mus. of Art, 1980-84; founding mem. G.A.T.E. Sch. Program, Santa Barbara, 1980-85; mem., group leader City/County Disaster Svcs., Santa Barbara, 1980-89. Recipient Honor for Bravery World Secret Svc. Orgn., 1960; grantee Calif. Cattlemen's Assn., 1956, Fed. Defender Program, Washington, 1978. Mem. World Assn. Detectives, Assn. Brit. Detectives, Coun. Internat. Investigators, Calif. Assn. Lic. Investigators (co-founder 1966, Svc. award 1969), Inst. Personal Injury Investigators (dir., co-founder 1966—), Def. Investigators Assn. Avocations: printing, designing, amateur radio, lecturing, acting.

SHELTON, RICHARD W. academic administrator, writer; b. Boise, Ind., June 24, 1933; s. Leonard Pryor and Hazel Shelton; m. Lois D. Bruce; 1 child Brad Scott. MA, U. Ariz., Tucson, Ariz., 1961; BA, Abilene Christian U., Abilene, Tex., 1956. Prof. U. Ariz., Tucson, 1991—. Author: (book) Going Back to Bisbee, 1992 (western states award), (poetry) 13 books. Office: Dept Eng U Ariz Tucson AZ 85721

SHELTON, ROBERT NEAL, physics educator, researcher; b. Phoenix, Oct. 5, 1948; s. Clark B. and Grace M. (McLaughlin) S.; m. Adrian Ann Millar, Aug. 30, 1969; children: Christian, Cameron, Stephanie. BS, Stanford U., 1970; MS, U. Calif., San Diego, 1973, PhD, 1975. Postdoctoral researcher U. Calif.-San Diego, La Jolla, 1975-76, asst. rsch. physicist, 1976-78; asst. prof. Iowa State U., Ames, 1978-81, assoc. prof., 1981-84, prof. physics, 1984-87; prof. physics, chmn. dept. U. Calif.-Davis, 1987-90, vice chancellor for rsch., 1990-96, vice provost for rsch., 1996-2001; exec. vice chancellor, provost U. North Carolina, Chapel Hill, 2001—. Contbr. over 200 articles to profl. jours. Fellow Am. Phys. Soc., Calif. Coun. on Sci. and Tech.; mem. AAAS, Materials Rsch. Soc., Sigma Xi. Office: U North Carolina 104 South Bldg CB#3000 Chapel Hill NC 27599-3000 E-mail: robert_shelton@unc.edu.

SHELTON, ROBERT WARREN, marketing executive; b. Albuquerque, Apr. 26, 1943; s. Eugene and Rusty M. (Jentsch) S.; children: Elise Straus, Samantha; m. Ginger Lee Rapp, Feb. 14, 1984. BBA in Mktg., St. Mary's U., San Antonio, 1969; postgrad., Ga. State U., 1972-73, postgrad. in fin. and internat. bus., 1973. Field mgr. Ford Motor Co., Atlanta, 1969-78; dir. fleet ops. Rollins, Inc., 1978-81; v.p. sales and ops. Lease Plan U.S.A., 1981-85; v.p. mktg. Spencer Services, Inc., Roswell, Ga., 1985-87; v.p. FX-10 Corp., 1987-88; pres. Shiloh Capital Corp., 1989—, Innovators.Com, Inc., 2000—. Pres. Victory Svcs., Inc., 1989—. Mem. Lost Forest Civic Assn. (pres. 1980-81). Mem. Nat. Assn. Fleet Adminstrs., Am. Fleet and Leasing Assn., NRA. Republican. Christian. Avocations: golf, racquetball, tennis, shooting. E-mail: rshelton@innovators.com.

SHELTON, SONJA C. musician, music educator; b. Sumner, Mo., Sept. 1, 1940; d. Earl W. and Claire C. Louden; m. Wayne A. Shelton, June 25, 1966; children: Robert D., David M. B in Music, Oberlin Coll. Conservatory, 1962; MA, Kent State U., 1963. Pvt. piano tchr., 1968—; music instr. Coll. Wooster, Ohio, 1963-67; piano tchr. Eastman Sch., Rochester, N.Y., 1967-68; pianist, choral asst. Penfield (N.Y.) Ctrl. Schs., 1975-81; asst. prof. music Roberts Wesleyan Coll., Rochester, 1981—. Pianist Rochester Piano Quintet, 1976-95. Tchrs. Performance Inst. fellow Rockefeller Found., 1967, 69, Yale U. fellow, 1964. Mem. Nat. Guild Piano Tchrs. (adjudicator). Episcopalian. Avocation: travel. Office: Robert Wesleyan Coll 2301 Westside Dr Rochester NY 14624-1933

SHELTON, STEPHANI, broadcast journalist, consultant, freelance producer; b. Boston; d. Phil and Babette (Belloff) Saltman; m. Frank Herold. BS, Boston U. Corr. CBS News, N.Y.C., 1973-84; news corr. WWOR-TV, 1984-88; corr., anchor Fin. News Network, 1989-91. Freelance reporter Sta. WPIX-TV, 1991-95, Sta. WNBC-TV, 1993-96, WWOR-TV, 1999—; cons. trainer Ctrl. and Eastern Europe broadcast journalists, 1998—; med. health prodr.-reporter PBS, The Learning Channel, 1997—; co-owner The Fred Group Ltd., TV prodn. co., 1998—; freelance radio documentary writer Westinghouse Group W Broadcasting, N.Y.C., 1970-73. Recipient Peabody award, 1972, N.J. Best Spot News award AP, 1987, 88, N.J. Working Press award, 1992-94; Emmy nominee, 1994-95. Mem. Soc. Profl. Journalists (award 1999), Radio and TV News Dirs. Assn., N.Y.C. Press Club, Investigative Reporters and Editors, Com. to Protect Journalists. E-mail: backbay38@aol.com., fredgroup@aol.com. *Guiding principles: a questioning mind, a refusal to take no for an answer and the memory of 28 marathons. The important thing is to survive well.*

SHELTON, THOMAS ALFRED, pastor; b. Kansas City, Mo., Dec. 6, 1951; s. Thomas and Savanna S.; m. Phyllis Annette White, Aug. 18, 1979; children: Thomas, Reginald, Veronica. AA, Penn Valley Community, 1975; BA, U. Mo. Kansas City, 1983; MDiv. Cen. Bapt. Theol. Seminary, 1988. Cert. secondary tchr., social scis., Mo. Dean MidWest Dist. Congress, Kansas City, Mo., 1984-95; pres. Black Student Fellowship, 1985-87; regional v.p. Nat. Conf. Black Seminarians, N.Y.C., 1986-88; asst. pastor Kansas City, 1985-95; resource tchr. Kansas City Sch. Dist., 1988—; pastor Ward Meml. Missionary Bapt. Ch., Sedalia, Mo., 1995—. Pres. Mt. Sinai Day Care Bd., Kansas City, 1989-95; tchr. Five State Laymens Meeti ng, St. Louis, 1989. Bd. dirs. Kansas City Youth Ct., 1989—. Master sgt. USAF Res., 1979-93. Mem. Tchrs. Union, ASCD. Home: 1706 E 60th St Kansas City MO 64110-3550 also: Ward Meml Miss Bapt Ch Sedalia MO 65301 Office: PO Box 565 Sedalia MO 65302-0565

SHEMCHUK, MARY ELIZABETH, occupational therapist; b. Meriden, Conn., Dec. 17, 1954; d. Paul John and Rose Virginia (Piccolo) S. AS, Middlesex C.C., Middletown, Conn., 1977; BS, Eastern Mich. U., 1983. Registered occupl. therapist Minn., Conn. Staff occupl. therapist Gaylord Rehab. Hosp., Wallingford, Conn., 1985-89, sr. staff occupl. therapist, 1989-95; clin. supr. occupl. therapy Sundance Rehab. Corp., East Berlin, 1995; lead therapist in occupl. therapy Symphony Rehab. Svcs., Minnetonka, Minn., 1995—. Guest spkr. Bridgeport (Conn.) Arthritis Support Group, 1992; cons. for hearing impaired Gaylord Hosp., Wallingford, 1992-94. Former church organist Our Lady of Mt. Carmel Ch., Meriden, Conn.; guest spkr. Quota Club of Hamden (Conn.), 1986; vol. St. Vincent DePaul Soc. of Meriden Shelter, Inc., 1988. Mem. Am. Occupl. Therapy Assn. (cons. on hearing impaired 1992—), Minn. Occupl. Therapy Assn., Conn. Occupl. Therapy Assn., Self Help for Hard of Hearing, Inc., Minn. Arthritis Found. Avocations: horseback riding, nature walks, playing piano and organ, handicrafts. Home: 42 Antonio Ave # 3 Meriden CT 06451-2806

SHEMIN, BARRY L. insurance company executive; b. Bklyn., Dec. 17, 1942; AB magna cum laude, Brown U., 1963; MA, U. Mich., 1964. With John Hancock Life Ins. Co., Boston, 1968—, sr. v.p., corp. actuary. Bd. dirs. Hancock Natural Resource Group. Bd. dirs. ARC of Mass. Bay, Chair, Harvard Pilgrim Health Care. Fellow Soc. Actuaries; mem. Am. Acad. Actuaries, Phi Beta Kappa, Sigma Xi, Brown U. Club (Boston). Office: John Hancock Mut Life Ins Co PO Box 111 Boston MA 02117-0111

SHEMKOVITZ, GREG, playwright; b. Buffalo, June 20, 1979; s. Paul and Justine Shemkovitz. Author: (short story) Paul (Pub. in Gihon River Rev., 2002); author: (playwright) (one act play) Slide Show (2002 New Voices Competition), Venison (Pub. in Gt. Lake Rev., 2002). Recipient Phi Kappa Phi Nat. Honor Soc., Phi Kappa Phi, 2002; scholar Girgis B. Ghobrial Award in English, Oswego State U., 2002. Mem.: Phi Kappa Phi Nat. Honor Soc. (life).

SHEMWELL, MARY ANNE, adapted physical education specialist; b. Shreveport, La., Mar. 16, 1942; d. James Dee Jr. and Frances (Oden) Youngblood; children from previous marriage: Dee Wade, Charles James. BS, Centenary Coll., 1965; postgrad., La. Poly. Inst. Phys. edn. tchr. Midway Jr. H.S., Shreveport, 1965-69; adapted phys. edn. specialist Caddo Parish Pub. Schs., 1982—. Phys. edn. tchr. for track and field events for physically handicapped State of La. Coach United Cerebral Palsy of La.; mem. Rep. Women's Orgn., 1989—; treas. Rep. Profl. Women's Club, 1993—94. Named G.U.M.B.O. coach of the Yr., State of La., 1994. Mem.: La. Fedn. Tchrs., La. Assn. Heath Phys. Edn. and Recreation, Coun. Exceptional Children, Jr. League Shreveport, Plantation Club, Cotillion Club. Republican. Methodist. Avocations: reading, tennis, walking, swimming, coaching handicapped students. Home: 4431 Fern Ave Shreveport LA 71105-3103

SHEN, CE, sociologist, researcher; b. Haicheng, Liaoning Province, China, Sept. 16, 1942; arrived in U.S., 1988; s. YuShi Shen, ZhiDuo Hao; m. Wenzhen D. Du, Dec. 24, 1948; children: Liangbi, Liangyin. Student, Andover and Newton Theol. Sem., 1988—89; MA, Boston Coll., 1991, PhD in Sociology, 1996. Prof. Shenyang Archtl. and Civil Engring. Coll., Shenyang, China, 1980—87; rsch. fellow Royal Inst. Tech., Stockholm, 1987—87; rsch. asst. Brandeis U., 1990—93; rsch. assoc. Sch. Edn. Boston Coll., Chestnut Hill, Mass., 1993—96, rsch. assoc. Internat. Study Ctr., 1996—2000, acad. rsch. assoc. Rsch. and Instrnl. Tech. Svcs., 2000—. Mem.: New Eng. Sociology Assn. Avocations: soccer, blush and ink painting. Office: Boston Coll Acad and Instrnl Tech Svc 140 Commonwealth Ave Chestnut Hill MA 02467 Office Fax: 617-552-2836. Business E-Mail: shenc@bc.edu.

SHEN, CHIA THENG, former steamship company executive, religious institute official; b. Chekiang, China, Dec. 15, 1913; came to U.S., 1952, naturalized, 1964; s. Foo Sheng and Wen Ching (Hsai) S.; m. Woo Ju Chu, Apr. 21, 1940; children: Maria May Shen Jackson, Wilma Way Shen George, David Chuen-Tsing, Freda Foh. BEE, Chiao Tung U., 1937; LittD (hon.), St. John's U., 1973. With Central Elec. Mfg. Works, China, 1937-44, factory mgr., 1942-44; dep. coordinating dept. Nat. Resources Commn., Govt. of China, 1945-47; pres. China Trading and Indsl. Devel. Corp., Shanghai, 1947-49; mng. dir. China Trading & Indsl. Devel. Co. Ltd., Hong Kong, 1949-53; with TransAtlantic Financing Corp., 1954-62, pres., 1958-62, Pan-Atlantic Devel. Corp., N.Y.C., 1955-70; with Marine Transport Lines Inc., 1958-70, sr. v.p., 1964-70; with Am. Steamship Co., Buffalo, 1967-80, chmn. bd., chief exec. officer, 1971-80. Trustee Inst. Advanced Studies World Religions, N.Y., 1970—, chmn. bd., chief exec. officer, 1970-92, pres., 1970-84, 90—; trustee China Inst. in Am., N.Y.C., 1963-90, vice chmn., 1970-79, chmn., 1979-80, mem. exec. com., 1963-84; trustee, v.p. Buddhist Assn. U.S., N.Y.C., 1964—. Mem. Chinese Inst. Engring. Home and Office: 2020 Route 301 Carmel NY 10512-3426 Fax: (845) 225-0447. E-mail: chiatshen@yahoo.com. *To benefit all human beings and to work toward freeing them from fear is my goal. The collective wisdom of all world religions furnishes us the direction and means to achieve that goal. To introduce such wisdom into the daily life of mankind in general and America in particular, is therefore what I devote my energy to.*

SHEN, DINGGANG, computer sciences educator; b. Ningbo, Zhejiang, China, Feb. 6, 1969; s. Guoging Shen and Ruiju Mi; m. Qijun Wang, Apr. 6, 1994; 1 child, Siyuan. BS, Shanghai Jiao Tong U., China, 1990, MS, 1992, PhD, 1995. Rsch. asst. The Hong Kong U. Sci. and Tech., 1994-95; lectr. Shanghai Jiao Tong U., Shanghai, 1995-96; rsch. fellow City U. of Hong Kong, 1996-97, Nanyang Techol. U., Singapore, 1997—. Contbr. articles to profl. jours. Named to Top Ten Youth Scientists, Shang-hai Jiao Tong U., 1994, recipient scholarship, 1993. Mem. Assn. of China Image and Graphics. Avocations: swimming, running, chess, badminton. Home: Jurong West ST 81 640853 Singapore Singapore Office: Nanyang Technol Univ Nanyang Ave 639798 Singapore Singapore

SHEN, GANGSHU, metallurgist; b. Beijing, June 29, 1955; came to U.S., 1987; s. Jiang Shen and Yun Sa; m. Fang Wen, Apr. 8, 1983; children: Lisa, Michael. BE, Beijing U. Aero/Astronautics, 1982; MS in Engring., Ohio State U., 1990, PhD, 1994. Engr. China Precision Engring. Inst., 1982-87; vis. scientist ERC Ohio State U., Columbus, 1987-88, rsch. assoc. ERC, 1988-94, staff engr. ERC, 1994; prin. metall. engr. Ladish Co., Inc., Cudahy, Wis., 1994—. Contbr. articles to profl. jours. Mem. Materials Soc. Avocations: travel, swimming, ice skating, tennis. Office: Ladish Co Inc PO Box 8902 Cudahy WI 53110-8902

SHEN, GENE GIIN-YUAN, organic chemist; b. Taipei, Taiwan, Apr. 12, 1957; came to U.S., 1981; s. Chi and Su-Chin Shen; m. Grace Hsiao-Fen Shen, July 31, 1982; 1 child, Jennifer Iting. BS in Chemistry, Nat. Taiwan U., 1979; PhD in Organic Chemistry, U. Calif., Riverside, 1986; MBA, Calif. State U., Fullerton, 1998. Postdoctoral fellow U. Calif., Riverside, 1986-87; rsch. chemist Nucleic Acid Rsch. Inst. ICN, Costa Mesa, Calif., 1987-88; prin. investigator Pharm-Eco Labs., Inc., Simi Valley, 1988-91; staff scientist Beckman Instruments, Inc., Brea, 1991—. Contbr. articles to Jour. Am. Chem. Soc., Jour. Steroid Biochemistry and Molecular Biology, Tetrahetron Letters, Nucleosides and Nucleotides, others. Mem. Am. Chem. Soc., Phi Beta Kappa. Achievements include research in antisense oligonucleotides, near infrared fluorescent dyes and their applications to fluoroimmuno assay and DNA sequencing, dideoxynucleosides and deoxynucleosides as anti-AIDS drugs, highly sulfated cyclodextrins as chiral drugs separators using capillary electrophoresis, avidin-biotin chemistry, turbidimetric and nephelometric immunoinhibition assay, Vitamin A and Vitamin D analogs as cancer chemopreventive and chemotherapeutic agents, sigmatropic rearrangement of vinyl-allenes. Office: Beckman Instruments Inc 200 S Kraemer Blvd Brea CA 92821-6228

SHEN, HUNG TAO, hydraulic engineering educator; b. Shanghai, China, May 4, 1944; s. Chin Mei and Ai-Yuan (Chen) S.; m. Hayley Hsi, May 26, 1973; children: Scott P., June P. BSCE, Chung Yuan U., Chungli, Taiwan, 1965; ME, Asian Inst. Tech., Bangkok, 1969; PhD in Mechanics and Hydraulics, U. Iowa, 1974. Engring. analyst Sargent & Lundy, Chgo., 1974-76; asst. prof. Clarkson U., Potsdam, N.Y., 1976-81, assoc. prof., 1981-83, prof. civil and environ. engring., 1983—, chair fluid mechanics and thermal sci. program, 1980-88. Monbusyo spl. vis. prof. Min. Edn. Iwate U., Hokkaido River Disaster Prevention Rsch. Ctr., Japan, 1998-99; expert, cons. U.S. Army Cold Regions Rsch. and Engring., Hanover, N.H., 1984—; vis. prof. Lulea (Sweden) U., 1990-91; advisor China Inst. Water Resources and Hydropower Rsch., Beijing, 1994—; chmn. 14th Internat. Ice Symposium. Editor: Frontiers in Hydraulic Engineering, 1983, Ice in Surface Waters, 1998; assoc. editor Jour. Cold Regions Engring. ASCE, 1994-97, editor, 1997—; mem. editorial bd. Jour. Hydraulic Rsch., 1993—; contbr. articles to Jour. Hydraulic Engring., Geophys. Rsch., Hydraulic Rsch., Fluid Mechanics. Bd. dirs. Asian Inst. Tech. Found., N.Y., 1984-90. U.S. Nat. Acad. Sci. vis. scholar, 1991; grantee NSF, U.S. Army Rsch. Office, NOAA, Dept. Transp., World Bank. Mem. ASCE (tech. coms. 1980—, Can.-Am. Civil Engring. Amity award 2000, Harold R. Peyton award 2000), Am. Geophys. Union, Internat. Assn. Hydraulic Rsch. (mem. ice rsch. and engring. com. 1986-94, 98—, chmn. 2000—, chair 14th Internat. Symposium on Ice), Internat. Assn. Great Lakes Rsch. Achievements include development of first comprehensive computer model on river ice, and theories on frazil jam evolution, and dynamic transport and jamming of surface ice in rivers; computer models on oil/chemical spills in rivers. Office: Clarkson U Dept Civil-Environ Engring PO Box 5710 Potsdam NY 13699-0001

SHEN, JEROME TSENG YUNG, retired pediatrician; b. Shanghai, China, Aug. 5, 1918; came to U.S., 1947; s. John G.K. and Agnes (Yao) S.; m. Theresa D.S. Yao, Oct. 10, 1938; children: Jerome L., Elizabeth Burke, Frances Schuman, Li Poppen, Thomas. BS, St. John's U., Shanghai, 1942, MD, 1945; MS in Pediatrics, St. Louis U., 1949. Diplomate Am. Bd. Pediatrics 1951. Instr. dept. pediatrics St. Louis U. Sch. Medicine, 1949-52, sr. instr., 1952-60, asst. clin. prof., 1960-70, assoc. clin. prof., 1970-76, clin. prof., 1976-93, clin. prof. emeritus, 1994—; grad. fellow adolescent medicine Harvard Grad. Sch., Boston, 1958-59. Vis. prof. Nat. Coll. Juvenile Ct. Judges, Reno, Nev., 1973, adj. prof. jud. adminstrn., 1981-82; cons. adolescent medicine St. Louis State Hosp. and Mo. Inst. Psychiatry, St. Louis, 1973-80; head dept. pediatrics St. Louis City Hosp., 1959-63; chief dept. pediatrics and outpatient dept. Scott Field Air Force Hosp., Belleville, Ill., 1956-58; chief dept. pediatrics St. Louis Labor Health Inst., 1967-90; sr. cons. adolescent clinic Cardinal Glennon Children's Hosp., St. Louis, 1977-90; hon. staff Cardinal Glennon Children's Hosp., St. Mary's Health Ctr., St. John's Mercy Health Ctr.; emeritus staff Jewish Hosp. St. Louis, 1993—; chmn., Expert Advisors Medicine and Pub. Health Rep. China (Taiwan), 1978; bd. dirs., mem. exec. com. Children's Lobby, Washington, 1972; mem. planning com. Mo. State Conf. on Crime, Delinquency and System of Justice; mem. adv. com. Mo. Divsn. Family Svcs., 1973-80; pres. Bi-State Interagy. Coun. on Smoking and Health, 1971-74; Mo. del. to White House Conf. on Children and Youth, 1970; mem. Gov. Com. for Children and Youth, chmn. subcom. on health, 1972-81; chmn. Midwest Regional Conf. Smoking and Health, 1972. Author, editor: Clinical Practice of Adolescent Medicine, 1980, Spanish edit., 1983; editorial bd. Postgrad. Medicine, 1977-88; contbr. articles to profl. jours. Coord. Mother Teresa's Gift of Mary Ctr., St. Louis; founder, bd. dirs. past pres. Pro Life Citizens Polit. Action Com., St. Louis, 1986—; chmn. Mo. Task Force on Unwed Adolescent Sexual Activity and Pregnancy, Jefferson City, 1987; hon. mem. Nat. Coun. Juvenile and Family Ct. Judges, Reno, 1982—; bd. dirs. Birthright Counseling, 1965—; Westminster Day Ctr. for the Poor, St. Louis, 1969-72, St. Louis Archdiocesan Pro Life Com., 1974—, co-chmn. 1981-82; bd. dirs.; Mo. and Nat. Drs. for Life, 1980—; mem. Bd. of Health, City of University, 1974-80; bd. dirs. Our Lady's Inn, St. Louis, 1981—; chmn. Midwest Regional Conf. on Smoking and Health, 1972. Maj. USAF, 1956-58. Recipient Cardinal Carberry Pro Life award Archdiocese of St. Louis, 1978, Citation for Outstanding Achievement Senate State of Mo., Jefferson City, 1988, Svc. award St. Louis U. Fellow Am. Acad. Pediat. (now emeritus; liaison rep. to various couns., mem. Nat. Com. on Youth 1970-76, com. on adolescence 1977-80, chmn. Mo. com. on youth 1969-70, co-chmn. youth and sch. com. 1971); charter mem. Soc. Adolescent Medicine (treas. 1973-75, chmn. pvt. practice com. 1969-75, historian 1982-90), Am. Life League, Inc. (Am. bioethics adv. commn. 1997—). Republican. Roman Catholic. Avocations: photography, insects, collection of miniatures, stamps, coins. Home: 7132 Kingsbury Blvd University City MO 63130-4306

SHEN, JIANPING, education educator; b. Shanghai, 1965; came to U.S., 1991; MA, East China Normal U., Shanghai, 1990; PhD, U. Wash., 1995. Tchr. Fengtang Sch. Dist., Shanghai, 1984—86; lectr. East China Normal U., 1988—91; postdoctoral rschr. U. Wash., Seattle, 1995—96; asst. prof. Western Mich. U., Kalamazoo, 1996—99, assoc. prof., 1999—2001, prof., 2001—. Author: The School of Education, 1999; editor: Education and Educational Science, 1997; contbr. over 60 articles to profl. jours. Spencer postdoctoral fellow Nat. Acad. Edn., 1998. Mem. Am. Ednl. Rsch. Assn., Comparative and Internat. Edn. Soc.

SHEN, JOHN JIANYUE, fuel cell company executive; b. Shanghai, Sept. 21, 1960; arrived in Can., 1988; s. P.Z. and Qiaozin (Xie) S. BS, ECUST, Shanghai, 1982; MS, SRICI, Shanghai, 1985; PhD, Laval U., Que., Can., 1992. Registered profl. engr., Can. Engr. SRICI, 1985-88; vis. rschr. NIMCR, Japan, 1993; rschr. Simon Fraser U., Vancouver, B.C., Can., 1993; v.p. Palcan Envirotech Ltd., 1994-95; chief engr. Nexcel Power Sys. Corp., Richmond, B.C., Can., 1995-98; founder, pres. Palcan Fuel Cell Co. Ltd., Burnaby, Can., 1998—. Patentee in applied surface sci., applied spectroscopy, others. Mem. AIChE, Am. Chem. Soc., Internat. Ziolite Assn. Christian. Avocations: hockey, fishing, pop music. Office: Palcan Fuel Cell Co Ltd 8624 Commerce Ct Burnaby BC Canada V5A 4N6 E-mail: jshen55089@aol.com.

SHEN, MASON MING-SUN, medical center administrator; b. Shanghai, China, Mar. 30, 1945; came to U.S., 1969; s. John Kaung-Hao and Mai-Chu (Sun) S.; m. Nancy Hsia-Hsian Shieh, Aug. 7, 1976; children: Teresa Tao-Yee, Darren Tao-Ru. BS in Chemistry, Taiwan Normal U., 1963-67; MS in Chemistry, S.D. State U., 1971; PhD in Biochemistry, Cornell U., 1977; postgrad., U. Calif., Berkeley, 1977-79, Lawrence Livermore Nat. Lab., 1979-80; MS in Chinese Medicine, China Acad., Taipei, Taiwan, 1982; OMD, San Francisco Coll Acupuncture, 1984; D Acupuncture Medicine (hon.), Asian Am. Acupuncture Coll., San Diego, 1985; MD (Medicina Alternativa), Internat. U., Colombo, Sri Lanka, 1988. Diplomate Nat. Commn. for Cert. of Acupuncturists; lic. acupuncturist, clin. chemist technologist, Calif. Rsch. assoc. Lawrence Livermore (Calif.) Lab., 1979-80; assoc. prof. Nat. Def. Med. Coll., Taipei, 1980-82; prof. Inst. of Chinese Medicine China Acad., 1981-82, San Francisco Coll. Acupuncture, 1983-85, Acad. Chinese Culture and Health Scis., Oakland, Calif., 1985-86, U. No. Calif., 2001—. Pres. Florescent Inst. Traditional Chinese Medicine, Oakland, Calif., 1995—2001; adminstr. Am. Ea. Med. Inst., Pleasanton, Calif., 1993—, chmn. adminstrn. subcom., 1991—92; acupuncture com. State of Calif., 1988—92; chief acupuncturist Acupuncture Ctr. Pleasanton, 1993—2000, Acupuncture Ctr. Tracy, 1995—98, Ea. Med. Ctr. Danville, Calif., 1996—99; v.p. Modern Medicine, Hayward, Calif., 1997—98, U. Health Sci., Honolulu, 1997—99; adminstrv. officer Rsch. Inst. Chinese Medicine, San Francisco, 1998—; chief acupuncturist Ea. Med. Ctr. Pleasanton, Calif., 2000—; bd. dir. Am. Inst. Acupuncture Orthopedics & Traumatology, San Francisco. Contbr. over 50 articles to profl. jours. Mem. Danville Rep. Com., 1988-93; bd. dirs. Asian Rep. Assembly, 1989-98; mem. presdnl. adv. com. Republican Presdl. Task Force, 1992-99; mem. chmn's. adv. bd. Republican Nat. Com., 1993—; pres. Internat. Congress Chinese Medicine, Calif., 1987—. Recipient Nat. Rsch. Svc. award NIH, 1977, Presdl. Order of Merit, Pres. of the U.S., 1991. Mem.: AAAOM (pres. 1988—89), Ea. Med. Assn. (pres. 2002—), United Calif. Practioners Chinese Medicine (bd. dir. 1995—98, dep. supr. 1998—2001, hon. cons. 2001—), Internat. Congress Chinese Medicine (pres. 1997—), Presdl. Round Table (presdl. adv. com.), Am. Assn. Traditional Chinese Medicine (exec. dir. 1997—), Nat. Acupuncture Detoxification Assn. (cons. 1987—), Am. Assn. Acupuncture & Oriental Medicine (bd. dir. 1987—92, pres. 1989—90, Acupuncturist of Yr. 1998), Am. Acupuncture Assn. (bd. dir. 1986—90, v.p. 1987—89), Calif. Cert. Acupuncturists Assn. (pres. 1985—86, mem. polit. action com. 1995—, supr. 1999—), NY Acad. Sci. (bd. dir. 1984—93), Hong Kong & Kowloon Chinese Med. Assn. (hon.; life pres. 1985). Republican. Avocations: travel, horse back riding. Home: 3240 Touriga Dr Pleasanton CA 94566-6966 Office: Eastern Med Ctr 3510 Old Santa Rita Rd Ste D Pleasanton CA 94588-3466 Fax: 925-847-4180. E-mail: masonmshen@yahoo.com.

SHEN, MICHAEL, lawyer; b. Nanking, Jiangsu, Peoples Republic of China, Aug. 15, 1948; came to U.S., 1951; s. James Cheng Yee and Grace (Pai) S.; m. Marina Manese (div.); m. Pamela Nan Bradford, Aug. 12, 1983; 1 child, Jessica Li. BA, U. Chgo., 1969; MA, U. Pa., 1970; JD, Rutgers U., 1979. Bar: U.S. Dist. Ct. N.J. 1979, N.Y. 1980, U.S. Dist. Ct. (so., no. and ea. dists.) N.Y. 1980, N.J. 1981, U.S. Ct. Appeals (2d cir.) 1987, U.S. Supreme Ct. 1988, U.S.

Ct. Appeals (3rd cir.) 1996. Staff atty. Bedford Stuyvesant Legal Svcs., Bklyn., 1979-80, Com. for Interns and Residents, N.Y.C., 1980-81; ptnr. Shneyer & Shen, P.C., N.Y.C. 1981—. Pres. bd. dirs. Asian Am. Legal Def. and Edn. Fund, N.Y.C.; of counsel 318 Restaurant Workers Union, N.Y.C., 1984—. Bd. dirs. Nat. Asian Pacific Am. Legal Consortium, N.Y.C., Nat. Employment Law Project; past bd. dirs. N.Y. Civil Liberties Union, N.Y.C., 1987-98. Mem. Internat. Platform Assn., Nat. Employees Lawyers Assn., N.Y. State Bar Assn., N.Y. County Bar Assn., Nat. Lawyers Guild. Avocations: arts, reading. Office: Shneyer & Shen PC 2109 Broadway Ste 206 New York NY 10023-2106 also: 1085 Cambridge Rd Teaneck NJ 07666-1901 E-mail: shenlaw@compuserve.com.

SHEN, SIN-YAN, physicist, conductor, acoustics specialist, music director; b. Singapore, Nov. 12, 1949; came to the U.S., 1969, naturalized, 1984; s. Shao-Quan and Tien-Siu (Chen) S.; m. Yuan-Yuan Lee, Aug. 4, 1973; children: Jia, Jian. BSc, U. Singapore, 1969; MS, Ohio State U., 1970, PhD, 1973. Concert recitalist on Erhu Chinese fiddle, 1963—; instr. math. U. Singapore, 1969; asst. prof. physics Northwestern U., Evanston, Ill., 1974-77, assoc. prof., 1977-81; faculty assoc. Argonne (Ill.) Nat. Lab., 1974-77, scientist, 1977-83, sr. rsch. leader, 1983—. Dir. rsch. Divsn. Natural Resource Mgmt., SUPCON Internat., 1988—; prof. Harvard U., 1989—; meeting series reviewer NSF, Washington, 1981—; coord. Tech. Rev., Argonne, Atlanta, Phoenix, Portland, Oreg., 1983—; dir. Global Warming Internat. Ctr., 1991—, chmn. Internat. Conf. Chgo., 1990-93, San Francisco, 1994-95, Vienna, 1996, Columbia U., N.Y.C., 1997, Hong Kong U. Sci. and Tech., 1998, Yamanashi Inst. Environ. Scis., 1999, Harvard U., 2000, Cambridge U., 2001; Chinese Music Internat. Conf., 1991, 94; advisor Internat. Energy Agy., 1986—, Gas Rsch. Inst., 1984—, SUPCON Internat., 1986—, Nat. Geog., 1986—, Intenrat. Boreal Forest Rsch. Assn., 1991—, Electric Power Rsch. Inst., 1992—, UN Devel. PRogram, 1993—, World Bank, 1994—, U.S. Dept. Energy and U.S. EPA, 1995—; prof. Chinese Acad. Forestry, 1986—; mem. panel on biol. diversity Nat. Acad. Scis., Smithsonian Instn., 1986; chmn. internat. program com. Austrian Acad. Scis., 1995-96, Columbia U., 1996-97, Japan Environ. Agy., 1998-99, Intergovt. Panel on Climate Change, 1999—; music dir. Orch. of Chinese Music Soc. N.Am., 1976—, The Silk & Bamboo Ensemble, 1981—; adv. Ctrl. Traditional Orch., 1984—; del. leader, UN Conf. Environ. and Devel., Rio, 1992; del. chmn. Third All China Arts Festival, Kunmin, 1992; panelist Nat. Endowment for Arts, 1981—, New Eng. Found. for Arts, 1987—, Arts Midwest, 1985—, Ill. Arts Coun., 1982—, Chgo. City Arts, 1990—, Ill. Art's Alliance Found., adv. coun., 1992—, bd. dirs., 1988—, mem. adv. coun. Mid-Am. Arts Alliance, 1992—; tech. adv. Shanghai Nat. Musical Instrument Co., 1985—; adv. West Lake Qin Soc., Hangzhou, China, 1991—. Author: Superfluidity, 1982, Acoustics of Ancient Chinese Bells, 1987, Chinese Music and Orchestration: A Primer om Principles and Practice, 1991, Global Warming Science and Policy, 1992, The Boreal Forests and Global Change, 1993, Global Warming Eludidated, 1994, Chinese Musical Instruments, 1999, Global Warming and Public Health, 1999, China: A Journey through Its Musical Art, 1999, Chinese Music in the 20th Century, 2001; editor-in-chief Chinese Music Internat. Jour., 1978—; mem. internat. editl. bd. World Resource Rev., 1989—, Internat. Boreal Forest Rsch., 1992—, Ency. of Life Support Sys., 1994—; adv. Ency. Brit., 1983—; contbr. over 300 articles to profl. jours.; patentee molten liquids, 1974, 80. Recipient Mich. Heritage award, 1992; Fulbright scholar U.S. State Dept., 1969; merit scholar Govt. Singapore, 1967; named Artistic Treasure Gov. Jim Edgar of Ill., 1998. Mem. AAAS, Am. Phys. Soc., Ops. Rsch. Soc. Am., Acoustical Soc. Am., Chinese Music Soc. N.Am. Achievements include current work on renewable energy and materials techs.; global change and global warming; extreme event index; indsl. sonic techs.; energy policy, planning and economics; acoustics; cultural acoustics. Office: Chinese Music Soc N Am 2329 Charmingfare Dr Downers Grove IL 60517-2910 also: SUPCON Internat PO Box 5275 Woodridge IL 60517-0275

SHEN, THOMAS TO, environmental engineer; b. Chia-Shing, Chekiang, China, Aug. 14, 1926; m. Cynthia Shen; children: Grace, Joyce. BS in Civil Engring., St. John's U., Shanghai, China, 1948; MS in Sanitary Engring., Northwestern U., 1960; PhD in Environ. Engring., Rensselaer Poly. Inst., 1971. Registered profl. engr., Wash., N.Y. Assoc. engr. Boeing Co., Renton, Wash., 1961-63; sanitary engr. Wash. State Health Dept., Seattle, 1963-66; sr. sanitary engr. N.Y. State Health Dept., Albany, 1966-70; sr. rsch. scientist N.Y. State Dept. Environ. Conservation, 1970-93. Adj. prof. Columbia U., N.Y.C., 1981-93; mem. U.S. EPA Sci. Adv. Bd., 1987-90; cons. UN's Environ. Protection Program, various Asian cities, 1983—; lectr. various U.S. and fgn. univs., 1978—; cons. World Bank, 1990; tech. reviewer Annual Pres. Bush's Environ. and Conservation Challenge awards, 1991, 92. Author: Air Pollution and Its Control, 1985, Hazardous Waste Incineration, 1982, Assessment and Control of VOC Emissions from Waste Treatment and Disposal Facilities, 1993, Industrial Pollution Prevention, 1995, 2d edit., 1999; author: (with others) Electrostatic Precipitator, 1979, Air Quality Assessment, 1989; contbr. articles to profl. jours. Bd. dirs. Internat. Ctr. of the Capital Region, Albany, 1984-88, Am. Bur. Med. Advancement ot China, N.Y.C., 1985—. Recipient Svc. award Phi Tau Phi, 1986, Nat. award Indsl. Wast. Minimization Taiwan Environ. Protection Adminstrn., Ministry Fgn. Affairs, 1993, Man of Yr. award N.Y. State Capital Region Chinese Am. Alliance, 1995; Named for Outstanding Editorial Contbn. on Pollution Engring., Chgo., 1978, 81. Fellow ASCE (chmn. N.Y. State Coun. 1979-80); mem. Am. Acad. Environ. Engrs. (diplomate 1973), Air and Waste Mgmt. Assn. (com. chmn. 1985—, Frank Chamber award for Outstanding Achievement in Sci. of Air 1993), Delmar Club (pres. 1979-80), Rotary. Avocations: travel, music appreciation. Home: 146 Fernbank Ave Delmar NY 12054-4215

SHEN, TIANSHENG, research scientist; b. Mizhi, Shaanxi, People's Republic of China, Mar. 3, 1965; d. Changzhong Shen and Shaoping Ye; m. Shaogang Lu, Feb. 10, 1988; 1 child, Yunhe Lu. MD, Xi'an Med. U., People's Republic of China, 1985, MS, 1988; PhD in molecular and cellular pharmacology, U. Pierre and Marie Curie (Paris VI), 1997. MS candidate Xi'an Med. U., People's Republic of China, 1985-88, rsch. assoc. Rsch. Lab. Keshan Disease People's Republic of China, 1988-93; trainee French lang. Beijing Foreign Lang. U., 1993-94; PhD candidate, INSERM U-99 Henri Mondor Hosp., France, 1994-97; postdoctoral rschr. Lankenau Med. Rsch. Ctr., Pa., 1997-98; postdoctoral rschr. dept. oral biology Ohio State U., 1998—. Contbr. numerous articles to profl. jours. Xi'an Med. U. fellow, 1985-88, Chinese Nat. Edn. Com. fellow, 1994-97. Mem. AchemS Assn. Chemoreception Scis., Sigma Xi. Home: 690 Riverview Dr Apt 104 Columbus OH 43202-3240 Office: Ohio State U PO Box 182357 305 W 12th Ave Columbus OH 43218 E-mail: tianshengs@hotmail.com.

SHEN, TSUNG YING, medicinal chemistry educator; b. Beijing, China, Sept. 28, 1924; came to U.S., 1950; s. Tsu-Wei and Sien-Wha (Nieu) S.; m. Amy T.C. Lin, June 20, 1953; children: Bernard, Hubert, Theodore, Leonard, Evelyn, Andrea. B.Sc., Nat. Ctrl. U., Chongqing, China, 1946; diploma, Imperial Coll. Sci. and Tech., London, 1948; PhD, U. Manchester, Eng., 1950, D.Sc., 1978. Research assoc. Ohio State U., Columbus, 1950-52, MIT, Cambridge, 1952-56; sr. research chemist Merck, Sharp & Dohme Research Labs., Rahway, N.J., 1956-65, dir. synthetic chem. research, 1966-76, v.p. membrane chem. research, 1976-77, v.p. membrane and arthritis research, 1977-86; A. Burger prof. medicinal chemistry U. Va., Charlottesville, 1986-96, emeritus and rsch. prof., 1996—. Vis. prof. U. Calif., Riverside, 1973, U. Calif., San Francisco, 1985, Harvard Med. Sch., 1986; adj. prof. Stevens Inst. Tech., Hoboken, N.J., 1982-85; hon. prof. Beijing Med. U., Chinese Acad. Med. Sci., Inst. Material Medica, China Pharm. U.; mem. sci. bd. CytoMed, 1989-96, T Cell Sci, 1988-93, Gene Labs., 1989-94, Osteo Arthritis Sci, 1993-95, Argonex, 1994-98. Mem. editl. bd. Clinica Europa Jour., 1977, Prostaglandins and Medicine, 1978, Medicinal Rsch. Revs., 1979-94, Jour. Medicinal Chemistry, 1980-83, Medicinal Chem. Rsch., 1991; patentee in field. Recipient Outstanding Patent award N.J. Research and Devel. Council, 1975, Rene Descartes medal U. Paris, 1977, medal of Merit Giornate Mediche Internazionali del Collegium Biologicum Europea, 1977, cert. of merit Spanish Soc. Therapeutic Chemistry, 1983, achievement award Chinese Inst. Engrs.-U.S.A., 1984. Mem. AAAS, Am. Chem. Soc. (1st Alfred Burger award in medicinal chemistry 1980), N.Y. Acad. Scis., Acad. Pharm. Assn. (hon.), Chinese Am. Chem. Soc. (bd. dirs. 1995-97). Home: 10013 Park Royal Dr Great Falls VA 22066-1847 Office: U Va Dept Chem Charlottesville VA 22901

SHEN, VIRGINIA SHIANG-LAN, Spanish and Chinese language educator; b. Kaosiung, Taiwan, July 30, 1955; d. Mu-hsing and Ah-hsin (Huang) Li; m. Eric Yao-chu Shen, May 15, 1983; children: Andrew David, Alan Michael. BA in Spanish, Fu-Jen Cath. U., 1977; MA in Latin Am. Lit., Inst. Caro y Cuervo, 1983; PhD in Spanish, Ariz. State U., 1988. Instr. Wen Tzao Jr. Coll., Kaosiung, 1982-83; tchg. assoc. Ariz. State U., Tempe, 1983-87; asst. prof. N.Mex. State U., Las Cruces, 1987-88, La. State U., Shreveport, 1988-91, Chgo. State U., 1991-94, assoc. prof., 1994-99, prof., 1999—. Author: Encyclopedia of World Literature in the Twentieth Century, 3rd. edit., 1999, El Teatro Español del siglo XX y su contexto, 1994, Critical Perspectives of the Works of Enrique Jaramillo-Levi, 1996, Literatura y Cultura, 2000, Literatura y cultura Narrativa Colombiana del siglo XX, 2000; contbr. articles. Mem. Am. Assn. Tchrs. Spanish and Portuguese, Am. Coun. on Tchg. of Fgn. Langs., Ill. Coun. Tchg. of Fgn. Langs. Office: Chgo State U 9501 S King Dr Chicago IL 60628-1598 E-mail: vs-shen@csu.edu.

SHEN, XIAOHUI, application developer, researcher; s. Decheng Shen and Youfen Liang; married. MS, Tsinghua U., Beijing, 1994; PhD, Northwestern U., 2001. Rsch. asst. Northwestern U., Evanston, Ill., 1997—2001; sr. software engr. Motorola Inc., Libertyville, 2001—. Program com. mem., session chair numerous internat. confs. Contbr. articles to profl. jours. Recipient Guanghua prize, Guanghua Edn. Found., 1990. Mem.: IEEE (sr.). Home: 15 S Bristol Ct Mundelein IL 60060 Office: Motorola Inc 1000 Technology Way Libertyville IL Home Fax: 847-523-2854; Office Fax: 847-523-2854. Personal E-mail: shen_xh@yahoo.com. Business E-Mail: axs095@email.mot.com.

SHEN, XIAOPING, mathematician, educator; d. Jianhua Shen and Yaqin Wang. PhD, U. Wis., Milw. From asst. prof. to assoc. prof. Ea. Conn. State U., Willimantic, 1999—2000; asst. prof. Ohio U., Athens, 2001—. Vis. prof. Narasuan U., Thailand, 1999—. Author: (book) Wavelets and Other Orthogonal Systems, 2d edit., 2001; translator: Spectral Approximations of Linear of Operators, 1987. Fellow ONR/VIGRE, U. Calif., Davis, 2001—. Mem.: Am. Math. Soc. Office: U Calif Davis One Sheilds Ave Davis CA 95616 E-mail: xashen@math.ucdaiv.edu.

SHEN, YING, chemist, educator; b. Changshu, Jiangsu Province, China, Sept. 14, 1924; d. Tung Wu Shen and Yun Quei. BS in Chemistry, Tsing Hua U., Peking, China, 1947; MA in Sci., Peabody Coll., 1959; MS in Chemistry, Ohio State U., 1972; postgrad., Standford U., 1963, U. Okla., 1980—. Tchr., Taipei, Puli, Taiwan, 1947—60; asst. to UNESCO expert UNESCO, Taipei, 1960—62; grad. tchg. asst./assoc. Ohio State U.; lectr. Cen. State U., Edmonds, Okla., 1978—79; lab. scientist/chemist Okla. Dept. Environ. Quality, Oklahoma City, 1980—. Seminar lectr. Beijing Meteorol. Coll., 1999. Sec. Chinese Assn. Greater Oklahoma City, 1982—83. Scholar, Internat. Coop. Adminstrn., 1958—59, Fulbright schol, U.S Dept. State, 1962, Ford Found. scholar, Ford Found./Stanford U., 1963. Mem.: Asia Assn. Okla., Pi Lambda Theta. D-Liberal. Avocations: music, sports, reading. Home: Apt 40 6616 Lyrewood Ln Oklahoma City OK 73132 Office: Okla Dept of Environ Quality 707 N Robinson Oklahoma City OK 73102 Office Fax: 405-702-1111. Personal E-mail: yshen10346@aol.com. Business E-Mail: yshen10346@aol.com.

SHEN, YUEN-RON, physics educator; b. Shanghai, China, Mar. 25, 1935; came to U.S. BS, Nat. Taiwan U., 1956; MS, Stanford U., 1959; PhD, Harvard U., 1963; DSc (hon.), Hong Kong U. Sci. and Tech., 1997, Nat. Chiao-Tung U., Taiwan, 1998. Rsch. asst. Hewlett-Packard Co., Palo Alto, Calif., 1959; rsch. fellow Harvard U., Cambridge, Mass., 1963-64; asst. prof. U. Calif., Berkeley, 1964-67, assoc. prof., 1967-70, prof., 1970—, chancellor's prof., 1997-2000. Prin. investigator Lawrence Berkeley Nat. Lab., 1967—. Author: The Principles of Nonlinear Optics, 1984. Recipient Charles Hard Townes award Am. Phys. Soc., 1986, Arthur L. Schawlow prize Am. Phys. Soc., 1992, DOE Alexander von Humboldt award, 1984, DOE Outstanding Rsch. award DOE-MRS Rsch., 1983, DOE Sustained Outstanding Rsch. award, 1987, Max Planck Rsch. award, 1996, Materials Sci. award Solid State Physics, 1997; Sloan fellow, 1966-68, Guggenheim Found. fellow, 1972-73. Fellow Am. Phys. Soc. (disting. traveling lectr. Laser Sci. Topical Group 1994-96, Frank Isakson prize 1998), Photonics Soc. Chinese-Ams., Optical Soc. Am.; mem. AAAS, NAS, Acad. Sinica, Chinese Acad. Scis. (fgn.). Achievements include research in nonlinear optics and condensed matter physics. Office: U Calif Berkeley Dept Physics Berkeley CA 94720-0001

SHEN, YU-MIN, molecular biologist; b. Shanghai, Peoples Republic of China, Sept. 4, 1939; s. Wei-Ji Shen and Wan-Jin Liu; m. Zhi-An Yuan; 1 child, Ying Shen. BS, Nanjing (China) U., 1962; PhD, Acad. Sinica, Inst. Biophysics, Beijing, 1966. Rsch. asst. prof. Acad. Sinica Inst. Biophysics, Beijing, 1966-80, sr. rsch. asst. prof., 1984-87; vis. scholar dept. pathology Temple U., Phila., 1980-83, rsch. assoc. dept. microbiology, thrombosis rsch. ctr., 1988-91; sr. rsch. investigator dept. pharmacology U. Pa., 1991—. Contbr. articles to sci. and profl. jours. Office: U Pa Dept Pharmacology 135 John Morgan Bldg Philadelphia PA 19104 E-mail: yumin@spirit.gcrc.upenn.edu.

SHENDRIKAR, ARUN DHONDOPANT, environmental scientist, chemist; s. Dhondopant Datatrya and Vachala Bai Narayan Rao Shendrikar; m. Rajani Arun Boramanikar, Dec. 26, 1945; children: Rita Karaoguz, Atul. PhD, Durham U., England, 1966. Sr. chemist Rsch. Triangle Inst., Rsch. Triangle Pk., NC, 1980—82; inorganics mgr. Compuchem Lab., 1982—86; gen. mgr. Beta Laboratories, Durham, England, 1986—88; mgr. analytical svc. EIRA, Inc., Saint Rose, England, 1988—89; dir. of environ. affairs Litho Industries, Raleigh, NC, 1989—93; chemist N.C. Divsn. of Air Quality, 1997—. Cons. N.C. State U., Raleigh, 1984—86, Sumitomo, Rsch. Triangle Pk., 1995—96. Contbr. chapters to books. Bd. of dir. Hindu Soc. of N.C., Morrisville, NC, 1981—82; mem. Colo. air pollution bd. Gov. Colo. Recipient Excellence in Waste Mgmt. & Pollution Abatement award, N.C. Gov., 1993. Mem.: Am. Chem. Soc. (none). Home: 1011 West Saint Helena Place Apex NC 27502

SHENEFELT, ARTHUR B. transportation executive, consultant; b. Boston, May 5, 1920; s. Arthur Merle and Martha Marion (Baird) S.; m. Gloria Mae Willis, Apr. 28, 1948; 1 child, Michael Baird. BA, Miami U., Oxford, Ohio, 1942; student, Garrett Theol. Sem., Evanston, Ill., 1942-44, Columbia U., 1946-47. Dir. pub. rels. Brotherhood of Locomotive Engrs., Cleve., 1951-56; dir. press rels. N.Y. Ctrl. R.R., N.Y.C., 1956-57; transp. editor Jour. of Commerce, 1957-59; asst. tp pres. for pub. affairs Freight Forwrders Inst., Washington, 1959-71; dir. comms. N.Y. State Trucking Assn., N.Y.C., 1960-61, Trucking Employers Inc., Washington, 1970-71; press sec. to chmn. U.S. Senate Transp. Com., 1971-73; personal transp. adviser to Gov. of Pa., Harrisburg, 1973-77. Cons. Fed. Appalachian Regional Commn., Harrisburg and Washington, 1977-79, Japanese Nat. Ry., N.Y.C. and Tokyo, 1980-85; chmn. Bucks HUB Conf., Bristol, Pa., 1985—; chmn. Super Mag. Coalition, Washington, 1988—; chmn. Amtrak for Profit Coalition, Washington, 1995-97; pres. Interstate Maglev Inc., Bristol, 1992—; dir., chmn. Office of Transp. Tech., Strategy and Planning, 1998—. Contbr. articles, stories and features to most maj. Am. newspapers and trade jours. Lt. (j.g.) USN, 1944-46, PTO. Avocation: music. Office: Bucks HUB Conf 1200 New Rodgers Rd Bristol PA 19007-2525 E-mail: shenefelt@surface.transportation.com.

SHENEFELT, PHILIP DAVID, dermatologist; b. Colfax, Wash., July 31, 1943; s. Roy David and Florence Vanita (Cagle) S.; m. Debrah A. Levenson; children: Elizabeth, Sara, Shaina. BS with honors, U. Wis. Madison, 1966, MD, 1970, MS in Adminstrv. Medicine, 1984. Intern U.S. Naval Hosp., Bethesda, Md., 1970-71; gen. practice Oreg. (Wis.) Clinic, 1975; resident in dermatology U. Wis. Hosp., Madison, 1975-78, mem. staff, 1978-87; asst. prof. dermatology sect. Dept. Internal Medicine U. South Fla., Tampa, 1987-97, assoc. prof., 1997—. Chief dermatology sect. VA Hosp., Bay Pines, Fla., 1987-89, asst. chief, Tampa, 1988-2002, chief, 2002—; dermatologist Univ. Health Svc., U. Wis.-Madison, 1978-87, VA Hosp., Madison, 1982-85. Served to lt. comdr. USN, 1969-74; capt. USNR (ret.). Kellogg fellow, 1980-82. Mem. AMA, Am. Acad. Dermatology, Fla. Dermatol. Soc., Fla. West Coast Dermatol. Soc., Am. Coll. Physician Execs., Am. Soc. Clin. Hypnosis. Home: 15919 Notting Hill Dr Lutz FL 33548-6147 Office: U South Fla Internal Medicine/Dermatol 12901 Bruce Downs Blvd #79 Tampa FL 33612-4742 E-mail: pshenefe@hsc.usf.edu.

SHENG, GANG (GANG CHEN), engineer, scientist; b. Wuhan, Hubei, China, Mar. 26, 1963; arrived in Singapore, 1993; s. Yukuen and Yilan (Chen) Zhang; m. Linda Juan Zhang, May, 1989; 1 child, Hanlu Chen. B of Engring., Shanghai Jiao Tong U., 1984, M of Engring., 1987; PhD, Nanyang Tech. U., Singapore, 1997. Asst. prof., lectr. Huazhong U. Sci. and Tech., Hubei, China, 1987-92; engr. Magnetic Tech. Ctr., Singapore, 1996; sr. engr. Data Storage Inst., Singapore, 1997-98, prin. engr. Singapore, 1999-2000; leader HDI group Singapore Rsch. Lab. Sony Electronics, 2000—01; adv. engr. and scientist storage tech. divsn. IBM, San Jose, Calif., 2001—. Author: Dynamic Modeling of Mechanical Systems, 1991, Mechanical Vibration Systems, Vol. I and II, 1992 (award Nat. Ednl. Coun. 1994); contbr. articles to profl. jours. Grad. scholar Nanyang Tech. U., Singapore, 1993-96. Mem. ASME, IEEE. Achievements include patents in field. Avocations: Qigong, tennis. Home: 272 Palm Valley Blvd #207 San Jose CA 95123 Office: STD IBM 5600 Cottle Rd N76A/050 San Jose CA 95193 Fax: 408-256-2410. E-mail: shenggc@yahoo.com., gschen@us.ibm.com.

SHENG, QIN, mathematics educator; b. Suzhou, Jiangsu, China, Nov. 22, 1956; s. Ren Sheng and Shang Hui Hu; m. Sheng Lun Huang, Nov. 9, 1990; children: Andrew De Kai, Daniel De Yuan. BS, Nanjing (China) U., 1982, MS, 1984; PhD, U. Cambridge, Eng., 1990. Lectr. in math. Suzhou (China) U., 1984-85; asst. prof. math. Nat. U. Singapore, 1990—. Numerical cons. U. Ariz., Tucson, 1987-88. Recipient ORS award U.K. Ministry of Edn., 1986, 87, 88, J.T. Knight prize Cambridge U., 1987; Schlumberger scholar, 1986, 87, 88, King's Coll. scholar, 1987-88. Mem. Am. Math. Soc., Soc. for Indsl. and Applied Math., Internat. Fedn. Nonlinear Analysts, S.E. Asian Math. Soc., Singapore Math. Soc., Cambridge Philos. Soc. Avocations: music, paintings, sight-seeing, mountain walks. Office: Nat U Singapore Dept Math Kent Ridge Crescent Singapore 0511 Singapore

SHENG, QUAN, chemist; b. Changzhou, China, Nov. 7, 1947; came to U.S., 1997; s. Benyu Sheng and Yuru Lu; m. Chimin Jiang, Oct. 28, 1982; 1 child, Yiqing. BSc, Nanjing U., Nanjing, China, 1982, MSc in Polymer Chemistry, 1985; MSc, Laurentian U., Sudbury, Ont., Canada, 1992; PhD in Polymer Chemistry, McMaster U., Hamilton, Ont., Canada, 1997. Technician Jiangsu Jintan Pharm. Factory, Jintan, China, 1973-78; lectr., vice dir. Polymer Chemistry Inst. Dept. Chemistry Nanjing (China) U., 1985-91; rsch. chemist postdoctoral fellow Nat. Ctr. for Agrl. Utilization Rsch. USDA, Peoria, Ill., 1997-98; chemist OMG Ams., Research Triangle Park, N.C., 1998—. Vice dir. Polymer Chemistry Inst. Nanjing U., China, 1985-91. Contbr. articles to profl. jours.; solder paste trade secrets and patents. Coord. Canada-China Friendship Assn., Hamilton, Ont., Canada, 1995-97. Mem. Am. Chem. Soc. Achievements include selective functionalizations of polymers, developments of anti-corrosive coating, no-clean solder paste, water-soluble solder paste, and lead free solder paste. Avocations: Chinese finger calligraphy, play table tennis, travel, reading. Home: 807 Bristol Blue St Apex NC 27502 Office: OMG Ams 2601 Weck Dr Research Triangle Park NC 27709

SHENG, YEA-YI PETER, oceanographic engineer, educator, researcher; b. Shanghai, Republic China, Aug. 3, 1946; came to U.S., 1969; s. Ting and Yu-Sen (Yuan) S.; m. Ruth Chou, Aug. 31, 1970; 1 child, David. BSME, Nat. Taiwan U., Taipei, 1968; MS, Case Western Res. U., 1972, PhD, 1975. Research assoc., then sr. research assoc. Case Western Res. U., Cleve., 1975-78; assoc. cons. Aero. Research Assocs. Princeton, N.J., 1978-80, cons., 1980-84, sr. cons., 1984-86, mgr. coastal oceanography, 1985-86; assoc. prof. engring. U. Fla., Gainesville, 1986-88, prof., 1988—. Mem. Marine Resources Council, Melbourne, Fla., 1987—; invited prof. Inst. de Mecanique Grenoble, France, 1987; vis. prof. U. Western Australia, 1992-93. Grantee numerous govt. agys. and industries, 1979—. Mem. Am. Geophys. Union, ASCE, ASME, Am. Soc. Engring. Edn. Lutheran. Avocations: tennis, music. Office: U Fla Dept Coastal & Oceanographic Engring 345 Weil Hall Gainesville FL 32611-6580 E-mail: pete@coastal.ufl.edu.

SHENG, YIHUA PHILIP, information scientist, computer scientist; m. Qin Li, June 20, 1998. Student, So. Ill. U., 2000—. Cert. sys. engr., Microsoft, 1995. V.p. for tech. Shanghai TianFang Computer Tech. Ltd., Shanghai, 1995—98; computer info. specialist Computer Sci. Dept., So. Ill. U., Carbondale, Ill., 2000—. Dir. networking and image processing group computer sci. dept. Shanghai Tchr. U., Shanghai, 1995—98. Author: (book) The Networking and Multimedia Technology of Windows 95, 1996, Exercise Book of Computer Application, 1997, Computer Application Tools, 1998. Mem.: INFORMS. Office: Department of Computer Science Southern Illinois University Carbondale IL 62901

SHENK, GEORGE H. lawyer; b. N.Y.C., Sept. 10, 1943; BA, Princeton U., 1965; M in Internat. Affairs, Columbia U., 1967; JD, Yale U., 1970. Bar: N.Y. 1971, Calif. 1985. Assoc. Coudert Bros., Paris, 1970, N.Y.C., 1970-73, Hong Kong, 1973-75, Tokyo, 1975-78, ptnr. N.Y.C., 1978-91, San Francisco, 1991-94, Heller Ehrman, White & McAuliffe, 1994—. Exec. dir. San Francisco Com. on Fgn. Rels. Contbr. articles to publs. Mem. Bar Assn. City of N.Y., Calif. State Bar Assn., Coun. Fgn. Rels., Pacific Coun. on Internat. Policy. Office: Heller Ehrman White & McAuliffe 333 Bush St San Francisco CA 94104-2806

SHENK, LOIS ELAINE, writer; b. Ephrata, Pa., May 30, 1944; d. Raymond Earle and Esther May (Forry) L.; m. John Barge Shenk, June 12, 1965; children: Philip Jon, Matthew Alan. BA in English, Eastern Mennonite Coll., 1966; MSc in Edn., Temple U., 1984. English mistress Githumu Secondary Sch., Thika, Kenya, 1966-68; English tchr. Kraybill's Jr. High, Mount Joy, Pa., 1976-77; freelance writer, 1978—; religious news corr. Gospel Herald, Scottdale, Pa., 1978-82. Observer, corr. The U.S. Senate, Washington, 1987—. Author: Out of Mighty Waters, 1982 (R.I.M. excellence award 1983), The Story of Ephrata Mennonite School, 1996; (one act play) A House for David in (anthology) Swords into Plowshares, 1983; (study guide for Christian edn.) Hebrews, 1988; contbr. poems, stories & features to jours.; editl. work Mennonite Ctrl. Com., Akron, Pa., 1977. Cmty. living advisor Friendship Cmty., Lititz, Pa., 1997-99; Sunday sch. tchr. Ephrata (Pa.) Mennonite Ch., 1997-99. Recipient Rep. Senatorial Medal of Honor, many other honors and awards. Avocations: reading, swimming, cooking, music, public service. Home and Office: 301 E Church St Stevens PA 17578-9456

SHENK, WILLIS WEIDMAN, newspaper executive; b. Manheim, Pa., Nov. 2, 1915; s. John Horst and Amanda (Weidman) S.; m. Elsie Sherer, Aug. 31, 1940; 1 son, J. David. Acct. Raymond D. Shearer, Lancaster, Pa., 1937-39; sr. acct. Lancaster Newspapers, Inc., 1940-50, sec.-controller, 1950-61, v.p., sec., 1961-76, pres., 1977-83, chmn. bd., 1984—. Pres. United Way of Lancaster County, 1961; pres., bd. trustees Lancaster Country Day Sch., 1971-72; trustee Franklin and Marshall Coll., Lancaster, 1977-85; sec. Pequea Twp. Planning Commn., 1965-77. Mem. Nat. Assn. Accts., Pa. Inst. CPAs, Lancaster Country Club. Clubs: Hamilton, Masons. Lutheran. Office: Lancaster Newspapers Inc PO Box 1328 8 W King St Lancaster PA 17603-3824

SHENKER, JOSEPH, academic administrator; b. N.Y.C., Oct. 7, 1939; s. George and Isabelle (Schwartz) S.; m. Adrienne Green (div. 1979); children: Deborah, Karen; m. Susan Armiger, Jan. 2, 1988; children: Sarah Gabrielle, Jordan. BA in Psychology, Hunter Coll., 1962, MA in Econ., 1963; EdD in High Edn., Tchrs. Coll., 1969. Dean, community coll. affairs CUNY, 1967-69; acting pres. Kingsborough Community Coll., N.Y.C., 1969-70; chief negotiator for mgmt. CUNY, 1977; acting pres. Hunter Coll., N.Y.C., 1979-80; founding pres. LaGuardia Community Coll., 1970-88; pres. Bank St. Coll. Edn., 1988-95; provost C.W. Post Campus, L.I. U., 1995—. Bd. dirs. Sch. & Bus. Alliance, N.Y.C.; ptnr. N.Y.C. Partnership, 1990—; advisor Consortium for Worker Edn., 2001--; bd. dirs. DeWitt Wallace Reader's Digest Fund, 2001--. Chmn. Liberty Scholarship Adv. Com., Albany, N.Y., 1989—; co-chmn. Task Force on Early Childhood Edn., N.Y.C., 1989—, Agenda for Children Tomorrow, 1989—; chmn. Chancellor's Com. on U./Sch. Collaboratives, N.Y.C., 1988. Recipient Distinguished Alumni award Tchrs. Coll. Columbia, N.Y.C., 1990. Office: C W Post Campus Long Island U 720 Northern Blvd Greenvale NY 11548-1319

SHENKER, YORAM, endocrinologist; b. Wroclaw, Poland, Mar. 25, 1949; s. Joseph and Eve (Katz) Shenker; m. Lucyna Rozmaity, Sept. 10, 1972; children: Dana, Anat, Ross. MD, Hebrew U., 1973. Diplomate Am. Bd. Internal Medicine, Am. Bd. Endocrinology and Metabolism. Resident internal medicine Kaplan Hosp., Rehovot, Israel, 1979-82; fellow endocrinology U.

Mich., Ann Arbor, 1982-85, instr. in medicine, 1986; dir., endocrine fellowship program U. Wis., Madison, 1989—; chief endocrine sect. VA Hosp., 1986—; asst. prof. medicine U. Wis., 1986-91, assoc. prof. medicine, 1991—, interim sect. head endocrinology, diabetes and metabolism, 1998—2000. Author: DeGroot's Endocrinology, 1994; contbr. articles to profl. jours. Fellow High Blood Pressure Rsch. coun., Am. Heart Assn.; mem. Endocrine Soc., Cen. Soc. for Clin. Rsch., Am. Soc. Hypertension. Avocations: opera, theater, classical music, lit. Office: VA Hosp 2500 Overlook Ter Madison WI 53705-2254

SHENKIN, HENRY ARNOLD, retired neurosurgeon; b. Phila., June 25, 1915; s. Julius and Rose (Rosenbaum) S.; m. Renee Friedenberg, Jan. 12, 1940 (dec. Nov. 1989); children: Budd, Robert, Katherine Shenkin Seal, Emily Shenkin Simon. AB, U. Pa., 1935; MD, Jefferson Med. Coll., 1939. Diplomate Am. Bd. Neurol. Surgery. Pvt. practice, 1946-88; internship Phila. Gen. Hosp., 1939-41; fellow dept. of Physiology Yale U. Sch. Medicine, 1941-42; residency Hosp. Univ. of Pa., 1942-45; instr., asst. prof. neurosurgery U. Pa. Sch. Medicine, Phila., 1945-60, assoc. prof., 1960-67; clin. prof. Temple U. Sch. Medicine, 1967-74; prof. Med. Coll. Pa., 1974-82; ret., 1982. Dir. neurosurgery and ind. residency program in neurosurgery Episcopal Hosp., Phila., 1960-82. Author: Clinical Practice and Cost Containment, 1986, Medical Ethics: Evolution, Rights and the Physician, 1991, Medical Care Reform: A Guide to Issues and Choices, 1994, Current Dilemmas in Medical-Care Rationing: A Pragmatic Approach, 1996; contbr. articles to profl. jours. Avocation: study of influence of Darwinian evolution on social issues. Home: 3300 Darby Rd Apt 3101 Haverford PA 19041-1069

SHENKIR, WILLIAM GARY, business educator; b. Three Rivers, Tex., June 27, 1938; s. William and Lydia (Jancik) S.; m. Missy Smith, Jan 1, 1973. BBA, Tex. A & M U., 1960; postgrad. (Rockefeller Bros. Theol. fellow), Drew U. Sem., 1960-61; MBA, U. Tex., 1962, PhD, 1964. Asst. prof. McIntire Sch. Commerce, U. Va., Charlottesville, 1967-69, assoc. prof., 1969-72, prof., 1972-73, dean, 1977-92, Paul Goodloe McIntire prof., 1977—82; William Stamps Farish prof. McIntire Sch. Commerce U. Va., 1982—. Project dir. Fin. Acctg. Stds. Bd., Stamford, Conn., 1973—76; vis. prof. NYU Grad. Sch. Bus., N.Y.C., 1976—77; bd. dirs. ComSonics Corp., Harrisburg, Va. Editor: Carman Blough: His Professional Career and Accounting Thought, 1978; co-author: The University of Virginia's McIntire School of Commerce: The First 75 Years, 1921-96, 1996, Open-Book Management: Creating an Ownership Culture, 1998, Making Enterprise Risk Management Pay Off, 2001, Making Enterprise Risk Management Pay Off: How Leading Companies Implement Risk Management, 2002, Enterprise Risk Management: Putting It All Together, 2002; contbr. articles to profl. jours. Served to lt. USAF, 1964-67. Mem. AICPA, Am. Acctg. Assn. (former v.p.), Acctg. Edn. Change Commn. (former vice chmn.), Am. Assembly Collegiate Schs. of Bus. (former bd. dirs., pres. 1990-91), Fin. Execs. Inst., Va. Soc. CPAs, Raven Soc., Landfall Club, Farmington Country Club, Phi Delta Kappa, Beta Gamma Sigma, Phi Kappa Phi. Presbyterian. Home: 420 Rookwood Dr Charlottesville VA 22903-4732 E-mail: wgs2Z@virginia.edu.

SHENKMAN, MARK RONALD, investment and finance executive; b. Providence, Aug. 17, 1943; s. George and Florence (Littman) S.; children: Andrew Harris, Gregory Alexander; m. Rosalind Schmidt, Aug. 10, 1997; 1 stepchild, Justin Warren Slatky. BA, U. Conn., 1965; MBA, George Washington U., 1967. Security analyst New Eng. Mchts. Bank, Boston, 1969-71; fin. analyst Stone & Webster Securities Corp., 1971-73; rsch. analyst, portfolio mgr. Fidelity Mgmt. & Research Co. , 1973-79; v.p. Lehman Bros. Kuhn Loeb, N.Y.C., 1979-83; pres. First Investors Asset Mgmt. Co., 1983-85; pres., chief exec. officer Shenkman Capital Mgmt. Inc., 1985—. Vice chmn. bd. trustees Wilbraham (Mass.) and Monson Acad.; bd. dirs. U. Conn. Found.; bd. visitors George Washington U. Sch. Bus.; mem. bd. advisors Coll. William and Mary Sch. Bus. 1st lt. U.S. Army, 1967-69. Mem. Am. Bankruptcy Inst., N.Y. Soc. Security Analysts, Boston Security Analysts Soc., Am. Statis. Assn., Assn. Investment Mgmt. and Rsch. Home: Gaston Farm Rd Greenwich CT 06831 Office: 461 Fifth Ave New York NY 10017-6234

SHENNUM, ROBERT HERMAN, retired telephone company executive; b. Scobey, Mont., Apr. 12, 1922; s. Joseph M. and Nellie M. Shennum; m. Doris Postlewait; children: Sharon, Keith, Marsha Shennum Burns. BSE.E., Mont. State U., 1944, MSE.E., 1948, D. Eng. (hon.), 1963; PhD in Physics and Elec. Engring., Calif. Inst. Tech., 1954. Instr. engring. Mont. State U., Bozeman, 1946-50; rsch. assoc. engring. Calif. Inst. Tech., Pasadena, 1950-54; cons. Kelman Electric Co., Los Angeles, 1954; mem. tech. staff AT&T Bell Labs., Murray Hill, N.J., 1954-85, also dir. Parsippany. Mem. adv. com. Internat. Telecommunications Energy Conf., 1974-87. Contbr. articles to profl. jours.; patentee pulse code modulation Served to 1st lt. Signal Corps, U.S. Army, 1944-46, ETO. Recipient cert. of appreciation for patriotic services U.S. Army, 1975 Fellow IEEE (chmn. N.C. sect. 1973), Greensboro C. of C. (chmn. continuing edn. 1970-74) Republican. Home: 2888 Swan Hwy Bigfork MT 59911-6414

SHENON, PHILIP, journalist; b. San Francisco, June 26, 1959; s. Peter and Philippa (Richards) S. BA in English Lit., Brown U., 1981. Reporter N.Y. Times, N.Y.C., 1983-1985, corr. Washington, 1985-1990, S.E. Asia corr. Bangkok, 1991-95, def. corr. Washington, 1996-97, diplomatic corr., 1997—99, investigative corr., 2000—. Office: NY Times Washington Bur 1627 I St NW Washington DC 20006-4007

SHENOY, GOPAL, physicist, researcher; b. Kasaragod, Kerala, India, Jan. 26, 1940; s. Devadas and Yamuna Shenoy; m. Ravibala Kasbekar; children: Shami Kini, Lakshmi. PhD, U. Bombay, 1966. Postdoctoral fellow Argonne (Ill.) Nat. Lab., 1967—70, physicist, 1974—81, sr. scientist/group leader, 1981—86, assoc. divsn. dir. - APS, 1986—89, divsn. dir., 1989—99, sr. sci. dir. - APS, 1999—2001, sr. sci. advisor - APS, 2001—; vis. scientist Tech. U. Munich, 1970—72; sr. rschr. Centre de Nucleaire, Strasbourg, France, 1972—74. Author, editor: Mossbauer Isomer Shifts, 1974 (U. Chgo. Disting. Performance award, 1987) exec. prodr.: Reviews of Scientific Instruments, 1986—88. Fellow: AAAS, Am. Phys. Soc. Office: Argonne Nat Lab 9700 S Cass Ave Argonne IL 60439 Business E-Mail: gks@aps.anl.gov.

SHENTON, MARTHA ELIZABETH, research psychologist, educator; b. Concord, N.H., Nov. 11, 1952; d. Enoch and Loretta Marie (Halle) S., m. George Santiccioli; 1 child, Jessica. AB, Wellesley Coll., 1973; MS, Tufts U., 1976; MA, Harvard U., 1981, PhD, 1984. Research fellow Mclean Hosp. Mailman Research Ctr., Belmont, Mass., 1979-84; lecturer Brandeis U., Walton, 1984-85; postdoctoral rsch. fellow Harvard Med. Sch., Mass. Mental Health Ctr., Boston, 1984-86; instr. Harvard Med. Sch., VA Med. Ctr., 1986-88, 1986-88; asst. prof. psychology dept. psychiatry Harvard Med. Sch., 1988-93, assoc. prof, 1993-2000, prof., 2000—. Contbr. articles to profl. jours. Mem. Am. Psychol. Assn., Mass. Psychol. Assn., Phi Beta Kappa. Office: VA Med Ctr Dept Psychiatry 116A 940 Belmont St Dept 116A Watertown MA 02472-1025 E-mail: martha_shenton@hms.harvard.edu.

SHEON, AARON, art historian, educator; b. Toledo, Oct. 7, 1937; s. Benjamin William and Katherine (Rappoport) S.; m. Martine Bruel, Jan. 26, 1963 (div. 1986); children: Sandrine, Nicolas; m. Jill Belasco, Nov. 11, 2000. BA, U. Mich., 1959, MA, 1960; M.F.A. (Wilson fellow), Princeton U., 1962, PhD, 1966; postgrad., U. Paris, 1962-63. Staff officer, dir. gen.'s cabinet UNESCO, Paris, 1963-66; asst. prof. U. Pitts., 1966-69, asso. prof., 1969-78, prof. art history, 1979—, acting chmn. dept. fine arts, 1969, 79-80, dir. univ. program France, 1974-75; vis. prof. Carnegie-Mellon U., 1981. Vis. exhbn. curator Mus. Art, Carnegie Inst., Pitts., 1977-81; program cons. Nat. Endowment Arts and Humanities, 1978-85; visual arts cons. Pa. Arts Council, 1981; vis. mem. Inst. for Advanced Study, Princeton, 1984-85 Author: The Gosman Collection, 1969, Monticelli, His Contemporaries, His Influence, 1978, Organic Vision, The Architecture of Peter Berndtson, 1980, Monticelli, 1986, Paul Guigou, 1987. Recipient Charles E. Merrill faculty award, 1968; Chancellor Bowman award, 1976; Honor award Pa. Soc. Architects, 1982, Innovation award in tchg. Art History Course for Blind Students U. Pitts., 2001; grantee Ford Found., 1967, NEH, 1979; Gould Arts Found. fellow, 1986; Bellet Teaching award, 2002. Mem. Coll. Art Assn., Société de l'histoire de l'art français, Am. Assn. of Mus. Office: U Pitts Dept History Arts & Arch Pittsburgh PA 15260

SHEON, AMY RUTH, biomedical researcher; b. Cleve., Sept. 15, 1960; d. Robert Phillip and Irma Shainberg Sheon; m. Marvin Krislov, Aug. 25, 1991; children: Zachary Jacob, Jesse Harris, Eve Rose. BA with honors, Cornell U., 1983; MPH, U. Mich., 1984; PhD in Health Policy and Mgmt., Johns Hopkins U., 1996. Rsch. cons. com. on population NRC, Washington, 1985; country monitor Demographic and Health Surveys Program, Columbia, Md., 1985-89; sr. prevention scientist, health specialist NIH, Rockville, 1989-97; sr. study dir. Westat, Inc., 1997-98; dir. for programs Ctr. for Clin. Investigation and Therapeutics U. Mich., 1999—2000, assoc. dir. life scis. values and soc. program, 2000—. Contbr. articles to profl. jours. Office: U Mich Life Scis Values and Soc Program 837 Greene St Box 3213 Ann Arbor MI 48104-3213 E-mail: asheon@umich.edu.

SHEP, ROBERT LEE, editor, publisher, textile book researcher; b. L.A., Feb. 27, 1933; s. Milton and Ruth (Miller) Polen S. BA, U. Calif., Berkeley, 1955; student, Royal Acad. Dramatic Art, London, 1956; B Fgn. Trade, Am. inst. Fgn. Trade, 1960. Asst. area mgr. fgn. dept. Max Factor, Hollywood, Calif., 1960-65; editor, pub. The Textile Booklist, Lopez Island, Wash., 1980-84; freelance writer/book reviewer/libr. appraiser/book repairer. Sponsor Triannual R.L. Shep Symposium, L.A. County Mus. Art, R.L. Shep Book award Textile Soc. Am. Author: Cleaning and Repairing Books, 1980, Cleaning and Care for Books, 1983, Bhutan - Fibre Forum, 1984, Civil War Gentleman, 1994, Late Victorian Women's Tailoring, 1997, Regency Etiquette, 1997, Early Victorian Men, 2001; co-author: (annotated editl) The Costume or Annals of Fashion, 1986, Dress and Cloak Cutter: Women's Costume 1877-1882, 1987; Federalist and Regency Costume: 1790-1819, 1998, Shirts and Men's Haberdashery 1840's to 1920's; editor: The Handbook of Practical Cutting, 2d rev. edit., 1986, RAGS: Quarterly Revs. Costume, Clothing & Ethnic Textile Books; pub. Ladies' Guide to Needle Work, 1986, Edwardian Ladies' Tailoring, 1990, Art of Cutting and History of English Costume, 1987; editor, pub. Tailoring of the Belle Epoque, 1991, Late Georgian Costume, 1991, Civil War Cooking, 1992, Art in Dress, 1993, Minister's Complete Guide to Practical Cutting, 1993, Freaks of Fashion, 1993, 1999, The Great War Fashions of the 1910s; pub. Civil War Era Etiquette, 1988, Ladies Self Instr., 1988; mem. editl. bd. The Cutter's Rsch. Jor. Bd. dirs. AIDS Care and Edn. Svcs., Pacific Textiles. Mem. Costume Soc. London, Costume Soc. Am. (bd. dirs. 1985-87, bd. dirs. region V 2000—), Costume Soc. Ont., Mendocino County HIV Consortium (mem. steering com.), Australian Costume and Textile Soc., U.S. Inst. Theatre Tech., Textile Soc. Am., Seattle Textile and Rug Soc. E-mail: rlshep@centurytel.net.

SHEPARD, BEATRICE L. retired microbiologist, historian; b. Hillsdale, Mich., May 15, 1919; d. James Wesley Shepard and Ona Ola Kinney. AB in Zoolog., U. Calif., Berkeley, 1940. Regional lab. dir. L.A. County Health Dept., L.A., 1945-46; sr. biologist, sr. chemist S.E. Regional Lab., Juneau, Alaska, 1946-67; acting chief of labs. Alaska Dept. Health & Social Svcs., 1967-70; microbiologist in charge S.E. Regional Lab., Alaska Dept. Heath and Social Svcs., 1967-77; ret., 1977. Chemist L.A. County Health Dept., 1944-45, L.A. County Gen. Hosp., 1943-44; dir. pub. health lab. Health Dept. Riverside (Calif.) County, 1942-43. Author: Praise the Lord and Pass the Penicillin, 1979; co-author: Have Gospel Tent, Will Travel, History of 100 Years of Alaskan Methodism, 1986; editor: (newsletter) Western Cir. Rider, 1998—, Eagle River United Meth. Camp, 1998—; contbr. articles to profl. jours., chapters to books. Docent Alaska State Mus., 1992—; mem. Juneau Borough Commn. on Aging, 1997—; mem. gen. commn. archives and history United Meth. Ch. Archives Ctr., Madison, NJ, 1988—96; historian Alaska Meth. Ch., Alaska Missionary Conf., Anchorage, 1980—; bd. dirs., advocacy chair Mus. Alaska, 1992—; sec. bd. dirs. Eagle River Meth. Camp, 1955—; bd. dirs. Western Jurisdictional Commn. on Archives and History, 1984—; chair Alaska Missionary Conf. Commn. on Archives and History, 1980—. Named Outstanding Lay Person of Yr. award Alaska Missionary Conf. of United Meth. Ch., 1986; recipient Meritorious Health Svc. award Alaska Pub. Health Assn., 1990. Mem.: Friends of Alaska State Mus. (hon.; life), Museums Alaska (hon.; life). Avocation: photography. Home: 12585 Glacier Hwy Juneau AK 99801 E-mail: BShep98308@aol.com.

SHEPARD, BRUCE M. retired anesthesiologist; b. Leadville, Colo., Nov. 15, 1911; AB, U. Ill., 1932; MD, Harvard U., 1940. Diploamte Am. Bd. Anesthesiology. Commd. 2d lt. USN, 1941, ret., 1961; intern Bellevue Hosp., N.Y.C., 1941-42; resident in anesthesiology Univ. Hosps. Minn., Mpls., 1956-58; pvt. practice; anesthesiologist St. Bernardine Med. Ctr., San Bernardino, Calif.; ret., 1999. Fellow Am. Coll. Chest Physicians; mem. AMA, Am. Soc. Anesthesiologists. Office: St Bernardine Med Ctr 2101 N Waterman Ave San Bernardino CA 92404-4836

SHEPARD, COLLEEN, elementary school educator, art educator; b. Chardon, Ohio, Mar. 28, 1966; d. Charles Irvin and Shirley Ann (Weinstein) Hewins; m. Clifford Stephan Shepard, June 31, 1989; 1 child, Christopher. BFA, Fla. Atlantic U., 1989. Art tchr. Logger's Run Mid. Sch., Boca Raton, Fla., 1989-91, Omni Mid. Sch., Boca Raton, 1991-94, J.C. Mitchell Elem. Sch., Boca Raton, 1994—, sponsor Art Club, 1995—. Site coord. Project Leap, West Palm Beach, 1996-98. Artist numerous shows. Nominee William Dwyer award, 1997. Mem. Nat Art Edn. Assn., Fla. Art Edn. Assn., FAU Potter's Guild (pres. 1989-91). Roman Catholic. Avocations: painting, sculpting, gardening, breeding birds, cooking. Office: JC Mitchell Elem 2401 NW 3rd Ave Boca Raton FL 33431-7428

SHEPARD, DAVID HASPEL, film restoration specialist; b. N.Y.C., Oct. 22, 1940; s. Bertram David Shepard and Marjorie (Haspel) Markley; m. Kimberly Fetter, Mar. 26, 1977 (div.); 1 child, Benjamin Baker. AB, Hamilton Coll., 1962; MA, U. Pa., 1963. Asst. prof. theatre Pa. State U., State College, 1965-68; film acquisitions mgr., programmer Am. Film Inst., Washington, 1968-73; v.p. Blackhawk Films, Inc., Davenport, Iowa, 1973-76; spl. projects officer Dirs. Guild Am., Hollywood, Calif., 1976-87; adj. prof. cinema-TV U. So. Calif., L.A., 1982-95; owner Film Preservation Assocs., Hat Creek, Calif., 1989-2000; managing dir. Film Preservation Assocs., Inc., 2000—. Trustee Internat. Film Seminars, N.Y.C., 1972-82; mem. adv. bd. Hollywood (Calif.) Entertainment Mus., 1984—. Prodr. (video restoration series) Chaplin: A Legacy of Laughter, 1992-93, Masterworks of D.W. Griffith, 1992/2002, Landmarks of Early Soviet Cinema, 1992-97, Great British Documentary Movement, 1993, Golden Age of German Cinema, 1994-2002, Art of Buster Keaton, 1995, Douglas Fairbanks: King of Hollywood, 1996, Cecil B. De Mille: The Visionary Years, 1997, Slapstick encyclopedia , 1998, Les Vampires (1915 serial), 1998, Lon Chaney: Behind the Masks, 1997-2002, others. Recipient Preservation award Soc. Cinephiles, 1970, 95, 2 Emmy awards Acad. TV Arts & Scis., 1973, Scholarship and Preservation award Internat. Documentary Assn., 1989, Prix Jean Mitry, Giornate des Cinema Muto, Pordenone, Italy, 1993, Saturn award Acad. Sci. Fiction, Horror and Fantasy Films, 1999, Mel Novikoff award San Francisco Internat. Film Festival, 2000. Mem. Acad. Motion Picture Arts and Scis. Home: PO Box 71 Hat Creek CA 96040-0071 E-mail: DShepFilm@aol.com.

SHEPARD, GEOFFREY CARROLL, insurance executive; b. Santa Barbara, Calif., Nov. 7, 1944; s. James J. and Barbara (Hoose) S.; m. Saundra Gayle Carlton, Jan. 10, 1973; children: Jonathan Pettus, William Dabney. BA, Whittier Coll., 1966; JD, Harvard U., 1969. Bar: Wash. 1970, D.C. 1972, Pa. 1977, U.S. Supreme Ct. 1973. White House fellow, 1969-70; staff asst. to Pres. White House, 1970-72, assoc. dir. domestic coun., 1972-75; sr. assoc. Steptoe & Johnson, Washington, 1975-77; sr. v.p., assoc. gen. counsel CIGNA Corp., Phila., 1977-91; sr. v.p., gen. counsel, corp. sec. Reliance Ins. Group, 1991-94; pres. corp. divsn. Karr Barth Assocs., 1994—. Mem. pvt. security adv. coun. Dept. Justice, 1975-77. Adv. coun. on gen. govt. Rep. Nat. Com., 1977-78; Phila. Cmty. Leadership Seminar, 1978-79, exec. com. Boy Scouts Am., Phila, 1981-83, exec. bd. Valley Forge Coun., 1994-96; mem. exec. bd. Cradle of Liberty Coun., 1996-2001; bd. dirs. Sacred Heart Med. Ctr., 1983-85, Swarthmore Presbyn. Ch., 1984-86, 97-2000, Wallingford Hills Civic Assn., 1983-85, Com. of 70, 1985-87, Acad. Natural Scis., Phila., 1987-93, Pub. Affairs Coun., Washington, 1986-89, Episc. Acad., 1987-90; mem. exec. com. White House Fellows Regional Selection Panel, 1987-93; prin. counsel Excellence in Govt., 1994-96; bd. dirs. White House Fellows Found., 1997-2000. Mem. ABA, Assn. for Advancement Life Underwriting, Pa. Bar Assn., Phila. Assn. of Life Underwriters, D.C. Bar Assn., White House Fellows Alumni Assn., Met. Club (Washington), Union League Club (Phila.), Harvard Club (N.Y.C.). Office: Karr Barth Assocs Inc Corp Divsn 40 Monument Rd Bala Cynwyd PA 19004-1797

SHEPARD, GEORGE LEO, sales and marketing executive, consultant; b. Balt., Sept. 18, 1947; s. George Wesley and Naomi S.; m. Eleanor Sheila Fitzpatrick, June 29, 1985; children: Jeffrey Stewart, David George. BS, U. Md., 1974; MS in Pub. Rels., Am. U., 1979; MBA, U. Balt., 1990; postgrad., U. Md., 1993—. Key account rep. Chesebrough-Ponds Inc., Greenwich, Conn., 1969-71, Armour-Dial Inc., Phoenix, 1971-74; ter. mgr. Am. Optical Corp., Southbridge, Mass., 1974-76, Norton Co., Worcester, 1976-83; dist. mgr. Childs Corp., Newport, Del., 1983-86; sales and mktg. mgr. Nat. Capital Industries, Bladensburg, Md., 1987-90; mgr. sales adminstrn. Locke Insulators, Balt., 1990-93; asst. prof. mgmt. U. Balt., 1990—; rsch. asst. U. Md., 1993—. Vol. Balt. Symphony Orch., 1985—. Mem. U. Balt. Alumni Assn. (mentor 1991—), U. Md. Alumni Assn., Am. U. Alumni Assn., Blue Key, Phi Kappa Phi, Alpha Sigma Lambda, Sigma Iota Epsilon. Avocations: classical music, running. also: 6 Ginger View Ct Apt F Cockeysville Hunt Valley MD 21030

SHEPARD, HENRY BRADBURY, JR. lawyer; b. Exeter, N.H., Oct. 29, 1927; s. Henry Bradbury and Frances Gardner (Dudley) S.; m. Klaudia Ockert Steidle, July 26, 1958; children: Katherine Shepard Alexander, Emily Perry, Julia Bradbury Shepard Stenzel. BA with honors, Yale U., 1949; postgrad., U. Goettingen, Germany, 1951-52; LLB with honors, Harvard U., 1957. Instr. Am. U. in Cairo (Egypt), 1949-51; asst. dir. Fridtjof Nansen Internat. Student House, Goettingen, Germany, 1951-52; instr. Interpreters Inst., Germany, 1951-52; assoc. Goodwin, Procter & Hoar, Boston, 1957-64, ptnr., 1965-93, counsel, 1994-99, of counsel, 1999—. Dir. Mass. Venture Capital Corp., Boston, 1973-88, The C.T. Main Corp., Boston, 1975-85, Neworld Bancorp, Inc., Boston, 1986-92, Neworld Bank, Boston, 1968-92. Author: Handbook of Recent Developments in Massachusetts Banking Law, 1983, Obligations and Liabilities of Bank Directors and Trustees, 1990. Trustee George R. Wallace Found., Boston, 1978—, N.H. Hist. Soc., Concord, 1991-99; hon. trustee Deree-Pierce Coll., Athens, Greece, 1970—; dir. Am. Congregational Assn., 1998—; chmn. Seminarians, 1998-2000, pres. Harvard Law Sch. class of 1957—. With U.S. Army, 1952-54. Mem. ABA (chmn. subcom. on regulatory liaison mut. savs. banks 1980-85), Mass. Bar Assn., Boston Bar Assn., Greater Boston C. of C. (bd. dirs. 1974-80, pres. 1979-80, hon. v.p. 1980-93), The Hamilton Trust (v.p. 1989, pres. 1990-91), New Bedford Yacht Club, The Country Club, Harvard Travellers Club, Elizabethan Club of Yale U., Phi Beta Kappa. Independent. Office: Goodwin Procter & Hoar Exch Pl Boston MA 02109

SHEPARD, IVAN ALBERT, securities and insurance broker; b. Springfield, Mass., Sept. 28, 1925; s. Albert Joseph and Mary (Harrigan) S.; m. Miriam Murray, May 20, 1950; children: Kirk, Robin, Mark. BS in Edn., Ohio State U., 1949. Registered rep. Divisional mgr. Confedn. Life, Columbus, Ohio, 1953-62; regional v.p. Western Res. Life, Cleve., 1962-69; v.p. Computer Life-Pan Western, Columbus, 1969-74; ins. broker Shepard and Assocs., Rocky River, Ohio, 1974—. Bd. dirs., v.p., sec. Computer Life Ohio, 1969-72. With U.S. Navy, 1943-45. Home: 29318 Lake Rd Cleveland OH 44140-1321 Office: Shepard and Assocs 20525 Center Ridge Rd Cleveland OH 44116-3424 E-mail: 9281925@msn.com.

SHEPARD, JEAN HECK, publishing company consultant, author, agent; b. N.Y.C., Feb. 2, 1930; d. Chester Reed and Anna S. (Charig) Heck; m. Lawrence Vaeth Hastings, Mar. 29, 1950 (div. 1953); 1 child, Lance Clifford Hastings; m. Daniel A. Shepard, July 26, 1954 (div. 1981); 1 child, Bradley Reed. BA, Barnard Coll., 1950; postgrad., Columbia U., 1952. Mem. sch. and libr. svc. Viking Press, N.Y.C., 1956-57; asst. dir. sch. and libr. promotion E.P. Dutton, 1957-58; dir. advt. publicity and promotion Thomas Y. Crowell Co., 1958-62; dir. advt. and promotion Charles Scribner's Sons, 1962-67; cons. Stephen Greene Press, Brattleboro, Vt., 1970-73; mktg. mgr. A&W Publishers, N.Y.C., 1979-80, Franklin Watts Publ., N.Y.C., 1980-82; pub. 2 mags., divsn. advt. & promotion mgr. McGraw Hill Book Co., 1983-85; cons. Monitor Publ. Co., 1988-2000. Author: Simple Family Favorites, 1971, Herb and Spice Sampler, 1972, Cook With Wine!, 1973, Earth Watch: Notes on a Restless Planet, 1973, Harvest Home Steak Cookbook, 1974, Fresh Fruits and Vegetables, 1974, Yankee Magazine, 1972, Let Them be Sea Captains. Mem. Authors Guild, Pub. Ad Club, Am. Libr. Assn., Women's Nat. Book Assn. Methodist. Avocations: the dance, reading, writing, travel, music. Home: 73 Kingswood Dr Bethel CT 06801-1834 Office Fax: 845-279-3239. E-mail: shepardagcy@mindspring.com.

SHEPARD, JON MAX, sociologist, educator; b. Ashland, Ky., July 15, 1939; s. Maxwell Irwin and Mabel Louise S.; m. Virginia Kay Vogel, July 16, 1961; 1 son, Jon Mark. BA, Georgetown (Ky.) Coll., 1961; MA, U. Ky., 1963; PhD, Mich. State U., 1968. Rsch. assoc. MIT, 1968-69; from asst. prof. to prof. sociology U. Ky., 1969-78, prof. mgmt. and sociology, 1978-88; head dept. mgmt. and prof. mgmt. and sociology Va. Poly. Inst. and State U., Blacksburg, 1989—, head dept. mgmt. and Pamplin prof. mgmt. Author: Automation and Alienation, A Study of Office and Factory Workers, 1971, Organizational Issues in Industrial Society, 1972, (with H. Voss) Social Problems, 1978; contbr. articles to profl. jours. Recipient Gt. Tchr. award U. Ky., 1978 Mem. Am. Acad. Mgmt., Am. Sociol. Assn. Home: 2817 Newton Ct Blacksburg VA 24060-4122 Office: Va Poly Inst & State U Pamplin Hall Blacksburg VA 24061

SHEPARD, KATHRYN IRENE, public relations executive; b. Tooele, Utah, Jan. 6, 1956; d. James Lewis and Glenda Verleen (Slaughter) Clark; m. Mark L. Shepard, June 5, 1976. BA in History, Boise State U., 1980. On-air writer Sta. KTTV, Channel 11, L.A., 1982-85; publicity dir. Hollywood (Calif.) C. of C., 1985-87; pres. Kathy Shepard Pub. Rels., Burbank and Portland, 1987-93; dir. public relations Las Vegas Hilton, 1993-94; dir. comms. Hilton Gaming, 1994-96; dir. corp. comms. Hilton Hotels Corp., 1996—97, v.p. corp. comms., 1997—. Instr. pub. rels. ext. program UCLA, 1991-92. Contbr. articles to profl. publs. Mem.: Pub. Rels. Assn. Am., Pub. Communicators L.A. (pres. 1991—92, bd. dirs. 1987—91). Avocations: genealogy, film, travel. Office: Hilton Hotels Corp PR Dept 9336 Civic Center Dr Beverly Hills CA 90210-3604 E-mail: kathy_shepard@hilton.com.

SHEPARD, RANDALL TERRY, state supreme court chief justice; b. Lafayette, Ind., Dec. 24, 1946; s. Richard Schilling and Dorothy Ione (Donlen) S.; m. Amy Wynne MacDonell, May 7, 1988; one child, Martha MacDonell. AB cum laude, Princeton U., 1969; JD, Yale U., 1972; LLM, U. Va., 1995; LLD (hon.), U. So. Ind., 1995. Bar: Ind. 1972, U.S. Dist. Ct. (so. dist.) Ind. 1972. Spl. asst. to under sec. U.S. Dept. Transp., Washington, 1972-74; exec. asst. to mayor City of Evansville, Ind., 1974-79; judge Vanderburgh Superior Ct., Evansville, 1980-85; assoc. justice Ind. Supreme Ct., Indpls., 1985-87, chief justice, 1987—. Instr. U. Evansville, 1975-78, Indiana U., 1995, 99 Author: Preservation Rules and Regulations, 1980; contbr. articles to profl. publs. Bd. advisors Nat. Trust for Hist. Preservation, 1980-87, chmn. bd. advisors, 1983-85, trustee, 1987-96; dir. Hist. Landmarks Found. Ind., 1983—, chmn., 1989-92, hon. chmn., 1992—; chmn. State Student Assistance Commn. on Ind., 1981-85; chmn. Ind. Commn. on Bicentennial of U.S. Constn., 1986-91; vice chmn. Vanderburgh County Rep. Ctrl. Com., 1977-80. Recipient Friend of Media award Cardinal States chpt. Sigma Delta Chi, 1979, Disting. Svc. award Evansville Jaycees, 1982, Herbert Harley award Am. Judicature Soc., 1992. Mem. ABA (coun. mem. sect. on legal edn. 1991—, chair sect. on legal edn. 1997—, immediate past chair appellate judges conf. 1997-98), Ind. Bar Assn., Ind. Judges Assn., Princeton Club (N.Y.), Capitol Hill Club (Washington), Columbia Club (Indpls.). Republican. Methodist. Home: 3644 Totem Ln Indianapolis IN 46208-4171 Office: Ind Supreme Ct 304 State House Indianapolis IN 46204-2213*

SHEPARD, ROBERT M. lawyer, investment banker, engineer; b. Amityville, N.Y., Feb. 15, 1932; s. Sidney M. and Undine L. (Lehmann) Shapiro; m. Barbara S. Stannard, June 25, 1955 (div. 1980); children: Karen Michele Shepard Sweer, Daniel Robert; m. Joanne E. Devlin, May 16, 1981 (div. 1993); m. Martha Kothe, Nov. 24, 1999. B.C.E., Cornell U., 1954; MBA, Hofstra Coll., 1960; LL.B., Yale U., 1963; LLM, NYU, 1988. Bar: N.Y. 1964; registered profl. engr., N.Y., Conn. Project engr. Lockwood Kessler & Bartlett, Syosset, N.Y., 1956-60; assoc. atty. Cravath, Swaine & Moore, N.Y.C. and Paris, 1963-70; gen. ptnr. Kuhn, Loeb & Co., N.Y.C., 1970-77; sr. v.p.

Donaldson, Lufkin & Jenrette, 1977-83; gen. ptnr. Donovan Leisure Newton & Irvine, 1983-89, Adler & Shepard, N.Y.C., 1989-91, Shepard & van Essche, N.Y.C., 1991, Ballon Stoll Bader & Nadler, P.C., N.Y.C., 1992—. Note and comment editor: Yale Law Jour., 1962-63. Bd. dirs. N.Y. Grand Opera, Regency Whist Club. Recipient Fuertes Medal Cornell U., 1953 Mem. ABA, Am. N.Y. State Bar Assn., Pub. Power Assn., Nat. Assn. Bond Lawyers, Order of Coif, Union League Club, Regency Whist Club, Inc., Tau Beta Pi, Chi Epsilon. Home: 750 Park Ave Apt 2C New York NY 10021-4252 Office: Ballon Stoll Bader & Nadler 1450 Broadway New York NY 10018-2201

SHEPARD, ROGER NEWLAND, psychologist, educator; b. Palo Alto, Calif., Jan. 30, 1929; s. Orson Cutler and Grace (Newland) S.; m. Barbaranne Bradley, Aug. 18, 1952; children: Newland Chenoweth, Todd David, Shenna Esther. BA, Stanford U., 1951; PhD, Yale U., 1955; AM (hon.), Harvard U., 1966; ScD (hon.), Rutgers U., 1992. Rsch. assoc. Naval Research Lab., 1955-56; rsch. fellow Harvard, 1956-58; mem. tech. staff Bell Telephone Labs., 1958-66, dept. head, 1963-66; prof. psychology Harvard U., 1966-68, dir. psychol. labs., 1967-68; prof. psychology Stanford U., 1968-98, Ray Lyman Wilbur prof. social sci., 1989-96, Ray Lyman Wilbur prof. emeritus social sci., 1996—. Guggenheim fellow Center for Advanced Study in Behavioral Scis., 1971-72; recipient, N.Y. Acad. Scis. award, 1987, Nat. Medal of Sci., 1995, Gold medal Am. Psychol. Found., 2000. Fellow AAAS, APA (pres. exptl. div. 1980-81, Disting. Sci. Contbn. award 1976); mem. Am. Acad. Arts and Scis., Nat. Acad. Scis., Psychometric Soc. (pres. 1973-74), Psychonomic Soc., Soc. Exptl. Psychologists (Howard Crosby Warren medal 1981), Am. Philos. Soc., Yale Grad. Sch. Alumni Assn. (Wilbur Cross medal 2001).

SHEPARD, STEPHEN BENJAMIN, journalist, magazine editor; b. N.Y.C., July 20, 1939; s. William and Ruth Shepard; m. Lynn Povich, Sept. 16, 1979; children: Sarah, Ned. BS, CCNY, 1961; MS, Columbia U., 1963. Reporter, editor, writer Business Week, N.Y.C., 1966-75; asst. prof., dir. Walter Bagehot fellowship program econs. and bus. journalism Columbia U., 1975-76; sr. editor Newsweek, 1976-81; editor Saturday Rev., 1981-82; exec. editor Business Week mag., 1982-84, editor in chief, 1984—. Mem. bd. of visitors Columbia Grad. Sch. of Journalism. Recipient Lifetime Achievement award, Gerald Loeb Found., 1999, Henry Johnson Fisher award, Mag. Publs. Am., 2000. Mem. Am. Soc. Mag. Editors (v.p. 1990-92, pres. 1992-94; Hall of Fame 1999), Coun. Fgn. Rels., Century Assn. Home: 322 Central Park W New York NY 10025-7629 Office: Business Week McGraw Hill Inc 43rd Fl 1221 Ave Of The Americas New York NY 10020-1001

SHEPARD, STEVEN LOUIS, graphic artist, painter; b. Port Arthur, Tex., Mar. 23, 1955; Student, Workshops Contemporary Art, Santa Fe, 1976; BFA with honors, U. South Ala., 1977. Exhibited in group shows Chgo. Pub. Libr., 1987, Wake Forest U., Winston-Salem, N.C., 1988, Am. Cultural Ctr., Ouagadougou, Burkina Faso, 1988, Mus. Soc. (Book) Illustrators, N.Y.C., 1991, Southeastern Ctr. for Contemporary Art, Winston-Salem, 1997, U. West Fla., 1998, Miss. Mus. Art, 1999; represented in permanent collections Miss. Mus. Art, Jackson, Mobile (Ala.) Mus. Art; murals commd. by J.L. Scott Marine Edn. Ctr., Biloxi, Miss., George Ohr Mus., Biloxi; works pub. in various publs.; author, illustrator: Elvis Hornbill: International Business Bird, 1991. Mem. Nat. Assn. Ind. Artists. Address: America Oh Yes Gallery care Joe Adams PO Box 3078 Hilton Head Island SC 29928-0078 E-mail: shepart@datasync.com.

SHEPARD, THOMAS HILL, physician, educator; b. Milw., May 22, 1923; s. Francis Parker and Elizabeth Rhodes (Buchner) S.; m. Alice B. Kelly, June 24, 1946; children: Donna, Elizabeth, Ann. AB, Amherst Coll., 1945; MD, U. Rochester, 1948. Intern Strong Meml. Hosp., Rochester, N.Y., 1948-49, resident, 1950-52, Albany (N.Y.) Med. Center, 1949-50; pediatric endocrine fellow Johns Hopkins Hosp., 1954-55; pediatrician U. Wash., Seattle, 1955-61; embryologist dept. anatomy U. Fla., 1961-62; teratologist U. Wash., 1961—, prof. pediatrics, head central lab. for human embryology, 1961-93, prof. emeritus, 1993—; rsch. assoc. dept. embryology Carnegie Inst., 1962, U. Copenhagen, 1963. Cons. NIH, FDA, EPA, 1971— ; vis. prof. pediatrics U. Geneva, 1972, 73-74. Author: A Catalog of Teratogenic Agents, 1973, 10th edit., 2001; contbr. articles to profl. jours. Served with U.S. Army, 1946-48; Served with USAF, 1952-54. Mem. Teratology Soc. (hon. mem. 1993, pres. 1968), Western Soc. Pediatric Rsch. (pres. 1970), Am. Pediatric Soc., Japanese Teratology Soc. (hon. 1998), Orgn. for Teratogen Answering Svcs. (hon.). Home: 3015 98th Ave NE Bellevue WA 98004-1818 Office: U Wash Sch Medicine Dept Pediatrics Seattle WA 98195-0001

SHEPARD, WILLIAM SETH, government official, diplomat, writer; b. Boston, June 7, 1935; s. Robinson and Myra Ellen (Foster) S.; m. Lois Rosalie Burke, June 25, 1960; children— Stephanie Lee, Cynthia Robin, Warren Burke (dec.) AB cum laude, Wesleyan U., Middletown, Conn., 1957; JD, Harvard U., Cambridge, Mass., 1961. Bar: N.H. 1961, U.S. Ct. Mil. Appeals 1962 U.S. Supreme Ct., 1970. Aide to ambs. Henry Cabot Lodge and Ellsworth Bunker, Am. embassy, Saigon, Vietnam, 1966-67; staff officer Exec. Secretariat Dept. of State, Washington, 1967-69; consul, polit. officer Am. Embassy, Budapest, Hungary, 1970-73; desk officer Hungarian affairs Dept. State, Washington, 1973-75; desk officer Singapore and Malaysian affairs Dept. of State, 1975-77; dep. polit. counselor Am. embassy, Athens, Greece, 1978-80; consul gen. Am. Consulate Sen., Bordeaux, France, 1983-85; dir. Office Congl. Affairs, ACDA, Washington, 1987-89; cons. to gen. counsel USDA, 1991-92. Lectr. internat. law U. Singapore, 1965-66; CEO The Shepard Internat. Group, Inc., 1994—. Author: Consular Tales, 2001, Murder on the Danube, 2001, Vintage Murder, 2002, Foreign Service Tales, 2002; wine editor: Bonjour Paris, 2002—. Candidate for Rep. nomination 8th Md. Congl. Dist., 1985-86, Rep. nominee for Gov. of Md., 1990, candidate, 1994; del. Rep. Nat. Conv., 1992; Md. co-chmn. Dole Presdl. Campaign, 1996. Recipient Pro Libertate Hungariae Commemorative medallion, 1981, Pub. Svc. Leadership award U.S.-Baltic Found., 1996; French Govt. teaching asst. and Fulbright travel grantee, 1957-58; Congl. fellow Am. Polit. Sci. Assn. and fgn. policy legis. asst. to Senator Robert Dole, 1982-83. Mem. Am. Fgn. Service Assn., Soc. Mayflower Desc., Gov. Bradford Compact, Soc. Desc. Colonial Govs. (chancellor gen. 1993-95), Soc. Desc. Colonial Wars; corr. mem. Montesquieu Acad. France Clubs: City Tavern (Washington), Flagon and Trencher, Les Chevaliers de Bretvin, Ordre des Compagnons de Bordeaux, Connetablie de Guyenne, La Jurade de St. Emilion, Bontemps Medoc et des Graves. Republican. Unitarian Universalist. Avocations: reading, vintage Bordeaux wines, travel, gastronomy. Home: 4540 Boone Creek Dr Oxford MD 21654 *I remember Himalayan peaks, Asian sunsets, Greek islands and Bordeaux vineyards. Along the way, hard work in a principled cause is its own reward. In the end, family life and friends, a foyer, pets, a book worth reading, and a glass of wine matter most.*

SHEPARD-TAGGART, GLORIA HARVEY, communications company executive; b. Ridgeland, S.C., June 20, 1932; d. Leroy Everett and Addie Gertrude (Gray) Harvey; m. Ray Lester Shepard (dec.); children: Michael Ray, Glenn Eric; m. Eugene Sheppard Taggart, June 1, 1986. Student Armstrong Coll., 1950-52. Head bookkeeper Liberty Nat. Bank, Savannah, Ga., 1952-55; v.p. Hargray Telephone Co., Inc., Hilton Head Island, S.C., 1953-82, pres., 1982—; bd. dirs. Citizen & So. Nat. Bank of S.C. Bd. dirs. Hilton Head Heart Assn. Mem. U.S. Telephone Assn., S.C. C. of C., S.C. Indsl. Developers Assn., Nat. Assn. Female Execs., Am. Mgmt. Assn., Ind. Telephone Pioneers, Profl. Women's Club, Beta Kappa. Baptist. Club: Christian Women's. Avocations: biking, cards, dancing. Office: Hargray Telephone Co Inc PO Box 5519 Hilton Head Island SC 29938-5519

SHEPHARD, BRUCE DENNIS, obstetrician, educator, medical writer; b. San Francisco, Apr. 21, 1944; s. Richard G. and Madelyn (Rogers) S.; children: Christopher, Carleton, Elizabeth. BA in History, U. Calif., Berkeley, 1966; MD, U. Calif., San Francisco, 1970. Diplomate Am. Bd. Obstetrics and Gynecology. Intern Jackson Meml. Hosp.-U. Miami (Fla.), 1970-71, resident in ob-gyn., 1971-74; obstetrician Tampa (Fla.) Ob-Gyn Assocs., 1976-94; clin. assoc. prof. obstetrics U. So. Fla. Sch. Medicine, Tampa, 1976—. Bd. dirs. Ctr. of Excellence, 1983-90, Humana Women's Hosp., Tampa, Fla., 1983-90, Gulf Coast Health Systems Agy., 1980-83; mem. midwifery adv. com. Fla. Dept. Health and Human Resources, Tallahassee, 1982-86. Author: (with Carroll Shephard) The Complete Guide to Women's Health, 1982, 3d rev. edit., 1997; prin., writer, spokesperson (series of TV commls.) The Healthy Woman (Gold Link award 1987); mem. med. adv. bd. Baby Talk mag., 1995—; contbr. articles to profl. jours. and women's mags. Served as maj. USAF, 1974-76. Mem. AMA, Am. Coll. Obstetricians and Gynecologists (patient edn. com. 1984-86, John McCain fellow 1981), Sta. WEDU, Tampa, Phi Beta Kappa. Democrat. Lutheran. Avocations: tennis, photography, golf, antique collecting, running. Home: 8649 N Himes # 1123 Tampa FL 33614 Office: 4302 N Habana Ave Ste 300 Tampa FL 33607-6316

SHEPHARD, DOREEN LOY, retired community health nurse, educator; b. York, Nebr., Apr. 16, 1936; d. Daniel R. Friesen and Marie Mildred (Janzen) Friesen Siebert; m. Raymond C. Shephard, Aug. 24, 1985. Diploma in nursing, Lincoln Gen. Hosp. Sch., 1957; student, U. Nebr., 1954-57, Portland State Coll., 1961-63; BSN, U. Oreg., 1963; postgrad., Tex. Christian U., 1964-65, U. Tex., 1965-66; MPH, U. Hawaii, 1975; PhD, Tex. Woman's U., 1987. RN, Tex. Staff nurse Lincoln (Nebr.) Gen. Hosp., 1957-59, VA Hosp., Fargo, N.D., 1959-61; clinic nurse Kaiser Permanente Clinic, Portland, Oreg., 1962-63; staff nurse VA Hosp., 1963-64; night float nurse All Saints Hosp., Ft. Worth, 1965; missionary nurse United Christian Missionary Soc., Indpls., 1966-73; oper. rm. instr. Christian Med. Coll. Hosp., Ludhiana, Punjab, India, 1966-67; instr. Mid-India Bd. Examiners Sch. for Grad. Nurses, Indore, India, 1968, Sch. of Nursing Mission Hosp., Tilda, India, 1969-71; cmty. health nurse Holy Family Hosp., Cmty. Health Project, New Delhi, 1971-72; staff nurse St. Elizabeth's Health Care Ctr., 1973; pub. health nurse II Lincoln Lancaster Health Dept., 1973-74; instr. U. Hawaii Coll. Nursing, Honolulu, 1975-77; tester, reader U. Hawaii Rsch. Corp., 1980; vis. nurse Tabitha Home Health Care, Lincoln, 1980; night staff nurse York (Nebr.) Gen. Hosp., 1980-81; instr. nursing Kearney (Nebr.) State Coll., 1981-84; supr. North Ctrl. Tex. Home Health Agy., Ft. Worth, 1986-87; asst. prof. nursing West Tex. State U., Canyon, 1987-88; assoc. prof. nursing U. Guam, Mangilao, 1988; asst. prof. nursing Stephen F. Austin State U., Nacogdoches, Tex., 1989-93; asst. prof. U. Tex. Pan Am., Edinburg, 1994-97, ret., 1997. Attendee numerous nursing confs., seminars and workshops. Contbr. articles to profl. jours. Home: 3956 Parkhaven Dr Denton TX 76210-3424

SHEPHARD, FRANK CONNELL, science writer, publishing executive; b. Knoxville, Tenn., July 11, 1944; s. Lester C. and Dean (Moody) S.; m. Susan C. Race, July 20, 1968; children; Jennifer, John, Jillian. BS, Rutgers U., 1966; postgrad., Columbia U., 1968. Vol. Peace Corps., Kenya, 1968-72, trainer Iran, 1972; editor oceanography Pergamon Press, Oxford, Eng., 1973-84; CEO Woods Hole (Mass.) Data Base, 1984—. Founding editor Oceanography Lit. Rev., 1978, Sea Grant Abstracts, 1984, Resource/Environ. Rev., 1990. Founder, pres. Citizens for Sound Planning, Falmouth, Mass., 1988; active Cape Code Commn., 1997-2002, chmn., 2000-01. Mem. AAAS, Soc. Scholarly Publishing, Am. Soc. Info. Sci., Nat. Orgn. Retired Peace Corp Vols. Avocations: outdoor sports, music, travel. Office: Woods Hole Data Base PO Box 712 Woods Hole MA 02543-0712 E-mail: whdb@capecod.net.

SHEPHARD, NEIL, economist, educator; b. Plymouth, Eng., Oct. 8, 1964; s. Thomas F. and Tydfil Shephard; m. Heather L. Bell. BA, York U., 1986; MSc, London Sch. Econs., 1987, PhD, 1990. Lectr. London Sch. Econs., 1988-93; rsch. fellow Nuffield Coll., Oxford U., 1991-93, ofcl. fellow, 1993—. Office: Nuffield Coll Oxford OX1 1NF England E-mail: neil.shephard@nuf.ox.ac.uk.

SHEPHARD, WILLIAM DANKS, physicist, educator; b. Ind., July 8, 1933; m. Barbara Ann Parker, July 25, 1959 (dec. Apr. 26, 1996). BA, Wesleyan U., 1954; MS, U. Wis., 1955, PhD, 1962. Asst. prof. U. Ky., Lexington, 1960—63; Fulbright sr. rsch. fellow Max Planck Inst. fur Physik und Astrophysik, Munich, 1962—63; asst. then assoc. prof. U. Notre Dame, Ind., 1963—73, prof., 1973—; guest prof. U. Nijmegen, Netherlands, 1975—76. Vis. scientist Fermilab, Batavia, Ill., 1971—; guest scientist SLAC, Palo Alto, Calif., 1980—; vis. scientist Brookhaven Nat. Lab., Upton, NY, 1960—; guest physicist and cons. Argonne Nat. Lab., Ill., 1963—80; organizer XII Internat. Symposium on Multiparticle Dynamics, Notre Dame, 1981. Editor: (book) Multiparticle Dynamics 1981, 1982; contbr. articles to profl. jours. Elder 1st Presbyn. Ch., South Bend, Ind., 2000—02, deacon, 1997—99. Fellow Predoctoral fellow, NSF, 1954—55, 1956—57; grantee Rsch. grantee, 1963—; scholar Fulbright Sr. Rsch. scholar, U.S. Govt., 1962—63. Mem.: Am. Phys. Soc., Sigma Xi (pres., Notre Dame chpt. 1977—78), Phi Beta Kappa (pres. Epsilon chpt. Ind. 1991—93). Office: Univ Notre Dame Dept Physics 225 Nieuwland Notre Dame IN 46556-5670 Personal E-mail: shephard.1@nd.edu. E-mail: shephard.1@nd.edu.

SHEPHERD, CHARLES CLINTON, real estate executive; b. Westport, Conn., May 25, 1929; s. J. Clinton and Gail Fleming (English) S.; m. June Stalls, June 19, 1956; children: Gail Paige, Susan Arlen, Richard Clinton. B in Landscape Arch., U. Fla., 1954, M in City Planning, 1956. Lic. real estate broker. Pres. Kendree and Shepherd, Phila., 1958-72; regional pres. Robino-Ladd Co., Palm Beach, Fla., 1972-75; v.p. Hovnanian Co., Lake Worth, 1975-78; pres. Gamina Co., 1978-92, Charles Shepherd, Ent., Palm Beach, 1992—. Chmn. Whitpain Planning Commn., Blue Bell, Pa., 1967-72; mem. land use adv. bd. Palm Beach County, 1989-91. Contbr. articles to profl. jours. Mem. Palm Beach County Task Force, 1984, Downtown Devel. Authority, Lake Worth, 1985-88, chmn., 1988. 1st lt. arty. U.S. Army, 1952-54. Mem. Am. Soc. Planners, Home Builders Assn. Home: 400 Country Club Dr Lake Worth FL 33462

SHEPHERD, DANIEL MARSTON, executive recruiter; b. Madison, Ind., Apr. 8, 1939; s. Marston Vincent and Edith America (Brunson) S.; m. Bonnie Lynn Brawley, June 27, 1970 (div. Nov. 1987); children: Vincent, David, Christopher, Megan; m. Gail Lenore Sanborn, Oct. 3, 1989; children: Heather, Shannon. BS in Civil Engring., U. Ky., 1962; MBA, Harvard Bus. Sch., 1964. Mfg. and distbn. mgr. Procter & Gamble Co., Staten Island, N.Y., 1966-70; distbn. and ops. mgr. Mattel, Inc., Gardenia, Calif., 1970-73; gen. mgr., dir. ops. Fuqua Industries, Inc., Atlanta, 1973-76; v.p. product/market mgmt. Masonite Corp., Chgo., 1976-78; v.p. Heidrick & Struggles, 1978-82, Lamalie Assocs., Chgo., 1982-86; prin. Sweeney Shepherd Bueschel Provus Harbert & Mummert, 1986-91, Shepherd Bueschel & Provus, Inc., Chgo., 1991—. Capt. U.S. Army, 1964-66. Decorated Army Commendation medal, 1966; recipient Am.'s Top 150 Recruiters award Harper Bus., N.Y.C., 1992. Mem. Assn. Exec. Search Cons., Inc., Harvard Bus. Sch. Club. Republican. Episcopalian. Avocations: coin and art collecting, skiing, baseball, food, wine. Home: 100 Buckboard Pl Pagosa Springs CO 81147 Office: 401 N Michigan Ave Ste 3020 Chicago IL 60611-4257 E-mail: sbp401@aol.com.

SHEPHERD, ELIZABETH POOLE, health science facility administrator; b. Bulape, Kasai, Congo, Mar. 16, 1937; (parents Am. citizens); d. Mark Keller and Sara Amelia (Day) Poole; m. Donald Ray Shepherd, June 6, 1958; children: Lisa, Stephanie, Leslie, Don Poole. BA magna cum laude, Austin Coll., 1958. Cert. secondary and elem. tchr., Tex. Tchr. Thomas Jefferson High Sch., Dallas, 1958, Edward H. Cary Jr. High Sch., Dallas, 1959-60; bus. mgr. Donald R. Shepherd, M.D., P.A., Conroe, Tex., 1972-96; bus. mgr., co-owner Profl. Labs, Inc., Houston, 1975-82; bus. mgr. Profl. Pathology Labs., Ltd., Conroe, 1997-2000, ret., 2000. Brownie leader Girl Scouts Am., 1967-69; dist. chmn. San Jacinto council Boy Scouts Am., Conroe, 1977; pres. Women of Ch. First Presbyn. Ch., Conroe, 1973-74, Montgomery County Med. Soc. Aux., Conroe, 1974-75; bd. dirs. ARC, Conroe, 1970-80; bd. dirs., officer Med. Ctr. Hosp. Vols., Conroe, 1978-81. Mem. AAUW, Alpha Chi, Alpha Delta. Republican. Presbyterian. Avocations: gardening, reading. Home: 175 Granite Point Rd Tow TX 78672

SHEPHERD, ELSBETH WEICHSEL, supply chain consultant; b. Youngstown, Ohio, Dec. 5, 1952; d. Richard Henry and Lesley Frances (Lynn) Weichsel; m. Gordon Ray Shepherd, Aug. 28, 1976. BS in Math, Carnegie-Mellon U., 1974; MBA, U. Cin., 1979. Asst. indsl. engr. Armco, Inc., Middletown, Ohio, 1974-76, assoc. indsl. engr., 1976-78, indsl. engr., 1978-82, sr. ops. engr., 1982-86, supr. process planning, 1986-88; project mgr. Integrated Mfg., 1988-91, supt. primary ops. scheduling, 1991-92; sr. assoc. Coopers & Lybrand, Cin., 1992-93, mng. assoc., 1993-94; sr. cons. CSC Consulting, 1995—2002, prin., 1998. Vol. Miami Purchase Assn. Am. Iron and Steel Inst. Fellow, 1978-81; mem. news mag. staff Jr. League Cin., 1980-81. Mem. Soc. Women Engrs. (pres. sect. 1981-82, provisional regional dir. 1983-84), Assn. Computing Machinery, Am. Inst. Indsl. Engrs. (v.p. services, pres. 1985-86), Tech. Socs. Coun. Cin. (pres. 1986-87, 1st v.p. 1985-86, 2d v.p. 1984-85, treas. 1983-84), Engrs. and Scientists of Cin. (sec. 1986-87, pres. elect 1987-88, pres. 1988-89, treas. 1990-95). Home: 7382 Ridgepoint Dr Cincinnati OH 45230-4398 Office: 27th Flr 255 E 5th St Ste 27 Cincinnati OH 45202-4700 E-mail: eshepherd@cinci.rr.com., eshepher@csc.com.

SHEPHERD, GAAL, artist; b. Gainesville, Fla., Jan. 25, 1951; d. Charles Claypoole and Ruby Frances (Grogan) S.; m. John Allen Crowl. Student, Stella Adler Theater Studio, 1968-73, U. Tampa, 1974-75, Corcoran Sch. Art, 1985-88. Artist, Atlanta, Tampa, Ga., Fla., 1973-76; graphic designer Art Prodn., Inc., Washington, 1976-79; art dir., illustrations editor Chronicle Higher Edn., 1979-88; painter, sculptor South Woodstock, Vt., 1988—. Exhbn. agt. The Carving Studio, West Rutland, Vt., 1996—. One-woman shows include Pierre Antoine Gallery, Washington, 1987, 1989, Beside Myself Gallery, Arlington, Vt., 1993, Bromfield Gallery, Boston, 1993, Colby-Sawyer Coll., New London, NH, 1993, Lyndon State Coll., Lyndonville, Ct., 1993, Chaffee Art Ctr., Rutland, Vt., 1994, 1997, 1998, 2002, Vt. Coun. on Arts, Montpelier, 1995, Clarke Galleries, Stowe, Vt., 1995, Between the Muse Gallery, Rockland, Maine, 1996, No B.I.A.S. Gallery, Bennington, Vt., 1997, Steinway Gallery, Chapel Hill,NC, 1998, Red Mill Gallery, Johnson, Vt., exhibited in group shows at Middletown (NY) Arts Ctr., 1994, Vt. State Craft Ctr. at Frog Hollow, Middlebury, 1994, Attleboro (Mass.) Mus., 1996, Helen Day Art Ctr., Stowe, 1996, Vt. Coun. on Arts, West Rutland, 1996, AVA Gallery, Lebanon, NH, 1996, Harvard U., Cambridge, Mass., 1996, Ashuah-Irving Gallery, Boston, 1996, Ctr. for Contemporary Arts, Santa Fe, N.Mex., 1997, Guadalupe Fine Arts, Santa Fe, 1997, State Capitol Rotunda, 1997, Vt. Inst. Natural Sci., Woodstock, 1997, Beside Myself Gallery, Arlington, Vt., 1998, Maine Coast Artists, Rockport, 1999, Shelburne Farms, Vt., 2001, N.Mex. State Capitol, Santa Fe, 2002, two-person shows. Democrat. Avocations: mycology, gardening. Home: Thistle Hill Rd PO Box 307 North Pomfret VT 05053-0307

SHEPHERD, GILLIAN MARY, physician; b. Mar. 12, 1948; d. John Thompson and Helen (Johnston) S.; m. Eduardo Goar Mestre, Aug. 4, 1973; children: Laura Elena, Cristina Alicia, Eduardo Goar. BA, Wheaton Coll., Norton, Mass., 1970; postgrad., Tufts U., 1970-73; MD, N.Y. Med. Coll., 1976. Diplomate Am. Bd. Internal Medicine, Am. Bd. Allergy and Immunology. Intern, resident Lenox Hill Hosp., N.Y.C., 1976-79; fellow in allergy and immunology N.Y. Hosp./Cornell Med. Sch., 1979-81; assoc. prof. medicine Cornell U. Med. Coll., 1988—, clin. assoc. prof. medicine, 1995—. Assoc. attending physician N.Y. Hosp., N.Y.C.; cons. allergy and immunology dept. medicine Meml. Sloan-Kettering Cancer Ctr., N.Y.C., 1982—. Contbr. articles in field to profl. jours. Fellow ACP, Am. Acad. Asthma, Allergy and Immunology (chair Edn. and Rsch. Trust 1999-2001, bd. dirs. 2000—); mem. AAAS, Am. Fedn. for Clin. Rsch., Joint Coun. Allergy and Immunology, N.Y. Allergy Soc. (exec. com. 1982-94, pres. 1991-92), N.Y. County Med. Soc. Office: 235 E 67th St Rm 203 New York NY 10021-6040

SHEPHERD, GORDON GREELEY, space physics educator, researcher; b. Senate, Sask., Can., June 19, 1931; s. George Fredrick and Irene Eleanor (Thompson) S.; m. Marian Margaret Morgenroth, Aug. 15, 1953; children—Theodore Gordon, David Michael, Paul Ronald; m. Marianna Genova Gerdjikova, Dec. 19. 1987. B.Sc. in Engring. Physics, U. Sask., Saskatoon, Can., 1952; M.Sc. in Physics, U. Sask., 1953; PhD in Physics, U. Toronto, Ont., Can., 1956. Asst. prof. physics U. Sask., 1957-64, assoc. prof., 1964-69; prof. York U., Toronto, 1969—, dir. Ctr. for Rsch. in Earth and Space Sci., 1994—. Fellow Royal Soc. Can., Can. Aeronautics and Space Inst., Am. Geophys. Union; mem. Optical Soc. Am., Can. Assn. Physicists Mem. United Ch. of Can. Avocations: swimming; diving; skiing. Home: 14 E Humber Dr King City ON Canada L7B 1B6 Office: York Univ/Ctr Rsch E/S Sci 4700 Keele St Toronto ON Canada M3J 1P3

SHEPHERD, JOHN MICHAEL, lawyer; b. St. Louis, Aug. 1, 1955; s. John Calvin and Bernice Florence (Hines) S.; m. Deborah Tremaine Fenton, Oct. 10, 1981; children: Elizabeth White, Katherine Tremaine. BA, Stanford U., 1977; JD, U. Mich., 1980. Bar: Calif. 1981, D.C. 1991, U.S. Dist. Ct. (no. dist.) Calif. 1981. Assoc. McCutchen, Doyle, Brown & Enersen, San Francisco, 1980-82; spl. asst. to asst. atty. gen. U.S. Dept. Justice, Washington, 1982-84, dep. asst. atty gen., 1984-86; assoc. counsel to The President The White House, 1986-87; sr. dep. comptroller of the currency Dept. Treasury, 1987-91; spl. counsel Sullivan & Cromwell, N.Y.C., 1991-93, Washington, 1993; exec. v.p., gen. counsel Shawmut Nat. Corp., Boston, 1993-95; ptnr. Brobeck, Phleger & Harrison LLP, San Francisco, 1995-2000; exec. v.p., gen. counsel and sec. Bank of New York Co., Inc., N.Y.C., 2001—. Contbr. articles to profl. jours. Asst. dir. policy Reagan-Bush Presdl. Transition Team, Washington, 1980-81; bd. dirs. Reagan Dep. Asst. Secs., Washington, 1985-90, Episc. Charities N.Y., Mus. Law, Common Good; trustee New Eng. Aquarium, 1994-96. Named one of Outstanding Young Men Am., U.S. Jaycees, 1984; Wardack Research fellow Washington U., 1976. Mem. ABA (chmn. fin. markets and ins. com., antitrust law sect. 1992-95, banking law com. 1983—, vice chair 1998—, chmn. bank holding co. acquisitions subcom. 1995-98, bus. law sect., standing com. on law and nat. security 1984-96), D.C. Bar Assn., New Eng. Legal Found. (bd. dirs. 1994-96), Pacific Coun. Internat. Policy, Coun. Fgn. Rels., Chevy Chase Club, Univ. Club, Met. Club, Olympic Club, Wilson Coun, Woodrow Wilson Internat. Ctr. for Scholars, 2000—. Office: Bank of NY Co Inc One Wall St New York NY 10286 E-mail: mshepherd@bankofny.com.

SHEPHERD, JOHN THOMAS, music educator, educational association administrator; b. Martinsburg, W.Va. s. Howard A and Rachel Ruth Shepherd. Bachelor Music Edn., W.Va. U., Morgantown, West Virginia, 1966—70, Master Music Edn., 1970—71. Music tchr. Ohio county schools, Wheeling, W.Va., 1971—; dir. music ministry Edgewood Evan-Lutheran Ch., 1990—. Bd. diretors WVACC, W.Va., 1988—2002. Recipient Ohio county tchr. yr., Ohio county schools, 1995. Mem.: WVMEA, NEA. Home: 8 Hubbard Place Wheeling WV 26003-5523 Office: Ohio county schools 100 Clark Lane Wheeling WV 26002 Office Fax: 304-243-0357. E-mail: allegrojf@aol.com.

SHEPHERD, JOHN THOMPSON, physiologist; b. No. Ireland, May 21, 1919; s. William Frederick and Matilda (Thompson) S.; m. Helen Mary Johnston, July 28, 1945; children: Gillian Mary, Roger Frederick John; m. Marion G. Etzwiler, Apr. 22, 1989. Student, Campbell Coll., Belfast, No. Ireland, 1932-37; MB, BCh, Queen's U., Belfast, 1945, MChir, 1948, MD, 1951, DSc, 1956, DSc (hon.), 1979; MD (hon.), U. Bologna, 1984, U. Gent, 1985. Lectr. physiology Queen's U., 1948-53, reader physiology, 1954-57; assoc. prof. physiology Mayo Found., 1957-62, prof. physiology, 1962—, chmn. dept. physiology and biophysics, 1966-74; bd. govs. Mayo Clinic, 1966-80; trustee Mayo Found., 1969-81, dir. rsch., 1969-77, dir. for edn., 1977-83, chmn. bd. devel., 1983-88; dean Mayo Med. Sch., 1977-83; assoc. dir. Gen. Rsch. Ctr. Mayo Clinic, Rochester, 1992-94. Chmn. U.S. Nat. Com. for the Internat. Union of Physiol. Scis., 1991-95; vis. prof. U. Auckland, New Zealand, 1997; vis. prof. cardiovasc. divsn. U. Minn., 1995; Soma Weiss meml. lectr. Third Internat. Congress WHMA, Pecs, Hungary, 1996. Author, editor: Physiology of the Circulation in Human Limbs in Health and Disease, 1963, Cardiac Function in Health and Disease, 1968, Veins and Their Control, 1975, Human Cardiovascular System, 1979, Handbook of Physiology, The Cardiovascular System Peripheral Circulation and Organ Blood Flow, 1983, Vascular Diseases in the Limbs, 1993, Nervous Control of the Heart, 1996; co-editor: Exercise: Regulation and Integration of Multiple Systems. Handbook of Physiology, 1996; mem. editl. bd. Hypertension, 1973—, Am. Jour. Physiology, Am. Heart Jour., Microvascular Rsch.; cons. editor Circulation Rsch., 1981—; editor-in-chief News in Physiol. Sci., 1988-94; mem. editl. adv. bd. Clin. Autonomic Rsch., 1990—, Jour. Autonomic Nervous Sys., 1994—, Exptl. Physiology, 1994—, Vascular Medicine, 1995—, Internat. Angiology Adv. Com., 1994—, Cardiovasc. Rsch., 1997—; contbr. more than 590 sci. articles to profl. jours. Recipient NASA Skylab Achievement award, 1974, A. Ross McIntyre medal for achievement, 1991; Brit. Med. Assn. scholar, 1949-50, Fulbright scholar, 1953-54; Anglo-French Med. exch. bursar, 1957; Internat. Francqui chair, 1978; Einthoven lectr. 1981, Volhard lectr., 1990. Fellow Am. Coll. Cardiology (hon.), Royal Coll. Physicians (London), Royal Acad. Medicine (Belgium); mem. NAS (space sci. bd. 1973-74, chmn. com. space biology and medicine 1973), Am. Physiol. Soc. (Disting. Svc. award 1990, Ray G. Daggs award 1997), Louis Rapkine Assn., Am. Heart Assn. (dir. 1968—, pres. 1975-76, chmn. vascular medicine and biology task force 1990, hon. fellow coun. clin. cardiology), Physiol. Soc. Gt.

Brit., Med. Rsch. Soc. London, Assn. Am. Physicians, Internat. Union of Angiology (hon.), Worldwide Hungarian Med. Acad. (hon.), Rappaport Inst. Israel (sci. adv. bd.), Sigma Xi. Office: Mayo Clinic Plummer Bldg N-10 Rochester MN 55905

SHEPHERD, KAREN, former congresswoman; b. Silver City, N.Mex., July 5, 1940; m. Vincent P. Shepherd. BA, U. Utah, 1962; MA, Brigham Young U., 1963. Former instr. Brigham Young U., Am. U., Cairo; former pres. Webster Pub. Co.; former adminstr. David Eccles Sch. Bus., U. Utah; former dir. Salt Lake County Social Svcs., Utah; former dir. continuing edn. Westminster Coll.; former mem. Utah Senate; mem. 103d Congress from 2d Utah dist., Washington, 1993-95, Nat. Common Cause Governing Bd., Washington, 1995-96; exec. dir., U.S. rep. European Bank for Reconstruction Devel., 1996—2002; mem. exec. com., chair East West Trade and Investment Forum Am. C. of C., England, 1998—2002; dir. EMILY's List, 2002—. Founder Karen Shepherd Fund; founding mem. Utah Women's Polit. Caucus, Project 2000; mem. Internat. Delegation to Monitor Elections in West Bank and Gaza, Israel; trustee KeyBank Victory Funds. Former mem. United Way, Pvt. Industry Coun.; former mem. adv. bd. U.S. West Grad. Sch. Social Work; trustee Westminster Coll. Recipient Women in Bus. award U.S. Small Bus. Assn., Woman of Achievement award, Pathfinder award, YWCA Leadership award, 1st place award Nat. Assn. Journalists, Disting. Alumni award U. Utah Coll. Humanities. Fellow Inst. Politics Kennedy Sch Govt., Internat. Women's Forum; Salt Lake Area C. of C. (pub. rels. com.), Coun. on Fgn. Rels. Home: PO Box 1049 Salt Lake City UT 84110-1049 Office: 21 G St Salt Lake City UT 84103-2949

SHEPHERD, MARK, JR. retired electronics company executive; b. Dallas, Jan. 18, 1923; s. Mark and Louisa Florence (Daniell) S.; m. Mary Alice Murchland, Dec. 21, 1945; children: Debra Aline Shepherd Robinson, MaryKay Theresa, Marc Blaine. BSEE, So. Meth. U., 1942; MSEE, U. Ill., at Urbana, 1947. Registered profl. engr., Tex. With GE, 1942-43, Farnsworth TV and Radio Corp., 1947-48, Tex. Instruments, Dallas, 1948-88, v.p., gen. mgr. semicondr.-components div., 1955-61, exec. v.p., chief operating officer, 1961-66, pres., chief operating officer, 1967-69, pres., chief exec. officer, 1969-76, chmn. bd. dirs., chief exec. officer, 1976-84, chmn. bd. dirs., chief corp. officer, 1984-85, chmn., 1985-88; ret. Hon. trustee Com. for Econ. Devel.; councillor conf. Bd.; mem. Bus. Coun. Lt. (j.g.) USNR, 1943-46. Fellow IEEE; mem. NAE, Sigma Xi, Eta Kappa Nu.

SHEPHERD, MARY ANNE, elementary education educator; b. Washington, Jan. 26, 1950; d. Edwin Joseph and Louise Therese (McKay) Zabel; m. Robert A. Shepherd, June 25, 1988. BS, U. Md., 1972; MEd, George Mason U., 1976; postgrad., U. Akron, 1991-93. Cert. mid. childhood generalist tchr., tchr. Nat. Bd., 2000. Tchr. elem. schs. Montgomery County Public Schs., Rockville, Md., 1972-74, Fauquier County Pub. Schs., Warrenton, Va., 1974-76, Wooster (Ohio) Pub. Schs., 1976—; mem. faculty East Region Ohio Sch. Net, 1996-98. Master tchr, 1998-99; vestrywoman St. Paul's Episcopal Ch., Akron, Ohio, Ohio, 1996-99, jr. warden, 1998-99 Mem. Wooster Edn. Assn. (treas. 1984-91). Republican. Avocations: needlecrafts, exercising, gardening. Home: 4872 Medina Rd Akron OH 44321-1122 Office: Wooster City Schs 144 N Market St Wooster OH 44691-4810

SHEPHERD, MARY ELIZABETH, dermatologist; b. Beaumont, Tex., Sept. 2, 1948; d. Albert Anthony and Addie (Moore) S.; m. George Maurrye Munchus, Mar. 21, 1970 (div. Sept. 1979); 1 child, Damon George. BS, Tex. Women's U., 1970, MS, 1972, PhD, 1975; MD, U. Ill., Chgo., 1988. Cert. Am. Bd. Dermatology. Instr. N. Tex. State U., Denton, 1975-76; rsch. assoc. U. Ala., Birmingham, 1976-80; asst. prof. U. Ill., Chgo., 1980-84; intern in internal medicine U. Tex. Med. Br., Galveston, 1988-89, resident in dermatology, 1989-92; attending physician Cook County Hosp., Chgo., 1995-96; with dept. medicine Mt. Sinai Hosp. Med. Ctr., 1996—. Maj. USAF, 1990-95, USAFR, 1995—. Fellow Am. Acad. Dermatology; mem. NAACP, Nat. Med. Assn., Women's Dermatol. Soc., Chgo. Dermatol. Soc., Sierra Club. Office: Dreyer Med Clinic Dermatology Dept 1870 W Galena Blvd Aurora IL 60506-4356 E-mail: mary.shepherd@dreyermed.com.

SHEPHERD, PAUL H. elementary school educator; b. Salt Lake City, Sept. 6, 1955; s. Richard Lawrence and Janis (Hoskings) S.; m. Marlene Wade, Aug. 31, 1978; children: Janice, Faith, Matthew, Andrew, Luke, Christian. BS in Elem. Edn., U. Utah, 1981, MEd, 1985. Cert. elem. tchr., Utah. Printer Transamerica Film Svc., Salt Lake City, 1978-81; tchr. Granite Sch. Dist., 1981—. Pres. Granite Fedn. Tchrs., 1985-87, treas., 1990-92. Active mem. State House of Reps., 1992-94; Bishop LDS Ch., West Jordan, Utah, 1988; mem. Oquivrh Shadows Community Coun., West Jordan, 1987; chmn. rels. com. Boy Scouts Am., 1972—. Recipient Outstanding Tchr. award Excel Found., 1985, Elem. Tchr. of Yr. award Utah Fedn. Tchrs., 1991. Mem. ASCD, Utah Assn Gifted Children. Democrat. Avocations: fishing, guitar. Home and Office: 6644 W 5095 S West Jordan UT 84084-7728 E-mail: shepfam@concentric.net., paul.shepherd@granite.k12.ut.us.

SHEPHERD, REGINALD, writer, educator; b. N.Y.C., Apr. 10, 1963; s. Goldburn Shepherd and Blanche Althea Berry. BA, Bennington (Vt.) Coll., 1988; MFA, Brown U., 1991, U. Iowa, 1993. 1asst. prof. No. Ill. U., DeKalb, 1995—99; asst. prof. Cornell U., Ithaca, NY, 1999—2002. Lit. fellowship panelist Nat. Endowment for the Arts, 1998. Author: Some Are Drowning, 1994 (award in poetry Associated Writing Programs 1993), Angel, Interrupted, 1996, Wrong, 1999. Recipient "Discovery"/The Nation award Poetry Ctr. of the 92d St. Y, N.Y.C., 1993; Poetry Travelling scholar Amy Lowell Trust, 1994-95; Creative Writing fellow Nat. Endowment for the Arts, 1994, Poetry fellow Ill. Arts Coun., 1998, Poetry fellow Constance Saltonstall Found., 2000. Mem. Associated Writing Programs. Home: 741 Cornell Ave Pensacola FL 32514

SHEPHERD, STEVEN STEWART, auditor, consultant; b. Pauls Valley, Okla., Aug. 7, 1956; s. Lloyd Thomas and Barbara Lou (Garton) S.; m. Dawn Rachelle Godwin, Aug. 22, 1981; children: Shane, Lauren. BBA, U. Tex., 1981, MBA, 1990. Internal auditor Ark-La. Gas Co., Shreveport, La., 1982-84; sr. constrn. auditor Cen. & S.W. Svcs., Inc., Dallas, 1984-87; constrn. audit supr. City of Ft. Worth, 1987-96; city auditor City of Garland, Tex., 1996—. Cons. Constrn. Mgmt. Svcs., Arlington, Tex., 1990—, Eagle Tax Svcs., Arlington, 1990—; mem. adv. com. for acctg. program Tarrant County Jr. Coll., 1995-97; mem. internal audit adv. bd. U. North Tex., 1993-96. Contbr. articles to profl. jours. Mem. allocation com. Tarrant County United Way, Ft. Worth, 1991; bd. dirs. Charlotte Anderson Elem. Sch. PTA, Mansfield, Tex., 1990-91. Mem. Inst. Internal Auditors (bd. govs. Ft. Worth chpt. 1990-96, sec. 1990-91, treas. 1991-92, v.p. 1992-93, pres. 1993-94), Mansfield Youth Baseball Assn. (bd. dirs. 1993-95), Delta Upsilon (bd. dirs. 1991-96, sec. 1994-95). Republican. Mem. Ch. of Christ. Avocations: little league coach, horseback riding, water skiing, snow skiing, scuba diving.

SHEPHERD, WILLIAM M. astronaut; b. Oak Ridge, Tenn., July 26, 1949; s. George R. and Barbara Shepherd; m. Beth Stringham. BS in Aerospace Engring., U.S. Naval Acad., 1971; degree in ocean engring., MSME, MIT, 1978. Commd. USN, 1971, advanced through grades to capt., with underwater demolition team ELEVEN, with SEALS Team One and Two, with spl. boat unit 20; astronaut candidate NASA, 1984, various mgmt. positions space sta. program, 1993—96, comdr. flight crew Expedition-1 on Internat. Space Sta., 2000—01. Mem.: AIAA. Achievements include over 159 days in space; 3 shuttle flights as mission specialist in 1988, 1990 and 1992. Office: Astronaut Office/CB NASA Johnson Space Ctr Houston TX 77058*

SHEPLER, DEBRA LYNN, artist, secondary education educator; b. Huntington, Ind., June 30, 1955; d. Dwight Elmer and Barbara Ann Jennings; m. Scott Shepler, June 23, 1979; children: Heather N. Shepler Smith, Ashlae Dawn. BS, Ind. Wesleyan U., 1977; MA, Ball State U., 1988. Lic. tchr., Ind. Graphic designer Graphic Menus Inc., Eaton, Ind., 1977-78; mem. advt./display staff J.C. Penney, Marion, 1978-80; tchr. art Marion Cmty. Schs., 1985—. Author, illustrator: Glimpses, 1988; solo shows Marion H.S. Auditorium, 1993, 99; group shows at Marion Pub. Libr., 1992, 96, 97, 98, 2000. Mem. Ave Maria choir Marion Easter Pageant, 1980—; former pres., mem. Quilters Hall of Fame Friends, Marion, 1992—; instr. art Marion Cmty. Sch. of Arts, 1995—. Recipient Gold Key award Scholastic Arts, Ft. Wayne, Ind., 1973, Best of Show award Marion Pub. Libr., 1992, several 1st and 2d place awards. Mem. Art Educators' Forum, Grant County Art Assn. (bd. dirs.). Avocations: photography, drawing, painting, gardening, antiquing. Home: 101 North D St Marion IN 46952

SHEPLER, JOHN EDWARD, engineering executive; b. Freeport, Ill., June 23, 1950; s. Edward Charles and Joyce Margaret (Wagner) S.; m. Barbara Jeanne Heinrich, Sept. 11, 1976. BSEE, Milw. Sch. Engring., 1972. Lic. FCC gen. class radiotelephone operator. Disc jockey, chief engr. Sta. WACI, Freeport, 1972-73, owner, ops. mgr., 1974-75; asst. chief engr. Sta. WROK, Rockford, Ill., 1973-74, chief engr., 1975-79; project engr. Martin Automatic, 1979-80; engring. mgr. Pacific Scientific, 1984-86; design engr. Sundstrand Corp., 1980-84, engring. mgr., 1986-99; Internet entrepreneur, 1998—; owner LongDistanceRateFinder.com, 2001—. Tech. instr. Rock Valley Coll., Rockford, 1981-84; tech. cons. various broadcasters, 1979-94; columnist Electronic Servicing and Tech. Mag., 1990-94. Author: Sensational Sound Handbook, 1981, Shepler's Weekly News and Views, Celebrating Great People Doing Great Things, 1993-98, John Shepler's Writing in a Positive Light, 1998—; columnist Radio World mag., 1982-94; tech. illustrator, cartoonist, 1989-94; contbg. reviewer Epinions, 2000—; mem. poetry rev. bd. Rockford Rev., 1997-99; contbr. articles to profl. jours.; patentee in field. Named Outstanding Alumnus Milw. Sch. Engring., 1987. Mem.: Broadcast (v.p. 1971-72). Avocations: nature photography, parrots, poetry, tech. and fiction writing. Home and Office: 5653 Weymouth Dr Rockford IL 61114-5544

SHEPLEY, HUGH, architect; b. Boston, Mar. 17, 1928; s. Henry Richardson and Anna Lowell (Gardiner) S.; m. Mary Waters Niles, Dec. 27, 1950; children: Hamilton Niles, Philip Foster. BA, Harvard U., 1951; BArch., Boston Archtl. Ctr., 1958; postgrad., Mass. Inst. Tech., 1958-59. Mem. archtl. firm Shepley, Bulfinch, Richardson & Abbott, Boston, 1955-63, ptnr., 1963-91. Bd. dirs. Greater Boston Red Cross, 1967-73, mem. exec. com., 1968-69; bd. dirs. Cmty. Music Ctr., Boston, 1968-72, Boston Ctr. for Blind Children, 1979-87; trustee New Eng. Conservatory Music, 1978-83, overseer, 1983—; trustee Univ. Hosp., 1980-96, mem. exec. com., 1981-92, vice chmn. bd. dirs., 1985-89, chmn. bd. dirs., 1989-92; trustee Am. Coll. of Greece, 1983-92, treas., 1986-88; trustee, sec. Rotch Travelling Scholarship, 1987-93, v.p., 1993—; mem. adv. coun. Boston U. Med. Ctr., 1990-96, Corp. Old South Assn., 1993—; bd. dirs. Manchester (Mass.) Hist. Soc., 1994—. Fellow AIA; mem. Mass. Assn. Architects (pres. 1972), Boston Soc. Architects (pres. 1974), Boston Archtl. Ctr. (pres. 1969-71). Clubs: Tavern (Boston); Manchester Yacht (commodore 1985-87). Republican. Episcopalian. Home: 22 Forster Rd Manchester MA 01944-1420

SHEPLEY, MARDELLE MCCUSKEY, architect, educator; b. Bethesda, Md., June 28, 1949; d. E. Scott McCuskey (father) & James R. and Yvonne Hudson S.; m. Laurence Berger, 1974 (div. 1978); m. Michael Curtice Blair, Sept. 5, 1981; children: Colin, Ian, Teal. BA, Columbia U., 1971, MArch, 1974; MA, U. Mich., 1979, DArch, 1981. Registered architect, Calif. Urban designer N.Y.C. Dept. City Planning, 1972-74; planner Min. Planning & Econ. policy, Panama, Panama, 1975-77; lectr., teaching asst. U. Mich., Ann Arbor, 1977-81; assoc. Tai Assocs. Architects, San Francisco, 1981-85, The Design Partnership, San Francisco, 1985-93; asst. prof. Tex. A&M U., College Station, 1993-97, assoc. prof., 1997—. coord. PhD program, 1999-2001, assoc. dean for students, 2001—. Rsch. com. Ctr. Health Design, Martinez, Calif., 1993—; assoc. dir. Ctr. Health Sys. and Design, 1995—. Co-author: Healthcare Environments for Children and Their Families, 1998. Bd. dirs. Assn. for Care of Children's Health, Mt. Royal, N.J., 1998-2000; mem. parent bd. Oakland (Calif.) Montessori Sch., 1991-93. Recipient Health Facilities Rsch. award AIA, 1992; Tex. A&M U. scholar, 1998; Tex. A&M U. faculty fellow, 2001—. Office: Tex A&M U Dept Architecture College Station TX 77843-3137

SHEPP, BRYAN EUGENE, psychologist, educator; b. Cumberland, Md., Sept. 13, 1932; s. Bryan Evert and Dorothy Lorene (Stell) S.; m. June Lee Langeluttig, Jan. 31, 1953; children— Karen Suzanne, David Bryan. BS, U. Md., 1954, MS, 1956, PhD, 1960; MS with honors, Brown U., 1966. Rsch. prof. U. Conn., 1961-63; asst. prof. psychology George Peabody Coll., Nashville, 1963-64, Brown U., Providence, 1964-66, assoc. prof., 1966-69, prof., 1969-98, prof. emeritus, 1998—, chmn. dept., 1983-88, assoc. dean faculty, 1988-91, dean faculty, 1991-96. Cons. in field; vis. scientist Oxford (Eng.) U., 1970 Contbr. numerous articles to profl. publs.; ad hoc editor for several psychol. jours. Served with USN, 1955-59. Decorated letter of commendation Sec. of Navy; USPHS postdoctoral fellow, 1959-61; Nat. Inst. Child Health and Human Devel. grantee, 1965— Fellow APA (founder); mem. AAAS, AAUP, Psychonomic Soc., Univ. Club. Clubs: Univ. E-mail: bjshepp@gwi.net.

SHEPPARD, ANNE THOMSON, elementary school educator; b. Charlotte, N.C., Feb. 23, 1932; d. William Francis and Nina Hunter Thomson; m. George Edwin Sheppard, Sept. 11, 1954 (dec. Sept. 15, 1996); children: George Francis, Thomas Keim, Martha S. Wills, Margaret S. Slaton. BA, Agnes Scott Coll., 1953; MAT, Converse Coll., 1965. Cryptographer Nat. Sec. Agy., Washington, 1953—54; tchr. Dist. 55, Laurens, SC, 1963—88. Mem. State Bd. Edn., Columbia, SC, 1991—93; trustee Coll. Charleston, 1994—2002. Book sale chmn. Friends of Libr., Laurens, 1995—; outreach co-chmn. First Steps, Laurens County, 2001—; treas. Laurens County Cmty. Concert Assn., 2001—. Named Woman of Yr., Bus. and Profl. Women, Laurens, 1979—80. Mem.: NEA. Presbyterian. Avocations: reading, travel. Home: 210 Ball Dr Laurens SC 29360

SHEPPARD, CLAUDE-ARMAND, lawyer; b. Ghent, Belgium, May 26, 1935; m. Claudine Proutat; children— Jean-Pierre, Michel, Marie-Claude, Stephane, Annabelle. BA, McGill U., 1955; B.C.L., 1958. Bar: Que. 1959. Sr. partner firm, head litig. sect. Robinson, Sheppard & Shapiro, Montreal, 1965—. Legal commentator for French and English radio and television networks in, Can.; lectr. various instns.; counsel various royal commns.; counsel to com. Canadian Ho. of Commons; legal supr. Que. Commn. of Inquiry Lang. Rights; dir. various orgns. and founds. Author: The Law of Languages in Canada, 1965, The Organization and Regulation of the Health and Social Welfare Professions in Quebec, 1970, Language Rights in Quebec, 1973, also numerous papers. Past pres. Canadian Civil Liberties Union; former mem. Canadian Adv. Council on Status of Women; pres. Internat. Music Festival of Lanaudière, 2000—. Fellow C.B.A. Found. for Legal Rsch. Mem. ABA (assoc.), Can. Bar Assn. (nat. com. continuing legal edn.), Can. Inst. for Adminstrn. Justice, Internat. Law Assn. Office: Robinson Sheppard & Shapiro 800 Place Victoria Ste 4600 Montreal QC Canada H4Z 1H6 E-mail: cdus@rsslex.com., dove@rsslex.com.

SHEPPARD, DEBORAH CODY, hearing handicapped educator, clinician; b. Atlanta, Aug. 4, 1959; d. Jack Benar and Wilma (Shoffner) Cody; m. Kenneth Louis Sheppard, Nov. 14, 1987. BA in Speech Correction, Columbia (S.C.) Coll., 1981; MS in Edn. of Hearing Handicapped, U. Tenn., 1983; EdS in Spl. Edn. and Early Childhood, U. S.C., 1991, postgrad., 1998—. Cert. speech pathologist, S.C., cert. early childhood edn. tchr., cert. in hearing handicapped, S.C. Speech/lang. clinician Dist. 60 of Abbeville, S.C., 1981-82, Dist. of Pickens (S.C.) County, 1984-85; tchr. hearing handicapped Dist. 50 of Greenwood, S.C., 1985-88; speech/lang. clinician Saluda (S.C.) Dist. 1, 1989-91; tchr. hearing impaired Millbrook Elem. Sch., Aiken, S.C., 1991—. Tchr. Am. sign lang. Saluda Dist. 1, 1989-91, 91—. Grantee, 1993-94, 94-95, 95-96, 96-97, 97-98. Mem.: Nat. Assn. of the Deaf. Baptist. Avocations: aerobics, gardening, travel. Home: 301 Chime Bell Church Rd Aiken SC 29803-9365 Office: Millbrook Elem Sch Aiken SC 29803

SHEPPARD, HOWARD REECE, accountant; b. Monmouth, Ill., Mar. 1, 1926; s. Loren Ernest and Ruby Pearl (Magee) S.; m. Mary Kathryn Hofstetter, June 8, 1951 (div.); children: Stephen, Peter, Jean Elizabeth; m. Maxine Dolores Johnson, Nov. 28, 1974. BSBA, Northwestern U., Evanston, Ill., 1946. CPA, Calif. Chief cost acct. Sunkist Growers Plant, Corona, Calif., 1946-52; fiscal officer U.S. Guided Missle Test Ctr., Pt. Mugu, 1952-54; internal auditor Sunkist Growers Plant, Corona, 1954-58; auditor Eadie & Payne CPAs, San Bernardino, 1958-61; pvt. practice Corona, 1961-63, 87—; ptnr. Sheppard, Reynolds & Sholl, 1963-85, Sheppard, Reynolds & Green, Corona, 1985-87. Faculty expert Hastings Law Sch., U. Calif., San Francisco, 1986-98; lectr. Dept. Water and Power, L.A., 1986. Author: Litigation Services Resource Directory, 1989, 5th edit., 1994; co-author: Litigation Services Handbook, 1990, 3d edit., 2001. Lt. USNR. Mem. AICPA, Calif. Soc. CPAs. Avocation: sailing. Home: 6370 Percival Dr Riverside CA 92506-5139 Office: Howard Reece Sheppard 1485 Spruce St Ste P Riverside CA 92507-2445

SHEPPARD, JACK W. retired career officer; b. Parkersburg, W.Va., Aug. 8, 1931; s. James Lee and Audrey Irene (Heiney) S.; m. Norma Ann Stutler, Sept. 4, 1953; children— Bradley, Gregory BAC, U. Akron, Ohio, 1955; MA in Pub. Adminstrn., George Washington U., 1965. Commd. lt. U.S. Air Force, 1955, advanced through grades to maj. gen.; vice comdr. 60 Mil. Airlift Wing, USAF, Travis AFB, Calif., 1977-79; comdr. 1606 Air Base Wing, USAF, Kirtland AFB, N.Mex., 1979-81; dir. internat. staff Inter Am. Def. Bd., USAF, Washington, 1981-82; dep. chief staff for personnel USAF Mil. Airlift Command, Scott AFB, Ill., 1982-83, chief of staff, 1983-85; comdr. Twenty First Air Force, McGuire AFB, N.J., 1985-87; asst. dep. chief staff programs and resources Hdqrs. USAF, Washington, 1987-88, ret., 1988. Mem. Albuquerque Armed Forces Adv. Assn., Order of Daedalians, Air Force Assn., Airlift Assn., USAF Order of the Sword, USAF Order of the Bayonet, Theta Chi. Presbyterian. Home: PO Box 908 21 Beaver Ln Cedar Crest NM 87008-0908 E-mail: jackgenusaf@cs.com.

SHEPPARD, THOMAS RICHARD, lawyer; b. Pasadena, Calif., Aug. 8, 1934; s. James Carroll and Ruth Mary (Pashgian) S.; m. Arlene Clubb, June 23, 1956; children— Eileen Diana, Pamela Lynn, Thomas Richard. AB, Stanford U., 1956; LL.B., Harvard U., 1961. Bar: Calif. bar 1962. Assoc. firm Sheppard, Mullin, Richter & Hampton, Los Angeles, 1961-66, ptnr., 1966—. Dir. numerous small corps.; pres. Legal Aid Found. Los Angeles, 1973 Trustee Harold Lloyd Found., Los Angeles, 1971-87, Della Martin Found., 1979—. Served to lt. (j.g.) USN, 1956-58. Mem. Am. Bar Assn., State Bar Assn. Calif., Los Angeles County Bar Assn., Am. Law Inst., Am. Coll. Real Estate Lawyers, Beta Theta Pi. Clubs: Calif. (Los Angeles) (bd. dirs. 1985-87, sec. 1987). Home: 1680 Oak Grove Ave San Marino CA 91108-1109 Office: Sheppard Mullin Richter & Hampton 333 S Hope St Ste 4800 Los Angeles CA 90071-3056

SHEPPARD, WILLIAM STEVENS, investment banker; b. Grand Rapids, Mich., Apr. 29, 1930; s. James Herbert and Emily Gilmore (Stevens) S.; m. Jane Steketee, 1956 (dec. 1975); children: Stevens C., Elizabeth W., Emily R.; m. Patricia Gillis Bloom, Dec. 2, 1978. BA in Econs, U. Va., 1953. Trainee J.P. Morgan & Co., Inc., N.Y.C., 1955-58; investment adv. Delafield & Delafield, 1958-71; from salesman to sr. v.p. and dir. F.S. Smithers & Co., 1971-76; sr. v.p., dir. successor Paine, Webber, Jackson & Curtis, Inc., 1976-81; pres., chief exec. officer, dir. Paine Webber Real Estate Securities Inc., 1980-85; mng. dir. Paine Webber Capital Markets, N.Y.C., 1985-88, Berkshire Capital Corp., N.Y.C., 1988-95, adv. dir., 1995—2001; adminstr. Pequot Investment Advisors, Inc., Southport, Conn., 1995—; ret. Chmn. bd. dirs. Ea. Bancorp; adv. dir. Putnam Trust Co., Greenwich, Conn. An editor: Ginny Mae Manual, 1979; contbr. to handbooks. Trustee, treas. Riot Relief Fund City N.Y., 1970—. Served to lt. USNR, 1953-55. Mem. N.Y. Yacht Club, Country Club of Fairfield (Conn.), Pequot Yacht Club, Mashomack Fish and Game Club, North Haven Casino Club, Cruising Club of Am., Mountain Lake Club. Republican. Home: 167 Salt Meadow Rd Fairfield CT 06430-6370 Office: HGK Asset Mgmt Inc PO Box 139 Southport CT 06490-0139 E-mail: pequotshep@aol.com.

SHEPPE, JOSEPH ANDREW, surgeon; b. Huntington, W.Va., Sept. 24, 1953; m. Kathy Chapman; children: Sheree Nicole, Natalee Marie, Brittany Lee. BS summa cum laude in Chemistry and Zoology, Marshall U., 1975; MD, W.Va. U., 1979. Diplomate Am. Bd. Surgery, Am. Bd. Colon and Rectal Surgery. Intern in gen. surgery Charleston (W.Va.) Area Med. Ctr., 1979-84; fellow in colon and rectal surgery William Beaumont Army Med. Ctr., Royal Oak, Mich., 1984-85; pvt. practice Columbia, S.C., 1985—. Physician Bapt. Med. Ctr., Columbia, Providence Hosp., Columbia, Richland Meml. Hosp., Columbia, Lexington Med. Ctr., West Columbia, S.C.; clin. instr. in gen./colorectal surgery U. S.C. Med. Sch. Mem. FACS, Fellow Am. Soc. Colon and Rectal Surgery, S.C. Med. Soc., Columbia Med. Soc. Home: 204 Leaning Tree Rd Columbia SC 29223-3009 Office: 1333 Taylor St Ste 4-a Columbia SC 29201-2949

SHEPPERD, SUSAN ABBOTT, special education educator; b. Pekin, Ill., May 12, 1942; d. Robert Fred and Martha Mae (Abbott) Belville; m. Thomas Eugene Shepperd, Oct. 7, 1960; children: Scott Thomas, Allison Marie Shepperd-Henry, Michele Lea. BA, Maryville Coll., 1990; MEd, U. Mo., 1994. Cert. elem. edn. tchr. grades 1-8, spl. reading tchr. grades K-12. Resource tchr. reading grades K-8 St. Joseph Sch., Ardiocese of St. Louis, Cottleville, Mo., 1990-98. Mem. Pi Lambda Theta (pres. 1992-94), Assn. in Edn. (Gamma Zeta chpt.), Phi Kappa Phi, Delta Epsilon Sigma. Episcopalian. Avocations: golfing, music, swimming. Home: 15977 Chamfers Farm Rd Chesterfield MO 63005-4717

SHEPPERD, THOMAS EUGENE, accountant; b. Pekin, Ill., Aug. 19, 1941; s. William Thomas and Marguerite Louise (Meisinger) S.; m. Susan Abbott Belville, Oct. 7, 1960; children: Scott Thomas, Allison Marie Shepperd-Henry, Michele Lea. BS in Acctg., U. Ill., 1964. CPA, Ill., Mo., Iowa, Ind. From jr. acct. to mgr. Haskins & Sells, St. Louis, 1964-74, mgr. Washington, 1974-75, ptnr., 1975-77, Deloitte Haskins & Sells (formerly Haskins & Sells), St. Louis, 1977-89, Deloitte & Touche (merger Deloitte Haskins & Sells and Touche Ross & Co.), St. Louis, 1989—. Treas. Shepley concert com. Christ Ch. Cathedral, St. Louis, 1989; bd. dirs. Care & Counseling, Inc., Howard Park Early Childhood Ctr.; trustee Diocesian of Mo. Investment Trust. Mem. AICPA (various coms.), Mo. Soc. CPAs (adminstrv. v.p., bd. dirs. 1988-92, treas. 1992-95, v.p. 1996-97, pres.-elect 1997-98, pres., 1998—, chair long range fin. planning com. and the office location com., terms on the tech. standards peer review exec., profl. ethics coms., legislation com., acctg. and auditing procedures com.), U. Ill. Press. Coun., David Kinley Assn., Noonday Club (treas., bd. dirs. 1977-81), Glen Echo Country Club. Republican. Episcopalian. Avocations: golf, travel, sports. Home: 15977 Chamfers Farm Rd Chesterfield MO 63005-4717 Office: Deloitte & Touche LLP 1 City Ctr Ste 2200 Saint Louis MO 63101-1819

SHER, GEORGE ALLEN, philosophy educator; b. N.Y.C., Nov. 10, 1942; s. Daniel and Clara (Landesberg) S.; m. Emily Fox Gordon, July 10, 1972; 1 child, Sarah Landesberg. BA, Brandeis U., 1964; PhD, Columbia U., 1972. Instr. philosophy Fairleigh Dickinson U., Teaneck, N.J., 1966-72, asst. prof. philosopy, 1972-74; assoc. prof. philosophy U. Vt., Burlington, 1974-80, prof., 1980-91; Herbert S. Autrey prof. philosophy Rice U., Houston, 1991—, chmn. dept. philosophy, 1993-2000. Mem. Inst. for Advanced Study, Princeton, N.J., 1987-88. Author: Desert, 1987, Beyond Neutrality: Perfectionism and Politics, 1997, Approximate Justice: Studies in Non-Ideal Theory, 1997; editor: Moral Philosophy: Selected Readings, 1989, 2d edit., 1996; contbr. articles to profl. jours. Named fellow Nat. Humanities Ctr., Rsch. Triangle Park, N.C., 1980-81. Mem. Am. Philos. Assn. Home: 2425 Dryden Rd Houston TX 77030-1001 Office: Rice U Dept Philosophy MS 14 6100 Main St Houston TX 77251-1892

SHER, LEO, psychiatrist; b. Kiev, Ukraine, June 13, 1961; s. Alexander and Ivetta (Iokhved) Sher. MD summa cum laude(hon.) , Ukrainian Nat. Med. U., Kiev, 1985. Sr. staff fellow NIMH, Bethesda, Md., 1997—2000; asst. clin. prof. psychiatry and behavioral scis. The George Washington U., Washington, 2000—; rsch. psychiatrist N.Y. State Psychiat. Inst., Columbia Presbyn. Med. Ctr., N.Y.C., 2000—; asst. clin. prof. psychiatry Columbia U. Coll. of Physician and Surgeons, 2001—; asst. attending physician The N.Y. Presbyn. Hosp., Columbia Presbyn. Med. Ctr., 2001—. Contbr. Recipient Charlotte Marker Zitrin, M.D. award, Albert Einstein Coll. of Medicine Psychiatry Residency Program at L.I. Jewish Med. Ctr., 1997. Mem.: Am. Psychiat. Assn. Jewish. Achievements include patents for in field. Personal E-mail: drleosher@aol.com.

SHER, NORMAN, physician, psychiatrist, consultant; b. Phila., Jan. 21, 1931; s. Max and Emma (Friedman) S.; m. Joanna Hollenberg, Dec. 27, 1955 (dec. July 1992); children: Jonathan, Katherine Sher Baker. BA, Swarthmore Coll., 1952; MD, U. Chgo., 1956. Rotating intern Kings County Hosp./SUNY, Bklyn., 1956-57, resident in psychiatry, 1957-58, Manhattan Psychiat. Ctr., N.Y.C., 1960-62; fellow in child psychiatry Bklyn. Psychiat. Ctr., 1962-64; dir. child psychiatry Maimonides Med. Ctr., Bklyn., 1964-68, dir. child psychiatry tng., 1968-78, dir. gen. residency tng., 1973-82; pvt. practice child and adult psychiatry, 1964—. Contbr. articles to profl. jours. Capt. M.C., U.S. Army,

1958-60. Fellow Am. Psychiat. Assn. (life), Bklyn. Psychiat. Soc. (Disting. life, pres. 1975-76), Am. Acad. Child Psychiatry (life); mem. Soc. Adolescent Psychiatry (life). Democrat. Jewish. Avocations: reading, swimming, squash, gardening, theater-going. Home: Apt 202 1801 Susquehanna Rd # 202 Abington PA 19001-4620

SHER, RICHARD B. historian, educator; b. Newark, Mar. 29, 1948; m. Doris S. Holstein, Jan. 4, 1977; 1 child, Jeremy. BA, George Washington U., 1970; MA, U. Chgo., 1971, PhD, 1979. Spl. lectr. N.J. Inst. Tech., Newark, 1979-85, asst. prof. history, 1985-86, assoc. prof. history, 1986-92, prof. history, 1992-2000, disting. prof. history, 2000—, assoc. dean coll. sci. and liberal arts, dir. honors program, 1985-91, chair dept. history, 1999—; mem. grad. faculty Rutgers U., 1991—. Vis. prof. N.Y.U., 1982; with grad. faculty Rutgers U., New Brunswick, N.J., 2000—. Author: Church and University in the Scottish Enlightenment, 1985; editor: Eighteenth-Century Scotland, 1987—, Scotland and America in the Age of the Enlightenment, 1990, Sociability and Society, 1991, The Glasgow Enlightenment, 1995, Works of William Robertson, 1997. Fellow Royal Hist.Soc.; mem. Eighteenth Century Scottish Studies Soc. (exec. sec. 1986—). Office: NJ Inst Tech Dept History University Heights Newark NJ 07102-1982

SHER, STEVEN J. writer, educator; b. Bklyn., Sept. 28, 1949; s. Albert and Miriam R. S.; m. Nancy G. Sher, Mar. 11, 1978; children: Kyla, Ari. BA, CCNY, 1970; MA, U. Iowa, 1973; MFA, Bklyn. Coll., 1978. Dir. creative writing humanities Spalding U., Louisville, 1979-81; instr. English/Journalism Oreg. State U., Corvallis, 1981-86; asst. prof. English U. N.C., Wilmington, 1986-89; vis. writer, adj. U. Oreg., 1989—, Linn-Benton C.C., 1989—, Willamette U., 1989—, Western Oreg. U., 1989—. Editor, staff writer, media Observer Quar., Albany, Oreg., 1972—; cons., literary mag. Aronson, Ch2M Hill, 1989-97; staff prodn. editor Appleton-Century-Crofts, 1977, Swan Publs., 1976-78, People and Places, 1974-75, Fin. mag., 1972, The Wilmington Rev., others. Author: Flying Though Glass, 2001, Traveler's Advisory, 1994, Man with a Thousand Eyes, 1989, Northwest Variety, 1987, Trolley Lives, 1985, Caught in the Revolving Door, 1980, Thirty-Six, 2002; contbr. poetry to numerous profl. publs. Mem. Willamette Literary Guild (pres. 1992-2000). Jewish. Avocations: biking, organic gardening, cooking, Tai chi. E-mail: ssher@eudoramail.com.

SHERA, REX A. financial executive; b. Crawfordsville, Ind., June 24, 1959; s. Thomas H. and Rachel E. Shera; m. Amanda J. Shera, May 31, 1997; children: Thomas K., Deborah A. BS, Ind. State U., 1981. CPA. Sr. Blue Cross Blue Shield, Indpls., 1981-86; prin. Ernst & Young, 1986—. Pres. United Cerebral Palsy Assn. of Greater Ind., Inc. Fellow Health Care Fin. Mgmt. Assn.; mem. AICPA, Ind. CPA Soc. Office: 111 Monument Cir Indianapolis IN 46204-5100 E-mail: rex.shera@ey.com.

SHERAR, MICHAEL D. science educator; Grad. in physics, Oxford U. With Ontario Hydro; sr. scientist, rsch. coord. Ontario Cancer Inst./Princess Margaret Hosp.; assoc. prof. Dept. Radiation Oncology, Dept. Med. Biophysics U. Toronto. Office: Dept Med Biophysics Ontario Cancer Inst Prin Margaret Hosp 610 University Ave Rm 7-414 Toronto ON Canada M5G 2M9*

SHERARD, RODNEY MERLE, retired military officer, educator; b. Grand Island, Nebr., Dec. 21, 1942; s. Howard Laverne and Sylvia Gertrude (Hurlbert) S.; m. Kathleen Ann Meis, Oct. 6, 1962 (div. Apr. 1979); children: Jeanette R., Gilbert J., Gregory H., Joanne E., Todd A.; m. Betty Jane Fultz, Nov. 16, 1985. AS, Vincinnes U., 1978; B in Gen. Studies, Ind. U., Indpls., 1993; grad., Armor Officer Candidate Sch., 1967, Command and Gen. Staff Coll., 1982. Commd. 2d lt. U.S. Army, 1967, advanced through grades to maj., 1979, ret., 1990; JROTC instr. Manual H.S., Indpls., 1990—. Author: The Descendants of William Henry Hurlbert and Amy Adeline Austin, 1995, (booklet) The Descendents of Merle Adam Sherard and Ida Eleanor Waddington, 1992, revised, 1997, The Descendants and Ancestors of Samuel Waddington, 2002,(newsletter) Hurlbert Family Reunion Annual, 1994—. Decorated Bronze Star, Combat Inf. badge, others. Mem. VFW, Am. Legion, N.G. Assn. Ind., 38th Inf. Divsn. Assn., Nebr. State Hist. Soc. Mem. Ch. of Christ. Avocations: travel, computers. E-mail: RodSherard@aol.com.

SHERBELL, RHODA, artist, sculptor; b. Bklyn. d. Alexander and Syd (Steinberg) S.; m. Mervin Honig, Apr. 28, 1956; 1 child, Susan. Student, Art Students League, 1950-53, Bklyn. Mus. Art Sch., 1959-61; also; pvt. study art, Italy, France, Eng., 1956. Cons., coun. mem. Emily Lowe Gallery, Hofstra U., Hempstead, N.Y., 1978, pres., 1989-81, instr., 1991—, life mem. bd. friends, pres. bd. trustees; tchr. instr. Mus. Modern Art, N.Y.C., 1959, NAD Art Sch., N.Y.C., 1985—, Art Students League, N.Y.C., 1980—; Nat. Portrait Gallery Mus. rep. to 150th anniversary Smithsonian Instn., Washington, 1996. Exhibited one-woman shows Country Art Gallery, Locust Valley, N.Y., Bklyn. Mus. Art Sch., 1961, Adelphi Coll., A.C.A. Galleries, N.Y.C., 1967, Capricorn Galleries, Rehn Gallery, Washington, 1968, Huntington Hartford Mus., N.Y.C., 1969, Morris (N.J.) Mus. Arts and Scis., 1980, Bergen Mus. Arts and Scis., N.J., 1984, William Benton Mus., Conn., 1985, Palace Theatre of the Arts, Stamford, Conn., Bronx Mus. Arts, 1986, Hofstra Mus. Art, L.I., N.Y., 1989, 90, 97-98, County Art Gallery, N.Y.C., 1990, Hecksher Mus., 2000; one-woman retrospective at N.Y. Cultural Ctr., 1970, Nat. Arts Collection, Washington, 1970, Montclair Mus. of Art, 1976, Nat. Art Mus. of Sport, 1977, Jewish Mus. of N.Y.C., 1980, Black History Mus., 1981, Queens Mus., 1981, 82, Nat. Portrait Gallery, Smithsonian Inst., Washington, 1981, 82, Bronx Mus., N.Y., Bklyn. Mus., Mus. Modern Art, N.Y.C., Country Art Gallery, 1990, Port Washington Library, Nat. Mus. Am. Art, The Smithsonian Instn., 1982, Nat. Acad. Design, N.Y.C., 1984, 89, Castle Gallery Mus., N.Y.C., 1987, Emily Lowe Mus., N.Y.C., 1987, Heckshire Mus., N.Y.C., 1989, Islip Art Mus., N.Y.C., 1989, Gallery Emanuel, N.Y.C., 1993, Sundance Gallery, Bridgehampton, N.Y., 1995, Castiron Gallery SoHo Show, 1995, Nat. Acad. Design Exhibition, 1995; 2 person exhibition, Works on Paper, Hofstra Mus., 1997-98; exhibited group shows Heckscher Mus., 1989, Islip Mus., 1989, Nassau Dept. Recreation and Parks, 1989, Downtown Gallery, N.Y.C., Maynard Walker Gallery, N.Y.C., F.A.R. Gallery, N.Y.C., Provincetown Art Assn., Detroit Inst. Art, Pa. Acad. Fine Arts, Bklyn. and L.I. Artists Show, Old Westbury Gardens Small Sculpture Show, Audubon Artists, NAD, Allied Artists, Heckscher Mus., Nat. Art Mus. Sports, Mus. Arts and Scis., L.A., Am. Mus. Natural History, Post of History Mus., 1987, 88, Caslte Gallery Mus., N.Y.C., 1987, Emily Lowe Gallery, N.Y., 1987, Bronx Mus. Arts, 1987, Chgo. Hist. Soc., Mus. of Modern Art, N.Y.C., 1988, Sands Point Mus., L.I., NAD, Hofstra Mus., 1990, Nat. Mus. Sports Art, 1991, Indpls. Art Mus., Phoenix Mus. Art, Corcoran Mus. Art, Washington, IBM, N.Y.C., Fire House Gallery Mus. Nassau Cmty. Coll., L.I., 1992, Nat. Arts Club Ann. Exhbn., 1992, Sports in Art From Am. Mus. at IBM, N.Y.C., 1992, Nat. Sculpture Soc. and The Regina A Quick Ctr. for The Arts Fairfield U.Centennial Anniversary Exbn., 1993, Mus. Modern Art, N.Y.C., Nat. Sculpture Soc. 100 Anniversary Exhbn., 1993, 97, Italy, 1994, 98, Provincetown Assn. and Art Mus., 1993, Kyoto (Japan) Mus. Sculpture Guild, 1993, Nat. Sculpture Soc. Exhbn. in Italy, Lucca, 1994, Sculptures Guild, N.Y.C., 1994-95, Cline Gallery, Santa Fe, 1995, Smithtown Township Art Coun., N.Y.C., 1997, Hofstra Mus. Art, Hempstead, 1997, Hofstra Mus., 1997—, Smithsonian Inst. 150th Celebration Nat. Portrait Gallery, 1997, Nat. Sculpture Soc, 1997, (From Maquette to Monument portrait of Eleanor Roosevelt), 98, Nature Arts Club, 1999, Molloy Coll. Art Gallery, 1999, Nat. Acad. Art, 1999, Nat. Acad. Group Show, 1999, Nat. Sculpture Soc., 1999, Portrait in bronze of Senator Norman J. Levy for Merrick Train Station, 2000, Aaron Copland's America, Heckscher Mus. of Art, 2000, Work From N.Y. Studios, Nat. Sculpture Soc., 2001; represented permanent collections, Stony Brook Hall of Fame, William Benton Mus. Art, Colby Coll. Mus., Oklahoma City Mus., Montclair (N.J.) Mus., Schonberg Library Black Studies, N.Y.C., Albany State Mus., Hofstra U., Bklyn. Mus., Colby Coll. Mus., Nat. Arts Collection, Nat. Portrait Gallery, Smithsonian Instn., Baseball Hall of Fame Cooperstown, N.Y., Nassau Community Coll., Hofstra U. Emily Lowe Gallery, Art Students League, Jewish Mus., Queens Mus., Black History Mus., Nassau County Mus., Stamford Mus. Art and Nature Ctr., Jericho Pub. Library, N.Y., African-Am. Mus., Hempstead, N.Y., 1988, Stamford (Conn.) Mus. Art and Scis., Silvermine Artists North East exhibition, 1989, Nassau Community Coll. Fire House Gallery Exbn., 1992, Nat. Portrait Gallery Smithsonian Instn., 1996, Monument Work, Base Ball Club, The Family Grp., The Sea Dogs, 1999, MTA, Pub. Monument for Senator Norman J. Levy Merrik Railroad Sta., N.Y., 1999, Yogi Berra Portrait, Nat. Gallery Smithsonian Inst., 2001, Raphare Soyer Portrait, 2001, others; also pvt. collections, TV shows, ABC, 1968, 81; ednl. TV spl. Rhoda Sherbell-Woman in Bronze, 1977; important works include Seated Ballerina, portraits of Aaron Copland (Bruce Stevenson Meml. Best Portrait award Nat. Arts Club 1989), Eleanor Roosevelt, Variations on a Theme (36 works of collaged sculpture), 1982-86; appeared several TV shows; guest various radio programs; contbr. articles to newspapers, popular mags. and art jours.; mem. Conservation Art Group Coun. City of N.Y., 1994, 95, 96, 97. Council mem. Nassau County Mus., 1978, trustee, 1st v.p. council; assoc. trustee Nat. Art Mus. of Sports, Inc., 1975—; cons., community liaison WNET Channel 13, cultural coordinator, 1975-83; host radio show Not for Artists Only, 1978-79; trustee Women's Boxing Fedn., 1978; mem. The Art Comm of The City of New York, 1993. Recipient Gold medal Allied Artists of Am., 1989, Alfred G. B. Steel Meml. award Pa. Acad. Fine Arts, 1963-64; Helen F. Barnett prize NAD, 1965, Jersey City Mus. prize for sculpture, 1961, 1st prize sculpture Locust Valley Art Show, 1966, 67, Ann. Sculpture prize Jersey City Mus., Bank for Savs. 1st prize in sculpture, 1950, Ford Found. purchase award, 1964, 2 top sculpture awards Mainstreams 77, Cert. of Merit Salmagundi Club, 1978, prize for sculpture, 1980, 81, award for sculpture Knickerbocker Artists, 1980, 81, top prize for sculpture Hudson Valley Art Assn., 1981, Sawyer award NAD, 1985, Gold medal of honor Audubon Artists, 1985, 39th Ann. Silvermine Exhbn. award, Gold medal Allied Artists Am., 1990, Pres' award Nat Arts Club N.Y.C.; MacDowell Colony fellow, 1976, Am. Acad. Arts and Letters and Nat. Arts and Letters grantee, 1960, Louis Comfort Tiffany Found. grantee, 1962, Ford Found. grantee, 1964, 67, also award; named one of top 5 finalist World Wide Competition to do Monument of Queen Catherine of England, 1991; named to represent Nat. Portrait Gallery at Smithsonian Mus. 150th Anniversary Party, 1996, sculpture selected to represent Nat. Portrait Gallery Mus., 1997. Fellow Nat. Sculpture Soc.; mem. Sculpture Guild (dir.), Nat. Assn. Women Artists (Jeffery Childs Willis Meml. prize 1978), Allied Artists Soc. (dir., Gold medal 1990, The Pietro and Alfrieda Montana Meml. award 2000, award 2001), Audubon Artists (Greta Kempton Walker prize 1965, Chaim Gross award, award for disting. contbr. to orgn. 1979, 80, Louis Weskeem award, dir.), Woman's Caucus for Art, Coll. Art Assn., Am. Inst. Conservation Historic and Artistic Works, N.Y. Soc. Women Artists, Artists Equity Assn. N.Y., Nat. Sculpture Soc. (E.N. Richard Meml. prize 1989), Internat. Platform Assn., Profl. Artists Guild L.I., Painters and Sculptors Soc. N.J. (Bertrum R. Hulmes Meml. award), Am. Watercolor Soc. (award for disting. contbn. to orgn.), Catharine Lorillard Wolfe Club (hon. mention 1968), Nat. Arts Club (N.Y.C., Stevenson Meml. award 1989, Pres. award 1992, Robert Sayford award 2000, Bruce Stevenson Meml. award for Portrait 2000, Siegfort award 2000), NAD Design (Leila Gordon Sawyer prize 1989; The Dessle Green Prize 1993). Home: 64 Jane Ct Westbury NY 11590-1410

SHERBERT, SHARON DEBRA, financial services executive; b. Bklyn., Aug. 18, 1953; d. Joseph George and Leah (Katzman) Goldstein; m. Robert Fisher, Oct. 20, 1973 (div. Nov. 1981); 1 child, Meredith Audra Fisher; m. Michael Sherbert, Apr. 4, 1982; 1 child, Jared Alan. Grad. high sch., Bklyn. Cert. fin. planner; registered fin. cons. Real estate agent Century 21 R.E., Sepulveda, Calif., 1976-80; life ins. agt. Prudential Life Ins., North Hollywood, 1980-82; sr. v.p. Profl. Planning, Encino, 1982-90; exec. v.p. Comprehensive Fin. Svcs., Burbank, 1992—. Columnist on Internet Web site Women in Tech., Inc., Van Nuys, Calif., 1996—. Co-host: (TV show) You and Your Money, 1993—. Mem. NAFE, Nat. Assn. Women Bus. Owners, Internat. Assn. for Fin. Planners, Inst. Cert. Fin. Planners, Zonta Club of Santa Clarita Valley (sunshine sec. 1992-93). Office: Comprehensive Fin Svcs 3811 W Burbank Blvd Burbank CA 91505-2116

SHERBORNE, ROBERT, editor; b. Fairborn, Ohio, Mar. 26, 1950; s. Henry Hall and Lauramay (Rider) S.; m. Pamela Saunders, Apr. 16, 1988; children: Laura, Sophie. BS in Comms., U. Tenn., 1976. Reporter Clarksville (Tenn.) Leaf Chronicle, 1976, Tullahoma (Tenn.) News, 1976-77, The Tennessean, Nashville, 1977-92, regional editor, 1993-94, special project editor, 1995—. Recipient Nat. Gold Mass Media award Nat. Conf. Christians & Jews, 1983; special citation Nat. Headliners award Press Club of Atlantic City, N.J., 1983. Office: The Tennessean 1100 Broadway Nashville TN 37203-3134

SHERBY, KATHLEEN REILLY, lawyer; b. St. Louis, Apr. 5, 1947; d. John Victor and Florian Sylvia (Frederick) Reilly; m. James Wilson Sherby, May 17, 1975; children: Michael R.R., William J.R., David J.R. AB magna cum laude, St. Louis U., 1969, JD magna cum laude, 1976. Bar: Mo. 1976. Assoc. Bryan Cave, St. Louis, 1976-85; ptnr. Bryan Cave LLP, 1985—. Contbr. articles to profl. jours. Bd. dirs Jr. League, St. Louis, 1989-90, St. Louis Forum, 1992-99, pres., 1995-97; chmn. Bequest and Gift Coun. of St. Louis U., 1997-99; jr. warden Ch. of St. Michael and St. George, 1998-2000; bd. dirs. Bistate chpt. ARC, 2000—; bd. trustees St. Louis Sci. Ctr., 2000—. Fellow Am. Coll. Trust and Estate Coun. (regent 1997—), Estate Planning Coun. of St. Louis (pres. 1986-87), Bar Assn. Met. St. Louis (chmn. probate sect. 1986-87), Mo. Bar Assn. (chmn. probate and trust com. 1996-98, chmn. probate law revision subcom. 1988-96). Episcopalian. Home: 47 Crestwood Dr Saint Louis MO 63105-3032 Office: Bryan Cave LLP 1 Metropolitan Sq Ste 3600 Saint Louis MO 63102-2733

SHERBY, LOUISE SHARON, librarian; b. Bridgeton, N.J., Feb. 2, 1947; d. David and Edith (Fisher) S. BA, Hofstra U., 1969; MA in Libr. Sci., U. Denver, 1970; DLS, Columbia U., 1988. Adult svcs. libr. Chgo. Pub. Libr., 1970-73; reference libr. R.I. Coll. Libr., Providence, 1973-77, head reference libr., 1977-82; reference libr. Columbia U. Librs., N.Y.C., 1982-87, dep. head for adminstrn., 1987-88; asst. dir. for pub. svcs. U. Mo.-Kansas City Librs., 1988-96; chief libr. Hunter Coll., N.Y.C., 1996—. Adj. prof. U. R.I. Grad. Libr. Sch., Kingston, 1981-82, U. Mo. Sch. Libr. and Info. Sci., 1989-96. Co-editor: P.G. Wodehouse: A Comprehensive Bibliography, 1990, Who's Who of Nobel Prizes, 1901-95, 1996, Who's Who of Nobel Prizes, 1901-2000, 2002; contbr. chpt. to Basic Bus. Libr., 1983, 89, 95. Mem. Am. Libr. Assn., Assn. Coll. & Rsch. Librs. (bd. dirs. univ. libr. sect. 1994-97, exec. bd. reference and adult svcs. divsn., 1991-92, vice chair univ. libr. sect. 2001-2002, chair 2002—), Reference and Users Svcs. Assn. (vice-chair mgmt. and ops. of user svcs. sect. 1996-97, chair, 1997-98), Phi Kappa Phi. Office: Hunter Coll Librs 695 Park Ave New York NY 10021-5024

SHERE, DENNIS, retired publishing executive; b. Cleve., Nov. 29, 1940; s. William and Susan (Luskay) S.; m. Maureen Jones, Sept. 4, 1965; children: Rebecca Lynn, David Matthew, Stephen Andrew. BS in Journalism, Ohio U., 1963, MS in Journalism, 1964; postgrad., DePaul U., 2001—. Staff writer Dayton (Ohio) Daily News, 1966-69; asst. prof. Sch. Journalism Bowling Green (Ohio) State U., 1969-70; fin. editor Detroit News, 1970-72, city editor, 1973-75; editor Dayton Jour. Herald, 1975-80; pub. Springfield (Ohio) Newspapers Inc., 1980-83, Dayton Newspapers, Inc., 1983-88; gen. mgr. Media Group Moody Bible Inst., 1989—2001; ret., 2001. Served with AUS, 1964-66. Mem. Sigma Alpha Epsilon, Omicron Delta Kappa.

SHEREDOS, CAROL ANN, rehabilitation clinical specialist; b. N.Y.C., Jan. 29, 1944; d. Robert J. and Margaret M. (Adams) Ross; m. Saleem J. Sheredos, July 14, 1973; children: Emily Joy, Douglas Joseph. BS, Ithaca Coll., 1967; MA in Studies in Aging, Coll. of Notre Dame, Balt., 1994. Lic. phys. therapist, N.Y., Md., Fla., N.J. Staff phys. therapist Glen Cove (N.Y.) Cmty. Hosp., 1967—68, Nassau County Health Dept., Mineola, NY, 1968—70; rsch. phys. therapist VA, N.Y.C., 1970—71, prosthetics rsch. and edn. specialist, 1971—73; chief phys. therapist Medicus, Wappingers Falls, 1983—88; dir. Meridian Rehab. Svcs., Towson, Md., 1989—92; rehab. svcs. dir. Prism Rehab. Sys. at North Charles Healthcare Ctr., Balt., 1993—98; dist. mgr. Mariner Rehab. Svcs., 1995—96; rehab. clin. resource specialist Prism Rehab. Sys., Towson, Md., 1998; mid-atlantic regional mgr. Theracor Rehab Svcs., 1998—99; pres., founder CAS Resources, LLC, Towson, Md., 2000—; rsch. fellow, program specialist NCMRR/NICHD NIH, Bethesda, 2000—. Pvt. practice phys. therapy, N.Y., 1967-83; cons. in disability and aging Alliance, Inc., Balt., 1990-93; co-instr. course The Challenge of Geriat. Rehab., 1994-98. Contbr. articles to profl. jours. Host minister St. Joseph's Ch., Tex., Md., 1990-97; mem. Gov.'s Adv. Coun. Individuals with Disabilities, 1996—, chair, 1997—. Named One of Ten Most Outstanding Handicapped Americans, Pres.' Com. on Employment of Handicapped, 1971. Mem. Am. Phys. Therapy Assn., Md. Coalition for Assistive Tech., Assn. Christian Therapists, Christian Phys. Therapists Internat., Am. Soc. Aging, Resna, Amputee Coalition Am., Am. Assn. Persons with Disabilities. Republican. Roman Catholic. Avocations: gardening, travel, internet. Office: CAS Resources LLC 919 Metfield Rd Towson MD 21286-1622 also: 6100 Executive Blvd Rockville MD 20852 E-mail: carolannpt@aol.com.

SHERER, DAVID MATTHEW, clinical pathologist, laboratory director; b. N.Y.C., Mar. 19, 1943; s. Leslie and Fay (Spiwak) S.; m. Barbara Rose Franco, Feb. 14, 1976; children: Robert H., Charles I., Margaret E. BS in Math. and History, NYU, 1963; MD, SUNY, Buffalo, 1969. Diplomate Am. Bd. Pathology. Intern U. Calif., San Diego, 1969-70; resident in viral oncology NIH, Bethesda, Md., 1970-72; resident, chief resident clin. pathology Bellevue Med. Ctr., NYU, N.Y.C., 1972-74; staff physician Schaefer Brewery, Bklyn., 1973-74; dir. clin. labs. Group Health Coop. of Puget Sound, Seattle, 1974—. Tchr. math. N.Y.C. Sch. System, 1962-65; mem. clin. adv. bd. Shoreline Community Coll., Seattle, 1976—; chmn. infection control com. Group Health Coop. of Puget Sound, 1976-78, transfusion com., 1979—, staff pension com., 1975—, mem. deferred compensation com., 1976—, lab. com., 1974—, info. policy com., 1978-82, 95—; asst. clin. prof. sch. medicine Univ. Wash., 1989—. Mem. Town of Clyde HIll (Wash.) Community Activities Group, 1984—; bd. dirs. Bellevue (Wash.) and Sun Valley (Idaho) Homeowners Assn., Group Health Credit Union, 1987-96, chmn. 1989-94; choir dir. Herzl Ner Tamid Conservative Congregation, Mercer Island, 1976-82, 84—; tenor Seattle Opera Aux. Chorus, 1976-85, Seattle Chorale, 1975-78; patroller Snoqualmie (Wash.) Summit Ski Patrol, 1975-78, 85—; sec., bd. dirs., treas. Boy Scouts Troop 600, 1989—; pres. Bellevue West Little League, 1991-92. Recipient Winthrop Ranney award NYU, 1972. Fellow Am. Soc. Clin. Pathology, Am. Assn. Blood Banks; mem. A.P.P.L.E. Coop., Glendale Country Club (Bellevue; bd. dirs., v.p. 1993-94, pres. 1994-95). Jewish. Avocations: reading, gardening, skiing, golf, computers. Home: 1900 94th Ave NE Bellevue WA 98004-2524 Office: Group Health Coop Puget Sound 200 15th Ave Seattle WA 98122-5604

SHERER, SAMUEL AYERS, lawyer, urban planning consultant; b. Warwick, N.Y., June 17, 1944; s. Ernest Thompson and Helen (Ayers) S.; m. Dewi Sudewinahidah, June 28, 1980 (dec. Dec. 2000). AB magna cum laude, Oberlin Coll., 1966; JD, Harvard U., 1970; M in City Planning, MIT, 1970. Bar: D.C. 1972, U.S. Supreme Ct. 1979. Atty., advisor HUD, Boston, 1970; sr. cons. McClaughry Assoc., Washington, 1970-71, 74-76; cons. Urban Inst., 1971-72; atty., urban planner IBRD Jakarta (Indonesia) Urban Devel. Study, 1972-74; atty., advisor Office Minority Bus. U.S. Dept. Commerce, Washington, 1976-77; ptnr. Topping & Sherer, 1977-90; pres. Sherer-Axelrod-Monacelli, Inc., Cambridge, Mass., 1978-99; prin. The Washington Team, Inc., 1992—, Richardson & Sherer, LLC, 2000—. Bd. dirs. EnviroClean Solutions, Inc., The Urban Agr. Network; rep. Internat. Devel. Law Inst., Washington, 1983-90; sr. fellow Climate Inst., 1988—; cons. in field. Co-author: Urban Land Use in Egypt, 1977; editor: Important Laws and Regulations Regarding Land, Housing and Urban Development in the Arab Republic of Egypt, 1977, Important Laws and Regulations Regarding Land, Housing and Urban Development in the Hashemite Kingdom of Jordan, 1981. Bd. dirs. MIT Enterprise Forum of Washington-Balt., 1980-82; mem. D.C. Rep. Cent. Com., 1984-88; mem. nat. governing bd. Ripon Soc., Washington, 1977-83. Urban Studies fellow HUD, 1969-70. Mem. ABA, D.C. Bar Assn., Am. Planning Assn., The Am. Soc. of Internat. Law, Asia Soc., Phi Beta Kappa. Avocations: tennis, reading. Home: 4600 Connecticut Ave NW Apt 205 Washington DC 20008-5702 Office: 7 Brookes Ave Gaithersburg MD 20877-2754 E-mail: washteam@aol.com.

SHERER, VALORI MULVEY, battered women's shelter director; b. Perth Amboy, N.J., Dec. 11, 1958; d. Manuela Rivera Mulvey; m. Steven Theodore Sherer, Apr. 16, 1988; children: Jessica Elizabeth, David Layden, Patrick Steven. AA, County Coll. Morris, 1978; BA, Rutgers U., 1984. Dir. mktg. and pub. rels. Greenleaf Ctr. Inc., Valdosta, Ga., 1984-86; dir. mktg. New Horizons Inc., 1986-87; freelance mktg. profl., 1987-93; v.p. Theo's Inc., 1990-93; dir. Salvation Army Blackbelt Region Abuse Haven, Selma, Ala., 1992-94; exec. dir. battered women's shelter The Haven, Valdosta, 1994—. Victim response team, 1996-98; active Christ the King Episcopal Ch.; chmn. so. jud. cir. Domestic Violence Task Force, 1997-98; Ga. coalition on Family Violence (pres. 1996-98). Mem. victim response team Diocese of Ga., 1996-97; v.p. So. Ctrl. Ga. Coalition to End Homelessness, 1995-97. Mem. Quota Internat. Valdosta. Avocations: opera, symphony, painting and drawing, skiing, boy scouting. Office: The Haven Battered Womens Shelter Inc PO Box 5382 Valdosta GA 31603-5382

SHERIDAN, CHRISTOPHER FREDERICK, human resources executive; b. Syracuse, N.Y., June 7, 1953; s. Frederick John and Patricia Ann (McCormick) S.; m. Diane Marie Harman, Dec. 31, 1977; children: Ryan, Kelly. BS in Indsl. Relations, LeMoyne Coll., 1975. Employee rels. trainee Anaconda Co., Buffalo, 1975-76, employee rels. rep. Los Angeles, 1976-78; pers. mgr. HITCO, Gardena, Calif., 1978-80; labor rels. rep. Miller Brewing Co., Fulton, N.Y., 1980-82, labor rels. mgr. Los Angeles, 1982-90; employee rels. mgr. Ryder Distbn. Resources, Anaheim, Calif., 1990-91; dir. human resources Alta-Dena Cert. Dairy Inc., City of Industry, 1991-99; regional human resources dir. west/southwest Dean Foods Co., 1999—. Mem. Soc. Human Resources Mgmt., Am. Mgmt. Assn. Roman Catholic. Avocations: golf, basketball, reading, music. Email: chris. Office: Dean Foods Co 17637 Valley Blvd La Puente CA 91744-5731 E-mail: chris_sheridan@deanfoods.com.

SHERIDAN, DIANE FRANCES, public policy facilitator; b. Wilmington, Del., Mar. 12, 1945; d. Robert Kooch and Eileen Elizabeth (Forrest) Bupp; m. Mark MacDonald Sheridan III, Dec. 7, 1968; 1 child, Elizabeth Anne. BA in English, U. Del., 1967. Tchr. English Newark (Del.) Sch. Dist., 1967-68, Lumberton (Tex.) Ind. Sch. Dist., 1969-71, Crown Point (Ind.) Sch. Dist., 1972-75; sr. assoc. The Keystone (Colo.) Ctr., 1986-98; facilitator cmty. adv. panels to chem. plants and refineries Taylor Lake Village, Tex., 1986—. Facilitator cmty. adv. panels to chem. plants and refineries, Tex., Kans.; chair Keystone Siting Process Local Rev. Com.; mem. pub. adv. panel Chem. Mfrs. Assn. Responsible Care, 1989-97. 1st v.p. LWV, Washington, 1992-94, sec. treas. voters edn. fund, sec. treas. Nat. LWV, 1994-96, bd. dirs. 1996-98; pres. LWV of Tex., 1987-91, chair edn. fund, 1987-91, bd. dirs., 1983-87; pres. LWV of the Bay Area, 1981-83; mem. adv. com. Ctr. for Global Studies of Houston Advanced Rsch. Ctr., The Woodlands, Tex., 1991-97, Ctr. for Conflict Analysis and Mgmt., bd. advisors Environ. Inst.; mem. U. Houston-Clear Lake Devel. Adv. Coun., 1989-95; mem. Bay Area Cmty. Awareness and Emergency Response Local Emergency Planning Com., 1988-92; active Tex. House-Senate Select Com. on Urban Affairs Regional Flooding Task Force, 1979-80, Congressman Mike Andrews Environ. Task Force, 1983-85, Gov.'s Task Force on Hazardous Waste Mgmt., 1984-85; dir. local PTAs, 1981-91; coord. Tex. Roundtable on Hazardous Waste, 1982-87; sec., v.p. Tex. Environ. Coalition, 1983-85; co-chair Tex. Risk Commn. Project, 1986-89; mem. Leadership Tex., Class of 1988; mem. cmty. adv. bd. U. Tex. Med. Br. Ctr. Nat. Inst. Environ. Health Studies, 1998—. Mem. LWV (nat. bd. dirs. 1992-98, trustee nat. edn. fund 1992-98), Assn. for Conflict Resolution, Internat. Assn. for Pub. Participation, Mortar Board, East Harris County Mfrs. Assn. (risk mgmt. comm. com. 1994-99), Pi Sigma Alpha, Kappa Delta Pi. E-mail: DBSheridan@aol.com.

SHERIDAN, EDWARD PATRICK, college dean; b. Detroit, Dec. 2, 1937; s. Geoffrey Francis and Mary Ann (Beirne) S.; m. Kathleen Gentile, June 3, 1967. BA, U. Windsor (Ont., Can.), 1961; MA, U. Detroit, 1964; PhD, Loyola U., Chgo., 1968. Lic. psychologist, Ill., Fla. Intern clin. psychology Hines (Ill.) VA Hosp., 1963-65, Westside VA Outpatient Clinic, Chgo., 1965-66; asst. prof. U. Windsor, 1966-67; sr. psychologist Oakland County CMHC, Birmingham, Mich., 1967-68; asst. prof., coord. tng. U. Ill., Chgo., 1968-73; assoc. prof. Northwestern U. Med. Sch., 1973-81, chief psychiatry outpatient svcs., 1973-81, prof., chmn., 1981-90; dean Coll. Arts & Scis. U. Cen. Fla., Orlando, 1990—. Cons. Ill. Dept. Mental Health, Chgo., 1982-86, First Nat. Bank Chgo., 1987—, State of N.Y. Dept. Higher Edn., N.Y.C., 1988—, Edward Hines Jr. VA Hosp., Hines, 1985-90. Editorial bd. Psychology and Health: An Internat. Jour., 1987—; contbr. articles to profl. jours. Fellow APA (chair accreditation com. 1991, chair bd. ednl. affairs 1994-95). Office: U Cen Fla Hfa # 511 Orlando FL 32816-0001

SHERIDAN, GEORGE GROH, elementary education educator, adult education educator, English educator; b. Balt., Mar. 18, 1947; s. Edward Walter and Mary Jane (Groh) S.; m. Catherine Elizabeth Heinz, May 25, 1968; children: Michael Edward, Elizabeth Makepeace, Peter Carlos, Tiffany Anne, Danielle Rebecca, Nicholas George. BA in Polit. Sci., Loyola U., L.A., 1969; MS in Edn., U. So. Calif., 1970. Std. elem. and secondary tchg. credentials, bilingual cert. competence. Acad coun. Loyola U., 1967-68; tchr. intern Tchr. Corps Rural-Migrant, Tulare County, Calif., 1968-70; boycott organizer United Farm Workers AFL-CIO, Ohio, Mass., Conn., Cal., 1970-78; bilingual tchr. Lenox Sch. Dist., L.A., 1978-81; 5th-6th grade tchr. Black Oak Mine Unified Sch. Dist., Georgetown, Calif., 1981-87, 7th-8th grade tchr., mentor Cool, 1987-97, 2d grade tchr., mentor, 1997—. tchr. Beginning Tchr. Support and Assessment Program, 1998-2000, mem. profl. devel. leadership team, 2001—. Fellow Area 3 Writing Project, Davis, 1986—; tchr. leader, inst. dir. Calif. Reading & Lit. Project, Sacramento, 1987—; mem. State Instrnl. Resources Evaluation Panel, Sacramento, 1988, 94, 96; mem. State Lang. Arts Framework Com., Sacramento, 1996-97. Author: First Papers in Migrancy and Rural Poverty, 1970; prin. author: Seeking Excellence in Education K-12, 1987; contbg. author: Picture Yourself in Local Government, 1995. Mem. Dem. State Ctrl. Com., 1999-2000. L.A. Times scholar, 1964-68. Mem. ASCD, NEA, NAACP, NOW, ACLU, Nat. Coun. Tchrs. English, Calif. Tchrs. Assn. (state coun. of edn. 1998—), Black Oak Mine Tchrs. Assn. (pres. 1996—), Sierra Club, Georgetown Divide Dem. Club. Avocations: family activities, walking, gardening, reading, home improvement. Home: 4467 Meadowbrook Rd Garden Valley CA 95633-9403 Office: Northside Sch 860 Cave Valley Rd Cool CA 95614-9441 E-mail: gsheridan@bomusd.k12.ca.us., learn@jps.net.

SHERIDAN, JAMES EDWARD, history educator; b. Wilmington, Del., July 15, 1922; s. Phillip Lambert and Ida Alverna (Green) S.; m. Sonia Landy, Sept. 27, 1947; 1 son, Jamy. BS, U. Ill., 1949, MA, 1950; PhD, U. Calif. at Berkeley, 1961. Lectr. Chinese history Stanford U., 1960; mem. faculty Northwestern U., 1961—, prof. history, 1968—, chmn. dept., 1969-74, assoc. dean Coll. Arts and Scis., 1985-89, prof. emeritus, 1992—. Author: Chinese Warlord: The Career of Feng Yu-hsiang, 1966, China: A Culture Area in Perspective, 1970, China in Disintegration: The Republican Era in Chinese History, 1912-1949, 1975, A Community of Caring: An Introduction to Kendal at Hanover, 1998; editor: The Transformation of Modern China series, 1975— . Served to ensign USN, 1941-46. Fulbright fellow France, 1950-51; Ford Found. fellow, 1958-60; grantee Am. Council Learned Socs.-Social Sci. Research Council, 1966-67, 71-72 Home: 80 Lyme Rd Apt 438 Hanover NH 03755-1236 Office: Northwestern Univ Dept History Evanston IL 60201 E-mail: james.e.sheridan@valley.net.

SHERIDAN, JIM, director, screenwriter; b. Dublin, Ireland, 1949; Student, Univ. Coll., Dublin, NYU. Artistic dir. Project Arts Theatre, 1976-80, N.Y. Irish Arts Ctr., 1982-87; founder Children's Theatre Co., Dublin. Screenwriter: Into the West, 1993, screenwriter: My Left Foot, 1989; dir.: My Left Foot, 1989, The Field, 1990, In the Name of the Father, 1993, The Boxer, 1997, East of Harlem, 2001; prodr.: exec. prodr.: Some Mother's Son, 1996, Agnes Browne, 1999, On the Edge, 2000, Borstal Boy, 2000, Bloody Sunday, 2001. Office: Hells Kitchen Ltd 21 Mespil Rd Dublin 4 Ireland also: CAA 9830 Wilshire Blvd Beverly Hills CA 90212-1804 E-mail: hellskit@isl.ie.

SHERIDAN, MARK WILLIAM, mechanical engineer, strategic planner; b. Bryn Mawr, Pa., July 9, 1959; s. Phillip Frederick and Shirley (Frazer) S. BSME, Lafayette Coll., 1981; MBA, Cornell U., 1987, M. Engring. (Mech.), 1988. Registered profl. engr., Ohio. Project engr. Internat. Paper Co., Mobile, Ala., 1981-83, sr. process engr., 1983-85; assoc. Booz-Allen & Hamilton, Cleve., 1988-90; coord. long range planning appliance motor divsn. Emerson Electric Co., St. Louis, 1990-93, resident engr. Paragould Plant, 1993-96; dir. mfg. Thermodisc, Mansfield, Ohio, 1996—. Summer intern Saturn Corp., Troy, Mich., 1986, 87. Patentee in field. Bd. dirs. ABC Condominium Assn., St. Louis, 1992-94; chmn. JGSM Student Faculty Com./Quality of Life Com., Ithaca, N.Y., 1985-87; pres. Mobile Soap Box Derby, 1983-85; v.p. ways and means, bd. dirs. Mobile Jaycees, 1984-85; active YMCA; treas. First Presbyn. Ch. of Mansfield, 1998—. Lester B. Knight scholar Cornell U., 1986-88, J. Stanford Smith scholar Cornell U., 1985-87; named Outstanding Young Man of Am., 1984, 85, 87. Mem. ASME, Inst. Indsl. Engrs., The Planning Forum, Soc. Indsl. Archaeology, World Future Soc., St. Louis Jaycees (bd. dirs. 1992-94), Am. Mensa. Republican. Avocations: biking, golf, reading, tennis, computing. Home: 2403 Ranchwood Dr Mansfield OH 44903-9044 Office: Thermodisc 1320 S Main St Mansfield OH 44907-5500

SHERIDAN, PATRICK MICHAEL, finance company executive, retired; b. Grosse Pointe, Mich., Apr. 13, 1940; s. Paul Phillip and Frances Mary (Rohan) S.; m. Diane Lorraine Tressler, Nov. 14, 1986; children: Mary, Patrick, Kelly, Kevin, James. BBA, U. Notre Dame, 1962; MBA, U. Detroit, 1975. Acct. Peat, Marwick, Mitchell & Co., Detroit, 1962-72, audit mgr., 1969-72; exec. v.p. fin. Alexander Hamilton Life Ins. Co., Farmington, Mich., 1973-76; sr. v.p. ops. Sun Life Ins. Co. Am., Balt., 1976-78, exec. v.p., 1978-79; pres. Sun Ins. Services, Inc., 1979-81; pres., chief exec. officer Am. Health & Life Ins. Co., Balt., 1981-85; chief exec. officer Gulf Ins. Co., 1985-86; sr. v.p., chief fin. officer Comml. Credit Co., 1985-86, sr. v.p. audit, 1987; exec. v.p., chief fin. officer Anthem, Inc., Indpls., 1987-99, ret., 1999. Rep. candidate for U.S. Congress, 1972; past pres. Charlesbrooke Cmty. Assn.; past. v.p. Jr. Achievement of Met. Balt., 1984-85; bd. dirs. Goodwill Industries of Balt., 1986, bd. govs. 1994; bd. dirs. Family Svcs. Assn., 1994, Goodwill Industries of Indpls., 1994; mem. adv. coun. Clowes Meml. Hall. Capt. AUS, 1963-65. Recipient various Jaycee awards. Fellow Life Mgmt. Inst.; mem. Am. Mgmt. Assn. (pres.'s assn.), AICPAs, Mich. Assn. CPAs, Md. Assn. CPAs, Am. Soc. CLUs, U.S. Jaycees (treas. 1973-74), Mich. Jaycees (pres. 1971-72), Detroit Jaycees (pres. 1968-69), Balt. C. of C. (bd. dirs.), Mensa, Notre Dame Club, Skyline Club.

SHERIDAN, PHILP HENRY, pediatrician, neurologist; b. Washington, June 29, 1950; s. Andrew James and Mildred Adele (Stohlman) S.; m. Margaret Mary Williams, Oct. 3, 1987; children: Gerard Andrew, Philip Henry, Kathleen Mary, Patrick Gerard, Mary Margaret Gerard, Mary Anne Gerard, Mary Claire Gerard, Andrew James. BS magna cum laude, Yale U., 1972; MD cum laude, Georgetown U., 1976. Resident in pediat. Children's Hosp., Phila., 1976-79; fellow in pediat. neurology Hosp. U. Pa., 1979-82; med. staff fellow NIH, Bethesda, Md., 1982-84; neurologist epilepsy br. Nat. Inst. Neurol. Disorders and Stroke, 1984—; neurologist Divsn. Children's Splty. Svcs., Fairfax, Va., 1984—; health scientist admsntr., guest worker rschr., 1984-89; chief devel. neurology br., 1989-95; chief epilepsy br. NIH, 1995-2000; med. reviewer Ctr. for Drug Evaluation and Rsch. FDA, 2000—. Cons., lectr. Nat. Naval Med. Ctr., Bethesda, 1984—; med. dir. U.S. Pub. Health Svc.; adj. assoc. prof. Uniformed Svcs. U. Health Scis., Bethesda. Contbr. articles on clin. and rsch. neurology to med. jours. Diplomate Am. Bd. Pediatrics, Am. Bd. Psychiatry and Neurology, Am. Bd. Qualification in Electroencephalography. Mem. Am. Acad. Neurology, Child Neurology Soc. (invited reviewer), Soc. Neurosci., Am. Epilepsy Soc., Alpha Omega Alpha. Roman Catholic. Achievements include current work planning and administering a comprehensive research program concerning epilepsy, pediatric neurology, developmental neurobiology, neuroimmunology and neuromuscular disorders. Subspecialties include neurology and pediatrics. Office: FDA CDER HFD-120 Rm 4057 1451 Rockville Pike Rockville MD 20857

SHERIDAN, ROBERT LEO, surgeon; b. Boston, Sept. 6, 1955; s. Sylvester Robert and Joanne Marie (Laporte) S.; m. Martha Mae Grunewald, Apr. 21, 1979; children: Kevin, Daniel, Anna. BA, Boston U., 1973, MD, 1979. Diplomate Am. Bd. Surgery, Nat. Bd. Med. Examiners. Intern Madigan Army Med Ctr., 1979-80; commd. 2d lt. U.S. Army, 1980, 1975, lt. col., 1991; flight surgeon Stuttgart, Fed. Republic of Germany, 1980-82; surg. resident Walter Reed Army Med. Ctr., Washington, 1982-86; surgeon Honduras, 1986-87, Colorado Springs, Colo., 1987-90, Inst. Surg. Rsch., San Antonio, 1990-91, Shriners Burns Inst., Boston, 1991—, Mass. Gen. Hosp., Boston, 1991—, Harvard Med. Sch., Boston, 1992—. Asst. chief of staff Shriners Burns Inst., Boston, 1991—; assoc. prof. surgery Harvard Med. Sch., Cambridge, Mass., 1992—; chief trauma surgery Mass. Gen. Trauma Svc., Boston, 1991—, Mass. Gen. Burn Svc., Boston, 1991—. Author textbook chpts., 1993, 94; contbr. articles to profl. jours. Recipient Rsch. grant Shriners Hosps. for Crippled Children, 1993. Fellow ACS; mem. Am. Burn Assn., Am. Assn. for Surgery of Trauma, Ea. Assn. for Surgery of Trauma, Soc. Critical Care Medicine, Assn. Acad. Surgery. Avocations: running, woodworking, music. Office: Shriners Burns Inst 51 Blossom St Boston MA 02114-2623 E-mail: rsheridan@partners.org.

SHERIDAN, SONIA LANDY, artist, retired art educator; b. Newark, Apr. 10, 1925; d. Avrom Mendel and Goldie Cornelia (Hanon) Landy; m. James Edward Sheridan, Sept. 27, 1947; 1 son, Jamy. AB, Hunter Coll., 1945; postgrad., Columbia U., 1946-48; MFA with high honors, Calif. Coll. Arts and Crafts, 1961. Tchr. art public high schs., Calif., 1951-57; chmn. dept. art Taipei (Taiwan) Am. Sch., 1957-59; instr. Calif. Coll. Arts and Crafts, 1960-61; asst. prof. art Sch. Art Inst. Chgo., 1961-67, assoc. prof., 1968-75, prof., 1976-80, prof. emeritus, 1980—, founder, head generative sys. program, 1970-80. Artist-in-residence 3M Corp., 1970, 76; cons. French Ministry of Culture, 1986; artist-in-residence Xerox Corp., 1981; lectr., univs., museums, art schs., workshops; lectr. Hungarian Acad. Scis. Symposium Collected Essays & Exhbn., Budapest, 1989, Internat. Soc. of Electronic Arts, Liverpool, UK. One-woman shows include Rosenberg Gallery, Chgo., 1966, Visual Studies Workshop, Rochester, N.Y., 1973, Iowa Mus. Art, Iowa City, 1976, Mus. Sci. Industry, Chgo., 1978; two-person show Mus. Modern Art, N.Y.C., 1974; exhibited in group shows at Print Ann, Boston Mus., 1963, Software, Jewish Mus., N.Y.C., 1969-70, Photography into Art, London, 1972-73, Photokino, Cologne, Germany, 1974, San Francisco Mus. Art, 1975, U. Mich. Mus. Art, 1978, Toledo Mus. Art, 1982-83, Mus. Modern Art, Paris, 1983, Siggraph, U.S., Japan, France, 1982, 83, Reina Sofia Mus., Madrid, Spain, 1986, Smithsonian Instn., 1990, Tokyo Met. Mus. Photography, 1991, Madrid City Cultural Ctr., 1992, Karl Ernst Osthaus Mus., Hagen, Germany, 1992, Circulo des Belles Artes, Madrid, 1992, Yale U. Art Gallery, 1995, Tokyo Intercom. Ctr., 1995, U. Montreal, 1995, Internat. Soc. Electronic Arts, Liverpool, Eng., 1998, Hungarian Art Mus., 1995 Scripton Mus., Netherlands, 1997, Video Gallery, Hungary, 2000, Mus. for Kommunikation, Frankfort, Germany, 2001; represented in permanent collections Art Inst. Chgo., San Francisco Mus. Art, Mus. Sci. and Industry, Chgo., U. Iowa Mus. Art, Nat. Gallery Art, Ottawa, Can., Visual Studies Workshop, Rochester, Tokyo Met. Mus. Photography, Fundacion Arte y Technologia, Madrid, Tweed Mus., Univ. Minn., 1997, Scryption Mus., Tilburg, Netherlands, 1998; author: Energized Artscience: Sonia Landy Sheridan, 1978; co-editor Leonardo jour., hon. editor, 2000; contbr. articles, essay to profl. jours. Guggenheim fellow, 1973; Nat. Endowment for Arts workshop grantee 1974, pub. media grantee, 1976, artist grantee 1981; Union Ind. Colls. Art grantee 1975. Mem. Coll. Art Assn., Internat. Soc. for Interdisciplinary Study of Symmetry, Internat. Soc. of Electronic Arts. E-mail: sonia.sheridan@valley.net.

SHERIDAN, THOMAS BROWN, mechanical engineering and applied psychology educator, researcher, consultant; b. Cin., Dec. 23, 1929; s. Mahlon Brinsley and Esther Anna (Brown) S.; m Rachel Briggs Rice, Aug. 1, 1953; children: Paul Rice, Richard Rice, David Rice, Margaret Lenore. BS, Purdue U., 1951; MS, UCLA, 1954; ScD, MIT, 1959; Dr. (hon.), Delft U. Tech., The Netherlands, 1991. Registered profl. engr., Mass. Asst. prof. mech. engring. MIT, Cambridge, 1959-65, assoc. prof., 1965-70, prof., 1970-78, prof. engring. and applied psychology, 1978-94, prof. aeronautics and astronautics, 1994—, Ford prof., 1995—. Lectr. U. Calif., Berkeley, Stanford U., 1968; vis. prof. U. Delft, The Netherlands, 1972, Stanford U., 1989, Ben Gurion U., Israel, 1995; chmn. com. human factors, mem. com. aircrew-vehicle interaction, com. on commercially developed space facility, com. on human factors in air traffic control, NRC, mem. com. on nat. automated hwy. sys., com. on setting and enforceing speed limits, com. on intelligent vehicle initiative; mem. adv. com. on applied phys., math. and biol. scis. NSF; mem. life scis. adv. com., study group on robotics, oversight com. flight telerobotic servicer NASA; mem. task force on appropriate tech. U.S. Congress Office Tech. Assessment; mem. study sect. accident prevention and injury control NIH; mem. Def. Sci. Bd. Task Force on Computers, Tng. and Gaming, Nuclear Regulatory Commn. on Nuclear Safety Rsch. Rev. Com. Author: Telerobotics, Automation and Human Supervisory Control, 1992; co-author: Man Machine Systems, 1974; editor: (with others) Monitoring Behavior and Supervisory Control, 1976; assoc. editor Automatica, 1982-94; co-editor: Perspectives on the Human Controller, 1997; mem. edtl. adv. bd. Tech. Forecasting and Social Change, Computer Aided Design, Advanced Robotics, Robotics and Computer Integrated Mfg.; sr. editor Presence: Telerobots and Virtual Environments, 1991—. Served to 1st lt. USAF, 1951-53. Recipient Nat. Engring. award Am. Assn. Engring. Socs., 1997, Rufus Oldenburger medal ASME, 1997. Fellow IEEE (pres. Systems, Man and Cybernetics Soc. 1974-76, Centennial medal 1984, Norbert Wiener award 1993, Joseph G. Wohl award 1995, Millenium medal 2000), Human Factors Soc. (Paul M. Fitts award 1977, Arnold Small award 2000, pres. 1990-91, Pres. Disting. Svc. award 2000), Nat. Acad. Engring. Democrat. Mem. United Ch. of Christ. Office: MIT 77 Massachusetts Ave Cambridge MA 02139-4307

SHERIF, S. A. mechanical engineering educator; b. Alexandria, Egypt, June 25, 1952; came to U.S., 1978; s. Ahmed and Ietedal H. (Monib) S.; m. Azza A. Shamseldin, Feb. 6, 1977; children: Ahmed S., Mohammad S. BSME (hon.), Alexandria U., 1975, MSME, 1978; PhD in Mech. Engring., Iowa State U., 1985. Tchg. asst. mech. engring. Alexandria U., 1975-78; tchg. assoc. mech. and environtl. engring. U. Calif., Santa Barbara, 1978-79; rsch. asst. mech. engring. Iowa State U., Ames, 1979-84; asst. prof. No. Ill. U., Dekalb, 1984-87, mem. grad. faculty, 1985-87, U. Miami, Coral Gables, Fla., 1987-91, asst. prof. civil, archtl. and mech. engring., 1987-91; assoc. prof. mech. engring. U. Fla., Gainesville, 1991-2001, prof. mech. engring., 2001—, mem. doctoral rsch. faculty, 1992—, dir. Wayne K. and Lyla L. Masur HVAC Lab., 1995—; asst. dir. Indsl. Assessment Ctr., 2001—. ABET coord. for mech. engring., 1997-; coord. for mech. engring. So. Assn. Colls. and Schs., 2001-; affiliate Inst. for Sci. and Health Policy U. Fla., 2001-; cons. Solar Reactor Techs., Inc., Miami, 1988-91, Dade Power Corp., Miami, 1988-91, Ind. Energy Sys., Miami, 1988-91, Carey Dwyer Eckhart Mason Spring & Beckham, P.A. Law Offices, Miami, 1988-89, Michael G. Widoff, P.A., Attys. at Law, Ft. Lauderdale, Fla., 1989-93, Law Offices Pomeroy and Betts, Ft. Lauderdale, 1991-92, Ctr. for Indoor Air Rsch., 1994-2000; cons. Fla. Power and Light Co., 1996—; cons. U. Roorkee, 1994-95, 98—; adj. faculty cons. Kennedy Western U., Thousand Oaks, Calif., 1994-97; resident assoc. Argonne (Ill.) Nat. Lab., Tech. Transfer Ctr., summer 1992; faculty fellow NASA Kennedy Space Ctr., Cape Canaveral, Fla., summer 1993; rsch. assoc. summer faculty rsch. program USAF Office Sci. Rsch., Arnold Engring. Devel. Ctr., Arnold AFB, Tenn., 1994; faculty fellow NASA Marshall Space Flight Ctr., Huntsville, Ala., 1996, 97. Co-editor: Industrial and Agricultural Applications of Fluid Mechanics, 1989, The Heuristics of Thermal Anemometry, 1990, Heat and Mass Transfer in Frost and Ice, Packed Beds, and Environmental Discharges, 1990, Industrial Applications of Fluid Mechanics, 1990, rev. edit., 1991, Mixed Convection and Environmental Flows, 1990, Measurement and Modeling of Environmental Flows, 1992, Industrial and Environment Applications of Fluid Mechanics, 1992, rev. edit., 1998, Thermal Anemometry-1993, 1993, Developments in Electrorheological Flows and Measurement Uncertainty-1994, 1994, Heat, Mass and Momentum Transfer in Environmental Flows, 1995, Thermal Anemometry, 1996, Fluid Measurement Uncertainty Applications, 1996, Devices for Flow Measurement and Analysis, 1997, Heat and Mass Transfer in Environmental Flows, 1998, Industrial and Environmental Applications of Fluid Mechanics, 1999, rev. edit., 2001; reviewer more than 35 internat. jours., more than 150 conf. procs.; mem. editl. com. SECTAM XXI, 2001—; book rev. editor ASME Applied Mech. Revs., 2001-; contbr. numerous articles to profl. jours. NASA ambassador, 1996-98, lab. host student sci. tng. program Ctr. for Precollegiate Edn. and Tng., 1997—; mem. environ. awareness adv. com., Dade County Pub. Schs., 1989-91, lab. dir. cmty. lab. rsch. program, 1989-91, also faculty liaison design svcs. dept.; active Com. for Nat. Inst. for Environ., 1992—; mem. senate U. Fla., 1994-95, mem. OUTREACH Spkrs. program, 1996-98. Fellow ASME (mem. energy resources bd. 2001-, steering com. internat. energy conversion engring. conf., 2002-, coord. group fluid measurements, fluids engring. divsn. 1987—, vice chmn. 1990-92, chmn. 1992-94, fluids engring. divsn. adv. bd. 1994—, fed. honors and awards com. 1995-2001, mem. fluid mechs. tech. com. 1990—, fluid mech. com. 1987-90, K-19 environ. heat transfer com. heat transfer divsn. 1987—, mem. K-6 com. on heat transfer in energy systems, 2001-, mem. fluid applications and systems tech. com. 1990—, systems analysis tech. com. advanced energy sys. divsn. 1989—, newsletter editor advanced energy sys. divsn. 1995-98, exec. com., 1999—, mem.-at-large honors awards 1999-2000, sec., treas. 2000-2001, vice chmn., 2001-02, chmn., 2002-03, fundamentals and theory tech. com. solar energy divsn. 1990-97, chmn. CGFM nominating com. 1992-94, mem. 1994-98, chmn. profl. devel. com. Rock River Valley sect. 1987, tech. activities operating com. Gator sect. 1994-96, MFFCC subcom. 1 on uncertainties in flow measurements 1995-2000), ASHRAE (mem. heat transfer fluid flow com. 1988-92, 93-97, corr. mem. 1992-93, 97—, mem. thermodynamics and psychrometrics com. 1988-92, 96-2002, corr. mem. 1992-96, vice chmn. 1990-92, mem. liquid to refrigerant heat exchs. com. 1989-93, 96-97, sec. 1990-92, corr. mem. 1993-96, 97-2001, corr. mem. air-to-refrigerant heat transfer com., 1999-; chmn. stds. project com. on measurement of moist air properties 1989-95, corr. mem. refrigeration load calculations, 1999-), AIAA (assoc. fellow, assoc. terrestrial energy systems tech. com. 2001—), AIChE (sr.); mem. Internat. Assn. Hydrogen Energy, Internat. Solar Energy Soc., Am. Solar Energy Soc., Internat. Energy Soc. (mem. sci. coun.), European Assn. Laser Anemometry (ASME/FED rep., mem. steering com.), Internat. Inst. Refrigeration (U.S. nat. com.), ABI (hon. mem. rsch. bd. adv. 1994—), Sigma Xi. Moslem. Avocations: reading, soccer, basketball, history, astronomy. Home: 3544 NW 88th Ter Gainesville FL 32606-3802 Office: U Fla Dept Mech Engring 228 MEB PO Box 116300 Gainesville FL 32611-6300 E-mail: sasherif@ufl.edu.

SHERIFF, KENNETH WAYNE, social services administrator; b. Carthage, Mo., Dec. 27, 1942; s. Albert Edward and Veda Marie (Holcomb) S.; m. Shirley Ann Wingler, Oct. 3, 1964; children: Wendy Ann, Bradley Wayne. BA, Greenville Coll., 1965; MSW, U. Mo., 1970; M in Pub. Adminstrn., U. Ill., 1983. Lic. clin. social worker, Ill. Social worker Ill. Dept. Pub. Aid, Centralia, 1965-70, social svcs. cons., 1970-71, asst. regional dir. Springfield, 1971-72, sect. supr., 1972-79, program mgr., 1979-82, asst. bur. chief, 1982-97, sr. pub. svc. adminstr., 1997-2000; clin. counselor Killian & Assocs., 2000—. Bd. dirs. Woodstock (Ill.) Christian Care Inc., 1981-94; exec. dir. Christian Counseling and Ednl. Ministries, Springfield, 1985-87; exec. dir. Keep In Touch Svcs., Inc., Springfield, 1983-2000. Bd. edn. Community Unit Dist. 8, Pleasant Plains, Ill., 1981-87; com. chmn. Citizens Com. for Better Schs., Pleasant Plains, 1979-80; bd. dirs. ministerial edn. and guidance Free Meth. Gateway Conf., Greenville, 1980—; alumni bd. mem. Greenville Coll., 1975-78. Mem. NASW, Am. Assn. of Christian Counselors. Free Methodist. Avocations: canoeing, camping, traveling. Home: 1201 Larchmont Dr Springfield IL 62704-2109

SHERIN, EDWIN, theatrical and film director, actor; b. Danville, Pa., Jan. 15, 1930; s. Joseph and Ruth (Berger) S.; m. Jane Alexander, Mar. 29, 1975; children: Anthony J., Geoffrey B. (dec.), Jonathan E.; 1 stepchild, Jason E. AB in History and Polit. Sci., Brown U., 1952. Acting tchr. Am. Theatre Wing, N.Y.C., 1962-64; acting tchr. Am. Theatre Tng. Inst. Southeastern Mass. U., South Dartmouth, 1974; Lucille Lortel Disting. guest artist U. Bridgeport (Conn.), 1980; dir. Sch. Theatre Arts Boston U., 1981; acting tchr. Okla. Summer Arts Inst., 1985-86, One on One, L.A., 1989, 90; exec. v.p. Altion Prodns., 1985-93; pres. Pumpkin House Prodns., 1993—. Mem. nat. adv. for Mus. Am. Theatre; instr. Okla. Summer Arts Inst., guest dir. Calif. Inst. Arts. Actor with Houseman's troupe Phoenix Theatre, N.Y.C., 1957-58, actor N.Y. Shakespeare Festival, 1956-60; appeared as: Octavius Caesar in, Anthony and Cleopatra, 1958; appeared in Broadway plays Come Blow Your Horn, 1960, Desert Incident, 1961, Romulus, 1962, Face of a Hero, 1963; TV films Playhouse 90, 1956-58, Studio One, 1956-58, Omnibus, 1957-60, East Side/West Side, 1960; dir. Broadway plays including The Great White Hope, 1968, Glory Hallelujah, 1969, 6 RMS RIV VU, 1973, Find Your Way Home, Of Mice and Men, 1974, Red Devil Battery Sign, 1975, Sweet Bird of Youth, 1976, Eccentricities of a Nightingale, 1976, The First Monday in October, 1978, Goodbye Fidel, 1980, The Visit, 1992; assoc. producing dir. Washington's Arena Stage, 1964-68; dir. Cosi Fan Tutte, N.Y. City Opera Co., 1972, A Streetcar Named Desire, Piccadilly Theatre, London, 1973, Semmelweiss, Studio Arena Theatre, Buffalo, N.Y., 1978, Outrage, Kennedy Ctr., Washington, 1982; films including Valdez is Coming, 1970, My Old Man's Place, 1971; producing artistic dir. Showdown at Adobe Hotel, Semmelweiss, Hedda Gabler, Night Must Fall, A Streetcar Named Desire, Hartman Theatre, Stamford, Conn., 1980-85; dir. Chelsea Walls, Naked Angels, N.Y.C., 1990, TV programs Hill Street Blues, Moonlighting, WIOU, L.A. Law, Tour of Duty, MEN; co-exec. prodr. Law and Order, 1993-94, exec. prodr., 1994-2000, (TV films) The Father Clements Story, Lena, My 100 Children, Daughter of the Streets, Getting Even, A Marriage: Georgia O'Keeffe and Alfred Stieglitz, 1991. With USN, 1952-56, Korea. Recipient Outer Circle award, 1969; New Eng. Theatre award, 1969; Recipient N.Y. Drama Critics award, 1969, Drama Desk award, 1969, L.A. Drama Circle award, 1971, Recipient Tony nomination, 1974, London Evening Standard citation, 1973, Joseph Jefferson award, 1976, Buffalo drama award, 1978, Emmy award, 1997; New Eng. Theatre Conf. award; Ford Found. grantee, 1965-66. Mem. AFTRA, SAG, Actors Equity Assn., Dirs. Guild Am. nat. v.p. 1997—), Dramatists Guild, Soc. Stage Dirs. and Choreographers (v.p. 1970-80), Lincoln Soc., Phi Gamma Delta.

SHERIN, ROBIN, artist; b. Bklyn., May 22, 1955; d. Leonard and Shirley (Smookler) S. BS, NYU, 1976. One-woman shows include Washington Place Artists' Gallery, N.Y.C., 1981; group exhbns. include Haggin Mus., Stockton, Calif., 1982, SUNY, Potsdam, 1982, U. N.D., Grand Forks, 1982, Boston Printmakers, Decordova Mus., Lincoln, Mass., 1982, Atlantic Gallery, N.Y.C., 1983, Clemson (S.C.) U., 1983, 85, Emerging Collector, N.Y.C., 1986, U. Mo., Columbia, 1986, Trenton (N.J.) State Coll., 1986, 50 West Gallery, N.Y.C., 1986, Somerstown Gallery, Somers, N.Y., 1990, Eleven East Ashland Gallery, Phoenix, 1990, Chattahoochie Valley Art Assn., La Grange, Ga., 1990, Fine Arts Inst., San Bernadino Cty. Mus., Redlands, Calif., 1991, West Nebr. Arts Ctr., Scottsbluff, 1991, Hill Country Arts Found., Ingram, Tex., 1991, Galesburg (Ill.) Civic Art Ctr., 1991, Boston Printmakers, Decordova Mus., Lincoln, Mass., 1991, d'Art Ctr., Norfolk, Va., 1992, Haggin Mus., Stockton, Calif., 1992, Mus. Without Walls, Bemus Point, N.Y., 1992, Trenton State Coll., 1992, Acad. Arts, Easton, Md., 1992, Pleiades Gallery, N.Y.C., 1992, 1708 East Main Gallery, Richmond, Va., 1992, Amos Eno Gallery, N.Y.C., 1992, Art Assn. Harrisburg, Pa., 1992, Austin Peay St. U., Trahern Gallery, Clarksville Tenn., 1993, Cmty. Coun. for Arts, Kinston, N.C., 1993, Cooperstown (N.Y.) Art Assn., 1993, Warren St. Gallery, Hudson, N.Y., 1993, Allentown (Pa.) Mus., 1994, Main Line Art Ctr., Haverford, Pa., 1994, Harper Coll., Palatine, Ill., 1994, Chattahoochee Valley Art Mus., LaGrange, Ga., 1994, Womens Caucus for Art, Owen Patrick Gallery, Phila., 1994, Pa. State U., University Park, 1994, Hill Country Arts Found., Ingram, Tex., 1994, Fine Arts Inst., San Bernardino County Mus., Redlands, Calif., 1994, Erector Square Gallery, New Haven, 1994, Chautauquea (N.Y.) Galleries, 1995, Ottawa Gallery, Sylvania, Ohio, 1995, Wenatchee (Wash.) Valley Coll., 1995, Art Assn. Harrisburg, Pa., 1995, Women's Found. Genesee Valley, Shoestring Gallery, Rochester, N.Y., 1995, Galesburg (Ill.) Civic Art Ctr., 1995, Austin Peay State U., Trahern Gallery, Clarksville, Tenn., 1995, Carnegie Art Ctr., North Tonawanda, N.Y., 1996, 1708 Gallery, Richmond, Va., 1996, Mable Cultural Ctr., Mableton, Ga., 1996, Cooperstown (N.Y.) Art Assn., 1996, Artlink, Fort Wayne, Ind., 1996, Pa. State U., University Park, 1996, Nat. Art League, Douglaston, N.Y., 1996, QCC Art Gallery, Queensborough C.C., CUNY, Bayside, N.Y., 1996, Cedar City Art Com., Braithwaite Fine Arts Gallery, So. Utah U., Cedar City, 1996, Artist Coun., Palm Springs (Calif.) Desert Mus., 1996, Muscarelle Mus. Art, Coll. William & Mary, Williamsburg, Va., 1996, Del Mar Coll., Corpus Christi, Tex., 1996, Nightingale Gallery, Eastern Oreg. State Coll., La Grande, 1996, Carrie Haddad Gallery, Hudson, N.Y., 1997, University Gallery, St. John's U., Jamaica, N.Y., 1997, Calif. Soc. Printmakers, Richmond (Calif.) Art Ctr., 1997, Bank of Am. World Hdqs., San Francisco, 1997, Michael Ingbar Gallery, N.Y.C., 1998, Saddleback Coll. Art Gallery, Mission Viejo, Calif., 1999. Studio: 27 W 24th St Ste 506 New York NY 10010-3204

SHERIS, STEVEN JAY, physician; b. Queens, N.Y., Jan. 17, 1962; s. Harold and Sandra (White) S.; m. Ilene Ruth Strumeyer, May 5, 1988; children: Arielle, Daniel, Jordan. BA, Rutgers Coll., 1984; MD, U. Med. Dentistry N.J., 1988. Diplomate Am. Bd. Internal Medicine (subsplty. in cardiology), Nat. Bd. Med. Examiners. Commd. lt. USN, 1988, advanced through grades to comdr., 1998; intern Nat. Naval Med. Ctr., Bethesda, Md., 1988-89; asst. divsn. surgeon 2d Marine Divsn., Camp Lejeune, N.C., 1989-91; resident in internal medicine Nat. Naval Med. Ctr., Bethesda, Md., 1991-93, chief medicine resident, 1993-94, fellow in cardiology, 1994-97; fellow in advanced cardiac ultrasound Georgetown U. Med. Ctr., 1997-98; dir. cardiac ultrasound, staff cardiologist Naval Med. Ctr., Portsmouth, Va., 1998—2001. Fellow ACP, Am. Coll. Cardiology. Office: Assocs in Cardiovasc Disease 33 Overlook Rd Ste 305 Summit NJ 07970 Home: 6 Essex Ct Livingston NJ 07039

SHERK, GEORGE WILLIAM, lawyer; b. Washington, June 23, 1949; s. George William and Lorraine Martha (Meyer) Sherk; m. Patricia F. Sherk, Oct. 27, 2001. AA, St. Louis C.C., 1970; BA, Colo. State U., 1972, MA, 1974; JD, U. Denver, 1978; DSc, George Washington U., 2002. Bar: Am. Samoa 1978, Colo. 1979, U.S. Dist. Ct. Colo. 1979, U.S. Ct. Claims 1984, U.S. Supreme Ct. 1985. Cons. office of legis. counsel Govt. of Am. Samoa, Pago Pago, 1978-79; atty. advisor western area power adminstrn. U.S. Dept. Energy, Colo., 1979-80; pvt. practice law Denver, 1980-82; staff assoc. Nat. Conf. State Legis., 1980-82; spl. asst. office of water policy U.S. Dept. Interior, Washington, 1982-83; atty. land and natural resources div. U.S. Dept. Justice, 1984-90; of counsel Will & Muys, 1990-93; pvt. practice Alexandria, Va., 1993—, Vis. scholar U. Wyo. Coll. Law, 1993; vis. prof. Ga. State U. Coll. Law, 1994-95, Ga. State U. Policy Rsch. Ctr., 1995-96; assoc. professorial lectr. George Washington U. Sch. Engring. and Applied Sci., Washington, 1997—; hon. assoc. water law and policy programme Ctr. for Energy, Petroleum and Mineral Law Policy, U. Dundee, Scotland, 1998—; lectr. various colls. and univs.; mem. assoc. faculty Va. Inst. Marine Sci., Coll. of William and Mary, Gloucester Pt., Va., 1989-94; dep. dir. Ctr. Risk Sci. & Pub. Health Sch. Pub. Health & Health Svcs. George Washington U., 2000-01. Author, co-author or editor numerous books and articles on water law and alternative energy law; book review editor Rivers: Studies in the Science, Environmental Policy and Law of Instream Flow, 1989-2000. Mem. ABA, ASCE, Water Environ. Fedn., State Bar Colo. Avocations: automobile racing and rallying, sports, reading, outdoor activites, sailing. Home and Office: 801 N Pitt St # 1708 Alexandria VA 22314-1765

SHERK, KENNETH JOHN, lawyer; b. Ida Grove, Iowa, Feb. 27, 1933; s. John and Dorothy (Myers) Sherk; children: Karin Fulton, Katrina, Keith, Kyle. BSC, U. Iowa, 1955; JD, George Washington U., 1961. Bar: Ariz. 1962, U.S. Dist. Ct. Ariz. 1962, U.S. Ct. Appeals (9th cir.) 1966, U.S. Supreme Ct. 1974. Assoc. Moore & Romley, Phoenix, 1962-67, ptnr., 1967-79, Romley & Sherk, Phoenix, 1979-85; dir. Fennemore Craig, 1985—. 1st lt. U.S. Army, 1955-58, Korea. Recipient Profl. Achievement Svcs. award George Washington Law Assn., 1986, Ariz. Judges Assn., 1989, Disting. Svc. award Phoenix Assn. Def. Counsel, 1990; named Mem. of Yr. State Bar of Ariz., 1994. Fellow Am. Coll. Trial Lawyers, Am. Acad. Appellate Lawyers, Am. Bar Found., Ariz. Bar Found. (Walter E. Craig award 1999); mem. ABA (ho. of dels. 1990-93), Ariz. Bar Assn. (pres. 1985-86), Maricopa County Bar Assn. (pres. 1978-79). Republican. Congregationalist. Avocations: fishing, hiking, bicycling. Home: 1554 W Las Palmaritas Dr Phoenix AZ 85021-5429 Office: Fennemore Craig 3003 N Central Ave Ste 2600 Phoenix AZ 85012-2913

SHERLIN, JERRY MICHAEL, retired hydro meteorological technician; b. Chattanooga, Oct. 8, 1938; s. Chester Wallace and Eva Pearl (Scruggs) S; m. Susan Loxie Doenhoefer, July 22, 1993. BGS, U. Nebr., 1971; MA, Ball State U., 1976. Advanced through grades to master sgt. USAF, 1959, ret., 1981; rsch. asst. Sacramento Peak Solar Observatory, Sunspot, N.Mex., 1981-82; meteorological technician Nat. Weather Svc., Sioux City, Iowa, 1982-89, coop. program mgr. Denver, 1989-94, hydrometeorological technician, 1994-99; ret. Adj. instr. astronomy Aurora Arapahoe CC, 2001—. Co-editor: Observe-and Understand the Sun, 1976; contbr. articles to profl. jours. Vol. Denver Mus. of Natural History, Denver, 1990—; chmn. Astronomical League 50th Ann. Nat. Conv., Copper Mountain, Colo., 1997. Recipient G. R. Wright Svc. award Astronomical League, 1992; decorated Air Force Commendation medal with 2 oak leaf clusters, 1974, 79, 81. Fellow Royal Astron. Soc.; mem. AAAS, Am. Astron. Soc., Am. Assn. Variable Star Observers, Astron. Soc. of the Pacific, Astronomical League and Internat. Dark-Sky Assn. Home: 17002 E Prentice Dr Centennial CO 80015-2412 Fax: 303-693-3503. E-mail: sherlinj@aol.com., jsherlin@spd.aas.org.

SHERMAN, ALAN ROBERT, psychologist, educator; b. N.Y.C., Nov. 18, 1942; s. David R. and Goldie (Wax) S.; m. Llana Helene Tobias, Aug. 14, 1966 (div. 1989); children: Jonathan Colbert, Relissa Anne; m. Ann Marie Redington, Aug. 22, 2002. BA, Columbia U., 1964; MS, Yale U., 1966, PhD, 1969. Lic. psychologist, Calif. Faculty psychology U. Calif., Santa Barbara, 1969—; clin. psychologist in pvt. practice, 1981—. Cons. in field. Author: Behavior Modification, 1973; contbr. articles to profl. jours. and chpts. in books. Pres. Santa Barbara Mental Health Assn., 1978, 84-85, 91, Mountain View Sch. Site Coun., Santa Barbara, 1978-84. Recipient Vol. of Yr. award Santa Barbara Mental Health Assn., 1979, Tchg. Excellence awards Delta Delta Delta, Alpha Chi Omega, Gamma Phi Beta, Santa Barbara; NIMH predoctoral rsch. fellow, 1964-69; grantee in field. Fellow Behavior Therapy and Rsch. Soc.; mem. APA, AAUP (chpt. pres. 1978-79), Calif. Psychol. Assn., Assn. for Advancement of Behavior Therapy, Santa Barbara County Psychol. Assn. (pres. 1985), Phi Beta Kappa (chpt. pres. 1977-78), Sigma Xi, Psi Chi (chpt. faculty advisor, 1979—). Office: Univ of Calif Dept Psychology Santa Barbara CA 93106-9660 E-mail: sherman@psych.ucsb.edu. *Pursuing a creative profession which allows one to help improve the condition of others, provides intrinsic rewards that make the work process satisfying in itself. I am fortunate to be involved in two such professions, college teaching and psychotherapy. When you genuinely enjoy what you are doing, you are likely to be successful at it.*

SHERMAN, ALAN THEODORE, computer science educator; b. Cambridge, Mass., Feb. 26, 1957; s. Richard Beatty and Hanni Fey (Fechenbach) Sherman; m. Tomoko Shimakawa, Aug. 2, 1986; m. Pamela C. Steele, Oct. 20, 2001. ScB in Math. magna cum laude, Brown U., 1978; SM in Elec. Engring and Computer Sci., MIT, 1981, PhD in Computer Sci., 1987. Instr. Tufts U., Medford, Mass., 1985-86, asst. prof., 1986-89, U. Md. Balt. County, Catonsville, 1989-95, assoc. prof., 1995—; mem. Inst. for Advanced Computer Studies U. Md., College Park, 1989-92, 95-98. Rsch. affiliate MIT Lab. for Computer Sci., Cambridge, 1985-88. Author: VLSI Placement and Routing: The PI Project, 1989; co-editor: Advances in Cryptology: Proceedings of Crypto 82, 1983; contbr. articles to profl. jours. Mem. Assn. for Computing Machinery, IEEE, Internat. Assn. for Cryptologic Rsch., AAUP, Soc. for Indsl. and Applied Maths., Phi Beta Kappa, Sigma Xi. Avocations: tennis, Aikido, piano, chess. Home: 3618 Ordway NW Washington DC 20016 Office: U Md Baltimore County Dept Comp Sci Elec Engring Baltimore MD 21250-0001 E-mail: sherman@umbc.edu.

SHERMAN, ARTHUR, theater educator, writer, actor, composer; b. Dec. 5, 1920; s. Herman and Fay (Epstein) S.; m. Margery Frost Sherman, Apr. 15, 1974 (div. Sept. 1989); children: Claudia, Andrew Jay. MusB, Juilliard Sch. Music, 1955; M in Music Edn., Manhattan Sch. Music, 1957; Doctoral Equivalency, CUNY, 1969. Dir. performing arts N.Y.C. (N.Y.) Tech. Coll., 1964-72; prof. speech and theatre John Jay Coll., N.Y.C., 1990—, Borough Man C.C., N.Y.C., 1990—. Judge Film Award Com., Australia, 1972-89, Acad. Awards, 1990; cons. Min. for Edn., Tasmania, Australia, 1977; presenter in field. Author: (screenplays) Thistle and Thorn, 1982, Same Difference, 1983, (book and lyrics) Lenore and the Wonder House, 1964, (children's novel) Paradise Lagoon, 1989, (book) Picture Book for Young Adults Paintings, Music and Lyrics, 1998, An Adventure in the New Mythology, 1999, (philos. study) Our Species Ethical Dilemma, 1998, (book) Songwriting Is Easy and Fun, 1996, (comedy theater) But Its Not Chekhov, 1999, (comic screenplay) Weaning, 1999, (7-book novel) The Pleiades, Burning in Heaven, Freezing in Hell, Bloody Mooring, Scoring in Limbo, Chasing the Phoenix, The Pleiades and Beyond Adventure Etc., The Ethical Dilemma, (with Edward Mapp) The Road to Mainstream, 1999, Anyone for Eagle Wings?, 1999, (polit. satire play) To Hell with Buffalo Wings-Anyone for Eagle Wings?, 1999, The Pleiades, 2000, Warsaw Ghetto Uprising, 2001; composer : (book, music lyrics) Prisms in the Looking Glass, 1993, Once Upon a Crime, We the Common Earth (cantata); actor, dir. films, TV, theater in U.S. and Australia; actor: (films) The Punisher, 1979, Death of a Soldier, 1985, Les Patterson Saves the World, 1988, The Last Bastion, 1987; sculptures displayed YWCA, Hamilton, Ont., Can., 1967, Lincoln Ctr., N.Y.C., 1969, State Bank, Sydney, Australia, 1974; bust of Louis Armstron Meml. Mus. and House, Dame Judith Anderson Australian Consulate N.Y. Pres. United Fedn. Coll. Tchrs., N.Y.C., 1971. With USN, 1943-46. Grantee Australian Film Commn., 1981. Mem. ASCAP, Australasian Performing Rights Assn., Actors' Equity U.S. and Australia. Home: 315 W 57th St New York NY 10019-3158 Office: John Jay Coll 58th St 10th Ave New York NY 10019 E-mail: asherman@jjaycuny.edu.

SHERMAN, BARBARA JANE, social worker; MSW, Fordham U., 1973. Lic. social worker, Conn. Pvt. practice, Cheshire and Fairfield, Conn., 1980—. Cons. in field. Mem. Child Care Action Campaign; mem. Bd. Edn., 1997—. Mem.: APWA, LWV (2d v.p. 1995—), NASW (regional rep. 1983, invitational abstract reviewer conf. social workers in bus. and indust 1984), Conn. Assn. Bds. Edn. (bd. dirs., area rep.), Lions Club Internat. Office: 577 S Main St Cheshire CT 06410-3146 also: 1088 Black Rock Tpke Fairfield CT 06432-4107

SHERMAN, BARNET, financial services executive; b. Bklyn., Sept. 27, 1958; s. Meyer and Naomi Gertrude (Ullman) S.; m. Colleen T. McSpirit, 1990; 1 child, Ryan Alexander. BA with honors, Syracuse U., 1980; M in Pub. Adminstrn., Columbia U., 1982. Legis. aide U.S. Rep. Thomas J. Downey, Washington, 1982-83; mcpl. specialist Prudential-Bache Securities, N.Y.C., 1983-84; sr. analyst mcpl. and fixed income research group Smith, Barney, Harris, Upham & Co., 1984-89; assoc. portfolio mgr. Colonial Mgmt. Assocs., Boston, 1989-91, asst. v.p., 1991-92, v.p., 1992—, dir. mcpl. rsch., 1993-94; v.p., assoc. portfolio mgr. VanKampen Investments, 1994-2000, portfolio mgr., 2000—. Bd. dirs. fin. com. MetroWest Med. Ctr., Framingham, Mass., 1994-96; trustee MetroWest Health Ptnrs., Inc., 1996—. Mem. Smith's Rating & Rsch., Boston Mcpl. Analysts Soc., Mass. Striped Bass Assn., New Eng. Outdoor Writers Assn., Pi Sigma Alpha. Avocations: American art, salt/fresh/fly fishing.

SHERMAN, BEVERLY ROBIN, medical, surgical, pediatric, and maternity nurse; b. Boston, July 24, 1960; d. Lawrence and Frances D. (Weiner) Smith; m. Richard A. Sherman, Aug. 21, 1982; children: Rebecca Lynn, Craig Adam. BSN, Northeastern U., 1983. Nurse Caritas Good Samaritan Med. Ctr., Brockton, Mass. Home: 31 Marion Ave Brockton MA 02301-6524

SHERMAN, BRAD JAMES, congressman; b. L.A., Oct. 24, 1954; s. Maurice H. and Lane (Moss) S. BA summa cum laude, UCLA, 1974; JD magna cum laude, Harvard U., 1979. Bar: Calif. 1979; CPA, Calif. Pvt. practice, L.A., 1980-91; chmn. Calif. Bd. Equalization, Sacramento, 1991-95; mem. U.S. Congress from 24th Calif. dist., 1997—; mem. banking and fin. svcs. com., internat. rels. com. Lectr. on tax law and policy; mem. Calif. Franchise Tax Bd., 1991-95. Contbr. articles to legal jours. Bd. dirs., rep. on tax issues Calif. Common Cause, 1984-89; mem. exec. com. Calif. Dem. Com., 1991—. Mem. Calif. State Bar. Jewish. E-mila. Office: US Ho Reps 1524 Longworth HOB Washington DC 20515-0524 E-mail: brad.sherman@mail.house.gov.*

SHERMAN, CAROL, poet, educator; b. N.Y.C., N.Y., Oct. 20, 1935; d. Albert and Betty Sherman; m. Eugene M. Cooper, Sept. 5, 1971 (dec. June 1982). BA, Hunter Coll., 1957; AAS, Fashion Inst. Tech., 1962. Cert. tchr. N.Y. Bd. Edn., N.Y.C., N.Y. State . Assoc. prof. fashion design Fashion Inst. Tech., N.Y.C., 1964—68; writer Butterick Fashion Mktg. Co., 1971—72; fashion designer, 1965—70, 1976—82; poet Bridgehampton, 1976—. Examiner N.Y. Bd. Edn., N.Y.C., 1975; prodr. LTV, E. Hampton, NY, 1997, 2000, dir., 1996, 2000. Author: Bronx Ballads, 2001; contbr. chapters to books. Fellow, Vt. Studio Ctr., 2001. Mem.: Poets & Writers, Southampton Players (best supporting actress award 1999). Democrat. Buddhist. Avocations: community theater, swimming, cooking, dancing, travel. E-mail: muffinmama@yahoo.com.

SHERMAN, CHARLES DANIEL, JR. surgeon; b. Avon Park, Fla., Oct. 5, 1920; s. Charles Daniel and Mary Alice (Oliver) S.; m. Jean Riebling, Aug. 13, 1943 (dec.); children: Rachel, Charles Daniel, Edward. BS, U. Fla., 1942; MD, Johns Hopkins U., 1945. Diplomate: Am. Bd. Surgery. Intern Duke U. Hosp., Durham, N.C., 1945-46; resident U. Rochester Med. Center, 1948-52, instr., 1952-56, asst. prof., 1956-64, clin. assoc. prof. surgery, 1964-70, clin. prof., 1970—; fellow Meml. Center for Cancer, 1951; practice medicine specializing in cancer surgery Rochester, 1953-98; mem. staff Highland Hosp., N.Y. V.p. Redd Labs., Clearwater, Fla., 1961-70; advisor N.Y. State Bur. Cancer Control, 1964-75; sec.-treas. Monroe County Health Planning Coun., 1967-69; mem. Monroe County Bd. Health, 1966-79; advisor to WHO, 1971, dir. Internat. Network of WHO Collaborating Ctrs. for Cancer Edn., 1996—; mem. advisory com. Nat. Cancer Insts.; dir. Internat. Union Against Cancer Project to Survey Cancer Edn. in L.Am., 1976, Asia, 1977; mem. hosp. adv. com. to Joint Com. on Accreditation of Hosps., 1980-88; organizer WHO/Internat. Union Against Cancer European Congress on Cancer Edn., 1981; mem. Accreditation Coun. for Continuing Med. Edn., 1983-89, vice-chmn., 1988, chmn., 1989; organizer Coordinating Coun. on Cancer Edn. in L.Am., 1986, in Asian-Pacific region, 1987; chmn. Coordinating Coun. for Cancer Edn. in Europe, 1987-88; bd. dirs. Nat. Resident Matching Plan, 1988-92, treas., 1989-90; mem. organizing com. Internat. Med. Scholar Program, 1987-89; keynote spkr. Internat. Cancer Congress, 1992; lectr. in field. Author: Clinical Concepts in Cancer Management, 1976; co-author: Clinical Oncology, 1974; editor, pub.: Directory of U.S. Oncologists, 1983-98; editor: (with others) Programmed Instruction in Medical Education; Newsletter in Cancer, 1968-80; chmn. editorial bd. for 2d , 3d and 4th edits. Clinical Oncology (monograph): (with others) Internat. Union against Cancer, 1978-86; mem. editorial bd. Jour. Cancer Edn., 1984—, Greek Jour. Continuing Med. Edn., 1986—; participant movie on esophogeal reconstrn., 1957; producer exhibits on cancer treatment and cancer edn.; co-contbr. articles to profl. jours. Mem. adv. com. on Continuing Edn. in Oncology of the European Community, 1993; advisor European Sch. Oncology, European Med. Student Assn.; mem. internat. adv. com. Asian Pacific Cancer Congress, Beijing, 1991, Bangkok, 1993, Singapore, 1995, Malaysia, 1996. Recipient Health Edn. award N.Y. State Pub. Health Assn., 1973; cert. of merit. Rochester Acad. Medicine, 1982, John P. McGovern award Houston Acad. Medicine, 1998, Kaiser award Rochester Acad. Medicine, 2001; Fulbright fellow, Mendoza, Argentina, 1963. Mem. ACS, AMA (N.Y. state del. to Ho. of Dels., coun. on med. edn. 1983-92, com. on med. liability 1984-85, com. on fgn. grads. 1984, com. on cancer 1970-74, exec. com. 1989-90), Am. Radium Soc., Soc. Head and Neck Surgeons, Royal Soc. Medicine, Am. Assn. Cancer Edn. (pres. 1975-76), Am. Fedn. Clin. Oncologic Socs. (bd. govs. 1974-77), Am. Soc. Gen. Surgeons (trustee 1994—, James E. Davis award 1998), N.Y. State Med. Soc. (councillor 1973-79, asst. treas. 1980-83, treas. 1983-85, v.p. 1986, pres.-elect 1987, pres. 1988-89, trustee 1990-95, chair trustees 1994-95, liaison com. on med. edn. 1992-94, Fineburg award disting. svc. 1997, Sherman award as adv. to med. student sect. 1997), N.Y. Acad. Sci., N.Y. State Cancer Programs Assn. (pres. 1970-71, chmn. UICC prof. edn. program 1986-94, exec. coun. 1986-94), Monroe County Med. Soc. (pres. 1965, Edward Mott Moore award 1978), Monroe County Cancer and Leukemia Assn. (pres. 1962-66), European Assn. Cancer Edn. (bd. dirs. 1987-92), Soc. Surg. Oncology (chmn. residents award com. 1963-66), Am. Soc. Preventive Oncology, U.S. Squash Rackets Assn. (dir. 1963-65), Argentine Anti-Smoking Union (hon.), Blue Key Soc., Genesee Valley Club, Univ. Club, Phi Beta Kappa, Alpha Phi Omega. Home: 127 Southern Pky Rochester NY 14618-1052

SHERMAN, DANIEL ADAM, psychiatrist; b. N.Y.C., Oct. 21, 1948; s. Morris R. and Dorothy (Salomon) S. BA in Human Biology, Johns Hopkins U., 1969, MD, 1972. Diplomate Am. Bd. Psychiatry and Neurology, 1977. Intern then resident in psychiatry Denver Gen. Hosp., 1972-75; staff psychiatrist Am. Lake VA Hosp., Tacoma, 1975-76; program dir. Harborview Med. Ctr., Seattle, 1976-77; acting instr. U. Wash. Sch. Medicine, 1976-77; psychiat. med. dir. Providence Med. Ctr., 1977-81; practice medicine specializing in psychiatry, 1977—. Research asst. Md. Psychiat. Research Ctr., Catonsville, 1971. Former planning commr. City of Des Moines, Washington, former mem. coun.; former voting mem. Bd. of Health, Seattle/King County. Mem. Am. Psychiat. Assn., Wash. State Psychiat. Assn. (sec. Seattle chpt. 1979-80), King County Med. Soc. Office: 550 16th Ave Ste 300 Seattle WA 98122-5655

SHERMAN, DEANE MURRAY, culture organization administrator; b. Beulah, N.D. m. John F. Sherman, Feb. 8, 1944; children: Betsy Deane, Mary Ann. Student, N.D. State U., George Washington U. Bd. dirs. Arts Coun. Montgomery County, Md., Md., 1978-2000, emeritus, 2000—. Bd. trustees Internat. Conservatory of Music, 1981—, sponsor Phia Berghout Harp Series, 1996-97. Decorated chevalier Ordre des Palm Academiques;recipient Hornbook award Montgomery County Tchrs. Assn., 1967, Leadership award Am. Biog. Inst., 1995, Strathmore Hall Found. award, 1998; honored guest Fukui Harp Festival, 1982, Internat. Harp Contest, Israel, 1988-94, U.S., 1991-95, Perugia Classico IV, 1998, Russian Internat. Festival and Harp Competition, 2000. Mem.: Friends of Franklin (v.p. 1990—, devel. com. 1992—98), Help and Resource Porject (chmn. 1989—), World Harp Congress (founder, v.p. 1990—), Women's Com. for Nat. Symphony, Md. Congress PTA (life), Nat. Congress PTA (life), Western Club Glasgow, Elstophos Sci. Club Washington. Home: 11016 Ardwick Dr North Bethesda MD 20852-3204

SHERMAN, DEMING ELIOT, lawyer; b. Providence, July 22, 1943; s. Edwin Fisk and Martha Amy (Parkhurst) S.; m. Jane Catherine Bauer, Dec. 20, 1966; children: Melissa Jane, Nicholas Deming. BA, Amherst (Mass.) Coll., 1965; JD, U. Chgo., 1968. Bar: R.I. 1968, U.S. Dist. Ct. R.I. 1970, U.S. Supreme Ct. 1974, Mass. 1985, U.S. Dist. Ct. Mass. 1985. Ptnr. Edwards & Angell, Providence, 1969—, mng. ptnr., 1986-94. Trustee First Night Providence, 1988-93, 2001—, pres., 1991-93; bd. dirs. R.I. Philharm. Orch., 1985—, pres., 1993-95; trustee Providence Preservation Soc., 1990—, pres. 1996-99; mem. R.I. Com. on Jud. Tenure and Discipline, 1992-2000; bd. dirs. Providence YMCA, 1975-85, Blackstone Pk. Improvement Assn., 1979—, Nope's Island Conservation Assn., 1992-98 , New Eng. Legal Found., 1994—, R.I. Legal Edn. Partnership, 2000—, Grow Smart RI, 1998—, sec., 1998—; corporator R.I. Hosp., 1989—; bd. dirs. Friends of Blackstone Pk. and Blvd. 2001--, pres., 2001--. Fellow R.I. Bar Found.; mem. ABA, R.I. Bar Assn., Amherst Alumni Assn. R.I. (pres. 1980-91), Greater Providence C. of C. (bd. dirs. 1991-94). Home: 254 Irving Ave Providence RI 02906-5544 Office: Edwards & Angell LLP 2800 Financial Plz Providence RI 02903 E-mail: dsherman@ealaw.com.

SHERMAN, ERIC, director, writer, educator; b. Santa Monica, Calif., June 29, 1947; s. Vincent and Hedda (Comorau) S.; m. Eugenia Blackiston Dillard, Apr. 1, 1978; children: Cosiimo, Rocky. BA cum laude, Yale U., 1968. Film prodr., dir., writer, photographer, editor. Pres. Film Transform; film tchr. Art Ctr. Coll. Design, Cal Arts, L.A. Film Sch., Pepperdine U., UCLA; guest lectr. Yale, Calif. Inst. Tech., U. So. Calif.; Andrew Mellon lectr. on arts Calif. Inst. Tech., 1977; chief cons. (motion picture industry) Gallup Orgn. Films include: Charles Lloyd-Journey Within, 1968; Paul Weiss-a Philospher in Process, 1972; Waltz, 1980; Inside Out, 1982; Measure of America, 1983; Michael Reagan's Assault on Great Lakes, 1983, Futures, 1990 (Peabody Broadcast award 1990), Pep Squad, 1998, Mystic Nights, 1998, After Freedom, 2000; represented in film festivals N.Y.C. Cine Golden Eagle, Melbourne, Australia, Bilbao, Spain, others; books include: (with others) The Director's Event, 1970; Directing the Film, 1976; Frame by Frame, 1987, Selling Your Film, 1990; contbr. numerous articles to film publs. and distbn. catalogues, book dedication; works include three oral h istories for Am. Film Inst. under Louis B. Mayer Found. grant. Trustee Am. Cinematheque; bd. dir. Film Forum. Mem. Soc. Motion Picture and TV Engrs. (assoc.), Assn. I nd. Video Filmmakers, Univ. Film Assn., Assn. Visual Communicators, Nat. Alliance Media Arts Ctrs. Home and Office: 316 N Maryland Ave Apt 208 Glendale CA 91206-3512 E-mail: ericsfilm@aol.com.

SHERMAN, ETHAN, contractor, publisher; b. N.Y.C., June 23, 1941; s. Frank Issac and Jean (Abel) S.; m. Irene Linder, Oct. 31, 1965; children: Adam Howard, Rachael Suzanne. BS, Rider U., 1963. With Style-Master, Poughkeepsie, N.Y., 1971—, pres., 1979—. *Ethan Sherman believes that the procedure he discovered for straightening the spinal column and limbs by using the senses, just might be a non-surgical cure for scoliosis and muscular dystrophy.* Author, pub.: How I Straightened My Spine, 1991. Trustee The Ethan Sherman Found., Poughkeepsie, N.Y., 1995—. With USAF, 1969-71. Mem. Knights of Pythias (chancellor comdr. 1989, 2000). Avocations: sailing, camping, gardening. Home: 37 Hornbeck Rd Poughkeepsie NY 12603-1121 Office: Style-Master Home Products Inc 37 Hornbeck Rd Poughkeepsie NY 12603

SHERMAN, EUGENE JAY, retired marketing executive, economist; b. N.Y.C., Jan. 10, 1935; s. Samuel and Sarah (Lavinsky) S.; m. Mary Eileen Van, Apr. 22, 1966; 1 child, Rebecca. BA, CCNY, 1956; MBA, NYU, 1959, postgrad., 1959-63. Economist Fed. Res. Bank N.Y., 1959-62, Chase Manhattan Bank, N.Y.C., 1962-65; v.p. Bank of N.Y., 1965-72; sr. v.p., exec. dir., dir. rsch. Merrill Lynch and Co., 1972-78; v.p., chief economist, mgr.internat. investment Internat. Gold Corp., 1980-86; sr. v.p., chief economist Fed. Home Loan Bank N.Y., 1986-93; sr. v.p., dir. rsch. M.A. Schapiro & Co., Inc., N.Y.C., 1993-96. Gold cons., N.Y.C., 1986—; adj. prof. Touro Coll., N.Y.C., 1997-98; exec.-in-residence, adj. prof. Baruch Coll., N.Y.C., 1997—, mem. faculty senate. Author: Gold Investment: Theory and Application, 1986; contbr. articles to profl. jours. Mem. Money Marketeers (pres. 1971-72. honored fellow 1987), Downtown Economist Club (chmn. 1988-89), Forecasters (winner 1986, 95), Treasury Securities Luncheon (pres. 1995-96), Nat. Assn. Bus. Econs., N.Y. Assn. Bus. Econs. Avocations: mountaineering, performing arts. Home: 115 E 9th St New York NY 10003-5414

SHERMAN, FRANCIS GEORGE HARRY, advertising agency executive; b. Croydon, Eng., Apr. 12, 1924; came to U.S. 1947, naturalized 1950. s. Frank Edward and Amelia Elizabeth (Oddy) S.; m. Barbara Opal Blick, May 3, 1947 (dec. 1975); children: Christopher Randolph, Dawn Madeline Ann; m. Elaine Roemisch Crane, Feb. 6, 1977; 1 child, Elizabeth Courtney Crane. Student, U. Durham, Eng., 1942-43, Harvard Coll., 1947-48; MBA, Harvard U., 1950. Sales rep. Eagle-Ottawa Leather Co., Grand Haven, Mich., 1951-55; automotive sales mgr. Detroit, 1955-58; regional mgr. Rogers Publ. Co., Pitts., 1958-59; exec. v.p. Penn & Hamaker, Inc., Cleve., 1959-71; v.p. mktg. Soc. Nat. Bank, 1971-77, McKinney Great Lakes Co., Cleve., 1977-79, pres., 1979-83; v.p. internat. ops. McKinney, Inc., Cleve., Chgo. and Phila., 1983-86, sr. v.p., 1986-89; pres. Ted Sherman Mktg. Comm., Inc., Willoughby Hills, Ohio, 1989—. Bd. dirs. Minority Econ. Developers Council, Cleve., 1973-90; past pres. West Shore Symphony Orch., Muskegon, Mich., 1955-56; mem. pub. rels. com. Cleve. Orch., 1974-86; mktg. dir. Harvard Bus. Sch. 2001 Global Alumni Conf., 1998-2001; bd. dirs. Breckenridge Village, Ohio Presbyn. Retirement Svcs., 2002—; mktg. dir. Cleve. Coun. on World Affairs, 2002—. Served to flight lt. RAF, 1947. Mem. Indsl. Marketers Cleve. (trustee 1980-83, best programs award 1981), Affiliated Advt. Agys. Internat. (trustee 1981-83), Am. Assn. Advt. Agys., Cleve. World Trade Assn. (bd. dirs. 1985-97, chmn. mktg. and communications com. 1985-92), Assn. Ohio Commodores (life mem.), Soc. Automotive Engrs., Am. Foundrymen's Soc., Lake County Profl. Communicators (trustee 1984-90, pres. 1988), Harvard Bus. Sch. Club Northeastern Ohio (pres. 1964-65, trustee 1965-66, 66-68, 75-79, 87-2001, trustee emeritus 2001—), Harvard U. Club Northeastern Ohio, Kirtland Country Club, Royal Air Force Club (London). Office: 37355 Rogers Rd Willoughby OH 44094-9482 E-mail: tedsherman@earthlink.net.

SHERMAN, FRANK WILLIAM, engineer; b. Ft. Dodge, Iowa, Nov. 15, 1946; s. Frank LaSalle and True Rosemary (Miller) S.; m. Joan Frances Van Bruaene, Aug. 21, 1971; children: Emma Daun, Joshua Frank. BS, Iowa State U., 1970; MS, So. Ill. U., 1991. Registered profl. engr., Ill. Air pollution engr. Ill. Environ. Protection Agy., Springfield, 1970-84; mgr. Ill. Vehicle Emission Test Program, 1984-89; self-employed internat. environ. engring. practice Ill., 1990-92; bd. dirs., pres. Sherman Engring., Inc., 1992—. Chmn. Air Quality Adv. Com. Chgo. Area Transp. Study, 1976-84; bd. dirs., pres. Decatur Bicycle Shoppe Ltd. Contbr. articles to profl. jours. Pres. Pasfield Neighborhood Assn., Springfield, 1979; active St. Agnes Ch., Springfield, 1985-88, host sponsor Youth for Understanding Fgn. Lang., 1987-88; vol. capt. Am. Heart Assn. Mem. Am. Assn. Motor Vehicle Adminstrs. (chmn. vehicle emissions subcom. 1988-90), Nat. Soc. Profl. Engrs., Ill. Soc. Profl. engrs., Air Waste Mgmt. Assn., Ctrl. Ill. Air Waste Mgmt. Assn. (bd. dirs.). Avocations: bicycling, bridge. E-mail: frank.sei@warpnet.net. *Personal philosophy: Life is a journey, not a destination.*

SHERMAN, FRED, biochemist, educator; b. Mpls., May 21, 1932; s. Harry and Ann (Kaufman) Sherman; m. Revina Freeman, July 25, 1958 (div.); children: Aaron, Mark, Rhea; m. Elena Rustchenko Bulgac, May 5, 2001. BA, U. Minn., Mpls., 1953; PhD, U. Calif., Berkeley, 1958. Postdoctoral fellow U. Wash., Seattle, 1959—60; 60postdoctoral fellow 61Lab. Genetique Physiol., Gif-sur-Yvette, France, 1960-61; sr. instr. U. Rochester, NY, 1961—62, asst. prof., 1962—66, assoc. prof., 1966—71, prof. dept. biochemistry Sch. Medicine & Dentistry, 1971—, chmn. dept. biochemistry, 1982—99. Instr. Cold Spring Harbor Lab., NY, 1970—87; Wander Meml. lectr., 1975; Wilson prof. U. Rochester, 1982. Co-author: Cold Spring Harbor Manual on Yeast Genetics and Molecular Biology, 1970—87; assoc. editor: Genetics, 1975—82, assoc. editor: Molecular Cell Biology, 1979—88. Fellow NIH,

1959—61; grantee, 1963. Mem.: AAAS, NAS, Am. Soc. Microbiology, Genetic Soc. Am. (bd. dirs. 1983—85). Home: 69 Westminster Rd Rochester NY 14607-2223 E-mail: fred_sherman@URMC.Rochester.edu.

SHERMAN, FREDERICK HOOD, lawyer; b. Deming, N.Mex., Aug. 9, 1947; s. Benjamin and Helen (Hood) S.; m. Janie Carol Jontz, Oct. 23, 1973; children: Jerah Elizabeth, Frederick Jakub. BBA, Southern Meth. U., 1970, JD, 1972. Bar: Tex. 1972, N.Mex. 1973, U.S. Dist. Ct. N.Mex. 1973, U.S. Dist. Ct. (we. dist.) Tex. 1974, U.S. Supreme Ct. 1979; cert. mediator. Assoc. Sherman & Sherman, Deming, 1973-74, ptnr., 1974-78, prin., 1978—, owner, 1998—. Mem. spacialization com. N.Mex. Supreme Ct., 1986—94; liaison N.Mex. Supreme Ct. and Workers Compensation Bd., 1991—94; apptd. guardian Assets State Fiscal Acctg. State N.Mex., 1992—; state coord. Nat. Bd. Trial Advocates for Bd. Cert. Trial Specialist, 1994—98. Contbr. articles to profl. jours. Chmn. Luna County Planning Commn., Deming, 1976-78; apptd. visitor to U. N.Mex. Law Sch., 1983—; treas. Luna County Econ. Devel. PSS, 1987-88, also bd. dirs.; bd. dirs. Luna County Hosp., 1991-94; bd. mem. Deming Pub. Sch., 1991-94, pres., 1991-92, elected bd. mem. 1991-95; chmn. bd. dirs. Luna County Charitable Found., 1991—; hon. dir. Deming Art Coun., 1989—; pres. Luna County Sch. Bd., 1991-92; pres., chmn. of the bd. Sherman Family Charitable Found., 1991—; mem. N. Mex. High Sch. Task Force, 1993-94. Recipient Svc. award, N.Mex. Bd. Legal Specialization, 1994, Cert. Advocacy, Nat. Coll. Advocacy, 2001. Mem.: Supreme Ct. Com. Professionalism, Col. Albert Fountain Inns of Ct. (charter), Coll. State Bar Tex. (pro bono 1995—), Am. Inns of Ct. (master atty. 1995—, officer 1997—), 6th Jud. Bar Assn., Tex. Bar Assn., State Bar N.Mex. (commr. 1978—86, com. on alt. dispute resolutions practice 1980—90, jud. selection com. 1985, com. legal retreat 1989, med. rev. com. 2000, arbitration com. 2000, mem. jud. selection com. 1985—88, legal retreat com. 1986—88, co-chair 1986—87, alternative dispute resolution com. 1980—91, Outstanding Svc. award 1986, Dedication award 1986), N.Mex. Bar Assn., N.Mex. Trial Lawyers Assn. (bd. dirs. 1986—, sec. 1989, 1997, officer 1997—98, designgated mentor in personal injury/auto and social security 1998—, Notably Large award 1983, 1984, 1985, Amicus Curiae award 1991), ATLA (del. 2000—, state del. 2000—, pub. edn. com. 2001—). Democrat. Roman Catholic. Avocations: skiing, investments, camping, farming, wine making. Office: Sherman & Sherman PO Box 850 Deming NM 88031-0850

SHERMAN, FRIEDA FRANCES, writer; b. N.Y.C., Oct. 21, 1929; d. Benjamin and Anna (Brown) Jeffe; m. Alan Morton Sherman, Feb. 21, 1952; children: Steven, Daniel, Elizabeth, Richard. BA, Hunter Coll., 1951. Market researcher Am. Broadcasting Co., N.Y.C., 1953-55, Am. Inst. Mgmt., N.Y.C., 1955-56; tchr. dance Palo Alto (Calif.), 1960-70; co-founder Workshop Unltd., Palo Alto, 1970-74; dir. client support Prognostics, 1982-85; dance therapist pvt. practice, 1975-90. Cons. Market Intelligence Rsch., Palo Alto, 1985. Author of poems and short stories; sr. rschr., editor: The Workshop Unlimited, Non-Profit Innovation in the 21st Century, 1998-2002. Coord. cmty. outreach Lively Arts Stanford (Calif.) U., 1990-92; bd. dirs. SPCA, Santa Cruz, Calif., 1994; judge Nat. Poetry Contest, Santa Cruz, 1994. Mem. Nat. Writers Union, Phi Beta Kappa. Avocations: dancing, hiking, music. Home: 900 Glen Canyon Rd Santa Cruz CA 95060-1619

SHERMAN, GERALD, nuclear physicist, financial estate adviser, financial company executive; b. Bklyn., Sept. 7, 1938; s. Saul and Claire S.; m. Annette Ellen Drasin, Aug. 29, 1965; children: Rochelle Heidi, Sondra Nicole. BA in Physics, UCLA, 1960, MS in Nuclear Physics, 1962; PhD in Physics, Columbia Pacific U., 1985. Cert. Nat. Assn. Securities Dealers, Series 6 and 63, Investment Co. Products/Variable Contracts, registered rep.; lic. in securities and health and life ins. Calif.; lic. Fed. Securities Series 7. Physics instr., lower divsn. Lab. UCLA, 1960-62, physics instr. upper divsn. nuclear physics, 1961-62; nuclear ion engine rocket physicist Rocketdyne, Canoga Park, Calif., 1961; sr. scientist Advanced Tech. Co., L.A., 1965-66; physicist, principle superconductivity investigator Northrop Space Sci. Lab., Hawthorne, Calif., 1966-70; pres. Sherman Ins. Agy., Inc., L.A., 1970-84; pres., CEO Sherman Fin. Svcs., Inc., Thousand Oaks, Calif., 1984—. Cons. TRW, 1970; spkr. sci. seminars for NASA, U.S. Air Force, Lockheed; speaker fin. seminars, 1972—; developer bus. plan between Bank of China and New USA-China Project; create internet interactive website bus. plan, 1998—. Author: Microwave Phenomenological Theory of Superconductivity, 1965, Superconductive Antennas, 1966, Estate Tax Savings of 90%, 1992, Financial Security for Life, 1993; creater original internet interactive ins. investment website bus. plan, 1998-99. Recipient AEC Time Reduction Analysis award Am. Electronics, 1960, Top Prodr. Nationwide award U.S. Life Ins. Co. Calif., 1978, Leading Disability Prodr. Nationwide award Chubb Life Ins. Co. Am., 1983-85, 90, Leading Combined Life and Disability Prodr. award Chubb, 1987, Leading Combined Disability and Life Ins. Producer award Chubb, 1989, Internat. Life and Health Ins. awards Chubb Corp./Summit Club Calif., 1979, 88, 89, 92, 94, Hawaii, 1982, 92, 94, Italy, 1984, 93, Greece, 1984, Bermuda, 1985, 72, 88, England, 1985, Scotland, 1985, Mex., 1986, Monaco 1987, Switzerland, 1987, Hong Kong, 1988, Thailand, 1988, France, 1989, Africa, 1989, Puerto Rico, 1990, 95, Ariz., 1991, Australia, 1992, Fla., 1993, Austria, 1994, Securities Acad. Award, 1997, Stock Option award Jefferson Pilot Fin., 1999, Locust Street Securities award, Hawaii, 1999, Summit award Jefferson Pilot Fin., Eng./Scotland, 1999; PhD Rsch. fellow UCLA, 1962-64. Mem. Calif. Assn. Life Underwriters, Westlake Art Guild, UCLA Physics Honor Soc. (v.p. 1959, exec. v.p. 1960), Sigma Pi Sigma. Avocations: seascape/landscape artist, gallery and bank exhibitions, 1991; played trumpet and drums, 1956-58, USAF ROTC marching band; arranger and composer of ballad/symphonic music; planetary astrophotography. One of the first to design the NASA crystal experiment for astronauts; originated and performed first superconductive non-destructive test to determine aircraft titanium alloy strength; created concept and experimentally performed the first superconductive short antenna for very low frequency communication. Office: Sherman Financial Svcs Inc 2158 Calle Riscoso Thousand Oaks CA 91362-1141

SHERMAN, GERALD HOWARD, lawyer, educator; b. N.Y.C., Aug. 29, 1932; s. Abraham and Jean (Rose) S.; m. Lola Barbara Kay, Mar. 19, 1961; children: Jonathan, Ann. BBA, CCNY, 1953; LLB, Harvard U., 1958. Bar: N.Y. 1959, D.C. 1960. Mem. firm Cooper & Silverstein, Washington, 1958-61; ptnr. Silverstein & Mullens, 1961-99; shareholder Buchanan Ingersoll, P.C., 2000—. Adj. prof. Georgetown U. Law Center, 1974-87, also mem. Adv. Bd. Tax Mgmt., 1960—, BNA Pension Reporter, 1975-81. Bd. dirs., v.p. Jewish Found. for Group Homes, 1982-90; bd. dirs. Am. Digestive Disease Soc., 1983-87, Washington Conservatory Music, 1995—. Mem. ABA, Bar Assn. D.C. Home: 3804 Klingle Pl NW Washington DC 20016-5433 Office: 1776 K St NW Washington DC 20006-2304

SHERMAN, HAROLD, lawyer; b. Newark, Oct. 19, 1921; s. Myron H. and Mollie (Zell) S.; m. Sylvia Selikowsky, Feb. 20, 1943; children: Ralph, Neal. AB, Bklyn. Coll., 1942; PhD, NYU, 1956; JD, Pace U., 1986. Bar: Conn. 1987, U.S. Dist. Ct. Conn. 1988. Physicist Premier Crystal Labs., N.Y.C., 1944-47, Schlumberger-Doll Rsch., Ridgefield, Conn., 1956-83; instr. physics St. Peter's Coll., Jersey City, 1949-51; rsch. assoc. NYU, 1952-56; pvt. practice Ridgefield, 1987--. Cons. Teleco Oilfield Svcs., Meriden, Conn., 1985-92. Patentee (5) in field. Vol., Conn. Legal Svcs., 1988-97. Mem. Conn. Bar Assn., Am. Phys. Soc., Soc. Profl. Well Log Analysts, Sigma Xi. Avocations: gardening, photography. Home and Office: 24 Webster Rd Ridgefield CT 06877-4308 Fax: 203-438-6870. E-mail: attyharoldsherman@msn.com.

SHERMAN, HOWARD D. financial consultant; b. Tuscon, May 25, 1961; s. Donald J. and Elaine (Schwartz) S. BA, George Washington U., 1982; MBA, U. Pa., 1986. Rsch. asst. Fed. Res. Bd., Washington, 1982—84; sr. analyst Investor Responsibility Rsch. Ctr., 1986—88; sr. v.p., dir. Inst. Shareholder Svcs., 1988—97, pres., CEO, 1997—99; pres. Thomson Fin. Investor Rels., NYC, 1999—2000; COO Governance Metrics Internat. LLC, 2001—. Spkr. in field. Contbr. articles to profl. jours. Mem. Phi Beta Kappa.

SHERMAN, IRWIN WILLIAM, biological sciences educator; b. N.Y.C., Feb. 12, 1933; s. Morris and Anna (Ezaak) S.; m. Vilia Gay Turner, Aug. 25, 1966; children: Jonathan Turner, Alexa Joy. BS, CCNY, 1954; MS, Northwestern U., 1959, PhD, 1960. Asst. prof. U. Calif., Riverside, 1962-67, assoc. prof., 1967-70, prof. biology, 1970—, chmn. biology dept., 1974-79, dean Coll. Natural and Agrl. Scis., dir. agrl. expt. sta., 1981-88, exec. vice chancellor, 1993-94. Instr. marine biol. lab., Woods Hole, Mass., 1963-68; mem. study sect. tropical medicine NIH, 1970-73; cons. Agy. Internat. Devel., 1978-90; mem. ad hoc study group U.S. Army, 1975-78. Author: The Invertebrates: Function and Form, 1976, Biology: A Human Approach, 1989, Malaria: Parasite Biology, Pathogenesis, Protection, 1998, Chemotherapy of Malaria. Steering com. World Health Orgn., 1978-87. With U.S. Army, 1954-56. USPHS fellow Rockefeller Inst., 1960-62, Guggenheim fellow, 1967, NIH/Nat. Inst. Med. Rsch. fellow 1973-74, Walter and Eliza Hall Inst. for Med. Rsch. fellow, 1986; Wellcome Trust lectr. Brit. Soc. Parasitology, 1987, Scripps Rsch. Inst. fellow 1991. Mem. AAAS, Am. Soc. Tropical Medicine and Hygiene, Soc. Protozoology, Soc. Parasitology, Sigma Xi. Democrat. Jewish. Avocations: painting, reading. Office: U Calif Riverside Dept Biology Riverside CA 92521-0001 E-mail: sherman@mail.ucr.edu.

SHERMAN, JANE, author; b. Beloit, Wis., June 14, 1908; d. Horace Humphrey and Florentine (St. Clair) Sherman; m. Ned Lehac, Feb. 8, 1940 (dec.). Grad., Newtown H.S., Elmhurst, N.Y., 1925. Mem. Far East tour Ruth St. Denis-Ted Shawn Denishawn Dancers, 1925-26, mem. U.S. tour, 1926-27, mem. U.S. Ziegfeld Follies tour, 1927-28; mem. Doris Humphrey-Charles Weidman Co., 1928-29; appeared in Broadway musicals, 1929-31; mem. Radio City Music Hall Rockettes, 1934-35. Artistic advisor Denishawn Repertory Dancers, Trenton, N.J., 1981—; adv. bd. Vanaver Caravan, Rosendale, N.Y., 1981—; lectr. in field; re-created dances for the Martha Graham Co., the Vanaver Caravan, the Phila. Dance Co., others. Author: Soaring: The Diary and Letters of a Denishawn Dancer in the Far East, 1976 (de la Torre Bueno prize), The Drama of Denishawn Dance, 1979, Denishawn: The Enduring Influence, 1983; co-author: Barton Mumaw, Dancer, 1986, paperback edit., 2000; contbr. numerous articles on dance to Ballet Rev., Dance Chronicle, Dance Mag., 1976—. Avocation: reading. Home: Actors Fund Residence 155 W Hudson Ave Englewood NJ 07631-1609

SHERMAN, JEFFREY ALAN, dentist; b. Bklyn., June 16, 1947; s. Joseph G. and Gertrude P. S.; m. Roslyn B. Tillis, Aug. 15, 1970; children: Jodi Heather, Brett Andrew. BA, Adelphi U., 1969; DDS, Howard U., 1973. Diplomate Am. Bd. Oral Electrosurgery. Resident in gen. dentistry Del. State Hosp., 1974; pvt. practice, Oakdale, N.Y., 1975—. Mem. faculty Albert Einstein Coll. Medicine; vis. lectr. Tufts U.; dir. Greater L.I. Dental Meeting, 1990—. Author: Oral Electrosurgery: An Illustrated Clinical Guide, 1992, Oral Radiosurgery, 2d edit., 1997; contbr. to profl. publs. Fellow Internat. Coll. Dentists, Am. Coll. Dentists; mem. ADA (lectr. ann. meetings 1978—), Suffolk County Dental Soc. (bd. dels. 1989—, dental lab and trades com. 1989—, edn. com. 1989-91, photographer dental meeting 1990—, sec. 1997-98, pres. 2000—), Acad. Gen. Dentistry (membership com. 1992—, area v.p. 1991-92), Am. Acad. Dental Electrosurgery (co-editor, pres. 1987), N.Y. State Acad. Gen. Dentistry (pub. info. officer 1992). Office: 1237 Montauk Hwy Oakdale NY 11769-1434

SHERMAN, JEFFREY WAYNE, physician, clinical researcher; b. Chgo., Nov. 15, 1954; s. Ben and Stella (Kwiatkowski) S.; m. Mary Ann Bryan, Aug. 9, 1980; two children. BA, Lake Forest Coll., 1976; MD, Chgo. Med. Sch., 1981. Diplomate Nat. Bd. Med. Examiners; diplomate in internal medicine and infectious diseases Am. Bd. Internal Medicine. Intern, resident, chief resident internal medicine Northwestern Med. Ctr., Chgo., 1981-85; fellowship in infectious disease U. Calif., San Francisco, 1985-88, rsch. assoc. Howard Hughes Med. Inst., 1986-88; from asst. dir. to assoc. dir. clin. pharmacology The Squibb Inst. Med. Rsch., Princeton, N.J., 1988-90; dir. clin. rsch. The Bristol-Myers Squibb Pharm. Rsch. Inst., 1990-92; from dir. clin. rsch. to exec. dir. clin. rsch. Searle/Monsanto, Skokie, Ill., 1992-99; head oncology global med. ops. Global Med. Mktg./Oncology Franchise, 2000; chief med. officer, exec. v.p. NeoPharm, Lake Forest, Ill., 2000—. Fellow: ACP, Am. Assn. Neuro-Surg., Am. Assn. Cancer Rsch.; mem.: APHA, European Assn. Neuro-Oncology, Soc. Neuro-Oncology, Am. Coll. Physician Execs., Am. Soc. Preventive Oncology, Soc. for Biol. Therapy, Am. Acad. Pharm. Physicians, Am. Coll. Gastroenterology, Am. Gastrointestinal Assn., Drug Info. Assn., Am. Soc. Blood and Marrow Transplantation, Am. Soc. Clin. Oncology, Am. Soc. Hematology, European Soc. Med. Oncology, Infectious Disease Soc. Am., European Soc. Clin. Microbiology, Am. Soc. Microbiology, Am. Soc. Clin. Pharmacology and Therapeutics, Am. Fedn. Clin. Rsch., Am. Coll. Clin. Pharmacology, Internat. Soc. Antiviral Rsch. Office: 150 Field Dr Ste 195 Lake Forest IL 60045 Fax: (847) 295-8854. E-mail: jsherman@neophrm.com.

SHERMAN, JEROME KALMAN, retired anatomy educator; b. Bklyn., Aug. 14, 1925; s. Murray and Beatrice Freilich S.; m. Hildegard Schroeder, Dec. 26, 1952; children: Karen, Marc, Keith. AB, Brown U., 1947; MS, Western Res. U., 1949; PhD, U. Iowa, 1954. Teaching asst. Brown U., Providence, 1946-47; grad. asst. Western Res. U., Cleve., 1947-49; from rsch. asst. to rsch. assoc. U. Iowa, Iowa City, 1949-54; rsch. assoc. Am. Found. for Biol. Rsch., Madison, Wis., 1954-58; from asst. to assoc. prof. U. Ark. for Med. Sci., Little Rock, 1958-67, prof., 1967-92, prof. emeritus, 1992—; spl. chair prof. Nat. Chung Hsin U., Taichung, Taiwan, 1973-74; Fulbright prof. U. Munich, 1965-66. Cons. Animal Breeders Svc., 1956-57, Winrock Farm Semen Storage Project, 1960; sci. adv. Idant Corp., 1971-73; rsch. cons. Naval Med. Rsch. Unit II, Taipei, Taiwan, 1973-74, Dow Chemical Co., 1977-89; cons. Human Frozen Semen Banks (various states), 1972—. Contbr. articles to profl. jours., chpts. to books. Pres. Forest Heights Lions Club, Little Rock, 1978-79; bd. trustees Agudah Achim Synagogue, Temple B'Nai Israel, Little Rock, 1965, 76; chmn. adv. bd. Amelia Ives Day Care Ctr., Little Rock, 1970-90; vice-chmn. Nat. Med. Exploring Com. Boy Scouts Am., Dallas, 1978-81; bd. dirs. Cmty. Org. for Prevention of Poverty, 1993-98; mem. Douglas MacArthur Mil. Mus. Commn., 1995-2000. Lt. comdr. USN, 1943-46. Recipient Lederle Med. Faculty award Am. Cyanamid Co., 1961-64, Fulbright Sr. Rsch. award Fulbright Found., Munich, 1965-66, Nat. Sci. Coun. award Taiwan, Republic of China, 1973-74, Vol. Svc. Project Head Start award U.S. Dept. Health and Human Svcs., 1988, 89, Outstanding Vol. Svc. award V.A., 1989, 90, 91, Judge Gubow Nat. Americanism award Jewish War Veterans, 1991, Faculty Vol. Svc. award, Disting. Faculty award U. Ark. for Med. Sci., 1991, 92, Nat. Shofar award Boy Scouts Am., 1978, Whitney M. Young Svc. award, 1992, Golden Rule Cmty. Svc. award, 1995; named to Sr. Arkansas Hall of Fame, 1995. Mem. Am. Assn. Tissue Banks (founding, chmn. reproduction coun., bd. govs. 1976-93, Disting. Svc. award 1994), Soc. Exptl. Biology and Medicine, Am. Physiological Soc., Am. Soc. Anatomists, Am. Soc. Zoologists, Soc. for Cryobiology (charter, bd. govs. 1964-66), Soc. for Cryosurgery (hon.), Seven Sci. Soc., Sigma Xi (pres. Little Rock chpt. 1975-76). Democrat. Jewish. Avocations: fishing, camping, hiking, tennis, home repair. Home: 3012 N Grant St Little Rock AR 72207-2820

SHERMAN, JOHN FOORD, biomedical consultant; b. Oneonta, N.Y., Sept. 4, 1919; s. Henry C. and Ruth (Foord) Sherman; m. Betsy Deane Murray, Feb. 8, 1944; children: Betsy Deane, Mary Ann. BS, Albany Coll. Pharmacy/Union U., 1949, DSc, 1970; PhD, Yale U., 1953. With NIH, 1953—74; assoc. dir. extramural programs Nat. Inst. Neurol. Diseases and Blindness, 1961—62, Nat. Inst. Arthritis and Metabolic Disease, 1962—63; assoc. dir. for extramural programs Office Dir. NIH, 1964—68, dep. dir., 1968—74; v.p. Assn. Am. Med. Colls., Washington, 1974—91, exec. v.p., 1987—91, spl. cons., 1991—94. Bd. advisors Am. Bd. Internal Medicine, 1991—98; sr. advisor Rsch!Am., 1994—. Asst. surgeon gen. USPHS, 1964—68; spl. rsch. chemotherapy and neuropharmacology; panel on data and studies NRC, 1976—87; biomed. libr. rev. com. NIH, 1981—98; bd. dirs. Spinal Cord Injury Edn. and Tng. Found., 1986—92, Musculoskeletal Transplant Found., 1987—. With U.S. Army, 1941—46. Decorated Bronze Star; recipient Meritorious Svc. award, USPHS, 1965, Disting. Svc. award, HEW, 1971, Sec.'s Spl. Citation award, 1973, Nat. Civil Svc. League award, 1973, Disting. Alumnus award, Union U.-Pharmacy Coll. Coun., 1974, Lifetime Achievement award, Nat. Assn. for Biomed. Rsch., 1990, Spl. Recognition award, Assn. Am. Med. Colls., 1996. Fellow: AAAS; mem.: Inst. Medicine NAS, Cosmos Club, Sigma Xi. Congregationalist. E-mail: johnfsherman@msn.com.

SHERMAN, JOHN JUDSON, public relations executive, writer; b. Portland, Ind., Apr. 3, 1944; s. John F. and Dorothy I. Sherman; m. Lois Marie McGowan, Apr. 13, 1944; children: Chizoma, David. BA in Journalism and English, Ind. U., 1966; MA African Studies, U. Ghana, Legon, 1974; cert. in French studies, Alliance Francaise, Kinshasa, Zaire, 1974. Tchr. Ascension H.S., Eleme, Nigeria, 1966—67, Mlanje Day Secondary Sch., Mlanje, Malawi, 1967—68, West Side H.S., Gary, Ind., 1969—70; placement officer U.S. Peace Corps, Washington, 1970—71, asst. dep. dir. Accra, Ghana, 1971—73; nat. dir. Am. Field Svc., Ghana, 1973—73; tchr. Ecole de Langue Anglaise, Kinshasa, 1973—74, Zaire-American Language Inst., Kinshasa, 1974—75; instr. Georgetown U.- Am. Language Inst., Washington, 1975—75, Federal City Coll., Washington, 1975—75; from African programs coord. to programmer U.S. Peace Corps, 1975—77; dir. pub. rels. and devel. St. Catherine Indian Sch., Santa Fe, 1978—83; editor El Palacio Mag.-Mus. N.Mex., 1984—85; mng. editor Ind. Bus. Mag., Indpls., 1985—86; acct. exec. Borshoff Ketchum Pub. Rels., 1986—86; mgr. Travel Agy. Mktg. RCI, 1986—89; mgr. pub. rels. Resort Condominiums Internat., Indpls., 1989—91; Owner Sherman & Co. Public Relations, 1991—. Food/med. team Internat. Com. the Red Cross, Lagos, Nigeria, 1968—69. Author: It Give You Something To Think About, 1977, America Is A Negro Child: Race Poems, 1981, Santa Fe: A Pictorial History, 1983 (Governor's Award of Honor for Historic Preservation, 1985), Taos: A Pictorial History, 1990, Marjorie Main: Rural Documentary Poetry, 1999, War Stories: A Memoir of Nigeria and Biafra, 2002; editor: Resumes! Resumes! Resumes!, 1995. Nat. adv. com. Am. Field. Svc., N.Y.C., NY, 1995—97; mktg. com. Am. Pianists Assn., Indpls., 1991—98; hon. dir. Ind. State Mus. Found., 2000—; pub. rels. coord. Am. Field Svc. Ctrl. Ind., 1991—97; mktg. com. Historic Landmarks Found. Ind., 1994; pres., bd. dirs. Ind. State Mus. Soc., 1996—98; bd. dirs. Internat. Ctr. Indpls., 1992—94. Recipient 1st prize Poetry in the Gallery, Writers' Ctr. Indpls., 1999, 1st prize Poetry, Indpls.-Marion County Public Libr., 1989; grantee Poetry Reading grant, Fla. Endowment for the Humanities, 1981, Individual Artist Grant, Ind. Arts Commn., 2000. Mem.: Authors' Guild, Indpls. Press Club, Fairview Cemetery Preservation Assn. (bd. dirs. 1983—85). Avocations: travel, photography. Home: 4175 Central Ave Indianapolis IN Office: Sherman & Co Public Rels 4175 Central Ave Indianapolis IN 46205 Fax: 317-924-4160. Personal E-mail: shermco@earthlink.net.

SHERMAN, JONATHAN HENRY, lawyer; b. Washington, Jan. 4, 1963; s. Gerald Howard and Lola (Kay) Sherman; m. Catherine Sara Foot, Nov. 4, 2000; 1 child Benjamin Ashton. BA in History magna cum laude, U. Rochester, 1984; MA in History, Yale U., 1989; JD, Stanford U., 1991. Bar: N.Y. 1992, U.S. Dist. Ct. (so. dist.) N.Y. 1992, U.S. Supreme Ct. 1995, U.S. Dist. Ct. (ea. dist.) N.Y. 1996, U.S. Ct. Appeals (11th cir.) 1996, U.S. Dist. Ct. (we. dist.) N.Y. 1998, D.C. 2000. Assoc. Cahill Gordon & Reindel, N.Y.C., 1991-2000; ptnr. Boies, Schiller & Flexner LLP, Washington, 2001—. Lectr. Stanford U., Palo Alto, Calif., 1991, Yale Coll., New Haven, 1993; adj. assoc. prof. law Fordham Law Sch., N.Y.C., 1998-2001. Sponsor, mentor Student-Sponsor Partnership, N.Y.C., 1992-96; contbr. The Cornerstone Sch., Jersey City, 1994. Mem. ABA, N.Y. State Bar Assn. (media law com. 1997-99), Phi Beta Kappa. Home: 1700 19th St NW Apt 3 Washington DC 20009-1669 Office: Boies Schiller & Flexner LLP Ste 800 5301 Wisconsin Ave NW Washington DC 20015-2061 E-mail: jsherman@bsfllp.com.

SHERMAN, JOSEPH OWEN, pediatric surgeon; b. Chgo., Aug. 15, 1936; s. Joseph Owen and Mary Elizabeth (Kelly) S.; m. June Marie Martin, Mar. 16, 1963; children: Brian William, Lee Ann. Student, U. Ill., 1955-58; BS, Northwestern U., 1959, MD, 1962. Diplomate Am. Bd. Surgery, Am. Bd. Pediatric Surgery; lic. physician, Ill. Rotating intern Passavant Meml. Hosp., Chgo., 1963-64; resident in gen. surgery VA Rsch. Hosp., 1964-65, 67-68; Am. Cancer Soc. clin. fellow Northwestern U. Med. Sch., 1965-66; resident in pediatric surgery Children's Meml. Hosp., 1966, 68-69; resident in thoracic surgery Mcpl. Tb San., 1967; from instr. to assoc. prof. surgery Northwestern U. Med. Sch., 1967-86, prof. clin. surgery, 1986—. Emeritus staff dept. surgery Children's Meml. Hosp., 1995—, Evanston (Ill.) Hosp., 1995—. Contbr. articles to profl. jours. Served with Ill. Army N.G., 1953-69, Ill. Air N.G., 1966-67. Fellow ACS; mem. AMA, Am. Pediat. Surg. Assn., Assn. for Acad. Surgery, Chgo. Med. Soc., Chgo. Surg. Soc., Ill. Pediat. Surg. Assn., Ill. State Med. Soc. Avocations: photography, computer programing, indoor and outdoor gardening.

SHERMAN, JUDITH DOROTHY, producer, recording company owner, recording engineer; b. Cleve., Nov. 12, 1942; d. William Paul and Laverne (Speerke) Luekens; m. Kenneth Sherman, Aug. 1, 1964 Idiv. Aug. 1972); m. Max Wilcox, Jan. 1, 1981 (div. Jan. 1988); m. Curtis Macomber, Apr. 29, 1988. BA, Valparaiso U., 1964; MFA, SUNY, Buffalo, 1971. Rec. engr. Edward at the Moog, N.Y.C., 1971-72; producer-music dir. WBAI-FM, 1972-76; owner-producer Judith Sherman Prodns., 1976—. Rec. engr. Marlboro (Vt.) Music Festival, 1976-94; adminstrv. dir. La Musica di Asolo, Sarasota, Fla., 1986-88; vocalist Steve Reich and Musicians, 1971-72. Recipient Corp. Pub. Broadcasting award, 1976, two Grammy award nominations, 1991, Grammy award, Classical Prodr. of Yr., 1993, Grammy award nominations, 1994, 95, 97, 98. Mem. NAFE, Chamber Music Am. (bd. dirs. 2000—), NARAS. Democrat. Home and Office: 645 W 239th St Apt 2A Bronx NY 10463-1236

SHERMAN, KATHRYN ANN, communications professional; b. Phila., Mar. 12, 1964; d. Edward and Ann Elizabeth (Shields) S. AA, Bucks County C.C., Newtown, Pa., 1988; BBA, Temple U., 1993. Waitress Posh Nosh, Newtown, Pa., 1985-89, Blue Fountain Diner, Langhorne, 1989-93; comm. assoc. The Vanguard Group, Valley Forge, 1993—. Mem. Inst. Mgmt. Accts. (bd. dirs., dir. membership acquisition), Golden Key, Beta Alpha Psi, Phi Theta Kappa. Republican. Lutheran.

SHERMAN, LAWRENCE JAY, lawyer; b. Pitts., May 20, 1942; s. Ben E. and Leonora C. (Weill) S.; m. Iris Shapiro, Aug. 19, 1967; children: Rachel L., Jessica S. BA in Polit. Sci. with honors, U. Pitts., 1963; JD, U. Mich., 1966. Bar: D.C. 1967, Calif. 1967, Md. 1984, U.S. Dist. Ct. D.C., U.S. Dist. Ct. Md., U.S. Claims Ct., U.S. Ct. Appeals (D.C., 1st, 3rd, 4th, 5th and 6th cir.). Appellate atty. NLRB, Washington, 1966-69; assoc. Cohen & Berfield, 1969-70; exec. dir. Migrant Legal Action Program, 1970-75; assoc. Lichtman, Abeles, Anker & Nagle, P.C., 1975-77; pvt. practice, 1977-81; ptnr. Sherman & Lapidus, 1981-86; counsel Deso, Thomas, Spevack, Weitzman & Rost PC, 1991-2000; ptnr. Brown & Sherman, LLP, 2000—01; prin. Law Offices of Lawrence J. Sherman, P.C. , 2002—. Adj. prof. George Meany Ctr. for Labor Studies, Silver Spring, Md. 1988-2000; prin. Mng. Human Resources For 21st Century, Washington, 1990-99. Contbr. articles to profl. jours. Fellow Am. Bd. Trial Advocates; mem. ABA (labor and employment law sect., litig. sect.), D.C. Bar (labor and employment law sect., litig. sect., co-chmn. steering com., 1981-85, labor law sect. 1978-84, co-chmn. labor law sect. 1983-84, lawyers coord. com.), Met. Lawyers Assn., Md. Lawyers Assn., Nat. Employment Lawyers Assn. Democrat. Avocations: tennis, racquetball, running, travel, reading. Office: Lawrence J Sherman PC 1400 K St NW Washington DC 20005-2403 E-mail: jdlarry@aol.com.

SHERMAN, LAWRENCE WILLIAM, criminologist; b. Schenectady, Oct. 25, 1949; s. Donald Lester and Margaret (Heckman) Sherman; m. Eva Fass Fass; children: Eliot, Katharine. BA, Denison U., Granville, Ohio, 1970; MA, U. Chgo., 1970; Diploma in Criminology, Cambridge U., Eng., 1973; PhD, Yale U., 1976; MA, U. Pa., 1999. Program rsch. analyst N.Y.C. Police Dept., 1971—72; asst. to assoc. prof. criminal justice SUNY, Albany, 1976—82; dir. rsch., v.p. Police Found., Washington, 1979—85; pres. Crime Control Ins., 1985—95; assoc. prof. to Disting. univ. prof and chair dept. criminology and criminal justice U. Md., College Park, Md., 1982—99; Albert M. Greenfield prof. human relations, dept. sociology, dir. Lee Ctr. of Criminology and dir. Fels Ctr. of Govt. U. Pa., Phila., 1999—. Pres. Crime Control Rsch. Corp., Phila., 1981—; mem. panel on rsch. policies NRC-NAS, Washington, 2000—; lead co-chmn. transition com. on pub. safety Office of the Mayor, Phila., 1999—2000; lectr. FBI Acad., Quantico, 1980—2000; adj. prof. law and sci. dir. reintegrative shaming experiments Rsch. Sch. Social Scis., Australian Nat. U., , Canberra, ACT, Australia, 1993—; dir. Justice Rsch. Consortium, Oxford, 2000—. Author: (book) Scandal and Reform: Controlling Police Corruption, 1978, Policing Domestic Violence: Experiments and Dilemmas, 1992 (American Sociological Association Distinguihsed Scholarship Award in Crime, Law and Deviance, 1973); editor: (Book) Police Corruption: A Sociological Perspective, 1974; contbr. articles. Recipient Bruce Smith award for disting. contbn. to criminal justice, Acad. of Criminal Justice Scis., 1994; fellow N.Y.C. Urban fellow, Alfred P. Sloan Foun., 1970—71. Fellow: Am. Soc. Criminology (pres. 2001—, E.H. Sutherland Award for Disting. Contbn. to Criminology 1999); mem.: Acad. of Exptl. Criminology (pres. 1999—2001), Internat. Soc. Criminology (pres. sci. commn. 1995—99, pres.

2000—), Am. Acad. Polit. and Social Sci. (pres. 2001—). Home: 3507 Baring St Philadelphia PA 19104 Office: University of Pennsylvania 3814 Walnut St Philadelphia PA 19104 Office Fax: 215-898-1202. Personal E-mail: lws@sas.upenn.edu. Business E-Mail: lws@sas.upenn.edu.

SHERMAN, LESTER IVAN, retired lawyer; b. Flagler, Colo., June 1, 1936; s. Lester B. and Helen E. S.; m. Lois E. Hafling, July 19, 1958 (div. Mar. 1986); children: Kathi, Scott, Brett; m. Kay A. Swanson, Dec. 21, 1993. Student, Colo. State U., 1954-55; BSBA, U. Denver, 1958, JD, 1961. Bar: Colo. 1961, U.S. Dist. Ct. Colo. 1961. Pvt. practice, Durango, Colo., 1965-67, 79-81, 1986-97; ret., 1997; ptnr. Hamilton, Sherman, Hamilton & Shand, P.C., 1967-78, Sherman, Rhodes & Wright, P.C., Durango, 1981-86; judge La Plata County (Colo.) Ct., 1966-76. Cons. in field; mem. Colo. Commn. on Jud. Qualifications, 1974-76. Mem. La Plata County Bd. for Mentally Retarded and Seriously Handicapped, Inc., 1968-75, pres., 1970-73; bd. dirs. Colo. County Judges Assn., 1973-74. Mem. S.W. Colo. Bar (pres. 1969-70), Colo. Bar Assn. (gov. 1970-72, 74-76), ABA, Petroleum Club, Elks, Phi Delta Phi, Sigma Chi. Republican. Home: 320 N Skylane Dr Durango CO 81303-6040

SHERMAN, LINDA ANN, infectious disease physician, pathologist, researcher; b. Rochester, N.Y. BA, U. Rochester, N.Y., 1970; MS, Hahnemann U., 1975; MSE, Temple U., 1975; MD, Jefferson Med. Coll., 1979; DTM&H, London Sch. Tropical Medicine, Eng., 1982; MPA, American U., 1998. Diplomate Am. Bd. Internal Medicine, Am. Bd. Infectious Diseases, Am. Bd. Clin. & Anatomic Pathology, Am. Bd. Pathology. Dir. adv. com. oversighta nd mgmt. staff FDA, Rockville, Md., 1990—. Fellow Infectious Disease Soc. Am. Office: FDA 5600 Fishers Ln # HF-4 Rockville MD 20857-0001

SHERMAN, MARY ANGUS, public library administrator; b. Lawton, Okla., Jan. 3, 1937; d. Donald Adelbert and Mabel (Felkner) Angus; m. Donald Neil Sherman, Feb. 8, 1958; children: Elizabeth, Donald Neil II. BS in Home Econs., U. Okla., 1958, MLS, 1969. Br. head Pioneer Libr. System, Purcell, Okla., 1966-76, regional libr. Norman, 1976-78, asst. dir., 1978-80, dir., 1987—. Bd. dirs. McClain Bank, chair audit com., 1997—. Mem. bd. visitors U. Okla. Coll. Arts and Scis., 1998—; bd. dirs. Women's Resource Ctr., Norman, 1998—, pres., 2002—. Named one of Disting. Alumni, Sch. Home Econs. U. Okla., 1980; recipient award of merit, Okla. Sch. Libr. and Info. Sci., 2000. Mem. ALA (councilor 1988-96, planning and budget assembly 1990-91, internat. rels. com. 1992-96, 2001—, internat. rels. round table 1989—, orientation com. 1998-99, mem. com. 1999-2000, chair sister libr. com. 2000-02, first mem., exec. bd. 2000-02), Pub. Libr. Assn. (divsn. of ALA, pres. pub. policy for pub. librs. sect. 1995-96), Internat. Rels. Comm.(chair 2002-03), Tech. in Publ. Librs. Com. 2002-04, Internat. Fedn. Libr. Assns. (standing com. on pub. librs. 1999—), AAUW (pres. Okla. chpt. 1975-77, nat. bd. dirs. 1983-87, S.W. ctrl. region dir. 1983-85, v.p. nat. membership 1985-87, Woman of the Yr. Purcell chpt. 1982), Okla. Libr. Assn. (pres. 1982-83, interlibr. cooperation com. 1993-95, chair 1994-95, Legal Comm. 1998-, Disting. Svc. award 1986), Norman Soc. Internat. Affairs (v.p. 1998-99, pres. 1999-2001), Norman C. of C. (bd. dirs. 1988-96, pres. 1994-95), Rotary (program chair 1991-92, 99—, bd. dirs. 1993-97, pres. 1995-96, 99—, Paul Harris fellow, group study exch. leader to Iceland 1998, dist. literacy chair 1998-2000, dist. group study exch. chair 2001—), Norman Assistance League Club (cmty. assoc.), Norman Sister City Com. 1994-98, Delta Gamma Mothers (pres. 1978-79), Kappa Alpha Theta (pres. Alpha Omicron House Corp. 1984-87, nat. dir. house corps. 1987-88), Beta Phi Mu, Phi Beta Kappa. Democrat. Methodist. Office: Pioneer Libr System 225 N Webster Ave Norman OK 73069-7133 E-mail: mary@pls.lib.ok.us.

SHERMAN, MICHAEL FRANCIS, professional football coach; b. Norwood, Mass., Dec. 19, 1954; m. Karen Sherman; children: Sarah, Emily, Matthew, Benjamin. Student, Ctrl. Conn. State U., 1974, 76-77. Coach U. Pitts., 1981-82, Tulane, 1983-84; offensive coord. Holy Cross, 1985-88; offensive line coord. Tex. A&M, 1989-93, 95-96, UCLA, 1994; tight ends/asst. offensive line Green Bay Packers, 1997-98, head coach, 2000—; offensive coord. Seattle Seahawks, 1999; exec. VP & gen. mgr. Green Bay Packers, 2001—. Office: care Green Bay Packers PO Box 10628 Green Bay WI 54307-0628 also: Green Bay Packers, Inc 1265 Lombardi Ave. Green Bay WI 54304*

SHERMAN, MICHAEL SCOTT, healthcare executive, anesthesiologist; b. Bklyn., June 20, 1961; m. Heather Sherman, Dec. 28, 1996. BA, MS, U. Pa., 1982; MD, Yale U., 1986; MBA, Harvard U., 1997. Diplomate Am. Bd. Anesthesiologist, Am. Bd. Cardiac Anesthesiology, Am. Bd. Med. Mgmt. Intern St. Luke's/Roosevelt Hosp. Ctr., N.Y.C., 1986-87, resident in gen. surgery, 1987-88; resident in anesthesiology SUNY Health Sci. Ctr., Bklyn., 1990-93; emergency medicine attending physician Comty. Hosp. Bklyn., 1988-90; anesthesiologist Good Samaritan Regional Med. Ctr., Phoenix, 1993-95; dir. corp. devel., managed care and integrated programs Total Renal Care, 1997-99; mng. dir. physician network devel. Total Nephrology Care Network, 1997-99; v.p. provider bus. devel. and product mgmt. HealthAllies.com., Glendale, Calif., 1999—2001; v.p. med. and clin. affairs Immusol, Inc., San Diego, 2001—. Mem. AMA, Am. Soc. Anesthesiologists, Am. Coll. Healthcare Execs., Am. Coll. Physician Execs. (diplomate), Am. Coll. Legal Medicine, Calif. Soc. Anesthesiologists, Calif. Med. Assn. E-mail: msherman@immusol.com.

SHERMAN, MILDRED MOZELLE, music educator, singer, actress, opera director; b. Mt. Grove, Mo., Nov. 21, 1932; d. William Husley and Jessie Claire (Faulkner) Clark; m. Louis Leroy Sherman, Aug. 14, 1954; children: Clark Michael, Gayla Dawn. MusB, Bethany Coll., Lindsborg, Kans., 1953; MusM, Ind. U., 1955; PhD, U. Wis., 1971; postgrad., U. Wis., Stevens Point, Kans. U., Baylor U. Instr. music Kans. State U., Manhattan, 1962-66; prof. music Howard Payne U., Brownwood, Tex., 1973-80, Grand Canyon U., Phoenix, 1980-84; prof. ch. music, dir. ch. music, drama, theatre So. Bapt. Theol. Sem., Louisville, 1984-2001, founding dir. Ch. Music Drama Theatre, sr. prof. ch. music, 2001—. Instr., rep. Inst. Pan Americano, Panama City, 1955-56; vis. prof. Belem and Rio Bapt. Sems., Brazil; owner Sherman Svcs., 2000—, Ky. Opera Roster, 2001—; vis. lectr. Staley, Cambridge, Union, Furman, Stetson, and Fla. Bapt. univs., 1990-99. Performer, dir. over 1000 operas, musicals, and plays including Women of the Bible, 1986-97; author: The Vocal Technician, 1991, also short stories; translator Mozarts Obligation of the 1st Commandment, 1986, Debussy's Prodigal Son, 1987, Massenet's Herodiade, 1997, Two from Galilee prodn. kit, 1996; also monologues; contbg. author: New Christian Dictionary, 2001. Recipient Orpheus award Phi Mu Alpha Sinfonia, 1978; Lily Found. grantee, 1988-90; Baylor Univ. fellow, 1990-91. Mem. Nat. Opera Assn., Nat. Assn. Tchrs. Singing, Met. Opera Guild, Ch. Music Conf., DAR, Ea. Star, Christian Opera Assn. Bd., Sigma Alpha Iota. Baptist. Avocations: geneology, handwork, animals, travel. Home: 3602 Coronado Dr Louisville KY 40241-2611 Office: So Bapt Theol Sem 2825 Lexington Rd Louisville KY 40280-0001 E-mail: msherman@sbts.edu., SherServ@hotmail.com.

SHERMAN, M(ORTON) EUGENE, cardiologist, health care consultant; b. Memphis, Aug. 4, 1944; s. Jerry E. and Sarah (Feldman) S.; m. Susan Ann Shapiro, July 3, 1966; children: Jonathan, Jill. BS in Life Scis., MIT, 1966; MD, U. N.C., 1970; M in Healthcare Systems, U. Denver, 1992. Diplomate in internal medicine and cardiovascular diseases Am. Bd. Internal Medicine. Cardiologist Aurora (Colo.) Med. Assn., P.C., 1977—, pres., 1989—. Pres. med. staff Aurora Presbyn. Hosp., 1993-95, medi dir. intensive care unit, 1980-97; divisional med. adminstr. Rocky Mountain divsn. Sports Car Club Am., Denver, 1990—; bd. dirs. Pacificare of Colo., Aurora. Bd. dirs. Denver Mobility, 1990-95, Colo. Med. Soc. Lt. comdr. USN, 1975-77. Fellow Am. Coll. Cardiology; mem. Am. Heart Assn., Colo. Med. Soc. (chair managed care task force, bd. dirs. 1999—), Am. Soc. Nuclear Cardiology. Avocations: sports car racing (regional champion 1999), divisional champion 1999), hiking, skiing. Office: Aurora Med Assocs PC 750 Potomac St Ste L5 Aurora CO 80011-6742 E-mail: aurmedcardendo@aol.com.

SHERMAN, NANCY, philosophy educator; b. Passaic, N.J., June 20, 1951; d. Seymour and Beatrice (Hoffman) S.; m. Marshall Presser, June 22, 1980; children: Kala, Jonathan. AB in Philosophy magna cum laude, Bryn Mawr Coll., 1973; postgrad., Boston U., 1973; MLitt in Philosophy, U. Edinburgh, Scotland, 1976; PhD, Harvard U., 1982. Tchg. asst. in philosophy Harvard U., Cambridge, Mass., 1980-81; asst. prof. Yale U., New Haven, 1982-88, assoc. prof., 1988-89, Georgetown U., Washington, 1989-94, prof., 1994—, univ prof. Vis. rsch. scholar King's Coll., Cambridge (Eng.) U., spring 1978; vis. prof. Johns Hopkins U., Balt., spring 1995, U. Md., College Park, spring 1995, 96; cons. on ethics to undersec. Dept. Navy, 1994; vis. disting. chair of ethics U.S. Naval Acad., Annapolis, Md., 1997, 98; participant numerous confs., symposia, colloquia; lectr., spkr. in field. Author: The Fabric of Character: Aristotle's Theory of Virtue, 1989, paperback edit., 1991, Making a Necessity of Virtue: Aristotle and Kant on Virtue, 1996; editor: Aristotle's Ethics: Critical Essays, 1999; contbr. articles and revs. to profl. jours. Vans Dunlop scholar U. Edinburgh, 1974-76; Teschemacher fellow Harvard U., 1976-81, Newcombe fellow, 1981-82, fellow NEH, 1984-85, 96, Am. Coun. Learned Socs., 1987, Mellon fellow Yale U., 1988, Whitney Humanities fellow Yale U., 1987-88, fellow Kennedy Inst. Ethics, 1991-96, Mellon summer fellow, 1992, Georgetown U. summer fellow, 1990, 91, 94, 95; Am. Philos. Soc. fellow, 2002. Mem. APA (program com. ea. divsn. 1995-97), Soc. for Ancient Greek Philosophy, N.Am. Kant Soc., Am. Philos. Assn., Washington Psychoanalytic Found. Office: Georgetown U Dept Philosophy 224 New North St NW Washington DC 20057-0001

SHERMAN, NORMAN MARK, advertising agency executive; b. N.Y.C., June 19, 1948; s. Sol and Rhoda (Kaplan) S.; m. Michelle Petnov, Jan. 8, 1978; 1 child, Michael Isaac. BA, U. Buffalo, 1970; MBA, Columbia U., 1972. Cert. tchr., N.Y. Product mgr. RCA Records, N.Y.C., 1972-73; dir. mktg. Shelter Records, 1973-74; account exec. Rosenfeld Sirowitz & Lawson, 1974-76, Benton & Bowles, N.Y.C., 1976-78, v.p. account supr., 1978-81, sr. v.p., mgmt. supr., 1981-84; exec. v.p., dir. account mgmt. Avrett, Free & Ginsberg, N.Y.C., 1984-85; sr. v.p., group account dir. D'arcy, Masius, Benton & Bowles, 1985-93, mng. dir., bd. dirs., 1993-96, corp. exec. v.p., 1996-98; mng. dir. The Sr. Network, Stamford, Conn., 1998-99; pres. N.Am. Gundersen Ptnrs. LLC, N.Y.C., 1999—2001; exec. v.p., dir. healthcare Hill, Holliday, Connors, Cosmopulos, 2002—. Home: 330 W 72nd St New York NY 10023-2641 Office: Hill Holliday 345 Hudson St New York NY 10014 E-mail: nsherman@hhny.com.

SHERMAN, RICHARD ALLEN, lawyer; b. Atlanta, Mar. 16, 1946; s. Robert Hiram and Olivia Mae (Latham) S.; m. Mary Margaret Sawyer, June 23, 1973 (div. June 1994); children: Richard A. Jr., Jill Mary, James Warren. BA, Tulane U., 1968, JD, 1972. Bar: Fla. 1974, La. 1973, U.S. Ct. Appeals (5th cir.) 1978, U.S. Ct. Appeals (11th cir.) 1981, U.S. Supreme Ct. 1981. Ptnr., head appellate divsn. Wicker, Smith, Blomqvist, Davant, Tutan, O'Hara, McCoy et al, Miami, 1973-83; pvt. practice Ft. Lauderdale, Fla., 1983—; practice limited to handling appeals in Fla. Active Rep. Nat. Com. Mem. ABA (vice-chmn. U.S. Ct. Appeals 5th cir. com. 1981), Fla. Bar Assn. (appellate rules com. 1979-81), Dade County Bar Assn. (chmn. appellate cts. com. 1982-83), Mensa, Pres. Club, Lauderdale Yacht Club, Upper Keys Sailing Club (bd. dirs.). Avocations: yacht racing, boating, scuba diving, travel, theatre. Office: 1777 S Andrews Ave Ste 302 Fort Lauderdale FL 33316-2517

SHERMAN, ROBERT, broadcaster; b. N.Y.C., July 23, 1932; s. Isaac Jacob and Nadia (Reisenberg) S.; m. Veronica Jean Bravo; children: Steven J., Peter M. BA, NYU, 1952; MA, Columbia U., 1953. Music dir. Sta. WQXR-FM, N.Y.C., 1960-70, program dir., 1970-85, exec. prodr., 1985-93, sr. cons., 1993—. Faculty The Julliard Sch., N.Y.C., 1988—, Manhattan Sch. Music, N.Y.C., 1995—; artistic advisor Pulvermann Found., Rye, N.Y., 1993—; artistic dir. Beethoven Festival, 1985—; narrator West Point Band, Rye, 1994—; bd. dirs. Naumburg Found., The Mannes Coll. of Music.; pres. adv. coun. Pa. Acad. Music. Co-author: Nadia Reisenberg, 1986, Complete Idiot's Guide to Classical Music, 1997; contbr. reviews and articles The New York Times, 1964—. Bd. dirs. Tisch Ctr. for the Arts, 1996-97. With U.S. Army, 1953-56. Recipient Verdi medal Met. Opera Nat. Coun., 1987, Sanford medal Yale U., 1994, Appreciation award ASCAP, 1993, radio competition prizes N.Y. festivals, 1994. Home: 5 Tavano Rd Ossining NY 10562-3105 Office: WQXR 122 5th Ave New York NY 10011-5605

SHERMAN, ROBERT B(ERNARD), composer, lyricist, screenwriter; b. N.Y.C., Dec. 19, 1925; s. Al and Rosa (Dancis) S.; student UCLA, 1943; BA, Bard Coll., 1949; MusD (hon.) Lincoln U., 1990; m. Joyce Ruth Sasner, Sept. 27, 1953; children: Laurie Shane, Jeffrey Craig, Andrea Tracy, Robert Jason. Popular songwriter, 1950-60, including Tall Paul, Pineapple Princess, You're Sixteen (Gold Record); songwriter Walt Disney Prodns., Beverly Hills, Calif., 1960-68, for 29 films including The Parent Trap, 1961, Summer Magic, 1963, Mary Poppins, 1964, That Darn Cat, 1965, Winnie The Pooh, 1965, Jungle Book, 1967, Bedknobs and Broomsticks, 1971; co-composer song It's A Small World, theme of Disneyland, Walt Disney World, Fla., Disneyland, Tokyo, Disneyland, Paris; composer, lyricist United Artists, Beverly Hills, 1969—, songs for film Chitty, Chitty, Bang, Bang, 1969, Snoopy, Come Home!, 1972; song scores Charlotte's Web, 1972, Cabbage Patch Kids, 1974, Little Nemo, 1992, The Mighty Kong, 1996, The Tigger Movie, 1999; composer for Walt Disney's Wonderful World of Color, TV, 1961—; co-producer NBC-TV spl. Goldilocks, 1970; v.p. Musi-Classics, Inc.; co-producer, composer, lyricist stage musical Victory Canteen, 1971; composer-lyricist Broadway show Over Here, 1975, Busker Alley, 1995; screenplay and song score Tom Sawyer, United Artists, 1972, Huckleberry Finn, 1974, The Slipper and the Rose, 1977, The Magic of Lassie, 1978. Served with inf. AUS, 1943-45; ETO. Decorated Purple Heart; recipient 2 Acad. awards best score for Mary Poppins, 1964, best song for Chim Chim Cheree, 1964; Grammy award, 1965; Christopher medal, 1965, 74; nine Acad. award nominations; Acad. award nomination for song score Bedknobs and Broomsticks, 1971, for best song The Age of Not Believing, 1971, others; 16 golden, 4 platinum and one diamond record album, 1965-83; first prize best composer song score Tom Sawyer, Moscow Film Festival, 1973, B.M.I. Pioneer award, 1977; Golden Cassette awards for Mary Poppins, Jungle Book, Bed Knobs and Broomsticks, 1983, Mouscar award Disney Studios, Disney Legend award, 1990, BMI Richard Kirk Lifetime Achievement award, 1991. Mem. Acad. Motion Picture Arts and Scis. (exec. bd. music br. 12 yrs.), AFTRA, Nat. Acad. Rec. Arts and Scis., Composers and Lyricists Guild (exec. bd.), Dramatists Guild, Authors League. Office: 9030 Harratt St West Hollywood CA 90069-3858

SHERMAN, ROBERT LEE, JR. chemist, educator; b. Mt. Carmel, Ill., Dec. 24, 1974; s. Robert Lee and Nancy Joan Sherman; m. Crystal Lynn Kirby, July 26, 1997. BS in Chemistry, So. Ill. U., 1997, MS in Chemistry, 2000; postgrad., Okla. State U., 2000—. Lab. technician Ctrl. State Analytical Co., Evansville, Ind., 1996, 97; tchg. asst. dept. chemistry So. Ill. U., Carbondale, 1997-2000; tchg. asst. Okla. State U., Stillwater, 2000, rsch. asst. in chemistry, 2002—; rsch. asst. Ohio State U., 2002—. C. David Schmulbach tchg. scholar So. Ill. U., 1997-98. Mem. Am. Chem. Soc. (assoc.). Baptist. Avocations: U.S. Civil War history, models. Home: 608 Copp Ave Mount Carmel IL 62863-1716 Office: Okla State Univ Chemistry Dept Stillwater OK 74075 E-mail: rlschem@aol.com.

SHERMAN, ROGER, economics educator; b. Jamestown, N.Y., Sept. 10, 1930; s. Claire Blanchard and Margaret Gertrude (Burke) S.; m. Charlotte Ann Murphy, Apr. 4, 1953 (div. Feb. 1995); children: Claire Randall, Thomas Allen; m. Geraldine Szott Moohr, May 25, 1996. BS in Math., Grove City Coll., 1952; MBA in Fin., Harvard U., 1959; MS in Econs., Carnegie-Mellon U., 1965, PhD, 1966. Mgr. mfg. control IBM Corp., N.Y.C., 1956-62; asst. prof., assoc. prof., prof. U. Va., Charlottesville, 1965-72, Brown Forman prof. econs., 1982—, chmn. dept. econs., 1982-90. Vis. scholar Oxford U., 1987, Sydney U., 1988. Author: Oligopoly: An Empirical Approach, 1972, The Economics of Industry, 1974, Antitrust Policies and Issues, 1978, The Regulation of Monopoly, 1989; editor: Perspectives on Postal Service Issues, 1980; contbr. articles to profl. jours. Bd. dirs. McGuffey Art Ctr., Charlottesville, 1984-92. Lt. USNR, 1953-62. U. Bristol fellow, 1968-69; Fulbright lectr., Madrid, 1972; Sci. Ctr. Berlinfellow, 1975, 79, 80; Rockefeller Found. Vis. scholar, 1985 Mem. Am. Econ. Assn., Royal Econ. Soc., Econometric Soc. Office: U Va Rouss Hall Charlottesville VA 22903-3288

SHERMAN, ROGER TALBOT, surgeon, educator; b. Chgo., Sept. 30, 1923; s. Joseph Bright and Alice Elizabeth (Baur) S.; m. Ruth Kathryn Thieman, Aug. 23, 1952; children: Nann, Alice, Nina, John, Julie. AB, Kenyon Coll., 1946; MD, U. Cin., 1948. Diplomate Am. Bd. Surgery (mem.). Intern, fellow in pathology St. Luke's Hosp., Chgo., 1948-50; resident in surgery Cin. Gen. Hosp., 1950-56; chief dept. exptl. surgery Walter Reed Army Med. Center, 1956-59; asst. prof. to prof. surgery U. Tenn., Memphis, 1959-72; prof., chmn. dept. surgery U. South Fla., Tampa, 1972-82; prof. surgery Emory U. Sch. Medicine, Atlanta, 1983-93; chief surgery Grady Meml. Hosp., 1983-92; Whitaker prof. surgery Emory U. Sch. Medicine, 1993-97, prof. emeritus, 1997—; dir. surg. edn. Piedmont Hosp., 1993-97. Mem. editorial bd. Am. Surgeon, 1970-91, Jour. Trauma, 1970-93; contbr. articles to profl. jours., chpts. to books. Served to maj. M.C. AUS, 1956-59. Recipient Golden Apple Tchr. of the Yr. award, 1972, Williams Disting. Teaching award Emory U., 1984, Curtis P. Artz award, 1988. Fellow ACS (gov.); mem. Am. Assn. Surgery of Trauma (pres. 1979), Am. Surg. Assn., So. Surg. Assn., Southeastern Surg. Congress (pres. 1985), Internat. Surg. Soc., Soc. Surgery of Alimentary Tract, Am. Burn Assn., Shock Soc., Am. Trauma Soc., Ga. Surg. Soc. (pres. 1997), Sigma Xi, Psi Upsilon, Alpha Omega Alpha. Home: 3747 Peachtree Rd NE Apt 807 Atlanta GA 30319-1352 *Surgery. The opening, exploration and repair of the living human body is an awesome responsibility afforded to only a few. To be privileged to be counted among those is a high honor, surpassed only by being trusted to teach others this demanding, and marvelous craft.*

SHERMAN, RUTH TENZER, artist, fixtures company executive; b. Chgo., Sept. 11, 1920; d. Philip and Jennie (Greitzer) Tenzer; m. Samuel Sherman, May 18, 1946 (dec. Nov. 1974); children: Patricia (dec.), Randy Mitchell. Art student, Pratt Inst., 1938-42, Art Students League, N.Y.C., 1942-45; studies with Raphael Soyer, N.Y.C., 1943, studies with Harold Baumbach, 1947-49; studies with Ruth Connery, Mamaroneck, N.Y., 1955; studies with Rudolph Baranik, White Plains, N.Y., 1961-63, studies with George Koras, 1966. Cert. artist Dept. Cultural Affairs. Pres. Pioneer Fixture Corp., Paterson, N.J., 1975-86. Exhbns. include Mamaroneck Artists Guild, 1963, Jr. League Artists of North Westchester, 1964, Westchester C.C., Valhalla, N.Y., 1964, The New Rochelle (N.Y.) Art Assn., 1964, Silvermine Guild Artists, New Canaan, Conn., 1964-88, Westchester Art Soc., White Plains, 1964-72, Hudson River Mus., Yonkers, N.Y., 1965, First Westchester Nat. Bank, New Rochelle, 1967, Conn. Acad. Fine Arts, Hartford, 1967, Stern Bros., N.Y.C., 1967, Nat. Jewish Hosp. Denver, Woodmere, N.Y., 1968, Quaker Ridge Sch., Scarsdale, N.Y., 1970, Gallery Shop, Westport, Conn., 1978, Mari Gallery, Woodstock, N.Y., 1978, The Village Gallery, Ardsley, N.Y., 1979, Todd Gallery, Kiamesha Lake, N.Y., 1980, Norwalk Mchts. Bank, New Canaan, 1980, Mchts. Bank, Norwalk, 1980, Emery Air Freight Hdqrs., Conn., 1981, Mari Hube Gallery, N.Y., 1990, Helio Gallery, N.Y.C., 1991, Maska Gallery, Seattle, 1991, Rockefeller Town House, N.Y.C., 1992, Denise Bibro Fine Art Gallery, Soho, N.Y., 1993, Museè D'Art Moderne, Tonniens, France, 1993, Salon du Vieux Colombier, Paris, 1993, Md. Fedn. Art, Cardinal Gallery Md. Hall, Annapolis, 1993, Mus. Modern Art, Coral Gables, Fla., 1994, Wirtz Gallery, South Miami, Fla., 1994, U.S. Dept. State-Art in Embassies, 1995. Recipient Merit award Westchester Art Soc., 1964, Cert. of Honor Museè d'Art Moderne, 1994, Disting. Visitor award Mayor of Miami, 1994, U.S. Dept. of State, Art in Embassies Program, 1995; FIBA fellow, Cambridge, Eng., 1995. Avocations: golf, opera, classical and contemporary music, travel.

SHERMAN, SANDRA BROWN, lawyer; b. Galesburg, Ill., May 14, 1953; d. Charles Lewis and Lois Maria (Nelson) Brown; m. Robert Sherman, June 10, 1979; children: Michael Wesley, Stephen Averill, Alexander Joseph. B of Music Edn., Ind. U., 1975; JD, U. Ill., 1979, LLM, 1981. Bar: Ill. 1979, Tex. 1982, N.J. 1984, U.S. Tax Ct. 1988, N.Y. 1997. Instr. law U. Ill., Champaign, 1979-81; assoc. Law Offices of William E. Remy, San Antonio, 1984, Gutkin Miller Shapiro & Selesner, Millburn, N.J., 1985-88, ptnr., 1989-91; counsel Riker Danzig Scherer Hyland & Perretti LLP, Morristown, 1991-95; ptnr. Riker Danzig Scherer Hyland & Perretti, LLP, 1996—. Contbr. articles to profl. jours. Trustee, sec. Found. U. Medicine and Dentistry N.J., 1998—; trustee Jersey Battered Women's Svc., 1999—. Scholar Ind. U., 1971-75, U. Ill., 1977-79. Mem. ABA (probate and trust law divsn.), N.J. Bar Assn., Estate Planning Coun. No. N.J., Estate Planning Coun. N.Y.C., Park Ave. Club. Avocation: music. Home: 15 Hawthorne Dr New Providence NJ 07974-1111 Office: Riker Danzig Scherer Hyland & Perretti LLP Headquarters Plz 1 Speedwell Ave Ste 2 Morristown NJ 07960-6823 E-mail: ssherman@riker.com.

SHERMAN, SIGNE LIDFELDT, portfolio manager, former research chemist; b. Rochester, N.Y., Nov. 11, 1913; d. Carl Leonard Broström and Herta Elvira Maria (Tern) Lidfeldt; m. Joseph V. Sherman, Nov. 18, 1944 (dec. Oct. 1984). BA, U. Rochester, 1935, MS, 1937. Chief chemist Lab. Indsl. Medicine and Toxicology Eastman Kodak Co., Rochester, 1937-43; chief rsch. chemist Chesebrough-Pond's Inc., Clinton, Conn., 1943-44; ptnr. Joseph V. Sherman Cons., N.Y.C., 1944-84; portfolio strategist Sherman Holdings, Troy, Mont., 1984—. Author: The New Fibers, 1946. Fellow Am. Inst. Chemists; mem. AAAS, AAUW (life), Am. Chem. Soc., Am. Econ. Assn., Am. Assn. Ind. Investors (life), Fedn. Am. Scientists (life), Union Concerned Scientists (life), Earthquake Engring. Rsch. Inst., Nat. Ctr. for Earthquake Engring. Rsch., N.Y. Acad. Scis. (life), Cabinet View Country Club. Office: Sherman Holdings Angel Island 648 Halo Dr Troy MT 59935-9415 E-mail: creative@libby.org.

SHERMAN, SPENCER ERWIN, ophthalmologist; b. Jersey City, Apr. 8, 1936; AB cum laude, Princeton U., 1958; MD, Columbia Coll. Physicians & Surgeons, 1962. Diplomate Am. Bd. Ophthalmology. Intern Mt. Sinai Hosp., N.Y.C., 1962-63, attending ophthalmologist, 1968—, resident in ophthalmology, 1965-68; asst. clin. prof. ophthalmology NYU Sch. Medicine; staff Mt. Sinai Hosp., 1998—. Attending ophthalmologist Manhattan Eye & Ear Hosp., N.Y.C., 1968—, Lenox Hill Hosp., N.Y.C., 1968—, N.Y. Eye and Ear Infirmary, Mt. Sinai Hosp., 1970—. Capt. USAMC, 1963-65. Named one of Best Drs. in N.Y., Castle Connolly Group, 1980—, Top Drs. in U.S., Ctr. for Study of Svcs. Fellow ACS, Internat. Coll. of Surgeons, Am. Acad. of Ophthalmology (Honor and Svc. award); mem. AMA, Nat. Soc. Prevention Blindness, Found. Children with Learning Disabilities, Am. Soc. Refractive Surgeons, N.Y. Acad. Medicine, N.Y. Ophthalmologic Soc., Internat. Soc. Refractive Surgery, Am. Soc. Catarect & Refractive Surgery, Harmonie Club, Sunningdale Country Club, Maidstone Gun Club, Peconic Sportsman Club, East Hampton Tennis Club, Sigma Xi. Office: 166 E 63rd St New York NY 10021-7636 Fax: (212) 752-4285. E-mail: sesmdpc@aol.com.

SHERMAN, STEPHEN MICHAEL, lawyer; b. N.Y.C., Dec. 9, 1946; s. Arthur and Marjorie Elizabeth Sherman; m. Sue Lynn Gould, Oct. 10, 1965 (div. Oct. 1983); children: Michael Aaron, Laura Elizabeth Sherman Getz; m. Kathryn Sue Davis, June 1, 1985. BA, Ind. U., 1968, JD, 1972. Bar: Ind. 1972, U.S. Dist. Ct. (so. dist.) Ind. 1972, U.S. Ct. Appeals (6th cir.) 1975. Clk. chief justice Ind. Supreme Ct., Indpls., 1972-73; dep. atty. gen. Ind. Atty. Gen., 1973-74; pvt. practice law, 1974—. Staff counsel Legis. Coun. Adminstrv. Rules, Indpls., 1978-79; pres. Marion County Juvenile Detention Ctr. Adv. Bd., Indpls., 1987—; chmn. bd. Omega Concepts, Inc., Indpls., 1993—. Recipient Dawson award Tabernacle Presbyn. Ch., Indpls., 1988. Mem. ABA, Ind. State Bar Assn., Indpls. Bar Assn. (mem. grievance com. 1978—, mem. legal awareness com. 1985—). Democrat. Avocations: grandchildren, RV camping, travel, spectator sports. Home: 6021 Winnpeny Ln Indianapolis IN 46220-5252 Office: PO Box 20576 Indianapolis IN 46220-0576

SHERMAN, SUSAN JEAN, writer, educator, editor, educator; b. N.Y.C., Oct. 30, 1939; d. Monroe and Gertrude (Horn) S.. BA, Sarah Lawrence Coll., 1969, MA in Lit., 1971. Tchr. English Dwight-Englewood, 1970-72, Riverdale Country Sch., NY, 1972-97; writer Riverdale, 1997—. Author: Give Me Myself, 1961, (rec.) Promises to Be Kept, 1962; editor: Forward Into the Past, 1992, May Sarton: Among the Usual Days, 1993, May Sarton: Selected Letters, 1916-1954, 1997, To Bid Us Still Rejoice, 1998, Dear Juliette: Letters of May Sarton to Juliette Huxley, 1999, May Sarton: Selected Letters, 1955-1995, 2002, May Sarton: Catching Beauty, The Earliest Poems (1924-1929), 2002, May Sarton: At Fifteen: A Journal, 2002.

SHERMAN, THOMAS FRANCIS, education educator; b. Salamanca, N.Y., Dec. 20, 1946; s. Harry and Ione (Schultz) S.; m. Janice Ann Wade, Aug. 17; children: Piper Lee, Wade Thomas. AA, Paul Smith's Coll., 1967; BA, SUNY, Buffalo, 1970; MEd, Colo. State U., 1975; EdD, U. Colo., 1980. Tchr. Buffalo Pub. Schs., 1970, Poudre R.I. Pub. Schs., Ft. Collins, Colo., 1971, tchr., reading specialist, 1973-80; sr. resident supr. Lookout Mountain Schs. for Boys, Golden, 1972; faculty, dir. reading ctr. Ea. N.Mex. U., Portales, 1981-84; faculty Bemidji (Minn.) State U., 1985-90, Winona State U., Rochester, Minn., 1990-92; interim asst. v.p. acad. affairs S.W. State U., Marshall, 1992-93; interim asst. vice chancellor acad. affairs Minn. State Univ. System, St. Paul, 1993; prof. Winona State U., Rochester, 1994-2000; disting. faculty fellow Sheldon Jackson Coll., Sitka, Alaska, 2001—. Mem. system quality facilitator team Minn. State U.; chair Winona State Outcomes/Indicators, 1990-92; coord. WSU/Minn. High Success Consortium Grad. Program; mem. Minn. State Colls. and Univs. Grad. Coun., 2000--. Contbr. articles on reading edn. to profl. jours. Bd. mem. Dodge/Fillmore/Olmstead Counties Corrections Bd., 1990-93; elder Presbyn. Ch. Mem. Internat. Reading Assn. (pres. Minn. Coun., cert. of merit, sub chair evaluation team Nat. Coun. Accreditation Tchr. Edn., mem. nat. media award com.), Rochester Kiwanis (bd. dirs. 1992-95), Alpha Upsilon Alpha Internat. (chair steering com.). Democrat. Avocation: former profl. skier. Home: 1735 Walden Ln SW Rochester MN 55902-0901 Office: Winona State U Highway 14 E Rochester MN 55904

SHERMAN, THOMAS WEBSTER, JR. environmental company executive; b. Newark, Oct. 17, 1929; s. Thomas Webster and Myrtle Agnes (Benson) S.; m. Marilyn Margaret Noss, Nov. 15, 1952; children: Susan, Catherine, Thomas, Janet. BS in Engring., U.S. Naval Acad., 1951; MS in Bus. Adminstrn., George Washington U., 1964. Commd 2d lt. USAF, 1951, advanced through grades to col., 1969, retired, 1981; engring. coord. Systems Mgmt. Am., Washington, 1984-85; dir. govt. mktg. Sullair Corp., Michigan City, Ind., 1985-90; pres. Aquacide LLC, 1996—, MGS Technology LLC. Cons. in field; guest lectr. Purdue U. Contbr. articles to profl. jours. Coord. Round Table, Michigan City, 1997; bd. dirs. Mil. Mus., Michigan City, 1996-97, Civil War Club, Michigan City, 1995-97. Decorated DFC. Mem. AAAS, Air Force Assn., Naval Inst., Air Commd. Assn., Partnership for Sustainability with Russia, Nat. Shipbuilding Rsch. Program, Doctors for Disaster Preparedness. Avocations: conversation, reading, golf. Home: 12255 Clipper Dr Woodbridge VA 22192 Office: Aquacide 2 Devonshire Ct Ste 9 Michigan City IN 46360-1584

SHERMAN, WILLIAM FARRAR, lawyer, former state legislator; b. Little Rock, Sept. 12, 1937; s. Lincoln Farrar and Nancy (Lowe) S.; m. Carole Lynn Williams, Sept. 2, 1967; children: John, Anna, Lucy. BA in History, U. Ark.-Fayetteville, 1960; LLB, U. Va., 1964. Bar: Ark. 1964, U.S. Supreme Ct. 1970. Assoc. Smith, Williams, Friday & Bowen, Little Rock, 1964-66; asst. U.S. atty. Ea. Dist. Ark., 1966-69, Ark. Securities Commr., Little Rock, 1969-71; ptnr. Jacoway, Sherman & Pence, 1971—. Legal counsel Voice of the Retarded, 1991-2001, BBB Ark., 1971-2001; mem. Ark. Ho. of Reps., 1974-84; spl. assoc. justice Supreme Ct., 1991; del. Constnl. Conv. Ark., 1979. With U.S. Army, 1960-61, now brig. gen. U.S. Army ret. Mem. ABA, Ark. Bar Assn., Pulaski County Bar Assn., Ark. Bar Found. Democrat. Methodist. Office: 221 W 2nd St Little Rock AR 72201-2505 E-mail: clsherman@aristotle.net.

SHERMAN, WILSON, poet, foundation administrator; b. Conn. s. Robert Sherman, Patricia Wilson. Pres. Automobile Safety Found., La Jolla, Calif., 1988—. Founder Poetry Band, 1995—. Mem.: ASCAP. Mailing: Automobile Safety found PO Box 12183 La Jolla CA 92039

SHERMAN, ZACHARY, civil and aerospace engineer, consultant; b. N.Y.C., Oct. 26, 1922; s. Harry and Minnie (Schulsinger) S.; m. Bertha Leikin, Mar. 23, 1947; children: Gene Victor, Carol Beth. BCE, CCNY, 1943; MCE, Polytech. U. N.Y., Bklyn., 1953, PhD in Civil Engring. & Mechanics, 1969; MME, Stevens Inst. Tech., 1968. Registered profl. engr., N.Y., N.J. Stress analyst Gen. Dynamics, San Diego, 1943-45; sr. stress analyst Republic Aviation, Farmingdale, N.Y., 1945-47, 59-62; prof. civil engring. U. Miss., Oxford, 1954-59; lectr. civil engring. Stevens Inst. Tech., Hoboken, N.J., 1962-67, CUNY, 1967-69; assoc. prof. aerospace engring. Pa. State U., State College, 1969-73; prin. Dr. Zachary Sherman Cons. Engrs., Santa Monica, Calif., 1973—; aerospace engr. FAA, N.Y.C., N.Y., 1980-86. Designated cons. engr. rep., FAA, 1986—. Contbr. articles to profl. jours. NSF grantee, 1972. Fellow ASCE; mem. AIAA (v.p. Western Conn. chpt. 1977-78), N.Y. Acad. Scis., Sigma Xi. Achievements include development of beam/beam-column deck suspension bridge, prestressed aircraft wing. Home and Office: 2021 California Ave Apt 7 Santa Monica CA 90403-4531 Fax: 310-264-5990.

SHERMAN-APPEL, LORI RAE, nursing administrator; b. Newark, Oct. 16, 1955; d. Albert Paul and Janice E. (Waldholz) S.; m. Carl Aaron Appel. BSN, Adelphi U., 1977; MPA, Fairleigh Dickinson U., 1993. RN N.J., cert. advanced practice nurse; diabetes educator. Program dir. Internat. Diabetes Ctr., East Hanover, N.J., 1985-88; coord. diabetes edn. St. Mary's Hosp., Orange, 1988-89; dir. Daibetes Ctr. N.J., Muhlenberg Regional Med. Ctr., Plainfield, 1989-96; corp. dir. profl. devel. Insulin Infusion Specialities, New Orleans, 1996-97; program dir. Diabetes Treatment Ctrs. Am., Newark Beth Israel Med. Ctr., Newark, 1997—2001, Med. Ctr. at Princeton, 1997—2001; dir. APN/Diabetes Ctr. Newark Beth Israel Med. Ctr., , 2001—. Spkr. in field. Various v.p. positions Sisterhood Temple Beth O'R/Beth Torah, Clark, NJ, 1994—98. Mem.: Garden State Assn. Diabetes Educators (bd. trustees 1995—, pres. 1992—93, pres.-elect 1991—92, mem. chair 1990—91), Orgn. Nurse Execs., N.J. State Nurses Assn., Am. Assn. Diabetes Educators. Avocations: baking, walking, reading. Home: 357 Ellen Ln Bridgewater NJ 08807-5690 Office: Beth Israel Med Ctr Diabetes Ctr 201 Lyons Ave Newark NJ 07112-2094 E-mail: sugarrn@aol.com.

SHERN, DAVID LEN, educator, dean; b. Pueblo, Colo., Feb. 23, 1951; s. Lennox Lyle and Louise Marie Shern; m. Karen Sue Westerman, Nov. 5, 1977 (div.). BA in Psychology, U. Colo., 1973, MA in Social Psychology, 1977, PhD in Social Psychology, 1980; cert. in advanced epidemiologic methods, NIMH Staff Coll., 1980. Asst. dir. research and evaluation sect. Denver Dept. Health and Hosps. Mental Health Programs, 1981-82; research assoc. evaluation services sect. Colo. div. Mental Health, Denver, 1982-84, mgr. sponsored research program, 1984-88, project dir., investigator estimating residential services for chronically mentally ill, 1983-87; investigator validation models for estimating mental health need U. Denver, 1983-88; dir. bur. evaluation and svcs. rsch. N.Y. Office of Mental Health, Albany, 1988-95; dean, prof. Louis de la Parte Fla. Mental Health Inst., U. South Fla., Tampa, 1995—. Cons. several health facilities, Denver, 1976—88; chmn. Fla. Commn. Mental Health and Substance Abuse, 1999—2000; prin. investigator Treatment Outcome Study, 1988; prin. investigator rsch. grants NIH Substance Abuse and Mental Health Svcs. Adminstrn., 1988—2000; dir. NIMH Ctr. for Sudy Issues in Pub. Mental Health, 1993—95. Contbr. articles to profl. jours. Bd. dirs. Travelers Aid of Denver, 1981-83, Karis Cmty., 1986-88, pres. 1988; founding mem. Albany County Land Conservancy, 1992-95, pres., 1992-95. Mem. APA, APHA (chair mental health sect. 1992-93, governing coun. 1995-97), Orgn. for Program Evaluation in Colo. (pres. 1982-83, assoc. editor bull.), Am. Evaluation Assn., Sigma Xi. Democrat. Avocations: hiking, gardening, travel. Office: Louis de la Parte Fla Mental Health Inst U South Fla 13301 Bruce B Downs Blvd Tampa FL 33612-3807

SHERNICOFF, MARK B. accountant; b. Bklyn., Aug. 2, 1942; s. William Shernicoff and Pauline Chayt; m. Judy Frankel, June 27, 1965; children: Stephen Howard, Barry Isaac, Daniel Michael. BBA, Pace U., 1965. CPA. Tax acct. Eltra Corp., Bklyn., 1965; asst. to commr. N.Y.C. Dept. Markets, 1966-67, N.Y.C. Dept. Sanitation, 1967-68; budget analyst N.Y.C. Mayor's Office of Mgmt. and Budget, 1968-74, asst. budget dir., 1974-76; chief acct. N.Y.C. Comptroller's Office, 1976-82; dir. audits N.Y.C. Health and Hosps. Corp., 1982-86; ptnr. Zucker & Shernicoff, CPAs, N.Y.C., 1986—. Contbr. articles to profl. jours. Treas. Coun. N.Y. Coops. and Condominiums, N.Y.C., 1982—; Nat. Assn. Housing Coops., Washington, 1995— Mem. AICPA, N.Y. State Soc. CPAs. Jewish. Office: Zucker & Shernicoff 1700 Broadway New York NY 10019

SHERONY, CHERYL ANNE, dietitian; b. Lincoln, Nebr., Dec. 5, 1948; d. John Eugene and Hazel Ethel (Stites) Howe; m. Bruce Carl Sherony, Aug. 11, 1973; children: Thomas Carl, Michael Bruce. BS in Dietetics, U. Wis., Stevens Point, 1971, MS, 1979. Registered dietitian. Dietitian Marquette (Mich.) Gen. Hosp., 1979-80, self employed, 1980-85, 89-90, Alger Marquette C.C., Marquette, 1982-87, Upper Peninsula Home Nursing, Marquette, 1989-93; dietititian self employed, 1989-93; dietitian, owner Superior Dietetic Svcs. of the Upper Peninsula Inc., 1996-99; pvt. practice dietitian dietitian, 1999—. Citizen amb. to China, People to People Program, 1995. Sect. reviewer Pediat. Manual of Clin. Dietetics, 1998. Capt. USAF, 1972-90. Mem. Am. Dietetic Assn., Mich. Dietetic Assn., Upper Peninsula Dietetic Assn. Roman Catholic. Avocations: reading, water skiing, cross country skiing. Home and Office: 1781 M-28 East Marquette MI 49855

SHERPA, FRAN MAGRUDER, geography educator; b. Midland, Tex., Aug. 20, 1952; d. Edwin Howard Magruder and Barbara June Cowden; m. Ang Kazi Sherpa; children: Sarah, Susie, Sonia, Tsowang. BS Geography, S.W. Tex. State U., 1995, M Applied Geography, 1998. Owner, operator Himalayan Excursions, Nepal, 1983—85; investor, mgr. office Nepal Internat. Clinic , Nepal, 1989—91; adj. prof. geography U. Tex. Permian Basin, Odessa, Tex., 2000—. Sec. Am. Women of Nepal, Nepal, 1989—93; mem. United Nations Women's Orgn., Nepal, 1989—93; mem. audio visual acom. Road Users Nepal, Nepal, 1992—93. Mem.: Am. Assn. Geographers. Avocations: polo, photography, travel. Home: 2201 Neely Midland TX 79705 E-mail: fransherpa@cleansed.net.

SHERR, DAVID LLOYD, radiation oncologist, educator; b. N.Y.C., Oct. 11, 1956; s. Joseph and Marjorie Sherr. AA, BA, Yshiva U., 1977; MD, Albert Einstein, 1981. Diplomate Am. Bd. Radiology. Resident Columbia-Presbyn. Med. Ctr., 1983-86; radiation oncologist North Shore Univ. Hosp., Manhasset, N.Y., 1986-2001, Presbyn.-Weill Cornell Med. Ctr., N.Y.C., 2001—, asst. clin. prof., 2001—. Asst. prof. Cornell U. Med. Coll., N.Y.C., 1988-95, NYU Sch. Medicine, 1996—; com. mem. Radiation Therapy Oncology Group, Phila., 1988—. Mem. Am. Coll. Radiology, Am. Soc. Neuro-Oncology, Am. Soc. Therapeutic Radiology and Oncology, Am. Soc. Clin. Oncology, Radiol. Soc. N.Am., N.Y. Roentgen Soc. Office: NY Presbyn Hosp Stich Radiation Oncology 525 E 68th St Box 575 New York NY 10021

SHERR, SYLVIA, artist, educator; b. Zamosc, Poland, Jan. 1, 1931; came to U.S., 1938; d. Isadore and Edna (Rifer) Feldstein; m. Allan E. Sherr, Sept. 11, 1955; children: Susan Matalon, Carol Cunn, Evan Sherr. BS, U. Wis., 1953; MA, Kean Coll., 1977. Cert. tchr., Conn., N.J. Tchr. Wilton (Conn.) Bd. Edn., 1958-59, Bound Brook (N.J.) Bd. Edn., 1975-90, chairperson gifted and talented com., 1980-85. One-woman shows include N.J. Ctr. for Visual Art, 1998, Johnson & Johnson World Hdqs., 2002, exhibitions include Polo Gallery, Edgewater, N.J., 1994—99, The Collector, Merrick, L.I., 1995—99, Lincoln Ctr., N.Y.C., 1995, Gallery 402, 1999, Belles Artes, San Miguel de Allande, Mex. Fellow Geraldine Dodge Found., Vt. Studio Ctr., 1998. Mem. Orgn. Ind. Artists, 1998. E-mail: sylsplace@msn.com.

SHERRARD, JAMES ROBERT, nuclear engineering educator; b. Portsmouth, Va., Aug. 6, 1942; s. Guy Wright Sherrard and Sara Lee (Whitehead) McKibben; m. Penelope Palmer, July 8, 1972. BS in Gen. Engring., USCG Acad., New London, Conn., 1964; MS in Nuclear Engring./Naval Arch., MIT, 1970; MS in Mech. Engring., U. Conn., 1972; MS in Nuclear Sci., PhD in Nuclear Engring., Cath. U. Am., Washington, 1978. Registered profl. engr., Md. Commd. ensign USCG, 1964, advanced through grades to comdr., 1978, shipboard engr., 1964-68, with R&D, 1974-78, 81-85; with U.S. Arms Control and Disarmament Agy., 1978-81; engring. faculty UCG Acad., New London, Conn., 1970-74, Cath. U. Am., Washington, 1974-78, U. Conn. Avery Point Campus, Groton, Conn., 1982-85; chmn. nuclear dept. Three Rivers Comm. Tech. Coll., Norwick, 1987—. Alt. commr. Technology Accreditation Commn. of Accrediation Bd. for Engring. and Technology, N.Y.C., 1993, 94, 2000, commr., Balt., 1995-99; alt. commr. Engring. Accreditation Bd., 2000; program advisor WPI Nuclear Program, Worcester, Mass., 1987—, U. Mass. Lowell (Mass. Nuclear Program, 1989—). Co-author: Basic Naval Architecture, 1972, Nuclear Reactor Simultator, 1992; contbr. articles to profl. jours. Mem. Groton Town Planning Commn., 1987—, chmn., 1994—; tennis coach USCG Acad., New Conn., 1970-74; golf coach Three Rivers Cmty. Tech. Coll., Norwich, 1987—; chmn. standing adv. com. Conn. Bd. of Govs. for Higher Edn., 1999—; mem. Nuclear Energy Adv. Coun. Conn., 2001—; mem. adv. com. Millstone Nuclear Complex, 2000. Recipient Innovation in Edn. award ABET, 1993; named Tech. Educator of Yr. Am. Tech. Edn. Assn., 1995. Mem. Am. Nuclear Soc., Soc. Naval Archiects and Marine Engrs., Am. Soc. Engring. Edn., Am. Tech. Edn. Assn., Am. Indian Sci. and Engring. Soc., Health Physics Soc., New Eng. Tng. Assn., Nuclear Engring. Dept. Head Orgn. Republican. Presbyterian. Avocations: golf, racketball, tennis, travel, jigsaw puzzles. Home: 66 Algonquin Dr Mystic CT 06355-1721 Office: Three Rivers Comm Tech Coll 574 New London Tpke Norwich CT 06360-6500 E-mail: jsherrard@trcc.commnet.edu.

SHERRARD, RAYMOND HENRY, retired federal agency agent; b. Chgo., Mar. 8, 1944; s. Henry Loren and Minnie Valeria (Elrod) S.; m. Marsha L. McDermid, 1967 (div. 1971). AA, Long Beach City Coll., 1965; BA, Calif. State U., 1967; grad., Treasury Dept. Law Enforcement, Washington, 1970. Spl. dep. U.S. Marshal, L.A., 1970; pres. RHS Enterprises, Cypress, Calif., 1981—; criminal investigator criminal investigation div. IRS, Santa Ana, 1969-94. Story cons. Charles Fries Prodns., Hollywood, Calif., 1976—; instr. Fed. Law Enforcement Tng. Ctr., Glynco, Ga., 1977—; screenwriter Orion TV, Century City, Calif., 1984—; tech. advisor Paramount Pictures, Hollywood, 1987—; dir. speaker panel IRS, Laguna Niguel, Calif., 1984-92. Author: Federal Law Enforcement Patches, 1983, vol. 2, 1987, About Badges, 1987, Badges of the United Marshals, 1990, The Centurions Shield-A History of the Los Angeles Police Department, Its Badges and Insignia, 1996, The Encyclopedia of Federal Law Enforcement Patches, 2000; columnist Police Colector News; contbr. articles to profl. jours. Recipient Presidential Commendation, Pres. U.S.A., Washington, 1980, Spl. Act award U.S. Treasury Dept., L.A., 1978, 87. Mem. Nat. Assn. Treasury Agts. (v.p. 1995-98), Fed. Criminal Investigators Assn. (life, regional v.p. 1978-80), Assn. Fed. Investigators, Fed. Law Enforcement Officers Assn., Calif. Narcotic Officers Assn. (life, sec. 1974). Republican. Avocations: Korean Tae Kwon Do, screenwriting, film and TV cons./rsch. Home: PO Box 5779 Garden Grove CA 92846-0779

SHERRATT, GERALD ROBERT, retired university president; b. Los Angeles, Nov. 6, 1931; s. Lowell Heyborne and Elva Genevieve (Lamb) S. BS in Edn., Utah State U., 1953, MS in Edn. Adminstrn., 1954; PhD in Adminstrn. Higher Edn., Mich. State U., 1975. Staff assoc. U. Utah, Salt Lake City, 1961-62; dir. high sch. relations Utah State U., Logan, 1962-64, asst. to pres., 1964-77, v.p. for univ. relations, 1977-81; pres. So. Utah U., Cedar City, 1982-97; mayor Cedar City, UT, 2002—. Dir. Honeyville Grain Inc., Utah; mem. coun. pres. Utah Sys. Higher Edn., 1982-97; chmn. bd. Utah Summer Games, Cedar City, 1984-97; chmn. pres.'s coun. Rocky Mountain Athletic Conf., Denver, 1984-85 Author hist. pageant: The West: America's Odyssey, 1973 (George Washington Honor medal 1973); musical review: How the West Was Won, 1998. Chmn. Festival of Am. West, Logan, Utah, 1972-82; chmn. bd. Utah Shakespearean Festival, Cedar City, 1982-86; chmn. bd. dirs. Salt Lake City Br. of the Fed. Res. Bank of San Francisco, 1996-98; bd. trustees Salt Lake Organizing Com. Winter Olympics 2002. 1st lt. USAF, 1954-57. Recipient Editing award Indsl. Editors Assn., 1962, Robins award Utah State U., 1967, Disting. Alumnus award Utah State U., 1974, So. Utah U., 1991, Total Citizen award Cedar City C. of C., 1993, Minuteman award Utah Nat. Guard, 1997; named to Utah Tourism Hall of Fame, 1989; Centennial medal So. Utah U., 1997; Imperial Order Utah Shakespearean Festival, 1997; named to Hall of Honor Utah Summer Games, 1997, Utah Educators Hall of Fame, 1999. Mem. Am. Assn. State Colls. and Univs., Cache C. of C. (bd. dirs. 1980-82), Cedar City Civic Club (pres.), Phi Kappa Phi, Phi Delta Kappa, Sigma Nu (regent 1976-78) Mem. Lds Ch.

SHERREN, ANNE TERRY, chemistry educator; b. Atlanta, July 1, 1936; d. Edward Allison and Annie Ayres (Lewis) Terry; m. William Samuel Sherren, Aug. 13, 1966. BA, Agnes Scott Coll., 1957; PhD, U. Fla., Gainesville, 1961. Grad. tchg. asst. U. Fla., Gainesville, 1957-61; from instr. to asst. prof. Tex. Womans U., Denton, 1961-66; rsch. participant Argonne Nat. Lab., 1973-80, 93-94; assoc. prof. chemistry North Cen. Coll., Naperville, Ill., 1966-76, prof., 1976-2001, prof. emeritus, 2001—. Contbr. articles to profl. jours. Ruling elder Knox Presbyn. Ch., 1971—, clk. of session, 1976-94. Mem. Am. Chem. Soc., Am. Inst. Chemists, Sigma Xi, Delta Kappa Gamma (chpt. pres. 2002-), Iota Sigma Pi (nat. pres. 1978-81, nat. dir. 1972-78, nat. historian 1989—). Presbyterian. Office: North Ctrl Coll Dept Chemistry Naperville IL 60566 Office Fax: 630-637-5180. E-mail: ats@noctrl.edu.

SHERRER, CHARLES DAVID, college dean, clergyman; b. Marion, Ohio, Sept. 21, 1935; s. Harold D. and Catherine E. (Fye) S. AB, U. Notre Dame, 1958, MA, 1965; S.T.L., Gregorian U., 1962; PhD, U. N.C., 1969; HHD, King's Coll., 1997. Ordained priest Roman Cath. Ch., 1961. Instr. English U. Portland, Oreg., 1963-64, asst. prof., 1969-74, prof., 1990—, chmn. dept., 1970-74, dean Grad. Sch., 1982-87, mem. Bd. Regents, 1986-87, acad. v.p., 1987-96; pres. King's Coll., Wilkes Barre, Pa., 1974-81. Bd. trustees Stonehill Coll., 1992-98; dir. studies Holy Cross Fathers, Ind. Province, 1979-88.

SHERRER, GARY, state lieutenant governor; m. Judy Waller, 1965; children: Stuart, Nancy. Grad., Emporia State U. Sec. Kans. Dept. Commerce and Housing, 1995—; lt. gov. State of Kans., 1996—. Vice chmn. Gov.'s Cabinet. Recipient Disting. Alumni award Emporia State U., 1994, award of excellence, 1995, Carl Perkins Humanitarian award, 2000; Toll fellow, 1999. Mem. Nat. Conf. Lt. Govs. (chmn.).

SHERRICK, DANIEL NOAH, real estate broker; b. Greenup, Ill., Mar. 28, 1929; s. Conrad Donovan and Helen Lorene (Neeley) S.; m. Dora Ann Moore, Aug. 11, 1957; children: Renata Ann Sherrick McBride, Sherrie Dee Sherrick Sierra. BS in Edn., Eastern Ill. U., Charleston, 1956. Owner Midwest Ins. Agy., Greenup, 1956-60; supt. agys. Midwest Life Ins. Co., Lincoln, Nebr., 1960-62; asst. v.p. Gulf Life Ins. Co., Jacksonville, Fla., 1962-71; pres. Bank of Carbondale, Ill., 1971-74, Prescription Learning Corp., Springfield, 1974-76; exec. v.p. Imperial Industries, Inc., Miami Lakes, Fla., 1976-88, pres., chief exec. officer, 1988-90; broker, salesman Coldwell Banker Residential Real Estate, 1990-91, 93—; pres., bd. dirs. Palmer State Bank, Taylorville, Ill., 1991-93; broker-salesman Coldwell Banker Highlands Properties, 1993—. Pres. Alderman Park Civic Assn., Jacksonville, 1968, Heritage Hills Home Owners Assn., Carbondale, 1973. With USAF, 1948-52. Mem. Am. Legion, Greater Sebring C. of C., VFW, Internat. Torch Club, Masons, Elks. Presbyterian. Home: 6228 Aquavista Dr Sebring FL 33876 Office: Coldwell Banker Highlands Properties 2617 US Hwy 27 S Sebring FL 33870-2127

SHERRIE, LAUREL ELIZABETH, artist; b. Hammond, Ind., June 24, 1949; d. Robert Michael and Ruth Marie S.; m. Robert Earl Harvey, Nov. 24, 1983. Student, Ea. Ill. U., 1968. One woman shows include Gallery 113, 1994, Buenaventura Gallery, Ventura, 1995, Interiors by Amanda, 1998, Village Art, Arroyo Grande, 1998, Jamaica You Salon, San luis Obrspo, 2000, 01; exhibited in group shows at Santa Barbara County Fair, 1992 (1st and 4th pl. awards), Danica House Art Assn. Show, Santa Barbara, 1992, Faulkner Gallery, Santa Barbara, 1992, Buenaventura Gallery , 1992, 94, (merit award), Mus. of History and Art, Ventura, Calif., 1993, May, Faulkner Gallery Show, Santa Barbara, 1993, Ventura County Fair, 1994, Thousand Oaks Art Assn., 1994, Membership Show, 1994, San Luis Obispo Art Ctr. and Acrylics Show, 1996, 97, Castoro Cellars, Templeton, Calif., 1997, Laetitia Winery, Arroyo Grande, Calif., 1998, 2000, San Luis Obispo Art Ctr., 1998, Brassiere Show, 1999, Castoro Cellars, Templeton, 1999, Old World Charm, Arroyo Grande, 1999, El Camino Art Assn. Show, 2000, 2001, Village Art Mini-Show, 2000, Open Studios Tour, Jonathan's at Peirano's, Branch Street Deli, Arroyo Grande, Environ. Def. Fund Fundraiser exhibit, 2000, Cottonwood Canyon Winery, Santa Monica, 2000, Botanic Garden, 2001 (award San Luis Obispo 2001), Galaxy, 2001, Paso Robles, 2001; represented in permanent collections. Mem. Oil Painters of Am., El Camino Art Assn., San Luis Obispo Art Ctr., Oil, Pastel and Acrylic Group. Scientology. Avocations: exotic bird breeding, gardening, interior decorating, traveling. E-mail: laurel@laurelsherrie.com.

SHERRILL, BARBARA ANN BUKER, elementary school educator; b. Hamilton, Mont., July 11, 1952; d. Emery Orville and Helen (Hackett) Buker; m. Mark Warren Sherrill, Oct. 7, 1978; children: Kristopher Kain, Ashley Ann. BS in Elem. Edn., Western Mont. Coll., 1973, postgrad., 1984; M. Human Svcs., U. Gt. Falls, 1991. Cert. tchr., Mont. Tchr. elem. grades Ramsay (Mont.) Sch., 1974-90; tchr. Sch. Dist. 1, Butte, Mont., 1990-2000; media coord. Creativity Factory Presch., 1974-87; ednl. coord. R.O.C.K.I.E.S. Grant for Sch. Dist. 1, 2000—. Sci. mentor West Elem. Sch., 1997-2000; facilitator labor history workshop Internat. Brotherhood Teamsters, U. Wis., 1987, U. Calif., Berkeley, 1988; writer, rschr., 1987-88; Mont. Keystone Project mentor, 1997—; mem. Exploratium Inst. for Inquiry, 1998; early career mentor, 1999—; adult edn. instr. Butte Sch. Dist., 2002—; cmty. outreach instr. U. Mont. Western, 2002—; mem. Mont. Out-of-Sch. Time task force, 2001—. Co-author: Teaching Labor Studies in the Schools, vol. 1, 1988, Gezel Developmental Tester, 1991—. Parent vol. Silver Bow Amateur Wrestling Assn. Butte, pairings master. Mem. AAUW, Am. Fedn. Tchrs., Mont. Fedn. Tchrs., AFL-CIO, Ramsay Fedn. Tchrs. (pres. 1975-79), Butte Tchrs. Union, Mont. Energy Edn. Coun. (bd. dirs. 1991, v.p. 1995—, presenter workshop, negotiating com. 1999—), Alpha Delta Kappa (pres. Mu chpt. 1994-96, corr. sec. Mont. chpt. 1996-98, scholarship com. 1998-2000). Democrat. Avocations: reading, skiing, swimming, computers. Office: Curriculum Office 119 N Montana St Butte MT 59701-9219

SHERRILL, BILLY NORRIS, record producer, songwriter; b. Phil Campbell, Ala., Nov. 5, 1936; s. Clyde Rivers and Ora Lucille (Thompson) S.; m. Charlene Evans, Jan. 30, 1961; 1 child, Catherine Eve Sherrill Lale. Recording engr. Sam Phillips Studio, Nashville, 1961-62; staff prodr. Columbia/Epic Records, 1962—. Songwriter: Almost Persuaded, Stand by Your Man, I Don't Wanna Play House, Your Good Girl's Gonna Go Bad, My Elusive Dreams, He Loves Me All the Way, The Ways to Love a Man, A Picture of Me (Without You), The Grand Tour, The Door, We're Gonna Hold On, We Loved It Away, A Very Special Love Song, The Most Beautiful Girl, Southern California, Two-Story House, numerous others; prodr. Tanya Tucker's early hits, also Charlie Rich, David Allan Coe, Ray Charles duets, Tammy Wynette, George Jones, Barbara Mandrell. Elected to Nat. Songwriter's Assn. Internat. Hall of Fame, 1984; recipient Nashville Entertainment Assn. Master award, 1986, Nat. Acad. Rec. Arts and Scis. Grammay awards for best songwriter for Best Country and Western Song, Almost Persuaded, 1966, best country song A Very Special Love Song, 1974, Country Music Assn. prodr. awards for albums of the yr. Behind Closed Doors, 1973, A Very Special Love Song, 1974, singles of the yr. Behind Closed Doors, 1973, He Stopped Loving Her Today, 1980, Broadcast Music Inc. Writer Performance awards, 1985, Billboard Mag. Favorite Country Single award, 1966, Top Country Song of Yr. for Most Beautiful Gir, 1974, Ala. Music Hall of Fame Mus. Creator's award, 1985, Acad. Country Music prodr. awards for single record of year Behind Closed Doors, 1973, album of yr. Behind Closed Doors, 1973, single of yr. He Stopped Loving Her Today, 1980, , Songwriter of Century award BMI, 1999. Office: 1022B 18th Ave S Nashville TN 37212-2105

SHERRILL, THOMAS BOYKIN, III, retired newspaper publishing executive; b. Tampa, Fla., Nov. 19, 1930; s. Thomas Boykin Jr. and Mary Emma (Addison) S.; m. Sandra Louise Evans, Dec. 27, 1969; children: Thomas Glenn, Stephen Addison. Circulation dir. Tampa (Fla.) Tribune, 1962-67, Sarasota (Fla.) Herald-Tribune, 1967-75; v.p. circulation The Dispatch Printing Co., Columbus, Ohio, 1975-78, v.p. mktg., 1978-97, bd. dirs., 1977-97; v.p., bd. dirs. Ohio Mag., Inc., 1979-97; ret., 1997. Bd. dirs., past chmn. bd. dirs. Salvation Army; trustee, past chmn. bd. dirs. Better Bus. Bur. Ctrl. Ohio, Inc.; bd. dirs. Ctrl. Ohio Ctr. Econ. Edn.; v.p., trustee Columbus Dispatch Charities; exec. bd. mem. Simon Kenton coun. Boy Scouts Am.; past pres. Wesley Glen United Meth. Retirement Ctr.; pres.'s adv. bd. Meth. Theol. Sch. With USN, 1951-56. Recipient Disting. Svc. award Editor and Pub. Mag., 1978; named hon. pres. Troy State U., 1979, hon. Ky. Col., 1980, hon. lt. col. aide-to-camp to Gov. State of Ala., 1984. Mem. Internat. Circulation Mgrs. Assn. (pres. 1975, Pres's. award 1989), Internat. Newspaper Mktg. Assn., Ohio Newspaper Assn. (bd. dirs. 1984-97, pres. 1986-88, Pres.'s award 1990), So. Circulation Mgrs. Assn. (life; pres. 1967-68, C.W. Bevinger Meml. award 1972), Audit Bur. Circulations (bd. dirs. 1980-90), Am. Advt. Fedn., Navy League, Ohio Newspapers Found., Ohio Circulation Mgrs. Assn (life; Pres.' award 1989), Columbus Area C. of C., SAR, Internat. Platform Assn., Athletic Club of Columbus, Muirfield Village Country Club, Kiwanis Club of Columbus (life, pres. 1982, George F. Hixon fellow). Republican. Home: 5215 Hampton Ln Columbus OH 43220-2270

SHERRINGTON, PAUL WILLIAM, marketing communications executive; b. Champaign, Ill., Oct. 7, 1949; s. P. William and Quirine (Kinate) S.; m. Nancy Sherrington; children: Gregg, Sally. BS in Communications, U. Tenn., 1971. Staff writer News Palladium, Benton Harbor, Mich., 1971-72; copywriter Retail Credit Co., Atlanta, 1972-75; asst. advt. dir. Equifax Inc., 1975-79, mgr. advt., 1979-83; mgr. communications Equifax, 1983-88, dir., advt. and sales promotion, 1988-93, asst. v.p. mktg. comm., 1993-95; dir. sales and mktg. Fernbank Mus. Natural History, 1996-98; v.p. adminstrn. Elrick & Lavidge, Atlanta, 1998—. Author (book) What Communicators Must Know About Service Marketing, 1991; co-author (book) Business-to-Business Advertising, 1991. Bd. dirs. Atlanta Arthritis Found., 1991-95. Recipient Addy award, 1985-86. Mem. Bus. Mktg. Assn. (chmn. 1988, 95-96, vice chmn. 1987, 94-95, internat. bd. dirs. 1984-88, 93-96, pres. Atlant chpt. 1983-84, 92-93, Atlanta bd. dirs. 1980-84, 91-93, Peach award 1986-88, 95). Republican. Roman Catholic. Avocations: golf, marketing, military history. Home: 1920 Barnes Mill Rd Marietta GA 30062-2941

SHERROD, LLOYD BRUCE, nutritionist; b. Goodland, Kans., Mar. 5, 1931; s. Charles and Helen S.; m. Judith Harms Sherrod, Dec. 21, 1963; children: Donna J., Barbara E. BS, S.D. State U., Brookings, 1958; MS, U. Ark., Fayetteville, 1960; PhD, Okla. State U., Stillwater, 1964. Rsch. assoc. Okla. State U., Stillwater, 1963; asst. prof. U. Hawaii, Hilo, 1964-67; from assoc. prof to prof. Tex. Tech. U. Ctr., Pantex, 1967-79; nutrition-chemistry instr. Frank Phillips Coll., Borger, Tex., 1979-88; part-time nutrition instr. Amarillo (Tex.) Coll., 1989-95; ret., 1995. Rschr. in field. Contbr. articles to sci. jours. Served with U.S. Army, 1951-53. Mem. AAAS, Am. Soc. Animal Science, Am. Dairy Science Assn., Am. Soc. Agronomy, Am. Inst. Biol. Scis., Tex. Jr. Coll. Tchrs. Assn., Am. Men and Women of Sci., Plains Nutrition Coun., Sigma Xi., Phi Kappa Phi, Gamma Sigma Delta. Home: PO Box 1017 Panhandle TX 79068-1017

SHERRY, GEORGE LEON, political science educator; b. Lodz, Poland, Jan. 5, 1924; came to U.S., 1939, naturalized 1945; s. Leon G. and Henrietta (Mess) S.; m. Doris H. Harf, Mar. 6, 1947; 1 child, Vivien Gail Sherry Greenberg. BA summa cum laude, CCNY, 1944; MA, Columbia U., 1951, MA, cert. Russian Inst., 1955, PhM, 1959. Reporter, radio news writer The N.Y. Times, N.Y.C., 1944-46; editor, interpreter, then sr. interpreter UN, 1946-59, from polit. officer to dir. and dep. to under sec.-gen. for spl. polit. affairs, 1959-84; polit. advisor to missions Congo, Cyprus, India and Pakistan, 1962-66; asst. sec.-gen. for spl. polit. affairs UN (office in charge peacekeeping forces which won Nobel Peace Prize, 1988), N.Y.C., 1984-85; Stuart Chevalier prof. diplomacy and world affairs Occidental Coll., Los Angeles, 1985—. Dir. Occidental at-the-UN program, N.Y.C., 1986-2002; U.S. del. staff Dartmouth Soviet-Am. confs., 1961-94; assoc. seminar on problem of peace Columbia U., N.Y.C.; cons. UN dept. peacekeeping ops., 1992, 93; leader UN tech. mission to Ga., 1993; UN envoy to follow Russian elections, 1993; cons. Internat. Peace Acad., 1993-97. Author: The United Nations Reborn: Conflict Control in the Post-Cold War World, 1990; editorial adv. bd. Polit. Sci. Quar., N.Y.C., 1973-89; contbr. articles and revs. to profl. jours. Recipient Townsend Harris medal CCNY, 1993; UN Inst. for Tng. and Rsch. sr. fellow, 1985-93. Mem. Coun. on Fgn. Rels., Acad. Coun. on UN Sys., UN Assn.-USA. Democrat. Avocations: piano playing; skiing; sailing. Home: 185 E 85th St Apt 3-c New York NY 10028-2172

SHERRY, JOHN SEBASTIAN, lawyer; b. Homestead, Pa., Apr. 18, 1946; s. Sebastian John and Margaret Josephine (Coyne) S.; m. Joan Carol Paulsen, Aug. 9, 1969; children: Brendan P., Michael S., Conor J. BA, U. Dayton, 1968; JD, Duquesne U., 1971. Bar: Pa. 1971, U.S. Dist. Ct. (we. dist.) Pa. 1971, U.S. Supreme Ct. 1975, U.S. Ct. Appeals (3d cir.) 1976, U.S. Tax Ct. 1977, U.S. Claims Ct. 1977, U.S. Ct. Mi. Appeals 1977, U.S. Ct. Internat. Trade 1977. Pvt. practice, Pitts., 1971—; mng. atty. The Travlers Ins. Co., 1972-78; mng. trial atty. The CNA Ins. Cos., 1978-88, sr. mgr. staff counsel, 1988-94, mng. trial atty., 1994-96, asst. v.p. claims litigation, 1996-98; pvt. practice John S. Sherry & Assocs., 1999—; prin. Sherry Dispute Resolution Svcs., 2001—. Lectr. Trial Advocacy Found., Pitts., 1984, Nat. Inst. for Trial Advocacy, 1997, 98. Assoc. opinion editor Pitts. Legal Jour., 1977-78, editor YLS newsletter, 1980. Chmn. Bd. Auditors, South Park, Pa., 1977-85. Fellow: Acad. Trial Lawyers Allegheny County (bd. govs. 1997—98); mem.: South Park C. of C., Western Pa. Trial Lawyers Assn., Pa. Bar Assn. (jud. adminstrn. com. 1992—, ADR com. 2001), Pa. Trial Lawyers Assn., Allegheny County Bar Assn. (CLE com. 1978—, coun. civil litigation sect. 1985—87, treas. 1988—2001, vice chmn. 1989, civil procedure rules com. 1999—, ADR com. 2001, chmn. 1990), ATLA, ABA, Lions, Pine Lake Trout Club, Rivers Club. Democrat. Roman Catholic. Avocations: fishing, hunting, literature. Address: 1302 Grant Bldg Pittsburgh PA 15219 Home: 113 Stroneygate Dr Mc Murray PA 15317-2766 E-mail: jsherryesq@msn.com

SHERRY, PAUL HENRY, minister, religious organization administrator; b. Tamaqua, Pa., Dec. 25, 1933; s. Paul Edward and Mary Elizabeth (Stein) S.; m. Mary Louise Thornburg, June 4, 1957; children: Mary Elizabeth, Paul David. BA, Franklin and Marshall Coll., 1955; ThM, Union Theol. Sem., N.Y.C., 1958, PhD, 1969; hon. doctorate, Ursinus Coll., 1981, Elmhurst Coll., 1990, Defiance Coll., 1991, Lakeland Coll., Sheboygan, Wis., 1991, Reformed Theological Acad., Debrecen, Hungary, 1994, United Theol. Sem. Twin Cities, 1995, Eden Theol. Sem., St. Louis, 2000, Chgo. Theol. Sem., 2000. Ordained to ministry United Ch. of Christ, 1958. Pastor St. Matthew United Ch. of Christ, Kenhorst, Pa., 1958-61, Community United Ch. of Christ, Hasbrouck Heights, N.J., 1961-65; mem. staff United Ch. Bd. Homeland Ministry, N.Y.C., 1965-82; exec. dir. Community Renewal Soc., Chgo., 1983-89; pres. United Ch. of Christ, Cleve., 1989-99, pub. policy cons., 2000—. Mem. gen. bd. Nat. Coun. Chs., N.Y.C., 1989-99; mem. ctrl. com. World Coun. Chs., 1990-99, del. 8th Assembly, Harare, Zimbabwe, 1998, del. 7th Assembly, Canberra, Australia, 1991. Editor: The Riverside Preachers; editor Jour. Current Social Issues, 1968-80; contbr. numerous articles to religious jours.; host weekly radio programs local sta., 1974-78, 84-85, 93-97. Bd. dirs., cons. Nat. Campaign for Jobs and Income Support, 2000—; bd. dirs. Nat. Interfaith Com. for Worker Justice, 2000—. Mem. Soc. Christian Ethics. Democrat. Avocations: reading, hiking, cultural events. Home and Office: 12700 Lake Ave Apt 1612 Lakewood OH 44107- E-mail: psher973@aol.com

SHERRY, PRISCILLA MAE, retired music educator; b. Hagerstown, Ind. d. Ray C. and Ruth P. (Cromer) S. BS, Ball State U., 1952, MA, 1964. Cert. elem. and music tchr. Tchr. vocals,instruments Richmond (Ind.) Community Schs., 1953-90—. Instr. pvt. music lessons, 1950-62; organist 1st United Meth. Ch., 1948-68, pianist 1st Ch. Christ Scientist, Hagerstown, Ind., 1958-68. Mem. Profl. Educators Assn., Ind. State Music Assn. Clubs: Hartley Hills Country (sec. bd. dirs.), Hartley Hills Ladies' Golf Assn., Eastern Ind. Ladies' Golf Assn., Ind. Women's Golf Assn. Methodist. Avocation: needlepoint. Home: 11 Es Mkt Hagerstown IN 47346 E-mail: lots-a-dots@msn.com

SHERRY, WILLIAM F. airport executive; Asst. city mgr., Vero Beach, Fla.; mgr. Vero Beach Airport, 1987—; dir. aviation Fla. Dept. of Transp., 1996-97; mgr. airports Broward County, Ft. Lauderdale, Fla., 1997-98, aviation dir., 1998—. Office: Aviation Dept Ft Lauderdale/Hollywood Internat Airport 320 Terminal Dr Fort Lauderdale FL 33315*

SHERTZER, BRUCE ELDON, education educator; b. Bloomfield, Ind., Jan. 11, 1928; s. Edwin Franklin and Lois Belle S.; m. Carol Mae Rice, Nov. 24, 1948; children: Sarah Ann, Mark Eldon. BS, Ind. U., 1952, MD, 1953, EdD, 1958. Tchr., counselor Martinsville (Ind.) High Sch., 1952-56; dir. div. guidance Ind. Dept. Pub. Instrn., 1956-58; assoc. dir. project guidance of superior students North Central Assn. Coll. and Secondary Sch., 1958-60; asst. prof. Purdue U., 1960—, assoc. prof., 1962-65, prof., 1965-95, head dept. ednl. studies, 1989-95, prof. emeritus of counseling, 1995—. Vis. prof. ednl. psychology U. Hawaii, 1967; Fulbright sr. lectr., Reading, Eng., 1967-68; vis. prof. U. So. Calif. Overseas Grad. Program, 1975, 82; chmn. Nat. Adv. Council for Career Edn., 1976 Author: Career Exploration and Planning 1973, 2d edit., 1976, Fundamentals of Counseling, 3d edit., 1980, Fundamentals of Guidance, 4th edit., 1981, Individual Appraisal, 1979, Career Planning, 3d edit., 1985, also articles. Chmn. bd. trustees Found. Am. Assn. of Counseling and Devel., 1986-87. With AUS, 1946-47. Mem. Am. Counseling Assn. (pres. 1973-74, Disting. Profl. Svc. award 1986). Home: 1620 Western Dr West Lafayette IN 47906-2236 Office: Purdue U Liberal Arts Edn Bldg West Lafayette IN 47907

SHERTZER, HOWARD GRANT, health educator; b. N.Y.C., Oct. 9, 1945; s. Sidney Maurice and Terry June (Rosenbaum) S.; m. Ellen Lea Shertzer, June 22, 1968; children: Kyle William, Kevin Maurice. BS in Physiology, U. Mich., 1967; PhD in Cell Biology, UCLA, 1973. Postdoctoral fellow Cornell U., Ithaca, N.Y., 1973-75; asst. prof. environ. health Tex. A&M U., College Station, 1975-79; assoc. prof. environ. health U. Cin., 1979—. Vis. prof. Karolinska Inst., Stockholm, 1989; cons. in field. Contbr. articles to profl. jours., chpts. to books. NIH grantee, 1976—. Mem. Am. Bd. Master Educators (bd. dirs. 1980—), Am. Soc. Pharmacology and Exptl. Therapeutics, Soc. Toxicology. Avocations: soccer, racquetball, banjo, music. Office: U Cin Med Ctr 3223 Eden Ave Cincinnati OH 45267-0001

SHERTZER, KENNETH EUGENE, accountant; b. Lancaster, Pa., May 3, 1973; s. Daniel and Mary Ellen (Myer) Shertzer. BBA, minor in computer sci., Millersville (Pa.) U., 1995. CPA Pa. Fin. analyst, internal auditor Cardinal Technologies, Inc., Lancaster, Pa., 1995-97; sr. acct. Flinchbaugh Engring. Inc., York, 1997-99; staff acct. Beard, Miller and Co., LLP, Lancaster, 1999—. Avocations: rock climbing, hockey. Home and Office: 212 Locust St Lancaster PA 17602

SHERVA, DENNIS G. retired investment company executive; b. Mpls., Dec. 3, 1942; s. Garfield Theodore and Dorothy Genevive (Oberlander) S.; m. Cathleen Marybeth Tischer, Oct. 15, 1965 BA, U. Minn., 1964; MA, Wayne State U., 1965. Chartered fin. analyst. Fin. analyst 1st Nat. Bank, Mpls., 1965-67; fin. analyst Honeywell, Inc., 1967; v.p. Smith, Barney & Co., N.Y.C., 1967-71, Baker, Weeks & Co., N.Y.C., 1971-77; mng. dir. Morgan Stanley & Co., Inc., 1977—2000. Bd. dirs. Morgan Stanley Ventures, San Francisco, Morgan Stanley Venture Capital, N.Y.C., Morgan Stanley Asset Mgmt. Inc., N.Y.C. Recipient All-Am. Research Team 1st place award Instl. Investor Mag., 1979, 81, 83, 84, 85, 87 Mem.: Nat. Assn. Securities Dealers (instl. com. 1985—90), PGA West Club, Torrington Country Club. Home: 42 Old South Rd PO Box 30 Litchfield CT 06759-0030 Home (Winter): 54-087 Southern Hills La Quinta CA 92253

SHERVE-OSE, ANNE, music educator; b. Minot, N.D., Feb. 11, 1953; d. Albin Gustav and Alvhild Margaret (Slen) Sherve; m. Alan Kent Ose, Jan. 19, 1980; children: Samuel Sherve Ose, Rachel Sherve Ose. BA in Phys. Edn. and Health, St. Olaf Coll., 1975; MusB in Music Composition, Iowa State U., 1982; MA in Music Edn., U. St. Thomas, 1998. Cert. tchr., Iowa. Asst. instr. Minn. Outward Bound Sch., Ely, 1977; tchr. phys. edn. and music Am. Girls Sch., Izmir, Turkey, 1978-79; tchr. elem. music N.E. Hamilton Schs., Blairsburg, Iowa, 1985-88, St. Thomas Aquinas Sch., Webster City, 1992-98; dir. music Ellsworth C.C., Iowa Falls, 1998—. Tchr. Blairsburg Community Presch., 1982-85, Iowa. Church organist Blairsburg United Ch. of Christ, 1980—; cmty. chorus dir. Williams (Iowa) Cmty. Chorus, 1988—; bd. dirs. William Pub. Libr., 1990-98; asst. scout leader Girl Scout Troop 234, Webster City, 1992-97. Home: 2230 Wilson Ave Williams IA 50271-7571 Office: Ellsworth CC 1100 College Ave Iowa Falls IA 50126

SHERVHEIM, LLOYD OLIVER, insurance company executive, lawyer; b. Kensington, Minn., June 22, 1928; s. Lewis and Ruth Amanda (Thronson) S.; m. Ruth Elaine Rhodes, Oct. 29, 1950; children: Daniel, Anne, Heidi, Garold, Robette, Shanna, Bryce. Student, Gustavus Adolphus Coll., 1948-50, U. Minn., 1950-52; BS, LL.B., William Mitchell Coll. Law, 1958. Bar: Minn. 1959. Supr., asst. to corp. sec. Investors Diversified Services, Inc., 1952-59; legal counsel Investors Syndicate Life Ins. Co., Mpls., 1959-66; gen. counsel Western Life Ins. Co., St. Paul, 1966-72; corporate sec. St. Paul Cos., Inc., 1969-82, chief legal officer, 1972-78, v.p. legal affairs, 1978-85, sr. v.p. law, corporate sec., 1985-89. Corporate sec. St. Paul Fire and Marine Ins. Co., 1969-82; dir. St. Paul Ins. Co., Tex., St. Paul Surplus Lines Ins. Co., St. Paul Mercury Ins. Co., St. Paul Guardian Ins. Co., St. Paul Ins. Co., Ill. Charter patron Minn. Theatre Co., 1958; mem. Lake Elmo City Council, 1970-78; past chmn. protection open space task force Met. Open Space Adv. Bd., 1969-70; trustee William Mitchell Coll. Law, 1981-92, vice chmn., 1983-86, chmn., 1986-89; dir. Minn. Citizens Council on Crime and Justice, 1986-89. With U.S. Army, 1946-48. Mem. ABA, Minn. Bar Assn. (chmn. ins. com. 1964-65, gov. 1980-81), Fed. Bar Assn. (pres. Minn. chpt. 1978-79), Ramsey County Bar Assn. (ethics com. 1978-80), Assn. Life Ins. Counsel, Am. Soc. Corp. Secs., Am. Life Conv. (v.p. Minn. chpt. 1969-71), Am. Judicature Soc., Corp. Counsel Assn. Minn. (dir., pres. 1979-80), Pool and Yacht Club (St. Paul). Lutheran (chmn. bd. trustees). Died July 20, 2001.

SHERWIN, JAMES TERRY, lawyer; b. N.Y.C., Oct. 25, 1933; s. Oscar and Stella (Zins) S.; m. Judith Johnson, June 21, 1955 (div. Apr. 1984); children—Miranda, Alison, Galen; m. Hiroko Inouye, June 15, 1985. BA, Columbia U., 1953, LLB (Stone scholar), 1956. Bar: N.Y. 1956, U.S. Supreme Ct. 1963. Assoc. Kaye, Scholer, Fierman, Hays & Handler, N.Y.C., 1957-60; with GAF Corp., 1960-83, 84-90, assoc. counsel, gen. mgr. European ops., 1969-71, group v.p. photography, 1971-74, exec. v.p. fin. and adminstrn., legal and investment svcs., 1974-83, vice chmn., chief adminstrv. officer Wayne, N.J., 1984-90; exec. v.p., CFO Triangle Industries, Inc., 1983-84, Hunter-Douglas N.V., 1991-99, bd. dirs., 1999—. Bd. dirs. Internat. Rescue Com., chmn. exec. com., v.p. to 1990; mem. coun. U. Bath, 2001--. Lt. comdr. USCGR, 1956-57. U.S. intercollegiate chess champion, 1951-53, N.Y. State champion, 1951, U.S. speed champion, 1956-57, 59-60, internat. master. Mem. Am. Chess Found. (pres., bd. dirs. to 1990), Marshall (N.Y.) Chess Club (pres. 1967-69, gov. to 1990), Phi Beta Kappa. Home: The Chase Winsley Nr Bradford-on-Avon Wiltshire BA15 2LX England E-mail: jsherwin@thechase99.freeserve.co.uk

SHERWOOD, ALLEN JOSEPH, lawyer; b. Salt Lake City, Sept. 26, 1909; s. Charles Samuel and Sarah (Abramson) Shapiro; m. Edith Ziff, Jan. 19, 1941; children— Mary (Mrs. John Marshall), Arthur Lawrence Student, UCLA, 1927-30; AB, LLB, U. So. Calif., 1933. Bar: Calif. 1933, U.S. Supreme Ct. 1944. Pvt. practice law, L.A., 1933-54, Beverly Hills, 1954-95. Legal counsel Internat. Family Planning Rsch. Assn., Inc., 1970-76; bd. dirs. Family Planning Ctrs. Greater L.A., Inc., 1968-84, pres., 1973-76 Mem. editorial bd. So. Calif. Law Rev., 1932-33. Contbr. articles to profl. jours. Mem. Calif. Atty. Gen.'s Vol. Adv. Coun. and its legis. subcom., 1972-78 Mem. Med.-Legal Soc. So. Calif. (bd. dirs. 1966-74), ABA, L.A. County Bar Assn., Beverly Hills Bar Assn., State Bar of Calif., Am. Arbitration Assn. (nat. panel arbitrators 1965—), Order of Coif, Tau Delta Phi, Brentwood Country Club (L.A.), Masons. Home: 575 Moreno Ave Los Angeles CA 90049-4840

SHERWOOD, ARTHUR MORLEY, lawyer; b. Buffalo, Oct. 3, 1939; s. Frederick T. and Neva E. (Merrill) S.; m. Karen H. Hilstad, Apr. 2, 1964; children: Laurel Ann, Carolyn Margaret. BA, Harvard U., 1961; JD, U. Mich., 1964. Bar: Mich. 1965, N.Y. 1967, U.S. Supreme Ct. 1989. Law clk. to Hon. Ralph M. Freeman U.S. Dist. Ct. (ea. dist.) Mich., Detroit, 1964-66; pntr. Phillips, Lytle, Hitchcock, Blaine & Huber, Buffalo, 1971-99. Contbr. articles to Trusts and Estates, N.Y. State Bar Jour. and N.Y. Tax Svc. Mem. adv. com. N.Y. State Legislature on N.Y. Estates, Powers and Trusts Law, Surrogate's Ct. Procedure. Fellow Am. Coll. Trust and Estate Counsel, N.Y. Bar Found.; mem. N.Y. State Bar Assn. (chairperson trusts and estates law sect. 1987). Home: 3770 Windover Dr Hamburg NY 14075-6322 Office: Phillips Lytle Hitchcock Blaine & Huber 3400 HSBC Ctr Buffalo NY 14203-2887

SHERWOOD, DONALD LEWIS, congressman; b. Nicholson, Pa., Mar. 5, 1941; s. Walter A. and Doris (Williams) S.; m. Carol Evans, 1973; children: Jesse, Dana, Maria. BA in Econs., Dartmouth Coll., 1963. Founder, pres. Sherwood Chevrolet, Tunkhannock, Pa., 1967—; mem. U.S. Congress from 10th Pa. dist., 1999—; mem. appropriations com. Expanded Sherwood Chevrolet to include Horiacher-Sherwood Forestry Equipment; ptnr. in Sun Auto Group, Clarks Summit, Sun Buick/Pontiac/GMC, Moosic. Appointed to Tunkhannock Area Sch. Bd, 1975; subsequently elected 6 times; served as pres., 1992-98. Pres. Wyoming County Indsl. Found., Wyoming County UnitedFund; bd. dirs. Triton House Fireman's Relief Assn., Wyoming County C. of C. Elected to Ho. Reps. Nov. 3, 1998, replacing Joseph M. McDade (R-Clarks Summit)who retired after 36 yrs. in Congress. 10th Congl. Dist. includes the counties of Bradford, Lackawanna, Pike, Sullivan, Susquehanna, Wayne and Wyoming and portions of Lycoming and Monroe counties. Dir. Pa. Chevrolet Dealers Area Mktg. Group; v.p. N.E. Pa. Chevrolet Dealers Assn.; mem. Pa. Hardwood Lumber Mfrs. Assn., Pa. Farmers Assn. Republican. Avocation: raises and shows Belgian horses. Office: 1223 Longworth Ho Office Bldg Washington DC 20515-0001*

SHERWOOD, JAMES ALAN, physician, scientist, educator; b. Oneida County, N.Y., Jan. 4, 1953; s. Robert Merriam and Sally (Trevett-Edgett) S. AB, Hamilton Coll., 1974; MD, Columbia U., 1978. Diplomate Nat. Bd. Med. Examiners, Am. Bd. Internal Medicine. Intern Duke U. Med. Ctr., Durham, N.C., 1978-79; resident physician Strong Meml. Hosp., Rochester, N.Y., 1979-81; fellow U. Rochester Sch. Medicine and Dentistry, 1981-83, NIH, Bethesda, Md., 1983-86; rsch. investigator Walter Reed Army Inst. Rsch., Washington, 1986-92; vis. scientist Clin. Rsch. Ctr., Kenya Med. Rsch. Inst., Nairobi, 1987-92; physician Saradidi Rural Health Programme, Nyilima, Kenya, 1987-92; rsch. cons. Rockville, Md., 1992-93; physician St. Mary's Hosp., Waterbury, Conn., 1993—; clin. instr. Sch. Medicine, Yale U., 1993-98; pvt. practice Conn., 1998—. Founding donor Yale Univ.-Kazan State Medical Univ. Russian Fedn. fellow exchange program. Contbr. chpt. to book, articles to profl. jours. Cmty. svc. vol. The Door, N.Y.C., 1976-77; vol. physician Washington Free Clinic, 1985-87; charity Sisters of St. Joseph of Chambery, 1993-98. Lt. col. Med. Corps, USAR, 1986-92. Recipient Norton prize in chemistry, 1974, Underwood prize in chemistry, 1974. Fellow Am. Coll. Physicians; mem. Med. Soc. D.C., Am. Fedn. Clin. Rsch., Am. Soc. Tropical Medicine and Hygiene, Conn. State Med. Soc., New Haven County Med. Assn., Muthaiga Club, Phi Beta Kappa, Sigma Xi. Avocations: drawing, book collecting. Office: PO Box 112 Waterbury CT 06720-0112

SHERWOOD, JAMES WEBSTER, III, author, limousine company owner; b. Hollywood, Calif., May 18, 1936; s. James Webster Sherwood Jr. and Vesta Graybeal Hughes; m. Valdi Hiesinger, Apr. 17, 1964 (div. 1972); m. Marylou Coddington Lemke, July 4, 1972 (div. 1989); m. Karyn Virginia Lindig, Mar. 18, 1990; children: Veronica E.C. Sherwood, Alexandra C.E. Sherwood Patterson, Roxanna Z.S.R., Christopher Michael De Santis, James Webster IV, George Marshall De Santis. Student, Choate Sch., U. Chgo., 1954-55; BL, U. Paris, 1963. Reporter, columnist San Mateo (Calif.) Times, Burlingame Advance, 1951-52; mng. editor Chgo. Rev. Mag., 1954-55; producer Myers-Sherwood Pictures, Inc., Chgo., 1955; editor Trans World Pictures, Inc., 1955; editor, columnist Westchester News-Advertiser, L.A., 1956-57; prodn. asst. Cecil B. DeMille-Paramount Pictures, Hollywood, Calif., 1957-59; v.p., gen. mgr. Smith Limousine, N.Y.C., 1977-85; pres., owner Sherwood Justice & Barton Limousine Corp., 1985—; dir. Hamilton Manf. Corp., Holland, Ohio. Producer, dir. Sherwood Films, Hollywood, 1958-60; cons. on Tom Jones, 1961; adaptor The Sicilian Clan, 1966; producer After Laughter, 1968, others; founder, pub. Opus Books. Author: Dining on Thorns, 1996, Some Sonnets of Flame & Flower, 1998; syndicated columnist 11 western states for Christian Sci. Monitor, Hungry Horse (Mont.) News, Hellenic Rev., 1956-58; editor Popular Libr., 1970-72; biographic researcher Holt, Rinehart & Winston, 1970-72; journalist Ladies Home Jour., Village Voice, N.Y., 1972-73; author: (verse play) The Wooed Wife, 1957; author: 101 Sonnets of Sex, God, The Circus and Love, 2d edit., 1959, (novel) Stradella, 1961, others. Trustee Shakespeare Oxford Soc. Recipient Nat. Book award for best translation preface to (with Ralph Manheim/Castle to Castle), 1970, John Dos Passos award for Creative Writing, 1987. Republican. Episcopalian. Avocation: walking. Home: Grand Central Five Central Dr Plandome NY 11030-1408 Office: Sherwood Limousines PO Box 925 Plainview NY 11803-0925

SHERWOOD, JOAN KAROLYN SARGENT, retired career counselor; b. Wichita, Kans., July 11, 1934; d. James Wirth and Ann K. (Freeburg) Sargent; m. Howard Kenneth Sherwood, Jan. 26, 1956 (div. 1966); children: Diane Elizabeth, Karolyn Sherwood, David Matthew. BS, Kans. State U., 1956; MA, Wichita State U., 1964; PhD, U. Kans., 1978. Asst. dir. student fin. aid U. Kans., Lawrence, 1973-78, asst. vice chancellor/student affairs, 1978-81, U. Mo., Kansas City, 1981-84; v.p. student affairs Western Wash. U., Bellingham, 1984-87; pres./owner Corp. Tng. Assurance, Kansas City, 1987-95; career coord. Park Univ., Parkville, Mo., 1995-01; ret., 2001. Program chair Phi Delta Kappa, Lawrence, 1983-84; initiation chair Phi Kappa Phi, Kansas City, 1983-84; organizer Singles Connection, Kansas City, 1983-84; creator SummerStart, Bellingham, 1988-89. Contbr.: Theatre Companies of the World, 1986; female voice: (film) Junction City, 1973; editor Case Studies in the Governance of Higher Edn., 1982, Nat. Assn. of Student Personnel Adminstrs. Alcohol Policies and Practices Among Colls. and Univs., 1987. Long range planning coord. Ch. Redeemer, Kansas City, 1994; workshop facilitator South Side Jr. C. of C., Kansas City, 1991; presenter Centurians, Kansas City, 1982; spkr. Pi Lambda Theta, 1983; vol., resident mgr. Hillcrest Ministries, 1996-99. NDEA fellow, 1969. Mem. ASTD, Phi Kappa Phi. Democrat. Roman Catholic. Avocations: creative writing, reading, films. Home: Unit 2204 2421 Yellowstone Wichita KS 67215 Office: Vista Vols Cmtys in Schs Alcott Acad 3400 E Murdock Wichita KS 67208

SHERWOOD, KENNETH WESLEY, information technology executive, consultant; b. Denver, Nov. 15, 1943; s. Richard Wesley Sherwood and Mary Ellen (Sorling) McClure; m. Virginia Kay Betts, June 24, 1966; children: Jeremy James, Pamela Ann. BS summa cum laude, Met. State Coll., Denver, 1971. Missile mechanic helper Martin Marietta, Littleton, Colo., 1963-64, electronics technician, 1964, communications ctr. operator, 1968-69; systems rep. Burroughs Corp., Denver, 1971-76, systems supr. Las Vegas, Nev., 1976-79, dept. mgr. Atlanta, 1979-83, mgr. support ctr., 1983-85; sr. mgr. profl. svcs. UNISYS, 1985-2000; project mgr. Micromuse, 2000—. Cons. in pers. computer and check processing fields. Sgt. U.S. Army, 1964-68, Tokyo. Methodist. Avocations: computers, handyman activities, fishing. Office: Micromuse 5271 Lanford Springs Ct SW Lilburn GA 30047-6551 E-mail: ken.sherwood@attbi.com

SHERWOOD, LOUIS MAIER, physician, scientist, pharmaceutical company executive; b. N.Y.C., Mar. 1, 1937; s. Arthur Joseph and Blanche (Burger) S.; m. Judith Brimberg, Mar. 27, 1966; children: Jennifer Beth, Arieh David. AB with honors, Johns Hopkins U., 1957; MD with honors, Columbia U., 1961. Diplomate Am. Bd. Internal Medicine, Subsplty. Bd. in Endocrinology and Metabolism. Intern Presbyn. Hosp., N.Y.C., 1961-62, asst. resident in medicine, 1962-63; clin. assoc. research fellow Nat. Heart Inst., NIH, Bethesda, Md., 1963-66; NIH trainee endocrinology and metabolism Coll. Physicians and Surgeons, Columbia U., N.Y.C., 1966-68; assoc. medicine Beth Israel Hosp. and Harvard Med. Sch., Boston, 1968-69; chief endocrinology Beth Israel Hosp., 1968-72; asst. prof. medicine Harvard U., 1969-71, assoc. prof., 1971-72; physician-in-chief, chmn. dept. medicine Michael Reese Hosp. and Med. Ctr., Chgo., 1972-80; prof. medicine, div. biol. scis. Pritzker Sch. Medicine, U. Chgo., 1972-80; Ted and Florence Baumritter prof. medicine and biochemistry Albert Einstein Coll. Medicine, 1980-88, vis. prof. medicine, 1989—, chmn. dept. medicine, 1980-87; physician-in-chief Montefiore Hosp. and Med. Ctr., N.Y.C., 1980-87; adj. prof. medicine U. Pa., 1993—. Sr. v.p. med. and sci. affairs Merck, Sharp & Dohme Internat., 1987-89; exec. v.p. worldwide devel. Merck, Sharp & Dohme Rsch. Labs., 1989-92, sr. v.p. U.S. Med. and Sci. Affairs Merck Human Health, 1992-2002; pres. Medsa, LLC, 2002—; Josiah Macy Jr. Found. fellow and vis. scientist Weizmann Inst., Israel, 1978-79; assoc. mem. bd. on subspecialty endocrinology and metabolism Am. Bd. Internal Medicine, 1977-83; bd. dirs. UROCOR Inc.; med. adv. bd. HPR, 1996-99; pres., chief med. officer Bone Measurement Inst., 1996-2002. Editor: Beth Israel seminars New Eng. Jour. Medicine, 1968-71; mem. editorial bd. Endocrinology, 1969-73; assoc. editor Metabolism, 1970-85, Gen. Medicine B Study Sect., NIH, 1975-79; mem. editorial bd. Yr. in Endocrinology, 1976-86, Calcified Tissue Internat., 1978-80, Internal Medicine Alert, 1979-89; contbr. numerous articles on endocrinology, protein hormones, calcium metabolism and ectopic proteins to jours. Trustee Michael Reese Med. Ctr., 1974-77; mem. vis. council CUNY Med. Sch., 1986—; mem. alumni council Columbia Coll. Physicians and Surgeons, 1986—; bd. dirs. Jewish Fedn. Phila., 1997—, Alliance on Aging Rsch., 1997-2002. Served as surgeon USPHS, 1963-66. Recipient Joseph Mather Smith prize for outstanding alumni research Coll. Physicians and Surgeons, Columbia U., 1972, Sr. Class Teaching award U. Chgo., 1976, 77, Spl. Achievement award Assn. Profs. Medicine, 2002; grantee USPHS, 1968-88. Fellow: ACP (Outstanding Contbn. to Internal Medicine award 1987); mem.: AAAS, Nat. Rsch. Adv. Com. (com. on rsch. integrity 2001—02), Clin. Rsch. Roundtable (IOM 2000 2000—03), Chgo. Soc. Internal Medicine, Assn. Program Dirs. Internal Medicine (coun. 1979—85, pres. 1983—84), Ctrl. Soc. Clin. Rsch., Mass. Med. Soc., Am. Soc. Hypertension (bd. dirs. 1992—97), N.Y. Acad. Medicine (bd. dirs. 1991—95), Am. Acad. Pharm. Physicians (trustee 2000—, v.p. strategic alliances and planning 2000—, Lifetime Achievement award in Pharm. Medicine 2001), Am. Physicians Fellowship for Medicine in Israel (pres. 1993—97, Disting. Med. Svc. award 1998), Endocrine Soc., Assn. Am. Physicians, Am. Soc. Clin. Investigation (pres. 1982—83), Am. Soc. Biol. Chemists, Am. Inst. Chemists, Am. Acad. Pharm. Physics (v.p. and dir. strategic planning 1999—), Am. Fedn. Clin. Rsch. (bd. dirs. Found. 1989—92, Spl. Recognition award 1992), Interurban Clin. Club, Alpha Omega Alpha, Phi Beta Kappa. Achievements include research in protein and polypeptide hormones: structure, function and regulation of secretion; molecular studies of hormone biosynthesis; clinical pharmacology, new drug development, outcomes research and disease management. Office: Medsa 7598 Playa Rienta Way Delray Beach FL 33446 E-mail: lou@medsa.org., sherwool@earthlink.net. *To be a successful leader, you must be willing to surround yourself with outstanding individuals, give them your full support and enjoy their growth.*

SHERWOOD, PATRICIA WARING, artist, educator; b. Columbia, S.C., Dec. 19, 1933; d. Clark du Val and Florence (Yarbrough) Waring; widowed; children: Cheryl Sherwood Kraft, Jana Sherwood Kern, Marikay Sherwood Taitt. BFA magna cum laude, Calif. State U., Hayward, 1970; MFA, Mills Coll., Oakland, Calif., 1974; postgrad., San Jose State U., 1980-86. Cert. tchr., Calif. Tchr. De Anza Jr. Coll., Cupertino, Calif., 1970-78, Foothill Jr. Coll., Los Altos, 1972-78, West Valley Jr. Coll., Saratoga, 1978—. Artist-in-residence Centrum Frans Masereel, Kasterlee, Belgium, 1989. One-woman shows include Triton Mus., Santa Clara, Calif., 1968, 2002, RayChem Corp., Sunnyville, Calif., 1969, Palo Alto (Calif.) Cultural Ctr., 1977, Los Gatos (Calif.) Mus., 1992, Stanford U. faculty club, Palo Alto, 1993, d.p. Fong Gallery, San Jose, Calif., 1995, 97, Heritage Bank, San Jose, 1997, City Jr. Coll., d.p. Fong Gallery, San Jose, 1997, City Coll., San Jose, Calif., 1997, West Valley Coll., Saratoga, Calif., 1998, Mus. West, Palo Alto, 2000-2001, Triton Mus., Santa Clara, 2001; exhibited in group shows at Tressider Union Stanford U., 1969, Oakland (Calif.) Mus. Kaiser Ctr., 1969, Sonoma (Calif.) State Coll., 1969, Bank Am., San Francisco, 1969, Alrich Gallery, San Francisco, U. Calif. Santa Clara, 1967, Charles and Emma Frye Mus., Seattle, 1968, Eufrat Gallery DeAnza Coll., Cupertino, 1975, San Jose Mus. Art, 1976, Lytton Ctr., Palo Alto, 1968 (1st award), Zellerbach Ctr., San Francisco, 1970, Works Gallery, San Jose, 1994, Inst. Contemporary Art, San Jose, 1997, Triton Mus. Art, Santa Clara, Calif., 1997, 98, San Jose Inst. Contemporary Art, 1998, San Jose City Coll. Artists Forum, 1998, West Valley Jr. Coll., Saratoga, Calif., 1998 ; represented in permanent collections Mills Coll., Bank Am., San Francisco, Heritage Bank, San Jose, Stanford U., Palo Alto, Calif., San Jose U., Smithsonian Inst. Nat. Mus. Am. Art, WAshington, 2002. Art judge student show Stanford U., Palo Alto, 1977; mem. d.p. Fong Gallery, San Jose, Calif., 1994, J.J. Brooking Gallery, San Francisco, Mus. West Gallery, Palo Alto, Calif. Nat. Endowment for Arts/We. States Art Fedn. fellow, 1994. Mem. Calif. Print Soc., Womens Caucus for Arts, Internat. Platform Assn. Home: 1500 Arriba Ct Los Altos CA 94024-5956

SHERWOOD, ROBERT PETERSEN, retired sociology educator; b. Black Diamond, Wash., May 17, 1932; s. James Brazier and Zina (Petersen) S.; m. Merlene Burningham, Nov. 21, 1951; children: Robert Lawrence, Richard William, Rolene, RaNae. BS, U. Utah, 1956, MS, 1957; EdD, U. Calif., Berkeley, 1965. Tchr. Arden-Carmichael Sch. Dist., Carmichael, Calif., 1957-59, vice prin. jr. high, 1960-61, prin. jr. high, 1962-65; v.p., prin. San Juan Unified Sch. Dist., Sacramento, 1966-70; assoc. prof. Calif. State U., 1966-71; dir. outreach progs. Am. River Coll., 1971-73, acting assoc. dean of instrn., 1973-74, prof. sociology, 1970-92, chmn. sociology/anthropology dept., 1980-86, retired, 1992. Pres. acad. senate Am. River Coll., 1990-91. With USN, 1953-55. Recipient Merit Recognition award, Boy Scouts Am., 1989. Mem. NEA, Calif. Tchrs. Assn., Faculty Assn. Calif. Community Colls., Western Assn. Schs. and Colls., Calif. Fedn. Coll. Profs., Phi Delta Kappa (life). Mem. Lds Ch. Avocations: reading, writing, woodworking, travel. Home: 4053 Esperanza Dr Sacramento CA 95864-3069

SHERWOOD, SHARON DEE, association executive; b. Chadron, Nebr., Oct. 24, 1944; d. George Meredith and Franell (Fritts) Porter; m. William H. Sherwood, Nov. 11, 1976; children: Lynette M., Dawn D., T.J. BS in Biology, U. Wyo., 1971, BA in Edn., 1972; MBA in Healthcare, City U. Bellevue, Wash., 1989. Instr. Griffin Bus. Coll., Bellevue, 1987-88; acct. Mended Hearts #143, Redmond, 1987-89; mktg. intern ARC, Seattle, 1989; site coord. Group Health Coop., 1988-90; area recruitment coord. Campfire, Bellevue, 1990-91; asst. adminstr. Exeter House, Seattle, 1991-92; program coord. med. Amasia Coll., 1992-93; ind. mgmt. cons. Sherwood Cons., Portland, Oreg.; transp. coord. Advocates for Women in Sci., Engring. & Math. Oreg. Health Sci. U., 1997—. Distbr./mgr. Retail Showcase Internat., 1998—. Contbr. articles to profl. jours. Chmn. pre-parade banquet Seafair Torchlight Parade, Seattle, 1988-91; banquet chmn. Masquerade Ball, Bellevue Community Coll., 1986-87; workshop leader Coord. Expanding Horizons Workshop, Bellevue, 1986-87; dist. capt. March of Dimes, Redmond; area chmn. Nat. Heart Assn., Seattel; sec. 2d v.p. PTA; rec. sec. city coun. meetings, Kirkland, Wash., 1989-92; park ranger Wind Cave Nat. Park; forester Bur. Land Mgmt., Soil Conservation Svc.; hosp. vol. Recipient Cert. Teaching Excellence, Griffin Bus Coll., 1988, letter of commendation for rescuing visitors from flooded cave. Mem. AAUW (Nat. Recognition award., v.p., sec.), Portland Rose Soc. Avocations: camping, crocheting. Home: 2923 113th Ave SE Everett WA 98205-2945

SHERZER, HARVEY GERALD, lawyer; b. Phila., May 19, 1944; s. Leon and Rose (Levin) S.; m. Susan Bell, Mar. 28, 1971; children: Sheri Ann, David Lloyd. BA, Temple U., 1965; JD with honors, George Washington U., 1968. Bar: D.C. 1970, U.S. Ct. Appeals (D.C. cir.) 1970, U.S. Ct. Fed. Claims 1970, U.S. Ct. Appeals (fed. cir.) 1970, U.S. Supreme Ct. 1974. Law clk. to trial judges U.S. Ct. Fed. Claims, Washington, 1968-69; law clk. to chief judge U.S. Ct. Appeals for Fed. Cir., 1969-70; assoc. Sellers, Conner & Cuneo, 1970-75, ptnr., 1975-80, McKenna, Conner & Cuneo, Washington, 1980-82, Pettit & Martin, Washington, 1982-85, Howrey & Simon, Washington, 1985-2000, Howrey Simon Arnold & White, Washington, 2000—. Adv. bd. The Govt. Contractor, 1996-99. Author: (with others) A Complete Guide to the Department of Defense Voluntary Disclosure Program, 1996; contbr. articles to profl. jours. Office: Greenberg Trourig LLP 1750 Tysons Blvd Ste 1200 Mc Lean VA 22102 E-mail: sherzerh@gtlaw.com.

SHESTACK, ALAN, museum administrator; b. N.Y.C., June 23, 1938; s. David and Sylvia P. (Saffran) S.; m. Nancy Jane Davidson, Sept. 24, 1967. BA, Wesleyan U., 1961, DFA (hon.), 1978; MA, Harvard U., 1963. Mus. curator graphic art Nat. Gallery Art, Washington, 1965-67; assoc. curator prints and drawings Yale Art Gallery, New Haven, 1967-68, curator prints and drawings, 1968-71, dir., 1971-85; adj. prof. history of art Yale U., 1971-85; dir. Mpls. Inst. Art, 1985-87, Boston Mus. Fine Arts, 1987-93; dep. dir. Nat. Gallery of Art, Washington, 1994—. Mem. adv. com. Art Mus., Princeton, 1972-75; mem. vis. com. Harvard U. Art Mus., 1990-95, Davis Mus. Wellesley Coll., 1997—; mem. mus. panel Nat. Endowment for the Arts, 1974-77; mem. com. prints and illustrated books Mus. Modern Art, N.Y.C., 1972—; mem. Fed. Arts and Artifacts Indemnification Panel, 1979-83. Author: Fifteenth Century Engravings of Northern Europe, 1967, The Engravings of Martin Schongauer, 1968, Master LCZ and Master WB, 1971, Exhibitions Organized and Catalogued: Master E.S, 1967, The Danube School, 1969, Hans Baldung Grien, Prints and Drawings, 1981, (exhbn. catalog) Art for the Nation, 2000; contbr. articles to profl. jours. Woodrow Wilson fellow Harvard U., 1963, David E. Finley fellow, 1963-65. Mem. Print Coun. Am. (bd. dirs., v.p. 1970-71), Coll. Art Assn. (bd. dirs. 1972-76), Am. Assn. Mus., Am. Fedn. Arts (trustee 1981-94), Alpha Delta Phi, Phi Beta Kappa. Office: Nat Gallery Of Art Washington DC 20565-0001

SHESTACK, JEROME JOSEPH, lawyer; b. Atlantic City, Feb. 11, 1925; s. Isidore and Olga (Shankman) Shestack; m. Marciarose Schleifer, Jan. 28, 1951; children: Jonathan Michael, Jennifer. AB, U. Pa., 1944; LLB, Harvard U., 1949; LLD (hon.) , Dickinson Coll. Law, 1997, Stetson Sch. of Law, 1998, Whittier Coll. Law, 1998. Bar: Ill. 1950, Pa. 1952. Tchg. fellow Northwestern U. Law Sch., Chgo., 1949—50; asst. prof. law, faculty editor La. State Law Sch., Baton Rouge, 1950—52; dep. city solicitor City of Phila., 1952, 1st dep. solicitor, 1952—55; ptnr. Schnader, Harrison, Segal & Lewis, Phila. and Washington, 1956—91, Wolf, Block, Schorr & Solis-Cohen, Phila., 1991—. Adj. prof. law U. Pa., 1956; U.S. amb. to UN Human Rights Commn., 1979—80; U.S. del. to ECOSOC, UN, 1980; sr. U.S. del. to Helsinki Accords Conf., 1979—80; mem. U.S. Commn. on Improving Effectiveness of UN, 1989—; chmn. Internat. League Human Rights, 1973—94, hon. chmn., 1994—; U.S. del. to CSCE Conf., Moscow, 1991; founder, chmn. Lawyers Com. Internat. Human Rights, 1978—80, Jacob Blaustein Inst. Human Rights, 1988—92; mem. nat. adv. com. legal svcs. OEO, 1965—72; bd. dirs., exec. com. Lawyers Com. Civil Rights; mem. coun. Holocaust Mus., 1999—, exec. com., chair com. on conscience. Editor (with others): Rights of Americans, 1971, Human Rights, 1979, International Human Rights, 1985, Bill of Rights: A Bicentennial View, 1991, Understanding Human Rights, 1992, Thomas Jefferson: Lawyer, 1993, Francis Scott Key, 1994, Abraham Lincoln, Circuit Lawyer, 1994, The Holocaust, 1997, Moral Foundations of Human Rights, 1997, The Philosophy of Human Rights, 1997, W.B. Yeats, Poet of Passionate Intensity, 1997. Mem. exec. com. Nat. Legal Aid and Defender Assn., 1970—80; trustee Eleanor and Franklin Roosevelt Inst., 1986—; bd. govs. Tel Aviv U., 1983—, Hebrew U., 1969—; chmn. bd. dirs. Am. Poetry Ctr., 1976—91; trustee Free Libr. Phila., vice chmn., 1989—96; v.p. Am. Jewish Com., 1984—89. With USNR, 1943—46. Fellow Rubin, Columbia U. Law Sch., 1984, hon., U. Pa. Law Sch., 1980. Mem.: ABA (ho. of dels. 1971—73, 1977—, mem. jud. com. 1985—90, bd. govs. 1992—95, exec. com. 1994—95, pres.-elect 1996, pres. 1997—98, pres. ALI-ABA 1997—98), Nat. Conf. Bar Found. (bd. dirs. 1998—), Am. Soc. Internat. Law, Internat. Assn. Jewish Lawyers and Jurists (Am. Soc. pres. 2000—02), Am. Acad. Appellate Lawyers, Am. Coll. Trial Lawyers, Am. Arbitration Assn. (bd. dirs. 1999—), Am. Law Inst., Am. Soc. Internat. Law (exec. com. 1993—95, internat. com. jurists exec. com. 1998—, counsellor 1999—), Internat. Acad. Trial Lawyers, Internat. Bar Assn. (chmn. com. on human rights 1990—94, chmn. com. profl. ethics 2000—), Order of Coif. Home: Parkway House 2201 Pennsylvania Ave Philadelphia PA 19130-3513 Office: Wolf Block Schorr & Solis-Cohen 1650 Arch St Fl 20 Philadelphia PA 19103-2029 E-mail: jshestack@wolfblock.com.

SHETABI, HOUSHANG, physician; b. Rasht, Gilan, Iran, Nov. 26, 1939; came to U.S., 1968; s. Esmail and Hajar (Shamsi) S.; m. Parvin Sadighi, Sept. 14, 1965; children: makan, Barmak, Pegah. MD, U. Tehran, 1965. Diplomate in internal medicine, med. oncology and hematology Am. Bd. Internal Medicine. Intern Northeastern Hosp., Phila., 1968-69; resident in internal medicine Nassau Hosp., Mineola, N.Y., 1969-71, resident in endocrinology, 1971-72, fellow in med. oncology/hematology, 1972-74; chief divsn. oncology Am. Hosp., Teheran, 1975-78; med. oncologist and hematologist Affiliated Health Svcs. Hosp., Mt. Vernon, Wash., 1979—; attending hematologist/oncologist United Gen. Hosp., Sedro Woolley, 1979—, Skagit Valley Hosp., Mt. Vernon, 1979—. Co-founder North Puget Oncology, Skagit County, Wash., 1979. Contbr. articles to profl. jours. Fellow ACP; mem. AMA, Wash. State Med. Oncology Soc. (trustee 1993-96), Am. Soc. Clin. Oncology, Am. Soc. Hematology, S.W. Oncology Group, Assn. Cmty. Cancer Ctrs. Avocations: fishing, political debates, chess. Home: 406 Briar Rd Bellingham WA 98225-7810 Office: North Puget Oncology 1971 Hospital Dr Sedro Woolley WA 98284-9317

SHETH, JAGDISH NANCHAND, business administration educator; b. Rangoon, Burma, Sept. 3, 1938; came to U.S., 1961, naturalized, 1975. s. Nanchand Jivraj and Diwaliben Sheth; m. Madhuri Ratilal Shah, Dec. 22, 1962; children: Reshma J., Raju J. B.Com. with honors, U. Madras, 1960; MBA, U. Pitts., 1962; PhD, 1966. Research asso., asst. prof. Grad. Sch. Bus., Columbia U., 1963-65; asst. prof. M.I.T., 1965-66, Columbia U., 1966-69; asso. prof. bus. adminstrn. U. Ill., Urbana, 1969-71, acting head dept., 1970-72, prof. and research prof., 1971-73, I.B.A. Disting. prof. and research prof., 1973-79, Walter H. Stellner Disting. prof. and research prof., 1979-83; Robert E Brooker Disting. prof. mktg. and research U. So. Calif., Los Angeles, 1983-91; Charles H. Kellstadt prof. mktg. Emory U., Atlanta, 1991—. Founder, dir. Ctr. for Telecommunications Mgmt. U. So. Calif, 1985—, Ctr. Relationship Mktg. Emory U., 1992; vis. prof. Indian Inst. Mgmt., 1968; vis. lectr. Internat. Mktg. Inst., Harvard U., 1969; Albert Frey vis. prof. mktg. U. Pitts., 1974; condr. seminars for industry and govt.; cons. to industry. Author: (with John A. Howard) The Theory of Buyer Behavior, 1969, (with S.P. Sethi) Multinational Business Operations: Advanced Readings, 4 vols, 1973, (with A. Woodside and P. Bennett) Consumer and Industrial Buying Behavior, 1977; (with Bruce Newman): A Theory of Political Choice Behavior, 1986; (with Dennis Garrett) Marketing Theory, 1986; (with S. Ram) Bringing Innovation to Market; (with Gary Frazier) Theories of Marketing Practice; (with Milind Lele) The Customer is Key; editor: Models of Buyer Behavior, 1964, (with Peter L. Wright) Marketing Analysis for Societal Problems, 1974, Multivariable Methods for Market and Survey Research, 1977, Winning Back Your Market, 1984, (with David Gardener and Dennis Garrett) Marketing Theory: Evolution and Evaluation, 1988, also (with Abdol Reza and Goli Eslghi) 9 vols. on global bus., 1989-90, (with Bruce Newman and Barbara Gross) Consumption Values and Choice Behavior, 1990; (with Bruce Newman and B. Miltal) Customer Behavior: Consumer Behavior and Beyond, 1998; (with Banwari Mittal) Value Space, 2001; (with Rajendra Sisodia) The Rule of Twice, 2002; series editor Research in Marketing, 1978— , Research in Consumer Behavior, 1984—, Clients for Life, 2000, Handbook of Relationship Marketing, 2000, Internet Marketing, 2000; contbr. articles profl. jours. Recipient Viktor Mataja medal Austrian Rsch. Soc., 1976, Mktg. Educator award Sales and Mktg. Execs. Internat., 1991, 99; Mgmt. Program for Execs. fellow, S & H Green Stamps fellow, 1963-64, Disting. fellow Internat. Engring. Consortium, 1997. Fellow APA, Acad. Mktg. Sci. (Disting. fellow 1996, Mktg. Educator award 1989); mem. Am. Mktg. Assn. (P.D. Converse award 1992). Home: 1626 Mason Mill Rd NE Atlanta GA 30329-4133

SHETTY, JAYAKARA, surgeon; b. India, 1949; MD, Mysore U., India, 1973. Diplomate Am. Bd. Surgery. Intern U. Rochester, N.Y., 1977-78, resident, 1978-79, Waterbury (Conn.) Hosp., 1979-82; fellow in vascular surgery United Hosp.-N.J. Sch. Medicine, Newark, 1982-83; pvt. practice Waterbury. Mem. staff WaterburyHosp., St. Mary's Hosp., Watrbury. Fellow ACS, Royal Coll. Surgeons (Can.). Office: Waterbury Med Arts Bldg 134 Grandview Ave Ste 209 Waterbury CT 06708-2507

SHETTY, KAUP RAJMOHAN, endocrinologist, educator; b. Kaup, Karnataka, India, Mar. 3, 1942; came to U.S., 1966; s. Muddanna and Girija M. Shetty; m. Vasanthi R. Shetty; children: Sandeep, Suparna. MB BChir, Mysore Med. Coll., Karnataka, 1965. Diplomate Am. Bd. Internal Medicine, cert. in internal medicine, endocrinology and metabolism, geriatric medicine. Resident in internal medicine VA Med. Ctr., Chgo. and Milw., 1967-70; fellow in endocrinology and metabolism Med. Coll. Wis. and Affiliated Hosps., Milw., 1970-72, attending physician in endocrinology and metabolism, 1972—; attending physician in geriatrics and gerontology VA Med. Coll., 1991—; assoc. prof. medicine Med. Coll. Wis., 1991-95, prof. medicine, 1995-2000, prof. medicine emeritus, 2000—. Contbr. 10 chpts. to books, articles and abstracts to profl. jours. Fellow ACP, Royal Coll. Physicians Can., Am. Coll. Endocrinology; mem. Am. Diabetes Assn., Endocrine Soc., Am. Geriatric Soc., N.Y. Acad. Scis. Achievements include research in hormones and aging, post-polio syndrome, metabolic accompaniments of inactivity. Avocation: tennis. Office: VA Med Ctr 5000 W National Ave Milwaukee WI 53295-0001

SHETTY, MULKI RADHAKRISHNA, retired oncologist, consultant; b. Hiriadka, Karnataka, India, July 10, 1940; arrived in U.S., 1974; s. Sunderram and Kusumavati Shetty. MBBS, Stanley Med. Coll., Madras, 1964; DTM, U. Liverpool, Eng., 1968; LMCC, Med. Coun., Can., 1975. House surgeon and physician Bombay Hosp., 1965-66; sr. house officer Manor Pk. Hosp., Bristol, Eng., 1966-67, Torbay Hosp., 1967-68, St. Lukes Hosp., Huddersfield, 1969-70; sr. resident Gen. Hosp. Meml. U., New Foundland, 1971-72; intern Ottawa Gen. Hosp., 1972-73; fellow in chemotherapy Ont. Cancer Found., Ottawa, Can., 1973-74; fellow in clin. oncology U. Fla., Gainesville, 1974-75; attending oncologist N.W. Community Hosp., Arlington Heights, Ill., 1975-2000; ret., 2000. Cons. N.W. Cmty. Hosp., Arlington Heights, Ill., 1975—2000. Author: (book) Lung Cancer, 1980, Recent Advanced in Chemotherapy, 1985, Wildlife Adventures, 1997, Chicago, 1997; contbr. chapters to books, articles to profl. jours.; coined new word calcifectomy. Recipient Cert. for Oustanding Svc., Am. Cancer Soc., 1982. Hindu. Achievements include Reached the North Pole by icebreaker YAMAL, Aug. 5, 2001.

SHETTY, SANTOSH KUMAR, physician; b. Mangalore, India, 1942; came to U.S., 1965; MD, Govt. Med. Coll. Mysore U., India, 1965. Intern St. Peters Hosp., Albany, 1966-67; resident U. Presbyn. U. Hosp., Pitts., 1967-68, Boston City Hosp., 1968-70; with Holy Family Hosp. Cancer Mgmt. Ctr., Methuen, Mass., 1991—; asst. prof. Boston U., 1980—. Mem. AMA, Am. Coll. Surgeons, MassM, MassRA, NEROncS. Office: 70 East St Methuen MA 01844-4597

SHETTY, SUGANDH DASU, urological surgeon, researcher; b. Elinje, Karnataka, India, June 4, 1951; came to the U.S., 1991; s. Dasu and Meenakshi Shetty; m. Behroze Shetty, June 28, 1980; children: Varun, Zubin. MBBS, U. Bombay, 1975, MS, 1978; D in Urology, U. London, 1986. Gen. surgery resident King Edward Meml. Hosp., U. Bombay, 1975-78, lectr. surgery, 1978-79; gen. surgery resident Nat. Health Svc. Hosps., Wakefield, Manchester, Rhyl, U.K., 1979-84; urology residency Princess Royal Hosp., Hull, U.K., 1984-86; asst. prof. urology King Saud U., Abha, Saudi Arabia, 1986-91; urol. oncology fellow Henry Ford Hosp., Detroit, 1991-93, urology resident, 1993-98, sr. staff urologist, urol. rschr., 1998-2000; attending urologist William Beaumont Hosp., Royal Oak, Mich., 2000—. Contbr. articles to profl. jours. Fellow: Royal Coll. Surgeons Glasgow, Royal Coll. Surgeons Edinburgh; mem.: AMA, Am. Urol. Assn. Avocations: tennis, music, travel. Office: William Beaumont Hosp 3535 W 13 Mile Rd #501 Royal Oak MI 48073 E-mail: sshetty@beaumont.edu.

SHETTY, TARANATH, neurologist, educator; b. Mangalore, India, Apr. 29, 1938; s. Shankar and Bhavani Shetty; m. Urmila Shetty, Dec. 1972; children: Neeta, Teena, Geema. MBBS, Madras U., 1962; MD, Lucknow U., 1965. Diplomate Am. Bd. Pediatrics; diplomate in neurology with spl. competence in child neurology Am. Bd. Psychiatry and Neurology; diplomate with added qualification in clin. neurophysiology Am. Bd. Electroencephalography. Resident in pediatrics Children's Hosp. Med. Ctr., Boston, 1967-68, fellow in neurology, 1968-69; rsch. fellow in neurology Harvard U., 1968-69, tchg. fellow, 1971-72; resident in neurology Boston City Hosp., 1969-72; instr. Brown U., Providence, 1973-74, asst. prof., 1974-79, clin. assoc. prof., 1979—; dir. pediatric neurology R.I. Hosp., 1976—. Fellow Am. Acad. Neurology, Royal Coll. Physicians Can., Neurology Soc., Univ. Cub (Providence). Hindu. Home: 80 Clarendon Ave Providence RI 02906-5826 Office: 120 Dudley St Providence RI 02905-2436 E-mail: tara_shetty@hotmail.com.

SHEU, CHWEN, finance educator; b. Tainan, Taiwan, Dec. 21, 1956; arrived in U.S., 1983, naturalized, 2001; s. Hsing-ming Sheu and Su-jen Chen; m. Litzang Hsu; children: Scott, Shawn. PhD, Ohio State U., 1990. Prof. Kans. State U., Manhattan, 1990—. Author: (rsch. and tchg. materials) Introduction to Operations Management, 1999, (video course) Theory of Constraints - Introduction, 2000. Recipient Best Paper award, Acad. Mgmt. Ops. Divsn., 2001; fellow, Kans. State U., 1999. Mem.: Decision Scis. Inst. (Instrnl. Innovation award 2001), Alpha Delta (hon.). Office: Kans State U 101 Calvin Hall Manhattan KS 66506 Fax: 785-532-7024. Business E-Mail: csheu@ksu.edu.

SHEVACH, ETHAN MENAHEM, immunologist; b. Brookline, Mass., Oct. 16, 1943; s. Benjamin Jacques and Anne (Pollack) S.; m. Ruth Schneider, May 30, 1967; children: Matthew, Seth. BA, MD, Boston U., 1967. Diplomate Am. Bd. Internatl Medicine, Am. Bd. Allergy/Immunology. Resident physician Bronx (N.Y.) Mcpl. Hosp. Ctr., 1967-69; fellow Lab. Clin. Investigation, NIH, Bethesda, Md., 1969-72; sr. staff fellow Lab. of Immunology, NIAID, 1972-73, sr. investigator, 1973-87, head cellular immunology sect., 1987—. Adv. bd. Am. Leprosy Found., Rockville, Md., 1988. Author: Immunophysiology, 1990; editor: Current Protocols in Immunology, 1990; editor-in-chief Jour. of Immunology, Bethesda, 1987-92. Capt. USPHS, 1973—. Recipient Pub. Health Svc. Commendation medal 1978, Pub. Health Svc. Meritorious Svc. medal 1986, Disting. Svc. medal 1993. Mem. Am. Assn. Immunologists, Am. Soc. Clin. Investigation, Assn. Am. Physicians, Am. Fedn. Clin. Rsch., Coun. Biology Editors. Office: NIH Niaid Rm 11 N 315 Bldg 10 Bethesda MD 20892-0001

SHEVCHENKO, SERGEY MARKOVICH, organic chemist; b. Leningrad, USSR, Apr. 19, 1952; s. Tatiana S. (Shitova) Shevchenko; m. Tatiana S. Rotnova, June 22, 1978; children: Anna, Sergey. BS in Chemistry, Leningrad U., 1974, PhD in Organic Chemistry, 1980; DSc in Wood Chemistry, Acad. Forestry, St. Petersburg, Russia, 1992. Engr. Leningrad U., 1974-80, jr. rsch. assoc., 1981-82; sr. rsch. assoc. Acad. Forestry, St. Petersburg, 1982-89, prin. rsch. assoc., 1990-93; sr. rsch. assoc. Environ. Rsch. Lab. US EPA, Athens, Ga., 1993-96; rsch. assoc. U. Victoria (Can.), 1996—97, U. B.C., Canada, 1997—98; staff scientist ONDEO Nalco Co., Naperville, Ill., 1999—. Vis. scientist Rugjer Boskovic Inst., Zagreb, Yugoslavia, 1986—87, Comenius U., Bratislava, Czech Republic, 1989, N.C. State U., Raleigh, 1990—91; referee Jour. Molecular Structure (Theochem), Wood Chemistry; cons. East European Tour TAPPI, Atlanta, 1990—91; exec. sec. UNESCO Internat. Expert Coun. on Chemistry of Vegetal Resources. Author: A Molecule in Space, 1986, The Image of a Molecule, 1989; satiric columnist Novostii NMR v Pismakh, Moscow, 1990-93, Jour. Irreproducible Results, 1994—; contbr. over 150 articles to sci. jours. Chmn. Coun. Employees, Acad. Forestry, St. Petersburg, 1988-90. Recipient award Internat. Sci. Found., U.S. NRC. Fellow: Internat. Acad. Wood Sci.; mem.: TAPPI, Am. Chem. Soc. Achievements include first synthesis of simplest hydrazinothiol, reaction of thiiranes with hydrazones, minimal conformational graph, new conformational effects; chemistry of quinone methides, quantum chemistry, conformational and morphological analysis, HI-splitting and C-13 NMR ionization chemical shift techniques in lignin and humic substances; development of computational molecular soil chemistry, new methods of scale monitoring and control and brightness enhancement in pulp and paper industry. Home: 931 Park Hill Cir Aurora IL 60504 E-mail: sshevchenko@ondeo-nalco.com.

SHEVCHUCK, HARRY, retired image systems consultant; b. Jerome, Pa., Sept. 24, 1924; s. Nickolai and Anastana (Emilianovich) S.; (div.), remarried Joyce E. Shevchuck; children: Robert N., Gregory A., Cathleen E. (dec.), Susan D., Ivan P., Lisa M. BS in Geology, W.Va. U., 1949; AS in Electronics, Temple U., 1960. Warehouse supr. Owens Ill. Glass Co., Fairmont, W.Va., 1949-50; polymer structural analyst E.I. DuPont de Nemours & Co., Wilmington, Del., 1950-73, electronic imaging equipment specialist, 1973-86, cons., 1986—; now ret. Asst. to scout master Boy Scouts Am., Wilmington, 1960. Served with inf. U.S. Army, 1943-45, ETO, prisoner of war, Germany. Mem.: Ceasar Rodney. Roman Catholic. Home: 602 Stanton Rd Wilmington DE 19804-3636

SHEVIN, DAVID A. English literature educator; b. June 1, 1951; MFA, Bowling Green State U., 1976; PhD, U. Cin., 1986. Assoc. prof. English Miami U., Oxford, Ohio, 1985-87; prof. English Tiffin (Ohio) U., 1987—. Address: Apt 6 1453 N Broad St Fairborn OH 45324-5576

SHEVIN, ROBERT LEWIS, b. Miami, Fla., Jan. 19, 1934; s. Aaron and Pauline (Bott) S.; m. Myrna Bressack, Jan. 27, 1957; children: Laura Dawn, Hilary Beth, Harry Alan. BA, U. Fla., 1955; JD magna cum laude, U. Miami, 1957. Bar: Fla. 1957, U.S. Dist. Ct. (so. and mid. dists.) Fla. 1963, U.S. Supreme Ct. 1971, U.S. Ct. Appeals (5th cir.) 1971, U.S. Dist. Ct. (no. dist.) Fla. Ptnr. Shevin, Goodman and Holtzman, 1957-67, Shevin and Shevin, 1967-70; mem. Fla. Ho. of Reps., 1963-65, chmn. interim com. on crime and law enforcement, 1965; mem. Fla. State Senate, 1966-70, chmn. select com. to investigate organized crime and law enforcemnt, 1967, mem. interim study com. on urban affairs, 1968; atty. gen. State of Fla., 1971-79; ptnr. Sparber, Shevin, Rosen, Shapo & Heilbronner, Miami, 1979-87, Stroock & Stroock & Lavan, Miami, 1988-96; judge 3d Dist. Ct. Appeals, 1996—. Mem. Fla. Tax Reform Commn., 1968, Fla. Constl. Revision Commn., 1978; city atty. City of Miami Beach, Fla., 1979-80; apptd. to Fla. Jud. Mgmt. Coun., 1999—, chmn. jury trial innovations com., 1999—; mem. Supreme Ct. Workload Study Commn., 2000. Chmn. Housing Fin. Authority Dade County, Fla., 1980-82, Fla. State Athletic Commn., 1984-87; mem. exec. com. Miami Citizens Against Crime; bd. dirs. Fla. Citizens Against Crime, 1985-90; mem. Fla. Senate's Sunshine Adv. Com., 1988; chmn. Ptnrs. for Safe Neighborhoods, 1994; vis. com. U. Miami Law Sch. Recipient Allen Morris award, 1969, Intergovtl. award HUD, 1969, Conservationist of Yr. awards Fla. Wildlife Fedn., 1973, Audubon Soc., 1974, Furtherance of Justice award Fla. Prosecuting Attys. Assn., 1974, Disting. Svc. award Fla. Sheriff's Assn., 1976, Peace award State of Israel, 1977, Jud. Cmty. Svc. award Greater Miami Jewish Fedn., 1998, Statewide Jud. Achievement award Acad. Fla. Trial Lawyers, 2000; named one of 10 Most Valuable Mems. Fla. Legislature Capital Press Corps, 1965, Fla. Freedom Info. Hall Fame, 1997. Mem.: ABA, Nat. Assn. Attys. Gen. (chmn. So. region 1981), Am. Judicature Soc., Dade County Bar Assn., Fla. Bar Assn., Internat. Bar Assn., Fla. Blue Key, Iron Arrow, Sertoma, Omicron Delta Kappa, Phi Kappa Phi, Pi Lambda Phi, Phi Delta Phi. Democrat. Jewish. Home: 7171 SW 56th St Miami FL 33155-5616 Office: Third Dist Ct of Appeal 2001 SW 117th Ave Miami FL 33175-1799

SHEVIS, JAMES MURDOCH, journalist; b. Brattleboro, Vt., Oct. 2, 1929; s. James Allan and Frances (Ritchie) S.; divorced; children: Heidi Shevis Clark, Holly Shevis Markwood, Andrew. BA in English, U. Mass., 1951; M in

Liberal Studies, Georgetown U., 1977; postgrad., Am. U., 1978-83. Bur. mgr. UPI, Lubbock Tex., Springfield, Mass., 1964-65; mng. editor Airline Pilot, Washington, 1985-86, Courier, Fairfax County, Va., 1986-88; editor N.Am. Newspaper Alliance, N.Y.C., 1965-67, Newhouse Nat. News Svc., Washington, 1967-68, AFL-CIO News, Washington, 1972-85; writer, reporter Worcester (Mass.) Telegram & Gazette, 1961-63, UPI, various locations, 1962-65, Reuters and Bur. Nat. Affairs, Washington, 1968-69; sr. writer, reporter, editor USIA, 1988-94. Lectr. writing George Mason U., Fairfax, 1987-95; lectr. feature writing USDA Grad. Sch., Washington. Columnist The Observer, 1990-91; contbr. articles to consumer mags. and profl. jours. Mem. Soc. Environ. Journalists (charter), Soc. Profl. Journalists, Nat. Assn. Govt. Communicators, Nat. Press Club, Washington Ind. Writers, Freelance Cons. Assn. (v.p.), Tree Action. Home: 2587 Viking Dr Herndon VA 20171-2422

SHEVORY, THOMAS CARLSON, political studies educator; b. Boston, June 5, 1955; s. Joan Peterson Shevory; m. Tamara Lizabeth DiVasto, July 31, 1999. BA, Hobart and William Smith Coll., 1976; PhD, U. iowa, 1983. Asst. prof. Marshall U., Huntington, W.Va., 1984-88; assoc. prof. Ithaca (N.Y.) Coll., 1988—. Author: (books) John Marshall's Law, 1994, Body/Politics, 2000; editor: John Marshall's Achievement, 1989. Fulbright scholar, 1994-95. Avocations: songwriting, piano, running, biking. Office: Ithaca Coll Dept Politics Ithaca NY 14850 E-mail: shevory@ithaca.edu.

SHEVSHENKO, LLADOOW "SCOOTER", scuba instructor; b. Tomaston, Ga., Apr. 30, 1956; s. Elon Ausbon Woodall, Edith Bertha Shevshenko. Degree in Computer Info. Sys., Macon U., 1997. Cert. 101 Basic Firefighter Ga. Fire Acad., 1989, Rescue Diver PADI, 1990. Instr. Robins Air Force Base, Warner Robins , Ga., 1985—86; SCUBA instr. Internat. Diving Educators, Jacksonville, Fla., 1990—. Composer: Taras: A New Poetic Form, 1995; author: R0B Amsterdam, 1996, Ice House, 1998. Pvt. U.S. Army, Camp LeJuene N.C. Recipient Outstanding Performance award, Macon Coll., 1996—97, First Place award, Georgia Coll. Press Assn., 1997, Third Place award, 1997. Native American. Avocations: pool, chess, scuba diving, swimming, Karate. Home: 1841 General Twiggs Dr. Macon GA 31217 Office: L.S. Shevshenko 4008 Kemper Ave. Macon GA 31206 Home Fax: 478-784-8260. Personal E-mail: shevshenko@excite.com. Business E-Mail: scootabb@mylink.net.

SHEVY, ALLEN EARL, JR. publishing executive; b. Mar. 23, 1959; s. Allen Earl Shevy Sr. and Myra Lee (Cone) Muller. Sales rep. Police Benevolent Assn., Tampa, Fla., 1974-79, Fox and Fink Inc., Tampa, 1979-85; pub. World of Fandom Mag., 1985—. Sales and mktg. rep. Fla. Spl. Olympics, 1979-85, U. South Fla. Basketball, 1979-85, U. South Fla. Baseball, 1979-85, U. South Fla. Soccer, 1979-85, U. South Fla. Volleyball, 1979-85, U. South Fla. Student Calendar of Events, 1979-85, Internat. Motor Sports Assn., 1979-85, Sports Car Off Road Events, 1979-85, Gasperilla Distance Classic, 1979-85, Saint Pete Grand Prix, 1979-85, Bucaneer Mag., 1989-93; pub. Rat Fink Comics, 1989-91, Comic Collectors Guide, 1989-91. Office: World of Fandom Mag PO Box 9421 Tampa FL 33674-9421

SHEW, ROSE JEAN, nurse; b. Clinton, Ind., June 21, 1952; d. Paul James and Norma Jean (Bonomo) Duchene; m. Robert Morgan Roberts, Aug. 26, 1972 (div. May 1979); children: Joy Lynn, Robert John; m. Howard Edward Shew II, May 4, 1987 (div. Mar. 1994); 1 child, Sara Rose. Student, Ind. Vocat. Tech. Coll., Terre Haute, 1982-83. Float nurse Union Hosp., Terre Haute, 1983-88, ob.-gyn. nurse, 1988—; intensive coronary care Vermillion Country Hosp., Clinton, 1984-88; sec. Shew Excavating, Universal, Ind., 1987-93; obstet. nurse Union Hosp., 1990-97, Nurse Health Check, 1997—; owner Rose's Rental's Houses for Rent. Chmn. Boy Scouts Am., 1985; troop leader Girl Scouts U.S.A., 1991-92. Mem. Daus. of Nile, Kappa Delta Phi. Roman Catholic. Home: 1440 S 4th St Clinton IN 47842-2232

SHEWAN, ANDREW FRASER, actuary; b. Edinburgh, Scotland, June 28, 1944; came to the U.S., 1976; s. Henry Alexander and Ann Fraser Shewan; m. Jacquelyn Jovita Foryst, Aug. 28, 1979. MA, Cambridge (Eng.) U., 1965. Various positions Scottish Widows Fund, Edinburgh, 1965-71; investment analyst and portfolio mgr. Ivory and Sime, 1971-73; portfolio mgr. and mng. dir. Stewart Fund Mgrs. (now Stewart, Ivory & Co.), 1973-76; cons. actuary and prin. William M. Mercer Inc., N.Y.C., 1976-87; pvt. practice cons. actuary, 1987—. Author: Trustees of Posterity, 1989. Fellow Faculty of Actuaries in Scotland; mem. Am. Acad. Actuaries, Soc. Actuaries (assoc.), New Club Edinburgh. Avocations: traveling, reading.

SHEWARD, DAVID JOHN, newspaper editor and critic; b. Wilamatic, Conn., May 7, 1959; s. John Albert and Marjorie Patricia (Berry) S. Student, Carnegie-Mellon U., 1977-79; BA, Temple U., 1982. Actor, dir. stock and regional theatres, Phila., N.Y.C., 1982—; mng. editor, critic Back Stage newspaper, N.Y.C., 1984—. Author: It's A Hit: The Back Stage Book of Broadway's Longest Running Hits 1884 to the Present, 1994, The Big Book of Show Business Awards, 1997; contbg. corr. weekly TV program New York-1 On Stage; contbr. articles to theatrical publs.; actor in Long Day's Journey into Night, The Crucible, A Midsummer Night's Dream; dir. As Is, Talking With, Plaza Suite. Mem. Drama Desk (treas. 1994-96, nominating com. 1995—, pres. 1996—), N.Y. Drama Critics Circle, Outer Critics Circle, Am. Theatre Critics Assn. Avocations: acting, directing, travel. Office: Back Stage 770 Broadway New York NY 10003-9522 E-mail: dsheward@backstage.com.

SHEWCHUK, ROBERT JOHN, television executive; b. Passaic, N.J., Oct. 2, 1950; s. Frank Russel and Adele (Sweetman) Shewchuk. BFA, Rochester Inst. Tech., 1972; Cert in Advt., Fairleigh Dickinson U., 1972. Assoc. producer, tech. dir. TV Ctr. Rochester (N.Y.) Inst. Tech., 1970-72; prodn. cons., writer ABC TV Network/Daphne Don Lipp Prodns., N.Y.C., 1975-76; pres., producer, dir. Bob Shewchuk Prodns., Clifton, N.J., 1972-76; dir., editor, prodn. mgr. AT&T Long Lines, Bedminister, 1976-80; sr. prodr. Gen. Foods Corp., White Plains, N.Y., 1980-82; v.p., dir. TV services, pub. affairs dept. Citicorp, N.Y.C., 1982-94; producer, dir. World Cycling Championships, 1986; pres., CEO Bob Shewchuk Enterprises/Video Vanguard Prodns., N.Y.C., 1977—. Mem ed adv bd: Int TV Orgn, Corp TV Mag, 1987—89; producer, photographer, writer Penthouse Mag, Playboy Mag, 1974—75; prodr.: Vocal Extravaganza in Black Music Special, 1997, Summer Slam, charity sports spec, 1994, 50th Anniversary Human Rights live telecast Franklin & Eleanor Roosevelt Inst, 1998. Recipient Medals, Chicago Indust Film Festival, 1985, Int Film and TV Festival, New York City, 1985—87, Telly Awards, 1986, Cine Gold Eagle, Coun Int Non-Theatrical Events, 1987. Mem.: Nat Acad TV Arts and Scis (2 Emmy Awards 1987), Soc Motion Picture and TV Engrs, Int TV Asn (Medals winner). Avocations: tennis, racquetball, cartooning, boating, bicycling. Home: 52 Woodland Dr West Paterson NJ 07424-3706 Office: Bob Shewchuk Enterprises Video Vanguard Prodns 630 9th Ave Ste 308 New York NY 10036-3708 E-mail: shewchuk99@aol.com.

SHEWMAKER, KENNETH EARL, history educator; b. L.A., June 26, 1936; s. James Virgil and Jeanette M. (Greenberg) S.; m. Elisabeth L. Spalteholz, June 12, 1960; children: Richard Glenn, Nancy Jeanette. BS, Concordia Tchrs. Coll., 1960; MA, U. Calif., Berkeley, 1961; PhD, Northwestern U., 1966. Instr. Northwestern U., Evanston, Ill., 1965-66; asst. prof. Coll. William and Mary, Williamsburg, Va., 1966-67; from asst. prof. to assoc. prof. Dartmouth Coll., Hanover, N.H., 1967-78, prof. history, 1978—, acting chair dept. history, 1985-86, chmn. dept. history, 1986-89. Author: Americans and Chinese Communists, 1927-45: A Persuading Encounter, 1971 (Stuart L. Bernath prize 1972); editor: Papers of Daniel Webster, Diplomatic Papers, Vol. 1, 1841-1843, 1983, Vol. 2, 1850-1852, 1987, Daniel Webster, The Completest Man, 1990; contbr. articles to profl. jours. Recipient Disting. Tchg. awards Dartmouth Coll., 1986, 96. Mem. N.H. Hist. Soc., Orgn. Am. Historians, Soc. Historians Am. Fgn. Rels. Lutheran. Avocations: fly fishing, fly tying. Office: Dept History Dartmouth Coll Hanover NH 03755

SHI, CAIJUN, materials engineer, researcher; b. Yixing, Jiangsu, China; BEng, Southeast U., China, 1984; PhD, U. Calgary, Can., 1992. Registered profl. engr. Engr., sr. engr. Wastewater Tech. Ctr., Burlington, NY, 1993—99; v.p. Advanced Materials Technologies LLC, Hamburg, 1990—. Fellow Indsl. Rsch. fellow, NSERC, 1993—95. Fellow: Internat. Energy Found. Achievements include invention of high early strength steel self-sealing, self-healing liners, ultra-lightweight concrete. Office: Advanced Materials Technologies LLC 5225 Southwestern Blvd Hamburg NY 14075 Business E-Mail: caijunshi@yahoo.com.

SHI, FENG SHENG, mathematician; b. Shanghai, China, Sept. 28, 1935; came to U.S., 1990; s. Jing Long and Xu Wenzheng Shi; m. Dorothy Shi, May 30, 1992. Degree of engr., 1957. Prof. math. and physics U. Industry, Shanghai, 1961-64; ship designer Govt. of China, 1964; rschr., business liaison Hong Kong of U.S.A. Liaison for Bus. Investment; owner, editor Pendulum Math. Jour. in Libr. of Congress. Trustee, founder, dir. Chinese Math. Students Orgn., Miami, Fla., 1993—; dir. Chinese Internat. Math. Students Orgn., 1994—; mem. bd. intellectuals, Oxford Internat. Dictionary; trustee Nat. Heritage Found. Author: (math. solutions) Exist, 1991 (Libr. of Congress), Solving the Fermat Problem and Goldbach's Conjecture, 1993. Recipient Son of Yr. award Sons and Daus. Found., 1990, Internat. award for poetry, Nat. award for Poetry, Gold Star award for knowledge. Mem. All Nations (trustee, bd. dirs. 1990-93, Internat. Man of Yr. 1991). Home and Office: 1000 8th St N Saint Petersburg FL 33701-1510

SHI, JIALAN, pathologist, educator; b. Harbin, China, Feb. 1, 1957; s. Ruyou and Jingzhen (Zhang) S.; m. Yingli Yang, Aug. 1, 1987; 1 child, Yinan. MD, Harbin Med. U., China, 1978-83; MS, Harbin Med. U., 1986-89; PhD, Tokyo Med. and Dental U., 1993-97. Tchg. asst. Harbin Med. U., China, 1983-88, asst. prof. China, 1988-91, dir., 1989-91; rsch. fellow Tokyo Med. & Dental U., 1991-93, tchg. asst., 1996-98; postdoctoral fellow Harvard Med. Sch., Boston, 1998—. Contbr. articles to profl. jours. Grantee, Japanese Govt., Tokyo, 1991; 3rd prize Acad. Sci., Harbin, China, 1991, 2nd prize Dept. Health, Harbin, 1991. Mem. Japanese Soc. Immunology, N.Y. Acad. Scis., Am. Assn. Advancemsnt Sci., Am. Soc. of Hematology, Am. Chem. Soc. Avocations: swimming, skiing, classical music, travel. Home: 56 Cypress St Apt 2 Newton Center MA 02459 Office: Brigham and Women's Hosp 75 Francis St Boston MA 02115-6110 E-mail: jialan_shi@hms.harvard.edu., jshi@rics.bwh.harvard.edu., shi_jialan@yahoo.com.

SHI, JONATHAN JINGSHENG, engineering educator; b. Huangmei, Hubei, China, June 19, 1962; arrived in Canada, 1992; s. Haitao and Xingmei (Xiong) S.; m. Junli Bai; children: Sandy, David, Kevin. BSc, Wahan U., China, 1982, MSc, 1985; PhD, U. Alta., 1995. Lectr. Wuhan U., China, 1985-92; rschr. Constrn. Rsch. Inst., China, 1985-92; rsch. assoc. U. Alta., 1992-95; asst. prof. City U. Hong Kong, 1995-98, assoc. prof., 1999, Ill. Inst. Tech., Chgo., 1999—. Contbr. articles to profl. jours. Province of Alta. Grad. fellow U. Alta., 1995. Mem. Am. Soc. Civil Engrs., Hong Kong Instn. Engrs., Constrn. Mgmt. Assn. Am. Home: 1100 Columbian Ave Oak Park IL 60302-1226 E-mail: jonathan.shi@iit.edu.

SHI, LEIYU, educator, researcher; b. Shanghai, China, July 7, 1961; s. Yongchun Shi and Zhengku Guan; m. Lirong Shi, Jan. 29, 1991; children: Sylvia M., Jennifer T. BA, Shanghai Fgn. Lang. U., 1982; M of Pub. Adminstrn., Seton Hall U., 1986; MBA, D of Pub. Health, U. Calif., Berkeley, 1990. Health adminstr. Shanghai Pub. Health Dept., 1982-84; rsch. assoc. U. Calif., Berkeley, 1986-90; asst. prof. U. S.C., Columbia, 1991-94, assoc. prof. dept. health adminstn., 1995-97, chair dept. health adminstn., 1995-97; assoc. dir. Primary Care Policy Ctr., Balt., 1997—; assoc. prof. Johns Hopkins U., 1997—. Cons. U.S. Dept Health and Human Svcs., Washington, 1991—, Grad. Coun. of Med. Edn., Washington, 1994, various health orgns., 1986—; adv. bd. Ryan White Title II Care Act Svcs., S.C., 1994-98. Author: Delivering Health Care in America, 1998, Health Services Research Methods, 1997, Physician Recruitment and Retention, 1993; contbr. numerous articles to profl. jours. Grantee Managed Care and Cmty. Health Ctr., 1998—, Robert Wood Johnson Found., 1999—, Bur. of Primary Health Care, HRSA, 1996—, Ctrs. for Disease Control, 1995-99. Mem. Am. Pub. Health Assn., Assn. for Health Svcs. Rsch. Office: Johns Hopkins U 624 N Broadway Rm 409 Baltimore MD 21205-1900 Home: 3708 Font Hill Dr Ellicott City MD 21042 E-mail: lshi@jhsph.edu.

SHI, MING FENG, engineer; b. Ningbo, Zhejiang, China, Apr. 5, 1960; came to U.S., 1984; s. Benfa and Xuachai S.; m. Haoming Li, July 24, 1986; children: Lucy Z., Jennifer S., Michael S. BS, Hehai U., Nanjing, China, 1982; MS, Mich. Tech. U., 1986, PhD, 1989. Project engr. Nat. Steel Corp., Livonia, Mich., 1989-90, sr. engr., 1991-93, staff specialist, 1994-96; tech. specialist U.S. Steel, Troy, 1997-99, tech. mgr., 2000—. Presenter in field. Author: (papers) Zinc-Based Steel Coating Systems Metallurgy and Performance, 1990, Automotive Stamping Technology, 1993, 95, 99. Treas. Chinese Sch. of Greater Detroit, 1996-97. Named to Outstanding Young Men of Am., 1996. Mem. Soc. Automotive Engr., Am. Soc. for Metals (Outstanding Young Mem. award 1995-96), The Minerals, Metals, Materials. Avocations: basketball, ping-pong, golf. E-mai. Home: 5470 White Hall Cir West Bloomfield MI 48323-3459 E-mail: mfshi@uss.com.

SHI, SHAN-RONG, research pathology educator; b. Jiangan, Sichuan, China, Feb. 6, 1936; came to U.S., 1989; s. Sheng-Zhi and Xing-Rui (Liu) S.; m. Shou-Xian Wang, Feb. 15, 1969 (div. Oct. 1991); 1 child, Yan Shi. MD, West China U. Med. Scis., Chengdu, Sichuan, 1957. Attending physician ear, nose, and throat Sichuan Med. Coll., Chengdu, 1967-75, instr. ear, nose, and throat pathology, 1976-79; rsch. fellow pathology Harvard U. Med. Sch., Boston, 1982-84; assoc. prof. ear, nose, and throat Sichuan Med. Coll., 1980-87; asst. prof. pathology U. So. Calif., L.A., 1992—. Mem. editl. bd.: Jour. Histochemistry & Cytochemistry, 1993—; contbr. articles to profl. jours. Recipient Chinese Sci. award Chinese Govtl. Rsch. Found., 1986. Mem. Internat. Otopathology Soc., Histochem. Soc., Nat. Soc. Histotech. Taoist. Achievements include patent for heating antigen retrieval (AR) technique, first inventor for nonheating AR technique. Avocations: swimming, ballroom dancing, music, movies. Office: Dept Pathology Hmr 310A 2011 Zonal Ave Los Angeles CA 90089-0110 E-mail: sshi@hsc.usc.edu.

SHI, YONG, information science educator; b. Chengdu, Sichuan, China, Aug. 24, 1956; came to U.S., 1985; s. Yuanqing Shi and Guihua Li; m. Bailing Gong, Aug. 30, 1984; 1 child, Christopher S.B. BS in Math., S.W. Petroleum Inst., Nanchong, China, 1982; PhD in Bus., U. Kans., 1991. Disting. chair, prof. info. tech. U. Nebr., Omaha, 1999—. Contbr. articles to profl. jours. Mem. IEEE (Disting. Visitor Program 1997—). Home: 16024 Wakeley St Omaha NE 68118-2080 Office: Coll Info Sci and Tech U Nebr-Omaha Omaha NE 68182

SHI, ZHI-QING, endocrinologist; b. Shanghai, China, July 19, 1951; came to US, 1996; s. Yu-Qi Shi and Ai-Yi Zou; m. Ai-Ping Xu, May 9, 1982; 1 child, Andrew Bei-Hong. MD, Shanghai No. 2 Med. U., 1975; PhD, McGill U., 1986. Resident surgeon Shanghai 9th Mcpl. Hosp., 1975-78; rsch. fellow Shanghai No. 1 Med. U., 1978-80; dir. surg. rsch. ctr. Zhong Shan Hosp., Shanghai, 1987-89; postdoct. fellow U. Toronto, 1989-93, asst. prof. physiology and surgery, 1993-96; rsch. scientist Amgen, Inc., Thousand Oaks, Calif., 1996—. Invited lectr. physiology Canadian Meml. Chiropractic Coll., Toronto, 1993-95. Contbr. more than 40 research articles to profl. jours., chpts. to books. Recipient Outstanding Young Med. Profl. award City of Shanghai, 1988. Mem. Am. Diabetes Assn. Avocations: Western and Oriental classical music, literature. Home: 819 Cayo Grande Ct Newbury Park CA 91320-1944 Office: Amgen Inc One Amgen Ctr Dr Thousand Oaks CA 91320

SHIAU, BOR-JIER (BEN SHIAU), environmental scientist, researcher; b. Taipei, Taiwan; came to U.S., 1988; s. Su and Lee Chin-Lan Shiau; m. L.Y.C. June Shiau. BSChemE, Chung Yuan Christian U., Taiwan, 1983; MSChemE, U. Okla., 1990, MS in Civil Engring., 1991, PhD in Civil Engring., 1995. Rsch. asst. Chung Shan Inst. Sci. and Tech., Lung-Tan, Taiwan, 1983-88; grad. rsch. asst. U. Okla., Norman, 1988-95, rsch. assoc., 1995-97; sr. scientist ManTech Environ. Rsch. Svcs. Corp., Ada, Okla., 1997-99; dir. surfactant tech. Surbec-ART Environ., LLC, Norman, 1999—. Manuscript reviewer Environ. Sci. and Tech. jour., 1995-2000; contbr. articles to profl. jours. Mem. Am. Chem. Soc., Am. Geophys. Union, Nat. Ground Water Assn., Chi Epsilon. Home: 4311 Monticello Rd Norman OK 73072 Office: Surbec-ART Environ 3200 Marshall Ave Ste 200 Norman OK 73072 Fax: 405-329-1602. E-mail: bshiau@msn.com.

SHIAU, JOHN SOU-CHENG, neurosurgeon; b. Taiwan, Nov. 18, 1965; came to U.S., 1967; s. Hsing-Shong and Jaw-Huey (Wu) S. BS in Biomed. Scis., U. Mich., 1987, MD, 1990. Diplomate Am. Bd. Neurosurgery, Nat. Bd. Med. Examiners. Rsch. fellow Mt. Sinai Med. Ctr., N.Y.C., 1990-91, intern in gen. surgery, 1991-92, resident in neurosurgery, 1992-96, chief resident, 1996-97; keyhole and neuroendoscopic surgery fellow Johannes Gutenberg U. Hosp., Mainz, Germany, 1997. Presenter in field. Contbr. articles, abstracts and revs. to med. jours., including Neurosurgery, Jour. Epilespy, Jour. Neurosurgery, chpt. to book. Angell scholar U. Mich., 1983-87. Mem. Am. Assn. Neurol. Surgeons, Congress Neurol. Surgeons. Democrat. Avocations: scuba diving, skiing, running, cooking. Office: Healthcare Assocs in Med 1099 Targee St Staten Island NY 10304-4310

SHIBAMOTO, TAKAYUKI, food scientist; b. Shizuoka, Japan, Sept. 28, 1940; s. Reizo and Ima Shibamoto; m. Tomoko Shibamoto; 1 child Erica Zizak 1 child Reizo. PhD, U. Calif., Davis, 1974. Prof. U. Calif., Davis, 1979—. Regional dir. USDA, Davis, 1992—. Author: Introduction to Food Toxicoloy, 1993. Recipient Fellow award, Am. Chem. Soc., 1991. Office: U Calif 1 Shields Ave Davis CA 95616 Office Fax: 530-752-3394. Business E-Mail: tshibamoto@ucdavis.edu.

SHIBASAKI, YOSHIO, chemistry educator, researcher; b. Gyoda, Japan, Mar. 21, 1934; s. Reiji and Shige (Kobayashi) S.; m. Teiko Ishizuka Shibasaki, Apr. 15, 1967; children: Hideaki, Miki. BS, Saitama U., Japan, 1959; DSc, U. Tokyo, 1980. Tech. official U. Tokyo, Japan, 1960-63, asst. Japan, 1963-67; lectr. Saitama U., Urawa, Japan, 1967-70, assoc. prof. Japan, 1970-92, prof. Japan, 1992-99, ret. Japan, 1999. Inventor: Kobunshi Kagaku, 1964, J. Polymer Science, 1967, 80, 98, 99. Internat. Conf. Thermal Analysis & Calorimetry, Japan Soc. Calorimetry & Thermal Analysis. Mem. AAAS, N.Y. Acad. Sci. Avocations: appreciation of pictures. Home: 1642 Tsutsumine Gyoda 361-0035 Japan

SHIBLEY, RALPH EDWIN, JR. special education and vocational educator; b. Columbus, Ohio, Dec. 31, 1944; s. Ralph Edwin and Dorothy Ann (Evans) S.; m. P. Kathleen Phillips, July 23, 1966; children: Christine Marie, Margot Marie. BSc in Edn., Ohio State U., 1971, MA, 1981, PhD, 1984. Cert. spl. edn. supr., Ohio. Spl. edn. tchr. Columbus City Schs., 1974-80; dir. rsch. and devel. Six Pence Sch., Columbus, 1980-81; grad. rsch. assoc. Ohio State U., 1980-84, program dir. Nisonger Ctr., 1984-87; prof. U. Rio Grande, Ohio, 1987—, dir. Vocat. Tchr. Edn. Program, 1998—. Adj. prof. Bowling Green State U., 1994—, Ohio Dominican Coll.; vis. prof. W.Va. U., 1997; cons. Gallipolis (Ohio) Devel. Ctr., 1989-90; project site coord. U. Cin., Gallipolis, 1990-91. Author articles and textbook revs. Apptd. State of Ohio Com. Practitioners for Career-Tech. and Adult Edn., 2000-2002; mem. 1st Class Nat. Leadership Inst. Career Tech. Edn. Named Tchr. of Yr. Cen. Ohio Soc. for Autistic Children, 1977; recipient cert. of appreciation Coalition of Handicapped Students, 1988; Ohio Career Tech. Leadership Inst. fellow, 1999. Mem. ASCD, Coun. for Exceptional Children (past pres., editor Ohio fedn. tchr. edn. divsn.), Ohio Fedn. Coun. for Exceptional Children (past pres.), Interuniv. Coun. for Tchr. Edn., Am. Career-Tech. Assn., Epsilon Pi Tau (Laureate citation). Democrat. Roman Catholic. Avocations: photography, golf, fishing. Bus. Home: 3590 Milton Ave Columbus OH 43214-4045 Office: U Rio Grande Sch of Edn Rio Grande OH 45674 E-mail: rshibley@rio.edu., rshibley@columbus.cs.com.

SHICK, JOHN EARL, retired radiologist; b. Chgo., Feb. 24, 1926; BA, Harvard U., 1947; MD, Northwestern U., Chgo., 1951. Diplomate Am. Bd. Radiology. Intern St. Luke's Hosp., Chgo., 1951-52; resident in radiology Thomas Jefferson U. Hosp., Phila., 1954-55, Barnes Hosp., St. Louis, 1955-57; pvt. practice Henry Ford Hosp., Detroit, 1957-61, Grossmont Hosp., La Mesa, Calif., 1961-81; ret., 1981. Mem. AMA, Am. Coll. Radiology, Radiol. Soc. N.Am.

SHICK, RICHARD ARLON, academic dean; b. DuBois, Pa., July 17, 1943; s. Arlon Elmer and Melva Elizabeth (Bartell) S.; m. Linda B. Shick; children: Richard Arlon, Charles, Elizabeth. BS, SUNY, Buffalo, 1966, MBA, 1968, PhD, 1972. Asst. prof. banking and fin. U. Ga., Athens, 1970-75; assoc. prof. fin. St. Bonaventure (N.Y.) U., 1975-78, chmn. fin. dept., 1975-78, acting chmn. mktg. dept., 1976-99; assoc. prof. fin. Canisius Coll., Buffalo, 1978-99, prof. fin., 1999—, dean Richard J. Wehle Sch. Bus., 1979—. Bd. dirs. Better Bus. Bur., 1990-95, Statler Culinary program Emerson H.S., buffalo, 1992—; sec., treas., bd. dirs. Chautauqua Brick Co. Mem. editl. bd. Jour. Bus. Rsch., 1973-76, Jour. Fin. Rsch., 1977-81, Jour. Econs. and Bus., 1984-88, Fin. Rev., 1976-87, editor, 1981-82; contbr. articles to profl. jours. Chmn. mayor's rev. com. Buffalo Bd. Edn.; bd. dirs. Buffalo Alliance Edn., Old Ft. Niagara; bd. dirs. Buffalo Philharm. Orch., 1995-97, treas., 1996-97; mem. N.Y. State Com. to Promote Pub. Trust and Confidence in the Legal System, 1999; bd. dirs. Studio Arena Theatre, 2001-, v.p. bd. NDEA fellow, 1966-68; U.S. Savs. and Loan League grantee, 1974, St. Bonaventure U. grantee, 1976, U.s. Govt. Title III grantee, 1999. Mem. Am. Fin. Assn., Ea. Fin. Assn., Southwestern Fin. Assn., So. Fin. Assn., Western Fin. Assn., Am. Mgmt. Assn., Jusuit Colls. and Univs. Deans of Bus. Schs. (treas. 1983-84, v.p. 1985-89, pres. 1987-88), Middle Atlantic Assn. Colls. and Schs. Bus. Adminstrn. (v.p. 1985-86, pres. 1986-87), Am. Assembly of Collegiate Schs. of Bus., Country Club Buffalo, Town of Jamestown Club, Buffalo Club (bd. dirs. 1995-97, 2001, 1st v.p. 1997), Automobile Club Western N.Y. (bd. dirs. 1995-99, exec. com. 1998-99, 2001), Beta Gamma Sigma, Alpha Kappa Psi, Di Gamma, Alpha Sigma Lambda, Alpha Signa Nu. Republican. Home: 157 Crestwood Ln Buffalo NY 14221-1508 Office: Canisius Coll 2001 Main St Buffalo NY 14208-1035 E-mail: shick@canisius.edu.

SHICKLEY, MARGARET S. librarian; b. Armstrong County, Pa., Mar. 11, 1938; d. Oscar Henry and Ella Margaret (Titus) Fry; m. Roger Clair Storms, Aug. 24, 1963 (dec. 1980); children: Ethel Charis, Eric Malcolm; m. Nelson W. Shickley Sr., June 23, 1996. BA in Christian Edn., Eastern Coll., 1961; MSLS, Clarion U., 1991. Organist, pianist Lee Bapt. Ch., Maine, 1965-78; tchr. sewing Beth Eden Bapt. Sch., Wheatridge, Colo., 1978-81; organist, pianist Evang. Meth. Ch., Altoona, Pa., 1984-91; libr. Manahath Sch. Theol., Hollidaysburg, 1984-90; piano tchr. Altoona, 1986-90; cataloging libr. Lancaster (Pa.) Bible Coll., 1991—. Music libr. Blair Concert Chorale, Altoona, 1987-90; choir dir. Bapt. Ch., New Bethlehem, Pa., 1990-91. Nat. sec. Nat. Temperance and Prohibition Coun., 1983-89, del., sec. Prohibition Nat. Com., Denver, 1979-95; trustee Prohibition Trust Assn., 1992—. Mem. Am. Theol. Libr. Assn., Harmony Club (pres. 1977), Assn. Christian Librs., Lee Lit Club (community project chmn. 1976-77). Avocations: music, needlework, sewing, knitting, reading. *The building of today is not finished. Each day influences the next. Yesterday was the foundation that set the general outline for today's framework of living—built with solid materials of learning, experiences, relationships and memories. The life materials of today include a possibility of change and involvement with others as essential to our life building. Today's building influences the interior decorating of Tomorrow and its beauty to be revealed. Thus God's blueprint will be made visible.*

SHIDELER, ROSS PATRICK, foreign language and comparative literature educator, writer, translator, poet; b. Denver, Apr. 12, 1936; BA, San Francisco State U., 1958; MA, U. Stockholm, 1963; PhD, U. Calif., Berkeley, 1968. Instr. in comparative lit. U. Calif., Berkeley, 1967-68; asst. prof. English Hunter Coll., N.Y.C., 1968-69; asst. prof. Scandinavian lang. and comparative lit. UCLA, 1969-73, assoc. prof., 1973-79, prof., 1979—; chmn. program in comparative lit., 1979-86, 92-96. Author: (monograph) Voices Under the Ground: Themes and Images in the Poetry of Gunnar Ekelof, 1973, Per Olov Enquist-A Critical Study, 1984; translator: (plays) The Night of the Tribades (Per Olov Enquist), 1977, The Hour of the Lynx (Per Olov Enquist), 1990; co-editor (with Kathleen L. Komar): Lyrical Symbols and Narrative Transformations, Essays in Honor of Ralph Freedman, 1998; co-editor: Questioning the Father: From Darwin to Zola, Ibsen, Strindberg and Hardy, 1999; U.S. assoc. editor Swedish Book Rev., 1984—98. Fellow NDFL, 1964; fellow NDEA, 1965; Fulbright-Hays fellow, 1966-67 Mem. MLA (exec. com. divsn. Scandinavian Langs. and Lits. 1993-97), Soc. Advancement Scandinavian Studies (exec. coun. 1985-89, v.p. 1997-99, pres. 1999-2001), Am. Comparative Lit. Assn., Assn. Depts. and Programs Comparative Lit. (exec. com. 1993-94, 94-98). Office: UCLA Dept Comparative Lit Los Angeles CA 90024

SHIDELER, SHIRLEY ANN WILLIAMS, lawyer; b. Mishawaka, Ind., July 9, 1930; d. William Harmon and Lois Wilma (Koch) Williams; 1 dau., Gail Shideler Frye. LLB, Ind. U., 1964. Bar: Ind. 1964. Legal sec. Barnes, Hickam, Pantzer & Boyd, Indpls., 1953-63; assoc. Barnes & Thornburg, 1964-70, ptnr., 1971-92, of counsel, 1993—. Participant fund drives Indpls. Symphony, 1968-81, Indpls. Mus. Art, 1969-79, Marion County Libr. Restoration, 1985-88, Goodwill Industries, 1988-89; bd. dirs. Bus. Unit Gals Indpls. Mus. Art, 1973-80; bd. dirs. Indpls. Legal Aid Soc., 1982-93, Cmty. Hosp. Found., 1986-94, Ctrl. Newspapers Found., 1979-99. Fellow Am. Coll. Trust and Estate Counsel, 1981-96; mem. Ind. Bar Assn. (sec. 1975-76, chmn.

probate, trust and real property sect. 1982), Nat. Conf. Bar. Founds. (trustee 1988-94), Indpls. Bar Assn. (bd. mgrs. 1968-72, v.p. charge affairs 1972), Ind. Bar Found. (bd. mgrs. 1980-92, sec. 1981-82, treas. 1981-86, v.p. 1986-88, pres. 1988-90), Indpls. Bar Found. (bd. mgrs. 1970-82, sec. 1972-77), Women's Rotary (pres. Indpls. club 1969-71, dir. 1968-79). Home: 2224 Boston Ct Apt C Indianapolis IN 46228-3257 Office: Barnes & Thornburg 11 S Meridian St Ste 1313 Indianapolis IN 46204-3535

SHIDHAM, VINOD BABURAO, pathologist, cytopathologist, surgical pathologist; b. Wani, India, Mar. 23, 1954; s. Baburao T. and Sunanda Baburao Shidham; m. Anjani Vinod Shidham, Dec. 31, 1983; children: Sushrut, Anushree. MBBS with honors in Physiology, Govt. Med. Coll., Nagpur, India, 1975, MD in Pathology, 1979. Diplomate Am. Bd. Pathology Cytopathology. Rotating intern Govt. Med. Coll., 1976, resident in pathology, 1977, lectr., 1977-83; assoc. prof. Grant Med. Coll., Mumbai, India, 1983-85; dir. pathology, cons. histo/cytopathology Ghamed Nat. Clinic, 1985-92; hematologist Al-Ymamah Specialist Hosp., Riyadh, Saudi Arabia, 1992-94; resident, chief resident, then cytopathology fellow Allegheny U. Health Scis. (now MCP-Hahnemann U.)_, Phila., 1994-98; asst. prof., dir. cytopathology tng. program Med. Coll. Wis., Milw., 1998—2002, assoc. prof., 2002—, assoc. prof. dept. pathology, 2002—, also dir. fine needle aspiration biopsy svc., 1998—2002. Founder Siddham Diagnostics, Nagpur, India. Mem. editl./adv. bd. Jour. of Cytology; contbr. chpt. to book; contbr. or co-contbr. articles to profl. jours., including Acta Cytologica, Diagnostic Cytopathology, Am. Jour. Clin. Pathology, Archives of Pathology and Lab. Medicine, Am. Jour. Clin. Oncology, Am. Jour. Ophthalmology, Lab. Medicine. Fellow: Am. Soc. Clin. Pathologists, Coll. Am. Pathologists (molecular biology workshop stipend 1996), Internat. Acad. Cytology (editl. bd., ethics com.); mem.: Papanicolau Soc. Cytopathology (task force on standards of practice), Royal Coll. Pathologists London, Assn. Indian Pathologists N.Am. (treas. 2000—01), Hematology Assn. Ctrl. India (joint sec. 1991—94), Wis. Soc. Pathologists (program chair 2001—), Assn. Indian Pathologists in N.Am., Am. Assn. for Cancer Rsch., Am. Soc. Cytopathology, Am. Assn. for Cancer Rsch., Am. Soc. Cytopathology (budget and fin. com.), U.S. and Can. Acad. Pathologists. Hindu. Avocations: gardening, photography, painting, crafts. Office: Med Coll Wis Dept Pathology 9200 W Wisconsin Ave Milwaukee WI 53226-3522 Fax: 414-8058444. E-mail: vshidham@mcw.edu.

SHIEH, FRANCIS, economics educator, consultant, researcher; b. Shanghai, People's Republic of China, Feb. 7, 1926; came to U.S., 1947; s. Wei-yu and Pei-ying (Chen) S.; m. Agnes Li, Nov. 26, 1955; children: Grace, Joseph, Michael, F. Christopher. Instr. Loyola Coll., Shanghai, 1945-47; statistician Farmers Ins. Group, L.A., 1951-52; instr. Chinese lang. U.S. Army Lang. Sch., Monterey, Calif., 1953-56; acct. IBM, San Jose, 1957-58; instr. bus. adminstrn. Immaculate Heart Coll., L.A., 1958-61; asst. prof. Aquinas Coll., Grand Rapids, Mich., 1961-64; mem. rsch. staff RAND Corp., Santa Monica, Calif., 1964-65; chief compiler project NSF, 1965-66; assoc. prof. econs. Prince George's Coll., Largo, Md., 1966-71, head econs. dept., 1967-69, prof., chmn. dept. econs., 1971-73, prof., 1973-84; adj. prof. Montgomery Coll., Takoma Park, Md., 1987—. Fulbright sr. scholar Lignan Coll., Hong Kong, Coun. Internat. Exch. of Scholars, USIA, 1989-90; cons. GE TEMPO, Santa Barbara, 1966; economist U.S. Dept. Labor, Washington, 1967. Author: Economics, 1971, 76, 78; 10 works listed in the Libr. of Congress, Washington. Mem. Atlantic Econ. Soc. Democrat. Roman Catholic. Avocation: travel. Home and Office: 11201 Woodlawn Blvd Upper Marlboro MD 20774-2361

SHIEH, JOHN TING-CHUNG, economics educator; b. 1935; BS, Chung-hsing U., Taiwan, 1956; MS, Kans. State U., 1960; MA, U. Calif., Riverside, 1981. Asst. prof. Northwestern State Coll., Alva, 1964-67; asst. prof. econs. Calif. State Poly. U., Pomona, 1967-70; assoc. prof. Calif. STate Poly. U., 1970-81; prof., chmn. dept. econs. Calif. State Poly. U., 1982-85, prof., 1981-98, prof. emeritus, 1999—. Prof., dir. Inst. Mainland China Studies, 1994-98, dean student affairs, 1997-99, Nat. Dong-hua U., Hwalian, Taiwan, 1994-2001; cons. to small bus., So. Calif., Taiwan, 1975—; vis. prof. Tax Inst., U. So. Calif., L.A., 1977-84, U. Calif., Irvine, 1978-79, U. So. Calif., 1978-81, UCLA, 1983—. Contbr. rsch. articles to publs. in field. NSF fellow, 1965, 66, 67, 73, fellow seminars in econs. and math. U. Wyo., summer 1972. Mem. Am. Econ. Assn., Omicron Delta Epsilon, Omega Rho. Home: 10556 Ilona Ave Los Angeles CA 90064-2313

SHIEH, WEI T. senior hardware design engineer; b. Keelung, Taiwan, Jan. 22, 1934; came to U.S., 1961; m. Mei W. Huang, Dec. 30, 1961; children: Karl, Karen, Denise. BASc, U. Toronto, 1961; MS, U. Ill., 1963, PhD, 1968. Rsch. metallurgist Timcen Co. Rsch. Ctr., Canton, Ohio, 1968-69, rsch. specialist, 1969-72, rsch. mission leader, 1972-77; engr. Gen. Electric Co., Utica, N.Y., 1977-87, sr. engr., 1988-91; cons. Ford Electronics, Lansdale, Pa., 1992-93; sr. hardware design engr. Lockheed Martin Corp., Pittsfield, Mass., 1993-96, Gen. Dynamics, Pittsfield, 1997—2001; cons. FAPRE Engring., New Hartford, NY, 2002—. Contbg. author: Resistance Welding Manual, 1997; editor: Microelectronic Packaging Technology, 1989; contbr. tech. articles to profl. jours. including Corrosion Jour., Jour. Applied Physics, Internat. Jour. Fracture, Engring. Fracture Mechs., Metallurg. Trans., Internat. Inst. Weld Conf. Mem. ASM Internat. (chmn. electronic packaging and interconnect group of 4 tech. coms. 1987-90, session chmn. microelectronic packaging confs. 1987-88, conf. chmn. electronic packaging conf. 1989), Am. Welding Soc. (chmn. resistance welding/test methods subcom. 1979—). Achievements include development of world's first maximum shear fatigue test method to observe crack initiation and propagation by inclusion in bearing steels. Avocations: swimming, skiing, fishing, concerts, plays. Home and Office: 7 Upper Woods Rd New Hartford NY 13413-5523

SHIEKMAN, LAURENCE ZEID, lawyer; b. Phila., Feb. 13, 1947; s. Morton and Roberta (Zeid) S.; m. Marjorie Kershbaum, Dec. 25, 1970; children: Wendy K., Thomas K. BS in Econs., U. Pa., 1968, JD, 1971. Bar: Pa. 1971. Law clk. to Hon. A. Leon Higginbotham, Jr. U.S. Dist. Ct. (ea. dist.) Pa., 1971-73; asst. prof. Fla. State U. Coll. Law, Tallahassee, 1973-75; assoc. Pepper, Hamilton & Scheetz, Phila., 1975-78, ptnr., 1978—. Chmn. 20th Yr. reunion com. U. Pa. Law Sch., Phila., 1995. Mem. ABA, Pa. Bar Assn., Phila. Bar Assn. Office: Pepper Hamilton LLP 3000 Two Logan Sq 18th & Arch Sts Philadelphia PA 19103-2799

SHIEL, LAUREL ELIZABETH, interior designer; b. Benton, Ill., Nov. 4, 1955; d. Suzanne (Reinardy) McReynolds; m. William A. Shiel, Dec. 27, 1980. B.S. in Interior Design with honors, U. Wis.-Madison, 1977. Interior designer Carson Pirie Scott & Co., Chgo., 1978-79, Walgreen Co., Deerfield, Ill., 1979-80, J. Cotey Inc., Northbrook, Ill., 1980-83; facilities planner Teradyne, Deerfield, 1983— ; mem. ednl. assistance com. Inst. Bus. Designers, Chgo., 1982-83. Mem. Internat. Facility Mgmt. Assn. (affiliate). Episcopalian. Avocations: reading; running; tennis; travel; modern dance; Home: 40 Warwick Rd Winnetka IL 60093-4257

SHIELDS, ALLAN EDWIN, writer, photographer, retired educator; b. Columbus, Ohio, July 3, 1919; s. Richard Edwin and Eloessa (Smith) S.; m. Bernice Clark, Aug. 2, 1941; children— Allan Oakley, Richard Minter, Larry Michael, Catherine Marie AB, U. Calif.-Berkeley, 1941; MA, U. So. Calif., 1947, PhD, 1951. Prof. philosophy San Diego State U., 1949-68, 70-78; emeritus prof. San Diego State Coll., 1978—; dean Coll. Humanities and Fine Arts U. No. Iowa, 1968-70; owner, pub. Jerseydale Ranch Press, 1992-98. Seasonal ranger naturalist Nat. Park Service, Yosemite Nat. Park, 1955-60; freelance writer, photographer, 1978— ; violinist-violist, frequent recitalist; mem., sometime concertmaster Merced Symphony Orch., Calif., 1979-91; founder, with wife, Jerseydale Ranch Press, 1992. Author: Guide to Tuolumne Meadows Trails, 1960, rev. edit., 1973, (with Herbert Searles) A Bibliography of the Works of F.C.S. Schiller, 1969, (with Richard Shields) Tuolumne Profile: Yosemite, 1967, (novella) The Tragedy of Tenaya, 1974, new version 1992, A Bibliography of Bibliographies in Aesthetics, 1974, (poetry) A Horse in the House, 1985, Mariposa Now and Then, 1993, Tuffy, an Angel Hid in a Cloud, 1994, What Animals Taught Me, 1995, (with Bernice Shields) Into the Valley: A Brief History of Jerseydale Ranch, 1995, (with John Sharsmith) Climb Every Mountain: A Portrait of Carl Sharsmith, 1996, The Spirit of Rin-Tin-Tin, 2001, also numerous poems and articles; editor: A Yosemite Adventure in 1863, 1992, Wild Bill Neely and the Pagan Brothers' Golden Goat Winery, 1993, The Song of Sonora, 1993, O.S.S.: One Sad Sack—Pvt. Neely Disciplines the Military, 1994, A Yosemite Naturalist's Odyssey, 1994, Wilderness Treks by Foot, Canoe, and Adobe Rocket, and Father's Far-Flung Fables, 1995, Dream Temple and Other Visions, 1997; pub. various profl. jours. Bd. dirs. San Diego Symphony. Served with USAAF, 1942-45 Mudd fellow in philosophy U. So. Calif., 1948-49 Mem. Am. Soc. for Aesthetics (trustee), Phi Beta Kappa, Phi Kappa Phi, Phi Mu Alpha Sinfonia (hon.). Home: 2444 Beverly Ave Clovis CA 93611-5927 E-mail: ashields@csufresno.edu. *My greatest satisfactions have come with tasks completed to the best of my abilities. Whether raising children, building a building, nurturing a marriage, learning the violin, or writing, all have inherent standards demanding recognition. Though there is always joy in the process of doing, joy can be transformed into satisfaction only in completion evaluated against the standards of worth for that kind of undertaking.*

SHIELDS, ANTHONY FRANK, oncologist, hematologist; b. Highland Park, Mich., 1952; MD, Harvard U., 1979; PhD, MIT, 1979. Diplomate Am. Bd. Internal Medicine, Am. Bd. Oncology, Am. Bd. Hematology. Intern U. Wash. Hosp., 1979-80, resident internal medicine, 1980-81; fellow hematology/oncology U. Wash., 1981-84; mem. staff VA Med. Ctr., Seattle, 1987-95, Harper Hosp., Detroit, 1995—, Karmanos Cancer Inst., Mich., 1995—; asst. prof. U. Wash., 1987-93, assoc. prof., 1993-95, Wayne State U., 1995-99, prof. medicine and oncology, 1999—. Mem. Am. Assn. Cancer Rsch., Am. Soc. Clin. Oncology, Am. Soc. Hematology, Soc. Nuclear Medicine. Office: Harper Hosp 534 Hudson 3990 John R St Detroit MI 48201-2097 E-mail: shieldsa@karmanus.org.

SHIELDS, BRUCE MACLEAN, management consultant; b. Wilkinsburg, Pa., Sept. 27, 1922; s. Edwin Bruce and Edith Barbara (Kennedy) S.; m. Nancy Garwood Adams, June 2, 1951; children: Duncan, Gordon A. BSMetE, Carnegie-Mellon U., 1944; MS in Metallurgy, MIT, 1952; cert., U. Pitts., 1959, U.S. Steel Adv. Mgmt. Sch., 1976. Registered profl. engr., Pa. With U.S. Steel Corp., various locations, 1942, 46-56, chief metallurgist Duquesne, Pa., 1956-60, Chgo., 1960-65, mgr. process metallurgh Pitts., 1965-68, mgr. tubular product metallurgy, 1968-72, gen. mgr. product metallurgy, 1972-76, gen. mgr. customer tech. svc., 1976-77, gen. mgr. metall. svcs., 1977-78, dir. metall. engring., 1978-83, cons., 1983—; pvt. practice mgmt. cons., 1983—. Presenter to tech. confs. Contbr. articles to profl. jours.; patentee in field. Cubmaster, scoutmaster, dist. chmn., mem. exec. bd., bd. dirs. Boy Scouts Am., Chgo. and Pitts., 1962-87; elder, deacon, budget chmn., pres. bd. trustees Southminster Ch., Pitts.; pres. USS Goodfellowship Club, Pitts., 1983. 1st lt. U.S. Army Corps Engrs., 1943-46. Recipient Silver Beaver award Boy Scouts Am., 1978. Fellow Am. Soc. Metals (life); mem. AIME (life), Am. Iron and Steel Inst. (life, chmn.'s award 1983), Am. Petroleum Inst. (mem. pipe standardization com.), Am. Iron and Steel Engrs. Republican. Presbyterian. Avocations: golf, sailing, music, reading, computers. Home and Office: 100 Tall Pine Ln Apt 1104 Naples FL 34105-2615

SHIELDS, CAROL ANN, writer, educator; b. Oak Park, Ill., June 2, 1935; came to Can., 1957, naturalized, 1974. d. Robert Elmer and Inez Adelle (Sellgren) Warner; m. Donald Hugh Shields, July 20, 1957; chldren: John, Anne, Catherine, Margaret, Sara. BA, Hanover Coll., 1957; MA, U. Ottawa, Ont., Can., 1975; hon. degree, U. Ottawa, 1995, Hanover Coll., 1996, Queen's U., 1996, U. Winnipeg, 1996, U.B.C., 1996, U. Western Ont., 1997, U. Toronto, 1998, Concordia U., 1998, Carleton U., 2000, Mount St. Vincent, 2000, Wilfred Laurier U., 2000. Editl. asst. Can. Slavonic Papers, Ottawa, 1972-74; lectr. U. Ottawa, 1976-77, U.B.C., Vancouver, Can., 1978-80; prof. U. Man., Winnipeg, Can., 1980-2000, prof. emerita Can., 2000—; chancellor U. Winnipeg, 1996-2000; chancellor emerita, 2000—. Author: (poems) Others, 1972, Intersect, 1974, Coming to Canada, 1991, (novels) Small Ceremonies, 1976, The Box Garden, 1977, Happenstance, 1980, A Fairly Conventional Women, 1982, Swann: A Mystery, 1987, The Republic of Love, 1992, The Stone Diaries, 1993 (Nat. Book Critics Circle award for fiction, 1995, Pulitzer Prize for fiction, 1995), Larry's Party, 1997 (Orange prize for fiction, 1998), Unless, 2002, (biography) Jane Austen, 2000, (plays) Women Waiting, 1983, Departures and Arrivals, 1984, Thirteen Hands, 1993; author: (with Catherine Shields) Fashion Power Guilt; author: (with David Williamson) Anniversary, 1998; author: (story collections) Various Miracles, 1985, The Orange Fish, 1989, Dressing Up for the Carnival, 2000; co-editor (with Marjorie Anderson): Dropped Threads, 2001; author: (novels) Unless, 2000. Named Order of Can., Can. Booksellers Author of Yr., 2001; recipient prize, CBC, 1983, 1984, Nat. Mag. award, 1985, Arthur Ellis award, 1987, Can. Book Sellers' award, 1994, Manitoba Book of the Yr., 1994, Marian Engel award, 1990, Gov. Gen's award, Can. Coun., 1993, Nat. Book Critics Circle award, 1995, Pulitzer prize, 1995, Chevalier de l'Ordre des Arts et des Lettres, 2000, Order of Manitoba, 2001; fellow Guggenheim, 1999; grantee, Can. Coun., 1973, 1976, 1978, 1986, Man Arts Coun., 1984, 1985. Mem. PEN, Writers Union Can., Writers Guild Man., Jane Austen Soc., Royal Soc. Can. Mem. Soc. Of Friends.

SHIELDS, CRAIG M. lawyer; b. Oceanside, N.Y., Nov. 28, 1941; s. John Anderson and Lillian Ethel (Hagen) S.; m. Candia Atwater Shields, July 13, 1963 (div. 1985); children: Mark, Christopher, Evan; m. Norma Magor Peters, Apr. 25, 1998. Bar: N.Y. 1967, U.S. Dist. Ct. (so. and ea. dists.) N.Y. 1967, U.S. Ct. Appeals (2d cir.) 1967, U.S. Supreme Ct. 1976. Assoc. Clark, Carr & Ellis, N.Y.C., 1966-69; ptnr. Borden & Ball, 1969-76, Sage, Gray, Todd & Sims, N.Y.C., 1976-80; counsel Conboy, Hewitt, O'Brien & Boardman, 1980-83; ptnr. Collier, Cohen, Shields & Bock, 1983-92, Quinn & Suhr, White Plains, N.Y., 1992-95; v.p., gen. counsel United Vanguard Homes, Inc., Glen Cove, 1992—. Contbr. articles to profl. jours. Bd. dirs. Group House of Port Washington (N.Y.) Inc., 1973-85, Children's House, Inc., Mineola, N.Y., 1985-89, Resources for Program Devel., Inc., Port Washington, 1982—; pres. Port Washington Community Action Coun., 1968-69; committeeman Dem. Party, Port Washington, 1967-71. Mem. ABA, Assn. of Bar of City of New York, N.Y.State Bar Assn. Democrat. Methodist. Home: 103 E 86th St Apt 7A New York NY 10028-1058 Office: United Vanguard Homes Inc 4 Cedar Swamp Rd Glen Cove NY 11542-3744 E-mail: afeck@uvhco.com.

SHIELDS, DAVID JONATHAN, English educator; b. Seattle, July 22, 1956; s. Milton and Hannah (Bloom) S.; m. Laurie McCallum, Sept. 1, 1990; 1 child, Natalie McCallum. BA in Brit. and Am. Lit., Brown U., 1978; MFA in Fiction, U. Iowa, 1980. Vis. asst. prof. St. Lawrence U., Canton, N.Y., 1985-88; asst. prof. U. Wash., Seattle, 1988-92, assoc. prof., 1992-97, prof. dept. English, 1997—. Mem. faculty Warren Wilson Coll. low-residency MFA program for writers, Asheville, N.C., 1996—; guest spkr. and guest lectr. in field; numerous readings. Author: Heroes, 1984, Dead Languages, 1989, A Handbook for Drowning, 1992, Remote, 1996, Black Planet: Facing Race During an NBA Season, 1999, Baseball Is Just Baseball, 2001, Enough About You, 2002; contbr. essays, stories and articles to mags. Recipient fellowships Nat. Endowment for Arts, 1982, 91, N.Y. Found. for Arts, 1988, PEN/Person Found., 1992; recipient award Ingram-Merrill Found., 1983; recipient grant Ludwig Vogelstein Found., 1986; residence fellowships include Corp. of Yaddo (3), MacDowell Colony (2), Va. Ctr. for the Creative Arts (3), Ragdale Found. (2), Millay Colony (Edna St. Vincent Millay award), Cummington Cmty. of the Arts, Centrum, 1982-91; book reviewer. Mem. MLA, Authors Guild, Writers Guild, Poets and Writers, Assoc. Writing Programs, Poets, Editors, Novelists. Jewish. Office Fax: (206) 547-6363. Business E-Mail: eshields@u.washington.edu.

SHIELDS, DONALD GRAHAM, speech pathology/audiology services professional; b. New Haven, June 8, 1925; s. Andrew Graham and Marjorie Agard Shields; m. Kathleen Hamilton Shields, Mar. 6, 1975 (div. Mar. 1980); children: Judith Allison, Mark Agard, Nancy Hamilton Shields Goodhue; m. Janet Witcher Cole (dec. June 1990). BA, U. Denver, 1965, MA, 1966, PhD, 1977. Pvt. practice, 1967—. Contbr. articles to profl. jours., poetry to mags. Docent Dubuque Mus. Art, 1998—; mem. Jackson County (Iowa) Dem. County Com.; lector, singer 1st Luth. Ch., Maquoketa, Iowa; bd. dirs. Jackson County Humane Soc., 1997—99. Hosp. corps USNR, 1943—46. Mem.: Iowa Speech and Hearing Assn. (life; cert.), Am. Speech Lang./Hearing Assn. (life; cert.), Dubuque Area Writers' Guild. Democrat. Achievements include development of integrated therapy approach to aphasia, stuttering and dysphagia therapy under scoring rate and rhyme as common elements of improvement. Avocations: photography, poetry reading. Home: PO Box 1122 Maquoketa IA 52060

SHIELDS, DONALD JAMES, communications educator; b. Paris, Oct. 28, 1937; s. John and Harriet Ann (Francis) S.; divorced; children: Donald Gary, Christina Shields-Proctor. BS, Ea. Ill. U., 1959; MS, Purdue U., 1961, PhD, 1964. Asst. prof. Cornell U., Ithaca, N.Y., 1964-65; prof. Ind. State U., Terre Haute, 1965-2000. Adj. prof. Rose-Hulman Inst. Tech., Terre Haute, 1975—, Edison C.C., 2000—. Precinct committeeperson, ward chair Ind. Dem. Party, Indpls., 1989-97; chair Lee County (Fla.) Dem. Campaign Com., 2000. Mem. AAUP (state bd. dirs. 1995-97), Ind. Comm. Assn., Centera States Comm. Assn., Speech Comm. Assn. Methodist. Avocations: golf, scuba, water sports. Home and Office: 3593 Knollwood Rd Fort Myers FL 33919-6414

SHIELDS, JAMES JOSEPH, education administrator, educator, author; b. Phila., Feb. 11, 1935; s. James Joseph and Lena Josephine (Dyer) S. (dec.). BS in Polit. Sci., Saint Joseph's U., 1956; EdM, Temple U., 1959; EdD, Columbia U., 1963. Asst. dir. internat. studies Tchrs. Coll., Columbia U., N.Y.C., 1961, field rschr., Tchrs. for East Africa Program N.Y.C. and Kampala, Uganda, 1961-62; asst. prof. history and philosophy of edn. SUNY, New Paltz, 1962-64; asst. prof. comparative and internat. edn. CUNY, N.Y.C., 1964-69, assoc. prof., 1969-75, prof., 1975-98, prof. emeritus, 1998, head, Sch. Adminstrn. Program, 1983-85, chair dept. social and psychol. founds., 1988-90; dir. Japan Initiative, 1986-98; spl. projects dir. Ctr. for Edn. Outreach and Innovation Tchrs. Coll. Columbia U., 1998—. Cons. Inst. for Ednl. Devel., N.Y.C., 1968-71, Equitable Life Ins. Co., N.Y.C., 1981, N.Y.C. Bd. Edn. Dist. 4, 1996-97, Time Mag., 1998, Inst. Internat. Edn., 1998-99; vis. rsch. prof. Tokyo Met. U., 1986-95; vis. prof. Tchrs. Coll., Columbia U., 1965-67, 93-95, 98, 2000—, Yale U., 1997; mem. evaluation bd. Nat. Coun. on Accreditation of Tchr. Edn., Washington, 1970-75; assoc. Columbia U., Univ. Seminar on Modern Japan, N.Y.C., 1987—, chair, 1990-91. Author: Education in Community Development: Its Function in Technical Assistance, 1967, Problems and Prospects in International Education, 1968, Foundations of Education: Dissenting Views, 1974, Japanese Schooling: Patterns of Socialization Equality and Political Control, 1989, rev. edit. 1993; author numerous book chpts., monographs and book reviews; contbr. numerous articles to profl. jours. Mem. Pub. Edn. Assn. Task Force on a Reconstructed Ednl. Sys., N.Y.C., 1977-78, Pub. Edn. Assn. Task Force on Tchr. Selection, N.Y.C., 1981; mem. N.Y. Urban Coalition, 1982-84, Alumni Coun., Tchrs. Coll. Columbia U., 1993-99, 2000—. With USAR, 1959-59. Grantee SUNY Rsch. Found., 1964, Fulbright Travel grantee, 1964, N.Y. State Edn. Dept., 1969-72, Rsch. Found. CUNY, 1980-81, Japan-U.S. Friendship Commn., 1986-89, The City Coll. Provost Fund, 1988-89, 89-90; Japan Found. Ctr. for Global Partnership, 1994, The U.S.-Japan Found., 1994-96, The Tokyo Found, 1998-2000; recipient Wyo. Gov.'s Youth Coun. award, 1974, Higher Edn. award Holy Family Coll., Phila., 1990, Ann. Gertrude Langsam Ednl. Reconstrn. award Adelphi U., 1992; postdoctoral fellow Yale U., New Haven, 1967-68. Hon. fellow Comparative and Internat. Edn. Soc. (N.E. region conf. coord. 1984, bd. dirs. 1992-95); mem. Am. Ednl. Studies Assn. (pres. 1973-74, exec. coun. 1970-75), Carnegie Coun. on Ethics and Internat. Affairs (bd. trustees 1998—, vice chmn. 2001—), Japan Soc. of N.Y., Internat. House of Japan, Soc. for Ednl. Reconstrn. (exec. com. 1973—), N.Y. Athletic Club (N.Y.C.), Beaux Arts Alliance. Avocations: collecting Long Island painters (1850-1950), travel, gardening. Address: Trump Pl 200 Riverside Blvd Apt 11N New York NY 10069-0911 also: 42 Old Town Xing Southampton NY 11968-5015 E-mail: jshieldsII@juno.com.

SHIELDS, JOHN CHARLES, American studies and African American studies and literature educator; b. Phoenix, Oct. 29, 1944; s. Granville Blaine and Elizabeth Merle (Hartgraves) S. BA, U. Tenn., Knoxville, 1967, MA in Coll. Teaching, 1969, PhD, 1978; EdS, George Peabody Coll., 1975. Tchr. English Sevier County High Sch., Sevierville, Tenn., 1967-68; head dept. English Battle Ground Acad., Franklin, 1969-71; dir. academics Brentwood Acad., Nashville, 1971-73, Columbia (Tenn.) Mil. Acad., 1973-74; instr. U. Tenn., Knoxville, 1978-79; asst. prof. Ill. State U., Normal, 1979-86, assoc. prof. English, 1986-93, prof. English, 1993—. Cons. Ency. Britannica, Oxford Companion to African Am. Lit., Norton Anthology African American Literature, others; project dir. conf. on Phillis Wheatley NEH, 1983-85; faculty advisor Native Am. Student Soc. Ill. State U., 1990—. Assoc. editor Style, DeKalb, Ill., 1988-90, guest editor, 1990—; editor: The Collected Works of Phillis Wheatley, 1988, paperback, 1989; adv. editor, contbr. Oxford Companion to African Am. Lit., 1997—, Am. Nat. Biography, 24 vols., 1994—; contbr. New Dictionary of Nat. Biography, Great Britain, 1995—; author: The American Aeneas: Classical Origins of the American Self, 2001 (nominated for Ralph Waldo Emerson prize, John Hope Franklin award, Susan M. Glasscoch Interdisciplinary Book prize and Lora Romero First Book prize); contbr. articles to lit. jours. and chpts. to books; manuscript reviewer various presses and jours. Spokesperson for Native Am. citizens, 1990—. Ford Found. fellow, 1968-69, Soc. for Humanities fellow Cornell U., 1984-85, NEH fellow, 1983, 84, 89, 93, John C. Hodges Teaching Excellence award, 1969. Mem. MLA, Internat. Soc. for 18th-Century Studies, Am. Studies Assn., Melville Soc., Coll. Lang. Assn., Phi Mu Alpha Sinfonia, Alpha Phi Omega, Sigma Nu. Unitarian Universalist. Avocations: piano, singing, Native American culture, archaeology, rare book collecting. Home: 1412 Donegal Dr Normal IL 61761-5416

SHIELDS, JOHN HUGH, postmaster, writer; b. Lorain, Ohio, June 20, 1942; s. John Henry and Huldah Dunning Shields; m. Sara Elizabeth Irvin Shields, July 24, 1965; children: Stefanie Ruth, John Henry, Dylan Frederick, Benjamin Roon. BA, Coll. of Wooster, Ohio, 1964; MA, U. Iowa, 1967. Instr. English Lorain (Ohio) County C.C., 1968—70; asst. head alumni svcs. U. Alaska, Fairbanks, 1970—71; log builder Jamieson Constrn., Ester, 1971—75; postmaster U.S. Postal Svc., Owyhee, Nev., 1981—. Author: (novel trilogy) Letters from Alaska, 1971—93; contbr. short story to Sewanee Rev. Home: PO Box 99 Owyhee NV 89832 E-mail: jhshields@msn.com.

SHIELDS, LAWRENCE THORNTON, orthopaedic surgeon, educator; b. Boston, Oct. 2, 1935; s. George Leo and Catherine Elizabeth (Thornton) S.; m. Karen S. Kraus, Sept. 21, 1968; children: Elizabeth Coulter, Laura Thornton, Sarah Daly, Michael Lawrence. AB, Harvard U., 1957; MD, Johns Hopkins U., 1961. Diplomate Am. Bd. Orthopedic Surgery. Intern Barnes Hosp., Washington U., St. Louis, 1961-62, resident, 1962-63; resident orthopedic surgeon Children's Hosp. Med. Ctr., Boston, 1966-67, Mass. Gen. Hosp., Boston, 1967-68, Peter Bent Brigham, Robert Breck Brigham Hosps., Boston, 1968-69, Harvard Med. Sch., Boston, 1965-69, instr., 1969—; orthopedic surgeon Peter Bent Brigham & Women's Hosp., Children's hosps., 1969—, Waltham (Mass.)-Weston Hosp. and Med. Ctr., 1969—, also chief orthopedic surgery, pres. med. staff. Mem. Waltham-Weston Orthop. Assocs.; proprietor Boston Athenaeum; mem. staff Hahnemann Hosp., Boston, Newton-Wellesley (Mass.) Hosp.; cons. orthop. surgeon VA Hosp., Boston; mem. faculty Harvard Med. Sch.; vis. scholar Trinity Hall Cambridge U., 1987; hon. prof. New Eng. Coll., Henniker, NH, Sussex, England, 1995; bd. dirs. Wal-West Health Sys., 1986—; pres. Mass. Bay Investment Trust; dir. Waltham Investment Group. Contbr. articles to med. jours. Bd. dirs. Mass. Acad. Emergency Med. Technicians, Waltham Boys' Club; bd. of overseers Boston Lyric Opera, 1993—; trustee, exec. com. Waltham-Weston Hosp. and Med. Ctr. Lt. M.C. USNR, 1963-65. Fellow: ACS, Mass. Hist. Soc. Libr., Am. Acad. Orthop. Surgeons, Mass. Hist. Soc.; mem.: Thomas B. Quigley Sports Medicine Soc. (v.p., pres.-elect, pres. 2001), R. Austen Freeman Soc. (v.p.), Mass. Med. Soc. (v.p. 1982—83, councillor), Mass. Orthop. Assn. (sec. 1986—, bd. dirs.), Royal Soc. Medicine, N.Y. Acad. Scis., Cox & Co., Boston Lyric Opera (bd. overseers 1993), English Speaking Union (bd. dirs.), Academie Brillat-Savarin, Confrerie de La Chaine des Rotisseurs (elected 1996), Waltham Hist. Soc., Trollope Soc. (founding mem., bd. dirs., London), Thoreau Soc., Internat. Consular Corps (hon.), Charles River Dist. (treas., exec. com., pres. 1982—83), Titanic Hist. Soc., Boston Opera Assn. (bd. dirs.), Harvard Mus. Assn., Emerson Soc., Handel and Hayden Soc. (bd. overseers), Les Amis d'Escoffier Soc., L'Ordre Mondial (elected 1999), St. Crisplin's Soc. Boston (founding mem., pres. 1991—), USS Wasp CV-19 Assn., Theodore Roosevelt Assn. New Eng. (founding), East India, Devonshire Sports and Pub. Schs. Club (London), New Eng. Orthop. Club, Boston Orthop. Club, St. Botolph Club (Boston), Bull Dog Terries, Clover Club Boston, Union Club Boston, Harvard Club, Algonquin Club Boston (bd. dirs., pres. 1990—), Rotary, Pi Eta (Harvard). Home: 9 Beverly Rd Newton MA 02461-1112 Office: 721 Huntington Ave Boston MA 02115-6010 also: 20 Hope Ave Ste 314 Waltham MA 02453-2717 E-mail: ltshields@mcb.harvard.edu.

SHIELDS, MARGARET AGNES, land surveyors association executive; b. Bloomsburg, Pa., Apr. 21, 1946; d. Robert James Alexander and Isabel Corley (Davey) S. BS in Music Edn., Susquehanna U., 1967. Tchr. music Boyertown (Pa.) Area Schs., 1967-68; tchr. jr. high sch. music Abington (Pa.) Schs., 1969; tchr. instrumental music Ft. Washington Sch. Dist., Upper Dublin, Pa., 1969-70, Warwick Sch. Dist., Lititz, 1970-73, Pittsford (N.Y.) Cen. Schs., 1973-76; v.p., bus. mgr. Dengler Studios Inc., Rochester, N.Y., 1976-81; owner MAS Enterprises, Syracuse, 1981—; exec. adminstr. N.Y. State Assn. Profl. Land Surveyors, Albany, 1982—2002. Mem. Nat. Soc. Profl. Surveyors (chmn., editor 1987-99), Vt. Soc. Land Surveyors (adminstrv. sec. 2001—), Sigma Alpha Iota. Avocations: home remodeling, reading, music, writing, camping. Home and Office: 223 Crown Dr Groton VT 05046 E-mail: vermontpeace@aol.com., megshields@kingcon.com.

SHIELDS, MARLENE SUE, elementary school educator; b. Denver, Apr. 7, 1939; d. Morris and Rose (Sniderman) Goldberg; m. Charles H. Cohen, Dec. 22, 1957 (dec.); children: Lee, Richard, Monica; m. Harlan Shields. BA magna cum laude, Met. State Coll., 1980; MA, U. No. Colo., 1986. Preschool tchr. Temple Emanuel, Denver, 1970-75; tchr. Kindergarten Temple Sinai, 1975-80; tchr. pre-Kindergarten St. Mary's Acad., Englewood, 1980-83; tchr. Beach Court Elem., Denver, 1983-86, Valverde Sch., Denver, 1984-85; tchr. third grade Brown Elem., 1985-86; tchr. learning disabilities Cowell Elem. Sch., 1986-87, Sabin Elem. Sch., Denver, 1987-88; tchr. second grade Sabin Elem., 1988—. Mem. curriculum com. Denver Pub. Sch., 1989—, pers. subcom., 2000-02; citizen amb. Spain joint tchr. conf., 1995. Mem. personal subcom. Sabin Elementary Sch., 2000. Mem. Colo. Copun. Internat. Reading Assn., Nat. Assn. for Young Children, Nat. Tchrs. Colo. Math., Internat. Reading Assn., Carousel of Intervention, Delta Kappa Gamma (sec., v.p., grade level chair), PRIDE (lang. curriculum com., math. curriculum com., impact com., CDM rep. 1994-95), Delta Kappa Gamma (state 2d v.p. 2001-02). Home: 5800 Big Canon Dr Englewood CO 80111-3516

SHIELDS, MARTHA BUCKLEY, elementary school educator; b. Ridley Park, Pa., Mar. 4, 1942; d. John Edward and Anne Josephine (Hayes) Buckley; m. James F. Shields, Aug. 22, 1964; children: James F., Martha S. Runzer, Katherine Anne Landaiche, John Edward. BA, Wheeling (W.Va) Jesuit U., 1964; postgrad., Widener U., Chester, Pa., 1975-76. Cert.: (paralegal). Exec. asst. Economy Engring. and Machine Works, Chester, 1970-77; tchr. gifted program RoseTree-Media S.D., Media, 1979-80; tchr. grade 5 St. Kevin Sch., Springfield, 1980-85; tchr. honors math. grades 4-8 St. Thomas the Apostle Sch., Glen Mills, 1985-97, tchr. 7th grade, 1997—. Bd. dirs. Chester County Voices Abroad, 1994—. Sec. vice-chair adv. com. Children and Youth Svcs. Delaware County, Media, 1979—, chmn. adv. com., 1999—2001; bd. dirs. St. Thomas the Apostle CYO, Glen Mills, 1977—, volleyball and track coach, 1977—; mem. alumni bd. Wheeling Jesuit U., 1996—. Named Educator-Vol. of the Yr., Leadership Delaware County Alumni Assn., 1992; named to Harry Watson Track Hall of Fame, KC, 1996; recipient Clifford M. Lewis Alumnus award, Wheeling Jesuit U., 1976, Coaches award for christian leadership, Archdiocese Phila.-Cath. Youth Orgn., 1989, Julia Forst award, Archdiocese Phila., 1999, Father Francis Griffin award, St. Thomas the Apostle Parish, 1999. Roman Catholic. Avocations: travel, sewing, reading. Home: 190 Andrien Rd Glen Mills PA 19342-1168 Office: St Thomas the Apostle Sch 430 Valleybrook Rd Glen Mills PA 19342-9440 E-mail: mopsys@comcast.net.

SHIELDS, MARY ANN HOUFF, library director; b. Hopewell, Va., Oct. 10, 1948; BA, Ga. State U., Atlanta, 1973, MA, 1977. Creative dir. Hydrick/Calhoun, Columbus, Ga., 1980-86; dir. devel. The Devereux Ctr. Ga., kennesaw, 1986-97; mgr. capital campaigns pandas Atlanta Zoo, 1998-99; dir. devel. First Montessori Sch. Atlanta, 1999—2001, IUPUI Univ. Libr., Indpls., 2001—. Conf. com. Assn. Healthcare Philanthropy Region IV, 1997-98. Recipient 6 gold and silver awards Healthcare Mktg. Report, 1994-96, Showcase award in Planned Giving Assn. Healthcare Philanthropy, 1996. Mem. Assn. Fundraising Execs. (cert. fundraising exec., bd. dirs., conf. cha

SHIELDS, PATRICIA LYNN, educational broker, consultant; b. Bklyn. BS in Biology, Bucknell U., 1984; postgrad., Rutgers U., 1985; MAT in Biol. Scis., Rutgers U., 2002. Pres., CEO Buttercup's Internat., Inc., Middletown, N.J., 1988—. Office: Buttercup's Internat Inc PO Box 148 Middletown NJ 07748-0148

SHIELDS, RANA COLLEEN, special education educator; b. Midland, Tex., Oct. 2, 1951; d. Robert Campbell and Edith Sue (Alexander) S.; m. Micheal Leggett; children: Daniel Robert Tilly, Casey Michelle Leggett; 1 stepchild, Laurie Ayn Leggett. B of Journalism, U. Tex., 1974; JD magna cum laude, South Tex. U., 1984; MEd in Spl. Edn., S.W. Tex. State U., 1993. Bar: Tex., 1985; cert. generic spl. edn., reading, Tex. City editor Huntsville (Tex.) Item, 1976-78; asst. county atty. Travis County Atty.'s Office, Austin, Tex., 1986-87; tchr. spl. edn. Liberty Hill (Tex.) H.S., 1990-91, Tex. Sch. for the Blind, Austin, 1991-93; grad. rsch. asst. in spl. edn. U. Tex., spring 1994, tchg. asst. spl. edn., 1995-96; tchr. spl. edn. Liberty Hill Middle Sch., 1997-98; contract spl. edn. monitor Tex. Edn. Agy., 1998—. Asst. casenotes editor: South Tex. Law Jour., 1983. Recipient 1st Pl. Spot News Photography award AP Mng. Editors, 1978, Am. Jurisprudence awards, 1979, 82, 83; named Outstanding Sophomore Journalist, Women in Comm., 1971; Univ. fellow, 1996-97. Mem. Assn. Tex. Profl. Educators, Kappa Delta Pi, Phi Kappa Phi, Pi Lambda Theta.

SHIELDS, ROBERT EMMET, merchant banker, lawyer; b. Ridley Park, Pa., May 18, 1942; s. Joseph Leonard and Kathryn J. (Walsh) S.; m. Mary Katherine Reid, July 22, 1967; children: Christopher D., David R., Kevin M., Kathleen. AB, Coll. Holy Cross, 1964; LLB cum laude, NYU, 1967. Bar: Pa. bar 1968. Mem. faculty Boalt Hall Sch. Law U. Calif., Berkeley, 1967-68; assoc. Drinker Biddle & Reath, Phila., 1968-74, ptnr., 1974-94, mng. ptnr., 1979-83, 85-94, head corp. and securities group, 1983-93, CFO, 1993-94; mng. dir., prin., ptnr., COO Questor Gen. Ptnr., L.P., 1995—, Questor Ptnrs. Funds, L.P. and Questor Mgmt. Co., 1995—. Sec. Wallquest Inc. Author: (with Eliot B. Thomas) Federal Securities Act Handbook, 4th edit, 1977; (with Robert H. Strouse) Securities Practice Handbook, 1987. Mem. ABA, Am. Law Inst., Pa. Bar Assn., Phila. Bar Assn. Home: 206 Atlee Rd Wayne PA 19087-3836 Office: Questor Mgmt Co 2000 Town Ctr Ste 2450 Southfield MI 48075-1406 also: 1 Logan Sq Ste 2000 Philadelphia PA 19103-6933 E-mail: rshields@questorfund.com.

SHIELDS, ROBERT FRANCIS, stockbroker; b. Chgo., Oct. 22, 1923; s. Francis Hugh and Adele Marie (Melcher) S.; children: Debra, Cynthia, Judith. BS in Econs., St. Joseph's Coll., 1944; MBA in Fin., Governors' State U., 1970. Registered fin. cons., investment adviser. With instl. bonds dept. Bear Stearns & Co., Chgo., 1946-49; resident mgr. Reynolds & Co., Chicago Heights, Ill., 1952-62; v.p., resident mgr. Dempsey Tegeler & Co., 1962-70; sr. v.p., resident mgr. Stifel Nicolaus & Co., 1970-93; sr. v.p. Everen Securities (formerly known as Prin. Fin. Securities), Munster, Ind., 1993—, First Union Securities, Munster. Maj. USMC, 1943-46, 50-52. Decorated Purple Heart. Mem. Olympia Fields Country Club. Roman Catholic. Home: 1910 Winfield Dr Munster IN 46321- Office: Wachovia Securities 8317 Calumet Ave Munster IN 46321-1723

SHIELDS, ROBERT MICHAEL, state agency administrator; b. Buffalo, Nov. 14, 1952; s. George Henry and Rose Mary (Reznik) S.; m. Michele Jean Kantor, Sept. 18, 1982. BA, U. Notre Dame, Ind., 1974; M of Regional Planning, Syracuse (N.Y.) U., 1976. Assoc. planner Dept. Devel. and Planning, Gary, Ind., 1976-78; sr. planner Dept. Urban and Econ. Devel., Utica, N.Y., 1978-79, dep. planning dir., 1980-82, planning dir., 1982-84; rep. housing and community devel. N.Y. State Div. Housing and Community Renewal, Albany, 1984-85, program mgr., 1985-89, dir. contract adminstrn., 1989-91, asst. dir. housing assistance programs, 1992-98, asst. dir. community devel., 1998—. Bd. dirs. Sculpture Space, Inc., Utica, 1980-84. Mem. Am. Planning Assn., Am. Inst. Cert. Planners, Notre Dame Club Mohawk Valley (sec., treas. 1979-81, v.p. 1981-83, pres. 1983-85), Notre Dame Club N.E. N.Y. (sec. 1990-93), Optimists (bd. dirs. Downtown Utica club 1980-83, v.p. 1980-82). Roman Catholic. Avocations: sports, music. Home: 5 Linda Ln Niskayuna NY 12309-1911 Office: NY State Div Housing and Community Renewal 38-40 State St Albany NY 12207-2867 E-mail: rshields@dhcr.state.ny.us.

SHIELDS, THOMAS CHARLES, lawyer; b. Evergreen Park, Ill., Apr. 26, 1941; s. Thomas James and Adelaide (McElligott) S.; m. Nicoline M. Murphy, Sept. 14, 1974; children: Thomas James II, Nicoline M.E., Suzanne Adelaide, Kerry Anne. AB, Georgetown U., 1963; JD cum laude, Northwestern U., 1966. Bar: Ill. 1966, U.S. Dist. Ct. (no. dist.) Ill. 1966, U.S. Ct. Appeals (7th cir.) 1966, U.S. Tax Ct. 1968, U.S. Supreme Ct. 1977. Assoc. Hopkins & Sutter, Chgo., 1966-73, ptnr., 1973-93; ptnr., chair health law dept. Bell, Boyd & Lloyd, Chgo., 1994—; chief counsel Cath. Health Assn. U.S., St. Louis, 1994—. Mem. adv. bd. Health Law Inst. Loyola U. Sch. Law, Chgo., 1984-89, Health Law Inst. DePaul U. Sch. Law, Chgo., 1985-96; lectr. Ill. Inst. Continuing Legal Edn., 1973; bd. dirs. Ill. Health Facilities Authority, 2000—; trustee Village of Riverside, Ill., 2001—. Contbr. articles to profl. jours., chpt. to book; mng. editor Northwestern Law Rev., 1965-66. Bd. dir. Cancer Rsch. Found., Chgo., 1987—, Brother Louie and Fannie Roncoli Found., 1994—, Chgo. Zool. Soc., Cath. Charities Chgo.; trustee Village of Riverside, 2001—. Mem.: Chgo. Bar Assn., Ill. Assn. Healthcare Attys. (bd. dir. 1983—89, pres. 1987—88), Ill. Bar Assn., Am. Hosp. Assn. (tax adv. group 1987—90), Am. Soc. Law and Medicine, Am. Health Lawyers Assn. (bd. dir. 1983—91, pres. 1989—90), Mid-Am. Club Chgo., Law Club Chgo., Exec. Club Chgo., Order of Coif. Avocations: skiing, bicycling, golf, tennis. Office: Bell Boyd & Lloyd 3 First Nat Plz Ste 3200 Chicago IL 60602

SHIELDS, THOMAS WILLIAM, surgeon, educator; b. Ambridge, Pa., Aug. 17, 1922; s. John Jr. and Elizabeth (Flanagan) S.; m. Dorothea Ann Thomas, June 12, 1948; children: Thomas William, John Leland, Carol Ann. BA, Kenyon Coll., 1943, DSc (hon.), 1978; MD, Temple U., 1947. Resident surgery Northwestern U. Med. Sch., Chgo., 1949-55, prof. surgery, 1968-92, prof. Emeritus of surgery, 1992—; practice medicine specializing in surgery Chgo., 1956—; chief of surgery VA Lakeside Hosp., 1968-87; chief thoracic surgery VA Lakeside Med. Ctr., 1987-90. Editor: General Thoracic Surgery, 1972, 5th edit., 2000, Bronchial Carcinoma, 1974, Mediastinal Surgery, 1991; assoc. editor Surgery, Gynecology and Obstetrics, Annals of Thoracic Surgery, 1993-2002; mem. editl. bd. Annals of Thoracic Surgery, Lung Cancer; contbr. articles to profl. jours. Served with U.S. Army, 1951-53. Mem. ACS, AMA, Am. Assn. for Thoracic Surgery, Soc. Thoracic Surgery, Central, Western Surg. Assns., Société Internationale de Chirurgie, Soc. for Surgery of Alimentary Tract, Internat. Assn. for Study Lung Cancer, Japanese Assn. Thoracic Surgery (hon.), Pan Pacific Surg. Assn., Phi Beta Kappa, Sigma Xi, Alpha Omega Alpha. Home: 10513 E Cinnabar Ave Scottsdale AZ 85258-4908 Office: Northwestern U Feinberg Sch Medicine Galter 10-105 201 E Huron St Chicago IL 60611

SHIELDS, V. SUE, federal magistrate judge; b. 1939; AB, Ball State U., 1959; LLB, Ind. U., 1961. Atty. Office of the Regional Counsel, IRS, 1961; dept. atty. gen. Office of the Atty. Gen. of Ind., 1962-64; judge Hamilton Superior Ct., 1965-78, Ind. Ct. Appeals, 1978-94; magistrate judge U.S. Dist. Ct. for So. Dist. Ind., Indpls., 1994—. Office: 256 US Courthouse 46 E Ohio St Indianapolis IN 46204-1903

SHIELDS-CASSIDY, GLORIA ANN, adult education educator, poet; b. Cherow, SC, Aug. 16, 1948; d. Henry Elijah and Annie Tillman Shields; divorced; children: Kulcey Lolanda Cassidy, Kenesha Latessa Cassidy. Diploma, Northeastern Tech. Coll., Cheraw, SC, 1976, Lincoln Sch. Practical Nursing, 1969; cert., Nat. Inst. Govtl. Purchasing, 1985, Pan Parenting Assn., 2000. Cert. Laubach tutor. Procurement officer Northeastern Tech. Coll., Cheraw, 1976—88; mega contract coord. Dept. Health Environ. Control, Chesterfield, 1993—2000; recruiter, parent educator Pee Dee Healthy Start, Cheraw, 2000—01; parent educator Darlington (SC) County Sch. Dist., 2001—. Regional dir. SCAGPO, Columbia, SC, 1986—89. Contbr. poetry to profl. publs. Treas. Chesterfield County Lit. Coun., Cheraw, 2001—; bd. dirs. Boys and Girls Club, 1988—93. Recipient plaque, LHS Cmty., Cheraw, 1986, Chesterfield Marlboro Tech. Coll., 1988, medallion, JC Penney Cmty. Citizen, Florence, SC, 1994. Avocations: youth activities, writing, mentoring, senior citizens. Home: 27 Tote Rd Cheraw SC 29520 Office: Darlington County Sch Dist 501 Spring St Darlington SC 29532

SHIELY, JOHN STEPHEN, company executive, lawyer; b. June 19, 1952; s. Vincent Robert and Mary Elizabeth (Hope) S.; m. Helen Jane Pauly, Aug. 29, 1981; children: Michael, Erin, Megan. BBA, U. Notre Dame, 1974; JD, Marquette U., 1977; M of Mgmt., Northwestern U., 1990. With Arthur Andersen & Co., Milw., 1977-79, Hughes Hubbard & Reed, Milw., 1979-83, Allen-Bradley Co., Milw., 1983-86, Rockwell Internat. Corp., Milw., 1985-86, Briggs & Stratton Corp., Milw., 1986—, gen. counsel, 1986-90, v.p., gen. counsel, 1990-91, pres., COO, 1994-2001, pres., CEO, 2001—. Bd. dirs. Briggs & Stratton Corp., Marshall & Ilsley Corp., Milw., Quad/ Graphics, Inc., Pewaukee, Wis., 1996—. Mem. Greater Milw. Com., 2000—; chmn. bd., dir. Children's Hosp. of Wis., 1992—; mem. bd. regents Milw. Sch. Engring., 1995—. Mem.: Wis. Mrfs. and Commerce (bd. dirs. 2002—), Assn. for Corp. Growth (past pres., bd. dirs. Wis. chpt. 1988—). Office: Briggs & Stratton Corp PO Box 702 Milwaukee WI 53201-0702

SHIENTAG, FLORENCE PERLOW, lawyer; b. N.Y.C. d. David and Ester (Germane) Perlow; m. Bernard L. Shientag, June 8, 1938. BS, NYU, 1940, LLB, 1933, JD, 1940. Bar: Fla. 1976, N.Y. Law aide Thomas E. Dewey, 1937; law sec. Mayor La Guardia, 1939-42; justice Domestic Relations Ct., 1941-42; mem. Tchrs. Retirement Bd., N.Y.C., 1942-46; asst. U.S. atty. So. dist. N.Y., 1943-53; cir. ct. mediator Fla. Supreme Ct., 1992; pvt. practice N.Y.C., 1960—, Palm Beach, Fla., 1976—. Lectr. on internat. divorce; mem. Nat. Commn. on Wiretapping and Electronic Surveillance, 1973—, Task Force on Women in Cts., 1985-86. Contbr. articles to profl. jours. Candidate N.Y. State Senate, 1954; bd. dirs. UN Devel. Corp., 1972-95, Franklin and Eleanor Roosevelt Inst., 1985—; bd. dirs., assoc. treas. YM and YWHA; hon. commr. commerce, N.Y.C. Mem. ABA, Fed. Bar Assn. (exec. com.), Internat. Bar Assn., N.Y. Women's Bar Assn. (pres., dir., Life Time Achievement award 1994, special award 2002), N.Y. State Bar Assn., N.Y.C. Bar Assn. (chmn. law and art sect.), N.Y. County Lawyers Assn. (dir.), Nat. Assn. Women LAwyers (sec.). Home: 737 Park Ave New York NY 10021-4256 *Success is a product of self respect and hard work at what you do well.*

SHIER, GLORIA BULAN, mathematics educator; b. The Philippines; came to U.S., 1966. d. Melecio Cauilan and Florentina (Cumagun) Bulan; m. Wayne Thomas Shier; children: John Thomas, Marie Teresita, Anna Christina. BS, U. Santo Tomas, Manila, Philippines; MA, U. Ill., 1968; PhD, U. Minn., 1986. Tchr. Cagayan (Philippines) Valley Coll., St. Paul Coll., Manila, Manila Div. City Schs.; asst. prof. U. of East, Manila; rsch. asst. U. Ill., Urbana, 1968-69; instr. Miramar Community Coll., San Diego, 1974-75, Mesa Community Coll., San Diego, 1975-80, Lakewood Community Coll., St. Paul, 1984, U. Minn., Mpls., 1986-87, North Hennepin Community Coll., Brooklyn Park, 1987—. Cons. PWS Kent Pub. Co., Boston, 1989—. Chairperson Filipino Am. Edn. Assn., San Diego, 1978-79. Fulbright scholar U.S. State Dept., U. Ill., 1966-70; fellow Nat. Sci. Found., Oberlin Coll., 1967; recipient Excellence in Teaching award UN Ednl. Scientific Cultural Organ., U. Philippines, Cert. Commendation award The Gov. of Minn., 1990, Outstanding Filipino in the Midwest Edn. Cat. award 1992, Cavite Assn., 1998, Gintong Pamana Found.; Outstanding Filipino-Am. in Edn. Mem.: Am. Statis. Assn., Minn. Math. Assn. of Two Yr. Colls., Minn. Coun. Tchrs. Math., Internat. Group for Psychology of Math. Edn., Am. Math. Assn. for Two Yr. Colls., Nat. Coun. Tchrs. Math., Philippine-Am. Acad. Sci. and Engring., Math. Assn. Am., Am. Math. Soc., Fil-Minnesotan Assn. (bd. dirs. 1991—), Cultural Soc. Filipino-Ams. (pres. 2001—), Sigma Xi, Phi Kappa Phi. Roman Catholic. Avocation: piano. Home: 210 Wexford Heights Dr New Brighton MN 55112-3144 E-mail: gloria.shier@nhoc.mnacu.edu.

SHIER, SHELLEY M. production company executive; b. Toronto, Mar. 15, 1957; d. Harry Shier and Rosaline (Cutler) Sonshine; m. Hank O'Neal, May 14, 1985. Student, H.B. Studio, N.Y.C., 1975-76, Stella Adler Conservatory, 1976-80. Company mem., actor Soho Artists Theater, N.Y.C., 1976-81; casting dir. Lawrence Price Prodns., 1981-82; pres. Hoss, Inc., 1983—; v.p. Chiaroscuro Records, 1987—; pres. Broadway Bound, Inc., 1998—. Cons. Peter Martin Assocs., N.Y.C., 1983, Norwegian Cruise Line, Miami, Fla., 1983-98, Floating Jazz Festival, 1983—, Big Bands At Sea, Rhythm & Blues Cruise, Dixieland At Sea, 1991—, The Blues Cruise, 1991—, Oslo (Norway) Jazz Festival, 1986—, New Sch. for Social Rsch., N.Y.C., 1989—, Beacons In Jazz Awards Ceremony, A Tribute to the Music of Bob Wills and The Texas Playboys, Mardi Gras at Sea. Talent acquisition agt. Save the Children, N.Y.C., 1986, Tomorrow's Children, N.Y.C., 1990, Royal Caribbean Internat., Miami, 1994-96, Ultimate Caribbean Jazz Spectacular, Country Music Festival in the Caribbean, CUNARD N.Y.C., 1994—, Barcelona Olympics, NBC, 1992, Broadway at Sea, 1996, Millennium at Sea, 1999—, Broadway Bound, 1999—, others. Avocations: karate, photography, riding, fishing, weightlifting. Office: HOSS Inc 830 Broadway New York NY 10003-4827 E-mail: broadwayboundinc@aol.com.

SHIERSHKE, NANCY FAY, artist, educator, property manager; b. St. Helens, Oreg., May 10, 1935; d. David Cline and Matilda Ruth (Pearce) Morrison; m. H. McNeal Kavanagh, Sept. 4. 1955 (dec. Dec. 1978); children: Marjorie L. Wood, David M. Kavanagh, Katherine F. Fiske; m. Richard M. Shiershke, Nov. 29, 1980. AA, Pasadena (Calif.) City Coll., 1956; BA, UCLA, 1965. Substitute elem. sch. tchr., Buena Park, Calif., 1967-69; property mgr. Pky. Cts., Arcadia, 1977—; libr. Reading Rm., 1979-87; freelance artist Kavanagh-Shiershke Art St., Calif., 1985—; art gallery hostess Descanso Gardens, La Canada, Flintridge, 1990—; display and sales person Village Fine Arts Gallery, Arcadia, 1991-92; art instr. Tri Cmty. Adult Edn., Covina, Calif., 1994—, Claremont (Calif.) Art Edn., 1998—. Art instr. Claremont (Claif.) Adult Edn. Group shows include Pasadena Presbyn. Ch., 1985—, Hillcrest Ch., 1992—, Descanso Gardens, 1994—, San Gabriel Fine Arts, 1994—. Named Artist of the Yr. Mid Valley Art League, 1990; Recipient Best of Show San Gabriel Fine Arts, 1991, Hulsebus award Pasadena Prebyn. Ch., 1996. Mem. Nat. Watercolor Soc., San Gabriel Fine Arts, Mid Valley Arts League (Artist of Yr. 1998), East Valley Art Assn., Valley Watercolor Soc., Foothill Creative Arts Group, Water Color West. Home: 505 Vaquero Rd Arcadia CA 91007-6045 Office: 614 E Vine Ave West Covina CA 91791

SHIFFER, JAMES DAVID, retired utility executive, consultant; b. San Diego, Mar. 24, 1938; s. Kenneth Frederick and Thelma Lucille (Good) S.; m. Margaret Edith Rightmyer, Sept. 5, 1959 (div. July 1986); children: James II, Elizabeth, Russell; m. Esther Zamora, Sept. 13, 1986; stepchildren: Bryan Boots, Jeremy Hellier, Marisol Boots. BS ChemE, Stanford U., 1960, MS ChemE, 1961. Registered profl. engr., Calif. Nuclear engr. Pacific Gas & Electric Co., Humboldt Bay Power Plant, Eureka, Calif., 1961-71; tech. mgr. Pacific Gas & Electric. Co., Diablo Canyon Power Plant, Avila Beach, 1971-80; mgr. nuclear ops. Pacific Gas & Electric Co., San Francisco, 1980-84, v.p. nuclear power generation, 1984-90, sr. v.p., gen. mgr. nuclear power generation bus. unit, 1990-91; exec. v.p. Pacific Gas & Electric, 1991-97; ret., 1997; pres., CEO PG&E Enterprises, San Francisco, 1994-95, also bd. dirs. Bd. dirs. Math., Engring., Sci. Achievement. Mem. AIChE, Am. Nuclear Soc., Commonwealth Club of Calif. (bd. govs. 1992-97). Republican. Episcopalian. Avocations: golf, music. Home: 2550 Royal Oaks Dr Alamo CA 94507-2227 E-mail: jshiffer@msn.com.

SHIFFMAN, BERNARD, mathematician, educator; b. N.Y.C., 1942; s. Max and Bella S.; m. Doris Judith Yaffe, July 11, 1965; children: Jonathan, Daniel. BS, MIT, 1964; PhD, U. Calif., Berkeley, 1968. C.L.E. Moore instr. MIT, 1968-70; asst. prof. math. Yale U., 1970-73; assoc. prof. Johns Hopkins U., Balt., 1973-77, prof., 1977—, chair dept. math., 1990-93. Mem. Inst. Advanced Study, Princeton, NJ, 1975, Math. Scis. Rsch. Inst., Berkeley, Calif., 1996, 99; series lectr. U. Kaiserslautern, West Germany, 1977, Inst. Math., Academia Sinica, Beijing, 1978, U. Paris VI, 1979, Nordic Summer Sch., Joensuu, Finland, 1981, U. Tokyo, 2000; mem. Inst. des Hautes Etudes Scientifiques, Bures-sur-Yvette, France, 1979; vis. prof. U. Paris VI, 1981, 85, U. Grenoble, 1992, 95, 2001. Editor Forum Mathematicum, 1989-95; assoc. editor Am. Jour. Math., 1990-92, editor, 1992-93, editor-in-chief, 1993—; rschr. publs. in complex analysis. Hon. Woodrow Wilson fellow, 1964, NSF fellow, 1968, Alfred P. Sloan rsch. fellow, 1973-75; recipient Woodrow Wilson Faculty Devel. award, 1979. Mem. Am. Math. Soc. Office: Johns Hopkins U Dept Math Baltimore MD 21218

SHIFFMAN, LESLIE BROWN, management executive; b. Fresno, Calif., Dec. 9, 1936; d. Albert Brown and Marion Jean (Riese) Brown-Propp; married, Jan. 20, 1957 (div. 1972); m. Sydney Shiffman, July 4, 1993; children: Susan, Steven, David, Thomas. BS, U. So. Calif., 1958. Office mgr. pvt. practice physician, Long Beach, Calif., 1971-73; cost acct. Panavision, Inc., Tarzana, 1974-76; exec. sec. Hartman Galleries, Beverly Hills, 1976-78; adminstrv. exec., corp. treas. Galanos Originals, L.A., 1978-98; adminstrv. asst., rabbinic asst., dir. adult edn. Sinai Temple, 1998—2002. Named L.A. Alumnae Panhellenic Assn. Women of Yr., 2000. Mem. Alpha Epsilon Phi (nat. pres. 1985-89, 99—, trustee, sec. Found. Inc. 1990-91, pres. 1991-95, treas. 1996-98, Woman of Distinction award 1993), Order of Omega. Republican. Jewish. Avocation: designing and hand knitting sweaters. Home: 1745 S Bentley Ave Apt 1 Los Angeles CA 90025-4323 E-mail: lbshiffman@aol.com.

SHIFFMAN, SAUL, psychologist, consultant; b. Bogota, Colombia, Nov. 27, 1951; s. Morris Shiffman, Bella Shiffman; m. Joan Susan Wagman; children: Miriam, Eliza. PhD, UCLA, 1981. Lic. clin. psychology 1982. Asst. prof. U. South Fla., Tampa, 1981—84; prof. U. Pitts., 1984—. Sr. sci. advisor Pinney Assocs., Pitts., 1993—; chief sci. officer Invivodata, Inc., Pitts., 1999—. Contbr. articles to profl. jours. Fellow: APA, Am. Psychol. Soc., Soc. Behavioral Medicine. Office: U Pitts 130 N Bellefield Pittsburgh PA 15260 Office Fax: 412-687-4855. Business E-Mail: shiffman@pitt.edu.

SHIFRIN, HARRIS DAVID, physician; b. Washington, June 4, 1936; s. William and Rose (Wein) S.; m. Sydney Helene Hannon, Oct. 27, 1978; children: Arthur, Roger, Renee. BS in Chemistry, George Washington U., 1958, MD, 1962. Intern Montefiore Hosp., Bronx, N.Y., 1962-63; internal medicine resident U. N.C., Chapel Hill, 1965-67; gastro-intestinal fellow Jackson Meml. Hosp., Miami, Fla., 1967-68; gastroenterologist Hollywood, 1969—. Author: Gastrointestinal Endoscopy, 1972, Gastroenterology, 1995; contbr. articles to profl. jours. Capt. USAF, 1963-65. Fellow ACP, Am. Coll. Gastroenterology; mem. Am. Gastrointestinal Assn. Republican. Jewish. Avocation: collecting watches. Home: 737 N South Lake Dr Hollywood FL 33019-1626

SHIGETOMI, KEITH SHIGEO, lawyer; b. Honolulu, Oct. 16, 1956; s. Samson Shigeru and Doris (Ogawa) S.; m. Ann Keiko Furutomo, Oct. 29, 1985; children: Samson Shigeru II, Marisa Mae. BSBA magna cum laude, Drake U., 1978; JD, U. Hawaii, 1983. Bar: Hawaii, 1983, U.S. Dist. Ct. Hawaii 1983, U.S. Ct. Appeals (9th cir.) 1986. Dep. pub. defender Office of Pub. Defender, Honolulu, 1983-88; pvt. practice, 1988-90, 94—; ptnr. Shigetomi & Thompson, 1990-94. Ind. grand jury counsel Cir. Ct., State of Hawaii, Honolulu, 1988-89. Finalist Three Outstanding Young Persons Hawaii Jaycees, 1994; named Criminal Def. Lawyer of Yr. Consumer Bus. Rev., 1996, 97, 99. Mem. Hawaii Bar Assn., Nat. Asian Pacific Bar Assn., Beta Gamma Sigma, Beta Alpha Psi, Phi Eta Sigma. Office: 711 Kapiolani Blvd Ste 1440 Honolulu HI 96813-5238

SHIGO, ALEX LLOYD, biologist, educator, publishing executive; b. Duquesne, Pa., May 8, 1930; s. Alex Shigo and Helen Szilagyi; m. Marilyn A. Paul, May 22, 1954; children: Judy Ruth, Robert Paul. BS in Biology, Waynesburg Coll., 1956; MS in Plant Pathology, W.Va. U., 1958, PhD in Plant Pathology, 1960. Rsch. scientist U.S. Forest Svc., Laconia and Durham, NH, 1959—85; pub., educator Shigo and Trees, Assocs., Durham, 1985—, cons., expert witness, 1985—95. Author (16 langs.): A New Tree Biology, 1986; author: Tree Anatomy, Tree Pruning, 1987—95, Modern Arboriculture (6 booklets). 1st clarinet Pitts. Youth Symphony, 1945—45; sgt., solo clarinet sect. Ofcl. USAF Band, Washington, 1951—56. Recipient awards (30) for rsch. on tree biology, U.S. Forest, Svc., Padua U. , Italy, ARS, 1974—2000. Fellow: Am. Phytopathological Soc., Internat. Acad. World Sci. Republican. Achievements include development of new tree biology based on successions and compartmentalization concepts; first to explain how branches are attached to trees leading to worldwide changes in pruning methods and featured on the front page of the Wall Street Journal. Avocations: music, reading, walking, walking with my dog in the woods, writing. Office: Shigo and Trees Assocs PO Box 769 Durham NH 03824 Home Fax: 603-868-1045.

SHIGYO, TETSUO TED, emergency physician; b. Newell, Calif., 1944; BA in Zoology, U. Calif., Santa Barbara, 1969; MD, U. Calif., San Francisco, 1973. Intern Valley Med. Ctr., Fresno, Calif., 1973-74, resident, 1974-76, asst. chief emergency medicine, 1976-78; emergency physician Fresno Cmty. Hosp. and Med. Ctr., 1978-80, St. Agnes Med. Ctr., Fresno, 1980—, ACLS med. dir., 1983-94, chmn. CME com., 1988-90, 92-94. Med. dir. paramedic program Fresno County, Calif., 1976-78. Fellow Am. Coll. Emergency Physicians; mem. Calif. Med. Assn. Office: 1303 E Herndon Ave Fresno CA 93720-3309 E-mail: shigyu@earthlink.net.

SHIH, IE-MING, medical educator, researcher; b. Taipei, Mar. 8, 1963; came to U.S., 1989; s. I-Fang Shi and Chiu-Sheh Yeh; m. Tian-Li Wang, Jan. 1, 1995; 1 child, Janie. MD, U. Pa., 1988, PhD, 1993. Bd. cert. Am. Bd. Pathology. Resident physician Johns Hopkins Hosp., Balt., 1994-2000; faculty Johns Hopkins U., 2000—. Prin. investigator Johns Hopkins U., Balt., 2000—. Contbr. articles to sci. jours.; inventor in field. Recipient Invest award, Internat. Assn. Gynecol. Pathologists, 2000; grantee, Dept. of Def., Am. Cancer Soc., 2000. Mem. AMA, Internat. Soc. for Study of Trophoblastic Disease, Internat. Assn. Gynecologic Pathologists (Young Investigator award 2000), Internat. Fedn. of Placental Assns., Am. Assn. for Cancer Rsch. Office: Johns Hopkins Med Inst Rm B315 418 N Bond St Baltimore MD 21231

SHIH, JOHN YOZEN, osteopathic physician; b. Hsinchu, Taiwan, Dec. 1, 1962; came to U.S., 1969; s. Joe Minching and Jean C. Shih; m. Nina Pauline Dipietro, Nov. 29, 1997. BA, U. South Fla., 1986; DO, Nova Southeastern U., 1991. Diplomate Am. Bd. Family Practice, Nat. Bd. Osteo. Med. Examiners. Intern Columbia Hosp., West Palm Beach, Fla., 1991-92; resident in family medicine Med. Coll. Ga., Augusta, 1992-94; resident in gen. surgery U. Medicine and Dentistry, Stratford, N.J., 1994-95; pvt. practice family/sports medicine and urgent care Macon, Ga., 1995-97, Duluth, 1997-98, Cumming, 1998-2000, Suwanee, 2000—. Fellow Am. Acad. Family Physicians; mem. AMA, Am. Osteo. Assn., Am. Coll. Osteo. Family Physicians, Am. Acad. Family Physicians, Ga. Acad. Family Physicians, mED. aSSN. gA. Office: Suwanee Family Physicians 960 Peachtree Industrial Blvd Suwanee GA 30024 E-mail: jyshih@pol.net.

SHIH, MICHAEL MING-YU, lawyer; b. Stanford, Calif., May 23, 1966; s. Kwang K. and Marion C. Shih; m. Melissa S. Marks, Nov. 23, 1997. BS, Cornell U., 1988; MS, U. Ill., 1990; JD, Fordham U., 1994. Bar: N.Y. 1995, U.S. Dist. Ct. (so. and ea. dists.) N.Y. 1995. Assoc. Kaye, Scholer, Fierman, Hays & Handler, LLP, N.Y.C., 1994—97, Kalow, Springut & Bressler, N.Y.C., 1997—99, The Beanstalk Group, Inc., N.Y.C., 1999—2001, Patterson, Belknap, Webb & Tyler LLP, N.Y.C., 2001—. Merck & Co., Inc. Patent Dept. fellow, 1991. Mem. ABA, N.Y. State Bar Assn., N.Y. Intellectual Property Law Assn., Assn. Bar City N.Y. Office: Patterson Belknap Webb & Tyler 1133 Ave of the Americas New York NY 10036

SHIH, WEI, astrophysicist; b. Shanghai, China, May 5, 1943; came to U.S., 1959; s. Frank I. and Emily Kwong S. BS in Physics, Nat. Taiwan U., 1956; MS in Physics, U. Del., 1963; PhD in Physics, NYU, 1969. Rsch. assoc. Union Indsl. Rsch. Inst., Hsinchu, Taiwan, 1956-59; rsch. microwave physicist Frequency Engrng. Lab., Farmingdale, N.J., 1968-71; rsch. physicist Atomic Energy Coun., Taipei, Taiwan, 1972-74; prof. physics Soochow U., 1972-78. Adj. prof. physics Tam Kang U., Tamsui, Taiwan, 1972-78. Author: Accretion Power and Mechanism for Conversion of Gravitational Potential to Radiative Energy in Active Galactic Nuclei, 1980; co-author: Magnetohydrodynamics of Viscous Gas Accreting on Highly Magnetized Neutron Stars and White Dwarfs, 1974, Dynamics and Accretion Column Structure for Neutron Stars, 1989. Rsch. grantee NASA, Goddard Space Flight Ctr., Greenbelt, Md., 1968. Mem. Am. Assn. for Advancement of Sci., Am. Phys. Soc., Nat. Geographic Soc., N.Y. Acad. Scis. Avocations: piloting, boating, fishing, travel. Office: Fortuna-CRX Inc 50 Bayard St Apt 7K New York NY 10013-4918

SHIH-CARDUCCI, JOAN CHIA-MO, cooking educator, biochemist, medical technologist; b. Rukuan, Chunghua, Taiwan, Dec. 21, 1933; came to U.S., 1955; d. Luke Chiang-hsi and Lien-chin (Chang) Shih; m. Kenneth M. Carducci, Sept. 30, 1960 (dec. July 1988); children: Suzanne R., Elizabeth M. BS in Chemistry, St. Mary Coll., Xavier, Kans., 1959; intern in med. tech., St. Mary's Hosp., Rochester, N.Y., 1960. Med. rschr. Strong Meml. Hosp. U. Rochester, 1960-61; pharm. chemist quality control Strasenburgh Labs., Rochester, 1961-62; cooking tchr. adult edn. Montgomery County Pub. Schs., Rockville, Md., 1973-79; tchr. The Chinese Cookery Inc., 1975-86, Silver Spring, Md., 1986—, pres., bd. dirs., 1975—; chemist NIH, Bethesda, 1987-2000; analytical chemist NIH/WRAIR, Rockville, Md., 1994-96. Author: The Chinese Cookery, 1981, Hunan Cuisine, 1984, Vegetarian Cuisine, 2000, The Art of the Chinese Cookery, 2001. Mem. Am. Chem. Soc., Internat. Assn. Cooking Profls. (Woman of Yr. 1994-2000). Republican. Roman Catholic. Avocations: piano, music, dance, flowers, vegetables. Home and Office: The Chinese Cookery Inc 14209 Sturtevant Rd Silver Spring MD 20905-4448 E-mail: joahshih@aol.com., chinesecookery@aol.com.

SHIKINA, SEIJI, educator, consultant; b. Naha, Okinawa, Japan, Mar. 2, 1940; s. Seitoku and Kiku (Zukeran) S.; m. Shikego Inamine, Mar. 31, 1968; children: Alice Yuko, Helen Ai, Edward Tatsuji, Robert Tetsuo. BA in English Lit., U. of Ryukyus, Japan, 1965; BA in Social Welfare, U. Nebr., 1973; MA in English, N.W. Mo. State U., 1975; PhD in English, U. S.W. La., 1986. Translator U.S. Counterintelligence, Okinawa, Japan, 1965-67; writer, editor Today's Ryukyus, Japan, 1967-70; family counselor Cath. Diocese of Lafayette, La., 1978-79; mgr. St. Francis Found., Lafayette, La., 1976-85; human resources exec. T.S. Trim Industries, Columbus, Ohio, 1987-91; prof. English Alcorn State U., Lorman, Miss., 1985-87; acad. dean U. Rio Grande, Tokyo, Japan, 1992-93, provost, 1993-94, cons. to pres., 1994-95. Univ. ombudsman U. S.W. La., Lafayette, 1983-85; owner cons. Bilingual Columbus, Ohio, 1991-99. Author: Requiem for a Toddler, 1995. Scholarship to U.S. Coll., Miami Rotary Club, Okinawa, Japan, 1970. Mem. Am. Translators Assn. Roman Catholic. Avocations: Shakuhachi, karate, chess, golf, swimming. Home: 2985 Upton Rd E Columbus OH 43232-5241

SHIKORA, SCOTT ALAN, surgeon; b. N.Y.C., Jan. 3, 1959; s. Jay and JoAnne (Garey) Shikora; m. Susan Ruth Musicant, Dec. 18, 1983; children: Jonathan Max, Katie Nicole, Samuel Ari. BS, Muhlenberg Coll., 1981; MD, Columbia U., 1985. Diplomate Am. Bd. Surgery, Am. Bd. Surg. Critical Care. Intern New England Deaconess Hosp., Boston, 1985-86, fellow in nutrition/metabolism, 1988-89, resident in gen. surgery, 1986-91; assoc. prof. surgery Sch. Medicine Tufts U.; mem. staff New England Med. Ctr., Boston. Editor: Nutrition Support Theory and Therapeutics, 1996. Fellow ACS, Am. Soc. Parenteral and Enteral Nutrition (chmn. clin. congress com. 1997-98), Soc. for Crit. Care Medicine, Am. Soc. Bariatric Surgery, Am. Soc. Clin. Nutrition. Office: New England Med Ctr Box 900 750 Washington St Boston MA 02111-1526

SHIKUMA, EUGENE YUJIN, travel agency executive; b. Tokyo, Nov. 18, 1948; came to U.S., 1957; s. Mitsuo and Yukiko (Kanaoka) S. BSEE, U. Hawaii at Manoa, Honolulu, 1971, MS in Computer Sci., 1975. Lab. test engr. and scientist McDonnell Douglas Astronautics, Inc., 1971-72; systems engr. Lear Siegler Astronics, 1972-73; jr. coord. Japan Travel Bur. Hawaii, Inc., Honolulu, 1978-83, sr. coord., 1983-84, supr., 1984-89, mgr., 1989—. Bd. dirs. Maui United Way, Kahului, Hawaii, 1988-89, Maui Hui Malama, Waiulku, 1989-90; bd. dirs., sec. Kamoa Views Apt. Owners Assn., 1991-96; mem. Maui County Visitor Task Force, 1995—; adv. bd. mem. Maui Acad. Travel and Tourism. Mem. Maui C. of C., Maui Japanese C. of C. Avocations: swimming, coin collecting, fine art, antique prints.

SHILEPSKY, ARNOLD CHARLES, mathematics educator, computer consultant; b. Norwalk, Conn., Dec. 10, 1944; s. Morris Jacob and Rose (Pfeffer) S.; m. Carol Irene Carter, June 15, 1968; children: Lisa Ruth, Beth Carter. AB, Wesleyan U., Middletown, Conn., 1966; PhD, U. Wis., 1971. Asst. prof. Ark. State U., Jonesboro, 1971-74; asst. prof. dept. math. Wells. Coll., Aurora, N.Y., 1974-79, assoc. prof., 1979-85, prof., 1985—, Herbert E. Ives prof. of scis., 1985-91, John D. Wilson Presdl. prof., 2000—. Cons. Digicomp Rsch. Corp., 1992-2000. Pres. Cmty. Devel. Fedn., S.W. Cayuga County, N.Y., 1987-92. Mem. Am. Math. Soc., Math. Assn. Am., Assn. for Women in Math. Home: Main St 295 Aurora NY 13026 Office: Wells Coll Dept Math Aurora NY 13026

SHILLADY, DONALD DOUGLAS, chemist, educator; b. Norristown, Pa., Aug. 27, 1937; s. John Nelson and Orpha Lillian (Schaefer) Shillady; m. Nancy Lee Knopf; children: Lucinda Teachey, Douglas, Amy. BS in Chemistry, Drexel Inst. Tech., 1962; MA, Princeton U., 1964; PhD in Chemistry, U. of Va., 1970. Postdoctoral assoc. U. of Va., Charlottesville, 1969—70; prof. chemistry Va. Commonwealth U., Richmond, 1970—. Pres. Quantum Mechanics LLC, Ashland, 2000—. Co-author, editor: update chemistry text Chemical Materials in the News, 1998 (Disting. Svc. award Va. sect. Am. Chem. Soc., 1992); editor (with M. Allen, S. Cleary and A. Sowers): (editl. conf. procs.) Charge and Field Effects in Biosystems-3, 1992; contbr. numerous articles to refereed publs. Elder Brandermill United Meth. Ch., Brandermill Planned Community, 1996—99. Mem.: Am. Chem. Soc. (chmn. Va. sect. 1986—87, Disting. Svc. Award 1992). Republican. Methodist. Avocation: sailing. Home: 10500 Old Telegraph Rd Ashland VA 23005 Office: Va Commonwealth U 1001 West Main St Richmond VA 23284 Office Fax: 804-828-8599. Personal E-mail: quantummechanicsllc@msn.com. Business E-Mail: dshillad@vcu.edu.

SHILLADY, WILLIAM SCOTT, minister; b. Reading, Pa., Aug. 22, 1956; m. Judith Amy Maneval, Sept. 20, 1948. BA in Religion and Econs. and Bus. Adminstrn., Lebanon Valley Coll., 1978; MDiv, Duke U., 1981; D of Ministry, Drew U., 1992. Cert. elder United Meth. Ch. Assoc. pastor Asbury Crestwood United Meth. Ch., Tuckahoe, NY, 1982—88; sr. pastor Mamaroneck United Meth. Ch., Mamaroneck, 1988—99, Pk. Ave. United Meth. Ch., N.Y.C., 1999—. Pres. Clergy of Yonkers, NY, 1986—88, Larchmont-Mamaroneck Hunger Task Force, Mamaroneck, 1990—99; religious adv. coun. Planned Parenthood of Peconic-Hudson, Yonkers, 1982—99; legis. dir. N.Y. Ann. Conf., White Plains, 1988—97; registrar, chairperson Bd. Ordained Ministry, N.Y.C., 1994—; cons. Partnership of Faith, N.Y.C., 1999—. Advisor Congressperson, Nita Lowey, White Plains, 1988—99; bd. dirs. Food-Patch Westchester Food Bank, 1994—99, Habitat for Humanity, N.Y.C., 1999—2002. Named Bnai Brith Man of Yr., Westchester Jewish Ctr., 1996; recipient Marzella Garland Cmty. Svc. award, Washingtonville Housing Alliance, 1997. Mem.: Duke Alumni Assn. (life), Kiwanis (pres. 1986—87). Liberal. Methodist. Avocations: tennis, travel, reading. Home: 21 East 87th St New York NY 10128 Office: Park Ave United Methodist Church 106 East 86th St New York NY 10028 Personal E-mail: hatpastor@aol.com. E-mail: pastorbill@parkavemethodist.org.

SHILLER, ROBERT JAMES, economist, educator; b. Detroit, Mar. 29, 1946; s. Benjamin P. and Ruth R. (Radzville) S.; m. Virginia M. Fualstich, June 13, 1976; 2 sons. BA, U. Mich., 1967; SM, MIT, 1968, PhD, 1972. Asst. prof. U. Minn., 1972-74; rsch. fellow Nat. Bur. Econ. Rsch., Cambridge, Mass., 1974-75; vis. scholar dept. econs. MIT, 1974-75, vis. prof., 1981-82; assoc. prof. dept. econs. U. Pa., Phila., 1974-81, prof. econs., 1981-82; prof. fin. Wharton Sch., 1981-82; prof. econs. Yale U., New Haven, 1982—. Co-founder Case, Shiller, Weiss Inc., Cambridge, Mass.; vis. scholar dept. econs. Harvard U., Mass., 1980; mem. academic adv. panel Fed. Reserve Bank of N.Y. Fgn. editor Rev. Econ. Studies, 1981-84; assoc. editor Jour. Econometrics, 1980-83; author: Market Volatility, 1989, Macro Markets, 1993, Irrational Exuberance, 2000. Grantee NSF, 1976—; Guggenheim fellow. Fellow Econometric Soc., Am. Acad. Arts and Scis. Office: Yale U Cowles Found New Haven CT 06520-8281

SHILLESTAD, JOHN GARDNER, financial services company executive; b. Oak Park, Ill., Oct. 31, 1934; s. John Nelson and Isabel Blanche (Gardner) Shillestad; m. Astri Cedervall; children: Christine C, Annette. BBA, Northwestern U., 1964, MBA, 1967. CLU, CPCU; ChFC. Mktg. dir. spl. plans CNA Ins., Chgo., 1958-66; asst. v.p. Montgomery Ward Life, 1966-69; pres., CEO Fort Dearborn Life Ins. Co., 1969-79; sr. v.p. Hartford Life Cos., Conn., 1979-85, also bd. dirs., 1985-87; pres. JGS Fin. Svcs., Inc., 1987—, Columbian Mut. Life Ins. Co., Binghamton, NY, 1987—. Chmn. Columbian Life Ins Co, Washington Nat. Life NY; with Golden Eagles Sales Corp., 1997—; bd. dirs. Reassure Am. Mem Bd Educ, Dist 30, Northbrook, Ill., 1976—79; mem adv bd SUNY Sch Mgt, Binghamton, Kellogg Sch Bus, Northwestern Univ; bd dirs Salvation Army, Binghamton, Partnership 2000, Southern Tier Equity Fund. With U.S. Army, 1954—56. Mem.: Broome County CofC (bd dirs), Pelican Marsh Golf Club (Naples, Fla), Sunset Ridge Club (Northfield, Ill). Republican. Congregationalist. Home: 3 Regentwood Rd Northfield IL 60093-2728 also: Unit 304 1600 Clermont Dr Naples FL 34109 E-mail: sjackshil@aol.com.

SHILLING, A. GARY, economic consultant, investment advisor; b. Fremont, Ohio, May 25, 1937; s. A. Vaughn and Lettie E. (O'Harrow) S.; m. Margaret E. Bloete, Dec. 22, 1962; children: Geoffrey B., Andrew J., Stephen E., Jennifer E. AB in Physics magna cum laude, Amherst (Mass.) Coll., 1960; MA in Econs., Stanford (Calif.) U., 1962, PhD in Econs., 1965; LLD (hon.), Tiffin U., 1999. Economist Standard Oil Co. (N.J.), N.Y.C., 1963-67; chief economist Merrill Lynch, Pierce, Fenner & Smith, 1967-71; rsch. dir. Estabrook & Co., 1971-72; sr. v.p., chief economist White, Weld & Co., 1972-78; chmn., pres., dir. A. Gary Shilling & Co., Inc., Springfield, N.J., 1978—; pres. Lakeview Econ. Svcs., Inc., 1979—; owner Lakeview Svcs., Inc., 1993—. Bd. dirs. Nat. Life Vt., Montpelier, Am. Productivity and Quality Ctr., Houston; adv. dir. Austin (Tex.) Trust Co., 1988—; informal econ. advisor Former Pres. George Bush, 1978—; mem. Nat. Com. on Jobs and Small Bus., 1986-87; dir. The Heartland Group of Mutual Funds, 1995—, Palm. Harbor Homes, 1995—. Author: Is Inflation Ending? Are You Ready?, 1983, The World Has Definitely Changed: New Economic Forces and Their Implications for the Next Decade, 1986, After the Crash: Recession or Depression? Investment and Business Strategies for a Deflationary World, 1988, Deflation: Why it's coming, whether it's good or bad, and how it will affect your investments, business, and personal affairs, 1998, Korean and Chinese edits., 2000, Deflation: How to Survive and Thrive in the Coming Wave of Deflation, 1999, Chinese edit., 2000; creator bd. game The Deflation Game, 1989; columnist Forbes, 1983—, Nihon Keizai Shimbun Jour. Bd. dirs. Aim Packaging Inc., 1986-89, Episcopal Ch. Found., Springfield, NJ, 1989-97; chmn. Episcopal Preaching Found., N.Y.C., 1988—; trustee Bates Coll., Lewiston, Maine, 1988-91, Kent Pl. Sch., Summit, N.J., 1983-89, Henry J. Kessler Found., 1987-95; bd. dirs. The Gen. Theol. Episcopal Sem., N.Y.C., 1988-2001, treas., 1994-2001; chmn. N.J. State Revenue Forecasting Adv. Commn., 1995—; bd. dirs. Am. Rep. Ins. Co. of N.Y., 1978-81, N.J. Shakespeare Festival, 1987-96, chmn., 1994-96. Named Wall St. Top Econs., Instl. Investor Mag., 1975, 76, Top Commodity Trading Advisor, Futures Mag., 1993. Mem. Nat. Assn. Bus. Economics, N.Y. Soc. Security Analysts, Short Hills Club, Phi Beta Kappa, Sigma Xi. Republican. Episcopalian. Avocations: tennis, travel, gardening, hunting, fishing, beekeeping. Home: 33 Lakeview Ave Short Hills NJ 07078-2264 Office: A Gary Shilling & Co Inc 500 Morris Ave Springfield NJ 07081-1020 E-mail: shil@ixnetcom.com.

SHILLING, MONICA JILL, lawyer; b. Kansas City, Kans., Dec. 17, 1969; d. David Randall Shilling and Shelia Jan Brown. BA in Creative Writing and French, U. Redlands, 1992; JD magna cum laude, Georgetown U., 1995. Bar: Calif. 1995. Assoc. Skadden, Arps, Slate, Meagher & Flom LLP, L.A., 1995—. Mem.: ABA, L.A. County Bar Assn., Calif. Bar Assn., Order of Coif, Phi Beta Kappa. Office: Skadden Arps Slate Meagher & Flom LLP 300 S Grand Ave Los Angeles CA 90071-3109 E-mail: mshillin@skadden.com.

SHILLING, ROY BRYANT, JR. academic administrator; b. Enville, Okla., Apr. 7, 1931; s. Roy Bryant and Lila M. (Prestage) S.; m. Margaret Riddle, Oct. 16, 1952; children: Roy Bryant III, Nancy Gale. BA, McMurry U., 1951, HHD, 1982; BD, So. Meth. U., 1957; MS, Ind. U., 1966, PhD, 1967. Presdl. asst. McMurry U., Abilene, Tex., 1959-61; asst. to pres. Tenn. Wesleyan Coll., 1961-64; asst. in devel. Ball State U., 1964-65; rsch. assoc. Ind. U., 1965-67; dir. planning and rsch. Baldwin Wallace Coll., 1967-68; exec. v.p. Southwestern U., 1968-69, pres., 1981-2000, pres. emeritus, 2000—; pres. Hendrix Coll., 1969-81. Mem. Nat. Commn. on United Meth. Higher Edn., 1975-77. Mem. Ark. Arts and Humanities Coun., 1970-76, chmn., 1974-75; bd. dirs. Ark. Children's Hosp., 1981; mem. bd. higher edn. and ministry United Meth. Ch., 1972-80, mem. univ. senate, 1980-88, v.p. 1983-84, pres., 1984-88; chmn. Gulf dist. Rhodes Scholarship Selection Com., 1992, Ark. chmn., 1973-74, Tex. chmn., 1985-91; mem. Young Pres. Orgn., 1975-81; mem. bd. visitors Air U., 1991-94. With U.S. Army, 1952-54. Recipient Disting. Alumnus award McMurry U., 1980, Perkins Disting. Alumnus award So. Meth. U., 1987, Owen B. Sherrill award for leadership in econ. devel. Georgetown, 1988; named one of Top 100 Most Effective Coll. Pres. in Nation, Bowling Green State U./Exxon Edn. Found., 1986. Mem. North Ctrl. Assn. Colls. and Schs. (vice chmn., chmn. elect 1980-81), Nat. Assn Schs. and Colls. of United Meth. Ch. (v.p. 1975-76, pres. 1976-77), Nat. Coun. Ind. Colls. and Univs. (bd. dirs. 1984-88), So. U. Conf. (exec. com. 1974-78), 79-86, sec.-treas. 1979-86, v.p. 1991-92, pres. 1992-93), Am. Coun. Edn. (bd. dirs. 1989-91; mem. commn. on govt. and pub. rels. 1999-2000), Inst. for Humanities (bd. dirs. Salado, Tex. chpt. 1985-91, mem. internat. coun. advs. 1994), NCAA Divsn. III Pres.'s Coun., 1998-2000, Philos Soc. Tex., Rotary, Masons, Alpha Chi, Phi Delta Kappa. Office: 1405 Mesa Ridge Ln Austin TX 78735-1639 E-mail: shilling@southwestern.edu.

SHILLINGBURG, HERBERT THOMPSON, JR. dental educator; b. Mar. 21, 1938; s. Herbert Thompson and Stefi Marie (Schuster) Shillingburg; m. Constance Joanne Murphy, June 11, 1960; children: Lisa Grace, Leslie Susan, Lara Stephanie. Student, U. N.Mex., 1955-58, 65-66; DDS, U. So. Calif., 1962. Gen. practice dentistry, Albuquerque, 1964-67; asst. prof. fixed prosthodontics sect. UCLA Sch. Dentistry, 1967-70, chmn., 1970-72; chmn. dept. fixed prosthodontics U. Okla. Coll. Dentistry, Oklahoma City, 1972—, David Ross Boyd Disting. prof., 1983. Cons. VA Hosp., Muskogee, Okla., 1975—84, Oklahoma City, 1977—93, U.S. Army Dental Activity, Ft. Knox, Ky., 1980—94. Author: (also in Japanese, German, Greek, Spanish, Italian, French, Portuguese, Polish, and Korean) Preparations for Cast Gold Restorations, 1974, Fundamentals of Fixed Prosthodontics, 1976, Fundamentals of Fixed Prosthodontics, 2d edit., 1981, Fundamentals of Fixed Prosthodontics, 3d edit., 1997, Guide to Occlusal Waxing, 1979, Guide to Occlusal Waxing, 2d edit., 1984, Guide to Occlusal Waxing, 3d edit., 2000, Restoration of the Endodontically Treated Tooth, 1984, Fundamentals of Tooth Preparations for Cast Metal and Porcelain Restorations, 1987; co-editor: Quintessence of Dental Technology, 1984—88. Capt. U.S. Army, 1962—64. Named Disting. Lectr., O U Assocs., 1989; recipient Award for tchg. excellence, UCLA Sch. Dentistry, 1969, 1972, 1973, Okla. Coll. Dentistry, 1976, 1978, 1982, 1987, 1993, 1994, 1997, 1st prize, Am. Med. Writers Assn., 1998, La Mèdaille de la Ville de Paris (èchelon Argent), 1990. Fellow: Am. Coll. Dentists; mem.: ADA, Okla. State Dental Assn., Internat. Assn. Dental Rsch., Am. Coll. Prosthodontists (hon.), Am. Acad. Restorative Dentistry, Am. Acad. Fixed Prosthodontics (George H. Moulton award 1998), Acad. Operative Dentistry, Phi Kappa Phi, Omicron Kappa Upsilon (Stephen H. Leeper award for tchg. excellence 2000). Republican. Episcopalian. Avocation: travel, photography. Home: 1312 Brixton Rd Edmond OK 73034-3314 Office: U Okla Coll Dentistry PO Box 26901 Oklahoma City OK 73190-0001

SHILLINGLAW, GORDON, accounting educator, consultant; b. Albany, N.Y., July 26, 1925; s. James McCombe and Margaret Blanche (Stephens) S.; m. Barbara Ann Cross, June 24, 1950; children— James McCombe, Laura Cross AB magna cum laude, Brown U., 1945; MS, U. Rochester, 1948; PhD, Harvard U., 1952. Asst. prof. Hamilton Coll., Clinton, N.Y., 1951-52; cons. assoc. Joel Dean Assocs., Yonkers, 1952-55; asst. prof. MIT, Cambridge, 1955-61; assoc. prof. Columbia U., N.Y.C., 1961-66, prof. acctg., 1966-90, prof. emeritus, 1991—. Vis. prof. Mgmt. Devel. Inst., Lausanne, Switzerland, 1964-65, 67-69; mem. U.S. Cost Acctg. Stds. Bd., 1978-80, U.S. R.R. Acctg. Prin. Bd., 1985-87; cons. in field. Author: Managerial Cost Accounting, 1961, 5th edit., 1982, Accounting: A Managment Approach, 1964, 9th edit., 1993, Financial Accounting: Concepts and Applications, 1989; contbr. articles to profl. jours. Mem. bd. advisors Fund Directions, 1990-96; bd. dirs., treas. Feris Found. Am., Stamford, Conn., 1970-94. Served with U.S. Navy. 1943-46. Recipient Disting. Tchr. award, Columbia U., 1970, Lifetime Achievement award, Instnl. Investor Newsletter, 2002. Mem. Am. Acctg. Assn. (v.p. 1966-67), Phi Beta Kappa, Beta Gamma Sigma. Avocations: tennis, travel, family history. Home: 115 Live Oak Ln Largo FL 33770-2657 E-mail: gslive25@aol.com.

SHILLINGTON, AUDREY MENGWASSER, educator; b. Jefferson City, Mo. d. Norbert F. and Carolyn Ann Mengwasser; m. Stephen Shillington, Mar. 31, 1990; children: John, Kaleb BA in Psychology & History, Drury Coll., 1982; MSW, Washington U., St. Louis, 1987, PhD, 1991, M of Psychiat. Epidemiology, 1993. Asst. prof. Utah State U., Logan, 1994, San Diego State U., 1997—. Contbr. articles to profl. jours. Rsch. grantee; Nat. Inst. Mental Health Postdoctoral fellow Washington U., St. Louis, 1991-94. Office: San Diego State U 5500 Campanile Dr San Diego CA 92182-4119 Fax: 619-594-5991. E-mail: ashillin@mail.sdsu.edu.

SHILOH, ALLEN, writer, postal employee; b. Bastrop, La., May 24, 1947; s. Al and Rosia B (Davis) S.; children: Datoya Moneake Penn. Grad. high sch., Bastrop; student, Cal/Arts, 1966-68. Mail handler U.S. Postal Svc., Bell, Calif., 1972—. Author: (novels) The Brotherhood, Terror, 1973, Bayou Girl, 1990, (paperback) The Real First United States President, 1983, (short stories pub.) New Cosmic Star, 1968. Sgt. USAF, 1968-72, Vietnam. Avocations: photography, drawing. Home: 305 S Essey Ave Compton CA 90221-3417

SHILS, EDWARD B. management educator, lawyer; b. Phila., May 29, 1915; s. Benjamin and Dinah (Berkowitz) S.; m. Shirley Seigle, July 31, 1942; children: Ronnie Lois, Nancy Ellen, Edward Barry. BS in Econs., U. Pa., 1936, MA in Polit. Sci., 1937, PhD, 1940, JD, 1998, LLM, 1990, SJD, 1997; LLD (hon.), Phila. U., 1975; PhD (hon.), Tel-Aviv U., Israel, 1990. Bar: Pa. 1988, U.S. Dist. Ct. (ea. dist.) Phila. 1988, Pa. Supreme Ct. Research assoc. Pa. Economy League, 1938—42; cons. job classification and wage adminstrn. Phila. City Council, 1942—43; chief coordination and planning VA, Phila., 1947—48; cons. tchr. salary schedules Phila. Bd. Pub. Edn., 1948—50; dir. pub. edn. survey Greater Phila. Movement, 1950—51; sr. dept. head U.S. Wage Stabilization Bd., Phila., 1951; methods cons. Budget Office Gov. Pa., 1951—55; cons., dir. Dental Mfrs. of Am., Inc., 1952—; cons. Phila. County Med. Soc., 1955—56; chmn. social sci. dept. Community Coll., Temple U., Phila., grad. lectr. pub. adminstrn., 1948—56; mem. faculty Wharton Sch. U. Pa., 1956—, prof. mgmt., chmn. mgmt dept., 1968—76, George W. Taylor prof. emeritus entrepreneurial studies, 1979, prof. emeritus polit. sci., 1985—, dir. Wharton Entrepreneurial Ctr., 1973—86, dir. emeritus, 1986—; judicial adminstr. U. Pa., 1986—90; pvt. practice law Phila., 1988—; of counsel Sarner and Assocs.; disting. prof. entrepreneurial studies Tel Aviv U., 1991—95; atty., cons. Office Phila. Dist. Atty., 2001—. Pers. cons. Phila. Bd. Pub. Edn., 1946-75; cons. Phila. Psychiat. Ctr., 1971-76, Am. Bd. Internal Medicine, 1973-77, Girard Coll., 1974, Royal Coll. Physicians and Surgeons Can., 1977-80; cons. on sports and econs., major league baseball, football, hockey and basketball, 1985-; cons. labor rels. Phila. Pub. Sch. Dist., 1951-68; cons. econ. Phila. New Cnv. Ctr., 1988-90; mgmt. advisor to Phila. Dist. Atty., 1992-93; bd. trustees Dental Sch. U. Pa., 2002-. Author: Finances and Financial Administration of Philadelphia's Public Schools 1923-1939, 1940, Automation and Industrial Relations, 1963, Teachers, Administrators and Collective Bargaining, 1968, Industrial Peacemaker: George W. Taylor's Contribution to Collective Bargaining, 1979; co-editor: Frontiers of Entrepreneurship Research, 1985, The Shils Report, Impact of Mega Retail Chains on Small Enterprise, 1997. V.p. Fedn. Jewish Agys. for Phila., 1976-84, Life Trust fed. Jewish Agys., 1990—; pres. Jewish Publs. Soc. Am., 1978-81, Hon. pres., 1982-; Life trustee, hon. chmn. trustee com. on edn. Phila. U.; chmn. bd., hon. pres. Pathway Sch., Jeffersonville, Pa., 1970-84; pres. Philadelphians for Good Govt., 1991-93, hon. pres., 1992-95. Served as officer Signal Corps U.S. Army, 1943-46. Honored with a chair in his name at U. Pa. Law Sch., The Edward B. Shils Professorship in Arbitration and Alternative Dispute Resolution, 1991, Wharton Sch. U. Pa., Edward B. and Shirley R. Shils Term Professorship Entrepeneurial Mgmt., 2001; recipient Alumni Merit award U. Pa., 2001. Mem. Union League Pa., Faculty Club U. Pa. (pres. 1966-69, 87-92), Green Valley Country Club (Plymouth, Pa.), Masons (32 degree), Shriners. Home: 335 S Woodbine Ave Narberth PA 19072-1525 Office: U Pa Wharton Sch Philadelphia PA 19104 Also: 123 S Broad St Philadelphia PA 19109-1029

SHILS, MAURICE EDWARD, physician, scientist, educator; b. Atlantic City, Dec. 31, 1914; s. Samuel L. and Sarah (Harris) S.; m. Cylia Finkiel, Feb. 19, 1939 (dec. Sept. 1987); children: Loraine J., Jonathan R.; m. Betty Ann Bell, Sept. 24, 1988. BA, Johns Hopkins U., 1937, ScD, 1940; MD, NYU, 1958. Intern joint program Cornell divsn. Bellevue Hosp. and Meml. Hosp., N.Y.C., 1958-59; fellow in physiology Meml. Hosp., 1959-60; instr., asst. prof. nutrition Sch. Pub. Health Columbia U., N.Y.C., 1946-54; instr. biochemistry Sch. Hygiene Johns Hopkins U., Balt., 1940-42; head Ctrl. Metabolic Lab. Sloan Kettering Inst., N.Y.C., 1960-72; from asst. to assoc. attending physician Meml. Hosp., 1962-72, attending physician, 1972-85; asst. prof. biochem. Sloan-Kettering divsn. Med. Coll. Cornell U., 1959-62, from asst. prof. to prof. medicine Med. Coll., 1962-85, prof. emeritus, 1985—. Adj. prof. nutrition dept. pub. health scis. Wake Forest U. Sch. Medicine, Winston-Salem, N.C., 1989-94, cons., 1994-97. Author, sr. editor: Modern

Nutrition in Health and Disease, 9th edit., 1998; contbr. more than 200 rsch. and review articles to profl. jours. Fellow Am. Coll. Physicians, N.Y. Acad. Medicine (Acad. Plaque award 1987), Soc. Nutritional Scis.; mem. AMA (chmn. nutrition adv. group 1974-77, Goldberger award 1983), Am. Soc. Clin. Nutrition (pres. 1985-86, Excellence in Med. Sch. award 1994), Am. Bd. Nutrition, Phi Beta Kappa, Alpha Omega Alpha. E-mail: mshils@triad.rr.com.

SHIM, SANG KOO, state mental health official; b. Tokyo, Japan, Oct. 1, 1942; came to U.S., 1968; s. Sang Taek and Kum Ryon (Bae) S.; m. Jae Hee Lee, July 12, 1972; children: Tammy, David. BS, Seoul Nat. U., Korea, 1967; MBA, No. Ill. U., 1970; MS, U. Wis., 1975. CPA, Ill., cert. govt. fin. mgr., Assn. Govt. Accts. Acct. Vaughn Mfg. Co., Chgo., 1970-72, Stewart-Warner Corp., Chgo., 1972-73; fin. cons. Cen. Acctg. Assn., New Baden, Ill., 1977-79; auditor Ill. Dept. Mental Health, Springfield, 1980-82, CFO, 1983-97; chief bureau gen. acctg. Ill. Dept. Human Svcs., 1997—. Treas. Korean Assn. Greater St. Louis, 1982. Mem. Ill. CPA Soc., Assn. Govt. Accts. (cert. govt. fin. mgr.), Korean-Am. C. of C. (v.p. Greater St. Louis chpt. 1994-95). Home: 5 Settlers Ln Springfield IL 62707-7725 Office: Ill Dept Human Svcs Bur Gen Acctg 100 S Grand Ave E Springfield IL 62762 E-mail: skshim@aol.com.

SHIMADA, HARUO, physical chemistry educator; b. Himeji, Hyōgo, Japan, Mar. 27, 1935; s. Shigeyoshi and Shige (Okamoto) S.; m. Ikuko Tanaka, Sept. 21, 1968; children: Yōko, Kenichiro. Grad., U. Tokyo, 1958, doctorate, 1968. Rschr. Yawata (Japan) Iron & Steel Co., 1958-72; sr. rschr. Nippon Steel Corp., Kawasaki, Japan, 1973-80, chief rschr., 1980-90; prof. Sci. U. Tokyo, Shinjuku, Japan, 1990—. Editorial mem.: (monthly jour.) Chem. Industry, 1972—; contbr. articles to profl. jours. Mem. AAAS, Nat. Assn. Corrosion Engrs., Internat. Tech. Inst. (life mem.). Avocations: jogging, swimming. Home: Chuō 5-3-5 Tokyo Ota 143-0024 Japan Office: Sci Univ Tokyo 1-3 Kagurazaka Shinjuku 1628601 Japan

SHIMADA, KATSUNORI, retired electrical engineer; b. Tokyo, Mar. 12, 1922; arrived in U.S., 1950; s. Katsujiro and Mume Shimada; m. Ikuko Ueno, Oct. 30, 1975; m. Kazuko Matsumoto; children: Karl, Keiko Shimada Stearns. BSEE, U. Tokyo, 1945; MSEE, U. Minn., 1954, PhD, 1958. Engr. Toshiba Japan, Kawasaki, Japan, 1945—50; instr. U. Minn., Mpls., 1950—58; asst. prof. engring. U. Wash., Seattle, 1958—64; supr. JPL, G&C Rsch. Group, Pasadena, Calif., 1964—80; mgr., Field Ctr. Integration JPL, 1980—85, supr. Celestrial Sensors, 1985—89; ret., 1989. Cons. Boeing Co., Seattle, 1960—63, NASDA of Japan, L.A., 1987—91; invited prof. engring. U. Tokyo, 1973; invited lectr. NEDO of Japan, Tokyo, 1983. Contbr. articles to profl. jours., tech. reports and memoranda. Com. mem. Nat. Parents Day Coalition, L.A., 1996—99, RSVP of Pasadena, 1993—95, Assoc. Retirees of Caltech/JPL, Pasadena, 1998—. Fellow Resident rsch., JPL, 1963—64. Mem.: AIAA, IEEE (sr.), Sigma Xi, Eta Kappa Nu. Achievements include patents for Cavity Emitter for Thermionics, 1969; Thermionic Diode Switch, 1975; Solid State Power Converter, 1979. Avocations: photography, computers, golf, travel. Home: 3840 Edgeview Dr Pasadena CA 91107

SHIMANDLE, SHARON ANNE, medical/surgical nurse; b. Cleve., Mar. 12, 1959; d. Harry William and Dorothy May (McGivney) Dowdell; m. James Edward Shimandle Jr., Dec. 22, 1979; children: Jason Michael, Jillian Lyn. ADN, Cuyahoga C.C., Parma, Ohio, 1980; MSN, Case Western Reserve U., 1990; grad. nurse anesthesia, Akron U., 2001. RN, Ohio; cert. ACLS, BLS instr. Staff nurse SICU St. Vincent Charity Hosp., Cleve., 1980; staff nurse ICU Kaiser Hosp., Parma, 1981-82, staff nurse oper. rm., 1982-85; staff nurse post anesthesia care unit/ambulatory surgery unit Deaconess Hosp., Cleve., 1985-86, asst. dir. post anesthesia care unit/ambulatory surgery unit, 1986-87, critical care educator, 1987-90; critical care instr. Mt. Sinai Med. Ctr., 1990-92; critical care educator Lorain (Ohio) Cmty. Hosp., 1992-94, Cmty. Health Ptnrs., 1994—2001; clin. nurse specialist for critical care EMH Regional Med. Ctr., Elyria, Ohio, 1996-98, CRNA MetroHealth Med. Ctr., Cleve., 2001—. Mem. AACN, Nat. Assn. Clin. Nurse Specialists. Avocations: boating, arts and crafts. Home: 11713 Akins Rd North Royalton OH 44133-4500

SHIMBERG, ELAINE FANTLE, writer; b. Yankton, S.D., Feb. 26, 1937; d. Karl S. and Alfreda (Edelson) Fantle; m. Mandell Shimberg, Oct. 1, 1961; children: Karen, Scott, Betsy, Andrew, Michael. BS, Northwestern U., 1958. Freelance writer, 1961—. Co-hostess WFLA-TV talk show Women's Point of View, Tampa, Fla., 1976-81; tchr. Writing for Publication and Profit, Hillsborough C.C., Tampa 1980-82. Author: How to be A Successful Housewife/Writer, 1979, Two for the Money: A Woman's Guide to a Double Career Marriage, 1981; contbg. author: The Complete Guide to Writing Non-Fiction, 1983, Coping with Kids and Vacation, 1986, Relief From Irritable Bowel Syndrome, 1988, Strokes: What Families Should Know, 1990, Depression: What Families Should Know, 1992, Gifts of Time, 1993, Living with Tourette Syndrome, 1995, How to Get Out of the Hospital Alive, 1997, Blending Families, 1999, Write Where You Live, 1999, Coping with Chronic Heartburn, 2001; contbr. articles to various mags. Mem. pub. info. com. Fla. divsn. Am. Cancer Soc., 1974-89; bd. dirs. United Way, 1986-89; bd. mem. St. Joseph's Hosp., Tampa. Mem. Am. Soc. Journalists and Authors, Am. Med. Writers Assn., Fla. Med. Assn. (coun. ethical and jud. affairs 1993—). Office: 611 W Bay St Tampa FL 33606-2703 E-mail: efshimberg@aol.com.

SHIMEK, JOHN ANTON, legal investigation business owner, educator; b. Chgo., Sept. 1, 1925; s. John Anton Sr. and Florence Marie (Redman) S.; m. Corinne Gladys Hornburg, Mar. 1, 1947 (div. June 1988); m. Janet Lea Ingham Snyder, Sept. 10, 1988; children: Ronald Wayne, Scott Anthony, Brian Dean Snyder. AA, Phoenix Coll., 1963; BS, Grand Canyon Coll., 1967; M of Phys. Edn., Sussex (Eng.) Coll., 1974. Cert. sch. adminstr. Am. Police Acad.; cert. aquatic dir.; lic. pvt. investigator; lic. ins. agt. Patrolman Chgo. Police Dept., 1946-51; agt. Met. Life Ins., Colorado Springs/Phoenix, 1951-61; owner, head coach Ariz. Swim Devils, Phoenix, 1967-80; phys. dir., assoc. dir. Phoenix YMCA, 1957-67; sch. adminstr. Cartwright Sch. Dist., Phoenix, 1967-88; pres., owner Shimek & Assocs., Inc., Glendale, Ariz., 1988—. Adj. prof. Grand Canyon Coll., Phoenix, 1963-83; spl. agt Internat. Intelligence and Organized Crime Investigations Assn., Washington, 1981-83; mem. AAU Regional Swimming Com., 1967-68; mem. coach AAU State Swim Com., chmn., 1966-67. Author: Physical Education Handbook, 1979, 80, Shimek Heritage, 1998, Swimming Today, 1998, revised, 2000, So You Want To Be a P.I., Vols. I, II & III, 1999, IV, 2000, A Family Cook Book, 2000, A Boys Dream, 2001; co-author: An Annotated Bibliography of Experimental Research Concerning Competitive Swimming, 1970, (video) Desert Survival, 1983; contbr. articles to mags. Commdr., instr. search and rescue team Maricopa County Sheriff's Office, Ariz., 1980-89; counselor police acad. Ariz. Dept. Pub. Safety, Tucson, 1982. With USN, 1942-47, WWII, USNR, 1965-80, ret., 1980. Named to Swimming Hall of Fame, Internat. Swimming Hall of Fame, 1971-72. Mem.: Fraternal Order of Police (life; trustee 1980—, v.p. 2001—02), Palm Brook Country Club, Am. Legion (comdr. 1980—, Americanism citation 1980—81). Republican. Methodist. Home: 7101 W Beardsley Rd #1604 Glendale AZ 85308-5691 E-mail: pvtdickusa@netscape.net, jashimek@msn.com.

SHIMEK, ROSEMARY GERALYN, medical/surgical nurse; b. Manitowoc, Wis., Oct. 12, 1952; d. Raymond James and Margaret Rita (Zinkel) Trainor; m. Richard Joseph Shimek, May 23, 1987. Diploma, Lakeshore Tech. Inst., Sheboygan, Wis., 1972; ADN, Lakeshore Tech. Coll., Cleveland, Wis., 1989; BSN, Marian Coll., 1998. RN Wis., cert. in med-surg. nursing, ANCC, LPN. Nurse Holy Family Meml. Med. Ctr., Manitowoc, 1972-89, student nurse intern, 1988-89, unit clk., 1988-89, charge nurse med. fl., 1989—. Scholar Charles E. Wall, Lakeshore Tech. Coll., 1989, Karen Deehr, Holy Family Meml. Med. Ctr., 1997. Home: 925 N 24th St Manitowoc WI 54220-2448

SHIMER, ALICE MARIE, retired educator; b. Decatur, Ill., Apr. 24, 1926; d. George Henry and Grace Lovawn (Burkard) S. Student, Millikin U., 1944-46; BS, U. Ill., 1948; MS, SUNY, Buffalo, 1963. Cert. health ins. councellor, N.Y. Chemist Clarks Microanalytical Lab., Urbana, Ill., 1949-51; rsch. microanalytical chemist Olin Mathieson Labs., Niagara Falls, N.Y., 1951-60, Thiokol Labs., Huntsville, Ala., 1960-61; tchr. Niagara Falls Bd. Edn., 1961-84. Tax coord. and counselor AARP, Niagara Falls and Lewiston, N.Y., 1984—; vol. St. Mary's Hosp., Lewiston, N.Y., 1986-99. Mem. Niagara Falls Ret. Tchrs. Assn. (pres. 1988-92, 98—), Delta Kappa Gamma (past treas.). Republican. Lutheran. Avocations: weaving, travel, photography, singing, dogs. Home: 5105 Dana Dr Lewiston NY 14092-2015 E-mail: elealice@yahoo.com.

SHIMER, DANIEL LEWIS, corporate executive; b. San Angelo, Tex., July 30, 1944; s. Lewis V. and Mary A. (Slick) S.; married. BS in Acctg. and Mktg., Ind. U., 1972; postgrad., Loyola U., New Orleans, 1977. CPA. Sr. acct. Peat, Marwick, Mitchell & Co., Indpls., 1973-75; asst. treas. LTV Corp., Dallas, 1975-79; v.p. fin. Stoller Chem. Co., Houston, 1979-81; v.p., CFO Petro-Silver, Inc., Denver, 1981-83; v.p., treas. FoxMeyer Corp., 1983-86; v.p., treas., sec. CoastAmerica Corp., 1986-88; exec. v.p. Bard & Co., 1989-90; pres. nat accounts divsn. I Can't Believe It's Yogurt/ Brice Foods, Inc., Dallas, 1991-93; exec. v.p., CFO COREStaff Inc., Houston, 1994-96; pres. Shimer Capital Ptnrs., Inc., Dallas, 1996—; venture ptnr. Austin Ventures, 1996—; vice-chmn. ePartners, Inc (formerly Tex Sys RD Corp.), 1996—. Mem. AICPA, Nat. Assn. Corp. Treas. Methodist. Avocations: sailing, carpentry, snow skiing, fishing. Home: 6441 Norway Rd Dallas TX 75230-5146

SHIMIZU, KAZUHIKO, education educator; b. Akeno, Japan, Jan. 20, 1952; s. Kazuyoshi and Toyoko S.; m. Tsurumi Tamagawa, March 30, 1979; children: Kazutaka, Kazuma, Kazuki. BA, Tokyo U. Edn., 1974, MA, 1976; PhD, U. Tsukuba, Japan, 1997. Rsch. fellow Japan Soc. for the Promotion of Sci., Tokyo, 1980-81; asst. prof. Seisen Women's Jr. Coll., Nagano, Japan, 1983-86, assoc. prof., 1986-88; asst. prof. U. Tsukuba, 1988-91, assoc. prof., 1991-99, prof., 1999—. Vis. assoc. prof. U. Hiroshima, 1992-96; vis. scholar U. Pa., Phila., 1995-96, U. Minn., Mpls.; spl. lectr. Yonsei U., Seoul, Korea, 1996; guest lectr. Nat. Edn. Commn., Beijing, 1998, East China Normal U., Shanghai, 2001. Author: Comparative and Hist. Study of Univ. Credit Sys. Between USA and Japan, 1998, Univ. Reform in Japan, 1999; author and editor: A Databook of Edn. Statistics, 2000. Mem. Coun. for Univ. Chartering and Sch. Judicial Person (Monbusho), 2000—; mem. Japanese Univ. Accreditation Assn., 1994-2000; trustee Assn. for the Advancement of Colls. in Japan, 1994—; mem. Inter-Univ. Seminar House, Tokyo, 1997-2002. Recipient rsch. fund Assn. Internat. Edn., Japan, 1990, grant-in-aid for scientific rsch. Ministry of Edn., Sci., Sport and Culture (Monbusho), Tokyo, 1998, 2000, 01. Mem. Comparative and Internat. Edn. Soc., Chgo., Japan Assn. Lifelong Edn. (office dir. 1998-2000), Japan Soc. for Ednl. Sys. and Orgn., Tsukuba (office dir. 1999—). Avocation: gardening. Home: 9015 Uede 407-0204 Yamanashi-ken Japan Office: Faculty of Edn U Tsukuba 1-1-1 Tennodai 305-8572 Tsukuba-shi Japan E-mail: shimizuk@sakura.cc.tsukuba.ac.jp.

SHIMIZU, YOSHIAKI, art historian, educator; b. Tokyo, Feb. 27, 1936; came to U.S., 1953, naturalized, 1999; s. Mamoru and Michiko (Hayasaka) S.; children: Karen Akiko Marie, Kenneth Cuyler Norio, Katherine Kimie, Kei Robert. BA, Harvard U., 1963; MA, U. Kans., 1968; MFA, Princeton U., 1971, PhD, 1974. Asst. prof. dept. art and archaeology Princeton (N.J.) U., 1973-75, prof., 1984—, chmn. dept. art and archaeology, 1990-92, Marquand prof. art & archaeology, 1992—; asst. prof. U. Calif., Berkeley, 1975-78, assoc. prof., 1978-79; curator Japanese art Freer Gallery, Smithsonian Instn., Washington, 1979-84; guest curator Nat. Gallery Art, 1982-89; guest prof. U. of Heidelberg, 1993. Guest prof. Ritsumeikan U., 1996; vis. fellow dept. art history U. Tokyo, 1996; mem. art adv. com. Japan Soc. Gallery, 1984—, adv. com. Asia Soc. Galleries, N.Y.C., 1992—, chmn. adv. com., 1999—; vis. fellow dept. comparative culture Sophia U., Tokyo, 1993. Author: (with John M. Rosenfield) Masters of Japanese Calligraphy, 1984; editor: (with Carolyn Wheelwright) Japanese Ink Paintings, 1976; author, editor: Japan: The Shaping of Daimyo Culture 1185-1858, 1988; mem. editorial bd. Archives of Asian Art, 1979-89. Adv. bd. Asian Art, Smithsonian Inst., 1985-93; mem. vis. com. Arthur M. Sackler Gallery, Washington, 1984-94. Smithsonian Inst. fellow, 1967, Social Sci. Rsch. Coun./Am. Coun. Learned Socs. fellow, 1977-78, Asian Cultural Coun. fellow, 1995. Mem. Coll. Art Assn. (bd. dirs. 1987-91), Japan Art History Assn., Japan Soc. N.Y., Ctr. for the Study of Japanese Woodblock Prints (mem. internat. adv. bd. 1983—) Home: 2 College Rd Princeton NJ 08540-5108 Office: Princeton U Dept Art and Archaeology Princeton NJ 08540 E-mail: shimizu@princeton.edu.

SHIMKHADA, DEEPAK, philosopher, educator; b. Darkha, Nepal, Sept. 5, 1945; s. Ratna Prasad and Kausalya Shimkhada; m. Kanti Koirala, July 7, 1970; children: Leepi, Riti. BFA, U. Of Baroda, 1968; MFA, U. Of Baroda, Baroda, India, 1970; MA, U. Of So. Calif., 1974; PhD, Claremont u., 2001. Prof. Rio Hondo Coll., Whittier, Calif., 1995—96, Mt.san Antonio Coll., Walnut, 1997—98; asst. prof. Claremont Mckenna Coll., Claremont, California, 1999—. Pres. Found. For Indic Philosophy & Culture, Claremont, 2001—; vis. lectr. Scripps Coll., Claremont, 1981—82. Editor: (book) Himalayas At A Crossroads: The Portrait Of A Changing World, 1988, (compilation) Original Buddhist Mantras In Sanskrit, 1985 (grantee N.Am. Buddhist Found., 1984); contbr. book; author: (exhibition catalog) NEPALI ART; Author, Man, Woman, and Nature in Asian Art, exhibition catalog, 1982, 1973; contbr. exhibition catalog. Founder Himalayan Arts Coun. of Pacific Asia Mus., Pasadena, Calif., 1986—94. Recipient Cert. award, Nepal Assn. of Fine Arts; 1966, 1969, Grad. Students Alumni Rsch. award, Ohio State U., 1980; fellow Fulbright fellow, U.S. Dept. Of State, 1972—74, Tuition fellowship, U. Of Chgo., 1974—77; grantee Sr. Cultural fellow, Govt. Of India, 1968—70, Jr. Rsch. fellow, Am. Inst. Of Indian Studies, 1978—79. Mem.: Am. Nepal Soc. Calif. (pres. 1998—2000), Art Historians of So. Calif., South Asia Soc., Assn. For Asian Studies, Assn. for Asian Studies (grantee 1989). Home: 1682 Lowell Avenue Claremont CA 91711

SHIMKUS, JOHN MONDY, congressman; b. Collinsville, Ill., Feb. 21, 1958; s. Gene Louis and Kathleen (Mondy) S.; m. Karen Kay Muth; children: David, Joshua. BS, U.S. Mil. Acad., 1980; MBA, So. Ill. U., Edwardsville, 1997. Advanced through grades to capt. U.S. Army, 1980-86; stationed at U.S. Army Base, Columbus, Ga., 1980-81, 85, served at Bamberg, Germany, 1981-84, stationed at Monterey, Calif, 1985-86; tchr. Metro East Luth. H.S., Edwardsville, Ill., 1986-90; treas. Madison County, 1990-96; mem. U.S. Congress from 20th Ill. dist., 1997—, mem. energy and commerce com. Liaison officer U.S. Mil. Acad., 1987-96; treas. So. Ill. Law Enforcement Commn., 1990-96. Bd. dirs. Sr. Citizen Companion Program, Belleville, Ill., 1991; trustee Collinsville Twp., Ill., 1989-93; Rep. precinct committeeman, Collinsville, 1988—. Maj. USAR. Mem. Nat. Assn. County Treas. and Fin. Officers (bd. dirs.), Ill. County Treas. Assn., Am. Legion Post 365. Lutheran. Home: 504 Sumner Blvd Collinsville IL 62234-1934 Office: US Ho of Reps 513 Cannon HOB Washington DC 20515-1320 also: 3130 Chatham Rd Ste C Springfield IL 62704*

SHIMM, MELVIN GERALD, law educator; b. N.Y.C., Jan. 30, 1926; s. Joseph George and Sadie Rosalie (Rosenblatt) Shimm; m. Cynia Brown, Aug. 15, 1948; children: David Stuart, Jonathan Evan. AB, Columbia U., 1947; LLB, Yale U., 1950. Bar: NY 50. Assoc. Cahill, Gordon, Zachry & Reindel, N.Y.C., 1950—51; atty. Wabe Stblzn. Bd., Washington, 1951—52; Bigelow fellow U. Chgo., 1952—53; asst. prof. Duke U. Law Sch., Durham, NC, 1953—56, assoc. prof., 1956—59, prof., 1959—96, prof. emeritus, 1996—, assoc. dean, 1978—83. Vis. prof. NYU, 1957, U. So. Calif., 1965, U. Mich., Ann Arbor, 1973, U. Tex., Austin, 1976; chmn. Durham (NC) Bd. Adjustment, 1966—70; dir. Assn. Am. Law Schs. Orientation Program in Am. Law, 1968—70, Duke Inst. in Transnat. Law, 1987—92; cons. The Brookings Instn., 1965—67; mem. NC Gen. Statutes Commn., 1984—88. Editor-in-chief: Law & Contemporary Problems, editor-in-chief: Jour. Legal Edn., editor-in-chief: Am. Editor Jour. Bus. Law; editor: Yale Law Jour. Bd. dirs., vice-chmn. Lucy Daniels Found., 1989—; bd. advisors Ctr. for Law, Ethics and Nat. Security, 1993—; pres. Beth El Congregation, Durham, NC, 1967—70, 1975—78; chmn. Jewish Fedn. Durham/Chapel Hill, 1996—. Lt. U.S. Army, 1943—46. Mem.: Order of Coif, Phi Beta Kappa. Office: Duke U Sch Law PO Box 90360 Durham NC 27708-0360 E-mail: shimms@earthlink.net., shimm@law.duke.edu.

SHIMMIN, MARGARET ANN, women's health nurse; b. Forbes, N.D., Oct. 26, 1941; d. George Robert and Reba Aleda (Strain) S. Diploma in Nursing, St. Luke's Hosp. Sch. Nursing, Fargo, N.D., 1962; BSW, U. West Fla., 1978; cert. ob-gyn nurse practitioner, U. Ala., Birmingham, 1983, MPH, 1986. Lic. nurse, Fla., N.D., Ala. Head nurse, emergency room St. Luke's Hosps., Fargo, 1962-67; charge nurse, labor and delivery, perinatal nurse educator Sacred Heart Hosp., Pensacola, Fla., 1970-82; ARNP Escambia County Pub. Health Unit, 1983-89; cmty. health nursing cons. Dist. 1 Health and Rehab. Svcs., 1989-96; sr. cmty. health nursing supr. Escambia County Health Dept., 1996—. Capt. nurse corps U.S. Army, 1967-70, Japan. Mem. NAACOG (cert. maternal-gynecol.-neonatal nursing 1978, ob-gyn nurse practitioner 1983), Fla. Nurses' Assn., ANA, N.W. Fla. ARNP (past sec./treas.), Fla. Perinatal Assn., Nat. Perinatal Assn., Healthy Mothers/Healthy Babies Coalition, Fla. Pub. Health Assn., U. West Fla. Alumni Assn., U. Ala. at Birmingham Sch. of Public Health Alumni Assn., Phi Alpha. Republican. Presbyterian. Avocations: cooking, music, travel, photography, reading. Home: 8570 Olympia Rd Pensacola FL 32514-8029 Office: Escambia County Health Dept 1295 W Fairfield Dr Pensacola FL 32501-1107

SHIMMYO, THEODORE TADAAKI, international consultant; b. Shiokawa-machi, Japan, Aug. 13, 1944; came to U.S. 1973; s. Shizuo and Tomiko (Saito) S.; m. Sumie Kurihara, Oct. 21, 1970; children: Keijo, Tatenaga, Keishin, Keika. BS in Nuclear Engring., U. Tokyo, 1971; diploma in religious edn., Unification Theol. Sem., Barrytown, N.Y., 1977; MPhil in Christian Theology, Drew U., Madison, N.J., 1981, PhD in Christian Theology, 1984. Asst. prof. theology Unification Theol. Sem., Barrytown, N.Y., 1984-96, asst. dean faculty, 1987, asst. acad. dean, 1987-94, pres., 1994-2000, assoc. prof. theology, 1996—; cons. Interreligious and Internat. Fedn. for World Peace, Tarrytown, NY, 2000—. Author: Addressing Some of the Criticisms About the Divine Principle, 1985, Explorations in Unificationism, 1997; translator: The Divine Principle Study Guide Part II, 1975; contbr. articles to profl. jours. Mem. Family Fedn. for World Peace and Unification, Soc. for Study of Process Philosophies, Karl Barth Soc. of N.Am. Mem. Unification Ch. Avocations: harmonica, classical guitar. Home: 20 Browning Ln Tarrytown NY 10591-6202 Office: Interreligious and Internat Fedn for World Peace 155 White Plains Rd Ste 204 Tarrytown NY 10591

SHIMNOSKI, GAYLORD FRANCIS, Catholic priest, psychologist, consultant; b. Manistee, Mich., Feb. 10, 1934; s. Harry and Julia Marie (Olejniczak) S. PhB, U. Montreal, 1955; BA, St. John's Sem., Plymouth, Mich., 1959; MA in Psychology, Human Rels., U. Detroit, 1972; PhD, Ind. Profl. Sch. Mgmt., 1974. Ordained priest, 1959. Parish priest Roman Cath. Chs., Muskegon, Grand Rapids, Mich., 1959-69; tchr. h.s. Roman Cath. Schs., 1959-69; clergy, psychologist Ecumenical Ctr., N.Y.C., 1974-96. Cons. Thomas More Ctr., N.Y.C., 1975-94, dir., 1982-94; corp. cons. Carlson Learning Co.; interfaith faculty mem. pastoral psychiatry The Rabbinical Acad., Woodmere, N.Y., 1998. Author Transactional Analysis Work Shops.; Theolog. lectrs. on Ecumenism, Marriages, Vatican II. Elected Fellow Nat. Alliance of Family Life, N.Y.C., 1990; Hon. Canon Anglican Cath. Ch., 1982. Mem. Nat. Assn. Ednl. Psychologists, (clinician), Am. Counselor Assn. (clin. mem.). Avocations; golf, tennis. Home: 1014 Vine St Manistee MI 49660-3145

SHIMODA, JERRY YASUTAKA, retired national historic park manager; b. Haleiwa, Hawaii, Mar. 21, 1930; s. Tamotsu and Sasai Shimoda; m. Clara H. Segawa, Aug. 7, 1954; children: Karen Marie K., Randall T., Shaun T., Teri Ellen H., Jacqueline Y., David Y. BA in Govt., U. Hawaii, 1952, MA in Far Ea. Area Studies, 1957; postgrad., St. Louis U., 1957-59. Historian Jefferson Nat. Expansion Meml. Nat. Hist. Site, St. Louis, 1957-60; chief historian, in charge hist. rsch. and visitor svcs. Saratoga Nat. Hist. Park, Stillwater, N.Y., 1960-66; chief historian Home of Franklin D. Roosevelt Nat. Hist. Site and, Frederick Vanderbilt Nat. Hist. Site, Hyde Park, N.Y., 1966-69; instr. Nat. Park Svc. Stephen T. Mather Tng. Ctr., Harpers Ferry, W.Va., 1969-72; supt. Pu'uhonua o Honaunau (Hawaii) Nat. Hist. Park, 1972-96, Puukohola Heiau Nat. Hist. Site, Kawaihae, 1972-96; ret., 1996. Lectr. environ. edn. Pa. State U., U. W.Va., Shepard Coll., 1969-72; acting supt. Kaloko-Honokohau Nat. Hist. Park, 1988-90; instr. environ. edn., interpretive and basic instructing techniques U. Hawaii, Hilo, Kapiolani C.C.; instr. Japanese culture U. Hawaii, Hilo, 1994; U.S. del. U.S.-Japan Panel on Nat. Parks and Equivalent Res., 1968-97, World Conf. on Marine Parks, Tokyo, 1975; Japanese translator U.S. Nat. Park Svc.; mem. internat. bd. dirs. Heritage Interpretation Internat., 1989-98; presenter in field. Author booklets on nat. parks, mgmt. and history; contbr. numerous articles to profl. publs., mags. and newspapers. Bd. dirs. Volcano Art Ctr.; mem. adv. com. Wailoa State Ctr.; mem. Hawaii Gov.'s Task Force on Ocean and Recreation; chmn. restoration com. St. Benedict's Ch., Honaunau, 1982-95; chmn. bd. dirs. Kahua Na'au 'Ao, 1996-97; vol. training cons. to Nat. Pk. Svc., 1996-2001; cons. Nat. Park Svc., 2001-. Recipient Spl. Achievement award Nat. Park Svc., 1964, 68, 70, resolution W.Va. Senate, 1971, Hawaii Ho. of Reps., 1982, sec.'s cert. Dept. Interior, 1971, Exec. of Yr. award West Hawaii chpt. Profl. Secs. Internat., 1981, cert. Govt. of Japan, 1981, staff plaque Pu'uhonua o Honaunau Nat. Hist. Park, Puukohola Heiau Nat. Hist. Site and Kaloko-Honokohau Nat. Hist. Park, 1988, cert. Japan Nat. Parks Assn., 1989, cert. of appreciation South Kona Aloha Lions Club, 1990, Meritorious Svc. award Sec. Interior, 1996, others. Mem. Hawaii Mus. Assn. (bd. dirs. 1988-92), Kona Hist. Soc. (bd. dirs. 1988-92), Big Island Ocean Recreation and Tourism Assn. (exec. com.), Kona Judo Club (pres. 1977-96), Rotary (pres. Kona Mauka 1978-79, co-founder Volcano chpt. 2001, Paul Harris fellow 1991, Disting. Svc. award 1992). Avocations: writing, reading, travel, teaching.

SHIMOKUBO, JANICE TERUKO, marketing professional; b. Chgo. d. Paul Kazuso and Tsugiye Jane (Fujii) Shimokubo; m. Ronald Theodore Spreigl, Jan. 3, 1982; 1 child, Elizabeth Shimokubo Spreigl. BA, U. Ill., 1973; MBA, Loyola U., Chgo., 1976. Sales rep. 3M Co., Rockford, Ill., 1976-79, mktg. coord. St. Paul, 1979-81, mktg. supr., 1981-83, mktg. mgr., 1983-88, sales and mktg. mgr., 1988-90; mktg. dir. U S WEST Comms., Inc., Phoenix, 1990-95, exec. dir. Denver, 1995—. Advisor Jr. Achievement, St. Paul, 1980-82; mem. 3M Women's Adv. Coun., St. Paul, 1984-87. Commr. Colo. Civil Rights commn., Denver, 1997—; bd. dirs. Ariz. Kidney Found., Phoenix, 1994-95, Phoenix Fire Pals, 1990-92, Melpomene Women's Health, St. Paul., 1986, YWCA USA, 1998—. Recipient Unity award KWGN-TV, 1997; Asian Pacific Am. Women's Leadership Inst. fellow, 1996. Fellow Internat. Women's Forum, 1998-99; mem. Am. Mktg. Assn. (nat. bd. dirs. 1999—), Women in Cable and Telecomms., Japanese Am. Citizens League, U. Ill. Alumni Assn., Alpha Omicron Pi. Avocations: golf, yoga, travel, needlework. Home: 5641 S Lima St Englewood CO 80111-4119

SHIMOMURA, ROGER Y. artist, educator; b. Seattle, June 26, 1939; s. Eddie K. and Aya (Tanagi) S.; children: Mark Aaron, Johanna Mariko, Yoko Allison; m. Janet Davidson-Hues, Jan. 9, 1995. BA, U. Wash., 1961; MFA, Syracuse (N.Y.) U., 1969. Disting. prof. art U. Kans., Lawrence, 1969—. Over 100 solo exhbns., 1965-99. Recipient award Archives of Am. Art, Smithsonian, Washington, 1990, Gov.'s artist award State Kans., Topeka, 1992, more than over 25 grants, 1965-69. Mem. Coll. Art Assn. (bd. dirs. 1995-98). Home: 1424 Wagon Wheel Rd Lawrence KS 66049-3544 E-mail: shim@ukans.edu.

SHIMP, KAREN ANN, accountant, municipal financial executive; b. Atlantic, Iowa, July 17, 1959; d. Emerson Arnold and Verna Louise (Schmeling) Fett; m. Philip Kenneth Shimp, Jan. 30, 1988 (div.); 1 child, Keith Emerson. BSBA, Drake U., 1981. Acct. Midwest Mut. Ins. Co., West Des Moines, Iowa, 1981-84; staff acct. Deborah J. Kent, CPA, Palm Desert, Calif., 1985; fin. analyst Massey Sand & Rock Co., Indio, 1986-88; supr. interline Greyhound Lines, Inc., West Des Moines, 1989-93; fin. dir. City of Pella, Iowa, 1994-2000; dir. fin. orgnl. svcs. Cedar Falls (Iowa) Utilities, 2000—. Coord. Drake U. Bus. Aid Soc., 1980; mem. Inland Soc. Tax Consultants, 1987-91. Treas. Luth. Women's Missionary League, Indio, 1986-88, sec., 1988-89; v.p. Aid Assn. for Lutherans, Indio, 1988-89; bd. dirs. After School Kid's Klub, 1995-97. State of Iowa scholar, 1977. Mem. Inst. Mgmt. Accts., Kiwanis Internat (pres. 1996-97). Democrat. Avocations: sewing, reading, aerobics, taxes. Home: 1303 College Street Cedar Falls IA 50613 Office: CVU Utility Pkwy PO Box 769 Cedar Falls IA 60613 E-mail: kshimp@cfunet.net.

SHIMP, ROBERT EVERETT, JR. academic administrator, historian; b. Phila., Mar. 1, 1942; s. Robert Everett Sr. and Vivian (Myrtetus) S.; m. Marilyn Hopkins, Aug. 3, 1963; children: Gregory, Cecily, Jennifer. BA, Thiel Coll., 1964; MA, Ohio State U., 1965, PhD, 1970. Instr. history Ohio Wesleyan U., Delaware, Ohio, 1968-70, asst. prof., 1970-76, assoc. prof., 1976-82, prof. history, 1982-84, dir. off campus program, 1979-84; acad. dean Ky. Wesleyan Coll., Owensboro, 1984-88; provost, v.p. for acad. affairs Millikin U., Decatur, Ill., 1988-93; pres. McMurry U., Abilene, Tex., 1993—. Vis. assoc. prof. Ohio State U., Columbus, summer 1978, Coll. of V.I., St. Croix, fall 1982; mem. Inst. for Ednl. Mgmt. Harvard U., 1985; reader and table leader European history AP, Princeton, N.J. 1976-83; dir. Newberry Libr. Program in the Humanities, Chgo., 1976-77. Contbr. articles to profl. jours. Active Leadership Owensboro, 1986-87; capt. drives United Way, Owensboro and Delaware, 1981-85, bd. dirs., Decatur and Abilene; trustee for Sears Retirement Systems, Thiel Coll., Abilene Higher Edn. Found.; bd. dirs. Abilene C. of C., Ind. Coll., U. Tex., Nat. Assn. of Schs. and Colls. of the United Meth. Ch. Fellow Ohio State U., 1968, Newberry Libr., Chgo., 1976-77; named Disting. Alumnus Thiel Coll., 2000. Mem. Ohio Acad. History, Conf. on Brit. Studies. Democrat. Methodist. Avocations: fishing, reading. Office: McMurry U Office of Pres PO Box 98 Abilene TX 79604-0098

SHIMPOCK, KATHY ELIZABETH, lawyer, writer; b. Mooresville, N.C., July 20, 1952; d. Charles Walter and Minna Ethel (McLean) S.; m. David Edward Vieweg, Sept. 3, 1983 (div. Mar. 1997); children: Jessica Kim Vieweg, Jayme Elise Kyung Vieweg. BA, Colo. Coll., 1973; JD, U. Wyo., 1977; MLL, U. Denver, 1979; MBA, Ariz. State U., 1992. Bar: Ariz. 1977. Asst. librarian Stanford (Calif.) U. Coll. Law, 1979—82; law librarian, asst. prof. law U. Bridgeport (Conn.) Coll. Law, 1982—83; dir. Law Libr. Adminstrv. Svcs., Mountain View, Calif., 1983—85; exec. asst. to dean Ariz. State U. Coll. Law, Tempe, 1985—87; dir. Law Libr. Adminstrv. Svcs., Mesa, Ariz., 1987—95; dir. libr. svcs. Jennings, Strouss & Salmon, Phoenix, 1988—89; dir. rsch. svcs. O'Connor, Cavanagh et al, 1989—95; pres. Juris Rsch., Mesa, 1995—96; counsel Muchmore & Wallwork, Phoenix, 1995—98; pres. Juris Rsch., Tempe, 1998—2000; rsch. and legal info. mgr. Bryan Cave LLP, 2000—. Adv. bd. West Pub. Co., St. Paul, 1991-94; mediator Alternative Dispute Resolution Program, Maricopa County, Ariz. Author: Business Research Handbook: Methods and Sources for Lawyers and Business Professionals, 1996—; co-author: Arizona Legal Research Guide, 1992; contbr. chpts. to books, articles to profl. jours.; bi-monthly columnist AzALL News, 1996-97, Legal Assistant Today, 1993-96; contbr. book revs. to Libr. Jour., Legal Info. Alert, 1993-98; editor Southwest Assn. Law Librs. Bull., 1990, Ariz. State U. Coll. Law Law Forum, 1986, Juris Rsch. E-line, 1999—. Rsch. atty. Comml. Law Project for the Ukraine, Phoenix, 1995-96. Mem. ABA (co-chair law practice mgmt. environ. divsn. 1996-99), Am. Assn. Law Librs. (chair 1994-95), Ariz. Assn. Law Librs. (pres. 1996-97, pres.'s award 1997, Disting. Mem. award 1998), State Bar of Ariz. (chair 1996-98, Cont. Legal Edn. award 1998), Ariz. Women Lawyers Assn. (steering com. 1998-2000). Democrat. Unity. Avocations: reading, yoga, painting, drawing. Office: Juris Rsch PO Box 2157 Tempe AZ 85280-2157 E-mail: kshimpock@jurisresearch.com.

SHIN, BONGSIK, information systems educator; b. Seoul, Republic of Korea, Aug. 26, 1960; came to U.S., 1988; s. HyunJoo Shin and KyungLim Choi; m. Insook Jeong, Dec. 10, 1987. PhD, U. Ariz., 1997. Faculty U. Nebr., Omaha, 1997-99, San Diego State U., 1999—. Contbr. articles to profl. jours. Avocations: swimming, traveling. Office: San Diego State U 5500 Campanile Dr San Diego CA 92182 Office Fax: (619) 594-3675. E-mail: bshin@mail.sdsu.edu.

SHIN, HYUN KOOK, chemical engineer; b. Seoul, Korea, July 2, 1937; came to U.S., 1958; s. Jae Kyoon and Byung Sook (Yoon) S.; m. Sung Sook Park, May 20, 1966; children: Grace, Deena. BS in Chem. Engring., MIT, 1962, ScD, 1965. From rsch. engr. to sr. rsch. assoc. DuPont Co., Fibers, Wilmington, Del., 1965-80, rsch. fellow, 1980-89, sr. rsch. fellow, 1990-96, DuPont fellow, 1997—. Author articles on rheology. Mem. AIChE, Soc. Rheology, Am. Chem. Soc., Soc. Plastics Engrs. Methodist. Achievements include some 40 patents in area of synthetic fibers and nonwovens technology. Avocations: golf, classical music. Home: 134 Hitching Post Dr Wilmington DE 19803-1913 Office: DuPont Co DuPont Exptl Sta E302 Wilmington DE 19880 E-mail: hyunkook.shin@usa.dupont.com.

SHIN, JOHN JOONGSUNG, mechanical nuclear engineer, consultant; b. Keuchang-Gun, Kyongnam, Korea, Feb. 27, 1941; came to U.S., 1966; s. Jong-Hyup and Hyunpoong (Kwak) S.; m. Sooky C. Shin, Apr. 22, 1972; children: Michael P., Eric P. BS, Korea Maritime U., Pusan, 1963, Hanyang U., Seoul, Korea, 1965; MS, Syracuse U., 1968; PhD, U. Del., 1974. Tchg. asst. Korea Maritime U., Pusan, 1965-66; rsch. asst. Syracuse (N.Y.) U., 1966-68; design engr. Sargent, Webster, Crenshaw, Syracuse, 1968-69; rsch. asst. U. Del., Newark, 1969-73; engr., sr. engr., prin. engr. Ebasco Svcs., Inc., N.Y.C., 1973-93; prin. engr., cons., sr. cons. Raytheon Nuclear, Inc., 1993-2000; pres. Advanced Nucleartech, Kearny, N.J., 2000—. Tech. cons. Ebasco/Raytheon Nuclear, Inc., N.Y.C., 1973—; tech. cons., seminar Korea Atomic Energy Rsch. Inst., Taejon, 1993, Korea Power Engring. Co., Yongin, Korea, 1992—; condr. seminar Seoul Nat. U., Korea Advanced Inst. Sci. and Tech., Seoul and Taejon, 1992, 93; mem. adv. bd. Korea Next Generation Reactor Tech. Devel., 1992—. Contbr. articles to profl. jours. 2nd engring. officer on ocean going vessels Korea Maritime Bur. Recipient awards U.S. Dept. Energy, 1988, 93, shining star awards Ebasco Svcs., Inc., Entergy Ops., Inc., 1986, 97. Mem. ASME, Am. Nuclear Soc., Korean Scientists and Engrs. Am., Korea Maritime U. Alumni Assn. (pres. 1990-92, 96-98). Democrat. Achievements include research on passive containment cooling of new production reactor and advaned reactors following loss of coolant accident, advanced reactor analyses including incontainment refueling water storage tank during air bubble oscillation, condesnation-oscillation and chugging; hydrogen generation, hydrogen distribution, steam and hydrogen explosion, corium-concrete interaction and recritcality analyses following severe reactor accident of 100% reactor core meltdown, universal passive containment protection analysis for inherently safe advanced light water reactor, advanced neutron source reactor analyses, hydrogen ignitor location analyses inside reactor containments, boiling water reactor suppression pool analyses following loss of coolant accident; avocations: swimming, boating, hiking. Home: 314 Division Ave Hasbrouck Heights NJ 07604-1722 Office: Advanced Nucleartech 340 Kearny Ave Kearny NJ 07032

SHIN, WILLIAM DONG MOON, brokerage house executive; b. Seoul, Korea, Apr. 12, 1944; came to the U.S., 1970; s. Kyung Soon and Il Soon (Kim) S.; m. Jeanie C. Youn, Jan. 30, 1971; children: Laura, Melissa. BSBA, Youngstown State U., 1977, MBA, 1986. Cert. money mgr. Payroll auditor Gen. Motors, Lordstown, Ohio, 1978-82, steel cost analyst Mansfield, 1982-87; fin. cons. Merrill Lynch, Cleve., 1987-89, fin. mgr., 1989-90, asst. v.p., 1990-91, v.p., 1991-94, first v.p. Pepper Pike, Ohio, 1994—. Pvt. Korean Army, 1966-69. Presbyterian. Avocations: golf, skiing, swimming. Home: 32081 Meadow Lark Way Pepper Pike OH 44124-5507 Office: Merrill Lynch 30100 Chagrin Blvd Ste 200 Pepper Pike OH 44124-5705

SHINAGAWA, LARRY HATIME, American studies educator; b. Tokyo, Jan. 15, 1958; came to U.S., 1963; s. Roy Yonori and Fusaco Shinagawa; m. Sun Shinagawa, May 25, 1980; children: Nathan, Chiharu, Mitchell, Grant. AB in Ethnic Studies, AB in Sociology, U. Calif., Berkeley, 1983, MA in Sociology, 1986, PhD in Sociology, 1994. Lectr. U. Calif., Berkeley, 1984-87; mgr., statistician Census Bur., Washington, 1988-89; prof. dept. Am. multicultural studies Sonoma State U., Rohnert Park, Calif., 1990—. V.p. U. No. Calif., Novato, 1999-2000, Four Winds Rsch., San Francisco, 1994—. Author: Atlas of American Diversity, 1998, Multiracial Japanese, 2000; editor: Critical Perspectives, 1984, Asian Americans, 1998. Bd. dirs. Visions 2001, Santa Rosa, Calif., 2001, Accium, Santa Rosa, 1990—, Asian Americans for Marin, Santa Rosa, 1996-99, JACL, Santa Rosa, 1990-93; mem. Human Rights Commn., Santa Rosa, 1998. Rsch. fellow Stanford Law Sch., 1996. Mem. Assn. Asian Am. Studies, Am. Sociol. Assn. Democrat. Buddhist. E-mail: larry.shinagawa.sonoma.edu. Home: 1097 Pippin Cir Santa Rosa CA 95407 Office: Sonoma State U Dept Am Multicultural Study 1801 E Coleti Ave Rohnert Park CA 94928

SHINAGEL, MICHAEL, English literature educator; b. Vienna, Austria, Apr. 21, 1934; came to U.S., 1941; s. Emanuel and Lilly (Hillel) S.; m. Ann Birdsey Mitchell, Sept. 1, 1956 (div. 1970); children: Mark Mitchell, Victoria Stuart; m. Rosa Joanne Bonanno, Dec. 6, 1973 (div. 1993); m. Marjorie Lee North, May 26, 1995. AB, Oberlin Coll., 1957; A.M., Harvard U., 1959, PhD, 1964; Doctorate (hon.), Internat. U. Ecuador, 1997. Teaching fellow Harvard U., Cambridge, Mass., 1958-59, tutor in English, 1962-64, assoc. dir. career office, 1959-64, dean continuing edn., 1975—, lectr. extension, 1976—, sr. lectr. English, 1983—, master Quincy House, 1986—2001; asst. prof. English, Cornell U., Ithaca, N.Y., 1964-67; prof., chmn. dept. English, Union Coll., Schenectady, 1967-75. Bd. dirs. Harvard Coop. Soc., publ. Harvard Rev.; pres. bd. dirs. Ednl. Exch. Boston, 1982-87; editor Continuing Higher Edn. Rev., 1997—. Author: Defoe and Middle-Class Gentility, 1968; co-author: (handbook) Summer Institutes in English, 1965; editor: Concordance to Poems of Swift, 1972, Critical Edition of Robinson Crusoe, 1975 (revised 1993); co-editor: Harvard Scholars in English (1890-1990), 1991. Served with U.S. Army, 1952-54, Korea Woodrow Wilson fellow, 1957; NEH grantee, 1965 Mem. Univ. Continuing Edn. Assn., Assn. Continuing Higher Edn., Mass. Hist. Soc., Old South Meeting House, The Johnsonians, The Saturday Club, Harvard Faculty Club (pres. 1985-87), Phi Beta Kappa. Avocations: reading; cooking; music; tennis. Home: 22 Grozier Rd Cambridge MA 02138 Office: Harvard U Divsn Continuing Edn 51 Brattle St Cambridge MA 02138-3701 E-mail: shinagel@hudce.harvard.edu.

SHINBROT, RICHARD GARY, surgeon; b. Mineola, N.Y., May 19, 1961; BS magna cum laude, SUNY, Albany, 1983; DO, U. Health Scis., Kansas City, Mo., 1987. Diplomate Nat. Bd. Osteo. Med. Examiners, Am. Bd. Gen. Surgery. Intern Garden City (Mich.) Hosp., 1987-88, resident in surgery, 1988-91; chief resident in surgery N.Y. Coll. Osteo. Medicine, Peninsula Hosp. Ctr., Far Rockaway, N.Y., 1991-92; clin. instr. N.Y. Coll. Osteo. Medicine, 1992—. Attending surgeon Winthrop U. Hosp., New Island Hosp., North Shore Univ. Hosp., Good Samaritan Hosp.; assoc. co-dir. surgery New Island Hosp., 2000—. Recipient Allan Breakie resident med. writing award, 1990; grantee Mead Johnson, 1988. Fellow Am. Coll. Osteo. Surgeons; mem. Am. Osteo. Assn., N.Y. Osteo. Med. Soc.

SHINDELL, SIDNEY, medical educator, physician; b. New Haven, May 31, 1923; s. Benjamin Abraham and Freda (Mann) S.; m. Gloria Emhoff, June 17, 1945; children: Barbara, Roger, Lawrence, Judith. BS, Yale U., 1944; MD, L.I. Coll. Medicine, 1946; postgrad., Emory U., 1948-49; LLB, George Washington U., 1951. Diplomate Am. Bd. Preventive Medicine in Occupl. Medicine, Am. Bd. General Preventive Medicine. With USPHS, 1947-52; med. dir. Conn. Commn. on Chronically Ill and Aged, 1952-57, Am. Joint Distbn. Com., 1957-59; asst. prof. preventive medicine U. Pitts., 1960-65; dir. Hosp. Utilization Project Western Pa., 1965-66; prof. dept. preventive medicine Med. Coll. Wis., Milw., 1966-93, chmn. dept., 1966-89, dir. Office Internat. Affairs, 1989-93, prof. emeritus, 1993—; exec. dir. Health Svc. Data of Wis., 1967-73. Mem. bd. sci. advisors Am. Coun. Sci. and Health, 1978—87, 1992—, chmn., 1988—92; mem. Nat. Adv. Com. on Occupl. Safety and Health U.S. Dept. Labor, 1982—84; cons. Caribbean Epidemiology Ctr. Pan Am. Health Orgn./WHO, 1988; field edpiemiology tng. program Ctr. Disease Control, Thailand, 1989, Nat. Office Occupl. and Environ. Medicine Royal Thai Ministry of Pub Health, 1990; mem. gov.'s white paper com. on health care reform, Wis., 93; acad. cons. Facilities of Medicine Padjadjaran U., Airlangga U., Indonesia, 1993, 94. Author: Statistics, Science and Sense, 1964, A Method of Hospital Utilization Review, 1966, The Law in Medical Practice, 1966, A Coursebook on Health Care Delivery, 1976; contbr. 120 articles to profl. jours. Trustee Med. Coll. Wis., 1996—; mem. sch. bd. Fox Point-Bayside (Wis.), Sch. Dist., 1970-71; vice chmn. Citizens' Adv. Com. Met. Problems, 1971-72; bd. dirs. Med. Care Evaluation S.E. Wis., 1973-76; trustee Interfaith Caregivers Aliance, 2001--. With AUS, 1943-46. Recipient Frank L. Babbott Meml. award SUNY Health Sci. Ctr., Bklyn., 1996. Fellow Am. Coll. Preventive Medicine (mem. bd. regents 1982-85), APHA, Am. Coll. Occupl. and Environ. Medicine (Pres.'s award 1999), Am. Coll. Legal Medicine; mem. Am. Assn. Health Data Sys. (sec. 1972-73), Assn. Tchrs. Preventive Medicine (dir. 1973-74, pres. 1976-77, spl. recognition award 1992, Duncan Clark award 2002), Assn. Occupl. Health Profls. (pres. 1980-90), Wis. Med. Soc. (mem. coun. on health care financing and delivery, mem. coun. on govt. affairs, mem. ho. of dels., 50 Yr. recognition award 1996, svc. award 2000), Am. Coll. Physician Execs., Internat. Commn. on Occupl. Health, Aircraft Owners and Pilots Assn., Masons, CAP. Home and Office: One Polo Creek Unit 201 2400 Cherry Creek South Drive Denver CO 80209-3251

SHINDLEDECKER, JOSEPH GREGORY, programmer, analyst; b. Indiana, Pa., May 2, 1954; s. Robert F. and Joanne E. (Weigle) S.; m. Debra L. Caplan, Sept., 1976 (dec. Aug., 1984); children: Ian J., Eric M.; m. Angela J. Muscelli, Mar. 29, 1986. AA in Nuclear Medicine, Essex Community Coll., 1974; BS in Computer Sci., Towson State U., 1987. Staff, sr. staff tech. Johns Hopkins Hosp., Balt., 1974-78, chief tech. myocardial infarction rsch. unit, 1978-82; computer programmer/operator divsn. nuclear medicine St. Joseph Hosp., Towson, 1982-86; cons., prin. Med. Software Systems, Kingsville, Md., 1985-87; sr. software engr. Cricket Software, Malvern, Pa., 1987-89; sr. nuclear application specialist Centocor, Inc., 1989-90, image processing scientist, mgr. image processing ctr., 1990-92; assoc. dir. computer info. mgmt. Bio-Imaging Techs., Inc., West Trenton, N.J., 1992-94, dir. clin. sys. devel., 1994-98; dir. clin. oncology interactive comms. Quintiles, Inc., Research Triangle Park, N.C., 1998-99; dir. Info. Sys. Quintiles-Intelligent Imaging, Plymouth Meeting, Pa., 1999-2000; prin. M&D Cons. Assocs., Ltd., Downingtown, 2000-2001; dir. spl. projects Bio-Imaging Techs., Inc., Newtown, 2001—. Asst. scoutmaster troop 101 Boy Scouts Am., 1990-96, com. chair, 1996-97, asst. scoutmaster Venture Crew Troop 2, 1997-2000. Democrat. Avocations: model railroading, camping, bicycling, hiking, backpacking. Office: 826 Newtown-Yardley Rd Newtown PA 18940-1721 E-mail: gshindledecker@bioimaging.com.

SHINDLER, DONALD A. lawyer; b. New Orleans, Oct. 15, 1946; s. Alan and Isolene (Levy) S.; m. Laura Epstein, 1969; children: Jay, Susan. BSBA, Washington U., St. Louis, 1968; JD, Tulane U., 1971. Bar: La. 1971, U.S. Dist. Ct. (ea. dist.) La. 1971, U.S. Tax Ct. 1974, Ill. 1975, U.S. Dist. Ct. (no. dist.) Ill. 1975; CPA, La.; lic. real estate broker, Ill. Assoc. Pope, Ballard, Shepard & Fowle, Chgo., 1975-78, Rudnick & Wolfe, Chgo., 1978-81, ptnr., 1981-99; gen. counsel America's Second Harvest Nat. Food Bank Network, 1998-2000; ptnr. Piper Marbury Rudnick & Wolfe, Chgo., 1999—2002, Piper Rudnick, Chgo., 2002—. Seminar lectr. ABA, Chgo. Bar Assn., Ill. Inst. CLE, Profl. Edn. Sys., Inc., Internat. Assn. Corp. Real Estate Execs., Urban Land Inst., Am. Corp. Counsel Assn., Bldg. Owners and Mgrs. Assn., Internat. Assn. of Attys. and Execs. in Corp. Real Estate, others. Contbr. articles on real estate to legal jours. Trustee Glencoe (Ill.) Pub. Libr., 1981-87, pres., 1986-87; alumni bd. govs. Washington U., 1992-93; mem. Glencoe Zoning Commn./Bd. Appeals, 1994-2000. Lt. JAGC, USNR, 1971-75. Mem. ABA, La. State Bar Assn., Chgo. Bar Assn. (com. chmn. 1979-80, 83-84, 90-94, 96-99, editor land trust seminars 1984-96), Urban Land Inst. (mem. steering com. Chgo. dist. coun.), Internat. Assn. Corp. Real Estate Execs. (pres. Chgo. chpt. 1997-98, dir. 1991—), Internat. Assn. Attys. and Execs. in Corp. Real Estate, Union League Club (chair real estate group 1993-96), Order of Coif, Beta Gamma Sigma, Omicron Delta Kappa. Office: Piper Rudnick Ste 1800 203 N La Salle St Ste 1800 Chicago IL 60601-1210 E-mail: donald.shindler@piperrudnick.com.

SHINDLER, MERRILL KARSH, writer, radio personality; b. N.Y.C., July 2, 1948; s. Joseph and Miriam (Karsh) S. BA, CCNY, 1970; MFA, NYU, 1971. Entertainment editor San Francisco Bay Guardian, 1972-75; music editor Rolling Stone mag., San Francisco, 1976-79; film critic Los Angeles mag., 1979-89; restaurant critic L.A. Examiner, 1979-88; editor Zagat Los Angeles Restaurant Survey, 1986—; restaurant critic L.A. Reader, 1990-96, Daily Breeze, 1990—, Daily News, 1989-94, San Gabriel Valley Newspapers, 1994—. Author: Best Restaurants of L.A., 1989, Zagat, L.A. Restaurant Survey, 1986—, American Dish, 1996, El Cholo: A History, 1998; writer (radio shows) Am. Top 40, 1979-89, 98—, Casey's Top 40, 1989—, Casey's Biggest Hits, 1990—, USA Top 20, 1990—, (TV shows) Am. Top 10, 1980-93, Cinemattractions, 1990—, USA Music Today, 1990—; host radio show Feed Your Face with Merrill Shindler, KLSX-FM, 1988—; contr. to Gault-Millau Best of Los Angeles, 1988, Gault-Millau Best of Hong Kong, 1989; contbr. articles to jours. Avocations: restaurants, cooking, jogging, travel.

SHINDURLING, JON J. judge; b. Idaho Falls, Idaho, Apr. 13, 1947; s. Boyd Thomas and Donna Marie (Fullmer) S.; m. Christine Moss, May 24, 1974; children: Melissa, Marianne, Amanda, Alison. BA in English, Ariz. State U., 1972; JD, U. Idaho, 1977. Bar: Idaho. Ptnr. May & May Law Offices, Twin Falls, Idaho, 1977-88, Wright Law Offices, Idaho Falls, 1990-93; field dir. Sch. of Urban and Wilderness Survival, Shoshone, Idaho, 1988-90; dep. prosecuting atty. Bonneville County, Idaho Falls, 1994-2000, chief dep., 1995-2000; dist. judge 7th Jud. Dist., 2000—. Mem. continuing legal edn. com. Idaho Law Found., Boise, 1985-88; mem. civil jury instns. com. Idaho Supreme Ct., Boise, 1987-89, 96—. Mem. coun. exec. bd. Boy Scouts Am.-Snake River Area, Twin Falls, 1979-90; bd. dirs. Magic Valley YFCA, Twin Falls, 1988-90, Idaho Falls Opera Theatre, 1993-99. Mem. Idaho State Bar (mem. bar examination com. 1979-82, chmn. com. 1980-82, mem. fee disputes resolution com. 1991—). Mem. Lds Ch. Avocations: reading, fishing, scouting. Office: Office Dist Ct 605 N Capital Ave Idaho Falls ID 83402-3582 E-mail: JShindur@co.bonneville.id.us.

SHINE, DANIEL JOSEPH, JR. management consultant; b. Lawrence, Mass., Feb. 17, 1944; s. Daniel Joseph and Catherine Theresa (Mahoney) S.; Rosanne Marie Pingaro, Sept. 30, 1967; children: Matthew David, Jonathan Marc. BA in History, Merrimack Coll., 1965; MS in Fgn. Svc., Georgetown U., 1968. Mem. staff, intelligence officer CIA, Washington, 1967-76; dir. Sanders Assocs., Nashua, N.H., 1976-85; sr. v.p. Arthur D. Little, Inc., Cambridge, Mass., 1985-94; prin. EDS/Mgmt. Consulting, Plano, Tex., 1994-95; v.p./global practice leader A.T. Kearney, Inc., Chgo., 1995—. Bd. advisors Georgetown U. Admissions, Washington, 1976—; mem. pres.'s coun. Merrimack Coll., North Andover, Mass., 1995—. Home: 11 Granada Way Andover MA 01810-4201 Office: AT Kearney Inc 1 Memorial Dr Ste 14 Cambridge MA 02142-1346 E-mail: dan.shine@atkearney.

SHINE, KENNETH IRWIN, cardiologist, educator; b. Worcester, Mass., 1935; Grad., Harvard Coll., 1957; MD, Harvard U., 1961. Diplomate Am. Bd. Internal Medicine. Intern Mass. Gen. Hosp., 1961—62, resident, 1962—63, resident, 1965—66, fellow in cardiology, 1966—67; surgeon USPHS, 1963—65; instr. Harvard Med. Sch., 1968—; asst. prof. medicine UCLA Sch. Medicine, 1971—73, assoc. prof., 1973—77, prof., 1977—92, prof. emeritus, 1993—, dir. CCU, 1971—75, chief div. cardiology, 1975—79, vice chmn. dept. medicine, 1979—81, exec. chmn., 1981—86, dean, 1986—92; clin. prof. medicine Georgetown U. Med. Ctr., Washington, 1993—; provost for med. scis. UCLA Sch. Medicine, 1991—92; pres. Inst. of Medicine, Washington, 1992—2002; dir. RAND Center for Domestic and International Health Security. Mem.: Assn. Am. Med. Colls. (adminstrv. bd. coun. deans 1989—92, exec. bd. 1990—92, chmn. coun. deans 1991—92), Am. Heart Assn. (pres. 1986—87). Office: RAND Cntr 1200 S Hayes St Arlington VA 22202-5050*

SHINE, MARY TONISSEN, retired advertising executive; b. Jacksonville, Fla., Apr. 16, 1926; d. Otto John and Anna Ruth (Simms) T.; m. James Munnerlyn Shine, Mar.12, 1955; children: James Munnerlyn Jr., Wallace Tonissen. Student, Salem Coll., 1944-45, Greenleaf Bus. Coll., 1945-46. Sec. Morris Plan Bank, Jacksonville, 1945-46, Riverside Bank, Jacksonville, 1947; loan and discount teller Northwestern Bank, Hendersonville, N.C., 1947-48; sec. trust dept. Fla. Nat. Bank, Jacksonville, 1948-50; office mgr., sales asst. Harry E. Cummings Radio/TV Rep., 1950-62; traffic and billing clk. Sta. WJAX, 1963-64; media dir. William Cook Advt., Inc., 1966-90. Bd. dirs. Meth. Regional Hosp. System, Jacksonville, 1986-92, Morning Star Sch., Jacksonville, 1985-92; com. mem. Communications Com., Drug and Substance Abuse Com., Episcopal Diocese Fla., Jacksonville, 1984-88. Recipient Jack Philipps Gold medal 4th Dist. Am. Advt. Fedn., 1984. Mem. Jacksonville Advt. Fedn. (bd. dirs. 1972-81, treas. 1973-74, v.p. 1974-76, pres. 1976-77, 77-78, Silver medal 1988, life). Democrat. Avocations: oil painting, playing piano and organ. Home: 1984 Eventide Rd Switzerland Rte Jacksonville FL 32259

SHINE, NEAL JAMES, journalism educator, former newspaper editor, publisher; b. Grosse Pointe Farms, Mich., Sept. 14, 1930; s. Patrick Joseph and Mary Ellen (Conlon) S.; m. Phyllis Theresa Knowles, Jan. 24, 1953; children: Judith Ann, James Conlon, Susan Brigid, Thomas Patrick, Margaret Mary, Daniel Edward. BS in Journalism, U. Detroit, 1952; PhD (hon.), Cleary Coll., 1989, Siena Heights Coll., 1995, U. Mich., 1995, U. Detroit Mercy, 1996, Ctrl. Mich. U., 1996. Mem. staff Detroit Free Press, 1950-95, asst. city editor, 1963-65, city editor, 1965-71, mng. editor, 1971-82, sr. mng. editor, 1982-89, pub., 1990-95; prof. journalism Oakland U., Rochester, Mich., 1995—. Host, moderator Detroit Week in Rev., Sta. WTVS-TV, 1981-89, host Neal Shine's Detroit, 1989-91. Trustee, vice chmn. bd. trustees Youth for Understanding, 1973-75, chmn., 1975-78; mem. bd. for student publs. U. Mich.; bd. dirs. Children's Hosp., Econ. Club Detroit, Detroit Renaissance, New Detroit, Inc., Detroit Symphony Orch., Detroit Inst. Arts, Detroit Hist. Soc., United Way of Southeastern Mich., Met. Detroit Conv. and Visitors Bur., Operation ABLE, Detroit Press Club Found. With U.S. Army, 1953-55. Inducted Mich. Journalism Hall of Fame, 1990. Mem.: Soc. of Profl. Journalists, AP Mng. Editors, Mich. Press Assn. (bd. dirs. 1990—95), Am. Newspaper Pubs. Assn., Am. Soc. Newspaper Editors, Inc. Soc. Irish-Am. Lawyers, Sons of Whiskey Rebellion (comdr.-in-chief 1979), Detroit Press Club (charter, bd. govs. 1966—89, sec. 1957—68, v.p. 1969—71, pres. 1971—73). Home: 11009 Harbor Place Dr Saint Clair Shores MI 48080-1527 also: Carraig Rinn 13240 Crystal Beach Rd Pointe aux Roches ON Canada N0R 1N0

SHINEFIELD, HENRY ROBERT, pediatrician; b. Paterson, N.J., Oct. 11, 1925; s. Louis and Sarah (Kaplan) Shinefield; m. Jacqueline Marilyn Walker; children: Jill, Michael, Kimberley Putzer, Melissa Strome. BA, Columbia U., 1945, MD, 1948. Diplomate Diplomate: Am. Bd. Pediat. (examiner, 1975— , bd. dirs., 1979-84, v.p., 1981-84). 1949Rotating intern Mt. Sinai Hosp., N.Y.C., 1948; pediatric intern Duke Hosp., Durham, N.C., 1949-50; asst. resident pediatrician N.Y. Hosp. (Cornell), 1950-51, pediatrician to outpatients, 1953-59, instr. in pediatrics, 1959-60, asst. prof., 1960-64, asso. prof., 1964-65, asst. attending pediatrician, 1959-63, asso. attending pediatrician, 1963-65; pediatrician to outpatients Children's Hosp., Oakland, Calif., 1951-53; chief of pediatrics Kaiser-Permanente Med. Center, San Francisco, 1965-89, chief emeritus, 1989—; co-dir. Kaiser-Permanente Vaccine Study Ctr., 1984—; assoc. clin. prof. pediatrics Sch. Medicine U. Calif., 1966-68, clin. prof. pediatrics, 1968—, clin. prof. dermatology, 1970—; asso. attending pediatrician Paterson (N.J.) Gen. Hosp., 1955-59; chief of pediatrics Kaiser Found. Hosp., San Francisco, 1965-86; attending Moffitt Hosp., 1967-88; practice medicine specializing in pediatrics Paterson, 1953-59. Cons. San Francisco Gen. Hosp., 1967—88, Children's Hosp., San Francisco, 1970—88, Mt. Zion Hosp., San Francisco, 1970—88; mem. rsch. grants rev. br. NIH, HEW, 1970—74; med. dir. USPHSR, 1969—; bd. dirs. San Francisco Peer Rev. Orgn., 1975—81, sec., exec. com., 1976—81; chmn. Calif. State Child Health Disability Bd., 1973—82; mem. Inst. Medicine NAS, 1980—; cons. Bur. Drugs FDA, 1970, NIH, HEW, 1974—. Editl. bd. We. Jour. Medicine, 1968—80, Am. Jour. Diseases of Children, 1970—82; contbr. articles to profl. publs. Chmn. San Francisco Med. Adv. Com. Nat. Found. March of Dimes, 1969—80. Served USPHS, 1951—53. Fellow: Am. Acad. Pediat. (com. fetus and newborn 1969—76, com. on drugs 1978—82); mem.: AMA, Am. Pediatric Soc., We. Soc. Clin. Rsch., We. Pediatric Soc., Infectious Diseases Soc. Am., Soc. Pediatric Rsch., Phi Beta Kappa. Home: 2705 Larkin St San Francisco CA 94109-1117 Office: Kaiser Permanente 4131 Geary Blvd San Francisco CA 94118-3101 E-mail: henry.shinefield@kp.org.

SHINEMAN, EDWARD WILLIAM, JR. retired pharmaceutical executive; b. Canajoharie, N.Y., Apr. 9, 1915; s. Edward W. and Bertelle H. (Shubert) S.; m. H. Doris Thompson, Apr. 15, 1939; children: Edward T., Alan B. AB, Cornell U., 1937. With apparatus dept., acctg. dept. Gen. Electric Co., 1938-46, line auditor, 1942-46; with Beech-Nut, Inc. and predecessor cos., 1946-68, asst. treas., 1948-63, contr., 1959-63, treas., 1963-68; asst. sec.-treas. Squibb Corp., 1968-81. Bd. dirs. Fenimore Asset Mgmt., Inc., Taconic Farms, Inc. Trustee, pres. Arkell Hall Found.; mem. emeritus coun. Cornell U. Mem. Fin. Execs. Inst., Inst. Mgmt. Accts. Republican. Home: 420 E 51st St Apt 14E New York NY 10022-8022 E-mail: ESHINEMAN@AOL.com.

SHINEVAR, PETER O'NEIL, lawyer; b. Jackson, Mich., Oct. 3, 1955; m. Karen Kay Coats, Aug. 25, 1979. AB with high distinction, U. Mich., 1977, JD summa cum laude, 1980, postgrad., 1978-81. Bar: D.C. 1982, N.Y. 1994. Law clk. U.S. Ct. Appeals (D.C. cir.), Washington, 1981-82; assoc. Bredhoff & Kaiser, 1982-88, ptnr., 1989-92; assoc. dir. rsch. The Segal Co., 1992-95; spl. counsel O'Melveny & Myers LLP, 1995-2000, ptnr., 2000—. Mem. ABA (sec. labor and employment law employee benefits com., mgmt. co-chair, subcom. on welfare plans, sec. taxation, employee benefits com.), Order of the Coif, Phi Beta Kappa. Democrat. Office: O'Melveny & Myers LLP 153 E 53rd St Fl 54 New York NY 10022-4611 E-mail: pshinevar@omm.com.

SHINGLES, RICHARD D. political scientist, educator; b. Syracuse, NY, Apr. 20, 1944; s. David L. and Lucielle Shingles; m. Carol Shingles (div. 1981); children: Michael, Marc, Robert; m. Wendy Jacobson. BA, Wayne

State U., 1966, MA, 1968; PhD, U. Minn., 1973. Assoc. prof. Va. Poly. and State U., Blacksburg, 1971—. Contbr. articles to profl. jours., chapters to books. Named MacArthur fellow, Joint Ctr. for Polit. and Econ. Studies, 1989—90; grantee, NSF, 1985, Nat. Election Studies, 1985. Mem.: NAACP, Nat. Assn. Latino Elected Ofcls., Am. Polit. Sci. Assn. Office: Va Poly and State U Dept Polit Sci Blacksburg VA 24160 Office Fax: 540-231-6278. Business E-Mail: shingles@vt.edu.

SHINGLES, SAMUEL D, minister, music educator; b. Jex, Fla., 1970; s. John Ellis and Barbara Annette Shingles; m. Letonia Diane Shingles; children: Uriah Jumhl, Elijah R. Degree, Stetson U., Deland, FL, Bowling Green State U., Bowling Green, Ohio; D.ADegree, Univaersity of Miss., Oxford, MS. Music educator sch., Jacksonville, Fla., 2002—. Home: 4327 Timuquana Road Jacksonville FL 8537

SHINITZKY, HAROLD ELIOT, psychologist; b. Chgo., Mar. 10, 1960; s. Edwin Jerome and Charlotte Shinitzky. BS, U. Iowa, 1982; PsychD, Forest Inst., 1990. Lic. psychologist Fla., Md. Mem. faculty, psychologist Johns Hopkins U. Sch. Medicine, Balt., 1994—2000; mental health corr. ABC TV Network, Tampa, Fla., 1997—98, 1999—2000, Balt., 2000—; cons. psychologist Pinellas County Pub. Schs., Clearwater, Fla., 2000—, State of Md., Annapolis, 2000—; pvt. practice Clearwater, 2000—. Intern dept. psychology Sch. Medicine Johns Hopkins U., Balt., 1988—89; postdoctoral fellow Johns Hopkins U. Ctr. for Substance Abuse Prevention, Balt., 1995—98, Robert Wood Johnson, Balt., 1996—99; presenter UN Ann. Internat. Conf. Against Drugs, San Patrignano, Italy, 2000. Contbr. articles to profl. publs. Mem. nat. adv. bd. Com. for Drug Free Am., 2000—. Recipient Gov.'s Vol. and Svc. award, State of Md., 2000, Martin Luther King Jr. award for cmty. svc., 2000. Mem.: APA, Fla. Psychol. Assn., Psi Chi (Disting. Faculty award 1997, 1999). Avocations: tennis, drawing, travel. Office: 2531 Landmark Dr # 207 Clearwater FL 33761 E-mail: drshinitzky@yahoo.com.

SHINKAI, ICHIRO, chemist; b. Mie-Tsucity, Japan, Dec. 4, 1941; m. Yoshiko Shinkai; children: Gen, Kanade. PhD, Kyushu U., Fukuoka, Japan, 1971; MSc, Doshisha U., Kyoto, Japan, 1966, BSc, 1964. Chief sci. officer Beta-Chem, Tokyo, Japan, 2000—; mng. dir. Eirai Co., Ltd., Japan, 1997—2000; sr. v.p. Merck & Co., Ltd., NJ, 1990—96. Contbr. articles to profl. jours. Office: Beta-Chem Incorporated 1-2-1 Otemachi Tokyo Chiyoda-ku 100-0004 Japan Office Fax: 81-3-3214-2677. E-mail: shinkai.ichiro@beta-chem.com.

SHINN, CLINTON WESLEY, lawyer; b. Haworth, Okla., Mar. 7, 1947; s. Clinton Elmo and Mary Lucille (Dowdy) Shinn; m. Catherine Borne; children: Laura Kathryn, Clinton Wesley, Timothy Daniel. BS, McNeese State U., 1969; JD, Tulane U., 1972; LLM, Harvard U., 1973. Bar: La. 1972, U.S. Dist. Ct. (ea. dist.) La. 1975, U.S. Dist. Ct. (we. dist.) La. 1980, U.S. Ct. Appeals (5th cir.) 1981, U.S. Ct. Appeals (11th cir.) 1982, U.S. Tax Ct. 1982. Asst. prof. law Tulane U., New Orleans, 1973-75; assoc. Stone, Pigman et al, 1975-78, ptnr., 1979-97, Gill & Shinn, LLC, Covington, 1998-2000, of counsel, 2000—; assoc. prof. law Appalachian Sch. Law, 1999—2002, Miss. Coll. Sch. Law , 2002—. Co-founder, bd. dirs. Childhood Ctr. Families Network, 1987—90; co-founder Camp Challenge, 1988; team leader Campaign for Caring, Children's Hosp., New Orleans, 1989—91; bd. dirs. Greater New Orleans YMCA, 1989—98, 1999—2000, exec. com., 1991—98, asst. sec., 1994—95, sec., 1996—98, mem. fin. com., 1994—98, exec. dir. search com., 1996, 2d vice-chair, 1998; mem. Leadership Coun., 1997—98; active Indian Guides/Princesses; bd. dirs. West ST. Tammany YMCA, 1987—95, exec. com., 1988—95, chmn. bd. dirs., 1989—90, 1992—93; bd. dirs. La. Air & Waste Mgmt. Assn., 1993—99, chmn. corp. rels. com., 1992—93, vice chmn., 1996—97, chair, 1997—98, past chair, 1998—99; bd. dirs. Christ Episcopal Sch., Covington, 1988—91, chmn. long-range planning, 1990—91, mem. exec. com., 1989—91, chmn. legal com., 1989—91, chmn. admissions/recruitment com., 1988—90, mem. headmaster search com., 1993; bd. dirs. Christwood, 1992—, v.p. bd. dirs., 1997—99. Co-recipient Pals of the Yr. award, Greater New Orleans YMCA Indian Guides/Princesses, 1987—88; named Vol. of the Yr., West St. Tammany YMCA, 1990, 1992. Fellow: Northshore Estate Planning Coun., La. Bar Found., Am. Coll. Trust and Estate Counsel; mem.: ABA, Nat. Commn. Planning Giving (New Orleans chpt.), Air and Waste Mgmt. Assn., Nat. Wildlife Fedn. (life), New Orleans Estate Planning Coun., La. Forestry Assn., La. Bar Assn., Nat. Assn. Securities Dealers (bd. arbitrators), Order Coif. Avocations: backpacking, gardening. Home: 101 Aspen Dr Madison MS 39110 Office: Miss Coll Law Sch 151 E Griffith Jackson MS also: Appalachian Sch Law PO Box 2825 Grundy VA 24614-2825 *In all things be firm but fair.*

SHINN, DAVID HAMILTON, educator, former diplomat; b. Yakima, Wash., June 9, 1940; s. Guy Wilson and Ada Louise (Gelvin) S.; m. Judy Karen Rolfe, Sept. 9, 1961; children: Steven Hamilton, Christopher Rolfe. AA, Yakima Valley Coll., 1960; BA, George Washington U., 1963, MA, 1964, PhD, 1980; cert. African studies, Northwestern U., Evanston, Ill., 1969. With U.S. State Dept., 1964-2000; rotational officer U.S. Embassy, Beirut, Lebanon, 1964-66; polit. officer Nairobi, Kenya, 1967-68; desk officer East African affairs Washington, 1969-72; polit. officer Dar es Salaam, Tanzania, 1972-74; dep. chief of mission Nouakchott, Mauritania, 1974-76, Office of Mayor, City of Seattle, 1977-78; dep. coord. state and local govt. U.S. Dept. State, Washington, 1978-81; dep. chief of mission Yaounde, Cameroon, 1981-83, Khartoum, Sudan, 1983-86; U.S. ambassador Ouagadougou, Burkina Faso, 1987-90; diplomat-in-residence Southern U., Baton Rouge, 1990-91; diplomat State Dept., Washington, 1991-96; U.S. Amb. Addis Ababa, Ethiopia, 1996-99; diplomat-in-residence UCLA, 1999-2000. Adj. prof. George Washington U., 2001—. Sr. assoc. Internat. Ctr. for Religion and Diplomacy; mem. Pacific Coun. Internat. Policy; sr. assoc. Internat. Ctr. Religion and Diplomacy; bd. dirs. U.S. Cares for Ethiopia, People to People, Inc. Recipient Superior Honor award State Dept., 1980, 85, 94, Alumnus of Yr. award Am. Assn. Cmty. Colls., 1994, Phi Theta Kappa, 1995. Mem. Internat. Studies Assn., Am. Fgn. Service Assn., Am. Philatelic Soc., Rotary Internat. Methodist. Avocations: philately, skiing, physical fitness, antiques. Address: 23 8th St SE Washington DC 20003

SHINN, GEORGE LATIMER, investment banker, consultant, educator; b. Newark, Mar. 12, 1923; s. Leon Powell and Bertha Florence (Latimer) S.; m. Clara LeBaron Sampson, May 21, 1949; children: Deborah, Amy, Martha, Sarah, Andrew. AB, Amherst Coll., 1948; LLD (hon.), Denison U., 1975, Amherst Coll., 1982; MA, Drew U., 1990, PhD, 1992. Trainee Merrill Lynch, Pierce, Fenner & Beane, 1948-49; various exec. positions, 1949-75; pres. Merrill Lynch & Co., Inc., 1973-75; chmn. bd., chief exec. officer 1st Boston Corp., 1975-83; investment banking consultant, 1983—. Adj. prof. history Drew U., Madison, N.J., 1992—; mem. exec. com. President's Pvt. Sector Survey on Cost Control, 1982-84; exec.-in-residence Columbia U. Grad. Sch. Bus., 1983-85; bd. govs. Am. Stock Exch., 1970-74; bd. dirs., trustee Colonial Group Mut. Funds, 1983-98; bd. dirs. Kelso & Co., 1992—, N.Y. Stock Exch., 1975-83, vice chmn., 1979-83; bd. dirs. N.Y. Times Co., 1978-99, Philps Dodge Corp., 1983-95, N.Y. Life Ins. Co., 1983-94, Lehigh Press, 1983-91, Superior Oil Co., 1984-87, Congoleum Corp. Gen. chmn. United Hosp. Fund, N.Y.C., 1973-74; trustee Kent Pl. Sch., Summit, N.J., 1966-73, Carnegie Found. for Advancement Teaching, 1976-85, Pingry Sch., 1977-79, Lucille P. Markey Charitable Trust, 1985-97, Rockefeller Family Office Trust, 1989-97, N.J. Coun. for the Humanities, 1994-2000, Arts Coun. Morris Area, 1978-91, Philharmonic Symphony Soc. N.Y., 1983-91, Nat. Humanities Ctr., 1988-94; trustee emeritus Amherst Coll., 1968-82, chmn. bd. trustees, 1973-80; bd. dirs. Rsch. Corp., 1975-86. Capt. USMCR, 1943-52. Fellow Am. Acad. Arts and Scis., N.Y. Acad. Medicine, River Club, Century Assn., Morris County Golf Club.

SHINN, MICHAEL ROBERT, lawyer; b. Salem, Oreg., June 25, 1947; s. William Robert and Miriam Jean (Becke) S. BA, Willamette U., 1969, JD, 1973. Bar: Oreg. 1973, U.S. Dist. Ct. Oreg. 1973, U.S. Ct. Appeals (9th cir.) 1973. Law clk. to judge U.S. Dist. Ct., Portland, Oreg., 1974-75; pvt. practice, 1975—. Lectr. Masters at Trial Oreg., We. Trial Lawyers Assn., Oreg. State Bar, Mont. State Bar, Oreg. Law Inst., Nat. Bus. Inst. Editor Trial Lawyer Quar., 1988; dir., editor, producer: (videotape) (with Gerry Spence) Spence in Trial, 1989-90; co-producer, dir.: (videotape) Spence in Trial, Series for Trial Lawyers; cons. NBC mini-series Dead By Sunset, 1995. Pres. W. Hills and Island Neighbors Assn., Portland, 1983-84; del. Citizen to Citizen Legal Amb. Dels. to China, 1988; mem., bd. dirs. adv. coun. Oreg. Hearing Rsch. Ctr., 1992; bd. dirs. Portland Civic Theater. Inducted Willamette U. Athletic Hall of Fame, 1998. Mem. Oreg. Trial Lawyers Assn., (pres. 1980-81, edn. dir. 1984-89, svc. award 1986, 87), Am. Inns. of Ct. (master barrister 1988). Avocations: writing, wind surfing, skiing, water skiing, tennis, rugby. Office: 621 SW Morrison St Ste 1000 Portland OR 97205-3821 E-mail: michaelshinn@aol.com.

SHINNAR, SHLOMO, child neurologist, educator; b. Haifa, Israel, Nov. 11, 1950; s. Reuel and Miryam (Halpern) S.; m. Shoshana Ellen Cohen, Aug. 11, 1974; children: Ora Rivka, Aviva Batya, Avraham Ever. BA in Physics summa cum laude, Columbia Coll., 1971; PhD, Albert Einstein Coll. Medicine, 1977, MD, 1978. Diplomate Am. Bd. Pediat., Am. Bd. Psychiatry and Neurology, Am. Bd. Child Neurology and Clin. Neurophysiology. Intern, asst. resident in pediatrics, fellow Johns Hopkins Hosp., Balt., 1978-80, asst. resident, resident in neurology, fellow, 1980-83; from asst. prof. to prof. neurology and pediat. Albert Einstein Coll. Medicine, Bronx, 1983—; from asst. attending to attending neurology and pediat. Montefiore Med. Ctr., Bronx Mcpl. & North Ctrl. Bronx Hosps., 1983—. Dir. CERC Seizure Clinic R.K. Kennedy Ctr., Bronx, 1983—; co-dir. Epilepsy Mgmt. Ctr. Montefiore Med. Ctr. Albert Einstein Coll. Medicine, Bronx, 1983-86, dir., 1986—; mem. adv. bd. Epilepsy Inst., N.Y.C., 1984—, chair 1996—, instnl. rev. bd. protection of human subjects Montefiore Med. Ctr., Bronx, 1985—, vice-chmn., 1989—, prof. of neuroscience rsch., 2002—; adj. sch. scientist Gertrude Sergievsky Ctr. Columbia Coll. Physicians and Surgeons, N.Y.C., 1985—, Sergievsky Scholar, 1986—; cons. in field. Field editor Epilepsy Advances, 1987-93; editl. bd. The Neurologist, 1993—, Epilepsia, 1994-2000, Pediatric Neurology, 1996—; contbr. articles to profl. jours. N.Y. State Regents scholar, 1967-71; Martin and Emily L. Fisher fellow, 1991— Fellow Am. Acad. Pediats., Am. Acad. Neurology; mem. Am. Epilepsy Soc. (chmn. childhood onset epilepsy com. 1993-95, councillor 1992-95, Rsch. Recognition award 1989), Child Neurology Soc., Eastern EEG Soc., Internat. Child Neurology soc., Nat. Assn. Epilepsy Ctrs., Soc. for Pediat. Rsch., Am. Neurol. Assn. Office: Montefiore Med Ctr 111 E 210th St Bronx NY 10467-2401 E-mail: sshinnar@aol.com.

SHINNERS, STANLEY MARVIN, electrical engineer; b. N.Y.C., May 9, 1933; s. Earl and Molly (Planter) S.; m. Doris Pinsker, Aug. 4, 1956; children: Sharon Rose Cooper, Walter Jay, Daniel Lawrence. BEE, CCNY, 1954; MSEE, Columbia U., 1959. Equipment engr. Western Electric Co., N.Y.C., 1953-54; staff engr. electronics divsn. Otis Elevator Co., Bklyn., 1954-56; project engr. Consol. Avionics Corp., Westbury, N.Y., 1956-58; program mgr., fed. sys. Lockheed Martin Corp. (formerly Loral Corp., Unisys Corp.), Mitchel Field, 1958-99. Adj. prof. engrng. The Cooper Union, N.Y.C., 1966—, N.Y. Inst. Tech., Old Westbury, N.Y., 1972-92, Poly. Inst. Bklyn., 1959-72. Author: Control System Design, 1964, Techniques of Systems Engineering, 1967, A Guide to Systems Engineering and Management, 1976, Modern Control System Theory and Application, 1978, Modern Control System Theory and Design, 1992, 2d edit., 1998, Advanced Modern Control System Theory and Design, 1998. Recipient Career Achievement medal CCNY Alumni Assn., 1980. Fellow IEEE (life); mem. Am. Soc. for Engring. Edn., Eta Kappa Nu, Tau Beta Pi. Home: 28 Sagamore Way N Jericho NY 11753-2358 E-mail: shinnerssm@erols.com. *I was very poor financially as a child, but I received an abundance of love and encouragement from parents and family. I have always tried to succeed and to help others succeed. Above all, I have always tried to do what is right whether the decision had to be made in the business world or in private and family matters.*

SHINOLT, EILEEN THELMA, artist; b. Washington, May 18, 1919; d. Edward Lee and Blanche Addie (Marsh) Bennett; m. John Francis Shinolt, June 14, 1956 (dec. Aug. 1969). Student, Hans Hoffman Sch Art, 1949, Pa. Acad. Arts, 1950, Corcoran Sch. Art, 1945-51, Am. U., 1973-77. Sect. chief Dept. Army, Washington, 1940-73, retired, 1973. One-woman shows include various locations, 1982, 83, 85, 90, 94, 96; group shows include Perlmutter & Co., 1981, Fitch Fox and Brown, 1986, Foundry Gallery, 1987, Ann. Add Arts, 1986, Westminster Gallery, London, 1995; represented in permanent collections Women's Nat. Mus., Washington, Cameo Gallery, Columbia, S.C., Strathmore Hall Arts Ctr., North Bethesda, Md., 1997, 98, 99, 2000, Internat. Monetary Fund Members Show, Washington, 2000. Mem. Woman's Nat. Dem. Club, Washington, 1980—. Mem. Am. Art League (editor newsletter 1985-86, 1st pl. 1987, 2d pl. 1986), Arts Club Washington (exhbn. com. 1985—, admissions com. 1987-88), Miniature Painters, Sculptors & Gravers Soc. (historian 1989—, editor newsletter 1986-89). Roman Catholic. Avocations: reading, studying art periodicals, art galleries. Home: 4119 Davis Pl NW Apt 203 Washington DC 20007-1254

SHINOZAKI, TAMOTSU, retired physician, anesthesiologist; b. Dairen, Japan, Mar. 18, 1934; s. Yuichi and Shizue Shniozaki; m. Kazuko Sakanaka Shinozaki, Feb. 14, 1940; children: Aritomo, Yuji, Emiko. MD, Okayama U., Japan, 1958, D in Med. Scis., 1963. Diplomate Am. Bd. Anesthesiology; fellow critical care medicine; cert. spl. qualifications in critical care medicine. Intern St. Luke's Internat. Hosp., Tokyo, 1958-59; resident in anesthesiology Mary Fletcher Hosp., 1964-67; attending anesthesiologist Med. Ctr. Hosp. of Vt., Burlington, 1967-99; asst. prof. Med. Sch. U. Vt., 1967-72, assoc. prof., 1972-90, clin. prof., 1990-99, med. co-dir. surg. ICU, 1985-99, prof. emeritus, 2000—; adminstrv. dir. surg. ICU Fletcher Allen Healthcare, 1997-99. Cons. med. divsn. Hewlett Packard Co., Waltham, Mass., 1972-77, Intelligent Med. System, Carlsbad, Calif., 1987. Recipient Quality Cup award, Excellance in the Quality Movement, 1994. Fellow Am. Coll. Critical Care Medicine; mem. Sigma Xi. Home: 335 Dorset Hts South Burlington VT 05403

SHIONOIRI, HIDEO, computer technologist; b. Urawa, Saitama, Japan, July 15; came to U.S., 1996; m. Kimiko Sekine; 1 child, Yayoi. MSc in MIS, LaSalle U., La., 1998. Sys. designer Kawasaki Steel Corp., Japan, 1966-68; project mgr. CAC, Tokyo, 1968-71; project leader CSG, Can., 1971-77; IT mgr. Permanent Trust, Toronto, Ont., Can., 1977-83; v.p. info. sys. Barclays Bank of Can., 1983-96; sr. tech. advisor, prin. AMS Inc., N.Y.C., 1996—. Achievements include research in international and wholesale banking systems software development and integration. Office: AMS Inc 1 Chase Plz New York NY 10005

SHIORI MINAGAWA, STACEY, ballerina; b. L.A. Student, Tachibana Ballet Sch., Tokyo, San Francisco Ballet Sch., Princess Grace Acad., Monaco. Mem. Nat. Ballet Can., Toronto, Canada, 1995—2000, first soloist, 2000—. Dancer (ballets) Cinderella, The Nutcracker, The Merry Widow, Swan Lake, The Four Seasons, Désir, The Fairy's Kiss, Monotones I. Office: Walter Carsen Ctr for Nat Ballet Can 470 Queens Quay W Toronto ON Canada M5V 3K4 Office Fax: 416-345-8323.*

SHIPBAUGH, CALVIN LEROY, physicist; b. Huntington, Ind., Aug. 28, 1958; s. Paul and Marguerite (Pinkerton) S. BA, Rice U., 1980; PhD, U. Ill., 1988. Rsch. asst. U. Ill., Champaign-Urbana, 1981-88; analyst RAND Corp., Santa Monica, Calif., 1988—. Mem. space and surface power panel RAND support to NASA Project Outreach, Santa Monica, 1990; vis. scientist Fermilab, Batavia, Ill.,1982-85; workshop leader biotech. group RAND; team mem. POET, Arlington, Va., 1989-92; mem. bioscis. panel AAN Workshop, 1997; sr. assoc. Inst. Molecular Manufacturing. Contbr. articles to Phys. Rev. Letters, Physics Letters, RAND Pub. Series, others. Mem. Am. Phys. Soc., Internat. Meteoritical Soc. Achievements include research to measure charm particles' decay and hadronic production properties; evaluation of proposals from the public to the Space Exploration Initiative; policy analysis of nanotechnology; analysis of rotorcraft markets. Office: The RAND Corp 1700 Main St Santa Monica CA 90401-3297

SHIPLER, DAVID KARR, journalist, correspondent, author; b. Orange, N.J., Dec. 3, 1942; s. Guy Emery Jr. and Eleanor (Karr) S.; m. Deborah S. Isaacs, Sept. 17, 1966; children: Jonathan Robert, Laura Karr, Michael Edmund. AB, Dartmouth Coll., 1964; LittD (hon.), Middlebury Coll., 1988, Glassboro (N.J.) State Coll., 1988; AM (hon.), Dartmouth Coll., 1994. News clk. N.Y. Times, 1966-67, news summary writer, 1968, reporter met. staff, 1968-73, fgn. corr. Saigon bur., 1973-75, fgn. corr. Moscow Bur., 1975—, bur. chief Moscow Bur., 1977-79, chief Jerusalem bur., 1979-84, corr. Washington bur., 1985-87, chief diplomatic corr., 1987-88; sr. assoc. Carnegie Endowment for Internat. Peace, Washington, 1988-90. Guest scholar Brookings Instn., 1984-85; adj. prof. Am. U. Sch. Internat. Svc., Washington, 1990; Ferris prof. journalism and pub. affairs, Princeton U., 1990-91; Woodrow Wilson vis. fellow, 1990—; writer-in-residence U. So. Calif., 1998. Author: Russia: Broken Idols, Solemn Dreams, 1983 (Overseas Press Club award), revised, 1989, Arab and Jew: Wounded Spirits in a Promised Land, 1986 (Pulitzer prize for Gen. Nonfiction, 1987), revised, 2002; exec. prodr.: (documentaries) from Arab and Jew: Wounded Spirits in a Promised Land, 1989 (Alfred DuPont-Columbia U. award for Broadcast Journalism, 1990, Alfred DuPont-Columbia U. award for Broadcast Journalism, 2002); author: A Country of Strangers: Blacks and Whites in America, 1997; exec. prodr.: (documentaries) Arab and Jew: Return to the Promised Land, 2002; contbr. articles. Trustee Dartmouth Coll. With USNR, 1964-66. Recipient award for disting. reporting Soc. Silurians, 1971; award for disting. pub. affairs reporting Am. Polit. Scis. Assn., 1971; award N.Y. chpt. Sigma Delta Chi, 1973; co-recipient George Polk award, 1982. Office: 4005 Thornapple St Chevy Chase MD 20815-5037 *I have been governed professionally by the conviction that an open society needs open examination of itself to survive. Defining problems, inspecting blemishes, probing wounds, and exposing injustice are the required pastimes of a free people. Nothing intelligent can come from ignorance. If information does not guarantee wisdom, it is at least a prerequisite, for the only wise course is through knowledge. To write about current affairs, then, is to play a small role in a great endeavor. It is to measure one's own performance continually against the highest standards of honesty, fairness, thoroughness, intelligence, to search every day for a bit of truth, then share it. These are the ingredients of happiness, for such a job involves a life of constant learning, perpetual self-education. It keeps a man whole.*

SHIPLEY, ALDEN PEVERLY, broadcaster, broadcasting executive; b. Phila., Nov. 27, 1946; s. Alden Peverly and Selma Nadine (Smith) S.; m. Rose Marie Welsh, Dec. 27, 1969. Account exec. Sta. WAKY Radio/Multimedia Broadcast, Louisville, 1974-78; sales mgr. Sta. WGAC/Beasley Broadcast, Augusta, Ga., 1978-80; regional sales mgr. Stas. WVCG-WYOR/Insilco Broadcast, Coral Gables, Fla., 1980-83; gen. mgr. Sta. WMAD Radio, Madison, Wis., 1983-84; gen. sales mgr. Sta. WKAT Radio-Hernstadt Broadcast, Miami Beach, Fla., 1984-85; cons. Advanced Broadcast Mgmt., Washington, 1985-86; v.p. ops. Network Media Comm., N.Y.C., 1985-86; founder ABCI Prodns., Prospect, Ky., 1985—; founder, owner, dir. Automated Broadcast Cons., Inc., Miami Beach, 1986—. Corp. cons. Word Broadcasting. Co-author software Automated Cable Billing Sys.; prodr. TV programs Dance TV, Miss Robins Dance Class, World's Greatest Dancers, No Way with Ned and Joan Way. With USNR, 1965-67. Republican. Roman Catholic. Avocation: photography. Home: 7901 Barbourmeade Rd Louisville KY 40241-2621 Office: ABCI Prodns PO Box 768 Prospect KY 40059-0768 E-mail: abci@bigfoot.com.

SHIPLEY, MARTHA THERESA, social worker, educational and program consultant; b. Columbus, Ohio, May 16, 1960; d. Lucille (Shipley) Croy. BS in Edn., Ohio U., 1981; MSW, Ohio State U., 1990. Lic. social worker; cert. residential child care worker. Head tchr. Southside Day Care Ctr., Columbus, Ohio, 1981-84; social svc. coord. Southside Learning and Devel. Ctr., 1984-85; residential supr. St. Vincent Children's Ctr., 1985-89; case mgr. Columbus Area Cmty. Mental Health Ctr., 1989-90, program mgr. Multicultural Eastside Ctr., 1993—; prevention coord. Children's Hosp. Child Guidance Ctr., Columbus, 1990-93. Cons. John XXIII Head Start, Columbus, Ohio, 1991—, Columbus Met. Area Cmty. Action Orgn., Ohio, 1995—. Westside-Eastside Child Care Ctrs., Inc., Columbus, 1995—. Bd. mem. YWCA, 1996-98, co-chmn. for Bright Futures, 1995—. Recipient Warren H. Jennings award Alcohol Drug Addiction and Mental Health Bd., Columbus, Ohio, 1992, Women of Achievement/Racial Justice award YWCA, Columbus, 1995. Mem. Nat. Coun. Ohio State Women (vice-chmn. 1994-96), Nat. Assn. Black Social Workers (Columbus chpt. pres. 1993-97, treas. 1997-98). Avocations: walking, aerobics, working with yough children and youth, reading, horseback riding. Home: 3796 Dehner Dr Columbus OH 43227-3334 Office: Multicultural Eastside Ctr Columbus Area 1515 E Broad St Columbus OH 43205-1550

SHIPLEY, ROBERT ALLEN, lawyer; b. Chgo., May 3, 1953; s. William Walter and Bernice (Allen) S.; m. Denise L. Sark, Jan. 2, 1989; children: Allyson Paige, Remy Taylor. BA in History, U. Ill., 1975; JD, No. Ill. U., 1978; grad., DePaul U. Ctr. Dispute Resol. Bar: Ill. 1979, U.S. Dist. Ct. (no. dist.) Ill. 1979; cert. mediator. Assoc. Sheldon Oliver Zisook, Ltd., Chgo., 1979-80, Copeland Finn & Fieri, Ltd., Chgo., 1980-81, Gerald M. Sachs, Ltd., Chgo., 1981-82, Baskin Server Berke & Weinstein, Chgo., 1982-89; ptnr., pres. Shipley & Wilner Ltd., 1989-94, Shipley & Assocs. Ltd., 1994-99; ptnr., corp. sec. Franklin & Shipley, Ltd., Chgo., 1999—. Instr. Am. Inst. Paralegal Studies, Chgo., 1990-92; spkr. Casualty Adjusters Assn., 1995. Mem. ABA, Ill. State Bar Assn. (civil practice com. 1997-99, past chair interprofl. coop. com.), Ill. Assn. Def. Trial Counsel, Chgo. Bar Assn. Avocations: music, literature, athletics. Office: Franklin & Shipley Ltd 11 E Adams St Ste 700 Chicago IL 60603-6306 E-mail: robert.shipley@franklinshipley.com.

SHIPLEY, SAMUEL LYNN, advertising and public relations executive; b. Marlborough, Mass., Nov. 14, 1929; s. Clifford Lynn and Esther (Jacobs) S.; m. Sue Finucan, Sept. 5, 1955; children— Jeffrey Lynn, Beth Ann, Amy. Student, Charles Morris Price Sch. Advt. and Journalism, U. N.H., 1948-50. Exec. dir. Democratic Party N.H., 1953-56; pres., chmn. Shipley Assos., Inc., Wilmington, Del., 1962—; pres. Cable TV Advt. Inc., 1982—. Dir. Del. Devel. Dept., Dover, 1965-69; mem. bd. overseers Del. Coll. Art and Design. Nominee for U.S. Congress, 1976; pub. relations dir. Del. Democratic Com., 1964-68; chmn. Del. Dem. Com., 1982-90; bd. dirs. Blood Bank of Del., Jobs for Del. Grads., For Children; mem. Del. Heritage Commn.; trustee Grand Opera House; former chair Dem. State Com. With U.S. Army, 1951-53. Recipient Freedoms Found. Honor medal, 1966, Outstanding Grad. award Charles Morris Price Sch., 1974 Mem. Am. Advt. Fedn., Nat. Press Club, Wilmington Advt. Club, Masons. Home: 1196 Paper Mill Rd Newark DE 19711-2924 Office: 1300 Pennsylvania Ave Wilmington DE 19806-4311 E-mail: s.shipley@shipleyassociates.com. *The ingredients for success are good health, average intelligence, a giving spirit, positive thinking, good imagination, self-discipline, hard work, and persistence.*

SHIPLEY, TONY L(EE), software company executive; b. Elizabethton, Tenn., July 19, 1946; s. James A. and Edith J. (Crowder) S.; m. Lynda Anne Jenkins, Nov. 19, 1971; children: Blake Alan, Sarah Robyn. BS in Indsl. Engring., U. Tenn., 1969; MBA, U. Cin., 1975. Indsl. engr. Monsanto Co., Pensacola, Fla., 1969—72; mktg. mgr. SDRC, Cin., 1972—76; v.p. sales and mktg. Anatrol Corp., 1977—81; pres. Entek Sci. Corp., 1981—96; pres., CEO Entek IRD Internat. Corp., 1996—2000. Bd. dirs. ABT Corp., RM Waste, Ohio IT Alliance, CHMack, The Circuit. Named Small Bus. Person of Yr., Greater Cin. C. of C., 1994, Entrepreneur of Yr. in Cin., No. Ky. Region, 1996. Mem. ASME, The Exec. Com., Soc. Automotive Engrs., Greater Cin. Software Assn. (pres. 1996-97, chmn. 1997-99, bd. dirs.), Greater Cin. C. of C., Leadership Class XVIII, Terrace Park (Ohio) Country Club (bd. dirs., pres.). Republican. Avocations: golf, family activities, fishing. Home: 7825 Calderwood Ln Cincinnati OH 45243-1319 E-mail: tshipley@fuse.net.

SHIPLEY, VIRGINIA SEGAL, clinical social worker, psychotherapist, educator; b. N.Y.C., Mar. 23, 1941; d. Edward and Eudice (Brenner) Segal; m. Thorne Shipley; children: Neal, Jesse. BA, U. Wis., 1963; Diploma in Social Adminstrn., London Sch. Econ., Eng., 1969; MSW, Barry U., 1974, PhD, 1986. Bd. cert. diplomate Acad. Cert. Social Workers; lic. clin. social worker, Fla.; lic. marriage and family therapist, Fla. Clin. social worker Children's Psychiat. Ctr., Miami, Fla., 1974-83, pvt. practice, Coral Gables, 1979—, supr. social workers, 1981—. Adjunct prof. Fla. Internat. U., Miami, 1989, Barry U., Miami Shores, Fla., 1989-97; cons., supr. Crisis Nursery, Miami, 1990-91. Author: (book) Lambs, 1970. Mem. NASW, Clin. Social Work Assn. of S. Fla. (founding pres. 1986-88), Fla. Soc. for Clin. Social Work. Office: 1500 San Remo Ave Ste 178 Miami FL 33146-3041

SHIPLEY, WALTER VINCENT, retired banker; b. Newark, Nov. 2, 1935; s. L. Parks and Emily (Herzog) S.; m. Judith Ann Lyman, Sept. 14, 1957; children: Barbara, Allison, Pamela, Dorothy, John. Student, Williams Coll., 1954-56; BS, NYU, 1961. With Chem. Bank, N.Y.C., 1956-96; chmn., CEO, chmn. bd. dirs. Chase Manhattan Corp., 1996-99, ret., 2000. Bd. dirs. Exxon Mobil Corp., Verizon Comms., Wyeth. Bd. dirs. Goodwill Industries Greater N.Y. Inc. Mem. The Bus. Coun., Coun. Fgn. Rels., Links, Augusta Nat. Golf Club, Baltusrol Golf Club (Springfield, N.J.). Office: JP Morgan Chase & Co 270 Park Ave New York NY 10017-2070

SHIPLEY BIDDY, SHELIA, artist management executive; b. Scottsville, Ky., Oct. 2, 1952; d. Robert Shelby Davis and Pauline (Powell) Willoughby; 1 child, Michael; m. Ken Biddy. Student, U. Tenn., 1975-77, Nashville Tech. Inst., 1978-79. Adminstrv. asst. Monument Records, Nashville, 1976-79; promotion/sales coord. RCA Records, 1979-83; dir. career devel. Hallmark Direction Co., 1983-84; sr. v.p. nat. promotion MCA Records, 1984-93; sr. v.p., gen. mgr. Decca Records, 1994-99; pres., CEO Shipley Biddy Entertainment, Inc., 1999—. Author poetry. Pres. Leadership Music; bd. dirs. Acad. Country Music. Mem. NARAS, Country Music Assn., Acad. Country Music, Country Radio Bd. Dirs., Nat. Assn. Talent Buyers, Country Radio Broadcasters (v.p.), Source, Leadership Music, Leadership Nashville. Republican. Baptist. Office: Shipley Biddy Entertainment Inc 1400 South St Nashville TN 37212-2429

SHIPMAN, HARRY LONGFELLOW, astrophysicist, educator; b. Feb. 20, 1948; s. Arthur Leffingwell and Mary Dana Shipman; children: Alice Elizabeth, Thomas Nathaniel. BA summa cum laude, Harvard U., 1969; MS, Calif. Inst. Tech., 1970, PhD, 1971. Programmer Travelers Ins., 1966; rsch. asst. Smithsonian Astrophys. Obs., summer 1968, 69; tchg. asst. Calif. Inst. Tech., 1969-71; J.W. Gibbs instr. astronomy Yale U., 1971-73; asst. prof. U. Mo., St. Louis; astronomer McDonnell Planetarium, 1973-74; asst. prof. physics U. Del., 1974-77, assoc. prof., 1977-81, prof., 1981-99, prof. Annie Jump Cannon, 1999—. Dir. Ctr. Tchg. Effectiveness, 1988-94; vis. fellow sci. edn. U. Ga., 1994; Harlow Shapley vis. lectr. Am. Astron. Soc., 1975—; trustee, Mt. Cuba Obs., 1977—. Author: Black Holes, Quasars and the Universe, 2d edit., 1980, The Restless Universe: An Introduction to Astronomy, 1978, Space 2000-Meeting the Challenge of a New Era, 1987, Humans in Space-21st Century Frontiers, 1988; contbr. articles to profl. jours. NSF fellow, 1969-71, Guggenheim fellow, 1980-81; NASA grantee, 1975-80, 83—, NSF grantee, 1974-92, 96—. Mem. AAUP, AAAS, Internat. Astron. Union, Am. Astron. Soc. (task group on edn. in astronomy 1977-85, edn. officer 1979-85), Am. Assn. Physics Tchrs., Nat. Assn. for Rsch. in Sci. Tchg., Assn. Educators of Tchrs. of Sci., Phi Beta Kappa. Office: U Del Physics Dept Newark DE 19716 E-mail: harrys@udel.edu.

SHIPMAN, ROSS LOVELACE, petroleum executive; b. Jackson, Miss., Nov. 20, 1926; s. William Smylie and Jeanette Scott (Lovelace) S.; m. Lois Pegrim, June 6, 1948; 1 dau., Smylie Shipman Anderson. BA, U. Miss., 1950. Registered profl. geologist, Ark., chartered geologist, U.K. Geologist Humble Oil & Refining Co., West Tex., 1950-55; petroleum cons. Midland, Tex., 1955-60, Corpus Christi, 1960-67; asst. exec. dir. Am. Geol. Inst., Washington, 1967-71; assoc. dir. U. Tex. Marine Sci. Inst., Austin, 1971-79; assoc. v.p. for research U. Tex., 1979-85; pres., chief exec. officer Live Oak Energy, Inc., 1985-86; prin. Petroleum Investments/Worldwide, 1975—. Dir. Indsl. Assocs. program Coll. Nat. Scis. U. Tex., Austin, 1986-89; mem. Tex. Coastal and Marine Council, 1979-85; U.S.-Mexico Boundary Water Study Program, 1978-99; del. Argonne Univs. Assn., Chgo., 1982. Author numerous geol. reports and studies, 1955—; editor, pub. The AGI Report newsletter, 1968-70; editor Profl. Geologist, 1975-76. Served with U.S. Army, 1944-46, PTO. Fellow Geol. Soc. London; mem. Am. Inst. Profl. Geologists (cert. profl. geologist, Tex. pres. 1974, nat. editor 1975-76), Soc. Ind. Profl. Earth Scientists, Tex. Soc. SAR (pres., lectr. in Am. history), Soc. of Mayflower Descs. (gov. San Antonio colony), Petroleum Club of San Antonio, Jamestowne Soc. (gov. San Antonio co.), SCV (comdr. Hood's Tex. Brigade Camp), Order First Families Miss., Gen. Soc. Colonial Wars, Gov. Tex. Soc. Home: 1911 E Lawndale Dr San Antonio TX 78209-2043

SHIPP, DAN SHACKELFORD, lawyer; b. Yazoo City, Miss., Jan. 6, 1946; s. Dan Hugh and Anora Nona (Shackelford) A.; m. Carolyn Julie Perry, Nov. 30, 1974; children: Perry Lee, Clay Alexander. AA, Holmes Jr. Coll., 1966; BA, Miss. State U., 1968; JD, U. Miss., 1971. Bar: Miss. 1971, U.S. Dist. Ct. (no. dist.) Miss. 1971, U.S. Dist. Ct. (so. dist.) Miss. 1976, Colo. 1986, U.S. Ct. Appeals (5th cir.) 1982, U.S. Ct. Appeals (10th cir.) 1986, U.S. Dist. Ct. Colo. 1986. Pvt. practice, Yazoo City, Miss., 1974-83, Aspen, 1986—2001, Basalt, Colo., 2002—. Speaker in field. Recipient Master Advocate Cert. award Notre Dame Law Sch., 1993. Mem. ABA, Colo. Trial Lawyers Assn. (bd. dirs. 1986-88), Assn. Trial Lawyers Am., Colo. Bar Assn., Toastmasters Internat. Maroon Creek Club. Avocations: hunting, archery, traveling. Home: 0300 Vagneur Ln Basalt CO 81621-9103 Fax: 970-927-6633. E-mail: grand@rof.net.

SHIPP, MICKEY LYNN, county official; b. Carrollton, Mo., Dec. 30, 1952; s. William Jr. and Martorie Colleen Shipp; m. Carol A. Shipp, Sept. 15, 1979; children: Adam, Amy. BS in Bus., U. Mo., 1974. Dir. mktg., farm records coord. Farm Credit, Jefferson City, Mo., 1978-88; ins. specialist Mo. Bankers Assn., 1988-98; exec. dir. Literacy Coun. Macon County, Macon, Ga., 1998—. Bd. dirs. N.E. Cmty. Action Corp. Chmn. bd. trustees Union Hill Bapt. Ch., Holts Summit, Mo., 1997; pres. Human Resource Providers, Macon, 2001. Mem. Mo. Lit. Assn. (bd. dirs. 2000—), Macon C. of C., Laubach Literacy. Avocations: gardening, travel. Office: Literacy Coun Macon County 204 Crescent Macon MO 63552 E-mail: flc@istmacon.net.

SHIPP, THETA WANZA, educator, social service organization administrator, consultant, minister; b. Miami, Fla., June 19, 1948; d. James Willie and Fredericka Dean Wanza; m. Robert Glenn Shipp, June 28, 1970 (div. Aug. 1975); children: Tammi LaTrice, Eloria April Michelle. BA, Fisk U., 1970; MS, So. Ill. U., 1977; postgrad., Howard U. Ordained to ministry Christian Faith Ctrs., 1998. Asst. program dir. U. South Fla., Tampa, 1971-72; adminstr. City of Tampa, 1972-74; adminstrv. supr. Juvenile Svcs. Program, St. Petersburg, Fla., 1974-76; staff asst. City of Carbondale, Ill., 1976-77; tchg./rsch. asst., editl. asst. So. Ill. U., Carbondale, 1977-78; staff asst. U.S. Rep. Claude Pepper, Washington, 1978-82; legis./spl. asst. U.S. Rep. Mervyn M. Dymally, 1982-87; chief of staff U.S. Rep. Major R. Owens, 1987-88, U.S. Rep. Earl F. Hilliard, Washington, 1993-95; project dir. Nat. Assn. for Equal Opportunity in Higher Edn., 1998-99; asst. to v.p. for pub. policy Planned Parenthood Fedn. of Am., 2000—01; instr. D.C. Pub. Schs., 2001—. Ind. cons., 1989-98; part-time instr. dept. sociology Howard U., 1978-82. Campaign worker various congl. campaigns, 1976-2000, campaign fundraiser, 1978-97; mem. ministerial staff Michigan Park Christian Ch., Washington, 2000—; vol. Black Ch. Initiative, Religious Coalition for Reproductive Choice, Washington, 2000; ministerial cons. Soul Saving Sta., Miami, 1990—; campaign coord. Dem. Nat. Com. Office of African Am. Religious Outreach, Washington, 2000. Named one of Outstanding Young Women in Am.; recipient recognition United Negro Coll. Fund, Assn. Urban Univs., Southeastern Coun. on Ednl. Opportunity Assn., Internat. Bus. and Exec. Women, Women's Dept. Ministry of Help. Mem. NAACP, Nat. Urban League, Am. Sociol. Assn., Nat. Black Women's Agenda, Nat. Coalition on Black Civic Participation, Nat. Coalition for Black Voter Participation, Friends of Africa, Delta Sigma Theta, Alpha Kappa Delta, Phi Delta Lambda. Democrat. Avocations: reading, witnessing, movies, swimming, gardening. Home: 3924 18th St NE Washington DC 20018

SHIPP, WILLIAM WELDON, accountant; b. L.A., June 8, 1927; s. Pat and Mae (Harris) S.; m. Dorothy Forse, Sept. 23, 1967; children: Karyn, William. BS, U. San Francisco, 1952; MBA, Golden Gate U., 1963. CPA, Calif. Staff auditor Price Waterhouse, San Francisco, 1952-56; acctg. supr. CC Moore & Co., 1956-63; chief acct. Westland Life Ins. Co., 1963-66; audit mgr. Soule Steel Co., 1966-67; sr. acct. Bechtel Power Corp., 1967-82; pvt. practice Oakland, Calif., 1983—. Sgt. U.S. Army, 1945-46. Republican. Home: 5068 Dublin Ave Oakland CA 94602-2605 Office: 1964 Mountain Blvd Ste 199 Oakland CA 94611-2823

SHIPPER, DAVID W. lawyer; b. N.Y.C., Oct. 30, 1958; s. Herbert K. and Judith S. (Sigall) S. BA, NYU, 1979; JD, N.Y. Law Sch., 1982. Bar: N.Y. 1983, N.J. 1983, Fla. 1984; U.S. Dist. Ct. N.J. 1983, U.S. Dist. Ct. (so. and ea. dists.) N.Y. 1983; U.S. Tax Ct. 1989. Pvt. practice, N.Y.C., 1983—. Trustee N.Y. Law Sch., 1999—. Mem. ABA, N.Y. State Bar Assn., N.Y. Law Sch. Alumni Assn. (dir. 1983—, treas. 1991-95, v.p. 1995-99, pres. 1999—), Phi Delta Phi. Home: 201 E 69th St New York NY 10021-5471 Office: 567 3d Ave New York NY 10016

SHIPPER, TODD JEFFREY, communications executive; b. Detroit, Nov. 18, 1946; s. Norman N. Shipper and Evaline (Spring) Krasner; m. Sherry E. Brown, May 30, 1968 (div. 1969). AA, L.A. Valley Coll., 1970; student, Calif. State U., Northridge, 1970-72. Announcer various radio stas., 1967-73; salesman, mgr. Standard Shoes, Encino, Calif., 1973-76; asst. mgr. K-Mart, Westminster, 1976-77; salesman Contractors Lic. Sch., Van Nuys, 1977-80; dir. mktg. Columbia Sch. Broadcasting, Hollywood, 1980-84; owner, operator Nat. Broadcasting Sch., Sacramento, Portland, Seattle, 1984-92, Las Vegas, 1984-94, NBS Travel Tng. Sch., 1989-92, Nat. Career Tng. Ctr., Las Vegas, 1992-94; prin. Sound Ideas, Inc., 1994—. Contractor's License Svc., Las Vegas, 1999—; dir. ops. Waiters on Wheels, 1998-2000. Prin. Nat. Advt. Agy., Las Vegas, 1986—, Nat. Ednl. Cons., Las Vegas, 1986—. With USAF, 1965-67. Mem. Nat. Assn. Trade and Tech. Schs., Assn. Broadcasters. Democrat. Jewish. Office: Sound Ideas PO Box 29063 Las Vegas NV 89126-3063 E-mail: todd1271@aol.com.

SHIPPEY, SANDRA LEE, lawyer; b. Casper, Wyo., June 24, 1957; d. Virgil Carr and Doris Louise (Conklin) McClintock; m. Ojars Herberts Ozols, Sept. 2, 1978 (div.); children: Michael Ojars, Sara Ann, Brian Christopher; m. James Robert Shippey, Jan. 13, 1991; 1 child, Matthew James. BA with distinction, U. Colo., 1978; JD magna cum laude, Boston U., 1982. Bar: Colo. 1982, U.S. Dist. Ct. Colo. 1985. Assoc. Cohen, Brame & Smith, Denver, 1983-84, Parcel, Meyer, Schwartz, Ruttum & Mauro, Denver, 1984-85, Mayer, Brown & Platt, Denver, 1985-87; counsel western ops. GE Capital Corp., San Diego, 1987-94; assoc. Page, Polin, Busch & Boatwright, 1994-95; v.p., gen. counsel First Comml. Corp., 1995-96; legal counsel NextWave Telecom Inc., 1996-98; ptnr. Procopio, Cory, Hargreaves and Savitch, LLP, 1998—. Author: (article in The Secured Lender) Do We Need a License to Do that Deal?, 2001. Active Pop Warner football and cheerleading; bd. dirs. Southwestern Christian Schs., Inc., 2002—, San Diego Christian Found., 2001—. Mem. Phi Beta Kappa, Phi Delta Phi. Republican. Mem. Ch. of Christ. Avocations: tennis, golf, photography. Home: 15839 Big Springs Way San Diego CA 92127-2034 Office: Procopio Cory Et Al 530 B St Ste 2100 San Diego CA 92101-4496 E-mail: sls@procopio.com.

SHIPPY, CYNTHIA LESLIE, mental health nurse; ADN, Triton Coll., River Grove, Ill., 1983; BS, Coll. St. Francis, Joliet, Ill., 1988; MSN, U. Ill., Chgo., 1991. Cert. psychiat./mental health nurse; cert. chem. dependency counselor; cert. advanced practice nurse. Program nurse adminstr. HCA River Edge Hosp., Forest Park, Ill.; clin. nurse Elmhurst (Ill.) Meml. Hosp.; clin. nurse specialist adult psychiatry Good Samaritan Hosp., Downers Grove, Ill., clin. mgr. child/adolescent/adult and chem. dependency svcs.; mgr. psychiatry dept. Cedars-Sinai Med. Ctr., Beverly Hills, Calif.; DON Alexian Bros. Behavioral Health Hosp., Hoffman Estates, Ill. Mem. Am. Psychiat. Nurses Assn., Am. Heart Assn.

SHIPPY, DONNIE RAY, physical education educator; b. Windsor, Mo., Mar. 6, 1957; s. John Raymond and Dorothy May S.; 1 child, Carrie Amelia; m. Dianna Jo Shippy, Aug. 1, 1988; stepchildren: Stanley Darnell, Dallas Darnell. AA, Longview C.C., Lee's Summit, Mo., 1977; BS, Ctrl. Mo. State U., Warrensburg, 1980. Phys. edn. tchr., basketball, baseball coach Kingsville (Mo.) R-1 Sch., 1980—. Mem. Kingsville Booster Club. Eagle Scout, Boy Scouts Am., 1972; West Ctrl. Conf. all-conf. 1st team, basketball, 1975. Mem. AAHPERD, NEA, Mo. Assn. Health, Phys. Edn., Recreation & Dance, Optimist Club. Avocations: reading, playing and coaching basketball, fixing things around the house, collecting Larry Bird memorabilia. Home: 136 SW 1971st Rd Kingsville MO 64061-9217 Office: Kingsville R 1 School PO Box 7 Kingsville MO 64061-0007

SHIPTON, SIDNEY LAWRENCE, non-profit association consultant, solicitor; b. London, July 25, 1929; s. Harold and Rose (Horowitz) S.; m. Judith Scott, June 2, 1974; stepchildren: Jonathan Michael, Elana. LLB, U. London, 1951; MBA, Middlesex U., 1985. Pvt. practice law, London, 1956-72; gen. sec. Br. Zionist Fedn., 1972-82; dir. Jewish Nat. Fund, 1982-87; exec. dir. Ta'Ali, 1987-96; solicitor Supreme Ct. Judicature; coord. Three Faiths Forum, 1997—. Chmn. United Zionists of U.K., hon. v.p., chmn. ZF constn. com. Freeman City of London; former exec. Coun. Christians & Jews; former bd. mem. Middlesex U. Alumni. Fellow Royal Soc. Arts, Inst. Mgmt.; mem. Law Soc., Medico-Legal Soc., Brit. Acad. Forensic Sci., Mensa, B'nai B'rith (pres. Leo Baeck lodge). Jewish. Avocations: collecting books, lecturing, travel, cinema, theatre. Office: The Three Faiths Forum 104-8 Grafton Rd London NW5 4BD England Fax: 0207 485 4512. E-mail: sidney@sternberg-foundation.co.uk.

SHIPWAY, JOHN FRANCIS, career officer, retired; b. Cherry Valley, N.Y. m. Lynn Doe. MS in Chem. Engring., U. Louisville, 1965; attended, Basic Officer Nuclear Power, Bainbridge, Md., Naval Nuclear Power Tng. Unit, West Milton, N.Y., Naval Sub. Sch., Groton, Conn., Def. Syss. Mgmt. Coll., Ft. Belvoir, Va., 1988; grad., Navy War Coll., Newport, R.I. Commd. ensign USN, 1965; advanced through grades to rear admiral, 1994; communicator USS Cubera (SS 347), 1967; asst. damage control, main propulsion USS Von Steuben; exec. officer nuclear sub. NR-1, 1971-75; exec. officer USS Swordfish (SSN 579), 1971-78; asst. to program mgr. MK 48 torpedo acquisition program Naval Sea Sys. Cmd., 1978-81; comdr. USS Los Angeles (SSN 688), 1981-85; comdg. officer nuclear power tng. unit West Hamilton, N.Y., 1985-87; acquisition profl., 1985; program mgr. SSN 688 attack sub. acquisition program, 1988-91; program mgr. Seawolf, 1991-92; program exec. officer Dept. of Navy, 1992-95; dep. comdr. subs. naval sea sys. cmd., 1995-98; comdr. Naval Undersea Warfare Ctr., 1995-98; dir. strategic system programs Arlington, VA, 1998-2000. Decorated 4 Legion of Merit awards. Mem. Am. Soc. Naval Engrs., Assn. Scientists and Engrs., U.S. Naval Inst., Naval Sub. League. Office: Strategic Sys Dept Navy 3801 Nebraska Ave NW Washington DC 20393-0001

SHIRA, ROBERT BRUCE, university administrator, oral surgery educator; b. Butler, Pa., Dec. 2, 1910; s. Thomas Plummer and Erla (Brown) S.; m. Anne Eileen Anderson, Mar. 27, 1933; children: Sharon Lu, Mary Ann, Linda Kay. Student, Bartlesville (Okla.) Jr. Coll., 1927-28; D.D.S., U. Mo., Kansas City, 1932; D.Sc., Georgetown U., 1976, Tufts U., 1979, U. Mo., Kansas City, 1982, U. Detroit, 1987, Med. U. S.C., 2000. Diplomate: Am. Bd. Oral and Maxillofacial Surgery (pres. 1974-75). Pvt. practice dentistry, Pawhuska, Okla., 1932-38; commd. 1st lt., Dental Corps U.S. Army, 1938, advanced through grades to maj. gen., 1967; chief oral surgery Walter Reed Gen. Hosp., 1954-64; dir. dental activities Walter Reed Army Med. Center, 1966-67; dental surgeon Europe, 1964-66; asst. surgeon gen., chief Army Dental Corps, 1967-71; ret., 1971; prof. oral surgery Tufts U., Boston, 1971-93; dean Sch. Dental Medicine, Tufts U., 1972-78; sr. v.p., provost Tufts U., 1979-82, asst. to pres., 1982-93. Vis. prof. U. of Pacific, 1954-71, U. Pa., 1956-71; professorial lectr. Georgetown U., 1955-71 Contbr.: chpts. Textbook of Oral Surgery, 1973, Management of Office Emergencies, 1979, Improving Dental Practice through Preventive Measures, 1965; contbr. articles to profl. jours. Decorated D.S.M., Legion of Merit with 2 oak leaf clusters, Army Commendation medal, Army Disting. Svc. medal, Army Disting. Svc. medal; recipient Sword of Hope award Am. Cancer Soc., 1959; named Man of Yr. U. Mo., Kansas City, 1960. Mem. ADA (pres. 1975-76, cons. Council on Therapeutics, Disting. Service award), Am. Assn. Oral and Maxillofacial Surgery (pres. 1965-66), Am. Acad. Oral Pathology. Republican. Presbyterian. Home: Ste 814 3310 N Leisure World Blvd Silver Spring MD 20906

SHIRAI, SCOTT, communications executive; b. Honolulu, June 5, 1942; s. George Yoshio and Thelma Takeko (Tominaga) S.; m. Michelle M.; children: Todd, Kimberly, Lance, Lyle. MusB, U. Hawaii, 1983. Exec. dir. news, reporter Sta. KHON-TV, Honolulu, 1974—81; asst. gen. mgr. Vanguard Investments, Berkeley, Calif., 1976—79; newscaster Sta. KPOI, Honolulu, 1979—80; news dir. Sta. KGU, 1981—82; owner Visual Perspectives, 1980—; dir. pub. rels. Hawaiian Electric Co., Honolulu, 1982—90; dir. cmty. rels. Hawaiian Electric Industries, 1990—2000; vice chair, dir. Colo. Pub. Television, Denver, 2000—; exec. dir. Japan Am. Soc. of Colo., 2000—02; dir. The Samaritan Inst., 2000—; exec. dir. Combined Fed. Campaign, Mile High United Way, Denver, 2002—. Instr. U. Hawaii, 1984-99; pres. Hawaii Cmty. TV, 1993-2000; dir. BBB of Hawaii, 1995-2000. Author: Karaoke: Sing Along Guide to Fun & Confidence, 1997; dir., prodr. Gridiron, 1998, 99. Chair, dir. Hawaii Pub. TV Found., 1997-2000; bd. dirs., sec. Hawaii Com. for Freedom of Press, 1982-99; bd. dirs. Mental Health Assn. in Hawaii, 1981—, Moanalua Gardens Found., 1981-84, Health and Cmty Svcs. Coun., 1982-86, Friends of Father Damien, 1986; v.p. Mele Nani Singers, 1986—; mem. Mayor's Adv. Com. on Mcpl. TV, 1987, Office of hawaiian Affairs Pub. Rels. Adv. Com., 1987; sec., dir. Pro Geothermal Alliance, 1990-91. Recipient Jefferson award, Honolulu Advertiser, 1985, Gold award, Audio Visual Prodrs. Assn. Am., 1985, Audio Visual Dept. of Yr. award, Videography mag., 1986, Award of Excellence, Nat. Hospice Orgn., 1987, Intre award, Inst. Teleradial Atica P.R. Inc., 1988. Mem.: AFTRA (bd. dirs. 1980—83), ASTD, Hui Luna Club (bd. dirs. 1986—90), Hawaii Cmty. TV Assn. (pres. 1990—), Honolulu Cmty. Media Coun., Hawaii Film Bd., Hawaii Spkrs. Assn., Pub. Rels. Soc. Am. (past pres., nat. del. 1995—, Pub. Svc. award 2000, Pub. Rels. Profl. of Yr. award Hawaii chpt. 1999, Paul M. Lund Pub. Svc. award 2000, Coll. of Fellows), Am. Film Inst., Internat. TV Assn. (pres. 1983—), Honolulu Press Club (bd. dirs. 1984—). Avocations: martial arts, singing. Office: Visual Perspectives 1083 W 124th Dr Westminster CO 80234 E-mail: shirai2@msn.com.

SHIRAI, SHUN, law educator, lawyer; b. Tokyo, June 18, 1942; s. Kyo and Tomi Shirai; m. Junko Matsushita, Apr. 10, 1969; children: Akiko, Yuko, Jin. LLB, Hitotsubashi U., Tokyo, 1966, LLM, 1969. Cert. atty. at law. Asst. prof. criminal law Kokugakuin U., Tokyo, 1974-81, prof., 1981—, dean Grad. Sch., 1999-2001. Atty. Tokyo 2nd Bar Assn., 1992—. Author: Phenomenology of Crime, 1984, rev. edit., 1998, Thought on Criminal Law of Ancient India, 1985, Legal History on Criminal Law of Ancient India, 1990, Philosophy of Criminal Law in Ancient India, 1995, Phenomenology and Indian Philosophy for the Study on Ancient Indian Criminal Law, 1997, Prof. Shirai's Lectures on the Law of Criminal Procedure, 1998, Philosophy of Criminal Law in Bhagavad-gītā at Ancient India, 1998, Crime and Sorrowness of Human Being, 1999, Defence Lawyer's Statements in Criminal Court, 2000, Thoughts on Death Penalty in Ancient India, 2000, The Sanskrit, as a Legal Language, appearing in Judicial Documents of British India and Non-Violent Theory of Punishment, originated in Ancient India, 2000, Thought on Righteousness in Criminal Law, handed down by Tradition from Ancient India, 2002, On Basic Principles of Hindu Criminology, derived from Ancient Indian Legal Scriptures, 2002. Mem. Indian History Congress. Buddhist. Home: 703 Kinsen Bldg 2-16-1 Hanakawado Taito-ku Tokyo 111-0033 Japan Office: Kokugakuin U 4-10-28 Higashi Shibuya-Ku Tokyo 150-8440 Japan

SHIRANI, JAMSHID, internist, cardiologist, researcher; b. Sanandaj, Kurdistan, Iran, Feb. 28, 1955; came to U.S., 1984; s. Hossein and Pouran (Shahin) S.; m. Atarod R. Shirani, Sept. 30, 1980; children: Arshan, Tara. MD, Pahlavi Sch. Medicine, Shiraz, Iran, 1980. Diplomate Am. Bd. Internal Medicine, also Sub-bd. Cardiovascular Diseases. Resident in medicine St. Mary's Hosp., Waterbury, Conn., 1985-88; chief resident in medicine Yale U. Sch. Medicine, 1988-89; fellow in cardiology Michael Reese Hosp./U. Chgo., 1989-91; sr. staff fellow NIH, Bethesda, Md., 1991-93; clin. instr. medicine/cardiology Med. Coll. Va., Richmond, 1993-94; asst. prof. medicine Albert Einstein Coll. Medicine, N.Y.C., 1994-99, assoc. prof. medicine and pathology, 1999—. Recipient Luis Katz-Richard Langendorff award Michael Reese Hosp., 1991. Mem. ACP, AAAS, , Am. Coll. Cardiology, Am. Heart Assn., Am. Soc. Echocardiography, Soc. for Cardiovascular Pathology. Avocations: English and German literature, poetry. Office: Albert Einstein Coll Medicine 1300 Morris Park Ave Bronx NY 10461-1926 E-mail: jshirani@montefiore.org.

SHIRBROUN, RICHARD ELMER, veterinarian, cattleman; b. Coon Rapids, Iowa, Oct. 22, 1929; s. Francis Clyde and Clara Mable (Bell) S.; m. Treva Margaret Teter (div.), Sept. 9, 1951; children: Randal Mark, Camille Leean, James Bradley; m. Wava Lynne Frank, Nov. 11, 1989. DVM, Iowa State U., 1952. Owner, vet. Shirbroun Vet. Med. Ctr., Coon Rapids, 1955-2001; trust rep. Am. Vet. Med. Assn., Chgo., 2001—. Lt. USAF, 1952-55. Mem. AVMA (trustee 1982-2000), Am. Assn. Bovine Practitioners (bd. dirs. 1982-1990, Excellence Preventive Medicine award 1987), Am. Assn. Swine Practitioners, Iowa Vet. Med. Assn. (pres. 1981, Pres.' award 1985), Soc. for Theriogenology, N.Am. Limousin Found. (founding mem. 1968), Nat. Cattlemen Assn., Iowa Cattlemen Assn., Am. Legion, Rotary (pres. Coon Rapids 1965). Republican. Methodist. Home: 32104 Millard Circle Warrenville IL 60555-3988 Office: Am Vet Med Assn 55 E Jackson PO Box 1629 Chicago IL 60690-1629 E-mail: rshirbroun@mackparker.com.

SHIRCLIFF, JAMES VANDERBURGH, communications executive; b. Vincennes, Ind., Dec. 11, 1938; s. Thomas Maxwell and Martha Bayard (Somes) S.; m. Sally Anne Hoing, June 20, 1964; children: Thomas, Susan, Anne, Catherine, Caroline. AB, Brown U., 1961; postgrad., U. Va., 1963-64. Asst. gen. mgr. Pepsi Cola Allied Bottlers, Inc., Lynchburg, Va., 1964-65, v.p., divisional coord., 1966-68, v.p., dir. personnel, 1968-70; gen. mgr. First Colony Canners, Inc., 1965-66; v.p., gen. mgr. GCC Beverages, Inc., 1970-74, group v.p. Va., 1974-75; corp. v.p. Gen. Cinema Corp., Beverage Divsn., 1976-77; owner/mgr. WLLL-AM, WGOL-FM, 1977-86; pres. Jamarbo Corp., 1977-88. Chmn. bd. SignWaves, Inc., pres., The Shircliff Partnership, Ltd., presdl. interchange exec., 1975-76; exec. dir. Nat. Indsl. Energy Coun., Dept. Commerce, Washington, 1975-76. V.p. JOBS, Lynchburg, 1970; dir. Ctrl. Va. Health Planning Coun., 1974-75; mem. Govs. Indsl. Energy Adv. Coun., 1976—; dir. Piedmont coun., Boy Scouts Am., 1972-73; mem. City of Lynchburg Keep Lynchburg Beautiful Commn., 1974-75, chmn. emergency planning bd., 1974-75, chmn. overall econ. planning coun., 1977-88; bd. dirs. Lynchburg Broadway Theatre, 1973-75, Acad. Music, 1973-74, United Fund, Lynchburg, 1966-67, Ctrl. Va. Industries, 1971-72, VA. Pub. Telecomm. Coun.; former trustee Culver Ednl. Found.; chmn. campaign United Way, 1982, pres., 1983; co-founder, chmn. Citizens for a Clean Lynchburg; campaign chmn. United Way of Ctrl. Va., Dir., 1996; chmn. Arts Coun. Ctrl. Va., 1990-93; mem. nat. adv. coun. U.S. Small Bus. Adminstrn., 1990-93; past trustee Va. Episc. Sch.; past mem. pres.' coun. Randolph-Macon Women's Coll., Ctrl. Va. C.C. Found. Bd.; past mem. Va-Israel Commn.; dir. Lynchburg Hist. Found., 1996-99. Lt. (j.g.) USN, 1961-63. Recipient Cloyd Meml. award for outstanding svc., Greater Lynchburg C. of C., 1975; Va. Soft Drink Assn. citation, 1970, 73, 74; NCCJ Brotherhood citation; Pub. Svc. award RAdio-TV Commn. of So. Bapt. Conf., NCCJ State Adv. Bd., Exec. Com. Swensen's Owners Coun., 1988, Centurian award for bus. moral and leadership C. of C., 1999. Mem. Va. Soft Drink Assn. (pres. 1973-74), Va. Pepsi Cola Bottlers Assn. (pres. 1970-73), Nat., Va. (dir. 1974, pres. 1985-86) assns. broadcasters, Lynchburg Advt. Club (v.p.), Va. AP Broadcasters Assn. (pres.), Lynchburg Fine Arts Ctr. (pres.), Va. C. of C. (dir. 1976-79), Greater Lynchburg C. of C. (dir., v.p. 1973-74, chmn. cmty. appearance task force 1977-79), Culver Academies Alumni Assn. (pres.), Culver Cum Laude Soc. (award 1996, hon.), Mensa, Boonsboro Country Club, Navy League, The Pavane Club, Knight Sovereign Mil. Order Malta Fedn. Assn., Rotary (past pres., Paul Harris fellow 1982, dist. gov. 1986-87). Roman Catholic. Address: PO Box 10486 Lynchburg VA 24506-0486

SHIRE, DAVID LEE, composer; b. Buffalo, July 3, 1937; s. Irving Daniel and Esther Miriam (Sheinberg) S.; m. Talia Rose Coppola, Mar. 29, 1970 (div.); 1 child, Matthew Orlando; m. Didi Conn, Feb. 11, 1984; 1 child, Daniel Joshua. BA, Yale U., 1959. Film scores include The Conversation, 1974, The Taking of Pelham 1-2-3, 1974, Farewell, My Lovely, 1975, The Hindenburg, 1975, All the President's Men, 1977, Saturday Night Fever (adaptation and additional music), 1977, Norma Rae, 1979 (Acad. award for best original song It Goes Like It Goes), Only When I Laugh, 1981, The World According to Garp, 1982, Max Dugan Returns, 1983, 2010, 1984, Return to Oz, 1985, Short Circuit, 1986, 'Night, Mother, 1986, Vice Versa, 1988, Monkey Shines, 1988, Paris Trout, 1991, Bed and Breakfast, 1992, The Journey Inside (IMAX), 1993, One Night Stand, 1994, Ash Wednesday, 2002; TV scores include Raid on Entebbe, 1977 (Emmy nomination), The Defection of Simas Kudirka, 1978 (Emmy nomination), Do You Remember Love?, 1985 (Emmy nomination), Promise, 1986, Echoes in the Darkness, 1987, The Women of Brewster Place, 1989, The Kennedys of Massachusetts, 1990 (Emmy nomination), Common Ground, 1990, Sarah Plain & Tall, 1991, Last Wish, 1992, Broadway Bound, 1992, Skylark, 1993, Remember, 1993, The Companion, 1994, My Brother's Keeper, 1995, Serving in Silence, 1995, The Heidi Chronicles, 1995, My Antonia, 1995, The Streets of Laredo, 1995, Last Stand at Saber River, 1997, Rear Window, 1998 (Emmy nomination), Double Platinum, 1999, Small Vices, 1999, These Old Broads, 2001, Two Against Time, 2001; theatre scores include The Sap of Lie, 1961, Graham Crackers, 1962, The Unknown Soldier and His Wife, 1967, How Do You Do, I Love You, 1968, Love Match, 1970, Starting Here, Starting Now, 1977, Baby, 1983 (Tony nominee best mus. and best original score), Urban Blight, 1988, Closer Than Ever, 1989 (Outer Critics Circle award best off-Broadway musical and best score), Big, 1996 (Tony nominee best score); composer Sonata for Cocktail Piano, 1965;

recorded songs include Autumn, 1959, Starting Here, Starting Now, 1965, What About Today?, 1969, Manhattan Skyline, 1977, The Promise, 1978 (Acad. award nomination), It Goes Like It Goes, 1979 (Acad. award), With You I'm Born Again, 1979; albums include Saturday Night Fever, 1977 (Grammy award 1978), Starting Here, Starting Now, 1977 (Grammy nomination 1977), Baby, 1984, Return to Oz, 1985, Closer Than Ever, 1990, David Shire at The Movies, 1991, Big, 1996. With Army N.G., 1960-66. Mem. Composers and Lyricists Guild Am., Am. Fedn. Musicians, Broadcast Music Inc., Acad. Motion Picture Arts and Scis., Nat. Acad. Rec. Arts and Scis., Nat. Acad. TV Arts and Scis., Dramatists Guild Am. (coun. mem.). Jewish. Office: Ste 304 16501 Ventura Blvd Encino CA 91436-2067 E-mail: dshire@aol.com.

SHIRE, DONALD THOMAS, retired air products and chemicals executive, lawyer; b. Boston, Jan. 13, 1930; s. Thomas J. and Nellie M. S.; m. Anne Court Bither, Nov 21, 1953; children: Jennifer Anne, Andrew Carter, Daniel Orchard. BS in Bus. Adminstrn, Boston U., 1951, LL.B., 1953; postgrad., Harvard Bus. Sch., 1985; LLD (hon.), Muhlenberg Coll., 1997. Atty. Air Products and Chems., Inc., 1957-64, sec., atty., 1964-75, sec., asst. gen. counsel, 1975-78, v.p. energy and materials, 1978-85, v.p. human resources, 1986-90, sr. v.p. human resources and adminstrn., 1990-91, sr. v.p. adminstrn., 1991-93; ret., 1993; also bd. dirs. Air Products and Chems., Inc. Chmn. Air Products Found., 1991-93; bd. dirs. Lehigh Valley Bus./Edn. Partnership. Trustee Muhlenberg Coll., 1976-95, Lehigh Valley Hosp., 1983-99. Lt. USNR, 1954-57. Mem. Am. Arbitration Assn. Episcopalian. Home: 27 Drake Ln Scarborough ME 04074

SHIRE, HAROLD RAYMOND, law educator, writer, scientist; b. Denver, Nov. 23, 1910; s. Samuel Newport and Rose Betty (Herman) S.; m. Cecilia Goldhaar, May 9, 1973; children: David, Darcy, Esti. MBA, Pepperdine U., 1972, LLD (hon.), 1975; JD, Southwestern U., L.A., 1974; M in Liberal Arts, U. So. Calif., 1977; PhD in Human Behavior, U.S. Internat. U., San Diego, 1980. Bar: Calif. 1937, U.S. Dist. Ct. (so. dist.) Calif. 1939, U.S. Supreme Ct. 1978. Dep. dist. atty. L.A. County, Calif., 1937-38; asst. U.S. atty. So. Dist. Calif., L.A. and San Diego, 1939-42; pvt. practice L.A., 1946-56; pres., chmn. bd. Gen. Connectors Corp., U.S. and Eng., 1956-73; prof. mgmt. and law Pepperdine U., Malibu, Calif., 1974-75, U.S. Internat. U., San Diego, 1980-83; dir. Bestobell Aviation, Eng., 1970-74. Author: Cha No Yu and Symbolic Interactionism: Method of Predicting Japanese Behavior, 1980, The Tea Ceremony, 1984. Patentee aerospace pneumatics; invented flexible connectors; designed, manufactured flexible integrity systems. Advisor U. S.C. Gerontology Andrus Ctr., pre-retirement tng., 1976-80; bd. dirs. Pepperdine U., 1974-80; nat. bd. govs. Union Orthodox Jewish Congregations Am., 1973—; mem. Rep. Nat. Com.; pres. Jewish Nat. Fund Legion of Honor, 1991—; mem. Presdl. Roundtable, Washington, 1989-97; mem. Inner Cir., Pres. Regan and Bush, 1989-92; life mem. Rep. Nat. Com. With U.S. Army, 1942-46. Decorated chevalier du vieux moulin (France); companion Royal Aero. Soc. (U.K.); recipient Tea Name Grand Master Soshitsu Sen XV Urasenke Sch., Kyoto, Japan, 1976, Medal of Honor Jewish Nat. Fund, Legion of Honor, 1991, U.S. Senate Medal of Freedom. Mem. ABA, Am. Welding Soc., Soc. Material and Process Engrs., Am. Legion (svc. officer China #1 Shanghai), Calif. Symphony Soc. (pres. 1998—), Masons (32 degree, Hiram award 1994), Royal Arch, Shrine, Legion of Honor Jewish Nat. Fund (nat. chmn. bd. 1999). Achievements include design and manufacture of fluidic systems flexible integrity for Saturn IV and welding in Apollo XI landing on moon, 1969. Office: PO Box 1352 Beverly Hills CA 90213-1352

SHIREK, JOHN RICHARD, retired savings and loan executive; b. Bismarck, N.D., Feb. 5, 1926; s. James Max and Anna Agatha (Lala) S.; m. Ruth Martha Lietz, Sept. 22, 1950; children: Barbara Jo (Mrs. James A. Fowler), Jon Richard, Kenneth Edward. Student , U. Minn., 1944-46; BS with honors, Rollins Coll., 1978. Sports editor Bismarck (N.D.) Tribune, 1943-44; with Gate City Savs. and Loan Assn., Fargo, N.D., 1947-65, v.p., dir., 1960-65; exec. v.p., dir. 1st Fed. Savs. and Loan Assn., Melbourne, Fla., 1966-70, pres., dir. Cocoa, 1970-82; exec. v.p., dir. The First F.A. (formerly 1st Fed. Savs. and Loan Assn. of Orlando), 1982-91. Interim pres. Freedom Savs. and Loan Assn., Tampa, Fla., 1987-88; trustee Savs. & Loan Found., Inc., 1980-84; dir. Fin. Trans. Syss., Inc., Magnolia Svcs. Corp., 1st Cocoa Corp., Magnolia Realty Co., 1982-91. Chmn., dir. United Fund, Fargo, N.D., 1962-65; dir., exec. bd. mem. Boy Scouts Am., 1960-70, mem. adv. bd. cen. Fla. coun., 1983-85, 91-95, exec. bd., 1985-91, v.p. long-range planning, 1989-91; bd. assocs. Fla. Inst. Tech., founding pres., 1968; moderator St. Johns Presbytery, 1979, chmn. adv. coun., 1980-81; chair local arrangements com. 1993 Gen. Assembly Presbyn. Ch.; moderator Synod of Fla., 1983, Ctrl. Fla. Presbytery, 1991, coordinating coun., 1992; mem. adv. bd. Brevard Art Ctr. and Mus., 1980-82; bd. dirs., founding chmn. devel. coun. Holmes Regional Med. Ctr., Melbourne, 1981-84; bd. dirs. Orlando Regional Med. Ctr. Found., 1982-85, Jr. Achievement Cen. Fla., 1989-91; mem. fin. com. Mayor's Task Force on Housing, 1983-84; chmn. spl. com. on Nat. Coun. Chs./World Coun. Chs. rels. Presbyn. Ch. in U.S.A., 1983-86; pres. Ecumenical Ctr. Inc., Orlando, 1985-91, bd. dirs., 2001—; chmn. Fla. adv. com. Ctr. Theol. Studies Columbia Theol. Sem., 1991-95. Lt. (j.g.) USNR, World War II. Mem. Fla. Savs. and Loan League (past dir.), Fla. Savs. and Loan Svcs. (past dir.), Savs. and Loan Found. (state membership chmn. 1976), Fla. Savs. and Loan Polit. Action Com. (dir. 1976-82), U.S. Savs. and Loan League (chmn. advt. and pub. rels. com. 1969-70, dir. S.E. conf. 1975-80), Downtown Melbourne Assn. (past pres.), Cocoa Rotary (pres. 1979), Masons, Shriners, Elks, Beta Theta Pi, Omicron Delta Epsilon. Republican. Home: PO Box 568831 Orlando FL 32856-8831 E-mail: sjohnr@aol.com.

SHIREMAN, JOAN FOSTER, social work educator; b. Cleve., Oct. 28, 1933; d. Louis Omar and Genevieve (Duguid) Foster; m. Charles Howard Shireman, Mar. 18, 1967; 1 child, David Louis. BA, Radcliffe Coll., 1956; MA, U. Chgo., 1959, PhD, 1968. Caseworker N.H. Children's Aid Soc., Manchester, 1959-61; dir. research Chgo. Child Care Soc., 1968-72; assoc. prof. U. Ill., Chgo., 1972-85; prof. Portland (Oreg.) State U., 1985—, dir. PhD program, 1992-99; interim exec. dir. Partnership for Rsch., Tng. and Grad. Edn. in Child Welfare, 1994. Research cons. child welfare orgns., Ill., 1968-85, Oreg. 1985—; lectr. U. Chgo., 1968-72. Co-author: Care and Commitment: Foster Parent Adoption Decisions, 1985, Adoption: Theory, Policy and Practice, 1997; mem. editl. bd. Jour. Sch. Social Work, 1978-81, Social Work Rsch. and Abstracts, 1990-93, Children and Youth Svcs. Rev., 1990—, Jour. Social Work Edn., 1990-95; contbr. articles to profl. jours., chpts. to books. Bd. dirs. Oreg. chpt. Nat. Assn. for Prevention Child Abuse, 1985-87; bd. dirs. Friendly House, Portland, 1991-97, pres., 1995-96; mem. adv. com. children's svcs. divsn. State of Oreg., 1985-95. Grantee HEW, 1980-82, Chgo. Community Trust, 1982-86, Oreg. Children's Trust Fund, 1991-96. Mem. NASW, AAUP, Acad. Cert. Social Workers, Coun. on Social Work Edn., Phi Beta Kappa. Home: 2535 SW Sherwood Dr Portland OR 97201-1679 Office: Portland State U Grad Sch Social Work PO Box 751 Portland OR 97207-0751 E-mail: shiremj@rri.pdx.edu.

SHIRER, BRUCE EDWARD, pathologist; b. Chgo., Sept. 22, 1941; s. Benjamin Franklin and Thelma Katherine (Borgstrom) S.; m. Janett Margaret Jurasek, Sept. 16, 1967 (div. Nov. 1982); m. Linda Locke Sevcik, July 7, 1984; children: Brandt Stephen, Benjamin Stuart. Student, North Ctrl. Coll., Naperville, Ill., 1958-61; MD, U. Wis., 1965. Diplomate Am. Bd. Pathology. Resident internal medicine Northwestern U., Chgo., 1968-69, resident in pathology, 1969-73; pathologist, co-dir. San Diego Inst. Pathology, 1973-82; locum tenens pathologist various labs., San Diego, 1982-84; med. dir. Lab. Corp. Am., 1984—99; assoc. pathologist Yuma (Ariz.) Regional Med. Ctr., 1986—; pathologist Kaiser Permanente, Sacramento, 2000, U. Calif., San Diego, 2001, Kaiser Permanente, San Diego, 2001—. Lt. comdr. USNR, 1966-68, Vietnam. Fellow Coll. AM. Pathologists, Am. Soc. Clin. Pathologists; mem. AMA, Calif. Med. Assn., San Diego County Med. Soc. Libertarian. Avocations: travel, skiing, classical music, opera, reading. Office: 4647 Zion Ave San Diego CA 92120 Home: Unit D 3753 Balboa Ter San Diego CA 92117-5448

SHIRES, BRENT ALAN, music educator, musician; b. Santa Rosa, Calif., Mar. 26, 1968; s. Gerald R. and Karen M. Shires; m. Terrie Ann Barnes, June 6, 1992; children: Rebecca Joy, Rachel Hope. MusB in Music Edn., SUNY, Potsdam, 1990; MusM in Horn Performance and Pedagogy, No. Ill. U., 1992; postgrad., U. Ill., 1994—. Cert. music provisional grades K-12 N.Y., coll. cert. in horn Music Tchrs. Nat. Assn. Music tchr. grades K-8 Creston (Ill.) and Steward (Ill.) Schs., 1992—93; adj. asst. prof. music Millikin U., Decatur, 1993—95; vis. instr. horn/band So. Ill. U., Carbondale, 1996; asst. prof. music Silver Lake Coll., Manitowoc, Wis., 1996—99; lectr. horn U. Ctrl. Ark., Conway, 1999—; third horn Peoria (Ill.) Symphony Orch., 1991—94; from third horn to prin. horn Champaign-Urbana (Ill.) Symphony, 1994—96; prin. horn Green Bay (Wis.) Symphony Orch., 1996—2000; third horn Ark. Symphony Orch., Little Rock, 2000—. Ednl. specialist United Musical Instruments USA, South Bend, Ind., 1995—; at-large bd. mem. Assn. Wis. Symphony Orchs., 1997—99; regional workshop coord., Ark. rep. Internat. Horn Soc., Juneau, Alaska, 2001—. Editor: (newsletter) The Posthorn, 1995—96, The So. Bell, 2001—. Ch. planter, music dir. Harbor Cmty. Ch., Sheboygan, Wis., 1996—99; mem. steering com. Evang. Child and Family Agy., Green Bay, 1997—99. Named winner solo performance, U. Ill. Concerto Competition, Urbana, 1995, finalist winds/percussion divsn., Nat. Young Artists Competition, Midland, Tex., 1997; recipient award, Conway A&P Commn., Conway Ark. for the Midwest Horn Workshop, 2001. Mem.: Ark. Horn Club (founder, coord., dir. 2000—), Pi Kappa Lambda, Phi Kappa Phi, Phi Mu Alpha Sinfonia (life; pres. Theta Iota chpt. 1988—89, gov. province 4 2002—). Republican. Evangelical. Avocations: model railroading, bicycling, hiking, legos. Office: U Ctrl Ark Dept Music 201 Donaghey Ave Conway AR 72035

SHIRES, GEORGE THOMAS, surgeon, educator; b. Waco, Tex., Nov. 22, 1925; s. George Thomas and Donna Mae (Smith) S.; m. Robbie Jo Martin, Nov. 27, 1948; children: Donna Blain, George Thomas III, Jo Ellen. MD, U. Tex., Dallas, 1948. Intern Mass. Meml. Hosp., Boston, 1948—49; resident in surgery Parkland Meml. Hosp., Dallas, 1950—53; faculty U. Tex. Southwestern Med. Sch., 1953—60, assoc. prof. surgery, acting chmn. dept., 1960—61, prof., chmn. dept., 1961—74; surgeon in chief surg. svcs. Parkland Meml. Hosp., 1960—74; prof., chmn. dept surgery U. Wash. Sch. Medicine, Seattle, 1974—75; chief of service Harborview Med. Center, Univ. Hosp., Seattle, 1974—75; chmn. dept. surgery N.Y. Hosp.-Cornell U. Med. Coll., 1975—91; dean, provost for med. affairs Cornell U. Med. Coll., 1987—91, prof. emeritus, 1996—; prof., chmn. surgery Tex. Tech. U., Lubbock, 1991—95, Canizaro disting. prof. surgery, 1995—97; prof. surgery U. Nev. Sch. Medicine, Las Vegas, 1997—. Cons. Surgeon Gen., U.S. Army, 1965—75, Jamaica Hosp., 1978—91, Inst. Medicine Nat. Acad. Scis., 1975—; metabolism and trauma com. Nat. Acad. Scis.-NRC, 1964—71, com. trauma, 1964—71; rsch. program evaluation com., reviewer clin. investigation applications career devel. program VA, 1972—76; gen. med. rsch. program projects com. NIH NIH, 1965—69; mem. Surgery A study sect., 1970—74, chmn., 1976—78; mem. Nat. Adv. Gen. Med. Scis. Coun., 1980—84; cons. editl. bd. Jour. Trauma, 1968—88. Mem. editl. bd.: Year Book Med. Publs., 1970—92, Mem. editl. bd.: Annals of Surgery, 1972—, Mem. editl. bd.: Surg. Techniques Illustrated: An International Comparative Text, 1974—75, Mem. editl. bd.: Am. Jour. Surgery, 1968—, Mem. editl. bd.: Contemporary Surgery, 1973—89, assoc. editor-in-chief : Infections in Surgery, 1981, mem. editl. bd.: Jour. Clin. Surgery, 1980—82; editor: Surgery, Gynecology and Obstetrics, 1982—93. Lt. M.C. USNR, 1949—50, Lt. M.C. USNR, 1953—55. Fellow: Coll. Medicine South Africa (hon.); mem.: AMA, ACS (bd. regents 1971—82, chmn. bd. regents 1978—80, pres. 1981—82), James IV Assn. Surgeons (bd. dirs. 1980—81, sec. 1981—87, pres. 1987—91), Allen O. Whipple Surg. Soc., Western Surg. Assn., N.Y. Surg. Soc. (pres. 1981—82), So. Surg. Assn., Soc. Univ. Surgeons (chmn. publs. com. 1969—71), Soc. Surg. Chairmen (pres. 1972—74), Soc. Clin. Surgery, Soc. Surgery Alimentary Tract, Pan Pacific Surg. Assn., Pan-Am. Med. Assn. (surgery council 1971), Am. Burn Assn., Internat. Surg. Soc. (sec. 1978—81, v.p. 1982—83, pres. U.S. chpt. 1984—85), Internat. Soc. Burn Injuries, Halsted Soc., Digestive Disease Found. (founding mem.), Am. Surg. Assn. (sec. 1969—74, pres. 1980), Am. Burn Assn., Am. Assn. Surgery Trauma, Dallas Soc. Gen. Surgeons (pres.-elect, pres. 1972—74), Am. Bd. Surgery (dir. 1968—74, chmn. 1972—74, diplomate), Surg. Biology Club (sec. 1968—70), Phi Beta Pi, Alpha Pi Alpha, Alpha Omega Alpha. Office: U Nev Sch Medicine 2040 W Charleston Blvd Ste 501 Las Vegas NV 89102-2207 E-mail: gtshires@nvtrauma.com.

SHIREY, CONNIE MAE, secondary school educator; b. Cleve., Jan. 24, 1948; d. Raymond and Wilma Jean (Wood) DeOreo; m. Kenneth Walter Shirey, Aug. 29, 1970. BA, Cleve. State U., 1970; MA, Ashland (Ohio) U., 1994. Cert. tchr. English, Ohio. Tchr. English Hillside Jr. H.S., Seven Hills, Ohio, 1970-82, Normandy H.S., Parma, 1982—. Life mem. Ohio PTA, 1995—, Parma City Schs. Named Parma City Schs. Educator of Yr., 2001; Jennings scholar Martha Holden Jennings Found., 1990. Mem. Parma Edn. Assn. (chmn. instrn. and profl. devel. com. 1992-99, building rep. 1982—, chair scholarship com. 2000—), Alpha Delta Kappa. Avocations: collecting Disney products, dog-Magic, reading, movies. Home: 72 Wellsley Pl Brunswick OH 44212-1347 Office: Parma City Schs 6726 Ridge Rd Parma OH 44129-5703 E-mail: magyk@gte.net.

SHIREY, JOHN FREDERICK, local government administrator, lecturer, consultant; b. Muncie, Ind., July 10, 1949; s. John Mark and Chloie Marie (Harvey) S.; m. Marilyn Elaine Murden, Apr. 20, 1979; children: Jill Meredith, Gregory Mark, Elizabeth Anne. BSIE, Purdue U., 1971; MPA, U. So. Calif., 1973. Adminstrv. asst. City of Monterey Park, Calif., 1972-75; legis. analyst City of Long Beach, 1975-76, dir. intergovtl. rels., 1976-79, asst. city mgr., 1987-93; legis. counsel Nat. League Cities, Washington, 1979-82; asst. exec. dir. County of L.A. Cmty. Devel. Commn., Calif., 1982-85; asst. chief adminstrv. officer County of L.A., 1985-87; city mgr. City of Cin., 1993—2001; exec. dir. Calif. Redevelopment Assn., Sacramento, 2002—. Lectr. grad. ctr. for pub. policy and adminstrn., Calif. State U., Long Beach, 1977-79, 83-93, sch. pub. adminstrn. U. So. Calif, Los Angeles, 1986-93. Master track and field ofcl, USA Track and Field, So. Calif., 1974-93, Ohio, 1993—; mem. SCAPA Praetors, Sch. Pub. Adminstrn. U. So. Calif., L.A., pres. 1985-86; v.p.; bd. councilors Sch. Pub. Adminstrn., U. So. Calif., L.A., 1983-87, MPA adv. bd., 1998—; bd. dirs. Innovation Groups. Named Outstanding Young Man Am., U.S. Jaycees, 1980. Mem. Am. Soc. Pub. Adminstrn. (chpt. coun. 1978-79, 84-87, 94—, nat. chmn. sect. on intergovtl. adminstrn. and mgmt. 1979-80, chpt. pres. 1988, 98), Internat. City Mgmt. Assn. (program excellence award for outstanding partnerships 2001), Am. Soc. Assn. Execs., Internat. Econ. Devel. Coun., Mcpl. Mgmt. Assts. So. Calif. (pres. 1974-75), Urban Land Inst. Mem. Christian Ch. (Disciples of Christ, elder). Home: 7976 Pocket Rd #137 Sacramento CA 95831

SHIRILAU, MARK STEVEN, utilities executive; b. Long Beach, Calif., Dec. 13, 1955; s. Kenneth Eugene and Marjorie Irene (Thorvick) Shirey; m. Jeffery Michael Lau, Nov. 25, 1984 (dec. Aug. 1993). BSEE, U. Calif., Irvine, 1977, MS in Bus. Adminstrn., 1980, PhD, 1988; M in Engring., Calif. Poly. State U., 1978; diploma in theology, Episc. Theol. Sch., Claremont, Calif., 1984; MA in Religion, Sch. Theology at Claremont, 1985. Ordained priest Ecumenical Cath. Ch., 1987, consecrated bishop, 1991. Grad. asst. Electric Power Inst., 1977-78; pres., CEO M.S.E., Santa Ana, Calif., 1977-87; adminstrv. mgr. EECO Inc., 1979-83; fin. engr. So. Calif. Edison Co., Rosemead, 1983-84, conservation engr., 1984-85, conservation supr., 1985-89; exec. v.p. Aloha Sys., Inc., Villa Grande, Calif., 1989-93, pres., 1993—, also bd. dirs. Bd. dirs. Ewing Consol. Corp., Outrider Trucking, Inc.; part-time instr. Santa Ana Coll., 1982-84, Citrus Coll., Glendora, Calif., 2000-; lectr. engring. West Coast U., Orange, Calif., 1984-91; bd. dirs. Am. Electronics Assn. Credit Union, Sweetwater Springs Water Dist., Heat Pump Coun. So. Calif., AIDS Interfaith Network Sonoma County. Author: Triune Love: An Insight into God, Creation, and Humanity, 1983, Salvation, Scripture and Sexuality, 1992, History and Overview of the Ecumenical Catholic Church, 1993, Power 101, A Basic Introduction to Electric Utility Power, 1998, The Five Fatal Fears, 2002. Archbishop, primate Ecumenical Cath. Ch.; chief chaplain svcs. Nolanville (Tex.) Police Dept., 1998-2000; chaplain Jonestown (Tex.) Police Dept., 2001—. Mem. IEEE (sr.), ASHRAE, Internat. Assn. Chiefs Police, Assn. Energy Engrs. (sr.), Assn. Energy Svcs. Profls. (bd. dirs., charter mem., exec. v.p.), Am. Soc. Safety Engrs., Nat. Assn. Chiefs Police, Pacific Bears Club (v.p.), Dignity Integrity (life), Eta Kappa Nu. Democrat. Home: 20 Lincoln Irvine CA 92604-1947 Office: 2691 Richter Ave Ste 120 Irvine CA 92606-5124 E-mail: archbishop@ecchurch.org., mark@alohasys.com.

SHIRKEY, LINDA SUE, interior designer, film company executive, set designer; b. Denver, June 29, 1948; d. Roger L. and Virginia Ruth (Lee) Williams; m. Larry Wayne, May 2, 1972 (div. Aug. 1982); children Troy Lee, Ian Christopher. BFA, U. Colo., Denver and Boulder, 1970; AAS, Arapahoe C.C., Littleton, 1985. Figure skating coach, Denver, 1972-84; interior design Possibilities For Design, 1983-85; interior designer For Men Only, Inc., 1985-95; film prodn. mgr., set styling & interior design Desciose Prodns., 1991—. Prodn. mgr.: (public svc. announcement) Going Home-Colo. Christian Home, 1992 (Emmy nom. 1992). Mem. bd. dirs. Front Range Ctr. for Spiritual Growth, Denver, 1993-95, pres. 1995; treas. Spiritual Solutions, Denver, 1996; v.p. Sina Care Ctrs., Inc., holistic Healing & Teaching, 1997—. Mem. Internat. Interior Design Assn., Denver Mile High Rotary (chair cmty. svc. 1993-94, fellowship chair 1996-97). Avocations: figure skating, coaching figure skating, yoga. Office: Prodn & Design LLC PO Box 100865 Denver CO 80250-0865

SHIRKEY, WILLIAM DAN, writer; b. Roswell, N.Mex., Nov. 6, 1951; s. Robert Johnson and Joan (Savage) S.; m. Karel Kay Czanderna, May 4, 1985. BS in Physics, SUNY, Brockport, 1974; MS in Physics, Clarkson Coll., 1980; MBA, Cornell U., 1984; postgrad. sr. exec. program, MIT. Quality control engr. Corning Glass Works, Canton, N.Y., 1974-77, sr. process engr., 1979-80, devel. engr., 1980-81, sr. process/prodn. devel. engr., 1981-82, mktg. mgr. Corning, 1983; project mgr. Eastman Kodak Co., Rochester, 1984-87, tech. asst. to v.p. and gen. mgr. fed. systems div., 1987-88, strategic planning bus. imaging systems div., 1988, strategic planning bus. info. system div., 1988, mgr. bus. devel. advanced technology products Fed. Systems Div., 1988-90; dir. internat. trade, v.p. consumer products group Custom Bus. Solutions, Ltd., 1990-92; writer, cons., 1992—. Mem. Optical Soc. Am., Tech. Mktg. Soc. Am., Sigma Pi Sigma. Avocations: outdoor sports, martial arts, guitar. Home: 1732 Lake Rd Webster NY 14580-8517

SHIRLEY, CHARLES WILLIAM, insurance and investment advisor, farm owner; b. Norfolk, Va., Jan. 28, 1954; s. Norris Winfred and Margarie Elizabeth (Whedbee) S.; m. Carol Ruth Montgomery, May 21, 1977; children: Sarah Ruth, Daniel Talmadge. Student, U. S.C., 1972-74; BS in Bus. and Journalism, Old Dominion U., 1977, cert. profl. fin. planner, 1986; cert. land use planner, Va. Polytech. Inst., 1987; student, Am. Coll. CLU and ChFC Program, 1998—. Security lic. series 6, 7, 63 and 65; registered account rep., assoc. fin. planner Met Life, 1997—. Ptnr. N.W. Shirley Farms, Virginia Beach, Va., 1977-88; owner C.W. Shirley Farms, Chesapeake, 1982—; fin. svc. rep. Met. Life, 1997—2001, The C.W. Shirley Agy., 2001—. Dealer Northrup King, Chesapeake, Va., 1985-94, property and casualty coord., 1999; assoc. agt. Nationwide Ins., 1995-97. Contbr. articles to newspapers and mags., 1985—. Planning commr. City of Chesapeake, 1986-94; chmn. Planning Commn., 1991-92; mem. Chesapeake Growth Commn., 1993; chmn. Virginia Beach Young Farmers Com., 1983-85; cmn. food com. S.E. Young Farmer's Tractor Pull, 1984; bd. dirs. Chesapeake Crime Line, 1985-93. Recipient Young Farmer award and Discussion Meet award Va. Farm Bur., 1984; named Young Farmer of Yr., Virginia Beach Jaycees, 1984; winner Va. corn yield contest, 1993. Fellow Life Underwriters Tng. Coun.; mem. Nat. Assn. Profl. Fin. Planners, Nat. Assn. Ins. and Fin. Advisors, Va. Soybean Assn. (mem. com. chmn. 1991-92, v.p. 1992-93, pres. 1994, Young Leader Va. 1990), Nat. Assn. Life Underwriters, Nat. Assn. Ins. and Fin. Advisors (membership com. 2001), Virginia Beach Farm Bur. (v.p. 1990-92), Chesapeake Farm Bur. (v.p. 1994-95, pres. 1995), Creeds Ruritan Club (sec. 1987), Nat. Corn Growers Assn. (Va. Corn Contest winner 1993), Va. Small Grain Assn., Va. Citizen's Planners Assn., Va. Soybean Bd., Chesapeake Arboretum, Virginia Beach Bus. Exch., Blackwater Bapt. Ch. (usher, class tchr.). Baptist. Avocations: deer hunting, deep sea fishing, snow skiing. Office: CW Shirley Farms 2424 Carolina Rd Chesapeake VA 23322-1428 also: CW Shirley Agy 2420 Carolina Rd Chesapeake VA 23322-1428 E-mail: cwshirley@msn.com.

SHIRLEY, DAVID ARTHUR, chemistry educator, science administrator; b. North Conway, N.H., Mar. 30, 1934; m. Virginia Schultz, June 23, 1956 (dec. Mar. 1995); children: David N., Diane, Michael, Eric, Gail; m. Barbara Cerny, Dec. 26, 1995. BS, U. Maine, 1955, ScD (hon.), 1978; PhD in Chemistry, U. Calif.-Berkeley, 1959; D honoris causa, Free U. Berlin, 1987. With Lawrence Radiation Lab. (now Lawrence Berkeley Lab.), U. Calif., Berkeley, 1958-92, assoc. dir., head materials and molecular research div., 1975-80, dir., 1980-89, lectr. chemistry, 1959-60, asst. prof., 1960-64, assoc. prof., 1964-67, prof., 1967-92, vice chmn. dept. chemistry, 1968-71, chmn. dept. chemistry, 1971-75; sr. v.p. rsch., dean grad. sch. Pa. State U., University Park, 1992-96; dir. emeritus Lawrence Berkeley Nat. Lab., 1997—. Chair bd. overseers Fermilab. Contbr. over 400 rsch. articles. NSF fellow, 1955-58, 66-67, 70; recipient Ernest O. Lawrence award AEC, 1972, Humboldt award (sr. U.S. scientist); listed by Sci. Citation Index as one of the world's 300 most cited scientists for work published during 1965-78. Fellow Am. Phys. Soc.; mem. Nat. Acad. Scis., Am. Chem. Soc., AAAS, Am. Acad. Arts and Scis., Bohemian Club, Explorers Club, Sigma Xi, Tau Beta Pi, Sigma Pi Sigma, Phi Kappa Phi.

SHIRLEY, GRAHAM EDWARD, management executive; b. Starkville, Miss., Jan. 4, 1943; s. Herman Milford and Helen (Lang) S.; m. Deborah Kay Long, 1996; children: Jennifer, Caryn, Tyler. BS, USAF Acad., 1966; MA, U. So. Calif., 1973. Commd. 2d lt. USAF, 1966, advanced through grades to brig. gen., 1988; ops. officer 393d Bomb Squadron, Pease AFB, N.H., 1977-78; comdr. 84th Fighter Interceptor Squadron, Castle AFB, Calif., 1978-80, 86th Tactical Fighter Wing, Ramstein Air Base, Germany, 1984-85, 20th Tactical Fighter Wing, RAF Upper Heyford, Eng., 1985-88; with Hdqrs. USAF, Washington, 1980-83, dir. regional plans, 1988-90; assigned to Air War Coll., Maxwell AFB, Ala., 1983-84; vice comdr. Air Force Intelligence Command, San Antonio, 1990-92; ret. brig. gen. USAF, 1992; pres. The Pegasus Group, Washington, 1992-97; sr. mgr. KPMG, LLP (now KPMG Consulting), San Antonio, 1997—. Decorated DSM, Legion of Merit, DFC, Air medal. Mem. Air Force Assn., Internat. Inst. for Strategic Studies (London), Air Force Acad. Assn. Grads., Daedalians. Avocations: flying, reading, hunting, fishing, travel. Home: 13746 Bluff Villas Ct San Antonio TX 78216-1940 Office: KPMG Consulting 112 E Pecan St Ste 2400 San Antonio TX 78205-1528 E-mail: ettington@msn.com., gshirley@kpmg.com. *An enlightened and progressive society cannot exist unless the leadership at all levels has compassion, integrity and courage. Compassion for the less fortunate—integrity to know what is right—courage to do what is right regardless of the personal consequences.*

SHIRLEY, LAWRENCE HOYT, mathematician, educator; b. Flagstaff, Ariz., Nov. 13, 1947; s. Robert Albert and Shirley Amelia (Hoyt) S.; m. Alberta Ohenewah, Aug. 31, 1974; children: Jefferson, Emily. BS in Math., History, Calif. Tech., 1969; MEd in Comparative Edn., U. Ill., 1973; PhD in Math. Edn., Ahmadu Bello U., Zaria, Nigeria, 1984. Tchr. math. Bonthe (Sierra Leone) Secondary Sch./Peace Corps, 1969-71; advisor, peace corps math. Sierra Leone Ministry Edn., Bo, 1971-72; prof. math. edn. Ahmadu Bello U., 1974-88, dept. head., 1978-88; prof. math. edn. No. Ill. U., DeKalb, 1988-89, Towson U., Balt., 1989—, dept. vice chair, 1998-99,2000-01, acting dept. chair, 1999-2000, assoc. dean. grad. coll., 2001—. Cons., Nigeria Edn. Rsch. Coun., Lagos, 1978-88, Fed. U. Tech., Minna, Nigeria, 1986, Nat. Edn. Tech. Ctr., Kaduna, Nigeria, 1986-88, Peace Corps, 1995. Co-author, editor: Nigerian Primary Math, 1981; contbr. articles to profl. jours. Fellow Math. Assn. Nigeria; mem. Nat. Coun. Tchrs. Math., Md. Coun. Tchrs. Math., Internat. Study Group Ethnomath. (pres.), Internat. Study Group History Pedagogy Math., Amnesty Internat., Planetary Soc. Democrat. Avocations: African affairs, history, astronomy. Home: 854 Bosley Ave Baltimore MD 21204-2610 Office: Towson U Dept Math Towson MD 21252-0001 E-mail: lshirley@towson.edu.

SHIRLEY-QUIRK, JOHN, concert and opera singer; b. Liverpool, Eng., Aug. 28, 1931; came to U.S., 1990; s. Joseph Stanley and Amelia (Griffiths) S.-Q.; m. Patricia May Hastie, July 1955 (dec. Feb. 1981); children: Kate, Peter; m. Sara Van Horn Watkins, Dec. 29, 1981 (dec. Dec. 1997); children: Benjamin, Emily (dec.), Julia. BSc, Liverpool U., 1953, MusD (hon.), 1977; D Univ., Brunel U., 1981. Asst. lectr. Acton Tech. Coll., London, 1956-60; vicar choral St. Paul's Cathedral, 1960-61; profl. singer, 1960—; joint artistic dir. Aldeburgh Festival, 1981-84. Mem. voice faculty Peabody Conservatory, Balt., 1991—; vis. artist Carnegie-Mellon U., Pitts., 1994-98. Numerous recs. and 1st performances, especially works of Benjamin Britten. Mem. ct. Brunel U., 1977-81. Flying officer RAF, 1952-55. Decorated comdr. Order of Brit. Empire. Mem. Royal Acad. Music (hon.). Business E-Mail: jssq@peabody.jhu.edu.

SHIRTCLIFF, JOHN DELZELL, business owner, oil jobber; b. Roseburg, Oreg., Mar. 2, 1948; s. Henry Marion and Sheila Nell (Delzell) S.; m. Connie Lee Cantrell, June 13, 1975; children: Darcie, Danielle, Andrew. BS, Oregon State U., 1970. Pres. Shirtcliff Oil Co., Myrtle Creek, Oreg., 1971—. Engr. Myrtle Creek (Oreg.) Vol. Fire Dept., 1971—, emergency technician, 1981—; mem. Rep. Cen. Com., Roseburg, Oreg., 1982-88; chmn. Umpqua Community Coll. Budget Com., Roseburg, 1983-96; bd. dirs. Mercy Hospice, Roseburg, 1988-96. 2nd lt. U.S. Army, 1970-71. Named Citizen of Year, Myrtle Creek City, 1986, Vol. of Year, Douglas County C. of C., 1987. Mem. Petroleum Marketers Assn. Am. (dir. Oreg. 1988), Oreg. Petroleum Marketers Assn. (v.p. legis. chmn. 1986, pres. 1987, PMAA dir. 1988), Pacific Oil Conf. (bd. dirs., v.p. 1995, gen. chmn. 1997), Lions, Elks, Masons, Shriners. Republican. Avocations: landscaping, jogging, golf. Office: Shirtcliff Oil Co 283 SW Western Ave PO Box 6003 Myrtle Creek OR 97457-0051

SHIRTS, RANDALL BRENT, chemistry educator, researcher; b. Mt. Pleasant, Utah, Apr. 28, 1950; s. Morris Alpine and Dorothy Maxine (Baird) S.; m. Kathryn Adele Hanson, June 12, 1974; children: Michael, Brian, Caitlin, Peter, Kristen, Erica. BS in Chemistry, Brigham Young U., 1973; AM in Physics, Harvard U., 1978, PhD in Chem. Physics, 1979. Postdoctoral assoc. JILA, Boulder, Colo., 1979-81; asst. prof. chemistry Georgetown U., Washington, 1981-82, U. Utah, Salt Lake City, 1982-88, vis. assoc. prof. chemistry, 1990-91, Brigham Young U., 1991; scientific specialist EG & G Idaho, Inc., Idaho Falls, 1987-91; assoc. prof. chemistry Brigham Young U., Provo, 1991—. Prin. investigator INEL theoretical chemistry initiative, 1987-91. Contbr. articles to profl. jours. Grantee Nat. Sci. Found., 1985-88, Research Corp., 1982-84, Petroleum Research Fund, 1982-84. Mem. Am. Chem. Soc., Am. Phys. Soc., Sigmi Xi. Mem. Lds Ch. Office: Brigham Young Univ Dept Chemistry Provo UT 84602

SHIRTUM, EARL EDWARD, retired civil engineer; b. Montague, Mich., Feb. 20, 1927; s. Earl Willard and Elizabeth Caroline (Boelke) S.; m. Martha Louise Wright, June 19, 1953. BS in Civil Engring., Ind. Tech. Coll., Ft. Wayne, 1950. Bridge design squad leader Mich. Dept. Transp., Lansing, 1952-63, transp. planning engr., 1963-96. Mem. Bridge Replacement and Rehab. Com., Lansing, 1967-94. With U.S. Army, 1945-46, ETO. Mem. Mich. Profl. Engring. Soc. (rep. engr. in govt. 1974-77), Lansing Engr. Club (bd. mem. 1980-84). Republican. Methodist. Avocations: fishing, bridge. Home: 1617 Victor Ave Lansing MI 48910-6511

SHIRVANI, HAMID, architect, educator, author, administrator, philosopher; b. Tehran, Iran, Oct. 20, 1950; came to U.S., 1974, naturalized, 1986; s. Majid and Taji (Granpisheh) S. Diploma in architecture, Poly. of Cen. London, 1974; MArch, Pratt Inst., 1975; MS, Rensselaer Poly. Inst., 1977; MLA, Harvard U., 1978; MA, Princeton U., 1979, PhD, 1980. Project designer London Borough of Barnet, 1973-74; asst. prof. architecture Pa. State U., 1979-82; prof., dir. grad. studies SUNY, Syracuse, 1982-85; prof., dir. Sch. Urban Planning and Devel., U. Louisville, 1985-86; prof. architecture and urban design U. Colo., Denver, 1986-92, dean Sch. of Architecture and Planning, 1986-91; prof. philosophy, dean Coll. Arts and Scis. U. Mass., Lowell, 1992-95; v.p. grad. studies and rsch., prof. urban studies CUNY Queens Coll., Flushing, 1995-2000; provost, exec. v.p., Martha Masters prof. art/architecture Chapman U., Orange, Calif., 2000—. Mem. vis. faculty So. Calif. Inst. Architecutre, U. So. Calif.; lectr. numerous universities worldwide including U. Tex., San Antonio, Lehigh U., U. Waterloo (Can.), U. Sydney (Australia), Mo. State U., Columbia U., N.Y.C., Amsterdam Acad. Art, U. Venice (Italy), Chinese U. Hong Kong, So. China Inst. U., U. Calif., Irvine, Villanova U., Rutgers U., Ariz. State U., Duke U., U. Pa., Yale U., U. Colo., U. N.C. Author: Urban Design: A Comprehensive Reference, 1981, Urban Design Review, 1981, Urban Design Process, 1985, Beyond Public Architecture, 1990; editor Urban Design Rev., 1982-85, Urban Design and Preservation Quar., 1985-88; mem. editorial bd. Jour. Archtl. Edn., 1988-94, Avant Garde, 1988-93, Jour. Planning Edn. and Rsch., 1987-93, Art and Architecture, 1974-78, Jour. Am. Planning Assn., 1982-88. Recipient Gold Medal in Architecture and Urbanism, Faculty Honor award, Acad. Leadership award, Faculty Rsch. award. Fellow Am. Soc. Landscape Archs. (recognition award), Royal Geog. Soc., Royal Soc. Arts; mem. Am. Studies Assn., Am. Inst. Cert. Planners, Am. Planning Assn. (chmn. urban design divsn. 1987-89, Disting. award 1984, Urban Design award 1985), Sigma Xi, Omicron Delta Epsilon, Tau Sigma Delta (Silver medal in archtl. edn. 1988), Tau Beta Pi, Sigma Lambda Alpha. Office: Chapman U Orange CA 92866-1099 Fax: 714-997-6801. E-mail: Ham@chapman.edu.

SHIRZAD, FARYAR, federal agency administrator; married; 1 child. BS summa cum laude, U. Md.; JD, U. Va.; M in Pub. Policy, Harvard U. With Robins, Kaplan, Miller & Ciresi, Washington; internat. trade atty. Skadden, Arps, Slate Meagher & Flom; internat. trade counsel Senate Com. on Fin., 1997—2001; lead internat. trade policy coord. Bush-Cheney Transition Offices; asst. sec. for import adminstrn. U.S. Dept. of Commerce, Washington, 2001—. Office: US Dept of Commerce Import Adminstrn 14th & Constitution Ave Nw Washington DC 20230 Office Fax: 202-482-0947.*

SHITABATA, PAUL KENT, pathologist; b. Fukuoka, Japan, Sept. 20, 1962; s. George Joji and Janet Aiko (Ikeda) S.; m. Evangeline Chan Uy, Aug. 30, 1997. BA, Pomona Coll., 1984; MD, U. Hawaii, 1988. Diplomate Am. Bd. Pathology, Am. Bd. Dermatopathology. Med. dir. South Bay Surgicenter, Torrance, Calif., 1994-99, Long Beach (Calif.) Doctor's Hosp., 1996-99; with Pathology Cons. Med. Group, Torrance, 1994—; CEO, pres. The Doctor's Dr., 1999—. Contbr. articles to profl. jours. Mem. Alpha Omega Alpha. Avocation: jazz. Office: Pathology Cons Med Group 19951 Mariner Ave Ste 150 Torrance CA 90503

SHIUE, WEN-TSONG, computer scientist, educator; b. Tounan, Yunlin, Taiwan, Feb. 18, 1965; s. Chun-Ming Hsueh and Jui-Jung Shen; m. Shu-Ching Tu; children: Vivian, Stephen. MS, Western Mich. U., 1991; PhD, Ariz. State U., 2000. Adj. prof. Tamkang U., Taipei, Taiwan, 1991—96; chief electronics officer China Airlines, Taoyuan, Taiwan, 1991—96; rsch. assoc. Ariz. State U., Tempe, 1997—2000; sr. staff scientist Motorola Inc., Austin, Tex., 1999—2000; lead software scientist Silicon Metrics Corp., 2000—01; prof. Oreg. State U., Corvallis, 2001—. Contbr. articles to profl. jours. Recipient Travel Grant award, Ariz. State U., 1999; grantee, IEEE/ACM 36th Design Automation Conf., 1999; scholar, Motorola Inc., 1999, 2000. Mem.: IEEE Computer Soc., Assn. Computing Machinery, IEEE Circuits and Sys. Soc., Am. Soc. Engring Edn., Gamma Beta Phi. Avocations: swimming, travel. Home: 2645 NW Garryanna Dr #2 Corvallis OR 97330 Office: Oreg State Univ Dept ECE Corvallis OR 97331 Home Fax: 541-737-1300; Office Fax: 541-737-1300. Personal E-mail: shiue@ieee.org. Business E-Mail: shiue@ece.orst.edu.

SHIVAKUMAR, KUNIGAL NANJUNDAIAH, aerospace engineer, educator; b. Kunigal, Karnataka, India, Mar. 28, 1951; came to U.S., 1980; s. Kunigal H. Nanjundaiah; m. Netra D. Shivakumar, Nov. 1, 1984; children: Nishkala K., Nirmala K., Dhruva K. BE in Civil Engring., Bangalore (Karnataka) U., 1972; ME in Civil Engring., Indian Inst. Sci., Bangalore, 1974, PhD in Aeronautics, 1979. Rsch. assoc. Indian Inst. Sci., Bangalore, 1979, NRC, NASA Langley Rsch. Ctr., Washington, 1980-82; rsch. asst. prof. Old Dominion U., Norfolk, Va., 1982, rsch. assoc. prof., 1983-84; sr. scientist, group leader Analytical Svcs. & Materials, Hampton, 1985-89, group leader, 1989-91; rsch. prof. N.C. Agrl. and Tech. State U., Greensboro, 1991—; dir. Ctr. Composite Materials Rsch., 1999—. Cons. Bharat Heavy Elecs., Hyderbad, 1979, Aerotech, Lockheed Corp., Hampton, 1990, AS&M, NASA Langley Rsch. Ctr., Hampton, 1991. Contbr. over 130 articles to profl. jours. Com. mem. Kannada Sanga, Bangalore, 1978; pres. India Assn. of Peninsula, Hampton, 1984. Recipient 9 Tech. awards NASA, I.I. Sc. Assoc. Fellow AIAA (assoc., sr., bd. dirs. 1991, gen. chair 37th SDM Conf., chair long-range planning com. 1996-97, chair materials TC, assoc. editor jour., awards); mem. ASTM, ASME, ASC. Hindu. Avocations: tennis, gardening. Home: 5124 Hedrick Dr Greensboro NC 27410-9320 Office: NC A&T State U Fort Irc Bldg Rm 205 Greensboro NC 27411-0001 E-mail: kunigal@ncat.edu.

SHIVASHANKARA, TUMKUR S. physician; b. Channapatna, India, May 18, 1940; came to U.S., 1969; s. Chindiah P. Siddabasappa and Channapatna Meenekshi; m. Hemavathy Shivasankara, May 16, 1966 (div. 1981); 1 child Suparna ; m. Usha Shivashankara, Feb. 7, 1983. MB, BChir, Bangalore (India) Med. Coll., 1977. Diplomate Am. Bd. Internal Medicine. Lectr. in physiology Davanagere Med. Coll., India, 1967-68; geriat. ho. officer St. Mary's Hosp., Eng., 1969; intern Perth Amboy (N.J.) Gen. Hosp., 1970, Lakewood (Ohio) Hosp., 1971-72, resident, 1972-74, mem. med. staff, 1974-76, Wilmington (Ohio) Hosp., 1976-77; mem. med. core USAF, Barksdale AFB, La., 1979-84; mem. med. staff VA Hosp., Tuscaloosa, Ala., 1984—. Lt. col. USAF, 1979—. Home: 719 Petersburg Rd Tuscaloosa AL 35406-1783 Office: VA Med Ctr Loop Rd E Tuscaloosa AL 35404

SHIVE, RICHARD BYRON, architect; b. Cleve., Jan. 16, 1933; s. Roy Allen and Mary Elizabeth (Thompson) S.; m. Patricia Butler, Aug. 28, 1954; children: Lisa Ann, Laura Mary, John Thompson, Nancy Butler. BS, Rensselaer Poly. Inst., Troy, N.Y., 1954; postgrad., Newark (N.J.) Coll. Engring., 1957, Rutgers U., 1960-63. Registered architect, N.J., N.Y., Pa., Vt.; lic. profl. planner, N.J. Field engr. Wigton-Abbott Corp., Plainfield, N.J., 1954-55, The Glenwal Co., Rochelle Park, 1955; asst. supt. Wigton-Abbott Corp., Plainfield, 1955-57; archtl. draftsman Raymond B. Flatt, Architect, Bloomfield, N.J., 1957-58, chief draftsman, 1958-60; project architect Scrimenti/Swackhamer/Perantoni Architects, Somerville, N.J., 1960-66, assoc., 1966-69; ptnr. Scrimenti, Shive, Spinelli, Perantoni Architects, Somerville, 1969-86, Shive/Spinelli/Perantoni & Assocs., Architects & Planners, Somerville, 1986-97; prin. emeritus SSP Archtl. Group, 1998—. Adv. com. First Fidelity Bank, Bound Brook, N.J., 1989-91; chmn. bd. Somerset Health Care Corp., 1987-91. Contbr. articles to profl. jours. Bd. dirs., exec. com. N.J. Hosp. Assn., Princeton, 1986-92, 93-95; chmn. bd. trustees Somerset Med. Ctr., Somerville, 1973-96; mem. Nat. Trust for Hist. Preservation; bd. dirs. Ctr. for Health Affairs, Inc., 1992-93; mem. Borough of Bound Brook Planning Bd., 2000—; chmn. Borough of Bound Brook Redevel. Adv. Com., 2000—; mem. Somerset County Econ. Devel. Incentive Adv. Com., 1997—. Recipient award James F. Lincoln Arc Welding Found., 1973, President's award for outstanding svc. Rolling Hills coun. Girl Scouts U.S.A., 1988, Trustee of Yr. award N.J. Hosp. Assn., 1993, Outstanding Citizen of Yr. award Somerset County C. of C., 1993, Spirit of Somerset award, 2000; Paul Harris fellow Bound Brook-Middlesex Rotary Club, 1993. Mem. AIA, ASTM, ASHRAE, ACI (chpt. bd. dirs. 1978-83), N.J. Soc. Architects, Illuminating Engring. Soc., Nat. Fire Protection Assn., Greater Somerset County C. of C. (v.p. 1985-86, 92-93, Outstanding Citizen of Yr. award 1993), Rotary (pres. 1969-70, Paul Harris fellow 1993), Wash. Campground Assn. (pres. 1975-76, v.p. 1977-78, sec. 1978-97), Chi Phi (sec. 1973). Republican. Congregationalist. Avocations: fishing, photography, skiing, canoeing, backpacking. Home: 1786 Middlebrook Rd Bound Brook NJ 08805-1432 Office: SSP Archtl Group PO Box 758 148 W End Ave Somerville NJ 08876-1816 E-mail: rshive@ssparchitects.com.

SHIVELY, DANIEL JEROME, retired transportation executive; b. Akron, Ohio, Sept. 2, 1924; s. Richard Miles and Josephine (Pellicer) S.; m. Pamela Marion Kurfess, July 31, 1954; children: Jennifer, Laurie, Thomas. Grad., U.S. Mcht. Marine Acad., King's Point, N.Y., 1945. Chief officer (tanker) Trinidad Corp., N.Y.C., 1946-51; co-owner, mgr. Shively Bros. Jersey Farm, Quaker City, Ohio, 1952-54; staff asst. Gulf Oil Corp., Phila., 1955-57; distbn. coord. Standard Oil Co., Cleve., 1957-73; budget coord. BP Oil Co., Wilmington, Del., 1973-79; mgr. mktg. budget and planning Standard Oil Co., Cleve., 1979-85; owner, mgr. Shively & Assocs., 1985-88. Served to lt. (j.g.) USNR, 1945-61. Mem. Transp. Practitioners Assn. (exec. com. 1984-90, pres. local chpt. 1984-85), King's Point Club (treas. N.E. Ohio chpt. 1989-94, sec. 1999—), KC (chancellor 1986, dep. grand knight 1987-91). Republican. Roman Catholic. Avocations: farming, sailing. Home: 21347 Erie Rd Rocky River OH 44116-2133

SHIVELY, JOHN TERRY, business executive; b. Middletown, N.Y., July 1, 1943; s. Marvin Rathfelder and Esther (Manning) Westervelt; adopted child, Harold Eugene Shively. BA, U. N.C., 1965. Vol. worker VISTA, Bethel and Fairbanks, Alaska, 1965-68; health planner Greater Anchorage Area Cmty. Action Agy., 1968-69; health cons. Alaska Fed. Natives, Anchorage, 1969; dep. dir. Rural Alaska Cmty. Action Program, 1971-72; exec. v.p. Alaska Fedn. Natives, 1972-75; v.p. ops. NANA Regional Corp., Kotzebue, Alaska, 1975-77, NANA Devel. Corp., Anchorage, 1977-82; sr. v.p. NANA Regional Corp. Inc., 1986-92; pres. NANA Devel. Corp., 1992-94; commr. DNR, 1995-2000; chmn., CEO United Bar Corp., United Bank Alaska, 1987-88; sr. ptnr. Jade North, 2000—. Dir. Unicorp. Inc., United Bank of Alaska. Mem. Greater Anchorage Area Comprehensive Health Plan Coun., 1969-75, chmn., 1969-75; founding mem. bd. dirs. Alaska Pub. Interest Rsch. Group, 1974-75, 86-90, chmn. 1987-90; mem. Gov.'s Rural Affairs Coun., 1971-76, Gov.'s Manpower Commn., 1971, Greater Anchorage Health Bd., 1969-75, Alaska Pipeline Edn. Com., 1973-74; bd. regents U. Alaska, 1979-83; bd. trustees Alaska Permanent Fund Bd., 1999-2000. Democrat. Episcopalian. Home and Office: 2301 Loren Cir Anchorage AK 99516 E-mail: jtshively@att.net.

SHIVELY, JUDITH CAROLYN (JUDY SHIVELY), contract administrator; b. Wilkinsburg, Pa., Jan. 30, 1962; d. John Allen and Edith (Crowell) S. BA in English, U. Nev., Las Vegas, 1984. Circulation aide Charleston Heights Libr., Las Vegas, 1979-86; asst. food editor Las Vegas Sun Newspaper, 1985-88, asst. horse racing editor, 1985-90, features writer, page editor, 1988-89, editor youth activities sect., 1989-90; racebook ticket writer, cashier Palace Sta. Hotel Racebook, Las Vegas, 1989-92; contract adminstr. nat. accts. Loomis, Fargo & Co., 1992-2000; propr. Creative Computing, 1996—; content prodn. Preference Techs., Inc., 2000; data rsch. and processing PurchasePro.com, 2000; adminstrv. asst. Uinta Bus. Systems, 2001—. Horse racing historian, rschr., Las Vegas, 1985—; vol. rsch. asst. Dictionary of Gambling and Gaming, 1982-84; part-time clk. Hometown News, Las Vegas, 1994-96. Staff writer horse race handicaps, columns, articles, feature stories Las Vegas Sun Newspaper, 1985-90; freelance writer for monthly horse racing publ. Inside Track, 1992-94. Mem. Phi Beta Kappa. Republican. Avocations: collecting horse racing books, clippings, materials for personal library of horse racing, computers. Home: PO Box 26426 Las Vegas NV 89126-0426 E-mail: racehors1@aol.com.

SHIVELY, MERRICK LEE, pharmaceutical scientist, consultant; b. Alamagordo, N.Mex., Dec. 12, 1958; s. Milton Lee and Dorothy Jean (Garlock) S.; m. Maureen Lynch, Dec. 28, 1985; 1 child, Sierra Lange. BS in Pharmacy, U. Conn., 1982, PhD in Pharmaceutics, 1986. Registered pharmacist, Colo., Mass. Sr. rsch. assoc. Baxter Healthcare, Morton Grove, Ill., 1985-87; asst. prof. U. Colo., Boulder, 1987-93; sr. rsch. scientist Atrix Labs., Inc., Ft. Collins, Colo., 1993-94; sr. scientist Nexagen, Inc., Boulder, 1994-96; founder, mng. ptnr. Drug Delivery Solutions LLC, Louisville, 1996—. Pharm. cons. Glaxo, Synergen, Chemex, Cell Tech., Lilly; del. U.S. Pharmacopeia, 1988-94. Contbr. articles to Pharm. Rsch., Jour. Colloid Interface Sci., Drug Devel. and Indsl. Pharmacy, Internat. Jour. Pharmaceutics, others. Mem. Denver Econ. Com., 1989. Richardson-Vicks fellow, 1982-85. Mem. Am. Assn. Pharm. Scientists, Soc. of Controlled Release, Am. Chem. Soc., Rocky Mountain Devel. Forum (treas. 1989—), Phi Kappa Phi, Rho Chi. Achievements include patents in field; discovery and method of manufacture of solid state emulsions; findings that the formation of multi-molecular inclusion compounds are responsible for unique properties. Home and Office: 10ll Turnberry Cir Louisville CO 80027-9594

SHIVELY, WILLIAM PHILLIPS, political scientist, educator; b. Altoona, Pa., Mar. 31, 1942; s. Arthur and Ruth Shively; m. Barbara Louise Shank, Aug. 29, 1964; children: Helen, David. BA, Franklin and Marshall Coll., 1963; PhD, U. N.C., 1968. Mem. faculty U. Oreg., Eugene, 1967-68, Yale U., 1968-71; mem. faculty U. Minn., Mpls., 1971—, prof. polit. sci., 1979—, provost arts, scis. & engring., 1995-97. Author: Craft of Political Research, 1974, 5th edit., 2001, Research Process in Political Science, 1985, Power and Choice, 1986, rev. edit., 1989, 7th edit., 2001, Comparative Governance, 1995, Cross-Level Inference, 1995; editor Am. Jour. Polit. Sci., 1977-79; contbr. articles on elections and voting to profl. jours. Home: 1572 Northrop St Saint Paul MN 55108-1322 Office: U Minn Dept Polit Sci 1414 Social Scis Tower Minneapolis MN 55455 E-mail: shively@polisci.umn.edu.

SHIYANOVSKII, SERGIJ, physicist; b. Kiev, Ukraine, Dec. 1, 1955; s. Vladislav Ivanovich and Irina Efimovna S.; m. Irina Nestoyanova, Nov. 15, 1975; children: Natalie, Yuriy. MS in Physics/Theoretical Physics, Kiev Nat. U., 1977, PhD in Physics and Math., 1982, DSc, 1994. Lectr. of maths. and physics Lyceum of Natural Scis., Kiev, 1977-79; jr. rschr. Kiev Nat. U., 1977-79; sr. rschr. Inst. for Nuclear Rsch./Ukrainian Acad. of Scis., Kiev, 1979-93, prin. rsch. fellow, 1994—; vis. scientist, adj. assoc. prof. Liquid Crystal Inst./Kent State U., Ohio, 1997—. Vis. scientist U. Essen, Germany, 1996, Newton Inst. for Math. Scis., Cambridge, U.K., 1995; mem. rev. panel European INTAS, Brussels, Belgium, 1999, Ukrainian State Coun. for Sci. and Tech., Kiev, 1991—. Contbr. Travel grantee in field; grantee Sci. and Tech. Coun. of Ukraine, 1991-94, Cambridge U., 1995, German Rsch. Found., 1996, European INTAS, 1998; recipient award Soros Found., 1994, medal for Best Young Scientist Rsch. Work, Ukrainian Acad. Scis., 1978. Mem.: Soc. for Info. Display, Internat. Liquid Crystal Soc., Am. Phys. Soc. Avocations: tennis, soccer, kayaking. Office: Kent State U Liquid Crystal Inst Kent OH 44242-0001 E-mail: svshiyan@lci.kent.edu.

SHKLAR, GERALD, oral pathologist, periodontist, educator; b. Montreal, Que., Can., Dec. 2, 1924; came to U.S., 1950, naturalized, 1955; s. Louis and Ann (Schleifstein) S.; m. Judith Nisse, June 16, 1948 (dec. Sept. 18, 1992); children: David, Michael, Ruth; m. Se-Kyung Oh, July 13, 1997. BS, McGill U., 1947, DDS, 1949; MS, Tufts U., 1952; MA (hon.), Harvard U., 1971; D (hon.), U. Athens. Diplomate Am. Bd. Oral Pathology, Am. Bd. Periodontology. Asst. prof. oral pathology Tufts U. Sch. Dental Medicine, Boston, 1953-59, assoc. prof., 1960-61, prof., 1961-71, rsch. prof. periodontology, 1961-71, lectr. oral pathology, 1971—; Charles A. Brackett prof. oral pathology Harvard U. Sch. Dental Medicine, Boston, 1971-2000, Charles A. Brackett prof. oral pathology emeritus, 2000—, head dept. oral medicine and oral pathology, 1971-93; sr. clin. investigator Forsyth Dental Ctr., 1994—. Cons. oral pathology Children's Hosp. Med. Ctr., Brigham and Women's Hosp., Mass. Gen. Hosp. Author: Oral Cancer, 1984; co-author: (with Edmund Cataldo and Henry Goldman) Oral Pathology: An Atlas of Microscopic Pathology, 1975, (with Philip L. McCarthy) The Oral Manifestations of Systemic Disease, 1976, Diseases of the Oral Mucosa, 1982, (with David Chernin Libellus De Dentibus, 1563, of Bartholomaei Eustachii, 1999; contbr. over 350 articles to profl. jours.; contbr. numerous book chpts. Fellow AAAS, Am. Acad. Dental Sci., Am. Acad. Oral Medicine, Am. Acad. Oral Pathology, Am. Coll. Dentists, Internat. Coll. Dentists; mem. ADA, Internat. Assn. Dental Rsch., Am. Acad. Periodontology, Am. Cancer Soc., Am. Assn. Cancer Rsch., Am. Assn. Cancer Edn., Am. Acad. History Dentistry, History of Sci. Soc., Sigma Xi, Omicron Kappa Upsilon. Avocations: playing flute and harpsichord. Home: 154 Evelyn Rd Waban MA 02468-1042 Office: 188 Longwood Ave Boston MA 02115-5819 E-mail: gerald_shklzr@hms.harvard.edu.

SHKURKIN, EKATERINA VLADIMIROVNA (KATIA SHKURKIN), social worker, educator; b. Berkeley, Calif., Nov. 20, 1955; d. Vladimir Vladimirovich and Olga Ivanovna (Lisenko) S. Student, U. San Francisco, 1972-73; BA, U. Calif., Berkeley, 1974-77; MSW, Columbia U., 1977-79; postgrad., Union Grad. Sch., 1986, Calif. Coast U., 1994—. Social worker Tolstoy Found., N.Y.C., 1978-79, adminstr., 1979-80; program supr. Rehab. Mental Health Ctr., San Jose, Calif., 1980-81; dir. svc. counselor Kodiak (Alaska) Crisis Ctr., 1981-82; domestic violence counselor Abused Women's Aid in Crisis, Anchorage, 1982-85; pvt. practice social work Susitna Therapy Ctr., 1985-96; family therapist Anchorage Ctr. for Families, 1994-96; clin. supr., dir. New Parent Support Program, Ft. Lewis, Wash., 1997-99; asst. prof. St. Martin's Coll., Lacey, 1999—. Field instr. Abused Women's Aid in Crisis, Anchorage, 1983-88, Divsn. Family and Youth Svcs., State of Alaska, 1989-91, South Ctrl. Found.-Dena A. Coy Prematernal Alcohol Treatment Ctr., 1991-92; expert witness Anchorage Mcpl. Cts., 1982-96; interim faculty U. Alaska, Anchorage, summer 1985, fall 1988-95, LaVerne U., Anchorage, 1986-96. Coordinator Orthodox Christian Fellowship, San Francisco, 1972-76; pub. speaker Abused Women's Aid in Crisis, Anchorage, 1982-95; active nat. and local election campaigns, 1968—. Mem. NASW (cert.). Democrat. Russian Orthodox. Avocations: organic gardening, reading, crocheting, fine art. Home and Office: 3805 College St SE Unit 67 Lacey WA 98503-3567 E-mail: kshkurkin@stmartin.edu.

SHLADOVER, STEVEN ELLIOT, transportation research professional; b. N.Y.C., Feb. 15, 1950; s. Joel and Ida Shladover. SB, MIT, 1972, SM, 1974, ScD, 1978. Research asst. MIT, Cambridge, Mass., 1976-78, lectr., 1978; staff engr. Systems Control, Inc., Palo Alto, Calif., 1978-81; sr. engr. Systems Control Tech., Inc., 1981-84, program mgr., 1984-86, dir. CAE systems, 1986-89, mgr., transp. systems engr., 1987-89; tech. dir. PATH Program, dep. dir. U. Calif., Berkeley, 1989—. U.S. Expert to Internat. Standars Orgn. (tech. com. 204, working group 14). Assoc. editor Jour. of Dynamic Systems, Measurement and Control, 1980-85; contbr. articles to profl. jours. Nat. mem. Met. Opera Guild, N.Y.C., 1973—; mem. San Francisco Opera Guild, 1979—, Mus. Soc., San Francisco, 1979—, Common Cause, Washington, 1983—. Named one of the Outstanding Young Men of Am., U.S. Jaycees, 1983; fellow NSF, 1972-75. Mem. SAE (ITS div. 1992—), Intelligent Transp. Soc. Am. (chmn. AVCS com. 1990-97), ASME (assoc. editor 1980-85, program chmn. dynamic systems and control div. 1986, honors com. 1988-91, sec. 1989-92, exec. com. 1992-97, chmn. 1996), Transp. Rsch. Bd. (com. new transp. systems and tech. 1988, com. on study advanced vehicle and hwy. techs. 1990-91, com. intelligent transp. systems 1992—, task force on vehicle hwy. automation 1997—), MIT Alumni Assn., Calif. Alliance for Adv. Transp. Sys. (bd. dirs. 1994—). Democrat. Avocations: opera critic, tennis, international travel. Office: U Calif PATH Program 1301 S 46th St Bldg 452 Richmond CA 94804-4600 E-mail: ses@its.berkeley.edu.

SHLAES, JOHN B. consultant; b. L.A., Mar. 17, 1942; s. Burton L. and Jacquelyn (Metzger) Kramer; m. Kay Irene Edwards, Feb. 27, 1966; children: Darren, Katie. BS in Bus., U. So. Calif., 1963; MA in Internat. Transactions, George Mason U., 1993; cert. in internat. exec. mgmt., Georgetown U., 1995; adv. studies global trade strategies, Oxford U., 1996. Dir. spl. projects Chgo. Tribune, 1964-66; exec. dir. comms. Bellevue (Wash.) Pub. Schs., 1966-67; advt. mgr. Nixon for Pres. campaign, N.Y.C., 1967-69; cons. to dir. USIA, Washington, 1969; spl. asst. to dir. U.S. Peace Corps, 1970-72; dir. comms. Pres. Office of Emergency Preparedness, 1972; staff of counselor, staff asst. to pres., then dir. confs. White House, 1972-77; pres. John B. Shlaes Assocs., 1977-79; dir. govt. affairs Edison Electric Inst., 1979-92; exec. dir. Global Climate Coalition, 1991-97. Chmn., pres. Nat. Energy Resource Orgn., Washington, 1987-89. Mem. exec. com. Def. Adv. Com. Women in the Svcs., 1988-91; bd. dirs. Wash. Campus, 1980, Variety Clubs Internat., N.Y.C., 1988-92. Sgt. USAR, 1963-69. Avocations: skiing, SCUBA. Home: 5629 Lambeth Rd Bethesda MD 20814-1140 E-mail: jbsdcmd@aol.com.

SHLAUDEMAN, HARRY WALTER, b. L.A., May 17, 1926; s. Karl Whitman and Florence (Pixley) S.; m. Carol Jean Dickey, Aug. 7, 1948; children: Karl Frederick, Katherine Estelle, Harry Richard. BA, Stanford U., 1952. Joined U.S. Fgn. Svc., 1955; vice consul Barranquilla, Colombia, 1955-56; polit. officer Bogotá, Colombia, 1956-58; assigned lang. tng. Washington, 1958-59; consul Sofia, Bulgaria, 1960-62; chief polit. sect. Santo Domingo, Dominican Republic, 1962-64; officer charge Dominican Affairs State Dept., 1964-66; asst. dir. Office Caribbean Affairs, 1965-66; sr. seminar fgn. policy State Dept., 1966-67, spl. asst. to sec. state, 1967-69; dep. chief of mission Santiago, Chile, 1969-73; dep. asst. sec. state for Inter-Am. affairs Washington, 1973-75; amb. to Venezuela, 1975-76; asst. sec. state for Inter-Am. affairs, 1976-77; amb. to Peru, 1977-80; amb. to Argentina, 1980-83; exec. dir. Nat. Bipartisan Commn. on Central Am., 1983-84; spl. amb. to Cen. Am., 1984-86; amb. to Brazil Brasilia, 1986-89; amb. to Nicaragua, 1990-92; ret., 1992. Served with USMCR, 1944-46. Recipient Disting. Honor award Dept. State, 1966, Pres. Disting. Svc. award, 1988, Pres. Medal Freedom, 1992. Mem. Am. Acad. Diplomacy, San Luis Obispo Golf and Country Club, Phi Gamma Delta. Home: 7006 Pebble Beach Way San Luis Obispo CA 93401-8916 E-mail: harrywal@aol.com.

SHLIMOVICH, PAVEL, internist; b. St. Petersburg, Russia, June 9, 1941; came to U.S., 1988; s. Boris and Basia Shlimovich; m. Masha Shlimovich, Aug. 1, 1964 (div. Jan. 1990); children: Katia, Shira, Nira; m. Tamara Shlimovich, Feb. 15, 1991; 1 child, Miriam. MD, Leningrad Med. Sch., St. Petersburg, 1965; PhD, Inst. Physiology, St. Petersburg, 1969. Diplomate Am. Bd. Internal Medicine with subspecialties in endocrinology and geriatrics. Intern Montefiore Med. Ctr., N.Y.C., 1989-90, resident, 1990-92, fellow, 1992-94; asst. prof. medicine 2d Leningrad Med. Sch., 1969-79; attending physician City Hosp. # 4, 1980-88; cons. St. U. Clinic, St. Petersburg; attending physician Montefiore Med. Ctr., N.Y.C., 1994—, Maimonides Med. Ctr., N.Y.C., 1998—; asst. prof. Albert Einstein Coll. Medicine, Bronx,

1995—. Cons. Shorefront Jewish Geriat. Ctr., Bklyn., 1998—. Contbr. more than 65 articles to profl. jours. Fellow ACP; mem. Am. Geriat. Soc., Am. Diabetes Assn., Endocrine Soc. Avocations: reading, tennis.

SHMAGRANOFF, GEORGE L. physician; b. Benton, Ill., July 12, 1924; s. Lambro and Olga (Andreoff) S.; m. Helen Shmagranoff; children: George, Paula, Joan. AB, Washington U., 1948, MD, 1953. Diplomate Am. Bd. Internal Medicine. Intern Minn. Gen. Hosp., 1953-54; resident in medicine Jewish Hosp. of St. Louis, 1954-56; traineeship Stanford U. Sch. Medicine, 1956-57; pvt. practice Redwood City, 1959—; chmn. internal medicine Sequoia Hosp., Calif., 1963-64, chmn. dept. medicine, 1971-73; clin. assoc. prof. medicine Emeritus Stanford Med. Ctr., Palo Alto, 1988—. Tchg. asst. Stanford U. Sch. Medicine, 1957-62, clin. instr., 1962-71, clin. asst. prof., 1971-78, clin. assoc. prof., 1978-88, clin. assoc. prof. Emeritus, 1988—. Contbr. articles to profl. jours. Mem.: AHA, AMA, ACP, Am. Assn. Clin. Endorcinologists, Endocrine Soc., San Mateo County Med Soc., Calif. Soc. Internal Medicine, Am. Soc. Internal Medicine, Am. Diabetes Assn. Avocations: tennis, reading, golf. Office: 2950 Whipple Ave Ste 3 Redwood City CA 94062-2842

SHMAVONIAN, GERALD S. philanthropist, art collector; b. L.A., June 26, 1945; s. Sergius Neshan and Berje-Lucia (Hareutunyan) Shmavonian. Student, U. Calif., Berkeley, 1964-70. Leader archaeol. excavation team, Guatemala, Turkey, 1970-75; pub. City Mags., 1975-80; special advisor Bicentennial Commission, Washington, D.C., 1987; chmn. Am. Nationalities Coun., Stanford U., 1983-86; pres. Am. Talent, 1986—, Am. Documentary Film Acad., 2001—; ptnr. Assembly Plant Ptnrs. Recipient Intercollegiate Boxing Championship, 1965. Mem. Calif. Scholarship Fedn. (life, pres. 1963), Nat. Forensic League (pres. 1963, degree of honor). Home: 6219 N Prospect Ave Fresno CA 93711-1658

SHMIDOV, ANNA, music educator, piano teacher; b. Minsk, Belarus, Nov. 16, 1947; came to U.S., 1980; d. Fayba and Sheyna-Miriam Pikus; m. Semyon Shmidov, Nov. 25, 1967; children: Julia Shmidov-Latz, Valentin. BA in Piano and Music Edn., Music Tech. Coll., Minsk, 1962; M in Piano and Music Edn., State Conservatory of Music, Minsk, 1967. Music tchr. Music Sch. for Children and Adults, Minsk, 1964-67; dir. piano dept. in a music sch., 1967-80; owner piano studio, piano tchr., Mpls., 1980—; dir. music program in 5 northwestern cities, New Hope, Minn., 1990. Bd. dirs. Upper Midwest Music Festival, Mpls./St. Paul, 1985—96, exec. dir., 1996—. Mem. Minn. Music Tchrs. Assn., Music Nat. Tchrs. Assn. Avocations: theatre, travel, reading, concerts, art shows. Home and Office: Music for Everyone 8045 Narcissus Ln N Maple Grove MN 55311-1870

SHMUELI, ALFRED, accountant, educator; b. Bagdad, Iraq, Mar. 27, 1930; arrived in Eng., 1969; s. Oved and Naima (Sofer) S.; m. Rivka Polak, Nov. 27, 1956; children: Ehud, Aviya. LLM, Hebrew U., Jerusalem, 1956; MSc, City U., London, 1972, MPhil, 1973. Fin. analyst Ha'Aretz Newspaper, Tel Aviv, 1960-69; sr. lectr. N.E. London Poly., 1973-84, Southeastern U., London, 1988—. Author: Murder in the Kibbutz, 1993, In the Harem of the Sublime Porte, 1993, Withdrawal, 1994, The Murder of Selim III, 2000. Mem. Assn. Cert. Accts. Jewish. Mem. Labour Party. Avocations: writing, music. Home: 97 Geary Rd Dollis Hill London NW10 1HS England

SHMUKLER, STANFORD, lawyer; b. Phila., June 16, 1930; s. Samuel and Tessye (Dounne) S.; m. Anita Golove, Mar. 21, 1951; children: Jodie Lynne Shmukler Girsh, Joel Mark, Steven David. BS in Econs., U. Pa., 1951, JD, 1954. Bar: D.C. 1954, Pa. 1955, U.S. Ct. Appeals (2d cir.) 1959, U.S. Supreme Ct. 1959, U.S. Ct. Appeals (3d cir.) 1960, U.S. Ct. Mil. Appeals 1966. Atty. U.S. Bur. Pub. Roads, 1954-55, cons., 1955-57; sole practice Phila., 1955—. Lectr. Temple U. Law Sch., 1975-78; mem., past sec., exec. dir. crminal procedural rules com. Pa. Supreme Ct., 1971-87; mem. lawyers adv. com. Ct. Appeals for 3d cir., 1977-80, selection com. Criminal Justice Act Panel, 1979-84; chmn. selection com. Phila. Bar Ct. Appointments, 1988-91. Contbr. articles to profl. jours. Bd. dirs. Ecumenical Halfway House, 1967-71; bd. mgrs. Alumni Assn., Ctrl. High Sch., Phila. Served to col. JAGC, USAR, from 1955 (ret.). Recipient Phila. Bar Assn. Criminal Justice Sect. award, 1977, Justice Thurgood Marshall award, 1992; Legion of Honor, Chapel of the Four Chpalains, 1983. Mem. ABA, Pa. Bar Assn., Phila. Bar Assn. (bd. govs. 1971-73, past chmn. criminal justice com. and mil. justice com.), Fed. Bar Assn. (chmn. criminal law com. adminstrn. justice sect., co-chmn. criminal law com. Phila. chpt., Leadership award Phila. 1991, 94), Pa. Assn. Criminal Def. Lawyers, Nat. Assn. Criminal Def. Lawyers., Justice Lodge, B'nai B'rith. Democrat. Jewish. Home: 1400 Melrose Ave Elkins Park PA 19027-3155 E-mail: SSESQ1@aol.com.

SHMUNES, EDWARD, dermatologist; b. Jacksonville, Fla., July 24, 1940; s. Nathan and Anne Lillian (Berg) S.; m. Barbara Sue Mayson Hagen, Apr. 17, 1996; children: Stephanie, Marjorie, Jenifer. MD, U. Fla., 1965. Diplomate Am. Bd. Dermatology. Intern U.S. Pub. Health Hosp., New Orleans, 1965-66; epidemic intelligence officer svc. Ctr. for Disease Control, Atlanta, 1966-68; resident in dermatology U. Pa., Phila., 1968-71; ptnr. Columbia (S.C.) Skin Clinic, 1973—, pres., 1991—. Grantee NIH, 2 yrs., U. S.C., 1985. Mem. Greek Orthodox Ch. Office: Columbia Skin Clinic 3 Medical Park Rd Ste 500 Columbia SC 29203-6873

SHNAYERSON, ROBERT BEAHAN, editor, consultant; b. N.Y.C., Dec. 8, 1925; s. Charles and Madalene (Griffin) Beahan; m. Lydia Conde Todd, Dec. 23, 1950 (dec. Sept. 1973); children: Michael, Kate; m. Laurie Platt Winfrey, June 9, 1980; children: Maggie, Bonnie. AB, Dartmouth, 1950. Reporter N.Y. Daily News, 1946; reporter Life mag., N.Y.C., 1950-54; corr. Time-Life News Svc., 1954-56; contbg. editor Time mag., 1957-59, edn. editor, 1959-64, law editor, 1964-67, sr. editor, 1967-71; editor-in-chief Harper's Mag., N.Y.C., 1971-76; editor, pub. Quest mag., 1976-81, Technology mag., N.Y.C., 1981-82; editorial dir. Sci. Digest mag., 1986-87. Editl. cons. Lear's mag., 1987-90; cons. in mag. field; sr. advisor Travel Holiday mag., 1989-95. Author: Illustrated History of the Supreme Court, 1986; author, editor: Wordworks, 1995—; contbr. articles to various mags. With USNR, 1943-46. Home: 118 Riverside Dr New York NY 10024-3708

SHNEIDERMAN, BEN ABRAHAM, computer science educator, writer; b. N.Y.C., Aug. 21, 1947; s. Samuel Leib and Eileen (Szymin) S.; m. Nancy Helman, Mar. 25, 1973 (div. Dec. 1994); children: Sara Beth, Anna Rose. BS, CCNY, 1968; MS, SUNY, Stony Brook, 1972, PhD, 1973; hon. doctorate sci., U. Guelph, Ont., Can., 1995. Asst. prof. computer sci. Ind. U., Bloomington, 1973-76; asst. prof. U. Md., College Park, 1976-82, assoc. prof., 1982-89, prof., 1989—. Cons. Apple Computers, IBM, GE, Microsoft, Intel. Author: Software Psychology, 1980, Designing the User Interface, 1987, 2d edit., 1992, 3d edit., 1998, Hypertext Hands-On, 1989; co-author: Readings in Information Visualization, 1999; editor: Sparks of Innovation, 1992. Fellow ACM, AAAS. Avocation: skiing. Office: Univ Md Dept Computer Sci College Park MD 20742-0001 E-mail: ben@cs.umd.edu.

SHNEIDMAN, EDWIN S. psychologist, educator, thanatologist, suicidologist; b. York, Pa., May 13, 1918; s. Louis and Manya (Zukin) S.; m. Jeanne E. Keplinger, Oct. 1, 1944; children: David William, Jonathan Aaron, Paul Samuel, Robert James. AB, UCLA, 1938, MA, 1940; MS, U. So. Calif., 1947, PhD, 1948. Diplomate: Am. Bd. Examiners Profl. Psychology (past v.p.). Clin. psychologist VA Center, Los Angeles, 1947-50, chief research, 1950-53; co-dir. Central Research Unit for Study Unpredicted Deaths, 1953-58; co.-dir. Suicide Prevention Center, Los Angeles, 1958-66; chief Center Studies Suicide Prevention NIMH, Bethesda, Md., 1966-69; vis. prof. Harvard U., 1969; fellow Ctr. Advanced Study in Behavioral Scis., 1969-70; clin. assoc. Mass. Gen. Hosp., 1969, Karolinska Hosp., Stockholm, 1978; prof. med. psychology UCLA, 1970-75, prof. thanatology, 1975-88, emeritus, 1988—. Vis. prof. Ben Gurion U. of Negev, Beersheva, 1983 Author: Deaths of Man, 1973, Voices of Death, 1980; Definition of Suicide, 1985, Suicide as Psychache, 1993, The Suicidal Mind, 1996, Comprehending Suicide, 2001; editor: Thematic Test Analysis, 1951; editor: (with N.L. Farberow) Clues to Suicide, 1957, The Cry for Help, 1961, Essays in Self-Destruction, 1967, (with M. Ortega) Aspects of Depression, 1969, On the Nature of Suicide, 1969, (with N.L. Farberow, L.E. Litman) Psychology of Suicide, 1970, Death and the College Student, 1972, Death: Current Perspectives, 1976, 80, 84, Suicidology: Contemporary Developments, 1976, Endeavors in Psychology: Selections From The Personology of Henry A. Murray, 1981, Suicide Thoughts and Reflections, 1981 Served to capt. USAAF, 1942-45. Recipient Harold M. Hildreth award Psychologists in Pub. Service, 1966; Louis I. Dublin award Am. Assn. Suicidology, 1969. Mem. Am. Assn. Suicidology (founder, past pres.), Am. Psychol. Assn. (past div. pres., Disting. Profl. Contbn. to Pub. Svc. award 1987, Henry A. Murray award 1997), Melville Soc. Address: 11431 Kingsland St Los Angeles CA 90066-1329

SHNEIDMAN, J. LEE, historian, educator; b. N.Y.C., June 20, 1929; s. Bernard Wolf and Fannia Abramova (Raskin) S.; m. Conalee Levine, Sept. 3, 1961; children— Philip, Jack. BA, NYU, 1951, MA, 1952; PhD, U. Wis., Madison, 1957. Lectr. CCNY, 1956-57, U. Md. Overseas, 1957-58; asst. prof. Fairleigh Dickinson U., 1958-62; prof. history Adelphi U., 1963—2001, emeritus prof., 2001—. Chmn. seminar on hist., legal, and polit. thought Columbia U., 1985—. Author: Rise of the Aragonese-Catalan Empire, 2 vols, 1970, Spain and Franco, 1949-59, 1973, John F. Kennedy, 1974. Democratic N.Y. County committeeman, 1970—. Mem. Am. Hist. Assn., Medieval Acad. Am., Am. Philatel. Soc., Internat. Psychohist. Assn., Rossica Soc., China Soc. Jewish. Home: 161 W 86th St New York NY 10024-3411 Office: History Dept Adelphi University Garden City NY 11530 *Only by understanding from where we came can we understand where we are and where we are going.*

SHNEOUR, ELIE ALEXIS, biochemist, researcher, historian; b. Neuilly-sur-Seine, France, Dec. 11, 1925; came to U.S., 1941, naturalized, 1944; s. Zalman and Salomea (Landau) S.; m. Polly H. Henderson, Sept. 7, 1990; children from previous marriage: Mark Zalman, Alan Brewster. BA, Columbia U., 1947; DSc (hon.), Bard Coll., 1969; MA, U. Calif., Berkeley, 1955; PhD, UCLA, 1958. Tchr. and rsch. fellow U. Calif., Berkeley, 1953-55, Am. Heart Assn. rsch. fellow, 1958-62, tchg. and rsch. fellow L.A., 1958; rsch. fellow Nat. Cancer Inst., 1956-57; Am. Heart Assn. rsch. fellow NYU, 1958-59; rsch. assoc. genetics Stanford U., 1962-65; assoc. prof. biology and neuroscis. U. Utah, 1965-69; rsch. neurochemist City of Hope Nat. Med. Ctr., Duarte, Calif., 1969-71. Dir. rsch. Calbiochem., 1971-75; pres. Biosystems Insts., Inc., 1975—; dir. Biosystems Rsch. Inst., 1979—; mem. steering com. Nat. Acad. Sci. Study Group on Biology and the Exploration of Mars, 1964; chmn. Western Regional coun. Rsch. in Basic Bioscis. for Manned Orbiting Missions, Am. Inst. Biol. Scis., NASA, 1966-69; fellow Com. Sci. Investigation Claims of Paranormal, 1996—. Author: Extraterrestrial Life, 1965, (with Eric A. Ottesen) National Academy of Sciences, National Rsch. Coun., 1966, (with S. Moffat) Life Beyond the Earth, 1966, The Malnourished Mind, 1974; contbr. numerous articles to sci. and lay jours. Chmn. citizens adv. coun. San Diego Pub. Schs., 1971-72; mem. adv. coun. Cousteau Soc., 1977-98; bd. dirs. Am.-Ukraine Trade Coun., 1991-96, Lunar Power System Coalition, 1993-2002, Transinnova S.A. France, 1990—; chmn. sci. adv. bd. County of San Diego, 1995-2002. With U.S. Army, 1944-45. Recipient William Lockwood prize, 1947. Mem. IEEE, AAAS (chmn. So. Calif. Skeptics soc. Pacific divsn. 1988-90), Am. Chem. Soc., N.Y. Acad. Scis., Am. Inst. Biol. Scis., Am. Soc. for Biochemistry and Molecular Biology (chmn. sci. advisors program 1973-75, mem. com. on pub. policy 1974-76, congl. liaison 1992—), Am. Soc. Neurochemistry (mem. coun. 1971-73), Soc. Neurosci., Internat. Soc. Neurochemistry, U.S. C. of C. (bd. dirs. 1993—), La Jolla Chamber Music Soc. (bd. dirs. 1994-97), Internat. Coun. for Global Health Progress (N.Am. adv. bd. 1996—), Sigma Xi, Phi Sigma. Office: Biosystems Insts Inc 700 Front St MS CDM 608 San Diego CA 92101-6085

SHNIDER, BRUCE JAY, lawyer; b. Lansing, Mich., Oct. 16, 1950; s. Harold A. and Raynor (Seidner) Shnider; m. Patricia Lynn Strandness, Dec. 28, 1973; 1 child Ruth Strandness. AB magna cum laude, Dartmouth Coll., 1972; MPP, JD magna cum laude, Harvard U., 1977. Bar: Minn. 1977, U.S. Dist. Ct. Minn. 1977, U.S. Tax Ct. 1978, U.S. Ct. Appeals (8th cir.) 1980, U.S. Supreme Ct. 1981. Asst. to dir. Mich. Dept. Commerce, Lansing, 1972-73; law clk. United Mineworkers Am. Health/Retirement Funds, 1975; summer assoc. Robins, Davis & Lyon, Mpls., 1976; assoc. Dorsey & Whitney, 1977-82, ptnr., 1983—; chmn. diversity com., 1990-93; chmn. tax practice group, 1994-98. Bd. dirs. Minn. Justice Found., Mpls., 1989—91. Mem.: ABA, Hennepin County Bar Assn., Minn. State Bar Assn. Home: 1908 James Ave S Minneapolis MN 55403-2831 Office: Dorsey & Whitney 50 S 6th St Ste 1500 Minneapolis MN 55402-1498 E-mail: shnider.bruce@dorseylaw.com.

SHOAFF, THOMAS MITCHELL, lawyer; b. Ft. Wayne, Ind., Aug. 21, 1941; s. John D. and Agnes H. (Hanna) S.; m. Eunice Swedberg, Feb. 7, 1970; children: Andrew, Nathaniel, Matthew-John. BA, Williams Coll., 1964; JD, Vanderbilt U., 1967. Bar: Ind. 1968. Assoc. Isham, Lincoln & Beale, Chgo., 1967-68; ptnr. Baker & Daniels, Ft. Wayne, Ind., 1968—. Bd. dirs. Weaver Popcorn Co., Inc., Ft. Wayne, Dreibelbiss Title Co., Inc., Ft. Wayne, Am. Steel Investment Corp., Ft. Wayne. Bd. dirs. McMillen Found., Ft. Wayne, Wilson Found., Ft. Wayne. Mem. ABA, Allen County Bar Assn., Ind. State Bar Assn. Presbyterian. Avocations: golf, sailing. Office: Baker & Daniels 111 E Wayne St Ste 800 Fort Wayne IN 46802-2603

SHOAFSTALL, EARL FRED, entrepreneur, consultant; b. Des Moines, Jan. 26, 1936; s. Ralph Paul and Josephine E. (Carnes) S.; m. Sharon I. Vannoy, Mar. 21, 1962 (div. 1980); children: Michael E., Angela R.; m. Carlene Christenson, Dec. 11, 1980; 1 child, Trace Herman. BA, MBA, Drake U., 1962. Enlisted USAF, Des Moines, 1954, advanced through grades to sgt., 1961, resigned, 1962; underwriter Hawkeye Security Ins., Des Moines, 1962-65; mgr., owner B & B Transfer and Storage Inc., West Des Moines, Iowa, 1965-99; cons., owner B & B Mini Storage Inc., 1975-99. Inventor pressure gage, control valve for air and liquid. Mem. Mason (32 degree), Shriners. Republican. Avocations: flying, golf, hunting, fishing. Home: 12475 Douglas Pkwy Urbandale IA 50323-1813

SHOBE, NANCY, fundraising consultant, small business owner; b. Detroit, Oct. 3, 1961; d. Richard William and Barbara Ann (Williams) S.; 1 child, Allison Elizabeth Stelyn; m. William Wright Watling, Aug. 23, 1996. BA, Mich. State U., 1983. Copywriter Wickes Lumber Hdqr., Vernon Hills, Ill., 1983-85; asst. to prodr. Music Ctr. of L.A., 1985, mercado coord., 1985-86; dir. comms. Candlelight Pavilion, Claremont, Calif., 1987-88, corp. dir. mktg., 1988; asst. dir. devel. The Webb Schs., 1988-90; dir. devel. Crane Sch., Santa Barbara, 1991-96; owner Shobe Comm., 1996—. Contbr. chpts. to books. Mem. Coun. Advancement and Support of Edn. (heavy hitter spkr. 1993, cir. of excellence award for ednl. fund raising 1995). Democrat. Episcopalian. Avocations: antiques, travel, walking, swimming, reading.

SHOBER, (EDWARD) WHARTON, bioscience company executive; b. Bryn Mawr, Pa., Nov. 16, 1926; s. Edward Wharton and Catherine Mather S.; m. Sandra Metcalf, May 27, 1978; children: Jorie, Edward, Paula, Michael, Anne. Student, Princeton U., 1950; DSc, Wilkes U., 1975. Pres., CEO Atec Corp., N.Y.C., 1957-71, Hahnemann Med. Coll., Phila., 1971-77, pres. emeritus, 1977—; CEO, co-founder Gen. Arabian Medical, Riyadh, Saudi Arabia, 1978-88; London rep. Saudi Am. Ltd., 1988-92; chmn. Allergy Tech. Ltd., U.K., 1992—. Chmn. Drexel, Hahnemann, Jefferson Med. Coll. Pa. Cancer Ctr., 1973—; dir. Winfield Trust, 1996—. Author: Blood Lust, 1990, Royal Treachery, 1993. Dir. Old Phila. Devel. Corp., 1972-78, Bryn Mawr Hosp., Phila., 1965-72; hon. consul Nicaragua, Phila., 1960-75; dir. English Speaking Union, Newport, R.I., 1960-85; co-founder, chmn. Cuban Aide Relief, 1960. With USNR, 1944-46, 1st lt. C.E. mil., 1950-52. Home: 50A Elizabeth St London SWI W9PB England Fax: 44 1666 577942. E-mail: zacharias@blinternet.com.

SHOCHAT, STEPHEN JAY, pediatric surgeon; b. Balt., Dec. 17, 1938; s. Albert J. and Rose (Blechman) S.; m. Sheila Floam, July 1960 (div. July 1979); children: Francine Lynne, Alisa Joy; m. Carla Ann Centi, Jan. 26, 1980; children: David Robert, Sarah Elizabeth. BS, Randolph Mason Coll., 1959; MD, Med. Coll. Va., 1963. Surg. resident Washington U. Med. Ctr., St. Louis, 1963-68; pediatric surg. resident Boston Children's Hosp., 1968-70; thoracic surg. resident Queen Elizabeth Hosp., Birmingham, Eng., 1970, George Washington Hosp., Washington, 1972; chief pediatric surgery Hershey (Pa.) Med. Ctr., 1973-77, Stanford (Calif.) Med. Ctr., 1977-94; sr. surgeon Children's Hosp. Phila., 1994-96; surgeon-in-chief, chmn. dept. surgery St. Jude Children Rsch. Hosp., Memphis, 1996—; prof. pediats. and surgery U. Tenn., 1996-98. Lt. col. USAF, 1970-72. Office: St Jude Children Rsch Hosp Dept Surgery Memphis TN 38105

SHOCK, DAVID ROBERT, political science educator; b. Bucyrus, Ohio, June 2, 1973; s. Robert Eugene and Doris Mae Shock. BA, Kent State U., 1996; MA, Miami U., Oxford, Ohio, 1997, PhD in Polit. Sci., 2002. Grad. asst. Miami U., Oxford, Ohio, 1996-99, tchg. assoc., 1999—2002; asst. prof. polit. sci. Kennesaw State U., Ga., 2002—. Cand. U.S. Congress, 8th dist. Ohio, Libertarian Party, 2000. Mem. Am. Soc. for Pub. Adminstrn., Am. Polit. Sci. Assn. Lutheran. Avocations: travel. Home: 3900 Busbee Pkwy NW Apt 1011 Kennesaw GA 30144 Office: Miami U 218 Harrison Hall Oxford OH 45056 E-mail: davidshock@yahoo.com.

SHOCKEY, GARY LEE, lawyer; b. Casper, Wyo., Sept. 25, 1950; s. Bernis L. and Shirley E. (Diehl) Shockey; m. Dona K. Galles, June 1, 1979; children: Amber, Jeremy, Kimberly. AB in Polit. Sci. and Sociology, Yale U., 1973; JD, U. Wyo., 1976. Bar: Wyo. 1976, U.S. Dist. Ct. Wyo. 1976, U.S. Ct. Appeals (10th cir.) 1984, U.S. Ct. Appeals (9th cir.) 1988, U.S. Claims Ct. 1989, U.S. Supreme Ct. 1989, U.S. Ct. Appeals (fed. cir.) 1993, U.S. Dist. Ct. Ariz. 1994. Pub. defender State of Wyo. and City of Casper, 1976-78; pvt. practice Casper, 1976-79; assoc. Spence, Moriarty & Schuster, Casper and Jackson, 1978-82, ptnr. Jackson, 1982—. Mem. ATLA, ABA, Wyo. Trial Lawyers Assn. (bd. dirs. 1984—90), Wyo. State Bar (continuing legal edn. com. 1984—85, law and legis. reform com. 1986—88). Office: Spence Moriarty & Schuster PO Box 548 Jackson WY 83001-0548 E-mail: g_shockey@smswy.com.

SHOCKEY, MARTHA LUCILE, sociology educator; b. Villisca, Iowa, July 23, 1953; d. Harley B. and Wilma (Buffington) Bangston; m. William C. Shockey, Aug. 14, 1971; children: Christopher W., Amy M., Adam M., Benjamin D. BA, St. Ambrose U., 1987; MA, U. Iowa, 1991, PhD, 1994. Asst. prof. sociology St. Ambrose U., Davenport, Iowa, 1991—. Vis. asst. prof. criminal justice Appalachian State U., Boone, N.C., 1996-97; spkr. in field. Mem. exec. bd. AIDS Prevention Partnership, Davenport. Edwin Ford Piper Merit scholar, 1992. Mem. AAUP, Am. Soc. Criminology, Am. Sociol. Assn., Midwest Sociol. Soc., Acad. Criminal Justice Scis., Soc. Study Symbolic Interactronism. Democrat. Methodist. Home: 408 S 9th Ave Eldridge IA 52748-2001 Office: St Ambrose U 518 W Locust St Davenport IA 52803-2898

SHOCKEY, THOMAS EDWARD, real estate executive, engineer; b. Aug. 17, 1926; s. Verlie Draper and Margaret Ruth (Shuford) S.; m. Jacqueline McPherson, June 4, 1949; children: Cheryl Ann, Jocelyn Marie, Valerie Jean. BS, Tex. A&M U., 1950; postgrad., St. Mary's U., 1964, San Antonio Coll., 1972, Pacific Western U., 1981. With Petty Geophys. Survey, 1947-49, J.E. Ingram Equipment Co., 1950-51; co-owner, archtl. engr., realtor Moffett Lumber Co., Inc., San Antonio, 1952-76; cons. gen. contracting, gen. real estate, 1944—; retailer wholesale bldg. material, 1951—; v.p., 1959—. Real estate counselor, appraiser, 1972—; real estate appraiser Gill Appraisal Svc., San Antonio, 1977—; comml. loan appraiser, underwriter, analyst Gill Savs. Assn., Gill Cos., San Antonio, 1979; chief appraiser, underwriter, architect, engr., insp. Gill Cos., 1981, v.p., 1981-87, ret., 1987; v.p. La Hacienda Savs. Assn., 1988-91, ret., 1991. Fire chief Mico Vol. Fire Dept., 1993-95, tng. officer, 1996-2000. With inf. Signal Corps, U.S. Army, 1944-46, ETO. Davidson fellow Tau Beta Pi. Mem. San Antonio C. of C., Nat. Lumber Dealers, Nat. Home Builders, Nat. Real Estate Bd., Nat. Inst. Real Estate Brokers, Internat. Soc. Real Estate Appraisers, Tex. Assn. Real Estate Insps., Real Estate Appraisers Tex., Nat. Assn. Rev. Appraisers and Mortgage Underwriters, Internat. Inst. Valuers, Internat. Platform Assn., State Firemen's and Fire Marshal's Assn. of Tex. Home: 126 County Road 2620 Mico TX 78056-5213

SHOCKLEY, ANN ALLEN, librarian, writer; b. Louisville, June 21, 1927; d. Henry and Bessie (Lucas) Allen; children: W. Leslie Shockley Jr., Tamara Ann Shockley. BA, Fisk U., 1948; MSL.S., Case Western Reserve U., 1959. Asst. librarian Del. State Coll., Dover, 1959-60; asst. librarian U. Md. Eastern Shore, Princess Anne, 1960-66, assoc. librarian, 1966-69, Fisk U., Nashville, 1969-98. Author: (novels) Loving Her, 1974, Say Jesus and Come to Me, 1982, (short stories) The Black & White of It, 1980, (with E. J. Josey) Handbook of Black Librarianship, 1977, (with Sue P. Chandler) Living Black American Authors, 1973; editor: (anthology) Afro-American Women Writers 1746-1933, 1988 (Susan Koppelman Award 1989). Recipient Hatshepsut Award for Lit., N.Y., 1981, Martin Luther King Jr. Black Author award, Nashville, 1982. Mem. Authors Guild (Tenn. archivists), ALA (Black Caucus, Black Caucus award for editing caucus newsletter 1975, Black Caucus award for Extraordinary Achievement in Profl. Activities, 1992). Home: 5975 Post Rd Nashville TN 37205-3232

SHOCKLEY, EDWARD JULIAN, retired aerospace company executive; b. Augusta, Ga., Oct. 31, 1924; s. Julian P. and Margaret (Epps) S.; m. Dorothy Elizabeth Holley, Nov. 24, 1945; children: Edward J., Steven Holley. B.Aero. Engring., Ga. Inst. Tech., 1950; postgrad. (Sloan fellow), Stanford U. Grad. Sch. Bus., 1962-63. Flight test engr. Douglas Aircraft Co., 1950-53; with Lockheed-Ga. Co., 1953-80, dir. quality and safety, 1965-74, dir. mktg., 1974-78, v.p., 1978-80; pres. Lockheed Aircraft Service Co. div. Lockheed Corp., Burbank, Calif., 1980-86, sr. advisor to pres., 1986-87, ret., 1987; pres. Millimeter Wave Tech., Inc., Marietta, Ga., 1988-90, vice chmn. bd. dirs., 1991-92; ret., 1992. Dir. Aerosurge Mgmt. Cons., 1991-92; pres. Lockheed-Ga. Fed. Credit Union, 1971-74 Mem. bus. adv. coun. Ga. So. U.; mem. adv. coun. Sch. Bus. and Econs., Coll. of Charleston. Served with USN, 1941-46. Mem. Cherokee Town and Country Club. Republican. Methodist. E-mail: eshock@charter.net.

SHOCKLEY, JAMES JAY, elementary school administrator, choir director; b. Amarillo, Tex., Dec. 2, 1952; s. Warren Frederick Shockley and Margaret Agnes (Merriss) Shockley; m. Betty Jo Whitlow; children: Jaime (Shockley) Foland, Allyson (Shockley) Keo, Rachel. MS in Edn., Portland State U., 1990; BA in Music Performance, Columbia Christian Coll., Portland, OR, 1978. Prin., music tchr. Ophir Elem. Sch. Dist., Oreg., 1983—97; asst. prin., choral music tchr. Ctrl. Curry Sch. Dist., Gold Beach, 1997—2002. Bd. dirs., project chair Kiwanis Club of Gold Beach, 1997—2002; deacon Gold Beach Ch. of Christ, 1979—2002. Mem.: Am. Choral Dir.'s Assn., Oreg. Music Educator's Assn., Music Educators Nat. Conf., ASCD. Conservative. Mem. Ch. Christ. Avocation: golf, woodworking, singing, webpage design, stained glass. Home: 94242 7th St. Gold Beach OR 97444 Office: Riley Creek Elem Sch 94350 6th St Gold Beach OR 97444 Office Fax: 541-247-6484. Business E-Mail: jshockley@ccsd.k12.or.us.

SHOCKLEY, MILTON M., JR. real estate brokerage executive; b. Greenville, S.C., Jan. 1, 1954; s. Milton M. and Bea W. Shockley; m. Laraine Davis, June 16, 1979; children: Ashley, Carrie, Megan. AD, North Greenville Coll., Tigerville, S.C., 1974; student, Furman U., 1976. Cert. residential specialist; cert. residential broker; grad. Realator Inst. Pres. Merrill Lynch/C. Dan Joyner, Greenville, 1972-79; founder, pres. M. Shockley Builders, 1980; pres. Milton Shockley Co., Inc., 1986—; prin. Young Concrete Co., Inc., 1986—, SYS Assocs., Greenville, 1987—; pres. Century 21 Shockley Youngblood, Inc., 1987—. Bd. dirs. YMCA, Greenville, Goodwill Industries, 1986-89; mem. adv. bd. Greenville Tech. Coll. Named Realtor of Yr., Greenville Bd. Realtors, 1987, Realtor of Yr., Greenville Assn. Realtors, 1996. Mem. Commerce Club (pres. 1987), Greenville Rotary (legis. chair 1991, state treas. 1990, chair young life com. 1981-85), Thornblade Club, Million Dollar Club (life; sec. 1987), New Bus. Breakfast Club, Metro Civitan Club (past pres.). Avocations: skiing, water skiing, hunting, fishing, golf. Home: 212 Kilgore Cir Simpsonville SC 29681-4834 Office: Century 21/Shockley Youngblood PO Box 26537 333 Wade Hampton Blvd Greenville SC 29609-5738

SHOECRAFT, TIM HENRY, tax minimization strategist; b. Syracuse, N.Y., June 27, 1949; s. Byron Henry and Frances Genevive S.; m. Marianne T. Shoecraft, Aug. 15, 1982; children: Alison, Kellyn, Austin. BA, State U. N.Y., 1973; MBA, PhD, Columbia State U., 1997. Pres. Shoecraft & Assocs., Oswego, N.Y., 1976-80, Profl. Fin. Svcs., Bedford, 1980-98, chmn., CEO, 1998—. Spkr. in field; cons. to nat. law firms. Ave. chmn. Rotary, Oswego, N.Y., 1976-80; troop leader Boy Scouts Am., 1970-73. Mem. Internat. Forum, Internat. Assn. Fin. Planners, Top of Table, Million Dollar Round Table, Mensa, Assn. Advanced Life Underwriters. Republican. Office: Profl Fin Svcs LLC 762 N Bedford Rd Bedford NY 10507

SHOEMAKER, CAMERON DAVID JAMES, dean, educator; b. Honolulu, Dec. 15, 1940; s. John James and Belle Bird (Kellogg) S.; m. Catherine LaMoyne Prevost, May 23, 1966 (div. 1969); 1 child, David James; m. Leona

Martha Wohlwend, May 18, 1972; 1 child, Jennifer Lee. BA in Polit. Sci., The Citadel, 1963; MA in History, San Jose State U., 1973; EdD, U. San Francisco, 1990. Commd. 2d lt. U.S. Army, 1963, advanced through grades to maj., 1971, fgn. area officer U.S., Korea, Germany and Vietnam, 1972-84, ret., 1984; fin. cons. Merrill Lynch, Carmel, Calif., 1984-85; mgmt. analyst Def. Lang. Inst., Monterey, 1985, ednl. tech. project mgr., 1985-86, dir. info. resources mgmt., 1986-90; evening coll. adminstr., instnl. researcher Monterey Peninsula Coll., 1990-92; dean of bus. Sacramento (Calif.) City Coll., 1992-98; dean Vista Coll., Berkeley, Calif., 1999-2000; dir. ednl. svcs. Heald Coll., Roseville, 2000—01; project mgr. Little Hoover Commn. on Calif. State Govt. and Economy, 2002—. Instr., Chapman Coll., Monterey, 1982-84, Monterey Inst., 1987; chmn. Asian Employment Program Com., Monterey, 1983-84; guest lectr., Naval Postgrad. Sch., Monterey, 1986-87; mem. Handicapped Individual Program Com., Monterey, 1986-90, treas., 1989-90. Contbr. articles to various publs. Pres., Creekside Community Assn., Salinas, Calif., 1985-86; mem. County Svc. Area Adv. Bd., Salinas, 1985-87, Flood Control Dist. Planning Com., Salinas, 1986-87; active Leadership Monterey Peninsula, grad., 1992. Decorated Silver Star medal; recipient Comdrs. award for Civilian Svc. Dept. of Army, 1990; Carl D. Perkins fellow, 1993. Mem. Chief Instnl. Officers Calif. Cmty. Colls., Royal Asiatic Soc., Monterey Peninsula Scottish Soc. (treas. 1986-92), Los Rios Mgmt. Assn. (pres. 1995-96), Caledonian Club of Sacramento (treas. 1994-97, chief 1997-99). Republican. Roman Catholic. Home: 11577 Melones Cir Gold River CA 95670-7738 Office: Little Hoover Commn 925 L St Ste 805 Sacramento CA 95814 *Personal philosophy: Always do what is right, regardless of the personal cost.*

SHOEMAKER, CAROLYN SPELLMANN, planetary astronomer; b. Gallup, N.Mex., June 24, 1929; d. Leonard Robert and Hazel Adele (Arthur) Spellmann; m. Eugene Merle Shoemaker, Aug. 18, 1951 (dec. July 1997); children: Christine Shoemaker Abanto, Patrick Gene, Linda Shoemaker Salazar. BA cum laude, Chico State Coll., 1949, MA, 1950; ScD (hon.), No. Ariz. U., 1990. Vis. scientist Br. astrogeology U.S. Geol. Survey, Flagstaff, Ariz., 1980—; rsch. asst. Calif. Inst. Tech., Pasadena, 1981-85; rsch. prof. astronomy No. Ariz. U., Flagstaff, 1989—; mem. staff Lowell Obs., 1993—. Guest observer Palomar Obs., Palomar Mountain, Calif., 1982-94; Ruth Northcott Meml. lectrs. R.A.S.C., 1995; co-McGovern lectr. Cosmos Club Found., 1995. Co-recipient Rittenhouse medal Rittenhouse Astron. Soc., 1988, Scientist of Yr. award ARCS Found., 1995, James C. Watson medal NAS, 1998; recipient Woman of Distinction award Soroptimists, 1994, 20th Anniversary Internat. Women's Yr. award Zonta and 99s, 1995, NASA Exceptional Scientific Achievement medal, 1996, Woman of Distinction award Nat. Assn. Women in Edn., 1996, Shoemaker award Am. Inst. Profl. Geologists, 1997, plaque Internat. Forest Friendship, Atchison, Kans., 1997, Robert Burnham Jr. award Western Regional Astron. League, 2000; named Disting. Alumna of the Calif. State U., Chico, 1996. Fellow Am. Acad. Arts and Scis.; mem. AAAS, Astron. Soc. of Pacific, Am. Geophys. Union, Meteoritical Soc. Achievements include discovery of 32 comets including Periodic Comet Shoemaker-Levy 9 which impacted Jupiter in July 1994, more than 500 asteroids including 44 Earth approachers and approximately 68 Mars crossers, meteorites at Veevers Crater, Australia and impactites at Wolfe Creek Crater, Australia. Home: 5231 Hidden Hollow Rd Flagstaff AZ 86001-3821 Office: Lowell Obs 1400 W Mars Hill Rd Flagstaff AZ 86001-4499

SHOEMAKER, CLARA BRINK, retired chemistry educator; b. Rolde, Drenthe, The Netherlands, June 20, 1921; came to U.S., 1953; d. Hendrik Gerard and Hendrikje (Smilde) Brink; m. David Powell Shoemaker, Aug. 5, 1955; 1 child, Robert Brink. PhD, Leiden U., The Netherlands, 1950. Instr. in inorganic chemistry Leiden U., 1946-50, 51-53; postdoctoral fellow Oxford (Eng.) U., 1950-51; rsch. assoc. dept. chemistry MIT, Cambridge, 1953-55, 58-70; rsch. assoc. biochemistry Harvard Med. Sch., Boston, 1955-56; project supr. Boston U., 1963-64; rsch. assoc. dept. chemistry Oreg. State U, Corvallis, 1970-75, rsch. assoc. prof. dept. chemistry, 1975-82, sr. rsch. prof. dept. chemistry, 1982-84, prof. emerita, 1984—. Sect. editor: Structure Reports of International Union of Crystallography, 1967, 68, 69; co-author chpts. in books; author numerous sci. papers. Bd. dirs. LWV, Corvallis, 1980-82, bd. dirs., sec., Oreg., 1985-87. Fellow Internat. Fedn. Univ. Women, Oxford U., 1950-51. Mem. Metall. Soc. (com. on alloy phases 1969-79), Internat. Union of Crystallography (commn. on structure reports 1970-90), Am. Crystallographic Assn. (crystallographic data com. 1975-78, Fankuchen award com. 1976), Sigma Xi, Iota Sigma Pi (faculty adv. Oreg. State U. chpt. 1975-84), Phi Lambda Upsilon. Avocation: outdoor activities. Office: Dept Chemistry Oreg State U Corvallis OR 97331

SHOEMAKER, DANIEL WEYBRIGHT, lawyer; b. Harrisburg, Pa., Mar. 20, 1931; s. Norville Eugene and Victoria S.; m. Eleanor Boggs, Apr. 9, 1955 (div. 1987); children: Daniel W., William B.; m. Suzanne Leapley, July 3, 1987. BS, Millersville U., Pa., 1952; JD, George Washington U., D.C., 1956. Bar: D.C. 1956, U.S. Ct. Appeals (3rd cir.) 1956, Pa. 1957. Dist. atty. York County, Pa., 1962-65; pvt. practice law York, 1989—. Del. Pa. State Constl. Conv., 1976. With U.S. Army, 1949-52. Mem. York County Bar Assn. (pres. 1976), Pa. Bar Assn. (del. 978-88). Republican. Episcopalian. Avocations: fox hunting, farming, sailing, bridge. Home: 326 St George Ct Bermuda Club East Venice FL 34293 E-mail: dwshoe@aol.com.

SHOEMAKER, DOROTHY HAYS, technical writer; b. L.A., Nov. 4, 1959; d. David Glenn and Marguerite (Thompson) Hays; m. Lon Lawrence Shoemaker, Mar. 30, 1996. Student, Reed Coll., 1976-79; BA, Mills Coll., 1987; tech. writing cert., IBM, 1993. Tech. writer Mills C.C.M., Oakland, Calif., 1987; tchg. asst. Mills Coll., 1986-87; tech. sec. Hewlett-Packard, Palo Alto, Calif., 1988; tech. writer Cadre Techs., Saratoga, 1989-90, IBM R&D, San Jose, 1990-93, ret. Writer, editor: (tech. manuals) Programmer's Guides, 1987-93. Mem. Bay Area Action, Palo Alto, 1991—2000, trustee, 1995—98; mem. Portlanr Harbor Cmty. Adv. Group. Avocations: teaching and playing piano, computer programming, writing poetry. Home: 3652 SW Spring Garden St Portland OR 97219

SHOEMAKER, ELEANOR BOGGS, television production company executive; b. Gulfport, Miss., Jan. 20, 1935; d. William Robertson and Bessie Eleanor (Ware) Boggs; m. D. Shoemaker, April 9, 1955 (div. 1987); children: Daniel W. III, William Boggs. Student in protocol, Southeastern U., 1952-53; student, George Washington U., Washington, 1953-56; BA in Communications and Polit. Sci. with honrs, Goucher Coll., 1981; postgrad., Villanova U. Feature writer Washington Times Herald, 1951-54; dir. Patricia Stevens Modeling Agy., Washington, 1955-56; free-lance model Julius Garfinkel, Woodward & Lothrop, 1951-56; research analyst Balt. County Council, Towson, Md., 1980-81; feature news reporter Sta. WGCB-TV, Red Lion, Pa., 1980-99; pub. speaker, protocol The Reliable Corp., Columbia, Md., 1982-86; media cons. The Enterprise Found., 1985-86; faculty, TV prodn. and communication St. Francis Prep Sch., Spring Grove, Pa., 1985-88; owner Windswept Prodns. Co., Felton, 1984—; mktg. svcs. coord. Yorktowne, Inc., Red Lion, 1993-95. Mem. conservation bd. Pa. Parks and Recreation Soc., 1984—; prodr. The Pa. County TV Prodn., 1981; prodr., host Westar 4 Channel 9 half hour weekly news program Keystone Report. Prodr. The Pa. County TV Prodn., 1981, The Pa. County TV Prodn., 1981, documentary Human Rights: A Special Report, Sta. WGCB-TV, 1989; prodr., host Westar 4 Channel 9 half hour weekly news program Keystone Report, 1990. Bd. dirs. York (Pa.) County Parks and Recreation, 1972-87, YWCA, York, 1957-82, Hist. York, 1990—; mem. exec. com. York County Reps., 1972-82; accreditation adv. com. York Coll. of Pa.; instr. YWCA Women in Politics; founder, mem. Child Abuse Task Force, York, 1983—; mem. select com. Pa. Agrl. Zoning, 1988; mem. steering com. York Forum, 1989-96; co-chmn. Cross Mill Restoration, 1987—; mem. Displaced Homemaker's Bd., 1989—, pres., 1993—; bd. dirs. Hist. York, 1990-95; founder, host Old Rose Tree Pony Club, 1967—; chmn. camp com. U.S. Pony Club Inc., 1973-75; chair Spring Valley County Pk. Task Force, 1972; master of fox hounds Mrs. Shoemaker's Hounds, 1969—; master of beagles Mrs. Shoemaker's Weybright Beagles, 1988-96; edn. chair Jr. League of York, 1962-70. Recipient pro bono child legal representation grant Pa. Bar Assn., 1983, Pa. Tree Farmer of Yr. award, 1987, Outstanding Achievement in Broadcasting award Am. Women in Radio and TV, 1992, Lay Person of Yr. award Pa. Recreation and Parks Assn. and Gov. Thornburg, 1982, Jefferson award nominee, 1992, Matrix award Ctrl. Pa. Women in Comm., 1993, First pl. corp. video prodn. Ctrl. Pa. Women in Comm., 1993, Agrl. award C. of C., Cross Mill Restoration, 1999, Albright Care Found. Outstanding Vol. award, Ridge, Normandie, 1999, Daughters of Am. Revolution Outstanding Achievement award in preservation Nat. Resources, 2000, Game Commn. Recognition award farm game program, 2000, Albright Care Founders award; selected journalist for Novosti Press USSR-U.S. Press Exch. program, 1989. Mem. Am. Polled Hereford Assn., York Area C. of C., York County C. of C. (publicity com. 1985-90, agri. bus. com.), Masters of Foxhounds Assn. Episcopalian. Avocation: foxhunting, beagling. Home and Office: PO Box 167 Felton PA 17322-0167

SHOEMAKER, FRANK CRAWFORD, physicist, educator; b. Ogden, Utah, Mar. 26, 1922; s. Roy Hopkins and Sarah Parker (Anderson) S.; m. Ruth Elizabeth Nelson, July 11, 1944; children— Barbara Elaine, Mary Frances. AB, Whitman Coll., 1943, D.Sc. (hon.), 1978; PhD, U. Wis., 1949. Staff mem. Radiation Lab. MIT, 1943-45; instr. physics U. Wis., 1949-50; mem. faculty Princeton U., 1950-89, prof. physics, 1962-89, emeritus, 1989—; assoc. dir. Princeton U. Pa. Accelerator, 1962-66. Vis. scientist Rutherford High Energy Lab., 1965-66; main accelerator sect. head Nat. Accelerator Lab., 1968-69; prin. investigator Dept. of Energy High Energy Physics Contract, 1972-85. Co-author proposal for 3 billion electron volt Princeton-Pa. Accelerator, 1955. Fellow Am. Phys. Soc.; mem. Phi Beta Kappa, Sigma Xi Home: 49 Meadow Lakes 03 Hightstown NJ 08520-3351 E-mail: frankcs@princeton.edu.

SHOEMAKER, HAROLD LLOYD, infosystem specialist; b. Danville, Ky., Jan. 3, 1923; s. Eugene Clay and Amy (Wilson) S.; m. Dorothy M. Maddox, May 11, 1947 (dec. Feb. 1991). AB, Berea Coll., 1944; postgrad., State U. Ia., 1943-44, George Washington U., 1949-50, NYU, 1950-52. Rsch. physicist State U. Iowa, 1944-45, Frankford Arsenal, Pa., 1945-47; rsch. engr. N.Am. Aviation, L.A., 1947-49, Jacobs Instrument Co., Bethesda, 1949-50; assoc. head systems devel. group The Telerigister Corp., N.Y.C., 1950-53; mgr. electronic equipment devel. sect., head planning Hughes Aircraft Co., L.A., 1953-58; dir. command and control systems lab. Bunker-Ramo Corp., 1958-68; v.p. Data Systems, 1968-69, corp. dir. data processing, 1969-75; tech. staff R & D Assocs., Marina Del Rey, Calif., 1975-85; info. systems cons., 1985—. Patentee elec. digital computer. Served with AUS, 1945-46. Mem. IEEE, Ky. Cols. Home: PO Box 3385 Granada Hills CA 91394-0385 E-mail: haroldshoe@cs.com.

SHOEMAKER, HELEN E. MARTIN ACHOR, civic worker; b. Houston, Mar. 24, 1915; d. Earl L. and Blanche L. (Williams) Martin; m. Harold E. Achor, Oct. 11, 1935; children: Dianne Achor Johnston, Lana Achor Wolfe; m. Robert N. Shoemaker, May 19, 1972. AB, Anderson (Ind.) Coll., 1960, LLD, 1978. Resident dir. Anderson Coll., 1967-69, dir. alumni svcs., 1969-72; legis. counsel Ind. Colls. and Univ. Ind., 1970-72; spl. asst. Ctr. Pub. Svc., Anderson, 1973-77, spl. asst. to dean for acad. devel., 1977-78. Sec.-treas. Ind. State Libr. and Hist. Bldg. Expansion Commn., 1973-78; mem. com. region VII, Girl Scouts U.S.A., 1958-66; adv. coun. fin. aid to students Office Edn. HEW, 1976-78; mem. Ind. Ho. of Reps. from Madison County, 1968-70; v.p. Ind. Fedn. Women's Rep. Clubs, 1945-46; treas. Nat. Fedn. Women's Rep. Clubs, 1947-51; Rep. precinct vice chmn. Madison County, 1946-68, vice chmn., Anderson, 1967-68; bd. dirs. Urban League Madison County, 1969-76; adv. com. Georgetown U. Grad. Sch. Acad. in Pub. Svc., 1976-83; mem. adv. com. on sex discrimination Ind. Civil Rights Commn., 1978-83; bd. dirs. Anderson Symphony Orch. Women's Guild, 1987, hon. mem.; trustee Anderson Coll., 1978-85; bd. dirs. Opportunities Industrialization Ctr., Inc., Madison County, 1980-84, Ind. Acad. Pub. Svc., 1981-83, Women's Alternatives Inc., Anderson, 1982-93 (Elizabeth Howard McMahan award 1987); mem. exec. com. devel. bd. St. John's Med. Ctr., Anderson, 1981-92; bd. dirs. life enrichment Park Place Ch. God, 1989-94; bd. dirs. Anderson Symphony Womens Guild. Recipient William B. Harper award Urban League Madison County, 1975; named Sagamore of Wabash, State of Ind., 1979. Mem. LWV (dir. Madison County 1973-76, 78-84, 87), Anderson Coun. Women, Anderson Fine Arts Ctr. (treas.). Mem. Ch. of God. Home: 5801 W Bethel Ave Muncie IN 47304-9549

SHOEMAKER, INNIS HOWE, art museum curator; b. Reading, Pa. d. William Erety and Jean (Miller) S. AB, Vassar Coll., 1964; MA, Columbia U., 1968, PhD, 1975. Curator Vassar Coll. Art. Gallery, Poughkeepsie, N.Y., 1965-68, 73-76; asst. dir. Ackland Art Mus., U. N.C., Chapel Hill, 1976-82, dir., 1983-86; Audrey and William H. Helfand sr. curator prints, drawings and photographs Phila. Mus. Art, 1986—; adj. prof. U. Pa., 2001—. Fellow in art history Am. Acad. in Rome, 1971-73; adj. prof. U. N.C., Chapel Hill, 1983-86. Co-author: The Engravings of Marcantonio Raimondi, 1981, Paul Cézanne: Two Sketchbooks, 1989; author: Mad for Modernism: Earl Horter and His Collection, 1999, Jacques Villon and his Cubist Prints, 2001. Mem. vis. com. Lehman Loeb Art Ctr., Vassar Coll., 1993—; bd. advisors Ctr. for Advanced Studies in the Visual Arts, 2001—. Mem. Coll. Art Assn. Am., Am. Assn. Mus., Print Coun. Am. (bd. dirs. 1986-89). Office: Phila Mus Art PO Box 7646 Philadelphia PA 19101-7646

SHOEMAKER, MARJORIE PATTERSON, textbook editor, consultant; b. Cleve., Aug. 8, 1933; d. Franklin J. and Marjorie (Kennel) Patterson; children: Stephanie A. Veith, Timothy R. BS, Bowling Green (Ohio) State U., 1955, MA, 1968; postgrad., U. Pitts., 1972-74; PhD, Syracuse (N.Y.) U., 1980. Cert. supr. curriculum and instrn. Tchr. high sch. history/govt. Vanlue (Ohio) Schs., 1955-57; jr. high sch. tchr. history/govt./English tchr. Crestline (Ohio) Schs., 1963-65; elem. tchr. Galion (Ohio) City Schs., 1965-67; reading supr. Anthony Wayne Schs., Whitehouse, Ohio, 1968-70; instr. reading, ednl. psychology Heidelberg Coll., Tiffin, 1970-72; instr. reading Bowling Green (Ohio) State U., 1972-76; teaching fellow Syracuse U., 1976-79; reading cons. Macmillan Pub. Co., N.Y.C., 1980-88; editor Zaner-Bloser Ednl. Pub., Columbus, Ohio, 1988-90, sr. editor, 1990—, sr. curriculum editor, 1995, dir., 1995—. Cons. Ft. Wayne (Ind.) Schs., 1976-80, Las Cruces (N.Mex.) Schs., 1974-76; vis. prof. edn. N.Mex. State Coll., 1974, Ind.-Purdue U., 1976-80. Bd. trustees The Andrews Sch. for Girls, Willoughby, Ohio, 1978-81. Mem. Internat. Reading Assn. (editor newsletter 1974-76), Am. Soc. Curriculum and Devel., Edn. Press, Order Eastern Star.

SHOEMAKER, RICHARD L. retired physiologist; b. Cullman, Ala., Sept. 28, 1931; s. Edgar W. and Hester (Wisener) S.; children: Steven, Benjamin, William, Robert. MS, Auburn U., 1959; PhD, U. Ala., Tuscaloosa, 1967. Asst. prof. physiology U. Ala., Birmingham, 1967-72, assoc. prof., 1972-77, prof., 1977—. Cons. meteorologist Eastern Airlines, Atlanta, 1958-59. Office: U Ala Dept Physiology Uab Sta Birmingham AL 35294-0001

SHOEMAKER, ROBERT MORIN, retired army officer, county government official; b. Almont, Mich., Feb. 18, 1924; s. Uriah Beebe and Pomala (Morin) S.; m. Mary Alice Rickard, July 17, 1948. BS, U.S. Mil. Acad., 1946; postgrad., U.S. Army Command and Gen. Staff Coll., 1959, Army War Coll., 1967. Commd. 2d lt. U.S. Army, 1946, advanced through grades to gen., 1978, platoon leader, bn. staff officer, co. comdr. 18th Inf., Fed. Republic Germany, 1947-50, co. comdr., regtl. S2, S3, 23d Inf. Republic of Korea, 1953-54, staff officer inf. br. DA, 1954-56, student, faculty officer U.S. Army Aviation Sch. Ala., 1959-62, project officer Army Concept Team Vietnam, 1962-63, bn. comdr., asst. chief of staff, G-3, 11th Air Assault Div. Ga., 1963-65, bn. cmdr., squadron comdr. 1st Cav. Div., Vietnam, 1965-66, chief plans and programs Army Aviation DA, 1967-69, chief of staff, asst. div. comdr. 1st Cav. Vietnam, 1969-70, dep. comdr., chief. of staff III Corps and Ft. Hood, Tex., 1970, dept. comdr. MASSTER Tex., 1971-72, comdr. 1st Cav., 1973-75, comdr. III Corps, 1975-77, dep. comdr. FORSCOM Ft. McPherson, Ga., 1977-78; comdr. U.S. Army Forces Command, 1978-82; ret., 1982; county commr. Bell County, Tex., 1987-94. Decorated D.S.M., Silver Star medal with oak leaf cluster, Legion of Merit, D.F.C., Bronze Star, Air medal with 48 oak leaf clusters, Army Commendation medal with oak leaf cluster, Croix de Guerre (France), Gallantry Cross with palm (Republic of Vietnam), RVN Honor medal 1st class; Robert M. Shoemaker H.S., Killeen, Tex. named in his honor, Aug. 2001. Home: 111 Bluff Ln Belton TX 76513-9804

SHOEMAKER, SANDRA KAYE, aerospace executive; b. Dallas, July 13, 1954; d. Vondyl Claud and Billie Juanita (Pritchett) Willis; m. Carl Vernon Shoemaker, Aug. 16, 1975; children: Regan Amanda, Ryan Adam. BBA, Baylor U., 1975. Fin. coord. Tex. A&M U., College Station, 1975-77; from engrng. planner to mgr. adminstrv. support Gen. Dynamics Corp., Ft. Worth, 1977-90; dir. engrng. adminstrn. Lockheed Ft. Worth Co., 1990-94, dir. rsch. & engrng. svcs. & process support, 1994-96; dir. labs. and tech. support Lockheed Martin Tactical Aircraft Sys., 1996-97, dir. F-16 air vehicle, 1997-99, dir. and deputy ops. F-16 program, 1999-2000, dir. Aero Transition Team, 2000-01, dir. co. ops., 2001, v.p. integrated co. ops., 2001—. Republican. Baptist. Avocations: music, snow skiing, water skiing, racquetball, snorkeling and scuba diving. Home: 5100 Dewdrop Ln Fort Worth TX 76123-1931 Office: Lockheed Martin Tactical Aircraft Sys PO Box 748 Fort Worth TX 76101-0748

SHOEMAKER, SCOTT DAVID, network consultant, educator; b. Milw., Oct. 28, 1958; s. Alan Kent and Barbara Jean (Pepe) S.; m. Glenda Faye Coates, June 8, 1985; children: Brock, Paige, Leah. BA in Secondary Edn., Purdue U., West Lafayette, Ind., 1982; MEd, Ariz. State U., 1987; MS in Computer Sci. Edn., U. Evansville, Ind., 1988. Tchr. Monument Valley High Sch., Kayenta, Ariz., 1982-86; instr. computer sci. Grand Canyon U., Phoenix, 1986-90; systems analyst Bull NH Info. Systems, 1990-92; sr. network cons. Honeywell IAC, 1992—. Seminar instr. PCAI mag. Hands-On Seminars, Phoenix, 1985-90. Contbr. articles to profl. mags. Elder, Metro Presbyn. Ch., Glendale, Ariz., 1992—. Mem. Assn. Computing Machinery (sponsor student chpt. 1988-90). Republican. Presbyterian. Avocations: camping, hiking, photography. Home: 7843 W Topeka Dr Glendale AZ 85308-6134 Office: Ms Az15/le11 16404 N Black Canyon Hwy Phoenix AZ 85053-3033

SHOEMAKER, TROY, hazardous materials response team coordinator, firefighter; b. Alliance, Nebr., July 12, 1971; parent Freddie and Virginia Shoemaker. Cert. firefighter I 1992, apprentice fire protection specialist 1992, fire officer I 1995, airport firefighter 1995, hazardous materials technician 1997, advanced hazardous materials technician 1997, registered nat. emergency med. basic technician 2002. Damage controlman, firefighter USN, San Diego, 1989—94; sr. fire capt. Antarctic Support Assoc., Englewood, Colo., 1994—96; hazmat coord., firefighter Scottsbluff Fire Dept., Nebr., 1996—. Mem. Scotts Bluff County Local Emergency Planning Com., Nebr., 2002—, Nebr. Hazardous Materials Adv. Coun., Lincoln, 2000—. Contbr. articles. With USN, 1989—94. Mem.: Mo. Valley Assn. Fire Chiefs, Internat. Assn. Fire Chiefs. Office: Scottsbluff Fire Dept 1818 Ave A Scottsbluff NE 69361

SHOEMAKER, WILLIAM C. journalist; b. Simpson County, Miss., Nov. 19, 1931; s. William Ezra and Saleta (Roach) S.; m. Nell Slade, Apr. 12, 1957. Grad. high sch., Miss. Reporter Jackson (Miss.) Daily News, 1949-51, 54-65; editor, pub. The Star-Herald, Koscivsko, Miss., 1965-89; pres. Shoemaker Offset Inc., 1989—, Scott County Times, 1983-89, Simpson County News, 1983-87, Pontotoc Progress, 1985-89, Bulldog Pubs., 1983-90. Bd. dirs. Merchants and Farmers Bank. Chmn. Miss. Econ. Coun., 1996-97; chmn. Miss. svc. delivery area U.S. Job Tng. Partnership Act, 1983-95. With U.S. Army, 1951-54. Mem. Rotary. Independent. Office: PO Box 457 Kosciusko MS 39090-0457

SHOEMAKER, WILLIAM EDWARD, financial executive; b. Charleston, W.Va., Sept. 17, 1945; s. Robert Edward and Janet Elizabeth (Hoglund) S.; 1 child, Marcus. BBA, U. Notre Dame, 1967. Assoc. buyer Proctor & Gamble, Cin., 1971; gen. mgr. Eastwind Inc., Anchorage, 1972-73; pres., operator Golden Horn Lodge, Inc., Bristol Bay, Alaska, 1973-79; treas. Hawley Resource Group, Inc., Anchorage, 1979-88; treas., chief fin. officer Golden Zone Resources, Inc., Campbell, Calif., 1988-90; ptnr. Resort Mgmt. Corp., Anchorage, 1987-90; pres. Discovery Holdings, Inc., Ft. Lauderdale, Fla., 1991—. Bd. dirs. Pacific Art & Design Cons., Inc. Bd. dirs. Anchorage Econ. Devel. Corp., 1988-90, 4 Children's Sake, 1997—. Served to lt. (j.g.) USN, 1967-71. Republican. Avocations: boating, skiing, fishing. Home: 2301 Solar Plaza Dr Fort Lauderdale FL 33301-2601 Office: Discovery Holdings Inc Ste 120 2400 E Las Olas Blvd Fort Lauderdale FL 33301-1529 E-mail: weshoe@bellsouth.net.

SHOENBERGER, ALLEN EDWARD, law educator; b. Waynesburg, Pa., Sept. 18, 1944; s. Allen Edward and Evelyn S.; m. Cynthia Grant (div. 1975); 1 child, Michael Grant; m. Caroline Orzac, Aug. 3, 1980; 1 child, Elisa Orzac. BA with honors, Swarthmore Coll., 1966; JD with honors, Columbia U., 1969; LLM, NYU, 1972. Bar: Ill. 1973, U.S. Dist. Ct. (no. dist.) Ill. 1973, U.S. Ct. Appeals (7th cir.) 1977, U.S. Supreme Ct. 1977. Vis. lectr. U. Nairobi, Kenya, 1969-71; fellow Internat. Legal Ctr., Nairobi, 1969-71; asst. prof. Loyola U., Chgo., 1972-77, assoc. prof., 1977-85, prof., 1985—, chmn. faculty coun., 1983—. Cons. Adminstrv. Conf. U.S., Washington, 1988; mem. Ill. A.G. Task Force for Handicapped, 1982—; chmn. adv. bldg. com. Cir. Ct. of Cook County, Chgo., 1988-93. Editor Spina Bifida publ., 1985-93, East African Law Reports, 1969-71, Jour. Nat. Assn. Adminstrv. Law Judges, 1996—; contbr. articles to profl. publs. Mem. Ill. Spina Bifida Assn., Chgo., 1980-93; hearing officer Ill. Pollution Control Bd., 1974-97, U.S. Dept. Energy, Ill., 1984-89. Recipient various grants, including NIE, 1973; fellow Ford Found., 1972, NEH, 1987. Mem. ABA, Fed. Bar Assn., Chgo. Bar Assn. (chmn. adminstrv. law com. 1985-86). Office: Loyola Sch of Law 1 E Pearson St Chicago IL 60611-2055

SHOGAN, ROBERT, news correspondent; b. N.Y.C., Sept. 12, 1930; s. Albert and Millie (Jacobs) S.; m. Ellen Shrewsbury, May 26, 1959; children: Cynthia Diane, Amelia Ford. BA, Syracuse U., 1951; postgrad., U. Mich. Inst. Pub. Adminstrn., 1951, postgrad., 1952. Reporter Detroit Free Press, 1956-59; telegraph editor Miami (Fla.) News, 1959-61; asst. editor Wall St. Jour., N.Y.C., 1961-65; evaluation officer Peace Corps, Washington, 1965-66; corr. Newsweek, 1966-73; nation polit. corr. Los Angeles Times, 1973-99. Profl.-in-residence Annenberg Sch. Communication, U. Pa., 1993; adj. prof. Johns Hopkins U., Ctr. for Study of Am. Govt., Washington, 1999—. Author: Question of Judgement, 1972, Promises to Keep, 1977, None of the Above, 1982, The Riddle of Power, 1991, Hard Bargain, 1995, Fate of the Union, 1998, The Double-Edged Sword, 1998, Bad News, 2001, War Without End, 2002; co-author: (with Tom Craig) The Detroit Race Riot, 1964. Served with U.S. Army, 1952-54. Recipient 1st prize Feature Writing, Mich. AP, 1959, Disting. Reporting Pub. Affairs award Am. Polit. Sci. Assn., 1969, Scribes Book award, 1972; rsch. grantee Harry S Truman Presdl. Libr., 1989, Lyndon B. Johnson Presdl. Libr., 1989, Gerald R. Ford Presdl. Libr., 1989; McCormick fellow Hoover Presdl. Libr., 1993; fellow Media Studies Ctr., 1998. Mem. Phi Beta Kappa Home: 3513 Raymond St Chevy Chase MD 20815-3227

SHOHEN, SAUNDRA ANNE, health care communications and public relations executive; b. Washington, Aug. 22, 1934; d. Aaron Kohn and Malvina (Kleiman) Kohn Blinder; children: Susan, Brian. BS, Columbia Pacific U., 1979, MS in Health Svcs. Adminstrn., 1981. Adminstr. social work dept. Roosevelt Hosp., N.Y.C., 1978-79; adminstr. emergency dept. St. Luke's-Roosevelt Hosp. Ctr., 1979-83, assoc. dir. pub. rels., 1983-87; pres. Saundra Shohen Assocs., Ltd., 1987-92; v.p. Prism Internat., 1988-91; bd. dirs. Tureck Bach Inst., 1985—. Panelist ann. Emmy awards NATAS, N.Y.C., 1983, 84; tchr. healthcare mktg. Baruch Coll., N.Y.C., 1994. Author: Health Scripts for Radio, 1983, Voice of America, 1983 (Presdl. Recognition award, 1984); author: (with others) AIDS: A Health Care Management Response, 1987; author: EMERGENCY!, 1989. Mem. NATAS, Internat. Hosp. Fedn., Am. Soc. Hosp. Mktg. and Pub. Rels., Vols. in Tech. Assistance. Democrat. Jewish. Home: 240 Central Park S New York NY 10019-1413

SHOHET, JACK A. otolaryngologist; BS in Chemistry, U. Cin., 1986, MD, 1990. Resident in otolaryngology-head and neck surgery Vanderbilt U., Nashville, 1996; fellow in neurotology/skull base surgery Ear Found., Michael E. Glasscock, III, 1996; dir. neurotology/skull base surgery U. Calif.-Irvine Med. Ctr., Orange, 1997—, dir. residency program otolaryngology-head and neck surgery. Office: Dept Head and Neck Surgery 101 City Dr S # 25 Orange CA 92868-3201 also: 361 Hospital Rd Ste 327 Newport Beach CA 92663-3521 Fax: 949-631-2030. E-mail: jshohet@uci.edu.

SHOICHET, MOLLY, science educator; Founder matRegen, BoneTec Corp.; assoc. prof. chem. engring. and applied chemistry dept. chemistry U. Toronto; assoc. prof. Inst. Biomaterials and Biomed. Engring., U. Toronto. Spkr. in field. Office: Dept Chem Engring Applied Chem Rosebrugh Bldg U Toronto 4 Taddle Creek Rd Ste 407 Toronto ON Canada M5S 3G9*

SHOJI, HIROMU, orthopedic surgeon, educator; b. Chiba-Ken, Japan; Grad., Coll. Gen. Edn., 1959, U. Tokyo, Faculty Medicine, 1964. Diplomate Am. Bd. Orthopedic Surgery (examiner). Intern U. Tokyo Hosp., 1964-65, resident, 1965-67, Bklyn. Cumberland Med. Ctr., 1967-68, NYU Med. Ctr., 1968-69; bone tumor clin. fellow Meml. Sloan-Kettering Med. Ctr., N.Y.C., 1969-70; orthopedic fellow Hosp. Spl. Surgery, 1970-72; resident Bowman Gray Med. Sch., Winston-Salem, N.C., 1973-74; orthopedic surgeon pvt.

practice, Sacramento, 1974-76, New Orleans, 1976-90, Riverside, Calif., 1990—. Mem. staff Parkview Hosp., Riverside Comty. Hosp., Corona Regional Hosp.; asst. prof. dept. orthopedic surgery U. Calif., Davis, 1974-76; assoc. prof. dept. orthopedic surgery La. State U. Med. Ctr., 1976-80, prof., 1980-90; clin. prof. Loma Linda U., 1990—. Contbr. numerous articles to profl. jours. Bone tumor clin. fellow Meml. Sloan-Kettering Med. Ctr., N.Y.C., 1966-70, orthopedic fellow Hosp. Spl. Surgery, N.Y.C., 1971-72. Mem. AMA, NAS, Am. Acad. Orthopaedic Surgeons, Am. Assn. Hip and Knee Surgeons, Japanese Orthopedic Assn., Orthopedic Rsch. Soc., Japanese Soc. Connective Tissue Rsch., Japanese Rehab. Assn., Am. Orthopedic Assn., So. Med. Assn., Am. Rheumatism Assn., Calif. Orthopedic Assn., Internat. Soc. Orthopedics and Traumatology, Knee Soc., Internat. Soc. Knee Surgery. Office: 3838 Sherman Dr Riverside CA 92503-4001 E-mail: hiros65@aol.com.

SHOJI, JUNE MIDORI, import and export trading executive; b. Long Beach, Calif., June 21, 1957; d. Sam Masatsugu and Tomiyo (Kinoshita) S. BA in Psychology and Econs., UCLA, 1975-79; cert. Japanese, Waseda U., Tokyo, 1980-82; Grad. Gemologist, Gemol. Inst., Santa Monica, Calif., 1984. Mktg. rep. IBM Corp., L.A., 1982-84, Xerox Corp., El Monte, Calif., 1984-86; adminstrv. drilling analyst Arco Internat. Oil & Gas, L.A., 1986-89; asst. mgr. OEM components machinery and precious metals Honda Trading Am., Torrance, Calif., 1989-98; asst. mgr. CKD Parts and Ops., 1998-99, sr. asst. mgr. indsl. materials, 1999—. Home: 5959 E Naples Plz Long Beach CA 90803-5064

SHOKEIR, MARC OMAR, pathologist; b. Saskatoon, Sask., Can., Sept. 3, 1969; s. Mohamed H.K. and Donna J. (Nugent) S.; m. Cheryl Marie Dudar, June 19, 1992; children: Peter J., John G., Philip C., Emma A. MD with great distinction, U. Sask., 1991. Diplomate in anat. and clin. pathology Am. Bd. Pathology; cert. in gen. pathology Royal Coll. Phys. and Surg. Can. Intern Greater Victoria (B.C.) Hosp. Soc., 1991-92; resident in pathology U. B.C., Vancouver, 1992-96, chief resident, 1994-95; pathologist St. Joseph Hosp., Bellingham, Wash., 1996—, chair dept. pathology, 1997—; clin. instr. U. B.C., Vancouver, 1997—; pathologist St. Paul's Hosp., Vanvouver, 1997. Negotiator Profl. Assn. Interns and Residents of B.C., 1993-94, bd. dirs., 1993-94; internal reviewer cardiology residency program U. B.C., 1994, hematology residency program, 1994, examiner objective structured clin. exam., 1995, lectr., 1994—. Contbr. articles and abstracts to profl. jours. Recipient numerous undergrad. and med. sch. awards; Med. Coun. of Can. grantee, 1987, Boots Pharms. Ltd. grantee, 1994. Fellow Royal Coll. Physicians and Surgeons of Can., Coll. Am. Pathologists (ins. 1996—), Can. Assn. Pathologists (exec. com. sect. of anat. pathology 1994-96), Am. Soc. Clin. Pathologists (resident liaison 1994-96), Internat. Acad. Pathology, Wash. State Soc. Pathology, Pacific N.W. Soc. Pathologists, Wash. Med. Assn., Whatcom County Med. Soc. Office: Northwest Reg Pathologists Inc 2901 Squalicum Pkwy Bellingham WA 98225-1851 E-mail: mshokeir@peacehealth.org.

SHOKEIR, MOHAMED HASSAN KAMEL, medical geneticist, educator; b. Mansoura, Egypt, July 2, 1938; emigrated to Can., 1969, naturalized, 1974; s. Hassan Sayed and Lolia Nora (Kira) S.; m. Donna Jean Nugent, Feb. 27, 1968; children: Marc Omar, Vanessa May. MB, BChir, Cairo U., 1960, D in Surgery, 1963, D in Surgery in Orthop., 1964; MS, U. Mich., 1965, PhD, 1969. Intern Cairo U. Hosps., 1960-61, resident, 1961-64; Fulbright rsch. scholar dept. human genetics U. Mich., 1964-69; asst. prof. pediat. U. Sask., Saskatoon, Can., 1969-71, assoc. prof. Can., 1971-73, prof. Can., 1977—, dir. divsn. med. genetics Can., 1975-97, head dept. pediat. Can., 1979-96, Saskatoon Dist. Health Bd., 1993-96. Head sect. clin. genetics U. Man., Winnipeg, Can., 1973-75; mem. staffs Univ. Hosp., Saskatoon City Hosp., St. Paul's Hosp.; cons. Winnipeg Health Scis. Ctr., Regina Gen. Hosp. Contbr. articles to profl publs. Mem. Acad. Freedom and Tenure Com., Ottawa, Ont., Can., 1980-90, Queen Elizabeth II scientist, 1969-75. Med. Rsch. Coun. grantee, 1970-79; Can. Coll. Med. Geneticists Found. fellow, 1975— Fellow Can. Coll. Med. Geneticists, Can. Soc. Clin. Investigation (councillor 1974-76), Can. Med. Assn. (chmn., mem. adv. com. 1987-96); mem. APHA, Assn. Med. Sch. Pediat. Dept. Chairmen, Assn. Can. Univ. Dept. Chairmen, Am. Pediat. Soc., Soc. Pediat. Rsch., N.Y. Acad. Scis., Am. Geriat. Soc., Am. Fedn. Clin. Rsch., Mid-Western Soc. Pediat. Rsch., Western Pediat. Soc., Am. Soc. Human Genetics, Genetics Soc. Am., Genetics Soc. Can., Am. Genetic Assn. Home: 108 Riel Crescent Saskatoon SK Canada S7J 2W6 Office: U Sask Dept Pediatrics Saskatoon SK Canada S7N 0W8 E-mail: mshokeir@home.com. *Never tried to imagine what the future will bring, found the present and its implications enough to occupy me. The overriding passions in my life have been the love of man and the pity for his suffering. I have come to accept the futility of eliminating bias, even prejudice— mine or others'; my hope now is to recognize it and shield one's actions from it. What the world needs is more tolerance. Always found praise a bit embarrassing, confusing and altogether inhibiting— the most lavish for the least deserved accomplishment. Always thought the world is, at best, approximate. I now realize that in life one cannot have all bases covered.*

SHOKROLLAHI, MOHAMMAD AMIN, research scientist; b. Tehran, Iran, Mar. 21, 1964; s. Hasan Shokrollahi and Fatemeh Shokranian; m. Dorothe Doerholt, May 11, 1998. PhD, U. Bonn, Germany, 1991; degree in Math. and Computer Sci., U. Bonn, Germany, 1997. Mem. tech. staff Bell Lab., Lucent Tech., Murray Hill, NJ, 1998—2000; chief scientist Digital Fountain, Fremont, Calif., 2000—. Grantee, Deutsche Forschungsgemeinschaft, Germany, 1996—97. Mem.: IEEE. Office: Digital Fountain 39141 Civic Ctr Dr Fremont CA 94538 Office Fax: 510-284-1499. E-mail: amin@digitalfountain.com.

SHOL, KIM DURAND, accountant, computer programmer; b. Fergus Falls, Minn., Oct. 19, 1955; s. Robert Walter and Doris Ruby (Wahl) S.; m. Cheryl Renee Casmey, Sept. 18, 1992; children: Heidi Renee and Heather Kay (twins). AAS in Bus. Computer Systems, U. Minn., crookston, 1988. Program asst. Northwestern Apts., Crookston, 1982-86; jr. programmer U. Minn., 1988-90; acctg. technician Northwestern Mental Health Ctr., Inc., 1991—. Mem. computer adv. com. U. Minn., Crookston, 1989-90. Mpls. Tribune scholar, 1970. Mem. N.Y. Acad. Scis. Lutheran. Avocations: studying history and religion, painting still life and landscapes, collecting music. Office: Northwestern Mental Health Ctr 603 Bruce St Crookston MN 56716-0603 E-mail: kshol@webtv.net.

SHOLL, HOWARD GEORGE, JR. state official; b. Balt., July 14, 1944; s. Howard George and Elizabeth Mae (Sutton) S.; m. Rebecca Ann Eklund, Mar. 9, 1968 (div. Feb. 1975); 1 child, Barton C. (dec.); m. Marcia Mary Mitchell, Dec. 3, 1977; children: Elizabeth L., Howard G. III, John K., Robert M.S. BA in Polit. Sci., Va. Polytechnic Inst., 1966, MA in History, 1969; MBA, U. Mo., 1977. Grad. asst. dept. history Va. Polytechnic Inst., Blacksburg, Va., 1966-68; commd. 2nd lt. USAF, 1966, advanced through grades to col., 1989, intelligence officer, missile combat crew comdr. U.S., Germany, 1968-84, chief nuc. targets Supreme Hdqs. Allied Powers Europe Belgium, 1984-87, duty dir. of intelligence Def. Intelligence Agy., Pentagon Arlington, Va., 1987-88, chief Soviet/Europe divsn. Directorate of Current Intelligence, Def. Intelligence Agy., Pentagon, 1988-91, dir. intelligence resources Hdqs. USAF in Europe Ramstein AB, Germany, 1991-92; dep. adminstrv. dir. Dept. of Elections for New Castle County, Wilmington, Del., 1993—. Mgr. Waldorf (Md.) Little League, 1988, 89; treas., asst. cubmaster Cub Scouts, Waldorf, 1988-91; campaign worker Bush-Quayle, Wilmington, 1992; dir. Triangle Neighborhood Assn., Wilmington, 1994—. Decorated Legion of Merit. Mem. Air Force Assn. (pres. Diamond State chpt. 1993-96, Merit medal 1995, 99), Va. Tech Alumni Assn. (pres. First State chpt. 1995-96), The Election Ctr. (cert. electrion registration adminstr. 2002, mem. nat. task force on election reform), Internat. Assn. Clks., Recorders and Election Officers. Republican. Lutheran. Home: 606 W 19th St Wilmington DE 19802-3942 Office: Dept Elections for New Castle County 820 N French St Wilmington DE 19801-3531 Personal E-mail: delawarehokie@vt.edu. E-mail: hsholl@state.de.us.

SHOLL, JOHN GURNEY, III, physician; b. Phila., Mar. 6, 1915; s. John Gurney Jr. and Helen (Hare) S.; m. Marjorie Louise Hill, June 27, 1942 (dec. July 1999); children: John Douglas, Debora Sholl Humphreys, Robert Roy, David Gurney, Rebecca Sholl Baer. BS, Bucknell U., 1937; MD, Harvard U., 1941. Diplomate Am. Bd. Internal Medicine; cert. Nat. Bd. Med. Examiners. Intern Germantown Hosp., Phila., 1941-42; asst. resident in medicine Univ. Hosp., Cleve., 1942-43; pvt. practice in internal medicine, 1943-78; from demonstrator to assoc. clin. prof. medicine Case-Western Res. U., 1943-78, assoc. prof. principles of medicine Dental Sch., 1965-76; dir. med. edn. U. Suburban Health Ctr., 1973-78; chmn. edn. commn. Ohio Med. Assn., 1973-76; clin. prof. medicine U. Calif. San Diego, La Jolla, 1978-88, dir. internal medicine group, 1979-85; clin. prof. medicine St. Matthews U. Sch. Medicine, Windham, Maine, 2001—. Med. dir. E.F. Hutton Life Ins. Co., La Jolla, 1978-82; vol. cons. to med. staff Maine Vets. Homes, 1990-. Mem. editl. bd. Consultant mag., Greenwich, Conn., 1980-84, San Diego Physician, 1986-87. Capt. Army of US, 1944—46, ETO. Fellow ACP; mem. AMA, Calif. Med. Assn., VFW (life), Am. Legion (life), U. Calif. San Diego Emeriti Assn. Clubs: Rowfant (Cleve.). Republican. Baptist. Avocation: writing, golf, reading. Home: 1 Huntington Common Dr Apt 200 Kennebunk ME 04043-6564

SHOLLENBERGER, SHARON ANN, secondary school educator; b. Pottstown, Pa., Sept. 13, 1947; d. John Clayton Sr. and Betty Jean (Sands) Lefever; m. Dennis Lee Shollenberger, May 3, 1980; 1 child, Jessica Lea. EdB, Indiana U. Pa., 1969. Cert. master's equivalency, Pa. Tchr. Downingtown (Pa.) Sch. Dist., 1969—. Advisor student coun., supr. store Lionville Mid. Sch. Recipient Gift of Time tribute Am. Family Inst., 1993. Mem. NEA, Pa. Edn. Assn., Nat. Bus. Edn. Assn. Democrat. Lutheran. Avocations: reading, embroidery, computers. Home: 415 Estate Rd Boyertown PA 19512-2223 Office: 550 W Uwchan Ave Exton PA 19341

SHOLTIS, JOSEPH ARNOLD, JR. business owner, nuclear and aerospace engineer, consultant; b. Monongahela, Pa., Nov. 28, 1948; s. Joseph and Gladys (Frye) S.; m. Cheryl Anita Senchur, Dec. 19, 1970; children: Christian Joseph, Carole Lynne. BS in Nuc. Engring. Disting. Mil. Grad., Pa. State U., 1970; diplomas, Air Univ., 1975, 78; MS in Nuc. Engring., U. N.Mex., 1977, postgrad., 1978-80. Lic. sr. reactor operator NRC, 1980-84. Mathematician, statistician, mine safety analyst U.S. Bur. Mines, Pitts., 1968-70; commd. 2d lt. USAF, 1970, advanced through grades to lt. col., 1988, ret., 1993, nuc. rsch. officer Fgn. Tech. Divsn. Ohio, 1971-74, chief space nuc. sys. safety br. Air Force Weapons Lab. Kirtland AFB, N.Mex., 1974-78; mil. mem. tech. staff, project officer Sandia Nat. Labs., Albuquerque, 1978-80; chief radiation sources divsn., reactor facility dir. Armed Forces Radiobiology Rsch. Inst., Bethesda, Md., 1980-84; program mgr. SP-100 space reactor power sys. tech. devel. prog. Air Force Element U.S. Dept. Energy, Germantown, 1984-87; chief analysis and evaluation br. Air Force Safety Agy., Kirtland AFB, 1987-91, chief nuc. power and sources divsn., 1991-92, chief nuc. energy sys., 1992-93; dir. rsch. and engring., gen. mgr. N.Mex. ops. Oakton Internat. Corp., Va., 1993-96; cons. in field, 1993-96; owner, chief exec., prin. cons. Sholtis Engring. and Safety Consulting, 1996—. Tech. adv. Interagency A & B Nuc. Safety Rev. Panel evaluations Viking 1 & 2, Lincoln Exptl. Satellites 8 & 9, and Voyager 1 & 2 nuc.-powered space missions, 1974-77; space shuttle nuc. payload safety assessment officer Air Force Weapons Lab., Kirtland AFB, 1976-78; instr. med. effects nuc. weapons Armed Forces Radiobiology Rsch. Inst., Bethesda, 1980-84, mem. reactor and radiation facility safety com., 1980-85; faculty lectr. Uniformed Svcs. Univ. Health Scis., Bethesda, 1982-87; U.S. del., tech. advisor UN sci. and tech. subcom. and legal subcom. UN com. on peaceful uses outer space and working group on nuc. power sources in outer space, 1984-87; mem. Schreiber-Spence award com. Symposia on Space nuc. power and propulsion, U.N.Mex., 1987-90; instr. Inst. Space and Nuc. Power Studies U.N.Mex., 1987-91; chmn. Power Sys. Subpanel Interagency Nuc. Safety Rev. Panel risk assessments of Galileo and Ulysses nuc.-powered space missions, 1987-92; judge N.Mex. Sci. Fair, 1987-2000; mem. multimegawatt Space Reactor Power Project Safety working group, 1988-91; mem. U.S. contingent U.S. and USSR discussions on nuc. space power sys. safety, 1989-90; chmn. Dept. Def. Interagy. nuc. Safety Rev. panel evaluations of Ulysses and Cassini nuc.-powered space missions for Office of Pres., 1989-93; mem. adv. com. tech. program com. Space Tech. and Applications Internat. Forum U. N.Mex, 1989—; mem. NASA Space Exploration Initiative Nuc. Safety Policy Working Group, 1990-91; mem. SP-100 Space Reactor program safety adv. com., 1990-93; mem. safety com. USAF Thermionic Space Power program, 1990-93; mem. Ind. Evaluation Group, Strategic Def. Initiative Orgn., 1991-93; lectr. N.Mex. Acad. Sci. Vis. Scientist program, 1991—; mem. program com., reactor safety divsn. AM. Nuc. Soc., 1992-94; mem. ind. adv. U.S. Dept. Energy Safety assessment TOPAZ-II space reactor power sys., 1993; mem. Power Sys. Subpanel interagy. nuc. safety rev. panel evaluation Mars Pathfinder, Cassini, and Mars Exploration Rover nuc.-powered space missions, 1993—; mem. NASA ind. rev. team recert. evaluation Cassini space mission, Jet Propulsion Lab., 1994; edn. officer career enhancement officer Albuquerque sect. AIAA, 1997-2000; mem. outstanding paper award com. Space Tech. and Applications Internat. Forum U. N.Mex., 1999-2000, chmn., 2000—; mem. coord. com. flight safety working group N.Mex. Office Space Commercialization, 1999—; mem. NASA rsch. award adv. bd. N.Mex. Space Grant Consortium U. N. Mex., 2000—. Author: (with others) LMFBR Accident Delineation, 1980, Military Radiobiology, 1987, Power Systems Subpanel Reports for Galileo, Ulysses, Mars Pathfinder, and Cassini Space Missions, 1989-97, Safety Evaluation Report for Ulysses Space Mission, 1990, A Critical Review of Space Nuclear Power and Propulsion 1984-93, 1994, Test Plan for Pu-238 Oxide Coated Particle Fuel and Fuel Forms for Space Radioisotopic Heater Units and Radioisotope Power Systems, 1999; contbr. chpts. to books and over 90 articles to profl. publs. presented at nat. and internat. confs. Judge N.Mex. Sci. Fair, 1987-2000; charter mem. N.Mex. Edn. Outreach Com., 1989-93; group leader, Biblestudy discussions, Holy Child Parish, Tijeras, N.Mex., 1995-99; vol. Bros. of the Good Shepherd food kitchen, Albuquerque, 1997-2000; USGA sectional affairs com. mem. for N.Mex., 1996—, USGA course rating and chief rules ofcl., mem. bd. dirs., Sun Country Amateur Golf Assn., N.Mex., West Tex., 1996—, chmn. long range planning com., 1999-2000, mem., 2000—; edn. officer, career enhancement officer, Albuquerque sect. AIAA, 1997-2000; v.p. Engring. Alumni Assn., U. N.Mex., 1998—, pres. 2000—; pres. Tijeras Arroyo Golf Assn., Kirtland AFB, 1998-2000, v.p., 2000—, mem. golf adv. com., 1998—. Decorated Def. Meritorious Svc. medal (2), Air Force Meritorious Svc. medal (2), Air Force Commendation medal (3), Nat. Def. Svc. medal (2), Air Force Service medal (5), Marksmanship medal, USAF Master Space Sys. badge, U.S. Army Reactor Comdr. badge, USAF Missileman badge; recipient NASA Achievement awards (3), Dept. of Energy Achievement awards (3), Jet Propulsion Lab. Achievement awards (2), White House citation. Assoc. fellow AIAA; mem. ASME, AAAS, Am. Nuc. Soc. (Best Paper 1977), N.Mex. Acad. Sci., Engring. Alumni Assn. (v.p. 1998-2000, pres. 2000—), Planetary Soc., Nat. Space Soc., Nat. Orgn. Test, Rsch. and Tng. Reactors, Profl. Aerospace Contractors Assn. N.Mex., Sigma Xi. Republican. Achievements include the origination of an idea to advance and use coated particle fuel and fuel forms to enhance the design, performance, specific mass and volume, and safety of radioisotopic heaters and power systems for space and remote terrestrial applications, 1998. Avocations: hunting, camping, golfing. Office: Sholtis Engring PO Box 605 Tijeras NM 87059-0605 E-mail: sholtis@aol.com.

SHOM, JEAN, artist; b. Providence, Dec. 4, 1939; d. Eugene Francis Craven and Bertha Mary Cartier; m. Charles Louis Shom, Oct. 2, 1983; children: Bryan David Barr, Patrick Michael Barr. BS, Colo. Women's Coll., Denver, 1975; RN, St. Luke's Sch. Nursing, Denver, 1960, Taos (N.Mex.) Inst. Arts, 1998—; postgrad., Adams State Coll., 1996-98. RN St. Luke's Hosp., Denver, 1960-90. Exhibiting artist Abend Gallery, Denver, 1994—, Foothills II, Golden, Colo., 1995—, Morrison Art and Clay, Colo., 2001-. Artist subj mag. articles, 1998. Cover artist, Mayor's State of City Dinner, LWV, Denver, 1998. Mem. Am. Acad. Women Artists, Colo. Watercolor Soc. (signature mem., Winsor & Newton award 1997), Parkhill Art Club. Avocations: reading, gardening. E-mail: jeanshom@yahoo.com.

SHOMAKER, GORDON ALEXANDER, JR. poet, writer; b. Denver, Mar. 21, 1926; s. Gordon Alexander and Laura Louise Shomaker. MA, U. Colo., 1952; BA, U.S.C., , 1947. Instr. of various U. Theatres , 1957—67; instr. Quinnipiac Coll., Hamden, Conn., 1953—57; appliance repair clerk Shomaker Electric Co., Pueblo, Colo., 1950—51; insp. Steel Mill, 1947. Treas., playwright Theatre Original Plays, Pueblo, Colo., 1980—85; bd. dirs. Colo. Outdoor, 2000—. Playwright: plays Joshua, 1962, playwright: plays Literary Defectives, 1984, author numerous poetry. Rschr. Conn. Pub., Hartford, 1952, Expenditure Coun., Inc. Mem.: Nature Conservancy, NAACP, Native Am. Rights Fund., Acad. Am. Poets. Avocations: walking, music. Home: 900 W Abriendo Apt # 1020C Pueblo CO 81004-1158

SHOME, PARTHASARATHI, economist, educator; b. Calcutta, India, Oct. 12, 1950. B.A. with honours, Presidency Coll., Calcutta, 1970; M.A. in Econs., Delhi Sch. Econs., 1972; M.A. in Econs., U. Rochester (N.Y.), 1973; Ph.D. in Econs., So. Meth. U., 1975. Prof. econs. Am. U., Washington, 1975— ; cons. World Bank, Washington, 1976-83; vis. fellow Australian Nat. U., Canberra, 1982; acad. visitor London Sch. Econs., 1981-82; vis. fellow Delhi Sch. Econs., 1981; sr. economist Internat. Monetary Fund, Washington, 1983—. Author: Fiscal Issues in South East Asia, 1986; contbr. articles to profl. jours. Smithsonian Instn. Am. Inst. Indian Studies research and travel grantee, Chgo., 1981. Mem. Am. Econ. Assn., Nat. Tax Assn. (fed. taxation and fin. com. 1980-82), People for Ethical Treatment of Animals. Home: 1236 Eton Ct NW Washington DC 20007-3241 Office: Internat Monetary Fund 700 Internat Monetary Fund # 19T Washington DC 20431-0001

SHON, JOHN J. accounting executive, researcher; b. Seoul, Korea, Aug. 28, 1971; s. Sung D. Shon, Oka J. Shon. BS, MBA, PhD, U. Chgo., 2002. CPA 1996. Sr. acct. KPMG, New York, 1994—95, cons. risk mgmt., 1995—96; cons. UNext.com, Chgo., 2000—01. Cons. Andersen Consulting, Chgo., 2000—00. Personal E-mail: pjshon@hotmail.com.

SHONDEL, WILLIAM J. academic administrator; b. Barberton, Ohio, Oct. 18, 1943; s. John Robert Shondel and Helen Amelia Bidinger; m. Mary Frances Shondel. BA in History, Ohio State U., 1965, MA in History, 1966; MBA, Marshall U., 1983; postgrad., Squadron Officers Sch., 1968, Air Command and Staff Coll., 1975, Air War Coll., 1985. Commd. 2d lt. USAF, 1965, advanced through grades to brig. gen., 1996; individual equipment officer 862d Supply Squadron, Minot AFB, ND, 1967—70; supply officer 907th Supply Squadron, Rickenbacker AFB, Ohio, 1971—72; supply ops. officer 130th Supply Squadron, 130th Tactical Airlift Group, Charleston, W.Va., 1972—73, comdr., 1973—78, transp. staff officer, 1978—82, comdr., 1982—87, 130th Aerial Port Squadron, 130th Tactical Airlift Group, Charleston, 1982—87, 130th Resource Mgmt. Squadron, 130th Tactical Airlift Group, Charleston, 1987; dir. logistics W.Va. Air NG, 1987—94, asst. adj. gen. for air, 1994—96, chief of staff, 1996—99; dir. purchasing Marshall U., Huntington. Decorated Legion of Merit. Mem.: Nat. Assn. Ednl. Buyers, W.Va. Assn. Higher Edn. Purchasing Officers, NG Assn. W.Va., NG Assn. U.S., Air Force Assn., Ohio State U. Alumni Assn. (past pres. local chpt.), John Marshall Soc., Marshall U. Alumni Assn., Pres.' Club Ohio State U., Lions (past pres., former sec., former treas.). Avocations: farming, photography. Home: PO Box 10 Gallipolis OH 45631 Office: Marshall U One John Marshall Dr Huntington WV 25755

SHONEK, ARLENE, dietitian; b. N.Y.C., Mar. 22, 1944; d. Sidney and Lillian (Weiss) Speiser; m. Jack J. Shonek, Oct. 11, 1961 (dec. Apr. 1997); children: Chaim, Martin Aryeh, Sara Shayva, Esther Blima, Mina Tzivia. BA in Foods and Nutrition with honors, CUNY-Bklyn. Coll., 1978. Registered dietitian, Am. Dietetic Assn., Long Island Dietetic Assn., Greater N.Y. Dietetic Assn.; cert. dietitian-nutritionist. Clin. dietitian, dir. dietary Bezalel Nursing Home, Far Rockaway, N.Y., 1981—. Office: Bezalel Nursing Home 2938 Far Rockaway Blvd Far Rockaway NY 11691-1925

SHONK, ALBERT DAVENPORT, JR. advertising executive; b. L.A., May 23, 1932; s. Albert Davenport and Jean Spence (Stannard) S. BS in Bus. Adminstrn., U. So. Calif., 1954. Field rep. mktg. divsn. L.A. Examiner, 1954-55, asst. mgr. mktg. and field supr. mktg. divsn., 1955-56, mgr. mktg. divsn., 1956-57; account exec. Hearst Advt. Svc., L.A., 1957-59; account exec., mgr. keith H. Evans & Assocs., San Francisco, 1959-65; owner, pres. Albert D. Shonk Co., L.A., 1965-97; gen. ptnr. Shonk Land Co.LTD, Charleston, W.Va., 1989-00; dir. Shonk, LLC, Del., 2001—. Pres. Signet Cir. Corp., Inc., 1977-81, dir., 1962-81, hon. life dir., 1981—, treas., 1989-2002, pres., 2002—. Co-chair centennial com., founding chmn. Crittenton Assocs.; bd. dirs. Balboa Island Improvement Assn., 2000—, Balboa Island Mus. & Hist. Assn., 1999—, treas., 1999—; bd. dirs. Florence Crittenton Ctr., sec., 1978, 1st v.p., 1978—79, exec. v.p., 1979—81, pres., 1981—83, chmn. bd., 1983—85, hon. life dir., 1986—, treas., 1997, pres., 1997—2001, chmn. bd. dirs., 2002—. Recipient Medallion of Merit Phi Sigma Kappa, 1976, Founders award, 1961, NIC Interfraternal award, 1989. Mem.: Jr. Advt. Club L.A. (hon. life, dir., treas., 1st v.p.), Nat. Assn. Pubs. Reps. (past v.p. West Coast 1981—83), Pubs. Rep. Assn. of So. Calif., Advt. Club L.A., Town Hall, World Affairs Coun., Marshall Assocs. (bd. dirs. 1999—), U. S.C. Assocs., U. So. Calif. Alumni Assn. (bd. dirs. 2000—), U. S.C. Marshall Sch. Bus. Alumni Assn. (nat. bd. 1991—99, treas. 1995—99), Rotary (Paul Harris fellow), Trojan Club, Skull and Dagger, Alpha Kappa Psi, Phi Sigma Kappa (dir. grand coun. 1962—70, 1977—79, chancellor 1983—87, 1990—91, recorder 1995—, v.p. meml. found. 1979—84, pres. 1984, trustee pres. Phi Sigma Kappa found. 1984—95, trustee emeritus 1995—), Inter-Greek Soc. (cofounder, hon. life, dir., v.p. 1976—79, pres. 1984—86). Home and Office: 225 Sapphire Ave Newport Beach CA 92662-1148

SHONK, SCOTT LAMAR, architect, educator; b. Ephrata, Pa., July 12, 1967; s. Clyde Eugene and H. Elaine Shonk. BS in Architecture, BArch, Pa. State U., 1990; MArch, U. Pa., 1993. Registered architect, Pa., N.J., Del. Archtl. intern Althouse, Martin & Assocs., Ephrata, Pa., 1985-91; project mgr. Van Tilburg & Ptnrs., Santa Monica, Calif., 1993-94; project architect Beers & Schillaci, Ltd., Lancaster, Pa., 1995-97; project architect, assoc. Beers, Schillaci & Hoffman Ltd., 1998—. Adj. instr. Pa. Sch. of Art and Design, Lancaster, 1997-98. Contbr. articles to profl. jours. Bd. dirs. Ephrata Cloister Assocs., pres. 2001-; active James Buchanan Wheatland Found.; bd. dirs. Lancaster Twp. Hist. Commn., sec. 2001-; legis. activist Nat. Hemophilia Found., 1987—. Recipient 1st prize facade design, John Wingate Davidson FIBA, London, 1989. Mem. AIA (sec.-treas. Ctrl. Pa. chpt. 1997-98, v.p. 1999, pres. 2000, bd. dirs. 2000—), Hist. Preservation Trust of Lancaster, Nat. Trust for Hist. Preservation, Am. Mensa. Avocations: Beaux-arts renderings, water color painting, drawing portraits, playing piano. Home: 70 Spencer Ave Lancaster PA 17603-4855 Office: Beers Schillaci & Hoffman Ltd 20A E Roseville Rd Lancaster PA 17601-3800

SHONKOFF, JACK P. dean, educator; AB, Cornell U., 1968; MD, NYU Sch. Medicine, 1972. Intern, asst. resident, sr. resident in pediatrics Bronx Mcpl. Hosp. Ctr., Albert Einstein Coll. Medicine, 1972-75; clin. trainee divsn. child psychiatry Albert Einstein Coll. Medicine, Bronx, 1974-75, rsch. asst. child developmental psychology unit, 1974-75; fellow in medicine developmental eval. clinic Children's Hosp. Med. Ctr. and Harvard Med. Sch., Boston, 1975-76; coord. developmental consultation svc. Martha Eliot Health Ctr., Jamaica Plain, Mass., 1975-76; cons. cmty. eval. and rehab. ctr. Wrentham (Mass.) State Sch., 1975-76; asst. in medicine Children's Hosp. Med. Ctr., Boston, 1976-79; attending pediatrician U. Mass. Med. Ctr., Worcester, Mass., 1979-94; pediatric coord. masters program Wheelock Coll., Boston, 1981-90; coord. early intervention study group U. Mass., Brandeis U., Wellesley Coll, Mass. Dept. Public Health, 1982-84; prin. investigator, project dir. early intervention collaborative study U. Mass. Med. Sch., 1984-94, Florence Heller Grad Sch. Brandeis U., Waltham, Mass., 1994-98, dean, 1994—. Instr. pediatrics Harvard Med. Sch., 1976-79, lectr. 1997—, Simmons Coll., Boston, 1976-79, instr. dept. early childhood edn. Wheelock Coll., Boston, 1979-80, adj. asst. prof. grad. sch., 1980-85, adj. assoc. prof. grad. sch., 1985-90; asst. prof. pediatrics U. Mass. Med. Sch., Worcester, Mass., 1979-85, assoc. prof. 1985-89, prof. 1990-94; Samuel F. and Rose B. Gingold prof. human devel. Brandeis U., Waltham, Mass., 1994—; adj. prof. family medicine and cmty. health Tufts U. Sch. Medicine, Boston, 1997—; chair bd. on Children, Youth and Families Inst. Medicine and Nat. Rsch. Coun./Nat. Acad. Scis., com. on integrating the science of early childhood devel. bd.; bd. dirs. Zero to Three: Nat. Ctr. for Infants, Toddlers and Families; Robert Wood Johnson vis. rsch. prof. U. Rochester Sch. Medicine and Dentistry, Rochester, N.Y., 1986; Arthur L. Tuuri Interdisciplinary lectr. Mott Children's Health Ctr., Flint, MI, 1986; vis. prof. Sistema Nacional para el Desarrollo Integral de la Familia, Mexico City, Mexico, 1986, U. Puerto Rico Sch. Medicine, San Juan, Puerto Rico, 1988, A.I. Dupont Inst., Wilmington, Del., 1989, U. Vermont Sch. Medicine, Burlington, 1990, Koret vis. prof. pediatrics Pacific Presbyn. Med. Ctr., San Francisco, Calif., 1990, Harrie R. Chamberlin lectr. and vis. prof. U. N.C., Chapel Hill, 1991, vis. prof. in pediatrics Children's Hosp., Oakland, Calif.,

1991, Children's Nat. Med. Ctr., Washington, 1991, Omer H. Foust lectr. and vis. prof. Riley Hosp. for Children, Ind. U. Med. Ctr., Indpls., 1991, Dr. Louis W. Sauer lectr., vis. prof. Evanston Hosp., Ill., 1991, Sydney Rosen Commemorative lectr. Hosp. for Sick Children, Toronto, Ontario, 1992, vis. prof. Tel Aviv U., Israel, 1992, Felton Bequests' vis. lectr. Royal Children's Hosp. and Monash Med. Ctr., Melbourne, Australia, 1993, John B. Welsh Meml. lectureship and vis. prof. U. Calif. San Diego Med. Ctr., Calif., 1994, Warren Weiswasser lectr., vis. prof. Yale U. Sch. Medicine, New Haven, CT, 1995, Dr. Howard R. Rappaport Meml. lectureship, Mt. Sinai Sch. Medicine, N.Y.C., 1997, Raymond Keefe/Joseph Bellizzi Meml. lectr. St. Francis Hosp. and Med. Ctr., Hartford, Ct., 1998. Editl. bd.: Jour. Child Neurology, 1985-90, Jour. Early Intervention, 1989-94, Topics in Early Childhood Special Education, 1987-94, Infant Mental Health Jour., 1983-86; consulting editor: Child Development, 1983-90, Infant Mental Health Jour., 1993-95, Zero to Three, 1985—; assoc. editor: Infant Mental Health Jour., 19987-92, Rudolph's Pediatrics, 20th edit., 1993-94, 21st edit., 1998—; ad hoc manuscript review Am. Jour. Diseases of Children, Am. Jour. Pub. Health, Child Development, Clinical Pediatrics, Infant Mental Health Jour., Jour. of Am. Med. Assn., Jour. Child Psychology and Psychiatry, Jour. Devel. and Behavioral Pediatrics, Jour. Early Intervention, Jour. Division of Early Childhood, Jour. Special Edn., Pediatrics. Fellow W.K. Kellogg Found., 1980-83, Nat. Ctr. for Clin. Infant Programs, 1981-82; recipient Senator Gerard D'Amico award Mass. Early Intervention Consortium, 1986, award for Excellence Boston Inst. for Devel. of Infants and Parents, 1992, Disting. Contribution to Child Advocacy award APA Divsn. Child, Youth and Family Svcs., 1995; grantee in field. Mem. Am. Pediatric Soc. (elected mem.), Inst. Medicine (elected mem.). Office: Brandeis U Florence Heller Grad Sch PO Box 9110-MS 035 Waltham MA 02454-9110 Fax: (781) 736-3852. E-mail: shonkoff@brandeis.edu.*

SHONS, ALAN RANCE, plastic surgeon, surgical oncologist, educator; b. Freeport, Ill., Jan. 10, 1938; s. Ferral Caldwell and Margaret (Zimmerman) S.; m. Mary Ella Misamore, Aug. 5, 1961; children: Lesley, Susan. AB, Dartmouth Coll., 1960; MD, Case Western Res. U., 1965; PhD in Surgery, U. Minn., 1976. Diplomate Am. Bd. Surgery, Am. Bd. Plastic Surgery. Intern U. Hosp., Cleve., 1965-66, resident in surgery, 1966-67; rsch. fellow transplantation immunology U. Minn., 1969-72; resident surgery U. Minn. Hosp., 1972-74; resident plastic surgery NYU, 1974-76; asst. prof. plastic surgery U. Minn., Mpls., 1976-79, assoc. prof., 1979-84, prof., 1984; dir. divsn. plastic and reconstructive surgery U. Minn. Hosp., St. Paul Ramsey Hosp., Mpls. VA Hosp., 1976-84; cons. plastic surgery St. Louis Park Med. Ctr., 1980-84; prof. surgery Case Western Res. U., Cleve., 1984-93; dir. divsn. plastic and reconstructive surgery Case Western Reserve U., 1984-92; prof. surgery, assoc. dir. comprehensive breast program, H. Lee Moffitt Cancer Ctr. and Rsch. Inst. U. South Fla., Tampa, 1992—. Examiner Am. Bd. Plastic Surgery, 1987—. Author: (with G.L. Adams and D. McQuarrie) Head and Neck Cancer, 1986; (with R. Jensen) Plastic Surgery Review, 1993. Capt. USAF, 1967-69. Fellow ACS (chmn. Minn. com. on trauma 1978-84); mem. AMA, Am. Soc. Plastic and Reconstructive Surgeons, Am. Assn. Plastic Surgeons, Minn. Acad. Plastic Surgeons (pres. 1981-82), Soc. Head and Neck Surgeons, Transplantation Soc., Plastic Surgery Rsch. Coun., Am. Soc. Aesthetic Plastic Surgery, Am. Soc. Maxillofacial Surgeons, Am. Assn. Immunologists, Soc. Exptl. Pathology, Am. Cleft Palate Assn., Am. Soc. Craniofacial Surg. Assn., Fla. Soc. Plastic and Reconstructive Surgeons, Tampa Bay Soc. Plastic and Reconstructive Surgeons, Sigma Xi. Office: H Lee Moffitt Cancer Ctr & Rsch Inst 12902 Magnolia Dr Tampa FL 33612-9416

SHOOK, ANN JONES, lawyer; b. Canton, Ohio, Apr. 18, 1925; d. William M. and Lura (Pontius) Jones; m. Gene E. Shook Sr., Nov. 30, 1956; children: Scott, William, Gene Edwin Jr. AB, Wittenberg U., 1947; LLB, William McKinley Law Sch., 1955. Bar: Ohio 1956, U.S. Dist. Ct. (no. dist.) Ohio 1961, U.S. Ct. Appeals (6th cir.) 1981. Cost acct. Hoover Co., North Canton, Ohio, 1947-51; asst. sec. Stark County Prosecutor's Office, Canton, 1951-53; ins. adjuster Traveler's Ins. Co., 1953-56; ptnr. Shook & Shook, Toledo, 1958-62, North Olmsted, Ohio, 1962—. Mem. at large coun. Olmsted Community Ch., Olmsted Falls, Ohio, 1987-90; chmn. ways and means com. North Olmsted PTA, 1968; area chmn. United Way Appeal, North Olmsted, 1963; v.p. LWV, Toledo, 1960-62. Mem. Cleve. Bar Assn. Avocations: reading, boating, dancing, fitness. E-mail: shooklaw@worldnet.att.net.

SHOOK, C. DAVID, surgeon; b. Volga, S.D., Feb. 14, 1939; m. Wendy C. Shook, Dec. 26, 1964; children: David, Lori, Brian. MD, U. Cin., 1965. Intern Cin. Gen. Hosp., 1965-66; resident in gen. surgery U. Cinn. Med. Ctr., 1966-70, resident in cardiovasc. and thoracic surgery, 1970-72; pvt. practice Ohio Surg. Specialists, Inc., Ohio Vein Clinic, Mansfield, 1972—. Pres. Ohio Surg. Specialists, Inc., Mansfield, 1972—. Office: Ohio Surg Specialists Inc/Ohio Vein Clinic 370 Cline Ave Mansfield OH 44907-1057 E-mail: ossi370@aol.com.

SHOOK, JAMES CREIGHTON, real estate executive; b. Lafayette, Ind., May 19, 1931; s. Charles Wheeler and Jane Creighton (Peffer) S.; m. Mary Weil, Apr. 12, 1958 (dec. Jan. 1987); children: James C. Jr., Kathryn S. Bates, Stephen H., Sara Sullivan; m. Janice Warren, Feb. 13, 1988. BS in Bus., Ind. U., 1952. Ptnr. The Shook Agy., Lafayette, 1954-86; pres. The Shook Agy., Inc., 1986-2000. Bd. dirs. Crossmann Cmtys., Inc., Indpls. Pres. Greater Lafayette United Way, 1965-66, Lafayette Home Hosp., Inc., 1973-74; chmn. North Ctrl. Health Svcs., 1989-91. 1st lt. USAF, 1952-54. Mem. Ind. Acad., Ind. C. of C. (bd. dirs. 1975—), Lafayette Country Club (pres. 1969-70), Crystal Downs Country Club (Frankfort, Mich.), Bent Pine Golf Club (Vero Beach, Fla.). Republican. Avocations: golf, community activities. Office: Coldwell Banker Shook Agy Inc 427 Main St Lafayette IN 47901-1369 E-mail: janshoo@aol.com., jcshook@shook.com.

SHOOK, JOAN E. medical educator; b. Cleve., Mar. 27, 1954; m. Jeffery R. Starke, April 23, 1983; children: Nathan R., Matthew C., Hannah E. BA, Brown U., Providence, RI, 1976; MD, U. Cin., 1981; MBA, U. Houston, 1986. Asst. prof. pediat. Baylor Coll. Medicine, Houston, 1986-96, assoc. prof. pediat., 1996—, spl. asst. to chmn. dept. pediat., 1986—, head pediat. emergency medicine dept. pediat., 1993—; med. dir. emergency ctr. Tex. Childrens Hosp., 1986—, med. dir. short stay observation unit, 1994—, chief emergency med. svcs., 1994—. Chair com. Am. Acad. Pediat. Nat. Orgn., 1995—; adj. prof. adminstrv. sci. Rice U., Houston, 1998—. Editor: Seminars in Pediatric Infectious Diseases, 1995, 1996; contbr. chpt. to book. Bd. dirs. The Parrish Sch., Houston, 1986—, Houston Achievements Place, 1992; adv. bd. Huston C.C. Sys. Emergency, Med. Svc. Program, Houston, 1997—. Fellow Am. Acad. Pediat.; mem. Amulatory Pediat. Assn., Am. Coll. Emergency Physicians, Houston Soc. Emergency Medicine, Harris County Med. Soc., Am. Acad. Pediat. Nat. Orgn. (chair com. 1995—), Beta Gama Sigma. Office: Baylor College of Medicine Dept Pediatrics One Baylor Plaze Houston TX 77030

SHOOKSTER, LINDA ANNE, rheumatologist; b. N.Y.C., Jan. 10, 1956; d. George Raymond and Maria Antonia S. AB, Princeton U., 1977; MD, Columbia U., 1981. Diplomate Am. Bd. Internal Medicine. Intern, resident R.I. Hosp., Providence, 1981-84; fellow in rheumatology Hosp. Joint Diseases, N.Y.C., 1984-87; postdoctoral fellow Meml. Sloan Kettering Cancer Ctr., 1987-90; chief rheumatology St. Barnabas Hosp., Bronx, 1990-98; assoc. chief rheumatology Metro. Hosp., N.Y.C., 1998—2001. Lupus Found. fellow, 1985-87. Mem.: ACP-ASIM, AMA, N.Y. Rheumatism Assn., Am. Coll. Rheumatology. Office: Rheumatology Assocs So Westchester 421 Huguenot St New Rochelle NY 10801-7004

SHOOP, GLENN POWELL, investment consultant; b. Gracemont, Okla., Sept. 1, 1920; s. Roy Alonzo and Myrtle Nancy (Goodfellow) S.; m. Louise Wilhelmina Vollmer, Mar. 19, 1943; children: Merilou Love, Paul, Nancy Caver. Student, U. Okla., 1938-42. Pilot Braniff Internat. Airways, Dallas, 1946-80. Cons. bd. dirs. Braniff Inc., 1984-88. Bd. dirs. 1st Bapt. Ch. Dallas, 1950-2000; mem. devel. bd. Golden Gate Bapt. Sem., San Francisco, Southwestern Bapt. Sem., Fort Worth. Maj. USAF, 1942-46. Republican. Achievements include first U.S. pilot to fly Concorde in U.S. scheduled service. Avocations: farming, rebuilding and trading antique tractors.

SHOOSMITH, JOHN NORMAN, retired aerospace engineer; b. London, Eng., Oct. 9, 1934; arrived in U.S., 1959, naturalized, 1965; s. John Shoosmith, Louisa Doris (Corderoy) Shoosmith; m. June Elizabeth Pereira, Nov. 17, 1962 (div. Mar. 1986); children: John Philip, Ann Elizabeth Menandez, Virginia Alice Baldwin; m. Carolin Bloxsom, May 30, 1986. BS in Engring. Physics, Queen's U., 1956; MS in Math., Coll. William and Mary, 1967; PhD of Applied Math., U. Va., 1973. Computer specialist AVRO Aircraft Corp., Toronto, Canada, 1956—59; technologist aerospace NASA, Hampton, Va., 1959—62, technologist manned spacecraft , tech. mgr. Houston, 1962—65, br. head Langley Rsch. Ctr., 1965—89, divsn. chief scientist Langley Rsch. Ctr., 1989—95. Cons. Leads Corp., Arlington, Va., 2000; asst. lectr. George Washington U., 1974—79; instr. math. Coll. William and Mary, Williamsburg, Va., 1986—90, adj. prof. applied sci., 1990—98. Contbr. . Fellow: AIAA (assoc.); mem.: Soc. Indsl. and Applied Math., Assn. Computing Machinery. Avocation: Avocations: hiking, gardening, canoeing, sailing, skiing. Home: 105 Cambridge Ln Williamsburg VA 23185

SHOOTER, ERIC MANVERS, neurobiology educator, consultant; b. Mansfield, Eng., Apr. 18, 1924; arrived in U.S., 1964; s. Fred and Pattie (Johnson) Shooter; m. Elaine Staley Arnold, May 28, 1949; 1 child Annette Elizabeth. BA, Cambridge (Eng.) U., 1945, MA, 1949, PhD, 1950, ScD, 1986; DSc, U. London, 1964. Sr. scientist biochemistry Brewing Industry Rsch. Found., 1950—53; biochemistry lectr. Univ. Coll., London, 1953—63; assoc. prof. genetics Stanford U., 1963—68, prof. genetics and biochemistry, 1968—75, prof., chmn. neurobiology dept., 1975—87, prof. neurobiology, 1987—, chmn. Neurosci. PhD Program, 1972—82. Assoc. Neurosci. Rsch. Program, N.Y.C., 1979—89; mem. tchg. staff Internat. Sch. Neurosci., Praglia, Italy, 1987—93; sr. cons. Markey Charitable Trust, Miami, Fla., 1985—97; mem. sci. adv. bd. and dir. Regeneron Pharm., Inc., Tarrytown, NY, 1988—. Assoc. editor (book series) Ann. Rev. Neurosci., 1984—2001; contbr. articles. Recipient Wakeman award, Duke U., 1988, Award for Disting. Achievement in Neurosci. Rsch., Bristol-Myers-Squibb, 1997; scholar, Josiah Macy Jr. Found., N.Y.C., 1974—75. Fellow: AAAS, Am. Acad. Arts and Scis., Royal Soc. (London); mem.: NAS, Am. Philos. Soc., Internat. Brain Rsch. Orgn., Internat. Soc. Neurochemistry, Am. Soc. Neurochemistry, Am. Assn. Biol. Chemists, Soc. for Neurosci. (Ralph W. Gerard prize 1995), Biochem. Soc., Inst. Medicine of NAS, Alpha Omega Alpha (hon.). Avocation: travel. Home: 370 Golden Oak Dr Portola Valley CA 94028-7757 Office: Stanford U Sch Medicine Dept Neurobiology 299 Campus Dr Stanford CA 94305-5125

SHOPE, ROBERT ELLIS, epidemiology educator; b. Princeton, N.J., Feb. 21, 1929; s. Richard Edwin Shope and Helen Madden (Ellis) Flemer; m. Virginia Elizabeth Barbour, Dec. 27, 1958; children: Peter, Steven, Deborah, Bonnie BA, Cornell U., 1951, MD, 1954. Intern then resident Grace-New Haven Hosp., 1954-58; mem. staff Rockefeller Found., Belem, Brazil, 1959-65; dir. Belem Virus Lab., Brazil, 1963-65; from asst. to assoc. prof. epidemiology Yale Sch. Medicine, New Haven, 1965-75, prof., 1975-95; prof. pathology U. Tex. Med. Br., Galveston, 1995—. Adv. bd. Gorgas Inst., Panema City, 1972-90; mem. WHO Expert Panel Arboviruses, Geneva, Switzerland, 1974—, U.S. del. U.S.-Japan Coop. Med. Scis. Program, Washington, 1977—, Pan Am. Health Orgn. Commn. for Dengue, Washington, 1980—. Served to capt. U.S. Army, 1955-57, Southeast Asia Fellow Am. Acad. Microbiology; mem. Am. Soc. Tropical Medicine and Hygiene (pres. 1980, Bailey K. Ashford award 1974, Walter Reed award 1993), Am. Soc. Virology, Am. Soc. Epidemiology, Infectious Diseases Soc. Am. Democrat. Office: U Tex Med Br Dept Pathology 301 University Blvd Galveston TX 77555-0609 E-mail: rshope@utmb.edu.

SHOR, GEORGE G., JR. geophysicist, oceanographic administrator, engineer; b. N.Y.C., June 8, 1923; s. George Gershon and Dorothy (Williston); m. Elizabeth Louise Noble, June 11, 1950; children: Alexander Noble, Carolyn Elizabeth, Donald Williston. BS, Calif. Inst. Tech., 1944, MS, 1948, PhD, 1954. Joined Seismic Explorations, Inc., Houston, 1948, party chief, 1949-50; asst. research geophysicist to research geophysicist Scripps Inst. Oceanography, La Jolla, Calif., 1953-69, prof. marine geophysics, 1969-90, prof. emeritus, 1990—, assoc. dir., 1968-91; mgr. Calif. Sea Grant program, 1969-73. Mem. NAS-NRC panel on Mohole site selection, 1959; com. on underwater telecommunications, 1968, USN Marine Geophys. Survey Liaison Council, 1965-67; spl. adv. to Com. for Coordination of Joint Prospecting for Mineral Resources in Asian Offshore Areas, 1976-91; chmn. ship scheduling panel Univ. Nat. Oceanographic Lab. Systems, 1987-89; sci. leader oceanographic expdns. to various parts of Pacific and Indian oceans, 1955-82. Served to lt. (j.g.) USNR, 1943-46; now comdr. USNR Ret. Fellow Geol. Soc. Am., Am. Geophys. Union; mem. Soc. Exploration Geophyscists, Scholia Club, Am. Bamboo Soc. (pres. 1994-96). Home: 2655 Ellentown Rd La Jolla CA 92037-1147

SHOR, PETER W. mathematician, researcher; b. Aug. 14, 1959; BS, Calif. Inst. Tech.; PhD, MIT. Postdoc. fellow Mathematical Rsch. Ctr., Berkeley, Calif., 1985; mathematician AT&T Labs, Florham Park, N.J., 1986—. Contbr. articles to profl. jours. including Physics Rev. Letters, J. Combinational Theory, Algorithmica. Presenter at numerous conferences in field. Recipient King Faisal Inernat. prize Sci., 2002; fellow MacArthur Found. fellow, 1999. Office: AT & T Labs Rsch 180 Park Ave Rm C237 Florham Park NJ 07932-1004

SHOR, SAMUEL WENDELL WILLISTON, naval engineer; b. N.Y.C., June 25, 1920; s. George Gershon and Dorothy (Williston) S.; m. Joan Bopp, June 21, 1958; children: Peter Williston, Molly Hathaway. Student, Harvard U., 1937-39; BS, U.S. Naval Acad., 1942; Naval Engr., MIT, 1949; MS in Math., NYU, 1963. Commd. ensign U.S. Navy, 1942, advanced through grades to capt., 1962; served in cruisers Chicago, St. Louis, and Quincy, Pacific and Atlantic, 1942-46; assigned San Francisco Naval Shipyard, 1949-52, naval reactors br. AEC, 1952-53; AEC rep. for initial test of submarine nuclear propulsion in U.S.S. Nautilus and U.S.S. Seawolf, 1953-57; AEC rep. for startup testing of Shippingport Atomic Power Sta., 1957-58; design supt., prodn. engring. officer N.Y. Naval Shipyard, 1958-63; dir. sonar systems office Naval Ship Systems Command, 1963-67, exec. dir. plans, 1967-69, dep. comdr. for engring., 1969-71; project mgr. electronic warfare Naval Electronic Systems Commd., 1971-73; with Bechtel Power Corp., San Francisco, 1973—. Author tech. papers. Mem. Soc. Naval Architects and Marine Engrs., Soc. Naval Engrs., Am. Math. Soc., Am. Phys. Soc., Sigma Xi. Home: 318 Montford Ave Mill Valley CA 94941-3313 Office: Bechtel Corp 50 Beale St Ste 1 San Francisco CA 94105-1895

SHORB, GARY SEYMOUR, hospital administrator; b. Memphis, Sept. 7, 1950; married. B, Clemson U., 1972; M, Memphis State U., 1985. Acting dir. Regional Med. Ctr., Memphis, 1986-87, pres., CEO, 1987-90, Meth. Hosps. of Memphis, 1990—2001, Meth. Healthcare, 2001—. Contbr. articles to profl. jours. Chmn. Memphis Shelby Crime Commn.; mem. U. Memphis Bd. Visitors; bd. mem. United Way of the Med-South, Tenn. Hosp. Assn., Goals for Memphis. Home: 360 Bluff Ridge Cv Cordova TN 38018-7617 Office: Meth Hosps Memphis 1265 Union Ave Memphis TN 38104*

SHORE, HARVEY HARRIS, business educator; b. Cambridge, Mass., Apr. 14, 1940; s. Jacob and Freda Edna (Pearlman) S.; m. Roberta Ann Rogers, Jan. 29, 1967 (div. Oct. 1999); children: Nina Ellen, Elissa Amy. BA cum laude, Harvard U., 1961; MS, MIT, 1963; DBA, Harvard U., 1966. Asst. prof. indsl. adminstrn. U. Conn., Storrs, 1966-72, assoc. prof. indsl. adminstrn., 1972-77, dir. Hartford MBA prog., 1977-82, assoc. prof. mgmt. Storrs, 1982-95, assoc. prof. emeritus, 1995—. Contbr. articles to profl. jours.; editor Cubic Rev., 1975-78; author: Arts Administration and Management, 1987. Chmn. bus. adv. com. Tunxis Community Coll., Farmington, Conn., 1983-85; bd. dirs. Temple Beth Sholom, Manchester, Conn., 1987-90. Mem. Coll. and Univ. Bus. Instrs. Conn. (pres. 1975-76), Greater Nashua Human Resources Assn. (treas. 1997-98, pres. 1998-2000), Masons. Democrat. Jewish. Avocation: tennis.

SHORE, HERBERT, writer, poet, educator; b. Phila., June 6, 1924; s. Meyer and Frances (Smiler) S.; m. Yen Lu Wong, Dec. 23, 1977; children: Norman Jon, Pia Ilyen Griesenbeck, Maya Iming Richards. BA, U. Pa., 1942; postgrad., Columbia U., 1946-48, Dramatic Workship New Sch., 1946-48; postgrad, Stanford U., 1948-53; MA, Stanford U., 1958; PhD, Internat. Coll., 1983. Writer, poet, dramatist and dramaturg, 1956—; dir. Council Tech. and Cultural Transformation, UNESCO, 1974-88; prof., assoc. dean Sch. of Theatre U. So. Calif., 1979-93, prof. emeritus Sch. Theatre, 1996, prof. profl. writing program, 1996-99; founding dir. TNR: The New Repertory, 1972—; provost Internat. Coll., 1983-86; writer-in-residence Blue Mountain Centre, 1985, 86; dir. plays for theatre and TV, author plays, also cantatas. Cons. UNESCO, 1974—; disting. vis. fellow La Trobe U., Australia, 1990; artist in residence Eltham Coll., Australia, 1990; sr. affiliated scholar Multiethnic and Transnat. Studies, U. So. Calif., 1993—; fellow Mayibuye Ctr., South Africa, 1995; past mentor global studies Immaculate Heart Coll. Ctr.; bd. dirs. Eduardo Mondlane Meml. Found., 1996. Author: Come Back Africa, 1970, Ashes Dark Antigone, 1972, Toward the World of Tomorrow, 1978, Cultural Policy, 1981, Cicada Images, Moulting, 1983, No Future Wrapped in Darkness, 1984; Seek to Be Human, 1985, Beginnings are Born in Memory, 1986, Shime, 1986, Trees Die Standing, 1987, And the Dogs Are Silent, 1988, Should the Grain Perish, 1989, Namashawala, Santa Claus and the Bagamoyo Cock, 1990, South African Township Theatre, 1990, Southern Africa: A Dream Deferred, 1990, Apartheid's Waning and Dangerous Years, 1990, Sounds in the Wind, (poetry) 1991, Exile from El Salvador, Terra Infirma, 1992; co-author: (with George Houser) I Must Go Singing, An Oral History of Walter Sisulu, 1999, I Must go to the Gallows Singing, 1998; also articles, short stories, poems. Adv. council Internat. Symposium on Arts, Banff Centre, 1984—; exec. com. Internat. Inst. Audio-Visual Media, Vienna, 1985—; assoc. scholar Ctr. for African Studies, Eduardo Mondlane U., 1988—. Served with USMC, 1943-46. Named Herbert Shore Collection established, Immaculate Heart Coll. Ctr., 1991, Oberlin Coll., 1998, Jerome Lawrence Libr., 1995, Mayibuye Ctr., South Africa, 1995, Niebyl-Proctor Libr., Oakland, Calif., 1995; recipient Writers Digest prize for fiction, 1963, medal of Bagamoyo, Nat. Assembly, Mozambique, 1989; grantee, Ford. Found., 1978—79, 1996—97, Africa Fund, 1995—99, Rockefeller Found., 1966—67, NEH, 1979—81, Wurlitzer Found., 1958—60, Social Sci. Rsch. Coun., 1967—68, African and Am. Univs. Program, 1964—65, Kate Maremont Found., 1959—60, Centro Mexicano de Escritores, 1958. Mem. PEN Ctr. West, USA, LMDA, Assn. Theatre Higher Edn., Nat. Writers Union, Acad. Am. Poets, Soc. Writers and Poets, African Studies Assn. E-mail: hshore@urcad.org.

SHORE, JAMES H(ENRY), psychiatrist; b. Winston-Salem, N.C., Apr. 6, 1940; s. James Henry and Ellen Elizabeth (Hayes) S.; m. Christine Lowenbach, Aug. 24, 1963; children— Ellen Ottilie, James Henry. MD, Duke U., 1965. Diplomate Am. Bd. Psychiatry and Neurology. Intern U. Utah Med. Center, 1965-66; resident in psychiatry U. Wash., 1966-69; chief mental health office Portland (Oreg.) Area Indian Health Service, 1969-73; assoc. prof. psychiatry, dir. community psychiatry tng. program U. Oreg. Health Scis. Center, 1973-75, prof., chmn. dept. psychiatry, 1975-85; chmn. dept. psychiatry U. Colo. Health Scis. Ctr., Denver, 1985-99, interim chancellor, 1992-93, 98. Dir. Colo. Psychiatry Hosp., 1985-99; interim dir. U. Colo. Hosp., Denver, 1987-88, interim exec. vice chancellor, 1995-97, chancellor, 1999—; mem. exptl. and spl. edn. com. NIMH-Internal Rev. Group, 1976-80; cons. in field. Contbr. numerous articles to profl. publs. Mem. Various community bds. Served with USPHS, 1969-73. Decorated USPHS Commendation medal; various grants. Fellow Am. Psychiat. Assn., Am. Coll. Psychiatry; mem. Am. Assn. Chmn. Depts. Psychiatry (pres. 1989), Am. Bd. Psychiatry and Neurology (dir. 1987—, pres. 1994), Residency Rev. Com. for Psychiatry (chmn. 1991-92). Office: U Colo Health Scis Ctr PO Box A 095 4200 E 9th Ave Denver CO 80220-3706

SHORE, JENNIFER ANN, bank officer; b. N.J. d. Philip H. and Constance Michaels S. BA, Skidmore Coll., 1989; MA, NYU, 1990, George Washington U., 1996. With Internat. Media Ptnrs., 1990-94; spl. asst. Internat. Trade Adminstrn., U.S. Dept. of Commerce, Washington, 1994-96; assoc. Kissinger Assocs., N.Y.C., 1996-98; v.p. Citibank/Citigroup, 1998—. Bd. dirs. AUW Support Found. Mem. Coun. Fgn. Rels. (assoc.). Office: Citibank/Citigroup 3d Fl 399 Park Ave New York NY 10022 E-mail: shorej@citi.com.

SHORE, MILES FREDERICK, psychiatrist, educator; b. Chgo., May 26, 1929; s. Miles Victor and Margaret Elizabeth S.; m. Eleanor M. Gossard, July 4, 1953; children: Miles Paul, Rebecca M. Lewin, Susanna G. LeBoutillien. BA, U. Chgo., 1948; AB, Harvard U., 1950, MD, 1954. Intern U. Ill. Research and Edn. Hosp., Chgo., 1954-55; resident in psychiatry Mass. Mental Health Center, Beth Israel Hosp., Boston, 1956-61; asst. prof. psychiatry Tufts U. Sch. Medicine, 1964-68, assoc. prof., 1968-71, prof., 1971-75, prof. community health, 1972-75; founder, dir. Tufts Community Mental Health Center, 1968-74, asso. dean community affairs, 1972-75; mem. faculty Boston Psychoanalytic Inst., 1973—; Bullard prof. psychiatry Harvard Med. Sch., Boston, 1975—; supt. Mass. Mental Health Ctr., 1975-93; vis. scholar John F. Kennedy Sch. Govt. Harvard U., 1993—; cons. exec. edn. Harvard Med. Internat., 1999—, sr. cons., 2000—. Dir. program for chronic mental illness Robert Wood Johnson Found., 1985-92. Editl. bd. Psychat. Svcs. Jour., 1990; bd. editors Jour. Interdisciplinary History, 1975, Psycho History Rev., 1978; column editor Harvard Rev. Psychiatry, 1993; contbr. articles to profl. jours. Bd. dirs. Federated Dorchester Neighborhood Houses, Boston, 1975-78, tr. House, Boston, 1995—; bd. dirs. Med. Found., Boston, 1987—, chmn., 1999-2001; mem. Blue Ribbon Commn., Mass. Dept. Mental Health, 1979-80. Capt. U.S. Army, 1956-58. Community Mental Health Center grantee, 1964-75. Fellow Am. Psychiat. Assn. (life, joint commn. on pub. affairs, adminstrv. psychiatry award 1987), Am. Coll. Psychiatrists (chmn. fin. com. 1983-89, bd. regents 1988-90, 1st v.p. 1994, pres. 1996-97, Bowis award for svc. 1990, Arthur P. Noyes award 1994); mem. Assn. Am. Med. Colls. (coun. acad. socs. 1992—), Boston Psychoanalytic Soc. and Inst. (chmn. bd. trustees 1970-73), Mass. Psychiat. Soc. (pres. 1970-71), Mass. Hosp. Assn. (trustee 1980-85), Am. Hosp. Assn. (chmn. governing coun. for psychiat. and substance abuse svcs. 1992-93, ho. of dels. 1996—02, region I policy bd. 1997—2000), Roxbury Clinic Record Club, Aesculapian Club, Mass. Hist. Soc. Office: JFK Sch Govt 79 Jfk St Cambridge MA 02138-5801

SHORE, RICHARD ARNOLD, mathematics educator; b. Boston, Aug. 18, 1946; s. Philip M. and Miriam (Krensky) S.; m. Naomi J. Spiller, Aug. 3, 1969; children— Deena A., Aviva R. B. Jewish Edn., Hebrew Coll., 1966; AB, Harvard U., 1968; PhD, MIT, 1972. Instr. U. Chgo., 1972-74; asst. prof. Cornell U., Ithaca, N.Y., 1974-78, assoc. prof., 1978-83; asst. prof. U. Ill.-Chgo., 1977; vis. assoc. prof. MIT, Cambridge, 1980; vis. prof. Hebrew U., Jerusalem, 1982-83; prof. math. Cornell U., Ithaca, 1983—. Organizing com. Logic Yr. at MSRI, 1989-90, other internat. meetings. Author: (with A. Nerode) Logic for Applications; editor North-Holland, Studies in Logic and the Foundations of Mathematics, 1996—; cons. editor Jour. Symbolic Logic, 1980-83, editor, 1984-93, coord. editor, 1989-91; mng. editor: Bull. Symbolic Logic, 1993-2000; contbr. articles to profl. jours. V.p. for edn. Hillel Acad. Broome County, Binghamton, N.Y., 1985-89; treas. Beth David Synagogue, 1993-96; pres. Jewish Fedn. of Broome County, 1998-2000. NSF grantee, 1973— Mem. Am. Math. Soc., Spl. Interest Group in Algorithms and Computation Theory, Assn. for Computing Machinery, Assn. for Symbolic Logic (coun. 1984—, pres. 2001—). Jewish. Home: 14 Kenwood Ave Newton MA 02459 Office: Cornell U Dept Math Malott Hall Ithaca NY 14853 E-mail: shore@math.cornell.edu.

SHORE, RICHARD E. story teller, environmental educator; b. Visalia, Calif., July 5, 1937; s. Walter Evert and K. Madeline (Tillman) S.; m. Victoria P. Whiteside, June 7, 1957 (div. 1992); children: Melissa, John. AB in Zoology, Coll. of Pacific, 1959; PhD in Zoology, Duke U., 1963; MBA in Ops. Analysis, U. Toledo, 1974. Cert. quality engr. Am. Soc. for Quality. Mem. faculty dept. biology St. Louis U., 1963-66, U. Toledo, 1967-74; rsch. assoc. Oak Ridge (Tenn.) Nat. Lab., 1966-67; quality mgr. Owens-Ill., Perrysburg, Ohio, 1974-76, indsl. engr. Bardstown, Ky., 1976-78, Dayco, Herron, Ill., 1978-80, U.S. Army, Ft. Knox, Ky., 1981-98; chief R & D, Cepheus Labs., Marion, Ill., 1980—81; guide Whippoorwill Holler Ynstitute, Vine Grove, Ky., 1998-99, Lexington, 1999—. Instr. U. Louisville, 1987-99; storyteller first-person living history John Muir, 1988-2000; action officer Ft. Knox Hazardous Materials Ctr. Alternative Fuel Initiative, 1992-98 Mem. Ky. exec. com. Sierra Club, 1999—, also life mem.; lobbyist Ky. Conservation Com., Frankfort, Ky., 2000-01. Mem. Nat. Assn. for Interpretation (life). Avocations: hiking, poet, pianist. Home and Office: 205 Catalpa Rd Lexington KY 40502

SHORE, STEPHEN, photographer; b. N.Y.C., Oct. 8, 1947; m. Ginger Cramer Seippel, 1980; 1 child, Nicholas; 1 stepchild, Alex Seippel. Student, Minor White, Workshop, 1970. Photographer, 1953—. One-man shows, Met. Mus. Art, N.Y.C., 1971, Light Gallery, N.Y.C., 1972, 73, 75, 77, 78, 80, Phoenix Gallery, San Francisco, 1975, Mus. Modern Art, N.Y.C., 1976, Kunshalle, Dusseldorf, Germany, 1976, U. Akron, Ohio, 1978, Vision Gallery, Boston, 1978, La Photogaleria, Madrid, 1979, Ewing Gallery, Washington, 1979, Catskill Ctr. Photography, Woodstock, N.Y., 1980, Fraenkel Gallery, San Francisco, 1982, Mus. Arts and Scis., Daytona Beach, Fla., 1981, Polk Pub.

Mus., 1982, ARCO Ctr. Visual Arts, L.A., 1982, N. Mex. State U. Art Gallery, Las Cruces, 1982, Art Inst. Chgo., 1984, Pace Wildenstein MacGill, N.Y.C., 1989, 95, Sprengel Mus., Hannover, 1995, Würt. Kunstverein, Stuttgart, 1995, Amerika Haus, Berlin, 1995, George Eastman House, Rochester, N.Y., 1996, Skstiftung Kultur, Koln, Germany, 1999, Spazio Oberdan, Milan, Italy, 1999, 303 Gallery, N.Y.C., 2000, Galerie Conrads, Düsseldorf, 2001, 02; group shows include: Met. Mus. Art, N.Y.C., 1973, 82, 97, Internat. Mus. Photography, George Eastman House, 1975, Documenta 6, Kassel, W. Ger., 1977, Art Inst. Chgo., 1977, 79, 89, Mus. Modern Art, N.Y.C., 1978, 91, 2000, Corcoran Gallery, Washington, 1979, Kunsthaus, Zurich, Switzerland, 1980, U. Ariz. Mus. Art, Tucson, 1981, Nat. Gallery, Washington, 1989, Getty Mus., 1992, 97, Whitney Mus., N.Y.C., 1999, P.S. 1, N.Y.C., 1999, Victoria & Albert Mus., London, 1999, Sprenger Mus., Hannover, Germany, Uffizi Gallery, Florence, 2000; represented in permanent collections, Met. Mus. Art, N.Y.C., Mus. Modern Art, N.Y.C., Internat. Mus. Photography, George Eastman House, Rochester, N.Y., Mus. Fine Arts, Boston, Library of Congress, Washington, Art Inst. Chgo., Ctr. Creative Photography, U. Ariz., Tucson, Stedelijk Mus., Amsterdam, Netherlands, Neue Sammlung, Munich, W.Ger., Australian Nat. Gallery, Canberra; author: Andy Warhol, 1968, Uncommon Places, 1982, The Gardens at Giverny, 1983, Stephen Shore: Luzzara, 1993, Stephen Shore: Photographs 1973-1993, 1995, The Velvet Years, 1995, The Nature of Photographs, 1998, American Surfaces, 1999;, Essex County, 2002, Uncommon Places: 50 Unpublished Photographs, 1973-1978, 2002; portfolio 12 Photographs, 1976; contbr. articles to profl. jours. Nat. Endowment Arts grant, 1974, 79; Guggenheim fellow, 1975, Am. Acad. (Rome) Spl. fellow, 1980, MacDowell Colony fellow, 1993. Mem. Century Assn.

SHORE, STEVEN L. pediatrician; b. Phila., Mar. 3, 1942; s. Benjamin and Blanche Kay (Rothman) Shore; m. Mary Kathleen Garrity, Aug. 28, 1966 (div. Dec. 1984); children: Erika, Brian; m. Pamela Elaine Gary, June 20, 1987; children: Hannah, Colin, Adam. BA, MA, U. Pa., 1963; MD, Johns Hopkins U., 1967. Diplomate in pediat. and pediat. infectious diseases Am. Bd. Pediat. Intern in pediatrics Children's Hosp. Boston, 1966-67, resident in pediatrics, 1967-68; med. officer Ctrs. for Disease Control, Atlanta, 1968-77, chief cellular immunology br., 1977-81; chief dept. pediatric infectious diseases Scottish Rite Children's Hosp., 1981—2000; ptnr. Sandy Springs Pediatrics, 1981—. Contbr. Comdr. USPHS, 1968—81. Fellow: Am. Acad. Pediat. Avocation: Avocations: music, reading. Home: 1069 Hunters Brook Ct NE Atlanta GA 30319-4714 Office: Sandy Springs Pediatrics 993 Johnson Ferry Rd NE Atlanta GA 30342-1620

SHORE, THOMAS SPENCER, JR. lawyer; b. Akron, Ohio, Jan. 1, 1939; s. T. Spencer and Harriet G. (Delicate) S.; m. Margaret F. Kudzma, Aug. 12, 1961; children— Thomas Spencer III, John Christopher, Daniel Andrew, Mary Margaret. BA, Brown U., 1961; JD, Northwestern U., 1964. Bar: Ohio 1964. Assoc. Taft, Stettinius and Hollister, Cin., 1964-69; asso. Rendigs, Fry, Kiely & Dennis, 1969-71, partner, 1972—. Adj. asst. prof. Chase Law Sch., U. No. Ky. Bd. dirs. United Cerebral Palsy of Cin., 1978— ; bd. dirs., sec. Boys Club Am., Cin.; trustee emeritus Family Svc. of Cin. Area; past pres. Vis. Nurse Assn. of Cin., hon. trustee. Mem. Cin. Bar Assn., Ohio Bar Assn., Am. Bar Assn. Clubs: Cin. Country, Cin. Tennis, Queen City, Webhanet. Home: 3224 Columbia Pkwy Cincinnati OH 45226-1042 Office: 900 Central Trust Tower Cincinnati OH 45202 E-mail: t.shore@rendigs.com.

SHORENSTEIN, ROSALIND GREENBERG, internist; b. N.Y.C., Jan. 14, 1947; d. Albert Samuel and Natalie Miriam (Sherman) Greenberg; m. Michael Lewis Shorenstein, June 18, 1967; children: Anna Irene, Claire Beth. BA in Chemistry, Wellesley Coll., 1968; MA in Biochemistry and Molecular Biology, Harvard U., 1970, PhD in Biochemistry and Molecular Biology, 1973; MD, Stanford U., 1976. Diplomate Am. Bd. Internal Medicine. Resident in internal medicine UCLA Med. Ctr., 1976-79; pvt. practice internal medicine Santa Cruz, Calif., 1979—. Mem. dept. internal medicine Dominican Hosp., Santa Cruz, 1979—; co-dir. med. svcs. Health Enhancement & Lifestyle Planning Systems, Santa Cruz, 1983—. Contbr. articles to profl. journals. Dir. Santa Cruz Chamber Players, 1993-94, pres., bd. dirs., 1994—. Recipient Charlie Parkhurst award Santa Cruz Women's Commn., 1989; NSF fellow, 1968-72, Sarah Perry Wood Med. fellow Wellesley Coll., 1972-76. Mem. Am. Soc. Internal Medicine (del. 1994, 95), Calif. Soc. Internal Medicine (trustee 1994—, sec.-treas. 1996-2000), Am. Med. Women's Assn. (Outstanding Svc. award 1987, br. #59 pres. 1986—), Calif. Med. Assn. (com. on women 1987-93), Santa Cruz County Med. Soc. (mem. bd. govs. 1993—, sec. 1997-99, pres. 2000-01, sec. 2002-), Phi Beta Kappa, Sigma Xi. Jewish. Office: 700 Frederick St Ste 103 Santa Cruz CA 95062-2239

SHORENSTEIN, WALTER HERBERT, commercial real estate development company executive; b. Glen Cove, N.Y., Feb. 23, 1915; m. Phyllis J. Finley, Aug. 8, 1945 (dec.); children: Joan (Dec.), Carole, Douglas. Student, Pa. State U., 1933-34, U. Pa., 1934-36; D in Econs. (hon.), HanYang U., Seoul, Republic of Korea, 1988. With property sales mgmt. depts. Milton Meyer & Co., San Francisco, 1946-51, ptnr., 1951-60, owner, chmn. bd. dirs., 1960—, Shorenstein Group, San Francisco, Shorenstein Co., San Francisco, 1960—. Appt. by Pres. Johnson adv. del. UN Econ. Commn. for Asia and Far East, 1967, Pub. Advisory Com. U.S. Trade Policy; apptd. Pres. Carter Com. for Preservation fo White House; appt. by Pres. Clinton bd. dirs. Corp. Nat. Svc., 1994-96, adv.com. U.S. Commerce Dept. Industry, 1995-96. Past chmn. bd. trustees Hastings Law Ctr., U. Calif., San Francisco; founding mem. exec. adv. com. Hubert H. Humphrey Inst. Pub. Affairs, U. Minn.; bd. visitors; past pres., hon. life bd. dirs. San Francisco Park and Recreation Commn.; chmn. Vietnam Orphans Airlift; bd. dirs. San Francisco Performing Arts Ctr.; trustee Asia Found.; fin. chmn. Dem. Nat. Conv., 1984; founder Joan Shorenstein Ctr. on Press, Politics and Public Policy, Harvard U., 1986; apptd. by Pres. Clinton to Nat. Svc. Commn., 1994, Bd. of Americorp, founding mem. WWII Nat. Monument com., Nat. Endowment Arts, White House Endowment Fund; apptd. by Pres. Carter chair White House Preservation Fund; apptd. by Mayor Frank Jordon chair Save the San Francisco Giants com.; personal advisor Pres. Johnson, Carter, Clinton; chmn. Pacific Rim Econ. Coun., San Francisco; bd. visitors Internat. Studies Bd. Stanford U.; co-founder Orpheum, Curran and Golden Gate Theatres, San Francsico; founder Johnson Presdl. Libr., Carter Ctr.; chmn. San Francisco U. N50 nat. com., 1995, also numerous polit. activities. Maj. USAF, 1940-45. Named Leader of Tomorrow, Time mag., 1953, Calif. Dem. of Yr., 1985; recipient Nat. Brotherhood award NCCJ, 1982, Disting. Svc. award Dem. Nat. Com., 1983, Golden Plate award Am. Acad. Achievement, 1991, Svc. to Youth award Cath. Youth Orgn., 1994, Lifetime Achievement award Dem. Party, 1997; inducted Real Estate Legends Hall of Fame, 1997, Bay Area Coun. Bay Area Bus. Hall of Fame, 1998; Shorenstein award named in his honor Dem. Nat. Com., 1999. Mem. Calif. C. of C. (past bd. dirs.), San Francisco C. of C. (past chmn. bd. dirs., life bd. dirs.). Office: Shorenstein Co 555 California St Ste 4900 San Francisco CA 94104-1714

SHORR, SCOTT ALDEN, lawyer; b. N.Y.C., July 5, 1968; s. Ronald Philip and Jean Fishack Shorr. AB, Vassar Coll., 1990; JD, U. Calif., Berkeley, 1995. Bar: Oreg. 1996, U.S. Dist. Ct. Oreg. 1997, U.S. Ct. Appeals (9th cir.) 1998. Law clk. to Hon. Richard L. Unis Oreg. Supreme Ct., Salem, 1995-96; assoc. Stoll Stoll Berne Lokting & Shlachter, Portland, Oreg., 1996—. Contbr. articles to profl. jours. Pres. bd. dirs. Hands On Portland, 1998-2000; bd. dirs. Oreg. Pub. Affairs Network, 2000—. Mem. Oreg. Trial Lawyers Assn., Multnomah Bar Assn., Fed. Bar Assn. Democrat. Avocations: soccer, music, politics. Office: Stoll Stoll Berne Lokting & Shlachter 209 SW Oak St Ste 500 Portland OR 97204-2798 E-mail: sshorr@ssbls.com.

SHORS, CLAYTON MARION, cardiologist; b. Beemer, Nebr., June 10, 1925; s. Joseph Albert and Morva Edith (Clayton) S.; m. Arlene Towle, June 6, 1948; children: Susan Debra, Clayton Robert, Scott Towle BS, U. Nebr., 1950, MD, 1952. Diplomate Am. Bd. Internal Medicine (subspecialty cardiovascular disease). Intern Detroit Receiving Hosp., 1952-53, resident, 1953-56; practice medicine specializing in cardiology Detroit; chief cardiology St. John Hosp. Bd. dirs. Sedona Acad.; mem. Sedona 30. Served with U.S. Army, 1943-46 Fellow Am. Coll. Cardiology, Internat. Coll. Angiology, Am. Heart Assn. Council on Clin. Cardiology; mem. Alpha Omega Alpha Home: 44 Rue De La Rose Sedona AZ 86336-5970 Office: 1785 W Highway 89A Sedona AZ 86336-5567 also: 6562 E Crested Saguaro Ln Scottsdale AZ 85262-7373

SHORS, JOHN D. lawyer; b. Ft. Dodge, Iowa, July 21, 1937; s. George A. and Catherine (Shaw) S.; m. Patricia Ann Percival, Oct. 7, 1967; children: John, Tom, Matt, Luke. BSEE, Iowa State U., 1959; JD, U. Iowa, 1964. Bar: Iowa, U.S. Supreme Ct. Assoc. then shareholder Davis, Brown, Koehn, Shors & Roberts, P.C., Des Moines, 1964—. Co-author: Closely Held Corporations in Business and Estate Planning, 1982. Pres. Mercy Hosp. Found., Des Moines, 1981-84; chair Iowa State U. Found., Ames, 1989-92; bd. dirs. Mercy Housing, Denver, 1992—. Cpl. U.S. Army, 1960-61. Recipient Iowa State U. Alumni medal, YLS Merit award Iowa State Bar Assn. Mem. Iowa State Bar Assn. (pres. 1992) Iowa Women Profl. Corp. (Good Guy award 1987), Iowa Rsch. Coun. (bd. dirs. 1994—), Am. Judicature Soc. (bd. dirs. 1974-79), Polk County Bar Assn. (pres. 1986), Rotary (Des Moines chpt.), DM Club, Glenoaks C.C. Republican. Roman Catholic. Office: Davis Brown Koehn Shors & Roberts PC 666 Walnut St Ste 2500 Des Moines IA 50309-3904 E-mail: johnshors@lawiowa.com.

SHORT, ALEXANDER CAMPBELL, lawyer; b. Washington, July 26, 1940; s. Joseph Hudson and Beth (Campbell) S.; m. Patricia Graves Thompson, Aug. 24, 1968; children: Joseph Graves, Ashley Campbell, Justin Owen. BA, Amherst Coll., 1963; MA, U. Pa., 1968; JD, U. Va., 1972. Bar: Conn. 1972, Md. 1973. Field and site rep. U.S. Dept. of HUD, Phila., 1963-69; assoc. Reid & Riege P.C., Hartford, Conn., 1972-73, Piper & Marbury, Balt., 1973-79, Miles & Stockbridge, Balt., 1979-81, ptnr., 1981-94; pvt. practice, 1994-95; ptnr. Hooper, Kiefer & Cornell, LLP, 1995-96, Eastman & Short, LLP, Balt., 1996-2000; asst. atty. gen. State of Md., 2000—. Bd. dirs., pres. Handel Soc. adv. bd. to Handel Choir, Balt., 1983-87; pres. Handel Choir, Balt., 1987-88. Bd. dirs. Homeland Assn., Balt., 1984-85, Kernewood Assn., Balt., 1995—, Greater Homewood Cmty. Corp., 1997-2001; mem. bd. mgrs. Camp Dudley, YWCA, 1991-96, 1998-2001; pres. North Balt. Neighborhood Coalition, 1996-2000. Mem. Md. Bar Assn. (real property planning and zoning sect., coun. 1981-88, 96-98, sec. 1982-84, chmn. elect 1984-86, chmn. 1986-88. Democrat. Presbyterian. Avocations: choral singing, scouting, gardening. Office: Office of Atty Gen Ednl Affairs Divsn 200 St Paul Pl Baltimore MD 21202 E-mail: ashort@oag.state.md.us.

SHORT, ANN MARIE HEROLD, library director; b. Richmond, Ind., June 15, 1957; d. Clarence Ferdinand and Dorothy Joyce (Holaday) H.; m. Michael Estill Short, May 7, 1977 (div.); 1 child, Wenona Jeannette. BFA, Ind. U., Indianapolis, 1979; MLS, Ind. U., Bloomington, 1986. Cert. libr. I, Ind. Libr. dir. Rauh Meml. Libr. Indpls. Children's Mus., 1980; children's libr. Shelbyville-Shelby County (Ind.) Pub. Libr., 1981-84, reference libr., 1987-88, libr. dir., 1988-97, Rushville (Ind.) Pub. Libr., 1984-87; youth svcs. libr., dept. head Noblesville-Southeastern Pub. Libr., 1998—. Mem. Ind. Libr. Fedn. Avocations: vegetarian cooking, herbs, painting, drawing, calligraphy.

SHORT, BETSY ANN, elementary education educator; b. Macon, Ga., Mar. 18, 1958; d. Garland Brooks Jr. and Mary Eleanor (Jordan) Turner; m. Lynn Robin Short, July 21, 1984. BS in Early Childhood Edn., Ga. Coll., Milledgeville, 1981, M in Early Childhood Edn., 1993, EdS, 1995; cert. specialist in reading, U. West Ga., 2001; intech cert., Macon State Coll., 2001; degree in Adminstrn. and Supervision, Ga. Coll. and State U., 2002. Cert. elem. tchr. and tchr. support specialist, Ga. Tchr. 3d grade Stockbridge (Ga.) Elem. Sch., 1983-84, tchr. kindergarten, 1984-93; tchr. augmented spl. instructional assistance Locust Grove (Ga.) Elem. Sch., 1993-97, kindergarten tchr., 1997-99, first grade tchr., 1999-2000, early intervention reading tchr., 2000—02, 2000—02; student support specialist Unity Grove Elem. and Ola Elem., 2002—. Cons. Saxon Pub. Co.; v.p. Henry Heritage Reading Coun., 1999—; specialist in Reading, U. West Ga., Carrollton, 2001. Author: Spinning Yarns, 1995; mem. editl. adv. bd. Ga. Jour. Reading; contbr. articles to profl. jours.; artist oil painting/pen and ink drawing. V.p. Henry Heritage Reading Coun., 1999—2000. Mem. Profl. Assn. of Ga. Educators, Ga. Coun. Tchrs. Maths., Ga. Coun. Internat. Reading Assn., Ga. Coun. Social Studies, Ga. Sci. Tchrs. Assn., Henry Heritage Reading Coun. Baptist. Avocations: oil painting, cross-stiching, writing short stories, story telling. Office: Locust Grove Elem 95 LG Griffin Rd Locust Grove GA 30248 E-mail: bshort@henry.k12.ga.us.

SHORT, EARL DEGRAY, JR. psychiatrist, consultant; b. Talladega, Ala., Jan. 11, 1933; s. Earl DeGray and Adeline Eugenia (McWilliams) Short; m. Martha Burt Rossiter, Oct. 12, 1963; children: Earl D III, Philip A., Catherine E., William R. BS, The Citadel, 1956; MD, Med. U. S.C., Charleston, 1959. Commd. 2d lt. USAR, 1956; entered active duty U.S. Army, 1961, advanced through grades to col., 1976; bn. surgeon 4th Armored Bn., 8th Inf. div., Germany, 1961-62; resident psychiatry Walter Reed Army Med. Ctr., Washington, 1962-65; chief dept. psychiatry U.S. Army Hosp. and Mental Hygiene Consultation Svc., Ft. Polk, La., 1965-68, U.S. Walson Army Hosp. and Mental Hygiene Consultation Svc., Ft. Dix, N.J., 1968-70; student Command and Gen. Staff Coll., Ft. Leavenworth, Kans., 1970-71; divsn. surgeon, comdr. 2d Med. Bn., 2d Inf. divsn., Korea, 1971-72; chief psychiatry svc. Brooke Army Med. Ctr., Ft. Sam Houston, Tex., 1972-80; ret. U.S. Army, 1980; psychiatrist Mecklenburg County Mental Health Ctr., Charlotte, N.C., 1980-86; ret. Mecklenburg County, 1993; psychiatrist Behavioral Health Ctr.-Carolinas Med. Ctr.-Randolph, Charlotte, N.C., from 1986; pvt. practice Carolinas Med. Group, Psychiat. and Psychol. Assocs., from 1992. Psychiat. cons. Mecklenburg County, Charlotte, 1987—, Amethyst, Charlotte, 1993-95, Emergency Med. Svcs. Assocs., 1996-99, Murray Adolescent Tng. Acad., 1996—. Founder Philip Alexander Short Meml. Scholarship Fund, Wingate (N.C.) U., 1988, Short Endowment Fund, Wingate U., 1991, Philip Alexander Short Meml. Fund, Elon Homes for Children, Elon Coll., N.C., 1989. Decorated Meritorious Svc. medal with 1 oak leaf cluster, U.S. Army, 1972, 80, Army Commendation medal with 1 oak leaf cluster, U.S. Army, 1968, 70; recipient All Am. award The Citadel, 1956, and named Disting. Mil. Grad., 1956. Mem. AMA, Am. Psychiat. Assn., N.C. Med. Soc., N.C. Psychiat. Assn., Charlotte Psychiat. Soc., Assn. Mil. Surgeons, Mecklenburg County Med. Soc., Ret. Officers Assn., Am. Legion, VFW, Sons Am. Revolution, Nat. Assn. for Uniformed Svcs. Republican. Presbyterian. Avocations: genealogy, composing piano music, restoring ancestral homes, collecting stamps, books and coins. Died Sept. 10, 2001.

SHORT, ELIZABETH M. physician, educator, federal agency administrator; b. Boston, June 2, 1942; d. James Edward and Arlene Elizabeth (Mitchell) Meehan; m. Michael Allen Friedman, June 21, 1976; children: Lia Gabrielle, Hannah Ariel, Eleanor Elana. BA Philosophy magna cum laude, Mt. Holyoke Coll., 1963; MD cum laude, Yale U., 1968. Diplomate Am. Bd. Internal Medicine, Am. Bd. Med. Genetics. Resident internal medicine Yale New Haven Hosp., 1968-70; postdoctoral fellow in human genetics Yale Med. Sch., 1970-72; resident U. Calif., San Francisco, 1972-73; sr. chief resident Stanford (Calif.) Med. Sch., 1973-75; asst. prof. medicine Stanford Med. Sch., 1975-83, assoc. dean student affairs/med. edn., 1978-83; dep. dir. acad. affairs, dir. biomed. rsch. Assn. Am. Med. Colls., Washington, 1983-88; dep. assoc. chief med. dir. for acad. affairs VA, 1988-92, assoc. chief med. dir. for acad. affairs, 1992-96; health policy cons., 1996—2001. Vis. prof. human biology Stanford U., 1983-86; mem. Accreditation Coun. Grad. Med. Edn., 1988-97; mem. White House Task Force on Health Care Reform, 1993. Assoc. editor Clin. Rsch. Jour., 1976-79, editor 1980-84; contbr. articles to profl. jours. Mem. Nat. Child Health Adv. Coun., NIH, 1991-97; mem. com. edn. and tng. Office Sci. and Tech. Policy, 1991-96. Recipient Maclean Zoology award; Munger scholar, Markle scholar, Sara Williston scholar Mt. Holyoke Coll., 1959-63, Yale Men in Medicine scholar, 1964-68; Bardwell Meml. Med. fellow, 1963. Mem. AAAS, Am. Soc. Human Genetics (pub. policy com. 1984-95, chmn. 1986-94), Am. Fedn. Clin. Rsch. (bd. dirs. 1973-83, co-chmn. com. status women 1975-77, editor Clin. Rsch. Jour., 1978-83, nat. coun., exec. com., pub. policy com. 1977-87), Western Soc. Clin. Investigation, Calif. Acad. Medicine, Phi Beta Kappa, Alpha Omega Alpha. Home and Office: 6807 Bradley Blvd Bethesda MD 20817-3004 E-mail: elizshort@aol.com.

SHORT, EUGENE MAURICE, JR. lawyer, accountant; b. San Francisco, Sept. 4, 1932; s. Eugene Maurice and Emeline Inez (Cox) S.; m. Ann Page, Sept. 4, 1953 (div. 1962); children: Lawrence, David, Dale; m. Karol Fageros, Dec. 1, 1963 (dec. Apr. 1988); children: Kristin, Karri; m. Mary Marhoefer Lynch, Apr. 2, 1992. BBA, City Coll. San Francisco, 1952, U. Miami, Fla., 1954; JD, U. Miami, 1959. Bar: Fla. 1959, U.S. Ct. Mil. Appeals 1960, U.S. Supreme Ct. 1963, U.S. Ct. Appeals (5th and 11th cir.) 1967, U.S. Tax Ct. 1971. Assoc. Carey, Goodman, Terry, Dwyer & Austin, Miami, Fla., 1959-62; ptnr. Peters, Maxey, Short & Maxey, P.A., Coral Gables, 1963—. Capt., U.S. Army, 1954-63. Mem. ABA, Dade County Bar Assn., Coral Gables Bar Assn., SAR, Royal Palm Tennis Club (dir.), Surf Club, Phi Alpha Delta, Sigma Nu. Avocation: bridge. Home: 7041 SW 92nd St Miami FL 33156-1614 Office: Peter Maxey Short & Maxey PA 3001 Ponce De Leon Blvd Miami FL 33134-6824

SHORT, FORREST EDWIN, lawyer; b. Ft. Scott, Kans., Aug. 3, 1928; s. Forrest Edwin Sr. and Laura Elizabeth Short; m. Sharon Lynn Miller, May 1, 1955; children: Stacey Lynn, Laurie Leigh. JD, U. Ala., Tuscaloosa, 1953. Bar: Kans. 1955, U.S. Dist. Ct. Kans. 1956, U.S. Dist. Ct. (so. dist.) Ala. 1953, U.S. Ct. Appeals (10th cir.) 1975, U.S. Supreme Ct. 1976. Sole practitioner, Ft. Scott, 1954-66; ptnr. Short & Short, 1966-77, Short & Gentry, Ft. Scott, 1977-83, Short, Gentry & Bishop, Ft. Scott, 1983-93; pres. Short, Gentry & Bishop, P.A., 1993—. Contbr. articles to profl. jours. 1st lt. JAG, U.S. Army, 1953-54. Mem. ABA, Kans. Bar Assn., Bourbon County Bar Assn., Ft. Scott Rotary Club (pres. 1996-97). Republican. Methodist. Avocations: golf, gardening. Office: Short Gentry & Bishop PA 4th and Judson Fort Scott KS 66701

SHORT, GEORGE OSCAR, III, accountant; b. Montgomery, Ala., Feb. 19, 1957; s. George Oscar Jr. and Jacqueline Hampton (Horne) S.; children: George Oscar IV, Caroline Elizabeth Coleman Short. BS in Accountancy, U. S.C., 1980. CPA, S.C. Ptnr. George O. Short & Assocs. CPAs, Greenville, S.C., 1980-91; pres., v.p. Oscar, Merald & Assocs., Inc., 1986-90; chief exec. officer Greenville Addictive Disease Assocs., 1989-90; v.p. Turn Key Leasing, Inc., Pompano Beach, Fla., 1990-92, 518 Corp., Savannah, Ga., 1992-96; exec. dir. New Party, Progressive Am., 1996—. Bd. dirs. Greenville Nat. Bank, Access, Inc.; steering com. Freedom Weekend Aloft, C. of C., Greenville, 1988. Bd. dirs., treas. Am. Cancer Soc., 1985-91; bd. dirs., v.p. Crimestoppers Greenville, 1985-87; bd. dirs. Big Bros. and Big Sisters, Greenville, 1987-90; diaconate mem., chmn. stewardship com. 1st Presbyn. Ch., Greenville, 1986-88; grad. Leadership Greenville, 1987; bd. dirs. New Party, Progressive Am., Working Families Party, 1996—. Mem. AICPA, S.C. Assn. CPAs (legis. com. 1983-91), Estate Planning Coun., Sigma Alpha Epsilon (bd. dirs., treas., v.p., pres. Greenville alumni 1986-91). Democrat. Avocations: hunting, fishing, golf, boating. E-mail: executivedirector@igc.org., gshort@igc.org.

SHORT, HAROLD ASHBY, imaging engineer; b. Cleve., Sept. 13, 1939; s. George Ashby and Irene June (Cibbs) S. BS in Photographic Sci., Rochester (N.Y.) Inst. Tech., 1961. Supr. quality control Cleve. Color Svc., 1959-61; assoc. engr. Lockheed Missiles & Space Co., Sunnyvale, Calif., 1961-63, micro photographer, 1970-74; photographic engr. Itek Corp., Palo Alto, 1963-68; project engr. Philco-Ford Corp., 1968-70; sr. staff engr. Fairchild Semiconductor Corp., Mountain View, Calif., 1974-87; mgr., maskmaking engr. Nat. Semiconductor Corp., Santa Clara, 1987-89. Instr. computer graphics, Carmel Found., 1999—. Editor The Engraving Art of Czeslaw Slania, 1987, 90, 96, 2001,Bay Phil, 1994—, Close-up, 1999—. Mem. North Coast Beaches Adv. Com., County Bd. Suprs., County of Santa Cruz., Calif., 1991—, chair, 1993—. Mem. Sierra Club (forestry task force), Friends of The Sea Otter (editor Coast Project Recovery Effort), Aubudon Soc., Cousteau Soc., Naturist Soc., Santa Cruz County Stamp Club (editor, treas. 1991-2001). Avocations: photography, stamp collecting, computer graphics and typesetting, environmental activism, woodworking. Home: 1575 Tindall Ranch Rd Corralitos CA 95076-0127

SHORT, JAMES FEREBEE, investment company executive; b. Norfolk, Va., Feb. 23, 1968; s. Richard Turner IV and Florence King (Timolat) S. Grad., Woodberry Forest Sch., 1986; BA, Coll. of William and Mary, 1990; MBA, U. Ga., 1996. CFP, CIMC, ChFC, RFC. Consumer lender Bank of Am., Virginia Beach, Va., 1990-91; investment advisor, fin. cons Merrill Lynch, VA Beach, VA, 1991-94; ind. investment advisor Athens, Ga., 1994-96; asst. v.p., portfolio mgr. Br. Banking & Trust Co., Investment Mgmt., Raleigh, N.C., 1996-98; v.p., sr. portfolio mgr. Kempner Capital Mgmt., Galveston, Tex., 1998-2001; v.p., portfolio mgr. Bank of Am., 2001—02; chief investment officer Waypoint Advisors, Norfolk, Va., 2002—. Delegate to congrl. and state conventions. Mem. Gubernatorial Adv. Com., 1992-93; vol. Am. Health Assn., Am. Cancer Soc., Westminster Canterbury Retirement Home, Surfrider Found. Mem. Richmond Soc. of Fin. Analysts, Assn. for Investment Mgmt. and Rsch., Fin. Planning Assn. (Hampton Rds. chpt. bd. dirs.), Princess Anne Country Club, The Revelers (bd. govs., v.p.), Theta Delta Chi, Sigma Iota Epsilon. Republican. Episcopalian. Avocations: collecting sports cards, surfing, baseball, volunteering, travel, politics. Home: 507 W Holly Rd Virginia Beach VA 23451-2829 Office: Waypoint Advisors 999 Waterside Dr Ste 2025 Norfolk VA 23510-3350 E-mail: jshort@waypointadvisors.net.

SHORT, JANET MARIE, principal; b. Boston, Sept. 18, 1939; d. Robert Emmet and Getta Agnes (Mills) S. BS in Edn., Boston State Coll., 1962, MEd, 1967; LLD (hon.), Regis Coll., 1991; doctorate in Pub. Svc. (hon.) , N.U., 2002. Tchr. Boston Pub. Schs., 1962-70, acting asst. dir. staff devel., 1970-71, tchr.-in-charge, 1971-75; prin. D.L. Barrett Sch., Boston, 1976-81; tchr. Boston Pub. Schs., 1981-82; prin. Maurice J. Tobin Sch., Boston, 1982—2001, lead cluster prin., 1995—2001; ret., 2001. Lectr. in field. Adv. bd. DiMaiti Stuart Found., Boston, 1990-97; adv. bd. Mission Hill and Camp Mission Posible, 1984-87; community adv. bd. Harvard Sch. Pub. Health, Boston, 1990—; adv. bd. Boston Against Drugs, 1990-94. Recipient Women of Achievement award Big Sister Assn. of Greater Boston, 1994, Thankful Recognition award Channel 5, Boston, 1987, Recognition award Boston Women's Mag., 1988, Pub. Svc. award Henry L. Shattuck, Bus. Mcpl. Bur. Rsch. award, 1988, Freedom's Found. Honor medal, 1990, Annual Excellence in Edn. award Alpha Gamma chpt. Pi Lambda Theta, 1993 and others; movie based on J.M. Short, "A Matter of Principal". 1990. Mem. ASCD, Mass. Middle Level Adminstrs. Assn., Boston Assn. Sch. Adminstrs. (exec. bd. 1984-93), Boston Middle Sch. Assn., Boston Elem. Prins. Assn., MESPA, Delta Kappa Gamma (chpt. pres. 1978-80). Roman Catholic. Avocations: travel, bowling, reading. Home: 39 Ridgeway Dr Quincy MA 02169-2321

SHORT, JOEL BRADLEY, lawyer, software publisher; b. Birmingham, Ala., Dec. 27, 1941; s. Forrest Edwin and Laura Elizabeth (Bradley) S.; m. Georgianna Pohl, June 5, 1965 (div. Apr. 1973); m. Nancy Ann Harty, Dec. 17, 1977; children: Christopher Bradley, Matthew Douglas. BA, U. Colo., 1963, LLB, 1966, JD, 1968. Bar: Kans. 1966, U.S. Dist. Ct. Kans. 1966, U.S. Ct. Appeals (10th cir.) 1975, U.S. Supreme Ct. 1976. Ptnr. Short & Short, Attys., Fort Scott, Kans., 1966-77, Nugent & Short, Overland Park, 1977-83; pvt. practice J. Bradley Short & Assoc., 1983-91; ptnr. Short & Borth, 1991—; owner Bradley Software. Mem. tech. adv. com. Kans. Jud. Coun., Topeka, 1991-95. Contbg. author: Practitioner's Guide to Kansas Family Law, 1997. 1st lt. U.S. Army, 1967-73. Fellow Am. Acad. Matrimonial Lawyers; mem. Johnson County Bar Assn. (ethics com. 1983-98, family law com. 1983—). Avocation: sailing. Office: Short and Borth 55/500 Corporate Woods 9300 W 110th St Overland Park KS 66210-1405 E-mail: brad@shortandborth.com.

SHORT, LINDA MATTHEWS, retired elementary education educator; b. Winston-Salem, N.C., Mar. 25, 1949; d. Edwin Kohl and Nannie Mae (Bowen) Matthews; m. James Coy Short, June 18, 1972. BS, Appalachian State U., 1971, MA, 1981. Cert. elem. edn. tchr. Tchr. Mt. Airy (N.C.) City Schs., 1971-72, 88-01, Surry County Schs., Dobson, N.C., 1972-88. Mem. Mt. Airy City Schs. Adv. Bd., 1994-95. Pres.-elect Foothills Reading Coun., 1992-93; active Mt. Airy Women's Club, 1970s, Mt. Airy Jaycettes, 1970s; mem. adv. bd. State Employees Credit Union, 1998-2001. Mem. Foothills Reading Coun. (pres. 1993-96), N.C. Reading Assn. (area dir. 1995-96, com. chair 1996-97, conf. coord. 1998, sec. 1998-00, v.p. 2000-01, pres.-elect 2001—), N.C. Assn. Educators (dist. sec. 1996-97, 98), Internat. Reading Assn., Mt. Airy N.C. Assn. Educators (treas. 1992-94, v.p. 1996-97), Altrusa Club, Mayberry Reading Coun. (pres. 2000-01). Democrat. Avocations: music, painting, crafts, collecting dolls, ceramic cats. Home: 125 Brentwood Dr Mount Airy NC 27030-1860

SHORT, R. J. DUKE, United States Senate official; b. Moultrie, GA., Mar. 31, 1934; s. Ernest A. and Eloise F. Short; m. Denise Powers, May 23, 1992; children: Sydne, Robert Jr., Coy. BS, North Ga. Coll., 1956; DC, Palmer Coll., 1965. Indsl. engr., 1956-57; spl. agt. Intelligence Divsn., Dept. Treasury, 1961-62, 65-72; sr. investigator Senate Subcom. on Internal Security, 1974-76; Rep. staff dir., chief investigator Senate Com. on the Judiciary, 1976-89; chief of staff to pres. pro tem U.S. Senate, 1989—, pres. Counselor to chief judge U.S. Mil. Ct. Appeals. With U.S. Army, 1957-61. Recipient USO Appreciation award, 1995, Employees Support of Guard and Res. Appreciation award, 1995; named one of 50 most Powerful Staffers in Congress, Roll Call, 1988-97, hon. judge U.S. Claims Ct.; Palmer Acad. Chiropractic fellow, 1994. Mem. Assn. Fed. Investigators, Combined Law Enforcement Intelligence Group, Assn. Former Intelligence Officers, Treasury Agts. Assn., U.S. Marshals Found., Nat. Adv. Coun., Internat. Chiropractic Assn., S.C. Chiropractic Assn., Ga. Chiropractic Assn., Fla. Chiropractic Assn., Asia Pacific Exch. Found. (adv. bd.), Sigma Theta. Office: Russell Senate Office Bldg Washington DC 20510-0001 E-mail: duke_short@thurmond.senate.gov.

SHORT, RAY EVERETT, minister, sociology educator emeritus, author, lecturer; b. Coffeyville, Kans., Jan. 5, 1919; s. Franklin Marion and Jennie (Messersmith) S.; m. Jeannette Louise Stephens, June 12, 1954 (dec. Jan. 2000); children: Glenn Alan, Linda Louise, Kenneth Ray, Timothy Wesley, Karen Amy; 1 stepdau., Mary Jennings. AB, Willamette U., 1944; postgrad., U. Chgo., 1946; BD, Duke, 1948, PhD, 1961; postgrad., U. Idaho, 1950-51. Ordained to ministry Meth. Ch., 1946. Dir. Westminster Found., Duke, 1944-46; co-pastor Interracial Meth. Ch., Durham, N.C., 1947; asst. prof. religion, dir. chapel programs Fla. So. Coll., Lakeland, 1947-48; exec. dir. Fla. br. United World Federalists, 1948-51; dir. Intermountain Region, 1953-54, Wesley Found., U. Idaho, 1950-51; exec. dir. Student YMCA-YWCA, U. Denver, 1951-53; pastor Fairmont Meth. Ch., Lockport, Ill., 1954-56; grad. asst. sociology Duke, 1956-57; assoc. prof. religion, head divsn. religion and philosophy, chaplain Tenn. Wesleyan Coll., 1957-60; assoc. prof. sociology and religion, head dept. sociology U. Dubuque, Iowa, 1960-65, acting chmn. div. social sci., 1962-65; assoc. prof. sociology, head dept. sociology and anthropology U. Wis., Platteville, 1965-70, prof. sociology, 1966-87, prof. emeritus, 1987—; prof. sociology and anthropology Copenhagen Study Ctr. U. Wis., spring 1974, nat. lectr., 1975—. Chmn. Peace and World Order divsn. North Iowa Meth. Conf., 1963-69; rep. U.S. Jr. C. of C. in testimony before U.S. Senate Com. on Fgn. Rels., 1950; Midwest region rep. Nat. Coun. World Federalist Assn., 1964-73, pres. Midwest region, 1967-69, chmn. nat. coun., 1971-72, nat. v.p., 1991—; (with wife) WFA dels. to NGO Forum and 4th UN Conf. on Women, Beijing, 1995; D.C. hdqrs. WFA property named Ray and Jeannette Short Peacemakers Bldg., 1997 (Presdl. WFA award 1998); co-chmn. Grenville Clark Club; mem. spl. Wis. Conf. called with Pres.'s Comn. for Observance of 25th Anniversary of UN, 1970-87; mem. Wis. U. Meth. Bd. on Ch. and Soc., 1973-80, chmn. World Peace divsn., mem. exec. com., 1975-80. Author: Sex, Love or Infatuation: How Can I Really Know?, 1978, on videocassete, 1987, 2nd edit., 1990 (Augsburg Bestseller), Sex, Dating and Love: Questions Most Often Asked, 1984, 2nd edit., 1994 (Augsburg Bestseller); contbr. articles to profl. jours. Dem. candidate for Wis. 3rd Dist. Congl. Seat, 1970, 72; del. Dist. and State Convs., 1969-87, mem. state platform com., 1975-87; bd. dirs. Dubuque Salvation Army, 1961-65; mem. nat. bd. Am. Freedom Assn.; nat. v.p. Campaign for UN Reform, 1983-87, 1st v.p., 1989—; dir., founder Wis. Ann. High Sch. World Peace Study Program, 1975-87. Recipient NSF grant Anthropology Inst., Fairmont State Coll., W.Va., 1962 Fellow Am. Sociol. Assn.; mem. AAUP, Nat. Coun. on Family Rels., Fedn. Am. Scientists, Nat. United Meth. Men (mem. peace adv. task force 1990—). Home: 505 S Miller Ave Lafayette CO 80026-1545 *Nuclear and chemical weapons, crises of environments. While my life has largely been spent helping others have a better future, I now know we have to help assure that they have a future at all by establishing limited democratic enforcible world law.*

SHORT, ROBERT, information technology executive; Graduate, CIT, Cork, Ireland; MS in Computer Sci., U. Wash. Sr. devel. mgr. Digital Equipment Corp.; from mem. devel. team to corp. v.p. Microsoft, Redmond, Wash., 1988, corp. v.p. windows core tech. Office: One Microsoft Way Redmond WA 98052-6399*

SHORT, SALLIE LEE, physical plant service worker; b. Knoxville, Tenn., Feb. 17, 1932; d. John J. and Louise Maude (Robertson) Bassett; children: Jacqueline, Carita, Paulette, Shelia, Marilyn, Regina, Panthea, Greta, Michael (dec.). Legal sec. Earl Rossin, Atty., Cleve., 1952-53; nursing technician Meharry Med. Hosp., Nashville, 1958-64; inspector May Hosiery Mill Corp., 1964-81; trustee sick leave bank Nashville State Tech. Inst., 1993—. Author poems; guest appearence Cable TV Channel 19 Read Poetry. Campaign worker Dem. Party, Nashville, 1975-80; mem. Com. on Svc. to Persons with Disabilities and Ams. with Disabilities Act. Recipient Poet of Merit award Internat. Soc. Poets, 1997; elected to Internat. Poetry Hall of Fame, 1998. Roman Catholic. Avocations: writing, hiking, reading, traveling. Home: 4113 Meadow Hill Dr Nashville TN 37218-1730 Office: Nashville State Tech Inst 120 White Bridge Rd Nashville TN 37209-4515

SHORT, SHENITA, writer; b. Columbus, Ga., June 8, 1965; d. Sam Brown, Jr. and Jessie Mae Richardson-Brown; m. Harry James Short, Sr., Mar. 31, 1999; children: Detavies Brown, Harry, Jr., LaBrandon Brown. Med. asst., Columbus Vocat.-Tech. Sch. Clk. typist, file clk. CETA, Ft. Benning, Ga., 1983—85; rm. attendant Holiday Inn, Courtyard by Marriot, Columbus, 1986—96; inspector printing plates Kodak Polychrome, 1996—99, online state operator, 1999—2000; freelance writer, 2000—. Author: (poetry) Natures Echoes, 2001, Poetic Odyssey, 2001, (CD, cassette) The Sound of Poetry, 2001. Recipient Honor and Recognition for outstanding achievement in poetry, Columbus Times Newspaper, Honor and Recognition of Disting. Achievement in Creative Writing, Jeff Roberts Pub. Co., Recognition for Outstanding Achievement in Poetry, Famous Poets Soc. Baptist. Avocations: writing poetry and songs, singing, sewing. Home: 808 35th St Columbus GA 31904-7555

SHORT, STEVE EUGENE, engineer; b. Crockett, Calif., Oct. 17, 1938; s. Roger Milton and Ida Mae (Mills) S.; m. Yumie Sedaka, Feb. 2, 1962; children: Anne Yumie, Justine Yumie, Katherine Yumie. BS in Gen. Engring. with honors, U. Hawaii, 1972, MBA, 1973; MS in Meteorology, U. Md., 1980. Registered profl. engr., Hawaii. With Nat. Weather Svc., NOAA, 1964—; pres. Short & Assocs., Inc., 1994—. Govt. exec. Silver Spring, Md., 1974-81, program mgr. ASOS,1981—, transition dir. 1991—; ind. tech. cons., 1994—; pres. Short & Assocs., Inc.; cons. engring. and mgmt.; cons. SBA. Contbr. articles to sci. jours. With USMC, 1956-60. Recipient Gold Medal award U.S. Dept. Commerce, 1992, Presdl. Meritorious Exec. award, 1992. Mem. VFW, Am. Meteorol. Soc., Japan-Am. Soc., Am. Soc. Pub. Adminstrn. Office: 3307 Rolling Rd Chevy Chase MD 20815-4033 E-mail: sshort@compuserve.com.

SHORTAL, TERENCE MICHAEL, systems company executive; b. St. Louis, Oct. 13, 1937; s. Harold Leo and Catherine margaret S.; m. Linda Margaret Elias, May 29, 1965; children: Jennifer (Mrs. Clay Morris Westbrook), Bradley Alexander. BSEE, U. Mo., 1961; MS, U.S. Naval Postgrad. Sch., 1966; grad. program execs., Carnegie Mellon U., 1979. Commd. ensign USN, 1961; advanced through grades to capt., 1980; ret., 1981; asst. officer in charge Engring. Duty Officer Sch. Vallejo, Calif., 1974-77; ship engring. mgr. AEGIS shipbldg. project Naval Ea Sys. Command, Washington, 1977-79; tech. dir. DDGX project, 1979-81; v.p., dir. Kastle Sys., LLC, 1981—. Trustee Cathedral Choral Soc., Washington, 1983-95, 97—, pres., 1986-88, 2000-2002; mem. vestry St. John's Episcopal Ch., McLean, Va., 1982-85; bd. dirs. Langley Sch., McLean, 1984-94, pres. 1986-88. Decorated Meritorious Svc. medal (2), Navy Commendation medal (2); recipient award of merit Cathedral Choral Soc., 1996. Mem. IEEE (br. award 1961), Am. Soc. Naval Engrs. (Flagship Sect. award 1979), Nat. Press Club (Washington), Tower Club, Gridiron Club (Washington), Sigma Xi, Phi Kappa Theta. Home: 858 Canal Dr Mc Lean VA 22102-1408 Office: 1501 Wilson Blvd Arlington VA 22209-2403 E-mail: mike@kastle.com.

SHORTELL, STEPHEN MICHAEL, dean, health services researcher; b. New London, Wis., Nov. 9, 1944; BBA, U. Notre Dame, 1966; MPH, UCLA, 1968; MBA, U. Chgo., 1970, PhD in Behavioral Sci., 1972. Rsch. asst. Nat. Opinion Rsch. Ctr., 1969; instr., rsch. assoc. Ctr. Health Adminstrv. Studies, 1970—72; acting dir. grad. program hosp. adminstrn. U. Chgo., 1973—74, from asst. prof. to assoc. prof., 1974—79; prof. health svc. Sch. Pub. Health and Cmty. Medicine, U. Wash., 1979—82; A.C. Buehler Disting. prof. health svc. mgmt. Northwestern U., Evanston, Ill., 1982—98; Blue Cross disting. prof. health policy and mgmt. Sch. Pub. Health, U. Calif., Berkeley, 1998—; dean Sch. Pub. Health, U. Calif, 2002—. Cons. VA, Robert Wood Found., Henry Kaiser Found.; asst. prof. Health Svcs. Orgn. U. Chgo., 1972—74; adj. asst. prof. dept. sociology U. Wash., 1975—76, dir. doctoral program dept. health svcs. Sch. Pub. Health and Cmty. Medicine, 1976—78; prof. sociology dept. sociology Northwestern U., 1982, prof. preventive medicine Sch. Medicine. Contbr. numerous articles to profl. jours. Recipient Baxter prize, Baxter-Allegiance Found., 1995. Fellow: Am. Coll. Healthcare Execs. (Gold medal 1998); mem.: Inst. Med.-NAS. Office: Univ Calif Berkeley Sch Pub Health 407 Warren Hl Berkeley CA 94720-0001*

SHORTEN, JAIME SUSAN, music educator; d. Barry N. and Sharon H. Shorten. MS in Edn., Hofstra U., 1995, BS in Edn., 1991. Cert. Music Edn. 1991, Spl. Edn. 1995. Dir. elem. orch. Hewlett Woodmere Sch. Dist., Hewlett, NY, 1991—95; dir. elem. and h.s. orch. West Babylon Sch. Dist., West Babylon, 1996—. Adjudicator N.Y. State Sch. Music Assn., 1996—. Guest condr. all dist. orch., 1997. Mem.: Nat. String Orch. Assn., L.I. String Festival Assn., Am. String Tchrs. Assn., Suffolk County Music Educators Assn., N.Y. State Sch. Music Assn., Music Educators Assn. Avocations: photography, travel, singing, reading. Personal E-mail: jaiviol@yahoo.com.

SHORTER, JAMES RUSSELL, JR. lawyer; b. N.Y.C., June 10, 1946; s. James Russell and Helen (Ibert) S. AB, Columbia Coll., 1968; JD, Harvard U., 1975; LLM in Taxation, NYU, 1979. Bar: N.Y. 1976, U.S. Dist. Ct. (so. and ea. dists.) N.Y. 1976, U.S. Tax Ct. 1987. Assoc. Thacher Proffitt & Wood, N.Y.C., 1975-84, ptnr., 1984—. Capt. USNR, 1968-98. Mem. ABA (tax, bus. law sect.). Clubs: Harvard (N.Y.C.). Republican. Home: 345 E 80th St Apt 26C New York NY 10021-0671 Office: Thacher Proffitt & Wood 11 W 42nd St 11th Fl New York NY 10036 E-mail: jshorter@tpwlaw.com.

SHORTER, NICHOLAS ANDREW, pediatric surgeon; b. London, Oct. 14, 1953; came to the U.S., 1961; s. Roy Gerrard and Rhiannon (Morris) S.; m. Sally Jo Trued, Aug. 28, 1982; children: Timothy Anders, Brittain David, Jaime Elizabeth Rhiannon. AB, AM, Harvard U., 1975; MD, Johns Hopkins U., 1979. Bd. cert. in surgery and pediatric surgery. Intern The Johns Hopkins Hosp., Balt., 1979-80, jr. asst. resident in surgery, 1980-81, sr. asst. resident in surgery, 1981-82, 83-84, chief resident in surgery, 1984-85; rsch. fellow in surgery The Children's Hosp. Med. Ctr., Boston, 1982-83; asst. chief resident in pediatric surgery The Children's Hosp., Phila., 1985-86, chief resident in pediatric surgery, 1986-87; hosp. staff Duke U. Med. Ctr., Durham, N.C., 1987-91; chief pediatric surgery Children's Hosp. at Dartmouth, Dartmouth-Hitchcock Med. Ctr., 1991-99, exec. com., 1991-99; assoc. attending surgeon Meml. Hosp., N.Y.C., 1999—2002; attending surgeon SUNY-Downstate Med. Ctr., Bklyn., 2002—, chief divsn. pediat. surgery, 2002—. Tchg. fellow biology Harvard U., Cambridge, Mass., 1974-75; asst. instr. pediatric surgery U. Pa., Phila., 1985-87, Duke U., Durham, 1987-91, asst. prof. pediat. surgery and pediat., 1987-91; asst. prof. pediat. Dartmouth Med. Sch., Hanover, N.H., 1991-94, asst. prof. surgery, 1991-94, assoc. prof. pediat., 1994-99, assoc. prof. surgery, 1994-99; hosp. staff The Children's Hosp., Phila., 1986-87, Dartmouth-Hitchcock Med. Ctr., Lebanon, N.H., 1991-99, Duke U. Med. Ctr., Durham, 1987-91, Meml. Hosp., N.Y., 1999-2002; dir. Kiwanis Affiliated Pediatric Trauma Ctr., Children's Hosp. at Dartmouth, Lebanon, 1993-99, SUNY Downstate Med. Ctr., Bklyn., 2002-; assoc. prof. surgery Cornell U., N.Y., 2001-2002; vis. prof. surgery, SUNY, Bklyn., 2002-. Referee Jour. Pediatric Surgery; contbr. chpts. to books and articles to profl. jours. Regular Clin. fellow Am. Cancer Soc., 1985-86. Fellow ACS, Am. Acad. Pediatrics, Southeastern Surg. Congress, Royal Soc. Medicine, Soc. Surg. Oncology; mem. Am. Pediatric Surg. Assn., Brit. Assn. Pediat. Surgeons, Internat. Soc. Pediat. Oncology, Internat. Pediatric Surg. Oncology, Am. Assn. for Cancer Rsch., Assn. for Acad. Surgery, N.Y. Acad. Scis., Royal Soc. Medicine, Cum Laude Soc., Phi Beta Kappa, Alpha Omega Alpha. Republican. Episcopalian. Avocation: collecting political memorabilia. E-mail: nicholas.shorter@downstate.edu.

SHORTESS, EDWIN STEEVIN, marketing consultant; b. Cedar Rapids, Iowa, Oct. 31, 1920; s. Edwin Stephen and Rita (Clemente) S.; m. Jane Elizibeth Gallagher, Dec. 27, 1941 (div. Apr. 1970); children: E. Stephen, Richard J., Mark Andrew, Cathy Shortess Pool; m. Mary Francis Kerns, May 28, 1970; children: Dana Menshing, Emil Bartsche, Roger Bartsche, Lisa Bartsche Coccia, Vincent Bartsche, Kirsten Bartsche Chirico. Student, North Iowa U., 1938-39; BSEE, Chgo. Tech. Coll., 1942. Engring. rsch. analyst Douglas Aircraft Corp., El segundo, Calif., 1942-44; liaison engr. Martin Aircraft Corp., Omaha, 1944-45; chief engr., dir. Burlington (Iowa) Instrument co., 1945-53; adminstrv. engr., dir. Hickok Elec. Instrument Co., Cleve., 1953-59, ea. sales mgr. Paramus, N.J., 1960-65; v.p., gen. mgr., dir. Wacline, Dayton, Ohio, 1959-60; v.p., gen. mgr. Colo. Hickok, Grand Junction, 1965-69; pres. Shortess Rawson & Assocs., Kenilworth, N.J., 1969-86, mktg. cons. Allenwood, 1986—. Bd. dirs. Federated Purchasers Inc., Kenelworth, N.J. Author: Design and Application of Electrical Industrial Instruments, 1964. Mem. Instrument Soc. Engrs. (sr.). Republican. Methodist. Avocations: golf, bridge. Home and Office: 123 Everest Dr S Brick NJ 08724-2027

SHORTLIFFE, EDWARD HANCE, internist, medical educator; b. Edmonton, Alta., Can., Aug. 28, 1947; s. Ernest Carl and Elizabeth Joan Shortliffe. AB, Harvard U., 1970; PhD, Stanford U., 1975, MD, 1976. Diplomate Am. Bd. Internal Medicine. Trainee NIH, 1971—76; intern Mass. Gen. Hosp., Boston, 1976—77; resident Stanford Hosp., Palo Alto, Calif., 1977—79; asst. prof. medicine Stanford U. Sch. Medicine, 1979—85, assoc. prof., 1985—90, prof., 1990—2000, chief div. gen. internal medicine, 1988—95, assoc. dean info. resources and tech., 1995—2000; pres. SCAMC, Inc. (Symposium on Computer Applications in Med. Care), Washington, 1988—89; assoc. chair medicine Primary Care, 1993—95; prof., chair dept. med. informatics Columbia U. Coll. Physicians and Surgeons, N.Y.C., 2000—; deputy v.p. Information Technology, Health Sciences, Columbia U., 2002—. Advisor Nat. Bd. Med. Examiners, Phila., 1987—93; mem. Nat. Fed. Networking Adv. Coun., NSF, 1991—93; mem. computer sci. and telecomm. bd. NRC, 1991—96; bd. regents ACP-Am. Soc. Internal Medicine, 1996—2002; mem. President's Info. Tech. Adv. Com., 1997—; chmn. com. on healthcare and next generation internet NRC, 1998—2000; mem. Nat. Com. on Vital Health Stats., 2000—. Editor: Rule-Based Expert Systems, 1984, Readings in Medical Artificial Intelligence, 1984, Medical Informatics: Computer Applications in Health Care, 1990, Medical Informatics: Computer Applications in Health Care and Biomedicine, 2d edit., 2000. Recipient Grace M. Hopper award, Assn. Computing Machinery, 1976, Young Investigator award, Western Soc. Clin. Investigation, 1987, Rsch. Career award, Nat. Libr. of Medicine, 1979—84; scholar, Kaiser Family Found., 1983—88. Fellow: Am. Coll. Med. Informatics (pres. 1992—94), Am. Assn. Artificial Intelligence; mem.: Am. Clin. and Climatol. Assn., Assn. Am. Physicians, Am. Med. Informatics Assn., Am. Soc. for Clin. Investigation, Inst. Medicine (mem. coun. 2000—), Soc. for Med. Decisionmaking (pres. 1989—90). Achievements include development of several medical computer programs including MYCIN. Avocation: skiing. Office: Columbia-Presbyn Med Ctr Vanderbilt Clinic Ste 550 622 W 168th St New York NY 10032-3720 E-mail: shortliffe@dmi.columbia.edu.

SHORT-MAYFIELD, PATRICIA AHLENE, business owner; b. Ft. Benning, Ga., Oct. 12, 1955; d. William Pressley and Ilse Marie (Hofmann) Short; m. Thomas Hicks Fort, June 2, 1973 (div. Jan. 1981); m. Michael Patrick Mayfield, Aug. 11, 1984; 1 child, William Zachary. Grad. high sch., Butler, Ga., 1973. Notary pub., Ga. Staff mem. Fairyland Day Care, Canton, Ga., 1973-74, Small World Child Care, Thomaston, 1974-77; nurses aide Kenneston Hosp., Marietta, 1978-80; staff worker Mental Health Ctr., Smyrna, 1980-81; dir. Kiddie Kollege, Marietta, 1981-85; bus. owner, mgr. Spiffy Clean by Mayfield, 1985-95; lead cashier Petsmart, Kennesaw, Ga., 1994—. Choir staff Eastside Bapt. Ch., Marietta, 1988-89; vol. East Valley Elem. Sch., 1989-95, chorus vol., 1994-95; vol. East Cobb Middle Sch., 1995—; active Nat. Congress Parents and Tchrs., Cobb County Humane Soc., 1991—. Mem. NAFE, Cobb County C. of C., Atlanta High Mus. Art, Dog Lovers Am. Republican. Baptist. Avocations: reading, walking, symphony, art, bicycling. Office: Spiffy Clean By Mayfield 2791 Georgian Ter Marietta GA 30068-3625

SHORTRIDGE, JUDY BETH, lawyer; b. Johnson City, Tenn., Feb. 17, 1954; d. George Edd and Anna Louise (Salmon) Copenhaver; m. Michael L. Shortridge, July 27, 1984; children: Sarah Elizabeth, Alexander Blake. BA, Va. Poly. Inst. and State U., 1976; MEd, U. Va., 1982; JD, U. Tenn., 1989. Bar: Va. 1990, U.S. Dist. Ct. (we. dist.) Va. 1990, Ea. Dist. Tenn., 1995. Tchr. Stafford County (Va.) Sch. System, 1976-84, Wise County (Va.) Sch. System, 1984-86; ptnr. Shortridge & Shortridge, P.C., Norton, Va., 1990—. Recipient Am. Jurisprudence award U. Tenn., 1989. Mem. Va. Bar Assn. Home: 340 Winterham Dr Abingdon VA 24211-3800 Office: Shortridge & Shortridge PC 170 Valley St NW Abingdon VA 24210-2836

SHORTRIDGE, MICHAEL L. lawyer; b. Grundy, Va., May 26, 1957; s. Leon and Mavis S.; m. Judy Beth Copenhaver, July 27, 1984. BA with distinction, U. Va., 1979, JD, 1982. Bar: Va. 1982, U.S. Dist. Ct. (we. dist.) Va. 1982, U.S. Ct. Appeals (4th cir.) 1984, U.S. Tax Ct. 1985, U.S. Supreme Ct. 1987, U.S. Dist. Ct. (ea. dist.) Tenn. 1995, Ky. 1996, U.S. Dist. Ct. (ea. dist.) Ky. 1996, U.S. Ct. Appeals (6th cir.) 1997. Assoc. Mullins, Winston, Keuling-Stout, Thomason & Harris, Norton, Va., 1982-84; pvt. practice, 1984-89; ptnr. Shortridge & Shortridge PC, Norton and Abingdon, 1989—. Adj. faculty Clinch Valley Coll., U. Va., 1996-97. Steering com. Appalachian Sch. Law, Grundy, Va. Mem. ATLA, Wise County Bar Assn. (pres. 1996), Va. Trial Lawyers Assn., Am. Bankruptcy Inst., Glenrochie Country Club. Home: 340 Winterham Abingdon VA 24211-3800 Office: Shortridge & Shortridge PC 170 W Valley St Abingdon VA 24210 Also: Shortridge & Shortridge PC 18 17th St Ste 300 Norton VA 24273-1946

SHORTZ, RICHARD ALAN, lawyer; b. Chgo., Mar. 11, 1945; s. Lyle A. and Wilma Warner (Wildes) S.; m. Jennifer A. Harrell; children: Eric, Heidi. BS, Ind. U., 1967; JD, Harvard U., 1970. Bar: Calif. 1971, U.S. Supreme Ct. 1980. Assoc. Gibson, Dunn & Crutcher, L.A., 1970-73; sr. v.p., gen. counsel, sec. Tosco Corp., 1973-83; ptnr. Jones, Day, Reavis & Pogue, 1983-95, Rogers & Wells, L.A., 1995-97, Morgan Lewis & Bockius, L.A., 1997—. Mem. L.A. World Affairs Inst., 1983—, Town Hall L.A., 1983—. 2nd lt. U.S. Army, 1970-71. Mem.: Calif. Bar Assn., L.A. Bar. Assn., ABA, Merion Golf Club (Ardmore, Pa.), Loch Lomond Golf Club (Scotland), L.A. Country Club, Beach Club (Santa Monica, Calif.), Calif. Club. Republican. Episcopalian. Home: 1343 Pavia Pl Pacific Palisades CA 90272-4047 Office: Morgan Lewis & Bockius 300 S Grand Ave Ste 2200 Los Angeles CA 90071-3132 E-mail: rshortz@morganlewis.com.

SHORTZ, WILL, puzzle editor; b. Crawfordsville, Ind., Aug. 26, 1952; s. Lyle A. and Wilma Warner (Wildes) S. AB, Ind. U., 1974; JD, U. Va., 1977. Editor Penny Press, Stamford, Conn., 1977-78; assoc. editor Games Mag., N.Y.C., 1978-82, sr. editor, 1982-89, editor, 1989-93; crossword editor N.Y. Times, 1993—. Founder, dir. Am. Crossword Puzzle Tournament, Stamford, Conn., 1978—, World Puzzle Team Championship, N.Y.C., 1992, Stamford, 2000; puzzlemaster Weekend Edit. Sunday, NPR, Washington, 1987—; U.S. team capt. Internat. Crossword Marathon, 1989-90, World Puzzle Championship, 1993-99; riddle writer Batman Forever, 1995; co-founder World Puzzle Fedn., 1999. Author: Brain Games, 1979, The American Quiz Book, 1979, Brain Games 2, 1980, The Bantam Great Masters Winning Crossword Puzzles, vol. 1-3, 1980, World Class Championship Crosswords, 1982, Brain Games 3, 1983, Games Mag. Book of Crossword Puzzles, 1985, American Championship Crosswords, 1990, Games Mag. Giant Book of Games, 1991, Will Shortz's Best Brain Busters, 1991, Games Mag. Best Pencil Puzzles, 1992, The World's Most Ornery Crosswords, vol. 1, 1992, Brain Twisters from the First World Puzzle Championships, 1993, N.Y. Times Daily Crossword Puzzles, vols. 40-60, 1995—, The Puzzlemaster Presents, 1996, Will Shortz's Tournament Crosswords, 1997; (with Ron Osher) Brain Twisters From the World Puzzle Championship, vol. 2-3, 1995-97, N.Y. Times Sunday Crossword Puzzles, vol. 24-27, 1998—, N.Y. Times Toughest Crossword Puzzles, vol. 7-9, 1998-. Mem. Am. Antiquarian Soc., Am. Cryptogram Assn., Authors Guild, Nat. Puzzlers' League (pres. 1977, 81, historian 1992—). Avocations: table tennis, book collecting. Office: NY Times 229 W 43rd St New York NY 10036-3959

SHORTZ, WILMA WILDES, writer, Arabian horse breeder; b. Kansas City, Mo., Dec. 16, 1910; d. John Henry Jr. and Viola Alberta (Warner) Wildes; m. Lyle Alton Shortz, Sept. 16, 1939 (dec. Nov. 1994); children: April Irene, Richard Alan, William Frederic. Grad. ct. reporter, Gregg Coll., Chgo., 1931. Freelance ct. reporter, Chgo., 1930-43, Crawfordsville, Ind., 1951; supr. Montgomery County Soil & Water Conservation Dist., 1970-85, chair, 1981-85, assoc. supr., 1986—. Contbg. author: Montgomery County Legend and Lore, 1988; spkr. weekly program on horses Sta. WCVL, 1980-81; contbr. horse articles, stories and humor to mags. Mem. Presbyn. Ch. Women's Assn., 1955—, pres., 1963—64, Crawfordsville H.S. PTA, 1961—63; mem. organizing com. Montgomery County 4-H Horse and Pony Club, 1960—61, officer, 1961—65; mem. Current Events Club, 1959—, pres., 1966—67, 2000—01. Mem. LWV (pres. Montgomery County 1965-67). Presbyterian. Avocations: writing, contests.

SHOSKY, JOHN EDWIN, communications consultant, speechwriter; b. Colorado Springs, Colo., Nov. 1, 1955; s. Alexander Matthew and Barbara Marie (Middelkamp) S. BA in Polic. Sci., Colo. Coll., 1979; MA in Philosophy, U. Wyo., 1987; PhD in Philosophy, Am. U., 1992. Dep. dir. media and sports commns. White House Conf. for Drug Free Am., Washington, 1987-88; sr. policy analyst White House Office Pub. Affairs, 1988; cons. to sec. HHS, Washington, 1984-91, cons. to Surgeon Gen., 1991-92; cons. to office of nat. drug control policy Exec. Office of the Pres., 1992-93; pres., sr. writer Roncalli Comm., 1991—; asst. prof. philosophy Am. U., Washington, 1996-97, asst. dir. honors program, 1999—. Speech writer for govt. ofcls., corp. execs., profl. athletes, congressmen, senators; lectr. in philosophy Am. U., 1987—2002; adj. prof. philosophy George Mason U., 1990—94; vis. sr. mem. Linacre Coll., Oxford, England, 1997—; vis. prof. Charles U., Prague, 1998; vis. scholar Ins. of Logic, Acad. Scis., Czech Republic, 1998; vis. fellow Acad. Scis., Czech Republic, 2002—. Contbr. numerous articles to acad. and profl. jours., trade publs., newsletters, regional and nat. newspapers. Mem. Austrian Wittgenstein Soc., Am. Philos. Assn., Hume Soc., Mind Assn., British Soc. for the History Philosophy, U. Wyo. Alumni Assn. Republican. Roman Catholic. Home: 1806 Rollins Dr Alexandria VA 22307-1613 Office: Am U Univ Honors Program Washington DC 20016

SHOSS, CYNTHIA RENÉE, lawyer; b. Cape Girardeau, Mo., Nov. 29, 1950; d. Milton and Carroll Jane (Duncan) S.; m. David Goodwin Watson, Apr. 13, 1986; 1 child, Lucy J. Watson. BA cum laude, Newcomb Coll., 1971; JD, Tulane U., 1974; LLM in Taxation, NYU, 1980. Bar: La. 1974, Mo. 1977, Ill. 1978, N.Y. 1990. Law clk. to assoc. and chief justices La. Supreme Ct., New Orleans, 1974-76; assoc. Stone, Pigman et al, 1976-77, Lewis & Rice, St. Louis, 1977-79, Curtis, Mallet-Prevost, et al, N.Y.C., 1980-82; ptnr. LeBoeuf, Lamb, Greene & MacRae, L.L.P., 1982—; mng. ptnr. London office LeBoeuf, Lamb, Leiby & MacRae, 1987-89. Assoc. editor Tulane Law Rev., 1972-74; frequent speaker before profl. orgns. and assns. Contbr. articles to profl. jours. Mem. ABA, Am. Mgmt. Assn. (ins. and risk mgmt. coun.), Corp. Bar Westchester and Fairfield, Power of Atty., Inc. (chair, bd. dirs.), Assn. Life Ins. Counsels. Office: LeBoeuf Lamb Greene Et Al 125 W 55th St New York NY 10019-5369

SHOSTAK, DEBRA BETH, English educator; b. Chgo., June 17, 1953; d. Irvin D. S. and Leila S. (Stuart) Rowe; m. Jeffrey A. Pinkham; children: Sarah, Michael. BA, Carleton Coll., 1975; MA, U. Wis., 1977, PhD, 1985. Mng. editor Contemporary Lit., Madison, Wis., 1982-87; instr. English U. Wis., Janesville, 1985, lectr. English Madison, 1987; asst. prof. English Coll. Wooster, Ohio, 1987-94, assoc. prof. English, 1994—2002, prof. English, 2002—. Judge new writers award Gt. Lakes Coll. Assn., 1996. Contbr. articles to profl. jours. Mem. MLA, Soc. Study Narrative Lit. E-mail: dshostak@wooster.edu.

SHOSTAK, S. RICHARD, lawyer; b. Omaha, July 16, 1931; s. Max Reubin and Reva Ruth (Gross) S.; m. Carole Ruth Blumenthal; children: Stuart Robert, Dennis Alan, Cynthia Robin. AB, U. Calif., Berkeley, 1951, BA, 1953, JD, 1956. Bar: Calif. 1956, U.S. Dist. Ct. (so. and cen. dists.) 1956, U.S. Ct. Appeals (9th cir.), U.S. Supreme Ct. 1960, U.S. Ct. Appeals (fed. cir.) 1960, D.C. 1980, U.S. Ct. Internat. Trade 1981. Assoc. Geary, Spridgen & Moskowitz, Santa Rosa, Calif., 1956-58; dep. dist. atty. Sonoma County Dist. Atty., 1958-59; ptnr. Stein and Shostak, L.A., 1960-76; v.p. Stein, Shostak, Shostak & O'Hara, Washington, San Diego, 1976—. Hearing examiner City of L.A. Police Commn., 1964-79; lectr. UCLA Ext., 1975-92. Author: U.S. Customs Laws and Regulations, 1978, 79, 80; contbr. articles to profl. jours. Chmn. World Trade Week, L.A., 1976; sec. Com. for 807, Washington, 1980-88, Com. for Prodn. Sharing, Washington, 1989-92. Mem. ABA, Wilshire Bar Assn., Fgn. Trade Assn. So. Calif. (pres., chmn. bd. 1976-78),

L.A. C. of C. Avocation: golf. Home: 4211 Clear Valley Dr Encino CA 91436-3315 Office: Stein Shostak Shostak O'Hara 515 S Figueroa St Ste 1200 Los Angeles CA 90071-3329 Fax: 213-486-0011. E-mail: dshostak@steinshostak.com.

SHOTKO, KURT JOSEPH, entrepreneur, music entertainer; b. Allentown, Pa., May 25, 1967; s. Karen Joy LaBella and Joseph Stanley Shotko. Student, Keystone Coll., 1985-87, East Stroudsburg U., 1989-90. Founder Hemp Expresses Rational Balance, Scranton, Pa., 1997—, An Idea Outlet, Moscow, 1996—, Earth Worship Nation, Scranton, 1997—. Founder Rhythm Against Rage, Scranton, 1997—. Contbr. articles to profl. jours. Green Party candidate 10th Dist. for U.S. Ho. Reps., Scranton, 1998, 2000, 2002; Green Party candidate for mayor, 2001; progressive activist, lobbyist Citizens for Common Sense, Scranton, 1995—; Lackawanna County chmn. for Ralph Nader, Green Party, 2000. Named N.E. Pa. Best Activist The Electric City, 2000. Avocations: musician, poet, photographer, sculptor, painter, urban gardener. Home: 542 Prescott Ave Scranton PA 18510 Office: An Idea Outlet 103 Van Brunt St Moscow PA 18444 E-mail: nation@epix.net.

SHOTT, SALLY RICHARD, otolaryngologist; b. Cin., 1956; Student, Williams Coll., 1974-76; BA, U. Chgo., 1978; MD, U. Cin., 1982. Diplomate Am. Bd. Otolaryngology. Resident gen. surgery U. Cin. Hosps., 1982-83, resident in otolaryngology, 1983-87; fellow in pediatric otolaryngology Children's Hosp., Cin., 1987; mem. staff Children's Hosp. Med. Ctr.; assoc. prof. U. Cin.; pvt. practice Cin. Mem.: S.E.N.T.A.C., AMA, Triologic Soc., Otolaryngol. Soc. N.Am., Am. Soc. Pediat. Otolaryngology, Am. Assn. Otolaryngology-Head and Neck Surgery. Office: 3333 Burnet Ave Bethesda and Elland Ave Cincinnati OH 45229

SHOTT, SUSAN, medical biostatistician, educator; b. Kalamazoo, June 17, 1954; d. Michael John and Peggy (Winifred) S. BA, Ctrl. Mich. U., 1976; MA, U. Chgo., 1977, MS, 1981, PhD, 1983. Tech. writer SPSS Inc., Chgo., 1980-81; asst. prof. preventive medicine Rush Med. Ctr., 1982-93, assoc. prof. med. oncology, 1994-95, assoc. prof. neurosurgery, 1995—. Statis. reviewer Jour. of Am. Vet. Med. Assn., 1984—. New Eng. Jour. Medicine, 1997—. Author: Statistics for Health Professionals, 1990 (Am. Jour. of Nursing Book of Yr. 1990); contbr. articles to profl. jours. NSF fellow, 1976-79. Mem. Am. Statis. Assn., Basenji Club Am., Sigma Xi. Jewish. Avocation: dog training. Office: Dept Neurosurgery Rush Med Ctr 1725 W Harrison St Ste 755 Chicago IL 60612-3863 E-mail: stattwit@aol.com.

SHOTTS, WAYNE J. nuclear scientist, federal agency administrator; b. Des Plaines, Ill., Mar. 20, 1945; s. Norman Russell Shotts and Winnifred Mae (Averill) Shotts Goeppinger; m. Melinda Maureen Antilla, June 24, 1967 (dec. Feb. 1975); children: Kenneth Wayne Shotts, Jeffrey Alan Shotts; m. Jacquelyn Francyle Willis, Aug. 11, 1979. BA in Physics, U. Calif., Santa Barbara, 1967; PhD, Cornell U., 1973. Rsch. physicist E.I. duPont deNemours & Co., Wilmington, Del., 1973-74; physicist U. Calif., Livermore, Calif., 1974—, Lawrence Livermore (Calif.) Nat. Lab., 1974-79; group leader, thermonuclear design divsn. Lawrence Livermore Nat. Lab., Livermore, Calif., 1979-85, divsn leader, nuclear chemistry, 1985-86, divsn. leader, prompt diagnostics, 1986-88, prin. dep. assoc. dir., military applications, 1988-92, prin. dep. assoc. dir. def. and nuclear techs., 1992-95, assoc. dir. nonproliferation arms control/internat. security, 1995—. Recipient Ernest Orlando Lawrence Meml. award U.S. Dept. Energy, Washington, 1990. Mem. Am. Phys. Soc., Am. Assn. Advancement Sci. Office: Lawrence Livermore Nat Lab PO Box 808 Livermore CA 94551-0808

SHOTWELL, MALCOLM GREEN, retired minister; b. Brookneal, Va., Aug. 14, 1932; s. John Henry and Ada Mildred (Puckett) S.; m. LaVerne Brown, June 19, 1954; children: Donna (dec.), Paula. BA in Sociology, U. Richmond, 1954; MDiv, Colgate Rochester Div. Sch., 1957; D Ministry, Ea. Bapt. Theol. Sem., 1990; DD (hon.), Judson Coll., 1990. Ordained to ministry Am. Bapt. Ch. in U.S.A., 1957. Student asst. Greece Bapt. Ch., Rochester, N.Y., 1954-57; pastor 1st Bapt. Ch., Cuba, 1957-62, sr. pastor Galesburg, Ill., 1962-71, Olean, N.Y., 1971-81; area minister Am. Bapt. Chs. of Pa. and Del., 1981-90; regional exec. minister Am. Bapt. Chs. of Great Rivers Region, Ill. and Mo., 1990-96; ret., 1997. Mem. Midwest Commn. on Ministry Am. Bapt. Chs. U.S.A., 1990—96, mem. task force for So. Bapt. Am. Bapt. Chs. Relationships, 1990—96; cons. for ch. growth and planning. Author: Creative Programs for the Church Year, 1986, Renewing the Baptist Principle of Associations, 1990; contbg. writer Baptists in the Balance, 1997; rschr., writer, performer: (dramatic monologue) Our Neighbors, the Lincolns: A Clergyman Remembers, 1999—. Trustee No. Bapt. Theol. Sem., Lombard, Ill., 1993-96; mem. gen. exec. coun., 1990-96, regional exec. ministers coun., 1990-96; trustee Judson Coll., 1990—, chmn., 1997-2000, chmn. presdl. search com., 1997-98; bd. dirs. Ctrl. Bapt. Theol. Sem., Kansas City, Kans., 1990-96; sec. bd. dirs. Shurtleff Fund, Springfield, Ill., 1990-96; tchr., libr. Ctrl. Bapt. Ch., Springfield, 1997—; mem. Hist. Commn. Am. Bapts. Ill. and Mo., 1998—; retreat leader in stress mgmt., 1985—; conf., spkr., pulpit supply preacher Bapt. Ch.; mentor ILCS Elem. Sch., Old State Capital Reenactment of Lincoln-Douglas Debates, 1999-2001. Walter Pope Binns fellow William Jewell Coll., 1995. Mem. Ministers Coun. Ill. and Mo., Coun. Ret. Execs.

SHOTWELL, SHEILA MURRAY, medical/surgical nurse; b. Alamance County, Dec. 27, 1963; d. Homer Banks and Betty Jane (Robertson) Murray; m. Tony Allen Shotwell, July 30, 1988; children: Brent Allen, Emily Beth. Diploma, Watt's Sch. Nursing, 1985. RN N.C., cert. case mgmt. . Staff nurse Durham (N.C.) County Gen. Hosp., 1985-91; home health nurse Home Care Providers, Burlington, N.C., 1992-98; utilization rev. case mgr. Jefferson Pilot Fin., Greensboro, 1998; disease mgr. Accordant Health Svcs., 1999—. Mem. Watt's Alumni Assn. Office: 4900 Koger Blvd Ste 300 Greensboro NC 27407-2710 E-mail: sshotwel@accordant.net.

SHOU, MAGANG, pharmacologist, researcher; b. ZhengZhou, China, Dec. 17, 1954; s. Hua-Shan Shou and Shu-Jie Ma; m. Ruiping Wang, Jan. 15, 1985; children: Louie, Jeffery X. BS in Pharmacy, Beijing U. Chinese Medicine, 1981; MS in Pharmacology, Henan Med. U., Zheng Zhou, 1985; PhD, Uniformed Svcs. U. Health Sci., Bethesda, Md., 1991. Rsch. assoc. Beijing Inst. Radiation Medicine, China, 1985-86; postdoctoral rschr. U. Pa. Med. Sch., Phila., 1991; vis. assoc. Nat. Cancer Inst., Bethesda, 1991-94, sr. staff fellow, 1994-96; rsch. fellow Merck Rsch. Labs., West Point, Pa., 1996—2001, sr. rsch. fellow, 2001—. Hon. prof. Henan Med. U., Zheng Zhou, 1994—. Author: Cytochrom P450 Protocols, 1998; mem. editl. bd. Pharmacogenetics, 1996—; contbr. articles to profl. jours. Mem. Internat. Soc. Study Xenobiotics, Am. Assn. Pharm. Scis., Soc. Chinese Biologists in Am. Office: WP75A-203 Dept Drug Metabolism Merck Rsch Labs 770 Sumneytown Pike West Point PA 19486 Fax: 215-652-2410. E-mail: magang_shou@merck.com.

SHOUN, ELLEN LLEWELLYN, retired secondary school educator; b. Germantown, Pa., Sept. 8, 1925; d. William Thomas and Ella (Hall) Llewellyn; m. Glenn Harte Shoun, June 25, 1949; children: Mary Deborah, Paul L., Eleanor C., Peter G., Elizabeth A. AB in Chemistry, Oberlin Coll., 1947; MA in Sci. Edn., Western Mich. U., 1972. Cert. libr. (ltd. profl.) Mich., secondary sch. tchr. Mich. Jr. chemist Am. Cyanamid, Stamford, Conn., 1947-49; Charles M. Hall Chem. instr. Oberlin (Ohio) Coll., 1949-51; br. libr. Bronson (Mich.) Pub. Libr., 1966-67; math. and sci. tchr. Bronson H.S., 1967-79; crew leader 1980 U.S. Census, Branch County, 1980; bus. mgr. Dr. C.F. Cole's Dental Office, Sturgis, 1982; reference aide Br. Dist. Libr., Coldwater, 1982-99; ret., 1999. Founder (with others) Bronson H.S. Cmty. Recycling Group, 1972—79. Trustee Bronson Pub. Libr., 1968—82, Housing Commn., 1975—; instr. CPR Cmty. health Ctr., Coldwater, 1978—80; cmty. chorus Cmty. Found., 1987—; chair refugee family com. Bronson United Meth. Ch., 1974—82, ch. choir, 1967—, sec. adminstrv. bd., 1987—, chair bd. dirs., 1984—86; bd. dirs., mgr. Food Pantry, 5 Ch. Coop., 1993—. Named Hon. Grand Marshal, Polish Festival Parade, Bronson, 2002; recipient Cmty. Vol. of Yr. award, Gleaner Life Ins. Soc., 2001. Mem.: Phi Beta Kappa. Democrat. Avocations: photography, knitting, Scrabble.

SHOUP, CHARLES SAMUEL, JR. chemicals and materials executive; b. Nashville, Dec. 10, 1935; s. Charles Samuel and Leola Ruth (Turner) S.; m. Frances Carolyn DiCarlo, June 7, 1958 (dec. Apr. 1999); children: Mark Steven, Elizabeth Ann Shoup Kehoe, Margaret Carol Shoup Meyer; m. Sara Jo Denkmann, May 5, 2001. AB, Princeton U., 1957; MS, U. Tenn., 1961, PhD, 1962. Rsch. chemist Oak Ridge (Tenn.) Natl. Lab., 1962-67; mgr. special projects Union Carbide Corp., N.Y.C., 1967-68; mgr. planning and controls Bell and Howell Co., Lincolnwood, Ill., 1968; v.p. Bell and Howell Sch. Inc., Chgo., 1968-69; mgr. tech. planning Cabot Corp., Boston and Cambridge, Mass., 1969-70, dir. corp. rsch., Mass., 1970-73, gen. mgr. E-A-R div., 1973-87, v.p., Indpls., 1984-87; pres. Alphaflex Ind. Inc., Indpls, 1987-88, bd. dirs., 1988, Cemkote Corp., Indpls., 1988-91. Chmn. bd. dirs. Blasterz Corp., Carmel, Ind., 1992-2001; mem. adv. bd. Technalysis, Inc., Indpls., 1996-99; bd. dirs. Exec. Svc. Corps, Indpls., 1993—, mem. exec. com., 1994—, vice chmn., sec., 1997-99, chmn. bd. dirs., 2001—; mem. bd. visitors Coll. Arts and Scis., U. Tenn., Knoxville, 1994—. Contbr. articles to profl. jours. Treas. Oak Ridge Arts Ctr., 1965-67; pres. Sherborn Edn. Found., 1974-76; chmn. Met. Div. United Way, 1982; bd. trustees, Ind. Safety Equipment Assn. 1978-81. Fellow Am. Inst. Chemists; mem. AAAS, Am. Chem. Soc., Noise Control Products and Materials Assn. (trustee 1977-87, pres. 1982-84), Sigma Xi. Presbyterian. Home: 13045 Abraham Run Carmel IN 46033-8618

SHOUP, JAMES RAYMOND, computer systems consultant; b. McKees Rocks, Pa., Apr. 9, 1932; s. Jacob Daniel and Violet May Shoup; m. Caren Michelle Gagner, Nov. 29, 1988; children: Emily Ruth, Rhonda Lou, Richard Eugene, Sean Jason, Amy Marisa, Rodney Warren. Student, U. Md., 1953-54, U. Miami, 1957-58, Palm Beach Jr. Coll., 1964-68; AA, Fla. Jr. Coll., 1978, AS, 1980. With Fla. Power and Light Co., Delray Beach, 1954-68; pres. JSE Corp., 1954-68; fin. cons. area bus., 1954-68; with FAA, 1968-72; with sales and mgmt. depts. Montgomery Ward Co., 1972-75; project mgr. JR Shoup & Assocs., Jacksonville, Fla., 1975-78; v.p. R&D JP Computing Co., Jacksonville Beach, 1981-86, AiKen Computer Sys. Co., Flower Mound, Tex., 1979-82; with U.S. Postal Svc., Jacksonville, 1975—; legislative delegate Nat. Assn Postal Spvs. Sys. instr. microcomputer sci. Duval County Cmty. Schs., Jacksonville, 1980-84; cons. on EDP acctg. applications analysis and EDP sys. engring., 1976-2001; fin. cons., 1967-87; legis. del. Nat. Assn. Postal Suprs., 1999—. Author manuals on computer applications in indsl. and transp. mgmt., 1975-84; oil painter represented in pvt. collections, Fla. Asst. chief, pres., dir. Tri-Cmty. Fire Dept., 1955-57; Sunday sch. tchr., deacon, treas., elder, local Presbyn. chs., 1955-80, chmn. pulpit com., 1990; pub. rels. officer N.B. Forrest H.S. Band Parents Assn., 1973-79; mem. Rep. Presdl. Task Force. With USAF, 1950-54. Mem. EDP Auditors Assn., Jacksonville C. of C. (com. of 100 1982), Confederate Point Civic Assn. (dir. 1998-99), Mensa. Achievements include designing Aiken computers, disk patch for tiny Pascal, system 8000 computers, IMAS and IMASNET acctg. sys. for microcomputers, MIC series computers. Home and Office: 4343 Charleston Ln Jacksonville FL 32210-7374 E-mail: j.m.shoup@worldnet.att.net.

SHOUSE, ROGER COLIN, education educator, researcher; b. Dearborn , Mich., Feb. 13, 1954; s. George Roger and Eva Roberta Shouse; m. Shiang-Jeou Shyu, Oct. 31, 1957. PhD, U. Chgo., 1994. Tchr. Southwestern H.S., Detroit, 1985—89; assoc. prof. Pa. State U., University Park, 1994—. Assoc. editor: Administrator's Notebook, 1993—94. Fellow postdoctoral fellow, Nat. Acad. Edn., 1996. Mem.: Am. Ednl. Rsch. Assn. Avocation: Music creation and performance. Office: Pa State U 302 Rackley Blvd State College PA 16802

SHOVER, JOAN, secondary school educator; b. St. Joseph, Mo., Apr. 7, 1948; d. Jay S. and Clara Lillian (Burkett) Marquis; m. Rolland Craig Shover, May 31, 1975; children: Terra Jayne, Thomas Jay. BS in Edn., Ctrl. Mo. State U., 1971, MS in Edn., 1976, postgrad., 1989-96. Cert. tchr., edn. specialist, Mo. Phys. edn. tchr. Worth County H.S., Grant City, Mo., 1971-73, Blue Springs (Mo.) H.S., 1973—. Mem. rev. com. Mo. Dept. Elem. and Secondary Edn., Jefferson City, 1993—; mem. Mo. Quality Health/Phys. Edn. Cadre, 1998—. Named Am. Cancer Soc. Educator of Yr., 1989, Top 36 Am. Tchrs. award, Disney Corp., 1992, Mo. State Secondary Physical Educator of Yr., 1996. Mem. AAHPERD (ctrl. dist. secondary phys. educator of yr. 1997), NEA, Am. Coun. on Exercise, Internat. Dance Exercise Assn., Mo. Assn. Phys. Edn., Health, Recreation and Dance (Kansas City rep. 1988—, pres. elect 1998-99, pres. 1998-99, past pres. 1999-2000, Kansas City Dist. Phys. Educator award 1989, Presdl. award 1988), Mo. State Tchrs. Assn., Delta Kappa Gamma. Avocations: reading, dancing, skiing, running. Home: 1418 NW A St Blue Springs MO 64015-3605 Office: 2000 Ashton Dr Blue Springs MO 64015 E-mail: jshover50@aol.com.

SHOVLIN, JOSEPH PATRICK, optometrist; BA in Psychology, Gettysburg Coll., 1974; BS in Physiol. Optics, Pa. Coll. of Optometry, 1978, D of Optometry, 1980. Cert. optometrist Pa., N.Y., Va., Md. Assoc. Morrison Assocs., Harrisburg Pa., N.Y.C., 1980-85; clin. assoc. Northeastern Eye Inst., Scranton, Pa., 1985-91; sr. optometrist Northwestern Eye Inst., 1991—. Cons. Lancaster County Blind Assn., Lancaster, Pa., 1980—85, State Bd. Optometry, 1988—90, Ophthalmic Devices' Adv. Panel, Ctr. for Devices and Radiological Health, FDA, 1987—88, 1992—93, voting mem., 1988—92; adj. faculty Pa. Coll. Optometry, 1981—; cons. and expert witness Bur. Profl. and Occupational Affairs, Pa., 1983—85; presenter over 500 formal lectures to major internat., nat., regional and state ophthalmic groups. Author: (with others) Problems in Optometry, 1990, Clinical Contact Lens Practice, 1991, Optometric Pharmacology, 1992, Anterior Segment Complications of Contact Lens Wear, 1994; contbr. numerous articles to profl. jours. including: Review of Optometry (contbg. editor 1984-88, assoc. clin. editor 1988—), Metabolic, Pediatric and Systemic Ophthalmology, Contact Lens Forum, Focus on Product News, International Contact Lens Clinic (contbg. editor 1988-93), Primary Care Optometry News, (cons. editor, 1995—), Contemporary Optometry, Contact Lens Spectrum (consulting editor 1988—), Optometric Management (contbg. editor 1992-95), Practical Optometry, Review of Ophthalmology, American Acad. of Optometry Newsletter; assoc. editor Making Contact, 1982-88, 94—; editl. bd. Contacto; mem. jour. rev. bd. Optometry Clinics, 1991—; cons. editor Primary Care Optometry News, 1995—; referee, mem. jour. review bd. Jour. Am. Optometric Assn. and Optometry and Vision Sci. Mem. sci. adv. com. Pa. Lions' Sight Conservation and Eye Rsch. Found., nat. adv. eye coun. Nat. Eye Inst. Nat. Insts. Health, 1992-96. Fellow Am. Acad. Optometry (diplomate cornea and contact lens sect. 1985, mem. exec. bd., sec., spkrs. bur., bd. dirs. Pa. chpt. past mem., numerous other coms.); mem. APHA, Internat. Soc. Refractive Surgery (assoc.), Am. Optometric Assn. (sec. contact lens sect. 1988-89, vice chair 1989-90, chair elect 1990-91, chair 1991-92, immediate past chair 1992-93, mem. jour. rev. bd., numerous other coms. and offices, Am. Optometric Recognition award 1980—), Pa. Optometric Assn. (chmn. continuing edn. com. 1993, Keystone contact lens conf. 1987—, com. on contact lenses 1986-94, others), The Assn. for Rsch. in Vision and Ophthalmology, Nat. Eye Rsch. Found., Am. Optometric Found. (bd. dirs. 1988-90), The Prentice Soc., Adv. Bd. Eye Vision Assocs., The Optometric Coun. of the State of N.Y. (Disting. Svc. award 1984). Home: 1308 Oakmont Rd Clarks Summit PA 18411-2061 Office: Northeastern Eye Inst 200 Mifflin Ave Scranton PA 18503-1982

SHOWALTER, BUCK (WILLIAM NATHANIEL SHOWALTER III), major league baseball team manager; b. DeFuniak Springs, Fla., May 23, 1956; Student, Chipola Jr. Coll., Fla., Miss. State U. Player various minor league teams N.Y. Yankee orgn., 1977-83, minor league coach, 1984, minor league mgr., 1985-89; coach N.Y. Yankees, 1989—92, mgr., 1992-95, Ariz. Diamondbacks, 1998—2000, Texas Rangers, 2002—. Named N.Y.-Pa. League Mgr. of Yr., 1985, Eastern League Mgr. of Yr., 1989, Am. League Mgr. of Yr., 1994. Office: Texas Rangers 1000 Ballpark Way #400 Arlington TX 76011

SHOWALTER, DAVID SCOTT, accounting executive; b. Harrisonburg, Va., May 23, 1953; s. Harold Marvin and Martha (Myers) Showalter; m. Elizabeth Allison, June 1, 1974; children: Braxton, Allison, Mason. AS, Ferrum Coll., 1973; BSBA, U. Richmond, 1975. CPA Ill, Mo, Wis, Ind. Asst. to nat. dir. KPMG, N.Y.C., 1981-84, asst. to vice-chmn., 1986-88, ptnr., 1986—, area ptnr. in charge Indpls., 1993-96; nat. industry dir. state, local govts., Chgo., 1996-98; nat. mng. ptnr. Assurance & Advisory Svcs. Ctr., Montvale, NJ, 1998—2002, industry sector leader pub. svc., 2002—. Dir KPMG Found, NY; vis prof Univ Ill. Editor: (newsletter) Govt Acct and Auditing Update. Pres Indianapolis Youth Hockey Asn, 1990—93; pres coun Boy Scouts Am, St Charles, Ill., 1995—97, chmn bd dirs, 1997—98, bd dirs, 1998—, Greater Indianapolis Rep Fin Comt, 1990—94. Named Ky Col, State of Ky, 1986, Sagamore of Wabash for Serv to State of Ind, 1990, D Scott Showalter Day named in his honor, City of Indianapolis, 1994; named one of Top 100 Most Influential in Acctg., Acctg. Today, 2001; recipient Silver Beaver Award, Boy Scouts Am, 1994, Dist Eagle Scout Award, 1998. Mem.: AICPA (mem. com. group of 100), Nat. Intergovtl. Audit Assn., Ill. CPA Soc., Am. Acctg. Assn., Assn. Sch. Bus. Ofcls. (mem. exec. com. cert. program), Govt. Fin. Officers Assn. (mem. com.). Presbyterian. Avocations: camping, jogging, backpacking, stamps. Home: 14 Forest Ridge Rd Upper Saddle River NJ 07458 Office: KPMG 3 Chestnut Ridge Rd Montvale NJ 07645-1842 E-mail: dsshowalter@kpmg.com.

SHOWEN JR. DONALD EUGENE, music educator; b. Charles Town, W.Va., Oct. 22, 1974; s. Donald Eugene and Carrie Alberta Showen; m. Tara Jenea Penick-Showen, Dec. 15, 2001. BA, Shepherd Coll., Shepherdstown, 1997. Coord. percussion studies Hancock H.S., Hancock, Md., 1993—94, Williamsport H.S., Williamsport, 1994—98; asst. band dir. Jefferson H.S., Shenandoah Junction, W.Va., 1998—99; grad. asst. U. of Fla. Sch. of Music, Gainesville, Fla., 1999—2000; dir. bands Jefferson H.S., Shenandoah Junction, W.Va., 2000—. Bd. directors New Hopewell Dance Studio, Shenandoah Junction, W.Va., 2001—. Mem.: Music Educators Nat. Conf., Phi Mu Alpha Sinfonia Frat. (pres. 1993—95). D-Liberal. Achievements include Jefferson High Jazz band won National Championship in 1999 and was named best hazz band in the state in 1999, 2001 and 2002; Symphonic and jazz bands received first place in a national competition in Orlando, Florida. Avocations: golfing, golfing, golfing. Office: Jefferson High School Band R1 1 Box 83 Shenandoah Junction WV 25442

SHOWER, ROBERT WESLEY, financial executive; b. Harvey, Ill., Sept. 5, 1937; s. Glenn Wesley and Chrissie Irene (Ford) S.; m. Sandra Marie Stough, June 27, 1959; children: David Wesley, Lynece Marie. BS, U. Tulsa, 1960; P.MD, Harvard Business Sch., 1972. Sr. auditor Arthur Andersen & Co., Tulsa, 1960-64; with The Williams Cos., 1964-86, asst. v.p., 1968-69, v.p. adminstrn., 1969-71, v.p., treas., 1971, v.p. fin., 1971-73, sr. v.p. fin., 1973-77, exec. v.p. fin. and adminstrn., dir., 1977-86; mng. dir. Shearson, Lehman, Hutton, Dallas, 1986-90; v.p. fin. Ameriserv Food Co., 1990-91; sr. v.p. fin., CFO Seagull Energy Co., Houston, 1992-94, exec. v.p., CFO, 1994-96. Mem. Okla. Soc. CPAs, Lambda Chi Alpha, Delta Sigma Pi. Home: 2922 S Lakeview Dr Cedar Hill TX 75104-8262 Fax: (972) 291-4131. E-mail: rshower@attglobal.net.

SHOWERMAN, CAREN CALAFATI, opera company administrator, educator; b. Huntington, N.Y., Oct. 13, 1952; d. Alan Russell and Dixie Rose (Mason) Calafati; m. John Kenneth Showerman, July 28, 1973 (div.); children: Derek Brent, Alex Reid. BA in Music and Music Edn., Keene (N.H.) State Coll, 1974; postgrad., U. Vt., 1987-88; MA in Liberal Studies, Dartmouth Coll., 1988. Cert. elem. and secondary music and art tchr., Vt.; cert. reality therapy Glasser Inst., L.A. Tchr. music Plainfield Sch., Meriden, 1974-78, Orange East Sch. Supervisory Union, Bradford, Vt., 1979-81; arts coord., tchr. music Hartland (Vt.) Elem. Sch., 1981-85; tchr. music and visual art Thetford (Vt.) Elem. Sch., 1981-86; coord. applied music, ensembles and arts Thetford Acad., Thetford Hill, Vt., 1986-92; founder, prodn. mgr., program developer Through the Opera Glass, Dartmouth Coll., Hanover, 1986—; mem. adj. faculty Thetford Acad., Thetford Hill, Vt., 1992-93; tchr. integrative arts Plainfield Sch., Meriden, NH, 1992—. Instr. Lebanon (N.H.) Coll., 1977-79, 1994—, Warren Sch., Vt., 1991-92, Vt. Coll. Preparatory Sch. Music and Dance, Montpelier, Vt., 1991-93; vis. lectr. SUNY, Cobleskill, 1978-79; dir. fine arts team Aloha Found., Fairlee, Vt., 1983; mem. faculty, instr. external degree program Johnson (Vt.) State Coll., 1987-88; edn. coord. Vt. Symphony Orch., Burlington, 1989-90; guest artistic dir. Vt. Opera Theater, Montpelier, 1993; fine arts edn. cons. various instns. throughout New England, 1990—; vocal/music workshop instr. cancer help program Wellspring Clinic, Lyme, N.H., 1994—, Women's Health Resource Network, Dartmouth, Hitchcock Med. Ctr., Hanover, N.H., 1996—; instr. U. N.H. Coll. Lifelong Learning, 1995-96; founder vocal studios, Woodstock and Thetford, Vt., 1995—. Mezzo soprano soloist, recitalist in New Eng. and N.Y. Bd. dirs. Friends of Ompompanoosuc, Thetford Center, 1985—, also past pres.; mem. MA in Liberal Studies alumni coun. Dartmouth Coll., 1993-95; mem. touring artists program N.H. Coun. on Arts, 1988—, Vt. Coun. on Arts, 1990-98, Artists in Edn. N.H. Coun. on Arts; mem. artists program Mass. Cultural Coun., Cambridge, 1991-96; profl. singer opera/Broadway style, N.Y.C., 1999—. Avocations: watercolors, traditional colonial design, sailing, reading, gardening. E-mail: c. Home: PO Box 357 296 Tucker Hill Rd Thetford Center VT 05075 Office: Through the Opera Glass PO Box 357 Thetford Center VT 05075-0357 E-mail: c_calafati@yahoo.com.

SHOWERS, KRISTA ANN, accountant; b. Lancaster, Pa., Apr. 8, 1968; d. Eugene Francis and Mary Ann Weisser. BA, Immaculata (Pa.) Coll., 1990; MBA, Lebanon Valley Coll., Annville, Pa., 1996. CPA, Pa. Acct. Trout, Ebersole & Groff, LLP, Lancaster, 1990—. Mem. AICPA, Pa. Inst. CPAs, Pa. Assn. Fed. Program Coords. Office: Trout Ebersole & Groff LLP 1705 Oregon Pike Lancaster PA 17601-4200 E-mail: kshowers@troutcpa.com.

SHOWS, LESA W. pharmaceutical executive; b. Glennville, Ga., Sept. 4, 1957; d. Garland Gene and Ronella (Haymans) Wilds; m. Henry Wyatt Shows Jr., Apr. 7, 1990; children: Henry Wyatt III, Alexa Gabrielle. AS in Acctg., S. Ga. Coll., 1977; BA in Bus. Adminstrn., Ga. So. U., 1981. Sales rep. Bristol-Myers Squibb, Macon, Ga., 1983-95, hosp. sales rep., 1995-96, regional sales trainer, 1996, dist. sales mgr., 1996-98; sr. dist. sales mgr. Pharmacia, Tampa, Fla., 1998—. Active Arthritis Found. Bd., 2002. Baptist. Avocations: reading, travelling. Home: 18416 Eastwyck Dr Tampa FL 33647-3184 E-mail: lesa.w.shows@pharmacia.com.

SHOWS, RONNIE, congressman; b. Moselle, Miss., Jan. 26, 1947; m. Johnnie Ruth, 1971; 4 children. BS, U. So. Miss., 1971. Tchr., coach various Jefferson County schs.; cir. ct. clk. Jefferson County, 1976-80; state senator, 1980-88; mem. So. Dist. Hwy. Commn., 1988—99, U.S. Congress from 4th Miss. dist., 1999—. Mem. transp. and infrastructure com., veterans affairs. com. In 1999 succeeded 5-term Rep. Mike Parker (Dem. turned Rep.); defeated Delbert Hosemann (R) for the seat in Congress. Democrat. Office: 1408 Longworth House Office Bldg Washington DC 20515-2404*

SHOWS, WINNIE M. speaker, author, consultant; b. L.A., Apr. 2, 1947; d. William Marion Arvin and Joan Catherine (Sperry) Wilson; m. George Albert Shows, Mar. 18, 1967 (div. May 1980); 1 child, Sallie; m. Michael P. Florio, Jan. 1, 1990 (div.). BA in English, UCLA, 1969; MEd, Calif. State U., Long Beach, 1976. Tchr. St. Joseph High Sch., Lakewood, Calif., 1969-71; tchr. high sch. Irvine (Calif) Unified Sch. Dist., 1972-79; freelance writer, 1979-80; mgr. pub. rels. Forth, Inc., Hermosa Beach, Calif., 1980-81; account mgr., account supr., dir. mktg. Franson & Assoc., San Jose, 1981-84; v.p., pres. Smith & Shows, Menlo Park, 1984-96; spkr., author, cons. in field; co-founder Spkrs. in the Mountains. Presenter seminar in field. Author: (newsletter) Smith & Shows Letter, 1989—94, Hairball and Other Poems of Trans Formation, 2000. Vol. Unity Palo Alto (Calif.) Cmty. Ch., 1989-99, Newcomers, Menlo Park, 1990-93, Kara, Palo Alto, 1991-98, Menlo Park Sch. Dist., 1993-95, Asistencia Para Latinos, 2000. Named Woman of Vision, Career Action Ctr., 1994; named one of Colorado Springs Most Dynamic Women, CS Bus. Jour., 2001. Mem.: Colorado Springs Women and Tech., Nat. Spkrs. Assn., Colorado Spring Women and Tech. (pres. 2001—02, founder, co-founder, pres. 2001—02), Nat. Spkrs. Assn. (treas., , Mem. of Yr. No. Calif. chpt. 1999, Mem. of Yr. 1999, Mem. of Yr. No. Calif. chpt. 1999, Mem. of Yr. 1999, SRI Organon Toastmaster of Yr. 1995, Karl Lind award 1996). Office: 1614 W Kiowa St Colorado Springs CO 80904 E-mail: winnie@wshows.com.

SHPIECE, MICHAEL RONALD, lawyer, educator; b. Detroit, Nov. 13, 1956; s. Harold Edwin and Rose Marie (Wheeler) S.; m. Tracy B. Schwartz; children: David E. Schwartz, Daniel E. Schwartz. PhB, Wayne State U., 1977; JD, U. Mich., 1984. Bar: Mich. 1985. Com. adminstr. Joint Legis. Com. on Aging, Lansing, Mich., 1979-81; policy analyst to commr. Mich. Ins. Bur., 1981; legis. cons Cmty. Action Program Mich. UAW, 1981-82; dep. dir. Mich. Dept. Licensing and Regulation, 1983-85; assoc., ptnr. Honigman Miller Schwartz & Cohn, Detroit, 1985-93; adj. prof. law Wayne State U. Law Sch., 1996—; of counsel Shapack, McCullough & Kanter, Bloomfield Hills, 1994-98; prin. Miller, Shpiece & Tischler, Southfield, 1998—. Pres. Friends of Child Abuse Prevention, Southfield, Mich., 1994—; bd. dirs. chmn. Mich. Freedom of Info. Com., Detroit, 1996-98. Contbr. articles to profl. jours. Pres. and trustee Farmington (Mich.) Bd. Edn., 1975-83; chairperson Farmington Hills Ad Hoc Com. on Ethids, 1990-96. Mem. Am. Statis. Assn., Econ. Club Detroit, ABA (vice chair employee benefit com. torts and ins. practice sect.

1996—), Oakland County Bar Assn. Democrat. Jewish. Home: 39372 Plumbrook Dr Farmington Hills MI 48331-2976 Office: Ste 200 26711 Northwestern Hwy Southfield MI 48034-2159 E-mail: mshpiece@msapc.net.

SHPILRAIN, VLADIMIR EVALD, mathematician, educator; b. Moscow, Sept. 11, 1960; arrived in Israel, 1991; s. Evald and Valentina (Titushina) S.; m. Elen Burov, Jan. 22, 1983. MA in Math., Moscow State U., 1982, PhD in Math., 1989. Asst. prof. Moscow Inst. for Computer Sci., 1982-86, Moscow State U., 1989-90; prof. Haifa, Israel, 1991—. Contbr. articles to profl. jours. Recipient scholarship Internat. Math. Union, Kyoto, Japan, 1990, Rsch. grants Israeli Acad. Sci., Haifa, 1991, '92, German-Israeli Found., Haifa, 1992, fellowship, Minerva Found. fellow, Bochum, Germany, 1993. Mem. Moscow Math. Soc., Moscow Club of Scientists, Am. Math. Soc. Avocation: Alpine skiing. Office: Technion Dept Math Haifa 32000 Israel

SHRADER, CHARLES REGINALD, historian; b. Nashville, July 3, 1943; s. Reginald Woodrow and Freda Olene (Presley) S.; m. Carole Anne Analore, Aug. 17, 1963; children: Peter Reginald, Sheila Lynne Shrader Bixby. BA cum laude, Vanderbilt U., 1964; MA History, Columbia U., 1970, M Phil, 1974, PhD History, 1976; Grad., U.S. Army Command/Gen. Staff, Coll., 1978, U.S. Army War Coll., 1982, NATO Def. Coll., 1984. Commd. 2d lt. U.S. Army, 1964, advanced through grades to lt. col., ret., 1987; asst. prof. history U.S. Mil. Acad., 1971-74; instr. European Divsn. U. Md., Pirmasens and Landstuhl, Germany, 1974-77; instr. U.S. Army Command and Gen. Staff Coll., 1977-80, U.S. Army War Coll., 1980-84; mem. staff NATO Def. Coll., Rome, 1984-85; independent historian, 1987—; exec. dir. Soc. for Mil. History, Carlisle, Pa., 1992-2000. Pres. Nat. Coalition Ind. Scholars, 2000—; adj. instr. Elizabethtown Coll., 1988-89, Penn State U.-Harrisburg, 1988-90; lectr. various Army svc. schs., CIA, U. Kans., U. Victoria/B.C., NATO Def. Coll. Mem. Carlisle Mcpl. Authority, 1993—. Mem. Army and Navy Club, Phi Kappa Psi, Phi Beta Kappa. Roman Catholic. Home and Office: 910 Forbes Rd Carlisle PA 17013-1721 E-mail: heriger@aol.com.

SHRADER, DOUGLAS WALL, JR. philosophy educator; b. Grundy, Va., May 22, 1953; s. Douglas Wall and Audrey Anne (Looney) S.; m. Barbara Frances Donahoe, June 15, 1975; children: Callie Hannah, Sterling Douglas. BA, Va. Polytech. Inst., 1974; MA, U. Ill., Chgo., 1975, PhD, 1979. Asst. to dean grad. studies U. Ill., Chgo., 1974-79; instr. philosophy U. Wis., Parkside, 1979; asst. prof. philosophy SUNY, Oneonta, 1979-85, assoc. prof. philosophy, 1985-92, prof. philosophy, 1992-99, chair dept. philosophy, 1988-91, 93—, dean humanities and fine arts, 1991-93, disting. teaching prof. philosophy, 1999—. Cons. Regents Coll., Albany, N.Y., 1994—, McGraw-Hill, N.Y., 1992-99, Prentice Hall, N.Y., 1997, Jones and Bartlett, 1998, Oxford, 2001, SUNY Press, 2000-2002. Author: Pathways to Philosophy, 1996; editor: Seeds of Wisdom, 1997, Language, Ethics and Ontology, 1998, The Fractal Self, 2000, Ethics, Theory and Practice, 1996, Children of Athena, 1999, Philosophy and the Public Realm, 2001, Thinking Outside the Box, 2002; mem. editl. bd., editor-in-chief Oneonta Philosophy Studies, 1991—, Ashgate World Philosophies Series, 1999—; mem. editl. bd. Ednl. Change, 1995—, Eidos: Studies in Ancient and Medieval Philosophy, 1991—, East-West Connections, 2000—. Bd. dirs. Catskill Area Hospice, Oneonta, 1985-88; troop treas. Boy Scouts Am., Oneonta, 1994-98, cubmaster, 1991-94; judge Odyssey of the Mind, Oneonta, 1994—. Rsch. grantee W.B. Ford Found., 1995, 98, 99, 2000, Henry Luce Found., 1999, 2002 Chinese Ministry of Edn., 2002; summer inst. fellow NEH, 1980, 85, 89, 95, 98; recipient Commendation for Acad. Excellence, SUNY-Oneonta Alumni Assn., 1995, Chancellor's award Excellence in Teaching, 1991 Mem. Soc. for Ancient Greek Philosophy, East-West Ctr. Assoc., N.Y. State Founds. Edn. Assn. Avocations: photography, music, construction, classic cars. Office: SUNY-Oneonta Ravine Pkwy Oneonta NY 13820-3414

SHRADER, WILLIAM WHITNEY, radar consulting scientist; b. Foochow, China, Oct. 17, 1930; came to U.S., 1932; s. Ralph Raymond and Elizabeth Talmadge (Hand) S.; m. Natalie Lucinda Hutchinson, July 21, 1984. BSEE, U. Mass., 1953; MSEE, Northeastern U., 1961. Rsch. engr. Boeing Airplane Co., Seattle, 1953-56; cons. scientist, tech. dir. numerous radar systems developed Raytheon Co., Wayland, Mass., 1956-1994; pvt. practice radar cons. Shrader Assocs. Inc., Stow, 1994—. Author: (with others) Radar Handbook, 1970, 2d edit., 1990; contbr. articles to profl. jours.; holder 10 U.S. patents, numerous fgn. patents. Fellow IEEE. Avocation: sports car rallying. Home and Office: 144 Harvard Rd Stow MA 01775-1070 E-mail: shrader@prodigy.net.

SHRAGE, LAURETTE, special education educator; b. Montreal, Jan. 15, 1951; d. Ivan and Adela (Zupnik) Benda; m. William Lee Shrage, Oct. 30, 1977; children: Robert, Jaclyn. BS in Elem. Edn., Adelphi U., 1972; MS in Reading, Coll. New Rochelle, 1994. Cert. elem. edn., spl. edn., reading, bilingual edn., N.Y. Mgr. Century Operating Corp., N.Y.C., 1973-82; substitute tchr. New Rochelle (N.Y.) Sch. Dist., 1992-93, bilingual spl. edn. tchr., 1993—; substitute tchr. Keller Sch., Yonkers, N.Y., 1992-93; spl. edn. tchr., 1993—; co-owner Pet Store, 1998—. Parent rep. New Rochelle Com. Presch. Spl. Edn., 1990-91, New Rochelle Com. Spl. Edn., 1991-92; mem. adv. coun. Jefferson Sch., New Rochelle, 1993—, mem. Magnet Think Tank com., 1994—; mem. Ptnrs. in Policy Making N.Y. State, 1992; Instr. Family Sci. Workshop, 1996—; co-owner full svc. pet store. Pres. PTA Augustus St. Gardens Sch., N.Y.C., 1987-90; advt. mgr. Mitchell Lama Apt., N.Y.C., 1983-86; telethon vol. Channel 13, N.Y.C., 1977; sponsor Sagamore Children's Sch., Suffolk, N.Y., 1974. Recipient Parent Leadership award Coun. Suprs. and Adminstrs. City of N.Y., 1990. Avocations: Spanish, French, tennis, piano, opera. Home: 110 Valley Forge Rd Weston CT 06883-1930 Office: Jefferson Sch 131 Weyman Ave New Rochelle NY 10805-1428

SHRAUNER, BARBARA WAYNE ABRAHAM, electrical engineer, educator; b. Morristown, N.J., June 21, 1934; d. Leonard Gladstone and Ruth Elizabeth (Thrasher) Abraham; m. James Ely Shrauner, 1965; children: Elizabeth Ann, Jay Arthur. BA cum laude, U. Colo., 1956; AM, Harvard U., 1957, PhD, 1962. Postdoctoral researcher U. Libre de Bruxelles, Brussels, 1962-64; postdoctoral researcher NASA-Ames Rsch. Ctr., Moffett Field, Calif., 1964-65; asst. prof. Washington U., St. Louis, 1966-69, assoc. prof., 1969-77, prof., 1977—. Sabbatical Los Alamos (N.Mex.) Sci. Lab., 1975-76, Lawrence Berkeley Lab., Berkeley, Calif., 1985-86; cons. Los Alamos Nat. Lab., 1979, 84, NASA, Washington, 1980, Naval Surface Weapons Lab., Silver Spring, Md., 1984. Contbr. articles on transport in semiconductors, hidden symmetries of differential equations, plasma physics to profl. jours. Fellow Am. Phys. Soc. (sr. divsn. plasma physics, exec. com. 1980-82, 96-98); mem. IEEE (sr.; sr. exec. com. of standing tech. com. on plasma sci. and applications 1996-98), AAUP (local sec.-treas. 1980-82), Am. Geophys. Union, Univ. Fusion Assn., Phi Beta Kappa, Sigma Xi, Eta Kappa Nu, Sigma Pi Sigma. Home: 7452 Stratford Ave Saint Louis MO 63130-4044 Office: Washington U 1 Brookings Dr Dept Elec Saint Louis MO 63130-4899 E-mail: bas@ee.wustl.edu.

SHRAYER, MAXIM D. writer, educator; b. Moscow, Russia, June 5, 1967; s. David and Emilia Shrayer; m. Karen E. Lasser, Aug. 26, 2000. BA, Brown U., Providence, RI, 1989; MA, Rutgers U., New Brunswick, NJ, 1990, Yale U., New Haven, CT, 1991—92, PhD, 1995. Asst. prof. Conn. Coll., New London, Conn., 1995—96, Boston Coll., Chestnut Hill, Mass., 1996—2001, assoc. prof. english Chestnut Hills, 2001—. Author: (book) The World of Nabokov's Stories (Outstanding Book, 1999), Russian Poet / Soviet Jew. Mem.: From the Other Shore (editl. bd. 2000—02), Am. Assn. Teachers Slavic and European Languages (program com. 2000—02), Am. Assn. Advancement Slavic Studies. Avocations: fishing, book collecting, book collecting. Office: Boston College 210 Lyons Hall Chestnut Hill MA 02467 E-mail: shrayerm@bc.edu.

SHREEVE, JEAN'NE MARIE, chemist, educator; b. Deer Lodge, Mont., July 2, 1933; d. Charles William and Maryfrances (Briggeman) S. BA in Chemistry, U. Mont., 1953, DSc (hon.), 1982; MS in Analytical Chemistry, U. Minn., 1956; PhD in Inorganic Chemistry, U. Wash., 1961; NSF postdoctoral fellow, U. Cambridge, Eng., 1967-68. Asst. prof. chemistry U. Idaho, Moscow, 1961-65, assoc. prof., 1965-67, prof., 1967-73, 2000—, acting chmn. dept. chemistry, 1969-70, 1973, head dept. and prof., 1973-87, v.p. rsch. and grad. studies, prof. chemistry, 1987-99. Lucy W. Pickett lectr. Mt. Holyoke Coll., 1976, George H. Cady lectr. U. Wash., 1993; mem. Nat. Com. Standards in Higher Edn., 1965-67, 69-73. Mem. editl. bd. Jour. Fluorine Chemistry, 1970—, Jour. Heteroatom Chemistry, 1988-95, Accounts Chem. Rsch., 1973-75, Inorganic Synthesis, 1976—; contbr. articles to sci. jours. Mem. bd. govs. Argonne (Ill.) Nat. Lab., 1992-98. Recipient Disting. Alumni award U. Mont., 1970; named Hon. Alumnus, U. Idaho, 1972; recipient Outstanding Achievement award U. Minn., 1975, Sr. U.S. Scientist award Alexander Von Humboldt Found., 1978, Excellence in Teaching award Chem. Mfrs. Assn., 1980; U.S. hon. Ramsay fellow, 1967-68, Alfred P. Sloan fellow, 1970-72. Mem. AAAS (bd. dirs. 1991-95), AAUW (officer Moscow chpt. 1962-69), Am. Chem. Soc. (bd. dirs. 1985-93, chmn. fluorine divsn. 1979-81, Petroleum Rsch. Fund adv. bd. 1975-77, women chemists com. 1972-77, Fluorine award 1978, Garvan medal 1972, Harry and Carol Mosher award Santa Clara Valley sect. 1992), Göttingen (Germany) Acad. Scis. (corr. mem.), Idaho Acad. Sci. (Disting. Scientist 2001, Idaho Hall of Fame, 2001), Phi Beta Kappa. Avocations: fishing, gardening. Office: U Idaho Dept Chemistry Moscow ID 83844-2343 Fax: 208-885-9146. E-mail: jshreeve@uidaho.edu.

SHREEVE, SUSANNA SEELYE, educational planning facilitator; BA in Dance, Arts and Humanities, Mills Coll.; MA in Confluent Edn., U. Calif., Santa Barbara, 1989; postgrad., U. Calif., 1990, San Diego State U., 1992. Cert. elem. tchr., C.C. adminstr., tchr., Calif. Comm. instr. Brooks Inst., 1982; initiator Santa Barbara County Arts and Aging Forum, 1982; co-planner PARTners "How Kids Learn" Conf., 1985; dir. Los Ninos Bilingual Head Start Program, 1986-87; writing counselor Am. and internat. students S.B. City Coll., 1988, U. Calif., Santa Barbara, 1989-90; writing counselor Upward Bound, 1989-90; edn. coord. Santa Barbara County Urban Indian Project, Santa Barbara, 1989-90; instr. Santa Barbara Youth Cultural Arts, 1993; planner/staff Tri-County Regional Team Youth Summit, 1993-94, staff/planner Discovering Individual Identity, 1993—; planner SIG confluent edn. AERA, 1994-98; DQ-U. math/sci. resources for tchrs. Indian Edn., 1992—; multicultural cmty. Regional Alliance Info. Network Internet Youth Programs, Santa Barbara, 1991—. Pro-Youth Coalition planner City Santa Barbara, NetDay 1996—, Native Ams., 1996—; planner, adv., website liaison Nuc. Age Peace Found, World Indigenous Peoples Edn. Confs. Networker Native Am. Rights Fund, mem. youth commn.; mem. steering com. Santa Barbara Cmty. Currency; charter mem. Smithsonian Mus. Am. Indians (Friends of the Lakota); active Adopt a (Oglala) Grandparent, 1994—; found., cons., facilitator, writer, spkr. William Samuel Friends, Native Am. Voices semi-ann. Circle of Sharing; rep. Am. Religions Spl. Collection Archives U. Calif.-Santa Barbara. Mem., Ctr. for Food Safety, Intertribal Bison Coop., SB's Foothills Coalition, Sensory Awareness Found., Native Am. Bus. and Econ. Devel., Cmty. Youth Journalists, Nat. Congress Am. Indians (life), Kappa Delta Pi. Office: PO Box 3887 Santa Barbara CA 93130-3887 E-mail: susanna@glimpsesandglimmers.com., susanna@rain.org.

SHREINER, CURT, educational technologist, consultant; b. Ephrata, Pa., June 27, 1952; s. Paul H. and Grace B. BS in Edn., Millersville U., 1974; MS in Integrative Edn., Marywood Coll., 1977; MEd in Tech. and Media, Temple U., 1982; EdD in Tech. and Media, Columbia U., 1989. Tchr. Lebanon (Pa.) Sch. Dist., 1974-76; instr., researcher Millersville (Pa.) State U., 1976-77; writer, pub. Instrnl. Design Assocs., Lancaster, Pa., 1977-80; tchr. trainer Mainland (Pa.) Inst., 1980-81; videodisc designer WNET/THIRTEEN, Pub. TV, N.Y.C., 1981-82; computer software designer Academic Tech., Inc., Moorestown, N.J., 1982-86; audio scriptwriter Learn Inc., Mt. Laurel, 1986-87; CAI curriculum developer Constructive Alternatives, Inc., Phila., 1987-88; GUI designer Resolute, Ltd., 1988-91; multimedia designer Remtech Svcs. Inc., Newport News, Va., 1991-92; database design and info. mgmt. trainer The Work Group, Pennsauken, N.J., 1992; multimedia project dir. Vocat. Rsch. Inst., Phila., 1993-95; owner Curt Shreiner Prodns., 1995-96; multimedia designer Galaxy Scientific Corp., Warminster, Pa., 1996—. Computer cons. Phila. Mayor's Commn. on Literacy, 1987-91; learning cons. for Pub. Health Videos, Phila. Dept. Pub. Health, 1989-90. Co-author: Straight Talk Parenting Series, 1988, Teacher Revitalization, 1982, The Giggle Kids Present, 1978; designer: Ollie and Seymour, 1986 (Media and Materials Portfolio award); prodr., writer Maria's Story, 1995 (Telly award). Mem. Am. Soc. Tng. & Devel., Soc. for Applied Learning Tech., Internat. Soc. Performance Improvement. Avocations: fine art, photography, travel. E-mail: curt.shreiner@galaxyscientific.com.

SHREM, CHARLES JOSEPH, metals corporation executive; b. Cairo, May 9, 1930; came to U.S., 1959; s. Joseph C. and Paula (Cadranel) S.; m. Vivian L. Chalom, Jan. 30, 1955; children: Jeff, Leslie Allen. Degree in bus. and economy, Coll. Français, Cairo, 1951. Export mgr. Stanton Ironworks U.K., Middle East, 1950-57; comml. mgr. Soc. Sovibor, Paris, 1957-59; purchasing dir. Montanore, Inc., N.Y.C., 1959-65; exec. v.p. Commonwealth Metal Corp., Englewood Cliffs, N.J., 1965-85, pres., CEO, 1985-2000, chmn., 2000—; bus. cons. Pompton Plains, NJ, 2002—. Bd. govs. Coll. Democracy, Arlington, Va. Bd. dirs. Adult Edn., Pequannock, N.J., 1970-80; bd. govs. Nat. Grad. U., Arlington, Va. Mem. U.S. C. of C. (econ. coun., exec. com. U.S. Polish Coun./U.S. C. of C.). Office: 560 Sylvan Ave Englewood Cliffs NJ 07632 also: 933 Rte 23 Pompton Plains NJ 07444

SHREMBEK, CAROL ROSE, critical care nurse, writer; b. Cleve., Oct. 27, 1957; d. Richard and Mary Rita Elchesen; m. David Edward Shrembek; 1 child Nicole. BA, Kent State U., 1981; diploma in nursing, MetroHealth Sch. Nursing, Cleve., 1986. Cert. ACLS; RN. Staff nurse Rainbow Babies and Childrens Hosp., Cleve., 1987—91, MetroHealth Med. Ctr., Cleve., 1986—87, 1991—93; asst. clin. mgr. Fairview Gen. Hosp., Fairview Park, 1992—93; staff nurse S.W. Gen. Health Ctr., Middleburg Heights, 1993—96, StarMed Staffing Svcs., Independence, Ohio, 1996—98, Initial Health Care Svcs., Beachwood, 1996—98; clin. nurse MetroHealth Med. Ctr., Cleve., 1998—2002; staff nurse MedSearch Staffing Svcs., Inc., Middleburg Heights, 2002—. Tchr. orientation classes Rainbow Babies and Childrens Hosp., Cleve., 1987—91, clin. preceptor, 1988—91; mem. flight team MetroHealth Med. Ctr. Neonatal ICU, Cleve., 1991—93, clin. preceptor; workshop leader, spkr. in field. Author: (novels) Cheri's Crossing, 2000, A Love Through Time, 2001. Mem.: Romance Writers of Am. Roman Catholic. Avocations: gardening, reading, weightlifting. Personal E-mail: lordc7591@earthlink.net.

SHRENSKER, WARREN LOUIS, information systems manager; b. Bklyn., Aug. 28, 1943; B Indsl. Engring., Pratt Inst., 1966. Cert. mfg. engr. Project mgr. advanced mfg. engring. GE Nuclear Energy Mfg., Wilmington, N.C., 1974-77, mgr. systems and projects, 1977-78; cons. mfg. systems GE Corp. Cons. Svcs., Schenectady, 1979-80; mgr. advanced system design GE Large Steam Turbine Generator, 1980-84; mgr. tech. div. info. systems GE Appliances, Louisville, 1984-88, mgr. IBM systems conversion, 1988-90, mgr. planning and resource mgmt., 1990-91, mgr. mktg. and tech. systems, 1991-93; mgr. Systems & Svcs. Info. Tech., Johnson Controls Inc., Milw., 1993—95, dir. IT ops., 1995—2000, dir. engring./IT svcs., 2000—01, dir. tech. integration, 2001—. Chmn. CAD/CAM Workshop GE, Louisville, 1984, advisor, 1985-88. Author, editor: CIM: A Working Definition, 1990; contbr.: 5th Generation Management, 1986, 5th Generation Management for 5th Generation Systems, 1987, Issues: Migrating to Team Work, 1991. Capt. U.S. Army, 1967-70. Mem. Computer and Automated Systems Assn. of Soc. Mfg. Engrs. (advisor 1990-94, chair 1993, Lead Team award 1984). Avocations: golf, fishing.

SHRENSKY, DON STEVEN, accountant, consultant; b. Jersey City, Jan. 30, 1944; arrived in Israel, 1981; m. Joan L. Berman, Nov. 25, 1967; 2 children. BA, Rutgers State U., 1967; JD, Seton Hall U. Law Sch., 1971. Bar: N.J. 1972; CPA, N.Y., Israel. Ptnr. Gross, Manford & Reinschreiber, N.Y.C., 1970-81; chief acct. Mennen Medical Ltd., Rohovot, Israel, 1982-88; ptnr. Feldman Shrensky Brody & Co., Jerusalem, Israel, 1988-96; propr. Don Shrensky & Co., 1997—. Speaker at conf., local groups and radio/TV. Treas. Assn. of Americans and Canadians in Israel, 1994-98, v.p., 1998-99; chmn. bd. Mercaz Harmony, 1985-95. Mem. AICPAs, Inst. of CPAs in Israel, N.Y. Soc. CPAs, Assn. Ams. and Canadians in Israel, Jerusalem Rotary Club (bd. dirs.), Jerusalem Rotary Found. (bd. dirs.). Office: Don Shrensky & Co PO Box 31570 Jerusalem 91001 Israel

SHRESTHA, ROSHAN, physician; b. Dec. 27, 1956; Assoc. prof. medicine, med. dir. liver transplantation U. N.C., Chapel Hill, 1998—. Office: U NC at Chapel Hill Cb 7080 Burnett Womack Blvd Chapel Hill NC 27599-0001

SHREVE, GENE RUSSELL, law educator; b. San Diego, Aug. 6, 1943; s. Ronald D. and Hazel (Shepherd) S.; m. Marguerite Russell, May 26, 1973. AB with honors, U. Okla., 1965; LLB, Harvard U., 1968, LLM, 1975. Bar: Mass. 1969, Vt. 1981. Appellate atty. and state extradition hearing examiner Office of Mass. Atty Gen., 1968-69; law clk. U.S. Dist. Ct., Dallas, 1969-70; staff and supervising atty. Boston Legal Assistance Project, 1970-73; assoc. prof. Vt. Law Sch., Royalton, 1975-81; vis. assoc. prof. George Washington U., Washington, 1981-83; assoc. prof. law N.Y. Law Sch., N.Y.C., 1983-84, prof., 1984-87; vis. prof. law Ind. U., Bloomington, 1986, prof., 1987-94, Richard S. Melvin Prof. Law, 1994—. Author: A Conflict of Laws Anthology, 1997; co-author: Understanding Civil Procedure, 2d edit., 1994; mem. editl. bd. Am. Jour. Comparative Law, 1994—, Jour. Legal Edn., 1998-2001; contbr. numerous articles to legal jours. Mem. Am. Law Inst., Am. Soc. for Pol. and Legal Phil., Assn. Am. Law Schs. (civil procedure sect. chair 1997, conflict of laws sect. chair 1998). Democrat. Episcopalian. Office: Ind U Sch Law Bloomington IN 47405

SHREVE, JACK, English and Spanish language educator; b. Youngstown, Ohio, Feb. 6, 1949; s. John F. and Evelyn (Sarcinella) S. BA, Pa. State U., 1970; MA, U. Pitts., 1972, PhD, 1976. Prof. English and Spanish, Allegany Coll., Cumberland, Md., 1975—, chmn. dept. lang. and lit., 1977-78, chmn. dept. humanities, 1984-85. Contbg. author: Magill Critical Survey of Literature, 1983-85, Beacham Research Guide and Fiction Series (5), 1985-86, Research Guide to American Historical Biography, 1988-91, Dictionary of Literary Biography: 20th Century Italian Poetry, 1992, Research Guide to European Historical Biography, 1993; contbr. over 400 book revs. in Choice, Libr. Jour., Modern Lang. Jour., Hispania, The Md. Hist. Mag., Book Rev. Digest, Names, Contemporary Literary Criticism Yearbook, 1991; book review editor DELOS, 1993, College Vocabulary Development, 1993, 3rd edit., 2000; asst. editor Md. English Jour., 1993. NEH seminar, 1979-80, 87, others. Fulbright Travel grantee, China, 1993. Democrat. Avocations: book collecting, translation of poetry, genealogy. Home: 308 Cumberland St Cumberland MD 21502-2008 Office: Allegany Coll 12401 Willowbrook Rd Cumberland MD 21502-2596 E-mail: jack@hereintown.net.

SHREVE, PEG, retired state legislator, retired elementary educator; b. Spencer, Va., July 23, 1927; d. Hubert Smith and Pearl (Looney) Adams; m. Don Franklin Shreve, June 17, 1950 (dec. Sept. 1970); children: Donna, Jennifer, John, Don. BA, Glenville State U., 1948. Cert. elem. tchr., Va., Wyo. Reading tchr. Wood County Bd., Parkersburg, W.Va., 1948—50; elem. tchr. Mt. Solon, Va., 1950—52, Bridgewater, 1952—53, Cody, Wyo., 1970—86; mem. Wyo. Ho. of Reps., 1983—98, chmn. com. travel, recreation and wildlife, 1983—91, majority whip, 1992—94, speaker pro tem, 1995—98; ret., 1998. Mem. coun. Girl Scouts U.S.A., White Sulpher Springs, W.Va., 1962-65; co-chmn. Legis. Exec. Conf., Wyo., 1987; mem. Nat. Com. State Legislatures, 1982—; co-chair Select Com. Sch. Fin., 1996-99. Named Legislator of Yr., Wyo. Outfitters Assn., 1989, Ofcl. of Yr., Wyo. Wildlife Assn., 1990, Alumna of Yr., Glenville State Coll., 1994. Mem. AAUW (exec. bd.), Nat. Women Legislators, Soroptimists (Women Helping Women award 1985), Beta Sigma Phi (Lady of Yr. award 1986). Republican. Presbyterian. Avocations: golf, walking, needlepoint, knitting, bridge. Home: PO Box 2257 Cody WY 82414-2257

SHREVE, SUE ANN GARDNER, retired health products company administrator; b. Bklyn., Jan. 26, 1932; d. Homer Frank and Grace Emily (Kohlhagen) Gardner; m. Eugene Sheldon Shreve II, Nov. 20, 1954; children: Pamela Ann, Cynthia Ann Shreve Richard. BBA, Hofstra U., 1955. Co. rep. N.Y. Tel. Co., Bay Shore, 1954-55; engr. Republic Aviation, Farmingdale, N.Y., 1955-58; substitute tchr. East Islip (N.Y.) Sch. Dist., 1966-71; mgr. Patchogue Surg. and Athletic Supplies, Sayville, N.Y., 1971-81, ret., 1981. Invited guest writer Nat. Geneal. Soc. newsletter, 1996, 99; lectr. in genealogy, 1997—; condr. genealogy workshops, 1996—. Author, editor, pub.: The Kohlhagen Family Genealogy, 1994, The Shreve Family Genealogy, an update from 1641, 1997, Hendrickson Genealogy England to Illinois before 1840, 1999, Piscitelli Genealogy Italy to NYC before 1912, 2000; compiler, editor newsletter Gardner/Gardiner Rschrs., 1993—, Amos F.F. Gardner His Maternal Ancestors—Kirkpatrick & Barkley & Descendants, 2001, The Coates Family Genealogy, 2002; issue reviewer Geneal. Helper Mag., 1995. Life mem. N.Y. State Congress of Parents and Tchrs., 1963—, past pres.; mem. Penataquit Aux. Southside Hosp., 1985—; mem., fundraiser Hospice of South Shore, 1983—; rec. sec. Bay Shore N.Y. Hist. Soc., 1997—, Bay Shore Beautification Soc., 2000—, Bradish Ln. Homeowners Assn., 1997—2002, treas., 2002—. Recipient Ofcl. proclamation Village of Frankfort, Ill., 1996; named one of Outstanding Young Women of Am., 1967. Mem. AAUW (charter, past pres., past treas. Islip area br., rsch. and project grantee 1989), DAR/Nat. Soc. DAR (vice regent 2001—), Daus. Union Vets. of Civil War, 1st Families of Ohio, Bay Shore Garden Club (past pres., treas., dir., 2d v.p. 2000—), Bay Shore C. of C., German Genealogy Group of L.I. Republican. Methodist. Avocations: tennis, gourmet cooking, gardening, needlework, international travel. Home: 5 Anderson Ct Bay Shore NY 11706-7701

SHREVE, SUSAN RICHARDS, author, English literature educator; b. Toledo, May 2, 1939; d. Robert Kenneth and Helen (Greene) Richards; children— Porter, Elizabeth, Caleb, Kate. BA, U. Pa., 1961; MA, U. Va., 1969. Prof. English lit. George Mason U., Fairfax, Va., 1976—. Vis. prof. Columbia U., N.Y.C., 1982—, Princeton U., 1991, 92, 93. Author: (novels) A Fortunate Madness, 1974, A Woman Like That, 1977, Children of Power, 1979, Miracle Play, 1981, Dreaming of Heroes, 1984, Queen of Hearts, 1986, A Country of Strangers, 1989, Daughters of the New World, 1992, The Train Home, 1993, Skin Deep: Women & Race, 1995, The Visiting Physician, 1995; (pseudonym Annie Waters) Glimmer, 1997, Plum & Jaggers, 2000; (children's books) The Nightmares of Geranium Street, 1977, Family Secrets, 1979, Loveletters, 1979, The Masquerade, 1980, The Bad Dreams of a Good Girl, 1981, The Revolution of Mary Leary, 1982, The Flunking of Joshua T. Bates, 1984, How I Saved the World on Purpose, 1985, Lucy Forever and Miss Rosetree, Shrinks, Inc., 1985, Joshua T. Bates In Charge, 1992, The Gift of the Girl Who Couldn't Hear, 1991, Wait for Me, 1992, Amy Dunn Quits School, 1993, Lucy Forever & the Stolen Baby, 1994, The Formerly Great Alexander Family, 1995, Zoe and Columbo, 1995, Warts, 1996, A Goalie, 1996, Joshua Bates in Trouble Again, 1997, Jonah, The Whale, 1997, Ghost Cats, 1999, The End of Amanda, The Good, 2000; co-editor: How We Want to Live: Narratives on Progress, 1996, (with Porter Shreve) Outside the Law: Narratives on Justice, 1997, How We Want to Live: Narratives on Progress, 1998, Tales Out of School: Narratives on Education, 1999, Blister, 2001. Recipient Jenny Moore award George Washington U., 1978; John Simon Guggenheim award in fiction, 1980; Nat. Endowment Arts fiction award, 1982. Mem. PEN/Faulkner Found. (pres.), Phi Beta Kappa. E-mail: srshreve@aol.com.

SHREVE, THEODORE NORRIS, construction company executive; b. St. Louis, Feb. 14, 1919; s. Truxtun Benbridge adn Beulah (Dyer) S.; m. Caroline Prouty, Jan. 7, 1943; children: Sara Ann Caile, Suzanne Shreve Foster, Theo Carol. BS, U. Colo., 1942. Registered profl. engr., Colo. Sec., treas. Trautman & Shreve, Inc., Denver, 1946-68, pres., 1965-86, chmn. bd., 1984—; pres. 4030 Corp., 1984—. Bd. dirs. Colo. U. Found., 1988—; rep. Country Assembly, 1962. Served with USNR, 1942-45. Mem. Colo. Soc. Profl. Engrs., Rotary, Gyro Club, Denver Country Club, Sigma Phi Epsilon. Republican. Episcopalian. Home: 420 S Marion Pkwy Apt 1403 Denver CO 80209-2549 Office: Trautman & Shreve 4406 Race St Denver CO 80216-3818 E-mail: tshreve333@aol.com.

SHRIER, ADAM LOUIS, investment firm executive, consultant; b. Warsaw, Poland, Mar. 26, 1938; came to U.S., 1943, naturalized, 1949; s. Henry Leon and Mathilda June (Czamanska) S.; m. Diane Kesler, June 10, 1961; children: Jonathan, Lydia, Catherine, David. BS, Columbia U., 1959; MS (Whitney fellow), MIT, 1960; D.Engr. and Applied Sci. (NSF fellow), Yale U., 1965; postdoctoral visitor, U. Cambridge, Eng., 1965-66; JD, Fordham U., 1976. With Esso Research & Engring. Co., Florham Park and Linden, N.J., 1963-65, 66-72, head. environ. scis. research area, 1969-72; coordinator pollution abatement activities, tanker dept. Exxon Internat. Co., N.Y.C., 1972-74; project mgr., energy systems Exxon Enterprises Inc., 1974-75, gen. mgr. solar energy projects, 1975-77, pres. solar thermal systems div., 1977-81; corp. planning cons., sec. new bus. investments Exxon Corp., N.Y.C., 1981-82; div. mgr. supply and transp. Exxon Internat. Co., 1983-86, mgr. policy and planning, 1986-88; mng. dir. Splty. Tech. Assocs., Washington, 1988-97; pres. Global Devel. Opportunities, LLC, 1997—. Adj. lectr. chem. egnring. Columbia U., N.Y.C., 1967-69; industry adv. bd. Internat. Energy Agy., 1984-88, Energy and Environ. Policy Ctr., Harvard U., 1986-88, Internat. Energy

Program, Johns Hopkins U., 1987-88; sr. assoc. Global Bus. Forum, 1988—, Cambridge Energy Rsch. Assocs., 1988—; adj. prof. internat. bus. Am. U., Washington, 2000—. Patentee in field; contbr. articles to profl. jours. Mem. AIChE, Internat. Assn. Energy Econs., Am. Chem. Soc., U.S. Energy Assn., Cosmos Club, Sigma Xi, Tau Beta Pi, Phi Lambda Upsilon. Office: 4000 Cathedral Ave NW Washington DC 20016-5249

SHRIER, DIANE KESLER, psychiatrist, educator; b. Mar. 23, 1941; d. Benjamin Arthur and Mollie (Wortman) Kesler; m. Adam Louis Shrier, June 10, 1961; children: Jonathan Laurence, Lydia Anne, Catherine Jane, David Leopold. BS in Chemistry/Biology magna cum laude, Queen's Coll., CUNY, 1961; postgrad., Washington U. Sch. Medicine, St. Louis, 1960-61; MD, Yale U., 1964. Diplomate Am. Bd. Psychiatry and Neurology. Pediat. intern Bellevue Hosp., N.Y.C., 1964-65; psychiat. resident Albert Einstein Coll. Medicine-Bronx Mcpl. Hosp. Ctr., 1966-68, child psychiatry fellow, 1968-70; staff cons. Family Svc. and Child Guidance Ctr. of the Oranges, Maplewood, Milburn-Orange, N.J., 1970-73, cons., 1973-79; pvt. practice Montclair, 1970-92, Washington, 1994—. Cons. Cmty. Day Nursery, East Orange, NJ, 1970—79, Montclair State Coll., 1976—78; psychiat. cons. Bloomfield (N.J.) pub. schs., 1974—75; clin. instr. Albert Einstein Coll. Medicine, 1970—73; clin. asst. prof. psychiatry U. Medicine and Dentistry N.J., 1978—82, clin. assoc. prof., 1982—89, prof. clin. psychiatry, 1989—92; vice-chmn., dir. clin. psychiat. svcs. dept. psychiatry Children's Nat. Med. Ctr., 1992—94, attending staff, 1994—; prof. psychiatry and pediats. George Washington U. Med. Ctr., 1992—94, clin. prof. psychiatry, behavioral scis. and pediat., 1994—; cons. Walter Reed Med. Ctr., 1994—. Contbr. articles to med. jours. Trustee Montessori Learning Ctr., Montclair, 1973-75. Regents scholar Queen's Coll., 1961. Fellow Am. Psychiat. Assn., Acad. Child Psychiatry; mem. Tri-County Psychiat. Assn. (exec. com., rec. sec. 1977-78, 2d v.p. 1978-79, 1st v.p. 1979-80, pres. 1977-81), N.J. Psychiat. Assn. (councillor 1981-84), Am. Acad. Child and Adolescent Psychiatry (councillor at large 1992-95), Phi Beta Kappa. Home: 4000 Cathedral Ave NW Apt 317B Washington DC 20016-5267 Office: Ste 104 1616 18th St NW Washington DC 20009-2521 E-mail: diane.shrier.med.64@aya.yale.edu.

SHRIMPTON, JAMES ROBERT, controller; b. St. Louis, Dec. 13, 1956; s. Robert Franklin and Mildred Lucille (Baxter) S.; m. Rhonda Jo Crabtree, July 23, 1983; children: Phillip Sean, Bradley James. BS, S.W. Bapt. Coll., 1978; CMA, So. Ill. U., 1982, MBA, 1983. CPA, Mo. Inventory supr. Edison Bros. Stores, St. Louis, 1978-79, asst. internal auditor, 1982-83, sr. acct., 1984; acctg. supr. Hill-Brehan Lumber Co., 1979-81; sr. regional auditor TG&Y Stores, Oklahoma City, 1984-85; asst. controller J&J Holding Co., Paola, Kans., 1985-90, corp. contr., 1990-93; contr. CISCO, 1993-94, KNAPPCO, 1994—99, dir. leadership, 2001; v.p. ops. Innovative Fulfillment Solutions, Riverside, Mo., 2000—. Mem. AICPA, Inst. Mgmt. Acctg. Home: 905 Walnut St Kearney MO 64060-7402

SHRINER, ROBERT DALE, economist, management consultant; b. Hobart, Okla., Nov. 28, 1937; s. William Dale and Mildred Ellen (Goodson) S.; m. Nancy Lee Thompson, June 6, 1961; 1 child, Leslie Annette. BA, U. Okla., 1965, MA, 1967; PhD, Ind. U., 1974. Asst. to chief ops. Gen. Dynamics Astronautics, Altus, Okla., 1961-63; dir. Wyo. tech. asst. program U. Wyoming, 1966-69; research assoc. Ind. U. Bur. Bus. Research, 1969-71; asst. prof. Ind. U. Sch. Pub. and Environ. Affairs, 1972-77; assoc. dir. resource devel. internship program Council of State Govt., 1970-72; dir. aerospace research application ctr. Ind. U., 1972-76; mng. assoc., sr. economist Booz Allen & Hamilton, Washington, 1977-79; dir. Washington ops. Chase Econometrics, 1979-82; mng. ptnr. Shriner-Midland Co., 1982—. Cons. Aerospace Industries Assocs., Assn. for Mfg. Tech., Nat. Endowment for Arts, Nat. Restaurant Assn., Presdl. Commn. on Social Security, U.S. Cath. Conf., YMCA of U.S., Nat. Industries for the Blind, Nat. Com. for Purchase from the Blind and Severely Disabled, YWCA of U.S.; also cons. to various major corps. and nat. assns. Editor, pub. Managing Technology and Change, 1972-75, 86-89; editor Aeroplus Update, 1993-2001; creator computer programs, 1982, 91; contbr. articles to profl. jours. Pres. grad. students assn. U. Okla., Norman, 1965-66; chmn. Rocky Mountain Tech. Svcs. Coun., Wyo., 1967-69; sci. advisor Wyo. Gov., 1968-69; vice-chmn. YMCA Fairfax County, Va., 1978-82; bd. dirs. YMCA of Metro Washington, 1982-89, treas., 1986-89, sr. v.p., 1989-91; exec. com. Gettysburg Coll. Parents Coun., 1985-89; mem. YMCA-USA Membership Standards Com., 1994—. With USAF, 1957-61. Recipient Disting. Svc. award YMCA Metro Washington, 1985, 91. Mem. AAAS, Nat. Assn. Bus. Economists, Am. Mgmt. Assn., Am. Econs. Assn., Va. Advanced Tech. Assn. (v.p. programs, 1986-89), Rotary (pres. 9176-77, 99-2000), Nat. Economists Club. Office: Shriner-Midland Co 6432 Quincy Pl Falls Church VA 22042-3117

SHRINER, THOMAS L., JR. lawyer; b. Lafayette, Ind., Dec. 15, 1947; s. Thomas L. Sr. and Margaret (Kamstra); m. Donna L. Galchick, June 5, 1971; children: Thomas L. III, John H. , Joseph P., James A. AB, Ind. U., 1969, JD, 1972. Bar: Wis. 1972, U.S. Ct. Appeals (7th cir.) 1972, U.S. Dist. Ct. (ea. dist.) Wis. 1973, U.S. Dist. Ct. (we. dist.) Wis. 1977, U.S. Supreme Ct. 1978, U.S. Ct. Appeals (8th cir.) 1989, U.S. Ct. Appeals (fed. cir.) 1990. Law clk to Hon. John S. Hastings U.S. Ct. Appeals (7th cir.), Chgo., 1972-73; assoc. Foley & Lardner, Milwaukee, Wis., 1973-79, ptnr., 1979—. Chmn. bd. trustees Cath. Charities of Archdiocese of Milw., 2001—. Fellow Am. Coll. Trial Lawyers; mem. 7th Cir. Bar Assn. (pres. 1993-94), Phi Beta Kappa. Republican. Roman Catholic. Office: Foley & Lardner 777 E Wisconsin Ave Ste 3800 Milwaukee WI 53202-5367 E-mail: tshriner@foleylaw.com.

SHRIVASTAVA, PRAKASH N. medical physicist, educator; b. Narsingpur, India, Sept. 5, 1940; came to U.S., 1963; s. Sunderlal and Vidyawati Shrivastava; m. Uma Devi Ravipaty, Mar. 7, 1968; children: Anil, Rashmi, Anupama. BSc, Nagpur (India) U., 1958, MSc, 1961; PhD, U. Tex., 1966; MPM, Carnegie Mellon U., 1992. Diplomate Am. Bd. Radiology, Am. Bd. Health Physics, Am. Bd. Med. Physics. Med. physicist Allegheny Gen. Hosp., Pitts., 1970-74, dir. divsn. med. physics, 1974-89; dir. Mideast CRP NIH Project, 1974-84; dir. hyperthermia Physics Ctr., NIH Project, 1983-92; prof. radiation oncology U. So. Calif., L.A., 1989—, prof. radiology, 1993—, prof. biomed. engrng., 1995—. Bd. dirs. Mideast Ctr. for Radiologic Physics, Pitts., 1974-87, Nat. Hyperthermia Physics Ctr., Pitts., 1983-92; dep. dir. U. So. Calif. Advanced Biotech. Consortium, L.A., 1994—; chief of med. physics Los Angeles County/U. So. Calif. Med. Ctr., L.A., 1989—. Author and editor in field. Pres. Hindu-Jain Temple, Pitts., 1980-83. Recipient Paranjpe Gold medal in physics Nagpur U., 1961; Govt. of Italy Internat. scholar, 1961-63; Outstanding Svc. award Hindu Temple, Pitts., 1986. Mem. Rotary Club of La Canada (pres. 1994-95). Avocations: tennis, swimming, drawing and painting. Home: 841 Greenridge Dr La Canada CA 91011-4206 Office: U So Calif 1175 N Cummings St Los Angeles CA 90033-1041 E-mail: pshriva@hsc.usc.edu.

SHRIVER, DONALD WOODS, JR. theology educator; b. Norfolk, Va., Dec. 20, 1927; s. Donald Woods and Gladys (Roberts) S.; m. Peggy Ann Leu, Aug. 9, 1953; children: Gregory Bruce, Lionel, Timothy Donald. BA, Davidson Coll., 1951; B.D., Union Theol. Sem. Va., 1955; S.T.M., Yale U., 1957; PhD (Rockefeller Doctoral fellow), Harvard U., 1963; L.H.D. (hon.), Central Coll., 1970, Davidson Coll., 1984, Union Medal, Union Theol. Sem. Am., 1991; D.D. (hon.), Wagner Coll., 1978, Southwestern Coll., Memphis, 1983, Colgate U., 1996; LHD (hon.), Jewish Theol. Sem., 1991; DD (hon.), Colgate U., 1996. Ordained to ministry Presbyterian Ch., 1955; pastor Linwood Presbyn. Ch., Gastonia, N.C., 1956-59; u. minister, prof. religion N.C. State U., Raleigh, 1963-72, dir. u. program on sci. and soc., 1968-72; prof. ethics and soc. Emory U., Atlanta, 1972-75; William E. Dodge prof. applied Christianity Union Theol. Sem., N.Y.C., 1975-96, pres. faculty, 1975-91. Adj. prof. bus. ethics Sch. Bus. Adminstrn., Columbia U., prof. ethics Sch. Internat. Affairs, 1995-98; sr. fellow freedom forum Sch. Journalism, Columbia U., 1992-93; adj. prof. ethics, 1994—; lectr. Duke U., Va. State U., Ga. State U., numerous colls. and univs. in Can., Kenya, India, Japan and Korea. Author: How Do You Do and Why: An Introduction of Christian Ethics for Young People, 1966, Rich Man Poor Man: Christian Ethics for Modern Man Series, 1972, (with Dean D. Knudsen and John R. Earle) Spindles and Spires: A Restudy of Religion and Social Change in Gastonia, 1976, (with Karl A. Ostrom) Is There Hope for the City?, 1977, The Social Ethics of the Lord's Prayer, 1980, The Gospel, The Church, and Social Change, 1980, The Lord's Prayer: A Way of Life, 1983, An Ethic for Enemies: Forgiveness in Politics, 1995; co-author: Redeeming the City, 1982, Beyond Success: Corporations and Their Critics in the Nineties, 1991; editor: The Unsilent South, 1965, Medicine and Religion: Strategies of Care, 1979. Dir. Urban Policy Study N.C. State U., 1971-73; precinct chmn. Democratic Party, Raleigh, N.C., del. to nat. conv., 1968; mem. Mayor's Com. on Human Relations, Raleigh, 1967-71; chmn. Urban Policy Seminar, Center for Theology and Public Policy, 1978-82. Served with Signal Corps U.S. Army, 1946-47. Recipient The Union medal, Union Theol. Sem., 1991; Kent fellow in religion, 1959; fellow Am. Acad. in Berlin, 1999. Mem. Am. Soc. Christian Ethics (pres. 1979-80), Soc. for Values in Higher Edn., Soc. for Health and Human Values, Soc. for Sci. Study of Religion, AAAS, Am. Sociol. Assn., Am. Soc. Engring. Edn. (chmn. liberal arts div. 1972-73), United Christian Youth Movement of Nat. Council of Chs. (nat. chmn. 1951-53), Council on Fgn. Relations. Home and Office: 440 Riverside Dr Apt 58 New York NY 10027-6830 E-mail: dwshriver@aol.com. *Modern people need to recover connections between memory and hope. The past we applaud pre-enacts the future we hope for, and the past we deplore forms our obligation, in the present, to make a different future. In a time when young people find it hard to envision a long human future, the connections of history and ethics are indispensable. The forging of such connections is my vocation as an educator.*

SHRIVER, DUWARD FELIX, chemistry educator, researcher, consultant; b. Glendale, Calif., Nov. 20, 1934; s. Duward Laurence and Josephine (Williamson) S.; m. Shirley Ann Clark; children: Justin Scott, Daniel Nathan. BS, U. Calif., Berkeley, 1958; PhD, U. Mich., 1961. From instr. to assoc. prof. chemistry Northwestern U., Evanston, Ill., 1961-70, prof., 1970-87, Morrison prof. of chemistry, 1987—, chmn. dept. chem., 1992-95; mem. Inorganic Syntheses Inc., 1974—, pres., 1982-85. Vis. staff mem. Los Alamos (N.Mex.) Nat. Lab., 1976-85, cons., 1985-92; vis. prof. U. Tokyo, 1977, U. Wyo., 1978, U. Western Ont., Can., 1979. Author: The Manipulation of Air-Sensitive Compounds, 1969, edit., 1987; co-author: Inorganic Chemistry, 1990, 2d edit., 1994, 3d edit., 1998; editor-in-chief Inorganic Syntheses, vol. 19, 1979; co-editor: The Chemistry of Metal Cluster Complexes, 1990; editl. bd. Inorganic Synthesis, 1979—, Advances in Inorganic Chemistry, 1986—, Jour. Coordination Chemistry, Inorganic Chimca Acta, 1988—, Chemistry of Materials, 1988-90, 92—, Jour. Cluster Sci., 1990-97, Organometallics, 1993-95; contbr. articles to profl. jours. Alfred P. Sloan fellow, 1967-69; Japan Soc. Promotion of Sci. fellow, 1977; Guggenheim Found. fellow, 1983-84. Fellow AAAS; mem. Am. Chem. Soc. (Disting. Svc. in Inorganic Chemistry award 1987), Royal Soc. Chemistry London (Ludwig Mond lectr. 1989), Electrochem. Soc., Materials Rsch. Soc. (medal 1990). Home: 1100 Colfax St Evanston IL 60201-2611 Office: Northwestern U Dept Chemistry Evanston IL 60208-0001 E-mail: shriver@chem.nwu.edu.

SHRIVER, ELIZABETH, computer scientist, researcher; b. L.A., Nov. 12, 1966; d. Bruce and Beverly Shriver; m. Tom Swartz. PhD, NYU, 1997. Mem. tech. staff Lucent Techs., Murray Hill, NJ, 1997—2002. Office: Lucent Techs 2A-316 600 Mountain Ave New Providence NJ 07974 Personal E-mail: shriver@cs.nyu.edu.

SHRIVER, LOREN J. astronaut; b. Jefferson, Iowa, Sept. 23, 1944; m. Susan Diane Hane; children: Camilla, Melinda, Rebecca, Jered. BS in Aero. Engring., USAF Acad., 1967; MS in Astronautical Engring., Purdue U., 1968; grad., USAF Test Pilot Sch., 1975. Commd. 2d lt. USAF, 1967, advanced through grades to col.; acad. instr. pilot Vance Air Force Base, Okla., 1969—73; pilot Thailand, 1973—74; with 6512th Test Squadron, Edwards Air Force Base; test pilot F-15 Joint Test Force; astronaut NASA, Houston, 1978—97, 1992, space shuttle program mgr., launch integration, 1993—, dep. dir. launch and payload processing John F. Kennedy Space Ctr., 1997—. Decorated DFC; recipient Flight Achievement award, Am. Astronautical Soc., 1990, Haley Space Flight award, AIAA, 1990. Achievements include logged over 6,200 hours in jet aircraft; logged 386 hours in space; pilot STS-51C (1985), STS-31 (1990) and STS-46 (1992). Office: Astronaut Office/CB NASA Johnson Space Ctr Houston TX 77058*

SHRIVER, MARIA OWINGS, news correspondent; b. Chgo., Nov. 6, 1955; d. Robert Sargent and Eunice Mary (Kennedy) S.; m. Arnold Schwarzenegger, Apr. 26, 1986; children: Katherine Eunice, Christina Aurelia, Patrick. BA, Georgetown U. Coll. Am. Studies, Washington, 1977. News producer Sta. KYW-TV, 1977-78; producer Sta. WJZ-TV, 1978-80; nat. reporter PM Mag., 1981-83; news reporter CBS News, Los Angeles, 1983-85; news correspondent, co-anchor CBS Morning News, N.Y.C., 1985-86; co-host Sunday Today, NBC, 1987-90; anchor Main Street, NBC, 1987; co-anchor Yesterday, Today, and Tomorrow, NBC, 1989; anchor NBC Nightly News Weekend Edition, 1989-90, Cutting Edge with Maria Shriver, NBC, 1990, First Person with Maria Shriver, NBC, 1991—. Co-anchor summer olympics, Seoul, Korea, 1988; substitute anchor NBC News at Sunrise, Today, NBC Nightly News with Tom Brokaw; contbg. anchor Dateline, NBC. Appeared in Last Action Hero, 1993; correspondent TV series The American Parade, 1984. Recipient Christopher award for "Fatal Addictions", 1990, Exceptional Merit Media award Nat. Women's Political Caucus, first-place Commendation award Am. Women in Radio and TV, 1991, Emmy nomination. Democrat. Roman Catholic. Office: NBC News First Person with Maria Shriver 3000 W Alameda Ave Burbank CA 91523-0002*

SHRIVER, PHILLIP RAYMOND, academic administrator; b. Cleve., Aug. 16, 1922; s. Raymond Scott and Corinna Ruth (Smith) S.; m. Martha Damaris Nye, Apr. 15, 1944; children: Carolyn (Mrs. William Shaul), Susan (Mrs. Lester LaVine), Melinda (Mrs. David Williams), Darcy, Raymond Scott II. BA, Yale U., 1943; MA, Harvard U., 1946; PhD, Columbia U., 1954; LittD, U. Cin., 1966; LLD, Heidelberg Coll., 1966, Eastern Mich., 1972, Ohio State U., 1973; DH, McKendree Coll., 1973; DPS, Albion Coll., 1974; LHD, Central State U., 1976, No. Ky. State U., 1980, Miami U., 1984, U. Akron, 1988. Mem. faculty Kent (Ohio) State U., 1947-65, prof. Am. history, 1960-65; dean Coll. Arts and Scis., 1963-65; pres. Miami U., Oxford, Ohio, 1965-81, pres. emeritus, prof. Am. history, 1981-99. Pres. Ohio Coll. Assn., 1974-75; chmn. coun. pres.'s Mid-Am. Conf., 1971-77; chmn. Ohio Bicentennial Commn. for NW Ordinance and U.S. Constn., 1985-89, Ohio Tuition Trust Authority, 1989-92; chmn. coun. pres.'s Nat. Assn. State Univs. and Land Grant Colls., 1975-76, mem. exec. coun., 1976-78. Author: The Years of Youth, 1960, George A. Bowman: The Biography of an Educator, 1963, (with D.J. Breen) Ohio's Military Prisons of the Civil War, 1964, A Tour to New Connecticut: The Narrative of Henry Leavitt Ellsworth, 1985, Miami University: A Personal History, 1998, (with C.E. Wunderlin Jr.) The Documentary Heritage of Ohio, 2000, (with E.F. Puff) The History of Presbyterianism in Oxford, Ohio, 2000. Bd. dirs. Cin. Ctr. Sci. and Industry, 1965-70; trustee Ohio Coll. Library Center, 1968-74; chmn. bd. Univ. Regional Broadcasting, 1975-76, 78-79. Served to lt. (j.g.) USNR, 1943-46, PTO. Decorated Order of Merit Grand Duchy of Luxembourg, 1976; recipient Disting. Acad. Svc. award AAUP, 1965, Gov.'s award 1969, A.K. Morris award, 1974, Ohioana Career medal, 1987, Converse award, 1990, Award of Merit, Am. Assn. for State and Local History, 1993, Bjornson award Ohio Humanities Coun., 2001. Mem. Orgn. Am. Historians, Ohio Acad. History (pres. 1983-84, Disting. Svc. award 1991), Archaeol. Inst. Am., Ohio Hist. Soc. (trustee 1982-91, v.p. 1983-84, pres. 1984-86), Ohio Humanities Council (Bjornson award 2001), Am. Studies Assn., Mortar Board, Phi Beta Kappa, Omicron Delta Kappa, Phi Alpha Theta, Alpha Kappa Psi, Kappa Delta Pi, Phi Eta Sigma, Phi Kappa Phi, Kappa Kappa Psi, Alpha Lambda Delta, Beta Gamma Sigma, Sigma Delta Pi, Alpha Phi Omega, Delta Upsilon (Disting. Alumni Achievement award 1985) Clubs: Rotary. Presbyterian. Home: 5115 Bonham Rd Oxford OH 45056-1428 Office: Miami U Oxford OH 45056 E-mail: shrivepr@muohio.edu.

SHRIVER, ROBERT SARGENT, JR. lawyer; b. Westminster, Md., Nov. 9, 1915; s. Robert Sargent and Hilda Shriver; m. Eunice Mary Kennedy, May 23, 1953; children: Robert Sargent III, Maria, Timothy, Mark Kennedy, Anthony Paul Kennedy. Student, Canterbury Sch.; BA cum laude, Yale U., 1938, LLB, 1941; LLD, St. Procopius Coll., 1959, Notre Dame U., DePaul U., Seton Hall Coll., 1961, St. Louis U., Kansas State U., Brandeis U., 1962, St. Michael's Coll., Vt., Fordham U., Boston Coll., Yale U., Duquesne U., N.Y.U., Wesleyan U.; DCL, U. Liberia, 1963; HHD, Salem Coll., 1963, Bowling Green State U.; LHD, Springfield (Mass.) Coll., 1963, U. Scranton, Providence Coll.; D in Polit. Sci., Chulalongkorn U., Bangkok, Thailand. Bar: N.Y. 1941, Ill. 1959, U.S. Supreme Ct. 1969, D.C. 1971. With Winthrop, Stimson, Putnam & Roberts, 1940—41; asst. editor Newsweek, 1945—46; assoc. Joseph P. Kennedy Enterprises, 1947—48; asst. gen. mgr. Merchandise Mart, Chgo., 1948—61; dir. Peace Corps., Washington, 1961—66, Office Econ. Opportunity, 1964—68; U.S. ambassador to France, 1968—70; spl. asst. to the Pres., 1965—68; sr. ptnr. law firm Fried, Frank, Harris, Shriver & Jacobson, N.Y.C., Washington, L.A., London, Eng., 1971—86, of counsel, 1986—; pres. Spl. Olympics, Washington, 1986—90, chmn., CEO, 1990—96, chmn. bd. dirs., 1996—. Mem. Am. Com. on East-West Accord, 1978—, Ams. for SALT, 1979—. Author: Point of the Lance, 1964. Pres. Chgo. Bd. Edn., 1955—60; mem.-at-large Nat. Coun. Boy Scouts Am.; chmn. Internat. Orgn. Patrons on Israel Mus., 1972—75; bd. dirs. The Arms Control Assn., 1983—; Dem. candidate for v.p., 1972; ran for Dem. presdl. election, 1976; pres. Cath. Interracial Coun. Chgo., 1955—60. Lt. comdr. USNR, 1940—45. Named Lay Churchman of Yr., Religious Heritage Am., 1963; recipient Yale U. medal, 1957, Chgo. medal of merit, 1957, James H. Hoey award, Cath. Interracial Coun. N.Y., 1958, Golden Heart Presdl. award, Philippines, 1964, Laetare medal, U. Notre Dame, 1968, Franklin D. Roosevelt Freedom from Want award, 1993, Presdl. Medal of Freedom, 1994, Equal Justice award, Nat. Ctr. on Poverty Law, 1999, William O. Douglas award, Pub. Counsel Law Ctr., 1999. Mem.: Chgo. Coun. Fgn. Rels. (dir.), Yale U. Law Sch. Assn. (exec. com.), Navy League (life), Yale Club (N.Y.C.), Onwentsia Club (Lake Forest, Ill.), Execs. Club (Chgo.), Econ. Club, Serra Club, Racquet Club, Delta Kappa Epsilon. Roman Catholic. Achievements include extensive world travel to visit Peace Corps projects, 1961-1966. Office: Spl Olympics Internat 1325 G St NW Ste 500 Washington DC 20005-3104

SHRIVER, SARGENT, sports association executive; m. Ethel Kennedy Shriver; children: Robert Sargent Shriver III, Maria Owings Schwarzenegger, Timothy Perry, Mark Kennedy, Anthony Paul Kennedy. BS, Yale U.; JD, Yale Law Sch.; D (hon.) , Brandeis U., Boston Coll., Yeshiva U., U. Liberia, Chulalongkom U. Organizer, dir. Peach Corps, 1961—66; amb. France, 1968—70; ptnr. Fried, Frank, Harris, Shriver and Jacobson, 1970—86; pres. bd. Spl. Olympics, Inc., Washington, 1984—90, chmn. bd., 1990—. Lt. comdr. USN. Named Nat. Father of Yr., 1964; recipient Vet. of Yr., 1956, Lay Churchman of Yr., 1963, Hannah G. Solomon award, Nat. Coun. Jewish Women, 1972, Order of Smile, 1989, Notre Dame Patriotism award, 1965, Nat. Brotherhood award, 1966. Mem.: KC, VFW, Navy League, Nat. Interreligious Task Force on Soviet Jewry, Nat. Cath. Conf. for Interracial Justice (James J. Hooey award N.Y. chpt. 1958). Office: Special Olympics Inc 1325 G St NW Ste 770 Washington DC 20005*

SHRIVER, TIMOTHY P. sports association executive; m. Linda Potter Shriver; 5 children. BS, Yale U.; M in Religion and Religious Edn., Cath. U.; DEd, U. Conn.; D (hon.) , New Eng. Coll, Albertus Magnus Coll., Loyola U. Balt. Tchr. New Haven Pub. Schs., New Haven; supr. Pub. Schs. Social Devel. Project, 1987—96; pres., CEO Spl. Olympics, Inc. Co-prodr.(film): Amistad, 1997, The Loretta Claiborne Story, 2000. Bd. dirs. Compact for Learning and Citizenship, Frank Porter Child Devel. Ctr. at U. N.C.; co-chair Am.'s Promise Task Force on Youth Svcs., 1997—; chmn. Collaborative for Advancement of Social and Emotional Learning at U. Ill., 1994—; bd. dirs. John F. Kennedy Libr. Found., Boston. Recipient Medal of City of Athens, Order de Manuel Amador Guerrera, Pres. of Panama, Conn. Citizen of Yr.; fellow Yale Child Study Ctrs. Sch. Devel. Program, 1984. Office: Special Olympics NAm 1325 G St NW Ste 770 Washington DC 20005*

SHRIVER, WILLIAM RUSSELL, secondary education educator; b. Garfield Heights, Ohio, Aug. 15, 1950; s. William Washington and Olive Elizabeth (Doutt) S.; m. Karen Ann Wolfe, June 20, 1987; children: Lauren, Matthew. BA, Coll. of Wooster, 1972; MA, U. Chgo., 1973; postgrad., Cleve. State U., 1973-74. Cert. tchr., Ohio. Summer staff Philmont Scout Ranch, Cimarron, N.Mex., 1968-76; tchr. Mt. Vernon (Ohio) Sr. H.S., 1974—. Tchr. Kenyon Acad. Partnership Kenyon Coll./Mt. Vernon Sr. H.S., 1983—; vice chair state tchr. edn. cert. adv. commn. Ohio Bd. Edn., Columbus, 1991-99, state tchr. cert. standards revision com., 1992-95; mem. bd. examiners Nat. Coun. Accreditation of Tchr. Edn., Washington, 1993-02; mem. Ohio Gov.'s Commn. on Tchg. Success, 2001-02. Bd. of session First Presbyn. Ch., Mt. Vernon, 1980-87, 89-95, 2001—. Eagle Scout Boy Scouts Am., 1966. Mem. NEA (assembly del. 1983-99), Ohio Edn. Assn. (exec. com. 1987-93, 96-2002), North Ctrl. Ohio Edn. Assn. (pres. 1984-85, exec. sec. 1993—), Mt. Vernon Edn. Assn. (pres. 1976-78). Avocation: photography, geneology. Office: Mt Vernon HS 300 Martinsburg Rd Mount Vernon OH 43050-4246 E-mail: wshriver@mt-vernon.k12.oh.us.

SHRODER, MARK DAVIS, economist; b. Washington; s. Morris Shroder, Florence Davis Shroder; m. Susan Keller; 1 child Deborah Alexandra. BA in History, Yale U., 1975; MS in Econs., U. Wis., PhD in Econs., 1991. Economist HUD - Policy Devel. & Rsch., Washington, 1991—. Co-author: The Digest of Social Experiments, 1997. Coun. mem. City of College Park, Md., 1999—. Home: 4909 Muskogee St College Park MD 20740 Office: HUD--Policy Devel and Rsch 451 7th St SW Washington DC 20410-6000 Personal E-mail: shroder_keller@yahoo.com. Business E-mail: Mark_D._Shroder@hud.gov.

SHROFF, FIROZ SARDAR, merger and acquisition professional; b. Karachi, Pakistan, Feb. 27, 1950; s. Sardar Mohammad Shroff and Kulsum (Bano) Dhanji; m. Munira Firoz, Oct. 27, 1977; children: Khurram, Sara, Ally, Kassim, Anushae. Grad. high sch., Nairobi, Kenya. Apprentice, duty incharge Empire Investment Ltd., Nairobi, 1966-67; asst. mgr. to mgr. Trade Aids Inc., Karachi, 1967-69, asst. gen. mgr., 1969-72; gen. mgr. Canorient Overseas Distbrs. Ltd., London, 1972-74; dir., gen. mgr. Westland Securities Ltd., Nairobi, 1974-75; dep. mng. dir. Sasi Ltd., Karachi, 1975-78; dir. internat. expansion Sasi Group Cos., 1978-80, mng. dir., 1984—; dir. operation Key Internat. S.A., London, 1980-84. Participant Nat. Book Devel. Council, Singapore, 1980, Arthur D. Little Mgmt. Edn. Inst. and Pakistan Inst. Mgmt., 1986; trustee Sasi Found., Karachi, 1985; developer bus. info. and rsch. ctr.; advisor/cons. various corp. bodies on takeover acquisition of bus. in U.S., U.K. and the Pacific; involved in group discussions on internat. bus. opportunities, contacts in fin. circles. Recipient Cert. Recognition Asia-Pacific Real Estate Congress, 1987. Mem. Pakistan Pubs. and Booksellers Assn. (copyright com. 1975-80), Internat. Real Estate Fedn., Assn. Builders and Developers (convenor 1985), Internat. Real Estate Inst. (chpt. head 1986), Inst. Dirs., Pakistan C. of C. and Industry, United Coop. Credit Soc. (bd. dirs. 1977-79), Property Cons. Soc., Internat. Airline Passengers Assn., Karachi Golf Club, Defense Club, Rotary. Avocations: reading, travel, research and participating in discussion group on global investment opportunities. Office: Sasi House G/2 Block 9 Main Clifton Rd Karachi 75600 Pakistan also: 1201 S Courthouse Rd # 220 Arlington VA 22204 E-mail: firoz55@hotmail.com.

SHROPE, NANCY RUTH, academic administrator; b. Pocatello, Idaho, May 21, 1951; d. Roy Edward and Patricia Ruth Taylor; m. Gerald Don Shrope, June 3, 1972; children: Kelli Michelle, Melissa Kay. BA in Instrnl. Media, U. Idaho, 1972. Escrow-mortgage teller Old Nat. Bank, Pullman, Wash., 1973-76; prin. Pullman Nursery Sch., 1979-82; office asst. Inst. Biol. Chemistry, Washington State U., Pullman, 1982-83, program material specialist Office Grant and Rsch. Devel., 1983-92, mgr. adminstrv. and regulatory affairs, 1992—. Adv. mem. Commn. on Status of Women, Pullman, 1985-87. Econ. devel. liaison Bus. and Profl. Women's Assn., Pullman, 1985-87. Mem. Soc. Rsch. Adminstrs., Applied Rsch. Ethics Nat. Assn., Nat. Assn. IRB Mgrs., Beta Sigma Phi (life, Woman of Yr. Pullman chpt. 1978, 85, 93), Alpha Omicron Pi (life, corp. v.p. 1983—). Office: Wash State U Office Grant & Rsch Devel PO Box 643140 Pullman WA 99164-3140 Office Fax: 509-335-1676. E-mail: nshrope@wsu.edu.

SHROPSHIRE, DONALD GRAY, hospital executive; b. Winston-Salem, N.C., Aug. 6, 1927; s. John Lee and Bess L. (Shouse) S.; m. Mary Ruth Bodenheimer, Aug. 19, 1950; children: Melanie Shropshire David, John Devin. BS, U. N.C., 1950; Erickson fellow postgrad., U. Chgo., 1958-59; LLD (hon.), U. Ariz., 1992; EdD (hon.), Tucson U., 1994. Personnel asst. Nat. Biscuit Co., Atlanta, 1950-52, asst. personnel mgr. Chgo., 1952-54; adminstr. Eastern State Hosp., Lexington, Ky., 1954-62; assoc. dir. U. Md. Hosp., Balt., 1962-67; adminstr. Tucson Med. Ctr., 1967-82, pres., 1982-92, pres. emeritus, 1992—; pres. Tucson Hosps. Med. Edn. Program, 1970-71, sec., 1971-86; pres. So. Ariz. Hosp. Council, 1968-69; bd. dirs. Ariz. Blue Cross, 1967-76, chmn. provider standards com., 1972-76; chmn. Healthways Inc., 1985-92. Mem. bd. La Posada at Park Centre, Inc., Green Valley, Ariz., 1996-2000, chmn. bd., 1996-99, mem. emeritus, 2000—. Bd. dirs. Health Planning Coun.

Tucson, mem. exec. com., 1969-74; chmn. profl. divsn. United Way, Tucson, 1969-70, vice chmn. campaign, 1988, Ariz. Health Faciltities Authority, bd. dirs., 1992—; chmn. dietary svcs. com., vice chmn., 1988, Md. Hosp. Coun., 1966-67; bd. dirs. Ky. Hosp. Assn., 1961-62, chmn. coun. profl. practice, 1960-61; past pres. Blue Grass Hosp. Coun.; trustee Assn. Western Hosps., 1974-81, pres., 1979-80; mem. accreditation Coun. for Continuing Med. Edn., 1982-87, chair, 1986; bd. govs. Pima C.C., 1970-76, sec., 1973-74, chmn., 1975-76, bd. dirs. Found., 1978-82, Ariz. Bd. Regents, 1982-90, sec., 1983-86, pres., 1987-88; mem. Tucson Airport Authority, 1987—, bd. dirs., 1990-95, pres., 1995; v.p. Tucson Econ. Devel. Corp., 1977-82; founder, dir., bd. dirs. Vol. Hosps. Am., 1977-88, treas., 1979-82; mem. Ariz. Adv. Health Coun. Dirs., 1976-78; bd. dirs. Tucson Tomorrow, 1983-87, Tucson Downtown Devel. Corp., 1988-95, Rincon Inst., 1992-97, Sonoran Inst., 1992-97; dir. Mus. No. Ariz., 1988—; nat. bd. advisors Coll. Bus. U. Ariz., 1990—, mem. Dean's Bd. Coll. Fine Arts, 1992—, chmn., 1992-96, pres. Ariz. Coun. Econ. Edn., 1993-95; vis. panel Sch. Health Adminstrn. and Policy Ariz. State U., 1990-92; bd. dirs. Cmty. Found. So. Ariz., 1996-2001; mem. adv. bd. Steele Meml. Rsch. Ctr., U. Ariz. Coll. Medicine, 1996—. Named to Hon. Order Ky. Cols.; named Tucson Man of Yr. 1987, Tucson Father of Yr. 1997; recipient Disting. Svc. award Anti-Defamation League B'nai B'rith, 1989, Humanitarian award Arthritis Found. S.Am., 2001. Mem. Am. Hosp. Assn. (nominating com. 1983-86, trustee 1975-78, ho. dels. 1972-78, chmn. coun. profl. svc. 1973-74, regional adv. bd. 1969-78, chmn. joint com. with NASW 1963-64, Disting. Svc. award 1989), Ariz. Hosp. Assn. (Salisbury award 1982, bd. dirs. 1967-72, pres. 1970-71), Ariz. C. of C. (bd. dirs. 1988-93), Assn. Am. Med. Colls. (mem. assembly 1974-77), Tucson C. of C. (bd. dirs. 1968-69), Nat. League for Nursing, Ariz. Town Hall (bd. dirs. 1982-92, chmn. 1990-92, treas. 1985), Pima County Acad. Decathlon Assn. (dir. 1983-85), The Rotary Club of Tucson (pres. 1993-94), U. Ariz. Alumni Assn. Coll. Nursing (hon. alumnus 1998). Baptist/Presbyterian (ch. moderator, chmn. finance com., deacon, ch. sch. supt., trustee, bd. dirs. ch. found.) Home: 6734 N Chapultepec Cir Tucson AZ 85750-1001 Office: Tucson Med Ctr 5301 E Grant Rd Tucson AZ 85712-2805 *It seems important to put something back into life - for all we take from it.*

SHROPSHIRE, WALTER, JR. biophysicist emeritus, pastor; b. Washington, Sept. 4, 1932; s. Walter and Mary Virginia (Anderson) S.; m. Audrey Marie McConkey, June 28, 1958; children— Janet Marie, Susan Lynn, Edward Allen. BS in Physics, George Washington U., 1954, MS in Botany, 1956, PhD in Plant Physiology, 1958; MDiv summa cum laude, Wesley Theol. Sem., 1990; postdoctoral fellow biophysics, Calif. Inst. Tech., 1957-59. Ordained to ministry United Meth. Ch., 1977. Physicist Smithsonian Instn., Washington, 1954—63; asst. dir. Smithsonian Environ. Rsch. Ctr., 1963-86; Gast prof. U. Freiburg, Germany, 1968-69; biophysicist, dir. Omega Lab., Cabin John, Md., 1986—. Professorial lectr. botany George Washington U., 1960-85; Gast prof. U. Zurich, Switzerland, 1985-86; part-time adj. prof. Practice Min. and Mission Wesley Theol. Sem., 1990—. Editor: Phytochrome, 1972, Joys of Research, 1981, Photomorphogenesis, Vol 16A, 16B, 1983, Photobiology, 1984-85; Contbr. 50 articles to profl. jours. Pastor, Foundry United Meth. Ch., Washington, 1991—. Recipient Smithsonian Outstanding Performance award, 1967, Smithsonian Research award, 1968, Merit award Soc. John Wesley, 1997, Templeton Sci. and Religion Course prize, 1999, 2002; NSF grantee, 1960-66. Fellow Explorers Club, Am. Solar Energy Soc. Office: Omega Lab PO Box 189 Cabin John MD 20818-0189 E-mail: wshrop@erols.com. *The world is an incredible place, rich with unexplored and unexplained interconnections between the biological and physical domains. I am fortunate to have been born when science has begun to unravel some of the mysteries of these interconnections and especially fortunate to have had teachers who shared their enthusiasm for learning. I also have benefited from mystical religious experiences of others and my own that enable me to work at the interface between science and religion. My belief is that the pursuit of both subjective and objective knowledge of ourselves and the universe we live in is necessary to enable humanity to develop to its fullest potential. This is an exciting pursuit I hope to continue to participate in a long time.*

SHROUT, MICHAEL KIRBY, dental educator, researcher; b. Detroit, July 28, 1945; m. Carol Margaret Weber Shrout, June 8; children: Catherine E., Margaret M. BS, U. Tulsa, Oklahoma, 1967; DMD, Washington U., St. Louis, 1975. Mo. Dental Bd., 2001, Ga. Dental Bd., 2001. Pvt. practice, Clayton, Mo., 1976-83; asst. prof. Washington U. Sch. Dental Medicine, St. Louis, 1983-89; prof. Med. Coll. Ga., Augusta, 1989—. Edtl. bd. Oral Surgery, Oral Medicine, Oral Pathology, Oral Radiology and Endodontics, St. Louis, 1998-; scientific adv. bd. Alara, Hayward, Calif., 1995-; reviewer Dento Maxillo Dacial Radiology, Basingstoke, Hampshire, Great Britain and Northern Ireland, 1992-2001, Jour. Am. Dental Assn., Chgo., 1995-, Jour. Prosthodontics, 1999-2001, mem. faculty assembly Med. Coll. Ga., 1998, 2000. Author: (chpt.) Clinical Dentistry, 1991, 1995; contbr. articles to profl. jours. Mem. SOc. for Preservation and Encouragement of Barber Shop Quartet Singing in Am., Kenosha, Wi., 1996-2000. Named Gov.'s Teaching fellow Ga. Inst. Higher Edn. andOffice of Instrnl. Devel., U. Ga., 1998, chmn. Gen. Faculty Assembly, Med. Coll. Ga., 1998; recipient Disting. Svc. award Med. Coll. Ga. Acad. Coun., 1995, 2000, fellow Acad. Gen. Dentistry, 1985. Mem. Acad. Gen. Dentistry, Internat. Assn. Dento-Maxillo-Facial Radiology, Am. Acad. Oral and Maxillofacial Radiology, Am. Assn. Dental Rsch. Home: 4587 Mulberry Creek Dr Evans GA 30809 Office: Med Coll Ga 1459 Laney Walker Blvd Augusta GA 30912-1241 Fax: 706-721-6276. E-mail: mshrout@mail.mcg.edu.

SHROYER, THOMAS JEROME, lawyer; b. Morris, Minn., Mar. 18, 1952; s. Virgil Ernest and Muriel June (Hanson) S.; m. Nan Kenwood Sorensen, June 30, 1979; children: Eric Sorensen, Peter Thomas. BA in Polit. Sci., U. Minn., 1974, JD, 1977. Cert. civil trial specialist Minn. State Bar Assn. With Thoma, Schoenthal, Des Moines, 1977-78; assoc. Chadwick Johnson & Bridell, Bloom, Minn., 1978-80; shareholder, bd. dirs., pres., CEO Moss & Barnett, Mpls., 1980—. Author: Accountant Liability, 1991. Address: 90 S 7th St 4800 Wells Fargo Ctr Minneapolis MN 55402-3903 *Notable cases include: Cooley vs. CBS, Inc., which achieved def. verdict for CBS, Inc. on a $1.2 million claim of pirating a video tape of a heavyweight boxing match; Hagert vs. Glickman, 520 F. Supp., D. Minn, 1981; which defended accts. in maj. securities and tax cases; Burns vs. Ersek, 591 F. Supp. 837 D. Minn., 1984, which successfully moved to limit the "tolling" effect of a putative class action.*

SHRUM, L. J. finance educator; b. Paragould, Ark., Dec. 25, 1955; s. Joe W. and Jean Shrum; m. Tina M. Lowrey. PhD, U. of Ill., 1992. Assoc. prof. Rutgers U., New Brunswick, NJ, 1992—2002, U. of Tex., San Antonio, 2002—. Office: University of Texas San Antonio 6900 North Loop 1604 West San Antonio TX 78249 Business E-Mail: LJShrum@utsa.edu.

SHTENGOLD, YEFIM SHELICHOVICH, medical educator, researcher; b. Novograd Volinsk, Russia, Apr. 16, 1927; came to U.S., 1996; s. Shelik David and Basya (Grushko) S.; m. Liliya Nikitichna Vasilevskaya, Feb. 16, 1961; 1 child, Ekaterina Gribanova. MD, Med. Inst., Kishinew, Moldova, 1954; PhD, Inst. Clin. and Exptl. Surgery, Moscow, 1974. Intern in oncology Regional Med. Ctr., Grodno, Belarus, 1954-58; surgeon Regional Med. Ctr. Oncology, Moscow, 1958-62; anesthesiologist Inst. Child Surgery, 1962-64; head Organ Preservation Lab., Inst. Clin. and Exptl. Surgery, 1964-74; head Artificial Heart Lab., Inst. Transplantology and Artificial Organs, 1974-80; head dept. biophysics, biomechanics and biomed. engring. Inst. Problems in Mechanics-Russian Acad. Sci., 1980-96, prof., 1992—. Author: Mathematical Simulation of the Physiological Systems, 1971, Organ Preservation, 1975, Biomechanics of the Myocardial Muscle, 1981, Stress-Deformed Cardiovascular System and Hypertension, 1990; contbr. over 300 articles to sci. publs.; patentee in field. Home: 7549 Lexington Ave Los Angeles CA 90046-5563

SHTOHRYN, DMYTRO MICHAEL, librarian, educator; b. Zvyniach, Ukraine, Nov. 9, 1923; came to U.S., 1950; s. Mykhailo and Kateryna (Figol) S.; m. Eustachia Barwinska, Sept. 3, 1955; children: Bohdar O., Liudoslava V. Student, Ukrainian Free U., Munich, 1947-48, U. Minn., 1954; MA in Slavic Studies, U. Ottawa, Can., 1958, B.L.S., 1959, PhD in Slavic Studies, 1970. Slavic cataloger U. Ottawa, 1959; cataloger NRC Can., Ottawa, 1959-60; Slavic cataloger, instr. library adminstrn. U. Ill., Urbana, 1960-64, head Slavic cataloging, asst. prof. library adminstrn., 1964-68, head Slavic cataloging, assoc. prof., 1968-75, head Slavic cataloging, prof., 1975-85, lectr. Ukrainian lit., 1975-91, assoc. Slavic librarian, prof., 1985-95, prof. Ukrainian lit., 1991-95, prof. emeritus, 1995—. Vis. prof. Ukrainian lit. U. Ottawa, 1974; assoc. prof. Ukrainian lit. Ukrainian Cath. U., Rome, 1978— ; prof. Ukrainian lit. Ukrainian Free U., Munich, 1983—, Ukrainian lang. and lit., U. Ill., 1991-95, Ukrainian culture, 1996—; chmn. Ukrainian Research Program U. Ill., 1984—. Editor: Catalog of Publications of Ukrainian Academy of Sciences, 1966, Ukrainians in North America: A Bibliographical Directory, 1975; author: Ukrainian Literature in the U.S.A.: Trends, Influences, Achievements, 1975, The Rise and Fall of Book Studies in Ukraine, 1986, Oleh Kandyba-Olzhych: Bibliography, 1992; editor: Bull. Ukrainian Libr. Assn. Am., 1982-88; mem. editl. bd. Ukrainian Historian, 1985-98, Ethnic Forum, 1985-95, Crossroads, 1986-97, Ukrainian Quar., 1993—, Ukrainian Problems, 1997—, Ukrainian Rev., 1997-99. Counselor Boy Scouts Am., Champaign, Ill., 1967-85; bd. dirs. Ukrainian-Am. Found., Chgo., 1978-87. Recipient Grant Future Credit Union Toronto, 1956, Grant U. Ill., 1977, 1982, Silver medal, Parliament of Can. Librarian, Ottawa, 1959, award, Glorier Soc. Can., 1959, citation plaque, Ukrainian Congress Com. Am., Chgo., 2000, Medal, V. Stefanyk Subcarpathian State U., 2001. Fellow Shevchenko Sci. Soc. (exec. com., M. Hrushevsky medal 1998); mem. ALA (chmn. Slavic and East European sect. 1968-69), Ukrainian Libr. Assn. Am. (pres. 1970-74, 82-87), Ukrainian Acad. and Profl. Assn. (charter, sec. 1985-89, pres. 1989—), I. Franko Internat. Soc. (founding mem., pres. 1978-79, 81-82), Ukrainian-Am. Assn. Univ. Profs. (exec. com. 1981-96), Ukrainian Hist. Assn. (exec. com. 1983-97), Ukrainian Acad. Arts and Scis. in U.S. (exec. com. 1993-98), Ukrainian Congress Com. of Am. Scholarly Coun., Ukrainian Writers' Assn. Slovo, Libr. Congress Assocs. (charter mem.). Ukrainian Catholic. Home: 403 Park Lane Dr Champaign IL 61820-7729 Office: Dept Slavic Langs & Lits 3092 Fgn Langs Bldg 707 S Mathews Ave Urbana IL 61801-3625 E-mail: shtohryn@uiuc.edu.

SHTURMAKOV, ALEXANDER JOSEPH, automotive industry executive; b. Moscow, Apr. 15, 1953; came to U.S., 1991; s. Joseph Boris and Eugenia Shturmakov; m. Olga Nikoshkova, Aug. 1, 1986; 1 child, Marina. BSME in Foundry with highest honors, Moscow State Tech. U., 1974, MSME in Foundry with highest honors, 1975, PhD in Metallurgy and Materials Sci., 1982. Sr. rsch. engr. Moscow R&D Inst. of Automotive Industry, 1975-80, head of rsch., 1980-85, chief rsch. engr., 1985-91; quality assurance mgr., metallurgist ME Internat. (GS Techs. Group), St. Cloud, Minn., 1992-95; tech. dir. Iroquois Foundry Co./Citation Corp., Browntown, Wis., 1995-99; dir. tech. and devel. Internat. Truck and Engine Corp., Chgo., 1999—2002; engr. mgr. Burgess-Norton Mfg. Co. (Amsted Industries), Beaver Dam, Wis., 2002—. Contbr. chpts. in books, numerous articles to profl. jours.; inventor in field. Recipient Bronze medal for tech. and sci. achievements Coun. Mins. Russia, 1986, Inventor of USSR award Soc. of Inventors of USSR, 1990. Mem. Am. Foundrymen's Soc. (mem. 5-H com. Gray Iron Rsch. 1996—), ASM Internat., ASM Heat Treating Soc. (founding mem.). Avocations: photography, swimming, ping pong, golf, tennis. Office: Burgess-Norton Mfg Co 201 Industrial Dr PO Box 220 Beaver Dam WI 53916 E-mail: ajshturmakov@burgessnorton.com.

SHU, CHI-WANG, mathematics educator, researcher; b. Beijing, People's Republic of China, Jan. 2, 1957; arrived in U.S., 1982, naturalized, 1993; s. Kuang-Yao and Ding-Zhen (Shi) Shu; m. Din-Sui Loh, May 1, 1984; 1 child Hai-Shuo. BS, U. Sci. and Tech. of China, 1982; PhD, UCLA, 1986. Rsch. assoc. U. Minn., Mpls., 1986-87; asst. prof. applied math. Brown U., Providence, 1987-91, assoc. prof., 1992-96, prof., 1996—, chmn., 1999—. Cons. ICASE, NASA Langley Rsch. Ctr., Hampton, Va., 1988—. Mng. editor: Math. of Computation, 2002—, co-chief editor: Jour. Sci. Computing, 2000—; contbr. Recipient Pub. Svc. Group Achievement award for pioneer work in computational fluid dynamics, NASA, 1992, First Feng Kang prize of Sci. Computing, Chinese Acad. Sci., 1995; grantee, NSF, NASA, Army Rsch. Office. Mem.: Soc. for Indsl. and Applied Math., Am. Math. Soc. Achievements include research in in numerical solutions for discontinuous problems. Home: 135 Woodbury St Providence RI 02906-3511 Office: Brown U Div Applied Maths 182 George St Providence RI 02912-9056

SHU, PETER H.C. research scientist; b. Nanjing, China, Feb. 6, 1948; s. Jyr-Chi and Huei-Chung (Chang) Shu; m. Chun Wan Liu; 1 child Janet E. BS, Nat. Taiwan U., Taipei, 1970; MS, Ohio State U., 1974; MBA, SUNY, 1984; PhD, Rensselaer Poly. Inst., 1978. Rsch. fellow U. Mass., Amherst, 1979; project leader GE Co., Selkirk, N.Y., 1979-85; materials specialist Bayer Corp., Pitts., 1985-90; dep. gen. mgr. Bayer Taiwan Co., Ltd., Taipei, 1990—98; regional tech. mgr. Asia Pacific region Bayer China Co., Ltd., Hong Kong, 1998—2001; bus. devel. mgr. Bayer Corp., Pitts., 2001—. Patentee in field. Chmn. Chinese Sch. Bd., Pitts., 1984; bd. dirs. Overseas Chinese Assn., Pitts., 1984. Lt. Taiwan mil., 1970-71. Merit scholar Ministry of Edn., Taiwan, 1966-70; named Tchg. Officer of Yr., First NC Mil. Sch., Taiwan, 1971. Mem. Am. Chem. Soc., Soc. Plastic Engrs. (sr. mem.), Soc. Automotive Engrs. Avocations: Chinese arts, photography. Office: 206 Doubletree Dr Venetia PA 15367-1438 E-mail: peter.shu.b@bayer.com.

SHU, WENLONG, environmental engineer, educator; b. Shanghai, China, Nov. 28, 1932; s. Junde and Yuying (Wang) S.; m. Manqing Chen, Mar. 10, 1957; children: Minmin, Hongmin. B in Engring., Qing Hua U., Beijing, China, 1953; MS in Environ. Engring., U. N.C., 1982. Cert. sr. engr. in water and wastewater engring. Bur. Staffs of Sci. and Tech., State Coun. China. Asst. tchr. Harbin (China) U. Tech., 1953-56; engr. Rsch. Inst. Bldg. and Constrn., Beijing, 1956-80; vis. scholar U. N.C., Chapel Hill, 1980, rsch. assoc., 1981-82; sr. engr. and vice chief engr. Rsch. Inst. Environ. Protection, Beijing, 1982-90, rsch. prof., 1990—. Presenter in field; appraiser for proposals in environmental sciences of the Natl. Natural Science Found. of China, 1984—. Contbr. articles to profl. jours.; inventor in field. Recipient Lifelong Achievement award State Coun. China, Beijing, 1993—; Continuation Edn. grantee Ministry of Edn., Beijing, 1980-82; grantee UNEP Asia & Pacific Region Office, Bangkok, 1992. Mem. Am. Water Works Assn., Pacific Basin Consortium for Hazardous Waste Rsch., Chinese Soc. Water and Wastewater Engring. (com. 1985—), Rsch. Inst. Environ. Protection Metall. Industry (advisor to grads. 1984—). Avocations: travel, writing, handiwork. Home: 33 Xitucheng Rd Beijing 100088 China Office: Rsch Inst Environ Protect 33 Xitucheng Rd Beijing 100088 China E-mail: wenlong_shu@yahoo.com.

SHU, YU-JEN, mathematician; b. Taipei, Taiwan, Apr. 23, 1976; d. Sh-chin Lin. MS, Nat. Taiwan U., 2000. Tchg. asst. dept. math. SUNY, Stony Brook, 2000—. Office: SUNY at Stony Brook Dept Math Stony Brook NY 11794 E-mail: yjshu@math.sunysb.edu.

SHUART, JAMES MARTIN, retired academic administrator; b. College Point, N.Y., May 9, 1931; s. John and Barbara (Schmidt) S.; m. Marjorie Strunk, Apr. 5, 1953; children: James Raymond, William Arthur. BA, Hofstra U., 1953, MA, 1962; PhD, NYU, 1966; D (hon.), L.I. U., 2000. Group rep. Home Life Ins. Co., 1955-57, N.Y. Life Ins. Co., 1957-59; adminstr. Hofstra U., Hempstead, N.Y., 1959-70, asst. dir. admissions, asst. dean faculty, asst. pres., exec. dean student services, assoc. dean liberal arts scis., trustee, 1973-75, v.p. adminstrv. svcs., 1975-76, pres., 1976-2001, pres. emeritus, 2001—. Mem. higher edn. adv. com. N.Y. State Senate, 1979-95; trustee Commn. on Ind. Colls. and Univs., N.Y. State, 1982-89, 92-95, chmn., 1988-89; mem. Am. Coun. on Edn.'s Labor/Higher Edn. Coun., 1983-88, Am. Coun. on Edns. Commn. on Leadership Devel., 1987-89, Peat Marwick Higher Edn. Pres.'s Adv. Com., 1988-96; bd. dirs. European Am. Bank, 1990-2001; chair Nassau County Property Tax Relief Commn., 1990-92; co-chair N.Y. State Temporary Commn. for L.I. Tax Relief, 1990-93. Trustee Molloy Coll., 1973-77; mem. adv. bd. Adelphi U. Sch. Social Work, 1973-84; dep. county exec. Nassau County, 1973-75, commr. social svcs., 1971-73, commr. L.I. Reg. Planning Bd., 1978-83, chmn., 1981-83; bd. dirs L.I. Assn., 1986-90; trustee Uniondale (N.Y.) Pub. Libr., 1966-68, L.I. Hosp. Planning Coun., 1971-75; pres., bd. dirs. Health Welfare Coun. Nassau County, 1971-80; chmn. Nassau Bd. Social Svcs., 1971-73; bd. dirs. Winthrop U. Hosp., 1979-86; mem. Nassau County Charter Revision Commn., 1993-96. Decorated officer Order of Orange Nassau (The Netherlands); recipient Founders Day award NYU, 1967, Alumnus of Yr. award Hofstra U., 1973, George M. Estabrook Disting. svc. award Alumni Assn., 1974, Leadership in Govt. award C.W. Post coll., L.I. U., 1978, Man of Yr. award Hempstead C. of C., 1978, L.I. Pers. and Guidance Assn., award, 1977, Lincoln Day award Syosset-Woodbury Rep. Club, 1981, L.I. Bus. disting. Leadership award 1982, 96, Joseph Giacalone award 1986, Medal of Honor L.I. Assn., 1988, L.I. Achievement award Pub. Rels. Profls. of L.I., 1995, Award L.I. Bus. Devel. Coun., 1994, 98, WLIWCh21 Educator of the Yr. award, 1999, Lifetime Achievement award L.I. Assn., 2001, L.I. Software and Tech. Network award L.I. Software and Tech. Network, 2001; others; named to L.I. Hall of Fame, 1985, Lifetime Achievement award Met. Lacrosse Found., 2001. Home: 111 Cherry Valley Ave # M35 Garden City NY 11530-1570

SHUBART, DOROTHY LOUISE TEPFER, artist, educator; b. Ft. Collins, Colo., Mar. 1, 1923; d. Adam Christian and Rose Virginia (Ayers) Tepfer; m. Robert Franz Shubart, Apr. 22, 1950; children: Richard, Lorenne. AA, Colo. Women's Coll., 1944; grad., Cleve. Inst. Art, 1946; student, Western Res. U., 1947-48; BA, St. Thomas Aquinas Coll., 1974; MA, Coll. New Rochelle, 1978; student, Santa Fe C.C., 2001—02. Art tchr. Denver Mus., 1942-44; art tchr. adults and children Cleve. Recreation Dept., 1944-50; adult edn. art tchr. Nanuet (N.Y.) Pub. Schs., 1950-65, Pearl River (N.Y.) Adult Edn., 1950-51. Rec. sec. Van Houten Fields Assn., West Nyack, NY, 1969—74. Exhibited in group shows at Hopper Ho., Rockland Ctr Arts, CWC, Cleve. Inst. Arts, Coll. New Rochelle, Rockland County Ann. Art Fair, Gonzalez Sr. Ctr.; co-author, photographer: Windmills & Dreams, 1997. Leader 4-H Club, Nanuet, 1960—80, Girl Scouts U.S., Nanuet, 1961—68; mem. scholarship com., gen. com. PTA, 1964—68; rec. sec. Van Houten Fields Assn., West Nyack, NY, 1969—74; com. mem. Eldorado Cmty. Improvement Assn.-Arterial Rd. Planning Com., Santa Fe, 1992—94, Environ. Def. Fund, Union Concerned Scientists, Nat. Com. to Preserve Social Security and Medicare; capt., organizer Neighborhood Watch; mem. Eldorado chpt. Security Com.; mem. Eldorado Conservation Greenbelt Com., 1996—97; campaign vol. Jim Baca for Gov., N.Mex., 1996, Tom Udall for Congress, 1999—, Gore for Pres., Santa Fe, 2000; mem. Eldorado Hist. Com., 1995—97, Shakespeare in Santa Fe Guild, 1998, Mil. Hist. Found., 2000—; vol. Santa Fe Libr., 1998—, Eldorado's Vista Grande Libr., 2001—, Cerro Grande Food Bank, 1998—. Scholar Gund, Cleve. Inst. Arts, 1946. Mem.: NOW, AAUW, Audubon Soc., Action on Smoking and Health, Union Concerned Scientists, Am. Dem. Action, Envrion. Def. Fund, Wilderness Club, Phi Delta Kappa, Delta Tau Kappa. Democrat. Avocations: books, gardening, photography, bicycling, writing. Home: 8 Hidalgo Ct Santa Fe NM 87508-8898

SHUBB, WILLIAM BARNET, judge; b. Oakland, Calif., May 28, 1938; s. Ben and Nellie Bernice (Fruechtenicht) S.; m. Sandra Ann Talarico, July 29, 1962; children: Alisa Marie, Carissa Ann, Victoria Ann. AB, U. Calif., Berkeley, 1960, JD, 1963. Bar: Calif., 1964, U.S. Ct. Internat. Trade 1981, U.S. Customs Ct. 1980, U.S. Ct. Appeals (9th cir.) 1964, U.S. Supreme Ct. 1972. Law clk. U.S. Dist. Ct., Sacramento, 1963-65; asst. U.S. atty., Sacramento, 1965-71; chief asst. U.S. atty. (ea. dist.) Calif., 1971-74; assoc. Diepenbrock, Wulff, Plant & Hannegan, Sacramento, 1974-77, ptnr., 1977-80, 81-90; U.S. atty. Eastern Dist. Calif., 1980-81; judge U.S. Dist. Ct. (ea. dist.) Calif., 1990-96, chief judge, 1996—; chmn. com. drafting of local criminal rules U.S. Dist. Ct. (ea. dist.) Calif., 1974, mem. speedy trial planning com., 1974-80; lawyer rep. 9th Cir. U.S. Jud. Conf., 1975-78; mem. faculty Fed. Practice Inst., 1978-80; instr. McGeorge Sch. Law, U. Pacific, 1964-66. Mem. ABA, Fed. Bar Assn. (pres. Sacramento chpt. 1977), Calif. Bar Assn., Assn. Def. Counsel, Am. Bd. Trial Advs., Sacramento County Bar Council.

SHUBERT, DENNIS L. neurosurgeon, medical administrator; b. Bangor, Maine, Dec. 27, 1947; BS, Tufts U., 1969, MS, 1970; MD, George Washington U., 1975; PhD, U. Minn., 1981; MA in Health Care Mgmt., Harvard U., 2002. Diplomate Am. Bd. Neurol. Surgery. Chmn. dept. surgery Ea. Main Med. Ctr., Bangor, 1991—. Bd. dirs. Merrill Merchants Bank, Bangor. Home and Office: 404 State St Bangor ME 04401-6604

SHUBERT, GUSTAVE HARRY, research executive, consultant, social scientist; b. Buffalo, Jan. 18, 1929; s. Gustave Henri and Ada Shubert (Smith) S.; m. Rhea Brickman, Mar. 29, 1952; children: Wendy J., David L. BA, Yale U., 1948; MA, NYU, 1951. Staff mem. Lincoln Lab., MIT, 1955-57; adminstr. sys. engring. Hycon Ea., Inc., Paris, 1957-59; with RAND Corp., Santa Monica, Calif., 1959—, corp. v.p. domestic programs, 1968-75, sr. corp. v.p. domestic programs, 1975-78, sr. corp. v.p., 1978-89, trustee, 1973-89, sr. fellow, corp. advisor and adv. trustee, 1989—; founding dir. Inst. Civil Justice, 1979-87; trustee mutual funds Neuberger Berman, N.Y.C., 1989—. Cons. Keene Corp., N.Y.C., 1990-92; pres. N.Y.C. Rand Inst., 1972-73, trustee, 1972-79; trustee Housing Allowance Offices Brown County, Wis. and South Bend, Ind., 1973-80; mem. adv. coun. Sch. Engring., Stanford U., 1976-79; mem. policy adv. com. clin. scholars program UCLA, 1975-88; mem. adv. group evaluation and methodology divsn. GAO, 1986-96; mem. adv. commn. on professionalism ABA, 1985-87; mem. Calif. jud. system com. Los Angeles County Bar Assn., 1984-85; mem. com. on evaluation of poverty rsch. NAS. Mem. Pacific Coun. of Fgn. Affairs, 1991; mem. U.S. adv. com. Internat. Inst. Applied Sys. Analysis, 1998—; mem. history dept. adv. bd. Carnegie Mellon U., 1995—. With USAF, 1951-55. Decorated Air medal with 3 oak leaf clusters, Commendation medal. Mem. AAAS, Am. Judicature Soc. (bd. dirs. 1987-90), Inst. Strategic Studies (London), Coun. of Fgn. Rels. Home: 13838 W Sunset Blvd Pacific Palisades CA 90272-4022 Office: RAND Corp 1700 Main St Santa Monica CA 90401-3297 E-mail: shubert@rand.org.

SHUBERT, JOSEPH FRANCIS, librarian; b. Buffalo, Sept. 17, 1928; s. Joseph Francis and Lena M. (Kohn) S.; m. Dorothy Jean Whearty, Feb. 5, 1955 (div. Feb. 1980); children: Julia Ellen, Alan Joseph. BS, State U. Tchrs. Coll., Geneseo, N.Y., 1951; MA, U. Denver, 1957. Reference and extension librarian Nev. State Library, Carson City, 1951-57, library cons., 1957-59, state librarian, 1959-61; asst. dir. internat. relations office ALA, 1962-66; state librarian Ohio, 1966-77; state librarian, asst. commr. libraries N.Y. State Edn. Dept., 1977-96, state libr. emeritus, 1996—, sec., treas. chief officer state Library Agys., 1973-76, chmn., 1976-78; mem. adv. council to U.S. Pub. Printer, 1974-77; adv. com. White House Conf. Library and Info. Services, 1977-79; chmn. steering com. for survey of state libr. agys. U.S. Nat. Ctr. for Edn. Stats., 1992—. Bd. dirs.Capital Dist. Regional Info. Svc. Network State U. Albany, 1994—97; trustee Ohio Coll. Libr. Ctr., 1976—78; mem. adv. com. Ctr. for the Book, Libr. of Congress, 1979—82, mem. network adv. coun., 1981—96; Disting. Alumnus lectr. U. Denver, 1979; mem. adv. coun. Sch. Libr. and Info. Sci., Pratt Inst., 1980—2000; bd. dirs. N.E. Document Conservation Ctr., 1980—82, treas., 1986—89; chmn. chief officers State Libr. in the N.E., 1987—89; mem. design task force White House Conf. on Libr. and Info. Svcs., 1985. Editor: The Bookmark, 1987-96; contbr. to numerous periodicals. Mem. adv. com. U. Wis. Inst. on Edn., Federally Funded Literacy Program, 1992-94; dir. The Friends of the N.Y. State Libr., Inc., 1998—; co-chair 58th Anniversary com. Coll. Geneseo, 2001. Recipient Hall of Fame award Ohio Libr. Assn., 1991, Exceptional Achievement award ALA Assn. Specialized and Coop. Library Agy. Assn., 1985, Disting. Pub. Service award SUNY-Albany, Nelson A. Rockefeller Coll. of Pub. Affairs and Policy, 1987, Velma K. Moore award NY. State Assn. Libr. Bds., 1996; named Disting. Alumnus, SUNY-Geneseo, 1985, named to Alumni Honor Roll., 1997. Mem. ALA (grass roots advocate 1996), Nat. Ctr. for Ednl. Stats., Nat. Commn. on Librs. and Info. Svcs., Task Force on Pub. Libr. Stats. (adv. com. 1990-96), chair steering com. for NCES Survey of State Libr. Agencies, 1993—, Assn . of Specialized and Coop. Lit. Agys. (pres. 1988-89), Nev. Libr. Assn. (pres.), North Collins Libr. Assn. (N.Y.), Meml. Libr. Assn., N.Y. Libr. Assn. (hon. chair capital campaign 1999-2000, Outstanding Svc. award 1996), Chief Officers State Libr. Agys. (chmn. 1977-78), Nev. Congress Parents and Tchrs., Torch Club of Albany Roman Catholic. Home: 494 Madison Ave Albany NY 12208-3601 Office: NY State Libr State Edn Dept 33 Cultural Edn Ctr # 10A Albany NY 12230-0001

SHUBIK, MARTIN, economics educator; b. N.Y.C., Mar. 24, 1926; s. Joseph Louis and Sara S.; m. Julia Kahn, Aug. 11, 1970; 1 child, Claire Louise. BA, U. Toronto, 1947, MA, 1949; PhD, Princeton U., 1953. Rsch. asst. Princeton U., 1950—53, rsch. assoc., 1953-55; fellow Ctr. for Advanced Study in Behavioral Scis., Palo Alto, Calif., 1955-56; cons. mgmt. consultation svcs. Gen. Electric Co., 1956-60; adj. rsch. prof. Pa. State U., 1957-59; vis. prof. econs. Yale U., New Haven, 1960-61, prof. econs. of orgn., dept. adminstrv. sci., 1963-75, Seymour H. Knox prof. math. instl. econs., 1975—. Bd. dirs. Equity Strategies, Third Avenue Funds; mem. staff T.J. Watson Rsch. Labs., IBM Corp., 1961-63; vis. prof. Escuela de Estudios Económicos U. Chile, Santiago, 1965, Inst. Advanced Studies, Vienna, Austria, 1968, 70, U. Melbourne, Australia, 1973; cons. Rand Corp., Santa Monica, Calif., 1963; dir. Cowles Found. for Rsch. In Econs., Yale U., 1973-76; external faculty Santa

Fe Inst., 1994—, sci. bd. 1996—; cons. in field. Author or co-author: numerous books, including The War Game, 1979, (with G. Brewer) The Aggressive Conservative Investor, 1979, (with M.J. Whitman) Market Structure and Behavior, 1980, (with R.E. Levitan) Game Theory in the Social Sciences, vol. 1, 1982, vol. 2, 1984, The Theory of Money and Financial Institutions, vols. 1 and 2, 1999; mem. editorial bd. Conflict Resolution; mem. editl. adv. bd. Internat. Studies Series; assoc. editor Mgmt. Sci, 1965-81; contbr. articles to profl. jours. Served to lt. Royal Can. Navy. Recipient Lanchester prize, 1983, Koopman prize mil. ops. rsch., 1996; named hon. prof. U. Vienna Fellow Econometric Soc., World Acad. Arts and Scis.; mem. Am. Acad. Arts and Scis., Conn. Acad. Arts and Scis. Home: 140 Edgehill Rd Hamden CT 06517-4011 Office: PO Box 208281 30 Hillhouse Ave New Haven CT 06520-8281 E-mail: martin.shubik@yale.edu.

SHUBIN, MIKHAIL A. mathematics educator; b. Kuibyshev, Russia, Dec. 19, 1944; came to U.S., 1991; s. Alexandr M. Shubin and Maria A. Shubina; m. Maria D. Shaposhnikova, June 11, 1969; children: Anna, Galina. MS in Math., Moscow State U., Moscow, 1966, PhD in Math., 1969; DSc in Physics and Math., Steklov Inst., Leningrad, Russia, 1981. Asst. prof. Math. Moscow State U., Moscow, 1969-75, assoc. prof. Math., 1975-90; prin. researcher Inst. of New Techs., 1990-91; prof. Math. MIT, Cambridge, 1991-92, Northeastern U., Boston, 1992—, Matthews disting univ. prof., 2001—. Author (books) Pseudodifferential Operators and Spectral Theory, 1987, The Schrödinger Equation, 1991, others; mem. editorial bd. (jours.) Potential Analysis, 1991—, Russian Jour. of Math. Physics, 1993—, Annals of Global Analysis and Geometry, 2001-; contbr. over 100 articles to profl. jours. NSF grantee, 1993-96, 97—. Mem. Moscow Math. Soc. (bd. dirs. 1990-92), Russian Acad. Natural Scis., Am. Math. Soc., Internat. Assn. Mathematical Physics. Office: Northeastern U Dept Math 360 Huntington Ave Dept Math Boston MA 02115-5000 E-mail: shubin@neu.edu.

SHUBIN, SEYMOUR, writer; b. Phila., Sept. 14, 1921; s. Isadore and Ida (Barsh) S.; m. Gloria Amet, Aug. 25, 1957; children: Neil, Jennifer. BS, Temple U., 1943. Mng. editor Ofcl. Detective Stories mag., Phila., Psychiat. Reporter, Phila., J.B. Lippincotte Pub., Phila. Author: Anyone's My Name, 1953, Manta, 1958, Wellville, U.S.A., 1961, The Captain, 1982, Holy Secrets, 1984, Voices, 1985, Never Quite Dead, 1989, Remember Me Always, 1994, Fury's Children, 1997, My Face Among Strangers, 1999, The Good and the Dead, 2000, A Matter of Fear, 2002. Recipient Edgar Allen Poe Spl. award Mystery Writers Am., 1983, Spl. Citation for Fiction, Athenaeum of Phila., 1984. Mem. PEN, Am. Ctr., Mystery Writers Am. (Edgar Allen Poe Spl. award 1983), Authors Guild. Home: 122 Harrogate Rd Wynnewood PA 19096-3533 E-mail: sishu@aol.com.

SHUBSDA, STANLEY RICHARD, retired computer engineer; b. Niagara Falls, N.Y., Sept. 23, 1941; s. Stanley R. and Jane F. (Rutkowski) S.; m. Winifred A. Chatterton, June 28, 1969; children: Stanley, Mary, Michael, Carol, Patrick, David. BS, Canisius Coll., 1963; MS, Rensselaer Poly. Inst., 1965. Instr. N.D. State U., Fargo, 1969-75; software engr. Power Authority State of N.Y., Niagara Falls, 1975-77; sr. ednl. specialist Digital, Tewksbury, Mass., 1977-79; prin. software design engr. Lockheed Martin, Syracuse, NY, 1979—2002; ret., 2002. Mem. Assn. Intelligent Systems Tech. (bd. dirs. Syracuse 1987-95), Assn. Computer Machinery, Assn. Symbolic Logic, Math. Assn. Am., Am. Math. Soc. Home: 7727 Lemontree Ln Liverpool NY 13090-2403

SHUCART, WILLIAM ARTHUR, neurosurgeon; b. St. Louis, Oct. 23, 1935; s. Frank M. and Beatrice S.; m. Laura Huber, Dec. 16, 1971. AB, Washington U., 1957; MD, U. Mo., 1961. Diplomate Am. Bd. Neurol. Surgery. Intern U. Utah Hosp., Salt Lake City, 1961-62; resident in surgery Peter Bent Brigham Hosp., Boston, 1963-64; resident in neurosurgery Columbia-Presbyn. Hosp., N.Y.C., 1967-70, Hosp. for Sick Children, Toronto, Ont., Can., 1970-71; mem. faculty dept. neurosurgery Med. Sch. Tufts U., Boston, 1971-76, assoc. prof., 1976; prof., chmn. dept. neurosurgery SUNY, Downstate Med. Ctr., Bklyn., 1976-81; neurosurgeon Tufts-New England Med. Ctr., Boston, 1972-76, prof., chmn. dept. neurosurgery, 1981—; chief neurosurgery Beth Israel Hosp., 1996-97. Vis. prof. surgery Harvard Med. Sch., 1996-97. With U.S. Army, 1964-67. Mem. ACS, Am. Assn. Neurol. Surgeons, Soc. Neurol. Surgeons. Home: 100 Meadowbrook Rd Weston MA 02493-2406 Office: New England Med Ctr PO Box 178 750 Washington St Boston MA 02111-1526

SHUCK, ANNETTE ULSH, education educator; b. Harrisburg, Pa., Apr. 4, 1946; d. David Addison and Florence (Scholl) Ulsh; children: Ryan David Summers, Kirsten Annette Shuck. BS, Bloomsburg U., 1967; MS, W.Va. U., 1968, EdD, 1976; cert., Albert Ellis Inst., 1993. Cert. elem., secondary, spl. edn. tchr., Pa., W.Va., sch. psychologist, W.Va. Elem. tchr. Pa. and W.Va. schs., 1968-70; instr. W.Va. U., Morgantown, 1972, grad. asst., 1972-75, instr. spl. edn. dept., 1976-77, asst. prof., 1977-83, assoc. prof., 1983-87; vis. assoc. prof. divsn. edn. U. V.I., Charlotte Amalie, St. Thomas, 1987-88, assoc. prof., 1988, prof. divsn. edn., 1989—. Instr. Lebanon Valley Coll. and Temple U., Harrisburg, Pa., 1970-72; cons. sch. psychology program Coll. Grad. Studies, Institute, W.Va., 1986; mem. Gov. of V.I. Spl. Edn. Task Force, 1988—. Author: International Family Interventionist Booklet, 1976, 1988, rev. edit., 1997; contbr. chpt. to book and articles to profl. jours. Active Environ. Awareness and Action Com., St. Thomas, 1991—; bd. dirs. V.I. Women's Bus. Ctr; hearing officer State Dept. Spl. Edn.; family edn. interventionist, 1979—. NDEA fellow, 1967-68. Mem. Coun. for Exceptional Children, Am. Assn. Coll. Tchr. Edn., Phi Delta Kappa (v.p. 1975-76, pres. 1976-77). Avocations: research, writing, snorkeling, sailing, architectural design. Office: U VI Tchr-Edn-209 Saint Thomas VI 00802

SHUCK, JERRY MARK, surgeon, educator; b. Bucyrus, Ohio, Apr. 23, 1934; s. James Edwin and Pearl (Mark) S.; m. Linda Wayne, May 28, 1974; children: Jay Steven, Gail Ellen, Kimberly Ann, Lynn Meredith, Steven James. BS in Pharmacy, U. Cin., 1955, MD, 1959, DSc, 1966. Intern Colo. Gen. Hosp., Denver, 1959-60; resident in surgery U. Cin. Integrated Program, 1960-66; mem. faculty dept. surgery U. N.Mex., Albuquerque, 1966-80, prof., 1974-80; Oliver H. Payne prof. dept. surgery Case-Western Res. U., Cleve., 1980—, chmn. dept., 1980-2000, prof. anatomy, 1999—, interim v.p. for med. affairs, 1993-95. Cons. FDA, 1972-77 Contbr. articles to profl. jours. Served to capt. U.S. Army, 1966-68. Mem. ACS, Am. Surg. Assn., Am. Bd. Surgery (bd. dirs., chmn. 1993-94, residency rev. com. for surgery 1994-2000, vice chmn. 1997-2000), Soc. Univ. Surgeons, Am. Ass n. S urgery Trauma, Am. Trauma Soc. (founding mem.), Univ. Assn. Emergency Medicine (founding mem.), Am. Burn Assn. (founding mem.), We. Surg. Assn., Ctrl. Surg. Assn. (pres. 1996-97), Assn. Acad. Surgery, S.W. Surg. Assn., Cleve. Surg. Soc. (pres. 1988-89), Ohio Med. Assn., Acad. Medicine Cleve., Halsted Soc., Surg. Infection Soc. (founding mem.), B'nai B'rith, Jewish Cmty. Ctr. Club, The Temple Club. Democrat. Jewish. Office: Case Western Reserve U Dept Surgery 11100 Euclid Ave Cleveland OH 44106-2602

SHUCK, L. ZANE, research scientist; BSME, W.Va. Inst. Tech., 1958; MSME, W.Va. U., 1965, PhD, 1970. Registered profl. engr., W.Va.; cert. Nat. Coun. Engring. Examiners. Sales engr. W.Va. Armature Co., 1958-59; assoc. prof., chmn. mech. engring. dept. W.Va. Inst. Tech., 1959-68; NSF sci. faculty fellow, rsch. engr. W.Va. U., Morgantown, 1968-70, assoc. dir. Engring. Expt. Sta., prof. mech. engring., 1976-80; supervisory mech. engr. ERDA Morgantown Energy Rsch. Ctr., 1970-76; pres. Tech. Devel. Inc., 1980—. Sci. advisor to W.Va. gov. Jay Rockefeller; adj. prof. W.Va. U. Coll. Engring., 1980-88; engring. cons. FMC Corp., South Charleston, W.Va., United Fuel Gas Co., Charleston, W.Va.,So. Pub. Svc. Co., Montgomery, W.Va., W.Va. Air Pollution Control Commn., Charleston, Gravely Tractor Divsn., Studebaker corp., Dunbar, W.Va., METC-Dept. of Energy, Mound Labs., numerous oil and gas cos.; mem. State of W.Va. Coal and Energy Adv. Com. Prodn. 4 tech. films for U.S. Dept. Energy; editl. bd. In Situ Jour.; assoc. editor ASME Trans. Jour. Energy Resources Tech.; editor 2nd Underground Coal Gasification Symposium Procs.; contbr. articles to profl. jours. Sci. and tech. coord. W.Va. Legislature, 1979-80; founder, pres., WMAC Found., 1997—; founder, chmn. Appalachian Rivers Conf. and Exhibit, 1999, 2000, 2001; apptd. to W.Va. Region VI planning and devel. coun., 2000; vis. com. W.Va. U. and Tech. Coll. Engring., 2002. Recipient 4 Ford Found. fellowships, 2 NSF fellowships, Iowa State U. and Wayne State U, NSF sci. faculty fellowship W.Va. U., Materials Testing award ASTM, 1970. Mem. ASME (energy tech. com., The WMAC Found. (pres. 1998—), Ralph James nat. award 1980), Sigma Xi, Tau Beta Pi. Achievements include 13 patents, others pending; first to hypothesize the discrete jump nature of fracture growth in such materials as sandstones, limestone and shales during hydraulic fracturing and experimentally proved it in the laboratory; first to analyze and predict the 3-dimensional stress distribution in the earth's crust during hydraulic fracturing and demonstrate the feasibility of re-orienting the earth's stress field sufficiently to control the orientation of new induced fractures; development of a process for controlling fracture orientations in the earth's crust. Home: 401 Highview Pl Morgantown WV 26505-4715

SHUE, SHYH-PYNG JACK, aerospace engineer, electrical engineer, researcher, consultant; b. Taipei, Taiwan, China; came to U.S., 1991; s. Wan-Fung Shue and Chin Huan Lin; m. Wei-Chen Janus, Apr. 26, 1991; 1 child, Francis. BS in Marine Engring., Nat. Taiwan Ocean U., Keelung, China, 1986; MSME, Poly. U. Bklyn., 1992; PhD in Aerospace Engring., Wichita State U., 1997, PhD in Elec. and Computer Engring., 2000. Project engr. Even Fair Enterprise Co., Taipei, 1988-89; plant mgr. Casetek Internat. Co., 1989-91; tech. support Hampel Techs. Inc., Tustin, Calif., 1992; rsch. asst. Wichita (Kans.) State U., 1993-98; rsch. assoc. Nat. Inst. Aviation Rsch., Wichita, 1997-98; engring. specialist Raytheon Aircraft Co., 1998—. Pres. Inter Networking Corp., 2001—. Contbr. more than 50 tech. papers to jours. Engring. fellow Wichita State U., 1995-96. Mem. AIAA (Best Paper 1995), Sigma Gamma Tau, Phi Kappa Phi. Avocations: golf, swim, fishing, boating, badminton. Office: Raytheon Aircraft co B99 PO Box 85 Wichita KS 67201-0085

SHUER, LAWRENCE MENDEL, neurosurgery educator; b. Toledo, Apr. 12, 1954; s. Bernard Benjamin and Estelle Rose (Drukker) S.; m. Paula Ann Elliott, Sept. 4, 1976; children: Jenna, Tammy, Nichole. BA with high distinction, U. Mich., 1975, MD cum laude, 1978. Diplomate Am. Bd. Neurol. Surgery, Nat. Bd. Med. Examiners. Fellow in neurology Inst. Neurology, London, 1979; intern in surgery Stanford (Calif.) U. Sch. Medicine, 1978-79, resident in neuropathology, 1980, resident in neurosurgery, 1980-84, clin. asst. prof. surgery and neurosurgery, 1984-90, assoc. prof., 1990—, acting chmn. dept. neurosurgery, 1992-95, 96—, assoc. dean, 1996—, chief of staff Stanford Health Sys., 1996—; chief of staff Stanford U. Hosp. and Clinics, 1999—. Numerous presentations in field. Contbr. articles and abstracts to med. jours., chpts. to books. Recipient Kaiser tchr. award Stanford U., 1993; James B. Angell scholar. Mem. AMA, Am. Assn. Neurol. Surgeons, Congress Neurol. Surgeons, Western Neurosurg. Soc., Calif. Assn. Neurol. Surgeons (bd. dirs., treas. 1995—98, 2nd v.p. 1998-99, 1st v.p. 1999-2000, pres.-elect 2000-01, pres. 2002—), Calif. Med. Assn., Am. Heart Assn. (fellow stroke coun.), Santa Clara County Med. Assn., San Francisco Neurol. Soc., Alpha Omega Alpha. Avocations: skiing, swimming, travel. Office: Stanford U Med Ctr 300 Pasteur Dr R229 Palo Alto CA 94304-2203 E-mail: lshuer@stanford.edu.

SHUEY, JAMES FRANK, lawyer; b. Shreveport, La., May 17, 1953; s. John Miller and Mary Abbie S.; m. Susan Elizabeth Harmon, Dec. 29, 1979 (div. Jan. 1995); children: Kate Harmon, Rachel Ferguson. AB, Duke U., 1975; JD, La. State U., 1980. Bar: La. 1980, Tex. 1994; U.S. Dist. Ct. (ea. and we. dists.) La. 1981, U.S. Dist. Ct. (mid. dist.) La. 1982; U.S. Supreme Ct. 1991. Law clk. La. Supreme Ct., New Orleans, 1980-81; assoc. to ptnr. Lemle Kelleher, 1981-94; ptnr. Frilot Partridge, 1995—. Office: Frilot Partridge Kohnke et al 1100 Poydras St New Orleans LA 70163-1101

SHUEY, RICHARD LYMAN, engineering educator, consultant; b. Chgo., May 7, 1920; s. Ralph Clement and Abbie Miriam (Strong) S.; m. Frances Barbara Fortier, Sept. 22, 1944; children: Roy Fortier, Marie Frances. BS in Engring., BSE in Math., U. Mich., 1942; PhD in Elec. Engring., U. Calif., Berkeley, 1950. Registered engr. N.Y., Calif. Engr. U. Calif. Radiation Lab., Berkeley, 1946-50; rsch. staff, br. mgr. GE Rsch. Lab., Schenectady, N.Y., 1950-84; adj. prof. Rensselaer Polytech. Inst., Troy, 1985—; cons. Schenectady, 1985—. Author: The Architecture of Distributed Computer Systems, 1997; contbr. articles to profl. jours. Bd. dirs. Self Help for Hard of Hearing N.Y. Assn., 1996-2001. Sr. mem. IEEE (various coms., offices 1952-87, Donald McLellan Cmty. Svc. award, 3d Millennium medal), AAAS, Am. Auditory Soc., Soc. Mfg. Engrs., Assn. Computing Machines, Sigma Xi, Tau Beta Pi. Avocations: golf, bridge, photography. Office: Computer Sci Dept RPI Troy NY 12180 Home: 242 Glen Eddy Dr Schenectady NY 12309-4967 E-mail: shueyrl@juno.com.

SHUFFELTON, FRANK CHARLES, educator; b. St. Marys, Ohio, Mar. 10, 1940; s. Frank B. and Dorothy A. S.; m. Jane Ballow Weiss, Apr. 20, 1963; children: Amy Ballou, George Gordon. AB, Harvard U., 1962; MS, Stanford U., 1968, PhD, 1972. Instr. U. Rochester (N.Y.), 1969-72, asst. prof., 1972-77, assoc. prof., 1977-87, prof., 1987—, dir. coll. writing, 1997—. Author: Thomas Hooker, 1586-1647, 1977, Thomas Jefferson: A Complete Bibliography, 1983, Thomas Jefferson: 1981-90, 1992; mem. editl. bd. Early Am. Lit., 1984-87, 90-93. Lt. USCGR, 1963-67. NEA Sr. fellow, 1988-89; Nat. Merit scholar, 1958-62. Mem. Northeast Am. Soc. 18th Century Studies (pres. 1994-95), Modern Lang. Assn. (chair divsn. Am. lit. to 1800 exec. com. 1996-98), Soc. 18th Century Am. Studies (pres. 1997-99). Office: U Rochester Dept English Rochester NY 14627 Fax: 716-442-5769.

SHUGART, CECIL GLENN, retired physics educator; b. Ennis, Tex., Oct. 13, 1930; s. Clifford Clarence and Ethel Hazel (Venable) S.; m. Theresa Lively, Aug. 26, 1955 (div. July 1981); children: David Neal, Peter Gregory; m. Anita Brumbelow, Dec. 14, 1985. Student, Navarro Coll., Corsicana, Tex., 1954-55; BA, N. Tex. State U., 1957; MA, U. Tex., 1961, PhD, 1968. Rsch. scientist Def. Rsch. Lab., Austin, 1958-61; assoc. engr. IBM, San Jose, Calif., 1961-62; asst. prof., head dept. physics Hardin-Simmons U., Abilene, Tex., 1962-65; dir. Soc. Physics Students Am. Inst., N.Y.C., 1968-70; rsch. assoc. U. Tex.-Austin, 1967-68; prof. physics, chmn. Northeast La. U., Monroe, 1970-77; prof. chmn. physics U. Memphis, 1977-97; ret., 1997. Cons. Tech. Legal Assocs., Memphis, 1978— Author: (with Bedell and Genusa) Experiments for General Physics, 1975; co-author: (with Johnston) The Phenomena of Physics, 1982, Phenomenal Physics and Astronomy, 1991; editor: (with P. Barker) After Einstein, 1981, (with J. Payne) Scientists and Public Policy, 1982. Served with USAF, 1948-52. NSF fellow, 1966-67; NSF grantee, 1974-75, 79-80 Fellow AAAS; mem. Am. Assn. Physics Tchrs., Am. Phys. Soc. (vice chmn. southeastern sect. 1982-83, sect. chmn. 1983-84, sect. sec., 1991-95, sec. ea. region 1991-95), Sigma Pi Sigma (pres. 1972-76). Republican. Methodist. Home: 11483 Front Beach Rd # A112 Panama City FL 32407-3659

SHUGART, HOWARD ALAN, physicist, educator; b. Orange, Calif., Sept. 21, 1931; s. Howard Ancil and Bertha Elizabeth (Henderson) S.; m. Elizabeth L. Hanson, Feb. 6, 1971. BS, Calif. Inst. Tech., 1953; MA, U. Calif.-Berkeley, 1955, PhD, 1957. Teaching asst. physics U. Calif.-Berkeley, 1953-56, assoc., 1957, lectr., 1957-58, acting asst. prof., 1958-59, asst. prof., 1959-63, assoc. prof., 1963-67, prof., 1967-93, prof. emeritus, 1993—, vice chmn. 1968-70, 79-87, 89-2001, acting chmn., summer 1979, 80, 81, 83, 84,87; atomic beam group leader Lawrence Berkeley Lab. Lawrence Berkeley Nat. Lab., 1965-79. Cons. Convair divsn. Gen. Dynamics Corp., 1960-61; mem. com. nuclear constants NRC, 1960-63. Recipient Donald Sterling Noyce prize for excellence in undergrad. tchg. U. Calif., 1988, Berkeley citation, 1993. Fellow Am. Phys. Soc. (acting sec. Pacific Coast 1961-64, exec. com. div. electron and atomic physics 1972-74), Nat. Speleological Soc. (gov. 1954-56); mem. Sigma Xi. Office: U Calif Dept Physics Berkeley CA 94720-7300

SHUGHART, DONALD LOUIS, lawyer; b. Kansas City, Mo., Aug. 12, 1926; s. Henry M. and Dora M. (O'Leary) Shughart; m. Mary I. Shughart, July 25, 1953; children: Susan C. Hogsett, Nancy J. Goede. AB, U. Mo., Columbia, 1949, JD, 1951. Bar: Mo. 1951, U.S. Dist. Ct. (we. dist.) Mo. 1951, U.S. Tax Ct. 1979. With Shughart, Thompson & Kilroy, PC, Kansas City, Mo., 1951—. Mem. Mo. Motor Carriers Assn. Planned giving com. Rockhurst U.; adv. bd. St. Joseph Hosp. With AC, U.S. Army, 1944-47. Mem. Kansas City Bar Assn. (chmn. bus. orgns. com. 1990-91), Mo. Bar Assn. (chmn. corp. com. 1980-81, 82-83), Lawyers Assn. Kansas City, Am. Judicature Soc., Mo. Orgn. Def. Lawyers (pres. 1971-72), U. Mo. Law Soc., Phi Delta Phi, Sigma Chi. Republican. Roman Catholic. Home: 1242 W 67th Ter Kansas City MO 64113-1941 Office: Shug Thom Kilroy 12 Wyandotte Pla 120 W 12th St Kansas City MO 64105-1917

SHUGRUE, JAMES LEONARD, bookseller, writer, educator; b. Chgo., Mar. 22, 1948; s. Leonard Eugene Shugrue and Anne Mannion; m. Lisa Malinowski Steinman, July 23, 1984. Bookbuyer Powell's Books, Portland, Oreg., 1983-97; arts adminstr. Mountain Writers Ctr., 1998-99; bookbuyer/seller Gt. N.W. Bookstore, 1999-2000; bookbuyer Reed Coll. Bookstore, 2000—. Founder, editor: Hubbub Mag., Portland, 1983—; workshop dir./reader various colls., 1987—. Author: Small Things Screaming, 1995 (Oreg. Book award finalist 1995), Icewater, 1997; contbr. poetry to mags. and anthologies. Bd. dirs. Portland Poetry Festival, 1982-86. Recipient Carolyn Kizer award Calapooya Coll., 1988, Open Voice award Writers' Voice Series, 1988; poetry fellow Oreg. Arts Commn., 1987. Mem. PEN (elected). E-mail: jim.shugrue@reed.edu.

SHUHAN, JANICE-LYNN NAZZIOLA, educator; b. Passaic, N.J., Sept. 11, 1959; d. Gabriel Anthony and Camille Mary (Monisera) Nazziola. BS in Math., Montclair State U., 1981, MA in Adminstrn. and Supervision, 1999. Cert. tchr. Substitute tchr. Belleville (N.J.) High Sch., 1977-81, long-term substitute tchr., 1981—, secondary math. tchr., 1986—. Sch. choreographer Belleville Mid. and High Schs., 1978—; dir. mus. Belleville H.S., 1991—; performer nat. tour U.S. Coast, 1979-80; performer off-Broadway and dinner theatres, N.Y. and N.J., 1977-86; presenter N.J. Sch. Bds. Curriculum Fair at Conv. Hall, 1989, 90, 91, 92; profl. performer, actress, singer, dancer. Author (poem): Selections of the Heart, 2000, External Songs, 2000, Between Darkness and Light, 2000; co-author: Math Essentials, Selected Strategies of Teaching Math Essentials, 1992, 93; contbr. articles to profl. jours.; appeared in motion pictures Other People's Money, A Fire in the Dark, Carlito's Way, and nat. commls. Campaign mgr. Belleville B.O.E., 1989; judge Bell/Nutley Columbus Day Parade Bella Signorina, 1988-91; dance classes Nutley Italian Am. Club, 1988; bd. dirs. Cranford Dramatic Club Theatre, mem. bd. govs. Recipient Steven's Leadership award Steven's Inst., Hoboken, N.J., 1990, Outstanding Math Nat. Educator award Tandy Corp., 1991; named Mrs. West Paterson N.J. America, Essex County Tchr. of Yr. 1999-00. Mem. NEA, ASCD, Nat. Coun. Tchrs. Math., Assn. Math. Tchrs. N.J., Belleville Edn. Assn., N.J. Edn. Assn. Republican. Roman Catholic. Avocations: acting, singing, dancing, writing poetry. Office: Belleville High Sch 100 Passaic Ave Belleville NJ 07109-1898 E-mail: janicelyn1@aol.com.

SHUHLER, PHYLLIS MARIE, physician; b. Sellersville, Pa., Sept. 25, 1947; d. Raymond Harold and Catherine Cecilia (Virus) S.; m. John Howard Schwarz, Sept. 17, 1983; 1 child, Luke Alexander. BS in Chemistry, Chestnut Hill Coll., 1971; MD, Mich. State U., 1976; diploma of Tropical Medicine and Hygiene, U. London, 1980. Diplomate Am. Bd. Family Medicine. With Soc. Cath. Med. Missionaries, Phila., 1966-82; ward clk., nursing asst. Holy Family Hosp., Atlanta, 1971-72; resident in family practice Somerset Family Med. Residency Program, Somerville, N.J., 1976-79; physician East Coast Migrant Health Project, Newton Grove, N.C., 1980; physician, missionary SCMM, Diocese of Sunyani, Berekum, Ghana, West Africa, 1980-81; emergency rm. physician Northeast Emergency Med. Assn., Quakertown, Pa., 1981-82; founder, physician Family Health Care Ctr., Inc., Pennsburg, 1982-90; physician Lifequest Med. Group, 1990-93; pvt. practice, 1993-99; physician Tri-Valley Primary Care Group, 1999—. Fellow Royal Soc. Tropical Medicine and Hygiene; mem. Am. Acad. Family Practice, Am. Bd. Family Practice, Am. Med. Women Assn. Pa. Acad. Family Practice, Lehigh Valley Women Med. Assn. Roman Catholic. Avocations: guitar, reading, bicycling, hiking. Office: 101 W 7th St Ste 2C Pennsburg PA 18073-1512

SHULA, DON FRANCIS, former professional football coach, team executive; b. Painesville, OH, Jan. 4, 1930; s. Dan and Mary (Miller) S.; children: David, Donna, Sharon, Anne, Michael; m. Mary Anne Shula. BS, John Carroll U., Cleve., 1951, H.H.D. (hon.), 1972; MA, Case Western Res. U., 1953; Sc.D. (hon.), Biscayne Coll., 1974, St. Thomas U., 1976, U. Miami, 1992, Fla. Atlantic U., 1999. Profl. football player Cleve. Browns, 1951-52, Balt. Colts, 1953-56, Washington Redskins, 1957; asst. coach U. Va., 1958, U. Ky., 1959, Detroit Lions, 1960-62; head coach Baltimore Colts, 1963-69, Miami (Fla.) Dolphins, 1970-96; vice chmn. Miami Dolphins, 1996—; owner, pres. Shula Enterprises. Author: The Winning Edge, 1972, (with Ken Blanchard) Everyone's A Coach, 1995. Fla. crusade chmn. Nat. Cancer Soc., 1975; co-chmn. Jerry Lewis March Against Dystrophy, 1975; nat. bd. dirs. Boy's Hope; mem. nat. sports com. Multiple Schlerosis Soc., Muscular Dystrophy Assn.; bd. dirs. Heart Assn. Greater Miami; established Don Shula Found., breast cancer rsch., 1991—; sponsor Don Shula Scholarship, 1978—. Coached 6 Superbowl teams, winning teams 1972, 73; recipient Coach of Yr. awards 1964, 66, 70, 71, 72, Coach of decade Profl. Football Hall of Fame, 1980, Pro Football's All-Time Winningest Coach, 1994, Brotherhood award Fla. region NCCJ, 1977, Light of Flames Leadership award Barry Coll., 1977, Concern award Cedars Med. Ctr., 1992, Solheim Lifetime Achievement award, 1992, Jim Thorpe award, 1993,Sportsman of Yr. Sports Illustrated, 1993, Horrigan award Pro Football Writers,1994, Horatio Alger award, 1995, Vince Lombardi Award of Excellence, 1999; named Balt. Colts Silver Anniversary Coach, 1977, elected to Pro Football Hall of Fame, 1997. Roman Catholic. Office: Shula Enterprises Inc 16 Indian Creek Is Miami Beach FL 33154-2904 *Success is never final; defeat is never fatal.*

SHULA, ROBERT JOSEPH, lawyer; b. South Bend, Ind., Dec. 10, 1936; s. Joseph Edward and Bertha Mona (Buckner) S.; m. Gaye Ann Martin, Oct. 8, 1978; children: Deirdre Regina, Robert Joseph II, Elizabeth Martin. BS in Mktg., Ind. U., 1958, JD, 1961. Bar: Ind. 1961. Ptnr. Bingham Summers Welsh & Spilman, Indpls., 1965-82, sr. ptnr., 1982-89; ptnr. Price & Shula, 1989-91, Lowe Gray Steele & Darko, Indpls., 1991—. Mem. faculty Nat. Inst. Trial Advocacy; guest lectr. Brit. Medicine and Law Soc., 1979, Ind. U. Sch. Law; medico-legal lectr. Ind. U. Schs. Medicine, Dentistry, and Nursing. Bd. dirs. Arts Ind., Indpls., 1995-99; pres. Oriental Arts Soc., Indpls., 1975-79, Meridian Women's Clinic, Inc., Indpls.; trustee Indpls. Mus. Art, 1975-78, life trustee, 1984—; bd. dirs. Ind. Repertory Theatre, Indpls., 1982-92, chmn. bd. dirs., pres., 1985-89; pres. Repertory Soc., 1993-96; v.p., bd. dirs. Flanner House of Indpls., Inc., 1977-88, chmn., 1988-99; pres. Internat. Ctr. of Indpls., Inc., 1993-96. Maj. JAGC, USAFR, 1961-65. Maj. JAGC, USAFR, 1961—65. Recipient Gov.'s award of Sagamore of the Wabash, 1998. Master Am. Inns of Ct.; fellow Internat. Soc. Barristers; mem. ABA, FBA, Ind. Bar Assn., Indpls. Bar Assn., Am. Bd. Trial Advs. (pres. 2000), Am. Law Inst., Am. Coll. Legal Medicine, Def. Trial Counsel Ind. (diplomate), Confrerie Chevaliers du Tastevin, Woodstock Country Club. Democrat. Episcopalian. Home: 7924 Beaumont Green Pl Indianapolis IN 46250-1663 Office: Bank One Ctr 111 Monument Cir Ste 4600 Indianapolis IN 46204-5402 E-mail: bob.shula@lgsd.com.

SHULDINER, ALAN RODNEY, physician, endocrinologist, educator; b. Irumagawa, Japan, Feb. 5, 1957; parents Am. citizens; s. Julius and Janet (Gursky) S.; m. Jill Francie Bresman, June 27, 1984; children: Seth David, Scott Ross. AB in Chemistry magna cum laude, Lafayette coll., 1979; MD with honors, Harvard U., 1984. Diplomate Am. Bd. Internal Medicine, Am. Bd. Endocrinology and Metabolism. Intern in medicine Columbia-Presbyn. Hosp., N.Y.C., 1984-85, resident in medicine, 1985-86; med. staff fellow Diabetes Br. Nat. Inst. Diabetes and Digestive and Kidney Diseases NIH, Bethesda, Md., 1986-88, sr. staff fellow, 1988-90; asst. prof. div. geriatric medicine and gerontology Sch. Medicine Johns Hopkins U., Balt., 1990-91, assoc. prof. div. geriatric medicine and gerontology. Guest rschr. Nat. Inst. on Aging NIH, Balt., 1991—96; prof., head divsn. diabetes, obesity and nutrition U. Md. Sch. Medicine, 1997—99; dir. Joslin Diabetes Ctr, 1997—, head divsn. endocrinology, diabetes & nutrition, 1999—; lectr. Endocrine Soc. meetings, 1996, 99, Japan Diabetes Soc. meeting, 1996, Am. Heart Assn. meeting, 1996, FASEB meeting, 1997, Am. Diabetes Assn. meeting, 1997, 99, VII Internat. Symposium on Insulin Action, 1998, with, 2000, NAASD, 2001, FASEB, 2002. Co-author: Current Therapy in Endocrinology and Metabolism, 3d edit., 1988, 4th edit., 1991, Handbook of Endocrine Research Techniques, 1993, Diabetes Mellitus: A Fundamental and Clinical text, 1996, 2d edit., 2000; contbr. articles to profl. jours. including Archives Biochem. Biophysics, Jour. Biol. Chemistry, New Eng. Jour. Medicine, Diabetes, Analytical Biochemistry, Endocrinology, Gene, Nucleic Acids Rsch., Procs. NAS, Biotechniques, Jour. Clin. Endocrinology Metabolism, Diabetes. Recipient Paul Beeson Physician Faculty Scholar award Am. Fedn. Aging Rsch., 1996. Mem. AAAS, AMA, Am. Diabetes Assn., Endocrine Soc. Office: Univ of Maryland 660 W Redwood St Rm 494 Baltimore MD 21201-1009 E-mail: ashuldin@medicine.umaryland.edu.

SHULER, ELLIE GIVAN, JR. retired military officer, military museum administrator; b. Raleigh, N.C., Dec. 6, 1936; s. Ellie Givan and Berta (Williams) S.; m. Annette Fontaine Maury, Mar. 22, 1961; children— Ellie Givan III, Franklin Maury, Gray Hays. BSCE, The Citadel, 1959; MS in Mgmt., Rensselaer Poly. Inst., 1967; grad., Squadron Officer Sch., Maxwell AFB, Ala., 1964; postgrad., Naval War Coll.; grad. command and staff course, Nat. War Coll., 1976; grad. cen. flight instr. course, Castle AFB, Calif. Engr. in tng., S.C. Commd. 2d lt. U.S. Air Force, 1959, advanced through grades to lt. gen., 1988, various positions and locations, 1959-68, F-4C pilot, asst. flight comdr. 558th Tactical Fighter Squadron Republic of Vietnam, 1968-69, indsl. engr., then asst. dep. chief Engring. Mgmt. Div., Hdqrs. 2d Air Force Barksdale AFB, La., 1969-71; asst. exec. officer to comdr. in chief U.S. Air Force in Europe, Lindsey Air Sta., West Germany, 1972-73, base civil engr., comdr. 86th Civil Engring. Squadron Ramstein Air Base, Fed. Republic Germany, 1973-75; dir. ops. 3902d Air Base Wing, comdr. 3902d Ops. Squadron Offutt AFB, Nebr., 1976; dir. programs Office Dep. Chief of Staff for Engring. and Services SAC, 1976-77, exec. to comdr. in chief, 1977-79; vice comdr., then comdr. 19th Bombardment Wing Robins AFB, Ga., 1979-80; comdr. 42d Bombardment Wing Loring AFB, Maine, 1980-81; comdr. 4th Air Div. F.E. Warren AFB, Wyo., 1981-84; comdr. 3rd Air Div. SAC, Andersen AFB, Guam, 1984-86; asst. dep. then dep. chief of staff, ops. SAC Hqrs., Offutt AFB, Nebr., 1986-88; comdr. 8th Air Force SAC, Barksdale AFB, 1988-91; retired, 1991; chmn. bd., CEO 8th Air Force Heritage Mus., 1992—98. Bd. trustees, vice chair bd. dirs. Longs Peak coun. Boy Scouts Am., 1983-84; trustee Falcon Found., USAF Acad., 8th Air Force Heritage Mus., 1992—. Decorated D.S.M. with oak leaf cluster, Legion of Merit with oak leaf cluster, D.F.C., Air medal with five oak leaf clusters, Air Force Commendation medal with oak leaf cluster. Mem. Soc. Am. Mil. Engrs. (chpt. pres. 1971), Am. Def. Preparedness Assn. (regional bd. dirs. 1981-84), Order of Dadaelians (hon. flight capt. 1981-85), Council on Am.'s Mil. Past, Mil. Order of World Wars, Kiwanis, Tau Beta Pi. Republican. Episcopalian. Avocations: numismatics, golf, hunting, fishing, military history. Office: 675 Willow Way W Alexander City AL 35010-6253

SHULER, GEORGE NIXON, JR. social worker, writer; b. Houston, Apr. 17, 1952; s. George Sr. and Anna Isabel (Huebner) S.; m. Lois Laverne Byram, June 16, 1979. BA, U. Tex., 1977; MSW, U. Houston, 1992. Lic. Master Social Worker, Advanced Clin. Practitioner, Tex. Mgr. Law Book Co. of Tex., San Antonio, 1973-74; mgr. store Elliot Garner Enterprises, 1974-77; child protective svcs. specialist Karnes County (Tex.) Child Welfare, Karnes City, 1978-80, Atascosa County Child Welfare, Jourdanton, Tex., 1980, Bexar County Child Welfare, San Antonio, 1980-84; supr. Child Protective Svcs. Brazoria County Child Welfare, Angleton, Tex., 1984-86; specialist Child Protective Svcs. Harris County Child Welfare, Houston, 1986-92; respite specialist Galveston County Children's Protective Svcs., Texas City, 1993-95; clin. social worker social work dept. Army Family Advocacy Program, Ft. Hood, Tex., 1995-99; project supr. New Parent Support Program, Ft. Polk, La., 1999-00; social worker Behavioral Health Ctr., Bayne-Jones Army Cmty. Hosp., 2000—. Adj. faculty Upper Iowa U., 2000—. Columnist Leon Valley Leader newspaper, San Antonio, 1981-87; contbr. articles to profl. pubs. Dir. state exec. com. Tex. State Employees Union, Austin, 1983-84; del. ctrl. labor coun. AFL-CIO, San Antonio, 1981-84, Tex. Dem. Conv., 1974, 76, 78, 82, 84, 86, 90, 92, 96, 98, 2000, 02; permanent chair Newton County Dem. Conv., 2000, 02; campaign aide Dem. Com. Bexar County, San Antonio, 1974; campaign mgr. Jon Roland for U.S. Congress, San Antonio, 1974; chmn. resolutions com. Brazoria County Dem. Conv., Angleton, 1986; mem. rules com. Galveston County Dem. Conv., 1994; mem. exec. bd. North Galveston County Dems., 1994-95; lay min. Ch. of Subgenius of Gulf Coast, 1986-95, hierarchy candidate, 1990, initiate, 1993; min. Universal Life Ch., 1994—; founder Texian Natashaphile Team, 2000. Recipient Service award Tex. State Employees Union, 1984. Mem. NASW, Masons (Master Mason Tex. City Lodge), Shriners (noble Galveston 1995—). Avocations: woodworking, reading. Home: RR 1 Box 212 Newton TX 75966-9728 Office: Bayne-Jones Army Cmty Hosp Behavioral Health Ctr 1505 3d St Fort Polk LA 71459-5110 E-mail: GeorgeShuler2@CEN.AMEDD.army.mil., Kingfish1928@hotmail.com.

SHULER, JAMES MANNIE, health physicist; b. Orangeburg, S.C., Oct. 23, 1951; s. Ellie Grier Shuler and Gerdene Rickenbaker Shuler. BS in Botany, Clemson U., 1974; MA in Mgmt. and Supervision, Ctrl. Mich. U., 1977; MS in Radiation Sci., Georgetown U., 1988; MPA in Public Adminstrn., U. So. Calif., 1997, DPA in Public Adminstrn., 1999. Regstered radiation protection technologist, environ. profl., environ. mgr.; cert. hazard control mgr., hazardous materials mgr., environ. trainer transp. of hazardous materials and waste occupl. health and safety. Health physics technician Allied-General Nuclear Svcs., Barnwell, S.C., 1975-79; supr. health physics Chem-Nuclear Sys., Inc., 1979, customer and compliance rep., 1979; radioactive materials enforcement specialist U.S. Dept. Transp., Washington, 1979-81, 83-88; radwaste/transp. specialist Applied Tech. of Barnwell, Inc., 1981-83; phys. scientist U.S. Dept. Energy, Germantown, Md., 1988-89, health physicist Aiken, S.C., 1989-93, from sr. health physicist to phys. scientist Washington, 1993-96, health physicist, 1996—. Assoc. staff instr. U.S. Dept. Transp./Transp. Safety Inst., Oklahoma City, 1981-89; vis. instr. Georgetown U., Washington, 1988-89; assoc. grad. faculty Ctrl. Mich. U., 2001—. Contbr. over 100 articles to profl. jours. and tech. publs. Mem. ASTM (sect. 6 leader radiation protection methods verification 1993), Nat. Environ. Tng. Assn., Assn. of MBA Execs., Am. Nuclear Soc., Health Physics Soc. (environ. radiation sect., govt. sect. 1993—). Home: 12835 Locbury Cir Apt I Germantown MD 20874-3858 Office: US Dept Energy EM-5 Gtn Washington DC 20585-0001 E-mail: James.Shuler@hq.doe.gov.

SHULER, JON EMMETT, securities industry professional; b. Aiken, S.C., Sept. 21, 1946; s. Cyril Ovierre and Elizabeth Carolina (Smith) S.; m. Virginia Rose Harris, Aug. 1, 1981; children: Jon Emmett Jr., Kline Martin. BA in Econs., Clemson U., 1968; MBA, U. S.C., 1970. CFP. Broker J.C. Bradford & Co., Spartanburg, S.C., 1972-81, br. mgr., 1981-88, Raymond James & Assocs., Spartanburg, 1988-94; owner, pres., reg. investment adv. Wealth Mgmt. Assocs., Inc., 1994—. Co-author: Getting to the Heart of the Matter, 1999. Bd. dirs. Habitat for Humanity, Spartanburg, 1990; mem. ARC State Pub. Support Com., Columbia, S.C., 1993; trustee Spartanburg Day Sch., 1997—; v.p. endowments Palmetto coun. Boy Scouts Am., 1999—. Mem. Rotary (pres. North Spartanburg chpt. 1990, Paul Harris fellow 1989), Soc. Mayflower Descendants. Republican. Presbyterian. Avocations: snow skiing, antique collecting, woodworking. E-mail: jeshuler@hotmail.com.

SHULER, KURT EGON, chemist, educator; b. Nuremberg, Germany, July 10, 1922; came to U.S., 1937, naturalized, 1944; s. Louis and Donie (Wald) Schulherr; m. Beatrice Gwyn London, Nov. 11, 1944. BS, Ga. Inst. Tech., 1942; PhD, Cath. U. Am., 1949. Fellow Johns Hopkins U., 1949-51; sr. staff mem., asst. group supr., chem. physics group Applied Physics Lab., Johns Hopkins, 1951-55; supervisory phys. chemist Nat. Bur. Standards, 1955-58, cons. to dir., 1958-61, asst. dir., sr. research fellow, 1963-68; rsch. staff, sci. adviser to v.p. rsch. Gen. Motors Corp., 1958; spl. asst. to dir. rsch. Inst. Def. Analyses, 1961-63; vis. prof. chemistry U. Calif., San Diego, 1966-67, prof. chemistry, 1968-91, prof. emeritus, 1991—, chmn. dept., 1968-70, 84-87. Cons. in field; mem. Solvay Conf., 1962, 78; mem. adv. panel, chemistry div. NSF, 1973-75. Author, editor tech. books; assoc. editor: Jour. Math. Physics, 1963-66; bd. editors: Jour. Statis. Physics, 1968-80; mem. adv. bd.: Chem. Engring. News, 1967-70; contbr. articles to profl. jours. Served with U.S. Army, 1944-46. Recipient Distinguished Service award Nat. Bur. Standards, 1959, Gold medal award Dept. Commerce, 1968; Solvay Found. fellow, 1975 Fellow Am. Inst. Chemists, AAAS, Am. Phys. Soc., Washington Acad. Sci.; mem. Am. Chem. Soc., Washington Philos. Soc. Clubs: Rancho Santa Fe Golf. Home: PO Box 1504 Rancho Santa Fe CA 92067-1504 Office: Univ Calif San Diego Dept Chemistry La Jolla CA 92093

SHULER, MICHAEL LOUIS, biochemical engineering educator, consultant; b. Joliet, Ill., Jan. 2, 1947; s. Louis Dean and Mary Clara (Boylan) S.; m. Karen Joyce Beck, June 24, 1972; children: Andrew, Kristin, Eric, Katherine. BSChemE, U. Notre Dame, 1969; PhDChemE, U. Minn., 1973. Asst. prof. biochem. engring. Cornell U., Ithaca, N.Y., 1974-79, assoc. prof., 1979-83, prof., 1984-91, Samuel B. Eckert prof. chem. engring., 1992—, dir. bioengring. program, 1994—, dir. sch. chem. and biomolecular engring., 1998—. Vis. scholar U. Wash., Seattle, 1980-81; vis. scientist U. Wis., Madison, 1988-89; guest prof. ETH, Zurich, Switzerland, 1995; bd. dirs. Phyton Inc., Ithaca. Editor 6 books; contbr. articles to profl. jours., chpts. to books. Bd. dirs., treas., sec., v.p. Advs. for the Handicapped, Ithaca, 1978-88; sec., bd. dirs. Tompkins County Human Rights Commn., Ithaca, 1985-87; coach Spl. Olympics, 1994—; adv. bd. Carnegie-Mellon Chem. Engring., Princeton U. Chem. Engring., Cambridge U. Press. Recipient Outstanding Paper award Am. Oil Chemist Soc., 1984, Coll. of Engring. Honor award U. Notre Dame, 1989, Amgen award Biochem. Engring., 1997. Fellow Am. Inst. Med. and Biol. Engrs. (founder, v.p. edn. com.); mem. NAE (exec. com. bioengring. sect.), AIChE (editor Biotech. Progress 1985-88, cons. editor jour. 1986—, mem. publ. com. 1988—, awards com. 1993-98, bd. dirs. 2001—, chmn. Food Pharm. and Bioengring. divsn. 1994, Food, Pharm., Engring. award 1989, Prof. Progress award 1991), Am. Acad. Arts and Scis., Am. Chem. Soc. (M.J. Johnson award 1986), Am. Soc. Microbiology, Am. Soc. Pharmacognosy, Biomed. Engring. Soc. Roman Catholic. Avocation: fishing. Office: Cornell U Sch Engring 270 Olin Hall Ithaca NY 14853-5201 E-mail: mls@cheme.cornell.edu.

SHULER, SALLY ANN SMITH, retired media consultant; b. Mt. Olive, N.C., June 11, 1934; d. Leon Joseph and Ludia Irene (Montague) Simmons; m. Henry Ralph Smith Jr., Mar. 1, 1957 (div. Jan. 1976); children: Molly Montague, Barbara Ellen, Sara Ann, Mary Kathryn; m. Harold Robert Shuler, Aug. 2, 1987 (div. Mar. 1997). BA in Math., Duke U., 1956; student, U. Liège, Belgium, 1956-57; postgrad., Claremont Grad Sch., 1970-72. Mgr. fed. systems GE Info. Svcs. Co., Washington, 1976-78, mgr. mktg. support Rockville, Md., 1978-81; dir. bus. devel. info. tech. group Electronic Data Sys., Bethesda, 1981-82, v.p. mktg. optimum systems div. Rockville, 1982-83, v.p. planning and comm. Dallas, 1983-84; exec. dir. comml. devel. U.S. West Inc., Englewood, Colo., 1984-90; v.p. mktg. devel. Cin. Bell Info. Sys. Inc., 1990-92; mgmt. cons. in mergers and acquisitions Denver, 1992-93, 1995—2002; v.p. major accounts U.S. Computer Svcs., 1993-95; ret., 2002. Bd. dirs. Rotary-Denver Tech. Ctr., 2000—01, Seeking Common Ground, 2001—02. Recipient GE Centennial award, Rockville, 1978. Mem. Women in Telecommunications, Rotary (Found. fellow, prest. Denver Tech. Ctr. 1999-2000, amb. scholar 1956-57), Phi Beta Kappa, Tau Psi Omega, Pi Mu Epsilon. Democrat. Presbyterian. Office: 1626 S Syracuse St Denver CO 80231-2691 Home Fax: 303-745-0183.

SHULER, SCOTT CORBIN, art educator; b. Detroit, Nov. 23, 1953; s. John Hays and Marilyn (Corbin) S.; m. Monica Ascui, Aug. 13, 1977; children: Stephanie Ascui, Nathan Corbin. BMus in Instrumental Music, U. Mich., 1975; MS in Edn., U. Ill., 1976; PhD in Music Edn., Eastman Sch. Music, 1987. Cert. music tchr. presch.-12. Music tchr. The Tatnall Sch., Wilmington, Del., 1976-78, Kohler (Wis.) Pub. Schs., 1978-83; vis. instr. Eastman Sch. Music, Rochester, N.Y., 1983-85; assoc. prof., music edn. coord. Calif. State U., Long Beach, 1985-88; arts cons. Conn. Dept. Edn., Hartford, 1988—; prof. music edn. New Eng. Conservatory, Boston, 1992-93. Adj. prof. U. Del., Newark, 1977-78, Hartt Sch. Music, West Hartford, Conn., 1990—; vis. prof. Ctrl. Conn. State U., New Britain, 1989-90; co-chair Nat. Assessment Ednl. Progress Planning Com., Washington, 1993-96, State Collaborative on Assessment, Washington, 1993-98; mem. task force Nat. Stds. in the Arts, Washington, 1992-94. Author: (monograph) Music Educators Nat. Conf. Words of Note series, 1990; editor, author: (spl. focus issue) Music Educators Jour., 1992 (Edn. Press Assn. Am. award 1992); contbr. articles to profl. jours. V.p., pres. Edn. Adminstrs. Union, Hartford, 1989-94; assoc. music dir. Cmty. United Meth. Ch., Huntington Beach, Calif., 1985-88; dir. of music Grace United Ch. of Christ, Kohler, Wis., 1981-82; co-chair bd. trustees Congregational Ch. in South Glastonbury, Conn., 1996-97. Recipient Disting. Svc. award Conn. Art Edn. Assn., 1993, 2000, Young Writers award Design for Arts in Edn., 1988, Disting. Svc. award Conn. Drama Assn., 2001, Outstanding Music Educator award Nat. Fedn. Interscholastic Music Assn., 2001. Mem. ASCD, Nat. Art Edn. Assn., Conn. Music Educators Assn. (exec. bd. dirs. 1988—, Outstanding Adminstr. award 1992), Conn. State Employees Assn. (v.p., pres., Pres.'s award for commitment and svc. 1993), Nat. Coun. State Suprs. Music (pres.-elect 1996-98, pres. 1998-2000), Conn. Alliance for Arts Edn. (exec. bd. dirs. 1990—), Phi Delta Kappa. Office: Conn Dept Edn 165 Capitol Ave Rm 205 Hartford CT 06106-1659 E-mail: scott.shuler@po.state.ct.us.

SHULER DONNER, LAUREN, film producer; b. Cleveland, OH; BS in Film and Broadcasting, Boston U. TV films include: Amateur Night at the Dixie Bar and Grill, 1979; films include: Thank God It's Friday, 1978 (assoc. prodr.), Mr. Mom, 1983, Ladyhawke, 1985, St. Elmo's Fire, 1985, Pretty in Pink, 1986, Three Fugitives, 1989, Radio Flyer, 1992, Dave, 1993, Free Willy, 1993, The Favor, 1994; (producer) Free Willy 2: The Adventure Home, 1995, Assassins, 1995, You've Got Mail, 1998, Any Given Sunday, 1999, XMen, 2000; exec. prodr.Free Willy 3, 1997, Volcano, 1997. Office: The Donners' Co Ste 420 9465 Wilshire Blvd Beverly Hills CA 90212

SHULEVITZ, URI, author, illustrator; b. Warsaw, Poland, Feb. 27, 1935; came to U.S., 1959, naturalized, 1965; Student, Tel-Aviv Art Inst., 1953-55; Tchrs. Cert., Tchrs. Coll. Israel, 1956; student, Bklyn. Museum Art Sch., 1959-61. Instr. illustrating and writing children's books The New Sch., 1970-86; dir. illustrating and writing children's books Hartwick Coll., 1974-92. Author, illustrator: The Moon In My Room, 1963, One Monday Morning, 1967, Rain Rain Rivers, 1969, Oh What a Noise, 1971, The Magician, 1973, Dawn, 1974, The Treasure, 1978, (Caldecott honor Book 1979), The Strange and Exciting Adventures of Jeremiah Hush, 1986, Toddlecreek Post Office, 1990, The Secret Room, 1993, Snow, 1998 (Caldecott Honor book 1999), What is a Wise Bird like you Doing in a silly tale like this?, 2000; author: Writing with Pictures: How to Write and Illustrate Children's Books, 1985; illustrator: The Fool of the World and the Flying Ship, 1968 (Caldecott medal 1969), The Twelve Dancing Princesses, 1966, Soldier and Tsar in the Forest, 1972, The Fools of Chelm, 1973, The Touchstone, 1976, Hanukah Money, 1978, The Lost Kingdom of Karnica, 1979, The Golem, 1982, Lilith's Cave: Jewish Tales of the Supernatural, 1988, The Diamond Tree, 1991, The Golden Goose, 1995, Hosni The Dreamer, 1997. Served with Israeli Army, 1956-59. Guggenheim fellowship, 1999. Mem Authors Guild. Address: PO Box 123 Treadwell NY 13846-0123 Office: care Farrar Straus & Giroux Inc 19 Union Sq W New York NY 10003-3304

SHULGASSER-PARKER, BARBARA, writer; b. Manhasset, N.Y., Apr. 10, 1954; d. Lew and Luba (Golante) S.; m. Norman Parker, Sept. 1999. Student, Sarah Lawrence Coll., 1973-74; BA magna cum laude, CUNY, 1977; MS, Columbia U., 1978. Feature writer Waterbury (Conn.) Rep., 1978-81; reporter, feature writer Chgo. Sun Times, 1981-84; film critic San Francisco Examiner, 1984-98; freelance book critic N.Y. Times Book Rev., N.Y.C., 1983—; film critic Chgo. Tribune, 1999—. Author: Funny Accent, 2001; co-author: (screenplay, with Robert Altman) Ready to Wear, 1994; freelance video columnist N.Y. Times Sunday Arts & Leisure, 1989, features for Vanity Fair, Glamour and Mirabella mags.

SHULL, CLAIRE, documentary film producer, casting director; b. N.Y.C., Oct. 26, 1925; d. Barnet Joseph and Fannie (Florea) Klar; m. Leo Shull, Aug. 8, 1948; children: Lee Shull Pearlstein, David. Student, Am. Acad. Dramatic Arts, N.Y.C., 1943-44, NYU, 1973-74. Editor, assoc. pub. Show Bus. Publs., N.Y.C., 1957-85; owner, founder Claire/Casting, N.Y.C. and Miami, Fla., 1972—, Claire/Casting Film Prodns., N.Y.C. and Miami, 1978—; cons. dir., prodr., dir. film and TV, The Bass Mus., Miami Beach, Fla., 1992—. Miami corr. film, TV, theatre Show Bus. Weekly, 1999—. Actress in The Front Page, USO European tour, 1945-46, (on Broadway) Tenting Tonight, 1947; prodr., dir. HBO TV series How To Break into Show Business, 1980-81, Cable-TV series, Join Us at the Bass, 1993-97. Recipient gold award and distinctive merit TV award Advt. Club. Hartford, Conn., 1984, Clio award, 1989. Mem. Ind. Casting Dirs. Assn. N.Y., Actors Equity Assn., Drama Desk.

SHULL, HARRISON, chemist, educator; b. Princeton, N.J., Aug. 17, 1923; s. George Harrison and Mary (Nicholl) S.; m. Jeanne Louise Johnson, 1948 (div. 1962); children: James Robert (dec.), Kathy, George Harrison, Holly; m. Wil Joyce Bentley Long, 1962; children: Warren Michael Long, Jeffery Mark Long, Stanley Martin, Sarah Ellen. AB, Princeton U., 1943; PhD, U. Calif. at Berkeley, 1948. Assoc. chemist U.S. Naval Research Lab., 1943-45; asst. prof. Iowa State U., 1949-54; mem. faculty Ind. U., 1955-79, research prof., 1961-79, dean Grad. Sch., 1965-72, vice chancellor for research and devel., 1972-76, dir. Research Computing Center, 1959-63, acting chmn. chemistry dept., 1965-66, acting dean arts and scis., 1969-70, acting dean faculties, 1974; mem. faculty, provost, v.p. acad. affairs Rensselaer Poly. Inst., 1979-82; chancellor U. Colo., Boulder, 1982-85, prof. dept. chemistry, 1982-88; provost Naval Postgrad. Sch., 1988-95; asst. dir. rsch., quantum chemistry group Uppsala (Sweden) U., 1958-59; vis. prof. Washington U., St. Louis, 1960, U. Colo., 1963; founder, supr. Quantum Chemistry Program Exchange, 1962-79; chmn. subcom. molecular structure and spectroscopy NRC, 1958-63; chmn. Fulbright selection com. chemistry, 1963-67; mem. adv. com. Office Sci. Personnel, 1957-60; chmn. First Gordon Research Conf. Theoretical Chemistry, 1962; mem. com. survey chemistry Nat. Acad. Sci., 1964-65; mem. adv. panel chemistry NSF, 1964-67; mem. adv. panel Office Computer Activities, 1967-70, cons. chem. information program, 1965-71, mem. adv. com. for research, 1974-76; mem. vis. com. chemistry Brookhaven Nat. Lab., 1967-70; mem. adv. com. Chem. Abstracts Service, 1971-74. Dir. Storage Tech. Corp., 1983-99; chief of Naval Ops. Exec. Panel, 1984-88. Assoc. editor: Jour. Chem. Physics, 1952-54; editorial adv. bd.: Spectrochimica Acta, 1957-63, Internat. Jour. Quantum Chemistry, 1967—2001, Proc. NAS, 1976-81; contbr. articles to profl. jours. Trustee Argonne U. Assn., 1970-75, Asso. Univs., Inc., 1973-76, U. Rsch. Assn., 1984-89, Inst. Defense Analysis, 1984-96. Served as ensign USNR, 1945. NRC postdoctoral fellow phys. scis. U. Chgo., 1948-49; Guggenheim fellow U. Uppsala, 1954-55; NSF sr. postdoctoral fellow, 1968-69; Sloan research fellow, 1956-58 Fellow AAAS, Am. Acad. Arts and Scis. (v.p. 1976-83, chmn. Midwest Ctr. 1976-79), Am. Phys. Soc.; mem. Nat. Acad. Scis. (com. on sci. and pub. policy 1969-72, coun., exec. com. 1971-74, chmn. U.S.-USSR sci. policy subgroup for fundamental rsch. 1973-81, naval studies bd. 1974-79, 96-2001, chmn. Commn. on Human Resources, 1977-81, nominating com. 1978), Am. Chem. Soc., Royal Swedish Acad. Scis. (fgn. mem.), Royal Acad. Arts and Scis. Uppsala (corr. mem.), Cosmos Club (Washington), Old Capital Club (Monterey), Phi Beta Kappa, Sigma Xi, Phi Lambda Upsilon. Home: 2 Cramden Dr Monterey CA 93940-4144

SHULL, MICHAEL SLADE, lecturer, writer, researcher; b. Balt., Sept. 20, 1949; s. Edward Slade and Beatrice Mary (Parker) S. BA in History, U. Md., 1972; postgrad. in internat. studies, Am. U., Washington; MA in Radio, TV and Film, U. Md., 1983, PhD in Mass Comm., 1994. Legal rschr., investigator Mitchell Assocs., 1973-77; cataloger Libr. Congress, Washington, 1980-82; cons. pub. rels. Skuce & Assocs., 1983-87; ind. scholar and writer, Silver Spring, Md., 1987—; politics and media cons. Gaithersburg, 1990—. Lectr. Washington Ctr., 1995-2001; film columnist, cons. The 1940s Preservation Trust, Balt., 1997-99; cons., talking head film documentary Cartoons Go to War, 1995; adj. faculty Frederick Coll., Md., 1998—, Towson U., Md., 2000-01. Author: Doing Their Bit: Wartime American Animated Short Films, 1939-1945, 1987, Hollywood War Films, 1937-1945, 1996, Radicalism in American Silent Films, 1909-1929, 2000. Mem. Am. Hist. Assn., Historians Am. Communism, Popular Culture Assn., Soc. Cinema Studies, Internat. Assn. Media Historians, U.S. Naval Inst. Avocations: film, bridge, rugby, jazz. Home: 90 Waverley Dr LL210 Frederick MD 21702-3809 E-mail: shullms@aol.com.

SHULL, MIKKI, media consultant; b. Cleve. d. Lois Biles; life ptnr. Jerome China. BS, Carnegie-Mellon U., 1983. Bus. transformation cons. PriceWaterhouseCoopers, N.Y.C., 1986-97; media and entertainment cons. IBM Global Svcs., 1997—. Mem. Advt. Women N.Y. Republican. Office: IBM 590 Madison Ave New York NY 10022 E-mail: shull@us.ibm.com.

SHULLICH, ROBERT HARLAN, systems analyst; b. Bklyn., Feb. 20, 1954; s. William and Vivian (Polowitz) S.; m. Phyllis Elaine Strickland, June 4, 1979 (dec. Oct. 1991). AS in Liberal Arts, Staten Island C.C., 1976; BS in Computer Sci., Coll. Staten Island, 1985, MS in Computer Sci., 1988; MBA in Mgmt., Baruch Coll., 1993; MS in Telecom. Network, Polytech U., 1998. Cert. computer programmer, systems profl., data processor; Microsoft cert. sys. engr. Sr. systems analyst in ednl. adminstrv. systems Coll. of Staten Island, N.Y., 1981—. Mem. IEEE, Math. Assn. Am., Am. Mgmt. Assn., Assn. Computing Machinery, Data Processing Mgmt. Assn., Nat. Systems Programmer Assn., Tau Alpha Pi, Alpha Iota Delta. Roman Catholic. Avocations: bowling, concerts. Home: PO Box 021390 Brooklyn NY 11202-1390 Office: Coll Staten Island 2800 Victory Blvd Staten Island NY 10314-6609 E-mail: rshullic@bigfoot.com.

SHULMAN, ARNOLD, judge, lawyer; b. Phila., Apr. 12, 1914; s. Edward Nathaniel and Anna (Leshner) S.; m. Mary Frances Johnson, Nov. 26, 1943; children: Diane Shulman Thompson, Warren Scott, Amy Lynn Shulman Haney. Student, Emory U., 1931; JD, U. Ga., 1936. Bar: Ga. 1937. Mem. firm Shulman, Shulman, Bauer & Deitch (and predecessors), Atlanta, to 1977; judge Ga. Ct. Appeals, 1977-84, presiding judge, 1981-83, chief judge, 1983-84; of counsel Troutman, Sanders, Lockerman & Ashmore, Atlanta, 1984-87; appointed sr. appellate ct. judge, 1987—; chief judge settlement conf. div. Ct. Appeals Ga., 1989—; prof. Atlanta Law Sch., 1964-84; adj. prof. Ga. State U. Coll. Law, Atlanta. Author: (with Wiley H. Davis) Georgia Practice and Procedure, 1948, 3d edit., 1968, 4th edit., (with Warren S. Shulman), 1975; contbr. articles to legal jours. Chmn. DeKalb County (Ga.) Sch. Salary Commn., 1960-62, DeKalb County Sch. Study Commn., 1962-64; mem. Fulton County-Atlanta Ct. Study Commn., 1961-62. Served to capt. U.S. Army, 1941-46. Mem. ABA, Atlanta Bar Assn., Ga. State Bar, Lawyers Club (Atlanta). Home: 1527 September Chase Decatur GA 30033-1731 Office: 908 DeKalb County Courthouse Decatur GA 30030

SHULMAN, ARTHUR, communications executive; b. N.Y.C., Mar. 4, 1927; s. Jacob and Sarah (Hochman) S.; m. Jan. 30, 1958; children: James, Karen. BA, Syracuse U., 1950. Asst. to pub. TV Guide Mag., Radnor, Pa., 1958-72; pub. Seventeen Mag., N.Y.C., 1972-73; dir. regional ops. TV Guide, 1974-82; dir. comm. B'nai B'rith Internat., Washington, 1983-93. Author: How Sweet It Was, 1966, The Television Years, 1972. Dir. Penn Wynne (Pa.) Civic Assn., 1965-66. S/Sgt. US Army, 1945-46, Japan. Mem. Radio & TV Execs. Soc., Nat. Press Club, Overseas Press Club, Nat. Acad. TV Arts & Scis. Jewish. Address: 4017 Jardin Ln Sarasota FL 34238-4504 E-mail: ashulman@att.com.

SHULMAN, BARBARA, professional counselor; b. N.Y.C., Sept. 5, 1938; d. Jules and Mary (Lipcon) Peretz; m. Harold Shulman, Dec. 25, 1960; children: Amy Jill Feldman, Jeffrey Stuart. BS in Social Scis., Simmons Coll., 1959; MA in Edn., Columbia U., 1963; MA in Coll. Counseling and Student Devel., Hunter Coll., 1986. Nat. cert. counselor, nat. cert. career counselor; cert. profl. counselor, N.Y. Tchr. N.Y.C. Bd. Edn., 1959-61, Yonkers (N.Y.) Pub. Schs., 1961-65, Solomon Schechter Sch. of Westchester, White Plains, N.Y., 1981-85; head counselor Westchester Summer Day, Mamaroneck, 1975-80; vocat. counselor N.Y. Assn. for New Ams., N.Y.C., 1986-87; acad. counselor Adelphi U., Garden City, N.Y., 1987-96; career counselor WEBS Career and Ednl. Counseling Svc., Elmsford, 1989—; counselor Berkeley Coll., White Plains, 1996; career counselor Manhattanville Coll., Purchase, NY, 1996—99, assoc. dir. career svcs., 1999—. Pres. Tom Paine New Rochelle (N.Y.) B'nai B'rith, 1992-96, treas., 1990-92; pres., edn., v.p. New Rochelle Hadassah, 1975-78. Mem. ACA, Met. N.Y. Coll. Placement Officers Assn., N.Y. State Counseling Assn., Nat. Career Devel. Assn., Westchester Career Counselors Network. Democrat. Avocations: tennis, theatre, ballet, concerts, museums. Home: 9 Woodhollow Ln New Rochelle NY 10804-3419 Office: Manhattanville Coll Spellman Hall Purchase NY 10577 E-mail: shulman@bestweb.net., shulmanb@mville.edu.

SHULMAN, CORINNE EDWARDS LEWIS, mediator; b. Lynbrook, N.Y., Apr. 21, 1926; d. Wilbur Nelson and Ruth Pearl (McKenzie) Edwards; m. Paul Kenneth Lewis, Aug. 22, 1950 (div. June 1964); children: Paul K., Kim, Kevin, Kyle; m. William J. Lederer, 1965 (div. 1975); m. Nathan Shulman. BA, Hood Coll., 1948; MEd, U. Vt., 1972. Actuarial trainee Equitable Life Assurance, N.Y.C., 1948-51; pub. Pearl Harbor Pennysaver, Honolulu, 1954-57, Honolulu Beacon, 1957-65; dir. counseling Champlain Coll., Burlington, Vt., 1970-77; exec. dir. Hawaii Health Net, Honolulu, 1977-79; counselor Green Pastures Health Ctr., Scituate, Mass., 1979-83; mediator Neighborhood Justice Ctr., Honolulu, 1987—. Fundraiser Youth-at-Risk, Boston, 1979-85, Hawaii Youth-at-Risk, Honolulu, 1987-92; mem. Gov.'s Commn. Status Women, Burlington, 1973-75. Mem. AAUW. Home: 44-315 Kaneoke Bay Dr Kaneohe HI 96744

SHULMAN, DAVID GEORGE, economist; b. Forest Hills, N.Y., Feb. 22, 1943; s. Jack and Ann Shulman; m. Patricia E. Post, June 27, 1982; children: Rachel, Nathan, Rebecca. BBA, CUNY, 1964; MBA, UCLA, 1966, PhD, 1975. Assoc. prof. U. Calif., Riverside, 1975-83; dir. rsch. TCW Realty Advisors, L.A., 1983-85; mng. dir. real estate rsch., mgr. bond market rsch. Salomon Bros., Inc., N.Y.C., 1986-92, chief equity strategist, 1992—97; mem. Ulysses Mgmt. LLC, 1998—99; mng. dir. Lehman Bros., N.Y.C., 2000—. With U.S. Army, 1968-70.

SHULMAN, FRANK JOSEPH, librarian, bibliographer; b. Boston, Sept. 20, 1943; m. Anna See-ping Leon, Jan. 6, 1985. B.A. in History magna cum laude, Harvard U., 1964; postgrad. Hebrew U. Jerusalem, 1964-65, U. Minn., summer 1966, Inter-Univ. Ctr. Japanese Lang. Studies, Tokyo, 1967-68; M.A. in E. Asian Studies, U. Mich., 1968, M.L.S., 1969, doctoral candidate, 1974. Bibliographer/librarian Ctr. Japanese Studies, U. Mich., Ann Arbor, 1970-75; curator, head E. Asia Collection and Gordon W. Prange Collection, U. Md. Libraries, College Park, 1976-92, spl. asst. to assoc. dir. pub. svcs., 1992—; bibliographer, editor and cons. reference publs. in Asian Studies, 1976—; founder, curator Asian Studies Newsletter Archives, 1970—; library cons. Groupe d'Etudes et de Documentation sur le Japon Contemporain, Ecole Pratique des Hautes Etudes, Sciences Economiques et Sociales, Paris, 1974, Woodrow Wilson Internat. Ctr. for Scholars, Smithsonian Instn.; adv. editor G. K. Hall & Co.; mem. editorial adv. bd. New Asia Review; mem. editorial bd. Mid-Atlantic Bulletin of Korean Studies; mem. Washington and Southeast Regional Sem. on Japan. Recipient several found. grants and awards for bibliog. work; Carnegie Library Sci. fellow, 1969; Nat. Def. Fgn. Lang. fellow, 1965-69. Mem. Asiatic Soc. Japan, Assn. Asian Studies (asst. editor Bibliography of Asian Studies 1970-72, contbr. ann. vols. 1988-90, bd. dirs 1983-86, mem. council of confs. 1983-86, mem. com. E. Asian libraries, v.p. Mid-Atlantic region 1980-81), Assn. Bibliography History, European Assn. Japanese Studies, Internat. Assn. Orientalist Librarians, Japan-Am. Soc. of Washington, Middle East Librarians Assn., Phi Kappa Phi, Beta Phi Mu. Author: Japan and Korea: An Annotated Bibliography of Doctoral Dissertations in Western Languages, 1877-1969, 1970; (with Leonard H. D. Gordon) Doctoral Dissertations on China: A Bibliography of Studies in Western Languages, 1945-1970, 1972; American and British Doctoral Dissertations on Israel and Palestine in Modern Times, 1973; (with Robert E. Ward) The Allied Occupation of Japan, 1945-1952: An Annotated Bibliography of Western-Language Materials, 1974; (with others) East Asian Resources in American Libraries, 1977; Doctoral Dissertations on China, 1971-1975, 1978; (with others) Mid-Atlantic Directory to Resources for Asian Studies, 1980; Doctoral Dissertations on Japan and on Korea, 1969-79: An Annotated Bibliography of Studies in Western Languages, 1982; Burma: An Annotated Bibliographical Guide to International Doctoral Dissertation Research, 1898-1985, 1986; Japan (World Bibliographical Series, vol. 103), 1989; Directory of Individuals Interested in the Jews and the Jewish Communities of East, Southeast and South Asia, 1993; others; editor Doctoral Dissertations on Asia: An Annotated Bibliog. Jour. of Current Internat. Research, 1975— ; contbr. numerous articles and revs. to scholarly jours.; presenter numerous papers at internat., nat. and regional scholarly confs. Home: 9225 Limestone Pl College Park MD 20740-3943

SHULMAN, LAWRENCE EDWARD, biomedical research administrator, rheumatologist; b. Boston, July 25, 1919; s. David Herman and Belle (Tishler) S.; m. Pauline K. Flint, July 19, 1946; 1 son, Lawrence E.; m. Reni Trudinger, Mar. 20, 1959; children: Kathryn Verena, Barbara Corina. AB, Harvard U., 1941, postgrad., 1941-42; PhD, Yale U., 1945, MD, 1949. Diplomate Nat. Bd. Med. Examiners. Intern Johns Hopkins Hosp., 1949-50, resident and fellow in internal medicine, 1950-53; dir. connective tissue div. Johns Hopkins U., 1955-75, assoc. prof. medicine, 1964—; assoc. dir. div. arthritis, musculoskeletal and skin diseases NIH, Bethesda, Md., 1976-86, dir., 1982-86, dir. Nat. Inst. Arthritis, Musculoskeletal and Skin Diseases, 1986-94, dir. emeritus, 1994—, emissary for clin. rsch., 1995—. Chmn. med. adminstrn. com. Arthritis Found., Atlanta, 1974-75, exec. com., 1972-77; dir. Lupus Found. Am.; med. adv. bd. United. Scleroderma Found., Watsonville, Calif., 1977-88; chmn. sci. group rheumatic diseases WHO, 1989; W.R. Graham meml. lectr., 1973; Cochrane disting. lectr., 1993. Discoverer: Eosinophilic Fasciitis, 1974, new med. sign friction rubs in scleroderma, 1961. Recipient Sr. Investigator award Arthritis Found., 1957-62, Disting. Svc. award, 1979, Heberden medal for rsch., London, 1975, Superior Svc. award USPHS, 1985, master Am. Rheumatism Assn., 1986, Spl. Recognition award Nat. Osteoprosis Found., 1991, Spl. award Am. Acad. Orthop. Surgeons, 1992, Presdl. citation for leadership Am. Acad. Dermatology, 1993, Leadership award Lupus Found. Am., 1994, Career Achievement award Am. Coll. Rheumatology, 1994, Outstanding Support Rsch. award Am. Soc. Bone Mineral Rsch., 1994, Gold medal Am. Coll. Rheumatology, 1995, 1995 Award of Merit, NASA. Fellow ACP, AAAS; mem. Am. Rheumatism Assn. (pres. 1974-75), Pan-Am. League Against Rheumatism (pres. 1982-86, Morine Gold medal award 2002), Soc. Investigative Dermatology. Home: 6302 Swords Way Bethesda MD 20817-3350 Office: NIH 9000 Rockville Pike Bethesda MD 20892-0003

SHULMAN, LEON J. retired obstetrician, gynecologist; b. L.A., Sept. 22, 1913; BA, UCLA; MD, U. So. Calif., 1940. Diplomate Am. Bd. Ob-Gyn. Intern Los Angeles County Hosp., 1939-41; resident M. Hague Maternity Hosp., Jersey City, 1942-45; pvt. practice, 1945-80; obstetrician Santa Monica (Calif.) Hosp., 1980—; clin. prof. emeritus U. So. Calif., 1980—. Hon. staff mem. St. Johns Hosp. Fellow AMA, ACS, Pacific Coast Ob-Gyn Soc.; mem. Am. Coll. Ob-Gyn.

SHULMAN, MICHAEL GEOFFREY, physician; b. Paterson, N.J., May 8, 1940; s. Raymond and Clara Cecile (Schneider) S.; m. Peggy Marlene Alterman, Dec. 27, 1961 (div. 1971); 2 children. Student, U. N.C.; MD, Columbia U., 1965. Diplomate Am. Bd. Internal Medicine subspecialty nephrology. Med. dir. Northside Dialysis Ctr., Atlanta, 1980-91; assoc. dir. Sandoz Pharm. Corp., East Hanover, N.J., 1991-94, Syntex Devel. Rsch., Palo Alto, Calif., 1994; med. dir., cons. SangStat Med. Corp., Menlo Park, 1995-96; med. safety cons. Genentech, Inc., South San Francisco, 1996; v.p. clin. devel. Anergen, Inc., Redwood City, Calif., 1997-99; acting med. dir., cons. Corixa Corp., 1999. Biopharm. cons., San Francisco; med. monitor cons. Chiron Corp. HBV program, 2001. Contbr. chpt. to book. Chmn. med. adv. bd. Greater Atlanta Lupus Found. Maj. Med. Corps U.S. Army, 1969—72. Mem.: Am. Soc. Hypertension, Am. Coll. Rheumatology, Am. Soc. Nephrology, Am. Soc. Transplantation, Phi Beta Kappa, Alpha Omega Alpha. Jewish. Avocations: golf, cross country skiing, cycling, fly fishing, writing poetry. Office: 1360 Jones St Apt 401 San Francisco CA 94109-0302

SHULMAN, MILDRED, artist, inventor; b. Perth Amboy, N.J., Aug. 13, 1927; d. Abraham and Estelle (Golub) S.; m. Ben Spina, Feb. 20, 1947 (div. Aug. 1954). Student, Sch. Indsl. Arts, N.Y.C., 1942-45, McDowell Sch. Art, 1946-47, NYU, 1961-62, Art Student's League, 1991-95. Controller Continental Mdse. Co., Inc., N.Y.C., 1959-65, Famous Fashion Shops, N.Y.C., 1966-69; owner, pres. Luminere Creations, Inc., 1969-91; self-employed artist, 1991—. Author: Barter*The Silent Giant, 1985; co-inventor and patentee elec./sculptural lighting design; inventor, patentee sculpturing method. Mem.: Am. Soc. Portrait Artists, Nat. Mus. Women in the Arts, Art Students League. Avocations: hiking, swimming. Fax: (212) 242-2846.

SHULMAN, ROBERT GERSON, biophysics educator; b. N.Y.C., Mar. 3, 1924; s. Joshua S. and Freda (Lipshay) S.; m. Saralee Deutsch, Aug., 1952 (dec. Oct. 1983); children: Joel, Mark, James; m. Stephanie S. Spangler, May 11, 1986. AB, Columbia U., 1943, MA, 1947, PhD, 1949. Rsch. assoc. Columbia U. Radiation Lab., N.Y.C., 1949; AEC fellow in chemistry Calif. Inst. Tech., Pasadena, 1949-50; head semicondr. research sect. Hughes Aircraft Co., Culver City, Calif., 1950-53; mem. tech. staff Bell Labs., Murray Hill, N.J., 1953-66, head biophysics rsch. dept., 1966-79; prof. molecular biophysics and biochemistry Yale U., 1979-94, dir. divsn. biol. scis., 1981-87, Sterling prof. molecular biophysics and biochemistry, 1994—. Rask Oersted lectr. U. Copenhagen, 1959; vis. prof. Ecole Normale Superieur, Paris, 1962; Appleton lectr. Brown U., 1965; vis. prof. physics U. Tokyo, 1965; Reilly lectr. U. Notre Dame, Ind., 1969; vis. prof. biophysics Princeton U., 1971-72; Regents lectr. UCLA, 1978 Lt. (j.g.) USNR, 1944-46. Guggenheim fellow in lab. molecular biology MRC Cambridge (Eng.) U., 1961-62; recipient Havinga medal Leiden U., 1983, Gold medal Soc. Magnetic Resonance in Medicine, 1984, Mem. Nat. Acad. Scis., Inst. Medicine. Achievements include research in spectroscopic techniques applied to physics, chemistry and biology. Office: Dept Molecular Biophysics Biochemistry Yale Univ PO Box 208024 New Haven CT 06520-8024 E-mail: Robert.Shulman@Yale.edu.

SHULMAN, ROBERT JAY, physician; b. Newark; s. Irving Jack and Shirley (Weinstock) S.; children: David Ian, Hannah Rachel. BA, Emory U., 1972; MD, Chgo. Med. Sch., 1976. Asst. prof. pediat. Baylor Coll. Medicine, Houston, 1982-89, assoc. prof., 1989-96, prof., 1996—; dir. nutritional support team Tex. Children's Hosp., 1982—. Mem. sub-bd. pediatric gastroenterology Am. Bd. Pediatrics, 2000—. Author: Young Chef's Nutrition Guide and Cookbook, 1990, Keys to Child Nutrition, 1991, (with others) Principles and Practice of Pediatrics, 1998, Physiology of the Gastrointestinal Tract, 1994, Pediatric Parenteral Nutrition, 1997; editor: Nutrition in Your Pocket, 2002; mem. editl. bd. Jour. Pediat. Gastroenterology and Nutrition, 1994-96. Fellow Am. Acad. Pediat.; mem. Am. Gastroent. Soc., Am. Soc. Patenteral and Enteral Nutrition (chmn. pediatric sect. 1997-99, pres. 1997-99), Am. Inst. Nutrition, N.Am. Soc. Pediat. Gastroenterology and Nutrition (exec. coun. 1997-99), Soc. Pediat. Rsch. Avocation: guitar. Office: Baylor Coll Medicine 1100 Bates Ave Houston TX 77030-2600

SHULMAN, STEPHEN NEAL, lawyer; b. New Haven, Apr. 6, 1933; s. Harry and Rea (Karrel) S.; m. Sandra Paula Still, Aug. 14, 1954; children—Harry, Dean, John. BA, Harvard, 1954; LL.B. cum laude, Yale, 1958. Bar: Conn. 1958, D.C. 1960. Indsl. relations Bendix Aviation Corp., 1954-55; law clk. to Justice Harlan, U.S. Supreme Ct., 1958-59; vis. asst. pro. U. Mich. Law Sch., 1959; asso. firm Covington & Burling, Washington, 1959-60; asst. U.S. atty., 1960-61; exec. asst. to sec. labor, 1961-62; dept asst. sec. of def., 1962-65; gen. counsel U.S. Air Force, 1965-66; chmn. Equal Employment Opportunity Commn., 1966-67; mem. Kane, Shulman & Schlei, Washington, 1967-70; mem. firm Cadwalader, Wickersham & Taft, N.Y.C., also Washington, 1971-95, Freedman, Levy, Kroll & Simonds, Washington, 1995-99, O'Connnor & Hannan, L.L.P., Washington, 1999—. Vis. prof. mgmt. U. Okla., 1965-66. Co-author: The Law of Equal Employment Opportunity, 1990; editor in chief Yale Law Jour., 1957-58. Mem. Book and Gavel, Order of Coif, Cum Laude Soc., Phi Alpha Delta. Home: 1332 Skipwith Rd Mc Lean VA 22101-1841 Office: O Connor & Hannan LLP 1666 K St NW Washington DC 20006-2803 E-mail: sshulman@oconnorhannan.com.

SHULMAN, YALE, urologist; b. Fort Dix, N.J., Dec. 19, 1953; m. Vivian Shulman, June 20, 1976. BA, Yeshiva U., 1973; MD, Albert Einstein Coll. Medicine, 1976. Diplomate Am. Bd. Urology. Pvt. practice urology, Jersey City, Bayonne, N.J., 1982—. Clin. assoc. prof. urology NYU Sch. Medicine; clin. asst. prof. surgery & urology Univ. Medicine & Dentistry of N.J. Fellow ACS; mem. AMA, Soc. Study Impotence, Am. Urol. Assn., Assn. Clin. Urologists, Soc. Reproductive Medicine. Office: 2255 Kennedy Blvd Jersey City NJ 07304-1428 E-mail: ycshulman@aol.com.

SHULMAN, YECHIEL, engineering educator; b. Tel Aviv, Jan. 28, 1930; came to the U.S., 1950; s. David and Rachel (Chonowski) S.; m. Ruth Danzig, June 29, 1950; children: Elinor D., Ron E., Orna L. BS in Aero. Engring., BS in Bus. and Engring. Adminstrn., MS in Aero. Engring., MIT, 1954, DSc Aero. and Astro., 1959; MBA, U. Chgo., 1973. Assoc. prof. mech. engring. Northwestern U., Evanston, Ill., 1959-67; v.p. adv. engring. Anocut, Inc., Elk Grove Vill., 1967-72; v.p. corp. devel. Alden Press, 1973-84; pres. MMT Environ., Inc., Shoreview, Minn., 1984-87; cons. Shulman Assocs., Mpls., 1987-89; prof. mech. engring. dept. U. Minn., 1989-2000, H. W. Sweatt chair in technol. leadership and dir. ctr. for devel. technol. leadership, 1989-2000, dir. grad. studies mgmt. of tech. program, 1990-2000, prof. emeritus mech. engring. dept., 2000—. Mem. ASME, Internat. Assn. for Mgmt. of Tech. Office: U Minn 109 ME Bldg 111 Church St SE Minneapolis MN 55455-0150

SHULMISTER, M(ORRIS) ROSS, lawyer; b. Atlanta, Jan. 6, 1940; s. Morris and Kathryn Sybella (Baker) S.; m. Benita Vee Rosin, Dec. 16, 1974. BEE, U. Fla., 1962, JD, 1973. Bar: Fla. 1973, U.S. Dist. Ct. (so. dist.) Fla. 1974, U.S. Dist. Ct. (mid. dist.) Fla. 1985, U.S. Ct. Appeals (5th and 11th cirs.) 1981. Pvt. practice, Broward County, Fla., Ft. Lauderdale, 1974-98, Pompano Beach, 1998—. Spl. master for code enforcement, Pompano Beach, Fla., 1991-92. Mem. Broward County Consumer Protection Bd., 1983-2001, chmn., 1999-2000; chmn. Charter Review Bd., Pompano Beach, Fla., 1994-97; dir. South Pompano Civic Assn., 1989-2000, v.p., 1989, pres., 1992-98. Lt. col. USAF, 1964-70, ret., USAFR, 1970-93. Mem. Fla. Bar (mem. constrn. law subcom., civil trial cert. 1984-99), Broward County Bar Assn. Office: 590 SE 12th St Pompano Beach FL 33060-9409

SHULTIS, ROBERT LYNN, finance educator, cost systems consultant, retired professional association executive; b. Kingston, N.Y., June 30, 1924; s. Albert H. and Dorothy Elizabeth (Jenkins) S.; m. Bernice Elizabeth Johnson, Jan. 20, 1946; 1 son, Robert Lee. BS, Columbia Univ. Sch. Bus., 1949, postgrad., 1949-51. Staff acct. Price Waterhouse, N.Y.C., 1949-52; credit mgr., controller Organon, Inc., West Orange, N.J., 1952-68; v.p., treas., chief fin. officer Arwood Corp., Rockleigh, 1968-72; v.p., controller Technicon, Tarrytown, N.Y., 1972-80; exec. dir. Inst. of Mgmt. Accts., Montvale, N.J., 1980-86; faculty, exec. dir. Ctr. for Exec. Devel. Coll. William & Mary, Williamsburg, Va., 1987-91. Instr. Rutgers U., 1964-74, Fairleigh Dickinson U., 1967-68; mem. Fin. Acctg. Standards Adv. coun., 1981-86; cons. Acctg. and Cost Sys. design, 1990—; lectr., seminar leader, cons. on controllership, activity-based costing, cost mgmt., cost sys. design U. Calif, Berkeley, U. Minn., Michigan State U., So. Meth. U., Baldwin Wallace Coll., George Mason U., James Madison U., U. N.C., Colo. State U., others, 1990—. Editor: Management Accountants' Handbook, and supplements, 1991-94. Mem. bd. advs. U. Fla. Sch. Accountancy, James Madison U. Sch. Accountancy; mem. fin. and budget com. Kingsmill Community Svcs. Assn. Served with USAF, 1943-45. Decorated Presdl. Unit Citation, ETO Ribbon, eight battle stars. Mem. AAUP, Fin. Execs. Internat., Inst. Mgmt. Accts., Am. Acctg. Assn., Ross Inst. Acctg. Rsch., Kingsmill Club, Beta Alpha Psi (adv. forum).

SHULTS, F. LERON, theology studies educator; b. Victoria, Tex., Feb. 5, 1965; s. Fount Lee Shults, Lynda Mae Shults; m. Elizabeth Mary Olczak; children: Sara, Lee Michael, Laura. DPhil, Princeton Theol. Sem., 1998. Prof. theology Bethel Theol. Sem., St. Paul, 1997—. Author: The Postfoundationalist Task of Theology, 1999 (Templeton Theology and Sci. award, 2001), Reforming Theological Anthropology, 2003, The Faces of Forgiveness, 2003. Office: Bethel Theol Sem 3949 Bethel Dr Saint Paul MN 55112

SHULTS, MARY J. retail store owner; b. El Reno, Okla., July 25, 1944; m. Ray D. Shults, Jan. 17, 1964; two children. Student, Boise Jr. Coll., 1963. Mgr. Highland Stables Tack Shop, Boise, Idaho, 1976-78, Horseman's Tac & Togs, Boise, 1978-79, Three Creek Ranch & Cattle Co., Ellensburg, Wash., 1982-84; co-owner Sagebrush Saddlery & Western Wear, 1982—. Res. dep. sheriff Kittitas County Sheriff's Office, Ellensburg, 1993—. Mem. N.W. Cutting Horse Assn., Cascade Cow Cutters. Avocations: horseback riding, camping, cow cutting, street rods, motorcycles. Home and Office: 1310 S Ruby St Ellensburg WA 98926-3762

SHULTZ, DELRAY FRANKLIN (LUCKY SHULTZ), management consultant, speaker; b. South Bend, Ind., Apr. 4, 1948; s. Jack Raymond and Georgina Martha (Johnston) S.; m. Catherine Elizabeth Yontz, June 6, 1970; children: Jeremy Frank, Eric Bruce, Jon Karl. BS, USAF Acad., 1970; MS, Air U., 1978. Commd. 2d lt. USAF, 1970, advanced through grades to capt., 1973, navigator, 1972-77, adminstrv. contracting officer L.A., 1978-81; mgr. purchasing, contracts supr. BP Exploration, Anchorage, 1981-92, internal cons. Bogotá, Colombia, 1992-93; mgr. contracts, internal cons. Alaska Petroleum Contractors, Anchorage, 1994-97; mgr. assurance and devel., internal cons. Natchiq Inc., 1997-2000; owner Pathways to Leadership, Seattle, 1999—. Adj. prof. U. Alaska, Anchorage, 1988-96. Bd. mem., vice chair bd. dirs. Family Connection, Inc., Anchorage, 1981-84; dir., bd. elders Bethany Christian Cmty., Anchorage, 1982-93; del. Rep. Party of Alaska, Anchorage, 1988, 96. Named Outstanding Young Men of Am., U.S. Jr. C. of C., 1978; recipient Silver medal Buckley Sch. Pub. Spkg., 1997. Mem. Nat. Contract Mgmt. Assn., Nat. Assn. Purchasing Mgrs., Am. Soc. for Quality. Avocations: commercial pilot, public speaker, personal development teacher, musician. E-mail: PTLWest@aol.com.

SHULTZ, GEORGE PRATT, former government executive, economics educator; b. N.Y.C., Dec. 13, 1920; s. Birl E. and Margaret Lennox (Pratt) S.; children: Margaret Ann Shultz Tilsworth, Kathleen Pratt Shultz Jorgensen, Peter Milton, Barbara Lennox Shultz White, Alexander George; m. Charlotte Mailliard, Aug. 15, 1997. BA in Econs., Princeton U., 1942; PhD in Indsl. Econs., MIT, 1949; Hon. degree, Yeshiva U., U. Tel Aviv, Technion-Israel Inst. Tech., Keio U., Tokyo, Brandeis U., U. Notre Dame, Princeton U., Loyola U., U. Pa., U. Rochester, Carnegie-Mellon U., Baruch Coll., Northwestern U., Tblisi State U., Columbia U. Mem. faculty M.I.T., 1949-57; assoc. prof. indsl. relations MIT, 1955-57; prof. indsl. relations Grad. Sch. Bus., U. Chgo., 1957-68; dean sch. Grad. Sch. Bus. U. Chgo., 1962-68, fellow Ctr. for Advanced Study in Behavioral Scis., 1968-69; U.S. sec. labor, 1969-70; dir. Office Mgmt. and Budget, 1970-72; U.S. sec. treasury, also asst. to Pres., 1972-74; chmn. Council on Econ. Policy, East-West Trade Policy com.; exec. v.p. Bechtel Corp., San Francisco, 1974-75, pres., 1975-81, vice chmn., 1977-81; also dir.; pres. Bechtel Group, Inc., 1981-82; prof. mgmt. and pub. policy Stanford U., 1974-82, prof. internat. econs., 1989-91, prof. emeritus, 1991—; chmn. Pres. Reagan's Econ. Policy Adv. Bd., 1981-82; U.S. sec. of state, 1982-89; Thomas W. and Susan B. Ford disting. fellow Hoover Instn., Stanford, 1989—. Bd. dirs. Charles Schwab & Co., Bechtel Group, Inc., Infrastructureworld; mem. GM Corp. Adv. Coun., Gilead Scis. Bd., Unext Bd.; chmn. J.P. Morgan Internat. Coun.; chmn. adv. coun. Inst. Internat. Studies, 1990-98, Calif. Gov.'s Econ. Policy Adv. Bd., 1995-98, Bechtel Group Inc. Author: Pressures on Wage Decisions, 1950, (with Charles A. Myers) The Dynamics of a Labor Market, 1951, (with John R. Coleman) Labor Problems: Cases and Readings, 1953, (with T.L. Whisler) Management Organization and the Computer, 1960, (with Arnold R. Weber) Strategies for the Displaced Worker, 1966, (with Robert Z. Aliber) Guidelines, Informal Controls and the Marketplace, 1966, (with Albert Rees) Workers and Wages in the Urban Labor Market, 1970, Leaders and Followers in an Age of Ambiguity, 1975, (with Kenneth W. Dam) Economic Policy Beyond the Headlines, 1977, 2d edition, 1998, Turmoil and Triumph: My Years as Secetary of State, 1993; also articles, chpts. in books, reports, and essays. Served to capt. USMCR, 1942-45. Recipient Medal of Freedom, 1989, Seoul Peace prize, 1992, Eisenhower medal for Leadership and Svc., 2001, Reagan Disting. Am. award, 2002, Ralph Bunch award for Diplomatic Excellence, 2002. Mem. Am. Econ. Assn., Indsl. Relations Research Assn. (pres. 1968), Nat. Acad. Arbitrators. Office: Stanford U Hoover Instn Stanford CA 94305-6010

SHULTZ, JEANNE MARIE, training director, workforce improvement analyst; b. Detroit, Oct. 27, 1954; d. Raymond Vincent and Helen Frances (Towne) S. AA, Wayne State U., 1975, BA, 1978. Catering, sales dir. Maxwell's Plum, San Francisco, 1982-84; sales rep. Heath Sign Co., Hayward, Calif., 1984-87; sales assoc. Cornish & Carey Real Estate, San Jose, 1987-88, Fox & Carskadon/ Better Homes & Gardens, Danville, 1988-95; sales, telesales and conf. mgr. Coun on Edn. in Mgmt., Walnut Creek, 1995-98; tng. dir. No. Calif. Tng. Coun., Monterey, 1998—; workforce improvement analyst Pacific Grove, 1998—. Advisor, cons. Internat. Inst. of Rsch., London, 1995-97; assoc. Calif. Dept. Real Estate, 1987—. Author: (book) Telesales Encyclopedia, 1996, (tng. manual) Complete Sales Successes, 1985, rev. edit. 1990; (short story) in Ladies Home Jour.; contbg. editor Law Update Monthly; publisher, editor: (newsletter) Lines of Fortune, 1995-98; radio talk show host, prodr. Sta. KNRY/KIEZ, Monterey, Calif. Tech. advisor Jr. Achievement U.S., N.Y.C., 1985-88; chair Bay Area Women in Bus., San Francisco, 1986-90; vol. Battered Women's Alternative, Contra Costa County, 1995-98, Monterey County Vols., 1988—, Friends of the Aquarium, Monterey, 1998; comm. coord City of Monterey, 1998; mem. Fairway Ptnrs. Salvation Army, Monterey County, Calif., 1998—. Mem. AAUW, Del Monte Women's Club, Toastmasters Group, Alliance on Aging Monterey County (sec.). Avocations: golf, golf tournament coord., storytelling, martial arts, rsch. Office: No Calif Tng Ctr 651 Cannery Row Monterey CA 93940-1035

SHULTZ, JOHN DAVID, lawyer; b. L.A., Oct. 9, 1939; s. Edward Patterson and Jane Elizabeth (Taylor) Shultz; m. Joanne Person, June 22, 1968; children: David Taylor, Steven Matthew. Student, Harvard Coll., 1960—61; BA, U. Ariz., 1964; JD, Boalt Hall, U. Calif., Berkeley, 1967. Bar: N.Y. 1968, Calif. 1978. Assoc. Cadwalader, Wickersham & Taft, N.Y.C., 1968—77; ptnr. Lawler, Felix & Hall, L.A., 1977—83, mem. exec. com., chmn. planning com., co-chmn. recruiting and hiring com.; ptnr. Morgan, Lewis & Bockius, 1983—, chmn. mgmt. com., mem. lateral entry com., chmn. profl. evaluation com., chmn. practice devel. com., chmn. recruiting com. Mem. adv. bd. Internat. and Comparative Law Ctr., Southwestern Legal Found., 1981—; active Practicing Law Inst. Adv. Bd., Corp. and Securities Law, 1992—; Trustee St. Thomas Ch., N.Y.C., 1969—72, Shore Acres Point Corp., Mamaroneck, NY, 1975—77. Mem.: N.Y. State Bar Assn., State Bar Calif., Assn. Bar City of N.Y., ABA, Jonathan Club (L.A.), Sigma Chi, Phi Delta Phi. Episcopalian. Office: Morgan Lewis & Bockius LLP 300 S Grand Ave Ste 22 Los Angeles CA 90071-3109

SHULTZ, LEONARD DONALD, research scientist; b. Boston, Apr. 16, 1945; s. Samson and Jean (Korim) S.; m. Kathy Louise Jacobs, Aug. 31, 1969; children: David Benjamin, Sarah Natalie. BA, Northeastern U., Boston, 1967; PhD, U. Mass., 1972. Rsch. asst. Tufts U. Sch. of Med., Boston, 1967-68; from grad. teaching asst. to predoctoral fellow U. Mass., 1968-72; from postdoctoral fellow to sr. staff scientist The Jackson Lab., Bar Harbor, Maine, 1972—. Editorial bd. In Vivo, 1991—. Contbr. numerous rsch. papers. Bd. Dirs. YMCA, Bar Harbor, Maine, 1989—. Mem. Am. Assn. Immunologists, Am. Soc Microbiology, Internat. Assn. Comparative Rsch. on Leukemia and related diseases. Achievements include development of numerous mouse models for human immunological diseases. Home: Box 2545 RR 1 Box 2545 Bar Harbor ME 04609-9751 Office: The Jackson Lab Main St Bar Harbor ME 04609

SHULTZ, LINDA JOYCE, retired library director; b. South Bend, Ind., Aug. 25, 1931; d. Justin Russell and Gladys Ernstine (Miller) Nash; m. Dale Jay Shultz, Apr. 20, 1952; children: Donald Jay, Sally Janine, William Justin, Alan Joel, Kent Jon. AA, Stephens Coll., 1951; BS in Edn., Ind. U., Ft. Wayne, 1971, Cert. I in Libr. Edn., 1975. Sec. John R. Worthman, Inc., Ft. Wayne, 1951-54; farm wife, mother Noble County, Ind., 1954-68; libr. Noble County Pub. Libr., Albion, 1968-97; ret., 1997. Mem. exec. bd. Tri-Alsa Libr. Svc. Authority, Ft. Wayne, 1988-90. Editor: Albion Memories, 1977. Mem. Albion Local Devel. Corp., 1989-92; sec. Cen. Noble Jr. Achievement, 1988-92. Named Albion Citizen of the Yr. Albion Rotary Club, 1977. Mem. DAR, Ind. Libr. Assn., Ind. Hist. Soc., Ind. Geneal. Soc., Order Ea. Star, Rotary (pres. Albion club 1993-94, Paul Harris fellow 1999), Toastmasters (pres. U.S. Six Shooters chpt. 1988-89), Gene Stratton Porter Meml. Soc., Ind. Soc. Mayflower Descendants, Geneal. Soc. (sec. 1985-95, pres. 1997—), Noble County Hist. Soc., Noble County Geneal. Soc. (pres.). Republican. Methodist. Avocation: genealogy.

SHULTZ, LOIS FRANCES CASHO, nursing supervisor; b. Phila., Apr. 29, 1936; d. Ellwood Francis Casho and Beatrice Mae Gunther Casho; m. Thomas Eugene Shultz, Aug. 15, 1959 (div. June 1983); children: David T., Patricia Shultz Bichefsky, Jeffrey A. Nursing diploma, Temple U. Hosp., 1957; BSN, U. Pa., 1961. RN; cert. gerontol. nursing, Pa. Staff nurse Temple U. Hosp., Phila., 1957, pvt. duty nurse, 1958-59; nursing instr. St. Luke's Hosp. Sch. Nursing, Bethlehem, 1959-61, Reading (Pa.) Area C.C., 1985-88; asst. DON Reading Nursing Ctr., West Reading, 1988-89; night supr. Berks County Home-BerksHeim, Leesport, Pa., 1989—. Mem. Berks County Bd. Assistance, Reading, 1980—, chmn., 1988-2001, chmn. cmty. rels. com., 2001—; pres., dir. Berks County Med. Soc. Aux.; bd. dirs., chmn. mem. children and youth com. Berks County Mental Health Assn.; bd. dirs., past bd. chmn. Berks County Children and Youth Svcs.; organizer, past dir. Reading Is Fundamental for Berks County; past mem., chmn., mem. programs and svcs. sub-com. United Way Home Health Care Study Com. Mem. Nat. Soc. DAR (1st vice-regent br. Berks County chpt.). Republican. Presbyterian. Home: 5 Wendy Rd Reading PA 19601-1031

SHULTZ, SUSAN F. executive search executive; b. N.Y.C., Mar. 25, 1943; d. L. Richard and Jane (Kent) Fried; m. Shas H. Shultz, Nov. 23, 1968 (dec. Jan. 1980). BA in Govt. and econs., U. Ariz.; postgrad., George Washington U. Legis. asst. to Rep. William Brock U.S. Congress, Washington, 1964-69; columnist, investigative reporter Phoenix Mag.; owner mktg. firm, SSA Exec. Search Internat., Ltd., Phoenix, 1981—. Presdl. del White House Conf. on

Small Bus.; participant symposia Coun. Fgn. Rels., Am. Assembly; past dir. Ariz. Dist. Export Coun.; founder The Bd. Inst., Inc., 2002—. Author: The Board Book, 2000, Beverly Hills Diet, How to Adopt the Baby You Want; contbr. articles to profl. jours.; featured: Wall St. Jour., featured: Dirs.' Monthly, featured: Directorship, Success, Employment Weekly, Inc. mag., featured: Working Women, Ariz. Rep., bus. jours., featured: N.Y. Times, featured: USA Today. Chair Phoenix Com. on Fgn. Rels.; mem. adv. bd. Nat. Small Bus. Devel. Ctr.; past mem. adv. coun. Ariz. State U. Sch. Agribus. and Resource Mgmt.; mem. Valley Leadership, Charter 100. Mem.: Ariz. Bus. Leadership Assn. (past pres.), Pacific Coun. Internat. Policy. Home: 6001 E Cactus Wren Rd Paradise Valley AZ 85253-4239 Office: SSA Exec Search Internat Ltd 4350 E Camelback Rd Ste 200B Phoenix AZ 85018-8335

SHULTZ, SUZANNE MARIE, medical librarian; b. Harrisburg, Pa., Feb. 27, 1947; d. Kenneth W. and Alice Julia (Zimmerman) S. BS in Edn., Shippensburg U., 1969; MA in Am. Studies, Pa. State U., Middletown, 1993. Med. libr. Polyclinic Med. Ctr. Libr., Harrisburg, Pa., 1969-96; dir. libr. svcs. York (Pa.) Hosp., 1996—. Author: Body Snatching, 1992; co-editor: Three Mile Island, 1988; mem. editorial bd. Med. Ref. Svcs. Quar., 1986—; contbr. articles to profl. jours. Mem. Pa. German Soc., Ctrl. Pa. Health Sci. Libr. Assn. (founding mem.), Med. Libr. Assn. Republican. Methodist. Avocations: cross-country skiing, handbell choir, antique collector. Office: York Hosp Philip A Hoover MD Libr 1001 S George St York PA 17403-3645 E-mail: sshultz@wellspan.org.

SHUM, HENRY, finance company executive; b. Hong Kong, 1960; BS, Cornell U., 1983, MSc, 1985, PhD, 1989. Sr. ops. analyst Internat. Paper, Hawthorne, NY, 1989—95; pres. Shum Ptnrs., Inc., Briarcliff Manor, 1995—. Office: Shum Ptnrs Inc 10 Summerland Ln Briarcliff Manor NY 10510

SHUMACKER, HARRIS B., JR. retired surgeon, educator, author; b. Laurel, Miss., May 20, 1908; s. Harris B. and Corinne (Teller) S.; m. Myrtle E. Landau, Dec. 1, 1933 (dec.); children: Peter D., James N.; m. Grace McConnel, Nov. 9, 1998. BS, U. Tenn., Chattanooga, 1927; A.M., Vanderbilt U., 1928; MD, Johns Hopkins U., 1932; D.Sc. (hon.), Ind. U., 1985. Diplomate Am. Bd. Surgery, Am. Bd. Thoracic Surgery. Asst. in surgery Johns Hopkins U., 1932-35, instr., 1938-41, asst. prof., 1941-46; asst. in surgery Yale U., 1936-37, instr., 1937-38, assoc. prof., 1946-48; prof. surgery Ind. U., 1948-70, chmn. dept., 1948-68, Disting. prof., 1970-78, Disting. prof. emeritus, 1978—. Prof., sr. advisor Uniformed Svcs. U. of Health Scis., Bethesda, Md., 1981-87, Disting. prof. surgery, 1988—; pres. Uniformed Svcs U. Assocs., 1987-88; hon. mem. surg. faculties in Peoples Republic of China, 1979— ; dir. sect. cardiovascular-thoracic surgery St. Vincent Hosp., 1973-78, sr. surg. cons., 1978-81. Served from capt. to lt. col. M.C., U.S. Army, 1942-46; cons. surgeon gen., 1949-60 Recipient Roswell Park award, 1968, Medal of Honor, Evansville U., 1970, Disting. Alumus award U. Tenn. at Chattanooga, Curtis medal, 1970, Spl. Alumnus award Johns Hopkins U., 1973, Disting. Svc. award Am. Soc. Abdominal Surgery, letter of commendation Surgeon-Gen. USN, 1987, Disting. Svc. medal Uniformed Svc. U. Health Scis., 1988, René Leriche prize Soc. Internat. de Chir., 1993. Fellow Royal Coll. Surgeons England (hon.); mem. Am. Assn. Surgery of Trauma, Am. Surg. Assn. (1st v.p. 1961, sec. 1964-68), So. Surg. Assn., Central Surg. Assn., Pan-Pacific Surg. Assn. (trustee 1961-64, v.p., 1964-75, 78— , pres. 1975-78), AMA (chmn. sect. gen. surgery), Internat. Surg. Soc., Internat. Soc. Cardiovascular Surgeons (v.p. 1957-59, pres. N.Am. chpt. 1956-58), Soc. Clin. Surgery (pres. 1961-63), ACS (chmn. forum com. 1955-60, chmn. nat. TV com. 1964-68, Disting. Service award 1968), Soc. U. Surgeons (pres. 1951), Soc. for Vascular Surgery (pres. 1958-59), Am. Thoracic Surg. Assn., Soc. Thoracic Surgeons (hon.), Internat. Surg. Group (v.p. 1974-75, pres. 1975-76), Polish Surg. Assn. (hon.), Sociedad Cubana de Angiologia (hon.), Societa Italiana di Chirurgia (hon.), Internat. Surg. Group (hon.), Phi Beta Kappa, Sigma Xi, Alpha Omega Alpha.

SHUMADINE, ANNE BALLARD, financial advisor, lawyer; b. Norfolk, Va., Mar. 8, 1943; d. William Pierce Ballard and Helen Caulfield Ballard Hoffman; m. Conrad Moss Shumadine, Sept. 1, 1965; children: John Ballard, James Hunter. AB, Wellesley Coll., 1965; JD, Coll. William and Mary, 1983. Bar: Va. 1983. Assoc. McGuire Woods Battle & Boothe, Norfolk, 1983-88; ptnr. Shumadine & Rose, P.C., 1988-94, McCandlish Kaine & Grant, 1994—; pres. Signature Fin. Mgmt., 1994—. Bd. dirs. CENIT Bancorp, Norfolk; co-chmn. Old Dominion Tax Conf., Norfolk, 1992; mem. adv. coun. William and Mary Tax Conf., 1997—. Trustee William and Mary Law Sch. Found., 1992—; chmn. Tidewater Scholarship Found., Norfolk, 1995—; rector, bd. visitors Old Dominion U., 1996-97. Fellow Va. Law Found., 1999—; named Vol. of Yr., Downtown Norfolk Coun., 1995. Office: Signature Fin Mgmt 999 Waterside Dr Ste 2220 Norfolk VA 23510-3306

SHUMAKE, JAMES MARTIN, emergency medicine physician; b. St. Louis, Mar. 31, 1957; s. Lindell Paul and Modesta Shumake; m. Tori Kei, Nov. 5, 1994; children: Elizabeth Mei Rose, James Winston, Theodore Nelson. BS in Biology, Northeast Mo. Sate U., 1980; DO, Kirksville Coll. Osteo. Med., 1984. Emergency medicine physician Nat. Emergency Service, 1985—, Healthline Mgmt. Inc., 1991—, EmCare, 1999—. Dir. emergency medicine St. Joseph's Hosp., Centerville, Iowa, 1995—. Mem. Am. Osteo. Assn., Am. coll. Osteo. Emergency Medicine. Avocations: cycling, tennis, jet skiing. Home: 1603 S Halliburton St Kirksville MO 63501-3019

SHUMAKER, ANNE WOLFE, social worker; b. Chattanooga, July 5, 1955; d. Thomas Elmer and Patricia Anne (Beene) Wolfe; m. David Kyle Shumaker, Aug. 20, 1977. BS, East Tenn. State U., 1977; MS in Social Work, U. Tenn., 1987. Cert. master social worker. Outpatient clinician Watauga Area Mental Health Ctr., Johnson City, Tenn., 1987-89; counselor, social work instr. Va. Intermont Coll.-Women's Resource Ctr., Bristol, 1989—. Cons. East Tenn. State U.-Counseling Ctr., Johnson City, 1989-90. Mem. NASW, Acad. Cert. Social Workers, Appalachian Peace Edn. Ctr. Democrat. Episcopalian. Avocations: bicycling, scuba diving.

SHUMAKER, HAROLD DENNIS, lawyer; b. Richmond, Va., July 8, 1946; s. Milton and Virginia (Grossman) S.; m. Lucy Jane Light, May 23, 1969. BS, U. Ala., 1969; JD, New England Sch. Law, 1983. Bar: Pa. 1983, U.S. dist. Ct. (mid. dist.) Pa. 1988. From br. fin. mgr. to regional fin. mgr. Sperry Univac, Harrisburg, Pa., 1970-80; sr. project adminstr. IOCS, Inc., Waltham, Mass., 1980-83; assoc. Sponaugle & Sponaugle, P.C., Lancaster, Pa., 1983-84; pres., gen. counsel, dir. Horizon Technologies, Inc., Marietta, 1984—; sr. staff atty. Commodore Bus. Machines, Inc., West Chester, 1985-87; pvt. practice Marietta, 1987—. Pres. Marietta-Maytown East Donegal Bicentennial, 1974-76, Marietta Restoration Assn., 1976; chmn. Marietta Housing Hearing Bd., 1984-2001; chmn. Marietta Planning Commn., 1996—. With USNG, 1969-75. With USNG, 1969—75. Mem. ABA, Pa. Bar Assn. (mem. unauthorized practice law com 1996-, elder law com. 2000-), Lancaster Bar Assn., Ctrl. Pa. U. Ala. Alumni Assn. (v.p. 1985-86, 95-96, 2000-01, pres. 1999-2000), Lions (pres. 1977-78, 89-90, 97-98, v.p. 1988-89, 93-97, bd. dirs. 1990—, Melvin Jones fellow for humanitarian work 1998). Democrat. Jewish. Home and Office: 402 W Market St Marietta PA 17547-1205 E-mail: hdshumaker@dejazzd.com.

SHUMAN, EARL STANLEY, songwriter, music publisher; b. Boston, Aug. 2, 1923; s. Benjamin Morris and Mildred Judith (Kaplan) S.; m. Margaret Stein, Nov. 25, 1956; children: Cathy Elizabeth, Daniel James, Steven Lewis. BA, Yale U., 1947. Owner, pres. Earl/Peg Music Co., N.Y.C., 1957—; pub. BMI, ASCAP, 1977—. Composer (lyric writer) popular songs including Seven Lonely Days, 1953 (Country and Western award 1970), Hey There Lonely Girl, 1970 (Gold record), Banjo's Back in Town, Caterina, Clinging Vine, Close to Cathy, Hotel Happiness, Left Right Out of Your Heart, Most people Get Married, My Shy Violet, The River, Starry-Eyed, Theme For a Dream, Young New Mexican Puppeteer; composer (musicals) Secret Life of Walter Mitty, 1964 (award 1965), (country song) Leaves are the Tears of Autumn, 1968 (Country and Western award 1969), (TV themes) Coronet Blue, ABC TV, 1967, Confidence/NFL-CBS, 1967-76, (Movie Title Songs) The Disorderly Orderly, Judith, Situation Hopeless But Not Serious, Barrabas, Monica (love theme from The Carpetbaggers), Love Me Longer (love theme from Arrivederci Baby); pub. Bat Out of Hell album, 1977 (platinum award 1979). Capt. USMCR, 1943-46, 50-51. Mem.: ASCAP. Avocations: music, baseball. Home and Office: 111 E 88th St Apt 3B New York NY 10128-1158 Fax: (212) 722-3698. E-mail: earlmusic@earthlink.net.

SHUMAN, JOSEPH DUFF, lawyer; b. Pitts., Dec. 27, 1942; s. Joseph and Anna Jane (Phillips) D.; m. Ann Stewart McMillan, Nov. 9, 1969; children: David Stewart, Lauren Forbes. BA, Yale U., 1964; LLB, Harvard U., 1967. Bar: Pa. 1968, U.S. Dist. Ct. (we. dist.) Pa. 1968. Assoc. Thorp, Reed & Armstrong, LLP, Pitts., 1967-73, ptnr., 1974—, co-chmn., corp. and bus. law dept., 1990-94, chmn., 1994-97. Republican. Presbyterian. Office: Thorp Reed & Armstrong LLP One Oxford Ctr 301 Grant St 14th Fl Pittsburgh PA 15219-1425

SHUMAN, LARRY MYERS, soil chemist; b. Harrisburg, Pa., Apr. 3, 1944; s. Mark P. and Opal I. (Myers) Shuman; m. Catherine A. Yost, Mar. 21, 1970; children: Karen, Rebecca. BS, Pa. State U., 1966, MS, 1968, PhD, 1970. Asst. prof. soil chemistry U. Ga., Experiment, 1972-79, assoc. prof., 1979-91, prof., 1991—. USDA-OICD Exch. scientist to People's Republic of China, 1992. Co-editor, contbg. author Micronutrients in Agriculture, 1991; contbg. author: Zinc in Soils, 1979, Plant Environment Interactions, 1994, Methods of Soil Analysis, Part 3 - Chemical Methods, 1996; contbr. articles to profl. jours. Capt. M.S., U.S. Army, 1970-72. U.S. Aid grantee, 1980-81, USDA-CSRS grantee, 1992-94, Dept. Energy, 1995-96, U.S. EPA, 2000--, NSF, 2000--. Fellow Soil Sci Soc. Am. (soil chemistry divsn. chair 1994, assoc. editor jour. 1986-91, tech. editor jour. 2000—); mem. Am. Soc. Agronomy, Coun. Agrl. Sci. and Tech., Soc. Environ. Geochemistry and Health. Home: 447 Trice Rd Milner GA 30257-3427 Office: U Ga Ga Experiment Sta Griffin GA 30223-1797

SHUMAN, NICHOLAS ROMAN, journalist, educator; b. Chgo., June 30, 1921; s. Roman William and Pauline (Stasevich) S.; m. Marilyn Elaine Johnson, Feb. 23, 1952; children— Kristin Mary, Elizabeth Carol, Mark Nicholas. BA, U. Ill., 1943. With Chgo. Jour. Commerce, 1938-46; mem. staff Herald-American, Chgo., 1946-51, asst. photo editor, 1947-51; mem. staff Chgo. Daily News, 1951-78, fin. editor, 1961-65, asst. mng. editor, 1965-69, nat. and fgn. editor, 1969-77, chief editorial writer, 1977-78; editorial writer Chgo. Sun-Times, 1978-84; prof. journalism Columbia Coll., Chgo., 1984-91, cons., 1992—; columnist Chgo. Reporter, 1985-90; sr. editor World Book Ency., 1965-66; profl. instr. Medill Sch. Journalism, Northwestern U., 1954-61; freelance mag. writer, 1951—. TV commentator, 1958-61 Founding pres. Arlington Heights (Ill.) Human Relations Com., 1965. Served to 1st lt. AUS, 1943-46, ETO. Recipient awards Ill. AP, UPI, John Howard Assn., Inland Press Assn., Chgo. Newspaper Guild; nominated for Pulitzer prize 3 times. Mem. Alpha Kappa Lambda, Sigma Delta Chi. Home: 1001 W Clarendon Rd Arlington Heights IL 60004-4507 E-mail: mjs124@aol.com.

SHUMAN, R. BAIRD, academic program director, writer, English language educator, educational consultant; b. Paterson, N.J., June 20, 1929; s. George William and Elizabeth (Evans) S. AB (Trustees scholar), Lehigh U., 1951; M.Ed., Temple U., 1953; PhD (Univ. scholar), U. Pa., 1961; cert. in philology, U. Vienna, Austria, 1954. Tchr. Phila. Pub. Schs., 1953-55; asst. instr. English U. Pa., 1955-57; instr. humanities Drexel U., Phila., 1957-59; asst. prof. English San José (Calif.) State U., 1959-62; asst. prof. English, edn. Duke U., 1962-63, assoc. prof., 1963-66, prof. edn., 1966-77; prof. English, dir. English edn. U. Ill., Urbana-Champaign, 1977-85, dir. freshman rhetoric, 1979-84, coord. Univ. Associates in Rhetoric Program, 1978-84, dir. devel., 1988-93, acting dir. Ctr. for Study of Writing, 1989-90, prof. emeritus, 1993—. Vis. prof. Moore Inst. Art, 1958, Phila. Conservatory Music, 1958-59, Lynchburg Coll., 1965, King Faisal U., Saudi Arabia, 1978, 81, Bread Loaf Sch. English, Middlebury Coll., 1980, East Tenn. State U., Johnson City, 1980, Olivet Nazarene Coll., 1984, 86, 88, U. Tenn., Knoxville, 1987; cons. Ednl. Testing Svc., 1970—, Am. Coll. Testing Svc., 1975-82; cons. in lang. and lit. Coll. Engring., U. Ill., 1980-97, Worldwide Youth in Sci. and Engring., 1995-97; mem. William Inge Nat. Festival Com., 1989—. Author: Clifford Odets, 1962, Robert E. Sherwood, 1964, William Inge, 1965, rev. edit., 1989, Strategies in Teaching Reading: Secondary, 1978, (with Robert J. Krajewski) The Beginning Teacher: A Guide to Problem Solving, 1979, Elements of Early Reading Instruction, 1979, The First R: Strategies in Early Reading Instruction, 1987, rev. edit., 1989, Classroom Encounters: Problems, Case Studies, Solutions, 1989, (with Eric Hobson) Reading and Writing in High School, (with Denny T. Wolfe Jr.) Teaching English Through the Arts, 1990, Resources for Writers, 1992, American drama 1918-1960, 1992, Georgia O'Keeffe, 1993; editor: Nine Black Poets, 1968, An Eye for an Eye, 1969, A Galaxy of Black Writing, 1970, Creative Approaches to the Teaching of English: Secondary, 1974, Questions English Teachers Ask, 1977, Educational Drama for Today's Schools, 1978, Education in the 80's—English, 1980, The Clearing House: A Closer Look, 1984, 70th anniversary issue The Clearing House, 1995, Great American Writers: 20th Century, 13 vols., 2002; exec. editor The Clearing House jour., 1976—; cons. editor Poet Lore, 1977-90, Cygnus, 1978—, Jour. Aesthetic Edn., 1978-82; contbg. editor Reading Horizons, 1975-85; editor quar. column Reading Horizons, 1975-85; editor Trends in English column Ednl. Leadership, 1989-96. Active Nat. Trust Hist. Preservation. NEH researcher Trinity Coll., Dublin, Ireland, 1985 Mem. MLA, Nat. Coun. Tchrs. English (evaluator ERIC Clearing House, com. alt. careers for English profls.), Internat. Fedn. Tchrs. English, Internat. Coun. Edn. of tchrs., Nev. Coun. Tchrs. English, Conf. English Edn. (exec. com. 1976-79), Internat. Reading Assn. (coord. symposium on cultural literacy, Queensland, Australia 1988), Internat. Assn. Univ. Profs. English, Nat. Soc. Study Edn., Am. Fedn. Tchrs., Union Profl. Employees (editor newsletter 1988-92, exec. com. 1988-92). Democrat. Home: PO Box 27647 Las Vegas NV 89126-1647 E-mail: rbaird@intermind.net. *An education that does not produce people who are vibrantly alive, intoxicated with the wonder of existence, has fallen short. Joy of learning is the fulcrum upon which the human equation is balanced. I have always believed that emotion prevails over intellect and have led my life accordingly with the inevitable result of being extraordinarily happy for most of my days.*

SHUMAN, SAMUEL IRVING, lawyer, law educator; b. Fall River, Mass., Aug. 7, 1925; s. Max and Fannie S.; children: Maxim Erric, Michael A. AB, U. Pa., 1947, MA, 1948, PhD, 1951; JD, U. Mich., 1954; S.JD, Harvard U., 1959. Bar: Mich. 1954, Tex. 1979. Research asst. Legis. Research Center, U. Mich., Ann Arbor, 1953-54, vis. prof. law, 1961; vis. prof. U. Rome, 1963-64; asst. prof. law Wayne State U., Detroit, 1954-55, assoc. prof., 1955-56, prof., 1957-80; prof. dept. psychiatry Wayne State U. Med. Sch. Lectr. Internat. Faculty Comparative Law, Luxembourg, 1964; prof. forensic psychiatry, spl. counsel Lafayette Clinic, Mich. Dept. Mental Health; gen. counsel Mich. Psychiat. Assn., Epilepsy Center Mich. Author: Legal Positivism: Its Scope and Limitations, 1963, (with N.D. West) Introduction to American Law: Cases and Materials, 1971, Psychosurgery and the Medical Control of Violence: Autonomy and Deviance, 1977; editorial bd.: Am. Jour. Jurisprudence, 1969-79. Bd. dirs. Tex. Modern Art Found. Recipient Wayne State U. Bd. Govs. Faculty Recognition award, 1978; Probus Club award Disting. Acad. Achievement in Humanities, 1963; Fulbright fellow Italy, 1961; Rockefeller Found. grantee, 1959, 61; Fulbright travel grantee Germany, 1961; Wayne State U. research grantee, 1960-64; Internat. Research & Exchanges Bd. grantee, 1973 Mem. Am. Law Inst. (life). E-mail: sishuman@aol.com.

SHUMAN, THOMAS ALAN, protective services official, consultant; b. Fairmont, W.Va., Dec. 31, 1946; BA, N.Mex. State U., 1969, 73; postgrad., U. N.Mex., 1988. Mgr. Drum Appliance, Inc., Las Cruces, N.Mex., 1971-75; classification supr. N.Mex. Corrections Dept., Santa Fe, 1976-80, mgmt. analyst supr., 1981-83, dir. classification, 1983-84, dep. sec., 1984-87; pres. Correctional Data Systems, 1987—; owner Desktop Publ. Co., 1988—; dir. N.Mex. Corrections Tng. Acad., 1991-95, probation, parole dir., 1995—; pres. Silicon Wizard Corp., 1989—. Cons. Nat. Inst. Corrections, Washington, 1988, Am. Correctional Assn., Md., 1987—. Mem. Smithsonian Inst., U.S. Naval Inst. Served to lt. U.S. Army, 1969-71, Vietnam. Decorated Bronze Star, Presdl. Commendation. Mem. NRA, N.Mex. State U. Alumni Assn. Republican. Presbyterian. Avocations: fishing, painting, photography, writing. E-mail: talans@aol.com.

SHUMATE, JAMES LEVON, psychotherapist; b. Meridian, Miss., Aug. 30, 1954; s. James Rolane and Evelyn Ruby (White) S. BA, Anderson U., 1976; MA, Calif. State U., Carson, 1983; PhD, U. So. Calif., 1992. Lic. marriage, family, child therapist. Grad. asst. U. So. Calif., L.A.; assoc. pastor S. Bay Ch. of God, Torrance, Calif.; clin. dir. S. Bay Ctr. for Counseling, Manhattan Beach; psychotherapist pvt. practice, Hermosa Beach, 1986-99; mem. faculty Ryokan Coll., L.A., 1997-99; psychologist I, dir. adolescent unit Alcohol/Drug program East Miss. State Hosp., Meridian, 1999-2000, psychologist II, dir. psychology dept. adolescent unit, 2000—. Mem. adj. faculty Miss. State U., Meridian. Mem. APA, Calif. Assn. Marriage, Family Therapists, Calif. State Psychol. Assn. Avocations: sailing, teaching. Office: Adolescent Unit East Miss State Hosp PO Box 4128 Meridian MS 39304-4128 E-mail: jshum30953@aol.com.

SHUMATE, JOHN PAGE, diplomat; b. El Paso, Tex., Sept. 18, 1934; s. John Page and Elizabeth (McWilliams) S.; m. Caroline Taylor, June 16, 1978. BA in Polit. Sci., UCLA, 1956; MAin Internat. Rels., U. So. Calif., 1970. Counsellor of Embassy, U.S. Embassy, Quito, Ecuador, 1970-72; dir. exec. tng. Fgn. Service Inst., Washington, 1972-75; dir. U.K. Affairs, Dept. State, 1975-78, exec. dir. Bur. Ednl. and Cultural Affairs, 1978-80, exec. dir. Bur. Adminstrn., Washington, 1981-84; staff dir. Sec. of State's Adv. Panel on Overseas Security, 1984-85; exec. v.p., CEO Am. Fgn. Svc. Protective Assn., 1986—, Assn. Fed. Health Orgns. (chmn. bd. dirs. 1992-97); co-pres. U.S.-Mexico Cultural Commn. com., 1978-80; exec. dir. sr. living found. Am. Fgn. Svcs. Recipient Superior Honor award U.S. Dept. State., 1981; Phi Kappa Phi Cert. of Honor, 1970. Mem. Am. Fgn. Service Assn., Nat. Assn. Sr. Living Industries, Phi Kappa Phi. Clubs: Ft. Meyer Officers, Fgn. Service, Dacor Bacon House, Bethany West Tennis. Office: Am Fgn Svc Protective Assn 1716 N St NW Washington DC 20036-2907

SHUMATE, MINERVA, risk management analyst; b. Akron, Ohio, Mar. 20, 1949; d. Everett Lee and Arthurine (Cole) S. BA, Ohio No. U., 1972. Comml. lines underwriter Home Ins. Co., N.Y.C., 1972-74, Chgo., 1974-75; sr. mktg. specialist Corroon and Black of Ill., Inc., 1975-77; risk analyst Reed Shaw Stenhouse, Inc., 1977-78; sr. property analyst Aetna Life & Casualty, Cleve., 1979-80, supervising sr. analyst, 1980-83, supr., 1983-84, underwriting unit mgr., 1984-89; underwriting specialist Kemper Ins. Group, Mansfield, 1990-93; risk mgmt. coord. Picker Internat., Inc., 1996-98; risk mgmt. analyst Philips Med. Sys., Highland Heights, Ohio, 1998—; owner Avrenim Funding Group, Hudson, 1993—. Mem. cmty. adv. bd. Northeastern Ednl. TV of Ohio, 1980-84, sec., 1981-83; reader Cleve. Soc. for Blind, 1980-84; pres. Ohio No. U. Minority Alumni Adv. Bd., 1990-95; mem. Mansfield br. Quality Initiative Task Force, 1991-93; mem. Hudson Mcpl. Planning Commn., 1995-2000; active Hudson Local Pub. Schs. Endowment Fund, 1996—, Hudson Pub. Sch. Endowment Fund. Recipient merit award, 1983; named Ins. Woman of the Yr., 1983. Mem. Ins. Women Cleve., Ins. Women of Orange County, Nat. Assn. Ins. Women, Ohio Ins. Inst., Ins. Women Orange County (pres.-elect 1988-89), Western Ins. Info. Svc., Hudson Heritage Assn., Links Club, Ohio Northern U. Alumni Assn. (bd. dirs. 1992-95). Presbyterian. Home: 5421 Lincoln Blvd Hudson OH 44236-2639 Office: 595 Miner Rd Highland Heights OH 44143-2131 E-mail: m.shumate@att.net.

SHUMICK, DIANA LYNN, computer executive; b. Canton, Ohio, Feb. 10, 1951; d. Frank A. and Mary J. (Mari) S.; 1 child, Tina Elyse. Student, Walsh Coll., 1969-70, Ohio U., 1970-71, Kent State U., 1971-77. Data entry clk. Ohio Power Co., Canton, 1969-70; clk. City of Canton Police Dept., 1971-73; sys. engr. IBM, Canton, 1973-81, adv. market support rep. Dallas, 1981-89, sys. engr. mgr. Madison, Wis., 1989-93, mktg. customer satisfaction mgr. Research Triangle Park, N.C., 1993; HelpCenter mgr. desktop and consumer sys. support IBM Personal Computer Co., 1993-96, call ctr. brand ops. mgr., 1996-97; solution mgr. product support svcs. IBM Global Svcs., Cary, N.C., 1997-98, tech. solutions mgr. profl. svcs. Boulder, CO, 1999—. Author: Technical Coordinator Guidelines, 1984. Mem. Western Stark County Red Cross, Canton, 1980; v.p. Parents Without Ptnrs., Madison, 1991; vol. ARC, 1985—, Paint-A-Thon, Dane County, 1990, Badger State Games Challenge, 1992, Cystic Fibrosis Found. Gt. Strides, 1992—2002, Cystic Fibrosis Found. Mother's Day Tea, 1991, 1992, 1993, 1994, 1995, 1996, 1998, 2002, N.C. Sr. Olympics, 1998—2002, The Dorcas Shop, Cary, NC, 1999—2001, Susan G. Komen Race for the Cure, 2000—02; active Strong Women Organizing Outrageous Projects, 1998—2001; mem. St. Philip Parish Coun., Lewisville, Tex., 1988—89; pres., bd. dirs. Big Bros. and Sisters of Denton (Tex.) County, 1989, v.p., 1988, sec., 1987; founding bd. mem. Single Parents Network, 1991; mem. bd. dirs. Rape Crisis Ctr., Dane County, sec., 1990—91; bd. dirs. Carolina chpt. Cystic Fibrosis, 1996—2002. Mem. Italian-Am. Women's Club of Cary. Office: IBM Global Svcs 5600 N 63rd St Boulder CO 80314-0001 E-mail: shumick@us.ibm.com.

SHUMWAY, ERIC, academic administrator; BA, Brigham Young U., 1964, MA, 1966; PhD, U. Va., 1973. Pres. Brigham Young U.-Hawaii, 1994—. Office: Brigham Young U-Hawaii 55-20 Kulanui St Laie HI 96762 Office Fax: 808-293-3329. Business E-Mail: shumwaye@byuh.edu.*

SHUMWAY, SARA JANE, cardiothoracic surgeon; b. Lake Charles, La., Dec. 21, 1952; BS in Biol. Scis., Stanford U., 1975; MD, Vanderbilt U., 1979. Diplomate Am. Bd. Surgery, Am. Bd. Thoracic Surgery; lic. physician, Minn. Resident in gen. surgery Vanderbilt U. Affiliated Hosps., Nashville, 1979-82, 83-85; resident in cardiothoracic surgery, chief resident The Johns Hopkins Hosp., Balt., 1985-88; asst. prof. surgery U. Minn. Hosp. and Clinic, Mpls., 1988-93, assoc. prof. surgery, 1993-96, assoc. mem. grad. faculty, 1996—, prof., 1996—. Author: (with Norman Shumway) Thoracic Transplantation, 1995; author numerous book chpts., abstracts, presentations in field; guest reviewer The Annals of Thoracic Surgery, 1992, mem. editl. bd. Clin. Transplantation, 1992—. Mem. Am. Assn. for Thoracic Surgery, Am. Surg. Assn. Home: 1925 James Ave S Minneapolis MN 55403-2852 Office: U Minn Mayo Mail Code 207 420 Delaware St SE Minneapolis MN 55455-0374

SHUNG, KOPING KIRK, engineering educator; b. Kiangsi, China, June 2, 1945; s. Fu-Ya and Hsueh-Quen (Li) S.; m. Linda M. Shaw, Mar. 20, 1971; children: Albert, Simon, May. BSEE, Cheng-Kung U., Tainan, Taiwan, 1968; MSEE, U. Mo., 1970; PhD, U. Wash., 1975. Rsch. engr. Providence Med. Ctr., Seattle, 1975-79; asst. prof. Pa. State U., University Park, 1979-85, assoc. prof., 1985-89, prof. bioenring., 1989-2000, disting. prof., 2001—02; prof. biomed. engring. U. So. Calif., L.A., 2002—. Study sect. mem. NIH, Bethesda, Md., 1998—2002. Author: Principles of Medical Imaging, 1992; editor: Ultrasonic Scattering in Tissues, 1993; assoc. editor IEEE Trans., 1998—; mem. editl. bd. Jour. Ultrasound in Med. Biology, 1999—. Fellow IEEE (early career achievement award 1985), Am. Inst. Ultrasound in Medicine, Acoustical Soc. Am., Am. Inst. Med. and Biol. Engring. Democrat. Baptist. Home: 881 Holladay Way Monterey Park CA 91754 Office: Univ So Calif 500 Olin Hall Los Angeles CA 90089 E-mail: kshung@bmsr.usc.edu.

SHUR, MICHAEL, electrical engineer, educator, consultant; b. Kamensk-Uralski, Sverdlovsk, USSR, Nov. 13, 1942; came to U.S., 1976. s. Saul and Anna (Katz) S.; m. Paulina Gimmelfarb, Sept. 25, 1966; children: Luba, Natasha. MS, Leningrad Elec. Tech. Inst., 1965; PhD, Ioffe Inst., Leningrad, 1967; DSc, Ioffe Inst., St. Petersburg, 1992; Hon. Doctorate, St. Petersburg State Tech. U., 1994. Scientist Ioffe Inst., 1965-75; asst. prof. Wayne State U., Detroit, 1976-77, Oakland U., Rochester, Mich., 1978; prof. U. Minn., Mpls., 1979-92; John Marshall Money prof. U. Va., Charlottesville, Va., 1989-96; Patricia W. and C. Sheldon Roberts prof. Rennselaer Poly. Inst., 1996—; assoc. dir., prof. physics. and info. tech. Ctr. Integrated Electronics and Electronics Mfg., 1997—. Author: 17 books; co-author; editor; editor-in-chief Internat. Jour. High Speed Electronics and Systems, mem. hon. editl. bd. Solid State Electronics, Internat. Semiconductor Device Rsch. Symposium; contbr. articles. Recipient Van Der Ziel award, ISDRS, 1999. Fellow: IEEE (v.p. pubs. IEEE Sensor Coun., assoc. editor IEEE Trans. 1990—93), Am. Phys. Soc.; mem.: ASEE, Internat. Soc. Optical Engring., Electrochem. Soc., Materials Rsch. Soc., Sigma Xi, Tau Beta Pi, Eta Kappa Nu. E-mail: shurm@rpi.edu. *When we were penniless refugees, the United States adopted me and my family with compassion and friendship, gave us work and citizenship. Our debt of gratitude to the American people who accepted us as their own we will never be able to repay.*

SHURBAJI, M. SALAH, pathologist; b. Cairo, 1957; came to U.S., 1984; BS with distinction, Am. U. Beirut, 1979, MS, 1981, MD with distinction, 1984. Diplomate Am. Bd. Pathology; cert. cytopathologist, anatomic and clin. pathologist; lic. physician Md., Tenn., Mich. Intern Am. U. Beirut Med. Ctr., 1983-84; resident pathology Johns Hopkins Hosp., Balt., 1984-87, resident dept. lab. medicine, 1987-89; clin. fellow dept. pathology Johns Hopkins U. Sch. Medicine, 1984-89, rsch. fellow dept. pathology, 1989-90; asst. prof. pathology East Tenn. State U., Johnson City, 1990-94, assoc. prof. pathology, 1994-2000; prof. pathology, 2000—; staff pathologist Univ. Physicians Practice Group, Johnson City, 1990—. Staff pathologist Vets. Affairs Med. Ctr., Johnson City, 1990—, acting chief pathology and lab. medicine svc., 1993-94, chief pathology and lab. medicine svc., 1994—. Contbr. articles to profl. jours. Fellow Am. Soc. Clin. Pathologists, Coll. Am. Pathologists; mem. A.P. Stout Soc. Surg. Pathologists, Am. Soc. Cytopathology, U.S. and Can. Acad. Pathology, Papanicolaou Soc. Cytopathology, Internat. Soc. Urologic Pathology, Sigma Xi, Alpha Omega Alpha. Achievements include contribution to understanding of certain factors that affect the prognosis of neoplasms especially prostate cancer. Office: East Tenn State U Coll Med Dept Pathology PO Box 70568 Johnson City TN 37614-1707

SHURE, MYRNA BETH, psychologist, educator; b. Chgo., Sept. 11, 1937; d. Sidney Natkin and Frances (Laufman) Shure. Student, U. Colo., 1955; BS, U. Ill., 1959; MS, Cornell U., 1961, PhD, 1966. Lic. psychologist Pa. Asst. prof. U. R.I.; head tchr. Nursery Sch., Kingston, 1961-62; asst. prof. Temple U., Phila., 1966-67, assoc. prof., 1967-68; instr. Hahnemann Med. Coll., 1968-69, sr. instr. psychology, 1969-70, asst. prof., 1970-73, assoc. prof., 1973-80, prof., 1980—2002, Drexel U., Phila., 2002—. Spl. cons. PBS Children's TV Show The Puzzle Place. Author (with George Spivack): Social Adjustment of Young Children, 1974; author: (with George Spivack and Jerome Platt) The Problem Solving Approach to Adjustment, 1976; author: (with George Spivack) Problem Solving Techniques in Childrearing, 1978; author: (child curricula manual) I Can Problem Solve, 1992; author: (trade book) Raising a Thinking Child, 1994; author: (audiotape, workbook, paperback) Raising a Thinking Preteen, 2000 (Parents' Choice award, 2001). Recipient Lela Rowland Prevention award, Nat. Mental Health Assn., 1982, Sarah award, Women in Comm. (Phila. chpt., 1998, Psychology in the Media award, Pa. Psychol. Assn., 1999; grantee rsch. grant, NIMH, 1971—75, 1977—79, 1982—85, 1987, 1988—93. Fellow: APA (divsn. clin. psychology, child sect. 1994, Disting. Contbn. award divsn. cmty. psychology 1984, Task Force on Prevention award 1987, Task Force on Model Programs award 1994, U. Utah and Juvenile Justice Dept. of Delinquency Prevention award 1996, U.S. Dept. Edn. award 2001); mem.: Ctr. for Substance Abuse Prevention, Phila. Soc. Clin. Psychologists, Soc. Rsch. in Child Devel., Nat. Assn. Edn. Young Children, Nat. Assn. Sch. Psychologists. E-mail: mshure@drexel.edu.

SHUREN, JEFFREY ELIOT, behavioral neurologist, lawyer; b. Bklyn., June 19, 1963; m. Allison Weber, Aug. 31, 1991. BS, Northwestern U., Evanston, Ill., 1985; MD, Northwestern U., Chgo., 1987; JD, U. Mich., 1998. Diplomate Am. Bd. Psychiatry and Neurology. Asst. prof. dept. neurology U. Cin., Coll. Medicine; med. officer, Office Policy Food and Drug Adminstrn.; divsn. dir. coverage and analysis group Ctrs. Medicare and Med. Svcs. Mem. Am. Acad. Neurology, Internat. Neuropsychol. Soc., Alpha Omega Alpha. Office: 7500 Security Blvd Baltimore MD 21244-1850

SHURLEY, JAY TALMADGE, writer, retired psychiatrist, medical educator, administrator, behavioral scientist, polar explorer, genealogist; b. Sonora, Tex., Dec. 20, 1917; s. Ira L. and Jewell L. (Choate) S.; m. Erwina Bode Cornelison, Dec. 20, 1986. BA in Zoology, U. Tex.-Austin, 1940; MD, U. Tex. Med. Br., Galveston, 1942. Diplomate Am. Bd. Psychiatry and Neurology. Intern. Ind. U.-Indpls. Med. Ctr., 1943; Rockefeller fellow in neuropsychiatry dept. mental and nervous disease Inst. for Mental Hygiene Pa. Hosp., Phila., 1944-47; pvt. practice medicine specializing in psychiatry and psychoanalysis, 1947-51, Austin, 1951-52; pvt. practice medicine specializing in psychiatry San Antonio, 1952-54, Chevy Chase, Md., 1955-57; pvt. practice medicine specializing in psychiatry, psychoanalysis and sleep disorders medicine Oklahoma City, 1978-90; acting chief lab. adult psychiat. investigation, clin. investigations NIMH, NIH, Bethesda, 1955-57; chief psychiatry service and mental hygiene clinic VA Hosp., Oklahoma City, 1957-62; sr. med. investigator in psychiatry, research service, dept. medicine and surgery VA, 1962-76; founder and dir. behavioral sci. labs VA Med. Ctr., Oklahoma City, 1962-78; sci. dir. Oklahoma Mental Health Research Inst., Oklahoma Dept. Mental Health, 1988-89; cons.-liaison in geropsychiatry O'Donoghue Rehab. Inst., Okla. Med. Ctr., 1990-91; med. dir. emeritus Willow View Mental Health Ctr., Oklahoma City, 1985-87; prof. psychiatry Coll. Medicine U. Okla., 1957-77, prof. psychiatry and behavioral scis. Coll. of Medicine and Grad. Coll., 1977-81; prof. emeritus psychiatry and behavioral scis. U. Okla. Coll. Medicine, 1981—. Adj. prof. human ecology Coll. Health, U. Okla., 1967-81; mem. com. on polar rsch. NAS/NRC, 1970-74; U.S. rep. Working Group on Human Biology and Medicine XII Sci. Com. on Antarctic Rsch., Canberra and Melbourne, Australia, 1972; U.S. rep. Working Group on Human Biology and Medicine XIII Sci. Com. on Antarctic Rsch., Jackson Hole, Wyo., 1974; disting. vis. scientist program in human biology Acad. Scis. USSR, Moscow and Leningrad, 1972; Centennial Yr. vis. prof. dept. psychol. medicine U. Otago, Dunedin, N.Z., 1975; mem. Health Rsch. Com., Okla. Ctr. for Sci. and Tech., 1986-91, Okla. Alzheimer Rsch. Adv. Coun., 1990-92. Editor: Relating Environment to Mental Health and Illness: The Eco-psychiatric Data Base, 1979, Symposium on Man on the South Polar Plateau, 1970; mem. editorial bd. Jour. Clin. Psychology, 1970-80; contbr. more than 100 articles to sci. publs. Capt. M.C. U.S. Army, 1952-54. Recipient Antarctic Svc. medal NSF/NAS, 1970, Disting. Profl. Svc. award Okla. Psychol. Assn., 1972, Sustained Superior Achievement cert. VA, 1974, Disting. Psychiatrist award Mid-Continent Psychiat. Assn., 1986, Okla. Psychiat. Assn., 1990, Sealy Inc. prize Assn. Profl. Sleep Socs., 1991; Shurley Ridge, Pensacola Mountains Antarctica named in his honor. Fellow Am. Psychiat. Assn. (life), Am. Coll. Psychiatrists (life); mem. AMA, Oklahoma County Med. Soc., Okla. State Med. Assn. (life), Okla. Psychiat. Assn. (pres. 1968, chair ethics com. 1989-91), Faculty House Club, Sigma Xi, Alpha Omega Alpha, Alpha Epsilon Delta. Democrat. Address: 4400 N Indiana Oklahoma City OK 73118-2222 E-mail: jshurl441@cox.net.

SHURN, PETER JOSEPH, III, lawyer; b. Queens, N.Y., Aug. 30, 1946; s. Peter J. Jr. and Vivienne M. (Tagliarino) Shurn; m. Ingrid Kelbert; children: Steven Douglas, Vanessa Leigh, David Michael. BSEE magna cum laude, Poly. Inst. Bklyn., 1974; JD magna cum laude, New Eng. Sch. Law, 1977; LLM in Patent and Trade Regulation Law, George Washington U., 1981. Bar: N.C. 1977, Va. 1979, Tex. 1982. Rsch. scientist GTE Labs., 1965-77; pvt. practice Raleigh, NC, 1977-78; assoc. Burns, Doane, Swecker & Mathis, Alexandria, Va., 1978-80; tech. advisor to judge U.S. Ct. Appeals (fed. cir.), 1980-81; ptnr. Arnold, White & Durkee, Houston, 1981-2000, Howrey, Simon, Arnold and White LLP, Houston, 2000—01. Adj. prof. S. Tex. Coll. Law, 1984—88, 2000—; invited mem. nat. panel neutrals Am. Arbitration Assn., 1993—; arbitrator Nat. Patent Bd., 1999—. Contbr. articles to profl. jours. With U.S. Army, 1966—68. Fellow: Coll. State Bar Tex., Houston Bar Found. (life); mem.: IEEE, ABA, ATLA, Houston Patent Law Assn., Am. Patent Law Assn. (Robert C. Watson award 1981), Houston Patent Law Assn., Sigma Xi. Office: 14138 Heatherfield Dr Houston TX 77079-6805 E-mail: pjshurn@ieee.org.

SHURTLEFF, AKIKO AOYAGI, artist, consultant; b. Tokyo, Jan. 24, 1950; d. Kinjiro and Fumiyo (Sugata) Aoyagi; m. William Roy Shurtleff, Mar. 10, 1977 (div. Jan. 1995); 1 child Joseph Aoyagi. Grad., Women's Coll. Art, Tokyo, 1971; student, Acad. Art, San Francisco, 1991-92. Fashion designer, illustrator Marimura Co. and Hayakawa Shoji, Inc., Tokyo, 1970-72; co-founder, art dir. Soyfoods Ctr. consulting svcs., Lafayette, Calif., 1976-94; freelance illustrator, graphic designer. Lectr. U.S. Internat. Christian U., Tokyo, 1977, Japanese Tofu Mfrs. Conv., Osaka, 1978; presenter cooking demonstrations; tchr. cooking classes. Avocations: walking, running, dancing, designing company logos. Office: PO Box 443 Lafayette CA 94549-0443 E-mail: akiko1717@aol.com.

SHURTLEFF, C. MICHAEL, writer; b. Oslo, July 3, 1937; came to the U.S., 1940; s. Charles Joseph and Ruth (Mathison) S. BA, Lawrence U.; MFA, Yale U. Casting dir. David Merrick, Bob Fosse, Stuart Ostrow, Peter Glenville, Gower Champion, N.Y.C., 1959-79; pvt. Broadway casting cons.; ret. Lectr., tchr. various locations. Author: Audition, 1979 (Best Seller), Taking Care of Yourself, 1997; author (plays) Call Me By My Rightful Name, 1961, Sailing, 1996, Entertaining Angels, 1996, Driving Yourself Crazy, The Mischief Makers, (essays) Eclectics, 1999. Avocations: disco dancing, swimming, gardening. Home: 6619 Cahuenga Ter Hollywood CA 90068-2746

SHURTLEFF, DAVID, pediatrician, educator; b. Fall River, Mass., July 1, 1930; s. Bertrand Leolie Shurtleff and Hope Seal; m. Cynthia Helen Fuquet, June 10, 1952; children: Michael David, Hillary Anne, Matthew David. MD, Tufts U., 1955. Diplomate Am. Bd. Pediats. Resident in pediats. Mass. Gen. Hosp., Boston, 1955—57; chief pediat. resident U. Wash., Seattle, 1957—58, prof. dept. pediats., 1960—, head divsn. congenital defects, 1963—87, mem. grad. faculty, 1978—; mem. staff Children's Hosp. and Regional Med. Ctr., 1960—, Harbor View Med. Ctr., Seattle, 1960—, U. Wash. Med. Ctr., Seattle, 1960—. Chmn. profl. adv. com. Spina Bifida Assn. Am., 1978—91; vis. scientist Nat. Inst. Neurol. Diseases, Washington, 1970; vis. prof. Welch Nat. Sch. Medicine, Wales, 1969; Raimondi guest lectr. Am. Assn. Neurol. Surgeons, 1999; presenter, spkr., lectr. in field. Contbr. more than 100 articles to profl. publs.; author: 26 texts and chpts. in texts. Chmn. med. adv. com. Devel. and Disabilities Coun. Wash. State. Maj. Med. Corps U.S. Army, 1960, 58. Recipient Best Genetics Rsch. award, Soc. Perinatal Obs., 1989. Fellow: Soc. Rsch. into Spina Bifida Assn. (Casey Holter lectr.), Am. Acad. Pediats. (emeritus). Methodist. Achievements include research in management of patients with myelomeningocele and hydroencephalus. Avocations: fishing, hunting. Office: U Wash Sch Medicine Seattle WA 98195-0001

SHURTLEFF, JOHN HOWARD, lawyer; b. Wheaton, Ill., June 27, 1928; m. Joan Fagerburg, Oct. 17,1953; children: Karin, Robert Scot. BS in Chem. Engring., U. Ill., 1950; JD, DePaul, 1955. Bar: Ill. 1955, U.S. Patent Office, 1955, U.S. Dist. Ct. (no. dist.) Ill. 1965, U.S. Ct. Appeals (fed. cir.) 1965. Engr. Underwriters Labs., Chgo., 1950-51; assoc., ptnr. Marzall, Johnston, Cook & Root and succeeding firms., 1954-78; prin. Law Offices of John H. Shurtleff, 1978-2001; ret., 2002. Pres. Riverside (Ill.) Community Fund, 1964-65; mem. S.W. Suburban Mental Health Assn., Lyons and Riverside Twp., 1966-70; Riverside Zoning Commn. and Bd. Appeals, 1969-96, Community Family Service and Mental Health Ctr., Lyons and RiversideTwp. (v.p. 1970-71, pres. 1971-73); trustee Riverside Pub. Libr., 1974-78. With U.S. Army, 1952-54. Mem. ABA, Am. Patent Law Assn. (chmn. com. for indsl. design protection 1988-89), Am. Chem. Soc., Chgo. Bar Assn., Patent Law Assn. Chgo., Internat. Brotherhood Magicians, Masons, Sigma Phi Delta. Republican. Methodist.

SHURTLEFF, MALCOLM C. plant pathologist, consultant, educator, extension specialist; b. Fall River, Mass., June 24, 1922; s. Malcolm C. and Florence L. (Jewell) S.; m. Margaret E. Johnson, June 14, 1950; m. Freda L. Nothnagel, Aug. 1, 1998; children: Robert Glen, Janet Lee, Mark Steven. BS in Biology, U. R.I., 1943; MS in Plant Pathology, U. Minn., 1950, PhD in Plant Pathology, 1953. Asst. plant pathologist Conn. Agrl. Expt. Sta., New Haven, 1942, R.I. Agrl. Expt. Sta., Kingston, 1943; asst. extension prof. U. R.I., 1950-54; assoc. extension prof. Iowa State U., Ames, 1954-61; prof. plant pathology U. Ill., Champaign-Urbana, 1961-92, prof. emeritus, 1992—; cons., writer Urbana, 1992-98. Adj. prof. Tex. A&M U., College Station, 1998—. Author: How To Control Plant Diseases, 1962, 66 (award Am. Garden Guild 1962, 66), How To Control Lawn Diseases and Pests, 1973, How To Control Tree Diseases and Pests, 1975, Controlling Turfgrass Pests, 1987, 97, 2002, A Glossary of Plant Pathological Terms, 1997, The Plant Disease Clinic and Field Diagnosis of Abiotic Diseases, 1997, Diagnosing Plant Diseases Caused by Nematodes, 2000; editor-in-chief Phytopathology News, 1966-69, Plant Disease, 1969-72; contbr. numerous articles to encys., profl. publs. and mags. Lt. (j.g.) USN, 1943-46, PTO. Recipient Disting. Svc. award USDA, Washington, 1986, E.C. Stakman award U. Minn., 2000. Fellow Am. Phytopathological Soc. (councilor at large 1970-71, Excellence in Extension Plant Pathology award 1991); mem. Internat. Soc. Plant Pathology (chmn. extension com. 1975-80), Am. Phytopathological Soc. (mem. various coms.). Avocation: photography. Home: 6730 Heron Ln Pearland TX 77584-6618 E-mail: lmshurt@aol.com.

SHURTLEFF, MARK L. state attorney general; BA, Brigham Young U.; JD, U. Utah. Officer, atty. JAG USN, 1985—90; pvt. practice in law Calif., 1990—93; asst. atty. gen. State of Utah, 1993—97; dep. county atty. Salt Lake County, 1997—98; commr. Salt Lake County Commn., 1999—2000, chmn., 2000; atty. gen. State of Utah, 2001—. Leader Boy Scout troops, 1980—; anti-drug lectr., at-risk youth mentor. Office: State Capitol Bldg Rm 236 Salt Lake City UT 84114*

SHURTLIFF, MARVIN KARL, lawyer; b. Idaho Falls, Idaho, Nov. 6, 1939; s. Noah Leon and Melba Dorothy (Hunting) S.; m. Peggy J. Griffin, Nov. 23, 1963; 1 dau., Jennifer Karyl. BA, Idaho State Coll., 1962; JD, U. Idaho, 1968. Bar: Idaho 1968. Tchr. pub. schs., Jefferson County, Idaho, 1964-65; atty. U.S. Dept. Justice, Washington, 1968-74; commr. Idaho Pub. Utilities Commn., 1974-75, pres., 1975-76; spl. asst., legal counsel Gov. of Idaho, Boise, 1977; U.S. atty. for Dist. of Idaho, 1977-81; practice law, 1981—. Mem. Idaho Ho. of Reps., 1962-64 Mem. Idaho State Bd. Edn., 1990—95, Idaho Commn. on Redistricting, 2001. Mem. Idaho Bar Assn. Democrat. Home: 62 Horizon Dr Boise ID 83702-4419 Office: PO Box 1652 Boise ID 83701-1652

SHURTZ, STEVEN PARK, lawyer; b. Panquitch, Utah, Jan. 23, 1956; s. Doyle Park and Loree (Munson) S.; m. Jane Wanee Welch, Dec. 29, 1978; children: Thomas Park, Melissa Jane, Amy Marie, Timothy Evan, Stephanie Ann, Richard Steven, Kimberly Rae, Nathan Samuel. BS in Chem. Engring., U. Utah, 1980, JD, 1983. Bar: Ill. 1983, Utah 1997, U.S. Dist. Ct. (no. dist.) Ill. 1983, U.S. Dist. Ct. Utah 1997, U.S. Patent & Trademark Office 1984, U.S. Ct. Appeals (fed. cir.) 1989. Assoc. Brinks Hofer Gilson & Lione, Chgo., 1983-88, shareholder, 1989—. Mem. ABA, Am. Intellectual Property Law Assn., Chgo. Bar Assn. Mem. Lds Ch. Home: 1040 W Austin Ln Palatine IL 60067-5802 Office: Brinks Hofer Gilson & Lione Ste 3600 455 N City Front Plaza Dr Chicago IL 60611 E-mail: sshurtz@brinkshofer.com.

SHUSHKEWICH, KENNETH WAYNE, structural engineer; b. Winnipeg, Man., Sept. 22, 1952; m. Valdine Cuffe, Sept. 28, 1980. BSCE, U. Man., Winnipeg, 1974; MS in Structural Engring., U. Calif., Berkeley, 1975; PhD in Structural Engring., U. Alta., Edmonton, Can., 1985. Engr. Wardrop and Assocs., Winnipeg, 1974-78, Preconsult Can., Montreal, Que., 1978-80; prof. U. Alta., 1981-85, U. Man., 1985-87; engr. T.Y. Lin Internat., San Francisco, 1988-90, H.J. Degenkolb Assocs., San Francisco, 1990-92, Ben C. Gerwick, Inc., San Francisco, 1993-94, J. Muller Internat., Chgo., 1994-95, T.Y. Lin Internat., San Francisco, 1995—. Mem. bridge design com., prestressed concrete com. ASCE-Am. Concrete Inst. Prin. works include design of prestressed concrete segmental bridges, seismic strengthening of San Francisco Ferry Building damaged in Loma Prieta earthquake, seismic retrofit of Presidio Viaduct in San Francisco; design mgr. for long-span west approach bridge of Northumberland Strait Crossing in Can.; contbr. articles to profl. jours. Recipient award for design of Vierendeel truss bridge, Man. Design Inst., 1977. Mem. ASCE, Am. Concrete Inst., Prestressed Concrete Inst., Internat. Assn. Bridge and Structural Engrs. Office: PO Box 2590 San Francisco CA 94126-2590

SHUSS, JANE MARGARET, artist; b. Ost, Kans., Feb. 15, 1936; d. Leo and Mary Catharine Nett; m. Robert Hamilton Shuss, Feb. 19, 1954; children: Patric, Andrea, Matt, Lisa, Robert, Eric. Student, Otis Art Inst., L.A. Sec. Found. for Plein Air Painting, Avalon, Calif., 1995-97. One-woman shows include Challis Galleries, Laguna Beach, Calif., 1981, 1982, 1983, Esther Wells Gallery, 1984, 1985, 1986, 1987, exhibited in group shows at Plein Air Painters of Am., 1985, 1986, 1987, 1988, 1989, 1990, 1991, 1992, 1993, 1994, 1995, 1996, 1997, 1998—99, 2000, 2001, Western Acad. Women Artists, 1996, O'Brien's Gallery, Scottsdale, Ariz., 1996, Desert Caballeros Mus., 1997, 1998. Mem. Am. Acad. Women Artists (signature mem.), Soc. Am. Impressionists, Plein Air Painters Am. (treas. 1996-97, signature mem.), Calif. Art Club. Republican.

SHUSS, JOHN LOGAN, surgeon; b. Kansas City, Dec. 7, 1949; s. J. Logan and Marian Ruth (Brain) S.; m. Linda Lea Trower, Sept. 6, 1980; 1 child, Samantha Lea. BA, U. Kans., 1972; MD, U. Kans., Kansas City, 1975. Resident in gen. surgery La. State U., New Orleans, 1975-76, U. Kans. Coll. Health Scis., 1976-80; surgeon Garden City, Kans., 1980-85, Twin Falls (Idaho) Clinic and Hosp., 1985—2001, Magic Valley Regional Med. Ctr., 2002—. Fellow Am. Coll. Surgeons (pres. Idaho chpt. 1995-96), Southwestern Surg. Conf.; mem. Soc. Am. Gastrointestinal Endoscopic Surgeons, Soc. Laparoendoscopic Surgeons, Phi Beta Kappa. Avocations: skiing, white water rafting, tennis, golf. Home: 3185 Boehm Estate Dr Twin Falls ID 83301-8122 Office: Twin Falls Clinic & Hosp 660 Shoshone St E Twin Falls ID 83301-6110

SHUSTER, ALVIN, journalist, newspaper editor; b. Washington, Jan. 25, 1930; s. Fred and Dora (Levy) S.; m. Miriam Schwartz, June 22, 1952; children: Fred, Jessica, Beth. AB, George Washington U., 1951. Reporter Washington Bur. N.Y. Times, 1952-61, asst. news editor, 1961-66, reporter London Bur., 1967-70; bur. chief Saigon, Vietnam, 1970-71, London, 1971-75, Rome, 1975-77; dep. editor editorial pages L.A. Times, 1977-83, fgn. editor, 1983-95, sr. consulting editor, 1995—. Pres. Fgn. Corrs. Assn., London, 1973-74; trustee Monterey (Calif.) Inst. Internat. Studies, 1983-99; chmn. Pulitzer Prize Jury Internat. Reporting, 1999. Editor: The Witnesses, 1964, Washington: The New York Times Guide to the Nations' Capital, 1967, International Press Institute Report, 1995—; contbg. author: The Kennedy Years, 1964; contbg. editor Columbia Journalism Rev., 1999—. Nieman fellow Harvard U., 1966-67. Mem. Reform Club (London). Office: Los Angeles Times Times Mirror Sq Los Angeles CA 90053

SHUSTER, FRED TODD, journalist, commentator; b. Washington, Jan. 10, 1956; s. Alvin and Miriam (Schwartz) S. BA in English Lit., San Francisco State U., 1979. News asst. AP, L.A., 1985-87; reporter Simi Valley (Calif.) Enterprise, 1987-89; music critic L.A. Daily News, 1989—; instr. entertainment writing UCLA, 2002—. Radio corres. Greater London Radio, 1995-99; west coast bur. chief Down Beat Mag., Chgo., 1993-99. Recipient 2d pl. writing award Stuttering Found. Am., Memphis, 1996. Jewish. Avocation: playing jazz guitar. Office: LA Daily News 21221 Oxnard St Woodland Hills CA 91367-5015

SHUSTER, FREDERICK, retired internist, gastroenterologist; b. Newark, Sept. 12, 1933; s. Ralph and Ane (Weinstein) S.; m. Jane B. Block, June 11, 1958; children: Alan R., Robert G. BS, Rutgers U., 1955; MD, U. Chgo., 1959. Diplomate Am. Bd. Internal Medicine, Am. Bd. Gastroenterology. Intern U. Mich. Hosp., Ann Arbor, 1959-60, resident internal medicine, 1960-62; resident gastroenterology VA Hosp. U. Miami, Fla., 1962-63; pvt. practice N. Miami Beach, 1963-97; from clin. instr. to assoc. prof. medicine U. Miami, 1963—; pvt. practice Aventura, 1997-98; ret., 1998. Chmn. dept. medicine Parkway Regional Med. Ctr., N. Miami Beach, 1967, 70, chief of staff, 1974-75, chief divsn. gastroenterology, 1976-77, chmn. pharmacy and therapeutics com., 1978-98. Chmn. med. advisory com. Crohn's and Colitis Found., S. Fla. chpt., Miami, 1979-81. Major U.S. Army, 1967-69. Recipient Physician's Recognition award in Continuing Edn., AMA, Chgo., 1970—. Fellow Am. Coll. Physicians, Am. Coll. Gastroenterology, Alpha Omega Alpha. Jewish. Avocations: bowling, ballroom dancing. E-mail: fred991@att.net.

SHUSTER, JOHN A. civil engineer; b. Santa Fe, Jan. 18, 1939; s. William H. and Selma (Dingee) S.; m. Carol Habberley, July 1958 (div. Feb. 1960); m. Susan Handy, Aug. 20, 1962 (div. May 1992); children: David Brian, Karen; m. Barbara Yentzer, June 6, 1999. Student, U. N.Mex., 1961-63; BCE, U. Alaska, 1965; MCE, Stanford U., 1966. Registered profl. engr., Alaska, Calif., R.I., Mass., Va., Wash., Wis., Md., Del. Diplomate Am. Coll. Forensic Examiners. Project engr. Woodward Clyde Assocs., Oakland, Calif., 1966-67, sr. project engr., 1969-72; resident project engr. Soil Cons. of S.E. Asia, Bangkok, Thailand, 1967-69; v.p. engring. Am. Drilling Co., Providence, 1972-74, also bd. dirs.; exec. v.p. Terrafreeze Corp., Lorton, Va., 1974-79, also bd. dirs.; pres. Geocentric Engring. Corp., Newington, 1979-89; ind. profl. engr. Internat. Cons. Practice, Mason Neck, 1989-91; pres. Geofreeze, Inc., 1991—. Vis. lectr. on constrn. ground freezing and related techs., numerous univs. and profl. assns., 1975-88; bd. dirs. Geofreeze Corp., Lorton. Contbr. numerous tech. papers to internat. confs. Bd. dirs. Harbor View Civic Assn., Lorton, 1974-79; sect. dir. Operation Zap The Blackstone, Providence, 1972. Served with U.S. Army, 1957-61. Mem. ASCE, Internat. Soc. Soil Mechanics and Founds., Engring. Inst. Can., Am. Underground Space Assn. (charter), Deep Founds. Inst., Nat. Rsch. Coun. Transp. Rsch. Bd., Internat. Organizing Com. for Ground Freezing (internat. contractors rep.), Harbor View Recreation Club (bd. dirs. 1977-80). Democrat. Unitarian Universalist. Avocations: boating, fishing, skiing, motorcycling. E-mail: jshuster@geofreeze.com.

SHUSTER, MARGUERITE, minister, educator; b. Oxnard, Calif., Sept. 10, 1947; d. Carroll Lloyd and Grace Margaret (Hornbeck) S. BA (great distinction), Stanford U., 1968; MDiv, Fuller Sem., Pasadena, Calif., 1975; PhD, Fuller Grad. Sch. Psychology, Pasadena, Calif., 1977. Ordained to ministry Presbyn. Ch. (U.S.A.), 1980. From asst. to assoc. pastor Arcadia (Calif.) Presbyn. Ch., 1980-86; pastor Knox Presbyn. Ch., Pasadena, Calif., 1987-92; adjunct asst. prof. of preaching Fuller Sem., 1988-90; assoc. prof. preaching Fuller Theol. Sem., 1992-2001, prof. preaching, 2001. Del. gen. Assembly Mission Consultation Planning Team, 1984—85, Inst. Ecumenical and Cultural Rsch., Collegeville, Minn., 1985, Collegeville, 86; com. chair Gen. Assembly, 1988; Staley lectr. Sterling Coll., 2001. Author: Power, Pathology, Paradox, 1987; mem. editl. bd.: Theology, News and Notes, 1986—; contbr. articles sermons, and revs. in religious jours. and books; editor (contbr.): Perspectives on Christology, 1991—, Who We Are; Our Dignity as Human, 1996—. Named one of Outstanding Young Women in Am., 1979, 83. Mem. Presbytery of San Gabriel (chair, com. on ministry 1991, moderator, permenent jud. commn. 1993-95, moderator Presbytery 1996), Phi Beta Kappa. Home: 675 Mount Wilson Trl Sierra Madre CA 91024-1232 Office: Fuller Theol Sem 135 N Oakland Ave Pasadena CA 91182-0001 E-mail: shuster@fuller.edu. *A goal: so to trust in Jesus Christ, especially in times of sorrow and disappointment, that others might find it easier rather than more difficult to believe in a loving, omnipotent God.*

SHUSTER, ROBERT G. electronics company executive, consultant; b. N.Y.C., June 1, 1927; s. Robert Chandler and Therese G. (Giraud); m. Marianne B. Lynski, Apr. 20, 1970 (div. Jan. 1987); m. H. Elizabeth Young, May 20, 1989 (div. Dec. 1995); m. Erika Megas, May 5, 2002. BSEE, CCNY, 1948; MSEE, Columbia U., 1955, postgrad., 1959-64. Test engr. Elec. Testing Labs., N.Y.C., 1948-50; project leader Sperry Gyroscope Co., Great Neck, N.Y., 1950-59; project mgr. RCA Advanced Communications Lab., N.Y.C., 1959-67; prin. scientist Tracor, Inc., Rockville, Md., 1967-75, v.p. electronics systems div., 1975-87; pres. Tracor Tech. Resources, Inc., 1984-90, RGS Assocs., McLean, Va., 1990—; v.p. C-Cubed Corp., Alexandria, 1990-93, pres., 1993-95; sr. cons., 1996—. Mem. IEEE (sr.), N.Y. Acad. Scis. Avocations: photography, hiking.

SHUSTER, WILLIAM (BILL SHUSTER), congressman; b. McKeesport, Pa., Jan. 10, 1961; m. Rebecca Shuster; children: Ali, Garrett. BA, Dickinson Coll., Carlisle, Pa., 1983; MBA, American U., Washington, DC. Mgr. retail stores Goodyear Tire and Rubber Corporation; dist. mgr. Bandag Inc.; mem. U.S. Congress from 9th Pa. , 2001—. Mem. com. on Transp. & Infrastructure and Small Bus., subcommittees on Highway & Transit, Water Resources & Environment, Aviation, Rural Enterprises, Agriculture and Tech. Office: US House Representatives 2188 Rayburn House Office Building Washington DC 20515-3809*

SHUSTERMAN, NATHAN, life underwriter, financial consultant; b. Montreal, Que., Can., Aug. 27, 1927; came to U.S., 1950; s. Aaron and Annie (Nulman) S.; m. Norma Thalblum, Jan. 1950; children: Mark D., Claudia S. Student, Sir George Williams Coll., Montreal, 1944-47; grad., N.Y. Inst. Fin. CLU, chartered fin. cons. Retailing mgr. Jefferson Stores, Miami, Fla., 1950-65; gen. agt. Protective Life Ins. Co., 1965—. Chmn. emeritus field adv. coun., past pres. Protective Club; fin. and estate planning cons.; pres. Am. Fin. Counseling Corp., Miami; instr. in estate and tax planning Am. Coll., Bryn Mawr, Pa., 1972—, U. Miami, Coral Gables, Fla., 1972—; registered rep. Pro Equity Services Inc. Named Man of Yr., Gen. Agts. and Mgrs. Assn., Miami, 1965-67. Mem. North Dade-South Broward Estate Planning Coun., Million Dollar Round Table (life), Top of Table, Assn. Advanced Life Underwriting, Soc. Fin. Svc. Profls. (past pres. Miami chpt.), Nat. Assn. Ins. and Fin. Advisors (Nat. Sales Achievement award, Nat. Quality award), Fla. Assn. Ins. and Fin. Advisors, Miami Assn. Ins. and Fin. Advisors, Internat. Assn. Fin. Planners, Am. Soc. Pension Actuaries (assoc.), Optimists (pres. North Miami Beach, Fla. chpt. 1971), Masons, Shriners, B'nai B'rith (pres. Miami chpt 1950). Home: 2320 NE 196th St Miami FL 33180-2132 Office: Am Fin Counseling Corp 16121 NE 18th Ave Miami FL 33162-4749

SHUSTERMAN, NEAL DOUGLAS, writer, screenwriter; b. N.Y.C., Nov. 12, 1962; s. Milton and Charlotte Ruth (Altman) S.; m. Elaine Gale Jones, Jan. 31, 1987; children: Brendan, Jarrod, Joelle, Erin. BA in Psychology and Drama, U. Calif., Irvine, 1985. Author, screenwriter, 1987—. Author: Guy Talk, 1987, The Shadow Club, 1988 (Children's CHoice award Internat.

Reading Assn. 1989), Dissidents, 1989, Speeding Bullet, 1991 (Best Book for Teens award N.Y. Pub. Libr., nominated Calif. Young Reader Medal 1995-96), Kid Heroes, 1991, What Daddy Did, 1991 (Best Book for Young Adults award ALA, Outstanding Work of Fiction award So. Calif. Coun. Lit. for Children and Young People, Children's Choice award and Young Adult Choice award Internat. Reading Assn., Pick of the List award ABA, Best Book for Teens award N.Y. Pub. Libr., Okla. Sequoyah award 1994), The Eyes of Kid Midas, 1992 (ALA Best Book for Reluctant Readers), Darkness Creeping, 1993, Piggyback Ninja, 1994, Scorpion Shards, 1995 (N.Y. Pub. Libr. Best Book for the Teenaged), Darkness Creeping II, 1995, Mindquakes, 1996 (ALA YALSA Quick Pick), Mindstorms, 1996, Mindtwisters, 1997, The Dark Side of Nowhere, 1997 (ALA Best Book, ALA Quick Pick--Top 10 Book), Thief of Souls, 1999, Downsiders, 1999 (ALA Best Book, ALA Quick Pick), Mind-Benders, 2000, The Shadow Club Rising, 2002, Shattered Sky, 2002; screenwriter: Double Dragon, 1992, Evolver, 1993; dir. Heart on a Chain, 1991 (Golden Eagle award CINE), What About the Sisters, 1993 (Golden Eagle award CINE), Games: How to Host a Teen Mystery, Hot Times at Hollywood High, 1994, Barbecue with the Vampire, 1997, Roswell that Ends Well, 1999, How to Host a Murder: Roman Ruins, 1996, The Good, the Bad and the Guilty, 1997, The Tragical Mystery Tour, 1998, The Maiming of the Shrew, 2000, Saturday Night Cleaver, 2000, (TV) Goosebumps: The Werewolf of Fever Swamp, 1996, Goosebumps: Night of the Living Dummy III, 1997, Animorphs (staff writer), 1998. Mem. PEN, Writers Guild Am. West, Soc. Children's Book Writers and Illustrators. Avocations: swimming, tennis, storytelling. Office: PO Box 18516 Irvine CA 92623-8516 E-mail: NStoryman@aol.com.

SHUSTERMAN, NEIL HOWARD, internist, nephrologist; b. Phila., Dec. 18, 1955; BS, Pa. State U., 1976; MD, Jefferson Med. Coll., Phila., 1978. Diplomate Am. Bd. Internal Medicine. Intern Lankenau Hosp., Wynnewood, Pa., 1978-79, resident in internal medicine, 1979-81; fellow in nephrology U. Pa., Phila., 1981-83, dir. dialysis program, 1986-89; dir. clin. investigation GlaxoSmithKline, Collegeville, 1989-93, group dir. clin. rsch., 1993-96, v.p. clin. rsch. and devel., 1996—2001; exec. dir. internal medicine Forest Labs., N.Y.C., 2001—. Contbr. chpt. to book Angiotensin II Receptors, 1994. Fellow ACP; mem . Am. Heart Assn., Am. Soc. Nephrology. Avocations: photography. Office: Forest Labs 909 3d Ave New York NY 10022 E-mail: neil.shuster@frx.com.

SHUSTERMAN, VLADIMIR, medical researcher; b. Novosibirsk, Russia, Jan. 7, 1963; s. Rafael Shusterman and Evgenia Gershenzon. MD, PhD, Novosibirsk State Med. Inst., 1985. Dir. noninvasive cardiac electrophysiology labs. U. Pitts., 1996—. Contbr. articles to profl. jours. Grantee Scientist Devel. grantee, Am. Heart Assn., 2000—03, rsch. grantee, Competitive Med. Rsch. Fund of U. Pitts., 2001—02, Pitts. Mind-Body Ctr., 2001—02. Mem.: Cardiac Electrophysiology Soc., N.Am. Soc. for Pacing and Electrophysiology. Achievements include patents for for prediction of cardiac arrhythmias; for prediction of life-threatening cardiac arrhythmias; device for multi-scale analysis and representation of electrocardiographic data. Office: U Pitts Rm B535 200 Lothrop St Pittsburgh PA 15213 Office Fax: 412-647-7979. E-mail: shustermanv@msx.upmc.edu.

SHUTE, RICHARD EMIL, government official, engineer; b. Bklyn., May 1, 1938; s. William Leonard and Doris (Schlichting) S.; m. Linda Janan McElhiney, Mar. 7, 1960. BS in Mech. Engring., U. Miami, 1960; MBA, Fla. State U., 1970. Registered profl. engr., Fla. Engr. Pratt and Whitney Aircraft, West Palm Beach, Fla., 1960-62, Gen. Dynamics Corp., San Diego, 1962-64; aerospace engr. NASA/Kennedy Space Ctr., Fla., 1964-71; dir. planning and evaluation Fla. Dept. Health and Human Services, Tallahassee, 1971-76; dir. office program devel. Office Human Devel., HHS, Washington, 1976-87; dir. office of mgmt. and info. systems U.S. Dept. Commerce, 1987-90; pres. Richard E. Shute and Assocs. Mgmt. Cons., 1990—. Recipient Superior Achievement award NASA, 1966; recipient Spl. Achievement award HHS, 1977, Sr. Exec. award HHS, 1982 Mem. SAE, Nat. Assn. Security Dealers (bd. arbitrators).

SHUTLER, MARY ELIZABETH, academic administrator; b. Oakland, Calif., Nov. 14, 1929; d. Hal Wilfred and Elizabeth Frances (Gimbel) Hall; m. Richard Shutler Jr., Sept. 8, 1951 (div. 1975); children: Kathryn Allice (dec.), John Hall, Richard Burnett. BA, U. Calif., Berkeley, 1951; MA, U. Ariz., 1958, PhD, 1967. Asst., assoc., full prof. anthropology, chmn. dept. San Diego State U., 1967-75; prof. anthropology, dept. chmn. Wash. State U., Pullman, 1975-80; dean Coll. Arts and Scis., prof. anthropology U. Alaska, Fairbanks, 1980-84; vice chancellor, dean of faculty, prof. anthropology U. Wis. Parkside, Kenosha, 1984-88; provost, v.p. for acad. affairs, prof. anthropology Calif. State U., L.A., 1988-94; provost West Coast U., 1994-97; dean Sch. of Arts and Scis. Nat. U., La Jolla, Calif., 1997—. Mem. core staff Lahav Rsch. Project, Miss. State U., 1975-92. Co-author: Oceanic Prehistory, 1975, Deer Creek Cave, 1964, Archaeological Survey of Southern Nevada, 1963, Stuart Rockshelter, 1962; contbr. articles to jours. in field. Mem. coun. Gamble House. Fellow Am. Anthropol. Assn.; mem. Soc. for Am. Archaeology, Am. Schs. for Oriental Rsch., Am. Coun. Edn., Am. Assn. for Higher Edn., Am. Assn. State Colls. and Univs., Delta Zeta. Republican. Roman Catholic. Avocations: travel, gardening, cats. E-mail: eshutler@nu.edu.

SHUTTHANANDAN, VAITHIYALINGAM, research scientist; b. Jaffna, Sri Lanka, Nov. 14, 1962; , U.S., 1988; s. Elayathamby Vaithiyalingam, Eswary Vaithiyalingam; m. Janani Retnajothy; children: Swetha. BSc, U. Jaffna, Sri Lanka, 1985; MS, Mont. State U., 1990, PhD, 1994. Rsch. asst. prof. Tuskegee (Ala.) U., 1994—98; staff analyst Charles Evans and Assocs., Sunnyvale, Calif., 1998—99; sr. rsch. scientist Pacific Northwest Nat. Lab., Richland, Wash., 1999—. Contbr. articles to profl. jours. Recipient Cert. of Merit, Sci. Oratorical Contest, Sri-Lanka Assn. for the Advancement Sci., 1980; scholar Mahapola Higher Edn. scholar, 1981. Mem.: Materials Rsch. Soc., Am. Vacuum Soc. (bd. mem. Pacific N.W. chpt. 2000—). Hindu. Avocations: camping, basketball, college football. Home: 1981 Anna Ave Richland WA 99352 Office: Pacific Northwest Nat Lab PO Box 999 902 Battelle Blvd Richland WA 99352 Office Fax: 509-376-5106. Business E-Mail: shuttha@pnl.gov.

SHUTTLEWORTH, ANNE MARGARET, psychiatrist; b. Detroit, Jan. 17, 1931; d. Cornelius Joseph and Alice Catherine (Rice) S.; m. Joel R. Siegel, Apr. 19, 1959; children: Erika, Peter. AB, Cornell U., 1953, MD, 1956. Intern Lenox Hill Hosp., N.Y.C., 1956-57; resident Payne Whitney Clinic-N.Y. Hosp., 1957-60; practice medicine specializing in psychiatry Maplewood, N.J., 1960—. Cons. Maplewood Sch. System, 1960-62; instr. psychiatry Cornell U. Med. Sch., 1960; mem. Com. to Organize New Sch. Psychology, 1970. Mem. AMA (Physicians Recognition award 1975, 78, 81, 84, 87, 90, 93, 96, 99), Am. Psychiat. Assn., Am. Med. Women's Assn., N.Y. Acad. Scis., Acad. Medicine N.J., Phi Beta Kappa, Phi Kappa Phi. Home: 46 Farbrook Dr Short Hills NJ 07078-3007 Office: 2066 Millburn Ave Maplewood NJ 07040-3715

SHUTZ, BYRON CHRISTOPHER, real estate executive; b. Kansas City, Mo., Feb. 16, 1928; s. Byron Theodore and Maxine (Christopher) S.; m. Marilyn Ann Tweedie, Mar. 30, 1957; children: Eleanor S. Gaines, Byron Christopher, Collin Reid, Allison S. Moskow, Lindley Anne Baile. AB in Econs, U. Kans., 1949. Ptnr. Herbert V. Jones & Co., Kansas City, Mo., 1953-72; pres. Herbert V. Jones Mortgage Corp., 1967-72, The Byron Shutz Co., Kansas City, 1973—. Dir. 1st Am. Financial Corp., Rothschild's, Inc., Bus. Men's Assurance Co., Faultless Starch, Bon Ami Co. Chmn. bd. trustees U. Kansas City, 1979-81; trustee Pembroke-Country Day Sch., 1974-77, Midwest Rsch. Inst., 1980-89; chmn., bd. govs. Kansas City Art Inst., 1960-62; chmn. bd. dirs. Ctr. for Bus. Innovation, Inc., 1985-87; bd. dirs. Kansas City Crime Commn. 1st lt. USAF, 1951-53. Mem. Mortgage Bankers Assn. Am. (bd. govs. 1966-74), Am. Inst. Real Estate Appraisers. Clubs: Kansas City Country, University, Mercury (pres. 1978-79); Fla. Yacht (Jacksonville), Ocean Reef (Key Largo, Fla.). Home: 1001 W 58th Ter Kansas City MO 64113-1159 Office: 800 W 47th St Kansas City MO 64112-1251 E-mail: arrowrock@aol.com.

SHVETSOV, ALEXANDER ANATOLIEVICH, biochemist, researcher; b. Orel, Russia, July 25, 1960; s. Anatoly Ivanovich and Anna Yakovlevna (Tsytsarkina) S.; m. Tatiana Vasilevna Orlova, Feb. 26, 1988; 1 child, Oksana. MS in Agronomy, Agrl. Acad., Orel, 1983; PhD in Biochemistry, Inst. Biochemistry, Moscow, 1992, postgrad., 1992-95. Jr. rsch. assoc. Inst. Agrl. Industry, Orel, 1986-88; sr. rschr. Inst. Biochemistry, 1995-98; sr. rsch. investigator Plant Physiology Inst., Moscow, 1998-2000; postdoctoral fellow UCLA, 2000—. Reviewer Nat. Rsch. Initiative Grants Program, Washington, 1996-99; sec. Internat. Symposium on Stress and Inorganic Nitrogen Assimilation, Moscow, 1996. Patentee in field; contbr. numerous articles to profl. jours. Lt. USSR Military Svc., 1983-85. Mem. Russian Biochem. Soc., Russian Soc. Plant Physiologists. Russian Orthodox. Avocations: music, philosophy, painting. Home: 48 Pepvomalskaya Str Apt 14 303120 Orel Russia Office: UCLA Dept Chemistry 405 Hilgard Ave Los Angeles CA 90024-1569 E-mail: alexs@ucla.edu.

SHVIDLER, MARK JOSEPH, mathematician; b. Khmelnitsky, Ukraine, USSR, Mar. 25, 1931; s. Joseph Zuss and Lea Gersh (Gleyzer); m. Mariam Moses Mendelson, July 24, 1959; children: Irene, Eugene. MS in Applied Mechanics, Kiev State U., USSR, 1953; PhD, All-Union Rsch. Sci. Oil and Gas Inst., Moscow, 1958, DS, 1964. Scientist Sci. Rsch. Oil Inst., Ufa, USSR, 1953-58, dept. head, 1958-67; scientist All-Union Rsch.-Sci. Natural Gas Inst., Moscow, 1967-70; scientist, prof., dept. head All-Union Rsch.-Sci. Oil and Gas Inst., 1970-91; scientist Lawrence Berkeley Nat. Lab., Berkeley, Calif., 1991-92. Vis. scientist Atomic Energy of Can. Ltd., Chalk River, Ont., Can., 1993, Lawrence Berkeley Nat. Lab., Berkeley, 1994-2002. Author: (books) Filtration Flow in Heterogeneous Media, 1964, One-Dimensional Immiscible Flow Through Porous Media, 1970, Statistical Hydrodynamics of Porous Media, 1985; contbr. 160 articles to profl. jours. Mem. Am. Geophys. Union, Internat. Acad. Edn. Science Arts & Industry. Achievements include pioneer rsch. studies on statis. hydrodynamics of porous media and devel. of the theory. Avocations: chess, swimming. Home: 2951 Derby St Apt 228 Berkeley CA 94705-1350 E-mail: shvidler@earthlink.net.

SHWAYDER, TOR ADAM, dermatologist, pediatrician, musician; b. Detroit; BA, Harvard U., 1976; MD, U. Mich., 1980. Licentiate Royal Acad. Music (London). Resident in pediat. U. Mich., Ann Arbor, 1980-83; pvt. practice, 1983-84; resident in dermatology U. Rochester, N.Y., 1984-87. Dir. pediat. dermatology Henry Ford Hosp., Detroit, 1987—, Childrens Hosp. Mich., Detroit, 1995-2001. Contbr. articles to profl. jours. Violinist Birmingham (Mich.)-Bloomfield Symphony Orch., 1988—. Fellow Am. Acad. Pediat., Am. Acad. Dermatology. Avocations: violin, gardening. Office: Henry Ford Hosp Dept Dermatology K 16 Detroit MI 48202 E-mail: tshwayd1@hfhs.org.

SHYAM-SUNDER, SIVARAJ, structural engineer, researcher; b. Madras, India, Mar. 29, 1955; came to U.S., 1977; s. Krishnaswami and Vimala Sivaraj; m. Lakshmi Iyer Shyam-Sunder, Jan. 25, 1981; 1 child, Anushka M. Sunder. BTech with honors, Indian Inst. Tech., Delhi, 1977; MS, MIT, 1979, ScD, 1981. Asst. prof. engring. MIT, Cambridge, Mass., 1981-84, assoc. prof. engring., 1984-90, prin. rsch. scientist, 1990-94, sr. rsch. scientist, 1994; mgr. high-performance constrn. materials program Nat. Inst. Stds. and Tech., Gaithersburg, Md., 1994-96, program analyst, 1996-97, sr. program analyst, 1997, chief structures divsn., 1998—. Tech. cons. A/S Norske Shell, Norway, 1982-83, Stone & Webster Corp., Boston, 1984-85, Norwegian Seismic Array, 1984-85, U.S. Geol. Survey, Menlo Park, Calif., 1985, Can. Oil & Gas Adminstrn., Ottawa, 1990; mem. NAS/NRC com. on Cooperation with USSR on ice mechanics, 1991-92; mem. Naval Sea Systems Command ind. panel to evaluate USN's Submarine Arctic Strucures program, 1991-92; liaison mem. Constrn. Materials Coun., Civil Engring. Rsch. Found., 1994—, chair interagy. com. on seismic safety in constrn., 1998—, chair U.S.-Japan panel on wind and seismic effects, 1998—. Contbr. 60 articles and 20 papers to profl. publs. Mem. AAAS, ASCE (chair 2001 structures conf. 1998—, Walter L. Huber Rsch. prize 1991), Earthquake Engring. Rsch. Inst., Am. Concrete Inst. Avocations: current events, travel. Office: NIST Bldg 226 Rm B 164 100 Bureau Dr Stop 8610 Gaithersburg MD 20899-8610

SHYER, JOHN D. lawyer; b. Nashville, May 4, 1956; s. Michael and Hilda (Wertheim) S.; m. Marsha Anne Gisser, May 7, 1989; children: Allison Parcell, Michael Wertheim. AB, Princeton U., 1978; JD, Stanford U., 1981. Bar: N.Y. 1982, U.S. Ct. Appeals (2d cir.) 1983, U.S. Ct. Appeals (3d cir.) 1992. Assoc. Donovan, Leisure, Newton & Irvine, N.Y.C., 1981-85, Latham & Watkins, N.Y.C., 1985-89, ptnr., 1989—. Trustee Princeton (N.J.) Broadcasting Svc., 1985—. Mem. Assn. Bar City N.Y., Employment and Labor Lawcast (bd. editl. advisors 1994—). Avocations: travel, hiking, reading. Office: Latham & Watkins 885 3rd Ave Ste 1000 New York NY 10022-4834 E-mail: john.shyer@lw.com.

SHYERS, LARRY EDWARD, mental health counselor, educator; b. Middletown, Ohio, Aug. 16, 1948; s. Edward and Ruth Evelyn (Davis) S.; m. Linda Faye Shearon, July 31, 1970; children: Jami Lynn, Karen Lindsey. BA, David Lipscomb Coll., Nashville, 1970; MA, Stetson U., Deland, Fla., 1973; MEd, U. Ctrl. Fla., 1981; PhD, U. Fla., 1992. Lic. mental health counselor, Fla.; nat. cert. counselor, psychologist, approved clin. supr.; diplomate Nat. Registry Neurofeedback Providers; ordained to ministry non-denominational Ch. of Christ, 1969. Minister Ch. of Christ, Ocala, Fla., 1970-75, Mt. Dora, 1975-80; tchr. Christian Home and Bible Sch., 1970-77, dir. guidance, 1977-86; pvt. practice individual and family counseling, 1980—. Apptd. to state regulatory bd. for clin. social work, marriage, family therapy, mental heatlh counseling, 1987-95, vice-chmn., 1987-88, chmn., 1989-95, legis. liaison, 1988-95; adj. prof. Nova. U., 1986—, U. Ctrl. Fla., 1988—, psychology St. Leo Coll., 1985—, Rollins Coll., 1991—, Reformed Theol. Sem., 1995—; adj. instr. Lake Sumter C.C., 1989—, Stetson U., 1990—, Rollins Coll., 1991—; mem. individual manpower tng. sys. bd. Vocat.-Tech. Sch., Eustis, 1984-87; mem. adv. bd. U.S. Achievement Bd., 1983—; cons. in field. Dir. edn. Mt. Dora Ch. of Christ, 1983-86; mem. Leadership Lake County Class of 1999. Mem. Fla. Mental Health Counselors Assn. (chmn. award and profl. devel. coms. 1985, chmn. govt. rels. com., pres. 1986-87), ACA (govt. rels. com. 1990-95, publs. rev. com. 1991—), Am. Mental Health Counselors Assn. (govt. rels. com. 1987-90, chmn. 1988-90, publs. com. 1991—, PP&I com. 1992-95), Am. Orthopsychiat. Assn., Am. Assn. Christian Counselors, Internat. Assn. Marriage adn Family Counselors, Assn. of Assessment in Counseling, Am. Assn. Profl. Hypnotherapists, Lake Sumter Assn. for Counseling and Devel. (pres. 1987-88), Assn. for Applied Psychophysiology and Biofeedback, Mount Dora C. of C. (mem. youth com. 1984), Leadership Lake County Class of 1999, Kiwanis, Kappa Delta Pi, Pi Lambda Theta, Chi Sigma Iota. Republican. Avocations: amateur radio, target shooting. Office: 3750 Lake Center Loop Mount Dora FL 32757-2211

SHYLLON, PRINCE E.N. lawyer, law educator; b. Freetown, Sierra Leone, Nov. 3, 1943; came to the U.S. s. Henry W.O. and Lois (Johnson) S.; m. Millicent Boutchway, June 8, 1974; children: Nicky H., Selwyn A. BA in Economics, Shaw U., 1972; JD Sch. of Law, N.C. Ctrl. U., Durham, 1975. Bar: N.C. 1977, U.S. Dist. Ct. (ea. dist.), 1978, U.S. Ct. of Appeals (4th cir.), 1978. Ptnr. Shabica, Shyllon & Shyllon, Raleigh, N.C., 1977-79, Shyllon, Shyllon & Ratliff, Raleigh, 1979-85; prof. Bus. Law and Ins. Saint Augustines Coll., 1975-91; ptnr. Shyllon & Shyllon, 1986—. University counsel St. Augustines Coll., 1992—. Mem. ABA, N.C. Acad. of Trial Lawyers. Home: 1101 Athens Dr Raleigh NC 27606-2420 Office: Shyllon & Shyllon 4002 Barrett Dr Raleigh NC 27609-6618

SHYY, WEI, aerospace and mechanical engineering researcher, educator; b. Tainan, Taiwan, China, July 19, 1955; came to U.S. 1979; s. Chiang-Chen and June-Hua (Chao) S.; m. Yuchen Shih; children: Albert, Alice, Andrew Chang, Kevin Chang. BS, Tsin-Hua U., Taiwan, 1977; MSE, U. Mich., 1981, PhD, 1982. Postdoctoral rsch. scholar U. Mich., Ann Arbor, 1982-83; rsch. scientist GE Corp. Rsch. and Devel. Ctr., Schenectady, N.Y., 1983-88; faculty mem. of aeronautics and astronautics Nat. Cheng-Kung U., Taiwan, 1987; assoc. prof. aerospace engring., mechanics and engring. sci. U. Fla., Gainesville, 1988-92, prof. aerospace engring., mechanics and engring. sci., 1992—, chmn. dept. aerospace engring, mechs. and engring. sci., 1996—2002, chmn. dept. mech. and aerospace engring., 2002—. Cons. numerous pvt., fed. agencies U.S., Taiwan; lectr. in field. Author: Computational Modeling for Fluid Flow and Interfacial Transport, 1994; co-author: Computational Fluid Dynamics with Moving Boundaries, 1996, Computational Techniques for Complex Transport Phenemona, 1997; editor: Recent Advances in Computational Fluid Dynamics, 1989, Fluid Dynamics at Interface, 1999; mng. editor Cambridge U. Press: Aerospace Book Series, Jour. Applied Mechanics Revs., Computer Modeling in Engring. and Scis.; mem. editl. adv. bd. Numerical Heat Transfer Jour., Progress in Computational Fluid Dynamics. Recipient GE Rsch. and Devel. Ctr. 1986 Pubs. award, Chinese Soc. of Mech. Engrs. 1987 Rsch. Paper award, NASA/ASEE 1991 Cert. of Recognition. Fellow AIAA, ASME; mem. Minerals, Metals and Materials Soc., Am. Phys. Soc., Combustion Inst. Achievements include research in computational fluid dynamics, combustion and propulsion, gravity-induced thermofluid transport processes, materials processing and solidification, microgravity sciences and engring. contributions to gas turbine, hydraulic turbine, high pressure lamp and electronic cooling. Office: U Fla Dept Aerospace Engring 231 Aero Bldg Gainesville FL 32611

SIA, TINA, apparel executive; b. Hong Kong, Mar. 5, 1971; d. A. and M. S. BS, Fairleigh Dickinson U., 1994, MBA, 1996. Personal asst. Ace Style Internat. Ltd., Hong Kong, 1996-99, CEO Binan, Philippines, 1996—. E-mail: tina_sia@acestyle.com.ph.

SIAS, JOHN B. former multi-media company executive, newspaper publisher, publishing executive; b. 1927; AB, Stanford U., 1949. Group v.p. Metromedia Inc., 1962-71; with Capital Cities Communications, 1971-93; pres. Fairchild Pubs. Inc., 1971-75, exec. v.p., pres. pub. div., 1975-85; pres. ABC-TV Network Group, N.Y.C., 1986-93; also former exec. v.p. Capital Cities/ABC Inc.(parent); former pres., chmn Chronicle Pub. Co., San Francisco. Served with AUS, 1945-46. Office: Chronicle Pub Co 901 Mission St San Francisco CA 94103-2905 also: Capital Cities ABC Inc 24 E 51st St New York NY 10022-6801*

SIAS, JOHN WOLLENBURG, research scientist; BS, U. Ill., 1997, MS, 1999. Grad. rschr. U. Ill., Urbana-Champaign, 1997—. Mem.: IEEE. Office: Univ Ill Coord Sci Lab 1308 W Main St Urbana IL 61801-2307 Personal E-mail: sias@uiuc.edu. Business E-Mail: sias@uiuc.edu.

SIBBALD, JOHN RISTOW, management consultant; b. Lincoln, Nebr., June 20, 1936; s. Garth E.W. and Rachel (Wright) S.; m. Kathryn J. Costick; children: Allison, John, Wright. BA, U. Nev., 1958; MA, U. Ill., 1964. Office mgr. Hewitt Assocs., Libertyville, Ill., 1964-66; coll. rels. mgr. Pfizer Inc., N.Y.C., 1966-69; pres., CEO Re-Con Systems, 1969-70; v.p. Booz, Allen & Hamilton, 1970-73, Chgo., 1973-75; pres., founder John Sibbald Assocs., Inc., 1975. Mem. Nat. Advisory Coun., Nat. Club Assn. Author: The Career Makers, 1990, 92, The New Career Makers, 1995; pub. Club Leaders Forum; contbr. articles to profl. jours. Capt. AUS, 1958-64. Mem. Mid-Day Club Chgo., St. Louis Club. Episcopalian. Office: 7701 Forsyth Blvd Saint Louis MO 63105-1817

SIBBIO, MICHAEL GREGORY, promoter, concept developer, inventor technical consultant; b. Akron, Ohio, Feb. 2, 1955; s. Dominic Rocco Sibbio and Elizabeth Mari (Sadler) Parsons. Grad. high sch., Akron. Job supt. UNS Constrn. Co., Phoenix, 1973-75; gen. mgr. Staff Music Co., Akron, 1975-79; pres., sole propr. Mike's Music, Inc., 1979-88; pres., exec. producer, audio technician Sibcon Prodns., 1985-88; exec. dir., freelance producer Fastrac Comml. div. Akron Music Ctrs., 1988; staff cons. Akron Music Ctrs., 1988; dir. of promotions Western Park Model and RV, Inc., Mesa, Ariz., 1990-91; dir. promotions AAA Park Models Inc., 1991-92; mktg. cons. Polychrome Inc., Akron, Ohio, 1991; dir. market Color Burst, Inc., Simi Valley, Calif., 1992-94; pres. FASTRAC Communication, Phoenix, 1991-2001; CEO World Products Group Internat., Inc., San Clemente, Calif., 1996—. Cons. McDonald's Corp., North Royalton, Ohio, 1989, CMI Nashville, 1989, Motorola GEG, 1989, Pro Performance, 1992-94, Second Story Concepts, Canton, Ohio, 1993, Weyerhaeuser Corp., 1998-2000; exclusive ofcl. lic. holder Wilson Sporting Goods, Chgo., 1993—, Marvel Entertainment, 1996-98; mng. dir. Angel Visions LLC, 1998-99. Developer, inventor Wilson Power Squeez exercise concept, 1993, holder trademark; developer Heat Em Cool Ems, 2000, Wrap Ons-Mueller Sports Medicine, Wilson PowerFlex putty, Wilson Power V Glove System, Tru-Fit Medicine Ball; patentee in field. Fundraiser Am. Heart Assn., Easter Seal Soc. Mem. Nat. Sound Contractors Assn. (Sporting Goods Bus. Pub. Rookie of Yr. 1994), Phys. Edn. for Progress Fundraising. Avocations: songwriting, skiing, photography. Address: 1201 Via Catalina San Clemente CA 92672 E-mail: msibbio@cox.net.

SIBILLA, SUZANNE ROSE, training and organizational development consultant; b. San Jose, Calif., Oct. 15, 1961; d. Susan Pilar Asuzano; m. Michael E. Coutches. BA, Westmont Coll., 1983; MA, Antioch U., 1989. Registered drama therapist, Nat. Assn. Drama Therapists; lic. marriage, family, child counselor. Cons. tng. and orgnl. devel. Assn. Psychol. and Ednl. Counselors Asia, Thailand, Malaysia, Singapore; program dir. State of Oreg., Salem, 1988-93; cons. Hewlett Packard, Sun, Raychem, FEMA, CPC Hosps., San Jose, Fremont, Palo Alto, Calif., 1993-95; mgr. tng. and orgnl. devel. Tencor Instruments-KLA and TENCOR, Milpitas, Calif., 1995-97; mng. cons., tng. Sibilla & Assocs., Fremont, 1997—; orgnl. change specialist NEOPOST, 1998—; corp. tng. mgr. WebMD, 1999—2001; ind. cons. Hewlett Packard, 2001—, Compaq, 2001—, Right Mgmt. Cons., 2001—, Global Tng. & Cons., 2001—. Initiator mentorship program Tencor, Palo Alto, 1997. Guest (film and TV program) People Are Talking, 1993, (TV program) Mornings on Two, 1994. Dir. mentorship program for girls YWCA, Daly City, 1993-95. Mem. NAFE, ASTD, Assn. Psychol. and Ednl. Counselors Asia (cons. tng. and orgnl. devel. 1988-92, Key Presenter award 1992), Calif. Assn. Marriage, Family and Child Counselors (cert.), Women in Tech. Internat., Menttium 100 (chairperson steering com. 1996-97), Toastmasters (Palo Alto club). Avocations: acting, waterskiing, sailing, swimming, travel. E-mail: srsibilla@aol.com.

SIBLEY, CAROL MORSE, communications executive; b. San Antonio, Jan. 11, 1944; d. Edison Spencer and Cecile (Bernard) Morse; student U. Del., 1962-64; B.S., Hahnemann Med. Coll., 1966; m. Frederick Drake Sibley, Mar. 15, 1975; 1 child, Janet Bernard. Med. writer internat. div. Bristol-Myers, N.Y.C., 1968-72; assoc. biomed. communications Turner Assocs., Greenwich, Conn., 1972-73; clin. rsch. assoc. Pfizer Pharms., N.Y.C., 1974-76, mgr. sci. communications, 1976; cons. pharm. industry, Montclair, N.J., 1976-89; assoc. biomed. communications J.L. Shapiro Assocs., Metuchen, N.J., 1979-82; dir. sci. affairs Audio Visual Med. Mktg., N.Y.C., 1982-83, pres. Med.-Sci. Communications, Inc., Montclair, 1989—. Committeeman Rep. Party, Phila., 1965-66, Twp. of Montclair, 1989-90. Mem. Am. Soc. Microbiology, N.Y. Acad. Scis., Am. Soc. Clin. Pathologists, NAFE. Episcopalian. Home and Office: 92 Overlook Ter Bloomfield NJ 07003-2917

SIBLEY, HORACE HOLDEN, lawyer; b. Phila., Oct. 13, 1939; s. John Adams and Barbara (Thayer) S.; m. Beverly Bryan, Mar. 18, 1961; children: Clare, Holden, Eve. BA, Vanderbilt U., 1961; LLD, U. Ga., 1964; MBA, Ga. State U., 1971. Bar: Ga. 1964, U.S. Supreme Ct. 1975. Assoc. King and Spalding, Atlanta, 1968-72, ptnr., 1972—2001. Chmn. Ga. Ctr. for Advance Telecom. Tech., 1994-2000, So. Ctr. for Internat. Studies; bd. dirs. Woodruff Arts Ctr., Glenayre Technologies, Inc.; bd. advisors Carter Ctr., 1996-2001; bd. trustees Callaway Crarders Found.; hon. consul Dominican Republic. Trustee, mem. exec. com. Agnes Scott Coll., Atlanta, 1977; trustee Henrietta Egleston Hosp. for Children, Atlanta, 1974-77, trustee, mem. exec. com., 1977—, chmn. bd. dirs., 1983-90; mem. exec. com. Atlanta Organizing Com. Summer Olympics, 1989-90; bd. dirs. Atlanta Com. for Olympic Games, 1991-99; chmn. bd. dirs. Butler St. YMCA, Atlanta, 1981; past bd. dirs. United Way, Nat. Assn. of Childrens' Hosp. and various other charitable orgns.; participant Leadership Ga., 1978, Leadership Atlanta, 1973, Soc. Internat. Bus. Fellows, 1982—; elder Trinity Presbyn. Ch., 1969-73. Capt. inf. U.S. Army, 1965-68, Germany. Mem. ABA, Ga. Bar Assn., Atlanta Bar Assn., World Trade Club Atlanta (bd. dirs. 1988-92), Japan-Am. Soc. (bd. dirs. 1981-87), Rotary, Blue Key Svc. Soc., Phi Kappa Phi, Omicron Delta Kappa. Democrat. Presbyterian. Avocations: tennis, golf, fishing. Office: King & Spalding 191 Peachtree St NE Ste 40 Atlanta GA 30303-1740 E-mail: hsibley@kslaw.com.

SIBLEY, JAMES MALCOLM, retired lawyer; b. Atlanta, Aug. 5, 1919; s. John Adams and Nettie Whitaker (Cone) S.; m. Karen Norris, Apr. 6, 1942; children: Karen Mariea, James Malcolm Jr., Jack Norris, Elsa Alexandria Victoria, Quintus Whitaker. AB, Princeton U., 1941; student, Woodrow Wilson Sch. Law, 1942, Harvard Law Sch., 1945-46. Bar: Ga. 1942. Assoc. King & Spalding, Atlanta, 1942-47, ptnr., 1947-91. Bd. dirs. Summit Industries, Inc.; exec. com., mem. pub. affairs com. Coca-Cola Co., 1979-91; chmn. exec. com. John H. Harland Co., 1963-91; chmn. exec. com., mem. compensation com. Trust Co. of Ga., 1975-92; mem. exec. com., mem. compensation com. SunTrust Banks, Inc., 1985-92. Trustee Joseph B. Whitehead Found., Lettie

Pate Evans Found., A.G. Rhodes Home, Inc., Robert W. Woodruff Found., Inc. (formerly Trebor Found.), John H. and Wilhelmina D. Harland Charitable Found., Inc.; trustee emeritus Callaway Gardens Found, Emory U. With USAF, 1942-45. Mem. ABA, Ga. Bar Assn., Atlanta Bar Assn., Am. Coll. Probate Counsel, Am. Bar Found., Am. Law Inst. Clubs: Piedmont Driving, Commerce. Episcopalian. also: King & Spalding 191 Peachtree St NE Ste 40 Atlanta GA 30303-1740 Home: 3045 Slaton Dr NW Atlanta GA 30305-2006

SIBLEY, JAMES SCARBOROUGH, career officer; b. Sardis, Tex., Feb. 20, 1930; s. Fred Scarborough Sibley and Gladys Nell Middleton; m. Nancy Ann Deisher, May 26, 1956 (dec. July 1975); children: Wayne Scarborough, Charles Patrick, Steven Emerson, James Francis, Kenneth Richards. AS, North Tex. Agrl. Coll., 1948; BS, U.S. Mil. Acad., West Point, N.Y., 1953; MS in Civil Engring., Calif. Inst. Tech., 1957. Registered profl. civil engr., La. Commd. 2nd lt. U.S. Army, advanced through grades to col.; with U.S. Army Corps of Engrs., 1953-79; civil engr. Hdqs. Pusan Mil. Post, Korea, 1954-55; co. comdr., aide de camp 6th Armored Divsn., Fort Leonard Wood, Mo., 1955-56; co. comdr. 91st Engr. Bn. Combat, Fort Belvoir, Va., 1957-58; civil engr. U.S. Army Engr. Dist. Eastern Ocean Goose Bay Labrador, 1959-61; math. instr. U.S. Mil. Acad., West Point, N.Y., 1961-63, asst. prof., asst. to dean, 1963-65; sr. advisor 20th Engr. Brigade ARVN, Pleiku, Vietnam, 1965-66; plans officer Hqrs. U.S. Army Pacific, Fort Shafter, Hawaii, 1966-68; comdr. 3rd Engr. Bn. Combat, Fort Riley, Kans., 1968-69; chief engring. divsn., chief Cons. Divsn. Hqrs. U.S. Army, Long Binh, Vietnam, 1969-70; chief base devel. planning sect. J4 CINCPAC, Camp Smith, Hawaii, 1970-73; dep. engr. U.S. Army Forces Command, Fort McPherson, Ga., 1973-77; ret., 1979—. Dir. engrg. and housing, V Corps, Frankfurt, Germany, 1977-79. Author, pub. (2 vol. family genealogy): The Sibley Family in America, 1629-72, 2d edit., 1982. Precinct chmn. Republican Com., Ellis County, Tex., 1980-89; dir., sec.-treas. Sardis Cemetery Assn., Ellis County, Tex., 1988—, Sardis Lone Elm Water Supply Corp., Ellis County, 1982—; dir., sec. Ellis County Hist. Commn., 1984—; trustee Midlothian Ind. Sch. Dist., Tex., 1997-2000; Sunday sch. tchr. First United Meth. Ch., Midlothian, 1980—; host parent, area rep. Fgn. Exch. Student Program, Midlothian, 1991—. Decorated Legion of Merit, Bronze Star medal with oak leaf cluster, Commendation medal with oak leaf clusters, Air medal. Avocations: walking, biking, golfing, tennis. Home: 2620 Mount Zion Rd Midlothian TX 76065-6357

SIBLEY, LEWIS BRANCH, engineering executive; b. Lyons, N.Y., Apr. 13, 1931; s. Lewis Schollenberger and Hattie Elizabeth (Branch) S.; m. Clara Mary Carle, Oct. 17, 1953 (div. 1977); children: Russell Carle, Daniel Lee. Student, Ohio Wesleyan U., 1948-51; BSME, Rensselaer Poly. Inst., 1953; postgrad., Ohio State U., 1953-57. Prin. mech. engr. Battelle Meml. Inst., Columbus, Ohio, 1953-57, project leader, 1957-61; supr. mech. test SKF Industries, Inc., Phila., 1961-68; mgr. rsch. dept. SKF Tech. Svcs., King of Prussia, Pa., 1968-76, mgr. tribology, 1976-82; prin. Tribology Cons., Paoli, 1982—; CEO, chief tech. officer, owner Tribology Systems, Inc., Warminster, 1989—. Chmn. Computerized Tribology Info. Svcs. Planning Workshop, Gaithersburg, Md., 1985. Author: (with others) Role of Viscosity in Lubrication, 1960, Computer-Aided Design of Bearings and Seals, 1976, Wear Control Handbook, 1980 (ASME Centennial project award 1980); editor: Achievements in Tribology, 1990; contbr. articles to profl. jours.; patentee in field. Fellow ASME (life; chmn. rsch. com. on tribology 1981, Soc. Tribologists and Lubrication Engrs. (Alfred E. Hunt medal 1962); mem. ASTM, Am. Ceramic Soc. Avocations: biking, square dancing, hiking, travel, geneology. Home: 504 Foxwood Ln Paoli PA 19301-2010 Office: Tribology Systems Inc 239 K Madison Ave Warminster PA 18974-4864 E-mail: lew4tsi@aol.com.

SIBLEY, LYNN M. anthropologist, educator; b. Nashville, Mar. 4, 1949; d. James G. and Peggy L. Middleton; m. George J. Armelagos, June 21, 1991; children: Gabriel. PhD (Anthropology), U. of Colo., Boulder, Colorado, 1988—93; MS (Nursing), U. of Utah, Salt Lake City, Utah, 1978—80; BS (Nursing), U. of Colo., Denver, Colorado Health Sciences Center, 1970—73; MA (Anthropology), U. of Colo., Boulder, Colorado, 1986—87. Registered Nurse, Colo. State Bd. of Nursing, 1974, Certified Nurse Midwife, Am. Coll. of Nurse Midwives, 1980. Faculty U. of Colo. Sch. of Nursing, Denver, 1980—85; sr. tech. advisor Am. Coll. of Nurse-Midwives, Washington, 1995—; adj. asst. prof. of anthropology Emory U., Atlanta, 1995—; vis. clin. instr. Med. Coll. of Va., Richmond, Va. Cons. People's Clinic, Boulder, Colo., 1983—83; co-organizer, nsf nasa conf. on remote sensing U. of Colo., Boulder, Colo.; cons., tech. consultation on attendance at birth: cmty. birth attendants UNICEF and World Bank, New York City, NY, 1997; consultant-,global tech. consultation on safe motherhood Global Safe Motherhood Inter-Agency Working Group, Colombo, Sri Lanka, 1997; cons. Nat. Summit on Safe Motherhood, Centers for Disease Control and others, Atlanta, 2001; co-chair, workshop on home based life saving skills Am. Coll. of Nurse Midwives, Tucson; cons. Johns Hopkins Sch. of Pub. Health, Baltimore, Md., 2002—. Author: (journal article) Journal of Nurse-Midwifery; co-author (journal article) Current Anthropology, Obstetrics and Gynecology, Medical Anthropology; author: (journal article) American Journal of Physical Anthropology, Journal of Nurse Midwifery, Quickening, Journal of Women's Health and Midwifery; co-author (training manual) Home Based Life Saving Skills. Recipient Sigma Theta Tau, , Gamma Rho Chpt., 1980, Phi Kappa Phi, U. of Utah Chpt., 1980, Nat. Dean's List, A Nat. Honor Soc., 1980; fellow Grad. Tchg./Rsch. Asst., U. of Colo., 1986-1988, Fulbright Dissertation Fellowship, Belize, US Fulbright Program, 1989-1990; grantee Nurse Traineeship, US HHS, 1978-1980, NSF Doctoral Grant for Improving Dissertation Rsch., NSF, 1989-1990. Mem.: Am. Assn. of Phys. Anthropologists, Am. Anthrop. Assn., APHA, Am. Coll. of Nurse Midwives. Achievements include development of Co-team leader for development of Home Based Life Saving Skills, an innovative community based stragety to reduce maternal and neonatal mortality in developing countries; research in Traditional Birth Attendant Training Effectiveness, a meta-analysis of global TBA training programs spanning 30 years of publications; Analysis of paleo-obstetrics in ancient Sudanese Nubia. Avocations: sea kayaking, sea kayaking, sea kayaking. Home: 1327 Peachtree St NE #504 Atlanta GA 30309 Office: American College of Nurse-Midwives 818 Connecticut Ave NW Suite 900 Washington DC 20006 Office Fax: 202-728-9897. Personal E-mail: antls@learnlink.emory.edu. E-mail: antls@learnlink.emory.edu.

SIBLEY, ROBERT WHITMAN, printing company executive; b. Wilmington, Del., Dec. 11, 1944; s. Leonard Allen and Mabel (Rohrs) S.; m. Mary Patricia Evans, Sept. 6, 1969; children: Evelyn, Fernando, Katherine, Peter. BA, Shimer Coll., 1969; MBA, Phila. Coll. Textiles and Sci., 1991. V.p. mktg. Todays Sunbeam, Salem, N.J., 1969-82; mgr. comml. printing Bridgeton (N.J.) Evening News, 1982-94; v.p., gen. mgr. Evergreen Printing, Bellmawr, N.J., 1995—. Polit. cons. Salem County Dem. Com., Salem, N.J., 1971-84; activities chmn. So. N.J. Coun. Boy Scouts Am., Millville, 1993—; mgr. John Brandt Campaign Com., Carneys Point, N.J., 1997. Mem. Salem County Sportsmans Club. Christian Scientist. Avocations: church work, youth work, collecting books, cooking. Home: 121 Cypress St Carneys Point NJ 08069-2018 Office: Evergreen Printing & Pub Co Inc 101 Haag Ave Bellmawr NJ 08031-2535 E-mail: rsibley@egpp.com.

SIBLEY, WILLIS ELBRIDGE, anthropology educator, consultant; b. Nashville, Feb. 22, 1930; s. Elbridge and Elizabeth Reynolds (LaBarre) S.; m. Barbara Jean Grant, June 9, 1956; children: Sheila Katherine, Anthony Grant, Michael David. BA, Reed Coll., 1951; MA, U. Chgo., 1953, PhD, 1958. Instr. sociology and anthropology Miami (Ohio) U., 1956-58; asst. prof. anthropology U. Utah, 1958-60; from asst. prof. to prof. anthropology Wash. State U., 1960-71; prof. anthropology Cleve. State U., 1971—, chmn. dept., 1971-77, Cleve. (City) faculty fellow, 1987, interim chmn., 1989-90, prof. emeritus, 1990—; sr. program analyst EPA, Washington, 1977-78; Govtl. fellow Am. Coun. on Edn., 1978; Rockefeller Found. vis. prof. anthropology U. Philippines, Quezon City, 1968-69; postdoctoral fellow in society and tech. Carnegie-Mellon U., 1981-82. Fulbright grantee, 1954-55, 64; NIMH grantee, 1959-61; NSF grantee, 1964-71; Nat. Acad. Scis.-NRC travel grantee, 1966; Office Edn., HEW research grantee, 1967 Fellow AAAS, Assn. Profl. Anthropologists (pres. Washington chpt. 1999—), Am. Anthropol. Assn. (treas. 1989-91, com. on pub. policy 2000-2002), Soc. Applied Anthropology (sec. 1977-80, pres. 1981-82); mem. AAUP (treas. Wash. State U. chpt. 1962-63, v.p. 1963-64, pres. 1965-66, pres. Cleve. State U. chpt. 1979-80, treas. 1980-81, interim pres. 1989-90), ACLU (pres. Pullman chpt. 1963, 66), Ctrl. States Anthropol. Soc. (past mem. exec. bd., treas. 1986-89), Wash. Assn. Profl. Anthropologists, Edgewater Yacht Club (Cleve., commodore 1991), Chesapeake Yacht Club (Shady Side, Md.) (gov. 1999, 2000). Home: PO Box 484 Shady Side MD 20764-0484 Office: Cleve State U Dept Anthropology Cleveland OH 44115 E-mail: shadyside@aol.com.

SIBOLSKI, ELIZABETH HAWLEY, higher education administrator; b. Gt. Barrington, Mass., Aug. 18, 1950; d. William Snyder and Frances Harrington (Smith) Gallup; m. John Alfred Sibolski Jr., Aug. 15, 1970. BA, The Am. U., 1973, MPA, 1975, PhD, 1984. Acting dir. acad. adminstrn. Am. U., Washington, 1974, planning analyst, 1974-79, asst. dir. budget and planning, 1980-83, dir. instl. rsch., 1984-85, exec. dir. univ. planning and rsch., 1985-2000; exec. assoc. dir. Middle States Commn. on Higher Edn., Phila., 2000—. Trustee Mortar Bd. Nat. Found., 1989-95. Recipient Comencement award Am. U. Women's Club, 1973. Mem. Soc. Coll. and Univ. Planning (bd. dirs. 1995-2000, pres. 1998-99), Mortar Bd. (sect. coord. 1975-82), Pi Alpha Alpha, Phi Kappa Phi (chpt. officer 1986-92), Pi Sigma Alpha, Omicron Delta Kappa. Avocation: breed, raise and show Morgan horses. Home: 565 Wayward Dr Annapolis MD 21401-6747 Office: Middle States Commn on Higher Edn 3624 Market St Philadelphia PA 19104-2614 E-mail: esibolski@msache.org.

SIBOLSKI, JOHN ALFRED, JR. educational association executive; b. Nov. 4, 1946; S. John A. and Isabelle Barcaster S.; m. Elizabeth Gallup, Aug. 15, 1970. AA in Data Processing, Andover Inst. Bus., 1966; BS in Tech. of Mgmt., Am. U., 1967; cert. in data processing, 1974, grad. cert. in data processing, 1978. With Automated Systems Corp., Washington, 1969-71, KMS Tech. Ctr., Arlington, Va., 1971-72; ind. cons., 1972-73, 74-76; with Law Enforcement Asst. Adminstrn., Dept. Justice, Washington, 1973-74; D.A. Lewis, Assocs., Clinton, Md., 1974; with Bur. Nat. Affairs, Inc., Washington, 1976-80; mgr. systems. devel. NEA, 1980-90, Saturn Corp., Cheverly, Md., 1990-91, FBI, Washington, 1991—. Recipient spl. achievement award Dept. Justice, 1974. Mem. Fata Processing Mgmt. Assn., Am. Soc. for Info. Sci. Home: 565 Wayward Dr Annapolis MD 21401-6747 Office: FBI 10th St And Pa Ave Washington DC 20535-0001

SIBUL, LEON HENRY, electrical engineer; b. Voru, Estonia, Aug. 30, 1932; , U.S.49; s. Aleksander and Helene Sibul; m. Hele Mall Mandel, July 29, 1961; children: Eric Allan, Christina Linda. BEE, George Washington U., 1960; MEE, NYU, 1963; PhD, Pa. State U., 1968. Field engr. Engleman & Co., Inc., Washington, 1958—60; mem. tech. staff Bell Telephone Lab., Holmdel, NY, 1960—64; rsch. asst./assoc. Applied Rsch. Lab. Pa. State U., University Park, 1964—81, prof., sr. scientist Applied Rsch. Lab., 1981—. Cons. NAS, Washington, 1972—74; sr. tech. adv. USN, Washington, 1978—82. Editor: Adaptive Signal Processing, 1987; mem. editl. bd.: Multidimensional Signal Processing; contbr. articles to profl. jours., chpts. to books. Faculty advisor Pa. State Sailing Club, University Park, 1974—. Republican. Lutheran. Achievements include development of adaptive array processing techniques for underwater systems, use of wavelet transforms in optimum detectors; first to use application of group theory to signal processing, use info. theoretic concepts for sensor fusion and blind source separation; research in stochastic operator theory. Avocations: sailing, golf, basketball, cross-country skiing. Office: Pa State U Applied Rsch Lab PO Box 30 State College PA 16804-0030 E-mail: lh52@psu.edu.

SICA, JOHN, lawyer; b. Scranton, Pa., Jan. 23, 1962; s. John Anthony and Betty May (Sherbourne) S. BS, U. Md., Princess Anne, 1987; JD, No. Ill. U., 1989. Bar: Md. 1990. Mng. lawyer Sentinel Title Corp., Frederick, Md., 1989-90; pvt. practice, 1990—. Mem. Am. Agrl. Law Assn., Md. Bar Assn. (pub. svc. com.). Home: 329 S Jefferson St Frederick MD 21701-6206 E-mail: jsica80730@aol.com.

SICARD, GUILLERMO RAFAEL, dermatologist; b. LaVega, Dominican Republic, Oct. 25, 1937; came to U.S., 1963; s. Fausto A. and Margarita (Moya) S.; m. Emilia Cordova, Jan. 11, 1963; children: Fausto Antonio, Julia Margarita. BS, Norman Sch., La Vega, Dominican Republic, 1954; MD, U. St. Domingo, Dominican Republic, 1960. Diplomate Am. Bd. Dermatology, Am. Bd. Dermatopathology. Chief of health Health Dept., La Vega, 1960-63; intern Franklin Sq. Hosp., Balt., 1963-64; resident Cleve. Metro Gen. Hosp., 1966-69; ptnr. Gardner, Sicard DMD, Inc., Canton, Ohio, 1969-82; practice medicine specializing in dermatology, 1982—. Cons. Aultman Hosp., Canton, 1969—, Timken Mercy Hosp., Canton, 1969—, Massillow Community Hosp., 1982—; asst. prof. Northeastern Ohio U. Coll. Medicine, Rootswoen, 1984—, sect. chief dermatology, 1985— Investigator medication evaluation, 1984-85. Mem. Stark County Historical Soc., 1972—; sustaining mem. Republican Nat. Com., 1986—. Served to capt. U.S. Army, 1964-66. Fellow Am. Acad. Dermatology; mem. Canton Acad. Medicine (pres. 1981-82, Tennis Champion 1991), Stark County Med. Soc. (sec. 1979-80, pres. 1980-81), Smithsonian Inst., Ohio Dermatol. Assn., Cleve. Dermatol. Soc., Dermatology Found., Leaders Soc. Clubs: Hall of Fame Fitness (Canton). Roman Catholic. Avocations: tennis (Canton Acad. Medicine champion 1992, 93, other awards), camping, golf, swimming, music. Home: 1716 North Park Ave NW Canton OH 44708 Office: 4825 Munson St NW Canton OH 44718-3614

SICART, DANIEL SALOMON, investment counselor; b. Paris, Dec. 15, 1961; s. Abraham Alon and Regina (Meyer) Sicart; m. Eva Carolina Escobedo, June 13, 1989 (div. June 1995). BA, Columbia U., 1985. Registered rep. Tocqueville Asset Mgmt. Corp., N.Y.C., 1986-90; investment analyst, asst. v.p. Tocqueville Asset Mgmt. L.P., 1990-93, v.p., portfolio mgr., 1993—. Mem. Internat. Assn. Fin. Planning, Columbia U. Alumni Assn. Avocations: basketball, poetry, fine arts, tennis, Latin culture. Home: 6 W 77th St # 2A New York NY 10024-5125 Office: Sicart y Asociados Ave de Cas Naciones 38, 33 piso 14 Col Napoles 03810 Mexico

SICHEL, KIM DEBORAH, art history educator; b. N.Y.C., Dec. 31, 1955; d. E. Otto and Anne (Mayer) S.; m. Richard Leonard Brown, Oct. 9, 1988; children: David Sichel Brown, Alexandra Sichel Brown. AB, Brown U., 1977; MA, Yale U., 1981, MPhil in Art History, 1983, PhD in Art History, 1986. Part-time lectr. Yale U., New Haven, 1985-86; vis. asst. prof. Smith Coll., Northampton, Mass., 1986-87; dir. Boston Univ. Art Gallery, 1992-98; asst. prof. art history Boston U., 1987-2000, assoc. prof. art history, 2000—. Bd. trustees Photographic Resource Ctr., Boston, 1990-2000; mem. adv. coun. Addison Gallery of Am. Art, Phillips Acad., Andover, Mass., 1995—; lectr. in field. Author: Paris le jour, Paris la Nuit, 1988, Black Boston: Documentary Photographs, 1994, From Icon to Irony: German and American Industrial Photography, 1994, Germaine Krull: Photographer of Modernity, 1999, Photography in Boston 1955-85, 2000. Found. Singer-Polignac grantee, Paris, 1987, Councilium for West European Studies grantee, 1989-90; Nat. Mus. Act fellow Yale Art Gallery, 1982-83, Georges Lurcy fellow, 1983-84, NEH Tchrs. fellow, 1994-95, Bunting Inst., 1994-95. Mem. Coll. Art Assn. Office: Boston U 725 Commonwealth Ave Boston MA 02215-1401

SICHEL, WERNER, economics educator; b. Munich, Germany, Sept. 23, 1934; came to U.S., 1940; s. Joseph and Lilly (Greenwood) S.; m. Beatrice Bonne, Feb. 22, 1959; children: Larry, Linda. BS, NYU, N.Y.C., 1956; MA, Northwestern U., Evanston, Ill., 1960, PhD, 1964. Instr. Lake Forest (Ill.) Coll., 1959-62; asst. prof. Roosevelt U., Chgo., 1959-60; instr. Western Mich. U., Kalamazoo, 1960-64, asst. prof., 1964-67, assoc. prof., 1967-72, prof., 1972-85, prof., chair dept. econs., 1985—. Fulbright sr. lectr. U. Belgrade (Yugoslavia), 1968-69; vis. scholar Hoover Instn., Stanford, Calif., 1984-85; coord. Mich. Pub. Utility Confs., Ann Arbor, 1974-93; cons. Squire, Sanders and Dempsey, Cleve., 1980—. Author: Basic Economic Concepts, 1977, Economics, 1985, 87, 90, Economic Journalc, 1986 (Choice award 1987); editor 10 books and numerous jours., 1975—. Pres. Kalamazoo Jewish Fedn., 1989-93. Grantee NSF, 1966, Sperry & Hutchinson, 1963, Fulbright, 1968, W.E. Upjohn Inst., 1988. Mem. Am. Econ. Assn., Indsl. Orgn. Soc., Econs. Soc. Mich. (pres. 1975-76), Internat. J.A. Schumpeter Soc., Midwest Bus. Econ. Assn. (pres. 1989-90), Midwest Econ. Assn. (pres. 1995-96). Jewish. Home: 123 Merriweather Ln Kalamazoo MI 49006-4105

SICHERMAN, MARVIN ALLEN, lawyer; b. Cleve., Dec. 27, 1934; s. Harry and Malvina (Friedman) S.; m. Sue Kovacs, Aug. 18, 1957; children: Heidi Joyce, Steven Eric. BA, Case Western Res. U., 1957, LLB, 1960, JD, 1968. Bar: Ohio 1960. Mng. prin. Dettelbach, Sicherman & Baumgart, Cleve., 1971—. Editorial bd.: Case-Western Res. Law Rev, 1958-60; Contbr. articles to legal jours. Mem. Beachwood (Ohio) Civic League, 1972-92; mem. Beachwood Bd. Edn., 1978-86, pres., 1981, 85, v.p., 1984; trustee Beachwood Arts Council, 1977-84. Mem. Ohio Bar Assn. (lectr. truth in lending 1969, lectr. bankruptcy 1972, 81, 84, 99, 2000, Meritorious Service awards 1971, 77, 78, 79, 83, 84, 85, 86, 87), Cleve. Bar Assn. (lectr. practice and procedure clinic 1960-80, 82-87, chmn. bankruptcy ct. com. 1971-73), Jewish Chautauqua Soc., Tau Epsilon Rho, Zeta Beta Tau. Jewish (trustee Temple brotherhood 1968-76, sec. 1971-73). Home: 24500 Albert Ln Cleveland OH 44122-2302 Office: Dettelbach Sicherman & Baumgart 1100 Ohio Savings Plz Cleveland OH 44114 E-mail: msicherman@dsb-law.com.

SICHEWSKI, VERNON ROGER, physician; b. Winnipeg, Man., Can., Dec. 10, 1942; came to U.S., 1980; s. Nicholas and Helen (Sabanski) S. BS, U. Man., 1963; MD, Cairo U., 1979. Diplomate Am. Bd. Emergency Medicine. Resident Charity Hosp. La., New Orleans, 1980-83, Bellevue Hosp., N.Y.C., 1980-83; pvt. practice Broward Gen. Med. Ctr., Ft. Lauderdale, Fla., 1983-86, Trauma Care Assocs., North Miami, 1986—. Flight physician Nat. Jets, Ft. Lauderdale, 1986—; mem. Aero Jet Internat. Air Ambulance Profls., 1998; attending physician trauma unit Jackson Meml. Hosp. U. Miami, 1989-97; attending physician Cleve. Clin. Found. Hosp., Ft. Lauderdale, 1999—. Flight lt. RCAF, 1963-74. Fellow Am. Coll. Emergency Physicians; mem. AMA, So. Med. Assn. Republican. Roman Catholic. Avocations: stamp collecting, hunting, fishing, antiques. Home: 1108-2841 N Ocean Blvd Fort Lauderdale FL 33308 Office: Ste 941 1600 S Federal Hwy Pompano Beach FL 33062-7520

SICHUK, GEORGE, entrepreneur; b. Butler Twp., Pa., May 10, 1933; s. Stephan Nicholas and Eva (Hawranick) Sichuk; m. Georgiana Nadya Stroyen, July 27, 1968. BA, Drew U., 1954; PhD, Rutgers U., 1962. Rsch. assoc. Sloan-Kettering Inst. Cancer Rsch., N.Y.C., 1961—71; asst. prof. biology Montclair State Coll., Upper Montclair, NJ, 1972—75, William Paterson Coll., Wayne, 1975; lectr. interdisciplinary studies Bloomfield (N.J.) Coll., 1976; sci. tchr. Eastside H.S., Paterson, 1988—93; entrepreneur author Lincoln Park, 1993—. Author: Gabriel's Voice, 1996, Uriel's Light, 1997, One Man's Testament, 1998; contbr. articles to profl. med. jours. Good will amb. U.S. Govt., Cuba, 1960; coach Police Athletic League, Lincoln Park, 1977—79; exec. and coach Orthodox Christian Club, NJ, 1980—90. Achievements include clarification of relationship of th eendocrine and immune systems to cancer to direct atention to the nucleic acids (DNA and RNA); research in the role of sex hormones to thrombotic disease; clarification of transplantation immunology. Avocations: landscaping, house maintenance engineering, golf, cooking, pinochle. Home: 18 Sewanois Ave Lincoln Park NJ 07035-1710

SICILIAN, JAMES MICHAEL, research engineer; b. Bronx, N.Y., May 25, 1947; s. Leonard James and Veronica Patricia (Reinwald) S. BS, MIT, 1969; MS, Stanford U., 1970, PhD, 1973. Tech. editor C.S. Draper Lab., Cambridge, Mass., 1968-69; research analyst Savannah River Lab., Aiken, S.C., 1973-76; staff Los Alamos (N.Mex) Scientific Lab, 1976-79, asst. group leader, 1979-80; sr. scientist Flow Science, Inc., Los Alamos, 1980-96, sec. of corp., 1980-96, v.p., 1990-96; treas. LFD Techs., Inc., 1998—; mem. staff Los Alamos (N.Mex.) Nat. Lab., 2002—. Cons., Los Alamos, N.Mex., 1996—2002. Mem. Cultural Ctr. adv. com., Los Alamos, 1987-89; vice chmn. Park and Recreation Bd., Los Alamos, 1989-90; treas. N.Mex. Theater Assn., 1983-85; pres. Los Alamos Little Theater, 1978-79, v.p., 1997-98, sec., 2000-02; sec. Los Alamos Light Opera, 1990-91. Recipient AEC spl. fellowship, U.S. AEC, 1969-72. Mem. AAAS, AIAA, ASME, Sigma Xi. Avocations: theatrical productions, skiing. Office: Los Alamos Nat Lab MX K784 PO Box 1663 Los Alamos NM 87545 E-mail: sicilian@alum.mit.edu.

SICILIANI, ALESSANDRO DOMENICO, conductor; b. Florence, Italy; s. Francesco and Ambra Siciliani; m. Elizabeth Holleque; 1 child, Giacomo Francesco. Student, Giuseppe Verdi Milano Cons., Rome, Santa Cecilia; studied with, Franco Ferrara. Music advisor Columbus Symphony Orch., 1991—, music dir., 1992—. Condr. Nat. Radio Orchs. of Rome and Naples, Symphony of Abruzzi, Palermo Symphony Orch., Cagliari Symphony Orch., Bari Symphony Orch., N.Y. City Opera, Opera Co. of Phila., New Orleans Opera, Ky. Opera, Teatro San Carlo, Naples, Italy, Teatro dell'Opera, Rome, Teatro Massimo, Palermo, Italy, Verdi, Pisa, Italy, also Barcelona, Spain, Marseille, France, Avignon, and Liege; condr. revivals Cavalleria Rusticana, Pagliacci, N.Y. City Opera's revival La Rondine, Am. premiere Schubert's Fierrabras; appeared with Pitts. Symphony, Nat. Symphony, Washington, D.C., Munich Symphony Orch., Cologne Symphony Orch., Dresden Symphony Orch., Stockholm Symphony Orch., Goteborg Symphony Orch., Hong Kong Symphony Orch., Nat. Arts Ctr. Orch. of Ottawa, English Chamber Orch., Symphonia Varsovia, Perugia Chamber Orch., Padova Chamber Orch.; participant festivals including Schleswig-Holstein, Panatenee Pompeiane, Printemps Festival of Praha, Spring Festival in Saratoga Springs, Sagra Musicale Umbra; prin. guest condr. Orch. Teatro Colon, Buenos Aires, Teatro Mcpl. Sao Paulo. Recipient Amerigo Vespucci award, 1992. Office: Columbus Symphony Orch/Ohio Theater 55 E State St Columbus OH 43215-4203 also: Herbert Barrett Mgmt 1776 Broadway Ste 1610 New York NY 10019-2002*

SICILIANO, ROCCO CARMINE, institute executive; b. Salt Lake City, Mar. 4, 1922; s. Joseph Vincent and Mary (Arnone) S.; m. Marion Stiebel, Nov. 8, 1947; children: Loretta, A. Vincent, Fred R., John C., Maria. BA with honors, U. Utah, 1944; LL.B., Georgetown U., 1948; LHD, Hebrew Union Coll., Gettysburg Coll., 2000, U. Utah, 2001. Bar: D.C. bar 1949. Legal asst. to bd. mem. NLRB, Washington, 1948-50; asst. sec.-treas. Procon Inc., Des Plaines, Ill., 1950-53; asst. sec. labor charge employment and manpower Dept. Labor, Washington, 1953-57; spl. asst. to Eisenhower for personnel mgmt., 1957-59; ptnr. Wilkinson, Cragun & Barker, 1959-69; pres. Pacific Maritime Assn., San Francisco, 1965-69; undersec. of commerce Washington, 1969-71; pres., chmn. bd., chief exec. officer Ticor, Los Angeles, 1971-84, chmn., exec. com., 1984-85; of counsel Jones, Day, Reavis & Pogue, 1984-87; chmn. bd., chief exec. officer Am. Health Properties, Inc., 1987-88; chmn. Dwight D. Eisenhower World Affairs Inst., Washington, 1991-2001; apptd. mem. Eisenhower Meml. Commn., 2000, chmn., 2001—. Chmn. Ctr. for Govtl. Studies, 1992—; commr. Calif. Citizens Budget Commn.; mem. Fed. Pay Bd., 1971-73; trustee emeritus J. Paul Getty Trust. Past chmn. Calif. Bus. Roundtable; trustee Com. for Econ. Devel.; co-chmn. Calif. Commn. on Campaign Financing. 1st lt. AUS, 1943-46, MTO, ETO. Decorated Bronze Star, Combat Infantryman's badge; Order of Merit (Italy). Mem. Nat. Acad. Pub. Adminstrn., Met. Club (Washington), L.A. Philharm. Assn. (life dir.), Calif. Club (L.A.). Home: 612 N Rodeo Dr Beverly Hills CA 90210-3208

SICK, WILLIAM NORMAN, JR. venture capital company executive; b. Houston, Apr. 20, 1935; s. William Norman and Gladys Phylena (Armstrong) S.; m. Stephanie Anne Williams, Sept. 14, 1963; children: Jill Melanie, David Louis. BA, Rice U., 1957, BSEE, 1958. With Tex. Instruments Inc., various locations, 1958-87; exec. v.p. Tex. Instruments, Inc., Dallas, 1982-87; pres. semicondr. products group Tex. Instruments Inc., 1982-86; bd. dirs. Tex. Instruments, Inc., 1985-87; CEO Am. Nat. Can Co., Chgo., 1988-89; also bd. dirs. Am. Nat. Can. Co., 1988-89; mem. exec. com. Pechiney, Paris, 1989; bd. dirs. Pechiney Internat., 1989; vice, chmn., bd. dirs. Triangle Industries, N.Y.C., 1988—89; chmn., CEO, Bus. Resources Internat., Winnetka, Ill., 1989—; co-founder, mng. dir. Signature Capital Mgmt., LLC, Northfield, 1997—. Co-founder Metasolv, Dallas; bd. dirs. Acoustic Techs., Mesa, Ariz., VIRxSYS, Gaithersburg, Md.; former chmn. Aware, Bedford, Mass., Power Trends, Warrenville, Ill.; guest lectr. Sophia U., Tokyo, 1973. Trustee, past chmn. Shedd Aquarium, Chgo., 1990—; trustee Rice U., 1996—, Santa Fe Inst., 2000—. Mem. Chgo. Com., Exec. Club Chgo., Glenview Club, Sigma Xi, Tau Beta Pi, Sigma Tau. Episcopalian. Office: Bus Resources Internat PO Box 500 Winnetka IL 60093-0500

SICKAFUS, KURT EDWARD, materials scientist, researcher; b. Charlottesville, Va., Oct. 14, 1956; s. Edward Nathan and Mary Sue Sickafus; m. Talissa Kay Ralph, Sept. 13, 1983. BA, Ohio Wesleyan U., 1978; MS, PhD, Cornell U., 1985. Postdoctoral rsch. asst. Cavendish Lab. U. Cambridge, England, 1985—87; staff engr./scientist IBM, Tucson, 1987—88; project leader, mem. tech. staff Los Alamos (N.Mex.) Nat. Lab., 1989—. Fellow: The Am. Ceramic Soc.; mem.: Royal Microscopical Soc. (Gt. Britain), Inst. of Physics (Gt. Britain), Minerals, Metals, and Materials Soc., Electron Microscopy Soc. Am., Mineral. Soc. Am., Am. Phys. Soc., Am. Chem. Soc., Am. Nuc. Soc., Materials Rsch. Soc., Böhmische Phys. Soc. Avocations: horseback riding, photography, basketball. Home: Rt. 1 Box 28 Santa Cruz NM 87567 Office: Los Alamos Nat Lab PO Box 1663 MS-G755 Los Alamos NM 87545 Office Fax: 505-667-6802. Business E-Mail: kurt@lanl.gov.

SICKEL, EDWARD FRANCIS, surgeon; b. Reading, Pa., 1932; MD, U. Pa., 1958. Intern Harrisburg (Pa.) Hosp., 1958-59; resident Geisinger Med. Ctr., Danville, Pa., 1961-65; mem. staff Polyclin Med. Ctr., Harrisburg, 1965—, Holy Spirit Hosp., 1970—. Assoc. prof. surgery Pa. State U. With USN, 1959-61. Mem. AMA, Am. Acad. Otolaryngology-Head and Neck Surgery, Pa. Med. Soc. Office: 1000 N Front St Ste 400 Wormleysburg PA 17043-1034

SICKEL, JOAN SOTTILARE, foundation administrator; b. Jersey City, Dec. 29, 1941; d. Peter S. and Rose M. (Maresca) Sottilare; m. Walter F. Sickel Jr., Jan. 4, 1964 (div. July 1979); children: Walter F. III (dec.), Linda Hilaire. AB, Georgian Ct. Coll., 1963. Dir. ann. giving Tucson Med. Ctr. Found., 1980-87; dir. devel. and pub. rels. Ariz. Children's Home, Tucson, 1987-93; exec. dir. Ariz. Children's Home Found., 1993-94; curator edn. program devel. Ariz. Aerospace Found., 1995-96; tchr. Amphitheater Pub. Schs., 1997-98; pub. info. officer Ariz. Hist. Soc., 1998-2000, dir. pub. rels. & mktg., 2001—. Mem. women's studies adv. coun. U. Ariz. Mem. Nat. Soc. Fund Raising Execs., Nat. Assn. for Hosp. Devel., Pub. Rels. Soc. Am., Planned Giving Round Table of So. Ariz., AAUW, Ariz. Assn. for Hosp. Devel. (treas. 1986-88), U. Ariz. Presidents Club, U. Ariz. Wildcat Club, Soroptimists Internat. (chair fin. com. 1985). Home: 4151 N Camino Ferreo Tucson AZ 85750-6358 Office: Ariz Hist Soc 949 E 2nd St Tucson AZ 85719-4840

SICKELS, ROBERT JUDD, political science educator; b. Nyack, N.Y., June 26, 1931; s. Robert and Dorothy (Judd) S.; m. Alice Esterer; children: Stephen Judd, Wendy. BA, U. Chgo., 1950, MA, 1954; PhD, Johns Hopkins U., 1960. Asst. staff dir. Pres.'s Commn. on Registration and Voting Participation, Washington, 1963-64; asso. dir. exec. insts. U.S. CSC, 1964-65; asso. prof. polit. sci. Purdue U., West Lafayette, Ind., 1965-68; assoc. prof. polit. sci. U. N.Mex., Albuquerque, 1968-73, prof., 1973-95, prof. emeritus, 1995—, chmn. dept., 1976-81. Author: Race, Marriage, and the Law, 1972, Presidential Transactions, 1974, The Presidency, 1980, John Paul Stevens and The Constitution: The Search for Balance, 1988; contbr. articles to profl. jours. Home: 1514 Harvard Ct NE Albuquerque NM 87106-3712

SICKLES, CARLTON RALPH, employee benefit consultant; b. Hamden, Conn., June 15, 1921; s. Carlton Wilbur and Louise Edith (Torelli) S.; m. Simone Semailovna Shornick, Feb. 16, 1947 (dec. Jan. 1990); 1 child, Simone Louise Rockstroh; m. Jacqueline Bridewell Eig, Mar. 4, 1997. BSS cum laude, Georgetown U., 1943, JD, 1948. Bar: Md. Asst. gen. counsel United Mine Workers of Am. Welfare/Retirement Fund, 1949-51; atty., 1952-89; ptnr. Carday Assocs., Inc., 1952-59, part owner, v.p. and sec., 1960-70, pres., 1970-97, sr. v.p., 1997—; ptnr. Goldberg, Thompson, Pasternak & Sickles, 1979-86. Gen. counsel Internat. Assn. of Heat and Frost Insulators and Asbestos Workers, 1954-63; adj. prof. Georgetown U. Law Sch., 1960-67; mem. U.S. Congress, 1963-67, Md. Congress-at-Large; del. Md. Constnl. Conv., 1967-68, Md. Ho. of Dels., 1955-62, chmn. labor com., 1959-62; profl. neutral trustee United Mine Workers Combined Health Fund, 1993-98; pension reporter, mem. adv. com. Bur. Nat. Affairs, 1976-84. Bd. dirs. Washington Met. Area Transit Authority, 1967-73, chmn. 1971, alt. dir. 1975-78, 81—; commr. Washington Suburban Transit Commn., 1967-73, chmn. 1967, 75-79, chmn. 1977, 81—, chmn. 1992; mem. Internat. Met. R.R.s Com., Internat. Union of Pub. Transit, 1987—; commr. Md. State Planning Commn., 1969-80; mem. Washington Met. Coun. of Govts., chmn. 1962, 63; mem. Joint Commn. to Study Passenger Carrier Facilities in Met. Washington Area, 1955-66; chmn. Coun. of Govts. adv. com. on health info. systems, 1973-76; mem. U.S. Dept. HEW task force, 1974; bd. dirs. Prince George's Gen. Hosp. and Med. Ctr., 1974-76; chmn. Gov.'s Commn. to Study the Md. Pub. Svc. Commn., 1977-80; bd. dirs. Assn. of Pvt. Pension and Welfare Plans, Inc., 1969-79, pres., 1975-77, numerous others; bd. mem. Strathmore Found. Art Ctr., Montgomery County, 1980—, treas., 1989—; bd dirs. Internat. Found. Employee Benefit Plans, 1965-67, 69-74, pres., chmn. bd., 1974, mem. various coms., 1974—; mem. nat. coordinating com. Multi-Employer Plans, chmn. adminstrs. adv. com., 1976—. Served in U.S. Army, Inf., 1943-46, USAF, 1951-52, Korea. Mem. D.C. Bar assn., Prince George's County Bar Assn., Former Mems. of Congress (bd. dirs. 1965-67, 69-74, bd.d irs. 1965-67, 69-74, pres., chmn. bd. 1974, counselor 1983—), Cosmos Club Washington. Democrat. Roman Catholic. Avocations: music, photography. Office: 4600 Powder Mill Rd Ste 100 Beltsville MD 20705-2647 E-mail: carday@aol.com.

SICKLES, HELMA-JANE, museum executive; b. Knoxville, Tenn., Jan. 1, 1954; d. John William and Evelyn Joyce (Huff) Fawver; 1 child, Andrew Payne Shockley; m. James Thomas Sickles, 1997. BA in Speech Comm., U. Tenn., Knoxville, 1990. Cert. tourism profl., Tenn. Events coord. Affiliated Food Brokerage, Bristol, Tenn., 1989-96; exec. dir. Ramsey House Plantation, Knoxville, 1996-99; mgr., dir. Gateway Regional Visitor Ctr., 1999—2001. Travel columnist N.E. Knox Optomist. Bd. dirs. East Knox county Bus. and Profl. Assn., 1998-2000. Mem. Great Smoky Mt. Natural History Assn., S.E. Mus. Conf., Museums of Knoxville, Knox Area Mus. Edn. Roundtable, Knoxville Mus. Art, Historic Homes of Knoxville, Tenn. Tourism Roundtable, Vol. Landing Assn. (ops.). Republican. Avocations: theater, water sports, needlecrafts. Home: 397 Drummer Ln Knoxville TN 37924-2824 E-mail: hjsickles@aol.com.

SIDAMON-ERISTOFF, ANNE PHIPPS, community trust executive; b. N.Y.C., Sept. 12, 1932; d. Howard and Harriet Dyer (Price) Phipps; m. Constantine Sidamon-Eristoff, June 29, 1957; children— Simon, Elizabeth, Andrew. BA, Bryn Mawr Coll., 1954. Chmn. emerita Am. Mus. Natural History, N.Y.C.; dir.-at-large Black Rock Forest Consortium; chmn. N.Y. Cmty. Trust. Trustee God Bless Am. Fund, Hudson River Found., Sept. 11th Fund Bd. dirs. Greenacre Found., Highland Falls (N.Y.) Libr.; trustee World Wildlife Fund, Storm King Art Ctr., Mountainville, N.Y.; past bd. dirs. Scenic Hudson, St. Bernard's Sch., N.Y.C., Mus. Modern Art, N.Y.C., Mus. Hudson Highlands; trustee God Bless Am. Fund, Hudson River Found., Sept. 11th Fund Address: 120 E End Ave New York NY 10028-7552 E-mail: ananouri@aol.com.

SIDAMON-ERISTOFF, CONSTANTINE, lawyer; b. N.Y.C., June 28, 1930; s. Simon C. and Anne Huntington (Tracy) Sidamon-E.; m. Anne Phipps, June 29, 1957; children: Simon, Elizabeth, Andrew. BSE. in Geol. Engring. Princeton U., 1952; LL.B., Columbia U., 1957. Clk., then assoc. firm Kelley Drye Newhall Maginnes & Warren, N.Y.C., 1957-64; individual practice law, 1964-65, 74-77; exec. asst. to Congressman John V. Lindsay, 1964-65; city coordinator Lindsay Mayoral Campaign, N.Y.C., 1965; asst. to mayor City of N.Y., 1966, commr. hwys., 1967-68, transp. adminstr., 1968-73; ptnr. Sidamon-Eristoff, Morrison, Warren, & Ecker, N.Y.C., 1978-83; counsel Morrison & de Roos, 1984-88; pvt. practice N.Y.C., 1988-89; regional adminstr. Region II EPA, 1989-93; of counsel Patterson, Belknap, Webb & Tyler, 1993-99, Lacher & Lovell-Taylor P.C., N.Y.C., 1999—. Mem. N.Y. State Met. Transp. Authority Bd., 1974—89; commr. N.Y. State Jud. Commn. on Minorities, 1987—91; mem. Gov.'s Coun. on Hudson River Valley Greenway, 1989—89; trustee United Mut. Savs. Bank, N.Y.C., 1979—82, Phipps Houses, N.Y.C., 1974—, chmn., 1986—2001, chmn. emeritus, 2001—. Trustee Am. the Beautiful Fund, Washington, 1985—97; chmn. Audubon N.Y., 1999—; trustee Allaverdy Found., N.Y.C., 1962—, Am. Farm Sch., Thessaloniki, Greece, 1973—79, Carnegie Hall, N.Y.C., 1967—92, Millbrook (N.Y.) Sch., 1971—89, hon. trustee, 1989—, Orange County (N.Y.) Citizens Found., 1974—81; bd. dirs., mem. exec. com. Mid-Hudson Pattern for Progress, Poughkeepsie, NY, 1975—89, chmn., 1981—85; bd. dirs. Coun. on Mcpl. Performance, N.Y.C., 1979—87, chmn., 1981—85, vice chmn., 1986—87; mem. Orange County (N.Y.) Planning Bd., 1997—; N.Y. State Rep. committeeman, 1980—89; chmn. emeritus Tolstoy Found., N.Y.C., 2001—, bd. dirs., 1975—2002, chmn., bd. dirs., 1979—89, 1994—2001; bd. dirs. Caramoor Ctr. Music and Arts, Katonah, NY, 1961—80, Boyce Thompson Inst. for Plant Rsch., Ithaca, 1994—; emeritus Tolstoy Found., N.Y.C., 2001—. 1st lt. arty. AUS, 1952—54, Korea. Decorated Bronze Star; co-recipient Civic Leadership award (with wife), Citizens Union, 1997, Force for Nature award (with wife), Natural Resources Def. Coun., 1999, Environ. Leadership award (with wife), Nat. Audubon Soc., 2001; recipient Honor award, Kings County chpt. N.Y. State Soc. Profl. Engrs., 1969, Greater N.Y. coun. Girls Scouts U.S., 1973, Bd. Leadership award, Coun. Mcpl. Performance, 1984, Transp. Manof Yr. award, Greater N.Y. March of Dimes, 1985, award of excellence, Mid-Hudson Pattern for Progress, 1990, Honor award, Nat. and N.Y. Parks and Conservation Assn., 1992, Bronze medal, USEPA, 1993. Mem. ABA, N.Y. State Bar Assn., Assn. of Bar of City of N.Y., N.Y. County Lawyers Assn., Kent Moot Ct., AIME, Phi Delta Phi, Delta Psi. Clubs: Century Assn. (N.Y.C.), Knickerbocker (N.Y.C.), Racquet and Tennis (N.Y.C.). Eastern Orthodox. Office: Lacher & Lovell-Taylor PC 6th Fl 770 Lexington Ave New York NY 10021-8165 E-mail: cseristoff@lltlaw.com., ananouri@aol.com.

SIDAR, THOMAS WILSON, retail executive; b. New Brunswick, N.J., Nov. 21, 1949; s. Alexander George Jr. and Jean (Wilson) S.; m. Ellen Elizabeth Woods BA, Colby Coll., 1972. Sales rep. L.L. Bean, Inc., Freeport, Maine, 1975, retail buyer, 1976—82, asst. product mgr., 1982—85, product mgr., 1985—88, sr. product mgr., 1988—89, dir. product devel., 1990—, v.p. creative dept., 1991—98, sr. v.p., gen. mgr. of men's strategic bus. unit, 1998—2001, chief mktg. officer, mem. office of pres., 2001—. With L.L. Bean Inc. Trustee North Yarmouth Acad.; vice chair adv. commn., chair park use com. Acadia Nat. Park. Mem. Maine Inland Fisheries and Wildlife (adv. com. non-game), Leadership Maine (Maine Devel. Found.), Appalachian Mountain Club (bd. dirs., exec. com., chmn. capital campaign com., bd. advisors), Megantic Club, The Woodlands Club. Democrat. Episcopalian. Avocations: fly fishing, bird hunting, cross-country skiing, mountain climbing, canoeing. Home: 91 Glen Rd Yarmouth ME 04096-8136 Office: LL Bean Inc Casco St Freeport ME 04033-0001

SIDDAYAO, CORAZÓN MORALES, economist, educator, consultant; b. Manila, July 26, 1932; came to U.S., 1968; d. Crispulo S. and Catalina T. (Morales) S. Cert. in elem. teaching, Philippine Normal Coll., 1951; BBA, U. East, Manila, 1962; MA in Econs., George Washington U., 1971, MPhil, PhD, 1975. Cert. Inst. de Francais, France. Tchr. pub. schs., Manila, 1951-53; exec. asst. multinational oil corps., 1953-68; asst. pensions officer IMF, Washington, 1968-71; cons. economist, 1971-75; rsch. assoc. Policy Studies in Sci. and Tech. George Washington U., 1971-72, teaching fellow dept. econs., 1972-75; natural gas specialist U.S. Fed. Energy Adminstrn., 1974-75; sr. rsch. economist, assoc. prof. Inst. S.E.A. Studies, Singapore, 1975-78; sr. rsch. fellow energy/economist East-West Ctr., 1978-81, project dir. energy and industrialization, 1981-86; vis. fellow London Sch. Econ., 1984-85; sr. energy economist in charge energy program Econ. Devel. Inst., World Bank, Washington, 1986-94, ret., 1994. Affiliate prof. econs. U. Hawaii, 1979—94; co-dir. UPecon Inst. Resource Studies, 1995—; vis. prof. econs. U. Montpellier, France, 1992, France, 1995—96, France, 1997—; vis. prof. pub. policy Duke U., 1997; lectr. pub. policy George Mason U., 2000; tchr. coord. English for Hispanic program Parish; cons., spkr. in field. Author or co-author: Increasing the Supply of Medical Personnel, 1973, The Offshore Petroleum Resources of Southeast Asia: Some Potential Conflicts and Related Economic Factors, 1978, Round Table Discussion on Asian and Multinational Corporations, 1978, The Supply of Petroleum Resources in Southeast Asia: Economic Implications of Evolving Property Rights Arrangements, 1980, Critical Energy Issues in Asia and the Pacific: The Next Twenty Years, 1982, Criteria for Energy Pricing Policy, 1985, Energy Demand and Economic Growth, 1986; editor, co-author: Energy Policy and Planning series, 1990-92, Energy Investments and the Environment, 1993; co-editor: Investissements Energetiques et Environnement, 1993; co-editor: (series) Energy Project Analysis for the CIS Countries (Russian), 1993, Politique d'Efficacité de l'Énergie et Environnement, Expérience pratiques, 1994, Matérial Pedagogique sur la Politique d'Efficacité de l'Energie et Environnement, 1994; contbr. chpts. to books, articles to profl. jours. Grantee in field. Mem.: Alliance Francaise, Internat. Assn. Energy Economists (charter), Am. Econ. Assn., Eucharistic Frat. of St. P.J. Eymard, World Bank 1818 Soc. (bd. dirs. 1999—2000), John Carroll Soc., Omicron Delta Epsilon. Roman Catholic. Office: 1201 S Eads St Ste 1712 Arlington VA 22202-2845 *Power and money were never the stimuli to my endeavors. Spiritual and intellectual challenges are what drive me. In the end, all our achievements mean nothing if we have not learned to appreciate them as gifts and shared what we can with others.*

SIDDIQ, PATRICIA KAY, artist; b. Indpls., Oct. 1, 1937; d. Howard David and Miriam Cory (Beckley) Foley; m. Mir A.F. Siddiq, June 13, 1966 (div. Jan. 1992); children: Sharif, Tim, Bob. BA, DePauw U., 1959; MA, Ind. U., 1964. Cert. art tchr., Ind. Elem. art tchr. West Aurora (Ill.) Pub. Schs., 1959-63, Ahlman Acad., Kabul, Afghanistan, 1976-79, Bartholomew County Schs., Columbus, Ind., 1985-88; secondary art tchr. Arlington H.S., Indpls., 1964-66; K-12 art tchr. Am. Internat. Sch., Kabul, 1967-73; illustrator Mgmt. Signs for Health, 1972-79, Eric Pearson, Chico, Calif., 1982-85; mgr., owner Nashville Frame Co., 1988-95; self-employed artist Morgantown, Ind., 1995—. Illustrator: An Afghan Speakeasy, 1969, illustrator: No So Long Ago, 1970, illustrator: An Afghan Guide to How Vegetables Grow, 1974, illustrator: The Kabul Georgers, 1978, illustrator: Midwifery Guide, 1979;exhibitions include Hoosier Salon, Indpls., 1967, 1991, 1997. Active T.C. Steele Hist. Site, Belmont, Ind.; chairperson Art Around Town revolving exhibits Ind. Heritage Arts, Nashville, 1991—. Recipient oil painting award Fox River Valley Art Assn., 1963. Mem.: Brown County Libr. Assn., Brown County Art Gallery Assn. (gallery artist 1997—, oil painting award 1996, oil painting award 2000), Ind. Heritage Arts (bd. dirs., past pres. 1992—93), Brown County Art Guild Assn. (oil painting award 1997), Kappa Pi, Psi Iota Xi (philanthropic chmn. 1982—88). Methodist. Avocations: music, flute, reading, walking, travel. Home: 5764 N East Shore Dr Morgantown IN 46160-8694

SIDDIQEE, MUHAMMAD WAHEEDUDDIN, electrical engineer; b. Lahore, Pakistan, Aug. 23, 1931; s. Muhammad Nazeeruddin and Ayesha Humaira Siddiqee; m. Sabiha Sultana Siddiqee, Dec. 24, 1961; 2 children. BA in Physics, Forman Christian Coll., Lahore, Pakistan, 1951; BSEE, Engring. Univ., Lahore, 1955; MSEE, U. Tenn., 1960; PhD in Control Sci., U. Minn., 1967. Elec. engr. Siemens Pakistan, Lahore, 1955—56, Siemens Germany, Erlangen, 1956—58; sr. elec. engr. Siemens Pakistan, Karachi, 1958—61; staff scientist Stanford Rsch. Inst., Menlo Park, Calif., 1967—82; info. systems specialist Lockheed Missiles and Space Co., Sunnyvale, 1982—93; tchr. Sunnyvale Sch. Dist., 1995—. Project leader Stanford Rsch. Inst., Menlo Park, Calif., 1976—82. Contbr. articles. Pres. United Muslims of Am., Calif., 1991—93, San Francisco Islamic Ctr., 1981—83, Pakistan Assn., San Francisco, 1975—77. Recipient Lockheed Pub. award, Lockheed Missiles and Space Co., Calif., 1988. Mem.: Assn. Ret. Am. Muslims (pres., founder 1996—). Avocation: Sitar player, cmty. activism in human rights. Home: 1733 Banff Dr Sunnyvale CA 94087

SIDDIQUE, MUHAMMAD, poultry pathobiologist; b. Faisalabad, Punjab, Pakistan, Jan. 1, 1950; s. Ghulam Ahmad and Naziran Begum; m. Farkhanda Jamil, Oct. 17, 1976; children: Amir, Imran, Hina. DVM, West Pakistan Agrl. U., Faisalabad, 1972; MSc with honors, U. Agr., Faisalabad, 1978; PhD, Inst. Agron. N.B., Bucharest, Romania, 1984; postgrad., U. Ga. Vet. officer L&DD, Lahore, Pakistan, 1973-74; lectr. in vet. pathology U. Agr., Faisalabad, 1975-86, asst. prof. vet. pathology, 1986-89, asst. prof. vet. microbiology, 1989-90, assoc. prof. vet. microbiology, 1990-99, chmn. dept. vet. microbiology, 1990-93, 96-98, prof. vet. microbiology, 1999—. Author: Current Situation of Poultry Industry in Pakistan, 1979; contbr. articles to profl. jours. Mem. Pakistan Vet. Med. Assn. (life, pres. 1987-89, mem. coun., Spl. award 1995), Pakistan Sci. Forum. Avocations: reading scientific treatises, quiz and mentor challanges. Home: 62 Rachna Town Faisalabad Punjab Pakistan Office: U Agr Vet Microbiology Faisalabad Punjab 38040 Pakistan

SIDDIQUI, DILNAWAZ AHMED, communications educator, international communication planning advisor, consultant; b. Amroha, India, July 4, 1937; came to U.S., 1975; s. Aijaz Rosool and Safina (Begum) Khan; m. Narjis Bano Naqvi, May 18, 1963; children: Shajee Raza, Aamera. BEd, MA, Aligarh Muslim U., Aligarh, India, 1960; postgrad., U. London, 1968, CAS, 1977; PhD, Syracuse U., 1980. Asst. prof. MSG Coll., Malegaon, India, 1961-63; edn. officer H.H. The Aga Khan and Ministry of Edn., Dar-es-salaam, Tanzania, Lusaka, Zambia, 1963-71; chmn. Sir Evelyn Hone Coll. Can. Commn. Tech. Edn. and Vocat. Tng. CIDA later under, Ministry of Edn., 1971-75; rsch. asst. tchg. asst. Syracuse U., 1975-80; dir. Human Resource Planning and Devel. Action Programs Internat., Washington, 1980; prof. faculty commn. Clarion U., Pa.; pres. Siddiqui Assocs., Shippenville. Cons. Can. Commn. for Tech. Edn. and Vocat. Tng., Lusaka, 1971-75, IDD&E Syracuse U., 1977-78; chief U.S. adviser human resource planning and devel. Ctrl. Planning Orgn., Prime Minister's Office, Yemen Arab Repulic, Sana'a, 1980-82; adviser Mid-East/Africa API, Sheladia Assocs., 1983—; cons. Ariz. State U., 1983, chief of party U.S. evaluators' team to Hashemite Kingdom of Jordan Adminstrv. Tng. Project IV, 1992; human resource devel. master plan adviser to Govt. of Sudan, 1994-95. Author: Human Resources Development Master Plan for the Government of Sudan, 1995; co-author: A Proposed System of Managing Scholarships, 1983, An Analysis of Comparative Adult Education Methods, 1988, The Gulf War: Implications for Global Business and Media, 1992, Contributions of A.N. Charters To Field of Adult Education, 2000; contbr. articles to profl. jours., chpts. to books; mem. editl. bd. T & D Jour. ASTD, 1988-2000, Am. Jour. Islamic Social Scis.; mem. rev. bd. Jour. Internat. Acad. Bus. Disciplines; contbr. to Field of Adult Education, 2000. Active Internat. Congress for Univ. Adult Edn.; mem. U.S./NGO Delegation to World Congress on Adult Edn. UNESCO, Hamburg, Germany, 1997; advisor Interfaith Coun. Syracuse U., 1975-80; chief coord. Nat. Millenium Conf. on Muslim Contbn. to Human Civilization, Midway Hill Ch., Dallas, 2001. Recipient substantive contbn. to lit. for edn. ERIC award, 1977, rsch. and svc. East and Ctrl. Africa Disting. Contbn. to Edn. Adults award ICAE award, 1980, Aligarh Muslim U. improtu lit. writing competition Gold medal award, 1958, 1st prize award Anjuman-e-Taraqqui-Urdu, Amroha, India, 1957, VC award for rsch. in Africa Syracuse U., 1978-79, Profl. Excellence award Am. Fedn. Muslims from India, 1997; named Academician honoris causa Russian Acad. Humanities, 1996. Mem. Am. Assn. Tng. and Devel. (mem. editl. bd. jour.), Assn. Muslim Soc. Scis. (pres. 1993-95), Internat. Comm. Assn. (meml editl. bd. world-wide web jour. 1996—). Home: 510 Ridgewood Rd Marianne Est Shippenville PA 16254 Office: Clarion U Pa Dept Comm Clarion PA 16214 E-mail: siddiqui@clarion.edu., siddiqui37d@netscape.net., drdilnawazsiddiqui@hotmail.com.

SIDDIQUI, FAROOQ AHMAD, protein biochemist; b. Unnao, India, Jan. 1, 1951; came to U.S., 1976; s. Siddique Ahmad and Humra (Ahmad) S.; m. Yasmeen Siddiqui, June 24, 1979; children: Tazeen, Sanna. BS in Biology, M.U. Aligarh, India, 1969; MS in Biochemistry, M.U., Aligarh, India, 1971, MPhil in Biochemistry, 1972, PhD in Biochemistry, 1975. Sr. rsch. fellow in biochemistry Patel Chest Inst., Delhi, 1975—76; cancer rsch. affiliate Dept. Exptl. Therapeutics Roswell Park Meml. Inst., Buffalo, 1976—79; vis. assoc. in biology McGill U., Montreal, Canada, 1979—80; rsch. assoc. biochemistry Georgetown U., Washington, 1980—81; rsch. assoc. medicine Divsn. Hematology U. Miami, 1981—83, rsch. instr. medicine Divsn. Hematology, 1983—85, rsch. asst. prof. medicine Divsn. Hematology/Oncology, 1985—94, rsch. assoc. prof. medicine divsn. hematology/oncology, 1994—95; sr. scientist Walt Disney Meml. Cancer Inst., Fla. Hosp., Orlando, 1998—2000; chief scientist Fla. Hosp. Cancer Inst., 2000—. Presenter in field. Contbr. articles to profl. jours. Grantee NIH, 1988-93, Fla. Hosp. GALA Endowed Program for Oncologic Rsch., 2000-02; fellow Coun. Sci. and Indsl. Rsch., New Delhi, 1971-72, Indian Coun. Med. Rsch., 1972-75. Mem.: Sigma Xi. Home: 557 Sabal Palm Cir Altamonte Springs FL 32701-2668

SIDDIQUI, SHAHRAM MOHAMMAD, lawyer; b. Washington, Aug. 8, 1973; BSBA, Boston U., 1995; JD, U. Pitts., 1998. Bar: N.J. 1998, Pa. 1998. Assoc. Cozen O'Connor, Phila., 1998—. Office: Cozen O'Connor 1900 Market St Philadelphia PA 19103 Office Fax: (215) 701-2472. E-mail: veritas73@hotmail.com.

SIDDONS, SARAH MAE, chemist; b. Conway, S.C., July 20, 1939; d. Willie C. and Lelia (Parker) Crawford; m. John Lathan, June 26, 1958 (div.); m. Ronald Gladstone Siddons, June 26, 1965; 1 child, Ronald George. BA, Coll. New Rochelle, 1980; postgrad., Cornell U., 1975. Lab. technologist DC37-Local 144, Bronx, 1961-65, 65-82; jr. chemist DC37-Local 375, 1982-85, assoc. chemist, 1985-90, assoc. chemist, supr., 1990—. Del. DC37-Lcoal 144, 1962-84, DC37-Local 375, 1984—. Mem. Am. Assn. Clin. Chemistry, Dynamic Five Social Club (pres. 1988—, v.p. 1980-88). Home: 3924 Carpenter Ave Bronx NY 10466-3705 Office: Lincoln Med Ctr 234 E 149th St Rm 432 Bronx NY 10451-5504 E-mail: ssiddons@excite.com.

SIDDOWAY, HENRY RALPH, company executive; b. Vernal, Utah, Oct. 9, 1905; s. William Henry and Emily Jane (Dunster) S.; m. Marsale Eunice Eaton, Apr. 21, 1924; children: William Ralph, Lynn Irvin, Charyl Anita. BS with honors, U. Utah, 1928, postgrad., 1963, Brigham Young U., 1929-30. Cert. secondary tchr., music tchr., social svc. worker. Tchr. Uintah High Sch., Vernal, Utah, 1928-46, treas., 1928-44; acct., bus. mgr. Calder Motor Co.-S. Calder, 1930-34; dir. and owners self interest 3000 sheep Utah, 1946-80; bus. mgr., dir. Vernal Milling Co., 1933-56; stockholder, dir., sec., treas. Ashley Coop. Merc. Inst., 1943-96; office mgr., acct. Calder Bros. Creamers, Vernal, 1947-50; office mgr. Uintah Oil Refinery, 1950-54; dir. S. Raven Oil & Refining co., Rangely, Colo., 1960-65. Mem. U.S. Bur. Land Mgmt., Uintah, Duchesne Dagget County, Utah, 1943-60, sec., 3 County, 1943-60, mem. adv. bd., 1957-60. Mem. Utah State Adv. Bd.; mem. Uintah County Bd., Edn., 1942, pres., 1944-45; mayor City of Vernal, 1958-62; bd. dirs. Uintah County Coun. on Aging, 1970-78; dir. Area Agy. on Aging, 1978-89. Recipient Help Line Profl. Svc. award Dept. Social Svcs. Div. Alcohlism and Drugs, Salt Lake City, 1978. Mem. Lions Club (sec. 1945, pres. 1946, zone chmn. 1947). Republican. Mem. Lds Ch. Home: 673 N Vernal Ave Vernal UT 84078-3703 Office: Ashley Coop Merc Inst 22 W Main St Vernal UT 84078-2502

SIDEBOTTOM, WILLIAM GEORGE, communications executive; b. Greeley, Colo., July 21, 1948; s. William Carroll and Florence Elaine (Krusenstjerna) S.; m. Rosemary Russell, May 16, 1981; children: Faith Ann, William Jeremiah. BS in Mgmt. cum laude, U. West Fla., 1975; MA in Pub. Policy magna cum laude, Regent U., 1985. Mgr. Mgmt. Recruiters, Internat., Pensacola, Fla., 1976-79, divsn. mgr. Virginia Beach, Va., 1979-81; dir. comm. Rock Ch., 1981-83; dir. devel., v.p. comm. Nat. Freedom Inst., Chesapeake, Va., 1983; pres. William G. Sidebottom & Assocs., 1986—, InterAct Response Comms., 1997—. Co-founder, pres./CEO Common Good, Inc., 2001—. Author: Who Owns the Children, 1985; sr. editor: The Perspective Papers, 1985, Essential Lectures, 1985. Cons. Am. Ctr. for Law and Justice, 1990-2002, Christian Advocates Serving Evangelism, 1995-2002, Christian Coalition, 1999—; sr. flight instr. U.S. Navy Aviation Tng. Ctr. Capt. USMC, 1970-76. Mem. Phi Kappa Phi, Pi Kappa Delta. Mem. Assembly of God Church. E-mail: irc@infi.net.

SIDELSKY, PATRICIA LONEY, science educator; b. Hanover, N.H., Jan. 5, 1945; d. Charles Alexander and Mary (Zurbrugg) Loney; m. Richard W. Lippincott, Apr. 17, 1971 (div. Apr. 1980); 1 child, Richard Ryan; m. Michael G. Sidelsky, May 24, 1980; 1 child, Cory Charles. BS in Biology, Bucknell U., 1967; MS in Biology, Rutgers U., 1987. Cert. in comprehensive sci. tchr., N.J. Tchr. sci. Easton (Md.) Mid. Sch., 1972-79; med. technologist Easton Meml. Hosp., 1974-76; tchr. Easton Middle Sch., 1976-79; tchr. advanced placement biology and genetics Cherokee High Sch., Marlton, N.J., 1979—; med. technologist HIP of N.J., Medford, 1979-87, 90-92; lead tchr. Ctr. for Maths., Sci. and Computer Edn. Rutgers U., New Brunswick, N.J., 1988-93; lead tchr. Douglass Summer Sci. Inst., 1988-92. Mem. Douglass Coll. Bd. for Women in Maths. & Sci., 1988-92. Co-author: Molecular Approaches to the Study of Gene Activity, 1987—. Recipient Outstanding Tchr. award, N.J., Nat. Assn. Biology Tchrs., 1989, Tandy Tchr. Scholar award, 1991; Access Excellence fellow Genentech, 1994; grantee Ptnrs. in Sci. Rsch. Corp., 1994-95; named Tchr. of Yr. Lenape Regional H.S. Dist., 1996. Mem. Biology Tchrs. Assn. N.J. (v.p. 1990, pres. elect 1991-92, pres. 1992—), Nat. Sci. Tchrs. Assn., N.J. Sci. Tchrs. Assn., Nat. Biology Tchrs. Assn., Am. Soc. Clin. Pathologists, Am. Soc. Microbiology. Episcopalian. Home: 8 Rockledge Ct Marlton NJ 08053-9774 Office: Cherokee High Sch Wildwood Rd Marlton NJ 08053

SIDENER, MARGARET WEIL LEATHERS, foundation administrator; b. Princeton, Ind., Dec. 22, 1949; d. Albert J. and Nora Jewel (Franklin) Weil; m. Charles Leathers, 1971 (div. Dec. 1987); children: Juliana L. Leathers, Kevin Sean Leathers; m. A. Ritchie Sidener, 1998. AB, U. Ill., 1971; MS, Russell Sage Coll., 1979. Cert. tchr. N.Y., health edn. specialist. Employment counselor Snelling & Snelling, Schenectady, NY, 1972-76; substitute tchr. Monahasen High/Jr. HS, 1978-79; grant abstractor State of N.Y., Albany, 1979; program coordinator Am. Lung Assn. Santa Clara-San Benito Counties, San Jose, Calif., 1982-84, dir. programs, 1984-87, nat. clinic leader trainer, 1986—, acting exec. dir., 1987-88, exec. dir., 1988—. Author: (book) Camp Superstuff Workbook and Teachers Manual, 1983; contbr. articles to profl. publs. and mags. Leader explorer post Boy Scouts Am., San Jose, 1988; mem. citizen's oversight com. Local Transp. Commn. Santa Clara County,

1993—94; county chair No on 188 campaign, 1994; mem. adminstrv. bd. coun. ministries, trustee United Meth. Ch.; bd. dirs., officer Santa Clara Valley Coun. Parent-Participating Nursery Schs., 1980—81; resource vol. Lyceum Santa Clara Valley, 1983—87; mem. staff 1st asthma camp Young Tchrs. Health, Russia, 1989, Seattle, 1990, San Jose, 1996; mem. steering com. Measure A, 1992. Named Woman of distinction, Alpha Xi Delta, 1999. Mem.: APHA, Calif. Coun. Execs. (pres. 1995), Am. Lung Assn., Assn. United Way Agys. (exec. bd. 1993, 2000), Rotary. Avocations: bicycling, hiking, needlepoint, teaching creative drama. Home: 1810 Frobisher Way San Jose CA 95124-1725 Office: Am Lung Assn 1469 Park Ave San Jose CA 95126-2530

SIDER, RONALD J. theology educator, author; b. Stevensville, Ont., Can., Sept. 17, 1939; m. Arbutus Lichti Sider, Aug. 19, 1961; children: Theodore Ronald, Michael Jay, Sonya Maria. BA with honors, Waterloo Luth. U., 1962; MA in History, Yale U., 1963, BD, 1967, PhD in History, 1969; DDiv (hon.), Westminster Coll., 1998. Lectr., asst. prof., then assoc. prof. Messiah Coll., 1968-78, acting dir., dean, 1971-75; assoc. prof. theology Ea. Bapt. Theol. Sem., Wynnewood, Pa., 1978-84, prof. theology and culture, 1984—2002, Ronald J. Sider prof. theology, holistic mission and pub. policy, 2002—. Coord., chair, convenor workshops in field; coord. Internat. Consultation on Simple Lifestyle, London, 1980; lectr. in field. Editor: Preaching on Peace, 1982, Lifestyle in the Eighties: An Evangelical Commitment to Simple Life-Style, 1982, Evangelicals and Development: Toward a Theology of Social Change, 1982, Living More Simply, 1980, Cry Justice: The Bible on Hunger and Poverty, 1988, 91, For They Shall Be Fed, 1997; author: Christ and Violence, 1979, Karlstadt's Battle with Luther: Documents in a Liberal-Radical Debate, 1978, 82, Evangelism, 1985, Rich Christians in an Age of Hunger: A Biblical Study, 1977, rev. edit., 1984, 90, 97, German edit., 1979, Dutch edit., 1980, Portuguese edit., 1984, Japanese edit., 1989, Chinese edit., 1998, Korean edit., 1998, Andreas Bodenstein Von Karlstadt, 1974, Genuine Christianity, 1996, (with Richard K. Taylor) Nuclear Holocaust and Christian Hope, 1982, English edit., 1984, (with Oliver O'Donovan) Peace and War: A Debate About Pacifism, 1985, (in Chinese) Evangelical Faith and Social Ethics, 1986, Completely Pro-Life, 1987, (with Michael A. King) Preaching About Life in Threatening World, 1988, (with Kathleen Hayes), JustLife/88: A 1988 Election Study Guide for Justice, Life and Peace, 1988, Testing the Limits of Nonviolence, 1988, One-Sided Christianity? Uniting the Church to Heal a Lost and Broken World, 1993, Cup of Water, Bread of Life: Inspiring Stories About Overcoming Lopsided Christianity, 1994, Good News and Good Works: A Theology for the Whole Gospel, 1999, Living Like Jesus, 1999, Just Generosity: A New Vision for Overcoming Poverty in America, 1999, (with Philip N. Olson and Heidi Rolland Unruh) Churches That Make a Difference: Reaching Your Community with Good News and Good Works, 2002; co-editor: Transformation mag., 1984-99; editor, contbr.: The Chicago Declaration, 1974; pub. Prism mag., 1993—, Green Cross, 1994-98, Creation Care, 1998-2002; contbr. numerous articles to profl. publs., chpts. to books. Head voter registration dr., New Haven, 1967; pres. Diamont St. Cmty. Ctr., 1986-91; exec. dir. Evangelicals for Social Action, 1987-92, pres., 1992—; exec. dir. Just Life, 1987-91, pres., 1991-94; bd. dirs. Bread for the World, 1978-84, Mennonite Ctrl. Com., 1978-80; co-chair Nat. Workshop on Race and Reconciliation, Atlanta, 1975. Malcolm Chase fellow, 1962-63, R.E. Darling fellow, 1963-64, fellow Yale U., 1967-68, Inst. for Advanced Christian Studies, 1976. Mem. Nat. Assn. Evangelicals (mem. social action commn. 1975—). Mennonite. Home: 312 W Logan St Philadelphia PA 19144-4120 Office: Ea Bapt Sem 6 E Lancaster Ave Wynnewood PA 19096-3430 E-mail: ronsider@esa-online.org.

SIDERER, JACK PHILIP, engineering executive; b. May 3, 1946; BSME, Poly. U. N.Y., 1968; MS in Indsl. Engring., Pa. State U., 1980. Diplomate Am. Acad. Environ. Engrs.; lic. profl. engr., Pa. Design engr. Boeing Aircraft Co., 1968-70; dir. sanitation engring. and environ. planning Streets Dept. City of Phila., 1970—. Instr. math. and computer sci. C.C. of Phila., 1982—; cons., trainer in field, 1980—; environ. trainer U.S. Govt. overseas. Contbr. articles to profl. jours. Trustee Torah Acad., Phila., 1980—; bd. dirs. Congregation Beth Hamedrosh, 1985—. Mem. ASME, Solid Waste Assn. N.Am., Am. Pub. Works Assn., Tau Beta Pi, Pi Tau Sigma. Avocations: cycling, swimming, photography. Home: 7006 Sherwood Rd Philadelphia PA 19151-2325 Office: Streets Dept City of Phila 1401 JFK Blvd Philadelphia PA 19102-1617

SIDERIS, GINA, developer, fundraiser, vocalist; b. Livingston, N.J., Nov. 16, 1963; d. Panagiotis (Peter) and Wilma Maria (Virgil) S. BA, Montclair (N.J.) State Coll., 1986. Grants coord. N.J. Symphony Orch., Newark, 1988-93; dir. devel. Mental Health Assn. Essex County, Montclair, N.J., 1993—. Soprano soloist St. Luke's Episcopal Ch., Montclair, 1984—. Mem. Nat. Soc. Fund-raising Execs. Office: Mental Health Assn of Essex County 33 S Fullerton Ave Montclair NJ 07042-3358

SIDES, JACK DAVIS, JR. lawyer; b. Dallas, Sept. 18, 1939; s. Jack Davis Sr. and Edith Eugenia (Lowrie) S.; m. Nancy Pauline Cantwell, July 22, 1967 (div. Sept. 1976); children: Mary Katharine, Jack Davis III; m. Laura Gail Miller, Aug. 2, 1979; children: Susan Ashley, Stacy Anne. BBA, U. Tex., 1962, JD with honors, 1963. Bar: Tex. 1963. Assoc. Jackson, Walker, et al, Dallas, 1963-67, White, McElroy, White, Sides & Rector, Dallas, 1968-78; sole practice, 1978—. Editor: U. Tex. Law Review, 1963. With USAFNG, 1963-69. Fellow Dallas Bar Found., Tex. Bar Found. (life); mem. ABA, Tex. Bar Assn. (grievance subcom. 1979-86), Dallas Bar Assn. (ethics com. 1973-77, jud. com. 1988—), Tex. Assn. Def. Counsel, Dallas Assn. Def. Counsel (sec. 1973-74). Clubs: Brook Hollow Golf (Dallas). Republican. Methodist. Avocations: reading, tennis, exercising. Office: 2301 Cedar Springs Rd Ste 350 Dallas TX 75201-7803 E-mail: jacksides@aol.com.

SIDES, KERMIT FRANKLIN, furniture manufacturing company executive; b. Lee County, Miss., Feb. 13, 1932; s. Robert Franklin and Francis Jet (Cox) S.; grad. high sch., Wheeler, Miss.; m. Edna E. Heavener, Aug. 1, 1953; children: Connie Ann, Timothy Franklin. Mfg. supr. Futorian Mfg. Co., New Albany and Okolona, Miss., 1953-69; v.p. mfg., gen. mgr. Action Industries, Verona, Miss., 1969-79; exec. v.p., sec., treas. PeopLounger Inc., Nettleton, Miss., 1979—, also dir. Indsl. chmn. Lee United Neighbors div. United Way, Tupelo, Miss., 1969-73; v.p., bd. dirs. Northeast Miss. Community Relations Assn.; co-founder PeopLoungers, 1979. Recipient award for Outstanding Contbn. to Appearance of City, 1981. Baptist. Home: 2637 Saint Andrews Dr Belden MS 38826-9413 Office: PO Drawer PO Box 429 Nettleton MS 38858-0429

SIDES, LARRY EUGENE, advertising executive; b. Albany, Ga., Nov. 14, 1946; s. Robert N. and Florine (Stewart) S.; m. Kathy Ashworth, Aug. 13, 1950. BA in Radio and TV, U. La., 1970, MS in Communications, 1975. News reporter Sta. KATC-TV, Lafayette, La., 1970-71; account exec. Herbert S. Benjamin Assocs., 1971-76; pres. Sides & Assocs., 1976—. Vice-chmn. Crimestoppers, Lafayette, 1985; bd. dirs. Episcopal Sch. Acadiana, Lafayette, 1987; pres. Gateway Found., 1990; active Leadership La., 1989, 90; mem. Coun. for a Better La., 1991-94; bd. dirs. La. Coun. on Child Abuse, 1992-96; active Leadership Lafayette, 1995; mem. vestry Episcopal Ch. of the Ascension, 2002—, coord. Cuba project, 2001—, jr. warden, 2002.. Named one of Outstanding Young Men of Am., Lafayette Jaycees, 1976; recipient Disting. Alumni award dept. comms. U. La., 1995. Mem. Am. Assn. Advt. Agys. (pres. La. coun., 1989-90), Am. Soc. Hosp. Pub. Rels., Pub. Rels. Soc. Am., Pub. Rels. Assn. La., Acadiana Advt. Fedn., Lafayette C. of C. (pres. 1989, Entrepreneur of Yr. 1983), Sigma Nu (alumni pres. Lafayette chpt. 1977). Clubs: Beaver (pres. 1986, Outstanding Club Mem. award 1976). Home: 1015 W Saint Mary Blvd Lafayette LA 70506-3420 Office: 404 Eraste Landry Rd Lafayette LA 70506-2324

SIDEY, HUGH SWANSON, correspondent; b. Greenfield, Iowa, Sept. 3, 1927; s. Kenneth H. and Alice Margaret (Swanson) S.; m. Alice Anne Trowbridge, Dec. 5, 1953; children— Cynthia Anne, Sandra, Bettina, Edwin. BS, Iowa State U., 1950. Reporter Adair County (Iowa) Free Press, 1950, The Nonpariel, Council Bluffs, Iowa, 1950-51, Omaha World-Herald, 1951-55; reporter Life mag., 1955-58; corr. Time mag., 1958-96; columnist The Presidency, Time mag., Life mag., 1966—; chief Washington Bur., Time mag., 1969-78, Washington contbg. editor, 1978-96. Contbr. Time mag., 1996—. Author: John F. Kennedy, President, 1963, A Very Personal Presidency, Lyndon Johnson in the White House, 1966, These United States, 1975, Portrait of a President, 1975, The Presidency, 1991, Portraits of the Presidents, 2000; co-author: 1,000 Ideas for Better News Pictures, 1956, The Memories, 1961—JFK—1963, 1973; contbr.: The Kennedy Circle. Served with AUS, 1945-46. Mem. White House Hist. Assn. (chmn. 2000—). Office: Time 555 12th St NW Ste 600 N Washington DC 20004-1200

SIDGMORE, JOHN W. telecommunications executive; BA in Econs., SUNY, 1973. With Litton Industries; v.p., gen. mgr. GE Info. Svcs., Rockville, Md.; pres., CEO CSC Intelicom, Bethesda, 1991-94, UUNET Tech., Inc., Falls Church, Va., 1994-2000; chmn. bd. dirs. Strategy.com Personal Intelligence Network, Vienna, 2000—02; pres., CEO WorldCom, Clinton, Miss., 2002—. Office: Worldcom Inc 500 Clinton Center Dr Clinton MS 39056*

SIDHU, SANJIV, information technology executive; married; 2 children. B in Chem. Engring., Osmania U., Hyderabad, India; M in Chem. Engring., Okla. State U.; postgrad. in Systems and Control Engring., Case Western U., Cleve. Software developer Tex. Instruments, Dallas; founder, CEO, chmn. i2 Techs., Inc. Avocations: sailing (mem. India's nat. sailing team), surfing. Office: i2 Techs 1i2 Pl 11701 Luna Rd Dallas TX 75234*

SIDLIK, THOMAS W. automotive executive; b. New Britain, Conn., Nov. 14, 1949; BS with hon. in Econ. & Fin., N.Y.U., 1971; MBA in Fin., U. Chgo., 1973. With controller's office car product devel. Ford Motor Co., 1973—80; from mgr. car profuct fin. analysis to exec. v.p. Chrysler Corp., Auburn Hills, Mich., 1980—98; exec. v.p. procurement & supply Chrysler group & Jeep ops. Daimler Chrysler, 1998—. Mgmt. bd. Daimler Chrysler, 1998—. Office: Daimler Chrysler Corp 1000 Chrysler Drive Auburn Hills MI 48326-2766*

SIDMAN, MICHAEL DAVID, electrical engineer, consultant; b. Malden, Mass., Apr. 13, 1953; s. Seymour Harvey and Irene Rebecca (Bazman) S.; m. Renee Gabrielle Mock; children: Jessica, Adam. BSEE, MSEE, Northeastern U., Boston, 1975; PhD, Stanford (Calif.) U., 1986. Mgr. servo/mech. advanced devel. Digital Equipment Corp., Colorado Springs, Colo., 1975-92; ind. engring. cons., 1992—. Adj. assoc. prof. U. Colo., Colorado Springs, 1993—; instr. matlab/simulink/toolbox The MathWorks, Inc., Natick, Mass., 1992—; expert witness patent litig.; spkr., presenter in field. Contbr. articles to profl. jours. Chmn. Nat. Storage Industry Consortium Disk Mechanics/Servo Systems Task Force, 1991. Mem. IEEE (sr., control systems soc., industry applications soc.), ASME (dynamic systems and control divsn., assoc. editor jour. Advances in Information Storage Systems 1990-92, co-chmn. Pikes Peak sect. 2001-02, chmn. Pikes Peak sect, 2002-), Tau Beta Pi (pres. 1974-75), Phi Kappa Phi, Eta Kappa Nu. Achievements include patents for integral-cycling (solid state) relay, dynamic filter for a moving head disk storage system, adaptive misposition correcting method for magnetic disk servo system, velocity estimator in a disk drive positioning system, methods of automatic gain control basis selection half-track servoing, continuous-plus-embedded servo system for magnetic disk device, faulkt tolerant frame, guardband and index detection methods, embedded burst demodulation methods, track identification and counting in a disk drive positioning system, self-tuning adaptive bandwidth regulator, extended range servo system for positioning a disk drive head over a selected track, combination embedded and dedicated servo system, high speed switched automatic gain control, methods of writing and detecting dibit servo encoding, disk drive with constant bandwidth automatic gain control, automatic correction of position demodulator offsets, active disturbance compensation system for disk drives, robust active damping control system. Office: 6120 Wilson Rd Colorado Springs CO 80919-3579

SIDMAN, RICHARD LEON, neuroscientist, educator; b. Boston, Sept. 19, 1928; s. Manuel and Annabelle (Seltzer) Sidman; m. Ljiljana Lekic, 1974. AB, Harvard U., 1949, MD (Jeffries Wyman scholar), 1953. Intern in medicine Boston City Hosp., 1953—54; asst. resident in neurology Mass. Gen. Hosp., Boston, 1955—56; staff scientist NIH, Bethesda, Md., 1956—58; instr. to prof. neuropathology Harvard U. Med. Sch., Boston, 1959—69, Bullard prof., 1969—99, prof. emeritus, 1999—; chief div. neurogenetics New Eng. Regional Primate Rsch. Ctr. Harvard Med. Sch., Southborough, 1991—99; sr. rsch. assoc. dept. neurosurgery Brigham and Womens Hosp., Boston, 1999—; sr. rsch. assoc. dept. neurology Beth Israel Deaconess Med. Ctr., 2001—. Chief dept. neurosci. Children's Hosp., Boston, 1972—88; 1st Richard Stearns Meml.ml. lectr. Albert Einstein Coll. Medicine , 1958; Bailey Meml. lectr. U. Sask., Canada, 1978; Waisman Meml. lectr. U. Wis. Author (with M. Sidman): Neuroanatomy - A Programmed Text, vol. 1, 1965; author: (with others) Catalog of the Neurological Mutants of the Mouse, 1965; author: (with R.D. Adams) Introduction to Neuropathology, 1968; author: (with others) Atlas of the Mouse Brain and Spinal Cord, 1971; contbr. numerous articles, book chpts., revs. on neuroembryology. Mem. sci. adv. com. Retinitis Pigmentosa Found.; bd. sci. overseers Jackson Lab., Bar Harbor, Maine. Served with USPHS, 1956—58. Recipient Soma Weiss student rsch. prizes, Harvard U. Med. Sch., 1951—53, Boylston Soc. Essay prize, 1953; fellow Harvard U. Mosley Travelling fellow, 1954—55, Neuroscis. Rsch. Program fellow, 1971—79. Fellow: Nat. Acad. Sci., Am. Acad. Arts and Scis.; mem.: AAAS, Tissue Culture Assn., Soc. Neurosci., Soc. Devel. Neurosci., Internat. Soc. Devel. Neurobiology, Soc. Devel. Biology, Internat. Brain Rsch. Orgn., Histochem. Soc., Am. Soc. Cell Biology, Am. Assn. Neuropathologists, Am. Assn. Anatomists, Am. Acad. Neurology. Office: Longwood Med Rsch Ctr 221 Longwood Ave Ste 118 Boston MA 02115-5804 E-mail: richard_sidman@hms.harvard.edu.

SIDMAN, ROBERT JOHN, lawyer; b. Cleve., Aug. 4, 1943; s. Charles Frances and Louise (Eckert) S.; m. Mary Mato, July 29, 1967; children: Christa Mary, Alicia Mary. BA, Benedictine Coll., 1965; JD, U. Notre Dame, 1968. Bar: Ohio 1968, U.S. Dist. Ct. (so. dist.) Ohio 1970, U.S. Ct. Appeals (6th cir.) 1971, U.S. Supreme Ct. 1971. Law clk. U.S. Dist. Ct. (so. dist.) Ohio, Columbus, 1968-70; assoc. Mayer, Tingley & Hurd, 1970-75; judge Bankruptcy Ct. U.S. Dist. Ct. (so. dits.) Ohio, 1975-82; ptnr. Vorys, Sater, Seymour & Pease, 1982—. Prof. Ohio State U. Law Sch., Columbus, 1984, 85, 86. Mem. Nat. Conf. Bankruptcy Judges (bd. dirs. 1981-82), Assn. Former Bankruptcy Judges (bd. dirs. 1983-89, treas. 1986-87, pres. 1988-89). Office: Vorys Sater Seymour & Pease PO Box 1008 52 E Gay St Columbus OH 43215-3161 E-mail: rjsidman@vssp.com., rsidman843@aol.com.

SIDNAM, ALAN NORTHCOTE, retired advertising executive, venture capitalist; b. Kalamazoo, July 14, 1916; s. William Northcote and Esther Lulu (Humphrey) S.; m. Shirley S. Meeker, Dec. 31, 1947 (div. Sept. 1975); 1 child, Caroline; m. Gloria Delli-Bovi, Oct. 10, 1975. BA, Kalamazoo Coll., 1937. Apprentice Staake-Schoonmaker, Kalamazoo, 1937-38; acct. exec., copywriter Winternitz & Cairns, N.Y.C., 1938-39, Robert Winternitz, Advt., N.Y.C., 1939-42; acct. exec., exec. v.p. Benton & Bowles, Advt., 1945-61; vice chmn. Ogilvy & Mather, 1963-68, cons., 1968-70; venture capitalist, 1970—. Founding investor, dir. Lindblad Travel, N.Y.C., 1961-75; investor, dir. Kelley Oil Corp., Houston, 1970-87. Vestryman St. George's Episcopal Ch., N.Y.C., 1964-65; trustee Kalamazoo Coll., 1971-82, Ch. Heavenly Rest Day Sch., N.Y.C., 1973-79; bd. dirs. Mus. Tower, N.Y.C., 1999—. 1st lt. USAF, 1942-45, PTO. Mem. Univ. Club (coun. 1986-88), Waccabuc Country Club (pres. 1955-56). Republican. Episcopalian. Avocations: tennis, golf.

SIDON, CLAUDIA MARIE, psychiatric and mental health nursing educator; b. Bellaire, Ohio, Feb. 6, 1946; d. Paul and Nell (Bernas) DePaulis; m. Michael Sidon; children: Michael II, Babe. Diploma, Wheeling (W.Va.) Hosp. Sch., 1966; BSN summa cum laude, Ohio U., Athens, 1979; MSN, W.Va. U., Morgantown, 1982. Lic. cert. social worker Bd. Social Worker Examiners, W.Va. Various staff positions Bellaire City Hosp., 1966-67, 72-77; adj. nursing faculty W.Va. No. C.C., Wheeling, 1977-82; nurse clinician, psychotherapist Valley Psychol. and Psychiat. Svcs., Moundsville, W.Va., 1984; psychotherapist, nurse clinician, case mgr. No. Panhandle Behavioral Health Ctr., Wheeling, 1984-88; assoc. prof. ADN program Belmont Tech. Coll., St. Clairsville, Ohio, 1988—. Presenter in field. Mem. Tri-State Psychiat. Nursing Assn. (past pres., v.p., program chmn.), Nat. League for Nursing (presenter), Phi Kappa Phi, Sigma Theta Tau. Home: 52295 Sidon Rd Dillonvale OH 43917-9538 Office: Belmont Tech Coll 120 Fox Shannon Pl Saint Clairsville OH 43950-9766

SIDOR, MICHAEL LOUIS, orthopedic surgeon; b. Johnstown, Pa., May 24, 1961; s. Bernard Stephen and Helen Marie (DeBarto) S.; m. Francesca DiLeonardo, July 22, 1997; children: Alexander, Matthew. BS, Allegheny Coll., 1983; MD, Temple U., 1987. Surg. intern Pa. Hosp., Phila., 1987-88; orthopaedic surgery resident Hosp. for Joint Diseases, N.Y.C., 1988-92; arthroscopic surgery fellow Temple U., Phila., 1992-93; pvt. practice N.J. Knee and Shoulder Ctr., Mt. Laurel, N.J., 1995—, King of Prussia, Pa., 1997—. Assoc. dir. U. Pa. Sports Medicine Ctr., 1995—97; asst. prof. dept. orthopaedic surgery U. Pa. , 1995—97, arthroscopy fellow dept. orthopaedic surgery, 1995—97; clin. instr. dept. orthopaedic surgery Temple U. Cons., reviewer Jour. Musculoskeletal Medicine; contbr. chpts. to books, articles to profl. jours. Head team physician U. Pa. Ivy League athletic teams, 1995-97; asst. team physician Temple U. Divsn. 1 athletic teams, 1992-93. Recipient John Lachman award Temple U. Sch. Medicine, 1987, Sloane Clin. Rsch. award Hosp. for Joint Disease, 1992; named one of Am. Top Surgeons, Consumers Rsch. Coun. Am. Fellow: Am. Acad. Orthopaedic Surgeons, Arthroscopy Assn. N.Am.; mem.: Hosp. for Joint Diseases Alumni Assn., Am. Assn. Physicians & Surgeons, Phila. Orthopaedic Soc. for Sports Medicine, Phila. Orthopaedic Soc., NJ Orthopaedic Soc., Pa. Orthopaedic Soc., Ivy League Team Physician Assn. (U. Pa. rep.), Phi Beta Kappa. Office: Pa Knee and Shoulder Ctr Renaissance Corp Park 3400 Horizon Dr Ste 130 King Of Prussia PA 19406 also: NJ Knee & Shoulder Ctr Ste 100 1288 Rt 73 South Mount Laurel NJ 08054

SIDOTI, DANIEL R. food technologist; b. North Bergen, N.J., Jan. 17, 1921; s. John and Dora (Disposti) S.; m. Gloria V. Tressler, Mar. 24, 1951; 1 child, Lisa Stephanie. BA, Union Coll., Schenectady, N.Y., 1947; MS, Stevens Inst. Tech., 1959. Sect. head Gen. Foods Corp., Tarrytown, N.Y., 1947-66; group leader Monsanto Co., St. Louis, 1966-69; rsch. mgr. Anheuser-Busch Co., Inc., 1969-91; cons. Food Product R&D, Ballwin, Mo. Patentee in field. Loaned exec. United Way of Greater St. Louis, 1992—; area coord. U.S. Congressman, 2d Congl. Dist., 1994-2000. Lt. (j.g.) USN, 1942-46. Mem.: St. Louis Acad. Sci. (nat. councilor 1976—89), Inst. Food Technologists (chmn. St. Louis sect. 1973), U.S. Naval Inst., U.S. Navy League, U. Mo. Extension Coun. (St. Louis County Region). Republican. Presbyterian. Avocations: gardening, reading. Home: 500 Wellshire Ct Ballwin MO 63011-2550 E-mail: drsidoti@earthlink.net.

SIDWELL, ROBERT WILLIAM, virologist, educator; b. Huntington Park, Calif., Mar. 17, 1937; s. Robert Glen and Eva Amalie (Gordy) S.; m. Rhea Julander, May 31, 1957; children: Richard Dale, Jeanette Kathleen, David Eugene, Cynthia Diane, Michael Jason, Robert Odell. BS, Brigham Young U., 1958; MS, U. Utah, 1961, PhD, 1963. Head serology, ricketts and virus research Epizoology Lab., U. Utah, 1958-63; head virus div. So. Research Inst., Birmingham, Ala., 1963-69; head dept. virology ICN Nucleic Acid Research Inst., Irvine, Calif., 1969-72, head div. chemotherapy, 1972-75, dir. inst., 1975-77; prof. animal, dairy and vet. scis. Utah State U., Logan, 1977—; mem. faculty U. Ala. Med. Sch., 1968-69; dir. Inst. Antiviral Rsch. Utah State U., Logan, 1992—. Lectr. in field. Editor: ISAR News, 1992—; mem. editorial bd. Antimicrobial Agts. and Chemotherapy, 1972—, Chemotherapy, 1974—, Antiviral Research, 1980—, Internat. Antiviral News, 1992—; Contbr. articles to profl. jours. Mem. Nibley (Utah) City Planning and Zoning Commn., 1978-80; mem. steering com. Irvine Sch. Bd., 1972, chmn. health edn. awareness forum, 1975; chmn. basic rsch. subcommittee div. AIDS Nat. Inst. Allergy Infectious Diseases, NIH, 1990. Recipient E. Wynne Thorne Research award Utah State U., 1987, Silver Beaver award Boy Scouts Am., 1987; Gov.'s medal for Sci. and Tech., Utah State U., 1988; scholar Order of Eagles, 1954, Dept. Interior, 1954; named Coll. Agr. Prof. of Yr., 1989. Fellow Infectious Disease Soc. Am.; mem. AAAS, Am. Assn. Immunologists, Soc. Exptl. Biology and Medicine, Pan Am. Med. Assn., Internat. Soc. Chemotherapy (exec. com. 1991—), Inter-Am. Soc. Chemotherapy, Am. Soc. Microbiology, Am. Soc. Virology, Nat. Assn. Colls., Tchrs. in Agriculture, Am. Assn. U. Profs., Internat. Soc. Antiviral Rsch., Sigma Xi. Home: 162 Quarter Cir Logan UT 84321-6313 Office: Utah State U Inst Antiviral Rsch Logan UT 84322-0001

SIDWELL, WILLIAM G. military officer, hospital administrator; b. San Diego, 1958; Student, U.Tenn., 1975—77, Hosp. Corps "A" Sch., Great Lakes, Field Med. Svc. Sch., Camp Johsnon, N.C., 1977; grad., Navy Sr. Enlisted Acad., Newport, R.I., 1994. Commd. USN, 1977; assigned to USS ASPRO (SSN 648), 1986—91; comdr. submarine sq. one Pearl Harbor, Hawaii, 1991—94; force corpsman submarine force U.S. Pacific Fleet, 1994—97; sr. Pacific Fleet corpsman, 1997; command master chief Nat. Naval Med. Ctr., Bethesda, Md., 2000—. Office: 8801 Wisconsin Ave Bethesda MD 20889-5600*

SIEBEL, MATHIAS PAUL, mechanical engineer; b. Witten, Germany, Mar. 6, 1924; came to U.S., 1957, naturalized, 1962; s. Franz and Marie-Luise S.; m. Katherine Elizabeth Jente, May 27, 1960. BS in Mech. Engring, U. Bristol, Eng., 1949, PhD, 1952. From research and devel. engr. to asst. plant mgr. Tube Investments Ltd., Birmingham, Eng., 1952-57; research asso. Columbia U., N.Y.C., 1958-59; mgr. pressure equipment Pall Corp., Glen Cove, N.Y., 1959-64; v.p. ops. RDI Co., Westbury, 1964-65; dir. mfg. engring. lab., then mem. sci. staff Marshall Space Flight Center, NASA, Huntsville, Ala., 1965-79; mgr. NASA Michoud Assembly Facility, New Orleans, 1979-87, cons., 1987—. Assoc. dean Coll. Engring. U. New Orleans, 1989-92, adj. prof. mech. enring., 1993-2001. Patentee in field. Mem. Sigma Xi. Home: 5204 Janice Ave Kenner LA 70065-3238

SIEBEN, J(OHN) KENNETH, retired humanities educator, writer, editor; b. Irvington, N.J., Mar. 10, 1939; s. Oscar August and Dorothy Maude (Burke) S.; m. Regina Marie Monks, June 18, 1960; children: Joseph Richard, Mark Thomas, Ann Karen, Gregory Paul, Laura Jean Jerry. BS, Seton Hall U., 1960, MA, 1962; PhD, NYU, 1971. French and English tchr. Essex Cath. H.S., Newark, 1960-62; English tchr. Middleton Twp. (N.J.) H.S., 1962-65; supr. remedial reading ctr. Kilmer Job Corps Ctr., Edison, N.J., 1965-67; curriculum coord. pub. svc. career program CUNY, N.Y.C., 1967-68; dean continuing edn. Essex County Coll., Newark, 1968-70, prof. humanities, 1970-00, ret., 2000. Spkr., presenter Nat. Coun. Tchrs. English, Coll. English Assn. Author: (textbook) Communication Skills Lab, 1976, 83, Composition Five, 1982, 85; and short stories; fiction editor Northwoods Jour., 1992-2002. Lt. USNR, 1956-74. Summer scholar NEH, 1974. Avocations: sailing, fishing, hiking, cooking. E-mail: kensieben@home.com.

SIEBENALER, RITA REILLY, clinical social worker, consultant; b. Bklyn., June 12, 1943; d. Edward Thomas and Rita (Farrell) Reilly; m. Donald L. Siebenaler, June 12, 1965; children: Sharon L., Kristin R. BA, St. Joseph's Coll., Bklyn., 1964; MSW, NYU, 1966. Lic. clin. social worker, Va., D.C. Social worker Child and Adolescent Clin. Kings County Hosp., Bklyn., 1966; sch. social worker Internat. Sch., Bangkok, Thailand, 1969-70; social worker Child Guidance Clinic, Heidelberg, Fed. Republic of Germany, 1975-76, No. Va. Family Svc., Falls Ch., 1966-67, 76-77; sch. social worker Fairfax (Va.) County Pub. Schs., 1977-78, 89-90; dir. Community Mental Health Program, Moscow, USSR, 1980-82; family counselor Luth. Svcs., Camp Hill, Pa., 1982-84, Family Life Ctr., Ft. Leavenworth, Kans., 1988-89; clin. social worker med. div. U.S. Dept. State, Washington, 1984-94; social worker/counselor Arlington (Va.) Pub. Schs., 1994—. Lectr. Foreign Svc. Inst. Overseas Briefing Ctr. Rosslyn, Va., 1984—, cons. 1989—. Mem. adv. bd. Fairfax County Juvenile and Domestic Rels. Ct., 1986-89; counselor Borromeo Housing, Inc., Arlington, Va., 1990. Grantee, HEW, 1964, '65. Fellow Am. Orthopsychiatry Assn.; mem. Acad. Cert. Social Workers (bd. cert. diplomate).

SIEBENMORGEN, PAUL, retired family physician, lay church worker; b. Terre Haute, Ind., Sept. 16, 1920; s. Louis and Ruby E. (Curtis) Siebenmorgen; m. Jane Maxine Waggoner, June 20, 1948; children: Paul Stephen, Elizabeth Ann Siebenmorgen Brentlinger, Susan Lynn Siebenmorgen Amos. BS in Edn., Ind. State Teacher's Coll., 1941; MD, Ind. U., 1944. Pvt. practice, Terre Haute, 1947-2000; pres. med. and dental staff Terre Haute Regional Hosp., 1974-75, 96, trustee, 1975-81; assoc. clin. faculty Sch. Medicine, Ind. U., Inpls., 1975-2000. Deacon Cen. Christian Ch., Terre Haute, 1947, elder, 1948—2000, elder emeritus, 2001—, trustee, 1966—86, chmn. bd., 1957—59; mem. bd. Ind. Region Christian Ch. (Disciples of Christ), 1966—76, pres.-elect, 1972—74, moderator, 1974—76; mem. exec. com. Conf. Regional Mins. and Bd. Chmn., 1974—76; bd. dirs. Med. Assurance Ind., 1982—2001, chmn., 1986—91, pres., 1986—88; trustee Ind. State U., Terre Haute, 1975—83; mem. alumni coun. Ind. U. Sch. Medicine, 1989—97, pres., 1993, bd. dir. dean's coun., 1997—2001; mem. U. So. Ind. Found. Bd., 1976—86; mem. Gov.'s Commn. for the United Way of Ind. Centennial Observance, 1986; sec.

Vigo County Comprehensive Health Planning Coun.; bd. dir. So. Ind. Health Sys. Agy., 1975—78, Ind. Med. Polit. Action Com., 1988—94; mem. Ind. Statewide Health Coord. Coun., 1977—89, mem. exec. com., 1982—84; pres. Vigo County Heart Assn., 1965—66; hon. parade marshall Ind. State U. Homecoming, 1990; hon. mem. Ind. State U. Found. Bd., charter mem. pres.'s soc., 1990. Pres. Vigo County Bd. Health, 1967—68, 1971—75, 1980—81, v.p., 1976—79; trustee Ind. State U., Terre Haute, 1975—83; mem. alumni coun. Ind. U. Sch. Medicine, 1989—97, pres. alumni coun., 1993, bd. dirs. dean's coun., 1997—2000; mem. U. So. Ind. Found. Bd., 1976—86; mem. Gov.'s Commn. United Way Ind. Centennial Observance, 1986; sec. Vigo County Comprehensive Health Planning coun.; bd. dirs. So. Ind. Health Sys. Agy., 1975—78, Ind. Med. Polit. Action Com., 1988—94; mem. Ind. Statewide Health Coord. Coun., 1977—89, mem. exec. com., 1982—84; pres. Vigo County Heart Assn., 1965—66; hon. parade marshall Ind. State U. Homecoming, 1990; hon. mem., charter mem. pres.'s soc. Ind. State U. Found. Bd., 1990. Recipient Sustained Outstanding Svc. award, Scottish Rite Valley Terre Haute, 1972, Meritorious Svc. award, Ind. State U. Alumni Assn., 1972, Disting. Alumni award, Ind. State U., 1993, Hand Clasp award, Kiwanis Club Terre Haute, 1991, Disting. Alumni award, Ind. U. Sch. Medicine, 1994, Excellence in Health Care award, Columbia Terre Haute Regional Hosp. Found., 1997, Bowen award for Leadership, Ind. U., 1996. Fellow: Am. Acad. Family Physicians (charter); mem.: AMA, Ind. Acad. Family Physicians (dir. 1973—82, dist. pres. 1961, 1971, pres. 1981, Lester Bibler award 1989), Aesculapian Soc. Wabash Valley, Vigo County Med. Soc. (pres. 1970), Ind. State Med. Assn. (chmn. bd. trustees 1981—84, pres., chmn. delegation to AMA Ho. Dels. 1985), Terre haute C. of C., Elks, Phi Rho Sigma, Kappa Delta Pi, Alpha Phi Omega, Sigma Alpha Epsilon. Home: 1241 Watertree Rd Terre Haute IN 47803-7712 *Though we have precious memories and lessons from the past, it is the future, a new frontier experienced by no one, that holds exciting new discoveries, challenges, opportunities, hope, and progress. Under God let us proceed with diligence and in confidence.*

SIEBERT, CALVIN D. economist, educator; b. Hillsboro, Kans., Feb. 11, 1934; s. Ira and Margaret (Everett) S.; m. Valerie Dawn Nanninga, Feb. 18, 1960; children— Douglas Erik, Derek Christopher. BA, U. Kans., 1958, MA, 1960; PhD in Econs., U. Calif., Berkeley, 1966. Asst. prof. econs. U. Iowa, 1965-68, assoc. prof., 1968-75, prof., 1975—, chmn. dept., 1969-71, 75-79. Rockefeller Found. vis. asso. prof. U. Philippines, 1971-72 Contbr. articles to profl. jours. With U.S. Army, 1954-56. Ford Found. grantee, 1964-65 Mem. Am. Econ. Assn., Phi Beta Kappa. Home: 341 N 7th Ave Iowa City IA 52245-6003 Office: U Iowa Dept Econs S318 Pbb Iowa City IA 52242 E-mail: calvin_siebert@uiowa.edu.

SIEBERT, DEBORAH ANN, public relations and marketing executive; b. Hoisington, Kans., Nov. 12, 1952; d. Kenneth Theodore and Mildred Marie (Steiner) Siebert; m. Donald Raymond McLaughlin, July 17, 1976 (div. Oct. 2001); 1 child, Kalla Dawn. AS, Barton County Coll., Great Bend, Kans., 1972; BS, Kans. State U., 1975. News editor Great Bend Tribune, 1975-76; deposition indexer Turner & Boisseau, Great Bend, 1976-77; feature editor Mid-Kans. Ruralist, Hoisington, 1977-78; copywriter, audio-editor Advt. Assocs., Great Bend, 1978-79; photographer, sales mgr. Clay Ward Color Portraits, 1979-80; news editor, photographer St. John (Kans.) News, 1980-83; freelance writer, photographer Great Bend, 1984-85; pres., owner McLaughlin Pub. Rels. Agy., 1985-87; owner Cen. Kans. Sunrise mag., 1987-88, Creative Mktg. Svcs., Great Bend, 1988—; dir. pub. info. Unified Sch. Dist. 428, 1991-93; editor Ellinwood Leader, 1995-97; acct. exec. Multimedia Cable Ad Sales, 1998-99, Cox Comms., 2000—. Contbr. articles and photographs to various publs. Mem. Coalition for Prevention Child Abuse, Great Bend, 1986-87; mem. 75th anniversary com. Kansas State U. Coll. Journalism and Mass Communications, Manhattan, 1986. Mem. Kans. State U. Alumni Assn. Roman Catholic. Avocations: yoga, gardening, gourmet cooking, interior decorating. Home: 381 Grove Ter Great Bend KS 67530-9710

SIEBERT, DIANE DOLORES, author, poet; b. Chgo., Mar. 18, 1948; m. Robert William Siebert, Sept. 21, 1969. RN. Author: Truck Song, 1984 (Notable Childrens Book award ALA 1984, Sch. Libr. Jour. one of Best Books 1984, Outstanding Childrens Book award N.Y. Times Book Rev. 1984, Reading Rainbow Selection book 1991), Mojave, 1988 (Childrens Editors Choice 1988, Internat. Reading Assn. Tchrs. Choice award 1989, others), Heartland, 1989 (award Nat. Coun. for Social Studies/Childrens Book Coun. 1989, on John Burroughs List Nature Book for Young Readers 1989, Ohio Farm Bur. Women award 1991), Train Song, 1990 (Notable Childrens Book award ALA, 1990, Redbook Mag. one of Top Ten Picture Books 1990, one of Best Books award Sch. Libr. Jour. 1990, others), Sierra, 1991 (Outstanding Sci. Trade Book for Children award NSTA 1991, Notable Childrens Trade Book in Field Social Studies award Nat. Coun. Social Studies 1991, Beatty award Calif. Libr. Assn. 1992), Plane Song, 1993 (Outstanding Sci. Trade Book for Children 1994, Platinum award Oppenheim Toy Portfolio, Tchrs. Choice award Internat. Reading Assn. 1994), Cave, 2000 (named to John Burroughs List of Nature Books for Young Readers 2000), Mississippi (named to John Burroughs List 2001), 2001, Motorcycle Song, 2002. Avocations: environmental affairs, running, classical guitar, motorcycle, animals. Home: 9676 SW Jordan Rd Culver OR 97734-9567

SIEBERT, HORST, economics educator, institute administrator; b. Neuwied, Germany, Mar. 20, 1938; s. Fritz and Anna (Heini) S.; m. Christa Causemann, Apr. 29, 1965. MA in Econs., U. Cologne, Fed. Republic Germany, 1963; PhD, U. Muenster, Fed. Republic Germany, 1965, habilitation, 1969. Asst. prof. Tex. A&M U., 1967-68; prof. econs. U. Mannheim, Fed. Republic Germany, 1969-84, U. Konstanz, Fed. Republic Germany, 1984-89; prof. theoretical econs. U. Kiel, Fed. Republic Germany, 1989—; pres. Kiel Inst. World Econs., 1989—. Mem. Coun. Econ. Advisors, Germany, 1990—. Author: Economics of the Environment, 1987, 5th revised edit., 1998, Aussenwirtschaft, 7th edit., 2000, The New Economic Landscape in Europe, 1991, Geht den Deutschen die Arbeit aus?, 1995, Weltwirtschaft, 1997, The World Economy, 1999, 2d edit., 2002. Mem. Am. Econ. Assn., European Econ. Assn., Verein Fuer Socialpolitik. Office: Kiel Inst World Econs Duesternbrooker Weg 120 24105 Kiel Germany

SIEBERT, MURIEL, brokerage house executive, former state banking official; b. Cleve. d. Irwin J. and Margaret Eunice (Roseman) Siebert. Student, Western Res. U., 1949-52; DCS (hon.), St. John's U., St. Bonaventure U., Molloy Coll., Adelphi U., St. Francis Coll., Mercy Coll., Coll. New Rochelle, St. Lawrence U., Manhattan Coll., Seton Hall Coll., Case Western Res. U., Marymount Manhattan Coll., Hofstra U. Security analyst Bache & Co., 1954-57; analyst Utilities & Industries Mgmt. Corp., 1958, Shields & Co., 1959-60; ptnr. Stearns & Co., 1961, Finkle & Co., 1962-65, Brimberg & Co., N.Y.C., 1965-67; individual mem. (first woman mem.) N.Y. Stock Exch., 1967; chmn., pres. Muriel Siebert & Co., Inc., 1969-77; trustee Manhattan Savs. Bank, 1975-77; supt. banks, dept. banking State of N.Y., 1977-82; dir. Urban Devel. Corp., N.Y.C., 1977-82, Job Devel. Authority, N.Y.C., 1977-82, State of N.Y. Mortgage Agy., 1977-82; chmn., pres. Muriel Siebert & Co., Inc., N.Y.C., 1983—. Assoc. in mgmt. Simmons Coll.; mem. adv. com. Fin. Acctg. Stds. Bd., 1981-84; guest lectr. numerous colls. Former mem. women's adv. com. Econ. Devel. Adminstrn., N.Y.C.; former trustee Manhattan Coll.; v.p., former mem. exec. com. Greater N.Y. Area coun. Boy Scouts Am.; mem. N.Y. State Econ. Devel. Bd., N.Y.C. Coun. Economy; bd. overseers NYU Sch. Bus., 1984-88; former bd. dirs. United Way of N.Y.C.; trustee Citizens Budget Commn., L.I. U.; mem. bus. com. Met. Mus., bus. com. of N.Y. State Bus. Coun.; advive Women's Campaign Fund.; bd. dirs. N.Y. Women's Agenda; bd. dirs. Guild Hall Mus. EH; current appointee Commn. Jud. Nomination; founding mem. The Mus. Women-The Leadership Coun. Recipient Spirit of Achievement award Albert Einstein Coll. Medicine, 1977, Women's Equity Action League award, 1978, Outstanding Contbns. to Equal Oppty. for Women award Bus. Coun. UN Decade for Women, 1979, Silver Beaver award Boy Scouts Am., 1981, Elizabeth Cutter Morrow award YWCA, 1983, Emily Roebling award Nat. Women's Hall of Fame, 1984, Entrepreneurial Excellence award White House Conf. on Small Bus., 1986, NOW Legal Def. and Edn. Fund award, 1981, Brotherhood award NCCJ. 1989, Women on the Move award Anti-Defamation League, 1990, Bus. Philanthropist of Yr. award So. Calif. Conf. for Women Bus. Owner's, 1990, award Borough of Manhattan, 1991, Benjamin Botwinick prize Columbia Bus. Sch., 1992, Women in Bus. Making History award Women's Bus. Coun. N.Y. C. of C., 1993, Disting. Woman of Yr. award Greater N.Y. Boy Scouts of Am., 1993, Corning Excellence award N.Y.C. Bus. Coun., 1993, Woman of Yr. award Fin. Women's Assn. N.Y., 1994, Medal of Honor award Ellis Island, 1994, Star award N.Y. Women's Agenda, 1994, N.Y. Urban Coalition's Achievement award, 1994, Women of Distinction award Crohn's and Colitis Found., 1994, Entrepreneurial Leadership award Nat. Found. Tchg. Entrepreneurship, 1994, Athena award, 1997, USO Women of Yr. award, 1998, Sara Lee Frontrunner award, 1998, Mattel/Barbie Ambassador of Dreams award, 1999; inductee Nat. Woman's Hall of Fame, Seneca Falls, N.Y., 1994, Internat. Women's Forum Hall of Fame, 1994, Ohio Women's Hall Fame, 1994; N.Y. Univ.'s Stern Sch. Bus. 1st Woman Stovall fellow, 1992; Established Siebert Entrepreneurial Philanthropic Program, 1990. Mem. Women's Forum (founding mem., pres.), Com. 200, Fin. Women's Assn. (Cmty. Svc. award 1993), River Club, Doubles Club, Westchester Club, West Palm Beach Polo and Country Club, Nat. Assn. Women Bus. Owners (NAWBO's Veuve Clicquot Bus. Women of Yr. award 1992, Mayor's Lifetime Achievement award for Women Bus. Owners 1993), Econ. Club (exec. com.), Southampton Bath and Tennis Club (founding mem. , bd. dirs.), River Club, Doubles Club, Westchester County Club, West Palm Beach Polo and Country Club (former mem.). Home: 435 E 52nd St New York NY 10022-6445 Office: Muriel Siebert & Co Inc 885 3rd Ave Ste 1720 New York NY 10022-4834

SIEBERT, SEPTEMBER J. marketing and communications executive; b. Seattle, Sept. 6, 1956; d. Gordon Douglass and Patricia Johnson; m. Gary F. Seibert, June 19, 1976; children: Jennifer Anne, Rachel Lynn, Erica Michelle. Cert. employee benefit specialist, U. Pa. Acct. adminstr. Trusteed Plans Svc. Corp., Tacoma, 1978-84; mktg. rep. Group Health, Seattle, 1984-86; supr. health plans PACCAR, Inc., Bellevue, 1986-89; exec. dir. Associated Risk Mgrs., Everett, 1989-2000, Ins. Mktg. Comm. Assn., Mukilteo, 2000—. Leader Snohomish County 4-H Program, Everett; bd. dirs. Elliott Point Homeowners Assn., Mukilteo, Shilshole Bay Yacht Club, Seattle; active Mukilteo Schs. PTA. Mem. Am. Mktg. Assn., Wash. Soc. Assn. Execs. (bd. dirs. 1990-2001), Am. Soc. Assn. Execs. Lutheran. Avocations: gardening, sewing, writing, boating, biking. Office: Ins Mktg Comm Assn PO Box 983 Mukilteo WA 98275 E-mail: imcassn@cs.com.

SIEBERT, THOMAS L. lawyer, diplomat; b. Cleve., May 2, 1946; m. Deborah Simpson; 4 children. BA, JD, Georgetown U. Intern Rep. Robert E. Sweeney, 1965—66; vol. Senator Robert F. Kennedy, 1966—68; aide Senator Carl Hayden, 1968—70; assoc. Pittman, Lovett, Ford & Hennessey, Washington, 1971—78; ptnr. Lovett, Ford, Hennessey, Stambler & Siebert, 1978—87; of counsel Besozzi & Gavin, 1987—93, Besozzi, Gavin & Craven, Washington, 1993; U.S. amb. to Sweden, Am. Embassy, Stockholm, 1993—97; mem. Patton Boggs LLP, Washington. Chmn. Plenipotentiary Conf., Internat. Telecom. Union, 1998; chmn., pres. U.S. Telemetry Corp., 1999—. Bd. regents Cath. U.; bd. visitors St. John's Coll., Georgetown U. Law Ctr.; mem. bd. visitors and govs. Washington Coll.; active U.S. Naval Acad. Midshipmen Program, Md. Hall for the Creative Arts. Mem.: ABA, Annapolis Assn., Fed. Comm. Bar Assn., D.C. Bar. Office: Patton Boggs LLP 2550 M St NW Ste 500 Washington DC 20037-1350

SIEBERT, WILLIAM ALAN, lawyer; b. Royal Oak, Mich., Jan. 25, 1955; s. William Edward and Mary Elizabeth (Northrup) S. BA, Albion Coll., 1977; JD, U. Detroit, 1980. Bar: Mich. 1980, U.S. Dist. Ct. (ea. dist.) Mich. 1981, U.S. Dist. Ct. (we. dist.) Mich. 1995. Gen. counsel RARE Realty, Beaverton, Mich., 1983-85; sole practice Gladwin, 1985—. Exec. com. Gladwin County Reps., 1983-92; candidate for Gladwin County Prosecuring Atty., 1984, 88. Mem. Mich. Bar Assn. (real property sect. title ins. com. 1984-2002), Clare-Gladwin Trial Lawyers, Masons (v.p. Gladwin Temple Assn. 1988-92, worshipful master 1992), Albion Coll. Alumni Bd., Phi Alpha Delta (chpt. clk. 1980). E-mail: wsiebert@voyager.net.

SIEBOLD, E. F. JOSEPH, pediatrician; b. Phila., Dec. 4, 1943; s. Ernest Frederick and Veronica Bernadette (O'Hagan) S.; m. Elaine M. Siebold, May 27, 1972; children: Damian, Alexis, Maura. AB, LaSalle Coll., 1965; DO, Phila. Coll. Osteo. Medicine, 1969. Diplomate Am. Bd. Pediatrics and Adolescent Medicine. Intern Detroit Osteo. Hosp., 1970; resident Hahnemann Med. Coll., Phila., 1970-73; chmn. dept. pediatrics Langley (Va.) AFB Hosp., 1973-75; dir. student health svc. U. Del., Newark, 1975—. Instr. pediatrics Jefferson Med. Coll., Phila.; instr. phys. therapy U. Del. Maj. USAF, 1973-75. Fellow Am. Acad. of Pediatrics; mem. AMA, Soc. for Adolescent Medicine, New Castle County Med. Soc. Roman Catholic. E-mail. Home: 41 Hidden Valley Dr Newark DE 19711-7463 Office: Student Health Svc U Del Newark DE 19716-8101 E-mail: jsiebold@udel.edu.

SIEBURTH, RICHARD, literature educator, translator; BA, U. Chgo., 1970; PhD, Harvard U., 1976. Prof. French and Comparative Lit. NYU, 1983—. Author: Instigations, 1978; editor: Ezra Pound, A Walking Tour in Southern France, 1992; translator: Walter Benjamin, Moscow Diary, 1986, Friedrich Hölderlin, Hymms & Fragments, 1984, Gerard de Nerval, Selected Writings, 1999. Decorated chevalier Ordre des palmes academiques (France); recipient Book of the Month-Translation prize PEN USA.

SIECK, ROBERT, aerospace engineer; Mem. Aerospace Safety Adv. Panel NASA, Washington; meteorologist USAF, 1960—64; Gemini spacecraft sys. engr. NASA, Kennedy Space Ctr., 1964—76, Apollo spacecraft test team project; engring. mgr. sulttle approach and landing tests Dryden Flight Rsch. Facility, Calif., 1976—78; chief shuttle project engr. NASA, Kennedy Space Ctr., 1978—83, shuttle flow dir., 1983—84, dir. launch and landing ops., 1984—92, dep. dir. shuttle ops., 1992—95, dir. shuttle processing; cons. Aerospace Adv. Panel NASA, Washington, 1999—. Office: Aerospace Safety Adv. Panel NASA Hdqrs 300 E St SW Washington DC 20546

SIEDBAND, MARC A. military officer; b. Balt., Aug. 7, 1953; s. Melvin Paul and Dorothy Dee Siedband; m. Deborah Roberta Schuckit, Feb. 1, 1976; children: David Samuel, Michael Adam. BSME, US Naval Acad., 1975; MSME, US Naval Postgrad. Sch., 1987. Registered profl. engr. Calif. Commd. ensign USN, 1971, ship supt., type desk Puget Sound Naval Shipyard Wash., 1987—90, asst. ship material officer San Diego, 1990—93, chief engr. USS Constellation, 1994—95, br. head, ship maintenance Office of Chief of Naval Ops. Washington, 1995—98, asst. chief of staff, maintenance and engring. Comdr. Naval Surface Force San Diego, 1998—2000, comdr. Naval Surface Warfare Ctr. Indian Head, Md., 2000—. Recipient Woelfel award, Woelfel Family-Naval Pg Sch., 1987. Avocations: running, kayaking, bicycling, motorcycling. Office: Naval Surface Warfare Ctr Indian Head 101 Strauss Ave Indian Head MD 20640

SIEDE, WOLFRAM, research scientist; b. Darmstadt, Germany, Sept. 10, 1958; s. Werner Heinrich and Ilse (Schütt) S. PhD, U. Frankfurt, Germany, 1986. Postdoctoral rsch. fellow Stanford (Calif.) U. Med. Ctr., 1986-90; instr. in pathology U. Tex. Southwestern Med. Ctr., Dallas, 1990-94, asst. prof. pathology, 1994-96; asst. prof. radiation oncology Emory U. Sch. Medicine, 1996—. Editl. bd. Jour. Mutation Rsch. DNA Repair, 1994—; co-author DNA Repair and Mutagenesis, 1995. Office: Emory U Sch Medicine Winship Cancer Ctr 1365 Clifton Rd NE # B Atlanta GA 30322-1013

SIEDEL, GEORGE JOHN, III, law educator; b. Medina, Ohio, Feb. 17, 1945; s. George Joseph and Justine Elizabeth (Johnson) S.; m. Helen Louise Haeck, June 28, 1969; children: Joseph, Kathryn, John. BA, Coll. Wooster (Ohio), 1967; JD, U. Mich., 1970; DCLS, U. Cambridge, 1971. Bar: Mich. 1971, Fla. 1974, Ohio 1974, U.S. Supreme Ct. 1976. Assoc. Robertson, Bartlow and Des Chenes, Adrian, Mich., 1971-73; asst. prof. bus. law Bowling Green (Ohio) State U., 1973-74; prof. bus. law U. Mich., Ann Arbor, 1974—; assoc. dean, 1993—98; dist. chair in Humanities and Social Scis. Fulbright Program, 2001. Vis. fellow U. Cambridge, Eng., 1981, 89; vis. prof. Harvard U., Cambridge, Mass., 1998Stanford U., Palo Alto, Calif., 1985, China U. Polit. Sci. and Law, 1992; Parsons fellow U. Sydney, Australia, 1991; Thurnau prof. U. Mich., 1992-95; Williamson family prof. of bus. adminstrn. U. Mich., 1996—. Author: Business Law and the Legal Environment, 1992, Using the Law for Competitive Advantage, 2002, Real Estate Law, 2002, The Lawyer and Business, 1976; spl. editor Am. Bus. Law Jour., Athens, Ga., 1987-88; editor-in-chief Mich. Real Property Rev., 1976—. Corp. sec., dir. Medic Alert Found. Internat., Turlock, Calif., 1979-87; dir. William Davidson Inst., 1992—, AIESEC U.S., Inc., 1994-98. Recipient Excellence award Midwest Bus. Law Assn., 1982, Hoeber award Acad. Legal Studies in Bus., 1993; Ford Found. fellow, 1970-71, Ralph Bunche award, Acad. Legal Studies in Bus., Internat. Case Writing award, 2000. Fellow Mich. State Bar Found. (life); mem. ABA, Am. Corp. Counsel Assn. (bd. dirs. Mich. chpt. 1984-85), Am. Bus. Law Assn. Presbyterian. Home: 2103 Devonshire Rd Ann Arbor MI 48104-4059 Office: U Mich Bus Sch Ann Arbor MI 48109-1234

SIEDLE, ROBERT DOUGLAS, management consultant; b. Canton, Ohio, Aug. 08; BA in Econs., Hiram Coll., 1956; profl. cert. edn., Kent State/Western Res. Univs., 1963. Tchr., prin. Ohio secondary schs., 1957-65; salesman, area rep. visual products divsn. 3M Co., 1966-68; mgr. market devel. and tng. AV divsn. Bell & Howell, 1968-69; Chgo. br. mgr. info. systems divsn. Am. Std., 1969-72; mgr. edn. systems divsn. Audiotronics Corp., 1972-76; gen. mgr. Niles Entertainment/Wardway Films, 1977-80; pres. The Ultimate Image, Lakeland, Fla., 1985—. *Robert Siedle is the youngest passenger to fly in the original prototype B-17 Fling Fortress (held on the lap of one of the test crew), his love for aviation was thus born leading to a life of participation and political involvement, both civilian and military. He actively supported and aided in getting both the Air Force Memorial and World War II Memorial projects started. General aviation safety and designing an aviation museum for military memorabilia occupy most of his spare time.* Producer: (films) New Dimensions in Learning II, 1969, District 65: The Exceptional Child, 1969, Career Exploration: Health, 1976, The Wide World of Work, 1976; author: Multisensory Learning: A Training Guide, 1973, Alphabet Zoo, 1973, City of Boston Young Adult Alternate Career Program, 1974, The Quick Job Hunt Guide, 1991; author, producer, dir.: (multimedia rd. show) "Rap" With Students, 1975; producer, editor: (film) Stampin' Ground, 1977; author poetry appearing in books and mags., 1991—; appeared on nat. radio and TV programs in U.S. and Can. Recipient Internat. Peace prize United Cultural Conv., 2002; named to Nat. Aviation and Space Exploration Wall of Honor Smithsonian Nat. Air and Space Mus. Dulles Ctr., 2000. Mem. U.S. Naval Aviation Mus. (life), U.S. Naval Inst. (life), Navy League of U.S. (life), Internat. Platform Assn., Sun 'n Fun Air Mus. (life), Am. Air Mus. in Britain (founding mem.), Aircraft Owners and Pilots Assn. (life), Aircraft Owners and Pilots Assn. Safety Found. (life), Exptl. Aircraft Assn., Warbirds of Am., Great Lakes Hist. Soc. (life), Air Force Assn. (life), Steamship Hist. Soc. Am. (life), Palm Springs Air Mus., Airship Assn. Ltd., World War II Meml. Soc. (charter), Air Force Meml. Found. (charter), Vintage Aircraft Assn., Defenders of Wildlife (pres.' coun.), Living Planet Soc. World Wildlife Fund, Century Soc., St. Labre Indian Sch. Ednl. Assn., Soc. for Prevention of Cruelty to Animals, Inc., Defenders of Wildlife (pres.' coun.), Living Planet Soc., World Wildlife Fund, Helper Soc. St. Labre, Indian Sch. Edn. Assn., SPCA, Inc. Baptist. Office: The Ultimate Image PO Box 91388 Lakeland FL 33804-1388 E-mail: Office22@webtv.net.

SIEDLECKI, NANCY THERESE, lawyer, funeral director; b. Chgo., May 30, 1954; d. LeRoy John and Dorothy Josephine (Wilczynski) Schielka; m. Jonathan Francis Siedlecki, June 18, 1977; children: Samantha Ann, Abigail Marie. Student Triton Jr. Coll., 1971-73; grad. funeral dir., Worsham Coll., 1974; student Loyola U., Chgo., 1974-76., U. Ill.-Chgo., 1976-77; JD with honors, Chgo.-Kent Coll. Law, 1980. Bar: Ill. 1980. Paralegal in real estate Rosenberg, Savner & Unikel, Chgo., 1974-77; pvt. practice law, Burr Ridge, Ill., 1980—; cons. probate and various small bus. corps., Chgo., 1980—. Mem. ABA, Ill. State Bar Assn., Chgo. Bar Assn. Roman Catholic. Office: 5300 Main St Downers Grove IL 60515-4846

SIEDLECKI, PETER ANTHONY, English language and literature educator; b. North Tonawanda, N.Y., May 19, 1938; s. Anthony Paul and Mary Barbara (Litwin) S.; m. Rose Mary Murphy, June 25, 1960 (div. 1978); children: Christopher, Gregory, Jeffrey, William; m. Lynnette Noreen Mende, Apr. 26, 1980; children: Peter Emmanuel Mende-Siedlecki. BA, Niagara U., 1960, MA, 1966; PhD, SUNY, Buffalo, 1982. Tchr. English Lewiston-Porter Sr. H.S., Youngstown, NY, 1960—64, Grand Island (N.Y.) Sr. H.S., 1964—65; prof. English Rosary Hill Coll., Amherst, NY, 1965—74, Daemen Coll., Amherst, 1974—, dean, divsn. arts and scis., 2001—; chair div. humanities and social scis.; prof. Am. Lit. Jagiellonian U., Krakow, Poland, 1982-84, Friedrich-Schiller U., Jena, 1988-89. Commentator pub. radio, 1995-98. Author (poetry) Voyeur; contbr. articles to profl. jours. Fulbright Sr. lectr., Council for Internat. Exchange of Scholars, 1982-84, 88-89. Mem. MLA, Fulbright Alumni Assn. Democrat. Home: 249 Winspear Ave Buffalo NY 14215-1035 Office: Daemen College 4380 Main St Buffalo NY 14226-3592

SIEDLER, ARTHUR JAMES, nutrition and food science educator; b. Milw., Mar. 17, 1927; s. Arthur William and Margaret (Stadler) S.; m. Doris Jean Northrop, Feb. 23, 1976; children: William, Nancy Siedler Wilhite, Sandra Siedler Lowman, Roxanne Rose Butler, Randy Rose. BS, U. Wis., 1951; MS, U. Chgo., 1956, PhD, 1959. Chief div. biochemistry and nutrition Am. Meat Inst. Found., Chgo., 1959-64; group leader Norwich (N.Y.) Pharmacal Co., 1964-65, chief physiology sect., 1965-69, chief biochemistry sect., 1969-72; acting dir. div. nutritional scis. U. Ill., Urbana, 1978-81, head dept. food sci., 1972-89, prof. food sci., internal medicine and nutritional scis., 1972-94, prof. emeritus, 1994—. Patentee in field. With USCG, 1945-46, PTO. NIH research grantee, 1960-63; Nat. Livestock and Meat Bd. grantee, 1959-64 Mem. Inst. Food Technologists, Am. Chem. Soc., Am. Soc. Nutritional Scis., Coun. for Agrl. Sci. and Tech., Eagles, Moose, Sigma Xi. Home: 8 Stanford Pl Champaign IL 61820-7620 Office: 382M Ag Eng Sci 1304 W Pennsylvania Ave Urbana IL 61801-4713 E-mail: asiedler@uiuc.edu.

SIEDZIKOWSKI, HENRY FRANCIS, lawyer; b. Chester, Pa., Dec. 27, 1953; s. Henry W. and Virginia (Szymanski) S. BA cum laude, Juniata Coll., 1975; JD magna cum laude, Villanova U., 1979. Bar: Pa. 1979, U.S. Dist. Ct. (ea. dist.) Pa. 1979, U.S. Ct. Appeals (3d cir.) 1979, U.S. Ct. Appeals (8th cir.) 1981, U.S. Dist. Ct. (we. dist.) Pa. 1986. Assoc. Dilworth, Paxson, Kalish & Kauffman, Phila., 1979-86; ptnr. Baskin Flaherty Elliott & Mannino P.C., 1986-90, Elliott Bray & Riley, Phila., 1990-92, Elliott, Vanaskie & Riley, 1992-94, Elliott, Reihner, Siedzikowski & Egan, 1994—. Mem. hearing com. disciplinary bd. Supreme Ct. Pa., 1985—91. Mem. ABA (chmn. Lanham act subcom. of bus. torts com. of litigation sect. 1986—, rotating editor newsletter of antitrust sect. franchisee com.), Pa. Bar Assn., Phila. Bar Assn. (chmn. subcom. disciplinary rules for profl. responsibility com. 1984-90). Democrat. Roman Catholic. Office: Elliott Reihner et al 925 Harvest Dr Blue Bell PA 19422-1956 E-mail: hfs@erse.com.

SIEFERT, DAVID MICHAEL, computer manufacturing company executive; b. Dayton, Ohio, Apr. 8, 1951; s. Raymond Joseph and Laura Jayne (Blanford) S.; m. Rita Marlene Kuenle, Dec. 12, 1970; children: Christina Marie, Joel David, Jamie Michael, Matthew David, Caroline Marie. BA in Mgmt. Info. Sys., Capital U., 1988; MA in Bus., Antioch U., 1994. Cert. sys. profl., quality analyst; cert. assessment profl. Mgr. computer sys. ops. Koehring Bomag, Springfield, Ohio, 1974-77; gen. mgr. bus. ops. Mead Corp., Dayton, 1977-79, mgr. internat. support, 1979-81; sr. cons. computer applied sys. engring., lifestyle methodologies software engring. edn. systems, software reliability and quality engring. NCR Corp., 1981-86, mgr. advanced quality sys., 1986-89, dir. advanced quality tech., 1988-89, dir. strategic processes, 1990-91, program mgr. mergers and qcquisitions, 1991, dir. rsch. and tech., 1992-94, dir. R&D corp. global adv. sys. warehouse, access and libr., 1996, dir. global learning strategy and arch., 1999—, dir. corp. learning tech., 1996-98. Inventor Continuous Learning Sys., VISIONet, Knowledge Ctr.; developer, reviewer internat. computer stds. Nat. Inst. Stds. and Tech.; founder NCR U., 1998, asst. v.p. 1999-2000; dir. strategic programs Sinclair C.C.; mgr. NSF grant; founder IT@Sinclair; mem. Nat. Blue Ribbon Panel, chmn. AIAA; cons. in field; profl. paper referee Nat. Computer Conf., 1983, 88, 89; disting. lectr. U.S. Commerce Dept., NIST. Author books on software reliability, customer satisfaction and continuous improvement of software; contbr. articles to profl. jours.; 25 patents pending or issued. Recipient invention disclosure awards AT&T, 1994, Eureka award for best patent, best patent award AT&T, NCR, 1997-99. Mem. IEEE (sr., profl. paper reviewer IEEE Software Jour. 1988—, sr. mem. stds. com.), Assn. for Computing Machinery, Am. Soc. for Quality Control, Quality Assurance Inst. Address: 831 Buckingham Rd Dayton OH 45419-3645 E-mail: siefert@worldnet.att.net.

SIEFERT-KAZANJIAN, DONNA, corporate librarian; b. N.Y.C. d. Merrill Emil and Esther (Levins) S.; m. George John Kazanjian, June 15, 1974; 1 child, Merrill George. BA, NYU, 1969; MSLS, Columbia U., 1973; MBA, Fordham U., 1977. Asst. librarian Dun & Bradstreet, N.Y.C., 1969-73; research assoc. William E. Hill & Co., 1973-76; sr. info. analyst Info. for Bus.,

1976-77; librarian Handy Assocs., 1979-90; mgr. Infoserve Fuchs Cuthrell & Co., Inc., 1991-94; libr. Heidrick & Struggles, Inc., 1994-2001; learning media specialist St. Mary's Elem. Sch., Manhasset, NY, 2002—. Mem. Spl. Librs. Assn., Rsch. Roundtable, Am. Mensa Ltd. Roman Catholic.

SIEFKEN, MARK W, small business owner; b. Hawkinson, Nd, Oct. 3, 1939; s. Carl Hobart Siefken and Thelma Sylvia Stutlien; m. Sharon Yvonne Heinzenoth, June 3, 1961; children: Pamela, Michael, Tanya. Bachelor sci. chemistry, ND State U., Fargo, North Dakota, 1957—61; fulbright, Tech. Huchsale, Stuttgart, Germany, 1961—62; PhD organic chemistry, U. Wis., Madison, Wisconsin, 1962—67. Rsch. chemist 3M Corporatioin, Saint Paul, Minn., 1969—77; v.p. rsch. devel. Diversal, Chicago, Ill., 1977—81; divsn. mgr. Diversey, Wyandotte, Mich., 1981—89; v.p. Taxo/Nalco, Cincinatti/Saint Paul, Minn., 1990—96; pres. Manpro, Saint Paul, 1996—98; area mgr. Brelin, 1998—2002. Contbr. articles AC Society. Campaign mgr. Rep. Party, Saint Paul, Minn., 1974—74, del., 1970—76. Cpt U.S. Army, 1961—67, Maryland. Recipient fulbright, Fulbright Com., 1961. Mem.: Am. Chemistry Soc. R-Consevative. Lutheran. Achievements include patents for Alkoxy Silame Materials. Avocations: golf, fishing, hunting. Home: 462 Holly Lane North Saint Paul MN 55128-7035

SIEG, ALBERT LOUIS, photographic company executive; b. Chgo., Mar. 25, 1930; s. Albert Fredrick and Louise Augusta (Strege) S.; m. Irma Alice Spencer, Sept. 3, 1955; children— Karen, Diane, Susan BS in Chemistry, U. Ill., 1951; PhD in Organic Chemistry, U. Rochester, 1954; P.MD, Harvard Bus. Sch., 1971. Supr. emulsion Eastman Kodak Co., Rochester, N.Y., 1970-72, corp. mgr. instant., 1972-76, mgr. paper mgt., 1976-81, v.p., dir., 1981-84; pres. Kodak Japan K.K., Tokyo, 1984-89; pres., rep. dir. Eastman Kodak Japan, 1989-91, also bd. dirs.; pres., rep. dir. Eastman Chems. Japan Ltd., 1989-91; v.p., dir. strategic resources, sec. imaging bd. Eastman Kodak Co., Rochester, 1991-92, ret., 1992; prin., cons. Albert L. Sieg Assocs., 1992—. Bd. dirs. Kodak Japan Industries, Ltd., XM Corp.; mem. adv. bd. Worldscape, Inc., 2001--; sr. lectr. U. Rochester, 1960-69 Co-author: 8th Here's How, 1972; co-author (with S. Bennett, Oliver Wight) Tokyo Chronicles, 1994; inventor in field. Bd. dirs., St. John's Home Found., 2000—; chmn. corp. gifts Rochester Philharm. Orch., 1982-84, corp. gifts Internat. Mus. Photography at George Eastman House, 1993, 94; pres. Reformation Luth. Ch., Rochester, 1978-83; bd. dirs. St. John's Home for the Aging, 1994-99, vice chmn. bd. dirs., 1997-99; bd. dirs. St. John's Nursing Home, 1994-99, vice chmn. bd. dirs., 1997-99, chmn., 1999-2001; bd. dirs. St. John's Sr. Svcs., 1997-2001, chair elect, 1997-99, chair, 1999-01, pres., 1997-01. Served with Med. Svc. Corps, U.S. Army, 1955-57. Recipient George Eastman Medal Kodak Camera Clubs, 1980; Kiwanis Club Chgo. fellow, U. Ill., 1947-51; Am. Cyanamide fellow, 1953-54 Fellow Am. Inst. Chemists, Photog. Soc. Am. (v.p. 1969-84, Harold Lloyd award 1978, exec. v.p. 1995, progress medal 1995); mem. Am. Chem. Soc., Soc. Photog. Scientists and Engrs., AAAS, Rochester C. of C., Am. C. of C. in Japan (bd. govs. 1988-91, v.p. 1989-91), Internat. Stereoscopic Union (pres. 1993, 94), Photographic Soc. of Am. (bd. dirs. 1992—, exec. v.p. 1995-99, pres. 1999—). Clubs: American (Tokyo); Fgn. Correspondence. Republican. Avocations: skiing; photography; gardening. Home and Office: 159 Hillhurst Ln Rochester NY 14617-1938 E-mail: albert4182@aol.com.

SIEG, ELIZABETH A. medical professional; b. Griffin, Ga., May 20, 1971; d. Mark Anthony and Sandra Roddy Jungers; m. Paul Jonathan Sieg, Sept. 12, 1998. BA in Biology, Randolph-Macon Woman's Coll., 1993; M in Med. Sci., Emory U., 1995. Cert. anesthesiologist asst. Physician's asst. Pediat. Anesthesia Specialists, Atlanta, 1995—. Mem. Am. Acad. Anesthesiology Assts., Sierra Club. Episcopalian. Avocations: quilting, cross-stitching, snow skiing. Home: 3050 E Ramble Ln Decatur GA 30033-1121 Office: Pediat Anesthesia Specialists PC 1001 Johnson Ferry Rd NE Atlanta GA 30342-1605

SIEGAL, ALLAN MARSHALL, newspaper editor; b. N.Y.C., May 1, 1940; s. Irving and Sylvia Norma (Wrubel) S.; m. Gretchen M-P. Leefmans, May 31, 1977; children— Anna Marianita, Peter Bert Grad., NYU, 1962. With New York Times, 1960—, editor Pentagon Papers, 1971, asst. fgn. editor, 1971-76, asst. to exec. editor, 1976-77, news editor, 1977-87, asst. mng. editor, 1987—, founding editor nat. edit., 1980; tchr. journalism NYU, 1966, Columbia U., 1967-69. Juror Pulitzer Prize Nominating Com., 1987-89. Co-author: The New York Times Manual of Style and Usage, 1999. Mem. Century Assn., Am. Soc. Newspaper Editors. Office: NY Times Co 229 W 43rd St New York NY 10036-3959

SIEGAL, BARBARA LEATRICE, visual artist; b. Bklyn., Oct. 14, 1931; d. Harry and Rachel Wank; m. George H. Friedman, Apr. 29, 1977; 1 child, Cindy Leesha. BA cum laude, CUNY, 1976. Exhibited works in one-person show at La Jolla Art Assn. Gallery; group show at Watercolor Soc. Houston, 1997, 98, San Diego Watercolor Soc., 1999, 2001, 02, Lyceum Theater, San Diego, 1999. Exhibited in group shows at Coronado (Calif.) Art Assn., 1986 (Best of Show), Del Mar Art Fair, 1995, 99 (Hon. Mention); contbr. art to corp. calendars, art publs. Mem.: Clairemont Art Guild, Artists Guild of the San Diego Mus. of Art, Different Strokes (pres. 1997—), La Jolla Art Assn. (pres. 1992—94), San Diego Watercolor Soc. (pres. 1988—89). Home: 3783 1st Ave Apt 3 San Diego CA 92103-4045

SIEGAL, BURTON LEE, product designer, consultant, inventor; b. Chgo., Sept. 27, 1931; s. Norman A. and Sylvia (Vitz) S.; m. Rita Goran, Apr. 11, 1954; children: Norman, Laurence Scott BS in Mech. Engring., U. Ill., 1953. Torpedo designer U.S. Naval Ordnance, Forest Park, Ill., 1953-54; chief engr. Gen. Aluminum Corp., Chgo., 1954-55; product designer Chgo. Aerial Industries, Melrose Park, Ill., 1955-58; chief designer Emil J. Paidar Co., Chgo., 1958-59; founder, pres. Budd Engring. Corp., 1959—. Dir. Dur-A-Case Corp., Chgo.; design cons. to numerous corps. Holder more than 125 patents in more than 40 fields including multimemory for power seats and electrified office panel sys., Piezo ink jet valves; contbr. articles to tech. publs. Mem. math., sci. and English adv. bds. Niles Twp. High Schs., Skokie, Ill., 1975-79; electronic cons. Chgo. Police Dept., 1964 Winner, Internat. Extrusion Design Competition, 1975; nominated Presdl. Medal Technology Sen. Paul Simon and Rep. Dan Rostenkowski, 1986; named Inventor of Yr. Patent Law Assn. Chgo., 1986. Mem. ASME, Soc. Plastics Engrs., Soc. Mfg. Engrs., Inventor's Coun., Soc. Automotive Engrs., Pres.'s Assn. Ill. *A true professional can perform any time, any place, independent of his mood.*

SIEGAL, GENE PHILIP, pathology educator; b. Bronx, N.Y., Nov. 16, 1948; s. Murray H. and Evelyne (Philips) S.; m. Sandra Helene Meyerowitz, Aug. 3, 1972; children: Gail Deborah, Rebecca Stacey. BA, Adelphi U., Garden City, N.Y., 1970; MD, U. Louisville, 1974; PhD, U. Minn., 1979; cert. in hosp. mgmt., U. N.C., 1988. Diplomate Nat. Bd. Med. Examiners, Am. Bd. Pathology. Intern, resident, rsch. fellow Mayo Clinic Found., Rochester, Minn., 1974-79; rsch. assoc. Lab. Pathophysiology, Nat. Cancer Inst., NIH, Bethesda, Md., 1979-81; fellow surg. pathology U. Minn., Mpls., 1981-82; asst. prof. pathology U. N.C., Chapel Hill, 1982-88, assoc. prof. pathology, 1988-90; mem. Lineberger Comprehensive Cancer Ctr., 1983-90; prof. pathology U. Ala., Birmingham, 1990—, sr. scientist/group leader breast, ovary, prostate program, Comprehensive Cancer Ctr., 1990—, prof. pathology, prof. cell biology, prof. surgery, 1991—. Mem. Children's Cancer Study Group, 1987-90, Pediatric Oncology Group, 1990—, mem. osteosarcoma pathology com.; sr. scientist Ctr. for Aging, Cell Adhesion and Matrix Rsch. Ctr., 1995—, Ctr. Metabolic Bone Disease, 1997—. Co-editor: Molecular Antibodies in Diagnostic Immunohistochemistry, 1988; assoc. editor Archives of Pathology and Lab. Medicine, 1989-90; mem. editl. bd. Yearbook of Pathology, 1983-91, Archives of Pathology and Laboratory Medicine, 1990-91, Am. Jour. Clin. Pathology, 1990—, Modern Pathology, 1996—, Advances in Anat. Pathology, 1999--, Am. Jour. Surg. Pathology, 2001--, Annals Diagnostic Pathology, 2001--. With USPHS, 1979-81. Clin. fellow Am. Cancer Soc., Chapel Hill, 1981-82, jr. faculty fellow, 1983-86, Jefferson-Pilot fellow in acad. medicine, U. N.C., Chapel Hill, 1985-86. Fellow Am. Soc. Clin. Pathologists (coun. on edn. and rsch.), Coll. Am. Pathologists (inspector 1990—), Royal Soc. Medicine (London); mem. AMA, AAAS, Internat. Skeletal Soc., AOA, Am. Soc. for Investigative Pathology (councilor 2002--), U.S. and Can. Acad. Pathology (abstract rev. bd. 1989-91, 99—), A.P. Stout Surg. Pathologists (mem., sec. exec. bd.), Metastasis Rsch. Soc., Am. Assn. Cancer Rsch., Assn. Dirs. Anatomic and Surg. Pathology (coun. 2000--), Sigma Xi (pres. U. N.C. chpt. 1989-90), Phi Beta Delta. Democrat. Jewish. Office: Univ Ala Dept Pathology 506 Kracke Birmingham AL 35233

SIEGAL, JACOB J. management and financial consultant; b. Phila., Apr. 4, 1929; s. Louis and Henrietta (Greenberg) S.; m. Dolores Berg, June 8, 1952; children: Marla, Karen, Leslie. BS, Temple U., 1951, LLB, 1954; postgrad., U. Chgo., 1973. Bar: Pa. 1955, Ill. 1973. With City of Phila., 1954-61, chief counselor, 1959-61, dep. city solicitor, 1958-61; pvt. practice law, partner firm Meltzer & Schiffrin, Phila., 1961-72; v.p., gen. counsel, dir. Bluebird Inc., 1972-74, exec. v.p., 1974-78, pres., 1978-79, chmn., chief exec. officer, 1979. Chmn. bd. Armen Cadillac-Osmobile, Inc. Mem. Am. Meat Inst. (dir., conv. speaker 1978) Home: 101 Cheswold Ln Haverford PA 19041-1865 Office: PO Box 193 Plymouth Meeting PA 19462-0193

SIEGAL, JOEL DAVIS, lawyer; b. Plainfield, N.J., Feb. 9, 1937; s. Samuel and Florence (Ravitz) S.; m. Ronny J. Greenwald, Oct. 16, 1972; children: Samuel Jesse, Evan Charles. BA in Polit. Sci., U. Pa., 1958; JD, Yale U., 1961; MA in Internat. Rels., U. Stockholm, 1963. Bar: N.J., 1962, N.Y., 1965; U.S. Dist. Ct. N.J., 1962, U.S. Ct. Appeals (3rd cir.), 1963, U.S. Supreme Ct., N.Y., 1969, U.S. Dist. Ct. (so. and ea. dist.) N.Y., 1975. Law clk. to Hon. Arthur S. Lane, Newark, 1961-62; law clk. to Hon. Phillip Forman, 1963-64; assoc. Hellring Lindeman Goldstein & Siegal, Newark, 1967-70, ptnr., 1970—. Commr. Nat. Conf. Commrs. on Uniform Laws, 1991-98; mem. U.S. Dist. Ct. Adv. Bd., Newark, 1991-92. Contbr. articles to profl. jours. Mcpl. chmn. Dem. Party, Borough of Alpine, N.J., 1983-86. Fellow Am. Bar Found.; mem. ABA, N.J. Bar Assn., Essex County Bar Assn., Bergen Bar Assn., Assn. Fed. Bar N.J. (nat. del. N.J. 1974, pres. 1990-92, adv. bd. 1993—), Harmonie Club of N.Y.C. Democrat. Jewish. Office: Hellring Lindeman Goldstein Siegal 1 Gateway Ctr Fl 8 Newark NJ 07102-5386 Fax: (973) 621-7406. E-mail: jdsiegal@hlgslaw.com.

SIEGAL, RITA DENA, interior plantscaper, florist; b. Jersey City, Feb. 24, 1947; d. Arthur and Shirley Estelle (Klemons) S.; m. James Lee D'Angelo, Aug. 1, 1971 (div. May 1983). Student U. S.C., 1967; A.A. in Retailing, Vernon Ct. Jr. Coll., 1968. Fashion coordinator Simplicity Pattern Co., N.Y.C., 1968-70; asst. to pub. Crane Communications, N.Y.C., 1970-71; pres., owner Dandelion, Ltd., Myrtle Beach, S.C., 1975— . Chmn. house and grounds com. Arcadian II Homeowners Assn., Myrtle Beach, 1984— ; pres. Grand Strand Tips Club, Myrtle Beach, Myrtle Beach chpt. Hadassah; active Myrtle Beach Women's Club. Mem. Landscape Contractors Am. Jewish. Avocations: running; cooking; reading. Home: Arcadian II 7-D Myrtle Myrtle Beach SC 29577 Office: Dandelion Ltd 515 W Broadway St Myrtle Beach SC 29577-3970

SIEGAL, RITA GORAN, engineering company executive; b. Chgo., July 16, 1934; d. Leonard and Anabelle (Soloway) Goran; m. Burton L. Siegal, Apr. 11, 1954; children: Norman, Laurence Scott. Student. U. Ill., 1951-53; BA, DePaul U., 1956. Cert. elem. tchr., Ill. Tchr. Chgo. Public Schs., 1956-58; founder, chief exec. officer Budd Engring. Corp., Skokie, Ill., 1959—; founder, pres. Easy Living Products Co., 1960—; pvt. practice in interior design, Chgo., 1968-73; dist. sales mgr. Super Girls, Skokie, 1976. Lectr. Northwestern U., 1983; guest speaker nat. radio and TV, 1979—. Contbr. to profl. jours. Mem. adv. bd. Skokie High Schs., 1975-79; advisor Cub Scouts Skokie coun. Boy Scouts Am., 1975; bus. mgr. Nutrition for Optimal Health Assn., Winnetka, Ill., 1980-82, pres., 1982-84, v.p. med./profl., 1985-93; leader Great Books Found., 1972; founder Profit Plus Investment, 1970; bd. dirs. Noha, Internat. Named Prominent Alumni, Sullivan H.S., 2001; recipient Cub Scout awards, Boy Scouts Am., 1971—72, Nat. Charlotte Danstrom award, Nat. Women of Achievement, 1988, Corp. Achievement award, 1988. Mem. North Shore Women in Mgmt. (pres, 1987-88), Presidents Assn. Ill. (bd. dirs 1990-94, membership chair 1991-93), Inventors Coun., Oriental Art Soc. Chgo. (publicity chair). *Believe in yourself, if others can do it so can you. Prioritize so you are not overwhelmed by your responsibilities.*

SIEGAL, RONNY JO, lawyer; b. N.Y.C., July 16, 1947; d. Irwin Daniel and Doris Rae (Lewin) Greenwald; m. Joel Davis Siegal, Oct. 14, 1972; children: Samuel, Evan. Ba, Syracuse U., 1968; JD, Fordham U., 1972. Bar: N.Y. 1973, U.S. Dist. Ct. (so. and ea. dist.) N.Y. 1974, N.J. 1978, U.S. Dist. Ct. N.J. 1978, U.S. Ct. Appeals (3d cir.) 1983, U.S. Supreme Ct. 1994. Asst. dist. atty. Bronx Dist. Atty.'s Office, 1972-77, dep. bur. chief appeals, 1976-77; ptnr. Hellring, Lindeman, Goldstein & Siegal, Newark, 1978—. Mem planning bd. Borough of Alpine, 1992-95, chairperson, 1993-94; vice-chair Legalized Gambling Policy Study Commn., 1993-94; mem. bd. adjustment Borough of Alpine, 1980, sec., 1981, 82, vice-chair, 1983-86; Dem. committeewoman, Alpine, 1983—. Mem. ABA, N.J. Bar Assn., Bergen County Bar Assn., Women in Fed. Practice in N.J., N.J. Women Lawyers Assn., Women Lawyers in Bergen, Assn. of Fed. Bar State N.J. (v.p. 1991-93, trustee 1994—), Shelter Our Sisters (governing bd. 1997-98, sec. 1999-2000, v.p. 2000-01, pres. 2001—). Democrat. Jewish. Avocation: running. Office: Hellring Lindeman Goldstein & Siegal One Gateway Ctr Newark NJ 07102

SIEGAN, BERNARD HERBERT, lawyer, educator; b. Chgo., July 28, 1924; s. David and Jeannette S.; m. Sharon Goldberg, June 15, 1952 (dec. Feb. 1985); m. Shelley Zifferblatt, Nov. 19, 1995. AA, Herzl. Jr. Coll., Chgo., 1943, 46; Student, Roosevelt Coll., Chgo., 1946-47; JD, U. Chgo., 1949. Bar: Ill. 1950. Practiced in, Chgo.; partner firm Siegan & Karlin, 1952-73; pres., sec. various small corps. and gen. partner in partnerships engaged in real estate ownership and devel., 1955-70; weekly columnist Freedom newspaper chain, other papers, 1974-79. Cons. law and econs. program U. Chgo. Law Sch., 1970-73; adj. prof. law U. San Diego Law Sch., 1973-74, Disting. prof., 1975—; adj. scholar Cato Inst., Washington, 1991—, Heritage Found., 1992—; cons. windfalls and wipeouts project HUD, 1973-74; cons. FTC, 1985-86, U.S. Justice Dept., dir. constl. bibliog. project, 1986-88; keynote speaker 5th Internat. Conf. on Urbanism, Porto Alegre, Brazil, 1989; nominated by Pres. Reagan to U.S. Ct. Appeals (9th cir.) Feb. 2, 1987, confirmation denied July 14, 1988 by party line vote Senate Judiciary Com. Author: Land Use Without Zoning, 1972, Spanish edit., 1995, Other People's Property, 1976, Economic Liberties and the Constitution, 1980, The Supreme Court's Constitution: An Inquiry Into Judicial Review and Its Impact on Society, 1987, Drafting a Constitution for a Nation or Republic Emerging into Freedom, 1992, 2d edit., 1994, Portuguese, Ukrainian, Polish and Spanish edits., 1993, Property and Freedom: The Constitution, Supreme Court and Land Use Regulation, 1997, Adapting a Constitution to Protect Freedom and Provide Abundance (in Bulgarian), 1998, Property Rights: From Magna Carta to the Fourteenth Amendment, 2001; editor: Planning without Prices, 1977, The Interaction of Economics and the Law, 1977, Regulation, Economics and the Law, 1979, Government, Regulation and the Economy, 1980. Mem. pres.-elect's Task Force on Housing, 1980-81; mem. Pres.'s Commn. on Housing, 1981-82; mem. Nat. Commn. on bicentannial of U.S. Constn., 1985-91; chmn. adv. com. Affordable Housing Conf., San Diego, 1985, Rights of Regulated Conf., Coronado, Calif., 1976; chmn. Conf. on the Taking Issue, 1976; mem. Houston Regional Urban Design Team, Study of Houston, 1990; mem. U.S. team Bulgarian Econ. Growth and Transition Project, 1990; mem. devel. bd. Mingei Internat. Mus. World Folk Art, 1981-84. Served with AUS, 1943-46. Research fellow law and econs. U. Chgo. Law Sch., 1968-69; Urban Land Inst. research fellow, 1976-86; recipient Leander J. Monks Meml. Fund award Inst. Humane Studies, 1972, George Washington medal Freedom Founds. at Valley Forge, 1981, Spl. award Liberal Inst. of Rio Grande do Sul, Porto Alegre, Brazil, 1989, Thorsnes award for outstanding legal scholarship, 1998; named Univ. Prof., U. San Diego, 1997-98.

SIEGEL, ARTHUR HERBERT, finance executive; b. N.Y.C., Jan. 5, 1938; s. Joseph Kenneth and Gertrude Sylvia (Hecker) S.; m. Eleanor Novick, June 5, 1960; children: Joan Aileen, Linda Beth, Mark Eric. AB, Columbia U., 1958, MBA, 1960. With Price Waterhouse, N.Y.C., 1960-97, mgr. L.I., 1961-72, ptnr. Boston, 1972-83, nat. dir. acctg. svcs. N.Y.C., 1984-88, vice chmn. bus. adv. and auditing svcs., 1988-95; mem. Fin. Acctg. Stds. Bd. Emerging Issues Task Force, 1985-88, Fin. Acctg. Stds. Adv. Coun., 1985-90; mem. adv. coun. Sch. Acctg., U. So. Calif., 1987-89. Active World ABS Exec. Com., 1988—95, chmn., 1990—95, U.S. Mgmt. Com., 1988—95, World Mgmt. Coms., 1990—95; exec. dir. Independence Stds. Bd., 1997—2001. Past trustee, treas., 1st v.p. Temple Beth Avodah, Newton Centre, Mass.; bd. dirs. Nat. Multiple Sclerosis Soc., treas. exec. com., chmn. fin. com., 1990-98. Mem. AICPA (chmn. task force on risks and uncertainties 1985-87, chmn. SEC practice exec. com. 1994-97), N.Y. Soc. CPAs (Silver Medal award), Mass. Soc. CPAs (pres.-elect 1983), Beta Gamma Sigma. Home: Apt 3A 179 E 70th St New York NY 10021-5109 E-mail: ASiegs@ix.netcom.com.

SIEGEL, BARRY, reporter; b. St. Louis, Sept. 7, 1949; m. Marti Devore; 1 child Alexandra Nicole. BA in English, Pomona Coll., 1971; MS in Journalism, Columbia U., 1972. Stringer L.A. bur. Newsweek, L.A., 1973; news editor West Coast Women's Wear Daily, 1973—76; writer View sect. L.A. Times, 1976—78, writer spl. assignment, 1979, corr. Nat., 1980—83, corr./sr. writer, 1983—. Vis. lectr. U. So. Calif., 1988. Author: A Death in White Bear Lake, 1990, Shades of Gray, 1992, The Perfect Witness, 1998, Actual Innocence, 1999; contbr. Recipient USA West Lit. award in Journalism, PEN Ctr., 2000, USA West Journalism award, 1987, Silver Gavel award, ABA, 1985, Golden Medallion Media award, State Bar Calif., 1984, Paul Tobenkin Meml. award, 1997. Office: LA Times 202 W 1st St Los Angeles CA 90012*

SIEGEL, BARRY ALAN, nuclear radiologist; b. Nashville, Dec. 30, 1944; s. Walter Gross Siegel and Lillian B. Ivener; m. Pamela M. Mandel, Aug. 18, 1968 (div. Mar. 1981); children: Peter A., William A.; m. Marilyn J. Siegel, Jan. 29, 1983. AB, Washington U., St. Louis, 1966, MD, 1969. Diplomate Am. Bd. Nuclear Medicine, Am. Bd. Radiology. Intern Barnes Hosp., St. Louis, 1969-70; resident in radiology and nuc. medicine fellow Mallinckrodt Inst. Radiology, Washington U., 1970-73, dir. div. nuc. medicine, 1973—, asst. prof., 1973-76, assoc. prof., 1976-79, prof. radiology, 1979—, assoc. prof. medicine, 1980-83, prof. medicine, 1983—. Dir. Am. Bd. Nuc. Medicine, L.A., 1985-90, sec., 1990; chmn. adv. com. on med. uses of isotopes NRC, Washington, 1990-96; chmn. radiopharm. drugs adv. com. U.S. FDA, Rockville, Md., 1982-85, radiol. devices panel, 1992-95; mem. U.S. Pharmacopeia Adv. Panel on Radiopharms., 1975-2000, Armed Forces Radiobiol. Rsch. Inst., Bethesda; coun. experts, chair Radiopharm. Expert Com., U.S. Pharmacopoeial Conv., 2000—. Author, editor 33 books; contbr. articles to profl. jours., chpts. in books. Maj. USAF, 1974-76. Recipient Commr.'s Spl. citation U.S. FDA, 1988, Honor citation U.S. Pharmacopeial Conv., 1995, 2000. Fellow ACP, Am. Coll. Radiology (vice chmn. commn. on nuc. medicine 1981-93, editor in chief profl. self evaluation program 1988-2002), Am. Coll. Nuc. Physicians; mem. AMA, Am. Roentgen Ray Soc., Assn. Univ. Radiologists, Radiol. Soc. N.Am., Soc. Nuclear Medicine (trustee 1981-85, 87-91), Acad. Molecular Imaging (chair Inst. Clin. PET coun. 2001-). Office: Washington U Mallinckrodt Inst Radiology 510 S Kingshighway Blvd Saint Louis MO 63110-1016 E-mail: siegelb@mir.wustl.edu.

SIEGEL, BERNARD LOUIS, lawyer; b. Pitts., Sept. 15, 1938; s. Ralph Robert and Frieda Sara (Stein) S.; m. Marcia Margolis, Sept. 3, 1961 (div. Aug. 1983); children: Jonathan, Sharon; m. Susan Erickson, Aug. 31, 1997 (div. June 2001). BA, Brandeis U., 1960; JD, Harvard U., 1963. Bar: Pa. 1964, U.S. Dist. Ct. (we. dist.) Pa. 1964, U.S. Dist. Ct. (ea. dist.) Pa. 1985, U.S. Ct. Appeals (3d cir.) 1985, U.S. Supreme Ct. 1985. Assoc. Silin, Eckert & Burke, Erie, Pa., 1963-66; ptnr. Silin, Eckert, Burke & Siegel, 1966-73; 1st asst. dist. atty. Erie County, 1972-76; dep. atty. gen. Pa. Dept. Justice, Phila., 1976-78; dep. dist. atty. Dist. Atty. of Phila., 1978-86; pvt. practice Phila., 1986—. Adj. prof. La Salle U., Phila., 1986-98; lectr. Fed. Law Enforcement Tng. Ctr., Glynco, Ga., 1986-97, Mercyhurst Coll., Erie, 1974-76, Nat. Coll. Dist. Attys., Houston, 1978-85; adj. prof. Temple U. law sch., 1995—; mem. criminal rules com. Pa. Supreme Ct., Phila., 1976-85; commr. Pa. Crime Commn., Harrisburg, 1976-79. Author: (with others) Pennsylvania Grand Jury Practice, 1983, By No Extraordinary Means, 1986. Mem. ABA, Nat. Assn. Criminal Def. Lawyers, Pa. Assn. Criminal Def. Lawyers (bd. dirs. 1988—), Pa. Bar Assn. (chmn. criminal law sect. 1988-91), Phila. Bar Assn. (chmn. criminal justice sect. 1990-91). Democrat. Jewish. Avocations: bicycling, reading, hiking. Office: 1515 Market St Ste 1915 Philadelphia PA 19102-1920 E-mail: blsesq@snip.net.

SIEGEL, CHARLES, lawyer, investment banking and brokerage executive; b. N.Y.C., June 6, 1944; s. Edward and Ann (Aronson) S.; m. Francine Marie Prioli, Sept. 26, 1970; children— David Aaron, Stefanie Joy BS in Econs., U. Pa., 1965; JD, Boston U., 1968. Bar: N.Y. 1969, U.S. Dist. Ct. (so. and ea. dists.) N.Y. 1976, U.S. Ct. Appeals (2nd cir.) 1975, U.S. Ct. Appeals (8th cir.) 1978, U.S. Supreme Ct. 1979. Asst. arbitration dir. N.Y. Stock Exchange, Inc., N.Y.C., 1968-72, arbitrator, 1979—; v.p., asst. sec., asst. legal counsel Blyth Eastman Dillon & Co. Inc., 1972-80; sr. v.p., spl. counsel E.F. Hutton & Co. Inc., 1980-86; assoc. dir. Bear, Stearns, & Co. Inc., 1986-88; sr. v.p., sr. assoc. gen. counsel PaineWebber Inc., 1988-94, Kelley Drye & Warren, N.Y.C., 1995-98; gen. counsel Fleet Securities, Inc., 1998—. Lectr. Securities Industry Assn., N.Y.C., 1985, 86 Mem. ABA Office: Fleet Securities Inc 26 Broadway New York NY 10004-1703

SIEGEL, EDWARD M. lawyer; b. N.Y.C., Apr. 14, 1934; s. Charles and Rose (Fritzhand) S.; m. Elyse R. Roth, Mar. 9, 1969; children: Eric, Eve-Lynn. BA, Columbia Coll., 1955; MA, Columbia U., 1957, JD, 1960. Bar: N.Y. 1961. Legal asst. to dean Columbia U. Law Sch., N.Y.C., 1960-65; gen. counsel Transp. Displays, Inc., 1965-75, corp. sec., 1968-75, v.p., 1972-73, sr. v.p., 1973-75; pub. affairs mgr. J.C. Penney Co., 1975-77; gen. counsel, corp. sec. Electro Audio Dynamics, Inc., Great Neck, N.Y., 1977-85, v.p., 1981-85; v.p. legal affairs East View Co., N.Y.C., 1985-87; ptnr. Bangser Klein Rocca & Blum (formerly Bangser & Weiss), 1988-92; sr. v.p., gen. coun., corp. sec. Nat. Med. Funding Corp., 1992-94; atty pvt. practice, 1994—. Mem. N.Y. State Bar Assn., Columbia Law Sch. Alumni Assn. (dir. 1966-70). Home: 1036 Park Ave Apt 6D New York NY 10028-0971 Office: 7 Penn Plz Ste 505 New York NY 10001-3900

SIEGEL, FREDERIC RICHARD, geology educator; b. Chelsea, Mass., Feb. 8, 1932; s. Louis and Eva (Minsky) S.; m. Felisa Matilde Puszkin, Mar. 3, 1962; children: Gabriela Davina, Galia Dinah. BA, Harvard U., 1954; MS, U. Kans., 1958, PhD, 1961. Prof. titular Universidad Nacional de Tucuman, Argentina, 1961-63; head geochemistry divsn. Kans. Geol. Survey, Lawrence, 1963-65; assoc. prof. geochemistry George Washington U., Washington, 1965-69, prof., 1969-99, prof. emeritus geochemistry, 1999—, dir. geochemistry program, 1965-99, chmn. dept. geology, 1976-86. Tech. cons. UN Devel. program, Havana, Cuba, 1980. Author: Applied Geochemistry, 1974, Geoquimica Aplicada, 1992, Natural and Anthropogenic Hazards in Development Planning, 1996, Environmental Geochemistry of Potentially Toxic Metals, 2001; editor: Review of Research on Modern Problems in Geochemistry, 1979. With U.S. Army, 1954-56; ETO. Recipient Erasmus Haworth award Dept. Geology, U. Kans., 1958; Fulbright prof., 1970, Best Paper award Energy Minerals divsn. Am. Assn. Petroleum Geologists, 1989. Mem. Assn. Exploration Geochemists (councillor 1988-95), Geochem. Soc., Internat. Assn. Geochemists and Cosmochemists, Soc. Environ. Geochemistry and Health. Jewish. Home: 4353 Yuma St NW Washington DC 20016-2027 Office: George Washington U 2029 G St NW Washington DC 20052-4211 E-mail: nzkara@research.circ.gwu.edu.

SIEGEL, GEORGE HENRY, international business development consultant; b. Bklyn., Oct. 8, 1926; s. Samuel S. and Sara Siegel; m. Lenore D. Greenberg, Oct. 28, 1951; children: Arthur B., Ellen S. BEE, CCNY, 1948; MS in Indsl. Engring, NYU, 1951. Registered profl. engr., N.Y. From engr. to gen. mgr. Gen. Electric Corp., Syracuse, Utica and Binghamton, N.Y., 1951-74; v.p., gen. mgr. flight systems div. Bendix Corp., 1974-77, chief tech. officer, 1977-79, v.p., gen. mgr. diesel engine controls, 1979-82; v.p., group exec. Bendix Automation Co., Cleve., 1983-84; v.p. tech. Allied-Signal Internat., Morristown, N.J., 1984-90; v.p. Volt Tech. Svcs. Co., N.Y.C., 1991-93; pres. Point North Assocs., Inc., Madison, N.J., 1990—. Invited guest lectr. UCLA, 1960-63. Bd. visitors Oakland U., Rochester, Mich., 1977-83. Served with AUS, 1944-46. Mem. IEEE (sr., life, sect. chmn. 1965), Soc. Automotive Engrs. Office: Point North Assocs Inc PO Box 907 Madison NJ 07940-0907 E-mail: siegelgh@att.net.

SIEGEL, GEORGE LEWIS, endocrinologist; b. Bklyn., June 2, 1934; s. Harry and Bertha (Safier) S.; m. Jean Gellis, May 29, 1964; children: Robert, Steven, Laura. AB, Colgate U., 1955; MD, Albany Med. Coll., 1959. Diplomate Am. Bd. Internal Medicine, Am. Bd. Endocrinology and Metabolism. Asst. clin. prof. Hahneman Sch. of Medicine, Phila., 1968-71, Mt. Sinai Sch. Medicine, N.Y.C., 1971—; attending physician of endocrinology Beth Israel Med. Ctr., 1971—; chief endocrinology sect. Beth Israel North, 1989—. Contbr. articles to profl. jours. Capt. M.C., US. Army, 1966-68. Fellow Am. Coll. Endocrinology; mem. ACP, Am. Assn. Clin. Endocrinologists, Endocrine Soc., Am. Diabetes Assn., N.Y. Acad. Scis., Clin. Diabetes Soc. N.Y., N.Y. County Med. Soc. Avocations: skiing, reading, music. Home: 40 E 80th St New York NY 10021-0230 Office: 240 E 82nd St New York NY 10028-2703

SIEGEL, HERBERT BERNARD, management consultant; b. N.Y.C., Mar. 10, 1934; s. Jacob and Clara Dora (Goldgeier) S.; m. Joan Miriam Goodkin, Nov. 6, 1955; children— Jeffrey Roy, Lori Robin, Amy Hope, Jonathan Stuart. Degree, N.Y. U., 1959, postgrad. in bus., 1960-63, Harvard U., 1975; PhD in Internat. Law, Columbia U., 1999. Diplomate Am. Acad. Cons. and Forensic Experts; cert. profl. mgmt. cons.; chartered cons., U.K.; accredited profl. cons. With William Iselin & Co., Inc., N.Y.C., 1957-67; treas. Bates Mfg. Co., Inc., 1968; pres. Emle Industries, Inc., 1968-72; fed. pres. trustee Toys R Us, 1973-78; pres. Nat. Silver Co., 1973-78, F.B. Rogers Silver Co., N.Y.C., 1979-82; pres., chief exec. officer Quaker City Steel Co., 1980-86, Seal-Kap Packaging Co., N.Y.C., 1980-90, J. Ramsey Reese, Inc., Tarrytown, N.Y., 1980-87; pres. Deerhill Devel. Corp., 1980-87; exec. v.p. Columbia Profl. Baseball Club, Inc., 1980-87; pres., chief exec. officer J.R. Reese Enterprises, Ltd. et al, 1989-90; prin. officer Whitestone Cons. Group, Ltd., 1991—. Trustee Dime Savs. Bank of Williamsburg, N.Y.C.; thesis examiner Grad. Sch. Banking, Rutgers U., 1963-64; chmn. Fin-Tec Corp.; lectr. Grad. Sch. Mgmt. and Orgn., Yale U.; bd. dirs. Motorcycle Malls of Am., Inc., Advanced Rehab. Ctrs., Inc., N.Y. Pacific Exch. Ltd., Silvergull Industries Inc., Havemeyer Equities, Inc., Lionville Packing Co., Coast-to-Coast Mktg. Am., Inc.; trustee Neisner Bros. Dept. Stores, United Cerebral Palsey, Nassau; counsellor internat. bus. law. Author: A Trustee's View of Chapter Ten, 1981, Tomorrow's America, Made Today in the U.S.A., 1993, The Entropy of Government Deficits, 1995, Corporate Rehabilitation After Bankruptcy, 1995, The Masquerade of Cost Cutting, 1996, Market Economics for Multinational Corporations, 1997, International Trade and the Competitive Environment, 1997, Accounting Strategies for Multinational Corporations, 1998, Statistics That Measure the Wealth of Multinational Companies, 1998, Developments and Organizational Behavior in International Business Environments, 1998, Privatization: A Social Milestone or Millstone?, 1999. Served with AUS, 1955-57. Mem. ABA, Internat. Bar Assn., Internat. Studies Assn., Am. Mgmt. Assn., Am. Bankruptcy Inst., Am. Acad. Profl. Cons. and Experts, N.Y. Acad. Sci., NYU Alumni Club, Turnaround Mgmt. Assn., Soc. of Profls. in Dispute Resolutions, Prime Raters Fin. Club (pres.), Am. Mensa Soc., Am. Cons. League. Office: 854 E Broadway #2F Long Beach NY 11561 E-mail: herb515@rcn.com.

SIEGEL, HERBERT JAY, communications executive, director; b. Phila., May 7, 1928; s. Jacob and Fritzi (Stern) S.; m. Ann F. Levy, June 29, 1950; children: John C., William D. BA in Journalism, Lehigh U., 1950. Sec., dir. Official Films, Inc., N.Y.C., 1951-54; v.p., dir. Bev-Rich Products, Inc., Phila., 1955-56; chmn. bd. Westley Industries, Inc., Cleve., 1955-58; v.p. Phila. Ice Hockey Club, Inc., 1955-60; chmn. bd. Fort Pitt Industries, Inc., Pitts., 1956-58, Seeburg Corp., 1958-60, Centlivre Brewing Corp., Ft. Wayne, Ind., 1959-61; dir. Baldwin Rubber Co., Pontiac, Mich., Mono-Sol Corp., Gary, Inc., 1959-62; chmn. bd. Baldwin-Montrose Chem. Co., 1960-67; pres., chmn. bd. Gen. Artists Corp., 1960-64, chmn., 1960-62; chmn. bd., pres. Chris-Craft Industries, Inc., 1968—; chmn. bd. BHC Comm. Inc., 1977—, pres., 1977-96; chmn. bd. dirs. United TV, Inc., 1982—, chmn. bd., 1982-96, CEO, 1983-90; bd. dirs. Warner Communications, Inc., 1984-89. Bd. dirs. Piper Aircraft Corp., 1971-77, Paramount Pictures, 1963-64, Harvard-Mahoney Neurosci. Inst., 2000. Bd. dirs. Friends of Israel Defense Forces, 1996—, Research to Prevent Blindness, 2000—, Phoenix House, 1978-81; bd. advisors Vets. Bedside Network, 1980-90; v.p. Friars Nat. Assn. Found., 1980—, Chas. A. Dana Found., Inc., 1996—; trustee Lehigh U., 1989-92, Blair Acad., 1985-92. Office: News America Inc 767 5th Ave Fl 46 New York NY 10153-0023*

SIEGEL, HOWARD JEROME, lawyer; b. Chgo., July 29, 1942; s. Leonard and Idele (Lehrner) S.; m. Diane L. Gerber; children: Sari D., Allison J., James G. BS, U. Ill., 1963; JD, Northwestern U., 1966. Bar: Ill. 1966, U.S. Dist. Ct. (no. dist.) Ill. 1967. Assoc. Ancel, Stonesifer & Glink, Chgo., 1966-70; ptnr. Goldstine & Siegel, Summit, Ill., 1970-75; sole practice Chgo., 1975-77; pres. Wexler, Siegel & Shaw, Ltd., 1978-82; ptnr. Keck, Mahin & Cate, 1982-95, Neal Gerber & Eisenberg, Chgo., 1995-99; counsel Fagel & Haber, 1999—. Bd. dirs. various corps. Mem.: ABA, Chgo. Bar Assn., Ill. Bar Assn., Twin Orchard Country Club (Long Grove. Ill.). Office: FabelHaberLLC 55 E Monroe 40th Fl Chicago IL 60603 E-mail: hsiegel@fagelhaber.com.

SIEGEL, IRA T. publishing executive; b. N.Y.C., Sept. 23, 1944; s. David Aaron and Rose (Minsky) S.; m. Sharon Ruth Sacks, Sept. 5, 1965. BS, NYU, 1965; MBA, L.I. U., 1968. Bus. mgr. Buttenheim Pub. Co., N.Y.C., 1965-72; corp. v.p. rsch. Cahners Pub. Co. div. Reed Pub. USA, Boston, 1972-86; pres., COO, R.R. Bowker Pub. Co. div. Reed Pub. USA, New Providence, N.J., 1986-91; pres. Martindale-Hubbell div. Reed Pub. USA, 1990-91; pres., CEO Reed Reference Pub. (includes R.R. Bowker Co., Martindale-Hubbell, Nat. Register Pub. Co., The Salesman's Guide, Marquis Who's Who), 1991-95, Lexis-Nexis, Dayton, Ohio, 1995-97. Bd. dirs. Seisint (formerly eData.com), Boca Raton, Fla. Address: 16589 Senterra Dr Delray Beach FL 33484-6948

SIEGEL, JACK MORTON, retired biotechnology company executive; b. Sioux City, Iowa, June 11, 1922; s. Harry and Rose (Perlman) S.; m. Betty Virginia Collins, Feb. 22, 1946 (dec. Feb. 1986); children: Jennifer L. Mastricola, Marjorie G., Thomas A.; m. Dolores E. Williams Kinert, Dec. 20, 1991. BS in Chemistry, UCLA, 1944; PhD in Chemistry, Washington U., St. Louis, 1950. Chemist The Clinton Labs., Oak Ridge, Tenn., 1944-46; asst. prof. chemistry U. Ark. Sch. Medicine, Little Rock, 1950-55; chemist, v.p. P-L Biochems. Inc., Milw., 1955-82; v.p., gen. mgr. Pharmacia P-L Biochems. Inc., 1982-87, pres., 1987-89. Contbr. articles to profl. jours. Mem. AAAS, Am. Chem. Soc. Democrat. Jewish.

SIEGEL, JEFFREY NORTON, lawyer; b. N.Y.C., Nov. 27, 1942; s. George Siegel and Rose (Friedman) Gerber; m. Judith Sharon Chused, June 11, 1966; children: Daniel, Linda. AB, Brown U., 1964; LLB, Harvard U., 1967. Bar: N.Y. 1968. Assoc., ptnr. Golenbock & Barell, N.Y.C., 1967-89; ptnr. Whitman & Ransom, 1990-93, Shack Siegel Katz Flaherty & Goodman P.C., N.Y.C., 1993—. Mem. bus. com. The Jewish Mus. Mem. ABA, Assn. Bar City N.Y. (com. securities regulation 1987-90, com. profl. responsibility 1979-84), Phi Beta Kappa. Home: 975 Park Ave New York NY 10028-0323 Office: Shack Siegel Katz Flaherty & Goodman PC 530 5th Ave New York NY 10036-5101

SIEGEL, JOEL STEVEN, television news correspondent; b. Los Angeles, July 7, 1943; s. Robert and Libby (Kantor) S.; m. Jane Kessler, Nov. 21, 1976 (dec. 1982); m. Melissa Nina De Mayo, Aug. 27, 1985 (div.); m. Ena Swansea, June 21, 1996; 1 child, Dylan. BA, UCLA, 1965, postgrad., 1966-67. Copywriter, producer Carson & Roberts Advt., Los Angeles, 1967-72; freelance writer Rolling Stone mag., Los Angeles Times, others, 1967-77; news anchorman Sta. KMET-FM, Los Angeles, 1972; corr. Sta. WCBS-TV, N.Y.C., 1972-76; corr., film critic Sta. WABC-TV, 1976—, Good Morning America, N.Y.C., 1980—. Author: (Broadway mus.) The First, 1981 (Tony award nomination 1981). Dir. voter registration drive SCLC/Dr. Martin Luther King, Macon, Ga., 1965; joke writer Robert F. Kennedy, 1968. Served with USAR, 1967-73. Recipient 6 Emmy awards, numerous nominations Nat. Acad. TV Arts and Scis. (N.Y. chpt.), Freedom award B'nai Brith/Anti-Defamation League, 1976. Mem. AFTRA, Dramatists Guild, Drama Desk, Gilda's Club (founding pres.). Democrat. Jewish. Office: Good Morning Am 147 Columbus Ave New York NY 10023-5900

SIEGEL, JUDITH S. music educator; b. Richmond, Va., June 27, 1940; d. Meyer Harry and Mildred (Meyers) Salsbury; m. Murray Siegel, June 18, 1960; children: Lisa Siegel Machlin, Sheri Siegel Cohen, Harry. Student, U. N.C., Greensboro, 1958-60, Smithdeal-Massey Coll., Richmond, 1960-61, Columbia U. Tchrs. Coll., 1965-68, U. Richmond, 1968-79, Columbia U. Tchrs. Coll., 1970. Nat. cert. tchr. of music. Dir. The Pianoforte Sch. of Music, Va., Md., 1965—. Contbr. over 300 articles to profl. jours. books; composer of music and poetry. Avocations: performing arts, journalism, gourmet cooking. Home: 7113 Feldspar Ct Middletown MD 21769-7439 E-mail: PianoSchool@xecu.net.

SIEGEL, JULIAN LEE, lawyer; b. Washington, July 22, 1928; s. Harry Alec and Etta (Schofer) S. BS, George Washington U., 1954, JD, 1959. Bar: D.C. 1960, U.S. Ct. Appeals (D.C. cir.) 1960, Mass. 1969, U.S. Supreme Ct. 1980, U.S. Ct. Appeals (fed. cir.) 1982; registered patent atty. U.S. Patent and Trademark Office. Mathematician U.S. Naval Obs., Washington, 1954-62; patent atty. USAF, Waltham, Mass., 1962-76, Hanscom AFB, 1976-97; chief patent and data br. Electronics Sys. Ct., 1997—. Chief intellectual property law. With USN, 1946-48. Mem. Boston Patent Law Assn., North Medford Club (pres. 1976-78). Republican. Home: 56 Fifer Ln Lexington MA 02420-1225 Office: ESC/JAZ 40 Wright St Hanscom AFB MA 01731-2903 E-mail: julian.siegel@hanscom.af.mil.

SIEGEL, KRISTI ELLEN, English educator; b. Breckenridge, Minn., Jan. 2, 1951; d. Dennis Elton and Cleo Ardell Hjalmer; m. Ronald Siegel, Sept. 30, 1978; children: Aaron, Adam, Ross, Elizabeth. PhD, U. Wis., Milw., 1991. Lectr. Mt. Mary Coll., Milw., 1992-99, asst. prof., 1999—. Author: Word 97 Fundamentals for the Workplace, 1998, Women's Autobiographies, Culture, Feminism, 1999, 2d edit., 2001, Excel 97/Power point 97 for the Workplace, 1999; editor: Empire, Spectacle, and Displacement, 2002; series gen. editor: Travel Writing Across the Disciplines: Theory and Pedagogy; contbg. author: Special Needs Adoption Network: A Series on Adoption and Foster Care Issues, 2000. Mem. Nat. Coun. Tchrs. English, Modern Lang. Assn., Autobiography Assn., Soc. for Tech. Comm. Avocations: writing, music, tennis. Office: Mt Mary Coll 2900 N Menomonee River Pky Milwaukee WI 53222 Home: W223n2257 Meadowood Ln Waukesha WI 53186-1182 E-mail: siegelkr@mtmary.edu.

SIEGEL, LLOYD HARVEY, architect, real estate developer, consultant; b. N.Y.C., Nov. 27, 1928; s. Saul M. and Lillian (Bell) Siegel; m. Margot Kopsidas Phillips, Oct. 25, 1987. BArch, Princeton U., 1949; MArch, MIT, 1953. Registered architect, N.Y., N.J., Conn., Ohio, Ill., Mich., cert. Nat. Coun. Archtl. Registraion Bds. Designer Skidmore, Owings & Merrill, then I. M. Pei & Assocs., then Antonin Raymond, N.Y.C., 1955-60; assoc. Kelly & Gruzen, 1960-66; dep. health services adminstr. City of N.Y., 1966-70; dep. exec. dir. health and hosps. governing commn. Cook County, Chgo., 1970-76; prin. L.H.S. Cons. in Health Planning, Facility Design & Mgmt., Washington, 1976—, Siegel & Schroeder, P.C., Chgo., 1983-87; dir. Office Architecture & Engring. VA, Washington, 1987-94, dir. Facilities Quality Office, 1994-98, dir. Facilities Mgmt. Svc. Delivery Office, 1999-2001; dir. facilities Strategic Mgmt. Office, 2001—. Prin. Yacht Harbor Devel. Co., South Haven, Mich., 1983—88, Siegel & Schroeder Developers Inc., Chgo., 1983—88; mem. adv. coms. HEW; mem. pub. adv. panels GSA; mem. adv. com. Legislature State of Ill.; mem. fellowship evaluation com. AIA-Am. Hosp. Assn.; mem. tech. adv. com. Northeastern Ill. Planning Commn.; chmn. Com. Architecture for Health, 1984. Author: (book) Hidden Asset? Interstitial Space, A Critical Evaluation, 1987; Represented in permanent collections Met. Mus. Art, N.Y.C., Mus. Modern Art, others, prin. works include N.Y. World's Fair Spanish Pavillion, N.Y.C. (N.Y. chpt. AIA award, 1964), Williams Meml. Residence, Flushing, N.Y. (Queens C. of C. award, 1964), Hebrew Home for Aged, Riverdale, N.Y. (Bronx C. of C. award, 1966). Fellow Fulbright, Università di Roma, 1954, Politecnico di Milano, 1955. Fellow: AIA (Presdl. Fed. Design Achievement award); mem.: Urban Land Inst., Univ. Club, Cosmos Club, Arts Club. Avocations: micology, macrophagy, oenology. Home: 3133 Connecticut Ave NW Washington DC 20008-5147 Office: VA 810 Vermont Ave NW Washington DC 20420-0001

SIEGEL, LOUIS PENDLETON, forest products executive; b. Richmond, Va., Nov. 6, 1942; s. John Boschen Jr. and Francis Beale (Tyler) S.; m. Nancy Dicks Blanton, Apr. 10, 1974 (dec. July 1976); m. Nancy Northon, June 26, 1982; children: Kathryn Tyler. AB in Econs., Dartmouth Coll., 1967. Asst. cashier, security researcher First Nat. Citibank, N.Y.C., 1967-71; v.p. security rsch. Drexel Burnham Lambert, 1971-79; with Potlatch Corp., San Francisco and Spokane, Wash., 1979—, sr. v.p. fin. and adminstrn. San Francisco, 1989, group v.p. wood products and corp. planning, 1989-92, group v.p. pulp and paperboard and corp. planning, 1992-93, exec. v.p. pulp-based ops. and corp. planning, 1993-94, pres., COO San Francisco and Spokane, Wash., 1994-99, also bd. dirs. Spokane, chair, CEO, 1999—. Bd. dirs. San Francisco Fed. Corp., 1985-96. Pres., bd. dir. Bay Area Sci. Fair, San Francisco, 1989-90. With USCG, 1964-65. Republican. Episcopalian. Avocations: golf, tennis, fishing. Office: Potlatch Corp 601 W Riverside Ave Ste 1100 Spokane WA 99201-0603

SIEGEL, MARC MONROE, television and film producer, writer, director; b. N.Y.C., Dec. 8, 1916; s. Isaac and Annie N. (Natelson) S.; m. Anne Dorothy Fishman, Sept. 8, 1940; 1 son, Peter Kieve. BA, Washington Sq. Coll., 1936; MA, N.Y. U. Sch. Edn., 1938. Free-lance mag. writer, especially for: New Yorker mag, 1948-50; writer: Eternal Light radio series, NBC, N.Y.C., 1950-60; writer-dir-producer: Directions, ABC-TV, N.Y.C., 1961-78; exec. producer chief writer: Heritage: Civilization and the Jews, WNET, N.Y.C., 1978-84; author: feature screenplays A Child is Crying, 1961, The Young Adventurers, 1963; ABC News Bicentennial spls. Rendezvous With Freedom, 1973, The Right to Believe, 1975, The Will to Be Free, 1976; ABC News feature The Panama Canal, 1977 (Writers Guild award); (Recipient numerous awards, including: Edinburgh Film Festival award 1948, Venice Film Festival award 1962, Cannes Film Festival award 1964, Eternal Light award Jewish Theol. Sem. Am. 1969). Served with USAAF, 1943-45. Peabody award, 1979, 84; Gabriel award Nat. Assn. Catholic Broadcasters, 1979; Emmy award, 1984, Christopher award, 1984; also several awards Freedoms Found. Mem. Nat. Acad. TV Arts and Scis., Writers Guild Am. East (council 1972-73, 78-79, 84-88, awards 1959, 73, 78, 85, Jablow Meml. award 1988), Dirs. Guild Am. Democrat. Home: 75 Central Park W New York NY 10023-6011

SIEGEL, MARK BERNARD, surgeon; b. L.A., Dec. 19, 1948; Student, U. Calif., Berkeley, 1966-69; MD, UCLA, 1973. Diplomate Am. Bd. Surgery. Intern Barnes Hosp., St. Louis, 1973-74, resident in surgery, 1974-78; surgeon Grand Forks (N.D.) Clinic, 1978-97; med. dir. surg. svcs. Altru Health Sys., Grand Forks, 1997-99. Mem. staff Altru Hosp., Grand Forks, 1978—, chief of staff, 1991-93; assoc. prof. U. N.D. Sch. Medicine. Mem. AMA, ACS, Southwestern Surg. Congress. Office: Altru Clinic 1000 S Columbia Rd Grand Forks ND 58201-4032

SIEGEL, MARK JORDAN, lawyer; b. Dallas, Feb. 22, 1949; s. Jack H. and Zelda (Sikora) S.; m. Linda Siegel; children: Jenna, Jason, Jordan. BS in Psychology, North Tex. State U., 1972; JD, South Tex. Coll. Law, 1977. Bar: Tex. 1977, U.S. Dist. Ct. (no. dist.) Tex. 1980, U.S. Ct. Appeals (11th and 5th cirs.) 1982, U.S. Supreme Ct. 1982. Pvt. practice, Dallas, 1977-87. Bd. dirs. Scotch Corp., Dallas. Sponsor Civil Justice Found.; mem. North Dallas 40. Named one of Outstanding Young Men of Am. Mem. ATLA, Tex. Trial Lawyers Assn., Dallas Trial Lawyers Assn., Nat. Bd. Tril Advocacy (cert. civil trial specialist), Tex. Bd. Legal Specialization (cert. civl. trial law). Office: 3607 Fairmount St Dallas TX 75219-4710 E-mail: mjs@siegellegal.com.

SIEGEL, MARSHA ELLEN, medical administrator; b. Phila., Feb. 6, 1949; d. Albert Samuel and Annette Elizabeth (Cohen) Miller; m. June 18, 1972 (div. July 1978); 1 child, Evan Andrew. AS, Cherry Hill Sch. Med. Technology, 1968. Technologist, Thomas Jefferson U., Phila., 1968-69; supr. lab. Miami Heart Inst., Miami Beach, 1969-72; owner, v.p. Personnel Svc., North Miami Beach, Fla., 1976-78; v.p., dir. ops. Med. Group Mgmt., Hollywood, Fla., 1981—; bd. dirs., v.p., treas. Health Care of Greater N.Y.C., 1986—. Treas., v.p. Affiliated Med. Providers Assocs. Inc., North Miami Beach, Fla., 1986. Mem. Hollywood C. of C., Am. Med. Care and Rev. Assn., Group Health Assn. Am. Avocations: dancing, golf, fishing. Office: 680 6th Pl S Garden City NY 11530-5504 also: Health Care of Greater NY 680 6th Pl S Garden City NY 11530-5504

SIEGEL, MARVIN, newspaper editor; b. N.Y.C., June 23, 1935; s. Murray and Belle (Diamond) S.; 1 child, Joshua Murray. BA, U. Mich., 1957. Reporter The Record, Hackensack, N.J., 1957-59; free-lance writer Western Europe, 1960-62; reporter Fairchild Publs., N.Y.C., 1962-63; editor The World Telegram, 1963-66; copy editor The N.Y. Times, 1966-67, asst. met. editor, 1967-76, founding editor Weekend sect., 1976-82; founding editor World of N.Y., 1982-86; founding editor Edn. Life The N.Y. Times, 1986, dep. editor Week in Rev., 1987, culture news editor, 1988-92, dep. editor Book Rev., 1992-95; asst. to mng. editor, 1995—. Co-author: The World of New York, 1985, The New York Times Great Lives of the 20th Century, 1988; editor: Deadly Sins, 1994, The Last Word: The New York Times Book of Obituaries and Farewells, 1997. Pfc. U.S. Army. Jewish. Office: NY Times Co 229 W 43d St New York NY 10036-3913

SIEGEL, MARY ANN GARVIN, writer; b. Louisville, Apr. 3, 1944; d. Samuel Hughes and Ann Wendell (Smith) Garvin; m. Charles Holladay Siegel, Sept. 2, 1967 (div.); children: Emily Hughes, Charles Holladay, Jr., Margaret Shafer. BA, Conn. Coll., 1966. Photog. rschr. Time Inc., NYC, 1966—67, Nat. Geog. Soc., Washington, 1967—68; content author and editor FundraisingINFO.com, 2000—01. Leadership Atlanta, 1993-94, exec. com., 1995-96. Trustee Conn. Coll., New London, 1985-90; chair Friends of Spelman Coll., Atlanta, 1990-92; active Atlanta/Fulton County adv. bd. United Way Met. Atlanta, 1994-96; Olympic Envoy to Republic of Nauru, Atlanta Com. Olympic Games, 1994-96; formerly active adv. bd. N.C. Outward Bound Sch., Asheville. Recipient Agnes Berkeley Leahy award Conn. Coll. Alumni Assn., 1991.

SIEGEL, MARY-ELLEN, social worker, psychotherapist, author; b. N.Y.C., Feb. 12, 1932; d. Monroe E. and Miriam (Baum) Greenberger; m. Edgar Kulkin, Nov. 4, 1951 (div. 1978); children: Betsy Kulkin Baldwin, Peter, Vicki Kulkin Beckerman; m. Walter Siegel, Aug. 24, 1980. BA, CUNY, 1974; MSW, Columbia U., 1976. Lic. social worker, N.Y. Pvt. practice, N.Y.C., 1978—. Social worker Mt. Sinai Hosp., N.Y.C., 1976-82; clin. instr. cmty. and preventive medicine Mt. Sinai Sch. Medicine, N.Y.C., 1983—; cons. Chemotherapy Found., N.Y.C., 1978—. Author, co-author: Her Way, rev. edit., 1984, More Than a Friend: Dogs with a Purpose, 1984, Reversing Hair Loss, 1985, The Cancer Patient's Handbook, 1986, The Nanny Connection, 1987, Finger Tips, 1988, Dr. Greenberger's What Every Man Should Know About His Prostate, 1989, 2d edit., 1998, Behind the 8-Ball, 1992, Safe in the Sun, rev. edit., 1995, Feeling Dizzy, 1995, Living With Shingles, 1998; mem. editl. bd. numerous jours. Mem. NASW, Nat. Assn. Profl. Geriatric Care Mgrs., Assn. Oncology Social Workers, Am. Soc. Journalists and Authors, Am. Med. Writers Assn., Authors Guild. Avocations: family activities, theatre. Home and Office: 75-68 195th St Fresh Meadows NY 11366-1842 E-mail: herway2@aol.com.

SIEGEL, MELVYN HARRY, financial consultant, securities company executive; b. Bronx, N.Y., Oct. 19, 1944; s. Herbert and Minnie Siegel; m. Nancy S. Levine (div.); m. Inna Traytel. BBA, CCNY, 1965; MBA, U. Chgo., 1974. CPA Ill. Asst. prof. bus. and econs. Calumet Coll., East Chicago, Ind., 1967-71, mgmt. cons., 1971-75, 77-79; mgr. mgmt. adv. service Naron, Wagner, Voslow, CPA's, Balt., 1975-77; pres. Stone Mill Assocs., Ltd., 1980—, Stone Mill Co., Inc., Balt., 1982—, Stone Mill Group, Balt., 1986—. Bd. advisors H.C. Wainwright & Co., Econs., Inc., Wainwright & Co. Econs., 1997—. Bd. dirs. Pro Musica Rara, Balt., 1978-89, Sinai Hosp., Balt., 1986-92, Beth Am Synagogue, 1985-87, The Handel Choir Balt., 1999—; chmn. Friends of Symphony, Balt., 1984-86. Mem. AICPA, Md. Assn. CPAs. Jewish. Office: The Stone Mill Group 300 W Pratt St Ste 520 Baltimore MD 21201-6500 E-mail: stonemill@worldnet.att.net.

SIEGEL, MICHAEL ELLIOT, nuclear medicine physician, educator; b. N.Y.C., May 13, 1942; s. Benjamin and Rose (Gilbert) S.; m. Marsha Rose Snower, Mar. 20, 1966; children: Herrick Jove, Meridith Ann. AB, Cornell U., 1964; MD, Chgo. Med. Sch., 1968. Diplomate Nat. Bd. Med. Examiners. Intern Cedars-Sinai Med. Ctr., L.A., 1968-69, resident in radiology, 1969-70; NIH fellow in radiology Temple U. Med. Ctr., Phila., 1970-71; NIH fellow in nuclear medicine Johns Hopkins U. Sch. Medicine, Balt., 1971-73, asst. prof. radiology, 1972-76; assoc. prof. radiology and medicine U. So. Calif., L.A., 1976—, prof. radiology, 1989—, dir. divsn. nuclear medicine, 1982-99. Dir. Sch. Nuclear Medicine, Los Angeles County-U. So. Calif. Med. Ctr., 1976-99; dir. divsn. nuclear medicine Kenneth Norris Cancer Hosp. and Rsch. Ctr., L.A., 1983-99; dir. dept. nuclear medicine Orthopaedic Hosp., L.A., 1981—, Intercmty. Hosp., Covina, Calif., 1981—, U. So. Calif. Univ. Hosp., L.A., 1993—; clin. prof. radiology U. Calif., San Diego, 2000—. Author: Textbook of Nuclear Medicine, 1978, Vascular Surgery, 1983, 88, numerous other textbooks; editor: Nuclear Cardiology, 1981, Vascular Disease: Nuclear Medicine, 1983. Mem. Maple Ctr., Beverly Hills. Served as maj. USAF, 1974-76. Recipient Outstanding Alumnus award Chgo. Med. Sch., 1991. Fellow Am. Coll. Nuclear Medicine (sci. investigator 1974, 76, nominations com. 1980, program com. 1983, trustee 1993, disting. fellow, 1993, bd. reps. 1993—, bd. dirs. 1994—, treas. 1996—, chmn. ann. sci. program 1996—, pres.'s award 1997, v.p. 1997-98, pres. 1999—); mem. Soc. Nuclear Medicine (sic. exhbn. com. 1978-79, program com. 1979-80, Silver medal 1975), Calif. Med. Assn. (sci. adv. bd. 1987—), Radiol. Soc. N.Am., Soc. Nuclear Magnetic Resonance Imaging, Friars So. Calif., Alpha Omega Alpha. Achievements include research on development of nuclear medicine techniques to evaluate cardiovascular disease and diagnose and treat cancer; clinical utilization of video digital displays in nuclear medicine development; invention of pneumatic radiologic pressure system. Office: U So Calif Med Ctr Rm 5250 1200 N State St Los Angeles CA 90033-1029

SIEGEL, MICHAEL ERIC, judicial center official; b. Newark, June 1, 1950; s. Aaron and Mindy (Schulman) S.; m. Anne Paula Solotar, Nov. 11, 1984; 1 child, Sophie Elaine. BA, Am. U., 1972; MA, Tufts U., 1975, PhD, 1976. Asst. prof. govt. U. Va., Wise, 1977-78, Am. U., Washington, 1978-82, dir. credit programs and continuing edn., 1982-84; coordinator faculty devel. U. Md., College Park, 1984-87, asst. dean faculty devel., 1987-88; sr. tng. specialist divsn. ct. edn. Fed. Jud. Ctr., Washington, 1988—. USIA speaker on judicial independence Buenos Aires, 1995; cons. Coun. of Ind. Colls., Washington, 1986-87, Am. Coll. of Cardiology, Bethesda, Md., 1986-87, Loyola U., Balt., 1987—; chmn. Commn. Juvenile Justice, Montgomery County, Md., 2001—. Contbr. articles to profl. jours. Chmn. commn. on internat. affairs Am. Jewish Congress, Washington, 1985—. Recipient Tchng. Excellence award U. Tex., 1985, Outstanding Tchng. award for Adj. Faculty, Am. U., 1993; fellow Ctr. for Study Am. Govt., Johns Hopkins U., 1997. Mem. Nat. U. Continuing Edn. Assn. (sec. region II 1986-87), Am. Polit. Sci. Assn. Democrat. Avocations: karate, tennis, singing, playing guitar. Home: 10500 Rockville Pike Apt 702 Rockville MD 20852-3342 Office: Fed Jud Ctr Divsn Ct Edn and Tng One Columbus Cir NE Washington DC 20002 E-mail: msiegel@fjc.gov.

SIEGEL, MORTON KALLOS, religious organization administrator, educational administrator; b. N.Y.C., Dec. 5, 1924; s. Samuel William and Esther (Sackin) S.; m. Pearl Fox, June 28, 1949; children: Deborah Siegel Eisenstadt, Daniel, Deenah Siegel Speiser. BA summa cum laude, Yeshiva U., 1945; MA in Philosophy and History, Columbia U., 1946, PhD, 1952. Ednl. dir. Laurelton Jewish Ctr., Queens, N.Y., 1945-49; ednl. dir., dir. educator placement United Synagogue Am., N.Y.C., 1949-51, dir. youth activities, 1951-64, exec. dir., 1970-75, ednl. dir., 1964-88, dir. regional and extension activities, 1988-98, sr. vp., 1998—. Adj. asst. prof. Sch. Edn., NYU, 1971-76; lectr. in field. Contbr. articles to profl. jours. Home: 43 Crossbow Ln Commack NY 11725-1214 Office: 155 5th Ave New York NY 10010-6802

SIEGEL, NATHANIEL HAROLD, sociology educator; b. Bklyn., May 17, 1929; s. Victor and Yetta (Kogel) S.; m. Annabelle Replansky, Mar. 3, 1958; children— Anthony, Jennifer. AB, Bklyn. Coll., 1950; A.M., N.Y.U., 1952, PhD, 1956. Asst. prof. sociology Columbia, 1956-59; sociologist Hillside Hosp., Queens, N.Y., 1958-63; assoc. dir. behavioral research N.Y.C. Dept. Health, 1963-64; chief social sci. tng. sect. NIMH, 1964-67, cons., 1970-79; prof. sociology Queens Coll., 1967-79, chmn. dept., 1967-70, v.p., dean faculty, 1970-74, provost, 1974-77, acting pres., 1977-78; sr. v.p. acad. affairs SUNY Purchase, 1979-94; prof. sociology SUNY, 1979-2000. Served with M.C. AUS, 1950-51. Home: 8 Birchfield Rd Larchmont NY 10538-1505

SIEGEL, NED LAWRENCE, real estate developer; b. Newark, Sept. 26, 1951; s. Howard and Esther (Facher) S.; m. Stephanie Moak, Aug. 7, 1976; children: Justin, Joshua, Jillian. BA, U. Conn., 1973; JD, Dickinson Sch. Law, 1976. Law clk. U.S. Dist. Ct., Camden, N.J., 1976-77; assoc. Kimmelman, Wolff & Samson, Roseland, 1977-78; v.p. Howard Siegel Cos., Manalapan, 1978-80; pres. The Weingarten-Siegel Group, 1980-88, Weingarten Siegel Group of Fla., Inc., Boca Raton, Fla., 1985-91, Weingarten, Siegel, Fletcher Group, La Mesa, Calif., 1985-91, The Siegel Schoor Orgn. Fla., INc., Boca Raton, 1991-98. Pres. SGS Communities Inc., Manalapan, N.J., Boca Raton, 1992— (exec. com. Republican Jewish Coalition, 1995—), NLS Cmtys., Inc., 1996—; dir. Marietta Corp., 1996, Blue Lake Ltd., 1997—, Miami One Ctr., L.P., 1998—; chmn. The Siegel Group, 1997—, Siegel-Moskin Realty Group, 1998—; bd. dirs. Palm Beach Internat. Film Festival. Bd. govs. Solomon Schechter Sch., West Orange, N.J., 1986-88; mem. bd. adv. Pine Crest Sch. at Boca Raton, 1989-93, mem. bd. dirs. 1992—; bd. trustees Saint Andrew's Sch.; mem. task force City of Boca Raton Affordable Housing, 1995—; founding mem. Treve Brogan Ednl. Inst.; co-chmn. Palm Beach County Gov. George W. Bush Presdl. Exploratory com., Palm Beach County Jeb Bush for

Governor Campaign, 1998, Palm Beach County Phil Gray for Pres., 1996. Named Bldr. of the Yr., N.J. Shore Bldrs. Assn., 1986. Mem. Nat. Assn. Homebuilders, Gold Coast Builder's Assn., Fla. Homebuilder's Assn., Internat. Coun. Shopping Ctrs., Found. Fla.'s Future (chmns. adv. bd.), Econ. Coun. Palm Beach County, The Beacon Coun. (Miami chpt.), Republican Eagles, Republican Party of Fla., N.J. Bldrs. Assn., N.J. Shore Bldrs. Assn. (v.p. 1986-88), Urban Land Inst., N.J. Bar Assn., Greater Miami C. of C., Greater Boca Raton C. of C., Phi Beta Kappa. Republican. Jewish. Avocations: tennis, sailing. Office: 5000 Blue Lake Dr Ste 150 Boca Raton FL 33431-4469

SIEGEL, NORMAN JOSEPH, pediatrician, educator; b. Houston, Mar. 8, 1943; m. Rise Joan Ross, Dec. 24, 1967; children: Andrew, Karen. BA, Tulane U., 1964; MA, MD, U. Tex. Med. Br., Galveston, 1968. Intern, resident Yale-New Haven Hosp., 1968-70; fellow Sch. Medicine, Yale U., New Haven, 1970-72, asst. prof. pediat. and medicine, 1972-76, assoc. prof., 1976-82, prof., 1982—, vice chmn. pediatrics, 1979—; acting chmn. pediats, Yale U., 1995-97, 2000—; physician-in-chief Yale-New Haven Children's Hosp., 1996—. Contbr. articles to profl. jours., chpts. to books. Grantee NIH, Am. Heart Assn., Hood Found. Mem. Am. Pediat. Soc. (sec.-treas. 1993-99), Am. Soc. Pediatric Nephrology (pres. 1988-89), Am. Soc. Nephrology (mem. coun. 1997—), Nat. Kidney Found. (chmn. com. on pediatric nephrology and urology 1987-91, grantee, scientific adv. com. 1988-91), Soc. Pediatric Rsch. (membership sec. 1979-85), Am. Soc. Nephrology (coun. 1999—, pres.-elect 2001), Nat. Bd. Med. Examiners (pediatric test com. 1993-95), Phi Beta Kappa, Mu Delta. Office: Yale U Sch Medicine Dept Pediatrics PO Box 208064 New Haven CT 06520-8064

SIEGEL, PAUL, judge; b. Troy, N.Y., May 7, 1938; s. Benjamin and Mary (Silverman) S.; 1 child, Mark Aron; m. Janique Auvertin, Apr. 30, 1994. BS in Physics magna cum laude, U. Miami, 1958, LLB cum laude, 1962. Bar: Fla. 1963, D.C. 1964, U.S. Supreme Ct. 1967, U.S. Ct. Appeals (5th cir.) 1967, U.S. Ct. Appeals (11th cir.) 1982; cert. civil trial lawyer Fla. Bar. Mem. gen. counsel's office AEC, Washington, 1962-65; ptnr. Sinclair, Louis, Siegel, Heath, Nussbaum & Zavertnik, P.A., Miami, Fla., 1972-91; judge Dade County Cir. Ct., 1991—. Editor in chief, exec. editor U. Miami Law Rev. Chmn. bd. dirs. Alliance Francaise of Dade County, 1983-87, pres., 1990-92; pres. Pro-Mozart Soc. Greater Miami, 1984-92. Home: 235 E San Marino Dr Miami FL 33139-1151 Office: Dade County Courthouse 73 W Flagler St Ste 412 Miami FL 33130-1707 E-mail: psiegel@jud11.flcourts.org.

SIEGEL, RACHEL JOSEFOWITZ, writer, social worker; b. Berlin, Aug. 13, 1924; d. Zachar and Frieda (Shur) Josefowitz; m. Benjamin M. Siegel, June 15, 1944 (dec. 1990); children: Charles Ellis, Hyam Barry, Ruth Vivian. BS, Simmons Coll., 1944; MSW, Syracuse (N.Y.) U., 1973. Bd. cert. social worker. Staff social worker Tompkins County Mental Health Clinic, Ithaca, N.Y., 1973-76; cons. Tompkins County Task Force for Battered Women, 1976—; pvt. practice, 1976—. Editor: (with Joan Hamerman Robbins) Women Changing Therapy: New Assessments, Values and Strategies in Feminist Therapy, 1983; (with Ellen Cole) Seen But Not Heard, Jewish Women in Therapy, 1991, (with Ellen Cole) Celebrating the Lives of Jewish Women, 1997, (with Ellen Cole and Susan Steinberg-Oren) Jewish Mothers Tell Their Stories, 2000; author: Midlife Marriage, 1981, Old Women as Mother Figures, 1990, Silencing the Voices of Older Women, 1999. Mem. NASW, Feminist Therapy Inst., Assn. for Women in Social Wk., Assn. for Rsch. on Mothering. Home: 11 Spruce Ln Ithaca NY 14850-1766

SIEGEL, RICHARD DAVID, lawyer, former government official; b. Lewistown, Pa., Oct. 13, 1939; s. Robert and Pearl Eleanor (Nieman) S.; m. Marjorie Esther Greenwald, Mar. 13, 1966; children—Andrew, Jonathan, Michele BA, U. Pa., 1960; JD, Harvard U., 1963. Bar: Pa., D.C., U.S. Supreme Ct. Staff writer Phila. Inquirer, 1964-66; spl. asst. U.S. Rep. Richard Schweiker, Washington, 1966-69; legis. counsel U.S. Senator Richard Schweiker, 1969-71; assoc. minority counsel Senate Com. on Labor and Human Resources, 1971-73; sole practice, 1978-79; mem. various firms, 1973-78, 80-81; dep. asst. sec. for natural resources and environment USDA, 1981-87; pvt. practice, 1987—. Contbr. articles to profl. jours. Treas. Com. for Senator Schweiker, Washington, 1974; mem. nat. coun. Am. Israel Pub. Affairs Com., Washington, 1974-77; v.p. Tifereth Israel Congregation, Washington, 1980-82, 93-99; sec.-treas. North Am.-Israel Hort. Found., 1987-95. With USCGR, 1963-64. Mem. ABA, FBA, Pa. Bar Assn., Assn. Former Senate Aides. Republican. Jewish. Home: 3141 Aberfoyle Pl NW Washington DC 20015-2325 Office: 1400 16th St NW Washington DC 20036-2220 E-mail: rsiegel@ofwlaw.com.

SIEGEL, RICHARD ALLEN, economist; b. Chgo., Mar. 11, 1927; s. Mandel Irving and Mary Marsha (Shulman) S.; m. Shirley Platin, Dec. 17, 1950 (dec. 1980); children: Joel, Robert, Peter; m. Rosalyn Sandra Miller, June 28, 1981. AB, UCLA, 1953, MBA, 1959, PhD, 1961. Asst. prof. econs. SUNY, Buffalo, 1962-64; economist Bank of Am., San Francisco, 1964-66, Calif. Dept. Fin., Sacramento, 1967-68, Arthur D. Little, Inc., Cambridge, Mass., 1968-70; pres., economist Richard Siegel Assocs., Boston, 1970-79; prin., economist Econ. Research Assocs., 1979-83; pres., economist Applied Econs., Inc., 1983—. Contbr. articles to profl. jours. Served with USN, 1945-46, PTO. Mem.: Appalachian Mountain (chmn. Boston chpt. 1983-84). Jewish. Avocations: sailing, skiing, motorcycle touring. Office: Applied Econs Inc 220 Boylston St Chestnut Hill MA 02467-2077 E-mail: appencon@aol.com.

SIEGEL, RICHARD ALLEN, corporate management consultant; b. N.Y.C., Dec. 30, 1942; s. Harold J. and Thelma (Seidman) S.; m. Marcia G. Fellner, Sept. 15, 1968; children: Joshua S., Rana A. BS, Syracuse U., 1964; postgrad., Hofstra U., 1964-66. Cons. various orgns., N.Y.C., 1966-71; v.p. Furn-A-Kit, Inc., East Rutherford, N.J., 1971-73; pres. Gallery 2000, Inc., N.Y.C., 1973-76; v.p. Innotech, Inc., Trumbull, Conn., 1976-82; pres., CEO ISIS Internat., Inc., Monroe, 1982—; exec. dir. SICO Internat. Tech., LLC, 1986—, SICO/FinnEast, Monroe, Moscow, Helsinki, 1989-92. Tech. transfer agt. SICO/Finneast-Soviet Tech., Moscow, 1988-92. Contbg. editor Tech. Bus. Mag., 1998—; patentee hort. display, 1981. Mem. Lic. Execs. Soc. Avocations: video photography, writing, fishing. Office: ISIS Internat Inc 588 Monroe Tpke Monroe CT 06468-2363 E-mail: rsiegel@isisusa.com.

SIEGEL, RICHARD CHARLES, biochemist; b. N.Y.C., Jan. 25, 1952; s. Lawrence Irwin and Betty June (Cohen) S.; m. Lily Max, Oct. 19, 1975; children: Jill Leah, Jamie Rebecca. BA in Chemistry cum laude, Boston U., 1974; PhD in Biochemistry, Tufts U., 1980. Postdoctoral scholar UCLA, 1979-81; scientist Technicon Instruments Corp., Tarrytown, N.Y., 1981-83; group leader Cytogen, Corp., Princeton, N.J., 1983-87; v.p. pharm. devel. Centocor, Inc., Malvern, Pa., 1987—. Contbr. articles to profl. publs.; patentee in field. Mem. AAAS, Am. Chem. Soc., Am. Assn. Immunologists. Home: 367 Harshaw Chester Springs PA 19425-9609 E-mail: siegelr@centocor.com.

SIEGEL, RICHARD LAWRENCE, allergist, immunologist; b. Miami, Fla., Jan. 22, 1949; MD, Washington U., St. Louis, 1977; also PhD. Diplomate Am. Bd. Allergy and Immunology, Am. Bd. Diagnostic Lab. Immunology, Am. Bd. Pediats. Resident in pediats. Children's Hosp. Med. Ctr., Boston, 1977-79, fellow in allergy and immunology, 1979-81; allergist U. Comm. Hosp., Tampa, Fla. Fellow AIS, Am. Coll. Allergy, Asthma and Immunology; mem. Am. Acad. Pediats., Am. Acad. Allergy and Immunology. Office: 3450 E Fletcher Ave Ste 210 Tampa FL 33613-4600

SIEGEL, ROBERT CHARLES, broadcast journalist; b. N.Y.C., June 26, 1947; s. Joseph and Edith Ruth (Joffe) S.; m. Jane Claudia Schwartz, June 17, 1973; children: Erica Anne, Leah Harriet. BA, Columbia U., 1968, postgrad. sch. journalism, 1969-70. Newscaster Sta. WGLI, Babylon, N.Y., 1968-69; reporter, news dir. Sta. WRVR-FM, N.Y.C., 1971-76; assoc. producer, editor Nat. Pub. Radio, Washington, 1976-78, sr. editor, 1976-79, dir. news and info., 1983-87, host All Things Considered, 1987—, sr. editor London, 1979-83. Host Ea. Europe: Breaking with the Past, The Learning Channel, Washington, 1990, Earth Scope, Arlington, Va., 1990-91. Editor: The NPR Interviews. Recipient DuPont-Columbia award Columbia U., 1984. Jewish. Avocations: reading, golf, baseball. Home: 1340 19th Rd S Arlington VA 22202-1637 Office: Nat Pub Radio All Things Considered 635 Massachusetts Ave NW Washington DC 20001-3753 E-mail: rsiegel@npr.org.

SIEGEL, ROBERT ERROL, internist, pulmonologist, educator; b. N.Y.C., Aug. 6, 1953; s. Raymond and Roslyn (Weissen) S.; m. Lisa P. Vetrano, June 30, 1985; children: Julia V., Gregory V. BA, CUNY, 1975; MD, Columbia U., 1979. Diplomate Am. Bd. Internal Medicine, Am. Bd. Pulmonary Disease, Am. Bd. Critical Care Medicine. Intern, resident in internal medicine St. Luke's Hosp., N.Y.C., 1979-82; chief resident in internal medicine Booth Meml. Med. Ctr., 1982-83; pulmonary fellow Bronx (N.Y.) Mcpl. Hosp., 1983-85; assoc. chief pulmonary sect. Bronx VA Med. Ctr., 1992—; clin. assoc. prof. medicine Mt. Sinai Sch. Medicine, N.Y.C., 1990—; dir. critical care patient ctr. Bronx VA Med. Ctr., 1999—. Contbr. articles to med. jours. Fellow Am. Coll. Chest Physicians; mem. ACP, Am. Thoracic Soc., Soc. Critical Care Medicine, Infectious Disease Soc. Am., European Respiratory Soc., Phi Beta Kappa. Democrat. Jewish. Principle areas of rsch. include treatment of pneumonia nd bacterial resistance. Avocations: tennis, cross-country skiing. Office: Bronx VA Med Ctr 130 W Kingsbridge Rd Bronx NY 10468-3904 Fax: (718) 741-4623. E-mail: Robert.siegel@med.va.gov.

SIEGEL, ROBERT HAROLD, English literature educator, writer; b. Aug. 18, 1939; married; 3 children. Student, Denison U., 1957-59; BA in English, Wheaton Coll., 1961; MA, Johns Hopkins U., 1962; PhD in English, Harvard U., 1968. Instr. Dartmouth Coll., 1967-68, asst. prof., 1968-75; vis. lectr. Princeton (N.J.) U., 1975-76; poet-in-residence, McManes vis. prof. Wheaton (Ill.) Coll., 1976; asst. prof. U. Wis., Milw., 1976-79, assoc. prof. English, 1979-83, prof., 1983—. Poet on faculty Summer Writers' Inst., Wheaton Coll., 1980, Wesleyan U., 1982, 83; vis. prof. J. W. v. Goethe U., Frankfurt, Fed. Republic Germany, 1985; lectr., reader various univs. Author: (fiction) Alpha Centauri, 1980, Whalesong, 1981, The Kingdom of Wundle, 1982, White Whale, 1991, The Ice at the End of the World, 1994; (poetry) The Beasts and the Elders, 1973, In A Pig's Eye, 1980; contbr. poems to Atlantic Monthly, Sewanee Rev., other jours. Recipient Margaret O'Loughlin Foley award Am. mag., 1970, award Cliff Dwellers' Arts Found., 1974, Chgo. Poetry prize Soc. Midland Authors, 1974, Poetry prize Prairie Schooner, 1977, Jacob Glatstein Meml. prize Poetry mag., 1977, award Ingram Merrill Found., 1979, Gold medallion ECPA, 1981, Book of Yr. award Campus Life mag., 1981, 1st Pl. prize for juvenile fiction Coun. for Wis. Writers, 1981, 1st Pl. prize poetry Soc. Midland Authors, 1981, Matson award Friends of Lit., 1982, Golden Archer award Sch. Libr. Sci., U. Wis., Oshkosh, 1986; Gilman fellow Johns Hopkins U., 1961-62; tchg. fellow Harvard U., 1965-67, Dartmouth Coll., 1971, Yaddo Artists' Colony, 1974, 75, Transatlantic Rev. fellow Bread Loaf Writers Conf., 1974, Nat. Endowment for Arts, 1980; grantee U. Wis., 1978, 84, 88-89, 96-97. Office: U Wis English Dept Milwaukee WI 53201 E-mail: siegelrh@uwm.edu.

SIEGEL, ROBERT JAMES, communications executive; b. N.Y.C., Feb. 26, 1929; s. Hiram and Regina (Goldstein) S.; m. Gonnie McClung, Jan. 8, 1953; children: William Laird, Richard Joseph. BS in Econs., Marietta Coll., 1950. With copy desk N.Y. Times, 1951-53; assoc. editor Lorain (Ohio) Jour., 1953-56; reporter Cleve. Press, 1956-61; with IBM, Armonk, N.Y., 1961—, data processing div. press rels. mgr., corp. info. mgr., corp. pub. affairs mgr., 1979—, dir. info., dir. internal communications, 1988-89; mng. dir., mktg. comm. agy. Metaphor, Inc., Atlanta, 1989-90; pres. Siegel Assocs., Communications Cons., Bal Harbour, Fla., 1991—. Mayor Key Colony Beach, Fla., 1995-98; bd. dirs. Fla. Keys Land and Sea Trust. Mem. Nat. Press Club, Overseas Press Club, Deadline Club of N.Y., Sigma Delta Chi. Home: 4427 SW 91st Dr Gainesville FL 32608-7137 E-mail: bobsiegel@att.net.

SIEGEL, SAMUEL, metals company executive; b. Elizabeth, N.J., Oct. 30, 1930; s. Morris and Anna (Fader) S.; m. Raenea Kershenbaum, Mar. 29, 1953; children: Daryl Lynn, Annie Roslyn. BBA, CUNY, 1952. CPA, N.Y. Cost accountant Seaporcel Metals, Inc., Long Island City, N.Y., 1955-56; asst. to controller Deltown Foods, Inc., Yonkers, 1956-57; sr. accountant DeLoitte & Touche, N.Y.C., 1957-61; vice chmn., chief fin. officer, treas., sec., dir. Nucor Corp., Charlotte, NC, 1961-99, vice chmn. emeritus, CFO emeritus, 2000—. Mem. AICPA, Am. Soc. Corp. Secs., Fin. Execs. Inst. Home: 3421 Windbluff Dr Charlotte NC 28277-9850 Office: Nucor Corp 2100 Rexford Rd Charlotte NC 28211-3484

SIEGEL, SARAH ANN, lawyer; b. Providence, Aug. 29, 1956; BA in History cum laude, Brandeis U., 1978; JD, Washington U., St. Louis, 1981. Bar: Mo. 1982, U.S. Dist. Ct. (ea. dist.) Mo. 1983. Assoc. atty., St. Louis, 1982-83; staff atty. Land Clearance for Redevel. Authority, 1983-85, gen. counsel, 1985-88, Econ. Devel. Corp., St. Louis, 1988-90, St. Louis Devel. Corp., 1990-91; spl. counsel for devel. City of St. Louis, 1991-92; assoc. Suelthaus & Walsh, P.C., St. Louis, 1992-95, prin., 1995-99; v.p., gen. counsel Dierbergs Mkts. Inc., 1999—. Exec. com. Friends of the Sheldon Concert Hall, 2001—; pres. Ctrl. Reform Congregation, St. Louis, 1991—93, v.p., 1989—91, bd. dir., 1987—89, St. Louis Art Fair, 2001—, Friends of the Sheldon Concert Hall, 1997—. Mem. ABA, Mo. Bar Assn. (vice chair com. on eminent domain 1990-91, steering com. 1987-89, 95-96), Women's Lawyer Assn. (bd. dirs. 1985-90, v.p. 1989-90), Am. Corp. Counsel Assn. (bd. dirs. 2000-, v.p. 2000-). Avocations: hiking, swimming. E-mail: siegels@dierbergs.com.

SIEGEL, SEYMOUR, internist; b. Phila., Aug. 10, 1920; s. Maurice and Ida (Spear) S.; m. Rose Myers, June 10, 1985; children: Kenneth, Karen. BA in Chemistry, Temple U., 1942, MD, 1945. Intern Jewish Hosp./Albert Einstein Med. Ctr., 1945-46; resident Wadsworth Gen. VA Hosp., L.A., 1948-49, Episc. Hosp. PHC, 1950-51; pvt. practice Jenkintown, Pa., 1951—; emeritus Einstein Medical Ctr., Phila. Assoc. chmn. dept. medicine Einstein Med. Ctr., Phila., 1979-86l faculty dept. internal medicine Grad. Sch., U. Pa., Phila., 1949-65. Capt. U.S. Army, 1946-48. Fellow ACP. Democrat. Jewish. Avocations: golf, tennis, music. Home: 1431 Academy Ln Elkins Park PA 19027-2514 Office: 201 York Rd Jenkintown PA 19046-3707

SIEGEL, SHELDON C. pediatrician, allergist, immunologist; b. Mpls., Jan. 30, 1922; s. Carl S.; m. Priscilla Rikess, Mar. 3, 1946; children— Linda, Nancy. AA, Va. Jr. Coll., 1940; BA, BS, U. Minn., 1942, MD, 1945. Intern U. Minn. Hosp., 1946, resident in pediatrics, 1947-48; fellow in pediatric allergy Rochester, N.Y., 1949-50; practice medicine specializing in pediatric allergy and pediatrics St. Paul, 1950-52, San Antonio, 1952-54, Los Angeles, 1954—; clin. instr. pediatrics U. Rochester, 1949-50, U. Minn., 1950-51; asst. prof. pediatrics U. Tex., 1952-54; asst. clin. prof. U. Calif. at Los Angeles Med. Sch., 1955, clin. asso. prof., 1957-62, clin. prof., 1963—, co-chief pediatric allergy clinic, 1957—; mem. staff Harbor Gen. Hosp., Torrance, Calif., Daniel Freeman Hosp., Inglewood, Centinela Valley Community Hosp., Inglewood, Hawthorne (Calif.) Community Hosp. Editorial bd.: Jour. Allergy, 1973-75; contbr. articles to med. jours. Fellow Am. Acad. Allergy (pres. 1974), Am. Coll. Allergists, Am. Acad. Pediatrics; mem. AMA, Allergy Found. Am. (pres. 1976), Calif., Los Angeles County med. assns., Los Angeles Pediatric Soc., Calif., Los Angeles socs. allergy, Western Pediatric Research Soc., Am. Bd. Med. Specialists, Sigma Xi. Office: 11620 Wilshire Blvd Los Angeles CA 90025-1706

SIEGEL, STANLEY, lawyer, educator; b. N.Y.C., Mar. 2, 1941; s. David Aaron and Rose (Minsky) S. BS summa cum laude, NYU, 1960; JD magna cum laude, Harvard U., 1963. Bar: N.Y. 1963, D.C. 1964, Mich. 1970, Calif. 1976; CPA, Md. Atty. Office Sec. of Air Force, 1963-66; asst. prof. law U. Mich., Ann Arbor, 1966-69, assoc. prof., 1969-71, prof., 1971-74; ptnr. Honigman, Miller, Schwartz & Cohn, Detroit, 1974-76; prof. law UCLA, 1976-86, NYU, 1986—, assoc. dean, 1987-89. Vis. prof. Stanford Law Sch., 1973, Ctrl. European U., Budapest, 1993—2001, U. Konstanz, Germany, 1996, Tel Aviv U., 1998; fellow Max-Planck Inst., Hamburg, 1988; cons. reorgn. U.S. Postal Svc., 1969—71; exec. sec. Mich. Law Revision Commn., 1973; mem. bd. examiners AICPA, 1980—83. Author: (with Schulman and Moscow) Michigan Business Corporations, 1979, (with Conard and Knauss) Enterprise Organization, 4th edit., 1987, (with D. Siegel) Accounting and Financial Disclosure: A Guide to Basic Concepts, 1983, (with others) Swiss Company Law, 1996; mem. edit. bd. Lexis Electronic Author's Press, 1996-98. Served to capt. USAF, 1963-66. Mem. ABA, D.C. Bar Assn., Calif. Bar Assn., Assn. of Bar of City of N.Y., Am. Law Inst., AICPA. Office: NYU Law Sch 40 Washington Sq S New York NY 10012-1099 E-mail: stanleysiegel@nyu.edu.

SIEGEL, STEPHEN B. real estate company executive; b. N.Y.C., Sept. 13, 1944; children: Kenneth, Jonathan, Jared, Cassandra. Student, NYU. With Cushman & Wakefield, Inc., N.Y.C., 1961—, mgr. Lyndhurst office N.J., 1970-80, mem. nat. mgmt. com., 1979—, pres., chief exec. officer, chief operating officer, 1980—, N.E. regional dir., 1980—, dir., 1980—, chmn. bd., 1984-88; pres., chief exec. officer Chubb Realty, Inc., 1988—. Bd. dirs. of adv. bd. NYU Real Estate Inst.; adv. bd. The Wharton Sch. Bd. dirs. N.Y. couns. Boy Scouts Am., Benjamin N. Cardozo Sch. Law, Realty Found. N.Y.; mem. exec. com. of real estate coun. Met. Mus. Art, adv. bd. Wharton Sch.; gen. chmn. Assn. for Help of Retarded Children. Mem. Indsl. Real Estate Brokers Assn., Real Estate Bd. N.Y., Coll. Real Estate Cons., Meadowland C. of C. (dir.). Office: Insignia Financial Group Inc PO Box 1089 Greenville SC 29602

SIEGEL, STEVEN L. finance company executive, consultant; b. New Rochelle, N.Y., Feb. 21, 1962; s. Stuart A. Siegel and Stephanie (Kaplita); m. Elizabeth Ellen Starr, Dec. 12, 1987 (div. Jan. 1993). BS in Fin., MBA in Internat. Fin., Calif. Coast U.; D in Bus. Adminstrn. magna cum laude, So. Calif. U. Fin. analyst Am. Express, Plantation, Fla., 1982-84; investment banker Kidder Peabody & Co., Ft. Lauderdale, 1985-87, Shearson Lehman Hutton, Boca Raton, 1987-89; pres. internat. divsn. Cabe Internat. Cons., Inc., 1989-92; fin. and adminstv. dir. Ensec, Inc., 1994-95, Art Collectors Internat., Miami, Fla., 1995-96; CFO, COO Enternet Entertainment Group, Inc., Ft. Lauderdale, 1996—97, S.L. Siegel and Assoc. Consulting Group, 1997—. Mng. dir. Federal Group Ltd., 2001—, bd. dirs., Bought Deal, Inc.; pres., CEO Champion Accessories, 2002—. Mem. Lambda Alpha Epsilon. Avocations: golf, sailing. Address: 2460 Deercreek CC Blvd Deerfield Beach FL 33442

SIEGEL, STUART ELLIOTT, physician, pediatrics educator, cancer researcher; b. Plainfield, N.J., July 16, 1943; s. Hyman and Charlotte Pearl (Freinberg) S.; m. Linda Wertkin, Jan. 20, 1968; 1 child, Joshua. BA, MD, Boston U., 1967. Diplomate Am. Bd. Pediatrics, Am. Bd. Pediatric Oncology. Intern U. Minn. Hosp., Mpls., 1967-68, resident, 1968-69; clin. assoc. NIH, Bethesda, Md., 1969-72; asst. prof. pediatrics U. So. Calif. Sch. Medicine, L.A., 1972-76, assoc. prof., 1976-81, prof., 1981—, vice chmn. dept. pediat., 1994—; head div. hematology-oncology Childrens Hosp. L.A., 1976—, dep. physician-in-chief, 1987-90; dir. Childrens Ctr. for Cancer and Blood Diseases, L.A., 1996—. Mem. clin. cancer program project com. NIH, Nat. Cancer Inst., HEW, Bethesda, Md., 1978-82; pres. So. Calif. Children's Cancer Services, L.A., 1977-95. Bd. dirs. Nat. Leukemia Broadcast Coun., 1987—, Ronald McDonald Children's Charities, 1988-95, Make-A-Wish Found., 1987-95, Children's Hosp. L.A. Found., 1994-2000, Ronald McDonald House Charities, 1995—, L.A. Regional Coun. Am. Cancer Soc., 1996—, Nat. Childhood Cancer Found., 1995—; pres. Ronald McDonald House Charities So. Calif., 1996—; bd. trustees, Children's Hosp., L.A., 2000—. Surgeon USPHS, 1969-72. Fellow Am. Acad. Pediatrics. Office: Childrens Hosp LA Divsn Hematology Oncology MS#54 PO Box 54700 Los Angeles CA 90054-0700 E-mail: ssiegel@chla.usc.edu.

SIEGEL, WILMA BULKIN, oncologist, educator, artist; b. Phila., Dec. 2, 1936; d. Morris and Minnie (Staffin) Bulkin; m. Jesse Sanders Siegel, Nov. 11, 1976 (div. 1975); children: Hillary Siegel Levin, Nancy Siegel Jaffee. BA, U. Pa., 1958; MD, Women's Med. Coll. Pa., 1962; student, Nat. Acad. Design, N.Y., 1989-93, New Sch., 1974-84; studied with Rowena Smith, Ft. Lauderdale, 1991-94. Lic. physician, Pa., N.Y. Rotating intern Mt. Sinai Hosp., N.Y.C., 1963; resident in internal medicine Temple U. Hosp., 1964-65; fellow in hematology Mt. Sinai Hosp., N.Y.C., 1966; fellow in cancer chemotherapy Meml. Sloan Kettering Hosp., 1967; asst. attending physician divsn. neoplastic medicine Montefiore Med. Ctr., N.Y.C., 1967-74; clin. asst. physician Mt. Sinai Hosp., 1974-75; pvt. practice Extra Greenspan, M.D. and Assocs., 1974-75; attending physician Trafalgar Hosp., N.Y.C., 1975; asst. attending physician Montefiore Med. Ctr., 1976-81, attending physician, 1981—; med. dir. Beth Abraham Hosp., Ritter-Scheuer Hosp., 1983-87; dir. hospice edn. and rsch. Beth Abraham Hosp., 1988—. Asst. prof. medicine dept. oncology Albert Einstein Coll. of Medicine, Bronx, 1979-90, asst. prof. medicine dept. epidemiology and social medicine, 1988—, emeritus prof., 1990—; mem. cancer com. Montefiore Med. Ctr., mem. adv. com. home care dept.; mem. adv. com. Bronx Comty. Home Care, Hospice Visiting Nurse Svc. of the Bronx. One-person shows include AIDS Resource Ctr. of Wis., Hotel Pfister, Milw., 1997; exhibited in group shows Bailey Hall Exhibits, Ft. Lauderdale, 1992-97, Ft. Lauderdale City Hall, 1992, Lauderhill Libr., Ft. Lauderdale, 1993, LeGrange (Ga.) Mus., 1995, Marcella Geltman Gallery, No. N.J., 1995, Women for the Visual Arts, Boca Raton, Fla., 1995, Northwood U. Art Gallery, West Palm Beach, Fla., 1995-97, Gwinnett Fine Arts Ctr., Duluth, Ga., 1996, San Diego Watercolor Soc. Internat. Exhbn., 1996, North Valley Art League Nat. Show, Redding, Calif., 1997, San Bernardino (Calif.) Art Assn. Nat. Show, 1997, Hollywood (Fla.) Art and Culture Ctr., 1997, Ky. Watercolor Soc., Elizabethtown, 1997; represented in pvt. collections; contbr. articles to med. jours. Mem. AMA, Am. Soc. Clin. Oncology, Ea. Pain Assn., Acad. Hospice Physicians, Found. Thanatology, Found. for Rsch. on Sexually Transmitted Diseases, N.Y. Cancer Soc., N.Y. County Med. Soc., Ea. Clin. Oncology Group, Bronx PSRO, Nat. Assn. Women Artists Inc. (juried, 1st Place award 1999, Moore Greenblatt Meml. award 1995), 2+3 Artist Group Inc. (juried), Fla. Artist Group Inc. (juried), Gold Coast Watercolor Soc. (Dick Blick award 1994), Ga. Watercolor Soc., Fla. Watercolor Soc., Catherine Lorillard Wolfe Assn. (assoc.), Internat. Arts-Medicine Assn., Am. Physicians Art Assn. Home: 2504 Lajune Terr Fort Lauderdale FL 33316

SIEGELMAN, DON EUGENE, governor; b. Mobil, Ala., Feb. 24, 1946; m. Lori Allen; c. Dana, Joseph. BA, U. Ala., 1968; JD, Georgetown U., 1972; postgrad., Oxford U., Eng., 1972-73. Bar: Ala. 1972. Sec. of state State of Ala., Montgomery, 1979-87, atty. gen., 1987-94, lt. gov., 1996-98, gov., 1999—. Office: Office of Gov State Capitol 600 Dexter Ave Montgomery AL 36130-2751*

SIEGENDORF, ARDEN M. judge; BBA, U. Miami, 1960, JD, 1963. Diplomate Fla. Acad. Profl. Mediators. Asst. atty. gen. State of Fla., 1963-71; county ct. and cir. judge, 1971-81; commr. City of Miami, 1971; pvt. practice, 1981-89; mediator, arbitrator, 1989—. Past pres. Tallahassee Mediation Ctr., Inc., 1992-2000; spkr. in field. Contbr. articles to profl. jours. Named Outstanding Young Man of Miami, 1973; recipient excellence award Fla. Conflict Resolution Consortium, 2000. Fellow Am. Coll. Civil Trial Mediators; mem. Fla. Bar, Soc. for Profls. in Dispute Resolution, Tallahassee Bar Assn., Fla. Govtl. Bar Assn. (past v.p.), Iron Arrow Honor Soc., Bar and Gavel Legal Soc. (past pres., Roger Sorino award), Soc. of Wig and Robe, U. Miami Law Alumni Assn. (past pres.), Phi Alpha Delta, Phi Alpha Delta Alumni Assn. (past pres.), Omicron Delta Kappa. Address: 108 Lakeshore Dr #1139 North Palm Beach FL 33408 E-mail: ams@compaq.net.

SIEGENTHALER, WALTER ERNST, internal medicine educator; b. Davos, Switzerland, Dec. 14, 1923; s. Walter and Anna Siegenthaler; m. Gertrud Siegenthaler, Dec. 31, 1957. MD, U. Zurich (Switzerland), 1948; Dr.h.c., Martin Luther U., Halle, Germany, 1991. Chief resident in internal medicine, St. Gallen, Switzerland, 1954-58; prof. internal medicine, chmn. dept. U. Bonn, Fed. Republic Germany, 1969-71; asst. in pathology U. Zurich, 1949-50, asst. in internal medicine, 1950-54, chief resident, 1958-61, lectr., 1961-67, asst. prof., 1967-69, assoc. prof., 1971-91, chmn. dept., dean Med. Sch., 1978-80. Pres. Conf. Clinic Dirs., Zurich, 1980—91, 10th Internat. Congress Chemotherapy, Zurich, 1977, Swiss Rsch. Inst. for Climate and Medicine, Davos, 1992—; vis. prof. Baylor Med. Coll., Houston, 1981. Contbr. Bd. dirs. EMDO Found., Zurich, 1974—, Jung Found., Hamburg, 1982—95, Zurich, 1994—2000, Swiss Found. for Promotion of Young People, 1995—2002, Col. Swiss Army, 1941—88. Col. Swiss Army, 1941—88. Named Acad. Naturforscher Leopoidina, 1981; recipient Ernst von Bergmann plaque, 1972, Ludwig Hellmeyer Gold medal, 1984, Sci. and Rsch. Gold medal for medicine, Jung Found., 1997, Crystal of Davos, 1998, Hon. Medal of Charitè, U. Berlin, 1999, Walter Siegenthaler prize, German Med. Jour., 2000—. Fellow: Infectious Diseases Soc. Am. (corr.), Am. Acad. Microbiology (hon.); mem.: Soc. for Progress in Internal Medicine (bd. dirs., pres. 1990—), Swiss Soc. Internal Medicine (bd. dirs. 1993), Assn. German Internists (hon.), Paul Ehrlich Soc. (hon.; pres. 1969—71, 1973—75, 1975—77), Swiss Soc. Infectious Diseases (hon.), German Soc. Internal Medicine (pres. 1983—84, bd. dirs. 1992, Gustav von Bergman Gold medal 2000). Home: Forsterstrasse 61 CH-8044 Zurich Switzerland Office: Univ Hosp Rämistrasse 100 CH-8091 Zurich Switzerland

SIEGER, CHARLES, librarian; b. Fountain Hill, Pa., Dec. 9, 1944; s. Charles Franklin and Kathryn (Farny) S.; m. Deborah Day Malone, May 13, 1972; children: C. Alexander, Meredith Kathryn. BA History, Wesleyan U., 1969; student, Duke U., 1969-71; MS Libr. Sci., UNC, 1979. Reference, U.S. Documents libr. Fairleigh Dickinson U., Rutherford, N.J., 1980-83, asst. dir. tech. svcs., 1983-85, assoc. dir., 1985-92, dir., 1992-94, Lyndhurst (N.J.) Free Pub. Libr., 1994—. Contbr. articles to World Book ency., libr. jours; contbr. chpts. to books. Coach, v.p., then pres. Lyndhurst Youth Soccer Club; trustee Meadowlands United Soccer Club; sec. Metro Youth Soccer League; mem. parent adv. com. Lyndhurst H.S. With U.S. Army, 1966-68, Vietnam. Mem. ALA, Nat. Soccer Coaches Assn. Am., Lyndhurst Lions Club, Vietnam Vets. of Am. Avocation: soccer. Home: 227 Tontine Ave Lyndhurst NJ 07071-1819 Office: Lyndhurst Free Pub Libr 355 Valley Brook Ave Lyndhurst NJ 07071-1810

SIEGERT, BARBARA (BARBARA MARIE SIEGERT), health care administrator; b. Boston, May 22, 1935; d. Salvatore Mario and Mary Kathleen (Wagner) Tartaglia; m. Herbert C. Siegert (dec. Apr. 1974); children: Carolyn Marie, Herbert Christian Jr. Diploma, Newton-Wellesley (Mass.) Hosp. Sch. Nursing, 1956; MEd, Antioch U., 1980. Diplomate Am. Bd. Med. Psychotherapists. Supr. nursing Hogan Regional Ctr., Hathorne, Mass., 1974-78; community mental health nursing advisor Cape Ann area office Dept. Mental Health, Beverly, 1978-79, dir. case mgmt., 1979-87, dir. case mgmt. north shore area office, 1988-91; dir. case mgmt. Dept. Mental Health-north shore area-Lynn (Mass.) site, Lynn, Mass., 1991-92. Mem. interdisciplinary faculty, profl. cons. com., lecture staff clin. pastoral counseling program Danvers State Hosp./Hogan/Berry Regional Ctrs., Hathorne, Mass., 1982-86; nursing edn. adv. com. North Shore Community Coll., Beverly, 1983-91; tng. staff Balter Inst., Ipswich, Mass., 1987-88. Mem. Internat. Cultural Diploma Honor, 1989—. Recipient Spl. Recognition award Lexington (Mass.) Pub. Schs., 1973, Peter Torci award Lexington Friends of Children in Spl. Edn., 1974. Home: 63 Willow Rd # B Boxford MA 01921-1218

SIEGFRIED, DAVID CHARLES, retired lawyer; b. N.Y.C., Feb. 15, 1942; s. Charles Albert and Marjorie Claire (Young) S.; m. Meri Stephanie Smith; children: Karin Elisabeth, Christine Elise. AB summa cum laude, Princeton U., 1964; JD, Harvard U., 1967. Bar: N.Y. 1970. Assoc. Milbank, Tweed, Hadley & McCloy, N.Y.C., 1968-76, ptnr. 1977-79, 83-85, 88-98, resident ptnr. Hong Kong and Singapore, 1979-83, 85-88. Bd. dirs. PALS; speaker in field. Bd. dirs. Cmty. Agys. Corp. N.J., Inc., v.p. found. 1st lt. USAR, 1967-74. Mem.: ABA, Princeton U. (exec. com. alumni coun.), Millburn-Short Hills Hist. Soc. (pres.), Millburn N.J. Hist. Preservation Commn. (vice chmn.), Assn. of Bar of City of N.Y., N.Y. State Bar Assn., Princeton (New York), Short Hills (N.J.), Am. (Hong Kong/Singapore), Tanglin (Singapore), Cricket. Congregationalist. Avocations: running, tennis, historic reading. Home: 30 Western Dr Short Hills NJ 07078-3230

SIEGFRIED, JOHN, association officer; BS, Rensselaer Polytechnic Inst., Troy, N.Y., 1967; MA, Pa. State U., 1968; PhD, U. Wis., 1972. Instr. in econs. Pa. State U., 1968-69; lectr. in econs. U. Wis., 1970-72; asst. prof. to full prof. econs. Vanderbilt U., Nashville, 1972-75, 81—, chmn. dept. econs., 1980-86; sec., treas. Am. Econ. Assn., 1997—. Vis. prof. U. Adelaide, South Australia, 1986, 91-92, 93-96, adj. prof. econs., 1996—; vis. prof. U. Leeds, Eng., 1987-88, Simon Fraser U., B.C., 1992; economist U.S. Fed. Trade Commn., Bur. of Econs., 1975-76; sr. staff economist, Pres.'s Coun. of Econ., 1976-77; econs. cons. numerous orgns. Bd. editors: The Quarterly Rev. of Econs. and Fin., 1985-97, Rev. of Indsl. Orgn., 1976-80, 83—, Jour. of Econ. Edn., 1990—; contbr. more than 140 articles to profl. jours. Recipient Marvin Bower award Nat. Coun. on Econ. Edn., 1995, Fulbright Sr. Scholar award/Australia, 1991-92, others. Mem. Nat. Bur. Econ. Rsch. (bd. dirs. 1997—), Am. Coun. Learned Socs. (mem. coun. adminstrv. officers 1997—), others. Office: Am Econ Assn 2014 Broadway Ste 305 Nashville TN 37203-2425 Fax: 615-343-7590.

SIEGFRIED, TOM, newspaper editor; b. Lakewood, Ohio, Dec. 23, 1950; s. Ivan T. and Marian (Griffin) S.; m. Anna Christine Beckelhymer, June 24, 1978. BA, Tex. Christian U., 1974; MA, U. Tex., 1981. Sci. editor Dallas Morning News. Author: The Bit and the Pendulum, 2000, Strange Matters, 2002. Office: The Dallas Morning News AH Belo Corp PO Box 655237 Dallas TX 75265-5237 E-mail: tsiegfried@dallasnews.com.

SIEGLER, MARK, internist, educator; b. N.Y.C., June 20, 1941; s. Abraham J. and Florence (Sternlieb) S.; m. Anna Elizabeth Hollinger, June 4, 1967; children:Dillan, Alison, Richard, Jessica. AB with honors, Princeton U., 1963; MD, U. Chgo., 1967. Diplomate Am. Bd. Internal Medicine. Resident, chief resident internal medicine U. Chgo., 1967-71; hon. sr. registrar in medicine Royal Postgrad. Med. Sch., London, 1971-72; asst. prof. medicine U. Chgo., 1972-78, assoc. prof. medicine, 1979-85, acting dir. div. gen. internal medicine, 1983-85, dir. MacLean Ctr. Clin. Med. Ethics, 1984—, prof. medicine, 1985—, Lindy Bergman prof., 1997-2000, Lindy Bergman Disting. Svc. prof., 2000—, dir. fellowship tng. program in clin. med. ethics, 1986—. Vis. asst. prof. medicine U. Wis., Madison, 1977; vis. assoc. prof. medicine U. Va., Charlottesville, 1981-82. Co-author: Clinical Ethics, 1981, 2d edit., 1986, 3d edit., 1992, 4th edit., 1998, 5th edit., 2002, An Annotated Bibliography of Medical Ethics, 1988, Institutional Protocols for Decisions About Life-Sustaining Treatment, 1988; co-editor: Changing Values in Medicine, 1985, Medical Innovations and Bad Outcomes, 1987; editl. bd.: Am. Jour. Medicine, 1979—94, editl. bd.: , 1997—, editl. bd.: Archives Internal Medicine, 1979—90, editl. bd.: Bibliography of Bioethics, Jour. Med. Philosophy, 1978—89, editl. bd.: Jour. Med. Philosophy, 1978—89, editl. bd.: Jour. Clin. Ethics , 1989—, editl. bd.: Jour. Med. Ethics (London), 2002—; contbr. articles. Mem. adv. bd. Bioethics Inst., Madrid, Notre Dame Ctr. for Ethics and Culture. Grantee Andrew W. Mellon Found., Henry J. Kaiser Family Found., Pew Charitable Trusts, Field Found. Ill., Ira De Camp Found., Gaylord & Dorothy Donnelley Found.; Phi Beta Kappa vis. scholar, 1991-92, Chirone prize Italian Nat. Acad. Medicine, 1996; mem. NAS Cloning Panel, 2001-02, others. Fellow ACP (human rights com., ethics com. 1985-90), Hastings Ctr.; mem. ACS (ethics com. 1992—), Assn. Am. Physicians, Chgo. Clin. Ethics Program (pres. 1989-90). Office: Univ Chgo MC 6098 MacLean Ctr Clin Med Ethics 5841 S Maryland Ave Chicago IL 60637-1463

SIEGLER, NICHOLAS, astrophysicist; b. Tel Aviv, July 29, 1964; s. Marcel and Eveline (Caciularu) S. B of Engring., Stevens Inst. Tech., 1985; MBA, Rotterdam (The Netherlands) Sch. Mgmt., 1993; postgrad., U. Ariz., 2001—. Project engr. Nat. Starch and Chem., Plainfield, N.J., 1985-86, plant supr. Kansas City, Mo., 1986-89, project engr. Milan, 1990-91, project mgr. Johannesburg, South Africa, 1993, site mgr. Villefranche, France, 1994-96; European ops. mgr. Permabond, Eastleigh, U.K., 1997; concentrator in physics Harvard U., Cambridge, Mass., 1998-2001. Mem. Boston Jr. Chamber (membership dir. 1998-2000), Southampton Jr. Chamber (project mgr. 1997), Lyon Jr. Chamber, Milan Jr. Chamber (founder 1990-91), Kansas City Jr. Chamber (project mgr. 1986-89). Avocations: hiking, reading, travelling. Home: 2102 E Hawthorne St Tucson AZ 85719

SIEGRIST, BRENT, state legislator; b. Council Bluffs, Iowa, Sept. 30, 1952; m. Valerie Siegrist; children: Evan, Harriet. BA, Dana Coll., 1974; postgrad., U. Nebr. Former govt. tchr. Mo. Valley High Sch.; mem. 84th dist. Iowa House of Reps., Des Moines, 1984—, speaker, 1999—. Asst. minority leader 73rd and 74th Gen. Assembly Iowa House of Reps., majority leader 75th and 76th Gen. Assembly, mem. adminstrn. & rules com. Active ISEA, NEA, Bluffs Arts Coun., St. Patrick's Cath. Ch.; past pres. Mo. Valley Edn. Assn.; mem. adv. bd. Ret. Vols. Program, Southwest Iowa Regents Grad. Resource Ctr. Republican. Home: 204 Lori Ln Council Bluffs IA 51503 Office: State Capitol Des Moines IA 50319 E-mail: brent_siegrist@legis.state.ia.us.*

SIEJKA, GEORGE JOHN, artist; b. Vienna, Austria, June 24, 1946; came to U.S., 1950; Cert. Fine Arts, Sch. Visual Arts, N.Y.C., 1969; BS in Art Edn. cum laude, NYU, 1974, MA in Fine Arts, 1975. Represented by Nancy Hoffman Gallery, N.Y.C. Group exhbns. include Fitchburg (Mass.) Art Mus., Anchorage (Alaska) Mus. Art, Rockford (Ill.) Coll. Art Gallery. Recipient Founders Day award NYU, 1974. Mem. N.Y. Artists Equity Assn. E-mail: siejka@bellsouth.net.

SIEKERT, ROBERT GEORGE, neurologist; b. Milw., July 23, 1924; s. Hugo Paul and Elisa (Kraus) S.; m. Mary Jane Evans, Feb. 17, 1951; children: Robert G. Jr., John E., Friedrich A.P. BS, Northwestern U., 1945, MS, 1947, MD, 1948. Diplomate Am. Bd. Psychiatry and Neurology. Instr. anatomy U. Pa., Phila., 1948-49; fellow neurology Mayo Found., Rochester, Minn., 1950-54; cons. Mayo Clinic, 1954-91, head neurology sect., 1966-76, bd. govs., 1973-80, prof. neurology med. sch., 1969-91, prof. emeritus neurology, 1991—. Chmn. Internat. Stroke Conf. Am. Heart Assn., 1976-80. Editor Mayo Clinic Procs., 1982-86; cons. editor Jour. Stroke, 1992-2001; contbr. articles to profl. jours.; described transient cerebral ischemic attacks. Trustee Mayo Found., Rochester, 1973-81, chmn. emeritus com., 1997-98. Served to lt. j.g. M.C., USNR, 1950-52. Recipient Disting. Achievement award, Am. Heart Assn., 1984, Merit award, 1989, Robert G. Siekert Young Investigator award Am. Heart Assn., 1986. Fellow Am. Coll. Physicians; mem. Am. Neurol. Assn., Northwestern U. Med. Sch. Alumni Assn. (Service award 1983), Swiss Neurol. Soc. (corr.), Alpha Omega Alpha. Avocation: philately. Office: Mayo Clinic 200 1st St SW N-10 Rochester MN 55905-0002

SIEKMANN, DONALD CHARLES, accountant; b. St. Louis, July 2, 1938; s. Elmer Charles and Mabel Louise (Blue) S.; m. Linda Lee Knowles, Sept. 10, 1966; 1 child, Brian Charles. BS, Washington U., St. Louis, 1960. CPA, Ohio, Ga. Regional mng. ptnr. Arthur Andersen & Co., Cin., 1960-98. Columnist Cin. Enquirer, 1983-86, Gannett News Services, 1983-86; editor "Tax Clinic" column Tax Advisor mag., 1974-75. Mem. bd. Cin. Zool. Soc., 1985-88; officer, bd. dirs. Cin. Found. for Pub. TV, 1984-88, Cin. Symphony Orch., 1973-85, Cin. Ballet Co., 1973-88, Atlanta Symphony Orch., 1988-91, The Atlanta Opera, 1988-91, Cin. Theatrical Assn., Jewish Hosp., 1993—, Cin. Assn. for Performing Arts, 1992—, Cin. United Way, 1992-99, Cin. Pk. Bd. Found., 1995-98; pres. Greater Cin. Arts and Edn. Ctr., 1996-99; mem. Friends of Sch. for Creative and Performing Arts, 1996-99, Cin. Arts Festival, 1992-96, Ronald McDonald House, 1998—. Mem. AICPA, Ohio Soc. CPAs, Cin. Country Club (trustee 1983-88), Optimists Club (pres. Queen City chpt. 1986). Clubs: Cin. Country (trustee 1983-88). Lutheran. Home: 5495 Waring Dr Cincinnati OH 45243-3933 Office: Arthur Andersen & Co 425 Walnut St Ste 1500 Cincinnati OH 45202-3946 E-mail: dsiekmann@aol.com.

SIELCZAK, MAREK WLODZIMIERZ, pathologist, researcher; b. Warsaw, Poland, Jan. 28, 1935; came to U.S., 1977; s. Kazimierz and Stefania (Rukec) S. MD, Med. Acad. Warsaw, 1962, PhD in Hematopathology, 1972. Med. asst. Med. Acad., Warsaw, 1954-62; rsch. assoc. Inst. Hematology, 1962-65, sr. rsch. assoc., 1970-76, asst. prof., 1976-78; rsch. staff assoc. U. Miami Sch. Medicine at Mt. Sinai Med. Ctr., Miami, Fla., 1978—. Cons. in field. Contbr. articles to profl. jours. Mem. Am. Assn. Exptl. Pathologists, Nat. Soc. for Histotech., N.Y. Acad. Scis. Democrat. Avocations: traveling, fishing, antique glass collecting. Home: 400 Golden Isles Dr Apt 51 Hallandale FL 33009-7508

SIELICKI-KORCZAK, BORIS ZDZISLAW, political educator, investigative consultant; b. Wilno, Lithuania, Poland, Feb. 11, 1939; came to U.S., 1980; s. Wiltold and Antonina (Arciszewski) Sielicki-Korczak; m. Barbara Maria Kaniewski, May 29, 1971; children: Robert, Sandra. MSC, Warsaw U., 1964, Kunstindustriskole, Copenhagen, 1971; PhD, Basel (Switzerland) U., 1973. Pres. Impolex Ltd., Copenhagen, 1970-79; field operative Europe CIA, 1983-90; pres., educator Anti-Soviet Rsch. Ctr., McLean, Va., 1981-84; export dir. Worldwide Investment Ltd., Arlington, 1985-87; pres. Amexim Internat. Co. Ltd., 1986-89, BK & Assocs., Arlington, 1990—, Boris S. de Korczak, Inc., Fairfax Station, Va., 1986—. Pres. R.R. Internat. Ltd., Copenhagen, 1983-89; mng. dir. Securitas Inc., Arlington, 1986-87; multiple appearance on U.S. and fgn. TV shows as expert on terrorism, USSR and Russian intelligence and its ops.; crime scene analyst, 1986—. Author: A Man From Atlantis, 1976; designer anti-drug poster. Dir. Nat. Lyric Opera Co., Washington, 1981-91; chief investigator Nat. Police Def. Found., 1995-98; legis. asst. to Congl. James A. Traficant, U.S. Congress, 2001; sr. analyst 17th Dist. Ohio Congl. Office, Washington. Republican. Avocations: chess, classic music, travel, art, history. Office: PO Box 7153 Fairfax Station VA 22039-7153 E-mail: bkorcz@worldnet.att.net.

SIEMENS, MARK C. agricultural engineer; b. Ithaca, N.Y., July 11, 1965; s. John Cornelius and Jean Emily Siemens; m. Olga Luz Moreno-Urquiza, Sept. 27, 1997. BS, U. Ill., 1988, MS, 1990; PhD, U. Ariz., 1996. Engr.-in-tng., Ill. Coop. edn. student engr. GE Co., Cleve., 1984-88; rsch. engr. Caterpillar Inc., Peoria, Ill., 1988-89; tchg. asst. U. Ill., Urbana, 1988-90; tchg./rsch. asst. U. Ariz., Tucson, 1990-96; asst. prof./ext. engr. U. Ga., Tifton, 1997-98; pres. Smartnet Electronic Pubs., 1997-98; agrl. engr. USDA Agrl. Rsch. Svc., Pendleton, Oreg., 1999—. Patentee flexible ground-driver residue mgmt. wheel; contbr. articles to profl. jours. Recipient Acad. Achievement award Am. Inst. Plant Engrs., 1989. Mem. Am. Soc. Agrl. Engrs. (com. sec. 2000—), Pacific N.W. Direct Seed Assn. Avocations: hiking, soccer, bicycling, golf, hunting. Office: USDA-ARS PO Box 370 Pendleton OR 97801

SIEMENS, PHILIP JOHN, physicist, educator; b. Elgin, Ill., Nov. 13, 1943; s. Jacob John and Dorothea Bau Siemens. BSc, MIT, 1965; PhD, Cornell U., 1970. Lectr. Niels Bohr Inst., Copenhagen, 1973—80; prof. Tex. A&M U., Coll. Sta., Tex., 1980—86; disting. prof. U. of Tenn., Knoxville, Tenn., 1986—88, 1986—88; prof. Oreg. State U., Corvallis, Oreg., 1988—. Chmn. nuc. sci. adv. com. Lawrence Berkeley Lab., Berkeley, Calif., 1983—86; organizer NSF Nat. Summer Sch. in Nuc. Physics, Corvallis, Oreg.; disting. sci. Oak Ridge Nat. Lab., Oak Ridge, Tenn., 1986—88. Author: Elements of Nuclei, 1988. Fellow: AAAS, Am. Phys. Soc. Avocation: music. Office: Physics Dept Oregon State Univ 301 Weniger Hall Corvallis OR 97331 E-mail: siemens@physics.orst.edu.

SIEMENS, RICHARD ERNEST, retired metallurgy administrator, researcher; b. Coeur d'Alene, Idaho, July 7, 1938; s. John Charles and Ruth Eva (Schumaker) S.; m. Louise Irene Niehaus, June 21, 1959; children: Rhonda Kaye, Leann Marie. BS, Oreg. State U., 1960, postgrad., 1961-65, 70-71, Linfield Coll., McMinnville, Oreg., 1960-61. Rsch. physicist Albany (Oreg.) Rsch. Ctr. U.S. Bur. Mines, 1961-77, metallurgist, 1977-80, group supr., 1980-84, rsch. supr., 1984-89, sr. tech. monitor, contract officers' rep. pilot plant, 1980-81, acting rsch. dir. Tuscaloosa (Ala.) Rsch. Ctr., 1988, rsch. dir. Reno Rsch. Ctr., 1989-94; ret., 1994. Mem. adv. com. Profl. Coun. Fed. Scientists and Engrs., 1990-94, MacKay Sch. Mines, U. Nev., Reno, 1991-94; presenter numerous tech. mtgs. Contbr. over 50 articles to profl. jours. and internal publs. Pres. Fed. Metals Cen. Credit Union, Albany, 1976-89; bd. trustees Oreg. Tech. Found., Oreg. Inst. Tech., Klamath Falls, Oreg., 1999—. Recipient Meritorious Svc. award U.S. Dept. Interior, 1981, Raiffeisen award Nat. Credit Union Assn., 1988; NDEA fellow Oreg. State U., 1960-63. Mem. AIME, Sigma Xi. Achievements include patents for Process for Recovery of Non-Ferrous Metal from Oxide Ores and Concentrates, for Reduction of Laterite Ores, for Recovery of Valuable Organic and Aqueous Phases from Metallurgical Solvent Extraction Emulsions, for Process for Recovering Ni(II), Cu(II), and Co(II) from Ammoniacal-Ammonium Sulfate Leach Liquor; research on phase relations of metal alloy systems, on phase relations and superconductivity in metal alloys and compounds, and on hydrometallurgical process development. Home: 39416 Highway 62 Chiloquin OR 97624-7752

SIEMER, DEANNE CLEMENCE, lawyer; b. Buffalo, Dec. 25, 1940; d. Edward D. and Dorothy J. (Helsdon) S.; m. Howard P. Willens; 1 child, Jason L. BA, George Washington U., 1962; LLB, Harvard U., 1968. Bar: N.Y. 1968, D.C. 1969, Md. 1972. Economist Office of Mgmt. and Budget, Washington, 1964-67; assoc., then ptnr. Wilmer, Cutler & Pickering, 1968-77, 80-90; ptnr. Pillsbury, Madison & Sutro, 1990-95; mng. dir. Wilsie Co., Washington and Saipan, M.P., 1995—. Gen. counsel U.S. Dept. of Def., Washington, 1977—79; spl. asst. to sec. U.S. Dept. of Energy, Washington, 1979—80. Author: Tangible Evidence, 1984, 3d edit., 1996, National Security and Self-Determination: United States Policy in Micronesia, 1999, Corel Presentations for Litigators, 2000, PowerPoint for Litigators, 2000, Judges' Handbook on Courtroom Technology, 2001, An Honorable Accord: The Covenant Between the Northern Mariana Islands and the United States, 2001, Effective Use of Courtroom Technology: A Lawyer's Guide to Pretrial and Trial, 2002, Easy Tech: Cases and Materials on Courtroom Technology, 2002. Mem. Lawyers Com. for Civil Rights, Washington, 1973—; mediator D.C. Superior Ct., Washington, 1986—, U.S. Ct. Appeals, Washington, 1988—; trustee Nat. Inst. Trial Advocacy, 1989—, Am. Law Inst., 1990—; arbitrator Atty. Client Arbitration Bd., NASD. Recipient Citation Air Force Assn., 1977, Dist. Pub. Service medal Sec. of Def., 1979, Commendation Pres. of U.S. 1981. Mem. ABA, D.C. Bar Assn., No. Marianas Bar Assn. Episcopalian.

SIEMON, JOYCE MARILYN, lawyer, writer; b. Bridgeport, Conn., Dec. 4, 1944; d. George Lewis and Rita (Siegel) Nissenson; m. Robert G. Cash, Oct. 7, 2001; 1 child Alyssa Karen. BA in English, Carnegie Inst. Tech., 1966; JD with high honors, Fla. State U., 1980. Bar: Fla. Tech. writer Computer Sci. Rsch. Ctr. Carnegie Inst. Tech., Pitts., 1966-67; tchr. Leesville (La.) Jr. High Sch., 1967-68; mag. editor VanTrump, Zeigler and Shane, Pitts., 1969; news editor Pitts. Press, 1970; staff writer Dade County Pub. Safety Dept., Miami, 1971-75; reporter North Dade Jour., 1977; freelance writer, 1977—; instr. legal writing and rsch. Coll. Law Fla. State U., Tallahassee, 1979-80; intern Fla. Supreme Ct., 1980; law clk. Office Gen. Counsel Fla. Dept. Gen. Svcs., Tallahassee, 1980; assoc. Young, Stern & Tannenbaum, P.A., North Miami Beach, 1981, Greenberg, Traurig, Askew, Hoffman, Lipoff, Quentel & Wolff, Miami, 1981—82, Hornsby & Whisenand, Miami, 1982-85; pvt. practice North Miami Beach, 1985-92, Boca Raton, Fla., 1992—. Author: employee manual, advtsg. brochures, newspaper articles and ads, book revs.; editor: Lawrenceville: A Short History, 1969; columnist Siemon Says North Dade Jour., 1977; contbr. Mem. Dade County Coord. Network, 1983. Mem.: ABA, Dade County Bar Assn., Fla. Bar Assn., Internat. Platform Assn., Am. Jewish Congress (v.p. S.E. region), Am. Judicature Soc., Kiwanis Internat., West Boca Toastmasters Club, Order of the Coif, Phi Alpha Delta.

SIEMON-BURGESON, MARILYN M. education administrator; b. Whittier, Calif., Nov. 15, 1934; d. John Roscoe and Louise Christina (Secoy) Mason; m. Carl J. Siemon, Aug. 18, 1956 (div. Oct. 1984); children: Timothy G., Melanie A. Siemon Imes; Troy M.; m. James K. Burgeson, Jan. 24, 1987. BA, U. Redlands, 1956; MA, Pacific Oaks Coll., 1975; postgrad., Point Loma Coll., 1979-80. Cert. adminstr., elem. and early childhood tchr. Tchr. Sierra Madre (Calif.) Cmty. Nursery Sch., 1970-77; tchr. parent edn. and music Pasadena (Calif.) Unified Schs., 1977-79, project coord., 1980-82, tchr. curriculum resource dept., 1982-83, adminstr. Washington Children's Ctr., 1983-99; endorsed trainer High Scope Found. Register, 1990—; cons. staff devel. and tng. Pasadena. Trainer Program for Infant/Toddler Caregivers; instr. Citrus Coll., 1996-98; conf. chair Calif. High Scope Educators, 1995—. Active Arcadia (Calif.) Bicentennial Commn., 1974-76; mem. policy coun. for cmty. housing svcs. Pasadena Head Start, 1992-95; life mem. Sierra Madre Sch. PTA; mem. Child Care Coalition, Pasadena; Altar Guild, lay Eucharistic minister St. Edmunds, San Marino, Calif. Ednl. Professions Devel. fellow Pacific Oaks Coll., Pasadena, 1969. Mem.: AAUW (co-chair Math.-Sci. Conf. 1983, chair coll./univ. rels. 1988—, v.p. ednl. found. 1996—98, Calif. state divsn. program co-v.p. 2002—, past pres., grantee 1982—83), Calif. Child Devel. Adminstrs. Assn. (bd. dirs. 1994—), Women's Ednl. Leadership (asst. program v.p.), Child Care Info. Svc. (chair parent edn. and family affairs 1986—, bd. dirs.), Nat. Assn. Edn. Young Children (grantee 1970), Pasadena Women's City Club (dir. membership 2000—02, chmn.), Coun. Women's Clubs (pres. 1995—98), Pasadena Coll. Women's Club (pres. 2000—02, 2000—02), Delta Kappa Gamma (pres. Omicron chpt. 1986—88, 1992—94). Republican. Episcopalian. Avocation: music. Home: 2266 Kinclair Dr Pasadena CA 91107-1022 E-mail: mburgeson@earthlink.net.

SIEMSEN, SUSAN ANNE, physician assistant; b. Monnett, Mo., Nov. 26, 1963; d. Norman Lee Snook and E. Avis Foster; m. Wayne Fredrick Siemsen, May 28, 1982; 1 child, Natalie Marie. B of Health Sci., Wichita State U., 1987. Nat. certified and state registered phys. asst. Phys. asst. to William Henderson, MD, Albuquerque, 1988-89; subspecialty in pediatric GI/hematology/oncology KUMC Pediatrics, Kansas City, Kans., 1989-92; phys. asst. South Federal FP, Denver, 1992-97, Lawrence (Kans.) Family Practice Ctr., 1997—. Proctor for phys. asst. students, Colorado/Denver program, 1992-97, KUMC NP program, Lawrence, 1997—. Presbyterian. Avocations: golf, skiing, family. Home: 2820 Meadow Dr Lawrence KS 66047-3240 Office: Lawrence Fam Practice Ct 3510 Clinton Pkwy Ste 320 Lawrence KS 66047-2145

SIENKIEWICZ, RAYMOND JEROME, lawyer, retired army officer; b. Travis AFB, Calif., Dec. 4, 1952; s. Henry Vincent and Elizabeth Eloise (Elston) S.; m. Sook Park, May 27, 1983; 1 child, Raymond Matthew. BS in Chemistry, Tex. A&M U., 1975, BA in Russian, 1976; MS in Bus. Adminstrn., Boston U., Heidelberg, Germany, 1983; JD, Lewis and Clark Coll., 1999. Bar: Oreg. 1999. Commd. 2d lt. U.S. Army, 1975, advanced through grades to lt. col., 1994; platoon leader 1st Cavalry Divsn., Ft. Hood, Tex., 1976-80; ops. officer 3rd Armored Divsn., Buedingen, Germany, 1980-81, co. comdr. Hanau, Germany, 1981-83; R&D officer U.S. Army Chem. Sch., Ft. McClellan, Ala., 1984-87; left active duty U.S. Army, 1987; material specialist U.S. Army Chem. Sch., Ft. McClellan, Ala., 1987-90; mil. analyst 7th Army Tng. Ctr., Hohenfels, Germany, 1990-93; test and evaluation specialist U.S. Army Chem. Sch., Ft. McClellan, Ala., 1993-96; atty. Oreg., 1999-2001, Social Security Adminstrn., 2001—. Pres. Parish Coun. St. Michael's Parish, Hohenfels, 1992-93; asst. scoutmaster, 1999—. Mem. ABA, Oreg. State Bar, Multnomah County Bar Assn., Assn. U.S. Army, U.S. Army Armor Assn., KC. Roman Catholic. Avocations: cross-country skiing, camping, bicycling, reading. Home: 4398 Glacier Lily St Lake Oswego OR 97035-1841 E-mail: SienkRJ@abanet.org., raymond.sienkiewicz@ssa.gov.

SIENKO, LEONARD EDWARD, JR. lawyer; b. Hancock, N.Y., Aug. 24, 1946; s. Leonard Edward and Louise Albina (Gaudor) S. BA, Boston Coll., 1968, JD, 1977; MDiv, Andover-Newton Theol., 1971. Bar: N.Y. 1978, U.S. Dist. Ct. (no. dist.) N.Y. 1980, U.S. Supreme Ct. 1982. Estate tax atty. Del. County N.Y. State Dept. Taxation & Fin., Delhi, 1983-93; ct. atty. trial part Del. County Ct., N.Y., 1993—; town atty. Town of Hancock, 1990—. County chair Del. County Dem. Com., N.Y., 1987-93. Mem. Del. County Bar Assn. (pres. 1993-95), N.Y. State Bar Assn. (Ho. Dels. 1993-97, N.Y. Law Net com. 1995—, mem. President's Task Force on Electronic Comm. 1996—). Democrat. Unitarian Universalist. Avocations: computers. Office: PO Box 579 12 E Main St Hancock NY 13783-1126 Home: PO Box 425 Hancock NY 13783-0425 E-mail: lennyesq@hancock.net., sienkolawoffice@yahoo.com.

SIEPI, CESARE, opera singer; b. Milan, Italy, Feb. 10, 1923; Operatic debut in Rigoletto, Schio, 1941, Il Nabucco, LaScala Opera, Milan, 1946, Don Carlo, Met. Opera, N.Y.C., 1950; soloist debut in, Carnegie Hall, N.Y.C., 1951; sang in Mozart and Verdi requiems, Edinburgh Festival, Albert Hall, London; leading bass at, Salzburg Festival, LaScala, Milan; appeared in: play Bravo Giovanni, 1962; appeared: play Vienna Staatsoper; made many opera recordings for, London Records. (Winner Nat. Singing Competition, Florence 1941, recipient Italy's Orfeo award 1956). Achievements include making operatic debut, Rigoletto, Schio, at age of 18. Home: 12095 Brookfield Club Dr Roswell GA 30075-1261

SIEPMANN, JAMES PATRICK, research company executive, retired physician; b. Rochester, Minn., Jan. 16, 1960; s. Richard James and Mary Margaret Siepmann; m. Victoria Lynn Ewert, Sept. 4, 1982; children: Jeffrey Michael (dec.), Justine Nicole, Jennifer Ashley, Jessica Raquel, Joelle Kristina, Jarett James. BA, U. St. Thomas, St. Paul, 1982; MD, Mayo Med. Sch., Rochester, Minn., 1986. Diplomate Am. Bd. Family Practice. Resident in family practice Mayo Grad. Sch. Medicine, Rochester, 1986-89; pvt. practice, Oshkosh, 1989-2000; founder, chmn. LightTime, Winnebago, Wis., 2000—. Med. dir. United Health Wis., Appleton, 1993-95; chmn. dept. family practice Mercy Med. Ctr., Oshkosh, 1992-94; team physician Lourdes H.S., Oshkosh, 1993-99. Editor Jour. Theoretics, 1999—. Founding pres. sch. bd. Oshkosh Area Cath. Sch. Sys. (now consol.), 1991-93 Mem. IEEE, AMA, Wis. Med. Soc. (del. 1994-98, bd. dirs. polit. action com. 1994—, Wis. Physician-Citizen of Yr. award 1993). Roman Catholic. Achievements include patentee of humidifier; patents pending in optoelectronic field. Avocations: inventing, theoretics, writing, computer science, collecting fine wines and cigars. Home: 2941 Prairie Wood Dr Oshkosh WI 54904-8478 Office: 375 City Ctr Oshkosh WI 54901 E-mail: james@siepmann.org., mail@lighttime.com.

SIEPSER, STUART LEWIS, cardiologist, internist; s. Jesse and Miriam (Spector) S.; children: Gabrielle, Craig, Amy. BA, Columbia Coll., 1964; MD, NYU, 1968. Diplomate Am. Bd. Internal Medicine, Am. Bd. Cardiology, Certifying Bd. Nuclear Cardiology. Intern Bellevue Hosp., 1968-69, resident in medicine, 1969-70; fellow in cardiology NYU Med. Ctr., 1970-72; ptnr.

Cardiology Assocs. North Jersey, PA, Wayne, N.J., 1974—; clin. asst. prof. N.J. Med. Sch. Coll. Medicine and Dentistry N.J., 1976—; pres. med. dental staff Chilton Meml. Hosp. Cardiology liaison Morristown (N.J.) Meml. Hosp., 1993—; mem. med. care appraisal com. Chilton Meml. Hosp., 1980—, hosp. pharmacy and therapeutics com., 1980-84, 93—, chmn. sect. cardiology, 1993—. Maj. U.S. Army, 1972-74. Fellow Am. Coll. Cardiology, Am. Coll. Physicians; mem. AMA, Soc. Internal Medicine, Passaic County Med. Soc., Alpha Omega Alpha. Avocations: skiing, running, mountain biking. Home: 173 Fritz Ln Bloomingdale NJ 07403-1402 Office: Cardiology Assocs North Jersey PA 1777 Hamburg Tpke Wayne NJ 07470-5243 E-mail: stuartls@aol.com.

SIERLES, FREDERICK STEPHEN, psychiatrist, educator; b. Bklyn., Nov. 9, 1942; s. Samuel and Elizabeth (Meiselman) S.; m. Laurene Harriet Cohn, Oct. 25, 1970 (div. Aug. 1990); children: Hannah Beth Alterson, Joshua Caleb. AB, Columbia U., 1963; MD, Chgo. Med. Sch., 1967. Diplomate Am. Bd. Psychiatry and Neurology. Intern Cook County Hosp., Chgo., 1967-68; resident in psychiatry Mt. Sinai Hosp., N.Y.C., 1968-69, Chgo. Med. Sch., 1969-71, chief resident, 1970-71; staff psychiatrist U.S. Reynolds Army Hosp., Ft. Sill, Okla., 1971-73; assoc. attending psychiatrist Mt. Sinai Hosp., Chgo., 1973-74; instr. psychiatry Chgo. Med. Sch., North Chicago, 1973—, asst. prof., 1974-78, assoc. prof., 1978-88; prof. Finch U. Health Scis., Chgo. Med. Sch., 1988—, vice chmn., 1990-94, acting chmn., 1994-95, chmn., 1995—2002, chmn. ednl. affairs com., 1983-85, 86-01, residency dir., 1999-2001. Cons. psychiatry Cook County Hosp., 1974-79, St. Mary of Nazareth Hosp., 1979-84, Gt. Lakes Naval Hosp., 1987-90, Jackson Park Hosp., 1987-89, Mt. Sinai Hosp., 1988—, Elgin Mental Health Ctr., 1997—; chief mental health clinic, North Chicago VA Hosp., 1982-85, chief psychiatry svc., 1983-85. Author: (wth others) General Hospital Psychiatry, 1985, Behavioral Science for the Boreds, 1987, rev. 2d edit., 1989, rev. 3d edit., 1993; editor: Clinical Behavioral Science, 1982, Behavioral Science for Medical Students, 1993, USMLE Behavioral Science Made Ridiculously Simple, 1998; editl. bd. Acad. Psychiatry, 2000—; contbr. articles to profl. jours. Coach Glenview (Ill.) Youth Baseball, 1987-89, mgr. 1990 (age 10-12 Glenview World Series winner 1990), Glenview Tennis Club, 1986-90 (3.5 Men's Doubles League winner 1989-90). Maj. M.C., U.S. Army, 1971-73. N.Y.State Regents scholar, 1959-63; NIMH grantee, 1974-83, Chgo. Med. Sch. grantee, 1974-83. Fellow Am. Psychiat. Assn. (coun. edn. and career devel. 1993-95); mem. Am. Coll. Psychiatrists, Ill. Psychiat. Soc. (fellowship com. 1985-99), Columbia Coll. Alumni Secondary Schs. Com., Assn. Dirs. Med. Student Edn. in Psychiatry (exec. coun. 1985-99, chmn. program com. 1987-88, treas. 1989-91, pres-elect 1991-93, pres. 1993-95, immediate past pres. 1995-99), Alliance for Clin. Edn., Am. Assn. Chmn. Depts. Psychiatry, Chgo. Consortium for Psychiat. Rsch. (sec. 1996-97, treas. 1997-99), Am. Assn. Dirs. Psychiat. Residency Tng. (exec. coun. 2000—, chair workforce coalition 2000—), Sigma Xi, Alpha Omega Alpha, Phi Epsilon Pi. Office: Finch U Health Sci Chgo Med Sch 3333 Green Bay Rd North Chicago IL 60064-3037 E-mail: sierlesf@finchcms.edu.

SIESS, ALFRED ALBERT, JR. engineering executive, management consultant; b. Bklyn., Aug. 16, 1935; s. Alfred Albert and Matilda Helen (Suttmeier) S.; m. Gale Murray Scholes, Dec. 17, 1966; children: Matthew Alan, Daniel Adam. BCE, Ga. Inst. Tech., 1956; postgrad. in bus., Boston Coll., 1968; MBA, Lehigh U., 1972. With fabricated steel constrn. divsn. Bethlehem (Pa.) Steel Corp., 1958-76, project mgr., 1969-76, engr. projects and mining divsn., 1976-86; sr. cons. T.J. Trauner Assocs., Phila., 1986-87; assoc. S.T. Hudson Internat., 1987-90; dir. mktg. SWIN Resource Sys., Inc., Bloomsburg, Pa., 1989-90; mem. adj. faculty Drexel U., 1976-96. Weekly columnist Economic and Environmental Issues, East Pa. edit. The Free Press, 1981-86; co-patentee suspension bridge erection equipment. Founder S.A.V.E. Inc., Coopersburg, Pa., 1969, pres., 1970, 75, 81, bd. dirs. 1970—. Served with C.E., USN, 1956-58. Recipient Environ. Action award S.A.V.E., Inc., 1975. Mem. ASCE (chmn. environ. tech. com. Lehigh Valley sect. 1971-83, life), Lions, Chi Epsilon. Republican. Mem. United Church of Christ. Home: 6460 Blue Church Rd Coopersburg PA 18036-9371 Office: C E Resource Group PO Box 39 Coopersburg PA 18036-0039 E-mail: siess@quixnet.net.

SIESS, CHESTER PAUL, civil engineering educator; b. Alexandria, La., July 28, 1916; s. Leo C. and Adele (Liebreich) S.; m. Helen Kranson, Oct. 5, 1941; 1 dau., Judith Ann. BS, La. State U., 1936; MS, U. Ill., 1939, PhD, 1948. Party chief La. Hwy. Commn., 1936-37; research asst. U. Ill., 1937-39; soil engr. Chgo. Subway Project, 1939-41; engr., draftsman N.Y.C. R.R. Co., 1941; mem. faculty U. Ill., 1941—, prof. civil engring., 1955-78, emeritus, head dept. civil engring., 1973-78. Mem. adv. com. on reactor safeguards Nuclear Regulatory Commn., 1968-92, chmn., 1972 Recipient award Concrete Reinforcing Steel Inst., 1956, Alumni Honor award for disting. service in engring. U. Ill., 1985, Disting. Service award NRC, 1987; named to Engring. Hall of Distinction, La. State U., 1979. Mem. ASCE (hon. mem., Rsch. prize 1956, Howard medal 1968, Reese award 1970), Nat. Acad. Engring., Am. Concrete Inst. (pres. 1974-75, Wason medal 1949, Turner medal 1964, hon. mem.), Reinforced Concrete Rsch. coun. (chmn. 1968-80, Boase award 1974), Internat. Assn. Bridge and Structural Engring., Sigma Xi, Tau Beta Pi, Phi Kappa Phi, Omicron Delta Kappa, Gamma Alpha, Chi Epsilon (chap. hon., nat. hon.). Achievements include research in reinforced and prestressed concrete structures and hwy. bridges. Home: 401 Burwash Dr Savoy IL 61874-9215 E-mail: c-siess@uiuc.edu.

SIEVER-HENDERSON, PATRICIA, history university educator; b. L.A., July 21, 1937; d. Raymond and Barbara Gammage; m. Daniel Siever, Sept. 22, 1969 (div. Apr. 1, 1991); 1 child, A. Joshua Siever; m. Dr. Luther L. Henderson, Jan. 1, 1995; children: Melanie, Robert, Stephanie Pinkard. BA, UCLA, 1971, MA, 1973. Rsch. tech. John Wesley Hosp., L.A., 1963; med. asst. Dr. Harry Breetwor, 1964-67; grad. tchg. asst. in history UCLA, 1971-73; prof. history L.A. Mission Coll., San Fernando, Calif., 1975-86, L.A. Pierce Coll., Woodland Hills, 1989—. Chair Commn. for Advancement of Tchg., 1986-88; pres. bd. dirs. Calif. Assn. C.C., Sacramento, 1989-90; pres. Dist. Acad. Senate, L.A. C.C. Dist., 1986-89; v.p. State Acad. Senate, Sacramento., 1991-92; mem. bd. Govt. Calif. Commn. Colls., Sacramento, 1997-2002, v.p. 2001-2002. Editor, creator: The Anvil and Quill, 1995-99, The Faculty Forum, 1977-85. Mem. AB3409 Task Force Calif. State Legis., Sacramento, 1986-87, Assn. Calif. C.C., L.A., 1977-85; treas. Calif. Black Faculty and Staff, L.A., 1980-82. Named Outstanding Black Educator Black Assn. Calif. C.C., Sacramento, 1989; recipient Golden Apple award Assoc. Student Orgn., L.A., 1989-99, Spl. Recognition, USA Today, 1994. Mem. United African Am. Student Assn. (faculty adv.), Asilomar Women's Leadership. Republican. Avocations: chess, tennis, dance. Office: LA Pierce Coll 6201 Winnetka Ave Woodland Hills CA 91371-0001 E-mail: sieverpg@aol.com.

SIEVERS, ANN ELISABETH FURIEL, clinical nurse specialist in otolaryngology; b. Utica, N.Y., Mar. 26, 1950; d. Ralph Edward and Mary Paula (Delahunt) Furiel; m. Mark Scott Sievers, Apr. 29, 1979; children: Elisabeth Ann, Katherine Tanner. BSN, Russell Sage Coll., 1972; MA in Human Resource Devel., George Washington U., 1979. Cert. in otorhinolaryngology nursing; RN, Calif., D.C., N.Y. Staff/charge nurse Rome (N.Y.) Murphy Meml. Hosp., 1972-73; staff/charge nurse ICU George Washington U. Hosp., 1973-74, respiratory clin. specialist, 1974-79; otolaryngology clin. nurse specialist U. Calif. Davis Med. Ctr., Sacramento, 1979—, staff Skull Base Surgery Ctr., 1990—. Adj. clin. prof. U. Calif., San Francisco; lectr., presenter in field; mem. nursing rsch. com. U. Calif., Davis, 1982-89, mem. nursing ethics and practice com., 1983-92, mem. instnl. rev. bd., 1984-90, chmn. hospice adv. bd., 1984-87, mem. skull base surgery programmatic subcom., 1990-97, mem. home care hospice quality care com., 1997—, mem. nutrition com. Contbr. articles and chpts. to profl. jours. and books. Bd. dirs., vol. D.C. Lung Assn., 1974-79; vol. Am. Cancer Soc. Asian of Immigrant Trails, Sacramento, 1980—; fundraiser Calif. hospice North Bay Med. Ctr., 1987—. Recipient Nursing Excellence award Nurse Week Mag., 2000, UC Dairs Nursing Excellence award, 2002 Mem. AACN, Soc. Otorhinolaryngology Head and Neck Nurses (coord. nat. rsch. project 1990—, nat. bd. dirs. 1989-92, nat. v.p. 1992-94, chmn. rsch. com. 1980-90, 96-98, edn. com. 1990, 92-94, Nat. Honor award 1991, 94, chair 5th internat. congress head and neck cancer nursing, Nat. Clin. Excellence award 1995, chmn. nat. nursing practice com. 2001—), Ear, Nose and Throat Nursing Found. (founder, chair rsch.), Sigma Theta Tau (Clin. Excellence award Zeta Eta chpt. 1982). E-mail: ann.sievers@ucmc.ucdavis.edu.

SIEVERTS, FRANK ARNE, association executive; b. Frankfurt, Fed. Republic Germany, June 19, 1933; s. Helmut J. and Cecile M. (Behrendt) S.; m. Jane Woodbridge, Dec. 31, 1957 (div.); children: Lisa, Michael; m. Sue Hubbell, Feb. 13, 1988; 1 stepchild, Brian. BA, Swarthmore Coll., 1955; M in Philosophy (Rhodes Scholar), Balliol Coll. Oxford U., 1957; postgrad., Nuffield Coll., 1957-59. News corr. Time mag., London and Washington, 1959-60; legis. asst. U.S. Senator Washington, 1960-62; with Dept. of State, 1962-86, spl. asst. to ambassador at large Averell Harriman, 1966-68, adviser on prisoner of war matters to U.S. delegation to Vietnam peace talks, spl. asst. to dep. sec. of state for prisoner of war matters, 1969-75, dep. asst. sec. for prisoner of war and missing in action matters, 1976—, dep. asst. sec. for refugee and migration affairs, 1978—; minister-counselor for humanitarian affairs U.S. Mission, Geneva, 1980-81; spl. asst. for refugee programs, 1982-86; spokesman for Com. on Fgn. Relations U.S. Senate, 1987-95; asst. to head of delegation for U.S., Can. Internat. Com. Red Cross, Washington, 1995—. Mem. advance team for release Am. prisoners of war, Hanoi, 1973. Mem. U.S. delegation to 20th Internat. Conf. Red Cross, Vienna, 1965, 21st Conf., Istanbul, 1969, 22d Conf., Tehran, 1973; chmn. 23d Conf., Bucharest, 1977, 24th Conf., Manila, 1981, 25th Conf., Geneva, 1986; U.S. del. Diplomatic Conf. on Humanitarian Law in Armed Conflicts, Geneva, 1974-77, to exec. com. of UN High Commn. for Refugees, 1978, 79, 80; staff dir. Indochinese Refugee panel, 1986. Mem. Am. Assn. Rhodes Scholars (bd. dirs.). Office: Internat Com Red Cross 2100 Pennsylvania Ave NW Washington DC 20037-3202 E-mail: washington.was@icrc.org.

SIEVING, PAUL A. federal agency administrator; B in physics and history, Valparaiso U.; MS in physics, Yale U.; postgrad., Yale Law Sch.; MD, U. Ill. Med. Sch.; PhD in biomedical engring., U. Ill. Grad. Sch. Resident in ophthalmology U. Ill.; post-doctoral fellow in retinal physiology U. Calif., San Francisco; fellow in inherited retinal degenerations Mass. Eye and Ear Infirmary, Harvard Med. Sch.; Paul R. Lichter prof. of ophthalmic genetics Dept. Ophthalmology and Visual Scis., U. Mich. Kellogg Eye Ctr., Ann Arbor, dir. Ctr. Retinal and Macular Degeneration; dir. Nat. Eye Inst., 2001—. Office: 2020 Vision Pl Bethesda MD 20892*

SIEWERT, EDGAR ALLEN, retired military non-commissioned officer; b. Slayton, Minn., Nov. 9, 1927; s. Albert William and Matilda Ernestine (Zahn) S.; m. Irene Phyllis Zevenbergen, Apr. 6, 1950; 1 child, Kevin Lee. Grad., Sgt. Maj. Acad., 1974, El Paso (Tex.) Community Coll., 1978. Lic. real estate agent; cert. pilot, airframe mechanic. Electrician USS Philippine Sea USN, 1945-48; aircraft mechanic Sevedy & Sornsen Aviation, Worthington, Minn., 1948-51; tank platoon sgt. U.S. Army, Ft. Rucker, Ala., 1951-52; aircraft electrician Douglas Aircraft, Tulsa, Okla., 1952-56; self-employed, 1956-61; adminstrn. and supply technician Okla. Nat. Guard, Claremore, 1961-72, ops., tng. and readiness specialist Tulsa, 1972-76, tng. technician Oklahoma City, 1976-87, ret., 1987. State command sgt. maj., 1976-78; comdt. Okla. Nat. Guard Non-Commd. Officers Acad., Oklahoma City, 1978-83; chief ops. sgt. Okla. Mil. Dept., Oklahoma City, 1983-87; sgt. maj. acad. selection bd. Nat. Guard Bur., Edgewood Arsenal, Md., 1979. Scout master Boy Scouts Am., Tulsa, 1962-65; vol. various orgns., 1989—. Mem. Okla. Real Estate Investors Assn., Nat. Guard Assn. (bd. dirs.), Nat. Guard Enlisted Assn. (pres., v.p. 1976-78), Nat. Guard Assn. Okla. (bd. dirs. 1976-77, 83-84), 45th Infantry Div. Assn., USS Philippine Sea Assn., Dale Carnegie Alumni Assn. (pres. 1956-57). Republican. Presbyterian. Avocations: sailing, swimming, marksmanship, traveling. Home: 1313 SW 106th Pl Oklahoma City OK 73170-4213

SIEWERT, ROBIN NOELLE, chemical engineer; b. Heidelberg, Fed. Republic Germany, Dec. 14, 1956; (parents Am. citizens); d. Orville Ray and Norma Idella (Sprink) S. BSChemE, U. Tex., 1979; MA in Christian Edn., So. Bapt. Theol. Sem., 1993. Registered profl. engr. Start-up engr. Cen. Power and Light Co., Fannin, Tex., 1979-81, chem. engr. Corpus Christi, 1981-85, performance analysis engr., 1985-87, performance analysis supr., 1987-91; budget analyst Louisville Gas & Electric, 1992-93, chem. engr., 1994-2000, systems analyst, 2000—01, planning engr., 2001—. Republican. Baptist. Avocations: piano, singing, walking, traveling, photography. Home: 9304 Smyrna Pkwy Louisville KY 40229-1418

SIEWICKI, JEAN ANN, school administrator; b. Balt., May 31; d. Joseph E. and June R. (Bensenburg) Balthazar; m. Thomas C. Siewicki, July 19, 1975; children: Tiffany A., Jeffrey R. BA, U. Md., 1975; M Elem. Edn., U. Charleston, 1995. Art tchr. Moultrie Mid. Sch., Mt. Pleasant, S.C., 1978-80, Harborview Mid. Sch., Charleston, 1980-83, Ft. Johnson Mid. Sch., Charleston, 1983-86, writing lab. coord., 1992-95, English educator, 1995—; cen. staff adminstr. Charleston County Sch. Dist., 2000—, accountability specialist, 2001. Asst. dir. Charleston Area Writing Project, 1997; mem. Sch. Governance Coun., Charleston, 1997; mentor New Tchr. Induction Program, Charleston, 1995-96; co-dir. Lowcounty Writing Project, 1999—. Contbr. articles to profl. jours. Pres. Redeemer Evang. Luth. Ch. Am., Charleston, 1996, pres. Women's Cir., 1997; mem. Sch. Improvement Team, Charleston, 1992-95. Recipient Innovator in Edn. award Lowcountry Edn. Coop., 1995; named Honor Roll State Tchr. Yr. 2000, S.C. Dept. Edn., Charleston County Tchr. Yr., 1999. Mem. Nat. Coun. Tchrs. English, Coun. Internat. Reading Assn. (named to Top 10 Reading Tchrs. 1996, Innovator grantee 1998). Avocations: rollerblading, canoeing, hiking. Office: Moutrie Dist 1 and 2 665 Coleman Blvd Mount Pleasant SC 29464 E-mail: jeansiewicki@charleston.k12.sc.us.

SIFF, MARLENE IDA, artist, designer; b. N.Y.C. d. Irving Louis and Dorothy Gertrude (Lahn) Marmer; m. Elliott Justin Siff, July 11, 1959; children: Bradford Evan, Brian Douglas. BA, Hunter Coll., 1957. Cert. tchr. elem. edn., N.Y., N.J. Tchr. Stewart Manor (N.Y.) Sch. Sys., 1957-59, Teaneck (N.J.) Sch. Sys., 1959-60; freelance interior designer Westport, Conn., 1966-70; designer Varo Inertial Products, Trumbull, 1970; designer signature collections J.P. Stevens & Co. Inc., N.Y., 1974-78, J.C. Penney Co., 1978, C.R. Gibson Co., Norwalk, Conn., 1980. Corp. sec., treas., bd. dirs. Belmar Corp., Westport, 1972—; chmn. bd. Marlene Designs Inc., Westport, 1973-77; owner Marlene Siff Design Studio, Westport, 1978—; aesthetic cons. Alcide Corp., Norwalk, 1980-88. One-person shows include David Segal Gallery, N.Y.C., 1987, Conn. Pub. TV Gallery, Hartford, 1987, Paul Mellon Art Ctr., Choate Rosemary Hall, Wallingford, Conn., 1989, Conn. Nat. Bank Hdqs., Norwalk, 1990, Michael Stone Collection, Washington, 1992, Bergdorf Goodman Men, N.Y.C., 1993, Joel Kessler Fine Art, Miami Beach, Fla., 1994, Park Pl., Stamford, Conn., 1995, Westport Arts Ctr., 1995, Mitchells, Westport, 1998, NIH, Bethesda, Md., 1999, Durst Lobby Gallery, N.Y.C., 1999; represented in permanent collections B'nai Brith Klutznick Nat. Jewish Mus., Washington, 1997. Decorator Easter Seal Home Svc. Charity Ball, 1976; bd. dirs. United Jewish Appeal, Westport, 1982-86; com. mem. Levitt Pavillion of the Performing Arts, Westport, 1982-89. Recipient award for creating the most beautiful working environment in an indsl. facility in lower Conn., Lower Conn. Mfrs. Assn., 1970. Mem. LWV, Nat. Coun. Jewish Women, Anti Defamation League, Kappa Pi. Jewish. Avocations: tennis, swimming, race walking, gardening. Home: 15 Broadview Rd Westport CT 06880-2303

SIFFERT, JOHN SAND, lawyer, educator, writer; b. N.Y.C., Mar. 26, 1947; s. Robert Spencer and Miriam (Sand) S.; m. Goldie Alfasi-Siffert, June 1, 1975; children: David Alfasi, Matthew Alfasi. BA, Amherst Coll., 1969; JD, Columbia U., 1972. Bar: N.Y. 1973, U.S. Dist. Ct. (so. dist.) N.Y. 1974, (ea. dist.) N.Y. 1974, U.S. Ct. Appeals (2d cir.) 1974, U.S. Supreme Ct. 1979. Law clk. to Hon. Murray I. Gurfein U.S. Dist. Ct. (so. dist.) N.Y., 1972-74; asst. U.S. atty. (so. dist.) N.Y., 1974-79; ptnr. Fulop & Hardee and predecessor firm Barovick, Konecky et al, N.Y.C., 1979-83, Lankler & Siffert, N.Y.C., 1983-84, Lankler, Siffert & Wohl, N.Y.C., 1984—. Adj. prof. NYU, 1979—; mem. adv. coun. procurement policy bd. City of N.Y., 1991-95; bd. dirs. N.Y.C. Off-Track-Betting, 1995—, NYLPI, 1998—; spl. master First Dept. Appellate Divsn., 1999—. Co-author: Business Crime, 1981, Modern Federal Jury Instructions-Criminal, Modern Federal Jury Instructions-Civil. Fellow: Am. Coll. Trial Lawyers (chair com. on admission to fellowship 2001—); mem.: ABA, Fed. Bar Coun. (pres. Inns of Ct. 2001—02), Assn. of Bar of City of N.Y., N.Y. State Bar Assn. Democrat. Jewish. Office: Lankler Siffert & Wohl 500 5th Ave Fl 33 New York NY 10110-3398 E-mail: jsiffert@lswlaw.com.

SIFFERT, ROBERT SPENCER, orthopedic surgeon; b. N.Y.C., June 16, 1918; s. Oscar and Sadye (Rusoff) S.; m. Miriam Sand, June 29, 1941; children: Joan, John. AB in Biology with honors, NYU, 1939, MD, 1943. Diplomate Am. Bd. Orthop. Surgery, Nat. Bd. Med. Examiners. Intern Kings County Hosp., Bklyn., 1943; resident in orthop. surgery Mt. Sinai Hosp., N.Y.C., 1946-49, fellow in pathology, 1949-52, mem. staff, 1949—, dir. orthor. surgery, orthop. surgeon in chief, 1960-86, Lasker/Siffert Disting. Svc. prof., 1986—; pvt. practice, 1949—. Dir. dept. orthops. City Hosp., Elmhurst, 1965-86; sr. orthop. cons. N.Y.C. Dept. Health, 1952-60; attending orthop. surgeon Blythedale Children's Hosp., Valhalla, N.Y., 1960-86, cons., 1986-90; prof., chmn. dept. orthops. Mt. Sinai Sch. Medicine, 1966-86, Dr. Robert K. Lippman prof., 1983-86, acting chmn., 1993-94. Author: See How They Grow, 1985; co-author: (with J.F. Katz) Management of Hip Disorders in Children, 1983; contbr. over 100 articles to profl. jours. Mem. adv. bd. CARE-MEDICO, 1972-83, bd. dirs., 1981-83, chmn., 1981-83; bd. dirs. CARE, 1983-90; adv. bd. Orthopaedics Overseas, 1981-93; bd. dirs., mem. profl. adv. com. Easter Seal Soc. for Crippled Children and Adults, 1st v.p., 1977-79. Capt. USAAF, 1944-46, CBI. Decorated 4 Battle Stars; recipient annual award medicine N.Y. Pub. Health Assn., 1958, annual award medicine N.Y. Philanthropic League, 1959, Richman award for humanism in medicine Mt. Sinai Sch. Medicine, 1989. Fellow ACS, APHA; mem. Am. Orthop. Assn., Am. Acad. Orthop. Surgery (chmn. com. on care of handicapped child), Assn. Bone and Joint Surgeons, Internat. Soc. Orthop. Surgery and Traumatology, Internat. Skeletal Soc., Orthop. Rsch. Soc., N.Y. Acad. Medicine (fellow orthop. sect. 1952, sec. 1962-63, chmn. 1963-64), N.Y. State Med. Soc. (chmn. orthop. sect. 1967-68), Century Assn. (N.Y.C.), Phi Beta Kappa, Alpha Omega Alpha. Office: 955 5th Ave New York NY 10021-1738

SIFFORD, JASON, music educator; b. St. Louis, Apr. 29, 1972; s. Jack Sifford and Anne Schubert. B Music, Southwest Mo. State U., 1995; M Music, La. State U., 1997; D Musical Arts, U. Mich., 2001. Music instr. Schoolcraft Coll., Livonia, Mich., 1998—2001; asst. prof. music Tex. Tech. U., Lubbock, 2001—. Music instr. Blue Lake Fine Arts Camp, Twin Lake, 2001. Mem.: Music Tchrs. Nat. Assn. Home: 7001 Utica Ave #1401 Lubbock TX 79424 Office: Tex Tech U Sch Music PO Box 42033 Lubbock TX 79409 Personal E-mail: jason.sifford@ttu.edu.

SIFNEOS, PETER EMANUEL, psychiatrist, educator; b. Greece, Oct. 22, 1920; came to U.S., 1941, naturalized, 1944; s. Demitrios Z. and Mary E. (Lucas) S.; divorced; children: Ann Lucas Callahan, Peter Gray, Jean Coit Sifneos Schafer. B.Sc., Sorbonne, 1940; MD, Harvard U., 1946; PhD (hon.), U. Athens, Greece, 1998. Diplomate: Am. Bd. Psychiatry. Intern Boston City Hosp. and Harvard Med. Svc., 1946-47; resident in psychiatry McLean Hosp., Belmont, Mass., 1950-52; chief resident Mass. Gen. Hosp., Boston, 1952-53, mem. staff, chief psychiat. clinic, 1954-68; fellow Harvard U. Sch. Public Health, 1953-54; mem. faculty Harvard U. Med. Sch., 1952—, prof. psychiatry, 1973-91, prof. emeritus, 1991—; staff, assoc. dir. psychiatry dept. Beth Israel Hosp., Boston, 1968-94. Author: Ascent from Chaos, 1964, Short-Term Psychotherapy and Emotional Crisis, 1972, Short-Term Dynamic Psychotherapy Evaluation and Technique, 1979, 2d edit., 1987, Short-Term Anxiety Provking Psychotherapy, 1992, Escape?, 1998; editor-in-chief Psychotherapy and Psychosomatics, 1974-91; contbr. over 125 articles to profl. jours. Served with AUS, 1944-46, 47-50. Fellow Am. Psychiat. Assn. (life); mem. AMA, Internat. Fedn. Med. Psychotherapy (v.p. 1976-88, bd. dirs. 1988-94), Am. Psychosomatic Soc., Boston Psychoanalytic Soc. (life), Hellenic Psychosomatic Soc. (hon.), Italian Psychosomatic Soc. (hon.). Democrat. Home and Office: 59 Common St Belmont MA 02478-3022 Fax: 617-484-3496. E-mail: pesifneos@aol.com. *The principles which helped me most have been a belief in good education, a fierce sense of non-conformity, a strong sense of independence, an admiration of creativity and new ideas, a love of writing, teaching, reading, classic music, traveling, lecturing and conducting workshops, seminars all over North and South America and Europe, swimming, and luck in being healthy.*

SIFONTES, JOSE E. pediatrics educator; b. Arecibo, P.R. s. Jose E. and Josefa M. (Fontan) S.; m. Iris J. Sotomayor, Dec. 20, 1952; children: J. Jaime, Mariat, Iris, J. Roberto, Myrta, J. Ricardo, Beatriz. MD, Syracuse U., 1948. Diplomate Am. Bd. Pediatrics. Dir. USPHS TB Rsch., San Juan, Puerto Rico, 1958-66; dean U. Puerto Rico Sch. of Medicine, 1966-71; chief of pediatrics U. Puerto Rico Sch. Medicine, 1974-77, chief pediatric pulmonary program, 1960-66, prof. pediatrics, 1966—. Specializing in pulmonary pediatrics, San Juan, 1982—; cons. to many nat. and internat. health orgns. including WHO, UN, PAHO, CARE, 1954-82. Author: (Spanish textbook) Neumologia Pediatrica, 1974; contbr. over 100 articles to profl. jours. and pediat. texts. Vol. Am. Thoracic Soc. ATS, ALA, 1953—. Surgeon USPHS, 1957-59. Grantee USPHS, NIH, 1954-82. Mem. Am. Acad. Pediatrics (fellow chest sect., nat. chmn. 1964-65), Am. Pediatric Soc., Alpha Omega Alpha. Roman Catholic.

SIFTON, CHARLES PROCTOR, federal judge; b. N.Y.C., Mar. 18, 1935; s. Paul F. and Claire G. S.; m. Susan Scott Rowland, May 20, 1986; children: Samuel, Tobias, John. AB, Harvard U., 1957; LL.B., Columbia U., 1961. Bar: N.Y. 1961. Assoc. Cadwalader, Wickersham & Taft, 1961-62, 64-66; staff atty. U.S. Senate Fgn. Rels. Com., 1962-63; asst. U.S. atty. N.Y.C., 1966-69; ptnr. LeBoeuf, Lamb, Leiby and MacRae, 1969-77; judge U.S. Dist. Ct. (ea. dist.) N.Y., Bklyn., 1977—, chief judge, 1995-2000, sr. judge, 2000—. Mem.: Bar Assn. City of NY. Office: US Dist Ct US Courthouse 225 Cadman Plz E Rm 244 Brooklyn NY 11201-1818

SIFTON, DAVID WHITTIER, magazine editor; b. N.Y.C., Sept. 12, 1940; s. David William and Dorothy (Whittier) S. BA, Trinity Coll., Hartford, Conn., 1962; MA, Stanford U., 1967. Editor Inside Edn., N.Y. State Edn. Dept., 1968-70; adminstrv. editor Med. Econs., Oradell, N.J., 1970-72; editor Drug Topics, 1972-75; editor in chief Current Prescribing, 1975-78, RN mag., Oradell, 1978-83; dir. spl. editorial projects Med. Econs. Co., 1983-90; editor PDR Pubs., Montvale, 1990—. Founder Physicians' Desk Reference on CD-ROM, PDR's Drug Interactions and Side Effects Index, PDR's Indications Index, Pocket PDR (handheld electronic database), The PDR Family Guide to Prescription Drugs, The PDR Family Guide to Women's Health, The PDR Family Guide to Nutrition and Health, The PDR Family Guide to Lifelong Health, The PDR Family Guide Encyclopedia of Medical Care, The PDR Family Guide to Over-the-Counter Drugs, The PDR Family Guide to Natural Medicines and Healing Therapies, The PDR Family Guide to Common Ailments, The PDR Family Guide to Nutritional Supplements, The PDR Guide to Biological and Chemical Warfare Response, The PDR Guide for Mental Health Professionals. Served to 1st lt. USAF, 1963-66. Decorated Air Force Commendation medal; grantee Ford Found., 1967 Mem. Am. Bus. Press (chmn. editorial com. 1975-76) Republican. Episcopalian. Office: Med Econs Co Inc 5 Paragon Dr Montvale NJ 07645-1725

SIFTON, ELISABETH, book publisher; b. N.Y.C., Jan. 13, 1939; d. Reinhold and Ursula (Keppel-Compton) Niebuhr; m. Charles P. Sifton, 1962 (div. 1984); children: Peter Samuel, Charles Tobias, John Paul Gustav; m. Fritz R. Stern, 1996. BA magna cum laude, Radcliffe Coll., Cambridge, Mass., 1960; postgrad., U. Paris, 1960-61. Asst. to dep. asst. sec. of state U.S. Dept. of State, Washington, 1961-62; editorial asst., assoc. editor, editor, sr. editor Frederick A. Praeger Pubs., N.Y.C., 1962-68; editor, sr. editor, editor-in-chief The Viking Press, 1969-83; v.p., pub. Elisabeth Sifton Books, Viking Penguin, 1984-87; exec. v.p. Alfred A. Knopf, Inc., 1987-92; sr. v.p. Farrar, Straus & Giroux, 1993—; pub. Hill & Wang, 1993—. Fulbright fellow, 1960-61 Democrat. Episcopalian. Home: 15 Claremont Ave New York NY 10027-6802 Office: Farrar Straus & Giroux 19 Union Sq W Fl 4 New York NY 10003-3304

SIGAL-IBSEN, ROSE, artist; b. Bucharest, Romania, Aug. 22; arrived in U.S., 1957; d. Joseph and Tilly (Eckstein) Cohen; m. Albert D. Sigal, Dec. 25, 1941 (dec. May 1970); 1 child, Daniel M.; m. Joseph Ibsen, Oct. 1973 Diploma, Fashion Inst. Technology, N.Y.C., 1978; Parson, Sch. of Design, N.Y.C., 1985-86; student, Koho Sch. of Sumi-E, N.Y.C., 1979-90, Zhejiang Acad. Fine Arts, China, 1990. Curator Metro N.Y. Chpt. of Sumi-E Soc., 1990—, v.p., 1990—. One-woman shows include China-Gallery Weizhi Schubert, Hanover, Germany, 1991, Manhattan Savs. Bank, N.Y.C., 1993—94, Chem. Bank, 1993—95, N.Y. Pub. Libr., 1996, Bankers Fed., N.Y.C., 1996, Rep. Bank for Savs., 1996, Roumanian Cultural Found., Bucharest, 1998, World Fine Art Gallery, N.Y.C., 1998, Romanian Embassy, Washington, 2000, others, exhibited in group shows at China Nat. Acad. of Fine Arts, Hangzhou, 1994, Fourth World Conf. on Women, Beijing, 1995, Steinhardt Conservatory, Bklyn. Bot. Garden, 1996, Nat. Mus. of Women in the Arts, Washington, 1996, 80 Washington Square East Galleries, N.Y.C., 1996, Seton Hall U., South Orange, N.J., 1996, Golden West Coll. Fine Arts

Gallery, Huntington Beach, Calif., 1995, Seton Hall Gallery, South Orange, N.J., 1996, Wesleyan U., Middletown, Conn., 1998, Taipei Gallery Chinese Info. and Culture Ctr. and the Chinese-Am. Arts Coun., 1998, Cork Gallery/Lincoln Ctr., N.Y.C., 1998, Pen and Brush, (All-sections award), Sumi-e Soc. Am., Inc., 1999, Japanese Am. Cultural & Cmty. Ctr. at Doizaki Gallery, 1999, Broome St. Gallery, N.Y.C., 1999, 2001—02, Nat. Mus. of Women in Arts, 1999, Asia Soc. Store, 1999, ASCA, 1999—2000, Japanese Cultural Ctr., L.A., 1999, Pen and Brush All Media Millennium Celebration, 2000, Pen and Brush Ann. Watercolor, 2000, Broome St. Gallery Invitational, 2000, Contemporary Artists Guild, 2000, Newark Mus. and Taiwan Art Edn. Inst., 2000, Sumi-e Soc. Am. Inc. at Courthouse Galleries of Portsmouth Va., 2001 (Hallie Hazen Meml. award, 2001), Pen and Brush Ann. Mixed Media, 2002, Korean Cultural Ctr., L.A., 2002, Japanese Artists Assn. N.Y., 2002, others; artwork Courage Card design, 1998. Recipient Manhattan Arts award Cover Art Competition, N.Y.C., 1992, 94, 95, 97, King Point award, Fla., 1991, Tenth Japanese Internat. Calligraphy Exhbn. award, N.Y.C., 1996, Manhattan Arts Internat. Showcase award, Emily N. Hatch Meml. award Pen and Brush, Inc., Spring Watercolor Exhbn., 1998, Hallie Hazen Meml. award Sumi-e Soc. Am., Inc., 2001. Mem. Nat. Mus. of Women in the Arts, Artist Equity of N.Y., Am. Soc. Contemporary Artists, Art of Ink in Am., The Oriental Brushwork Soc. of Am., Surui-e Soc. (hon.). Avocations: sculptor in clay, dancing. Home: One Irving Pl #222B New York NY 10003-9741

SIGALL, HAROLD FRED, psychology educator; b. N.Y.C., June 29, 1943; s. Walter and Regine (Goldenberg) S.; m. Brenda Ann Alpert, Aug. 8, 1965; children: Elana, Jennifer, Emily. BS, CUNY, 1964; PhD, U. Tex., 1968. Asst. prof. psychology U. Rochester, N.Y., 1968-72; assoc. prof. U. Md., College Park, 1972-78, prof., 1978—, dir. grad. program in social psychology, dir. grad. studies dept. Psyc., 2000—; cons. editor Jour. Applied Social Psychology, 1992—. Cons. social rsch. and decision making to numerous orgns., lectr. Smithsonian Inst., Washington, 1984, 85; vis. prof. U. Bologna, 1997. Editor Personality and Social Psychology Bull., 1977-81. Bd. dirs. Columbia (Md.) Jewish Congregation, 1985-87, Howard County (Md.) Jewish Cmty. Sch., Columbia, 1986-87; mem. Human Rights Commn., Howard County, 1994-99. NDEA fellow, 1967-68, Danforth Found. fellow, 1970-71. Fellow APA, Am. Psychol. Soc.; mem. Soc. Exptl. Social Psychology. Home: 5060 Castle Moor Dr Columbia MD 21044-1871 Office: U of Md Dept Psychology College Park MD 20742-0001 E-mail: hsigall@psyc.umd.edu.

SIGBAND, NORMAN BRUCE, management communication educator; b. Chgo., June 27, 1920; s. Max and Bessie S.; m. Joan C. Lyons, Aug. 3, 1944; children: Robin, Shelley, Betsy. BA, U. Chgo., 1940, MA, 1941, PhD, 1954; LHD (hon.), DePaul U., 1986. Asst. prof. bus. communication De Paul U., 1946-50, assoc. prof., 1950-54, prof., 1954-65; prof. mgmt. communication U. So. Calif., 1965—, chmn. dept. mktg., 1970-72; assoc. dean U. So. Calif. (Sch. Bus.), 1975-80, Disting. prof. emeritus, 1989—. Disting. Centennial lectr. U. Tex., Austin, 1986; cons. to industry; speaker, condr. workshops, seminars in field; Scholar in Residence, Va. Commonwealth U., 1987, DePaul U., 1988; Disting. emeritus prof. U. So. Calif., 1989., Author books including: Practical Communication for Everyday Use, 25th edit., 1954, Effective Report Writing for Business, Industry and Government, 1960, Communication for Management, 1970, Communicacion Para Directivos, 1972, Management Communication for Decision Making, 1972, Communication for Management and Business, 1976, Communication for Managers, 6th edit., 2001, Communicating in Business, 1987, 3d edit., 1989, in Chinese, 2001, Patient-Pharmacist Consultation: A Communication Skills Approach, 1993, Communication for Pharmacists and Other Health Professionals, 1995, 2d edit., 1996, (with J. Biles) The American University in the New Millennium: Problems and Opportunities, 2001; movies include: Communication Barriers and Gateways, 2d edit., 1993, Listening: A Key to Problem Solving (award winner), 2d edit., 1993, The Grapevine, The Power of a Minute, 1992; gen. editor books including: Harcourt Brace Jovanovich Bus. series; contbr. numerous articles to profl. jours., mags. Served to capt. AUS, 1942-46, ETO. Decorated Bronze Star; recipient recognition award City of L.A., 1985, hon. alumnus award U. So. Calif., 1991. Fellow Am. Bus. Communication Assn. (pres. 1964-65); mem. Internat. Communication Assn., Acad. Mgmt., Anti-Defamation League, Hadassah Assocs., Blue Key, Phi Kappa Phi, Alpha Kappa Psi, Beta Gamma Sigma. Democrat. Jewish. Home: 3109 Dona Susana Dr Studio City CA 91604-4355 Office: 1985 Zonal Ave Los Angeles CA 90089-0105

SIGEL, MARSHALL ELLIOT, financial consultant; b. Hartford, Conn., Nov. 25, 1941; s. Paul and Bessie (Somer) S.; m. Sybil R. Miller, Nov. 23, 1995. BS in Econs., U. Pa., 1963; JD, U. Miami, 1982, LLM in Taxation, 1983. Exec. v.p. Advo-System div. KMS Industries, Inc., Hartford, 1963-69, pres., 1969-72; pres. Ad-Type Corp., Hartford, 1963-69, Ad-Lists, Inc., Hartford, 1963-69; fin. cons. Hartford, 1972-83, Boca Raton, Fla., 1987—; pvt. practice law, 1983-87. Bd. dirs. Wharton Sch. Club of South Fla. Mem. FOPA, World Pres.' Orgn., citizens bd. U. Miami, Boca Grove Club, 100 Club of So. Palm Beach County. Home and Office: PO Box 273408 Boca Raton FL 33427-3408

SIGERSON, CHARLES WILLARD, JR. insurance agency executive; b. Biloxi, Miss., Mar. 6, 1945; s. Charles Willard and Eugenia (Linstad) S.; m. Elizabeth Ann Moss, Dec. 9, 1967; children: Anthea Louise, Andrew Charles. B in Gen. Studies, U. Nebr., Omaha, 1971. Pres., owner Sigerson Ins. Agy., Inc., Omaha, 1973—. Pres. Floyd Rogers Diabetic Found., Lincoln, Nebr., 1981—; mem. Douglas County Stand-by Draft Bd., Omaha, 1982—; chmn. Douglas County Rep. Com., Omaha, 1982-83, 90-93; mem. exec. com. Nebr. Rep. Com., Lincoln, 1982-83, 86-88, 90—; chmn. Nebr. Rep. Party, 1995-2001. Staff sgt. USAF, 1964-71. Recipient Cosmopolitan of Yr.award I-80 Cosmopolitan Club, 1982, Patrick hodgins award I-80 Cosmopolitan Club, 1983, Legion of Honor ward State Farm Ins. Co., 1984. Mem. Nat. Assn. Health Underwriters, Nat. Assn. Ins. and Fin. Advisors, Soc. Fin. Svc. Profls., Nat. Assn. Life Underwriters, Rotary Internat., Masons, Christian Missionary Alliance. Presbyterian. Avocations: genealogy, antique book and newspaper collecting, coin collecting. Home: 11435 Grand Cir Omaha NE 68164-2109 Office: Sigerson Ins Agy Inc 10766 Fort St Omaha NE 68134-1230*

SIGETY, CHARLES BIRGE, investment company executive; b. N.Y.C., Sept. 30, 1952; s. Charles Edward and Katharine Kinne (Snell) S.; m. Elizabeth Ross Pennington, Nov. 27, 1976; children: Austin Douglas, Katharine Colyer, Alexander Birge. BA in English Lit., Bates Coll., 1975. Lic. nursing home adminstr. Adminstr. in tng. Florence Nightingale Nursing Home, N.Y.C., 1972, asst. dir. facility ops., 1975, dir. facility ops., 1975-78, assoc. adminstr., 1978-81, exec. dir., 1981-82; pres., CEO Profl. Med. Products, Inc., Greenwood, S.C., 1982-96; dir. Upper Savannah Internat. Trade Assn., 1993-94, pres., 1993; CEO Bison Investments, Inc., Tampa, Fla., 1996—, Aerial Machine & Tool Corp., Vesta, Va., 1998—2000, Polyten Plastics, LLC, Washington, 1998-2000, Coeur Acquisition, LLC, Washington, 1999—, Polyten, LLC, Washington, 2000—. Mem. adv. bd. Liberty Mut. Ins. Cos. S.C., 1986—96, NationsBank (Bank of Am.), Greenwood, SC, 1984—96; vice chmn. Upper Savannah Bus. Group on Health Care, 1981—87, S.C. Bus. Roundtable for the Initiative for Work Force Excellence, Columbia, 1988—92; dir. exec. com. Osteo Am., Inc., 1993—96; dir. Victory Ship, 1999—2000; bd. dirs. MD Internat., Inc., Miami, Fla., 2000—01. Bd. visitors Med. U. S.C., 1988; YPO HealthCare Focus Forum, 1997; active Soc. of Internat. Bus. Fellows, 1999—. Mem. Health Industry Mfrs. Assn. (ofcl. rep. 1982-96, 99—), Upper Savannah Internat. Trade Assn. (pres. 1993), Young Pres.'s Orgn. Presbyterian. Avocations: hunting, sailing. Office: Bison Investments Inc 3225 S Macdill Ave # 236 Tampa FL 33629-8171

SIGETY, CHARLES EDWARD, lawyer, family business consultant; b. N.Y.C., Oct. 10, 1922; s. Charles and Anna (Toth) S.; m. Katharine K. Snell, July 17, 1948; children: Charles, Katharine, Robert, Cornelius, Elizabeth. BS, Columbia U., 1944; MBA, Harvard U., 1947; LLB, Yale U., 1951; LHD (hon.), Cazenovia Coll., 1994. Bar: N.Y. 1952, D.C. 1958. With Bankers Trust Co., 1939-42; instr. adminstrv. engring. Pratt Inst., 1948; instr. econs. Yale U., 1948-50; vis. lectr. acctg. Sch. Gen. Studies Columbia U., N.Y.C., 1948-50, 52; rapporteur com. fed. taxation for U.S. coun. Internat. C. of C., 1952-53; asst. to comm. fed. taxation Am. Inst. Accts., 1950-53; with Compton Advt. Agy., N.Y.C., 1954; vis. lectr. law Yale U., 1952; pvt. practice law N.Y.C., 1952-67; pres., dir. Video Vittles, Inc., 1953-67; dep. commr. FHA, 1955-57; of counsel Javits and Javits, 1959-60; 1st asst. atty. gen. N.Y., 1958-59; dir., mem. exec. com. Gotham Bank, N.Y.C., 1961-63; dir. N.Y. State Housing Fin. Agy., 1962-63; chmn. Met. Ski Slopes, Inc., N.Y.C., 1962-65; pres., exec. adminstr. Florence Nightingale Health Ctr., 1965-85; dir. Schaerer AG, Wabern, Switzerland, 1982-88; chmn. Kenbar Group, N.Y.C., 1997—, Internat. Bioimmune Sys., Inc., Great Neck, NY, 1999—2002. Professorial lectr. Sch. Architecture, Pratt Inst., N.Y.C., 1962-66; mem. Sigety Assocs., cons. in housing mortgage financing and urban renewal, 1957-67; ho. cons. Govt. of Peru, 1956; mem. missions to Hungary, Poland, Fed. Republic Germany, Malta, Czechoslovakia, Russia, Israel, Overseas Pvt. Investment Corp., 1990-92; owner, operator Peppermill Farms, Pipersville, Pa., 1956—. Bd. dirs., sec., v.p., treas. Nat. Coun. Health Ctrs., 1969-85; bd. dirs. Am.-Hungarian Found., 1974-76, Pritikin Rsch. Found., 1991—, Stratford Arms Condo Assn., 1992-93, 2002–, Global Leadership Inst., 1993—; founding mem., bd. dirs., Natl. Assn. for Continence, 1982, trustee Cazenovia (N.Y.) Coll., 1981-2002, Delaware Valley Coll. Sci. and Agr., Doylestown, Pa., 1998—; trustee, v.p. Woodmere Art Mus. Phila., 2000—, Navy Supply Corps Found., Athens, Ga., 2000—; del. White House Conf. on Aging, 1971, White House Conf. on Mgmt. Tng. and Market Econs. Edn. in Ctrl. and Ea. Europe, 1991; bd. visitors Lander Coll., U. S.C., Greenwood, 1982-84; mem. fin. com. World Games, Santa Clara, 1981, London, 1985, Karlsruhe, 1989, The Hague, 1993, Confrerie des Chevaliers du Tastevin, Confrerie de la Chaine des Rotisseurs, Wine and Food Soc., Wednesday 10. Lt. (j.g.) Supply Corps, USNR, 1942-46. Recipient President's medal Cazenovia Coll., 1990, George Washington laureate Am. Hungarian Found., 1996; named Prin. for Day, Townsend Harris H.S. N.Y.C. Bd. Edn., 1997-2001, Disting. Alumnus U.S. Navy Supply Corps Sch., Athens, Ga., 1998; Baker scholar Harvard U., 1947. Mem. DOCA (Defense Orientation Conf. Assn.). Presbyterian. Office: 7155 Old Easton Rd Box 156 Pipersville PA 18947-9701 E-mail: sigety@msn.com.

SIGETY, CORNELIUS EDWARD, office manager; b. N.Y.C., June 6, 1958; s. Charles Edward and Katharine (Snell) Sigety; m. Virginia White, Oct. 28, 1995; children: Charles Edgar, Bradford Earle, Cornelia Ring. BA, U. Rochester, N.Y., 1980; MBA, Harvard U., Boston, 1985. Asst. adminstr. Florence Nightingale Health Ctr., N.Y., 1980-83; v.p. Profl. Med. Products, Greenwood, S.C., 1985-88; mng. dir. Kenbar Group, N.Y., 1988—. Bd. dirs. Heritage Conservancy. Mem. Union Club, Doylestown Country Club, Mantoloking Yacht Club. Presbyterian. Avocations: sailing, golf, skiing. Home: PO Box 369 Pipersville PA 18947-0369 Office: Kenbar Group 1760 3rd Ave New York NY 10029-6810 E-mail: cesigety@hotmail.com.

SIGGINS, JAMES E. chemist; b. Salt Lake City, Oct. 14, 1928; s. Ernest L. and Mabel G. Siggins; m. Martha J. McIntire, Aug. 15, 1983; m. Joyce Y. Kangas, June 15, 1959 (div.); children: Cecile, Karen, Theodore. PhD, Univ. Chgo., Chicago, IL, 1960. Chemist NY State Health Labs, Albany, NY. Home: 107 Van Dyke Place Apt 10 Guilderland NY 12084-9699

SIGINER, DENNIS A. mechanical engineering educator, university dean; b. Ankara, Turkey, July 10, 1946; came to U.S., 1976; s. Kazim Siginer and Emine Turkoz. BS, MS with honors, Tech. U. Istanbul, 1969, ScD, 1971; PhD, U. Minn., 1982. Rsch. assoc. U. Minn., Mpls., 1976-80; asst. prof. U. Ala., Tuscaloosa, 1981-83; assoc. prof. Auburn (Ala.) U., 1984-92, prof. mech. engring., 1992-97; prof., head dept. mech. engring. N.J. Inst. Tech., Newark, 1998-2000; dean Coll. Engring., Wichita (Kans.) State U., 2000—. Organizer, chmn. several internat. and nat. confs.; invited spkr. several countries, fgn. and nat. instns., internat. and nat. meetings; reviewer for numerous profl. archival jours. and fed. and pvt. funding agys. including NSF; book reviewer pubs. in field. Editor procs. of 1st East-West Conf. on advances in structured and heterogeneous continua, Moscow, 1993; editor numerous books on devels. in non-Newtonian flows, electrorheol. fluids and fluid mechanics phenomena in microgravity, rheology and fluid mechanics of nonlinear materials; editor-in-chief: Advances in the Flow and Rheology of Non-Newtonian Fluids, 1999; assoc. editor Jour. of Applied Mechanics, 1997—; guest editor Jour. Non-Newtonian Fluid Mechanics, 1999; author books in field; contbr. more than 120 articles to profl. jours. Recipient 3 univ.-wide teaching awards; Summer faculty fellow NASA, 1991, 92. Fellow: Sci. and Tech. Rsch. Coun. Turkey, ASME (lectr. 2000, svc. award 1993, 1995, 1996, 1997); mem.: N.Y. Acad. Scis., Soc. Engring. Sci., Am. Inst. Physics, Am. Acad. Mechanics, Soc. Rheology (organizer ann. meeting), Am. Soc. Engring. Edn. (organizer 16 symposia, editor 16 procs. vols., rsch. award 1992), Sigma Xi, Pi Tau Sigma (hon.). Home: 13211 Edgewood Dr Wichita KS 67230 Office: Wichita State U Coll Engring 105 Wallace Hl 1845 Fairmount Wichita KS 67260-0044 E-mail: dennis.siginer@wichita.edu.

SIGLER, HOLLIS, artist, educator, author; b. Gary, Ind., Mar. 2, 1948; Studied in Florence, Italy, 1968-69; BFA, Moore Coll. Art, 1970, DFA (hon.), 1994; MFA, Sch. Art Inst. Chgo., 1973. Mem. faculty Columbia Coll., Chgo., 1978—, instr. painting and drawing, 1984—. One-woman shows include Akron (Ohio) Art Mus., 1986, S.W. Craft Ctr., San Antonio, 1989, Nat. Mus. Women Arts, Washington, 1991, 93, Printworks Gallery, Chgo., 1991, 93, Priebe Art Gallery, U. Wis., Oshkosh, 1992, Susan Cummins Gallery, Mill Valley, Calif., 1992, 94, Steven Scott Gallery, Balt., 1993, 94, Hartman Ctr. Gallery, Bradley U., Peoria, Ill., 1994, Mus. Contemporary Art, Chgo., 1994, Suburban Fine Arts Ctr., Highland Park, Ill., 1994, Lakeview Mus. Arts and Sci., Peoria, 1994, Decordova Mus. and Sculpture Park, Lincoln, Mass., 1994, Leedy-Voulkos Art Ctr. Gallery, Kansas City, Mo., 1995, Ark. Art Ctr., Little Rock, 1996, Elvehjem Mus. Art., U. Wis., Madison, 1997, Palo Alto Cultural Ctr., Calif., 1998, Carl Hammer Gallery, Chgo., 1998, Printworks Gallery, Chgo., 1999; exhibited in group shows Whitney Mus. Art, N.Y.C., 1981, Walker Art Mus., Mpls., 1982, Mus. Modern Art, N.Y.C., 1984, Corcoran Gallery Art, Washington, 1985, Chgo. Cultural Ctr., 1992, The Drawing Ctr., N.Y.C., 1993, The Contemporary Mus., Honolulu, 1994, Butler Inst. Am. Art, Youngstown, Ohio, 1995, Nat. Mus. Am. Art, Smithsonian, Washington, 1996, Corcoran Sch. of Art and U.S. Senate, Russell Rotunda Gallery, Washington, 1998; represented in permanent collections Mus. Contemporary Art, Chgo., Indpls. Mus. Art, Seattle Art Mus., Madison Art Ctr., High Mus. Art, Atlanta, Nat. Mus. Am. Art, Smithsonian, Nat. Mus. Women in the Arts, Washington, John D. and Catherine T. MacArthur Found., Johns Hopkins Hosp. Oncology Ctr., Balt.; pub.: Hollis Sigler's Breast Cancer Journal, 1999; also others. Recipient cash award Southwestern Ctr. for Contemporary Art, Winston-Salem, N.C., 1987, Childe Hassam purchase award AAAL, 1988; grantee Ill. Arts Coun., 1986, Nat. Endowment for Arts, 1987. Office: Columbia Coll 600 S Michigan Ave Chicago IL 60605-1900

SIGLER, LOIS OLIVER, retired educator; b. Piney Flats, Tenn., Sept. 8, 1923; d. Willie Campbell and Lillie (Brown) Oliver; m. William Virgil Sigler Jr., Aug. 25, 1962; 1 child, William Oliver. BS, East Tenn. State U., 1944; MS, U. Tenn., 1952; postgrad., Memphis State U., U. Tenn. Home econs. tchr. Buchanan (Va.) pub. schs., 1944-46; area supr. home econs. edn. and sch. lunch prog. State Dept. Edn., Commonwealth of Va., 1946-54; asst. nat. advisor Future Homemakers of Am./New Homemakers of Am., HEW, Washington, 1954-56, nat. advisor, 1956-63; family living coord. Ohio State Dept. and Columbus (Ohio) Pub. Schs., Columbus Met. Housing Authority, 1963; tchr. Millington (Tenn.) High Sch., 1966-92; ret., 1992. Mem. Pres. Kennedy's Food for Peace Coun., Pres. Eisenhower's Adv. Com. on Youth Fitness. Named Tenn. Home Econs. Tchr. of Yr., 1975, Woman of Yr., 1991, Twentieth Century award for achievement, 1991, One of Top 2000 Outstanding People of 20th Century, 1998. Mem. NEA, Am. Home Econs. Assn., Tenn. Home Econs. Assn., Am. Voc. Assn., Tenn. Voc. Assn., Nat. Voc. Home Econs. Tchrs. Assn., Tenn. Voc. Home Econs. Tchrs. Assn. (hon. 1992, past sec.-treas., Outstanding Svc. award 1986), W. Tenn. Home Econs. Edn. Assn. (past sec.), Tenn. Edn. Assn. (bd. dirs. 1977-80), W. Tenn. Edn. Assn., Shelby County Edn. Assn. (past sch. rep.), Future Homemakers Am. (nat. hon. 1956, state hon. 1991, master advisor award 1988, advisor mentor 1991), Omicron Nu, Pi Lambda Theta. Home: 4785 Rolling Meadows Dr Memphis TN 38128-4868

SIGMAN, STUART J. communications educator; b. Bklyn., Jan. 29, 1955; s. Harvey M. and Pauline (Balasiano) S. BA, CUNY, 1976; MA, U. Pa., 1979, PhD, 1982. Asst. prof. W.Va. U., Morgantown, 1981-82, Pa. State U., University Park, 1982-84, SUNY, Buffalo, 1984-87, assoc. prof. Albany, 1987-97; dean comms. Emerson Coll., Boston, 1998—. Mem. adv. bd. Health Edn. Svcs. Network, Albany, 1991-92; mem. editl. bd. Comm. Theory jour., 1989-98; manuscript cons. SUNY Press, Lawrence Erlbaum Assocs., others. Author: A Perspective on Social Communication, 1987; editor: The Consequentiality of Communication, 1995; founding editor jour. Rsch. on Lang. and Social Interaction, 1987; co-editor book series: Everyday Communication: Case Studies, 1995. Vol. Compeer, Albany, 1994-97; vice chmn. bd. dirs. Cornell Coop. Extension, Schenectady, N.Y., 1997. Grantee N.Y. State Edn. Dept., 1993-94; Ea. Comm. Assn. scholar, 1993-94. Office: Emerson Coll 120 Boylston St Boston MA 02116-4624 E-mail: stuart_sigman@emerson.edu.

SIGMON, JOYCE ELIZABETH, professional society administrator; b. Stanley, N.C., Oct. 4, 1935; d. Rome Alfred and Pearl Elizabeth (Beal) S. BS, U. N.C., 1971; MA, Loyola U., 1980. Cert. dental asst., assn. exec. Dental asst. Dr. Paul A. Stroup, Jr., Charlotte, N.C., 1953-63; instr. Wayne Tech. Inst., Goldsboro, 1963-65, Ctrl. Piedmont Community Coll., Charlotte, 1965-69; dir. Dental Assisting Edn. ADA, Chgo., 1971-85, asst. sec. Coun. Prosthetics Svcs., 1985-87, mgr. Office Quality Assurance, 1987—90, exec. dir. Aux., 1990-92; dir. adminstrv. activities Am. Acad. of Implant Dentistry, 1993—; exec. sec. Am. Bd. of Oral Implantology/Implant Dentistry, 1993-99. Deacon 4th Presbyn. Ch., 1973-75, elder 1975-77, 88-91, 2002—, trustee, 1991-94; moderator Presbyn. Women in 4th Ch., 1987-91, Stephen min., 1997-99. Mem. Am. Soc. Assn. Execs., Chgo. Soc. Assn. Execs. (chair CAE com. 1991-92), Am. Dental Assts. Assn., N.C. Dental Assn. (pres. 1968-69), Charlotte Dental Assts. Soc. Presbyterian. Home: 260 E Chestnut St Chicago IL 60611-2401 Office: Am Acad Implant Dentistry 211 E Chicago Ave Chicago IL 60611-2637

SIGMON, SCOTT B. psychologist; b. Newark, Dec. 30, 1946; s. Henry and Shirley (Juffe) S. BA, Bloomfield Coll., 1973; MA, Montclair State Coll., 1975; profl. diploma in sch. psychology, Kean Coll., 1977; EdD, Rutgers U., 1985. Sch. psychologist Middlesex Borough Pub. Schs., N.J., 1976-77, Milton Sch., Millburn, 1977-78; sch. psychologist, chair child study team Irvington Pub. Schs., 1978-87; psychotherapist Family Svc. Bur. Newark, 1987; supr. child study East Orange (N.J.) Sch. Dist., 1987-88; sch. psychologist Elizabeth (N.J.) Pub. Schs., 1988-89; sch. psychologist, child study team chairperson Carlstadt-East Rutherford Regional H.S. Dist., N.J., 1989-2001; pvt. practice Union, 1991—. Adj. prof. grad. psychology, Kean Univ. N.J., 1986, adj. prof. grad. psychology and spl. edn. Seton Hall U. (N.J.), 1988-90; asst. prof. coun. svcs. program William Paterson U. of N.J., 1992-95. Author: Radical Socioeducational Analysis, 1985, Radical Analysis of Special Education: Focus on Historical Development and Learning Disabilities, 1987; author, editor: Critical Voices on Special Education: Problems and Progress Concerning the Mildly Handicapped, 1990; editor The N.J. Sch. Psychologist newsletter, 1986-88; contbr. articles to profl. jours. With USMC, 1966-69. Mem. APA, Internat. Sch. Psychology Assn., N.Am. Soc. of Sport Psychology and Phys. Activity, Assn. for the Advancement of Applied Sport Psychology, Am. Ednl. Rsch. Assn., N.J. Assn. Sch. Psychologists, N.J. Psychol. Assn. Office: 1945 Morris Ave Union NJ 07083-3526

SIGMOND, CAROL ANN, lawyer; b. Phila., Jan. 9, 1951; d. Irwin and Mary Florence (Vollmer) S. BA, Grinnell Coll., 1972; JD, Cath. U., 1975. Bar: Va. 1975, D.C. 1980, Md. 1988, N.Y. 1990, U.S. Dist. Ct. (ea. dist.) Va. 1975, U.S. Dist. Ct. (so. and ea. dist.) N.Y. 1991, U.S. Ct. Appeals (4th cir.) 1976, U.S. Ct. Appeals (fed. cir.) 1987, U.S. Ct. Appeals (2d cir.) 2000. Asst. gen. counsel Washington Met. Area Transit Authority, 1978-85; acting assoc. gen. counsel for appeals and gen. law, 1985-86; assoc. Patterson, Belknap, Webb & Tyler, Washington, 1986-89, Berman, Paley, Goldstein & Kannry, N.Y.C., 1991-93; prin. Law Offices of Carol A. Sigmond, 1993-97; of counsel Pollack & Greene, LLP, 1998-2000; pvt. practice, 2000—. Mem. Women's Nat. Dem. Club. Active Womens Nat. Dem. Club. Mem. ABA, D.C. Bar Assn., Arlington County Bar Assn., Va. State Bar Assn., Md. State Bar Assn. Democrat. Mem. Lds Ch. Avocations: piano, bridge. Office: 733 3d Ave Fl7 New York NY 10017 E-mail: c.sigmond@inetmail.att.net.

SIGMOND, RICHARD BRIAN, lawyer; b. Phila., Dec. 7, 1944; s. Joseph and Jean (Nissman) S.; children: Michael, Catherine, Alina; m. Susan Helen Peteraf, Dec. 24, 1984. BS, Phila. Coll. Textiles & Sci., 1966; JD, Temple U., 1969. Bar: Pa. 1969, U.S. Supreme Ct. 1973, U.S. Dist. Ct. (ea. dist.) Pa. 1975, U.S. Ct. Appeals (3d cir.) 1975, N.Y. 1982, D.C. 1995. Atty. Pub. Defender Assn., Phila., 1969-70; ptnr. Meranze, Katz, Spear & Wilderman, 1970-84; sr. ptnr. Spear, Wilderman, Sigmond, Borish & Endy, 1985-89, Sagot, Jennings & Sigmond, Phila., 1989—; gen. counsel Internat. Brotherhood Painters and Allied Trades, 1997-2000. Chmn., bd. dirs. Gatehouse Phila., 1972-83; lectr. Pvt. Industry Coun., Phila., 1985—, labor studies div., Pa. State U., 1978-82, 85-86; gen. counsel Stabilization Agreement, Sheet Metal Industry Trust Fund, 1994—, Internat. Painters and Allied Trades Industry Pension Fund, 1997—. Mem. ABA (labor law com., litigation com.), AFL-CIO (lawyers coordinating com.), Pa. Bar Assn. (labor law com.), Phila. Bar Assn. (labor com.), Phi Alpha Delta. Avocations: sailing, writing. Office: Penn Mutual Towers 510 Walnut St Fl 16 Philadelphia PA 19106-3601

SIGNORI, JACQUELINE M. writer, educator; b. Waterbury, Conn., Dec. 16, 1947; d. Samuel and Agnes Signori. BA, Western Conn. State U., 1973; postgrad., U. New Orleans, 2002. 74counselor Alternative House, McLean, Va., 1973, asst. dir., 1974—75; tchr. World Plan Exec. Coun., Washington, 1976-85; freelance writer Fairfield, Iowa, 1998—; instr. Virtual U., 2000-2001. Co-author: Alternative House, 1975; author: 5046 MacArthur Boulevard, 1990; contbr. articles to profl. jours.; columnist Fairfield Ledger, 1992. Regional rep. Nat. Network Runaway and Youth Svcs., Washington, 1974-75; treas. Divine Mother Charities, Fairfield, 1995-2001; vol. Bradley Presdl. Primary Campaign, N.H., 2000; mem. Jefferson County Dem. Com., Fairfield, 2000-01. Mem. Internat. Women's Writing Guild (Iowa rep. 1998—), Writers Revelations. Avocations: walking, reading, cooking, drawing, traveling. E-mail: jmms51@hotmail.com.

SIGNORILE, VINCENT ANTHONY, lawyer; b. Jersey City, Mar. 22, 1959; s. Ralph R. and Rita (DeRosa) S. BS, St. Peter's Coll., Jersey City, 1981; JD, Seton Hall U., 1985. Bar: N.J. 1985, Pa. 1985. Aide Jersey City Mcpl. Coun., 1980-81, Office of Mayor, City of Jersey City, 1981; law clk. Corp. Counsel Jersey City, 1981-85; law sec. Superior Ct. N.J. for Hudson County, Jersey City, 1985-86; assoc. atty., 1986-89; ptnr. Signorile & Saminski, 1989-97; atty. Jersey City Zoning Bd. Adjustment, 1994-97, Bayonne City Ethics Bd., 1995-97; judge Jersey City Mcpl. Ct., 1996—99, chief judge, 1999—. Judge Jersey City Mcpl. Ct., 1996—. Mem. Hudson County Dem. Com., 1977-81, Jersey City Environ. Com., 1989-93, Jersey City Planning Bd. Com., 1991-93, Jersey City Ins. Fund Com., 1989-93; co-chmn. Hudson County Columbus Parade, 1984-85; elected to Mcpl. Coun. Jersey City, 1989-93. Mem. ABA, N.J. Bar Assn., Pa. Bar Assn., Hudson County Bar Assn. (treas. Young Lawyer's Assn. 1987-88, scholar 1984-85), Assn. Trial Lawyers Am. Roman Catholic. Home: 1691 John F Kennedy Blvd Jersey City NJ 07305-1841 Office: Jersey City Municipal Ct 365 Summit Ave Jersey City NJ 07306

SIGNOROVITCH, DENNIS J. communications executive; b. Norristown, Pa., July 23, 1945; s. James and Regina S.; m. Susan M. McLaughlin, 1968; children: James Edward, Sarah Elizabeth. BS in Fgn. Svc., Georgetown U., 1967; MA, Old Dominion U., 1972. Instr. U. Toledo, 1972-77; writer/editor Doehler Jarvis div. NL Industries, Toledo, 1977-78; mgr. pub. rels. Eltra Corp., N.Y.C., 1979, mgr. planning, 1980; various assignments AlliedSignal Corp., Morristown, N.J., 1980-92; v.p. pub. affairs AlliedSignal Inc., Torrance, Calif., 1992-98; v.p. mktg. and comm. AlliedSignal Aerospace, 1998-99; v.p. comms. Honeywell Aerospace, 1999—. Mem. Exec. Comm. Forum. With U.S. Army, 1967-70. Decorated Bronze Star with oak leaf cluster. Mem. The Conf. Bd. (corp. comm. coun. 1991), Arthur W. Page Soc., San Francisco Acad. (trustee), Aerospace Industries Assn. (chmn. comms. coun. 2001—). Office: Honeywell Aerospace 2525 W 190th St Torrance CA 90504-6002

SIGULER, GEORGE WILLIAM, financial services executive; b. Cleve., Apr. 26, 1947; s. John Frederick and Helen Alice (Popp) S.; m. Pamela Ann Mallon, Oct. 31, 1981; children: George William Jr., Emily Ann, Charles Arthur, Mary Elizabeth, Andrew Cooper. AB, Amherst Coll., 1970; MBA, Harvard U., 1972. Ptnr. Harvard Mgmt. Co., Boston, 1974-83; chief of staff HHS, Washington, 1983-84; exec. v.p. Monarch Capital Corp., Springfield, Mass., 1984-87, vice chmn. bd., 1987-91; pres. Associated Capital Investor, San Francisco, 1990-91; mng. dir. Mitchell Hutchins Instl. Investors, Inc., N.Y.C., 1991-95; founder Siguler Guff & Co., 1995—. Assoc. treas. Harvard U., 1973-88; bd. dirs. Venture Lending and Leasing, Inc., Russia Ptnrs., L.P. Mem. vis. com. Harvard U. Med. Sch., Boston, 1986—; mem. nat. adv. com. on community health resources HHS, Washington, 1985-90; trustee Perkins

Sch. for Blind, Watertown, Mass., 1976-83, New Eng. Aquarium, 1989-91. Recipient Disting. Svc. award HHS, 1984. Republican. Presbyterian. Office: Siguler Guff & Co 630 5th Ave New York NY 10111-0100

SIH, CHARLES JOHN, pharmaceutical chemistry educator; b. Shanghai, China, Sept. 11, 1933; s. Paul Kwang-Tsien and Teresa (Dong) S.; m. Catherine Elizabeth Hsu, July 11, 1959; children: Shirley, Gilbert, Ronald. AB in Biology, Caroll Coll., 1953; MS in Bacteriology, Mont. State Coll., 1955; PhD in Bacteriology, U. Wis., 1958. Sr. research microbial biochemist Squibb Inst. for Med. Research, New Brunswick, N.J., 1958-60; mem. faculty U. Wis.-Madison, 1960—, Frederick B. Power prof. pharm. chemistry, 1978, Hilldare prof., 1987—. Recipient 1st Ernest Volwiler award, 1977; Roussel prize, 1980, Am. Pharm. Assoc. award 1987. Mem. Am. Chem. Soc., Soc. Am. Biol. Chemists, Acad. Pharm. Scis., Soc. Am. Microbiologists. Home: 10 Coyote Ct Madison WI 53717-2736

SIHLER, WILLIAM WOODING, finance educator, educator; b. Seattle, Nov. 17, 1937; s. William and Helen Alice (Wooding) S.; m. Mary Elizabeth Unwin, Aug. 21, 1963; children: Edward Wooding, Jennifer Sihler Zysman. AB summa cum laude in Govt. (Sheldon traveling fellow), Harvard U., 1959, MBA with high distinction, 1962, DBA, 1965. Instr., asst. prof. Harvard U. Bus. Sch., 1964-67; asso. prof. Darden Grad. Bus. Sch., U. Va., Charlottesville, 1967-72, prof., 1972-76, A.J. Morris prof., 1976-84; R.E. Trzcinski prof., 1984—; dir. D.B.A. Program, 1971-73; assoc. dean acad. affairs, 1972-77; exec. dir. BAFT/Ctr. for Internat. Banking Studies, 1977-91. Bd. dirs. Curtiss-Wright Corp.; pres. Southeastern Cons. Group, Ltd. Co-author: Financial Management: Text and Cases, 2d edit., 1991, The Troubled Money Business, 1992, Financial Service Organizations: Cases in Strategic Management, 1993, Cases in Applied Corporate Finance, 1994, Building Valve with Capital-Structure Strategies, 1998, Financial Turnarounds--Preserving Value, 2001; editor: Classics in Commercial Bank Lending, vol. 1, 1981, vol. 2, 1985; contbr. articles to profl. jours. Vis. com. Sch. Mgmt., Case Western Res. U., 1976-86, bd. overseers, 1980-86. Recipient DeL. K. Jay prize Harvard U., Disting. Prof. award U. Va. Alumni Assn., 1982; C.J. Bonaparte scholar Harvard U. Mem. Fin. Mgmt. Assn., Am. Econ. Assn., Am. Fin. Assn., Eastern Fin. Assn., Univ. Club (N.Y.C.), Harvard Club (N.Y.C.), Greencroft Club (Charlottesville), Phi Beta Kappa, Beta Gamma Sigma. Home: 202 Sturbridge Rd Charlottesville VA 22901-2116 Office: PO Box 6550 Charlottesville VA 22906-6550

SIIROLA, JEFFREY JOHN, chemical engineer; b. Patuxent River, Md., July 17, 1945; s. Arthur Raymond and Nancy Ellen (Harris) S.; m. Sharon Ann Atwood, Apr. 24, 1971; childen: John Daniel, Jennifer Ann. BS in Chem. Engring., U. Utah, 1967; PhD, U. Wis., 1970. Rsch. engr. Eastman Chem. Co., Kingsport, Tenn., 1972-74, sr. rsch. engr., 1974-80, rsch. assoc., 1980-88, sr. rsch. assoc., 1988-95, tech. fellow, 1995—. Trustee CACHE Corp., Austin, Tex., 1983--. Co-author: Process Synthesis, 1973. Appalachian tr. maintenance Eastman Hiking Club, Kingsport, 1973—. With U.S. Army, 1970-72. Fellow AIChE (A.E. Marshall award 1967, Computing Practice award 1991, bd. dirs. 1999-2001); mem. Nat. Acad. Engring., Accreditation Bd. for Engring. and Tech., Am. Chem. Soc., Am. Soc. for Engring. Edn., Am. Assn. for Artificial Intelligence, Kingsport C. of C. Achievements include development of the AIDES chem. process flowsheet invention procedure. Home: 2517 Wildwood Dr Kingsport TN 37660-4748 Office: Eastman Chem Co 200 S Wilcox Dr PO Box 1972 Kingsport TN 37662-5150 E-mail: siirola@eastman.com.

SIKER, EPHRAIM S. anesthesiologist; b. Port Chester, N.Y., Mar. 24, 1926; s. Samuel S. and Adele (Weiser) S.; m. m . Eileen Mary Bohnel, Aug. 5, 1951; children— Kathleen Ellen, Jeffrey Stephen, David Alan, Paul William, Richard Francis. Student, Duke U., 1943-45; MD, N.Y.U., 1949. Diplomate: Am. Bd. Anesthesiology (dir. 1971— , sec.-treas. 1974-82, pres. 1982-83) Nat. Bd. Med. Examiners. Intern Grasslands Hosp., Valhalla, N.Y., 1949-50, resident in anesthesia, 1950; resident dept. anesthesiology Mercy Hosp., Pitts., 1952-53, assoc. dir. dept., 1955-62, chmn., 1962-92; practice medicine, specializing in anesthesiology Pitts., 1954—; pres. Pitts. Anesthesia Assocs., Ltd., 1967-89; dir. anesthesia services Central Med. Ctr., Pitts., 1973-89. Courtesy staff St. Clair Meml. Hosp., Pitts., 1954—89, St. Margaret Meml. Hosp., 1992—; clin. prof. dept. anesthesiology U. Pitts. Sch. Medicine, 1968—; mem. exec. com. Am. Bd. Med. Spltys., 1978—81; Exch. cons. Welsh Nat. Sch. Medicine, Cardiff, 1955—56; mem. Pa. Gov.'s Commn. on Profl. Liability Ins., 1968—70; mem. adv. panel U.S. Pharmacopeia, 1970—76; mem. Am. Acupuncture Anesthesia Study Group NAS to Peoples Republic China, 1974; mem. adv. com. on splty. and geog. distbn. of physicians Inst. Medicine NAS, 1974—76; trustee Ednl. Coun. for Fgn. Med. Grads., 1980—82, Mercy Hosp. Found., 1983—95; bd. dirs., sec. Anesthesia Patient Safety Found., 1985—89, mem. exec. com., 1985—92, exec. dir., 1992—97. Author: (with F.F. Foldes) Narcotics and Narcotic Antagonists, 1964; sect. on narcotic: (with F.F. Foldes) numerous other publs. in med. lit. Ency. Brittanica. Served to lt. M.C. USNR, 1950-52. USPHS postdoctoral research fellow, 1954; hon. fellow faculty anaesthetists Royal Coll. Surgeons, Eng., 1974; hon. fellow faculty anesthetists Coll. Medicine South Africa, 1983; recipient Hippocratic award Mercy Hosp., 1982 Fellow Royal Coll. Surgeons Ireland, Faculty Anaesthetists (hon. 1988); mem. Am. Soc. Anesthesiologists (pres. 1973—, bd. dirs. Disting. Svc. award l984), AMA (alt. del. 1962), Pa. Med. Soc., Allegheny County Med. Soc., Pa. Soc. Anesthesiologists (pres. 1965, Disting. Svc. award 1986), Royal Soc. Medicine (Eng.), Pitts. Acad. Medicine, Am. Coll. Anesthesiologists (bd. govs. l969-7l), World Fedn. Anesthesiologists (chmn. exec. com. 1980-84, v.p. 1984-88), Assn. Anesthesia Program Dirs. (pres. 1987-89), Japanese Soc. Anesthesiologists (hon.). Achievements include developing Siker Laryngoscope, 1956. Home: 185 Crestvue Manor Dr Pittsburgh PA 15228-1814 Office: 1400 Locust St Pittsburgh PA 15219-5114 E-mail: r.siker@worldnet.att.net. *If you have to tell someone who you are, then you probably aren't. People are measured by more than their deeds, and such estimations are frequently made on the basis of their inter-personal relationships. While achievement and effort usually bear a linear relationship to each other, the impact that the achiever has on society depends upon the impact he makes on individuals.*

SIKES, CYNTHIA LEE, actress, singer, advocate; b. Coffeyville, Kans., Jan. 2, 1954; d. Neil and Pat (Scott) S.; m. Alan Bud Yorkin, June 24, 1989. Student, Am. Conservatory Theater, San Francisco, 1977-79. Actor: (TV series) St. Elsewhere, 1981—83, L.A. Law, 1989, JAG, 2000—01, (TV movies) Oceans of Fire, 1986, His Mistress, 1990; (films) Man Who Loved Women, That's Life, Arthur on the Rocks, Love Hurts, 1988, Possums, 1998, Shopping, 2001; prodr., actor: Sins of Silence, 1996, (Broadway musical) Into the Woods, 1988—89. Active Hollywood Women's Polit. Com.; apptd. Pres. Clinton's Adv. Com. on Arts John F. Kennedy Ctr. for Performing Arts, 1999. Recipient Gov.'s Medal of Merit, Kans., 1986. Democrat. Avocations: hiking, writing, reading.

SIKES, MARY TAGGART, librarian; b. Oceanside, Calif., Aug. 29, 1964; d. Billy Ray and Joycln Ruth Taggart; m. Clay Daniel Sikes, Dec. 17, 1995; 1 child, Victoria Celeste. AA, Weatherford (Tex.) Coll., 1984; BA, U. N. Tex., 1987, MLS, 1993. Receiving clk. Walden Books, Denton, Tex., 1986, asst. store mgr. Denton, Irving, 1986-90, store mgr. Sherman, 1990-93; reference libr. Ft. Worth (Tex.) Pub. Libr., 1993-95, reference asst. mgr., 1995-98, interlibrary loan supr., 1998—. Vol. Meals on Wheels, Tarrant County, Big Bros. Big Sisters, Tarrant County. Mem.: ALA, Tex. Libr. Assn. (alt. counsilor interlibr. loan roundtable 1999—2000, counsilor interlibr. loan roundtable 2001—), Phi Theta Kappa, Beta Sigma Phi. Republican. Home: 820 Parkwest Blvd Saginaw TX 76179-3416 Office: Fort Worth Pub Libr 500 W 3d St Fort Worth TX 76102 Fax: 817-332-1160.

SIKKEMA, KENNETH R. state legislator; b. Cadillac, Mich., Feb. 10, 1951; s. Peter John and Kathryn Mae (Laarman) S.; m. Carla Chase, Oct. 12, 1985; 1 child, Zachary Chase. BA in History cum laude, Harvard U., 1974; MBA with distinction, U. Mich., 1984. Legis. asst. Mich. Ho. of Reps., Lansing, 1974-75; adminstrv. asst. Mich. State Senate, 1975-79; mktg. mgr. Herman Miller, Inc., Zeeland, Mich., 1984-86; exec. dir. West Mich. Environ. Action, Grand Rapids, 1979-82; mem. Mich. Ho. of Reps., Lansing, 1987-98, Mich. Senate from 31st dist., Lansing, 1999—. Republican. Mem. Reformed Ch. in Am. Home: 4309 Del Mar Ct Grandville MI 49418 Office: State Senate Capitol Bldg Lansing MI 48913-0001 E-mail: senksikkema@senate.state.mi.us.

SIKORA, BARBARA JEAN, library director; b. Passaic, N.J., Apr. 12, 1943; d. Stanley Francis and Jean (Sobczyk) S. BA in Edn., English, William Paterson Coll., 1969, MEd in Learning Disabilities, 1978; MLS, Rutgers U., 1978; Cert. in Fundraising Mgmt., Fairleigh Dickinson U., 1990. Profl. libr. N.J. Tchr. Clifton (N.J.) Pub. Schs., 1969-73; office mgr. Singer/TRW, Fairfield, N.J., 1974-76; prin. libr. Passaic Pub. Libr., 1978-88; asst. libr. dir. Pub. Libr. Livingston, N.J., 1989-90, libr. dir., 1991—. Adj. faculty William Paterson Coll., 1977-90; trustee Wayne Pub. Libr., 1986-88; bd. dirs. Polish and Slavic Fed. Credit Union, 1999—. Mem. Polish Heritage Festival Com., Holmdel, N.J., 1987—, gen. chmn., 1999; trustee, bd. dirs. Livingston Area C. of C., 1998—; pres. Libr. Pub. Rels. Coun., 1997; West Essex br. YMCA of the Oranges, 1997—; mem. Polish Children's Heartline, Inc. Grantee U.S. Dept. Edn. libr. literacy program, 1987, N.J. State Libr. Leadership Inst., 1988, Christopher Leadership Inst., 1997; Paul Harris fellow Rotary Internat., 1999. Mem. ALA (ethics com. 1995-99), AAUW, N.J. Libr. Assn., Nat. Spkrs.' Assn., Rotary (pres. Livingston chpt. 1994-96, 2000), Rutgers Sch. Comm. and Info. Libr. Studies Alumni Assn. (pres. 1991-94), Beta Phi Mu. Avocations: writing, speaking, adult education, psychology, leadership skills training. Home: The Mill 300 Main St Apt 314 Little Falls NJ 07424-1359 Office: Pub Libr Livingston 10 Robert Harp Dr Livingston NJ 07039 E-mail: sikora@bcols.org.

SIKORA, JAMES ROBERT, educational business consultant, financial analyst; b. Sacramento, July 8, 1945; s. George Robert and Marian Frances (Fears) S.; m. Marie Lynore Nyarady, June 22, 1968. BEE, U. Santa Clara, 1967; postgrad., U. Calif., Santa Cruz, 1979—, personal fin. planning cert., 1998. Electronic engr. GTE-Sylvania, Santa Cruz, 1967-69, sys. analyst, 1969-71, sr. support analyst Calif., 1971-73; coord. bus. sys. Santa Clara County Office Edn., San Jose, 1973-76, dir. dist. payroll, pers. svcs., 1976-85, dir. dist. bus. svcs., 1985-95; self-employed sch. bus. cons. Omniserve, Ben Lomond, 1995—; interim dir. fin. San Jose Unified Sch. Dist., 2001, spl. fiscal asst., 2001—. Cons. records mgmt. County Santa Clara, San Jose, 1982; cons. Sonoma County Office of Edn., Santa Rosa, 1995, Union Sch. Dist., San Jose, 1996—99, San Jose Unified Sch. Dist., 1997, 2000, Santa Clara County Office of Edn., San Jose, 1997, San Jose, 1998—2000, Milpitas Unified Sch. Dist., 1995—97, Los Altos Sch. Dist., 1998—99; interim bus. mgr. Healdsburg Unified Sch. Dist., 1999—2000; interim dep. supt. adminstrv. svcs. Gilroy Unified Sch. Dist., 1999; interim bus. mgr. Moraga Sch. Dist., 1999; interim asst. supt. bus. svcs. Mountain-View/Los Altos Union H.S. Dist., Mountain View, 1997; interim asst. supt. fiscal svcs. Cupertino Union Sch. Dist., 1997—98; interim CFO Union Sch. Dist., San Jose, 1998; spl. asst. Milpitas Unified Sch. Dist., 1998—2000; interim bus. mgr. Los Gatos Sch. Dist., 1997; interim budget mgr. Saint Helena Unified Sch. Dist., 2000; interim AB1200 coord. Napa County Office Edn., 2000; vice-chmn. Edn. Mandated Cost Network Exec. Bd., 1991—95; mem. Schs. Fin. Svcs. subcom., 1987—94, Maui Arts and Cultural Ctr. Ohia Club; life mem. Napa Valley Wine Libr. Assn. Author, co-editor Howdy Rowdy Memorial, 1979. Mem. Ballet Master's Circle, Ballet San Jose/Silicon Valley; sponsor Dixieland Monterey; patrons cir. Monterey Bay Aquarium; angel, seat donor San Jose Repertory Theater; sustaining mem. Bay Shore Lyric Opera Co.; patron Second Harvest Food Bank; active Ctr. Photog. Arts; charter mem. Long Marine Lab.; mem. Team Shakespeare, Shakespeare Santa Cruz; treas. Mountain Parks Found., 1997—99, bd. dirs., 1997—. Mem.: Montalvo Assn. (patron), Santa Cruz Mus. Art and History, Am. Assn. Ret. Persons, Friends of Santa Cruz Pub. Librs., ARC Cmty. Friend, Nature Conservancy, Felton Cmty. Hall (supporter), Planned Parenthood, Waddell Creek Assn. (sponsor), Point Lobos Natural History Assn., Calif. State Parks Found., Trout Unltd., Calif. Trout, Amnesty Internat., Wine Investigation for Novices and Oenephiles, Santa Cruz Fly Fisherman, Golden Gate Nat. Park Assn., Norwegian Elkhound Assn. (pres. 1977—79), Calif. Assn. Sch. Bus. Ofcls. (subsect. pres. 1984—85, state risk mgmt. com. 1985—87, sect. bd. dirs. 1987—93, state legis. com. 1989—2000, sect. pres. 1991—92, state bd. dirs. 1991—92, state schs. employer adv. com. rep. 1991—, state strategic planning com. 1994—2001, state risk mgmt. com. 1996—97, state bd. dirs. 1999—2002, state risk mgmt. com. 1999—2002, state purchasing com. 1999—2002), Am. Diabetes Assn., Pub. Agy. Risk Mgmt. Assn., Am. Assn. Individual Investors (life), Rotary Internat. (club svcs. dir. 2000—, San Lorenzo Valley chpt.), Monterey Hot Jazz Soc., Am. Dog Owners Assn., Redwood Coast Brewers Assn., Easter Seals Ctrl. Calif. Century Club, Cabrillo Music Festival New Century Club, Sierra Club (life). Libertarian. Roman Catholic. Avocations: photography, travel, oenophilia, fishing, snorkelling. Home and Office: 400 Coon Heights Rd Ben Lomond CA 95005-9711

SIKORA, RIYAZ T. finance educator; b. Hyderabad, India, May 23, 1966; s. Tajammul A. and Ateka T. Sikora; m. Farzana Riyaz Hafizee, May 28, 1998; children: Tamanna. B in Engring., Osmania U., India, 1987; diploma in mgmt., Indian Inst. of Mgmt., Calcutta, 1988; PhD, U. Ill., Urbana-Champaign, 1994. Asst. prof. U. Mich., Dearborn, 1994—97, U. Ill., Champaign, 1997—. Chair Decision Sciences Inst., Atlanta, 2001; chair cluster on evolutionary algorithms at informs ann. meeting Inst. for Ops. Rsch. and Mgmt. Sci., Linthicum, Md., 2000; chair spl. interest group on enterprise integration INFORMS Coll. Artificial Intelligence, Linthicum, Md., 1994—. Author: (book chapter) Business Modeling: A Multidisciplinary Approach Essays in honor of Andrew B. Whinston, 2001; contbr. articles; mem. editl. bd.: Jour. Database Mgmt., 1998—, mem. editl. bd.: Jour. Info. Sys. and E-Bus. Mgmt., 1999—. Fellow, Coll. Commerce and Bus. Adminstrn., U. Ill., Urbana-Champaign, 1990—92; scholar State Merit scholar, Bd. of Higher Edn., State of Andhra Pradesh, India, 1981—87. Mem.: Decision Sciences Inst., Inst. Ops. Rsch. and Mgmt. Sci., IEEE Computer Soc., Am. Assn. Artificial Intelligence, Assn. Computing Machinery. Office: Univ Ill Dept Bus Adminstrn 1206 S 6th St Champaign IL 61820 Office Fax: 217-244-7969. E-mail: rtsikora@uiuc.edu.

SIKORA, ROSANNA DAWN, emergency physician, educator; b. Weirton, W.Va., Nov. 16, 1955; d. Edward and Dorothy Ann (Wade) S.; m. Odus E. Brown, Nov. 25, 1994; stepchildren: Aza, Katherine, Hannah. AB in Biology, W.Va. U., 1978, MD, 1982. Cert. in emergency medicine; cert. in pediats., specialty in pediat. emergency medicine; cert. in internal medicine. Resident in pediat. internal medicine W.Va. U. Hosps. Inc., Morgantown, 1982-86, with. Assoc. prof. emergency medicine, pediats., internal medicine W.Va. U. Sch. Medicine, 1996—; mem. pediat. advanced life support subcom. Am. Heart Assn., Charleston, 1987-97, mem. pediat. advanced life support affiliate faculty, 1987-97. Physician men's/women's varsity swim/diving team W.Va. U., Morgantown, 1994—. Fellow Am. Coll. Emergency Physicians (bd. dirs. 1990—, sec.-treas. 1995-96, v.p. 1996-97, pres.-elect 1997-98); mem. AMA, ACP, Am. Acad. Pediats., Alpha Omega Alpha. Democrat. Roman Catholic. Office: W Va U Dept Emergency Medicine PO Box 9149 Morgantown WV 26506-9149

SIKORA, SUZANNE MARIE, dentist; b. Kenosha, Wis., Dec. 4, 1952; d. Leo F. and Ida A. (Dupuis) S. BS, U. Wis., Parkside, 1975; DDS, Marquette U., 1981. Assoc. Paul G. Hagemann, DDS, Racine, Wis., 1981-84; pvt. practice dentistry, 1984—. Cons. Westview Health Care Ctr., Racine, 1981—89, Lincoln Luth. Home, Racine, 1981—2001, Becker-Shoop Ctr., Racine, 1981—2000, Lincoln Village Convalescent Ctr., Racine, 1986—2000, Lincoln Luth Cmty. Care Ctr., 1989—2000. Mem. ad hoc study com. County Health Dept., Racine, 1982—83. Mem.: ADA, Racine County Dental Soc. (pres.-elect 2001, v.p. 2002), Wis. Dental Assn. (coun. on access preventiona and wellness com. 1984—86, impaired provider program intervenor 1990—2001, del. 1993—, Dental Care for Older Persons award 2000). Office: 1900 Lathrop Ave Racine WI 53405-3707

SIKOROVSKY, EUGENE FRANK, retired lawyer; b. Jackson, Mich., Nov. 27, 1927; s. Frank Joseph and Betty Dorothy (Malik) S.; m. Patricia O'Byrne, July 11, 1953; children: Paul, Charles, Catherine, Elizabeth, Emily. BSEE, U. Mich., 1948; LLB, Harvard U., 1951. Bar: N.Y. 1952, Va. 1970, Ill. 1978. Assoc. predecessor firms Cahill, Gordon & Reindel, 1954-63, prin., 1964-68; v.p., gen. counsel, dir. Reynolds Metals Co., Richmond, Va., 1969-76; gen. counsel Gould Inc., Rolling Meadows, Ill., 1977-79, v.p., 1977-81; dep. gen. counsel Bell & Howell Co., Skokie, Ill., 1981-83, v.p. Chgo., 1983-88, gen. counsel, 1983-92, sec., 1984-92, sr. v.p., dir., 1988-92. Lt. USNR, 1951-54. Mem. Ill. State Bar Assn., Tau Beta Pi, Eta Kappa Nu, Phi Eta Sigma, Phi Delta Theta. Episcopalian. Home: 720 Grandview Ln Lake Forest IL 60045-3953 E-mail: genesik@aol.com.

SIKORSKY, ROBERT BELLARMINE, syndicated columnist; b. Pitts., July 1, 1936; s. Anthony Joseph and Frances Dorothy (Latsko) S.; m. Rogga Bowie, May 26, 1972; 1 child, Kyle Joseph. BA, U. Ariz., 1965. Writer Ariz. Daily Star, Tucson, 1984-86; syndicated columnist N.Y. Times Syndicate, N.Y.C., 1984—. Automotive cons. to govt. and pvt. industry, Tucson, Ariz., 1965—; lectr., leader seminars on car care and safety driving; keynote spkr. nat. convs. including Automotive Svc. Assn., Hughes Aircraft Co., nat. new car dealer assns.; co-founder U.S. Dept. Energy Driver Energy Conservation Awareness Tng. Program, 1978-79. Author: How to Get More Miles Per Gallon, 1978, Drive It Forever, 1983, 3d rev. edit., 1997, Break It iN Right, 1984, revised edit., 1988, Rip-Off Tip-Offs: Winning the Auto Repair Game, 1990, Car Tips for Clean Air, 1991, From Bumper to Bumper, 1991, How to Get More Miles Per Gallon in the 90s, 1991; (booklets) Ease the Squeeze, Drive-Wise; (video) Avoid Repair Rip-offs: How to Find an Honest Mechanic, 1988; contbr. articles to Reader's Digest, Parade Mag., Family Circle, can. Reader's Digest, others; appeared on nat. and local radio and TV shows including the Tonight Show, Today, Hour Mag., Regis and Kathy Lee Show, CNBC's Smart Money, Steals and Deals and more. With USMC, 1957-58. Recipient 12 MOTO awards ann. Automotive Journalism Conf., Las Vegas, Nev., awards from journalism groups, State of Ariz., various cities. Mem. Soc. Automotive Engrs., Soc. Tribologists and Lubrication Engrs., Svc. Technicians Soc. Office: NY Times Syndicate 122 E 42nd St Fl 14 New York NY 10168-1401

SILA, CATHY ANN, neurologist; b. Cleve., Apr. 21, 1955; d. Andrew Lee and Mary Florence (Patrick) S.; m. Gene H. Barnett, Dec. 9, 1990; children: Austin Andrew, Addison Edgar. BA Chemistry, Zoology summa cum laude, Miami U., 1977; MD, Case Western Res. Sch. Med., 1981. Intern, resident in neurology Cleve. Clinic, 1981-83; resident in neurology Mayo Clinic, Rochester, Minn., 1983-85; rsch. fellow in cerebrovascular rsch. studies Cleve. Clinic, 1985-86; assoc. med. dir. cerebrovascular ctr. Cleve. Clin. Found., 1987—. Examiner Am. Bd. Psychiatry and Neurology, 1987—; mem. expert panel Agy. for Health Care Policy and Rsch., 1995-96; presenter in field; mem. stroke adv. bd. several pharm. firms; clin. events com. mem. multiple clin. trials; chmn. clin. events com. Abest9; mem. adv. bd. Nat. Women's Health Resource Ctr. Mem. editl. bd. Stroke, Jour. Stroke and Cerebrovascular Disease, Jour. Thrombosis and Thrombolysis, Cleve. Clinic Jour. Medicine; contbr. articles to profl. jours., chpts. to books. Mem. adv. bd. Astra-Zeneca Stroke Specialists; mem. BMS-Sanofi Stroke Adv. Bd. Fellow Am. Heart Assn. (brain-stroke peer rev. com. 1998-2001, women and minorities com. 1993-95, operaton stroke med. subcom. 1999—, sci. programs com. 1999-2000, sci. programs com. 2001-), Am. Acad. Neurology (editl. panel Brain Matters Stroke Initiative 1997-98, exec. com. Vascular Neurology section, quality stds. subcom. 1989-98); mem. AMA (name bank for divsn. rsch. grants 1995—, cons. file project 1996—), Nat. Stroke Assn., Internat. Stroke Soc., Phi Kappa Phi. Office: Cleve Clinic Found S91 9500 Euclid Ave Cleveland OH 44195-0001 E-mail: silac@ccf.org.

SILAGI, BARBARA WEIBLER, corporate administrator; b. Chgo., June 26, 1930; d. Carleton Thomas and Catherine Josephine (Wolph) Weibler; m. Joseph Edward Sturgulewski (Sturgus), Feb. 12, 1953 (div. Aug. 1954); 1 child, Mariann Catherine; m. John Louis Silagi, Jr., July 2, 1960 (div. July 1968). BM in Edn., Northwestern U., 1958; MS in Edn., No. Ill. U., 1965. Cert. K-14 supervisory teaching, spl. edn. tchr., airline transport pilot, FAA dispatcher. Elem. sch. tchr. St. Mary's Sch., Chgo., 1947-49, Kingman, Ariz., 1949-52; legal sec. Judge Edward J. Mahoney, Quincy, Ill., 1954-55; elem. sch. tchr. C.M. Bardwell Sch., Aurora, 1955-76; flight instr. flight schs. Chgo., Aurora and Frankfort, Ill., Clinton, Iowa, 1970-77; aircraft dispatcher Transcontinental Airlines, Zantop Internat. Airlines, Ypsilanti, Mich., 1977-81; airline pilot Mannion Air Charter, 1977-80; head night auditor Howard Johnson, Quality Inn, Travelodge, BestWestern, others, Ocala, Fla., Silver Springs, Fla., 1983-87; sec.-treas. Diamond Design Svcs., Inc., Ocklawaha, 1985—. Pub. Forest Shopper, Springs Shopper, Belle Shopper. Author: Dispatch Training, 1989; editor tng. manuals, 1977-85. Violist Chgo. Suburban Symphony, Naperville, Ill., 1956-60; contralto Palestrina A capella Choir, Aurora, Ill., 1956-60; life mem. Ill. PTA, Aurora, 1974—; apptd. vice chmn. adv. bd. Dunellon Airport and Indsl. Park, 1992-96. Recipient 1st place Suburban Aviation Assn., Chgo., 1975, 5th place Illi-Nines Air Derby, Chgo., Moline, Ill., 1973, 2d place Leg prize Powder Puff Derby, McLean to Lincoln, Nebr., 1971; Eckstein scholar Northwestern U., 1952. Mem. AAUW (life), NEA (life), Ill. Edn. Assn., Ninety Nines Internat. (life), Illi-Nines Air Derby (handicap chmn. 1972-76, air marking chmn. 99's Chgo. chpt. 1972-76, corr. sec. Chgo. chpt. 1976-77, 1st pl. achievement awards 1972-78), Pi Lambda Theta (charter, life, rsch. chmn. Beta Delta chpt. 1962-63). Roman Catholic. Avocations: needlework, gardening, reading, music. Home: 6305 SE 158th Ct Ocklawaha FL 32179-2988 Office: Diamond Design Svcs Inc PO Box 186 Ocklawaha FL 32183-0186

SILAK, CATHY R. former state supreme court justice; b. Astoria, N.Y., May 25, 1950; d. Michael John and Rose Marie (Janor) S.; m. Nicholas G. Miller, Aug. 9, 1980; 3 children. BA, NYU, 1971; M in City Planning, Harvard U., 1973; JD, U. Calif., 1976. Bar: Calif. 1977, U.S. Dist. Ct. (no. dist.) Calif. 1977, D.C. 1979, U.S. Ct. Appeals (D.C. cir.) 1979, U.S. Dist. Ct. (so. dist.) N.Y. 1980, Idaho 1983, U.S. Dist. Ct. Idaho 1983, U.S. Ct. Appeals (2nd cir.) 1983, U.S. Ct. Appeals (9th cir.) 1985. Law clk. to Hon. William W. Schwarzer U.S. Dist. Ct. (no dist.), Calif., 1976-77; pvt. practice San Francisco, 1977-79, Washington, 1979-80; asst. U.S. atty. So. Dist. of N.Y., 1980-83; spl. asst. U.S. atty. Dist. of Idaho, 1983-84; pvt. practice Boise, Idaho, 1984-90; judge Idaho Ct. Appeals, 1990-93; justice Idaho Supreme Ct., Boise, 1993—2000; ptnr. Hawley, Troxell, Ennis, and Hawley. Assoc. gen. counsel Morrison Knudsen Corp., 1989-90; mem. fairness com. Idaho Supreme Ct. and Gov.'s Task Force on Alternative Dispute Resolution; instr. and lectr. in field. Assoc. note and comment editor Calif. Law Rev., 1975-76. Land use planner Mass. Dept. Natural Resources, 1973; founder Idaho Coalition for Adult Literacy; bd. dirs. Literacy Lab., Inc.; mem. adv. bd. Boise State U. Legal Asst. Program. Recipient Jouce Stein award Boise YWCA, 1992, Women Helping Women award Soroptimist, Boise, 1993. Fellow Idaho Law Found (ann., lectr.); mem. ABA (nat. conf. state trial judges jud. adminstrn. divsn.), Nat. Assn. Women Judges, Idaho State Bar (corp./securities sect., instr.), Am. Law Inst., Fellows of the Am. Bar Found, Am. Judicature Soc. (bd. dirs.). Office: Hawley Troxell Ennis & Hawley PO Box 1617 Boise ID 83702-1617*

SILAS, CECIL JESSE, retired petroleum company executive; b. Miami, Fla., Apr. 15, 1932; s. David Edward and Hilda Videll (Carver) S.; m. Theodosea Hejda, Nov. 27, 1965; children: Karla, Peter, Michael, James. BSChemE, Ga. Inst. Tech., Atlanta, 1953. With Phillips Petroleum Co., Bartlesville, Okla., 1953-94, pres. Europe-Africa, Brussels and London, 1968-74, mng. dir. natural resource group Europe/Africa, 1974-76, v.p. gas and gas liquids div. natural resources group Bartlesville, 1976-78, sr. v.p. natural resources group, 1978-80, exec. v.p. exploration and prodn., minerals, gas and gas liquids, 1980-82, pres., chief operating officer, 1982-85, chmn., CEO, 1985-94. Bd. dirs. Reader's Digest Assocs., Inc., bd. dirs. of Halliburton Co., Boys/Girls Clubs Am., Atlanta, parton councillor Atlantic Coun. of the U.S.; bd. dirs. Okla. Found. for Excellence, Ga. Tech. Found.; trustee Frank Phillips Found. Served to 1st lt. Chem. Corps, AUS, 1954-56. Decorated comdr. Order St. Olaf (Norway); inducted into Ga. Inst. Tech. Athletic Hall of Fame, 1959, recipient Former Scholar-Athlete Total Person award, 1988; inducted into Okla. Bus. Hall of Fame, 1989; named CEO of Yr., Internat. TV Assn., 1987. Mem. Am. Petroleum Inst., U.S. C. of C. (past chmn. bd. dirs.), 25 Yr. Club, Phi Delta Theta. Avocations: fishing, golf, hunting. Office: PO Box 2127 Bartlesville OK 74005-2127

SILAS, NANCY, small business owner; b. Gainesville, Fla., Sept. 6, 1943; d. Joseph N Simmons and Roberta Walker Simmons. Bechelor of sci., Fl.a&m. U., Tallahassee, Fl, 1964—65; Work on MS degree, U;niv Of South Fl., Tampa Florida, 1969—77; work on MS degree, Hillsbough Cc, Tampa, Fl, 1974. Tchr. jr high Hillsbourgh Counnty, Tampa, Fla., 1965—82; interior decorator Interior Show Rm., 1986—89; self employed clothes/accessories, 1989—93; bus. owner Source Innova Concepts Intl Inc, 2000—02. Bd. of directors Source Innova, Gainseville, Fla., 1999—2002; pres. exc.director Concepts Intl, Inc, Gainesville, Fla., 1999—2002; advocacy cons. For Youth /Women, Gainesville, Fla., 202. Vol. youth Weed And Seed Program, Gainesville, Fla., 2000—02. Grantee Bus. Grant, state of Fla. GAINESVILLE,FL, 2000. Mem.:

Partners Cmty. (assoc.; parliamentarian 2002). Avocations: interior design, community prohects, fine carfts, fine carfts. Office: Source Innova Concepts Itl Inc 904-A Sw 62nd Ter Gainesville FL 32607 Office Fax: 352-332-8041. E-mail: nssilas@bellsouth.net.

SILAS, PAUL, professional basketball coach; b. Prescott, Ariz. m. Carolyn Silas; children: Paula, Stephen. Student, Creighton U. Mem. St. Louis Hawks, 1964, Phoenix Suns, Boston Celtics, Denver Nuggets, Seattle Supersonics; head coach San Diego Clippers, 1980-83; asst. coach N.J. Nets, 1988-89, 92-95, N.Y. Knicks, 1989-92, Phoenix Suns, Charlotte Hornets, 1997-98, head coach, 1999—. Host ann. corp. basketball tournament for Spl. Olympics, N.Y. Named NBA All-Star, NBA All-Defensive first team, 1975, 76, NBA All-Defensive second team, 1971, 72, 73. Achievements include rank of 14th on the all-time list with 12,357 career boards. Office: New Orleans Hornets 1501 Girod St New Orleans LA 70113*

SILBAJORIS, FRANK RIMVYDAS, Slavic languages educator; b. Kretinga, Lithuania, Jan. 6, 1926; came to U.S., 1949; s. Pranas and Elzbieta (Bagdonaviciute) S.; m. Milda Zamzickaite, Aug. 27, 1955; children: Victoria, Alex BA, Antioch Coll., 1953; MA, Columbia U., 1955; PhD, Columbia U., 1962; D Philology (hon.), Latvian Acad. Scis., Riga, 1991. Instr. to asst. prof. Oberlin Coll., Ohio, 1957-63; assoc. prof. Ohio State U., Columbus, 1963-67, prof. Slavic langs., 1967-91, chmn. dept., 1986-89, prof. emeritus, 1991. Cons. NEH, 1978-79, exchange fellow, USSR, 1977-79; dir. NEH summer seminars, 1975, 77, 83, 84, 86, 88. Author: Russian Versification: The Theories of Trediakovskij, Lomonosov and Kantemir, 1968, Perfection of Exile: Fourteen Contemporary Lithuanian Writers, 1970, Tolstoy's Aesthetics and His Art, 1991, War and Peace. Tolstoy's Mirror of the World, 1995; editor: The Architecture of Reading, 1976, Mind Against the Wall, 1983; contbr. articles to profl. jours. Cons., lectr., organizer cultural events Lithuanian-Am. Community Orgn., 1949— Antioch Coll. scholar, 1950-53; fellow John Hay Whitney Found., 1953-54, Ford Found., 1954-56, Woodrow Wilson Ctr., 1984, IREX, USSR, 1963-64 Mem. Inst. Lithuanian Studies (pres. 1977-82), Assn. Advancement Baltic Studies (pres. 1973-74). Avocations: photography; bicycling; swimming; travel. Home: 4082 Ruxton Ln Columbus OH 43220-4046 also: Ohio State U Dept Slavic Langs Columbus OH 43210 E-mail: silbajoris.1@osu.edu.

SILBER, ALBERT J. lawyer; b. Detroit, Mar. 15, 1912; s. Ben Baruch Silber and Ida (Kogut) S.; m. Merry J. Kurtz, June 9, 1935; children: Michael D., Marc S., Julie E. BA, Wayne State U., 1930; JD magna cum laude, U. Mich., 1932. Bar: Mich. 1933, U.S. Dist. Ct. Mich. 1933. Sec., gen. counsel, dir. Barley Earhart Co., Portland, Mich., 1938, 2B Systems Inc., Sterling Heights, 1976-96; mng. ptnr. Venoy Palmer Ctr., Westland, 1958—, King Investment Co., Dearborn, 1979—. Del. World Jewish Congress, Montreux, Switzerland, 1948; pres. Mich. coun. Am. Jewish Congress, 1949. Inductee Mich. Jewish Sports Hall of Fame, 1993. Fellow: The Order of the Coif; mem.: Mich. Bridge Assn. (pres. 1953—54), Am. Contract Bridge League (Gold Life master), Tau Epsilon Rho (nat. pres. 1950—51). Avocation: playing bridge. Office: Silber and Silber 21700 Northwestern Hwy Ste 900 Southfield MI 48075-4985 Fax: 248 557-1238.

SILBER, JEFFREY LEE, physician; b. Bklyn., June 25, 1958; s. Harry and Charlotte (Bernstein) S.; m. Cynthia Grossel, Nov. 30, 1985; children: Mason Daniel, Ilana Sara. BA, Harvard U., 1980; MD, Albert Einstein Coll. Medicine, 1984. Bd. cert. internal medicine and infectious diseases Am. Bd. Internal Medicine. Intern and resident internal medicine NYU Med. Ctr./Bellevue Hosp. Ctr., N.Y.C., 1984-87; med. dir. Salomon Bros., 1987-88; fellow infectious diseases U. Pa. Med. Ctr., Phila., 1988-90; attending physician Cooper Hosp./UMC, Camden, N.J., 1990-97; assoc. dir. biologics clin. rsch. Merck & Co. Inc., West Point, Pa., 1997-99, dir. biologics clin. rsch., 2000—. Asst. prof. medicine U. Medicine and Dentistry N.J./Robert Wood Johnson Med. Sch., Camden, 1990-97. Grantee Ctrs. for Disease Control and Prevention, Atlanta, 1994-97. Mem. ACP, Infectious Diseases Soc. Am. Office: Merck and Co Inc PO Box 4 Mail Stop UN-C141 West Point PA 19486-0004 E-mail: jeffrey_silber@merck.com.

SILBER, JOHN ROBERT, university chancellor, philosophy and law educator; b. San Antonio, Aug. 15, 1926; s. Paul G. and Jewell (Joslin) S.; m. Kathryn Underwood, July 12, 1947; children: David Joslin (dec.), Mary Rachel, Judith Karen, Kathryn Alexandra, Martha Claire, Laura Ruth, Caroline Jocasta. BA summa cum laude, Trinity U., 1947; postgrad., Northwestern U., summer 1944, Yale Div. Sch., 1947-48, U. Tex. Sch. Law, 1948-49; MA, Yale, 1952, PhD, 1956; L.H.D., Kalamazoo Coll., 1970; many others. Instr. dept. philosophy Yale U., 1952-55; asst. prof. U. Tex., Austin, Austin, 1955-59, asso. prof., 1959-62, prof. philosophy, 1962-70, chmn. dept. philosophy, 1962-67, Univ. prof. arts and letters, 1967-70, chmn. (Comparative Studies Program), 1967, dean (Coll. Arts and Scis.), 1967-70; Univ. prof., prof. philosophy and law Boston U., 1971—, pres., 1971-96, prof. internat. rels., 1996—, chancellor, 1996—. Vis. prof. Bonn U., 1960; fellow Kings Coll. U. London, 1963-64; bd. dirs. Mut. Am. Inst. Funds, Inc. Author: The Ethical Significance of Kant's Religion, 1960, Straight Shooting: What's Wrong With America and How to Fix It, 1989, Ist Amerika zu retten?, 1992; editor: Kant's Religion Within the Limits of Reason Alone, 1960, Works in Continental Philosophy, 1967— ; assoc. editor: Kant-Studien, 1968-87; contbr. to profl. jours. Chmn. Tex. Soc. to Abolish Capital Punishment, 1960-69; mem. Nat. Commn. United Meth. Higher Edn., 1974-77; exec. bd. Nat. Humanities Inst., 1975-78; trustee Coll. St. Scholastica, 1973-85, U. Denver, 1985-89, WGBH Ednl. Found., 1971-96, Adelphi U., 1989-97; bd. visitors Air U., 1974-80; bd. dirs. Greater Boston coun. Boy Scouts Am., 1981-93, v.p. fin., 1981-93, Silver Beaver award, 1989, Disting. Eagle, 1997; mem. Nat. Humanities Faculty, 1968-73, Nat. Captioning Inst., 1985-94; bd. advisors Matchette Found., 1969-70; mem. Nat. Bipartisan Commn. on Ctrl. Am., 1983-84, Presdl. Adv. Bd. Radio Broadcasting to Cuba, 1985-92; adv. bd. Schurman Libr. of Am. Hist., Ruprecht-Karl U., Heidelberg, 1986—, Jamestown Found., 1989—; mem. def. policy bd. U.S. Dept. Def., 1987-90; mem. internat. coun.advisors Inst. for Humanities at Salado, 1988—; bd. dirs. New Eng. Holocaust Meml. Com., 1989—, Brit. Inst. of U.S., 1989—, Bette Davis Found., 1997—, Boston Police Found., 1997—; Dem. gubernatorial candidate of Mass., 1990; vice chmn. U.S. Strategic Inst.; bd. dirs., vice chmn. Americans for Med. Progress, 1992—, chmn., 1994-95, mem. exec. com. 1995—; chmn. Mass. Bd. Edn., 1996-99; bd. advisors Nat. Assn. Scholars. Recipient E. Harris Harbison award for disting. tchg. Danforth Found., 1966, Wilbur Lucius Cross medal Yale Grad. Sch., 1971, Outstanding Civilian Svc. medal U.S. Army, 1985, Disting. Pub. Svc. award Anti-Defamation League of B'nai B'rith, 1989, Horatio Alger award, 1992, Am.-Swiss Friendship award, 1991, Israel Peace medal, 1985, Ehrenmedaille U. Heidelberg, 1986, White House Small Bus. award for entrepreneurial excellence, 1986, Cross of Paideia, Greek Orthodox Archdiocese of North and South Am., 1988, Pro Bene Meritis award U. Tex., Austin, 1997; Fulbright rsch. fellow Germany, 1959-60; Guggenheim fellow Eng., 1963-64; decorated with Knight Comdr.'s Cross with Star of Order of Merit Fed. Republic of Germany, 1983; commandeur Nat. Order of Arts and Letters (France), 1985. Fellow Royal Soc. Arts; mem. Am. Philos. Assn., Am. Soc. Polit. and Legal Philosophy, Royal Inst. Philosophy, Am. Assn. Higher Edn., Nat. Assn. Ind. Colls. and Univs. (dir. 1976-81), Phi Beta Kappa. Office: Boston U 147 Bay State Rd Boston MA 02215-1708*

SILBER, NORMAN JULES, lawyer; b. Tampa, Fla., Apr. 18, 1945; s. Abe and Mildred (Hirsch) Silber; m. Linda Geraldine Hirsch, June 10, 1979; 1 child Michael Hirsch. BA, Tulane U., 1967, JD, 1969; postgrad. in bus. adminstrn., NYU, 1970—72. Bar: Fla. 1970, U.S. Dist. Ct. (so. dist.) Fla. 1975, U.S. Tax Ct. 1975, U.S. Ct. Appeals (5th cir.) 1975, U.S. Ct. Appeals (11th cir.) 1981. With legal dept. Fiduciary Trust Co. N.Y., N.Y.C., 1969—72, asst. trust officer, 1971—72; exec. v.p. I.R.E. Fin. Corp., Miami, Fla., 1972—76; mng. atty. Norman J. Silber, P.A., 1973—85; ptnr. McDermott, Will & Emery, 1985—2001, Ruden, McClosky, Smith, Schuster & Russell, P.A., 2001—. Mem.: Fla. Bar (chmn. 11th jud. cir. grievance com. 1982—84). Republican. Jewish. Home: 1232 Palermo Ave Miami FL 33134-6327 Office: Ruden McClosky Smith Schuster & Russell PA 701 Brickell Ave Fl 19 Miami FL 33131

SILBERBERG, DONALD H. neurologist; b. Washington, Mar. 2, 1934; s. William Aaron and Leslie Frances (Stone) S.; m. Marilyn Alice Damsky, June 7, 1959; children: Mark, Alan. MD, U. Mich., 1958; MA (hon.), U. Pa., 1971. Intern Mt. Sinai Hosp., N.Y.C., 1958-59; clin. assoc. in neurology NIH, Bethesda, Md., 1959-61; Fulbright scholar Nat. Hosp., London, 1961-62; NINDB spl. fellow in neuro-ophthalmology Washington U., St. Louis, 1962-63; assoc. neurology U. Pa., 1963-65, asst. prof., 1965-67, assoc. prof., 1967-71, prof., 1971-73, acting chmn. dept., 1973-74, prof., vice chmn. neurology, 1974-82, chmn., 1982-94, sr. assoc. dean, dir. internat. programs, 1994—. Active staff U. Pa. Med. Ctr., Phila.; cons. Children's Hosp., Phila.; pres., CEO Betasteron Found., Inc., 1994—. Contbr. articles to profl. jours., abstracts, chpts. in books. Recipient grants in study of multiple sclerosis. Mem.: World Fedn. Neurology, Soc. Neurosci., Phila. Neurol. Soc. (pres. 1978—79), Assn. Univ. Profs. Neurology (pres.-elect 1993), Nat. Multiple Sclerosis Soc. (trustee 1997-99 2001—), John Morgan Soc. U. Pa. (pres. 1974—75), Internat. Soc. Neurochemistry, Internat. Soc. Devel. Neuroscis., Internat. Brain Rsch. Orgn., Coll. Physicians Phila., Am. Soc. Neurochemistry, Am. Neurol. Assn., Am. Acad. Neurology, Alpha Omega Alpha. Office: U Pa Med Ctr Dept Neurology 3400 Spruce St Philadelphia PA 19104-4206

SILBERBERG, INGA, dermatologist; b. Kassel, Germany, Sept. 16, 1934; came to U.S., 1938; d. Willi and Erna (Rosenbaum) S.; m. Herbert M. Sinakin, Feb. 16, 1969; 1 child, William Elias. BA, Hunter Coll., 1955; MD, SUNY, 1959; MS in Dermatology, NYU, 1965. Diplomate Am. Bd. Dermatologists, 1964. Instr., clin. dermatology NYU Med. Ctr., N.Y.C., 1963-65, clin. asst. prof., 1965-66, asst. prof. dermatology, 1966-71, clin. assoc. prof. dermatology, 1971-76; cons., dermatology Newcomb Hosp., Vineland, N.J., 1975-98. Recipient Henry Silver award Dermatologic Soc. Greater N.Y., 1962, 65, Dermatology Found. Discovery award, 1993, Dr. Rose Hirschler award Women's Dermatologic Soc., 1999; Jonas Salk scholar, City of N.Y., 1955-59. Fellow Am. Acad. Dermatology; mem. AMA. E-mail: hmsina@pol.net.

SILBERBERG, RICHARD HOWARD, lawyer; b. N.Y.C., Feb. 20, 1951; BA, U. Wis., 1972; JD, NYU, 1975. Bar: N.Y. 1976, U.S. Dist. Ct. (so. and ea. dists.) N.Y., 1976, U.S. Ct. Appeals (2d cir.) 1982, U.S. Ct. Internat. Trade 1983, U.S. Ct. Appeals (3d cir.) 1991, U.S. Supreme Ct. 1994, U.S. Ct. Appeals (11th cir.) 1996, U.S. Ct. Appeals (1st cir.) 1997. Assoc. Delson & Gordon, N.Y.C., 1975-83, ptnr., 1983-87, Dorsey & Whitney, N.Y.C., 1988—, mng. ptnr., 1994-97. Mem. panel arbitrators U.S. Dist. Ct. for Ea. Dist. N.Y., 1987—; mem. panel mediators U.S. Dist. Ct. for So. Dist. N.Y., 1992—; trustee Lawyers Com. for Civil Rights Under Law, 1992—; dir. Fund for Modern Cts., 1999—, High 5 Tickets to the Arts, 1999—. Mng. editor NYU Jour. Internat. Law and Politics, 1974-75. Office: Dorsey & Whitney LLP 250 Park Ave New York NY 10177-0001 Business E-Mail: silberberg.richard@dorseylaw.com.

SILBERFARB, PETER MICHAEL, psychiatrist, educator; b. Jersey City, Oct. 28, 1938; m. Anne Wagner, 1962; children: Benjamin, Leah S. BS, Bucknell U., 1960; postgrad., NYU, 1960-61; MD, Hahnemann Coll., 1965; MA (hon.), Dartmouth Coll., 1986. Diplomate Nat. Bd. Med. Examiners, Am. Bd. Psychiatry and Neurology (pres. 1998). Intern Hahnemann Med. Coll. Hosp., Phila., 1965-66; resident in internal medicine Dartmouth Affiliated Hosps., Hanover, N.H., 1966-68, resident in internal medicine and psychiatry, 1968-69, psychiatry resident, 1971-72, chief resident in psychiatry, 1972-73; instr. in psychiatry Med. Sch., Dartmouth Coll., 1972-73, asst. prof. of psychiatry, 1973-77, dir. tng. and edn., 1976-86, assoc. prof. clin. psychiatry, assoc. prof. clin. medicine, 1977-80, dir. grad. edn. and residency tng., 1978-86, assoc. prof. psychiatry, assoc. prof. medicine, 1980-82, dir. tng. and edn., 1984—, prof. psychiatry, prof. medicine, 1986—, chmn. dept. psychiatry, 1986—, Raymond Sobel prof. psychiatry, 1993. Cons. psychiatrist Mary Hitchcock Meml. Hosp., Hanover, 1973—; dir. psychiat. in-patient svc. Dartmouth-Hitchcock Med. Ctr., 1973-75, dir. cancer psychiatry program Norris Cotton Cancer Ctr., 1975—, acting dir. psychiatry consultation svc., 1977-79, assoc. dir. cancer control Norris Ctr., 1981-86; sec. psychiatry com. Cancer and Leukemia Group B, 1976-79, vice chmn., 1979—; mem. grant rev. com. for cancer control Nat. Cancer Inst., 1979, 80, mem. spl. grant rev. com., 1981, 82, 85, cons. to bd. sci. counselors, 1982, mem. cancer control grant rev. com., 1986-90; vice chmn. adv. com. for psychosocial and behavioral rsch. Am. Cancer Soc., 1982-88, chmn., 1988-89; cons. collaborative ctr. for cancer pain relief WHO, Milan, 1985; mem. accreditation coun. for grad. med. edn. Appeals Bd. for Psychiatry, Chgo., 1983, specialist site visitor, 1985-90, mem. residency rev. com. for psychiatry, 1991—; dir. Am. Bd. Family Practice, 1996—; mem. exec. com. Am. Bd. Med. Specialties, 1996-99. Author chpts. to books; mem. editl. bd. Jour. Psychosocial Oncology, 1983-91, Internat. Jour. Psychiatry in Medicine, 1986-90, Contemporary Psychiatry, 1987-91, Psychooncology, 1991—; referee numerous manuscripts; contbr. articles to profl. jours. Surgeon USPHS, 1969-71. Fellow Am. Psychiat. Assn. (cons. to task force on treatment if psychiat. disorders 1989), Am. Coll. Psychiatrists; mem. AMA, Am. Soc. Psychiat. Oncology/AIDS, Am. Soc. Clin. Oncology, Am. Assn. Dirs. Psychiat. Residency Tng. (mem. curriculum com. 1979-88, mem. task force on med. students and residents, chmn. com. regional dirs. 1984-88, mem. exec. com. 1984-88), Am. Psychosomatic Soc., N.H. Psychiat. Soc. (chmn. membership com. 1974-76, chmn. continuing edn. com. 1977-79), N.H. Med. Soc., Assn. Rsch. in Nervous and Mental Disease, Assn. Acad. Psychiatry, Benjamin Rush Soc. Home: Bragg Hill Norwich VT 05055 Office: Dartmouth Coll Med Sch Dept Psychiatry Lebanon NH 03756-0001

SILBERFARB, STEPHEN RUSSELL, lawyer; b. Washington, Feb. 16, 1962; s. Robert Michael and Marcia Cohan Silberfarb; m. Laura Anne Oliven, May 30, 1993; children: Rebecca Avital, Gauriela Channah. BA in Govt., U. Md., 1987; JD, Columbus Sch. Law, 1997. Bar: Md. 1997, D.C. 1998, Minn. 1999. Legis. liaison Am. Israel Pub. Affairs Com., Washington, 1984-91; legis. dir. U.S. Rep. Wayne Owens, 1991-93, U.S. Rep. Peter Deutsch, Washington, 1993; spl. asst. U.S. Office Personnel Mgmt., 1993-96; pvt. practice, 1997-99; dep. exec. dir., gen. counsel Nat. Jewish Dem. Coun., 1996-99; exec. dir. Jewish Cmty. Rels. Coun. of Minn. and the Dakotas, 1999—. Pro bono counsel Hoop Dreams, Washington, 1998. Md. State Senatorial scholar U. Md., 1980-84. Mem. Internat. Assn. Jewish Lawyers and Jurists, Jewish Cmty. Coun. (chair Israel and Internat. affairs commn. 1994-97, officer 1997-99). Avocations: ice hockey, carpentry. Office: 12 N 12th St Ste 480 Minneapolis MN 55403 E-mail: stephen@minndakJCRC.org.

SILBERG, CAROL ANN SCHWARTZ, cultural organization administrator, consultant; b. Balt., June 8, 1948; d. Aaron Huron and Reba Isabel (Gottlieb) Schwartz; m. Steven Edward Silberg, Aug. 10, 1968; 1 child, Elizabeth Ellis Silberg. BS, U. Md., 1971, PhD, 1990; MA, Cen. Mich. U., 1980. Freelance journalist, 1968-74; sci. editor Raytheon Svc. Co., Hyattsville, Md., 1974-75; press sec. U.S. Congress, Washington, 1975; pres. Silberg & Assocs., Inc., Balt. and Washington, 1976-82; dir. coll. rels. Prince George's Community Coll., Largo, Md., 1982-86; exec. dir. Prince George's Community Found., Inc., Bowie, 1986-94, Nat. Fund for Patuxent Wildlife Visitor Ctr., Largo, 1988-92, Prince George's Community Found., Inc., Bowie, 1994—; asst. prof. grad. sch. U. Md. U. Coll., 1992—. Adj. asst. prof. U.Md., 1992—; mgmt. cons. in field, 1982—; fundraising cons. in field, 1986—. Author, co-author: Talking the Mystery Out of Cable TV, 1984. Member Israeli friendship com. Sisters Cities Program, Upper Marlboro, Md., 1991; pres. College Park (Md.) Bus. and Profl. Women, 1980; bd. dirs. Prince Georgians on Camera, Largo, 1982-87; chair local bd. Selective Svc. System, Bowie, 1991. Exxon Corp. grantee, 1985, Ind. U. grantee, 1991; recipient Citation, Gov. of Md., 1982. Mem. Nat. Soc. Fund Raising Execs., Ind. Soc. Fund Raising Execs. (assoc.), Nat. Fedn. Bus. and Profl. Women (Nat. Program award 1983, 84), Prince George's County Pub. Rels. Assn., Prince George's C. of C. Jewish. Avocations: swimming, walking, photography, travel. Home: 13203 Marthas Choice Cir Bowie MD 20720-4705

SILBERGELD, ARTHUR F. lawyer; b. St. Louis, June 1, 1942; s. David and Sabina (Silbergeld) S.; m. Carol Ann Schwartz, may 1, 1970; children: Diana Lauren, Julia Kay. BA, U. Mich., 1968; M in City Planning, U. Pa., 1971; JD, Temple U., 1975. Bar: N.Y. 1976, Calif. 1978, D.C. 1983, U.S. Ct. Appeals (2nd cir.), U.S. Ct. Appeals (9th cir.), U.S. Ct. Appeals (D.C. cir.), U.S. Supreme Ct. 1999. Assoc. Vladeck, Elias, Vladeck & Lewis, N.Y.C., 1975-77; field atty. NLRB, L.A., 1977-78; ptnr., head employment law practice group McKenna, Conner & Cuneo, 1978-89; ptnr. Graham & James, 1990-96; labor ptnr. Sonnenschein Nath & Rosenthal, 1996-99; ptnr. Proskauer Rose LLP, 1999—. Instr. extension divsn. UCLA, 1981-89. Author: Doing Business in California: An Employment Law Handbook, 2nd edit., 1997, Advising California Employers, 1990, 91, 93, 94, 95 supplements; contbr. articles to profl. jours. Founding mem. L.A. Mus. Contemporary Art; bd. dirs. Bay Cities unit Am. Cancer Soc., Calif., 1981-85, Jewish Family Svc., L.A., 1981-85, So. Calif. Employers Roundtable, Leadership coun., So. Poverty Law Ctr., L.A., Child Devel. Ctr., 1998—, Leadership Task Force, Drs. Without Borders; pres. Mo. Valley Fedn. of Temple Youth, 1959-60. Mem. L.A. County Bar Assn. (chair labor and employment law sect. 1999-2000, trustee 2000-01), Mus. Modern Art (N.Y.C.), Aperture Found., Coll. of Labor and Employment Lawyers. Office: Proskauer Rose LLP 2049 Century Park E Fl 32 Los Angeles CA 90067-3101

SILBERGELD, CAROL A. clinical social worker, psychotherapist; b. Bklyn., July 10, 1948; d. Albert Schwartz and Alice Halperin Sachs; m. Arthur F. Silbergeld, May 1, 1970; children: Diana, Julia. BA cum laude, Goucher Coll., 1969; MSS, Bryn Mawr Coll., 1973. Lic. clin. social worker. Psychiatric social worker Balt. City Hosps., 1969-70; Hahnemann Hosp., Phila., 1970-75; clin. social worker, cons. Jewish Family and Children's Svcs., N.Y.C., 1975-77; pvt. practice, 1975—; supr., therapist Reiss-Davis Child Study Ctr., L.A., 1977-83, dir. children divorce clinic, 1980-98, co-dir. postgrad. tng., 1983-94, dir. clin. social work, 1983-95, mem. faculty, supervising cons., 1995—; dir. children divorce project L.A. Child Devel. Ctr., 1998—; dir. program devel. Safety Zone, Santa Monica, Calif., 1999—2002. Contbg. author: Social Work in Health Settings, 1993; author: Meeting Children on Their Own Grounds, 1999. Fellow Calif. Soc. Clin. Social Work; mem. ACSW, NASW. Office: 2730 Wilshire Blvd Ste 250 Santa Monica CA 90403-4749

SILBERGELD, ELLEN KOVNER, environmental epidemiologist, researcher, toxicologist; b. Washington, July 29, 1945; d. Joseph and Mary (Gion) Kovner; m. Alan Mark Silbergeld, 1969; children: Sophia, Nicholas. AB, Vassar Coll., 1967; PhD, Johns Hopkins U., 1972. Kennedy fellow Johns Hopkins Med. Sch., Balt., 1974—75; scientist NIH, Bethesda, 1975—81; chief toxics scientist Environ. Def. Fund, Washington, 1982—90; prof. epidemiology, toxicology and pharmacology U.Md., Balt., 1990—2001, affil. prof. environ. law, 1990—2001, dir. program in human health and environ., 1996—2000, prof. dept. pathology toxicology, 1995—2000, adj. prof. dept. pharmacology and exptl. therapeutics, 1995—2000; Prof. Environ. Health Scis. Bloomberg School of Public Health, Johns Hopkins U., 2002—. Scientist NIH, 1982—84; mem. sci. adv. bd. EPA, 1983—89, 1993—99, Dept. Energy, 1994—95; mem. bd. on environ. sci. and toxicology NAS-NRC, 1983—89; mem. com. geosci. environment and resources, 1994—98; mem. bd. biotech. and agr., 1999—; mem. bd. sci. counselors Nat. Inst. Environ. Health Scis., 1987—93; cons. Oil and Chem. Atomic Workers, 1970, NSF, 1974—75, OECD, 1987—90. Mem. editl. bd.: Neurobehavioral Toxicology, 1979—87, mem. editl. bd.: Am. Medicine, 1980—, mem. editl. bd.: Neurotoxicology, 1981—86, mem. editl. bd.: Environ. Health, 1986—, mem. editl. bd.: Environ. Rsch., 1983—, editor-in-chief: , 1994—. Mem. Homewood Friends Meeting. Recipient Wolman award, Md. Pub. Health Assn., 1991, Barsky award, APHA, 1992, Md. Gov. Excellence citation, 1990, 1993, Fulbright fellow, London, 1967; fellow Woodrow Wilson and Danforth fellow, 1967, NAS exch. fellow, Yugoslavia, 1976, MacArthur Found. fellow, 1993—98; scholar Baldwin scholar, Coll. Notre Dame. Mem.: APHA, AAAS, Soc. for Neurosci., Soc. Toxicology, Soc. for Occupl. and Environ. Health (sec.-treas. 1983—85, pres. 1987—89), Am. Soc. Tropical Med. Hygiene, Am. Soc. Pharmacology and Exptl. Therapeutics, Collegium Ramazzini, Phi Beta Kappa (councillor). Office: Bloomberg School of Public Health 615 N. Wolfe St. Baltimore MD 21205

SILBERGELD, JEROME LESLIE, art historian, educator; b. Highland, Ill., Apr. 25, 1944; s. David and Sabina Silbergeld; m. Michelle DeKlyen, June 27, 1970; children: David, Emily. BA in History, Stanford U., 1966, MA in History, 1967, PhD in Art History, 1974; MA in Art History, U. Oreg., 1972. Vis. asst. prof. dept. art history U. Oreg., Eugene, 1974-75; from asst. prof. to prof. U. Wash., Seattle, 1975-2001, chmn. art history dept., 1988-92, dir. sch. art, 1992-96; Donald E. Petersen prof. arts, 2000-01; vis. prof. dept. fine arts Harvard U., Cambridge, Mass., 1996; P.Y. and Kinmay W. Tang family of Chinese art history Princeton U., 2001—, dir. Tang Ctr. for Chinese and Japanese Art, 2001—. Author: Chinese Painting Style, 1982 (Soc. for Tech. Achievement award 1983), Mind Landscapes: The Painting of C.C. Wang, 1987, Contradictions: Artistic Life, the Socialist State, and the Chinese Painter Li Huasheng, 1993 (among N.Y. Times Notable Books of 1993), China into Film: Frames of Reference in Contemporary Chinese Cinema, 1999; editor, translator: Chinese Painting Colors (Yu Fei'an) 1988; contbr. articles to profl. jours. Grantee Nat. Endowment for Humanities, 1981, 92, J. Paul Getty Trust, 1987. Mem. Assn. Asian Studies, Coll. Art Assn. Avocations: classical piano, long-distance running. Office: Princeton U Dept Art & Archaeology Princeton NJ 08544-0108 E-mail: jsil@princeton.edu.

SILBERGLEIT, ALLEN, surgeon, researcher, medical educator; b. Springfield, Mass., Mar. 8, 1928; s. Harry and Frances Bennett Silbergleit; m. Ina Richman; children: Richard, Nina, Robert. BA, U. Mass., 1949, MS, 1951; MD, U. Cin., 1955; PhD, Wayne State U., 1965. Diplomate Am. Bd. Surgery, Am. Bd. Thoracic Surgery. Tchg. fellow in zoology U. of Mass., Amherst, Mass., 1949—50; fellow and resident in surgery U. of Minn., Mpls., 1955—60; from instr. surgery to prof. surgery & physiology Wayne State U. Sch. Medicine, Detroit, 1962—88, prof. surgery & physiology, 1988—. Program dir. surg. residency St. Joseph Mercy Oakland, Pontiac, Mich., 1966—, dir. dept. of surgery, 1984—; chmn. surgery com. OHEP-Wayne State U. Consortium, Detroit, 1980—; mem. inst. rev. bd. Oakland U., Rochester, Mich., 1987—. Associate editor: Detroit Med. News, 2002; contbr. articles to profl. jours. Judge Detroit & Mich. Sci. Fairs, Detroit, 1999, 2000 Intel Internat. Sci. & Engring. Fair, Detroit, 2000. Capt. USAF, 1960—62, Shepard AFB, Wichita Falls, Tex. Named one of Top Twenty Milestones - 20th Century World/Nat. Firsts, Am. Coll. Cardiology, Mich. chpt., 2000. Fellow: ACS (gov. 1990—96); mem.: Am. Trauma Soc. (founding mem.), Mich. Soc. of Thoracic & Cardiovasc. Surgeons (pres. 1990). Avocations: socializing, dancing, active and spectator sports. Office: St Joseph Mercy Oakland 44405 Woodward Avenue Pontiac MI 48341-2985 Fax: 248-858-3244., 248-858-3244. Personal E-mail: Silberga@trinity-health.org. Business E-Mail: silberga@trinity-health.org.

SILBERLING, STEPHEN PIERCE, lawyer; b. Far Rockaway, N.Y., Feb. 14, 1950; s. Edwyn and Margaret Ann Silberling; 1 child, Beverly June. BA, Haverford Coll., 1971; MA, U. Toronto, Ont., Can., 1973; JD, Vanderbilt U., 1979. Bar: Tenn. 1979, U.S. Dist. Ct. (mid. dist.) Tenn. 1979, U.S. Dist. Ct. (we. dist.) Tenn. 1980, Mo. 1980, U.S. Ct. Appeals (6th and 8th cirs.) 1980, N.Y. 1985, U.S. Dist. Ct. (ea. dist.) N.Y. 1985, U.S. Supreme Ct. 1991. Co-author: (book) Shopping the Insiders Way, 1985. Office: Silberling & Silberling Fed Plz 300 Rabro Dr Hauppauge NY 11788-4256

SILBERMAN, ALAN HARVEY, lawyer; b. Chgo., Oct. 22, 1940; s. Milton J. and Mollie E. (Hymanson) S.; m. Margaret Judith Auslander, Nov. 17, 1968; children: Elena, Mark. BA with distinction, Northwestern U., 1961; LLB, Yale U., 1964. Bar: Ill. 1964, U.S. Dist. Ct. (no. dist.) Ill. 1966, U.S. Ct. Appeals (7th cir.) 1970, (5th and 9th cir.) 1977, (D.C. cir.) 1979, (4th cir.) 1980, (11th cir.) 1981, (3rd cir.) 1982, (8th and 10th cirs.) 1993, U.S. Supreme Ct. 1978. Law clk. U.S. Dist. Ct., Chgo., 1964-66; assoc. Sonneschein Nath & Rosenthal, 1964-71, ptnr., 1972—. Mem. antitrust adv. bd. Bur. Nat. Affairs, Washington, 1985—; mem. Ill. Atty. Gen. Franchise Adv. Bd., 1996—. Contbr. articles to profl. jours. Bd. dirs., v.p., sec. Camp Ramah in Wisc., Inc., Chgo., 1966-86, pres., 1986-94; bd. dirs. Nat. Ramah Commn., Inc. of Jewish Theol. Sem. Am., N.Y.C., 1970—, v.p., 1986-94, pres., 1994-99, sr. v.p., 1999—; mem. U.S. del. 33d World Zionist Congress, Jerusalem, 1997, 34th World Zionist Congress, Jerusalem, 2002. Mem. ABA (chmn. antitrust sect. FTC com. 1981-83, chmn. nat. insts. 1983-85, mem. coun. antitrust sect. 1985-88, fin. officer 1988-90, sect. del. ho. of dels. 1990-92, chmn.-elect 1992-93, chmn. 1993-94), Ill. Bar Assn. (chmn. antitrust sect. 1975-76), Northwestern U. 1851 Soc. (chair 1994-97). Home: 430 Oakdale Ave Glencoe IL 60022-2113 Office: Sonnenschein Nath 233 S Wacker Dr Ste 8000 Chicago IL 60606-6491

SILBERMAN, CHARLOTTE SCHATZBERG, retired lawyer, artist; b. N.Y.C., Oct. 15, 1918; d. Louis and Annie (Hammerman) Schatzberg; m. Bernard Silberman, Sept. 24, 1942 (dec. Mar. 1991); children: Adela Wagman, Margery Miller Moores. BA, Hunter Coll., 1938; LLB, JD, Bklyn. Law Sch.,

1940; postgrad., SUNY, Albany, 1977-84, Fla. Atlantic U., 1984—. Bar: N.Y. 1941. Pvt. practice law, N.Y.C., 1940-43, Albany, N.Y., 1947-57; atty. State N.Y., 1957-63; assoc. counsel SUNY, 1963-74, dir. paralegal studies, 1975-77. Works exhibited Soc. of Four Arts, 1990, Cornell Mus., Delray Beach, Fla., 1994, 95. Home: 7076 Huntington Ln Apt 401 Delray Beach FL 33446-2554

SILBERMAN, EDWARD KENNETH, physician, educator; b. N.Y.C., Dec. 28, 1944; s. Alfred D. and Lillian J. (Simon) S.; m. Barbara Warnick, Sept. 21, 1975; children: Michael John, Peter Warnick. BA, Yale U., 1965; MD, Tufts U., 1974. Diplomate Nat. Bd. Med. Examiners, Am. Bd. Psychiatry and Neurology. Clin. assoc. Nat. Inst. Mental Health, Bethesda, 1977-82; resident in psychiatry Mass. Mental Health Ctr., Boston, 1974-77; clin. fellow in psychiatry Harvard Med. Sch., 1974-77; asst. to assoc. prof. psychiatry USUHS, Bethesda, Md., 1982-86; dir. residency edn., assoc. prof. psychiatry Med. Coll. of Pa., Phila., 1986-92; dir. of residency edn., clin. prof. psychiatry Jefferson Med. Coll., 1992—. Editor: (book) Successful Psychiatric Practice; co-editor: Handbook of Psychiatric Education and Faculty Development, 1999; contbr. numerous articles to profl. jours., publs. and textbooks. Surgeon USPHS, 1977-82. Recipient Outstanding Svc. medal Uniformed Svcs. Univ. of the Health Scis., Bethesda, 1986. Fellow: Am. Psychiat. Assn.; mem.: Assn. for Acad. Psychiatry (pres.-elect 2002), Am. Assn. of Dirs. of Residency Tng. in Psychiatry (mem. exec. coun. 1988—), Am. Coll. Psychiatrists. Home: 619 W Upsal St Philadelphia PA 19119-3627 Office: Jefferson Med Coll 1020 Sansom St Philadelphia PA 19107-5002 E-mail: edward.k.@mail.tju.edu.

SILBERMAN, ENRIQUE, physics researcher and administrator; b. Buenos Aires, Dec. 9, 1921; came to U.S., 1966; m. 1949; 2 children. PhD in Engring., U. Buenos Aires, 1945. Investigator physics Argentina Atomic Energy Commn., Buenos Aires, 1953-58; head dept. Arg AEC, 1958-63; prof. U. Buenos Aires, 1963-66; prof. physics Fisk U., Nashville, 1966—; dir. photonic materials and devices NASA Ctr., 1992—. Guest prof. U. Notre Dame, 1963; cons. Arg Nat. Coun. Sci. Rsch., 1964; vis. prof. Vanderbilt U., 1967—. Mem. AAAS, Am. Assn. Physics Tchrs., Am. Phys. Soc., Arg Physics Assn. Office: Fisk U Dept Physics Nashville TN 37208-3051

SILBERMAN, H. LEE, public relations executive, editorial consultant; b. Newark, Apr. 26, 1919; s. Louis and Anna (Horel) S.; m. Ruth Irene Rapp, June 5, 1948; children: Richard Lyle, Gregory Alan, Todd Walter. BA, U. Wis., 1940. Radio continuity writer Radio Sta. WTAQ, Green Bay, Wis., 1940-41; reporter Bayonne (N.J.) Times, 1941-42; sales exec. War Assets Adminstrn., Chgo., 1946-47; copy editor Acme Newspictures, 1947; reporter, editl. writer Wichita (Kans.) Eagle, 1948-55; reporter Wall St. Jour., N.Y.C., 1955-57, banking editor, 1957-68; 1st v.p., dir. corp. rels. Shearson-Hamill & Co., N.Y.C., 1968-74; N.Y. corr. Economist of London, 1966-72; from contbg. editor to editor in chief Finance mag., 1970-76; from v.p., dir. to exec. v.p. Fin. Svcs. Group, Carl Boyir & Assos., Inc., N.Y.C., 1976-86, exec. v.p., 1981-86; sr. counselor Hill & Knowlton, Inc., 1986-93, sr. v.p., 1993-96, sr. mng. dir., 1996; pres. LSA Media Cons., 1997—. Cons. in field. Contbr. articles to profl. jours. Capt. C.E. AUS, 1942-46. Recipient Loeb Mag. award U. Conn., 1965; Loeb Achievement award for disting. writing on fin. Gerald M. Loeb Found., 1968 Mem. Soc. Profl. Journalists, Soc. Silurians, N.Y. Fin. Writers Assn., Deadline Club N.Y., Zeta Beta Tau. Republican. Home and Office: 475 E 2nd St Clayton NC 27520-2558

SILBERMAN, HAROLD REITER, retired internist; b. Newark, June 6, 1931; MD, Washington U., 1956. Diplomate Am. Bd. Internal Medicine, Am. Bd. Hematology, Am. Bd. Oncology. Intern Duke Univ. Hosp., Durham, N.C., 1956-57, resident, 1960-61, Durham VA Hosp., 1961-62; fellow in rheumatology Duke U. Hosp., 1957-58, fellow in hematology/oncology, 1962-64; clin. dir. Fed. Prison Hosp., 2000—02; ret. Fellow Am. Coll. Physicians; mem. Am. Soc. Hematology, Alpha Omega Alpha. Office: 4 Chiswell Ct Durham NC 27705-6441

SILBERMAN, LAURENCE HIRSCH, federal judge; b. York, Pa., Oct. 12, 1935; s. William and Anna (Hirsch) S.; m. Rosalie G. Gaull, Apr. 28, 1957; children: Robert Stephen, Katherine DeBoer Balaban, Anne Gaull Otis. BA, Dartmouth Coll., 1957; LLB, Harvard U., 1961. Bar: Hawaii 1962, D.C. 1973. Assoc. Moore, Torkildson & Rice and Quinn & Moore, Honolulu, 1961-64; ptnr. Moore, Silberman & Schulze, 1964-67; atty. appellate divsn. gen. counsel's office NLRB, Washington, 1967-69; solicitor of labor U.S. Dept. Labor, 1969-70, undersec. labor, 1970-73; ptnr. Steptoe & Johnson, 1973-74; dep. atty. gen. U.S., 1974-75; amb. to Yugoslavia, 1975-77; mng. ptnr. Morrison & Foerster, Washington, 1978-79, 83-85; exec. v.p. Crocker Nat. Bank, San Francisco, 1979-83; judge U.S. Ct. Appeals (D.C. cir.), Washington, 1985—. Lectr. labor law and legis. U. Hawaii, 1962—63; adj. prof. adminstrv. law Georgetown U., Washington, 1987—94, Washington, 1997, Washington, 1999—2001, NYU, 1995, 96, Harvard U., 1998; lectr. labor law Georgetown U., Washington, 2001; Pres.' spl. envoy on ILO affairs, 1976; gen. adv. com. on Arms Control and Disarmament, 1981—85; mem. Def. Policy Bd., 1981—85; vice-chmn. State Dept.'s Commn. on Security and Econ. Assistance, 1983—84. Bd. dirs. Com. on Present Danger, 1978-85, Inst. for Ednl. Affairs, 1981-85; vice chmn. adv. coun. on gen. govt. Rep. Nat. Com., 1977-80. With AUS, 1957-58. Am. Enterprise Inst. sr. fellow, 1977-78, vis. fellow 1978-85. Mem. U.S. Fgn. Intelligence Surveillance Act Ct. of Rev., Coun. on Fgn. Rels.

SILBERMAN, ROBERT A. S. lawyer; b. Lebanon, Pa., Mar. 4, 1945; s. Henry T. and Genevieve (Mensh) S.; m. Nancy D. Netzer, Nov. 10, 1974. BA magna cum laude, Yale U., 1967; JD, Harvard U., 1970. Bar: Mass. 1970, Pa. 1984. Assoc. Csaplar & Bok, Boston, 1970-78, ptnr., 1978-90, Gaston & Snow, Boston, 1990-91, Edwards & Angell, Boston, 1991-2000, Erickson Schaffer Peterson Israel & Silberman PC, Wellesley, Mass., 2000—. Mem. editl. bd. Managed Care Law Strategist, monthly newsletter/Am. Lawyer Media, 1999-2001. Mem. citizens rev. com. United Way Massachusetts Bay, Boston, 1981-89; dir. All Newton (Mass.) Music Sch., 1994-96, v.p., 1995-96; bd. overseers Boston Baroque, 1998-2000; bd. dirs., chair bd. overseers Boston Baroque, 2000—. Mem. ABA (vice chmn. health law com. sect. bus. law 1992-95, chmn., 1995-99), Internat. Bar Assn., Boston Bar Assn., Nat. Health Lawyers Assn., Phi Beta Kappa. Office: Erickson Schaffer et al Ste 150 20 William St Wellesley MA 02481 Office Fax: 781-235-1571. E-mail: rass@esplaw.com.

SILBERSACK, MARK LOUIS, lawyer; b. Cin., Dec. 27, 1946; s. Joseph Leo and Rhoda Marie (Hinkler) S.; m. Ruth Ann Schwallie, Sept. 7, 1985. AB, Boston Coll., 1968; JD, U. Chgo., 1971. Bar: Ohio 1971, U.S. Dist. Ct. (so. dist.) Ohio 1973, U.S. Ct. Appeals (6th cir.) 1974, U.S. Supreme Ct. 1975. Atty. Dinsmore & Shohl, Cin., 1971—. Lectr. Ohio CLE Inst., Columbus, 1981-91. Co-author: Managed Care: The PPO Experience, 1990, Information Sharing Among Health Care Providers, 1994. Bd. dirs. United Way, Cmty. Chest, 1985-89, 2001—, chmn. pub. policy com., 1998—; vice-chmn. Ohio United Way, Columbus, 1989-94, chmn. bd. dirs., 1994-96; pres. Hyde Park Neighborhood Coun., Cin., 1989-91, Hyde Park Ctr. for Older Adults, 1989-91; active Cin. Bd. Health, 1991-97, chmn., 1995-97; bd. dirs. Cath. Social Svcs. of S.W. Ohio, 1998--. Mem. ABA, Ohio State Bar Assn. (bd. govs., antitrust sect.), Cin. Bar Assn., Fed. Bar Assn., Hyde Park Golf And County Club. Republican. Roman Catholic. Avocations: reading, travel, theater . Home: 3465 Forestoak Ct Cincinnati OH 45208-1842 Office: Dinsmore & Shohl 1900 Chemed Ctr 255 E 5th St Cincinnati OH 45202-4700

SILBERSTEIN, EDWARD BERNARD, nuclear medicine educator, researcher, oncologist; b. Cin., Sept. 3, 1936; s. Bernard Gumpert and Harriet Louise (Kahn) S.; m. Jacqueline Rose Mervis, Oct. 2, 1988; children: Scott, Lisa. BS magna cum laude, Yale U., 1958; MD, Harvard U., 1962. Intern Cin. Gen. Hosp., 1962-63, resident in internal medicine, 1963-64; resident Univ. Hosps. Cleve., 1966-67; NIH fellow in hematology New Eng. Med. Ctr., Boston, 1967-68; asst. prof. radiol. medicine U. Cin. Med. Ctr., 1968-72, assoc. prof. radiol. medicine, 1972-76, prof. radiol. medicine, 1976—, Eugene L. and Sue R. Saenger prof. radiol. scis., 1998—; chmn. Am. Bd. Nuclear Medicine, Los Angeles. Assoc. dir. E.L. Saenger Radioisotope Lab., 1980—; chmn. Environ. Safety Health Com. Dept. Energy Fernald Facility, 1986-91; mem. U.S. Pharmacopeia Com. of Revision, 1990—; mem. Nat. Coun. on Radiation Protection and Measurement, 1997—; cons. Nuclear Regulatory Commn., 1988—; dir. divsn. nuclear medicine Jewish Hosp., 1976-95; cancer pain panel Agy. for Health Care Planning and Rsch., 1992-93. Author: Differential Diagnosis in Nuclear Medicine, 1984, Bone Scintigraphy, 1984, Diagnostic Patterns in Nuclear Medicine, 1998; contbr. articles to profl. jours. Active Race Rels. Commn. Greater Cin., 1995—2000; trustee Cin. Opera Assn., 1993—; active Jewish Cmty. Rels. Coun., 1992—; trustee Isaac M. Wise Temple, 1992—2000, treas., 1997—2000; bd. dirs. Talbert House, 1969—, Air Pollution Control League, Cin., 1980—95. Capt. U.S. Army, 1964—66. Mem.: Am. Bd. Nuclear Medicine (chmn. 1999), Soc. Nuc. Medicine (sec. 1989—92, bd. dirs. 1989—99, pres. S.E. chpt. 1990—91, chair sci. program 1992—94). Jewish. Avocations: tennis, history of art, archaeology, travel. Office: U Cin Med Ctr Mont Reid Pavilion G026 234 Goodman St Cincinnati OH 45219-2364 E-mail: silbereb@healthall.com.

SILBERSTEIN, MARK ALAN, conservationist, biologist; b. L.A., Apr. 18, 1950; s. J. Harold and Lillian Silberstein; m. Jane King, Nov. 27, 1997; children: Joshua, Ian. BA in Zoology, San Jose State U., 1972; MA in Marine Sci., Moss Landing Marine Labs., 1987. Rsch. zoologist N.Y. Ocean Sci. Lab., Montauk, 1973-74; pres. Asociacion de Biologos Ambulantes, Pacific Grove, Calif., 1974-77; rsch. assoc. Moss Landing (Calif.) Labs., 1978-83; rsch. and edn. coord. Elkhorn Slough Nat. Estuarine Rsch. Res., Watsonville, 1983-87; exec. dir. Elkhorn Slough Found., Moss Landing, 1987—. Author: Elkhorn Slough, 1989. Bd. dirs. Santa Cruz (Calif.) Mus. Assn., 1988-94; pres. Sunset Beach Water Co., Watsonville, Calif., 1990-99, Friends of Moss Landing Labs., 1995-99; colleague Monterey Bay (Calif.) Nat. Marine Santuary, 1992—. Recipient Environ. Hero award Monterey Bay Nat. Marine Sanctuary, 2000. Mem. Soc. Wetland Scientists, Estuarine Rsch. Fedn. Avocations: music, surfing, history. Office: Elkhorn Slough Found 1700 Elkhorn Rd Watsonville CA 95076 E-mail: silbermud@aol.com.

SILBEY, JOEL HENRY, history educator; b. Bklyn., Aug. 16, 1933; s. Sidney and Estelle (Mintzer) S.; m. Rosemary Johnson, Aug. 13, 1959; children: Victoria, David. BA, Bklyn. Coll., 1955; MA, U. Iowa, 1956, PhD, 1963. Asst. prof. San Francisco State Coll., 1960-64, U. Md., College Park, 1965-66; asst. prof. Am. History Cornell U., Ithaca, N.Y., 1966-67, assoc. prof., 1967-68, prof., 1968-86, Pres. White prof. history, 1986—. Vis. asst. prof. history U. Pitts., 1964-65. Author: The Shrine of Party, 1967, The Transformation of American Politics, 1968, A Respectable Minority: The Democratic Party in the Civil War Era, 1977, The Partisan Imperative: The Dynamics of American Politics before the Civil War, 1985, The American Political Nation, 1838-1893, 1991, The American Party Battle, 1828-1876, 1999, Martin Van Buren and the Emergence of American Popular Politics, 2002; editor: (with others) Voters, Parties and Elections, 1972, American Political Behavior, 1984, The History of American Electoral Behavior, 1978; editor-in-chief: Encyclopedia of the American legislative System, 1993; editorial cons. numerous publs.; contbr. numerous articles to profl. jours. Am. Philos. Soc. fellow, 1969-70; NSF fellow, 1970-74; NEH fellow, 1980-81; vis. fellow Ctr. for Advanced Study in the Behavioral Scis., 1985-86; vis. scholar Russell Sage Found., 1988-89; John Simon Guggenheim Meml. fellow, 1989-90. Mem. Am. Hist. Assn. (program com. 1977), Orgn. Am. Historians (chmn. program com. 1983), So. Hist. Assn., Social Sci. History Assn. (co-chmn. membership com., mem. exec. com). Home: 105 Judd Falls Rd Ithaca NY 14850-2715 Office: Cornell U 452 Mcgraw Hall Ithaca NY 14853-4601

SILBEY, ROBERT JAMES, chemistry educator, researcher, consultant; b. N.Y.C., Oct. 19, 1940; s. Sidney Richard and Estelle (Mintzer) S.; m. Susan Sorkin, June 24, 1962; children: Jessica, Anna. BS, CUNY Bklyn. Coll., 1961; PhD, U. Chgo., 1965. From asst. prof. to assoc. prof. MIT, Cambridge, 1966-76, prof., 1976—, chmn. dept. chemistry, 1990-95, dir. ctr. for materials sci. and engring., 1998-2000, dean of sci., 2000—. Vis. prof. U. Utrecht, The Netherlands, 1972-73, 97, U. Grenoble, France, 1983; cons. Exxon Rsch., Clinton, N.J., 1984-98. Author: Physical Chemistry, 1991, 2d edit., 1997, 3rd edit., 2000; editor: Conjugated Polymers, 1991; contbr. articles to profl. jours. Recipient Alexander von Humboldt Found. Sr. Scientist award, 1989, Max Planck award, 1992; Alfred P. Sloan fellow, 1968, John S. Guggenheim fellow, 1972; Dreyfus Found. Tchr.-Scholar grantee, 1969. Fellow AAAS, Am. Acad. Arts and Scis., Am. Phys. Soc. Avocations: swimming, sailing. Office: MIT Dept Chemistry 77 Mass Ave Cambridge MA 02139-4307 E-mail: silbey@mit.edu.

SILBIGER, MARTIN L. radiologist, medical educator, college dean; b. Ravenna, Ohio, Mar. 17, 1938; s. Alfred James and Evelyn Norma (Cheswick) Silbiger; m. Ruth Hope Steele, June 4, 1957; children: Martin, Eve, Jonathan, Holly, Wendy. BA, U. Pa., 1958; MD, Western Reserve U., 1962; MBA, U. South Fla., 1989. Diplomate Am. Bd. Radiology, Am. Bd. Nuc. Medicine. Intern Univ. Hosps. Cleve., 1962—63; resident Johns Hopkins Hosp., 1963—66; with NIH, 1966—68; radiologist Tampa (Fla.) Gen. Hosp., 1968—; prof. U. South Fla., Tampa, 1982—; chief of staff Tampa Gen. Hosp., 1978—80; chmn. dept. radiology U. South Fla. Coll. Medicine, 1982—95; dean coll. medicine U. South Fla., 1995—2000, v.p. health scis., 1995—2000. Founder Hillsborough County Med. Assn. Found., Tampa, 1992; treas. Cmty. Found. Tampa, 1993—95; bd. dirs. Moffitt Cancer Ctr., Tampa, 1985—2000, Moffitt Cancer Ctr. Found., 1994—2000. Avocations: reading, rollerblading, golf, tennis. Home: 1827 Bayshore Blvd Tampa FL 33606-3210 Office: 3301 Alumni Dr Tampa FL 33612-9413 also: 1209 Bruce B Downs Blvd PO Box 66 Tampa FL 33601-0066

SILCOX, FRANCES ELEANOR, museum and exhibits planning consultant; b. Orange, Calif., Sept. 26, 1956; d. William Henry and M. Eleanor (Saulpaugh) S.; m. David William Smith, June 21, 1986; children: Lena Celeste, Reid Whitney. BA in English, U. San Francisco, 1979; MA in Mus. Studies, George Washington U., 1984. Intern divsn. performing arts Smithsonian Instn., Washington, 1978; adminstrv. asst. exhibits dept. Calif. Acad. Scis., San Francisco, 1979-81; gallery coord. The George Washington U., Washington, 1981-83; intern art dept. aide Smithsonian Instn., 1983-84; asst. dir. Torpedo Factory Arts Ctr., Alexandria, Va., 1983-84; accreditation coord. Am. Assn. Mus., Washington, 1984-86; interpretive planner Design and Prodn. Inc., Lorton, Va., 1986-88; mus. planner West Office Exhbn. Design, San Francisco, 1988-91; ind. mus. and exhibits planner, owner Dallas, 1991—2000; prin., owner Moraga, 2000—02, ExhibiTree, Calif., 2002—. Bd. mem. St. Gerard Circle, St. Rita Cath. Cmty., Dallas, 1995-98; contbr. numerous natural and cultural resources orgns. Scholar Nat. Endowment for the Arts-Am. Law Inst.-ABA, Washington, 1982. Mem. Am. Assn. for State and Local History, Am. Assn. Mus., Archaeol. Inst. Am., Internat. Coun. Mus., Nat. Assn. for Mus. Exhibition, Tex. Assn. Mus. Democrat. Avocations: travel, correspondence, photography, reading, walking. Home and Office: 463 Fernwood Dr Moraga CA 94556-2119

SILEN, WILLIAM, physician, surgery educator; b. San Francisco, Sept. 13, 1927; s. Dave and Rose (Miller) S.; m. Ruth Heppner, July 13, 1947; children: Stephen, Deborah, Mark. BA, U. Calif., Berkeley, 1946; MD, U. Calif., San Francisco, 1949; MA (hon.) (hon.) , Harvard U., 1966. Diplomate Am. Bd. Surgery. Intern U. Calif., San Francisco, 1949—50, asst. resident gen. surgery, 1950—56, chief resident gen. surgery, 1956—57; asst. chief surgery Denver VA Hosp., 1957—59, chief surgery, 1959—60; asst. chief surgery San Francisco Gen. Hosp., 1960—61, chief surgery, 1961—66; surgeon-in-chief Beth Israel Hosp., Boston, 1966—94; instr. surgery, asst. prof. surgery U. Colo. Med. Sch., Denver, 1957—60; asst. prof. then assoc. prof. surgery U. Calif. Sch. Medicine, San Francisco, 1960—66; prof. surgery Harvard Med. Sch., Boston, 1966—, Johnson and Johnson prof. surgery, 1966—94, Johnson & Johnson disting. prof. surgery, 1994—, faculty dean faculty devel. & diversity, 1995—2000; adj. prof. biology Brandeis Univ. Dir. Harvard Digestive Diseases Ctr. NIH, Bethesda, Md., 1984—94; adj. prof. biology Brandeis U., 2000—. Author: Cope's Early Diagnosis of the Acute Abdomen, 1995, Conservative Management of Breast Cancer, 1983, Atlas of Techniques in Breast Surgery, 1995. With USAF, 1950—52. Mem.: ACS, AMA, H.C. Naffziger Surg. Soc., Soc. Univ. Surgeons, Phi Beta Kappa. Avocation: bonsai cultivation. Office: Harvard Med Sch Faculty Dev & Diversity 25 Shattuck St # A-151 Boston MA 02115-6027

SILER, EUGENE EDWARD, JR. federal judge; b. Williamsburg, Ky., Oct. 19, 1936; s. Eugene Edward and Lowell (Jones) Siler; m. Christy Dyanne Minnich, Oct. 18, 1969; children: Eugene Edward, Adam Troy. BA cum laude, Vanderbilt U., 1958; LLB, U. Va., 1963; LLM, Georgetown U., 1964. Bar: Ky. 1963, Va. 1963, D.C. 1963. Pvt. practice, Williamsburg, 1964—65; atty. Whitley County, Ky., 1965—70, U.S. Dist. Ct., Ea. Dist., Lexington, 1970—75; judge U.S. Dist. Ct., Ea. and We. Dists., Ky., 1975—91; chief judge U.S. Dist. Ct., Ea. Dist., 1984—91; judge U.S. Ct. Appeals (6th cir.), 1991—. Trustee Cumberland Coll., Williamsburg, 1965—73, 1980—88; campaign co-chmn. Congressman Tim L. Carter, 1966, 5th Congl. Dist., U.S. Senator J.S. Cooper, 1966; 1st v.p. Ky. Bapt. Convention, 1986—87; bd. dirs. Bapt. Healthcare System Inc., 1990—. With USN, 1958—60, with USNR, 1960—83. Recipient Freedom's Found. medal, 1968; fellow E. Barrett Prettyman fellow, 1963—64. Mem.: Va. State Bar, D.C. Bar Assn., Ky. Bar Assn. (Judge of Yr. 1992), Fed. Bar Assn. Republican. Baptist. Home: PO Box 129 Williamsburg KY 40769-0129 Office: US Ct Appeals 310 S Main Street Room 333 London KY 40741

SILER, J. BERNARD, lawyer, educator; b. Washington, Nov. 11, 1951; s. H. Bernard and Frances (Hickman) S.; children: Brandon A., Max J., Joshua B. BA, U. Dayton, 1972; JD, U. Cin., 1978. Bar: Ohio, D.C., U.S. Army Ct. Criminal Appeals. Legal advisor U.S. Bd. Vets. Appeals, Washington, 1980-84; pros. atty. D.C. Corp. Counsel, 1984—. Adj. prof. Montgomery Coll., Takoma Park, Md., 1992—; lectr. Am. history various colls., univs., civic assns., 1990—. Bd. dirs. Police and Firefighters Retirement Bd., Washington, 1985-88. Maj., U.S. Army, 1997, Germany. Mem. Nat. Bar Assn., Kappa Alpha Psi. Avocations: whitewater kayaking, hiking, Civil War reenactment. Home: 1207 Sheridan St NW Washington DC 20011-1103

SILER, SUSAN REEDER, communications educator; b. Knoxville, Tenn., May 31, 1940; d. Claude S. Jr. and Mary Frances (Cook) Reeder; m. Theodore Paul Siler Jr., Sept. 3, 1960; children: Mary Siler Walker, Theodore Paul III. BS in Communications and Journalism, U. Tenn., Knoxville, 1988, MS in Mass Comms., 1994, postgrad. 2d grade tchr. Lawton (Okla.) Pub. Schs., 1961-62, substitute tchr., 1963-64; with By Design, 1987-88; English tutor, 1991-95; adj. instr. comm. U. Tenn., 1994—, U. Tenn., Pellissippi State Tech. C.C., Knoxville, Tenn. Bd. dirs. Hlen Ross McNabb Mental Health Ctr., Knoxville. Tutor Episc. Ch. Ascension, Knoxville, 1990—; instr. United Meth. Ch., Knoxville, 1985-92; chmn. Dogwood Arts Festival, Knoxville, 1980-85; chmn. Bd. Govs . of East Tenn. Presentation Soc., 1988-96, Dogwood Trails; chmn., sec. bd. dirs. YWCA, Knoxville, 1982-88, editor newsletter, membership chmn., placement adv., sec.; Knoxville Jr. League, 1979-95; bd. dirs. Knoxville Women's Ctr., 1993-94; spl. events chmn. St. Mary's Med. Ctr. Found., 1986-89; Pres. Knoxville area Literacy Assn., 1989-92, tutor Episcopal Ch. Literacy program, Knoxville, 1990-95. Mem. Internat. Mass Comm. Assn., Soc. Profl. Journalists, Am. Journalism Historians Assn., Assn. for Edn. in Journalism and Mass Comms., Kappa Tau Alpha, Golden Key. Home: 717 Kenesaw Ave Knoxville TN 37919-6662

SILESKY, BARRY T. writer, educator; b. Mpls., July 1, 1949; s. Sidney Lyle Silesky and Layah Berneice Schneider; m. Loren Madelina Delorenzo (div.); m. Sharon Dee Solwitz, June 13, 1982; children: Seth, Jesse(dec.). BA, Northwestern U., 1971; MA, U. Ill., Chgo., 1976. Adj. assoc. prof. Sch. Art Inst. Chgo., 1984—. Poet in schs. Urban Gateways, Chgo., 1984-98. Author: The New Tenants, 1991, Ferlinghetti: The Artist in Hist Time, 1991, One Thing That Can Save Us, 1992, Greatest Hits, 2000. Home: 3709 N Kenmore Chicago IL 60613

SILETS, HARVEY MARVIN, lawyer; b. Chgo., Aug. 25, 1931; s. Joseph Lazarus and Sylvia Silets; m. Elaine L. Gordon, June 25, 1961; children: Hayden Leigh, Jonathan Lazarus (dec.), Alexandra Rose. BS cum laude, DePaul U., 1952; JD (Frederick Leicke scholar), U. Mich., 1955. Bar: Ill. 1955, U.S. Dist. Ct. (no. dist.) Ill. 1955, N.Y. 1956, U.S. Tax Ct. 1957, U.S. Ct. Mil. Appeals 1957, U.S. Ct. Appeals (7th cir.) 1958, U.S. Supreme Ct. 1959, U.S. Ct. Appeals (6th cir.) 1965, U.S. Ct. Appeals (2d cir.) 1971, U.S. Ct. Appeals (5th cir.) 1972, U.S. Ct. Appeals (11th cir.). Assoc. Paul, Weiss, Rifkind, Wharton & Garrison, N.Y.C., 1955-56; asst. atty. U.S. Dist. Ct. (no. dist.) Ill., 1958-60; chief tax atty. U.S. atty. No. Dist. Ill., Chgo., 1960-62; ptnr. Harris, Burman & Silets, 1962-79, Silets & Martin, Ltd., Chgo., 1979-92, Katten Muchin Zavis, Chgo., 1992—. Asst. advance tng. program IRS, U. Mich., 1952-53; law lectr. advance fed. taxation John Marshall Law Sch., 1962-66; adj. prof. taxation Chgo.-Kent Coll. Law, 1985—; gen. counsel Nat. Treasury Employees Union, 1968-92; mem. adv. com. tax litigation U.S. Dept. Justice, 1979-82; mem. Tax Reform Com., State of Ill., 1982-83; mem. Speedy Trial Act Planning Group U.S. Dist. Ct. (no. dist.) Ill., 1976-79; mem. civil justice reform act adv. com. U.S. Dist. Ct. (no. dist.) Ill., 1991-94; lectr. in field. Contbr. articles to profl. jours. Trustee Latin Sch., Chgo., 1970-76; active Chgo. Crime Commn., 1975-93, Govv.'s Commn. Reform Tax Laws, Ill., 1982-83. With AUS, 1956-58. Fellow Am. Coll. Trial Lawyers (chmn. com. on fed. rules of criminal procedure 1982-91, fed. rules of evidence com. 1988-93, jud. com., fed. criminal procedures com., Upstate Ill. com. chmn. 1990-91), Am. Coll. Tax Counsel, Internat. Acad. Trial Lawyers, Soc. Advanced Legal Studies; mem. ABA (active various coms.), Bar Assn. 7th Fed. Cir. (chmn. com. criminal law and procedure 1972-82, bd. govs. 1983-86, sec. 1986-88, v.p. 1989-90, pres. 1990-91), NACDL, FBA (bd. dirs. 1971—, pres. 1977-78, v.p. 1976-77, sec. 1975-76, treas. 1974-75, active various coms.), Chgo. Bar Assn. (tax com. 1958-66, com. devel. law 1966-72, 78-88, com. fed. taxation 1968—, com. evaluation candidates 1978-80, exec. com. tax sect. 1994—), Am. Bd. Criminal Def. Lawyers, Decalogue Soc. Lawyers, Bar Assn. N.Y. City, Standard Club, Cliff Dwellers Club, Chgo. Club, Phi Alpha delta, Pi Gamma Mu. Office: Katten Muchin Zavis Rosen Man 525 W Monroe St Ste 1600 Chicago IL 60661-3693 E-mail: harvey.silets@kmzr.com.

SILIN, DMITRY BORISOVITCH, mathematics educator; b. Moscow, Apr. 29, 1957; s. Boris Michaelovitch and Alexandra Petrovna (Konyaeva) S.; m. Vera Vladislavovna Sorokina, June 14, 1980; children: Gregory, Michael. B of Math., Moscow State U., 1979, Candidate of Physics and Math., 1982; Dr. Physics & Math., 1993. Asst. prof. Faculty of Computational Math./Cybernetics/Moscow State U., 1982-90, assoc. prof., 1990—. Reviewer on optimal control and real functions, Referativny Jour. math—, Moscow, 1981—; researcher Moscow State U., 1982—. Contbr. articles to profl. jours. Recipient award for new tech. devel. Ministry of Higher Edn. of USSR, Moscow, 1988, All-Union prize in Techniques and Scis. for Young Specialists, All-Union Komsomol, Moscow, 1990. Avocation: tourism. Home: Universitetsky Prospect 23 4 130 117330 Moscow Russia Office: Faculty of Computational Math and Cybernetics Moscow State U 119899 Moscow Russia

SILIPIGNI, ALFREDO, opera conductor; b. Atlantic City, Apr. 9, 1931; s. Alfredo and Elisabeth (Calhoun) S.; m. Gloria Rose DiBenedetto, Apr. 11, 1953; children: Marisa, Elisabetta Luisa, Afredo Roberto. Student, Westminster Choir Coll., 1948, Juilliard Sch. Music, 1953; HHD (hon.), Kean Coll. N.J., 1978. Prin. condr., gen. dir., artistic dir. N.J. State Opera, Newark, 1965—, founder Young Artist Program, 1969—. Guest lectr. Glassboro (N.J.) State Coll. Carnegie Hall debut with Symphony of the Air, 1956; condr. NBC Symphony, Boston, Bklyn. and Conn. operas, Newark Symphony; guest condr. Vienna State Opera, 1976, Grand Liceo di Barcelona, Spain, 1976, London, 1977, also numerous cos. Eng., Venezuela, France, Italy, Mex. and Can. with frequent appearances at L'Opera de Montreal; made recs. of Zaza by Leoncavallo, "Adriana Lecouvrer" by Cilea; prin. guest condr. and advisor Bellas Artes, Mex., 1993-94; guest condr. Opera Colo., 1997-98, largest prodn. Aida anywhere in world, Shanghai, 2000. Decorated cavliere Order of Merit (Italy); recipient Centennial medal St. Peter's Coll., 1972, Disting. Svc. to Culture award City of San Remo, Columbia Found. award, Boys Town of Italy award, Music award N.J. Edn. Assn., 1988. Office: NJ State Opera 50 Park Pl Ste 10 Newark NJ 07102 E-mail: newjerseystateop@aol.com.

SILJAK, DRAGOSLAV D. engineering educator, researcher; b. Belgrade, Yugoslavia, Sept. 10, 1933; came to U.S. 1964, naturalized; s. Dobrilo T. and Ljubica Z. (Zivanovic) S.; m. Dragana T. Todorovic, Sept. 28, 1967; children— Ana, Matija. BSEE, U. Belgrade, 1958, MSEE, 1961, ScD, 1963. Docent prof. U. Belgrade, 1963-64; assoc. prof. U. Santa Clara, Calif., 1964-70, prof. engring., 1970-84, B. and M. Swig Univ. chair, 1984—. Author: Nonlinear Systems, 1969, Large Scale Systems, 1978, Decentralized Control of Complex Systems, 1991; mem. editl. bd. Jour. Difference Equations, Nonlinear World, Comm. in Applied Analysis, Internat. Jour. Computer Rsch., Theory, Methods and Applications, Dynamics of Cont., Disc. and Impulsive

Systems, Math. Problems in Engring., Stability and Control: Theory and Applications. Disting. prof. Fulbright Found., 1984. Fellow IEEE (life); mem. Serbian Acad. Scis. and Arts (hon.) Mem. Christian Orthodox Ch. E-mail: dsiljak@scu.edu.

SILK, ALVIN JOHN, business educator, management consultant; b. Winnipeg, Manitoba, Can., Dec. 31, 1935; came to U.S., 1959, naturalized, 1975; s. John Edward and Bertha Lena (Kirton) S.; m. Diane D. Wilson; children: Jonathan, Andrea, Stephanie. BA, U. Western Ont., 1959; MBA, Northwestern U., 1960, PhD, 1968. Asst. prof. mgmt. UCLA, 1963-66; asst. prof. U. Chgo., 1966-68; from assoc. prof. to prof. Sloan Sch. Mgmt., MIT, Cambridge, 1968-88; dep. dean MIT Sloan Sch. Mgmt., 1981-87; Lincoln Filene prof. Grad. Sch. Bus. Adminstrn. Harvard U., Boston, 1988—. Vis. rsch. fellow Mktg. Sci. Inst., Cambridge, Mass., 1970-71, trustee, 1984-96, Disting. rsch. assoc., 2001–; Ford Found. vis. prof. European Inst. for Advanced Studies in Mgmt., Brussels, 1975-76, Harvard Bus. Sch., 1987—; bd. dirs. Reed and Barton, Inc., Taunton, Mass., AdPilot, Inc. Co-editor: Behavioral and Management Science in Marketing, 1978; assoc. editor: Mgmt. Sci., 1969-77; co-editor: Quantitative Mktg. Absracts, Social Sci. Rsch. Network; mem. editl. bd. Jour. Mktg. Rsch., 1969-73, Jour. Mktg., 1978-81, Mktg. Sci., 1980-93; author, co-author numerous articles to profl. jours. Mem. Am. Mktg. Assn. (O'Dell award 1983), INFORMS (Achievement award 1982, 83), Psychometric Soc., Beta Gamma Sigma, Zeta Psi. Home: 464 Starboard Ln Osterville MA 02655-1432 E-mail: asilk@hbs.edu.

SILK, FREDERICK C.Z. financial consultant; b. Pretoria, Transvaal, South Africa, July 29, 1934; arrived in Canada, 1964; s. Frederick Charles and Edythe D'Olier (Ziervogel) S.; m. Margaret Colbourne, May 12, 1962; children: Michael, Alison, Jennifer. BS, Rhodes U., Grahamstown, Republic South Africa, 1954; cert. acctg. theory, U. Witwatersrand, Johannesburg, Republic South Africa, 1957. Acct., cons. Deloitte, Plender, Haskins & Sells, Johannesburg, London and N.Y.C., 1954-64; mgmt. cons. P.S. Ross & Ptnrs., Montreal, Que, Can., 1964-68; v.p. fin. and adminstrn. J&P Coats Ltd., Can., 1968-74; treas. Standard Brands, Ltd., Can., 1974-75; asst. treas. Standard Brands, Inc., N.Y.C., 1975-78; treas. Harlequin Enterprises, Ltd., Toronto, Ont., Can., 1978-82; v.p., treas. Nabisco Brands, Ltd., 1982-95; pvt. treas. cons., 1995—. Fellow Inst. Chartered Accts. (Eng., Wales), Inst. Chartered Accts. (South Africa), Fin. Execs. Inst. Avocations: music, choral music, Gilbert and Sullivan operettas. Office: 80 Front St E Ste 602 Toronto ON Canada M5E 1T4 E-mail: fczsilk@hotmail.com.

SILKENAT, JAMES ROBERT, lawyer; b. Salina, Kans., Aug. 2, 1947; s. Ernest E. and Mildred R. (Iman) S.; children: David Andrew, Katherine Anne. BA, Drury Coll., 1969; JD, U. Chgo., 1972; LLM, NYU, 1978. Bar: N.Y. 1973, D.C. 1980. Assoc. Cravath, Swaine & Moore, N.Y.C., 1972-80; counsel Internat. Fin. Corp., Washington, 1980-86; ptnr. Morgan, Lewis & Bockius, N.Y.C., 1986-89, Morrison & Foerster, N.Y.C., 1989-92, Pillsbury, Winthrop, N.Y.C., 1992—2002, Arent Fox, N.Y.C., 2002—. Chmn. Council N.Y. Law Assocs., 1978-79, Lawyers Com. Internat. Human Rights, 1978-80. Editor ABA Guide to Fng. Law Firms, Moscow Conf. on Law Bilateral Econ. Rels., ABA Guide to Internat. Bus. Negotiations; contbr. articles to profl. jours. Capt. U.S. Army, 1972-73. Fellow NEH, 1977, U.S. Dept. State, 1981. Fellow Am. Bar Found.; mem. ABA (chmn. internat. law and practice sect. 1989-90, chmn. sect. officer's conf. 1990-92, mem. ho. of dels. 1989—, bd. govs. 1994-97). Office: Arent Fox 1675 Broadway New York NY 10019

SILL, GERALD DE SCHRENCK, hotel executive; b. Czech Republic, Dec. 11, 1917; arrived in U.S., 1948, naturalized, 1953; s. Edward and Margaret (Baroness von Schrenck-Notzing) S.; m. Maria Countess Draskovich, May 11, 1946; children: Susan, Gabrielle. BS, Budapest Tech. U., 1944. With econs. divsn. U.S. Hdqs., Vienna, 1945-48; exec. hotel positions N.Y.C., 1948-52; managerial positions with Hilton Hotel Corp., 1953-61; exec. v.p. Houston Internat. Hotels, Inc., 1961-72, pres., CEO, 1972-74, chmn. bd., 1984-86, v.p., bd. dirs., 1986-88; chmn. emeritus, adv. dir. Preferred Hotels Worldwide, 1989; pres., CEO GdSS Mgmt. and Cons., Inc., Houston, 1989—. Mem. Am. Arbitration Assn. (panel arbitrators), River Oaks Country Club (Houston). Home: 2227 Pelham Dr Houston TX 77019-3530

SILL, MELANIE, editor; m. Bennett Groshong. Grad. in journalism, U. N.C., 1981. Mng. editor, 1998; asst. metro editor, 1988; with The Transylvania Times , Brevard, NC, United Press Internat. , Raleigh; project editor Boss Hog; exec. editor, sr. v.p. The News & Observer, Raleigh , NC, 2002—. Recipient Pulitzer prize, Boss Hog, 1996; fellow Nieman, Harvard U., 1993—94. Office: 215 S McDowell St Raleigh NC 27601*

SILLARS, MALCOLM OSGOOD, communication educator; b. Union City, N.J., Feb. 12, 1928; s. Malcolm Osgood and Dorothy Edna (Browning) S.; m. Charlotte Jane Grimm, June 1, 1948; children— Paul Louis, Bruce Malcolm, Alan Leslie. BA, U. Redlands, 1948, MA, 1949; PhD, U. Iowa, 1955. Asst. prof. communication Iowa State U., Ames, 1949-53; asst. prof. Calif. State U., Los Angeles, 1954-56, prof., dean Northridge, 1970-71, pres., 1969-70; prof. U. Mass., Amherst, 1971-74; prof. communication U. Utah, Salt Lake City, 1974-97, dean humanities, 1974-81, ret., 1998. Author: Speech: Content and Communications, 6th edit., 1991, Argumentation and Critical Decision Making, 5th edit., 2001, Communication Criticism, 2d edit., 2001; contbr. articles to profl. jours. Recipient Silver Beaver award Boy Scouts Am. Mem. ACLU, Nat. Comm. Assn. (pres.), We. States Comm. Assn. (pres.). Democrat. Home: 3508 Eastoaks Dr Salt Lake City UT 84124-3811

SILLER, STEPHEN I. lawyer; b. May 8, 1949; m. Helen Seewald, June 6, 1971. BA, Bklyn. Coll., 1970, JD cum laude, 1973; LLM, NYU, 1978. Bar: N.Y. 1974, U.S. Dist. Ct. (so. and ea. dists.) N.Y. 1974, U.S. Ct. Appeals (2d cir.) 1974. Assoc. Fried, Frank, Harris, Shriver & Jacobson, N.Y.C., 1973-78, Feit & Ahrens, N.Y.C., 1978-80, ptnr., 1981-87; founder, sr. ptnr. Siller Wilk LLP, 1987—. Mem. ABA (partnership law com., negotiated acquisitions com.), Internat. Bar Assn., Assn. Bar City of N.Y. (transp. com. 1978—, U.S. in global economy com. 1996-97). Office: Siller Wilk LLP 675 3rd Ave Fl 9 New York NY 10017-5704 E-mail: ssiller@sillerwilk.com.

SILLERUD, ARLEN ROGER, retired educator; b. Nov. 28, 1934; BS, Moorhead State U., 1958; postgrad., Bemidji State U., 1969-70, U. Minn., 1988-90. Tchr. Ada School Dist., Ada, Minn., 1958-90. Chmn. Norman County Reps., Ada, Minn., 1996—, county, dist., and state del., 1994-2000, , 2002—, state ctrl. del., 1997-2001, alt., 2000—; elder Zion Luth. Ch., Ada, 1994—, Gideon spkr., 1971—. Achievements include advancement of idea that heart fibrillation should not be considered fatal, but that the heart can be restarted by electric shock; creator five solutions to clean up oil spills. Home: 807 3rd Ave E Ada MN 56510-1120

SILLIMAN, JOHN PARKS, JR. national guard officer, engineering consultant; b. Rochester, Minn., Mar. 15, 1943; s. John Parks and Sylvia (Davidson) S.; m. Janet Marie English, July 10, 1971; children: Jennifer Sage, John Prks III. BA in Psychology, Hamline U., 1965. Admissions counselor Hamline U., St. Paul, 1965-68, dir. fin. aid, 1970-74; officer USAF, 1968-70; commd. 2d lt. Minn. Air N.G., 1968, advanced through grades to brig. gen., ops. officer, pilot 133d Airlift Wing, 1974-95, wing comdr., 1995-98; comdr., chief staff Hdqs. Minn. Air N.G., 1998—2001. Mem. air directorate fiedl adv. coun. Nat. Air N.G., Washington, 1995-98; mem. adv. bd. Starbase, MN, Inc., St. Paul, 1995—; cons. on human engring. design Litton Guidance and Control Sys., Northridge, Calif., 1998-2000, Boeing, Wichita, Kans., 2001-. Ordained elder North Como Presbyn. Ch., Roseville, Minn., 1998—; mem. vulcan krewe 2001 St. Paul Winter Carnival, 2000—. Decorated Legion of Merit. Mem. N.G. Assn., Air Force Assn., St. Paul Club (bd. dirs. 1997—). Avocations: golf, alpine skiing, sailing, mountain biking. E-mail: jpsill@attglobal.net.

SILLIMAN, RICHARD GEORGE, retired lawyer, retired farm machinery company executive; b. Elgin, Ill., Aug. 11, 1922; s. Charles B. and Mabel Ellen (Winegar) S.; m. Mary L. Yost, June 12, 1945; children— Martha Jane, Charles R. BA in History, Cornell Coll., Mt. Vernon, Iowa, 1946; JD, Northwestern U., 1949. Bar: Ill. 1949. Atty. various U.S. agys., Chgo., 1949-52; atty., asst. sec. Elgin Nat. Watch Co., Ill., 1952-59, sec., gen. atty., 1959-62; asst. gen. counsel Deere & Co., Moline, 1962-75, assoc. gen. counsel, 1975-82, sec., assoc. gen. counsel, 1982-87. Mem. editorial bd. Ill. Law Rev., 1948-49. Contbr. articles to profl. jours. Past pres., hon. dir. Quad-City Symphony Orch., Moline and Davenport, Iowa, 1968-87; bd. dirs., trustee Upper Rock Island County YMCA, Moline, 1965-87; bd. dirs. Police-Fire Commn., Elgin, 1957-61; bd. dirs., sec. Elgin YMCA, 1955. Served with USN, 1943-46 Mem. Ill. State Bar Assn. (past chmn. com. on corp. law dept.), Short Hills Country Club (Moline), Union League (Chgo.). Avocations: golf, music. Home: 4817 6th Street Ct East Moline IL 61244-4274

SILLMAN, ARNOLD JOEL, physiologist, educator; b. N.Y.C., Oct. 10, 1940; s. Philip and Anne L. (Pearlman) S.; m. Jean Fletcher Van Keuren, Sept. 26, 1969; children: Andrea Jose, Diana Van Keuren. AB, U. Calif., Los Angeles, 1963, MA, 1965, PhD, 1968. Asst. prof. U. Calif., L.A., 1969-73, Davis, 1975-78, assoc. prof., 1978-85, prof., 1985—; asst. prof. U. Pitts., 1973-75, interim dir. aquaculture and fisheries program, 1994—95, vice chair sect. neurobiology, physiology and behavior, 1998—, acting chair, 2001. Contbr. articles to profl. jours. USPHS trainee, UCLA, 1966-67; fellow NSF, 1967-68, Fight for Sight, Inc., 1968-69. Recipient Acad. Senate Disting. Tchg. award, 1996. Mem. Am. Physiol. Soc., Soc. Gen. Physiologists, Am. Soc. Zoologists, Assn. Rsch. in Vision and Ophthalmology, AAAS, N.Y. Acad. Sci. Jewish. Home: 1140 Los Robles St Davis CA 95616-4927 Office: U Calif Sect Neurobiology Physiology & Behavior Divsn Biol Scis Davis CA 95616 E-mail: ajsillman@ucdavis.edu.

SILLMAN, GEORGE DOUGLAS, computer programmer analyst; b. Dayton, Ohio, Mar. 13, 1957; s. Herbert Carl Sillman and Martha Carolyn Stump-Greene. AA, Santa Monica City Coll., 1978; BA, Calif. State U., Northridge, 1981; AA, Pierce Coll., Woodland Hills, Calif., 1988. Programmer analyst Transamerica Ins. Group, Woodland Hills, 1989-92, Wellmark Inc., Westlake Village, Calif., 1993, Korn/Ferry Internat., L.A., 1993-96, Pentel of Am., Ltd., Torrance, Calif., 1996-98; systems analyst PacifiCare Health Systems, Cypress, 1998-99; programmer analyst Bally Total Fitness Corp., Norwalk, 1999—. Freelance computer cons., L.A., 1992—. Author software products. Avocations: old movies, sports, music, gourmet dining, the outdoors. Home: 486 Palos Verdes Blvd Redondo Beach CA 90277-6514 Office: Bally Total Fitness Corp Ste 300 12440 E Imperial Hwy Norwalk CA 90650-3178 E-mail: gsillman@hotmail.com.

SILLS, ERIC SCOTT, infertility surgeon, reproductive endocrinologist; b. Oak Ridge, Tenn., Apr. 27, 1965; s. James L. and Linda Carmack Sills; m. Carol Wells, Mar. 10, 1990; children: Charles Alton Carmack, Ann-Marie Carter. AB, Vanderbilt U., 1987; MD, U. Tenn., Memphis, 1992. Diplomate Nat. Bd. Med. Examiners, Am. Bd. Obstetrics and Gynecology. Resident Meml. Sloan-Kettering Cancer Ctr., N.Y.C., 1993; chief resident NYU Downtown Hosp., 1995-96; asst. attending physician N.Y. Hosp.-Cornell Med. Ctr., 1996-98; sr. fellow Cornell U. Med. Coll., 1997-98; pvt. practice, Atlanta, 1999—. Chmn. resident med. bd. N.Y. Downtown Hosp., 1994-96; editor Internat. Coun. for Infertility Info. Dissemination, Arlington, Va., 1998; co-chair infertility and endometriosis working group 15th FIGO World Congress of Gynecology and Obstetrics, Copenhagen, 1995; mem. sci. adv. bd. Vicor Techs., Ingenix Pharms., Datamonitor Corp. PLC, London. Contbr. articles to profl. jours. Trustee Tenn. State Dept. Health, Nashville, 1986-92. Recipient Meritorious Patient Svc. award Cooper Inst. for Advanced Studies in Medicine and the Humanities, 1999. Fellow AAAS, Soc. for Reproductive Endocrinology, Royal Soc. Medicine London, Am. Soc. for Reproductive Medicine; mem. AMA (nat. chmn. resident credentials com. 1995, physicians recognition award in med. edn. with commendation 2001-03), UN Assn. of USA, Med. Assn. Atlanta. Office: Ga Reproductive Specialists LLC Ste 270 5445 Merdian Mark Rd Atlanta GA 30342 E-mail: dr.sills@ivf.com.

SILLS, NANCY MINTZ, lawyer; b. N.Y.C., Nov. 3, 1941; d. Samuel and Selma (Kahn) Mintz; m. Stephen J. Sills, Apr. 17, 1966; children: Eric Howard, Ronnie Lynne Sills Lindberg. BA, U. Wis., 1962; JD cum laude, Albany Law Sch. Union U., 1976. Bar: N.Y. 1977, U.S. Dist. Ct. (no. dist.) N.Y. 1977, U.S. Tax Ct. 1984. Asst. editor fin. news Newsweek mag., N.Y.C., 1962-65; staff writer, reporter Forbes mag., 1965; rsch. assoc. pub. rels. Ea. Airlines, 1965-67; asst. editor Harper & Row, 1968-69; freelance writer, editor N.Y.C., Albany, 1967-70; confidential law sec. N.Y. State Supreme Ct., Albany, 1976-79; assoc. Whiteman, Osterman & Hanna, 1979-81, Martin, Noonan, Hislop, Troue & Shudt, Albany, 1981-83; ptnr. Martin, Shudt, Wallace & Sills, 1984; of counsel Krolick and DeGraff, 1984-89; ptnr. Hodgson, Russ, Andrews, Woods & Goodyear, 1990-91; pvt. practice, 1991—2001; of counsel Lemery & Reid, Albany and Glens Falls, NY, 1993—94, O'Connell and Aronowitz, Albany, 2002—. Asst. counsel N.Y. State Senate, 1983-88; cons. The Ayco Corp., 1975; jud. screening com. Third Jud. Dept., 1997—. Editor: Reforming American Education, 1969, Up From Poverty, 1968; rschr.: The Negro Revolution in America, 1963; contbr. articles to mags. Bd. dirs. Jewish Philanthropies Endowment, 1983-86, United Jewish Fedn. N.E. N.Y. Endowment Fund, 1992-96, Daus. Sarah Found., 1994-97, Albany Jewish Cmty. Ctr., 1984-87; mem. Guilderland (N.Y.) Conservation Adv. Coun., 1993-96; mem. planned giving tech. adv. com. Albany Law Sch., Union U., 1991-95, chmn., 1992-95; mem. regional cabinet State of Israel Bonds Devel. Corp. for Israel, 1991-92; surrogate decision making com. N.Y. State Commn. Quality of Care for Mentally Disabled. Mem. ABA, N.Y. State Bar Assn., Albany County Bar Assn., N.Y. Criminal and Civil Cts. Bar Assn. (dir. 2000-), Estate Planning Coun. Ea. N.Y., Aux. Albany County Med. Soc., Capital Dist. Trial Lawyers Assn., Capital Dist. Women's Bar Assn., Phi Beta Kappa, Sigma Epsilon Sigma. Republican. Home: 16 Hiawatha Dr Guilderland NY 12084-9526 Office: O'Connell and Aronowitz 100 State St Albany NY 12207-1885 E-mail: nmsills@capital.net.

SILLS, RICHARD REYNOLDS, scientist, educator; b. N.Y.C., Sept. 19, 1946; s. Leonard Harold and Carol (Rudin) S. BA, Boston U., 1968. Tchr. N.Y.C. Pub. Schs., 1968-70, 79-81; v.p. Plutronics, Inc., N.Y.C., 1981-85; pvt. practice, 1985—. Author: (children's book) Jonny the Jester, 1977; contbr. articles to profl. jours.; patentee method and apparatus for encoding and decoding signals, method and apparatus for modifying synthesized sound signals, analog processing system. Mem. Rep. Nat. Com., Washington, 1981—, Rep. Presdl. Task Force, Washington, 1982—, Rep. Senatorial Inner Cir., 1987—, Rep. Senatorial Trust, 1999—; founding mem. Chmn.'s Club, Ronald Reagan Presl. Found., 1997—. Named Educator of Decade, Found. for Universal Brotherhood Inc., 1978; recipient Rep. Senatorial Medal of Freedom, 1999. Mem. AAAS, N.Y. Acad. Scis., Union of Concerned Scientists. Avocations: running, weight lifting.

SILLS, STEPHEN JOEL, ophthalmologist; b. N.Y.C., Mar. 1, 1939; s. Reuben and Edna Henrietta (Epstein) S.; m. Nancy Mintz, Apr. 17, 1966; children: Eric Howard, Ronnie Lynne. BS, Rensselaer Poly. Inst., Troy, N.Y., 1972; MD cum laude, Albany Med. Coll., 1962. Lic. physician, N.Y.; diplomate Am. Bd. Ophthalmology. Surg. intern Columbia-Presbyn. Med. Ctr., N.Y.C., 1962-63, resident Inst. Ophthalmology, 1965-69; pvt. practice ophthalmology Albany, 1969—; attending ophthalmologist Albany Med. Ctr. Hosp.; chmn. med. staff Albany Med Ctr./South Clin. Campus; chief ophthalmology St. Peters Hosp. Clin. prof. ophthalmology Albany Med. Coll. Mem. hwy. safety med. com. N.Y. State Dept. Health, Albany, 1976; mem. med. adv. bd. N.Y. State Athletic Commn., N.Y.C., 1980-93. Capt. M.C. USAF, 1963-65. Fellow Am. Acad. Ophthalmology; mem. AMA, N.Y. State Ophthal. Soc. (dir. 1975-78), Eastern N.Y. Eye, Ear, Nose and Throat Assn. (pres. 1987), Med. Soc. State N.Y. (chmn. sect. on ophthalmology 1976), Albany County Med. Soc., Lake George Club. Avocations: tennis, sailing. Home: 16 Hiawatha Dr Guilderland NY 12084-9526 Office: 632 New Scotland Ave Albany NY 12208-1919

SILLS, THOMAS W. physical science educator; b. Hartford City, Ind., Oct. 13, 1947; s. Ivan D. and F. Virginia Sills. BS in Physics and Chemistry, Ball State U., 1969; MS in PHysics, Purdue U., 1971, PhD in Physics and Edn., 1977. Instr. Ball State U., Muncie, Ind., 1967-69, Purdue U., West Lafayette, 1969-77; head product devel. Psychol. Testing Stoelting Co., Chgo., 1977-79; prof. City Colls. of Chgo., 1981—. Faculty coord. PBS Channel 20 TV, Chgo., 1986—; pub. Dearborn Resources, Chgo., 1995—; cons. PBS Adult Learning Svc., Alexandria, Va., 1987-88, Mus. of Sci. and Industry, Chgo., 1988-89, Sci. and Arts Acad., Des Plaines, Ill., 1988-92, also for various pubs. Author: Science Is..., 1985, Science Fun in Chicagoland, 1995, Science Fun with Toys, 1999, Science Fun in Chicagoland, 1999; mem. editl. bd. Discourse: Focus on Curriculum, 1984-96; developer psychol. tests. Prodn. advisor Granada TV Ltd., Manchester, Eng., 1984-86; mem. math. and sci. com. Ford Found., Chgo., 1985-87; developer employment test Ill. Ball/Office of Mayor of Chgo., 1989. Mem. Nat. Sci. Tchrs. Assn., Ill. Sci. Tchrs. Assn., Manuscript Soc. Avocations: collecting books, television history, portrait artist. Home: PO Box 59667 Chicago IL 60659-0667 Office: Wilbur Wright Coll 4300 N Narragansett Ave Chicago IL 60634-1591 E-mail: tsills@ccc.edu.

SILLS, WILLIAM HENRY, III, investment banker; b. Chgo., Jan. 2, 1936; s. William Henry II and Mary Dorothy (Trude) Sills; children: William Henry IV, David Andrew Henry. AB, Dartmouth Coll., 1958; MA, Northwestern U., 1961. Stockbroker Bache & Co., Chgo., 1961—64; co-founder, investment banker Chgo. Corp., 1964—84, First of Mich. Corp., Chgo., 1984—86, Sills & Co., Inc., Zenda, Wis., 1986—. With Chgo. Harvard and Geneva Lake R.R. Co., 1962—, Wis. River Rail Transit Commn., 1995—; vice chmn., bd. dirs. Honduras-Am. Securities Ltd.; dir. Honduran-Am. Real Estate Programs; chmn. bd. dirs., pres. Cen. Am. Fund, Ltd., INVI, S.A., Honduras, San Pedro Sula, Cortes, 1990—; cons. in field; chmn., pres. Ferro Carreal Nacional de Honduras Acquiring Cmrp., 1993—; pres. PRC, U.S., Cen. Am. Transp. Co., 1988—. Commodore Sea Scout flotilla Ctrl. Region Boy Scouts Am., 1987—99, nat. vice commodore Nat. Sea Scout Fleet, 1992—; chmn. Geneva Lake (Wis.) Area Joint Transp. Commn., 1965—86, 1990—92, sec., 1992—. With USMC, 1955—61. Mem. Am. Soc. Traffic and Transp., Am. Short Line R.R. Assn., U.S. Yacht Racing Union (sr. judge), Inland Lake Yachting Assn. (sr. judge), Lake Geneva Yacht Club (commodore), Lake Geneva Country Club, Skeeter Ice Boat Club. Republican. Forward In Faith Episcopal. Address: PO Box 40 Zenda WI 53195-0040

SILTON, BARBARA J. educational center administrator BA, Calif. State U., 1972; MA, U. San Francisco, 1980, Internat. Coll., 1984; PhD, William Lyon U., 1990. Cert. lifetime tchr., Calif; lic. clin. psychologist. Counselor Yakima Indian Center, Santa Rosa, Calif., 1974-75; cons. hosp.-home instrn. multi-handicapped Los Angeles Unified Sch. Dist., Berenece Carlson Sch., 1975-80; cofounder, dir. Noble Ednl. Center, Woodland Hills, Calif., 1975—, pres. Noble Found., 1981—; cons. pvt. schs., including Montessori Schs. Santa Monica, Agoura, Woodland Hills; co-founder, pres. Silton-Read Learning Systems, Woodland Hills, 1985—. Contbr. articles to profl. jours. Mem. Am. Psychol. Assn., Council Exceptional Children, Assn. Ednl. Therapists, L.A. County Psychol. Assn. Office: 22008 Del Valle St Woodland Hills CA 91364-1637

SILTON, RONALD HELMUT, electrical engineer; b. Erfurt, Germany, May 11, 1951; arrived in U.S., 1953; s. William Frederick Siegel and Gerda Alma (Röhrborn) S.; m. Christine Marie Theresa Spinde, Aug. 24, 1985; children: John, James. BSEE, Fairleigh Dickinson U., 1973. Reg. prof. engr., fireman-in-charge (high pressure boilers). Field engr. Fla. Power & Light, West Palm Beach, 1973-77; assoc. engr. Pub. Svc. Elec. & Gas, Linden, N.J., 1977-78; staff engr. Gilbert Assoc., Reading, Pa., 1978-89; sr. engr. Combustion Engring., Aiken, S.C., 1989, Westinghouse Savannah River Co., Aiken, 1989—. Cons. Gilbert Assoc., Jackson, Mich., 1983-89, lead auditor, 1983-86, level III elec. inspector, 1987-89. Author, contbr. Jackson Edge, 1979-83; editor Cygnus, 1972. Charter orgn. rep. Boy Scouts Am., Augusta, 1994-98, asst. scoutmaster, Aiken, 1997-99, troop com., 1999-2000. Recipient Award of Merit, Boy Scouts Am., 1995. Mem. IEEE (regional dir. 1982-84), NSPE (chpt. pres. 1997-01, bd. dirs. 1994-01, engr. of yr. 1995), SCSPE (edn. found. vice-chmn. 1998—, state chpt. bd. dirs. 1999-2001), Jackson Ski Club (pres. 1978-82). Home: 211 Pebble Ln Aiken SC 29801-1200 Office: Westinghouse Savannah River Bldg 703-45A Aiken SC 29808-0001 E-mail: ron.silton@srs.gov., silton@ieee.org.

SILVA, BEVERLY, literature educator; b. L.A., May 12, 1932; d. Cecilio Cruz and Marian Langstaff; children: Geof, Carla, Madelyn, Joy. BA in English, San Jose State U., 1971, MA in English, 1976. Tchr. Met. Adult Edn., San Jose, Calif., 1977—88; adj. prof. Evergreen Coll., Ceilton, 1978—91, Gavion Coll., San Jose, 1978—91; prof. Mesa (Ariz.) C.C., 1991—. Author: (poetry) The Second St. Poems, 1983, The Cat and Other Stories, 1986, Nosotras: Latina Literature Today, 1985. Home: 6745 E Superstition Springs Blvd Mesa AZ 85206-4315

SILVA, CHERYL LYNN, financial economist; b. Providence, Sept. 26, 1968; d. Alfred and Shirley Elaine (Bennett) S. BA, Bowdoin Coll., Brunswick, Maine, 1990; MA, Northwestern U., 1992. Staff economist Chgo. Board of Trade, 1992-94, fin. economist, 1994-99; product mgr. Bus. Logic, Chgo., 1999-2000; sys. engr. Trading Techs., Evanston, 2000—01; sr. bus. sys. analyst Abbott Labs., Abbott Park, 2001—. Mem. Northwestern U. Chorus, Evanston, Ill., 1992-94. Recipient Noyes prize in Polit. Economy, Bowdoin Coll., 1990; Northwestern U. fellow, 1990-92. Mem. Futures Industry Assn. (info. tech. and rsch. divsns.). Avocations: playing tennis and golf, collecting sports memorabilia. Office: Abbott Labs Bldg J41-3 Dept R5YT2 200 Abbott Park Rd Abbott Park IL E-mail: clynnsilva@alumni.bowdoin.edu.

SILVA, JOANNE RIZZO, family nurse practitioner; b. Boston, Feb. 20, 1950; d. Anthony M. and Barbara A. Rizzo. BS, Northeastern U., 1972; MS, U. Colo., Denver, 1976. ACLS; cert. family nurse practitioner. RN pediat. Mass. Gen. Hosp., Boston, 1972—75; family nurse practitioner Frontier Nursing Svc., Hyden, Ky., 1976—78; nurse practitioner migrant health program U. Colo., Alamosa, 1978—79; family nurse practitioner, clinic mgr. Plan de Salud del Valle, Ft. Lupton, Colo., 1979—82; family nurse practitioner Family Health Svc., Worcester, Mass., 1982—89; fgn. svc. nurse practitioner State Dept., Washington, 1989—, Am. Embassy, Bucharest, Romania, 1989—91, Lima, Peru, 1991—96, fgn. svc. Kathmandu, Nepal, 1996—98, Am. Embassy Quito, Ecuador, 1998—2001; family nurse practitioner, Fla. Regional Ctr. Dept. of State, Ft. Lauderdale, 2002—. Nurse practitioner preceptor Robert Wood Johnson plan de salud del valle, Platteville, Colo., 1980-81, U. Lowell, Worcester, 1984-88, U. Wash., 1995. Recipient Cert. of Appreciation, Agy. Internat. Devel., Romania, 1990, Meritorious Honor award & Group Valor award, Romania, 1990, Dept. of State Health Practitioner of Yr. award, 1995. Mem. Sigma Theta Tau. Avocations: reading, scuba diving, traveling, photography. Address: 4511 S Ocean Blvd # 701 Highland Beach FL 33487 Office: Fla Regional Ctr Dept State 4000 N Andrews Ave Fort Lauderdale FL 33309

SILVA, JOSEPH, JR. dean, medical educator; BS , Rutgers U., 1962; MD, Northwestern U., 1966. Dean sch. medicine U. Calif., Davis, 1997—; prof. and chair. of internal med. U. of Calif. at Davis, 1980—. Office: U Calif Sch Medicine Office of Dean 2315 Stockton Blvd Rm 1501 Sacramento CA 95817*

SILVA, LAWRENCE KEHINDE, physical education educator; b. Lagos, Nigeria, June 27, 1948; s. Jacob Olawumi and Leah Adetunmibi Rotimi0Silva; m. Moji Silva, Mar. 8, 1980; children: James, Emmanuel, Daniel, Grace. BS, Benedict Coll., 1976; MAT, U. S.C., 1978; PhD, Ahmadu Bello U., Zaria, Nigeria, 1987. Asst. edn. officer Ministry of Edn., Govt. of Nigeria, Kaduna, 1971-78; lectr. Ahmadu Bello U., Zaria, 1979-90; assoc. prof. Bowie (Md.) State U., 1990—. Chmn. phys. edn. dept. Advanced Tchrs. Coll., Zaria, 1982-86; phys. edn. specialist Inst. of Edn., Zaria, 1986-90; faculty athletic rep. Bowie State U., 1998-98. Author: Community and Public Health, 1988; contbr. articles to sci. and profl. jours. Mem. AAUP, AAHPERD, Md. Assn. for Health, Phys. Edn., Recreation and Dance, Internat. Coun. for Health, Phys. Edn. (aging commn. 1992—). Democrat. Baptist. Avocations: music, athletics, Christian activities. Home: 9104 6th St Lanham MD 20706 Office: Bowie State U 14000 Jericho Park Rd Bowie MD 20715 E-mail: lsilva@bowiestate.edu.

SILVA, OMEGA LOGAN, physician; b. Washington, Dec. 14, 1936; d. Louis Jasper and Ruth (Dickerson) Logan; m. C. Francis A. Silva, Oct. 25, 1958 (div. 1981); 1 child, Frances Cecile; m. Harold Bryant Webb, Nov. 28, 1982. BS cum laude with honors in chemistry, Howard U., Washington, 1958, MD, 1967. Bio-chemist NIH, Bethesda, Md., 1958-63; asst. chief endocrinology Vets. Affairs Med. Ctr., Washington, 1977-96; physician Mitchell-Trotman Med. Group, P.C., 1996-97; assoc. prof. endocrinology George Washington U., 1975-91, prof., 1991-98, prof. emeritus, 1999—; prof. Howard U., 1977-96. Mem. exec. com. Health Care Coun. Nat. Capital Area, 1995—, bd. dirs.; med. rev. officer Employee Health Programs, Bethesda, 1998—. Author: (with others) Endocrinology, 1990; contbr. articles to profl. jours. Charter mem. Nat. Mus. of Women in the Arts, Washington, 1986; trustee Howard U., 1991-97. Recipient Disting. Alumni award Howard U. Coll. Medicine, 1997. Fellow ACP (Best Sci. Presentation award 1974); mem. Am. Chem. Soc., Am.

Med. Women's Assn. (br. I v.p. 1986-87, pres. 1987-88, anti-smoking task force 1989-92, chair govtl. affairs, 1992-96, mem. nominations com. 1992, gov. region III 1996-97, v.p. program 1997-99, chmn. leadership com. 1996-97, pres. elect 1999-2000, pres. 2000-2002), Howard U. Med. Alumni (pres. 1983-88, bd. dirs. 1983—), Alpha Omega Alpha. Avocations: dress and hat design, furniture design, home construction.

SILVA, PAUL DOUGLAS, reproductive endocrinologist; b. Durban, Natal, Republic South Africa, Oct. 29, 1956; came to U.S., 1968; s. George Douglas and Georgette Marie (Schedivetz) S.; m. Diane Elisabeth Deterville, June 28, 1980; children: Julie Renee, Jennifer Marie, Dawn Elisabeth. BA in Biology, UCLA, 1976; MD, U. Calif., Davis, 1981. Diplomate Am. Bd. Ob-Gyn, Am. Bd. Reproductive Endocrinology. Resident in ob-gyn. U. Calif., Irvine, 1981-85; fellow in reproductive endocrinology U. So. Calif., L.A., 1985-87; reproductive endocrinologist Gundersen/Luth. Med. Ctr., La Crosse, Wis., 1987—; med. rschr. Gundersen Med. Found., 1987—. Cons. St. Francis Med. Ctr., La Crosse, 1988—. Contbr. articles to Jour. Am. Acad. Dermatology, Am. Jour. Ob-Gyn., Jour. Clin. Endocrinology and Metabolism, Acta Endocrinology, others. Lectr. to cmty. orgns. Recipient Geog. Acad. award U. Calif., Irvine, 1984, rsch. award Soc. for Gynecologic Investigation, 1987, svc. award Pacific Coast Fertility Soc., 1987; Gundersen Med. Found. grantee, 1989—. Fellow ACOG, Am. Fertility Soc.; mem. Am. Assn. Gynecologic Laparoscopists, Soc. Reproductive Endocrinologists. Roman Catholic. Achievements include development of outpatient methods for surgical treatment of reproductive diseases which were previously treated by inpatient methods; demonstration that androstenedione may be a more important androgen in women than testosterone. Office: Gundersen Clinic 1836 South Ave La Crosse WI 54601-5494

SILVAGNI, ANTHONY JOSEPH, dean, osteopath; b. Atlantic City, Apr. 18, 1940; s. Anthony Serafino and Madeline (Valentino) S.; m. Marlene Scherr, Mar. 12, 1961 (div. July 1977); children: Paul, Michelle; m. Dianna Poole, Oct. 1, 1977. BS in Pharmacy, Phila. Coll. of Pharmacy and Sci., 1963, MS in Hosp. Pharmacy, 1966, PharmD, 1970; postgrad., Purdue U., 1963-64; DO, Phila. Coll. Osteo. Medicine, 1982. Resident in hosp. pharmacy Thomas Jefferson U. Hosp., Phila., 1965-66, assoc. dir. pharmacy services, 1969-73; chief pharmacist prescription div. cen. pharm. services Appalachian Regional Hosp., Williamson, W.Va., 1966-67, asst. dir. cen. pharm. services, 1967-68; dir. pharmacy services Presbyn. U. Pa. Hosp., Phila., 1968-69; dir. pharmacy programs Lake Area Health Edn. Ctr., Erie, 1973-74; assoc. dir. clin. pharmacy services Peter Bent Brigham Hosp., Boston, 1974-76; clin. pharmacist U. Ariz., Tucson, 1976-78; faculty Health Care Edn. Programs Am., Chestnut Hill, Mass., 1980-82; intern Tucson Gen. Hosp., 1982-83; physician Dakota Family Practice, Parkston, S.D., 1983—; dean Nova Southeastern Univ. Coll. of Osteopathic Med., 1998—. Instr. in clin. pharmacy Phila. Coll. Pharmacy and Sci., 1969-73; asst. profl clin. pharmacy U. Ariz., 1977-78; chmn. dept. clin. practice Mass. Coll. Pharmacy, Boston, 1974-76; cons. clin. pharmacy Tucson Gen. Hosp., 1977-78, dir. clin. pharmacy services, 1977-78, vis. cons. staff dept. medicine, 1978; vis. faculty hypertension, Smith, Kline & French, Phila., 1980-82; lectr. to nat., state, county and local health profl. orgns. Contbr. articles to profl. jours. Mem. curriculum com. Mass. Coll. Pharmacy, 1974-76, chmn. PharmD admissions com., 1975-76; mem. bldg. com. U. Ariz. Coll. Pharmacy, 1976-78, grad. thesis com., 1977-78, faculty voting rights com., 1978, chmn. grade grievance com, 1978. Served with U.S. Army, 1961-62. Pa. State U. grantee, VA grantee, Lakes Area Regional Med. Program grantee, Smith, Kline and French grantee; Merck Sharp and Dohme scholar, 1979, Nat. Student Osteo. Med. Assn. scholar, 1980. Fellow Am. Found. for Pharm Edn.; mem. AMA, Am. Acad. Gen. Practitioners, Am. Osteo. Assn. (grantee), Am. Pharm. Assn. (review panel for handbook 1975—, practitioner panel 1973—), Am. Soc. Hosp. Pharmacists (adv. panel on student membership 1975-76), Am. Pharm. Assn. Acad. of Pharmacy Practice (charter), S.D. Med. Assn., Dist. 6 Med. Soc., Kappa Psi, Phi Sigma Gamma, Rho Chi. Avocations: flying, skiing, motorcycling, camping. Office: Nova Southeastern Univ Coll of Med 3200 S Univ Drive, Rm 1401 Terry Bldg Fort Lauderdale FL 33328*

SILVA POTTS, MARGARITA, counselor; b. El Paso, Tex., June 28, 1950; d. Virgil Irwin and Estella (Silva) Mohler; m. Charles Ray Leeth, June 28, 1970 (dec. Jan. 1978); 1 child, Aimée N.; m. Steven Dale Potts, Jan. 4, 1980; 1 child, Elliott S. AA, Fresno City Coll., 1970; student, Fresno State U., 1970-72; BS, Western Mich. U., 1988, MA, 1992. Lic. profl. counselor, Mich. Dietitian's asst. Albion (Mich.) Cmty. Hosp., 1972-80; field rep. Assn. for Child Devel., Lansing, Mich., 1985-91; home/sch. liaison Western Sch. Dist., Parma, 1988-91; supr. client svcs. Guardian, Inc., Battle Creek, 1992-97; program supr. Starr Commonwealth, Jackson, 1998—2001; pres. Doches Inc., 2001—. Presenter in field. Contbr. articles to profl. jours. Commr. Human Rels. Commn., Jackson, Mich., 1988-93; mem. coun. Regiona. Inter-agy. Coord. Coun., Battle Creek, 1995-96; cons. Families for Kids, Kellogg Found., Battle Creek, 1993. Recipient Oneness of Human Kind Leadership award, 2000; grantee Thurgood Marshall Profl. grantee, Western Mich. U., 1991—92. Mem. ACA, Nat. Assn. Human Rights Workers (profl. human rights worker), Mich. Counseling assn. (del. 1996-97, Human Rights award 2000), Mich. Counseling Assn., Mich. Assn. Multicultural Counseling and Devel. (bd. dirs. 1992—, Counselor of Yr. 1997), League United L.Am. Citizens (treas. Jackson dep. state dir. 1997—). Episcopalian. Avocations: reading, gardening, cooking. Home: 14500 Hanover Rd Hanover MI 49241 Office: Dochas Inc 209 E Washington Ste 246 Jackson MI 49201 E-mail: msilva_potts@hotmail.com.

SILVEIRA, AUGUSTINE, JR. chemistry educator; b. Mattapoisett, Mass., July 17, 1934; s. Augustine and Mildred (Lewis) S.; m. Beverly Ann Washburn, Aug. 20, 1960; children: Linda Ann, Karen Louise. BS, U. Mass., Dartmouth, 1957, ScD (hon.), 1975; PhD., U. Mass., Amherst, 1962. Research chemist Acushnet Process Co., Mass., 1957-58; instr. U. Mass., 1960-62; asst. prof. Rutgers U., 1962-63; assoc. prof. SUNY, Oswego, 1963-64, prof., 1964-67, chmn. dept. chemistry, 1967-2000, disting. tchg. prof., 1976-2000, disting. tchg. prof. emeritus, 2000—. Am. Coun. on Edn. fellow U. Calif., Irvine, 1969-70, vis. prof., 1976-77, 83-84, 91, 98; vis. prof. Calif. State U., Long Beach, 1976-77; cons. to edn. and industry; guest lectr.; evaluator SUNY Grad. Programs, 1968-70, Patent Policy Bd., 1971; mem. commn. higher edn. Middle States Assn., 1971—; mem. alumni adv. coun. U. Mass., 1971-75; mem. N.Y. State Bd. Optometry, 1981-91, N.Y. State Bd. Chiropractic, 1999—. Contbr. articles to profl. jours. Recipient N.Y. State/United Univ. Professions Excellence award, 1990; named to Fairhaven H.S. Hall of Fame Lifetime Achievement award; SUNY faculty exch. scholar, 1981—; SUNY rsch. grantee. Fellow Am. Inst. Chemists; mem. AAUP (v.p. 1965-66), Am. Chem. Soc. (Syracuse sect. award 1988, Syracuse sect. chair Citation award 2000), Sigma Xi (pres. 1972-73, 78-79), Delta Kappa Phi, Alpha Kappa Phi, Phi Kappa Phi. Office: SUNY Oswego Chemistry Dept Oswego NY 13126 Home: 61 Bayview Ave Fairhaven MA 02719-1801

SILVER, ANN-LOUISE SCHLESINGER, psychoanalyst, psychiatrist; b. Syracuse, N.Y., Mar. 3, 1942; d. Edward Ralph and Sylvia (Nelson) Schlesinger; m. Stuart Beal Silver, Apr. 2, 1962; children: Jean Lara Silver-Isenstadt, Daniel Joseph, Theodore Len. Student, Mt. Holyoke Coll., 1959-61; BA, Johns Hopkins U., 1963, MD, 1966; grad., Wash. Psychoanalytic Inst., 1989. Staff psychiatrist Springfield Hosp. Ctr., Sykesville, Md., 1974, Clifton T. Perkins Hosp. Ctr., Jessup, 1974-76, Chestnut Lodge Hosp., Rockville, 1976—2001, dir. edn. Chestnut Lodge, 1994—99. Clin. prof. U.S. U. of Health Scis., Bethesda, 1980—; clin. instr. Johns Hopkins U. Sch. Medicine, 1976—2001; civilian cons. Walter Reed Army Med. Ctr., Washington, 1987—; mem. faculty Wash. Sch. Psychiatry, 1984—, Wash. Psychoanalytic Inst., 1993—; pres. Columbia Study Group, 1978—; dir. Columbia Acad. Psychodynamics, 2001—. Editor: Psychoanalysis and Psychosis, 1989, Psychoanalysis and Severe Emotional Illness, 1990, Illness in the Analyst, 1990; contbr. articles to profl. jours. Fellow: Am. Psychiat. Assn., Am. Acad. Psychoanalysis (trustee 1993, pres. 1999—2000); mem.: Internat. Soc. Psychotherapy Schizophrenia (pres. U.S. chpt.), Internat. Psychoanalytical Assn., Am. Psychoanalytic Assn. Avocations: gardening, piano.

SILVER, BARNARD JOSEPH STEWART, mechanical and chemical engineer, consultant, inventor; b. Salt Lake City, Mar. 9, 1933; s. Harold Farnes and Madelyn Cannon (Stewart) S.; m. Cherry Bushman, Aug. 12, 1963; children: Madelyn Stewart Palmer, Cannon Farnes, Brenda Picketts Porter. BSME, MIT, 1957; MS in Engring. Mechanics, Stanford U., 1958; grad. Advanced Mgmt. Program, Harvard Grad. Sch. Bus., 1977. Registered profl. engr. Colo. Engr. aircraft nuclear propulsion divsn. GE Co., Evandale, Ohio, 1957; engr. Silver Engring. Works, Denver, 1959-66, mgr. sales and tech. svcs., 1966-71, pres., 1998-99, chmn. bd., 1999—; chief engr. Union Sugar divsn. Consol. Foods Co., Santa Maria, Calif., 1971-74; directeur du complex SODESUCRE Abidjan, Cote d'Ivoire, 1974-76; supt. engring. and maintenance U and I Inc., Moses Lake, Wash., 1976-79; pres. Silver Enterprise Denver, 1971—, Silver Energy Systems Corp., Moses Lake, 1980-98, chmn. bd., 1998—; pres., gen. mgr. Silver Chief Corp., 1983—; pres. Silver Corp., 1984—; chmn. bd. Silver Pubs., Inc., 1986-87, 90—; bd. mem., sec. Agronomics Internat., McLean and Salt Lake City, 1994—; exec. v.p. Cascadian Inulin L.L.C., Sedro-Wooley, Wash., 1996—; mgr. Silver Inulin LLC, Moses Lake, 1996-98; dir. processing rsch. Inula, Wyo., Lovell, 1999—, bd. mgrs.; v.p. Barnard J. Stewart Cousins Land Co., 1987-88, 92—; chmn. Mid. East Peace Inst., 1998—; founder Life Energy Foods, L.L.C., Salt Lake City, 2000—. Dir. Isle Piquant Sugar Found., 1993-94; mem. steering com. World Botanical Inst., 1993-99; instr. engring. Big Bend C.C., 1980-81. Patentee in field, including patent for extracting novel inulin fractions soluable substances from subdivided solids, 1995. Explorer adviser Boy Scouts Am., 1965-66, 89-90, chmn. cub pack com., 1968-74, 94-96, chmn. scout troop com., 1968-74, vice chmn. Columbia Basin Dist., 1986-87; pres. Silver Found., 1961-87, v.p., 1987-97, sec., treas. 1997—; ednl. conselor MIT, 1971-89; pres. Chief Moses Jr. H.S. Parent Tchr. Student Assn., 1978-79; missionary Ch. of Jesus Christ of Latter-day Saints, Can., 1953-55, Hawaii, P.R., Ctrl. and South Am., Asia, 1959-68, West Africa, 1988, Cote d'Ivoire, 1988-89, Zaire, 1989, Holladay North Stakes, 1991, 95,-97, Cheyenne, 1998-99, Salt Lake Inner-City Project Mission, 2000—; dist. pres. No. B.C., No. Alberta, Yukon and N.W. Ters., 1955; stake high counselor, Santa Maria, Calif., 1971-72, Moses Lake Wash., 1977-79; presiding elder Cote d'Ivoire, 1974-76, 88; 2d counsleor Moses Lake Stake Presidency, 1980-88; bd. dirs. Columbia Basin Allied Arts, 1986-88; mem. Health Sci. Coun. U. Utah, 1991—; mem. Sunday sch. gen. bd. Ch. of Jesus Christ of Latter-Day Saints, 1991-93, com. for mems. with Disabilities, 1992-93, CHOICE adv. bd., 1993-95; emergency preparedness dir. Holladay North Stake, 1993-95. Served with Ordnance Corps., U.S. Army, 1958-59. Decorated Chevalier Ordre National (Republic of Cote d'Ivoire). Mem. ASME, Assn. Energy Engrs., AAAS, Am. Soc. Sugar Beet Technolgists, Internat. Soc. Sugar Cane Technologists, Am. Soc. Sugar Can Technologists, Environ. Engrs. & Mgrs. Inst., Sugar Industry Technicians, Nat. Fedn. Ind. Bus., Utah State Hist. Soc. (life), Mormon Hist. Assn., G.P. Chowder and Marching Soc., Western Hist. Assn., Sons of Utah Pioneers (life), Univ. Archeol. Soc. (life), Kiwanis, Cannon-Hickley Study Group, Sigma Xi (life, sec., treas., Utah chpt. 1994-99), Pi Tau Sigma, Sigma Chi, Alpha Phi Omega. Republican. Mem. Lds Ch. also: Agronomics Internat 4390 South 2300 East Salt Lake City UT 84125-3651 also: Silver Pubs Inc 4390 S 2300 E Salt Lake City UT 84124-3501 E-mail: cbsilver@worldnet.att.net.

SILVER, BARRY MORRIS, lawyer, lay preacher; b. Mt. Vernon, N.Y., Nov. 18, 1956; s. Samuel Manuel and Elaine Martha (Shapiro) S. BA, Fla. Atlantic U., 1979; JD, Nova U., 1983. Bar: Fla. 1983. Law clk. to presiding justice 4th Dist. Ct. Appeals, West Palm Beach, Fla., 1982-83; pvt. practice Boca Raton, 1983—; sole practice, 1986—. Tchr. Hebrew and religion Temple Beth El, Boca Raton, 1979-84; tchr. bilingual edn. Palm Beach County Schs., Delray Beach, Fla., 1981-83; faculty Palm Beach Jr. Coll., Boca Raton, 1990—; atty. NOW, South Palm Beach County; mem. Fla. Ho. Reps., 1997-98. Vol. Haitian Refugee Ctr., Miami, 1982. Mem. Fla. Bar Assn., Palm Beach County Bar Assn., Sierra. Democrat. Jewish. Avocations: languages, tennis, Frisbee, chess, backgammon. Office: 7777 Glades Rd Ste 308 Boca Raton FL 33434-4150 Home: 18624 Cape Sable Dr Boca Raton FL 33498-6374 E-mail: barryboca@aol.com.

SILVER, BRIAN QUAYLE, broadcast journalist, musician, educator; b. Denver, Sept. 8, 1942; s. Harold Farnes and Madelyn Cannon (Stewart) S.; m. Shubha Sankaran, Dec. 4, 1988; adopted children: Laila Benazir Robinson, Zain Ganapathi Ramdas Sankaran. BA, Harvard Coll., 1964; postgrad., Sch. Oriental and African Studies U. London, 1969-70; PhD., U. Chgo., 1980. Asst. prof. Urdu U. Minn., 1971-74; assoc. prof. Urdu & Indo-Muslim studies Harvard U., 1974-83; lectr. music U. Va., Charlottesville, 1995; dir. internat. house, asst. dean study abroad Duke U., 1983-86; exec. dir. Internat. Music Assocs., Washington, 1982—; chief, Urdu svc. Voice of Am., 1986—. Dir. internat. exchange programs Pan Orient Arts Found., Manchester, N.H., 1968—, exec. dir., 1994—; bd. dirs. Archive Rsch. Ctr. Ethnomusicology, New Delhi, India, 1993—; South Asia coun. Assn. Asian Studies, Ann Arbor, Mich., 1983-86. Sitar performance in India, Pakistan, Bangladesh, Morocco, England, Peru, Canada and U.S., 1966—; contbr. numerous publs. on South Asian Music and Urdu Lit. Dir. Durham Chpt. UNICEF, 1984-86. Named Khansahib, All-Pakistan Music Conf., Lahore, 1988; recipient Gold medal, 1989; grantee in aid D.C. Commn. for Arts and Humanities/Nat. Endowment for Arts, 1991-92, 96-97; Fulbright grantee Inst. Internat. Edn., India, 1964-66; Ford fellow Am. Coun. Learned Socs., England, Pakistan, India, 1969-71, Am. Inst. Indian Studies, India, 1982-83. Mem. Soc. Ethnomusicology (New England chpt. v.p. 1978-80), Assn. Asian Music, Internat. Coun. Tradition Mus., Asia Soc., Assn. Asian Studies, Folklore Soc. Greater Washington. Avocations: cooking, gardening, films, travel. Home: 1730 C St NE Washington DC 20002-6661 Office: Internat Music Assocs PO Box 15526 Washington DC 20003-0526 E-mail: PanOrient@aol.com.

SILVER, CAROL RUTH, lawyer; b. Boston, Oct. 1, 1938; d. Nathan and Mildred S.; children: Steven Chao, Jefferson Chao Frensley; m. Stanley Mayerson, 1990 (div. 1994). BA, U. Chgo., 1960, JD, 1964. Bar: Calif. 1964, U.S. Supreme Ct. 1970, U.S. Dist. Ct. (so. dist.) La., U.S. Dist. (no. and cen. dists.) Calif. Dir. atty. Calif. Rural Legal Assistance, Delano, 1965-68; exec. dir. Berkeley (Calif.) Neighborhood Legal Svcs., 1968-71; tchr. Golden Gate Law Sch., San Francisco, 1970-73; legal counsel to sheriff City of San Francisco, 1972-75; elected ofcl. Bd. of Suprs., City and County of San Francisco, 1978-89; real estate broker San Francisco, 1985—, Carol Ruth Silver Real Estate, 1990—; pvt. practice law, 1978—. Spl. counsel ABRH Cons., Washington, 1988-90; cons. Nat. Legal Aid & Defender Assn., Washington, 1968-75; del. to ho. dels. Calif. Bar, Sacramento, 1972-74. Founder, editor, pub. Myers Flat News, 1996—; contbr. articles to profl. jours.; bd. editors Tikun. Pres. Golden Gate Bridge Dist., San Francisco, 1988, San Francisco Bay Area Air Pollution Control Dist., 1987, Friends of San Francisco Inmates and Deps., 1982, Golden Gate Dem. Club, San Francisco, 1976; founder Chinese Am. Internat. Sch., San Francisco, bd. dirs., 1980-2000; pres., co-founder Every Child A Wanted Child, San Francisco, 1989-95; bd. dirs. UN World Ctr., San Francisco, 1981—; chmn. bd. dirs. Jewish Ednl. Ctr., 1997-98; candidate for Dem. nomination U.S. Congress, 1996; bd. dirs. WildAid, 2001—; chair 1961 Freedom Riders 40th Reunion, Jackson, Miss.; co-chair San Francisco Friends Afghanistan, 2002—. Fellow Sch. Govt., Harvard U., 1973-74; recipient Cable Car award Tavern Guild, 1985, Award of Merit, Lawyers Constl. Def. Com., 1965. Mem. NOW, ACLU, Nat. Abortion Rights Action League. Jewish. Avocations: opera, family activities, travel, writing, hiking. E-mail: myersflat@aol.com.

SILVER, CHARLES MORTON, communications company executive; b. New Haven, Sept. 22, 1929; s. Sam and Rose (Fischman) S.; m. Rose Charek, Mar. 27, 1960; children— Ronni Ellen, Suzanne Paula, Steven Mitchell. BS, U Conn., 1954. With Arthur Andersen & Co., N.Y.C., 1954-61, ITT, N.Y.C., 1961-88, ret. as v.p. and assoc. treas., 1988. Served with U.S. Army, 1947-48, 50-51. Mem. AICPA, Roxbury Swim and Tennis Club. Home: 51 Akbar Rd Stamford CT 06902-1401 also: PO Box 420275 Summerland Key FL 33042-0275

SILVER, DAVID, b. N.Y.C., Jan. 27, 1931; s. Sol and Fannie (Stein) S.; m. Meryl Young, Sept. 14, 1952 (dec.); children: Daniel, Matthew, Joshua; m. Ann Schwartz, June 4, 1993. BA, CCNY, 1953; LL.B. cum laude, Harvard U., 1958. Bar: N.Y. 1958, D.C. 1979. Pvt. practice law, N.Y.C., 1960-61; spl. counsel SEC, Washington, 1961-65; gen. counsel Investors Planning Corp., N.Y.C., 1965-66; asst. counsel Investment Co. Inst., Washington, 1966-69, gen. counsel, 1969-77, pres., 1977-91, ICI Mut. Ins. Co., Bethesda, Md., 1987-2001. Cons. securities regulation Govt. of India, 1964; mutual fund regulation Govt. of China, 1999; lectr. Law Sch. Boston U., 1995—98; mem. individual investor adv. com. N.Y. Stock Exch., 1994—99. Served with U.S. Army, 1953-55. Mem. Fed. Bar Assn. (exec. council securities com., past chmn. investment co. com.). Home and Office: 9410 Brooke Dr Bethesda MD 20817-2110 E-mail: anndave@verizon.net.

SILVER, DONALD, surgeon, educator; b. N.Y.C., Oct. 19, 1929; s. Herman and Cecilia (Meyer) S.; m. Helen Elizabeth Harnden, Aug. 9, 1958; children: Elizabeth Tyler, Donald Meyer, Stephanie Davies, William Paige. AB, Duke U., 1950, BS in Medicine, MD, 1955. Diplomate Am. Bd. Surgery, Am. Bd. Gen. Vascular Surgery, Am. Bd. Thoracic Surgery. Intern Duke Med. Ctr., 1955-56, asst. resident, 1958-63, resident, 1963-64; mem. faculty Duke Med. Sch., 1964-75, prof. surgery, 1972-75; cons. Watts Hosp., Durham, 1965-75, VA Hosp., Durham, 1970-75, chief surgery, 1968-70; prof. surgery, chmn. dept. U. Mo. VA Med. Ctr., Columbia, 1975-98. Cons. Harry S. Truman Hosp., Columbia, 1975— ; mem. bd. sci. advisers Cancer Research Center, Columbia, 1975— ; mem. surg. study sect. A NIH; dir surg. svcs. U. Mo. Health System, 2001—. Contbr. articles to med. jours., chpts. to books; editorial bds.; Jour. Vascular Surgery, Postgrad. Gen. Surgery, Vascular Surgery. Served with USAF, 1956-58. James IV Surg. traveler, 1977 Fellow ACS (gov. 1995-99), Deryl Hart Soc.; mem. AMA, AAAS, Mo. Med. Assn., Boone County Med. Soc., Internat. Cardiovascular Soc., Soc. Univ. Surgeons, Am. Heart Assn. (Mo. affiliate rsch. com.), Soc. Surgery Alimentary Tract, Assn. Acad. Surgery, So. Thoracic Surg. Assn., Internat. Soc. Surgery, Soc. Vascular Surgery, Am. Assn. Thoracic Surgery, Am. Surg. Assn., Ctrl. Surg. Assn. (pres.-elect 1990-91, pres. 1991-92), Western Surg. Assn., Midwestern Vascular Surg. Soc. (pres. 1984-85), Ctrl. Surg. Assn. Found. (treas. 1992-93, 2d v.p. 1993-94, 1st v.p. 1994-95, pres. 1995-96). Home: 1050 W Covered Bridge Rd Columbia MO 65203-9569 Office: U Mo Med Ctr Dept Surgery N514 Columbia MO 65212-0001 E-mail: Silverd@health.missour.edu.

SILVER, EMILY ANN, artist, educator; b. Kremmling, Colo., July 13, 1951; d. Byron John and Halka Pattison Chronic; m. James Kevin Silver, June 6, 1980; children: Lindsay G., Dylan M. AB with distinction in art, Stanford U., 1973. Designer William O'Brien, Roy Ritola, Inc., San Francisco, 1973-75; prin. Emily Silver Illustration and Design, Menlo Park, Calif., 1975-80; sr. graphic designer Apple Computer, Cupertino, 1979-80; prin. Silver Fine Design, Pullman, Sedro Woolley, Wash., 1980-93; instr. fine art Wash. State U., Pullman, 1981-88; instr. art Skagit Valley Coll., Mt. Vernon, Wash., 1992-93, Western Nev. C.C., Carson City, 1993-98; contract artist Pelican Bay State Prison, Crescent City, Calif., 1998—. Artist-in-residence Wash. State Arts Commn., Olympia, 1991-92; art facilitator Pioneer Ctr. North, Sedro Woolley, Wash., 1992-93; roster artist, artist-in-residence Nev. Arts Coun., Carson City, 1993-99. One-woman shows include Sierra Arts Found., Reno, Nev., Morris Graves Mus. of Art, Eureka, Calif., 2000, Ink People, Eureka, Calif., 1999, Sun Mountain Gallery, Virginia City, Nev., 1999, City 2000 Gallery, Reno, 1996, Lucy Gallery, Spokane, Wash., 1984, NICA Gallery, Pullman, Wash., 1984, Hyde St. Pier Drawings, 1978, Western Nev. C.C. Gallery, 1994-96, Wiseman Gallery, Rogue River C.C., 1997, Nev. State Legis., 1997; group exhbns. include The Artists of Mt. St. Helens, 1983, Women in Wash.: The 1st 100 Years, 1989, N.W. Women, 1993, Biggest Little Art Show, 1996, Ink People, 1999, Laguna Art Mus., Laguna Beach, Maryhill Mus., Goldendale, Wash.; collections include Gov. Bob and Sandy Miller, Del Norte County Dept. Social Svcs., Western Nev. C.C., Wash. State U. Mus. of Fine Art, Spokane Sch. Dist. #81, Del Norte County Social Svcs., Northshorte Sch. Dist., State Senator Pat and Maxine Patterson, others. Artists grantee Sierra Arts Found., 1995, North Coast Cultural Trust, 2000, McLean Found., 2001. Mem. Sierra Arts Found., Humboldt Arts Coun., Ink People Ctr. for the Arts. Avocations: yoga, hiking, tennis. Home: 4278 Grizzly Bluff Rd Ferndale CA 95536-9771 E-mail: esilver713@aol.com.

SILVER, GARY L. chemist; married. PhD, U. N.C. Monsanto ellow Mound Lab., Miamisburg, Ohio, 1963—95; tech. staff mem. Los Alamos (Ohio) Nat. Lab., 1996—. Home: 868 Kristi Ln Los Alamos NM 87544 Office: Los Alamos Nat Lab PO Box 1663 Los Alamos NM 87545

SILVER, GEORGE, metal trading and processing company executive; b. Warren, Ohio, Dec. 17, 1918; s. Jacob and Sophie (Bradlyn) S.; m. Irene Miller, Aug. 5, 1945. Student, U. Ala., 1938; BA, Ohio U., 1940; postgrad. law sch., Ohio State U., 1940-41; grad., Adj. Gen. Sch., 1944. Pres. Riverside Indsl. Materials, Bettendorf, Iowa, 1947-70, Metalpel subs. Continental Telephone Co., Bettendorf, 1970-71, Riverside Industries Inc., Bettendorf, 1971—. Pres. Scott Resources Inc., Davenport, Iowa; v.p. Durbin Midwest, Davenport, 1987—90; mktg. dir. NAMCO Internat., Miami; cons. Waste Mgmt.-Non Ferrous Mktg., 1990—. Snyer Steel Casting, Iowa, Riverside Products, Ill., 1992—93, Tamron Internat. Ltd., Shanghai, 2002; founder Iowa Steel Mills (named changed to North Star Steel), Cargill and Wilton; mktg. dir. NAMCO Environ. Svcs. Corp., Miami, Fla., 1995—; bd. dirs. NAMCO Trading Co., Miami; cons. metal trading Cricket Club, Miami. Contbr. articles to profl. jours. Mem. Nat. UN Day Com., 1975-83. Capt. AC, USAF, 1941-46, 50-51, Korea. Named to Hon. Order Ky. Cols., 1991. Mem. Nat. Assn. Recycling Industries (co-chmn. nat. planning com., bd. dirs.), N.Y. Acad. Scis., Copper Club, Paper Stock Inst. Am. (exec. com.), Bur. Internat. de la Recuperation (chmn. adv. com.), Inter Global Trading Group (chmn. bd. dirs.), Mining Club N.Y.C., Outing Club, Hatchet Men's Chowder and Protective Assn., Copper Club, Jockey Club Miami, Williams Island Club, Rock Island Arsenal Officer's Club, Chemist Club (N.Y.C.), Crow Valley Country Club, Elks, Phi Sigma Delta. Fax: 305-891-0327.

SILVER, GEORGE ALBERT, physician, educator; b. Phila., Dec. 23, 1913; s. Morris M. and Sara (Tutelman) Silver; m. Mitzi Blieden, June 5, 1937; children: James David, Jane, Judith Ellen. BA, U. Pa., Phila., 1934; MD, Jefferson Med. Coll., Phila., 1938; MPH, Johns Hopkins U., Balt., 1948; MA (hon.) , Yale U., New Haven, 1969. Diplomate Am. Bd. Preventive Medicine. Asst. demonstrator Jefferson Med. Coll., Phila., 1939—42; health officer Balt. City Health Dept., 1948—51; asst. prof. Johns Hopkins U., Balt., 1948—51; chief divsn. social medicine Montefiore Hosp., N.Y.C., 1951—65; assoc. prof. health adminstrn. Columbia U., 1952—59; prof. social medicine Albert Einstein Coll. Medicine, 1959—65; dep. asst. sec. health and sci. affairs HEW, Washington, 1965—68; health exec. Nat. Urban Coalition, 1968—71; prof. pub. health Yale U., New Haven, 1969—84, prof. pub. health emeritus, 1984—. Chmn. com. on health policy Fedn. Am. Scientists, 2000. Author: Family Medical Care, 1963, Spy in the House of Medicine, 1974, Child Health: America's Future, 1978. Maj. M.C. U.S. Army, 1942—46. Named to Soc. of Scholars, Johns Hopkins U., 1993; recipient Superior Svc. award, HEW, 1966; fellow Branford Coll., Yale U. Fellow: APHA, N.Y. Acad. Medicine, Inst. Medicine NAS (sr.); mem.: Elizabethan Club, Sigma Xi. Democrat. Jewish. Home: 8100 Connecticut Ave Chevy Chase MD 20815-1636

SILVER, HARRY R. lawyer; b. Phila., Aug. 8, 1946; s. Jerome Benjamin Silver and Josephine Sandler (Steinberg) Furr; m. Jessica Dunsay, Nov. 23, 1972; children: Gregory, Alexander. BA, Temple U., 1968; JD, Columbia U., 1971. Bar: N.Y. 1972, D.C. 1973, U.S. Dist. Ct. D.C., U.S. Ct. Claims, U.S. Ct. Appeals (1st, 4th, 5th, 7th, 8th, 9th, 10th, fed. and D.C. cirs.), U.S. Supreme Ct. Law clk. to Hon. Harold R. Medina, U.S. Ct. Appeals (2d cir.), N.Y.C., 1971-72; assoc. Arent, Fox, Kintner, Plotkin & Kahn, Washington, 1972-74; atty. U.S. Dept. Justice, 1974-77, U.S. Dept. Energy, Washington, 1977-78; assoc. Akin, Gump, Strauss, Hauer & Feld, 1978-81, ptnr., 1981-88, Oppenheimer, Wolff & Donelly, Washington, 1988-91, Davis Wright Tremaine, Washington, 1991-94, Ober, Kaler, Grimes & Shriver, Washington, 1994—. Mem. ABA, Fed. Bar Assn. Avocations: running, music, travel. Home: 6829 Wilson Ln Bethesda MD 20817-4948 Office: Ober Kaler Grimes & Shriver 1401 H St NW Ste 500 Washington DC 20005-2175 E-mail: hrsilver@ober.com.

SILVER, HERBERT, physician; b. Bklyn., Feb. 18, 1932; s. Ben and Sylvia (Weinstock) S.; m. Judith Elaine Miller, Aug. 28, 1966; children: Rand Kenneth, David Jeffrey. BA, Adelphi U., 1953; MD, SUNY, Buffalo, 1957. Diplomate Am. Bd. Pathology. Intern Maimonides Med. Ctr., 1957-58; resident Nassau Univ. Med. Ctr., 1958-60, Hosp. of U. of Pa., 1960-62; assoc. pathologist, dir. blood bank/hematology Barnes-Jewish Hosp., St. Louis, 1964-70; dir. transfusion medicine Hartford (Conn.) Hosp., 1970—2001; assoc. prof. U. Conn. Med. Ctr., Farmington, 1970-90, U. Conn. Sch. of Allied Health, Storrs, 1977—2002. Cons. St. Francis Med. Ctr., Hartford, Conn., 1978-2002, Conn. Children's Med. Ctr., 1980-2002; med. dir. Hartford Med.

Lab, 1985-99. Author, editor: Probability of Inclusion in Paternity Testing, 1982, Problem Solving in Immunohematology, 1987; guest editor Transfusion Jour., 1992-96; contbr. articles to profl. jours. Bd. dirs. Emanuel Synagogue, West Hartford, Conn. Capt. U.S. Army Med. Corps, 1962-64. Mem.: AMA, Coll. Am. Pathologists, Am. Soc. Clin. Pathology, Am. Assn. Blood Banks (bd. dirs. 1987—92, Disting. Svc. award 1993, John Elliott Meml. award 2000). Democrat. Jewish. Avocations: bicycling, clarinet. Home: 32 Beacon Hill Dr West Hartford CT 06117-1003

SILVER, IAN ADAIR, pathology educator; b. Poona, India, Dec. 28, 1927; s. George James and Nora Adair (Seckham) S.; m. Marian Scrase, June 30, 1950 (dec. June 1994); children: Alison Janet, Fiona Marian, Alastair John, Robin Angus. m. Maria Erecinska, May 6, 1996. BA, Cambridge (Eng.) U., 1948, MA, 1952; DVM, London U., 1952. Demonstrator Cambridge U., 1952-57, lectr., 1957-70; prof. Bristol (Eng.) U., 1970—, chmn. dept. pathology and microbiology, 1980-93, dean of medicine, 1987-90, prof. emeritus pathology, 1993—, sr. rsch. fellow, 1995—; chmn. Southmead Hosp., Bristol, 1992-99, Inst. Clin. Neuroscis., Bristol, 2000—. Adj. prof. neurology U. Pa., 1976—. Editor numerous sci. books; contbr. articles to profl. jours. Lt. Brit. navy, 1944-46. Fellow Royal Coll. Vet. Surgeons (pres. 1985-87); mem. Internat. Soc. 02 Transport to Tissue (pres. 1977, 86), Brit. Vet. Assn. (Sir Frederick Hobday medal 1981, Dalrymple Champney medal 1985), Anat. Soc. U.K., Path. Soc. U.K., also others. 'vocations: farming, mountain climbing, fishing, reading. Office: Bristol U Vet Sch Southwell St Bristol BS2 8EJ England E-mail: ian.a.silver@bris.ac.uk.

SILVER, JACK MICHAEL, computer industry executive, consultant; b. Providence, Jan. 24, 1945; s. Ben and Mollie Zelda (Berman) S.; m. Marsha Diane Huttler, June 29, 1969; children: David Lee, Lauren Beth. BSBA, U. R.I., 1966, MBA in Fin., 1969. Underwriter Liberty Mut., Boston, 1966-67; data processing mgr. City and Sch. Sytem of Warwick, R.I., 1969-70; prof. mgmt. scis. U. R.I., Kingston, 1970-71; programming mgr. Am. Insulated Wire, Pawtucket, R.I., 1971-75; fin. systems supr. Raytheon Corp., Portsmouth, 1975-79; prin. Arthur Young and Co., Boston, 1979-83; v.p., gen. mgr. bd. dirs. ASA Internat. Ltd., Westboro, Mass., 1983—. Contbr. articles to profl. jours. Cons. R.I. Spl. Olympics, Warwick, 1986—. Jewish. Home: 2604 184th St Redondo Beach CA 90278-4509 Office: ASA Internat Ltd 10 Speen St Framingham MA 01701-4661

SILVER, JOAN, interior design consultant, artist; b. Port Huron, Mich., Jan. 12, 1927; d. Edwin Palmer and M. Jane (Hutchinson) Southard; m. Nov. 23, 1946 (div. Oct. 1972); children: Mark, Diane. Grad. high sch., Dearborn, Mich. Mgr. Systems, Inc., Traverse City, Mich., 1984-85, Ceramic Tile Sales, Southfield, 1978-83, Custom Tile Studio, Southfield, 1981-83, Broadway For Your Home, Kans. City, Mo., 1986-87, Midland Brick and Tile, Overland Park, Kans., 1987-88; pvt. practice, 1988—2001; ret., 2001—. Lectr. in field. Exhibited in group shows at Taos, N.M., 1985, travelling exhibit, 1985, Beijing China, 1995. Mem. Nat. Home Fashion League, Inc., Soc. Arts Crafts, Lawrence Art Guild. Home: PO Box 398 De Soto KS 66018-0398

SILVER, JOAN MICKLIN, film director, screenwriter; b. Omaha, May 24, 1935; d. Maurice David and Doris (Shoshone) Micklin; m. Raphael D. Silver, June 28, 1956; children: Dina, Marisa, Claudia. BA, Sarah Lawrence Coll., 1956. Writer, dir. (movies) Hester Street, 1975 (Writers Guild best screenplay nomination), Chilly Scenes of Winter, 1981, (TV film PBS) Bernice Bobs Her Hair starring Shelly Du Vall, 1975; dir. (TV films HBO) Finnegan, Begin Again with Robert Preston and Mary Tyler Moore, Parole Board, A Private Matter with Sissy Spacek and Aidan Quinn, (TV film Showtime) In The Presence of Mine Enemies, 1997, (films) Between the Lines, 1976, Crossing Delancey with Amy Irving, 1988, Loverboy, 1989, Stepkids, 1991; dir. stage plays and musicals including Album, Maybe I'm Doing It Wrong, Off-Broaday prodn. A...My Name is Alice; prod. On The Yard, (radio) Great Jewish Stories from Eastern Europe and Beyond, 1995; dir. (feature film) A Fish in the Bathtub, 1998, (TV film Lifetime) Invisible Child, 1999, (TV film Showtime) Charms for the Easy Life, 2001. Office: Silverfilm Prodns Inc 510 Park Ave New York NY 10022-1105

SILVER, JONATHAN M. physician; b. Paterson, N.J., May 10, 1953; s. Elihu Avigdor and Carol Ann Silver; m. Orli Silver, Mar. 4, 1979; children: Elliot, Benjamin, Leah. BA, Duke U., 1971-75; MD, Albert Einstein U., 1975-79. Diplomate Am. Bd. Psychiatry and Neurology. Intern in psychiatry Overlook Hosp., Summit, N.J., 1979-80; resident in psychiatry N.Y. State Psychiat. Inst., Columbia U., N.Y.C., 1980-83; rsch. fellow NIMH/N.Y. State Psychiat. Inst., Creedmoor, N.Y., 1983-84; attending psychiat. inpatient psychiatry svc. Columbia-Presbyn. Med. Ctr., N.Y.C., 1987-88, dir. psychiatry Allen Pavilion, 1988-93; dir. neuropsychiatry Columbia Presbyn. Med. Ctr., 1989-99; dir. psychiatry Columbia Presbyn. Psychiat. Assocs., 1993-99; chief Outpatient Ctr. for Mental Health, Lenox Hill Hosp., 1997—, asst. dir. clin. svcs. and rsch., dept. psychiatry, 1999—. Assoc. prof. clin. psychiatry Columbia U., 1994-98, lectr., 1998—; clin. prof. psychiatry NYU Sch. Medicine, 1998—. Editor: Neuropsychiatry of Traumatic Brain Injury, 1994; assoc. editor Jour. Neuropsychiatry; contbr. chpts. to books and articles to profl. jours. Recipient Laughlin award Nat. Psychiat. Endowment Fund, 1983. Fellow Am. Psychiat. Assn., Am. Neuropsychiat. Assn. (pres.-elect 2001—); mem. Phi Beta Kappa. Office: Lenox Hill Hosp 100 E 77th St New York NY 10021

SILVER, KATHLEEN FRANCES, rehabilitation counselor; b. Rochester, N.Y., May 5, 1947; d. Wilfred Laurier and Frances Pauline (Bidgood) Wyatt; divorced; children: Morgan Silver, Mark Orlando. BS, BA, U. Buffalo, 1971. Cert. rehab. counselor, disability mgmt., case mgr. Field dir. Am. Diabetes Assn., Buffalo, 1977-79; asst. dir. SPCC Home Health Svcs., Rochester, 1980-82; placement specialist Singer SS/VR, N.Y., 1982-84; sr. specialist Intracorp, Buffalo, 1984—. Sec. Auburn Crossroads Block Club, Buffalo, 1995-97; bd. dirs. Jellybean Junction Daycare, Buffalo, 1997-99; Ft. Erie Minor Lacrosse, v.p. 1995-99; bd. dirs. Buffalo Hornets Hockey, dir. of adminstrn., 1992-96; mem Parents Aux., North Buffalo Hockey Assn., 1998-2000; mem. religious edn. com. Unitarian-Universalist Ch., 2000—. Unitarian-Universalist. Office: Intracorp PO Box 1350 Buffalo NY 14240-1350 E-mail: ksilver@mail.intracorp.com.

SILVER, KATHRYN, health services executive; b. Belleville, Ill. d. Oliver and Bernice Knepper; m. Jules A. Silver (div. July 1986); children: Brett, Ryan. B of Health Care Adminstrn., U. Nev., 1994; MBA, U. Phoenix, 1996. Diplomate Am. Coll. Health Care Execs., cert. healthcare fin. profl. Regional dir. Maxi-Health IPA, Las Vegas, Nev., 1984-88; sr. assoc. adminstr. U. Med. Ctr., 1988-94; COO Lake Mead Hosp., North Las Vegas, Nev., 1994-96; CEO Oasis Health Sys., Las Vegas, 1996—2001; asst. adminstr. U. Med. Ctr., 2001—. Clin. asst. prof. hosp. adminstrn. U. Nev. Sch. Medicine, Reno. Mem. Healthcare Fin. Mgmt. Assn., Am. Assn. Integrated Health Care Delivery Systems, Am. Coll. Healthcare Execs. Republican. Roman Catholic. Avocations: golf, travel, shopping, gourmet dining. Office: Univ Med Ctr 1800 W Charleston Blvd Las Vegas NV 89102-4356 E-mail: ksilver928@aol.com.

SILVER, MALCOLM DAVID, pathologist, educator; b. Adelaide, South Australia, Apr. 29, 1933; s. Eric Bertram and Stella Louisa (Riley) S.; m. Meredith May Galloway, Jan. 19, 1957; children: Stuart Faulkner, Claire Eleanor, Caryl Louise. MD, U. Adelaide; PhD, McGill U. Diplomate: Am. Bd. Pathology. Resident med. officer Royal Adelaide Hosp., 1957-58; resident in pathology Royal Victoria Hosp.-Pathol. Inst., McGill U., Montreal, Que., Can., 1958-63; research fellow dept. exptl. pathology John Curtin Sch. Med. Research, Australian Nat. U., Canberra, 1963-65; asst. prof. pathology U. Toronto, 1965-68, assoc. prof., 1968-74, prof., 1974—79, chmn. dept. pathology, 1985-95, prof. dept. laboratory medicine and pathobiology, 1997-98; staff pathologist Toronto Gen. Hosp., 1965-72, sr. staff pathologist, 1972-79; prof., chmn. dept. pathology U. Western Ont., London, Can., 1979-85; chief pathology Univ. Hosp., London, 1979-85; pathologist in chief Toronto Gen. Hosp., 1985-89, The Toronto Hosp. (Toronto Gen. and Toronto Western Divs.), 1989-91, sr. staff pathologist, 1991-98. Prof. emeritus U. Toronto, 1998—. Contbr. articles to profl. jours. Fellow Royal Coll. Pathologists Australasia, Royal Coll. Physicians and Surgeons Can.; mem. Can. Assn. Pathologists, Ont. Assn. Pathologists, Internat. Acad. Pathology, Can. Cardiovascular Soc. E-mail: md.silver@utoronto.ca.

SILVER, MARC A. physician; b. Chgo., Oct. 14, 1949; s. Samuel and Ida (Reiter) S.; m. Laureen Dunne, Aug. 5, 1983. AB, U. Ill., Chgo., 1971; MD, Rush Med. Coll., Chgo., 1979. Instr. Rush Med. Coll., Chgo., 1979-82, instr. medicine and pathology, 1984-86; fellow NIH, Bethesda, Md., 1982-84; asst. prof. Loyola U. Med. Ctr., Maywood, Ill., 1986-88; assoc. prof. medicine and pathology Michael Reese Hosp. Med. Ctr., Chgo., 1988—, med. dir. cardiac surveillance unit, 1988—, chief div. cardiology and cardiovascular inst., 1988—, dir. heart failure programs, 1988—; prof. medicine Stritch Sch. Medicine Loyola U., 1994-98, dir. Heart Failure Ctr./assoc. dir. heart transplant program, 1994-98. Lectr. cardiac pathology Stritch Sch. Medicine; dir. Midwest Ctr. for Heart Failure, 1992-94; clin. prof. medicine U. Ill., 1998—; dir. cardiovascular disease fellowship Heart Failure Inst. Christ Hosp. and Med. Ctr., 1998—, chmn. dept. medicine, 2000—. Author: Success with Heart Failure, 1998; co-editor-in-chief Congestive Heart Failure; assoc. editor Angiogenesis and Myogenesis; contbr. articles to profl. jours.; mem. editl. bd. several jours. Manuscript Review Several Profl. Jours. Fellow ACP, Am. Coll. Cardiology, Am. Coll. Chest Physicians; mem. Internat. Soc. Heart Transplantatino, Am. Heart Assn., Soc. Cardiovasc. Pathology, Ctrl. Soc. Clin. Rsch., Alpha Omega Alpha. E-mail: marc.silver@advocatehealth.com.

SILVER, MARC LAURENCE, sales and marketing executive; b. Detroit, Oct. 10, 1953; s. Jerome and Muriel Silver; m. Rhonda Silver, Aug. 4, 1974; children: Bryan, Daniel. Student, Berklee Coll. Music, 1971-72, Wayne State U., 1973-75. With retail sales dept. Alexander Stationers, Los Angeles, 1976-77; instr. Dick Grove Sch. Music, L.A., 1977-79; owner Contemporary Guitar Workshop, 1979-80; sales rep. Ultra Systems, Detroit, 1980-81; with internal sales dept. David's Office Supply, Southfield, 1981-82; co-owner The Office Connection, Farmington Hills, 1982-84; account exec. United Stationers, Forest Park, Ill., 1984-85, vendor rels. mgr., 1985-86, internal sales mgr., 1986; midwest region mgr., nat. accounts mgr. Rubbermaid Office Products, Winchester, Va., 1986-88; dir. sales devel. Micro United Computer Products divsn. United Stationers, Des Plaines, Ill., 1988-90; dir. mktg., 1990-93; dir. furniture mktg. United Stationers, Des Plaines, Ill., 1993-94; v.p., creative dir. GlenHill Graphics, Glendale Heights, 1994—2002; exec. dir. market devel. The Systems House, Des Plaines, 2002—. Author: Contemporary Guitar Improvisation, 1977; co-patentee cutting system for document shredder, 1989, portable personal shredder, 1992. Small group leader and vol. musician, Willow Creek Cmty. Ch. Avocations: music performance and production, golf, tennis, softball, table tennis. Office: The Systems House 2250 E Devon Ave Ste 300 Des Plaines IL 60018

SILVER, MARVIN S. lawyer; b. Portland, Maine, Nov. 21, 1951; BS, Syracuse U., 1974; JD, Boston U., 1977, LLM, 1981. Bar: Mass. 1977, U.S. Dist. Ct. Mass. 1978, U.S. Tax Ct. 1983. Atty. Seder & Seder, Worcester, Mass., 1977-82, Seder & Chandler, Worcester, 1983—. Bd. dirs. Jewish Cmty. Ctr. of Worcester, Inc., Mass., 1982-84; mem. fin. com. Town of Shrewsbury, Mass., 1986-93, vice chmn., 1987-88, chmn. 1988-89; bd. dirs. Children's Friend Inc., 1990-99; bd. dirs. Westborough Edn. Found., Inc., 1996—, pres. 1999—, treas. 1996-99. Fellow Am. Coll. Trust and Estate Counsel; mem. Mass. Bar Assn. (chmn. estate planning com. tax sect. 1982-84, mem. tax sect. coun. 1983-86, mem. bus. law sect., probate law sect., taxation sect.), Worcester County Bar Assn. (co-chmn. tax law sect. 1981-84, 86-87, 97-98, bankruptcy and comml. law sect. 1987-88), Estate and Bus. Planning Coun. Worcester County (pres. 1990-91), Exch. Club of Tri-Towns, Inc. (pres. 1984-85) (Shrewsbury). Office: Seder & Chandler 339 Main St Ste 300 Worcester MA 01608-1585 E-mail: mssilver@sederlaw.com.

SILVER, MICHAEL, school superintendent; b. Landsberg, Germany, Jan. 30, 1948; came to U.S., 1949; s. Norman and Esther Silver; m. Beverley Ann Moss, May 16, 1971; children: Sabina, Joseph. AB, Washington U., 1970, MEd, 1973, PhD, 1982. Cert. supt. Mo., Wash. Tchr. Normandy Sch. Dist., St. Louis, 1970-72, Parkway Sch. Dist., St. Louis, 1972-75, asst. prin., 1976-79, adminstrv. asst., 1979-83, asst. to supt., 1983-84, asst. supt., 1984-86; supt. Tukwila Sch. Dist., Seattle, 1986—. Bd. dirs. Cities in Schs., Seattle; mem. adv. bd. Sta. KCTS, Seattle, 1990—; vis. exec. Seattle U. Sch. Edn., 1995. Author: Values Education, 1976, Facing Issues of Life and Death, 1976. Pres. SeaTac Task Force, Seattle, 1989; bd. dirs. Anti-Defamation League, Seattle, 1987—; mem. City of Tukwila (Wash.) 2000 Com., 1988-90. Recipient A Plus award Wash. Coun. Econ. Edn., 1992, Excellence in Ednl. Leadership award Univ. Coun. for Ednl. Adminstrn., 1998, Art Tribute award, Wash. Art Edn. Assn., 2001; named Exec. Educator, 100 Exec. Educator Mag., 1985, 1996 Assoc. for Inst. for Ednl. Inquiry Leadership Program; named to Homework Ctrl.; 100 Most Influential People in U.S. Pub. Edn.; I/D/E/A fellow Charles F. Kettering Found., 1978, 88, Title VI fellow Washington U., 1971-73; named Supt. of Yr. Wash. Libr. Media Assn., 2000. Mem. ASCD, Am. Assn. Sch. Adminstrs., Wash. Assn. Sch. Adminstrs. (met. chpt., pres. 1989-90), King County Supts. (chmn. adv. com. 1989-90, 95-96), Southcenter Rotary Club (Paul Harris fellow 1994), Southwest King County C. of C., Phi Delta Kappa. Home: 14127 SE 50th St Bellevue WA 98006-3409 Office: Tukwila Sch Dist 4640 S 144th St Seattle WA 98168-4134 E-mail: silverm@tukwila.wednet.edu.

SILVER, MORRIS, economist, educator; b. N.Y.C., July 9, 1931; s. Julius and Lilly S.; m. Sondra P. Hartman, Jan. 26, 1958; children: Gerald David, Ronald Alan. BA, CCNY, 1958; PhD (Earhart Found. fellow, Ford Found. fellow), Columbia U., 1964. Mem. faculty City Coll. CUNY, 1964—, assoc. prof. econs., 1968—, prof., 1972—, chmn. dept., 1969-95. Research asso. Nat. Bur. Econ. Research, 1967-71; cons crime deterrence and offender career Hudson Inst., 1974, Nat. Center for Health Services Research, 1970— Author: (with R.D. Auster) The State as a Firm, 1979, Affluence, Altruism, and Atrophy: The Decline of Welfare States, 1980, Prophets and Markets: The Political Economy of Ancient Israel, 1983, Enterprise and the Scope of the Firm, 1984, Economic Structures of the Ancient Near East, 1985, Foundations of Economic Justice, 1989, Taking Ancient Mythology Economically, 1992, Economic Structures of Antiquity, 1995. Served with AUS, 1953-55. Mem. Am. Econ. Assn. Jewish. Office: Dept Econs City Coll 133 D St New York NY 10031 E-mail: msilver12@nyc.rr.com.

SILVER, NEIL MARVIN, manufacturing executive; b. Bklyn., June 2, 1928; s. Jack and Rose (Eisenberg) S.; m. Leah Rebecca Coffman Silver, Sept. 4, 1949; children: Pamela Sue, Carole Beth. Student, U. Mich., 1945-46, 48-49; BS, Ind. U., 1951. Asst. mgr. Wolverine Parking Co., Lansing, Mich., 1951-54; treas. Capitol Parking Co., Indpls., 1955-60; controller, asst. to pres. Eberhart Steel Products, Inc., Mishawaka Tool & Die, Inc., Ind., 1961-63; PRES. Allied Quality Products, Inc., Mishawaka, Ind., 1964-67; treas. Allied Screw Products, Inc., 1968-88, chmn., sec., 1989—. Bd. dirs. Ind. State Anti-Defamation League, 1955-57; bd. dirs., treas., pres., chmn. Fin. Commn., Family and Children's Ctr., Inc., Mishawaka, Ind., 1957-77; bd. dirs., treas. Family Svc. Assn. St. Joseph County, Ind., 1955-57. With U.S. Army, 1946-48. Mem. AIAA, Soc. Mfg. Engrs., SAE Internat., Internat. Computing Soc., ASM Internat., B'nai B'rith. Avocations: photography, travel. Office: Allied Screw Products Inc PO Box 543 815 E Lowell Ave Mishawaka IN 46545-6480

SILVER, NINA GAIL, writer, educator, psychotherapist, singer-songwriter; b. Roslyn, N.Y., Oct. 15, 1951; d. David Louis Silverman and Dianne Kaplan. BA magna cum laude, Queens Coll., Flushing, N.Y., 1975; PhD in Transformational Psychology, The Union Inst., 1996. Performer (singer) Hosp. Audiences, Inc., N.Y.C., 1976-90. Contbr. articles to profl. jours.; author: Handbook of Rife Frequency Healing, 1999, revised edit., 2001. Meet the Composer grantee, 1982, 83; Broadcast Music Inc. scholar/grantee, 1976-77. Mem. Poets and Writers, Broadcast Music Inc. Avocation: jewelry crafting.

SILVER, PAUL ROBERT, marketing executive, consultant; b. Balt., Mar. 15, 1931; s. Harry and Frieda (Rosengarten) S.; m. Natalie Nessa Nechamkin, May 17, 1957; children; Geri Ellen, Steven Marc, Lawrence Alan. BA, U. Md., 1949; BS, U. Balt., 1958; postgrad., Eckerd Coll., 1984. Pres., CEO Sterling Prodns. Inc., Balt., 1950-51; advt. mgr. Hecht Co., Washington, 1951-53; pres., CEO Artists & Models, Inc., Washington and Balt., 1974-76, The Charles Agy. Inc., Washington and Balt., 1955-80, The Golden Triangle Agy., Clearwater, Fla., 1980-82; COO Bridgman Assocs. Inc., Annapolis, Md., 1985-86; dir. promotions Internat. Beverage Expn., Washington, 1986; pres., CEO Prasco Inc., Tampa, Fla., 1982—; CEO Kenaf Mktg. Worldwide, 1994—, Ode Paper Mill & Kenaf Farms Ltd., Ghana, 1999—. Cons. Lewis and Ptnrs., Inc., San Francisco, Corp. Vision, Inc., L.A., Computer Response, Inc., Balt., Themes and Schemes, Inc., Dunedin, Fla., San Diego, 1984—, J&B Mgmt. Co., 1991, Alberee Products, Inc., 1992; v.p. Coupon Am., Bel Air, Md., 1987-88; dir. mktg. Miles Homes, Inc., Cheshire, Conn., 1993; CEO Universal Industries, Inc., 1994—; ptnr. Drakeford & Drakeford, PA, 1995-96; v.p. Chapman Security Inc., 1995-98; ptnr. Global Mktg. Internat., 1997, CEO, also chmn. bd. dirs. Stoppit! Corp., New Port Richey, Fl., 1999—. Active in Radio Free Asia, 1972, Pinellas County Heart Savers, Clearwater, 1981; campaign mgr. for candidates for Balt. City Coun., U.S. Senate and U.S. Congress, 1968, 88, Fla. Commr. Agr., 1990. With U.S. Army, 1953-55, 72. Democrat. Jewish. Avocations: writing, art. Office: Prasco Inc PO Box 24461 Tampa FL 33623-4461 E-mail: prscoinc@verizon.net .

SILVER, RALPH DAVID, financial consultant and arbitrator; b. Chgo., Apr. 19, 1924; s. Morris J. and Amelia (Abrams) S.; m. Lois Reich, Feb. 4, 1951; children: Jay, Cappy. BS, U. Chgo., 1943; postgrad., Northwestern U., 1946-48; JD, DePaul U., 1952. Bar: Ill. bar 1952. Staff accountant David Himmelblau & Co. (C.P.A.'s), 1946-48; internal revenue agt. U.S. Dept. Treasury, 1948-51; practice in Chgo., 1952-55; atty. Lawrence J. West, 1952-55; fin. cons., bd. dirs. Barton Inc., Chgo., 1955-92. Bd. dirs. Stone Fin. Corp., Stone Fin. II Corp., 1992-95; arbitrator N.Y. Stock Exch., Cir. Ct. of Cook County, Ill. Bd. dirs., pres. Ralph and Lois Silver Found. Lt. (j.g.) USNR, 1943-46. Mem. ABA, Chgo. Bar Assn., AICPA. Clubs: Green Acres Country. Home: 1124 Old Elm Ln Glencoe IL 60022-1235

SILVER, RICHARD TOBIAS, physician, educator; b. Jan. 18, 1929; m. Barbara Silver; 1 son, Adam Bennett. BA, Cornell U., 1950, MD, 1953. Diplomate Nat. Bd. Med. Examiners, Am. Bd. Internal Medicine, Am. Bd. Clin. Oncology. Intern N.Y. Hosp.-Cornell Med. Ctr., N.Y.C., 1953-54, asst. resident in medicine, 1956-57, resident in hematology, 1957-58; clin. assoc. gen. medicine br. Nat. Cancer Inst., NIH, Bethesda, Md., 1954-56; asst. in medicine Cornell U. Med. Coll., N.Y.C., 1956-58, instr. medicine, 1958-62, clin. asst. prof., 1962-67, clin. assoc. prof., 1967-73, clin. prof., 1973—; pres. N.Y. State Soc. Med. Oncologists and Hematologists, 1991—; asst. attending physician N.Y. Hosp., 1964-67, assoc. attending physician, 1967-73, attending physician, 1973—; dir. clin. oncology & chemotherapy rsch. N.Y. Hosp. Divsn. Hemeotology & Med. Oncology. Asst. vis. physician 2d Cornell Med. div. Bellevue Hosp., N.Y.C., 1963-66; vis. Fulbright prof. U. Bahia Sch. Medicine, Brazil, 1958-59; vis. prof. Hershey Hosp.-Pa. State Hosp., 1976, Mayo Clinic, 1977, Upstate Med. Ctr., Binghamton, N.Y., 1977, Med. Coll. Va., 1979, Med. Sch. Colubia U., 1982, N.J. Coll. Medicine, New Brunswick, 1983, Meml. Med. Ctr. U. Ga., 1984, 86; invited lectr. Med. Coll. Shanghai and Chengchow, 1979, VIII Brazilian Hematology Congress, Salvador, 1981, 14th Internat. Congress Chemotherapy, Kyoto, Japan, 1985, XI Brazilian Congress of Cancerology, Florianoplis, Santa Catarina, 1987, 2d Internat. Conf. CML, Bologna, Italy, 1992, Internat. Symposium Myelo Proliferative Disorders, Mayo Clinic, Tochester Minn., 1994, 9th Internat. Symposium Molecular Biology Hematopolesis: Interferon in Myelo Proliferative Diseases, Genoa, Italy, 1995, The Myeloproliferative Dis. and Biol. Modifiers: Med. Grand Rounds, Sarasota Meml. Hosp. Fla., 1996; vis. faculty curriculum Devel., Annenberg Ctr. Rancho Mirage, Calif., 1994—; mem. rev. bd. NIH, Nat. Cancer Inst.; cons. Cancer Chemotherapy Investigative Rev. Bd., 1980, clin. trials com., 1979-81; mem. Cornell U. Coun., 1987—; spl. site visitor medicine A Roswell Park Meml. Inst., NIH-Nat. Cancer Inst., 1976, mem. combined modality com. divsn. cancer treatment, 1977-79, clin. trials com., 1979-81, cons. cancer chemotherapy rev. bd., 1980; vis. Fulbright lectr. Sch. Medicine U. Bahia, Brazil, 1958-59; lectr., presenter in field. Thor: Morphology of the Blood and Marrow in Clinical Practice, 1970; co-author: (with R.D. Lauper, C.I. Jarowski) A Synopsis of Cancer Chemotherapy, 1977, 2ndedit., 1986, monographs; editor: Clinical Topics in Cancer: Diagnosis and Treatment, 1982; cons. editor Am. Jour. Medicine, 1974—, mem. editl. adv. bd., 1984; editor, contbr.: Topics in Cancer, 1982; mem. editl. adv. bd. Cancer Investigation, 1983—; ad-hoc rev. New Eng. Jour. Medicine, Annals of Internal Medicine, Mayo Clinic Proceedings, Blood, Cancer, Am. Jour. Hematology, others; contbr. chpts. to books and articles to profl. jours., to nat. and internat. profl. confs., seminars and workshops in medicine. Trustee Frances and Edwin Cummings Meml. Fund, 1985-92; med. dir. Rsch. for Blood Health, Inc., 1968-85, Arnold K. Krakower Hematology Found., 1966-75, Cancer Rsch. and Treatment Fund, 1985—. Recipient Pasmantier award, Timothy Gee award for outstanding tchr., clinician, inventor and humanist, 2001; N.Y. State scholar for profl. study of medicine. Fellow ACP; mem. N.Y. State Soc. Med. Hematologists and Oncologists (pres. 1991—), Cornell U. Med. Coll. Alumni Assn. (pres. 1973-76, sr. advisor 1976—), Am. Soc. Clin. Oncology (mem. com. clin. practice 1976, com. on pub. affairs 1981-83, chmn. program com. 1977), Internat. Soc. Hematology (chmn. bone marrow biopsy wokshop XV congress 1974, internat. adv. com. XX Congress 1984, lectr.), Am. Soc. Hematology (chmn., guidelines com.), Leukemia Soc. Am. (med. dir., v.p. N.Y.C. chpt. 1968—), Chronic Myeloid Leukemia, Sass Found Hematologic Rsch. (bd. advs.), N.Y. Soc. Study of Blood, N.Y. County Med. Soc., N.Y. State Med. Soc. Oncologists and Hematologists (pres. 1991-93, mem. exec. com. 1991—), Harvey Soc., Am. Fedn. Clin. Rsch., Am. Assn. Cancer Rsch., Explorers Club (bd. dirs., chmn. sci. adv. com. 1987), Sigma Xi. Office: NY Presby Hosp ated Ctr Weill Cornell Med Ctr 525 E 68th St Box 581 New York NY 10021 also: 1440 York Ave New York NY 10021-2577 E-mail: rtsilve@mail.med.cornell.edu.

SILVER, RICK, marketing professional; Grad. cum laude, U. S.C., 1974. Pvt. practice as vice chmn., 1976—. Office: 801 Gervais St Columbia SC 29201*

SILVER, ROBERTA FRANCES (BOBBI SILVER), educator, writer; b. Sedalia, Mo., Oct. 11, 1941; d. Elvin Joshua and Hilda M. (Abrams) Gordon; m. Wayne E. Mason, July 19, 1959 (div. 1974); m. Burton B. Silver, June 3, 1989 (div. 1992); children: Lori Atkins, Philip A., Marc A. Mason. BA in Spl. Edn., Avila Coll., 1972; MA in Counselor Edn., U. Mo., 1974; MA in Spl. Edn., Santa Clara U., 1992. Cert. counselor, tchr., Calif.; specialist learning handicapped credential and multiple subject credential, 1992, C.L.A.D. Tchr. Learning Disabled Shawnee-Mission (Kans.) Sch. Dist., 1972-75; sch. counselor Hickman Mills Consolidated Sch. Dist. #1, Kansas City, Mo., 1975-77; tchr. Behavior Disorders Jefferson County Pub. Schs., Louisville, 1978-80; tchr. West Valley Ctr. for Edn. Therapy, Canoga Park, Calif., 1981-82, Ozanam Home for Boys, Kansas City, 1983-89; instr. in human svcs. and continuing edn. dept. Longview C.C., Lee's Summit, Mo., 1985-89; instr. learning handicapped Franklin-McKinley Sch. Dist., San Jose, Calif., 1990-95, chr. 2d grade, 1990—, lang. devel. tchr., art mentor. Writing and art mentor Gifted and talented (G.A.T.E.) program, coord. Author (as Roberta Gordon Silver) 3 novels; watercolorist; contbr. articles to pvt. in-house mag., poems to anthologies, short stories and articles to mags. Avocations: photography, painting, reading, hiking.

SILVER, ROSLYN O. federal judge; b. Phoenix, Feb. 28, 1946; m. Steven J. Silver. BA, U. Calif. Santa Barbara, 1968; JD, Ariz. State U., 1971. Law clk. Hon. Lorna E. Lockwood Ariz. Supreme Ct., Phoenix, 1971-72; advisor, litigator Navajo Nation Native Am. Rights Fund, 1974-76; legal counsel Dial Corp., 1976-78; ptnr. Logan and Aguirre, 1978-79; legal counsel EEOC, 1979-80; asst. U.S. Atty. Dist. Ariz., 1980-84; asst. atty. gen. Ariz. Atty. Gen.'s Office, 1984-86; acting 1st asst., chief criminal divsn. dist. Ariz. U.S. Atty. Office, 1986-94; judge Dist. Ariz. U.S. Dist. Ct., 1994—. Chair 9th Cir. Article III judges edn. com. Named one of 100 Significant Women and Minorities in Ariz.'s Legal History, 2000. Mem. ABA, Fed. Bar Assn., Nat. Assn. Women Judges, Ariz. Bar Assn. (Pub. Lawyer of Yr.), Ariz. Women Lawyers Assn. (outstanding legal practitioner award 1999), Ariz. State U. Alumni Assn. (outstanding alumnus award 1996). Office: US Dist Ct 401 W Washington SPC 59 Phoenix AZ 85003

SILVER, SHELLY ANDREA, media artist; b. N.Y.C., July 16, 1957; d. Reuben and Anita (Kuriloff) S. BA, BFA, Cornell U., 1980. Program fellow Japan/U.S. Friendship Commn. Artist Exch., 1994, Deutscher Akademischer Austauschdienst Berliner Kunstlerprogramm, 1992; vis. prof. Deutsche Film und Fernsehakademie, 1992; vis. artist Art Inst. Chgo., 1991; prof. Sch. Visual Arts grad. dept. photo and related media; Yaddo residency, 1999; freelance editor Sesame St., Frontline, Saturday Night Live, HBO, MTV, Showtime, others. Represented in exhbns. including The New Mus., N.Y.C., 1987, The Mus. of Modern Art, 1991, 95, 96, 97, The N.Y. Film Festival (video sect.),

1994, 96, The Mus. of Kyoto, Japan, 1994, The London Film Festival, 1991, Internat. Ctr. Photography, N.Y.C., 1989, 91, Portrait Gallery, Smithsonian Inst., 1998, Pulse, Serpentine Gallery, London, 1998, Mus. Art and History, Fribourg, Switzerland, 2000, Stadtgalerie Bern, Switzerland, Mus. Contemporary Art, Mexico City, 2001, Yokohama Portroid Gallery, 2002, Singapore Internat. Film Festival, 2002, Musée de L'Elysée, Lausanne, Switzerland, 2001. Japan Found. Film & Video grantee, 1995, N.Y. State Coun. Arts Project grantee, 1987, 89, 95, Checkerboard Found. grantee, 1990, Media Bur. Finishing Funds grantee, Anonymous Was A Woman grantee, 1998; fellow U.S./Japan Artists Exch., 1993, Nat. Endowment Arts, 1989, 91, N.Y. Found. Arts, 1986, 91, 99; Jerome Found. Media grantee, 2000. Home and Office: 22 Catherine St Apt 6 New York NY 10038-1025

SILVER, THELMA, social worker; b. Nfld., Can., Nov. 17, 1948; d. Mike and Monya Silver. BA, McGill U., 1969, MSW, 1971; PhD in Social Welfare, Case Western Res. U., 1995. Clin. supr. Neighboring: Supporting Svcs. for Mental Health, Mentor, Ohio, 1983-94; lectr. Case Western Res. U. Sch. Applied Social Sci., Cleve., 1990; asst. prof. social work D'Youville Coll., Buffalo, 1994-99; asst. prof. Youngstown State U., 1999—. Mem. Lake County Cmty. Crisis Intervention Team, Painesville, 1985-94; bd. dirs. Solomon Schechter Day Sch., Cleve., 1980-85. Mem. citizen's adv. bd. Northcoast Behavioral Healthcare Ctr., 2000—. Mem. NASW, Coun. on Social Work Edn., Am. Assn. for Advancement of Social Work with Groups. Avocations: walking, reading, gardening. Home: 24525 Penshurst Dr Cleveland OH 44122-1386 Office: Humanistic Counseling Ctr 4979 Mayfield Rd Lyndhurst OH 44124-2601 E-mail: doovil@aol.com.

SILVERBERG, DAVID STANLEY, financial consultant; b. Oelwein, Iowa, Mar. 3, 1936; s. Harold and Rose (Fishman) S.; m. Mary Ellen Silverberg, July 20, 1988; children: Laura, Sara, Stanley. Student, U. Minn.; LUTC, Life Underwriter Coll., Sioux City, Iowa, 1976; CFP, Coll. Fin. Planning, Denver, 1979. CFP. Fin. cons., 1st v.p. Smith Barney, Sioux City, 1978—. Instr. Western Iowa Tech. Coll., Sioux City, 1980-87, Inst. of Banking, Sioux City, 1990. Past pres. Sioux City Jewish Fedn., 1991-94; pres. Sioux City Jewish Cemetery Assn., 1990-2002; bd. dirs. Sioux City Symphony, 1991-2002, KWIT Pub. Radio Sta., 1997-2002. With U.S. Army, 1958-63. Recipient Young Leadership award Sioux City Jewish Fedn., 1984. Mem. Internat. Assn. Fin. Planners, Landmark Lodge AF&AM, Scottish Rite (32nd degree), Shriners, Sioux City Country Club. Avocations: golf. Home: 26 W 45th St Sioux City IA 51104-1002 Office: Smith Barney 600 4th St Sioux City IA 51101-1744

SILVERBERG, JAY LLOYD, lawyer; b. N.Y., Oct. 1, 1961; s. Sheldon and Elissa (Nenner) S.; children: Jennifer, Rebecca, Sabrina. BA, Brandeis U., 1983; JD, Boston U., 1986. Bar: N.Y. 1987, N.J. 1987, U.S. Dist. Ct. (so. dist.) N.Y. 1990, U.S. Dist. Ct. (ea. dist.) N.Y. 1991. Assoc. McCarter & English, Newark, 1986-87, Proskauer Rose, N.Y.C., 1987-91; mem. Silverberg, Stonehill & Goldsmith, P.C., 1991—. Lectr. Nat. Assn. Credit Mgmt., Columbia U. Sch. Bus., 1996. Editor: Annual Review of Banking Law, 1986. Paul J. Liacos scholar Boston U. Sch. Law, 1985, G. Joseph Tauro scholar, 1984. Mem. N.Y. Inst. Credit, Manhattan Credit Club (pres. 1998), Turnaround Mgmt. Assn. Office: Silverberg Stonehill & Goldsmith PC 111 W 40th St New York NY 10018-0968 E-mail: JLSilverberg@SSGPC.com.

SILVERBERG, LEWIS HENRY, legal consultant; b. L.A., Nov. 1, 1934; s. Milton Henry and Marjorie Vella (Coates) S.; children: Stephen, Richard, Donna; m. Alice Ellen Deakins, Mar. 9, 1979. BA, Pomona Coll., 1955; JD, UCLA, 1958. Bar: Calif. 1959, U.S. Supreme Ct. 1966. Pvt. practice, San Diego, 1959-89; bus. cons., 1993—. Bd. dirs. Internet C. and C., Inc. Trustee San Diego Zool. Soc., 1989-99; active various pub., charitable and ednl. orgns. Office: 1515 Merritt Dr El Cajon CA 92020-7847 E-mail: lewsilverberg@sbcglobal.net.

SILVERBERG, MARK VICTOR, lawyer, educator; b. Akron, Ohio, Sept. 26, 1957; s. Alvin Harold and Marilyn (Bierman) S.; m. Marsha Phyllis Mermelstein, Aug. 11, 1979; children: Samantha Michele, Marissa Jill. BS, Rider Coll., 1979; JD, Pace U., 1983. Bar: N.J. 1983, N.Y. 1984, U.S. Dist. Ct. (so. dist.) N.Y., U.S. Dist. Ct. N.J. Atty. Met. Life Ins. Co., N.Y.C., 1983-84; corp. counsel H & N Chem. Co., Totowa, N.J., 1984-85; pvt. practice East Brunswick, 1985-90; gen. coun. East Coast Title Ins., 1990-91; CEO New Century Mortgage Corp., 1991—. Prof. law Middlesex County Coll., Edison, N.J., 1985—, Mercer County Coll., Trenton, N.J., 1985—, Upsala Coll., East Orange, N.J., 1991—. Mem. ABA (real estate, probate and property law sect., corp. law sect.), N.Y. State Bar Assn., N.J. Bar Assn. (real estate, probate and property law sect., corp. law sect.), Middlesex County Bar Assn., Rotary. Republican. Jewish. Avocations: basketball, golf, hockey, woodworking, gardening.

SILVERBERG, MARTIN, educator; b. N.Y.C., Apr. 28, 1935; s. Louis and Freda S.; m. Joan, Dec. 23, 1956 (div. May 1980); children: Steven, Roni, Andrew; m. Bonnie, June 9, 1985. BA, Hunter Coll., 1956, MS, 1959; postgrad., Columbia Tchr. Coll., 1959-61. Tchr. DeWitt Clinton H.S., Bronx, 1956-73; asst. prin., supr., athletic dir. Harry S. Truman High Sch., 1973-91; aquatic dir. Town of Clarkstown (N.Y.), 1972-2000, Life Plex Health Club, Monsey, N.Y., 1997—; dir. Rockland County Swim Sch., N.Y.C., 1965—. Cons. Tech. Adv. Svc. Attys., Blue Bell, Pa., 1990—. Contbr. articles to swim jours.; inventor pool skimmer. Vol. ARC, N.Y.C., 1955—. Named N.Y. Athletic Club Coach of Yr., 1964-65, Hunter Coll. Athletic Hall Fame, 1987. Mem. ARC (water safety com.). Avocations: golf, boating, skiing, swimming, weight lifting. Home: 39 Crystal Hill Dr Pomona NY 10970 Office: Life Plex Health Club 18 College Rd Monsey NY 10952

SILVERBERG, MICHAEL BARRY, anesthesiologist; b. Bklyn., May 20, 1959; s. Norman and Florence (Berman) S.; m. Barbara Montana, Sept. 24, 1989. BA, Harvard U., 1979; MD, Yale U., 1983. Diplomate Am. Bd. Anesthesiology. Intern NYU Med. Ctr., N.Y.C., 1983-84, resident in internal medicine, 1983-86; resident in anesthesiology Hosp. U. Pa., Phila., 1986-89; anesthesia faculty Med. Coll. of Pa., 1989-91; anesthesia staff Staten Island U. Hosp., 1991—. Mem. staff Staten Island (N.Y.) U. Hosp. Mem. AMA, Am. Soc. Anesthesiologists, Internat. Anesthesia Rsch. Soc. Office: 475 Seaview Ave Staten Island NY 10305-3436

SILVERBERG, MICHAEL JOEL, lawyer; b. Rochester, N.Y., Aug. 12, 1932; s. Goodman and Minnie (Krovetz) S.; m. Charlotte Goldman, June 19, 1955; children: Mark (dec. 1999), Daniel. BA, U. Rochester, 1954; JD, Columbia U., 1957. Bar: N.Y. 1958, U.S. Dist. Ct. (so. dist.) N.Y. 1965, U.S. Dist. Ct. (ea. dist.) N.Y. 1990, U.S. Ct. Appeals (2d cir.) 1975, U.S. Supreme Ct. 1967. Instr. Columbia U. Law Sch., N.Y.C., 1957-58; assoc. Phillips, Nizer, Benjamin, Krim & Ballon, 1960-67, ptnr., 1967—. Pres. Nat. Alliance Mentally Ill N.C.Y., Inc., 1997—; cons. sci. program com. Am. Psychiat. Assn., 2000—01. Mem. exec. bd. N.Y. chpt. Am. Jewish Com.; bd. dirs. Nat. Alliance for Mentally Ill of N.Y. State, 1998—, pres., 1999—; mem. adv. bd. dept. psychiatry Columbia U.; mem. adv. bd. N.Y.C. Vis. Nurse Svc. Fulbright scholar U. Strasbourg, France, 1958-59. Mem. ABA, N.Y. State Bar Assn. (com. on internat. litigation), Assn. Bar City N.Y. Home: 205 W End Ave New York NY 10023-4804 E-mail: MSILVERBERG@PHILLIPSNIZER.COM.

SILVERBERG, MIRIAM, publicist, small business owner; b. Mineola, N.Y., June 14, 1949; d. Charles and Ann (Cutler) Silverberg. BA, Bklyn. Coll., 1969. Concierge Philipp Bros., N.Y.C., 1969—73; pres., founder Miriam Silverberg Assocs., 1973—. Instr. publicity course New Sch., 1980; adviser Light Opera Co. Manhattan, 1980—87; cons. to publicity office N.Y.C. Ballet, 1984—88; cons. Mayor Rudolph W. Giuliani's office of Spl. Projects and Cmty. Events, 1999—2001; cons. Park Art Exhibits, N.Y.C., 1985—86; party planner; restaurant cons.; cons., publicist N.Y.C. Fete de Cuisine, N.Y.C., 2002; cons., publicist fundraiser honoring former President Bill Clinton and former Sen. Bob Dole Citizens' Scholarship Found. Am., N.Y.C., 2002. Pres. chpt. Am. Red Magen David of Israel, N.Y.C., 1973—79; fundraiser, pres. Com. to Erect Monument to Duke Ellington, 1987—88. Recipient Pres.'s award Am. Red Magen David of Israel, 1978. Mem. Bklyn. Coll. Alumni Assn. Jewish. Avocations: ballet, theatre, art, fashion, restaurants. Home and Office: 400 E 57th St Apt 9F New York NY 10022-3024 E-mail: silverbergm@iopener.net.

SILVERBERG, ROBERT, author; b. N.Y.C., 1935; s. Michael and Helen (Baim) S.; m. Barbara Brown, 1956; m. Karen Haber, 1987. BA, Columbia U., 1956. Author: novels Thorns, 1967, The Masks of Time, 1968, Hawksbill Station, 1968, Nightwings, 1969, To Live Again, 1969, Tower of Glass, 1970, The World Inside, 1971, Son of Man, 1971, A Time of Changes, 1971, Dying Inside, 1972, The Book of Skulls, 1972, Born with the Dead, 1974, Shadrach in the Furnace, 1976, Lord Valentine's Castle, 1980, Majipoor Chronicles, 1982, Lord of Darkness, 1983, Valentine Pontifex, 1983, Gilgamesh the King, 1984, Tom O'Bedlam, 1985, Star of Gypsies, 1986, At Winter's End, 1988, To the Land of the Living, 1989, The New Springtime, 1990, (with Isaac Asimov) Nightfall, 1990, The Face of the Waters, 1991, (with Isaac Asimov) The Ugly Little Boy, 1992, Kingdoms of the Wall, 1993, (with Isaac Asimov) The Positronic Man, 1993, Hot Sky at Midnight, 1994, Mountains of Majipoor, 1995, Starborne, 1996, Sorcerers of Majipoor, 1997, The Alien Years, 1998, Lord Prestimion, 1999, The King of Dreams, 2001, The Longest Way Home, 2002; non-fiction The Face of the Lost Cities and Vanished Civilizations, 1962, The Great Wall of China, 1965, The Old Ones: Indians of the American Southwest, 1965, Scientists and Scoundrels: A Book of Hoaxes, 1965, The Auk, the Dodo and the Oryx, 1966, The Morning of Mankind: Prehistoric Man in Europe, 1967, Mound Builders of Ancient America: The Archaeology of a Myth, 1968, If I Forget Thee, O Jerusalem: American Jews and the State of Israel, 1970, The Pueblo Revolt, 1970, The Realm of Prester John, 1971. Recipient Hugo award World Sci. Fiction Conv., 1956, 69, 87, 90; Nebula award Sci. Fiction Writers Am., 1970, 72, 75, 86. Mem. Sci. Fiction Writers Am. (pres. 1967-68) Address: PO Box 13160 Oakland CA 94661-0160

SILVERBERG, STEVEN GEORGE, pathologist, educator; b. N.Y.C., Nov. 30, 1938; s. Bertram P. and Esther (Weintraub) S.; m. Kiyoe Ono, Nov. 16, 1968. *Wife Kiyoe Ono Silverberg was born in Nikko, Japan, to a family which traces its samurai roots back for generations. She attended Tokyo Women's College in Tokyo and worked as a laboratory administrator. In the United States she is known as a multicuisine gourmet cook and a student of history, and has inspired and assisted with many of her husband's projects.* AB, Bklyn. Coll., 1958; MD, Johns Hopkins U., 1962. Diplomate Am. Bd. Pathology. Intern in medicine Bellevue/Meml. Hosp., N.Y.C., 1962-63; resident in anatomic pathology Yale-New Haven Hosp., 1963-65; fellow in pathology Meml. Hosp. Cancer Allied Diseases, N.Y.C., 1965-66; asst., assoc. prof. pathology Med. Coll. Va., Richmond, 1968-72; assoc. prof., prof. pathology U. Colo., Denver, 1972-81; prof., dir. anatomic pathology George Washington U., Washington, 1981-96, U. Md., Balt., 1996—. Exec. dir. Colo. Regional Cancer Ctr., Denver, 1976-80. Co-author: Pathology in Gynecology and Obstetrics, 1969, 4th edit., 1993; editor: Principles and Practice of Surgical Pathology, 1983, 3d edit., 1997; editor-in-chief Internat. Jour. Gyn. Pathology, 1984-92, Pathology Case Revs., 1995—; contbr. 200 articles to profl. jours. Capt. USAF, Japan, 1966-68. Jonas Salk scholar CUNY, 1958. Fellow Am. Soc. Clin. Pathologists (life, coun. 1977—, Disting. Svc. award 1991, H.P. Smith Disting. Pathology Educator award 1997); mem. Internat. Soc. Gyn. Pathologists (pres. 1998-2001), Assn. Dirs. Anatomic and Surg. Pathology (pres. 1998-2000), Alpha Omega Alpha. Avocations: reading history, travel, collecting Japanese Edo period illustrated books, wine. Office: Dept Pathology U Md Med Sys 22 S Greene St Baltimore MD 21201-1544

SILVERBERG, STEVEN MARK, lawyer; b. Bklyn., June 7, 1947; m. Arlene Leopold, July 4, 1971; 2 children. BA, Bklyn. Coll., 1969; JD, NYU, 1972. Bar: N.Y. 1973, U.S. Dist. Ct. (so. and ea. dists.) N.Y. 1974, U.S. Supreme Ct. 1976, U.S. Ct. Appeals (2nd cir.) 1978. Asst. dist. atty. Kings County Dist. Atty., Bklyn., 1972-75; dep. town. atty. Town of Greenburgh, N.Y., 1975-79; ptnr. Stowell, Kelly & Silverberg, White Plains, 1979-83, Hoffman, Silverberg & Wachtell, Elmsford, 1983-86, Hoffman, Silverberg, Wachtell & Koster, White Plains, 1986-89; pvt. practice, 1989-92; ptnr. Kirkpatrick & Silverberg LLP, 1993-00, Wilson, Elser, Moskowitz, Edelman & Dicker LLP, White Plains, 2001—. Adj. assoc. prof. N.Y. Law Sch., 1990-93. Co-author: Wetlands and Coastal Zone Regulations and Compliance, 1993; contbr. to profl. publs. Counsel Greenburgh Housing Authority, 1979-84, Town of Mamaroneck, N.Y., 1984-96, Village of Mamaroneck, 1999—, planning and zoning bd. Town of Haverstraw, 2001—; bd. dirs. Temple Beth Torah, Upper Nyack, N.Y., 1977-89, 2000—, pres. 1984-86; bd. dirs. N.J. West Hudson Valley Region Union of Am. Hebrew Congregations, 1986-88, Westchester Mcpl. Planning Fedn. Mem. ABA, N.Y. State Bar Assn., Westchester County Bar Assn. (chair environtl. law com. 1997—). Office: Wilson Elser Moskowitz Edelman & Dicker LLP 3 Gannett Dr White Plains NY 10604

SILVERMAN, AL, editor; b. Lynn, Mass., Apr. 12, 1926; s. Henry and Minnie (Damsky) S.; m. Rosa Magaro, Sept. 9, 1951; children: Thomas, Brian, Matthew. BS, Boston U., 1949, LittD, 1986. Assoc. editor Sport mag., 1951-52; sports editor True mag., 1952-54; asst. editor Argosy mag., 1954-55; free-lance mag. writer, contbr. Saturday Evening Post, Coronet, Pageant, This Week, Am. Weekly, Am. Heritage, Saturday Review, others, 1955-60; editor-in-chief Saga mag., Impact mag., Sport Library, Sport mag., 1960-72; exec. v.p., editorial dir. Book-of-the-Month Club, 1972—, pres., chief operating officer, 1981—, chmn., chief exec. office, 1985-88; v.p., contbg. editor Viking Penguin, 1989-92, sr. v.p., pub., editor in chief, 1992—, sr. v.p., editor-at-large, 1994-97, editl. advisor, 1998—. Author: Warren Spahn, 1961, Best from Sport, 1961, (with Phil Rizzuto) The Miracle New York Yankees, 1962, The World of Sport, 1962, Mickey Mantle, Master Yankee, 1963, World Series Heroes, 1964, (with Paul Hornung) Football and the Single Man, 1965, The Specialist in Pro Football, 1966, Sports Titans of the 20th Century, 1968, (with Frank Robinson) My Life is Baseball, 1968, More Sport Titans of the 20th Century, 1969, Joe DiMaggio, The Golden Year, 1969, I Am Third, (with Gale Sayers), 1970, Foster and Laurie, 1974; editor: The Book of the Month, 1986; co-editor: The 20th Century Treasury of Sports, 1992. Mem. Authors Guild, PEN (bd. dirs.), The Merc. Libr. Home: 15 Woods Way White Plains NY 10605-5446

SILVERMAN, ALAN HENRY, lawyer; b. N.Y.C., Feb. 18, 1954; s. Melvin H. and Florence (Green) S.; m. Gretchen E. Freeman, May 25, 1986; children: Willa C.F., Gordon H.F. BA summa cum laude, Hamilton Coll., 1976; MBA, JD, U. Pa., 1980. Bar: N.Y. 1981, U.S. Dist. Ct. (so. and ea. dist.) N.Y. 1981, U.S. Ct. Internat. Trade 1981, D.C. 1986, U.S. Supreme Ct. 1990. Assoc. Hughes, Hubbard & Reed, N.Y.C., 1980-84; asst. counsel Newsweek, Inc., 1984-86; v.p., gen. counsel, sec., dir. adminstrn. Cable One, Inc., Phoenix, 1986—. Contbr. articles to profl. jours. Mem. prevention adv. com. Gov. Pa. Justice Commn., 1975-79; bd. dirs. Lawyers' Alliance for N.Y., 1982-85, N.Y. Lawyers Pub. Interest, 1983-85, Nat. Assn. JD-MBA Profls., 1983-85, Bus. Vols. for Arts, Inc., Phoenix, 1989-93, Ariz. Vol. Lawyers for the Arts, Inc., 1994-97, First Amendment Coalition Ariz., Inc., 1991—; mem. Maricopa County Citizens Jud. Adv. Coun., 1990-93; mem. citizens' bond com. City of Phoenix, 2000. Mem. ABA, Assn. of Bar of City of N.Y., D.C. Bar Assn., Phi Beta Kappa. Home: 5833 N 30th St Phoenix AZ 85016-2401 Office: Cable One Inc 1314 N 3d St Phoenix AZ 85004 E-mail: alan.silverman@cableone.net.

SILVERMAN, ALICE HOPE, interior designer; b. N.Y.C., Feb. 21, 1946; d. Jacob Grohman and Madeline Uris; divorced; children: Joshua, Jordan. BS, Fairleigh Dickinson U., 1965; degree interior designer, Pace U., 1983. Owner, pres. Creative Interiors Decorate-in-a-Day, Carmel, N.Y., 1983—. Mem. Am. Soc. Interior Designers (allied mem.), BBB. Democrat. Jewish. Avocations: antiquing, auctions. Home and Office: Creative Interiors 182 Mills Rd North Salem NY 10560 E-mail: decorateinaday@earthlink.net.

SILVERMAN, ARNOLD, pediatrician, educator; b. N.Y.C., Feb. 15, 1933; s. Sol and Gertrude (Cohen) S.; m. Bonnie J. Fenson, Aug. 28, 1955; children: Jeffrey R., Paul A., David E. BA, U. Colo., 1954, MA, 1957, MD, 1961. Diplomate: Am. Bd. Pediatrics. Intern Colo. Gen. Hosp., Denver, 1961-62; resident in pediatrics U. Minn. Hosp., Mpls., 1962-64; fellow in pediatric gastroenterology U. Colo. Med. Center, Denver, 1964-65, mem. faculty, 1965—, assoc. prof. pediatrics, 1975-80; prof. U. Colo. Med. Ctr. (Health Sci. Ctr.), 1980-93, prof. emeritus, 1994—. Dir. grad. edn. Denver Children's Hosp., 1967-75, chief gastroenterology svc., 1967-75; dir. pediat. svc. Denver Gen. Hosp., 1975-92; cons. Surgeon Gen. Fitzsimons Army Med. Hosp., 1976-95; mem. Nat. Commn. Digestive Diseases, 1979-80. Author: (with C.C. Roy and D. Alagille) Pediatric Clinic Gastroenterology, 4th edit., 1995. Recipient Silver and Gold Med. Alumni award U. Colo. Med. Sch., 2000. Mem. Am. Acad. Pediatrics, Am. Gastroenterology Assn., Am. Pediatric Soc., Am. Gastroenterology Assn., N.Am. Soc. Pediatric Gastroenterology, Am. Assn. Study Liver Disease, Denver Med. Soc., Alpha Omega Alpha. Jewish. Home: 3335 S Newport St Denver CO 80224-2823

SILVERMAN, ARNOLD BARRY, lawyer; b. Sept. 1, 1937; s. Frank and Lillian Lena (Linder) S.; m. Susan L. Levin, Aug. 7, 1960; children: Michael Eric, Lee Oren. B of Engring. Sci., Johns Hopkins U., 1959; JD cum laude, U. Pitts., 1962. Bar: U.S. Dist. Ct. (we. dist.) Pa. 1963, Pa. 1964, U.S. Patent and Trademark Office 1965, U.S. Supreme Ct. 1967, Can. Patent Office 1968, U.S. Ct. Claims 1975, U.S. Ct. Appeals (3d cir.) 1982, U.S. Ct. Appeals (fed. cir.) 1985. Patent atty. Alcoa, New Kensington, Pa., 1962-67, 68-72, sr. patent atty., 1972-76; ptnr. Price and Silverman, Pitts., 1967-68; v.p., gen. patent counsel Joy Mfg. Co., 1976-80; ptnr. Murray Silverman & Keck, 1980-81, Buell, Blenko, Ziesenheim & Beck, Pitts., 1984; ptnr. intellectual property dept. Eckert, Seamans, Cherin & Mellott, 1984—, chmn., 1992—, chmn. info. tech. practice group, 1992-97; spl. asst. atty. gen. State of W.Va., 1985—; spl. counsel patents U. Pitts., 1975—. Spkr. on patents, trademarks, copyright, computer law; nat. panel of arbiters Am. Arbitration Assn., 1987—. Contbr. articles to profl. jours. Mem. Churchill CSC (Pa.), 1967-90, chmn., 1975-90; mem. Pitts. law com. Anti-Defamation League, 1981—, regional adv. bd., 1982—, ch-chmn. Pitts. region ann. dinner, 1983, mem. chmn. by-laws com., 1983; bd. govs. Slippery Rock U. Found., 1985-91; Pitts. steering com. MIT Enterprise Forum, 1986-87. With U.S. Army, 1963-64. Recipient Am. Spirit Honor medal, Ft. Knox, 1963, Fellow: Mensa (lawyers in Mensa 1978—, nat. assoc. counsel patents and trademarks copyrights 1980—82, inventors' spl. interest group 1980—86); mem.: ASME, ABA, Assn. Corp. Patent Counsel (emeritus mem.), Intertel (treas. Pitts. Forum 1983—), Stratford Cmty. Assn. (v.p. 1966—67, gov. 1966—70, pres. 1967—68), Golden Panthers, U. Pitts. Law Alumni Assn. (bd. dirs. 1992—, treas. 1997—98, v.p. 1998—99, pres.-elect 1999—2000, pres. 2001—02), Johns Hopkins Soc. Engring. Alumni, Johns Hopkins U. Alumni Assn. (chmn. publicity com. 1963—66, exec. com. 1966—87, v.p. 1969—70, pres. 1971—72, nat. alumni coun. 1989—92, coun. mem. 2000—), Brit. Inst. Chartered Patent Agts. (fgn. mem.), Licensing Execs. Soc. (co-chmn. Pitts. chpt. 1994—96), Am. Chem. Soc. (chemistry and the law sect.), Nat. Assn. Coll. and Univ. Attys., Pa. Bar Assn. (co-chmn. sports/entertainment arts law com. 2001—), D.C. Bar Assn., U.S. Trademark Assn. (chmn. task force on advt. agys. 1981, membership com. 1987—89), Am. Intellectual Property Law Assn. (membership com. 1985—88, pub. rels. com. 1994—), Pitts. Patent Law Assn. (chmn. pub. rels. com. 1968—69, chmn. patent laws com. 1970—72, chmn. legis. action com. 1972—75, chmn. nominating com. 1973, bd. mgrs. 1974—88, newsletter editor 1974—88, sec.-treas. 1976—84, v.p. 1984—85, pres. 1985—86, pub. rels. com. 1994—95, program com. 1995—96), Allegheny County Bar Assn. (chmn. pub. rels. com. 1978—80, vice-chmn. intellectual property sect. 1981—83, chmn. 1984—85), Robert Bruce Assn. Law Fellows (life), U. Pitts. Gen. Alumni Assn. (life; bd. dirs. 2001—), Duquesne Club, Order of Coif, Psi Chi, Tau Epsilon Rho. Republican. Jewish. Home: 2019 High Pointe Ct Murrysville PA 15668-8515 Office: 600 Grant St 44th Fl Pittsburgh PA 15219-2703 E-mail: arnie@telerama.com., abs@escm.com. *Welcome challenge and perform all tasks with enthusiasm, in a moral manner and to the very best of your ability.*

SILVERMAN, ARTHUR CHARLES, lawyer; b. Lewiston, Maine, June 13, 1938; s. Louis A. and Frances Edith (Brownstone) S.; BS in Elec. Engring., BS in Indsl. Mgmt., MIT, 1961; JD, Columbia U., 1964; m. Donna Linda Zolov, June 18, 1961; children: Leonard Stephen, Daniel Edward. Bar: N.Y. 1965, U.S. Supreme Ct. 1971. Engr., engring. asst. Gen. Electric Co., Pittsfield, Mass. and Phila., 1958-62; assoc. Baer & Marks, N.Y.C., 1965-68; assoc. Golenbock and Barell, N.Y.C., 1968-72, ptnr., 1972-89; ptnr. Reid & Priest LLP, N.Y.C., 1989-98, dep. chair, 1996-98; ptnr. Thelen Reid & Priest LLP, N.Y.C., 1998—. Treas., trustee Ramaz Sch., 1977-84, vice chmn., 1984-85, 86-88, chmn., 1988-92, hon. chmn., 1992—; bd. govs. MIT Hillel Found., 1979-84; mem. Bd. Jewish Edn. of City of N.Y., 1981-84; mem. exec. com. Nat. Jewish Ctr. for Learning and Leadership, 1984-90. Mem. IEEE, ABA, NSPE, N.Y. State Bar Assn., Fed. Bar Council, Assn. Bar City N.Y., N.Y. Soc. Architects, Internat. Bar Assn., Inter-Pacific Bar Assn., Constrn. Mgmt. Inst., Constrn. Specifications Inst. Home: 200 E 74th St New York NY 10021-3618 Office: Thelen Reid & Priest LLP 40 W 57th St New York NY 10019-4097

SILVERMAN, BARRY G. federal judge; b. N.Y.C., Oct. 11, 1951; 1 child Bagel Ann. BA summa cum laude, Ariz. State U., 1973, JD, 1976. Bar: Ariz. 1976, U.S. Dist. Ct. Ariz. 1976, U.S. Ct. Appeals (9th cir.) 1976, U.S. Supreme Ct. 1980. Asst. city prosecutor, Phoenix, 1976—77; dep. atty. Maricopa County, 1977—79; ct. commr., 1979—84; judge Superior Ct. Ariz. Maricopa County, 1984—95; apptd. magistrate judge U.S. Dist. Ct. Ariz., 1995—98; judge U.S. Ct. Appeals 9th cir., 1998—. Instr. constnl. law Coll. Law, Ariz. State U., 1983, adj. prof. advanced criminal procedure, 89; lectr. cmty. property BAR/BRI Ariz., Idaho and Nev. Bar Rev. Courses, 1989—; mem. Ariz. Supreme Ct. Com. on Jud. Edn. and Tng., 1988—. Recipient Exel award, Soc. Nat. Assn. Publs., 1992. Mem.: ABA, Maricopa County Bar Assn. (Henry Stevens award 1991), State Bar Ariz. Avocations: magic, beagles, baseball, wine tasting. Office: US Ct of Appeals 401 W Washington St SPC 78 Phoenix AZ 85003*

SILVERMAN, BRUCE GARY, advertising executive; b. N.Y.C., Feb. 16, 1945; s. Edward E. and Lillian (Brill) S.; children: Jennifer, Matthew; m. Nancy Cole, 1996; children: Christen Cole, Larry Cole. BA, Adelphi U., 1965; JD, Albany Law Sch., 1967. Sr. v.p., exec. creative dir. Ogilvy & Mather Inc., N.Y.C., 1967-80; exec. v.p., exec. creative dir. Bozell & Jacobs Inc., Dallas, 1981-83, Batten, Barton, Durstine & Osborn Inc., L.A., 1984-85; exec. v.p., creative dir. Asher/Gould Advt. Inc., 1986-89, pres., chief creative officer, 1989-95, pres., COO, 1996-97; pres. Western Internat. Advocacy Group, 1997-98; exec. v.p., mng. dir. Initiative Media, 1998—; pres., CEO Initiative Ptnrs., USA, 1999—. V.p., bd. dirs. L.A. Children's Mus., 1984-88; chmn. Resource Devel. com. Starbright Pavillion Found., 1993. Mem. Acad. TV Arts and Scis., Am. Assn. Advt. Agys. (bd. dirs., vice chmn. western region). Home: 3168 Dona Mema Pl Studio City CA 91604-4264 Office: Initiative Media Worldwide 5700 Wilshire Blvd Los Angeles CA 90036-3659

SILVERMAN, BURTON PHILIP, artist; b. Bklyn., June 11, 1928; s. Morris Daniel and Anne (Firstenberg) S.; m. Claire Guss, June 12, 1969; children: Robert Arthur, Karen Lila. BA, Columbia Coll., 1949. Freelance illustrator Life, Fortune, Esquire, Time, Newsweek, Sports Illus., New York, The New Yorkers mags., 1959—; instr. Sch. Visual Arts, N.Y.C., 1964-67. *Mr. Silverman is a nationally known teacher and writer of art books, and his work is recognized for its ongoing contribution to the realist tradition in painting. He has lectured extensively to art schools, museums audiences and graduate art history programs on the vitality of realism as a valid artistic mode, even during the period before its recent renaissance. He has also been a role model for many aspiring, and currently accomplished, painters working in that idiom. A future dual traveling exhibition of his drawings of historic Montgomery Bus Boycott that elevated Martin Luther King to national prominence along with those by friends and colleague, Harvey Dinnerstein, is being planned.* Co-author: Abel, 1968, A Portfolio of Drawings, 1968, Sight and Insight: The Art of Burton Silverman, 1999; author: Painting People, 1977, Breaking the Rules of Watercolor, 1983; contbr. articles and drawings to profl. jours.; one-man exhbns. include Davis Gallery, N.Y.C, 1956, 58, 62, Kenmore Galleries, Phila., 1963, 67, 70, FAR Gallery, N.Y.C., 1965, 70, 75, 77, Genesis Gallery, N.Y.C., 1979, Sindin Galleries, N.Y.C., 1983, Capricorn Galleries, Bethesda, Md., 1979, 91, Gallery 52, South Orange, N.J., 1967, 70, 77, Harbor Gallery, L.I., 1971, 74, U. Utah, 1967, Doll and Richards, Boston, 1980, Grand Central Galleries, N.Y.C., 1988, Cudahy's Gallery, N.Y.C., 1990, Joseph Keiffer, Inc., N.Y.C., 1993, Gerold Wunderlich & Co., N.Y.C., 1996, 97, Merrill Gallery, Denver, 1996, 98, Butler Inst. of Am. Art, 1999, Brigham Young Mus., Provo, 1999, Gallery Henoch, N.Y.C., 2001; group exhbns. include Butler Inst. Am. Art, Youngstown, Ohio, 1954-71, 74, 76, 79, 88, 90, 93, 2002, NAD, N.Y.C., 1958-96, 98, 2001, Am. Watercolor Soc., N.Y.C., 1978-82, 84-87, 89-91, 95-96, 97, 99, 2002, Pa. Acad. Fine Art, 1949, New Britain (Conn.) Mus. Am. Art, 1964, Wadsworth Atheneum, Hartford, Conn., 1961, Am. Acad. Arts and Letters, 1967, 74, 76, 79, N.Y. Hist. Soc., 1976, Pa. State Mus. Art, Portsmouth (Va.) Mus. Art, 1976, 79-80, 82 (Purchase prize, 1979, 82), Mexico City Mus. Art, 1990, Nat. Portrait Gallery, Washington, 1993, Hofstra Mus., N.Y.C., 1993, South Bend (Ind.) Mus. Art, 1994, Old

Forge (N.Y.) Mus. and Gallery, 1994, Qgunquit Mus., 1997. With AUS, 1951-53. Named to Hall of Fame, Soc. of Illustrators, N.Y., 1990, Pastel Soc. Am., 1992; named Artist of Am., 1991, 94, 2000. Mem. NAD (numerous awards and prizes including Joseph Isidor Gold medal 1992, Ranger Purchase prize 1962, 84, Benjamin Altman figure prize 1969), Am. Watercolor Soc. (numerous awards and prizes including Gold medal 1979, Silver medal 1984, 95, annuals), Pastel Soc. Am. (hon.). Home: 324 W 71st St New York NY 10023-3502 E-mail: bpsart@aol.com. *In art I am wary of things too facile, or appealing. My painting is rooted in a realist tradition that is equally concerned with objective facts and subjective realities. It is a visual language that allows me to explore the tensions and ambiguities engendered by this dual aspect of human experience. Art is my life and my life is in my art.*

SILVERMAN, CATHY ALICE, indigenous culture researcher; b. Boston, Oct. 23, 1968; d. Kenneth Sherman and Barbara Helen Silverman. BA, Mary Washington Coll., Fredericksburg, Va., 1990; MFA, Calif. Inst. Arts, 1994. Co-founder, CEO, Nada Brahma Found., Danville, Calif., 1999—; mem. faculty, music, anthropology Franklin Pierce Coll., Concord, NH, 2000—; mem. faculty, philosophy, religion, anthropology So. N.H. U., 2001—; mem. faculty Emerson Coll., 2000—. Cons. Calif. Inst. Arts, Valencia, 2000, mem. Intercultural Arts project, 1995-2000, co-chair diversity com., 1999-2000; mem. FOOD (interdisciplinary arts ensemble), L.A., 1996-99. Prodr., videographer (video) Live FOOD Again, 1999, musician, performer Kecak: Balinese Monkey Chant, 2000; prodr.: (CD) Are You Full Yet?, 1998;. Grantee NARAS, L.A., 2000—. Home: 10 Crescent St Salem NH 03079 Office: Nada Brahma Found PO Box 1927 Danville CA 94526-6927 E-mail: cathy@nadabrahma.org.

SILVERMAN, CHARLOTTE, epidemiologist, educator; b. N.Y.C., May 21, 1913; d. Harry and Gussie (Goldman) S. BA, Bklyn. Coll., 1933; MD, Woman's Med. Coll. Pa., 1938; MPH, Johns Hopkins U., 1942, DrPH, 1948. Diplomate Am. Bd. Preventive Medicine. Intern Beekman Hosp., N.Y.C., 1939-40; resident Sea View Hosp., Staten Island, N.Y., 1940-41; asst. dir., dir. Bur. Tuberculosis Balt. City Health Dept., 1946-56; chief epidemiology, planning and rsch. Md. State Dept. Health, Balt., 1956-62; med. officer in various programs NIMH, Bethesda, Md., 1962-68; dep. dir. div. biol. effects and other positions Bur. Radiol. Health USPHS, Rockville, 1968-83; assoc. dir. for human studies FDA, 1983-92. Mem. faculty dept. epidemiology Johns Hopkins U. Sch. Hygiene and Pub. Health, Balt., 1950—. Author: Epidemiology of Depression, 1968; contbr. articles to profl. jours. Sr. Surg. USPHS, 1944-45. Recipient Mary Pemberton Nourse Meml. award AAUW, 1941-42, Merit award FDA, 1974, Alumni Life Achievement award Bklyn. Coll., 1994. Fellow APHA, Am. Coll. Preventive Medicine, Am. Orthopsychiat. Assn., Am. Coll. Epidemiology; mem. Delta Omega. Home: 4977 Battery Ln Apt 1001 Bethesda MD 20814-4927

SILVERMAN, ELLEN-MARIE, speech and language pathologist; b. Milw., Oct. 12, 1942; d. Roy and Bettie (Schlaeger) Loebel; m. Feb. 5, 1967 (div.); 1 child, Catherine Bette. BS, U. Wis., Milw., 1964; MA, U. Iowa, 1967, PhD, 1970. Rsch. assoc. U. Ill., Urbana, 1969-71; asst. prof. speech pathology Marquette U., Milw., 1973-79; assoc. clin. prof. otolaryngology Med. Coll. Wis., 1980—83; assoc. prof. speech pathology Marquette U., 1979-85; pvt. practice speech and lang. pathology, Milw., 1985—. Founder, pres. TSS-The Speech Source, Inc., 1995—. Author, illustrator: Jason's Secret; contbr. articles to profl. jours., chpts. to books. Marquette U. grantee, 1982. Fellow Am. Speech, Hearing, Lang. Assn.; mem. Wis. Speech, Hearing, Lang. Assn., Sigma Xi, Delta Kappa Gamma. Avocations: photography, painting, gardening, writing. E-mail: tsss920499@aol.com.

SILVERMAN, ENID, painter, stained glass artist; b. Chgo., Mar. 15, 1931; d. Frank Herbert and Idelle (Makowsky) Levy; m. Irv Silverman, Aug. 24, 1952 (dec.); children: Dan E., Susan Pritzker. BS, Ill. Inst. Tech., 1953; postgrad., Chgo. Acad. Fine Arts, 1951, Evanston Art Ctr., 1961-62, Northshore Acad. Art, 1963-68. Art instr. Steiner Gallery, Lincolnwood, Ill., 1971-80, Centre East Art Ctr., Skokie, 1980-92, Cambridge-on-the-Lake, Buffalo Grove, 1987-2001, Wheeling (Ill.) Park Dist., 1995—, Buffalo Grove Park Dist., 1998—. Host cable TV show Artist to Artist, 1989—. Stained glass windows designer A.G. Beth Israel, Chgo., 1991, Lincolnwood Jewish Congregation, 1992-97, Sanctuary-B'nai Jehoshua Beth Elohim, Glenview, Ill., 1992, Ark-Beth Tikvah Congregation, Hoffman Estates, Ill., 1995, Ner Tamid Congregation of North Town, Chgo., 2001; represented in Oak Brook (Ill.) Fine Art Invitational, Old Orchard (Ill.) Fine Art Promenade, Northwestern U. Dittmar Gallery, Ill., Harold Washington Cultural Ctr., Chgo.; created murals in oper. rms. and adjacent hallways Children's Meml. Hosp., Chgo., 1998. Charter mem. Nat. Mus. Women Arts. Grantee Skokie Cable Found., 1989. Mem. Oil Painters Am. (charter), Chgo. Artists Coalition, Am. Jewish Artists Club. Avocations: theatre, travel, music, dance. Home: 724 Picardy Cir Northbrook IL 60062-1719 E-mail: enidartist@aol.com.

SILVERMAN, FRANKLIN HAROLD, speech pathologist, educator; b. Providence, Aug. 16, 1933; s. Meyer and Reba (Sack) Silverman; m. Ellen-Marie Loebel, Feb. 1, 1967 (div. Feb. 1981); 1 child Catherine ; m. Evelyn Ellen Chanda, Nov. 13, 1983. BS in Speech, Emerson Coll., 1960; MA, Northwestern U., 1961; PhD, U. Iowa, 1966. Lic. speech-lang. pathologist Wis. Rsch. assoc. U. Iowa, Iowa City, 1965-67; asst. prof. U. Ill., Champaign, 1968-71; assoc. prof. Marquette U., Milw., 1971-77, prof., 1978—; clin. prof. Med. Coll. Wis., Wauwatosa, 1978—. Mem. adv. bd. Wis. Telecomm. Relay Svcs., Madison, 1991—; cons. USAID Palestinian Speech Pathology Tng. Program, Gaza City, 1993—, Joint Centre for Rsch. Prosthetics and Orthotics and Rehab. Programmes, Riyadh, Saudi Arabia, 1995—, Disables Children's Assn., Riyadh, Saudi Arabia, 1998—. Author: Speech, Language, and Hearing Disorders, 1995, Communication for the Speechless, 3d edit, 1995, Stuttering and Other Fluency Disorders, 2d edit., 1996, Computer Applications for Augmenting the Management of Speech, Language and Hearing Disorders, 1997, Research Design and Evaluation in Speech-Language Pathology and Audiology, 4th edit., 1998, Authoring Books and Materials for Students, Academics, and Professionals, 1998, Telecommunication Relay Service Handbook, 1999, Professional Issues in Speech-Language Pathology and Audiology, 1999, Fundamentals of Electronics for Speech-Language Pathologists and Audiologists, 1999, Publishing for Tenure and Beyond, 1999, Self-Publishing Books and Materials for Students, Academics and Professionals, 1999, Second Thoughts About Stuttering, 2000, Teaching for Tenure and Beyond, 2001; contbr. Fellow: Text and Acad. Authors Assn. (sec. 1993—94, pres.-elect 1996, pres. 1997), Am. Speech-Lang.-Hearing Assn. Jewish. Avocation: photography. Home: 5918 Currant Ln Greendale WI 53129-2427 Office: Marquette U Dept Speech Pathology Milwaukee WI 53201-1881

SILVERMAN, GARY WILLIAM, financial planner; b. L.A., Nov. 30, 1957; s. Albert and Anna Marie (Robinson) S.; m. Joanne Marie Robinson, Aug. 29, 1976. BS summa cum laude Psychology/Counseling, Miami (Fla.) Christian Coll., 1987; MBA, U. Dallas, 1992. CFP. Tng. supr. Tex. Utilities, Glen Rose, Tex., 1982-92; registered rep. Waddell & Reed, Ft. Worth, 1990-94; tng. dir. Howmet Refurbishment, Wichita Falls, Tex., 1992-94; owner, fin. planner Personal Money Planning, 1993—. Owner, cons. Sigma Edn. Sys., 1987—; adj. prof. Wayland Bapt. U., 1996—; fin. course instr. Midwestern State U., 1994—. Host, commentator TV show Falls Informer WFTV Vista Channel 15; editor: Personal Money Planning: editor fin. web site TexasInvest.com. Grad. Leadership Wichita Falls, 1993; loaned exec. Wichita Falls United Way, 1993; instr. ARC, 1983—; bd. dirs. North Tex. Workforce Devel. Bd. Mem. Fin. Planning Assn., Sigma Iota Epsilon. Office: Personal Money Planning 4245 Kemp Blvd Ste 806 Wichita Falls TX 76308-2822 E-mail: gary@personalmoneyplanning.com.

SILVERMAN, GERALD BERNARD, journalist; b. Mineola, N.Y., June 2, 1959; s. Martin and Esther S.; m. Robyn G. Silverman, Aug. 29, 1982; children: Rebecca, Joshua. BA in English, SUNY, New Paltz, 1981; Cert. in Labor Studies, Cornell U., 1987. Reporter Register-Star, Hudson, N.Y., 1981-83; N.Y. corrs. Bur. Nat. Affairs, Inc., Albany, 1982—; columnist The Saratogian, Saratoga Springs, N.Y., 1994—. Contbr. articles to profl. jours. Bd. dirs. Spring Hill Waldorf Sch., Saratoga Springs, N.Y., 1992-93, Temple Sinai, Saratoga Springs, 2002—. Mem. Soc. Profl. Journalists (pres. Empire State chpt. 1991—), The Newspaper Guild (shop steward 1992-95), Legis. Corrs. Assn. Avocations: cooking, jazz, camping, poetry. Home: 2 Frank St Ballston Lake NY 12019-2400

SILVERMAN, HAROLD IRVING, pharmaceutical executive; b. Lawrence, Mass., Apr. 27, 1928; s. Jack David and Norma (Illman) S.; m. Arlene Jacobowitz, Nov. 25, 1951; children: Robert L., Richard L. BSc, Phila. Coll. of Pharmacy, 1951, MSc, 1952, DSc, 1956. Instr. Phila. Coll. Pharmacy, 1952-56; prof. pharmaceutics L.I. U., Bklyn., 1956-64; sr. scientist Warner Lambert Rsch. Inst., Morris Plains, N.J., 1958-60; v.p. sci. dir. Knoll Pharm. Co., West Orange, 1964-68; prof., assoc. dean Mass. Coll. Pharmacy, Boston, 1968-85, prof. emeritus, 1985—; sr. v.p. Thompson Med. Co., N.Y.C., 1985-92; sr. v.p. for med. rsch. Bascomb Found. for Med. Rsch., Boston, 1992—. Lectr. Boston U. Sch. Medicine, 1971-73, New Eng. Coll. of Optometry, Boston, 1971-80. Contbr. numerous articles to sci. jours. Mem. human subcom. Peter Bent Brigham, Boston, 1980-85, Boston U., 1983-85; cons. Mass. Bd. Optometry, Boston, 1974-80, WHO, Washington, 1985. Named Man of Yr., Boston Assn. Druggists, 1977; recipient Disting. Svc. award Am. Optometric Assn., 1974. Fellow Soc. Cosmetic Chemists; mem. AAAS, Am. Pharm. Assn. (Phytochemistry award 1956), Am. Chem. Soc., Am. Oil Chemists Soc., Am. Assn. Pharm. Scientists. Avocation: investment banking. Home and Office: 45 Crest Rd Framingham MA 01702-5606 Fax: 508-875-4726.

SILVERMAN, HENRY RICHARD, diversified business executive, lawyer; b. N.Y.C., Aug. 2, 1940; s. Herbert Robert and Roslyn (Moskowitz) S.; m. Susan H. Herson, June 13, 1965 (div. Jan. 1977); children: Robin Lynn, Deborah Leigh; m. Nancy Ann Kraner, Jan. 22, 1978; 1 child, Catherine Anne Grad. cum laude, Hackley Sch., Tarrytown, N.Y., 1957; BA with honors, Williams Coll., 1961; LL.B., U. Pa., 1964; postgrad. in corp. fin. and taxation, NYU, 1965. Bar: N.Y. 1965, U.S. Tax Ct. 1965, U.S. Ct. Appeals (2d cir.) 1965. Practice law, 1965-66; with White, Weld & Co., beginning 1966; then gen. ptnr. Oppenheimer & Co., until 1970; pres., chief exec. officer ITI Corp., 1970-72; founder, pres. Trans-York Securities Corp., 1972; exec. v.p., chmn. exec. com. Ladenburg, Thalmann & Co., 1973; pres., CEO Vavasseur Am. Ltd., subs. U.K. mcht. bank, 1974-75; gen. ptnr. Brisbane Ptnrs., 1976-77; prin. various investment groups, 1977—, Silverman Energy Co., N.Y.C., 1977—, NBC Channel 20, Springfield, Ill., 1977-83, ABC Channel 9, Syracuse, N.Y., 1977-81; prin., dir. Delta Queen Steamboat Co., New Orleans, 1977-86; also prin. outdoor advt., music pub., motion picture prodn., radio broadcasting & hardware mfg. cos.; pres., CEO Reliance Capital Corp., subs. Reliance Group Holdings, Inc., N.Y.C., 1982—; sr. v.p. bus. devel. Reliance Group Holdings, Inc., 1982-90; chmn., CEO Days Inns Am., Inc., Atlanta, 1984-89; also dir.; pres., CEO Telemundo Group, Inc., N.Y.C., 1986-90; gen. ptnr. Blackstone Group, 1990-91; chmn., CEO, pres. HFS Inc., 1990—; chmn. CEO Cendant Corp., 1996—. Bd. dirs. N.Y. Univ. Hosp., N.Y.C., 1987—. Served to lt. USNR, 1965-73 Mem.: Harmonie (N.Y.C.). Republican. Jewish. Avocation: tennis. Office: Cendant Corp 9 W 57th St Fl 37 New York NY 10019-2701*

SILVERMAN, HERBERT R. corporate financial executive; b. N.Y.C., June 10, 1914; s. Jacob and Minnie (Stein) S.; m. Roslyn Moskowitz, Dec. 17, 1933 (dec. Dec. 1965); children: Karen Silverman Mayers, Henry; m. Nadia Gray, Oct. 17, 1967 (dec. June 1994). BS, NYU, 1932; JD, St. Lawrence U., 1935. Bar: N.Y. bar 1935. Organizer, pres. Centaur Credit Corp. (merged with James Talcott, Inc. of N.Y.), 1945; v.p. James Talcott, Inc., 1944-46, exec. v.p., 1956-58, dir., 1956-75, pres., 1958-64, chmn. bd., chief exec. officer, 1961-73; chmn., chief exec. officer Talcott Nat. Corp., 1968-73, also chmn. exec. com., dir., 1968-75. Pres. Nat. Comml. Fin. Conf., 1948-52, chmn., 1952-58; sr. advisor Bank Julius Baer; adj. prof. fin. NYU Coll. Bus. and Pub. Adminstrn., 1973—; trustee med. ctr., vice chmn. bd. NYU. Named Man of Yr. banking and finance Phi Alpha Kappa; recipient Golden Medallion for humanitarian services B'nai B'rith, Albert Gallatin award NYU, 1978 Mem. ABA, N.Y. Bar Assn., N.Y. Univ. Alumni Fedn. (pres. 1958-60), Phi Alpha Kappa, Iota Theta. Clubs: Harmonie (N.Y.C.); N.Y. Univ. (past pres.). Home: 150 Central Park S New York NY 10019-1566

SILVERMAN, IRA NORTON, news producer; b. Bklyn., May 17, 1935; s. Joseph and Mildred (Axelrod) S.; m. Elizabeth Parsons Aspray, June 16, 1979; children by previous marriage: Gary, Bruce; stepchildren: Elizabeth, Aime, Alison. AB, Columbia U., 1957. Newspaper, mag. and book editor, 1957—67; prodr., writer NBC News, 1967—79; sr. prodr. spl. projects NBC Nightly News, Washington, 1977—95; contbr. The New Yorker, N.Y.C., 1995—, editl. cons., 1995—96; cons. NBC News, 1998, PBS, 1999, 2002. Co-author: The Pleasant Avenue Connection, 1976. Recipient Nat. Headliner award, 1977, 78, 81, 87, Alfred I. DuPont-Columbia U. award, 1983-84, 85-86, Emmy award for news and documentary, 1985, 87, award Overseas Press Club Am., 1987, 90, George Polk award L.I. U., 1988, Excellence in TV award Channels mag., 1990, George Foster Peabody award U. Ga., 1991, Citation for Excellence Overseas Press Club, 1992.

SILVERMAN, JEREMY MARK, psychologist; b. Paterson, N.J., July 25, 1956; s. Robert Harris and Phyllis (Adolf) S.; m. Shaheen Rushd, Sept. 2, 1990; children: Arif Matin, Nadim Samuel. BA, Oberlin Coll., 1978; MA, NYU, 1981, PhD, 1987. Clin. psychology intern VA Med. Ctr., Bronx, N.Y., 1982-83; asst. prof. psychology Mt. Sinai Sch. Medicine, N.Y.C., 1987-95, assoc. prof., 1995—. Contbr. numerous articles to profl. jours. Office: Dept Psychiatry Mt Sinai Sch Medicine PO Box 1230 New York NY 10029-0313 Fax: 212-849-2505. E-mail: jeremy.silverman@mssm.edu.

SILVERMAN, JOSEPH, chemistry educator, scientist; b. N.Y.C., Nov. 5, 1922; s. Jakob and Mary (Chechick) S.; m. Joan Aline Jacks, Jan. 14, 1951; children: Joshua Henry, David Avrom. BA, Bklyn. Coll., 1944; A.M., Columbia U., 1948, PhD, 1951. Head research dept. Walter Kidde (nuclear labs.), Garden City, N.Y., 1952-54; v.p., tech. dir. RAI Research Corp., L.I. City, 1954-59; assoc. prof. chemistry State U. N.Y., Stony Brook, 1959-60; prof. dept. materials and nuclear engring. U. Md., College Park, 1960-92, prof. emeritus, 1992—. Cons. Danish AEC, Indsl. Research Inst., Japan, Boris Kidric Inst., Yugoslavia, Bechtel Co., GPU Nuclear Corp., GE, IAEA, Vienna; disting. vis. prof. Tokyo U., 1974; gen. chmn. 2d Internat. Meeting on Radiation Processing, Miami, Fla., 1978, 3d Tokyo, 1980, hon. chmn. 6th, Ottawa, 1987; trustee Washington Inst. Values in Pub. Policy, 1981-87. Editor Internat. Jour. Applied Radiation and Isotopes, 1973-78, Trans. 1st Internat. Meetings on Radiation Processing, 1977, 3d edit., 1981; mem. editorial adv. bd. Radiation Physics and Chemistry, 1978-95. Served with AUS, 1944-46. Recipient Founders award 6th Internat. Mtg. on Radiation Processing, 1987, Centennial medal U. Md. Coll. Engring., 1994; Rsch. fellow Brookhaven Nat. Lab., 1949-51; Guggenheim fellow, 1966-67. Fellow Nordic Soc. Radiation Chemistry and Tech., Am. Phys. Soc., Am. Nuclear Soc. (Radiation Industry award 1975); mem. Am. Chem. Soc., Sigma Xi. Home: 8101 Connecticut Ave Apt S407 Chevy Chase MD 20815-2839 Office: U Md Dept Materials And Nuclear College Park MD 20742-2115 E-mail: jagman@eng.umd.edu.

SILVERMAN, JOSEPH HILLEL, mathematics educator; b. N.Y.C., Mar. 27, 1955; s. Harry and Shirley (Seiner) S.; m. Susan Leslie Greenhaus, June 13, 1976; children: Deborah, Daniel, Jonathan. ScB, Brown U., 1977; MA, Harvard U., 1979, PhD, 1982. Moore instr. MIT, Cambridge, 1982-86; assoc. prof. Boston U., 1986-88; assoc. prof. math. Brown U., Providence, 1988-91, prof., 1991—. Founder and v.p. rsch., NTRU Cryptosystems, Inc., 1997—. Author: Arithmetic of Elliptic Curves, 1986; editor: Arithmetic Geometry, 1987, Rational Points on Elliptic Curves, 1992, Advanced Topics in Arithmetic of Elliptic Curves, 1995. Fellow NSF, 1983-86, Sloan fellow Sloan Found., 1987, Guggenheim Found. fellow, 1998. Mem. Am. Math. Soc. Avocation: bridge. Office: Brown U Dept Math PO Box 1917 Providence RI 02912-1917

SILVERMAN, JUDITH, human resource educational services director, author, consultant; b. Bklyn., Aug. 26, 1933; d. David and Shirley Beatrice (Maltz) Marks; m. Myron Bernard Silverman, July 3, 1955; 1 son, Brian Scott. B.A. cum laude, Bklyn. Coll., 1960; M.L.S., Pratt Inst., 1963; P.D., L.I.U. 1985. Sec. Fairchild Publs., N.Y.C., 1954-56; tchr., librarian N.Y.C. Bd. Edn., Bklyn., 1956-62; sr. librarian Bklyn. Pub. Library, 1964-68, Queens Borough Pub. Library, Queens, N.Y., 1973-76; asst. dir. personnel Baldwin (N.Y.) Pub. Library, 1976-80; dir. of personnel Bd. Cooperative Edn1. Services Nassau County, Westbury, N.Y., 1980—; cons. books R.R. Bowker Co., N.Y.C., 1971—. Author: Index to Collective Biographies for Young Readers, 1970, 3rd edit., 1979. Mem. N.Y. State/Sch. Personnel Adminstrs., L.I. Assn. Sch. Personnel Adminstrs., Nat. Assn. Ednl. Negotiators, N.Y. State Assn. Sch. Personnel Adminstrs. (Jay Greene award 1991), N.Y. State United Tchrs. (Friend of Edn. award 1993), N.Y. Library Assn. (mem. com.), Nassau County Library Assn., Beta Phi Mu. Office: Bd Coop Ednl Svcs Nassau County Valentines And The Pla Rd Westbury NY 11590

SILVERMAN, KENNETH EUGENE, English educator, writer; b. N.Y.C., Feb. 5, 1936; s. Gustave and Bessie (Goldberg) S.; children: Willa Zahava, Ethan Leigh. BA, Columbia U., 1956, MA, 1958, PhD, 1964. Instr. English U. Wyo., Laramie, 1958-59; preceptor in English Columbia U., N.Y.C., 1962-64; prof. English, co-dir. The Biography Seminar NYU, 1964-2001. Adv. council Inst. Early Am. History and Culture 1984-87. Author: Timothy Dwight, 1969, A Cultural History of the American Revolution, 1976, The Life and Times of Cotton Mather, 1984, Edgar A. Poe: Mournful and Never-ending Remembrance, 1991, Houdini!!! The Career of Ehrich Weiss, 1996; editor: anthology Colonial American Poetry, 1968; compiler: Selected Letters of Cotton Mather, 1976; mem. editorial bd.: Early Am Lit., 1969-72, 77-80, William and Mary Quar., 1984-87, Am. Lit. 1987-90. Recipient Bancroft prize in Am. history, 1985, Pulitzer Prize for biography, 1985, Edgar Allan Poe award Mystery Writers Am., 1992; grantee Bicentennial award NEH, 1972-74, Am. Philos. Soc., 1986, Am. Coun. Learned Socs., 1986; Guggenheim fellow, 1989-90. Mem. Am. Acad. Arts and Scis., Soc. Am. Historians, Am. Antiquarian Soc., Authors Guild, Soc. Am. Magicians. Jewish.

SILVERMAN, LAWRENCE IRA, music educator, musician; b. N.Y.C., Oct. 20, 1956; s. Adolphe Manny and Dorothy Silverman; m. Leslie Dawn Dixon, July 26, 1992; children: Alexis. M Music Edn., Hunter Coll., 1984. Cert. music tchr. NY, NJ. Band dir. Rye (NY) H.S., 1984—86; dir. of music Leonia (NJ) H.S., 1986—. Condr. Bergen County Band, Bergenfield, NJ, 1997. Contbr. articles to profl. publs. Condr. selection com. Bergen County Band, Bergenfield, 1998—2001. Mem.: Music Educators Nat. Conf. Office: Leonia HS 100 Christie Heights St Leonia NJ 07480 E-mail: leoniamusic@hotmail.com.

SILVERMAN, LESLIE E. federal agency administrator; b. Needham, Mass. Grad., U. Vt.; JD, Am. U.; M with distinction, Georgetown U. Bar: D.C., Mass. Law clk. U.S. Atty.'s Office; assoc. Keller and Heckman, 1990—97; labor counsel Senate Healtn, Edn., Labor and Pensions Com.; commr. Equal Opportunity Commn., Washington, 2002—. Office: EEOC 1801 L St NW Washington DC 20507*

SILVERMAN, LESTER PAUL, economist, energy industry consultant; b. N.Y.C., Feb. 28, 1947; s. Eli and Irene B. (Karp) S.; m. Janit Roslyn Smith, June 14, 1969 (dec.); children: Leigh, Stacy, Jenny; m. Patty Abramson, Jan. 7, 1995. BS in Adminstrn. and Mgmt. Sci., MS in Indsl. Adminstrn., Carnegie-Mellon U., 1969, PhD in Econs., 1973. Economist Ctr. for Naval Analyses, Arlington, Va., 1969-74; assoc. exec. dir. NAS, Washington, 1974-78; dir. policy analysis Dept. Interior, 1978-80; prin. dep. asst. sec. Dept. Energy, 1980-81; exec. v.p. Dist. Heat & Power, Inc., 1981-82; dir., head global nonprofit practice McKinsey & Co., Inc., 1982—. Author (with others) govt. report: Reducing U.S. Oil Vulnerability, 1981; editor: Population Redistribution and Public Policy, 1978; contbr. over 40 articles to profl. publs., op-ed pieces. Recipient Spl. Achievement award Dept. Interior, 1979, Outstanding Svc. award Dept. Energy, 1981. Mem. NAS (panel on natural gas stats., 1983-84, exploratory com. on future of nuclear power, 1984, alternative energy R&D com., 1989), Omicron Delta Epsilon, Omicron Delta Kappa. Home: 3005 0 St NW Washington DC 20007 Office: McKinsey & Co Inc 600 14th St NW Washington DC 20005

SILVERMAN, LINDA L. elementary educator; b. Balt., July 19, 1947; d. Benjamin and Doris (Abrams) Levin; m. Larry Ian Silverman; children: Ryan David, Michelle Alisa. BS in Elem. Edn., Towson State U., 1969, BS in Early Childhood, 1978; MEd, Johns Hopkins U., 1974; postgrad., Balt. County Dept. Curriculum, 1993. Cert. tchr., Md. 6th and 4th grade tchr. Baltimore County Bd. Edn., Balt., 1969-74, kindergarten tchr., 1985-86, 1st, 4th and 5th grade tchr., 1986—; camp counselor, tchr. Noah's Ark Nursery Camp, Jewish Cmty. Ctr., Owings Mills, Md., 1979-90; tchr., developer primary acad. program Balt. Actor's Theater, 1982-85. Cert. trainer Say Yes to Wellness Program, Genesee Valley Outdoor Learning Ctr., 1994—; supr. tchr. local colls., Baltimore and Carroll Counties, 1993—; curriculum devel.oper Baltimore County Bd. Edn., 1972, coord., merchandiser, trainer sch. store, 1987-96; gifted and talented program facilitator Ednl. Support Svcs., Baltimore County, 1995-96. Illustrator, editor mag. Randallstown Jaycees, 1980; author: (poems) A Muse to Follow, 1995. Fundraiser Randallstown (Md.) Jaycees, 1976-80, coord. safety town program, 1980-82; coord. fundraiser Johns Hopkins Children Ctr., Balt., 1996—. Recipient cert. of achievement Md. Assn. Elem. Sch. Adminstrs., 1993. Mem. NEA, Md. State Tchrs. Assn., Tchrs. Assn. Baltimore County, Pi Lambda Theta, Kappa Delta Pi. Democrat. Avocations: art and crafts, reading. Home: 2402 Hal Cir Baltimore MD 21209-2620 Office: Balt County Bd Edn 1711 Landrake Rd Towson MD 21204-1822

SILVERMAN, MARK, publisher; Pub. & editor Detroit News, 1997—. Office: Detroit News 615 W Lafayette Blvd Detroit MI 48226-3197*

SILVERMAN, MARTIN MORRIS BERNARD, secondary education educator; b. Boston, May 27, 1936; s. Joseph Lazarus and Sonya Lillian (Feldman) S.; m. Joseph Harvey. BS in Chemistry, U. Mass., 1960, MEd, 1962; EdM, Columbia U., 1974, EdD, 1985. Math. and sci. tchr. Northampton (Mass.) Pub. Schs., 1960-62, U.S. Dept. of Def., Korea and Bermuda, 1963-66; tchr. math, sci. N.Y.C. Bd. Edn., 1966-91. Rsch. scholar biophysics NYU, 1986—; biochemistry rsch. asst. Harvard U. Med. Sch., Boston, 1960; supr., dir. sci. fairs and competitions; cons. in field. Writer, musician, composer and performer; photographer Explorers Jour., U. Mo. Archives collection, Jour. Violin Soc. Am. Curator musical instrument collection , instrument restorer Abrons Arts Ctr., Henry Street Settlement, 2000—. Internat. Ctr. Photography scholar, N.Y.C., 1975. Mem. Violin Soc. Am., Jour. Violin Soc. Am., Nat. Assn. Watch Clock Collectors Assn., Musical Box Soc. Internat., Mensa, Explorers Club. Home: 25 Montgomery St New York NY 10002-6557

SILVERMAN, MARYLIN A. advertising agency executive; b. N.Y.C., Mar. 15, 1941; d. Morris George and Sophie (Betesh) Adler; m. Joseph Elias Silverman, May 30, 1965; children: Lisa, Jennifer. BA, Ind. U., 1962; postgrad., CUNY, 1963-65. Rsch. analyst Compton Advt., N.Y.C., 1962-63; account rsch. supr. Foote, Cone & Belding, 1963-68; self-employed market rsch. cons., 1968-78; rsch. group head Ogilvy & Mather, Inc., 1978-82; sr. v.p., assoc. rsch. dir. Backer Spielvogel Bates, Inc., 1982-88, exec. dir. strategic planning and internat. rsch., 1989-91; exec. v.p. strategic planning Bates Worldwide, 1991-97; exec. dir. strategic planning and rsch. Bates USA, 1997-99, exec. v.p. strategic planning, chief knowledge mgmt. officer, 1999—. Cons. Am. Assn. Advt. Agys., Boys Clubs Am., N.Y.C.; bd. dirs. Women at Risk; mem. conf. bd. Learning and Knowledge Mgmt. Coun. Co-author: Marketing Review, 1980, American Demographics, 1990, Marketing Review, 1997; mem. editl. adv. bd. Jour. Advt. Rsch. Mem. exec. coun. Washington Sq. Pk. Coun., 1969-74; mem. exec. bd. Friends Sem. PTA, N.Y.C., 1980-82, Advt. Rsch. Found., Children's Rsch. Coun. Devel. Com. Mem. Am. Mktg. Assn. (chair Effie awards), Women in Comm., Am. Assn. Advt. Agys. (rsch. com.), Grenwich Ho. Potters and Sculptors Assn. Office: Bates Worldwide 498 7th Ave New York NY 10018-6798 E-mail: msilverman@batesww.com.

SILVERMAN, MELVIN J. lawyer; b. Norwich, Conn., Apr. 2, 1939; s. Morris and Anna (Moyel) S.; m. Beverly Silverman, Aug. 12, 1963; children: Jonathan, Jason, Joel. BA in Math., U. Conn., 1960, JD, 1963. Bar: Conn. 1963, N.J. 1964. Assoc. Nevas & Nevas, Westport, Conn., 1965-67, Lepofsky & Lepofsky, Norwalk, 1967-76; pvt. practice, 1976—. Lectr. land use, contracts, continuing edu. Norwalk Community Coll., 1987—; atty., trial referee Conn. Jud. Dept., Bridgeport and Stamford, 1986—; spl. counsel Town of Ridgefield, Conn., Town of Wilton, Town of New Canaan; panelist numerous seminars; mem. chief justice's adv. com. on appellate rules 1993—. Contbr. articles to profl. jours. Pres., trustee Friends of Norwalk Pub. Lib., 1973-75; mem. coun. City of Norwalk, 1977-78, Wilton Solid Waste Study Commn., 1979. 1st lt. U.S. Army, 1963-65. Mem. Conn. Bar Assn. (exec. com. planning and zoning sect.) Democrat. Avocations: gardening, reading, racquetball. Office: 172 Deforest Rd Wilton CT 06897-1912

SILVERMAN, MERVYN F. health science association administrator, consultant; BS cum laude, Washington and Lee U., 1960; MD, Tulane U., 1964; MPH, Harvard U., 1969. Cert. Am. Bd. Preventive Medicine. Physician Peace Corps, Thailand, 1965-67, regional med. dir. East Asia and the Pacific, 1967-68; spl. asst. to commr. FDA, 1969-70, dir. Office of Consumer Affairs, 1970-72; dir. health Wichita (Kans.)-Sedgwick County Dept. Cmty. Health, 1972-77; med. dir. Planned Parenthood Kans., Wichita, 1976-77; dir. health Dept. Health, San Francisco, 1977-85; health care cons. Mervyn F. Silverman & Assocs., Inc., 1985—; dir. AIDS health svcs. program Robert Wood Johnson Found., 1986-92; nat. spokesperson Am. Found. for AIDS Rsch., 1986-96, pres., also bd. dirs. Resident physician Sta. KPIX-TV, San Francisco, 1979-85; dir., prodr., host weekly health program Sta. KMPX Radio, 1980-82; sr. tech. advisor Acad. Ednl. Devel.-AIDSCOM, 1990-92; former med. advisor to bd. dirs. Golden Gate chpt. ARC, San Francisco; past vice chmn. Adv. Health Coun., State of Calif.; former assoc. clin. prof. Wichita State U.; former assoc. clin. prof. U. Hawaii; former adj. assoc. prof. Sch. Pub. Health and Tropical Medicine Tulane U.; former adj. prof. Inst. Health Policy Studies, Sch. Medicine, U. Calif., San Francisco; former mem. nat. adv. coun. Harvard AIDS Inst.; spkr., presenter in field. Author: (with others) Humanistic Perspectives in Medical Ethics, 1972, What to Do About AIDS, 1986, AIDS and Patient Management: Legal, Ethical and Social Issues, 1986, AIDS: Facts and Issues, 1986, AIDS in Children, Adolescents and Heterosexual Adults: An Interdisciplinary Approach to Prevention, 1988, others; contbg. and consulting editor Modern Medicine Publs., Mpls., 1970-75; contbg. editor Healthline, 1983-85; contbr. articles to profl. jours. Bd. dirs., vice-chmn. U.S.-China Ednl. Inst. Recipient Award for Courageous Leadership, San Francisco Found., Award of Excellence, KAIROS Support for Care Givers, Civic Achievement award Bay Area Non-Partisan Alliance, Heroes in Medicine award Internat. Assn. Physicians in AIDS Care, Pub. Health Hero award U. Calif., Berkeley, 2001; Wear Found. fellow Wichita State U., scholar Kans. Newman Coll. Mem. APHA, AMA, Omicron Delta Kappa, Delta Omega. Address: 9 Crolona Heights Dr Crockett CA 94525

SILVERMAN, MITCHELL S. endocrinologist/diabetologist; b. Rockville Centre, N.Y., Sept. 11, 1954; s. Alvin and Doris S.; m. Elizabeth, June 13, 1993; children: Aliza, David, Jonathan. BA in Biochemistry magna cum laude, Harvard Coll., 1976; MD, Duke U., 1980. Diplomate Am. Bd. Internal Medicine, Am. Bd. Endocrinology and Metabolism. Res. internal medicine Emory U., Atlanta, 1981-83; endocrine rsch. fellow Meml. Sloan Kettering Cancer Ctr., N.Y.C., 1984-85; clin. endocrine fellow Cornell U. Med. Ctr., 1985-81; med. assoc. M.E.N.D., Union, N.J., 1988-90; pvt. practice, 1990—. Assoc. attending Newark Beth Israel Med. Ctr., St. Barnabas Med. Ctr., attending, chief endorcine divsn. Union Hosp.; attending Rahway Hosp., cons. Irvington Gen. Hosp., attending John F. Kennedy Med. Ctr., all 1990—; former Beth Israel asst. clin. prof. medicine U. Medicine and Dentistry N.J., Newark. Contbr. articles to profl. jours. and conf. procs. Fellow Am. Coll. Endocrinology, Assn. Clin. Endocrinologists; mem. AMA, ACP, Am. Diabetes Assn., Thyroid Soc., N.J. Med. Soc. Office: 2333 Morris Ave Ste B9 Union NJ 07083-5716

SILVERMAN, MORTON MAYER, psychiatrist, educator; b. Utica, N.Y., Aug. 15, 1947; s. Hirsch Lazaar and Mildred (Friedlander) S.; m. Kineret Shelli Jaffe, July 5, 1970; children: Ariana, Noah, Ethan. BA, U. Pa., 1969; MD, Northwestern U., 1974. Diplomate Am. Bd. Psychiatry and Neurology. Resident in psychiatry U. Chgo., 1975-78, asst. prof., 1978-80, assoc. prof., 1987—; asst. prof. Georgetown U., Washington, 1981-87; dir. Ctr. Prevention Rsch. NIMH, Rockville, Md., 1981-85; assoc. adminstr. prevention Alcohol, Drug Abuse & Mental Health Adminstrn., Washington, 1985-87. Temporary advisor WHO, Geneva, 1979-80, cons., 1998—; cons. forensic malpractice, 1992—; cons. U.S. Surgeon Gen., Washington, 1998—. Co-editor 4 books, 1995-2000; co-author: Comprehensive Textbook Suiciodology, 2000; contbr. articles to profl. jours. Bd. dirs. U. Chgo. Lab. Schs., 1992—. Recipient Spl. Recognition award USPHS, 1985; fellow Am. Coll. Forensic Examiners, 1997. Mem. Am. Psychiatric Assn. (fellow 1991), Am. Assn. Suicidology (editor-in-chief Suicide Jour. 1997—), Am. Found. Suicide Prevention, Internat. Assn. Suicide Prevention, Group Advancement Psychiatry, Sigma Xi. Jewish. Avocations: contemporary glass art collecting, opera, coin collecting. Home: 4858 S Dorchester Ave Chicago IL 60615-2012 Office: U Chgo 5737 S University Ave Chicago IL 60637-1507

SILVERMAN, MOSES, lawyer; b. Bklyn., Mar. 3, 1948; s. Bernard and Anne Silverman; m. Betty B. Robbins, Jan. 19, 1980; children: Benjamin, Rachel. AB, Colby Coll., 1969; JD, NYU, 1973. Bar: N.Y. 1974, U.S. Dist. Ct. (so. and ea. dists.) N.Y. 1974, U.S. Ct. Appeals (2d cir.) 1974, U.S. Ct. Appeals (D.C. cir.) 1977, U.S. Supreme Ct. 1977, D.C. 1982, U.S. Ct. Appeals (fed. cir.) 1985, U.S. Ct. Appeals (11th cir.) 2001, U.S. Dist. Ct. (D.C.) 2001, U.S. Ct. Appeals (9th cir.), U.S. Ct. Appeals (9th cir.) 2002. Assoc. Paul, Weiss, Rifkind, Wharton & Garrison, N.Y.C., 1973-81, ptnr., 1981—. Vol. U.S. Peace Corps., Istanbul, Turkey, 1969-70; bd. dirs. Legal Aid Soc., 1998—, Vols. Legal Svcs. Mem. ABA, N.Y. State Bar Assn., Assn. of Bar of City of N.Y. Home: 7 Gracie Sq New York NY 10028-8001 Office: Paul Weiss Rifkind Wharton & Garrison 1285 Ave of Americas New York NY 10019-6028 E-mail: msilverman@paulweiss.com.

SILVERMAN, NORMAN ALAN, cardiac surgeon; b. Boston, Dec. 19, 1946; BA, Dartmouth Coll., 1968; MD, Boston U., 1971. Prof. surgery U. Ill., Chgo., 1980-89; divsn. head Henry Ford Hosp., Detroit, 1989—; prof. surgery Case-Western Res. U., Cleve., 1992—. Contbr. 200 scientific articles to profl. jours. Lt. comdr. USPHS, 1973-75. Fellow Am. Coll. Surgeons, Am. coll. Cardiology, Am. Coll. Chest Physicians. Avocation: sailing. Office: Henry Ford Hosp 2799 W Grand Blvd Detroit MI 48202-2689

SILVERMAN, NORMAN HENRY, cardiologist, educator; b. Johannesburg, South Africa, Sept. 29, 1942; came to U.S., 1972; s. Simon Cecil and Jean (Krawitz) S.; m. Heather Silverman. DSc in Med., U. Witwatersrand, Johannesburg, 1985; postgrad., U. Witwatersrand. Diplomate Am. Bd. Pediatrics. Asst. prof. pediatrics Stanford U., Palo Alto, Calif., 1974-75; asst. prof. pediatrics U. Calif., San Francisco, 1975, assoc. prof. radiology, 1979, prof., 1985—. Co-author: Two Dimensional Echocardiography, 1982, Congenital Heart Disease, 1990; author: Pediatric Echocardiography, 1993. Lt. South African Def. Force, 1968-69. Grantee March of Dimes, 1977-79, Am. Heart Assn., 1978-80, 90-92. Fellow Am. Coll. Cardiology, Am. Acad. Pediatrics, Coll. Physicians South Africa, Soc. Pediatric Rsch., Am. Pediatric Soc. Achievements include research in echocardiography of congenital heart disease in infants and chiildren; fetal echocardiography and treatment. Avocations: classical music, opera, eonology. Office: Stanford U Med Ctr 750 Welch Rd #305 Palo Alto CA 94304 E-mail: nhsilverman@pedcard.ucsf.edu.

SILVERMAN, OZZIE, consulting strategist; b. Montreal, Que., Can., Jan. 30, 1939; s. Louis and Fanny (Black) S.; m. Sheela Marsha Zangwill, Aug. 22, 1962; children: Caroline, Marjorie. BSME, McGill U., Montreal, Que., 1963, diploma in mgmt., 1968, MBA, 1969. Cert. Que. Order of Engrs. Supr. quality control engring. Pratt and Whitney, Montreal, 1964-68; sr. mktg. rschr. United Aircraft, 1969-70; asst. chief internat. Dept. Industry, Trade and Commerce, Ottawa, Ont., Can., 1972-77; dir. industry projects Ministry of State for Sci. and Tech., 1978-85; dir. strategic techs. policy Industry, Sci. and Tech. Can., 1986-91; dir. gen. sci. strategy and innovation policy Industry Can., 1992-98, dir., 1998—. Chmn. com. for sci. and tech. policy Orgn. for Econ. Coop. and Devel., Paris, 1995-98. Avocations: Inuit and Japanese graphic art. Home: 112 Pigeon Terr Ottawa ON Canada K1V 9H7 Office: Ste 513 255 Albert St Ottawa ON Canada K1P 6AP E-mail: osilverman@secor.ca.

SILVERMAN, PAUL HYMAN, science administrator, former university official; b. Mpls., Oct. 8, 1924; s. Adolph and Libbie (Idlekope) S.; m. Nancy Josephs, May 20, 1945; children: Daniel Joseph, Claire. Student, U. Minn., 1942-43, 46-47; BS, Roosevelt U., 1949; MS in Biology, Northwestern U., 1951; PhD in Parasitology, U. Liverpool, Eng., 1955, DSc, 1968. Rsch. fellow Malaria Rsch. Sta., Hebrew U., Israel, 1951-53; rsch. fellow dept. entomology and parasitology Sch. Tropical Medicine, U. Liverpool, 1953-56; sr. sci. officer dept. parasitology Moredun Inst., Edinburgh, Scotland, 1956-59; head dept. immunoparasitology Glaxo, Allen & Hanbury, Ltd., Ware, Eng., 1960-62; prof. zoology and vet. pathology and hygiene U. Ill., Urbana, 1963-72, chmn., head dept. zoology, 1963-68; prof., chmn. dept. biology, v.p. for rsch. U. N.Mex., 1972-77; provost, rsch. and grad. studies Ctrl. Adminstrn. SUNY, Albany, 1977-79, pres. Rsch. Found., 1979-80; pres. U. Maine, Orono, 1980-84; biol. divsn. Lawrence Berkeley Lab. U. Calif., Berkeley, 1984-86; head biomed. divsn. Lawrence Berkeley Lab., 1986-87; adj. prof. med. parasitology Sch. Pub. Health U. Calif., Berkeley, 1986, assoc. lab. dir. for life scis., dir Donner Lab., 1987-90, dir. systemwide biotech. rsch. and edn. program, 1989-90; dir. Beckman's Scientific Affairs, Fullerton, Calif., 1990-93; assoc. chancellor Ctr. for Health Scis., adj. prof. medicine U. Calif., Irvine, 1993-96. Dir. Western Ctr., Am. Acad. Arts and Scis., 1997—; cons., Commn. Colls. and Univs., North Central Assn. Colls. and Secondary Schs., 1964—; chmn. Commn. on Instns. Higher Edn., 1974-76; Fulbright prof. zoology Australian Nat. U., Canberra, 1969; adjoint prof. biology U. Colo., Boulder, 1970-72; mem. bd. Nat. Council on Postsecondary Accreditation, Washington, 1975-77; dir. research in malaria immunology and vaccination US AID, 1965-76; bd. dirs. Inhalation Toxicology Research Inst., Lovelace Biomed. and Environ. Research Inst., Albuquerque, 1977-84, Hastings Ctr.; mem. N.Y. State Gov.'s High Tech. Opportunities Task Force; chmn. research and rev. com. N.Y. State Sci. and Tech. Found.; mem. pres.'s council New Eng. Land Grant Univs.; bd. advs. Lovelace-Bataan Med. Center, Albuquerque, 1974-77; adv. com. U.S. Army Command and Gen. Staff Coll., Ft. Leavenworth, Kans., 1983-84. Mem. editl. bd. Jour. Anti-Aging Medicine, 1997—; contbr. articles to profl. jours. Chmn. rsch. rev. com. N.Y. State Sci. and Tech. Found.; bd. dirs. Hastings Ctr., 1997—. Fellow Meridian Internat. Inst., 1992; assoc. The Hastings Ctr., 1995—. Fellow Royal Soc. Tropical Medicine and Hygiene, N.Mex. Acad. Sci.; mem. Am. Soc. Parasitologists, Am. Soc. Tropical Medicine and Hygiene, Am. Soc. Immunologists, Brit. Soc. Parasitology (coun.), Brit. Soc. Immunologists, Soc. Gen. Microbiology, Soc. Protozoologists, Am. Soc. Zoologists, Human Genome Orgn., Am. Inst. Biol. Scis., N.Y. Acad. Scis., N.Y. Soc. Tropical Medicine, World Acad. Art and Sci., B'nai B'rith, Sigma Xi, Phi Kappa Phi. Office: Am Acad Arts & Scis 3000 Berkeley Pl Irvine CA 92697-7425

SILVERMAN, RICHARD BRUCE, chemist, biochemist, educator; b. Phila., May 12, 1946; s. Philip and S. Ruth (Simon) S.; , Barbara Jean Kesner, Jan. 9, 1983; children: Matthew, Margaret, Philip. BS, Pa. State U., 1968; MA, Harvard U., 1972, PhD, 1974. Asst. prof. Northwestern U., Evanston, Ill., 1976-82, assoc. prof., 1982-86, prof., 1986—, Arthur Andersen teaching & rsch. prof., 1996-98, mem. Inst. Neurosci., 1990—, Charles Deering McCormick prof., 2001—. Cons. Procter and Gamble Co., Cin., 1984, Abbott Labs, North Chicago, 1987, Searle R&D, St. Louis, 1988-90, DuPont, 1991, Dow, 1991, Leytig, Voit & Mayer law offices, 1992—, DowElanco, 1993-95, G.D. Searle, 1995, Affymax, 1995, Kinetik Pharms., 1999, Guilford Pharms., 2001, Activ X Bioscis., 2001, Cytoclonal Pharms., 2001; mem. adv. panel NIH, Bethesda, Md., 1981, 83, 85, 87-91, 2001; expert analyst CHEMTRACTS; scientific adv. bd. Influx, Inc., 1998—. NIGMS adv. coun., 2002. Mem. editl. bd.: Jour. Enzyme Inhibition, 1988—2002, mem. editl. bd.: Archives Biochem. & Biophys., 1993—, mem. editl. bd.: Jour. Medicinal Chemistry, 1995—2000, mem. editl. bd.: Enzyme Inhibition and Medicinal Chemistry, 2002—; contbr. articles; mem. editl. bd.: articles Letters in Drug Desing & Discovery. Mem. adv. bd. Ill. Math. & Scis. Acad., 1988. With U.S. Army, 1969-71. Recipient Career Devel. award USPHS, 1982-87, E. LeRoy Hall award for tchg. excellence, 1999, Northwestern Alumni Tchg. award, 2000; postdoctoral fellow Brandeis U., Waltham, Mass., 1974-76, DuPont Young Faculty fellow, 1976, Alfred P. Sloan Found. fellow, 1981-85; grantee various govt. and pvt. insts., 1976—. Author: Co. Cope. Sr. Scholar, Award ACS. Fellow: AAAS; mem.: Am. Chem. Soc. (nat. elected nominating com. divsns. biol. chemistry 1993—96, long-range planning com. divsn. med. chem. 1999—2002), Am. Soc. Biochem. Molecular Biology, Am. Inst. Chemists. Avocations: tennis, family, golf. Office: Northwestern U Dept Chemistry 2145 Sheridan Rd Evanston IL 60208-3113

SILVERMAN, ROBERT ALAN, college official, historian; b. Phila., Dec. 22, 1947; s. Milton Edward and Rhoda (Pasternack) S.; m. Fran Stukelman, Mar. 30, 1969; 1 child, David. BS, Drexel U., 1969; MA, Harvard U., 1973, PhD, 1977. Fin. analyst Harvard U., Cambridge, Mass., 1977-78, v.p. Harvard real estate, 1978-84, dir. planning, 1984-88; sr. v.p. Watch Hill Co., 1988-89; mng. dir. Keystone Advisors, Inc., Cambridge, 1990-93; v.p. adminstrn. and fin. Emerson Coll., Boston, 1993—. Cons. in field. Author: Law and Urban Growth, 1981; editor: The Corporate Real Estate Handbook, 1987. With U.S. Army, 1969-72. Jewish. Office: Emerson Coll 120 Boylston St Boston MA 02116-4624

SILVERMAN, ROBERT JOSEPH, lawyer; b. Mpls., Apr. 4, 1942; s. Maurice and Toby (Goldstein) S.; 1 child, Adam Graham-Silverman; m. Suzanne M. Brown; 1 child, Thomas B. BA, U. Minn., 1964, JD, 1967. Bar: Minn. 1967. Assoc. Dorsey & Whitney, Mpls., 1967-72, ptnr., 1972—2001. Lectr. William Mitchell Coll. Law, St. Paul, 1977-78, Hamline Law Sch., St. Paul, 1990-96, Minn. Continuing Legal Edn., Mpls, 1985-99, Bd. dirs. Courage Ctr., Golden Valley, Minn., 1978-84, 85-95, v.p., 1983-86, pres., 1988-89. With USAR, 1967-73. Mem. ABA, Minn. Bar Assn., Hennepin County Bar Assn., Am. Coll. Real Estate Lawyers. Jewish. Office: Dorsey & Whitney 50 S 6th St Ste 1500 Minneapolis MN 55402-1498 E-mail: silverman.robert@dorseylaw.com.

SILVERMAN, SAM MENDEL, physicist, lawyer; b. N.Y.C., Nov. 16, 1925; s. Moshe Aaron and Gitel (Korenbaum) S.; m. Jacqueline Greenberg, Sept. 12, 1948 (div. Apr. 1965); children: Ann, William, Nancy; m. Phyllis Rolfe, June 26, 1966; children: Gila, Aaron. BChE, CCNY, 1945; PhD, Ohio State U., 1952; JD, Suffolk U., 1982. Bar: Mass. 1982, U.S. Dist. Ct. Mass. 1982, U.S. Ct. Appeals (1st cir.) 1982, N.Y. 1983, U.S. Supreme Ct. 1986. Assoc. Ohio State U., Columbus, 1952-55; asst. prof. chem. physics U. Toledo, 1955-57; rsch. physicist Air Force Cambridge Rsch. Labs., Bedford, Mass., 1957-80, chief polar atmospheric processes br. and dir. geopole obs., 1963-74, cons., 1980—. Vis. rsch. assoc. Queens U., Belfast, 1963-64; vis. prof. Osmania U., Hyderabad, India, 1965-66; mem. adv. bd. Inst. Space and Atmospheric Studies, U. Sask. (Can.), 1965-69; sr. rsch. physicist Boston Coll., 1981-97; co-chmn. interdivisional commn. history Internat. Assn. Geomagnetism and Aeronomy, 1987-91; lectr. palliative care courses, Poland, 1993, 94, 2000. Contbr. articles to profl. jours. Mem. Town Meeting Lexington, Mass., 1973-79, 84—; elected mem. Lexington Dem. Town Com., 1996—; legal counsel Internat. Work Group on Death, Dying and Bereavement. With USAAF, 1945-46. Fellow Am. Phys. Soc., Explorers Club; mem. Am. Geophys. Union (editor History of Geophysics newsletter 1983-91), Internat. Work Group on Death, Dying and Bereavement. Home: 18 Ingleside Rd Lexington MA 02420-2522 E-mail: smpr@ma.ultranet.com.

SILVERMAN, SHERRI LYNN, artist, educator; b. Atlanta, Apr. 19, 1951; d. Sigmund J. and Faye (Bloshtein) S. BA in English/Am. Lit., Emory U., 1971; MA in English/Am. Lit., Brandeis U., 1974; PhD in Art History and Humanities, The Union Inst., 1996. Instr. art history Front Range C.C., Boulder, Colo., 1999—2000; exec. dir. Arts and Humanities Assembly of Boulder Co., 2000—01. Adj. faculty fine arts, humanities and English Fla. C.C., Jacksonville, 1993; adj. faculty fine arts, humanities and English, lang. and lit. dept. U. North Fla. , Jacksonville, 1993—94; vis. faculty honors program U. North Fla., Jacksonville, 1994, U. N.Mex. , Albuquerque, 1996; seminar co-convener The Union Inst. , Cin., 1996; vis. faculty N.Mex. Highlands U., Las Vegas, Nev., 1997; seminar co-convener The Union Inst. , 1997; adj. faculty fine arts, humanities and English, lang. and lit. dept., art history and humanities dept. TVI C.C., Albuquerque, 1997—98; founder Women Artists and Art on the Move (WAAM), 1998; founder, pres. Santa Fe Coll. of Art and Creativity, 1998; adj. faculty humanities dept. Coll. Santa Fe, 1999; adj. faculty visual arts Naropa U., Boulder, Colo., 2000—; instr. Sahaj Samadhi Meditation and Art of Living Course, Internat. Art of Living Found. ; artist-in-residence Boulder Mus. Contemporary Art, 2001. One-woman shows include Santa Fe East, 1992, Vandroff Gallery, Jacksonville, 1993, Heaven on Earth, Atlantic Beach, Fla., 1994, The Book Mark, Atlantic Beach, 1994, Bank of Santa Fe Gallery, 1997, TVI C.C. Chambers Gallery, 1998, exhibited in group shows at First Nat. Bank, Santa Fe, 1992, 25th Ann. Mandarin Arts Festival, Jacksonville, 1993 (2d Pl. award, 1993), Ponte Vedra Beach , Fla., 1993, Jacksonville Coalition Visual Arts Gallery 88 , Ctr. Contemporary Arts , Santa Fe, 1995, Santuario de Guadalupe, 1995, Pensacola Mus. Art, 1996, North Moon Gallery, Telluride, Colo., 1997, Boulder Mus. Contemporary Art, 2001, Sonoma Mus. Visual Art, 2002, others, represented in numerous pub. and pvt. collections; contbr. poetry to various publs. Mem. Citywide Women's History Month Planning com., Jacksonville, 1993-94. Mem.: Am. Coun. for South Asian Art, Coll. Art Assn. Home: PO Box 2126 Boulder CO 80306-2126 Address: 4656 White Rock Cir #12 Boulder CO 80301 E-mail: shrisilver@aol.com.

SILVERMAN, STANLEY WAYNE, chemical company executive; b. Phila., June 18, 1947; m. Ellen J. Seligsohn, June 10, 1970. BSChemE, Drexel U., 1969, MBA, 1974; AMP, Harvard U., 1989. Process engr. Atlantic Richfield Co., Phila., 1969-71, PQ Corp., Phila., 1971-74, mgr. oper. planning Valley Forge, Pa., 1974-76, product mgr., 1976-80, mktg. mgr., 1980-82, nat. sales mgr., 1982-84, pres. Nat. Silicates Ltd. subs. Toronto, Ont., Can., 1984-87, pres. ind. chem. group Valley Forge, 1987-90, exec. v.p., COO, 1990-99, pres., CEO, bd. dirs., 2000—. Chmn. adv. coun. Drexel U. Coll. Engring, 1991-93, alumni bd. govs., 1998, bd. trustees, 2000—; bd. dirs. Phila. Acad., Inc., 1999—. Named among 100 most disting. grads. Drexel U., 1992; recipient Alumni Achievement award Drexel U., 1995. Mem. Soap and Detergent Assn. (vice chmn. bd. dirs. 2002—), Am. Chemistry Coun. (bd. dirs. 2001—). Office: PQ Corp 1200 W Swedesford Rd Berwyn PA 19312-1078

SILVERMAN, SUSAN JOY, lawyer; b. N.Y.C., Sept. 11, 1954; d. Sidney G. and Belle Silverman; m. Mark F. Montalbano, Dec. 21, 1980; children: Victoria Jo, Zachary Lucas. BA, CCNY, 1975; JD, Temple U., 1978. Bar: Fla. 1981, U.S. Ct. Appeals (11th cir.), U.S. Supreme Ct. Assoc. Marlow, Shofi et al, Miami, Fla., 1981-84, Branning, Breslau et al, Sarasota, 1987-92; pvt. practice, 1992—. Pres. Gulf Gate Elem. Sch. PTA, Sarasota, 1995, 98. Mem. Fla. Bar Assn., Acad. Fla. Trial Lawyers, Sarasota County Bar Assn. Office: 3400 S Tamiami Trl Fl 2D Sarasota FL 34239-6093

SILVERMAN, TREVA, writer, producer, consultant; b. N.Y.C. d. Nathan and Janno (Harra) S. Student, U. Chgo., 1956; BA, Bennington Coll., 1958. Staff writer: (TV) The Entertainers, 1964, The Monkees, 1966, 67, 68, Captain Nice, 1968, Room 222, 1969, The Mary Tyler Moore Show, 1970-75 (Emmy award Best Comedy Writer 1974, Writer of Yr. 1974); episode writer He and She, 1968, Get Smart, 1968; writer: (TV pilots) Dates from Hell, 1991, Boy, Girl, Boy, 1991, Home Again, 1992, Ladies Night, 1992, The Rev, 1995, San Diego Presents, 1996; (features) A Nice Girl, 1980, Going All the Way, 1986, Act One, 1987; writer, prodr. children's musicals Theatre East, N.Y.C., 1960-63, Scandal, 1985, Hearts' Desire: Out of Town, 1992; contbg. writer: Julius Monk's Upstairs at the Downstairs, 1962-64; cons. Columbia pictures TV comedy devel., 1985-86, MTM Prodns., 1986, Just in Time, ABC-TV, 1987. Named one of TV Women of Yr., Ladies Home Jour., 1975. Mem. Writers Guild Am. (Best Writer of a Spl. award 1969), Dramatists Guild, Acad. TV Arts and Scis. Democrat. Office: 8827 Beverly Blvd Los Angeles CA 90048-2405

SILVERMAN, VICTORIA LILLIAN, not-for-profit fundraiser; b. St. Louis, July 2, 1961; d. Thomas and Eva Alice (Hasko) Schiff; m. Lloyd Alan Silverman, Dec. 31, 1995; children: Anyu Isabella, Emmanuelle Snow. BA, Washington U., 1983; postgrad., St. Louis U., 1985-86. Assoc. dir. devel. Jewish Cmty. Ctr., St. Louis, 1983-85; assoc. dir. engring. Washington U., 1986-89; dir. engring. fund Stanford (Calif.) U., 1989-92; dir. major gifts and planned giving U. Calif., Santa Barbara, 1992-95; v.p. devel., exec. dir. found. St. Francis Med. Ctr., 1995; dir. devel. Am. Film Inst., L.A., 1995—2001; v.p. external affairs St. Louis Symphony Orch., 2001—. Cons. Stanford Engring. Sch., 1992, other various orgns., 1992—. Bd. dirs. Santa Barbara Ballet, 1990-92; vol. fundraiser Walter Capps for Congress, Santa Barbara, 1991. Mem. Coun. Advancement Support Edn. (presentor 1992—, conf. dir. 1995). Democrat. Jewish. Avocations: percussionist, dance and film enthusiaist. Office: 718 N Grand Blvd Saint Louis MO 63103

SILVERMAN, WARREN, physician; b. N.Y.C., Nov. 16, 1954; s. Leon and Ruth S.; m. Jean Marie Ogburn, Apr. 11, 1981 (div. Sept. 1990); 1 child, Arone Yacov; m. Elena Gennadievna Kiyatkina, Oct. 13, 1997; children; Inessa, Danielle Nicole, Samantha Leah. BS in Biology, Rensselaer Polytech Inst., 1978; MD, Albany Med. Coll., 1978. Bd. cert. internal medicine, occupational medicine, forensic medicine. Med. dir. Ocrancoke (N.C.) Health Ctr., 1981-85; asst. prof. Albany Med. Coll., 1985-87; dir. emergency dept. Cmty. Hosp., Cobleskill, N.Y., 1989-91; med. dir. Workplace Health & Safety Assn., Latham, 1986-95, dir., 1995-97, Access Case Mgmt. Svcs., Latham, 1998—, Access Health Systems, Latham, 1999—. Profl. adv. bd. Ctr. for Disabled, Albany, 1994—; exec. dir. Northeast N.Y. Fed. Safety & Health Coun., Albany, 1998—; sr. aviation med. examiner FAA, Latham, 1989—; med. dir. N.Y.S. PPO Corvel Corp., 2000—; cons. in field. Editor Nat. Safety Data Sheets, 1989-91. Exec. dir. Theater Dance Network, Voorheesville, N.Y., 1998; med. officer Civil Air Patrol, Albany, 1988-91; dir. Voohheesville Cmty. Sch. Found., 1990. Lt. comdr. USPHS, 1981-85. Fellow Am. Coll. Forensic Medicine, Am. Coll. Forensic Examiners; mem. Am. Coll. Occupational & Environ. Medicine, Internat. Soc. Police Surgeons. Jewish. Home: 547 New Salem Rd Voorheesville NY 12186-4829 Office: Access Health Systems 776A Watervliet Shaker Rd Latham NY 12110-2296

SILVERMINT, ANDREI, digital media and imaging facility executive; b. Minsk, Russia, May 6, 1973; came to the U.S., 1982; s. Emanuel H. and Faina May (Dvorkin) S.; m. Irina Vladi Levis, June 16, 1996. Cert. 16mm film prodn., Columbia Coll., 1992; student, Mpls. Coll. Art and Design, 1994; A in Multimedia Design, Sch. Comm. Arts, 1995. Microsoft cert. profl. Mgr. United Artists Theatres, Roseville, Minn., 1988-92; multimedia developer Wilson Learning Corp., Eden Prairie, 1992-93; animator, multimedia developer Badiyan Prodns., Bloomington, 1993-95; founder, pres. Cyberspatial Labs., Inc., St. Louis Park, 1996-98; photographer Draelants Design, Brussels & Paris, 1997; photospin Drake Morton Studios, L.A., 1998; photographer J18/Tan Holdings, Saipan, China, 1997—, CNMI, Hong Kong, 1997—, Kimberly Franson Agy., Mpls., 1998—; founder, pres. Andrei Photography Co., 1998—. Cons., analyst GB Lumima Corp., Golden Valley, Minn., 1995-96. Author: (CD ROM) Repacking Your Bags, 1994; contbr. photographs to pubs. Mem. Minn. Film Bd., Assn. Internet Profls., Ilfo Pro Photographers' Assn., Microsoft Sitebuilder Network, Mpls. Athletic Club (bus. roundtable mem. 1997—), U.S. Chess Fedn., Minn. State Chess Assn., Minn. Sword Club. Jewish. Avocations: independent and foreign films, Japanese anime, science-fiction, fencing, yoga, Djing. Address: PO Box 95426 Seattle WA 98145-2426

SILVERS, ANN, peri-operative nurse, educator; b. Omaha, Mar. 1, 1943; d. John Stephen and M. Georgina Marie Mary McNeil; m. Ralph L. Silvers, Oct. 30, 1993. Diploma, St. Joseph Hosp. Sch. Nursing, Phoenix, 1966; BS in Health Care Scis., Chapman Coll., Travis AFB, Calif., 1979. RN Ariz. Pvt. scrub nurse Drs. Nelson, Brown, Cornell, Phoenix, 1969; staff nurse operating room St. Joseph Hosp., 1966-69, 70, Tucson, 1970—71, Washoe Med. Ctr., Reno, 1976—77; staff nurse U. Ariz. Med. Ctr., Tucson, 1971—75, asst. oper. rm. supr., 1975—76; oper. rm. staff nurse David Grant Med. Ctr., Travis AFB, Calif., 1977—81; coord. oper. rm. edn. Seton Med. Ctr., Daly City, 1981—85; staff nurse operating room Yavapai Regional Med. Ctr., Prescott, Ariz., 1985—88, John C. Lincoln Hosp., Phoenix, 1988—2000. Instr. surg. technician program and perioperative nurse program Gateway C.C., Phoenix, 1989-91, also extern preceptor. Capt. USAF, 1977-81. Mem. Assn. Operating Room Nurses (cert.), Sigma Theta Tau.

SILVERS, GERALD THOMAS, publishing executive; b. Cin., Aug. 26, 1937; s. Steve Allen and Tina Mae (Roberts) S.; m. Ann Gregory Woodward, July 25, 1964. BA, U. Ky., 1960. Asst. research svcs. mgr. Cin. Enquirer, 1963-72, research svcs. dir., 1972-74, research dir., 1974-90, v.p. mktg. svcs., 1990-94, v.p. market devel., 1994—. Mem. U. Ky. Devel. Coun., Lexington, 1986—; trustee Neediest Kids of All, 1991—; mem. region 5 exec. com. Ohio Sch. to Work, 1997-2000; mem. corps. com. St. Elizabeth Med. Ctr. Found., 1998; mem. bd. overseers Taft Mus. Art, 1999—, treas., bd. govs., 2002—. 1st lt. U.S. Army, 1960-62. Recipient Thomas H. Copeland award of merit, 1991. Mem. U. Ky. Alumni Assn. Cin. Chpt. (pres. 1985), Newspaper Research Council (pres. 1985,86), Internat. Newspaper Market Assn., Am. Mktg. Assn., Am. Art Soc. Cin. (pres. 1999-2001). Presbyterian. Home: 229 Watch Hill Rd Fort Mitchell KY 41011-1822 Office: Cin Enquirer 312 Elm St Cincinnati OH 45202-2739 E-mail: gsilvers@enquirer.com.

SILVERS, LAWRENCE WYNN, surgeon; b. Bklyn., Dec. 6, 1950; s. Ralph Irving and Jean (Sosne) S.; m. Robin Diane Boxer, June 6, 1976; children: Ashley Danielle, Myles Nolan. BA, Colgate U., 1972; MD, Albany Med.

Coll., 1976. Gen. surg. intern R.I. Hosp., Providence, 1976-77; resident Brown U., 1977-78, Roosevelt Hosp., Columbia U., N.Y.C., 1978-81; vascular fellow Henry Ford Hosp., Detroit, 1981-82; surgeon, ptnr. Lakewood (N.J.) Surg. Group, 1982—; chief surgery Kimball Med. Ctr., Lakewood. Attending surgeon Cmty. Med. ctr., Toms River, N.J., 1990—. Contbr. articles to profl. jours. Fellow Am. Coll. Surgeons; mem. AMA, NJ. Vascular Soc., Ea. Vascular Soc. Avocation: golf. Home: 725 Woodchuck Ln Toms River NJ 08755-2170

SILVERS, ROBERT B. editor; b. N.Y., Dec. 31, 1929; s. James J. and Rose (Roden) S. AB, U. Chgo., 1947; cert., Ecole de Sci. Politiques, Paris, 1956. Paris editor Paris Rev., 1954-59; asst. editor Harpers Mag., N.Y.C., 1959-63; co-editor N.Y. Rev. of Books, 1963—. Editor: Writing in America, 1962, Hidden Histories of Science, 1995, Doing It: Five Performing Arts, 2001; co-editor: The Legacy of Isaiah Berlin, 2001, Striking Terror: America's New War, 2002. Trustee N.Y. Pub. Libr., 1997—, Ditchley Found., 1996—, Am. Acad. in Rome, 1998-. Decorated Legion d'Honneur. Mem. Am. Acad. Arts and Scis., Coun. Fgn. Rels., Century Assn. Office: NY Rev of Books 1755 Broadway New York NY 10019-3743 Home: 655 Park Avenue New York NY 10021

SILVERS, SALLY, choreographer, performing company executive; b. Greeneville, Tenn., June 19, 1952; d. Herbert Ralston and Sara Elizabeth (Buchanan) S.; life ptnr. Bruce Erroll Andrews. BA in Dance and Polit. Sci., Antioch Coll., 1975. Artistic dir. Sally Silvers & Dancers, N.Y.C., 1980—. Mem. faculty Leicester Poly., 1986, 87, 89, summer choreography project Bennington Coll., 1988-92, Chisenhale Dance Space, London, 1989, 91, Am. Dance Festival, Durham, N.C., 1990, 92; guest tchr. European Dance Devel. Ctr., Arnhem, The Netherlands, 1992—. Choreographer (performances) Politics of the Body Microscope of Conduct, 1980, Social Movement, 1981, Connective Tissue, 1981, Less Time You Know Praxis, 1981, Don't No Do And This, 1981, Lack of Entrepreneurial Thrift, 1982, Celluoid Sally and Mr. E, 1982 , Mutate, 1982, Being Red Enough, 1982, Disgusting, 1982, Bedtime at the Reformatory, 1982, Eat the Rich, 1982, They Can't Get It in the Shopping Cart, 1982, Blazing Forceps, 1982, And Find Out Why, 1983, Choose Your Weapons, 1984 , Extend the Wish for Entire, 1985, No Best Better Way, 1985, Every All Which is Not Us, 1986, Swaps Ego Say So, 1986, Be Careful Now, You Know Sugar Melts in Water, 1987, Fact Confected, 1987 , Both, Both, 1987, Tizzy boost, 1988, Moebius, 1988, Whatever Ever, 1989, Get Tough, Sports and Divertissement, 1989, Flap, 1989, Swan's Crayon, 1989, Fanfare Tripwire, 1990, Harry Meets Sally, 1990 , Along the Skid Mark of Recorded History, 1990, Matinee Double-You, 1991, Grand Guignol, 1991, Dash Dash Slang Plural Plus, 1992, The Bubble Cut, 1992, Vigilant Corsage, 1992, Oops Fact, 1992, Small Room, 1993, Exwhyzee, 1993 , Elegy, 1993, Now That It Is Now, 1994, Give Em Enough Rope, Swoon Noir, 1994, Radio Rouge, 1995, Braceletizing, 1995, Hush Comet, 1995, Bite the Pillow, 1995, Pandora's Cake Stain, 1996, Secrets Of, 1997, HUSHHUSH, Sugar Raised, 1998 Capture, Teddy Growl, 1999, Storming Heaven, 2000, Swaphot Trouble, 2001, Strike Me Lightning, 2002 ; (video and performance filmmaker): (films) Little Lieutenant , 1993 (Silver); N.Y. Dance on Camera Festival, Mechanics of the Brain, 1997; co-author: (book) Resurgant New Writings By Women, 1992; contbr. articles to profl. jours. Grantee Nat. Endowment Arts, 1987, 89, 90, 91, 98, Jerome Found., 1993, Meet the Composer N.Y. Found. for the Arts, 1995; Guggenheim Found. fellow, 1988; Found for Contemporary Performance Arts, 2001. Mem. Segue Found. (bd. dirs. Segue Performance Space 1992-2002). Avocations: reading, writing, art events, costume design. Home: 303 E 8th St Apt 4F New York NY 10009-5212

SILVERS, WILLYS KENT, geneticist; b. N.Y.C., Jan. 12, 1929; s. Lewis Julian and Miriam Elizabeth (Rosenzweig) S.; m. Abigail M. Adams, Sept. 29, 1956; children: Deborah Elizabeth, Willys Kent. BA, Johns Hopkins U., 1950; PhD, U. Chgo., 1954. Assoc. staff scientist Jackson Lab., Bar Harbor, Maine, 1956-57; assoc. mem. Wistar Inst., Phila., 1957-65; mem. faculty U. Pa. Med. Sch., 1965—, prof. genetics, 1967-98, prof. emeritus, 1998—. Mem. allergy and immunology study sect. NIH, 1962-66, adv. bd. primate rsch. ctrs., 1968-71, com. cancer immunobiology Nat. Cancer Inst., 1974-78, bd. sci. overseers Jackson Lab., Bar Harbor, 1980-89. Author: The Immunobiology of Transplantation, 1971, The Coat Colors of Mice: A Model for Mammalian Gene Action and Interaction, 1979; mem. editorial bd. Transplantation, 1963-71, Jour. Exptl. Zoology, 1965-70, 81-86, Jour. Immunology, 1973-77, Jour. Reticuloendothelial Soc., 1974-77; contbr. articles to profl. jours. Mem. Am. Genetic Assn. (coun. 1980-83, pres. 1983). Home: 210 Millcreek Rd Ardmore PA 19003-1506 Office: U Pa Dept Genetics Sch Medicine Philadelphia PA 19104

SILVERSTEIN, ALLEN, neurologist, educator; b. N.Y.C., Sept. 13, 1931; s. Max and Jean (Goldschlager) S.; m. Pamela Newson, Nov. 5, 1960; children: Suzanne, Russell, Robin Paul. Student, Cornell U.; MD, NYU, 1956. Rotating intern to chief resident neurology Mt. Sinai Hosp., N.Y.C., 1956-60; neurologist Green Point Hosp., Bklyn., 1962-64; asst. attending neurologist Mt. Sinai Hosp., N.Y.C., 1962-70; attending neurologist Valley Hosp., Ridgewood, N.J., 1966—; assoc. attending neurologist Mt. Sinai Hosp., 1970—; clin. assoc. prof. neurology Mt. Sinai Sch. Medicine, N.Y.C., 1970—. Cons. in field. Contbr. articles to profl. jours. Lt. comdr. USNR, 1960-62. Fellow Am. Acad. Neurology; mem. Am. Neurologic Assn., Assn. Rsch. Nervous and Mental Diseases. Avocation: music related to medicine. Home: 215 Blauvelt Ave Ho Ho Kus NJ 07423-1013 Office: 127 Union St Ridgewood NJ 07450-4436 also: 133 E 73d St New York NY 10021-3556

SILVERSTEIN, ARTHUR MATTHEW, ophthalmic immunologist, educator, historian; b. N.Y.C., Aug. 6, 1928; s. Sol and Beatrice (Pearl) S.; m. Frances Swimmer, 1950; children— Alison, Mark, Judith AB, Ohio State U., 1948, M.Sc., 1951; PhD, Rensselaer Poly. Inst., 1954; D.Sc. (hon.), U. Granada, Spain, 1986. Research asst. Sloan Kettering Inst., N.Y.C., 1948-49; biochemist N.Y. Health Research Lab., 1949-52, sr. biochemist Albany, 1952-54; chief immunobiology Armed Forces Inst. Pathology, Washington, 1956-64; assoc. prof. Johns Hopkins Sch. Medicine, Balt., 1964-67, prof., 1967-89, prof. emeritus, 1989—. Cons. NIH, 1963-77. Author: Pure Politics and Impure Science: The Swine Flu Affair, 1981, A History of Immunology, 1989; mem. editorial bd. various sci. jours.; contbr. articles to profl. jours. Served to 1st lt. U.S. Army, 1954-56. Recipient Doyne Meml. medal Oxford Ophthal. Congress, Eng., 1974, Endowed Professorship Ind. Order Odd Fellows, 1964-89; Congl. Sci. fellow Fedn. Am. Socs. Exptl. Biology, 1975-76. Mem. AAAS, Am. Assn. Immunologists, Brit. Soc. Immunology, Assn. Research in Vision and Ophthalmology (trustee 1984-87, pres. 1988), Phi Beta Kappa, Sigma Xi. Home: 2011 Skyline Rd Baltimore MD 21204-6442 Office: Johns Hopkins Inst History Medicine 1900 E Monument St Baltimore MD 21205-2113 E-mail: arts@jhmi.edu.

SILVERSTEIN, BARBARA ANN, conductor, artistic director; b. Phila., July 24, 1947; d. Charles and Selma (Brenner) S.; m. Bernard J. Taylor II, Aug. 19, 1978. Student, Bennington Coll., 1965-67; BMus, Phila. Coll. Performing Arts, 1970; MA, U. Del., 1997. Assoc. music dir. Suburban Opera Co., Chester, Pa., 1967-75; asst. condr. Toledo Opera Assn., 1975-76; asst. condr., coach Curtis Inst. Music, Phila., 1973-77; asst. condr. Phila. Lyric Opera, 1971-74, Des Moines Opera Festival, Indianola, Iowa, 1974-78; music dir., condr. Savoy Co., Phila., 1977-80, Miss. Opera, Jackson, 1979-82; artistic dir., condr. Pa. Opera Theater, Phila., 1976-93; guest condr. Anchorage Opera, 1982, Opera Del., Wilmington, 1981, 83, Utah Festival Opera Co., 1993-96, Lyric Opera Kansas City, 1995—, Opera Roanoke, Va., 1995, 98, Hollins U., 1999; mng. editor Epotec Inc., 1999-2000, dir. comm., 2000—. Recipient alumni award U. of Arts. Mem. Am. Fedn. Musicians, Jusic Fund Soc., Pa. Coun. on the Arts (adv. panel 1987-90, OPERA Am. (bd. dirs. 1987-93, exec. com. 1988-93). Jewish. Avocations: scuba diving, reading.

SILVERSTEIN, LOUIS, art director, designer, editor; b. Bklyn., Oct. 10, 1919; s. Hyman and Yetta (Brodsky) S.; m. Helen Abby Becker, May 23, 1951; children: Jamie Richard (dec.), Anne Leith. B.F.A., Pratt Inst., Bkyln., 1940; MA credit, Inst. of Design, Chgo., 1948-50. Art. dir. Denhard & Stewart Advt., N.Y.C., 1942-43, 46-47; art. dir. Amerika (Russian lang. mag. distbn. USSR), Dept. State Publs., 1947-48; promotion art dir. N.Y. Times, 1952-67, corporate art dir., 1967-85, asst. mng. editor, 1969-85; cons. art director, 1985—; designer, cons. various newspapers, mags., U.S. and fgn. lectr. Am. Press Inst., Reston, Va., 1978-85; tchr. Sch. Visual Arts, N.Y.C., 1958-59; lectr. in field. Bd. dirs. Am. Inst. Graphic Arts, N.Y.C., 1958-59, Soc. Publ. Designers, 1976-78; cons. Toronto Star, 1988—; founder Louis Silverstein Design Assn.; lectr. Ctr. Ind. Journalism, Prague, Czechoslovakia, 1991; cons. art dir.-editor La Nación, Buenos Aires, 1997—; design cons. Coun. of Fgn. Rels., 1998—, Internat. Herald Tribune, Paris, 2000; designer, cons., editor Coun. on Fgn. Rels., N.Y.C., 1999—, The Nairobi (Kenya) Nation, 2000; cons., designer World Econ. Forum, Davos, Switzerland, 2000—, Agha Khan Found. Nation Newspaper Chain, Chantilly, France, Nairobi, Kenya, 2000—. Co-author: America's Taste, 1961; editor, art dir.: The Earth Times, 1993—, exec. editor, 1994—; exhibited in group shows and galleries, 1951—, Am. Fedn. Arts, 1963, USIA Exhbn., USSR, 1964; designer film strips Am. Fedn. Labor, 1950-52; one-man shows include Cooper Union, 1988, U. Montreal, 1988, Walker Art Ctr., Mpls.; author: Newspaper Design for the Times, 1989; design cons.: The Hill, 1994—, The American, 1996. Served with USAF, 1943-46 Recipient Spl. Gold award N.Y. Times Op-Ed Page, N.Y. Arts Dirs. Club, 1972, Hall of Fame, 1984, Gold Medal Lifetime Achievement award Soc. Publ. Designers, N.Y.C., 1984, Am. Inst. Graphic Arts Design Leadership award, Spl. medal for best design of Am. publs., 1989, Pulitzer prize nominee, 1984, 94, numerous awards Art Dir. Clubs, other profl. groups. Mem. Alliance Graphique Internationale, N.Y. Art Dirs. Club (bd. dirs. 1978-80, 82-84, 86—), Internat. Soc. Newspaper Designers (2001 Lifetime Svc. award), Am. Abstract Artists. Avocations: tennis; amateur poker. Home: 54 Remsen St Brooklyn NY 11201-2304 also: 36 Highland Rd Southampton NY 11968-3612 E-mail: helenabby7@aol.com.

SILVERSTEIN, MARTIN ELLIOT, surgeon, consultant, writer; b. N.Y.C., Sept. 6, 1922; s. Louis and Ethel (Statman) S.; m. Mabelle A. Cremer, Dec. 10, 1962. AB cum laude, Columbia U., 1945; MD, N.Y. Med. Coll., 1948. Instr. bacteriology N.Y. Med. Coll., 1953-57, asst. to dean for clin. scis., 1953-58, instr. surgery, 1953-55, asst. dean, 1958, assoc. dean, 1959—62; asst. vis. surgeon Bird S. Coler Hosp., N.Y.C., 1953-57, assoc. vis. surgeon, 1957-60; asst. vis. surgeon Met. Hosp., 1953-57, assoc. vis. surgeon, 1957-60; asst. attending surgeon Flower and 5th Ave. Hosps., 1953-57; asst. attending surgeon Monorah Med. Ctr. U. Kans. Sch. Medicine, 1963-65, exec. dir. Monorah Med. Ctr. Kansas City, 1963-65, exec. dir. Danciger Inst. for Health Scis. Mo., 1963-66, chmn. dept. exptl. surgery Danciger Inst. for Health Scis., 1963-66; chmn. dept. Surgery Menorah Med. Ctr. U. Kans. Sch. Medicine Affiliate, 1963-66; assoc. clin. prof. surgery U. Kans. Sch. Medicine, 1966-67; surgeon courtesy staff N.Y. Infirmary, 1969; surgeon Grand Canyon Med. Group and Hosp., 1969-70; chief sect. on surgery of trauma, dept. surgery U. Ariz. Coll. Med., Tucson, 1974-80, adj. assoc. prof. optical scis., 1979-83, assoc. prof. surgery, 1974-83, dir. quality assurance Univ. Hosp., 1983-84, rsch. prof. family and community medicine, internat. medicine, 1984-85, rsch. prof. surgical biology, 1984-85; sr. fellow in sci. and tch. Ctr. for Strategic and Internat. Studies Georgetown U., Washington, 1983-87. Pres. Claude Gips Found. Inc., N.Y.C., 1967-93; disting. vis. prof. Uniformed Svcs. U. Health Scis., 1984, adj. prof. surgery, 1999—; clin. prof. surgery F. Edward Hebert Sch. Medicine, 1984-99; disting. vis. prof. Tulane U. Med. Sch., 1984; mem. internat. adv. bd. Univ. Microfilms Internat. Collections on Terrorism, 1987—; internat. cons. Disaster Mgmt. and Disaster Medicine, Australia, India, others, 1983—; gov. emeritus Internat. Coun. for Computer Comm., 1996—, exec. com., v.p., 1972-92; bd. rep. Am. Coll. Nuclear Med., 2001—. Author: Disaster: Your Right to Survive, 1991; mem. editorial bd. Terrorism, 1976—, Prehosp. and Disaster Medicine, 1989—; assoc. editor Jour. Prehosp. Care, 1984-85; contbr. articles to profl. jours. With U.S. Army, 1943-45; lt. (j.g.) USNR, 1946-53. Fgn. fellow NSF, 1974. Fellow ACS (chmn. Ariz. State com. on trauma 1979-84), Am. Assn. for Surgery of Trauma, Am. Coll. Emergency Physicians, Am. Coll. Gastroenterology, Am. Coll. Nuc. Medicine (bd. reps. 2001—); mem. World Assn. for Emergency and Disaster Medicine (exec. com. 1987-92), Critical Care Soc., Internat. Coun. Computer Comm. (co-founder).

SILVERSTEIN, NEAL TERRY, pediatrician; b. Chgo., Sept. 7, 1948; s. Isaac and Anne Silverstein; m. Rosa Silverstein, June 25, 1972; children: Leonard J., Brian S., Mitchell S. BS, U. Ill., 1970; MD, U. Ill., Chgo., 1974. Diplomate Am. Bd. Pediatrics. Attending physician Cook County Hosp., Chgo., 1977-84; pediatrician Ravenswood Med. Group, 1979-84, Cigna Healthcare, Orlando, Fla., 1984-95, Fla. Physicians Med. Group, Orlando, 1995—. Chmn. pediats. Fla. Hosp., Orlando, 1988-94. Bd. dirs. Juvenile Diabetes Found., Orlando, 1987-99; pres. CPR for Citizens, Orlando, 1990-92, Congregation Beth Am, Longwood, Fla., 1990-91; bd. dirs. Freedom Ride, Orlando, 1999-2000. Fellow Am. Acad. Pediats; mem. AMA, Ctrl. Fla. Pediat. Soc. (exec. bd. 1988—). Jewish. Avocation: horseback riding. Office: Pediat Care of Altamonte 661 E Altamonte Dr Ste 217 Altamonte Springs FL 32701 E-mail: nehi8200@aol.com.

SILVERSTEIN, ROBERT SELNICK, lawyer; b. Englewood, N.J., July 8, 1956; s. William Bernard and Sylvia (Selnick) S.; m. Wanda Jean Olson, June 6, 1981; children: Joshua Olson, Erica Olson. BA magna cum laude, Brown U., 1978; JD, NYU, 1981. Bar: N.J. 1981. Assoc. Riker Danzig Scherer Hyland & Perretti, Morristown, N.J., 1981-86; v.p. corp. counsel Lincoln Property Co., Parsippany, 1986-91; gen. counsel, sr. v.p. SJP Properties, 1991—. Office: SJP Properties 379 Interpace Pky Parsippany NJ 07054-1050

SILVERSTEIN, SAMUEL CHARLES, cellular biology and physiology educator, researcher; b. N.Y.C., Feb. 11, 1937; s. Paul Robert and Jeanette (Kamen) S.; m. Jo Ann Kleinman, Apr. 2, 1967; children: David Paul, Jennifer Kate. AB, Dartmouth Coll., 1958; MD, Albert Einstein Coll. Medicine, 1963. Intern in medicine U. Colo. Med. Center, 1963-64; postdoctoral fellow dept. cell biology Rockefeller U., 1964-67, asst. prof. cellular physiology and immunology, 1968-71, assoc. prof., physician, 1972—; John Dalton prof. physiology, prof. medicine Columbia U. Coll. Physicians and Surgeons, N.Y.C., 1983—, chmn. dept., 1983—. Editor: Transport of Macromolecules in Cellular Systems, 1979; chmn. editl. bd. Jour. Cell Biology, 1979-82, editor, 1978-89. Bd. dirs. Arnold P. Gold Found., 1998, Cancerr Rsch. Fund, Damon Runyon Found., 1990; bd. dirs. Rsch.!Am., 1993, mem. exec. com., 1996. Recipient John Oliver LaGorce medal, Nat. Geog. Soc., 1967, Marie Bonazinga Rsch. award, Soc. Leukocyte Biology, 1984, Disting. Alumnus award, Albert Einstein Coll. Medicine, 1987; fellow Helen Hay Whitney, 1964—67, John Simon Guggenheim, 2002, Pres. Lasker/Funding First, 2001—. Fellow: AAAS (chair sect. medicine 1998), N.Y. Acad. Sci. (edn. com.), Am. Soc. Microbiology; mem.: Inst. Medicine Nat. Acad. Scis., Fedn. Am. Socs. for Exptl. Biology (bd. dirs. 1991—96, v.p. 1993—94, pres. 1994—95, chmn. pub. affairs adv. com. 1995—96), Practitioners Soc. N.Y., Assn. Am. Physicians, Am. Physiol. Soc., Am. Soc. Biol. Chemists, Infectious Diseases Soc. Am., Am. Assn. Immunologists, Am. Soc. Clin. Investigation, Am. Soc. Cell biology, Am. Alpine (dir. 1963-64, 69-74), Explorers, Century Assn., Explorers Club, Am. Alpine Club (dir. 1963—64, 1969—74). Achievements include research and numerous publications in field of virology, cell biology, immunology, science policy and mountaineering. Home: 110 Riverside Dr New York NY 10024-3715 Office: Columbia U Coll Physicians & Surgeons 630 W 168th St New York NY 10032-3795 E-mail: scs3@columbia.edu.

SILVERSTONE, DAVID EDWARD, ophthalmologist; b. N.Y.C., Feb. 16, 1948; s. Sidney Milton and Estelle (Cohen) S.; m. Linda Carol Thalberg, June 19, 1969; 1 child, Scott; m. Barbara Lester Dunn, Dec. 5, 1999. AB, Columbia Coll., 1969; MD, NY Med. Coll., 1973. Cert. Ophthalmology, Am. Bd. Ophthalmology, 1977. Acad. internat. eye fellow Albert Schweitzer Hosp., Deschapples, Haiti, 1976; instr. dept. ophthalmology and visual scis. Yale Sch. Medicine, New Haven, 1976-77, asst. clin. prof. Dept. Ophthalmology and Visual Scis. Newhaven, 1977-86, assoc. clin. prof. Dept. Ophthalmology and Visual Scis., 1986-91, clin. prof. Dept. Ophthalmology and Visual Scis., 1991—; chief ophthalmology VA Hosp., West Haven, 1977-85; attending physician Yale-New Haven Hosp., New Haven, 1976—, asst. chief ophthalmology, 1988—. Dir. continuing edn. Am. Soc. Cataract and Refractive Surgery, Washington, 1991—; mem. Bd. Permanent Officers Yale Sch. Medicine, New Haven, 1991—. Author: Automated Visual Field Testing, 1986; contbr. articles to profl. jours. Recipient Med. Student Essay award Am. Sc. Pharmacology and Experimental therapeutics, 1971, Moshy Book award N.Y. Med. Coll., N.Y.C., 1973, Physician's regognition award AMA, Chgo., 1976, 79, 82, 85, 96, Honor award Am. Acad. Ophthalmology, San Francisco, 1990. Fellow Am. Acad. Ophthalmology; mem. New England Ophthalmological Soc., AMA, ASCRS (dir. continuing edn. 1992—), Conn. State Med. Soc., Conn. Soc. Eye Physicians, New Haven County Med. Assn., Yale Alumni Ophthalmology, Assn. for Rsch. in Vision and Ophthalmology. Avocation: computers. Office: Temple Eye Physicians 60 Temple St New Haven CT 06510-2716

SILVERSTONE, HARRIS J. chemistry educator; b. N.Y.C., Sept. 18, 1939; s. Sidney M. and Estelle Silverstone; m. Ruth C. Federman, 1960; children: Robert, Aron, Nancy, Murray. AB, Harvard U., 1960; PhD, Calif. Inst. Tech., 1964. Asst. prof. Johns Hopkins U., Balt., 1965-68, assoc. prof., 1968-71, prof., 1971—. Contbr. articles to profl. jours. NSF Postdoctoral fellow Yale U., 1964. Mem. Am. Phys. Soc., Am. Chem. Soc., Internat. Soc. Theoretical Chem. Physics. Office: Johns Hopkins U 3400 N Charles St Baltimore MD 21218-2680

SILVERSTONE, LEON MARTIN, neuroscientist, cardiologist, educator, researcher; b. London, May 21, 1939; came to U.S., 1976; s. Jack Stanley and Sadie (Osen) S.; children from previous marriage: Samantha, Frances, Mark; m. Deborah Advani, Sept. 13, 1998. Student, U. London, 1958-59; L.D.S., U. Leeds, U.K., 1963, B.Ch.D., 1964, D.D.Sc., 1971; L.D.S., Royal Coll. Surgeons, Eng., 1964; PhD, U. Bristol, Eng., 1967; postgrad., U. London, 1969-76. House surgeon Leeds Dental Hosp., Eng., 1963-64; rsch. fellow med. rsch. coun. unit Bristol Med. and Dental Sch., 1964-67; lectr. in dental surgery U. Bristol, 1967-68; sr. lectr. child dental health Med. Coll., Royal London Hosp., 1969-75, reader in preventive and pediat. dentistry, 1975-76; cons. Royal London Hosp., 1973-76; vis. Lasby prof. Dental Sch. U. Minn., Mpls., 1974-75; prof., head divsn. cardiology Dows Inst. Dental Rsch., Coll. Dentistry, U. Iowa, Iowa City, 1976-82; assoc. dean rsch. Dental Sch. U. Colo. Health Scis. Ctr., Denver, 1982-89, dir. Oral Scis. Rsch. Inst., 1986-89; biomed. cons., 1990; v.p. R & D The Synaptic Corp., La Jolla, Calif., 1990-95; dir. R&D BioSciences Systems LLC, 1995—. Vis. Nicholaysen prof. U. Oslo, 1972; cons. Pan Am. Health Orgn., WHO, 1973-85, dental rsch. Va, 1978-85; mem. study sect. and program adv. com. NIH-Nat. Inst. Dental Rsch., 1976-84, chmn. subcom. on dental caries, 1982-83, chmn. program adv. com., 1983-84; pres. Neura Corp., La Jolla, Calif., 1997-98. Mem. editorial bd. Caries Rsch., 1976-86; contbr. chpts. to books, articles in field to profl. publs. Recipient Nobel-Pharma A.B. Bofors prize, 1971, ORCA-ROLEX rsch. prize, 1973, Disting. award in child dental health, 1981; NIH/Nat. Inst. Dental Rsch. grantee, 1976-89. Mem. European Orgn. Caries Research (mem. bd., sci. councillor 1971-83, pres. 1977-79), Internat. Assn. Dental Research (pres. cariology group 1982-83, Disting. Scientist award 1984), Am. Assn. Dental Research (pres. cariology group chpt. 1982-83, chmn. publs. com. 1985-86), Brit. Dental Assn., Internat. Assn. Dentistry for Children (exec. com. 1972-79, jour. editor 1971-79), AAAS, Soc. Exptl. Biology and Medicine, Space Medicine Com., AAUP, Am. Acad. Pedodontics, Omega Kappa Upsilon, Sigma Xi. Office: 3248 Brant St San Diego CA 92103 E-mail: neuromod@cox.net.

SILVERTHORNE, MICHAEL JAMES, classics educator; b. Bristol, Eng., Dec. 20, 1941; emigrated to Can., 1966; s. Frederick J. and Freda (Fox) S.; m. Ann Frances O'Malley, Aug. 6, 1966; children: Christopher, Stephen, Katherine. BA, Oxford U., 1964, B.Litt., 1966, MA, 1967, D.Phil., 1973. Lectr. McGill U., Montreal, 1966-68, asst. prof., 1968-74, assoc. prof. dept. classics, 1974—, chmn. dept., 1981-86, 88-91, 94-97. Editor: On the Duty of Man and Citizen, 1991, On the Citizen, 1998, The New Organon, 2000, Natural Rights on the Threshold of the Scottish Enlightenment, 2002. Can. Council fellow, 1969-73; Social Sci. and Humanities Research Council Can. grantee, 1980-83, 92-95. Mem. Internat. Soc. Classical Tradition, Classical Assn. Can. (sec. 1991-95), Conf. Social and Polit. Thought. Office: McGill U Classics Dept 855 Sherbrooke St W Montreal QC Canada H3A 2T7 Home: 35 Wolseley Ave S Montreal West QC Canada M4X 1T7 Business E-Mail: michael.silverthorne@mcgill.ca. E-mail: silverth@po-box.mcgill.ca.

SILVESTRI, ALAN ANTHONY, film composer; b. N.Y.C., Mar. 26, 1950; s. Louis and Elizabeth (Clarke) S.; m. Sandra Dee Shue; children: Alexandra, Joseph, James. PhD in Music (hon.), Berklee Coll. Music, Boston, 1995. Film scores include The Doberman Gang, 1972, The Amazing Dobermans, Las Vegas Lady, 1976, Romancing the Stone, 1984, Par ou t'es rentre? On t'as vu sortir, 1984, Fandango, 1984, Cat's Eye, 1984, Back to the Future, 1985 (Grammy award nominations best instrumental composition and best album of original score for a motion picture, 1985), Summer Rental, 1985, Clan of the Cave Bear, 1986, The Delta Force, 1986, American Anthem, 1986, Flight of the Navigator, 1986, No Mercy, 1986, Critical Condition, 1987, Outrageous Fortune, 1987, Predator, 1987, Overboard, 1987, Who Framed Roger Rabbit?, 1988 (Grammy award nominations best instrumental composition and best album of original score for a motion picture, 1988), My Stepmother Is an Alien, 1988, Mac and Me, 1988, She's Out of Control, 1989, Downtown, 1989, The Abyss, 1989, Back to the Future II, 1989, Back to the Future III, 1990, Young Guns II, 1990, Predator II, 1990, Soapdish, 1991, Dutch, 1991, Ricohet, 1991, Shattered, 1991, Father of the Bride, 1991, Ferngully: The Last Rainforest, 1992, Death Becomes Her, 1992, Stop! Or My Mom Will Shoot, 1992, The Bodyguard, 1992, Cop and a Half, 1993, Sidekicks, 1993, Super Mario Bros., 1993, Judgment Night, 1993, Grumpy Old Men, 1993, Clean Slate, 1994, Blown Away, 1994, Forrest Gump, 1994 (Academy award nomination best original score, Grammy award nomination best instrumental performance for "Feather Theme from Forrest Gump," Golden Globe award nomination best original score), Richie Rich, 1994, The Quick and the Dead, 1994, The Perez Family, 1995, Judge Dredd, 1995, Father of the Bride II, 1995, Sgt. Bilko, 1995, Grumpier Old Men, 1995, Eraser, 1996, Long Kiss Goodnight, 1996, Fools Rush In, 1996, Volcano, 1997, Contact, 1997, Mousehunt, 1997, Odd Couple II, 1998, Parent Trap, 1998, Holyman, 1998, Practical Magic, 1998, Siegfried & Roy, The Magic Box, 1999, Stuart Little, 1999, Reindeer Games, 2000, What Lies Beneath, 2000, What Women Want, 2000, Cast Away, 2000 (Grammy award winner for best instrumental composition for "Theme from Cast Away"), The Mexican, 2001, The Mummy Returns, 2001, Serendipity, 2001, Showtime, 2002, Lilo & Stitch, 2002, Stuart Little 2, 2002; TV themes include CHiPs, 1978-83, Manimal, 1983. Recipient ACE award Nat. Acad. Cable Programming for Tales from the Crypt - All Through the House, 1990, Saturn award Acad. Arts and Sci. for fantasy and horror film, 1987.

SILVESTRI, ROBERT, electric company executive; b. New Haven, Nov. 9, 1954; s. Danny and Helen (Turek) S.; m. Debra Ann Summa, Oct. 4, 1980; 1 child, Jason Dante. BS, Fairfield (Conn.) U., 1976; MS, U. New Haven, 1986. Cert. lab. dir. State of Conn. Dept. Health Svcs., cert. safety profl., cert. hazardous materials mgr. Lectr., rschr. Yale U., New Haven, 1976; sr. chemist Mitchell-Bradford Internat., Milford, Conn., 1977-81; dir. C.A.L., Inc., Hamden, 1981-89; supr. environ. reporting and support svcs. United Illuminating, New Haven, 1989-90, mgr. environ. licensing and regulatory affairs, 1990-94, mgr. environ. ops. and safety, 1994-99; environtl. ops. leader Wisvest-Conn., LLC, Bridgeport, Conn., 1999—. Chair Bus. Recycling Coun., New Haven, 1990-94; lectr. Middlesex C.C., Middletown, Conn., 1992-95, So. Conn. State U., New Haven, 2000; dir. Bus. Environ. Coun., Bristol, Conn., 1993-95; mem. adv. coms. Conn. Dept. Environ. Protection, 1989—. Co-author comty. planning report; contbg. author: Connecticut's Environment, 1995, 97, 98. Judge Conn. Sci. Fair, 1993—; mem. State of Conn. Environ. Permitting Task Force, Hartford, 1992-94; lobbyist United Illuminating, New Haven, 1991-99, Wisvest-Conn., Shelton, 1999—; dir. Eli Whitney Mus., 1994-97. Recipient Keynote Speaker award Conn. Forum of Regulated Environ. Profls., 1991, cert. of merit for bus. recycling Conn. Dept. Environ. Protection, 1991, Green Ribbon award Greater New Haven C. of C., 1991, Dedicated Svc. award Conn. Sci. Fair, 2002. Mem.: Conn. Environ. Forum (sec. 1993—96, v.p. 1996—), Conn. Bus. and Industry Assn. (steering com. 1995—, air quality task foce chair 1997—2000, vice chair 1999—2000, chair 2000—), Electric Coun. New Eng., Air and Waste Mgmt. Assn. (dir. 1993—, vice chair 1996—98, chair 1998—2000), Am. Indsl. Hygiene Assn., Am. Chem. Soc., Am. Electroplater's Soc. (cert. electroplater finisher), Civitan (dir. New Eng. dist. 1992—95), State of Conn. L.I. Sound Couns. (Hamden rep. 2000—), Nat. Soccer Coaches Assn. Am., Orange Soccer Assn. (asst. coach 1999—, women's soccer coach Conn. State Games, silver medalist 2001), Hamden Soccer Assn. (asst. coach 1996, coach 1997—, referee 1997—). Avocations: woodworking, music, antique automobiles. Home: 1140 Mount Carmel Ave Hamden CT 06518-1610 Office: Wisvest Connecticut LLC Bridgeport Harbor Sta 1 Atlantic St Bridgeport CT 06604-5513

SILVESTRO, CLEMENT MARIO, museum director, historian; b. New Haven, Sept. 7, 1924; s. Joseph and Rose (Griego) S.; m. Betty C. Mack, June 26, 1950; 1 dau., Elizabeth J. Silvestro Casner. BS, Central Conn. State Coll., 1949; MS, U. Wis., 1951; PhD, 1959. Asst. to dir. Wis. Hist. Soc., 1956-57; dir. Am. Assn. State and Local History, 1957-64; editor History News, 1957-64; assoc. dir. Chgo. Hist. Soc., 1964-65, dir., 1965-74, sec., 1970-74; dir. Mus. of Our Nat. Heritage, Lexington, Mass., 1974-92. Mem. exec. com. Am. Assn. Museums, 1965-71, v.p., 1966-71; vis. lectr. Northeastern U., 1983-85 Co-author: A Decade of Collecting: Maps, 1985 Mem. Chgo. Archtl. and Landmark Com., 1968-74; mem. Ill. Historic Sites Adv. Council, 1970-74, U.S. ICOM, Nat. Com., 1970-74; chmn. Pres.'s Adv. Council on Historic Preservation, 1974-77; mem. adv. bd. Eleutherian Mills-Hagley Found., 1973-76; U.S. rep. to UNESCO Internat. Adv. Com. to Safeguard City of Venice, 1975; trustee U.S. Capitol Hist. Soc.; trustee, pres. Fruitlands Mus., 1982-85. Served with USAAF, 1943-45. Decorated Air medal with oak leaf clusters. Mem. Am. Assn. Mus., Orgn. Am Historians (chmn. hist. sites com. 1973-78), Chgo. Hist. Soc., Colonial Soc. Mass., Bostonian Soc., Mass. Hist. Soc. (resident), Union Club Boston, Masons. Home: PO Box 119 Hancock ME 04640-0119 E-mail: clements@panax.com.

SILVEY, ANITA LYNNE, editor; b. Bridgeport, Conn., Sept. 3, 1947; d. John Oscar and Juanita Lucille (McKitrick) S.; m. Bill Clark, 1988. BS in Edn., Ind. U., 1965-69; MA in Comm. Arts, U. Wis., 1970. Editorial asst. children's book dept. Little Brown and Co., Boston, 1970-71; asst. editor Horn Book Mag., 1971-75; mng. editor, founder New Boston Rev., 1975-76; mktg. mgr. children's books, libr. svcs. mgr. trade divsn. Houghton Mifflin, Boston, 1976-84; editor-in-chief Horn Book Mag., 1985-95; v.p., pub. Children's Books Houghton Mifflin Co., 1995—2001. Editor: Children's Books and Their Creators, 1995, Help Wanted: Stories About Young People and Work, 1997, Essential Guide to Children's Books and their Creators, 2002. Named one of 70 Women Who Have Made a Difference, Women's Nat. Book Assn., 1987. Mem. ALA (chmn. children's librs., Laura Ingalls Wilder award 1987-89), Internat. Reading Assn. (mem. IRA Book award com. 1985-87), Assn. Am. Pubs. (libr. com.), New England Round Table (chmn. 1978-79).

SILVEY, EDGAR H. health services administrator; b. Nov. 22, 1946; BA, La. State U., 1969; MPH, Tulane U., 1971, MBA, 1988. Exec. v.p. Baton Rouge Gen. Med. Ctr., 1982-83, pres., 1983-86; exec. v.p. Gen. Health Sys., Baton Rouge, 1986-88; CEO Baton Rouge Clinic, 1988—. Fellow: Am. Coll. Health Care Execs.; mem.: Am. Coll. Med. Practice Execs. (cert., Adminstr. of Yr. 2001). Office: Baton Rouge Clnic 7373 Perkins Rd Baton Rouge LA 70808

SILVEY, LEANNE ELIZABETH, social welfare administrator, consultant; b. Ypsilanti, Mich., July 23, 1958; d. James Lee and Rose Lauretta (Ramage) S. BS, Ea. Mich. U., 1979; MSW, Western Mich. U., 1984. Lic. social worker, Mich. Asst. to dir. Mich. Dept. of Indian Affairs, Detroit, 1977; case mgr. Monroe (Mich.) County Community Health Life Cons. Ctr., 1978; child care worker Northwestern Guidance Clinic/Romulus (Mich.) House, 1979; respite care worker Northwestern Guidance Clinci, Garden City, Mich., 1979; housing social worker Kent Client Svcs., Grand Rapids, 1979-81; counselor Bridge for Runaways, 1982-83; therapist, social work intern Kent Oaks Psychiat. Hosp., 1983-84; caseworker Mich. Indian Child Welfare Agy., Lansing, 1984-88, exec. dir., 1988—. Mem. ad. bd. social work Grand Valley State U., Allendale, Mich., 1987—; mem. task force Mich. Dept. Social Svcs., Lansing, 1988-89; bd. dirs. Family Outreach Ctr., Grand Rapids. Vol. Anonymous Santas, Grand Rapids, 1982-90; mem. N.Am.-Indian Assn., Detroit, 1977-79, Grand Rapids AIDS Task Force, 1987-89, Children's Advocacy Group, Grand Rapids, 1990. Mem. NASW, Acad. Cert. Social Workers, Mich. Fedn. Pvt. Child and Family Agys. Avocations: cross-country skiing, music, Am.-Indian culture, tennis, reading. Office: Mich Indian Child Welfare Agy 6425 S Pennsylvania Ave Ste 3 Lansing MI 48911-5975

SILVEY, MURL L. psychologist; b. Sanford, Tenn., June 25, 1941; s. William Lloyd and Evelyn Louise S.; m. Bev J., Oct. 25, 1963; children: Brian, Barbie. BA, Calif. State U., San Francisco, 1966; MS, Calif. State U., Fresno, 1975; PhD, Pacific U., 1986. Probation officer Merced County Probation Dept., Calif., 1966-77; psychologist Mt. Hood Counseling Svc., Sandy, Oreg., 1980—. Bd. dirs. Sandy Family Svcs., 1984-99. Mem. APA, Am. Counseling Assn., Oreg. Psychol. Assn. Office: Mt Hood Counseling Svc PO Box 1237 Sandy OR 97055-1237

SILVEY, TONY LEE, music educator; b. Gadsden, Ala., Aug. 13, 1959; s. Thomas L and Bonnie M Silvey. BS, Jacksonville State U., Jacksonville, AL, 1982; MA, U. West Ala., Livingston, AL, 1995. Band dir., tchr. North Sand Mtn Sch., Higdon, Ala., 1982—85; band dir., choir, drama Glencoe H.S., Glencoe, 1985—90; band dir. Etowan H.S., Attalla, 1990—91; band dir., elem music Oneonta H.S., Oneonta, 1991—92; band, choir, dance Dora H.S., Dora, 1992—98; band, elem music, choir, dance West Point H.S., Cullman, 1998—. Chmn. Etowan Band Directors Assoc, Gadsden, Ala., 1985—85, Walker Band Directors Assoc, Jasper, Ala., 1996—96. Mem. Straight Mtn Water Commn., Altoona, Ala., 1991—91. Mem.: Nat. Band Assoc, Ala. Cullman Cnty Edn. Assoc, Am. Music Educators Assoc, Ala. Bandmasters Assoc, Ala. Farmers Fedn. Avocations: farming, nature conservation, furniture restoration. Office: West Point School 4314 County Rd 1141 Cullman AL 35057-6651

SILVIA, DAVID ALAN, insurance broker; b. Taunton, Mass., Mar. 5, 1953; s. Edward J. and Loretta (Sousa) S.; m. Janet E. McMahon, Apr. 16, 1988 (div. Jan. 1996); 1 child, David. BA, Roger Williams U., 1975. Sales rep. New England Brass, Taunton, Mass., 1976-81; ins. agt. Prudential Ins., Raynham, 1981-82; owner, ptnr. CS Assocs., North Attleboro, 1982-86; broker Fin. Mktg. Assocs., North Dighton, 1986—. Pres. United Meth. Mens Club, Taunton, 1994, pres., 1995—. Independent. Office: Fin Mktg Assocs 495 Somerset Ave North Dighton MA 02764-1809

SIM, CRAIG STEPHEN, retired investment banker; b. Bklyn., Apr. 23, 1942; s. William Henry Craig and Lenore (Overton) S.; m. Susan Hart; children: Brandon Craig William, Stephanie Brooke. BA, Gettysburg Coll., 1965. Account exec. Francis I. duPont & Co., N.Y.C., 1969-72; v.p. E.F. Hutton & Co., 1972-75; sr. v.p. Donaldson, Lufkin & Jenrette, 1975-83; exec. v.p. Shearson Am. Express, 1983-84; mng. dir. Donaldson, Lufkin & Jenrette, 1984-2001, Credit Suisse First Boston, 2001—. Trustee Gettysburg Coll. Served to capt. USMC, 1965-69. Mem. Bond Club N.Y. (gov. 1979-80, 84-85, 90-93), Lawrence Beach Club (gov.), The Leash, India House, St. Andrew's Soc. (N.Y.C.), Burns Soc. City of N.Y. (trustee), L.I. Wyandanch Club, Seawanhaka Corinthian Yacht Club, Army and Navy Club (Washington), Union Club. Address: PO Box 57 Charlotte VT 05445

SIM, ROBERT WILSON, accountant; b. Three Rivers, Quebec, Can., June 10, 1944; came to U.S., 1955; s. James Wilson and Winnifred May (Stephenson) S.; m. Maureen Ann McCune, Mar. 28, 1970; children: Patricia Marie, Catherine Ann, Jennifer May. BSBA, U. Fla., 1966. CPA, Fla., Mo. Staff acct. Arnold and Co., Sarasota, Fla., 1964-66; audit supr. Ernst and Ernst, Atlanta, 1968-74; audit mgr. Tornwall, Lang and Lee, St. Petersburg, Fla., 1974-76; ptnr. Grant Thornton, 1976-80, Kansas City, Mo., 1980-85, Miami/Ft. Lauderdale, Fla., 1985-90; owner, practitioner Robert W. Sim, CPA, Hollywood, 1990—. Treas. Mental Health Assn. Pinellas County, Inc., St. Petersburg, 1976-80; sec./treas. Suncoast Rotary Club St. Petersburg, 1976-80; organizer Chinese/Am. Soc. Kansas City, 1983-85. With U.S. Army, 1966-68. Recipient Cert. of Appreciation, St. Petersburg C. of C., 1975, Univ. Fla., 1992; plaque CPA Club Miami, 1990, Youth Orch. Fla., 1992. Mem. Fla. Inst. CPAs (chmn. com. on Univ. Fla. Acctg. Conf. 1993), Women in Distress of Broward County, Inc. (fund raising com. 1992, vol. cons. 1975-80), Miami Fin. Group. Republican. Presbyterian. Avocations: golf, travel/camping, weight lifting, car buff, spectator sports. Office: Robert W Sim CPA 6565 Taft St Ste 211 Hollywood FL 33024-4000 E-mail: rsimcpa@prodigy.net.

SIMA, ANDERS ADOLPH FREDRIK, neuropathologist, neurosciences researcher, educator; b. Jönköping, Sweden, Dec. 3, 1943; came to the U.S., 1990; s. Karl Jonas Simon and Svea Gunhild (Nilsson) S.; children: Patricia, Alexander, Vanessa. BS, U. Vienna, Austria, 1967; MD, U. Göteborg, Sweden, 1973, PhD, 1974. Asst. prof. pathology U. Goteborg, Sweden, 1973-83, U. Toronto, Ont., 1978-81, assoc. prof. pathology, 1981-82, U. Manitoba, Winnipeg, 1982-85, prof. pathology, 1985-90, dir. Diabetes Rsch. Ctr., 1988-90; prof. pathology U. Mich., Ann Arbor, 1990-96, prof. internal medicine, 1991-96; dir. neuropathology core MADRC Mich. Alzheimer Disease Rsch. Ctr., 1992—; prof. pathology and neurology Wayne State U., Detroit, 1996—, dir. Morris Hood Jr. Comprehensive Diabetes Ctr., 1998—. Hon. prof. neurosci. Med. Univ., Shanghai, China, 1988; cons. Pfizer, Inc., N.Y.C., 1987—, FDA, Washington, 1988—, Miles Pharm. Inc., West Haven, Conn. 1990—; mem. internat. adv. bd. Hoffman La Roche, Basel, Switzerland, 1992—. Assoc. editor: Jour. PNS, Internat. Jour. Diab.; editor-in-chief Frontiers in Animal Diabetes Research, Internat. Jour. Exptl. Diabetic Rsch., Internat. Jour. Diabetes Rsch.; assoc. editor Diabetes/Metabolism Rsch. and Revs.; mem. editl. bd. mem. for 8 nat. and internat. jours.; contbr. numerous articles to profl. jours. Recipient Chinese Acad.'s award for Sci. Achievement, 1981, Acad. Achievement award Toku Med. Soc., Sendai, Japan, 1985, Gold medal Consiglio Nat. delle Ricerche, Rome, 1987, Internat. Order of Merit, 1999, Order of Internat. Ambs., 1999; Diabetes Rsch. grantee NIH, Bethesda, Md., 1991, 92, Dementia Related grantee NIH, Bethesda, Md., 1994, Ednl. Tng. grantee Pfizer, Inc., N.Y.C., 1994. Fellow Royal Coll. Physicians and Surgeons Can., Internat. Study Group on Diabetes in Animals, Am. Assn. Pathologists, Juvenile Diabetes Found. (hon. chmn. 1984, Appreciation award 1984, Spl. Achievement award 1989, 97). Achievements include major contributions to the pathogenesis of diabetic neuropathy; description of genetically linked senile dementias. Avocations: international civic history, medical history, visual arts, linguistics. Office: Wayne State U Dept Pathology 540 E Canfield St Detroit MI 48201-1928 E-mail: asima@med.wayne.edu.

SIMAAN, MARWAN, electrical engineering educator; b. July 23, 1946; m. Rita Simaan. MSEE, U. Pitts., 1970; PhDEE, U. Ill., 1972. Registered profl. engr., Pa. Rsch. engr. Shell Devel. Co., Houston, 1974-76; assoc. prof. elec. engrng. U. Pitts., 1976-85, prof., 1985-89, Bell of Pa./Bell Atlantic prof., 1989—, chmn. dept. elec. engrng., 1991—. Cons. Gulf Rsch. and Tech., Pitts., 1979-85, ALCOA, Pitts., 1986-89. Editor: Vertical Seismic Profiles, 1984, Two-dimensional Transforms, 1985, Artificial Intelligence in Petroleum Exploration, 1989, Expert Systems in Exploration, 1991, (series) Advances in Geophysical Signal Processing; co-editor jour. Multidimensional Sys. and Signal Processing; mem. editl. bd. profl. jours., including IEEE Procs., IEEE Transactions on Cirs. and Sys., IEEE Transactions on Geosci. and Remote Sensing, Jour. Optimization Theory and Applications, Jour. Cirs., Sys. and Computers; contbr. over 225 articles on signal processing and control to profl. publs. Grantee NSF, ONR, Def. Advance Rsch. Project Adminstrs., Ben Franklin, Westinghouse, Gulf, ALCOA; recipient Outstanding ECE Alumnus U. Ill. Fellow IEEE (Best Paper award 1985, 99), AAAS; mem. NAE, Am. Soc. Engrng. Edn., Soc. Exploration Geophysics, Am. Assn. Artificial Intelligence, Eta Kappa Nu, Sigma Xi (Best Paper award ALCOA chpt. 1988). Achievements include patent in application of signal processing technology in aluminum manufacturing. Office: Univ Pitts Dept Elec Engring Pittsburgh PA 15261-0001 E-mail: simaan@ee.pitt.edu.

SIMAI, MIHALY, economics and business educator; b. Budapest, Hungary, Apr. 4, 1930; s. Mátyas and Jolan (Rosenberg) S.; m. Vera Bence, Apr. 28, 1954; 1 child, Anna-Maria. MA, Budapest U. Econs., 1952, PhD, 1957. Asst. prof. Budapest U. Econs., 1952-57, assoc. prof., 1957-59, 61-64, prof., 1970—, dir. grad. studies, 1992—; staff mem. UN Econ.Commn. for Europe, 1959-60; staff mem., 1st officer UN Centre for Projections, N.Y.C., 1964-69; dir. Inst. World Econs., Budapest, 1987-91; Peace fellow U.S. Inst. Peace, Washington, 1991-92. Dir. World Inst. Devel. Econs. Rsch. of UN U., 1993-96; rsch. prof. Inst. World Econs., Hungarian Acad. Scis.; prof. internat. econ. and bus. studies, dir. grad. program on internat. econ. cooperation and bus. strategy Budapest U. Econ. Scis; mem., chmn. coun. UN Univ., Tokyo, 1986-92, dir. World Inst. for Devel. Econs, Helsinki, 1993-95; mem. adv. bd. UN Staff Coll; spl. advisor sec. gen. UN. Author: Interdependence and Conflicts in the World Economy, 1982, Power, Technology and the World Economy, 1990, The Future of Global Governance, 1994, The New Global Environment for the Development Process, 1995, Global Employment, The Future of Work, 2 vols., 1995, International Business Policy, 1996, The Democratic Process and the Market, 1999, The Reintegration of the Former Socialist Countries in Europe, China and Vietnam into the Global Economy, 2000, others; contbr. articles to profl. jours.; mem. editl. bd. Transnational, Geneva, Global Governance, N.Y., Internat. Affairs, London, Devel. Studies, Geneva, Environment and Resource Econs., Amsterdam. Pres. World Fedn. UN Assn., Geneva, 1979-84, hon. pres., 1985—; pres. Nat. Com. UNICEF, Budapest, 1980—. Named to Order of the Flag of Hungarian Republic, Pres. of Republic of Hungary, Budapest, 1990. Mem. Hungarian Acad. Scis. (former dir. gen. Inst. World Econs.), Internat. Studies Assn. Avocations: hiking, skiing. Office: Inst World Econs Orszaghaz St 30 1014 Budapest Hungary Fax: 361 224 67-65. E-mail: msimai@vki.hu.

SIMAIE, JOSEPH R. dentist; b. Tehran, Iran, Jan. 18, 1970; s. Simon and Silva Simaie. BS cum laude, U. Calif., Riverside, 1992; DDS, U. So. Calif., 1996. Pvt. practice, Beverly Hills, Calif., 1997—. Mem.: L.A. Dental Soc., Am. Acad. Implant Dentistry, ADA, Am. Acad. Cosmetic Dentistry. Avocations: investing, hiking, travel.

SIMANDLE, JEROME B. federal judge; b. Binghamton, N.Y., 1949; s. Paul R. Sr. and Mary F. Simandle; married; children: Roy C., Liza Jane. BSE magna cum laude, Princeton U., 1971; JD, U. Pa., 1976; diploma in Social Scis., U. Stockholm, 1974-75. Bar: Pa. 1977, N.J. 1978. Law clk. to Hon. John F. Gerry U.S. Dist. Ct., N.J., 1976-78; asst. U.S. atty. Dist. N.J., 1978-83; U.S. magistrate judge U.S. Dist. Ct., N.J., 1983-92, judge, 1992—. Mem. lawyers adv. com. U.S. Dist. Ct. N.J., 1984-95; ct. adminstrn. case mgmt. com. Jud. Conf. U.S., 1991-97, mem. joint adv. coucil of Adminstrv. Office of U.S. Courts, 2002; mem. CPR Inst. for Dispute Resulution Commn. on Ethics and Stds. in Alternative Dispute Resolution, 1996—. Internat. grad. fellow Rotary Found., 1974-75. Fellow Am. Bar Found.; mem. Fed. Judges Assn. (bd. dirs. 1997—), Am. Judicature Soc., Camden County Bar Assn., Camden Inn of Ct. (master 1987—, program chmn. 1990-93, vice chmn. 1996—). Office: 1 John F Gerry Pl Camden NJ 08101-0888

SIMARI, NANCI JOAN, herbalist; b. N.Y.C., Mar. 12, 1965; d. Frank P. and Rosalie B. S. BFA, NYU, 1989; postgrad., Pacific Coll. of Oriental Medicine. Intern Late Night with David Letterman, N.Y.C., 1988-89; video technician Video Transfer Ctr., San Francisco, 1990-92; video editor CNN, N.Y.C., 1994-95; tech. asst. Prodigal Sound, 1987—; camera operator John Barry Video Svcs., 1993—; writer Astrology Column/Fashion Market, 1997-98; artists' agt., 1997-99. Contbr. poetry to Poetry Jour.

SIME, ELISSA CHRISTINE, healthcare company official; b. Tacoma, Jan. 22, 1970; d. James Alexander Harris and Durive (Shafer) Croake; m. Eric Wayne Sime, June 20, 1995; children: Braden Eric, Nathan William. BA in Pub. Rels., Ctrl. Wash. U., 1995. Provider rels. liaison N.W. Physicians Network, Tacoma, 1995—. Avocations: reading, travel, music, fitness.

SIMENDINGER, THEODORE JOHN, writer, publishing executive; b. Phila., Oct. 6, 1954; s. Theodore John and Margaret Smith Simendinger; m. Bonita Ann Kolish; 1 child Grace. BS, Jacksonville U., 1976. Founder, chmn. Pro Leisure Tour, Inc., Greenwood Village, Colo., 2000—; bus. devel. mgr. Western USA Xerox Corp., Denver, 1979—2000. Career devel. cons. Airplane Reader Pub., Greenwood Village, 2000—02. Author: (book) Rich Without Money, 2002, (book and movie) 12 Miles to Paradise, 2002, (book) Critters, Fish & Other Troublemakers, 1999 (Writer's Digest Cert. Achievment, 2000). Founder, chmn. No Bats Baseball Club Global Ambassadors for the Good of the Game, Greenwood Village, Colo., 1991—2002; founding donor Jacksonville U. Scholarship Fund Peggy Smith Simendinger Scholarship Fund, 1998—2002. Republican. Roman Catholic. Avocations: reading, writing, comedy, fishing. Office: Pro Leisure Tour Inc PO Box 4434 Englewood CO 80111-5233 Home Fax: 303-221-2766; Office Fax: 303-221-2766. Personal E-mail: theo@richwithoutmoney.org. Business E-Mail: theo@richwithoutmoney.org.

SIMEON, GEORGE PRODROM, healthcare company executive; b. St. Louis, Jan. 10, 1971; arrived in Belgium 1997, France, 1994, 98; s. Jovan George and Susan Diane (Kramer) S.; m. Beatrice Michel Dauvier, July 6, 1996; children: Eleni, Constantinos. B in Social Sci., U. Ottawa, Can., 1992; MPH, Yale U., 1994; MBA, INSEAD, Fontainebleau, France, 1999. Mgr. Novartis, Basel, Switzerland, 1994-97; dir. Cordis Europe, Brussels, 1997-98, Cordis Endovascular, Paris, 1999-2000; v.p. Cordis Neurovascular (divsn. of Johnson & Johnson), 2000—. Contbr. articles to profl. jours. including Jour. Hypertension, Jour. Clin. Psychiatry, Quality of Life Rsch., others. Mem. INSEAD Alumni Assn. Avocations: sailing, writing, chess, theatre. Home: 56 rue des Petits Bois 92370 Chaville France Office: Cordis Neurovascular Dreve Richelle 161 H 1410 Waterloo Belgium Fax: 32 2 352 1591. E-mail: george.simeon@aya.yale.edu., gsimeon@crdbe.jnj.com.

SIMEONE, FREDERICK ANTHONY, neurosurgeon, researcher; b. Phila., June 8, 1936; s. Anthony and Emma Celeste (Grimaldi) S.; m. Catherine Eliz Walsh, Oct. 4, 1975 (div. 1989); 1 child, Christina. BA, Temple U., 1956; MD, Temple Med., 1960. Neurosurgical fellow Mayo Clinic, Rochester, Minn., 1961-63; neurosurgical resident U. Pa., Phila., 1963-65; asst. prof. Harvard Med., Boston, 1965-68; prof. U. Pa., Phila., 1968-94; prof., chmn. neurosurgery Jefferson Med. Coll., 1994—. Chmn. Neurosurgery Pa. Hosp., 1969—, Jefferson Med. Coll., 1994, Wills Neurosurgery, 1994—. Author: The Spine, 1972—; contbr. articles to profl. jours. Major U.S. Army, 1961-78. Mem. Am. Assoc. of Neurosurgeons, Am. Acad. Neurol. Surgeons, Congress of Neurosurgeons, Soc. Neurol. Surgeons. Republican. Roman Catholic. Avocations: sports car historical collection, automobile history writing. Home: 8700 Seminole St Philadelphia PA 19118-3708 Office: Penn Hosp 800 Spruce St Philadelphia PA 19107-6130

SIMERAL, WILLIAM GOODRICH, retired chemical company executive; b. Portland, Oreg., May 22, 1926; s. Claire Cornelius and Geneva G. Simeral; m. Elizabeth Louise Ross, June 25, 1949; children: Linda Simeral McGregor, Karen Simeral Schousen, William Goodrich Jr., John David; m. Marion Poore Anderson, Nov. 3, 2001. BS in Physics, Franklin and Marshall Coll., Lancaster, Pa., 1948; PhD in Physics, U. Mich., 1953. With E.I. duPont de Nemours and Co., Inc., 1953-87, v.p., gen. mgr. plastics dept. Del., 1974-76, v.p., gen. mgr. plastic products and resins dept., 1976-77, sr. v.p., dir., mem. exec. com., 1977-81, exec. v.p., dir., mem. exec. com., 1981-87; vice chmn. bd., chief operating officer Conoco Inc., 1984-85. Trustee Franklin and Marshall Coll., 1977—, chmn. bd., 1991-94; trustee, bd. dirs. Wilmington Med. Ctr., 1978-93, chmn. bd., 1982-86; bd. dirs. YMCA Wilmington and New Castle County, 1978-81. Mem. Chem. Mfrs. Assn. (vice chmn. bd. 1980-81, chmn. exec. com. 1981-82, chmn. bd. 1982-83), Am. Phys. Soc., Phi Beta Kappa, Sigma Xi, Wilmington Country Club, The Club Pelican Bay.

SIMEROTH, DEAN CONRAD, chemical engineer; b. Marysville, Calif., Mar. 21, 1946; s. Raphael Conrad and Mary Beatrice (Watson) S.; m. Phyllis Deborah Minakowski, Feb. 7, 1971 (div. Nov. 1994); 1 child, Brian Conrad. BS in Chem. Engring., U. Calif., Davis, 1968. From air pollution specialist to chief engr. evaluation br. Calif. Air Resources Bd., Sacramento, 1969-87, chief criteria pollutant br., 1987—. Served in U.S. Army, 1969-71, Korea. Mem. AIChE, Air Waste Mgmt. Assn., Kiwanis (treas. Woodland, Calif. chpt. 1988-96). Democrat. Roman Catholic. Avocations: hunting, fishing, tennis, history. Office: Calif Air Resources Bd PO Box 2815 1010 I Street Sacramento CA 95814-4219

SIMES, DIMITRI KONSTANTIN, international affairs expert and educator; b. Moscow, Oct. 17, 1947; came to U.S., 1973; s. Konstantin M. and Dina (Kaminsky) S.; m. Anastasia Ryurikov, May 27, 1993; 1 child, Dimitri Alexander. MA, Moscow State U., 1969. Sr. research fellow Ctr. for Strategic and Internat. Studies, Washington, 1973-76, dir. Soviet studies, 1976-80; prof. Soviet studies, exec. dir. Soviet and East European research program Sch. Advanced Internat. Studies, Johns Hopkins U., 1980-83, lectr., 1983-90; sr. assoc. Carnegie Endowment for Internat. Peace, 1983-94; pres. The Nixon Ctr., 1994—; co-pub. The Nat. Interest, 2001—. Vis. prof. polit. sci. U. Calif., Berkeley, 1982; adj. prof. govt. Columbia U., N.Y.C., 1985, 92; cons. CBS News, N.Y.C., 1985-87, NBC News, 1987-94. Author: Detente and Conflict: Soviet Succession: Leadership in Transition, 1978, After the Collapse: Russia Seeks Its Place as a Great Power, 1999; columnist: Christian Sci. Monitor, Boston, 1983-87, L.A. Times Syndicate, 1987-89, Newsday, 1991—; contbr. articles to newspapers and jours. Mem. Coun. on Fgn. Rels. Office: The Nixon Ctr 1615 L St NW Ste 1250 Washington DC 20036-5651 E-mail: dsimes@nixoncenter.org.

SIMES, STEPHEN MARK, pharmaceutical products executive; b. N.Y.C., Nov. 23, 1951; s. Herbert H. and Mimi (Maurer) S.; m. Anita H. Herzog, Aug. 23, 1975. BS in Chemistry, Bklyn. Coll., 1973; MBA in Mktg., NYU, 1980. Sales rep. G.D. Searle and Co., N.Y.C., 1974-78, supr. sales tng. Chgo., 1978-79, dist. sales mgr. N.Y.C., 1979-81, product mgr. Chgo., 1981-82, sr. product mgr., 1982-83, dir. pub. affairs and communications, 1983-84; v.p. Gynex Inc., 1984-88; dir. Gynex Pharms. Inc., Deerfield, 1985-93; pres., dir. Gynex Labs., Chgo., 1985-88; pres., CEO Contracap Inc., Ill., 1988-89, Gynex Pharms., Inc., Chgo., 1989-93, chmn., 1992-93; sr. v.p., dir. Bio-Technology Gen. Corp., 1993-94; pres., CEO, dir. Unimed Pharms., Inc., 1994-97; bd. dirs., CEO, pres. Simes Pharm. Cons., 1997-98. Vice chmn., CEO, pres., BioSante Pharms., Inc., Lincolnshire, Ill., 1998—. Mem. Chgo. Coun. Fgn. Rels., Licensing Exec. Soc. Office: 111 Barclay Blvd Lincolnshire IL 60069 Office Fax: 847-478-9260.

SIMÉUS, DUMAS M. food products executive; b. Pont-Sondé, Haiti, Sept. 11, 1939; Degree in Elect. Engring., Howard U.; MBA with honors, U. Chgo. Pres., CEO TLC Beatrice Internat. Foods, Mansfield, Tex., prior to 1996; chmn., CEO, controlling stockholder Siméus Foods Internat., Inc., 1996—. Mem. bd. dirs. TGIF. Pres. Dumas M. Siméus Found.; chmn. Caribbean Am. Leadership Coun.; pres. Dumas M. Siméus Found. to provide med. care, food and clothing to the less fortunate; active Haitian Am. Bus. Devel. Coun., Nat. Orgn. for Advancement of Haitians, Dallas Urban League, Inc., Dallas Together Forum, Dallas/Ft. Worth Minority Bus. Devel. Coun. Named Entrepreneur of Yr. for the Southwest Region by Ernst & Young, LLP; finalist Horatio Alger award. Mem. Internat. Foodservice Mfrs. Assn. (bd. dirs.), Caribbean/Am. Leadership Coun. (chmn.), Haitian/Am. Bus. Devel. Coun., Nat. Orgn. Advancement Haitians, Dallas Urban League, Inc., DF/W Minority Bus. Devel. Coun. Office: Siméus Foods Internat 812 S 5th Ave Mansfield TX 76063-2210 E-mail: dsimeus@simeusfoods.com.

SIMIC, CHARLES, English language educator, poet; b. Beograd, Yugoslavia, May 9, 1938; came to U.S., 1954, naturalized, 1971; s. George and Helen (Matijevich) S.; m. Helen Dubin, Oct. 1964; children: Anna, Philip. BA, NYU, 1967. Editl. asst. Aperture, Quar. of Photography, N.Y.C., 1966-69; prof. English Calif. State U., Hayward, 1970-73, U. N.H., Durham, 1973—. Vis. tchr. Boston U., spring 1975, Columbia U., fall 1979. Author: (poems) What the Grass Says, 1967, Somewhere Among us a Stone is Taking Notes, 1969, Dismantling the Silence, 1971, White, 1972, Return to a Place Lit by a Glass of Milk, 1974, Biography and a Lament, 1976, Charon's Cosmology, 1977, Classic Ballroom Dances, 1980, Austerities, 1982, Weather Forecast for Utopia and Vicinity, 1983, Selected Poems, 1985, Unending Blues, 1986, The World Doesn't End, 1989 (Pulitzer Prize for poetry 1990), The Book of Gods and Devils, 1990, Hotel Insomnia, 1992, A Wedding in Hell, 1994, Walking the Black Cat, 1996, Jackstraws, 1999, Night Picnic, 2001; (prose) The Uncertain Certainty, 1985, Wonderful Words, Silent Truth, 1990, The Unemployed Fortune Teller, 1994, Orphan Factory, 1997, A Fly in the Soup, 2000; translator, editor: (with C.W. Truesdale) poems Fire Gardens, 1970, (with Mark Strand) Another Republic, 1976, (with others) Selected Poems of Tomaz Salamun, 1987, RollCall of Mirrors, 1987; translator: Four Modern Yugoslav Poets, 1970, (with P. Kastmiler) Atlantis, 1983; contbr. poems to mags. and anthologies. With U.S. Army, 1961-63. Recipient PEN Internat. award for translation, 1970, 80, Edgar Allan Poe award Am. Acad. Poets, 1975, Nat. Inst. Arts and Letters and AAAL award, 1976, Harriet Monroe poetry award U. Chgo., 1980, DiCastignola award Poetry Soc. Am., 1980, Pulitzer prize for poetry, 1990; Guggenheim fellow, 1972-73; Nat. Endowment for Arts fellow, 1974-75, 79-80; Fulbright Travelling fellow, 1982, Ingram Merrill fellow, 1983-84; Mac Arthur fellow, 1984-89. Mem. Am. Acad. Arts and Letters. Home: PO Box 192 Strafford NH 03884-0192 Office: U NH Dept English Durham NH 03824

SIMINI, JOSEPH PETER, accountant, financial consultant, author, former educator; b. Buffalo, Feb. 15, 1921; s. Paul and Ida (Moro) S.; m. Marcelline McDermott, Oct. 4, 1968. BS, St Bonaventure U., 1940, BBA, 1949; MBA, U. Calif.-Berkeley, 1957; DBA, Western Colo. U., 1981. CPA, Calif. Insp. naval material Bur. Ordnance, Buffalo and Rochester, N.Y., 1941-44; mgr. Paul Simini Bakery, Buffalo, 1946-48; internal auditor DiGiorgio (Fruit) Corp., San Francisco, 1950-51; tax acct. Price Waterhouse & Co., 1953; sr. acct. Richard L. Hanlin C.P.A., 1953-54; prof. acctg. U. San Francisco, 1954-79, emeritus prof., 1983—. Mem. rev. bd. Calif. Bd. Accountancy,

1964-68; host The Bus. Doctor Stas. WALE and KCCF, 1998. Author: Accounting Made Simple, 1967, rev. edit., 1987, Cost Accounting Concepts for Nonfinancial Executives, 1976, Become Wealthy! Using Tax Savings and Real Estate Investments, 1982, Balance Sheet Basics for the Nonfinancial Managers, 1989, Petals of the Rose, 1990, How to Become Financially Independent, 1996, 10 Steps to Financial Independence Guaranteed, 2000; tech. editor Accounting Essentials, 1972; patentee Dial-A-Trig and Verbum Est card game. Mem. coun. com. Boy Scouts Am., Buffalo, San Francisco, 1942-65, Souters Key, San Francisco coun.; bd. dir. Nat. Italian Am. Found., Washington, 1979-85. Lt. j.g. USNR, 1944-46. Recipient Bacon-McLaughlin medal St. Bonaventure U., 1940, Laurel Key, 1940; Outstanding Tchr. award Coll. Bus. Adminstrn., U. San Francisco, 1973, Disting. Tchr. award U. San Francisco, 1975, Joseph Per Simini award, 1977, Crown Zellerbach Found. fellow, 1968-69, Gold Medal Associazione Piemontese nel Mondo, Turin, Italy, 1984; decorated Knight Order of Merit, Republic of Italy, 1982. Mem. AICPA's, Calif. Soc. CPAs (past chmn. ednl. stds., student rels. com. San Francisco chpt.), Inst. of Mgmt. Accts. (past pres. San Francisco chpt.), Am. Acctg. Assn., Am. Mgmt. Assn. (lectr. 1968-78), Serra (past pres. Golden Gate chpt.), Il Cenacolo (past pres.), Toastmasters (past pres. Magic Word, treas. Dist. 4, 1996-97), K.C., Rotary (past pres. Daly City), Delta Sigma Pi (past pres. San Francisco alumni club), Beta Gamma Sigma. Roman Catholic. Home: 977 Duncan St San Francisco CA 94131-1800 Office: PO Box 31420 San Francisco CA 94131-0420 *Personal philosophy: You can succeed! but you must program yourself for success and know what you want.*

SIMIS, THEODORE LUCKEY, investment banker, information technology executive; b. N.Y.C., June 17, 1924; s. Theodore William Ernest and Helen (Luckey) S.; m. Laura Cushman Ingraham, Sept. 8, 1946; children— Nancy Simis Ricca, Theodore Steven, Karen Simis Woods, June Simis Sobocinski BS, NYU, 1950, MBA, 1952. With Bell System, 1941-79; various positions to officer level with N.Y. Telephone Co., N.J. Telephone Co., and AT&T; v.p. Warner Amex Cable Co., 1980-81; sr. v.p. E.F. Hutton, Sarasota, Fla., 1982-87; vice chmn., bd. dirs. XMX Corp., Burlington, Mass., 1986-2000; pres. Pvt. Transatlantic Telecommunication System Inc., McLean, Va., 1987-89; chmn. Value Added Network System, Inc., Sarasota, Fla., 1990-91; vice-chmn., bd. dirs. OPIX Corp., Burlington, Ma., 2000—. Dir. Liebenzell Mission, Schooleys Mountain, N.J.; vis. Nieman fellow Harvard U., 1977. Mem. Republican Nat. Com., 1981—. 1st lt. U.S. Army, 1942-53, ETO Mem. N.Y. Acad. Scis., U.S. C. of C., NYU Club. Lutheran. Home: 6025 Manasota Key Rd Englewood FL 34223-9245 Fax: 941-475-1128. E-mail: tlslns@cs.com.

SIMITIS, SPIROS, legal educator; b. Athens, Greece, Oct. 19, 1934; s. George and Fanny (Christopoulo) S.; m. Ilse Grubrich, Aug. 3, 1963. JD, U. Marburg, Fed. Republic Germany, 1956. Assoc. prof. U. Frankfurt, Fed. Republic Germany, 1963, prof., 1969, U. Giessen, Fed. Republic Germany, 1964-69; vis. prof. London Sch. Econs., U. Calif. - Berkeley, 1976, U. Pa., 1980, U. Strasbourg, France, 1987-88, Paris, 1990—, Yale U., New Haven, 1981—. Sec. gen. Internat. Civil Status Commn., 1966—80; chmn. Data Protection Experts Com. of the Coun. of Europe, Strasbourg, 1982—86; with Hesse Data protect commr., 1975—91; mem. rsch. coun. European Univ. Inst.; chmn. social rights com. European Commn., 1998; chmn. German Nat. Ethic Coun., 2000—. Contbr. numerous articles to legal publs. Mem.: Nat. Bioethics Council (chmn.), European Group on Ethics in Sci. and New Techs., Info. Soc. Forum of European Union, German Coun. Pvt. Internat. Law, German Lawyers Assn. (bd. dirs. 1970—82). Office: Johann Wolfgang Goethe U Senckenberganlage 31 Postfach 111932 60054 Frankfurt Germany E-mail: simitis@jur.uni-frankfurt.de.

SIMITSES, GEORGE JOHN, retired engineering educator, consultant; b. Athens, Greece, July 31, 1932; came to U.S., 1951, naturalized, 1963; s. John G. and Vasilike (Goutoufas) S.; m. Nena Athena Economy, Sept. 11, 1960; children: John G., William G., Alexandra G. BS in Aerospace Engring., Ga. Tech. Inst., 1955, MS in Aerospace Engring., 1956; PhD in Aeronautics and Astronautics, Stanford U., 1965. From instr. to prof. engring. Ga. Inst. Tech., Atlanta, 1956-89; prof., head dept. aerospace engring., interim dean engring. U. Cin., 1989-2000, retired, 2000. Cons. Lockheed-Georgia Co., Marietta, Ga., 1965-70, King & Gavaris Engrs., N.Y.C., 1977-79, Ga. Power Co., Atlanta, 1971-72. Author: Stability of Elastic Structures, 1976, Dynamic Stability of Suddenly Loaded Structures, 1989; contbr. chpts. to books, articles to profl. jours. Cmty. rep. Am. Hellenic Inst., Washington, 1976-91; del. Ga. State Dem. Conf., Macon, 1969. Fellow AIAA (various coms. 1974—), ASME (coms. 1976—), Am. Acad. Mechs.; mem. Hellenic Soc. Theoretical and Applied Mechs. (founding hon. mem.), AHEPA (v.p. chpt. 1978-79, coms. 1975-90), Acad. Athens (corr.), Sigma Xi (Sustained Rsch. award 1980, Best Paper award 1985). Office: Ga Inst Technology Aerospace Enging Atlanta GA 30332-0150 E-mail: george.simitses@aerospace.gatech.edu.

SIMJEE, AISHA, ophthalmologist, educator; b. Surat, India, Jan. 23, 1944; came to U.S., 1970; d. Yusuf Esmail Simjee and Amina Ahmed Badat; m. Sabbir A. Dadabhai, Apr. 28, 1978; children: Alia Dadabhai, Sufia Dadabhai. Intermediate Sci. degree, Rangoon (Burma) U., 1963; MB, BS, Inst. Medicine, Rangoon, 1968. Diplomate Am. Bd. Ophthalmology. Intern Rangoon Gen. Hosp., 1968-69, South Balt. Gen. Hosp., 1970-71; rschr. in ophthalmology Johns Hopkins Hosp., Balt., 1971-72; resident in ophthalmology Eye Dept. Howard U. Hosp., D.C. Gen. Hosp., Armed Forces Inst. Pathology, Washington, 1972-75; fellow in cornea external diseases Wills Eye Hosp., Phila., 1975-76; fellow in ophthalmic pathology and med. retina Scheie Eye Inst., 1976-77; asst. prof. ophthalmology Howard U., Washington, 1977-78; clin. assoc. prof. ophthalmology U. Calif., Irvine, 1978—; pvt. practice Orange, Calif. Mem. med. adv. bd. Orange County Eye & Tissue Bank, 1990—; attending physician St. Joseph Hosp., Orange, 1978—, U. Calif. Irvine Med. Ctr., 1978—. Contbr. articles to profl. jours. Vol. ophthalmologist La Amistad de Jose Clinic, Sponsor Care Program of St. Joseph Hosp., 1988—, Testing 1-2-3 Screening Clinic St. Joseph Hosp., ann. eye screening for local sch. children, Project Orbis, S.E.E. Internat., Santa Barbara. Named Woman of Achievement, Rancho Santiago Coll., Santa Ana, 1990; recipient certs. of recognition Calif. state senator John Seymour, Calif. congressman Christopher Cox, Calif. lt. gov. Leo McCarthy. Fellow ACS, Am. Acad. Ophthalmology (Nat. Eye Care Project 1986—); mem. Calif. Med. Assn., Orange County Med. Assn. (bd. dirs. 1995—), Orange County Soc. Ophthalmology (exec. com. 1992—). Office: 1310 W Stewart Dr Ste 501 Orange CA 92868-3856

SIMKANICH, JOHN JOSEPH, lawyer, engineer; b. Clairton, Pa., 1941; BSEE, Drexel Inst. Tech., 1964; MSEE, Purdue U., 1966; JD, George Washington U., 1972. Bar: U.S. Patent Office 1970, Pa. 1973, U.S. dist. Ct. (ea. dist.) Pa. 1977, U.S. Supreme Ct. 1977, U.S. Ct. Appeals (Fed. cir.) 1982, U.S. Ct. Appeals (3d cir.) 1992. Elec. engr. U.S. Steel Co., 1963-65; engr. Westinghouse Aerospace, Balt., 1966-69; sys. developer TRW Sys. Inc., Washington, 1969-70; patent atty. Burroughs Corp., Paoli, Pa., 1970-74, Johnson & Johnson, New Brunswick, N.J., 1974-77; pvt. practice intellectual property law Newtown, Pa., 1977—. Adv. Soup, Inc., Washington, 1970-72; introduced to FTC truth-in-advt. law; presenter in field. Patentee in field; product developer and licensing; analog and digital computer designer, programmer. Mem. IEEE (sr.), Pa. Bar Assn., Bucks County Bar Assn., Phila. Intellectual Property Law Assn., Am. Intellectual Property Law Assn., Delta Theta Phi, Eta Kappa Nu. Roman Catholic. Republican. Office: PO Box 671 Newtown PA 18940-0671

SIMKHOVICH, SEMEN LASAREVICH, engineering educator, researcher; b. Cherven, Minsk, USSR, July 25, 1940; came to U.S., 1994; s. Lasar A. and Liliya S. (Rosengaus) S.; m. Marianna M. Fridman, Sept. 3, 1966; 1 child, Galina. MS in Hydromechanics, Novosibirsk State U., USSR, 1965; PhD in Hydromechanics, Inst. Physics and Optics, Moscow, 1974. Asst. prof. Poly. Inst., Omsk, USSR, 1965-67, Bauman's Tech. U., Moscow, Russia, 1967—74, assoc. prof. Russia, 1974—90, prof. Russia, 1990—94; sr. rschr. Inst. Cryogenic Engring., Russia, 1973-81, lead rschr. Russia, 1981-90; ind. cons. Bklyn., 1994-97; technical specialist Guardian Life Ins. Co. Am., N.Y.C., 1997-2001; ind. cons., 2001—. Contbr. numerous articles to profl. jours. Recipient USSR Inventor award USSR State Com. Inventions & Discoveries, 1981. Achievements include over 30 patents in field of cryogenic engineering and space technology; research in fields of hydrodynamics and cryogenics; participation in Soviet Space Exploration program. Home: 80 Timber Ridge Dr Staten Island NY 10306-1105 E-mail: s.simkhovich@worldnet.att.net.

SIMKIN, JACQUELINE, real estate developer; b. Winnipeg, Manitoba, Can., Nov. 14, 1942; came to U.S., 1985; d. Saul and Claribel (Katz) S.; m. Archie Cham, Aug. 15, 1961; divorced. LLB, U. Manitoba, 1967; LLM, U. London, 1969. Sole practice, 1971-76; developer Nine Island Ave. Assoc., Ltd., Miami, Fla., 1976—, v.p. Bd. dirs. Atico Savs. Band, Miami, Intercontinental Bank, Bass Mus., Miami Beach, Fla. Mem. Law Soc. B.C., Israel Bar Assn.

SIMKIN, PETER ANTHONY, internist, educator; b. Morgantown, W.Va., Nov. 22, 1935; s. William Edward and Ruth Helen (Commons) S.; m. Penelope Hart Payson, Aug. 9, 1958; children— Andrew, Caroline, Mary, Elizabeth. BA, Swarthmore Coll., 1957; MD, U. Pa., 1961. Intern N.C. Meml. Hosp., Chapel Hill, 1961-62, resident, 1962-63, Univ. Hosps. Cleve., 1965-66; fellow in medicine U. Wash., Seattle, 1966-69, asst. prof., 1969-74, assoc. prof., 1974-84, prof., 1984—. Mem. editorial bd.: Arthritis and Rheumatism, 1981-85, BIMR Rheumatology, 1980-84; contbr. articles to profl. jours. Bd. dirs. Wash. chpt. Arthritis Found., 1974-90, chmn. med. and sci. com., 1974-78. Served with U.S. Army, 1963-65. Fellow Am. Coll. Rheumatology; mem. Osteoarthritis Rsch. Soc. Internat. Mem. Soc. Of Friends. Office: U Wash Rheumatology 356428 Seattle WA 98195-0001

SIMKO, JAN, English, foreign language and literature educator; b. Zlaté Moravce, Slovakia, Oct. 30, 1920; came to U.S., 1967; s. Simon Simko and Terezia Simkova; m. Libusa Safarikova, Dec. 20, 1950 (div. 1970); children: Jan, Vladimir (dec.). Diploma in English, U. Bratislava, 1942, Diploma in German, 1943, PhD in English, 1944; MPhil in English, U. London, 1967. Tchr. English and German various bus. schs., 1942-45; asst. depts. English and German U. Bratislava, 1945-46; instr. English Econom U., 1946-47; faculty U. Bratislava, 1950-68, from asst. prof. to assoc. prof. English, 1957-68; prof. English Rio Grande Coll., Ohio, 1968-75. Instr. Shakespeare Georgetown U., 1982-84; vis. prof. English, scholar-in-residence W. Va. U., Parkersburg, 1989-90; instr. Slovak Fgn. Svc. Inst., Washington, 1974, 96, fed. govt., 1989, 91-93, IMF & World Bank, 1994-95; examiner critical langs. program Kent (Ohio) State U., 1974-91; feature writer Voice of Am., 1983-94; translator U.S. Dept. State, 1997—; bd. linguistics Slovak Acad. of Scis., 1957-67 Author: 3 English textbooks, 2 bilingual dictionaries, 1 linguistic monograph; editor: Lectures in the Circle of Modern Philology, 2 vols., 1965-66; chief consulting editor: textbooks of Slovak and Czech, 1993-96; contbg. writer: The Review, 1995—; Am./Can.-Slovak press; contbr. articles to profl. jours. With inf. Czecho-Slovak Army, 1946. Grantee Brit. Coun., 1947-49, Folger Shakespeare Libr./U.S. Dept. State, 1967-68; Internat. Rsch. and Exch. Bd., 1982, others; recipient awards W.Va. U., 1990, Bratislava U., 1995. Mem. MLA (life), Slovak Studies Assn., Soc. for Scis. and Arts, Met. Opera Guild, Shakespeare Theater Guild, Nat. Symphony Orch. Assn., English-Speaking Union. Roman Catholic. Avocations: classical music, opera, theatre, fine arts, hiking, swimming. Home: 1356 E Capitol St NE Washington DC 20003-1533

SIMMANG, CLIFFORD LILES, surgeon; b. Bryan, Tex., Dec. 6, 1953; s. Clifford Max and Elnora (Liles) S.; m. Karen Janette Black, May 19, 1979; children: Clifford Jonathan, Marc Alan. BS, Tex. A&M U., 1976, MS, 1978; MD, U. Tex. Med. Br., 1982. Diplomate Am. Bd. Surgery, Am. Bd. Colon and Rectal Surgery. Categorical surgery intern Brooke Army Med. Ctr., Ft. Sam Houston, Tex., 1981-82, resident in gen. surgery, 1982-87; resident in colon and rectal surgery Jewish Hosp.-Washington U., St. Louis, 1991-92; chief gen. surgery svc. Frankfurt Army Regional Med. Ctr., Germany, 1987-91; chief colon & rectal surgery Madigan Army Med. Ctr., Tacoma, 1992-95; med. dir. aston surg. svcs., assoc. prof. surgery U. Tex. SW Med. Ctr., Dallas, 1995—, program dir. colon and rectal surgery residency. Surg. adv. bd. 3M Corp., St. Paul, 1993-95. Assoc. editor Diseases of the Colon and Rectum, 1997—. Decorated Meritorious Svc. medal with oak leaf cluster. Fellow ACS, Am. Soc. Colon and Rectal Surgeons (stds. task force 1994—, armed forces task force 1992-94); mem. AMA, Soc. Am. Gastrointestinal Endoscopic Surgeons, Soc. Surgery Alimentary Tract, S.W. Surg. Congress, Soc. for Surgery Alimentary Tract, Soc. Am. Gastrointestinal Endoscopic Surgeons, Southwest oncology Group, Tex. Soc. Colon and Rectal Surgeons, Dallas Soc. Gen. Surgeons, N.W. Soc. Colon and Rectal Surgeons, Midwest Soc. Colon and Rectal Surgeons (pres.), Soc. U.S. Army Flight Surgeons, Soc. for Surg. Oncology. Baptist. Avocations: parenting, water skiing, snow skiing, golf, tennis. Office: U Tex SW Med Ctr 5323 Harry Hines Blvd Dallas TX 75390-7208

SIMMER, RITA, retired public relations executive; Dir. pub. rels. Supervalu, Inc., Mpls., 1997—, ret., 2002—. Office: Supervalu Inc PO Box 990 Minneapolis MN 55440-0990

SIMMERMON, JAMES EVERETT, credit bureau executive; b. Arnold, Pa., Mar. 23, 1926; s. Joseph C. and Melba J. (McGeary) S.; m. Lois Bowden, Apr. 19, 1952; children: James, Thomas, John, Lisa, William. BS in Bus. Adminstrn, Ashland (Ohio) U., 1949. Chmn. Collection Service Ctr., New Kensington, Pa., 1955—. Mem. adv. bd. Associated Credit Bus., Houston, 1965-73, bd. dirs., 1984—; bd. dirs. Consumer Credit Counseling Svc. of Western Pa., 1975—; vice chmn. Citizens Gen. Enterprises Inc., 1986—. Trustee Ashland (Ohio) U., 1986—; bd. dirs. Citzens Gen. Hosp., New Kensington, Pa., 1972—. With USNR, 1944-46. Mem. Rotary Club of Fox Chapel (past dist. gov. dist. 7300, 1982-83, Oakmont Country Club, Union Club B.C. Home: 302 Fox Chapel Rd Apt 316 Pittsburgh PA 15238-2337

SIMMONDS, JIMMIE NEIL, theatre educator; b. Battle Creek, Mich., Jan. 16, 1949; s. Deland M. and Frances J. S; divorced; 1 child, Jayme Allen. BS in Art Edn., Bowling Green (Ohio) State U., 1971, MA, 1989; MA in Christian Ministry, Internat. Sch. Theology, San Bernardino, 1986. Nat. dir. for drama Campus Crusade for Christ, San Bernardino, Calif., 1972-88; graphic artist Lamb's Theatre, N.Y.C., 1987-88; tchr. Union County H.S., Lake Butler, Fla., 1989-91; prof. Daytona Beach (Fla.) C.C., 1989-91; performing arts prof. Savannah Coll. of Art and Design, Ga., 2001—. Varsity forensica coach Bowling Green State U., 1988-89; regional selection team Am. Coll. Theatre Festival Kennedy Ctr. for Performing Arts, Washington, 2000. Actor, dir. many community plays. Arby Flynn Meml scholarship Kellogg C.C., 1968. Mem. Fla. C.C. Activity Assn. (dir. theatre divsn., adjudicator, dir. 1995-2001), Phi Kappa Delta. Home: 2200 E Victory D Savannah GA 31404 Office: Savannah Coll of Art and Design PO Box 8146 Savannah GA 31402 E-mail: simmondsj@bdcc.cc.fl.us.

SIMMONDS, RAE NICHOLS, musician, composer, educator; b. Lynn, Mass., Feb. 25, 1919; d. Raymond Edward and Abbie Iola (Spinney) Nichols; m. Carter Fillebrown, Jr., June 27, 1941 (div. May 15, 1971); children: Douglas C. (dec.), Richard A., Mary L., Donald E.; m. Ronald John Simmonds, Oct. 9, 1971 (dec. Nov. 1995). AA, Westbrook Coll., Portland, Maine, 1981; B in Music Performance summa cum laude, U. Maine, 1984; MS in Edn., U. So. Maine, 1989; PhD, Walden U., 1994. Founder, dir. Studio of Music/Children's Studio of Drama, Portsmouth, N.H., 1964-71, Studio of Music, Bromley, Eng., 1971-73, Bromley Children's Theatre, 1971-73, Oughterard Children's Theatre, County Galway, Ireland, 1973-74, Studio of Music, Portland, Maine, 1977-96, West Baldwin, 1997—; resident playwright Children's Theatre of Maine, Portland, 1979-81; organist, choir dir. Stevens Ave. Congl. Ch., 1987-95; field faculty advisor Norwich U., Montpelier, Vt., 1995. Field advisor grad. program Vt. Coll., Norwich U., 1995; cons./educator mus. tng. for disabled vets. VA, Portsmouth, N.H., 1966-69; show pianist and organist, mainland U.S.A., 1939-59, Hawaii, 1959-62, Rae Nichols Trio, 1962—; mus. dir. Theatre By the Sea, Portsmouth, N.H., 1969-70. Author/composer children's musical: Shamrock Road, 1980 (Blue Stocking award 1980), Glooscap, 1980; author/composer original scripts and music: Cinderella, If I Were a Princess, Beauty and the Beast, Baba Yaga - A Russian Folk Tale, The Journey - Musical Bible Story, The Perfect Gift - A Christmas Legend; original stories set to music include: Heidi, A Little Princess, Tom Sawyer, Jungle Book, Treasure Island; compositions include: London Jazz Suite, Bitter Suite, Jazz Suite for Trio, Sea Dream, Easter (chorale), Rae Simmonds Jazz Trio Songbook Series, (CD) Fascinatin' Gershwin Rae Simmonds Jazz Trio, 2000; contbr. Maine Women Writers Collection. Recipient Am. Theatre Wing Svc. award, 1944, Pease AFB Svc. Club award, 1967, Bumpus award Westbrook Coll., 1980; Nat. Endowment for Arts grantee, 1969-70; Women's Lit. scholar, 1980, Westbrook scholar, 1980-81, Nason scholar, 1983; Kelaniya U. (Colombo, Sri Lanka) rsch. fellow, 1985-86. Mem. ASCAP, Internat. Soc. Poets, Internat. League Women Composers, Music Tchrs. of Maine, Am. Guild of Organists, Music Tchrs. Nat. Assn., Internat. Alliance for Women in Music, Doctorate Assn. N.Y. Educators, Inc., Delta Omicron, Phi Kappa Phi. Democrat. Episcopalian. Avocations: travel, philately. Home: 230 Douglas Hill Rd West Baldwin ME 04091-9715

SIMMONDS, ROBERT MAURER, engineering educator; b. Beaver Falls, Pa., Apr. 16, 1947; s. Harold Maurer and Mary Simmonds; m. Deborah Lynne Carawan, June 25, 1977; children: Stephen Maurer, Kent Hayes. BS, Youngstown State U., 1972, MS, 1975; advanced cert. edn., Coll. William and Mary, 1983, EdD, 1985. Regional planner Southeastern Va. Planning Dist. Commn., Norfolk, 1977-78; statis. rsch. analyst Nat. Ctr. for State Cts., Williamsburg, Va., 1978-82; assoc. prof. St. Leo Coll., Ft. Eustis, 1982-85; ops. rsch. analyst U.S. Army Transp. Sch., 1985-88; dept. chmn. sys. engring. dept. U.S. Army Logistics Mgmt. Coll., Ft. Lee, Va., 1988—. Cons. Dep. Chief of Staff for Tng., Ft. Monroe, Va., 1992, Picatinny Arsenal, N.J., 1994-96, Concepts and Analysis Agy., Washington, 1999—. Contbr. articles to profl. jours. Mem. bus. adv. coun. Chesterfield (Va.) Tech. Ctr., 1999—; faculty advisor for FIRST Robotics Competition, Chesterfield, 1999—. With USN, 1965-68. Recipient Dubach Scholarship award Sigma Phi Epsilon, Youngstown State U., 1972. Mem. Mil. Ops. Rsch. Soc. (Coin for Excellence 1998). Avocations: walking, golf. Office: US Army Logistics Mgmt Coll 2401 Quarters Rd Fort Lee VA 23801-1705 E-mail: simmondr@lee.army.mil.

SIMMONS, ANNE L. federal official; b. Spencer, Iowa, Jan. 4, 1964; d. Donald Lewis and Lois Amber (Blass) S. B in Spl. Studies, Cornell Coll., 1986. Intern for Congressman Berkley Bedell, Washington, 1986; field staff Iowans for Clayton Hodgson, Sioux City, Iowa, 1986; exec. sec. Atomic Indsl. Forum, Bethesda, Md., 1986-87; staff asst. House Armed Svcs. Com., Washington, 1987; legis. asst. to Congressman Tim Johnson, 1988-93; staff dir. gen. farms commodities subcom. House Agriculture Com., 1993, staff dir. environ., credit and rural devel. subcom., 1994, minority resource conservation rsch. and forestry subcom., 1995-96. Profl. Staff Ho. Com. on Agrl., 1997—. Music scholar Cornell Coll., 1982-86. Mem. Delta Phi Alpha. Democrat. Office: House Agriculture Com 1301 Longworth House Ofc Bldg Washington DC 20515-0001 E-mail: anne.simmons@mail.house.gov.

SIMMONS, BETH A. political science educator; b. Sacramento, Apr. 11, 1958; d. Charles N. and Barbara A. (Terrell) S.; m. Bruce Vincent Jackan, Dec. 29, 1987. BA, U. Redlands, 1979; MA, U. Chgo., 1982, Harvard U., 1987, PhD, 1991. Asst. prof. polit. sci. Duke U., Durham, N.C., 1991—. Author: Domestic Sources of Foreign Economic Policy, 1923-1939, 1993. MacArthur fellow, 1990-91, Ford Found. fellow, 1989-90, Krupp fellow, 1987-88; recipient Morris Abrams award for Internat. Rels., Jewish Vocat. Soc., 1987-88. Mem. Am. Polit. Sci. Assn., Phi Beta Kappa. Office: Duke U Polit Sci Dept 214 Perkins Libr Durham NC 27706

SIMMONS, BONNIE ANDERSON, management information systems educator, accountant; b. Amarillo, Tex., July 21, 1943; d. James Franklin Strader and Wanda Lou (Wood) Anderson; m. A. Frank Simmons, Aug. 19, 1961 (div. Feb. 1983); children: Daniel, Brian, Stephanie, Joanna. BA, No. Cen. Coll., 1978; MBA, Ill. Inst. Tech., 1982; postgrad., No. Ill. U., 1984—. CPA, Ill. Taxpayer svc. rep. IRS, Chgo., 1977-78; reporter Dun & Bradstreet, Glen Ellyn, 1978; sr. programmer No. Trust Bank, Chgo., 1978-82; assoc. prof. MIS and acctg. No. Cen. Coll., Naperville, 1982—99, chair acctg. dept., 1983-85, chair bus. dept., 1985-91, coord. MIS program, 1988-92; healthcare cons. Simmons Cons., 2002—. Vis. assoc. prof. Elmhurst Coll., DePaul U. Treas. Boy Scouts Am., DuPage, Ill., 1982-83. Mem. Ill. CPA Soc., Sigma Iota Epsilon, Delta Pi Epsilon. Home: 2 S 341 Seneca Dr Wheaton IL 60187 Office: No Cen Coll 30 N Brainard St Naperville IL 60540-4607

SIMMONS, CAROLINE JENNERMANN, biomedical researcher, writer; d. Donald L. and M. Ann Jennermann; m. Kirt E. Simmons, Nov. 29, 1996. BS, Purdue U., 1989; MS, Ind. U., 1993. Sr. rsch. technician Ind. U., Indpls., 1989—93; scientist Glaxo Wellcome, Inc., Rsch. Triangle Pk., NC, 1993—97; program adminstr. Ark. Cancer Rsch. Ctr., Little Rock, 1998—2000; biomedical rsch. editor Ark. Ctr for Birth Defects Rsch., 2000—. Grant reviewer Mar. of Dimes, Little Rock, 2001—; rsch. mentor NIH: Minority Rsch. Apprenticeship Prgm., Indpls., 1992; tchg. asst. dept. biol. sci. Purdue U., West Lafayette, Ind., 1989. Contbr. articles to profl. jours. (Best of Conf. in Category: Surveillance award, 2002); reviewer: Jour. Young Investigators, 2001—. Vol. Ark. Children's Hosp., Little Rock, 1999—2000; vol. youth music program St. James United Meth. Ch., 2000. Mem.: Nat. Orgn. for Rare Disorders, The ARC of Ark., The Magic Found., Coun. of Sci. Editors, Bd. of Editors in the Life Sciences, Am. Med. Writers Assn. (regional dir. Ark. chpt. 2001—), Nat. Birth Defects Prevention Network. Avocations: miniatures, antiques, cooking. Office: Ark Ctr for Birth Defects Research 11219 Financial Centre Parkway Ste 250 Little Rock AR 72211 Home Fax: 501-320-5107; Office Fax: 501-320-5107. Personal E-mail: simmonscarolinej@uams.edu. E-mail: simmonscarolinej@uams.edu.

SIMMONS, CAROLINE THOMPSON, civic worker; b. Denver, Aug. 22, 1910; d. Huston and Caroline Margaret (Cordes) Thompson; m. John Farr Simmons, Nov. 11, 1936; children: John Farr (dec.), Huston T., Malcolm M. (dec.). AB, Bryn Mawr Coll., 1931; MA with honors, Amherst Coll. Chmn. women's com. Corcoran Gallery Art, 1965-66; vice chmn. women's com. Smithsonian Assocs., 1969-71; pres. Decatur House Coun., 1963-71; mem. bd. Nat. Theatre, 1979-80; trustee Washington Opera, 1955-65; bd. dirs. Fgn. Student Svc. Coun., 1956-79; mem. Washington Home Bd., 1955-60; bd. dirs. Smithsonian Friends of Music, 1977-79; commr. Nat. Mus. Am. Art, 1979-89; mem. Folger com. Folger Shakespeare Libr., 1979-86, trustee emeritus, 1986—; mem. Washington bd. Am. Mus. in Britain, 1970-93; bd. dirs. Found. Preservation Historic Georgetown, 1975-89; trustee Marpat Found., 1987—, Amherst Coll., 1979-81, Dacor-Bacon House Found., Phillips Collection, 1990—, Georgetown Presbyn. Ch., 1989-91; v.p. internat. coun. Mus. Modern Art, N.Y.C., 1964-90, emeritus trustee. Recipient award for eminent svc. Folger Shakespeare Libr., 1986. Mem. Soc. Women Geographers, Sulgrave Club, Chevy Chase Club. Address: 1508 Dumbarton Rock Ct NW Washington DC 20007-3048

SIMMONS, DAVID JEFFREY, real estate executive; b. Greenville, S.C., Oct. 12, 1961; s. Wilbur Bernard and Grace (Duncan) S.; m. Georgie Ann Lollis, June 8, 1985. BS in Fin. and Mgmt., U. S.C., 1983. Lic. real estate broker, S.C. V.p. W.B. Simmons and Co., Greenville, 1983—; pres. Simmons Realty and Devel., 1983—; v.p. Greenville Turf and Tractor, 1987-94, Foothills Turf and Tractor, Easley, S.C., 1987-94; pres., chief exec. officer Simmons Chevrolet-Geo Inc., Pendleton, 1989-92. Active March of Dimes, Greenville. Mem. NRA, Nat. Assn. Realtors, S.C. Assn. Realtors, Aircraft Owners and Pilots Assn. Clubs: Poinsett, Commerce (Greenville). Republican. Baptist. Office: PO Box 1315 Greenville SC 29602-1315

SIMMONS, DAVID NORMAN, lawyer; b. Denver, Aug. 29, 1957; s. David Lee and Janet Thelma (Meseroll) S.; m. Neri Alcocer Argáez, Mar. 15, 1986; children: Chester Rolando, Laura Victoria. BA, U. Denver, 1980, JD, 1985. Bar: Colo. 1986, U.S. Dist. Colo. 1987, U.S. Ct. Appeals (10th cir.) 1993. Pvt. practice, Denver, 1986—. Hon. legal counsel Mex. Consulate Gen., Denver, 1987—. Bd. dirs. Justice Info. Ctr., Denver, 1997—, Mexican Cultural Ctr., Denver, 1992-95; elder Presbyn. Ch. U.S.A., Denver, 1986-99; with CAP Aux. USAF, 1971—. Colo. Wing legal officer, 1992-96, nat. legal officer, 1998-2001. Mem. Colo. Bar Assn. (diversity com. 1997—), Denver Bar Assn., Am. Immigration Lawyers Assn. (exec. com. Colo. chpt. 1993-97, pres. 1996-97), Denver Law Club (asst. sec. 1997-98, co-sec. 1998-99, treas. 1999-2000, v.p. 2001-2002, pres. 2002—). Democrat. Avocations: pilot, choral singing, bicycling. Office: 333 W Hampden Ave Ste 703 Englewood CO 80110-2337 E-mail: dnsimmons@uswest.net.

SIMMONS, DEBORAH JO, pharmacy executive; b. Houston, July 31, 1953; d. Joe George Haskovec and Olga Norma (Clifton) Kirkland; m. Dennis Edwin Simmons, Mar. 24, 1979 (div. May 1988). BS, U. Tex., 1975. Registered pharmacist, Tex., Fla. Pharmacy intern Eckerd Drug Co., Dallas County, Tex., 1976, pharmacist, 1976-82, pharmacy area mgr. north Tex. Garland, 1982-86, pharmacy svcs. mgr. north Tex., 1986-90, pharmacy svcs.

mgr. Largo, Fla., 1990-92; dir. pharmacy devel. Eckerd Corp., 1992—. Dir. Eckerd Credit Union, Largo, 1993, 96, 98, vice-chair, 1994-95, 97. Mem. Am. Pharmacy Assn. (adminstrv. practice mem.-at-large 1997-99, chair-elect 2000, chair 2001, nominating com. 1999, 2000, publs. com. 1997-98, awards com. 2000, pharmacy practice com. 2001), Tex. Pharmacy Assn. (pub. affairs com. 1988-91, vice-chair ho. dels. 1990-91, chair 1991-92), Fla. Pharmacy Assn. (orgnl. affairs coun. 1999-2001, profl. affairs coun. 2001--), Dallas County Pharmacy Soc. (pres. 1989-90), Am. Heart Assn. (bd. dirs. Pinellas County, 1999--). Avocations: travel, reading. Office: Eckerd Corp 8333 Bryan Dairy Rd Largo FL 33777-1230 E-mail: dsimm9@cs.com.

SIMMONS, DEBRA LYNN, physician, educator; b. Dallas, Aug. 27, 1954; d. Marvin Gene and Dorothy (Lee) Simmons; m. Robert Edmund Doran Jr., Nov. 26, 1989. BA with high honors, U. Tex., 1976; MS, Cornell U., 1980; MD, U. Tex., Dallas, 1982. Diplomate in internal medicine and endocrinology, diabetes and metabolism Am. Bd. Internal Medicine. Resident in internal medicine Ind. U. Med. Ctr., Indpls., 1982-85; fellow in endocrinology and metabolism U. Calif., San Diego, 1985-88, instr. dept. medicine, 1989-90, asst. clin. prof. medicine, 1991-94; endocrinologist, dir. diabetes edn. program Sharp Rees-Stealy Med. Group, 1988-94; pvt. practice endocrinology, Ft. Worth, 1994-96; asst. prof. medicine U. Ark. for Med. Scis., Little Rock, 1997—, dir. Ark. Diabetes Program, 1998—, dir. tng. program in endocrinology, diabetes and metabolism, 1997—. Med. dir. North Hills Hosp. and Diabetes Edn. Program, Ft. Worth, 1994-96. Mem., vol. Am. Diabetes Assn., San Diego County, 1988-94, Pulaski County, 1998—. Mem. ACP, AMA, Am. Coll. Endocrinology, Am. Diabetes Assn., Am. Assn. Clin. Endocrinolgoy, Assn. Program Dirs. Endocrinology and Metabolism, Phi Beta Kappa. Avocations: hiking, birdwatching. Office: U Ark for Med Sci 4300 W 7th St Little Rock AR 72205-5446

SIMMONS, DEIDRE WARNER, performing company executive; b. Easton, Pa., May 11, 1955; d. Francis Joseph and Irene Carol (Burd) Mooney; m. Robert D. Jacobson, June 27, 1981 (div. Mar. 1989); m. William Richard Simmons, Aug. 18, 1990; children: Caitlin Dawn, Abigail Patricia, Samantha Irene. BA in Music, Montclair State Coll., 1978. Music tchr. Warren Hills Regional Sch., Washington, 1978-80; devel. dir. N.J. Shakespeare Festival, Madison, 1981-83; dir. contbns. Parent Found., Lancaster, Pa., 1983-86; exec. dir. Fulton Opera House, 1986—, capital campaign counsel, 1990-95, dir. theatre advancement, 2000—. Mem. adv. bd. WITF, 2000—. Vice chmn. bd. dirs. Ind. Eye, Lancaster, 1986—89; bd. dirs. Pa. Dutch Conv. and Visitors Bur., The Lancaster Campaign. Mem. Theatre Communications Group, League Hist. Theatres. Avocations: piano, singing. Office: Fulton Opera House 12 N Prince St PO Box 1865 Lancaster PA 17608-1865 E-mail: dsimmons@atthefulton.org.

SIMMONS, DOLORES BROWN, finance officer, accountant; b. Alexandria, La., Mar. 23, 1937; d. Edward Eugene and Anita Marie (Chaudoir) Brown; m. Gordon E. Simmons, July 13, 1956 (dec. Apr. 1982); children: Gordon E. II, Steven E. Student, La. State U., 1954-55, 73-74, La. Coll., 1955-56. Acctg. clk. La. State U., Baton Rouge, 1956-58; real estate assoc. Realty Mart, Syron Real Estate, 1971-73; acct. Tchr.'s Retirement System of La., 1973-76, chief acct., 1976-87, fiscal officer, 1987—. Mem. adv. com. La. Pub. Employees Deferred Compensation Plan, Baton Rouge, 1985—; mem. acctg. adv. com. State Dept. of Civil Svc., Baton Rouge, 1987. Vol. Our Lady of Lake Hosp., Baton Rouge, 1980-81, Tax Preparation for Elderly, Baton Rouge, 1984-85. Named Hon. Citizen of New Orleans, 1977. Mem. Nat. Assn. Govtl. Accts., Govtl. Fin. Officers Assn. Am. (Excellence in Fin. Reporting award 1990-91), Govtl. Fin. Officers La., La. Sch. Bus. Officials, Am. Assn. Individual Investors (steering com. Baton Rouge chpt. 1987-91). Democrat. Roman Catholic. Avocation: bowling. Home: 10343 Ridgely Rd Baton Rouge LA 70809-3223 Office: Tchrs Retirement System La 8401 United Plaza Blvd Baton Rouge LA 70809-7017

SIMMONS, DWAYNE DEANGELO, neuroscience educator; b. Toledo, Oct. 31, 1959; s. Johnnie Clarance Simmons and Carleen Reid; m. D'Nisa Dell Hoover. BS, Pepperdine U., 1980; PhD, Harvard U., 1986. Harvard teaching fellow Harvard U., Cambridge, Mass., 1982-85, Harvard resident tutor, 1983-85; asst. prof. biology Pepperdine U., Malibu, Calif., 1985-90; asst. prof. physiol. scis. UCLA, 1994-95, assoc. prof., 1995-97, assoc. prof. neurobiology, 1997-99; rsch. assoc. prof. Washington U., St. Louis, 1998—; assoc. scientist Ctrl. Inst. for Deaf, 1998—. Guest lectr. L.A. Elem. Schs., 1986; trustee Mission Jour.; participant seminars Harvard U., Mich. State U., Swarthmore Coll., Calif. Inst. Tech., Duke U. Med. Sch., Montpellier Cedex, France; mem. review com. NIH, 1993—, NSF, 1995; mem. postgrad. com. Ford Found., 1995—. Contbr. articles to profl. jours. Sci. Team Leader Lynwood Unified Sch. Dist., 1991—, part-time min. Recipient minority rsch. initiation award NSF, 1987, NSF grant awards, 1988, 91; Soc. Neurosci. travel fellow, 1987; Alfred P. Sloan rsch. fellow, 1990; recipient NIH 1st award, 1992, Christian svc. award Pepperdine U. Alumni, 1993, Rsch. Career Devel. award NIH, 1997. Mem. Pepperdine U. Alumni Bd. (assoc., sec. 1986), Assn. Research in Otolaryngology, Soc. for Neurosci., N.Y. Acad. Scis., Sigma Xi, Sigma Chi, Alpha Chi. Mem. Ch. of Christ. Office: Ctrl Inst Deaf 4560 Clayton Ave Saint Louis MO 63110-1504 E-mail: dsimmons@cid.wustl.edu.

SIMMONS, EARL W. music educator, vocalist; b. Phoenix, Oct. 24, 1965; s. Wilbur N. and Maxine M. Simmons; m. Lori K. Maxwell. Dr. of Musical Arts, U. of Oreg., Eugene, OR, 1994—98; MA and MusB, U. of Calif., Santa Barbara, CA, 1986—89. Tchg. asst. U. of Calif., Santa Barbara, Calif., 1988—89; gen. music tchr., choral dir. Sunriver Prep. Sch., Bend, Oreg., 1992—94; grad. tchg. fellow U. of Oreg., Eugene, 1994—96; voice faculty NW Christian Coll., 1995—96; voice faculty chair Summer Vocal Inst., U. of Calif., Santa Barbara, Calif., 1994—95; asst. prof. of music Grand Canyon U., Phoenix, 1996—99; elem. gen. music tchr., choral dir. Deer Valley Unified Sch. Dist., 2000—. Adjudicator-arizona all-state choir Ariz. Music Educators Assn., Phoenix, 1997, adjudicator-arizona regional solo and ensemble festival, 98; adjudicator and clinician North Ea. Ariz. Regional Choral Festival, Pinetop, Ariz., 1998; adjudicator Nat. Assn. of Teachers of Singing State Auditions, Phoenix, 1996—99. Singer (figaro): (santa barbara chamber orchestra) The Marriage of Figaro; singer: (ottone) (opera performance in goettingen, germany) L'Incoronazione di Poppea; singer: (tenor soloist) (an evening in vienna) Sunriver Music Festival, OR; singer: (ferrando) (university of oregon opera theatre) Cosi fan tutte; singer: (gastone) (eugene opera, or) La Traviata; singer: (gherardo) (eugene opera) Gianni Schicchi; singer: (oregon bach festival chorus) (professional recording) Messiah - Handel; singer: (phoenix bach choir) A Southwest Christmas; singer: (the knight) (premiered at aspen opera theater, co) The Knights Tale. Recipient Winner of Young Artist Competition, Apprentice Divsn., LA Chpt. of Nat. Assn. of Teachers of Singing, 1989, Semi-finalist (top 25), Wash., D.C. Internat. Voice Competition held at The Kennedy Ctr., 1989, 2nd Pl. Winner, Opera Guild of So. Calif. Voice Competition, 1989, 3rd Pl. Winner, Oreg. Chpt. of Nat. Assn. of Teachers of Singing Young Artist Competition, 1995, nominated for creative tchg. in Music, Disney's Am. Teachers Awards, 2002, Outstanding Grad. Student in Voice, Voice Faculty at the U. of Oreg., 1997; fellow Fulbright Fellow, studied opera with Iris Corradetti (La Scala), researched 18th century Italian vocal pedagogy, culminated in dissertation, 1998, William J. Fulbright Commn., 1991-1992; scholar Rotary Scholar, studied German Lied at the Hochschule fur Musik in Hamburg, Germany; lang. at U. of Hamburg and Goethe Inst., Rotary Internat., Evanston, IL, 1989-1990, Britten-Pears Sch. in Eng., studied title role of opera Billy Budd with Ted Uppman who premiered the role under Britten at Covent Garden,1951, Am. Friends of the Aldeborough Festival, NY, 1989. Mem.: Ariz. Music Educators Assn., Music Educators Nat. Conf. Office: Mirage Elementary School 3910 W Grovers Avenue Glendale AZ 85308-3006 E-mail: esimmons@me.dvusd.org.

SIMMONS, EDWIN HOWARD, marine corps officer, historian; b. Paulsboro, N.J., Aug. 25, 1921; s. Edwin Lonsdale and Nettie Emma (Vankirk) S.; m. Frances Bliss, Apr. 25, 1962; children: Edwin Howard, Clarke Vankirk, Bliss, Courtney. BA, Lehigh U., 1942; MA, Ohio State U., 1955; postgrad., Amphibious Warfare Sch., 1949-50, Nat. War Coll., 1966-67. Commd. 2d lt. USMC, 1942, advanced through grades to brig. gen., 1967; asst. prof. NROTC, Ohio State U., 1952-55; with Hdqrs. Marine Corps, 1955- 59; naval attache Dominican Republic, 1959-60; with Hdqrs. Marine Corps and Joint Staff, 1962-65, 3d Marine Div., 1965-66, 1st Marine Div., Vietnam, 1970-71; dep. fiscal dir. Marine Corps, 1967-70; dir. Marine Corps history and museums USMC Hdqrs., Arlington, Va., 1971-95, dir. emeritus, 1996—. Pres. Am. Mil. Inst., 1979; v.p. U.S. Commn. Mil. History, 1979-83; exec. v.p. Marine Corps Hist. Found., 1979-96; pres. Coun. Am. Mil. Past, 1991-95. Author: The United States Marines, 1974, 76, 98, 2002, Marines, 1987, Dog Company Six, 2000, Frozen Chosin, 2002; editor: The Marines, 1998; mng. editor: Marine Corps Gazette, 1946-49; sr. editor: Publs. Group, Marine Corps Schs., 1960-61; Contbr. to numerous books, encys., mags., jours. and annuals. Decorated D.S.M., Silver Star, Legion of Merit with two gold stars, Bronze Star with gold star, Meritorious Service medal, Navy Commendation medal, Purple Heart; knight Nat. Order of Vietnam, Vietnamese Cross of Gallantry with 2 palms and silver star; recipient Centennial Disting. Grad. medallion Ohio State U., 1970 Fellow Co. Mil. Historians; mem. Am. Soc. Mil. Comptrollers (nat. v.p. 1967-69, pres. 1969-70), Nat. War Coll. Alumni Assn. (v.p. 1969-70, 74-75), Phi Beta Kappa, Omicron Delta Kappa, Phi Sigma Kappa. Home: 9020 Charles Augustine Dr Alexandria VA 22308-2822 Office: Marine Corps Historical Ctr Navy Yard 1254 Charles Morris St SE Washington DC 20374-5040 E-mail: ehsimmons@envista.com.

SIMMONS, ELROY, JR. retired utility executive; b. Johnstown, Pa., Sept. 23, 1928; s. Elroy and Hazel Maria (Shomo) S. BS in Bus. Adminstrn., U. Pitts., 1951. With Pa. Electric Co., Johnstown, 1953, system treasury asst., 1969-71, system coordinator, treasury services, 1971-74, asst. treas., 1974-79, sec., treas., 1979-90; ret., 1990. Bd. dirs. Community Arts Ctr. of Cambria County, 1987-95. With CIC, U.S. Army, 1951-53. Mem. Pa. Electric Assn. (customer relations com. 1965-69), Nat. Corp. Cash Mgmt. Assn., Nat. Assn. Accts., Nat. Assn. Corp. Treas. Republican. Methodist. Home: 1023 Hillside Trl Johnstown PA 15905-1234

SIMMONS, EMMY B, federal agency administrator; b. Suring, Ws. m. Roger Simmons. B, U. Wis., Milw.; M Agrl. Econs., Cornell U. Vol. Peace Corps, agrl. rschr. Nigeria, Liberia; agrl. economist USAID, 1978—91, supv. program economist regional office East and So. Africa, 1991—94, sr. program officer mission in Moscow, 1994—97, deputy asst. adminstr., 1997—2002, asst. adminstr. bus. econ. growth, agrl. and trade, 2002—. Office: USAID RRB 1300 Pannsylvanis AVe NW Washington DC 20523-3900*

SIMMONS, GARY M. writer, small business owner; b. Chgo., Dec. 21, 1961; s. Larry Franklin S. and Carol T. Berry. Student, W. Ky. Tech., 1982-83. Respiratory therapist Lourdes, Paducah, Ky., 1982-96; owner Pets Plus, Sympsonia, 1990-91; retail mgr. Dippin' Dots Inc., Paducah, 1991-95; owner Pen, Inc., 1995—; founder A Time of Reflection mag. Spkr. Kingsbury Enterprises, 1994, Bus. Events Internat., Escondido, Calif., 1995-96, Visionary Voices, Mission Viejo, Calif., 1997—; cons., websited designer Debco Software, Paducah, Ky.; screenwriter represented by Shirley Hamilton Agy., Inc., Chgo.; pub. (periodical) A Time of Reflection, Nashville; rep.KMA Record Label, Madison, Tenn. Author: Nature's Impressions, 1995, The Bahamian Inheritance: Under Friendly Fire, 1997, Children's Expressions: A Time of Reflection, 1998; assisted (video, cassette, book) BECOMING (Donna Loesh and Jack Canfield); Internet and radio columnist (advice column) "Mr. Businessman"; screenwriter; country single: Where Does Your Love Park, 1999; sung written songs include Thinking of Us, 1999, Meant to Be, 2000, Memory Lane, 2000, Regrets and Gone Fishin, 2000; appeared on record label KMA. Mem. Am. Rivers (Washington), Poets of the Western Rivers (Paducah, Ky.), Philosophy Round Table (Paducah, Ky.), Club Theatrical Arts (pres. 1981-82). Avocations: piano, swimming, weight lifting, fishing.

SIMMONS, GEOFFREY STUART, physician; b. Camp Gordon, Ga., July 28, 1943; s. Ted R. and Jane A. (Lavander) Simmons; m. Sherry Simmons, Sept. 7, 1985; children: Bradley, Anais. BS, U. Ill., 1965, MD, 1969. Intern U. So. Calif., L.A., 1969-70, resident, 1971-74; pvt. practice Astoria, Oreg., 1974-77, Eugene, 1977—; chmn. internal medicine dept. Peace Health Med. Group, 1996-98, 2000—. Med. corres. KUGN Radio, 1993—95. Author: (book) The Z Papers, 1977, The Adam Experiment, 1978, Pandemic, 1980, Murdock, 1982, The Glue Factory, 1995, To Glue or Not to Glue, 1997; med. commentator KABC Radio, 1970. Mem.: Lane County Med. Soc. (chmn. task force for disaster preparedness 2001—, bd. dirs., chmn. bioterrorism task force 2001—, pres.-elect 2002—). Avocation: writing.

SIMMONS, GEORGE FINLAY, mathematics educator; b. Austin, Tex., Mar. 3, 1925; s. George Finlay and Armede Victoria (Hatcher) S.; m. Hope Bridgeford, Sept. 11, 1954; 1 child, Nancy Bingham. BS, Caltech, 1946; MS, U. Chgo., 1948; PhD, Yale U., 1957. Instr. U. Chgo., 1947-50, U. Maine, Orono, 1950-52, Yale U., New Haven, 1952-56; asst. prof. U. R.I., Kingston, 1956-58, Williams College, Williamstown, Mass., 1958-62; assoc. prof. math. Colo. Coll., Colorado Springs, 1962-65, prof., 1965-90, prof. emeritus, 1990—. Author: Introduction Topology and Modern Analysis, 1962, Differential Equations, 1972, 2d edit., 1991, Precalculus Mathematics in a Nutshell, 1981, Calculus with Analytic Geometry, 1985, 2d edit., 1995, Calculus Gems: Brief Lives and Memorable Mathematics, 1992. Mem. Math. Assn. Am. Avocations: travel, cooking, trout fishing, billiards. Home: 1401 Wood Ave Colorado Springs CO 80907-7348 Office: Colorado College Dept Math Colorado Springs CO 80903

SIMMONS, HARRY DADY, pathologist; b. Chgo., June 10, 1938; s. Harry Dady and Ruth (Finkelberg) S. BS, U. Ill., 1950; PhD in Chemistry, MIT, 1966; MD, SUNY, Bklyn., 1977. Resident Mt. Sinai Med. Ctr., N.Y.C., 1985-87; staff pathologist, clin. asst. prof. Huntington (W.Va.) VA Med. Ctr., Marshall U. Med. Ctr., 1991-93; staff pathologist Timken Mercy Med. Ctr., Canton, Ohio, 1994-95, ProED Comms. Corp., Beachwood, 1996-97, New Hope Alt. Therapy Rsch., Cleve., 1997—. Rsch. fellow Rensselaer Polytech Inst., Troy, N.Y., 1981-85, Montefiore Med. Ctr., Bronx, 1987-91. Mem. AMA, Am. Soc. Clin. Pathologists, Coll. Am. Pathologists.

SIMMONS, HOWARD L. education educator; b. Mobile, Ala. BS in Secondary Edn., Spring Hill Coll., 1960; MAT in Slavic langs. and Lit., Ind. U., 1965; PhD in Design and Mgmt. of Postsecondary Edn., Fla. State U., 1975; LHD (hon.), Sojourner-Douglass Coll., 1995; HHD (hon.), King's Coll., 1998. Assoc. dir., asst. exec. sec. Commn. on Higher Edn. Middle States Assn. of Colls. & Schs., Phila., 1974-95, exec. dir., 1988-95; prof. edn. leadership in higher edn. Ariz. State U., Tempe, 1996-2000, prof. emeritus, 2000—, assoc. dean, 1996-97; prof., coord. higher edn. doctoral program Morgan State U., Balt., 2001—. Vis. lectr. Russian Lafayette Coll., Easton, Pa., 1970—71; part-time Russian/Spanish instr. Clayton (Mo.) High Sch., 1965—67; dean instructional servs. Northampton Community Col. , Bethlehem, Pa., 1969—74; chmn. dept. fgn. language Forest Park Community Col., Mo., 1964—69; sr. researcher Ariz. State Univ., 1986—87, Nat. Ctr. Postsecondary Governance and Finance , 1986—87; cons. in field including cons./evaluator N. Cent. Asn. Cols. and Schs. , 1997—; prin. cons. Global Consults. in Higher Educ.; keynote speaker in field; researcher on accreditation and blacks in higher educ. ; app. Bd. Behavioral Health Examiners State Ariz., 1999; mem. comn. accreditation Coun. Chiropractic Educ., 2000, 05. Contbr. articles to profl. jours. Gov. apptd. mem. Bd. Behavioral Health Examiners. NDEA grantee Spring Hill Coll., 1958-60, grantee Japan-U.S. Friendship Commn., 1993-94; NDEA fellow Ind. U., 1963-64, Edn. Professions Devel. Act fellow Fla. State U., 1973-75, fellow Am. Coun. Edn., 1972-73; USIA Acad. Specialist grantee, Quito, Ecuador, 1996. Mem. Am. Ednl. Rsch. Assn., Am. Assn. for Community and Jr. Colls. (assoc.), Assn. for the Study of Higher Edn., Assn. of Tchrs. of Slavic and East European Langs., Assn. Caribbean Tertiary Instn., Internat. Accreditation Specialist, 1996—, Am. Assn. for Higher Edn. (exec. bd. black caucus, nat. cultural diversity award by caucuses 1992), Lang. Labs. and Faculty Assn. Pres. (dir.), Phi Delta Kappa, Kappa Delta Pi. Home: 218 N Charles St Apt 604 Baltimore MD 21201 Office: Morgan State U Jenkins Hall 325 1700 E Cold Spring Ln Baltimore MD 21251 E-mail: simmons421@aol.com., global.che@verizon.net.

SIMMONS, JAMES GREGG, statistician; b. Newton, Miss., June 6, 1948; s. John Clint and Carrie Amanda (Horton) S. BS in Math., Miss. State U., 1971, MS Psychology, 1972; PhD in Psychology, U. R.I., 1976; AS in Computer Tech., East Ctr. C.C., 1997. Cons. Dept. Justice, Bur. Prisons, Memphis, 1979, Ashland, Ky., 1982; cost estimator Precision Stud Welding, L.A., 1983; transp. planner Miss. Dept. Transp., Jackson, 1984-90; applications programmer/analyst La. Dept. Labor, Baton Rouge, 1999-2000; acclaim sys. cons. to Pa. Dept. Environ. Protection, Harrisburg, 2000—02; programmer, analyst Social Scienrific Systems, Silver Spring, Md., 2002—. U. R.I. tchg. fellow, 1974. Mem. N.Y. Acad. Scis., Miss. Acad. Scis., Libr. Congress Assn., Phi Theta Kappa.

SIMMONS, JANET BRYANT, writer, publisher; b. Oakland, Calif., Apr. 22, 1925; d. Howard Pelton and Janet Horn (McNab) Bryant; m. William Ellis Simmons, May 17, 1944 (div. 1979); children: William Howard, Janet Margaret Simmons McAlpine. BA, San Jose State U., 1965; MA, U. San Francisco, 1979. Social worker Santa Clara County Social Svcs., San Jose, Calif., 1965-91; editor, pub. Enlightenment Press, Santa Clara, 1994—. Author: The Mystical Child, 1996. Mem. AAUW, Am. Booksellers Assn., Pubs. Mktg. Assn., Bay Area Ind. Pubs. Assn., Audubon Soc., Jacques Cousteau Soc. Avocations: playing piano, swimming, Tai Chi, travel, gardening. Office: Enlightenment Press PO Box 3314 Santa Clara CA 95055-3314 E-mail: enlightenmentpress@home.com.

SIMMONS, J.K. See SIMMONS, JONATHAN

SIMMONS, JOHN DEREK, retired financial consultant; b. Essex, Eng., July 17, 1931; came to U.S., 1952; s. Simon Leonard and Eve (Smart) S.; m. Rosalind Wellish, Mar. 5, 1961; children: Peter Lawrence, Sharon Leslie. BS, Columbia U., 1956; MBA, Rutgers U., 1959; postgrad., NYU, 1959-62. Chief cost acct. Airborne Accessories, Hillside, N.J., 1952-57; sr. cost analyst Curtiss-Wright Corp., Wood Ridge, 1957; sr. fin. analyst internat. group Ford Motor Co., Jersey City, 1958-60; rsch. assoc. Nat. Assn. Accts., N.Y.C., 1960-64; asst. to v.p. fin. Air Reduction Co., Inc., 1965-67; mgr. corp. planning Anaconda Wire & Cable Co., N.Y.C., 1968; ind. fin. cons., 1968-71; assoc. cons. Rogers, Slade & Hill, Inc., N.Y.C., 1969-71; v.p., security analyst, economist Moore & Schley, Cameron & Co. (name now Fourteen Rsch. Corp.), 1972-81; v.p., security analyst Merrill Lynch Capital Markets, N.Y.C., 1981-88; security analyst Arnhold and S. Bleichroeder, Inc., 1988-89; v.p., security analyst, corp. fin. specialist Smith Barney, Harris Upham & Co., Inc., 1989-90; sr. cons. Carl Byoir & Assocs., 1991-94; assoc. mng. dir. Commonwealth Assocs., 1994-95; mng. dir. State St. Capital Markets Corp., 1996; v.p. GKN Securities Corp., 1996-97; dir. instnl. sales Gabelli & Co., Rye, N.Y., 1997; assoc. Manning, Selvage & Lee, N.Y.C., 1998-2001; ret., 2001. Lectr. profl. socs. and confs.; lectr. econs., mgmt., polit. sci. Rutgers U., 1957-64. Contbr. articles on econs. of underdeveloped nations, polit. sci., mgmt., fin. to U.S. and fgn. publs. Served to 1st lt. Brit. Army, 1950-52. Granted personal coat of Arms by Queen Elizabeth II: manorial Lord of Ash., Suffolk, Eng. Mem. Knight Templar Sovereign Mil. Order Temple of Jerusalem. Home: 360 E 72d St New York NY 10021-4753

SIMMONS, JON L. music educator; b. Cleve., Oct. 22, 1962; s. James L. and Ruth S. Simmons; m. Amy C. Morgan, June 5, 1968; children: Charlotte, Benjamin. MusM, Longy Sch. of Music, 1995. Cert. K-12 music tchr. Mass. Music tchr. Meford (Mass.) Pub. Schs., 1993—95; dir. of vocal music Peabody (Mass.) Veterans Meml. H.S., 1995—. Recipient Masterworks Concert funding, Mass. Cultural Coun., 2000, 2001. Mem.: Music Educators Nat. Conference, Mass. Music Educators Assn., Am. Choral Dirs. Assn. Avocations: bicycling, cooking. Home: 47 Pioneer Tr Marlborough MA 01752 Office: Peabody Vets Meml HS 485 Lowell St Peabody MA 01961 Personal E-mail: simmons_jon@hotmail.com.

SIMMONS, JONATHAN KIMBLE (J.K. SIMMONS), actor; b. Detroit, Jan. 9, 1955; d. Donald William and Patricia (Kimble) Simmons; m. Michelle Schumacher, 1996. Student, Ohio U., Athens, Ohio State U., Columbus; BMus, U. Montana, Missoula, 1978; student, HB Studios, N.Y.C. Studied acting with Jacqueline Barton; studied voice with Mario Alch, Esther England and John Mount. Actor: (plays) The Fantasticks, 1981, (touring musical) Doonesbury, 1984; (mem. of theatre co.): Seattle Repertory Theatre, 1984—85; actor: (TV films) Popeye Doyle, 1986, (Off-Broadway musical) Birds of Paradise, 1987; (Broadway plays) A Change in the Heir, 1990, (Broadway and touring revival) Peter Pan, 1991—92; (Broadway plays) Guys and Dolls, 1992—95; (featured): (documentaries) Guys and Dolls Off the Record, 1992; actor: (Broadway plays) Laughter on the 23rd Floor, 1993; (films) The Ref, 1994, The Scout, 1994; (plays) Das Barbecu, 1994; (TV series) Homicide: Life on the Street, 1996; (films) The First Wives Club, 1996, Extreme Measures, 1996, Crossing Fields, 1998, The Jackal, 1997; (voice): Anastasia, 1997; actor: (TV films) Face Down, 1997; (TV series) Oz, 1997—; actor, actor: (TV series) Law & Order, 1994; (films) Celebrity, 1998, For Love of the Game, 1999, The Cider House Rules, 1999; (TV series) Law & Order: Special Victims Unit, 2000—; (films) Above Freezing, 2000, The Gift, 2000, Autumn in New York, 2000, Hit and Runaway, 2001, The Mexican, 2001, Spider-Man, 2002.*

SIMMONS, JOY LOUISE, activist; b. Torrington, Wyo., Sept. 9, 1946; d. Jack Mervin and Betty Case Thompson; foster parents William R. and Ruth Martin; m. Richard L. Simmons, Sept. 9, 1971; children: Cheleen L. Simmons-Morgan, Michael L. Grad. H.S., Cheyenne, Wyo. Cocktail waitress, Las Vegas, Nev., 1967-78; casino dealer Laughlin, 1979-85; owner Trifles of Arizona, 1985-92. Author: This of Joy, Celestial Arts, 1975. Activist Civil Rights, Wyo, Colo., Nev., 1962—, Feminist Movement ERA, Comty. Action Against Rape, Nev., 1969—, Worker's Rights, Nev., 1985-87, Silicone, 1991-92, Anti-Nuke; spearheaded class action suit against Dow Chem. for liquid injections of silicone. Mem. ACLU, Common Cause, Halt, Pub. Citizen. Democrat. Home: 3129 Palo Verde Dr Laughlin NV 89029-0118

SIMMONS, KAREN ELAINE, artist; b. Bremerton, Wash., Feb. 2, 1937; d. Arthur William Hardy and Marjorie Jollie; m. George Carroll Simmons, Sept. 4, 1972; children: Kristan Dodge, Kerryn Araiza. BBA, U. Ark., Fayetteville, 1962; BS in Social Sci., U. Ark., 1973. Chief dep., assessor, recorder, clk. County of San Diego, 1974-96. Adv. bd. Regional Urban Info. Sys., San Diego, 1985-96. One-woman shows include The Gathering, 1995, Point Loma Cultural Ctr., 1995, Paige Hardy & Assocs., 1996, Southwestern Coll., 1996, 97, 98, County Libr., 1996, San Diego County Adminstrn. Ctr., 1997, San Diego City Info. Ctr., 1998, Little Italy Assn., 1998, Sony Artwalk, 1998, 99, 2000, Galeria Del Centro Cultural De La Raza, 1998. Bd. dirs. City Hosp., Siloam Springs, Ark., 1960-71. Recipient Achievement awards Nat. Assn. Counties, 1980-96; grantee Campbell Soup Co., Inc., 1960, First Nat. Bank, Dale Carnagie & Assocs., 1962, Am. Banker's Assn., 1964-65, U.S. Law Enforcement Adminstrn., 1973; scholar Whitman Coll., 1955, Outstanding Freshman scholar U. Ark., 1956, Baldwin Piano Co. scholar, 1957-58, Urrutia Green scholar, 1997. Mem. Nat. Assn. Fine Artists, San Diego Mus. Art, Nat. Mus. Women in the Arts, The Athenaeum. Avocations: travel, skiing, scuba diving, horses, dogs.

SIMMONS, LORNA WOMACK, elementary school educator, educator; b. Enid, Okla., Dec. 25, 1954; d. Doyle Alex and Ruth Phyllis (Wiens) Nunneley; m. Daniel Bruce Womack, June 7, 1975 (widowed Jan. 1981); children: Zachary Womack, Travis Womack, Shawn Simmons, Shayla Simmons; m. H. Lynn Simmons, Feb. 14, 1982. BS cum laude, U. Tex., 1977. Spl. edn. tchr. Sand Springs (Okla.) I.S.D., 1977-78; pvt. therapist Alphabetic Phonics, Big Spring, Tex., 1981-87; dyslexia cons. Big Spring (Tex.) I.S.D., 1987-88; chpt. I tchr. Forsan I.S.D., Big Spring, Tex., 1988-91; cons. Classroom Phonics, 1991—. Author: Classroom Phonics, 1989, Classroom Phonics II, 1991, Classroom Phonics Spelling, 1991, Classroom Phonics Kid Cards, 1994, Classroom Phonics Comprehension Tests, 1994, Saxon Phonics K, 1996, Saxon Phonics 1, 1996, Saxon Phonics 2, 1996, Saxon Homestudy Phonics K, 1998, Saxon Homestudy Phonics 1, 1998, Saxon Homestudy Phonics 2, 1998, Saxon Phonics Intervention, 2000. Mem. Internat. Reading Assn., Assn. Tex. Profl. Educators. Republican. Mem. Ch. of God. Home: 15650 CR BB Childress TX 79201

SIMMONS, MARGUERITE SAFFOLD, pharmaceutical sales professional; b. Montgomery, Ala., Oct. 21, 1954; d. Arthur Edward and Gwendolyn Jane (Saffold) S. BS in Communications, U. Tenn., 1976. Press sec. Mt. Mayor's Office, Nashville, 1977-78; advt. copywriter United Meth. Pub. House, 1976-77; sales rep. No Nonsense Pantyhose, Houston, 1978-81, Breon Labs., Houston, 1981-82; profl. sales rep. Janssen Pharmaceutica, Inc., 1982-88, sr. sales rep., 1988-97; territory sales mgr. Bristol-Myers Squibb Co., 1997-2001, sr. territory bus. mgr., 2001—, longterm cae specialty rep., 2002—. Vol. Dem. Nat. Conv., Atlanta, 1988. Named to Outstanding Young Women in Am., 1981, 87. Mem. NAFE, U. Tenn. Alumni Assn. (bd. dirs.

Atlanta chpt. 1989-90, v.p. 2000—), U. Tenn. Black Alumni Assn. (bd. dirs. Atlanta chpt. 1989—, pres. Atlanta chpt. 1995-96, bd. govs. dist. 5 rep. 1995-2000), Ga. Trust Hist. Soc., Ala. Geneal. Soc., Ga. Geneal. Soc., Nat. Trust Hist. Preservation, Delta Sigma Theta. Baptist. Avocations: reading, genealogical research, personal computing.

SIMMONS, MARK, state representative; m. Joni Simmons; children: Lindy, Holly. With Boise Cascade, Oreg.; mem. Oreg. Ho. of Reps., 1997—, House Majority Whip, 1999, House Majority Leader, 1999, speaker, 2002—. Republican. Office: Speaker of the House 900 Court St NE Rm 269 Salem OR 97301*

SIMMONS, MARSHA THRIFT, science and reading educator, musician; b. Brunswick, Ga., Jan. 18, 1953; d. James Russell II and Ouida (Tyre) Thrift; m. Samuel Leland Simmons, Aug. 2, 1975; 1 child, Natalie Renee. BA, Agnes Scott Coll., 1975; MEd, Coll. of Charleston, 1980; postgrad., Regent U., 1998—. Cert. tchr., Tenn., postgrad. profl. lic., Va. Organist Epworth United Meth. Ch., Atlanta, 1975-76; tchr. 3d grade Hanahan (S.C.) Acad., 1976-77; grad. asst. Coll. of Charleston, S.C., 1977-78, sub. tchr. Early Childhood Devel. Ctr., 1978-79; owner, tchr. Marsha's Music (Studio and Store), S.C., Ga., Tex., Tenn., Va., 1979—; tchr. presch. Sykes Daycare, Lawrenceville, Ga., 1994; sub. tchr. Glynn County Schs., Brunswick, 1994; tchr. 6th grade sci. and reading Jackson (Tenn.)-Madison County Schs., 1995-97; sub. tchr. Virginia Beach (Va.) City Pub. Schs., 1997—. Treas. Kingwood (Tex.) Music Tchrs. Assn., 1985-87; mem. local sch. adv. com. Gwinnett County Bd. Edn., Lawrenceville, Ga., 1993-94; Odyssey of the Mind coord., coach N.E. Mid. Sch., Jackson, 1995-97; lead tchr. sci. stds. implementation Jackson-Madison County Schs., 1996-97. Leader Girl Scouts Am., St. Simons Island, Ga., 1988-89; PTA v.p. and cultural arts chmn. Benefield Elem. Sch., Lawrenceville, 1991-93; chmn. cmty. outreach West Tenn. Music Tchr.'s Assn., Jackson, 1996-97. Recipient Spl. Svc. award Girl Scouts Am., 1989, Outstanding Woman in Bus. and Edn. award Parker Chapel Christian Meth. Episcopal Ch., Tenn., 1996, Lockheed Martin fellow Lockheed Martin Corp., 1997. Mem. ACA, Am. Guild Organists, Music Tchrs. Nat. Assn., Am. Assn. of Christian Counselors. Avocations: reading, cooking, sewing, crafts, drawing, painting. Home: 313 Chase Arbor Ct Virginia Beach VA 23462-7407

SIMMONS, MARVIN GENE, geophysics educator; b. Dallas, May 15, 1929; s. Burt H. and Mable (Marshall) S.; m. Dorothy Richter; children by previous marriage: Jon Eric, Debra Lynn, Sandra Kay, Pamela Jean. BS, Tex. Agrl. and Mech. Coll., 1949; MS, So. Methodist U., 1958; PhD, Harvard U., 1962. Registered profl. geologist, NH. Petroleum engr. Humble Oil Co., 1949-51; propr. gravel business, 1953-58; asst. prof. So. Meth. U., 1962-65; prof. geophysics MIT, 1965-89, prof. emeritus, 1989—; prin. Hager-Richter Geoscience Inc., 1989—. Cons. NASA, 1965-72; chief scientist NASA (Manned Spacecraft Center), Houston, 1969-71; cons. on siting of nuclear facilities; sec. Internat. Heat Flow Com., 1967-71; chmn. com. drilling for sci. purposes Nat. Acad. Scis., 1965; Mem. geophysics panel NSF. Served with USAF, 1951-53. NSF postdoctoral fellow, 1961-62 Fellow Geol. Soc. Am., Am. Geophys. Union; mem. ASTM (com. C-18 on dimension stone 1986—), Boston Geol. Soc. (pres. 1967-68), Soc. Exploration Geophysicists, Sigma Xi, Tau Beta Pi. Achievements include research on physical properties of materials, lunar exploration, marine geophysics, temperature of earth, regional geophysics, engineering geology and geophysics. Home: 180 N Policy St Salem NH 03079-1916 Office: 8 Industrial Way Unit D10 Salem NH 03079-2837

SIMMONS, MOLLIE LAWANNA, association administrator, computer system manager; b. Atlanta, Dec. 11, 1962; d. John Edward and Joy (Suddath) S. Student, Oglethorpe U., 1980-82, Clayton State U., 1984-90. Payroll mgr. Delta Life Ins. Co., Atlanta, 1982-83; CFO Pinkerton's, 1983-84; acctg. mgr. Northside Airport Express/Travel, 1984-87; controller, office mgr. O'Kon & Co. Structural Engrs., 1987-90; dir. acctg. Ga. Tech. Athletic Assn., 1990—. Active Walk Am. AIDS Fundraising, Atlanta, 1990—. Mem. Am. Payroll Assn. Republican. Methodist. Avocations: piano, remodeling, softball. Home: 3440 Rugby Cir College Park GA 30337-1630 Office: Ga Tech Athletic Assn 150 Bobby Dodd Way NW Atlanta GA 30313-2551

SIMMONS, NAOMI CHARLOTTE, poet; b. Amarillo, Tex., Aug. 28, 1923; d. Thomas Elmer and Louise Irene (Babek) Stroud; m. Malcolm J. Simmons, Apr. 6, 1943; children: Judy Ann, Katherine Lee, Mary Martha, Michael Leo, Barbara Dell. AS, Amarillo (Tex.) Coll., 1942. Sec. Drs. Puckett-Puckett, Amarillo, 1940-42, Pamtex Ordinance Pl., Amarillo, 1942-43. Author: (poetry books) It's About Time, 1992, Lite Verse for Express Lane, 1992, Hooks, Lines and River Rhymes, 1994, I Will Miss You Gently, 1997. Docent Amon Carter Mus., Ft. Worth, 1975-2001; vol. Food Bank of Greater Tarrant County, Ft. Worth, 1985-94; vol. musician James L. West Presbyn., Ft. worth, 1990-94; pres. Women of All Saints, Ft. Worth, 1964-66. Recipient Svc. award Amon Carter Mus., 1975-2001, Ann. Poetry award Nat. Fedn. State Poetry Socs., 1995-2002. Mem. Poetry Soc. Tex. (dir. and program dir. 1991-2002, libr. 1991-2000, Promoting Poetry in Schs. award 1991, Ann. Poetry awards 1988, 91-92, 95-97, 1999-2001), Poets of Tarrant County (pres., mem. programs com. 1988-92), Ft. Worth Poetry Soc. (v.p. 2001, pres. 2002), Composers, Authors and Artists of Am. Avocations: music, art. Home: 3721 Lenox Dr Fort Worth TX 76107-1711

SIMMONS, OTTO DEBRUHL, III, microbiologist, researcher; b. New Bern, N.C., Dec. 23, 1967; s. Otto DeBruhl Simmons, Jr. and Brenda Register Simmons. BA, U. N.C., 1990, MSPH, 1995, PhD, 2001. Environ. lab. rsch. technician U. N.C., Chapel Hill, 1989—92, grad. rsch. asst., 1993—2001, rsch. asst., 2001—; environ. lab. intern Weyerhauser Co., New Bern, 1992—93. Contbr. chapters to books. Mem.: Am. Water Works Assn., Am. Soc. for Microbiology, Sigma Xi, Delta Omega. Avocations: sports, fishing, basketball. Home: 108 Locust Ct. Chapel Hill NC 27516 Office: University of North Carolina-Chapel Hill Rosenau Hall, CB# 7400 Chapel Hill NC 27599-7400 Business E-Mail: osimmons@email.unc.edu.

SIMMONS, PETER, law and urban planning educator; b. N.Y.C., July 19, 1931; s. Michael L. and Mary A. S.; m. Ruth J. Tanfield, Jan. 28, 1951; children: Sam, Lizzard. AB, U. Calif., Berkeley, 1953, LL.B., 1956; postgrad. (Alvord fellow), U. Wis., 1956-58. Prof. SUNY, Buffalo, 1963-67; mem. faculty Ohio State U., 1967-75, U. Ill., 1972, Case Western Res. U., 1974-75; prof. law and urban planning Rutgers U. Coll. Law, Newark, 1975—, dean, 1975-93; university prof. Rutgers U., 1993—. Contbr. articles to profl. jours. Mem. Ohio Housing Commn., 1972-74; commr. Ohio Reclamation Rev. Bd., 1974-75; chmn. N.J. Criminal Disposition Commn., 1983-84; mem. N.J. Law Revision Commn., 1987—. Mem. Am. Planning Assn., Urban Land Inst., Am. Law Inst., AAUP (nat. council 1973-75). Office: Rutgers U Law Sch 15 Washington St Newark NJ 07102-3192 E-mail: psimmons@andromeda.rutgers.edu.

SIMMONS, PETER LAWRENCE, lawyer; b. N.Y.C., May 1, 1965; s. John Derek and Rosalind (Wellish) S. AB magna cum laude, Columbia U., 1985, JD, 1987. Bar: N.Y. 1987, U.S. Dist. Ct. (so. and ea. dists.) N.Y. 1988, U.S. Ct. Internat. Trade 1991, U.S. Spreme Ct. 1991, U.S. Ct. Appeals (2d cir.) 1992, U.S. Ct. Appeals (1st cir.) 1993. Law clk. to Hon. Lawrence W. Pierce U.S. Ct. Appeals (2d cir.), N.Y.C., 1987-88; assoc. Fried, Frank, Harris, Shriver & Jacobson, 1988-94, ptnr., 1994—. Treas., sr. editor Columbia Law Rev., 1985-87. Harlan Fiske Stone scholar, 1985-87. Mem.: ABA, Assn. Bar City NY (profl. responsibility com. 1998—2001, civil rights com. 1989—92), NY Bar Assn., Fed. Bar Coun., Phi Beta Kappa. Home: 91 West Rd Short Hills NJ 07078 Office: Fried Frank Harris Shriver & Jacobson 1 New York Plz Fl 22 New York NY 10004-1980 E-mail: peter.simmons@ffhsj.com.

SIMMONS, RAYMOND HEDELIUS, lawyer; b. Salinas, Calif., May 27, 1958; s. Raymond Hedelius and Antoinette (Lynch) S. BA magna cum laude, U. Calif., San Diego, 1979; JD magna cum laude, U. Calif., San Francisco, 1982. Bar: Calif. 1982, U.S. Dist. Ct. (no. dist.) Calif. 1982, Ga. 1987. Assoc. Farella, Braun & Martel, San Francisco, 1982-85; atty., v.p. Barnett-Range Corp., Atlanta, 1985-86; counsel Nationwide Capital Corp. subs. HomeFed. Bank, 1986, HomeFed. Bank, San Diego, 1987-90; gen. counsel, sr. v.p., sec. ITT Fed. Bank, San Francisco, 1990-95; also ITT Residential Capital Corp., ITT Residential Capital Servicing Corp.; pvt. practice, Newport Beach, Calif., 1995—. Mem.: ABA, Calif. Bar Assn., Calif. Scholarship Fedn. (life), Thurston Soc., Order of Coif. E-mail: rsimmons@simmonslawoffices.com.

SIMMONS, RICHARD DE LACEY, mass media executive; b. Cambridge, Mass., Dec. 30, 1934; s. Ernest J. and Winifred (McNamara) S.; m. Mary DeWitt Bleecker, May 20, 1961; children: Christopher DeWitt, Robin Bleecker Turner. Grad., 1951; AB, Harvard Coll., 1955; LLB, Columbia U., 1958. Bar: N.Y. 1959. V.p., gen. counsel Dun & Bradstreet Corp., N.Y.C., 1969-73, exec. v.p., 1976-79, vice chmn., 1979-81; pres. Moody's Investors Svc. , 1973-75, Dun & Bradstreet, Inc., N.Y.C., 1975; pres., chief oper. officer Washington Post Co., Washington, 1981-91; pres. Internat. Herald Tribune, Paris, 1989-96. Bd. dirs. Washington Post Co.; mem. equity adv. bd., dir. The Directorship Group. Mem., dir. coun. White Burkett Miller Ctr. Pub. Affairs, U. Va. Office: 105 N Washington St Ste 202 Alexandria VA 22314-3022

SIMMONS, RICHARD L. surgeon; b. Boston, Feb. 23, 1934; s. Nathanial J. and Anne Dorothy (Levenson) S.; widowed (Feb. 1993); children: Nicole, Janine. AB in Biochem. Scis. magna cum laude, Harvard U., 1955; MD summa cum laude, Boston U., 1959. Diplomate Am. Bd. Surgery. Intern, resident in surgery Columbia Presbyn. Med. Ctr., N.Y.C., 1959-66; clin. and rsch. fellow Mass. Gen. Hosp., Boston, 1965; rsch. fellow in surgery Harvard Med. Sch., 1965; instr. surgery Columbia U. Coll. P&S, N.Y.C., 1965-68; from asst. prof. to assoc. prof. surgery U. Minn., Mpls., 1968-72, prof. surgery and microbiology, 1972-87; George V. Foster prof. surgery U. Pitts., 1987—; chmn. dept. surgery U. Pitts. Med. Ctr., 1987-98; assoc. dean for clin. affairs Sch. Medicine U. Pitts., 1989-92, prof. molecular genetics and biochemistry, 1992—; med. dir. U. Pitts. Med. Ctr., 1996—. Chief of surgery Presbyn.-Univ. Hosp., Pitts., 1987—; staff Children's Hosp. of Pitts.; cons. staff VA Med. Ctr. Author/co-author 11 books; contbr. more than 1200 articles to profl. jours. Recipient Disting. Svc. Prof. Surgery, 1994, other awards and grants. Mem. AMA, AAAS, ACS (pres. Southwestern Pa. chpt. 1992), NAS Inst. Medicine, Am. Soc. for Microbiology, Am. Soc. Transplant Physicians (pres. 1980-81), Am. Assn. Immunologists, Am. Assn. Pathologists, Am. Surg. Assn. (chmn. program com. 1990), Assn. for Acad. Surgery, Ctrl. Surg. Assn., Cell Transplant Soc., Halsted Soc., Infectious Diseases Soc. Am., Midwest Surg. Soc. (hon.), Reticuloendothelial Soc., Soc. for Leukocyte Biology, Soc. for Microbiology, Soc. Clin. Oncologists, Surg. Infection Soc. (pres. 1988), Soc. Surg. Chmn., Soc. Univ. Surgeons (exec. coun. 1973-81, pres. 1977-78), Allegheny County Med. Soc., Transplantation Soc. (councillor 1974-80), others. Office: U Pitts Sch Medicine 497 Scaife Hall Pittsburgh PA 15219

SIMMONS, ROBERT BURNS, history and political science educator; b. Gadsden, Ala., Dec. 27, 1937; s. Burns Hunter and Grace Barbara (Armstrong) S.; m. Eleanor Conner, Nov. 11, 1959 (dec.); children: Kathleen D., Mary Ellen. BS in Chemistry, U. Ala., 1961; BA in Biology and History, Athens State Coll., 1968, MA in Tchg., 1969; EdS (Coll. Scholar, PhD, George Peabody Coll., 1976; MAS, U. Ala., 1978. Quality control chem. lab. supr. Goodyear Tire & Rubber Co., Gadsen, 1961-65; sect. leader, R&D chem. labs. Thiokel Chem. Corp., Redstone Arsenal, Huntsville, Ala., 1966-69; prof. history, polit. sci. and mgmt. John C. Calhoun State C.C., Decatur, 1969—. Adj. prof. Athes (Ala.) State Coll., 1988—, asst. coord. instnl. devel. grant, 1983-84; asst. acad. dean Vol. State C.C., Gallatin, Tenn., 1974; cons. Ala. govs. office, 1987; attended Internat. Rels. Conf. U.S. State Dept., 1989; program presenter Conf. Tchg. Excellence, U. Tex., 1991, found. grant award; presenter Ala. Geog. Assn., 1998, 99; del. Ala. Edn. Assn. Post Secondary Com. Conf., 1990-98, Ala. Edn. Assn. Del. Assembly, 1997-98. Author: texts on world regional geography and on western civilization. Chmn. coms. Decatur Band Boosters; program com. coord. Congressman James Martin of Ala.; mem. acad. affairs com. Commn. on Instnl. Self Study, chmn. Instnl. Effectiveness, Exec. Com. on Articulation Post Secondary Insts. Ala., Calhoun's Instnl. Effectiveness Com., 1998-2000; chmn. Post Secondary Social Sci. Articulation Com., 1996-99, Faculty Senate, 1989-2000, chmn. faculty senate, 1999-2000. Woodrow Wilson fellow Athens State Coll., 1968; E. U.S. Office Edn. grantee, 1970-71, grantee, 1985—, Master Tchr. award NISOD U. Tex., 1990. Mem. Am. Hist. Assn., So. Hist. Assn., Ala. Hist. Assn. (mem. post secondary polit. action com. 1990—), Ala. Coll. Assn. (history chmn. 1990-93, coord. 1990-95, mem. curriculum com. 1993-95, instnl. effectiveness 1993-94, mem. Calhoun pres. cabinet 1994—), C.C. Humanity Assn., Am. Assn. Higher Edn., Am. Chem. Soc., Archaeol. Inst. Am., Burningtree Country Club, Decatur C. of C., Beta Beta Beta, Phi Delta Kappa. Achievements include patent for missile propellants. Home: PO Box 2328 Decatur AL 35602-2328 Office: Calhoun C C PO Box 2216 Bldg Decatur AL 35609-2216

SIMMONS, ROBERT RUHL, Congressman; b. N.Y.C., Feb. 11, 1943; s. Charles Herbert Jr. and Roxane Page (Ruhl) S.; m. Edith Heidi Paffard, June 22, 1974; children: Jane Adams, Robert Waldo Ruhl. BA, Haverford Coll., 1965; MPA, Harvard U., 1979. Ops. officer CIA, Washington, 1969-79; legis. asst. U.S. Senator John H. Chafee, 1979-81; staff dir. intelligence com. U.S. Senate, 1981-85; vis. lectr. Yale U., New Haven, 1985-95; mem. Conn. Gen. Assembly, Hartford, 1991—2001; mem. 107th session 107th Congress from Conn. 2nd Dist., Washington, 2001—. Contbr. articles to profl. jours. Mem. Republican Nat. Com. Col. USAR, 1970-99. Decorated Bronze Star with 1 oak leaf cluster, Meritorious Svc. medal, Army Commendation medal with 1 oak leaf cluster, Vietnam Svc. medal with four campaign stars, Nat. Def. medal, Army Res. Achievement medal, Vietnam Civilian Svc. medal. Episcopalian. Avocations: Chinese art, forestry. Home: 268 N Main St Stonington CT 06378-2910 Office: 511 Cannon House Office Bld Washington DC 20515 also: 2 Courthouse Square, 5th Floor Norwich CT 06360

SIMMONS, ROGER CRAIG, lawyer, writer; b. Fort Lauderdale, Fla., Nov. 21, 1952; s. John Luther Simmons, Jr. and Iris Simmons; m. Ilene Gail Shaine; children: Brittany Berkowitz, Jordan Berkowitz, Sean; m. Barbara Joan Flanagan (div. May 29, 1983); children: Matthew, Michael. AA, Broward C.C., 1972; BA, U. of Fla., 1974; JD, St. Thomas U., 1993. Assoc. Hoffman, Larin, Agnetti & Karas, Miami, Fla., 1999—2002, Neale, de Almeida & Snowden, Fort Lauderdale, 2002—. Author: (novels) ReUnion, 2001. Republican. Avocation: coaching soccer and football. Office: Neale, de Almeida & Snowden 221 West Oakland Park Boulevard Fort Lauderdale FL 33311 Fax: 954-565-3556. Personal E-mail: rcsesq@excelonline.com.

SIMMONS, ROGER K. environmental services administrator; b. Weatherford, Tex., Nov. 25, 1953; s. Bernard W. and Betty Jean Simmons; m. Beverly G. Nelms, May 22, 1987; children: Angele, Alexandria, Ashley. DD(hon.) , Christ Eternity Fellowship Intl. Cert. energy mgr. Environ. protection specialist Red River Army Depot, Texartkana, Tex., 1972—. Author poems. Mem.: Assn. Energy Engrs. Home: 122 Akins Rd Texarkana TX 75501 Office: Red River Army Depot AMSTA-RR-OL Bldg 421 N Texarkana TX 75507-5000

SIMMONS, RULON ANDRUS, internist; b. Idaho Falls, Idaho, Sept. 1, 1939; s. Rulon Lee and Sarah Jane (Andrus) S.; m. Helen Elaine Niederhauser, Aug. 16, 1963; children: David Rulon, Lori Ann Simmons Conder. AS, Ricks Coll., 1959; BS, U. Utah, 1963, MD, 1968. Diplomate Nat. Bd. Med. Examiners, Am. Bd. Internal Medicine. Intern Latter-Day St. Hosp., Salt Lake City, 1968-69, resident in gen. surgery, 1971-72, resident in internal medicine, 1972-75; internal medicine specialist Internal Medicine Assocs., 1975-89, Bryner Clinic, Salt Lake City, 1989—. Asst. clin. instr. U. Utah Med. Sch., Salt Lake City, 1975-85, asst. prof. clin.medicine, assoc. prof. clin. medicine, 1997—. Mem. Salt Lake City/County Bd. of Health, 1980-90. Capt. U.S. Army, 1969-71, Vietnam. Decorated Bronze star. Mem. AMA, ACP, Am. Soc. Internal Medicine, Utah Med. Assn. (alt. del.), Salt Lake County Med. Soc. Republican. Mem. Lds Ch. Avocations: piano, organ, golf, old movies, traveling. Office: IHC-Bryner 745 East 3d South Salt Lake City UT 84102

SIMMONS, RUTH J. academic administrator; b. Grapeland, Tex., July 3, 1945; 2 children. Student, Universidad Internacional, Saltillo, Mex., 1965, Wellesley Coll., 1965-66; BA, Dillard U., 1967; postgrad., Universite de Lyon, 1967-68, George Washington U., 1968-69; AM, Harvard U., 1970, PhD in Romance Langs., 1973; LLD (hon.), Amherst Coll., 1995; LHD (hon.), Howard U., 1996, Dillard U., 1996; LLD (hon.), Princeton U., 1996, Lake Forest Coll., 1997; LHD (hon.), U. Mass., 1997; LLD (hon.), Dartmouth Coll., 1997. Interpreter lang. svcs. divsn. U.S. Dept. State, Washington, 1968-69; instr. French George Washington U., 1968-69; admissions officer Radcliffe Coll., 1970-72; asst. prof. French U. New Orleans, 1973-75, asst. dean coll. liberal arts, asst. prof. French, 1975-76; adminstrv. coord. NEH liberal studies project Calif. State U., Northridge, 1977-78, acting dir. internat. programs, vis. assoc. prof. Pan-African studies, 1978-79; asst. dean grad. sch. U. So. Calif., 1979-82, assoc. dean grad. sch., 1982-83; dir. studies Butler Coll. Princeton (N.J.) U., 1983-85, acting. dir. Afro-Am. studies, 1985-87, asst. dean faculty, 1986-87, assoc. dean faculty, 1986-90, vice provost, 1992-95; provost Spelman Coll., 1990-91; pres. Smith Coll., Northampton, Mass., 1995-2001; pres Brown Univ., Providence, 2001—. Peer reviewer higher edn. divsn. NEH, 1980-83, bd. cons., 1981; mem. grad. adv. bd. Calif. Student Aid Commn., 1981-83; chair com. to visit dept. African-Am. studies Harvard U., 1991—; mem. strategic planning task force N.J. Dept. Higher Edn., 1992-93; mem. nat. adv. commn. EQUITY 2000, Coll. Bd., 1992-95; mem. adv. bd. ctrl. N.J. NAACP Legal Def. Fund, 1992-95; mem. Mid. States Assn. Accreditation Team, Johns Hopkins U., 1993, chmn. accreditation team, Bryn Mawr Coll., 1999; chair rev. panel for model instns. planning grants NSF, 1993; mem. Conf. Bd., 1995—; bd. dirs. MetLife, JSTOR, Pfizer Inc., COFHE; bd. dirs. Com. for Econ. Devel., 1996—; mem. adv. coun. dept. Romance Langs. and Lit., Princeton U., 1996—. Mem. editl. bd. World Edn. series Am. Assn. Collegiate Registrars and Admissions Officers, 1984-86; contbr. articles to profl. jours.; presenter, speaker and panelist in field. Mem. adv. bd. N.J. Master Faculty program Woodrow Wilson Nat. Fellowship Found., 1987-90, bd. trustees, 1991-96; trustee Inst. for Advanced Study, 1995-98, The Clarke Sch. for the Deaf, 1995—; chmn. bd. trustees Acad. Music, 1995-98; mem. adv. com. Healthy Steps for Young Children Program, 1996-98; mem. bd. advisors 1st Internat. Conf. on AIDS, Ethiopia, 1998—. KYOK scholar, 1963; Worthing Found. scholar, 1963-67; Danforth fellow, 1967-73; Fulbright scholar U. de Lyon, 1967-68; Sr. Fulbright fellow, 1981; recipient Disting. Svc. award Assn. Black Princeton Alumni, 1989, Dillard U., 1992, Pres.'s Recognition award Bloomfield Coll., 1993, TWIN award Princeton Area YWCA, 1993, Women's Orgn. Tribute award Princeton U., 1994, Leadership award Third World Ctr. Princeton U., 1995, Tex. Excellence award Leap Program, 1995, Benjamin E. Mays award A Better Chance, 1995, Achievement award Nat. Urban League, 1998, Centennial medal Harvard U. Grad Sch. Arts & Scis., 1997; named Woman of the Year CBS, 1996, Glamour Mag., 1996, Fin. Women's Assn., N.Y., 1997, NBC Nightly News Most Inspiring Woman, 1996, NASA Woman of World, 1998, named Disting. Fulbright Alumna, Inst. Internat. Edn., 1997. Fellow Am. Acad. Arts & Scis.; mem. AAAS, Am. Philos. Soc. Office: Office of the President Brown University 1 Prospect Street, Campus Box 1860 Providence RI 02912 Mailing: Brown University President's Office Box 1860 Providence RI 02912-1860*

SIMMONS, SCOTT MARTIN, information specialist; b. Albany, N.Y., Aug. 21, 1957; s. William Everett and Dorothy (McQueen) S.; m. Angela Koschelew, Feb. 14, 1985; children: Alexandra, Elizabeth. BS in Biology, U. Calif., Davis, 1978; MS in Zoology, U. Nev., 1981; MBA in Mgmt., So. Ill. U., 1985. Database adminstr. SAIC, O'Fallon, Ill., 1986-89; prin. cons. Sybase, Phoenix, 1989-95; prin. engr. Illustra, Denver, 1995; worldwide specialist Informix, 1996-98; prin. arch. Vitria, 1998-2000; dir. tech. solutions Extricity/Peregrine, 2000—02; bus. integration arch. IBM, 2002—. Grad. tchg. asst. U. Nev., Reno, 1979-81; presenter numerous speeches. Contbr. articles to profl. jours. Vol. EMT, Reno, 1979-81. Sgt. USAF, 1982-86. Mem. St. Louis Oracle Users Group (founder, pres. 1987-89), Beta Gamma Sigma. Avocations: guitar, skiing, hiking. E-mail: scottsim@starband.net.

SIMMONS, SHERWIN PALMER, lawyer; b. Bowling Green, Ky., Jan. 19, 1931; AB, Columbia U., 1952, LLB, 1954, JD, 1969. Bar: Tenn. 1954, Fla. 1957. Assoc. Fowler, White, Collins, Gillen, Humkey & Trenam, Tampa, Fla., 1956-60, ptnr., 1960-70, Trenam, Simmons, Kemker, Scharf & Barkin, Tampa, 1970-77; stockholder, pres. Trenam, Simmons, Kemker, Scharf, Barkin, Frye & O'Neill, PA, 1977-94; ptnr., chair tax group Steel Hector & Davis, LLP, Miami, Fla., 1994—. Atty. adv. U.S. Tax Ct., Washington, 1954-56, mem. nominating commn., 1978-81; mem. adv. group Commr. of IRS, 1978-79, 89-90, U.S. Dept. Justice, 1979-80; adj. prof. U. Miami, 1995—. Author: Federal Taxation of Life Insurance, 1966; bd. of advisors mag. The Tax Times, 1986-87; contbr. articles to legal jours. Trustee Hillsborough County Soc. Crippled Children & Adults, 1956-65, pres., 1960-61; treas., chmn. Hillsborough County Pub. Edn. Study Commn., 1965-66; mem. adv. bd. Salvation Army, 1959-62, 64-66, sec., 1960-61; chmn., bd. dirs. The Fla. Orch., 1987-89; founding trustee, pres. Am. Tax Policy Inst., 1996-99; trustee Tampa Bay Performing Arts Ctr., Inc., 1984-93, program adv. com., 1985-89, investment com., 1986-91. Fellow Am. Coll. Trust and Estate Counsel (bd. regents 1982-88), Am. Bar Found. (fellow 1969—, devel. com. 1992-94), Am. Coll. Tax Counsel (regent 1987-93, vice chmn. 1989-91, chmn. 1991-93); mem. ABA (vice chmn. adminstrn. taxation sect. 1972-75, chmn. 1975-76, ho. of dels. 1985-90, bd. govs. 1990-93, chmn. bd. govs. fin. com. 1992-93, chmn. commn. on multidisciplinary practice 1998-2000), Am. Bar Retirement Assn. (bd. dirs. 1984-90, v.p. 1987-88, pres. 1988-89), Am. Law Network ABA-Am. Law Inst. (com. continuing profl. edn. 1973—), FBA, Fla. Bar Assn. (chmn. taxation sect. 1964-65), Am. Judicature Soc., So. Fed. Tax Inst. (trustee, pres. 1974, chmn. 1975 trustee emeritus 1999—), Internat. Acad. Estate and Trust Law, Internat. Fiscal Assn., Am. Law Inst. (mem. coun. 1985—, exec. com. 1994-97, 99—, mem. com. 1997—, chmn. 1999—). Office: 200 S Biscayne Blvd Ste 4100 Miami FL 33131-2362 Personal E-mail: spshome@msn.com. Business E-Mail: spstax@steelhector.com.

SIMMONS, STEPHEN GREGORY, accountant; b. Milledgeville, Ga., Dec. 8, 1958; s. John Sidney and Glenda Faye Simmons; m. Mary Sue Simmons, Feb. 22, 1958; children: Melissa, Christopher, Matthew. BBA in Acctg., Ga. Coll., 1980. CPA, Ga. Staff acct. Powell, Booth & Thombley, P.C., Atlanta, 1980-83; mgr. Powell, Booth & Grace, P.C., 1983-87, ptnr., 1987-88; mgr. John S. Thombley P.C., Marietta, Ga., 1988-94; ptnr. Thombley & Simmons, P.C., 1994—. Treas., bd. dirs. MUST Ministries, Inc., Marietta, Ga., 1998—. Mem. AICPA, Ga. Soc. CPAs, Delta Sigma Pi (life). Republican. Baptist. Avocations: golf, hunting, fishing, hiking. Home: 3305 Burnham Way Kennesaw GA 30152 Office: Thombley & Simmons PC 305 Lawrence St Ste 100 Marietta GA 30060 E-mail: sgs1258@bellsouth.net.

SIMMONS, STEPHEN JUDSON, lawyer; b. Columbus, Ohio, Feb. 19, 1946; s. Samuel A. and Jane A. (McGrath) S.; m. Claire Maxine Schriber, Aug. 15, 1970; children: Darren, Judson. BA, Ohio State U., 1968; JD, U. Cin., 1972. Bar: Ohio 1973, Tex. 1982. Sr. law clk. U.S. Dist. Ct. (ea. dist.) Tenn., Knoxville, 1972-74; asst. atty. gen. Office of Atty. of Ohio, Columbus, 1974-75; assoc. McGrath & Shirey, 1975; corp. counsel Wendys, Inc., 1975-79; sr. v.p., gen. counsel Precision Tune, Inc., Beaumont, Tex., 1979-87, also dir.; sr. v.p. adminstrn., dir. Kwik-Kopy Corp., Cypress, Tex., 1988-90; v.p. Deli Mgmt., Inc., 1990-94; pvt. practice Houston, 1994—. Bd. editors U. Cin. Law Rev., 1971-72. Mem. Tex. Bar Assn. Roman Catholic. Home: 13603 Balmore Cir Houston TX 77069-2703 Office: 3845 Fm 1960 Rd W Ste 250 Houston TX 77068-3548 Fax: 281-586-0088. E-mail: sjsimmons@aol.com.

SIMMONS, TED CONRAD, writer; b. Seattle, Sept. 1, 1916; s. Conrad and Clara Evelyn (Beaudry) S.; m. Dorothy Pauline Maltese, June 1, 1942; children: Lynn, Juliet. Student, U. Wash., 1938-41, UCLA and L.A. State U., 1952-54, Oxford (Eng.) U., 1980. Drama critic Seattle Daily Times, 1942; indsl. writer, reporter-editor L.A. Daily News, 1948-51; contbr. Steel, Western Metals, Western Industry, 1951—. Past poetry dir. Watts Writers Workshop; instr. Westside Poetry Center; asst. dir. Pacific Coast Writers Conf, Calif. State Coll. Los Angeles. Author: (poetry) Deadended, 1966; (novel) Middlearth, 1975; (drama) Greenhouse, 1977, Durable Chaucer, 1978, Rabelais and other plays, 1980, Dickeybird, 1981 (nominated TCG Plays-in-Progress award 1985), Alice and Eve, 1983, Deja Vu, Deja Vu, 1986, The Box, 1987, Ingrid Superstar, 1988, Three Quarks for Mr. Marks, 1989, Ingrid: Skier on the Slopes of Stromboli, 1990, A Midsummer's Hamlet, 1991, Hamlet Nintendo, After Hours, Dueling Banjoes, Viva el Presidente, Climate of the Sun, 1992, Nude Descending Jacob's Ladder, 1993, Almost an Opera, 1994, Landscape with Inverted Tree and Fred Astaire Dancing, 1995, O.J. Othello, Fast Track, Searching for Alice Liddell, Mr. Blue of Freaky Animals, Inc., 1997, Rosenstern & Guildencrantz II, 1997, Rosa/Rosa of the Centuries/Rosa of the Thorns, 1997, Joyce, 1997, Joyce-After Hours, 1997, Amadeus & da Cultchur Club, 1997, Wonderland: Alice's New Adventures, 1998, The Brilliant Life of an Intelligent Orchid-A Play About Ingrid Bergman, 1998, Chekhov Off-Broadway, The Premiere, Good Night Sweet Prince, The Scare, 1999, 18 Mini-Micro Dramas, BloomsDay, The Scream, The Bird, 2000, Will, Jean "n" Jim—A Play, 2001; writer short story, radio verse; book reviewer Los Angeles Times; contbr. poetry to the Am. Poet, Prairie Wings, Antioch Rev., Year Two Anthology; editor: Venice Poetry Company Presents, 1972. Served with USAAF, 1942-46. Grantee Art Commn. King County, 1993.

SIMMONS, TIMOTHY DONALD, protective services official; b. Oklahoma City, May 10, 1954; s. Donald George and BetteRuth (Reeder) S.; m. Jean (Kashitsina) Simmons, Aug. 8, 1997; 1 child, Helena. AA, Phoenix Coll., 1975; BA in Journalism, Ariz. State U., 1978. With Phoenix Fire Dept., 1985—. Author: Up From the Ashes, 1986, Brothers of the Pine, 1995; contbr. articles to profl. publs. Vol. capt. Nogales (Sonora, Mex.) Fire Dept., 1988—. Mem. Nat. Writers Assn., Soc. Profl. Journalists, Western Writers Am. Home: 4840 W Kaler Cir Glendale AZ 85301-1538

SIMMONS, VAUGHAN PIPPEN, medical consultant; b. Balt., Nov. 19, 1922; s. Harry S. and Sarah Jane (Pippen) S.; m. Marguerite Carolyn Massino, Dec. 27, 1947 (dec. 1990); children: Malynda Sarah, Jefferson Vaughan. Student, Ill. Inst. Tech., 1943-44; BS, U. Chgo., 1947, MD, 1949. Diplomate Am. Bd. Life Ins. Medicine. From instr. to asst. prof. Marquette U. Sch. Medicine, Milw., 1950-56; asst. med. dir. Northwestern Mut. Life Ins. Co., 1956-60; med. dir. Fidelity Mut. Life Ins. Co., Phila., 1961-73, v.p., 1968-73; v.p., med. dir. Colonial Penn Life Ins. Co., 1973-84. Vis. lectr. ins. medicine Temple U. Sch. Medicine, Phila., 1966-84; asst. prof. anatomy Jefferson Med. Coll., Phila., 1977-88, hon. asst. prof. anatomy, 1988—. Patentee in field (3); contbr. articles to profl. jours. Mem. ofcl. bd. St. Luke United Methodist Ch., Bryn Mawr, Pa., 1963-83, chmn. commn. membership and evangelism, 1963-71, trustee, 1968-83. Served with M.C., U.S. Army, 1943-45, as lt. (j.g.) USNR, 1952-54; Korea Fellow Coll. Physicians Phila. (chmn. pub. health sect. 1967-68, ins. medicine sect. 1970-72, planning com. 1981-82, adv. bd. Francis C. Wood Inst. History of Medicine 1984-88), Milw. Acad. Medicine, Am. Geriatrics Soc., N.Y. Acad. Medicine; mem. Am. Acad. Ins. Medicine (founding editor Ins. Medicine 1969-71, exec. coun. 1970-72, publs. com. 1967-75), Am. Life Ins. Assn. (sec. med. sect. 1974-77), Pa. Hist. Soc., Am. Assn. Automotive Medicine (dir. 1980-83), Am. Legion, Sigma Xi, Alpha Kappa Kappa. Clubs: Union League (bd. dirs. 1982-85, v.p. 1985-86), Sketch (Phila.). Avocations: photography, amateur radio, drawing, painting, medical research and writing. Home: 4665 S Landings Dr Fort Myers FL 33919-4683 E-mail: vaughanps@aol.com.

SIMMONS, WARREN HATHAWAY, JR. retired retail executive; b. Indpls., May 10, 1927; s. Warren Hathaway and Jane (Jillson) S.; m. Nancy Lynn Sullivan; 1 child, Warren Hathaway III. AB in English, Princeton U., 1948. From mgr. tour ops. to supr. employees svcs. NBC, 1949-53; various positions in pers., labor rels. and store ops. Bamberger's, a divsn. of R.H. Macy and Co., Inc., 1953-63; v.p., dir. pers. and labor rels. Bamberger's divsn. R.H. Macy and Co., Inc., 1963-65; sr. v.p., dir. Bamberger's, Inc., 1965-70; sr. v.p. pers. and indsl. rels. R.H. Macy and Co., Inc., 1970-83, cons., 1983-89; ltd. practice in human resource cons. and project mgmt. Princeton, N.J., 1983-87. Mem. Plainfield Planning Bd. and Traffic/Parking Commn.; mem., former chmn. and life gov. Muhlenberg Regional Med. Ctr.; life trustee Muhlenberg Found.; trustee, former chmn. Huntington Found.; mem., former chmn. bd. Nat. Captioning Inst., Vienna, Va., former co-chmn. bd.; trustee emeritus Wardlaw/Hartridge Sch.; trustee Rider U., Lawrenceville, N.J., Princeton/Blairstown Ctr., Prospect Found., Princeton; past trustee McCarter Theatre Co., Princeton, 1981-88, N.J. Symphony Orch., Symphony Hall, Newark, United Way of Essex and Union County, Mental Health Assn. Essex County, Robert Treat coun. Boys Scouts Am.; trustee, past pres. Friends of Pub. Broadcasting in N.J.; commr. Pub. Broadcasting Authority in N.J; former trustee David Lawrence Found. for Mental Health, Naples, Fla.; pres. Class of 1984 Princeton U., 1988-93; mem. Pub. Employee Rels. Commn., Naples, 1992-98. With USN, 1945-46. Mem. Am. Mgmt. Assn. (human resources coun.), U.S. C. of C., (bus. adv. com. on white collar crime). Home: 508 Terhune Rd Princeton NJ 08540-3656 E-mail: hathasim@aol.com.

SIMMONS, WILLIAM, physicist, retired aerospace research executive; b. Chgo., Apr. 24, 1932; s. Walter Garfield and Edna Dean (Winch) S.; m. Barbara Millet Haury, Oct. 4, 1954; children: Sheryl Lee, Cynthia Jane, Shelly Jean. BA in Physics, Carleton Coll., 1953; MS in Physics, U. Ill., 1955, PhD in Physics, 1960. Mem. tech. staff Space Tech. Labs., Redondo Beach, Calif., 1960-62; sr. rsch. scientist Gen. Tech., Torrance, 1962, TRW, Redondo Beach, 1962-71, dir. rsch., 1984-89, chief engr. spl. projects assigned to Lawrence Livermore (Calif.) Labs., 1989-92; engring. mgr. Lawrence Livermore Labs., 1972-84, rsch. reviewer, 1985-89; prof. engring. UCLA, 1968-72. Tech. panel mem. U. Calif., Berkeley, 1985; tech. reviewer Dept. Energy, Washington, 1986—, mem. rev. com., 1987—; cons. in field, 1992-99. Editor, reviewer 2 books, 1982, 83; contbr. numerous articles to profl. jours. 10 patents in electro-optics devices. Named Disting. Engring. Prof. of Yr. UCLA, 1972, one of Top 100 Innovators in U.S.A, Sci. Digest, 1986; George F. Baker Found. scholar Carleton Coll., 1949-53. Mem. IEEE (sr., life, gen. chmn. symposia 1988, 89, Simon Ramo Major medal 1987), Laser Inst. Am., Laser Engring. and Optical Soc., Am. Phys. Soc., Soc. of Photographic and Instrumentation Engrs., U.S. Chess Club, Phi Beta Kappa, Sigma Xi. Republican. Avocations: chess, table tennis, bridge. Office: Sys Solutions 1621 W 25th St Ste 231 San Pedro CA 90732-4300

SIMMONS SCOTT, VANESSA ANN, lawyer; b. Bronx, N.Y., Sept. 15, 1971; d. Chillie Ann Simmons; m. Quentin E. Scott, Oct. 3, 1998. BA, Duke U., 1993; JD, Vanderbilt U., 1997. Bar: Ala. 1997, U.S. Dist. Ct. (no. and mid. dists.) Ala. 1997, U.S. Ct. Appeals (11th cir.) 1997. Law clk. to Hon. Alfred Robbins, N.Y. Supreme Ct., Mineola, 1995; assoc. Lange, Simpson, Robinson & Somerville LLP, Birmingham, Ala., 1997-2000, Haskell, Slaughter and Young, LLC, Birmingham, 2000—. Mem. jr. bd. dirs. YWCA of Birmingham. Mem. ABA (Amb. bus. law sect.), Birmingham Bar Assn. (exec. bd. women's sect.), Magic City Bar (v.p. young lawyers sect.), Alpha Kappa Alpha. Office: Haskell Slaughter et al 1200 Am S Harbert Plz 1901 6th Ave N Birmingham AL 35203 E-mail: vas@hsy.com.

SIMMONS SMITH, MONA JEAN (MONICA SIMMONS), special education educator, writer; b. Sharon, Pa., Sept. 23, 1952; d. James Pearman and Michaelina (Votino) Simmons; children: Manley Taylor Smith, Rachael Christina Smith. BS, Ga. Coll., 1973; MEd, U. Ga., 1975, postgrad. Cert. tchr. T-5 learning disorders, hosp.-homebound edn., T-5 multi-physically handicapped edn., T-5 leadership in edn., Ga. Tchr. Clayton County Bd. of Edn., Jonesboro, Ga., 1973-74; fellow, instr. U. Ga., Athens, 1974-75, instr., 1978-80; tchr. self-contained learning disabilities Cobb County Bd. of Edn., Marietta, Ga., 1976-78; ednl. coord. Physicians and Surgeons Hosp., Atlanta, 1981-83, Parkway Regional Hosp., Atlanta, 1984-89; hosp. homebound tchr. DeKalb County Bd. of Edn., 1980-86; mktg. mgr., 1987-88. Ednl. cons. 1977-80; mem. psycho ednl. testing Ednl. Evaluations, Atlanta, 1976-80; ednl. cons. Comprehensive Care Corp., Atlanta; field based rschr. Prep Sch., Hilton Head, S.C., 1993; lectr. in field. Author: (with Susan Brown) 50 Strategies for Positive Single Parenting, 1996, The Lowcountry Child, 1996, The Island Child, 1997, The AsterPlanet Chronicles 1-5, 1998, Vol. 1, Uniworld, Vol. II, Aster Jungle, 1998, Vol. III, Aster Desert, 1998, AsterJungle, 1998, Vol. 2, 1998, AsterOcean, 1998, Vol. 5, Aster City, 1998; co-author: 365 Positive Strategies for Single Parenting, 1998. Mem. Atlanta Ballet Guild (life), 1988—; vol. North Arts Ctr. Docent, 1989-91. U. Ga. teaching assistantship, 1976. Mem. Coun. for Exceptional Children (divsn. Children Learning Disabilities), Reynolds Plantation Club, Phi Delta Kappa. Avocations: snow skiing, fishing, travel, dancing, water skiing. Home: 4804 Calais Ct NE Marietta GA 30067-4078

SIMMS, FRANCES BELL, retired elementary education educator; b. Salisbury, N.C., July 29, 1936; d. William Taft and Anne Elmira (Sink) Bell; m. Howard Homer Simms, June 24, 1966 (dec. Oct. 1993); 1 child, Shannon Lara. AB in English, U. N.C., 1958; MEd, U. Fla., 1962; postgrad., Boston U., 1963—, U. Va., Queen's Coll., Cambridge, U.K. Playroom attendant dept. neurology Children's Hosp., Boston, 1958-60; reading clinician Mills Ctr., Inc., Ft. Lauderdale, Fla., 1960-61; reading/lang. arts tchr. Arlington (Va.) Pub. Schs., 1962-99. Cons. Arlington Pub. Schs. curriculum devel.; adv. bd. mem. ad hoc com. Edn. Tech., Arlington, 1965-67; reading instr. Va. Poly. Inst. and State U., Arlington, 1974; prodr., dir. Barcroft Newsbag-CATV, Arlington, 1982—; chair self-study Elem. Sch., Arlington, 1987, 93; adv. bd. Reading is Fundamental of No. Va., Arlington, 1988—; guest lectr. Marymount U., cons.; lectr., presenter in field; bd. dirs. Cen. European Leadership Inst., 2001. Exhibitions include Lee Heights Gallery. Laborer Christmas in April, Arlington, 1990—; tutor, vol. instr. Henderson Hall Marine Corps, 1990—; organizer, instr. Better Beginnings, 1994—, The Reading Connection, PR, 1994—; usher Kennedy Ctr., Washington; mem. Spkrs.' Bur. with Hospice; lay leader, choir mem. Cherrydale Meth. Ch., Arlington, 1976—. Recipient Literacy award, Margaret McNamara award Reading is Fundamental of No. Va., 1994-95. Mem. Va. State Reading Assn. (mem. conf. coms.), Arlington Edn. Assn. (contbg. editor newsletter 1967-69), Art League of Alexandria, Arlington Artist's Alliance, Greater Washington Reading Coun. (com. chairperson 1962—, Tchr. of Yr. 1995-96), Delta Kappa Gamma (Alpha Omicron former news writer, v.p., program chairperson, news editor). Avocations: water color, singing in choir, writing poetry, traveling, producing children's musicals. Home: 6110 23rd St N Arlington VA 22205-3414 E-mail: fsimms@starpower.net.

SIMMS, JOHN WILLIAM, retired foreign service officer, consultant; b. Upland, Pa., Jan. 2, 1924; s. Earle and Katharyn Hamilton (Van Roden) S.; m. Ronda Jean Motter, Sept. 11, 1965; children: Llewellyn Earle Simms, Eric Marion Simms. Student, U. Pa., 1941-43; BA in Govt., George Washington U., 1948; postgrad., Georgetown U., 1948-50, Am. U., Washington, 1959-60, 63-64. U.S. foreign svc. officer, various cities, Germany, 1950-53, 56-58; staff aide to amb. Tokyo, Japan, 1953-55; U.S. foreign svc. officer Bureau Internat. Orgns. Affairs, Washington, 1958-61; consul, prin. officer Kisangani, Zaire, 1962; U.S. fgn. svc. officer Bureau African Affairs, Washington, 1963, Bureau European Affairs, Washington, 1964-65; staff aide to sec. gen. NATO, Paris, 1965-67, Brussels, Belgium, 1967-68; chief polit. sect. U.S. Embassy, Port-au-Prince, Haiti, 1968-71; chief polit. sect. U.S. Embassy Asuncion, Paraguay, 1971-73; U.S. foreign svc. officer Bureau Inter-Am. Affairs, Washington, 1973-74; from dep. chief of mission to charge d'affaires Bridgetown, Barbados, 1974-77; congl. liaison officer Office Congl. Rels., Washington, 1977-78; polit. counselor Bogotá, Colombia, 1978-80; sr. officer Bureau Pers., Washington, 1980-81; v.p. COMEX, 1981-82; cons. Profl. Mgmt. Assocs., Bethesda, Md., 1986-90; sr. crisis mgmt. assoc. Rsch. Planning, Inc., Arlington, Va., 1990-93. Mem. Fairfax County (Va.) Republican Com., 1983-85. Warrant Officer (j.g.) U.S. Army, 1943-46, ETO, lt. col. res. ret. Recipient Orden de la Democracia, Congress of Rep. Colombia, Bogotá, 1980. Republican. Avocations: drawing, painting, traveling in the U.S. and abroad.

SIMMS, MARIA ESTER, health services administrator; b. Bahia Blanca, Argentina; came to U.S., 1963; d. Jose and Esther (Guays) Barberio Esandi; m. Michael Simms, July 15, 1973 (dec. Aug. 1993); children: Michelle Bonnie Lee Carla, Michael London Valentine, Matthew Brandon. Degree medicine, Facultad del Centenario, Rosario, Argentina, 1962; Physician Asst. Cert. (hon.), U. So. Calif., 1977. Medical diplomate. Pres. Midtown Svcs. Inc., L.A., 1973—; dir. internat. affairs, speaker Gov. of Papua, New Guinea, 1996—; dir., CFO, pres. World Film Inst., 1996—; commr. Inmate Welfare Commn. L.A. County Sheriff's Dept., 1977—. Dir. internat. affairs, spkr. on humanitarian, cultural and econ. matters Govt. of Papua New Guinea; advocate, internat. spkr. for women, children and animal rights; bd. mem. Kohtakt, Raduga, L.A. Chmn. bd. Am.'s Film Inst., Washington; chmn. bd. trustees World Film Inst, Dir. Intl. Affairs, speaker-Humanitarian, Economic and Cultural Consulate of Papua New Guinea, Los Angeles, Calif.; bd. dirs. Glendale Symphony Orch.; mem. Tumate Welfare Commn., L.A. County Sheriff Dept. (commissioner). Fellow Am. Acad. Physicians' Assts.; mem. World Film Inst. (pres. 1997--), Bus. for Law Enforcement (northeast divsn.), Physicians for Social Responsibility, Mercy Crusade Inc., Internat. Found. for Survival Rsch., Noetic Scis. Soc., Inst. Noetic Scis., So. Calif. Alliance for Survival, Supreme Emblem Club of U.S., Order Eastern Star, Flying Samaritans, Shriners. Avocations: coin collecting, designing, writing, oil painting, flying. Fax: 323-256-3372. E-mail: msimms1234@aol.com.

SIMMS, MARIA KAY, writer, non-profit organization executive; b. Princeton, Ill., Nov. 18, 1940; d. Frank B. and Anna (Haurberg) S.; m. Neil F. Michelsen, Oct. 2, 1987 (dec. 1990); children: Shannon Sullivan Stillings, Molly A. Sullivan, Elizabeth Maria Jossick; m. James l. Jossick, July 12, 1998. BFA, Ill. Wesleyan U., 1962. Cert. cons. profl. astrologer; ordained min. L.A. Cmty. Ch. of Religious Sci. Elder priestess Covenant of the Goddess; art tchr. elem. and jr. high pub. schs., Dundee, Northbrook, Ill., 1962-65; H.S. art tchr. Danbury, Conn., 1975-76; freelance gallery painter various cities, 1962-77; free-lance comml. illustrator, 1972-74, 86-87; shop, gallery, café owner Conn., 1976-79; art dir. ACS Pubs., Inc., San Diego, 1987-90; pres. Astro Comm. Svcs., Inc. (formerly ACS Pubs.), 1990-98, dir., 1990-2000; acquisitions editor, 1998-2000; cons., 2000—. Bd. dirs. Omni Techs. Corp.; conf. lectr. Author: Twelve Wings of the Eagle, 1988, Dial Detective, 1989, 2d edit., 2001; co-author: Search for the Christmas Star, 1989, Circle of the Cosmic Muse, 1994, Your Magical Child, 1994, Future Signs, 1996, The Witch's Circle, 1996, Millenium: Fears, Fantasies and Facts, 1998, A Time for Magick, 2001; contbr. articles to popular mags.; columnist Moon Magich, www.starcraftsbob.com. High priestee Cir. of the Cosmic Muse; elder priestess Covenant of the Goddess, 2d officer Calafia Local Coun., 1995-96, pub. info. officer, 1996-98; mem. adv. bd. Kepler Coll., 1998—. Recipient numerous art awards. Mem. Nat. Coun. Geocosmic Rsch. Inc. (dir., pubs. dir. 1981-92, editor jour. 1984-92, chairperson bd. 1999—), Am. Fedn. Astrologers, Internat. Soc. Astrol. Rsch., New Age Pubs. Assn., Alpha Gamma Delta. Office: Astro Comm Svcs Inc 5521 Ruffin Rd San Diego CA 92123-1314

SIMMS, MICHAEL ARLIN, poet, publishing executive; b. Houston, Apr. 6, 1954; s. Harry William and Jane Lu Simms; m. Cassandra Garcia (div. Dec. 1984); m. Eva Maria Spork, Sept. 29, 1987; children: Nicholas, Lea. Cert., Sch. Irish Studies, Dublin, Ireland, 1974; BA, So. Meth. U., 1976; MFA, U. Iowa, 1978. Lectr. in rhetoric So. Meth. U., Dallas, 1979-87; lectr. in English C.C. of Allegheny, Pitts., 1988-96; mng. ptnr. Michael Simms Real Estate, 1988—; lectr. in English Duquesne U., 1997—; poet-in-residence Carnegie Mellon U., 1998; exec. dir. Autumn House Press, 1998—. Author: Migration, 1985, The Fire-eater, 1990; co-author (reference text) Longman Dictionary of Poetry, 1985; contbg. editor: Pitts. Quar., 1997—. Mem. adv. bd. Southwestern Pa Reg. Planning Commn., Pitts., 1992-96; advisor to bd. Waldorf Sch. of Pitts., 1996-2000; mem. com. in Solidarity with People of El Salvador, 1980-84. Grantee NEH, 1984, Internat. Poetry Forum, 1995—; fellow So. Meth. U., 1975; poetry fellow Sewickley Acad., Pitts., 1997-2001. Mem. Internat. Poetry Forum (assoc., bd. dirs. 1999—). Avocations: history, economics. Office: Autumn House Press 219 Bigham St Pittsburgh PA 15211-1431 E-mail: simms@duq.edu.

SIMMS, PAULETTE ANDREA HATCHETT, management analyst; b. Clearwater, Fla., Aug. 29, 1948; d. Paul Andrew Sr. and Pearlie (M.Y.) Hatchett; m. Howard Gray Simms Sr., Dec. 23, 1972 (div. Oct. 1981); 1 child, Howard Gray II. BS, Hampton U., 1970; cert., U. D.C., 1974; MA in Tchg., Trinity Coll., 1975; cert., Fla. A&M U., 1991. Tchr. D.C. Pub. Schs., Washington, 1970-75; substitute tchr. Dependent Schs., Camp LeJeune, N.C., 1976; substitute tchr., tchr. Leon County Schs., Tallahassee, 1977-78; investigator, unit supr. Fla. Commn. on Human Rels., 1978-79, adminstr. Office Employment Investigations, 1979-88, investigation supr., 1988-89; planning mgr. Fla. Dept. Law Enforcement, 1989-96, sr. mgmt. analyst II, 1996—. Mktg. exec. Melaleuca Inc., Idaho Falls, 1995—; ind. cons. D'essence Designer Fragrances, Santa Ana, Calif., 1996-98. Mem. Internat. Assn. Law Enforcement Profls., Fla. Assn. Law Enforcement Profls., Soc. Govt. Meeting Profls., Delta Sigma Theta (sec. 1987-89, v.p. 1992-93, pres. 1993-95). Methodist. Avocations: instrumental music, reading, travel. Home: 1905 Doomar Dr Tallahassee FL 32308-4805 Office: Fla Dept Law Enforcement PO Box 1489 2331 Phillips Rd Tallahassee FL 32308-5333

SIMMS, ROBERT D. former state supreme court justice; b. Tulsa, Feb. 6, 1926; s. Matthew Scott and Bessie L. (Moore) S.; m. Patricia C., Feb. 16, 1950; 1 son, Robert D. Student, Milligan Coll., Phillips U.; LLB, U. Tulsa. Bar: Okla. 1950. Pvt. practice law, Sand Springs, Okla., from 1950; asst. county atty. Tulsa County, 1953-54; chief prosecutor County Atty.'s Office, 1955-58, county atty., 1958-62; judge Okla. Dist. Ct., Dist. 14, 1962-71, Okla. Ct. Criminal Appeals, 1971-72; justice Okla. Supreme Ct., 1985—2000. Mem. Okla. Crime Commn. Mem. Gov.'s Spl. Com. on Drug Abuse, 1970; sponsor and coach Pee-Wee Baseball. Served with USN, 1943-46. Mem. Tulsa County Bar Assn., Okla. Bar Assn. (chmn. dist. atty. sect. 1959)*

SIMO, GLORIA ANNE, public administration educator; b. Evergreen Park, Ill., Dec. 30, 1946; d. John Robert and Bessie Pearl (McGrew) Stancik; children: Matthew John, Melissa Leigh. BA, Elmhurst Coll., 1988; MA in Pub. Adminstrn., No. Ill. U., 1991; PhD, No. Ill. U, 1997. Field rep. DuPage County Housing Authority, Wheaton, Ill., 1989-90; adminstrv. intern Village of Addison, 1990-91; presdl. mgmt. intern NIH, Bethesda, Md., 1991-92; rsch. asst. Ctr. for Govtl. Studies No. Ill. U., DeKalb, 1992-93; spl. projects coord. City of St. Charles, Ill., 1993-94; tchg. asst. No. Ill. U., De Kalb, 1993-96; adj. prof. Elmhurst (Ill.) Coll., 1993-96; MPA program coord. No. Ill. U., 1994-95; asst. prof. Inst. Govt., U. Ark., Little Rock, 1996-2000; asst. prof. grad. program publ svcs. DePaul U., Chgo., 2000—; acting dir. Chaddick Inst. for Met. Devel., 2002—, Chaddick Inst. Met. Affairs, 2002—. Mem. adv. b d. Jamal Place, 2002. Mem. ASPA, Am. Planning Assn., Pi Alpha Alpha, Psi Chi, Pi Gamma Mu. Lutheran. E-mila. Office: O'Malley Bldg Ste 1250 25 E Jackson Blvd Chicago IL 60604 E-mail: gsimo@depaul.edu.

SIMOES, ERIC ARUN FRANCIS, pediatrics educator; b. Bombay, India, Sept. 17, 1956; B Medicine B Surgery, Madras U., Vellore, India, 1980, diploma in child health, 1982, MD, 1984. Lectr. gen. pediats. U. Madras, Christian Med. Coll., Vellore, 1984-86; instr. in pediat. infectious diseases U. Colo. Sch. Medicine, Denver, 1989-90, asst. prof. pediat. infectious diseases, 1991-96, assoc. prof. pediat. infectious diseases, 1997—2002, prof., 2002—; med. officer divsn. child and adolescent health WHO, Geneva, 1999. Hon. sr. lectr. divsn. pediats., ob-gyn Imperial Coll. Sci. and Tech. and Medicine, St. Mary's Hosp., Eng., 1999—; cons. WHO, 1989—; fellowship dir. infectious diseases program U. Colo. Health Scis. Ctr. Sch. Medicine, Denver, 1995-99. Editor: Manual of Pediatric Emergencies for House Officers, 1987; contbr. chpts. to books in field. Mem. AAAS, Am. Soc. Microbiology, Western Soc. Pediat. Rsch. Office: Children's Hosp 1056 E 19th Ave # B70 Denver CO 80218-1088 Fax: (303) 764-8117. E-mail: simoes.eric@tchden.org.

SIMOES, RONALD ALAN, mortgage company executive; b. Lawrence, Mass., Apr. 21, 1949; s. Caesar R. and Irene (Sousa) S.; m. Cathy Gail Arsenault, Oct. 25, 1970; children: Scott, Chad, Cristen, Keith. BSBA, New Hampshire Coll., 1980. Advt. salesperson Lawrence Eagle Tribune, North Andover, Mass., 1970-72; sales rep. Eagle Tribune Printing Co., 1972-74; asst. v.p. Arlington Trust Co., Lawrence, 1974-82; v.p., mgr. bus. devel. Bank of New Eng., 1982-85; sr. mktg. rep. Northeastern Mortgage Co., Inc., Cambridge, Mass., 1985-88; pres. Golden Gate Mortgage Co., Inc., Andover, 1986—, Northland Mortgage Co., Inc., Andover, 1988—. With U.S. Army, 1968-70, Vietnam. Avocation: golf. Office: Northland Mortgage Co 240 Pleasant St Methuen MA 01844-7134

SIMOKAITIS, FRANK JOSEPH, air force officer, lawyer; b. St. Louis, Dec. 12, 1922; s. Frank and Constance (Ladish) S.; m. Mary Jane Feeny; children: Peggy, Mary, Frank (dec.). Student, Washington U., St. Louis, 1945-47; LL.B., St. Louis U., 1950, JD, 1970. Bar: U.S. Supreme Ct. U.S 1950, Mo. 1950, also other fed. cts. 1950. Commd. 2d lt. USAAF, 1943; advanced through grades to maj. gen. USAF, 1973; plans and ops. officer Hdqrs. Pacific Air Force, 1960-63; staff officer Hdqrs. USAF, Washington, 1963-69, exec. asst. to sec. air force, 1969-73; comdt. Air Force Inst. Tech., 1973-78; dir. Dept. Def. affairs Hdqrs. NASA, Washington, 1978-83, cons., 1983—. Bd. dirs. Dayton chpt. ARC, Greater Miami chpt., arbitrator Better Bus. Bur. Decorated D.S.M. with oak leaf cluster, Legion of Merit, Air medal with 4 oak leaf clusters, Air Force Commendation medal. Mem. Miami Air Force Assn. (bd. dirs.), Navy League (v.p. U.S. Miami coun.), Ft. Myer Officers Club. Home: 1594 Frontier Dr Melbourne FL 32940

SIMON, ANDREW L. educational publishing executive; b. Bklyn., June 17, 1942; s. Sidney Simon and Ruth Kornblum; m. Andrea Judith Wollman, June 30, 1968; children: Alexandra, Rachel. BA, Washington U., 1963; MBA, Columbia U., 1965. Account exec. Ogilvy & Mather, N.Y.C., 1967-71, Benton & Bowles, N.Y.C., 1971-73; group product mgr. L'Oreal, 1973-74, Norcliff-Thayer, Tuckahoe, N.Y., 1974-78; group head consumer products Lederle Labs., Pearl River, 1978-79; v.p. Citibank, N.Y.C., 1980-83; v.p., divsn. head Bankers Trust, 1983-86; cons. investor, 1986-94; chmn. bd., pres., CEO Touchstone Applied Sci. Assocs., Inc., Brewster, N.Y., 1994—. Bd. govs. Washington U. Alumni, 1970-73; trustee City of Poughkeepsie (N.Y.) Partnership, 1987-93, The Harvey Sch., Katonah, N.Y., 1989-2000, Nat. Coun. Edn. & Human Devel., George Washington U., 2000—. With USNR, 1964-70. Avocations: tennis, riding, skiing. Home: 1905 Hunter Brook Rd Yorktown Heights NY 10598-6233 Office: Touchstone Appl Sci Assoc Inc PO Box 382 Brewster NY 10509-0382

SIMON, ARTHUR, pharmacologist, research laboratory executive; b. Bklyn., June 1, 1942; s. Harry and Ann S.; m. Sandra Goldberg, July 10, 1966; children— Brett David, Kira Denise BS in Biology, Phila. Coll. Pharmacy and Sci., 1965; MS cum laude, Fairleigh Dickinson U., 1969; PhD in Pharmacology (NIH fellow), U. Cin., 1972. Lab. technician La Wall and Harrisson Research Lab., Phila., 1962-63; research asst. toxicology dept. Wyeth Labs., Paoli, Pa., 1965-66; research assoc. pharmacology dept. Warner Lambert Research Inst., Morris Plains, N.J., 1966-69; research investigator Squibb Inst. for Med. Research, Princeton, 1972-74; sr. cardiovascular pharmacologist USV Pharm. Corp., Tuckahoe, N.Y., 1974-76; dir. cardiovascular clin. research Bristol Myers Co. Internat. Div., 1974-82; pres., chief exec. officer Research Testing Labs., Inc., Great Neck, N.Y., 1982—. Mem.: Regulatory Affairs Profl. Soc., Drug Info. Assn. Home: 52 Tamarack Ln Pomona NY 10970-2012 Office: Rsch Testing Labs Inc 255 Great Neck Rd Great Neck NY 11021-3308

SIMON, BERNECE KERN, social work educator; b. Denver, Nov. 27, 1914; d. Maurice Meyer and Jennie (Bloch) Kern; m. Marvin L. Simon, Feb. 26, 1939; 1 dau., Anne Elizabeth. BA, U. Chgo., 1936, MA, 1942. Social worker Jewish Children's Bur. Chgo., 1938-40, U. Chgo. Hosps. and Clinics, 1940-44; mem. faculty U. Chgo., 1944-81, instr., 1944-48, asst. prof., 1948-60, prof. social casework, 1960—, Samuel Deutsch prof. Sch. Social Service Adminstrn., 1960-81, emeritus, 1981—. Mem. bd. editors 17th Edit. Ency. Social Work, 1975-77, Social Svc. Rev., 1975-99; bd. editors: Social Work, 1978-82, book rev. editor, 1982-87; cons. editor Journal of Social Work Education, 1991-94; contbr. articles to profl. jours., book chpts., monographs. Mem. NASW, Coun. Social Work Edn. (mem. nat. bd., sec. 1972-74), Acad. Cert. Social Workers, Nat. Acads. Practice: Social Work Office: U Chgo Sch of Social Svc Adminstrn 969 E 60th St Chicago IL 60637-2677

SIMON, BOB, news correspondent, anchor; b. Bronx, May 29, 1941; m. Francoise Simon; 1 child. Degree in history, Brandeis U., 1962. Reporter CBS News, N.Y.C., London, Saigon, 1967-81, and Tel Aviv, Dept. State corr. Washington, 1981-82, nat. corr. N.Y.C., 1982-87, chief Mid.-Ea. corr., 1987—; contbr. 60 Mins., N.Y.C., 1996—; corr. 60 Mins. II, 1999—. Officer Am. Fgn. Svc., 1964-67. Recipient Emmy awards, Peabody award, Edward Weintal prize Georgetown U., 1997; Fulbright scholar, France, Woodrow Wilson scholar. Office: c/o 60 Minutes II 524 W 57th St New York NY 10019-2902*

SIMON, DANIEL JACK, entertainment executive; b. Chgo., Mar. 25, 1949; s. Ralph David and Marigene Simon; m. Carey Susan Simon, Mar. 18, 1949; 1 child, Jane Alexandra. BA in History, U. Denver, 1971, MA in Mass Comms., 1974; postgrad., U. Manchester, 1973. V.p. licensing and promotion Lorimar Prodns., L.A., 1975-79; v.p. licensing 20th Century Fox, 1979-84, Loriman Telepictures, L.A., 1984-88; pres. licensing Cancolo Pictures, 1988-92; pres., CEO Licensing Group, 1992—. Expert witness in field for various law firms; tchr. UCLA Extension; lectr. in field of licensing. Contbr. articles to profl. publs. Mem. Licensing Industry Merchandisers Assn. (v.p. West Coast 1986-95, 2001—, pres. 1995-97). Republican. Office: Licensing Group Ltd 8455 Beverly Blvd Ste 508 Los Angeles CA 90048-3416

SIMON, DAVID ROBERT, lawyer; b. Newton, Mass., June 21, 1934; m. Myrna B. Kiner, June 28, 1959; children— Marianne, Geoffrey. A.B., Harvard U., 1956, LL.B., 1960. Bar: Mass. 1960, N.J. 1963, N.Y. 1980. Law sec. to judge U.S. Dist. Ct., Newark, 1961-63; assoc. Newark Law Firm, 1964-68; ptnr. Simon & Allen, Newark, 1968-86; ptnr. Kirsten, Simon, Friedman, Allen, Cherin & Linken, Newark, 1987-89; ptnr. Whitman & Ransom, Newark, 1989-93; sole practitioner, 1994—. Served with USAR, 1956-64. Mem. ABA, N.J. State Bar Assn., Essex County Bar Assn. Home: 875 Fifth Ave 11E New York NY 10021-4952 Office: One Riverfront Plz Newark NJ 07102

SIMON, DIANE, music educator, writer, poet; b. Appleton, Wis., Oct. 19, 1945; d. Raymond George and Violet Beatrice (Behnke) Rippl; m. Ronald Phillip Simon, Sept. 18, 1938; children: David Clarence, Mary Anne. BMus, Ariz. State U., 1969, postgrad., 1971—94, Stevens Point State Tchrs. Coll.,

Wis., 1966, Union Coll., Schenectady, N.Y., 1970; student saxophone, Paris Am. Acad., 1970; student, Westminster Choir Coll., Princeton, N.J., 1979, Grand Canyon Coll., Phoenix, 1992, Inst. of Children's Lit., West Redding, Conn., 1998—2002, Poetry Laureate Program, Owings Mills, Md., 2002. Band dir., chorus, gen. music Wellton Elem. Sch. Dist., Ariz., 1969—70; saxophone instr. Ariz. Western Coll., Yuma, 1969—70; woodwind specialist Yuma Sch. Dist., 1970—72; band dir. Balsz Sch. Dist., Phoenix, 1972—76, Paradise Valley Sch. Dist., Phoenix, 1976—77; band dir., chorus, gen. music Mesa Pub. Schs., 1978—94; ret., 1994. Saxophone clinician, adjudicator Ariz. Music Educators Assn., 1972—76, 2002—; dir. saxophone ensembles Yuma Sch. Dist. #1, 1970—72. Author: Family Treasures, 1998, Expressions of the Heart, 1997, With a Giggle and a Tear, 1998, Butterflies in the Meadow, 1999, Into the Millennium, 2000; pub. Beneath the Mesquite, 1999, Sunrise Over the Desert, poet (poetry) pub. numerous anthologies (Editors Choice Award cert., 1996, Editors Choice Award cert., 1997, Editors Choice Award cert., 1998). Recipient The Muse of Fire trophy, medallion, The Famous Poets Soc., 2000. Mem.: Internat. Libr. of Poetry (Internat. Poetry Hall of Fame 1996), Internat. Soc. Poets (Disting. Membership 1996, Internat. Poet of Merit award Medallion and Commemorative Plaque 1996, 1998). Republican. Roman Catholic. Avocations: hiking, cross stitch, embroidery, tennis, bicycling. Home: 732 W Curry St Chandler AZ 85225

SIMON, DIANE MEYER, environmental company executive; b. South Bend, Ind., Apr. 2, 1946; d. Orlando Lott Meyer and Irene Elizabeth (Speheger) Best; m. N. Stuart Grauel, Aug. 2, 1969 (div. Nov. 1976); m. Herbert Simon, Nov. 25, 1981; children: Sarah, Rachel, Asher Benjamin. BA in Psychology, Butler U., 1968; postgrad., IUPUI. Press/media staff U.S. Senator Robert F. Kennedy, 1968; presdl. campaign adminstr. U.S. Senator Birch Bayh, Washington and Indpls., 1968-79; pres. Meyer Simon Group, Indpls., 1981-89; prin. ECO Ptnrs., Inc., 1990—, ECO Educators, Indpls., 1990-94. Founder, pres. emeritus Global Green USA, Santa Monica, Calif., N.Y.C. and Washington, 1993—; exec. bd. Green Cross Internat., Geneva, 1993—. Bd. dirs. Hollywood Policy Ctr. Found., Calif., Sadat Peace Found., N.Y., Sundance Inst., Indpls. Children's Mus., Indpls. Symphony Orch., United Way Indpls., WFYI Channel 20 (PBS); co-founder Dialogue Today (Coalition of Black and Jewish Women); bd. sponsors Ind. Planned Parenthood; mem. Ind. U. Found., Indpls. Clean City Com., Indpls. Human Rels. Task Force; capital campaign co-chair Madame C.J. Walker Urban Life-Ctr.; bd. govs. Orchard Country Day Sch.; trustee YMCA; fin. chair Baron Hill for U.S. Senate, Ind.; mem. fin. com. Evan Bayh for Gov., Ind.; presdl. appointment to adv. com. on arts and JFK Ctr. for Performing Arts; committeewoman Dem. Nat. Com. Recipient Ind. State award for design ASID, Ind., 1986, Mary Mcleod Bethune award Nat. Coun. Negro Women, Ind., 1986, Wilma Rudolph Found. award, Indpls., 1988, King, Walker, Wilkins, Young award, Indpls., 1989, Millennium award Green Cross Internat., Geneva, 1997, Founders award Global Green USA, Santa Monica and Washington, 1997; named Woman of Yr., City of Indpls., 1985, Soroptomist Internat. Woman of Distinction for Environment, Indpls., 1988. Mem. Internat. Womens Forum. Jewish. Home: 1570 E Mountain Dr Montecito CA 93108-1407 also: 616 Alverna Dr Indianapolis IN 46260 Office: Global Green USA 227 Broadway Ste 302 Santa Monica CA 90401-2370

SIMON, DOLORES DALY, copy editor; b. San Francisco, Nov. 18, 1928; d. Francis Edward and Jeannette (Cooke) Daly; m. Sidney Blair Simon, Aug. 24, 1952 (div. Nov. 1955); children: John Roderick, Douglas Brian. BA in Journalism, Pa. State U., 1950. County editor Centre Daily Times, State College, Pa., 1950-51; soc. editor Bradford (Pa.) Era, 1951-52; copy editor Harper & Bros., Pubs., N.Y.C., 1955-60; copy chief Harper & Row, Pubs., 1960-88; freelance editor, copy editor Warwick, N.Y., 1988—. Co-author: Recipes into Type, 1993 (Best Food Reference 1994). Mem. James Beard Found., Phi Mu. Democrat. Avocations: book collecting. Office: Editl Svcs 63 Blooms Corners Rd Warwick NY 10990-2403

SIMON, DONALD JOHN, employee benefits administrator, insurance and investment broker; b. Chgo., July 16, 1947; s. Nicholas J. and Alice R. (Vaughan) S.; 1 child, Joshua K. BSBA, Oglethorpe U., 1969. CFP, CLU, ChFC. Sales rep. D. W. Shaw, Inc., Berlin, 1969-74; owner Simon Fin. Co., Silver Spring, Md., 1975—. Mem. Nat. Assn. Ins. and Fin. Advisors. Avocations: music, cycling, boating. Home: 12600 Eastbourne Dr Silver Spring MD 20904-2041

SIMON, ECKEHARD (PETER), foreign language educator; b. Schneidemühl, Germany, Jan. 5, 1939; came to U.S., 1955, naturalized, 1960; s. Herbert and Doris (Keiler) S.; m. Eileen Higginbottom, Dec. 19, 1959; children: Anders, Conrad (dec.), Matthew, Frederick. AB, Columbia U., 1960; A.M., Harvard U., 1961, PhD, 1964. Instr., German Harvard U., Cambridge, Mass., 1964-65, asst. prof., 1965-69, assoc. prof., 1969-71, prof., 1971—, Victor S. Thomas prof. Germanic langs. & lits., 1996—, head tutor and lang. coordinator, 1965-76, chmn. dept. German 1976-82, 85-86, 96-99, chmn. com. on medieval studies, 1992—95, 2001—02. Author: Neidhart von Reuental: Geschichte der Forschung und Bibliographie, 1968, Neidhart von Reuental, 1975, The Türkenkalender (1454) Attributed to Gutenberg and the Strasbourg Lunation Tracts, 1988; editor: The Theatre of Medieval Europe, New Research in Early Drama, 1991; mem. editorial adv. bd.: Dictionary of the Middle Ages, 1982-89; contbr. articles to profl. jours. Woodrow Wilson fellow, 1960-61; NEH Younger Scholar fellow, 1968-69; research fellow, 1977-78; Guggenheim fellow, 1968-69; Fulbright fellow U. Cologne, 1983; Sr. Exchange fellow Dumbarton Oaks, Washington, 2001. Mem. MLA, Am. Assn. Tchrs. German, Medieval Acad. Am. (asst. editor Speculum 1981-94, book review editor 1994-2000). Home: 11 Hayes Ave Lexington MA 02420-3521 Office: Harvard U Barker Ctr 345 Cambridge MA 02138-3879 E-mail: simon2@fas.harvard.edu.

SIMON, EDGAR HARMON, interior designer; b. Cleve., Apr. 12, 1919; s. Sigmund E. and Rose (Klineman) S.; m. Shirley Jean Schwartz, Mar. 1, 1942; children: Allen Harold, Ruth Esther McRae. Student, We. Res. U., 1939-44, Cleve. Inst. Art, 1968-74. Furniture showroom mgr., prodn. mgr. Lincoln Lounge Co., Cleve., 1952-53; interior designer Tom Sinks Furniture Showroom, 1955-55, Ed Simon Interiors, Cleve., 1955—. Pottery exhibns. include Mt. Sinai Hosp., 1968-72 (Ceramics award 1973), Chagrin Valley Art Show, 1971, Cleve. Mus. Art, 1973, Butler Inst. Art, 1976. Mem. Shaker Sq. Devel. Corp., 1998—. Capt. USAF, 1942-46. Mem. ASID (life, chmn. historic preservation com. 1978-79, participant Designer Showcase Cleve. Home and Flower Show 1978, treas. Ohio north chpt. 1988-89, nat. bd. dirs. 1971-76), Jewish Cmty. Ctr. Cleve. (Ceramics award 1970, 72), Cleve. Mus. Art, Cleve. City Club, Cleve. Inst. Music, Cleve. Art Inst. Alumni Assn., Smithsonian Instn. Avocations: pottery, silversmithing, swimming, walking, skiing. Home: 13800 Shaker Blvd Apt 1008 Cleveland OH 44120-1585 Office: Ed Simon Interiors 13800 Shaker Blvd Apt 1008 Cleveland OH 44120-1585

SIMON, ELINOR DEE, music educator; b. L.A., Jan. 28, 1942; d. Arthur August and Bessie (Feldman) Neuser; m. Harold Marvin Gerstein, Oct. 1, 1966 (dec. Sept. 1992); children: Michael, Steven; m. Richard Simon, Aug. 20, 1998. AA, L.A. City Coll., 1961; BA, UCLA, 1963. Cert. tchr., Calif. Elem. sch. tchr. Kirk of the Valley Sch., Reseda, Calif., 1972-89; music specialist The Buckley Sch., Sherman Oaks, 1989-95, Music Rhapsody, Manhattan Beach, 1995-98. Pvt. piano instr.; past pres., bd. mem. LACAOSA, 1978-99. Composer: (children's music) Holiday Gift of Love, 1990. Mem. Univ. Concert Singers, L.A. U. Judaism, 1997, L.A. Zimriyah Chorale, 1998, Valley Beth Shalom Choir, 1999. Named Tchr. of Yr. The Buckley Sch., Sherman Oaks, Calif., 1994. Mem. Am. Orff Schulwerk Assn. (v.p.), So. Calif. Choral Soc. Democrat. Jewish. Avocation: jazz music. Home: 3924 Alla Rd Los Angeles CA 90066-4114 E-mail: ethon@aol.com.

SIMON, ERIC JACOB, neurochemist, educator; b. Wiesbaden, Germany, June 2, 1924; came to U.S., 1938, naturalized, 1945; s. Joseph and Paula (Meyer) S.; m. Irene M. Ronis, Aug. 9, 1947; children: Martin A., Faye Ruth, Lawrence D. BS, Case Inst. Tech., Cleve., 1944; MS, U. Chgo., 1947, PhD, 1951; hon. doctorate, U. René Descartes Sorbonne, Paris, 1982. Postdoctoral trainee in biochemistry Columbia U. Coll. Physicians and Surgeons, 1951-53; lectr. in chemistry CCNY, 1952-59; research assoc. Cornell U. Med. Coll., 1953-59; asst. prof. medicine NYU Med. Center, 1959-64, assoc. prof. exptl. medicine, 1964-72, prof. exptl. medicine, 1972-80, prof. psychiatry and pharmacology, 1980—. Harry Williams Meml. lectr. Dept. Pharmacology Emory U., Atlanta, 1986; mem. initial rev. com. Nat. Inst. Drug Abuse, 1976-80, chmn. 1979-80, mem. Nat. Adv. Coun. on Drug Abuse, 1989-92; Sterling-Winthrop lectr. Albany Med. Coll., 1977; vis. prof. Coll. de France, Paris, 1990; vis. lectr. Shanghai and Beijing, 1985. Trustee Teaneck (N.J.) Bd. Edn., 1975-79. Served with U.S. Army, 1944-46. Recipient Rsch. Pace Setter award Nat. Inst. Drug Abuse, 1977, Louis and Bert Freedman Found. award N.Y. Acad. Scis., 1980, Nathan B. Eddy Meml. award Com. on Problems of Drug Dependence, Lexington, Ky., 1983, Alumni Profl. Achievement award U. Chgo., 1986; Health Rsch. Coun. N.Y.C. career scientist, 1959-75 Fellow AAAS, N.Y. Acad. Scis. (trustee 1986-89); mem. Am. Soc. Biol. Chemists, Am. Soc. Neurochemistry, Am. Soc. Pharmacology, Internat. Soc. Neurochemistry, Am. Chem. Soc., Sigma Xi. Lodges: B'nai B'rith. Research, publs. on opiate receptors, endorphins, biochemistry of analgesic action, vitamin E metabolism, acyl-coenzyme A synthesis. Office: 550 1st Ave New York NY 10016-6402 E-mail: eric.simon@nyu.edu.

SIMON, EVELYN, lawyer; b. N.Y.C., May 13, 1943; d. Joseph and Adele (Holzschlag) Berkman; m. Fredrick Simon, Aug. 18, 1963; children: Amy Jocelyn, Marcie Ann. AB in Physics, Barnard Coll., 1963; MS in Physics, U. Pitts., 1964; JD, Wayne State U., 1978; LLB, Monash U., Melbourne, Australia, 1980. Bar: Mich. 1980, Victoria (Australia) 1981. Supr. engring. Chrysler Corp., Detroit, 1964-72; edn. and profl. mgr. Engring. Soc. Detroit, 1972-78; solicitor Arthur Robinson & Co., Melbourne, 1980-81; sr. atty. Ford Motor Co., Detroit, 1981-89; assoc. gen. counsel Sheller-Globe Corp., 1989-90; v.p. planning, gen. counsel United Techs. Automotive Inc., Dearborn, Mich., 1991-94, v.p. bus. devel. and legal affairs, 1995-96, v.p. Asian bus. devel., 1997-98. Cons. internat. bus. devel., 1998-99. Mem. Mich. Bar Assn. Office: 1787 Alexander Dr Bloomfield Hills MI 48302-1204 E-mail: evelynsimon@prodigy.net.

SIMON, GARY B. health care manager, investor; b. Honolulu, Oct. 15, 1960; s. Benedict Joseph and Frances (Seno) S.; m. Akemi Hata, July 9, 1993; 1 child, Seth Carlos Hisao. BS in Chemistry, U. Hawaii, 1985. Notary public, Hawaii. Vol. U.S. Peace Corps, Sierra Leone, 1985-87; exec. asst. to pres. Focus Techs., Inc., Washington, 1989-90; office mgr. St. Francis Hospice, Honolulu, 1990-95, bus. mgr., 1995—. Achievement award St. Francis Med. Ctr., 1998—, Mother Marianne award St. Francis Healthcare Sys. Hawaii, 2001. Mem. Health Care Info. Sys. Hawaii User Group (pres. 1996—). Republican. Office: St Francis Hospice 24 Puiwa Rd Honolulu HI 96817-1127 E-mail: GARYS@sfhs-hi.org.

SIMON, GARY LEONARD, internist, educator; b. Bklyn., Dec. 18, 1946; s. Bernard and Dorothy (Ligeti) Simon; m. Vicki Thiessen, Aug. 29, 1970; children: Jason, Jessica. BS, U. Md., 1968; PhD, U. Wis., 1972; MD, U. Md., 1975. Diplomate Am. Bd. Internal Medicine, Am. Bd. Infectious Diseases. Resident internal medicine U. Md. Hosp., Balt., 1975—78; fellow infectious diseases Tufts-New Eng. Med. Ctr., Boston, 1978—80; asst. prof. dept. medicine George Washington U., Washington, 1980-84, assoc. prof., 1984-89, assoc. chmn. medicine, 1984-97, prof., 1989—, dir. divsn. infectious diseases, 1993—, vice chmn. medicine, 1997—. Cons. on AIDS Assn. Am. Med. Coll., Washington, 1990—. Contbr. articles to profl. jours. Fellow: ACP (Laureate award 2000), Infectious Disease Soc.; mem.: Internat. Aids Soc., Assn. Subspecialty Profs., Am. Soc. Microbiology. Office: George Washington U 2150 Pennsylvania Ave NW Washington DC 20037-3201 E-mail: gsimon@mfa.gwu.edu.

SIMON, HANK, information science executive; b. Charleston, S.C., Jan. 2, 1955; BS, Clemson U., 1977; MS, Tex. A&M U., 1983, PhD, 1985. Cons. in field. Author: XML Foundations, 2001, Bluetooth, A Manager's Guide, 2001; contbr. chpt. to book. Welch Found. fellow, Tex., 1980-84. Avocations: knowledge management, data discovery, website design, origami, gardening. Home: 3712 Pimlico Dr Arlington TX 76017-2422

SIMON, HAROLD, radiologist; b. Trenton, N.J., May 13, 1930; s. John and Rae B. (Gilinsky) S.; m. Jane L. Ludwig, Feb. 25, 1956; children— Steven Gregg, John Gregory. MD, Duke U., 1955. Diplomate Am. Bd. Radiology, Am. Bd. Nuclear Medicine. Intern U.S. Naval Hosp., Chelsea, Mass., 1955-56; med. officer U.S. Navy, Newport, R.I., 1956-58; resident in radiology Mass. Gen. Hosp., Boston, 1958-61, Oak Ridge Inst. Nuclear Medicine, 1959; instr. radiology Med. Sch., Tufts U., Boston, 1961-63, clin. asst. prof. radiology, 1965, assoc. clin. prof., 1971-77, clin. prof. radiology, 1977-98; practice radiology and nuclear medicine Newton Lower Falls, Mass., 1963-95; hon. mem. staff Newton Wellesley Hosp., Newton, assoc. chief radiology, 1977—, radiologist-in-chief, 1987-95. Dir. Sch. Nuclear Med. Tech.; bd. dirs. Grove Bank for Savs.; bd. dirs., mem. CRC com., mem. audit. com. Grove Bank, chmn. audit com. 1995-96; bd. dirs., treas. Newell Physicians, Inc., 1986-93; bd. overseers Newell Health Corp.; cons. in radiology VA Hosp., Boston, 1996—, Charitas Norwood (Mass.) Hosp.; mem. staff Intracoaatal Med. Sys., West Palm Beach, Fla. Contbr. articles to med. jours. Served with USNR, 1955-58. Fellow Am. Coll. Radiology; mem. Radiol. Soc. N.Am., Am. Roentgen Ray Soc., New Eng. Roentgen Ray Soc., Mass. Med. Soc. (mem. ins. com.), Mass. Radiology Soc., Pinebrook Country Club (pres. 1982-85), Belmont Country Club, Banyon Country Club, Presdl. Country Club, Phi Beta Kappa, Phi Eta Sigma. Home: 252 Atlantic Ave Palm Beach FL 33480-3709

SIMON, HERBERT, professional basketball team executive; b. Bronx; Grad., CCNY. With Albert Frankel Co., Indpls., 1959; co-founder Melvin Simon and Assocs., Inc., 1959—, pres., 1973—; owner Ind. Pacers (Nat. Basketball Assn.), 1983—. Office: Ind Pacers 125 South Pennsylvania St Indianapolis IN 46204*

SIMON, H(UEY) PAUL, lawyer; b. Lafayette, La., Oct. 19, 1923; s. Jules and Ida (Rogére) S.; m. Carolyn Perkins, Aug. 6, 1949 (dec. Dec. 1999); 1 child, John Clark. BS, U. Southwestern La., 1943; JD, Tulane U., 1947. Bar: La. 1947; CPA, La. 1947. Pvt. practice, New Orleans, 1947—; asst. prof. advanced acctg. and taxation U. Southwestern La., 1944-45; staff acct. Haskins & Sells (now Deloitte & Touche), New Orleans, 1945-53, prin., 1953-57; ptnr. Deutsch, Kerrigan & Stiles, 1957-79; sr. founding ptnr. Simon, Peragine, Smith & Redfearn, 1979—. Mem. New Orleans Bd. Trade. Author: Community Property and Liability for Funeral Expenses of Deceased Spouse, 1946, Income Tax Deductibility of Attorney's Fees in Action in Boundary, 1946, Fair Labor Standards Act and Employee's Waiver of Liquidated Damages, 1946, Louisiana Income Tax Law, 1956, Changes Effected by the Louisiana Trust Code, 1965, Gifts to Minors and the Parent's Obligation of Support, 1968; co-author: Deductions—Business or Hobby, 1975, Role of Attorney in IRS Tax Return Examination, 1978; assoc. editor: The Louisiana CPA, 1956-60; mem. bd. editors Tulane Law Rev., 1945-46, adv. bd. editors, 1992—; estates, gifts and trusts editor The Tax Times, 1986-87. Bd. dirs., mem. fin. com. World Trade Ctr., 1985-86; mem. New Orleans Met. Crime Commn., Coun. for a Better La., New Orleans Met. Area Com., Bur. Govtl. Rsch., Pub. Affairs Rsch. Coun.; co-chmn. NYU Tax Conf., New Orleans, 1976; mem. dean's coun. Tulane U. Law Sch. Fellow Am. Coll. Tax Counsel; mem. ABA (com. ct. procedure tax sect. 1958—), AICPA, La. Bar Assn. (com. on legis. and adminstrv. practice 1966-70, bd. cert. tax atty.), New Orleans Bar Assn., Internat. Bar Assn. (com. on securities issues and trading 1970-88), Am. Judicature Soc., So. La. CPAs, New Orleans Assn. Notaries, Tulane U. Alumni Assn., New Orleans C. of C. (coun. 1952-66), Tulane Tax Inst. (program com. 1960-96, emeritus 1997--), Internat. House (bd. dirs. 1976-79, 82-85), Internat. Platform Assn., City Energy Club, Press Club, New Orleans Country Club, Phi Delta Phi (past pres. New Orleans chpt.), Sigma Pi Alpha. Roman Catholic. Home: 6075 Canal Blvd New Orleans LA 70124-2936 Office: 30th Fl Energy Ctr New Orleans LA 70163 E-mail: hpsimon@aol.com., hpsimon@spsr-law.com. *Developing and maintaining consistency and constancy in feeling and showing genuine respect towards others nourish and stimulate an individual to become day by day a better person. Whether alone or in the presence of others, one who daily abides by the guidance and rules he would advocate to others invariably finds the greatest reward of all-true respect for one's self.*

SIMON, JACK AARON, geologist, former state official; b. Champaign, Ill., June 17, 1919; s. Abraham and Lenore (Levy) S. BA, U. Ill., 1941, MS, 1946; postgrad., Northwestern U., 1947-49, D.Sc. (hon.), 1981. Tech. and research asst. Ill. State Geol. Survey, Urbana, 1937-42, asst. to assoc. geologist, 1945-53, geologist, head, coal sect., 1953-67, prin. geologist, 1967-74, asst. chief, 1973-74, chief, 1974-81, prin. scientist, 1981-83. Occasional cons.; asso. prof. dept. metallurgy and mining engring. U. Ill., 1967-74, prof., 1974-77, 80-85, adj. prof. dept. geology, 1979-86. Served with F.A. AUS, 1942-43, F.A., USAAF, 1943-45. Decorated Air Medal with 4 oak leaf clusters; recipient Disting. Svc. award So. Ill. U., Edwardsville, 1982, Coal Day award So. Ill. U., Carbondale, 1982, Alumni Achievement award U. Ill. dept. geology, 1994. Fellow AAAS (sect. E chmn. 1980), Geol. Soc. Am. (chmn. coal geology div. 1962-63, Gilbert H. Cady award 1975, mem. council and exec. com. 1979-81); mem. Am. Assn. Petroleum Geologists (ea. sect. Gordon M. Wood Jr. Meml. award 1991), AIME (chmn. Midwest coal sect. 1966, Percy W. Nicholls award 1981), Am. Inst. Profl. Geologists (v.p. 1973), Am. Mining Congress, Assn. Am. State Geologists (hon.), Ill. Mining Inst. (hon. life; exec. sec.-treas. 1963-68, v.p. 1980-81, pres. 1981-82), Ill. Soc. Coal Preparation Engrs. and Chemists, Ill. Geol. Soc., Ill. Acad. Sci., Soc. Econ. Geologists (councillor 1982-84), B'nai Brith, Sigma Xi. Clubs: Exchange (Urbana) (pres. 1969). Home: 101 W Windsor Rd # 4204 Urbana IL 61802-6697 E-mail: coaljack@hotmail.com.

SIMON, JACQUELINE ALBERT, political scientist, journalist; d. Louis and Rose (Axelroad) Albert; m. Pierre Simon; children: Lisette, Orville. BA cum laude, NYU, MA, 1972, PhD, 1977. Adj. assoc. prof. Southampton Coll., 1977-79; mng. editor Point of Contact, N.Y.C., 1975-76; assoc. editor, U.S. bur. chief Politique Internationale, Paris, 1979—. Sr. vis. scholar Inst. French Studies, NYU, 1980—, assoc. prof. govt., 1982-83; assoc. Inst. on the Media for War and Peace; frequent appearances French TV and radio. Contbg. editor Harper's, 1984-92; contbr. numerous articles to French mags., revs., books on internat. affairs. Bd. dirs. Fresh Air Fund, 1984—, v.p., 1998-2000, treas., 2000—. Mem. Women's Fgn. Policy Group, Women in the Media, Overseas Press Club of Am. (v.p. 1996-2000, treas. 2001—), Phi Beta Kappa. Home: 988 5th Ave New York NY 10021-0143 E-mail: jasimon@ixnetcom.com.

SIMON, JAMES, writer; b. Long Island, N.Y., Feb. 12, 1950; s. Joseph Simon, Harriet Feldman; m. Jany Simon. BA, Stony Brook U., 1973; student, Sch.of Visual Arts, N.Y.C. Author: The Comic Book Makers, 1990, The Monster Channel, 1997, Crane's Neck, 2000, The Far Away, 2002. Mem.: Authors Guild. Office: Information Builders 2 Penn Plaza New York NY 10121 Personal E-mail: privatename1@yahoo.com. Business E-Mail: jim_simon@ibi.com.

SIMON, JAMES LOWELL, lawyer; b. Nov. 8, 1944; s. K. Lowell and Elizabeth Ann (Unholz) S.; m. RuthAnn Beck, July 4, 1997; children: Heather Lyn Small, Brandon James; stepchildren: Gary G. Mower, Richard M. Nazareth II, Juliet A. Nazareth. Student, U. Ill., 1962-63, JD with honors, 1975; BSEE magna cum laude, Bradley U., 1967. Bar: Fla. 1975, Utah 1999, U.S. Dist. Ct. (mid. dist.) Fla. 1976, U.S. Ct. Appeals (11th cir.) 1981, U.S. Patent Office 1983, U.S. Dist. Ct. Utah 1999. Engr. Pan Am. World Airways, Cape Kennedy, Fla., 1967-68; assoc. Akerman, Senterfitt & Eidson, Orlando, 1975-80; ptnr. Bogin, Munns, Munns & Simon, 1980-87, Holland & Knight, LLP, 1987-99; corp. counsel Agilent Technologies, Palo Alto, Calif., 2000—. With Seminole County Sch. Adv. Coun., Fla., 1981-88, chmn., 1982, 83; with Forest City Local Sch. Adv. Com., Altamonte Springs, Fla., 1981-84, Code Enforcement Bd., Altamonte Springs, 1983-84, Cen. Bus. Dist. Study com., Altamonte Springs, 1983-85, Rep. Coun. of '76, Seminole County, 1982-87; mem. Seminole County Libr. Adv. Bd., 1989-92, sec., 1990, pres., 1991, Seminole County Citizens for Quality Edn., 1990-92; mem. Seminole County Sch. Dist. Strategic Planning Com., 1991-99, Leadership Orlando Alumni, 1992-99; bd. dirs. Found. for Seminole County Pub. Schs., Inc., 1992-95, chmn., 1993-94; bd. dirs. Greater Seminole C. of C., 1993; active Lake Brantley H.S. Band Boosters, 1995-2000, Lake Brantley H.S. PTSA, 1995-2000, Chorus Boosters, 1997, Leadership Club-Heart of Fla. United Way, 1997; sponsor concerts Orlando Philharm. Orch. for Boys and Girls Clubs. Cen. Fla., 1996-97; regional dir. region 5 Holocaust Remembrance Project, 1997-99. Capt. USAF, 1968-72. Mem. ABA, Orange County Bar Assn. (jud. rels. com. 1982-83, fee arbitration com. 1983-99), Greater Orlando C. of C., Seminole County Bar Assn. (sec. trial lawyers sect. 1993-94), U. Ill. Alumni Club, Phi Kappa Phi, Tau Beta Pi, Sigma Tau, Eta Kappa Nu. Republican. E-mail: jim. Home: 1675 Tupolo Dr San Jose CA 95124-4754 E-mail: jsimon@agilent.com.

SIMON, JAMES M. federal agency administrator; Grad., U. Ala., So. Calif. Joined CIA, 1975—, asst. dir. adminstrn., 1998—. With U.S. Army. Office: CIA Office of Dir Washington DC 20505*

SIMON, JANE, psychiatrist, educator; d. John L. and Ruth (Briedenbach) S.; m. 1967 (div. 1976); children: Claire Simon-Lanks, Belinda Elizabeth Simon-Lanks. Student, Columbia U., 1960-63, U. P.R., 1963-65; MD, Temple U., 1967; cert., Am. Inst. Psychoanalysis, 1982. Diplomate Am. Bd. Psychiatry and Neurology, Am. Bd. Forensic Pathology, Am. Bd. Anatomic Pathology. Inter, resident in pathology Columbia-Presbyn. Hosp., N.Y.C., 1967-71, fellow dept. pathology, 1971-73; resident in psychiatry Roosevelt Hosp., 1973-75, fellow in child psychiatry, 1975-77; pvt. practice, 1977—; med. dir. Blanton-Peale Counseling Ctr., Blanton-Peale Inst., 1978—. Instr. dept. forensic medicine NYU Sch. Medicine, 1971-73; cons. Odyssey House, 1971-75; jr. med. examiner Office Chief Med. Examiner, City of N.Y., 1971-72, assoc. med. examiner, 1972-73; staff psychiatrist Jewish Meml. Hosp., 1977-78; asst. attending dept. psychiatry and assoc. attending outpatient svc. child and adolescent divsn. St. Luke's-Roosevelt Med. Ctr., N.Y.C.; mem. Faculty Columbia U.; med. dir. Blanton-Peale Grad. Inst.; presenter in field. Author: (poetry) Incisions, 1989; editor Am. Jour. Psychoanalysis; contbr. articles and revs. to med. jours., poems to poetry jours. Vol. psychiatrist Project for Psychiat. Outreach to Homeless, 1992-96. Fellow Am. Acad. Psychoanalysis (Editor Acad. Forum), 1995-2000; mem. Am. Psychiat. Assn., Internat. Karen Horney Soc., Poets and Writers, Poetry Soc. Am., Am. Physicians Poetry Assn., Acad. Am. Poets, Road Runners Assn. Avocations: piano, running. Office: 145 Central Park W Ste 1A New York NY 10023-2004 Fax: (212) 877-3566. E-mail: js145@msn.com.

SIMON, JANOS, computer science educator; b. Budapest, Hungary, June 11, 1946; came to U.S., 1976; s. Sandor and Ilona (Neufeld) S.; married; children: Sandor, Kyle, Trevor. BS in Physics, U. São Paulo, Brazil, 1968, diploma in engring., 1969; PhD, Cornell U., 1975. Instr. State U. São Paulo, 1969-75; asst. prof. U. at Campinas, Brazil, 1975-76, assoc. prof. computer sci. dept. Brazil, 1976-79, head dept. Brazil, 1975-79; asst. prof. computer sci. dept. Pa. State U., State College, 1979-83, assoc. prof., 1983-85, prof., 1985, U. Chgo., 1985—. Editor-in-chief Chgo. Jour. Theoretical Computer Sci.; contbr. articles to profl. jours. Recipient Jabuti prize Brazilian Pubs. Assn. Mem. Assn. for Computing Machinery, IEEE (com. on theory of computing).

SIMON, JIMMY LOUIS, pediatrician, educator; b. San Francisco, Dec. 27, 1930; s. Sylvain L. and Hilda H. (Netter) S.; m. Marilyn S. Wachter, June 21, 1953; children: Kent, Nancy. AB, U. Calif.-Berkeley, 1952; MD, U. Calif.-Berkeley, San Francisco, 1955. Diplomate Am. Bd. Pediats. Intern U. Calif., San Francisco, 1955-56; resident Grace-New Haven Hosp., 1956-57; sr. asst. resident Boston Children's Hosp., 1957-58; instr., asst. prof. pediats. U. Okla., Oklahoma City, 1960-64; assoc. prof. U. Tex. Med. Br., Galveston, 1966-72, prof. pediatrics, 1972-74; prof., chmn. pediats. Bowman Gray Sch. Medicine, Wake Forest U., Winston-Salem, N.C., 1974-96; prof., chmn. emeritus Wake Forest U. Sch. Medicine, 1996—. With USAF, 1958-60. Mem. Am. Pediat. Soc., Am. Acad. Pediats., Am. Bd. Pediats., Ambulatory Pediat. Assn., Alpha Omega Alpha. Office: Wake Forest U Sch Medicine Dept Pediatrics Medical Center Blvd Winston Salem NC 27157-0001 E-mail: jsimon@wfubmc.edu.

SIMON, JOHN BERN, lawyer; b. Cleve., Aug. 8, 1942; s. Seymour Frank and Roslyn (Schultz) S.; children: Lindsey Helaine, Douglas Banning. BS, U. Wis., 1964; JD, DePaul U., 1967. Bar: Ill. 1967. Asst. U.S. atty. U.S. Justice Dept., Chgo., 1967-70, dep. chief civil div., 1970-71, chief civil div., 1971-74; spl. counsel to dir. Ill. Dept. Pub. Aid, 1974-75; legal cons. to Commn. on Rev. of Nat. Policy Toward Gambling, 1975-76; ptnr. firm Friedman & Koven, 1975-85, mem. exec. com., 1983-85; ptnr. firm Jenner & Block, 1986—. Spl. cons. to adminstr. DEA Dept. Justice, 1976-77; counsel to Gov.'s Revenue Study Commn. on Legalized Gambling, 1977-78; spl. counsel Ill. Racing Bd., 1979-80; lectr. tng. seminars and confs.; instr. U.S. Atty. Gen.'s Advocacy Inst., Washington, 1974; lectr. Nat. Conf. Organized Crime, Washington, 1975, Dade County Inst. Organized Crime, Ft. Lauderdale, Fla., 1976; faculty Cornell Inst. Organized Crime, Ithaca, N.Y., 1976, judge Miner Moot Ct. competition Northwestern U., 1971-73; mem. law coun. DePaul U., 1974-83, mem. alumni assn., 1984-85, chmn., 1975-79; adj. prof. DePaul U. Coll. Law, 1977, 81; faculty Practising Law Inst., Chgo., 1984. Contbr. articles to profl. jours. Bd. dirs. Lawyer's Trust Fund of Ill., 1998—, treas., 2000—, Cmty. Film Workshop of Chgo., 1977-90, Friends of Glencoe Parks, 1977-78, sec., 1978-79; mem. nominating com. Glencoe Sch. Bd., 1978-81, chmn. rules com., 1980-81; pres. Glencoe Hist. Soc., 1979-82; mem. Glencoe Zoning Bd. Appeals, Zoning Commn., Sign Bd. Appeals, 1981-86, chmn., 1984-86; mem. Ill. Inaugural Com., 1979, 83, 87, 95; bd. dirs., mem. exec. com. Chgo. World's Fair 1992 Authority, 1983-85; mem. Chancery divsn. task force Spl. Commn. on Adminstrn. of Justice in Cook County, 1985-87; trustee De Paul U., 1990, chair phys. plant and property com., 1992-94, vice chair, 1995—; commr. Ill. Racing Bd., 1990—; gen. trustee Lincoln Acad. Ill., 1993—, regent, 1999—, chancellor, 2001—; mem. Ill. Supreme Ct. Planning and Oversight Com. for Jud. Performance Evaluation Program, 1997-98, 2000—. Recipient Bancroft-Whitney Am. Jurisprudence award, 1965, 66, Judge Learned Hand Human Rels. award Am. Jewish Com., 1994, award for outstanding svc. to legal profession DePaul U. Coll. Law, 1996, Am. ORT Jurisprudence award, 1999. Mem. ABA (com. on liaison with the judiciary 1983-95), FBA (fed. civil procedure com. 1979-85, chmn. 1985-86, bd. mgrs. 1987-89, chmn. house com. 1989-90, treas. 1990-91, 2d v.p. 1991-92, 1st v.p. 1992-93, pres. 1993-94), Ill. State Bar Assn., Women's Bar Assn., Ill. Police Assn., Ill. Sheriffs Assn., U.S. Treasury Agts. Assn., Chgo. Bar Assn., DePaul U. Alumni Assn. (pres. 1985-87, chmn. spl. gifts com. campaign, chmn. Simon Commn. 1989-91, nat. chair for ann. giving 1991-94), Std. Club. Office: Jenner & Block One IBM Plz 42nd Fl Chicago IL 60611

SIMON, JOHN ERNEST, psychiatrist; b. Lincoln, Nebr., Jan. 21, 1951; s. Ralph Irwin and Eleanor Flora (Hubbard) S.; m. Penne Lynn Simon, Aug. 17, 1982; children: Christopher S. Morlan, Jessie F. Simon. BS, U. Nebr., Lincoln, 1973; MD, U. Nebr., Omaha, 1976. Psychiatrist, 1982—. Author: Sasquach Journal, 1997. Avocation: rock climbing. Office: Clinic of Psychopharmacology 701 25th Ave S Ste 303 Minneapolis MN 55454-1490 E-mail: jesimonmd@quest.net.

SIMON, JOHN OLIVER, poet, educator; b. N.Y.C., Apr. 21, 1942; m. Frances Kehrlein Adler; 1 child, Kia. BA, Swarthmore Coll., 1964; MA, U. Calif., Berkeley, 1966. Staff poet Calif. Poets In The Schs., 1971-78, exec. dir., 1978-81; dir. Calif. Heritage Poetry Curriculum, Oakland, 1981-86; bilingual thcr. La Escuelita, 1986-95. Author: (books of poems) Roads to Dawn Lake, 1968, Rattlesnake Grass, 1976, Neither of Us Can Break the Others Hold, 1982, Lord of the House of Dawn, 1991, Velocities of the Possible, 2000, Caminante, 2001. Calif. Arts Coun. individual artist fellow, 1989, Nat. Endowment of the Arts Lit. fellow in transl., 2001.

SIMON, JOHN ROBERT, cell biologist; b. Abington, Pa., Sept. 23, 1958; s. Werner and Erminia Cecilia (Grano) S.; m. Keiko Ozaki, Mar. 12, 1988; children: Emily Jean, Sarah Claire. BS in Biology, Drexel U., 1981; PhD in Biology, Carnegie-Mellon U., 1988. Speaker Internat. Conf. on Video Microscopy, 1989. Contbr. articles to Methods in Enzymology, Biophys. Jour., Jour. Cell Sci., Optical Microscopy for Biology, Jour. Organic Chemistry. NIH/NIGMS grantee, 1989-91. Mem. Am. Soc. Cell Biology, Biophys. Soc., Sigma Xi. Achievements include co-design of organic synthesis of alpha-acrylic fatty acids; discovery of fluorescent actin filaments as being susceptible to photodamage; characterization of kinetic parameters of microtubules assembled from non-neural tubulin. Home: 1942 Lafayette Rd Lansdale PA 19446-5519 Office: Tulip BioLabs Inc PO Box 334 West Point PA 19486

SIMON, JOSEPH PATRICK, food services executive; b. Phila., Nov. 9, 1932; s. Joseph Patrick and Elizabeth Gertrude (McLaughlin) S.; m. Vera Cornelia Steiner, Sept. 15, 1956; children: Joseph Walter, Walter Joseph, Leslie Vera, Ernest William. BS, Cornell U., 1955. With Slater Systems, 1955-59; with ARA Services, Inc., Phila., 1959-72, regional v.p., 1964-66, area v.p., 1966-68, group v.p. and sr. v.p., 1968-70, pres. community and school food service div., 1970-71, gen. mgr., pres. internat. ops., 1971-72; v.p., gen. mgr. airline services div. Dobbs Houses Inc., Memphis, 1972-73; group v.p. Service Systems Corp., Buffalo, 1973-79, pres., 1980-85, also nat. dir.; group v.p. P.J. Schmitt subs. Loblaw Ltd., 1984, sr. v.p., 1985-88, also bd. dirs., 1986, 87. Dist. chmn. Detroit United Fund, 1966-67, Nat. Alliance of Businessmen, 1969; mem. adv. bd. McComb Jr. Coll.; mem. council Cornell U., 1980-83; chmn. bd. Sheehan Emergency Hosp., Buffalo, 1984-85; trustee D'Youville Coll.; bd. dirs. United Fund, Buffalo, 1981-82, CODE Inc., 1986-87. Served as 1st lt. U.S. Army, 1955-56. Mem. Assn. Food Svc. Mgmt. (dir.), Nat. Automatic Merchandising Assn. (dir.), Buffalo C. of C. (dir. 1982-84), Cornell Hotel Soc. Mich. (pres.), Memphis Athletic Club, Detroit Athletic Club, Buffalo Club, Park County Club, The Meadows Country Club, Zeta Psi. Episcopalian. Home: 4422 Whisperwood Sarasota FL 34235-6924

SIMON, JULIAN LINCOLN, economics educator; b. Newark, Feb. 12, 1932; s. Philip Mordechai and Mae (Goodstein) S.; m. Rita Mintz James, June 25, 1961; children: David Meyer, Judith Debs, Daniel Hillel. BA, Harvard U., 1953; MBA, U. Chgo., 1960, PhD, 1961. Advt. copywriter William Douglas McAdams Inc., N.Y.C., 1956; with sale promotion Ziff-Davis Pub. Co., 1957-61; owner Julian Simon Assocs., Newark, 1961-63; prof. econs., mktg. and advt. U. Ill., Urbana, from 1963; now prof. mgmt. U. Md., College Park, 1983—. Prof. Hebrew U., Jerusalem, 1968, 70-71, 74-75. Author: How to Start and Operate a Mail-Order Business, 1965, 4th edit., 1986, Basic Research Methods in Social Science, 1969, 3d edit., 1985; (with Herman H. Fussler) Patterns of Use of Books in Large Research Libraries, 1969; Issues in the Economics of Advertising, 1970, The Management of Advertising, 1971, The Effects of Income on Fertility, 1974, Applied Managerial Economics, 1975, The Economics of Population Growth, 1977, The Ultimate Resource, 1981, Theory of Population and Economic Growth, 1986, Effort, Opportunity, and Wealth, 1987, The Economic Consequences of Immigration, 1989, Population Matters: People, Resources, Environment and Immigration, 1990; editor: Research in Population Economics, Vol. I, 1978, Vol. II (with Julie daVanzo), 1978, Vol. III (with Peter Lindert), Vol. IV (with Peter Lindert), 1982, (with Herman Kahn) The Resourceful Earth: A Response to the Global 2000 Report, 1984. Served to lt. (j.g.) USN, 1953-56. Mem. Am. Statis. Assn., Am. Econ. Assn., Pop Assn. Am., Population Assn. Am. Jewish. Home: 110 Primrose St Bethesda MD 20815-3325 Office: U Md Dept Mgmt College Park MD 20742-0001

SIMON, KATHRYN ALLYN, fashion designer, textile designer; b. Nov. 11, 1953; d. Kenneth Paul Simon and Elaine Doris (Rosenberg) Simon Post; m. Robin Poppelsdorff, Oct. 31, 1972 (div. July 1979). Student Rudolf Steiner Inst., Emerson Coll., Sussex, Eng., 1973-74. Clothing and sweater designer Elaine Post Ltd., N.Y.C., 1969-71; textile designer Ascher Fabrics, London, 1972-73, Galleon Fabrics, N.Y.C., 1974-75; freelance textile designer New Wave, N.Y.C., Los Angeles, N.Y.C., 1975-79, Paris, 1979-80; owner Kathryn Simon Inc., designer and mfr. women's high fashion clothing, N.Y.C., 1981—. Work featured in Woman's Wear Daily, Harpers Bazaar, Vogue, Elle, N.Y. Times. High sch. coordinator Vietnam Moratorium Com., N.Y.C., 1969. Mem. Fashion Council. Avocations: African/Brazilian dance, painting.

SIMON, LEONARD SAMUEL, banker; b. N.Y.C., Oct. 28, 1936; s. Nathaniel and Lena (Pasternack) S.; m. Marion Appel, Sept. 1, 1957; children: Andrew, Jonathan. BS, MIT, 1958; MS, Columbia U., 1959, PhD, 1963. Mem. faculty Grad. Sch. Mgmt., U. Rochester, 1962-79, prof., 1974-79; v.p. Community Savs. Bank, Rochester, N.Y., 1969-74, sr. v.p., 1974-77, exec. v.p., 1977-83, Rochester Community Sav. Bank, 1983-84, chmn., chief exec. officer, 1984-97; chmn., CEO, pres. RSCB Fin., Inc., 1995-97; vice. chmn. charter One Financial Inc., 1997—; chmn. Captial Internet Grp., 1997—2000; vice chmn. Charter One Fin. Inc., 1997—. Bd. dirs. Gateway Am. Bank, Integrated Nano Tech., Inc.; chmn. Telephone Computing Svc. Corp., 1974—79; trustee Tchrs. Ins. Annuity Assn. Editor-in-chief, founding editor: Interfaces, 1970-76; Author books and articles in field. Past chmn. Rochester-Monroe County chpt. ARC, Rochester Area Ednl. TV Assn., Career Devel. Svcs. of Rochester; past trustee Ctr. for Govt. Rsch.; mem. Urban Policy Conf., Brookings Instn., 1972-73, 64th Am. Assembly; bd. dirs. Cmty. Preservation. Ford Found. grantee, 1964; recipient MIT Corp. Leadership award, 1987. Mem. Cmty. Bankers Assn. N.Y. State (bd. dirs.), Am.'s Cmty. Bankers, Genesee Valley Club, Beta Gamma Sigma.

SIMON, LOTHAR, publishing company executive; b. Wuppertal, Germany, Sept. 17, 1938; came to U.S., 1961, naturalized, 1973; s. Fritz and Erna (Backhaus) S.; m. Jeannine Rechtman, Oct. 30, 1964; 1 child, Charles. Mgr. book dept. Franz Bader Book Shop and Globe Book Shop, Washington, 1961-66; sales mgr. Humanities Press Inc., N.Y.C., 1966-73; pres. Longman Inc., 1973-81; pub. cons., 1981-82; pres., chief exec. officer Sheridan House, Inc., Dobbs Ferry, N.Y., 1982—. Mem. Assn. Am. Pubs. Clubs: Town (Scarsdale, N.Y.). Democrat. Office: Sheridan House Inc 145 Palisade St Dobbs Ferry NY 10522-1617

SIMON, MARGARET B(ALLIF), elementary school educator, writer; b. Washington, Sept. 12, 1942; d. Paul Shirvington and Lucy White (Grasty) Ballif; m. Roger Tillison, 1964 (div. 1965); 1 child Melle Broaderick ; m. Bruce Boston, Apr. 7, 2001. BA, U. No. Colo., 1969, MA, 1970. Art tchr. Marion County Sch. Sys., Ocala, Fla., 1973—. Author: Eonian Variations, 1995; illustrator: CD-ROM Extremes 2, 2001 (Bram Stoker award, 2002); illustrator Consumed, Reduced to Beautiful Gray Ashes, 2001 (Bram Stoker award, 02); illustrator: Thy Kingdom Come, 2002, illustrator, editor: Mystic Hoofbeats, 1988; editor: Poets of the Fantastic, 1992; art/poetry editor: Small Press Writers/Artists Orgn. Internat. Showcase, 1987—92. V.p. Marion Art Educators Assn., Ocala, 1987. Mem.: Horror Writers Assn. (membership chmn. 1999—), Sci. Fiction Poetry Assn. Internat. (editor Star*Line 1993—96, pres. 1996—2000, Rhysling Best Long Poem award 1995), Small Press Writers/Artists Orgn. Internat. (pres. 1988—90, Best Artist award 1991, Dale Donaldson award 1991). Home: 1412 NE 35th St Ocala FL 34479

SIMON, MARTIN STANLEY, commodity marketing company executive, economist; b. St. Louis, Sept. 6, 1926; s. Elmer Ellis and Bee Marion (Werner) S.; m. Rita Edith Scheinhorn, June 18, 1950; children: Deborah, Richard. BBA, CCNY, 1949; MA, NYU, 1953. Econ. statistician Indsl. Commodity Corp, N.Y.C., 1949-52; agrl. econ. statistician Dept. Agr., Washington, 1952-58; commodity analyst Connell Rice & Sugar Co., Inc., Westfield, N.J., 1958-62, asst. to pres., 1962-67, v.p., 1967-74; sr. v.p. Connell Rice & Sugar Co., Inc. (now The Connell Co.), 1974-99; pres. Eureka Group, LLC, 1999—, The Rice Econs. Group, LLC, Westfield, 1999—; cons. AID, Jamaica, 1963; mem. Rice Insp. Industry Adv. Com., Washington, 1971-72; adv. U.S. Del. to UN FAO Intergovtl. Meetings on Rice, 1981; export dir., bd. dirs. Assn. Adminstrn. Rice Quotas, Inc., 1997-99. Served with U.S. Army, 1944-46, ETO. Recipient Class of 1920 award for merit in econ. stats. CCNY, 1949 Mem. Am. Econ. Assn., Rice Millers Assn. (chmn. legis. options working group 1984-86, govt. programs com. 1986-87, chmn. PL480 subcom. 1988-90), Nat. Economists Club. Office: The Rice Econs Group LLC PO Box 2446 Westfield NJ 07091-2446 E-mail: rice.economics@prodigy.net.

SIMON, MARVIN B. investment company executive, real estate broker; b. Chgo., Dec. 18, 1931; s. Abe and Ida Simon; m. Patty G. Simon, Aug. 1, 1954; children: Rachel, Mark, Craig. BS, Roosevelt U., 1954. CPA, Ill.; lic. real estate broker, Colo. Exec. v.p. Datronic Rental Corp., Chgo., 1971-76; mng. broker Just Relax Realty, Vail, Colo., 1978—; pres. MBS Devel. Corp., Denver, 1979—, Grand Eagle Investment Corp., Denver, 1979—. Host Just Relax Bed & Breakfast, Avon, Colo., 1996-99. With U.S. Army, 1954-56. Mem.: Denver Bd. Realtors. Avocations: skiing, golf. Home: 16888 W 67th Pl Arvada CO 80007

SIMON, MARVIN KENNETH, electrical engineer, consultant; b. N.Y.C., Sept. 10, 1939; s. Sidney and Belle (Cone) S.; m. Anita Joyce Sauerhof; children: Brette, Jeffrey. BEE, CCNY, 1960; MSEE, Princeton U., 1961; PhD, NYU, 1966. Mem. tech. staff Bell Telephone Labs., Holmdel, N.J., 1961-63, 66-68; sr. rsch. engr. Jet Propulsion Lab., Pasadena, Calif., 1968—. Adj. prof. Calif. Inst. Tech., Pasadena, 1986-87, 88-90. Author: Telecommunications Systems Engineering, 1973, Phase-Locked Loops and Their Application, 1978, reprinted, 1991, Spread Spectrum Communications, Vols. I, II, III, 1984, Introduction to Trellis--Coded Modulation with Application, 1990, Digital Communication Techniques, Vol. I: Signal Design and Detection, 1994, Spread Spectrum Communications Handbook, 1994, Mobile Communications Handbook, 1995, Digital Communications over Fading Channels: A Uniform Approach to Performance Analysis, 2000; also numerous articles; patentee in field. Recipient NASA Exptl. Svc. medal, 1979, NASA Exptl. Engring. Achievement medal, 1995. Fellow IEEE (Bicentennial medal 1984, Armstrong Achievement award 1997, 3d Millennium medal 2000), Inst. for Advancement Engring. Avocation: computer games. Office: Jet Propulsion Lab Mail Stop 238-343 4800 Oak Grove Dr Pasadena CA 91109-8001

SIMON, MELVIN, real estate developer, professional basketball executive; b. Oct. 21, 1926; s. Max and Mae Simon; m. Bren Burns, Sept. 14, 1972; children: Deborah, Cynthia, Tamme, David, Max. Bs in Acctg., CCNY, 1949, M in Bus., Real Estate, 1983; PhD (hon.), Butler U., 1986, Ind. U., 1991. Leasing sgt. Albert Frankel Co., Indpls., 1955-60; pres. Melvin Simon & Assocs., 1960-73, co-chmn. bd. dirs., 1973—; co-owner Ind. Pacers, 1983—. Adv. bd. Wharton's Real Estate, Phila., 1986—. Adv. bd. dean's council Ind. U., Bloomington; bd. dirs. United Cerebral Palsy, Indpls., Muscular Dystrophy Assn., Indpls., Jewish Welfare Found., Indpls.; trustee Urban Land Inst., Internat. Council Shopping Ctrs. Recipient Horatio Alger award Boy's Club Indpls., 1986; named Man of Yr., Jewish Welfare Found., 1980. Democrat. Jewish. Office: Indiana Pacers 125 South Pennsylvania St. Indianapolis IN 46204*

SIMON, MICHAEL PAUL, general contractor, realtor; b. Madison, Wis., Sept. 23, 1941; s. Michael Francis and Ferne Doris (DeBower) S.; m. Sharon Lee Hackbart, Aug. 31, 1963; children: René M., Michael V. BS in Bldg. Constrn., Bradley U., 1964. Designer, estimator Michael F. Simon Builders, Inc., Waunakee, Wis., 1964-67, v.p., 1967-73, pres., 1973—. Commentator St. John's Cath. Ch., Waunakee, 1975-93. Named Bus. Man of Yr., Waunakee C. of C., 1980, One of Top Dane County Execs., Madison Mag. Poll, 1994. Mem. Nat. Assn. Home Builders (bd. dirs. 1985—), Wis. Builders Assn. (bd. dirs. 1980-85, membership chair 1981), Madison Area Builders Assn. (pres. 1980, chair arbitration com. 1992-94, Builder of Yr. 1980). Roman Catholic. Avocations: boating, golf, travel.

SIMON, MICHAEL RICHARD, allergist, immunologist, internist; b. N.Y.C., Oct. 12, 1943; MD, NYU, 1969; MA, Stanford U., 1973. Diplomate Am. Bd. Allergy and Immunology, recert.; diplomate Am. Bd. Internal Medicine, recert.; diplomate Am. Bd. Med. Lab. Immunology. Intern SUNY-Downstate Med. Ctr., Bklyn., 1969-70; resident in internal medicine Wayne State U., 1973-75; fellow in allergy and immunology U. Mich. Med. Ctr., Ann Arbor, 1975-77; chief sect. allergy and immunology VA Med. Ctr., Detroit, 1977-2000; assoc. prof. medicine Wayne State U., 1990-98, assoc. prof. pediats., 1992-98, tng. program dir. allergy and immunology, 1991-2000; assoc. tng. program dir. allergy and immunology Henry Ford Health Sys., 2000—. Prof. pediatrics and internal medicine Wayne State U., Detroit, 1998—. Fellow ACP, Am. Acad. Allergy Asthma and Immunology, Am. Coll. Allergy Asthma and Immunology, Royal Coll. Physicians Can. Office: Henry Ford Health Sys Allergy and Immunology 1 Ford Pl Detroit MI 48202 E-mail: mrsimonmd@ameritech.net.

SIMON, MICHAEL SCOTT, lawyer; b. Bronx, N.Y., Feb. 9, 1954; s. Philip and Miriam C. (Feller) S.; m. Elayne Robin Baer, May 26, 1974; children: Joshua Seth, Sarah Emily, Rachel Melissa. BA, SUNY, Stony Brook, 1976; JD, Boston U., 1979. Bar: N.Y. 1980, U.S. Dist. Ct. (ea. and so. dists.) N.Y. 1980, U.S. Ct. Appeals (2d cir.) 1981, U.S. Tax Ct. 1983, U.S. Supreme Ct. 1983; Fla. 1987. Asst. corp. counsel N.Y.C. Law Dept., 1979-82; assoc. Tenzer, Greenblatt, Fallon & Kaplan, N.Y.C., 1982-88; ptnr. Tenzer, Greenblatt L.L.P., 1989-99, Blank Rome Tenzer Greenblatt, LLP, N.Y.C., 2000—. Mem. ABA, N.Y. State Bar Assn., Fla. Bar Assn., N.Y. County Lawyers Assn., Assn. Bar City N.Y., Pi Sigma Alpha. Avocations: travel, music. Home: 4 Talon Way Dix Hills NY 11746-6239 Office: Blank Rome Tenzer Greenblatt LLP 405 Lexington Ave New York NY 10174-0002 E-mail: msimon@blankrome.com.

SIMON, MORDECAI, religious association administrator, clergyman; b. St. Louis, July 19, 1925; s. Abraham M. and Rose (Solomon) S.; m. Maxine R. Abrams, July 4, 1954; children: Ora, Eve, Avrom. BA, St. Louis U., 1947; MA, Washington U., St. Louis, 1952; MHL, Rabbi, Jewish Theol. Sem. Am., N.Y.C., 1952, DD (hon.), 1977. Ordained rabbi, 1952. Rabbi in, Mpls., 1952-56, Waterloo, Iowa, 1956-63; exec. dir. Chgo. Bd. Rabbis, 1963-80, exec. v.p., 1980-95, exec. v.p. emeritus, 1995—. Nat. chaplain Jewish War Vets., 1977-78. Host: (weekly program) What's Nu?, Sta. WGN-TV, 1973-92. With AUS, 1943-46. Recipient citation Jewish War Vets., 1967, Boy Scouts Am., 1966, 74, 88, Chgo. chpt. Am. Jewish Congress, 1973, Chgo. Conf. Jewish Women's Orgns., 1973, Chgo. Bd. Rabbis, 1973, Rabbinical Svc. award of Appreciation, Jewish Theol. Sem. Am., 1988, Raoul Wallenberg Humanitarian award, 1989, citation and commendation Ill. Ho. Reps., 1995, Order of Merit, The Equestrian Order of the Holy Sepulchre of Jerusalem, 1996; Rabbi Mordecai Simon Day proclaimed by Gov. James Edgar, State of Ill., 1995. Mem. Rabbinical Assembly. Home: 621 County Line Rd Highland Park IL 60035-5220 Office: 1 S Franklin St Chicago IL 60606-4609

SIMON, NANCY RUTH, lawyer; b. Gary, Ind. BSEE, Iowa State U., 1985; MBA, U. Dallas, 1988; JD, So. Meth. U., 1991. Bar: Tex. 1991, Calif. 1994, U.S. Patent and Trademark. Elec. engr. Tex. Instruments, Dallas, 1986-88; law clk. to pvt. law firms, 1989-91; law clk. U.S. Attys. Office, 1991; assoc. Felsman, Bradley, Gunter & Dillon, LLP, Ft. Worth, 1991-93; patent counsel Apple Computer, Inc., Cupertino, Calif., 1993-2000; ptnr. Simon & Koerner, LLP, 2000—. Realtor Coldwell Banker, San Jose, Calif., 1997—98. Co-author: (book) Attorney's Fees in IPL Cases; mem.: So. Meth. U. Law Rev. Jour. Air Law and Commerce, 1990—91. Bd. dirs. Sunset Pk. Sunnyvale Homeowners Assn., 1998—. Mem.: ABA, Am. Inn of Ct., San Francisco Bay Area Intellectual Property, State Bar Calif., State Bar Tex., Am. Intellectual Property Law Assn., Iowa State U. Student Alumni Assn. (mem. career awareness com. 1984—85), Mensa, Phi Delta Phi, Zeta Tau Alpha (social chmn. 1982—83, ho. mgr. 1983—84, chmn. jud. bd. 1984—85), Sigma Iota Epsilon. Avocations: reading, music, scuba diving. Office: Simon & Koerner LLP 10052 Pasadena Ave Ste B Cupertino CA 95014-5945

SIMON, NEIL, playwright, television writer; b. N.Y.C., July 4, 1927; s. Irving and Mamie Simon; m. Joan Baim, Sept. 30, 1953 (dec.); m. Marsha Mason, 1973 (div.); m. Diane Lander, 1987. Student, NYU, 1946; LLD (hon.), Hofstra U., 1981, Williams Coll., 1984. Author materials for Tamiment (Pa.) revues, 1952-53; author: (with brother Danny) sketches Catch a Star, 1955, (with brother Danny) for New Faces of '56; book for musicals Little Me, 1962, Sweet Charity, 1966 (Evening Standard Drama award 1967), Promises, Promises, 1968 (Tony award nomination 1969), They're Playing Our Song, 1979, Little Me (Tony award nomination 1963 version, rev. version), 1982, The Goodbye Girl, 1993, Rewrites: A Memoir, 1996; plays include Come Blow Your Horn, 1961, Barefoot in the Park, 1963 (Tony award nomination 1963), The Odd Couple, 1965 (Tony award 1965), The Star-Spangled Girl, 1966, Plaza Suite, 1968 (Tony award nomination 1968), Last of the Red Hot Lovers, 1969 (Tony award nomination 1970), The Gingerbread Lady, 1970, The Prisoner of Second Avenue, 1971 (Tony award nomination 1972), The Sunshine Boys, 1972, The Good Doctor, 1973, God's Favorite, 1974, California Suite, 1976, Chapter Two, 1977, I Ought to be in Pictures, 1980, Fools, 1981, Brighton Beach Memoirs, 1983, Biloxi Blues, 1985 (Tony award for Best Playwright 1985, Best Play 1985), The Odd Couple (female version), 1985, Broadway Bound, 1986 (Tony award nomination 1987), Rumors, 1988, Lost in Yonkers, 1991 (Pulitzer Prize for drama 1991, Tony award Best Play 1991), Jake's Women, 1992, Laughter on the 23rd Floor, 1993, London Suite, 1995, Proposals, 1997; wrote screenplays adapted from own plays: Barefoot in the Park, 1967, The Odd Couple, 1968, Plaza Suite, 1971, Last of the Red Hot Lovers, 1972, The Prisoner of Second Avenue, 1975, The Sunshine Boys, 1975, California Suite, 1978, Chapter Two, 1979, Only When I Laugh (adapted from play The Gingerbread Lady), 1981, I Ought to be in Pictures, 1982, Brighton Beach Memoirs, 1986, Biloxi Blues, 1988, Broadway Bound, 1992 (TV motion picture), Lost in Yonkers, 1993, (TV motion picture) Jake's Women, 1996; other screenplays include After the Fox, 1966, The Out-of-Towners, 1970, The Heartbreak Kid, 1973, Murder by Death, 1976, The Goodbye Girl, 1977, The Cheap Detective, 1978, Seems Like Old Times, 1980, Max Dugan Returns, 1983, The Lonely Guy (adaptation), 1984, The Sluggers Wife, 1984, The Marrying Man, 1991, The Odd Couple II, 1997, The Out-of-Towners, 1999; other motion pictures based on his stage plays: Come Blow Your Horn, 1963, Sweet Charity, 1969, The Star-Spangled Girl, 1971; wrote for TV shows: The Phil Silvers Arrow Show, 1958, The Tallulah Bankhead Show, 1951, The Sid Caesar Show, 1956-57 (Emmy award 1956-57), Phil Silvers Show, 1958-59 (Emmy award 1958-59), Garry Moore Show, 1959-60; also NBC spl. The Trouble with People, 1972. Served to cpl. USAAF, 1945-46. Recipient Sam S. Shubert award 1968, Writers Guild screen awards, 1968, 70, 75, Writers Guild Laurel award, 1979. Mem. Dramatists Guild, Writers Guild Am. (Laurel award 1979, screen awards 1968, 70, 75). Address: care Albert DaSilva 502 Park Ave New York NY 10022-1108*

SIMON, NORMA PLAVNICK, psychologist; b. Washington, Sept. 20, 1930; d. Mark and Mary Plavnick; m. Robert G. Simon, Dec. 18, 1949; children: Mark Allan, Susan. BA, NYU, 1952, cert. in psychoanalysis, 1977; MA, Columbia U., 1953, EdD, 1968. Diplomate Am. Bd. Profl. Psychology, 1988, Counseling Psychology, Psychoanalysis, 1997. Psychologist Queens Coll. Counseling Ctr., Flushing, N.Y., 1968-70, asst. dir., 1970-76, dir., 1976; gen. practice psychology N.Y.C., 1970—. Faculty, supr. New Hope Guild, Bklyn., 1976—, dir. child and adolescent tng. prog., 1988-98; adj. prof. clin. psychology Columbia U., N.Y.C., 1986—; supr. NYU Postdoctoral Prog. in Psychoanalysis, 1988—. Author: (with Robert G. Simon): Choosing a College Major: Social Science, 1981; co-author 3 book chpts. on licensure and ethics in psychology; mem. editl. bd. The Counseling Psychologist jour., 1986-89, Profl. Practice and Rsch. in Psychology, 1994-99, Jour. Infant, Child and Adolescent Psych Therapy, 1999—. Vice chairperson N.Y. State Bd. for Psychology State Edn. Dept., Albany, 1978-82, chairperson, 1982-88; bd. dirs. Pelham (N.Y.) Guidance Coun., 1980-83; pres.-elect Assn. State and Provincial Psychology Bds., 1990, pres., 1991. Recipient Karl Heiser award, 1993, Morton Berger award Assn. State and Provincial Psychology Bds., 1998. Fellow: APA (mem. bd. profl. affairs 1987—89, chair bd. profl. affairs 1989—90, policy and planning bd. 1991—93, mem. ethics com. 1995—98, vice chair ethics com. 1996—97, chair ethics com. 1997, workgroup on telehealth 1998—2000, John Black award 1994), Am. Bd. Counseling Psychology (bd. dirs. 1992—2000, pres.-elect 1999, pres. 2001—), Nat. Acads. of Practice (elected disting. practitioner), Am. Bd. Profl. Psychology (trustee 1998—2001, pres.-elect 2001—); mem.: Nat. Register Health Svc. Providers in Psychology. Office: 500A E 87th St # 5A New York NY 10128-7626 E-mail: normasimon@aol.com.

SIMON, PETER E. publishing executive; b. Bklyn., July 29, 1953; BA in English, CCNY, 1971; MA in Libr. Sci., Columbia U., 1980. Database mgr. R.R. Bowker, N.Y.C., 1982-84; v.p. R.R. Bowker/Reed Reference Pubs., 1984-93; sr. v.p. Reed Reference Pub., New Providence, N.J., 1993-95, exec. v.p., 1995-97; v.p. bus. devel. Nat. Info. Svcs./Lexis-Nexis, Horsham, Pa., 1997-98; v.p. new product planning and devel. The Gale Group, Farmington Hills, Mich., 1998—, v.p. product mgmt., 1999, v.p. bus. devel., 1999-2000; dir. content lic. The Deal, LLC, N.Y.C., 2000-2001; v.p. strategic devel. Digital Owl, Orlando, Fla., 2001—02; dir. new bus. devel. Nstein Techs. Corp., 2002—. Mem. Info. Industry Assn. (chmn. content divsn., bd. dirs.), Phi Beta Kappa.

SIMON, PHILIP GEORGE, music educator, musician; b. Quincy, Mass., Sept. 13, 1947; s. George Louis and Maryrita Elizabeth Simon; m. Lucinda May Simpson, July 7, 1990; children: Rebecca, Elizabeth, Benjamen; m. Martha Ann Bonney, July 24, 1969 (div. Feb. 10, 1987). BMus, Boston U., 1969; MEd in Music Edn., U. Md., 1975. Cert. K-12 music tchr. Md., Va. Tubist First U.S. Army Band, Ft. George G. Meade, Md., 1969—71; band dir. Friendly H.S., Oxon Hill, 1971—85; dir. of bands Thomas Jefferson H.S. for Sci. and Tech., Alexandria, Va., 1985—2001; adj. prof. of instrumental music Southwestern Adventist U., Keene, Tex., 2001—. Guest condr./clinician numerous schools, colleges, and profl. ensembles, throughout the U.S., and internationally, 1969—. Arranger, transcriber: Concerto for French Horn in E-flat, Rondo, K.496, arranged for Wind Ensemble, 1976. With U.S. Army, 1969—71. Mem.: Music Educators Nat. Conf., Nat. Band Assn. (Citation of Excellence 1994, 1997, 2000, citation of excellence 1994, 1997, 2000), Internat. Assocation of Jazz Educators (pres., va. unit 1995—97). Home: 1030 Dallas Dr Apt 1428 Denton TX 76205 Home Fax: same. Personal E-mail: tubasrus@yahoo.com.

SIMON, ROBERT G. lawyer; b. N.Y.C., Feb. 21, 1927; s. Monroe and Claire S. S.; m. Norma Plavnick, Dec. 18, 1949; children: Mark A., Susan. BA, Cornell U., 1947; LLB, JD, Georgetown U., 1950; LLM, NYU, 1961. Bar: D.C. 1950, N.Y. 1951, U.S. Supreme Ct. 1955. Assoc. firms in, N.Y.C., 1950-52; legal sec. to judge U.S. Dist. Ct. So. Dist. N.Y., 1953-58; assoc. Jaffe & Wachtell, N.Y.C., 1958-61; legal adv. TV series The Verdict Is Yours, 1958-60; successively dir. bus. affairs, v.p., sr. v.p., mgr. bus. affairs dept. McCann-Erickson, Inc., N.Y.C., 1961-80; sr. broadcast atty. The Interpublic Group of Cos., 1980-95. Adj. faculty Manhattan Community Coll., 1967, Baruch Coll., 1968, CCNY, 1968, New Sch. Social Research, 1972-73; speaker in field. Author: (with Norma Simon) Choosing a College Major: The Social Sciences, 1981; contbr. articles to profl. jours. Dem.-Liberal candidate for county clk. Westchester County, N.Y., 1952; chmn. Narcotics Guidance Coun., Pelham, N.Y., 1973; mem. Nat. Media Coun. on Disability, 1986-90; bd. dirs., gen. counsel Nat. Challenge Com. on Disability, 1986-88; mem. adv. bd. The Caption Ctr. WGBH Found., 1987—; mem. state bd. for podiatry N.Y. State Dept. Edn., 2000—. With USAAF, 1944-46. Mem.: NATAS (chpt. gov. 1972—85, treas. 1976—81, 1st v.p. 1981—83, nat. trustee 1981—85, pres. 1983—85, chpt. gov. 1996—97, nat. trustee 1996—98), Am. Assn. Advt. Agy.s (com. on broadcast adminstrn. policy 1985—93), N.Y. County Lawyers Assn. (com. on comms. and entertainment law 1990—, not-for-profit orgns., alternate dispute resolution com. 1998—), Hemlock Soc. N.Y. (bd. dirs. 2000—02). Home: 2 Garden Pl Pelham NY 10803-3207

SIMON, ROBERT STEPHEN, artist; b. Flushing, N.Y., Nov. 4, 1939; s. Benjamin and Clara (Helsel) S. BA, Ill. Wesleyan U., Bloomington, 1962; degree in Fine Arts, Arts Students League, N.Y.C., 1965. Landscape, portrait artist, N.Y.C., 1965-82; sports and portrait artist, 1983—. Sports artist: more than 500 paintings in last 10 yrs.; displayed in Baseball's Hall of Fame, Nat. Acad. Fine Art, Madison Sq. Garden, Downtown Athletic Club, Sports Immortals Mus., as well as in the personal collections of Mickey Mantle, Sylvester Stallone and Joe DiMaggio; The 70 Karat Diamond depicting 70 of baseball's greatest players on a diamond-shaped canvas will be displayed at the entrance of a baseball mus. that will open in Orlando, Fla., in 2001; recent completion of Masters of the Millenium a 50x50 oil painting depicting over 50 of the greatest golfers in history of game proving to be 1st of its kind. Sports Artist of Yr. U.S. Sports Acad. of Art, 1992; People's Choice 1st prize Broward Art Guild, 1997; 1st Prize Oil Norwood U., 1998; nominated for Disting. Alumni award Ill. Wesleyan U., 1999; Color Trend award for Disting. Artwork in Lithography, 1998. Mem. Nat. Soc. of Illustrators, Am. Soc. of Classical Realism, Internat. Soc. Artists, Allied Artists of Am., Salmagundi Club, Norton Mus. Fine Art Guild. Home: 2700 S Oakland Forest Dr Fort Lauderdale FL 33309-7527

SIMON, ROGER FRANK, law educator; b. Ft. Worth, Oct. 17, 1961; s. Richard Uriah Jr. and Bayla Handler Simon. BA, Rice U., 1984; MA, NYU, 1986; JD, U. Tex., 1997. Bar: Tex. 1997. Rschr. Am. Film Inst., L.A., 1989—90; dir. exhbns. Southwestern Alt. Media Project, Houston, 1991—93; briefing atty. Tex. Ct. Criminal Appeals, Austin, 1998, staff atty., 1999—2002; legal writing prof. Tex. Wesleyan U. Sch. Law, Ft. Worth, 2002—. Contbr. articles to profl. jours. Allen Lane Roberts Endowed Presdl. scholar, Austin, 1996-97; Tex. Law fellow, Austin, 1995. Mem. ABA, Tex. Bar. Home: 3720 Murray Ct Ft Worth TX 76107-6845 Office: Tex Wesleyan U Sch Law Legal Writing Dept Ft Worth TX 76102 E-mail: rsimon@law.tx.wes.edu.

SIMON, RONALD CHARLES, curator; b. Phila., Feb. 23, 1951; s. Samuel Charles and Emily (Luzenberg) Simon. BA, Dickinson Coll., 1973; postgrad., Brit. Film and TV Inst., Stirling, Scotland, 1973, Columbia U., 1973-75. Researcher NBC, N.Y.C., 1976—77; mgr. media prodn. 1st Boston Corp., 1979; curator TV, Mus. TV and Radio, 1979—. Adj. prof. Hunter Coll., CUNY, 1987—, Columbia U., N.Y.C., 1991—; cons., lectr. to mus. and colls. including Smithsonian Instn., Whitney Mus. Am. Art, NYU, Cooper Hewitt Mus., 1985—. Author: Worlds Without End: The Art and History of Soap Opera, 1997. Mem.: NATAS (panelist and juror for numerous awards 1985—, mem. editl. bd. TV Quar. 1987—), TV Ltd. (bd. dirs. 2002—). Home: 141 E 17th St New York NY 10003-3402 Office: Television & Radio 25 W 52nd St New York NY 10019-6104 E-mail: ronsimonnyc@yahoo.com., rsimon@mtr.org.

SIMON, RONALD I. financial executive; b. Cairo, Nov. 4, 1938; came to U.S., 1942; s. David and Helene (Zilkha) S.; m. Anne Faith Hartman, June 19, 1960; children: Cheryl, Eric, Daniel. BA, Harvard U., 1960; MA, Columbia U., 1962, PhD, 1968. V.p. Harpers Internat., N.Y.C., 1959-62; fin. analyst Amerace Corp., 1965-66; v.p. Am. Foresight Inc., Phila., 1966-67; asst. to pres. Avco Corp., Greenwich, Conn., 1967-70; exec. v.p. Avco Community Developers Inc., La Jolla, Calif., 1970-73; pres. Ronald I. Simon Inc., 1973—99; pres., CEO Delta Data Systems Corp., Phila., 1980-81; exec. v.p. Towner Petroleum Corp., Houston, 1983-85; mng. dir., chief fin. officer The Henley Group Inc., La Jolla, 1986-90; pvt. practice fin. cons., 1990—2000. Vice-chmn. bd. dirs. Softnet Corp., San Francisco, Calif., 1998-2001, acting chmn. and CEO, 2001; CFO Wingeast LLC, San Diego, 2001—; bd. dirs. Collateral Therapeutics, Inc., San Diego, Softnet Sys., Inc., San Francisco; exec. v.p., CFO/bd. dirs. Western Water Co., San Diego, 1997-2000. Bd. dirs. San Diego Opera Co., 1988-90; bd. dirs. Univ. Art Gallery U. Calif., San Diego, 1991-95. Ford Found. fellow, 1963-65. Office: 10251 Vista Sorrento Pky San Diego CA 92121-2706

SIMON, SEYMOUR, lawyer, former state supreme court justice; b. Chgo., Aug. 10, 1915; s. Ben and Gertrude (Rusky) S.; m. Roslyn Schultz Biel, May 26, 1954; children: John B., Nancy Simon Cooper, Anthony Biel. BS, Northwestern U., 1935, JD, 1938; LLD (hon.), John Marshall Law Sch., 1982, North Park Coll., 1986, Northwestern U., 1987. Bar: Ill. 1938. Spl. atty. Dept. Justice, 1938-42; practice law Chgo., 1946-74; judge Ill. Appellate Ct., 1974-80; presiding justice Ill. Appellate Ct. (1st Dist., 3d Div.), 1977, 79; justice Ill. Supreme Ct., 1980-88; ptnr. Piper Marbury Rudnick & Wolfe, Chgo., 1988—. Former chmn. Ill. Low-Level Radioactive Waste Disposal Facility Siting Commn.; former dir. Nat. Gen. Corp., Bantam Books, Grosset & Dunlap, Inc., Gt. Am. Ins. Corp. Mem. Cook County Bd. Commrs., 1961-66, pres., 1962-66; pres. Cook County Forest Preserve Dist., 1962-66; mem. Pub. Bldg. Commn., City Chgo., 1962-67; Alderman 40th ward, Chgo., 1955-61, 67-74; Democratic ward committeeman, 1960-74; bd. dirs. Schwab Rehab. Hosp., 1961-71, Swedish Covenant Hosp., 1969-75. With USNR, 1942-45. Decorated Legion of Merit; recipient 9th Ann. Pub. Svc. award Tau Epsilon Rho, 1963, Hubert L. Will award Am. Vets. Com., 1983, award of merit Decalogue Soc. Lawyers, 1986, Judge Learned Hand award Am. Jewish Com., 1994, Frances Feinberg Meml. Crown award Associated Talmud Torahs of Chgo., 1995, Bill of Rights in Action award Constl. Rights Found., 1997, Civic Contbn. award LWV Chgo., 2000; named to Sr. Citizen's Hall of Fame, City of Chgo., 1989, Hall of Fame Jewish Comty. Ctrs. Chgo., 1989, Laureate Lincoln Acad. Ill., 1997, Chgo. Coun. Lawyers and the Appleseed Fund Justice Commitment to Justice award, 1998. Mem. ABA, Ill. Bar Assn., Chgo. Bar Assn., Chgo. Hist. Soc., Decalogue Soc. Lawyers (Merit award 1986), Izaak Walton League, Chgo. Hort. Soc., Comml. Club Chgo., Std. Club, Variety Club, Order of Coif, Phi Beta Kappa, Phi Beta Kappa Assocs. Home: 1555 N Astor St Chicago IL 60610-1673 Office: Piper Marbury Rudnick & Wolfe 203 N La Salle St Ste 1800 Chicago IL 60601-1210

SIMON, SHELDON WEISS, political science educator; b. St. Paul, Jan. 31, 1937; s. Blair S. and Jennie M. (Dim) S.; m. Charlann Lilwin Scheid, Apr. 27, 1962; 1 child, Alex Russell BA summa cum laude, U. Minn., 1958, PhD, 1964; MPA, Princeton U., 1960; postgrad., U. Geneva, 1962-63. Asst. prof., then prof. U. Ky., 1966-75; prof. polit. sci. Ariz. State U., 1975—, chmn. dept., 1975-79, dir. Ctr. Asian Studies, 1980-88. Vis. prof. George Washington U., 1965, U. B.C., Can., 1972-73, 79-80, Carleton U., 1976, Monterey Inst. Internat. Studies, 1991, 96, Am. Grad. Sch. Internat. Mgmt., 1991-92; cons. USIA Rsch. Analysis Corp., Am. Enterprise Inst. Pub. Policy Rsch., Hoover Instn., Orkand Corp.; cons., dir. S.E. Asian Projects, Nat. Bur. Asian Rsch., 1998. Author: Asian Neutralism and U.S. Policy, 1975, The ASEAN States and Regional Security, 1982, The Future of Asian-Pacific Security Collaboration, 1988; editor: The Military and Security in the Third World, 1978, East Asian Security in the Post-Cold War Era, 1993, Southeast Asian Security in the New Millenium, 1996, The Many Faces of Asian Security, 2001; also others; contbr. articles to profl. jours., chpts. to books. Mem. Com. Fgn. Relations, Phoenix, 1976— ; bd. dirs. Phoenix Little Theater, 1976-79 Grantee Am. Enterprise Inst., 1974, Earhart Found., 1979, 81, 92, 84, 88, U.S. Inst. Peace, 1994-96, 2000-01, Nat. Bur. Asian Rsch., 1998, W. Alton Jones Found., 2000; Hoover Instn. fellow, 1980, 85. Mem. Am. Polit. Sci. Assn., Assn. Asian Studies, Internat. Studies Assn. (profl. ethics com. 1987-91, v.p. 1991-93), Asia Soc. (contemporary affairs com. 1987—), U.S. Coun. for Asia-Pacific Security (exec. bd. 1998—), Phi Beta Kappa. Democrat. Jewish. Avocations: acting, singing, tennis. Home: 5630 S Rocky Point Rd Tempe AZ 85283-2134 Office: Ariz State U Polit Sci Dept Tempe AZ 85287 E-mail: shells@asu.edu.

SIMON, SHERYL JOY, writer, astrologer; b. Paris, Oct. 4, 1956; d. Morton and Arlene (Rogoff) Kranich; m. David Andrew Simon; child, Brenna. Student, Holy Family Coll., Atlantic C.C., Hunter Coll. Pres. Astro Depot, Fla., 1997—. Cons. HB Studio. Author: (children's books) Clean Your Room, Nancy Lee, 1997, Nancy Lee, 1997, (astrology book) Astro Star Kards, 1998. Recipient Mike Nichols Scholarship, 1989, 90, 91. Mem. Nat. Coun. Geocosmic Rsch., Am. Fedn. Astrologers. Avocations: acting, poetry, directing. Office: Astro Depot PO Box 167 Livingston NJ 07039 Fax: 973-243-9870. E-mail: Astrodepot@aol.com.

SIMON, SIDNEY, osteopathic physician, educator; b. N.Y.C., Aug. 6, 1924; DO, Phila. Coll. Osteopathic Medic, 1950. Intern Met. Hosp., Phila., 1950-51; prof. medicine N.Y. Coll. Osteo. Medicine, Old Westbury, 1977-83, chmn. dept. allergy, immunology and rhematology, 1977—, clin. prof. medicine, 1983—; pvt. practice specializing in adult allergy and immunology Bronx, N.Y., 1952—. Lectr. to sci. and profl. groups. Contbr. articles to profl. jours. Fellow Am. Coll. Allergy, Immunology and Asthma, Am. Acad. Allergy, Immunology and Asthma, Am. Osteo. Coll. Allergy and Immunology (past pres.). Office: 1846 Victor St Bronx NY 10462-3510

SIMON, THEODORE RONALD, physician, medical educator; b. Hartford, Conn., Feb. 2, 1949; s. Theologos Lingos and Lillian (Faix) S.; m. Marcia Anyzeski, Apr. 5, 1974; children: Jacob T., Theodore H., Mark G. BA cum laude, Trinity Coll., Hartford, 1970; MD, Yale U., 1975. Diplomate Am. Bd. Nuclear Medicine, Diplomate Nat. Bd. Med. Examiners; lic. Calif., Tex. Intern in surgery Strong Meml. Hosp., Rochester, N.Y., 1975-76; resident in diagnostic radiology U. Calif., San Francisco, 1976-78; resident in nuclear medicine Yale-New Haven Hosp., Conn., 1978-80, chief resident, 1979-80; asst. prof. nuclear medicine U. Tex. Southwestern Med. Ctr., Dallas, 1980-88, assoc. prof., 1990—. Cons. nuclear medicine St. Paul's Hosp., Dallas, 1981-88; cons. internal medicine Presbyn. Hosp., Dallas, 1981-88, 90, Med. City Hosp., Dallas, 1989—; cons. nuclear medicine VA Med. Ctr., Dallas, 1981-82, chief nuclear medicine svc., 1982-88; nat. dep. dir. nuclear medicine VA, 1985-88; dep. chief nuclear medicine NIH, Bethesda, Md., 1988-90; mem. del. Taiwan Atomic Energy, U.S. State Dept., 1990. Mem. editorial bd. Jour. History of Med. and Allied Scis., 1974-75; contbr. articles to Internat. Jour. Radiol. Applications, Jour. Nuclear Medicine, Am. Jour. Cardiology, Clin. Nuclear Medicine, Circulation, Yale Jour. Biol. Medicine, Radiology, Surg. Radiology, and others. Pres. Christ Lutheran Ch., University Park, Tex. Mem. Soc. Nuclear Medicine (treas. correlative imaging coun. 1988-90, mem. exec. com 1988—). Achievements include patent for Complex Motion Device to Enhance Single Photon Emission Computed Tomography Uniformity; research in single photon emission computed tomography as it related to substance abuse, schizophrenia, depression, neurotoxicity and chronic fatigue syndrome. Home and Office: 4429 Southern Ave Dallas TX 75205-2622

SIMON, WILLIAM, biomathematician, educator; b. Pitts., May 27, 1929; m. Maxine Check, June 27, 1965; children: Robert, Steven, Alan. BS in Physics, Carnegie Inst. Tech., 1950; MA in Applied Physics, Harvard U., 1952, PhD, 1958. Staff physicist Comstock & Wescott, Inc. (cons. engrs.), Cambridge, Mass., 1951-53; head instruments sect. Spencer Kennedy Lab., Boston, 1953-57; sr. systems engr. Nat. Radio Co., Malden, Mass., 1957-59; chief physicist Image Instruments, Inc., Newton Lower Falls, 1959-60; mem. staff M.I.T. Lincoln Lab. and Center for Computer Tech. in Biomed. Scis., 1961-64; research asso. dept. physiology, dir. biomed. tech. cons. group Harvard U. Med. Sch., 1964-68; asso. prof., head div. biomath. U. Rochester Sch. Medicine and Dentistry, 1968-77, prof., head div. biomath., 1977-82, prof. biochemistry and biophysics, 1982—, prof. med. info., 1989. Vis. assoc. prof. dept. elec. engring. MIT, 1974-75 Author: Mathematical Techniques for Physiology and Medicine, 1972, Mathematical Techniques for Biology and Medicine, 1977; contbr. articles to profl. jours. Office: U Rochester Box BPHYS Rochester NY 14642 E-mail: william_simon@urmc.rochester.edu.

SIMON, WILLIAM LEONARD, film and television writer and producer, writer; b. Washington, Dec. 3, 1930; s. Isaac B. and Marjorie (Felsteiner) S.; m. Arynne Lucy Abeles, Sept. 18, 1966; 1 child, Victoria Marie; 1 stepson, Sheldon M. Bermont. BEE, Cornell U., 1954; MA in Ednl. Psychology, Golden State U., 1982, PhD in Comm., 1983. Writer features and TV movies, documentary and indsl. films, TV programs, 1958—; lectr. George Washington U., Washington, 1968-70. Juror Coun. on Nontheatrical Events Film Festival, 1975-90, Cindy Festival Blue Ribbon Panel, 1985—; jury chmn., bd. dirs. CINE film festival, 1990—. Writer more than 600 produced works for motion pictures and TV, including (screenplays) Fair Woman Without Discretion, Majorca, Swindle, A Touch of Love, (teleplays and documentaries) From Information to Wisdom, Flight of Freedom II, Missing You, (home video) Star of India, Combat Vietnam series, writer, prodr. The Star of India: Setting Sail; co-author: Profit from Experience-The Story of Transformation Management , 1995, Lasting Change, 1997; author: Beyond the Numbers, 1996; co-author: On the Firing Line, My 500 Days at Apple Computer, 1998, High Velocity Leadership--The Mars Pathfinder Approach to Faster, Better, Cheaper, 1999, Driving Digital--What Microsoft is Learning from its Customers about Thriving in the Digital Revolution, 2000, The Afterlife Experiments--Breakthrough Scientific Evidence of Life After Death, 2002. Pres. Foggy Bottom Citizens Assn., 1963-65, mem. exec. bd., 1965-69; v.p. Shakespeare Summer Festival, 1966-67, trustee, 1965-70; mem. interview com. Cornell U., 1987-88. Lt. USN, 1954-58. Recipient 12 Golden Eagle awards Cine Film Festival, gold medal N.Y. Internat. Festival, gold medal Freedoms Found., IFPA Gold Cindy; awards Berlin, Belgrade and Venice film Festivals, numerous others. Mem. Nat. Acad. TV Arts and Scis. (gov. D.C. chpt. 1970-73, gov. San Diego chpt. 1998—), Silver Cir., Writers Guild Am., Am. Film Inst., Internat. Documentary Assn., Rotary (bd. dirs., program chmn.), Eta Kappa Nu (chpt. pres. 1953-54), Tau Beta Pi. Republican. Avocations: crew member square-rigged brig Pilgrim, San Diego Museum ship Star of India, tennis. Home: 6151 Paseo Delicias PO Box 2048 Rancho Santa Fe CA 92067-2048

SIMONAITIS, RICHARD AMBROSE, chemist; b. Chgo., Dec. 7, 1930; s. George Peter and Sofija Constance (Woijkiewicz) S.; m. Vera Sandra Hall, Sept. 17, 1960; children: Steven, Rachel, Laura. Student, Loyola U., Chgo., 1948-50; BS, U. Ill., 1952; MS, Ohio State U., 1957, PhD, 1962. Chemist Aerojet-Gen. Corp., Nimbus, Calif., 1962-64; rsch. chemist Gulf Oil Corp., Merriam, Kans., 1964-66; analytical chemist Gen. Electric Co., Liverpool, N.Y., 1966-69; rsch. chemist, rsch. leader, lead scientist Agrl. Rsch. Svc.-U.S. Dept. Agr., Savannah, Ga., 1970—. Chemist; b. Chgo., Dec. 7, 1930; s. George Peter and Sofija Constance (Woijkiewicz) S.; m. Vera Sandra Hall, Sept. 17, 1960; children: Steven, Rachel, Laura. Student Loyola U., Chgo., 1948-50; BS, U. Ill., 1952; postgrad. Ohio State U., 1952-55, MS, 1957, PhD, 1962. Chemist, Aerojet-Gen. Corp., Nimbus, Calif., 1962-64; rsch. chemist, Gulf Oil Corp., Merriam, Kans., 1964-66; analytical chemist, Gen. Electric Co., Liverpool, N.Y., 1966-69; rsch. chemist, rsch. leader, lead scientist Agrl. Rsch. Svc., U.S. Dept. Agr., Savannah, Ga., 1970—; abstractor, Chem. Abstracts, 1965-85. Bd. dirs. Savannah coun. Girl Scouts U.S.A., 1978-84, exec. com., 1980-84, neighborhood chmn., Oleander Neighborhood, 1980-89; booth chmn., Night in Old Savannah Ethnic Festival, 1977-91; usher, Nativity of Our Lord Ch., 1974—, capt. ushers, 1977—, sec., Men's Club, 1976, Sunday sch. tchr., 1977-81; bd. dirs., Savannah Young People's Theater, 1980-85, treas., 1983-85; bd. dirs., Savannah Theatre Co., 1990-94, treas., 1991-95, house mgr., 1986—. With U.S. Army, 1955-56. Mem. Am. Chem. Soc. (exec. com. 1979-83, sec., treas., 1979, chmn. elect., 1980, chmn., 1981, counselor, 1981, disting. contbn. plaque 1978, cert. recognition Chem. Abstract Svc. 1975), Entomol. Soc. Am., Rsch. Soc. Am., Ga. Entomol. Soc., Assn. Ofcl. Analytical Chemists, ASTM, Chem. Analysts Central N.Y., Wilmington Island Pleasure and Improvement Assn. (treas. 1975—), Tybee Light Power Squadron, KC, Sigma Xi, Phi Lambda Upsilon. Roman Catholic. Contbr. numerous articles to sci. jours. Abstractor Chem. Abstracts, 1965-85; contbr. articles to profl. jours. Bd. dirs. Savannah coun. Girl Scouts U.S.A., 1978-84, exec. com., 1980-84; neighborhood chmn. Oleander Neighborhood, 1980-89; booth chmn. Night in Old Savannah Ethnic Festival, 1977-91; usher Nativity of Our Lord Ch., 1974-2000, capt. ushers, 1977-2000, sec. Mens Club, 1976, Sunday sch. tchr., 1977-81; bd. dirs. Savannah Young Peoples Theater, 1980-85, treas., 1983-85; bd. dirs. Savannah Theatre Co., 1990-95, treas., 1991-95, house mgr., 1986-99. With U.S. Army, 1955-56. Mem. ASTM, Am. Chem. Soc. (exec. com. 1979-83, sec.-treas. 1979, chmn.-elect 1980, chmn. 1981, counselor 1981, Disting. Contbn. plaque 1978, Cert. Recognition Chem. Abstract Svc. 1975), Entomol. Soc. Am., Rsch. Soc. Am., Ga. Entomol. Soc., Assn. Ofcl. Analytical Chemists, Chem. Analysts Ctrl. N.Y., Wilmington Island Pleasure and Improvement Assn. (treas. 1975—), Tybee Light Power Squadron, KC, Sigma Xi, Phi Lambda Upsilon. Roman Catholic. Office: USDA Agrl Rsch Svc PO Box 22909 3401 Edwin Ave Savannah GA 31405-1607 E-mail: mrsimi@aol.com.

SIMONDS, CHARLES FREDERICK, artist; b. N.Y.C., Nov. 14, 1945; s. Robert and Anita I. (Bell) S. BA, U. Calif., Berkeley, 1967; MFA, Rutgers U., 1969. One man shows include Ctr. nat. d'Art contemporain, Paris, 1975, Mus. Modern Art, N.Y.C., 1976, Westfälischer Kunstverein, Munster, 1978, Mus. Ludwig, Cologne, 1979, Mus. Contemporary Art, Chgo., 1981, Phoenix (Ariz.) Mus. Art, 1982, Brooks Meml. Art Gallery, Memphis, 1982, Solomon R. Guggenheim Mus., N.Y., 1983, Leo Castelli Gallery, N.Y., 1984, Architekturmuseum, Bâle, 1985, Corcoran Gallery Art, Washington, 1988, Fundació "la Caixa," Barcelona, 1994, Galerie nat. Jeu Paume, Paris, 1994; exhibited in group shows Whitney Mus. Am. Art, N.Y., 1975, 77, Mus. d'Art moderne Ville de Paris, 1975, Stedelijk Mus., Amsterdam, 1978, Mus. Modern Art, N.Y., 1979, Hayward Gallery, London, 1980, Tate Gallery, London, 1983, Solomon R. Guggenheim Mus., N.Y., 1985, 87, 89; works included in publs. including Artforum, 1980, Art/Cahier, 1977, Sprache im Technischen Zeitalter, 1978, Art in America, 1983, Images and Issues, 1982, ARTnews, 1978, Beaux Arts, 1986. Fellow Am. Acad. Rome. Home: 26 E 22nd St New York NY 10010-6107

SIMONDS, JOHN EDWARD, retired newspaper editor; b. Boston, July 4, 1935; s. Alvin E. and Ruth Angeline (Rankin) S.; m. Rose B. Muller, Nov. 16, 1968; children— Maximillian P., Malia G.; children by previous marriage— Rachel F. Cobb, John B. BA, Bowdoin Coll., 1957. Reporter Daily Tribune, Seymour, Ind., 1957-58, UPI, Columbus, Ohio, 1958-60; reporter, asst. city editor Providence Jour. Bull., 1960-65, Washington Evening Star, 1965-66; corr. Gannett News Svc., Washington, 1966-75; mng. editor Honolulu Star Bull., 1975-80, exec. editor, 1980-87, sr. editor, editorial page editor, 1987-93; exec. Hawaii Newspaper Agy., Honolulu, 1993-99; reader rep. The Honolulu Advertiser, 1999—2002; ret., 2002. Served with U.S. Army, 1958. Mem. Am. Soc. Newspaper Editors, AP Mng. Editors, Soc. Profl. Journalists, Nat. Conf. Editl. Writers, Orgn. News Ombudsmen. Home: 5316 Nehu Pl Honolulu HI 96821-1941 Office: The Honolulu Advertiser 605 Kapiolani Blvd Honolulu HI 96813-5195 E-mail: simondsj001@hawaii.rr.com.

SIMONDS, JOHN ORMSBEE, landscape architect; b. Jamestown, N.D., Mar. 11, 1913; s. Guy Wallace and Marguerite Lois (Ormsbee) S.; m. Marjorie C. Todd, May 1, 1943; children: Taye Anne, John Todd, Polly Jean, Leslie Brook. BS, Mich. State U., 1935, DSc hon.; MLandscape Architecture (Eugene Dodd medal), Harvard U., 1939. Landscape architect Mich. Dept. Parks, 1935-36; ptnr. Simonds and Simonds, Pitts., 1939-70, Collins, Simonds and Simonds, Washington, 1952-70, The Environ. Planning and Design Partnership, Pitts., also Miami Lakes, 1970-82, emeritus, 1983—. Cons. Dept. Pks., Collier County, Fla., 1986-90, Land and Nature Trust, Lexington, Ky., 1987-92, SW Fla. Water Mgmt. Dist., 1987-89; lectr., vis. critic urban and regional planning Carnegie-Mellon U., 1955-67; vis. critic Grad. Sch. Planning, also Sch. Architecture, Yale, 1961-62; Cons. Chgo. Cen. Area Com., 1962, Allegheny County Dept. Regional Pks., 1961-74; U.S. cons. community planning Inter-Am. Housing and Planning Ctr., Bogota, Colombia, 1960-61; mem. jury Am. Acad. Rome, 1963, 65, 66, 69; mem. jury projected pilgrim's reception Cultural Ctr., Mecca, 1995; mem. Nat. Adv. Com. on Hwy. Beautification; chmn. panel on pks. and open space White House Conf. on Natural Beauty; mem. Interprofl. Commn. on Environ. Design; mem. and report editor urban hwy. adv. bd. U.S. Bur. Pub. Rds., 1965-68; mem. landscape architecture adv. panel U.S. C.E., 1968-71, Pres.'s Task Force on Resources and Environ., 1968-70; mem. design adv. panel Operation Breakthrough, HUD, 1970-71; mem. Mid-Atlantic regional adv. bd. Nat. Park Svc., 1976-78; assoc. trustee U. Pa., 1962-66, mem. bd. fine arts, 1962-66; chmn. joint com. planning Carnegie-Mellon U. and U. Pitts., 1959-60; overseer's vis. com. Harvard Grad. Sch. Design, 1962-68, exec. coun. alumni assn., 1960-63; adv. com. Sch. Design, N.C. State U., 1965-67; mem. Fla. Gov.'s Task Force on Natural Resources, 1979-80, Chgo. Bot. Garden 25th Anniversary, 1991, keynote address, 1991, Internat. Fedn. Landscape Architects, Seoul, Korea, 1992; speaker keynote address Internat. Congress Urban Green, Geneva, 1986. Author: Landscape Architecture, the Shaping of Man's Natural Environment, 1961, 2d rev. edit., 1997, Earthscape, a Manual of Environmental Planning, 1978, revised edit. 1986, Garden Cities 21, Creating a Livable Urban Environment, 1994; editor: Virginia's Common Wealth, 1965, The Freeway in the City, 1968; contbr. sect. on urban design Ency. Architecture, 1990, sect. on landscape architecture Ency. Urban Planning, 1980, Lessons, 1999. Maj. works (with others) include master plans for Chgo. Bot. Garden, Mellon Sq., Pitts., Equitable Plaza, (with others) Miami Lakes New Town, Va. I-66 Corridor, Fairfax and Arlington counties, Va., Pelican Bay Community, Fla., Weston New Town, Fla. Bd. dirs. Hubbard Ednl. Trust, 1974—. Recipient citation Top Men of Year Engring. News-Record, 1973; Charles L. Hutchinson medal Chgo. Hort. Soc., John R. Bracken medal Dept. Landscape Architecture, Pa. State U., 1985, Sigma Lambda Alpha award Coun. Educators in Landscape Architecture, 1979. Fellow Am. Soc. Landscape Architects (mem. exec. com. 1959-67, pres. 1963-65, pres. Found. 1966-68, recipient medal 1973, Centennial Pres.'s medal 1999), Royal Soc. Arts (Gt. Britain); mem. Nat. Acad. (US), Archtl. League N.Y., Royal Town Planning Inst. (hon. corr.), Landscape Arch. Found., Am. Soc. Landscape Archs.; hon. assoc. Pa. chpt. AIA, Harvard-Yale-Princeton Club. Presbyterian (ruling elder). Home: 17 Penhurst Rd Pittsburgh PA 15202-1023 Office: The Loft 17 Penhurst Rd Pittsburgh PA 15202 *Perhaps the most important lesson in life is to learn to address oneself with intensity to each person, object and event. One may be with friends without awareness of either friend or friendship, live with family as an almost stranger, partake of food and drink without savor, pass burgeoning tree, splashing stream, or splendid view without appreciation . . . unless one learns to address all powers of perception-first consciously, and then by habit, to the subject at hand. Only thus may each experience be made rich and rewarding, and life, the sum of experience, be lived to the full.*

SIMONDS, MARIE CELESTE, architect; b. Miami, Fla., Mar. 30, 1947; d. Hinton Joseph and Frances Olivia (Burnett) Baker; m. Albert Rhett Simonds, Jr., Oct. 9, 1974; children: Caroline Lamar, Frances Rhett. BA, U. Pa., 1968; BArch, U. Md., 1973. Registered architect, Va. Architect Harry Weese & Assocs., Washington, 1973-75; pvt. practice Alexandria, Va., 1976—. Mem. Jr. League Washington, 1978—. NSF grantee, 1972; recipient Design award No. Va. Chpt. AIA, 1990. Mem. AIA (scholar 1971, Design award No. Va. 1990), Va. Soc. AIA, Severn Sailing Assn. (Annapolis, Md.). Episcopalian. Avocations: sailboat racing, horseback riding. Home and Office: 624 S Lee St Alexandria VA 22314-3820

SIMONDS, MARTHA MUÑOZ, musician, educator; b. Washington, Nov. 26, 1960; d. Roger Tyrell and Peggy (Muñoz) S.; m. David Robert Teeters, May 5, 1996. MusB, Juilliard Sch., 1982; MusM, Eastman Sch. Music, 1984. Tchg. asst. Eastman Sch. Music, Rochester, N.Y., 1984; violinist Santa Fe Opera Orch., 1984; 1st violin San Francisco Ballet Orch., 1984—; assoc. prin. 2nd violin San Francisco Opera Orch., 1985—; assoc. concertmaster New Century Chamber Orch., San Francisco, 1993—; violinist Due Voci Duo, 1993—. Pvt. music tchr., Oakland, Calif., 1985—; performer Earplay, San Francisco, 1985—, Berkeley (Calif.) Contemporary Players, 1998—. Cmty. activist Cmty. Action Network, Oakland, 1991—. Touring grantee Calif. Arts Coun., 1992. Mem. Musicians Union Local 6. Democrat. Avocations: gardening, rescues animals, improvisational acting, Qi Gong, salsa dancing. Home: 1427 Paru St Alameda CA 94501-2532

SIMONDS, RICHARD KIMBALL, investment executive; b. Detroit, June 7, 1927; s. Ralph Warner and Bernardine (Kimball) S.; M. Judith Holland, Jan. 27, 1956 (div. Nov. 1985); m. Barbara Wood, Oct. 4, 1986; children: Lisa, Todd. BS, U. Vt., 1952. Chartered fin. analyst. Pres. Baker Simonds & Co., Detroit, 1954-59, Investment Counsel Inc., Grosse Pointe, Mich., 1960-91. Contbr. articles to profl. publs. Bd. dirs. Boys Republic, Farmington Hills, Mich., 1961-73; trustee Liggett Sch., Grosse Pointe, 1962-71. Avocation: boating. Home: 19789 Wedgewood Dr Grosse Pointe Woods MI 48236-2732

SIMONDS, STEPHEN PAIGE, former state legislator; b. Franconia, N.H., Nov. 25, 1924; s. Stephen Moses and Gertrude Martha (Jesseman) S.; m. Judith Cole, Sept. 13, 1952; children: Scott, Mark, Laura, Jane. BA, U. N.H., 1948; MA in Social Svcs. Adminstrn., U. Chgo., 1953. Caseworker N.H. Dept. Pub. Welfare, Woodsville, 1950-51, dist. supr. Conway and Woodsville, 1953-56; field supr. Conn. Dept. Welfare, Hartford, 1958-60; dir. social welfare Maine Dept. Health and Welfare, Augusta, 1960-67; commr. Assitance Payments Adminstrn. HEW, Washington, 1967-69; commr. Cmty. Svcs. Adminstrn. HEW, 1968-71; founder, dir. Human Svcs. Devel. Inst., U. So. Maine, Portland, 1971-86, dir. Office Internat. Programs, 1986-92; mem. Maine Ho. of Reps., Augusta, 1990-94, mem. human resources com., edn. com. Past pres. World Affairs Coun. of Maine, Cmty. Counseling Ctr.; trustee SALT Inst. Documentary Studies, 1998—. Recipient Disting. Svc. award World Affairs Coun. Maine, 1991; Fulbright scholar, Eng., 1957-58. Mem. Ptnrs. of Ams. (pres. 1997—), Chinese and Am. Friendship Assn. (founder). Democrat. Avocations: flying, boating, canoeing, gardening. Home: 18 Brentwood Rd Cape Elizabeth ME 04107-2210 E-mail: ssimonds@maine.rr.com.

SIMONDS, VALERIE DEVERSE, prehospital educator; b. Greensburg, Pa., Jan. 23, 1943; d. John Young and Margaret (McCommons) Woods. Diploma in nursing, Shady Side Hosp., 1963; BS, Johns Hopkins U., 1976, MS with honors, 1979. RN, Md., Pa.; CEN NREMT-P. Health educator U. Md. Sch. of Pharmacy, Balt., 1979-80; EMT dept. chair Anne Arundel C.C., Arnold, 1979-2000; health educator, cons. Johns Hopkins Inst. Policy Studies, Balt., 2000—02. Developed and implemented 1st EMT-Paramedic program, Md.; mem. Md. Region III EMS adv. bd., Balt., 1986-98. Recipient Disting. Program award Md. State Dept. of Edn., 1986. Mem. Emergency Nurses Assn. Home: 285 Laguna Cir Severna Park MD 21146-1360

SIMONE, ALBERTINA, accountant; b. Briey, France, Nov. 30, 1962; came to U.S., 1994; d. Americo and Maria Antonia (Santavicca) S. B in Commerce with honors, U. Windsor, Ont., Can., 1985. Chartered acct., Can. Acct. Clarkson Gordon-Ernst & Young, Windsor, 1985-88; mgr. internal audit Allied Domecq, 1988-90; mgr. sales svcs. Hiram Walker & Sons, Inc. (subs. of Allied Domecq), Southfield, Mich., 1990-92, asst. contr., 1992-93, contr., 1993-96, dir. fin. and adminstrn., 1996-97, v.p. comml. fin., 1998—. Office: Hiram Walker & Sons Inc 355 Riverside Ave Westport CT 06880-4810

SIMONE, GAIL ELISABETH, manufacturing administrator; b. Boston, Dec. 3, 1944; d. Hugh Nelson and Louise Amelia (Shedrick) Saunders; m. Edburnne R. Hare, Sept. 7, 1968 (div. 1974); m. Joseph R. Simone, June 27, 1987. BA, The King's Coll., 1966; postgrad., Harvard U., 1976-77, N.H. Coll., 1991—. Placement dir. Boston Bar Assn., 1966-67; pub. relations Emerson Coll., Boston, 1967-69; asst. to v.p. Vance, Sanders, Inc., 1969-70; office mgr. Trans. Displays, Inc., 1970-71; seminar coordinator Assn. Trial Lawyers Am., Cambridge, Mass., 1971-74; writer, researcher Ednl. Expeditions Internat., Belmont, 1975-76; analyst United Brands Co., N.Y.C., 1976-80, Mil. Sealift Commd., USN, Washington, 1980-84, legis. affairs officer, 1984-88; rsch. analyst Bath (Maine) Iron Works Corp., 1988—. Free-lance writer, editor, Boston, 1970-73. Active New Missions, Haiti, 2000—; mem. Amnesty Internat., N.Y.C., 1987—; bd. dirs. Coastal Transp.; various other orgns. Mem. AAUW, NAFE, People for the Ethical Treatment of Animals. Avocations: ballet, writing, gardening. Office: Bath Iron Works 700 Washington St Stop 1 Bath ME 04530-2556

SIMONE, JOSEPH, clergyman, educator; b. Bridgeport, Conn., Jan. 13, 1924; s. Dominic and Anna (Mastrianni) S.; B.A., Elon Coll., 1958; M.A., Andover Newton Theol. Sch., 1968; m. Viola Ruskay, June 27, 1953; children— J. Scott, Zachary D., Claudia A. Ordained to ministry Congl. Ch., 1960; pastor Congl. Ch., Chicopee Falls, Mass., 1958-61, 1st Congl. Ch., Farmington, N.H., 1961-63, Hope Congl. Ch., East Providence, R.I., 1963-65, All Souls Ch., Lowell, Mass., 1965-69; tchr. English, also guidance counselor, 1969-87 . Chmn. ecumenical commn. Greater Lowell Council Chs., 1967-68; founder Ecumenical Dialogue with Clergymen and Laymen, Lowell, 1966, Radio Ministry on Ecumenism, Lowell, 1966-69; chaplain Roger Hall Sch. for Girls, Lowell, 1965-69. Bd. dirs. Jewish-Arab Ednl. Fund, Lowell Served with AUS, 1942-45. Mem. Andover Assn. Ministers United Ch. of Christ (adv. com. 1966-87), Assn. Clin. Pastoral Edn., Am., Mass. sch. counselors assns., N.E.A., Nat. Vocational Guidance Assn., Am. Personnel and Guidance Assn., Sigma Mu Sigma (v.p. 1957). Mason. Home: 117 Jenkins Rd Andover MA 01810-2303

SIMONE, JOSEPH R. lawyer; b. N.Y.C., Jan. 7, 1949; m. Virginia E. Simone, May 29, 1971; children: Jacquelyn, Robert. BA cum laude, Queens Coll., 1971; LLM in Taxation, NYU, 1977; JD cum laude, Fordham U., 1974. Bar: N.Y. 1975, U.S. Dist. Ct. (so. dist.) N.Y. 1975, U.S. Ct. Appeals (2d cir.) 1975. Ptnr. Patterson, Belknap, Webb & Tyler, N.Y.C., 1982-88, Schulte, Roth & Zabel, N.Y.C., 1988—; spl. prof. law Hofstra U. Sch. Law, 1998-2001. Author: (textbooks) Pension Answer Book, 5th edit., 1990, Essential Facts: Pension and Profit-sharing Plans, 1999; editl. advisor Jour. of Pension Planning. Mem. Am. Arbitration Assn. (panel on multiemployer pension plans, employee benefits law adv. com, co-chair symposium employee benefits), Phi Beta Kappa. Office: Schulte Roth & Zabel 919 3rd Ave Fl 19 New York NY 10022-4774 E-mail: joseph.simone@srz.com.

SIMONEAU, CYNTHIA LAMBERT, newspaper editor, journalism educator; b. Central Falls, R.I., May 18, 1958; d. Roland and L. Jean Simoneau; m. Paul E. Lambert, Oct. 24, 1981; children: Thomas S. Lambert, Marc S. Lambert. BA, U. R.I., 1980. Asst. news editor Newtown (Conn.) Bee, 1980-82; reporter Bridgeport (Conn.) Post & Telegram, 1982-83, bur. chief, 1983-91; editor Woman Wise Conn. Post, Bridgeport, 1991-97, asst. mng. editor, 1997—. Adj. prof. So. Conn. State U., New Haven, 1993—. Eucharistic min., mem. parish adv. coun., religious edn. tchr., St. Thomas Aquinas Ch., Fairfield, Conn. Mem. Soc. Profl. Journalists (bd. dirs. Conn. chpt. 1983—, past treas. Conn. chpt. 1985-95, past pres. Conn. chpt. 1995-97, Journalism Excellence awards for news stories and columns, Pres.'s award Conn. chpt.). Avocation: reading. Office: Conn Post 410 State St Bridgeport CT 06604 E-mail: csimoneau@ctpost.com.

SIMONEAU, DANIEL ROBERT, accountant, watercolorist, educator, application developer; b. Lewiston, Maine, Aug. 3, 1962; s. Robert Eugene and Rolande Muriel (Plante) S. BFA, U. So. Maine, 1984. Reconciling specialist Fleet/Norstar Bank of Maine, Lewiston, 1981-84, acct., 1984-88, Sterling Engineered Products, Auburn, Maine, 1988-89; fin. analyst Pioneer Plastics Corp., 1989-91; acct. Aeroquip Corp., New Haven, 1992, adminstrv. sys. coord. Maumee, Ohio, 1992-93, acct., 1993-94, Trinova Corp., Maumee, 1994-96, chmn. employee activities com. ann. outing Toledo, 1995; fin. edn. specialist PeopleSoft, Inc., Westchester, Ill., 1996-98, master tech. instr., 2000—02; sr. cons. The Revere Group, Deerfield, 1998-2000, functional specialist, 2000; PeopleSoft developer Robert W. Baird, Milw., 2002—. Dir. Spectrum Gallery, 1995-96; pres. Pioneer Mgmt. Assn., 1991. Contbr. article to mag. Chmn. award winners show Spectrum Friends of Fine Art, Toledo, 1995. Recipient Recognition award Spectrum Friends of Fine Art, 1994, Com. award Spectrum Gallery, 1994, 3d pl. award Toledo Fedn. Art Socs., 1992, 3d Judge's award Lewiston Art Festival Com., 1988, 90, 91, Purchase award Portland Art Festival Com., 1981, 91. Mem. Northwestern Ohio Watercolor Soc., Coll. Art Assn., Friends of the Arts (Chgo.). Office: Robert W Baird 777 E Wisconsin Ave Milwaukee WI 53201-0672 Home: 9507 74th St Kenosha WI 53142-8194

SIMONEIT, BERND ROLF TATSUO, geochemistry educator; b. Heilbronn, Republic of Germany, Sept. 7, 1937; came to U.S., 1952; s. Kurt Erich and Anna (Dietrich) S.; m. Lynda J. Wells, June 17, 1961 (div. Mar. 1966); m. Doreen Joy Gee, Sept. 7, 1968; 1 adopted child, Amanda Jane Houlding. BS, U. R.I., 1960; postgrad., MIT, 1961, 64; PhD, U. Bristol, Eng., 1975. Chemist A.C. Lawrence Leather Co., Peabody, Mass., 1962-63; spectroscopist space sci. lab. U. Calif., Berkeley, 1965-70, assoc. specialist space sci. lab., 1970-72, specialist space sci. lab., 1972-73; assoc. rsch. geochemist UCLA, 1976-81; assoc. prof. sch. oceanography Oreg. State U., Corvallis, 1981-83, prof. coll. oceanography, 1983-93, prof. coll. oceanic and atmospheric scis., 1993—2002, prof. emeritus, 2002—. Cons. EG&G Idaho, Inc., Idaho Falls, 1983-92, Refineria de Petroleo, SA, Concon, Chile, 1990—, Chevron Petroleum Tech. Co., La Habra, 1992-97; mem. NASA Exobiology Adv. Panel, Washington, 1980-85; mem., chmn. deep sea drilling project Joint Oceanographic Instns. for Deep Earth Sampling Orgn. Geochemisty Adv. Panel, Washington, 1978-83; vis. faculty assoc. Calif. Inst. of Tech., Pasadena, 1995-2002; vis. prof. Ctr. d'Investigacio Desenvolupament, Consell Superior d'Investigacions Sci., Barcelona, Spain, 1996-97; adj. prof. U. Utah, Salt Lake City, 1998-2002; vis. prof. Hokkaido U., Saporo, Jappan, 2002. Editor: Organic Geochemistry, 1982-87, 90-2001, Applied Geochemistry, 1992—; co-editor: Gulf and Peninsular Province of the Californias, 1990; contbr. articles to profl. jours. Recipient Best Paper of Yr. award Geochemical Soc., 1977, 81. Mem. AAAS, Internat. Assn. Geochemistry and Cosmochemistry, Am. Assn. for Aerosol Rsch., Internat. Soc. for the Study of the Origin of Life, Am. Assn. Petroleum Geologists, Am. Chem. Soc., Am. Geophys. Union, Am. Soc. for Mass Spectrometry, European Assn. for Organic Geochemistry. Office: Oreg State U Coll Oceanic and Atmospheric Scis Oceanography Adminstrn Bldg 104 Corvallis OR 97331-5501 E-mail: simoneit@coas.oregonstate.edu.

SIMONELLI, MAGGIE, artist; b. N.Y.C., Jan. 18, 1966; d. Donald and Caroline S.; m. John Pilling Manderson, Oct. 15, 1994. BA in Studio Art, Conn. Coll., 1987; MS in Art History, MFA in Painting, Pratt Inst., 1994. Asst. prof. art history Art and Pratt Inst., Bklyn., 1996-98. Lectr. in field. One-woman shows include Sara Nightingale Gallery, Watermill, N.Y., 1999—2001, Provincetown (Mass.) Group Gallery, 1999, Axel Raben Gallery, N.Y.C., 2001, U. S.C., Beaufort, 2001, exhibited in group shows at Sara Nightingale Gallery, 1999—2002, Gallery Bershad, Boston, 1999—2001, Provincetown Group Gallery, 1999, Dieu Donne Paper Mill, 2000, Inman Gallery, Houston, 2001, Mus. Edits., N.Y.C., 2001, Tribeca Temporary, 2002, Porter Troupe Gallery, San Diego, 2002, Contemporary Gallery, N.Y.C., 2002, Represented in permanent collections Jennison Assocs., DoubleTree. Office: 401 Washington St 6G New York NY 10013 E-mail: maggiesimonelli@yahoo.com.

SIMONIAN, LANE PETER, history and environmental educator; b. Walnut Creek, Calif., Nov. 14, 1960; s. Simon and Cecelia (Arkelian) S. BA, U. Nev., Reno, 1982; MA, U. Calif., Davis, 1984; PhD, U. Calif., Santa Barbara, 1992. Tchg. asst. U. Calif., Davis, 1982-85, Santa Barbara, 1986-90; instr. Truckee Meadows C.C., Reno, 1993-99; instr. corr. course U. Nev., 2000—. Coor. access to seccess scholarship program, Truckee Meadows Cmty. Coll., 1998-00. Author: Defending the Land of the Jaguar: A History of Conservation in Mexico, 1995; contbr. articles to profl. jours. U.S.-Mexus grantee, 1990. Mem. Am. Soc. for Environ. History, L.Am. Studies Assn. Democrat. Avocations: hiking, tennis, golf, satire writing. Home: 2800 W Moana Ln Reno NV 89509-7811

SIMONIAN, SIMON JOHN, surgeon, scientist, educator; b. Antioch, French Ter., Apr. 20, 1932; came to U.S., 1965, naturalized, 1976. s. John Simon and Marie Cecile (Tomboulian) S.; m. Arpi Ani Yeghiayan, July 11, 1965; children: Leonard Armen, Charles Haig, Andrew Hovig. MD, U. London, 1957; BA in Animal Physiology, St. Edmund Hall, U. Oxford, Eng., 1964; MA in Animal Physiology, U. Oxford, Eng., 1969; MSc in nutrition, immunology & genetics, Harvard U., 1967, ScD in nutrition, immunology & genetics, 1969; DSc (hon.), Nat. Acad. Scis., Republic of Armenia, 1998. Diplomate Am. Bd. Surgery. Rsch. asst. immunology unit Lister Inst. Preventive Medicine, Elstree, Essex, U.K., 1952; intern in medicine Univ. Coll. Hosp., London, 1957; intern in surgery Edinburgh (Scotland) Royal Infirmary, 1957-58, resident in surgery, 1961-62; clin. clk. Nat. Hosp. & Inst. of Neurology, 1958; resident Edinburgh Western Gen. Hosp., 1958-59, City Hosp., Edinburgh, Birmingham Accident and Burns Hosp., U. Birmingham, Eng., 1959-60; demonstrator dept. anatomy Edinburgh U., 1960-61; rsch. fellow surgery and biochemistry Am. U. Beirut, Lebanon, 1964-65; rsch. fellow in pathology Lab. Chem. Pathology Harvard U., Boston, 1965-68, trainee NIH, 1967; instr. immunology Harvard Med. Sch., Boston, 1966-70, instr., assoc. in surgery, 1968-70, surg. dir. course on transplantation, biology and medicine, 1968-70; vis. prof. Harvard Med. Sch., Mass. Gen. Hosp., Brigham and Womens Hosp., New Eng. Deaconess Hosp., 1982; dir. transplantation immunology unit, asst. in surgery Brigham and Womens Hosp., Boston, 1968-70; resident in surgery Boston City Hosp., 1970-74; attending surgeon in transplantation and gen. surgery services U. Chgo. Med. Ctr., 1974-77; asst. prof. surgery, mem. com. immunology U. Chgo., 1974-77; head div. renal transplantation Hahnemann U. Sch. Medicine and Hosp., 1978-87, prof. surgery, 1978-88, chmn. Transplantation Com., 1983-88, chmn. quality assurance of surgery com., 1986-88; dept. surgery coord. with joint commn. for accreditation of hosps. Hahnemann U. Sch. Medicine, 1986; chief and chmn. dept. surgery St. John Hosp. and Med. Ctr., Detroit, 1988-89, chmn. credentials com. of surgery and oper. rm. com., 1988-89, assoc. v.p. for med. affairs, 1989-90; pres., CEO Vein Inst. of Met. Washington, Inc., 1990—; assoc. Fairfax Hosp., Falls Church, Va., 1990-92, active faculty, 1992—; guest lectr., 1994, 99; clin. assoc. prof. surgery Georgetown U. Sch. Medicine, Washington, 1992-95, guest lectr., 1994—, clin. prof. surgery, 1995—. Lectr. in the field; vis. prof. Vanderbilt U., 1968, Cedars-Sinai Med Ctr., UCLA, 1977, Addenbroke's Hosp., Cambridge U., 1977, Karolinska Inst., 1977, Huddinge Hosp. U. Stockholm, 1977, Med. Coll. Pa. and Hosp., 1980, 81, 85, Grad. Hosp., U. Pa., 1981, 85, U. Athens , 1981, U. Coll. Hosp., U. London, 1981, VA Hosp., Tufts U., 1982, John Radcliffe Hosp. U. Oxford, 1982, Nat. Acad. Scis. , Yerevan, Armenia, 1995, St. Edmund Hall, U. Oxford, 1997, Christ Ch. Hosp., Chgo., South Chgo. Hosp., Del. Med. Ctr., Wilmington, Wilkes Barre (Pa.) Gen. Hosp., Robert Packer Hosp., Guthrie Clin., Sayre, Pa., Brigham & Women's Hosp. and Harvard Med Sch. , Boston, Abington Meml. Hosp., Phila., Crozer Chester Med. Ctr., Pa., Cath. Med. Ctr., Manchester, NH, Burlington County Med. Ctr., Mount Holly, NJ, St. Agnes Hosp. Med. Ctr., Phila., Riverview Hosp., Red Bank, NJ, Easton (Pa.) Hosp. , Allentown, Sacred Heart Hosp., Newcombe Med. Ctr., Vineland, NJ; cons. Michael Reese Hosp., Chgo., 1976—77; cons. gen. surg. City of Phila., 1986—88; cons. vascular surg. Coll. Podiatry , Phila., 1986—88; cons. venous vascular surg. Podiatry Residence Program, No. Va. Med. Coll., Richmond, 1994—; cons. surg. John F. Kennedy Meml. Hosp., Stratford , NJ, St. Agnes Hosp. Med. Ctr., Phila.; cons. Am.-Armenian Cultural Assn., 2001—; chief med. team support U.S. Presdl. visits to Detroit, 1988—89; vis. surg. Inst. Vein Disease , Mich., 1989—90; vis. scientist Argonne (Ill.) Nat. Lab., 1969, 1974—77; mem. sci. bd. regenerative biology Ind. U. Ctr., 2001—; guest lectr., panelist 4th Internat. Dialogue Transition to Global Soc., U. Md., College Park, 1995; chmn. session 5th Armenian Med. World Congress , Paris, 1992; eminent scholar external assessor U. Zambia, Lusaka, 1994; mem. Internat. Consensus Panel The Investigation Chronic Venous Insufficiency , Paris, 1997; mem. Internat. Consensus Panel Thromboembolism , Rhodes, Greece, 1999; guest lectr. 3rd Clin. Workshop of Vein Clin. Kansas City , 1998, Am. Soc. Phlebology, 1998, 7th Armenian Med. World Congress, Lyon, France, 20th Anniversary GefassKlinic , Blaustein, Germany, 1998, 8th Pan Am. Congress Phlebology and Lymphology , Campo Grande, Brazil, 1998, 9th Pan Am. Congress Plebology and Lymphology, Cordoba, Argentina, 2000; mem. sci. bd. Ind. U. Ctr. for Regenerative Biology, 2001—; mem. 9th Pan-Am. Congress Phlebology and Lymphology, Cordoba, Argentina, 2000. Co-author: Manual of Vascular Access Procedures, 1987; cons. to editorial bd. dateline: Issues in Transplantation, 1985-87; mem. editl. bd. Phila. Medicine, 1988, Transplantation Proc., 1987-96, Jour. Transplantation Abstracts, 1968-70, Internat. Angiology, 1998—, Am. Coll. Phlebology Newsline, 2000—, Am. Soc. Lymphology Newsletter 2000—; reviewer Jour. Oncology and Dermatologic Surgery, 1993, Jour. Dermatologic Surgery, 1997, Jour. Vascular Surgery, 2000-, Venous Digest, 2002; translator Short Saphenous Vein issue, Jour. de Phlebologie, 1999; contbr. articles to profl. jours. and books; appeared in med. movie Giving. Co-founder Armenian Youth Soc., Eng., 1953, pres. 1953-54; Armenian Studies Program U. Chgo., 1975; bd. govs. Friends Sch., London, 1964-65; Mass. del., co-founder Armenian Assembly, Washington, 1970-74; fellow-trustee, co-founder Entry into Manhood of Armenian Youth at Age 13, 1981; co-founder Armenian Am. Health Assn. of Greater Washington, 1992, mem. pharms. com. 1992—, chmn. nominating com., 1993; mem. Am. Friends of St. Edmund Hall, U. Oxford, 1992—, U.S. Campaign for St. Edmund Hall, 1995—, Rep. Presdl. Task Force, leader, 1998—, mem. bd. advisors, 1999—, mem. campaign steering bd., 2000—; mem. St. Mary's Armenian Apostolic Ch., Washington, guest preacher, 1994, 95, 96; guest spkr. Armenian Ch. Youth Orgn. Am., Washington, 1998; mem. Am. Friends Am. U. Armenia, Yerevan, 1994, bd. dirs. mammography unit, 1997—; bd. dirs. Arlington (Va.) Symphony Orch., 1992-96, sci. com. Armenia-U.S.A., 1996—; mem. regional com. U.S. Campaign for Univ. Oxford, 1993; bd. dirs. First Western Found., Inc., 1994; active amphitheatre endowment fund Boston City Hosp., 1994; dist. benefactor, fundraiser Eurasia Found., 1996; sci. advisor, chmn. session Internat. Union Plebology, World Congress, London, 1995, Sydney, 1998, Rome, 2001; sci. advisor, chmn. session Internat. Union Angiology World, London, 1995, Tokyo, 1998, N.Y., 2002. Nairn scholar, 1949-52; Middlesex scholar, 1952-57; recipient Suckling prize, 1956, Brit. Med. Research Council award, 1962-64, Alt prize, 1973, Thompson award, 1974-77, Johnson award, 1975-77, Upjohn award, 1982, Presdl. Rep. Medal of Merit, 1982, U.S. Presdl. Seal and Medal, 1988, Kabakjian award Armenian Student Assn. Am., 1986, Disting. Alumni award St. Edmund Hall, U. Oxford, 1997, Kaken award, 1998, STD award, 2000; named outstanding new citizen of Citizenship Coun. of Met. Chgo. and Dept. Justice, Washington, 1976-77, Jonathan E. Rhoads ann. orator, 1984; co-endowed The John and Marie J. Simonian Award, St. Nerces Sem., 1981, John R. Pfeifer, MD, Rsch. Award, Providence Hosp., Southfield, Mich., 1992; endowed Marie J. Simonian Prize, Georgetown U. Med. Sch., 1991 (prize com. 1991—); established The John N.D. Kelly Prize in Med. Studies St. Edmund Hall, U. Oxford, 1992, The Simon J. and Arpi A. Simonian Prize for scholastic excellence for doctoral candidates, Harvard U., 1992; recognized for philanthropy to Hahnemann U. by placques in med. sch. and hosp. lobbies., Simon and Arpi Simonian plasma physics room Sch. of Humanities and Scis. U. Yerevan, Armenia, 1994, plaque in Cyrus Vesuna Auditorium and Conf. Ctr., Fairfax Hosp., Falls Church, Va., 1995; grantee U.S. Govt., industry cos., founds. Fellow Royal Coll. Surgeons Edinburgh, ACS (Phila., Mich. and Washington chpts.), Phila. Acad. Surgery (Jonathan E. Rhoads ann. orator 1984—); mem. AAAS, AMA, AAUP, Nat. Acad. Scis. Armenia (fgn. mem. 2001-), Internat. Forum Minisurgery Varicose Veins (hon. mem. 2000-), Royal Coll. Surgeons of Eng., Royal Coll. Physicians of London Licentiates, Nat. Assn. Armenian Studies and Rsch. (rep. Midatlantic region 1994—), Armenian Gen. Benevolent Union (pres.' club 1990—, guest lectr.), Am. Armenian Med. Assn. (co-founder 1972, 25th Anniversary co-founder award 1997), Brit. Med. Assn., Immunology Club Boston, Cancer Rsch. Assn. Boston, Physicians for Social Responsibility, Am. Pub. Health Assn., Assn. for Study of Med. Edn., Armenian Med. and Dental Assn. Greater Phila. (co-founder 1983, pres. 1983-85, Outreach award 1986), Assn. Acad. Surgery, Transplantation Soc., Am. Fedn. Clin. Rsch., N.Y. Acad. Scis., Am. Soc. Transplant Surgeons (co-founding mem. 1974), Am. Venous Forum (chair Internat. Rels. Com. 2001—), Am. Venous Found. (dir. 2002-), Assn. of Ill., Transplant Surgeons, Chgo. Assn. Immunologists, Chgo. Soc. Gastroenterology, Phila. Acad. Scis., Greater Delaware Valley Soc. Transplant Surgeons (pres. 1982-85), Phila. Med. Soc. (pres. 1984), Pa. Med. Soc., Samuel Hahnemann Surg. Soc., Am. Technion Soc., Am. Soc. Artificial Internal Organs, European Soc. Organ Transplant, Internat. Cardiovascular Soc. (N.Am. chpt.), Am. Assn. Vascular Surgery, Am. Coll. Phlebology (curriculum devel. projects com. 1992—, faculty 1993—, panelist 10th ann. congress 1996, membership com. 1998—, co-chmn. symposiums and session 1998-, chmn. sci. program com. 13th ann. congress 1999, program chair 14th ann. congress 2000), End Stage Renal Disease Network 24, Am. Coll. Physician Execs., Detroit Acad. Surgery, Detroit Surgical Assn., Transplantation Soc. Mich., Organ Procurement Agy. Mich., Wayne County Med. Soc., Mich. State Med. Soc., Fairfax County Med. Soc., Med. Soc. Va., Soc. Brigham Surg. Alumni, Greater Washington Telecomm. Assn. (pres.'s club 1994), Am. Soc. Lymphology (nat. adv. bd 1999—, pres.-elect 2000-2001, pres. 2001-), Am. Soc. Phlebectomy (chmn. program com. 1999—, chmn.-elect 2000-2001, chmn. bd. 2001-2002), Med. Club (Phila.), Sigma Xi. Mem. Soc. Of Friends. Achievements include bilateral lung reimplantation, reversal of renal allgraft rejection, prevention and treatment of massive gastroduodenal hemrrhage from hemorrhagic gastritis; co-discovery essential aminoacids phenylalanine and tryptphan are essential for antibody formation, participated in the lyophilization of the smallpox vaccine which was used by the WHO in 1966; to vaccinate everybody resulting in eradication of smallpox in 1978; co-discovery of immunogenetic control of antibody formation, rsch. advantages and disadvantages and pervention of splenectomy in renal transplant recipients; stage-enmasse cardiopulmonary reimplantation, zinc deficiency depresses the action of zinc dependent enzymes, priming the recipient with donor antigen improves kidney transplant survival; combined surgery and sclerptherapy corrects; abnormal structure, function and aesthetics of leg varicose veins; pioneering conversion of arteriovenous shunt to arteriovenous fistula for hemodialysis, needle phlebectomy in USA; beaver microblade phlebectomy, bupivicaine wound infiltration in venous surgery wounds to minimize post operative pain; abolition of concurrent deep and perforator vein incompetence by surgical correction of superficial vein incompetence; treatment of the varicose giacomini vein. Office: The Vein Inst 3301 Woodburn Rd Ste 102 Annandale VA 22003-6889

SIMONS, ALBERT, III, lawyer; b. Charleston, S.C., Nov. 22, 1950; s. Albert Jr. and Caroline Pinckney (Mitchell) S.; m. Theodora Bonnell Wilbur, Jan. 28, 1970; children: Albert IV, Charles A., Theodora B. BA, U. Va., 1972, JD, 1976. Bar: S.C. 1977, N.Y. 1978. Ptnr. Orrick, Herrington & Sutcliffe, N.Y.C., 1984—. Mem. S.C. Bar Assn., N.Y. State Bar Assn. Office: Orrick Herrington & Sutcliffe 666 5th Ave Rm 203 New York NY 10103-1798

SIMONS, BARRY, underwriter, insurance consultant; b. London, Aug. 18, 1927; came to U.S., 1990; s. Elkan Simons and Sylvia (Norris) Bonner-May; m. Susan Hoffman-Simons, Aug. 12, 1990. BA, Marlborough (Eng.) Coll., 1944, MA. Police sgt. Scotland Yard, London, 1970-83; pres., CEO Elkan & Barry Simons Ltd., 1947-90; underwriting mem. Lloyd's of London, 1978; incorporator Eastern Health Network, 1996—; supr., trainer H.P. Koppleman, Inc., Hartford, Conn., 1996-98. Dir. media and pub. rels. New Britain (Conn.) Symphony, 1992—; mem. adv. bd., corborator Rockville Bank, Conn., 1992—. (writer, dir.): (stage plays). 1st chmn. London Young Conservatives, 1950-53. Capt. Brit. Army, 1944-47. Ennobled by Prince Regent to Sir Barry Simons. Fellow Inst. Ins. Cons., Brit. Inst. Mgmt. Avocations: auto racing, wild animal training, photography. Home: 44 Glenn Dr Tolland CT 06084-4019

SIMONS, BERNARD PHILIP, lawyer; b. N.Y.C., Nov. 14, 1942; s. Harold J. and Lila (Orchant) S.; m. Eve C. Steinberg, Nov. 28, 1971; 1 child, Caroline A. BA, Rutgers U., 1964; JD, Hastings Coll. of Law, San Francisco, 1967. Ptnr. Gendel, Raskoff, Shapiro & Quittner, L.A., 1969-87; prin. Sanders, Barnet, Goldman, Simons & Mosk, 1988-2000; now ptnr. Crosby Heajey Roach & May, 2000—. Capt. U.S. Army, 1967-69, Vietnam. Decorated Bronze Star. Mem. ABA, Calif. Bar Assn., L.A. County Bar Assn., Order of Coif. Office: Crosby Heajey Roach & May 1901 Ave of the Stars # 700 Los Angeles CA 90067-6078 Fax: 310-734-5299. E-mail: bsimons@chrm.com.

SIMONS, CAROL LENORE, magazine editor; b. Bklyn., Feb. 2, 1942; d. Paul and Grace (Rotwein) Seiderman; m. Lewis M. Simons, Feb. 7, 1965; children: Justine, Rebecca, Adam. BA, Tufts U., 1963; MS, Columbia U., 1964. Rschr. Newsweek mag., N.Y.C., 1964-65, CBS News, N.Y.C. and Saigon, Vietnam, 1967-68; reporter Denver Post, 1965-67; editor Pres. Commn. on Marijuana and Drug Abuse, Washington, 1971-72; assoc. editor Smithsonian mag., 1978-82; dir. publs. Am. C. of C. in Japan, Tokyo, 1991-96; mng. editor Modern Maturity mag., Washington, 1997—. Office: Modern Maturity 601 E St NW Washington DC 20049-0001

SIMONS, DENNIS, performing company executive; b. Port Alberni, B.C., Can., Apr. 05; Student, Royal Acad. Music, Eng. Conducter, coach, tchr. violin Chethams Sch. Music, Manchester, Eng., Royal No. Coll. Music, Manchester; founder, music dir. Altrincham Youth Chamber Orch.; concertmaster British Broadcasting Co. Philharmonic Orch., 1977-93; joint concertmaster London Philharmonic Orch.; artistic dir., conductor Saskatoon Symphony, 1993-97; music dir., conductor Shreveport (La.) Symphony, 1996—. Founder, leader Alberni String Quartet; preliminary juror Banff Internat. String Quartet Competition, 1995; juror for finals Banff Internat. String Quartet Competition, 1998. Guest conductor Toronto Symphony, Thirteen Strings of Ottawa, Victoria Symphony, Orch. London Ontario, Manitoba Chamber Orch.; recordings include Mozart Concert Arias; videos include The Maestro and the Diva. Fellow Royal Acad. Music. Office: Strand Theatre PO Box 205 Shreveport LA 71162-0205 E-mail: dsimons@aol.com.*

SIMONS, DOLPH COLLINS, JR. newspaper publisher; b. Lawrence, Kans., Mar. 11, 1930; s. Dolph Collins and Marie (Nelson) S.; m. Pamela Counseller, Feb. 7, 1952; children: Pamela, Linda, Dolph Collins, Dan. AB, U. Kans., 1951; LLD (hon.), Colby Coll., 1972. Reporter Lawrence Jour.-World, 1953, asso. pub., 1957, pub., 1962—, editor, 1978—, pres., 1969—; reporter The Times, London, 1956, Johannesburg (South Africa) Star, 1958; pres. World Co. Mem. Pulitzer Awards Jury, 1977, 78, 80, 81. Trustee, past pres. William Allen White Found.; trustee Midwest Rsch. Inst., Menninger Found., Nat. Parks and Conservation Assn.; former mem. governing bd. Children's Mercy Hosp., Kansas City, Mo.; trustee, chmn. U. Kans. Endowment Assn.; past bd. dirs. Greater Kansas City Cmty. Found., Commerce Bancshares, Kansas City, Mo.; former trustee The Freedom Forum, Kans. Nature Conservancy. Served to capt. USMRC, 1951-53. Recipient Elijah Parish Lovejoy award, 1972; Fred Ellsworth award for significant service to U. Kans., 1976; Disting. Service citation, 1980 Mem. Newspaper Advt. Bur. (past dir.), Am. Soc. Newspaper Editors, Inland Daily Press Assn. (past dir.), Kans. Press Assn. (past pres., dir.), AP (past dir.), Am. Newspaper Pubs. Assn. (past dir., past nat. sec.), Lawrence C. of C. (past pres., dir.), U. Kans. Alumni Assn. (past pres., dir.), Lawrence Country Club, Kansas City Country Club, Kansas City River Club, Masons, Rotary, Sigma Delta Chi, Phi Delta Theta. Republican. Episcopalian. Home: 2425 Vermont St Lawrence KS 66046-4761 Office: 609 New Hampshire St Lawrence KS 66044-2243 E-mail: dsimonsjr@ljworld.com.

SIMONS, DONA, artist; b. Bryn Athyn, Pa., Aug. 10, 1953; d. Keneth Alden and Reta Isabel (Evens) S.; m. John Louis Vigo, May 17, 1986. Student, Phila. Coll. Art, 1974, Moore Coll. Art, 1976, Pa. Acad. Fine Arts, 1977-79. One-woman shows include Frank Tanzer Gallery, Boston, 1975, The Curaçao Mus., Netherlands Antilles, 1991, The Curaçao Seaquarium, 1991, Sylvia Schmidt Gallery, New Orleans, 1992, 1999, 2001, Mobil Oil Co. bldg. lobbies, 1997, exhibited in group shows at Berg Gallery, Jenkintown, Pa., 1973, United Artisans Gallery, Chalfont, Pa., 1974—75, Arthur Roger Gallery, New Orleans, La., 1980, Arts Coun. New Orleans Acad. Fine Arts, La., 1982, Am. Italian Renaissance Found., New Orleans, 1985, Found. Prince Pierre de Monaco, Monaco, 1985, The Rittenhouse Galleries, Phila., 1993—94, Sylvia Schmidt Gallery, New Orleans, 1993—2002, Allentown (Pa.) Mus. Art, 1998, Pa. Acad. Fine Arts, Chester Springs, Pa., 1999, 1999, 2000, 2002, New Orleans Art Assn., Hanson Gallery, New Orleans, 2001, commns., Represented in permanent collections Percent for Art Program, City of New Orleans. Mem. Pa. Acad. Fine Arts. Office: Sylvia Schmidt Gallery 400 Julia St # A New Orleans LA 70130-3606

SIMONS, ELIZABETH R(EIMAN), biochemist, educator; b. Vienna, Austria, Sept. 1, 1929; came to U.S., 1941, naturalized, 1948; d. William and Erna Engle (Weisselberg) Reiman; m. Harold Lee Simons, Aug. 12, 1951; children: Leslie Ann Mulert, Robert David. BChemE, Cooper Union, N.Y.C., 1950; MS, Yale U., 1951, PhD, 1954. Rsch. chemist Tech. Ops., Arlington, Mass., 1953-54; instr. chemistry Wellesley (Mass.) Coll., 1954-57; rsch. asst. Children's Hosp. Med. Ctr. and Cancer Rsch. Found., Boston, 1957-59, rsch. assoc. pathology, 1959-62; rsch. assoc. Harvard Med. Sch., 1962-66, lectr. biol. chemistry, 1966-72; tutor biochem. scis. Harvard Coll., 1971-94; assoc. prof. biochemistry Boston U., 1972-78, prof., 1978—. Contbr. articles to profl. jours. Grantee in field. Mem.: AAAS, Soc. for Neurosci., Biophys. Soc., Am. Soc. Hematology, Am. Soc. Cell Biology, Am. Soc. Biol. Chemists, Am. Heart Assn., Am. Chem. Soc. Office: Boston U Sch Medicine 80 E Concord St Roxbury MA 02118-2307 E-mail: esimons@bu.edu.

SIMONS, ELWYN LAVERNE, physical anthropologist, primatologist, paleontologist, educator; b. Lawrence, Kans., July 14, 1930; s. Verne Franklin and Verna Irene (Cuddeback) S.; m. Friderun Annursel Ankel, Dec. 2, 1972; children: Cornelia Verna Mathilde, Verne Franklin Herbert; 1 child by previous marriage: David Brenton. BS in Biology, Rice U., 1953; MA, Princeton U., 1955, PhD in Paleobiology, 1956; D.Phil., Oxford (Eng.) U., 1959; MA (hon.), Yale U., 1967; DSc, Oxford U., 1995. Demonstrator, exhibitor Oxford U., 1956-58; lectr. geology Princeton (N.J.) U., 1958-59; asst. prof. zoology U. Pa., Phila., 1959-61; vis. assoc. prof. geology, curator vertebrate paleontology Yale U., New Haven, 1960-61, head divsn. vert. paleontology, 1961-77, prof. paleontology, 1967; prof. geology, curator charge div. vertebrate paleontology Peabody Mus., 1965-77; prof. biol. anthropology, anatomy Duke U., Durham, NC, 1977-82, 1982—, prof. zoology, dir. Duke Primate Center, 1977-91, sci. dir., 1991—2001. Dir. Paleontol. Expdns., Egypt, 1961—68, Egypt, 1977—2001, sci. dir., Egypt, 1991—2001, dir., India, 1968—69, India, 1996, India, 98, India, 1999—2000; rsch. expdns. for fossil mammals, Wyo., 1960—96, Wyo., 1998—99, Iran, 1970, Spain, 71, Madagascar, 86, Madagascar, 1987—2000; Barbour-Schramm Meml. lectr. U. Nebr., 1974; David French lectr. Claremont Coll., 1974; traveling lectr. French Bur. Fgn. Affairs, 1976; bd. dirs. Ctr. Tropical Conservation, NC. Author: Primate Evolution: An Introduction To Man's Place In Nature, 1972; co-editor: Macmillan Series in Physical Anthropology; A Simons Family History in England and America, 1975; contbr. numerous articles to profl. publs. Decorated chevalier Ordre Nat. (Madagascar); named hon. citizen, Fayum Province of Egypt, 1981; recipient Annadale Meml. medal, Asiatic Soc. Bengal, 1973, Sr. U.S. Scientist award, Alexander von Humboldt Found., 1975. Mem. AAAS, Am. Philos. Soc., Nat. Acad. Scis., Soc. Vertebrate Paleontology, Inst. Human Paleontology, Am. Assn. Zool. Parks and Aquariums (primate specialist group, advisor prosimian taxon group), Assn. Phys. Anthropology (Charles R. Darwin award 2000), Madagascar Fauna Group (bd. dirs.), Internat. Assn. Human Biologists, Sigma Xi. Democrat. Achievements include research in on early mammals, prosimians and primate and human evolution, with special interest in living prosimians, higher primate and human origin and evolution; discovery of of 1st tarsiers and 1st marsupials in Africa; naming of earliest known ape Aegyptopithecus in Oligocene of Africa; discovery of of Gigantopithecus in India, 1968; naming of earliest anthropoids Oligopitheucs, 1962, Qatrania, 1983, Serapia and Arsinoea, 1992; discovery of and naming of new species of Propithecus: Golden Crowned Sifaka in Madagascar, 1989; conservation of lemurs and rain forest of Madagascar. Office: Duke Primate Ctr Divsn Fossil Primates 1013 Broad St Durham NC 27705 Fax: (919) 490-5394. E-mail: esimons@duke.edu.

SIMONS, ERIC WARD, financial executive; b. N.Y.C., Sept. 21, 1958; s. Theodor Leonard and Jean Lenore (Farbman) S. BS in Mgmt. and Internat. Bus., NYU, 1980. Sales cons. Paris Health Club, N.Y.C., 1979-81; registered rep. First Investors Corp., 1981-82; fin. courses instr. Learning Annex, 1981—; cert. aquatics dir. West Side YMCA, 1973—99; founder, pres. Simons Fin. Network, 1982—; former exec. v.p. wealth mgmt. group Ramirez & Co. Chmn. bd. dirs. Found. in Motion, N.Y.C., 1983-85; dir., treas. Rockville Dance Co., N.Y.C., 1984-86. Mem., spl. activities coord. West 83d St. Block Assn., N.Y.C., 1970-76; retired mem. bd. mgrs. McBurney YMCA, 1996-98. Named to Million Dollar Round Table, First Investors Corp., N.Y.C., 1982; recipient Highest Sales award Paris Health Club, N.Y.C., 1981. Mem. Fin. Planning Assn. (bd. dirs., officer 1984-99), Assn. Divorce Fin. Planners (founding, bd. dirs., chmn. 1999-2000), NYU Tax Soc. (retired bd. dirs.), Psi Upsilon (chmn. traditions and edn. com., Resolution of Appreciation exec. coun. 1987). Democrat. Jewish. Avocations: physical fitness, travel, karate, numerology. Home: 175 W 93rd St Apt 1D New York NY 10025-9314 Office: Simons Fin Network 175 W 93d St New York NY 10025 E-mail: SFN@juno.com.

SIMONS, GAIL S. artist, educator, librarian; b. Elgin, Ill., Aug. 13, 1963; d. James Philip and Vivian Faith (Ewalt) S. Cert. Christian edn., Lincoln Christian Coll., 1986; BFA, Judson Coll., 1991. Tchg. asst. Pub. Sch. Dist. 300, Dundee, Ill., 1986-89; illustrator computer clip art Media Mktg. Svcs., St. Charles, 1989; computer data plant ops. Judson Coll., Elgin, 1990-91, watercolor painting instr., 1991—; libr. Dundee Twp. Pub. Libr., East Dundee, Ill., 1994—, staff artist, 1997—. Youth/adult choral dir. First Congl. Ch., Carpentersville, Ill., 1986-96; stop motion animator, Chgo., 1991. Exhibited works at Ruth M. Wendt Gallery, East Dundee, 1997-99, Agora Gallery, N.Y.C., 1999—, Incognito Gallery, Fox Lake, Ill., 2001; actress, asst. dir., set/prop designer various musicals and plays. Deaconess/Sunday sch. dir. Congl. Ch., Carpentersville, 1986-96; watercolor/craft tchr. Pub. Libr, East Dundee, 1997—; wildlife adv.; youth leader. Mem. Christians in the Visual Arts, N.W. Area Arts Coun., Dundee Twp. Fine Arts Coun., Alpha Chi Soc. Avocations: collecting, gardening, writing, entomology, old movies. Office: Dundee Twp Pub Libr Dist 555 Barrington Ave East Dundee IL 60118-1422

SIMONS, GALE GENE, nuclear and electrical engineer, educator; b. Kingman, Kans., Sept. 25, 1939; s. Robert Earl and Laura V. (Swartz) S.; m. Barbara Irene Rinkel, July 2, 1966; 1 child, Curtis Dean. BS, Kans. State U., 1962, MS, 1964, PhD, 1968. Engr. Argonne Nat. Lab., Idaho Falls, Idaho, 1968-77, mgr. fast source reactor, head exptl. support group, 1972-77; prof. nuclear engring. Kans. State U., Manhattan, 1977—, assoc. dean for rsch., dir. rsch. coun. Coll. Engring., 1988-97, bd. dirs. Rsch. Found., 1988-97, Presdl. lectr., 1983-96, career counselor, 1984-96. Cons. to pvt. and fed. agys., 1983—; bd. dirs. Kans. Tech. Enterprise Corp., Topeka; com. mem. Kans. Gov.'s Energy Policy Com., Topeka, 1992-97; numerous presentations in field; reviewer proposals fed. agys. Contbr. over 100 articles to sci. jours.; patentee radiation dosimeter. Expert witness State of Kans., Topeka, 1986. Fellow AEC, 1964-67; numerous grants from fed. agys., 1979—. Mem. AAAS, IEEE, Am. Nuclear Soc., Health Physics Soc., Am. Soc. for Engring. Edn., Masons, Rotary, Phi Kappa Phi, Tau Beta Pi, Pi Mu Epsilon. Home: 2395 Grandview Ter Manhattan KS 66502-3729 Office: Kans State U Durland Hall Rm 261 Manhattan KS 66506-5103

SIMONS, GERALD T. physician assistant; b. May 26, 1970; BS, SUNY, Stony Brook, 1993; Physician Asst., Cornell U., 1995. Physician asst. Hyperbaric Svcs. Am., Great Neck, NY, 1998—; physician asst. East End Assocs./HPC, East Hampton, 1995—; acad. coord. Cornell U. Physician Asst. Program, N.Y.C., 1998—. Mem. editl. bd. Surg. PA Jour.; contbr. articles. Fellow: Am. Assn. Surg. Physician Assts. (v.p. 1998—2000, pres. 2000—, Kirklin award 1998), Am. Acad. Physician Assts. (del.); mem.: N.Y. State Soc. Physician Assts. (dir. 1994—95, chair com. 1995—98, 1999—2000). Office: 139 Springs Fireplace Rd East Hampton NY 11937-2016 E-mail: cornellspa@aol.com.

SIMONS, HELEN, school psychologist, psychotherapist, educator; b. Chgo., Feb. 13, 1930; d. Leo and Sarah (Shrayer) Pomper; m. Broudy Simons, May 20, 1956 (May 1972); children: Larry, Sheri. BA in Biol., Lake Forest Coll., 1951; MA in Clin. Psychology, Roosevelt U., 1972; D of Psychology, Ill. Sch. Profl. Psychology, 1980. Intern Cook County Hosp., Chgo., 1979-80; pvt. practice psychotherapist, 1980—; sch. psychologist Chgo. Bd. Edn., 1974-79, 80—. Faculty Internat. Soc. for Prevention of Child Abuse and Neglect; lectr., presenter at workshops. Contbr. articles to profl. jours. Mem.: APA, Internat. Soc. for Prevention of Child Abuse and Neglect, Internat. Coun. Psychologists, Chgo. Sch. Psychol. Assn., Chgo. Psychol. Assn., Ill. Sch. Psychologists Assn., Nat. Sch. Psychologists Assn. Avocations: music, dancing, reading. Home: 6145 N Sheridan Rd Apt 29D Chicago IL 60660-6855 Office: Brennemann Sch 4251 N Clarendon Ave Chicago IL 60613-1593 E-mail: hpompers@aol.com.

SIMONS, LAWRENCE BROOK, lawyer; b. N.Y.C., Oct. 19, 1924; s. Harry A. and Marion B. (Brook) S.; m. Annalou Kadin, Aug. 24, 1947; children: Barbara Flexner, Kenneth. Student, Duke U., 1941-43, 46-47; JD, Columbia U., 1949. Bar: N.Y. 1949, D.C. 1984, U.S. Dist. Ct. (so. dist.) N.Y. 1949, U.S. Supreme Ct. 1987. Assoc. Spring & Eastman, N.Y.C., 1949-53; v.p., gen. mgr. Caribe Knitting Mills, San Juan, P.R., 1953-58; pres. LBS Constrn. Co. Inc., S.I., N.Y., 1958-77; asst. sec. housing FHA commn. HUD, Washington, 1977-81; ptnr. Powell, Goldstein, Frazier & Murphy, 1981—. Mem. Task Force on Quality of Life, Dept. of Def., 1995. Trustee Bayley Seton Hosp., S.I., 1981-90, NHP Found., Inc., 1991—; chmn. bd. dirs. N.Y. State Urban Devel. Corp., 1975-77, Nat. Housing Conf., 1981—, Pa. Ave. Devel. Corp., 1981-87; mem. Nat. Housing Task Force, 1988, Nat. Housing Trust, 1990—; trustee Affordable Housing Found., 1990-92, Ctr. for Democracy, 1990-96; pres. Ctr. for Housing Policy, 1992-96, bd. dirs., 1996—; commr. Beaufort (S.C.) Housing Authority, 1997—, Affordable Housing Commn. Hilton Head, S.C., 1997-99. With U.S. Army, 1943-46, ETO. Named Man of Yr. Nat. Housing Conf., Washington, 1985. Mem. ABA, Nat. Assn. Home Builders (named to Housing Hall of Fame 2002), Army Navy C. of C., Sea Pines Country Club, Lambda Alpha. Democrat. Jewish. Avocation: golf. Home: 40 Plantation Dr Hilton Head Island SC 29928-4402 Office: Powell Goldstein Frazier Murphy 1001 Pennsylvania Ave NW Washington DC 20004-2505 E-mail: simons@digitel.net.

SIMONS, LEWIS MARTIN, journalist; b. Paterson, N.J., Jan. 9, 1939; s. Abram and Goldie (Fleisher) S.; m. Carol Lenore Seiderman, Feb. 7, 1965; children: Justine, Rebecca, Adam P.D. BA, NYU, 1962; MS, Columbia U., 1964. Corr. AP, Kuala Lumpur, Singapore, Saigon, Denver, 1965-70, Washington Post, Bangkok, New Delhi, Washington, 1971-82; bur. chief Knight-Ridder Newspapers, Tokyo and Beijing, 1982-95; fgn. policy corr. Time mag., 1996-97; freelance writer, 1997—. Author: Worth Dying For, 1987; contbg. author: Crimes of War, 1999, The World of Islam, 2001; contbr. to Nat. Geog. mag., Smithsonian mag., Atlantic Monthly, N.Y. Times. With USMC, 1962-64. Recipient Grand prize and Investigative Reporting award Am. Newspaper Guild, 1981, Citation for Excellence, Overseas Press Club Am., 1983, Jessie Meriton White award Friends World Coll., 1986, Investigative Reporters and Editors award U. Mo., 1986, Award of Excellence, World Affairs Coun., 1984, 86, 89, 92, Pulitzer Prize, 1986, George Polk award, 1985, Malcolm S. Forbes award Overseas Press Club Am., 1986, 92, Gerald Loeb award UCLA, 1993; Edward R. Murrow fellow Coun. of Fgn. Rels., 1970-71. Mem. Fgn. Corrs. Club Japan (bd. dirs. 1991-92, pres., 1993-94). E-mail: clsimons@ix.netcom.com.

SIMONS, LYNN OSBORN, educational consultant; b. Havre, Mont., June 1, 1934; d. Robert Blair and Dorothy (Briggs) Osborn; m. John Powell Simons, Jan. 19, 1957; children: Clayton Osborn, William Blair. Tchr. Midvale (Utah) Jr. H.S., 1956-57, Sweetwater county Sch. Dist. 1, Rock Springs, Wyo., 1957-58, U. Wyo., 1959-61, Natrona County Sch. Dist. 1, Casper, Wyo., 1963-64; credit mgr. Gallery 323, 1972-77; Wyo. state supt. pub. instrn. Cheyenne, 1979-91; sec.'s regional rep. region VIII U.S. Dept. Edn., Denver, 1993—2001; mem. Denver Fed. Exec. Bd., 1995-2001; mem. exec. bd. combined Fed. campaign, 1994—2001; ednl. cons., 2001—. Mem. State Bds. Charities and Reform, Land Commrs., Farm Loan, 1979-91; mem. State Commns. Capitol Bldg., Liquor, 1979-91; Ex-officio mem. bd. trustees U. Wyo., 1979-91; ex-officio mem. Wyo. Community Coll. Commn., 1979-91; mem. steering com. Edn. Commn. of the States, 1988-90; mem. State Bd. Edn., 1971-77, chmn., 1976-77; advisor Nat. Trust for Hist. Preservation, 1980-86. Mem. LWV (pres. 1970-71). Democrat. Episcopalian. E-mail: simonov@worldnet.att.net.

SIMONS, RICHARD DUNCAN, lawyer, retired judge; b. Niagara Falls, N.Y., Mar. 23, 1927; s. William Taylor and Sybil Irene (Swick) S.; m. Muriel (Penny) E. Genung, June 9, 1951 (dec. 1992); m. Esther (Esi) Turkington Tremblay, May 21, 1994; children: Ross T., Scott R., Kathryn E., Linda A. AB, Colgate U., 1949; LLB, U. Mich., 1952; LLD (hon.), Albany Law Sch., 1983. Bar: N.Y. 1952. Pvt. practice, Rome, 1952-63; asst. corp. counsel City of Rome, 1955-58, corp. counsel, 1960-63; justice 5th jud. dist. N.Y. Supreme Ct., 1964-83, assoc. justice appellate divsn. 3d dept., 1971-72, assoc. justice appellate divsn. 4th dept., 1973-82; assoc. judge N.Y. Ct. Appeals, 1983-96, acting chief judge, 1992-93; counsel McMahon, Grow & Getty, Rome, 1997-00; dir. N.Y. State Capital Defender Office, 1997-2000; chief appellate judge Oneida Indian Nation, 1997—. Jurist in residence Syracuse U. Law Sch., 1998; mem. Law Sch. Admission Svcs., Bar Passage Study Com. Editorial staff: N.Y. Pattern Jury Instructions, 1979-83. Chmn. Republican City Com., 1958-62; vice chmn. Oneida County Rep. Com., 1958-62; bd. mgrs. Rome Hosp. and Murphy Meml. Hosp., 1953; mem. Chief Judge's Commn. on Fiduciary Appointments, Chief Judge's Com. to Promote Trust and Confidence in the Legal Sys., N.Y. Fair Elections Project, Inc., Campaign for Effective Justice. Served with USN, World War II. NEH fellow U. Va. Law Sch., 1979 Fellow Am. Bar Found., N.Y. State Bar Found. (chmn. 1997-98); mem. ABA, N.Y. State Bar Assn. (chair task force on ct. reorganization 1999-2002, Disting. Svc. award 2000), Oneida County Bar Assn., Rome Bar Assn., Am. Law Inst., Inst. Jud. Adminstrn. Home: 6520 Pillmore Cir Rome NY 13440-7337 Office: McMahon Grow & Getty 301 N Washington St Ste 4 Rome NY 13440-5152

SIMONS, STEPHEN, mathematics educator, researcher; b. London, Aug. 11, 1938; came to U.S., 1965; s. Jack Isidore Simons and Ethel Esther (Littman) Harris; m. Jacqueline Mania Berchadsky, Aug. 13, 1963; 1 son, Mark. BA, Cambridge U., Eng., 1959, PhD, 1962. Instr. U. B.C., Vancouver, Can., 1962-63; asst. prof. U. BC., Can., 1964-65, U. Calif., Santa Barbara, 1965-67, assoc. prof., 1967-73, prof., 1973—, chmn. dept., 1975-77, 88-89. Trustee Math. Scis. Rsch. Inst., Berkeley, Calif., 1988-94. Peterhouse rsch. fellow, Cambridge U., 1963-64. Mem. Am. Math. Soc. Office: Univ Calif Dept Math Santa Barbara CA 93106

SIMONS, THOMAS W., JR. educator; b. Crosby, Minn., Sept. 4, 1938; s. Thomas Winston and Mary Jo (Enochs) S.; m. Margaret Eleanor Quinn, Dec. 23, 1963; children: Suzanne Deirdre, Benjamin Thomas. BA, Yale U., 1958; MA, Harvard U., 1959, PhD, 1963. Joined Fgn. Svc., Dept. State, 1963; sec. del., tech. sec. U.S. Del. to 6th round trade negotiation in GATT, 1964-67; consular officer, polit. officer Am. Embassy, Warsaw, Poland, 1968-71; Coun. on Fgn. Rels. fellow Hoover Instn., Stanford, Calif., 1971-72; internat. rels. officer Bur. Politico-Mil. Affairs, 1972-74, mem. policy planning staff, 1974-75; chief external reporting unit, polit. sect. Am. Embassy, Moscow, 1975-77, dep. chief of mission Bucharest, Romania, 1977-79, counselor for polit. affairs London, 1979-81; dir. for Soviet Union affairs Dept. State, 1981-85; mem. Sr. Seminar in Fgn. Policy, 1985-86; dep. asst. sec. for European and Can. affairs Dept. State, 1986-89; diplomat-in-residence, adj. prof. history Brown U., Providence, 1989-90; amb. extraordinary and plenipotentiary Poland, 1990-93. Coord. U.S. assistance to new ind. states of former Soviet Union, Washington, 1993-95; amb. extraordinary and plenipotentiary, Pakistan, 1995-98; cons. prof. history Stanford U., 1998-2002, Ctr. Internat. Security and Coop., Stanford U., 1998—; program dir. Davis Ctr. for Russian and Eurasian Studies, Harvard U., 2002—; vis. diplomat-scholar Wellesley Coll., 2002-2003. Author: The End of the Cold War?, 1990, Eastern Europe in the Postwar World, 2d edit., 1993. Home: 11 Buena Vista Park Cambridge MA 02140 Office: 625 Massachusetts Ave Cambridge MA 02139

SIMONS, WILLIAM W. lawyer, mediator, arbitrator; b. N.Y.C., Mar. 13, 1928; s. Abraham R. and Yetta (Lubow) S.; m. Marilyn Frankel, May 23, 1953; children: Amy Joan Abramovich, Richard Anderew Simons. BA, NYU, 1950, JD, 1954. Bar: N.Y. 1954, Mass. 1960, U.S. Dist. Ct. (so. dist.) N.Y. 1962, U.S. Dist. Ct. (no. dist.) N.Y. 1963, U.S. Dist. Ct. Mass. 1963. Assoc. Moses & Singer, N.Y.C., 1954-60, Albert Silverman, Pittsfield, Mass., 1960-62; ptnr. Simons, Cook & Shepard, 1962-78; justice Superior Ct. Mass., Boston, 1978-93; of counsel Reder & Simons, Pittsfield, 1993—. Asst. dist. atty. Western Dist. Mass., Pittsfield/Springfield, 1968-73. Sgt. U.S. Army, 1946-47, Korea. Mem. N.Y. State Bar Assn., Mass. Bar Assn., Berkshire County Bar Assn. (pres. 1971-72). Office: Simons Smith & Gerrard 75 North St Pittsfield MA 01201-5116 E-mail: wsimons@ssandg-law.com.

SIMONSEN, ROBERT ALAN, marketing executive; b. Cherokee, Iowa, Apr. 8, 1956; s. Earl Dean and Betty (Gabrielson) S.; m. Shawn Marie Beck, June 11, 1983; children: Adam David, Patrick Robert, Brian Matthew. BS in Bus. with honors, BA in Econs. with honors, Iowa State U., 1978; MBA in Mktg. with honors, U. Colo., 1982. Cost acct. Simonsen Mfg. Co., Quimby, Iowa, 1978-81, mktg. mgr., 1983-87; mgr. corp. mkt. Simonsen Mill, Simonsen Mfg., Simonsen Propane, 1987-94; pres. Simbec, Inc., Cherokee, Iowa, 1994—; mktg. mgr. R.J. Thomas Mfg. Co., Inc., 1995—. Fin. chmn. Cherokee County Rep. Party, 1992—; chmn. Quimby Centennial Com., 1983-87; precinct chmn. Cherokee County Reps., Quimby Twp., 1980, 88, Cherokee Twp., 1990—; trustee Quimby United Meth. Ch., 1983-89; bd. dirs. Cherokee Area Econ. Devel. Corp., 1993—, We. Iowa Tech. C.C. Found., 1998—. Recipient First Pl. award for Radio Advt. Cen. Iowans in Radio and TV, 1988, Iowa chpt. of Nat. Agr. Mktg. Assn., 1990, Addy Citation of Excellence award Advt. Profls. of Des Moines, Inc., 1989, First Pl. for Radio Series and Best Show award, Nat. Agr. Mktg. Assn., 1990, Merit award for Print Advt. Iowa chpt., 1992. Mem. Cherokee C. of C. (bd. dirs. 1995—), Iowa State U. Alumni Assn., Beta Gamma Sigma. Home: 1567 520th St Cherokee IA 51012-7228 Office: Simbec Inc 1401 N 2nd St Cherokee IA 51012-2201

SIMONSON, BRUCE MILLER, geologist, educator; b. Washington, May 13, 1950; s. Roy Walter and Susan (Miller) S.; m. Sue Mareske, June 28, 1974; children: Joseph Walter, Sonja Anne, Maya Beth. BA with high honors, Wesleyan U., Middletown, Conn., 1972; PhD, Johns Hopkins U., 1982. Field mapper Nat. Geog. Inst., Honduras, 1973-74; instr. dept. geology Oberlin (Ohio) Coll., 1979-81, asst. prof., 1982-85, assoc. prof., 1986-88, prof., 1989—, Biggs prof. natural scis., 2001—, chmn. dept. geology, 1986-89, 93-97, 2000—. Adj. faculty Case Western Res. U., Cleve., 1983—2000; vis. scientist Geol. Survery Western Australia, summers, 1985—87, 1989, 93; tchr. U.S. Geol. Survey, Reston, Va., 1985, vis. prof., Denver, 1992—93. Contbr. articles to profl. jours. Recipient Bradley award Geol. Soc. Washington, 2000; grantee Nat. Geog. Soc., 1986-89, 93-94, 96-97, 99-2000, NSF, 1977-79, 84, 91-94, Rsch. Corp., 1983, Petroleum Rsch. Fund, 1982-84. Mem.: Meteoritical Soc., Soc. for Sedimentary Geology (sec. Gt. Lakes sect. 1986—90), No. Ohio Geol. Soc., Geol. Soc. Australia, Geol. Soc. Am. Office: Oberlin Coll Dept Geology Oberlin OH 44074-1044 E-mail: bruce.simonson@oberlin.edu.

SIMONSON, DAVID C. retired newspaper association executive; b. N.Y.C., May 9, 1927; s. Simon and Rebecca (Coolman) S.; m. Lois E. Sneider, Nov. 1, 1952; children: Peter, Eric, John Frederick. BA, Hamilton Coll., 1948; postgrad., U. Vt., 1949, Art Student League of N.Y., 1949. Copywriter Forwell & Mart Advt., N.Y.C., 1949-50; reporter, editor Croton-Cortlandt News, Croton, N.Y., 1950-52; gen. mgr. Colony Publs., N.Y.C., 1952-54; editor, mgr. County Press Newspapers, Croton, 1955-59; promotion dir. Amcrete Corp., Peekskill, N.Y., 1959-60; various positions in mgmt. Patent Trader, Mt. Kisco, 1960-72, pub., 1972-77; pres./pub. Pioneer Press Newspapers, Wilmette, Ill., 1977-86; exec. v.p., chief exec. officer Nat. Newspaper Assn., Washington, 1987-92; retired, 1992. Bd. dirs. Christian Herald Assn., N.Y.C., NY; lectr. Medill Sch. Journalism, Meridian House, U.S.A., numerous state press assns.; media cons.; seminar leader Ea. Europe for World Pres Freedom Com.; cons. to Slovakian publs. for U.S. Info. Agy., 1993—94; cons. to Slovakian publs. for USIA, 1995; cons. to African publs. for UNESCO, 95; cons. to Bulgarian Publs. for USIA, 96, 97, Croatian Publs. for USIA, 1999; seminar leader Voice of Am. for Bulgarian Publs., 1997, Bosnian pubs., 2000, Albanian pubs., 2000; U.S. rep. Media Conf., Prague, 2001; DUTV U.S. rep. with Chinese journalists, 01; participant Freedom Forum Roundtables. Chmn. planning bd. Town of Croton-on-Hudson, N.Y., 1962-67, trustee, 1967, mayor, 1969. With USNR, 1945-46. Recipient Lesher award Suburban Newspapers of Am., 1998. Mem. Suburban Newspapers Am. (pres. 1984-85, bd. dirs. 1980-84), Ill. Press Assn (bd. dirs. 1980-84, 1st v.p. 1986), N.Y. Press Assn. (bd. dirs. 1966-76, 1st v.p. 1976), Nat. Newspaper Assn. (bd. dirs. 1985-86), Cook County Pubs. Assn. (pres. 1983-84). Avocations: painting, cartooning. Home: 1805 28th St S Arlington VA 22202-1536

SIMONSON, LEE J. small business owner; b. Niagara Falls, N.Y., Sept. 5, 1953; s. Marvin W. and Mamie C. (Maroon) S.; m. Brenda J. Wright, July 3, 1976; children: Jill, Robin. AAS Bus. Adminstrn., Niagara County Community Coll., 1974; BS in Commerce, Niagara U., 1978. Asst. to dir. United Way Niagara, Niagara Falls, 1973; dir. small bus. program Medaille Coll., Buffalo, 1977-79; pub. Investible Growth Letter, Lewiston, 1977-89; owner, pres. Am. Collectibles, 1979-96. Bd. dirs. Niagara Ednl. Found., Niagara Falls; exec. dir. Excel Comms., 1996—; founder, pres. Heartwarmers.com, 1998—; founder, pres. Conf. Solutions, 2002—. Author: How to Run for Public Office, 1977. County legislator Niagara County, Lockport, N.Y., 1974—, chmn. jud. and laws and legis. com., 1978, chmn. edn. com. 1979, 87-88, chmn. social svcs. com. 1982, chmn. waste mgmt. com., 1989, chmn. of the legis., 1990-93, chmn. health com., 1998-2001; bd. dirs. sml. bus. resource ctr. Niagara County C.C., 1986-90; chmn. Western N.Y. Chalk Walk, Lewiston Com. on the Arts, 1984-97. Named Rep. of Yr. Lewiston Rep. Com., 1984, 92, Leader of the Yr. Leadership Niagara, 1991; 40 Under 40 award Bus. First Western N.Y., 1991. Roman Catholic. Office: Am Collectibles 504 Morgan Dr Lewiston NY 14092-1106

SIMONSON, LEE STUART, broadcast company executive; b. Balt., July 3, 1948; s. Theodore and Sara (Silver) S.; m. Nancy Paula Levin, Mar. 25, 1973; children: Laura Todd, Michael Theodore. BA, U. Md., 1970. Acct. exec. WGMS-AM-FM (subs. RKO Gen.), Washington, 1971-73, retail sales mgr., 1973-76; sales mgr. WFYR-FM (subs. RKO Gen.), Chgo., 1976-80; v.p., gen.

mgr. WRKS-FM (subs. RKO Gen.), N.Y.C., 1980-84, WOR-AM (subs. RKO Gen.), N.Y.C., 1984-88; vice chmn., COO, owner radio stas. Broadcasting Ptnrs., Inc., 1988-95; chmn., CEO Broadcasting Ptnrs. Holdings, LP, 1997-2000; pres. Simonson Assocs., 2000—. Bd. dirs. N.Y.C. chpt. March of Dimes, 1982—; Broadcast Pioneers Libr. Washington, 1995—; IRTS Found., 1995—98. With U.S. Army, 1970—76. Jewish. E-mail: SIMONSONLS@aol.com.

SIMONSON, PATRICIA LOU HOFFMAN, director health, fitness and recreation programs, grants writer; b. Buffalo, Feb. 2, 1954; d. Norman Richards and Evelyne (Ghnassia) H. BS, Canisius Coll., 1976; MA, Adelphi U., 1978; postgrad., SUNY, Buffalo, 1978-79. Pool supr. Town of Tonawanda Recreation Dept., Kenmore, N.Y., 1973-77; grad. asst. Adelphi U., 1977-78, SUNY, Buffalo, 1978-79; health and phys. edn. asst. Jewish Ctr. of Greater Buffalo, 1979-80, supr., 1980-81, asst. dir. health and phys. edn., 1981-83, assoc. dir. health and phys. edn., 1983-86, dir. health, fitness and recreation, 1986—. Cons. Computer Task Group, Buffalo, 1984—, Scot Architects, Fitness Facility Design ; lectr. on fitness; profl. golf instr.; mem. Gross-Schuman Facility Design, 1998. Contbr. articles to profl. jours. Grants Writer grantee JM Found., N.Y.C., 1978, Erie County Svcs. to Srs., 1995, N.Y. State Mary Laskey Heart Inst., 1995, 96, Merck Pharms., 1999, Buffalo Firefighters, 2000. Mem. AAHPERD, U.S. Golf Assn., Internat. Dance Exercise Assn., Am. Coll. Sports Medicine, N.Y. State Assn. for Health Phys. Edn. Recreation and Dance (pres. recreation/leisure sect. 1988-91), Assn. Jewish Ctr. Workers (chair ea. states chpt. 1981-83), Canisius Coll. Phys. Edn. Alumni Assn. (pres. 1975-76), Exec. Womens Golf Assn. Democrat. Jewish. Avocations: golf, harness racing. Home: 1420 Maple Rd Apt 7 Buffalo NY 14221-3543

SIMONSON, STEVEN NEIL, psychotherapist; b. New London, Ct., Apr. 25, 1960; s. Alvin Harris and Marilyn Simonson. BA in English, U. Pa., 1982; MA in Clin. Psychology, Conn. Coll., 1986; MS in Psychiat. Social Work, Columbia U., 1996. Intern in psychology VA Med. Ctr., Newington, Conn., 1984-85; psychotherapist Hartford (Conn.) Cmty. Mental Health Ctr., 1987-89, Ledyard (Conn.) Youth Svcs., 1992, Assocs. for Behavioral Change, Norwich, Conn., 1992-95, The Care Clinic, New London, 1993-94; resident in psychiat. social work Cath. Family Svcs., Milford, Conn., 1995-96; lic. psychotherapist South Shore Mental Health, Charlestown, R.I., 1996-2000, Family Ctr. Svcs., Westport, Conn., 2000—02, Conn. Behav. Health Assn., Stonington, 2002—. Mem. APA, NASW, ACA, AMHCA, NBCC, ACSW, BCD. Democrat. Avocations: reading, writing, music, art, exercise.

SIMONSON, SUSAN KAY, hospital clinical care coordinator; b. La Porte, Ind., Dec. 5, 1946; d. George Randolph and Myrtle Lucille (Opfel) Menkes; m. Richard Bruce Simonson, Aug. 25, 1973. BA with honors, Ind. U., 1969; MA, Washington U., St. Louis, 1972. Perinatal social worker Yakima Valley Meml. Hosp., Yakima, Wash., 1979-81, dir. patient support program, 1981—, dir. social svc., 1982-98; instr. Spanish, ethnic studies, sociology Yakima Valley Coll., 1981—. Pres. Yakima Child Abuse Council, 1983-85; developer nat. patient support program, 1981. Contbr. articles to profl. jours. Mem. adv. council Robert Wood Johnson Found. Rural Infant Health Care Project, Yakima, 1980, Pregnancy Loss and Compassionate Friends Support Groups, Yakima, 1982—, Teen Outreach Program, Yakima, 1984—. Recipient NSF award, 1967, discharge planning program of yr. regional award Nat. Glasrock Home Health Care Discharge Planning Program, 1987; research grantee Ind. U., 1968, Fulbright grantee U.S. Dept. State, 1969-70; Nat. Def. Edn. Act fellowship, 1970-73. Mem. Soc. Med. Anthropology, Soc. Hosp. Social Work Dirs. of Am. Hosp. Assn. (regional award 1989), Nat. Assn. Social Workers, Phi Beta Kappa. Office: Yakima Valley Meml Hosp 2811 Tieton Dr Yakima WA 98902-3799

SIMONTACCHI, CAROL NADINE, nutritionist, writer; b. Bellingham, Wash., July 6, 1947; d. Ralph Eugene and Sylvia Arleta (Tyler) Walmer; m. Bob Simontacchi, Oct. 3, 1981; children: Caryl Anne, Bobbie Anne, Melissa Anne, Laurie Anne. BS in Social Sci., Columbia Pacific U., 1996, MS in Social Sci., 1997; postgrad. The Union Inst., 2000—. Cert. clin. nutritionist Wash. CEO The Health Haus, Inc., Vancouver, Wash., 1985-98; host radio program Back to the Beginning, 1990-97; CEO The Natural Physician Ctr., Beaverton, Oreg., 1995-97. Author: Your Fat is Not Your Fault, 1994, 1997, The Sun Rise Book: Living Beyond Depression, 1996, All About Chitosan, 1999, The Crazy Makers, 2000, Heart Health for Women, 2000; author, designer Wings: Weight Success for a Lifetime, 2001, host Here's To Your Health, 1999—2000; columnist: Health Products Business, 1999—2000. Mem.: Internat. and Am. Assn. Clin. Nutritionalists, Nat. Nutritional Foods Assn. (chmn. edn. com. 1996—2001), Soc. Cert. Nutritionists (pres. bd. 1992—93), Autograph Soc. (chmn. 1999—). Republican. Christian Ch. Office: 533 Kinzie Isle Ct Sanibel FL 33957 E-mail: csimontacchi@cs.com.

SIMONTACCHI, JOHN FRANCIS, business executive; b. Boston, Apr. 10, 1946; BS in Engring. Physics, Merrimack Coll., 1968; MBA, Ind. U., 1976. Mktg. and sales mgr. Westinghouse, Pitts., 1968-88; gen. mgr. Square D Co./Group Schneider, Monroe, N.C., 1988-93; asst. v.p. NCR/AT&T, Columbia, S.C., 1993-95; v.p., gen. mgr. Barber-Colman Co./Siebe, Rockford, Ill., 1995-98; pres. Robertshaw Indsl. Products divsn. Invensys, Knoxville, Tenn., 1998—. Home: 4214 Waterford Dr Charlotte NC 28226-7835 Office: 1602 Mustang Dr Maryville TN 37801-3766

SIMONTON, DEAN KEITH, psychology educator; b. Glendale, Calif., Jan. 27, 1948; s. Dean Clarence Simonton and Laverne (Merkobrad) Williams; m. Susan Youel, June 21, 1971; (div. 1982); m. Melody Boyer, Dec. 29, 1984. BA in Psychology magna cum laude, Occidental Coll., 1970; MA in Social Psychology, Harvard U., 1973, PhD with distinction, 1975. Asst. prof. psychology U. Ark., Fayetteville, 1974-76; asst. prof. U. Calif., Davis, 1976-81, assoc. prof., 1981-85, prof., 1985—. Cons. Wissenschaftzentrun, Berlin, 1979, Ctr. for Creative Leadership, Greensboro, N.C., 1983, NATO, Brussels, Belgium, 1980-81, Dept. Def., Washington, 1983, Creative Problem Solving Inst., 1984, Arvin Perlmutter, Inc., 1992, Milken Family Found., 1994. Author: Genius, Creativity and Leadership, 1984, Why Presidents Succeed, 1987, Scientific Genius, 1988, Psychology, Science, and History, 1990, Greatness, 1994, Genius and Creativity, 1997, Origins of Genius, 1999; editor Jour. Creative Behavior, 1993-99; contbr. numerous articles to profl. jours. Recipient Excellence award Mensa Adn. and Rsch. Found., 196, Francis Galton award Internat. Assn. Empirical Aesthetics, 1996. Fellow AAAS, Am. Psychol. Soc., Am. Assn. Applied and Preventive Psychology, Am. Psychol. Assn. (mem.-at-large 1979-82, pres. psychology and the arts divsn. 1985-86, Rudolf Arnheim award Outstanding Contbn. to Psychology and the Arts, 1996, George A. Miller award 1997); mem. Phi Beta Kappa, Sigma Xi. Home: 2903 Solito St Davis CA 95616-0274 Office: U Calif Dept Psychology Davis CA 95616

SIMOS, EVANGELOS OTTO, economist, editor; b. Patras, Achia, Greece, May 18, 1947; came to U.S., 1972; s. Otto Evangelos and Demetra E. Dervenis; m. Louisa E., Apr. 18, 1972; children: Demetra E., Maria E. BS, Athens (Greece) Grad. Sch. Bus. and Econs., 1972; MA, No. Ill. U., 1975, PhD, 1977. V.p., economist D-Glass Co., Piraeus, Greece, 1969-72; instr. econs. No. Ill., Dekalb, 1976-77; prof. econs. U. N.H., Durham, 1977—, chmn. econs. program, 1987-90; v.p., chief Economist Infometrica, Inc., 1993—; sr. ptnr., founder Global Numis. Prognostications, 1987-94; v.p. econ. devel. World Trade Group N.H., 1989-91; editor, chief economist IBR, Inc., Dover, N.H., 1982-85. Chief editor Internat. Bus. Conditions Digest, 1983-85; editor for internat. affairs Jour. of Bus. Forecasting, 1987—, Quar. Domestic and Global Forecasts of Key Econ. Indicators, 1987—; editorial rev. bd. Rev. of Bus.; mem. bd. dirs. Internat. Assn. Bus. Forecasting, 1988-89; contbr. articles to profl. jours. Mem. Beta Gamma Sigma, Omicron Delta Epsilon. Home: 67 Newmarket Rd Durham NH 03824-3127 Office: Univ NH WSBE Durham NH 03824

SIMOVIC, DRASKO, neurologist; b. Belgrade, Yugoslavia, Aug. 13, 1964; MD, U. Belgrade, 1988. Diplomate Am. Bd. Neurology, Am. Bd. Electrodiagnostic Medicine, Am. Bd. Clin. Neurophysiology. Resident in medicine, postdoctoral fellow Belgrade U., 1989-91; intern in medicine Cabrini Med. Ctr., N.Y.C., 1991-92; resident in neurology Boston U. Med. Ctr., 1992-95; clin. fellow in neurophysiology St Elizabeth's Med. Ctr./Tufts U., Boston, 1995-97; clin. rsch. assoc. in neurology St Elizabeth's Med. Ctr., 1997—. Instr. neurology Tufts U. Sch. Medicine, 1998-99, asst. prof. neurology, 2000—. Mem. AMA, Am. Acad. Neurology, Am. Assn. Electrodiagnostic Medicine. Home: 12 Stoneholm St Apt 615 Boston MA 02115-2915 Office: St Elizabeth's Med Ctr Divsn Neurology 736 Cambridge St Boston MA 02135-2907 Fax: (617) 267-3156. E-mail: simovic@rcn.com.

SIMOVIC, LASZLO, architect; b. O Becej, Yugoslavia, May 11, 1957; s. Mihaly and Eva (Daku) S. BArch, Ill. Inst. Tech., 1982; postgrad., Mass. Inst. Tech., 1984. Architect Marton Sass & Assoc., Chgo., 1974-82, Imre & Anthony Halasz Inc., Boston, 1984-85, Skidmore, Owings & Merrill, N.Y.C., 1985-86, Chgo., 1986-87, Loebl, Schlossman & Hackl, Chgo., 1987-89; pvt. practice, 1989—. Home: 6512 N Artesian Ave Chicago IL 60645-5328 Office Fax: 773-338-2226. E-mail: laszloarch@aol.com.

SIMPKINS, LUCILLE ANGELIQUE, personnel administrator; b. New Orleans, May 26, 1944; d. Robert Aunding and Addie Grace (Frazier) Elmore; m. Leonard W. Simpkins, Jr., Nov. 22, 1960; children: Terri, Leonard W. BA, Coppin State Coll., 1979; MEd, Temple U., 1982. Cert. pers. adminstr. Clk. stenographer Unemployment Compensation Bd. Rev., Phila., 1964-66; sec. to br. mgr. West Br. OIC, 1967-69; adminstrv. asst. to pres. external affairs U. Pa., 1969-70; sec. III fiscal dept. Nat. Progress Assn. Econ. Devel., 1970-72; office mgr., pers. adminstr. Opportunities Acad. Mgmt. Tng. Inc./Opportunities Industrialization Ctrs. Am., Inc., 1975—. Bd. mem. YWCA North Cen. Br., 1984—; v.p. St. Barbara's Parish Coun., 1989—. Mem. ASTD, Soc. Human Resource Mgmt., Educators' Roundtable Inc. (co-editor 1985-88), Indsl. Human Svcs. Coun. (bd. mem. 1985-89). Roman Catholic. Avocations: fishing, reading, skiing, writing, listening to music. Home: 2235 Georges Ln Philadelphia PA 19131-2326 Office: OAMT Inc 1415 N Broad St Philadelphia PA 19122-3323

SIMPLICIO, JOSEPH S.C. education educator; b. Long Branch, N.J. s. Philip L. and Angelina (Scott) S.; m. Mary Joan Carnera, July 16, 1972; 1 child, Angela Marie. BA, Seton Hall U., 1971; MA in Teaching, Montclair State U., 1976; PhD, NYU, 1989. Cert. social studies tchr., N.J. Prof. Caldwell (N.J.) Coll., 1992—. Mem. curriculum com. King of Kings Pvt. Sch.; panelist N.J. ASCD Ednl. Forum, 1994, Leadership Inst., 1994, The Pres.'s Forum, 1994; presenter in field. Contbr. articles to profl. jours. Dir. exec. bd. Coalition Adoptive Parents; mem. fundraising & orgnl. planning coms. Monmouth County Adoptive Parents Orgn., pub. rels. com. St. Mary's Sch. Adv. Coun. Named Honoree, Ednl. Opportunity Fund, 1995; recipient Excellence in Edn. award West Essex C. of C., 1994. Roman Catholic. Home: PO Box 877 New Monmouth NJ 07748-0877 Office: Caldwell Coll 9 Ryerson Ave Caldwell NJ 07006-6109

SIMPSON, ALLAN BOYD, real estate company executive; b. Lakeland, Fla., Nov. 24, 1948; s. Alfred Forsythe and Ruth Jeanette (Coker) S.; m. Melody Elaine Mann; 1 child, Lauren Leigh. B in Indsl. Ingring., Ga. Inst. Tech., 1970; MBA, U. Pa., 1972. Cert. rev. appraiser; lic. realtor, Ga. Dir. mortgage banking Ackerman & Co., Atlanta, 1972-73; v.p. B.F. Saul & Co., 1973-79; pres. L.J. Hooker, 1979-88; also bd. dirs. Hooker/Barnes. Bd. dirs. Hooker Holdings (USA), Inc., Century Ins. Co., Hooker Internat. Devels. Ltd., Hooker Internat. Fin. BV, Charter Credit Corp. Ltd., Simpson Spring, Inc., Strategic Land, Inc., Dunwoody Retail, Inc., 750 Park Ave.; bd. dirs., treas. Midtown Bus. Assn., 1979-88; chmn., CEO The Simpson Orgn., Inc., Coker Capital Corp., 1989—. Bd. dirs. YES Atlanta, 1991—, Atlanta Coll. Art, Theatrical Outfit. Mem. Am. Inst. Indsl. Engrs., MBA Execs. Assn., Bldg. Owners and Mgrs. Assn., Nat. Assn. Realtors, U.S. C. of C., Atlanta C. of C., Internat. Coun. of Shopping Ctrs., Urban Land Inst., Nat. Assn. of Office and Indsl. Pks., Ctrl. Atlanta Progress, Cherokee Town and Country Club, Amelia Island Club, Mystic Krewe of Ga. (capt.), Loch Lomond Golf Club, Pinehurst Country Club. Democrat. Methodist. Home: 750 Park Ave NE Atlanta GA 30326-3266 Office: 1401 Peachtree St Ste 400 Atlanta GA 30309-3607

SIMPSON, ANDREA LYNN, communications executive; b. Altadena, Calif., Feb. 10, 1948; d. Kenneth and Barbara Simpson; 1 child, Christopher Ryan Myrdal. BA, U. So. Calif., 1969, MS, 1983; postgrad., U. Colo., Boulder Sch. Bank Mktg., 1977. Mktg. officer United Calif. Bank, L.A., 1969-73; asst. v.p. mktg. 1st Hawaiian Bank, Honolulu, 1973-78; v.p. corp. comms. Pacific Resources Inc., 1978-89, BHP Hawaii, Inc., 1989-98; v.p. corp. rels. Tesoro Petroleum Corp., San Antonio, 1998-2000; v.p. corp. comms. Edison Internat., Rosemead, Calif., 2000—. Bd. dirs. Arts Coun., Hawaii, 1977-81, Hawaii Heart Assn., 1978-83, Coun. Pacific Girls Scouts USA, 1982-85, Child and Family Svcs., 1984-86, Honolulu Symphony Soc., 1985-91, Sta. KHPR Hawaii Pub. Radio, 1988-92, Kapiolani Found., 1990-95, Hanahauoli Sch., 1991-98, Hawaii Strategic Devel. Corp., 1991-98, Children's Discovery Ctr., 1994-98, Pacific Asian Affairs Coun., 1994-96, adv. dir. Hawaii Kids at Work, 1991-98, Hawaii MADD, 1992-96; bd. dirs., 2d v.p. Girl Scout Coun. Hawaii, 1994-96, mem. adv. bd., 1996-98; trustee Hawaii Loa Coll., 1984-86, Kapiolani Women's and Children's Hosp., 1988-97, Hawaii Sch. for Girls at LaPietra, 1989-91, Kapiolani Med. Ctr. at Pali Momi, 1994-98; bd. dirs. Aloha coun. Boy Scouts Am., 1998-2000, Alamo coun., Hawaii Pub. TV, 1998, bd. dirs., San Pedro Playhouse, 1999-2000; bd. dirs. Red Cross of San Antonio, 1999-2000; commr. Hawaii State Commn. on Status of Women, 1985-87, State Sesquecentennial of Pub. Schs. Commn., 1990-91. Named Advt. Woman of Yr., Honolulu Advt. Fedn., 1982, Pub. Rels. Profl. of Yr., Honolulu Pub. Rels. Soc., 1993, Communicator of Yr., Utilities Communicators Internat., 1983; recipient Silver Anvil award Pub. Rels. Soc. Am., 1983, 97. Mem. Internat. Pub. Rels. Assn. (Golden World award 1997), Am. Mktg. Assn., Pub. Rels. Soc. Am. (bd. dirs. Honolulu chpt. 1984-86, Silver Anvil award 1984, Pub. Rels. Profl. Yr. 1991), U. So. Calif. Alumni Assn. (bd. dirs. Hawaii 1981-83), Outrigger Canoe Club, Pacific Club, Rotary (pub. rels. chmn. 1988-97, Honolulu chpt., bd. dirs. 1998), Rotary Club of San Antonio, Alpha Phi (past pres., dir. Hawaii), Hawaii Jaycees (Outstanding Young Person of Hawaii 1978).

SIMPSON, CAROL, educator; b. Galesburg, Ill., Nov. 7, 1945; d. William Lawrence Bailey and Ruby Elaine Peterson; m. Robert Carter Simpson, Aug. 28, 1965; 1 child, Bradley William. BS in Elem. Edn., Western Ill. U., 1971, MS in Edn. Adminstrn., 1974. Tchr. 1st grade Cooke Sch., Galesburg, 1971-75, Silas Willard Sch., Galesburg, 1975-76, 79-82, tchr. 2d grade, 1976-79; tchr. 1st grade Gale Sch., 1982-94; tchr. Title 1 reading and math. Steele Accelerated Sch., 1994—. Spkr. in field. Author: Daily Journals, 1993, Daily Poetry, 1995, Daily Guided Writing, 1998, Daily Writing Prompts, 1999. Sec., precinct comitteeman Knox County (Ill.) Rep. Ctrl. Com., 1998—. Mem. Australian Literacy Educators Assn., Ill. Title 1 Assn. (sec. 1997-2000), Western Ill. Reading Coun. (pres. 1997-98), Internat. Reading Assn., Alpha Delta Kappa (newsletter editor 1998—). Republican. Avocations: travel, writing poetry and childrens stories. Office: 1480 W Main St Galesburg IL 61401-3318

SIMPSON, CAROL CAGNON, library director; m. Lowell, Dec. 5, 1965; children: Andrew Lloyd, Peter Charles. BS in English Edn., Simmons Coll.; MS, L.I. U. Head reference and adult svcs. Babylon (N.Y.) Pub. Libr., 1976-87; dir. North Babylon Pub. Libr., 1987-94, Lindenhurst Meml. Libr., 1994—. Treas. Suffolk Libr. Consortium, Inc., 1991-92, pres. 1993-94; conf. co-chairperson L.I. Libr. Resources Coun., 1993, 94; chairperson L.I. Libr. Conf., 1986. Parents edn. com. North Babylon Sch. Dist., spkr. Internat. Festival Week 1993, 94, environmental concerns com., sponsored supt. schs.; mem. bd. dirs. Literacy Vols. Am.-Suffolk County, Inc., 1994—. Recipient appreciation award Friends of the North Babylon Pub. Libr., 1992, Distbrv. Edn. Clubs Am., 1992-92. Mem. Pub. Libr. Dir.'s Assn. (v.p. 1990), Suffolk County Libr. Assn. (pres. 1989), Babylon Rotary Club (sec. 1993-94), Beta Phi Mu.

SIMPSON, CAROL LOUISE, investment company executive; b. Phila., Jan. 30, 1937; d. William Hoffingum and Hilda Agnes (Johnston) S. Student, Community Coll., 1985, 86, 87, U. Minn., 1986, 87, 88. Cert. Nat. Assn. Securities Dealers, Inc., Washington; registered options, mcpl. securities, gen. securities, fin. and ops. prin.; lic. life, accident, health ins. Exec. asst. Germantown Fed. Savs., Phila., 1954-67; asst. sec. Am. Med. Investment Co., Inc. (formerly Cannon and Co., Inc.), Blue Bell, Pa., 1967-91; also bd. dirs. Cannon & Co., Inc., 1986; v.p., sec. AMA Investment Advisers, Inc. (formerly Pro Svcs., Inc.), Blue Bell, Pa., 1967-91; also bd. dirs. AMA Investment Advisers, Inc. (formerly PRO Svcs., Inc.), 1984-86; fin. svcs. compliance cons., 1991; exec. v.p., sec. Rutherford Fin. Corp., Phila., 1991-2000, Rutherford, Brown & Catherwood Inc., Phila., 1991-2000, Walnut Asset Mgmt. Inc., Phila., 1991-98. Mem. Investment Co. Inst. (fed. legis. com. 1984-91, investment advisers com. 1988-2000, compliance com. 1990-2000), Pa. Assn. Notaries, VNA Cmty. Svcs. Found. (bd. dirs. 1995-2001), Vis. Nurse Assn. Cmty. Svcs. (bd. dirs. 1997-2000), Whitemarsh Valley Country Club. Republican. Home: 7701 Lawnton St Philadelphia PA 19128-3105

SIMPSON, CAROLYN MARIE, critical care nurse; b. Boise, Idaho, Mar. 1, 1950; d. Thomas Michael and Eva Lucille (Hieter) Sliman; m. Jon E. Simpson, Feb. 17, 1973; children: Christy Lynn, David Jon. Diploma, St. Elizabeth Sch. Nursing, 1971. Cert. utilization rev. and managed care ACLS, CCRN; cert. trauma nurse. Staff nurse St. Elizabeth's Hosp., Yakima, Wash., 1971-72, Vancouver Meml. Hosp., 1972-73; relief house supervisor Tri-State Meml. Hosp., Clarkston, Wash., 1973-75; charge nurse VA Hosp., Vancouver, 1975-83, Bess Kaiser, Portland, Oreg., 1984-96; house supr. Kaiser Ambulatory Care, 1998—; staff nurse S.W. Wash. Med. Ctr., Vancouver, 1995-99. Med.-legal cons., lectr. Bess Kaiser, AACN; owner And All That Stuff. Leader Girl Scouts U.S., Portland. Mem. AACN, Eagles Aux., Women of the Moose. Roman Catholic. Avocations: sewing, cooking, reading. Home: 5017 NE 139th Ave Vancouver WA 98682-6388 E-mail: carolm96@yahoo.com.

SIMPSON, CHAD W. pharmacist, educator; s. Sharon Janine Park, David Henry Simpson, Robert Frank Park, Jr. (Stepfather); life ptnr. C. S. Corning. BS Pharmacy, Southwestern Okla. State U., 1996. Registered pharmacist Tex., 1996. Pharmacist Eckerd, San Antonio, 1996—96, Wal-Mart, 1996—98; educator Amarillo Coll., Amarillo, 1999—; clinical pharmacist Baptist St. Anthony's Health Sys., 1998—. Mem. adv. com. Amarillo Coll. Pharmacy Tech. Adv. Com., Amarillo, 1999—; bd. dirs. Tex. Soc. Health Sys. Pharmacists; mem. Tex. State Bd. Pharmacy Taskforce on Technician Registration. Author: (poster with abstract) Texas Society of Health System Pharmacists 53rd Annual Seminar, 2001. Mem.: Panhandle Soc. Health System Pharmacists (pres. 2002—), Tex. Soc. Health System Pharmacists. Avocations: writing, cooking, reading. Office: Baptist St Anthonys Health System 1600 Wallace Blvd Amarillo TX 79106

SIMPSON, CHARLES REAGAN, retired judge; b. Danville, Ill., June 16, 1921; s. Frank and Mamie (Moreland) S.; m. Ruth V. Thomason, June 5, 1948. BA with highest honors, U. Ill., 1944, JD with high honors, 1945; LL.M., Harvard U., 1950. Bar: Ill. 1945. Practiced in, Champaign, Ill., 1946-49; atty. OPS, 1951-52; with legislation and regulations div. Office Chief Counsel, IRS, 1952-65, dir. office, 1964-65; judge U.S. Tax Ct., 1965-88, ret., 1988. Teaching fellow Harvard Law Sch., 1950-51 Chmn. Champaign County chpt. Nat. Found. Infantile Paralysis, 1947-49; Mem. Ill. Gen. Assembly from 24th Dist., 1947-50. Recipient Justice Tom C. Clark award Fed. Bar Assn., 1964 Mem. ABA, Am. Law Inst., Am. Judicature Soc., Phi Beta Kappa, Order of Coif, Phi Kappa Phi. Office: US Tax Ct 400 2nd St NW Washington DC 20217-0002 E-mail: crsimpson2@comcast.net.

SIMPSON, CHARLES EDMOND, crop science educator; b. Winters, Tex., Aug. 19, 1940; s. Robert Charles and Rosalie Helen Simpson; m. Lynann Kruse, Aug. 29, 1964; children: Melissa E. Hinga, Shay L. BS in Agrl. Edn., Tex. A&M U., 1963, MS in Plant Breeding, 1966, PhD in Plant Breeding, 1967. From asst. prof. to assoc. prof. Tex. Agrl. Exptl. Sta., Tex. A&M U., Stephenville, 1967-84, prof., 1984—. Contbr. 8 chpts. to books, numerous articles to profl. jours. Fellow Am. Peanut Rsch. and Edn. Soc. (pres. 1991-92); mem. Am. Soc. Agronomy, Am. Genetics Assn., Crop Sci. Soc. Am. (Frank N. Meyer medal 1993), Am. Peanut Coun. (Rsch. and Edn. award 2001). Lutheran. Avocation: peanut germplasm preservation and collection. Office: Tex A&M U Tex Agrl Exptl Sta PO Box 292 Stephenville TX 76401-0292 E-mail: c-simpson@tamu.edu.

SIMPSON, CURTIS CHAPMAN, III, lawyer; b. Leonia, N.J., Apr. 19, 1952; s. Curtis Chapman Simpson Jr. and Marguerite (Johnson) Host; m. Joy D.; children: Ashley Blake, Curtis Chapman. BA, George Washington U., 1977; JD, Calif. Western U., 1980. Bar: Calif. 1981, U.S. Dist. Ct. (cen. dist.) Calif. 1983, U.S. Ct. Claims 1991. Pres. Curtis C. Simpson, III, P.C., Santa Barbara, Calif., 1981-84; assoc. Schurmer & Drane, 1984-90; prin. Curtis Simpson Law Offices, Santa Barbara, Oxnard, Calif., 1991—. Ct.-appointed arbitrator superior cts. Santa Barbara County, Ventura County, San Luis Obispo County, all Calif., 1991—; guest lectr. U. Calif., Santa Barbara, 1997. Contbr. to profl. jours. Co-chmn. youth group leader, coach Montecito YMCA, 1992, 97—; bd. dirs. Montecito Ednl. Found., 1993—; co-pres. Montecito Ednl. Found., 1994-97. Mem. Assn. Trial Lawyers Am., Consumer Attys. Calif. (cert. recognition 1991—), State Bar Calif., Santa Barbara County Bar Assn., Ventura County Bar Assn., Hon. Order Ky. Cols., Coral Casino Beach and Cabana Club. Episcopalian. Office: Ste 1-252 1187 Coast Village Rd Santa Barbara CA 93108-2761

SIMPSON, DANIEL H. ambassador; b. Wheeling, W.Va., July 9, 1939; married; 4 children. BA, Yale U., 1961; cert. in African studies, Northwestern U., 1973. Joined Fgn. Svc., U.S. Dept. State, Washington, 1966—, staff asst. Bur. Security and Consular Affairs, 1966-67, speech writer for asst. sec. state for African affairs, 1968, desk officer for Rhodesia, Botswana, Lesotho, and Swaziland, 1973-74; tng. officer USIA, 1967-68; polit., econ. and consular officer Am. Embassy, Bujumbura, Burundi, 1968-70, polit. officer Pretoria, Republic South Africa, 1970-72, dep. chief mission Beirut, until 1989; amb. to Cen. African Republic, Bangui, 1989-92; dep. comdr. Army War Coll., Carlisle, Pa., 1993-94; ambassador to Somalia Mogadishu, 1994-95; ambassador to Congo Kinshasa, 1995-98; v.p. Nat. Def. U., Washington, 1998-2000; regional dir. OSCE, Bosnia-Herzegovina, 2000—01; fgn. editor Pitts. Post-Gazette, 2001—. Address: Pitts Post-Gazette 34 Blvd of the Allies Pittsburgh PA 15222 Home: 112 Washington Pl #20A Pittsburgh PA 15219 E-mail: dsimpson@post-gazette.com.

SIMPSON, DANIEL REID, lawyer, mediator; b. Glen Alpine, N.C., Feb. 20, 1927; s. James R. and Margaret Ethel (Newton) S.; m. Mary Alice Leonard, Feb. 25, 1930; children: Mary Simpson Beyer, Ethel B. Simpson Todd, James R., II. BS, Wake Forest U., 1949, LLB, 1951. Bar: N.C. 1951, U.S. Dist. Ct. (we. dist.) N.C. 1951, U.S. Ct. Appeals (4th and 5th cirs.) 1980; cert. mediator. Former ptnr. Simpson Aycock PA, Morganton, N.C.; of counsel Simpson, Kuehnert, Vinay & Bellas, P.A. Author: American Angels, 2001. Mem. N.C. Ho. of Reps., 1959-65; mem. N.C. Senate, 1984-96; del. Rep. Nat. Conv., 1968, 76; mem. N.C. Rep. Exec. Com. Served with AUS, 1943-45, PTO. Recipient Guardian Small Bus. award Order of Longleaf Pine; named to NRA Legion of Honor; sports complex named in his honor by Town of Glen Alpine, N.C. Mem. N.C. Bar Assn., Burke County Bar Assn., Masons. Baptist. Home: 2358 E Point Rd Nebo NC 28761-9694 Office: Simpson Kuehnert Vinay & Bellas PA 216 N Sterling St Morganton NC 28655 also: PO Box 1329 Morganton NC 28680-1329

SIMPSON, DAVID ALLEN, osteopath; b. Highland Park, Mich., Mar. 29, 1955; s. Fred Raymond and Mary Theresa (Rossi) S.; m. Anne M. Pawlak, Oct. 20, 1984. BS in Biology with distinction, Wayne State U., 1977, MS in Anatomy, 1979; DO, Kirksville Coll. Osteo. Medicine, 1983. Diplomate Am. Bd. Neurology and Psychiatry (examiner), Electrodiagnostic Medicine (examiner). Commd. 2d lt. U.S. Army, 1979, advanced through grades to maj., 1988; resident in neurology Botsford Gen. Hosp., Farmington Hills, 1988-91; staff neurologist Mich. Inst. for Neurologists, 1991—; asst. clin. prof. U. Mich., Mich. State U., 1991—. Dir. fellowship tng. in neuromuscular disease Mich. Inst. for Neurol. Disorder, U. Mich., MDA Clinic, Mich. State U.; co-dir. Muscular Dystrophy Clinic of Southeastern Mich., Mich. Inst. for Neurol. Disorders; physician Wheel-Chair Hockey League, 1999—; lectr. in field. Patentee in field; contbr. articles to profl. jours.; chief editor: Jour. of Am. Coll. of Neurologists and Psychiatrists. 2nd lt. USAR, 1979—84, with U.S. Army, 1988—97. Decorated Meritorious Svc. medal, DSM, Army Commendation medal, Humanitarian Svc. medal, Army Achievement medal, Good Conduct medal, Army Res. medal. Mem. Am. Osteo. Assn., Mich. Assn. Osteo. Physicians and Surgeons, Am. Coll. Neuropsychiatrists, Psi Sigma Alpha, Sigma Sigma Alpha. Roman Catholic. Avocation: golf. Home: 19550 Laurel Dr Livonia MI 48152-1141 Office: Mich Inst Neurologic Disord Dept Neurology Farmington Hills MI 48045

SIMPSON, DAVID WILLIAM, artist, educator; b. Pasadena, Calif., Jan. 20, 1928; s. Frederick and Mary Adeline (White) S.; m. Dolores D. Debus, July 30, 1954; 1 stepchild, Gregory C. Vose; 1 child, Lisa C. B.F.A., Calif. Sch. Fine Arts, 1956; MA, San Francisco State Coll., 1958. Instr. art Am. River Jr. Coll., Sacramento, 1958-60, Contra Costa Jr. Coll., San Pablo, Calif., 1960-65;

prof. art U. Calif., Berkeley, 1967-91, prof. emeritus, 1991—. Exhibited in one-man shows including Robert Elkon Gallery, N.Y.C., 1961, 63, 64, San Francisco Mus. Art, 1967, Henri Gallery, Washington, 1968, Oakland Mus., 1978, Modernism, San Francisco, 1980-81, 84, 86, 2001, Sheldon Meml. Art Gallery, Lincoln, Nebr., 1990, Mincher/Wilcox Gallery, San Francisco, 1991, 92, 93, Angles Gallery, Santa Monica, Calif., 1991, 92, 94, 99, Bemis Found., Omaha, Nebr., 1991, Anthony Ralph Gallery, N.Y.C., 1992, John Berggruen Gallery, San Francisco, 1994, Charlotte Jackson Fine Art, Santa Fe, 1995, Laguna Art Mus., Laguna Beach, Calif., 1995 Haines Gallery, San Francisco, 1997, 99, 2000, Studio La Citta, Verona, Italy, 1998, 2002, Renate Schröder Gallery, Cologne, Germany, 2000-02, Artothek, Cologne, 2002; group shows include Mus. Modern Art, N.Y.C., 1963, Carnegie Internat., Pitts., 1961-62, 66-67, L.A. Mus. Art, 1964, U. Ill., 1969, Expo '70, Osaka, Japan, 1970, Josly Art Mus., Omaha, 1970, John Berggruen Gallery, San Francisco, 1979, Angles Gallery, Santa Monica, 1988, 90, John Good Gallery, N.Y., 1992, John Berggruen Gallery, San Francisco, 1993, Cheryl Haines Gallery, San Francisco, 1996, Museo di Arte Moderna e Contemporanea, Trento, Italy, 1996, Studio La Citta, Verona, Italy, 1996, Llonja, Palma De Majorca, Spain, 1997, Museo Cantonale d'Arte, Lugano, Switzerland, 1997, Studio La Citta, Verona, Italy, 1997, Haines Gallery, San Francisco, 1997, Palazzo Ducale, Gubbio, Italy, 1999, Palazzo Ducale, Sassuolo, Panza Collection, Italy, 2002, Palazzo Della Gran Guardia, Verona, Italy, 2002, Panza Collection Gran Guardia, Verona, Italy, 2002; represented in permanent collections including Phila. Mus. Art, Nat. Collection Fine Arts, Washington, Seattle Art Mus., La Jolla (Calif.) Mus. Art, Mus. Modern Art, N.Y.C., San Francisco Mus. Art, Oakland (Calif.) Mus., Panza Collection, Italy, Laguna Art Mus., Laguna Beach, Calif., Univ. Art Mus., Berkeley, Calif., Museo Cantonale d'Arte Lugano, Switzerland. Home: 565 Vistamont Ave Berkeley CA 94708-1244 Office: U Calif Dept Art Berkeley CA 94720

SIMPSON, DENNIS DWAYNE, psychologist, educator; b. Lubbock, Tex., Nov. 9, 1943; s. Homer Arnold and Georgie Lee (Barrett) S.; m. Sherry Ann Johnson, Aug. 20, 1965; children: Jason Renn, Jeffrey Todd, Jennifer Lynn. BA, U. Tex., 1966; PhD, Tex. Christian U., 1970. Asst. prof. psychology Tex. Christian U., Ft. Worth, 1970-74, assoc. prof., 1974-79, prof., 1979-82, dir., prof., 1989—, S.B. Sells prof. psychology, 1992—; dir., prof. Tex. A&M U., College Station, 1982-89. Sci. adv. bd. NIDA Rsch. Ctrs., Washington, 1992—; adv. bd. Nat. Drug Treatment Evaluation Studies, Washington, 1992—; expert advisor U.S. Acctg. Office, Health and Human Svcs., others; cons. WHO, fgn. govts. regarding drug rsch. Mem. editl. bd. Am. Jour of Drug and Alcohol Abuse, 1992, Internat. Jour. of the Addictions, 1995, Substance Use and Misuse; contbr. over 225 articles to profl. jours.; author 5 books. Recipient Disting. Rsch. Achievement award Tex. Commn. on Alcohol and Drug Abuse, 1987; recipient numerous grants. Mem. APA, Am. Psychol. Soc., Am. Evaluation Assn., Soc. of Psychologists in Addictive Behaviors, Southwestern Psychol. Assn., Sigma Xi. Achievements include research emphasis on the process of treatment service delivery in relation client attributes and how they related to retention rates, relapse, posttreatment outcomes; research on drug use in the workplace, other areas. Office: Tex Christian U Inst Behavioral Rsch PO Box 298740 Fort Worth TX 76129-0001 E-mail: ibr@tcu.edu.

SIMPSON, DIANE JEANNETTE, school social worker, counselor, adoption home study worker; b. Denver, Sept. 20, 1952; d. Arthur Henry and Irma Virginia (Jordan) S.; 1 child, Shantè N. BS, Nebr. Wesleyan U., 1974; MSW, U. Denver, 1977. Asst. Mile Hi coun. Girl Scouts U.S.A., Denver, 1971-77; social worker asst. Denver Pub. Schs., 1974-75, social worker, 1977—. Field instr. Grad. Sch. of Soc. Work, U. Denver, 1984—. Tour leader Kenyan Safari to Kenya, East Africa, 1988. V.p. United Meth. Women, Christ United Meth. Ch., Denver, 1989-91; chmn. Christian action com., 1985-88; active Girl Scouts U.S.A., 1959—; mem. collaborative decision making com. Denver Pub. Schs., 1993-95; mem. Shorter A.M.E. Ch., sr. usher bd. and edn. and scholarship com., 1996—. Mem. NASW, Delta Kappa Gamma. Democrat. Avocations: reading, health and fitness, travel, genealogy. Home: 6865 E Arizona Ave # D Denver CO 80224-1829 Office: Denver Pub Schs 900 Grant St Denver CO 80203-2907

SIMPSON, DICK WELDON, political science educator; b. Houston, Nov. 8, 1940; s. Warren Weldon and Ola Ela (Felts) S.; m. Sarajane Avidon, Mar. 22, 1987; children: Kate Donley, August Donley. BA, U. Tex., 1963; MA, Ind. U., 1964, PhD, 1968; MDiv, McCormick Theol. Sem., 1984. Ordained to ministry United Ch. of Christ, 1985. Rsch. asst. Ind. U., Bloomington, 1965; fgn. area fellow Ford Found., Africa, 1966-67; instr. U. Ill., Chgo., 1967-68, asst. prof., 1968-71, assoc. prof. polit. sci., 1972-96, prof., 1996—. Exec. dir. Inst. on Ch., Chgo., 1984-86, Clergy and Laity Concerned, Chgo., 1987-89. Author: Winning Elections, 1972, 74, 81, 96, Strategies for Change, 1976, Politics of Compassion, 1989; editor: Chicago's Future, 1976, 80, 83, 88, 93, Rogues, Rebels, and Rubber Stamps, 2001. Alderman Chgo. City Coun., 1971-79; campaign mgr. McCarthy for Pres., Ill., 1967-68; transition team Mayors Washington and Byrne, 1979, 83, State's Atty. O'Malley and County Clk. Orr, 1990, 91; congl. candidate, 1992, 94. Humanities Inst. fellow U. Ill., Chgo., 1985-86; rsch. grantee Joyce, Amoco, Woods, Wieboldt Founds., 1972-80; recipient award Clarence Darrow Cmty. Ctr., Clergy and Laity Concerned, IVI-IPO. Mem. Am. Polit. Sci. Assn., Midwest Polit. Sci. Assn., Ill. Polit. Sci. Assn. (past pres.), City Club Chgo. (v.p., award). Office: Dept Polit Sci U Ill M/C 276 1007 W Harrison St Chicago IL 60607-7137 E-mail: simpson@uic.edu.

SIMPSON, ETHEL CHACHERE, archivist; b. Opelousas, La., July 22, 1937; d. John Elliott and Annie Margaret (Trahan) Chachere; m. Roy Vergil Simpson Jr., Sept. 5, 1959; children: Michael, Christopher. BA, U. Southwestern La., 1958; MA, U. Ark., 1960, PhD, 1977. Bibliographer libr. U. Ark., Fayetteville, 1974—, archivist, 1991-95, head archives and manuscripts, 1995—. Author: Image and Reflection, 1990; editor: Simpkinsville and Vicinity, 1983, Tulip Evermore, 1985, Arkansas in Short Fiction, 1986, Selected Letters of John Gould Fletcher, 1996. Avocations: travel, cooking, Gregorian chant. Office: U Ark U Libr Fayetteville AR 72701

SIMPSON, FREDERICK JAMES, retired research administrator; b. Regina, Sask., Can., June 8, 1922; s. Ralph James and Lillian Mary (Anderson) S.; m. Margaret Christine Simpson, May 28, 1947; children: Christine Louise, Steven James, Leslie Coleen, Ralph Edwin, David Glen. B.Sc., U. Alta., Can., 1944, M.Sc. in Agr., 1946; PhD in Bacteriology, U. Wis., 1952. With Nat. Research Council Can., 1946-84; asst. dir. Atlantic Research Lab., Halifax, N.S., 1970-73, dir., 1973-84; sci. cons., 1985-90. Vis. scientist U. Ill., Urbana, 1955-56, vis. prof., 1964; mem. exec. council Atlantic Provinces Interuniv. Com. on Scis., 1976-79, chmn., 1981-84; pres. Fed. Inst. Mgmt., Halifax, 1981-82 Contbr. numerous articles to profl. jours. Treas. Lunburg Condominium Corp. No. 1, 1998—. Decorated Queen's Silver Anniversary medal. Fellow Royal Soc. of Arts (London); mem. Can. Soc. Microbiologists (hon., sec.-treas. 1969-70, v.p. 1971-72, pres. 1972-73), Nova Scotian Inst. Sci. (v.p. 1975-76, pres. 1977-78), Internat. Phycological Soc., Aquaculture Assn. Can., Sigma Xi. Mem. United Ch. of Canada.

SIMPSON, GARY LAVERN, public health medical executive; b. St. Louis, Jan. 3, 1947; m. Sandra Cheryl Lapham; children: Cassandra Alyn, Courtney Meredith. BS, U. Ill., 1969, MS, 1970, PhD, 1973; MD, Rush Med. Coll., Chgo., 1974; MSc in Clin. Medicine, U. Oxford, Eng., 1977; MPH in Tropical Pub. Health, Harvard U., 1978. Diplomate Mass. Bd. Med. Examiners, Am. Bd. Internal Medicine, Calif. Bd. Med. Examiners, N.Mex. Bd. Med. Examiners. Intern Peter Bent Brigham Hosp., Boston, 1974-75, resident, 1975-76; sr. registrar in internal medicine/infectious diseases U. Oxford, Clin. Med. Sch., Radcliffe Infirmary, Eng., 1976-77; fellow infectious diseases divsn. infectious diseases Stanford (Calif.) U., 1978-79; asst. prof. medicine divsn. infectious diseases U. N.Mex., Albuquerque, 1979-83, clin. assoc. prof. medicine, 1983-88; attending physician Presbyn. Healthcare Svcs., 1987-89; med. dir. infectious diseases Pub. Health divsn. Dept. Health, State of N.Mex., Santa Fe, 1992—. Teaching asst. U. Ill., Champaign-Urbana, 1969-70, rsch. assoc., 1970-72; rsch. cons. U. N.Mex., Albuquerque, 1973-74, adj. assoc. prof. dept. biology, 1986-87; rsch. prof. dept. biology U. N.Mex., 1996—; rsch. scientist Rush Med. Sch., 1973-74; clin. fellow Harvard Med. Sch., Boston, 1974-76; dir., chief medicine Raymond Hosp., Wrentham, Mass., 1976; staff physician Children's Hosp. Med. Ctr., Boston, 1976; vis. prof. Instituto Nacional de Salud, Bogota, Colombia, 1979-80; attending physician U. N.Mex. Hosp., 1979-87, VA Med. Ctr., Albuquerque, 1980-87; assoc. scientist Lovelace Med. Found., Albuquerque, 1983-86; med. dir. Cottonwood de Albuquerque, Residential Treatment Ctr., Los Lunas, N.Mex., 1983-84, Jim Kelly Counseling Assocs., Albuquerque, 1984-86, Presbyn. Alcohol and Drug Treatment Ctr., Northside Presbyn. Hosp., Albuquerque, 1987-89; sr. cons. bur. communicable diseases AID, Dept. State, Washington, 1984—; cons. Am. Inst. Biol. Scis., Washington, 1984—; Eagleson lectr. Am. Biol. Safety Assn. 36th Annual Conf., Albuquerque, lectr. in field; vis. prof. dept. med. microbiology and sec. of infectious diseases Faculty of Medicine U. Man., Winnipeg, Can.; adj. prof. dept. biology U. M.Mex., Albuquerque, 1996—. Contbr. articles to profl. jours. Recipient Cert. award U.S. Indian Health Svc., 1995; Robert Wood Johnson fellow, 1977, Agy. for Internat. Devel. Edn. fellow, 1978, Palo Alto Med. Rsch. Found. fellow, 1979; hon. I award U. Ill. Fellow ACP, Am. Soc. Addiction Medicine (cert.); mem. AAAS, Oxford. Soc., Royal Soc. Tropical Medicine and Hygiene, Am. Soc. Microbiology, Am. Soc. Tropical Medicine and Hygiene, Am. Fedn. Clin. Rsch., Infectious Diseases Soc. Am. Home: 18 Senda Aliento Placitas NM 87043-9530

SIMPSON, GEORGE EUGENE, music educator, director; b. Toronto, Ontario, Canada, May 5, 1972; s. George Earnest and Carolyn Irene Simpson. MusB, EdB, U. We. Ont., London, Can., 1997; degree in Jazz Studies, Humber Coll., 1996. Dir., instrumental music divsn. Boston Arts Acad., 1999—; dir., city music prep. sch. Berklee Coll. of Music, 2000—. Advisor Boston Classical Orch., 2000—. Musician: Band of the Ceremonial Guard, 1993—95. Mem.: Mass. Music Educator's Assn., Music Educator's Nat. Conf., Internat. Assn. for Jazz Edn. Democrat. Avocations: travel, composition, activism. Home: 92 Draper #3 Boston MA 02122 Office: Boston Arts Acad 174 Ipswich St Boston MA 02215 Home Fax: 617-635-8854; Office Fax: 617-635-8854. E-mail: gsimpson@artsacad.boston.k12.ma.us.

SIMPSON, GEORGE TRUE, surgeon, educator; b. Aurora, Colo., Apr. 29, 1943; s. George True and Meryle Flora (Moore) S.; m. Sharon Louise Mason, Mar. 9, 1944; children: Amber-Louise Elizabeth, George True III. BA in History, LaSierra U., 1969; MD, Loma Linda U., 1973, MPH, 1975. Diplomate Am. Bd. Otolaryngology, Am. Bd. Laser Surgery, Nat. Bd. Med. Examiners. Surgery resident U. Ala. Hosp. & Clinics, Birmingham, 1973-75; surgeon Kalabo Hosp., Zambia, 1975; otolaryngology resident UCLA Head/Neck Surgery, L.A., 1975-78; pediatric otolaryngology fellow Children's Hosp, Boston, 1978-79; assoc. prof., acting chair Boston (Mass.) U., 1979-90; dir. dept. otolaryngology Boston (Mass.) City Hosp., 1979-90; otolaryngologist-in-chief U. Hosp., Boston, 1984-90; chmn. dept. otolaryngology SUNY, Buffalo, 1991-97, prof. otolaryngology, 1997—; chmn. dept. otolaryngology Sisters of Charity Hosp., 1991—; pres. U. Head/Neck Surgery, 1991—. Cons. Ministry Pub. Health, State of Kuwait, 1976, MIT, Cambridge, 1979—, Gillette Corp., Boston, 1984-90; pres. Boston City Hosp. Med. Staff, 1983, 85; bd. dirs. Voice Found. Sci. Adv., Phila.; chmn. otolaryngology sect. 10 Internat. Congress on Lasers in medicine and Surgery, Taipei, Taiwan, 1989; examiner Am. Bd. Otolaryngology, Chgo., 1992, 93, 94. Author: Lasers in Otolaryngology, 1985; author, editor: Textbook of General Medicine, 1987; editor: Lasers in Otolaryngology: OTOL Clinics of N.Am., 1990; contbr. articles to profl. jours. With U.S. Army, 1964-66. Recipient Caring Physician award Mass. Nursing Assn., Mass. Med. Assn., 1989. Fellow ACS, Am. Acad. Otolaryngology-Head/Neck Surgery (Honor award 1987), Am. Acad. Pediatrics, Am. Soc. Head/Neck Surgery, Am. Broncheosophagological, Am. Acad. Facial Plastic and Reconstructive Surgery, Am. Acad. Cosmetic Surgery, Royal Soc. Medicine, Am. Bd. Laser Surgery; mem. Am. Assn. Acad. Depts. Otolaryngology, Assn. for Rsch. in Otolaryngology, Soc. Univ. Otolaryngologist, Internat. Soc. for History Otolaryngology (sec./treas. 1984-87, v.p. 1987—), Buffalo Otolaryngology Soc., Buffalo Canoe Club, Buffalo Club, Orchard Park Country Club, Alpha Omega Alpha. Avocations: medical history, personal computing, music, running, boating. Office: SUNY Buffalo-VA Med Ctr Dept Otolaryngology 3495 Bailey Ave Buffalo NY 14215-1129

SIMPSON, H. RICHARD (DICK SIMPSON), retailer; b. Oct. 10, 1928; s. Bert M. and Violet K. (Mathias) S.; m. Marion Welty, 1950; children: Carla Sue, Barry Nelson, Richard Drew, Catherine Irene; m. Joan Rose Marshall, March 22, 1970; m. Charlotte S. Fox, Dec. 12, 1999. *Mr. Simpson's wife, Charlotte, R.N., is now Heart Transplant Coordinator for Seaton Hospital. She is also pursuing her masters degree. His son, Barry, just opened his third auto dealership, which is doing great. Mr. Simpson's kid's all have solid A's in high school, with two scholarships already offered.* Student, U. Akron, 1949-50; BS, U. Md., 1955. Mgr. Tex. GMC, Detroit, 1959-62. Pres. Friendly Pontiac, Friendly Toyota, Derrick Chrysler, Simpson Oil Corp., Corp. S., Dick Tiger Homes, Austin, 1962-85, Simpson Hill Country Realty and Builders, 1989-98. Served to lt. col. USAF, 1953-75; Korea. Decorated D.F.C., Air Medal. Mem. Soc. Automotive Engrs., Res. Officers Assn., Horseshoe Bay Yacht Club, Horseshoe Bay Country Club, Rotary Internat., Masons. Methodist. Office: PO Box 8186 Horseshoe Bay TX 78657-8186 E-mail: csinfinity@281-com..

SIMPSON, JACK BENJAMIN, medical technologist, business executive; b. Tompkinsville, Ky., Oct. 30, 1937; s. Benjamin Harrison and Verda Mae (Woods) S.; m. Winona Clara Walden, Mar. 21, 1957; children: Janet Lazann, Richard Benjamin, Randall Walden, Angela Elizabeth. Student, Western Ky. U., 1954-57; grad., Norton Infirmary Sch. Med. Tech., 1958. Asst. chief med. technologist Jackson County Hosp., Seymour, Ind., 1958-61; chief med. technologist, bus. mgr. Mershon Med. Labs., Indpls., 1962-66; founder, dir., officer Am. Monitor Corp., 1966-77; founder, pres., dir. Global Data, Inc., Ft. Lauderdale, Fla., 1986—. Mng. ptnr. Astroland Enterprises, Indpls., 1968—, 106th St. Assocs., Indpls., 1969-72, Keystones Ltd., Indpls., 1970-82, Delray Rd. Assoc. Ltd., Indpls., 1970-71, Allisonville Assocs. Ltd., Indpls., 1970-82, Grandview Assocs. Ltd., 1977—, Rucker Assocs. Ltd., Indpls., 1974—; mng. ptnr. Raintree Assocs. Ltd., Indpls., 1978—, Westgate Assocs. Ltd., Indpls., 1978—; pres., dir. Topps Constrn. Co., Inc., Bradenton, Fla., 1973-91, Acrovest Corp., Asheville, N.C., 1980—; dir. Indpls. Broadcasting, Inc.; founder, bd. dirs. Bank of Bradenton, 1986-92; founder, CFO Biomass Processing Tech., Inc., West Palm Beach, Fla., 1996—; also bd. dirs. Mem. Am. Soc. Med. Technologists (cert.), Indpls. Soc. Med. Technologists, Fla. Soc. Med. Technologists, Am. Soc. Clin. Pathologists, Am. Assn. Clin. Chemistry, Royal Soc. Health (London), Internat. Platform Assn., Am. Mus. Natural History, Columbia of Indpls. Club, Harbor Beach Surf Club, Fishing of Am. Club, Marina Bay Club (Ft. Lauderdale), Elks. Republican. E-mail: jack_simpson@msn.com.

SIMPSON, JACQUELINE ANGELIA, legal administration; b. Battersea, Eng., Apr. 19, 1965; d. Headley Emmanuel and Paula Hermeone Simpson. Cert. in French/Can. studies, U. Laval, Que., Can., 1986; BA, SUNY, Stony Brook, 1986; MLS, SUNY, Albany, 1988. White House conf. on libr. and info. svcs. cert. Grad. asst. SUNY, Albany, 1986-88; bibliographer libr. svcs. divsn. Libr. of Congress, Congl. Rsch. Svc., 1987-88; asst. libr. Squire, Sanders and Dempsey, Washington, 1988-90, assoc. libr., 1990-95; libr. East Coast Squire, Sanders and Dempsey, LLP, 1995-99, east coast/regional support mgr., 1999—. Louise Giles Minority scholar ALA; exch. student scholar Can. Govt. Mem. Am. Assn. Law Librs., Law Librs. Soc. of Washington. Avocations: church, reading, singing, dining at different restaurants. Office: Squire Sanders & Dempsey LLP 1201 Pennsylvania Ave NW Washington DC 20004-2401 E-mail: jsimpson@ssd.com.

SIMPSON, JAMES ALBERT, surgeon; b. Little Rock, July 29, 1939; MD, U. Ark. Sch. Medicine, 1964. Diplomate Am. Bd. Surgery. Intern Hennepin County Gen. Hosp., Mpls., 1964-65; resident in surgery U. Ark. Hosp., Little Rock, 1965-69; chief of surgery Forbes AFB Hosp., Topeka, 1969-71; staff Ctrl. Ark. Gen. Hosp., Searcy, White County Meml. Hosp, Searcy. Fellow Am. Coll. Surgeons. Home: 1300 S Main St Searcy AR 72143-7341

SIMPSON, JOANNE MALKUS, meteorologist; b. Boston, Mar. 23, 1923; d. Russell and Virginia (Vaughan) Gerould; m. Robert H. Simpson, Jan. 6, 1965; children by previous marriage: David Starr Malkus, Steven Willem Malkus, Karen Elizabeth Malkus. BS, U. Chgo., 1943, MS, 1945, PhD, 1949; DSc (hon.), SUNY, Albany, 1991. Instr. physics and meteorology Ill. Inst. Tech., 1946-49, asst. prof., 1949-51; meteorologist Woods Hole Oceanographic Instn., 1951-61; prof. meteorology UCLA, 1961-65; dir. exptl. meteorology lab. NOAA, Dept. Commerce, Washington, 1965-74; prof. environ. scis. U. Va., Charlottesville, 1974-76, W.W. Corcoran prof. environ. scis., 1976-81; head Severe Storms br. Goddard Lab. Atmospheres, NASA, Greenbelt, Md., 1981-88, chief scientist for meteorology, 1988—; Goddard sr. fellow, earth scis. dir. Goddard Space Flight Ctr., NASA, 1988—; project scientist tropical rainfall measuring mission, 1986-98. Mem. Bd. on Atmospheric Scis. and Climate, NRC/NAS, 1990-93, 97-2000, Bd. on Geophys. and Environ. Data, 1993-96, com. on climate, ecosystems, infectious diseases and human health, 1998-2000; mem. sr. adv. bd. NOAA, 1998—. Author: (with Herbert Riehl) Cloud Structure and Distributions Over the Tropical Pacific Ocean; assoc. editor: Revs. Geophysics and Space Physics, 1964-72, 75-77; contbr. articles to profl. jours. Mem. Fla. Gov.'s Environ. Coordinating Coun., 1971-74. Recipient Disting. Authorship award NOAA, 1969, Silver medal Dept. Commerce, 1967, Gold medal, 1972, Vincent J. Schaefer award Weather Modification Assn., 1979, Cmty. Headliner award Women in Comm., 1973, Profl. Achievement award U. Chgo. Alumni Assn., 1975, 92, Lifetime Achievement award Women in Sci. Engring., 1990, Exceptional Sci. Achievement award NASA, 1982, William Nordberg award NASA, 1994, NASA Medal Outstanding Leadership, 1998, I.M.O. prize World Meteorol. Orgn., 2002; named Woman of Yr. L.A. Times, 1963; Guggenheim fellow, 1954-55, Goddard Sr. fellow, 1988-94. Fellow Am. Geophys. Union, Am. Meterol. Soc. (mem. coun. 1975-77, 79-81, mem. exec. com. 1977, 79-81, commr. sci. and tech. activities 1982-88, pres.-elect 1988, pres. 1989, publs. commr. 1992-98, hon. mem. 1995, Meisinger award 1962, Rossby Rsch. medal 1983, Charles Franklin Brooks award 1992, Charles E. Anderson award 2001), Explorers Club; mem. Nat. Acad. Engring., Royal Meteorological Soc. (hon.), Cosmos Club, Phi Beta Kappa, Sigma Xi. Home: 540 N St SW Washington DC 20024-4557 Office: NASA Goddard Space Flight Ctr Earth Scis Dir Greenbelt MD 20771-0001 E-mail: nasajoanne@earthlink.net., simpson@agnes.gsfc.nasa.gov.

SIMPSON, JOE LEIGH, obstetrics and gynecology educator; b. Birmingham, Ala., Apr. 4, 1943; s. Robert S. and Winnie (Leigh) S.; m. Sandra A. Carson, May 6, 1978; children: Scott, Reid MD, Duke U., 1968. Diplomate Am. Bd. Ob-Gyn, Am. Bd. Med. Genetics. Fellow in ob-gyn Cornell Med. Coll., N.Y.C., 1968-73; clin. assoc. N.Y. Blood Ctr., 1969-73; asst. clin. prof. ob-gyn U. Tex., San Antonio, 1973-75; assoc. prof., head ob-gyn Northwestern U. Med. Sch., Chgo., 1975-79, prof. ob-gyn, 1979-86; Faculty prof. chmn. dept. ob-gyn U. Tenn., Memphis, 1986-94; Ernst W. Bertner chmn. and prof. dept. ob-gyn., prof. dept. molecular and human genetics Baylor Coll. of Medicine, Houston, 1994—. Mem. genetics grant rev. and adv. bd. HHS, 1979-82; mem. clin. rsch. panel March of Dimes, 1986-94, chmn. adv. panel reproductive hazards, 1988-92, mem. sci. adv. bd., 1994—; mem. accreditation coun. grad. med. edn. Residency Rev. Com. Med. Genetics, 1993-98; mem. adv. com. Nat. Inst. Child Health and Devel., 1994-97. Author: Disorders of Sexual Development, 1976; author: (with others) Genetics in Obstetrics and Gynecology, 1982, 2d edit., 1992, Obstetrics: Normal and Problem Pregnancies, 1986, 2d edit., 1991, 3d edit., 1996, 4th edit., 2001; co-editor: Genetic Diseases in Pregnancy, 1981, Material Serum Screening for Fetal Genetic Disorders, 1992, Essentials of Prenatal Diagnosis, 1993; contbr. articles to profl. jours. and chpts. to books. Maj. U.S. Army, 1973-75. Recipient numerous awards Nat. Insts. Child Health and Devel., March of Dimes, Wyeth-Ayerest pub. recognition award Assn. Profs. Ob-Gyn, 1992. Fellow Am. Coll. Obstetricians and Gynecologists (chmn. genetics subcom. 1981-84), Am. Coll. Med. Genetics (treas. 1996-02), Am. Gynecol. and Obstet. Soc. (mem. coun. 1997-99), Am. Fertility Soc. (bd. dirs. 1984-87, pres. 1993-94), Soc. Gynecologic Investigation (pres. 1998-99, mem. coun., Pres.'s Achievement award 1986, Pres. Disting. Scientist award 2002), Soc. Advancement Contraception (pres. 1995-98), Am. Soc. Human Genetics (mem. program com. 1988-91), Internat. Soc. Prenatal Diagnosis (pres. 1994-98), U.S. Nat. Acad. Scis., Inst. Medicine. Office: Baylor Coll of Medicine Dept Ob/Gyn 6550 Fannin St Ste 729A Houston TX 77030-2717

SIMPSON, JOHN AROL, retired government executive, physicist; b. Toronto, Ont., Can., Mar. 30, 1923; came to U.S., 1926; naturalized, 1938; s. Henry George and Verna Lavinia (Green) S.; m. Arlene Badel, Feb. 11, 1948; 1 child, George Badel. BS, Lehigh U., 1946, MS, 1948, PhD, 1951. Rsch. physicist Nat. Bur. Standards, Washington, 1948-62, supervisory physicist, 1962-69, dep. chief optical physics div., 1969-75, chief mechanics div., 1975-78, dir. Ctr. for Mfg. Engring. Gaithersburg, Md., 1978-91; dir. Mfg. Engring. Lab., Nat. Inst. Standards and Tech., 1991—; ret. Contbr. articles on electron optics to profl. jours. With U.S. Army, 1943-46. Recipient Silver medal Dept. Commerce, 1964, Gold medal, 1975; Allen V. Austin Measurement Sci. award, 1984; Disting. Exec. award Sr. Exec. Svc., 1985, Am. Machinist award, 1986. Fellow Am. Phys. Soc.; mem. NAE, Sigma Xi. Home: 312 Riley St Falls Church VA 22046-3310

SIMPSON, JOHN M. lawyer; b. Ponca City, Okla., Sept. 26, 1950; AB, Harvard U., 1972; JD, Columbia U., 1978. Bar: D.C. 1979, N.C. 1988. Mem. Fulbright & Jaworski L.L.P., Washington. Office: Fulbright & Jaworski LLP Market Square 801 Pennsylvania Ave NW Washington DC 20004-2615 E-mail: jsimpson@fulbright.com.

SIMPSON, JOHN NOEL, healthcare administrator; b. Durham, N.C., Feb. 27, 1936; m. Virginia Marshall, June 27, 1959; children: John Noel, William M. Asst. adminstr. Riverside Health Sys., Newport News, Va., 1962-65, assoc. adminstr., 1965-70, Richmond (Va.) Meml. Hosp., 1970-74, sr. v.p., adminstr., 1974-77, exec. v.p., 1977-80, pres., 1980-85, Health Corp. Va., 1985-96; chmn. bd. Bon Secours-Richmond Health System, 1996-97, regional v.p., CEO, 1997-2000, divisional cons., 2000—. Preceptor Sch. Health Adminstrn. Duke U. and Med. Coll. Va., Washington U., St. Louis; bd. dirs. Sun Health, Inc./Sun Alliance, 1979-92, vice-chmn., 1984, chmn., 1985-87; vice-chmn. Med./Bus. Coalition, 1981-83; participant Leadership Met. Richmond; bd. dirs. Ctrl. Va. Health Sys. Agy., 1980-84, Richmond chpt. ARC, 1980-83; mem. Va. Bd. Med. Assistance, 1980-84; mem. joint subcom. studying Va. med. malpractice laws divsn. legal svcs. Gen Assembly of Comm. of Va., 1984; chmn. Va. Health Network, 1989-91; chmn. Hanover Bus. Coun., 1994-95; mem. Gov. Regional Econ. Devel. Adv. Coun., 1994-95. Served with Med. Svc. Corps U.S. Army, 1959-62. Fellow Am. Coll. Healthcare Execs. (Coun. of Regents 1976-82, Edgar C. Hayhow award 1976, bd. govs. 1990-94, regents award sr. exec. level 1995). Fellow Am. Coll. Healthcare Execs. (coun. of regents 1976-82, Edgar C. Hayhow award 1976, bd. govs. 1990-94, regents award sr. exec. level 1995); mem. Am. Hosp. Assn. (chmn. RPBIII 1994-97, del. 1989-93, mem. bd. trustees 1994-97, Va. Hosp. Assn. (dir. 1974-97), del. 1989-93, mem. bd. trustees 1994-97, Va. Hosp. Assn. (dir. 1974-97, chmn.-elect, chmn. 1984-85, Disting. Svc. award 1998), Va. Ins. Reciprocal (chmn. 1977-79), Met. Richmond C. of C. (bd. dirs), Richmond Acad. Medicine (Disting. Svc. award 2000). Republican. Presbyterian. E-mail: JSIMP22736@aol.com.

SIMPSON, JOHN WISTAR, energy consultant, former manufacturing company executive; b. Glenn Springs, S.C., Sept. 25, 1914; s. Richard Caspar and Mary (Berkeley) S.; m. Esther Slattery, Jan. 17, 1948; children: John Wistar, Carter B., Patricia A., Barbara J. Student, Wofford Coll., 1932-33, DSc, 1972; BS, U.S. Naval Acad., 1937; MS, U. Pitts., 1941; DSc (hon.), Seton Hill Coll., 1970. With Westinghouse Electric Corp., 1937-77; mgr. Navy and Marine switchboard engring., switchgear div., on leave as mgr. nuclear engring. Daniels pile group, Oak Ridge Nat. Lab., successively as Westinghouse Electric Corp. (Bettis Atomic Power div.), 1949-58; v.p. Westinghouse Electric Corp.; gen. mgr. Westinghouse Electric Corp. (Bettis atomic power lab.), 1958-59, v.p., gen. mgr. atomic power divs., 1959-62, v.p. engring. and research, 1962-63, v.p. electric utility group, 1963-69, pres. power systems, corp. exec. v.p., dir., 1971-77; chmn. bd. Internat. Energy Assocs. Ltd., 1976-80; pres. Simpson Bus. Services, Inc., 1980-86; v.p. Sea Pines Assocs., Hilton Head Island, S.C., 1989-91, also bd. dirs., 1987-91; bd. dirs. Sea Pines Real Estate Cos., 1987-91. Pvt. energy cons.; mem. adv. bd. Lawrence Livermore Nat. Lab. Fusion, 1975-88; mem. Naval Tech. Mission to Japan, 1945; del. 1st Internat. Conf. on Peaceful Uses Atomic Energy, Geneva, Switzerland, 1955, Conf. on Peaceful Uses Atomic Energy (2d Internat. Conf.), 1958; chmn. Atomic Indsl. Forum, 1974-75; mem. energy research adv. bd. Dept. Energy, 1981-83; chmn. com. on outlook for fusion hybrid and tritium breeding fusion reactors NRC; mem. sci. adv. bd. Notre Dame, 1974-86. Author: Nuclear Power from Underseas to Outer Space, 1994. Mem. governing bd. Nat. Coun. Chs., 1979-81; trustee Seton Hall Coll., 1969-76, Point Park Coll., 1973—, Wofford Coll., 1973-87. Recipient Navy cert. of merit for civilian svc. in World War II, 1947, Gold medal for advancement of rsch. Am. Soc. Metals, 1973, Disting. Alumnus award U. Pitts., 1975. Fellow

IEEE (Edison medal 1971), ASME (hon. mem., George Westinghouse Gold medal 1975), Am. Nuclear Soc. (pres. 1973, Henry Dewolf Smyth Nuclear Statesman award 1997); mem. Nat. Acad. Engring., Franklin Inst. (Newcomen Gold medal), Rolling Rock Club (Ligonier, Pa.), Daufuskie Island Club, Bear Creek Golf Club, Sea Pines Club (Hilton Head, S.C.). Home and Office: 36 E Beach Lagoon Rd Hilton Head Island SC 29928-5714 E-mail: jws@hargray.com. *The guiding principles of my career have been to work in an area I considered to be of major importance, to have the most competent people working for me, to know enough technically that I could properly evaluate performance and, as far as possible, always make my position clear to all.*

SIMPSON, JUDITH WHITING, art education educator, artist; b. Beverly, Mass., Sept. 27, 1936; d. Paul Whiting and Winifred Irene (Greene) Warren; m. George Irving French (div.); children: Jeffrey Warren, Jonathan Carr; m. Joseph John Simpson, Apr. 18, 1977. BS, U. N.H., 1972; MS in Art Edn., Mass. Coll. Art, 1975; PhD, U. Wis., Milw., 1992. Cert. K-12 art edn. tchr., Mass. Tchr. art Amesbury (Mass.) Pub. Schs., 1972-79; art cons., designer Environs., Chgo. and Nashua, N.H., 1980-86; staff asst. Art Inst. Chgo., 1987-89; teaching asst. U. Wis., 1989-92; asst. prof. art edn. SUNY, Buffalo, 1992-96; assoc. prof. visual arts Boston U., 1996—. Mem. Nat. Art Edn. Assn., Mass. State Art Tchrs. Assn., U.S. Edn. Through Art Assn., Internat. Soc. for Edn. Through Art, Mass. Alliance for the Arts in Edn. Office: Boston U Coll Fine Arts 855 Commonwealth Ave Boston MA 02215-1303

SIMPSON, LINDA ANNE, retired protective services official, municipal official; b. Greensburg, Pa., Oct. 23, 1953; d. Henry Theodore and Marceline (Krempasky) S.; m. Gail Montgomery, Jan. 10, 1977 (div. May 1981); m. Jeri Anne Sheely, July 10, 1981; children: Jessica Ann, Alexander Richard, Allison Dawn. BA, Calif. U. Pa., 1976, 78; cert., Pa. Police Acad., 1978. Asst. security supt. Rouse Svc. Co., Greensburg, 1971-77; asst. police chief Ellsworth (Pa.) Borough Police Dept., 1977-78; police officer Fallowfield Twp. Police Dept., Charleroi, Pa., 1978-80; police detective, trainer, instr., coord. field tng., supr. sex crimes unit Rock Springs (Wyo.) Police Dept., 1980-96, ret., 1996; security officer ACSS Microsoft Co., Redmond, Wash., 1997-99; control rm. supr. Guardsmark at Microsoft, 1999-2000; quality assurance analyst, software engr. test lead Sierra-On-Line, Bellevue, Wash., 2000—. Rsch. asst. centennial com. Rock Springs Police Dept.; police instr. State of Wyo., 1982—; instr. Women's Inst., Western Wyo. Coll., Rock Springs, 1996—, actor, cons. tng. film series theater dept., 1987-88. Editor quar. newsletter Blue Knights News Wyo., 1986-92. Asst. basketball coach Spl. Olympics, Rock Springs, 1987; mem. Sweetwater County Child Protection Team, 1995-96; mem. Domestic Violence Coun., 1995-96, Harry Benjamin Internat. Gender Dysphoria Assn., 1997—, City of Seattle Sexual Minorities Commn., 1996—; regional dir. Transgendered Officers Protect and Serve (TOPS), 1999-2000, web mistress on-line internet mag. and website, 1999-2000; bd. dirs. Ingersoll Gender Ctr., 1999—. Recipient numerous commedations Rock Springs Police Dept., 1980-96, Outstanding Law Enforcement Officer award, 1985, Disting. Svc. medal, 1987, Svc. medal 1988. Mem. Internat. Found. for Gender Edn., Nat. Assn. Field Tng. Officers, Police Protective Assn. (v.p. 1984-85, treas. 1990-94), Western Alliance Police Officers (v.p. 1985-87), Svcs. and Comm. Dirs., Calif. U. Pa. Alumni Assn., Intermountain World War II Reenactment Assn., Shooting Stars Motorcycle Club (pres. 1980-84), Blue Knights Internat. Law Enforcement Motorcycle Club (pres. Wyo. chpts. 1985-92, bd. dirs. Wyo. chpt. 1 1992-96), High Desert Riders, Motorcycle Club (legis. officer 1991-94), Salt Lake Gender Consortium (mem. bd. protectors 1995-96). Avocations: camping, reading, gender studies. Home: 4306 156th Ave NE # FF120 Redmond WA 98052 Office: Sierra On Line 3060 139th Ave SE Ste 500 Bellevue WA 98005 E-mail: lasimpson@hotmail.com., ltr@lasimpson.org.

SIMPSON, LISA ANN, government agency administrator, physician; b. Lagos, Nigeria, Feb. 9, 1958; (parents Am. citizens); d. Howard Russell and Mary Alice (Turner) Simpson; m. Richard L. Wittenberg; children: Ethan Simpson Wittenberg, Sydney Simpson Wittenberg. MB, B of Surgery, Trinity Coll., Dublin, Ireland, 1981; MPH, U. Hawaii, 1986. Diplomate Am. Bd. Pediat. Resident in pediat. U. Hawaii, Honolulu, 1982-85; resident in preventive medicine U. N.C., Chapel Hill, 1987-88; dir. Maternal and Child Health Bur. State Dept. Health, Honolulu, 1988-90, acting dir. family health svcs. divsn., 1990; policy advisor Office of Asst. Sec. for Health HHS, Washington, 1993-94, sr. advisor Agy. for Health Care Policy and Rsch. Rockville, Md., 1994-95, acting dep. adminstr. Agy. for Health Care Policy and Rsch., 1995-96, dep. adminstr. Agy. for Health Care Policy and Rsch., 1996-99; dep. dir. Agy. Healthcare Rsch. & Quality, 1999—. Mid-career fellow Inst. Health Policy Studies, San Francisco, 1991-93; adj. faculty dept. health policy and mgmt. Johns Hopkins U., Balt., 1995—; vis. prof. U. Wash., 2000, U. Mich., 2000. Mem. editl. bd. Future Children, Maternal and Child Health Jour.; contbr. articles to profl. jours. Recipient Preventive Medicine traineeship Pub. Health Svc., 1986, Dir. Disting. Svc. award AHRQ, 2001, Sec. Disting. Svcs. award Dept. HHS, 2000. Fellow: Am. Acad. Pediat. (Excellence in Pub. Svc. award 2002); mem.: APHA (governing coun. 1994—96), Nat. Acad. for Social Ins., Ambulatory Pediats. Assn., Assn. Health Svcs. Rsch. Avocations: hiking, cuisine, gardening. Office: Agy Health Care Rsch & Quality 2101 E Jefferson St Rockville MD 20852-4908 E-mail: lsimpson@ahrq.gov.

SIMPSON, LOUIS A. insurance company executive; b. Chgo., Dec. 23, 1936; s. Irving and Lillian (Rubin) S.; m. Margaret Rowley, Dec. 16, 1959; children: Irving, Kenneth, Edward Student, Northwestern U., 1954-55; BA, Ohio Wesleyan U., 1958; AM, Princeton U., 1960. Instr. econs. Princeton U., 1961-62; assoc., ptnr. Stein Roe & Farnham, Chgo., 1962-69; v.p. Shareholders Mgmt., Los Angeles, 1969-70; sr. v.p., exec. v.p., pres. Western Asset Mgmt., 1970-79; vice chmn. bd. Geico Corp., Washington, 1979-93, pres., chief exec. officer capital ops., 1993—. Bd. dirs. AT & T, Pacific Am. Income Shares, Western Asset Funds, Inc., HNC Software, ResMed, Inc. Mem. endowments com. Ohio Wesleyan U.; trustee Woodrow Wilson Nat. Fellowship, Cate Sch. Woodrow Wilson fellow, 1958 Mem. San Diego Soc. Fin. Analysts, Calif. Club, Arts Club Chgo., Chevy Chase Club, Met. Club. Episcopalian. Office: Geico Corp 1 Geico Plz Washington DC 20076-0005

SIMPSON, LOUIS ASTON MARANTZ, English educator, author; b. Jamaica, W.I., Mar. 27, 1923; s. Aston and Rosalind (Marantz) S.; m. Jeanne Claire Rogers, 1949 (div. 1954); 1 child, Louis Matthew; m. Dorothy Mildred Roochvarg, 1955 (div. 1979); children: Anne Borovoi, Anthony Rolf; m. Miriam Butensky Bachner, 1985 (div. 1998). Higher schs. certificate, Munro Coll., Jamaica, 1939; BS, Columbia U., 1948, A.M., 1950, PhD, 1959; D.H.L., Eastern Mich. U., 1977; DLitt, Hampden Sydney Coll., 1990. Editor Bobbs-Merrill Pub. Co., N.Y.C., 1950-55; instr. Columbia U., 1955-59; prof. English U. Calif., Berkeley, 1959-67, SUNY, Stony Brook, 1967-91, Disting. prof., 1991—. Author: (poems) The Arrivistes, 1949, Good News of Death, 1955, A Dream of Governors, 1959, At the End of the Open Road, 1963 (Pulitzer prize for poetry 1964), Selected Poems, 1965, Adventures of the Letter I, 1971, Searching for the Ox, 1976, Caviare at the Funeral, 1980, The Best Hour of the Night, 1983, People Live Here: Selected Poems 1949-83, 1983, Collected Poems, 1988, In the Room We Share, 1990, Jamaica Poems, 1993, There You Are, 1995, Nombres et poussière, 1996, (translation) Modern Poets of France, 1997, Kaviar pä begravningen, 1998, François Villon: The Legacy and the Testament, (prose) Riverside Drive, 1962, James Hogg: A Critical Study, 1962, North of Jamaica, 1972, Three on the Tower: The Lives and Works of Ezra Pound, T.S. Eliot and William Carlos Williams, 1975, A Revolution in Taste: Studies of Dylan Thomas, Allen Ginsberg, Sylvia Plath and Robert Lowell, 1978, A Company of Poets, 1981, The Character of the Poet, 1986, Selected Prose, 1989, Ships Going into the Blue, 1994, The King My Father's Wreck, 1995; editor: The New Poets of England and America, 1957, An Introduction to Poetry, 1967. Served with AUS, 1943-45. Decorated Purple Heart, Bronze Star with oak leaf cluster; Hudson Rev. fellow, 1957, Guggenheim fellow, 1962, 70; Am. Coun. Learned Socs. grantee, 1963; recipient Prix de Rome, 1957, Millay award, 1960, Distinguished Alumnus award Columbia U., 1960, medal for excellence Columbia U., 1965; American Acad. of Arts and Letters award in literature, 1976; Centenary medal Inst. of Jamaica, 1980, Jewish Book Coun. award for poetry, 1981, Elmer Holmes Bobst award, 1987, Harold Morton Landon award for translation, 1997. Fellow Am. Acad. in Rome. Home: PO Box 119 Setauket NY 11733-0119

SIMPSON, LYLE LEE, lawyer; b. Des Moines, Oct. 15, 1937; s. R. Clair and Martha B. (Accola) S. BA, Drake U., 1960, JD, 1963. Bar: Iowa 1963, U.S. Dist. Ct. (so. and no. dists.) Iowa 1963, U.S. Ct. Appeals (8th cir.) 1963, U.S. Tax Ct. 1963, U.S. Supreme Ct. 1970, U.S. Ct. Mil. Appeals 1972. Pvt. practice, Des Moines, 1963; mem. Beving and Swanson, 1964-68; sr. ptnr. Peddicord, Simpson & Sutphin, 1968-83; pres. Dreher, Simpson & Jensen, PC, 1984—. Gen. counsel campaign com. Gov. Iowa, 1978-98. Contbr. articles to profl. jours. Chmn. bd. trustees Broadlawns Med. Ctr., 1974-80; mem. Iowa Inaugural Com., 1983, 87, 89, 91, 95; bd. dirs. YMCA Boys Camp, 1967-86, Home, Inc., 1981-85, Project H.E.L.P.E.R., 1983-87, Batten Found.; pres., bd. dirs. Polk County Health Svcs., 1972-88; chmn. Iowa Health Facilities Coun., 1988-93; pres. First Unitarian Ch., 1958-70, Iowa Humanities Bd., 1988-94, Humanist Found., 1980—, East High Alumni Found., 1992—; treas. Iowa Humanities Found., 1994-99, vice-chmn., Iowa Health Found.; investment com., fin. com. Iowa Health Sys., 2000—. Recipient Oren E. Scott award, Class of 1915 award in liberal arts Drake U., 1960. Mem. ABA, Iowa Bar Assn., Polk County Bar Assn., Am. Arbitration Assn., Am. Humanist Assn. (pres. 1979-89), Prairie Club (pres. 1992), Morning Club (pres. 1965), Le Chevaliers de vin Club (pres. 1976-85), YMCA Heritage Club (pres.), Masons, Scottish Rite (Shriner, 33 degree), Rotary. Republican. Congregationalist. Address: 1500 Hub Tower Des Moines IA 50309-3940 E-mail: lsimpson@dreherlaw.com.

SIMPSON, MARK EDWARD, educational administrator; b. Saginaw, Mich., July 29, 1958; s. Frank E. and Beverly Jean S. MA in Christian Edn., Denver Sem., 1984; MA in Edn., DePauw U., Greencastle, Ind., 1989; PhD in Ednl. Studies, Trinity Evang. Div. Sch., Deerfield, Ill., 1992. Min. Christian edn. and discipleship First Bapt. Ch., Greencastle, 1985-89; coord. acad. doctorate programs Trinity Evang. Div. Sch., Deerfield, 1990-94; assoc. dean nontraditional edn. Coll. Liberal Arts and Scis., Trinity Internat. U., 1994-95; Gaines S. Dobbins prof. leadership and ch. ministry, assoc. dean doctoral studies So. Bapt. Theol. Sem. Sch. Edn., Louisville, 1995—. Website mgr. Sch. Leadership and Ch. Ministry So. Bapt. Theol. Sem. Sch. Edn., 1997—. Author book chpts. and jour. articles in field; editor sect. in book. Sec. AIDS adv. coun. Greencastle Cmty. Sch., 1988; pub. policy dir. bd. dirs. Puy Mental Health Assn., 1989. Mem. N.Am. Profs. Christian Edn. (Cert. Recognition 1984). Republican. Avocations: computer database design, digital imaging. Office: So. Baptist Theological Seminary 2825 Lexington Rd Louisville KY 40280-0001

SIMPSON, MARY MICHAEL, priest, psychotherapist; b. Evansville, Ind., 1925; d. Link Wilson and Mary Garrett (Price) S. BA, BS, Tex. Women's U., 1946; grad., N.Y. Tng. Sch. Deaconesses, 1949, Westchester Inst. Tng. in Psychoanalysis and Psychotherapy, 1976; S.T.M., Gen. Theol. Seminary, 1982. ordained priest Episcopal Ch., 1977. Missionary Holy Cross Mission, Bolahun, Liberia, 1950-52; mem. Order of St. Helena, 1952—; acad. head Margaret Hall Sch., Versailles, Ky., 1958-61; sister in charge Convent of St. Helena, Bolahan, 1962-67, dir. novices, 1968-74; pastoral counselor on staff St. John the Divine, N.Y.C., 1974-87, canon residentiary, canon counselor, 1977-87, hon. canon, 1988—. Pvt. practice psychoanalyst, 1974—; dir. Cathedral Counseling Svc., 1975-87; cons. psychotherapist Union Theol. Seminary, 1980-83; bd. dirs. Westchester Inst. Tng. in Psychoanalysis and Psychotherapy, 1982-84; priest-in-charge St. John's Ch., Wilmot, New Rochelle, N.Y., 1987-88; trustee Coun. Internat. and Pub. Affairs, 1983-87;interim pastor St. Michael's Ch., Manhattan, 1992-94; cons. Diocese of N.Y., 1990—. Author: The Ordination of Women in the American Episcopal Church: The Present Situation, 1981; contbg. author: Yes to Women Priests, 1978. Mem. Nat. Assn. Advancement of Psychoanalysis, N.Y. State Assn. Practicing Psychotherapists, N.Y. Soc. Clin. Psychologists. Home and Office: 151 E 31st St Apt 8H New York NY 10016-9502

SIMPSON, MELVIN DION, quality assurance professional; b. Killen , Ala., July 8, 1974; s. Robert Lee and Geneva M. Simpson; m. Dionne Eileen Adams; children: Cailin, Jordan. Degree in quality mgmt., U. Man., Can., 2001. Cert. ASQ quality techinician, ASQ mech. inspection. Dir. quality Ozark Electronic Repairs Inc., Siloam Springs, Ark., 2000—02; quality engr. OECA, Cullman, Ala., 2000; mech. inspector Adtran Inc., Huntsville, 1995—98, quality technician, 1998—2000. Author: (book) Win-Win Leadership, 2002. Recipient ISO 9000 Internal Quality Auditing award, GLF Quality Assocs., 1998, ISO 9001:2000 for Ozark Electronics Repair Inc. award, NSF Internat. Strategic Registrations Ltd.200, 2001, ISO 9000 Internal Quality Auditing award, GLF Quality Assocs., 1999, 2000, 2001. Mem.: APICS, Am. Soc. for Quality (Inspector of Yr. 1998). Office: Ozark Electronics Repair Inc 501 N Lincoln Siloam Springs AR 72761 Business E-Mail: msimpson@oe-inc.com.

SIMPSON, MICHAEL, metals service center executive; b. Albany, N.Y., Dec. 10, 1938; s. John McLaren Simpson and Constance (Hasler) Ames; m. Barbara Ann Bodtke, Jan. 5, 1963; children: Leslie Ann, Elizabeth S. Wessel. BA, U. Mich., 1965, MBA, 1966. Product mgr. Armour & Co., Chgo., 1966-68; with A.M. Castle & Co., Franklin Park, Ill., 1968—, pres. Hy-Alloy Steels Co. divsn., 1974-79, v.p. Midwestern region, 1977-79, chmn. bd., 1979—, also bd. dirs. Trustee Rush-Presbyn.-St. Luke's Med. Ctr., Chgo., 1978—, mem. exec. com., 1980—, vice chmn., 1991—; trustee Oldfields Sch., Glencoe, Md., 1982-87, 95—, chmn. bd., 1998-2000; bd. dirs. Lake Forest (Ill.) Hosp. Found. and Lake Forest Hosp., 1998—; chmn. bd. overseers Rush U., Chgo., 1996-. Office: AM Castle & Co 3400 N Wolf Rd Franklin Park IL 60131-1319 E-mail: msimpson@amcastle.com.

SIMPSON, MICHAEL K. congressman; b. Burley, Idaho, 1950; m. Kathy Johnson, 1971. Student, Utah State U.; DDS, Washington U., St. Louis, 1978. Dentist, Blackfoot, Idaho, 1978—; mem. from 2d Idaho dist. U.S. Ho. Reps., Washington, 1999—. Serves on Agr., Resources, Transp. and Infrastructure and Veterans Affairs coms. Served as spkr. majority caucus chmn. and asst. majority leader in the Idaho Ho. Reps.Elected to U.S. Ho. Reps. in 1998, when 3-term Rep. Michael Crapo was elected to the U.S. Senate. Elected to Blackfoot City Coun., 1980, Idaho Ho. Reps., 1984; asst. majority leader, 1989-91; spkr. of the house, 1991-97. Mem. Idaho's Rep. Party Hall of Fame. Recipient Friend of Edn. award, 1994, Citizen of the Yr. award Idaho Family Forum, 1996, Boyd A. Martin award Assn. Idaho Cities. Mem. Idaho State Dental Assn. (Pres.'s award 1998), Am. Legis. Exch. Coun. (state chmn., nat. bd. dirs., Jefferson award 1994). Republican. Avocations: golf, chess, painting. Office: US Ho Reps 1440 Longworth Hob Washington DC 20515-0001*

SIMPSON, MICHAEL MARCIAL, science specialist, consultant; b. Honolulu, Sept. 24, 1954; s. Marcial Tolentino and Beatrice (Martin) S. AB in Biol. Scis., U. Calif., Berkeley, 1976; MS in Biol. Scis., U. San Francisco, 1977; MS in Energy and Resources, U. Calif., Berkeley, 1979; PhD in Environ. Scis. and Engring., UCLA, 1986. Assoc. researcher NASA, Moffett Field, Calif., 1973; radio program host, producer Sta. KUSF-FM, San Francisco, 1976-78; rsch. asst. Lawrence Berkeley Lab., Berkeley, Calif., 1977-79; rsch. assoc. UCLA/U.S. Dept. Energy, 1979-81; congl. fellow, environ. health U.S. Congress, Washington, 1981-82; head biomed. policy sect. U.S. Congl. Rsch. Svc., 1982—, specialist in environ. techs., terrorism and life scis., environ. technologies and terrorism, 1982—. Adv. bd. Banbury Ctr., Cold Spring Harbor, N.Y., 1985—; adj. faculty The Washington Ctr., 1992—. Contbr. articles to profl. jours. Values clarification educator, Alexandria, Va., 1985—. Fellow AAAS (Named Congl. Sci. fellow 1981-82); mem. Washington Acad. Sci., Library of Congress Profl. Assn., UCLA in Washington (exec. steering com. 1986-92). Avocations: photography, bicycle touring, short story writing, travel. Office: US Congl Rsch Svc Crs Rsi Lm423 Washington DC 20540-7450 E-mail: msimpson@crs.loc.gov.

SIMPSON, MINNIE PEACH, interior designer; b. Kinston, N.C., Apr. 8, 1949; d. Michael Joseph and Margie (Philips) Peach; m. John Wimberly Simpson, Aug. 1974 (div. Dec. 1980). BFA in Interior Design, U. Ga., 1973. Interior designer Hinson Galleries, Columbus, Ga., 1974-79; interior designer, sales rep. Crabapple Galleries, 1980-81; interior designer kitchen and bath design Larry Bussey, Inc., 1981-85; mem. staff sales/designer dept. Mansours, 1985-86; mgr. interior design/space planning AFLAC, 1986—. Coord. March of Dimes, Columbus, 1993-96, Salisbury Fair, Columbus, 1996, Volunteers for Cortea. Mem. U.S. Tennis Assn., Am. Soc. Interior Designers, Internat. Interior Design Assn., Columbus Regional Tennis Assn. (mem. corta bd., 1999-2001). Avocations: tennis, crafts, antiquing. Office: AFLAC 917 Brown Ave Columbus GA 31906-3631

SIMPSON, MURRAY, engineer, consultant; b. N.Y.C., July 27, 1921; s. George and Sonia (Vernov) S.; m. Ethel Gladstein, June 29, 1947; children: Anne Simpson Ozsan, David, Mindy, Jonathan. BEE, CCNY, 1942; MEE, Polytech. Inst. of N.Y., 1952. Engr. Internat. Tel.&Tel., N.Y.C., 1942-44; sr. engr. Raytheon Co., Waltham, Mass., 1946-48; sect. mgr. Fairchild Guided Missles div., Farmingdale, N.Y., 1948-50; v.p. Maxson Elec. Co., N.Y.C., 1950-62; pres. SEDCO Systems Inc. subs. Raytheon Co., Melville, N.Y., 1963-86; cons. M. Simpson Assocs., Ft. Lauderdale, Fla., 1986—. Former chmn. bd. dirs. Radyne Corp. Contbr. articles to profl. jours. Former bd. dirs. United Way of L.I., N.Y., 1984-87. Served to lt. (j.g.) USNR, 1944-46, PTO. Fellow IEEE (chmn. L.I. sect. 1963-64). Avocations: boating, skiing, golf, tennis. E-mail: msimp@aol.com. *Don't be afraid to take risk in the hope of great reward and satisfaction. The worst that could happen is that you may fail. A much greater loss is that you never tried and perhaps missed the great opportunity of your life.*

SIMPSON, PATRICIA ELAINE, education educator, dean; b. Ponca City, Okla., Nov. 9, 1945; d. Loy Lee and Mildred E. (Walker) Stockburger; m. David L. Simpson, Mar. 30, 1964; children: Scott, Steve. AA, York Coll., 1972; BS in Edn., U. Nebr., 1975; MEd, Tex. Tech. U., 1981, EdD, 1989. Cert. elem. tchr. grades K-8; cert. profl. reading specialist; cert. adminstr. Elem. tchr. York (Nebr.) Pub. Schs., 1975-79; asst. prof. edn., dir. acad. counseling Lubbock (Tex.) Christian U., 1981-82; elem. tchr. Lubbock (Tex.) Ind. Sch. Dist., 1979-81, reading specialist, 1982-84, instrnl. specialist, 1984-85, curriculum coord., 1985-90; assoc. prof. edn. York (Nebr.) Coll., 1991-93, chair edn. dept., asst. acad. dean, 1993-95. Cons. Macmillan Pubs., De Soto, Tex., 1992—. Named Alumnus of Yr., York (Nebr.) Coll., 1987, Tex. Elem. Prins. and Suprs. Assn. of the Yr., Tex. Elem. Prins. and Suprs. Assn., Lubbock, 1987, Adminstr. of Yr., Lubbock (Tex.) Classroom Tchrs. Assn., 1989. Mem. ASCD, Internat. Reading Assn., S.E. Nebr. Reading Coun. (chair scholarship com.), Tex. Assn. for the Improvement Reading (pres. 1989), Nat. Coun. Tchrs. Math., Phi Delta Kappa, Delta Kappa Gamma. Avocations: writing poetry, reading, antique collecting, camping. Home: 2069 Fm 89 Buffalo Gap TX 79508-2123 Office: York Coll 9th and Kiplinger York NE 68467

SIMPSON, RICHARD LEE, sociologist, educator; b. Washington, Feb. 2, 1929; s. Donald Dake and Lottie (Lee) S.; m. Ida Ann Harper, July 10, 1955; children: Robert Donald, Frank Daniel. AB, U. N.C., 1950, PhD, 1956; MA, Cornell U., 1952. Instr. Pa. State U., University Park, 1956-57; asst. prof. sociology Northwestern U., Evanston, Ill., 1957-58; asst. prof. U. N. C., Chapel Hill, 1958-61, assoc. prof. sociology, 1961-65, prof., 1965-80, Kenan prof. sociology, 1980-2000, disting. prof. sociology, 2000—; acting dir. Inst. Rsch. Social Sci., 1966-67. Author numerous research papers, articles and book chpts. in field; editor: Social Forces, 1969-72, 83— ; co-editor Research in Sociology of Work, 1981-96. Mem. Am. Sociol. Assn., So. Sociol. Soc. (pres. 1971-72), Sociol. Research Assn. Methodist. Home: 604 Brookview Dr Chapel Hill NC 27514-1406 Office: Univ NC Dept Sociology Hamilton Hall Chapel Hill NC 27599-3210 E-mail: social_forces@unc.edu.

SIMPSON, ROBERT GLENN, lawyer; b. Seattle, June 27, 1932; s. Harold Vernon and Anna Rondeau (McCabe) S.; m. Josephine Anne Heald, June 7, 1959; children: Jenifer Jane, Thomas Glenn, Mary Elizabeth. BS, U. Oreg., 1954; LLB, Willamette U., 1959. Bar: Oreg. 1959. Assoc. William B. Adams Law Office, Portland, Oreg., 1959-67; ptnr. Adams McLaughlin & Simpson, 1967-70, Schwabe Williamson & Wyatt, Portland, 1970—. Trustee, sec. Legacy Good Samaritan Hosp. and Med. Ctr., Portland, 1983-89, mem. cmty. bd., 1989-98; trustee, chancellor Episcopal Diocese of Oreg., Portland, 1988—. Mem. Oreg. State Bar (exec. com. health law sect. 1987-90), Am. Health Lawyers Assn. (program com. 1987-88), Oreg. Acad. Healthcare Attys. (pres. 1977-78, legis. com. 1989), Multnomah Athletic Club, Univ. Club. Home: 13345 SW Iron Mountain Blvd Portland OR 97219-9306 Office: Schwabe Williamson & Wyatt 1211 SW 5th Ave Ste 1800 Portland OR 97204-3713 E-mail: rsimpson@schwabe.com.

SIMPSON, ROBERT LEE, university official, biology educator; b. San Francisco, Apr. 3, 1942; s. Robert Lee and Valerie Brinley (Serrick) S.; m. Penelope Sue Flint, June 12, 1970; children: Robert Lee III, Elizabeth Jean. BA in Zoology, Fresno State Coll., 1965, MA in Biology, 1967; PhD in Limnology, Cornell U., 1971. Instr. Cornell U., Ithaca, N.Y., 1970; from asst. prof. to prof. biology Rider Coll., Lawrenceville, N.J., 1970-85, chairperson biology dept., 1972-80; acting dean sch. health professions and nursing William Paterson Coll., Wayne, N.J., 1986-87, prof. biology, 1985-91, dean sch. sci. and maths., 1985-91; provost, vice chancellor acad. affairs U. Mich., Dearborn, 1991—, prof. biology, 1991—. Adj. grad. prof. Rutgers U., Camden, N.J., 1976-91; vis. scientist Smithsonian Environ. Rsch. Ctr., Edgewater, N.J., 1977; mem. grad. degree adv. com. N.J. Dept. Higher Edn., Trenton, 1989-91. Editor: (with D. Whigham, R. Good) Freshwater Wetlands: Ecological Processes & Management Potential, 1978, (with M. Leck, V.T. Parker) Ecology of Soil Seed Banks, 1989; contbr. articles to profl. jours. Mem. N.J. Wetlands Mitigation Coun., Trenton, 1988-91; trustee Chilton Meml. Hosp., Pompton Plains, N.J., 1989-91; bd. dirs. Granville Acad., Detroit, 1991-93; chair acad. affairs affairs subcom. Pres. Coun. of State Univs. of Mich., 1997—. Rsch. grantee Office Water Rsch. & Tech., 1975, 79, U.S. EPA, 1976, 78, NSF, 1975, 80, U.S. Geol. Survey, 1983, Challenge to Excellence grantee N.J. Dept. Higher Edn., 1987. Mem. N.J. Acad. Sci. (pres. 1983-85, Outstanding Svc. award 1989), Ecol. Soc. Am., Brit. Ecol. Soc., Soc. Wetland Scientists, Am. Soc. Limnology and Oceanography, Sigma Xi. Home: 2470 Harness Dr West Bloomfield MI 48324-3733 E-mail: rslamd@umich.edu.

SIMPSON, RUSSELL AVINGTON, retired law firm administrator; b. Greybull, Wyo., June 19, 1935; s. William Avington and Margaret E. (Draper) S.; m. Margarita A. del Valle, Dec. 19, 1960; children: Margaret E., Robert A., Alexandra P., Christina M. BS with honors, U. Wyo., 1957; LLB, Harvard U., 1965. Bar: Tex. 1965, Mass. 1966. Assoc. Bonilla, de Pena, Read & Bonilla, Corpus Christi, Tex., 1965-66; asst. dean, dir. admissions Harvard Law Sch., Cambridge, Mass., 1966-75, asst. dean, dir. fin. aid, 1972-78, asst. dean for fin. and gen. adminstrn., 1978-84; dir. adminstrn. Hill & Barlow, Boston, 1984-90; v.p., treas. The Archs. Collaborative, Cambridge, 1991-92, ret., 1992. Chmn. devel. com. Law Sch. Data Assembly Service, 1969; pres. bd. dirs. Law Sch. Admissions Services, Newtown, Pa., 1979-80, bd. dirs., 1989-91; trustee Law Sch. Admission Coun., 1968-70, 72-78, 81-82, chmn. svcs. com. 1972-74, chmn. test devel. and rsch. 1976-78; founder Grad. and Profl. Sch. Fin. Aid Coun. Mem. Belmont (Mass.) Town Meeting, 1975-96, Belmont Sch. Com., 1977-83. Capt. USAF, 1957-62. Mem. Tex. Bar Assn., Rotary (bd. dirs. Belmont 1978-80), Phi Kappa Phi. Democrat. Home: 49 Elizabeth Rd Belmont MA 02478-3819 E-mail: russsmpsn@earthlink,net.

SIMPSON, RUSSELL GORDON, lawyer, former mayor, counselor to not-for-profit organizations; b. Springfield, Mass., May 22, 1927; s. Archer Roberts and Maude Ethel (Gordon) S.; m. Bickley F. Flower, Sept. 11, 1954; children: Barbara G., Elisabeth Pires-Fernandes, Helen Blair. BA, Yale U., 1951; JD, Boston U., 1956; postgrad., Parker Sch. Internat. Law, 1962. Bar: Mass. 1956, U.S. Dist. Ct. (fed. dist.) Mass. 1957, U.S. Ct. Appeals (2d cir.) 1958, U.S. Supreme Ct. 1980. Advt. mgr. Burden Bryant Co., Springfield, 1951-53; assoc. Goodwin, Procter & Hoar, Boston, 1956-64, ptnr., 1965-87, of counsel, 1987—. Sr. advisor to pres. World Learning, Inc., Brattleboro, Vt., 1988-89, exec. v.p., 1989-90, sr. v.p., 1990-91, trustee, 1991—, exec. com., 1994—; trustee, mem. exec. com., Save the Children Fedn., Westport, Conn., 1995—; mem. exec. group Internat. Save the Children Alliance, Geneva, Switzerland and London, Eng., 1996—; dir., vice chmn., mem. exec. com., Cmty. Found. Palm Beach and Martin Counties, West Palm Beach, Fla., 1994-2000; counselor to not-for-profit orgns., 1991-2000. Author: The Lawyer's Basic Corporate Practice Manual, 1971, rev. edit., 1978, 84, 87. Mayor Jupiter Island, Fla., 1993-99; hon. consul New Eng. of Bolivia, 1958-82, mem. spl. com. to revise Mass. Corrupt Practices Act, 1961-62; bd. govs. Jupiter Island Club, 2000—; mem. blue ribbon commn. Martin County Fla. Econ. Coun. Named Outstanding Young Man of Greater Boston, 1963. Fellow Am. Bar Found., Mass. Bar Found.; mem. Mass. Bar Assn. (chmn. banking and bus. law sect. 1980-83, bd. dels., exec. com. 1983-87, v.p. 1985-87), ABA (corp. banking and bus. law sect., com. on law firms, co-chmn. com. on law firm governance, panel on corp. law ednl. programs), Hobe Sound Yacht Club (gov., sec. 2001—). Home: 101 Harbor Way PO Box 1106 Hobe Sound FL 33475-1106

SIMPSON, SANDRA KAY, logistics management specialist; b. Rutland, Vt., Feb. 26, 1949; d. Freeman Edward and Ruth Gail (Smith) Campbell. BA, U. Vt., 1971; M of Pub. Adminstrn., Troy State U., Europe, 1988, MSc in Internat. Rels., 1991. Isntr., trainer U.S. Govt., Ft. McClellan, Ala., 1975-79, asst. logistics officer Kitzingen, Germany, 1979-82, property acctg. officer Ft. Hood, Tex., 1982-86, Wiesbaden, Germany, 1986-93; exec. mgmt. asst. Sport and Sound, Mainz Kastel, Germany, 1993-94; maintenance mgmt. coord. U.S. Govt., Wiesbaden, 1994—, dep. dir. internal logistics, 1999—2002, item mgr. theater level logistics, 2002—. Cons. U.S. Govt., Heidelberg, Germany, 1994—. Served with U.S. Army, 1973-93. Mem. Women in Mil. Svc. to Am. Found. (charter mem.), USAREUR Retiree Coun., Wiesbaden/Mainz Retiree Coun. (sec. 1994—), Oxford Club. Avocations: photography, ultra-marathons. Home: Cmr 430 Box 1505 APO AE 09096-1505 E-mail: sandra.simpson@200mmc.21esc.army.mil.

SIMPSON, STEVEN DREXELL, lawyer; b. Sturgis, Mich., Sept. 20, 1953; s. Rex and Lorraine Simpson; m. Peggy Deibert, Apr. 28, 1979; children: Andrew Drexell, Christine Elizabeth, Marianne Tyner. BA, Hillsdale (Mich.) Coll., 1975; JD, Wake Forest U., 1978; LLM in Taxation, Georgetown U., 1981. Bar: Fla. 1978, D.C. 1980, N.C. 1984. Assoc. Bradford, Williams et al, Miami, Fla., 1978-80, Webster & Chamberlain, Washington, 1980-82, Fisher, Wayland et al, Washington, 1982-84, Maupin, Taylor & Ellis, P.A., Raleigh, N.C., 1984-98; ptnr. Law Offices of Steven D. Simpson P.A., 1998—. Author: Taxation of Broadcasters, 1984, Tax-Exempt Organizations: Organizational and Operational Requirements, 2000, Tax-Exempt Organizations: Reporting, Disclosure and Other Procedural Aspects, 2000, Taxable Expenditures, 2000, Tax Compliance for Tax-Exempt Organizations, 2002; contbr. articles to profl. jours. Mem. ABA (exemp orgns. com.). Republican. Methodist. Avocations: golf, running. Home: 409 Hillandale Dr Raleigh NC 27609-7036 Office: Landmark Center II 4601 Six Forks Rd Ste 530 Raleigh NC 27609-5286 E-mail: s.simpsonlaw@verizon.net.

SIMPSON, VINSON RALEIGH, manufacturing company executive; b. Chgo., Aug. 9, 1928; s. Vinson Raleigh and Elsie (Passeger) S.; m. Elizabeth Caroline Matte, Sept. 9, 1950; children: Kathleen Simpson Zier, Nancy Simpson Ignacio, James Morgan. SB in Chem. Engring, MIT, 1950; MBA, Ind. U., 1955. With Trane Co., LaCrosse, Wis., 1950-75, mgr. mktg. services, 1957-64, mgr. dealer devel., 1964-66; mng. dir. Trane Ltd., Edinburgh, Scotland, 1966-67; v.p. internat. Trane Co., LaCrosse, Wis., 1967-68, exec. v.p., 1968-70; exec. v.p., gen. mgr. comml. air conditioning div., 1970-73; pres., 1973-75, Simpson and Co., La Crosse, 1975-76; pres., chief operating officer Marathon Electric Mfg. Corp., Wausau, Wis., 1976-80; chmn., pres., chief exec. officer Marion Body Works, Inc., 1980-93, chmn., 1993—. Bd. dirs. Clintonville Area Found. Past trustee, treas. Fox Valley Tech. Coll.; bd. dir., past pres. Fox Valley Tech. Coll. Found.; past pres., bd. dir. Wausau Area Jr. Achievement; mem. Marion Minutemen; past 20 yr. trustee, chair endowment com., trustee emeritus Northland Coll.; past dir. Wis. Mfrs. and Commerce; dir. Wis. Family Bus. Forum, Wis. Found. for Ind. Colls. Decorated Korean War Commendation ribbon. Mem. Fire Apparatus Mfrs. Assn., Nat. Truck Equipment Assn., Am. Legion, Kappa Kappa Sigma, Alpha Tau Omega, Beta Gamma Sigma (dirs. table). Lodges: Masons, Shriners, Jesters, Rotary (past. pres. Marion club, Paul Harris fellow). Congregationalist. Avocations: running, snorkeling, water skiing, cross country skiing, playing the trombone. Home: 171 Fairway Dr Clintonville WI 54929-1071 Office: Marion Body Works Inc 211 W Ramsdell PO Box 500 Marion WI 54950-0500

SIMPSON, W(ILBURN) DWAIN, physicist, corporate executive, computer systems, telecommunications, environmental, and advanced fueling systems consultant; b. Long Grove, Okla., Oct. 4, 1937; s. Joseph Charles and Wilma Ruby (Smith) S.; m. Ann Marie Coratello, Aug. 27, 1967; children: Ketah Marie, Rebecca Elizabeth. BS, U. Miss., 1959, MS, 1961; MA, Rice U., 1963, PhD, 1965. Rsch. assoc. Rice U., Houston, 1965-67; asst. physicist Brookhaven Nat. Lab., Upton, N.Y., 1967-69; v.p., sec., founder Periphonics Corp., Bohemia, 1969-80, dir. R&D, 1972-78; v.p., sec., founder, dir. R&D Alta Tech. Inc., Stamford, Conn., 1980-85; pres., founder W.D. Simpson Tech., Inc., Wilton, 1985-91; v.p., founder Saber Equipment Corp., Fairfield, 1989-97; pres., founder Synergetic Techs. Inc., Wilton, 1996—. Cons. Ayentka Cons. Corp., Bay Shore, N.Y., 1980-81; founder, mgr. Saber Techs., LLC, Austin, Tex., 1997—. Author: New Techniques in Software Project Management, 1987; patentee in computers and electronically controlled advanced fueling systems; over 15 patents issued. Fellow NSF, 1961; NASA, 1963; named Inventor of Yr., U.S. Patent Office, 1973. Mem. AAAS, IEEE, Am. Phys. Soc., N.Y. Acad. Scis. Methodist. Avocations: robotics, computer controlled systems. Home and Office: Synergetic Techs Inc 32 Bay Dr Center Barnstead NH 03225-3300 E-mail: dwainsimpson@aol.com., saberllc@aol.com.

SIMPSON, WILLIAM KELLY, curator, Egyptologist, educator; b. N.Y.C., Jan. 3, 1928; s. Kenneth Farrand and Helen L.K. (Porter) S.; m. Marilyn E. Milton, June 19, 1953; children: Laura Knickerbacker Simpson Thorn, Abby Rockefeller Simpson Mydland. BA, Yale U., 1947, MA, 1948, PhD, 1954. Asst. in Egyptian art Met. Mus. Art, 1948-54; rsch. fellow Center Middle East Studies, Harvard U., 1957-58; mem. faculty Yale U., New Haven, 1958—, prof. Egyptology, 1965—, chmn. dept. Near Eastern langs., 1966-69; curator Egyptian and ancient Near Eastern art Mus. Fine Arts, Boston, 1970-86; ltd. partner Kin and Co., 1967-69; ltd. ptnr. Venrock, 1970—. Dir. editor of papers Penn-Yale Archaeol. Expdn. to Egypt, 1960— ; mem. adv. council fgn. currency program Smithsonian Instn., 1966-69 Author: Papyrus Reisner I-Records of a Building Project, 1963, Hekanefer and the Dynastic Material from Toshka, 1963, Papyrus Reisner II-Accounts of the Dockyard Workshop, 1965, Papyrus Reisner III: Records of a Building Project in the Early Twelfth Dynasty, 1969, The Terrace of the Great God at Abydos, 1974, The Mastabas of Qar and Idu, 1976, The Offering Chapel of Sekhem-ankh-ptah, 1976, The Offering Chapel of Kayemnofnet in the Museum of Fine Arts Boston, 1992, The Inscribed Material from the Pennsylvania-Yale Excavations at Abydos, 1995, (with others) The Ancient Near East, A History, 2d edit., 1998, The Literature of Ancient Egypt, 1972, The Mastaba of Queen Mersyankh III, 1994. Trustee Am. Sch. Classical Studies, Athens, Am. U. in Cairo; mem. internat. council Mus. Modern Art, N.Y.C.; pres. Wrexham Found., 1965-67. Fulbright fellow Egypt, 1955-57; Guggenheim fellow, 1965 Mem. Am. Oriental Soc., Am. Philos. Soc., Archaeol. Inst. Am., Internat. Assn. Egyptologists, Egypt Exploration Soc., Soc. française d'egyptologie, German Archaeol. Inst., Foundation egyptologique Reine Elisabeth. Clubs: Century (N.Y.C.), Met. Opera (N.Y.C.), University (N.Y.C.), Union (N.Y.C.), River (N.Y.C.); Bedford (N.Y.); Golf and Tennis. Home: 129 Katonah Woods Rd Katonah NY 10536-3846 E-mail: william-simpson@yale.edu.

SIMPSON-STEEKER, MARYBETH, educator; b. Bayonne, N.J., Mar. 17, 1966; d. David B. and Rosanne L. (Setaro) S. BA, Douglass Coll., 1987; MEd, Rutgers U., 1988. Cert. tchr. Coord., day camp, art tchr. Y.W.C.A., Bayonne, N.J., 1984-87, tchr., group, 1987-88; substitute tchr. Bayonne Bd. Edn., 1985-87; tchr. South Bound Brook (N.J.) Bd. Edn., 1988—. Mem. N.J. Edn. Assn., Phi Beta Kappa, Kappa Delta Pi. Roman Catholic. Office: South Bound Brook Bd Edn 1 Zimmerman Pl South Bound Brook NJ 08880-1209

SIMS, ANDREW HARLEY, JR. engineering executive, public administrator; b. Tacoma, Aug. 10, 1937; s. Andrew Harley and Mary Leone (Maguire) S.; m. Dianna Lynn Glass, May 28, 1994; children from previous marriage: Christopher, Gregory. BS with honors, USCG Acad., New London, Conn., 1959; BSEE, MIT, 1971. Registered profl. engr., 40 states. Rsch. assoc. psychology dept. MIT, Cambridge, Mass., 1968-75, sr. teaching asst. elec. engring. dept., 1970-71; project engr. R. G. Vanderweil Engrs., Boston, 1971-76; pres. Sims Engring., South Hampton, N.H., 1976—; city engr. New London City, Conn., 1976-89; exec. dir. South Essex Sewerage Dist., Salem, Mass., 1989-96; sr. engr. Duke Solutions, Boston, 1996-99, corp. dir. environ., health and safety, 1999—. Arbitrator Am. Arbitration Assn., Hartford, 1979-89; instr. East Conn. State U., Willamantic, Conn., 1986. Author, editor: Supervisor's Guide to Safety, 1992 (Water Environment Fedn. Svc. award 1992), MOP-1 Occupational Health & Safety, 1993 (Water Environment Fedn. Svc. award 1994); contbr. articles to profl. jours. Regional coord. MIT Edn. Coun., New London, 1976-90; trustee St. Bernard High Sch., Montville, Conn., 1980-88; treas., dir. Ea. Conn. Symphony Orch., New London, 1980-90; exec. bd., commr. Yankee Clipper Coun., Boy Scouts Am., Middleton, Mass., 1990-96. Lt. USCG, 1959-68. Recipient High Note award Ea. Conn. Symphony Orch., New London, 1990. Mem. Am. Acad. Environ. Engrs. (diplomate), Water Environment Fedn. (safety com.), Am. Waterworks Assn. (equal employment opportunity com.), U.S. Naval Inst., Inst. for Profl. Environ. Practice (qualified environ. practitioner), Nat. Safety Coun. Roman Catholic. Avocations: scouting leader, symphony volunteer. Office: Duke Solutions Inc One Winthrop Sq Boston MA 02110 E-mail: ahsims@duke-energy.com.

SIMS, BENNETT JONES, minister, educator; b. Greenfield, Mass., Aug. 9, 1920; s. Lewis Raymond and Sarah Cosette (Jones) S.; children: Laura (Mrs. John P. Boucher), Grayson, David. AB, Baker U., 1943, LHD (hon.), 1985; postgrad., Princeton Theol. Sem., 1946-47; B.D., Va. Theol. Sem., 1949, D.D., 1966, U. of South, 1972; Merrill fellow, Harvard U., 1964-65; postgrad., Cath. U., 1969-71. Ordained to ministry Episc. Ch. as deacon, 1949, priest, 1950. Rector Ch. of Redeemer, Balt., 1951-64; dir. continuing edn. Va. Theol. Sem., 1966-72; bishop of Atlanta, 1972-83; vis. prof. theology Emory U., Atlanta, 1980-88, founder Inst. for Servant Leadership, 1988—; priest-in-charge St. Alban's Ch., Tokyo, 1962, 69. Author: Invitation to Hope, 1976, Purple Ink, 1982, Servanthood: Leadership for the Third Millennium, 1997. Trustee U. of South. With USNR, 1943-46. Named Young Man of Yr. Balt. C. of C., 1953; Disting. Alumnus of Yr., Baker U., 1972 Office: Inst Servant Leadership 5 Macon Ave Asheville NC 28801-1522

SIMS, CHRISTOPHER ALBERT, economics educator; b. Washington, Oct. 21, 1942; s. Albert Gladstone and Ruth Bodman (Leiserson) S.; m. Catherine Averill Sears, Feb. 4, 1967; children: Benjamin Hayden, Jody Ruth, Nancy Averill. BA, Harvard U., 1963, PhD, 1968; postgrad., U. Calif., Berkeley, 1963-64. Instr., asst. prof., dept. econs. Harvard U., Cambridge, Mass., 1967-69; research fellow Nat. Bur. Econ. Research, N.Y.C., 1969-70; asst. prof., prof., dept. econs. U. Minn., Mpls., 1970-90; prof. dept. econs. Yale U., New Haven, 1990—. Research assoc. Nat. Bur. Econ. Research, Cambridge, Mass. Fellow Econometric Soc.; mem. NAS, Am. Econ. Assn., Am. Statis. Assn., Inst. Math. Stats. Home: 276 Dodds Ln Princeton NJ 08540-4108 Office: Yale U Dept Econs 37 Hillhouse Ave New Haven CT 06511-3703

SIMS, DAVID BRYSON, JR. engineer; b. Memphis, Aug. 12, 1947; s. David Bryson and Ruth (Gnuse) S.; widowed; children: Jennifer Braddock, David Bryson III. BSChemE, U. Tenn., 1969; MS Mech. Engring., U. Memphis, 1972, MS Civil Engring., 1974. Registered profl. engr., Ga., Mi., Va., Kans., N.C., Tenn., S.C., La., Ohio, Ind., Fla., Md. Engr. DuPont, Memphis, 1969-73; cons. engr. Elles, Reaves, Fanning & Oakley, 1973-75; engr. W.R. Grace, 1975-79, engring. mgr. Wilmington, N.C., 1979-85; prin. David Sims & Assocs., 1985—. Trustee Cape Fear Acad., Wilmington, 1987-92; part-time instr. Cape Fear C.C., Wilmington, 1981-86. Bd. dirs., pres. Bradley Creek Boatominium, Wilmington, 1990-97. Mem. NSPE, ASHRAE, AIChE (sec. 1972, pres. 1973), Nat. Fire Protection Assn. Republican. Presbyterian. Home: 108 N Korr Ste K-1 Wilmington NC 28405 Office: David Sims & Assocs 108 N Kerr Ave Ste K-1 Wilmington NC 28405-3401

SIMS, DOUGLAS D. bank executive; b. 1946; Grad., U. Ill., Urbana, 1968. With St. Louis Bank for Cooperatives, St. Louis, 1969-74; v.p. Ctrl. Bank for Coops., 1974-78; pres. St. Louis Bank for Coops., 1978-84; exec. v.p. Farm Credit Banks of St. Louis, 1984-86, pres., 1986-88, Nat. Bank for Cooperatives, Englewood, Colo., 1988-93; CEO CoBank, 1994—. Office: CoBank 5500 S Quebec St Greenwood Village CO 80111-1914

SIMS, EDWARD HOWELL, editor, publisher; b. Orangeburg, S.C., May 29, 1923; s. Hugo Sheridan and Jesse Lucile (Howell) S.; m. Frances Dell Hartt, Jan. 5, 1946; m. Martha Lurene Bass, July 18, 1960; children— Edward H., Robert; m. Bente Thorlund Christensen, Oct. 4, 1969; children— Edward Christian, Frederik. AB, Wofford Coll., 1943; postgrad., Emory U., 1946-47. Mng. editor Orangeburg Times and Democrat, 1946, editor, 1952—; Washington corr., founder Washington bur. for number S.C. dailies, 1947. Dir. Sims Pub. Co., Orangeburg. Columnist: Looking South From Washington, 1948— ; Washington Bur. chief: Editor's Copy syndicate, 1950-52; editor-pub., 1952— ; radio news analyst: The News of The Week In Washington, 1951— ; Author: American Aces, 1958, Greatest Fighter Missions, 1962, The Fighter Pilots, 1967, Fighter Tactics 1914-70, 1972, Aces Over the Oceans, 1987; contbr. articles to pubs. White House corr. covering Pres.''s confs., 1948—; mem. Senate and House press galleries, 1947—; Am. consul Munich, Germany, 1963-65; cons. Exec. Office of White House, 1966-67; consul gen. Zurich, 1992; apptd. mem. Commn. to Preserve Am. Heritage Abroad, 1987. Served to 1st lt. USAF, World War II. Recipient Young Man of the Year award S.C. Jr. C. of C., 1959 Mem. White House Corrs. Assn., Am. Legion, V.F.W. Clubs: Rotary, Nat. Press; Metropolitan (Washington); R.A.F. (London). Methodist. Home: 3803 Pin Oaks St Sarasota FL 34232-1241 also: PO Box 400 Fairview NC 28730-0400 Office: PO Box 532 Orangeburg SC 29116-0532

SIMS, ELIZABETH LANEAL, association executive; b. Manila, May 22, 1948; d. Aaron Neal and Mary Elizabeth (Butler) Shedd; m. Jared Preston Sims, Aug. 31, 1968; children: Jared Neal, David Paul, Christopher Wayne. BA in English, James Madison U., 1974. Tchr. English Buffalo Gap H.S., Augusta County, Va., 1977—79, Wilson Meml. H.S., 1981—88, tchr., sponsor, high sch. yr. book The Hornet's Nest, 1981—88; vol. coord., case mgr. Family Children's Svc., Richmond, 1989—93, program adminstr. sr. svcs., 1993—98; exec. dir. Hanover Mental Health Assn., Inc., Ashland, 1998—. Pres. bd. dirs. Hanover Mental Health Assn., 1996-98; bd. dirs. Va. Coalition for Aging. Bd. dirs. United Way, Richmond, 1995-97, campaign cabinet, 1998-2000; v.p. bd. dirs. Urban League Greater Richmond, 1999—; bd. dirs. Urban League Found., 2002--; mem. adminstrv. bd. Ctrl. United Meth. Ch., 1981-83. Recipient Cert. of Appreciation, Urban League, 1998, Cert. of Appreciation, United Way Svcs., 1997, 99, 2000. Mem. NASW, Internat. Assn. Psychosocial Rehab. Svcs., Mental Health Assn. Va. (bd. dirs. 1998—). United Methodist. Avocations: Boy Scout counselor, first aid CPR instructor.

SIMS, EZRA, composer; b. Birmingham, Ala., Jan. 16, 1928; s. Ezra G. and Kathryn W. (Wallace) S. BA, Birmingham So. Coll., 1947; postgrad., Birmingham Conservatory Music, 1945-48; MusB in Composition, Yale U. Sch. Music, 1952; MA in Composition, Mills Coll., 1956. Librarian Harvard Music Library, Cambridge, Mass., 1958-62, 65-74; music dir. New Eng. Dinosaur Dance Theatre, Boston, 1968-78; instr. theory New Eng. Conservatory Music, 1976-78; instr. microtonal theory Mozarteum, Salzburg, 1992-93; freelance composer Cambridge, 1974—. Dir. Dinosaur Annex Music Ensemble, Cambridge, pres. 1977-81; guest composer 23d Ann. Contemporary Music Festival, Ill. Wesleyan U., 1977; lectr. various colls. including Warwick U., Cleve. Inst. Music, Internat. Christian U., Westport Friends of Music, Schlumberger-Doll Rsch., Webster U., Mozarteum, Northwestern U., Hochschule für Musik, Hamburg. Composer over 100 works, predominantly microtonal music for various mediums including Chamber Cantata on Chinese Poems, 1954, Mass, 1955, Two Folk Songs, 1958, String Quartet, 1959, Sieben-Spencer Lieder, 1960, Sonate Concertanti, 1961, Third Quartet, 1962, Buchlein for Lyon, 1962, Cantata III, 1963, Octet for Strings, 1964, In Memoriam Alice Hawthorne, 1967, Antimatter: Three Dances for Toby, 1968, A Frank Overture: Four Dented Interludes and Coda, 1969, Pastorale, 1970, Clement Wenceslaus Lothaire Nepomucene, Prince Mettermich (1773-1859), In Memoriam, 1970, Real Toads, 1970, Interlope, 1971, Tango Variations, 1971, Museum Piece, 1972, Where the Wild Things Are, 1973, String Quartet #2 1962, 1974, After Lyle or Untitled, 1975, When the Angels Blow Their Trumpets, 1976, Celebration of Dead Ladies, 1976, Elegie-nach Rilke, 1976, Collage XIII, 1977, Aeneas on the Saxophone, 1977, Come Away, 1978, Midorigaoka, 1978, 5 Songs, 1979, -And, As I Was Saying..., 1979, Two for One, 1980, Sextet, 1981, All Done From Memory, 1980, Phenomena, 1981, Solo After Sextet, 1981, Quartet, 1982, Pictures for an Institution, 1983, Tune and Variations, 1983, Brief Elegies, 1983, String Quartet #4, 1984, The Conversions, 1985, Wedding Winds, 1986, Quintet, 1987, Chase, 1987, Solo in four movements, 1987, AEDM in memoriam, 1988, Flight, 1989, Night Piece: IN Girum Imus nocte et Consuminur Igni, 1989, Concert Piece, 1990, Duo, 1992, Invocation, 1992, Stanzas, 1995, If I Told Him, 1996, Duo, 1996, 97, Kumo Sudare, Encores: Three Parlor Songs, 2000, String Quartet #5, 2000; contbr. articles to profl. jours. Served as pvt. U.S. Army, 1952-54. Recipient Composers Forum award, 1959, Koussevitzy Found. commn., 1983, Am. Acad. Arts and Letters award, 1985; grantee Cambridge Arts Coun., 1975, 76, Martha Baird Rockefeller Found., 1977; fellow Guggenheim Found., 1962, McDowell Colony, 1966, Nat. Endowment for Arts, 1976, 78, Mass. Artists Found., 1979, Djerassi Found., 1990, Fulbright Sr. Scholar, 1992, Wurlitzer Found., 1998, Camargo Found., 2000. Mem. Broadcast Music, Inc. Home and Office: 229 Hurley St Cambridge MA 02141-2133 E-mail: ezrsims@aol.com.

SIMS, GERALD KEITH, minister; b. Cheboygan, Wis., Mar. 31, 1951; s. Eugene Robert and Betty Ruth Sims; m. Lorraine Dale White, Jan. 7, 1972; children: Mindy Baker, Christa Kemp, Erica. BA, Bethel Coll., 1973, MA, 1982. Sr. pastor Calif. Rd. Missionary Ch., Elkhart, Ind., 1977—83, Davison (Mich.) Missionary Ch., 1983—89; ch. planter Santa Maria (Calif.) Missionary Ch., 1989—93; sr. pastor Sturgis (Mich.) Missionary Ch., 1993—98, Locust Grove Mennonite Ch., Burr Oak, 1998—2001, New Hope Missionary Ch., Lapeer, 2000—, dir. ch. planting, 2001—. Ch. planting cons. Providence Ch. of God, Shelton Township, Mich., 2001—02. Pres. alumni assn. Bethel Coll., Mishawaka, Ind., 1982; pres. Sturgis Ministerial Assn., 1998—2001. Avocation: writing novels, screenplays and stage plays. Home: 1582 Heather Dr Lapeer MI 48446 Office: New Hope Missionary Ch 1009 N Saginaw Lapeer MI 48446

SIMS, HENRY P., JR. management educator; Prof. mgmt. U. Md., College Park. Author: The Thinking Organization: Dynamics of Organizational Social Cognition, 1986, SuperLeadership: Leading Others to Lead Themselves, 1989, The New Leadership Paradigm: Social Learning and Cognition in Organizations, 1992, Business Without Bosses: How Self-Managing Teams Are Building High-Performance Companies, 1993, Company of Heroes: Unleashing the Power of Self Leadership, 1996, Team Work and Group Dynamics, 1999, The New Superleadership: Leading Others to Lead Themselves, 2001. Office: U Md Van Munching Hall College Park MD 20742-0001 E-mail: hsims@rhsmith.umd.edu.

SIMS, JANETTE ELIZABETH LOWMAN, educational director; b. Lincolnton, N.C., July 21, 1934; d. Lee Hobson and Myrtle Elizabeth (Travis) Lowman; m. Mickey Ray Sims, Feb. 2, 1951; children: Carol Lee, Rickey Ray. BS, Lenoir-Rhyne Coll., 1968; MAT, U. N.C., 1973; EdD, U. N.C., Greensboro, 1989. N.C. "G" tchg. cert; cert. devel. edn. specialist. Quality control supr. Kiser Roth Hosiery, Inc., Maiden, N.C., 1959-63; 9th grade phys. sci. and math. tchr. Cherryville (N.C.) Jr. H.S., 1968; phys. sci., chemistry and astronomy tchr. Maiden (N.C.) H.S., 1968-75; dir. studies lab. coord. Catawba Valley C.C., Hickory, N.C., 1975-79, physics, chemistry, math. and computer sci. instr., 1979-90, dir. developmental studies and learning assistance ctr., 1990-2001; ret., 2001. Apprentice program instr. Meredith/Burda Corp., Newton, NC, 1979—88; part-time instr. math. and physics Catawba Valley C.C. Mem. Conover Planning Bd., 2001—; trustee Catawba County Assn. for Spl. Edn., Conover, 1978—79, Catawba Valley Found., Hickory, 1993—96, chair, 1996; tchr., mem. choir Faith Luth. Ch., Conover, 1980—, mem. ch. coun., 1995—97, pres. congregation and ch. coun., 1997—98, v.p. congregation and ch. coun., 2001—. Mem. NEA, N.C. Assn. Educators (local unit pres.), Nat. Assn. Developmental Educators, N.C. Assn. Developmental Educators (regional chair 1990), Atlantic Assn. Physics Tchrs. (chair nominations com. 1992), N.C. Math. Assn. Two-Yr. Colls. (chairperson devel. math. com. 1991-93, sec. 1996-2000), Am. Legion Aux., Delta Kappa Gamma. Avocations: sewing, cooking. Home and Office: 300 Parlier Ave NE Conover NC 28613-9312 E-mail: jsims721@conninc.com.

SIMS, JOHN ROGERS, JR. lawyer; b. Red Star, W.Va., Apr. 10, 1924; s. John Rogers and Myrtle (Hutchison) S.; m. Geraldine L. Bucklew, Oct. 8, 1966; children: John Rogers III, Joyce Rebecca. BS in Commerce, U. Va., 1950, LLB, 1952. Assoc. Dow, Lohnes & Albertson, Washington, 1953-57; gen. counsel D.C. Transit Sys., Inc., 1957-65; individual practice law, 1965-68; ptnr. Wrape and Hernly, Arlington, Va., 1968-71, Sims, Walker & Steinfeld (and predecessor firm), Washington, 1972-95; pvt. practice Nellysford, Va., 1995—. Chmn. bd. dirs. John Sims Assocs., Inc., 1978-2000, Purnell Bros. Transport, Ltd., 1981-91; co-founder, bd. dirs., gen. counsel A Presdl. Classroom for Young Ams., Inc., chmn. bd. dirs., 1979-83; dir., v.p., gen. counsel, sec. SunWorld Internat. Airways, Inc., 1984-88; chmn. corp. bd. adv. Omniplex World Svcs. Corp. Vice chmn. Falls Church (Va.) Planning Commn., 1958-64; pres. Falls Church Republican Party, 1961-62; bd. dirs. Heart Assn. No. Va., Inc., pres., 1963-64; bd. dirs., v.p., gen. counsel Commonwealth Doctors Hosp., Fairfax, Va., 1967-74; bd. dirs. Jefferson Area Bd. for Aging. Served with Armed Forces, 1943-45. Mem. ABA, W.Va. Bar Assn., D.C. Bar Assn., Va. State Bar, Motor Carrier Lawyers Assn. (nat. pres. 1971-72), Assn. for Transp. Law, Logistics and Policy, Va. Trial Lawyers Assn., Rotary, Masons (Shriner), Washington Golf and Country Club, Farmington Country Club (Charlottesville, Va.). Presbyterian. Home: 31 Sawmill Creek Dr Nellysford VA 22958-9538 E-mail: sims@firstva.com.

SIMS, JOHN WILLIAM, lawyer; b. Vicksburg, Miss., Mar. 25, 1917; s. John Ernest and Helen Ross (Moore) S.; m. Marie Elise Hebert, Sept. 28, 1940; 1 dau., Helen Moore. BA, Tulane U., 1937, LL.B., 1939. Bar: La. 1939. Of counsel Phelps Dunbar; mem. permanent adv. bd.-planning com. Admiralty Law Inst., Tulane U., New Orleans, 1966—, chmn., 1985-91, adj. prof. law, 1981-95. 1st chmn. USCG Lower Mississippi River Waterway Safety Adv. Com., chair, 1983-94. Assoc. editor Am. Maritime Cases, 1974-96; mem. editl. bd. Lloyd's Maritime and Comml. Law Quar., 1984-92; mem. bd. adv. editors Tulane Law Rev., 1985-93, Maritime Advisor-Ct. Case Digest, 1985-96; contbr. articles to profl. jours. Trustee Gulf South Rsch. Inst., 1965-68, Children's Hosp., 1975-78; bd. dirs. Coun. for Better La., Bur. Govt. Rsch., 1973-84, USCG Found., 1986-91, La. World Expn., Inc., 1980-84, World Trade Ctr., 1985—; bd. dirs., v.p. New Orleans Opera Assn., 1974-93; mem. men's adv. bd. Christian Woman's Exch. Lt USCGR, 1942-45. Named Rex, King of Carnival Mardi Gras, New Orleans, 1981; recipient Disting. Pub. Service award Dept. Transp. U.S. Coast Guard, 1985, 88. Fellow Am. Coll. Trial Lawyers; mem. Am., La. (past sec.-treas.), New Orleans Bar assns., Maritime Law Assn. U.S. (2d v.p. 1976-78, 1st v.p. 1978-80, pres. 1980-82, com. Supreme Ct. admiralty rules 1963-69, com. limitation of liability 1963-96, com. Comite Maritime Internat. 1965-80, com. uniformity admiralty law 1975-92, com. liquified natural gas transp. 1978-80, del. Comite Maritime Internat. conv. N.Y.C. 1965, Rio de Janeiro, 1977, Montreal, 1981, adv. cons. Hamburg 1974, titular mem. Comite Maritime Internat. 1979—, del. Comite Maritime Internat. Lisbon Conv., 1985), SAR, Soc. Colonial Wars, Order of Coif, Phi Beta Kappa, Omicron Delta Kappa, Phi Delta Theta, Phi Delta Phi. Clubs: Boston, Louisiana. Office: Canal Place Ste 2000 365 Canal St New Orleans LA 70130-6534

SIMS, KAREN ANN, public defender; b. St. Louis, May 21, 1957; BA in Comms. and Pub. Rels., William Jewell Coll., 1990; JD, Washburn U., 1994. Asst. pub. defender State Pub. Defender's Office, Liberty, Mo., 1995—. Mem. ABA, Kans. Bar, Mo. Bar Assn., Clay County Bar Assn. Avocations: photography, travel. Office: Clay County Pub Defender 234 W Shrader St Liberty MO 64068-2448

SIMS, KENT OTWAY, economist; b. Chickasha, Okla., Nov. 2, 1940; s. Jesse Otway and Mable Vela (Bear) S.; m. Jeanette McCollum, June 9, 1961; children: Marketa, Adam. BA, U. Colo., 1963, PhD, 1966. registered investment advisor. Economist Urban Renewal Authority, Denver, 1965-66, U.S. Dept. State mission to Pakistan, 1966-69, Fed. Res. Bank of San Francisco, 1969-71, asst. v.p., 1971-72, v.p., dir. research, 1972-74, sr. v.p., 1974-82, exec. v.p., chief fin. officer, 1982-85; fin. advisor, investment mgr., mgmt. cons. Theodore R. Seton, 1985-86; ptnr. C&K Partnership, 1987-89. Pres. Her Equal Share, Inc., 1986-89, San Francisco Econ. Devel. Corp., 1988-91; dir. econ. planning and devel. Mayor's Office, San Francisco, 1992-93, San Francisco Redevel. Agy., 1993-96; dir. spl. projects City Mgr.'s Office, Oakland, Calif., 1997; dep. dir. Com. Econ. Devel., Oakland, 1997-98; cons. Bay Area Life Scis. Alliance, 1999, San Francisco Planning and Urban Rsch. Assn., 2000, Golden Gate Restaurant Assn., 2001-02. Bd. govs. Econ. Lit. Coun. Calif., Long Beach, 1983-88; trustee Strybing Arboretum Soc. Golden Gate Park, San Francisco, 1993-96; bd. dirs. Jewish Community Mus., San

Francisco, 1986-93, Design Coun. San Francisco Bay Area, 1989-90, Career Resources Devel. Ctr., 1991-92; adv. bd. St. Lukes Hosp., San Francisco, 1988-96. Mem. Am. Econs. Assn., Nat. Audubon Soc. Am. Clubs: Sierra. E-mail: kentsims@aol.com.

SIMS, MARTHA J. library director; b. Portsmouth, Va., Oct. 29, 1946; m. Hunter Sims; children: Hunter, Clara. BA in English, Mary Baldwin Coll., 1968; MS in Libr. Sci., U. N.C., 1969; MBA in Pub. Adminstrn., Old Dominion U., 1979. Reference asst. U. N.C., Chapel Hill, 1968-69; libr. art and music dept. Richmond Pub. Libr., 1969-71; br. libr. Virginia Beach Pub. Libr., 1971-74, asst. dir., 1974-76, dir., 1976—. Mem. adv. bd. New Va. Review, 1976-80. Contbr. articles to profl. jours. Bd. dirs. Va. Beach Arts Ctr., 1971-82, treas., 1974-75; mem. Va. Beach Bicentennial Commn., 1975-76, Jr. League Norfolk, Virginia Beach, 1976-82; sec. Tidewater Area Libr. Dir.'s Coun., 1984-85; bd. dirs. Boys Club Norfolk/Virginia Beach, 1986-90, Literacy Action South Hampton Roads, 1988—, Va. Ctr. for the Book, 1987—, pres. 1995—, Va. Literacy Found., 1989—; mem. steering com. Virginia Beach Roundtable, 1988-92; census chairperson Mayor's Complete Count Com. 1990, 1989-90; lead agt. region 12 literacy coord. com. State Office Adult Literacy, 1989-92; trustee, sec. Va. Beach Pub. Libr. Endowment Found., 1982—; mem. adv. bd. Tidewater Literacy Coun., 1984-90; tchr. Sunday sch. 1st Presbyn. Ch., 1988—; mem. steering com. Adult Literacy Lab, Adult Lng. Ctr. Va. Beach Pub. Schs., 1989—; keel divsn. leader United Way, 1991-92; bd. trustees Norfolk Acad., 1991—; keel club chairperson United Way, Virginia Beach, 1992-93; city chmn. United Way, Virginia Beach, 1995. Mem. ALA, Am. Soc. Pub. Adminstrs., Southeastern Libr. Assn., Va. Libr. Assn. (sec. 1976-78, legis. com. 1979-85, local arrangements 1982 conv. 1981-82, chmn. pub. libr. sect. 1982-84, state libr. bd. liaison com. 1984-88). Home: 1160 Cedar Point Dr Virginia Beach VA 23451-3864 Office: Virginia Beach Dept of Public Libraries Municipal Ctr Bldg 192nd Virginia Beach VA 23456-9115

SIMS, REBECCA GIBBS, accountant, certified fraud examiner, journalist, editor; b. Houston, Mar. 13, 1951; d. Shelton P. Gibbs and Elizabeth Gill Bisby; m. Morris Raymond Sims (div. 1977); children: Diana Elizabeth, Aaron Redding. BFA, U. Houston, 1977. Cert. fraud examiner. V.p. Lexley U.S.A., Inc., Houston and Mexico City, 1977-81; acct. self-employed, Houston, 1982-87, journalist/investigator, 1987—, fin. fraud investigator, 1991—; mng. ptnr. Boynton & Assocs., 1996—, expert witness, 1997—. V.p. Homa S.A., Texcoco, Mex., 1994—. Editor, rschr.: Mafia, CIA and George Bush, 1992, U.S. resident editor: Daily Hot News, 1998, screenwriter: , journalist: Bilanz mag., 1989—91. Childbirth instr. Houston Orgn. Parent Edn., Houston, 1974-77. Mem. Investigative Reporters and Editors, Nat. Writers Union, Assn. Cert. Fraud Examiners, Mensa. Democrat. Avocations: painting, gardening. Office: 6601 Kirby Dr Ste 671 Houston TX 77005-3943 E-mail: rebeccagsims@aol.com.

SIMS, REBECCA LITTLETON, lawyer; b. Macon, Ga., May 24, 1957; d. William Harvey and Carlan Patricia (Hammond) Littleton; m. Charles Neil Sims, Jr., Dec. 29, 1984; children: Charles Neil III, William Vickers, Caroline Greer. Student, Tex. A&M U., 1977, Baylor U., 1978, U. South, 1979; JD, Baylor U., 1981; BA in Polit. Sci. with honors, U. South, 1979. Bar: Ga. 1983, U.S. Dist. Ct. (so. dist.) Ga. 1984, U.S. Dist. Ct. (no. dist.) Ga. 1985, U.S. Dist. Ct. (mid. dist.) Ga. 1992, U.S. Supreme Ct. 2001. Law clk., Waco, Tex., 1981, Waycross Jud. Cir., Waycross and Douglas, Ga., 1982-83; asst. dist. atty. Waycross cir. Dist. Atty.'s Office, Douglas, 1983-84; spl. asst. to atty. gen. Dept. Family and Children's Svcs., Coffee County, 1988-90; pvt. practice Douglas, 1985-92; state ct. solicitor Coffee County, Ga., 1989-96; in-house counsel Sims Funeral Home, 1997-99; instr. polit. sci. South Ga. Coll., Douglas, 2000—. Mem Bar of United States Supreme Ct., 2001. Mem. altar guild St. Andrew's Episcopal Ch., Douglas, 1983-90, 2000—, vestryman, clk. of vestry, 1986-88; bd. dirs. Shelter for Abused Women, Waycross, 1986-87; trustee Diocese of Ga., U. South, Savannah, 1988-91; mem. First Meth. Ch., Douglas, Ga., 1991-99, United Meth. Women Cir. # 8, 1991-98; dir. Vacation Bible Sch., 1997, 98; legis. aid Charles Neil Sims, Jr., Ga. Ho. Reps., 1997—. Mem. State Bar Ga., Acad. Boosters Club (awards chmn. 1997-98), Beta Sigma Phi (pres. 1997-98). Avocations: gardening, reading, needlework, cooking, antiques. Office: PO Box 2352 Douglas GA 31534-2352 E-mail: rsims@mail.sgc.peachnet.edu., arcades57@aol.com.

SIMS, RICHARD LEE, hospital administrator; b. Columbus, Ohio, Jan. 6, 1929; s. Dorwin Delos and Christine Anna (Hanstein) S.; m. Marilyn Lou Atkinson, June 2, 1951; children: John Christopher, Steven Paul. BS, Ohio State U., 1951. Pres. Doctors Hosp. Found., Columbus, 1977-95; preceptor faculty Ohio State U. Coll. Health Care Adminstrn.; past chmn. Hosp. Coun. Franklin County; ret., 1995. Past chmn. Hosp. Shared Svc. Inc., Found. Osteo Health Svcs., 1989-93. Past pres. Franklin County chpt. ARC; past chmn. 1st Comty. Village Bd.; past chmn. governing bd. 1st Comty. Ch.; pres. Scioto Valley Health Systems Agy., 1999-2002; pres. Employment for Srs., 1999-2000; past chair Columbus area chpt. ARC, emeritus bd. dirs. Recipient Distinguished Service award Columbus Jr. C. of C., 1960-63 Fellow Am. Coll. Healthcare Execs. (life), Am. Coll. Osteo. Healthcare Execs. (life); mem. Am. Osteo. Healthcare Assn. (chmn. 1988), Ohio Soc. of Assn. Execs. (past pres.), Ohio Hosp. Assn. (past chmn. bd.), Ohio Osteo. Hosp. Assn. (past pres.), Am. Legion (past post comdr.), Rotary (pres. 1978-79), Columbus Club, Sigma Chi. Home: 1180 Kenbrook Hills Dr Columbus OH 43220-4941

SIMS, ROBERT BARRY, lawyer; b. N.Y.C., Aug. 20, 1942; s. Irving Zach and Laura (Levine) S.; m. Roberta Jane Donner, Nov. 17, 1973; children: Alexandra Lauren, Andrew Michael, Amanda Morgan. AB, Franklin and Marshall Coll., 1964; JD, George Washington U., 1967; MBA, NYU, 1969. Bar: N.Y. 1968, D.C. 1969, Conn. 1980, Tex. 1995, U.S. Dist. Ct. D.C. 1969, U.S. Dist. Ct. (so. and ea. dists.) N.Y. 1970, U.S. Dist. Ct. Conn. 1978, U.S. Dist. Ct. (we. dist.) Tex. 1997, U.S. Ct. Appeals (2d and D.C. cirs.) 1969, U.S. Ct. Appeals (5th cir.) 1997, U.S. Ct. Claims 1977, U.S. Ct. Customs and Patent Appeals 1978, U.S. Supreme Ct. 1979, U.S. Ct. Internat. Trade 1981, U.S. Ct. Appeals (5th cir.) 1997, U.S. Dist. Ct. (we. dist.) Tex. 1997. Assoc. Cahill, Gordon & Reindel, N.Y.C., 1967-69, Whitman & Ransom, N.Y.C., 1969-72; asst. counsel Gen. Signal Corp., N.Y.C., Stamford, Conn., 1972-76; v.p., sec., gen. counsel Raymark Corp. (formerly Raybestos-Manhattan, Inc.), Trumbull, Conn., 1976-82; assoc. gen. counsel Lever Bros. Co., N.Y.C., 1983; asst. to pres., corp. counsel Math. Applications Group, Inc., Elmsford, N.Y., 1984; sr. v.p., sec., gen. counsel Summagraphics Corp., Austin, Tex., 1984-95; atty. at law, mediator, pres. Counselcor LLC, 1995-2001; v.p., sec., gen. counsel. Novadigm, Inc., Mahwah, NJ, 2001—. Mem. ABA, N.Y. State Bar Assn., Assn. Bar City N.Y., D.C. Bar Assn., Conn. Bar Assn., Corp. Bar Assn., Tex. Bar Assn. Office: 6215 Northern Dancer Dr Austin TX 78746-2121

SIMS, ROBERT BELL, professional society administrator, public affairs official, newspaper publisher; b. Alamo, Tenn., Nov. 26, 1934; s. Robert Leslie and Lucille (Bell) S.; m. Patricia June Lytton, June 25, 1961; children—Jacqueline, James, Carolyn, William. BA, Union U., Jackson, Tenn., 1956; postgrad., U. Sydney, Australia, 1957; MA in Polit. Sci., MA in Journalism, U. Wis., Madison, 1971; Grad., Nat. War Coll. Reporter Jackson Sun, Tenn., 1955-56; dir. pub. rels. Union U., Jackson, 1958; commd. ensign USN, 1958, served to capt., 1984; spl. asst. to Pres., dir. pub. affairs NSC, Washington, 1982-83; spl. asst. to Pres., dep. press sec. for fgn. affairs The White House, 1983-85; asst. sec. def. pub. affairs Dept. of Def., 1985-87; v.p. comm. Nat. Geog. Soc., 1987-89, sr. v.p., 1989-97, sr. v.p. mag. pub. and comm., 1998-2000; exec. v.p. and pres. Mag. Group, 2000—01. Owner, pub. The Crockett Times, Alamo, Tenn., 1974— . Author: Pentagon Reporters, 1983. Bd. mem. Navy Meml. Found., Am. Cave Conservation Assn. Decorated Legion of Merit; Rotary Internat. Found. fellow, 1957; recipient Disting. Service award Union U., 1985. Mem.: Coun. on Fgn. Rels. Republican.

SIMS, ROGER W. lawyer; b. Cleve., Aug. 3, 1950; BA with high honors, U. Fla., 1972, JD, 1974. Bar: Fla. 1975. Mem. Holland & Knight, Orlando, Fla. Mem. Moot Ct. U. Fla.; contbr. to profl mags and jours. Mem. ABA (mem. standing com. on environ. law 2000—), Fla. Bar Assn. (chmn. environ., land use law sect. 1988-89), Phi Beta Kappa, Phi Kappa Phi, Omicron Delta Kappa, Phi Alpha Delta, Fla. Blue Key. Office: Holland & Knight PO Box 1526 200 S Orange Ave Ste 2600 Orlando FL 32801-3453

SIMS, TERRE LYNN, insurance company executive; b. Madison, Wis., Dec. 26, 1951; d. Roy Charles and Ruth Marie (McCloskey) Pierstorff; m. Gary Peter Laufenberg, Feb. 15, 1969 (div.); children: Amie, Monte, Tawna; m. Perry Allen Sims, May 3, 1994 (dec. Aug. 2000). Sales agt. Bankers Life and Casualty, Madison, 1977-80, asst. mgr., 1981-84, br. mgr. Peoria, 1984-91; co-owner Complete Ins. Svcs., Inc., Madison, Wis., 1991—; owner, operator Ohio Tavern, 1993—; co-owner Nu Brick Inn Bar and Grill, 2000—01. Office: 4521 Stein Ave Madison WI 53714-1731

SIMS, THOMAS AUBURN, retired shipbuilding company executive; b. Little Rock, Oct. 20, 1925; s. Thomas Alexander and Evie Jane (Riche) S.; m. Ruby Pearl Graham, Oct. 6, 1946; children: Gloria Jean, Judy Ann, Janet Lea. AA, East Central Jr. Coll., 1948; BS, U. Md., 1957; MBA, Babson Coll., 1962. Commd. 2d lt. U.S. Army, 1949, advanced through grades to lt. col., retired, 1967; asst. to purchasing agt. Ingalls Shipbuilding, Inc., Pascagoula, Miss., 1968-69, purchasing mgr., 1970-77, dir. procurement, 1978-93. Mem. Gov. of Miss. Minority Adv. Bd., Jackson, 1972-75; bd. dirs. Miss. Minority Supplier Devel. Coun., Jackson, 1980-93; deacon, Sunday sch. tchr. 1st Bapt. Ch., Ocean Springs, Miss., 1972—. With USN, 1943-46, PTO. Mem. Nat. Contract Mgmt. Assn. (bd. dirs. 1980-82, mem. coun. fellows 1993), Retired Officers Assn. Avocation: public speaking. Home: 6309 Prado Rd Ocean Springs MS 39564-2210

SIMS, VICTOR DWAYNE, lawyer; b. Middletown, Ohio, Aug. 1, 1959; s. Gerald Clifton and Ethel Ree (Bruce) S. Student, Am. U., 1980; BA, Heidelberg Coll., 1981; JD, Howard U., 1987. Bar: Ohio, 1989; U.S. Dist. Ct. (so. dist.) Ohio, 1990. Congl. intern U.S. Congress, Washington, 1980; fundraiser Telecommunications Rsch. and Action Ctr., 1984; assoc. Leslie I. Gaines & Assoc., Cin., 1989-91; pvt. practice Sims and Assocs., 1991—. Mng. atty. Leslie I. Gaines & Assoc., 1990—; ptnr. Sims and Asmah Law Firm. Author poetry. Mem. ABA, Ohio Bar Assn., Cin. Bar Assn. Avocations: writing, music, current events. Office: Centennial Plaza III #850 895 Central Ave Cincinnati OH 45202

SIMS, WATSON SHADRACK, research executive, journalist; b. Pembroke, Ga., July 9, 1921; s. John Elbert and Reeve (Garrick) S.; m. Elisabeth Sturdivant, Sept. 10, 1948; children: Elisabeth Hollister, Winfield Strickland. BS, Tufts U., 1946; MS, Columbia U., 1947. With AP, N.Y.C., 1947-71; editor Enquirer and News, Battle Creek, Mich., 1971-78, The Home News, New Brunswick, N.J., 1978-86; pres. Comm. Exch. Orgn., Princeton, 1988-93; scholar in comms. The George H. Gallup Internat. Inst., 1996—. Contbr. numerous articles to profl. jours. Bd. visitors Warren Wilson Coll. With USN, 1939-46. Decorated Silver Star, Bronze Star; Nieman fellow Harvard U., 1953. Mem. Overseas Press Club Am., Asheville Racquet Club. Avocations: tennis, fishing, birding. Home: 406 Crowfields Dr Asheville NC 28803-3274 Office: George H Gallup Intl Inst 47 Hulfish St Princeton NJ 08542-3713

SIMS, WILLIAM ARTHUR, orthopedist; b. Jefferson County, Tenn., Mar. 2, 1936; s. William Finlay and Madge Evelyn (Cates) S.; m. Betty Anne Brandon, June 20, 1959; children: Margaret Elizabeth, Sheryl Evelyn, William Arthur, Jr., Lisa Catherine. Degree, U. Tenn., 1958; MD, U. Tenn., Memphis, 1961. Diplomate Am. Bd. Orthopaedic Surgery. Rotating intern City of Memphis Hosp., 1961-62; surgical resident Bapt. Mem. Hosp., Memphis, 1962-63; resident in orthopaedics Campbell Clin., 1966; team physician Decatur (Ala.) H.S., 1972—95. Guest lectr. Calhoun C.C., 1980—; bd. dirs. Decatur Gen. Hosp. Found.; spkr. Decatur's Outreach Med. Program. Presenter seminars and profl. socs. Founder, bd. dirs. Nat. Com. for Quality Orthopaedic Health Care, 1994—; bd. trustees Orthopaedic Rsch. and Edn. Found., 2001—. Capt. U.S. Army, 1962—68. Fellow: Am. Acad. Orthopaedic Surgeons (bd. councilors 1990—96, exec. com. 1994—95, bd. dirs. 1998); mem.: AMA (chmn. orthopedic sect. and caucus 1999—), Orthopaedic Rsch. and Edn. Found. (trustees 2000), Ala. Orthopaedic Soc. (bd. dirs. 1974—96), Ala. Med. Assn., Nat. Rehab. Soc., Clin. Orthopaedic Soc., Am. Orthopaedic Soc. for Sports Medicine, So. Med. Assn., N.Am. Spine Soc. (del. to AMA), Hazbin's Orthopaedic Travel Club (pres. 1994), Lamplighters Orthopaedic Travel Club (pres. 2000), Willis C. Campbell Club (pres. 1993). Methodist. Avocations: hunting, fishing, sailing, tennis, snow skiing. Home: 4107 Indian Hills Rd SE Decatur AL 35603-5105 Office: Decatur Orthopaedic Clinic 1103 16th Ave SE Decatur AL 35601-3595 E-mail: wdocsims@cs.com.

SIMS, WILLIAM RILEY, design and facility management educator, consultant, architect; b. Gulfport, Miss., Dec. 17, 1938; s. William Riley and Hallie Pauline (Mills) S.; m. Jean Lee Booth, June 17, 1962; 1 child, Hallie Jean BArch, U. N.Mex., 1963; MArch, MCP, U. Pa., 1965; PhD, MIT, 1973. Cert. facility mgr. Internat. Facility Mgmt. Assn., 1993. Planner, urban designer Phila. City Planning Commn., 1964; planner, urban designer Wallace McHarg Assocs., Phila., 1965; lectr. dep. city and regional planning U. Calif., Berkeley, 1966-68; asst. prof. dept. urban planning U. Wash., Seattle, 1970-73; assoc. prof. dept. city and regional planning Ohio State U., Columbus, 1973-80; prof., Cornell U., Ithaca, NY, 1980—, chmn. dept. design and environ, analysis, 1980—97, dir. undergrad. studies, 1997—, co-dir. Internat. Facility Mgmt. program N.Y., 1989-93, co-dir. internat. workplace studies program, 1993—. Cons. Columbus, Ohio, 1978-80; prin. Orbit-II Study, Ithaca, 1984—, Becker-Sims Assocs. (formerly Facility Rsch. Assocs.), Ithaca, 1984—. Author: Neighborhoods, 1975, Managing the Reinvented Workplace, 1996, Team Space Strategies: Creating and Managing Environments to Support Teamwork, 1998; (with others) Taos Adobes, 1965; editor (jour.) Design Guidelines from Post Occupancy Evaluation, 1980; U.S. editor Internat. Jour. Facilities Mgmt.; contbr. articles to profl. jours.; mem. publs. bd. Jour. Interior Design Edn. and Research, 1986-89. Trustee Columbus Landmarks Found., 1978-80, IFMA Found., 1997—; mem. bldgs. and properties com. Cornell U. Trustees, Human Ecology Alumni bd. dirs. Cornell U., 2000—; mem. governing bd. Cornell Real Estate Program, 1996—; mem. adv. bd. Cornell Bus. and Tech. Park, 1986-. Fulbright scholar U.S. Inst. Internat. Edn., Norway, 1965-66; Mellon faculty fellow U. Wash., 1969, Ford faculty fellow Ohio State U., 1974 Fellow Internat. Facility Mgrs. Assn. (bd. dirs. 1984-87, cert. and accreditation task forces 1989—); mem. ASTM (chmn. assessing bldg. performance 1988-92), Environ. Design Rsch. Assn., Assn. for Study of Man and Environ. Rels. (editl. bd. 1978-86), Am. Assn. Housing Educators (editl. bd. 1978-85). Home: 735 Ridge Rd Lansing NY 14882-8805 Office: Cornell U Dept Design & Environ Analysis Ithaca NY 14853-4401 E-mail: wrs4@cornell.edu.

SIMS, WILLIAM RONALD, advertising executive; b. Coffeyville, Kans., Jan. 1, 1937; s. William Long and Mary Eloise (Lambe) S.; m. Greta Helene, July 12, 1958; children: Scott, Christopher, Douglas, Mark. BS, Northwestern U., 1958. Account exec. N.W. Ayer, Chgo., 1963-67, Leo Burnett Co., Inc., Chgo., 1967-73, account supr., 1973-76, account dir., 1976-77, sr. v.p., 1977—, retired, 1997; mktg. cons., pres., 1998—. Mktg. cons., pres. Lower Wacker LLC, 1996; writer in field. Active Chgo. Crime Commn. Mem. Chgo. Yacht Club (bd. dirs.), John Evans Club Northwestern U. (chair bd. dirs), Sheridan Shores Yacht Club. Clubs: Chgo. Yacht, Chgo. Athletic Assn. Republican. Presbyterian. Avocations: sailing. Home: 333 Harbour Dr Naples FL 34103-4078 also: Apt 103 333 Harbour Dr Naples FL 34103-4049 E-mail: rgsims@att.net.

SIMS IANNELLI, KIMBERLY, writer; b. Hereford, Tex., Mar. 9, 1964; d. Bob S. and Sue Hess Sims; m. Peter Carmine Iannelli, Sept. 6, 1997; 1 child, Sydney Iannelli. BS, Tex. A&M U., 1986, MPA, 1988, MA, 1999. Legis. aide, com. clk. Tex. Senate, Austin, 1993-95; dir. agr. and conservation policy Office of Gov. George W. Bush, 1995-97; interim exec. dir., sec. Tex. Water Found., 1998-2000; exec. dir. Environ. Edn. Found. Tex., 2000—01. Adj. faculty South Tex. C.C., McAllen, Tex., 2001—. Dir. Tex. Women's Alliance, Austin, 1995-2001; mem. adv. coun. Hidalgo County Hist. Mus., Edinburg, Tex., 2000-2001; dir. Friends of Wildlife Corridor, McAllen, 2001. Mem. Tex. Agrl. Lifetime Leadership, Jr. League of McAllen, Orgn. Women Execs., Daus. of the King. Episcopalian. Avocations: travel, fine dining, reading, hiking, scrapbooking.

SIMS-MCCALLUM, ROSALYN PATRICE, pharmacist; b. Detroit, June 16, 1968; d. William R. and Edna M. Sims; m. Anthony L. McCallum, Aug. 19, 1995; children: Christopher, Alicia. BA, Emory U., 1989; PharmD, Mercer-So. Sch. Pharmacy, 1993. Lic. pharmacist, Mich. Pharmacy technician North Fulton Regional Med. Ctr., Alpharetta, Ga., 1990-92, Egleston Children's Hosp., Atlanta, 1992-93; pharmacy practice resident Harper Hosp., Detroit, 1993-94; staff pharmacist Children's Hosp. of Mich., 1994-97, clin. pharmacy specialist in pediat. hematology/oncology, 1997—. Mem. Alpha Kappa Alpha. Avocations: reading, movies, travel, piano. Office: Children's Hosp Mich Pharmacy 3901 Beaubien Detroit MI 48201 E-mail: rsims_mccallum@hotmail.com.

SIMSON, BEVLYN, artist; b. Columbus, Ohio, Sept. 9, 1917; d. Amon and Fannie Florence (Gilbert) Thall; m. Theodore Richard Simson, Mar. 25, 1938; children: Sherran Blair, Douglas A. BFA, Ohio State U., 1969, MFA, 1972. Author, artist Prints and Poetry, 1969. One woman shows include J.B. Speed Art Mus., Louisville, 1970, Huntington Gallery, Columbus, Ohio, 1970, 73, United Christian Ctr., Columbus, 1970, Bodley Gallery, N.Y., 1971, 74, Gilman Galleries, Chgo., 1971, Gallery 200, Columbus, 1972, Hopkins Hall Gallery, Ohio State U., Columbus, 1972, Meth. Theol Sch., Deleware, Ohio, 1973, Columbus Public Lib., 1973, Garfinkels, Washington, 1973, City Hall, Mayor's Office, Columbus, 1974, 82, Capital U., Bexley, Ohio, 1977, Hillel Found., Ohio State U., 1978, Columbus Tech. Inst., 1979, Springfield (Ohio) Art Mus., 1980, Peace Luth. Ch., Gahanna, Ohio, 1981, Franklin U. Gallery, Columbus, 1981, Columbus Mus. Art Collectors Gallery, 1983; exhibited in juried and invitational shows at Columbus Mus. Art-Ohio Art League, 1968, 70, 71, 73, 74, 75, 77, 78, 79, 80, 86, Ohio Statehouse and State Office Tower, Columbus, 1968-78, Battelle Meml. Inst., Columbus, 1969-73, 75, 78, 81-82, Schumacher Gallery, Capital U., Columbus, 1969-85, 87, 88, Salles d'Exposition, Paris, 1969, Am. Cultural Ctr., Kyoto, Japan, J.B. Speed Art Mus. Collector's Gallery, Louisville, 1970-85, Studio San Guiseppe, Mt. St. Joseph Coll., Cin., 1971, Silver Anniversary Coll. Arts, 2d Biennial Alumni Exhbn., Hopkins Hall Gallery, 1972, 2nd Internat. Art Exhbn., Paramaribo, Serinam, 1974, Mansfield (Ohio) Art Ctr., 1971, Collector's Showroom, Chgo., 1971-82, Gov.'s MansionState of Ohio, 1972, 74, Western Ill. U., 1972, Albatross Gallery, Rome, 1972, Palazzo Dell Exprizioni, Rome, 1972, Place-Allrich Gallery, San Francisco, 1973-75, Chautauqua Assn., N.Y., 1973, Butler Inst. Am. Art, Youngtown, Ohio, 1973, 76, Huntington Gallery, Columbus, 1973, 74, Gallery 200, Columbus, 1972-76, Columbus C. of C., 1974, 75, Zanesville (Ohio) Art Ctr., 1976, Columbus Inst. Contemporary Art, 1978, Nationwide Plaza Gallery, Columbus, 1980, Franklin U., Columbus, 1980, Ohio State U., 1993, Ohio Art League, 1987, Jeffrey Mansion, Bexley, Ohio, 1996, 10th Ann. Women Artists Expo Seal of Ohio Girl Scout Coun., Inc. Columbus, 1996, Financial Group Gallery, Worthington, Ohio, 1997, Ohio Art League, 1997, 4th Hall Gallery, Ohio State U., 1997, Concourse Gallery, Upper Arlington, Ohio, 1998, 13th Ann. Women Artists Expo Art in The Nation Wide Atrium, Columbus, Ohio, 1999, Bexley (Ohio) Art League, Jeffrey Mansion, 2000;(Ohio) Art League Mem. Curated Exhbn., Structure/Consequences, 1997, Fourth Biennial Alumni Exhbn.:ReSiDivist, Hopkins Hall Gallery, Ohio State U., 1997, Concourse Gallery, Arlington Ohio, 1998, Bexley Art League, Precision Concepts, Dublin, Ohio, 1999, Art in the Atrium, Columbus, Ohio, 1999, Art on Main Street, Schumacher Gallery, 2002; represented in permanent collections Columbus Mus. Arts, J.B. Speed Art Mus., Louisville, Capital U., Bexley, Fordham U., N.Y.C., Kyoto City U. Fine Arts, Springfield (Ohio) Art Mus., Tyler (Tex.) Mus. Art, Wichita (Kans.) Mus. Art, Zanesville (Ohio) Art Ctr., Ohio State U., Columbus, Meth. Theol. Sch., Delaware, Ohio, Yerke Mortgage Co., Columbus, Marcorp, N.Y., Kresge Co., Detroit, IBM, Columbus, Chase Manhattan Bank, N.Y.C., Chase Bank Ohio, Am. Bancorp., Columbus, Ohio Nat. Bank Plaza, Columbus, Pan Western Life Ins. Co., Columbus, First Investment Co., Columbus, Children's Hosp., Phila., Franklin County Crippled Children's Ctr., Columbus, Zenith East, N.Y.C., First Cmty. Bank, Columbus, First City Bank, Columbus, Ohio, Ronald McDonald House, Columbus, Columbia Gas of Ohio, Columbus, Midland Title Security Co., Columbus, Huntington Nat. Bank Ctr., Columbus, Lehman Bros., N.Y.C., Columbus Sch. for Girls, Grand Prix Assocs., Inc., Columbus, Grant Hosp. Med Ctr., Columbus, Libr. and Rsch. Ctr. Nat. Mus. Women in Arts, Washington, D.C., Ohio State U. Libr. Rare Books Room Collection, Laredo (Tex.) Pub. Libr.; represented in private collections. Mem. Nat. League Am. Pen Women, Nat. Artists Equity Assn., Bexley Art League, Columbus Mus. Art, Ohio Art League (bd. dirs. 1965-96, treas., sec., pres. 1977), Ohio State U. Alumni Assn., Pres.'s Club (Ohio State U.), Winding Hollow Country Club, Phi Sigma Sigma. Avocations: golf, theater, symphony, travel. Studio: Bevlyn Simson Studio 4300 E Broad St 1st Cmty Bank Bldg Columbus OH 43213-1243 E-mail: trsimson@netwalk.com.

SIMSON, JO ANNE, anatomy and cell biology educator; b. Chgo., Nov. 19, 1936; d. Kenneth Brown and Helen Marjorie (Pascoe) Valentine; m. Arnold Simson, June 1961 (div.); 1 child, Maria; m. Michael Smith, Nov. 10, 1971 (div.); children: Elisabeth Smith, Briana Smith. BA, Kalamazoo Coll., 1959; MS, U. Mich., 1961; PhD, SUNY, Syracuse, 1969. Postdoctoral fellow Temple U. Health Sci. Ctr., Phila., 1968-70; asst. prof. Med. U. S.C., Charleston, 1970-76, assoc. prof., 1976-83, prof. anatomy and cell biology, 1983-96; prof. emerita, 1997—; with overseas program U. Md., 1999—2001. Featured in Smithsonian exhibit, Sci. in Am. Life, 1994—. Contbr. articles to profl. jours.; author short stories and poems. Active adult edn. Unitarian Ch., Charleston, 1973-75, social action, 1990-92. Grantee NSF, 1959-60, NIH, 1966-67, 72-87, 91-95. Mem. Am. Assn. Anatomists, Am. Soc. Cell Biology, Histochem. Soc. (sec. 1979-82, exec. com. 1985-89), Fogarty Internat. Fellowship Bioctr. (Basel, Switzerland, 1987-88), Amnesty Internat. (newsletter editor Group 168 1982-86), Phi Beta Kappa. Home: 1760 Pittsford Cir Charleston SC 29412-4110 *In the end, it is only what a person has created and given to the rest of the world that endures.*

SIMS-PERSON, LEANN MICHELLE, human resources specialist; b. Ft. Worth, Aug. 14, 1972; d. William Lee and Mildred Ann (Martin) Sims; m. Marc Anthony Person; children: Austin Person. BBA, Tex. Christian U., 1994; MBA, Tex. Wesleyan U., 2000. Cmty. devel. officer JPMorgan Chase, Ft. Worth, 1994—2000, human resources recruiter Dallas, 2000—. Composer Christian music. Named one of 50 Leaders of the Future, Ebony Mag., 1994; recipient Doer's award, City of Ft. Worth, 1997. Mem.: Minority Leaders and Citizens Coun. (v.p. 1996—98), The Links Inc., Delta Sigma Theta (life; asst. treas. 1994—98). United Methodist. Avocations: exercising, Bible studies, travel. Home: 6200 Brentwood Dr Fort Worth TX 76112 Office: JPMorgan Chase & Co Ste 720 2200 Ross Ave Dallas TX 75201 Office Fax: 214-965-2928. Business E-Mail: leann.sims@chase.com.

SIMUN, PATRICIA BATES, education educator, consultant; b. Pitts., Apr. 20, 1931; d. A.E. Griffith and Mary Effa (Casey) Bates; m. Richard Vincent Simun, Dec. 31, 1961; children: Mary Bates-Alt, Ann Eugenia Simun-Park. BS in Edn., W.Va. U., 1952; MA, U. Pitts., 1962, PhD, 1967. Cert. tchr., Calif., Pa., W.Va.; cert. counselor, Pa. Tchr. Avonworth Union Sch. Dist., Ben Avon, Pa., 1955-57; tchr. placement dir. Carnegie-Mellon U., 1957-61; rsch. asst. U. Pitts., 1961-62, rsch. assoc., 1962-63; chair ednl. founds. Calif. State U., L.A., 1983-84, assoc. chair adminstrn., counseling and founds. dept., 1985, prof. edn., 1967-91, dir. Costa Rica travel study, 1988-98, prof. emerita, 1991—. Vis. disting. prof. Universidad Autonoma, Guadalajara, Mex., summer 1975; cons., evaluation project sup[001b]port Calif. State U./L.A. Unified Sch. Dist., 1992-95; cons., evaluation integration L.A. Unified Sch.Dist., 1981-91; cons. ACLU, L.A., 1976-80; participant Alternative Edn. Exch., 1975, Internat. Options in Pub. Edn., Pasadena, Calif., 1975, others; discussion leader Am. Edn. Rsch. Assn. evaluation conf., San Francisco, 1977; speaker in field. Editor Excellence Through Equity, 1984-87; contbr. articles to profl. jours. Bd. dirs. Cmty. Child Care, Inc., L.A., 1985-88; mem. L.A. High Cmty. Adv. Voun., 1980-84; advisor Inst. Tchr. Leadership, L.A., 1978-80; mem. edn. com. Cmty. Rels. Conf. So. Calif., L.A., 1980-84. Recipient Cert. of Merit Human Rels. Commn., L.A., 1978, Cert. of Outstanding Svc. So. Poverty Law Ctr., 1984, Cert. of Appreciation L.A. Unified Sch. Dist., 1977, Outstanding Svc. award Mid-City Alternative Sch., 1982. Mem. Am. Ednl. Rsch. Assn. (SIG com. chair 1983-84, sec. 1984-89), Calif. Edn. Rsch. Assn., Phi Lambda Theta, Kappa Delta Pi, Phi Beta Delta. Avocations: hiking, stamp collecting, reading. Home: 1019 S Longwood Ave Los Angeles CA 90019-1755 Office: Calif State U 5151 State University Dr Los Angeles CA 90032-4226 E-mail: psimun@pacbell.net.

SINAGRA, JACK G. state legislator; b. Queens, N.Y., Mar. 18, 1950; m. Eileen Cook, 1978; children: Jacklyn, Alexandra, Patrick. Grad., Emporia Coll., 1972. Mem. N.J. Senate, Dist. 18, Trenton, 1992—2002; chmn. Port Author. Board of NY and NJ, 2001—. V.p. Turtle & Hughes, Linden, N.J. Mem. Assn. for a Better Middlesex County. Office: 225 Park Ave S New York NY 10003*

SINAI, ALLEN LEO, economist, educator; b. Detroit, Apr. 4, 1939; s. Joseph and Betty Paula (Feinberg) S.; m. Lee Davis Etsten, June 23, 1963; children: Lauren Beth, Todd Michael AB, U. Mich., 1961; MA, Northwestern U., 1966, PhD, 1969. From asst. prof. to assoc. prof. econs. U. Ill., Chgo., 1966-75; chmn. fin. info. group, chief fin. economist Data Resources, Lexington, Mass., 1971-83; chief economist, mng. dir. Lehman Bros. and Shearson Lehman Bros. Inc., N.Y.C., 1983-87; chief economist, exec. v.p. The Boston Co. Inc., 1988-93; pres., CEO The Boston Co. Econ. Advisors Inc., Boston and N.Y.C., 1988-93, Econ. Advisors, Inc., Boston, 1993-96; mng. dir., chief global economist, dir. global econs. Lehman Bros., N.Y.C., 1993-96; pres., CEO, chief global economist Decision Econs., Boston, N.Y., London, Tokyo, 1996—; chief global economist, vice-chmn. The WEFA Group, 1997-2000; global chief economist, exec. v.p. Global Insight, Inc., Lexington, Mass., 2001—. Cons. Laural Cons., Lexington and Evanston, Ill., 1966; vis. assoc. prof. econs. and fin. MIT, Cambridge, 1975-77; adj. prof. econs. Boston U., 1977-78, 81-83, NYU, 1984-88; adj. prof. econs. and fin. Lemberg Sch., Brandeis U., 1988-95; vis. faculty Sloan Sch., MIT, 1989-91; bd. dirs. Boston Pvt. Fin. Holdings, Inc. Contbr. articles to profl. jours. and books. Mem. reducing the fed. budget deficit task force Roosevelt Ctr., Washington, 1984; bd. govs. Com. on Developing Am. Capitalism, 1984-96, chmn., 1990-95; bd. economists Time Mag., 1991—. Recipient Alumnus Merit award Northwestern U., 1985 Mem. Am. Econ. Assn., Econometric Soc., Ea. Econs. Assn. (v.p. 1988-89, pres. 1990-91, Otto Eckstein prize 1988, fellow 1994), Western Econ. Assn. (exec. com.), Econometric Soc., Nat. Assn. Bus. Econs. Jewish. Avocations: tennis, skiing. E-mail: asinai@pdeco.com.

SINAISKY, NICHOLAS ALEKSEEVICH, mechanical engineer, researcher, consultant; b. Volgograd, Russia, Aug. 10, 1924; came to U.S., 1992; s. Aleksey Ivanovich and Klavdja Stepanovna (Krasukova) S.; m. Elizaveta Agapovna Kargina, Mar. 16, 1962 (div. Nov. 1984); children: Natalia, Nadezda, Julia; m. Valentina Alekseevna Pilgasova Pokrovskaya, Jan. 16., 1985. BME, Tomsk Poly. U., Russia, 1958; MME, USSR Acad. of Sci., Moscow, 1968; PhD in ME, USSR Acad. of Sci., Novosibirsk, Russia, 1980. Sr. designer combustion Siberian Sci. Rsch. Inst. for Aviation, Novosibirsk, Russia, 1958-60; lead engr. Inst. Theoretical and Applied Physics Siberian Dept. of USSR Acad. Sci., Russia, 1960-62, sci. worker Inst. for Physics and Chem. Russia, 1962-68, sr. rsch. assoc. Inst. for Solid Matter Russia, 1968-74; adj. prof., sr. rsc. assoc. Inst. for Constn. & Clinker, Novosibirsk-Krasnoyarsk, 1974-85; top mgr. in environ. protection Sci. Rsch. Inst. for Energy & Cavitator Enterprise, Baku, Azerbaijan, 1985-92; prin. rschr., cons. Cavitator LLC, Portsmouth, NH, 1992—. Patentee low temperature plasma and cavitation; contbr. numerous articles to Russian and Am. profl. jours. Polit. prisoner, north camps USSR, 1947-50, Kazakhstan, 1950-54. Recipient Vet. of Labour medal Presidium of the Supreme Ct. of the USSR, 1983, Golden medal and diploma 26th Salon Int. of Inventions, Geneva, Switzerland, 1998, Inventors laureate, Russia, 2000; named laureate in ecology Georgia Energo USSR, Tbilisi, 1990, 500 Leaders of Influence Presdl. Seal of Honor, 2001, Outstanding Scientists of 20th and 21st Century, Companion of Honor, Internat. Order of Merit, Am. Medal of Honor, 2002, World Lifetime Achievement award, 2002. Mem.: Assn. Victims Unlawful Polit. Repressions, Libr. Russian Acad. Scis. (hon.). Achievements include work in ballistic missile reentry radiation analysis, demonstrating short wave excitomic decay photoeffect in wide-gap insulators; atomization with atoms/molecules excitation/radiation through plural cumulative shock in spray used by means of cavitator to reduce boiler fouling, NOx/CO/SO2carbon emission and improve fossil fuel saving, including oil, coal-water slurries and orimulsion, coal-water slurries; leader in heavy cavitation assisted oil/orimulsion burning for power generation by North American, European, and Russian electric utilities. Home and Office: Cavitator LLC 20 Islington St #205 Portsmouth NH 03801-4242 Fax: 603-436-9720.

SINAY, HERSHEL DAVID, publishing executive; b. Chgo., Mar. 15, 1938; s. Irving Paul and Gertrude (Drucker) S. BA, U. So. Calif., 1960. Telecom. and Cinema account exec. Wall St. Jour., L.A., 1961-63; account exec. R.J. Friedman Assocs., 1963-66; dir. sales Performing Arts Mag., 1966-72; pub. East, West Network, 1972-79, 85-87; pres., pub. Calif. Bus. Mag., 1979-85; pub., editor-in-chief Ranch & Coast Mag., DelMar, Calif., 1987-88; pub. Am. Film. Mag., L.A., 1988-91; pres. Project Mktg. Custom Publ. Specialists divsn. Sinay Comm., Inc., 1991—. Pub. Am. Cinema Editors Tribute Program, 1993-97, Billboard Music Awards Tribute Book, 1993, 1st Ann. Thurgood Marshall Lifetime Achievement Award Tribute Book, NAACP Legal Def. and Ednl. Fund, 1993, 96. Recipient 32 Maggie awards Western Pub. Assn., 1979-2002, Pub Am. Film Inst. Life Achievement awards Tribute Book, 1991-2002. Mem. Am. Film Inst., Western Pub. Assn. (v.p., bd. dirs.), L.A. Advt. Club. Avocations: yachting, jogging, gardening, photography. Office: 810 S Hauser Blvd Los Angeles CA 90036-4726 E-mail: publish@attbi.com.

SINAY, JOSEPH, retail executive; b. Chgo., Dec. 5, 1920; s. Hyman and Ella S.; m. Ruth Milman, Mar. 7, 1961; 1 dau., Elise Sinay Spilker. Student, Herzl Jr. Coll., 1939. Gen. mgr. Fanchon & Marco Theatres, L.A., 1943-54; v.p., founder Interstate United, Chgo., 1953-56; ptnr. Josam Investment Co., L.A., 1956-97, Sinay Co. L.L.C., L.A., 1997—; pres., CEO R B Industries Inc., 1956-89, also chmn. bd. dirs., cons.; chmn. bd. dirs. Gorian Sinay Land Co., Inc., 1997—. Bd. dirs. Am. Acad. Dramatic Arts; pres. Variety Clubs Internat., 1985-87; gen. chmn. United Jewish Welfare L.A., 1976; pres. We. region Am. Friends Hebrew U., 1980; Calif. fin. chmn. Muskie for Pres., 1972; trustee Idyllwild Arts Found., 1968-73; bd. dirs. Constl. Rights Found., 1973-78. Mem. Nat. Home Furnishing Assn. Jewish. Office: Sinay Co LLC 1801 Century Park E Los Angeles CA 90067-2302

SINAY, TONY, economist, educator; b. Istanbul, Turkey, Aug. 1, 1963; s. Uluer and Zarif Sinay; m. Julie Swanston; children: Justin, Jack. PhD, St. Louis U., 1994. Asst. prof. U. Scranton, Pa., 1996—99; assoc. prof. Des Moines U., 1999—. Assoc. dir. healthcare mgmt. Des Moines U., 2001—. Contbr. articles to profl. jours. Fellow Accrediting Commn. Edn. for Health Svcs. Adminstrn., Washington, 2000—02. Recipient cert. of appreciation, State of Mo., 1994. Mem.: Healthcare Fin. Mgmt. Assn. Home: 1216 57th Pl West Des Moines IA 50266 Office: Des Moines U 3200 Grand Ave Des Moines IA 50312 Office Fax: 515-271-1614. Personal E-mail: tonysinay@aol.com. Business E-Mail: tony.sinay@dmu.edu.

SINCLAIR, ALASTAIR JAMES, geology educator; b. Hamilton, Ont., Can., Aug. 1, 1935; s. Burton Leslie and Grace (Isherwood) S.; m. Elizabeth Mary Sylvia Hill, June 13, 1964; children: Alison Trevena, Fiona Tamsin. BS, U. Toronto, 1957, MS, 1958; PhD, U. B.C., 1964. Asst. prof. U. Wash., Seattle, 1962-64, U. B.C., Vancouver, 1964-68, assoc. prof., 1968-74, prof., 1974-98, prof. emeritus, 1999—, head dept. geol. scis., 1985-90, dir. Geol. Engring., 1979-80, 81-82, 92-98. Pres. Sinclair Cons. Ltd., Vancouver, 1980—. Contbr. numerous articles to profl. jours. Fellow Killam Sr., 1990—91. Fellow Geol. Assn. Can. (treas. mineral deposits divsn. 1978-89, Disting. Svc. award 2001), Soc. Econ. Geologists; mem. Assn. Profl. Engrs. B.C., Internat. Assn. Math. Geologists, Assn. Exploration Geochemists (councillor 1992-96), Can. Inst. Mining, Metallurgy and Petroleum (life, disting. lectr. 1999-2000, Robert Elver award 1991), Geol. Soc. Brazil (hon. mem. sci.-tech. commn. geochemistry 1982), Brazilian Geochem. Soc. (hon. 1987). Avocations: classical music, skiing, golf. Home: 2972 W 44th Ave Vancouver BC Canada V6N 3K4 Office: U BC Dept Earth and Ocean Scis Vancouver BC Canada V6T 1Z4

SINCLAIR, BRIAN ROBERT, architect, educator; b. Calgary, Alta., Can., June 29, 1957; came to U.S., 1998; s. David Hickey and Evelyn Irene Sinclair; m. Lorraine Anne Marshall; children: Lauren, Brianne, Brennen. BSc in Psychology, U. Calgary, 1979, MSc in Psychology, 1981, MEd in Arch., 1987. Pres. Uptown Ave. Design, Calgary, 1983-98; architect Pendergast Group Architects, 1986-89; assoc. Arthur Erickson, AWA Architects, Vancouver, B.C., Can., 1989-92; asst. prof. U. Man., Winnipeg, Can., 1992-96, assoc. prof. Can., 1996-98, dir. CADLAB Can., 1993-98; prof., chair dept. arch. Ball State U., Muncie, Ind., 1998—. Cons. Sinclair Cons., Winnipeg, 1992; adj. prof. arch. U. B.C., Vancouver, 1990-92; mem. Ctr. Plan adv. bd. City of Winnipeg, 1992-98; bd. dirs. Archtl. Rsch. Ctrs. Consortium, Washington, 1997—, Intersymp, Baden-Baden, Germany; design and planning advisor Nepal Engring. Coll. and Inst. Engring., Kathmandu, 1998—, King Mongkut U., Bangkok, Thailand. Sect. author Frank Lloyd Wright project Digital UnBuilt, 1999; editor procs. in field; contbr. articles to profl. publs. Pres. Can. Assn. Computers in Design Edn., Toronto, Ont., Can., 1996-98; devel. cons. Can. Internat. Devel. Agy., Ottawa, 1996-98; design sector cons. Human Resource Devel. Can., Ottawa, 1995-98; mem. continuing edn. com. Man. Assn. Architects, 1992-98. Recipient Best Paper award Internat. Inst. Advanced Studies, UN Edn., Sci. and Culture Orgn., 1997, Outstanding Scholarly Contbn. award, 1997, Culture of Peace Disting. Scholar award, 1998, Millennium medal and award, 2000. Mem. AIA, Royal Archtl. Inst. Can., Environ. Design Rsch. Assn., Assn. for Computer Aided Design in Arch., Assn. for Computer Aided Design in Arch., Assn. Collegiate Schs. of Arch. (councilor 1992-98, chair Counterbalance, west ctrl. conf.), Archtl. Rsch. Ctrs. Consortium (bd. dirs. 1997—), Soc. Nepalese Architects. Office: Ball State U Dept Arch Ab 402 B Muncie IN 47306-0001

SINCLAIR, CAROLE, publisher, editor, author; b. Haddonfield, N.J., May 13, 1942; d. Earl Walter and Ruth (Sinclair) Dunham; 1 child, Wendy. Student, U. Florence, Italy, 1963; BA in Polit. Sci., Bucknell U. 1964. Advt. copywriter BBD&O Advertising, N.Y.C., 1966-67; sales promotion mgr. Macmillan Pub. Co., 1967-71; mktg. mgr. Doubleday & Co., Inc., 1972-74, promotion dir., 1974-76, advt. mgr., sales and promotion, chmn. mktg. com., 1976-80; v.p. mktg., editorial dir. Davis Pubs., 1980-83; founder, pub., editorial dir., sr. v.p. Sylvia Porter's Personal Fin. Mag., 1983-90; pres. The Sylvia Porter Orgn., Inc., 1980-91; founder, pres. Sinclair Media Inc., 1990—. Mktg. dir. Denver Pub. Inst., summers 1975-78; lectr. Columbia U. Bus. Sch. and Sch. of Journalism, 1976; host nationally syndicated TV show, Sylvia Porter's Money Tips, syndicated daily radio show, Sylvia Porter's Personal Fin. Report, audio cassette series on fin. topics. Author: Keys for Women Starting and Owning a Business, 1991, Keys to Women's Basic Professional Needs, 1991, When Women Retire, 1992; contbg. editor Pushcart Prize, 1977; contbr. The Business of Publishing, 1980. Renaissance Art Program fellow, Florence, Italy, 1963; White House intern, 1962. Mem. Women's Forum, Intercorp. Communications Group, Mag. Pubs.' Assn., Advt. Women in N.Y., Spence Sch. Parent's League. Clubs: Pubs. Lunch. Presbyterian. Avocation: boating.

SINCLAIR, DAISY, advertising executive, casting director; b. Perth Amboy, N.J., Mar. 22, 1941; d. James Patrick and Margaret Mary (McAniff) Nieland; m. James Pratt Sinclair, May 25, 1978; children: Duncan, Gibbons. BA, Caldwell Coll., 1962. Jr. copywriter Young & Rubican, N.Y.C., 1962-64; various positions in casting dept. Ogilvy & Mather, 1964-90, sr. v.p., dir. casting, 1990—. Mem.: Drama League N.Y. (3d v.p. 1982—), Am. Assn. Advt. (talent agt. com. 1972—), N.Y. Yacht Club, Union Club, Tuxedo Club, Chapaquoit Yacht Club, Edgartown Yacht Club, Knickerbocker Greys (pres.). Republican. Episcopalian. Avocations: opera, theater, sailing, skiing. Home: 4 E 95th St New York NY 10128-0705

SINCLAIR, DAVID GRANT, accountant; b. London, Feb. 12, 1948; s. Leslie and Zena Sinclair; m. Susan Carol Merkin, June 7, 1970; children: Alexander, Julian, Olivia. Sr. ptnr. Sinclair Silverman, London, 1972—; chmn. Motivision Worldwide PLC, 1993—2001, Investment Ventures Plc, 2000—; dir. Motivision Am., Inc., North Miami, Fla., 1996—2000, Auditfree Ltd., London, 1991—, Economic Group Plc., 1995—, Interest Plus Plc, 2001—; chmn. Sinclair Silverman Corp. Fin. Ltd., London, 2001—. Forensic acct., London, 1978—. Fellow Inst. Chartered Accts. Jewish. Office: Roman House 296 Golders Green Rd London NW11 9PT England E-mail: dgs@sinclairsilverman.com.

SINCLAIR, DAVID MACOWAN, marine surveyor; b. Phila., Aug. 6, 1928; s. John Stephens Sinclair and Mary Hewes (Biddle) Falconer; m. Susan Widmann, July 14, 1956; children: Timothy(dec.) , Craig, Margot. BA, Amherst Coll., 1946; MBA, NYU, 1957. Marine surveyor Theodore D. Helprin Inc., N.Y.C., 1950—. Sgt. USMC, 1951—53. Mem.: Nat. Assn. Marine Surveyors, Cruising Club Am., Noroton Yacht Club (commodore). Avocation: sailing. Home: 140 5 Mile River Rd Darien CT 06820-6236 Office: Theodore D Helprin Inc PO Box 153 Norwalk CT 06853

SINCLAIR, GLENN BRUCE, mechanical engineering educator, researcher; b. Auckland, New Zealand, Mar. 7, 1946; came to U.S., 1969; s. Alan John and Piri (Vincent) S.; m. Della Jane Sutton, Dec. 23, 1972; children— Heidi Lee, Heather Ann, Hillary Colleen, Christopher Alan B.Sc., U. Auckland, 1967, B.E., 1969; PhD, Calif. Inst. Tech., 1972. J. Willard Gibbs instr. mech. engring. Yale U., New Haven, 1972-74; lectr. U. Auckland, 1974-77; asst. prof. Carnegie-Mellon U., Pitts., 1977-80, assoc. prof., 1980-82, prof., 1982-2000, head, 1986-92; vis. prof. Cambridge U., England, 1981; prof., chmn. dept. mech. engring. La. State U., Baton Rouge, 2000—. Research scientist Dept. Sci. and Indsl. Research, Wellington, New Zealand, 1968-69; summer prof. Pratt & Whitney, Hartford, Conn., 1978, Aircraft Corp., West Palm Beach, Fla., 1979; cons. in field. Contbr. articles to profl. jours. Fulbright scholar, 1969-72. Mem. Am. Acad. Mechanics Office: La State U Dept Mech Engring Baton Rouge LA 70803

SINCLAIR, JAMES BURTON, retired plant pathology educator, consultant; b. Chgo., Dec. 21, 1927; s. James Lawrence Sinclair and Helen Marie (Thompson) Owens. BSc, Lawrence U., 1951; PhD, U. Wis., 1955. Grad. rsch. asst. U. Wis., Madison, 1951-55, grad. rsch. assoc., 1955-56; from asst. prof. to assoc. prof. La. State U., Baton Rouge, 1956-65, prof., 1965-68, adminstrv. asst. to chancellor, 1966-68; prof. U. Ill., Urbana, 1968-96, dir. nat. soybean rsch. lab., 1992-96; ret. Co-author: Basic Plant Pathology Methods, 1985, 1995, Principles of Seed Pathology, 1987, 1997, Anatomy and Physiology of Diseased Plants, 1991; contbr. articles to profl. jours. Pres. bd. dirs. W.R. and C.V. Spurlock Mus., Urbana, 1998-2000; sec., editor Greater Cmty. AIDS Project, 1996-2000. Sgt. U.S. Army, 1946-47. Recipient Soybean Rsch. Recognition award Am. Soybean Assn., 1983, Prodn. Rsch. award, 1989, Paul A. Funk award, 1984, Disting. Svc. award USDA, 1988, Disting. Svc. award Phytopathol. Soc. (north ctrl. divsn.), 1991, Rsch. award Land of Lincoln Soybean Assn., 1992. Fellow Am. Phytopathol. Soc., Nat. Acad. of Scis./India; mem. Ill. Crop Improvement Assn. (hon.), Am. Soc. Agronomy (hon.), Rotary (chmn. internat. com. Savoy chpt. 1990-91, v.p. 1991-93, pres. 1993-94). Home: 408 Arbours Dr Savoy IL 61874-9752 E-mail: jsinclai@uiuc.edu.

SINCLAIR, ROBERT DELANO, economics educator; b. Kingston, Jamaica, Apr. 26, 1969; s. Lyphroy Martin S. and Dorothy Merlene. BA in Econs. and Maths., N.Y., 1993; MA in Econs., Stanford U., 1998, PhD in Econs., 1999. Asst. to agronomist Cocoa Industry Bd. and Farms, Jamaica, 1986—89; tchg. asst. macroecons. dept. econs. Stanford U., 1994—99, rsch. asst. dept. econs., 1995—98, tchg. asst. coord., 1998—99, instr. dept. econs., 1999; asst. prof. dept. econs. Syracuse (N.Y.) U., 1999—. R.I.S.E. mentor and tutor Menlo-Atherton (Calif.) High Sch., 1993—98; presenter in field. Contbr. articles. Scholar Bertram Field Scholarship in Econ. Forecasting, 1993—94. Mem.: Golden Key. Office: Syracus U Dept Econs 1100 D Eggers Hall Syracuse NY 13244-1090 E-mail: rdsincla@maxwell.syr.edu.

SINCLAIR, ROLF MALCOLM, retired physicist; b. N.Y.C., Aug. 15, 1929; s. Nathan and Elizabeth (Stout) S.; m. Margaret Lee Andrews, June 13, 1959 (div. 1978); children: Elizabeth Ann, Andrew Caisley; m. Allyn J. Miner, July 29, 1991 (div. 1998). BS, Calif. Inst. Tech., 1949; MA (Reade scholar), Rice U., 1951, PhD (Inst. fellow), 1954. Physicist, Westinghouse Research Labs., 1953-56; vis. scientist U. Hamburg, Germany, 1956-57, U. Paris, 1957-58, U.K. Atomic Energy Authority, Culham Lab., Eng., 1965-66; research physicist Princeton U., 1958-69; program dir. NSF, Washington, 1969-98; ret., 1998. Mem. Solstice Project, 1978-91; NSF rep. U.S. Solar Eclipse Expdn. to Can., 1979, to India, 1980. Amundsen-Scott South Pole Sta., 1995, 96; Disting. vis. prof. N.Mex. State U., 1985; vis. prof. No. Ariz. U., 1986; vis. sci. Los Alamos Nat. Lab., 1988-89, guest scientist, 1989—; sr. advisor Ctr. Sci. Studies, Valdivia, Chile, 1999—; cons. to industry, 1960-69, 98—; sr. cons. Centro de Estudios Cientificos, Chile, 1999—. Fellow Am. Phys. Soc. (panel pub. affairs 1976-77, nominating com. 1988-90), AAAS (sec. physics sect. 1972-2000, mem. coun. 1972-73, nominating com. 1982-83); mem. Soc. Am. Archaeology, Sigma Xi. Achievements include research and publs. on physics, archaeoastronomy, tech. and instrumentation. Home: 7508 Tarrytown Rd Chevy Chase MD 20815-6027 E-mail: rolf@santafe.edu.

SINCLAIR, SARA VORIS, health facility administrator, nurse; b. Kansas City, Mo., Apr. 13, 1942; d. Franklin Defenbaugh and Inez Estelle (Figenbaum) Voris; m. James W. Sinclair, June 13, 1964; children: Thomas James, Elizabeth Kathleen, Joan Sara. BSN, UCLA, 1965. RN, Utah; lic. health care facility adminstr.; cert. health care adminstr. Staff nurse UCLA Med. Ctr. Hosp., 1964-65; charge nurse Boulder (Colo.) Meml. Hosp., 1966, Boulder (Colo.) Manor Nursing Home, 1974-75, Four Seasons Nursing Home, Joliet, Ill., 1975-76; dir. nursing Home Health Agy of Olympia Fields, 1977-79, Sunshine Terr. Found., Inc., Logan, Utah, 1980, asst. adminstr., 1980-81, adminstr., 1981-93; dir. divsn. health systems improvement Utah Dept. Health, Salt Lake City, 1993-97; CEO Sunshine Terr. Found., 1997—. Long term care profl. and tech. adv. com. Joint Commn. on Accreditation Healthcare Orgns., Chgo., 1987—91, chmn., 1990—91; adj. lectr. Utah State U., 1991—93, search com. for dir. major gifts, 2001; adj. clin. faculty Weber State U., Ogden, Utah; moderator radio program Healthwise Sta. KUSU-FM, 1985—93; del. White House Conf. on Aging, 1995; chmn. Utah Dept. of Health's Ethics, Instl. Rev. Bd. Com., 1995—97, Utah Dept. Health Rist Mgmt. Com., 1995—97; exec. com. Utah Long Term Care Coalition, 1995, chmn., 1997—2001; oversight com. and long term care tech. adv. group Utah Health Policy Commn., 1996—2000, Health Insight Utah State Coun., 1996—2001; adj. vol. faculty U. Utah Gerontology Ctr., 1997—; moderator Living Well Longer Utah Pub. Radio, 1998—; bd. dirs. Bridgerland Area Tech. Coll., Logan, Logan Regional Hosp., chair quality assurance, 2001—; mem. regional adv. bd. Zions Bank, 2001—; presenter in field. Contbg. author: Associate Degree Nursing and The Nursing Home, 1988; contbr. articles to profl. jours. Deans adv. coun. Coll. Bus. Utah State U., Logan, 1989—91, mem. presdl. search com., 1991—92; chmn., co-founder Cache Cmty. Health Coun., 1985, co-chair, 2000; bd. dirs. Bridgerland Area Tech. Coll., 2001—, Utah Assistive Tech. Found., 2001, vice chair; chmn. bd. Hospice of Cache Valley, Logan, 1986; apptd. chmn. Utah Health Facilities Com., 1989—91; chmn. health and human svcs. subcom. Cache 2010, 1992—93; mem. long term care tech. adv. group oversight com. Utah Health Policy Commn., 1997; dir. Health Insight, 1996; trustee Utah State U., 1997—2001; chmn. Utah State U. Trustee's Acad. Affairs Com., 1999—2001; co-chair Living Well Longer Coun., 1997—, Cache Cmty. Health Coun., 2000—; apptd. Utah State Bd. Regents, 2001; bd. dir. Utah Higher Edn. Assistance Authority, 2002—. Recipient Disting. Svc. award Utah State U., 1989. Fellow: Am. Coll. Health Care Adminstrs. (presenter 1992—93, convocation and edn. coms. 1992—93, v.p. Utah chpt. 1992—94, region IX vice gov. 1994—96, presenter 1995, 1996, bylaws com. 1996—2000, region IX vice gov. 1998—2000, presenter Winter Marketplace 1999, chmn. bylaws com. 1999—2000, chair edn. com. 2000, nominating com. 2000, presenter 2001, 2002, ann. convocations, bd. dirs. 2002—); mem.: Logan Bus. and Profl. Women's Club (pres. 1989, Woman of Achievement award 1982, Woman of Yr. 1982), Utah Gerontol. Soc. (bd. dirs. 1992—93, chmn. nominating com. 1993—94, bd. dirs. 1995—97, chmn. ann. conf. 1996, pres. 1997), Utah Health Care Assn. (pres. 1983—85, treas. 1991—93, pres. 2000—01, Disting. Svc. award 1991, Svc. award for long term care 1996), Am. Health Care Assn. (non-proprietary v.p. 1986—87, region v.p. 1987—89, presenter workshop conv. 1990—93, exec. com. 1993, presenter ann. convocation 1995, 1998—99), Cache C. of C. (pres. 1991, named Total Citizen of Yr. 2002), Rotary (Logan chpt. chair cmty. svc. com. 1989—90, pres. Logan club 1999—2000), Golden Key Nat. Honor Soc. (hon.). Avocations: walking, reading. E-mail: saras@sunshineterrace.com.

SINCLAIR, VIRGIL LEE, JR. judge, writer; b. Canton, Ohio, Nov. 10, 1951; s. Virgil Lee and Thelma Irene (Dunlap) S.; children: Kelly, Shannon; m. Janet Brahler Sinclair. BA, Kent State U., 1973; JD, U. Akron, 1976; postgrad., Case Western Res. U., 1939. Adminstr. Stark County Prosecutor's Office, Canton, 1974-76; mem. faculty Walsh Coll., 1976-78; asst. pros. atty. Stark County, 1976-77; ptnr. Amerman Burt Bones Co. LPA, 1976-91, Buckingham, Doolittle and Burroughs Co., L.P.A., Canton, 1991-95; judge Stark County Common Pleas Ct., 1995—, adminstrv. judge, 1996, presiding judge, 1999. Mem. faculty Ohio Jud. Coll., 1991—, lead faculty, 1998—; mem. legal adviser Mayor's Office, City of North Canton, Ohio, 1978-79; referee Stark County Family Ct., Canton, 1981, Canton Mcpl. Ct., 1991—; spl. referee Canton Mcpl. Ct., 1985-86. Author: Law Enforcement Officers' Guide to Juvenile Law, 1975, Lawy Manual of Juvenile Law, 1976, Handling Capital Punishment Cases, 1998, Ohio Jury Institutions, Capital Punishment Approved, Jury Instructions, 2000; editor: U. Akron Law Rev.; contbr. to Ohio Family Law, 1983, also articles to profl. jours. Mem. North Canton Planning Comm., 1979-82; bd. mgrs. North Canton YMCA, 1976—, Camp Tippecanoe, Ohio, 1981—; profl. adviser Parents Without Partners, 1980—; spl. sep. Stark County Sheriff Dept., 1983—; trustee Palace Theatre Assn., Canton, 1983—. Recipient Disting. Service award U.S. Jaycees, 1984; named to Hall of Distinction, Plain Local Schs., 1999, Jud. Hall of Fame, U. Akron Sch. Law, 2000. Mem. ABA, Ohio Bar Assn., Stark County Bar Assn. (lects. 1984), Ohio Trial Lawyers Assn., Assn. Trial Lawyers Am., Nat. Dist. Attys. Assn., Akron Law Sch. Alumni Assn. (trustee), Jaycees, Elks, Eagles, Masons, Delta Theta Phi (bailiff 1976, nat. key winner 1975-76). Republican. Methodist.

SINCLAIR, WILLIAM DONALD, state legislator, former church official; b. L.A., Dec. 27, 1924; s. Arthur Livingston and Lillian May (Holt) S.; m. Barbara Jean Hughes, Aug. 9, 1952; children: Paul Scott, Victoria Sharon. BA cum laude, St. Martin's Coll., Olympia, Wash., 1975; postgrad., Emory U., 1978-79. Commd. 2d lt. USAAF, 1944; advanced through grades to col. USAF, 1970; served as pilot and navigator Italy, Korea, Vietnam, Japan; ret., 1975; bus. adminstr. 1st United Mth. Ch., Colorado Springs, Colo., 1976-85, Village Seven Presbyn. Ch., 1985-87, Sunrise United Meth. Ch., 1987-89; vice chmn. coun. fin. and adminstrn. Rocky Mountain Conf., United Meth. Ch. U.S.A., 1979-83; mem. Colo. Ho. of Reps., Denver, 1996—, majority whip, 2001—. Bd. dirs. Chins-Up, Colorado Springs, 1983-86; chmn. bd. dirs. Pikes Peak Performing Arts Ctr., 1985-92; pres. Pioneers Mus. Found., 1985—; Rep. candidate for Colo. State Chmn., 1992-93. Decorated Legion of Merit with oak leaf cluster, DFC, Air medal with six oak leaf clusters, Dept. Def. Meritorious Svc. medal, Vietnam Cross of Gallantry with palms; named Legislator of Yr., Colo. Assn. Commerce and Industry, 1998, 1999, Colo. Sheriff's Assn., 2001; recipient Guardian Small Bus. award, Nat. Fedn. Ind. Bus., 1999, 2000, 2001, Frying Pan award, Colo. Restaurant Assn., 1999, Disting. Legislator award, United Vets. Com. of Colo., 2002. Fellow Nat. Assn. Ch. Bus. Adminstrn. (nat. dir., regional v.p., v.p. 1983-85, pres. 1985-87, Ch. Bus. Adminstr. of Yr. award 1983, inducted into Hall of Fame 1995), Colo. Assn. Ch. Bus. Adminstrs. (past pres.), United Meth. Assn. Ch. Bus. Adminstrs. (nat. sec. 1978-81), Christian Ministries Mgmt. Assn. (dir. 1983-85), USAF Acad. Athletic Assn., Colorado Springs Country Club, Garden of Gods Club, Met. Club (Denver), Winter Night Club, Rotary (pres. Colorado Springs 1985-86), Order of Daedalians. Home: 3007 Chelton Dr Colorado Springs CO 80909-1008

SINCLAIR, WILLIE THOMAS, civil engineer, consultant; b. Columbia, S.C., Sept. 17, 1946; s. Willie Nathaniel and Elise Rosa (Ray) S.; m. Doris Louise Dilworth, June 24, 1967; children: Charles Thomas, Karen Sinclair Heyman. BS in Civil Engring., Clemson U., 1973. Registered profl. engr., S.C., N.C. Assoc. field engr. Duke Power Co., Charlotte, N.C., 1973-80; divsn. mgr. constrn. svcs. Piedmont Olsen Hensley, Greenville, S.C., 1980-93; pres. Sinclair & Assocs., Duncan, 1993—. Bd. dirs. S.C. Soc. Profl. Engrs., Columbia, 1989-90, 99—. Staff sgt. USAF, 1966-70. Mem. ASCE, NSPE (pres. Piedmont chpt. 1990, Engr. of Yr. 1995), Ruritan Club (pres. Duncan, S.C. 1994, Man of Yr. 1994). Republican. Baptist. Avocations: hunting, fishing, golf. Home: PO Box 726 Duncan SC 29334-0726 Office: 128 S Main St Duncan SC 29334-9696

SINCOFF, MICHAEL Z. human resources and marketing professional; b. Washington, June 28, 1943; s. Murray P. and Anna F. (Jaffe) S. m. Kathleen M. Dunham, Oct. 9, 1983. BA, U. Md., 1964, MA, 1966; PhD, Purdue U., 1969. Instr. U. Tenn., Knoxville, 1968; asst. prof. Ohio U., Athens, 1969-74, dir. Ctr. for Comm. Studies, 1969-76, assoc. prof., 1974-76; vis. prof. U. Minn., St. Paul, 1974; dir. personnel devel. Hoechst-Celanese Corp. (formerly Celanese Corp.), N.Y., 1976-79; dir. employee comm. The Mead Corp., Dayton, Ohio, 1979-81, dir. edn., tng., 1981-83; assoc. dean Sch. of Bus. Adminstrn. Georgetown U., Washington, 1983-84; v.p. human resources ADVO, Sys., (formerly ADVO Inc.), Hartford, Conn., 1984-87; v.p. human resources, corp. officer DIMAC Direct Inc., St. Louis, 1987-88; sr. v.p. human resources and adminstrn., sr. corp. officer DIMAC Mktg. Corp. (parent of DIMAC Direct Inc.), 1988-97, also sec., asst. treas., exec. com., 1988-97; sr. v.p. human resources, exec. corp. officer Brooks Fiber Properties, Inc. (now Brooks WorldCom), 1997-98; pres., CEO Michaelson Group Ptnrs., Dayton, Ohio, 1969—. Vis. prof. Wright State U., Dayton, Ohio, 1999—; assoc. grad. faculty mem. Ctrl. Mich. U., Mt. Pleasant, 1999—. Author, editor human resources sect. Am. Mgmt. Assn. Mgmt. Handbook, 3d edit., 1994; author approximately

50 books and articles; mem. edtl. adv. bd. Jour. Applied Comm. Rsch., 1991-97. Life mem. Internat. Comm. Assn. (bus. mgr.-exec. sec. 1969-73, fin. com. 1982-85); mem. Am. Mgmt. Assn. (human resources coun. 1990-2000), Printing Industries of Am. (employer resources group 1989-97).

SINCOFF, STEVEN LAWRENCE, chemistry educator; b. N.Y.C., Apr. 17, 1948; s. Murray B. and Lillian (Goldberg) S.; m. Marcella Seay, June 12, 1993; children by previous marriage: Kristina Lynne, Carolyn Suzanne. BSChemE, N.J. Inst. Tech., 1969, MSChemE, 1972; PhD in Analytical Chemistry, Ohio State U., 1980. Commd. 2d lt. USAF, 1969, advanced through grades to lt. col., 1987, retired, 1991, fuels mgmt. officer, 1970-74; chem. engr. Aero. Systems Div., Wright-Patterson AFB, Ohio, 1974-77; assoc. prof. chemistry USAF Acad., Colorado Springs, Colo., 1980-84, dir. continuing edn. dept. chemistry, 1982-84; chief gas analysis lab. McClellan (AFB) Cen. Lab., Calif., 1984-88; exec. officer to comdr. Tech. Ops. Div. McClellan AFB, 1988-89, chief info. officer, 1989-91; gen. mgr. ChemWest Analytical Lab., Sacramento, 1991-92; dir. ops. Barringer Labs., Inc., Golden, Colo., 1992-94; instr. chemistry C.C. Aurora, 1995-98, Butte Coll., Oroville, Calif., 1998—. Reviewer chemistry textbooks Saunders Pub., Phila., 1983-84. Mem. Am. Chem. Soc., Air Force Assn. Jewish. Avocations: microcomputers, hiking. Home and Office: 14574 Carnegie Rd Magalia CA 95954-9647 Office: Butte Coll Dept Chemistry Oroville CA 95965 E-mail: sincoffst@butte.cc.ca.us.

SINCOSKIE, W. DAVID, computer engineer; Degree, U. Del. Rsch. scientist Bellcore; v.p. applied rsch. Internet Arch. Rsch. Lab. Telcordia Tech., Inc., Morristown, N.J. Cons. in field; adviser to Taiwan govt. on devel. of NII; mem. panel high performance computer and comm. initiative NRC; adj. prof. computer and info. sci. U. Del.; mem. adv. com. dean engring. U Pa. Fellow IEEE; mem. NAE, Internet Soc., Def. Advanced Rsch. Projects Agy., Info. Scis. and Tech. Com. Achievements include leading team that produced the experimental Sunshine ATM switch; building of ethernet-based packet telephones; inventor set of extensions to self-learning bridges known as VLANs. Office: Telcordia Techs 445 South St Morristown NJ 07960-6438

SINDELAR, JODY LOUISE, economics educator; b. Oak Park, Ill., June 17, 1951; s. Joseph C. and Margaret (Faulkner) S.; m. Roger G. Ibbotson, July 5, 1983; children: Tyler Ibbotson-Sindelar, Timothy Ibbotson-Sindelar. BA, MA, Stanford U., 1973, PhD, 1980. Economist HEW, Washington, 1975-77, Pub. Svc. Lab., Georgetown U., Washington, 1978; lectr. econs. U. Chgo., 1979; vis. asst. prof. Boston U., 1980; asst. prof. U. Chgo. Grad. Sch. Bus., 1980-84; asst. prof., assoc. prof. health Yale U., New Haven, 1985—. Assoc. dean Yale U., New Haven, 1995—. Chair Panel of Health Economist, N.Y.; bd. dirs. Shirley Frenchy Alcohol Treatment, New Haven, 1985—, Calvin Hill Daycare, New Haven, 1989—, Alcohol Svcs. Rsch. Orgn., 1991—. NIMH postdoctoral fellow, Chgo., 1978-80; grantee Rockefeller Foun., 1989-90, S.S. Huebner Found., 1982-83, Nat. Inst. Alcohol Abuse & Alcoholism, 1989—, Nat. Ctr. for Health Stats., 1990, Agy. Health Care Policy & Rsch., 1992—, Nat. Inst. for Alcohol & Alcohol Abuse, 1993—, Nat. Inst. for Drug Abuse, 1993—, Robert Wood Johnson, 1993—. Mem. Am. Econ. Assn., Am. Assn. Pub. Health. Home: 75 Old Hartford Tpke Hamden CT 06517-3524 Office: Yale U Sch Pub Health PO Box 3333 New Haven CT 06510-0333

SINE, WESLEY FRANKLIN, lawyer; b. Salt Lake City, Dec. 13, 1936; s. Ira F. and Dora Ann (Popp) S.; m. Barbara A. Belnap, June 6, 1958 (div. 1978); children: Barri Ann, Jeri Charlene, Wesley D., Anthony L.; m. Melva Carol Holmes, Dec. 30, 1978; children: Tammy Louise, Dorethea Ann, Christina Jean, Jared F., Katrina C., Joshua F., Kathryn M. JD, U. Utah, 1962. Bar: Utah 1962, U.S. Dist. Ct. Utah 1962, U.S. Ct. Appeals (10th cir.) 1962. Pvt. practice, Salt Lake City. Bd. dirs. Utah Hotel Motel Assn., Salt Lake City, 1963-79, pres. 1976; pres. Salt Lake Valley Inn, Salt Lake City, 1978, Utah Apt. Assn., 1977, Utah State Bowling Proprs., 1965, 83. Mem. Rep. Lincoln Day Club, Salt Lake City, 1985—. Mem.: Kiwanis (pres. Salt Lake City 1984—85, 1999—2000, dist. adminstr. collegiate orgn. Utah-Idaho dist. 1988—, lt. gov. divsn. 2 Utah 1989—90, George F. Hixon fellow award 2000). Mem. Lds Ch. Home: 451 Northmont Way Salt Lake City UT 84103-3322

SINEATH, TIMOTHY WAYNE, library educator, university dean; b. Jacksonville, Fla., May 21, 1940; s. Holcombe Asbury and Christine Marcel (Cook) S.; m. Patricia Ann Greenwood, June 8, 1962; children: Philip Greenwood, Paul Byron. BA, Fla. State U., 1962, MS, 1963; PhD (Higher Edn. Act fellow), U. Ill., 1970. Reference librarian U. Ga., 1963-64, catalog librarian, 1964-66; acad. coordinator continuing edn. in library sci. U. Ill., 1966-68; asst. prof. library sci. Simmons Coll., 1970-74, coordinator doctoral program, 1974-77; prof., dean Coll. Libr. Sci. and Info. Sci. U. Ky., Lexington, 1977-87, prof., 1987-97, dir. sch. Libr. and Info. Sci., 1997—. Cons. to libraries, schs., chs., industry; mem. Lexington (Ky.) Public Library Bd., 1978— Author profl. reports; contbr. articles on library and info. sci., gen. info. mgmt., organizational and small group behavior to profl. jours. Mem. ALA, Am. Soc. Info. Sci., Assn. for Libr. and Info. Sci. Edn. (pres. 1993). Episcopalian. Home: 3418 Bay Leaf Dr Lexington KY 40502-3804 Office: U Ky Mi King Bldg Lexington KY 40506-0039 E-mail: tsineath@uky.edu.

SINEGAL, JAMES D. wholesale distribution executive; b. 1936; With Fed-Mart Corp., 1954-77, exec. v.p.; v.p. Builders Enporium, 1977-78; exec. v.p. Price Co., 1978-79; with Sinegal/Chamberlin & Assocs., 1979-83; pres., COO Costco Wholesale Corp., Issaguah, Wash., 1983—, CEO, 1988—, bd. dirs. Address: Costco Wholesale PO Box 34331 999 Lake Dr Ste 200 Issaquah WA 98027-8982*

SINFELT, JOHN HENRY, chemist; b. Munson, Pa., Feb. 18, 1931; s. Henry Gustave and June Lillian (McDonald) Sinfelt; m. Muriel Jean Vadersen, July 14, 1956; 1 child Klaus Herbert. BS, Pa. State U., 1951; PhD, U. Ill., 1954, DSc (hon.) , 1981. Research engr. Exxon Research Engring. Co., Linden, NJ, 1954—57, sr. research engr., 1957—62, research assoc., 1962—68, sr. research assoc., 1968—72, sci. advisor, 1972—79, sr. sci. advisor, 1979—96, sr. sci. advisor emeritus, 1996—. Vis. prof. chem. engring. U. Minn., 1969; Lacey lectr. Calif. Inst. Tech., 1973; Reilly lectr. U. Notre Dame, 1974; Frontiers in Chemistry lectr. Case Western Res. U., Cleve., 1978; Matthew Van Winkle lectr. U. Tex., 1979, disting. vis. lectr. in chemistry, 81; Francois Gault lectr. catalysis Coun. Europe Rsch. Group Catalysis, 1980; Mobay lectr. in chemistry U. Pitts., 1980; Robert Welch Found. lectr. Confs. on Chem. Rsch., 1981; Camille and Henry Dreyfus lectr. UCLA, 1982; Edward Clark Lee Meml. lectr. U. Chgo., 1983; Dow disting. lectr. in chemistry Mich. State U., 1984; Arthur D. Little lectr. Northeastern U., 1985; Vollmer W. Fries lectr. Rensselaer Poly. Inst., 1986; disting. lectr. Ctr. Chem. Physics U. Fla., 1988; David M. Mason lectr. Stanford U., 1995, cons. prof. dept. chem. engring., 1996—. Contbr. articles to profl. jours. Named to N.J. Inventors Hall of Fame, 1991; recipient Dickson prize, Carnegie-Mellon U., 1977, Internat. prize for new materials, Am. Phys. Soc., 1978, Nat. medal of sci., 1979, Perkin medal in chemistry, Soc. Chem. Industry, 1984, Disting. Alumnus award, Pa. State U., 1985. Fellow: AIChE (Alpha Chi Sigma award 1971, Profl. Progress award 1975), Am. Inst. Chemists (Chem. Pioneer award 1981, Gold medal 1984), Am. Acad. Arts and Scis.; mem.: NAE, NAS (award for indsl. application of sci. 1996), Am. Philos. Soc., Catalysis Soc. (Emmett award 1973), Am. Chem. Soc. (Carothers lectr. Del. sect. 1982, Petroleum Chemistry award 1976, Murphree award 1986). Methodist. Achievements include development of bimetallic clusters as catalysts; invention of polymetallic cluster catalysts used commercially in petroleum reforming. Home: PO Box 364 Oldwick NJ 08858

SING, DORIS ANNE, music educator; b. Houston, Oct. 1, 1947; d. Theron Ponton Sr. and Anna Agnes (Dethlefsen) Spradley; m. William B. Sing, Sept. 1, 1967; children: Erin Elaine, Emily Elizabeth. BS in Edn. cum laude, U. Houston, 1970, BMus cum laude, 1990, MMus in Music Lit., 2000. Cert. tchr. elem. and spl. edn., Tex. Dir. children's choir St. Andrew's Presbyn. Ch., Houston, 1984-90; tchr. music St. Andrew's Presbyn. Sch., 1991-93; founder, dir. Arts a la Carte, 1993—. Elder St. Andrew's Presbyn. Ch., 1992-94. Mem. Early Childhood Music and Movement Assn., KinderMusik Educators Assn. (cert. tchr.), ORFF-Schulwerk Assn., Phi Kappa Phi, Kappa Delta Pi. Avocations: singing, listening to classical music, opera. Office: Arts a la Carte 3637 W Alabama St Ste 490 Houston TX 77027-5907 E-mail: dsing@hypercon.com., info@artsalacarte.com.

SING, ROBERT FONG, physician; b. Camden, N.J., May 29, 1953; s. William Fong and Elizabeth (Maxwell) S.; m. Lauren McNamee, May 11, 1991. BS in Biology, Ursinus Coll., 1975; DO, Coll. Osteo. Medicine, Surgery, 1978. Intern Met. Hosp., Phila., 1978-79, resident in family practice, 1979-80; dir. emergency dept. Springfield (Pa.) Hosp., 1984—; dir. sports medicine Sports Sci. Ctr., 1987—; med. dir. Emergency Ambulance Svcs., Inc., 1994-95; owner J. Enright Jewelers, Inc., Swarthmore, Pa., 1995-97. Owner, pres. Finish Line Sports, Inc., Phila., 1988-94; sch. and team physician Springfield Sch. Dist., 1989—, Rose Tree-Media (Pa.) Sch. Dist., 1987—; chief med. officer Kent Profl. Bicyling Tour of China, 1995, U.S. Olympic Cycling Trials, 1996. Author: Dynamics of the Javelin Throw, 1984. Med. dir. Springfield Ambulance Corp., 1988—. Named to Ursinus Coll. Athletic Hall of Fame, 1985. Fellow Am. Coll. Sports Medicine, Am. Osteo. Acad. Sports Medicine; mem. Am. Coll. Osteo. Emergency Physicians, Am. Coll. Emergency Physicians. Avocations: track and field, classical music, bicycling. Home: 1274 Gradyville Rd Glen Mills PA 19342-9614 Office: Sports Sci Ctr 166 Saxer Ave Springfield PA 19064-2335

SING, WILLIAM BENDER, lawyer; b. Houston, Oct. 16, 1947; s. William Bender Sr. and Alice Irene S.; m. Doris Anne Spradley, Sept. 1, 1967; children: Erin Elaine, Emily Elizabeth. BS cum laude, U. Houston, 1968, JD magna cum laude, 1971; MLA, U. St. Thomas, 1995. Bar: Tex. 1971. Assoc. Fulbright & Jaworski, LLP, Houston, 1973-80, ptnr., 1980—. Elder, trustee St. Andrew's Presbyn. Ch., Houston; past pres., bd. dirs. St. Andrew's Presbyn. Sch., Houston; past pres. Houston C.C. Place Civic Assn. 1st lt. U.S. Army, 1971-73. Mem. ABA, Tex. Bar Assn., Houston Bar Assn., Order of the Barons Law Honor Soc., U. Houston Alumni Orgn. (life), Phi Delta Phi (life), Phi Kappa Phi, Omicron Delta Epsilon. Presbyterian. Avocation: reading history and literature. Office: Fulbright & Jaworski LLP 1301 Mckinney St Houston TX 77010-3031

SINGARAJU, BHARADWAJA KESHAVA, electronics engineer; b. Secunderabad, Andhra Pradesh, India, June 20, 1945; came to the U.S., 1965; s. Subbarao and Subbamma (Gattupalli) S.; m. Camille H. Hamilton, Nov. 25, 1972; children: Raj, Ravi. BS, N.Mex. State U., 1968, MS, 1971, PhD, 1973. Rsch. engr. Dike Wood Corp., Albuquerque, 1976-78; electronics engr. Air Force Weapons Lab., Kirtland AFB, 1978-82, chief applications br., 1982-91; tech. dir. space electronics/software divsn. Phillips Lab., 1991-93, chief space electronics divsn., 1993-96, chief space mission tech. divsn., 1996-97, tech. dir. surveillance and control divsn., 1997—, tech. advisor integrated experiments divsn., 1997—. Tech. and program chmn. various nat. and internat. confs. Contbr. chpt. to book and articles to profl. jours. Recipient Nat. Rsch. Coun. associateship NSF, 1974-76. Fellow AIAA (assoc.); mem. IEEE (sr.), Sigma Xi, Eta Kappa Nu. Avocations: skiing, bicycling, hiking, wood working. Office: AFRL/VSE 3550 Aberdeen Ave SE Kirtland AFB NM 87117-5776

SINGER, ALAN DANIEL, artist; b. N.Y.C., June 19, 1950; s. Arthur B. and Edith (Goulfine) S.; m. Anna K. Sears, Sept. 1, 1979; 1 child, Nathaniel. BFA, Cooper Union, 1972; MFA, Cornell U., 1975; student, Yale U., 1971; postgrad., Pratt Inst., 1976-77. Artist, painter, freelance writer, educator, designer, illustrator and curator, 1974—; assoc. prof. dept. fine art Rochester Inst. Tech., 1987—; adult edn. instr. N.Y. Bot. Garden, 1985-88; instr. Asa Wright Nature Ctr., Trinidad, W.I., 1978-80. Designer program Franklin Mint Graphics for TDK/Impressions Illustration and Design Exhibits, Bklyn. Botanic Garden, 1987, designs and mechanicals for L.I. U. Brochures/N.C. Zool. Assn., 1986, others; designer, illustrator stamps U.S. Postal Svc., 1980-81. One-man shows include: Hobart William & Smith Coll., Geneva, N.Y., 2001, The Mill Art Ctr., Honeoye Falls, N.Y., 2001, Century Club, Rochester, 1999, Upstairs Gallery: Gallery Arabesque, Ithaca, N.Y., 1998, Germanow-Coffey Gallery, 1997, Angel Fire Gallery, Rochester, N.Y., 1993, 55 Mercer St. Gallery, N.Y.C., 1985, 1992, Haenah-Kent Gallery, N.Y.C., 1991, Bali Miller Gallery, N.Y.C., 1988, Smithsonian Mus. of Natural History, Washington, 1987, others; group shows include Everson Mus., Syracuse, N.Y., 1999, Norman Rockwell Mus., Stockbridge, Mass., 2000, Sonnenberg Gardens, Canandaigua, N.Y., 2000, Kew Gardens, Eng., 1997, Buffalo Mus. Sci., 1997, Monroe C.C., 1997, Meml. Art Gallery, Rochester, 1991, 93, Angel Fire Gallery, 1992, Rochester Inst. Tech., 1988, Nat. Acad. Design, N.Y.C., 1986, Community Gallery, Bklyn. Mus., 1985, Coffey Germanow Gallery, 1995, others; author: Wildlife Art, 1999, Botanica 2000, 2000—, Traveling the Erie Canal by Watercolor, 2001; author essays in mus. catalogs, newspapers and jours. Recipient cert. Merit Soc. Illustrators, 1985, Best of Yr. award Postal Commemorative Soc., 1983, Purchase award Nassau C.C., 1976, Pres.'s award Nat. Arts Club, N.Y.C., 1975; Robhester Inst. Tech. grantee, 1991, Faculty Devel. grantee, 1997. Mem. Rochester Print Club (pres.). Avocations: gardening, guitar, hiking. Office: Rochester Inst Tech One Lomb Memorial Dr Rochester NY 14623 E-mail: alan@singerarts.com.

SINGER, ALLEN MORRIS, lawyer; b. Mpls., Dec. 30, 1923; s. William and Ida (Simenstein) S. JD, U. Chgo., 1948; LLM, Harvard U., 1958. Bar: Ill. 1948, Calif. 1949. Pvt. practice, 1950-55, 59—; v.p., sec., gen. counsel ABM Industries, San Francisco, 1969-85. Assoc. prof. law U. Oreg., 1955-59; lectr. law Stanford (Calif.) U., 1960-62; of counsel Cooper, White & Cooper, San Francisco, 1970-97. Contbr. articles to profl. jours. Mem. U. Chgo. Nat. Alumni Cabinet, 1978-80. 2nd lt., USAAF, 1943-45. Mem. ABA, San Francisco Bar Assn., Calif. Bar Assn. Office: 1070 Green St Ste 703 San Francisco CA 94133-5414

SINGER, ARMAND EDWARDS, foreign language educator; b. Detroit, Nov. 30, 1914; s. Elvin Satori Singer and Fredericka Elizabeth (Edwards) Singer Goetz; m. Mary Rebecca White, Aug. 8, 1940; 1 child, Fredericka Ann Hill AB, Amherst Coll., 1935; MA, Duke U., 1939, PhD, 1944; diplôme, U. Paris, 1939; postgrad., Ind. U., summer 1964. Teaching fellow in sci. Amherst Coll., 1935-36; instr. French and Spanish, part-time Duke, 1938-40; teaching fellow Romance langs. W.Va. U., Morgantown, 1940-41, instr., 1941-47, asst. prof., 1947-55, assoc. prof., 1955-60, prof., 1960-80, prof. emeritus, 1980—, chmn. program for humanities, 1963-72, chmn. dept. integrated studies, 1963, acting chmn. dept. religion and program for humanities, 1973, dir. ann. colloquium on modern lit. and film 1976-80, 85-86, 96-97, 99-2001. Author: A Bibliography of the Don Juan Theme: Versions and Criticism, 1954, The Don Juan Theme, Versions and Criticism: An Annotated Bibliography, 1965, Paul Bourget, 1975, The Don Juan Theme: A Bibliography of Versions, Analogues, Uses, and Adaptations, 1993, The Armand E. Singer Tibet, 1809-1975, 1995, supplement, 1998, The Armand E. Singer Nepal, 1772-1961 and Beyond, 1997, The Officials of Tibet, 1999, (with J.F. Stasny) Anthology of Readings: Humanities I, 1966, Anthology of Readings: Humanities II, 1967, (with R.F. Gould) A Graded Catalog of Himalayan Mountaineering Correspondence, 2002; editor: West Virginia George Sand Conference Papers, 1981, (with Jürgen E. Schlunk) Martin Walser: International Perspectives, 1987, Doctor Faustus: Archetypal Subtext at the Millennium, 1999; editor W.Va. U. Philol. Papers, 1948-50, 53-55, editor-in-chief, 1951-52, 55—; editor: 1001 Horny Limericks by Ward Marden, 1996; editor, contbr. Essays on the Literature of Mountaineering, 1982; contbr. numerous articles to profl. and philatelic jours. Bd. dirs. Community Concert Assn., Morgantown, 1959-60, Humanities Found. W.Va., 1981-87. Recipient 4th Ann. Humanities award W.Va. Humanities Coun., 1990; the Armand E. and Mary W. Singer Professorship in Humanities named in honor of Armand Singer and wife Mary Singer, 1999. Mem. MLA (internat. bibliography com. 1956-59, nat. del. assembly 1975-78), So. Atlantic MLA (exec. com. 1971-74), Am. Assn. Tchrs. Spanish and Portuguese, Am. Philatelic Soc., Nepal and Tibet Philatelic Study Circle (pres. 2000—), Nepal Philatelic Soc., Collectors Club of N.Y., Phi Beta Kappa. Republican. Home: 248 Grandview Ave Morgantown WV 26501-6925 *In an age of deteriorating standards, I want to be counted among those educators who stand against the tide. We ask too little of others, we ask too little of ourselves; others ask too little of us. When we constantly encounter shoddy construction, shoddy merchandise, shoddy performances, shoddy ethics, shoddy education, we may be tempted to forswear our standards. But through our hands pass tomorrow's leaders. As teachers we must help stop this erosion of our national pride. If we fail, make no mistake: it could well destroy us all.*

SINGER, BARBARA HELEN, photographer; b. N.Y.C., Jan. 29, 1927; d. Robert and Rose (Kaplowitz) S.; m. Nat Herz, Jan. 15, 1956 (dec. Nov. 1964); m. Melvin C. Zalkan, Sept. 7, 1983 (dec. Nov. 1993). BA in Biology, NYU, 1947; studied with Eli Siegel, 1944-76. Radiographer, 1951-90; instr. Meth. Hosp. Sch. Radiologic Tech., Bklyn., 1968-72; asst. to Benedict J. Fernandez N.Y.C., N.Y., 1985-91; asst. to Lucien Clergue New Sch./Parsons, 1989; photographer, 1983—. Represented by John Stevenson Gallery, Bridgeman Art Library Internat. Ltd., Photonica; group exhbns. include Associated Artists Gallery, Winston-Salem, N.C., 1985, Donnell Libr., N.Y.C., 1986, Lincoln Sq. Gallery, N.Y.C., 1990, Konica Plz., Tokyo, 1990, Nikon House, N.Y.C., 1990, St. Margaret's House, N.Y.C., 1991, Duggal Downtown, N.Y.C., 1994, 97, Salmagundi Club, N.Y.C., 1989, 90, 91, 92, 94, 95, 96, Coll. New Rochelle, N.Y., 1994, Artists Talk on Art, N.Y.C., 1994, Gallery Cedar Hollow, Malvern, Pa., 1995, Columbia U., N.Y.C., 1995, Erector Sq. Gallery, New Haven, Conn., 1995, Hudson Pk. Libr., N.Y.C., 1996, Learning Alliance, N.Y.C., 1996, 97, Lever House, N.Y.C., 1996, Severoceske Mus., 1996, Nat. Mus. Asian, African & Am. Cultures, Prague, Czech Republic, 1996, Time Life Bldg., N.Y.C., 1996, 97, Wildlife Conservation Soc., N.Y.C., 1996, The Wildlife Gallery at Central Park, N.Y.C., 1996, The Stone Gallery, Ft. Collins, Colo., 1997, Nassau C.C., Garden City, N.Y., 1997, Fulcrum Gallery, N.Y.C., 1997, Independence Plz., N.Y.C., 1997, Ashforth-Warburg Downtown, N.Y.C., 1998, Fashion Inst. Tech., N.Y.C., 1998, John Stevenson Gallery, 1999, Pietra di Luna Gallery, Fla., 1999, 2000, Park Ave. Armory, N.Y.C., 1999, AIPAD, N.Y.C., 1999, George A. Spiva Ctr. for the Arts, Mo., 2000, Hist. Yellow Springs, Chester, Pa., 2000, Nat. League Am. Pen Women Art Exhbn., N.Y.C., 2000, AIR Gallery, NYC, 2000, Nat. Photo Competition, Pietra di Luna Gall., Hollywood FL., 2000, St. Francis Coll., NYC, 2001, Modernage, N.Y.C., 2001, Ashforth-Warburg Downtown, N.Y.C., 2002; CD-ROM Urbane Photography, 1996; photography published in The Murray Hill News, 1983, Profl. Women Photographers Newsletter, 1985, 95, Light and Shade, 1985, Best of Photography Annual 1990, Women of Vision, 1990, Tear Sheet, 1995, Wildlife Conservation Soc. Annual Report, Photonica 21, 1996, In Shape, 1996, Summer of Betrayal, Farrar Straus Giroux, 1997, Wildlife Conservation Mag., 1997, Worldcare Annual Report, 1997, Svenska Missions, 1997, Photonica 25, 1997, Fotophile, 1997, Photonica 34, 1998, Photonica 38, 44, 1999, 49, 2000, Shots, vol. 63, 1999, lit. published in PWP Newsletter, 2001, Tear Sheet, vol. 3, 1995, Today's Great Poems, 1994, Evangelism in America, 1988, Radiologic Tech., 1969, 71; edited and pub., The Impossible Landscapes of Nat. Hertz and Kurt Seligmann, 1999; slide lecture N.Y. Film Acad., N.Y.C., 2000; panel discussion The Phoenix Gallery, N.Y.C., 1999, St. Francis Coll., NYC, 2001. Photographers' Forum Finalist, 1990; recipient Photography award Beaux Arts Soc., 1994, fiscal sponsorship N.Y. Found. for the Arts, 2000, 2d pl. winner for poetry E.F.S. 1999 Ann. Writing Competition, 2000. Cert. by Women Pres. Ednl. Orgn., 2002. Mem.: Poetry Soc. Am., Am. Women's Econ. Devel. Corp., Nat. Assn. Women Bus. Owners, Women Presidents Ednl. Orgn., Am. Soc. Media Photographers, Aartists Talk on Art, Profl. Women Photographers (25th Anniversary Recognition award 2000), Am. Soc. Picture Profls., Art Dirs. Club, Nat. League Am. Pen Women, Women's Bus. Enterprise Nat. Coun., Internat. Platform Assn. Avocation: ballroom dancing. Office: Madison Sq Sta PO Box 1150 New York NY 10159-1150 Fax: (212) 684-1051. E-mail: barbara@barbarasinger.com .

SINGER, BERNARD ALAN, lawyer; b. Miami, Fla., Jan. 29, 1946; s. Arthur and Diane D. Singer; divorced; chldren: Steven, Barbara Ann; m. Karen Joyce Singer, June 3, 1995. BSBA, Northeastern U., 1968; JD, U. Miami, 1977. Bar: Fla., U.S. Tax Ct. Assoc. Abrams Anton, Hollywood, Fla., 1982-88; pres. Bernard A. Singer, P.A., 1988—. Served with U.S. Army Rex., 1968-74. Mem. North Dade-South Broward Estate Planning Coun., Greater Ft. Lauderdale Tax Coun. Avocation: boating. Office: 3107 Stirling Rd Ste 105 Fort Lauderdale FL 33312-2829

SINGER, BETH J. philosopher; b. Bklyn., Oct. 27, 1927; BA, U. Wis., Madison, 1949; MA, Columbia U., 1957, PhD, 1967. Instr. Manhattanville Coll., Purchase, N.Y., 1966-67, asst. prof., 1967-72, CUNY, Bklyn., 1972-73, assoc. prof., 1974-78, prof., 1979-96, chair dept. philosophy, 1991-95, prof. emerita, 1996—. Author: The Rational Society: A Critical Study of Santayana's Social Thought, 1970, Ordinal Naturalism: An Introduction to the Philosophy of Justus Buchler, 1983, Operative Rights, 1993, Pragmatism, Rights, and Democracy, 1999; editor (with Tom Rockmore) Antifoundationalism Old and New, 1992. Mem. Am. Philosophical Assn., Soc. Advancement Am. Philosophy (pres. 1986-88, Herbert W. Schneider award for Disting. Contbns. to Understanding and Devel. Am. Philosophy 1994), Metaphys. Soc. Am., Concerned Philosophers for Peace (pres. 1998-99), Alain L. Locke Soc. E-mail: 105152.1772.compuserve.com.

SINGER, CAREN BEBCHUCK, physician; b. Miami, Fla., June 10, 1955; d. Bernard and Marilyn Lois (Liebross) Bebchuck; m. Glenn Richard Singer, July 1, 1979; children: Melissa, Beth, Rebecca. BS, Emory U., 1976; MD, U. South Fla., 1980. Diplomate Am. Bd. Internal Medicine. Intern U. So. Fla., 1980-81, resident, 1981-83; pvt. practice pvt. practice, Ft. Lauderdale, Fla., 1984—. Fellow Am. Coll. Physicians. Avocations: golf, tennis, running. Home: 221 N Bel Air Dr Plantation FL 33317-2512 Office: 255 SE 14th St Ste 1B Fort Lauderdale FL 33316-1827

SINGER, CAROL ANN, librarian, researcher; b. Tarentum, Pa., Mar. 13, 1953; d. Richard Meade and Eleanor (Weir) S. BA, Bowling Green State U., 1975; MLS, Ind. U., 1979. Instr. info. svc. Wayne (Nebr.) State Coll., 1979-84; govt. documents libr. U. Nebr., Omaha, 1984-85, Kenyon Coll., Gambier, Ohio, 1985-91; sr. ref. libr. U.S. Dept. Energy, Washington, 1991-92; ref. libr. USDA, 1992-97; asst. libr. U.S. Dept. Justice, 1997-98; ref. libr. Bowling Green (Ohio) State U., 1998—. Temp. instr. Kent State U., Bowling Green, Ohio, 1999; researcher. Contbr. articles to profl. jours. Mem. ALA, Acad. Libr. Assn. Ohio, Ohio Govt. Documents Roundtable. Office: Bowling Green State U Jerome Libr Rm 152 Bowling Green OH 43403 E-mail: singerc@bgnet.bgsu.edu.

SINGER, CECILE DORIS, state legislator; BA, Queens Coll.; DHL (hon.), Pace U., 1997. Past rep. Spl. Svcs. for Children, N.Y.C.; past exec. dir. N.Y. State Assembly Social Svcs. and Judiciary Coms., Joint Legis. Com. on Corps., Authorities and Commns.; past pub. rep. Yonkers (N.Y.) Emergency Control Bd.; past coord. Westchester County Assembly Dels.; past chief of staff for dep. minority leader; mem. N.Y. State Assembly, Albany, 1988—94, leadership sec. Rep. Conf., mem. assembly children & families com., mem. various other coms. Past rep. Temp. Commn. to Revise Social Svcs. Law; mem. Presdl. Commn. on Privacy Conf., N.Y. State Senate Transp. Conf.; task force on substance abuse Am. Legis. Exch. Coun., task force on econ. devel., crime victims' rights, hosp. crisis, women's issues, com. on mass transit; sec. Rep. Conf. Nat. Adv. Panel Child Care Action Campaign; chmn. Westchester County Commn. on Pub. Financing of Campaigns; chmn. Lower Hudson Valley Adv. Com. N.Y. State Divsn. for Women.; past dir. commn. on poverty and pregnancy, Yonkers IDA, N.Y.; bd. dirs. Riverside Corp. Adv. bd. Legal Awareness for Women, Big Bros. and Big Sisters, Westchester C.C. Found., Westchester 2000 Rsch., Womens Adv. Bd. Westchester County; task force on certiorari Westchester County Sch. Bds. Assn.; sch. and cmty. chmn. Yonkers PTA; bd. dirs. Yonkers Gen. Hosp., Yonkers chpt. United Jewish Appeal; v.p. Westchester Sr. Housing; chair Women's Entrepreneurial Program, Women's Networking, Women in Bus. and the Professions; bd. dirs. Riverside health Care; v.p. Westchester Srs. Housing. Recipient Jenkins Meml. award, Nat. PTA award, Bus. and Profl. award Yonkers C. of C.; inducted Women's Hall of Fame, 1996, Sr. Citizens Hall of Fame, 1996. Mem. Mental Health Assn. (bd. dirs., v.p., nominating and pub. affairs coms. Westchester County chpt., Steering award), Rotary. Office: 21 Scarsdale Rd Yonkers NY 10707-3204 Home: 1 Scarsdale Rd Tuckahoe NY 10707-3215

SINGER, CRAIG, business executive, investor; b. N.Y.C., Aug. 13, 1947; s. Albert and Dorothy (Blackman) S.; m. Ellen Rappaport, Aug. 31, 1969; children: Chad Adam, Cara Danielle. BS, Cornell U., 1969; JD, Columbia U., 1972. Bar: N.Y. 1973. Exec. Continental Wingage Co., Inc., N.Y.C., 1972-74, Integrated Resources, Inc., N.Y.C., 1974-87; pres.bd. Westminster Fin. Group, Inc., 1989—. Chmn. bd. Integrated Resources Housing Corp., Integrated Funding, Inc., Resources Funding Corp., AIM Capital Mgmt. Corp., 1983-87; bus. exec., inventor, cons., broker, investor, Bedford Corners, N.Y., 1988—; reporter. Former dir. Assn. Govt. Assisted Housing, Inc., 1976-84; former mem. exec. com. Coalition for low and Moderate Income Housing; former mem. editl. adv. bd. Bur. Nat. Affairs Housing and Devel. Home and Office: 148 Meeting House Rd Bedford Corners NY 10549-4241

SINGER, DANIEL MORRIS, lawyer; b. Bklyn., Oct. 10, 1930; s. Samuel W. and Fannie G. (Sabloff) S.; m. Maxine Frank, June 15, 1952; children: Amy E., Ellen R., David B., Stephanie F. BA with honors, Swarthmore Coll., 1951; LLB, Yale U., 1954. Bar: N.Y. 1956, U.S. Dist. Ct. D.C. 1957, U.S. Ct. Appeals (D.C. cir.) 1957, U.S. Supreme Ct. 1959. Motions clk. U.S. Ct. Appeals for D.C. Circuit, Washington, 1956-57, law clk. to Judge George T. Washington, 1957-58; assoc. Fried, Frank, Harris, Shriver & Jacobson, 1958-64, ptnr., 1965-87, counsel, 1987—. Arbitrator complex comml. case and constrn. nat. panels; mediator US Dist. Ct., Washington; vol. atty. Lawyers Com. for Civil Rights Under Law, 1965, 66; mem. exec. com. Washington Lawyers Com. for Civil Rights Under Law, 1973—; spl. asst. corp. counsel, D.C., 1995-2000. Bd. mgrs. Swarthmore Coll., 1987—91; dir., sec.-treas. Coun. for a Livable World, 1962—64; dir. Am. Soc. for Protection of Nature in Israel, 1986—; mem. governing coun., mem. exec. com. Am. Jewish Congress, 1986—96, v.p., 1988—92; bd. dirs., sec.-treas. Nat. Com. Tithing in Investment, 1964—65; bd. dirs. D.C. Developing Families Ctr., 1999—, D.C. Appleseed Ctr., 1996—, bd. chair, 2000—. With Signal Corps U.S. Army, 1954—56. Mem.: ABA, D.C. Bar. Home: 5410 39th St NW Washington DC 20015-2902 Office: Fried Frank Harris Shriver & Jacobson 1001 Pennsylvania Ave NW Washington DC 20004-2596 E-mail: daniel.singer@ffhsj.com.

SINGER, DAVID MICHAEL, marketing and public relations company executive; b. Bklyn., Feb. 11, 1957; s. Seymour Allen and Ellen Sybil (Pavnick) S.; m. Pamela Rae Silton, July 20, 1986; children, Max!, Bobby. BA in History, NYU, 1978; MA in Comms., Syracuse U., 1979; MA in Media, New Sch. Social Rsch., 1983; JD, Yeshiva U., 1981. Cons. pub. rels. Burson-Marsteller, N.Y.C., 1979-81, The Haas Group, N.Y.C., 1981-84, Braff & Co., N.Y.C., 1987-89; pub., editor-in-chief Lodestone Pub., 1984-87; chief oper. officer Pentagon Ltd., 1989-91; v.p. pub. rels. Braff & Co., 1991-92; v.p. G.S. Schwartz & Co., 1993-97; v.p. mktg. comm. Imedia, Morristown, N.J., 1998-99; pres. S&S Mktg. Comms. Inc. Lectr. evening div. NYU, 1982-96; dir. media rels. Braff & Co. Contbr. articles and poems to profl. and consumer jours. and mags. Pres. Jewish Cultural Found., N.Y.C., 1976. Named to Outstanding Young Man of Am., Jaycees, 1977; recipient Cert. Recognition Am. Film Inst., 1982, ANDY Design award Advt. Club N.Y., 1983, Proclamation Bklyn. Borough Pres., 1987. Mem. Alpha Epsilon Pi (Bro. of Yr. 1976). Avocations: baseball, politics, ping-pong, films, theater.

SINGER, DEBORAH LOUISE, medical products company executive; b. Chgo., June 10, 1962; d. Theodore and Rochelle Fay (Kroan) S. BS in Bus. and Mktg., Ariz. State U., 1984; MS in Mktg. Comm., Roosevelt U., 1989. Mktg. asst. Versadata, Inc., Elk Grove Village, Ill., 1984-85; regional mktg. supr. McMaster Carr Supply, Elmhurst, 1985-88; v.p. sales and mktg. Singer Med. Products, Bensenville, 1988-94; regional sales mgr. Fresenius U.S.A., Lexington, Mass., 1994-2000; sr. territory mgr. Vasca, Inc., Tewksbury, 2000—. Mem. Mt. Sinai Hosp. Med. Inst. Coun., 1993-96, Mary Lawrence Children's Bur., 1994-95, 1414 Wells Condominium Bd., 1996-99. Mem. Am. Diabetes Assn., DL Fisher Found., Ariz. State U. Alumni Assn. (pres. Chgo. chpt. 1991-93). Avocations: biking, travel, tennis, reading, music. Home and Office: 1414 N Wells St # 501 Chicago IL 60610-7750

SINGER, DINAH, federal agency administrator, immunologist, researcher; MPhil, PhD, Columbia U. Dir. divsn. cancer biology Nat. Cancer Inst., 1999—. Mem.: Am. Assn. Immunologists. Office: Nat Cancer Inst Divsn Cancer Biology Executive Plaza North Ste 5000 Bethesda MD 20892*

SINGER, DONNA LEA, writer, editor, educator; b. Wilmington, Del., Oct. 6, 1944; d. Marshall Richard and Sara Emma (Eppihimer) S. BA in English cum laude, Gettysburg Coll., 1966; postgrad., Montclair State Coll., 1972-73, U. Birmingham, Eng., 1977; M of Letters, Drew U., 1985. Asst. to dir. student activities Fairleigh Dickinson U., Madison, crw., 1966-68; tchr., drama coach Morris Hills High Sch., Rockaway, N.J., 1968-84; free-lance editor Basic Books, Inc., N.Y.C., 1983-86; adj. instr. Fairleigh Dickinson U., Madison, 1986-87; free-lance writer, editor Visual Edn. Corp., Princeton, N.J., 1988—, Fact's on File, Bantam, Random House, Fodor's Travel Books, N.Y.C., 1990—, John Wiley & Sons, N.Y.C., 1990—; tchr. Sylvan Learning and Tech. Ctr., Sarasota, Fla., 1999—. Co-founder, co-dir. Traveling Hist. Troupe, Rockaway, 1976-78; tour leader Am. Leadership Study Groups, 1976, 78, 82; theatre studies participant Royal Shakespeare Co., Stratford, Eng., 1978, 79, 81; docent, lectr. acting co. Hist. Spanish Point, Osprey, Fla., 1989-2001. Contbg. author (poetry) Chasing Rainbows, 1987, An American Heritage, 1994, The Nitty Gritty, 1997, Doorways, 1997, The Best Poems of 1998, The Lasting Joy, 1998, Everlasting Dreams, 1998, America at the Millennium, 2000, The Sound of Poetry, 2001, (biography) Past and Promise: Lives of New Jersey Women, 1990, World Explorers and Discoverers, 1992, American Cultural Leaders, 1993, Structures That Changed the World, 1997, (articles) Writers Guidelines and News, 1999, The Antique Shoppe, 2000, 2001, (fiction) Thema , 2000, Tapestry, 2002. Big sister Big Bros./Big Sisters, Sarasota, Fla., 1990-98. Mem. Internat. Women's Writing Guild, West Coast Writers, Met. Mus. Art, Royal Shakespeare Company Assocs., Emerald Coast Writers, Travel Writers Internat. Network. Avocations: dance, theatre, travel, antiquing. E-mail: shakesds@aol.com.

SINGER, EDWARD NATHAN, radio engineer, consultant; b. Phila., Jan. 20, 1917; s. David and Esther (Levy) S.; (widowed Apr. 1965); 1 child, Gary L.; m. Hilda Gofstein, Sept. 7, 1966. BS, CCNY, 1938; MEE, Polytech. Inst. Bklyn., 1959. Registered profl. engr., N.Y. Electronic scientist Watson Labs., Eatontown, N.J., 1946-48; field engr. FCC, N.Y.C., 1948-54; radio engr. Naval Applied Sci. Lab., 1954-70, N.Y. Fire Dept., N.Y.C., 1970-85; pvt. practice, from 1985. Author: Land Mobile Radio Systems, 1989, 2d edit. 1994, 20th Century Revolutions in Technology, 1998. Pres. Home Owners Assn., S.I., 1987-88. Capt. USAF, 1941-46, CBI. Fellow Radio Club Am.; mem. IEEE, N.Y. Acad. Scis., Sigma Xi. Jewish. Achievements include patents for pulse statistical distribution analyzer, pulse percent indicator, time controlled switching system, adjustable cam, and automatic peak level indicator system; development of broad band antenna for field intensity meters. Died June 19, 2001.

SINGER, ELEANOR, sociologist, editor; b. Vienna, Austria, Mar. 4, 1930; came to U.S., 1938; d. Alfons and Anna (Troedl) Schwarzbart; m. Alan Gerard Singer, Sept. 8, 1949; children: Emily Ann, Lawrence Alexander BA, Queens Coll., 1951; PhD, Columbia U., 1966. Asst. editor Am. Scholar, Williamsburg, Va., 1951-52; editor Tchrs. Coll. Press, N.Y.C., 1952-56, Dryden-Holt, N.Y.C., 1956-57; rsch. assoc., sr. rsch. assoc., sr. rsch. scholar Columbia U., 1966-94; sr. rsch. scientist Inst. for Social Rsch. U. Mich., Ann Arbor, 1994—, acting assoc. dir., 1998-99, assoc. dir., 1999—2002; editor Pub. Opinion Quar., N.Y.C., 1975-86. Author: (with Carol Weiss) The Reporting of Social Science in the Mass Media, 1988, (with Phyllis Endreny) Reporting On Risk, 1993; editor: (with Herbert H. Hyman) Readings in Reference Group Theory and Research, 1968, (with Stanley Presser) Survey Research Methods: A Reader, 1989; contbr. articles to profl. jours. Mem. Am. Assn. Pub. Opinion Rsch. (pres. N.Y.C. chpt. 1983-84, pres. 1987-88, Exceptionally Disting. Achievement award 1996), Am. Sociol. Assn., Am. Statis. Assn. Office: U Mich Inst Social Rsch PO Box 1248 Ann Arbor MI 48106-1248 E-mail: esinger@isr.umich.edu.

SINGER, EMEL, staffing industry executive; b. Gaziantep, Turkey, Apr. 7, 1944; came to U.S., 1960; d. Mehmet Resit and Nesrin (Kescioglu) Tuzun; m. James Michael Singer, Apr. 28, 1968 (dec. 1987); children: Justin Michael, Jodi Michelle. BBA, Bradley U., 1968. Adminstrv. asst. U. Ky. Med. Ctr., Lexington, 1968; exec. sec. Hoffman Products/Cortron Industries, Chgo., 1968-70; co-founder, adminstr. Banner Pers. Svc., Inc., 1970-87, chmn., CEO, 1988—; co-founder Banner Temp. Svc., 1982—; founder Banner Tng. Ctrs., 1996—, Banner Acctg. and Fin., 1999—. Guest spkr. Chgo. Entrepeneurship Program, U. Ill., Chgo., 1993—; fund-raising co-chair U. Chgo., Divsn. Mid. Ea. Studies, 1993-95. Mem. parents bd. Bradley U., Peoria, Ill., 1989-90, assoc. trustee, 1992-93, alumni master, 1993, mem. Bradley coun., 1993-95, bd. trustees, 1995—. Listed in Crains Chgo. Bus. as a Top Woman-Owned Firm, 1989, 90, 91, Today's Chgo. Woman as one of 100 Women Making a Difference, 1997; named to Entrepreneurship Hall of Fame, 1993. Mem. ASTD, Chgo. Orgn. Data Processing Educators, Nat. Assn. Pers. Svcs., Nat. Assn. Temp. Svcs., Ill. Assn. Pers. Svcs., Ill. Assn. Temporary Svcs. Avocations: skiing, scuba diving, traveling, sailing. Home: 3750 N Lake Shore Dr Chicago IL 60613-4238 Office: Banner Personnel Svc Inc 122 S Michigan Ave Chicago IL 60603-6191

SINGER, ERIC T. investment banker; b. N.Y.C., 1952; s. Roger M. and Meredith Singer; m. Aet Paaro, Aug. 10, 1974; children: Brett A., Jamison P. BA, SUNY, Stony Brook, 1974; JD, Cornell U., 1977. Assoc. Barrett, Smith et al, N.Y.C., 1977-80; v.p. Smith Barney, 1980-84; sr. v.p. PaineWebber, 1984-88; exec. v.p. Metromedia Hotels, 1988-90; exec. v.p., dir. corp. fin. Gerard Klauer Mattison, 1990-99; co-head investment banking, mng. dir. H.C. Wainwright & Co., Inc., 1999—. Mem. Cornell Law Rev. Mem. U.S. Maccabiah Squash Team, 1997. Mem. Heights Casino Club, Yale Club, Phi Beta Kappa. Home: 72 Hicks St Brooklyn NY 11201-1709 Office: 44th Fl 245 Park Ave Fl 44 New York NY 10167-0002

SINGER, FREDERICK RAPHAEL, medical researcher, educator; b. St. Louis, June 27, 1939; s. Meyer and Lee (Minkle) S.; m. Sandra Joy Barnes, Aug. 16, 1964; children: Stefanie, Jeffrey. Student, UCLA, 1956-59; BS, U. Calif., Berkeley, 1960; MD, U. Calif., San Francisco, 1963. Diplomate Am. Bd. Internal Medicine, Am. Bd. Endocrinology and Metabolism. Intern UCLA Affiliated Hosp., 1963-64; resident VA Hosp., L.A., 1964-65, 68-69; instr. in medicine Harvard U., Boston, 1971-72; asst. prof. medicine UCLA, 1972-73, U. So. Calif., L.A., 1973-74, assoc. prof., 1974-78, prof., 1978-89, prof. orthopaedic surgery, 1980-89; dir. Bone Ctr. Cedars-Sinai Med. Ctr., 1989-92, clin. prof. medicine, 1993—. Dir. Osteoporosis/Metabolic Bone Disease program St. Johns Hosp. and Health Ctr., Santa Monica, 1992—; dir. Skeletal Biology Lab, John Wayne Cancer Inst., Santa Monica, 1992—; mem. endocrine and metabolic drug adv. com. FDA, USPHS, Bethesda, Md., 1983-87. Author: Paget's Disease of Bone, 1977; contbr. numerous articles, revs. to profl. jours. Vice chmn. cmty. adv. com. Univ. High Sch., L.A., 1984. Capt. USAF, 1965-67. Calif. State scholar, 1956-60; clin. investigator VA, 1971-73. Mem. Endocrine Soc., Am. Soc. Clin. Investigation, Am. Soc. Bone and Mineral Rsch. (chmn. pub. affairs 1981-86, coun. 1987, pres.-elect 1989, pres. 1990), Paget's Disease Found. (chmn. bd. dirs. 1990—). Office: John Wayne Cancer Inst 2200 Santa Monica Blvd Santa Monica CA 90404-2302 E-mail: singerf@yahoo.com.

SINGER, GEORGE MILTON, clinical psychologist; b. Phila., Oct. 13, 1924; s. Benjamin and Bessie (Podlisker) S.; m. Carol Ann Horton, June 15, 1977; children: Elizabeth Carol, Susan Theresa, Sonnet Marie-Anne. BA, Temple U., 1950, AM, 1952, PhD, 1958. Grad. asst. exptl. psychology lab. Temple U., Phila., 1950-51, grad. asst. psychol. clinic, 1951-53, lectr., 1953-54; chief psychologist Phila. State Hosp., 1953-56; dir. psychol. services Pennhurst State Hosp., Spring City, Pa., 1958-61; clin. psychologist Kern County Mental Health Dept., Bakersfield, Calif., 1961-68; project dir., coordinator Kernview Community Mental Health Ctr., 1968-70; pvt. practice clin. psychology, 1953—2001; ret., 2001. Mem. med. staff Kern View Mental Health Ctr. and Hosp., Bakersfield, Calif., 1988-92; mem. med. staff Meml. Ctr. for Behavioral Health, Bakersfield, 1992-97; affiliated med. staff Hoag Meml. Hosp., Newport Beach, Calif., 1972-73; cons. psychologist Pioneer Cmty. Hosp., 1976-83. Cons. editor Dictionary of Psychology, Corsini, 1999. Mem. Kern County Mental Health Adv. Bd., 1976-83, adv. bd. Patton State Hosp., 1979-85; bd. dirs. Orange County Child Guidance Clinic, 1973-74. Served with USAAF, 1943-46, ETO, MTO. Recipient Service award Psi Chi, 1952, Cert. of Achievement Southeast Pa. Mental Health Assn., 1956. Mem. AAAS, APA, Calif. Psychol. Assn., Am. Soc. Clin. Hypnosis, Kern County Soc. Clin. Psychologists (pres. 1993-94), Kern County Psychol. Assn. (pres. 1968-69), Internat. Soc. Hypnosis, Rotary of Spring City (pres. 1960-61). Home: 1805 Ridgewood Dr Bakersfield CA 93306-3829 E-mail: geo99sin@cs.com.

SINGER, HOWARD JACK, biology educator; b. Newark, Sept. 4, 1940; s. Nat I. and Rose (Alboum) S.; m. Helena Liisa Niskanen, May 29, 1986; children: Jamie Alexander Niskanen-Singer. BA, Oberlin Coll., 1962; MS, U. Minn., 1966; PhD, Tufts U., 1970. Prof. biology N.J. City U. (formerly Jersey City State Coll.), Jersey City, 1970—. Cons. Proforma Base Corp., Jersey City, 1985-87, Instructivision, Inc., Livingston, N.J., 1988-89; researcher SUNY Downstate Med. Ctr., Bklyn., 1987-89. Contbr. articles to profl. jours. Pres. Van Vorst Pk. Assn., Jersey City, 1977-78; treas. Environ. Voters Alliance, N.J., 1984-90; dir. Hudson County (N.J.) Toxic Task Force, 1980-86; active Scientists Com. for Pub. Info., N.Y.C., 1976-80. Am. Chem. Soc. scholar, 1958-62; fellow NIH, 1966-70, NSF, 1961. Mem.: Am. Fedn. Tchrs. (membership chmn. 1989—), Theobald Smith Soc. (chmn. program com., pres. 1996—97, alt. nat. councilor 1997—99, nat. councilor 2000—01), Am. Soc. for Microbiology. Avocations: skiing, art nouveau, scuba, tennis. Home: 297 York St Jersey City NJ 07302-4016 Office: NJ City U 2039 John F Kennedy Blvd Jersey City NJ 07305-1527 E-mail: hsinger@njcu.edu.

SINGER, IRVING, philosophy educator; b. N.Y.C., Dec. 24, 1925; s. Isidore and Nettie (Stromer) S.; m. Josephine Fisk, June 10, 1949; children— Anne, Margaret, Emily, Benjamin. AB summa cum laude, Harvard U., 1948, MA, 1949, PhD, 1952. Instr. philosophy Cornell U., 1953-56; asst. prof. U. Mich., 1956-59; vis. lectr. Johns Hopkins U., 1957-58; mem. faculty M.I.T., 1958—, prof. philosophy, 1969—. Author: Santayana's Aesthetics, 1957, The Nature of Love: Plato to Luther, 1966, rev. edit., 1984, The Goals of Human Sexuality, 1973, Mozart and Beethoven, 1977, The Nature of Love: Courtly and Romantic, 1984, The Nature of Love: The Modern World, 1987, Meaning in Life: The Creation of Value, 1992, The Pursuit of Love, 1994, The Creation of Value, 1996, The Harmony of Nature and Spirit, 1996, Reality Transformed: Film as Meaning and Technique, 1998, George Santayana: Literary Philosopher, 2000, Feeling and Imagination: The Vibrant Flux of our Existence, 2001, Sex: A Philosophical Primer, 2001, Explorations in Love and Sex, 2001. Served with AUS, 1944-46. Fellow Guggenheim Found., 1965, Rockefeller Found., 1970, Bollingen Found., 1966; grantee Am. Council Learned Socs., 1966; Fulbright fellow, 1955. Mem. Am. Philos. Assn., Am. Soc. Aesthetics. Office: MIT Rm E39-351 Cambridge MA 02139

SINGER, ISADORE MANUEL, mathematician, educator; b. Detroit, May 3, 1924; married; 5 children. BS, U. Mich., 1944; MS, U. Chgo., 1948, PhD in Math., 1950; ScD (hon.) , Tulane U., 1981; LLD (hon.) , U. Mich., 1989, U. Ill., Chgo. Moore instr. math. MIT, Cambridge, 1950—52, prof. math., 1956—70, Norbert Wiener prof., 1970—79, John D. MacArthur prof. math. (1st holder), 1983—, Inst. prof., 1987—; asst. prof. UCLA, 1952—54; vis. prof. math U. Calif., Berkeley, 1977—79, prof., 1979—83, Miller prof. math., 1982—83, prof. math., 1977—83. Vis. asst. prof. math. Columbia U., N.Y.C., 1954—55; mem. Inst. Advanced Study, 1955—56; past steering com. Ctr. for Non-Linear Scis., Los Alamos Nat. Labs.; adv. bd. Inst. Theoretical Physics, U. Calif., Santa Barbara; bd. dirs. Santa Fe Inst.; mem. various organizing coms. ; editor procs. for confs. in field. Former editor profl. jours. Recipient Nat. medal of Sci., 1983, Steele prize Lifetime Achievement, 2000; fellow Alfred P. Sloan, 1959—62, Guggenheim, 1968—69, 1975—76. Mem.: NAS (past councillor, former mem. com. math. and phys. scis., other coms.), Internat. Congress Mathematicians (program com.; 1986, Wigner prize 1989), Am. Phys. Soc., Am. Math. Soc. (v.p. 1970—72, past exec. com., Bocher Meml. prize 1969, Pub. Svc. award 1993), Am. Acad. Arts and Scis., Am. Philos. Soc. Office: MIT Dept of Math Bldg 2 Rm 387 77 Massachusetts Ave Cambridge MA 02139-4307

SINGER, J. DAVID, political science educator; b. Bklyn., Dec. 7, 1925; s. Morris L. and Anne (Newman) S.; m. C. Diane Macaulay, Apr., 1990; children: Kathryn Louise, Eleanor Anne. BA, Duke U., 1946; LLD (hon.), Northwestern U., 1983; PhD, NYU, 1956. Instr. NYU, 1954-55, Vassar Coll., 1955-57; vis. fellow social relations Harvard U., 1957-58; vis. asst. prof. U. Mich., Ann Arbor, 1958-60, sr. scientist Mental Health Research Inst., 1960-82, assoc. prof., 1964-65, prof. polit. sci., 1965—, coordinator World Politics Program, 1969-75, 81-90; vis. prof. U. Oslo and Inst. Social Research, 1963-64, 90, Carnegie Endowment Internat. Peace and Grd. Inst. Internat. Studies, Geneva, 1967-68, Zuma and U. Mannheim (W. Ger.), 1976, Grad. Inst. Internat. Studies, Geneva, 1983-84; U. Groningen, The Netherlands, 1991; Nat. Chengchi U., Taiwan, 1998. Author: Financing International Organization: The United Nations Budget Process, 1961, Deterrence, Arms Control and Disarmament: Toward a Synthesis in National Security Policy, 1962, rev. 1984, (with Melvin Small) The Wages of War, 1816-1965: A Statistical Handbook, 1972, (with Susan Jones) Beyond Conjecture in International Politics: Abstracts of Data Based Research, 1972, (with Dorothy La Barr) The Study of International Politics: A Guide to Sources for the Student, Teacher and Researcher, 1976, Correlates of War I and II, 1979, 80, (with Melvin Small) Resort to Arms: International and Civil War, 1816-1980, 1982, Models, Methods, and Progress: A Peace Research Odyssey, 1990, (with Paul Diehl) Measuring the Correlates of War, 1998, (with D. Geller) Nations at War, 1998; monographs; contbr. articles to profl. jours.; mem. editorial bd. ABC: Polit. Sci. and Govt., 1968-84, Polit. Sci. Reviewer, 1971— , Conflict Mgmt. and Peace Sci., 1978— , Etudes Polemologiques, 1978—, Internat. Studies Quar., 1989—, Jour. Conflict Resolution, 1989—, Internat. Interactions, 1989—. With USNR, 1943-66. Ford fellow, 1956; Ford grantee, 1957-58; Phoenix Meml. Fund grantee, 1959,, 1981-82; Fulbright scholar, 1963-64; Carnegie Corp. research grantee, 1963-67; NSF grantee, 1967-76, 1986-89, 1992-94; Guggenheim grantee, 1978-79 Mem. Am. Polit. Sci. Assn. (Helen Dwight Reid award com. 1967, 95, chmn. Woodrow Wilson award com., chmn. nominating com. 1970), Internat. Polit. Sci. Assn. (chmn. conflict and peace rsch. com. 1974—), World Assn. Internat. Rels., Internat. Soc. Polit. Psychology, Internat. Soc. Rsch. on Aggression, Social Sci. History Assn., Peace Sci. Soc., Internat. Peace Rsch. Assn. (pres. 1972-73), Consortium on Peace Rsch., Fedn. Am. Scientists (nat. coun. 1991-95), Union Concerned Scientists, Arms Control Assn., Internat. Studies Assn. (pres. 1985-86), Com. Nat. Security, Am. Com. on East-West Accord, World Federalist Assn. Office: U Mich Dept Polit Sci Ann Arbor MI 48104 *As a researcher, teacher, consultant and activist, my goal has been to bring rigorous scientific methods to bear on the causes of war question, and to encourage the integration of ethical concern and hard evidence.*

SINGER, JEFFREY, lawyer; b. Bklyn., Apr. 5, 1955; s. Stanley and May Singer; m. Carol Joan Gilbert, Nov. 23, 1991; 1 child, Tori Hannah; step-children: Matthew Hollander, Michael Hollander. BA, SUNY at Stony Brook, 1976; JD, Bklyn. Law Sch., 1979. Bar: N.Y. 1980, U.S. Dist. Ct. (so. dist. and ea. dist.) N.Y. 1980, U.S. Ct. Appeals (2d cir.) 1982, U.S. Supreme Ct. 1984. Law clk. Segan, Culhane, Nemerov & Geen P.C., N.Y.C., 1977-79, assoc., 1980-86, ptnr., 1986—. Mem. Am. Trial Lawyers Assn., N.Y. State Trial Lawyers, Assn. of Bar of City of N.Y. Avocations: scuba diving, golf, wine collecting. E-mial. Office: Segan Nemerov & Singer PC 112 Madison Ave Fl 6 New York NY 10016-7416 E-mail: jsinger@snslaw.com.

SINGER, JEFFREY ALAN, surgeon; b. Bklyn., Feb. 2, 1952; s. Harold and Hilda (Ginsburg) S.; m. Margaret Sue Gordon, May 23, 1976; children: Deborah Suzanne, Pamela Michele. BA cum laude, Bklyn. Coll., 1973; MD, N.Y. Med. Coll., 1976. Diplomate Am. Bd. Surgery. Intern Maricopa County Gen. Hosp., Phoenix, 1976-77, resident, 1977-81, mem. teaching faculty, 1981-96; trauma cons. John C. Lincoln Hosp., 1981-83; pvt. practice, 1981-87; group pvt. practice Valley Surg. Clinics, Ltd., 1987—, S.W. Surg. Clinics, P.C., Phoenix, 1996-97. Sec.-treas. med. staff Humana Desert Valley Hosp., Phoenix, 1987-89, chief surgery, 1985-87, 91-93, exec. com., 1993-95; adj. asst. prof. divsn. clin. edn. Ariz. Coll. Osteo. Med., Midwestern U., 1998—; mem. adj. clin. faculty Kirksville (Mo.) Coll. Osteo. Medicine. Assoc. editor Ariz. Medicine, 1994-2000, contbg. writer, 2001—. Rep. precinct committeeman, Phoenix, 1986-2000; mem. exec. com. bd. dirs. Goldwater Inst. for Pub. Policy Rsch., 2002—. Fellow: ACS, Am. Soc. Abdominal Surgeons, Southwestern Surg. Congress, Internat. Coll. Surgeons; mem.: Maricopa County Med. Soc. (v.p. 1998, bd. dirs. 1998—2002), Ariz. Med. Assn. (bd. dirs. polit. com. 1985—, legis com. 1986—, chmn. bd. dirs. polit. com. 1991—93), Ariz. Sch. Choice Trust (bd. dirs. 1998—). Avocations: philosophy, politics, history, travel, underwater sports, writing. Office: Valley Surg Clinics Ltd 16601 N 40th St Ste 216 Phoenix AZ 85032-3353

SINGER, JEFFREY MICHAEL, organic analytical chemist; b. N.Y.C., Feb. 2, 1949; s. Samuel and Theresa (Pohl) S.; m. Linda Arlene Prizer, Oct. 13, 1972; 1 child, Sarah. BA, CUNY, 1971; MS, Rensselaer Poly. Inst., 1976; MA, CUNY, 1979; PhD, Poly. U., Bklyn., 1987. Analytical chemist Equitable Environ. Health Inc., Woodbury, N.Y., 1979-80; group leader Chemtech Cons. Group, N.Y.C., 1980-81; sr. chemist, lab. supr. Revlon Health Care, Tuckahoe, N.Y., 1981-86; analytical devel. chemist Lederle Labs., Pearl River, 1986-87; sr. chemist PepsiCo Inc., Valhalla, 1987-89; lab. mgr. Pall Corp., Glen Cove, 1989-90; mgr. analytical tech. support Du Pont Pharms., Garden City, 1990-93; prin. scientist DuPont Pharms., 1993-94; mgr. analytical R & D Clay-Park Labs., Bronx, 1995-96, mgr. R & D contract product devel., 1996-97; mgr. analytical rsch. and methods devel. G & W Labs., South Plainfield, N.J., 1997-99; assoc. dir. quality support svcs. Emisphere Techs., Inc., Tarrytown, NY, 1999—2002; ind. pharm. devel. cons., 2002—. Author: Analytical Profiles of Drug Substances, 1985. Charter mem. N.Y. Hall of Sci., Flushing, 1985; judge borough competition N.Y.C. Annual Sci. Fair, Flushing, 1987-88, 90. Mem. AAAS, Am. Chem. Soc., Assn. Official Analytical Chemists Internat. (program chairperson 1988-90, pres. N.Y.-N.J. sect. 1991-92), Parenteral Drug Assn., Am. Soc. Quality Control, N.Y. Acad. Scis., Sigma Xi. Achievements include research in chromatographic analytical methods development and validation of biologically and pharmacological active molecules, pharmacognosy of novel natural products, lab. info. mgmt. systems, robotics, process optimization, computer validation and technology transfer.

SINGER, JON DOUGLAS, receptionist, writer; b. N.Y.C. s. Jerome Leonard and Dorothy Gottlieb Singer. BA, NYU, 1974, MA, 1978. Shelver libr. books Yale U. Med. Sch., New Haven, 1987-88, Wilbur Smith Assocs., New Haven, 1996; receptionist Fellowship Club, 2000—. Author: Lost Lands and Cities, 1987, Lost Lands and Cities Beneath the Sea, 1997, Ireland's Mysterious Lands and Sunken Cities, 2001. Campaign asst. Dem. Party, N.Y.C., 1980. Jewish. Avocations: archaeology, astronomy, quantum physics. Home: 305 Audubon Ct New Haven CT 06510

SINGER, JOYCE ZANDRA, physician; b. Bklyn., Jan. 12, 1950; d. Irving A. and Alice (Scondutto) S.; m. Peter B. Milburn, Aug. 11, 1974; children: Rebecca, Eleanor, Sarah, Deborah. AB, Barnard Coll., 1972; MD, Albert Einstein U., 1977. Diplomate Am. Bd. Internal Medicine. Med. resident Kings County Hosp., Bklyn., 1977-81; chief med. resident Bklyn. Vet. Hosp., 1981-82; rheumatology fellow SUNY, Bklyn., 1982-85, rheumatology faculty, 1985-90.

SINGER, KARL LAWRENCE, physician, health facility administrator; b. Detroit, June 20, 1942; s. David and Anne (Blum) S.; m. Paula Jane McCrensky, Aug. 21, 1967; children: Karen, Daniel, Holly, Matthew, Andrew. BA, Harvard U., 1963, MD, 1967. Diplomate Am. Bd. Family Practice, Am. Bd. Internal Medicine; added qualification in geriatrics. Intern U. Colo., Denver, 1967-68; resident Beth Israel Hosp., Boston, 1970-72; svc. unit dir. Pub. Health Svc., Chinle, Ariz., 1969-70; clin. dir. Exeter (N.H.) Clinic, 1972-79, pres., 1979-81; asst. prof. Ben Gurion U., Beer Sheva, Israel, 1981-82; pres. Exeter Family Medicine Assocs., 1982-95; med. dir. Exeter Family Medicine Lahey Hitchcock Clinic, 1995-97, Exeter Family Medicine Hitchcock Clinic, 1998, Exeter Family Medicine Assocs., 1999—. Med. dir. Rockingham Nursing Home, Brentwood, N.H., 1982—, Patient Care Mag., Montvale, N.J., 1989—. Fellow Am. Acad. Family Practice; mem. ACP-ASIM, N.H. Med. Soc. Avocations: viola, mathematics. Office: Exeter Family Medicine Assocs 9 Buzell Ave Ste 1 Exeter NH 03833-2595

SINGER, KATHRYN J. assistant principal; d. Walter and Elinor Katyryniuk; children: Joseph, Kristine. AA, Centralia (Wash.) Coll., 1963; BA, U. Puget Sound, 1965; MEd, Lesley Coll., 1991. Lic. adminstrv. edn. Nev., Wash. Sci. dept. chair Clark County Sch. Dist., Las Vegas, 1994-97, dean of students, 1997-99, asst. prin., 1999—. Chairperson Profl. Devel. Com., Las Vegas, 2000—; cons. Chapman U. State of Nev., 1998-2000, prof., 1998—; adv. bd. Nev. Sci. Project, Las Vegas, 1995-99. Named Outstanding Sci. Tchr. Clark County Sci. Tchrs. Assn., 1995, 96. Mem. Nat. Assn. of Secondary Sch. Prins., Assn. of Secondary Curriculum Devel., Phi Delta Kappa. Avocations: hiking, walking, books. Home: 113 Clifton Heights Dr Las Vegas NV 89145

SINGER, KATIE ELLEN, writer, medical educator; b. N.Y.C., Apr. 11, 1960; BA in Edn. and Lit., Antioch Coll., 1982. Cert. fertility educator. Writer in residence South Boston (Mass) H.S., 1983-89; cons. Writing Workshops for Tchrs., 1986-92; fertility educator Women's Health Svcs., Santa Fe, 1997—. Author: (book) The Wholeness of a Broken Heart, 1999 (selected for Barnes

& Nobles Discover Great New Writers Program, 1999); contbr. articles to profl. publs. Grantee, Vogelstein Found., 1992, Western State Arts Fedn., 1995. Mem.: PEN, Ovulation Method Tchrs. Assn., Authors Guild. Office: PO Box 6574 Santa Fe NM 87502

SINGER, KURT DEUTSCH, news commentator, writer, publisher; b. Vienna, Austria, Aug. 10, 1911; came to U.S., 1940, naturalized, 1951; s. Ignaz Deutsch and Irene (Singer) S.; m. Hilda Tradelius, Dec. 23, 1932 (div. 1954); children: Marian Alice Birgit, Kenneth Walt; m. Jane Sherrod, Apr. 9, 1955 (dec. Jan. 1985); m. Katherine Han, Apr. 8, 1989. Student, U. Zürich, Switzerland, 1930, Labor Coll., Stockholm, Sweden, 1936; PhD, Div. Coll. Metaphysics, Indpls., 1951. Escaped to, Sweden, 1934; founder Ossietzky Com. (successful in release Ossietzky from concentration camp); corr. Swedish mag. Folket i Bild, 1935-40; founder Niemöller Com.; pub. biography Göring in Eng. (confiscated in Sweden), 1940; co-founder pro-Allied newspaper Trots Allt, 1939; corr. Swedish newspapers in, U.S., 1940; editor News Background, 1942; lectr. U. Minn., U. Kans., U. Wis., 1945-49; radio commentator WKAT, 1950; corr. N.Am. Newspaper Alliance, N.Y.C., 1953—; pres. Singer Media Corp., 1987—. Dir. Oceanic Press Service, San Clemente, Calif. Author, editor: underground weekly Mitteilungsblätter, Berlin, Germany, 1933; author: The Coming War, 1934, (biog.) Carl von Ossietzky, 1936 (Nobel Peace prize), Germany's Secret Service in Central America, 1943, Spies and Saboteurs in Argentina, 1943, Duel for the Northland, 1943, White Book of the Church of Norway, 1940, Spies and Traitors of World War II, 1945, Who are the Communists in America, 1948, 3000 Years of Espionage, 1951, World's Greatest Women Spies, 1952, Kippie the Cow; juvenile, 1952, Gentlemen Spies, 1953, The Man in the Trojan Horse, 1954, World's Best Spy Stories, 1954, Charles Laughton Story; adapted TV, motion pictures, 1954, Spies Over Asia, 1955, More Spy Stories, 1955, My Greatest Crime Story, 1956, My Most Famous Case, 1957, The Danny Kaye Saga; My Strangest Case, 1958, Spy Omnibus, 1959, Spies for Democracy, 1960, Crime Omnibus Spies Who Changed History, 1961, Hemmingway-Life and Death of a Giant, 1961, True Adventures in Crime, Dr. Albert Schweitzer, Medical Missionary, 1962, Lyndon Baines Johnson-Man of Reason, 1964, Ho-i-man; juveniles, 1965; Kurt Singer's Ghost Omnibus, 1965; juvenile Kurt Singer's Horror Omnibus; The World's Greatest Stories of the Occult, The Unearthly, 1965, Mata Hari-Goddess of Sin, 1965, Daughter of Mata Hari, 1965, Lyndon Johnson-From Kennedy to Vietnam, 1966, Weird Tales Anthology, 1966, I Can't Sleep at Night, 1966, Weird Tales of Supernatural, 1967, Tales of Terror, 1967, Famous Short Stories, 1967, Folktales of the South Pacific, 1967, Tales of The Uncanny, 1968, Gothic Reader, 1968, Bloch and Bradbury, 1969, Folktales of Mexico, 1969, Tales of the Unknown, 1970, The House in the Valley, 1970, Hablan Los Artistas, 1970, Tales of the Macabre, 1971, Three Thousand Years of Espionage, 1971, El Mundo de Hoy, 1971, Cuentos Fantasticos del Mas, 1971, Aldous Huxley, El Camino al Infierno, 1971, Ghouls and Ghosts, 1972, The Unearthly, 1972, The Gothic Reader, 1972, Satanic Omnibus, 1973, The Plague of the Living Dead, 1973, Gothic Horror Omnibus, 1974, Dictionary of Household Hints and Help, 1974, Supernatural, 1974, They are Possessed, 1976, True Adventures into the Unknown, 1980, I Spied-And Survived, 1980, Great Adventures in Crime, 1982, The Oblong Box, 1982, Shriek, 1984, First Target Book of Horror, 1984, 2d, 1984, 3d, 1985, 4th, 1985, Solve A Crime, 1994, The Ultimate Quiz Book, 1994, The Complete Guide to Career Advancement, 1994, The Sex Quiz Book, 1994, The Marriage Quiz Book, The Psychology Quiz Book, The Teenage Quiz Book, Success Secrets, 1995, Conozcase Mejor y Triunfe, 1995, The Joy of Practical Parenting, 1995; editor: UN Calendar, 1959-58; fgn. corres. German mags., 1996-2000; contbr. articles to newspapers, popular mags., U.S., fgn. countries, all his books and papers in Boston U. Library-Spl. Collections, Awd Literatur Haus, Vienna, Austria. Mem. UN Speakers Research Com., UN Children's Emergency Fund, Menninger Found. Mem. Nat. Geog. Soc., Smithsonian Assos., Internat. Platform Assn. (v.p.), United Sch. Assemblies (pres.) *In the sunset years of my life, I feel stronger than ever that the most important contribution one makes in a lifetime is to plant as many seeds as possible with many people, and perhaps many countries. Who knows where the seeds of ideas survive and expand?.*

SINGER, MARCUS GEORGE, philosopher, educator; b. N.Y.C., Jan. 4, 1926; s. David Emanuel and Esther (Kobre) S.; m. Blanche Ladenson, Aug. 10, 1947; children: Karen Beth, Debra Ann. AB with high honors, U. Ill., 1948; PhD (Susan Linn Sage fellow), Cornell U., 1952. Asst. in philosophy Cornell U., Ithaca, N.Y., 1948-49, instr. philosophy, 1951-52, U. Wis.-Madison, 1952-55, asst. prof., 1955-59, assoc. prof., 1959-63, prof. philosophy, 1963-92, prof. emeritus, 1992—, chmn. dept. philosophy, 1963-68; chmn. philosophy dept. U. Wis. Center System, 1964-66; dir. pub. lectr. series Royal Inst. Philosophy, London, 1984-85. Vis. fellow Birkbeck Coll., U. London, 1962-63; research assoc. U. Calif.-Berkeley, 1969; vis. Cowling prof. philosophy Carleton Coll., Northfield, Minn., 1972; vis. prof. humanities U. Fla., Gainesville, 1975; vis. fellow U. Warwick, 1977, 84-85; vis. Francis M. Bernardin disting. prof. humanities U. Mo., Kansas City, 1979; hon. research fellow Birkbeck Coll., U. London, 1984-85; acad. visitor London Sch. Econs., U. London, 1984-85 Author: Generalization in Ethics, 2d edit., 1971, Verallgemeinerung in der Ethik, 1975, The Ideal of a Rational Morality, 2002; editor: Morals and Values, 1977, American Philosophy, 1986, Reason, Reality, and Speculative Philosophy, 1996, Essays on Ethics and Method, 2000; contbr. Essays in Moral Philosophy, 1958, Ency. of Philosophy, 1967, Law and Philosophy, 1971, Skepticism and Moral Principles, 1973, Morals and Values, 1977, Acad. Am. Ency., 1982, 84, 89, World Book Ency., 1984, 86, Gewirth's Ethical Rationalism, 1984, Morality and Universality, 1985, American Philosophy, 1986, New Directions in Ethics, 1986, The Handbook of Western Philosophy, 1988, Applying Philosophy, 1988, Moral Philosophy: Historical and Contemporary Essays, 1989, Key Themes in Philosophy, 1990, Essays on Henry Sidgwick, 1992, Ency. of Ethics, 1992, A History of Western Ethics, 1992, Ethics, 1993, Consequentialism, 1993, Cambridge Dictionary of Philosophy, 1995, 99, Biographical Dictionary of Twentieth Century Philosophers, 1996, Pragmatism, Reason, and Norms, 1998, Ratio Juris, 2000; co-editor: Introductory Readings in Philosophy, 2d edit., 1974, Reason and the Common Good, 1963, Belief, Knowledge and Truth, 1970, Legislative Intent and other Essays on Law, Politics and Morality, 1993. Served with USAAF, 1944-45. Am. Philos. Assn. Western Div. fellow, 1956-57; Summer Research grant Social Sci. Research Council, 1958; Guggenheim fellow, 1962-63; Inst. for Research in Humanities fellow U. Wis., 1984 Mem. AAUP, Am. Philos. Assn. (v.p. Western divsn. 1984-85, pres. Ctrl. divsn. 1985-86, bd. officers 1991-94), Royal Inst. Philosophy, Charles S. Peirce Soc, Soc. for Advancement Am. Philosophy, Wis. Acad. Scis., Arts and Letters, N.Y. Acad. Scis., Sidgwick Soc. (exec. dir.), Phi Beta Kappa, Phi Kappa Phi. Home: 5021 Regent St Madison WI 53705-4745

SINGER, MARKUS MORTON, retired trade association executive; b. N.Y.C., Dec. 20, 1917; s. Isadore and Nettie (Stromer) S.; m. Phyllis Berger, June 26, 1945; children— Fredric L., Robert B. B.C.S., NYU, 1939; postgrad., George Washington U., 1951-55. With Nat. Food Brokers Assn., Washington, 1946—, v.p., 1961-65, exec. v.p., 1965-71, pres., 1972-83, pres. emeritus, 1983—, acting pres., chief exec. officer, 1987-88. Lifetime hon. trustee Nat. Food Brokers Assn. Edn. and Tng. Found. Served with AUS, 1942-45. Recipient Pres.'s award as Man of Yr. Can. Food Brokers Assn., 1976 Mem. European Food Brokers Assn. (hon. life), Frozen Food Industry Disting. Order of Zerocrats. Jewish.

SINGER, MAXINE FRANK, biochemist, scientific institute executive; b. N.Y.C., Feb. 15, 1931; d. Hyman S. and Henrietta (Perlowitz) Frank; m. Daniel Morris Singer, June 15, 1952; children: Amy Elizabeth, Ellen Ruth, David Byrd, Stephanie Frank. AB, Swarthmore Coll., 1952, DSc (hon.) , 1978; PhD, Yale U., 1957, DSc (hon.) , 1994, Wesleyan U., 1977, U. Md.-Baltimore County, 1985, Cedar Crest Coll., 1986, CUNY, 1988, Brandeis U., 1988, Radcliffe Coll., 2000, Williams Coll., 1990, Franklin and Marshall Coll., 1991, George Washington U., 1991, NYU, 1992, Lehigh U., 1992, Dartmouth Coll., 1993, Harvard U., 1994, Yale U., 1994; PhD honoris causa (hon.) , Weizmann Inst. Sci., 1995. USPHS postdoctoral fellow NIH, Bethesda, Md., 1956—58, rsch. chemist biochemistry, 1958—74; head sect. on nucleic acid enzymology Nat. Cancer Inst., 1974—79; chief Lab. of Biochemistry, Nat. Cancer Inst., 1979—87, rsch. chemist, 1987—88; pres. Carnegie Inst. Washington, 1988—2002. Regents vis. lectr. U. Calif., Berkeley, 1981; bd. dirs. Johnson & Johnson. Mem. editl. bd.: Jour. Biol. Chemistry, 1968—74, mem. editl. bd.: Sci. mag, 1972—82, chmn. editl. bd.: Procs. of NAS, 1985—88; co-author (with Paul Berg): 3 books on molecular biology; contbr. Chmn. Smithsonian Coun., 1992—93; trustee Wesleyan U., Middletown, Colo., 1972—75, Yale Corp., New Haven, 1975—90; bd. govs. Weizmann Inst. Sci., Rehovot, Israel, 1978—; bd. dirs. Whitehead Inst., 1985—94. Named to Washington D.C. Hall of Fame, 2000; recipient award for achievement in biol. scis., Washington Acad. Scis., 1969, award for rsch. in biol. scis., Yale Sci. and Engring. Assn., 1974, Superior Svc. Honor award, HEW, 1975, Dirs. award, NIH, 1977, Disting. Svc. medal, HHS, 1983, Presdl. Disting. Exec. Rank award, 1987, U.S. Disting. Exec. Rank award, 1987, Mory's Cup, Bd. Govs. Mory's Assn., 1991, Wilbur Lucius Cross Medal for Honor, Yale Grad. Sch. Assn., 1991, Nat. Medal Sci., NSF, 1992, Pub. Svc. award, NIH Alumni Assn., 1995, Vannevar Bush award, Nat. Sci. Bd., 1999. Fellow: Am. Acad. Arts and Scis.; mem.: AAAS (Sci. Freedom and Responsibility award 1982), NAS (coun. 1982—85, com. sci., engring and pub. policy 1989—91, chmn. 1999—), Perlegen Scis. (bd. dirs. 2001), Biolabs (Nat. Adv. Bd. 2000), N.Y. Acad. Scis., Human Genome Orgn., Pontifical Acad. of Scis., Inst. Medicine of NAS, Am. Philos. Soc., Am. Chem. Soc., Am. Soc. Microbiologists, Am. Soc. Biol. Chemists. Home: 5410 39th St NW Washington DC 20015-2902 Office: Carnegie Inst Washington 1530 P St NW Washington DC 20005-1933

SINGER, MERLE ELLIOT, rabbi; b. Duluth, Minn., May 11, 1939; s. Samuel and Brenda (Naymark) S.; m. Myra Golden, Aug. 29, 1965; children: Jonathan, Jeremy, Michael, Mark. AB, U. Cin., 1961; BHL, MAHL, Hebrew Union Coll., Cin., 1966, DD (hon.), 1991; DHL, Gwynedd-Mercy Coll., 1978; D in Pub. Svc. (hon.), Fla. Atlantic U., 1999. Ordained rabbi. Rabbi Temple Sinai, Washington, 1966-71. Reform Congregation Beth Or, Phila., 1971-78; sr. rabbi Temple Beth El, Boca Raton, Fla., 1978—. Adj. prof. history, Judaic studies Fla. Atlantic U., Boca Raton,1978-79; adj. prof. Judaic studies Gwynedd Mercy Coll., Phila., 1975-78; instr. I.M. Wise div. Gratz Coll., Phila., 1971-76; chaplain Boca Raton Police Dept.; rabbinic and com. Camp Coleman, Union Am. Hebrew Congregations, Cleveland, Ga., 1978—; delegate to World Zionist Congress, Israel, 1997. Sponsor inter-faith and Holocaust seminars for the Sisters of Mercy, facuty and students of Gwynedd Mercy Coll., 1978; Jewish student affairs advisor Phila. Coll. of Textiles and Scis., 1976-77, Villanova U., 1976-77; Rabbinic bd. overseers Hebrew Union Coll., 1985—; campaign v.p. United Way of South Palm Beach County, 1986-87, pres., 1987-88; mem. adv. bd. Mae Volen Sr. Ctr., Boca Raton, 1981; clergy advisor Planned Parenthood of Palm Beach County, Inc., Boca Raton; bd. dirs. Edn. Found. Palm Beach County, Inc., 1986-88, Florence Fuller Child Devel. Ctr., Boca Raton, Am. Jewish Com., 1995—; past pres. Religious Leadres Assn. Boca Raton; mem. ethics com. Boca Raton Cmty. Hosp., 1992—; invitee Pres.'s Ann. Prayer Breakfast, Washington, 1996. Recipient nat. award for outstanding svc. Domestic Policy Assn./Nat. Issues Forum, 1985-86, Ben Gurion award for Israel bonds State of Israel, 1975, 85, Torch of Liberty Humanitarian award Anti-Defamation League, 1981, Cmty. Svc. award Boca Raton News, 1982, So Far award Boy Scouts Am., 1987, B'nai Avraham award Am. Jewish Com., 1991, citation Jewish Chautauqua Soc., 1993, Silver Medallion Brotherhood award NCCJ, 1992, Cmty. Svc. award Boys Town Jerusalem, 1993, Golden Shofar award Israel Bonds, 1997, Leading Man award Palm Beach County Cystic Fibrosis Found., 1998; named to Four Chaplains Legion of Honor, Phila., 1981; named Minister of Day, State of Fla., 1993; Merle E. Singer Day proclaimed in his honor, City of Boca Raton, 1991, 96; elected to Boca Raton's Walk of Recognition, 1999. Mem. South Palm Beach Bd. of Rabbis, Palm Beach Bd. of Rabbis (past. pres.), Union of Am. Hebrew Congregations (com. for winning the unaffiliated), Assn. Reform Zionists Am. (bd. dirs. 1983—), S.E. Ctrl. Conf. Am. Rabbis (pres. 1995—), Ctrl. Conf. Am. Rabbis (com. on relief, subvention and solicitation, nat. bd. 1995—), Israel Bonds (nat. rabbinic cabinet), Hebrew Union Coll. Inst. of Religion (presidents alumni assn. 1984—), Synagogue Coun. Am. (nat. bd. govs.). Office: Temple Beth El 333 SW 4th Ave Boca Raton FL 33432-5798

SINGER, MERTON, engineer; b. Superior, Wis., Aug. 21, 1913; s. Samuel N. and Lena H. (Dorf) S.; m. Jean Helen Eidelberg, Oct. 19, 1941; children: Stephen L., Robert E. BS, U.S. Mil. Acad., 1938; MS, U. Pitts., 1947; postgrad., Wharton Sch., U. Pa., 1955. Registered profl. engr. Commd. 2d lt. U.S. Army, 1938, advanced through grades to col., 1951, various comdg. officer positions worldwide, 1938-65; chief ops. divsn. Army-Navy petroleum bd. Joint Chiefs of Staff, Washington, 1947-48; army mem. Pacific command Petroleum office, comdr.-in-chief Pacific and Pacific Fleet, Pearl Harbor, 1949-53; prof. mil. sci. and tactics U. Pa., Phila., 1953-56; comdg. officer U.S. Army Petroleum Distbn. Command, Fontainebleau, France, 1956-60; commdr. Ft. Jay, Governors Island, N.Y., 1960-64; ret. U.S. Army, 1965; v.p. and asst. to the pres. United Bd. and Carton Corp., N.Y.C., 1964-70; exec. dir. R&D Assocs. for Mil. Food and Packaging Systems, 1970-89; CEO Merton Singer Assocs., San Antonio, 1989. Trustee Assn. of Grads., U.S. Mil. Acad., West Point, N.Y., 1961-67, 68-69. Inventor field method of distilling water, 1942, geologic calculator/U.S., 1950, geologic calculator/internat., 1955; contbr. articles to profl. jours. Founding chmn., bd. dirs. Jewish Cadet Chapel Fund, U.S. Mil. Acad. Decorated Legion of Merit, Bronze Star, Army Commendation medal, French Croix de Guerre with Palm, 1944, French Order of the Black Star, Pres. Charles DeGaulle, 1960, European Theater of Ops. medal with 1 silver svc. star, Army of Occupation medal with Germany clasp; recipient Royal Jugoslav Commemorative War Cross, King of Yugoslavia, 1945, Decoration for Disting. Civilian Svc., Sec. of Army, 1989, Disting. Civilian Svc. medal Comdr. U.S. Army Natick R&D Ctr., 1989; named to Hall of Fame, R&D Assocs. for Mil. Food and Packaging Systems, 1996. Mem. Assn. Grads. U.S. Mil. Acad., Mil. Order of World Wars (exec. com. 1960-70), Army Athletic Assn., U. Pitts. Alumni Assn., West Point Soc. of N.Y. (pres. 1966-68, bd. dirs. emeritus 1968), Am. Logistics Assn. (pres. Phila. chpt. 1951-52, pres. Orleans France chpt. 1954-55, pres. N.Y.C. chpt. 1960-61), West Point Soc. of South Tex. (bd. dirs. 1972-75), R&D Assoc. (exec. dir. 1970-89, exec. dir. emeritus 1989), McNay Art Inst., Masons, Club Giraud. Republican. Jewish. Achievements include development of Automatic Resupply for Petroleum Products adopted for ammunition that is universally used by department stores and companies for thousands of diversified products; development reduced paper work by 98% and guaranteed the supply of products at the right time and place. Home: 10119 N Manton Ln San Antonio TX 78213-1932 Office: Merton Singer Assocs Paper Bd Specialists 105 Biltmore San Antonio TX 78213-1832 E-mail: mert@mertsinger.com.

SINGER, MICHAEL HOWARD, lawyer; b. N.Y.C., Nov. 22, 1941; s. Jack and Etta (Appelbaum) S.; m. Saundra Jean Kupperman, June 1, 1962; children: Allison Jill, Pamela Faith. BS in Econs., U. Pa., 1962; JD, NYU, 1965, LLM in Taxation, 1968. Bar: N.Y. 1965, U.S. Ct. Claims 1968, U.S. Supreme Ct. 1969, U.S. Ct. Appeals (6th cir.) 1970, D.C. 1972, U.S. Tax Ct. 1972, Nev. 1973, U.S. Ct. Appeals (9th cir.) 1973. Law asst. Appellate Term Supreme Ct., N.Y.C., 1965-68; trial lawyer Ct. Claims Tax Div., Washington, 1968-72; tax lawyer Beckley, DeLanoy & Jemison, Las Vegas, 1972-74; ptnr. Oshins, Singer, Segal & Morris, 1974-87; pvt. practice, 1987; ptnr. Michael H. Singer Ltd., 1987-96, Singer, Brown, and Barringer, LLC, Las Vegas, 1996-99, Singer & Brown, LLC, 1999—. Settlement judge Nev. Supreme Ct., 1997—. Pres. Las Vegas chpt. NCCJ, 1980-82. Mem. ABA, ABI, Nev. Bar Assn., Las Vegas Country Club (bd. dirs. 1999—, v.p. 2001—). Democrat. Jewish. Avocations: golf, tennis. Home: 4458 Los Reyes Ct Las Vegas NV 89121-5341 Office: Singer & Brown LLC 520 S 4th St Fl 2 Las Vegas NV 89101-6524 E-mail: mhsinger@lvcm.com. *Personal philosophy: A reasonable settlement is more economically beneficial for the client than protracted litigation of a great lawsuit.*

SINGER, MYER R(ICHARD), lawyer; b. Everett, Mass., Oct. 24, 1938; s. Nathan and Celia (Rudin) Singer; m. Elaine Doris Ginesky, June 17, 1962; children: Andrew L., Stephen D., Jocelyn G. BSBA, Boston U., 1960, LLB, 1963. Bar: Mass. 1963, U.S. Ct. Appeals (1st cir.) 1963. Atty. Boston Legal Aid Soc., 1963-64; pvt. practice Dennis Port, 1965—. Trustee, corporator, mem. bd. investment Cape Cod Five Cents Savs. bank, Harwich Port, Mass.; trustee Cape Cod Mus. of Natural History, 2001—; faculty Mass. Continuing Legal Edn., Inc., 1985, 1990—98; program chmn. Real Estate Devel. Cape Cod-Mass. Bar Inst., 1999; spkr. in field. Co-author: (book) Creation and Care of Condominiums, 1985, Everything You Need to Know about the Cape Cod Commission Act, 1990. Pres. Dennis Yarmouth Band Parents, 1986—87; mem. adv. bd. Cape Mus. Fine Arts, Dennis, 1988—96; former trustee Cape Cod Synagogue; mem., clk. Yarmouth (Mass.) Zoning Bd. Appeals, 1980—86; former bd. dirs. Cape Cod and Island chpt. of Mass. Heart Assn.; former pres. Legal Svcs. of Cape Cod and Island, Inc. Mem.: ABA, Barnstable County Bar Assn. (mem. exec. com. 1999—), Mass. Bar Assn. (chmn. bar assn. program real estate devel. Cape Cod 1999). Avocations: boating, photography. Home: 238 Greenland Circle East Dennis MA 02641-1302 Office: PO Box 67 26 Upper County Rd Dennis Port MA 02639-0067 E-mail: singerlaw@capcod.net.

SINGER, NIKI, publishing executive, public relations executive; b. Rochester, N.Y., Sept. 10, 1937; d. Goodman A. and Evelyn (Simon) Sarachan; m. Michael J. Sheets, 1973; children: Romaine Kitty, Nicholas Simon Feramorz. BA cum laude, U. Mich., 1959. Mgr. advt. sales promotion Fairchild Publs., N.Y.C., 1959-67; acct. exec., acct. supr. Vernon Pope Co., 1967-69, v.p., 1969-71; pres. Niki Singer, Inc., 1971-93; sr. v.p. M. Shanken Comm., Cigar Aficionado, Wine Spectator, 1994—. Mem. Am. Inst. Wine and Food (bd. dirs.), Les Dames d'Escoffier. Home: 1035 5th Ave New York NY 10028-0135 Office: M Shanken Comm 387 Park Ave S Fl 8 New York NY 10016-8872 E-mail: nsinger@mshanken.com.

SINGER, NORBERT, health services professional, education consultant; b. Vienna, Austria, May 3, 1931; arrived in Eng., 1939; s. Salomon and Mina (Korn) S.; m. Brenda Margaret Walter, May 23, 1980. BSc in Spl. Chemistry, U. London, 1951, PhD in Phys. Chemistry, 1954; DSc (hon.), U. Greenwich, London, 1993. Project leader Morgan Crucible Co. Ltd., London, 1954-57; lectr., dept. head No. Polytechnic, 1958-70; prof., head dept. life scis. Polytechnic of Cen. London, 1971-74; asst., dep. dir. Polytechnic of North London, 1974-78; dir. Thames Polytechnic, London, 1978-92; vice chancellor U. Greenwich, 1992-93; chmn. Oxleas NHS Health Trust, Bexley, 1993-2001. Vis. prof. U. Westminster, 1996. Contbr. articles to profl. jours., including Jour. Chem. Soc. Chmn. Rose Bruford Coll., 1994-99. Decorated comdr. Order Brit. Empire; fellow Queen Mary and Westfield Coll., U. Coll., Northampton. Fellow Royal Soc. Chemistry. Home: Croft Lodge Bayhall Rd Tunbridge Wells TN2 4TP England

SINGER, PAUL RICHARD, ophthalmologist; b. N.Y.C., Feb. 1, 1947; m. Katherine W. Singer, June 13, 1970; children: Amy E., Evan P. BA with honors, U. Rochester, N.Y., 1969, MD, 1973. Diplomate Am. Bd. Ophthalmology. Internal medicine intern U. N.C., Chapel Hill, 1973-74, resident in neurology, 1974-75; resident in ophthalmology Washington U. Sch. Medicine, St. Louis, 1975-78, Fight for Sight postdoctoral rsch. fellow dept ophthalmology, 1978-79; pres. Hartford (Conn.) Eye Physicians, 1980—; sr. staff dept. ophthalmology Hartford Hosp., 1980—. Chmn. bd. dirs. Prevent Blindness Conn., Middletown, 1990-92, Combined Health Appeal, Hartford, 1993-95. Recipient Cmty. Svc. award Hartford County Med. Assn., 1993, Robert Polk award for outstanding vol. svc. Prevent Blindness Conn., 1993. Office: Hartford Eye Physicians 55 Nye Rd Ste 103 Glastonbury CT 06033-4394

SINGER, PHILIP CHARLES, environmental engineer, educator; b. Bklyn., Sept. 6, 1942; married Ellen Becker, 1965; children: Naomi, Elizabeth, Robert, Jennifer. BCE, Cooper Union, 1963; MS, Northwestern U., 1965; SM, Harvard U., 1965, PhD, 1969. Asst. prof. civil engring. U. Notre Dame, 1969-73; assoc. prof. environ. sci. and engring. U. N.C., Chapel Hill, 1973-78, prof., 1978—, dir. water resources engring., 1979-98, dir. drinking water rsch. ctr., 1999—. Mem. NAE, ASCE, Am. Chem. Soc., Am. Water Works Assn., Am. Acad. Environ. Engrs., Water Environment Fedn., Assn. Environ. Engring. Profs., Internat. Ozone Assn. Achievements include research on drinking water treatment, disinfection by-products formation and control, ozonation. Office: Univ North Carolina Dept Environ Sci & Engring CB7400 Chapel Hill NC 27599 E-mail: phil_singer@unc.edu.

SINGER, RENATA, publisher, writer, editor; b. Walbzych, Silesia, Poland, Feb. 8, 1946; arrived in Australia, 1952; d. Shmul-Itzack Diamond and Rysharda Kibberlain; m. Peter Albert Singer, Dec. 16, 1968; children: Ruth, Marion, Esther. BA with honors, U. Melbourne, Australia, 1967, diploma of edn., 1968; B of Edn., Monash U., Australia, 1975; grad. diploma in alt. dispute resolution, U. Melbourne, 1995. Tchr. secondary sch., Melbourne, N.Y., Oxford, 1969-82; comty. educator ethnic affairs Ecumenical Migration Ctr., Melbourne, 1983-87; dir. social rsch. consultancy Ellard & Assocs., 1988-89; sr. tribunal mem. Workcare Affairs Bd., 1990-92; equal opportunity officer Monash U., 1993; pub. Comty. Aid Abroad, 1994-99; adj. prof. N.J. City U., 1999—2000. Coord. Combating Racism in Edn., Project of Nat. Significance, Commonwealth Dept. of Edn., 1984-88; cons. Human Rights Commn. of Australia, 1986, Ctr. for Appropriate Tech., Alice Springs, 1997; Australasian del. UN High Commr. for Refugees Conf. on Refugee Documentation, Bonn, Germany, 1987. Author: Goodbye and Hello, 1985, True Stories from the Land of Divorce, 1997, (novel) The Front of the Family, 2001; editor: (quar. mags.) Migration Action, 1985-88, Horizons, 1994-99; contbr. articles and short stories to mags.; bd. dirs. Modern Times Mag., 1990-92. Chairperson Refugee Advice and Casework Svc., Melbourne, 1991-92, Statewide Cons. Women and Housing, Melbourne, 1989-91; convenor Women's Ethnic Network of Victoria, 1987-90; Victorian rep. Nat. Immigrant Women's Conf., Canberra, Australia, 1987; mem. Ministerial Adv. Com. on Women and Housing, Victoria, 1989-91; active Bottomless Closet, N.Y., 2000—, Citizens Com. for Children, 2000—. Avocations: bush walking, talking, films, reading novels. E-mail: renatasinger@hotmail.com.

SINGER, RICHARD BUNKER, physician, medical risk consultant; b. Phila., Mar. 22, 1914; s. Edgar A. and Helen (Bunker) S.; m. Margaret Henson, 1947; children: Elizabeth, Permelia, Richard H. AB, U. Pa., 1934, AM in Physics, 1935, MD, 1939. Intern Hosp. of U. Pa., Phila., 1939-41; NRC fellow in biochemistry Harvard Med. Rsch., Boston, 1941-42, 46-47; asst. prof. Sch. Medicine U. Pa., Phila., 1947-52; from asst. to assoc. med. dir. New Eng. Life Ins. Co., Boston, 1952-66, med. dir. rsch., 2d v.p., 1966-79; med. risk appraisal cons. Am. Acad. Ins. Medicine, Md., 1979—. Editor, author: (with L. Levinson) Medical Risks: Patterns of Mortality and Survival, 1976, (with M.W. Kita and J.R. Avery) Medical Risks--Compend of Mortality and Morbidity, 1994, A Descriptive Index of Mortality Studies from Selected Sources 1951-1995, 2001; contbr. articles to profl. jours. Mem. Town of Cohasset (Mass.) Bd. Health, 1963-67; trustee Cohasset Free Pub. Libr., 1963-79. Served to lt. comdr. USNR, 1942-46. Recipient Emmett Russell award Inst. Home Office Underwriters, 1996. Mem. Am. Acad. Ins. Medicine (chmn. mortality com. 1967-76, chmn. subcom. med. and mortality com. 1990-97, bd. med. ins. 1963-66, Dist. Physician's award 1980, 96). Episcopalian. Avocations: travel, sailing. Home and Office: 8 Blueberry Ln Apt C11 Falmouth ME 04105-1855 E-mail: rsinger1@maine.rr.com.

SINGER, SANDRA MARIA, forensic scientist; b. Wilkes-Barre, Pa., Sept. 9, 1964; d. Russell John and Anita Louise (Hovanec) S. BS in Chemistry, King's Coll., 1986; MS in Forensic Sci., George Washington U., 1989. Forensic analyst Collaborative Testing, Inc., Herndon, Va., 1988-89; forensic scientist Pa. State Police Crime Lab., Wyoming, 1990—. Mem. AAAS, Am. Acad. Forensic Sci., Am. Chem. Soc. Home: 203 Owen St Swoyersville PA 18704-2205 Office: Pa State Police Wyoming Regional Crime Lab 479 Wyoming Ave Wyoming PA 18644-1823

SINGER, SARAH BETH, poet; b. N.Y.C., July 4, 1915; d. Samuel and Rose (Dunetz) White; m. Leon Eugene Singer, Nov. 23, 1938; children: Jack, Rachel. BA, NYU, 1934; postgrad., New Sch. Social Research, 1961-63. Tchr. creative writing Hillside Hosp., Queens, N.Y., 1964-75, Samuel Field YMHA, Queens, 1980-82. Mem. Pacific N.W. Writers Conf.; prin. reader Frye Art Mus., 1998, 2000, 01. Author: Magic Casements, 1957, After the Beginning, 1975, Of Love and Shoes, 1987, The Gathering, 1992, contbr. poetry to anthologies, poetry mags. and quars. including Am. Women Poets, 1976, Yearbook Am. Poetry, 1981, The Best of 1980, 81, Filtered Images, 1992, the Croton Rev., The Lyric, Bitterroot, Judaism, Encore, The Jewish Frontier, Yankee, Hartford Courant, Poet Lore, N.Y.Times, Christian Sci. Monitor, Voices Internat., The Round Table, Orphic Lute, Brussels Sprout, Poetry and Medicine Column Jour. AMA, The Shakespeare Newsletter, Midstream (N.Y.C. Jewish Rev.), The Penwoman, Poets West, Showcase; cons. editor Poet Lore, 1975-81. Recipient Stephen Vincent Benet award Poet Lore, 1968, 71, Dellbrook award Shenandoah Valley Acad. Lit. and Dellbrook-Shenandoah Coll. Writers' Conf., 1978, 79, C.W. Post Poetry award, 1979-80, award for best poem Lyric quar., 1981, biennial award for achievement in poetry Seattle br. Nat. League Penwomen, 1988, award for traditional poetry

Wash. Poets Assn., 1989, 95, 97, 98, Traditional Poetry award Wash. Poets Assn., 1995, 98, four honorable mentions for structured verse, 1998, 2000, cert. of merit Muse mag., 1990, Editor's Choice award for Haiku Brussels Sprout, 1992, Carlin Aden award for structured verse Washington Poets Assn., 2001, 02, Hon. Mention, 2001, 2 Hon. Mentions, 2002; poem chosen for Met. Bus. Poetry Project, Seattle, 1992, 96, hon. mention Wash. Poets Assn., 1997, 98, 2000; poem Upon My Demise translated into Russian, recorded 1st prize Marj McAllistr award Voices Internat., 1993; poem chosen in top ten of structured verse category Writer's Digest, 1999, three honorable mentions in structured verse category, 1999, two honorable mentions, 2000; 2 hon. mentions for structured verse category Writer's Digest Contest, 2000. Mem. PEN, Poetry Soc. Am., Poets and Writers, Nat. League Am. Penwomen (poetry chmn. L.I. br. 1957-87, publicity chmn. 1990, sec. Seattle br. 1990, pres. 1992-94, v.p. 1994—, publicity chmn. State of Wash. 1992—, Marion Doyle Meml. award 1976, 3d place, 2000, 1st prize nat. poetry contest 1976, Drama award 1977, Poetry award 1977, 1st prize modern rhymed poetry 1978, Lectr. award 1980, Sonnet award Alexandria br. 1980, 81, Catherine Cushman Leach award 1982, 3d place, 2000; poetry award Phoenix br. 1983, Pasadena br. 1984, Alexandria br. 1985, 1st prize award Portland br. 1990, structured verse award Spokane br. 1992, Della Crowder Miller Meml. Petrarchan Sonnet award 1994, 2000, Della Crowder Meml. Free Verse award, 2000, Honorable Mention Anita Marie Boggs Meml. award 1994, 2000, Owl award and Ann. award for achievement in poetry Seattle br. 1994, Poet's Choice award Portland br. 1995, 2d prize Internat. Poetry Contest, Palomar br., 1996, 3d prize in internat. poetry 1997, Palomar Branch internat. poetry contest honorable mention, 1998, 1st prize Internat. Poetry Contest Palomar br., 1999, hon. mention, 1999, honorable mention Anne Marx Sestina award 2000, 3d pl. Catherine Cushman Leach Poetry award 2000, 3d pl. Marion Doyle Poetry award 2000, Della Crowder Meml. award for Petrarchan sonnet 2000, Della Crowder Meml. award for free verse 2000, Poetry Soc. Am. (v.p. 1974-78, exec. dir. L.I., 1979-83, James Joyce award 1972, Consuelo Ford award 1973, Gustav Davidson award 1974, 1st prize award 1975, Celia Wagner award 1976), Wash. Poets Assn., Northwest Writer's Conference. Address: 2360 43rd Ave E Apt 415 Seattle WA 98112-2703 E-mail: sarahsing2@aol.com. *As a poet, I have sought never to compromise my standards as to what constitutes poetry, despite fads that come and go. My goal has been to achieve whatever perfection I can in my work, and to preserve enough humility to realize that the best is never good enough. My life has truly been enriched by vision and aspiration. As a poet, the important thing for me is to create something moving and beautiful. Publication is a welcome by-product, but in itself, is not the goal for which I strive.*

SINGER, S(IEGFRIED) FRED, geophysicist, educator; b. Vienna, Austria, Sept. 27, 1924; came to U.S., 1940, naturalized, 1944; s. Joseph B. and Anne (Kelman) S.; m. Candace Carolyn Crandall, 1990. BEE, Ohio State U., 1943, DSc (hon.), 1970; AM, Princeton U., 1944, PhD in Physics, 1948. Instr. physics Princeton, 1943-44; physicist, applied physics lab. Johns Hopkins, 1946-50; sci. liaison officer Office Naval Research, Am. embassy, London, 1950-53; asso. prof. physics U. Md., College Park, 1953-59, prof., 1959-62; dir. Nat. Weather Satellite Center, Dept. Commerce, 1962-64; dean Sch. Environ. and Planetary Scis., U. Miami, 1964-67; dep. asst. sec. for water quality and research Dept. Interior, Washington, 1967-70; dep. asst. adminstr. EPA, 1970-71; prof. environ. scis. U. Va., Charlottesville, 1971-87; chief scientist U.S. Dept. Transp., Washington, 1987-89; pres. Sci. and Environ. Policy Project, 1989—; dir. rsch. prof. George Mason U., Fairfax, Va., 1999—. Vis. rsch. prof. Jet Propulsion Lab., Calif. Inst. Tech., 1961-62; Fed. Exec. fellow Brookings Instn., 1971; vis. Sid Richardson prof. J.B. Johnson Sch., U. Tex., 1978; sr. fellow Heritage Found., 1982-83; vis. eminent scholar George Mason U., 1984-86, disting. rsch. prof., 1994—; Wesson fellow Hoover Instn., Stanford, 1992, 98; head sci. evaluation group astronautics and space exploration com. U.S. Ho. of Reps., 1958; cons. U.S. Treasury Dept., GAO, Office Tech. Assessment, U.S. Congress; mem. bd. Nat. Com. on Am. Fgn. Policy; mem. White House Panel on U.S.-Brazil Sci. and Tech. Exch., 1987; guest scholar Nat Air and Space Mus., Smithsonian Instn., 1991, Woodrow Wilson Internat. Ctr. for Scholars, 1991, Hoover Instn., 1992; disting. rsch. rpof. Inst. for Space Sci. and Tech., Gainesville, Fla., 1989—; bd. dirs. AMREP Corp., Patent Enforcement Fund, Inc. Author: Geophysical Research with Artificial Earth Satellites, 1956, Manned Laboratories in Space, 1970, Global Effects of Environmental Pollution, 1970, Is There an Optimum Level of Population, 1971, The Changing Global Environment, 1975, Arid Zone Development: Potentialities and Problems, 1977, The Economic Effects of Demographic Changes, 1977, Energy, 1979, Price of World Oil, 1983, Free Market Energy, 1984, Global Climate Change, 1990, Origins of The Universe, 1990, The Ocean in Human Affairs, 1990, The Greenhouse Debate Continued, 1992, Hot Talk, Cold Science: Global Warming's Unfinished Debate, 1997; sci. adv. com. Dept State 1981; vice chmn. Nat. Adv. Com. Oceans and Atmosphere, 1981-86; contbr. articles on space, energy, environment and population problems to profl. publs. Served with USNR, 1944-46, USAFR, 1950-53. Recipient Presdl. commendation, 1958, gold medal for exceptional service Dept. Commerce, 1965; named Outstanding Young Man U.S. Jr. C. of C., 1959 Fellow AAAS (com. coun. affairs 1970), AIAA, Am. Geophys. Union, Am. Phys. Soc.; mem. Internat. Acad. Astronautics, European Acad. for Environ. Affairs, Pan Am. Med. Assn. (pres. sect. on environ. health scis. 1973—), Cosmos Club (Washington), Colonnade Club (Charlottesville). E-mail: singer@sepp.org.

SINGER, THOMAS KENYON, international business consultant, orchardist; b. Wilson, N.Y., Jan. 30, 1932; s. Harold Thomas and Grace (Kenyon) S.; m. Jacqueline Germain Moulin, June 8, 1957; children: Marc Andre, Vivianne Grace Singer Scott, Claire Anne, Michele Moulin Singer Ross, Gail Kenyon Singer Watson. BS in Econs., U. Pa., 1954. Dir. mktg. Europe Kaiser Aluminum & Chem. Corp., London, 1959-66; v.p. Kaiser LeNickel subs., Oakland, Calif., 1967-73, div. mgr., 1973-75; v.p. govt. relations Kaiser Aluminum & Chem. Corp., Washington, 1975-81, corp. v.p. Oakland, Calif., 1977-86; pres. Kaiser Internat. Corp., 1982-86, also dir.; chmn. Singer Farms, Appleton, N.Y. Dir., pres. IBA Inc., 1986-2000. Trustee United Way of Niagara County, trustee The Nature Conservancy of Central and Western N.Y., trustee Niagara Area Found. Capt. USAF, 1955-57. Mem. Army and Navy Club (Washington), Niagara Frontier Country Club. Republican. Episcopalian. Home: 6627 Hummingbird Ln Appleton NY 14008-9693 Office: 6730 Lake Rd Appleton NY 14008-9673 E-mail: applej65@hotmail.com.

SINGER, WILLIAM HARRY, interactive multimedia architect, software engineer, expert systems designer, consultant, entrepreneur, ceramic artist; b. Lancaster, Pa., Jan. 25, 1947; s. Wilbur Weitzel and Mildred (Myers) S.; m. Nanette Platt Willis, July 28, 1989. BS, U. Pitts., 1973; MS, Drexel U., 1982; postgrad., Pa. State U., 1994. Cert. in adult distance edn. Rsch. asst. Dept. Molecular Biology, E.P.P.I., Phila., 1976-81; rsch. fellow Dept. Biophys. Chemistry, Biozentrum, Basel, Switzerland, 1981-83; cons. to industry in applied artificial intelligence Palmyra, Pa., 1983-2000; ltd. ptnr. Tech. Systems Software, 1983-86; co-founder Singer, Stewart and New, Inc., 1987; gen. ptnr. Singer and Singer Assocs., 1993-2000; v.p. for sys. devel. Singer Cons., Inc.; retired, 1996. Software cons. REORG, Darmstadt, 1984, Kroeplin GmbH, 1983-86; co-founder, prin., ptnr. Singer Cons., Inc., 1993-96; adj. faculty lectr. in computer sci. Wilson Coll., Chambersburg, Pa., 1994-95, Cen. Pa. Bus. Sch., Summerdale, Pa., 1995, prodn. of functional and dysfunctional stoneware and porcelain, 2000—. Contbr. articles to profl. jours.; co-author: Diabetic's Daily Diary, 1987; world wide web site designer; prodr. abstract functional and nonfunctional ceramic art, 2000—. Swiss Nat. Sci. Found. fellow, 1981-83. Mem. ACM, IEEE Computer Soc., Math. Assn. Am., Am. Assn. for Artificial Intelligence, Okinawa Isshinryu Karate Assn. (life), Wasserfahrverein Horburg of Basel (Switzerland) (life mem.). Achievements include research in drug and chemically induced membrane fusion, design and production of various educational CD-ROM titles; design and production of various educational and business level worldwide web sites; statistical analysis and control of serum glucose levels in Type II diabetics; and design and production of ceramic works of art. Home: 1533 Cambridge Ct Palmyra PA 17078-9375 E-mail: singers@paonline.com.

SINGER-CHANG, GAIL LESLIE, science educator; d. Frank Max (Stepfather) and Rona Jane Singer; m. Anthony Chang. BA in Journalism, San Diego State U., 1988; MS in Counseling, Calif. State U., Fullerton, 1992; MA in Clin. Psychology, Calif. Sch. Profl. Psychology, 1994, D of Psychology in Clin. Psychology, 1996. Pupil pers. svcs. credential Calif. Asst. prof. family medicine, social and behavioral scis. Western U. of Health Scis., Pomona, Calif., 1999—. Orgnl. cons., Irvine, Calif., 1998—99; program dir., doctor-patient communication program Western U. of Health Sciences, Pomona, Calif., 1999—; post-doctoral psychology intern El Toro Marine Base Family Services Ctr., El Toro, Calif., 1997—99; psychology intern Kaiser Permanente, Tustin, Calif., 1995—96, Orange Coast Coll. Student Health Ctr., Costa Mesa, Calif., 1994—95; counseling intern Teen-Age Pregnancy and Parenting Program, Fullerton, Calif., 1991—91; adj. prof. Concordia U., Irvine, Calif., 1998—99, Calif. State U., Fullerton, 1999. Presenter (profl. presentation) Enabling Disability Education: The Value of Using Disabled Persons as Standardized Patients, 10th Internat. Ottawa Conf. Med. Edn., 2002 (Greatest Profl. Promise, 1992), Creative Use of Assessment and Feedback: Increasing Deep Learning and Professionalism, Western Assn. Schs. and Colls., 2002. Mem.: Assn. Profl. Cons., Am. Anthropol. Assn., Assn. for the Behavioral Scis. and Med. Edn., Soc. of Teachers of Family Medicine. Office: Western U Health Scis 309 East 2d St Pomona CA 91766 Office Fax: 909-469-5514. E-mail: gsingerchang@westernu.edu.

SINGER-MAGDOFF, LAURA JOAN SILVER (MRS. SAMUEL MAGDOFF), psychotherapist; b. N.Y.C., Mar. 21, 1917; d. Max David and Minnie (Stabsky) Silver; m. Edward I. Plotkin, 1938 (dec. 1945); 1 child, JoAnn Melanie; m. Arthur I. Singer, 1948 (div. 1962); m. Samuel Magdoff, Dec. 23, 1963. Student, NYU, 1936-38, U. Minn., 1938-39; BS, MA, Columbia U., 1946, EdD, 1961. Diplomate Am. Bd. Sexology; cert. sex educator, therapist Am. Assn. Sex Educators, Counselors and Therapists. Nursery and elem. sch. tchr., dir., Bronxville, N.Y., 1943-45; tchr. Cherry Lawn Sch., Darien, Conn., 1943-44, Columbia Grammar Sch., 1951-53, N.Y. Children's Colony, 1953-54; psychotherapist, marital, family counselor Community Guidance Service, N.Y.C., 1958-91; pvt. practice, 1958—. Founder, pres. Save A Marriage, Inc., 1974—; pres. Interpersonal Devel. Inst., Inc., 1983, co-producer Gleam Prodns., 1989; adj. prof. Tchrs. Coll., Columbia U., 1961-74; vis. faculty New Sch. for Social Research; faculty Am. Assn. for Psychoanalysis and psychotherapy; psychotherapist TV series Living Together; past mem. exec. bd. Sex Info. and Edn. Coun. of U.S., Cmty. Sec. Info.; adviser bd. trustees Nat. Accreditation Assn. for Psychoanalysis, Inc.; supr. dept. psychology CUNY, 1994-96. Co-author: (with Barbara L. Stern) Stages the Crises that Shape Your Marriage, 1980; (with JoAnn Magdoff) Sexual Relations and Therapeutic Practice; author: (with others) Human Sexuality, 1988, Family Therapy Collection: Aspen, 1989; cons. editor Jour. Sex and Marital Therapy; former mem. adv. bd. Jour. Marriage and Family Counselors; former mem. editorial bd. Jour. Divorce; co-producer (documentary film) Door of Hope, 1991. Fellow Am. Inst. Psychotherapy and Psychoanalysis, Am. Assn. Marriage and Family Therapists (past pres., supr.), Am. Orthopsychiat. Assn., Soc. Sci. Study Sex, Am. Acad. Clin. Sexologists (clin. fellow); mem. World Fedn. Mental Health, N.Y. Soc. Clin. Psychologists (past editor Newsletter, mem. exec. bd.), Am. Family Therapy Assn. (charter), Am. Psychol. Assn., Am. Soc. Psychologists in Pvt. Practice, Assn. Applied Psychoanalysis, Nat. Council Family Relations. Address: 1 Lincoln Plz New York NY 10023-7129

SINGERMAN, DONA FATIBENO, reading specialist; b. Cleve., July 6, 1939; d. Pasquale and Mary (Del Priore) Fatibeno; children: Camille Swartz, David E. BA, Lake Erie Coll., 1967; MEd, Cleve. State U., 1977; cert. in supervision, John Carroll U., 1985; student, Cambridge (Eng.) U., 1990-91. Cert. tchr. and supr., prin., Ohio. Tchr. Painesville-Mentor Schs., Ohio, Mentor (Ohio) Schs., tchr. chpt. I reading, 1986—. Mem. Gephart Symposium, U. Colo., summer 1992; chmn. Internat. Literacy, OCIRA, 1995, membership chair Lake coun., 2001-02; tchr. home instrn. grades 2-11; tchr. ESL Reynolds and Brentmoor Sch. k-8. Vol. Lake County Hist. Soc.; sec. Friends of Mentor Pub. Libr., 1990-91. Joseph Nemeth scholar (OCIRA), 1995. Mem. AAUW (legis. chair Mentor br. 1990-91, treas. 1991-93), Coun. Exceptional Children, Internat. Reading Assn. (v.p. Lake-Geauga unit 1990-91, 91-92, pres. 1992-93, 98-99, chair internat. lit. com. Ohio 1996-97), Phi Delta Kappa (program v.p. N.E. Ohio unit 1990-91, pres. 1991-92, Gerald Read Internat. scholar 1992)

SINGERMAN, PHILLIP A. corporate executive; BA, Oberlin Coll.; MA in Polit. Sci., PhD in Polit. Sci., Yale U. Past dir. mayor's office policy devel. City of Phila.; past exec. asst. to devel. adminstr. City of New Haven; pres., CEO Ben Franklin Tech. Ctr., Pa., 1983-95; pres. Md. Tech. Devel. Corp. (TEDCO), Balt., 1999—; asst sec. econ. devel. U.S. Dept. Commerce, 1995-99. Past policy devel. dir. Conn. Conf. Municipalities; past instr. urban policy and regional devel. Barnard Coll., U. Pa., Yale U.; past mem. gov.'s task force tech. transfer. Vol. Peace Corps, Colombia, 1965-67; past bd. dirs. Phila.-Israel C. of C. W. Phila. Empowerment Zone Cmty. Trust. Office: TEDCO 5575 Sternett Pl Ste 240 Columbia MD 21044 E-mail: psingerman@marylandtedco.org.

SINGH, AJIT, economist; b. Lahore, Punjab, Pakistan, Sept. 11, 1940; s. Gurbachan and Pushpa (Bawa) S. BA, Punjab U., Chandigarh, India, 1958; MA, Howard U., 1960; MA (hon.), Cambridge (Eng.) U., 1965; PhD, U. Calif., Berkeley, 1970. Coll. lectr. Queens' Coll., Cambridge U., 1965, dir. of studies in econs., 1975-94, sr. fellow, 1990—, prof., 1995—; Dr. William M. Scholl prof. econs. U. Notre Dame, Ind., 1987-95. Sr. econ. advisor Ministry of Oil and Natural Resources, Govt. of Mex., 1977-82, Ministry of Planning and Econ. Devel., Dar-es-Salaam, Tanzania, 1981-84; cons. various UN orgns., including ILO, UNCTAD, UNIDO, World Bank. Editor Cambridge Jour. Econs., 1975; author: Takeovers, 1971, Corporate Financial Structures in Developing Countries, 1993; co-author: Growth, Profitability and Valuation, 1968, Economic Crisis in Third World Agriculture, 1993; co-editor: (with C. Howes) Competitiveness Matters, 2000; contbr. articles and tech. papers to profl. jours. Mem. Soc. for Internat. Devel. World Hdqrs., Rome, 1987; mem. panel of eminent persons advising sec. gen. UN Conf. on Trade and Devel., Geneva, 1984. Mem. Royal Econ. Soc., Am. Econ. Assn., European Econ. Assn., European Assn. for Rsch. in Indsl. Econs. (chmn. programme com. 1985). Sikh. Avocations: table tennis, hiking. Home: 15 Westberry Ct Grange Rd Cambridge CB3 9BG England Office: Cambridge U Queens Coll Cambridge CB3 9ET England

SINGH, ANAND, application developer; b. Jaunpur, Uttar Pradesh, India, Nov. 25, 1974; s. Ashok Kumar and Tara Devi Singh; m. Samidha Singh, Jan. 21, 2001. MS, Purdue U., 1998. Cert. Java Profession 1999. Software engr. Ctr. for Devel. Advanced Computing, Pune, India, 1994—95; tchg. and rsch. asst. Purdue U., West Lafayette, Ind., 1996—98; sr. software engr. Silicon Graphics Inc., Eagan, Minn., 1997—98, Parametric Tech. Inc., Arden Hills, 2000—. Mem.: Upsilon Pi Epsilon. Home: 2735 Rice St #307 Roseville MN 55113 Office: Parametric Technology Corp 1200 W County Rd E Arden Hills MN 55112 Personal E-mail: anandsing@yahoo.com. E-mail: anandsingh@yahoo.com.

SINGH, BHRIGU NATH, engineering educator, researcher; b. Ballia, Uttar Pradesh, India, July 1, 1968; s. Sachchida Nand and Kunti Singh; m. Sudha Singh, Mar. 2, 1994; children: Aniket, Ichchita. B in Civil Engring., Motilal Nehru Regional Engring. Coll., Allahabad, India, 1990, M in Applied Mechanics, 1992; PhD in Aerospace Engring., Indian Inst. of Tech., Kanpur, India, 2001. Lectr. Motilal Nehru Regional Engring. Coll., Allahabad, India, 1993—98, sr. lectr., 1998—2001; vis. rschr. mech. and materials engring. Wright State U., Dayton, Ohio, 2002—. Dep. coord. admission com. Motilal Nehru Regional Engring. Coll., 1997—98. Inventor in field. Fellow, Govt. of India, 1990—92, Ministry of Human Resource Develop., India, 1998—2001. Mem.: Indian Soc. Tech. Edn. Office: 214 RC Dept Mech Engring Wright State Univ Dayton OH 45435 Office Fax: 937-775-5147. E-mail: bnsingh9@rediffmail.com.

SINGH, BRAHMA NAND, pharmaceutical scientist; b. Varanasi, Uttar Pradesh, India, May 10, 1969; came to U.S., 1995; s. Parma Nand and Vidya (Rai) S.; m. Priya Roy, Dec. 1, 1995. BPharm, Banaras Hindu U., Varanasi, 1991, MPharm, 1993; MS in Pharm. Scis., S.D. State U., 1997; postgrad., St. John's U. Trainee pharmacist R&D formulation Alkem Labs. Ltd., Mumbai, India, 1993-94; prodn. officer dept. tablets and capsules Hoechst Marion Roussel Ltd., Ankleshwar, India, 1994-95. Presenter in field. Jjour. reviewer Am. Jour. Physiology, Clin. Pharmacokinetics, Drugs; contbr. articles to profl. jours. Recipient First in Handwriting award Personality Devel. Soc., 1985; jr. rsch. fellow Banaras Hindu U., 1991-93; Doctoral fellow St. John's U., 1997-2002; Univ. Doctoral fellow St. John's U., 1999—; rsch. prizes, Internat. Soc. Preventive Oncology, 2000. Mem. Am. Assn. Pharm. Scientists, Controlled Release Soc., Crohn's and Colitis Found. Am. Avocations: reading, swimming, watching Indian and American movies. Office: St John's U 8000 Utopia Pky Jamaica NY 11432 Fax: 718-990-6316. E-mail: brahmasingh@hotmail.com.

SINGH, BRIJ NANDAN, electrical engineer, educator; b. Shahbur Charki, Uttar Praclesh, India, May 15, 1967; s. Heera Lal and Santi Kumari Singh; m. Meera Singh, June 17, 1989; children: Vibhav, Alka. BE, Gorakhbur U., Gorakhbur, India, 1989; ME, Indian Inst. Tech., Roorkee, India, 1991; PhD, Indian Inst. Tech., Delhi, India, 1996. Lectr. Jamia Milia Islama, New Delhi, India, 1995—96; post doctoral fellow ETS Montreal, Montreal, Canada, 1996—99; rsch. fellow Concordia U., Canada, 1999—2000; prof. elec. engring. Tulane U., New Orleans, 2000—. Ho. sec. IIT Delhi Vindyhostel, Delhi, India, 1994—95; dir. Hindi Que. Assn., Montreal, Canada, 1999—2000, educator Canada, 1997—99. Mem.: IEEE, IEEE PE/IE Societies (life). Achievements include research in IEEE Transactions on Industry Applications 1999; IEEE Transactions on Power Electronics 2000; European Transactions of Electrical Power (Germany) 2002. Avocations: reading, touring, touring. Office: Tulane University 6823 Saint Charles Aveune New Orleans LA 70118

SINGH, DALJIT, dean, business and public administration educator; b. Montgomery, Punjab, India, Apr. 13, 1942; came to U.S., 1960; s. Balwant Singh and Sant Kaur Dua; m. Katherine Lowe, Apr., 28, 1968; children: Nancy Kiran, John Norman Sher. BA, Calif. State U., 1965; PhD, Claremount U., 1970; LLM, Liecester U., 1997. Asst. prof. Adams State Coll., Alamosa, Colo., 1967-69; assoc. prof. Bemidji (Minn.) State U., 1969-72, Tuskegee (Ala.) U., 1972-75; chairperson polit. scis. dept. Fisk U., Nashville, 1976-79; dean, prof. U. Guam, Mangilao, 1979-96, prof. emeritus, 1996—. Dean U. D.C., 1989-91. Author: Government of Guam, 1981; editor: Small Business and Public Policy in America. Treas. dem. ctrl. com. Tulare County, Calif., 1998; mem. Dem. ctrl. com., Calif., 2000—; mem. affirmative action com. City of Visali, Calif., 1998, human resources adv. com., 1999. Recipient Ancient Order of Chamorri award Govt. Guam, 1996, Legis. Resolution award. Mem. Rotary (pres. 1984-85). Avocatons: travelling, tutoring, mentoring. Home: 1645 S Cedar St Visalia CA 93292 E-mail: deansingh2@yahoo.com.

SINGH, HARBACHAN, solicitor, barrister; b. Klang, Malaysia, Mar. 11, 1939; came to U.S., 1969; s. Kishen Singh and Than Kaur; m. Susil Kaur, Jan. 12, 1963; children: Sukhwant, Ramesh, Praveen. Barrister-at-law, Honorable Soc. Lincoln's Inn, London, 1967; MA, St. John's U., 1981. Police interpreter Royal Malaysian Police, Malaysia, 1957-63; advocate, solicitor Allen & Gledhill Law Firm, Kuala Lumpur, Malaysia, 1967-69; chief of travel UN, N.Y.C., 1969-79, chief of transp., 1979-90, chmn. hdqrs. com. on contracts, 1995—99, chmn. hdqrs. property survey bd., 1987—99; mng. dir. Triangle Mortgage Svcs., Inc., 2000—. UN team leader Return of Property from Iraq to Kuwait, UN Security Coun. Resolution, 1994-95; sr. exec. officer UN Mission East Timor, 1999; chmn. UN Appointments and Promotion Com., 1987-89; mem. UN Panel of Counsel Joint Appeals bd., 1987-92, Staff Union, 1979-86; mem. U.S. Presdl. Gateway Improvement Task Force. Mem. Queens Borough County Cmty. Bd. 8, 2000—. Mem. UN Appointments and Promotion com. (chmn. 1978-89). Home: 193-12 Foothill Ave Hollis NY 11423-1259 E-mail: hsing19@nyc.rr.com., Harbachan@hotmail.com.

SINGH, INDERJIT, nephrologist, internist, medical educator; b. Patiala, India, Oct. 17, 1962; arrived in U.S., 1987; s. Charanjit Singh and Pritinder Kaur; m. Toniya Cheema Singh, June 5, 1994; children: Kunaal Inder, Kabir Inder. MBBS, U. Delhi, 1986. Diplomate Am. Bd. Internal Medicine, Am. Bd. Nephrology. Cert. ACLS. Intern U. Delhi Affiliated Hosps., 1985-86, resident in internal medicine, 1986-87, Easton Hosp.-Hahnemann U. Hosp., 1990-92; rsch. assoc. in endocrinology U. Health Scis.-Chgo. Med. Sch., 1987-88; intern Nassau County Med. Ctr., N.Y., 1988-89; rsch. assoc. in med. transplantation Presbyn. Hosp.-U. Pitts., 1989-90; clin. fellow divsn. nephrology U. Mich., 1992-93, rsch. fellow, 1993-95; clin. asst. prof. internal medicine So. Ill. U. Sch. Medicine, Carbondale, 1995-97; clin. asst. prof. medicine St. Louis U. Sch. Medicine; with Metro Hypertension and Kidney Ctr.; staff nephrologist BMA Carbondale Dialysis Unit, 1995-97, Marion Nephroplex Dialysis Unit, 1996-97; assoc. med. dir. Jefferson County Dialysis, Festus, Mo., 1998—; med. dir. Washington County Dialysis, Potosi, 1999—. Med. dir. Arrowhead Point Med. Clinic, Harrisburg, Ill., 1995-97; staff nephrologist BMA Carbondale Dialysis Unit, 1995—. Marion (Ill.) Nephroplex Dialysis Unit, 1996—, Christian NE Hosp., St. Louis, DePaul Hosp., St. Louis, Jefferson Meml. Hosp., Crystal City, Mo., others; chmn. infection control com. Marion Meml. Hosp., 1995-97; instr. Washington U. Sch. Medicine. Contbr. articles to profl. jours., chpts. in books; presenter in field. Fellow ACP; mem. Am. Soc. Nephrology, Nat. Kidney Found., Am. Soc. Internal Medicine. Sikh. Avocations: travel, sports, tennis, opera, music, broadway. Home: 843 Courtwood Ln Ballwin MO 63011-5110 Office: Metro Hypertension and Kidney Ctr 11155 Dunn Rd Ste 315E Saint Louis MO 63136-6111 Fax: (314) 355-2669. E-mail: ising@worldnet.att.net., ijsinghmd@yahoo.com.

SINGH, LOREN CHAN, technical writing specialist; b. Palo Alto, Calif., Sept. 10, 1943; s. Shau Wing and Anna Mae Chan; m. Frances Anastasia Chow, Apr. 19, 1975 (div. Jan. 1988); children: Karen Monique Chan, Pierre Benedict Chan, Marc Henri Chan; m. Sandra Marie Miner, Mar. 14, 2000. AB, Stanford U., 1965, AM, 1966; MS, Golden Gate U., 1988; PhD, UCLA, 1971. Teaching asst. UCLA, 1968-69, teaching assoc., 1969-70; lectr. in history Calif. State U., Northridge, 1970-71, San Jose (Calif.) State U., 1971-72, asst. prof. history, 1972-76, assoc. prof. history, 1976-80; lectr. history Calif. State U., Hayward, 1980-81; prodn. test technician Nicolet Paratronics Corp., Fremont, Calif., 1982; computer svc. technician Bell-Northern Rsch., Mountain View, 1982-83; rsch. analyst Bell-No. Rsch., 1984-85, tech. writer, 1985-87; sr. tech. writer StrataCom, Inc., Campbell, Calif., 1987-88; tech. writer Sun Microsystems, Palo Alto, 1988-90, sr. tech. writer, 1990-2000; tech. writer Brocade Comms. Sys., Inc., San Jose, Calif., 2000—. Author: Sagebrush Statesman, 1973, SPARCstation 1 Installation Guide, 1989, Collected Technical Support Notes, 1988, SPARCstation 2 Installation Guide, 1990, Desktop Storage Pack Installation Guide, 1989-90, SPARCstation 10 Installation Guide, 1992, SPARCstation 10 Networking and Communication Guide, 1993, SPARCstation 10SX VSIMMs Installation, 1993, SPARCstation 20 HyperSPARC Module Upgrade, 1995, SPARCstation 20 SuperSPARC-II Module Upgrade, 1995, Sun Ultra 1 Reference Manual, 1995-96, Sun Ultra 2 Reference Manual, 1996, Sun Ultra 30 Installation Guide, 1997, Sun Ultra 30 Reference Manual, 1997, SPARCstorage FlexiPack Removable Storage Tray Installation Guide, 1997, Sun StorEdge Long Wave Gigabit Interface Converter Service Manual, 1999, Sun StorEdge PCI Dual Fibre Channel Host Adapter Installation, 2000; editor: Chinese-American History Reader, 1976; contbr. articles to profl. jours. Radio sta. trustee ARC, Menlo Park, Calif., 1975-80. Recipient Presdl. Sports award Pres.'s Coun. on Phys. Fitness and Sports, 1973. Mem. Nat. Geog. Soc., Am. Radio Relay League, Almaden Masters Swim Club. Democrat. Sikh. Avocations: masters swimming, amateur radio, philately. Home: 195 Blossom Hill Rd # 123 San Jose CA 95123-2348 E-mail: lsingh@brocade.com.

SINGH, MANMOHAN, orthopedic surgeon, educator; b. Patiala, Punjab, India, Oct. 5, 1940; came to U.S., 1969; s. Ajmer and Kartar (Kaur) S.; m. Manjit Anand, Jan. 1, 1974; children: Kirpal, Gurmeet. MB, BS, Govt. Med. Coll., Patiala, 1964; MSurgery, Panjab U., Chandigarh, India, 1968. Diplomate Am. Bd. Orthopaedic Surgery. Mem. vis. faculty Mayo Grad. Sch., Rochester, Minn., 1969; rsch. fellow Inst. Internat. Edn., Chgo., 1969-74; resident in orthopedic surgery Michael Reese Hosp. and Med. Ctr., 1974-78; pvt. practice, 1979—; mem. attending staff, dir. orthopedic rsch. Michael Reese Hosp. and Med. Ctr., 1979-94; fellow in orthopedic oncology Mayo Clinic and Mayo Found., Rochester, 1979; assoc. prof. U. Ill., Chgo., 1996—. Founder Quantum Health Ctr./Enterprises for Holistic Medicine. Developer x-ray method (Singh Index) and bone density method (Radius Index) for diagnosis of osteoporosis. Fulbright travel grantee, 1968. Fellow Am. Acad. Orthop. Surgeons, Am. Orthop. Foot and Ankle Soc.; mem. Orthop. Rsch. Soc., Am. Soc. for Bone and Mineral Rsch., Internat. Bone and Mineral Soc. Democrat. Sikh. Avocations: stamp collecting, photography, tennis. Office: 110 Ridge Rd Munster IN 46321

SINGH, RAJENDRA, mechanical engineering educator; b. Dhampur, India, Feb. 13, 1950; came to U.S., 1973; s. Raghubir and Ishwar (Kali) S.; m. Veena Ghungesh, June 24, 1979; children: Rohit, Arun. BS with honors, Birla Inst., 1971; MS, U. Roorkee, India, 1973; PhD, Purdue U., 1975. Grad. instr. Purdue U., West Layfayette, Ind., 1973-75; sr. engr. Carrier Corp., Syracuse, N.Y., 1975-79; asst. prof. Ohio State U., Columbus, 1979-83, assoc. prof., 1983-87, prof., 1987—, Donald D. Glower chair in engring., 2001—. Adj. lectr. Syracuse (N.Y.) U., 1977-79; pres.-elect, bd. dirs., v.p. tech. activities Inst. of Noise Control Engring., pres.-elect, 2002; gen. chmn. Nat. Noise Conf., Columbus, 1985; leader of U.S. delegation to India-U.S.A. Symposium on Vibration and Noise Engring., 1996; vis. prof. U. Calif., Berkeley, 1987-88; pres. Inter-Noise 2002 Congress; chmn. India-USA Symposium on Vibration and Noise, 2001; cons., lectr. in field. Author: Emerging Trends in Vibration and Noise Engineering, 1996; contbr. over 240 articles to profl. jours.; guest editor jours. Recipient Gold medal U. Roorkee, 1973, R. H. Kohr Rsch. award Purdue U., 1975, Excellence in Tchg. award Inst. Noise Control Engring., 1989, Rsch. award Ohio State U., 1983, 87, 91, 96, 2001, Educator of Yr. award GM Tech. Edn. Program, 1998. Fellow ASME, Acoustical Soc. Am.; mem. Soc. Auto Engring., Inst. Noise Control Engring.(cert.), Am. Soc. Engring. Edn. (George Westinghouse award 1993). Achievements include patent for rolling door; development of new analytical and experimental techniques in machine dynamics, acoustics, vibration and fluid control. Home: 4772 Belfield Ct Dublin OH 43017-2592 Office: Ohio State U 206 W 18th Ave Columbus OH 43210-1189 E-mail: singh.3@osu.edu.

SINGH, RIPUDAMAN, aerospace structure engineering researcher; b. Ambala, India, July 8, 1964; came to U.S., 1992; s. Manmohan Singh and Kuljit Kaur; m. Anupinder Kaur, Aug. 16, 1989; 1 child, Amanjot Singh. BE in Aero. Engring., Punjab Engring. Coll., Chandigarh, India, 1986; ME in Aerospace Engring., Indian Inst. Sci., Bangalore, 1988, PhD in Engring., 1992. Postdoctoral fellow Ga. Inst. Tech., Atlanta, 1992-94; asst. prof. aerospace engring. Indian Inst. Sci., Bangalore, 1994-98; program mgr. Karta Techs., Inc., San Antonio, 1998—. Rschr. in aircraft structural integrity and life extension. Editor: Life Extension Technologies for Aging Aircraft, 1998; contbr. Avocations: music, travel, dance, humor. Home: 11911 Ghostbride Helotes TX 78023-4456 Office: Karta Techs Inc 5555 Northwest Pkwy San Antonio TX 78249-3339 E-mail: rsingh@karta.com.

SINGH, RONALD, researcher; b. Vreed-en Hoop, Demerara, Guyana, Apr. 7, 1958; s. Heeraman and Rajmatti Singh; life ptnr. Dhanwatti Deochand, Oct. 16, 1967; children: Raymond Anthony D'Angelo. MS, Hunter Coll./CUNY, Manhattan, New York, 1998—99; Bachelor of Social Sci., U. of Guyana, Georgetown, Guyana, 1981—86. Trained Teacher's Certificate Edn. Ministry, Guyana, 1981. Planner State Planning Commision, Georgetown, Guyana, 1987—91; mgr. Internat. Devel. Consulting, Caracas, Venezuela, 1993—98. Dir./rsch. assoc. Liberty Tutoring Ctr./Rsch. Inst. for the Study of the Caribbean Diaspora, Queens, NY, 1999—. Author: (poetry writing) Fragrance of a Desert-Rose (Internat. Poet of Merit, 1997), (poetry) Universal Peace (Editor's Choice Award, 1995). V.p. Guyana Venezuela Friendship Assn., Caracas, Venezuela, 1995—98; rsch./editl. East Indian Diaspora, Inc, Queens, NY, 1998—2002; pres. U. of Guyana Assn. of NY, New York, 1999—2002; treas. Grad. Students' Assoc, Hunter Coll., Manhattan, 1998—99. Recipient Best Graduating Student in Edn., Cyril Potter Coll. of Edn., 1981. Fellow: Liberty Knights (pres. 2001—02). Office: Liberty Tutoring Center & RISCD 91-08 Liberty Avenue Queens NY 11417 Home Fax: 718-297-5687; Office Fax: 718-323-8406. Personal E-mail: daveronsingh@msn.com.

SINGH, SEOPAUL, security firm executive; b. Georgetown, Guyana, Apr. 26, 1946; s. Mooni and Deoki Singh; m. Gloria Indrouti Birbal, Nov. 6, 1972 (div.); children: Shelly Valini, Raul Rabindranauth, Sharlene Charisma Padmini. Diploma Pub. Adminstrn., U. Guyana, Georgetown, Guyana, 1981. Cert. Emergency Manager Va., 1998; Ordained Christian Minister Internat. Gospels Assemblies, 1977, Assemblies of God, 1979. Office mgr. UN Urban Planning, Georgetown, Guyana, 1977—78; trade intelligence exec. Ministry Trade and Consumer Protection, Guyana, 1978—83, chief allocation distbn. Guyana, 1978—83; exec. officer CD Commn., Guyana, 1983—88; resource person Partners Americas, Guyana, 1988—92; emergency mgmt. specialist UN Volunteers, Geneva, Switzerland, 1992—97; security supr. Morgan Stanley, New York, NY, 1991—. Advisor emergency relief Nat. Relief Com., Georgetown, Guyana, 1983—88; advisor emergency mgmt. Partners Americas, Guyana, 1988—92, Miss., 1988—92; presbyter, missions dir. Assembly God, Georgetown, Guyana, 1975—83. Author: (book of poetry) Changing Moods; contbr. articles to professional journals. Co-founder & sec. Guyanese-American Assn., Queens, NY, 1992; co founder & pub. rels. officer Assn. Arts & Writers, 1998. Fellow fellow, Ctrl. U.S. Earth Quake Consortium, 1992, Masonry Inst. Tenn., 1992, Harvard, 1994, Maj. Indsl. Accident Coun. Can. Mem.: Assn. Contingency Planners (Exec. Citation 1998), Internat. Assn. Emergency Managers (CEM 1995). D-Conservative. International Gospel Assembly. Achievements include development of First Integrated Disaster Response Mechanism, Office of the Prime Minister, Georgetown, Guyana; received Citation for Professionalism in high rise rescue of individual trapped in an elevator. Avocations: pool, dominoes, chess, poetry reading, christian ministry camping. Home: 139-20 89th Avenue Jamaica NY 11435 Office: Association Artists & Writers 105-27 Liberty Avenue Ozone Park NY 11417 Office Fax: 713-848-5957. Personal E-mail: seopauls@aol.com.

SINGH, SHASHI PRABHA, library and informations science educator; b. Muzaffarnagar, India, July 8, 1949; d. Raj and Satya (Kapil) Sharma; m. Narendra Pratap, Nov. 17, 1972; two children. MSc, Meerut U., 1971; M in Libr. Sci., U. Delhi, 1976, PhD, 1994. Documentation asst. Govt. India, 1976-78; prof. assist. U. Delhi, 1978-82, serials libr., 1982-87, lectr., 1987-94, reader, 1995—. Mem. Indian Libr. Assn., Indian Assn. Spl. Librs. and Info. Ctrs., Assn. Govt. India Librs. & Info. Sys. Home: F-507 Rashmi Appartments 110034 Shakti Vihar Delhi India

SINGH, SHIWENDRA PRASAD, civil engineer; b. Mukrera, Bihar, India, July 5, 1937; came to U.S., 1969; s. Ramchandra and Dhanna (Devi) S.; m. Sita Singh, Mar. 7, 1962; children: Sarita, Sabita, Kavita, Saket. BSc in Civil Engring., Bihar Coll. Engring., Patna, India, 1961; MSc in Civil Engring., U. Calgary, Alta., Can., 1968. Registered profl. engr., Pa. Asst. bridge engr. Bihar Pub. Works Dept., Patna, 1962-66; sr. project mgr. Pa. Dept. Transp., Clearfield, 1969—. Recipient Gov.'s Meritorious award Pa. State Gov., 1977, Outstanding Managerial Ability award Pa. Dept. Transp., 1982, Sec. award for excellence Pa. Dept. Transp., 1990. Mem. NSPE, Am. Soc. Hwy. Engrs. Home: 2537 Meadow Rd Clearfield PA 16830-1140 Office: Pa Dept Transp 1924 Daisy St Clearfield PA 16830-3224

SINGH, SUSAN MARIE, pediatrics, maternal and women's health nurse, women's health nurse; b. Mondovi, Wis., June 15, 1951; m. Jack Singh, Jan. 1, 1974 (dec.); 1 child, Devin. BSN, U. Wis., Milw., 1977. RN, Wis.; cert. neonatal intensive care nurse. Staff nurse pediat., neonatal ICU All Saints Healthcare, Racine. Mem. Nat. Assn. Neonatal Nurses. Home: 712 William St Racine WI 53402-4236

SINGH, YESH PAL, mechanical engineering educator, consultant; b. Muzaffarnagar, India, Jan. 1, 1940; came to U.S., 1970; s. Chhatar and Gyandevi Singh; m. Veera Singh, Feb. 27, 1963; children: Sveta, Vinay. BSME, Roorkee (India) U., 1962; MSME, Youngstown State U., 1974; postgrad., SUNY, Buffalo, 1974-75; DEng, U. Wis., Milw., 1984. Design engr., asst. engr. H.E.C. Ltd., Ranchi, India, 1962-70; design engr. Youjuralmashzavod, Orsk, USSR, 1964-65, Birdsboro (Pa.) Corp., 1970, 72-73; mech. engr. DES-ENG-Corp., Reading, Pa., 1971-72; engr. Allis-Chalmers Corp., Milw., 1975-77, sr. engr. I, 1977-84, sr. engr. II, 1984-85; assoc. prof. mech. engring. U. Tex., San Antonio, 1985—, chmn. mech. engring., 1993-96, chair mech. engring. grad. studies, adv. records, 1998—2001, dir. machine shop, 1998—2002. Chair mech. design group U. Tex., 1985-2000, chmn., advisor records ME grad. program, 1998-2001. Contbr. articles to profl. jours. Recipient Coll. Engring. and Applied Sci. Outstanding Alumni award U. Wis., Milw., 1996, Charles E. Balleisen Awd., 1999. Fellow ASME (treas. San Antonio sect. 1991-92, sec. 1992-93, vice-chmn. 1993-94, chmn. 1994-95, chair nomination and nat. agenda com. 1995-96, chair coll. rels. 1996-97, chair profl. practice 1997-98, Clifford H. Schumaker award Region X, 1998). Achievements include development of design procedures for very large spur and helical gears; of procedures and design programs for determining natural frequency and mode shapes of centrifugal pump systems; of designs for various units of high speed continuous slab casters; of finite element based design procedures for endodontic root canal instrument; of synthesis procedures for design of planar cam-link mechanisms. Home: 2615 Caravan Cir San Antonio TX 78258 Office: U Tex San Antonio 6900 N Loop 1604 W San Antonio TX 78249-0670 E-mail: ysingh@utsa.edu.

SINGHAL, RAKESH KUMAR, molecular biology educator, consultant, researcher; b. Khurja, India, Apr. 24, 1955; came to U.S., 1985; s. Pooran Mal Gupta and Shanti Devi; m. Mohanie Sookram, Sept. 7, 1991; 1 child, Krtin. BSc (hon.), Aligarh (India) Muslim U., 1975, MSc, 1977; PhD, Indian Inst. Tech., New Delhi, 1985. Sr. rsch. asst. Indian Inst. Tech., 1981-85; postdoctoral assoc. Cornell U. Med. Coll., N.Y.C., 1985-87; postdoctoral fellow U. Rochester, N.Y., 1987-91; vis. scientist U. Tex. Med. Br., Galveston, 1991-96; asst. prof. pediat. N.Y.-Presbyn. Hosp.-Cornell U. Weill Med. Coll., N.Y.C., 1996—. Author: DNA Damage and Repair, 1998, Genetic Instability and Hereditary Neurological Diseases, 1998; contbr. articles to sci. jours., including Biochemistry, Jour. Biol. Chemistry, Nature. Rsch. grantee Am. Lung Assn., 1998. Mem. AAAS. Hindu. Avocations: reading, cooking, worshipping, volleyball, hiking. Home: 500 Central Park Ave Apt 338 Scarsdale NY 10583-1081 Office: NY-Presbyn Hosp-Cornell U Weill Med Coll 1300 York Ave New York NY 10021-4805 E-mail: rsinghal@med.cornell.edu.

SINGHAL, VIVEK KUMAR, management consultant; b. Delhi, India, May 15, 1949; came to the U.S., 1970; s. Om Prakash Saraswati and Kirti Rani; m. Asha Garg; children; Ritu, Vikas. BSEE, Indian Inst. Tech., New Delhi, 1970; MSEE, U. Mich., 1971, MBA, 1973. Cert. mgmt. cons. Inst. Mgmt. Cons. Various positions Rockwell Internat., Troy, Mich., 1973-77; dir. strategic planning Sara Lee Corp., Chgo., 1977-84; v.p. Beatrice Cos., 1984-85; founder, pres. Strategic Bus. Mgmt. Co., Oakbrook Terrace, Ill., 1986—. Founder, CEO Global Outsource Bids, Oakbrook Terrace, 2000; adj. prof. Lake Forest Grad. Sch. Mgmt. Exec. com. mem. Assn. Indians in Am., Chgo., 1993-95; treas. Midwest Club, Oakbrook, Ill., 1994-96, dir. Inst. Mgmt. Cons., Chgo. Mem. U. Mich. Alumni Assn., World Future Soc. (v.p. Greater Chicagoland Futurists). Avocations: reading, travel, public speaking. Office: Strategic Bus Mgmt Co 2 Mid America Plz Oakbrook Terrace IL 60181-4451 E-mail: vsingha1@hotmail.com.

SINGHAL, YOG PAUL, engineer; b. Patiala, Panjab, India, Mar. 20, 1950; came to the U.S., 1971; s. Kundan Lal and Laj Wanti (Garg) S.; m. Kund Mala Bansal, Dec. 31, 1976; children: Richa, Sonal. BSEE, Kurukshetra (India) U., 1972; MS in Indsl. Engring., Lehigh U., 1974; MBA, Xavier U., 1980. Registered profl. engr., 1976. Corp. indsl. engr. Union Fork & Hoe, Columbus, Ohio, 1974-80; divsn. indsl. engr. Abbott Labs., North Chicago, Ill., 1980-81; joint venture mfg. mgr. Flowserve, Dayton, Ohio, 1981—. Mem. adv. bd. Huber Heights (Ohio) City Sch., 1988-94, Sinclair Coll.-Indsl. Engring. Tech. program, Dayton, 1990-96. Author: Metric System and Conversions, 1997. Mem. Inst. Indsl. Engrs. (ssr., pres. 1990-91, Best Performing Dayton chpt. in S.W. Ohio 1991), Am. Mgmt. Assn. Hindu. Avocations: chess, cards, soccer, swimming, golf. Office: Flowserve Corp 2200 E Monument Ave Dayton OH 45402-1362 E-mail: ysinghal@flowserve.com, ypsinghal@aol.com.

SINGHVI, SURENDRA SINGH, finance and strategy consultant; b. Jodhpur, Rajasthan, India, Jan. 16, 1942; came to U.S., 1962, naturalized 1986; s. Rang Raj and Ugam Kanwar (Surana) S.; m. Sushila Bhandari, July 7, 1965; children: Seema, Sandeep. B in Commerce, Rajasthan U., 1961; MBA, Atlanta U., 1963; PhD, Columbia U., 1967. CPA, Cert. Mgmt. Acct. Asst. prof. fin. Miami U., Oxford, Ohio, 1967-69, assoc. prof., 1969-70; adj. prof. fin., 1970-95; fin. mgr. ARMCO Inc., Middletown, Ohio, 1970-79, asst. treas., 1979-83, gen. fin. mgr., 1983-86; v.p. and treas. Edison Bros. Stores, Inc., St. Louis, 1986-90; pres. Singhvi & Assocs., Inc., Dayton, Ohio, 1990—. Bd. dirs. Columbia Indsl. Sales Corp., Hauer Music Co., Oasis Property Inc., Keystone Industries Ltd., Om Hospitality, Inc. Author: Planning for Capital Investment, 1980; co-editor: Frontiers of Financial Management, 4th edit., 1984, Global Finance 2000-A Handbook of Strategy and Organization (The Conference Board), 1996; contbr. over 90 articles to profl. jours. Bd. trustees South Ctrl. Ohio Minority Bus. Coun., 2000—. Recipient Chancellor's Gold medal Rajasthan U., Ahimsa (Non-Violence) award Fedn. Jaina Assns. in N.Am., 1999. Mem. Inst. Mgmt. Accts. (Bayer Silver medal 1978), Fin. Execs. Inst., Fin. Mgmt. Assn., Asian Am. Hotel Owners Assn., Asian Indian Am. Bus. Group in S.W. Ohio (pres. 1997, 98), Dayton Minority Supplier Devel. Coun. (dir. 1997—, chmn. 2000), Rotary (dir. internat. program Middletown chpt. 1973-86, Dayton chpt. 1995—, treas., dir. 2001—), India Club (pres. Dayton chpt. 1980). Avocations: swimming, kanasta, travel, hiking, writing. Home: 439 Ridge Line Ct Dayton OH 45458-9564 Office: Singhvi and Assocs Inc 515 Windsor Park Dr Dayton OH 45459-4112 E-mail: ssinghvi@att.net.

SINGLEHURST, DONA GEISENHEYNER, horse farm owner; b. Tacoma, June 19, 1928; d. Herbert Russell and Rose Evelyn (Rubish) Geisenheyner; m. Thomas G. Singlehurst, May 16, 1959 (dec.); 1 child, Suanna Singlehurst. BA in Psychology, Whitman Coll., 1950. With pub. rels. and advt. staff Lane Wells, L.A., 1950-52; staff mem. in charge new bus. Bishop Trust Co., Honolulu, 1953-58; mgr. Town & Country Stables, 1958-62; co-owner, v.p. pub. rels. Carol & Mary, Ltd., 1964-84; owner Stanhope Farms, Waialua, Hawaii, 1969—. Internat. dressage judge, sport horse breeding judge Am. Horse Shows Assn.; sr. judge Can. Dressage Fedn. Chmn. ways and means com. The Outdoor Cir., Hawaii, 1958-64, life mem.; pres. emeritus Morris Animal Found., Englewood, Colo., 1988—, pres., 1984-88; bd. dirs., pres. Delta Soc., Renton, Wash., 1994-97, chmn. emeritus 1998—, N.Y.C.; mem. Jr. League of Honolulu; mem. devel. com. Honolulu Symphony. Recipient Best Friends award Honolulu Vet. Soc., 1986, Spl. Recognition award Am. Animal Hosp. Assn., 1988, Recognition award Am. Vet. Med. Assn. Mem. NAFE, AAUW, Hawaii Horse Show Assn. (Harry Hutaff award 1985, past pres., bd. dirs.), Hawaii Combined Tng. Assn. (past pres. bd. dirs.), Calif. Dressage Soc., U.S. Dressage Fedn., U.S. Equestrian Team (area chmn. 1981-85), Hawaiian Humane Soc. (life), U.S. Pony Clubs (dist. commr. 1970-75, nat. examiner 1970-75), Pacific Club, Outrigger Canoe Club. Republican. Episcopalian. Avocations: music, travel. Home and Office: Stanhope Farms PO Box 546 Waialua HI 96791

SINGLETARY, ALVIN D. lawyer; b. Sept. 27, 1942; s. Alvin E. and Alice (Pastoret) Singletary; m. Judy Louise Singletary, Dec. 3, 1983; children: Kimberly Dawn, Shane David, Kelly Diane. BA, La. State U., 1964; JD, Loyola U., New Orleans, 1969. Bar: La. 1969, U.S. Dist. Ct. (ea. dist.) La. 1972, U.S. Ct. Appeals (5th cir.) 1972, U.S. Ct. Appeals (11 cir.) 1981, U.S. Ct. Internat. Trade 1981, U.S. Ct. Customs and Patent Appeals 1982, U.S. Supreme Ct. 1978. Instr. Delgado Coll., New Orleans, 1976—77; sole practice Slidell, 1970—. Spl. asst. dist. atty 22d Judicial Dist. Ct. , Parish of St. Tammany, La.; sec., treas. St. Tammany Pub. Trust Fin. Authority, 1978—2002. Chmn. sustaining membership enrollment Cypress dist. Boy Scouts Am., 1989—; treas. Slidell Centennial commn.; councilman-at-large City of Slidell, 1978—2002, interim mayor, 1985; mem. Dem. State Ctrl. Com., 1978—82; mem. Rep. State Ctrl. Com. Dist. 76, La., 1996—2000; del. La.Constl. Conv., 1972—73; chmn. Together We Build Program First Baptist Ch. of Slidell, La.; bd. dir. St. Tammany Coun. on Aging. Mem.: Lions, Delta Theta Phi. Baptist. Office: PO Box 1158 Slidell LA 70459-1158

SINGLETARY, CAGLAR JUAN, minister; b. Buffalo, July 7, 1972; s. David John and Desiree Elaine Singletary. Student, Elmira (N.Y.) Coll., 1992—95; Karate Tchr. Certificate, Dragon Kenpo Karate Acad., 1995; student, Corning C.C., 1996—97. Ordained minister World Christianship Ministries, 1998. Vol. Chs., librs., etc., Elmira, NY, 1995—. Republican. Roman Catholic. Home: 111 E Miller St Elmira NY 14901 Office: Applied Christianity Ch of God in Christ 407 W Church St Elmira NY 14901

SINGLETARY, JAMES, JR. school board administrator; b. Buffalo, Jan. 24, 1947; m. Carolyn Price, July 24, 1971; children: Airen, Craig, Brandon, Evan. Cert. sheet metal, Erie C.C., Buffalo, 1974; BS, SUNY, Buffalo, 1990; MS, Canisius Coll., 1993. Cert. tchr. permanent, 1988, sch. adminstr. and supr., 1993. Sheet metal worker Buffalo Sheets Metal, 1970-77; customer engr. IBM, Buffalo, 1977-83; sheet metal worker, drafting tchr. Buffalo Pub. Schs., 1983-93; asst. prin. Seneca Vocat. H.S., Buffalo, 1993-97; dir. Bur. Pers. Svcs., Buffalo Bd. Edn., N.Y.C., 1997—. 2d v.p. bd. dirs. Rev. Marvin W. Robinson Cmty. Ctr., Inc.; mem. Ctrl. Office Adminstrs. Adv. coun. mem. SUNY and Buffalo Vocat. Tech. Edn. Coun., 1988-91. With USN, 1964-70. Mem. Am. Edn. Rsch. Assn., Am. Fedn. Sch. Adminstrs., N.Y. State Fedn. Suprs. and Adminstrs., Vocat. Tech. Guild Buffalo, Buffalo Coun. Suprs. and Adminstrs. (mem. grievance com., v.p. exec. com. 1997—, mem. ctrl. office adminstrs.), Buffalo Secondary Asst. Prins. Assn. (v.p., pres. 1997—), Buffalo State Coll. Alumni Assn., Canisius Coll. Alumni Assn., Jack and Jill of Am., Inc., Phi Delta Kappa. Avocations: bowling, tennis, roller skating. Home: 273 Humboldt Pky Buffalo NY 14208-1044 Office: Buffalo Bd Edn Bur Pers City Hall Rm 719 Buffalo NY 14202-3331

SINGLETARY, OTIS ARNOLD, JR. university president emeritus; b. Gulfport, Miss., Oct. 31, 1921; s. Otis Arnold and May Charlotte (Walker) S.; m. Gloria Walton, June 6, 1944; children: Bonnie, Scot, Kendall Ann. BA, Millsaps Coll., 1947; MA, La State U., 1949, PhD, 1954. Mem. faculty U. Tex., Austin, 1954-61, prof. history, 1960-61, assoc. dean Sch. Arts and Scis., 1956-59, asst. to pres., 1960-61; chancellor U. N.C., Greensboro, 1961-66; v.p. Am. Council on Edn., Washington, 1966-68; on leave as dir. Job Corps, OEO, 1964-65; exec. vice chancellor acad. affairs U. Tex. System, 1968-69; pres. U. Ky., Lexington, 1969-87, prof. emeritus, 1987—. Bd. dirs. Howell Corp. Author: Negro Militia and the Reconstruction, 1957, The Mexican War, 1960; editor: American Universities and Colleges, 1968. Regional chmn. Woodrow Wilson Nat. Fellowship Found., 1959-61; chmn. N.C. Rhodes Scholarship Com., 1964-66; chmn. Ky. Rhodes Scholarship Com., 1970-71, 73-74, 77, 80-81, 84-86; mem. So. Regional Edn. Bd., 1969—; chmn. dept. Army history adv. com., 1972-80; bd. visitors Air U., Maxwell AFB, 1973-76. Served with USNR, 1943-46, 51-54. Recipient Scarborough Teaching Excellence award U. Tex., 1958, Students Assn. Teaching Excellence award, 1958, 59; Carnegie Corp. grantee, 1961 Mem. Am. Hist. Assn., So. Hist. Assn., Am. Mil. Inst. (Moncado Book Fund award 1954), Am. Assn. Higher Edn. (dir. 1969—), Phi Beta Kappa (senator 1977-94, v.p. 1985-88, pres. 1988-91), Phi Alpha Theta, Omicron Delta Kappa, Pi Kappa Alpha. Democrat. Methodist. Office: U of Ky 104 King Library N Lexington KY 40506-0001

SINGLETARY, PATRICIA ANN, minister; b. N.Y.C., Mar. 3, 1948; d. George and Minnie Juanita (Williams) Nickens; m. Edward Franklin Singletary, Feb. 5, 1966 (dec.); children: Erik Franklin, Don Andre. BTh, New World Bible Inst. & Sem., 1984, MRE, 1986; AS, BS, SUNY, 1991; AA, Va. Sem. and Coll., 1995; MDiv, New Brunswick Theol. Sem., 1995; DD, Tenn. Bapt. Sch. Religion, 1989. Sr. reorgn. underwriter Depository Trust Co., N.Y.C., 1968-90, acct. coord., 1990—. Nat. corr. sec. Nat. Bapt. Conv. U.S.A. Inc., 1984-87; vice chair Spiritual Life Commn. of Clergywomen, 1987—; assoc. minister Morning Star Missionsry Bapt. Ch. of Jamaica, N.Y. CEO, founder Adoni Econ. Enterprises, Inc., v.p. Queens County Young Pastors, Mins. Evangelist Ea. Bapt. Assn. Author: African-American Guide to Buying Stock Without a Broker; nat editor: Ekklesia, 1986. Pastor Elmendorf Reformed Ch., East Harlem, NY. Recipient Vol. Svcs. award City of N.Y., 1980. Mem. NAFE, Nat. Assn. Negro Bus. and Profl. Women, Interdenominational Bd. Clergywoman (gen. sec. 1985-91), Nat. Bapt. Women Ministers Xonv. (bd. mgrs. 1983-91), Ea. Bapt. Assn. (instr. 1981-83, v.p. evangelistic unit 1982-83, gen. dir. women's aux. 1988-91), Nat. Coun. Women U.S., Internat. Platform Assn., Bronx Bapt. Ministers Evening Conf. Greater N.Y. and Vicinity, Queens Bapt. Mins. Conf. Greater N.Y. and Vicinity, Assn. Black Seminarians (pres. 1993-95).

SINGLETARY, SONJA EVA, surgeon, educator; b. Coward, S.C., Dec. 23, 1952; 1 child Benjamin Harkrider. BS, Clemson U., 1973; MD, U. S.C., 1977. Resident in gen. surgery U. Fla., 1977-83; surg. oncology fellow M.D. Anderson Cancer Ctr., Houston, 1983-85; faculty assoc. U. Tex. M.D. Anderson Cancer Ctr., 1985-86, asst. prof. surgery, 1986-91, assoc. prof. surgery, 1991-96, prof., 1996—. Author: Breast Cancer, 1999, Breast Cancer-M.D. Anderson Solid Tumor Oncology Series, 1999. Named one of Good Housekeeping's Best Doctors in Am., 1995—2002; recipient Women on the Move award, Tex. Exec. Women, 1998, Ptnrs. in Courage award, 1999, Cancer Fighters Eagle award, 1999. Office: U Tex MD Anderson Cancer Ctr Box 444 1515 Holcombe Blvd Houston TX 77030-4009 Fax: 713-792-0722. E-mail: esinglet@mdanderson.org.

SINGLETERRY, ROBERT CLAY, JR. aerospace technologist, physicist; b. Fayetteville, N.C., Jan. 4, 1961; s. Robert Clay and Phyllis Lea (Donovan) S.; m. Maria Star Groshner, May 18, 1984. BS in Nuclear Engring., U. Ariz., 1984, MS, 1990, PhD, 1993; postgrad., U. Idaho, 1986-91, Coll. of William and Mary, 1998—. Software-reactor engr. Ga. Power Co., Baxley, 1984-85; software engr. Energy Inc., Idaho Falls, 1985-89; grad. rsch. asst. U. Ariz., Tucson, 1989-93; rsch. asst. Argonne Nat. Lab., Idaho Falls, summers 1989-93, staff nuclear engr., 1993-97; prin. mem. Quantum Solutions, LLC, 1995-97; aerospace technologist, physicist NASA Langley Rsch. Ctr., Hampton, Va., 1997—. Adj. prof. dept. nuclear sci. and engring. Idaho State U., Pocatello, 1994-97; vis. scientist program coord. Idaho Acad. Sci., 1997. Contbr. articles to profl. jours. Vice-chair Young Women's Conf., Idaho Falls, 1993-94, chair, 1994-95. Mem. Am. Nuc. Soc. (leader tech. working group on aerospace nuc. sci. tech.), Va. Acad. Sci. Avocations: golf, volleyball, teaching, community service. Home: 102 Chadwick Ct Yorktown VA 23693-5004 Office: NASA Langley Rsch Ctr Mail Ctr Stop 188B Hampton VA 23681-0001 Fax: 757-864-8094. E-mail: r.c.singleterry@larc.nasa.gov.

SINGLETON, DEAN, publishing executive; m. Adrienne Casale; children: William Casale, Paige Casale, Adam Casale. Chmn. Rocky Mountain News, Denver Newspaper Agy.; vice chmn., CEO MediaNews Group Inc., Denver; chmn., pub. Denver Post, 2001—. Bd. dirs. Associated Press. Mem. bd. trustees Rocky Mountain Multiple Sclerosis Ctr., Nat. Sports Ctr. Disabled Bd., Winter Park Recreational Assn. Bd. Mem.: Newspaper Assn. Am. (chmn. bd. dirs.). Office: Denver Post 1560 Broadway Denver CO 80202-1577*

SINGLETON, DONALD EDWARD, journalist; b. Morristown, N.J., Nov. 8, 1936; s. Edward Leslie and Charlotte (Angerbauer) S.; m. Maureen Ann McNiff, Aug. 8, 1959 (div. 1977); children: Nancy Ann, Mark Aram, Jill Susan. Student, Fairleigh Dickinson U., 1955-58. Reporter Dover (N.J.) Advance, 1959-61, Morristown Daily Record, 1961-63, Newark Eve. News, 1963-64; feature reporter-writer N.Y. Daily News, 1964—. Organizer Com. to Save Church Sq. Park, Hoboken, N.J.; vice chmn. Hoboken Environment Com.; mem. due process com. ACLU., Mem. bd. edn., City of Hoboken, 1974-77. Recipient Pub. Service award N.Y. Council Civic Affairs, 1967; President's Distinguished Service award N.Y.C. Council, 1969; Newspaper award merit Women's Press Club N.Y.C., 1970, 79; citation VFW, 1970; Heywood Broun Meml. award Am. Newspaper Guild, 1970; Silver medal for pub. service journalism N.Y. chpt. Pub. Relations Soc. Am., 1970; certificate merit Am. Bar Assn., 1971; Page One award Newspaper Guild N.Y., 1970; Feature award Newspaper Reporters Assn. N.Y., 1972; Consistent Excellence award Uniformed Firefighters Assn., 1991. Mem. Am. Newspaper Guild. Clubs: Press (N.Y.C.). Home: 366 Ogden Ave Jersey City NJ 07307-1115 Office: 220 E 42nd St New York NY 10017-5806 *In reporting, I try very hard to avoid gathering facts in such a way as to fulfill a preconception. I also attempt to force myself to review constantly my opinions about my subjects, and to keep my mind as open as possible. In writing, I try to ask myself the following questions regularly: "Is this what I really believe? Or am I simply writing this way because I believe that this is what some other person or group would like me to write?" Unless I can answer the first question in the affirmative, and the second in the negative, I am not satisfied with a particular story.*

SINGLETON, FRANCIS SETH, international educator; b. Phila., July 13, 1940; s. William Francis and Anna A. (Setian) S.; m. Margaret Neff, June 14, 1962 (div. 1983); children: William, Andrew; m. Charlotte T. Kennedy, Jan. 16, 1988. AB, Harvard U., 1962; MA, Yale U., 1963, PhD, 1968. Budget examiner Bur. of Budget, Washington, 1964-65; dean Pearson Coll. Yale U., New Haven, 1966-69; lectr. U. Dares Salaam, Tanzania, 1969-70; asst. prof. U. Alta., Edmonton, Can., 1970-71; from assoc. prof. to prof., chair politics and govt. Ripon (Wis.) Coll., 1972-83; rsch. assoc. Russian Ctr., Harvard U., Cambridge, Mass., 1983-84; dean arts and scis. Pacific U., Forest Grove, Oreg., 1984-91, prof. govt., 1991—; academic dean Espiritu Santo U., Guayaquil, Ecuador, 1994-97. Ampart lectr. U.S.I.A., Africa, 1983, Africa, 90; lectr. Ural U., Russia, 1991; cons. Russia Fedn. Govt., 1992; mem. Pacific Coun. on Internat. Policy, 1998—; chair nat. peer rev. com. for S.E. Asia Fulbright Scholars, 2001—. Author: (book) Africa in Perspective, 1968, Introduction to Vietnam and Kue; contbr. Bd. dirs. Com. Fgn. Rels., Portland,

1989-92; mem. adv. com. Light Rail Tri-Met, Portland, Oreg., 1989-94. Grantee Rockefeller Found., 1969-70, Nat. Coun. Soviet and E. Europe Rsch., 1983-84; U.S. Fulbright scholar, Vietnam, 1999-2000. Avocations: sailing, outdoor activities. E-mail. Home: 39 Hall Quarry Rd PO Box 185 Mount Desert ME 04660-0185 E-mail: ssinglet@pacificu.edu., sethsing@acadia.net.

SINGLETON, HARRY MICHAEL, lawyer; b. Meadville, Pa., Apr. 10, 1949; s. Getdins T. and Rose Ann (Fucci) S.; children: Harry M. Jr., Leah Rose DiFucci. BA, Johns Hopkins U., 1971; JD, Yale U., 1974. Bar: D.C. 1975, Pa. 1976, Calif. 1999, Md. 1999, U.S. Dist. Ct. D.C. 1975, U.S. Ct. Appeals (D.C. cir.) 1975, U.S. Ct. Mil. Appeals 1975. Assoc. Houston & Gardner, Washington, 1974-75, Covington & Burling, Washington, 1976-77; atty. FTC, 1975-76; dep. minority counsel Com. on D.C./U.S. Ho. of Reps., 1977-79, minority chief counsel, staff dir., 1979-81; dep. asst. sec. U.S. Dept. Commerce, 1981-82; asst. sec. U.S. Dept. Edn., 1982-86; pres. Harry M. Singleton & Assocs., 1986-91; pvt. practice law, 1991—; pres. Singleton Entertainment, LLC, 1999-2000. Legis. cons. Am. Enterprise Inst., Washington, 1975. Pres. bd. trustees Barney Neighborhood House, Washington, 1978-80; corp. bd. dirs. Children's Hosp. Nat. Med. Ctr., Washington, 1984-88; mem. crime com. Boys and Girls Clubs of Greater Washington, 1994-97; mem. D.C. Rep. State Com., 1991—, Rep. Nat. Com., 1992-2000, R.N.C. exec. coun., 1993-95, resolutions com., 1997-2000; mem. Rep. Nat. Hispanic Assembly Washington, 1991-92. Mem. Rep. Nat. Lawyers Assn. (bd. dirs. D.C. chpt. 1990-91), Coun. of 100 Black Reps. (bd. dirs. 1991-92), D.C. Black Rep. Coun. (chmn. 1992-93), Rep. Nat. African-Am. Coun. (nat. chmn. 1993-2001), D.C. Rep. Nat. African-Am. Coun. (chmn. 1993-2001). Republican. Presbyterian. Office: 2121 K St NW Ste 800 Washington DC 20037-1829

SINGLETON, JAMES KEITH, federal judge; b. Oakland, Calif., Jan. 27, 1939; s. James K. and Irene Elisabeth (Lilly) S.; m. Sandra Claire Hoskins, Oct. 15, 1966; children: Matthew David, Michael Keith. Student, U. Santa Clara, 1957-58; AB in Polit. Sci., U. Calif., Berkeley, 1961, LLB, 1964. Bar: Calif. 1965, Alaska, 1965. Assoc. Delaney Wiles Moore and Hayes, Anchorage, 1963, 65-68, Law Offices Roger Cremo, Anchorage, 1968-70; judge Alaska Superior Ct., 1970-80, Alaska Ct. Appeals, Anchorage, 1980-90, U.S. Dist. Ct. for Alaska, Anchorage, 1990-95, chief judge, 1995—. Chmn. Alaska Local Boundary Commn., Anchorage, 1966-69. Chmn. 3d Dist. Rep. Com., Anchorage, 1969-70. Mem. ABA, Alaska Bar Assn., Phi Delta Phi, Tau Kappa Epsilon. Office: US Dist Ct 222 W 7th Ave Unit 41 Anchorage AK 99513-7504

SINGLETON, LAVERNA, medical reviewere; b. Friend, Nebr., Nov. 14, 1940; d. Lester and Frances Anna M. (O'Dea) S. Diploma, St. Elizabeth Hosp., Lincoln, Nebr., 1961; BAAS, Midwestern State U., Wichita Falls, Tex., 1988, MA in Pub. Adminstrn., 1990. Quality control coord. Bethania Regional Health Care Ctr., Wichita Falls, head nurse, orthopedics, 1969-77, asst. dir. nursing adminstrn., 1977-90; regional rev. mgr. Tex. Peer Rev. Orgn., Tex. Med. Found., Dallas, 1991-93; quality mgmt. mgr. Vis. Nurse Assn. Tex., 1993-96; dir. quality mgmt. Compliants Cons. for the Home Care Industry, Garland, Tex., 1996; dir. quality mgmt. and regulatory compliance United In Home Nursing Svc., Arlington, 1996-97; med. reviewer Trailblazer Health Enterprises, LLC., Dallas, 2000—. Mem. Tex. Orgn. Nurse Execs., Dallas Area Healthcare Quality Assn., Pi Sigma Alpha.

SINGLETON, MARVIN AYERS, state legislator, otolaryngologist; b. Baytown, Tex., Oct. 7, 1939; s. Henry Marvin and Mary Ruth Singleton. BA, U. of the South, 1962; MD, U. Tenn., 1966. Diplomate Am. Bd. Otolaryngology. Intern City of Memphis Hosps., 1966-67; resident in surgery Highland Alameda City Hosp., Oakland, Calif., 1967-68; resident in otolaryngology U. Tenn. Hosp., Memphis, 1968-71; fellow in otolaryngic pathology Armed Forces Inst. Pathology, Washington, 1971; fellow in otologic surgery U. Colo. at Gallup (N.Mex.) Indian Med. Ctr., 1972; practice medicine specializing in otolaryngology/allergies Joplin, Mo., 1972—. Founder, operator Home and Farm Investments, Joplin, 1975—, staff mem. Freeman Hosp., St. John's Hosp., Joplin, Oakhill Hosp.; cons. in otolaryngology Mo. Crippled Children's Service, Santa Fe R.R.; pres. Ozark Mfg. Co., Inc., Joplin. Mem. Internat. Arabian Racing Bd., 1983-88; mem. Mo. State Senate, 1990—; del. Rep. Nat. Conv., 1988, 92. Served with USNG, 1966-72. Fellow Am. Coll. Surgery, Am. Acad. Otolaryngologic Allergy (past pres.), Am. Assn. Clin. Immunology & Allergy; mem. AMA (Mo. del.), Mo. State Med. Assn., Sthn. Med. Assn., Jasper County Med. Assn., Coun. Otolaryngology, Mo. State Allergy Assn., Ear Nose & Throat Soc. Mo. (past pres.), Joplin C. of C., Masons (32d degree), Sigam Alpha Epsilon, Phi Theta Kappa, Phi Chi. Methodist. Home: 4476 Five Mile Rd Seneca MO 64865-8357 Office: 114 W 32nd St Joplin MO 64804-3701 E-mail: DocSingleton@fivemileranch.com.

SINGLETON, ROBERT CULTON, graduate school administrator, Bible educator; b. Amarillo, Tex., Oct. 17, 1950; s. William Madison and Doris (Culton) S.; m. Stephanie Diane Lawrence, May 17, 1975; children: Kristin Michelle, Robert Culton Jr. BSEE, U. Tex., 1973; ThM in Bible Exposition, Dallas Theol. Sem., 1977; PhD in Higher Edn., U. Tex., 1993. Ordained to ministry Cmty. Bible Chapel, 1981. Campus staff Campus Crusade for Christ, Dallas, 1974-77; dean Nairobi (Kenya) Internat. Sch. Theology, 1978-83; grad. studies staff Campus Crusade for Christ, Austin, Tex., 1984-92; dean faculty East Asia Sch. Theology, Singapore, 1993-96; faculty The Orlando (Fla.) Inst., 1997—. Bd. dirs. Nairobi Internat. Sch. Theology, 1981-83. Contbr. articles to profl. jours. Mem. Kappa Delta Pi, Phi Kappa Phi. So. Bapt. Avocations: personal computers, tennis. E-mail: bsingleton@toi.edu.

SINGLETON, SAMUEL WINSTON, physician, pharmaceutical company executive; b. Blackpool, Eng., Nov. 17, 1928; came to U.S., 1953, naturalized, 1955; s. Samuel Smith and Jessica Constance M. (Knights) S.; m. Sheila Yolande C. Kershaw, Aug. 23, 1953; 1 child, Diane Jane. M.B., Ch.B., U. Manchester, 1952. Diplomate: Am. Bd. Pediatrics. Intern, Chester, Pa., 1953-54; pediatric resident Oakland, Calif., 1956-58; assoc. physician, dir. clin. investigation, med. dir., v.p. Burroughs Wellcome Co., Research Triangle Park, N.C., 1960-89; asst. clin. prof. pediatrics Duke U., Durham, 1972-90. Past dir. B.W. Fund. Served with M.C. USNR, 1954-60. Home: 429 Tranquility Rd Moneta VA 24121-3265 E-mail: wsing@cablenet-va.com.

SINGLETON, STELLA WOOD, nurse; b. Moore County, N.C., Nov. 3, 1948; d. Jay and Thelma A. Wood; children: Jennifer, Mike. Diploma, Hamlet Hosp. Sch. Nursing, Hamlet, N.C., 1975; postgrad., Appalachian State U., Boone, N.C., 1990—. RN, N.C. Dir. Hospice of Boone (N.C.) Area, 1982-83; Hospice dir. Hospice of Avery County, Newland, N.C., 1983-85; DON Toe River Health Dist., 1983-84; mental health nurse II New River Mental Health, 1977-82, 85-95; beauty cons. Mary Kay Cosmetics, 1986—; habilitation asst. Devl. Disabilities Svcs., Boone, N.C., 1995-98; personal care supr. HomeCare Mgmt. Corp., 1996-98; co-assoc., program mgr. Avery Citizens Against Domestic Abuse, 1998-2000; nurse Broughton Hosp., Morganton, N.C., 2000—. Instr. Mayland C.C., Spruce Pine, N.C., 1996-99. Co-facilitator Avery County Alzheimer's Support Group; group facilitator Cancer Support Group Svc., 1985-98; rehab. chmn. Am. Cancer Soc., 1977-99. Recipient Gov's. award for administrv. vol. Home: PO Box 483 Crossnore NC 28616-0483 Office: Broughton Hosp Morganton NC 28655

SINGLETON-WOOD, ALLAN JAMES, communications executive; b. Newport, Monmouthshire, Eng., Feb. 13, 1933; arrived in Can., 1968; s. Charles James and Violet Anne (Bond) S.-W.; m. Joan Davies, June 23, 1956; children: Ceri, Glendon. Student, London U., 1949-51. TV and radio musical dir., 1953-57; TV producer, 1957-61; freelance producer for BBC, 1962-64; indsl. advt. mgr. Western Mail, Cardiff, Wales, 1964; advt. dir. Voice of Brit. Industry Mags., London, 1966; mktg. svcs. exec. The Sun and The People, I.P.C. Newspapers, 1966-68; mktg. svcs. mgr. Fin. Post, Toronto, Ont., Can., 1969-71, rsch. mgr., 1971-76, nat. sales mgr., 1976-77; pub. Fin. Post Mag., 1978-79, dir. advt. sales Fin. Post divsn., 1980-83; pub. Small Bus. Mag., 1983-87; v.p. pub. Bedford House Ltd., Toronto, 1987-88; pub. Small Bus. mag., v.p. CB Media Ltd., 1988—; v.p. pub. Can. Bus. and Small Bus. mags., Who's Who in Can. Bus., Who's Who in Can. Fin., 1989—; corp. pub., gen. mgr. Sentry Comm., Willowdale, Ont., 1991-92; group pub. Bus. Publs. divsn. MacLean Hunter Ltd., Toronto, 1992-93; pres. Can. Productivity divsn. CB Media Ltd., 1994-96; pres., CEO Singleton-Wood Comm. Inc., 1996—. Lectr. at various univs.; cons. in field; pres., CEO, founder Can. Info. Productivity Awards, 1994—2001. Composer: contemporary music including title theme of Swing High, BBC nat. network series, 1953-57. Mem. Anglican Ch. Achievements include development of first computer media evaluation program for Canadian advertising industry.

SINGLEY, JOHN EDWARD, JR. retired environmental scientist, consultant; b. Wildwood, N.J., July 31, 1924; s. John Edward Singley and Dorothy Mae (Pfrommer) S.; children: Gladys, Ann, Margaret, Patricia; m. June Walden Calohan, Apr. 28, 2001; stepchildren: Daniel, C hristopher Calohan. BS, Ga. Inst. Tech, 1950; MS, Ga. Inst. Tech., 1952; PhD, U. Fla., 1966. Chemist Redstone Arsenal, Huntsville, Ala., 1950-51; dir. tech. svs. Tenn. Corp., College Park, Ga., 1951-64; lectr. chemistry Ga. State U., Atlanta, 1954-64, assoc. prof., 1964-67; prof. environ. engring. sci. U. Fla., Gainesville, 1967-90, prof. emeritus, 1990—; dir. TREEO Ctr., 1978-86; v.p. James M. Montgomery, Cons. Engrs., Inc., 1984-93, Montgomery Watson Cons. Engrs. Inc., Gainesville, 1993-96; sr. v.p. Environ. Scis. Engring. Inc., 1977-84; prin. Water and Air Rsch., 1970-77; v.p. Metcalf & Eddy, 1996-99; ret., 1999. Patentee in field of polymers. Mem. Fulton County Rep. Exec. Com., 1962-64; trustee Water for People, 1990-92. With USN, 1943-45. Recipient Donald R. Boyd award Met. Water Agys., 1992. Fellow Am. Inst. Chemists, Inst. Water and Environ. Mgmt.; mem. Am. Water Works Assn. (hon., life, bd. dirs. 1984-87, exec. com. 1986-87, 89-93, v.p. 1989-90, pres.-elect 1990-91, pres. 1991-92, Fuller award 1974, rsch. award 1983, Abel Wolman Excellence award 1995, Disting. Pub. Svc. award 1995, Water Industry Hall of Fame 2000), Fla. Water and Pollution Control Operators Assn. (Flanigan award 1979), Nat. Lime Assn. (Recognition award), Internat. Water Supply Assn., Nat. Assn. Corrosion Engrs., Internat. Ozone Assn. (bd. dirs. 1985-93). Clubs: Gainesville, Civitan (pres. 1972, lt. gov. Fla. dist. 1973-76). Presbyterian. Home: 1719 NW 23rd Blvd # Phe Gainesville FL 32605-3027 Office: 1719 NW 23rd Ave PHE Gainesville FL 32605-3079 E-mail: h20doceds@aol.com.

SINGSTOCK, DAVID JOHN, military officer; b. Oshkosh, Wis., July 19, 1940; s. Arnold William and Viola Rufine (Gerdener) S.; children: Susan, Brian, Elissa, Timothy. BS with distinction, Maine Maritime Acad., 1964; student, U.S. Merchant Marine Acad., 1959-62; BSBA with distinction, George Washington U., 1973, MS, 1975. Lic. profl. marine engr. Commd. ensign USN, 1964, advanced through grades to comdr., 1984, various sea assignments including combat duty in Vietnam, 1964-69, engr. officer USS Harold J. Ellison Va., 1969-71, ADP fin. mgr. Cinclantflt, 1971-73, planning and quality assurance officer supr. shipbuilding Portsmouth, 1973-76, prodn./repair officer supr. shipbuilding Bath, Maine, 1976-79, ship maintenance mgr. chief naval ops. Washington, 1980-83, dir. fleet modernization program space/naval warfare systems command, 1983-86, program mgr. USS Stark restoration naval sea systems command, 1986-88, tech. dir. dep. asst. sec. Navy for internat. programs, 1988-93; ships program mgr. ROH, Inc., Arlington, Va., 1993-95; ship self def. mgr. Vitro, Corp., 1996-97; theater ballistic missile def. R & D mgr. Tracor Sys. Techs., Inc., 1998-99; theater ballistic missile def. mgr. Marconi Sys. Techs., Inc., 1999—2001; dep. dir. Applied Ordnance Tech. Internat., 1999—2001; tech. dir. Anteon Corp., 2001—. Sr. tech. advisor Royal Saudi Naval Forces Ops. Desert Shield and Desert Storm, 1990-91; sr. naval tech. mem. to Sec. of Def. chartered delegation of sr. U.S. ofcls., Saudi Arabia, 1991; retired U.S. Navy, 1993. Asst. scoutmaster Boy Scouts Am., Dumfries, Va., 1985-90; coach Youth Soccer, Maine, Va., 1976-84; active local property owners civic orgns., Va., Maine, 1970—; instr. ARC, Seattle, 1967-68. Decorated Navy Commendation medal, Navy Achievement medal, Vietnamese Cross of Gallantry, Meritorious Svc. Medal, Joint Svc. Commendation medal, Bronze Star, Purple Heart; recipient Cert. of Appreciation and Gratitude, Comdr. of Saudi Arabian Armed Forces. Mem. Am. Soc. Naval Engrs. (dep. com. chmn., speaker 1988), Nat. Contract Mgmt. Assn. (cert. contracts mgr.), Ret. Officers Assn., Nat. Eagle Scout Assn., Mason (32 degree), Scottish Rite, Shriner. Presbyterian. Avocations: sailing, jogging, camping, golf, music. Home: 1125 Portner Rd Alexandria VA 22314-1314 Office: Anteon Corp 2231 Crystal Dr Ste 1000 Arlington VA 22202-3742

SINHA, AKHOURI A. research scientist, educator; b. Churamanpur, Bihar, India, Dec. 17, 1933; s. Akhouri Chandra B. and Bittan Devi Sinha; m. Dorothy Kay Parmer, Sept. 29, 1979. BSc, Allahabad (India) U., 1954; MSc, Patna (India) U., 1956; PhD, U. Mo., 1965. Lectr. Ranchi (India) U., 1956—61; asst. prof. U. Wis., Eau Claire, 1965—67; sr. scientist U. Minn., Mpls., 1967—69, prof., 1981—; rsch. scientist VA Med. Ctr., 1969—. Contbr. articles to profl. jours. Hindu. Avocations: riding, cross country skiing, photography, traveling, reading. Office: Rsch Svcs One Veterans Dr Minneapolis MN 55417

SINHA, BRAJRAMAN PRASAD, civil engineer, educator; b. Hazipur, Bihar, India, Dec. 20, 1936; s. B.N. and S. (Devi) S.; m. N. Sahay, June 2, 1962; children: Sangeeta, Saurabh, Shameek. BSc, Patna (India) U., 1957; postgrad. diploma in bldg. sci., Liverpool (England) U., 1964; PhD, U. Edinburgh, Scotland, 1967, DSc, 1998. Engring. asst. works dept. Patna U., 1957-59; asst. engr. Bihar Electricity Bd., Ranchi, India, 1959-60; asst. engr. dept. pub. works Bihar, 1960-63; design engr. dept. pub. works, 1968-69; demonstrator and rsch. asst. U. Edinburgh, 1966-68, from rsch. fellow to sr. lectr., 1969-95, reader, 1995—, prof., 1999. UNDP cons., Roorkee, Madras, India, 1986; vis. prof. Bihar Coll. Engring., 1984; vis. cons. and advisor dept. civil engring. U. Santa Catarina, Florianopolis, Brazil, 1991—; vis. prof. U. Ancona, Italy, 1999, Indian Inst. Sci., Bangalore, 2000. Co-author: Load-Bearing Brickwork Design, 1987; co-editor: Structural Masonry for Developing Countries, 1992; contbr. chpt.: Reinforced and Prestressed Masonry, 1989; contbr. articles to profl. jours. Active Lothian Racial Equality Coun., Edinburgh, 1984—; mem. senate Edinburgh U., 1984—; chmn. Hindu Temple and Cultural Ctr., Edinburgh, 1985-86; active Boroughmuir Sch. Coun., Edinburgh, 1981; pres. Indian Arts Coun., 1994. Recipient prize Instn. of Engrs. India, 1991-92. Mem. Internat. Masonry Engring. for Developing Countries (exec. dir. 1982), Internat. Coun. Bldg. Rsch. (mem. commn. W23A 1976). Hindu. Avocations: reading, overseas travel, photography, table tennis, writing. Office: U Edinburgh Dept Civil Engr Kings Bldgs Edinburgh EH9 3JN Scotland E-mail: B.Sinha@civ.ed.ac.uk.

SINHA, RAJ P. education educator, researcher; b. Pahsara, Bihar, India, Nov. 11, 1934; arrived in U.S., 1961; s. Kapilded P. and Kaushilya Sinha; m. Rani P. Sinha; children: Rajiv R., Nilu Sinha-Tiwari, Ena. BSc, Patna U., Bihar, India, 1957; MS, U. Wyo., 1963; PhD, U. Manitoba, Can., 1967. Fellow Carleton U., Ottawa, Canada, 1968—72; rsch. scientist Food Rsch. Inst., Canada, 1972—92; assoc. prof. Chgo. State U., 1992—. Contbr. articles to profl. jours. Recipient Proventia Govt. Ontario award, 1980. Office: Chgo State Univ Dept Biology 9501 S King Dr Chicago IL 60628-1598 Fax: 773-995-3759. E-mail: rp.sinha@csu.edu.

SINISE, GARY, actor, director; b. Blue Island, IL, Mar. 17, 1955; Co-founder, artistic dir. Steppenwolf Theatre, Chgo. Appeared in (plays) The Indian Wants The Bronx, 1977, Getting Out, 1980 (Joseph Jefferson award), Of Mice And Men, 1980, Loose Ends, 1982, True West, 1983 (also dir., Obie award best dir. 1982-83), Balm in Gilead, 1984, Streamers, 1985, The Caretaker, 1986, Grapes of Wrath, 1990 (Tony award and Drama Desk), (TV films) The Final Days, 1989, My Name is Bill W., 1989, The Stand, 1994, (theatrical films) Miles from Home, 1988, Of Mice and Men, 1991 (also actor); (actor) Jack The Bear, 1991, A Midnight Clear, 1991, Forrest Gump, 1994 (acad. award nominee, 1994, Disabled Am. Veterans Nat. Commanders award, 1994), The Quick and the Dead, 1995, Apollo 13, 1995, (TV) Truman, 1995 (Cable Ace award 1996, Golden Globe, 1996, Screen Actors Guild Award, 1996,), Ransom 1996, Albino Alligator, 1996, (play) Buried Child, 1996 (Tony award nominee, Joseph Jefferson award, 1996), (TV) George Wallace, 1997 (Emmy award, 1998, Screen Actors Guild award, 1998, Cable ACE award, 1997), Snake Eyes, 1998, That Championship Season, 1999, Being John Malkovich, 1999, Reindeer Games, 1999, Mission to Mars, 1999, Bruno, 1999, All the Rage, 1999, The Green Mile, 1999, A Gentleman's Game, 2001, Impostor, 2002, Made-Up, 2002, (TV) Path to War, 2002; various TV appearances including Crime Story (also dir.), Hunter, True West, Grapes of Wrath; dir. (plays) Frank's Wild Years, Action, The Miss Firecracker Contest, Waiting for the Parade, Tracers, Orphans, Landscape of the Body, 1984, (TV tapes) thirtysomething, 1989, China Beach, 1991. Office: care CAA 9830 Wilshire Blvd Beverly Hills CA 90212-1804 also: Licker & Ozurovich 2029 Century Park E Ste 1060 Los Angeles CA 90067-2919*

SINK, JOHN DAVIS, scientist, clergy member; b. Homer City, Pa., Dec. 19, 1934; s. Aaron Tinsman and Louella Bell (Davis) S.; m. Nancy Lee Hile, Nov. 9, 1956 (dec. Aug. 1961); 1 child, Lou Ann (dec. Aug. 1961); m. Claire Kaye Huschka, June 13, 1964 (div. Feb. 1987); children: Kara Joan, Karl John; m. Sharon Ferrando Padden, July 15, 1989; 1 child, Lisa Michelle Padden. BS in Animal/Vet. Sci., Pa. State U., 1956, MS in Biophys./Animal Sci., 1960, PhD in Biochem./Animal Sci., 1962; EdD in Higher Edn., U. Pitts., 1986; MDiv, Emory U., 2001. Adminstrv. officer, exec. asst. to sec. agr. State of Pa., Harriwburg, 1962; prof., group leader dept. food, dairy and animal sci. Inst. Policy Rsch. and Evaluation, Pa. State U., University Park, 1962-79; pres. Collegian, Inc., 1971-72; joint planning & evaluation staff officer Sci. & Edn. Adminstrn., U.S. Dept. Agr., Washington, 1979-80; prof., chmn. intercoll. program food sci. & nutrition U.W.Va., Morgantown, 1980-85; pres., CEO Pa. State U., Uniontown, 1985-92; pres. Sink, Padden & Assocs., Atlanta, 1992—; pastor Sardis United Meth. Ch., 1995—; prof. chemistry So. Polytech. State U., Marietta, Ga., 1997—. Dir. S.W. Inst. Uniontown, 1989-92; gen. mgr. Cavert Wire Co., Inc., Atlanta, 1993-97; exec. asst. naval rep. to gov. and adj. gen. State W.Va., Charleston, 1981-84; cons. Allied Mills Inc., Am. Air Lines, Am. Home Foods, Inc., Apollo Analytical Labgs., Armour Food Co., Atlas Chem. Industries, others. Author: The Control of Metabolism, 1974, Citizen Extraordinaire, 1993; contbr. articles to profl. jours. Mem. nat. adv. bd. Am. Security Coun., 1981-91; mem. nat. adv. coun. Nat. Commn. Higher Edn. Issues, 1980-82; bd. dirs. W.Va. Cattleman's Assn., 1981-83, W.Va. Poultry Assn., 1980-83, Pembroke Welsh Corgi Club, 1969-71, Greater Uniontown Idnsl. Fund, 1986-91, Fayette County Econ. Devel. Coun., 1985-93, Westmoreland-Fayette coun. Boy Scouts Am., 1986-91, Westmoreland-Fayette hist. Soc., 1986-91, Fayette County Soil Conservation Dist., 1990-93, Pa. Youth Found., 1989-93, Fayette County Coop. Extension Bd., 1992-93, Pa. Masonic Found., 1993, Ga. Meth. Commn. on Higher Edn. and Campus Min., 2000—. Capt. USNR, 1985-86, ret. Decorated Army commendation medal; recipient Nat. Merit Trophy award nat. Block and Bridle Club, 1956, Darbarker prize Pa. Aca.d Sci., 1967, W.Va. Disting. Achievement medal, Disting. Leadership award Am. Security Coun. Found., 1983; Pa. Meat Packers Assn. scholar, 1958-62; hon. fellow in biochemistry U. Wis., 1965, NSF postdoctoral fellow, 1964-65. Fellow AAAS, Am. Inst. Chemists, Inst. Food Technologists; mem. Am. Meat Sci. Assn. (pres. 1974-75), Pa. Air N.G. Armory (trustee 1968-80), Pa. Acad. Sci., U.S. Naval Inst., Res. Officers Assn., Armed Forces Comm. and Elecs. Assn., Acad. Polit. Sci. (world affairs coun. Pitts. chpt.), Am. Assn. higher Edn., Am. Assn. Univ. Adminstrs., Am. Chem. Soc., Am. Soc. for Biochemistry and Molecular Biology, Biophys. Soc., Am. Soc. Animal Sci., Inst. Food Technologists, Soc. Rsch. Adminstrs., Am. Cancer Soc. (bd. dirs. 1988-91), Greater Uniontown C. of C. (bd. dirs. 1989-93), Greater Connellsville C. of C. (pres., bd. dirs. 1989-91), North Fayette C. of C. (bd. dirs. 1986-89), Mon Valley Tri-State Network, Inc. (chmn. bd. dirs. 1989-92), Rotary (sec. State Coll. 1969-71, Paul Harris fellow 1991), Elks, Internat. Assn. Turtles, Consistory, Shriners, Masons, Alpha Zeta, Omicron Delta Kappa, Gamma Sigma Delta, Sigma Xi, Phi Lambda Upsilon, Gamma Alpha, Phi Tau Sigma, Phi Sigma, Phi Delta Kappa, Pi Sigma Phi. Republican. Office: 3725 Powers Ferry Rd NW Atlanta GA 30342-4422 E-mail: jsink@spsu.edu.

SINK, ROBERT C. lawyer; b. Racine, Wis., 1938; AB, Duke U., 1959, LLB, 1965. Bar: N.C. 1965. Ptnr. Robinson, Bradshaw & Hinson, P.A., Charlotte, N.C., 1965—. Assoc. editor Duke Law Jour., 1964-65. Trustee Pub. Libr. Charlotte and Mecklenburg County, 1985-90, chmn., 1989-90; bd. dirs. Mus. New South, 1991-97, chmn., 1996-97. Lt. USN, 1959-62, USNR. Mem. ABA (ho. dels. 2001—), N.C. State Bar (councilor 1988-96, pres. 1998-99), Mecklenburg County Bar (pres. 1986-87), Order of Coif, Phi Beta Kappa. Office: Robinson Bradshaw & Hinson PA 101 N Tryon St Ste 1900 Charlotte NC 28246-0103

SINKFORD, JEANNE CRAIG, dental association administrator, dentist, retired dean, educator; b. Washington, Jan. 30, 1933; d. Richard E. and Geneva (Jefferson) Craig; m. Stanley M. Sinkford, Dec. 8, 1951; children: Dianne Sylvia, Janet Lynn, Stanley M. III. BS, Howard U., 1953, MS, 1962, DDS, 1958, PhD, 1963; DSc (hon.), Georgetown U., 1978, U. Med. and Dentistry of N.J., 1992, Detroit Mercy U., 1996. Instr. prosthodontics Sch. Dentistry Howard U., Washington, 1958—60, faculty dentistry, 1964—, rsch. coord., co-chmn. dept. restorative dentistry, assoc. dean, 1968—75, dean, 1975—91, prof. Prosthodontics Grad. Sch., 1977—91, dean emeritus, prof., 1991—; spl. asst. Am. Assn. Dental Schs., 1991—93, dir. office women and minority affairs, 1993—97, assoc. exec. dir., 1998—. Instr. rsch. and crown and bridge Northwestern U. Sch. Dentistry, 1963—64; cons. prosthodontics and rsch. VA Hosp., Washington, 1965—; resident Children's Hosp. Nat. Med. Ctr., 1974—75; cons. St. Elizabeth's Hosp.; mem. attending staff Freedman's Hosp., Washington, 1964—; adv. bd. D.C. Gen. Hosp., 1975—; mem. nat. adv. dental rsch. coun. Nat. Bd. Dental Examiners; mem. ad hoc adv. panel Tuskegee Syphilis Study for HEW; sponsor D.C. Pub. Health Apprentice Program; mem. adv. coun. to dir. NIH; adv. com. NIH/NIDR/NIA Aging Rsch. Coun.; mem. dental devices classification panel FDA; mem. select panel for promotion child health, 1979—80; mem. spl. med. adv. group VA; bd. overseers U. Pa. Dental Sch., Boston U. Dental Sch.; bd. advisors U. Pitts. Dental Sch.; mem. anat. rev. bd. D.C. NRC Governing Bd.; cons. FDA; mem. Nat. Adv. Dental Rsch. Coun., 1993—96; active NRC Governing Bd. Mem. editl. bd. Jour. Am. Coll. Dentists, 1988—. Mem. Mayor's Block Grant Adv. Com., 1982; mem. parents' coun. Sidwell Friends, 1983; adv. bd. United Negro Coll. Fund, Robert Wood Johnson Health Policy Fellowships; mem. women's health task force NIH; bd. dirs. Girl Scouts U.S.A., 1993—. Fellow Louise C. Ball fellow grad. tng., 1960—63. Fellow: Internat. Coll. Dentists (Merit award), Am. Coll. Dentists (sec.-treas. Wash. met. sect.); mem.: ADA (chmn. appeal bd. coun. on dental edn. 1975—82), Links Inc., Dean's Coun., Smithsonian Assocs., N.Y. Acad. Scis., Am. Soc. Dentistry for Children, Inst. Medicine of NAS (coun.), Nat. Dental Assn., Fed. Prosthodontic Orgn., Am. Prosthodontic Soc., Am. Pedodontic Soc., Leadership in Acad. Medicine (adv. bd.), Health Professions Partnership Initiative (adv. bd.), Assn. Am. Women Dentists, Wash. Coun. Adminstrv. Women, So. Conf. Dental Deans (chmn.), Inst. Grad. Dentists (trustee), Am. Inst. Oral Biology, Dist. Dental Soc., Internat. Assn. Dental Rsch., Am. Soc. for Geriatric Dentistry (bd. dirs.), North Portal Civic League, Golden Key, Beta Kappa Chi, Psi Chi, Omicron Kappa Upsilon, Phi Beta Kappa, Sigma Xi (pres.). Address: 1765 Verbena St NW Washington DC 20012-1048

SINNECK, MICHAEL, information technology executive; married; 3 children. BA in Math., St. Francis Coll. Various positions IBM Global Svc.; corp. v.p. Microsoft, Redmond, Wash., 2001—. Avocations: scuba diving, skiing, playing piano. Office: One Microsoft Way Redmond WA 98052-6399*

SINNETT, WILLIAM MCNAIR, finance researcher; b. Chgo., Mar. 8, 1951; s. Carl Earl and Helen (McNair) S.; m. Eleanor Bush, Oct. 21, 1989. AA, Concordia Coll., Bronxville, N.Y., 1971; BA, Concordia Coll., Ft. Wayne, Ind., 1973; MBA, U. Pitts., 1975. Bus. mgr. No. Area Multi-Svc., Sharpsburg, Pa., 1975-77; sr. staff acct. Tube City Iron and Metal Co., Glassport, 1977-78; sec. lending mgr. Carnegie-Mellon U., Pitts., 1978-81, Mellon Bank, Pitts., 1981-83; fin. mgr. Eckankar, Menlo Park, Calif., 1984; mgr. acctg. then tech. assoc. Fin. Execs. Inst., Morristown, N.J., 1985-89; sr. rsch. assoc., then project mgr. Fin. Exec. Rsch. Found., 1989—. Office: Fin Execs Rsch Found 10 Madison Ave # 1938 Morristown NJ 07960-7303

SINNEX, CEIL, nonprofit foundation founder, newsletter publisher; b. Washington, Dec. 31, 1944; d. John Robertson and Mary Elizabeth (Titsworth) Deatherage; m. W. John McCormick, Feb. 16, 1985. BA, U. Tenn., 1966. Reporter local weekly papers, Washington, 1967, Houston Post, 1968-70; Washington correspondent small news burs., Washington, 1970-75; staff writer AP, Honolulu, 1975-76; pub. affairs writer East-West Ctr., 1978-82; prin. Ceil Sinnex Comm., 1983—; founder, exec. dir. Ovarian Cancer Prevention and Early Detection Found., Paauilo, Hawaii, 1991-94; 831. Speaker to various orgns. on ovarian cancer, 1991—. Editor, pub.: (newsletter) Ovarian Plus Internat.: Gynecologic Cancer Prevention Quarterly, 1995—; commr. (TV pub. svc. announcement) Silent Killer, 1992 (Telly award 1993); presenter U.S. Army Ovarian Cancer Rsch. Program Stakeholder's Meeting,

1997; contbr. articles to publs. Bd. dirs. Friends of the Waikiki Aquarium, Honolulu, 1980-90, Honolulu unit, Am. Cancer Soc., 1984-89. Recipient Outstanding Svc. cert. Montgomery County (Md.) Commn. on Status of Women, 1975, Jonquils award for efforts in the Fight Against Cancer, Duke U. Comprehensive Cancer Ctr., Durham, N.C., 1994. Avocations: photography, rare books, early rock 'n roll, outdoor activities, sketching. Office: PO Box 2831 Springfield VA 22152-1831

SINNING, MARK ALAN, thoracic and vascular surgeon; b. Holton, Kans., Apr. 24, 1953; s. Henry Harold andf Valere Madelene (Davey) S.; m. Kathy Diann Pugh, Sept. 25, 1982 (div.); children: Sarah, Emily, Mark, Rachel, Walter. BA, U. Kans., 1975; MD, U. Kans., Kansas City, 1978. Diplomate Am. Bd. Surgery, Am. Bd. Thoracic Surgery. Gen. surgery resident St. Luke's Hosp., Kansas City, Mo., 1978-83, thoracic surgery resident, 1983-85; pvt. practice Coastal Surg. Specialists, PA, New Bern, N.C., 1986—. Attending staff Danbury (Conn.) Hosp., 1985-86, Craven Regional Med. Ctr., New Bern, 1986—; asst. clin. prof. East Carolina U., Greenville, 1992—. Fellow ACS, Am. Coll. Chest Physicians; mem. AMA, Soc. Thoracic Surgeons, So. Assn. Thoracic Surgery, N.C. Med. Soc., Phi Beta Kappa, Alpha Omega Alpha. Avocations: golf, snow skiing, music. Office: Coastal Surgical Specialists 800 Hospital Dr Ste 10 New Bern NC 28560-3489

SINNOTT, JAN MARIE DYNDA, psychologist; b. Cleve., June 14, 1942; d. Edward Joseph and Dorothy Mary (Zurek) Dynda; children: James, Gwenn, Kiersten, Gavyn. BS, St. Louis U., 1964; MS, Cath. U., Washington, 1973, PhD, 1975. Lic. psychologist, Md. Rsch. psychologist Human Scis. Rsch. Inc., McLean, Va., 1975; rsch. psychologist, prof. Cath. U. Sch. Social Svcs., Washington, 1975-77; rsch. psychologist, pres. Human Devel. Rsch. Inc., Silver Spring, Md., 1977-80; rsch. psychologist U. Md. Ctr. on Aging, College Park, 1978-81; rsch. psychologist, guest scientist Gerontology Rsch. Ctr., Nat. Inst. Aging, NIH, Balt., 1980-89; prof. psychology Towson U., 1978—, dir. honors program in human devel. psychology, 1999—; dir. Ctr. for Study of Adult Devel. and Aging Towson State U., 1989-91. Steering com. Soc. for Rsch. in Adult Devel., 1987-91; bd. dirs. Inst. Noetic Scis. Editor: Everyday Problem Solving, 1989, Bridging Paradigms, 1991, Everyday Memory, 1991, Interdisciplinary Handbook of Adult Lifespan Learning, 1993; author: Sex Roles and Aging, 1986, Reinventing the University, 1996, Development of Logic in Adulthood: Postformal Thought & Its Applications, 1998; editl. bd. Jour. Adult Devel., 1992—, Internat. Jour. Adult Devel. and Aging, Jour. Aging and Human Develo[ment, 1999—; contbr. articles to profl. jours. Policy com. U. Md. System Women's Forum, College Park. Grantee NIH, 1980-89, Adminstrn. on Aging, 1979-82. Fellow APA, Gerontol. Soc. Am., Am. Psychology Soc.; mem. NOW, AAUP, Assn. for Women in Psychology, Philosophy of Psychology Study Group, Am. Assn. for Study Mental Imagery, Internat. Soc. Study of Energy Medicine, Ea. Psychol. Assn., Amnesty Internat., Planned Parenthood Internat. E-mail: (bus.). Office: Towson U Psychology Dept Baltimore MD 21252-0001 E-mail: jsinnott@towson.edu.

SINNOTT, JOHN PATRICK, lawyer, educator; b. Bklyn., Aug. 17, 1931; s. John Patrick and Elizabeth Muriel (Zinkand) Sinnott; m. Rose Marie Yuppa, May 30, 1959; children: James Alexander, Jessica Michelle. BS, U.S. Naval Acad., 1953; MS, USAF Inst. Tech., 1956; JD, No. Ky. U., 1960. Bar: Ohio 1961, NY 1963, NJ 1970, Ga 2000, US Patent Office 1963, US Supreme Ct 1977. Assoc. Brumbaugh, Graves, Donohue & Raymond, N.Y.C., 1961-63; patent atty. Bell Tel. Labs., Murray Hill, N.J., 1963-64, Schlumberger Ltd., N.Y.C., 1964-71; asst. chief patent counsel Babcock & Wilcox, 1971-79; chief patent and trademark counsel Am. Std. Inc., 1979-92; of counsel Morgan & Finnegan, 1992-99, Langdale, Vallotton, Linahan & Wetherington, L.L.P., Valdosta, Ga., 2000—. Adj lectr NJ Inst Technology, Newark, 1974—89; adj prof Seton Hall Univ Sch Law, Newark, 1989—98. Author: (book) Counterfeit Goods Suppression, 1998, World Patent Law and Practice, Vols 2-2P, 1999, A Practical Guide to Document Authentication, 2002; contbr. articles to profl jours. Mem. local Selective Serv Bd., Plainfield, NJ, 1971; bd dirs New Providence Community Swimming Pool, 1970. Capt. USAF, 1953—61, col. AUS ret., 1977—91. Decorated Legion of Merit, others. Mem. N.Y. Intellectual Property Law Assn. (bd. dirs. 1974-76), Squadron A Club, Cosmos. Republican. Roman Catholic. Home: 2517 Rolling Rd Valdosta GA 31602-1244 Office: Langdale Vallotton Linahan & Wetherington LLP 1007 N Patterson St PO Box 1547 Valdosta GA 31603 Fax: (229) 244-9646. E-mail: specan23@aol.com.

SINNOTT, JOHN THOMAS, internist, educator; b. Reading, Pa., May 16, 1948; s. John Thomas and Josephine (Mallon) S.; m. Barbara Ballentine, May 30, 1970. BA, Columbus (Ga.) Coll., 1971; MA, U. South Fla., 1973; MD, U. South Ala., 1978. Diplomate Am. Bd. Internal Medicine, Am. Bd. Infectious Diseases. Resident in internal medicine U. South Fla. Coll. Medicine, Tampa, 1978-81, infectious disease resident, 1981-83, prof. and dir. infectious diseases, 1991-2000, James Cullsion prof. medicine, 2000—, assoc. prof., 1987-92, asst. prof., 1983-87; mem. med. exec. bd. Tampa Gen. Healthcare, 1992—, vice chief staff, 1992-94, chief staff, 1994-96, dir. epidemiology, 1985—. Dir. S.W. Fla. Tissue Bank, 1987—. Editor jour. Infections in Medicine, 1994—. Recipient hon. alumnus award U. South Fla. Coll. Medicine, 1998, Outstanding Clin. Prof. award, 1986-92; Humanism in Medicine award NBI Healthcare Found., 1998, award For AIDS Care Today, 1998; John T. Sinnott Outstanding Clin Prof. award named in his honor U. So. Fla. Coll. Medicine, 1992. Fellow ACP, Infectious Disease Soc. Am. (fin. com. 1998—); mem. Soc. Hosp. Epidemiology (fin. com. 1998—), Alpha Omega Alpha. Avocations: fishing, flying. Home: 9666 Oak St NE Saint Petersburg FL 33702-2610 Office: Tampa Gen Hosp Dept Infectious Disease Tampa FL 33601-1289 E-mail: jsinnott@tgh.org.

SINNOTT, JOHN WILLIAM, lawyer; b. St. Louis, Jan. 5, 1966; s. John and Joan Martha Sinnott. AB, Dartmouth Coll., 1988; JD, Tulane U., 1995. Bar: La. 1995, U.S. Ct. Appeals (5th cir.) 1995, U.S. Dist. Ct. (ea., mid., and we. dists.) La. 1995. Assoc. Phelps Dunbar, New Orleans, 1995—97, Montgomery, Barnett, Brown, Read, Hammond & Mintz, New Orleans, 1997—2000, Irwin Fritchie Urquhart & Moore LLC, New Orleans, 2000—. Capt. USMC, 1988-92. Mem.: ABA, New Orleans Assn. Def. Counsel, La. Assn. Def. Counsel, Def. Rsch. Inst., La. State Bar Assn. Office: Irwin Fritchie Urquhart Moore LLC 400 Poydras St Ste 2700 New Orleans LA 70130 E-mail: jsinnott@irwinllc.com.

SINOFSKY, STEVEN, information technology executive; BA with hon., Cornell U., 1987; MS in Computer Sci., U. Mass., 1989. From software engr. to sr. v.p. Microsoft, Redmond, Wash., 1989, sr. v.p. Microsoft Office. Vis. scholar Harvard U. Bus. Sch., Cambridge, Mass., 1998. Office: One Microsoft Way Redmond WA 98052-6399*

SINOPOLI, THERESA ANN, government agency administrator; b. Rochester, N.Y., Oct. 2, 1975; d. Victor Michael and Cindra Lou Sinopoli; m. Gregory Seth Johnson. A in Gen. Studies-Sci., Monroe C.C., Rochester, NY, 1998; BA in Polit. Sci.-Pre-Law, St. John Fisher Coll., 1999; MPA, SUNY, Brockport, 2001. Staff asst. Office of Rep. Louise M. Slaughter, Washington, 1998—98, Office of the N.Y. State Atty. Gen., Rochester, 1999—2000; scheduler, dist. office mgr. Office of N.Y. State Assemblyman Joseph D. Morelle, 2000—00; rsch. asst. CGR, 2000—01; budget analyst N.Y. State Dept. Health, Albany, 2001—. Active Young Demos.Monroe County, Rochester, 1998—; active participant, fundraiser Monroe County Dem. Club, 1998—. Finalist Pub. Mgmt. Inst., N.Y. State Dept. Civil Svc., 2001; recipient Girl Scout Gold award, Girl Scouts Am., 1993; fellow N.Y. State Health Dept. Developmental fellow, N.Y. State Dept. Health, 2002. Mem.: ASPA, LWV. Roman Catholic. Avocations: walking, travel. Office: NY State Dept Health Corning Tower Albany NY 12237 Business E-mail: tas04@health.state.ny.us.

SINOR, DENIS, Orientalist, educator; b. Kolozsvar, Hungary, Apr. 17, 1916; s. Miklos and Marguerite (Weitzenfeld) S.; m. Eugenia Trinajstic (dec.); children: Christophe (dec.), Sophie. BA, U. Budapest, 1938; MA, Cambridge (Eng.) U., 1948; doctorate (hon.), U. Szeged, Hungary, 1971. Attache Centre National de la Recherche Scientifique, Paris, 1939-48; univ. lectr. Altaic studies Cambridge U., 1948-62; prof. Uralic and Altaic studies and history U., Bloomington, 1962-81, disting. prof. Uralic and Altaic studies and history, 1975-86, disting. prof. emeritus Uralic and Altaic studies and history, 1986—, chmn. dept. Uralic and Altaic studies, 1963-1981, dir. Lang. and Area Ctr., 1963-88, dir. Asian studies program, 1965-67, dir. Asian Studies Rsch. Inst., 1967-79, dir. Rsch. Inst. for Inner Asian Studies, 1979-1981, 85-86. Sec. gen. Permanent Internat. Altaistic Conf., 1961—; rsch. project dir. U.S. Office Edn., 1969-70; sec. Internat. Union Orientalists, 1954-64; vis. prof. Institut Nat. des Langues et Civilizations Orientales, Paris, spring 1974; scholar-in-residence Rockefeller Found. Study Ctr., Bellagio, 1975; vice chmn. UNESCO Commn. for History Civilization Cen. Asia, 1981—, mem. consultative com. UNESCO Silk Rd. Project, 1990-97; summer seminar dir. NEH, 1988. *An internationally recognized pioneer of Inner Asian studies. Former director ofthe federally funded Inner Asian and Uralic National Resource Center, founder and first chairman of the Department of Uralic and Altaic Studies and of the Research Institute for Inner Asian Studies, all three at Indiana University, he is credited with introducing this field into the United States as an academic discipline. Through his publications and activities at the Unesco and as Secretary General of the Permanent International Altaistic Conference (PIAC) he has been instrumental in the world-wide academic recognition of the historical and political importance of Inner Asia.* Author: Orientalism and History, 1954, History of Hungary, 1959, Introduction a l'ètude de l'Eurasie Centrale, 1963, Aspects of Altaic Civilization, 1963, Inner Asia, 1968, Inner Asia and Its Contacts with Medieval Europe, 1977, Tanulmányok, 1982, Essays in Comparative Altaic Linguistics, 1990, Studies in Medieval Inner Asia, 1997; editor, contbr.: Modern Hungary, 1977, Studies in Finno-Ugric Linguistics, 1977, Uralic Languages, 1988, Essays on Uzbek History, Culture and Languages, 1993, Cambridge History of Early Inner Asia, Handbook of Uralic Studies, Jour. Asian History, Ind. U. Uralic and Altaic Series; mem. Am. editl. rev. bd. Britannica-Hungarica. Served with Forces Françaises de l'Intérieur, 1943-44; with French Army, 1944-45. NEH grantee, 1981, 87, 88; recipient Jubilee prize U. Budapest, 1938, Barczi Geza Meml. medal, 1981, Gold medal Permanent Internat. Altaistic Conf., 1982, 1996, Arminius Vambery Meml. medal, 1983, The Thomas Hart Benton Mural Medallion, Hungarian Order of Star, 1986, UNESCO Avicenna medal, 1998; Am. Philos. Soc. Research grantee, 1963; Am. Council Learned Soc. research grantee, 1962; Guggenheim fellow, 1968-69, 1981-82, Amer. Oriental Soc. Med. of Hon., 1999. Fellow Kőrösi Csoma Soc. (hon.); mem. Royal Asiatic Soc. (hon. sec. 1954-64, Denis Sinor medal for Inner Asian Studies named in his honor 1992), Am. Oriental Soc. (pres. Midwest br. 1968-70, nat. pres. 1975-76, medal of honor 1999), Assn. Asian Studies, Am. Hist. Soc., Soc. Asiatique (hon.), Tibet Soc. (pres. 1969-74), Mongolia Soc. (pres. 1987-94), Correspondant de l'Académie des inscriptions et belles lettres (Paris), Hungarian Acad. Scis. (hon.), Acad. Europaea (fgn.), Deutsche Morgenlandische Gesellschaft, Suomalais-Ugrilaisen Seura (hon.), Soc. Uralo-Altaica (v.p. 1964-94, hon.), Internat. Union Oriental and Asian Studies (v.p. 1993—), Cosmos Club Washington, Explorers Club N.Y.C., United Oxford and Cambridge Club London. Home: 5581 E Lampkins Ridge Rd Bloomington IN 47401-8674 Office: Indiana U Dept Ctrl Eurasian Studies Goodbody Hall Bloomington IN 47405

SINOR, HOWARD EARL, JR. lawyer; b. New Orleans, Sept. 6, 1949; s. Howard E. and Beverly M. (Bourgeois) S.; children: Sally, Vera Sue, Sarah, Sadie. BA with honors, U. New Orleans, 1971; JD cum laude, Harvard U., 1975. Bar: La. 1975, U.S. Supreme Ct. 1983, U.S. Ct. Appeals (3rd, 5th and 11th cir.), U.S. Dist. Ct. (ea., middle, we.) Dist. La. Ptnr. Jones, Walker, Waechter, Poitevent, Carrere & Denegre, 1975-98, Gordon, Arata, McCollam, Duplantis & Eagan, New Orleans, 1999—. Contbg. author: La. Appellate Practice Handbook, 1990, 97; editor: CLE Manual of Recent Developments, 1985; contbr. articles to profl. jours. Recipient Pres.'s award, La. State Bar Assn., 1987. Fellow La. Bar Found.; mem. ABA, FBA, La. State Bar Assn. (chmn. antitrust sect. 1987-89). Avocations: golf, hiking. Office: Gordon Arata et al 201 Saint Charles Ave Fl 40 New Orleans LA 70170-4000

SINSHEIMER, ROBERT LOUIS, retired university chancellor and educator; b. Washington, Feb. 5, 1920; s. Allen S. and Rose (Davidson) S.; m. Flora Joan Hirsch, Aug. 8, 1943 (div. 1972); children: Lois June (Mrs. Wickstrom), Kathy Jean (Mrs. Vandagriff), Roger Allen; m. Kathleen Mae Reynolds, Sept. 10, 1972 (div. 1980); m. Karen Current, Aug. 1, 1981. S.B., MIT, 1941, MS, 1942, PhD, 1948. Staff mem. radiation lab. MIT, Cambridge, 1942-46; assoc. prof. biophysics, physics dept. Iowa State Coll., Ames, 1949-55, prof., 1955-57; prof. biophysics Calif. Inst. Tech., Pasadena, 1957-77, chmn. div. biology, 1968-77; chancellor U. Calif., Santa Cruz, 1977-87, chancellor emeritus, 1987—, prof. Santa Barbara, 1988-90, prof. emeritus, 1990—. Editor: Jour. Molecular Biology, 1959-67, Ann. Rev. Biochemistry, 1966-72. Named Calif. Scientist of Year, 1968; recipient N.W. Beijerinck-Virologie medal Netherlands Acad. Sci., 1969 Fellow Am. Acad. Arts and Scis.; mem. Am. Soc. Biol. Chemists, Biophys. soc. (pres. 1970), AAAS, Nat. Acad. Scis. (mem. council 1970-73, chmn. bd. editors Proc. 1972-80), Inst. Medicine. Achievements include discovery of single-stranded DNA, circular DNA; co-investigator in first in vitro replication of infective DNA. Office: U Calif MCD Biology Santa Barbara CA 93106

SINSHEIMER, WARREN JACK, lawyer; b. N.Y.C., May 22, 1927; s. Jerome William and Elizabeth (Berch) S.; m. Florence Dubin, Mar. 30, 1950; children: Linda Ruth, Ralph David, Alan Jay, Michael Neal. Student, Ind. U., 1943-47; JD cum laude, N.Y. Law Sch., 1950; LLM, NYU, 1957; MPhil, Columbia U., 1977; HLD (hon.) , Drew U., 2002. Bar: N.Y. bar 1950. Ptnr. Sinsheimer, Sinsheimer & Dubin, N.Y.C., 1950-78, Satterlee & Stephens, N.Y.C., 1978-86, Patterson, Belknap, Webb & Tyler, N.Y.C., 1986-91; counsel Patterson Belknap Webb & Tyler, 1991-96; pres., bd. dirs. Neighborhood Bagel Corp., 1994—. Pres. Plessey, Inc., N.Y.C., 1956-70, chmn., CEO, 1970-89; dir. oversees ops. and devel. The Plessey Co., Ltd., Illford, Essex, Eng., 1969-70, dep. chief exec., dir., 1976-89; dir. Plessey, Inc.; trustee NYU Sch. Law, 1996—; pres., bd. dirs. Legal Svcs. for Children, Inc., 1998—. Chmn. Com. of 68, 1964-67; Mem Westchester County Republican Com., 1956-73; chmn. Nat. Scranton for Pres. Com., 1964; mem. N.Y. State Assembly, 1965-66; Bd. visitors Wassaic State Sch., 1962-64; trustee Sch. Law, NYU, 1996—, bd. dirs. Shalom Hartman Inst., Jerusalem, 1991—, treas., 1996—; trustee City Bar Fund, 1998—. Served with USNR, 1944-45; with USAF, 1950-52. Mem. ABA, Assn. Bar City N.Y., Torch and Scroll, Century Club (Purchase, N.Y., gov., treas. 1997—), Century Assn. N.Y.C., Univ. Club, Zeta Beta Tau. Jewish. Home: 22 Murray Hill Rd Scarsdale NY 10583-2828 Office: 271 Madison Ave New York NY 10016-1001 E-mail: Sinsheimer@kidslaw.org.

SINTON, CHRISTOPHER MICHAEL, neurophysiologist, educator; b. Beckenham, Kent, Eng., Sept. 10, 1946; came to U.S., 1983; s. Leslie George and Evelyn Mabel (Burn) S. BA, Cambridge U., Eng., 1968, MA, 1977; BSc, London U., 1978; PhD, U. Lyon, France, 1981. Rsch. fellow U. Lyon, 1980-83; rsch. assoc. Princeton (N.J.) U., 1983-84; sr. scientist Ciba-Geigy Corp., Summit, N.J., 1984-88; dir. electrophysiology Neurogen Corp., Branford, Conn., 1988-94; asst. prof. U. Tex. Southwestern Med. Ctr., Dallas, 1994—. Rsch. asst. prof. medicine NYU, N.Y.C., 1986-94; vis. asst. prof. Harvard U. Med. Sch., Boston, 1999—. Contbr. Scholar Med. Rsch. Coun. France vis. scholar, Princeton U., 1983. Mem. N.Y. Acad. Scis., Soc. Neurosci., European Sleep Rsch. Soc., Sleep Rsch. Soc. Achievements include research on genetic basis of narcolepsy, fetal effects of in-utero caffeine exposure, possible functional role of REM sleep and neuropeptide modulation of synaptic input. Office: U Tex SW Med Ctr Dept Internal Medicine 5323 Harry Hines Blvd Dallas TX 75390-8874 E-mail: sinton@utsw.swmed.edu.

SINTROS, JAMES LEE, management consultant, foundation executive; b. Lowell, Mass., May 20, 1947; s. Constantine James and Martha Lou (Sawyer) S.; m. Effegenia Liakos, June 27, 1971 (div. Feb. 1993); 1 child, Sarah Gillian; m. Barbara Anne Kendall, Dec. 26, 1993; 1 child, Nathaniel David. BS, U. Mass., Lowell, 1970; JD, Suffolk U., 1974. Cert. registered arbitrator. Cons., 1974—; sr. cons. Cassidy & Assocs., Washington, 1985-95; clk. West of Ireland Edn. Fund, Inc., N.Y.C. and Galway, Ireland, 1990-96; dir. Mass. Ctr. for S.I.D.S., 1989—; clk., dir. S.I.D.S. Outreach Found., Inc., Mass., 1991—; exec. dir. Internat. Ednl. and Med. Alliance New Eng., Inc., 1989-96; exec. dir., treas. Joseph W. Stilwell Inst. Found., Ltd., Chongqing, China, 1989-99; pres. Stilwell Found., 1999—; v.p., dir. G.T.N.Y. Found., Inc., N.Y.C., 1991-95; pres., treas., clk., bd. dirs. Global Brokers Internat. Ltd., Dublin, 1993-97; pres., treas., bd. dirs. Multinat. Bus. Devel. Coalition, Ltd., Dakar, Senegal, 1990—. Internat. cons. Suffolk U., Boston, 1992—; spl. asst. to pres. New Eng. Coll. Optometry, Boston, 1992-96; automobile racer in U.S. and abroad, 1965-82; pres., CEO Phoenix Water Sys., Spokane, 1996-00; bd. dirs., sec. Amphion Internat. Ltd., British W.I., 1996-2000, Amphion Techs. Ltd., Dublin, 1996-2000; clk. Globus Internat. Ednl. Svcs., Inc., Mass., 1999-2000; ptnr. Blue Water Films, Ltd., Anguilla, Brit. W.I., 2000—; CEO FKSA Group Ltd., Saudi Arabia and Anguilla, 2001—. Bd. dirs., vice chair Young Audiences of Mass., 1979-82; bd. dirs. Boston Classical Orch., 1985-89, Critical Langs. and Area Studies Consortium, 1990-93; treas. Am.-Ireland Ednl. Found., N.Y.C., Dublin, Ireland, 1995—; clk. Irish R.R. and Transp. Heritage Found., Inc., N.Y.C., Dublin, 1999—. Home: Brickend Farm 134 Boston Rd Chelmsford MA 01824-3965 E-mail: jim@sintros.com.

SINTZ, EDWARD FRANCIS, librarian; b. New Trenton, Ind., Feb. 6, 1924; s. John and Edith E. (Rudicil) S.; m. Donna Norris, Apr. 12, 1952; children—Ann Kristin, Lesley Elizabeth, Julie Melinda. BA, U. Kans., 1950; MA in L.S, U. Denver, 1954; MS in Pub. Adminstrn, U. Mo., 1965. With Kansas City (Mo.) Pub. Library, 1954-66, asst. dir., 1964-66; asso. librarian St. Louis Pub. Library, 1966-68; dir. pub. libraries Miami, Fla., 1968-89, ret. Instr. Washington U., St. Louis, 1966-67; library surveys for Mo. State Library, 1967-68; library bldg. cons., 1965—. Editor: Mo. Library Assn. Quar, 1956-58. Served with USAAF, 1942-45. Mem. ALA, Fla. Library Assn. (pres. 1975-76), Southeastern Library Assn. Clubs: Kiwanian. Home: 7105 Lakeside Dr Charlotte NC 28215

SINYAK, YURI VLADIMIROV, engineer, economist; b. St. Petersburg, Russia, Jan. 7, 1936; s. Vladimir Stepanov and Antonina (Michailova) S.; m. Lia Mogilevskaya, Apr. 22, 1960 (div. 1980); 1 child, Maria; m. Svetlana Zabarinskaya, Feb. 22, 1981. MS, Moscow Power Inst., 1960; PhD, Moscow Acad. Mgmt., 1965; DSc, Russian Acad. Sci., Moscow, 1980. Jr. scientist Power Rsch. Inst., Moscow, 1960-65; sr. scientist ctrl. econs. math. inst. Russian Acad. Sci., 1965-72, chief dept. inst. planning, 1972-77, chief mgr. energy consulting group, 1977-89, chief rsch. fellow inst. econ. forecasting, 1996—; prin. investigator Internat. Inst. Applied Sys. Analysis, Vienna, Austria, 1989-95. Author: Economics of Metal Heating, 1965, Energy Balance: Construction and Analysis, 1974, PERT and Energy Systems, 1977, Long-Term Energy Perspectives, 1978, Industrial Energy Management, 1979. Avocation: nature, books. Home: Chelomeya St 2-115 117630 Moscow Russia Office: Inst Econ Forecasting RAS Nakchimovsky Ave 47 117418 Moscow Russia

SION, MAURICE, mathematics educator; b. Skopje, Yugoslavia, Oct. 17, 1928; came to Can., 1960; s. Max and Sarah (Alalouf) S.; m. Emilie Grace Chisholm, Sept. 15, 1957; children: Crispin, Sarah, Dirk. BA, NYU, 1947, MA, 1948; PhD, U. Calif., Berkeley, 1951. Mathematician Nat. Bur. Stds., Washington, 1951-52; instr. U. Calif., 1952-53; asst. prof. U. Calif., 1957-60; mem. Inst. for Advanced Study, Princeton, N.J., 1955-57, 62; asst. prof. U. B.C., Vancouver, Can., 1960, assoc. prof. Can., 1961, prof. Can., 1964-89, prof. emeritus Can., 1989—, head math. dept. Can., 1984-86, dir. Quadra Inst. Math. Can., 1970-89. Author: Introduction to Methods of Real Analysis, 1969, Theory Semi Group Valued Measures, 1973; contbr. articles to profl. jours. With U.S. Army, 1953-55. Mem. Am. Math. Soc., Can. Math. Soc. (v.p. 1972-74). Office: U BC Dept Math Vancouver BC Canada V6T 1Z2

SIOSON, EULOGIO R. physician; MD, Manila Ctrl. U. Diplomate Am. Bd. Internal Medicine, Am. Bd. Pulmonary Disease, Am. Bd. Geriatrics; cert. ind. med. examiner. Staff physician Metro Health Sys., Cleve. Co-inventor multipurpose syringe. Mem. ACP, Am. Geriatric Soc. Avocations: golfing, skiing. Office: 4200 Warrensville Center Rd Warrensville Heights OH 44122

SIPAHIOGLU, HATICE ELCIN, diplomat, interpreter/translator; b. Ankara, Turkey, Apr. 8, 1969; came to U.S., 1997; d. Vahdet and Nurten Sipahioglu. BA, Hacettepe U., Ankara, 1990; MA, Hacettepe U., 1995; MBA, U. St. Thomas, 2000. Translator, interpreter Turkish State Rlwys., Ankara, 1990-95; adminstrv. officer Ministry Fgn. Affairs, 1995-97; adminstrv. attaché Turkish Consulate Gen., Houston, 1997—. Scholar INst. for PUb. Adminstrn. for Turkey and Mid. East, Ankara, 1996-97. Mem. Houston World Affairs Coun., Houston Masterworks Chorus. Avocations: music, photography, yoga, hiking, travel. Home: 623 E 11 1/2 St Houston TX 77008 Office: Turkish Consulate Gen 1990 Post Oak Blvd Ste 1300 Houston TX 77056-3833

SIPCHEN, BOB, reporter; b. Chgo., June 13, 1953; m. Pamela Jean Sipchen; children: Ashley Rose-Anna, Emily Sage, Robert John III. BA in English, U. Calif. Santa Barbara, 1976. Freelance writer, 1980—87; staff writer Orange County Edit. LA Times, 1987—88, staff writer, 1988—98, sr. editor Mag., 1998—2001, assoc. editor Editl. Pages, 2001—. Author: Baby Insane and the Buddha, 1993. Recipient Pulitzer prize, 1993. Mem.: PEN, Nat. Writers Union, Soc. Profl. Journalists, Sigma Delta Chi. Office: LA Times 202 W 1st St Los Angeles CA 90012*

SIPER, CYNTHIA DAWN, special education educator; b. Bklyn., Apr. 16, 1965; d. Joel S. and Diana M. (Kessler) Rosenblatt; m. Alan Siper, Apr. 9, 1989; children: Rebecca Ruth, Daniel Louis. BS in Edn., SUNY, Plattsburgh, 1988; MEd, SUNY, New Paltz, 1992. Cert. K-12 spl. edn. tchr., N-6 elem. edn. tchr., N.Y. Tchr. spl. edn. Valley Cen. Sch. Dist., Montgomery, N.Y., 1988-90, Middletown (N.Y.) Enlarged City Sch. Dist., 1990—. Spl. edn. tchr. rep. Coun. on Spl. Edn., Middletown, 1990—. Mem. Coun. for Exceptional Children, Middletown Tchrs. Assn., Kappa Delta Pi. Avocation: collecting Disneyana.

SIPES, KAREN KAY, newspaper editor; b. Higginsville, Mo., Jan. 8, 1947; d. Walter John and Katherine Marie (McLelland) Heins; m. Joel Rodney Sipes, Sept. 24, 1971; 1 child, Lesley Katherine. BS in Edn., Ctrl. Mo. State U., 1970. Reporter/news editor Newton Kansan, 1973—76; sports writer Capital-Jour., Topeka, 1976—83, spl. sects. editor, 1983—85, editl. page editor, 1985—92, mng. editor/features, 1992—2002, asst. editl. page editor, 2002—. Co-chair Mayor's Commn. on Literacy, Topeka, 1995-96; mem. Act Against Violence Com., Topeka, 1995-96, Mayor's Task Force on Race Rels., 1998; mem. planning com. Leadership Greater Topeka, 1997; Great Am. Cleanup, 1999-2001, ERC/Resource and Referral, 2001—; mem. Martin Luther King Living the Dream Bus. Ptnrs. Com., 2001--. Mem. Ctrl. Mo. State U. Alumni Assn. (bd. dirs. 1996-2002, v.p. 1999, pres. 2000). Avocations: music, gardening, art. Office: The Capital-Journal 616 SE Jefferson St Topeka KS 66607-1194 E-mail: critterkaren@aol.com, ksipes@cjonline.com.

SIPFLE, DAVID ARTHUR, retired philosophy educator; b. Pekin, Ill., Aug. 29, 1932; s. Karl Edward and Louis Adele (Hinners) S.; m. Mary-Alice Slauson, Sept. 4, 1954; children: Ann Littlefield (dec.), Gail Elizabeth. BA in Math., Philosophy magna cum laude, Carleton Coll., 1953; MA, Yale U., 1955, PhD, 1958. Instr. philosophy Robert Coll., Istanbul, Turkey, 1957-58, Am. Coll. for Girls, Istanbul, 1957-60; asst. prof. Carleton Coll., Northfield, Minn., 1960-67, assoc. prof., 1967-70, chmn. dept., 1968-71, 89-92, prof., 1970-92, William H. Laird prof. philosophy and liberal arts, 1992-98. Vis. fellow Wolfson Coll., Cambridge U., 1975-76. Translator: (with Mary-Alice Sipfle) Emile Meyerson, The Relativistic Deduction: Epistemological Implications of the Theory of Relativity, 1985, Explanation in the Sciences, 1991; contbr. articles to profl. jours. NEH Younger Humanist fellow, Nice, France, 1971-72, NSF Sci. Faculty fellow, Cambridge, Eng., 1975-76; Carleton Coll. Faculty Devel. grantee, 1981-83, 86-87. Mem. Am. Philos. Assn., Metaphysical Soc. Am., Philosophy of Sci. Assn. Avocation: cross country skiing. Office: Carleton Coll 1 N College St Northfield MN 55057-4001 E-mail: dsipfle@carleton.edu.

SIPIORA, LEONARD PAUL, retired museum director, art appraiser; b. Lawrence, Mass., Sept. 1, 1934; s. Walter and Agnes S.; m. Sandra Joyce Coon, 1962; children— Alexandra, Erika. AB cum laude, U. Mich., 1955, MA, 1956. Dir. museums, City of El Paso, Tex., 1967-90; ret. Co-founder, pres. El Paso Arts Council, 1969-71; sec.-treas. El Paso Council Internat. Visitors, 1968-71; trustee El Paso Mus. Art; bd. dirs. Tex. Com. Humanities, Assn. Southwestern Humanities Council; adv. bd. S.W. Arts Found.; expert Antiques Roadshow-U.S.A. Bd. dirs. Community Concert Assn. El Paso, El Paso Symphony Orch., El Paso Hist. Soc. Mem. Assn. Mus. Dirs., Mountain Plains Mus. Assn. (pres. 1978-79), Tex. Assn. Museums (pres. 1977-79), Appraisers Assn. Am., Knights of Malta (decorated Grand Cross), Prior of Tex., Kappa Pi. Republican. Lutheran. Home: 1012 Blanchard Ave El Paso TX 79902-2727

SIPORIN, DAVID, human resources specialist; b. Detroit, June 8, 1954; s. Erwin and Ruth (Haase) S.; m. Maureen Lynn Wertheim, Sept. 4, 1977; children: Kaylyn Nellie, Ariana Molly. BA in Anthropology, Mich. State U., 1976, M in Labor and Indsl. Rels., 1978. Orgn. planning splst. Amoco Corp., Chgo., 1979-81; human resources rep. Amoco Prodn. Co., Denver, 1981-84, Chgo., 1984-88, human resources mgr., 1988-92, Amoco Chem.-Polymers,

Alpharetta, 1992-96; mng. dir. orgn. devel. Aristech Chem. Corp., Pitts., 1996-98, v.p. corp. svcs., 1999—2001; v.p. human resources Lord Corp., Cary, NC, 2001—. Mem. Soc. Human Resource Mgmt., Indsl. Rels. Rsch. Assn., Coun. Human Resource Execs. (conf. bd. 1997). Avocations: golf, skiing, gardening, excercise. Home: 109 Barkridge Ct Morrisville NC 27560-7069 Office: Lord Corp 111 Lord Dr Cary NC 27511

SIPORIN, SHELDON, lawyer, consultant; Bachelor's, CUNY; JD, U. Calif. Bar: N.Y., U.S. Dist. Ct. (ea. and so. dist.) N.Y., U.S. Ct. Appeals (2d. cir.). Asst. counsel Ctr. for Law and Health Care Policy, N.Y.C., 1983; assoc. Morgan, Melhuish & Monaghan, 1984; sole practice N.Y.C., 1985—. Cons. ADP-UCM, N.Y.C., 1986; of counsel various law firms, N.Y.C., 1985—. Vol. atty. Office of Aging, Legal Aid Soc., N.Y.C., 1985, Vol. Lawyers for Arts, 1990; arbitrator Am. Arbitration Assn., N.Y.C., 1983-86, small claims Civil Ct., N.Y.C., 1985-86, Civil Ct. Arbitration Panel, N.Y. County; trustee Lawyers Sq. N.Y., 1985. Mem. ABA (citizenship edn. com. young lawyers div. 1986-87), Am. Judges Assn., Soc. Profls. in Dispute Resolution (assoc.), N.Y. State Bar Assn. (com. fed. constn., film and video com. 1988—), N.Y. County Lawyer's Assn. (com. on entertainment law 1988—, arbitration and conciliation com. 1990-91, com. on legal tech. 1996—, com. on health and ins. law 2000—, com. on security law, 2001—), Assn. Computing Machinery, Bklyn. Bar Assn. (com. on arbitration 1994—, Assn. Ind. Video and Filmmakers, Phi Beta Kappa.

SIPPEL, WILLIAM LEROY, lawyer; b. Fond du Lac, Wis., Aug. 14, 1948; s. Alfonse Aloysious and Virginia Laura (Weber) S.; m. Barbara Jean Brost, Aug. 23, 1970; children: Katharine Jean, David William. BA, JD, U. Wis. Bar: Wis. 1974, U.S. Dist. Ct. (we. dist.) Wis. 1974, Minn. 1981, U.S. Dist. Ct. Minn. 1981, U.S. Ct. Appeals (10th cir.) 1984, U.S. Ct. Appeals (8th cir.) 1985. Research assoc. dept. agrl. econs. U. Wis., Madison, 1974-75; counsel monopolies and comml. law subcom. Ho. Judiciary Com., Washington, 1975-80; spl. asst. to asst. gen. antitrust div. U.S. Dept. of Justice, 1980-81; from assoc. to ptnr. Doherty, Rumble & Butler, Mpls. and St. Paul, Minn., 1981-99; ptnr. Oppenheimer, Wolff & Donnelly, LLP, Mpls., 1999—. Bd. dirs. Music in the Park, Inc.; mem. adj. faculty antitrust William Mitchell Coll. Law, spring of 2000, 2001. Co-author: The Antitrust Health Care Handbook, 1988. Mem. program com. Minn. World Trade Assn., Mpls., St. Paul, 1985-86, bd. dirs., 1986, Minn.; dir. Music in the Park, Mpls.; dir. Person to Person Inc.; vice-chmn., antitrust mktg. orders com. Nat. Coun. Farmer Cooperatives, 1999-00, chmn. 2001—. With USAR, 1971-77. Mem. ABA (vice chmn. ins. industry com. 1990-91, contbr. ABA Joint Ventures in Health Care), Minn. Bar Assn. (co-chmn. antitrust sect. 1986-88, internat. law sect. coun. 1986-89, treas. 1989-90, sec. 1990-91, vice chmn. 1995-96, chmn. 1996-97), Minn. Med. Alley Assn. (co-chmn. internat. bus. com. 1990-95, Hennepin County Office Internat. Trade (bd. dirs. 1988-93), Phi Beta Kappa. Roman Catholic. Avocations: reading, computers. Home: 2151 Commonwealth Ave Saint Paul MN 55108-1730 Office: Oppenheimer Wolff Donnelly LLP Plaza VII 45 S Seventh St Ste 3400 Minneapolis MN 55402-1609 E-mail: bsippel@oppenheimer.com.

SIPPEY, ROGER BOYD, corporate executive; b. Zanesville, Ohio, Feb. 6, 1942; s. Walter Boyd and Ruth Lillian Sippey; m. Janet Elsa Hoehn, Nov. 24, 1943; children: Michael, Nancy Denenburg. BS, Muskingum Coll., New Concord, Ohio, 1960—64. V.p. Feralloy Corp. , Chgo., 1968—2001; bd. dirs. Acero Prime Sa de Cv, San Louis Potosi, Mexico, 1998—2001. Bd. dirs. Feralloy Wheeling Specialty Processing Corp., Wheeling, W.Va., 1998. Mem.: Steel Svc. Ctr. Inst., Racquet Club Chgo. Republican. Episcopalian. Avocations: boating, travel. Home: 1366 N Dearborn Pkwy Chicago IL 60610 Office: Feralloy Corp. 5745 Higgins road Chicago IL 60645 Home Fax: 773-380-1500; Office Fax: 773-380-1812. Personal E-mail: rsippey@feralloy.com. Business E-Mail: rsippey@feralloy.com.

SIPPO, ARTHUR CARMINE, occupational medicine physician; b. Jan. 30, 1953; s. Carmine Constantine and Mildred Angela (Musto) S.; m. Katherine Velma Sager, Jan. 87, 1987; children: Sean, Tiffany, Courtney. BS in Chemistry magna cum laude, St. Peter's Coll., Jersey City, 1974; MD, Vanderbilt U., 1978; MPH, Johns Hopkins U., 1983. Diplomate Am. Bd. Preventive Medicine. Commd. 2d lt. U.S. Army, 1978, advanced through grades to lt. col., 1992; intern in ob-gyn. Walter Reed Army Med. Ctr., 1978-79; 1st brigade surgeon 101st Airborne Div., Ft. Campbell, Ky., 1979-81; resident in aerospace medicine USAF Sch. Aerospace Medicine, Brooks AFB, Tex., 1981-83; dir. biodynamics rsch. div. U.S. Army Aeromed. Rsch. Lab., Ft. Rucker, Ala., 1983-86; exch. officer RAF Inst. Aviation Medicine, Farnborough, Hants., Eng., 1986-90; ret., 1990; occupational medicine physicians Occupational Care Cons., Holland, Ohio, 1990-2000; comdr. 145th M.A.S.H., Camp Perry, 1992-94; dep. comdr. for clin. svcs. 112th Med. Brigade Ohio Army Nat. Guard, Columbus, 1994-95; asst. state surgeon Ohio Army N.G., 1995—2000; emergency medicine physician St. Joseph Hosp., Highland, Ill., 2001—; occupl. and emergency room physician St. Joseph's Hosp., 2002—. Med. dir. Libbey Glass, Inc., Toledo, 1990—, Clyde (Ohio) divsn. Whirlpool Corp., 1990—; mem. aerospace cons. adv. panel U.S. Army Surgeon Gen.'s Office. Author: Arthropometic Considerations of the U.S. Army, 1988. Mem. Ohio N.G., 1990—. Fellow Am. Coll. Occup. and Environ. Medicine, Am. Coll. Preventive Medicine, Aerospace Med. Assn.; mem. Soc. U.S. Army Flight Surgeons, Am. Coll. Emergency Physicians, Fellowship Cath. Scholars. Roman Catholic. Avocations: theology, philosophy, Biblical studies, patristics, paleontology. Office: PO Box 410 Sparta IL 62286 E-mail: artsippo@aol.com.

SIPPRELL, GEORGE SIDNEY, engineering professional; b. Buffalo, Jan. 10, 1949; s. George Gilbert and Eleanor M. Sipprell; m. Kathleen Ann Meyer, July 22, 1972; children: Jeffrey David, Benjamin Daniel. BS in Aero. Engring., Rensselaer Poly. Inst., 1970, MEng in Aero. Engring., 1972. Joined Sikorsky Aircraft Corp., Stratford, Conn., 1972, UH-60A Black Hawk project engr., 1972-76, engring. mgr. USCG SRR/S76, 1976-79, program mgr., engring. mgr. UH60A Black Hawk ESSS, 1979-83, engring. mgr. LHX Program, 1983-90, engr. mgr. LHX simulation and SHADOW program, 1988—91, dep. program mgr. RAH-66 Comanche Helicopter Program, 1990—. Recipient U.S. Army Chief of Staff award, AHS Grover Bell award, 1990, Bd. Dirs. Trophy award United Technologies Corp., 2001. Mem. Am. Helicopter Soc., Sikorsky Ski Club (pres. 1980-82, Outstanding Member award 1982). Avocations: 0-gauge model railroading, snow skiing, automotive restoration, toy collecting, historic homes. Office: Sikorsky Aircraft Corp M/S Z100A 6900 Main St PO Box 9729 Stratford CT 06615-9129 Home: 2956 Nichols Ave Trumbull CT 06611-5325 E-mail: gsipprell@sikorsky.com.

SIPPRELLE, DUDLEY GENE, investor; b. Compton, Calif., July 6, 1935; s. Foster and Dolores Lee (Dudley) S.; m. Linda Dekum Mills, Feb. 1, 1957; children: Dwight, Keith, Scott, Mark. BA, U. Redlands, 1957; postgrad., UCLA, 1957-59, Stanford U., 1960. Diplomatic & consular officer U.S. Dept. of State, Washington, 1963-93; investor pvt. practice, Santa Barbara, Calif., 1994—. Diplomat in residence Lehigh U., Bethlehem, Pa., 1980-81. Recipient Presdl. Meritorious Svc. award U.S. Dept. State, Washington, 1986. Mem. Coun. Fgn. Rels. Avocations: tennis, travel. Home: 222 Reef Ct Santa Barbara CA 93109-1958

SIPPY, DAVID DEAN, dentist; b. Waukesha, Wis., June 22, 1953; s. Lawrence Vern and Myrtle (Lawton) S.; m. Sharon Eleanor Komar, Jan. 8, 1977; children: Sharon Kay, Derek Bradley. MB, U. Wis., Milw., 1972; M in Dental Surgery, Marquette U., 1987. Dentist, New Glarus, Wis., 1988—. Owner Zenter Haus Bed and Breakfast Inn; part-time faculty Sch. Dental Hygiene Madison Area Tech. Coll. Bd. dirs. C. of C., 1989-91. Mem. ADA, Internat. Assn. for Orthodontics, Nat. Trust for Hist. Preservation, Oreg. Geneal. Soc., Am. Orthodontics Soc. (bd. dirs.). Mem. Seventh-Day Adventists. Avocations: geneology, history, historical architecture, astrophysics. Home: N8588 Zentner Rd New Glarus WI 53574-9720 Office: New Glarus Dental Clinic 119 6th Ave New Glarus WI 53574

SIPSKI, MARY LEONIDE, physician, healthcare administrator; b. Somerville, N.J., July 6, 1950; d. Joseph John and Sophia Barbara (Marcewicz) Sipski; m. Thomas Edward Lammertse, June 16, 1979; children: Meredith, Matthew, Evan. AB, Douglass Coll./Rutgers U., 1972; PhD in Phys. Biochemistry, Ohio U., 1976; MD, Ohio State U., 1979. Diplomate Am. Bd. Phys. Medicine and Rehab., Am. Bd. Managed Care Medicine, cert. in med. mgmt. Am. Coll. Physician Execs. and U. So. Calif., 2001. Intern, resident in phys. medicine and rehab. Ohio State U. Hosps., 1979-83; dir. phys. medicine and rehab. Gaylord Hosp., Wallingford, Conn., 1983-90; dir. brain injury program, dir. outpatient svcs. Kessler Inst. Rehab., Chester, NJ, 1990-97; chief med. officer Consumer Health Network, South Plainfield, 1997—, Selective Ins. Managed Care Solutions, Hamilton, 2002—. Med. dir. Gaylord/Yale-New haven Ctr. at Long Wharf, 1989-90; asst. clin. prof. dept. orthopedics and rehab. Yale U., New Haven, 1989-90; cons. Bur. Disability Determination, Columbus, Ohio, 1982-83; pvt. practice cons. in brain injury, disability, and expert medico-legal testimony, Far Hills, 1991—. Fellow Am. Acad. Phys. Medicine and Rehab. (sec. Conn. soc.); mem. AMA, Am. Coll. Physician Execs., Am. Coll. Managed Care Medicine, Soc. of Chief Med. Officers. Office: Consumer Health Network PO Box 708 South Plainfield NJ 07080 E-mail: dr.sipski@chnnetwork.com.

SIQUELAND, EINAR, psychology educator; b. Glasgow, Mont., Nov. 15, 1932; s. Harald and Anna Lydia (Kristensen) S.; m. Marian McGrail, Dec. 1960 (div. May 1970); children: Lynne Ruth, Beth Ann; m. Jillian E.A. Godfree, June 29, 1973. BA, Pacific Luth. U., 1954; MS, U. Wash., 1962, PhD, 1963. Rsch. assoc. pharmacology U. Wash., Seattle, 1958-59; clin. intern psychology VA Mental Hygiene Clinic, 1960-61; asst. prof. dept. psychology Brown U., Providence, 1965-69, assoc. prof., 1969-88, prof., 1988-99; rsch. scientist dept. Pediatrics Women's and Infants' Hosp., 1975-93; prof. emeritus Brown U., 1999—. Contbr. articles to profl. jours., chpts. to books. With U.S. Army, 1956-58, Korea. Predoctoral fellow USPHS, 1961-63, postdoctoral fellow, 1963-65. Fellow Am. Psychol. Soc.; mem. AAUP, APA, Soc. Rsch. in Child Devel., Sigma Xi. Office: Brown U Dept Psychology PO Box 1853 Providence RI 02912-1853

SIRABIAN, STEPHEN JAMES, business executive; b. N.Y.C., Nov. 15, 1955; s. Puzant and Violet Rose (Kacherian) S.; m. Karen Sirabian, Nov. 3, 1979; children: Stephanie, Christina. BSME, Tufts U., 1977; MBA, NYU, 1984. Mech. engr. Crawford & Russell, Stamford, Conn., 1977-79; mech. equip. engr. GE Environ. Svcs., N.Y.C., 1979-81; from sales/project engr. to bus. mgr. Werner & Pfeiderer Corp., Ramsey, N.J., 1981-87; gen. mgr. sales/ops. and process automation Glatt Air Techniques, 1987-93, sr. dir. sales/tech. ops., 1993-97, v.p. sales and tech. ops., 1997—2001, exec. v.p. sales and tech. ops., 2001—. Lectr./condr. seminars in field. Mem. bldg. com. St. James Ch., Harrison, N.Y., 1992-95; mem. N.J. Pharm. Discussion Group, 1995. Mem. Inst. Food Technologists, LWV. Avocations: running, boating, sports, automobiles. Office: 20 Spear Rd Ramsey NJ 07446-1221

SIRACUSANO, LOUIS H. communications company executive; b. N.Y.C., July 19, 1942; s. Luciano A. and Mafalda (Rossi) S.; m. Theresa Boegle, June 1, 1963; children: Marie, Louis H. Student, Bronx C.C., 1960-62. Electronics technologist Bendix Corp., Teterborough, N.J., 1962-68; broadcast engr. ABC Network, N.Y.C., 1968-70; field engr. AMPEX Corp., Hackensack, N.J., 1970-72, sales engr. Washington, 1972-75; pres., CEO Video Svcs. Corp., Northvale, N.J., 1975—. Mem. adv. bd. Key Bank, Westchester, N.Y., 1997; bd. dirs. Internat. Post Ltd., N.Y.C. Trustee Good Samaritan Hosp., Suffern, N.Y., 1988-94; chmn. Dem. Party, Washington Twp., N.J., 1969-75; bd. govs. CYO Youth Ministry, Newark, 1988-96. Recipient Medal of Honor, Good Samaritan Hosp., 1993, Outstanding Achievement awrd Vision Fund Am., 1992, Ellis Island Medal of Honor, 2000. Mem. KC (3d deg.). Roman Catholic. Avocations: golf, skiing. Home: 4 Concklin Ln Rockleigh NJ 07647 E-mail: usc.ceo@worldnet.att.net.

SIRAGUSA, CHARLES J. judge; BA, Lemoyne Coll., 1969; JD, Albany Law Sch., 1976. Judge U.S. Dist. Ct. (we. dist.) N.Y., 1997—. Office: 1360 US Courthouse 100 State St Rochester NY 14614-1350

SIRAGUSA, DONNA MARIE, pharmacist; b. Bklyn., Sept. 12, 1975; d. Joseph and Rosemary Ann Condon; m. Giuseppe Siragusa, Mar. 25, 2001. BS in Pharmacy cum laude, St. John's U., Jamaica, N.Y., 1998. Registered pharmacist, N.Y., Conn. Pharmacist Genovese Pharmacy, Howard Beach, NY, 1997—. Mem. Am. Pharm. Assn., N.Y. Soc. Pharmacists. Avocations: reading, biking, rollerblading. Office: Genovese Pharmacy 160-10 Cross Bay Blvd Howard Beach NY 11414 Home: 159-47 79th St Howard Beach NY 11414

SIRAGUSA, TULLIO, company executive, management consultant; b. Gerlafingen, Switzerland, Feb. 19, 1971; s. Giuseppe and Orazia (Salerno) S.; m. Josephine Casoria, Sept. 2, 1991; 1 child, Luca Joseph. BS in Info. Techs., U. Berkley, Mich., 1997, MBA in Mktg., 1998, PhD in Mgmt., 1999. Cert. profl. cons. The Cons. Inst. Sr. mgr. MCI Telecom., Inc., Boston, 1989-97; br. dir. LCI Internat. Worldwide Comm., Inc., 1997; gen. mgr. Call Scis., Inc., Edison, N.J., 1997-98; v.p. Softtek Integration Sys., Inc., Albany, N.Y., 1998-99; exec. bus. unit leader Softtek, White Plains, NY, 1999—. Mem. Am. Cons. League (accredited chartered cons.). Avocations: motorsports, reading, golf. Home: 302 Quaker Rd Pomona NY 10970-2833 Office: Softtek 75 S Broadway Fl 4 White Plains NY 10601-4413 Fax: (212) 386-6599. E-mail: siragusa@att.net.

SIRCY, BOB C., JR. accountant, financial executive; b. Nashville, May 1, 1951; s. Bobby Clay and Ophelia (Sloan) S.; m. Karen Lee West, Aug. 18, 1972; children: Laura, Clay, Reed. BS, David Lipscomb U., Nashville, 1974. From acct. to mgr. Deloitte Haskins & Sells (now Deloitte and Touche), Nashville, 1974-80; v.p. fin., sec.-treas. Advantage Cos., Inc., 1980-87; v.p., corp. contr. Southwestern/Great Amer., Inc., 1987—, bd. dirs., 2000—. Ptnr. Villa Properties, Nashville, WS Properties, Nashville; bd. dirs. BrightStone, Inc., treas., 2001—. Active United Way of Mid. Tenn., Nashville (fin. com. 1994—, treas., exec. com., bd. trustees, 1997—); Grace Sch., Nashville, 1986-87 (chmn. 1986-87, treas. 1985, bd. dirs. 1985-88); bus. adv. coun., David Lipscomb U., 1987—. Mem. AICPAs, Tenn. Soc. CPAs, Fin. Execs. Inst. (pres. 1995-96, bd. dirs. 1993-2000), Direct Selling Assn. (treas., exec. com., chmn. fin. com., bd. dirs. 1992-99),Metro. Govt. of Nashville (internal audit com. 1997-99), Exch. Club of Green Hills (past pres.), Direct Selling Edn. Found. (treas., bd. dirs., exec. com. 2001—). Republican. Ch. of Christ. Avocations: tennis, scuba diving. Home: 1209 Vintage Pl Nashville TN 37215-4706 Office: Southwestern/Great American Inc 2457 Atrium Way Nashville TN 37214-5102 E-mail: bsircy@southwestern.com.

SIRES, ALBIO, legislative staff member, business owner; BA in Spanish, Mktg. , St. Peter's Coll.; MA in Spanish, Middlebury Coll. Owner A.M. Title Agy., Inc.; mayor West N.Y., 1995—, gen. assembly, 2000—, acting gov., 2002, spkr., 2002—; Spkr. of Ho. State of N.J., Dist. 33, 2002—. Mem.: Legis. Svcs. Commn. Office: 303 58th St West New York NJ 07093*

SIRES, NORMAN GRUBER, JR. lawyer; b. Charleston, S.C., Sept. 14, 1942; s. N. Gruber and Emily (Neese) S.; m. Ann Jackson, Oct. 3, 1964; children: N. Gruber III, David Brian. BS in Bus. Adminstrn., U. S.C., 1967, JD, 1971. Bar: S.C. 1971, U.S. Dist. Ct. S.C. 1974. Pvt. practice, Seneca, S.C., 1971—; pub. defender Oconee County, 1972—; city atty. City of Clemson (S.C.), 1981-95. Pres. Oconee County Bar, 1978; commr. S.C. Indigent Def. Commn., 1992—. Mem. House Dels., S.C. Bar Assn. With U.S. Army, 1963-66. Coxain USCGR, 1996. Mem. S.C. Bar Assn., Oconee County Bar Assn. Republican. Methodist. Office: Commons Sq 123 PO Box 1277 Seneca SC 29679-1277

SIRI, WILLIAM E. physicist, consultant; b. Phila., Jan. 2, 1919; s. Emil Mark and Caroline (Schaedel) S.; m. Margaret Jean Brandenburg, Dec. 3, 1949; children: Margaret Lynn, Ann Kathryn. B.Sc., U. Chgo., 1942; postgrad. in physics, U. Calif.-Berkeley, 1947-50. Licensed profl. engr., Calif. Research engr. Baldwin-Lima-Hamilton Corp., 1943; physicist Manhattan Project Lawrence-Berkeley Lab., U. Calif., Berkeley, 1943-45, prin. investigator biophysics and research, 1945-74, mgr. energy analysis program, 1974-81, sr. scientist emeritus, 1981—; cons. energy and environment, 1982—. Lectr. U. Calif. Summer Inst., 1962-72; vis. scientist Nat. Cancer Inst., 1970; exec. v.p. Am. Mt. Everest Expdn., Inc.; field leader U. Calif. Peruvian Expdns., 1950-52; leader Calif. Himalayan Expdn., 1954; field leader Internat. Physiol. Expdn. to Antarctica, 1957; dep. leader Am. Mt. Everest Expdn., 1963. Author: Nuclear Radiations and Isotopic Tracers, 1949, papers on energy systems analyses, biophys. research, conservation and mountaineering. Pres. Save San Francisco Bay Assn., 1968-88; bd. dirs. Sierra Club Found., 1964-78; gov. gen. Mountain Medicine Inst., 1988-98; vice chmn. The Bay Inst., 1985—; bd. dirs. San Francisco Bay-Delta Preservation Assn., 1987-90. Lt. (j.g.) USNR, 1950-59. Co-recipient Hubbard medal Nat. Geog. Soc., 1963, Elsa Kent Kane medal Phila. Geog. Soc., 1963, Sol Feinstone Environ. award, 1977, Environ. award East Bay Regional Park Dist., 1984. Mem. Am. Phys. Soc., Biophys. Soc., Am. Assn. Physicists in Medicine, Sigma Xi. Clubs: Sierra (dir. 1955-74, pres. 1964-66, William Colby award 1975, John Muir award 1994), American Alpine (v.p.), Explorers (certificate of merit 1964). Democrat. Lutheran. Home: 1015 Leneve Pl El Cerrito CA 94530-2751

SIRICA, ALPHONSE EUGENE, pathology educator; b. Waterbury, Conn., Jan. 16, 1944; s. Alphonse Eugene and Elena Virginia (Mascolo) S.; m. Annette Marie Murray, June 9, 1984; children: Gabrielle Theresa, Nicholas Steven. MS, Fordham U., 1968; PhD in Biomed. Sci., U. Conn., 1977. Asst. prof. U. Wis., Madison, 1979-84; assoc. prof. Med. Coll. Va., Va. Commonwealth U., Richmond, 1984-90, prof. of pathology, 1990—, divsn. chair exptl. pathology, 1992-99, divsn. chair cellular and molecular pathogenesis, 1999—, Vis. prof., Pa. State U. Coll. Medicine, 2000, chmn. symposium on Pathobiology of Neoplasia, Am. Soc. Investigative Pathology, Richmond, Va., 1993; regular mem. sci. adv. com. on carcinogenesis and nutrition Am. Cancer Soc., Atlanta, 1989-92, metabolic pathology study sect., NIH, Bethesda, 1991-95, ad hoc mem. study sect., 1997, 98, 99, 2000; chmn. Fedn. Am. Socs. Exptl Biology Summer Rsch. Conf. on Growth Factor Receptor Tyrosine Kinases, Snowmass Village, Colo., 1999, 2001. Editor, author: The Pathobiology of Neoplasia, 1989, The Role of Cell Types in Hepatocarcinogenesis, 1992, Cellular and Molecular Pathogenesis, 1996; co-editor, author: Biliary and Pancreatic Ductal Epithelia: Pathobiology and Pathophysiology, 1997; mem. editl. bd. Pathobiology, 1990-99, Hepatology, 1991-94; rev. bd. In Vitro Cellular and Devel. Biology, 1987—, Exptl. and Molecular Pathology, 1999—; contbr. rsch. papers to Am. Jour. Pathology, Cancer Rsch., Hepatology, others. Mem.: AAAS, Soc. Toxicology, Hans. Popper Hepatopathology Soc., Soc. Exptl. Biology and Medicine, NY Acad. Scis., Am. Gastroenterological Assn., Am. Assn. Study Liver Diseases, Am. Soc. Investigative Pathology (chair program com. 1994—96), Assn. Clin. Scientists, Soc. for In Vitro Biology, Am. Assn. Cancer Rsch. (chmn. Va. state legis. com. 1992—95), Am. Soc. Cell Biology. Democrat. Roman Catholic. Achievements include development of collagen gel-nylon mesh system for culturing hepatocytes; first establishment and characterization of hyperplastic bile ductular epithelial cells in culture; research in hepato and biliary carcinogenesis, pathobiology of hepatocyte and biliary epithelial cells and molecular pathogenesis and experimental therapeutics of biliary cancer. Office: Med Coll Va Va Commonwealth U PO Box 980297 Richmond VA 23298-0297 E-mail: asirica@hsc.vcu.edu.

SIRIGNANO, WILLIAM ALFONSO, aerospace and mechanical engineer, educator; b. Bronx, N.Y., Apr. 14, 1938; s. Anthony P. and Lucy (Caruso) S.; m. Lynn Haisfield, Nov. 26, 1977; children: Monica Ann, Jacqueline Hope, Justin Anthony. B.Aero.Engring., Rensselaer Poly. Inst., 1959; PhD, Princeton U., 1964. Mem. research staff Guggenheim Labs., aerospace, mech. scis. dept. Princeton U., 1964-67, asst. prof. aerospace and mech. scis., 1967-69, assoc. prof., 1969-73, prof., 1973-79, dept. dir. grad. studies, 1974-78; George Tallman Ladd prof., head dept. mech. engring. Carnegie-Mellon U., 1979-85; dean Sch. Engring., U. Calif.-Irvine, 1985-94, prof., 1994—. Cons. indsutry and govt., 1966—; lectr. and cons. NATO adv. group on aero. rsch. and devel., 1967, 75, 80; chmn. nat. and internat. tech. congs.; chmn. acad. adv. coun. Indsl. Rsch. Inst., 1985-88; mem. space sci. applications adv. com. NASA, 1985-90, chmn. combustion sci. microgravity disciplinary working group, 1987-90; chmn. com. on microgravity rsch. space studies bd. NRC, 1991-94. Assoc. editor: Combustion Sci. and Tech., 1969-70, 2000—; assoc. tech. editor Jour. Heat Transfer, 1986-92; contbr. articles to nat. and internat. profl. jours., also rsch. monographs. United Aircraft research fellow, 1973-74; Disting. Alumni Rsch. award U. Calif. Irvine, 1992. Fellow: AAAS, ASME (Freeman scholar 1992), AIAA (Pendray Aerospace Lit. award 1991, Propellants and Combustion award 1992), Am. Phys. Soc.; mem.: NAE, Am. Electronics Assn. (recognition 1994), Orange County Engring. Coun. (Excellence award 1994), Soc. Indsl. and Applied Math., Combustion Inst. (treas. internat. orgn., chmn. ea. sect., Alfred C. Egerton Gold medal 1996), Inst. Dynamics Explosives and Reactive Sys. (v.p. 1991—95, pres. 1995—99, Oppenheim award 1993). Office: U Calif Irvine Sch Engring S3202 Engring Gtwy Irvine CA 92697-0001 E-mail: sirignan@uci.edu.

SIRILLA, MICHAEL GEORGE, theology studies educator; b. Washington, Jan. 7, 1970; s. George Michael and Floranne Sirilla; m. Laura Elizabeth Franzonello; children: Athanasius, Augustine. BA in Theology & Philos., The Franciscan U. of Steubenville, 1996, MA in Theology, 1998; student in Theology, The Cath. U. of Am., 1998—. Resident theologian Catholics United for the Faith, Steubenville, Ohio, 1996—97; prof. of systematic theology The Franciscan U. of Steuebenville, 2001, Christendom Coll., Front Royal, Va., 2002—. Rsch. asst. The Cath. U. of Am., Washington, 1998—2001. Scholar The Bd. of Trustees scholarship, The Cath. U. of Am., 1998—2001. Mem.: Am. Cath. Hist. Assn., Fellowship of Cath. Scholars, Alpha Chi (life). Republican. Roman Catholic. Avocation: family outings. Office: Christendom College 134 Christendom Drive Front Royal VA 22630 Office Fax: 540-636-1655.

SIRIS, SAMUEL GIDDING, psychiatrist; b. Phila., Aug. 28, 1944; s. Sydney Milton and Charlotte (Gidding) S.; m. Ethel Martha Silverman, June 2, 1971; children: Benjamin Avram, Sara Ann. BA in Biology, Lehigh U., 1966, MS in Biology, 1967; MD, Columbia U., 1970. Diplomate Am. Bd. Psychiatry and Neurology; cert. in adminstrv. psychiatry Am. Psychiat. Assn. Com. on Adminstriv. Psychiatry. Med. intern Mt. Sinai Med. Ctr., N.Y.C., 1970-71; psychiat. resident N.Y. State Psychiat. Inst., 1971-74; fellow in biol. psychiatry NIMH, Bethesda, Md., 1974-76; asst. prof. psychiatry Columbia U., N.Y.C., 1977-79, psychoanalytic tng., 1976-82; asst. prof. psychiatry Mt. Sinai Sch. Medicine, 1979-84, assoc. prof. psychiatry, 1984-88; dir. adult psychiat. day programs Hillside Hosp./L.I. Jewish Med. Ctr., 1988-97, dir. ambulatory psychiatry, 1995-97, dir. continuing psychiat. svcs. for schizophrenia and related conditions, 1997—; prof. psychiatry Albert Einstein Coll. Medicine, 1989—. Contbr. articles to profl. jours., chpts. to books; reviewer jours. in field. Lt. comdr. USPHS, 1974-76. Grantee NIMH, Rockville, Md., 1981-90, Nat. Inst. Drug Abuse, Rockville, 1987-91, others. Fellow Am. Psychopathol. Assn., Assn. Clin. Psychosocial Rsch.; mem. Am. Coll. Neuropsychopharmacology, Collegium Internat. Neuro-Psychopharmacologicum, Group for Advancement of Psychiatry. Office: Hillside Hosp 75-59 263rd St Glen Oaks NY 11004-1150

SIRITHARA, RAMANATHER, cardiologist; b. Jaffna, Ceylon, Feb. 23, 1946; MBBS, U. Sri Lanka - Ceyon Fac. Med., 1969. Diplomate Am. Bd. Internal Medicine and Cardiovasc. Diseases. Intern South Balt. Gen. Hosp., resident in medicine, 1972-74; fellow in cardiology Einstein Med. Ctr., Phila., 1975-77; cardiologist Harbor Hosp. Ctr., Balt., 1977—. Office: 3001 S Hanover St Baltimore MD 21225-1233

SIRKEN, MONROE GILBERT, statistician; b. N.Y.C., Jan. 11, 1921; s. Irving and Henrietta (Oram) S.; m. Blanche Skalak Horvitz (div. 1960); children: Robert, Philip. BA, UCLA, 1946, MA, 1947; PhD, U. Wash., 1950. Lectr. Med. Sch. U. Wash., Seattle, 1949; fellow Stats. Lab. U. Calif., Berkeley, 1950; statistician Census Bur., Suitland, Md., 1951-54, Pub. Health Svc., Washington, 1954-60, Nat. Ctr. Health Stats., Hyattsville, Md., 1961—. Cons. NIH, 1980-85, Nat. Inst. Drug Addiction, 1976-80, NSF, 1986—, Health Care Fin. Adminstrn., 1989-90. Contbr. articles to Jour. Am. Statis. Assn., Biometrics, Demography, Jour. APHA, Pub. Health Reports, also others. Home: 3309 Claridge Ct Silver Spring MD 20902-2201 E-mail: mgs2@cdc.gov .

SIRKIN, MICHAEL S. lawyer; b. Newark, Feb. 21, 1947; BSIE, Rutgers U., 1969; JD, Columbia U., 1972. Bar: N.Y. 1973. Mem. Proskauer Rose LLP, N.Y.C., 1989—. Office: Proskauer Rose LLP 1585 Broadway Fl 27 New York NY 10036-8299 E-mail: msirkin@proskauer.com.

SIRMAN, ROBERT, performing company executive; MA in Sociology, U. Toronto. Intern French Ministry of Culture, Paris; past speech writer Ont. Cabinet Min. Robert Welch; spl. asst., policy advisor Ont. Cabinet Min. Robert Welch, 1961—71; dir. ops. Ont. Arts Coun., Toronto, 1981—91; adminstrv. dir. The Nat. Ballet Sch., Canada, 1991—. Chair bd. dirs. Peggy Baker Dance Projects, Toronto; adv. com.arts adminstrn. co-op program U. Toronto, Scarborough Campus. Chmn. bd. dirs. Toronto PWA Found. Office: The Nat Ballet Sch 105 Maitland Toronto ON M4Y 1E4 Canada Office Fax: 416-964-5133.

SIROIS, CHARLES, communications executive; b. Chicoutimi, Que., Can., May 22, 1954; children: François-Charles, Marie-Hélène. Doctorate (hon.), U. Québec, Montréal, U. Ottawa (Can.), Concordia U., Montreal, Laval U., Que.; B Fin., Sherbrooke U., Qué.; M Fin., Laval U., Qué. Founder Telesystem Ltd., Montreal, 1984—, Nat. Pagette Ltd., Montreal, 1986-88; chmn., CEO BCE Mobile Comms. Inc., 1988-90, Teleglobe Inc., Montreal, 1992-2000, Telesystem Ltd., Montreal, 1990—; chmn. Microcell Telecomms. Inc., 1993—, Telesys. Internat. Wireless, 1997—. Bd dirs CGI Group Inc, Can Imperial Bank Commerce; mem adv bd Lazard Can; mem Global Info Infrastructure Comn, Can Info Hwy, Bus Coun Nat Issues. Co-author: (book) The Medium and the Muse, 1995, Organic Management-Creating a Culture of Innovation, 2000. Mem.: Knight Order nat du Que, Order Can (hon.). Office: Telesystem Ltd 38th Fl 1250 René Lévesque Blvd W Montreal QC Canada H3B 4W8 E-mail: csirois@telesystem.ca.

SIROKY, MIKE B. urologist, educator; b. Liberec, Czech Republic, Aug. 3, 1946; came to U.S., 1956; s. Jan and Lenka Siroky; m. Susan Weinstein, Aug. 20, 1972; children: David, Paul, Adam. AB, MD, Boston U., 1970. Diplomate Am. Bd. Urology. Rotating intern Albert Einstein, N.Y.C., 1970-71; surg. resident Harvard Med. Sch., Boston, 1971-73; urology resident Boston U., 1973-76; asst. prof. urology Boston VA Med. Ctr., 1976-86, assoc. prof. urology, 1986-92, prof. urology, 1992—, chief urology, 1983—. Editor: Male Sexual Dysfunction, 1983, Manual of Urology, 1990, Clinical Neuro-Urology, 1994, Clinical Urology, 1994. Major USAR, 1970-78. Republican.

SIROTA, PAUL RICHARD, music educator; b. Oceanside, NY, Feb. 18, 1974; s. Eileen Susan and Alan David Sirota, Terry Lou Sirota (Stepmother) and Michael Arthur Pecchioni(Stepfather). BS Music Edn., West Chester U., 1996; MS Ednl. Leadership, Barry U., 2002. Cert. K-12 music tchr. Fla. Resident asst. West Chester (Pa.) U., 1993—96; elem. sch. music tchr. Boca Raton (Fla.) Elem. Sch., 1999—2000; mid. sch. choral dir. Christa McAuliffe Mid. Sch., Boynton Beach, 2000—. Musical dir. Donna Klein Jewish Acad., Boca Raton, 1997—2000; theatrical advisor Little Palm Playhouse, Boca Raton, 1997—2000; tech. dir. dance prodn. workshop West Chester U. , 1993—97. Dir.: (musical theater prodn.) Pippin, 1998; (tech. dir.): Dance Production Workshop, 1998. Lobbyist Classroom Teachers Assn. of Palm Beach County, Tallahassee, 1999—2001, presdl. ballot recount observer West Palm Beach, 2000; com. mem. Fla. Retirement Sys., Tallahassee, 1999—2002. Mem.: NEA, Nat. League of Teachers, Nat. Tchr. Assn., Fla. Vocal Assn., Music Educators Nat. Conf., Am. Choral Directors Assn. Republican. Jewish. Avocations: travel, football, music. Home: 11208 Mahogany Dr Boynton Beach FL 33436 Office: Christa McAuliffe MidSch 6500 Le Chalet Blvd Boynton Beach FL 33437 Home Fax: 561-374-6656; Office Fax: 561-374-6656. Personal E-mail: mrsirota@aol.com. E-mail: mrsirota@aol.com.

SIROTA, ROBERT ALAN, physician, nephrologist; b. Bklyn., Apr. 22, 1948; s. Barney and Marjorie (Cohen) S.; m. Karen Foster; children: David, Jeffrey, Steven. BS summa cum laude, L.I. U., 1969; MD cum laude, Yale U., 1973. Diplomate Am. Bd. Internal Medicine, Am. Bd. Nephrology. Intern Yale-New Haven (Conn.) Hosp., 1973-74, resident, 1974-76, chief resident, 1976-77; fellow in nephrology Mass. Gen. Hosp., Boston, 1977-78; rsch. fellow Harvard U., 1977-79; fellow in nephrology Beth Israel Hosp., 1978-79; assoc. internal medicine Yale U. Sch. Medicine, 1976-77; clin. asst. prof. Hahnemann Med. Ctr., 1979—; tchg. attending physician Abington Meml. Hosp., 1979—, mem. residency adv. com., mem. dialysis com., 1979—, mem. radiology search com., 1981-82, mem. diet com., 1980-82, mem. instnl. rev. com., 1981-83, mem. transfusions com., 1985-86, mem. psychiatry search com., 1985-86. Presenter Nat. Kidney Found., 1987, 88, 90, Am. Soc. Artificial Internal Organs, 1992, among others; mem. dialysis com. Holy Redeemer Hosp., 1991—; mem. patient care com. Jeans Hosp., 1991—; mem. pharmacy and therapeutics com. Nazareth Hosp., 1991—. Contbr. articles to profl. jours. Trustee Meadow Brook Sch., 1980-86. Recipient Physician's Recognition award AMA, various yrs.; named Top Doc, Phila. Mag., 1994, 96, 99. Fellow ACP; mem. Am. Soc. Nephrology, Am. Soc. Hypertension (splst. in clin. hypertension 1999), Internat. Soc. Nephrology, Am. Soc. Internal Medicine, Internat. Soc. Peritoneal Dialysis, Phi Sigma, Alpha Epsilon Delta, Alpha Epsilon Delta, Alpha Omega Alpha. Avocations: rollerblading, photography, tropical fish. Home: 284 Wyndmoor Cir Huntingdon Valley PA 19006-7975 Office: Hypertension-Nephrology Assn 3940B Commerce Ave Willow Grove PA 19090-1705 E-mail: hna1@rcn.com.

SIROTKIN, PHILLIP LEONARD, education administrator; b. Moline, Ill., Aug. 2, 1923; s. Alexander and Molly (Berghaus) S.; m. Cecille Sylvia Gussack, May 1, 1945; children— Steven Marc, Laurie Anne. BA (McGregor Found. scholar), Wayne State U., 1945; MA, U. Chgo., 1947, PhD (Walgreen Found. scholar, Carnegie fellow), 1951. Lectr. U. Chgo., 1949-50; instr. Wellesley Coll., 1950-52, asst. prof. polit. sci., 1953-57; asso. dir. Western Interstate Commn. Higher Edn., Boulder, Colo., 1957-60; exec. asst. to dir. Calif. Dept. Mental Hygiene, Sacramento, 1960-63; asst. dir. NIMH, 1964-66, asso. dir., 1967-71, cons., 1971-73; exec. v.p., acad. v.p. State U. N.Y. at Albany, 1971-76; exec. dir. Western Interstate Commn. Higher Edn., Boulder, Colo., 1976-90, sr. adviser, 1990—, Midwestern Legis. Higher Edn. Steering Com., Boulder, 1990-91; sr. cons. Midwestern Higher Edn. Commn., 1991—; mem. oversight com. Hispanic Agenda, Larasa, 1992-98. Cons. Nebr. Post-Secondary Edn. Commn., 1994; mem. nat. adv. com. Soc. Coll. and Univ. Planning, 1976, adv. panel, rev. state system higher edn. in N.D., 1986, gov.'s com. on bi-state med. edn. plan for N.D. and S.D., 1988-90, Edn. Commn. States' Nat. Task Force for Minority Achievement in Higher Edn., 1989-91; cons. Bur. Health Manpower Edn., NIH, 1972-74, Nat. Ctr. Health Svcs. Rsch., 1975-85; spl. cons. AID, 1963-64; case writer Resources for the Future, 1954-55; mem. 1st U.S. Mission on Mental Health to USSR, 1967. Author: The Echo Park Dam Controversy and Upper Colorado River Development, 1959. Bd. dirs. Council Social Work Edn., 1959-60. Served to 1st lt. AUS, 1943-46. Recipient Superior Service award HEW, 1967; Wellesley Coll. Faculty Research award, 1956 Home: 299 Green Rock Dr Boulder CO 80302-4745

SIROTKO, THEODORE FRANCIS, priest, retired military officer; b. Muskegon, Mich., Oct. 5, 1936; s. Theodore Felix and Dorothy Mary (Bray) S.; m. Phyllis Anne Bourziel, May 5, 1962; children: Mary Anne, Kathleen, Stephen, Michael. BS, Ferris State U., 1958; MDiv, Nashotah House Theol. Sem., 1965; D in Ministry, San Francisco Theol. Sem., 1982; MSA, U. Notre Dame, 1982. Ordained to ministry Episcopal Ch., 1965. Vicar St. Matthew Ch., Sparta, Mich., 1965-68; rector St. Mark Parish, Howe, Ind., 1968-70; sr. chaplain Howe Mil. Sch., 1968-70; with U.S. Army, 1959-61, 70-93, advanced through grades to lt. col., 1985, chaplain, 1970-93, chief parish, profl. devel. Europe, 1982-85, chief pastoral ministry, counselling Chaplain Ctr. and Sch. N.J., 1985-88, asst. dir. dept. mil. ministry, 1988-89, dir., 1989, chief resource mgmt. br. Ky., 1989-91, chief adminstrn./ops. br., dep. post chaplain, 1991-93; ret., 1993; rector St. Peter's-by-the-lake, Montague, Mich., 1993—2002. Exec. coun. Diocese Western Mich., 1995-97. Bd. dirs. LaGrange County Mental Health Assn., Ind., 1969-70, Sch. Opportunity, LaGrange, 1969-70; chaplain Montague Fire Dept., 1995—; mem. Montague City Planning Commn., 2000-01. Decorated Bronze Star with 1 bronze oak leaf cluster, Air medal with 3 bronze oak leaf clusters, Meritorious Svc. medal with 3 bronze oak leaf clusters, Army Commendation medal with 1 oak leaf cluster. Mem. DAV (life), U.S. Army Chaplain Mus. Assn. (bd. dirs. 1986-88), Am. Soc. Mil. Comptrollers, Ret. Officers Assn. (life), Mil. Chaplains Assn., Evang. Cath. Mission, Confrater Order of St. Benedict. Home: 4788 S Shore Dr Whitehall MI 49461

SIROTY, WILLIAM CHARLES, physician; b. N.Y., June 9, 1951; s. Daniel Hirsch and Eileen (Gusman) S. BS, SUNY, Stony Brook, 1973; MD, Georgetown Univ., 1977. Diplomat Am. Bd. Internal Medicine, Am. Bd. Allergy-Immunology. Intern internal medicine Beth Israel Med. Ctr., N.Y.C., 1977-78, resident internal medicine, 1977-78; fellow allergy and immunology N.Y. Hosp.-Cornell U. Med. Ctr., 1980-82; pvt. practice N.Y.C., 1982-94; staff physician Nashua (NH) Med. Group, 1994—. Mem. adv. bd. Cmty. Rsch. Initiative, 1990-94, HIV Arts Network, 1994-95. Bd. dirs. Elizabeth Streb Righside Inc.; vol. Neighborhood Health Clinic; co-founder, first co-chair Gay People in Medicine Caucus Am. Med. Student Assn., 1976.; active N.H. State Dem. Com., 1998—, Hillsborough County Dem. Com., N.H., 1998—; delegate Democratic Nat. Convention, 2000. Mem. Am. Acad. Allergy, Asthma and Immunology, N.H. Med. Soc. Office: Nashua Med Group 173 Daniel Webster Hwy Nashua NH 03060-5224

SIROWER, BONNIE FOX, fundraising executive; b. Bklyn., Jan. 9, 1949; d. Stanley S. and Harriet (Fischer) Fox; m. Martin Alan Sirower, Sept. 20, 1970; children: Kenneth, Daniel. AB, Barnard Coll., 1970; MA, Columbia U., 1971. Tchr. United Cerebral Palsy, N.Y.C., 1970-73, Bergen County Bd. Spl. Svcs., Paramus, N.J., 1973-76; spl. events coord. Am. Heart Assn., Glen Ridge, 1979-81; dir. devel. Goodwill Industries, Astoria, N.Y., 1981-83; pres. Access Unltd., 1984-85; dir. devel. Cheshire Home, Inc., 1986-89, Barnert Hosp., Paterson, N.J., 1989-95; from dir. devel. to sr. v.p. United Way Passaic County, 1995-97; dir. devel. Cereral Palsy No. Jersey, 1997-99; dir. annual giving Union County Coll., Cranford, NJ, 1999—2001, Iona Coll., 2001—. Commr. Paterson (N.J.) Coun. for Disabled, 1994; trustee YMCA, Paterson, 1991; founder Pride in Paterson, 1993—; chair Youth in Philanthropy, 1995—; Paterson rep. Pres. Summit for Am. Future, 1997; dir. ann. giving Union County Coll. Found., 1999-2001; bd. dirs. Westchester Assn. of Devel. Officers, 2002—. Recipient Accolades Bronze Medal award CASE R4gion III, 2001; named Outstanding N.J. Fundraiser, Nat. Soc. of Fundraising Execs. of N.J., 1995. Mem. Nat. Assn. Fund Raising Profls. (seminars chmn. 1998-2000, 3d v.p. 2001), N.J. Soc. Fund Raising Execs. (bd. dirs. 1989, chmn. mentoring com., 3d v.p., nat. del., chmn. N.J. Conf. on Philanthropy 1994), Assn. Fund Raisers for Disabled (pres. 1981-83), N.J. Puzzlers' League (pres.), Barnard Coll. Class of '70 (pres. 1990-2000), Rotary Internat. (v.p. Paterson, past pres., asst. dist. sec., Outstanding fundraiser in N.J. 1995), Cranford Rotary (bd. dirs.), Cranford N.J. C. of C. (bd. dirs. 1999-2001), Bergen Women of Accomplishment, Cranford C. of C. (bd. dirs. 1999-2001), Phi Beta Kappa, Rotary (internat. svc. chair New Rochelle club 2002—). Jewish. Home: 69 Godfrey Ter Glen Rock NJ 07452-3510 E-mail: BSirower@iona.edu., Botzie@aol.com.

SIS, RAYMOND FRANCIS, veterinarian, educator; b. Munden, Kans., July 22, 1931; s. Frank J. and Edvie (Shimanek) S.; m. Janice L. Murphy, Aug. 31, 1953; children: Susan, Valerie, Mark, Michael, Amy. BS, Kans. State U., 1953, D.V.M., 1957; MS, Iowa State U., 1962, PhD, 1965. Clinician Blue Cross Animal Hosp., Albuquerque, 1957; asst. prof. small animal surgery Iowa State U., Ames, 1964-66; assoc. prof. anatomy Tex. A&M U., College Station, 1966-68, prof., 1968—, head dept. vet. anatomy, 1968-83. Served with USAF, 1957-61; mem. Res., 1961-91. Mem. Am. Vet. Med. Assn., Tex. Vet. Med. Assn. (dir. 1970-75), Tex. Assn. Lab Animal Sci. (pres. 1973), Am. Assn. Vet Anatomists (sec.-treas. 1973, pres. 1975), World Assn. Vet Anatomists, Brazos Valley Vet. Med. Assn. (pres. 1971), Tex. Acad. Vet. Practice (v.p. 1973), Internat. Assn. for Aquatic Animal Medicine (bd. dirs. 1984-86, pres. 1991-92), Serra Club (pres. 1985-86), Blue Key, Sigma Xi, Phi Zeta (exec. councilman 1969), Alpha Zeta, Phi Kappa Phi, Phi Sigma, Gamma Sigma Delta, Alpha Gamma Rho (adviser 1962-65, 77-85, pres. 1953, pres. alumni assn. 1976-83). Lodges: K.C. (trustee 1969, pres. 1968), Lions. E-mail: rsis@cvm.tamu.edu.

SISCO, JOSEPH JOHN, management consultant, corporation director, educator, government official; b. Chgo., Oct. 31, 1919; m. Jean Churchill Head, Mar. 26, 1946; children: Carol Bolton, Jane Murdock. Student, Morton Jr. Coll., 1937-39; AB magna cum laude, Knox Coll., 1941; MA, U. Chgo., 1947, PhD, 1950. Newspaper reporter, 1936-40; with City News Bur., Chgo., 1937; high sch. tchr., 1941; govt. service, 1950-51; staff Dept. State, 1951-76; successivley fgn. affairs officer, specialist internat. orgnl. affairs, officer-in charge Gen. Assembly, Security Council affairs, fgn. service officer, officer-in-charge UN polit. affairs, 1951-58; dep. dir. Office UN Polit. and Security Affairs, 1958-60, dir., 1960-63; dep. asst. sec. Bur. Internat. Orgn. Affairs, 1963-65, asst. sec. state internat. orgn. affairs, 1965-69; asst. sec. state Near East-South Asia, 1969-74; under sec. state for polit. affairs, 1974-76; pres. Am. U., Washington, 1976-80, chancellor, 1980-81; ptnr. Sisco Assocs. (mgmt. cons.), Washington, 1981—. Mem. U.S. delegation UN Collective Measures Com., 1952, U.S. delegations to UN Gen. Assembly, 1952-68; U.S. del. Spl. UN Gen. Assembly, session of Mid East, 1967; exec. officer, 1954=57; polit. adviser U.S. delegation Internat. Atomic Energy Agy., 1959; lectr. Fgn. Svc. Inst. Contbr. articles on internat. orgn., fgn. affairs to publs. Served as 1st lt., inf. AUS, 1941-45. Recipient Top Ten Career Service award Civil Service League, 1966, Rockefeller pub. service award, 1971; Silver Helmet Peace award Am. Vets. Com., 1973 Mem. Am. Acad. Diplomacy (chmn. bd. dirs.), Coun. Fgn. Rels. (pvt. sector coun.). Clubs: Cosmos (Washington). Home: 5630 Wisconsin Ave Chevy Chase MD 20815-4450 Office: 5335 Wisconsin Ave NW Washington DC 20015-2030

SISK, DANIEL ARTHUR, lawyer; b. Albuquerque, July 12, 1927; s. Arthur Henry and Myrl (Hope) S.; m. Katharine Banning, Nov. 27, 1954; children: John, Sarah, Thomas. BA, Stanford U., 1950, JD, 1954. Bar: N.Mex. 1955, Calif. 1954. Ptnr. firm Modrall, Sperling, Roehl, Harris & Sisk, Albuquerque, 1954-70, 71—; justice N.Mex. Supreme Ct., Santa Fe, 1970. Chmn. bd. Sunwest Fin. Svcs., Inc., Albuquerque, 1975-90. Pres. Legal Aid Soc., Albuquerque, 1960-61; trustee Sandia Sch., 1968-72, Albuquerque Acad., 1971-73, A.T. & S.F. Meml. Hosps., Topeka, 1966-82; bd. dirs. N.Mex. Sch. Banking Found., 1981-85. Served with USNR, 1945-46, PTO; to capt. USMCR, 1951-52, Korea. Mem. N.Mex. Bar Assn., Albuquerque Bar Assn. (dir. 1962-63), ABA, State Bar Calif. Presbyn. (elder). Office: 500 4th St NW Albuquerque NM 87102-5324

SISK, GREGORY CHARLES, lawyer, educator; b. Des Moines, May 29, 1960; s. James Anderson and Roberta Jean (Thornburg) S.; m. Melinda Fay Gilchrist, June 14, 1981; 1 child, Caitlin Anne. Student, Western Mont. Coll., 1978; BA in Polit. Sci., Mont. State U., 1981; JD, U. Wash., 1984. Bar: Wash. 1985, Iowa 1992, U.S. Ct. Appeals (3d cir. and 9th cir.) 1986, U.S. Ct. Appeals (2d, 5th, 11th and D.C. cirs.) 1987, U.S. Ct. Appeals (4th, 8th and fed. cirs.) 1988, U.S. Ct. Appeals (1st cir.) 1989, U.S. Supreme Ct. 1988. Legis. asst. U.S. Senate, Washington, 1984-85; jud. clk. U.S. Ct. Appeals (9th cir.), Seattle, 1985-86; appellate staff atty. civil div. U.S. Dept. Justice, Washington, 1986-89; assoc. Karr, Tuttle & Campbell, Seattle, 1989-91; asst. prof. Drake U., Des Moines, 1991-94, assoc. prof., 1994-97, prof., 1997—, Richard M. and Anita Calkins disting. prof., 1999—. Mem. ABA, Am. Law Inst., Fed. Bar Assn., Christian Legal Soc., Order of Coif, Nat. Order of Barristers, Law and Soc. Assn., Am. Polit. Sci. Assn. Republican. Roman Catholic. Office: Drake U Law Sch 2507 University Ave Des Moines IA 50311-4505 E-mail: greg.sisk@drake.edu.

SISK, JANE ELIZABETH, economist, educator; b. West Reading, Pa., Sept. 23, 1942; 2 children. BA with honors, Brown U., 1963; MA, George Washington U., 1965; PhD, McGill U., Montreal, Que., Can., 1976. Cons. Nat. Planning Assn., Washington, 1976; scholar VA, 1978-81; rsch. dir. Office Tech. Assessment, U.S. Congress, 1976-78, sr. analyst, 1981-84, sr. assoc., 1984-91. Vis. prof. Columbia U. Sch. Pub. Health, N.Y.C., 1990-91, prof., 1992— Co-author: Toward Rational Technology in Medicine, 1981; mem. editl. bd. Internat. Jour. Tech. Assessment in Health Care, 1987—, vol. editor, 1990, 98; asst. editor Am. Jour. Pub. Health, 1990-91; mem. editl. bd. Health Svcs. Rsch., 1994—; contbr. articles to profl. jours. Pres. Internat Soc. Tech. Assessment in Health Care, 1991-93, bd. dirs., 1987-95; mem. N.Y. State Task Force on Clin. Guidelines & Med. Tech. Assessment, 1994-96; mem. study sect. on health care quality and effectiveness rsch. U.S. Agy. for Health Care Policy and Rsch., 1997—. Elisah Benjamin Andrews scholar Brown U., 1961, 63; Bronfman fellow McGill U., 1971. Fellow Assn. for Health Svcs. Rsch.; mem. NAS (mem. cancer policy bd. 1997—), Phi Beta Kappa.

SISK, PAUL DOUGLAS, court official, lawyer; b. Colorado Springs, Colo., Mar. 30, 1950; s. Charles Ray Sisk and Patricia Joann (Linville) Botzler; m. Patricia Rizzo, Aug. 8, 1981; children: Hannah Elizabeth, Francesca Abigail. AB, Brown U., 1972; JD, Temple U., 1979; MA in Govt. Adminstrn., U. Pa., 1989. Bar: Pa. 1979, U.S. Ct. Appeals (3d cir.) 1980, U.S. Supreme Ct. 1983, U.S. Dist. Ct. (ea. dist.) Pa. 1985. Atty. U.S. Ct. Appeals (3d cir.), Phila., 1979-80, supervising atty., 1980-81, sr. staff atty., 1981-93, clk. of ct., 1993-2000, asst. dir. appellate mediation, 2000—. Lectr. U. Pa. Law Sch., 1989-95; reporter Joint Supreme Ct.-3d Cir. Death Penalty Task Force, 1989—. Acct., warden Episcopal Ch., Springfield, Pa., 1979-81; bd. dirs Springfield Pastoral Care Found., 1979-82; sr. warden, vestryman St. Giles Ch., Upper Darby, Pa., 1991-95. Mem. Com. Appellate Staff Attys. (exec. bd. 1986-88). Home: 409 Christian Dr Wallingford PA 19086-6912 Office: US Ct Appeals 3d Cir Appellate Mediation Program 601 Market St Philadelphia PA 19106-1713 Fax: (267) 299-4139. E-mail: Douglas_Sisk@ca3.uscourts.gov.

SISK, REBECCA BENEFIELD, retired secondary school educator, small business owner; b. Roanoke, Ala., Aug. 22, 1936; d. Arthur D. Benefield and Sollie Florence (Adcock) Riley; m. Rodney Ray Sisk, Jan. 8, 1931; children: Carlotta Rae, Kenneth Lamar. BS, Auburn U., 1957, MS, 1961. Tchr. Brentwood Jr. H.S., Pensacola, Fla., 1959-67, Woodham H.S., Pensacola, 1967; instr. Pensacola Jr. Coll., 1967-93, coord. fashion merchandising program, 1981-93; owner, sec., treas. Electronic Communications South, Inc., Pensacola, 1977-93, also bd. dirs. Author: Textiles Lab Manual and Study Guide, 1982, Fashion Internship Manual, 1983, Clothing Design, A Programmed Manual, 1990. Mem. Am. Home Econs. Assn. (del. 11th Lake Placid conf.), Am. Vocat. Assn., Am. Assn. Coll. Profs. of Textiles and Clothing, West Fla. Home Econs. Assn. (pres. 1982-84), AAUW, Omicron Nu, Delta Kappa Gamma, Phi Delta Kappa. Democrat. Mem. Christian Ch. (Disciples Of Christ). Avocations: remodeling older homes, tailoring, gardening, reading. Home: 1608 Spalding Cir Pensacola FL 32514-8301

SISK, WADE NAPOLEON, chemist, educator; b. Waterloo, Iowa, Aug. 17, 1962; s. James Arthur and Naomi Sisk; m. Avril Janine Ussery Judge, Apr. 17, 1962; children: Simone-Jeannelle V. BS in Chemistry, The U. of Iowa, 1984; PhD in Chemistry, The U. of Calif., 1990. Postdoctoral rschr. Tokyo Inst. of Tech., Tokyo, 1990—91; vis. rsch. scientist Hitachi Rsch. Lab., Hitachi-shi, Japan, 1991—92; postdoctoral rschr. Brookhaven Nat. Lab., Upton, NY, 1992—93; assoc. prof. of chemistry U. N.C., Charlotte, NC, 1993—. Vis. rsch. scientist The Inst. Physical & Chem. Rsch., Wako-shi, Saitama, Japan, 1997—98. Fellow, Sci. Tech. Agy. of Japan, 1996—98; grantee, NSF, 1996, CURSOR fellowship, Nat. Coun. of Undergraduate Rsch., 1996, NSF, 1998. Mem.: ACS (grant 1999—2001), Discovery Pl. Sci. Mus. (bd. dir. 1999—2002), Nat. Orgn. Profl. Advancement of Black Chemists & Chem. Engr. Avocations: Japanese culture, travel, weightlifting. Home: 6210 Corner Court Charlotte NC 28269 Office: Chem Dept UNC Charlotte 9201 University City Blvd Charlotte NC 28223-0001 Office Fax: 704-687-3151. Personal E-mail: sisk007@msn.com. Business E-Mail: wsisk@email.uncc.edu.

SISKA, MARY NOREEN, nursing administrator; b. Lima, Ohio, Apr. 17, 1952; d. Jacob Joseph and Gloria Ann (Mauch) Loggi; m. Edward Andrei Siska, Apr. 8, 1989. Assoc. degree, Lima Tech. Coll., 1972; BSN summa cum laude, Ohio U., 1985; MS, Ohio State U., 1988. CCRN; cert. nursing adminstr. Staff nurse, supr. Doctors Hosp., Columbus, Ohio, 1972-78; staff nurse Ohio State U. Hosp., 1978-80, Med. Pers. Pool, Columbus, 1980-82; staff nurse, head nurse Grant Med. Ctr., 1982-86; staff nurse, instr. Jewish Hosp., Cin., 1986-88; clin. nurse specialist St. Elizabeth Med. Ctr., Edgewood, Ky., 1988-89; nurse mgr.-dir. Morton Plant Hosp., Clearwater, Fla., 1989-94; mgmt. cons. Apache Med. Sys., McLean, Va., 1994-98; dir. patient care svcs. Brandywine Hosp., Coatesville, Pa., 1996-97; adminstrv. dir. Heart Inst. St. Joseph-Bapt. Health Sys., Tampa, Fla., 1998—2002; dir. nursing St. Anthony Hosp., St. Petersburg, 2002—. Disaster nurse ARC, Columbus, 1974; BLS instr. ARC, Columbus; ACLS instr., 1989—. Mem. AACN. Roman Catholic. Avocations: sailing, fishing, bicycling. Office: St Anthony's Hosp 1200 7th Ave N Saint Petersburg FL 33705-1300

SISKA, ROBERT JOHN, software developer, inventor; b. Evergreen Park, Ill., May 28, 1949; s. Emil Thomas and Marie Clara S.; m. Jane Suzan Dwyer, May 25, 1979; children: Johanna, Charlotte. BA, U. Mass., 1974. Advt. coord. Goldblatt Bros., Chgo., 1976-79; tech. writer Calif Fed., L.A., 1980-82; software engr. Informatics Gen. Corp., Canoga Park, Calif., 1982-84; software programmer Great We. Bank, Northridge, 1984-86; sr. software engr. Litton Computer Svcs., Woodland Hills, 1986-90; sr. software devel. Legent Corp., 1990-94; sr. systems programmer Nat. Computer Systems, Iowa City, 1994-97; sr. software devel. Storage Tek, Louisville, 1997—. Cons. advisor Johnson County, Iowa City, 1996-97. Creator/coord. Craven Maven Record Co., pres. 1995—. Cons. advisor Johnson County Computer Com., Iowa City, 1996-97. Mem. Network and System Profls. Assn., Colo. Blues Soc., Johnson County Blues Soc. Avocations: record company, marathon running, literature, music. Office: Storage Tek 1 Storage Tek Dr Louisville CO 80028-0001 E-mail: siskarj@louisville.stortek.com.

SISKE, ROGER CHARLES, lawyer; b. Starkville, Miss., Mar. 2, 1944; s. Lester L. and Helen (Cagan) S.; m. Regina Markunas, May 31, 1969; children: Kelly, Jennifer, Kimberly. BS in Fin. with honors, Ohio State U., 1966; JD magna cum laude, U. Mich., 1969. Bar: Ill. 1969. Assoc. Sonnenschein Nath & Rosenthal, Chgo., 1969-78, ptnr., 1978—. Chmn. nat. employee benefits and exec. compensation dept. Served to capt. U.S. Army, 1970-71. Decorated Bronze Star. Fellow Am. Coll. Employee Benefits Counsel (charter); mem. ABA (past chmn. tax sect. employee benefits com., past chmn. joint com. on employee benefits and exec. compensation and bus. law sect., employee benefits and exec. compensation com.), Chgo. Bar Assn. (past chmn. employee benefits com., mem. exec. coun. of tax com.), past chmn. employee benefits coun. ISBA, Order of Coif (editor law review), Phi Alpha Kappa. Republican. Office: Sonnenschein Nath Rosenthal 233 S Wacker Dr Ste 8000 Chicago IL 60606-6491

SISKIN, EDWARD JOSEPH, engineering and construction company executive; b. Bklyn., Apr. 30, 1941; s. Haskell and Sylvia (Steckler) S.; m. Patricia Ann Moore, June 26, 1965 (div. Apr. 1990); children: Candice P. Howard, Cristin Jo; m. Jean Elizabeth Bowen, Dec. 17, 1994. BSEE, U. Pa., 1963; cert., Bettis Reactor Engring. Sch., West Mifflin, Pa., 1965; postgrad., George Washington U., 1963-67. Registered profl. engr., Pa., Mass., N.Y., N.J., Ill., Mich., Fla., W.Va., Ind., S.C., Tex., La., Nebr., Calif., Ala. Engr. U.S. AEC, Washington, 1963-67, field office mgr. Pitts., 1967-70, Groton, Conn., 1970-77; project mgr. Stone & Webster Engring. Corp., Boston, 1977-78, asst. engring. mgr., 1978-79, engring. mgr. N.Y.C., 1979-83, v.p. & mgr., 1984-86, sr. v.p. & mgr. Cherry Hill, N.J., 1987-88, exec. v.p., 1988-90, dir. Boston, 1985-90; gen. mgr. Superconducting Supercollider Lab., Dallas, 1990-94; pres. Enerjoin Svcs., Inc., 1994—. Mem. adv. com. Inst. of Nuclear Power Ops., Atlanta, 1987-90, adv. bd. Ctr. for Chem. Plant Safety, N.Y.C., 1988-90. Bd. dirs. PenJerDel Coun., Phila., 1987-90. Lt. USN, 1963-69. Sr. mem. IEEE; mem. Am. Nuclear Soc., Am. Philatelic Soc. (State College, Pa.). Office: PO Box 17 Haddonfield NJ 08033-0016

SISKIND, ARTHUR, lawyer, director; b. N.Y., Oct. 11, 1938; s. William and Sylvia (Schuman) S.; m. Mary Ann Silverman, Nov. 10, 1962; children: Laura, Julie, Kenneth. BA in Liberal Arts, Cornell U., 1960, LLB with distinction, 1962. Ptnr. Squadron, Ellenoff, Plesent & Lehrer, N.Y., 1970-91; sr. exec. v.p., group gen. counsel, mem. exec. com., office chmn., dir. The News Corp. Ltd., 1991—; sr. exec. v.p., gen. counsel, dir. Fox Entertainment Grp. Inc., 1998—. Dir. Brit. Sky Broadcasting Group, PLC, Star TV Ltd., NDS plc. Active Cornell Law Sch. Adv. Coun., 1996—; nat. chmn. Cornell Law Sch. Alumni Fund, 1998-2001, Citizens Budget Commn. N.Y.C. Capt. U.S. Army, 1963-65. Mem. ABA, City Bar Assn., Cornell Club, Stockbridge Golf Club. Office: The News Corp Ltd Ste 300 1211 Avenue Of The Americas New York NY 10036-8795 E-mail: asiskind@newscorp.com.

SISKIND, DONALD HENRY, lawyer; b. Providence, Dec. 25, 1937; s. Samuel and Sadie (Wasserman) S.; m. Beth Mohel, July 15, 1962; children: Steven M., Edward M. BS, U. Pa., 1959; LLB, Columbia U., 1962. Bar: Mass. 1962, N.Y. 1963. Assoc. Marshall Bratter Greene Allison & Tucker, N.Y.C., 1962-69, ptnr., 1969-82, Rosenman & Colin, N.Y.C., 1982—. Bd. dirs. Chgo. Title Ins. Co.; chmn. various seminars Practicing Law Inst., 1974—; vis. lectr. Columbia U. Sch. Law, 1993—; mem. exec. com. of adv. bd. Wharton Real Estate Ctr. Adv. bd. Real Estate Fin. Jour.; contbr. articles to profl. jours. Pres. Greenville Community Coun., 1974-76; pres. bd. edn. Union Free Sch. Dist., Scarsdale, N.Y., 1978-81 Mem. ABA, Am. Coll. Real Estate Lawyers (past pres.), Anglo Am. Real Property Inst. (bd. govs.), N.Y. State Bar Assn., Assn. of Bar of City of N.Y., Phi Alpha Psi. Home: 876 Park Ave New York NY 10021-1832 Office: Rosenman & Colin 575 Madison Ave Fl 26 New York NY 10022-2585 E-mail: dhsiskind@rosenman.com.

SISLER, HARRY HALL, chemist, educator; b. Ironton, Ohio, Mar. 13, 1917; s. Harry C. and Minta A. (Hall) S.; m. Helen E. Shaver, June 29, 1940; children: Elizabeth A., David F., Raymond K., Susan C.; m. Hannelore L. Wass, Apr. 13, 1978. BSc, Ohio State U., 1936; MSc, U. Ill., 1937, PhD, 1939;

Doctorate honoris causa, U. Poznan, Poland, 1977. Instr. Chgo. City Colls., 1939-41; from instr. to assoc. prof. chemistry U. Kans., Lawrence, 1941-46; from asst. prof. to prof. chemistry Ohio State U., Columbus, 1946-56; Arthur and Ruth Sloan vis. prof. chemistry Harvard, fall, 1962-63; prof., chmn. dept. chemistry U. Fla., Gainesville, 1956-68, dean Coll. Arts and Scis., 1968-70, exec. v.p., 1970-73, dean grad. sch., 1973-79, dir. divsn. sponsored rsch., 1976-79, Disting. Svc. prof. chemistry, 1979-85, Disting. Svc. prof. chemistry emeritus, 1985—. Indsl. cons. W.R. Grace & Co., Martin Marietta Aerospace, Naval Ordnance Lab., TVA; chemistry adv. panel, also vis. scientists panel NSF, 1959-62; cons. USAF Acad., Battelle Meml. Inst., chmn. interinstl. com. nuclear research, Fla., 1958-64; mem. Fla. Nuclear Devel. Commn. Teaching Sci. and Math., 1958; chemistry adv. panel Oak Ridge Nat. Lab., 1965-69; dir. sponsored rsch. U. Fla., 1976-79. Author: Electronic Structure, Properties, and the Periodic Law, 2d edit, 1973, Starlight-A Book of Poems, 1976, Of Outer and Inner Space—A Book of Poems, 1981, Earth, Air, Fire and Water-A Book of Poems, 1989, (with others) Gen. Chemistry: A Systematic Approach, 2d edit, 1959, Coll. Chemistry: A Systematic Approach, 4th edit, 1980, Essentials of Chemistry, 2d edit, 1959, A Systematic Laboratory Course in Chemistry, 1950, Essentials of Experimental Chemistry, 2d edit, 1959, Semimicro Qualitative Analysis, 1958, rev. edit., 1965, Comprehensive Inorganic Chemistry, Vol. V, 1956, Chemistry in Non-Aqueous Solvents, 1961, The Chlorامination Reaction, 1977, Dying-Facing the Facts, 1988, Inorganic Reactions and Methods, Vol. 7, 1988, Encyclopedia of Inorganic Chemistry, Vol. 5, Nitrogen: Inorganic Chemistry, 1994, Autumn Harvest-A Book of Poems, 1996, Perspective-A Book of Poems, 1999; cons. editor: (with others) Dowden, Hutchinson & Ross, 1971-78; series editor: (with others) Phys. and Inorganic Textbook Series, Reinhold Pub. Corp, 1958-70; contbr. (with others) articles to profl. jours.; patentee in field. Decorated Royal Order North Star(Sweden); Named Outstanding Chemist in South, Am. Chem. Soc., 1969, Outstanding Chemist in Southeast, Am. Chem. Soc., 1960, James Flack Norris award Am. Chem. Soc., 1979; recipient Outstanding Centennial Achievement award Ohio State U., 1970. Mem. Am. Chem. Soc. (nat. chmn. div. chem. edn. 1957-58, exec. com. 1957-60, bd. publ. Jour. Chem. Edn. 1956-58), Phi Beta Kappa, Sigma Xi, Phi Delta Kappa, Phi Lambda Upsilon, Phi Kappa Phi, Alpha Chi Sigma. Methodist. Home: 6014 NW 54th Way Gainesville FL 32653-3265

SISLEY, EMILY LUCRETIA, retired psychologist, medical writer; b. North Charleroi, Pa., May 7, 1930; d. Frederick William and Harriet Watkins (Litman) S. PhD in Clin. Psychology, L.I. U., 1972. Diplomate Am. Bd. Med. Psychotherapists. Mng. editor Med. Jours., Harper & Row, N.Y.C., 1960-67; freelance med. writer-editor, 1967-95; supervising psychologist, dept. psychiatry Roosevelt Hosp., 1972-77; clin. instr. Columbia Univ. Coll. Physicians and Surgeons, 1975-77; chief psychologist Gramercy Park Inst., 1978-84; staff therapist MedcoBehavioral Care Sys., 1984-95; ret., 1995. Cons. Internat. Jour. Group Tensions, N.Y.C., 1968-72. Illustrator: You and Your Brain, 1963, Thomas Alva Edison award, 1963; co-author: The Vitamin C Connection, 1983; contbr. articles to profl. and lit. jours. Fellow Am. Bd. Med. Psychotherapists; mem. APA, N.Y. Acad. Scis. Democrat. Episcopalian. Avocations: music, golfing, skiing, sailing.

SISSEL, GEORGE ALLEN, manufacturing executive, lawyer; b. Chgo., July 30, 1936; s. William Worth and Hannah Ruth (Harlan) S.; m. Mary Ruth Runsvold, Oct. 5, 1968; children: Jenifer Ruth, Gregory Allen. BS in Elec. Engring., U. Colo., 1958; JD cum laude, U. Minn., 1966. Bar: Colo. 1966, Ind. 1973, U.S. Supreme Ct. 1981. Assoc. Sherman & Howard, Denver, 1966-70; with Ball Corp., Broomfield, 1970—, assoc. gen. counsel, 1974-78, gen. counsel, 1978-95, corp. sec., 1980-95, v.p., 1981-87, sr. v.p., 1987-95, pres., 1995-98, CEO, 1995-2001, chmn. bd., 1996—2002, also bd. dirs. Bd. advisors Bank One Equity Capital, 1995—; bd. dirs. First Merchants Corp. Assoc. editor: U. Minn. Law Rev., 1965-66. Served with USN, 1958-63. Mem. Colo. Bar Assn., Colo. Assn. Commerce & Industry, Order of Coif, MIT Soc. Sr. Execs., (bd. govs. 1987-95), Sigma Chi, Sigma Tau, Eta Kappa Nu. Lodges: Rotary. Methodist.

SISSOM, LEIGHTON ESTEN, engineering educator, dean, consultant; b. Manchester, Tenn., Aug. 26, 1934; s. Willie Esten and Bertha Sarah (Davis) S.; m. Evelyn Janelle Lee, June 13, 1953; children: Terry Lee, Denny Leighton. BS, Middle Tenn. State Coll., 1956; BS in Mech. Engring., Tenn. Technol. U., 1962; MS in Mech. Engring., Ga. Inst. Tech., 1964, PhD, 1965. Diplomate Nat. Acad. Forensic Engrs.; registered profl. engr., Tenn. Draftsman Westinghouse Electric Corp., Tullahoma, 1953-57; mech. designer ARO, Inc., 1957-58; instr. mech. engring. Tenn. Technol. U., Cookeville, 1958-62, chmn. dept. mech. engring., 1965-79, dean engring., 1979-88, dean of engring. emeritus, 1988—; prin. cons. Sissom & Assocs., Tenn., 1962—. Bd. dirs. Accreditation Bd. Engring. and Tech., N.Y.C., 1978-86, treas., 1982-86. Author: (with Donald R. Pitts) Elements of Transport Phenomena, 1972, Heat Transfer, 1977, 1,000 Solved Problems in Heat Transfer, 1991; contbr. An Attorney's Guide to Engineering, 1986; contbr. articles to various publs. Fellow ASME (sr. v.p. 1982-86, gov. 1986-88, Golden medallion), Am. Soc. Engring. Edn. (bd. dirs. 1984-87, pres. 1991-92), Accreditation Bd. Engring. and Tech.; mem. NSPE, Soc. Automotive Engrs., Nat. Engring. Deans Coun. (chmn. 1984-87), Order of the Engr. (chmn. bd. govs. 1994-96), Tau Beta Pi (v.p. 1986-89, councillor 1986-89). Home and Office: 1151 Shipley Church Rd Cookeville TN 38501-7730

SISSON, DOUGLAS LEE, pension fund executive; b. Gallipolis, Ohio, Sept. 6, 1959; s. Charles Elias and Martha Sue Sisson; m. Anne Blair Sisson, Dec. 27, 1980; children: Phillip, Laura, Andrew, Jeffrey. BA, Ohio State U., 1980, MBA, 1984. CPA, Ohio. Banking mgr. State Savs. Bank, Columbus, 1980-86; asset mgmt. officer State Tchrs. Retirement Sys. of Ohio, 1986-89, sr. asset mgmt. officer, 1989-96; investment officer Sch. Employees Retirement Sys. of Ohio, 1996-98, sr. investment officer, 1998-99, chief investment officer, 1999—. Mem. Columbus Soc. Fin. Analysts. Presbyterian. Avocations: golf, reading. Address: Sch Employees Retirement Sys of Ohio 300 E Broad St Ste 100 Columbus OH 43215-3602

SISSON, JEAN CRALLE, middle school educator; b. Village, Va., Nov. 16, 1941; d. Willard Andrew and Carolyn (Headley) Cralle; m. James B. Sisson, June 20, 1964 (div. Oct. 1994); 1 child, Kimberly Carol; m. donald Wimer (div. 1998). BS in Elem. Edn., Longwood Coll., 1964; MA in Adminstrn. and Supervision, Va. Commonwealth U., 1979. Tchr. 2nd grade Tappahannock (Va.) Elem. Sch., 1964-67; tchr. 2nd and 4th grades Farnham (Va.) Elem. Sch., 1967-71; tchr. 6th grade Callao (Va.) Elem. Sch., 1971-81; tchr. 6th and 7th grades Northumberland Mid. Sch., Heathsville, Va., 1981—. Sr. mem. Supt. Adv. Com., Heathsville, 1986-93. Author: My Survival, 1994; author of children's books, short stories and poetry. Lifetime mem. Gibeon Bapt. Ch., Village, Va., 1942—. Mem.: IDEA, ASCD, NEA, Nat. Wildlife Fedn., Nat. Coun. English Tchrs., Exercise Safety Assn., Va. Mid. Sch. Assn., Aerobics and Fitness Assn., PETA. Republican. Avocations: aerobics, dance, music, art, travel. Home: 1068 Lodge Rd Callao VA 22435-2105 Office: Northumberland Mid Sch PO Box 100 Heathsville VA 22473-0100 E-mail: jsisson@nucps.com.

SISSON, MARILYN SUE, writer; b. Paris, Dec. 15, 1947; d. Chester Wayne and Clara Katherine (Blaker) Kirby; m. Robert F. Sisson, Dec. 31, 1971. Grad. h.s., Paris, 1966; student, Famous Writer's Sch., 1970. Assembler Zenith, Paris, 1966-71; freelance writer, 1971—. Contbr. poetry to anthologies and lit revs., Tucumcar: Lit. Rev., Footprints mag., Adorations Christian Jour. Recipient Editor's Choice award Nat. Libr. Poetry, 1996, 97. Mem. VFW (aux.). Democrat. Methodist. Avocations: crochet, gardening, camping, reading, writing. Home: PO Box 152 630 Vance St Paris IL 61944-1156

SISSON, RAY L. retired dean, author; b. Pueblo, Colo., Apr. 24, 1934; s. William Franklin and Lillie Mae (Hall) S.; m. Dixie Lee McConnell, Oct. 5, 1952; children: Mark Lynn, Bryan Keith, Tammy Sue Ann. BSEE, U. Colo., 1960; MSEE, Colo. State U., 1966; AA, Pueblo Coll., 1958; EdD, U. No. Colo., 1973. Electronic technician TV Svcs. Co., Pueblo, 1958, Sid's Appliance Ctr., Tucson; from instr. engring. to asst. prof. So. Colo. State Coll., Pueblo, 1960-63, assoc. prof., 1963-76, engring., electronics dept. head, 1968-70; dean Sch. Applied Sci. and Engring. Tech. U. So. Colo., 1973-84, prof., 1976—, interim dean Coll. Engring. and Sci., 1984-85, dean Coll. Applied Sci. and Engring. Tech., 1985-96, dean, prof. emeritus, 1996—. Cons. Escuela Superior Politecnica del Litoral, Ecuador, 1979-82, SUNY, Alfred, Farmingdale, 1982, Moorhead U., 1985, N.Mex. Highlands U., 1985, 90, Kans. State U., Salina, 1994, Ministry Edn., Republic of Yemen, 1996, Min. Edn., State of Kuwait, 1998. Author: Pueblo Army Air Base 1942-46 A Chronological History, 2001. Bd. dirs. Colo. Transp. Inst., 1993-96; exec. dir. So. Colo. Bus. and Tech. Ctr., 1994-96. With USN, 1952-56. Recipient James H. McGraw award Am. Soc. Engring. Edn., 1990; NSF grantee, 1964, 65, 67, 68, 80-83. Mem. IEEE, ABET (tech. accreditation commn. 1990-96, chmn. definition com. 1991, vice chmn. tech. accreditation commn., 1993-96), Am. Soc. Engring. Edn. (active, spectrum com. 1989-90, chmn. definition com. 1991, fellow 1993), Engring. Tech. Leadership Inst. (founding mem., bd. dirs. 1983-88, chmn. 1984-85), Profl. Engrs. Colo. (So. chpt., assoc. mem., chair young engrs. 1969, scholarship, edn. com. 1969, chair state scholarship com. 1968), Pueblo Pachyderm Club (pres. 1986, 89, 98), Pueblo Hist. Aircraft Soc. (historian 1999—), Retirees Assn. (pres. 1998, 99), Phi Delta Kappa, Eta Kappa Nu, Tau Alpha Pi. Home: 403 Starlite Dr Pueblo CO 81005-2685 E-mail: sisson@uscolo.edu.

SISSON, ROBERT F. photographer, writer, lecturer, educator; b. Glen Ridge, N.J., May 30, 1923; s. Horace R. and Frances A. S.; m. Patricia Matthews, Oct. 15, 1978; 1 son by previous marriage, Robert F.H.; 1 stepson, James A. Matthews. With Nat. Geographic Soc., Washington, 1942-88, chief nat. sci. photographer, 1981-88; free-lance photographer, 1988—. Lectr. in field; mem. nature staff Sarasota Mag., 1989; owner Macro/Nature Workshops, Englewood, Fla. Photographer one-man shows, Nat. Geog. Soc., Washington, 1974, Washington Press Club, 1976, Berkshire (Mass.) Mus., 1976, Brooks Inst., Santa Barbara, Calif., 1980, U. Miami, 1993, Sea Ctr., Santa Barbara, Calif., 1993, Corcoran Gallery of Art's Spl. World Tour, 1988, permanent collections, Mus. Art, N.Y.C. Recipient 1st prize for color photograph White House News Photographers Assn., 1961; recipient Canadian Natural Sci. award, 1967, Louis Schmidt award, 1991. Fellow Biol. Photographers Assn.; mem. Biol. Photog. Assn. (awards for color prints 1967), Nat. Audubon Soc., Nat. Geog. Soc., Nat. Wildlife Fedn., Soc. Photog. Scientists and Engrs., N.Y. Acad. Scis., N.Am. Nature Photography Assn. (bd. dirs., Lifetime Achievement award 1999), Sigma Delta Chi. Office: Macro/Nature Photography PO Box 1649 Englewood FL 34295-1649 *The true wonders of the natural world gave me inspiration and a challenge. My cameras and I are privileged to share images of this world with all people.*

SISSON, VIRGINIA BAKER, geology educator; b. Boston, Apr. 8, 1957; d. Thomas Kingsford and Edith Virginia (Arnold) S.; m. William Bronson Maze, Oct. 14, 1989. AB, Bryn Mawr Coll., 1979; MA, Princeton U., 1981, PhD, 1985. Rsch. assoc. Princeton (N.J.) U., 1985-86, Rice U., Houston, 1986-87, lectr., 1987-92, asst. prof. geology, 1992-99, clin. prof., 1999-2001, rsch. scientist, 2001—. Cons. U.S. Geol. Survey, Anchorage, 1984-95; rsch. assoc. Am. Mus. Natural History, 2001—; rsch. assoc. prof. U. Utah, 2001—. Contbr. more than 35 articles to sci. publs. Trustee Geol. Soc. Am. Found. Rsch. grantee, NSF, Houston and Calif., 1988, Houston and Scotland, 1990, Alaska, 1990, Venezuela, 1996, Alaska, 1998, Nat. Geographic, 1998. Fellow Geol. Soc. Am.; mem. Assn. Women Geoscientists, Am. Women in Sci., Am. Geophys. Union, Mineral Soc. of Am., Mineral Assn. Can. Avocations: pilot, cross-country skiing, recorder playing, warbirds. Home: 4118 Lanark Ln Houston TX 77025-1115 Office: Rice U Dept Earth Sci MS-126 6100 Main St Houston TX 77005-1892 E-mail: jinnys@rice.edu.

SISTO, FERNANDO, mechanical engineering educator; b. La Coruña, Spain, Aug. 2, 1924; s. Fernando Cartelle and Clara (Reiss) S.; m. Grace Jeanette Wexler, June 27, 1946; children: Jane Caroll, Ellen Gail, Todd Frederic. Student, NYU, 1940-43; BS, U.S. Naval Acad., 1946; ScD, MIT, 1952; M Engring. (hon.), Stevens Inst. Tech., 1962. Registered profl. engr., N.J. Commd. ensign USN, 1946, service in the Pacific, ret., 1949; propulsion div. chief Curtiss-Wright Research, Clifton, N.J., 1952-58; prof. mech. engring. Stevens Inst. Tech., Hoboken, 1959-96, chmn. dept., 1966-79, George Meade Bond prof., 1978-96, prof. emeritus, 1996—, dean of the grad. sch. N.J., 1993-94. Bd. dirs., trustee Am. Capital Mut. Funds, Houston, 1960—, chmn. bd., 1992-95; co-chmn. merged bd. Van Kampen Am. Capital, 1995-97, dir. emeritus, 2001—; bd. dirs. Dynalysis of Princeton; cons. UN Devel. Program at Nat. Aero. Lab., Bangalore, India, 1978. Co-author: (textbook) A Modern Course in Aeroelasticity, 1978, 3d edit., 1995. Lt. USN, 1943-49. R.C. DuPont fellow MIT, 1951-52. Fellow ASME; mem. Adirondack Mountain Club. Avocations: skiing, tennis, woodworking, sculling. Office: Stevens Inst Tech Dept Mech Engring Hoboken NJ 07030-5991 E-mail: gsandfs@aol.com.

SISTO, GRACE WEXLER, social welfare consultant; b. N.Y.C. d. Theodore and Ruth (Sporty) Wexler; m. Fernando Sisto, June 27, 1946; children: Jane Sisto Long, Elena Sisto-Kirkpatrick, Todd. BA, Adelphi U., 1944; MS, Columbia U., 1946; EdD, Fairleigh Dickinson U., 1979. Mem. child welfare staff Childrens Aid and Adoption Soc. N.J., Hackensack, 1958-63, dist. supr., 1963-72, dir. spl. svcs., 1972-73, exec. dir., 1973-96, cons., 1996—. Mem. N.J. Gov.'s Blue Ribbon Panel, Trenton, 1997-98. Bd. dirs. Planned Parenthood, Hackensack, 1978-84; mem. strategic planning com. United Way Bergen County, Hackensack, 1984-88; mem. long range planning com. N.J. Divsn. Youth and Family Svcs., Hackensack, 1988-92; mem. nat. task force Child Welfare League, Washington, 1989-93. Recipient Social Worker of Yr. award NASW, N.J., 1991. E-mail: gsandfs@aol.com.

SIT, EUGENE C. investment executive; b. Canton, China, Aug. 8, 1938; s. Hom Yuen and Sue (Eng) S.; m. Gail V. Chin, Sept. 14, 1958; children: Ronald, Debra, Roger, Raymond, Robert, Richard. BSC, DePaul U., 1960; postgrad., Grad. Sch. Bus., 1962-65. CPA, Ill.; CFA. Fin. analyst Commonwealth Edison, Chgo., 1960-66, fin. asst. to chmn. finance com., 1966-68; assoc. portfolio mgr. Investors Stock Fund, Investors Diversified Svcs., Mpls., 1968-69; portfolio mgr. IDS New Dimensions, IDS Growth Fund., 1972-76; pres. IDS Adv., 1976-77, pres., CEO, 1977-81; CEO IDS Trust Co., 1979-81; chmn., CEO IDS Adv./Gartmore Internat. Ltd., 1979-81; chmn., CEO, global investment officer Sit Investment Assocs., Inc., Mpls., 1981—. Chmn. Sit/Kim Internat. Investment Assocs., Inc.; chmn., pres., dir. Sit Mut. Fund Group; trustee TIAA/CREF. Trustee Carleton Coll. Mem. Minn. Orchestral Assn. (trustee), Minn. Hist. Soc. (trustee), Univ. Club (N.Y.), Chgo. Club, Mpls. Club, Edina Country Club, World Trade Club (San Francisco), LaQuinta Country Club, Spring Hill Country Club. Home: 6216 Braeburn Cir Minneapolis MN 55439-2548 Office: 90 S 7th St Ste 4600 Minneapolis MN 55402-3903

SIT, HONG CHAN, minister; b. St. Louis, Nov. 25, 1921; s. Gan and Ying Foon (Wong) S.; m. Amy Wang, June 16, 1949; children: David, Daniel, Esteelle Joy, Mary. BS summa cum laude, U. Ill., 1943; BD, STM, Faith Theol Sem., 1950; ThD, No. Bapt. Theol. Sem., 1957. Ordained to ministry Blue Ch., Springfield, Pa., 1950. Missionary China Inter-Varsity Fellowship, Shanghai, 1947; pastor Chinese Evang. Ch., N.Y.C., 1950-51, Chinese Bapt. Ch., Houston, 1953-56, Grace Chapel, 1956-90, missionary pastor, 1990—; pastor Newlie Bapt. Ch., Houston, 2001—02. Pres. Chinese Fgn. Missionary Union, 1974, Chinese Full Gospel Fellowship Internat., Hong Kong, 1983-98; mem. bd. govs. Network of Christian Ministries, 1990—. Author: Your Next Step With Jesus, 1977, My View From a Bridge: Autobiography of Hong Sit, 1999; contbr. articles to profl. jours. Mem.: Phi Lambda Upsilon, Phi Beta Kappa. Office: PO Box 55664 Houston TX 77255-5664 E-mail: pasit@aol.com.

SIT, PING-FAI, research scientist; b. Hong Kong, Nov. 6, 1967; came to U.S., 1992; PhD, Case Western Res. U., 2001. Rsch. asst. dept. biomed. engring. Johns Hopkins U., Balt., 1992-94, Case Western Res. U., Cleve., 1994—; asst. rsch. prof., dept. of chemistry Rutgers U. Recipient Best Grad. Student Rsch. award Biomed. Engring. Soc., 1998. Mem. AAAS, ACS, Biophys. Soc., Soc. for Biomaterials. Office: Case Western Res U 319 Wickenden Bldg 10900 Euclid Ave Cleveland OH 44106 Office Fax: 732-445-0790.

SITA, MICHAEL JOHN, pharmacist, educator; b. Apr. 28, 1953; s. Julianne Gail Sita; m. Nora Ann Dillon, June 1, 1974 (div. 1996); children: Michael John, Paul Thomas, Julianne Joyce; m. Christine Elizabeth Nordmann, Aug. 22, 1997; children: Mary Elizabeth, April Christine. BS, St. Louis Coll. Pharmacy, 1976; MBA, So. Ill. U., 1983. Registered pharmacist, Mo., Ill. Staff pharmacist Luth. Med. Ctr., St. Louis, 1976-78, asst. chief pharmacist, 1978-81, adminstrv. coord. pharmacy svcs., 1981-85; dir. pharmacy svcs. Jefferson Meml. Hosp., 1985-98; pharmacist Mo. Bapt. Hosp., 1998-2000, Walgreen's, 2000—. Instr. St. Louis Coll. Health Careers, 1983-86; adj. instr. pharmacy practice St. Louis Coll. Pharmacy, 1980-98; relief pharmacist Dolgins Apothecary, St. Louis,1976-86, Best Pharmacy, 1986-88, Carraige Drugs, 1989-93, Medicine Shoppe, Festus, Mo., 1990-97, Otto (Mo.) Drug, 1997-2000. Author, editor: Pharmacy Capsule quar., 1977-85. Mem. St. Louis Soc. Hosp. Pharmacists (treas. 1985-87, pres. 1988-89, sec. 1990-92, Pharmacist of Yr. 1994-95), Mo. Soc. Hosp. Pharmacists, Am. Soc. Hosp. Pharmacists, Am. Pharm. Assn., Hosp. Assn. Met. St. Louis (chmn. pharmacy tech. adv. com. 1985-86). Avocations: carpentry, rehabbing. Home: 111 Ward Ter Crystal City MO 63019-1707 Office: Walgreens 101 Twin City Mall Crystal City MO 63019

SITARAMAN, SHANTHI VASUDEVAN, gastroenterologist, medical educator; MSc in Biochemistry, U. Madras, India, 1983; PhD in Pathology, U. Toronto, Can., 1989, MD with honors, 1992. Diplomate Am. Bd. Internal Medicine, Am. Bd. Gastroenterology. Internal medicine resident U. Toronto, Can., 1995; rsch. fellow Dept. Pathology Emory U., Atlanta, 1997-99; fellow in gastroenterology Mass. Gen. Hosp. Harvard U., Boston, 1996-99; asst. prof. dept. medicine, divsn. digestive diseases Emory U., Atlanta, 1999—. Tchg. asst. Dept. Pathology Sch. Medicine, U. Toronto, 1987-94. Contbr. articles, chpts. to profl. pubs. Recipient Stella Klotz award, 1985, Emmanuel Farber's award for Best Presentation, 1985, U. Toronto Open Doctoral Fellowship, 1986-87, Edward S. Reynold award for Best Rsch. in the Field of Pathology, Nat. Student's Rsch. Forum, 1987, Mead Johnson award for Overall Excellence in Rsch., Nat. Student's Rsch. Forum, 1987, Ontario Grad. Scholarship, 1986-88, Gladwin-Riding Meml. Scholarship, 1991, Med. Soc. Honor award, 1992, Kathleen Chambers Meml. award, 1992, Higgins Day Rsch. awrd, 1994, Crohn's and Coltis Found. of Am. Career Devel. award, 1999; grantee NIH. Fellow Royal Coll. Physicians and Surgeons of Can.; mem. Am. Gastroenterology Assn., Am. Assn. Cancer Rsch. Office: Emory U Sch Medicine 2101 Woodruff Meml Bldg 1639 Pierce Dr Atlanta GA 30322-0001 E-mail: ssitar2@emory.edu.

SITARZ, ANNELIESE LOTTE, pediatrics educator, physician; b. Medellin, Colombia, Aug. 31, 1928; came to U.S., 1935; d. Hans and Elisabeth (Noll) S. BA cum laude, Bryn Mawr (Pa.) Coll., 1950; MD, Columbia U., 1954. Diplomate Nat. Bd. Med. Examiners, Am. Bd. Pediatrics., Am. Bd. Pediatric Hematology and Oncology. Intern Children's Med. Ctr., Boston, 1954-55; resident in pediat. Babies Hosp.-Columbia-Presbyn. Med. Ctr., N.Y.C., 1955-57; mem. faculty Columbia U., 1957—, assoc. prof. clin. pediat., 1974-83, prof. clin. pediat., 1983-2000, prof. emerita clin. pediat., spl. lectr. in pediat., 2000—; attending in pediat. Babies and Children's Hosp., 1983—. Cons. pediatrics, hematology and oncology Harlem Hosp., N.Y.C., 1967—72, Overlook Hosp., Summit, NJ, 1975—2001. Contbr. numerous articles to profl. jours. Pres. Mt. Prospect Assn., Summit, 1987—. Fellow Am. Acad. Pediatrics; mem. Am. Assn. Cancer Rsch., Am. Soc. Clin. Oncology, Am. Soc. Hematology, Internat. Soc. Hematology, Harvey Soc. Republican. Episcopalian. Avocations: gardening, sewing, skiing, hiking, stamp collecting. Office: Childrens Hosp NY Irving Pavilion 161 Ft Washington Ave New York NY 10032-3710

SITARZ, PAULA GAJ, writer; b. New Bedford, Mass., May 25, 1955; d. Stanley Mitchell and Pauline (Rocha) Gaj; m. Michael James Sitarz, Aug. 26, 1978; children: Andrew Michael, Kate Elizabeth. BA, Smith Coll., 1977; MLS, Simmons Coll., 1978. Children's libr. Thomas Crane Pub. Libr., Quincy, Mass., 1978-84. Dir. Reader's Theatre Workshop Thomas Crane Pub. Library, Quincy Mass., 1985. Author: (book) Picture Book Story Hours: From Birthdays to Bears, 1986, More Picture Book Story Hours, 1989, The Curtain Rises: A History of Theater From Its Origins in Greece and Rome Through the English Restoration, 1991, The Curtain Rises Volume II: A History of European Theater from the Eighteenth Century to the Present, 1993, Story Time Sampler: Read Alouds, Book Talks, and Activities for Children, 1997; contbr. monthly column Bristol County Baby Jour., 1992-98, South Shore Baby Jour., 1992-98, First Tchr., 1992-98. Mem. New Eng. Libr. Assn., Libr. Sci. Honor Soc., Smith Club of Southeastern Mass. (v.p. 1987-89, pres. 1989-91), Dartmouth (Mass.) Arts Coun., Beta Phi Mu. Roman Catholic. Avocation: singer. Home and Office: 25 Stratford Dr North Dartmouth MA 02747-3843

SITES, JAMES PHILIP, lawyer, consul; b. Detroit, Sept. 17, 1948; s. James Neil and Inger Marie (Krogh) S.; m. Barbara Teresa Mazurek, Apr. 9, 1978; children: Philip Erling, Teresa Elizabeth. Student, U. Oslo, Norway, 1968-69; BA, Haverford Coll., 1970; JD, Georgetown U., 1973, ML in Taxation, 1979. Bar: Md. 1973, D.C. 1974, U.S. Supreme Ct. 1978, Mont. 1984, U.S. Tax Ct. 1984, U.S. Dist. Ct. Mont. 1984, U.S. Ct. Appeals (9th cir.) 1988. Law clk. to Hon. James C. Morton, Jr. Ct. Spl. Appeals Md., Annapolis, 1974-75; law clk. to Hon. Orman W. Ketcham Superior Ct. D.C., Washington, 1975-76; gen. atty. U.S. Immigration & Naturalization Svc., 1976-77; trial atty. tax divsn. U.S. Dept. Justice, 1977-84; ptnr. Crowley, Haughey, Hanson, Toole & Dietrich, Billings, Mont., 1984—; consul for Govt. of Norway State of Mont., 1987—. Instr. Norwegian Ea. Mont. Coll., 1987-88, Sons of Norway, 1989—, instr. polit. sci. Mont. State U., Billings, 1997—; v.p. Scandinavian Studies Found., 1989—; bd. dirs. Billings Com. on Fgn. Rels., Festival of Cultures; mem. Mont. Coun. for Internat. Visitors, The Norsemen's Fedn. Chmn. local exec. bd. Mont. State U., Billings, 1993—. Decorated knight 1st class Royal Norwegian Order of Merit; U. Oslo scholar, 1969. Mem. Md. Bar Assn., Mont. State Bar (co-chmn. com. on income and property taxes 1987-91, chair tax and probate sect. 1991-92, chair tax litigation subcom. 1992—), D.C. Bar Assn., Am. Immigration Lawyers Assn., Norwegian-Am. C. of C., Billings C. of C. (bd. dirs. 1998—, chair-elect), Hilands Golf Club, Kenwood Golf and Country Club, Billings Stamp Club, Elks, Masons. Avocations: philately, sports card collecting, hiking, Nordic skiing. Office: Crowley Haughey Hanson Toole & Dietrich Consulate for Norway 490 N 31st St Billings MT 59101-1256

SITILIDES, JOHN, government relations executive, policy analyst; b. Jersey City, Feb. 8, 1962; s. Louis and Frances Sitilides; m. Angela Beth Johnson, Oct. 11, 1997. BA, Queens Coll., 1984; M of Internat. Affairs, Columbia U., 1986. Campaign dir. Maltese for State Senate, Maspeth, N.Y., 1988; exec. asst. for comms. and legis. affairs U.S. Senator Alfonse M. D'Amato, N.Y.C., 1986-93; pres. The Sitilides Group, Sacramento, 1993-98; exec. dir. The Western Policy Ctr., Washington, 1994—; pres. JS Assocs, Alexandria, Va., 1998—. Exec. editor The Strategic Regional Report. Policy advisor Dole/Kemp '96, Calif., 1996; policy advisor Hellenic Am. Rep. Assn., N.Y.C., 1997—. Mem. Am.-Israel Pub. Affairs Com., Am. Soc. Assn. Execs., World Affairs Coun. Washington, Ahepa (chmn. Cyprus and Hellenic affairs com. 1994—). Republican. Greek Orthodox. Avocations: reading history current events, baseball, entertainment industry, creative writing. Home: 41 Alexander St Alexandria VA 22314-3872 Office: Western Policy Ctr 1990 M St NW Ste 610 Washington DC 20036-3434

SITNYAKOVSKY, ROMAN EMMANUIL, scientist, writer, inventor, translator; b. Kiev, Ukraine, Jan. 5, 1934; came to U.S., 1988; s. Emmanuil I. and Yevgeniya N. (Glazova) S.; m. Bella Baram, Oct. 4, 1968 (div. Mar. 1992); 1 child, Art. MS in Mech. and Heat Engring., Polytech. Inst., Kiev, Ukraine, 1956; PhD in Heat Theory/Engring., USSR Acad. Scis., Minsk, Belarus, 1967. Project engr. Ural Turbomotor, Sverdlovsk, USSR, 1956-58; mech. engr. Engring Factory, Kiev, Ukraine, 1958-61; project engr. Design Inst., Ukraine, 1961-63; sr. engr. Heat and Mass Transfer Inst., Minsk, Belarus, 1963-68; prin. engr. Thermophysics Inst., Kiev, Ukraine, 1968-87; project engr. Hirt Combustion Engring., Montebello, Calif., 1989-90. Cons. Socio-Econ. Sys., L.A., 1988-93; translator, Kiev, 1979-87, L. A., 1988—. Author: I Disagree with Guberman, 1995, Chernobyl is our Fate, 2000, What is Love?, 2002, Mollify, not harass hearts, 2002; contbr. numerous articles to jours., newspapers and mags.; patentee in field. Achievements include over 90 inventions, scientific discovers of discreteness property of internal heat-mass transfer processes in three-phase media; wave nature of moisture transfer into wet bodies; resonances at heat-mass transfer in three phase media.

SITOMER, SHEILA MARIE, television producer, director; b. Hartford, Conn., Aug. 25, 1951; d. George W. and Mary E. (Chaponis) Bowe; m. Daniel J. Sitomer, Aug. 25, 1985. BA, Smith Coll., 1973. Field producer, dir. Good Morning Am., ABC-TV, N.Y.C., 1981-86; field producer Evening Magazine, WWOR-TV, KDKA-TV, Pitts. and Secaucus, N.J., 1978-79, 88; supervising producer The Reporters, Fox Broadcasting, N.Y.C., 1988; producer Inside Edition, King World Prodns., 1988-95; co-exec. prodr. Inside Edition and Am.

Jour., 1995-98; exec. prodr. Extra, 1998-2000; exec. prodr. program devel. ABC News, N.Y.C., 2000—. Recipient 3 Emmys, New England chpt. TV Acad. Arts & Scis., 1975-78, 2 Emmys, N.Y. chpt. TV Acad. Arts & Scis., 1979, 89, recipient first prize Internat. Film & TV Festival N.Y., 1988, No. N.J. Press Club award, 1988, George Polk award, Sigma Delta Chi award, IRE award Nat. Headliners. Mem. Dirs. Guild Am., Actors Equity Assn. Office: ABC News 47 W 66th St New York NY 10023 E-mail: sheila.sitomer@abc.com.

SITRIN, DAVID, retired government official, educator; b. N.Y.C., Aug. 26, 1929; s. Max and Esther Sitrin; m. Gloria Liftman, Nov. 2, 1958; children: Elliot John, Joel Bennett. BSS, CCNY, 1951; MPA, Syracuse U., 1952. Mgmt. intern N.Y. State Rent Commn., N.Y.C., 1954—55; budget analyst Dept. Navy, Washington, 1955—63; budget examiner Office Mgmt. and Budget, 1963—66, tactical Air Forces unit chief, 1966—69, br. chief, 1969—71, dep. chief Nat. Security Divsn., 1971—74, chief Nat. Security Divsn., 1974—87; budget analyst Fairfax (Va.) County Office Mgmt. and Budget, 1987—94. Adj. prof. Georgetown U., Washington, 1995—. Mem. B'nai Brith; vol. U.S. Holocaust Meml. Mus., Washington, 1996—, pres. vol. adv. bd., 1999-2000. Capt. U.S. Army, 1952-54, Korea. Recipient Scantlebury award U.S. Govt., 1981, Disting. Civilian Svc. medal Dept. Def., 1987. Home: 4203 Webster Ct Annandale VA 22003

SITRUK-WARE, RÉGINE, research organization executive, educator; b. Tunis, Tunisia, Sept. 2, 1947; d. Simon and Simone (Cohen) S.; m. Claude Max Ware, Jan. 29, 1976; children: Cedric, Leslie. MD, U. Paris, 1975; Reproductive Endocrinologist, Paris, 1979. Resident Paris U. Hosps., 1972-76; clin. chief Univ. Hosps., Paris, 1976-83, assoc. prof., 1983-87; exec. cons. Population Coun., N.Y.C., 1984-89; internat. med. adviser Ciba Geigy, Basle, Switzerland, 1987-89, head internat. med. affairs Switzerland, 1989-95; head R&D Theramex, Monte Carlo, Monaco, 1995-97; head dept. medicine & R & D Exelgyn Labs., Paris, 1997-2000; exec. dir. devel. Population Coun., N.Y.C., 2000—. Cons. endocrinology Univ. Hosp., Basle, 1987-95, U. Hosp. Stantoine, Paris, 1996—; adj. prof. Rockefeller U., N.Y.C., 2000—. Editor, author: Menopause, 1986; co-editor: (textbook) Reproductive Medicine, 1986; editor: (book) Hormonal Replacement Therapy, 1991, Contraception, 1992, Progestins, 2000; contbr. over 200 articles to profl. jours. Mem. Assn. for Contraception Rsch. (head 1984-94), Internat. Soc. for Menopause (exec. mem. 1978-81, 84-94, 96—), Endocrine Soc., N.Y. Acad. Scis., Am. Soc. Reproductive Medicine. Avocations: writing books, reading, caring about my children. Home: 10 River Rd Manhattan Pk # 20A New York NY 10044 Office: Ctr Biomed Rsch Pop Coun 1230 York Ave New York NY 10021-6307 E-mail: rsitrukware@popcbr.rockefeller.edu.

SITTON, CLAUDE FOX, newspaper editor; b. Emory, Ga., Dec. 4, 1925; s. Claude B. and Pauline (Fox) S.; m. Eva McLaurin Whetstone, June 5, 1953; children: Lea Sitton Stanley, Clinton, Suzanna Sitton Greene, McLaurin. AB, Emory U., 1949, L.H.D., 1984. Reporter Internat. News Service, 1949-50; with U.P., 1950-55, writer-editor, 1952-55; information officer USIA, 1955-57; mem. staff N.Y. Times, 1957-68, nat. news dir., 1964-68; editorial dir. The News and Observer Pub. Co., Raleigh, N.C., 1968-90, dir., 1969-90, v.p., 1970-90; editor News and Observer, 1970-90; sr. lectr. Emory U., Atlanta, 1991-94. Active Pulitzer Prize Bd., 1985-94, chmn., 1992-93; bd. counselors Oxford Coll. Emory U., 1993-2001. Lay mem. Commn. on Evaluation of Disciplinary Enforcement, Ga. Supreme Ct., 1995-96; mem. Ga. First Amendment Found. Bd., 1994-97. With USNR, 1943-46, PTO. Recipient Pulitzer prize for commentary, 1983 Mem. Am. Soc. Newspaper Editors (dir. 1977-83). Home: PO Box 1326 Oxford GA 30054-1326

SITTON, MICHAEL, musician, educator; b. Hendersonville, NC, July 15, 1958; s. Clifford McKinley Sitton, Wilma (Whitaker) Sitton; life ptnr. Mark Martin; children: Trista Martin, Joshua Martin. DMA, U. Ill., 1991; MM, U. Ky., 1982; BM, Mars Hill Coll., 1980; Diplome de concert, Schola Cantorum, Paris, 1983. Piano tchr. Conservatory Ctrl. Ill., Urbana, 1985—87; asst. prof. music Coker Coll., Hartsville, RI, 1987—91; assoc. prof. music Hollins U., Roanoke, Va., 1991—2002, prof. , chmn. dept. music, 2002—. Contract player keyboard Roanoke Symphony Orch., 1992—. Vestry mem. Christ Episcopal Ch., Roanoke, 1995—97; mem. Gay and Lesbian Voters' League, 1998—2002, Human Rights Campaign, Washington, 1998—2002. Mem.: ASCAP, The Leschetizky Assn., Assn. Anglican Musicians, Coll. Music Soc., Music Tchrs. Nat. Assn. (cert. 1992, Jr. High Performance Chair, Virginia 1994—2000). Democrat. Episcopalian. Office: Hollins Univ Dept Music PO Box 9581 Roanoke VA 24020 Office Fax: 540-362-6648. Business E-Mail: msitton@hollins.edu.

SIU, WANG-NGAI, solicitor; b. Hong Kong, Feb. 14, 1938; s. Man-Wan and Wai-Ying (Cheung) S.; m. Yuen-Ling April Lee. Grad., St. Francis Xavier's Coll., 1959, Coll. Law, London, 1967. Solicitor T.S. Tong & Co., Hong Kong, 1971-73, Chan & Ho, Hong Kong, 1973-77, Gallant Y.T. Ho & Co., Hong Kong, 1993—95. Chmn. Fedn. Hong Kong-Macau Photographic Assns., Hong Kong. Author: Chinese Opera: Images and Stories, 1997; Hong Kong Ballet, 2002. Royal Photographic Soc. Gt. Britain fellow, Bath, 1985, 89. Mem. Law Soc. Hong Kong, Soc. Notaries. Avocations: classical music, go. Office: Gallant Y T Ho & Co 4th Fl Jardine House 1 Connaught Pl Hong Kong China

SIV, SICHAN AUN, ambassador; b. Phnom Penh, Cambodia, Mar. 1, 1948; came to U.S., 1976; s. Chham and Aun (Chea) S.; m. Martha Pattillo, Dec. 24, 1983. Diplome du Professorat, U. Phnom Penh, Cambodia, 1972; B. en Droit, U. Phnom Penh, 1974, Lic. es Lettres, 1975; M. Internat. Affairs, Columbia U., 1981. Flight attendant Royal Air Cambodge, 1969-70; tchr. high sch. Phnom Penh, 1972-74; program assoc. Care-Cambodia, Phnom Penh, 1974-75; statistician Lower Eastside Svc. Ctr., N.Y.C., 1977-78; staff asst. Lutheran Immigration & Refugee Svc., 1978-80; mgmt. assoc. Marine Midland Bank, 1981-82; adminstr., fin. officer Episcopal Ch., 1982-83; UN rep. Cambodian Non Communist Resistance, 1983-87; Asia-Pacific mgr. Inst. Internat. Edn., 1987-89; dep. asst. to The Pres. for pub. liaison The White House, Washington, 1989—93; U.S. repr. to econ. and social coun. of U.N. U.S. Dept. State , 2001—. Office: US Mission to the UN 799 United Nations Plaza New York NY 10017-3505*

SIVAKUMAR, KRISHNAMOORTHY, educator; B in Tech., Indian Inst. Tech., Bombay, 1991; MSEE, Johns Hopkins U., 1993, MS in Math. Scis., 1995, PhD, 1997. Vis. prof. Tex. A&M U., College Station, 1997-98; asst. prof. Wash. State U., Pullman, 1998—. Mem. editl. bd. Jour. Math. Imaging and Vision, 1999—; contbr. articles to profl. jours. Abel Wolman fellow Johns Hopkins U., Balt., 1991. Mem. IEEE (reviewer tech. articles 1993—). Office: Sch EECS Wash State Univ Pullman WA 99164-0001 E-mail: siva@wsu.edu.

SIVAKUMARAN, KUMARASWAMY, civil engineer, consultant; b. Inuvil, Sri Lanka, May 29, 1952; came to U.S., 1986; s. Thambipillai and Theivanayaki (Selliah) K.; m. Muthumanimoli Pakkirisamy, June 24, 1982; children: Karthikgeyan, Sathiyan. BS in Civil Engring., U. Sri Lanka, Moratuwa, 1976; MS in Civil Engring., U. Newcastle-upon-Tyne, Eng., 1985; PhD in Civil Engring., Colo. State U., 1989; JD, W.Va. U., 2001. Bar: W.Va. 2002. Irrigation engr. Irrigation Dept., Colombo, Sri Lanka, 1977-80; design engr. Group Engring. Consulting, 1981; sr. project engr. Samek Constrn. Co. Ltd., Aba, Nigeria, 1981-84; rsch. asst. Colo. State U., Ft. Collins, 1986-89; guest scientist GKSS Rsch. Ctr., Geesthacht, Germany, 1990-91; assoc., sr. water resources engr. TAMS Consultants, Inc., N.Y.C., 1991—. Adj. asst. prof. West Va. U., Morgantown, 1998—; pres. Sterling Legal Svcs., PLLC. Travel grantee Am. Pub. Works Assn., 1986. Mem. ASCE, U.S. Com. on Large Dams. Home: 154 Edgewood Dr Weston WV 26452-8540 Office: Earthtech 655 3d Ave New York NY 10017 E-mail: kumarsivakumaran@aol.com.

SIVAPRASAD, KONDAGUNTA N. electrical engineering educator; b. Madras, Tamilnadu, India, Mar. 3, 1935; s. Kondagunta and Venkaasubbu alladi Umamaheswaram; married, Dec. 15, 1966; 1 child, Rahul. PhD, Harvard U., 1963. Rsch. physicist AF Labs at Hanscon, Bedford, Mass., 1963-65; asst. prof. Indian Inst. Tech., Madras, 1965-68; lectr., postdoctoral fellow U. Houston, 1968-69; prof. elec. engring. U. N.H., Durham, 1969—. Cons. in field. Contbr. articles to profl. jours. Fulbright fellow NRC, 1997-98. Mem. IEEE (sr.). Home: 10F W Hartford Dr Portsmouth NH 03801-5824 Office: U NH Kingsbury Hall Durham NH 03824

SIVARAMAN, SMITHA, biochemist; b. Bombay, June 3, 1968; came to U.S., 1997; d. Sivaraman K. P. Pillai and Susheela Sivaraman Pillai; m. Charuhas G. Deshpande, Nov. 21, 2000. BSc, U. Bombay, 1988, MSc, 1990, PhD, 1996. Rsch. assoc. Nat. Ctr. Cell Scis., Poona, India, 1996-97, Tata Meml. Hosp., Bombay, 1997; scientist, lab mgr. Rush Cancer Inst., Chgo., 1997—. Recipient R. K. Anjaria Meml. award Seth G. S. Med. Coll. & King Edward Hosp., 1990. Mem. Am. Soc. Hematology, Internat. Soc. Hematology, Am. Assn. Cancer Rsch. (assoc.), Women Cancer Rsch. Avocations: reading, music, travel. Office: Rush Cancer Inst 2242 W Harrison St Ste 109 Chicago IL 60612 Office Fax: 312-563-4533. E-mail: smitha_sivaraman@rsh.net.

SIVCO, DEBORAH LEE, research materials scientist; b. Somerville, N.J., Dec. 21, 1957; d. Lawrence M. Skurkay and Elizabeth J. McCulla; m. Gregory Charles Sivco, July 11, 1981; children: Scott Gregory, Michelle Elizabeth, Carolyn Suzanne, David Charles. BA in chem. edn., Rutgers Univ., 1980; MS in material sci., Stevens Inst., 1988. III-V processing tech. Laser Diode Labs, New Brunswick, N.J., 1980-81; materials scientist Bell Labs. Lucent Technologies, Murray Hill, 1981—. Contbr. articles to profl. jours.; 15 patents in field. Recipient Newcomb Cleveland prize AAAS, 1993-94, Electronics Letters premium Instn. Elec. Engrs. U.K., 1995, Group Achievement award NASA, 2000. Office: Bell Labs Lucent Technologies 600 Mountain Ave New Providence NJ 07974-2008 E-mail: dls@lucent.com.

SIVE, REBECCA ANNE, public affairs company executive; b. N.Y.C., Jan. 29, 1950; d. David and Mary (Robinson) S.; m. Clark Steven Tomashefsky, June 18, 1972. BA, Carleton Coll., 1972; MA in Am. History, U. Ill., Chgo., 1975. Asst. to chmn. of pres.' task force on vocations Carleton Coll., Northfield, Minn., 1972; asst. to acquisitions librarian Am. Hosp. Assn., Chgo., 1973; rsch. asst. Jane Addams Hull House, 1974; instr. Loop Coll., 1975, Columbia Coll., Chgo., 1975-76; cons. Am. Jewish Com., 1975, Ctr. for Urban Affairs, Northwestern U., Evanston, Ill., 1977, Ill. Consultation on Ethnicity in Edn., 1976, MLA, 1977; dir. Ill. Women's History Project, 1975-76; founder, exec. dir. Midwest Women's Ctr., Chgo., 1977-81; exec. dir. Playboy Found., 1981-84; v.p. pub. affairs/pub. rels. Playboy Video Corp., 1985; v.p. pub. affairs Playboy Enterprises, Inc., Chgo., 1985-86; pres. The Sive Group, Inc., 1986—. Guest speaker various ednl. orgns., 1972— ; instr. Roosevelt U., Chgo., 1977-78; dir. spl. projects Inst. on Pluralism and Group Identity, Am. Jewish Com., Chgo., 1975-77; cons. Nat. Women's Polit. Caucus, 1978-80; bd. dirs. NOVA Health Systems, Woodlawn Community Devel. Corp.; trainer Midwest Acad.; mem. adv. bd. urban studies program Associated Colls. Midwest; proposal reviewer NEH Contbr. articles to profl. jours. Commr. Chgo. Park Dist., 1986-88; mem. steering com. Ill. Commn. on Human Rels., 1976; mem. structure com. Nat. Women's Agenda Coalition, 1976-77; del.-at-large Nat. Women's conf., 1977; mem. Ill. Gov.'s Com. on Displaced Homemakers, 1979-81, Ill. Human Rights Com., 1980-87, Ill. coordinating com., Internat. Womens Yr.; coord. Ill. Bicentennial Photog. Exhbn., 1977; mem. Ill. Employment and Tng. Coun.; mem. employment com. Ill. Com. on Status of Women; bd. dirs. Nat. Abortion Rights Action League and NARAL Found., Ill. div. ACLU, Midwest Women's Ctr. Recipient award for outstanding community leadership YWCA Met. Chgo., 1979, award for outstanding community leadership Chgo. Jaycees, 1988. Home: 1235 N Astor St Apt 3N Chicago IL 60610-5213 Office: The Sive Group Inc 1235 N Astor St Chicago IL 60610-5213

SIVERD, ROBERT JOSEPH, lawyer; b. July 27, 1948; s. Clifford David and Elizabeth Ann (Klink) S.; m. Bonita Marie Shulock, Jan. 8, 1972; children: Robert J. Jr., Veronica Leigh. AB in French, Georgetown U., 1970, JD, 1973; postgrad., The Sorbonne, Paris, 1969. Bar: N.Y. 1974, U.S. Dist. Ct. (so. and ea. dists.) N.Y. 1974, U.S. Ct. Appeals (2d cir.) 1974, U.S. Supreme Ct. 1980, U.S. Dist. Ct. (ea. dist.) Pa. 1984, U.S. Ct. Appeals (3d cir.) 1984, U.S. Ct. Appeals (6th cir.) 1985, Ohio 1991, Ky. 1992. Assoc. Donovan Leisure Newton & Irvine, N.Y.C., 1973-83; staff v.p., litigation counsel Am. Fin. Group, Inc., Greenwich, Conn., 1983-85, v.p. litigation counsel, 1986-87, v.p. assoc. gen. counsel Cin., 1987-92; sr. v.p., gen. counsel and sec. Gen. Cable Corp., 1992-94, exec. v.p., gen. counsel and sec., 1994—. Mem. ABA, Assn. of Bar of City of N.Y., Ky. Bar Assn. Republican. Office: Gen Cable Corp 4 Tesseneer Dr Newport KY 41076-9167

SIVERS, DENNIS WAYNE, physicist, real estate developer; b. Greeley, Colo., Jan. 20, 1944; s. Wendell Clifford and Elizabeth Elvera Sivers; m. Penny Kathleen Welch, June 18, 1966 (div. Aug. 1980); m. E. Anne Crider, June 3, 1985; children: Derek, Heidi. BS in Physics, MIT, 1966; PhD in Theoretical Physics, U. Calif., Berkeley, 1970. Physicist Argonne (Ill.) Nat. Lab., 1976-91; physicist Portland (Oreg.) Physics Inst., 1991—; pres./CEO Sivers Cos., Portland, 1986—. Adj. prof. U. Mich., 1997—. Contbr. articles to profl. jours. Fellow Am. Phys. Soc., Nat. Assn. Indsl. & Office Properties (nat. forum 1993—). Achievements include research in seminal calculations in perturbative quantum chromodynamics. Office: Portland Physics Inst 4730 SW Macadam Ave Portland OR 97201-6417 E-mail: densivers@sivers.com.

SIVERTSEN, LINDA JOYCE, writer, publishing consultant, editor; b. Stanford, Calif., Aug. 31, 1964; d. Alfred Eugene and Joanne Rose Tisch; m. Mark Duanne Sivertsen, Sept. 10, 1988; 1 child Tosh. Student, U. So. Calif., 1984—87. Life coach, L.A., 1987—89; owner pet sitting bus. Beverly Hills, 1989—94; cons. writing, nat. and internat., 1995—; author Health Comms., Deerfield Beach, Fla., 1998—; west coast editor Living in Balance Mag., Ft. Lauderdale, 2002—. Book proposal writer Illiani Co., L.A., 1999—; ghostwriter Jodere Pub. Group, San Diego, 2001, individuals, 2001—; spkr. in field; tchr. Learning Annex, L.A., 2001—02. Author: Lives Charmed: Intimate Conversations with Extraordinary People, 1998 (Earth Island Jour. award, 2000); contbr. columns in newspapers. Mem.: Nat. Assn. Women Bus. Owners, Delta Gamma (life). Avocations: tennis, gardening, hiking, painting, reading. Office: ILLIANI Co PO Box 41 1893 Los Angeles CA 90041

SIVITZ, WILLIAM IRVING, endocrinologist; b. Pitts., Aug. 17, 1945; MD, Hahnemann U., 1972. Clin. instr. Tufts U., Boston, 1977-80; asst. prof. endocrinology Marshall U., Huntington, W.Va., 1980-84, assoc. prof. endocrinology, 1984-85; assoc. med. dir. Shallowford Cmty. Hosp., Atlanta, 1985-87; assoc. in endocrine and metabolism U. Iowa Coll. Medicine, Iowa City, 1987-89, asst. prof. in endocrinology, 1989-91, assoc. prof. in endocrinology, 1993-2001, prof. endocrinology, 2001—. Recipient Hardin award for Outstanding Diabetes Health Care Profl., Am. Diabetes Assn., 1995, VA Merit grant VA Med. Ctr., NIH grant support. Office: U of Iowa Hosp 3E-17 Va Iowa City IA 52246

SIVOLI-KRAMER, DIANNE, management analyst, social worker; b. Kenosha, Wis., Dec. 28, 1958; d. Frank Phillip and Dusanka Rita (Hirsch) Sivoli; m. Thomas Matthew Kramer, May 23, 1996. BA in Sociology, U. Nev., Las Vegas, 1992, B of Social Work, 1994, MSW, 1998. Cashier supr. Tropicana Hotel, Las Vegas, Nev., 1986-90; cons. Clark County Dept. Family & Youth Svcs., 1992—, mgmt. analyst, 1995—. Com. mem. family advocates for cmty. empowerment, Las Vegas, 1996. Exemplery prog. award Ctr. for Substance Abuse, Nat. Assn. Substance Abuse & Drug Abuse, Washington, 1997. Mem. NASW. Democrat. Avocations: reading, gardening, swimming, yoga, needlepoint. Office: Clark County Family & Youth Svcs 601 N Pecos Rd Las Vegas NV 89101-2408

SIVY, MICHAEL, journalist; b. N.Y.C., May 30, 1953; s. Michael and Mary Frances (Waller) S. BA, Columbia U., 1974, MA, 1977. Chartered fin. analyst. Journalist Time, Inc., N.Y.C., 1985—. Author: Michael Sivy's Rules of Investing, 1996. Mem. N.Y. Soc. Security Analysts, Assn. Investment Mgmt. and Rsch. Office: Money Edit Rm 32-10 1271 Ave of Americas New York NY 10020

SIX, FRED N. state supreme court justice; b. Independence, Mo., Apr. 20, 1929; AB, U. Kans., 1951, JD with honors, 1956; LLM in Judicial Process, U. Va., 1990. Bar: Kans. 1956. Asst. atty. gen. State of Kans., 1957-58; pvt. practice Lawrence, Kans., 1958-87; judge Kans. Ct. Appeals, 1987-88; justice Kans. Supreme Ct., Topeka, 1988—. Editor-in-chief U. Kans. Law Review, 1955-56; lectr. on law Washburn U. Sch. Law, 1957-58, U. Kans., 1975-76. Served with USMC, 1951-53; USMCR, 1957-62. Recipient Disting. Alumnus award, U. Kans. Sch. Law, 1994, Disting. Alumni Achievement award, U. Kans. Coll. Liberal Arts and Sci., 2000—01. Fellow Am. Bar Found. (chmn. Kans. chpt. 1983-87); mem. ABA (jud. adminstrn. divsn.), Am. Judicature Soc., Kans. Bar Assn., Kans. Bar Found., Kans. Law Soc. (pres. 1970-72), Kans. Inn of Ct. (pres. 1993-94), Order of Coif, Phi Delta Phi. Office: Kans Supreme Ct 374 Kansas JudICIAL Center 301 SW 10th Ave Topeka KS 66612-1502 E-mail: fsix@kscourts.org.

SIYAN, KARANJIT SAINT GERMAIN SINGH, software engineer; b. Mauranipur, India, Oct. 16, 1954; came to U.S., 1978; s. Ahal Singh and Tejinder Kaur (Virdi) S. B in Tech. Electronics, Indian Inst. Tech., 1976, M in Tech. Computer Sci., 1978; MS in Engring., U. Calif., Berkeley, 1980; PhD of Computer Sci., Kennedy-Western U., Berkeley, 1994. Cert. enterprise netware engr.; cert. microsoft profl.; cert. master novell engr. Sr. mem. tech. staff Rolm Corp., San Jose, Calif., 1980-84; cons. Siyan Cons. Svcs., L.A., 1985-86, Emigrant, Mont., 1987—. Author, sr. instr. Learning Tree Internat., 1985—; author: Internet Firewalls and Network Security, Inside Java, Inside TCP/IP, Inside Active Dir. Svcs., Inside TCP/IP for Windows NT, Inside Visual J++ Netware-The Professional Reference, Windows NT Server: The Professional Reference, Netware Training Guide-Network 4 Update, Building Intranets with Netware Web Server, Netware Training Guide-Network 4 Update, Netware 4 Training Guide-Netware 4 Adminstration, CNE Training Guide-TCP/IP and NFS, Internetworking with Netware TCP/IP; co-author: Downsizing Netware, Implementing Internet Security, LAN Connectivity, Netware 4 for Professionals, Banyan Vines-The Professional Reference; author seminars on Novell Networking, TCP/IP Networks, Windows NT, Solaris-PC Network Integration. Mem. IEEE, Assn. for Computing Machinery, Enterprise, Network Profl. Assn., Kappa Omicron Phi.

SIZE, DENNIS MICHAEL, lighting and scenery designer; b. Scranton, Pa., Oct. 25, 1955; s. Michael Joseph and Virginia Mae (Nicholoff) S.; m. Patti McCormick; 1 child, Amanda Madison. BA in English, BA in Communications, U. Scranton, 1976; postgrad., Pa. State U., State Coll., 1976-79. Design Sta. WVIA-TV, Pittston, Pa., 1973-75; lighting designer White Birch Dinner Theater Co., Dalton, 1975-76; shop supr. dept. theater and film Pa. State U., State College, 1978-79; instr. theater design and prodn. U. Scranton, 1979-80; instr. theater Pa. State U., Scranton, 1980; lighting designer Disney/ABC-TV, N.Y.C., 1980-97; sr. lighting designer Lighting Design Gp., 1997—. Condr. master classes in lighting design for various colls., schs. and profl groups. Lighting designer numerous TV shows including All My Children, One Life To Live, Ryans Hope, As The World Turns, Oprah Winfrey Show, Ananda Lewis Show, Montel Williams Show, Dr. Joy Brown, Martha Stewart Living, Dick Clark's Rockin' New Year's Eve, Live With Regis & Kathie Lee, Gayle King Show, Good Morning America, several presidential convs., ABC Monday Night Football, Loving, 20/20; theatrical credits include Henhouse, My Old Friends with Imogene Coca, Ferocious Kisses, Dancing at Lughnasa; scenery designer: Peg O' My Heart, A Christmas Carol, The Time of Your Life, Philadelphia, Here I Come; columnist for TV Technology, 1984-85. Recipient Silver Screen award, Monitor award Internat. Teleproduction Soc., 1985, nomination, 1986, Emmy award nominations (6), Emmy award, 1989, 99, Axiem award, 1999-01. Mem. United Scenic Artists, Internat. Alliance Theatrical Stage Employees, Nat. Assn. Broadcast Employees and Technicians, Nat. Acad. TV Arts and Scis., Illuminating Engring. Soc., Soc. Motion Picture and TV Engrs., U.S. Inst. Theater Tech., Irish Am. Cultural Inst., Am. Film Inst., Internat. Assn. Lighting Designers. Roman Catholic. Avocations: architecture, photography, piano, dancing, fgn. traveling. Home: 163 Amsterdam Ave # 347 New York NY 10023-5001 Fax: 718-416-1964. E-mail: size@ldq.com.

SIZEMORE, BARBARA ANN, Black studies educator; b. Chgo., Dec. 17, 1927; d. Sylvester Walter Laffoon and Delila Mae (Alexander) Stewart; m. Furman E. Sizemore, June 28, 1947 (div. Oct. 1964); children: Kymara, Furman G.; m. Jake Milliones, Sept. 29, 1979 (div. Feb. 1992). BA, Northwestern U., 1947, MA, 1954; PhD, U. Chgo., 1979; LLD (hon.), Del. State Coll., 1974; LittD (hon.), Cen. State U., 1974; DHL (hon.), Bal. Coll. of Bible, 1975; D of Pedagogy (hon.), Niagara U., 1994. Tchr., prin., dir. Chgo. Pub. Schs., 1947-72; assoc. sec. Am. Assn. Sch. Adminstrs., Arlington, Va., 1972-73; supt. schs. D.C. Pub. Schs., Washington, 1973-75; ednl. cons. Washington and Pitts., 1975—; prof. Black studies U. Pitts., 1977-92; dean Sch. of Edn. DePaul U., Chgo., 1992-98, prof. emeritus Sch. Edn., 1998—. Author: The Ruptured Diamond, 1981; bd. mem. Jour. Negro Edn., 1974-83, Rev. Edn., 1977-85. Candidate city coun. Washington, 1977; mem. NAACP. Recipient Merit award Northwestern U. Alumni Assn., 1974, Excellence award Nat. Alliance Black Sch. Educators, 1984, Human Rights award UN Assn., 1985, Racial Justice award YMCA, 1995; named to U.S. Nat. Com., UNESCO, 1974-77. Mem. Nat. Coun. for Black Studies, African Heritage Studies Assn. (bd. mem. 1972—), Nat. Alliance Black Sch. Educators, Delta Sigma Theta. Democrat. Baptist. Avocations: reading, writing. Fax: 773-528-4485. E-mail: bsizemor@depaul.edu.

SIZEMORE, DEBORAH LIGHTFOOT, writer, editor; b. Lamesa, Tex., Mar. 18, 1956; d. Glenn Billy and Francis Earlene (Cable) Lightfoot; m. O.E. Gene Sizemore, June 19, 1981. BS in Agrl. Journalism summa cum laude, Tex. A&M U., 1977. Writer Tex. Agrl. Extension, College Station, 1976-77; copy editor Abilene (Tex.) Reporter-News, 1978; customer svc. rep. Motheral Printing Co., Ft. Worth, 1978-79; prodn. coord. Graphic Arts, Inc., 1980-81; writer, editor Crowley, Tex., 1981—; freelance writer, editor Boy Scouts Am., Irving, 1981—. Author: Your Future with the BSA, 1989, The LH7 Ranch, 1991, 2000, Trail Fever, 1992, co-author: (with Simon W. Freese) A Century in the Works, 1994; contbg. writer New Handbook of Texas, 1996; contbg. editor Dairymen's Digest, Arlington, Tex., 1981-89, 95-97, Longhorn Scene, Ft. Worth, 1982-84, Lone Star Horse Report, Ft. Worth, 1985-86; acting assoc. editor Boy's Life mag., Boy Scouts Am., 1995; writer, photographer Harvest Times, Dallas, 1983-84, Simbrah World, Ft. Worth, 1985-87; contbr. photographs to mags.; contbr. articles to mags. Women's issues chmn., v.p. membership, pub. info. officer, newsletter editor, yearbook editor AAUW of Tarrant County, 1981-86, 90-92, vice chmn. devel. com. Friends of Ft. Worth Pub. Lib., 1991-93, bd. mem., 1994-97, v.p. 1995-97. Recipient Sr. Merit award in Agrl. Journalism Tex. A&M U., 1978, Thomas S. Gathright Acad. Excellence award, 1976, Cert. of Merit Livestock Publs. Coun., 1984, 86, 2d place Nonfiction Book award Tex.-Wide Writers' Competition, 1988, 89, Publication awards San Antonio Conservation Soc., 1993, History and Heritage award Tex. sect. Am. Soc. Civil Engrs., 1997. Mem. Authors Guild, Soc. Children's Book Writers and Illustrators (publicity dir. North Ctrl. Tex. chpt. 1991-92, program dir. 1994-95), Sci. Fiction and Fantasy Workshop, Tex. Folklore Soc., Phi Kappa Phi, Gamma Sigma Delta. Office: PO Box 682 Crowley TX 76036-0682 E-mail: djls@compuserve.com.

SIZEMORE, NICKY LEE, computer scientist; b. N.Y.C., Feb. 13, 1946; s. Ralph Lee and Edith Ann (Wangler) S.; m. Frauke Julika Hoffmann, Oct. 31, 1974; 1 child, Jennifer Lee Sizemore; 1 stepchild, Mark Anthony Miracle. BS in Computer Sci., SUNY, 1989. Sgt. first class U.S. Army, 1964-68, 70-86; computer operator UNIVAC, Washington, 1968-69, programmer, 1969-70; programmer/analyst Ultra Systems, Inc., Sierra Vista, Ariz., 1986-87; computer scientist Comarco, Inc., 1987-92, ARC, Profl. Svcs. Group, Sierra Vista, 1992-93, Computer Scis. Corp., Ft. Huachuca, Ariz., 1994; sr. cons. Inference Corp., 1995; subject matter expert Northrop Corp., Sierra Vista, Ariz., 1995—; sr. info. sys. engr. Harris Corp., 1996—2001, EWA Svcs., Inc., Ft. Huachaca, 2002—. Speaker numerous confs., seminars, symposia; tech. columnist Sierra vista Herald. Mem.: IEEE, IEEE Computer Soc., Assn. Computing Machinery, Am. Assn. Artificial Intelligence (co-dir. workshop on verification, validation and test of knowledge-based sys. 1988). Avocations: chess, jogging/aerobics, karate. Home: 880 E Charles Dr Sierra Vista AZ 85635-1611

SIZEMORE, R. TOM, III, military officer, hospital administrator; b. Clay, W.Va. BS, U.S.Naval Acad., 1972; MD, W.Va. U., 1977. Lic. Calif., 1981. Commd. USN, 1972, advanced through grades to capt.; intern Naval Hosp., Oakland, Calif., 1977—78, resident in ophthalmology San iego, 1978—81, ophthalmologist, exec. officer NC, Phila., commdg. officer, Annapolis, Md.; fleet med. officer to comdr. in chief U.S. Naval Forces, Europe, 1998—2000; dep. comdr. Nat. Naval Med. Ctr., Bethesda, Md., 2000—. Decorated Legion of Merit (3), Meritorious Svc. medal, Def. Meritorious Svc. medal, Nat. Def. medal (2), NATO Svc. medal, numerous others. Fellow: Am. Acad. Ophthalmology, Am. Bd. Ophthalmology; mem.: Am. Coll. Physician Execs., Am. Coll. Healthcare Execs. (assoc.). Office: National Naval Med Ctr 8901 Wisconsin Ave Bethesda MD 20889-5600*

SIZEMORE, ROBERT CARLEN, immunologist, educator; b. Lexington, Ky., Sept. 30, 1951; s. Dewey and Juanita (Peel) S.; m. Katherine Killelea, Sept. 29, 1990; children: Katherine Peel, Robert Carlen Jr. BS, U. Ky., 1973, MS, 1975; PhD, U. Louisville, 1982. Postdoctoral rsch. assoc. U. Miss. Med. Ctr., Jackson, 1982-84; dir. immunology IMREG, Inc., New Orleans, 1984-94; adj. asst. prof. Tulane U. Sch. Medicine, 1985-99, asst. prof., 1994-96; assoc. prof. Alcorn State U., 1996—. Patentee in field; contbr. articles to profl. jours. Performer Alcorn State Jazz Ensemble. Recipient Project award U. Louisville, 1978, Grad. Dean's Citation U. Louisville, 1983; named Outstanding Young Men of Am., 1984. Mem. Am. Assn. Immunologists, Internat. AIDS Soc., Internat. Soc. Devel. and Comparative Immunology, Psychoneuroimmunology Rsch. Soc. Avocations: music, composing, photography, travel, writing poetry and short stories (published author). Home: 819 Washington St Natchez MS 39120-3565 Office: 1000 Alcorn Dr # 870 Alcorn State MS 39096-7510 E-mail: sizemore@lorman.alcorn.edu.

SIZEMORE, WILLIAM HOWARD, JR. journalist; b. South Boston, Va., Dec. 18, 1948; s. W. Howard and Genevieve T. (Walton) S.; m. Mary K. Lamont, Jan. 29, 1972; children: Justin, Jennifer, Julie. BA in Philosophy, Coll. William and Mary, 1971. Editor The Clarksville (Va.) Times, 1972-75; reporter The Roanoke (Va.) Times, 1975-76, The Times-Herald, Newport News, Va., 1976-81; editor, pub. The York Town Crier, Yorktown, 1981-88; copy editor The Ledger-Star, Norfolk, 1982-89, news editor, 1989-95; writer, editor The Virginian-Pilot, 1995—. Recipient various Journalism awards Va. Press Assn., 1972-2002. Avocations: tennis, music, bicycling, camping. Home: 4704 Yarrow Ct Williamsburg VA 23188-2427 Office: Virginian-Pilot 150 W Brambleton Ave Norfolk VA 23510-2075 E-mail: size@pilotonline.com.

SIZEMORE, WILLIAM CHRISTIAN, academic administrator; b. South Boston, Va., June 19, 1938; s. Herman Mason and Hazel (Johnson) S.; m. Anne Catherine Mills, June 24, 1961; children: Robert C., Richard M., Edward S. BA, U. Richmond, 1960; BD, Southeastern Bapt. Theol. Sem., Wake Forest, N.C., 1963; MLS, U. N.C., 1964; MLS (advanced), Fla. State U., 1971, PhD, 1973; postgrad., Harvard U., 1989. Library asst. U. N.C., Chapel Hill, 1963-64; assoc. librarian, instr. grad. research Southeastern Bapt. Theol. Sem., 1964-66; librarian, assoc. prof. South Ga. Coll., Douglas, 1966-71, acad. dean, prof., 1971-80, dean coll., prof., 1980-83, acting pres., 1982-83; pres. Alderson-Broaddus Coll., Philippi, W.Va., 1983-94, William Jewell Coll., Liberty, Mo., 1994-2000, chancellor, 2000—. Cons. Continental R&D, Shawnee Mission, Kans., 1987-92, So. Assn. Colls. and Schs., Atlanta, 1977, S.C. Commn. on Higher Edn., Columbia, 1975-76, State Coun. Higher Edn. for Va., Richmond, 1969-70, Software Valley Corp., 1989-94; adv. bd. Software Valley Found., 1991-94. Contbr. articles to profl. jours. Active Barbour County Devel. Authority, Philippi, 1984-94, Barbour County Emergency Food and Shelter Bd., 1985-94, Barbour County Extension Com., 1990-94; mem. exec. coun. Yellow Pine area Boy Scouts Am., Valdosta, 1974-76; pres. Satilla Librarians Ednl. Coun., Douglas, 1969-71; lectr., workshop leader on Bible studies various orgns., 1966—; bd. advisors Swatow Kakwang Profl. Acad., Peoples Republic China; pres. bd. dirs. W.Va. Intercollegiate Athletic Conf., 1985-86, coun. of pres. Nat. Assn. Intercollegiate Athletics; bd. dirs., mem. exec. com. Broaddus Hosp., Philippi, 1983-94; chmn. W.Va. Productive Industry Efforts Found., 1989-92; mktg. com. W.Va. Life Scis. Park Found., 1989-94, Gov.'s Partnership for Progress, 1989-94; mem. adv. panel W.Va. Rural Health Initiative, 1991-94; gov. bd., bd. dirs. W.Va. Alliance of Hosps., 1991-94; bd. dirs. Clay-Platte Econ. Devel. Coun., 1996—; exec. com. Am. Red Cross, Kansas City, 2000—; adv. com. Mo. Conservation Heritage Found. Discovery Ctr. Campaign, 1998—. Joseph Ruzicka scholar N.C. Library Assn., 1963; recipient Douglas Pilot Club Edn. award, 1981, Good Citizenship medal Nat. Soc. Sons of Am. Revolution, 1999. Mem. ALA, Am. Assn. for Higher Edn., Am. Assn. Univ. Adminstrs., Nat. Coun. Instrnl. Adminstrs., W.Va. Assn. Coll. and Univ. Pres. (exec. com., v.p., pres. 1992), Mountain State Assn. Colls., W.Va. Found. for Ind. Colls. (dir. 1983-84, v.p. 1988-92), Mo. Colls. Fund (exec. com. 1997-98), Barbour County C. of C. (bd. dirs. 1988-94, v.p. 1988-90, pres. 1990-92, chmn. bd. 1992-94), Liberty Area C. of C. (bd. dirs. 1995-97), Kansas City Club. Democrat. Baptist. Avocations: woodworking, gardening. Home: 1417 Woodbury Dr Liberty MO 64068-1266 Office: William Jewell Coll Office of the Chancellor 500 College Hl Liberty MO 64068-1843

SIZER, PHILLIP SPELMAN, consultant, retired oil field services executive; b. Whittier, Calif., Apr. 11, 1926; s. Frank Milton and Helen Louise (Saylor) S.; m. Evelyn Sue Jones, Aug. 16, 1952; children: Phillip Spelman Jr., Ves Warner. BSME, So. Meth. U., 1948. Registered profl. engr., Tex. With Otis Engring. Corp., Dallas, 1948-91, project engr., 1958-62, chief devel. engr., 1962-70, v.p. R & D, 1970-73, v.p. engring. and rsch., 1973-76, sr. v.p., tech. dir., 1977-91, bd. dirs., 1975-91; pres. Sizer Engring. Inc., 1992—; prin. Crawford-Sizer Devel. Co., 1996—. Bd. dirs. DHV Internat., Inc.; cons. in field; mem. exec. com. Offshore Tech. Conf., 1976-79. Patentee in field Mem. U. Tex. Mech. Engring. Dept. Vis. Com., 1977-83. Named to Hall of Achievement Coll. Engring., U. Tex., Arlington, 1983 Fellow ASME (chmn. exec. com. petroleum divsn. 1974-75, SPPE-1 chmn. main com. 1981-88, Engr. of Yr. award North Tex. sect. 1971, centennial medal 1980, OILDROP award petroleum divsn. 1982, Dedicated Svc. award 1985, Silver Patent award 1990, region x Clifford H. Shumaker award 1993); mem. Soc. Petroleum Engrs., S.W. Rsch. Inst. (trustee 1982—), Assn. Wellhead Eq. Mfrs. (pres. 1996), Petroleum Engrs. Club of Dallas, Rotary Internat., Kappa Sigma, Tau Beta Pi, Kappa Mu Epsilon. Home: 14127 Tanglewood Dr Dallas TX 75234-3851 E-mail: sizer26@attbi.com.

SIZER, REBECCA RUDD, performing arts educator, arts coordinator; b. Melrose, Mass., July 28, 1958; d. David William and Harriet Fay (Sart) Rudd; m. Theodore Sizer II, June 21, 1980; children: Caroline Foster, Lydia Catherine Rachel, Theodore Rudd. AB, Mount Holyoke Coll., 1980; MFA, Rochester Inst. Tech., 1983; postgrad., Eastman and Westminster Choir Coll. Cert. tchr. music and art K-12, N.J. Dir. music Christian Bros. Acad., Lincroft, N.J., 1991-93, Peddie Sch., Hightstown, 1993-94; chair dept. fine and performing arts, arts curriculum coord. Ranney Sch., Tinton Falls, 1994-97; tchr. music N.J. Ctr. for Performing Arts, 1997; tchr. music elem. schs. Lakewood Sch. Dist., N.J., 1997—; dir. music Christ Ch. United Meth., 1997—. Dir. after sch. art program Upstairs Youth Agy., Rochester, N.Y., 1984-85; music dir. Peninsula Opera Rep. Co., Rumson, N.J., 1986-88, local music. theatre, Red Bank, N.J., 1986—; freelance artist, musician. Illustrator: (books) China: A Brief History, 1981, Making Decisions, 1983. Joseph A. Skinner fellow Mt. Holyoke Coll., 1981, Dodge fellow Geraldine R. Dodge Found., 1993. Mem. Music Educators Nat. Conf., Local 399 Musicians Union. Avocation: tennis. Home: 385 Branch Ave Little Silver NJ 07739-1102

SJOERDSMA, ALBERT, research institute executive; b. Lansing, Ill., Aug. 31, 1924; s. Sam and Agnes S.; m. Fern E. MacAllister, Dec. 2, 1950; children— Leslie, Ann, Albert, Britt. Ph.B., U. Chgo., 1944, BS, 1945, PhD, 1948, MD, 1949. Research asst. U. Chgo., 1947-49, NIH postdoctoral research fellow, 1950; intern U. Mich. Hosp., Ann Arbor, 1949-50; resident physician Michael Reese Hosp., Chgo., 1951; resident in internal medicine USPHS Hosp., Balt., 1951-53; sr. investigator, chief exptl. therapeutics br. Nat. Heart and Lung Inst., Bethesda, Md., 1953-71; v.p. Merrell Internat. Co., Strasbourg, France, 1971-78; v.p. pharm. research and devel. Richardson-Merrell Inc., 1978-81; v.p. pharm. research Merrell Dow Pharms., Cin., 1981-83; pres. Merrell Dow Research Inst., 1983-89, pres. emeritus, 1989-94; med. scis. cons., 1994—. Vis. spl. fellow Gen. Hosp., Malmo, Sweden, 1959-60; spl. lectr. George Washington U., 1959-71; Anton Julius Carlson lectr. U. Chgo., 1984; hon. chmn. 2d World Conf. on Clin. Pharmacology and Therapeutics, Washington, 1983; clin. prof. medicine U. Cin. Med. Ctr., 1986-91. Mem. AAAS (Theobold Smith award med. scis. 1958), Am. Soc. Pharm. and Exptl. Therapeutics (Harry Gold award in clin. pharmacology 1977, Exptl. Therapeutics award 1990), Am. Soc. Clin. Pharmacology and Therapeutics (Oscar B. Hunter Meml. award in therapeutics 1981), Internat. Soc. Hypertension, Coun. High Blood Pressure Rsch., Am. Heart Assn., Am. Fedn. Clin. Rsch., Am. Soc. Clin. Investigation, Am. Soc. Exptl. Biology and Medicine, Assn. Am. Physicians, Am. Coll. Neuropsychopharmacology. Home and Office: 263 N Dogwood Trail Kitty Hawk NC 27949-3138

SJOGREN, DONALD ERNEST, farmer; b. Holdrege, Nebr., Jan. 3, 1932; s. Ernest V. and Ellen M. (Peterson) S. AA, Luther Jr. Coll., Wahoo, Nebr., 1951; BS in Agr., U. Nebr., Lincoln, 1953. Owner, farmer, Funk, Nebr., 1954—. Bd. dirs Nebr. Corn Devel. Utilization and Mktg. bd., Phelps Co. Livestock Feeders, 1975-78. Mem. Ch. Coun., 1962-65, 69-72, 75-78, 89-92, ch. coun., 1995-98; active Rep. Nat. Com., Washington, 1978—; bd. dirs. Phelps County Farm Bur., 1985-95, pres., 1989-91; mem. Phelps County Devel. Bd., 1998—. Mem. Holdrege C. of C., Nebr. Corn Growers Assn. (bd. dirs. 1974-90, Golden Ear award 1988), Nat. Corn Growers Assn. (v.p. rsch. 1982-85, bd. dirs. 1978-88), Lions, South. Cen. Nebr. Corn Growers Assn. (pres. 1988, Jerry Johnson Meml. Achievement award 1990). Republican. Lutheran. Avocations: football, sports. Home: PO Box 165 Funk NE 68940-0165

SJOGREN, ROBERT WILLIAM, internist; b. Ft. Collins, Colo., Aug. 4, 1919; s. John William and Flora Anne (Anderson) S.; m. Amenta Margaret Robeson, June 18, 1942; children: Robert Jr., Jane Durbin Fitch, Margaret Leigh. BS in Biology, Va. Poly. U., 1940; MD, U. Va., 1943. Diplomate Am. Bd. Internal Medicine. Intern U. Iowa Hosp., 1944, resident in internal medicine, 1994; resident in internal medicine and gastroenterology Lahey Clinic, Boston, 1948-51; pvt. practice internal medicine and gastroenterology Washington, 1951-81; chief of staff VA Med. Ctr., Martinsburg, W.Va., 1981-91; ret., 1991. With U.S. Army, 1945-47. Home: HC 73 Box 856B 119 Hillside Dr Locust Grove VA 22508-9572

SJOLANDER, RICHARD JAMES, marketing and economics educator; b. Dearborn, Mich., Aug. 5, 1946; s. Karl Gustaf and Margaret Jean (Lewis) S.; m. Elsa Marie Charlotte, June 23, 1972; children: Erik, Maria Lisa. BS in Pkg. Engring., Mich. State U., 1968, MS in Pkg., 1979, PhD in Resource Devel., 1984. Pkg. engr. Ford Motor Co., Livonia, Mich., 1968-70, TetraPak Devel., A.B., Lund, Sweden, 1972-76; asst. prof. mktg. and econs. U. West Fla., Pensacola, 1985-90, assoc. prof. mktg. and econs., 1990-98, prof. mktg. and econs., 1998—, chmn. mktg. and econs., 1995—2001. Vis. prof. mktg. U. Lund, 1991-92, Mikkeli Poly., Finland, 1999, 2000, Nyenrode U., The Netherlands, 1999, 2000; U.S.-EU export devel. program acad. project leader US US Dept. Edn., 1996-98; cons. in econs. Sjolander & Assocs., Pensacola, 1985—. Contbr. articles to profl. jours. Mem. Am. Mktg. Assn., Am. Acad. Econ. and Fin. Experts, Soc. Mktg. Advances, Mid South Mktg. Educators Assn., World Trade Coun. N.W. Fla. Avocations: sailing, international travel. Office: U West Fla 11000 University Pkwy Pensacola FL 32514-5750 Home: PO Box 9641 Pensacola FL 32513-9641

SJOLSETH, ROCHELLE M. organizational development specialist; b. Sioux Falls, S.D., May 13, 1952; Diploma, N.Mex. Sch. Radiology, 1972; BS in Health Svcs. Adminstrn., No. Ariz. U., 1982; MS in Orgnl. Devel., U. San Francisco, 1992. Registered radiologic technologist. Staff radiologic technologist Clovis (N.Mex.) Hosp., 1972-75, Presbyn. Hosp., Albuquerque, 1975-76; asst. mgr. radiology svc. Scottsdale (Ariz.) Meml. HOsp., 1976-82; adminstrv. dir. imaging svcs. Thunderbird Hosp., Phoenix, 1982-88; dir. radiology svc. Watsonville (Calif.) Cmty. Hosp., 1989-91, program dir. occupational health, 1991—. Orgnl. devel. cons. Monterrey Mushrooms, Watsonville, 1995-96, Easter Seals Santa Cruz County, 1996; wellness cons. City of Watsonville. Author articles, column and short stories. Grad. Leadership Santa Cruz County, 1993; bd. dirs. KUSP Pub. Radio, Santa Cruz County, 1995—. Recipient Bus. Excellence award Paradise Valley C. of C., 1992. Mem. Bay Area Orgnl. Devel. Specialists, Soc. Human Resource Profls., Nat. Assn. Occupational Health Profls. Mem. Soc. Of Friends. Avocations: writing, surfing, photography, reading. Home: 210 Kenneth Dr Aptos CA 95003-5010 Office: Orgnl Transformations PO Box 2553 Aptos CA 95003-5010

SJOSTRAND, FRITIOF STIG, biologist, educator; b. Stockholm, Sweden, Nov. 5, 1912; s. Nils Johan and Dagmar (Hansen) S.; m. Marta Bruhn-Fahraeus, Mar. 24, 1941 (dec. June 1954); 1 child, Rutger; m. Ebba Gyllenkrok, Mar. 28, 1955; 1 child, Johan; m. Birgitta Petterson, Jan. 23, 1969; 1 child, Peter. MD, Karolinska Institutet, Stockholm, 1941, PhD, 1945; PhD (hon.), U. Siena, 1974, North-East Hill U., Shillon, India, 1989. Asst. prof. anatomy Karolinska Institutet, 1945-48, assoc. prof., 1949-59, prof. histology, 1960-61; research assoc. MIT, 1947-48; vis. prof. UCLA, 1959, prof. zoology, 1960-82, prof. emeritus molecular biology, 1982—. Author: Über die Eigenfluoreszenz Tierischer Gewebe Mit Besonderer Berücksichtigung der Säugetierniere, 1944, Electron Microscopy of Cells and Tissues, Vol. I, 1967, Deducing Function from Structure, Vols. I and II, 1990; also numerous articles. Decorated North Star Orden Sweden; recipient Jubilee award Swedish Med. Soc., 1959, Anders Retzius gold medal, 1967; Paul Ehrlich-Ludwig Darmstaedter prize, 1971 Fellow Royal Micros. Soc. (hon., London), Am. Acad. Arts and Scis.; mem. Electron Microscopy Soc. Am. (hon., Disting. Scientist award 1992), Japan Electron Microscopy Soc. (hon.), Scandinavian Electron Microscopy Soc. (hon.). Achievements include development technique for high resolution electron microscopy of cells, fluorescence microspectrography; inventor ultramicrotome. E-mail: fsjostra@ucla.edu.

SKADEN, ANNE MARIE, library director; b. Emmetsburg, Iowa, Feb. 19, 1955; d. Dixon Wayne and Ruth Marie Parish; m. David M. Skaden, June 14, 1980; children: Erik, Mark, Mary. MLS, U. Wis., 1981. Reference/Young Adult Libr. Frank L. Weyenberg Libr., Mequon, Wis., 1982-85; media specialist St. James Sch., Washington, 1993-95; dir. Kalona (Iowa) Pub. Libr., 1994—. Bd. trustees Kalona Pub. Libr., 1986-94, pres., 1990-92. Mem. ALA, Iowa Libr. Assn., Iowa Small Libr. Assn. (sec.), Washington County Libr. Assn. (pres., v.p., sec., treas.), Iowa Libr. Assn., Libr. Adminstrn. and Mgmt. Assn. (sec., treas.). Office: Kalona Pub Libr PO Box 1212 Kalona IA 52247-1212 E-mail: kaloplib@kctc.net.

SKAFF, ANDREW JOSEPH, lawyer, public utilities, energy and transportation executive; b. Sioux Falls, S.D., Aug. 30, 1945; s. Andrew Joseph and Alice Maxine (Skaff) Skaff; m. Lois Carol Phillips, Oct. 4, 1971; 2 children. BS in Bus. Adminstrn, Miami U., Oxford, Ohio, 1967; JD, U. Toledo, 1970. Bar: Calif. 1971, U.S. Supreme Ct. 1974. Prin., sr. counsel Calif. Public Utilities Commn., 1977; gen. counsel Delta Calif. Industries, Oakland, 1977-82, sec., 1978-82; mem. Silver Rosen, Fischer & Stecher, San Francisco, 1982-84; sr. ptnr. Skaff and Anderson, 1984-90; pvt. practice Law Office of Andrew J. Skaff, 1990-95; ptnr. Knox Ricksen LLP, Oakland, 1995-97, Crosby, Heafey Roach & May, Oakland, 1997-99, Energy Law Group LLP, Oakland, 2000—. Officer Delta Calif. Industries and subs. Contbr. articles to legal jours.; contbg. mem. law rev. U. Toledo, 1970. Mem. ABA, Calif. Bar Assn., Conf. Calif. Pub. Utilities Counsel, Calif. Cogeneration Coun., Assn. Transp. Practitioners, Alameda County Bar Assn. Office: Energy Law Group LLP Lake Merritt Plz 1999 Harrison St Ste 2700 Oakland CA 94612-3582 E-mail: Askaff@energy-law-group.com.

SKAFF, JOSEPH JOHN, retired state agency administrator, army officer; b. Charleston, W.Va., June 13, 1930; s. Michael Joseph and Zahia S.; m. Maree A. Fleming, Aug. 4, 1957; children: Joseph M., Lynn M. Johnson, Gregory M., Nancy E. Kochman. BS, U.S. Mil Acad., 1955; MS, George Washington U., 1968. Commd. 2d lt. U.S. Army, 1955; commanded 1/27 FA battalion, 1968-69; advanced through grades to maj. gen.; dep. dir. internat. negotiations U.S. Army Joint Chiefs of Staff, Washington, 1979-81; mem. staff and faculty U.S. Mil. Acad., 1972-76; also dep. commr. U.S. Del. Standing Consultative Commn., Geneva, 1979-81; dep. dir. ops. readiness and moblzn. Hdqrs. Dept. Army, Washington, 1981-83; dep. comdr./chief staff U.S. Army in Japan, 1982-84; dep. commdg. gen., commdg. gen. 1st U.S. Army, Fort Devens, Mass., 1985-89, adj. gen. W.Va., 1989-95; cabinet sec. mil. affairs and pub. safety W.Va., 1989-97. Bd. dirs. Christian Internet Svc. Decorated DSM, Def. Superior Svc. medal, Legion of Merit, Bronze Star, Air medal, others; recipient Disting. West Virginian award. Mem. Assn. Grads. U.S. Mil. Acad., Assn. U.S. Army, Arty. Assn., Adj. Gens. Assn. U.S., N.G. Assn. U.S., Fellowship Christian Athletes (regional bd.). Eastern Orthodox.

SKAGGS, BEBE REBECCA PATTEN, college dean, clergywoman; b. Berkeley, Calif., Jan. 30, 1950; d. Carl Thomas and Bebe (Harrison) P. BS in Bible, Patten Coll., 1969; BA in Philosophy, Holy Names Coll., 1970; MA in Bibl. Studies New Testament, Wheaton Coll., 1972; PhD in Bibl. Studies New Testament, Drew U., 1976; MA in Philosophy, Dominican Sch. Philosophy & Theology, 1990; postgrad., U. Calif., Berkeley, 1991-92. Ordained to ministry Christian Evang. Ch., 1963. Co-pastor Christian Cathedral, Christian Evang. Chs. Am., Inc., 1964—; assoc. prof. Patten Coll., Oakland, Calif., 1975-82, dean, 1977—, prof. N.T., 1982—. Presenter in field. Author: Before the Times, 1980, The World of the Early Church, 1990; contbg. author: Internat. Standard Bibl. Ency., rev. edit., 1983, Women's Study Bible, Pneuma Faculty Dialogue. Active Wheaton Coll. Symphony, 1971-72, Drew U. Ensemble, 1971-75, Young Artists Symphony, N.J., 1972-75, Somerset Hill Symphony, N.J., 1973-74, Peninsula Symphony, 1977, 80-81, Madison Chamber Trio, N.J., 1973-75. Named one of Outstanding Young Women of Am., 1976, 77, 80-81, 82; St. Olaf's Coll. fellow, 1990. Mem. AAUP, Am. Acad. Religion, Soc. Bibl. Lit., Internat. Biographical Assn., Christian Evang. Chs. of Am., Inc. (bd. dirs. 1964—), Inst. for Bibl. Rsch., Soc. for Pentecostal Studies (pres. 1998-99), Phi Delta Kappa.

SKAGGS, KAREN GAYLE, elementary school educator; b. Campbellsville, Ky., Sept. 29, 1956; d. E. Edward and Mary Virginia (Kearney) Davis; m. Stephen Douglas Skaggs, July 30, 1976. BA in English, French and Journalism, Campbellsville Coll., 1977, elem. edn. endorsement 1-8, 1989; MA in Secondary Edn. and Psychology, Western Ky. U., 1980, reading specialist degree, 1986, rank 1 in edn., 1990. Cert. secondary tchr., Ky. Tchr. English, French, journalism Taylor County Bd. Edn., Campbellsville, 1978-81, adult edn. tchr., 1981-89; elem. tchr. Campbellsville Bd. Edn., 1989—. Bdlg. coord. Extended Sch. Svcs., 1998—. Mem. Campbellsville Site Based Coun., 1993-98, 99—, ESS coord., 1998—. Recipient Outstanding Tchr. award State Dept. of Edn. Mem. Internat. Reading Assn., Taylor County Lit. Coun. (pres.), Taylor County Bus. and Profl. Women's Club (chmn. young careerist com. 1987-88, Outstanding Young Career Woman award 1987, Tchr. of Yr. award 1993, Excellence in Tchg. award 1994). Democrat. Baptist. Avocations: reading, writing, decorating, internet. Home: 901 S Columbia Ave Campbellsville KY 42718-2410

SKAGGS, MELISSA M. elementary school educator; b. Elizabethtown, Ky., July 25, 1973; d. David Russell and Rita Copelin Miller; 1 child, Madeline Carrie. MusB in Music Edn., Campbellsville U., 1995; MAE in Sch. Counseling, Western Ky. U., 2001. Cert. music edn. grades K-12, instrumental music with vocal endorsement, Ky., rank I in elem. sch. counseling. Pvt. piano tchr., Glasgow, Ky., 1989—; music educator Marion County Bd. Edn., Lebanon, 1996, Barren County Bd. Edn., Glasgow, 1999—; elem. sch. counselor Park City (Ky.) Elem. Sch., 2001—. Dir. Hiseville (Ky.) Elem. Chorus, 1999, Park City (Ky.) Elem. Chorus. Mem. Music Tchrs. Nat. Assn., Music Educators Nat. Conf., Ky. Music Educators Assn., Ky. Music Tchrs. Assn., Ctrl. Ky. Music Tchrs. Assn., Ky. Counseling Assn., Ky. Sch. Counselor's Assn., S. Ctrl. Ky. Counseling Assn. Baptist. Home: 5417 Hiseville Rd Glasgow KY 42141 Office: Park City Elem Sch 45 Indian Mill Rd Park City KY 42160

SKAGGS, MERTON MELVIN, JR. environmental engineer; b. Kerrville, Tex., Nov. 16, 1953; s. Merton Melvin and Peggy LaNell (Dechert) S.; m. Susan Marie Frawley, Aug. 9, 1980; children: Alan, Marie, Bridget. BSChemE, Tex. A&M U., 1976; MS in Biology, U. Houston, Clear Lake City, Tex., 1979. Registered profl. engr., Tex. Process engr. Diamond Shamrock Chems. Co., Pasadena, Tex., 1976-78, environ. engr., 1979-80, sr. environ. engr., 1981-84; ctrl. ops. mgr. Maxus Energy Corp., Dallas, 1985-91, gen. mgr. environ. affairs, 1991-96. Pres. Chem. Land Holdings, Inc., Dallas, 1994-99, Maxus Agrl. Chems., Inc., Dallas, 1994-96; prs. InDepth Environ. Assocs., 1999—. Coach Odyssey of the Mind, Southlake, Tex., 1993-97. Mem. AIChE, Soc. Petroleum Engrs. (chmn. environ. study group 1993-96, sect. treas. 1996-97, edn. dir. 1997-98, chmn. edn. 1997-98, program chmn. 1998-88, social dir. 1999-00, dir. cmty. rels. 2000-01), Water Environ. Federation, Air and Waste Assn. Methodist. Achievements include management of projects to clean up and/or close five major hazardous waste disposal sites and 12 related publications. Home: PO Box 92653 Southlake TX 76092-0653 Office: InDepth Environ Assocs 320 W Highland Southlake TX 76092 E-mail: mmsnsl@aol.com.

SKAGGS, RICHARD WAYNE, agricultural engineering educator; b. Grayson, Ky., Aug. 20, 1942; s. Daniel M. and Gertrude (Adkins) S.; m. Judy Ann Kuhn, Aug. 25, 1962; children: Rebecca Diane Skaggs Ramsey, Steven Glen. BS in Agr. Engring., U. Ky., 1964, MS in Agr. Engring., 1966; PhD, Purdue U., 1970. Registered profl. engr., N.C. Grad. asst. U. Ky., Lexington, 1964-66; grad. instr. in rsch. Purdue U., West Lafaytte, Ind., 1966-70; asst. prof. agrl. engring. N.C. State U., Raleigh, 1970-74, assoc. prof., 1974-79, prof., 1979-84, William Neal Reynolds prof., 1984—, disting. univ. prof., 1991—. Cons. on drainage U.S. Aid, Egypt, 1989-97; cons., lectr. on water mgmt., India, 1992, Malaysia, 1993, 95, New Zealand, 1993, Turkey, 1998. Contbr. over 300 articles on water mgmt. and hydrology to profl. jours. Recipient Outstanding Young Scientist award N.C. State U. chpt. Sigma Xi, 1978; Alumni Rsch. award N.C. State U. Alumni Assn., 1983, Alumni Disting. Profl. award for grad. tchg., 1991, Alexander Q. Holladay Award for Excellence, N.C. State U., 1994, Superior Svc. award USDA, 1986, 90, O. Max Gardner award The U. of N.C. Sys., 1997, Alexander von Humbolt Found. award 1997, Gamma Sigma Delta award of merit N.C. State U., 1999, Internat. Disting. Achievement in Agr. award, 1999; inducted into Drainage Hall of Fame, Ohio State U., 1984, Engring. Hall of Distinction, U. Ky., 1994; named Outstanding Alumnus Agrl. Engr., U. Ky., 1985, Disting. Engring. Alumnus, Purdue U., 1997. Fellow: Am. Soc. Agrl. Engrs. (chmn. nat. drainage symposium com. 1976, mem. nominating com. 1979, 1995—96, pres. 2001—02, Hancor Soil and Water Engring. award 1986, John Deere Gold medal 1993); mem.: NAE, NRC (com. on wetland characterization). Avocations: basketball, golf, reading. Home: 2826 Sandia Dr Raleigh NC 27607-3150 Office: NC State U Dept Biol-Agrl Eng PO Box 7625 Raleigh NC 27695-0001 E-mail: wayne_skaggs@ncsu.edu.

SKAGGS, RONALD LLOYD, architect; b. Dallas, Nov. 7, 1942; s. Henry Lloyd and Willye Velle (Hill) S.; m. Sondra Lanette Garrett, June 25, 1965; children: David, Stephen, Jeffrey. BArch, Tex. A&M U., 1966, MArch, 1967. Registered architect, Tex., Ind., Kans., Minn., La., Ark., Tenn., Iowa, Ala., N.Mex., Mich., S.C., D.C., Idaho, Nebr. Architect/assoc. CRS Design assocs., Houston, 1970-73; architect HKS Architects, Dallas, 1973-74, assoc., 1974-75, sr. v.p., 1975-80, exec. v.p., 1980-88, chmn., CEO, 1988—. Adv. bd. Constrn. Industry Pres.'s Round Table, Washington, 1993-96. Author: Architecture for Long Term Care Facilities, 1993; co-author: Building Type Basics for Healthcare Facilities; editor: The Architecture of Healing, 1994; contbr. articles to profl. jours. Bd. advisors Salvation Army, Plano, Tex., 1995—; bd. trustees Tex. Scottish Rite Hosp. for Children, Dallas, 1990—; bd. dirs. Priority One Internat., Dallas, 1986-95; chmn. arch. devel. coun. Tex. A&M U., College Station, 1991—; regent Am. Archtl. Found., Washington, 1993—; mem. exec. bd. Cir. Ten coun. Boy Scouts Am. Decorated Army Commendation medal; recipient numerous design awards; named Disting. Alumnus Tex. A&M U., Outstanding Alumnus Coll. of Architecture Tex. A&M U., SIR award Assoc. Gen. Contractors. Fellow AIA (bd. dirs. 1995-97, v.p. 1998, pres. elect 1999, pres. 2000), Health Facilities Inst., Am. Coll. Healthcare Archs.; mem. Forum for Health Care Planning (pres. 1992-93), Masons (Scottish Rite 33 degree), Tau Sigma Delta (Silver medal). Republican. Baptist. Avocations: music, reading, art collecting, skiing, water sports. Office: HKS Architects 1919 Mckinney Ave Dallas TX 75201-1768

SKAGGS, SANFORD MERLE, lawyer; b. Berkeley, Calif., Oct. 24, 1939; s. Sherman G. and Barbara Jewel (Stinson) S.; m. Sharon Ann Barnes, Sept. 3, 1976; children: Stephen, Paula Ferry, Barbara Gallagher, Darren Peterson. BA, U. Calif., Berkeley, 1961; JD, U. Calif., 1964. Bar: Calif. 1965. Atty. Pacific Gas and Electric Co., San Francisco, 1964-73; gen. counsel Pacific Gas Transmission Co., 1973-75; ptnr. Van Voorhis & Skaggs, Walnut Creek, 1975-85, McCutchen, Doyle, Brown & Enersen, San Francisco and Walnut Creek, 1985—2002, Bingham McCutchen LLP, 2002—; dir. John Muir Mt. Diablo Health Sys., 1997—. Mem. Calif. Law Revision Commn., 1990—2001, chmn., 1993. Councilman City of Walnut Creek, 1972-78, mayor 1974-75, 76-77; bd. dirs. East Bay Mcpl. Utility Dist., 1978-90, pres., 1982-90. Mem. Calif. State Bar Assn., Contra Costa County Bar Assn., Urban Land Inst., Lambda Alpha, Alpha Delta Phi, Phi Delta Phi. Republican. Office: Bingham McCutchen 1333 N California Blvd Ste 210 Walnut Creek CA 94596-4585

SKAGGS, WAYNE GERARD, financial services company executive, retired; b. Bonneterre, Mo., Dec. 12, 1929; s. Jasper Pinkney and Lattie May (Duren) S.; m. Hana Kaneko, June 1, 1952; children: Robert Kenneth, Melody Jane, Joy Elizabeth. Student, Mo. Inst. Acctg. and Law, 1947-48, U. Mo., Columbia, 1954-55. With Advantage Capital Corp. (formerly Am. Capital Corp.), Houston, 1955-96, ret., 1996; pres., COO Mktg. Group of Cos., 1976-80, corp. v.p., cons., 1972-90. Served with USAF, 1950-54, Korea.

Mem. Nat. Assn. Securities Dealers (nat. vice chmn. 1977, dist. chmn. 1972), Nat. Bus. Conduct (gov., chmn. 1976), Investment Co. Inst. Clubs: Optimists (pres. club 1966, life mem.). Home: PO Box 726 Wimberley TX 78676-0726

SKAINS, TIMOTHY KARL, electrical engineer; b. Feb. 10, 1960; AS in Applied Sci. & Tech., Nat. Edn. Ctr., 1997; BS in Elec. Engring., Baylor U., 1999. Cert. control technician III, Instrument Soc. Am.; cert. engr. in tng., Tex. Head electrician Ideal Co., Waco, Tex., 1988-89; chief electrician Packless Industries, 1990; sr. technician M & M/Mars Inc., 1990-99; process/R&D engr. Pactiv Corp., Temple, 1999—. Mem. IEEE, NSPE, Instrument Soc. Am., Indsl. Computer Soc., Smithsonian Instn., Instrument Soc. Am., Tex. Soc. Profl. Engrs. Home: 4331 Harrison St Waco TX 76705-2627

SKALA, GARY DENNIS, electric and gas utilities executive management consultant; b. Bay Shore, N.Y, Oct. 15, 1946; s. Harry A. and Emily Skala. BS in Mgmt. Engring., Rensselaer Polytech. Inst., 1969; MA in Psychology, Hofstra U., 1972; postgrad., Chgo. Theol. Sem., 1996—. Engr. L.I. Lighting Co., Hicksville, N.Y., 1969-71, labor rels. coord., 1971-73; mgmt. cons. Gilbert/Commonwealth, N.Y.C., 1973-74; sr. mgmt. cons. Booz, Allen & Hamilton, San Francisco, 1974-78; mgr. utility cons. A.T. Kearney, Chgo., 1978-81; mng. cons. Cresap, div. Towers Perrin, 1981-85; pres. Gary D. Skala & Assocs. Mgmt. Cons., 1985—. Lectr. on utility bus. issues Edison Electric Inst., Utility Exec. Mgmt. Com., Internat. Maintenance Conf., Assn. Rural Electric Coops., Inst. Indsl. Engrs.; subcontracting cons. Arthur D. Little Inc., Liberty Cons. Group, Ernst & Young, Cresap, A.T. Kearney, Towers Perrin, Michael Paris Assocs. Ltd., Planmetrics. Contbr. articles to profl. jours. Bd. trustees Samaritan Inst. for Religious Studies, 1995-97, chair instnl. advancement com., 1995; bd. dirs. Bailiwick Repertory Theater, 1999—, pres., 2001-2002, chair mktg./pub. rels. com.; bd. dirs. Good Shepherd Parish Met. Cmty. Ch. of Chgo, 1995-99, vice moderator, 1996-97; mem. bd. Ordained Ministry o Gt. Lakes Dist. of Universal Fellowship Met. Cmty. Chs., 1996-99; vol. The Night Ministry of Chgo. Mem. Inst. Indsl. Engrs. (sr. mem. utility div. 1978—, charter), Am. Inst. Indsl. Engrs. (chmn. Midwest chpt. utility div. 1980-81). Office: Gary D Skala & Assocs PO Box 14838 Chicago IL 60614-0838

SKALAGARD, HANS MARTIN, artist; b. Skuko, Faroe Islands, Feb. 7, 1924; came to U.S., 1942, naturalized, 1955. s. Ole Johannes and Hanna Elisa (Fredriksen) S.; m. Mignon Diana Haack Haegland, Mar. 31, 1955; 1 child, Karen Solveig Sikes. Pupil, Anton Otto Fisher, 1947. Joined U.S. Mcht. Marine, 1942, advanced through grades to chief mate, 1945; ret., 1965; owner, operator Skalagard Sq. Rigger Art Gallery, Carmel, Calif., 1966—; libr. Mayo Hays O'Donnel Libr., Monterey, 1971-73; painter U.S. Naval Heritage series, 1973—. Lectr., bd. dirs. Allen Knight Maritime Mus., 1973—, mem. adv. and acquisitions coms., 1973-77. One-man shows include Palace Legion of Honor, San Francisco, 1960, J.F. Howland, 1963-65, Fairmont Hotel, San Francisco, 1963, Galerie de Tours, 1969, 72-73, Pebble Beach (Calif.) Gallery, 1963, Laguna Beach (Calif.) Gallery, 1969, Arden Gallery, Atlanta, 1970, Gilbert Gallery, San Francisco, Maritime Mus. of Monterey, 1993, 97, Rigger Art Gallery, Carmel, Stanton Ctr., Monterey, 1993, Monterey Mat. Mus., 1993, St. Francis Yacht Club, San Francisco, 1995, Ventura County Maritime Mus., Oxnard, Calif., 1998; exhibited in group shows at Am. Artists, Eugene, Oreg., Robert Louis Stevenson Exhibit, Carmel Valley Gallery, Biarritz and Paris, David Findley Galleries, N.Y.C. and Faroe Island, Maritime Mus., Calif., 1993, 94, 95, Pacific Coast Lumber Schooners, 1994, , San Francisco Art Expo, 2000, Herrschoff Marine Mus., Bristol, Pa., 2002numerous others; represented in permanent collections Naval Post Grad. Sch. and Libr., Allen Knight Maritime Mus., Salvation Army Bldg., Monterey, Robert Louis Stevenson Sch., Pebble Beach, Anenberg Art Galleries, Chestlibrook Ltd., Skalagard Art Gallery, Carmel; work represented in numerous books including Modern Masters of Marine Art, 1993; featured artist KTEH-TV On-Air Art Auction, 1998; profiled in profl. jours.; subject of cover and article Palette Talk, 1980, Compass mag., 1980. Chairperson Mayor's Choice Exhibit, Carmel, 1995; co-founder Carmel Gallery Alliance. Recipient Silver medal Tommaso Campanella Internat. Acad. Arts, Letters and Scis., Rome, 1970, Gold medal, 1972, Gold medal and hon. life membership Acad. Italia dell Arti e del Honoro, 1980, Gold medal for artistic merit Acad. d'Italia. Mem. Navy League (bd. dirs. Monterey), Internat. Platform Assn., Sons of Norway (cultural dir. 1974-75, 76-77). Home: 602 Stony Point Rd Petaluma CA 94952-1048 Fax: 707-776-4889. E-mail: skalagard@aol.com.

SKALKA, DOUGLAS SCOTT, lawyer; b. N.Y.C., Sept. 28, 1960; s. Philip and Margery Skalka; m. Susan Michelle Prince, MAy 12, 1985; children: Elizabeth, Rachel, Abigail. AB, Cornell U., 1982; JD, Boston U., 1985. Bar: Conn. 1985, N.Y. 1986, U.S. Dist. Ct. Conn. 1986, U.S. Dist. Ct. (so. and ea. dists.) N.Y. 1990, U.S. Ct. Appeals (2d cir.) 2001; cert. in bus. bankruptcy. Assoc. atty. Whitman & Ransom, Greenwich, Conn., N.Y.C., 1985-93; ptnr. Whitman Breed Abbott & Morgan, 1994-95; prin. Neubert, Pepe & Monteith, P.C., New Haven and Southport, Conn., 1995—. Mem. adv. bd. CPA/Law Forum of Fairfield County, Southport, Conn., 1996—. Contbg. editor: Bankruptcy, 1997, 98; editor-in-chief Probate Law Jour., 1984-85. Mem. exec. com. Southwestern Regional Planning Agy., Norwalk, Conn., 1996-2000; mem. Southwestern Corridor Action Coun., Bridgeport, Conn., 1998-2000. Recipient Bernard E. Farr Estate Planning award Boston U., 1985, Paul Liacos scholar, 1984. Mem. ABA (bus. law sect.), Conn. Bar Assn. (exec. com. of comml. law and bankruptcy sect. 1994—), Stamford/Norwalk Regional Bar Assn. (co-chair bankruptcy com. 1994-96), Am. Bankruptcy Inst., Conn. Turnaround Mgmt. Assn. (bd. dirs. 1996—, pres. 1999-2000), New Haven County Bar Assn. (chair bankruptcy com. 2002—). Office: Neubert Pepe & Monteith PC 195 Church St New Haven CT 06510-2009 E-mail: dss@npmlaw.com.

SKALKA, HAROLD WALTER, ophthalmologist, educator; b. N.Y.C., Aug. 22, 1941; s. Jack and Sylvia Skalka; m. Barbara Jean Herbert, Oct. 2, 1965; children: Jennifer, Gretchen, Kirsten. AB with distinction, Cornell U., 1962; MD, NYU, 1966. Intern Greenwich (Conn.) Hosp., 1966-67; resident in ophthalmology Bellevue Hosp., Univ. Hosp., Manhattan VA Hosp., 1967-70; fellow in retinal physiology and ultrasonography, 1970-71; cons. in ophthalmology St. Jude's Hosp., Montgomery, Ala., 1971-73; asst. prof. ophthalmology U. Ala., Birmingham, 1973-75, assoc. prof., 1975-80, prof., 1980-81, assoc. prof. dept. medicine, 1980—, chmn. combined program in ophthalmology, 1981-97, Nathan E. Miles prof., 1986—. Acting chmn. combined program ophthalmology U. Ala., 1974-76; ophthalmologist Lowndes County Bd. Health Community Health Project, 1972. Contbr. articles to Am. Jour. Ophthalmology, Eye, Ear, Nose and Throat Monthly, Annals of Ophthalmology, Ophthalmic Surgery, Jour. Clin. Ultrasound, Jour. Pediatric Ophthalmology and Strabismus, The Lancet, AMA Archives of Ophthalmology, Jour. So. Med. Assn., Acta Ophthalmologica, Metabolic and Pediatric Ophthalmology, Applied Radiology, Brit. Jour. Ophthalmology, Blood, Neuro-Ophthalmology; mem. editl. bd. Ala. Jour. Med. Sci. Major USAFMC, 1971-73. Mem. AAAS, AMA, ACS, SIDUO, Ala. Sight Conservation Assn., Ala. Conservancy, Ala. Wildlife Fedn., Eye Bank Bd., Am. Acad. Ophthalmology, Am. Inst. Ultrasound in Medicine, Internat. Soc. for Clin. Electrophysiology of Vision, Internat. Soc. on Metabolic Eye Disease, Assn. for Rsch. in Vision and Ophthalmology, AAUP, Am. Intraocular Implant Soc., Am. Assn. Ophthalmology, Pan Am. Assn. Ophthalmology, So. Med. Assn., Rsch. to Prevent Blindness, Ala. Acad. Ophthalmology, Ala. Med. Assn., Jefferson County Med. Soc., Contact Lens Assn. Ophthalmologists, Ala. Ultrasound Soc., Royal Soc. Medicine, N.Y. Acad. Scis., Am. Soc. Standardized Ophthalmic Echography (charter exec. bd. mem.), Am. Coll. Nutrition. Office: Eye Found Hosp U Ala 700 18th St S Ste 200 Birmingham AL 35233-3800 E-mail: hskalka@uabmc.edu.

SKALKO, RICHARD GALLANT, anatomist, educator; b. Providence, Apr. 10, 1936; s. Francis Charles and Emilie Margaret (Gallant) S.; m. Louise Marie Luchetti (div. 1982); m. Priscilla Ann Brown, 1985; children: Patricia, Margaret, Christine. AB, Providence Coll., 1957; MS, St. John's U., 1959; PhD, U. Fla., 1963. Instr. anatomy Cornell U. Med. Coll., 1963-66, asst. prof., 1966-67; asst. prof. anatomy La. State U. Med. Ctr., New Orleans, 1967-69, assoc. prof., 1969-70; dir. Embryology Lab. Birth Defects Inst., N.Y. State Health Dept., Albany, 1970-77; assoc. prof. anatomy and toxicology Albany Med. Coll., 1970-76, prof., 1976-77; prof. anatomy and cell biology Eas Tenn. State U. Coll. Medicine, Johnson City, 1977—, chmn. dept., 1977—. Mem. sci. adv. bd. NCTR, FDA, 1976-79; vis. prof. Institut fur Toxikologie und Embryonalpharmakologie, Freie U., Berlin, 1978; mem. human embryology and devel. study sect., NIH, 1990-94. Author: Basic Concepts in Teratology, 1985; editor: Heredity and Society, 1973, Congenical Defects, 1974. Mem. Am. Assn. Anatomists, Teratology Soc., Soc. Devel. Biology, European Teratology Soc., Soc. Toxicology. Democrat. Roman Catholic. Home: 3302 Pine Timbers Dr Johnson City TN 37604-4101 Office: East Tenn State U Coll Medicine Dept Anatomy and Cell Biology Johnson City TN 37614-0582

SKAMBIS, CHRISTOPHER CHARLES, JR. lawyer; b. Painesville, Ohio, Jan. 21, 1953; s. Christopher Charles and Anne (Haritos) S.; m. Susan Elaine Adrianson, Dec. 18, 1976 (div. Mar. 1997); m. Kathleen Louise Maloney, Feb. 1999; children: Adrianne Elaine, Christopher Roy. Student, U. Pa., 1970-72; BA, U. Conn., 1972-74; JD, Ohio State U. Coll. Law, Columbus, 1975-78. Bar: Fla. 1978, U.S. Dist. Ct. (mid. dist.), 1979, U.S. Dist. Ct. (no. and so. dists.) 1997, U.S. Ct. Appeals (5th and 11th cir.) 1981, U.S. Supreme Ct. 1989. Assoc. VandenBerg, Gay & Burke, Orlando, Fla., 1978-81, ptnr., 1982, VandenBurg, Gay, Burke, Wilson & Arkin, Orlando, 1982-85, Foley & Lardner, Orlando, 1985-96, Moran & Shams PA, Orlando, 1996-99, The Skambis Law Firm, Orlando, 2000—. Mem. Orange County Bar Assn., Orlando, Fla., 1978, Fla. Bar 9D Grievance Commn., Orlando, Fla., 1989; arbitrator Fla. Bar 9th Cir. Fee Arbitration Commn., Orlando, Fla., 1987; co-chair Federal and State Trial Practice Co., Orlando, Fla., 1992-93. Mem. Am. Judicature Soc., ABA. Avocation: amateur ham radio operator. Office: The Skambis Law Firm 715 Vassar St Orlando FL 32804-4920 Fax: (409) 649-0191. E-mail: cskambis@cfl.rr.com.

SKANTZE, PAT, model, consultant; b. Birmingham, Ala. m. Lawrence A. Skantze; children: Lawrence Michael, Patricia Anne, Vanessa Maria. BA in Speech and Drama, Birmingham So. Coll. Tchg. fellow U. Ala. Model, cons., commentator major dept. stores, N.Y.C., Washington, L.A.; spkr., lectr. image improvement and success motivation; advisor fgn. nats. through mil. cmty. Personality, spokesperson variety shows, talk show hostess, sitcoms, documentaries and commls. Past pres. bd. assocs. Nat. Rehab. Hosp.; past pres. Women's Com. of Washington Ballet; active Salvation Army Women's Aux., Welcome to Washington, Lab. Sch. Washington, Neediest Kids, Nat. Mil. Family Assn.; bd. trustees Nat. Aviation Hall of Fame. Mem. Capitol Spkrs. Club (pres.), Tower Club (bd. govs.). Home: 1703 Chesterbrook Vale Ct Mc Lean VA 22101-3244 E-mail: gen4las@aol.com.

SKARDA, LYNELL GRIFFITH, lawyer, banker; b. Clovis, N.Mex., Aug. 28, 1915; s. Albert S. and Bertha V. (Taylor) S.; m. Kathryn Burns Skarda, Dec. 25, 1939; children— Jeffrey J., Patricia Lyn, Katrina A., Gregory A.F. BS, U. Calif., Berkeley, 1937; JD, Washington & Lee U., 1941. Bar: N.Mex. 1941. Sole practice, Clovis, 1941— ; chmn. bd. Citizens Bank of Clovis 1968— ; mem. Uniform Jury Instrn. Com., 1963-83. Served to capt. JAG Corps, U.S. Army, World War II. Fellow Am. Coll. Trust and Estate Counsel; mem. ABA, N.Mex. Bar Assn., Am. Judicature Soc. Home: PO Box 400 Clovis NM 88102-0400 Office: Citizens Bank Bldg PO Box 400 Clovis NM 88102-0400

SKARDA, PATRICIA LYN, English literature educator; b. Clovis, N.Mex., Mar. 31, 1946; d. Lynell Griffith and Kathryn Rose (Burns) S. Student, Sweet Briar Coll., 1964-67; BA, Tex. Tech. U., 1969; PhD, U. Tex., 1973. Prof. English Smith Coll., Northampton, Mass., 1973—. Edn. dir. Girls Nation, Washington, 1973-75, A.P. Inst. Leader, U. No. Colo., Greeley, 1988-91, 94-2002. Editor: The Evil Image, 1981, Smith Voices, 1990, 99, Textured Lives: Celebrating Ada Comstock Scholars at Smith College, 2000, Instrumentum Laboris for the Third Continental Congress of Vocations, 2001; contbr. articles to profl. jours. Dir. Girls State, N.Mex., 1973. Fellow in Acad. Adminstrn., Am. Coun. on Edn., 1978-79, NDEA grad. fellowship, Disting. Vis. prof. USAF Acad., 1992-93. Mem. MLA, N.Am. Soc. Study Romanticism, Phi Beta Kappa, Sigma Tau Delta, Phi Kappa Phi. Democrat. Roman Catholic. Avocations: reading, swimming, playing piano, traveling, praying. Office: Smith Coll Dept English Northampton MA 01063-0001 E-mail: pskarda@smith.edu.

SKARDA, RICHARD JOSEPH, clinical social worker; b. Santa Monica, Calif., Jan. 2, 1952; s. Robert Ralph and Cathryn Marie (Tourek) S. AA, Los Angeles Valley Coll., Van Nuys, Calif., 1976; BA, U. Calif., Berkeley, 1978; MSW, UCLA, 1980. Lic. clin. social worker, Calif. Children's svcs. worker L.A. County Dept. Children's Svcs., Panorama City, Calif., 1980-82; children's services worker Ventura (Calif.) County Pub. Social Svcs. Agy., 1983-85; head social work dept. Naval Med. Clinic, Port Hueneme, Calif., 1985-94; pvt. practice, 1994—; med. social worker Valley Presbyn. Hosp., Van Nuys, Calif., 2000—. Subject matter expert Bd. Behavioral Scis., Calif., 1997—. With USN, 1970-74. Mem. NASW, Acad. Cert. Social Workers.

SKARE, ROBERT MARTIN, lawyer, director; b. Jan. 13, 1930; s. Martin Samuel and Verna Adelle (Forseth) S.; m. Marilyn Hutchinson, Aug. 28, 1954; children: Randolph, Robertson, Rodger, Richard. Student, St. Olaf Coll., 1947-48; BS, U. Minn., 1951, JD, 1954. Bar: Minn. 1956. Clk. Minn. Supreme Ct., 1953-54; assoc. Best and Flanagan, Mpls., 1956-60, ptnr., 1960-90, sr. ptnr., 1970-90, of counsel, 1990—. Founder, dir., gen. counsel, v.p. Luth. Brotherhood Mut. Funds, Mpls., 1969—93; corp. mcpl. counsel City of Golden Valley, Minn., 1963—88; bd. dirs. Norwest Bank Minn.-Wells Fargo Cmty. Bd., 1972—93, Vesper Soc. Group, San Francisco, 1985—; Son of Heaven, Inc.bd. dirs. Seattle, Wash., 1987—91, Aspen Inst. Cmty. Forum, 1997—, Nat. Coun. Search Inst. Youth Initiative, 1998—; nat. pres. Luth. Human Rels. Assn. Am., 1977—79; founder, dir. Episc. Found. of Aspen, Vinland Nat. Ctr.; founder Westwood Luth. Found. Trustee Am. Luth. Ch.; mem. bd. mgmt. U. Minn. YMCA. Recipient Pres. award Luth. Human Rels. Assn. Am., 1979, Presdl. Awd., Search Inst., 1997. Mem. ABA, Minn. State Bar Assn., Hennepin County Bar Assn., U. Minn. Alumni Club (charter), Mpls. Club, Torske Klubben, Sigma Alpha Epsilon (Disting. Alumni Svc. award 1978). Office: 4000 US Bank Pl Minneapolis MN 55402-4331 Home: 23165 Wild Rice Dr Canyon Lake CA 92587-7974

SKARSHAUG, DAVID PAUL, industrial engineer; b. Ames, Iowa, July 26, 1961; s. Paul Ernest and Eva Maude (Lindgren) S.; m. Jeanene Ann Powers, Aug. 11, 1984; children: Austin, Matthew, Zachary. BS in Journalism, Mass Comm., BS in Indsl. Engring., Iowa State U., 1984. Registered profl. engr., Iowa, Calif. Mfg. engr. Gen. Dynamics Convair Divsn., San Diego, 1985-86, indsl. engr., 1986-88; sr. indsl. engr. Plessey Electronic Sys. Divsn., San Marcos, Calif., 1988-89; sys. engr. Litton Automated Sys., San Diego, 1989-90; mfg. engr. Puritan-Bennett Foxs Divsn., Carlsbad, Calif., 1990-92; v.p. Skarshaug Testing Lab., Ames, Iowa, 1992—. Co-patentee reinforced catheter probe. Mem. Inst. Indsl. Engrs. (sr., newsletter editor 1986-90, pres. San Diego chpt. 1991-92, outstanding svc. award 1989, outstanding young engr. award 1991). Democrat. Lutheran. Avocations: drums, guitar, jogging, water skiing, snow skiing. Office: Skarshaug Testing Lab Inc 4803 Lincoln Way Ames IA 50014-3632

SKAU, MICHAEL W. English educator; b. Chgo., Jan. 6, 1944; s. Walter Francis and Martha Catherine (Marich) S. BA, U. Ill., 1965, MA, 1967, PhD, 1973. Rsch. asst. U. Ill., Urbana and Champaign, 1965-66, teaching asst., 1966-73; asst. prof. English U. Nebr., Omaha, 1973-78, assoc. prof. English, 1978-85, prof. English, 1985—, Jefferies chair, 1997—2000, dept. chair, 2001—. Author: Constantly Risking Absurdity: The Writings of Lawrence Ferlinghetti, 1989; Me and God Poems, 1990, A Clown in a Grave: Complexities and Tensions in the Works of Gregory Corso, 1999; author poems; contbr. articles to profl. jours. Mem. MLA, AAUP. Home: 4913 Chicago St Omaha NE 68132-2914 Office: U Nebr 60th & Dodge Sts Omaha NE 68182-0001 E-mail: mskau@mail.unomaha.edu.

SKAUEN, DONALD MATTHEW, retired pharmaceutical educator; b. Newton, Mass., May 14, 1916; s. Marcus and Mary A. (Duncan) S.; m. Rachel M. Burns, Oct. 25, 1942; children: Deborah Skauen Hinchcliffe, Bruce. BS, Mass. Coll. Pharmacy, 1938, MS, 1942; PhD, Purdue U., 1949. Dir. pharm. svc. Children's Hosp. Med. Ctr., Boston, 1940-46; teaching asst. Purdue U., West Lafayette, Ind., 1946-48; asst. prof. pharmaceutics U. Conn., Storrs, 1948-53, assoc. prof., 1953-59, prof., 1959-79, prof. emeritus, 1979—. Mem. del. of med. scientists to discuss biol. and pharm. uses of ultrasound Nat. Coun. U.S.-China Trade, People's Republic China, 1979. Co-author: American Pharmacy, 4th edit., 1955, 5th edit., 1961, 6th edit., 1966, Husa's Pharmaceutical Dispensing, 1959, 2d edit., 1966, Radioecology, 1963; contbr. numerous articles to Sci., Nature, Jour. Am. Pharm. Assn. Mem. Am. Pharm. Assn., Am. Soc. Hosp. Pharmacists, Sigma Xi. Achievements include research on effects of ultrasound on pharmaceutical and physical systems; radioecology, including gross beta levels in oysters and other organisms in Thames River, Connecticut, and zinc-65 levels in oysters. Home: 16 Storrs Heights Rd Storrs Mansfield CT 06268-2322

SKEDROS, CONSTANTINE J. retired secondary education educator; b. Salt Lake City, Mar. 9, 1923; s. James C. Skedros and Angeline G. Limberiou; m. Anna Kumarelas; children: Angela, Nia, James, Christina. BS, U. Utah, 1949, MA, 1951. Tchr. Granite Sch. Dist., Salt Lake City, 1950-52, Salt Lake Sch. Dist., 1952-87. Bd. dirs. Oral History Inst., Salt Lake City, 1985—, Utah Humanities Coun., Salt Lake City, 1988-94, Nat. Coun. Commn. Justice, Salt Lake City, 1995—; archivist Hellenic Cultural Mus., 1986—. Staff Sgt. USAF, 1942-45. Mem. DAV, Hellenic Cultural Assn. (v.p. 1986—), Greek Cmty. (historian 1995—), Masons. Greek Orthodox. Avocations: reading, travel. Home: 1818 Bryan Ave Salt Lake City UT 84108

SKEELS, JACK WILLIAM, economics educator, consultant; b. Wausau, Wis., Nov. 3, 1929; s. Lawrence John and Gertrude (Preuss) S.; m. Joyce Vivian Goldy, Jan. 29, 1956 (div. 1976); children: Jack Allen, Jennifer Joy; m. Barbara Ann Frick, June 19, 1999. BA, U. Wis., 1951, PhD, 1957. Asst. prof. econs. Mich. State U., East Lansing, 1957-59, Wayne State U., Detroit, 1959-63; assoc. prof. econs. No. Ill. U., DeKalb, 1963-65, full prof. econs., 1965-97, chmn. econs. dept., 1964-69, 77-82, assoc. provost, 1975-76, prof. emeritus, 1997—. Pvt. practice econs., DeKalb, 1972—. Contbr. articles to profl. jours. With USN, 1951-53, PTO. Mem. AAUP (state exec. coun.), Am. Econ. Assn., Assn. Comparative Econ. Studies (nat. exec. sec. 1971-73, nat. sec.-treas. 1964-71), Midwest Econ. Assn. (v.p. 1975-76). Avocations: fishing, tennis, jogging, gardening. Home: 3005 Oxford Rd Lawrence KS 66049-2830 Office: No Ill U Dept Econs Dekalb IL 60115

SKEELS, STEPHEN GLENN, civil engineer; b. Salem, Oreg., Mar. 8, 1951; s. Glenn Arthur and Shirley Belle (Brown) S. BS in Math., Oreg. Coll. Edn., Monmouth, 1974; cert., Computer Career Inst., Portland, Oreg., 1978. Profl. civil engr., 1994. Engring. aide Oreg. State Hwy. Dept., Coquille, 1974-76; programmer, analyst Northwest Area Sys., Inc., Salem, 1978-81, Interstate Fin. Svcs., Salem, 1981; engring. aide Oreg. Dept. Transp., Portland, 1983-84, engring. tech., 1985-86, assoc. transp. engr., 1986—. Active Rep. Presdl. Legion of Merit, 1992. Mem. ASCE, Math. Assn. Am., Am. Math. Soc., U.S. Chess Fedn. Libertarian. Avocations: chess, guitar.

SKEEN, AUTUMN ALEXANDER, child-passenger safety advocate, spokeswoman; b. Phila., Aug. 24, 1956; d. Daniel Wayne and Harriet Hill Alexander; m. Thomas Patrick Skeen, Aug. 7, 1987; children: Geneva Ruth Alexander Skeen, Anton Keith Jefferson (dec.). Student, St. Clares Hall, Oxford, Eng., 1976-77; BA, Macalester Coll., 1978. Cert. U. Wash. Cert. in Lit. Fiction, 2001. Lifestyles editor, writer, columnist Yakima (Wash.) Herald-Republic, 1990-94; freelance writer, 1995—; lobbyist Anton's Law booster-seat laws national, 2000—. Commentator N.W. Pub. Radio, Tri-Cities, Wash., 1994; ESL tchr. Walla Walla (Wash.) C.C., 1998—, Fuchu-Nishi H.S., Tokyo, 1998. Mem. LWV, Audubon Soc., Nat. Arbor Day Found. Avocations: gourmet cooking, ikebana, bird watching, music. Home: 625 S Park St Walla Walla WA 99362-3313

SKEEN, DAVID RAY, systems engineer, manager, consultant, educator; b. Bucklin, Kans., July 12, 1942; s. Claude E. and Velma A. (Birney) S.; m. Carol J. Stimpert, Aug. 23, 1964; children: Jeffrey Kent, Timothy Sean, Kimberly Dawn. BA in Math., Emporia State U., 1964; MS, Am. U., 1972; grad., Fed. Exec. Inst., 1983, Naval War Coll., 1984; DSc in Engring. Mgmt., George Washington U., 1998. Cert. office automation profl. Computer sys. analyst to comdr.-in-chief U.S. Naval Forces-Europe, London, 1967-70; computer sys. analyst Naval Command Sys. Support Activity, Washington, 1970-73; dir. data processing Office Naval Rsch., U.S. Navy Dept., Arlington, Va., 1973-78; dir. mgmt. info. sys. Naval Civilian Pers. Command, Washington, 1978-80; dep. dir. manpower, pers. tng. automated sys. Dept. Naval Mil. Pers. Command, 1980-85; dir. manpower, pers. tng. info. resource mgmt. Chief Naval Ops., 1985-91; assoc. dir. Office of IRM, USDA, 1992-96; dir. modernization of adminstrn. processes program, 1996-98; dep. dir. office of ops. USDA, Washington, 1998; sr. engring. manager, cons. Lockheed Martin, 1998—. Lectr. Inst. Sci. and Pub. Affairs, 1973-76; cons. Electronic Data Processing Career Devel. Programs, 1975—; detailed to Pres.'s Reorgn. Project for Automated Data Processing, 1978, spl. Navy IRM studies, SECNAV, 1991, USDA/Office of Mgmt. and Budget IRM, 1993, spl. USDA Field Structure Studies, 1997; adj. prof. Sch. Engring. and Applied Sci., George Washington U., 1985—; with Pres.'s Fed. Automated Data Processing Users Group, Washington, 1978-80. Contbr. articles to profl. jours. Capt. USNR, 1960-91. Recipient Outstanding Performance award Interagy. Com. Data Processing, 1976, Adminstrv. Staff Performance award, 1998, Sec.'s cert. Appreciation, 1998. Mem. IEEE, Internat. Coun. on Sys. Engring., Sr. Exec. Assn., Assn. Fed. IRM, Naval Res. Assn., Pres. Fed. Automated Data Processing Users Group. Home: 707 Forest Park Rd Great Falls VA 22066-2908 E-mail: david.r.skeen@lmco.com.

SKEEN, JOSEPH RICHARD, congressman; b. Roswell, N.Mex., June 30, 1927; s. Thomas Dudley and Ilah (Adamson) S.; m. Mary Helen Jones, Nov. 17, 1945; children: Mary Elisa, Mikell Lee. BS, Tex. A&M U., 1950. Soil and water engr. Ramah Navajo and Zuni Indians, 1951, 1951; rancher Lincoln County, N.Mex., 1952—; mem. N.Mex. Senate, 1960-70, 97th-103rd Congresses from 2nd N.Mex. dist., Washington, 1981—; mem. appropriations com., subcom. chair Interior, agr., chmn. appropriations com., subcom. def.; mem. subcom. interior. Chmn. N.Mex. Republican Party, 1963-66. Served with USN, 1945-46; Served with USAFR, 1949-52. Mem. Nat. Woolgrowers Assn., Nat. Cattle Growers Assn., N.Mex. Woolgrowers Assn., N.Mex. Cattle Growers Assn., N.Mex. Farm and Livestock Bur. Clubs: Elks. Republican. Office: House of Reps Rayburn House Office Building Rm 2302 Washington DC 20515-0001

SKEES, WILLIAM LEONARD, JR. lawyer; b. Indpls., Jan. 26, 1947; s. William Leonard and Marian Catherine (Fagan) S.; children: Kristina Suzanne Carlsen, Elizabeth Ann Garrison; children: Catherine Fagan, William Leonard III (dec.), Samuel Jackson. BA, Ball State U., 1969; JD, Ind. U., 1971. Bar: Ind. 1971, Ky. 1981. Law clk. U.S. Dist. Ct. (no. dist.), Fort Wayne, Ind., 1971-72; assoc. Ice, Miller Donadio & Ryan, Indpls., 1972-80; mem. Frost Brown Todd, LLC, Louisville, 1981—. Contbr. articles to jours. in field. Mem. bd. visitors Ind. U. Sch. Law, 1975-91; bd. dirs., past pres. Louisville Housing Partnership, 1978—; bd. dirs. Stage One, Louisville Children's Theatre, pres., 1990-91; bd. dirs. Ky. chpt. Nat. SIDS Found.; grad. Leadership Ky., 1996. Recipient Disting. Citizen award Mayor of Louisville, 1983, Cert. Merit Bd. Aldermen, Louisville, 1984, Cert. Appreciation Fiscal Ct., Louisville, 1986. Mem. ABA, Ky. Bar Assn., Ind. Bar Assn., Louisville Bar Assn., Nat. Assn. Bond Lawyers. Office: Frost Brown Todd LLC 400 W Market St Fl 32D Louisville KY 40202-3346 E-mail: bskees@FBTLaw.com.

SKELLAND, ANTHONY HAROLD PETER, chemical engineering educator; b. Birmingham, Eng., Feb. 21, 1928; came to U.S., 1959; s. Harold and Hilda Skelland. BSChemE, U. Birmingham, 1948, PhD in Chem. Engring., 1952. Mgr. Procter and Gamble, Eng., 1954-56, R&D engr. Eng., 1956-59; asst. prof. Ill. Inst. Tech., Chgo., 1959-62; assoc. prof. U. Notre Dame, South Bend, Ind., 1962-66, prof., 1966-69; Ashland prof. U. Ky., Lexington, 1969-79; prof. Ga. Inst. Tech., Atlanta, 1979—. Cons. Monsanto, Babcock and Wilcox, Union Carbide, E.I. duPont de Nemours, FMC Corp., Westinghouse and others. Author: Non-Newtonian Flow and Heat Transfer, 1967, Diffusional Mass Transfer, 1974; contbr. over 80 articles to profl. jours. Fellow AIChE, Inst. Petroleum; mem. Royal Soc. Chemistry (Eng.), Inst. Chem. Engrs. (Eng.). Avocations: tennis, theatre, dining out.

SKELLEY, DEAN SUTHERLAND, clinical laboratory administrator; b. Melrose, Mass., Mar. 27, 1938; s. Robert Henry and Roberta Jane (Morse) S.; m. Eleanor Bachofen, Dec. 21, 1966; children: Caroline, Rachel, Jonathan, Susanna. BS, Bates Coll., 1960; MS, Ohio State U., 1966, PhD, 1968. Asst. prof. Coll. Vet. Medicine Ohio State U., Columbus, 1968-70; asst. prof. ob-gyn. Baylor Coll. Medicine, Houston, 1970-76; clin. biochemist Meml. Hosp., 1976-83; dir. ops. Severance Reference Lab., San Antonio, 1983-84; v.p. ops. Cone Biotech., Inc., Seguin, Tex., 1984-86; dir. product devel.

MCLAS Techs. Inc., San Antonio, 1986-87; tech. dir. Lab Corp Am. (formerly, Nat. Health Labs., Inc.), 1989-99. Pres. Tech. and Profl. Svcs., Inc., San Antonio, 1973—; dir. lab. svcs. South Texas Blood and Tissue Ctr., San Antonio, 2000—; lab.-tech. dir. BioCom Clin. Labs., Weslaco. Tex. and Monterrey, Mex., 1999—. Editor: Internat. Bonhoeffer Soc., 2002-. Elder, Presbyn. Ch., San Antonio, 1994, Moderator, 2001-; mem. admissions com. Bates Coll., Lewiston, Maine, 1990—, mem. ann. alumni fund com., 1998—. Coalition Co-Chmn., New Tech. for Newborn Screening, Tex.; Mem. Safety Com., U. of Tex., Health Sci. Ctr., San Antonio, Tex.; With U.S. Army, 1961-63. Democrat. Mem. United Ch. of Christ. Avocations: reading, hiking, music, theology, calligraphy. Home: 16330 Hidden View St San Antonio TX 78232-2812

SKELLINGS, EDMUND, communications educator, poet; b. Ludlow, Mass., Mar. 12, 1932; s. Romeo Theodore Skellings and Lolita LaPlant; m. Louis Delores Noah, Aug. 17, 1962; 1 child, Sonnet. BA, U. Mass., 1957; PhD, U. Iowa, 1962; DFA (hon.), Internat. Fine Arts Coll., Miami, Fla. Dir., prof. Fla. Ctr. Electronic Comm., Fla. Atlantic U., Ft. Lauderdale, 1968—. Cons. IBM, Armonk, 1988-89. Author: Heart Attacks, 1976, Face Value, 1977, Showing My Age, 1978, Living Proof, 1985, Collected Poems, 1998; patent for computer colortext. Sgt. airborne divsn. U.S. Army, 1951-54, Ft. Bragg. Named Poet Laureate, Gov. of Fla. Avocation: computers. Office: Fla Atlantic U 220 SE 2d Ave Fort Lauderdale FL 33301 E-mail: skellings@earthlink.com.

SKELLY, JOHN JOSHUA, retired clergyman, fundraiser; b. Central Falls, R.I., Oct. 25, 1932; s. Joshua Essa and Catherine (Hermiz) S.; m. Una C. Meadowcroft, June 21, 1959 (div.); children: Timothy John, Joan Louise, Steven Allan. BSBA, Pepperdine U., 1956; BD, San Francisco Theol. Sem., 1959, DS in Theology, 1981; DD, Tarkio Coll., 1971. Asst. pastor First Presbyn. Ch., Granada Hill, Calif., 1959-61; pastor Port Hueneme (Calif.) Presbyn. Ch., 1961-65; v.p. devel. Pikeville (Ky.) Coll., 1967-69; sr. pastor Westminster Presbyn. Ch., Topeka, 1969-72; v.p. seminary rels. San Francisco Theol. Sem., 1972-83; pres. Pacific Homes Found., Woodland Hills, Calif., 1988-99; ret. Area counselor The Fifty Million Fund, United Presbyn. Ch., Kans.-Mo., 1965-67; mission devel. cons., 1967—; cons. Model Cities Program, Pikeville, 1968; campaign cons. United Way, L.A., 1986-87. V.p. student body Pepperdine U., L.A., 1955-56; pres. Hueneme-Oxnard Ministerial Assn., Port Hueneme, 1962; chmn. law enforcement com. Ventura County Grand Jury, 1964-65; chaplain of the day Ho. of Reps., State of Kans., 1970. Staff sgt. U.S. Army, 1950-52. Named Most Inspirational Player, Pepperdine Rugby Club, L.A., 1955, Outstanding Young Men of Am., U.S. Jr. C. of C., Port Hueneme, 1964. Democrat. Avocations: gardening, cooking Middle Eastern food, swimming, biking, golfing. Home and Office: 850 E Ocean Blvd Unit B4 Long Beach CA 90802-5446

SKELTON, BARBARA BURROWS, counselor, educator, artist; b. L.A., Dec. 26, 1928; children: Randolph, Marjorie, Thomas, Deborah; m. Gerald Skelton, 1989. BA, Calif. State U., San Bernardino, 1970; MA, Pacific Oaks Coll., 1974; postgrad., Claremont Coll., 1974—83. Lic. marriage, family and child counselor, Calif., 1974. Career devel., coord. Riverside County Head Start and Corono Norco Sch. Dist., Riverside, 1966-72; instr. Chaffey Community Coll., Alta Loma, Calif., 1971-82; class room coord., family counselor Casa Colina Hosp., Pomona, 1973-79; counselor LaVerne (Calif.) Ctr. for Edn. Counseling, 1976-82; social worker III San Andreas Regional Ctr., Salinas, Calif., 1984-87; pvt. practice family and individual counseling Medford, Oreg., 1987—92. Cons. Nat. Coun. Alcoholism, Covina, 1980-82; instr. U. LaVerne, 1976-82. Author: On Learning and Growing, 1974; co-author: Parent Advocacy Training, 1977, Creative Competency, 1978. Vol. Day Springs Hospice, Medford, 1987-90. Riverside County Headstart scholar, 1967, Ednl. Profl. Devel. Act scholar, 1971-74. Mem. Am. Assn. Marriage and Family Therapists, Upper Rogue Art Assn. Avocations: painting, pottery, horses. Home: 1851 Alta Vista Rd Eagle Point OR 97524 E-mail: barbsk@ccountry.net.

SKELTON, BYRON GEORGE, federal judge; b. Florence, Tex., Sept. 1, 1905; s. Clarence Edgar and Avis (Bowmer) Skelton; m. Ruth Alice Thomas, Nov. 28, 1931; children: Sue, Sandra. Student, Baylor U., 1923—24; AB, U. Tex., 1927, MA, 1928, LLB, 1931. Bar: Tex. 1931, U.S. Ct. Appeals 1937, U.S. Supreme Ct. 1946, FCC 1950, Tax Ct. U.S. 1952, U.S. Treasury Dept. 1952, ICC 1953. Practice of law, Temple, Tex., 1931—66; ptnr. Saulsbury & Skelton, 1934—42, Saulsbury, Skelton, Everton, Bowmer & Courtney, 1944—55, Skelton, Bowmer & Courtney, 1955—66; judge U.S. Ct. Claims, Washington, 1966—77, sr. fed. judge, 1977—82; sr. judge U.S. Ct. Appeals (fed. cir.), Washington, 1982—. County atty. Bell County, Tex., 1934—38; spl. asst. U.S. amb. to Argentina, 1942—45; atty. City of Temple, 1945—60; bd. dirs. First Nat. Bank of Temple. Past pres. Temple YMCA; pres. Temple Indsl. Found., 1966; Dem. nat. committeeman for Tex., 1956—64; del. Dem. Nat. Conv., 1948, 1956, 1960, 1964, Tex. Dem. Conv., 1946, 1948, 1950, 1952, 1954, 1956, 1960, 1962, 1964, vice-chmn., 1948, 1958; chmn. Dem. Adv. Coun. of Tex., 1955—57. Named Ky. Col. and Adm. in Tex. Navy, 1959; recipient Legion of Honor DeMolay, 1980, Temple Outstanding Citizen award, 1990. Mem.: ABA, Am. Judicature Soc., Am. Law Inst., State Bar Tex., Bell-Lampasas and Mills Counties Bar Assn. (past pres.), Ex-Students' Assn. U. Tex. (past pres., exec.coun.), Temple C. of C. (past pres., dir.), Masons (past worshipful master), Kiwanis (past pres.), Shriners, Delta Theta Phi, Sigma Delta Pi, Pi Sigma Alpha, Phi Beta Kappa. Democrat. Methodist. Home: 1101 Dakota Dr Temple TX 76504-4905 Office: US Ct Appeals 305 Fed Bldg Temple TX 76501

SKELTON, CAROL, member of parliament; b. Dec. 12, 1945; m. Noel Skelton; 3 children. Farmer, Harris, Canada; past coord. Can. Blood Svc.; mem. House of Commons, Ottawa, Canada, 2000—, dep. house leader ofcl. opposition, ofcl. opposition dep. critic health. Vice-chair leader's com. sr. issues Can. Alliance; adv. com. Min. of Health on Alcohol, Drugs and Youth, Saskatchewan; past bd. dirs. Saskatchewan Rsch. Coun., Can. 4-H Coun.; mem. mgmt. com. Saskatchewan Party. Can. Alliance Caucus. Office: House of Commons Rm 400 Justice Bldg Ottawa ON K1A 0A6 Canada Address: 940 E 22nd St E Saskatoon SK S7M 0S1 Canada Office Fax: 613-943-2010. E-mail: skelton@canadianalliance.ca.*

SKELTON, DON RICHARD, b. Des Moines, Dec. 9, 1931; s. Donald Harold and Wanda Mae (Johnson) S.; m. Barbara Joan Harris, Mar. 17, 1956 (dec. 1962); children: David, Janet; m. Alyce Mae Washington, May 15, 1964 (div. 1979); children: Laura, Lisa, James; m. Patricia Ann Matroni, July 10, 1981. BSBA, Drake U., 1953. Actuarial trainee Monarch Life Ins. Co., Springfield, Mass., 1953-57, mgr. group ins. dept., 1957-58, asst. actuary, 1958-64, group pensions actuary, 1964-67, asst. v.p., group actuary, 1967, v.p. R & D, 1967-83; v.p. Monarch Capital Corp., 1980-91; sr. v.p. Monarch Life Ins. Co., 1988-91; v.p. Monarch Fin. Svcs., Inc., 1989-91; pres., chief exec. officer First Variable Life Ins. Co., 1985-87, 91, also bd. dirs., ret., 1992; cons. actuary Longmeadow, Mass., 1992—98. Mem. budget com. Pioneer Valley United Way, Springfield, 1964-69, chmn. 1969-70. Fellow Soc. Actuaries; mem. Am. Acad. Actuaries. Republican. Avocations: golf, sailing, physical fitness. Home: 8 Althea Dr Longmeadow MA 01106-1707

SKELTON, EARL FRANKLIN, research physicist, engineering educator; b, Hackensack, N.J., Apr. 8, 1940; s. Floyd and Frances (Rucker) S.; m. Anita Patton, June 17, 1962 (div. 1984); children: Diana Lynn, Isaac Patton; m. Thelma Francesca Fried, Oct. 19, 1986. BS in Physics, Fairleigh Dickinson U., 1962; PhD in Physics, Rensselaer Polytechnic Inst., 1967. Rsch. physicist Benet Weapons Lab. Watervliet Arsenal, 1961-62; rsch. assoc. Rensselaer Polytechnic Inst., Troy, N.Y., 1967; postdoctoral assoc. NAS- Nat. Rsch. Coun. Naval Rsch. Lab., Washington, 1967-68, rsch. physicist, 1968-76, supervisory rsch. physicist, 1976-99; adj. prof. engring. dept. mech./astron. engring. Washington U., 1999-2000; prof. dept. physics George Washington U., 2000—. Liaison scientist Office Naval Rsch., U.S. Embassy, Tokyo, 1978; lectr. physics Prince George's C.C., 1968-73; assoc. professorial lectr. engring. George Washington U., 1974-79, professorial lectr., 1979—, adj. prof. dept. physics, 1996—; lectr. grad. sch. dept. chem. engring. U. Md., 1975-80, assoc. mem. lab. high presure sci., 1977-80; vis. scholar synchrotron radiation lab. Stanford U., 1980-81, elected mem. users exec. com., 1983; elected mem. users exec. com. nat. synchrotron light source Brookhaven Nat. Lab., 1989, 90, 91, 92; rsch. affiliate Hawaii Inst. Geophysics U. Hawaii, 1982-86. Contbr. over 300 articles to tech. and sci. jours.; patentee in field. Recipient Yuri Gargaran Satellite Communication award Fed. Commn. Radiosport, U.S.S.R., 1979, Best Family History Writing award Nat. Geneal. Soc., 1992, USN Tech. Transfer award, 1997; predoctoral scholar NIH, 1964-67. Fellow Am. Phys. Soc.; mem. SAR, Am. Crystallographic Assn., Mayflower Soc., Sigma Xi (Pure Sci. Rsch. award NRL chpt. 1995). Home: 6311 29th Pl NW Washington DC 20015-2221

SKELTON, GORDON WILLIAM, data processing executive, educator; b. Vicksburg, Miss., Oct. 31, 1949; s. Alan Gordon and Martha Hope (Butcher) S.; m. Sandra Lea Champion, May 1974 (div. 1981); m. Janet Elaine Johnson, Feb. 14, 1986; 1 stepchild, Brian Quarles. BA, McMurry Coll., 1974; MA, U. So. Miss., 1975, postgrad., 1975-77, MS, 1987; PhD, U. South Africa, 2001. Cert. in data processing. Systems analyst Criminal Justice Planning Commn., Jackson, Miss., 1978-80; cord. Miss. Statis. Analysis Ctr., 1980-83; data processing mgr. Dept. Adminstrn. Fed.-State Programs, 1983-84; mgr. pub. tech. So. Ctr. Rsch. and Innovation, Hattiesburg, Miss., 1985-87; internal cons. Sec. of State, State of Miss., Jackson, 1987; system support mgr. CENTEC, 1987-88; instr. dept. computer sci. Belhaven Coll., 1988—; v.p. info. svcs. Miss. Valley Title Ins. Co., 1988—. Adj. instr. engring. grad. program telecom. U. Miss., 1997—. Author: (with others) Trends in Ergonomics/Human Factors, 1986; contbr. articles to profl. jours. With U.S. Army, 1970-73, Vietnam. Recipient Cert. of Appreciation, U.S. Dept. Justice/Bur. Justice Stats., 1982. Mem. IEEE Computer Soc., Assn. Info. Tech. Profls. (chpt. pres. 1991, 92, program chair 1990), Assn. Computing Machinery, Am. Soc. Quality (cert. software quality engr.). Presbyterian. Avocations: gardening, collecting Civil War relics. Office: Miss Valley Title Ins Co 315 Tombigbee St Jackson MS 39201-4600

SKELTON, HELEN ROGERS, retired auditor; b. Bloomington, Tex., Sept. 23, 1917; d. Marshall Raymond and Clara Eva (Kennemer) Rogers; m. Clarance Carlton Skelton, Aug. 2, 1935; children: Doris Annette Skelton Swanson, Donald Melvin. Grad. high sch., Burkeville, Tex., 1935. Bookkeeper Am. Nat. Bank, Beaumont, Tex., 1944-56; auditor, payroll clerk Tex. Highway Dept., Austin, Dallas, 1956-76. Genealogist The Rogers Clan, Tex., 1975—. Author, editor: (with Clarance Carlton Skelton) Rogers/Skelton Allied Families, 1987. Mem. Internat. Porcelain Arts, DAR, Colonial Dames XVIIC, Am. Colonists, Huguenot Soc., Magna Charta Dames, Sons & Daus of Pilgrims, UDC, Soverign Colonial Soc. Ams. of Royal Descent, Colonial Order of the Crown, Soc. of Most Noble Order of the Garter. Avocations: crochet, embroidery, painting porcelain china, reading, genealogy. Home and Office: The Rogers Clan PO Box 340 Burkeville TX 75932-0340

SKELTON, ISAAC NEWTON, IV (IKE SKELTON), congressman; b. Lexington, Mo., Dec. 20, 1931; s. Isaac Newton and Carolyn (Boone) S.; m. Susan B. Anding, July 22, 1961; children: Ike, Jim, Page. AB, U. Mo., 1953, LLB, 1956. Bar: Mo. 1956. Pvt. practice, Lexington; pros. atty. Lafayette County, Mo., 1957-60; spl. asst. atty. gen. State of Mo., 1961-63; mem. Mo. Senate from 28th dist., 1971-76, 95th-107th Congresses from 4th Mo. Dist., 1977—, ranking minority mem. ho. armed svcs. com., mem. intelligence com. Active Boy Scouts Am. Mem. Phi Beta Kappa, Sigma Chi. Democrat. Mem. Christian Ch. Clubs: Masons, Shriners, Elks. Home: 6754 Towne Lane Rd Mc Lean VA 22101-2935 Office: US Ho of Reps 2206 Rayburn House Ofc Bldg Washington DC 20515-2876*

SKELTON, MARK ALBERT, lawyer; b. Kingsport, Tenn., Jan. 8, 1957; s. George Haskell and Mary Lucille (Berry) S.; m. Joanna Coffey, Sept. 8, 1979. BBA, U. Tenn., 1979, JD, 1982. Bar: Tenn. 1983, U.S. Dist. Ct. (ea. dist.) Tenn. 1984, U.S. Ct. Appeals (6th cir.) 1990, U.S. Supreme Ct. 1993. Sole practice, Rogersville, Tenn., 1983—. City atty. City of Surgoinsville, Tenn., 1984-98. Bd. dirs., v.p. Rogersville Heritage Assn., 1985-89; bd. trustees Surgoinsville First United Meth. Ch., 1992-96; chmn. bd. dirs. Surgoinsville Med. Ctr., Inc., 1994-99. Mem. ABA, ATLA, Tenn. Bar Assn., Tenn. Trial Lawyers Assn., Hawkins County Bar Assn., Nat. Assn. Criminal Def. Lawyers, Tenn. Assn. Criminal Def. Lawyers, Nat. Orgn. Social Security Claimants Reps., Nat. Assn. Consumer Bankruptcy Attys., Am. Bankruptcy Inst., Hawkins County C. of C., Phi Kappa Phi, Beta Gamma Sigma, Gamma Beta Phi, Pi Sigma Alpha. Methodist. Home: 903 Main St Surgoinsville TN 37873-6057 Office: 121 S Depot St Rogersville TN 37857-3303 Fax: 423-272-0712. E-mail: maslaw@usit.net.

SKELTON, WILLIAM DOUGLAS, physician; MD, EMory U., 1963. Sr. v.p. rsch. & health affairs Mercer U., Macon, Ga., 1985—. Office: Mercer Univ 1550 College St Macon GA 31207-1500 E-mail: skelton_wd@mercer.edu.

SKEMER, ARNOLD MARIUS, writer; b. Bronx, N.Y., Dec. 22, 1946; s. Alex Skemer and Lillian Farber; m. Leslie Helen Weiner, June 3, 1979; children: Roland Wells, Melanie Ann. BA, Queens Coll., 1968. Editor ZYX, Bayside, N.Y., 1990—. Author: The Famine, 1985, C, 1992, D, 1995, The Occupation, 1996, B, 1996, Momus, 1997, The Ruins of the City, 1998, Investigations of the Cyberneticist, 1999. Home: 58-09 205th St Bayside NY 11364

SKERRITT, TOM, actor; b. Detroit, Aug. 25, 1933; Student, Wayne State U., UCLA. Films: War Hunt, 1962, One Man's Way, 1964, Those Calloways, 1964, M*A*S*H, 1970, WIld Rovers, 1972, Fuzz, 1972, Big Bad Mama, 1974, Thieves Like Us, 1974, The Devil's Rain, 1975, The Turning Point, 1977, Up In Smoke, 1978, Alien, 1979, Ice Castles, 1979, Silence of the North, 1981, A Dangerous Summer, 1981, Savage Harvest, 1981, Fighting Back, 1982, The Dead Zone, 1983, Top Gun, 1986, Space Camp, 1987, The Big Town, 1987, Wisdom, 1987, Opposing Force, 1987, Maid to Order, 1987, Poltergeist III, 1988, Steel Magnolias, 1989, Big Man On Campus, 1990, The Rookie, 1991, Blue Movie Blue, 1991, Poison Ivy, 1991, A River Runs Through It, 1992, Contact, 1997, The Other Sister, Texas Rangers, 2000; TV shows: Ryan's Four, 1983, Contact, 1997, On The Edge, 1987, Cheers, 1987-88, Picket Fences, 1992-96 (Emmy award Outstanding Lead Actor in a Drama Series, 1993); TV movies: The Bird Man, The Last Day, Maneaters Are Loose!, Calendar Girl Murders, Miles to Go, True Believer, Parent Trap II, A Touch of Scandal, Poker Alice, Nightmare At Bitter Creek, Moving Target, The Heist, Red King White Knight, The China Lake Murders, Child of the Night, In Sickness and In Health, Getting Up and Going Home, Divided By Hate, 1997, What the Deaf Man Heard, The Heart of the Unicorn Killer, 1999, Aftershock, 1999, American Daughter, 2000, High Noon, 2000, Jacqueline Bouvier Kennedy Onassis: Alife, 2000, Path of War, 2002. Office: Guttman Assocs 118 S Beverly Dr Beverly Hills CA 90212-3003

SKIBA, AURELIA ELLEN, private school educator; b. Chgo., May 17, 1943; d. Anthony J. and Josephine (Cyza) Trojnar; m. Edward S. Skiba, June 11, 1966; children: Robert E. Randall A., Jeffrey W. BA, DePaul U., 1965; M.Math. Edn., U. Ill., Champaign, 1990. Cert. tchr., Ill. Tchr. Resurrection High Sch., Chgo., 1965-72, head math. dept., 1967-72, tchr., 1979—. Spkr. in field. Contbr. articles to profl. jours. Mem. parish liturgy bd. St. Isaac Jogues, Niles, Ill., 1990—. Recipient Ill. Presdl. award for excellence in math. tchg., 1997, Honorable Mention Presdl. award Ill. Coun. Tchrs. Math., 1996, Radio Shack Tchr. award, 2001; Geometry fellow U. Ill., 1987, stats. fellow U. Ill., 1988, calculus fellow U. Ill., 1989; NSF grantee, 1988, 91, 92, 93, 94, 95; Fulbright Meml. Fund award tchr. grantee, Japan, 1998. Mem. Nat. Coun. Tchrs. Math. (conf. speaker 1995), Ill. Coun. Tchrs. Math. (conf. speaker 1987, 93, 94, 95, 96-2001), Met. Math. Club Chgo., Math. Tchrs. Assn. Chgo. Roman Catholic. Avocations: choir, cake decorating, knitting, church lector, cantor, reading. Office: Resurrection High Sch 7500 W Talcott Ave Chicago IL 60631-3742

SKIBA, MARK A. computer company executive; BS in Computer Info. Sys., DeVry Inst. Tech., Ohio, 1987. Programmer Columbus (Ohio) Life Ins., 1987-88; pres., chmn. On-Line Sales and Info. Sys., Inc., Columbus, 1988—; assoc. C.W. Costello & Assocs., 1989-91; application programmer IV Franklin County Data Ctr., 1991—. Mem. Columbus Coun. on World Affairs. Mem. Ch. of God. Office: OSIS PO Box 32039 Columbus OH 43232-0039 E-mail: maskiba@aol.com., osis@earthlink.net.

SKIBELL, JOSEPH FREER, writer, educator; b. Lubbock, Tex., Oct. 18, 1959; s. Irvin Alfred and Shirlene Ruth (Lezan) S.; m . Barbara Freer, May 28, 1988; 1 child, Arianna Shirah Freer Skibell. BA in Humanities Plan II, U. Tex., 1981, MFA, 1996; postgrad., U. Chgo., 1982. Vis. writer dept. English U. Wis., Madison, 1996-98; asst. prof. English Emory U., Atlanta, 1999—. Author: A Blessing on the Moon, 1997; film projects include When Ezra Quilliam Came Home, 1987, Making Jack Wild, 1991-92; contbr. stories to Story Mag., Story Competition Winners, Many Mountains Moving, The Madison Rev.; several plays produced; journalist N.Y. Times, Chgo. Tribune. Bd. dirs. Hazzam Found. Recipient Joel Climenhaga Creative Writing award Kans. State U., 1994, Story Mag. Short Fiction award, 1994; Richard and Hinda Rosenthal Found. award Am. Acad. Arts and Letters, 1998, Steven Turner prize Tex. Inst. Letters, 1998; N.Mex. Arts Divsn./Nat. Endowment for Arts fellow, 1985-86, James A. Michener fellow Tex. Ctr. for Writers, U. Tex., Austin, 1993-96, Wis. Inst. for Creative Writing fellow, 1996-97; Helene Wurlitzer Found. grantee, Taos, N.Mex., 1982-83; Nat. Endowment for Arts lit. fellow, 2002. Mem. Writers Guild Am. West, Assoc. Writing Programs. Avocations: yoga, biking, hiking, Esperanto, saxophone.

SKIBINSKI, OLGA, artist, art conservator; b. Bucharest, Romania, Sept. 15, 1939; came to U.S., 1986; d. Alois Skibinski and Marina Barbulescu; divorced; 1 child, Stefan. BA, Fine Arts Coll., 1963; diploma in art conservation, Nat. Mus. Art, 1967. Sr. art conservator Nat. Mus. Art, Bucharest, 1964-86; freelance artist and art conservator N.Y.C., 1986—. Lectr. on art conservation. One woman shows at Orizont Gallery, Bucharest, Romania, 1978, Mus. Fine Arts, Craiova, Romania, 1981, Simeza Gallery, Bucharest, 1984, Romanian Cultural Ctr., N.Y.C., 1993; group shows in N.Y., Washington, Chgo.; contbr. articles to art mags. Mem. Internat. Inst. for Conservation London, Am. Inst. for Conservation, West Side Art Coalition. Republican. Avocation: classical music. Home: 78-12 35th Ave Apt 4A Jackson Heights NY 11372

SKIBO, JAMES M. anthropologist, educator; b. Crystal Falls, Mich., Jan. 7, 1960; s. Matthew L. and Rose Mae (Kania) S.; m. Rebecca G. Skibo, Dec. 27, 1981; children: Matthew, Sadie. BS, No. Mich. U., 1982; MA, U. Ariz., 1984, PhD, 1990. Asst. prof. anthropology Ill. State U., Normal, 1992-96, assoc. prof., 1996-2001, prof., 2001—. Author: Pottery Function, 1992, Ants for Breakfast: Archaeological Adventures Among the Kalinga, 1999; editor: Kalinga Ethnoarchaeology, 1994, Expanding Archaeology, 1995, Pottery and People, 1999, Jour. Archaeol. Method and Theory. Named Outstanding Young Alumni, No. Mich. U., 1996. Avocations: hiking, camping, biking. Home: 700 Sheridan Rd Normal IL 61761-4045 Office: Illinois State Univ Dept. Anthropology Normal IL 61790-4640 E-mail: jmskibo@ilstu.edu.

SKIDD, THOMAS PATRICK, JR. lawyer; s. Thomas Patrick and Anna Skidd; m. Judith Chase Roberts, Sept. 10, 1960; children: Suanne C., Sherry E., Thomas Patrick III, Jody E. BA in Econs. cum laude, Georgetown U., 1958; LLB, Yale U., 1961. Bar: Conn. 1961, U.S. Supreme Ct. 1963. Ptnr. Cummings & Lockwood, Stamford, Conn., 1961—. Mem. Conn. Bar Assn. (real estate sect. and land use sect.), Stamford-Norwalk Regional Bar Assn., Roton Point Club (Rowayton, Conn.). Roman Catholic. Avocation: phonograph record collector. Office: Cummings & Lockwood 107 Elm St 12th Fl Stamford CT 06902-3834

SKIDMORE, DONALD EARL, JR. government official; b. Tacoma, Apr. 27, 1944; s. Donald E. and Ingeborg (Johnsrud) S. BS, Evangel. Coll., 1968; grad., Bellevue (Wash.) Police Acad., 1992. With Dept. Social and Health Svcs. State of Wash., Yakima, 1967-74; quality rev. splst. Social Security Adminstrn., Seattle, 1974-76; program analyst Balt., 1976-79, Seattle, 1979-81; quality assurance officer, mgr. Satellite office Spokane, Wash., 1981-84; program analyst Seattle, 1984-90; mgmt. analyst, 1990—. V.p., trustee Norwood Village, 1987-90; vice chair ops. subcom., mem. citizen's adv. com. land use planning, Bellevue, Wash., 1988-90; pres., bd. dirs. Compton Ct. Condo Assn., 1980-81. Office: 701 5th Ave Seattle WA 98104-7097

SKIDMORE, JAMES ALBERT, JR. management, computer technology and engineering services company executive; b. Newark, June 30, 1932; s. James A. and Frances W. (Barker) S.; m. Peggy Ann Young, July 10, 1954; children: Jacqueline Sue, James Albert III. BA, Muhlenberg Coll., 1954; postgrad., Duke U., 1978. Customer sales rep. N.J. Bell Tel. Co., Newark, 1957-65, then dist. sales mgr., divsn. mktg. mgr.; asst. to pres. for pub. affairs Pepsi Co., Inc., N.Y.C., 1966-69; asst. to Pres. of U.S., 1968-69; v.p. Handy Assoc., N.Y.C., 1969—71, pres., 1972; pres., CEO Sci. Mgmt. Corp., Basking Ridge, N.J., 1972—; chmn. bd. dirs. Newark Brush Co., 1974-79. Bd. dirs. Franklin State Bank, Somerset, N.J., Franklin Bancorp, United Jersey Banks, United Jersey Bank Franklin State; mem. exec. com. UJB Fin.-Summit Bank, 1985-93, Blue Cross & Blue Shield N.J., Inc., Enterprise Holding Co., Inc.; exec. com., trustee Blue Cross of N.J., 1983—; dir. Coca Cola, N.Y., 1980-85, Mariner Comm., 1983-85, Horizon Blue Cross Blue Shield N.J., Pa., N.Y., Del., 1998—; mem., chmn. mktg. com. Seton Hall Commn., 1987; trustee Rutgers U. Grad. Sch. Mgmt., 1989—; trustee Pub. Affairs Rsch. Inst. N.J., 1988—; lectr. U. Amsteram, The Netherlands, 1967, U. Toronto, Ont., Can., U. Helsinki, Finland, 1967, Tokyo U.; bd. dirs. Ctr. Analysis of Pub. Issues. Guest columnist Rotary Internat. mag., 1966-68, Kiwanis mag., 1966-68, Japan Times on Cmty. Responsibility and Leadership, 1965-67. Mem. Nat. Commn. on Crime and Delinquency, 1965-66; mem. Nat. Commn. on Youth Employment, 1966-67; state chmn. N.J. Nat. Found. March of Dimes, 1966-73; mem. exec. bd. Watchung Area coun. Boy Scouts Am., 1972-77, dir. N.E. region, 1983-90; mem. Citizen's Adv. Bd. on Youth Opportunity, 1969-75; state chmn. United Citizens for Nixon-Agnew, N.J., 1968; nat. bd. govs. Alpha Tau Omega Found., 1967-73; bd. dirs. Muhlenberg Coll., Allentown, Pa., 1980-92, 2000, N.E. region Boy Scouts Am., 1983—; trustee Brick Twp. Hosp., Inc., Brick Town, N.J., 1976-80; bd. dirs. Am. Christmas Trains and Trucks, chmn., 1966; pres. Project Concern, San Diego, 1966-78; trustee The Scholarship Fund for Inner-City Children, 1997, Ctr. for Analysis of Pub. Issues, 1999—. Served to capt. USMC, 1954-57. Decorated Order of St. John (Eng.); recipient Internat. Understanding award, Brussels, 1966, Disting. Svc. award, St. Paul, 1966, Freedom Found. George Washington Medal of Honor award, 1965, Outstanding Achievement in Life award Muhlenberg Coll. Alumni, 1966, Amb. award U.S. Jaycees, 1977, Trinidad and Tobago award Prime Minister of Ireland, 1970, Human Rels. award Soc. Advancement of Mgmt., 1982, Statesman award N.J. Jaycees, 1983, Disting. Citizens award Boy Scouts Am., 1983, Pvt. Sector Initiative award Pres. Reagan, 1985; inducted into U.S. Jaycees Hall of Leadership, 1983. Mem. N.J. State C. of C. (bd. dirs.), Muhlenberg Coll. Alumni Assn., Alpha Tau Omega, Sky Club (N.Y.C.), Baltusrol Golf Club, Longboat Key Club. Home: 641 Ocean Ave Sea Girt NJ 08750 also: 1465 Gulf Of Mexico Dr Longboat Key FL 34228-3447 Office: Sci Mgmt Co LLC 721 Us Highway 202/206 Bridgewater NJ 08807-1760

SKIDMORE, JOYCE THORUM, public relations and communication executive; b. Dec. 30, 1926; d. Rolla Arden and Alice Luetta (Fox) Thorum; m. E. Douglas Jacobsen, Mar. 20, 1956 (dec.); 1 child, Kelly Douglas Jacobsen; m. Clarence E. Skidmore Jr., Aug. 9, 1969. BS, U. Utah, 1950, postgrad., 1953-55, U. So. Calif., 1964, U. Calif., Irvine, 1973-74, Cambridge (Eng.) U., 1992. Sales and promotion devel. JBL Internat., L.A., 1959-69; press sec. Utah Auditor's Office, Salt Lake City, 1979-81; pres., owner Joyce Skidmore Cons./Snowflake Prodns., 1980—. Adminstrv. asst. world hdqs. Toastmasters Internat., Santa Ana, Calif., 1973; adj. prof. comms. Pepperdine U., 1974; developer human resources, Oran, Algeria, 1975; promotions coord. Utah Bicentennial Project, Salt Lake City, 1976; adj. prof. Westminster Coll., 1978-79, 92-93, Brigham Young U., 1978—; cons., pub. rels. health costs and tourism C. of C. of Salt Lake Area; adj. prof. mktg. and comm. dept. and theater/film dept. Colo. Mountain Coll., 1985-86; bus. cons., prof. mktg. and comms. Mountainwest Coll. Bus. and Brigham Young U., Salt Lake City; cons. Hema U.S.A., Westline and Bunell Inc.; guest dir., writer Cablevision, Newport Beach, Calif., 1975; initiated use of old copper from Utah Capitol dome as collector's item, 1980; lectr. in field; writer pub. svc. announcements. Author: Happy Holidays, 1968; assoc. editor Utah Symphony newsletter; newsletter editor Nat. Auditor's Assn., 1979-81, State Auditor's Assn., 1979-81, Utah Health Fairs, 1982-83; journalist The Butler Banner; editor: Saga Weekly Post, Children's Page, Stavanger and Bergen, Norway, 1976-78; playwright, dir., author book and lyrics: (musical) They Came to Union Fort; playwright, dir. hist. musicals Shadows, Danish Dreams, A Perfect Picture; contbr. weekly columns to The Rifle Telegram; contbr. articles to Calif., Colo., Norwegian and Utah newspapers; author nat. bus. newsletters and family history newsletters. Utah dir. Nat. Health Screening Coun. for Vol. Orgns., Bethesda, Md., 1982-83; guest dir. Westminster Theatre, 1974; organizer Stavanger Theatre Guild and Workshops, 1977, Bookcliffs Arts and Humanities Coun., 1984-86; originator, organizer Hurlburt Days, Grand Valley and Parachute, Colo.; initiator, dir. Reader's Theatre, Comty. Christmas Festival; dir. Storytelling Festival, Neil Simon Night; promoter Salt Lake Arts Festival, Am. Geneal. Lending Libr. World Hdqs.; appearance Japanese condr. in Salt Lake City; Sister-City exch. Salt Lake and Matsumoto, Japan; fundraiser Utah Symphony Guild; dir. theater Art Barn, Salt Lake City; mem. steering com. 1st nat. competition Utah Playwriting Conf., Sundance, 1979-80; mem. local econ. devel. coun.; polit. dist. del., 1986; initiated invitation from Bergen Internat. Festival to Utah Symphony, 1981; campaign mgr. Mayor Lake Valley City, Utah, 1982; cons. Cottonwood Heights (Utah) Coun., 1982-83; cons. to Utah pres. Instrumentation Soc. Am.; co-chair advt. Utah Symphony Guild; winter and summer fundraisers Carousel Ball and Taste of the Town, 1988-89; guest dir., historian MMB Reading Arts Soc., 1988-89; promoter Utah Arts Orgns.; missionary leader Ch. of Jesus Christ of Latter-day Saints; v.p. Pub. Awareness RP Found. Fighting Blindness; dir. Internat. First Night Festival, Salt Lake City, 1993-2001; bd. dirs. Utah Centennial Commn., The Found. Fighting Blindness, 1st Night Festival of the Arts. Recipient Best Dir. statue, Colo., 2 Top Editor's awards Calif. Press Women, 1977, 4 writing awards 1977-78, Internat. Yr. of Child award Family Acad., San Francisco and Stavanger, 1979, Colo. Oscar award for Best Dir., 1986, Congl. Cup, Utah Polo Club; nat. Zeta Phi Eta scholar, 1948, So. Calif. Credit Assn. scholar, 1964; U. Utah fellow, 1953-55 Mem. LWV (dist. pres. 1976), Pub. Rels. Soc. Am. (student adv. 1980-82), Utah Press Women (6 writing awards 1979-81, 3d v.p. 1981-82), Instrument Soc. Am., Friendship Force Utah, MMB Reading Arts Soc. (v.p. devel.), Internat. Platform Assn., Daus. of Utah Pioneers (capt. Union Fort camp 1998-2000), Utah Polo Club (bd. dirs.), Japan-Am. Soc. (bd. dirs., with pub. affairs 1993-2000), Utah Storytelling Guild, UN Assn. Utah, Babcock Performing Readers (pres. 1996-2000), Internat. Soroptimist Club (pub. affairs dir.), Fima Voyagers France. Avocations: historian, extensive genealogical research, global business and education research programs, screenwriting for film and TV. Home and Office: 2629 Oak Creek Dr Sandy UT 84093-6522

SKIDMORE, MARK LAWRENCE, economist, educator; b. L.A., Dec. 30, 1964; s. Lawrence Kieth Skidmore; m. Kate Kareen Kenny; 1 child Jack. BA, U. Wash., 1987; MA, PhD, U. Colo., 1994. Methods analyst Boeing Comml. Airplane Co., Everett, Wash., 1987—89; instr. USAF Acad., Colorado Springs, 1993; prof. No. Ill. U., DeKalb, 1994—98; Fulbright scholar Nagoya City U. and Nanzan U., Japan, 1996—97; prof. U. Wis., Whitewater, 1998—. Pvt. cons., Whitewater, 1993—2002. Contbr. articles to profl. jours. Recipient Tchg. award, Mortar Bd. Nat. Honor Soc., 1998; fellow, Dept. Econs. U. Colo., 1993; grantee, Urban Inst., 2001. Mem.: Western Econ. Assn., Mid-Continent Regional Sci. Assn. (program com. chair 2000—02), Midwest Econ. Assn., Am. Econ. Assn. Avocations: mountain biking, cross country skiing, backpacking, basketball, home improvement. Home: N7593 State Pk Rd Whitewater WI 53190 Office: U Wis - Whitewater Carlson Hall 800 W Main St Whitewater WI 53190 Office Fax: 262-472-4863. Business E-Mail: skidmorm@mail.uww.edu.

SKIENS, WILLIAM EUGENE, electrical interconnect systems scientist, polymer engineer; b. Burns, Oreg., Feb. 21, 1928; s. William Poleman and Eugenia Glenn (Hibbard) S.; m. Vesta Lorraine Franz, Nov. 4, 1955; children: Rebecca, Beverly, Michael. Student, N.W. Nazarene U., 1946-48; BS in Chemistry, Oreg. State U., 1951; PhD in Phys. Chemistry, U. Wash., 1957. Chemist Dow Chem. Co., Pittsburg, Calif., 1951-53, rsch. chemist Midland, Mich. and Walnut Creek, Calif., 1957-58, 1958-73, E.I DuPont de Nemours, Wilmington, Del., 1955; sr. rsch. chemist Battelle Meml. Inst., Richland, Wash., 1973-84, also cons., 1984—; mgr. media system devel. Optical Data, Inc., Beaverton, Oreg., 1984-89; chief scientist Precision Interconnect, Portland, 1989—. Cons. WHO, Geneva, 1978-85, PI Med., Portland, 1991—. Contbr. chpts. to books, articles to profl. jours.; patentee in field. Com. chmn. Concord, Calif. council Boy Scouts Am., 1969-72; sec. Tri-Cities Nuclear Council, Richland, Wash., 1984. Named Alumni of Yr. N.W. Nazarene U., 1982. Mem. Am. Chem. Soc. (chmn. Richland sect. 1982), Soc. Plastic Engrs., Sigma Xi. Republican. Mem. Ch. Nazarene. Avocations: skiing, photography, backpacking, golf. Home: 31179 SW Country View Ln Wilsonville OR 97070-7479 Office: Precision Interconnect 10025 SW Freeman Dr Wilsonville OR 97070-9289 E-mail: gene.skiens@precisionint.com.

SKIEST, DANIEL JAY, medical educator, internist; b. Worcester, Mass., Jan. 9, 1962; s. Eugene Norman Skiest and Toby Anne Aisenberg; m. Suzette Evelyn Damboise, June 29, 1991; children: Hannah, Benjamin. BA in Govt., Dartmouth Coll., 1984; MD, Case We. Res., 1988. Diplomate Am. Bd. Internal Medicine and Infectious Diseases (assoc. chief infectious diseases). Asst. prof. U. Tex. Southwestern Med. Ctr., Dallas, 1994-2000, assoc. prof., 2000—. Editor: Parkland Guide to HIV Care, 1998; contbr. articles to profl. jours. Democrat. Jewish. Avocations: tennis, reading, traveling. Office: U Tex Southwestern Med Ctr Dallas TX 75390

SKIGEN, PATRICIA SUE, lawyer; b. Springfield, Mass., June 16, 1942; d. David P. and Gertrude H. (Hirschhaut) Skigen; m. Irwin J. Sugarman, May 1973 (div. Nov. 1994); 1 child Alexander David Sugarman ; m. Gary W. Guttman, May 2001. BA with distinction, Cornell U., 1964; LLB, Yale U., 1968. Bar: N.Y. 1968, U.S. Dist. Ct. (so. dist.) N.Y. 1969. Law clk. Anderson, Mori & Rabinowitz, Tokyo, 1966-67; assoc. Rosenman Colin Kaye Petschek Freund & Emil, N.Y.C., 1968-70, Willkie Farr & Gallagher, N.Y.C., 1970-75, ptnr., 1977-95; v.p., corp. fin. group legal dept. J.P. Morgan Chase & Co., 1995—2002, mng. dir., assoc. gen. counsel, 2002—. Dep. supt., gen. counsel N.Y. State Banking Dept., N.Y.C., 1975-77, first dep. supt. banks, 1977; adj. prof. Benjamin Cardozo Law Sch. Yeshiva U., 1979. Contbr. articles to profl. jours. Cornell U. Dean's scholar, 1960-64, Regent's scholar, 1960-64, Yale Law Sch. scholar, 1964-68. Mem.: ABA (corp. banking and bus. law sect.), Assn. of Bar of City of N.Y. (chmn. com. banking 1991—94, long range planning com. 1994—96, audit com. 1995—2001), Phi Kappa Phi, Phi Beta Kappa. Office: JP Morgan Chase and Co 270 Park Ave Fl 40 New York NY 10017-2014

SKIKNE, BARRY S. hematologist, educator; b. Brakpan, Transvaal, South Africa, Feb. 20, 1945; arrived in U.S., 1977; s. Harry and Rose Skikne; m. Marjorie L. Zucker, Dec. 16, 1969; children: Frances, Andrew, Sarah. MBBCh, U. Witwatersrand, Johannesberg, South Africa, 1969. Diplomate Am. Bd. Internal Medicine, Am. Bd. Hematology. Resident in internal medicine Johannesberg Gen. Hosp., 1972—74, cons., 1975—77; fellow in hematology U. Kans. Med. Ctr., Kansas City, 1977—78, from instr. to assoc. prof., 1978—89, prof., 1989—, dir. bone marrow transplant program, 1993—. Contbr. scientific papers to profl. jours. Grantee, various, 1979—. Fellow: ACP, South African Coll. Physicians; mem.: Am. Soc. Blood and Marrow Transplantation. Avocation: sailboat racing. Office: U Kans Med Ctr 3901 Rainbow Blvd Kansas City KS 66160 Office Fax: 913-588-3996.

SKILES, JAMES JEAN, electrical and computer engineering educator; b. St Louis, Oct. 16, 1928; s. Coy Emerson and Vernetta Beatrice (Maples) S.; m. Deloris Audrey McKenney, Sept. 4, 1948; children: Steven, Randall, Jeffrey. BSEE, Washington U., St. Louis, 1948; MS, U. Mo.-Rolla, 1951; PhD, U. Wis., 1954. Engr. Union Electric Co., St. Louis, 1948-49; instr. U. Mo.-Rolla, 1949-51; prof. elec. engring. U. Wis., Madison, 1954-89, prof. emeritus, 1989—, chmn. Dept. Elec. Engring., 1967-72, dir. Univ. Industry Rsch. program, 1972-75, dir. Energy Rsch. Ctr., 1975-95. Cons. in field Contbr. articles to profl. jours. Mem. Monona Grove Dist. Schs. Bd., Wis., 1961-69; mem. adv. com. Wis. Energy Office, Madison, 1979-80, Wis. Pub. Service Commn., 1980-81. Recipient Wis. Electric Utilities Professorship in Energy Engring. U. Wis., 1975-89; recipient Benjamin Smith Reynolds Teaching award, 1980, Kiekhofer Teaching award, 1955, Acad of Elec. Engring. award U. Mo.-Rolla, 1982 Mem. IEEE (sr.), Am. Soc. Engring. Edn. Home: 8099 Coray Ln Verona WI 53593-9073 Office: Univ of Wisconsin Dept Elec & Computer Engring 1415 Engineering Dr Madison WI 53706-1607 E-mail: skiles@engr.wisc.edu.

SKILLERN, FRANK FLETCHER, law educator; b. Sept. 26, 1942; s. Will T. and Vera Catherine (Ryberg) S.; m. Susan Schlaefer, Sept. 3, 1966; children: Nathan Edward, Leah Catherine. AB, U. Chgo., 1964; JD, U. Denver, 1966; LLM, U. Mich., 1969. Bar: Colo. 1967, Tex. 1978. Pvt. practice law, Denver, 1967; gen. atty. Maritime Adminstrn., Washington, 1967-68; asst. prof. law Ohio No. U., 1969-71, Tex. Tech U., Lubbock, 1971-73, assoc. prof. law, 1973-75, prof. law, 1975—, George W. McCleskey prof. water law, 1998—. Vis. prof. U. Tex. Law Sch., summer 1979, U. Ark. Law Sch., 1979-80, U. Tulsa Coll. Law, 1981-82; cons. and speaker in field. Author: Environmental Protection: The Legal Framework, 1981, 2d edit. published as Environmental Protection Deskbook, 1995, Regulation of Water and Sewer Utilities, 1989, Texas Water Law, Vol. I, 1988, rev. edit., 1992, Vol. II, 1991; contbr. chpts. to Powell on Real Property, Zoning and Land Use Controls, others; author cong. procs. and numerous articles. Mem. ABA (mem. publs. com. Sect. Natural Resources Law 1984—, vice chair internat. environ. law com. Sect. Natural Resources Law 1987). Office: Tex Tech U Sch Law PO Box 40004 Lubbock TX 79409-0004

SKILLING, MARIE L. music educator; b. Alma, Mich., Aug. 26, 1931; d. Dan Ernest and Florence Marie (Tolles) Harper; m. Darroll Dean Skilling, June 10, 1951; children: Ann Marie, James Dean, Stephen Richard. BS cum laude, U. Minn., 1974. Piano tchr., St. Paul. Scout leader Girl Scouts USA, St. Paul, 1958-64; ch. nursery dir. Presbyn. Ch., Wausau, Wis., 1956-60, ch. youth evening dir. weekly program, 1963-68. Mem. Nat. Music Tchrs. Assn., Minn. Music Tchrs. Assn. (test ctr. chmn., treas., constn. chair 1993-99, Disting. Svc. award 1998), St. Paul Piano Tchrs. Assn. (treas. 1975-78, pres. 1984-86, 1st v.p. 1982-84, 3d v.p. 1978-82). Avocations: sewing, needlework, sailing, camping, backpacking.

SKILLING, RAYMOND INWOOD, lawyer; b. Enniskillen, U.K., July 14, 1939; s. Dane and Elizabeth (Burleigh) S.; m. Alice Mae Welsh, Aug. 14, 1982; 1 child by previous marriage, Keith A. F. LLB, Queen's U., Belfast, U.K., 1961; JD, U. Chgo., 1962. Solicitor English Supreme Ct. 1966. Bar: Ill 1974. Assoc. Clifford-Turner (now Clifford Chance), London, 1963-69, ptnr., 1969-76; exec. v.p., chief counsel Aon Corp. (and predecessor cos.), Chgo., 1976—. Bd. dirs. Aon Corp. (and predecessor cos.). Commonwealth fellow, U. Chgo., 1961-62, Bigelow teaching fellow U. Chgo. Law Sch., 1962-63; Fulbright scholar U.S. Ednl. Commn., London, 1961-63; recipient McKane medal Queen's U., Belfast, 1961. Mem. ABA, Ill. Bar Assn., Chgo. Bar Assn., The Casino Chgo., Chgo. Club, Econ. Club Chgo., Racquet Club Chgo., Bucks Club London, The Carlton Club London, The City of London Club. Office: Aon Corp 200 E Randolph Chicago IL 60601

SKILLINGSTAD, CONSTANCE YVONNE, social services administrator, educator; b. Portland, Oreg., Nov. 18, 1944; d. Irving Elmer and Beulah Ruby (Aleckson) Erickson; M. David W. Skillingstad, Jan. 12, 1968 (div. Mar. 1981); children: Michael, Brian. BA in Sociology, U. Minn., 1966; MBA, U. St. Thomas, St. Paul, 1982. Cert. vol. adminstr.; lic. social worker; lic. real estate agt. Social worker Rock County Welfare Dept., Luverne, Minn., 1966-68, Hennepin County Social Svcs., Mpls., 1968-70, vol. coord., 1970-78, St. Joseph's Home for Children, Mpls., 1978-89, mgr. community resources, 1989-94; exec. dir. Mpls. Crisis Nursery, 1994-97; mem. cmty. faculty Met. State U., St. Paul and Mpls., 1980-97; faculty U. St. Thomas Ctr. for Non Profit Mgmt., 1990—2001; asst. adminstr. St. Joseph's Home Children, Mpls., 1997-98; asst. dir. Cath. Charities of Archdiocese of St. Paul and Mpls., 1998-2000; dir. mem. svcs. Minn. Coun. Founds., 2001—02; exec. dir. Family Support Network, St. Paul, 2002—; pres. Golden Girl Homes, Inc., 2001—. Trainer, mem. adv. commn. Mpls. Vol. Ctr., 1978-90, cons., 1980—, chmn. Contbr. articles to Jour. Vol. Adminstrn. Mem. adv. bd. Mothers Against Drunk Driving, Minn., 1986-88; vice chmn., chmn. adminstrv. coun., lay leader Hobart United Meth. Ch.; lay rep. to Minn. Ann. Conf. of Meth. Chs., 1989-92; chmn. social concerns. commn. Park Ave United Meth. Ch., 1992—; bd. dirs. Ctr. for Grief, Loss and Transition; mem. Initiative for Violence Free Families, 1998—. Named one of Oustanding Young Women Am., 1974, Woman of Distinction Mpls. St. Paul Mag./KARE-TV, 1995. Mem. Minn. Assn. Vol. Dirs. (pres. 1975, sec., ethics chmn. 1987—), Assn. for Vol. Adminstrn. (v.p. regional affairs 1985-87, mem. assessment panel 1986-94, coord. nat. tng. team, cert. process for vol. adminstrs. 1988-92, profl. devel. chair 1990-92), Minn. Social Svcs. Assn. (pres. 1981, 98-99, bd. dirs. 1996-2001, Disting. Svc. award 1987). Mem. Dem.-Farmer-Labor Party. Methodist. Avocations: bridge, volleyball, accordian, travel, reading. Office: Family Support Network Ste 202-S 1821 University Ave Saint Paul MN 55104 E-mail: cskillingstad@msn.com.

SKILLMAN, THOMAS GRANT, endocrinology consultant, former educator; b. Cin., Jan. 7, 1925; s. Harold Grant and Faustina (Jobes) S.; m. Elizabeth Louise McClellan, Sept. 6, 1947; children: Linda, Barbara. BS, Baldwin-Wallace Coll., 1946; MD, U. Cin., 1949. Intern Cin. Gen. Hosp., 1949-50, resident, 1952-54; instr. medicine U. Cin., 1952-57; asst. prof. medicine Ohio State U., Columbus, 1957-61, dir. endocrinology and metabolism Coll. Medicine, 1967-74, Ralph Kurtz prof. endocrinology, 1974-81, prof. emeritus, 1981—, cons. to v.p. med. affairs, 1981—. Asso. prof. medicine Creighton U., Omaha, 1961-67 Editor: Case Studies in Endocrinology, 1971; Contbr. numerous articles to med. jours. Served with USNR, 1943-45; 1950-52, Korea. Recipient Golden Apple award Student Am. Med. Assn., 1966 Mem. Am. Diabetes Assn., Central Soc. Clin. Investigation, Am. Fedn. for Clin. Research, Alpha Omega Alpha. Clubs: Ohio State Golf (Columbus). Home: 4179 Stoneroot Dr Hilliard OH 43026-3023 Office: Ohio State U Hosps McCampbell Hall 485 Columbus OH 43210

SKILLMAN, WILLIAM ALFRED, consulting engineering executive; b. Lakehurst, N.J., Jan. 22, 1928; s. Wilbur Newton and Greta Alfreda (Ekman) S.; m. Anne Marie Cavender, Sept. 19, 1948; children— Thomas R., Gregory A., Karen L. BS in Engring. Physics, Lehigh U., 1952; MS in Physics, U. Rochester, 1954. Assoc. engr. Westinghouse Electric Corp., Balt., 1954-56, engr., 1956-58, sr. engr., 1958-61, supervisory engr., 1961-64, advisory engr., 1964-73, sr. adv. engr., 1973-85, cons. engr., 1986-93, cons. electronic systems group, 1993—. Author: Radar Calculations Using the TI-59 Programmable Calculator, 1983; author: (with others) Radar Handbook, 2d edit., 1990. Patentee in field Served with USN, 1946-48 Fellow IEEE (life); mem. Aerospace and Electronic Sys. Soc. (Pioneer award 1995), Phi Beta Kappa. Republican. Methodist. Avocations: photography, travel, genealogy, programming. Home and Office: 605 Forest View Rd Linthicum Heights MD 21090-2819 E-mail: wskillman@aol.com.

SKILLRUD, DAVID MARK, pulmonologist, sleep specialist; b. Bloomington, Ill., Apr. 21, 1955; s. Harold C. and Lois A. Skillrud; m. Ann R. Stroink, June 22, 1974 (div. May 1991); children: Hans, Kirsten, Leif; m. Deborah Hattendorf, Nov. 27, 1992; children: Rikka, Meta, Linnea. BA in Chemistry summa cum laude, Ill. Wesleyan U., 1976; MD, So. Ill. U., 1979; MS, U. Minn., 1985. Diplomate Am. Bd. Internal Medicine, Am. Bd. Pulmonary Disease. Intern, resident Mayo Clinic, Rochester, Minn., 1979-82, fellow, 1982-85; pvt. practice Bloomington, 1985-94; dir. respiratory care and sleep medicine BroMenn Health Care, 1990—; staff pulmonologist Carle Clinic, 1994—. Staff physician St. Joseph's Hosp., Bloomington, St. James Hosp., Pontiac, Ill., Eureka (Ill.) Cmty. Hosp., Fairbury (Ill.) Hosp.; dir. McLean County TB Clinic, Bloomington-Normal, Ill., 1988—, Woodford County TB Clinic, Eureka, 1987-95; satellite med. dir. respiratory care program Parkland C.C., Champaign, Ill., 1988—; mem. Lorabid adv. com. Eli Lilly Co., 1992-93; physician case reviewer Ill. State Med. Ins. Svcs., Inc., 1993—; nat. faculty spkr. Glaxo-Wellcome Co., 1997; investigator in field. Mem. editl. bd. Pharmacy and Therapeutics, 1991—. Bd. dirs. Mennonite Coll. Nursing, 1987-96, chmn. nominating com., 1991, Am. Lung Assn. of Mid-Eastern Ill., 1986—, 2d v.p., 1990-93; bd. dirs. Bloomington-Normal Symphony Soc., chmn. nominating com., 1989, v.p. resource devel., 1990-93; bd. dirs., co-founder Franz Schubert Soc., 1986—; mem. physician's adv. com. McLean County Health Dept., 1986, AIDS Task Force, 1986; med. advisor Ill. Soc. Respiratory Care, 1988; activities dir. St. John's Luth. Ch., Bloomington, Ill., 1996—; mem. chorus Wesleyan Civic Orch. and Chorus, 1996; soloist St. John's Adult Choir, 1997; co-chmn. profl. divsn. United Way, 1990; mem. adv. coun. YWCA, 1996. Fellow ACP, Am. Coll. Chest Physicians; mem. AMA, Am. Thoracic Soc., Mayo Alumni Assn., Ill. Thoracic Soc., Nat. Assn. Med. Dirs. Respiratory Care, The Drs. Mayo Soc., Am. Sleep Disorders Assn., Assn. of Governing Bds. of Univs. and Colls., Phi Kappa Phi, Sigma Xi. Home: 1102 E Monroe St Bloomington IL 61701-3329 Office: Carle Clinic 1701 E College Ave Bloomington IL 61704-2100

SKILLRUD, HAROLD CLAYTON, minister, retired bishop; b. St. Cloud, Minn., June 29, 1928; s. Harold and Amanda Skillrud; m. Lois Dickhart, June 8, 1951; children: David, Janet, John. BA magna cum laude, Gustavus Adolphus Coll., 1950; MDiv magna cum laude, Augustana Theol. Sem., Rock Island, Ill., 1954; STM, Luth. Sch. Theology, Chgo., 1969; DD (hon.), Augustana Coll., 1978, Newberry Coll., 1988. Ordained to ministry Evang. Luth. Ch. in Am., 1954. Supply pastor Saron Luth. Ch., Big Lake, Minn., 1950-51; mem. staff 1st Luth. Ch., Rock Island, Ill., 1951-52; intern, organizer new mission Faith Luth. Ch., Syosset, N.Y., 1952-53; sr. pastor St. John's Luth. Ch., Bloomington, Ill., 1954-79, Luth. Ch. of the Redeemer, Atlanta, 1979-87; bishop Southeastern Synod Evang. Luth. Ch. in Am., 1987-95, regional rep. bd. pensions, 1995—. Del. to various convs. Luth. Ch. in Am., Luth. World Fedn. in Helsinki, 1963, mem. bd. publ., 1976-84, pastor-evangelist Evang. Outreach Emphasis program, 1977-79, mem. exec. bd. Ill. synod, 1977-79, pres. bd. publ., 1980-84, leader stewardship cluster Southeastern synod, 1983, mem. exec. bd. Southeastern synod, 1984-87; mem. exec. coun., Luth. Ch. in Am., 1984-87; mem. task force on new ch. design Commn. on New Luth. Ch., task force on ch. pub. house, 1985; del. constituting conv. Evang. Luth. Ch. in Am., 1987, del. assemblies Evang. Luth. Ch. in Am., 1989, 91, 93, 95; mem. commn. on clergy confidentiality Luth. Coun. in USA, 1987; co-chair USA Luth.- Roman Cath. Dialogue, 1990-97; mem. Task Force on Theol. Edn. Author: LSTC: Decade of Decision, 1969; co-editor Scripture and Tradition, Lutherans and Catholics in Dialogue, 1995; mem. edtl. bd. Partners mag., 1978-80; contbr. articles and sermons to religious jours. Former bd. dirs. Augustana Theol. Sem.; bd. dirs. Augustana Coll., 1969-77, chmn. bd., 1976-77; bd. dirs. Kessler Reformation Collection, Newberry Coll., Luth. World Relief, Augsburg Fortress; chmn. bd. dirs. Luth. Sch. Theology, Chgo., 1962-69; mem. Leadership Atlanta, 1980-81, United Way, Atlanta, 1980-81; mem. Bishop's Commn. on Econ. Justice, 1985-86; pres. bd. dirs. Atlanta Samaritan House, 1986-87. Recipient Alumni award Luth. Sch. Theology, Chgo., 1976, award Leadership Atlanta, 1981, The Rev. John Bachman award, Luth. Theol. Sem., Columbia, S.C., 1996. Mem. Luth. Sch. Theology Alumni Assn. (pres. 1975-77), Conf. of Bishops, Kiwanis (pres. Midtown chpt. 1984-85). Avocations: travel, photography. Home: 368 E Wesley Rd NE Atlanta GA 30305-3824 E-mail: hcskillrud@aol.com.

SKINGER, KENNETH ROBERT, communications executive, engineer, lawyer; b. New Britain, Conn., June 18, 1941; s. Dennis Leonard Skinger and Genevive (Buden) Backus; m. Nancy Lee Christien, July 6, 196 (div. 1984); children: Robin Lee, Todd Kristopher; m. Maryellen Kernen, Feb. 14, 1988; 1 child, Christopher D'Entremont. BS in Engring., U. Conn., 1963; JD cum laude, New Eng. Sch. Law, Boston, 1978. Bar: Mass. 1978, U.S. Dist. Ct. 1979, Mass. 1979, U.S. Ct. Appeals (1st cir.) 1979, U.S. Supreme Ct. 1982; profl. engr., Conn., Mass., N.Y., Tex., R.I., Fla. Sales engr. GE, N.Y.C., 1963-69, utility sales mgr. Albany, N.Y., 1969-74; elec. engr. Stone & Webster Engring. Corp., Boston, 1974-78, mgr. mktg. svcs., 1978-85, mgr. engring. svcs., 1985-86, prin. elec. engr., 1986-88, project mgr., 1989-95, v.p. comm. svcs. group, 1995—. Exec. com., bd. dirs. New Eng.-Can. Bus. Coun., Boston, 1993—, v.p., 1994-95. Contbr. articles to IEEE Transactions, FAA Tech. Forum, tech. mags. Mem. IEEE (sr. mem.). Avocations: sailing, cross country skiing. Office: Stone & Webster Engrg Corp 245 Summer St Ste 100 Boston MA 02210-1127

SKINNER, ALASTAIR, accountant; b. Hamilton, Ont., Can., Apr. 4, 1936; s. Allistair and Isabelle (Drysdale) S.; m. Patricia Skinner; children: Lisa, Iain, James, Graeme. CA, Queens U., Kingston, Ont., Can., 1959; MBA, Harvard U., 1963. Cert. mgmt. cons. Served to maj. Can. Army Res., 1954-71; nat. mng. ptnr. MacGillivray & Co. (name now Grant Thornton), 1977-83; ptnr.-in-charge Toronto (Ont.) Office, Spicer MacGillivray (name now Grant Thornton), 1984-86, 88-91; ptnr. Grant Thornton, Toronto, 1991—. Co-author: profl. manuals. Fellow Inst. Chartered Accts. of Ont. (pres. 1983-84), Soc. Mgmt. Accts. of Can. (bd. dirs.); mem. Inst. Mgmt. Cons. of Ont., Can. Tax Found. (bd. govs.), Pub. Accts. Coun. Ont. (pres. 1999-2000), Albany Club (Toronto), Devil's Glen Country Club (bd. dirs.). Avocations: skiing, bridge. Office: Grant Thornton Ste 1900 Royal Bank Plz Box 55 Toronto ON Canada M5J 2P9

SKINNER, ANDREW CHARLES, history educator, religious writer; b. Durango, Colo., Apr. 25, 1951; s. Charles La Verne and Julia Magdalena (Schunk) S.; m. Janet Corbridge, Mar. 22, 1974; children: Cheryl Lyn, Charles Lon, Kelli Ann, Mark Andrew, Holly, Suzanne. BA with distinction, U. Colo., 1975; MA with distinction, Iliff Sch. Theology, Denver, 1978; ThM, Harvard U., 1980; PhD, U. Denver, 1986. Group mgr. May Co. Dept. Store, Denver, 1980-83; assoc. studio dir. Talking Books Pub. Co., 1984-88; instr. history Metro. State Coll., 1984-88; prof. history Ricks Coll., Rexburg, Utah, 1988-92; prof. ancient scripture Brigham Young U., Provo, 1992—, chmn. ancient scripture, 1997—, dean Coll. of Religious Edn., 2000—. Vis. instr. ancient scripture Brigham Young U., Provo, Utah, 1987; vis. prof. Jerusalem Ctr. for Nr. Eastern Studies, Israel; cons. Univ. Without Walls, Loretto Heights Coll., Denver, 1985-88; mem. editorial staff Dead Sea Scrolls, publ. bd. Israel Antiquities Authority. Author chpts. numerous books including Gethsemane, 2002, Parables of the Latter Days; co-author: Jerusalem-The Eternal City, 1996, New Testament Apostles Testify of Christ, 1998, C.S. Lewis: The Man and His Message, 1999, Parables of the Latter Days, 2001, Discoveries in the Judaean Desert XXXIII-Qumran Cave 4; contbr. articles to profl. jours. Bishop Mormon Ch., Denver, 1986-88, Utah, 1996—; varsity scout leader Teton Parks coun. Boy Scouts Am., Rexburg, 1988-89; host Internat. Scholars Conf. on Holocaust and the Chs., 1995. Mil. history fellow U.S. Mil. Acad., 1989. Mem. Am. Hist. Assn., Soc. Bibl. Lit., Mormon History Assn., Phi Theta Kappa, Phi Alpha Theta. Mem. Lds Ch. Office: Brigham Young U Coll Religious Edn JSB 375-A Provo UT 84602

SKINNER, BRIAN ALLAN, writer, artist; b. Chgo., May 24, 1949; s. George Wendell and Elaine Elodie Skinner; m. Mary Weldi, May 7, 1972 (div. May 14, 1998); life ptnr. Anthony Chase Fountain. Student, U. Ill., Chgo., 1967-69. Owner Manhattan Group Pubs., N.Y.C., 1994—; editor Chgo. Quar. Rev., 1994—. Staff artist Chgo. Quar. Rev., 1994—; poetry reviewer Kirkus Reviews, 1999—. Author: Liars, Tattlers and Weavers, 1994, (short story) The Red Dress, 1999 (Ann. Fiction prize Rambunctious Review 1999); editor: Out of the Blue, 1996, Food for Thought, 1997; artist (illustration) Vision Quest, 1997 (Art in the Woods V award 1997). Mem. Ctrl. Park Conservancy, N.Y.C., 2000, Friends of Ft. Tryon Park, N.Y.C., 2000. Mem. Small Press Writers and Artists Orgn. Avocations: hiking, photography. Home and Office: Manhattan Group Pubs 120 Bennett Ave Ste 1-G New York NY 10033-2321 Personal E-mail: MGP_NYC@hotmail.com.

SKINNER, BRIAN JOHN, geologist, educator; b. Wallaroo, South Australia, Dec. 15, 1928; came to U.S., 1958, naturalized, 1963; s. Joshua Henry and Joyce Barbara Lloyd (Prince) S.; m. Helen Catherine Wild, Oct. 9, 1954; children: Adrienne Wild, Stephanie Wild, Thalassa Wild. B.Sc., U. Adelaide, Australia, 1950; A.M., Harvard U., 1952, PhD, 1955; D Engring. (hon.), Colo. Sch. Mines, 1998; DSc (hon.), U. Toronto, 1998. Lectr. U. Adelaide, 1955-58; research geologist U.S. Geol. Survey, 1958-62, chief br. exptl. geochemistry and mineralogy, 1962-66; prof. geology and geophysics, chmn. dept. Yale U., New Haven, 1966-73, Eugene Higgins prof., 1972—. Hugh Exton McKinstry Meml. lectr. Harvard U., 1978; Alex L. du Toit lectr. Combined Socs. South Africa, 1979; Cecil H. and Ida Green lectr. U. B.C., 1983; Thayer Lindsley Meml. lectr. Soc. Econ. Geologists, 1983; Soc. Econ. Geologists Overseas lectr., 1985; Hoffman lectr. Harvard U., 1986, Joubin-James lectr. U. Toronto, 1987; mem. exec. com. divsn. earth scis. NRC, 1966-69; chmn. com. mineral resources and the environ. Nat. Acad. Scis.-NRC, 1973-75; mem. Lunar Sample Analysis Planning Team, 1968-70, Lunar Sci. Rev. Bd., 1971-72, U.S. Nat. Com. for Geochemistry, 1966-67, U.S. Nat. Com. for Geology, 1973-77, 85-93, chmn., 1987-93, chmn. bd. earth scis. NRC, 1987-88, earth scis. and resources, 1989-90; mem. bd. Internat. Geol. Correlation Program, UNESCO-IUGS, 1985-89, 90-96, chmn., 1986-89; cons. Office Sci. and Tech. Policy, 1977-80, NSF, 1977-82; dir. Econ. Geology Pub. Co.; chmn. governing bd. Am. Jour. Sci., 1972—; pres. Econ. Geology Pub. Co., 1996—. Author: Earth Resources, 1969, 77, 86, Man and the Ocean, 1973, Physical Geology, 1974, 77, 87, Rocks and Rock Minerals, 1979, The New Iron Age Ahead, 1987, Resources and World Development, 1987, The Dynamic Earth, 1989, 92, 95, The Blue Planet, 1995, 99, 2000, Environmental Geology, 1996, Geology Today, 1999, Oxford Companion to the Earth, 2000; editor: Econ. Geology, 1969-96, Oxford Univ. Press Monographs in Geological Sciences, 1979—, Internat. Geology Rev., 1995—; editl. bd. Am. Scientist, 1974-90, chmn., 1987-90. Trustee Hopkins Grammar Sch., 1978-83. Recipient Disting. Contbns. award, Assn. Earth Sci. Editors, 1979, Silver medal, Soc. Econ.

Geologists, 1981, medal, Geol. Assn. Can., 1998, Futen's medal, Inst. of Mining and Metallurgy, London, 2002; fellow, Guggenheim fellow, 1970. Fellow Geol. Soc. Am. (councillor 1976-78, chmn. spl. publs. com. 1980-81, chmn. com. on coms. 1983, pres. 1985); mem. Geochem. Soc. (pres. 1972-73), Conn. Acad. Sci. and Engring. (div. chmn. 1978-80, council 1982-87), Soc. Econ. Geologists (pres. 1995). Home: PO Box 894 Woodbury CT 06798-0894

SKINNER, DANIEL THOMAS, language educator; b. Boston, May 1, 1916; s. Thomas Henson and Esther Hannetta (Jennings) Skinner; m. Vyna May Wingood, Oct. 15, 1944 (dec. Jan. 1995); children: David Edward, John Arnold. AB magna cum laude, Harvard U., 1938, PhD in Romance Lang., 1953; MA in Romance Lang., Boston Coll., 1939. Substitute instr. in French Va. State Coll., Ettrick, 1939—40; instr. in French and Spanish Dillard U., New Orleans, 1940—42; from asst. prof. to prof. French and Latin Morgan State Coll., Balt., 1946—81. Vis. prof. Tex. So. U., Houston, 1953—54, Houston, 1956, Towson State Coll., Balt., 1964; part-time prof. Sojourner-Douglass Coll., Balt., 1981—85, Coppin State Coll., Balt., 1985—90; mem. adv. bd. Directory of Am. Scholars, N.Y.C., 1970—80. Author: U.S. Teacher-Training Program: for France, 1959, Victor Hugo and L. Frechette, 1972, Ustaz Aswad (Black Professor), 1996. Pres. PTA, Balt., 1957. Named Rosenwald fellow, Rosenwald Found., Chgo., 1947—48, Fulbright prof. in France, Fulbright Found., Washington, 1956—57; recipient Nat. award, Urban League, Boston, 1949. Mem.: Frisby Hist. Soc. (fin. sec. 2001—02), Henson Family Soc., Phi Beta Kappa. Democrat. Roman Catholic. Avocations: movies, pinochle, sports, foreign travel. Home: 2033 Wheeler Ave Baltimore MD 21216-3225

SKINNER, DAVID BERNT, surgeon, educator, health facility administrator; b. Joliet, Ill., Apr. 28, 1935; s. James Madden and Bertha Elinor (Tapper) S.; m. May Elinor May Elinor Tischer, Aug. 25, 1956; children: Linda Elinor, Kristin Anne, Carise Berntine, Margaret Leigh. BA with high honors, U. Rochester, N.Y., 1958, ScD (hon.) (hon.), 1980; MD cum laude, Yale U., 1959; MD (hon.) (hon.) , U. Lund, 1994, Technishe U. Munich, 1995. Diplomate Am. Bd. Thoracic Surgery. Intern, then resident in surgery Mass. Gen. Hosp., Boston, 1959—65; sr. registrar in thoracic surgery Frenchay Hosp., Bristol, England, 1963—64; teaching fellow Harvard U. Med. Sch., 1965; from asst. prof. surgery to prof. Johns Hopkins U. Med. Sch., also surgeon Johns Hopkins Hosp., 1968—72; Dallas B. Phemister prof. surgery, chmn. dept. U. Chgo. Hosps. and Clinics, 1972—87; prof. orthopedic surgery Cornell U., 1987—. Pres., CEO, N.Y. Hosp., 1987—; vice chair, CEO N.Y. and Presbyn. Hosps., 1996—2000; dir. Omnis Surg. Inc., 1984—85, Churchill Livingston, 1990—93, Lab. Corp. Am.; mem. Pres.' Biomed. Rsch. Panel, 1975—76, pres. emeritus, 2000—. Author: Atlas of Esophageal Surgery, 1991; author: (with others) Gastroesophageal Reflux and Hiatal Hernia, 1972, Management of Esophageal Diseases, 1988; editor: Surgical Practice Illustrated, 1988—95, Current Topics in Surg. Rsch., 1969—71, Jour. Surg. Rsch., 1972—83; co-editor: Surg. Treatment of Digestive Disease, 1985, Esophageal Disorders, 1985, Reconstructive Surgery of the Gastrointestinal Tract, 1985, Primary Motility Disorders of the Esophagus, 1991; mem. editl. bd.: Jour. Thoracic and Cardiovasc. Surgery, mem. editl. bd.: ; contbr. Bd. visitors Cornell U. Med. Coll., 1980—87; trustee Fifth Ave. Presbyn. Ch., N.Y.C., 1999—2000; Elder Fourth Presbyn. Ch., Chgo., 1976—87, clk. of session, 1978—82, 1984—87. Maj. M.C. USAF, 1966—68. Decorated chevalier Nat. Order of Merit France, Cross of Honor Arts and Scis. 1st class Austria; scholar John and Mary Markle scholar acad. medicine, 1969—74. Mem.: AMA, ACS, Soc. Med. Adminstrs., Greater N.Y. Hosp. Assn. (chair 1996—97), Soc. Clin. Surgery (pres. 1986—88), Halsted Soc., Assn. Acad. Surgery, Internat. Soc. Diseases Esophagus (pres. 1992—95), Ctrl. Surg. Soc., Am. Coll. Chest Physicians, Collegium Internat. de Chirurgie Digestivae, Soc. Internat. de Chirurgie, Soc. Surgery Alimentary Tract, Soc. Pelvic Surgeons, Soc. Thoracic Surgery, Soc. Vascular Surgery, Am. Assn. Thoracic Surgery (pres. 1996—97), Soc. Surg. Chmn. (pres. 1980—82), Am. Soc. Artificial Internal Organs (pres. 1977), Soc. Univ. Surgeons (pres. 1978—79), Western So. Surg. Assn., Am. So. Surg. Assn., Internat. Surg. Group (pres. 1997—98), Am. Bd. Surgery (dir. 1974—80), River Club, Univ. Club, Cosmos Club (Washington), Quadrangle (Chgo.), Alpha Omega Alpha, Phi Beta Kappa. Home: 79 E 79th St New York NY 10021-0202 Office: NY Presbyn Hosp Office Pres 525 E 68th St New York NY 10021-4870

SKINNER, DELDA SMITH, artist, educator; b. Waco, Tex., Apr. 15, 1929; d. David Wilkes and Edith Arlene (Landrum) Smith; m. John Finley Skinner, May 27, 1948; children: John Lyle, Arlene, Eleanor, Sarah. BBA, Baylor U., 1949; BA, Dominican Coll., 1972; MA in Pastoral Ministry, Episcopal Sem. of S.W., 1999. Sec. LCRA, Austin, Tex., 1948-50; real estate agt. Houston, 1967-69; H.S. tchr., 1973-78; profl. visual artist, 1974-78, Wimberley, Tex., 1978-89, San Antonio, 1990-93, Austin, 1993—. Adj. prof. pastoral ministry Episcopal Theol. Sem. of the S.W., 2000—. Paintings included in In Harmony With Nature, 1990, Sowest Art Mag., 1992, Creative Collage Techniques, 1994, Best of Watercolor 2, 1997, Best of Watercolor in Textures, 1997, Best of Watercolor in Color, 1997, Best of Watercolor, 2002, Celebrate Your Creative Self, 2002, Stamping with Style, 2001. Bd. dirs. Tex. Watercolor, 1987-89, San Antonio Watercolor, 1991-93; lay eucharist min. Diocese of Tex. Episcopal Ch. Grantee McAshen Found., 1974, Nat. Collage Soc., 1988, Tex. Watercolor Soc., 1991. Mem. Nat. Watercolor Soc. (signature mem.), Nat. Collage Soc. (signature mem., regional dir. 1989-96), Soc. Layerists in Multimedia (bd. dirs. 1982—, v.p. 1999—), Internat. Assn. Paper Makers and Paper Artists (bd. dirs., treas. 1996-99), First Frontier Coll. Soc. (pres. 1999-00). Avocations: reading, travel, book making, paper making. Home: 8111 Doe Meadow Dr Austin TX 78749-2866

SKINNER, ELLIOTT PERCIVAL, anthropology educator; b. Port-of-Spain, Trinidad-Tobago, June 20, 1924; came to the U.S., 1943; s. Joseph McDonald Skinner and Ettice Geraldine Frances; m. Thelma Garvin, Dec. 15, 1946 (div. Dec. 1976); children: Victor, Gail, Sagha, Touray; m. Gwendolyn Yolande Mikell, May 28, 1982; 1 child, Luce Mikell Remy. BA in Biology, NYU, 1951; MA in Anthropology, Columbia U., 1952, PhD in Anthropology, 1955; LLD (hon.), Lincoln (Pa.) U., 1990. Rsch. asst. anthropology Columbia U., N.Y.C., 1954-55, vis. asst. prof. anthropology, 1957-59, asst. prof. anthropology, 1959-63, 63-69, Franz-Boas prof. anthropology, 1969—, chmn. dept. anthropology, 1972-75. Tchr. Sunrise semester courses on Africa, NYU/WCBS-TV, 1960, 62; U.S. amb. to Upper Volta, Burkina-Faso, 1966-69; mem. rsch. adv. com. USAID, 1978-81; mem. black forum on fgn. policy TRANSAFRICA, 1996—; dir. Pre-Freshman Inst. on Pub. Policy and Diplomacy, Lincoln, 1993; lectr. and cons. in field. Author: The Mossi of Upper Volta: The Political Development of a Sudanese People, 1964, (with D. Chu) A Glorious Age in Africa, 1974 (Melville J. Herskovits prize for best book 1975), African-Americans and U.S. Policy Towards Africa, 1992. Bd. dirs. Fulbright Assn., Washington, 1990-95; trustee U. Bridgeport, Conn., 1995—. With U.S. Army, 1943-46, ETO. Recipient Commandeur de l'Ordre Nat. Voltaique, Pres. of the Republic of Upper Volta, 1968, Spl. Svc. award Faculty of the Borough of Manhattan C.C., 1974, Disting. Africanist award African Studies Assn., N.Y., 1986; named hon. citizen State of Tenn., 1983; Opportunity fellow John Hay Whitney Found., 1953, Columbia U. Traveling fellow, N.Y.C., 1954, Fulbright fellow U. Abidjan, Cote d'Ivoire, 1987. Fellow Internat. African Inst.; mem. Assn. Black Am. Ambs. (pres. 1988-92), Coun. on Fgn. Rels., Coun. Am. Ambs. Home: 700 New Hampshire Ave NW # 317 Washington DC 20037-2406 Office: Columbia Univ Dept Anthropology 460 Schermerhorn Ext New York NY 10027 E-mail: eps1@columbia.edu.

SKINNER, G(EORGE) WILLIAM, anthropologist, educator; b. Oakland, Calif., Feb. 14, 1925; s. John James and Eunice (Engle) S.; m. Carol Bagger, Mar. 25, 1951 (div. Jan. 1970); children: Geoffrey Crane, James Lauriston, Mark Williamson, Jeremy Burr; m. Susan Mann, Apr. 26, 1980; 1 dau., Alison Jane. Student, Deep Springs (Calif.) Coll., 1942-43; BA with distinction in Far Eastern Studies, Cornell U., 1947; PhD in Cultural Anthropology, 1954; LLD (hon.), U. Hong Kong, 2001. Field dir. Cornell U. S.E. Asia program, also Cornell Research Center, Bangkok, Thailand, 1951-55; rsch. assoc. in Indonesia, 1956-58; asso. prof., then prof. anthropology Cornell U., Ithaca, N.Y., 1960-65; asst. prof. sociology Columbia, 1958-60; sr. specialist in residence East-West Ctr. Honolulu, 1965-66; prof. anthropology Stanford, 1966-89; Barbara Kimball Browning prof. humanities and scis., 1987-89; prof. anthropology U. Calif., Davis, 1990—. Vis. prof. U. Pa., 1977, Duke U., spring, 1978, Keio U., Tokyo, spring 1985, fall 1988, U. Calif.-San Diego, fall 1986; field rsch. China, 1949-50, 77, S.E. Asia, 1950-51, Thailand, 1951-53, 54-55, Java and Borneo, 1956-58, Japan, 1985, 88, 95; mem. joint com. on contemporary China Social Sci. Research Coun.-Am. Acad. Learned Socs., 1961-65, 80-81, internat. com. on Chinese studies, 1963-64, mem. joint com. on Chinese studies, 1981-83; mem. subcom. rsch. Chinese Soc. Social Sci. Rsch. Coun., 1961-70, chmn., 1963-70; dir. program on East Asian Local Systems, 1969-71; dir. Chinese Soc. Bibliography Project, 1964-73; assoc. dir. Cornell China Program, 1961-63; dir. London-Cornell Project Social Rsch., 1962-65; mem. com. on scholarly communication with People's Republic of China, Nat. Acad. Scis., 1966-70, mem. social scis. and humanities panel, 1982-83; mem. adv. com. Ctr. for Chinese Rsch. Materials, Assn. Rsch. Libraries, 1967-70; mem. policy and planning com. China in Time and Space, 1993-96. Author: Chinese Society in Thailand, 1957, Leadership and Power in the Chinese Community of Thailand, 1958; also articles; Editor: The Social Sciences and Thailand, 1956, Local, Ethnic and National Loyalties in Village Indonesia, 1959, Modern Chinese Society: An Analytical Bibliography, 3 vols, 1973, (with Mark Elvin) The Chinese City Between Two Worlds, 1974, (with A. Thomas Kirsch) Change and Persistence in Thai Society, 1975, The City in Late Imperial China, 1977, The Study of Chinese Society, 1979. Served to ensign USNR, 1943-46. Fellow Center for Advanced Study in Behavioral Scis., 1969-70; Guggenheim fellow, 1969; NIMH spl. fellow, 1970 Mem. NAS, AAAS, Am. Anthrop. Assn., Am. Sociol. Assn., Assn. Asian Studies (bd. dirs. 1962-65, chmn. nominating com. 1967-68, pres. 1983-84), Soc. for Cultural Anthropology, Internat. Union for Sci. Study of Population, Social Sci. History Assn., Am. Ethnol. Soc., Population Assn. Am., Siam Soc., Soc. Qing Studies, Soc. Econ. Anthropology, Phi Beta Kappa, Sigma Xi. Office: U Calif Dept Anthropology 1 Shields Ave Davis CA 95616-5270 E-mail: gwskinner@ucdavis.edu.

SKINNER, HELEN CATHERINE WILD, biomineralogist; b. Bklyn., Jan. 25, 1931; d. Edward Herman and Minnie (Bertsch) Wild; m. Brian John Skinner, Oct. 9, 1954; children: Adrienne, Stephanie, Thalassa. BA, Mt. Holyoke Coll., 1952; MA, Radcliffe/Harvard, 1954; PhD, Adelaide (Australia) U., 1959. Mineralogist sect. molecular structure Nat. Inst. Arthritis and Metabolic Diseases, NIH, 1961-65; with sect. crystal chemistry Lab. Histology and Pathology Nat. Inst. Dental Rsch., NIH, 1965-66; lectr. dept. geology and geophysics Yale U., 1967-69, rsch. assoc. dept. surgery, 1967-72, sr. rsch. assoc. dept. surgery Medical Sch., 1972-75; Alexander Agassiz vis. lectr. dept. biology Harvard U., 1976-77; lectr. dept. biology Yale U., 1977-83, assoc. prof. biochemistry in surgery, Medical Sch., 1978-84, lectr. dept. orthopaedic surgery, 1972—, lectr., rsch. affiliate in geology and geophysics, 1987—. Pres. Conn. Acad. Arts and Scis., 1986—94, publs. chair, 1994—2001; faculty affiliate in mineralogy Yale U. Peabody Mus., 2001—; mineralogist AEC, summer, 1953; master Jonathan Edwards Coll., Yale U., 1977—82; Alexander Agassiz vis. lectr. dept. biology Harvard U., 1976—77; vis. prof. sect. ecology and systematics dept. biology Cornell U., 1980—83; disting. prof. geology Adelaide U., 1990—91, disting .lectr., 1993; disting. prof. geology U. Wyo., 1996; mem. dental adv. com. Yale-New Haven Tchrs. Inst., 1983—99; chmn. site visit team Nat. Inst. Dental Rsch., 1974—75; mem. publs. com. Yale U. Press., 1979—84, Am. Geol. Inst., 1993—96; MSA del. Internat. Mineral. Commn. Applied Mineralogy, 1992—. Newsletter editor: Arlington County Tennis Assn., 1990—91, newsletter editor: On Campus With Women, Assn. Am. Colls. and Univs., 1996—2000; contbr. articles to profl. jours. and mags. Mem. bd. edn. com. Conn. Fund for Environ., 1983-89, mem. sci. adv. com., 1989-92; founder, pres. Investor's Strategy Inst., New Haven, 1983-85; trustee Miss Porter's Sch., Farmington, Conn., 1984-91, mem. edn. com., 1986-88, mem. salaries and benefits com., 1988-91; treas. YWCA, New Haven, 1983-84; trustee Geol. Soc. Am. Found., 1998—. Mem.: Mineralogical Soc. Am., Am. Soc. for Laser Medicine and Surgery, D.C. Sci. Writers Assn., Washington Ind. Writers, Nat. Press Club, Geol. Soc. Am. Found. (bd. dirs.), Sigma Tau Delta (founding mem. U. Va. chpt.). Home: 39 Temple Ct New Haven CT 06511-6820 Office: Yale U Dept Geology Geophysics PO Box 208109 New Haven CT 06520-8109 E-mail: catherine.skinner@yale.edu.

SKINNER, JAMES LAURISTON, chemist, educator; b. Ithaca, N.Y., Aug. 17, 1953; s. G. William and Carol (Bagger) S.; m. Wendy Moore, May 31, 1986; children: Colin Andrew, Duncan Geoffrey. AB, U. Calif., Santa Cruz, 1975; PhD, Harvard U., 1979. Rsch. assoc. Stanford (Calif.) U., 1980-81; from asst. prof. to prof. chemistry Columbia U., N.Y.C., 1981-90; Hirschfelder prof. chemistry, dir. Theol. Chemistry Inst. U. Wis., Madison, 1990—. Vis. scientist Inst. Theol. Physics U. Calif., Santa Barbara, 1987; vis. prof. physics U. Jos. Fourier, Grenoble, France, 1987, U. Bordeaux (France), 1995. Contbr. articles to profl. jours. Recipient Fresenius award Phi Lambda Upsilon, 1989, Camille and Henry Dreyfus Tchr.-Scholar award, 1984, NSF Presdl. Young Investigator award, 1984, Humboldt Sr. Scientist award, 1993; NSF grad fellow, 1975, NSF postdoctoral fellow, 1980, Alfred P. Sloan Found. fellow, 1984, Guggenheim fellow, 1993. Mem. AAAS, Am. Chem. Soc., Am. Phys. Soc. Achievements include fundamental research in condensed phase theoretical chemistry. Office: U Wis Dept Chemistry Theoretical Chem Inst 1101 University Ave Madison WI 53706-1322

SKINNER, JAMES LISTER, III, English language educator; b. Emory, Ga., Sept. 24, 1938; s. James Lister and Josephine Norvell (Fry) S.; m. Ramona Ann York Skinner, Apr. 2, 1961; 1 child, James Lister Skinner IV. AB in English, N. Ga. Coll., Dahlonega, 1960; MA in English, U. Ark., Fayetteville, 1962, PhD in English, 1965. Comdr. Headquarters and Headquarters Battery 28th Artillery Group, Selfridge AFB, Mich., 1964-65; assoc. prof. English Presbyterian Coll., Clinton, S.C., 1965-70, prof. English, 1970-92, Charles A. Dana prof. English, 1992—, chmn. The Russell Program, 1986-98; co-chmn. English dept. Presbyn. Coll., 1996-99, sr. faculty coun., 1995-98, chair sr. faculty coun., 1997-98, chair English dept., 1999-2001. NDEA fellow U. Ark., Fayetteville, 1960-63; NEH summer fellow Yale U., New Haven, Conn., 1976; hon. vis. fellow Leicester (Eng.) U., 1983; sec. Presbyterian Coll. Faculty, Clinton, S.C., 1995-98. Author: Boys Farm: A History, 2002; editor: The Autobiography of Henry Merrell: Industrial Missionary to the South, 1991; co-editor: The Death of a Confederate, 1996. 1st lt. U.S. Army, 1963-65. Recipient Commendation medal U.S. Army, 1965; named Presbyterian Prof. of Yr. Presbyterian Coll., Clinton, S.C., 1991, State Prof. of Yr. Coun. for Advancement and Support of Edn., 1991, Gov's. Prof. of Yr., Gov. of S.C., Columbia, 1991, DAR History Award medal, 1998. Mem. Phi Beta Kappa, Omicron Delta Kappa, Alpha Psi Omega, Phi Alpha Theta, Sigma Tau Delta. Democrat. Presbyterian. Home: 108 E Maple St Clinton SC 29325-2836 Office: Presbyterian Coll Broad St Clinton SC 29325 E-mail: jskinner@presby.edu.

SKINNER, JOHN VERNON, retail credit executive; b. Merryville, La., Aug. 21, 1938; s. Vernon and Margaret Skinner; m. Gail Grinnell, Sept. 1, 1960 (div. Sept. 1981); children: Sondra Skinner Keefer, Sherrin Skinner Mitzner, Stacey Skinner Schaefer, Jonathan; m. B. Jean Kevane, Nov. 1, 1983. Student, U. Houston, 1957-60. Cert. consumer credit exec. Mgr. collections, asst. mgr. Sears Roebuck & Co., Fitchburg, Mass., 1963-64; mgr. credit Torrington, Conn., 1964-65; mgr. collection/authorization Hartford, 1965-67; mgr. group collection Albany, N.Y., 1967-68; supr. credit field Boston, 1968; mgr. credit ctr. Balt., 1968-73, Washington, 1973-84; pres. Jewelers Fin. Svcs., Inc. sub. Zale Corp., Irving, Tex., 1984-96; pres., CEO Jewelers Fin. Svcs., Inc., 1987-96; sr. v.p. Zale Corp., 1984-96, exec. mgmt. com., 1993-96; cons., co-owner Profl. Alternatives, Dallas, Houston, Phoenix, Denver, Austin, Atlanta, 1996—, Albuquerque. Officer, bd. dirs. Consumer Credit Counseling and Edn. Svc., Washington and Balt., 1968-84, pres., 1978-84, vice chmn., 1989; mem. governing bd. dirs. Credit Rsch. Ctr., Purdue U., 1985—, chmn., 1990-91; credit cons., 1996, corp. credit mgr., Staffing Resources, 1997—. Contbr. numerous articles to profl. jours. Bd. dirs. Better Bus. Bur. of Met. Dallas, Inc., 1994-96. Recipient Disting. Svc. award Internat. Consumer Credit Assn., 1982, award of Excellence Assoc. Credit Burs., 1991. Mem. Fed. Reserve (mem. consumer adv. coun. 1992-94), Consumer Credit Assn. (pres. Greater Washington chpt. 1963-84, bd. dirs.), Internat. Credit Assn. (officer, bd. dirs. dist. XII chpt. 1975-84, bd. dirs., mem. exec. com. St. Louis chpt. 1980—, pres. dist. XII chpt. 1981, v.p. St. Louis chpt. 1985—, chmn. 1989-91, Outstanding Mem. award 1979, Greater Washington Outstanding Mem. award 1979, Svc. award 1985, Merit award 1988, Pinnacle award 1991), Nat. Found. for Consumer Credit (trustee, officer 1980-92, mem. exec. com. 1980-92, bd. dirs. 1980—, v.p., 1985—, chmn. 1991-92, Chmn.'s award 1982, Harry E. Fuller award 1985, Linkwilder award 1987), Nat. Retail Fedn. CMD divsn. (chmn. 1991-92, dirs. 1985—), Nat. Retail Mchts. Assn. (bd. dirs. 1985—, sec., treas. 1989). Republican. Methodist. Avocations: racquetball, golf, boating, tennis. Home: 2038 Wildwood Way Kemp TX 75143 E-mail: johnvskinner@aol.com.

SKINNER, KNUTE RUMSEY, poet, English educator; b. St. Louis, Apr. 25, 1929; s. George Rumsey and Lidi (Skjoldvig) S.; m. Jeanne Pratt; 1953; divorced 1954; 1 child, Frank; m. Linda Kuhn, Mar. 30, 1961 (div. Sept. 1977); children: Dunstan, Morgan; m. Edna Kiel, Mar. 25, 1978. Student, Culver-Stockton Coll., 1947-49; BA, U. No. Colo., 1951; MA, Middlebury Coll., 1954; PhD, U. Iowa, 1958. Instr. English U. Iowa, Iowa City, 1955-56, 57-58, 60-61; asst. prof. English Okla. Coll. for Women, 1961-62; lectr. creative writing Western Wash. U., Bellingham, 1962-71, asso. prof. English, 1971-73, prof. English, 1973-97; pres. Signpost Press Inc., nonprofit corp., 1983-95. Author: Stranger with a Watch, 1965, A Close Sky Over Killaspuglonane, 1968, 75, In Dinosaur Country, 1969, The Sorcerers: A Laotian Tale, 1972, Hearing of the Hard Times, 1981, The Flame Room, 1983, Selected Poems, 1985, Learning to Spell "Zucchini," 1988, The Bears and Other Poems, 1991, What Trudy Knows and Other Poems, 1994, The Cold Irish Earth: New and Selected Poems of Ireland, 1965-1995, 1996, An Afternoon Quiet and Other Poems, 1998, Stretches, 2002; editor: Bellingham Rev., 1977-83, 93-95; contbr. poetry, short stories to anthologies, textbooks, periodicals. Nat. Endowment for the Arts fellow, 1975 Mem. Am. Conf. Irish Studies, Wash. Poets Assn. E-mail: kielskin@eircom.net.

SKINNER, KRISTIN A. surgical oncologist; b. Newton, Mass., July 23, 1962; BS, U. Rochester, 1984; MD, Johns Hopkins U., 1988. Intern, jr. resident dept. surgery UCLA, 1988-90, surg. oncology postdoctoral fellow divsn. surg. oncology, 1990-92, sr. resident, chief resident dept. surgery, 1992-95; asst. prof. dept. surgery U. So. Calif., 1995—2002, assoc. prof. dept. surgery, 2002—. Dir. breast cancer program L.A. County/U. So. Calif., 1999—; dir. breast skills workshop Keck Sch. Medicine, U. So. Calif., 1997—. Contbr. numerous articles to profl. jours., chpts. to books. Fellow Clin. Oncology fellow, Am. Cancer Soc., 1990—92; grantee Rsch. Project grantee, 1998—2001, NIH/Nat. Cancer Inst., 1990—92, 2001—. Fellow ACS (bd. dirs. So. Calif. chpt. 2000—); mem. Soc. Surg. Oncology, Assn. for Acad. Surgery (chair com. on edn. 2000-01), Am. Assn. for Cancer Rsch., Am. Soc. Clin. Oncology, Soc. for Surgery of the Alimentary Tract, Internat. Assn. Surgeons and Gastroenterologists. Office: U So Calif/Norris Cancer Hosp 1441 Eastlake Ave # 7418 Los Angeles CA 90033

SKINNER, MARGARET SHEPPARD, pathologist; b. Jamaica, N.Y., May 8, 1938; d. Benjamin Sheppard and Thelma Ruth Burns; divorced; children: Scott Renton, David Renton. Student, U. Miami, Fla., 1955-58; MD, Emory U., 1962. Diplomate Am. Bd. Pathology. Med. intern Emory U., Atlanta, 1962-63, resident in pathology, 1963-65; fellow Tulane U., New Orleans, 1965-67, asst. prof., 1968-71, assoc. prof., 1971-73; pathologist Daniel Seckinger MDPA, Miami, 1973-89, Palm Beach Pathology, West Palm Beach, Fla., 1989—. Mem. Fla. State Bd. Medicine, Tallahassee, 1986-90, 92-97, chmn., 1990; chmn. bd. dirs. COLA, Balt., 2000—. Mem. med. adv. bd. Head Start, Palm Beach County, Fla., 1998-99; chmn. quality mgmt. com. Health Care Taxing Dist., Palm Beach County, 1998-2001. Fellow Am. Soc. Clin. Pathologists, Coll. Am. Pathologists (bd. govs. 1997—, Pres. medal 1999); mem. Am. Soc. Investigative Pathology, Alpha Omega Alpha. Office: PO Box 32609 Palm Beach Gardens FL 33420-2609

SKINNER, MICHAEL DAVID, lawyer; b. Jan. 5, 1950; s. Roger Gilman and Jerry Ann (Sneed) S.; m. Janet Louise Horaist, Jan. 7, 1978. JD, La. State U., 1976. Bar: La. 1977, U.S. Dist. Ct. (we. dist.) La. 1978, U.S. Ct. Appeals (5th and 11th cirs.) 1978, U.S. Dist. Ct. (mid. dist.) La. 1982, U.S. Supreme Ct. 1982, U.S. Dist. Ct. (so. dist.) Tex. 1983. Pvt. practice, Lafayette, La., 1976-84; ptnr. Guilliot, Skinner & Everett, 1984-86, Goode, Skinner & Hawkland, 1986-93; U.S. atty. West Dist. La., 1993-2000. Bd. dirs. Greater Lafayette C. of C. Mem. La. State Bar Assn. (mem. ho. of dels.). Democrat. Office: 102 Versailles Blvd Ste 600 Lafayette LA 70501-6700

SKINNER, PATRICIA MORAG, state legislator; b. Glasgow, Scotland, Dec. 3, 1932; d. John Stuart and Frances Charlotte (Swann) Robertson; m. Robert A. Skinner, Dec. 28, 1957; children: Robin Ann, Pamela. BA, NYU, 1953. Mdse. trainee Lord & Taylor, N.Y.C., 1955-59; adminstrv. asst. Atlantic Products, 1954-59; newspaper corr. Salem Observer, N.H., 1964-84; mem. N.H. Ho. of Reps., 1972-94, chmn. labor, human resources, and rehab. com., 1975-86, mem. House edn. com., 1987, chmn., 1989-94, exec. com. Nat. Conf. State Legislatures, 1987-90; chmn. N.H. Adv. Coun. Unemployment Compensation, 1984-94. Mem. State Libr. Adv. Coun., 2001—. Bd. dirs. Castle Jr. Coll., 1975, chmn. bd., 1988-96; v.p. bd. Swift Water coun. Girl Scouts U.S., v.p., 1987-92; N.H. Voc-Tech. Coll., Nashua, 1978-83; trustee Nesmith Libr., Windham, N.H., 1982—, chmn. bd. trustees, 1994-99; pres. N.H. Fedn. Rep. Women's Clubs, parliamentarian, legis. chmn., 1984-86, 94-96. Mem. Windham Woman's Club (pres. 1981-83), Order Ea. Star. Christian Scientist.

SKINNER, ROBERT EARLE, librarian, writer; b. Alexandria, Va., June 25, 1948; s. Earl Woodrow and Pearle Labar (Capper) S.; m. Linda Sue Long, June 12, 1970 (div. 1976); children: Christopher William, Kelly Sue; m. Patricia Ann Friedmann, Mar. 17, 1979 (div. 1996); children: Esme F., Werner H.; m. Bettye Jean Harrison, 2001. BA in History, Old Dominion U., 1970; MLS, Ind. U., 1977; postgrad. student, U. New Orleans, 1991-93. Search analyst Strughold Aeromed. Libr., Brooks AFB, Tex., 1977-79; from reference libr. to head med. edn. libr. La. State U. Med. Ctr., New Orleans, 1979-85; spl. cons. Robert L. Siegel & Assocs., 1985-87; univ. libr. Xavier U., 1987—; mng. editor Xavier Rev. Press, 1989—. Vis. lectr. in Am. studies U.S. Air Force Acad., 2002. Author: The Hard-Boiled Explicator, 1985, The New Hard-Boiled Dicks, 1987, rev. edit., 1995, Two Guns From Harlem, 1989, (with Michel J. Fabre) Chester Himes: An Annotated Primary and Secondary Bibliography, 1992, Fiction in Ellipsis, 1992, (with Thomas Bonner, Jr.) Above Ground, 1993, Immortelles, 1995, (with Michel J. Fabre) Plan B, 1993, (with Michel J. Fabre) Conversations with Chester Himes, 1995, Fiction in Hard Boiled, 1994, Fiction in Crime Yellow, 1994, Skin Deep, Blood Red, 1997, Cat-Eyed Trouble, 1998, Daddy's Gone-A-Hunting, 1999, Blood to Drink, 2000, Pale Shadow, 2001; guest editor La. Lit., spring 1998, Plots With Guns, 2002, The Righteous Cut, 2002; contbr. fiction in Xavier Rev., 2000. With USCG, 1970-74. Grantee Mellon Found., 1987-95, La. Divsn. of the Arts, 1993, 95, NEH, 1991—. Mem. ALA. Avocations: hiking, reading, book collecting, antique radios, shortwave listening. Office: Xavier Univ Libr 1 Drexel Dr New Orleans LA 70125-1056 E-mail: rskinner@xula.edu.

SKINNER, ROBERT EARLE, JR. civil engineer, engineering executive; b. Washington, Aug. 10, 1946; s. Robert Earle and Dorothy Inez (Ballance) S.; m. Dianne Lynette Sands; children: Martha, Jeffrey. BSCE, U. Va., 1969; MS in Civil Engring., MIT, 1971. Registered profl. engr., Va. Sr. assoc. PRC Voorhees, McLean, Va., 1971-79, v.p., 1979-83; sr. staff officer Transp. Rsch. Bd., Washington, 1983-86, dir. studies and info. svc., 1986-94, exec. dir., 1994—. Exec. com. Hwy. Innovative Tech. Evaluation Ctr., Washington, 1994—; adv. com. Ctr. for Transp. and the Environment, Raleigh, N.C., 1995—; bd. dirs. Innovation Pavement Rsch. Found., Washington, 1999—. Contbr. articles to profl. jours.; mem. editorial bd. Jour. Trans. and Stats., 1996. Mem. Md. Transp. Adv. Coun.; mem. adv. coun. U. Va., 1995—; bd. dirs. Innovative Pavement Rsch. Found., 1999—. With U.S. Army N.G., 1970-76. Mem. ASCE, Internat. Soc. Asphalt Pavements (ex-officio). Methodist. Avocations: woodworking, tennis. Office: Transportation Research Bd 2101 Constitution Ave NW Washington DC 20418-0007

SKINNER, SHARI L. dermatologist; b. Paducah, Ky., Nov. 11, 1964; d. William G. and Carolyn Ann (Englert) S. BS, Samford U., 1987; MD, U. Louisville, 1994. Pharmacist Bapt. Hosp., Paducah, 1987-88, Super X Pharmacy, Louisville, 1988-94; intern U. Louisville Med. Ctr., 1994-95; resident in dermatology Pa. State Geissinger Health Sys., Hershey, Pa., 1995-98; dermatologist Assocs. in Dermatology, Ft. Myers, Fla., 1998—. Primary investigator pharm. clin. trials SFBC, Ft. Myers, 2001—. Mem. small bus. adv. coun. Nat. Rep. Congl. Com., hon. co-chmn. physicians adv. bd., 2002. Grantee Am. Contact Dermatitis Soc., 1997; recipient Nat. Leadership award Nat. Rep. Congl. Com., 2002. Mem. AMA, NRA, Am. Acad. Dermatology, Fla. Med. Assn., Fla. Dermatol. Assn., Nat. Psoriasis Found., Lee County Med. Soc., Women's Dermatol. Soc., Am. Contact Dermatitis Soc.

SKINNER, THOMAS, broadcasting and film executive; b. Poughkeepsie, N.Y., Aug. 17, 1934; s. Clarence F. and Frances D. S.; m. Elizabeth Burroughs, June 22, 1957; children: Kristin Jon, Karin Anne, Erik Lloyd. BS, SUNY, Fredonia, 1956; MA, U. Mich., 1957, PhD, 1962. Instr. speech U. Mich., 1960; assoc. prof., exec. producer dept. broadcasting San Diego State U., 1961-66; asst. mgr. Sta. WITF-TV, Hershey, Pa., 1966-70; v.p. Sta. WQED-TV, Pitts., 1970-72; exec. v.p., COO QED Communications Inc. (WQED-TV, WQED-FM, Pittsburgh mag., WQEX-TV), 1972-93; founder, pres., exec. prodr. Windrush Assocs., 1993—; v.p. Programming Resolution Prodns., Burlington, Vt., 1996—; asst. dir. Inland Seas Edn. Assn., 2000—. Exec. prodr.: spls. and series including (for PBS) Nat. Geog. spls. Planet Earth, The Infinite Voyage, Conserving America, (for TBS) Pirate Tales, (for A&E) Floating Palaces, California and the Dream Seekers, The Story of Money, (for Discovery) Battleship, The Secret World of Air Freight. Recipient award as exec. prodr. DuPont Columbia, 1979, Oscar award as dir. Acad. Motion Picture Arts and Scis., 1967, Emmy award as exec. prodr. Nat. Acad. TV Arts and Scis., 1979, 83-84, 86-87, Peabody award as exec. prodr., 1980, 86. Episcopalian.

SKINNER, WALTER JAY, federal judge; b. Washington, Sept. 12, 1927; s. Frederick Snowden and Mary Waterman (Comstock) S.; m. Sylvia Henderson, Aug. 12, 1950; 4 children. AB, Harvard, 1948; JD, 1952. Bar: Mass. 1952, U.S. Dist. Ct. 1954. Assoc. firm Gaston, Snow, Rice & Boyd, Boston, 1952-57; pvt. practice law Scituate, Mass., 1957-63; asst. dist. atty. Plymouth County, 1957-63; town counsel Scituate, 1957-63; asst. atty. gen., chief Criminal Div., Commonwealth of Mass., 1963-65; mem. firm Wardwell, Allen, McLaughlin & Skinner, Boston, 1965-74; judge U.S. Dist. Ct. of Mass., 1974—; sr. status, 1992—. Bd. dirs. Douglas A. Thom Clinic, 1966-70. Mem. Mass. Bar Assn., Boston Bar Assn. Office: US Dist Ct 1 Courthouse Way Boston MA 02210-3002

SKINNER, WALTER WINSTON, journalist, minister; b. Newnan, Ga., Mar. 28, 1959; s. Walter Winston Sr. and Sara Jane (Trammell) S.; m. Deborah Lynn Strickland, Sept. 8, 1979; children: Sara Irene Skinner, Jane Golden Skinner. ABJ, U. Ga., 1980. Editor, publ. The Lee County Ledger, Leesburg, Ga., 1980-83; asst. news editor Newnan Times-Herald, Newnan, 1982—. Pastor Mt. Zion Bapt. Ch., Alvaton, Ga., 1986—. Author: Duty Patience and Endurance, 1977 (Louise Calhoun Barfield Local History Writing award 1977, Harris County Day award 1977), Wherein God Dwells, 1988, A Centennial History of Central Baptist Church, 1997, Sack of Turnips at Dinner on the Grounds, 2001. Chmn. Erskine Caldwell Mus., Moreland, Ga., 1992—; vol. fund drive Am. Heart Assn., Alvaton, 1993, March of Dimes, 1996-97. Recipient Ga. Press Assn. awards, 1985, 92. Mem. Moreland Cmty. Hist. Soc., Meriwether County Hist. Soc., Soc. Profl. Journalists, Bapt. Bivocat. Pastor's Assn. (Outstanding Town and Country award 1992), Ga. Bapt. Hist. Soc., Ga. Bapt. Hist. Commn., Newnan Civitan Club (sgt. at arms, 1994-95, chaplain 1995-96, 2001-, pres.-elect 1996-97, pres. 1997-98), Coneta Press Club (pres. 2001-). Democrat. Avocations: genealogy, creative writing, reading, travel. Home: 60 Temple Ave Newnan GA 30263-2023 Office: The Newnan Times-Herald PO Box 1052 Newnan GA 30264-1052 E-mail: winston@newnan.com.

SKINNER, WILLIAM FRENCH COCHRAN, JR. lawyer; b. Richmond, Va., June 18, 1943; s. W. French and Emma Sue (Linkous) S.; m. Judy Bryant, Aug. 28, 1965; children: Chip, Carey. BS in Commerce, Washington & Lee U., 1965; JD, Emory U., 1968. Bar: Ga. 1967, U.S. Dist. Ct. (no. dist.) Ga. 1973, U.S. Supreme Ct. 1974, U.S. Ct. Appeals (11th cir.) 1981. Assoc. Rich, Bass, Kidd & Broome, Decatur, Ga., 1968, 71-74; ptnr. Rich, Bass, Kidd & Skinner, 1974; pvt. practice, 1974—. Capt. U.S. Army, 1969-70, Vietnam. Mem. State Bar Ga., DeKalb Bar Assn., Inc. Episcopalian. Avocations: sports, family. Office: 315 W Ponce De Leon Ave Ste 956 Decatur GA 30030-2471 E-mail: wmskinner@aol.com.

SKINNER-LINNENBERG, VIRGINIA, English educator; b. Middletown, Ohio, Dec. 27, 1951; d. Bernard David and Joan (Koeppel) Skinner; m. Daniel M. Linnenberg, Aug. 22, 1975. BA, Bowling Green State U., 1974; MA, U. Louisville, 1983; PhD, Bowling Green State U., 1993. Instr. Brescia Coll., Owensboro, Ky., 1987-88; prof. English N. Ctrl. Mich. Coll., Petoskey, 1992-93, chair dept. comm. and humanities, 1993-97, asst. dean liberal arts, 1997-98; asst. prof. English Nazareth Coll., Rochester, N.Y., 1998—, dir. writing programs, 1999—. Author: Dramatizing Writing, 1997; mem. adv. bd. St. Martin's Guide to Writing Textbook, 1993-94, 96-97. Mem. Coll. Composition and Comm., Rhetoric Soc. Am., Soc. Tech. Comm. Episcopalian. Avocations: travel, reading, baseball. Office: Nazareth Coll 4245 East Ave Rochester NY 14618-3703 E-mail: vmskinne@naz.edu.

SKINSTAD, ANNE HELENE, psychologist, researcher; b. Bergen, Hordaland, Norway, July 8, 1949; d. Alfhild (Hektoen) and Leif Sigurd Skinstad; children: Siri Ødegaard. D in Psychology, U.of Bergen, Norway, 1977; PhD, U.of Bergen, 2001. Cert. Clin. Psychology 1985. Staff psychologist Hjellestad Clinic and Dr. Martens Clinic, Bergen, Norway, Norway, 1977—79; leading psychologist Blå-Kors Social Ctr., Bergen, Norway, 1979—83; faculty mem. U. Iowa, Iowa City, 1990—2001; asst. prof. Coll. of Pub. Health, 2001—. Rsch. fellow The U. of Bergen, Norway, 1983—87; leading psychologist Hjellestad Clinic, Bergen, Norway, 1987—90; program dir. Prairielands Addiction Tech. Transfer Ctr., Iowa City, 1995—2002. Contbr. articles to profl. jours. Mem.: APA, European Roschach Assn. (founding mem. 1989), Nat. ATTC Curriculum Com., Norwegian Psychol. Assn. Avocations: raising Australian sheppards, piano. Office: Coll of Public Health 2834 Steindler Bldg Iowa City IA 52242 Office Fax: 319-336-4068. Business E-Mail: anne-skinstad@uiowa.edu.

SKIPPER, ANNALYNN, dietitian, educator; b. El Paso, Tex., May 17, 1951; d. John Davis and Louise (Jarratt) S. BS, Tarleton State U., 1973; MS, Tex. Tech U., 1978. Registered dietitian; cert. nutrition support dietitian. Instr. nutrition Clarendon (Tex.) Coll., 1974-76; clin. dietitian Meth. Hosp., Lubbock, Tex., 1979-80, Hahneman Hosp., Phila., 1980; dietitian nutritional support, coord. Pa. Hosp., 1981-91; asst. prof. clin. nutrition, co-dir. nutrition cons. svc. Ruth-Presbyn.-St. Luke's Med. Ctr., Chgo., 1991—, dir. dietetic internship, 1999—. Cons. Nat. Bd. Nutritional Support Certification, Silver Spring, Md., 1997; panel mem. nutrition svcs. and quality care Food and Nutrition Bd., Washington, 1997, mem. com. on nutrition svcs. for Medicare beneficiaries, 1999. Editor: Dietitians Handbook of Enteral and Parenteral Nutrition, 1989, 2d edit., 1998; mem. editl. bd. Jour. Am. Dietetic Assn., 1989-92; assoc. editor Nutrition in Clin. Practice Jour., 1996-2001; contbr. articles to profl. jours. Grantee Phila. Dietetic Assn., 1990, Nat. Bd. Nutrition Support Cert., 1999. Fellow Am. Dietetic Assn. (media spokesperson 1982-85, Outstanding Svc. 1989, 92, 93, del. 2001—); mem. Am. Soc. Parenteral and Enteral Nutrition (certification com. 1987-90, dir. at large 1987-89, Cert. of Appreciation 1989, Disting. Achievement award 1999), Dietitians in Nutrition Support (treas. 1985). Avocation: travel. Office: Rush-Presbyn-St Luke's Med Ctr 1653 W Congress Pkwy Chicago IL 60612-3833

SKIPPER, WALTER JOHN, lawyer; b. Kenosha, Wis., Aug. 5, 1964; s. Walter J. Sr. and Marilyn A. Skipper; m. Irene P. Skipper, Oct. 6, 1996; 1 child, Jonathan Walter. BS in Acctg., Fin. and Econ., Marquette U., 1985; JD, U. Wis., 1990. Bar: Wis. 1990, Md. 1991. Assoc. Fried, Frank, Harris, Shriver & Jacobson, Washington, 1990-92, Quarles & Brady, Milw., 1992—. Author: Wisconsin Handbook for Securities Attorneys, 1994—. Mem. fin. com., Elm Grove, Wis., 1998—. Mem. Inst. Cert. Mgmt. Accts., Elm Grove Downtow Master Plan Com., Order of Coif, Alpha Sigma Nu, Beta Gamma Sigma. Home: 1035 Upper Ridgeway Elm Grove WI 53122-2405 Office: Quarles & Brady 411 E Wisconsin Ave Ste 2550 Milwaukee WI 53202-4497

SKIRBOLL, LANA R. federal health policy director; b. Balt., Dec. 7, 1949; m. Leonard Taylor, Feb. 19, 1986; 2 children. BA, NYU, 1970; MS in Zoology and Physiology, Miami U., 1972; PhD in Pharmacology, Georgetown U., 1977. Postdoctoral tng. in psychiatry and pharmacology Yale U. Sch. Medicine, New Haven, 1977-79; vis. scientist dept. histology and neurobiology Karolinska Inst., Stockholm, 1979-81; chief electrophysiology unit NIMH, 1981-87; dep. sci. advisor Alcohol Drug Abuse and Mental Health Adminstrn., 1987-88, exec. asst. to administr., 1989-91, assoc. adminstr. for sci., 1991-92; dir. office of sci. policy and program planning NIMH, 1992-95, 95—. Cons. Ctr. Environ. Health and Human Toxicology, 1985-87. Author: Pharmacology of Biochemical Behavior, 1988, Neuroanatomical Tract-Tracing Methods II: 1981-86, 1990, (with T. Hokfelt, G. Foster, O. Johannsson et alCentral Phenylethanolamine N-Methyltransferase Immunoreactive Neurons: Distribution Projections, Fine Structure, Ontogeny and Co-Existing Peptides, 1988, (with G.Stoner, S. Werkman, D. Hommer) Effects of Caffeine on the Substania Nigra, Biological Psychiatry, 1988, (with J.A. Stivers, R. Long, J. Crawley) Anatomical Analysis of Frontal Cortex Sites at Which Carbachol Induces Moteor Seizures in the Rat, (with T. Hokfelt, B. Robertson) Retrograde Flourescent Tracers with Immunohistochemistry, (with M. Palkovits, E. Mezey, T. Hokfelt) Adrenergic Projections from the Lower Brainstem to the Hypothalamic Paraventricular Nucleus, the Lateral Hypothalamic Area and the Central Nucleus of the Amygdala in Rats, vol. 1020, 1992. Biol. Scis. fellow in in psychiatry NIMH, 1977-79, Fogarty fellow, Internat. fellow Swedish Med. Rsch. Coun., 1979-81. Mem. AAAS, Am. Coll. Neuropsychopharmacology (Mead Johnson award), N.Y. Acad. Scis., Nat. Com. Edn. (Potomac chpt. pres. 1988-89), European Neurosci. Soc., Soc. Neurosci. Office: HHS NIH 9000 Rockville Pike Bldg 1 Bethesda MD 20892-0001

SKIRNICK, ROBERT ANDREW, lawyer; b. Chgo., Apr. 23, 1938; s. Andrew and Stella (Sanders) S.; children: Rebecca, David; m. Maria Ann Castellano, Oct. 4, 1974; 1 child, Gabriella. BA, Roosevelt U., 1961; JD, U. Chgo., 1966. Bar: U.S. Dist. Ct. (no. dist.) Ill. 1966, U.S. Ct. Appeals (7th cir.) 1968, U.S. Supreme Ct. 1970, U.S. Ct. Appeals (5th and 9th cirs.) 1982, N.Y. 1982, U.S. Ct. Appeals (3rd cir.) 1983, U.S. Dist. Ct. (ea. dist.) Mich. 1988, (so. and ea. dists.) N.Y. 1989, U.S. Ct. Appeals (2nd cir.) 1990, U.S. Dist. Ct. (no. dist.) Calif. 1992, U.S. Ct. Appeals (11th Cir.) 1992, U.S. Dist. Ct. (so. dist.) Tex. 1992, U.S. Dist. Ct. Ariz. 1993. Atty. office gen. counsel honors program HEW, Washington, 1966-68; ptnr. Fortes, Eiger, Epstein & Skirnick, Chgo., 1975-77, Much, Shelist, Freed, Chgo., 1977-79, Wolf, Popper, Ross, Wolf & Jones, N.Y.C., 1979-87, Kaplan, Kilsheimer & Foley, N.Y.C., 1988-89, Wechsler, Skirnick, Harwood, Halebian & Feffer, N.Y.C., 1989-95, Lovell & Skirnick, LLP, N.Y.C., 1995-97, Meredith Cohen Greenfogel & Skirnick, P.C., N.Y.C., 1997—. Instr. NYU, 1979-80; cons. Nat. Legal Aid and Def. Assn., Chgo., 1968-69; spl. asst. atty. gen. Ill. Atty Gen. Office, Chgo., 1972-73; spl. antitrust counsel State of Conn., 1976-77; mem. adv. bd. Small Bus. Legal Def. Commn., San Francisco, 1982—; lectr. Practicing Law Inst., N.Y.C., 1986-87; spl. master So. Dist. N.Y., 1988-91; ct. appted co-lead counsel NASDAQ market makers antitrust litigation, 1994—. Author: (with others) Federal Subject Matter Jurisdiction of U.S. District Courts, Federal Civil Practice, 1974, Antitrust Class Actions-Twenty Years Under Rule 23, 1986, The State Court Class Action-A Potpourri of Difference in the ABA Forum, Summer 1985; contbg. author: Multiparty Bargaining in Class Actions, Attorneys' Practice Guide to Negotiations, 2d edit., 1996; bd. editors Ill. Bar Antitrust Newsletter, 1969-73; topic and articles editor Jour. Forum Com. on Franchising, 1981-86. Atty. Office Gen. Counsel Honors Program, U.S. Dept. HEW, 1966-68; chmn. Ill. Legis. Com. Antitrust Section Ill. Bar., 1970-71; Topic and Articles Editor, Jour. Forum Com. on Franchising, 1981-86. Mem.: ATLA, ABA (co-chair securities law subcom. litigation sect. 1987, mem. com. on regulation of futures and derivative instruments, mem. forum com. on franchising, mem. com. on class actions and derivative suits, mem. internat. antitrust and fgn. competition laws com.), Nat. Assn. Pub. Interest Law (mem. fin. and investment com. 1998—, nomination and election com. 1998—99, chair nominations and elections com. 1999—2000, chair fin. and investment com. 2000—, bd. dirs. 1997—), Nat. Assn. for Pub. Interest Law Fellowships (mem. exec. com., mem. selection com., mem. investment and fin. com., bd. dirs. 1991—97, v.p. 1994—97, treas. 2000—, mem. budget com. 1998—, nomination and election coms. 1998—99, bd. dirs. 1997—), Ill. Bar Assn. (chmn. antitust sect. Ill. legis. com. 1970—71), N.Y. State Trial Lawyers Assn., N.Y. State Bar Assn. (mem. class action com.), Fed. Bar Coun. (mem. com. on second cir. cts. 1983—86), Navy League of U.S. (N.Y. coun., mem. jour. com. 1995—97), Plandome Country Club, Carlton Club. Office: Meredith Cohen Greenfogel & Skirnick 63 Wall St New York NY 10005-3001

SKJERVOLD, GERALDINE REID See REID, GERALDINE WOLD

SKLADAL, ELIZABETH LEE, retired elementary school educator; b. N.Y.C., May 23, 1937; d. Angier Joseph and Julia May (Roberts) Gallo; m. George Wayne Skladal, Dec. 26, 1956; children: George Wayne Jr., Joseph Lee. BA, Sweet Briar Coll., 1958; postgrad., U. Kans., 1966-67; EdM, U. Alaska, 1976. Choir dir. Main Chapel, Camp Zama, Japan, 1958-59, Ft. Lee, Va., 1963-65, Main Chapel and Snowhawk, Ft. Richardson, Alaska, 1968-70; tchr. Anchorage (Alaska) Sch. Dist., 1970-98; ret. Active Citizen's Adv. Com. for Gifted and Talented, Anchorage, 1981-83; mem. music com. Anchorage Sch. Dist., 1983-86; soloist Anchorage Opera Chorus, 1969-80, Cmty. Chorus, Anchorage, 1968-80; mem. choir First Presbyn. Ch., Anchorage, 1971—, deacon, 1988—, elder, 1996—, mission com. chair, 1996-99, mem. pastoral nominating com., 2001—; participant 1st cultural exch. from Anchorage to Magadan, Russia with Alaska Chamber Singers, 1992; participant mission trip to Swaziland, Africa with First Presbyn. Ch., Anchorage, summer 1995. Named Am. Coll. Theater Festival winner Amoco Oil Co., 1974; recipient Cmty. Svc. award Anchorage U. Alaska Alumni Assn., 1994-95. Mem. AAUW, Anchorage Concert Assn. Patron Soc. (assocs. coun. of dirs.), Alaska Chamber Singers, Am. Guild Organists (former dean, former treas., mem.-at-large), Local Delta Kappa Gamma (1st v.p.). Republican. Presbyterian. Avocations: camping, travel, cycling, fishing, cross-country skiing, gardening. Home: 1841 S Salem Dr Anchorage AK 99508-5156

SKLADAN, MARK D. music educator; b. Lorain, Ohio, Feb. 12, 1964; s. Douglas G. and Ruth J. Skladan; m. Jodi E. Skladan; children: Hannah K. , Noah W. MusB, Bowling Green State U., 1986. Cert. music edn. K-12 Ohio. Educator New London Schs., New London, Ohio, 1986—91, Midview Schs., Grafton, 1991—97, Amherst Schs., 1997—. Mem. bd. dirs. Oberlin Choristers, Oberlin, Ohio, 2000—. Named N.E. Tchr. of Yr., PTA, 1994. Mem.: Ohio Choral Dir.'s Assn., Ohio Music Educator's Assn., Elks. Republican. Episcopalian. Avocations: golf, bowling. Office: Amherst Steele HS 450 Washington St Amherst OH 44001 E-mail: mark_skladan@amherst.klz.oh.us.

SKLANSKY, DAVID BRUCE, gambling expert, writer; b. Teaneck, N.J., Dec. 22, 1947; s. Irving and Mae S.; 1 child, Mathew. Author: Theory of Poker, 1983, Getting the Best of It, 1985, Sklansky Talks Blackjack, 1998.

SKLANSKY, JACK, electrical and computer engineering educator, researcher; b. N.Y.C., Nov. 15, 1928; s. Abraham and Clara S.; m. Gloria Joy Weiss, Dec. 24, 1957; children: David Alan, Mark Steven, Jeffrey Paul. BEE, CCNY, 1950; MSEE, Purdue U., 1952; D in Engring. Sci., Columbia U., 1955. Research engr. RCA Labs., Princeton, N.J., 1955-65; mgr. Nat. Cash Register Co., Dayton, Ohio, 1965-66; prof. elec. and computer engring. U. Calif., Irvine, 1966—; pres. Scanicon Corp., 1980-89; prof. radiology Charles R. Drew U. of Medicine and Sci., L.A., 1995—. Author: (with others) Pattern Classifiers and Trainable Machines, 1981; editor: Pattern Recognition, 1973, (with others) Biomedical Images and Computers, 1982; editor-in-chief: Machine Vision and Applications, 1987. Recipient best paper award Jour. Pattern Recognition, 1977; rsch. grantee NIH, 1971-84, Army Rsch. Office, 1984-91, NSF, 1992-96, Office of Naval Rsch., 1995-97, Naval Air Warfare Ctr., 1997-98, Calif. Breast Cancer Rsch. Program, 1997-99, U.S. Army Med. Rsch. and Material Command, 1999—, Calif. Telehealth and Telemedicine Ctr., 2000—. Fellow IEEE, Internat. Assn. for Pattern Recognition; mem. ACM. Office: Charles R Drew Univ Med Sci Dept Rad Los Angeles CA 90059 E-mail: sklansky@uci.edu.

SKLAR, ALAN CURTIS, lawyer; b. N.Y.C., Aug. 19, 1959; s. Jerry and Martha (Kolin) S.; m. Linda Susan Catalan, Dec. 26, 1982; twins: Daniel Jay and Jennifer Rachel. BA summa cum laude, U. Pa., 1980, JD, 1982. Bar: Calif., Nev. Assoc. Wolf Block Schorr & Solis-Cohen, Phila., 1980, 81, Rifkind & Sterling, Beverly Hills, Calif., 1982-84, Mitchell Silberberg & Knupp, L.A., 1984-86; mng. dir. Coastal Investment Group, Beverly Hills, 1986-89; ptnr. Warren Clark & Sklar (and predecessor), L.A., 1989—, Gordon & Silver, Las Vegas, Nev., 1991-95, Sklar Warren Conway & Williams LLP, Las Vegas, 1995—. Bd. dirs. Consolidated Mgmt., Inc., N.Y.C., L.A., Las Vegas. Author: Tactics and Techniques in Mergers and Acquisitions, 1985, Recent Developments in Mergers and Acquisitions, 1985, California Corporate Securities Laws, 1985, Corporate Law Overview, 1985, Secured Real Estate Transactions, 1993. Bd. trustees Las Vegas Bowl Organizing Com., 1995, 96, So. Nev. Housing Corp., 1995—; mem. U. Pa. Alumni Secondary Sch. Com., 1998—; counsel Chabad of So. Nev., Las Vegas, 1991-2000. Named Top Corp. Atty., Nev. Bus. Jour. Mem. ABA, State Bar Nev., State Bar Calif., TPC Summerlin Country Club, World Zionist Orgn., Phi Beta Kappa, Phi Alpha Theta. Democrat. Jewish. Office: Sklar Warren Conway & Williams LLP 221 N Buffalo Dr Las Vegas NV 89145-0303 E-mail: asklar@sklar-law.com.

SKLAR, ALEXANDER, electric company executive; b. N.Y.C., May 18, 1915; s. David and Bessie (Wolf) S.; m. Hilda Rae Gevarter, Oct. 27, 1940; 1 dau., Carolyn Mae (Mrs. Louis M. Taff). Student, Cooper Union, N.Y.C., 1932-35; MBA, Fla. Atlantic U., 1976. Chief engr. Aerovox Corp., New Bedford, Mass., 1933-39; mgr. mfg., engring. Indsl. Condenser Corp., Chgo., 1939-44; owner Capacitron Inc., 1944-48; exec. v.p. Jefferson Electric Co., Bellwood, Ill., 1948-65; v.p., gen. mgr. electro-mechs. divsn. Essex Internat., Detroit, 1965-67. Advisor, bd. dirs. various corps.; vis. prof. mgmt. Fla. Atlantic U., Boca Raton, 1971-92, ret., 1993; lectr. profl. mgmt. UCLA, Harvard U. Grad. Sch. Bus. Adminstrn., U. Ill. Mem. Acad. Internat. Bus., Soc. Automotive Engrs. Address: 4100 Galt Ocean Dr #1505 Fort Lauderdale FL 33308-6030

SKLAR, CHARLES ARTHUR, pediatrician, educator; b. Wilmington, Del., May 16, 1948; s. Albert Sklar and Esther Rose Starr. BA, George Washington U., 1970; MD, U. So. Calif., 1974. Diplomate Am. Bd. Pediats., Am. Bd. Pediat. Endocrinology. Resident in pediat. Children's Hosp. of L.A., 1974-76; fellow in pediatric endocrinology U. Calif., San Francisco, 1976-79; asst. prof. pediat. U. Minn. Hosp., Mpls., 1979-81, NYU, 1982-90; assoc. prof. pediat. Cornell Med. Coll., N.Y.C., 1990—; assoc. attending physician Meml. Sloan-Kettering, 1990—. Contbr. articles to profl. jours. Multictr. grantee Genentech Found., 1996, ROI grantee NIH, 1998. Mem. Lawson Wilkins Pediat. Endocrine Soc., Endocrine Soc., Soc. Pediat. Rsch., Alpha Omega Alpha. Office: Meml Sloan Kettering 1275 York Ave New York NY 10021

SKLAR, GAIL JANICE, secondary special education educator; b. Phila., Nov. 10, 1949; d. Harold and Irma (Lusky) S.; m. David William Tucker, May 30, 1976 (div. May 1984); 1 child, Benjamin; m. Howard Rod Cohen, Jan. 2, 1997. BS in Edn., Temple U., 1971, MEd, 1974. Tchr. Simon Gratz High Sch., Phila., 1971—; ednl. diagnostician Phila./Ardmore, Pa., 1980—. Owner Buster & Kitty's Pet Pals. Recipient Dr. Ruth Hayre Svc. award. Mem. AAUW, Phila. Writing Project, Pa. Mid-Atlantic Seminar for Study of Women in Soc. Avocations: reading, researching women in history, orchid growing. Home: 402 Marple Rd Broomall PA 19008-2044 Office: Simon Gratz High Sch 18th & Hunting Park Ave Philadelphia PA 19140 E-mail: gailjsklar@erol.com.

SKLAR, HOLLY L. nonfiction writer; b. N.Y.C., May 6, 1955; BA, Oberlin Coll., 1977; MA in Polit. Sci., Columbia U., 1980. Rschr. UN Ctr. Transnat. Corps., N.Y., 1978; writer, rschr. N. Am. Congress Latin Am., 1981-82; exec. dir. Inst. New Communications, 1982-84; writer, lectr. N.Y., Boston. Review panelist NEH, Washington, 1989; del. Soviet-Am. Women's Summit, N.Y., Washington, 1990; dir. MediaVision, Boston, 1997—. Author, co-author (books) Trilateralism, 1980, Poverty in the American Dream: Women and Children First, 1983, Washington's War on Nicaragua, 1988, Streets of Hope: The Fall and Rise of an Urban Neighborhood, 1994, Chaos or Community? Seeking Solutions, Not Scapegoats for Bad Economics, 1995, Shifting Fortunes: The Perils of the Growing American Wealth Gap, 1999, Raise the Floor: Wages and Policies that Work for All of Us, 2001. Mem. adv. bd. The Progressive Media Project, Polit. Rsch. Assocs.; bd. dirs. United for a Fair Economy, 1996-2000; mem. steering com. Caribbean Basin Info. Project, 1982-85. Recipient Outstanding Book award Gustavus Myers Ctr. for Study Human Rights in U.S., 1988; Assocs. award Polit. Rsch. Assocs., Cambridge, 1991-97; fellow Columbia U. Grad. Sch. Arts and Scis., 1978-80. Mem. Nat. Writers Union, Acad. Polit. Sci. Office: 52 Parley Ave Boston MA 02130-1857 E-mail: Mediavi@aol.com.

SKLAR, KATHRYN KISH, historian, educator; b. Columbus, Ohio, Dec. 26, 1939; d. William Edward and Elizabeth Sue (Rhodes) Kish; m. Robert A. Sklar, 1958 (div. 1978); children: Leonard Scott, Susan Rebecca Sklar Friedman; m. Thomas L. Dublin, Apr. 30, 1988. BA magna cum laude, Radcliffe Coll., 1965; PhD, U. Mich., 1969. Asst. prof., lectr. U. Mich., Ann Arbor, 1969-74; assoc. prof. history UCLA, 1974-81, prof., 1981-88, chmn. com. to administer program in women's studies Coll. Letters and Sci., 1974-81; Disting. Prof. history SUNY, Binghamton, 1988—. Pulitzer juror in history, 1976; fellow Newberry Libr. Family and Community History Seminar, 1973; active Calif. Coun. for Humanities, 1981-85, N.Y. Coun. for Humanities, 1992—. Author: Catharine Beecher: A Study in American Domesticity, 1973 (Berkshire pri e 1974); editor: Catharine Beecher: A Treatise on Domestic Economy, 1977, Harriet Beecher Stowe: Uncle Tom's Cabin, or Life Among the Lowly: The Minister's Wooing, Oldtown Folks, 1981, Notes of Sixty Years: The Autobiography of Florence Kelley, 1849-1926, 1984, (with Thomas Dublin) Women and Power in American History: A Reader (2 vols.), 1991, (with Linda Kerber and Alice Kessler-Harris) U.S. History as Women's History: New Feminist Essays, 1995, Women's Rights Emerges within the Antislavery Movement: A Short History with Documents, 1830-1870, 2000; co-editor: The Social Survey Movement in Historical Perspective, 1992, Florence Kelley and the Nation's Work: The Rise of Women's Political Culture, 1830-1900, 1995 (Berkshire prize 1996). Social Justice Feminists in the United States and Germany: A Dialogue in Documents, 1885-1933, 1998; mem. editl. bd. Jour. Women's History, 1987—, Women's History Rev., 1990—, Jour. Am. History, 1978-81; contbr. chpts. to books. Fellow Woodrow Wilson Found., 1965-67, Danforth Found., 1967-69, Radcliffe Inst., 1973-74, Nat. Humanities Inst., 1975-76, Rockefeller Found. Humanities, 1981-82, Woodrow Wilson Internat. Ctr. for Scholars, 1982, 1992-93, Guggenheim Found., 1984, Ctr. Advanced Study Behavioral and Social Scis., Stanford U., 1987-88, AAUW, 1990-91; Daniels fellow Am. Antiquarian Soc., 1976, NEH fellow Newberry Library, 1982-83; Ford Found. faculty rsch. grantee, 1973-74; grantee NEH, 1976-78, UCLA Coun. for Internat. and Comparative Studies, 1983. Mem. Am. Hist. Assn. (chmn. com. on women historians 1980-83, v.p. Pacific Coast br. 1986-87, pres. 1987-88), Orgn. Am. Historians (exec. bd. 1983-86, Merle Curti award com. 1978-79, lectr. 1982—), Am. Studies Assn. (coun. mem.-at-large 1978-80), Berkshire Conf. Women Historians, Am. Antiquarian Soc., Phi Beta Kappa. Avocation: photography. Office: SUNY Dept History Binghamton NY 13902

SKLAR, LOUISE MARGARET, computer company executive; b. L.A., Aug. 12, 1934; d. Samuel Baldwin Smith and Judith LeRoy (Boughton) Nelson; m. Edwynn Edgar Schroeder, Mar. 20, 1955 (div. July 1975); children: Neil Nelson Schroeder, Leslie Louise Schroeder Grandclaudon, Samuel George Schroeder; m. Martin Sklar, Oct. 17, 1983. Student, U. So. Calif., 1952-54, UCLA, 1977-79. Acct. Valentine Assocs., Northridge, Calif., 1976-78, programmer, 1978-79; contr. Western Monetary, Encino, 1979-81; pres. Automated Computer Composition, Reno, 1984—. Mem.: DAR, Heart Am. Geneal. Soc., So. Calif. Assistance League, Conn. Soc. Genealogists, Greater L.A. Zoo. Assn., Am. Contract Bridge League (bd. govs. 1993—99, mem. nat. charity com. 1982—, mem. nat. goodwill com. 1994—), Assn. Los Angeles County Bridge Units (bd. dirs. 1990—2000, sec. 1984—86), Ky. Hist. Soc., Safari Club Internat., Zeta Tau Alpha. Republican. Avocations: tournament bridge, travel. Office: Automated Computer Composition Inc Reno NV 89511

SKLAR, RICHARD LAWRENCE, political science educator; b. N.Y.C., Mar. 22, 1930; s. Kalman and Sophie (Laub) S.; m. Eva Molineux, July 14, 1962; children: Judith Anne, Katherine Elizabeth. AB, U. Utah, 1952; MA, Princeton U., 1957, PhD, 1961. Mem. faculty Brandeis U., U. Ibadan, Nigeria, U. Zambia, SUNY-Stony Brook, UCLA; now prof. emeritus polit. sci. UCLA. Mem. fgn. area fellowship program Africa Nat. Com., 1970-73; Simon vis. prof. U. Manchester, Eng., 1975, Fulbright vis. prof. U. Zimbabwe, 1984; Lester Martin fellow Harry S. Truman Rsch. Inst., Hebrew U. Jerusalem, 1979; fellow Africa Inst. of South Africa, 1994—. Author: Nigerian Political Parties: Power in an Emergent African Nation, 1963, Corporate Power in an African State, 1975, African Politics in Postimperial Times, 2002; co-author: Postimperialism: International Capitalism and Development, 1987, African Politics and Problems in Development, 1991; co-editor: Postimperialism and World Politics, 1999; contbr. articles to profl. jours. Served with U.S. Army, 1952-54. Rockefeller Found. grantee, 1967 Mem. Am. Polit. Sci. Assn., African Studies Assn. (dir. 1976-78, 80-83, v.p. 1980-81, pres. 1981-82), AAUP (pres. Calif. Conf. 1980-81) Home: 1951 Holmby Ave Los Angeles CA 90025-5905

SKLAR, STANLEY LAWRENCE, judge; b. N.Y.C., Jan. 25, 1932; s. Julius and Rebecca (Skerker) S.; m. Margot Algase, Dec. 10, 1972; 1 child, Deborah. BA, Columbia U., 1953, LLB, 1956. Bar: N.Y. 1957, U.S. Supreme Ct. 1967. Assoc. Zipser & Levitt, N.Y.C., 1957-60, Wolf, Popper, Ross, Wolf & Jones, N.Y.C., 1960-64, Rubin, Baum, Levin, Constant & Friedman, N.Y.C., 1964-67, ptnr., 1967-76; judge N.Y.C. Civil Ct., 1977-78; acting justice N.Y. State Supreme Ct., N.Y.C., 1978-85, justice, 1986—. Author: Shoplifting: What You Need to Know About the Law, 1982; contbr. articles to profl. jours. Mem. Assn. Bar City N.Y., Am. Judicature Soc., Assn. Justices of the Supreme Ct. of City of N.Y. (pres. 2000-01), Bd. or Supreme Ct. Justices N.Y. County (chair 2001—). Office: NY Supreme Ct 60 Centre St Fl 1 New York NY 10007-1402

SKLAR, WILFORD NATHANIEL, retired lawyer, real estate broker; b. Salt Lake City, Dec. 13, 1916; s. Benjamin B. Sklar and Blanche Blau; m. Sarah Cohen, Jan. 16, 1945 (dec. Dec. 2000); children: Beth-Lynn (dec.), Teri Helene. BBA, U. Pitts., 1942; JD, Southwestern Sch. Law, 1960. Bar: Calif. 1960, U.S. Dist. Ct. Calif. 1962, U.S. Supreme Ct. 1965. Pvt. practice, Riverside, Calif., 1960-98; ret., 1998. Co-pub. worker's compensation books. Co-comdr. mil. affairs com. March AFB, Calif.; active Riverside Family Svcs., 1965-85. Sgt. USAF, 1942-46. Mem. B'nai B'rith (Akiba Dist. award 1970, 74), Riverside Jewish War Vets. Democrat. Jewish. Avocations: golf, coin collecting, real estate investments. Home: 5904 Copperfield Ave Riverside CA 92506-4510

SKLAR, WILLIAM PAUL, lawyer, educator; b. N.Y.C., Sept. 10, 1958; s. Morris and Helen (Meyers) S.; m. Lori Ann Hodges, Jan. 5, 1985. BBA magna cum laude, U. Miami, 1977, JD, 1980. Bar: Fla. 1980, N.Y. 1986, U.S. Dist. Ct. (so. dist.) Fla. 1981, U.S. Tax Ct. 1980, U.S. Ct. Appeals (5th cir.) 1980, U.S. Ct. Appeals (11th cir.) 1981. Assoc. Wood, Cobb, Murphy & Craig, West Palm Beach, Fla., 1980-85, ptnr., 1985-88, Foley & Lardner, West Palm Beach, 1989—, ptnr.-in-charge, 1995—2002. Chmn. Fla. Real Estate Dept., 1991—; adj. prof. law Sch. Law, U. Miami, Coral Gables, Fla., 1980—; dir. Inst. on Condo. and Cluster Devels., Inst. on Real Property Law, 1986—. Co-author: Cases and Materials in Condominium and Cluster Developments, 1980; author, co-editor; Florida Real Estate Transactions, 1983; contbr. articles to profl. jours. Atty. adv. bd. Morse Geriatric Ctr., West Palm Beach, 1984-88. Mem. ABA (chmn. subcom. on condominium and coop. housing sect. gen. practice 1983-88), Fla. Bar (com. condominium and planned devels. 1980—, bd. cert. real estate lawyer 1994, exec. coun. mem. real property, probate and trust law sect. 1997—), Palm Beach County Bar Assn., Coll. Cmty. Assn. Lawyers, Am. Coll. Real Estate Lawyers, Phi Delta Phi, Pi Sigma Alpha. Republican. Avocations: travel, tennis. Home: 7238 Montrico Dr Boca Raton FL 33433-6930 Office: Foley & Lardner West Tower 777 S Flagler Dr Ste 901 West Palm Beach FL 33401-6161

SKLAREW, MYRA, humanities educator, poet; BS in Biology, Tufts U., 1956; MA in Writing, Johns Hopkins U., 1970. Rsch. asst. Sch. Medicine Yale U., New Haven, 1955-57; tutor infant edn. project NIMH, 1960-64; dir. Montgomery County Coun. Coop. Nursery Schs., 1964-65; mem. English faculty George Washing U., 1970-71; mem. English faculty, co-dir. MFA creative writing program Am. U., Washington, 1970-87, prof. lit., 1992—; pres. Corp. Yaddo, 1987-91. Author: In the Basket of the Blind, 1975, From the Backyard of the Diaspora, 1981 (Jewish Book Coun. award 1977, Di Castagnola award 1972), Blessed Art Thou, No-One, 1982, The Science of Goodbyes, 1982, The Travels of the Itinerant Freda Ahron, 1985, Altamira, 1987, Like a Field Riddled by Ants, 1988, Eating the White Earth, 1994, Lithuania: New & Selected Poems, 1995, 2d printing, 1997, Yiddish edit., 2000 (Anna Davidson Rosenberg award Judah Magnes Mus. 1993), The Witness Trees, 2000, Over the Rooftops of Time, 2002; contbr. articles to profl. publs. Office: Am U Dept Lit 4400 Massachusetts Ave NW Washington DC 20016 E-mail: msklarew@erols.com.

SKLAREW, ROBERT JAY, biomedical research educator, consultant; b. N.Y.C., Nov. 25, 1941; s. Arthur and Jeanette (Laven) S.; m. Toby Willner, July 15, 1970; children: David Michael, Gary Richard. BA in Zoology, Cornell U., 1963; MS, NYU, 1965, PhD in Biology, 1970. Assoc. rsch. scientist NYU Sch. Medicine, N.Y.C., 1965-70, rsch. scientist, 1971-73, sr. rsch. scientist, 1973-79; rsch. asst. prof. pathology Goldwater Meml. Hosp. Sch. Medicine, 1979-87, rsch. assoc. prof. pathology, 1987-88; dir. cytokinetics and imaging lab. NYU rsch. svc. Goldwater Meml. Hosp., 1980-88; prof. cell biology, anatomy and medicine N.Y. Med. Coll., Valhalla, 1988-98. Rsch. assoc. dept. pathology Lenox Hill Hosp., N.Y.C., 1981-88; pres., CEO R.J. Sklarew Imaging Assoc., Inc., Larchmont, N.Y., 1990—; chmn. consensus panel for diagnostic cancer imaging Nat. Cancer Inst., 1994. Author: Microscopic Imaging of Steroid Receptors, 1990; sr. author: Cytometry, Jour. Histochem. Cytochem., Cancer, Exptl. Cell Rsch. Mem. Beth Emeth Synagogue, Larchmont, 1974—; group leader Boy Scouts Am., Larchmont, 1978-80; mem., bd. dirs. Pinelake Park Coop, 1998-2001. Grantee Am. Cancer Soc., Nat. Cancer Inst./NIH Conc. for Tobacco Rsch., R.J. Reynolds Industries Found., NYU; recipient Shannon award Nat. Cancer Inst., 1991. Mem. AAAS, Cell Kinetics Soc. (sec. 1983-85, 85-87, v.p. 1987-88, pres. 1988-89, chmn. nominations 1991, 93), N.Y. Acad. Sci., Soc. for Analytic Cytology, Soc. for Cell Biology, Tissue Culture Assn., Union Concerned Scientists, Kappa Delta Rho. Democrat. Achievements include development of methodology, algorithms and Receptogram analytic software for application of microscopic imaging in medical research and in pathodiagnosis of cancer, imaging methods for simultaneous densitometry and autoradiographic analysis; research in diagnostic imaging of steroid receptors, oncogenes and DNA ploidy in cancer, proliferative patterns and cell cycle kinetics of human solid tumors. Home: 8 Vine Rd Larchmont NY 10538-1247 Office: RJ Sklarew Imaging Assoc Inc 8 Vine Rd Larchmont NY 10538-1247 E-mail: rjsklarew@aol.com.

SKLARIN, ANN H. artist; b. N.Y.C., May 21, 1933; d. Sidney and Revera (Myers) Hirsch; m. Burton S. Sklarin, June 29, 1960; children: Laurie Sklarin Ember, Richard, Peter. BA in Art History, Wellesley Coll., 1955; MA in Secondary Art Edn., Columbia U., 1956. Art tchr. jr. high sch. N.Y.C. Sch. System, 1956-61, chmn. art. dept. jr. high sch., 1957-61. One-woman shows include Long Beach (N.Y.) Libr., 1973, Silvermine Guild Galleries, New Canaan, Conn., 1986, 98, Long Beach Mus. Art, 1986, Discovery Art Gallery, Glen Cove, N.Y., 1987, 92, 93, 94, Freeport (N.Y.) Libr., 1997; exhibited in juried shows at Nassau C.C., Garden City, N.Y., 1970, Nassau County (N.Y.) John F. Kennedy Ctr. Performing Arts, 1970 (1st Pl. award 1970), Long Beach Art Assn., 1970 (1st Pl. award 1970), Gregory Mus., 1973-74, L.I. Arts 76, Hempstead, N.Y., 1976, 5 Towns Music and Art Found., Woodmere, N.Y., 1980 (1st Pl. award 1981, Honorable Mention 1981, 3d Pl. award 1983), 85, Long Beach Art Assn. and Long Beach Mus. Art, 1982 (1st Pl. award), 84, 85 (3d Pl. award), Silvermine Guild Arts, 1984 (Richardson-Vicks Inc. award 1985, 87, Pepperidge Farm Inc. award 1987), Long Beach Mus. Art, 1985 (Best in Show-Grumbacher award 1985), Heckscher Mus., Huntington, N.Y., 1985, Fine Arts Mus. L.I., Hempstead, 1985, 91, Long Beach Art League and Long Beach Mus. Art, 1986 (2d Pl. award 1986), Wunsch Arts Ctr., Glen Cove, 1986, 87, Smithtown Twp. Arts Coun., St. James, 1989 (Honorable Mention award 1989), Chelsesa Ctr., Muttontown, NY, 2000; exhibited in group shows at Hewlett-Woodmere Libr., 1969, B.J. Spoke Gallery, Port Washington, N.Y., 1985, Shirley Scott Gallery, Southampton, N.Y., 1986, Smithtown Twp. Arts Coun., St. James, N.Y., 1988, 90, N.Y. Inst. Tech., Old Westbury, N.Y., 1989, Dowling Coll., Oakdale, N.Y., 1990, Discovery Art Gallery, 1992, 93, 94, 95, 96, Silvermine Guild Arts Ctr., 1984, 1992, 95, 97, 2000, Sound Shore Gallery, Stamford, Conn., 1993, Krasdale Foods Gallery, N.Y.C., 1993. Mem. exec. bd. 5 Towns Music and Art Found., 1960-2002, pres., 1971-74. Mem. Silvermine Guild Artists. Avocations: tennis, jogging, hiking, traveling, reading. Office: 501 Broadway Lawrence NY 11559-2501

SKLARIN, BURTON S. endocrinologist; b. N.Y.C., Feb. 28, 1932; s. Louis and Molla (Beiser) S.; m. Ann Hirsch, June 29, 1960; children: Laurie, Richard, Peter. AB, NYU, 1953, MD, 1957. Diplomate: Am. Bd. Internal Medicine, Am. Bd. Endocrinology and Metabolism. Intern Bellevue Hosp., N.Y.C., 1957-58, resident, 1958-61, asst. vis. clin. physician, 1961—; practice medicine specializing in endocrinology Lawrence, N.Y., 1961—; chief endocrinology St. John's Episcopal Hosp., 1961—, pres. med. staff, 1978-80, also chmn. med. exec. com.; asst. prof. clin. medicine NYU, 1961—, asst. in medicine Univ. Hosp., 1961; endocrinologist, staff physician L.I. Jewish Hosp. Contbr. articles on endocrinology to profl. publs. Vice pres. bd. trustees Woodmere Acad. Fellow ACP, Am. Coll. Endocrinology, N.Y. Acad. Medicine, Soc. Nuclear Medicine; mem. Nassau County Med. Soc., N.Y. Diabetes Assn., Endocrine Soc., Rockaway Med. Soc. (past pres.), Am. Assn. Clin. Endocrinologists. Home and Office: 501 Broadway Lawrence NY 11559-2501

SKLARSKY, CHARLES B. lawyer; b. Chgo., June 13, 1946; s. Morris and Sadie (Brenner) S.; m. Elizabeth Ann Hardzinski, Dec. 28, 1973; children: Jacob Daniel, Katherine Gabrielle, Jessica Leah. AB, Harvard U., 1968; JD, U. Wis., 1973. Bar: Wis. 1973, Ill. 1973, U.S. Dist. Ct. (no. dist.) Ill. 1973, U.S. Ct. Appeals (7th cir.) 1978, U.S. Ct. Appeals (2nd cir.) 1986. Asst. states atty. Cook County, Chgo., 1973-78; asst. U.S. atty. U.S. Dist. Ct. (no. dist.) Ill., 1978-86; ptnr. Jenner & Block, 1986—. Mem. ABA, Am. Coll. Trial Lawyers, Chgo. Bar Assn. Office: Jenner & Block One IBM Plz Chicago IL 60611-3586

SKLENAR, HERBERT ANTHONY, industrial products manufacturing company executive; b. Omaha, June 7, 1931; s. Michael Joseph and Alice Madeline (Spicka) S.; m. Eleanor Lydia Vincenz, Sept. 15, 1956; children: Susan A., Patricia I. BSBA summa cum laude, U. Omaha, 1952; MBA, Harvard U., 1954; LLD (hon.), Birmingham-So. Coll., 1996. CPA, W.Va. V.p., comptr. Parkersburg-Aetna Corp., W.Va., 1956-63; v.p., dir. Marmac Corp, Parkersburg, 1963-66; mgr. fin. control Boise-Cascade Corp., Idaho, 1966-67; exec. v.p. fin. and adminstrn., sec. Cudahy Co., Phoenix, 1967-72; chmn. emeritus Vulcan Materials Co., Birmingham, Ala., 1972-97, chmn. bd. dirs. emeritus, 1997—. Bd. dirs. Temple-Inland, Inc., Austin, Tex. Author: (with others) The Automatic Factory: A Critical Examination, 1955 Trustee Leadership Birmingham, Leadership Ala., Birmingham-So. Coll. Recipient Alumni Achievement award U. Nebr.-Omaha, 1977, cert. merit W.Va. Soc. CPAs, Elizah Watts Sells award AICPA, 1965, Brotherhood award NCCJ, 1993; inductee Ala. Acad. Honor, 1997. Mem.: Phi Eta Sigma, Birmingham Country Club, Shoal Creek Club, Phi Kappa Phi, Omicron Delta Kappa, Delta Sigma Pi. Republican. Presbyterian. Home: 2809 Shook Hill Cir Birmingham AL 35223-2618 Office: Vulcan Materials Co 1200 Urban Center Dr Birmingham AL 35242-2545 E-mail: sklenarh@vmcmail.com.

SKLENICKA, RUSSELL CHARLES, orthopaedic surgeon; b. Berwyn, Ill., July 20, 1947; s. Charles G. and Joan Barbara (Benco) S.; m. Betsy Sklenicka, Aug. 16, 1969;children: Kimberley, Scott. BA with distinction, DePauw U., Greencastle, Ind., 1969; MD with honors, U. Fla., 1973. Resident U. Fla. and Affiliated Hosps.; orthopaedic surgeon Watson Clinic, Lakeland, Fla., 1977—; mem. staff Lakeland Regional Med. Ctr., 1977—. Mem. ACS, AMA, Am. Acad. Orthopaedic Surgeons (bd. councillors 1988-94), Fla. Orthopaedic Soc. Avocations: jogging, snow skiing, computers, travel, railroad activities. Home: 1220 Lake Point Dr Lakeland FL 33813-2810 Office: Watson Clinic 1600 Lakeland Hills Blvd Lakeland FL 33805-3065 E-mail: rsklenicka@aol.com.

SKLOVSKY, ROBERT JOEL, naturopathic physician, pharmacist, educator; b. N.Y. BS, Bklyn. Coll., 1975; MA in Sci. Edn., Columbia U., 1976; PharmD, U. of Pacific, 1977; D in Naturopathic Medicine, Nat. Coll. Naturopathic Medicine, 1983. Intern Tripler Army Med. Ctr., Honolulu, 1977; prof. pharmacology Nat. Coll. Naturopathic Medicine, Portland, Oreg., 1982-85; pvt. practice Milwaukie, 1983—. Recipient Bristol Labs. award, 1983. Mem. Am. Assn. Naturopathic Physicians, Oreg. Assn. Naturopathic Physicians, N.Y. Acad. Sci. Avocations: classical and jazz music, tap dance, art, botany, acting. Office: 6910 SE Lake Rd Portland OR 97267-2101

SKODON, EMIL MARK, diplomat; b. Chgo., Nov. 25, 1953; s. Emil John and Anne (Soltes) S.; m. Dorothea Shaffer, Mar. 6, 1982; children: Catherine Marie, Christine Louise. BA, U. Chgo., 1975, MBA, 1976. Consular officer Am. Embassy, Bridgetown, Barbados, 1977-79, econ. officer East Berlin, Germany, 1979-81; econ. officer Office So. African Affairs, Dept. State, Washington, 1982-84; econ. officer Am. Embassy, Vienna, 1984-88, Kuwait City, Kuwait, 1989-91; consul gen. Am. Consulate Gen., Perth, Australia, 1991-94; dep. chief mission Am. Embassy, Singapore, 1995-98; dir. office Australia, New Zealand, Pacific Island Affairs Dept. State, Washington, 1998-2000, polit. advisor to USAF chief of staff, 2000—02; deputy chief of Mission Am. Embassy, Rome, 2002—. Recipient of U.S. Air Force decoration for exceptional civilian svc. Mem. Nat. Trust for Hist. Preservation. Avocations: visiting historic sites, good food, spending time with family. Office: Am. Embassy Rome Via Veneto 119A PSC 59 Box 70 APO AE 09624

SKOGEN, HAVEN SHERMAN, investment company executive; b. Rochester, Minn., May 8, 1927; s. Joseph Harold and Elpha (Hemphill) S.; m. Beverly R. Baker, Feb. 19, 1949; 1 child, Scott H. BS, Iowa State U., 1950; MS, Rutgers U., 1954, PhD, 1955; MBA, U. Chgo., 1970. Registered profl. engr., Wis. Devel. engr. E.I. duPont, Wilmington, Del., 1955-57; prof. Elmhurst (Ill.) Coll., 1957-58; chief engr. Stackpole, St. Marys, Pa., 1958-62; plant mgr. Magnatronics, Elizabethtown, Ky., 1962-65; mgr. Allen-Bradley, Milw., 1965-70; v.p. Dill-Clithrow, Chgo., 1970-74; oil co. exec. Occidental Oil Co., Grand Junction, Colo., 1974-92; ptnr. H&B Investment CO., 1992—. Author: Synthetic Fuel Combustion, 1984; inventor radioactive retort doping, locus retorting zone. Naval Rsch. fellow, 1951-55. Fellow Am. Inst. Chemists; mem. Internat. Platform Assn., Masons, Elks, Sigma Xi, Phi Beta Kappa, Phi Lambda Upsilon. Republican. Avocations: fly fishing, travel, reading, teaching. Home: 3152 Primrose Ct Grand Junction CO 81506-4147

SKOGLUND, ELIZABETH RUTH, marriage, child and family counselor; b. Chgo., June 17, 1937; d. Ragnar Emmanuel and Elizabeth Alvera (Benson) S. BA, UCLA, 1959; MA, Pasadena Coll., 1969. Cert. tchr., Calif.; cert. marriage, family and child counselor, Calif. Tchr. Marlborough Sch., Los Angeles, 1959-61; tchr., counselor Glendale (Calif.) High Sch., 1961-72; pvt. practice family counseling Burbank, Calif., 1972—. Author more than 28 books including It's OK to Be a Woman Again, 1988, Making Bad Times Good, 1991, Safety Zones, 1991, Harold's Dog Horace is Scared of the Dark, 1992, Life on the Line, 1992, The Welcoming Hearth, 1993, Amma: The Life and Words of Amy Carmichael, 1994, A Quiet Courage: Per Anger, Wallenberg's Co-Liberator of Hungarian Jews, 1997, Bright Days, Dark Nights: With Charles Spurgeon in Triumph over Emotional Pain, 2000, Secrets of the Second Half: Living Well for the Rest of Your LIfe, 2002. Mem. Calif. Assn. Marriage and Family Therapists, Simon Wiesenthal Ctr. Republican. Avocations: photography, scrapbooking, cooking.

SKOIEN, GARY, real estate company executive; BS cum laude, Colgate U., 1976; M Pub. Policy with honors, U. Mich., 1978. Asst. to James R. Thompson Gov. of Ill., Springfield, 1980-83; exec. dir. Ill. Capital Devel. Bd., 1983-90; sr. v.p., COO retail divsn. PGI (name now Prime Retail Inc.), 1991-92; exec. v.p., COO Prime Group, Inc., 1991—; chmn. bd., pres., CEO Horizon Group, Inc., Chgo., 1998—. Bd. dirs. Civic Fedn.; vice-chmn. bd. trustees No. Ill. U. Mem. Chicagoland C. of C. (bd. dirs.). Office: Horizon Group Inc 77 W Wacker Dr Ste 4200 Chicago IL 60601-1604

SKOK, PAUL JOSEPH, lawyer; b. Tarrytown, N.Y., Nov. 3, 1947; s. Paul Joseph Skok and Anna S. (Ruscigno) Barlow. BS, Purdue U., 1970; MA, Ball State U., 1974; JD, U. Denver, 1984. Bar: Colo. 1985, U.S. Dist. Ct. Colo. 1985. Prin. Law Office Paul Joseph Skok, Denver, 1985—. Lectr. in law U. Denver, 1990. Author: Trial Attorney's Guide to Insurance Coverage and Bad Faith, 1994. Mem. ABA, ATLA, Colo. Bar Assn., Denver Bar Assn., Colo. Trial Lawyers Assn. Office: 1720 Emerson St Denver CO 80218-1012 E-mail: skok@nilenet.com.

SKOL, MICHAEL, anti-corruption consultant; b. Chgo., Oct. 15, 1942; s. Ted and Rebecca (Williams) S.; m. Claudia Serwer, Sept. 29, 1973. BA, Yale U., 1964. U.S. fgn. svc. officer Dept. State, 1965-96; polit. officer U.S. Embassy, Buenos Aires, 1966-67, Saigon, Viet Nam, 1968-70; desk officer Dept. State, Washington, 1970-72; comml. attache U.S. Embassy, Santo Domingo, Dominican Republic, 1972-75; econ. comml. officer U.S. Consulate Gen., Naples, Italy, 1975-76; comml. attache U.S. Embassy, Rome, 1976-78, polit. counselor San Jose, Costa Rica, 1978-82; dep. dir. policy planning Inter-Am. Affairs Bur. Dept. State, Washington, 1982-85; dep. chief of mission U.S. Embassy, Bogota, Colombia, 1985-87; dir. Andean affairs Dept. State, Washington, 1987-88; dep. asst. sec. state for S.Am. U.S. Dept. of State, 1988-90; amb. U.S. Embassy, Caracas, Venezuela, 1990-93; prin. dep. asst. sec. for Latin Am./Caribbean Dept. State, Washington, 1993-96; sr. v.p. Diplomatic Resolutions, Inc., 1996-97; pres. Skol & Assoc. Inc., N.Y., Washington, Bogota, 1998—; chmn. US Colombian Bus. Ptnrshp., 1996-99; mng. dir. L.Am. Decision Strategies, N.Y.C., 1998—; pres. Skol, Ospina & Serna, N.Y.C., Washington and Bogota, 2001—. Mem. Coun. on Fgn. Rels., Coun. of the Americas, Yale Club of N.Y. Home: 400 E 54th St Apt 17B New York NY 10022 Office: Skol & Assocs Inc 33 E 33d St 4th fl New York NY 10019

SKOLER, CELIA REBECCA, art gallery director; b. Sioux City, Iowa, Apr. 7, 1931; d. Jacob and Flora (Gorchow) Stern; m. Louis Skoler, Aug. 24, 1952; children: Elisa Anne, Harry Jay. *In her early years, Celia Skoler's career path was centered on music; vocal performance and conducting held her total concentration. There is a reflection of this in son Harry, assistant professor at Berklee College, Boston, and featured jazz clarinetist on the Brownstone label. After marriage, an aptitude and love for visual art took precedence and was enthusiastically nurtured by husband Louis Skoler, noted architect and educator. New Acquisitions, created in 1981, combined Louis' spatial concepts and Celia's trained and intuitive aesthetics, along with her prior experience with public presentation. It also became a training ground for Syracuse University art majors.* BFA in Art and Music magna cum laude, Syracuse U., 1976. Fin. planner Architects' Partnership, Syracuse, N.Y., 1969-71; bus. mgr. Skoler & Lee Architects P.C., 1971-89; owner, dir. New Acquisitions Gallery, 1981-95, New Acquisitions, Syracuse, 1995—; ptnr. Gallery Metro, 1991-93, mng. ptnr., 1992-93; contbg. writer Syracuse Herald and Syracuse Newtimes, 1989-91. Art cons. Costello, Cooney & Fearon, Syracuse, 1981—83, IBM, Sracuse, Rochester, Albany, NY, 1989—91, Menter, Rudin & Trivelpiece, Syracuse, 1987—88, Blue Cross/Blue Shield, Ctrl. N.Y., Syracuse, 1990, Syracuse Newspapers, 1992—94, GTE Svcs. Corp., Syracuse, 1995; gallery supr. of sudent interns Syracuse U., 1981—93; dir. mayoral portrait City of Syracuse, 1983; dir. Gelling Meml. portrait U. Coll., 1984; dir. Levine Meml. Commn. Temple Concord, 1984; TV producer Syracuse U. Friends of Art, 1979—80; panelist for art critique Everson Mus. Art, Syracuse, 1989; lectr. on gallery mgmt. Syracuse U. Sch. of Art, 1989; juror fine art N.Y. State Fair, 1982, 89; panelist Onondaga County Cultural Resources Coun., 2001—, Cultural Resources Coun., Onondaga County, NY, 2001—. *New Acquistions Gallery took a new direction from 1995 forward. The enterprise was scaled back to concentrate on a more personal mode of help to a public that needs appraisals and guidance as much as art acquisitions. The nucleus of the gallery remains intact, and was moved to a home office site. This permits a more intensive one-on-one advisory service with the owner. In line with that change, the gallery name shortened to New Acquisitions. A network of artists is represented through portfolio, and the quality of client care remains exceptional.* One-man shows include Camillus Plaza, 1972, The Associated Artists Gallery, Syracuse, 1973, Library of Fayetteville, N.Y., 1974; exhibited in juried shows at N.Y. State Fair (1st prize 1974), U. Coll, 1967, 69, 71, Rochester Meml. Gallery, 1969, 70, 71, 72, 74, The Associated Artists, 1971, 72, Cen. N.Y. Art Open, 1970, 71, (Purchase prize 1970, 71), Munson Williams Protor Inst, Utica, N.Y., 1971, 72, Cayuga Mus., Auburn, N.Y., 1972, Oneida (N.Y.) Art Festival, 1969, (1st prize), Jewish Community Ctr., Syracuse, 1968 (1st prize 1969), St. David's Invitational, Dewitt, N.Y., 1970, 71, 72, 73, 74, 75, Cooperstown Art Inst., Nat. Show, 1973, 74, Arena Nat. Show, Binghamton, N.Y., 1975 (Purchase prize 1975); prodr.: (autobiographical CD-ROM) In Rehearsal, 1997; represented in permanent collection at Savannah (Ga.) Coll. Art and Design & Syracuse U. Peer counselor Univ. Coll., Syracuse, 1980-85; Tel-auc auctioneer Sta. WCNY-TV, Liverpool, N.Y., 1982; mem. steering and implementation com. Gelling Meml. Lounge U. Coll., 1984-85; exec. bd. Syracuse U. Friends of Art, 1977-80; fine art juror Downtown Com., Syracuse, 1982, Oswego (N.Y.) Art Guild, 1984. Recipient Purchase prize Marine Midland Bank, 1974, Crouse-Irving Hosp., 1971, 1974; named to Sioux City Ctrl. High Roster Hall of Fame, 1998. Mem. Everson Mus. Art (corp.) mem. Phi Kappa Phi, Alpha Sigma Lambda (pres. 1980-81). Home and Office: New Acquisitions 213 Scottholm Ter Syracuse NY 13224-1737

SKOLER, LOUIS, architect, educator; b. Apr. 5, 1920; s. Harry and Etta (Mitkoff) S.; m. Celia Rebecca Stern, 1952; children: Elisa Anne, Harry Jay. BArch, Cornell U., 1951. Maj. designer Sargent, Webster, Crenshaw & Folley, Syracuse, N.Y., 1951-59; design critic Cornell U., Ithaca, 1956-57; pvt. practice arch. Syracuse, 1956-69; faculty Sch. Arch. Syracuse U., 1959-92, prof. emeritus, 1990—. Head of MArch I Program, 1980-82, head undergrad. program, 1989-90, arch. programs abroad, London, 1977, Scandinavia, 1985, Japan, 1988; ptnr. Archs. Partnership, Syracuse, 1969-71; pres. Skoler & Lee Archs., P.C., Syracuse, 1971-89; lectr. Nanjing Inst. Tech., China, summer 1986; arbitrator Am. Arbitration Assn., 1980—. Named Best in Residential Design, Design-in-Steel, 1968-69. Mem. AIA. Home: 213 Scottholm Ter Syracuse NY 13224-1737 *A guiding-principle over many years of teaching and practice, is the interrelationship of theory and work-of idea and circumstance, of imagination and the forces generated by day to day life.*

SKOLFIELD, MELISSA T. public relations executive, former government official; b. New Orleans, June 25, 1958; m. Frank W. Curtis. BA in Econ. and Behavioral Sci., Rice U., 1980; MA in Pub. Affairs, George Washington U., 1986. Account exec. McDaniel & Tate Pub. Rels., Houston, 1981-84; press sec. Rep. Michael Andrews of Tex., 1985-87; press. sec. Senator Dale Bumpers of Ark., 1987-93; dep. asst. sec. for pub. affairs for policy and strategy Dept. Health and Human Svcs., Washington, 1993-95, asst. sec. pub. affairs, 1995—2001; sr. v.p., dir. healthcare practice group Golin/Harris Internat., 2001—. Press asst. Dem. Nat. Com., Dem. Nat. Conv., 1988, Clinton Pres. Campaign, Dem. Nat. Com., 1992. Mem. Senate Press Secs. Assn. (pres.), Assn. Dem. Press Assts., Pub. Rels. Soc. Am. Office: Golin/Harris Internat 2200 Clarendon Blvd Ste 1100 Arlington VA 22201*

SKOLL, JEFFREY, Internet company executive; BSEE, U. Toronto, 1987; MBA, Stanford U., 1995. Founder Skoll Engring., 1987, Micros on the Move Ltd., 1990; mgr. distbn. channels online news info. Knight-Ridder Info.; co-founder eBay Inc., San Jose, Calif. Office: eBay Inc 2145 Hamilton Ave San Jose CA 95125-5905

SKOLL, PEARL A. retired mathematics and special education educator; b. N.Y.C., Apr. 15, 1927; d. Samuel and Lillian Ruth Adler; m. Ralph Lewis Skoll (dec. 1959); children: Jeffrey A., Steve, Lyle. BA, Hunter Coll., 1950; MA in Adminstrn./Supervision, Calif. State U., Northridge, 1974. Math. tchr. various schs., L.A. and N.Y.C., 1954-71; program coord. The Mobilecomputer Math Lab L.A. Unified Sch. Dist., L.A., 1971-77, leader tchr. tng., 1967-83, mainstream tchr., 1977-83, spl. edn. vocat. assessment counselor, 1983-86; retired, 1986. Mem. task force State Dept. of Edn., Sacramento, Calif., 1976; instr. Calif. State U., Northridge, 1975-76, Pepperdine U., Malibu, Calif., 1975-76. Author (book) Coping with the Calculator, 1975; editor (book) The Calculator Book, 1975; contbr. articles to profl. jours. Reader tapes for literacy program U. Nev., Las Vegas, 1986-87; hon. mem. adv. coun. IBC, Cambridge, Eng. 3d Internat. Congress of Math. Edn. grantee U.S. Office of Edn., 1976, Internat. Biog. Ctr. (Cambridge, Eng.) 20th Century award for Meritorious Achievement, 1994, IB Citation of Meritorious Achievement in Math. Svcs., various miscellaneous honors from IBC, 1995; named Woman of Yr., Am. Biog. Inst., 1994. Mem. Calif. Math. Coun., Nat. Coun. of Tchrs. of Math., Calif. State U. Alumni Assn. Democrat. Jewish. Avocations: volunteer work, cooking, baking, jigsaw & crossword puzzles, gardening. Home: 7684 Keating Cir Las Vegas NV 89147-4908 E-mail: angel415@prodigy.net.

SKOLNICK, JEROME H. law educator; b. 1931; BBA, CCNY, 1952, MA, 1953; PhD, Yale U., 1957. Rsch. assoc. Yale U., New Haven, 1956-60, asst. prof., 1960-62, U. Calif.-Berkeley Law Sch., 1962-67, prof., 1970—; Claire Clements deans prof. law emeritus Jurisprudence and Social Policy, 1970—; disting. prof. sch. of law NYU, 1997—. Vis. assoc. prof. NYU, 1966; vis. prof. U. Denver, 1967; assoc. prof. U. Chgo., 1967-69; prof. U. Calif.-San Diego, 1969-70; dir. Ctr. Study of Law and Soc., 1972—; cons. Bd. dirs. Pres.'s Commn. on Causes and Prevention of Violence, 1968-69; disting. vis. prof. John Jay Coll. Criminal Justice, 1995-96; adj. prof., co-dir. Ctr. for Rsch. in Crime and Justice NYU Sch. Law, 1996-97; chmn. com. on law and justice NRC, 1994-97. Author: (with D. Bayley) The New Blue Line, 1986, Justice Without Trial, 1966, House of Cards, 1978, (with R.D. Schwartz) Society and the Legal Order, 1970, (with J. Fyfe) Above the Law, 1993, (with J. Kaplan and M. Feeley) Criminal Justice. Carnegie fellow, 1956-66, Guggenheim fellow, 1980; Rockefeller Found. fellow, Bellagio, 1991. Mem. Am. Sociol. Assn. (bd. dirs. 1971-74), ACLU, Am. Soc. Criminology (pres.), Law and Soc. Assn. (trustee). Office: NYU Sch Law 40 Washington Sq S New York NY 10012-1005

SKOLNICK, MALCOLM HARRIS, biophysics researcher, educator, lawyer, mediator; b. Salt Lake City, Aug. 11, 1935; s. Max Cantor and Charlotte Sylvia (Letman) S.; m. Lois Marlene Ray, Sept. 1, 1959; children: Michael, David, Sara, Jonathan. BS in Physics (with honors), U. Utah, 1956; MS in Physics, Cornell U., 1959, PhD in Theoretical Nuclear Physics, 1963; JD, U. Houston, 1986. Diplomate Am. Bd. Forensic Examiners. Staff scientist Elem. Sci. Study, Watertown, Mass., 1962-63; mem. Inst. for Advanced Study, Princeton, N.J., 1963-64; instr. Physics Dept. MIT, Cambridge, Mass., 1964-65; staff scientist dir. Edn. Devel. Ctr., Watertown, 1965-67; assoc. prof. physics Physics Dept. SUNY, Stony Brook, 1967-70; assoc. prof. dir. comm. Health Sci. Ctr. SUNY, 1968-71; prof. biophysics grad. sch. biomed. sci. U. Tex. Health Scis. Ctr., Houston, 1971-94, prof. biomedical comm., 1971-83, prof. health svcs. rsch., 1988-95, dir. neurophysiology rsch. ctr., 1985-91; dir office tec. mgmt. U. Tex. Health Sci. Ctr., 1991-96; prof. tech. and health law U. Tex. Sch. Pub. Health, 1994-2000, adj. prof., 2000—; of counsel Wisner & Assocs.; pres., CEO, chmn. bd. dirs. Cyto Genix, Inc., 1999—. Chmn. health care tech. study sect. nat. Ctr. Health Svcs. Rsch. HHS, 1975—79; editl. assoc. Cts., Health Sci. and Law, Washington, 1989—93; bd. dirs. Biodyne, Inc., Pub. Health Sys., Inc., S.W. Health Tech. Found. Patentee in field; contbr. numerous articles to profl. jours. With USNR, 1953-61, hon. discharge. Recipient Silver Beaver award Boy Scouts Am., 1978; Ford Found scholar, U. Utah, 1952; rsch. grantee Nat. Inst. for Drug Abuse, Brown Fund, Houston Endowment. Mem. ABA, APHA, Soc. Neurosci., Licensing Exec. Soc., Am. Intellectual Property Law Assn., Tex. Tech. Transfer Assn. (bd. dirs.), Houston Intellectual Property Law Assn., Houston Soc. Engring. in Medicine and Biology (bd. dirs.), Am. Bd. Forensic Examiners, Soc. Accident Reconstrn., Tex. Empowerment Network (pres., bd. dirs.), Soc. Automotive Engrs., Soc. Bioengring., Tex. Assn. Accid Reconstruction Specialists, Sigma Xi. Office: Cyto Genix Inc 9881 S Wilcrest Houston TX 77099 E-mail: mskolnick@cytogenix.com.

SKOLNICK, MARILYN, civic worker; b. N.Y.C., Jan. 17, 1925; d. Max and Annie Ruth (Stern) Kassel; n. Herbert Skolnick, Aug. 2, 1948; 1 child, Tamara. BA, Bklyn. Coll., 1946; MA, U. Okla., 1948; postgrad., State U. Iowa, 1948-52. Host, prodr. cable TV program Focus on Issues, 1983—; chair citizen participation com. Transp. Rsch. Bd., Nat. Acad. Sci., 1987-94; sec. local transp. fin. com., 1987—. Bd. dirs. Port Authority of Allegheny County, 1982-95; pres. Allegheny County Transp. Coun., 1997-99, v.p., 1999—. Chair Monroeville Planning Commn., 1983-85; bd. dirs. Pa. Planning Assn., 1983-85; mem. Allegheny County Hazardous Waste Task Force, 1983-85; bd. dirs. Group Against Smog and Pllution; mem. Pa. Transp. Adv. Com., 1983—; mem. air pollution ctrl. adv. com. Allegheny County Health Dept., 1985—; mem. Allegheny County Local Emergency Planning Com., 1987—. Mem. LWV (former bd. dirs.), N.Y. Acad. Scis., Pa. Acad. Scis., Sierra Club (bd. dirs. Pa. chpt. 1986—, chair Allegheny Group 1988-91), Sigma Xi. Home: 109 Southridge Dr Monroeville PA 15146-4739

SKOLNICK, S. HAROLD, lawyer; b. Woonsocket, R.I., June 17, 1915; s. David and Elsie (Silberman) S.; m. Shirley Marshall. AB cum laude, Amherst Coll., 1936; JD, Boston U., 1940. Bar: R.I. 1940, U.S. Supreme Ct. 1946, D.C. 1947, Fla. 1952, U.S. Dist. Ct. (so. dist.) Fla. 1953, U.S. Ct. Appeals (5th cir.) 1960, U.S. Ct. Appeals (11th cir.) 1981. Atty. Dept. of War, Washington, 1940-42; asst. gen. counsel, asst. chief legal dept. Office Chief Ordnance, Dept. of Army, 1947-50; assoc. Francis I. McCanna, Providence, 1951-52; ptnr. French & Skolnick, Miami, Fla., 1953-60; sole practice, 1961—. Served to lt. col. U.S. Army, 1942-47. Mem. ABA, Am. Judicature Soc., Nat. Def. Indsl. Assn. (life), R.I. Bar Assn., D.C. Bar Assn., Dade County Bar Assn., Estate Planning Coun. Greater Miami, Masons, Shriners. Home and Office: 6521 SW 122d St Miami FL 33156-5550

SKOLNICK, SHERMAN HERBERT, media host/producer, researcher, court reformer; b. Chgo., July 13, 1930; s. Max and Pauline (Lubelsky) S. Legal rschr., Chgo., 1958—; founder, chmn. Citizens Com. to Clean Up the Cts., 1963—. Instr., civic investigation Columbia Coll., 1969-70. Author: Secret History of Airplane Sabotage, 1973; radio talk show guest, 1967—, moderator, 1973-75; condr. univ. seminars in field; editor Hotline News, 1971—; prodr./panelist weekly pub. access Cable TV shows, Chgo., suburbs, 1991—, prodr., host, 1995—; writer Internet categories, websites, 1994—; writer/rsch. Japan Times Weekly, Tokyo, 1995. Home and Office: 9800 S Oglesby Ave Chicago IL 60617-4870 E-mail: skolnick@ameritech.net.

SKOLNIK, BARNET DAVID, retired lawyer; b. N.Y.C., Feb. 8, 1941; s. Jack and Edythe (Savitz) S.; m. Patricia L. Krohn; children: Sarah, Deborah, Daniel, Joseph, Benjamin, Rebecca, Zachary. AB in Am. Govt. cum laude, Harvard U., 1962, LLB, 1965. Bar: D.C. 1966, Md. 1984, Maine 1991. Atty. criminal div. U.S. Dept. Justice, Washington, 1966-68; asst. U.S. atty. for Dist. Md., Balt., 1968-78; chief public corruption unit U.S. Atty.'s Office, 1973-78; pvt. practice law Washington, 1978-83, 89-91, Balt., 1983-89, Portland, Maine, 1991-94; ret. Tchr., lectr. on trial practice, white collar criminality, public corruption. Recipient Spl. Achievement award Dept. Justice, 1972, 74, Spl. Commendation for Outstanding Svc., Dept. Justice, 1978, Younger Fed. Lawyer award Fed. Bar Assn., 1974, Atty. Gen.'s Disting. Service award, 1974, Legal award Assn. Fed. Investigators, 1977 E-mail: bskolnik@megalink.net.

SKOLNIK, DAVID ERWIN, financial analyst; b. Cleve., Oct. 31, 1949; s. Marvin and Ruth (Kovit) S.; m. Linda Susan Pollack, Mar. 31, 1973; children: Carla Denise, Robyn Laurel. BS in Acctg., Ohio State U., 1971. CPA, Ohio. Chief acct. Gray Drug Fair, Cleve., 1976-82, mgr. acctg. systems, 1982-84; fin. systems analyst Soc. Corp., 1984, fin. systems officer, 1984-86, fin. systems rsch. officer, 1986-90, sr. fin. systems officer, 1990-91, strategic rsch. officer, 1991-92; mgmt. acctg. officer Keycorp, 1992-96, asst. v.p., 1996—. Scoutmaster Boy Scouts Am., Cleve., 1971-77; coach Girls Softball League, South Euclid, Ohio, 1989-97. Mem. AICPAs, Ohio Soc. CPAs, Am. Inst. Banking, Am. Mgmt. Assn., Tau Epsilon Phi. Jewish. Avocations: golf, bowling, home repairs. Home: 33892 Hanover Woods Trl Solon OH 44139-4473 Office: Keycorp 127 Public Sq Cleveland OH 44114-1306

SKOLNIK, JONATHAN, economist; b. Schenectady, N.Y., Apr. 24, 1956; s. Willard and Sara Louise (Rosenbluth) S.; m. Ellyn Mary McKay, May 12, 1990; children: Julia McKay Skolnik, Kathlyn Ruth Skolnik. BS in Econs., U. Wis., 1978; M of Pub. Policy, Georgetown U., 1992. Sr. project dir. Jack Faucett Assocs., Inc., Bethesda, Md., 1979—. Contbr. articles to profl. jours. Mem. Interfaith Families Project, Takoma Park and Silver Spring, Md., 1997—. Mem. Nat. Acad. of Scis./Transp. Rsch. Bd., Assn. Sml. Bus. Govt. Contractors (exec. dir., founder 1999—). Democrat. Jewish. Avocations: volleyball, swimming, reading, softball, movies. Office: Jack Faucett Assocs Inc 4550 Montgomery Ave Ste 300N Bethesda MD 20814-3370 E-mail: skolnik@jfaucett.com.

SKOLNIK, MERRILL I. electrical engineer; b. Balt., Nov. 6, 1927; s. Samuel and Mary (Baker) S.; m. Judith Magid, June 4, 1950; children: Nachama, Martin Allen, Julia Anne, Ellen Charlotte. BEng, Johns Hopkins U., 1947, MSEng, 1949, DEng, 1951. Research scientist Johns Hopkins U., Balt., 1947-54, vis. prof., 1973-74; engring. specialist Sylvania Electric, Boston, 1954; staff mem. MIT Lincoln Lab., Lexington, Mass., 1954-59; research mgr. Electronic Communications, Timonium, Md., 1959-64, Inst. Def. Analyses, Arlington, Va., 1964-65; supr. radar div. Naval Research Lab., Washington, 1965-96, radar sys. cons., 1996—. Mem. bd. visitors Duke U. Engring. Sch., Durham, N.C., 1976-93; disting. vis. sci. Jet Propulsion Lab., 1990-92; mem. Md. Gov.'s Exec. Adv. Com., 1993-95. Author: Introduction to Radar Systems, 1962, 3d edit., 2001, Radar Handbook, 1970, 2d edit., 1990; editor: Radar Applications, 1988. Recipient Heinrich Hertz premium Instn. Electronic and Radio Engrs., London, 1964, Disting. Alumnus award Johns Hopkins U., 1979, Disting. Civilian Svc. award USN, 1982, Meritorious Exec. award Sr. Exec. Svc., 1986, Johns Hopkins Engring. and Applied Sci. Excellence in Tchg. award, 1998; named to Soc. of Scholars, Johns Hopkins U., 1975. Fellow IEEE (editor Proceedings 1986-89, Harry Diamond award 1983, Centennial medal 1984, Dennis J. Picard medal for radar technologies and applications 2000); mem. Nat. Acad. Engring. Home: 8123 McDonogh Rd Baltimore MD 21208-1005 Office: Naval Rsch Lab Washington DC 20375-0001 E-mail: skolnik@radar.nrl.navy.mil.

SKOLNIK, PHYLLIS, dermatologist; b. Bklyn., Sept. 16, 1947; d. Ben and Doris Skolnik; m. Marvin Lawrence Sussman, July 1, 1973; children: Jennifer Marnie Sussman, Andrew Jeremy Sussman. BS, Bklyn. Coll., 1968; MD, N.Y. Med. Coll., 1972. Diplomate Am. Bd. Dermatology. Intern Beth Isreal Med. Ctr., N.Y.C., 1972-73; rsch. fellow U. Miami (Fla.) Sch. Medicine, 1973-74, resident in dermatology, 1974-77; pvt. practice Miami, 1977—. Cons. S. Miami Hosp., Bapt. Hosp.; sr. active staff Miami Children's Hosp.; mem. courtesy staff Jackson Meml. Hosp.; clin. assoc. prof. U. Miami Sch. Medicine, 1991. Contbr. articles to profl. jours. Fellow Am. Acad. Dermatology (mem. adv. bd.); mem. AMA, Fla. Med. Assn., Fla. Soc. Dermatology, Miami Dermatol. Soc. (sec., treas. 1991-93, v.p. 1993-94, pres. 1994-95, rep. 1995-98), Dade County Med. Assn. Home: 5800 N Kendall Dr Miami FL 33156-2066 Office: 7800 SW 57th Ave Ste 102 South Miami FL 33143-5543

SKOLNIKOFF, EUGENE B. political science educator; b. Phila., Aug. 29, 1928; s. Benjamin H. and Betty (Turoff) S.; m. Winifred S. Weinstein, Sept. 15, 1957; children: Matthew, Jessica. BS, MS, MIT, 1950, PhD, 1965; BA, Oxford (Eng.) U., 1952, MA, 1955. Registered profl. engr. Rsch. asst. in elec. engring. Uppsala U., Sweden, 1950; prof. polit. sci. emeritus M.I.T., 1965—, chmn. polit. sci. dept., 1970-74; dir. Center for Internat. Studies, 1972-87. Vis. rsch. prof. Carnegie Endowment for Internat. Peace, Geneva, 1969-70; vis. fellow Balliol Coll., U. Oxford, 1989; vis. scholar Yale U., 1997; systems analyst Inst. for Def. Analyses, Washington, 1957-58; mem. White House staff Office Spl. Asst. to Pres. for Sci. and Tech., Washington, 1958-63; adj. prof. Fletcher Sch. Law and Diplomacy, Tufts U., Medford, Mass., 1965-72; sr. cons. White House Office of Sci. and Tech. Policy, 1977-81, also vice chmn. adv. com. on sci., tech. and devel.; mem. policy rev. com. on nat. low-level nuclear waste mgmt., 1980-86; cons. Dept. State, Office of Tech. Assessment, AID, OECD, Resources for the Future, Am. Soc. Internat. Law, Ford Found., Inst. Def. Analyses; chmn., pres. Sci. and Public Policy Studies Group, 1967-73; mem. Internat. Council Sci. Policy Studies; Montague Burton vis. prof. U. Edinburgh, 1977, mem. several Nat. Rsch. Coun. coms.; chmn. bd. UN U. Inst. on New Tech. (INTECH), Maastricht, Holland, 1998—; Michael Dukakis vis. prof. pub. policy Am. Coll. Thessaloniki, Greece, 2000. Author: Science, Technology and American Foreign Policy, 1967, International Imperatives of Technology, 1972, The Elusive Transformation: Science, Technology, and the Evolution of International Politics, 1993; co-editor: World Eco-Crisis, 1972, Visions of Apocalypse, End or Rebirth?, 1985, The Implementation and Effectiveness of International Environmental Commitments, 1998; contbr. articles to publs.; chmn. editorial bd. Pub. Sci., 1971-75; mem. editorial bd. Tech. Rev., 1976-78, Social Studies of Sci., 1970-75, Internat. Orgn., 1974-80, Internat. Rels. of Asia Pacific, 2000--; patentee hybrid circuits. Trustee German Marshall Fund, 1979-87, chmn., 1980-86; trustee UN Rsch. Inst. for Social Devel., 1979-85; bd. dirs. Saco Def., 1984-86; mem. Overseas Devel. Coun.; mem. U.S. del. UN Commn. for Social Devel., 1979; mem. State Dept. Adv. Com. on Sci. and Tech., 1987-90. Served with U.S. Army Security Agy., 1955-57. Rhodes scholar, 1950-52; Rockefeller Found. fellow, 1963-65; decorated Comdr.'s Cross Fed. Republic Germany, Order of Rising Sun, Golden Rays, Neck Ribbon, Japan. Fellow Am. Acad. Arts and Scis. (councillor 1973-77), AAAS (sec. sect. K 1967-69, mem. com. on sci. and pub. policy 1973-74, com. on sci., engring. and pub. policy 1984-89); mem. UN Assn., Fedn. Am. Scientists, (coun. 1981-85), Coun. Fgn. Rels., Am. Assn. Rhodes Scholars, Soc. for Social Studies of Sci., Sigma Xi, Tau Beta Pi, Eta Kappa Nu. Home: 3 Chandler St Lexington MA 02420-3601 Office: MIT E53-366 77 Massachusetts Ave Cambridge MA 02139-4307 E-mail: ebskol@mit.edu.

SKOLROOD, ROBERT KENNETH, lawyer; b. Stockton, Ill., May 17, 1928; s. Myron Clifford and Lola Mae (Lincicum) S.; m. Marilyn Jean Riegel, June 18, 1955; children: Cynthia, Mark, Kent, Richard. BA, Ohio Wesleyan U., 1952; JD, U. Chgo., 1957. Bar: Ill. 1957, Okla. 1981, D.C. 1987, U.S. Supreme Ct., 1982, Va. 1985, U.S. Dist. Ct. (no. dist.) Ill. 1959, U.S. Ct. Appeals (7th cir.) 1970, U.S. Dist. Ct. (no. dist.) Okla. 1982, U.S. Dist. Ct. Nebr. 1985, U.S. Dist. Ct. (so. dist.) Ala. 1986, U.S. Dist. Ct. (so. dist.) N.Y. 1986, U.S. Dist. Ct. (ea. and we. dists.) Va. 1986, U.S. Ct. Appeals (2nd, 4th, 6th, 7th, 8th 10th and 11th cirs.) 1986, U.S. Dist. Ct. D.C. 1987, Ptnr. Reno, Zahm, Folgate, Skolrood, Lindberg & Powell, Rockford, Ill., 1957-80; prof. O.W. Coburn Sch. Law, Oral Roberts U., Tulsa, 1980-81, gen. counsel, 1980-84; exec. dir., gen. counsel Nat. Legal Found., Virginia Beach, Va., 1984-95; with Law Firm of Scogins & Skolrood, Roanoke, Va., 1995—. Contbr. articles to legal jours.; lead counsel on several major constitutional cases. Pres., John Ericsson Rep. Club, 1964; trustee No. Ill. conf. United Meth. Ch., 1957-74, chmn., 1972-74; pres. Ill. Home and Aid Soc.; mem. Evangelical Free Ch. Served with U.S. Army, 1952-54, Korea. Fellow Am. Coll. Trial Lawyers; mem. Ill. Bar Assn., Okla. Bar Assn., Va., Bar Assn., Dist of Columbia Bar Assn, ATLA, Va. Trial Lawyers Assn., Tex. Trial Lawyers Assn., Ill. Trial Lawyers Assn., Okla. Trial Lawyers Assn., Christian Educators Assn. Internat. (bd. reference), Kappa Delta Pi, Pi Sigma Kappa. E-mail: skolrood@prodigy.net. Home: 5217 Dresden Ln Roanoke VA 24012-8576 Office: Scogins & Skolrood 3243 Electric Rd Ste 1A Roanoke VA 24018-6440

SKOMAL, EDWARD NELSON, aerospace company executive, consultant; b. Kansas City, Mo., Apr. 15, 1926; s. Edward Albert and Ruth (Bangs) S.; m. Elizabeth Birkbeck, Mar. 4, 1951; children: Susan Beth, Catherine Anne, Margaret Elaine; m. Joan Kerner, Apr. 9, 1988. BA, Rice U., Houston, 1947, MA, 1949. Engr., Socony Rsch. Labs., Dallas, 1949-51; asst. sect. head Nat. Bur. Standards, Washington, 1951-56; project engr. Sylvania Research Lab., Palo Alto, Calif., 1956-59; mgr. applications engring., chief applications engr. Motorola Solid State Systems Div., Phoenix, 1959-63; dir. communications dept. Aerospace Corp., El Segundo, Calif., 1963-86, ret., 1986; mem. Presdl. Joint Tech. Adv. Com. on Electromagnetic Compatibility, Washington, 1965-70, 71-75. Author: Man Made Radio Noise, 1978, Automatic Vehicle Locating Systems, 1980; Measuring the Radio Frequency Environment, 1985; contbr. articles to profl. jours. Patentee in field of radio systems, solid state devices, radar cross sect. reduction of ballistic rentry vehicles and sold state microwave components. Elder Riverside Presbytery. With USN, 1944-6. Fellow IEEE (asst. editor Trans. Electromatic Compatibility 1978-86, chmn. tech. adv. com. 1982-86, chmn. tech. com. electromagnetic environments 1976-82, standards com. 1980-86, nat. com. standards coordinating com. on definitions 1986—, Richard A. Stoddart award 1980, cert. of Achievement 1971, Paper of Yr. award 1970); mem. IEEE Electromagnetic Soc. (life), Am. Phys. Soc., Internat. Union Radio Scientists, Sigma Xi. Republican. Presbyterian. Home: 1802 Morning Dove Ln Redlands CA 92373

SKOMOROWSKY, PETER P. retired accounting company executive, lawyer; b. Leipzig, Germany, Nov. 14, 1932; BA, Columbia U.; MBA, CCNY; JD, N.Y. Law Sch. Ptnr. Grant Thornton LLP, N.Y.C.; now ret. Home: 25 E 86th St New York NY 10028-0553 Office: care Grant Thornton LLP 666 3rd Ave New York NY 10017-4011 E-mail: pskomorowsky@gt.com.

SKONEY, SOPHIE ESSA, educational administrator; b. Detroit, Jan. 29, 1929; d. George Essa and Helena (Dihmes) Cokalay; m. Daniel J. Skoney, Dec. 28, 1957; children: Joseph Anthony, James Francis, Carol Anne. PhB, U. Detroit, 1951; MEd, Wayne State U., 1960, EdD, 1975; postgrad., Ednl. Inst. Harvard Grad. Sch., 1986—. Tchr. elem. sch. Detroit Bd. Edn., 1952-69, remedial reading specialist, 1969-70, curriculum coord., 1970-71, region 6 article 3 title I coord., 1971-83, area achievement specialist, 1984-88; adminstrv. asst. Office Grant Procurement and Compliance, 1988-2000. Mem. dean's adv. coun. Coll. Edn. Wayne State U., 1995—; cons. in field. Editor newsletter Alliance to the Mich. Dental Assn., 1993-2000. Recipient Disting. Alumni award Wayne State U., 1993. Mem. ASCD, Wayne State U. Edn. Alumni Assn. (pres. bd. govts. 1979-80, newsletter editor 1975-77, 80—), Macomb Dental Aux. (pres. 1969-70), Mich. Dental Aux. (pres. 1980-81), Alliance Mich. Dental Assn. (pres. 1998-2000), Am. Assn. Sch. Adminstrs., Wayne State U. Alumni Assn. (dir., v.p. 1985-86), Internat. Reading Assn., Mich. Reading Assn., Mich. Assn. State and Fed. Program Specialists, Profl. Women's Network (newsletter editor 1981-83, pres. 1985-87, Anthony Wayne award for leadership 1981), Anthony Wayne Soc., Delta Kappa Gamma, Beta Sigma Phi, Phi Delta Kappa (v.p. 1988-90, pres. 1990-91, Educator of Yr. 1985, 91, 96, 2000). Roman Catholic. Home: 20813 Lakeland St Saint Clair Shores MI 48081-2104 E-mail: skoneys@aol.com.

SKOOG, DONALD PAUL, retired physician, educator; b. Sioux City, Iowa, Sept. 29, 1931; m. Mary Ann Bunn, 1955; children: Robert Eugene, David Alan (dec.), Kristin Marie. BA magna cum laude, Midland Lutheran Coll., Fremont, Nebr., 1953; MD cum laude, U. Nebr., 1958; DSci (hon.), Midland Luth. Coll., 1993. Diplomate Am. Bd. Pathology. Intern, then resident in pathology Bishop Clarkson Meml. Hosp., Omaha, 1958-62; resident in pathology Parkland Meml. Hosp., Dallas, 1962-63; fellow in pathology U. Tex. Southwestern Med. Sch., 1962-63; practice medicine specializing in pathology Omaha, 1963-92. Pathologist Bishop Carlson Meml. Hosp., 1963-88, chmn. dept. pathology, 1978-80, dir. dept., 1986-87, chmn. med. edn. com., 1978-83, sec.-treas. med. staff, 1982-87; prof. pathology and microbiology U. Nebr. Coll. Med., 1977-93, mem. dean's faculty adv. coun., 1977-79, mem. grad. and continuing edn. com., 1980-85, mem. coun. for affiliated instns., 1981-83, mem. admissions com., 1986-91, sr. cons. pathology and microbiology, 1993—; assoc. med. dir. ARC Blood Svcs., Midwest Region, Omaha, 1988, med. dir./dir. 1989-91, dir./prin. officer, 1991-92, mem. computer sys. selection com., 1991; med. affairs com. ARC Blood Svcs., Washington, 1991-92; mem. exec. com., chmn. loan com. Nebr. Med. Edn. Fund, 1983-91, sec., treas., 1984-91. Mem. editorial bd. Lab. Medicine, 1979— ; contbr. articles to med. jours. Councilman Luther Meml. Luth. Ch., Omaha, 1966-72, 87-91, vice chmn., 1969-72; trustee Midland Luth. Coll., 1968-87, chmn., 1973-75. Recipient Alumni Achievement award Midland Luth. Coll., 1972, Disting. Svc. award Sch. of Allied Health Program, U. Nebr. Med. Ctr., 1990, Disting. Alumnus award U. Nebr. Coll. Medicine Alumni Assn., 1998. Fellow Am. Soc. Clin. Pathologists (hematology profl. self-assessment com. 1972, 75,78, adv. coun. 1972-78, chmn. coun. hematology 1978-81, editor Hematology Check Sample 1983-88, Disting. Svc. award Commn. on Continuing Edn. 1985, mem. bd. censors 1987-89, mem. nat. meeting activities com. 1989-92, chmn. 1990-92, Israel Davidsohn disting. svc. award 1993), Coll. Am. Pathologists (hematology resource com. 1981-86, vice chmn. 1982-85); mem. AMA, Nebr. Assn. Pathologists, Nebr. Med. Assn., Met. Omaha Med. Soc. (coun. on grievances and profl. ethics 1983-91), Midland Luth. Coll. Alumni Assn. (pres. 1969-70), Alpha Omega Alpha (pres. U. Nebr. chpt. 1976-77, counsellor 1984-90). Home: 706 S 96th St Omaha NE 68114-4918 E-mail: dpsmd@aol.com.

SKOOG, DOUGLAS ARVID, retired chemistry educator, writer; b. Willmar, Minn., May 4, 1918; s. Arvid C. and Hilma E. (Erickson) S.; m. Judith Bone, Oct. 10, 1942; children: James Arvid, Jon Douglas. BS, Oreg. State U., 1940; PhD, U. Ill., 1943. Research chemist Standard Oil Co. of Calif., Richmond, Calif., 1943-47; asst. prof. chemistry Stanford (Calif.) U., 1947-53, assoc. prof., 1953-62, prof., assoc. exec. head dept. chemistry, 1963-76, prof. emeritus, 1976—; writer Stanford, 1976—. Author: Fundamentals of Analytical Chemistry, 7th rev. edit., 1996, Principles of Instrumental Analysis, 1998, 5th rev. edit., 1992, Analytical Chemistry, 7th rev. edit., 1994; contbr. articles to profl. jours. Fellow AAAS; mem. Am. Chem. Soc. (pres. Santa Clara Valley sect. 1962, Fisher award in analytical chemistry 1999), Sigma Xi, Phi Kappa Phi, Alpha Chi Sigma. Clubs: Bohemian (San Francisco). Avocations: flying, skiing. Home: #302 401 Webster St Apt 302 Palo Alto CA 94301-1249 E-mail: skoog@stanford.edu.

SKOOG, GERALD DUANE, science educator; b. Sioux City, Iowa, Feb. 27, 1936; s. Paul and Mary Ann Skoog; m. Elizabeth Ann Lee, Dec. 28, 1962; children: Jeffrey, John, Sarah. BS, U. Nebr., 1958; MA, U. No. Iowa, 1963; Ed.D., U. Nebr., 1969. Tchr. various schs., Nebr., Ill., 1958-69; instr. U. Nebr., Lincoln, summer 1969; asst. prof. curriculum and instrn. Tex. Tech U., Lubbock, 1969-72, assoc. prof., coordinator program, 1972-74, assoc. prof., chmn. secondary edn., 1976-80, prof., chmn. secondary edn., 1980-90, prof., chmn. curriculum and instrn., 1990-97, Helen DeVitt Jones prof., 1997-2001, pres. faculty senate, 1986-87, Paul Whitfield Horn prof., 2000—, dean Coll. Edn., 2002—. Vis. prof. Western Ill. U., summer 1972; lectr. in field; participant, facilitator numerous workshops; cons. Contbr. numerous articles to profl. jours., also reviewer articles and papers; co-author secondary sch. science textbooks. Bd. dirs. Gloria Dei Luth. Ch., Lubbock, 1971-74, 92-93; bd. dirs. Luth. Coun. Cmty. Action, 1970-71, Good Neighbor Ministry, 1982-84; leader Boy Scouts Am., 1978-79; foster parent Luth. Social Svcs. Tex.; bd. dirs. Triangle Coalition for Sci. and Tech., 1986-95. Recipient Pres.'s Faculty Achievement award Tex. Tech. U., 1986, Disting. Leadership award, 1996; named Notable Alumnus, U. Nebr., Lincoln, Tchrs. Coll., 1998; named to Tex. Sci. Hall of Fame, 2000. Fellow AAAS; mem. ASCD, Nat. Sci. Tchrs. Assn. (life, bd. dirs. 1977-79, pres. 1985-86, various coms., Disting. Svc. to Sci. Edn. award 1994), Nat. Assn. Rsch. Sci. Teaching, Assn. Edn. Tchrs. Sci., Sci. Tchrs. Assn. Tex. (hon. mem., past pres., Skoog Cup award), Nat. Assn. Biology Tchrs., Soc. Study Edn., Phi Delta Kappa. Home: 3214 67th St Lubbock TX 79413-6206 Office: Tex Tech U Coll Edn Lubbock TX 79409

SKOOG, WILLIAM ARTHUR, former oncologist, educator; b. Culver City, Calif., Apr. 10, 1925; s. John Lundeen and Allis Rose (Gatz) Skoog; m. Ann Douglas, July 17, 1949; children: Karen, William Arthur, James Douglas, Allison. AA, UCLA, 1944; BA with great distinction, Stanford U., 1946, MD, 1949. Intern in medicine Stanford Hosp., San Francisco, 1948-49, asst. resident in medicine, 1949-50, N.Y. Hosp., N.Y.C., 1950-51; sr. resideit in medicine Wadsworth VA Hosp., L.A., 1951, attending specialist in internal medicine, 1962-68; pvt. practice internal medicine Los Altos, Calif., 1959-61; pvt. practice hematology and oncology, Santa Monica, 1971-72; pvt. practice med. oncology, San Bernardino, 1972-94. Assoc. staff Palo Alto-Stanford Med. Ctr., 1959-61, U. Calif. Med. Ctr., San francisco, 1959-61; assoc. attending physician UCLA Hosp. and Clinics, 1961-78; vis. physicisn in internal medicine Harbor Gen. Hosp., Torrance, Calif., 1962-65, attending physician, 1965-71; cons. in chemistry Clin. Lab., UCLA Hosp., 1963-68; affiliate cons. staff St. John's Hosp., Santa Monica, 1967-71, courtesy staff, 1971-72; courtesy attending med. staff Santa Monica Hosp., 1967-72; staff physician St. Bernardine (Calif.) Hosp., 1972-94, hon. staff, 1994—; staff physician San Bernardino Cmty. Hosp., 1972-90, courtesy staff, 1990-94; chief sect. oncology San Bernardino County Hosp., 1972-76; cons. staff Redlands(Calf.) Cmty. Hosp., 1972-83, courtesy staff, 1983-94, hon. staff, 1994—; asst. in medicine Cornell U. Med. Coll., N.Y.C., 1950-51; jr. rsch. physician UCLA Atomic Energy Project, 1954-55; instr. medicine, asst. rsch. physician dept. medicine UCLA Med. Ctr., 1955-56, asst. prof. medicine, asst. rsch. physician, 1956-59; clin. assoc. in hematology VA Ctr., L.A., 1956-59; co-dir. metabolic rsch. unit UCLA Ctr. for Health Scis., 1955-59, 61-65; co-dir. Health Scis. Clin. Rsch. Ctr., 1965-68, dir., 1968-72; clin. instr. medicine Stanford U., 1959-61; asst. clin. prof. medicine, assoc. rsch. physician U. Calif. Med. ctr., San fRancisco, 1959-61; lectr. medicine UCLA Sch. Medicine, 1961-62, assoc. prof., 1962-734, assoc. clin. prof., 1973—. Contbr. articles to med. jours. Active duty USNR, 1943—46, lt. M.C. USNR, 1951—53. Fellow: ACP, Am Soc. Internal Medicine; mem.: AMA, San Bernardino County Med. Soc., Am. Soc Clin. Oncology, L.A. Acad. Medicine, Am. Fedn. Clin. Rsch., Western Soc. Clin. Rsch., So. Calif. Acad. Clin. Oncology, Calif. Med. Assn., Redlands Country Club, Alpha Omega Alpha, Sigma Xi, Alpha Kappa Kappa. Episcopalian (vestryman 1965-70). Home: 1119 Kimberly Pl Redlands CA 92373-6786 Fax: 909-798-5016. E-mail: wasredarrow@aol.com.

SKOOG, WILLIAM MELVIN, music/voice educator; b. St. Paul, Apr. 7, 1953; s. John Chester and Mary Edith S.; m. Elaine Ketter, March 1, 1986; children: Miles William, Rebekah Morgan, Jacquelyn Correlle. BA magna cum laude, Gustavus Adolphus Coll., 1975; MA in Music, U. Denver, 1981; ArtsD in Music, U. Northern Colo., 1992. Musical dir., conductor Littleton (Colo.) Chamber Orch., 1985-89, Longmont (Colo.) Chorale, 1989-90; dir. music and fine arts Littleton United Meth. Ch., 1981-85, St. Andrew United Meth. Ch., Littleton, 1985-89; asst. dir. choral and operatic activities U. No. Colo., Dowagiac, Mich., 1988-90; dir. choral activities, dept. chair Southwestern Mich. Coll., 1990-97; dir. choral activities dept. music Ind. U.-Purdue U., Fort Wayne, Ind., 1997—2001; coral condr. divsn. coral activities Bowling Green (Ohio) State U., 2001—. Mem. Robert Shaw Chorale, 1996, 97, 98. Guest soloist Carmina Burana, Blue Lake Music Camp, Mich., 1996, Ft. Collins Symphony, Colo., Garden City Symphony; guest conductor Elkart Chorale and Symphony, 1995, Northwest Ind. choral Festival, Denver, Ind., 1996, Fort Wayne Philharmonic Orch., 1997, Fort Wayne All City Choir, 1998, First Wayne St. United Meth. Ch., 2000, Ecumenical 2000 Svc., Ft. Wayne, 1999, Bridges Music Ministry, Littleton, 1999—, Northern Ind. Assn. Chs., Bethel Coll., 2000, European Tour of Germany and Prague, Sanctuary Choir,

2000; condr. INd./PUrdue Festival Chorus and Prague Radio Symphony Orch., 2001, Dvorak Festival, Prague and Vienna; rsch. and diagnostic, rsch. cons. Voice Care Ctr., Ft. Wayne, 2000. Pres. Ind. Opera North, South Bend, Ind., 1996-97, Fort Wayne Children's Choir, Inc., 1998—; bd. dirs. Encore Dance Co., Decatur and Dowagiac, Mich., 1995-97, Dowagiac Dogwood Fina Arts Festival, 1995-97. Mem. Nat. Assn. Tchrs. Singing, Nat. Otter Soc., Am. Choral Dirs. Assn. (Ind. chpt.), Am. Guild Organists and Choral Dirs., Nat. Music Educators Conf. (grantee 1999). Democrat. Methodist. Avocations: golf, jogging, biking, reading, fishing. Home: 1005 Lafayette Blvd Bowling Green OH 43402 Office: Bowling Green State U. Coll Musical Arts Bowling Green OH 43403 E-mail: skoogw@bgnet.bgsu.edu.

SKOOR, JOHN BRIAN, art educator, art consultant; b. Mount Vernon, Wash., Dec. 14, 1939; s. George Nephi and Marie Elizabeth (Collins) S.; m. Susan Diane Waugh, June 17, 1972; children: Marie Elizabeth, Christine Elaine. AA in Edn., Graceland Coll., Lamoni, 1960; BA in Art, Cen. Wash. U., 1962, BA in Edn., 1965, MA in Art, 1969. Art instr. Delta (Mich.) Coll., Saginaw, 1977-79; instr. Renton (Wash.) Vocat. Tech. Inst., 1981-83; art instr. Green River (Wash.) Community Coll., Auburn, 1988—; cons. staff and development instr. various Seattle sch. dists., 1988—; art instr. Higline Community Coll., Seattle, 1990—. Adj. faculty Cen. Wash. U., 1984—, Seattle Pacific U., 1986—; dir. sr. programs Highline C.C., 1992—, instr. sr.'s making art program, 1998—; guest speaker Wash. Art Educators Assn. Conv., 1990. Illustrator of religious curriculum texts, 1978-80; exhibited acrylic theol. paintings show, Independence, Mo., 1980. Guest speaker Alma (Mich.) Art Dept., 1977, Nat. Camping Assn., Detroit, 1979, Wash. Art Tchrs. Assn., 1990; coord. sr. programs Highline C.C., 1992-99; elder Reorganized Ch. of Jesus Christ of Latter Day Saints, Seattle, 1966—, pastor, 1987—, bd. dirs. creative arts festival, Mich., 1977; art instr. Srs. Making Art, Greater Puget Sound area. Mem. Wash. Alliance for Arts Edn. (commn. chmn. 1987—), Richland Art Tchrs. Assn. (pres. 1965-66), Tri-City Art Tchrs. Assn. (pres. 1966-67), Nat. Art Educators Assn. Avocations: public speaking, graphic design, calligrapher, performing artist, ministry. Home: 4830 S Morgan St Seattle WA 98118-3346

SKOPIL, OTTO RICHARD, JR. federal judge; b. Portland, Oreg., June 3, 1919; s. Otto Richard and Freda Martha (Boetticher) Skopil; m. Jane Rae Lundy, July 27, 1956; children: Otto Richard III, Casey Robert, Shannon Ida, Molly Jo. BA in Econs., Willamette U., 1941, LLB, 1946, LLD (hon.) , 1983. Bar: Oreg. 1946, U.S. Dist. Ct. Oreg., U.S. Ct. Appeals (9th cir.), U.S. Supreme Ct. 1946. Assoc. Skopil & Skopil, 1946—51; ptnr. Williams, Skopil, Miller & Beck (and predecessors), Salem, Oreg., 1951—72; judge U.S. Dist. Ct., Portland, 1972—79, chief judge, 1976—79; judge U.S. Ct. Appeals (9th cir.), 1979—85, sr. judge, 1986—. Chmn. com. adminstrn. of fed. magistrate sys. U.S. Jud. Conf., 1980—86; co-founder Oreg. chpt. Am. Leadership Forum; chmn. 9th cir. Jud. Coun. Magistrates Adv. Com., 1988—91; chmn. U.S. Jud. Conf. Long Range Planning Com., 1990—95. Hi-Y adviser Salem YMCA, 1951—52; appeal agt. SSS Marion County (Oreg.) Draft Bd., 1953—66; master of ceremonies 1st Gov.'s Prayer Breakfast for State Oreg., 1959; citizens adv. com. City of Salem, 1970—71; Gov.'s Com. on Staffing Mental Instns., 1969—70; pres., bd. dirs. Marion County Tb and Health Assn., 1958—61; bd. dirs. Willamette U., 1969—71; elder Mt. Park Ch., 1979—81; bd. dirs. Willamette Valley Camp Fire Girls, 1946—56, Internat. Christian Leadership, 1959, Fed. Jud. Ctr., 1979. Lt. USNR, 1942—46. Recipient Oreg. Legal Citizen of Yr. award, 1986, Disting. Alumni award, Willamette U. Sch. Law, 1988. Mem.: ABA, Internat. Soc. Barristers, Assn. Ins. Attys. U.S. and Can. (Oreg. rep. 1970), Def. Rsch. Inst., Oreg. Assn. Def. Counsel (bd. dirs.), Am. Judicature Soc., Marion County Bar Assn., Oreg. Bar Assn. (bd. dirs.), Prayer Breakfast Movement (fellowship coun.), Illahe Hills Country Club (pres., bd. dirs. 1964—67), Exchange Club (pres. 1947), Salem Club. Office: Sr Circuit Judge 827 US Courthouse 1000 SW 3rd Ave Portland OR 97204-2930

SKORA, SUSAN SUNDMAN, lawyer; b. Chgo., Jan. 5, 1947; d. Gordon Manley and Julia Walker (Firebaugh) Sundman; m. Alan Patrick Skora, May 1, 1977. AB, U. Ill., Chgo., 1970; JD, Ill. Inst. Tech., 1980. Bar: Ill. 1980, Mich. 1983, U.S. Dist. Ct. (we. dist.) Mich. 1983. Dir. Chgo. programs U. Ill. Found., 1973-79; asst. dir. bus. affairs U. of Ill., Chgo., 1980-81, exec. asst. to exec. v.p., 1981-83; 2d v.p. Nat. Bank of Detroit, Grand Rapids, 1983-88; v.p., dept. head bus. devel. NBD Grand Rapids Bank, 1985-88; v.p., trust divsn. head, mem. exec. com. First Bank, Davenport, Iowa, 1988-91; v.p., trust Firstar Bank, 1992-97; asst. prof. dept. bus. adminstrn. Black Hawk Coll., 1992; v.p. pvt. client svcs. Wells Fargo Bank, Davenport, 1998—. Author: Cuneen Linguist, 1975. Mem. Scott County Osteo. Physicians and Surgeons Aux., 1988-99, treas., 1989, 91-99, v.p., 1990; v.p. West Mich. U. Ill. Alumni Club, 1983-86; mem. Quad City Osteo. Found., 1988—, bequest and fin. com. mem., 1988-95, 97—, bd. dirs., 1992-95; lead gift com. mem. Davenport Mus. Art, 1988, endowment com. mem. St. Ambrose U., 1988, Quad City Arts, 1992-94; devel. and fin. com. CASI, 1998—, bd. govs., 1992-98, chair trustees com., 1994-98; bd. dirs. Cmty. Found. of the Great River Bend, 1998—, chair major gifts com., 1998, 2d v.p. 1998-2000, 1st vice chair, 2001, chair, 2002-; bd. dirs. Quad City Planned Giving Coun., 1998—, pres., 2000; mem. capital campaign com. Luth. Social Svcs., 1994; mem. Quad City Estate Planning Coun., 1988—; planned giving com. Am. Cancer Soc., 2000-. Mem. Bank Adminstrn. Inst. , U. Ill. Alumni Assn. (various offices to sec. 1989-91, exec. com. bd. dirs. 1985-91, nominating com. 1991), Quad City Employee Benefits Group (treas. 1993-95, 96-99), Davenport C. of C. (mem. com. 1996-97), Davenport Country Club (fin. com. 1996-2000), Exec. Women's Golf League, Classic Ladies Investment Club, Pi Alpha Tau. Avocations: gardening, reading, golf, auctions. Home: 1139 Brookview Dr De Witt IA 52742-9290 Office: Wells Fargo Bank 203 W 3rd St Davenport IA 52801-1977 E-mail: SusanSkora@mail.com., Susan.Skora@wellsfargo.com.

SKORA, WAYNE PHILIP, retired air force officer; b. Chgo., Jan. 16, 1944; s. Felix Anthony Skora and Lillie (Goshko) St. Thomas; m. Dorothy Mae Barrett, June 13, 1966; children: Tanya Christine, Christopher Michael. BS in Engring. Sci., USAF Acad., 1966; MS in Human Resource Mgmt., U. Utah, 1976. Commd. 2d lt. USAF, 1966, advanced through grades to col., 1988, F-4 pilot, 1967-69, 71-79; flight safety officer Hdqrs. Tactical Air Command, Langley AFB, Va., 1979-82; chief safety, A-10 pilot 23d Tactical Fighter Wing, England AFB, La., 1982-84; chief Office Mil. Cooperation, Am. Embassy, Manama, Bahrain, 1984-87; asst. chief logistics 507th Tactical Air Control Wing, Shaw AFB, S.C., 1987-88; dep. comdr. for ops. So. Air Div., Howard AFB, Panama, 1988-90; dep. for safety Air Force Devel. Test Ctr., Eglin AFB, Fla., 1990-92; pres. Skora Enterprises, Inc., Colorado Springs, Colo., 1994—. Decorated Legion of Merit, DFC with oak leaf cluster, Air medal with 21 oak leaf clusters, Def. Meritorious Svc. medal, AF Meritorious Svc. medal with oak leaf cluster, AF Commendation medal with oak leaf cluster. Mem. Order of Daedalians (sec. 1988-90), Sertoma. Roman Catholic. Home: 24 Luxury Ln Colorado Springs CO 80921-3300 E-mail: wayne@skorateam.com.

SKORD, JENNIFER LYNNE, patent lawyer; b. Chgo., Oct. 3, 1948; d. Joseph and Jean (Bobeyka) S. BA in Chemistry, Bradley U., 1970; cert. of summer law study, U. Exeter, Eng., 1978; JD, DePaul U., 1980. Bar: Ill. 1980, Ind. 1985, U.S. Dist. Ct. (no. dist.) Ill. 1980, U.S. Dist. Ct. (no. dist.) Ind. 1985, U.S. Patent Office 1982, U.S. Ct. Appeals (fed. cir.) 1983, U.S. Supreme Ct. 1984, S.C. 1990. Assoc. patent counsel Ladas & Parry, Chgo., 1980-83; patent counsel Eltech Systems, Chardon, Ohio, 1983-84; patent atty. Miles Labs., Elkhart, Ind., 1984-86, W.R. Grace & Co.-Conn. Cryovac div., Duncan, S.C., 1986—. Mem. AAUW, Ill. Bar Assn., Am. Intellectual Property Law Assn., S.C. Patent Copyright & Trademark Law Assn., Phi Alpha Delta. Avocations: aerobics, lifting weights. Office: University Tower 3100 Tower Blvd Ste 1401 Durham NC 27707-2563

SKORIKOV, VLADIMIR B, researcher, educator; b. Moscow, Russia, Apr. 6, 1959; s. Boris A Skorikov, Vladimira G Petrenko; life ptnr.. PhD in Psychology, State Academy of Management, Moscow, Russia. Professor State Academy of Management, Moscow, Russia, 1982—91; Instructor Pennsylavania State University, University Park, PA, 1993—97; Professor University of Hawaii at Hilo, Hilo, HI, 1997—2002. Editorial Board Member Career Development Quarterly, 1997—2003; Reviewer 4th National Counseling Psychology Conference, Houston, 2001, 7th Biennial Meeting of the Society for Research on Adolescence , San Diego, 1998; Ad hoc reviewer Journal of Adolescent Research, Health, International Journal of Behavioral Development , 1997—2000; Member American Psychological Association, Washington, 1997—2002, Society for Research on Adolescence, Chicago, IL, 1998—2002, Society for Research on Identity Formation, Miami, FL, 1999—2002, National Career Development Association , Columbus, OH, 1997—2002, Society for Vocational Psychology, Carbondale, IL, 1998—2002. Author: (research article) Journal of Adolescence , 1995, (2 research articles) Career Development Quarterly, 1997, (research article) Journal of Vocational Behavior, 1998, (research article) Journal of Career Assessment, 1998, (research aricle) Current Psychology, 2002, (research article) Educational and Psychological Measurement, 2002. Mem.: Society fro research on Identity Formation, Society for Vocational Psychology, Society for Research on Adolescence, Natioanl Career Development Association, American Psychological Association. Avocation: tennis, skiing, swimming. Office: University of Hawaii at Hilo 200 West Kawili Street Hilo HI 96720 Business E-Mail: skorikov@hawaii.edu.

SKORNEY, ROBERT CRAIG, secondary education educator; b. Portland, Oreg., Apr. 4, 1961; s. George John and Barbara Garrett S.; m. Mary Fitzpatrick, Apr. 21, 1990. BS, Wash. State U., 1988; MA, Pacific U., 1991. Cert. secondary education educator with advanced math., chemistry, and physics endorsements. Tchr. North Lake H.S., Silver Lake, Oreg., 1991—. Office: North Lake HS 57566 Ft Rock Rd Silver Lake OR 97638

SKORTON, DAVID JAN, academic administrator, internist, educator; b. Milw., Nov. 22, 1949; s. Samuel and Pauline (Millstein) Skorton; 1 child Joshua Samuel. BA, Northwestern U., 1970; MD, Northwestern U., Chgo., 1974. Diplomate Nat. Bd. Med. Examiners, Am. Bd. Internal Medicine, Am. Bd. Cardiovascular Disease. Resident UCLA, 1974-77, fellow in cardiology, 1977-80, chief resident in medicine, 1978-79, adj. asst. prof., 1978-80; instr. medicine U. Iowa, Iowa City, 1980-81, asst. prof., 1981-84, asst. prof. elec. and computer engring., 1982-84, assoc. prof. medicine and elec. and computer engring., 1984-88, prof. medicine, elec. and computer engring. and biomed. engring., 1988—; acting dir., then dir. div. gen. internal medicine U. Iowa Coll. Medicine, 1985-89, assoc. chmn. for clinical programs, 1989-92, v.p. for rsch. and external rels., 1992—. Dir. ochocardiology lab. VA Med. Ctr., Iowa City, 1980—89; mem. internat. and coop. projects study sect. NIH, 1988—92, chmn., 1990—92; lectr. in field numerous sci. sessions, nat. and internat. meetings; manuscript reviewer maj. jours. in field. Editor: (book) Cardiac Imaging and Image Processing, 1986, Cardiac Imaging, 1990, Cardiac Imaging, 2d edit., 1996; contbr. articles and abstracts to profl. jours., chapters to books. Named Intern-of-Yr., UCLA, 1975; recipient Rsch. Assoc. Career Devel. award, VA, 1981—84, Rsch. Career Devel. award, Nat. Heart Lung & Blood Inst., 1984—89; scholar Regents', UCLA, 1967—68. Fellow: ACP, Am. Physiol. Soc., Am. Heart Assn., Am. Coll. Cardiology; mem.: AAAS, Internat. Soc. Adult Congenital Cardiac Disease, Assn. Univ. Cardiologists, Am. Soc. Echocardiography. Jewish. Office: U Iowa VP for Rsch & External Rels 201 Gilmore Hall Iowa City IA 52242-1320 E-mail: david-skorton@uiowa.edu.

SKOTHEIM, ROBERT ALLEN, retired college and museum administrator; b. Seattle, Jan. 31, 1933; s. Sivert O. and Marjorie F. (Allen) S.; m. Nadine Vail, June 14, 1953; children— Marjorie, Kris, Julia. BA, U. Wash., 1955, MA, 1958, PhD, 1962; LLD (hon.), Hobart and William Smith Colls., Geneva, N.Y., 1975; LittD (hon.), Whitman Coll., 1988; LHD (hon.), Coll. Idaho, 1988, Occidental Coll., 1989, Ill. Wesleyan U., 1990; DFA (hon.), Willamette U., 1989, Whittier Coll., 2000, Gustavus Adolphys Coll., 2000. Prof. history U. Wash., 1962-63; prof. history Wayne State U., Detroit, 1963-66; prof. UCLA, 1966-67, U. Colo., Boulder, 1967-72; provost, dean faculty Hobart and William Smith Colls., 1972-75; pres. Whitman Coll., Walla Walla, Wash., 1975-88, Huntington Libr., Art Collections & Bot. Gardens, San Marino, Calif., 1988-2001; ret., 2001. Author: American Intellectual Histories and Historians, 1966, Totalitarianism and American Social Thought, 1971; Editor: The Historian and the Climate of Opinion, 1969; co-editor: American Social Thought: Sources and Interpretations, 2 vols, 1972. Guggenheim fellow, 1967-68 Mem. Phi Beta Kappa (hon.)

SKOUG, KENNETH NORDLY, JR. diplomat; b. Fargo, N.D., Dec. 2, 1931; s. Kenneth Nordly and Cecile Marjorie (Stevens) S.; m. Martha Gladys Reed, Sept. 13, 1958; children: Ms. Reed Stevens, Kenneth Nordly III. AB, Columbia Coll., 1953; MA, George Washington U., 1957, PhD, 1964. Technician Minn. Civil Svc. Dept., St. Paul, 1953-54; with Fgn. Svc., Dept. State, 1957-90; vice consul Am. Consulate Gen., Munich, 1959-61, Guadalajara, Mex., 1961-63; 1st sec. Am. Embassy, Prague, Czechoslovakia, 1967-69; dep. dir. Germany Dept. State, Wash., 1969-73, insp., 1974-76; counselor Am. Embassy, Moscow, 1976-79, Caracas, Venezuela, 1979-82; coord. for Cuba, Dept. State, Washington, 1982-88; min.-counselor, charge d'Affaires Am. Embassy, Caracas, 1988-90; ret., 1990. Author: Cuba as a Model and a Challenge, 1984, The United States and Cuba under Reagan and Shultz, 1996, Czechoslovakia's Lost Fight for Freedom, 1967-69, 1999. With U.S. Army, 1954-56. Recipient Orden del Libertador Pres. Venezuela, 1990. Mem. Humane Soc. of the U.S., World Wildlife Fund, Am. Fgn. Svc. Assn., Nat. War Coll. Alumni, Columbia Coll. Club of Washington, Concord Coalition, Fund for Animals, Brady Campaign to Prevent Gun Violence, League of Conservation Voters. Avocations: reading, writing, humane, environmental, travel. Home: 8320 Fort Hunt Rd Alexandria VA 22308-1812

SKOV, ARLIE MASON, petroleum engineer, consultant; b. Perry, Okla., Sept. 21, 1928; s. Arnold and Mary (Mason) S.; m. Luella Luticia Sloan, July 31, 1951; children: Gregory Morgan, Jeffrey Markham, Tamara Kay. BS in Petroleum Engring., U. Okla., 1956; postgrad., U. Va., 1966. Engr., Sohio Petroleum Co., Pauls Valley, Okla., 1958-66, mgr. spl. projects Oklahoma City, 1966-75; mgr. prodn. planning BP Alaska Inc., San Francisco, 1977-80; project advisor Sohio Gas Pipeline Co., 1980-81; mgr. new tech. devel. Sohio Petroleum Co., 1981-83; dir. prodn. tech. Sohio Petroleum Co. and Standard Oil Prodn., Dallas, 1983-88; sr. cons. BP Exploration, Inc., Houston, 1989-92; owner Arlie M. Skov, Inc. Petroleum Consulting, 1993—2001. Recipient Disting. Svc. award Okla. Petroleum Coun. 1973. Mem. AIME (bd. dirs. 1977-79, trustee 1990-92, 95-97) Soc. Petroleum Engrs. (bd. dirs. 1972-74, exec. com. 1990-92, pres. 1991, Disting. mem., hon. mem.), Nat. Petroleum Coun. Avocations: reading, travel. E-mail: askov@earthlink.com.

SKOVE, THOMAS MALCOLM, retired manufacturing company financial executive; b. Cleve., June 27, 1925; s. Thomas Malcolm and Ethel C. (Rush) S.; m. Helen Busing, June 12, 1948; children: Margaret, Thomas, Richard, Marcie, Douglas. BS, Bucknell U., 1949. Controller, treas. Cleve. Twist Drill Co., 1949-68; treas. Acme-Cleve. Corp., 1968-81, dep. treas., 1981-86, treas., 1986-88. Councilman, City of Aurora, Ohio, 1977-83; chmn. Aurora Meml. Library Trust, 1984-89. Served with USN, 1943-46. Mem. Sugar Mill Country Club (pres. 1993-94). Republican. Home: 209 Bromely Cir New Smyrna Beach FL 32168-2006 E-mail: tombuz209@yahoo.com.

SKOVIRA, ROBERT JOSEPH, information scientist, educator; b. Mt. Pleasant, Pa., May 4, 1943; s. Robert Joseph and Genevieve (Budney) S.; m. Mary Elizabeth Machuga, Aug. 21, 1971; 1 child, Suzanne Marie. BA, St. Vincent Coll., 1966; MA, U. Pitts., 1972, MS in Info. Scis., 1986, PhD, 1977. Cert. tchr., Pa.; cert. in computer programming and ops. Tchr. Greensburg (Pa.) Cen. Cath. High Sch., 1967-75; asst. visiting prof. U. Va., 1977-78; archives fieldworker U. Pitts., 1979; asst. vis. prof. U. Houston, Victoria, Tex., 1980-81; instr. St. Vincent Coll., Latrobe, Pa., 1982-84; prof. Robert Morris Coll., Coraopolis, 1983—. Web designer Imagining Info. Mem. Am. Soc. for Info. Sci. (chmn. spl. interest group FIS 1989-90, mem. spl. interest group cabinet steering com. 1989-92, chmn. Pitts. chpt. 1991), Decision Scis. Inst., Internat. Assn. for Computer Info. Sys., Assn. for Computing Machinery, Assn. for Info. Sys., Information Resources Mgmt. Assocs., Ohio Valley Philosophy Edn. Soc., Slovak Studies Assn. Democrat. Byzantine Catholic. Avocations: fishing, hiking, reading, gardening and growing Bonsai. Office: Robert Morris U Narrows Run Rd Coraopolis PA 15108-1189

SKOWRON, GAIL, medical educator, researcher; b. Bklyn., Oct. 15, 1956; d. Reynold John and Eleanore (Huber) S.; m. Edward Richard Isser, Mar. 28, 1982; children: Rachel Frances Isser, Micah David Isser. BS, Muhlenberg Coll., 1978; MD, Columbia U., 1982. Diplomate Am. Bd. Internal Medicine, Am. Bd. Infectious Diseases. Intern St. Luke's-Roosevelt Hosp. Ctr., N.Y.C., 1982-83, resident in internal medicine, 1983-85; infectious diseases fellow Stanford (Calif.) U., Stanford, Calif., 1986-89; asst. prof. medicine Brown U., Providence, 1989-98, assoc. prof. medicine, 1998-99, Boston U., 1999—. Assoc. dir. AIDS program Brown U., 1989—; lead investigator clin. study Annals of Internal Medicine, 1992; mem. AIDS and Related Rsch. Study Sec. NIH, Bethesda, Md., 1994-97; sci. adv. com. Am. Found. for AIDS Rsch., N.Y.C., 1992—. HIV immunology rsch. grantee NIH, 1991—. Fellow ACP; mem. Infectious Disease Soc. Am., Internat. AIDS Soc. Jewish. Avocations: swimming, rollerblading. Office: Roger Williams Hosp 825 Chalkstone Ave Providence RI 02908-4735

SKOWRON, TADEUSZ ADAM, physician; b. Czestochowa, Poland, Dec. 17, 1950; came to U.S., 1976; s. Stanislaw and Genowefa (Widera) Skowron; m. Elizabeth Sliwowska, Feb. 17, 1990; children: Sebastian Adam, Annette Kira, Christian Stanislaw, Alexander Mieczyslaw. MD, Med. Acad., Lodz, Poland, 1975. House physician Bklyn.-Cumberland Med. Ctr., 1979-80, fellow in neurology, 1981-83; resident in medicine Marshall U. Sch. Medicine, Huntington, W.Va., 1983-86, instr., 1986-87; pvt. practice bioenergy diagnosis & therapy Bridgeport, Conn., 1987—. Clin. specialist II, State Sch., Newark, 1981; advisor Congress Med. Polonia, Czestochowa, 1990—. Mem. Polish cultural events com. Sacred Heart U., Fairfield, Conn., 1990—. Mem. ACP, AMA, AAAS, N.Y. Acad. Scis. Home: 16 Williamsburg Ln Avon CT 06001-2987 Office: 50 Ridgefield Ave Ste 317 Bridgeport CT 06610-3106

SKOWRONSKI, FRANK STANLEY, foreign service officer, consulting executive; b. Plymouth, Pa., Feb. 27, 1925; s. Leon Skowronski and Leocadia Dudek; m. Marilyn Elsbeth Crane, Oct. 11, 1947. Student, Harvard U., 1946-47; AB, Oxford (Eng.) U., 1957, MA, 1960. Econ. advisor Harvard Adv. Group, Tehran, 1960-62; pvt. sector supervisory officer USAID, Cen. Am., 1964-90; CEO Bus. Adminstrn. and Sys. Info. Corp., McLean, Va., 1966; econ. cons. Washington, 1990—. 1st lt. U.S. Army, 1943—46, 1st lt. U.S. Army, 1950—53. Roman Catholic. Home: PO Box 60 Washington VA 22747-0060

SKOWRONSKI, VINCENT PAUL, concert violinist, recording artist, executive producer, producer classical recordings; b. Kenosha, Wis., Jan. 22, 1944; MusB, Northwestern U., 1966, MusM, 1968. V.p. Eberley-Skowronski, Inc., Evanston, Ill., 1973-92; internat. dir. mktg. and pub. rels. Vincent Skowronski: Producer of Classical Recordings, 1993—. Internat. broker rare instruments Strings & Things, Evanston, 1973-92; owner Vincent Skowronski: Fine Violins, Evanston, 1993—; internat. dir. mktg. and pub. rels. EB-SKO Prodns., Evanston, 1978-92; dir. media comm. E-S Mgmt., Evanston, 1985-92; instr. violin Northwestern U., 1969-71; asst. prof. violin U. Wyo., 1971-72; pvt. violin tchr., chamber music coach, lectr., master classes. Solo violinist debut Chgo. Youth Orch., 1959; soloist Chgo. Civic Orch., 1968, guest solo artist Am. Artist Gala, Nat. Puerto Rican TV, 1960, Peninsula Music Festival, Fish Creek, Wis., 1965, 66; solo guest artist Young Am. Musicians Sta. WKAR-TV Mich. State U., 1966, N.Am. premiere R. Nanes' Rhapsody Pathetique for violin and orch., Chgo. Cultural Ctr., 1994, Beijing, 1994, DePaul U. Ctr., Chgo., 1994, Skowronski in Recital: 20 Years Remembered, Northwestern U., Evanston, Ill., 1994, IV Internat. Tchaikovsky Competition Commemorative Recital-Moscow Remembered: 1970-95, Evanston, Ill., 1995, J.L. Kellogg Sch. Mgmt. Recital Northwestern Univ., Ill., 1996; featured solo artist Artist Showcase, Sta. WGN-TV Chgo., 1966-71; featured soloist Honors Concert-Northwestern U., 1966, guest solo artist A.M. Am., Sta. ABC-TV, 1977—; numerous concerts and recitals in Europe, Cen.Am., Mex. and U.S.; solo guest artist radio appearances include Continental Bank Concerts, Sta. WFMT-FM Chgo., 1983, 85-86, 88, 90, United Airlines Presents, Live!, Sta. WFMT-FM Chgo., Schumann, 1986, Szymanowski, 1987, Bloch, 1988, Saint-Saens, 1989, Grieg, 1991, Excursions in Music: The Artistry of Vincent P. Skowronski, Sta. KQED-FM San Francisco, 1979, Skowronski: Musical Giant, Interlake Profiles, Sta. WFMT-FM Chgo., 1980, Skowronski at 50: A Birthday Celebration Sta. WNIB-FM, Chgo., 1994; guest solo artist Chgo. Musicians Sta. WNIB-FM, 1996-97; Skowronski at 55: A Birthday Celebration, Station WNIB-FM, Chgo., 1999; guest solo artist, producer, annotator Separate But Equal, 1976, All Brahms, 1977; solo artist, exec. producer, annotator Gentleman Gypsy, 1978, Strauss and Szymanowski, 1979, Franck and Szymanowski, 1982, Skowronski Alone, 1996, Skowronski Plays, Strauss and Szymanowski, 1998, Skowronski Plays, Live in Concert, 2000, Skowronski Plays! Franck, Szymanowski, Bacewicz and Saint-Saens, 2002; producer, annotator Opera Lady I, 1978, Eberley Sings Strauss, 1980, American Girl, 1983, Opera Lady II, 1984; guest performances numerous TV stas. Bd. dirs. Chgo. Youth Orch., 1973-77, v.p., 1974-77; artistic cons. Classical and Protege Symphony Orchs., Chgo., 1994—; spl. cons. Beck Inst. for Arts, Schaumburg, Ill., 1998-2000; adjudicator ice skating shows and competitions Wilmette (Ill.) Park Dist., 1985-89; guest panelist classical performance-career forum Sch. of Music, Northwestern U., Evanston, 1992, 94; guest cons. career symposium Edwin G. Foreman High Sch., Chgo., 1989; mem. mayor's founding com. Evanston Arts Coun., 1974-75; pres. Vincent Skowronski Music Found., Evanston, 1997—. Recipient Excellence in Performance award Northwestern U., 1958, 59, 60, Nat. H.S. Inst., 1958-60, Roy Harris award Inter-Am. U., San German, P.R., 1960, award Am. Fedn. Musicians, 1961, award Soc. Am. Musicians, 1961, McCormick Found. award Chgo. Tribune, 1965, Wade Fetzer award for excellence in performance Northwestern U., 1966, award Crescendo Musical Club, 1967; selected as one of 7 violinists to represent U.S. in IV Internat. Tchaikovsky Competition, Moscow, 1970; nominated for Grammy award Best Chamber Music Performance, 2001; guest dignitary Papal Audience, The Vatican, 1995. Mem. Internat. Platform Assn. (voting mem.), Nat. Acad. Arts and Scis., Sigma Nu E-mail: skowviolinstudio@ameritech.net, skowronskirecordings@ameritech.net.

SKRAJEWSKI, DENNIS JOHN, health care executive; b. Trenton, N.J., Jan. 19, 1954; s. Raymond Joseph and Philomena Florence (Zook) S.; m. Debra Ann Fortin, Oct. 25, 1980; children: Diana Nicole, Danielle Marie, Dominic Raymond. BA in Biology, Lafayette Coll., 1977; cert. physician asst., Yale U., 1980; MBA in Health Care Mgmt., Boston U., 1985. Physician asst. Masonic Home and Hosp., Wallingford, Conn., 1980-84; adminstrv. resident/fellow Charlton Meml. Hosp., Fall River, Mass., 1984-86, mgr. clin. resource utilization, 1986-87; mgr. constrn. project Lakes Region Gen. Hosp., Laconia, N.H., 1987-88, v.p. adminstrv. and support svcs., 1988-95; acct. exec., project mgr. Shared Med. Systems, Malvern, Pa., 1995-97; support mgr. Shared Med. Sys., 1997-98; mgr. Century Date, 1998, nat. cons. mgr., 1998-2000; outsourcing ops. mgr. Siemens Health Svcs., 2000—01, mktg. mgr., 2001—. Mem. pastoral adv. coun. St. Joseph's Parish, Belmont, N.H., 1987-95, vice chmn., 1988-91, chmn., 1991-95, pastoral adv. coun., Downingtown, Pa., 1997-2000; mem. pastoral adv. bd. St. Elizabeth Parish, 2000—; bd. dirs. Cmty. Health and Hospice, Inc., Laconia, 1988-94, chmn. pers. com., 1989-90, chmn. bd. dirs., 1990-92. With USN, 1972-74. Mem. Am. Coll. Health Care Execs. (diplomate), Healthcare Info. Mgmt. Sys. Soc., Boston U. Health Care Mgmt. Alumni Assn., Beta Gamma Sigma. Republican. Avocations: athletics, personal fin. planning, computers, travel. Home: 261 Spring Run Ln Downingtown PA 19335-4409 E-mail: dennis.skrajewski@smed.com., dskrajewski@comcast.net.

SKRAMSTAD, ROBERT ALLEN, retired oceanographer; b. Montevideo, Minn., Apr. 3, 1937; s. Vernon Donald and Ann May (Tollefsen) S. Student, St. Olaf Coll., 1956, 60-61; BS in Geol. Engring., S.D. Sch. Mines and Tech., 1965. Geologist Naval Oceanographic Office, Washington, 1965-70, oceanographer, 1970-75, Bay St. Louis, Miss., 1975-82, phys. scientist, 1982-95; ret., 1995. With U.S. Army, 1957-60. Mem. Am. Soc. Photogrammetry and Remote Sensing, Nat. Geographic Soc. Republican. Avocations: photography, jogging, travel, mineral collecting. Home: Apt 105 601 Village Dr Marshall MN 56258-2548

SKRBIN, AARON T. social studies educator; b. Pitts., Dec. 16, 1974; s. Robert I. and Barbara A. Skrbin; m. Regina M. Sacco, July 28, 2001. BS in Edn., Duquesne U., 1997; M of Pub. Mgmt., Carnegie Mellon U., 2002. Tchr. social studies Woodland Hills H.S., Pitts., 1997—99, chairperson social studies dept., 1999—. Vol. firefighter Wilkins Twp. (Pa.) VFC #3, 1991—. Mem.: World Affairs Coun. Pitts., Nat. Coun. for Social Studies. Democrat. Home: 209 Twin Ponds Ln Bridgeville PA 15017 Office: Woodland Hills HS 2550 Greensburg Pike Pittsburgh PA 15221

SKRDLA, W. BLAKE, physician, psychiatrist; b. Atkinson, Nebr., Jan. 20, 1920; s. Frank Elmer and Olive (Blake) S.; m. Helen Patricia Muffly, May 1, 1948 (dec. Nov. 1996); children Robert Warren, Merri Patricia. AB, Nebr. Wesleyan U., 1942; MD, U. Nebr. Coll. of Medicine, 1948. Diplomate in psychiatry Am. Bd. Psychiatry and Neurology. Staff acute intensive treatment svc. Brentwood V.A. Hosp., L.A., 1955-57; admitting svc. L.A. County U. So. Calif. Med. Ctr., 1958-60; psychiat. panel L.A. Superior Ct., 1960—. Lt. USNR, 1951-53. Fellow Am. Acad. Forensic Scis.; mem. APA, Am. Acad. Psychiatry and Law, So. Calif. Psychiat. Soc.

SKRETNY, WILLIAM MARION, federal judge; b. Buffalo, Mar. 8, 1945; s. William S. and Rita E. S.; m. Carol Ann Skretny; 3 children. AB, Canisius Coll., 1966; JD, Howard U., 1969; LLM, Northwestern U., 1972. Bar: Ill. 1969, U.S. Dist. Ct. (no. dist) Ill. 1969, N.Y. 1972, U.S. Ct. Appeals (7th cir.) 1972, U.S. Dist. Ct. (we. dist.) N.Y. 1973, U.S. Ct. Appeals (2d cir.) 1976, U.S. Supreme Ct. 1980. Asst. U.S. atty. Office of U.S. Atty. No. Dist. Ill., Chgo., 1971-73, Office of U.S. Atty. We. Dist. N.Y., Buffalo, 1973-81, 1st asst., 1975-81; gen. ptnr. Duke, Holzman, Yaeger & Radlin, 1981-83; 1st dep. dist. atty. Office Dist. Atty Erie County, 1983-88; with Gross, Shuman, Brizdle and Gillfillan, PC, 1988, Cox, Barrell, Buffalo, 1989-90; judge U.S. Dist. Ct. (we. dist.) N.Y., 1990—. Mem. jud. conf. com. on security and facilities, 1994, chair subcom. on planning and space mgmt., com. liaison for long range planning. Bd. dirs. Sudden Infant Death Found. We. N.Y., 1979, Cerebral Palsy Foun. We. N.Y., 1985; chmn. major corps. divsn. Studio Arena Theatre, Buffalo, 1982; chmn. Polish Culture, Canisius Coll., 1985, trustee, 1989; pres. Canisius Coll. Alumni Assn., 1989; regional chmn. Cath. Charities Appeal, 1986-87. Named Citizen of Yr. Am Pol Eagle Newspaper, 1977, 90, Disting. Grad. Nat. Cath. Edn. Assn. Dept. Elem. Sch., 1991, Disting. Alumnus Canisius Coll., 1993; named to Wall of Fame Law Sch. Northwestern U. Mem. ABA, Fed. Judges Assn., Bar Assn. of Erie County, Di Gamma, Phi Alpha Delta, Alpha Sigma Nu. Republican. Roman Catholic. Office: US District Court 68 Court St Rm 507 Buffalo NY 14202-3405

SKRILOFF, ALEXIS ILENE, freelance/self-employed writer, editor, consultant; b. Torrance, Calif., Feb. 17, 1949; d. Alexander Eli and Selma Frances (Muschel) Skriloff; m. Frank Scott James, Nov. 9, 2001; children: Arthur Goldberg, Heidi Gorter, Michele Harvey, Lizabeth Merson, Nate Yelton. Degree(hon.) , Hollywood Film Inst., 1995. Freelance writer, editor, L.A., 1974—95; freelance writer Morgan City, La., 1995—96; mng. editor McCarthy Media, Plainfield, Ind., 1996, McCarty Media, 1997; owner, writer, editor AIS Publs., Indpls., 1996—. Cons. Efo, Chgo., 1997—2002; bd. dirs. Nsi. Online coord. Dems., 2001—02; online commr. Medicare, 2001—02. Named to Wall of Tolerance, Nat. Campaign Tolerance, 2001, 2002. Home and Office: PO Box 42603 Indianapolis IN 46242-0603 Personal E-mail: aispubs@indy.net.

SKROBELA, KATHERINE CREELMAN, music producer; b. N.Y.C., Jan. 18, 1941; d. George Douglas and Marjorie Ethel (Broer) Creelman; m. Paul John Skrobela, May 23, 1970 (dec. Feb. 1999). AB, Vassar Coll., 1962; MLS, Columbia U., 1964. Music cataloger Bklyn. Coll., 1964-71; music libr. Middlebury (Vt.) Coll., 1971-80; programmer ADT Co., N.Y.C., 1981-83; sr. cons. Marathon Software & Svcs. Inc., 1983-90; sr. programmer analyst Chase Manhattan Bank, 1990-2000. Pres. Miranda Music, Inc., 1995—. Editor Music Cataloging bull., 1970-75; prodr. Blame It On My Youth: Berri Blair Sings Ballads, 1999, Karen Oberlin: My Standards, 2000, Christopher Gines: The Way It Goes, 2001, Karen Oberlin: Secret Love, 2002. Treas., bd. dirs. Middlebury Farmers Market, 1979; dir. St. Stephen's Motet Choir, Middlebury, 1975-78. Mem. ALA, Music Libr. Assn. (chmn. com. on cataloging, rep. to ALA catalog code revision com.), Music OCLC Users Group, UFO-Cobol/XE Internat. Users Group (v.p. 1989-91), Country Dance and Song Soc. Am., Manhattan Assn. Cabarets and Clubs. Home and Office: 234 Lincoln Rd Brooklyn NY 11225-3432 E-mail: ceo@mirandamusic.com.

SKROCH, LARRY EUGENE, railway conductor; b. Oakes, N.D., Nov. 24, 1955; s. Peter Carl and Opal May (Peters) S. AS in Pre-law, N.D. State Sch. Sci., 1982; BA in Social Sci., U. N.D., 1984, MA in History, 1988. Warehouse laborer Internat. Multifoods, Forman, N.D., 1978-80; laborer Chicago Bridge and Iron, Grand Forks, 1987-88; brakeman, switchman Burlington No. Santa Fe, 1988-90, condr., 1990—. Co-publ. Valley Heritage Press, Grand Forks, 1994—. Co-author: (regional history books) Looking for Candles in the Window: The Tragic Red River Valley Blizzard of March 15, 1941, 1992, The Raging Red: The 1950 Red River Valley Flood, 1996. With U.S. Army, 1975-78, N.D. Nat. Guard, 1978-91. Mem. United Transp. Union local 525. Democrat. Avocations: avid reader, book collector, creating scrapbooks on political cartoons, Old West collectibles, playing softball. Home: 1918 Drees Dr Grand Forks ND 58201-8137 Office: Valley Heritage Press PO Box 12872 Grand Forks ND 58208-2872

SKROCKI, EDMUND STANLEY, II, health fair promoter, executive; b. Schenectady, N.Y., Sept. 6, 1953; s. Edmund Stanley I and Lorraine (Nocian) S.; m. Diane Carolyn Sittig, Sept. 6, 1976 (div. 1992); children: Carolyn, Michelle, Edmund III, Johnathan Edmund; m. Deborrah Anne Allen, June 4, 1998 (div. Mar. 2000). AA, LaValley Coll., 1981; BA, Sonoma State U., 1982, MA, 1987; postgrad., Am. Inst. Hypnotherapy, 1988. Pres. Skrocki's Philos. Svc., Lakeview Terrace, Calif., 1971-81, Redding, 1982—; pres., CEO Skrocki's Superior Svc., Lakeview Terrace, 1971-76, Redding, Calif., 1976—; pres., CEO, promoter, prodr. Realife Expositions, 1991—; producer Realife Expo Stars Over Hollywood, 1997. Prodr. Superstars of Excellence, 2000—. Bd. govs., deacon Ch. of Universal Knowledge, 1991—. Named one of Outstanding Young Men Am., 1980. Mem. Shasta Submarine Soc. (pres. 1984—). Avocations: chess, basketball, reading, health, fitness.

SKROMME, ARNOLD BURTON, educational writer, engineering consultant; b. Zearing, Iowa, Apr. 1, 1917; s. Austin and Belle (Holmedal) S.; m. Lois Lucille Fausch, Sept. 14, 1940; children: Roger, Keith, Deborah, Erik. Agrl. Engr., Iowa State U., 1941. Engr. Firestone Tire & Rubber Co., Akron, Ohio, 1941-45, Auto Splty. Mfg., St. Joseph, Mich., 1945-46; rsch. engr. Pineapple Rsch. Inst., Honolulu, 1946-50; asst. chief engr. John Deere, Ottumwa, Iowa, 1950-55; chief engr. John Deer Spreader Works, East Moline, Ill., 1955-70; mgr. value engring. John Deere Harvester Works, 1970-84; writer and cons., 1984—2002. Cons. to corps., 1984—. Author The 7-Ability Plan, 1989; The Cause and Cure of Dropouts, 1998; holder 44 patents. Chmn. Citizens Adv. Com., Moline, 1964-66. Mem. Am. Soc. Agrl. Engrs. (v.p. 1965-68, Honor Roll 1997). Lutheran. Avocation: research on children's education. Home: 2605 31st St Moline IL 61265-5309

SKROMME, LAWRENCE H. consulting agricultural engineer; b. Roland, Iowa, Aug. 26, 1913; s. Austin G. and Ingeborg B. (Holmedal) S.; m. Margaret Elizabeth Gleason, June 24, 1939; children: Cherlyn Sue Granrose, Inga Jean Hill, Karen Ann Sequino. BS with honors, Iowa State U., Ames, 1937. Registered profl. engr., Pa. Design and test engr. Goodyear Tire and Rubber Co., Akron, Ohio, 1937-41; project engr., asst. chief engr. Harry Ferguson Inc., Detroit, 1941-51; chief engr. Sperry New Holland div. Sperry Corp., New Holland, Pa., 1951-61, v.p. engring., 1961-78; cons. agrl. engr. Lancaster, 1978—. Mem. adv. bd. U.S. Congresss Com. on Sci. and Tech., 1989—93; cons. AID, World Bank, others, 1978—85, Saudi Arabia, 1985—86. Patentee; contbr. articles to profl. jours. Dir., pres. Farm and Home Found., Lancaster County, 1968—90, Lancaster County Agrl. Land Preservation Bd., 1978—2002, sec.-treas., 1989—99, dir. emeritus, 2002—; rsch. adv. com. U.S. Dept. Agr., Washington, 1964—68; gov.'s com. agr. and land preservation Gov. of Pa., 1969; bd. dirs. awards com. Engrs. Joint Coun., N.Y.C., 1967—75. Fellow: Am. Soc. Agrl. Engrs. (v.p. 1952—55, pres. 1959—60, Gold medal 1974); mem.: NAE (peer and membership com. 1978—82), Am. Soc. Engring. Edn., Internat. Assn. Agrl. Engrs. (v.p. 1974—79, pres. farm machine divsn.), Nat. Soc. Profl. Engrs., Tau Beta Pi, Alpha Zeta, Phi Kappa Phi. Republican. Methodist. Avocations: collecting old tools and antiques, farm machinery history. E-mail: lhsae@aol.com.

SKROWACZEWSKI, STANISLAW, conductor, composer; b. Lwow, Poland, Oct. 3, 1923; came to U.S., 1960; s. Pawel and Zofia (Karszniewicz) S.; m. Krystyna Jarosz, Sept. 6, 1956; children: Anna, Paul, Nicholas. Diploma faculty philosophy, U. Lwow, 1945; diploma faculties composition and conducting, Acad. Music Lwow, 1945, Conservatory at Krakow, Poland, 1946; L.H.D., Hamline U., 1963, Macalester Coll., 1972; L.H.D. hon. doctorate, U. Minn. Guest condr. in, Europe, S.A., U.S., 1947—; Composer, 1931—; pianist, 1928—; violinist, 1934—; condr., 1939—; permanent condr., music dir. Wroclaw (Poland) Philharmonic, 1946-47, Katowice (Poland) Nat. Philharmonic, 1949-54, Krakow Philharmonic, 1955-56, Warsaw Nat. Philharmonic Orch., 1957-59, Minnesota Orch., 1960-79; prin. condr., mus. adviser Halle Orch., Manchester, Eng., 1984-91; musical advisor St. Paul Chamber Orchestra, 1986-87. First symphony and overture for orch. written at age 8, played by Lwow Philharm. Orch., 1931. Composer: 4 symphonies Prelude and Fugue for Orchestra (conducted first performance Paris), 1948, Overture, 1947 (2d prize Szymanowski Concours, Warsaw 1947); Cantiques des Cantiques, 1951, String Quartet, 1953 (2d Prize Internat. Concours Composers, Belgium 1953), Suite Symphonique, 1954 (first prize, gold medal Composers Competition Moscow 1957), Music at Night, 1954, Ricercari Notturni, 1978 (3d prize Kennedy Center Friedheim Competition, Washington), Concerti for Clarinet and Orch., 1980, Violin Concerto, 1985, Concerto for Orch., 1985, Fanfare for Orch., 1987, Sextett for Oboe, Violin, Viola, Orchestra, 1980, String Trio for Violin, Viola, 1990, Triple Concerto for Violin, Clarinet, Piano, Orchestra, 1992, Fantasie per Tre (Flute, Oboe, Cello), 1993, Chamber Concerto, 1993, Passacaglia Immaginaria for Orch., 1995, Musica a Quattro for Clarinet, Violin, Viola, Cello, 1998; also music for theatre, motion pictures, songs and piano sonatas, English horn concerto; rec. by Mercury, Columbia, RCA Victor, Vox, EMI, Angel. Recipient nat. prize for artistic activity Poland, 1953; First prize Santa Cecilia Internat. Concours for Condrs., Rome, 1956, Comdr. Cross, Polonia Restituta, 1999. Mem. Union Polish Composers, Internat. Soc. Modern Music, Nat. Assn. Am. Composers-Condrs., Am. Music Center. Office: Orch Hall 1111 Nicollet Mall Minneapolis MN 55403-2406 Fax: 216-473-7384.

SKRYABINA, ZINA EDUARDOVNA, chemist, researcher; b. Ekaterinburg (Sverdlovsk), Russia, Nov. 23, 1957; came to U.S., 1996; d. Eduard Vladimirovich and Eya Diomidovna (Zapadnova-Lapshakova) Lipova; m. Dmitry Alexandvovich Skryabin, July 13, 1978 (div. Dec. 1985); 1 child, Anna Dmitrievna; m. David Alan Wilkinson, Aug. 15, 1996; 1 child, Jay Alexander. MSc in Chemistry, Ural State Tech. U., Ekaterinburg, 1980, PhD in Chemistry, 1988. Cert. chem. engr. and technologist. Sci. rschr. Ural divsn. Inst. Chemistry, SSSR Acad. Scis., Ekaterinburg, Russia, 1980—88; leader rschr. group Ural divsn. Inst. Organic Synthesis, Russian Acad. Scis., 1988—98. Dir. Alfa-Omega, Ltd., Ekaterinburg, 1994-96. Contbr. over 40 articles to sci. jours., including Jour. Fluorine Chemistry; patentee in field. Recipient young scientist's prize Ural divsn. SSSR Acad. Scis. and Sverdlovsk Regional Union Sci. and Edn., 1988, 89; grantee Internat. Sci. Found., Washington, 1993, Russian Found. Fundamental Rsch., 1995. Avocations: gardening, skiing, symphonic music. Home: 662 Stillwaters Dr SW Marietta GA 30064-2469 E-mail: dwilki8635@aol.com.

SKRZYPCZAK, JOZEF ALEKSANDER, education educator; b. Poznan, Poland, Mar. 1, 1938; s. Franciszek and Bronislawa (Kolodziejczyk) S.; m. Alina Sokolowska, Aug. 30, 1964 (div. 1980); 1 child, Liliana; m. Teresa Maresch, July 10, 1980; 1 child, Lidia. MA in Chemistry, Adam Mickiewicz U., Poznan, Poland, 1964, PhD in Chemistry, 1970, degree in Humanities, 1979. From asst. dept. magnetic chemistry to prof. Adam Mickiewicz U., 1964—89, prof., 1989—, vice head inst. pedagogy, 1978—82, head dept. adult edn., 1983—. Mem. sub-com. adult edn. Polish Acad. Sci., Warszawa, Poland, 1983—; mem. Univ. Senate, 1993—; expert Minister Edn. & Sport, 1995—; pres. Tech. Coll. Health & Beauty Treatment, Poznan, 2000—. Author: Model Assumptions of Audio-Visual Manual in Chemistry, 1977 (Ministry of Edn. award 1978), Didactic Film in Higher Education 1985 (Ministry of Edn. award 1986), Theoretical and Practical Problems of Research Methodology of a School Book, 1985 (Ministry of Edn. award 1986), Adult Education Strategies, 1991, Selected Aspects of Adult Education, 1991, 2d edit., 1993, The Construction and Evaluation of Handbooks, 1996 (Ministry of Edn. award 1996), Popular Encyclopaedia of Mass Media, 1999. Mem. Solidarity, 1980-89. Recipient The Gold Cross of Merit, Pres. Poland, 1984, Medal of Com. of Nat. Edn., Minister of Edn., 1995. Mem. Polish United Workers Party, Poznan, 1970-89. Avocations: films, chess, tourism, reading, videos. Home: Osiedle Boleslawa Chrobrego 11 m 224 60-681 Poznan Poland Office: Adam Mickiewicz U Szamakewskiego 89 60-569 Poznan Poland Fax: 0048 (61) 8292294., 0048 (61) 8292294. E-mail: andrago@main.amu.edu.pl.

SKUBBY, CHRISTOPHER DANIEL, political science educator, social sciences educator, department chairman; b. Cleve., Apr. 28, 1959; s. Daniel David and Mary Jane Skubby; m. Phyllis Ann Wargo, Aug. 17, 1959. BA magna cum laude, Cleve. State U., 1981; MA, Johns Hopkins U., 1984, PhD, 1995. Sr. lectr. Towson (Md.) State U., 1985-93; prof. Lakeland C.C., Kirtland, Ohio, 1993—. Instr. Cuyahoga C.C., Highland Hills, Ohio, 1996. Intern Coast Alliance, Washington, 1980; spkr. Lakeland Spkrs. Bur., Kirtland, Ohio, 1996—2001; bd. mem. Extended Housing, Inc., Painesville, 1999—2002; advisor Model UN Program; vol. Kennedy for Pres., Cleve., 1980. Hart fellow Johns Hopkins U., 1985-86. Mem. NEA, ACLU, Am. Polit. Sci. Assn., Acad. Polit. Sci., Am. Polit. Items Collectors, Ohio Assn. Economists and Polit. Scientists. Avocations: golf, collecting political memorabilia, travel, reading. Home: 91 Tuckmere Dr Painesville OH 44077 Office: Social Sci Divsn Lakeland CC Kirtland OH 44094 E-mail: phyllchris@nls.net.

SKUDDER, PAUL ALBERT, vascular surgeon; b. N.Y.C., Oct. 15, 1953; s. Paul Albert and Margaret Ann (Youmans) Skudder; m. Joanne Carol Moruzzi, May 31, 1980; children: Paul, Carolyn, Rebecca. BA, Williams Coll., 1975; MD, Cornell U. Med. Coll., 1979. Diplomate Am Bd Surgery, Am Bd Gen Vascular Surg, Am Bd Surg Critical Care. Intern, resident, chief resident in surgery U. Rochester, N.Y., 1979-84; fellow in vascular surgery Lahey Clinic, Burlington, Mass., 1984-85; asst. prof. surgery George Washington U. Sch. of Medicine, Washington, 1985-86; vascular and gen. surgeon, dir. vascular lab. Williamstown, Mass., 1986-91; clin. asst. prof. surgery Uniformed Svcs. U. of Health Scis., Bethesda, Md., 1991—; vascular, gen. surgeon Schenectady, N.Y., 1991—; asst. prof. surgery Vascular Inst. Albany Med. Coll., 2000—. Editor: (book) Visceral Vascular Surgery, 1987; contbr. articles to profl jours. Med vpres No Berkshire Unit Am Cancer Soc, 1987—89; mem exec bd Mt Greylock Ski Club, 1988—89; nat ski patrol Jiminy Peak, Hancock, Mass., 1988—97, Gore Mountain, North Creek, NY, 1997—; med advisor Williams Col Ski Patrol, 1990—; quality assurance comt Ellis Hosp, 1991—; chairperson Ellis-St Clare's Vascular Surg Clin Pathway Task Force, 1993—95; med advisor Western Mass Region, Nat Ski Patrol, 1993—97, Stephentown NY Fire Dept, 1994—; technical assessment comt Ellis Hosp, 1995—; bd dirs Inter-County Home Care, Albany, NY, 1995—. Nominee Golden Apple Clin Teaching Award, Georgetown Univ Med Sch, 1986; recipient Benedict Prize for Excellence in Biol, Williams Col, 1975, Resident Prize Paper, Upstate NY Vascular Surg Soc, 1983, Oustanding Sci Paper-Fourth Prize for Hemodynamics, 1987. Fellow: ACS; mem.: Chesapeake Vascular Soc, Mass Med Soc, Upstate NY Soc Vascular Surg, Peripheral Vascular Surgery Soc, Eastern Vascular Soc, New Eng Soc Vascular Surg, Soc Vascular Technology, Int Soc Cardiovascular Surg, Soc Critical Care Med. Roman Catholic. Avocations: National Ski Patrol, bicycling, running. Office: 1201 Nott St Ste 202 Schenectady NY 12308-2589 E-mail: skudder@pol.net.

SKUFCA, SHERRY LEE, newspaper editor; b. Bryan, Ohio, Mar. 15, 1955; d. Lewis Richard and Barbara Kay Kirkendall; m. John C. Skufca, Apr. 19, 1949. BS in Journalism, Bowling Green State U., 1977. Corr. The News-Messenger, Fremont, Ohio, 1976-77; reporter The Advocate, Newark, 1977-78; reporter, editor The Advertiser-Tribune, Tiffin, 1978-81; video text mgr., editor A-T Videotext, 1981-85; mng. editor Corona (Calif.)-Norco Ind., 1985-87; asst. mng. editor The Daily Record, York, Pa., 1987-89; mng. editor The Jour. Gazette, Ft. Wayne, Ind., 1989—. With Leadership Ft. Wayne, 1996; mem. journalism adv. bd. Bowling Green, 2002. Mem. Ind. Purdue Ft. Wayne Communicator (bd. mem. 1998—), Soc. Profl. Journalists, Investigative Reporters and Editors, AP Mng. Editors (com. mem. 1989—), Mid Am. Press Inst. (bd. mem., exec. bd. 1996—), Youth Leadership Ft. Wayne (com. mem. 1997—). Avocations: reading, sports, cooking, music. Office: The Jour Gazette 600 W Main St Fort Wayne IN 46802-1408 E-mail: sskufca@jg.net.

SKUJA, ANDRIS, physics educator; b. Riga, Latvia, Mar. 1, 1943; came to U.S., 1976; s. Edvins Martins and Rita (Ozolnieks) S. BSc, U. Toronto, Can., 1966; PhD, U. Calif., Berkeley, 1972. Rsch. officer U. Oxford, Eng., 1972-76; asst. prof. U. Md., College Park, 1976-81, assoc. prof., 1981-89, prof., 1989—; vis. prof. McGill U., Montreal, Que., Can., 1981; vis. scientist DESY, Hamburg, Fed. Republic Germany, 1983. Mem. instn. bd. CMS experiment Large Hadron Collider, CERN, 1994—. Contbr. articles to profl. jours. Fellow Am. Phys. Soc. Achievements include rsch. on the study of structure of nuclei by deep inelastic lepton scattering, study of the decay of the Zo; pioneer of the first electronic measurement of neutrino-electron scattering; study of gamma gamma interactions; lead scientist constrn. of forward muon sys. for solenoidal detector collaboration experiment at superconducting super collider; chair instn. bd. Hadron Calorimeter Subsy. for compact muon solenoid experiment at large Hadron collider, European Lab. for Particle Physics (CERN); pioneer construction of the forward sys. for the solenoidal detector collaboration experiment of the superconducting super collider. Home: PO Box 702 7711 Lake Glen Dr Glenn Dale MD 20769-2028 Office: U Md Dept Physics College Park MD 20742-0001

SKULINA, THOMAS RAYMOND, lawyer; b. Cleve., Sept. 14, 1933; s. John J. and Mary B. (Vesely) S. AB, John Carroll U., 1955; JD, Case Western Res. U., 1959, LLM, 1962. Bar: Ohio 1959, U.S. Supreme Ct. 1964, ICC 1965. Ptnr. Skulina & Stringer, Cleve., 1967-72, Riemer Oberdank & Skulina, Cleve., 1978-81, Skulina, Fillo, Walters & Negrelli, 1981-86, Skulina & McKeon, Cleve., 1986-90, Skulina & Hill, Cleve., 1990-97; atty. Penn Ctrl. Transp. Co., 1960-65, asst. gen. atty., 1965-78, trial counsel, 1965-76; with Consol. Rail Corp., 1976-78; pvt. practice Cleve., 1997—. Tchr. comml. law Practicing Law Inst., N.Y.C., 1970; practicing labor arbitrator Fed. Mediation and Conciliation Svc., 1990—; arbitrator Mcpl. Securities Rulemaking Bd., 1994-98, N.Y. Stock Exch., 1995—, NASD, 1996—; mediator NASD, 1997—, AAA Comml., 1997—; mediator vol. panel EEOC, 1997-99, contract panel, 1999-2000, v.p., 2001—; arbitrator Better Bus. Bur., 2000—. Contbr. articles to legal jours. Income tax and fed. fund coord. City of Warrensville Heights, Ohio, 1970-77; spl. counsel City of North Olmstead, Ohio, 1971-75, spl. counsel to Ohio Atty. Gen., 1983-93, Cleve. Charter Rev. Commn., 1988; pres. Civil Svc. Commn., Cleve., 1977-86, referee, 1986—; fact-finder State Employees Rels. Bd., Ohio, 1986—; hearing officer Human Resource Commn., Summit County, Ohio, 2000—. With U.S. Army, 1959. Mem. ABA (R.R. and motor carrier com. 1988-96, jr. chmn. 1989-96, alt. dispute resolution com. 1998—), FBA, Assn. Conflict Resolution, Cleve. Bar Assn. (grievance com. 1987-93, chmn. 1997-98, trustee 1993-96, ADR com. 1997—), Ohio Bar Assn. (bd. govs. litigation sect. 1986-98, negligence law com. 1989-96, ethics and profl. responsibility com. 1990-91, alt. dispute resolution com. 1996—), Am. Arbitration Assn. (practicing labor arbitrator 1987—), Nat. Assn. R.R. Trial Counsel, Internat. Assn. Law and Sci., Pub. Sector Labor Rels. Assn., Internat. Indsl. Rels. Rsch. Assn. Democrat. Roman Catholic. Home: 3162 W 165th St Cleveland OH 44111-1016 Office: 24803 Detroit Rd Cleveland OH 44145-2553 E-mail: tskulina@aol.com.

SKUP, DAVID ALAN, insurance company executive; b. Balt., Nov. 9, 1952; s. Murray and Elaine Betty (Goldberg) S.; m. Joan Elaine Earnest, Sept. 1, 1973; chidren: Brian Murray, Robert Ryan. BS, Fla. State U., 1974. Mgr. Deloitte Haskins & Sells, Jacksonville, Fla., 1974-84; v.p. Ind. Ins. Group, Inc., 1984-97; CFO Legacy Mktg. Group, Petaluma, Calif., 1997-2000; sr. v.p., COO AMOSC divsn. AON Corp., Ft. Wayne, Ind., 2000—. Commr. allocations United Way N.E. Fla., Jacksonville, 1987. Mem. AICPA, Ins. Acctg. and Sys. Assn. (bd. dirs. 1987—, pres. 1988-89), Inst. Internal Auditors (bd. dirs. 1984-86, pres. 1988—), Fin. Execs. Inst., Fla. Inst. CPAs, Fla. State U. Alumni Bd. (pres. Jacksonville chpt. 1986), Fla. State U. Bus. Sch. Alumni Bd., Pres.'s Club, Tournament Players, Chestnut Hills Country Club. Home: 10617 Indian Ridge Dr Fort Wayne IN 46814 Office: 8821 DuPont Cir Dr W # 300 Fort Wayne IN 46825 E-mail: dave_skup@amosc.com.

SKUPINSKI, BOGDAN KAZIMIERZ, artist; b. Poland, July 16, 1942; came to U.S., 1971, naturalized, 1976; s. Kazimierz Stanislaw and Jrena Lucja (Kanar) S. BA, Acad. Fine Arts, Krakow, Poland, 1969, MA, 1971; cert., Ecole Nationale Superieure de Beaux Arts, Paris, 1971. Pres. Bogdan & Assoc., N.Y.C. Graphic artist: painting Proclamation, 1968, Escape, 1968, Return, 1969, Good Journey, (permanent collection N.J. State Mus., 1971, The Stable, (permanent collection Library of Congress), 1971, Nouvel Ordre, 1970 (annual prize Ministry of Cultural Affairs of France), Gare du Nord, 1970 (award Commn. Fine Arts. Paris), anti-war themes, 1969-76; life and work of John F. Kennedy and Albert Michelson, 1969-76. Recipient Grand Prix, Nat. Salon Young Artists, 1968, People's Choice award 2d Nat. Graphic Rev., Karkow, 1969, ann. Bartoczek and Babrowski award Polish Ministry Art and Culture, 1970, lst prize for prints and drawings Nat. Conn. Acad. Exhbn., Hartford, 1971, medal Internat. Exhbn. Graphic Art, Frechen, Fed. Republic Germany, 1976, Presdl. Medal of Merit, 1990; fellow Ecole Nat. Superieure Beaux Arts. Fellow Pratt Inst.; mem. NAD (Cannon prize for graphics 1971), Kosciuszko Found., Rep. Presdl. Task Force. Roman Catholic. Home: Cathedral Sta PO Box 849 215 W 104th St New York NY 10025-4297

SKURA, MEREDITH ANNE, English educator; b. Bklyn., May 11, 1944; d. George and Esther (Ruth Feld) Skura.; m. Martin Joel Wiener, May 17, 1981; chdren: Rebecca, Vivian. BA, Swarthmore Coll., 1965; PhD, Yale U., 1971. With English dept. U. Bridgeport, Conn., 1968-69, 70-73, Yale U., New Haven, 1973-78, Rice U., Houston, 1978—. Author: The Literary Use of the Psychoanalytic Process, 1981, Shakespeare the Actor and the Purposes of Playing, 1993. Grantee Guggenheim Found., 1982-83, NEH, 1989-90, Folger Shakespeare Libr., 1998-99, Am. Coun. Learned Socs., 1981. Mem. MLA, Shakespeare Assn. Am. (v.p. 1999-2000, pres. 2000—). Jewish. Avocations: drawing, travel. Office: 6100 Main St Houston TX 77005-1827

SKURDENIS, JULIANN VERONICA, librarian, educator, writer, editor; b. July 13, 1942; d. Julius J. and Anna M. (Zilys) S.; m. Lawrence J. Smircich, Aug. 21, 1965 (div. July 1978); m. Paul J. Lalli, Oct. 1, 1978; 1 adopted child, Kathryn Leila Skurdenis-Lalli. AB with honors, Coll. New Rochelle, 1964; MS, Columbia U., 1966; MA, Hunter Coll., 1974. Young adult libr. Bklyn. Pub. Libr., 1964-66; periodicals libr., instr. Kingsborough C.C., Bklyn., 1966-67; acquisitions libr. Pratt Inst., 1967-68; acquisitions libr., asst. prof. Bronx (N.Y.) C.C., 1968-75, head tech. svcs., assoc. prof., 1975-97, prof., 1998—. Acting dir. Libr. Resource Learning Ctr., 1994-97. Author: Walk Straight Through the Square, 1976, More Walk Straight Through the Square, 1977; contbg. editor Internat. Travel News, 1989—, Travel Your Way/N.Y. Times, 1996-98; travel editor Archaeology mag., 1986-89; contbr. over 400 travel, hist., and archaeol. pieces. N.Y. State fellow, 1960-66, Columbia U. fellow, 1964-66, Pratt Inst. fellow, 1965. Mem. AAUP, Libr. Assn. CUNY (chairwoman numerous coms.), Archaeol. Inst. Am. Avocations: archaeology, travel, travel writing. Office: CUNY Bronx CC University Ave Bronx NY 10453-6994

SKURLA, LAURUS See LAURUS

SKUTNIK, BOLESH J. optics scientist, lay worker, lawyer; b. Passaic, N.J., Aug. 19, 1941; s. Boleslaw Stanley and Helen Marie (Dzierzynska) S.; m. Phyllis Victoria Wojciechowski, Sept. 2, 1967 (div. July 1991); children: Pam, Janeen, Todd; m. Anita Marie Bacon, Aug. 2, 1997. BS, Seton Hall U., 1962; MS, Yale U., 1964, PhD, 1967; JD, U. Conn., 1995. Bar: N.Y. 1996, Conn. 1996. Chief scientist Ensign Bickford Coating Co., Simsbury, Conn., 1979-91; prin. B.J. Assocs., New Britain, 1991-97, West Hartford, 1997—; patent atty., rsch. scientist Fiberoptic Fabrications, Inc., East Longmeadow, Mass., 1995-97; dir. rsch., dir. patents and licensing Sci. Fiberoptic Fabrications, Inc., 1997—. Lector, mem. parish coun. St. Catherine of Siena, West Simsbury, Conn., 1980-85, St. Maurice, New Britain, Conn., 1985-2000, St. Thomas Apostle, West Hartford, 2000—; chmn., del. synod Archdioces of Hartford, Conn., 1990-96; chmn. parish Holy Family Retreat League, New Britain, 1989-2000; pres. Enbic Employees Credit Union, Simsbury, 1988-91; asst. prof. chemistry Fairfield U., Conn., 1973-79. Patentees in field; contbr. articles to profl. jours. Interviewer Yale Alumni Schs. Com., L.I. and Hartford, Conn., 1969—; mem. Yale Assn. of Yale Alumni Rep., New Britain Club, 1997-2000. Mem. ABA (subcom. chair 1993, 94, 96), Conn. Bar Assn., N.Y. State Bar Assn., Conn. Patent Lawyers Assn., Am. Intellectual Property Lawyers Assn., Soc. Photo-optical Engrs., Am. Ceramic Soc., (coord. symposium 1991), Materials Rsch. Soc. (chair symposium 1987-89), Am. Chem. Soc. (alt. coun. 1988-90. sect. chair 1994, vice chair 1993, bd. dirs. 1985-2002), Porsche Club Am. (various positions Conn. Valley region), Yale Club New Britain (dir. 1994-2000), Yale Alumni (assoc.). Democrat. Roman Catholic. Home: 51 Banbury Ln West Hartford CT 06107-1102 Office: Fiber Optic Fabrications Inc 515 Shaker Rd East Longmeadow MA 01028-3126 *The human spirit is stronger than anything that can happen to it.*

SKVORECKY, JOSEF VACLAV, English literature educator, novelist; b. Nachod, Czechoslovakia, Sept. 27, 1924; arrived Can., 1969; s. Josef Karel and Anna (Kurazova) S.; m. Zdenka Josefa Salivarova, Mar. 30, 1958 PhD, Charles U., Czechoslovakia, 1951; LHD (hon.), SUNY, 1986; postgrad., Masaryk U., 1991, U. Calgary, 1992, U. Toronto, 1992. Vis. lectr. U. Toronto, Ont., Can., 1969-70, writer-in-residence, 1970-71, assoc. prof., 1971-75, prof. English, 1975-90; prof. emeritus, 1990—. Lectr. on lit. topics Voice of Am., 1973—; adv. to Pres. Vaclav Havel, 1990. Editor: Sixty Eight Publ. Corp., Toronto, 1972— ; author: The End of the Nylon Age, 1967, Republic of Whores, 1969, The Miracle Game, 1972, The End of Lieutenant Boruvka, 1975, The Swell Season, 1975, The Bass Saxophone, 1979, The Cowards, 1980, The Return of Lieutenant Boruvka, 1980, The Engineer of Human Souls, 1984, Miss Silver's Past, 1985, Dvorak in Love, 1986, The Bride from Texas, 1992, Headed for the Blues, 1996, The Two Murders in My Double Life, 1996, Narratio Questi, 1998, (with Z. Salivarova) Brief Encounter, With Murder, 1999, Brief Encounter After Many Years, with Murder, 2000, Brief Encounter at the End of an Era, With Murder, 2001; short story collections: The Menorah, 1964, The Life of High Society, 1965, The Mournful Demeanor of Lieutenant Boruvka, 1966, A Babylonian Story, 1967, The Bitter World, 1969, Sins for Father Knox, 1973, Oh, My Papa! 1972, The Edenvale Stories, 1996, When Eve Was Naked, 2001; plays: The New Men and Women CBC Radio 1977, God in Your House, 1980 (1st prize Multicultural Theatre Festival Hamilton 1980); films: The Tank Battalion, 1991, The Swell Season, 1994, Eine kleine Jazzmusik, 1996, Poe and the Death of a Beautiful Girl, 1997, The Legend of Emoke, 1998, The Detective Agency, 2000; essays: Reading Detecive Stories, 1965, They-Which Is We, 1968, All the Bright Young Men and Women, 1972, Working Overtime, 1979, Talkin' Moscow Blues, 1989. Decorated Order of the White Lion; apptd. mem. Order of Can., 1992; recipient Neustadt Internat. prize for lit., U. Okla., 1980, Gov. Gen. Can.'s award, 1985, lit. prize Echoing Green Found., 1990, Czech Republic's State Prize for Lit., 1999, Dangea prize 2001. Fellow Royal Soc. Can.; mem. Can. Writers' Union, Authors' League Am., Crime Writers Can., Mystery Writers Am., The Internat. PEN Club, Can. br. Czechoslovak Nat. Assn. Can. (mem. Presidium), Coun. Free Czechoslovakia (mem. Presidium), Order of Can. Progressive Conservative. Roman Catholic Avocation: swing music. Home: 487 Sackville St Toronto ON Canada M4X 1T6

SKWARA, ERICH WOLFGANG, novelist, poet, educator, literary critic; b. Salzburg, Austria, Nov. 4, 1948; came to U.S., 1975, naturalized, 1981. s. Alois Gaigg and Hermine Maria Skwara; m. Victoria Anne Dufresne, July 10, 1974 (div. Mar. 1978); m. Gloria Elaine Winniski, June 8, 1978; children: Gabriella Maria, Alexandra Felicitas. BA, U. Paris VII, 1970; MA, Salzburg U., 1972; PhD, N.Y. State U., Albany, 1985. Instr. U. Md., Balt., 1975-77; freelance author Balt. and Paris, 1977-82; vis. lectr. Georgetown U., Washington, 1982-84; freelance author Salzburg, 1984-86; prof. humanities, comparative lit. and German San Diego State U., 1986—. Dep. editor-in-chief for cultural affairs Die Welt, Berlin, 1993; cultural and lit. corr. for a number of German and Austrian newspapers and media, 1979—; worldwide readings and lecture tours. Author: (novels) Black Sails, 1979, 99, The Cool Million, 1990, Tristan Island, 1992, Die Heimlichen Könige, 1995, Plague in Siena, 1994, 95, Ice on the Bridge, 1997, Versuch einer Heimkehr, 1998, Nach dem Norden, 1998, The Angel of Death, 1998, Anruf aus Rom, 1999, Pest in Siena, 2001, Zerbrechlichkeit, 2002, Traumeerzahlen, 2002 others; translated (from English and French to German) works by T. Williams, Thomas Wolfe, J.J. Rousseau, Gustave Flaubert, others; own works translated into English, French, Japanese, Arabic, others. Mem. Internat. PEN Club, PEN Ctr. of German Speaking Authors Abroad (bd. dirs. 1985-2002), PEN Ctr. of Austria, PEN Ctr. of France. Roman Catholic. Avocations: fine wines, travel, walking. Office: San Diego State U Dept Classics Humanities San Diego CA 92182 also: Suhrkamp Verlag Linden Str 29-35 D60325 Frankfurt am Main Germany also: 264 rue Saint Honore F75001 Paris France E-mail: poetskwara@aol.com.

SKWARCZYŃSKI, HENRYK ADAM (HENRYK SKWAR), writer; b. Łódź, Poland, Aug. 13, 1952; came to U.S., 1980; s. Zdzislaw and Stanislawa Ewa (Laszczyk) S.; m. Eglé Juodvalkis, Sept. 2, 1989 MA, U. Warsaw, 1977; postgrad., Polish Acad. Sci., 1978-80, Sorbonne U. Free-lance writer, N.Y.C., 1980-81, Voice of Am., Washington, 1981-82; instr. Defense Lang. Inst., Monterey, Calif., 1982-84; staff writer Libertas, Paris, 1984-86; free-lance writer Radio Free Europe, Munich, 1987-95; writer Chgo., 1995—. Author: Man in a Cleft, 1979, The Anguish of Becoming American, 1989, Sweeney Among the Nightingales, 2000, The Straw Sea, 2002; editor-in-chief: Ephemeron, 1974—75; contbr. short stories to mags. Activist Solidarity Movement, 1980-89. Rotary Club grantee, 1982, Hoover Inst. grantee, 1985. Avocation: travel in Africa.

SKWARYK, ROBERT FRANCIS, judge; b. Erie, Pa., Nov. 4, 1948; s. Frank and Gloria (Hinkle) S. BS, Pa. State U., 1973; JD, U. Kans., 1977. Bar: Pa. 1977, U.S. Dist. Ct. (we. dist.) Pa. 1977. Legal intern legal svcs. Clallum and Jefferson Counties, Port Angeles, Wash., 1977; assoc. Galbo, McNelis, Restifo & Held, Erie, 1977-80; instr. bus. law Behrend Coll. Pa. State U., 1978-80; appeals referee Commonwealth of Pa., Harrisburg and Pottsville, 1981, Pitts. and Erie, 1985-88, adminstrv. law judge Allentown, 1988-96, Pitts., 1996—. Contbg. author ct. opinions Pa. Liquor Control Bd., 1988—. Mem. Behrend Coll. Soccer Alumni Assn., Erie, 1974-90. Sgt. USMC, 1967-70, lt. (j.g.) USN, 1981-85, lt. USNR, 1986-92, Saudi Arabia, lt. comdr. USNR, 1992-98, comdr., 1998—. Fellow Theatre-Sciptworks, Pa. Coun. Arts, 2002. Mem. ABA, Pa. State Bar Assn., Erie County Bar Assn., Pa. Conf. Adminstrv. Law Judges, First Marine Air Wing Assn., Pa. State U. Alumni Assn. Avocations: soccer, flying, orienteering. Home: 833 Greentree Rd Apt 2-6 Pittsburgh PA 15220-3418 Office: Commonwealth Pa Office Adminstrv Law Judge 875 Greentree Rd Pittsburgh PA 15220-3508

SKWERES, THOMAS W. advertising executive, writer; b. Chgo., May 11, 1929; s. Marion John and Sophie Regina (Rataiczyk) Skweres; children: Thomas Allan, Pamela Charmaine, Patricia Ann. AA, Wright Jr. Coll., Chgo.; student mktg., Northwestern U., Chgo. Prodn. mgr. Reincke, Meyer & Finn, Chgo., 1953—55; v.p., account exec. Hanson and Stevens, 1955—61; v.p. sales, gen. mgr. Ross & White, Wheeling, 1961—84; sales mgr. Graphics Plus, Lisle, 1984—89, Essig Printing, Lisle, 1989—91; CEO Tomco Printing, 1999—. Staff sgt. U.S. Army, 1951, Europe. Achievements include patents in field. Avocations: guidance, handicapping, poetry, teaching. Home: 5613 Snowdrop Lisle IL 60532 Office: Tomco Printing & Enterprise PO Box 475 Lisle IL 60532

SKWIERSKY, PAUL, accountant; b. N.Y.C., Aug. 14, 1925; s. Abraham and Dora (Rainer) S.; m. Gloria Evelyn Lederman, Dec. 27, 1947; children: Janet S., Denise C. Skwiersky Cohen. BS, NYU, 1948. CPA, N.Y., N.J. Mng. ptnr. Benjamin Nadel & Co., N.Y.C., 1942-87, Skwiersky, Alpert & Bressler, N.Y.C., 1987—. Bd. dirs. Philip & Janice Levin Found., North Plainfield, N.J., Darcy Found., Inc., N.Y.C., 1980-87, Levin Mgmt. Corp., North Plainfield, Allstate Constrn. Corp., North Plainfield; panelist, arbitrator Am. Arbitration Assn., N.Y.C. Dir. Birchwood Park Civic Assn., Syosset, N.Y., 1962. Sgt. U.S. Army, 1943-46. Mem. Fiber Producers Credit Assn., Textile Distbrs. Assn., Inc., N.Y. Credit & Fin. Mgmt. Assn., N.Y. State Soc. CPAs, Masons (master 1977-79), Fountains of Palm Beach Country Club. Avocations: reading, travel, golf. Office: Skwiersky Alpert Bressler 462 7th Ave New York NY 10018-7606

SKWIRUT, JOHN LAURENCE, computer company executive; b. Phila., July 27, 1965; s. Bernard Ludwig Skwirut and Lauretta Stella Gonsowski; m. Patricia Gail Sell, Nov. 23, 1991; children: Katie, William, Rachel. Cert. internat. bus., U. Copenhagen, 1986; BA in Econs. with honors, Franklin and Marshall Coll., 1987; cert. in bus., U. Pa., 1990, MS in Engring., 1994. Fin. mgr. mfg. ctr. Computer Scis. Corp., Integrated Sys. Divsn., Moorestown, N.J., 1988-90, sr. pricing specialist, 1991-94, pricing mgr., 1995-96, program control mgr., 1997-98; global dir. pricing Computer Scis. Corp., Chem. and Energy Group, Newark, 1998—. Bd. dirs., fin. advisor FAMCare, Bridgeton, N.J. Class pres. Danish Internation Study Program, U. Copenhagen, 1986. Mem. Wharton Club Phila. Republican. Avocations: basketball, sailing. Home: 128 Old Kings Hwy Salem NJ 08079-2014 Office: Computer Scis Corp Chem and Energy Group 400 Commerce Dr Newark DE 19713-6802 Fax: 302-391-7033. E-mail: jskwirut@worldnet.att.net.

SKY-EAGLE, MELISSA JEAN, musician, pianist; b. Waco, Tex., Nov. 2, 1978; d. William H. and Ivy Jean Sky-Eagle. Grad. summa cum laude, Tex. Christian U., 1997—2001; postgrad., Peabody Conservatory, 2001—. Pianist Bill Sky-Eagle Evangelistic Assoc., Arlington, Tex., 1989-96, Highland Bapt. Ch., Dallas, 1997, Springdale Bapt. Ch., Ft. Worth, 1998-99. Performer Inst. for Performing Arts, Moscow, 1996, Cliburn Inst., Ft. Worth, 1997, Chautauqua Inst., N.Y., 1998, Russian Piano Inst., Waco, Tex., 1999; performer, accompanist for numerous chs., clubs, sch. and cmty. activities, 1991-99. Recipient Cliburn award Am. Coll. Musicians, Austin, Tex., 1997; Eubie Blake scholar, 1999. Mem. Internat. Order Kings Daus., Alpha Lambda Delta, Phi Kappa Lambda, Mu Phi Epsilon (com. chair 1997-99). Republican. Baptist. Avocations: writing, accompanying vocalists and instrumentalists. Home: PO Box 170425 Arlington TX 76003-0425

SKYLER, MARC NORMAN, biology educator; b. Newark, Sept. 28, 1945; s. Morris and Ethel (Rabinowitz) S.; m. Aine Bray, June 11, 1972; children: David, Alexandra. BS, CCNY, 1967; MA, Hofstra U., 1969; MPhil, St. John's U., Queens, N.Y., 1984, PhD, 1986. Cert. soccer coach. Rsch. asst. Coll. Phys. and Surgs., N.Y.C., 1969; prof. biology N.Y.C. Tech. Coll., Bklyn., 1969—. Bd. dirs., advisor Acad. Sci. and Math., N.Y.C., 1990—; project dir. CUNY Collaborative Rsch. Grant. Developer rsch. course curriculum, author (lab. textbook) Introduction to Research, 2000. Resource person N.Y.C. Pub. Schs.; sci. resource judge N.Y. Acad. Sci., 1990. Mem. AAAS, N.Y. Acad. Sci., N.Y. State Assn. Two-Yr. Colls., Acad. for Humanities and Scis. CUNY. Democrat. Jewish. Achievements include research indicating that Vitamin E increases the amount of monounsaturation in the lipids of biomembranes. Office: NYC Tech Coll 300 Jay St Brooklyn NY 11201-1909 E-mail: mskyler@nyctc.cuny.edu.

SLAATTÈ, HOWARD ALEXANDER, minister, philosophy educator; b. Evanston, Ill., Oct. 18, 1919; s. Iver T. and Esther (Larsen) S.; m. Mildred Gegenheimer, June 20, 1951; children: Elaine Slaatte Quaddur, Mark, Paul. AA, Kendall Coll., 1940; BA cum laude, U. N.D., 1942; B.D. cum laude, Drew U., 1945, PhD, 1956; Drew fellow, Mansfield Coll., Oxford (Eng.) U., 1949-50. Ordained to ministry Meth. Ch. as elder, 1943. Pastor Detroit Conf. United Meth. Ch., 1950-65; assoc. prof. systematic theology Temple U., 1956-60; vis. prof., prof. philosophy and religion McMurry Coll. (now named McMurry U.), 1960-65; prof. dept. philosophy Marshall U., Huntington, W.Va., 1965-89, prof. emeritus, 1989—, chmn. dept., 1966-81, mem. grad. council, 1970-73, mem. research bd., 1974-76, mem. acad. standards and policy com., 1975-77, research grantee, 1976, 77; mem. bd. Campus Christian Center, 1973-75; prof. ethics St. Leo (Fla.) Coll., 1993. Lectr. Traverse City (Mich.) State Hosp., 1966-71, Am. Ontoanalytical Assn. internat. conf., Acapulco, Mex., 1970, World Congress Logotherapy, San Diego, 1980, other orgns. Author: Time and Its End, 1962, Fire in the Brand, 1963, The Pertinence of the Paradox, 1968, The Paradox of Existentialist Theology, 1971, Modern Science and the Human Condition, 1974, The Arminian Arm of Theology, 1977, The Dogma of Immaculate Perception, 1979, Discovering Your Real Self, 1980, The Seven Ecumenical Councils, 1980, The Creativity of Consciousness, 1983, Contemporary Philosophies of Religion, 1986, Time, Existence and Destiny, 1988, Critical Survey of Ethics, 1988; co-author: The Philosophy of Martin Heidegger, 1983, Religious Issues in Contemporary Philosophy, 1988, Our Cultural Cancer and Its Cure, 1995, A Re-Appraisal of Kierkegaard, 1995, Plato's Dialogues and Ethics, 1999, A Purview of Wesley's Theology, 2000; contbr. Analecta Frankliana, 1981; gen. editor: (series) Contemporary Existentialism; contbr. to theol. and philos. jours. Mem. W.Va. Conf. United Meth. Ch., 1966-87, ret., 1987; bd. dirs. Inst. for Advanced Philos. Research, 1979-90; chmn. bd. dirs. Salvation Army of Huntington, W. Va.; courtesy prof. U. South Fla., 1993-99. Recipient Outstanding Educators of Am. award, 1975, Profl. Excellence award Faculty Merit Found., State of W.Va., 1986, U. N.D. Found. award, 2000; named to Honorable Order of Ky. Colonels, W.Va. Ambassador of Good Will; named Internat. Man of Yr., 1993; NSF fellow, 1965, Benedum Found. rsch. grantee, 1970, NSF rsch.-grantee, 1965, 71. Mem. W.Va. Philos. Assn. (pres., 1966-67, 83-84), Am. Philos. Assn., AAUP, Am. Acad. Religion. Home: 300 Kildaire Woods Dr Apt 211 Cary NC 27511-7710 *Most knowledge is relative, a balanced existential position with empirical implications, except for the divine Absolute encountered by faith in existence. The revealed principles opened up thereby, especially the ultimacy of sacrifical love (Agape), give basis and motivation for vital morality and a healthy culture. True freedom springs from commitment to these principles.*

SLABACH, STEPHEN HALL, lawyer; b. Oklahoma City, Nov. 15, 1934; s. Carl Edward and Alvine A. (Woellner) S.; m. Elizabeth Havard Cartwright, Feb. 15, 1958; children: Elizabeth Slabach Schmit, Stephen Edward, William Cartwright. BSME, Northwestern U., 1957; postgrad. George Washington U. Sch. Law, 1957-59; LLB, Stanford U., 1961. Bar: Calif. 1962, U.S. Dist. Ct. (no. dist.) Calif. 1962, U.S. Ct. Appeals (9th cir.) 1973, U.S. Supreme Ct. 1976. Law clk. to judge Calif. First Dist. Ct. Appeal, San Francisco, 1961-62; assoc. Cooley, Crowley, Gather, Godward, Castro & Huddleson, San Francisco, 1962-65; assoc. Cushing, Cullinan, Hancock & Rothert, San Francisco, 1965-73, ptnr., 1973-75; sole practice, Burlingame, Calif., 1975-88, San Mateo, 88—; Legal aid vol. San Mateo County; trustee San Mateo County Law Libr. Com., 1993—, v.p. 1998—; pres. Pacific Locomotive Assn., 1988-90, gen. counsel, 1980—. Mem. State Bar Calif., ABA, Am. Judicature Soc., Kiwanis (Burlingame). Republican. Episcopalian. Office: 520 S El Camino Real Ste 700 San Mateo CA 94402-1720

SLABE, JAMES F. business executive; b. Johnstown, Pa., Nov. 29, 1940; s. Frank and Antoinette Marie (Draksler) S.; m. Elaine Werner, July 14, 1973. BA, Washington and Jefferson Coll., 1962; postgrad., U. Md., 1962-64. Div. contr. Pfizer, Inc., N.Y.C., 1967-72; treas., contr. Pharmacaps, Inc., Elizabeth, N.J., 1972-73; dir. profit planning McGraw-Hill, Inc., N.Y.C., 1973-78; v.p. fin. Parade Publs., Inc., 1978-79; pres. Exec. Enterprises, Inc., 1979-95, Sabor & Co., Inc., Mountainside, N.J., 1995—, 1995—. Pres. bd. dirs. Nat. Assn. Visually Handicapped; bd. dirs. Washington and Jefferson Coll., pres. Youth and Family Counseling Svc.; mem. investment com. Westfield YMCA. Capt. U.S. Army, 1964-66. Mem. Fin. Execs. Inst., Assn. Am. Planners, Assn. Am. Contrs., Phi Beta Kappa. Roman Catholic. Office: Sabor & Co 17 Mountainview Dr Mountainside NJ 07092-2510 E-mail: jfslabe@cs.com.

SLABY, LOUIS RICHARD, civil and mechanical engineer; b. Cleve., Dec. 13, 1941; s. Louis and Helen (Kovacs) S.; m. Virginia A. Slaby, Jan. 22, 1966; children: Richard, Laura. BSME, U. Pitts., 1965; MBA, Baruch Coll., N.Y.C., 1970. Registered profl. engr., N.J., Pa., Ohio, Del., N.Y.; cert. mcpl. engr., N.J.; profl. planner, N.J. Football player N.Y. Giants, N.Y.C., 1963-65, Detroit Lions, 1966; mech. engr. Havens & Emerson, N.Y.C., 1967-68; plant engr. T.J. Lipton Inc., Flemington, N.J., 1968-74; project engr. Alaimo Engring., Paterson, 1974-86; pres. L.R. Slaby Engring., Morris Plains, 1986—. Inductee Hall of Fame, City of Salem, Ohio, 1989. Mem. ASCE, ASME, NSPE, Am. Water Works Assn., N.J. Planning Ofcls., N.J. Soc. Mcpl. Engrs., Rotary (past pres.). Lutheran. Office: Louis R Slaby Engring Assoc 51 Gibraltar Dr Morris Plains NJ 07950-1254

SLACHTA, GREGORY ANDREW, urologist; b. Paterson, N.J., Mar. 17, 1946; s. Andrew Gregory and Mary Catherine (Shimko) S.; children: Gregory Andrew, Lara Ann, Andrea; m. Patricia A. Albano, Nov. 7, 1981. BS, Pa. State U., 1966; MD, Jefferson Med. Coll., 1968. Diplomate Am. Bd. Urology. Intern Lankenan Hosp., Phila., 1968-69; resident in urology Temple U. Hosp., 1969-70, 1973-75; pvt. practice, Springfield, Mass., 1975—97, Hilton Head (S.C.) Med. Group, 1997—99. Author: Inflammatory Diseases of the Male Genital Tract, 1982. Mem. City Council Com. for Health Ins., Springfield, 1984, Springfield Planning Bd., 1991. Maj. U.S. Army, 1971-73. Fellow ACS; mem. AMA, Am. Urol. Assn. (chmn. socioecon. com. 1986-91, del. to AMA 1991—), Mass. Med. Soc. (alt. del. to AMA 1986-91, vice chmn. legis. and nat. legis. affairs com. 1987-89), Hampden Dist. Med. Soc. (pres. 1986-88), Mass. Assn. Practicing Urologists (pres. 1985-87), Beaufort County med. Soc. (pres. 1998-2001). Democrat. Roman Catholic. Avocation: golf. Office: Hilton Head Clinics Med Office Bldg 25 Hospital Center Dr Ste 300 Hilton Head Island SC 29926-2730

SLACK, DONALD CARL, agricultural engineer, educator; b. Cody, Wyo., June 25, 1942; s. Clarence Ralbon and Clara May (Beightol) S.; m. Marion Arline Kimball, Dec. 19, 1964; children: Jonel Marie, Jennifer Michelle. BS in Agrl. Engring., U. Wyo., 1965; MS in Agrl. Engring., U. Ky., 1968, PhD in Agrl. Engring., 1975. Registered profl. engr., Ky., Ariz. Asst. civil engr. City of Los Angeles, 1965; research specialist U. Ky., Lexington, 1966-70, agrl. engring. advisor Tha Phra, Thailand, 1970-73, research asst. Lexington, 1973-75; from asst. prof. to assoc. prof. agrl. engring. U. Minn., St. Paul, 1975-84; prof. U. Ariz., Tucson, 1984—, head dept. agrl. and biosystems engring., 1991—. Mem. Mid. East and Mediterranean Desert Devel. Program, 1997—; vis. prof. dept. atmospheric sci. Fed. U. Paraiba, Campina Grande, Brazil, 1997; vis. prof. dept. irrigation Chapingo Autonomous U., Mexico, 2000; tech. adv. Ariz. Dept. Water Resources, Phoenix, 1985—, Tucson active mgmt. area, 1996—; cons. Winrock Internat., Morrilton, Ark., 1984, Water Mgmt. Synthesis II, Logan, Utah, 1985, Desert Agrl. Tech. Sys., Tucson, 1985—, Portek Hermosillo, Mexico, 1989—, World Bank, Washington, 1992—, Malawi Environ. Monitoring Project, 1996, Mex. Inst. for Water Tech., 1997, Nat. Agrl. Rsch. Inst., La Serema, Chile, 1997; dep. program support mgr. Rsch. Irrigation Support Project for Asia and the Near East, Arlington, Va., 1987—94; mem. adv. team Cearan Found. for Meteorology and Hydrology, Fortaleza, Brazil, 1995—; mem. internat. adv. panel Matrou Resources Mgmt. Project, World Bank, Egypt, 1996—2000; bd. dirs. Somoita Vineyards, Ltd. Contbr. articles to profl. jours. Fellow ASCE (Outstanding Jour. Paper award 1988), Am. Soc. Agrl. Engrs. (Ariz. sect. Engr. of Yr. 1993); mem. Am. Geophys. Union, Am. Soc. Agronomy, Soil Sci. Soc. Am., Am. Soc. Engring. Edn., SAR, Brotherhood of Knights of the Vine (master knight), Sigma Xi, Tau Beta Pi, Alpha Epsilon, Gamma Sigma Delta. Democrat. Lutheran. Achievements include 3 patents pending; developer of infrared based irrigation scheduling device. Avocations: hunting, camping, hiking, model railroading. Home: 9230 E Visco Pl Tucson AZ 85710-3167 Office: U Ariz Agrl Biosystems Engring Tucson AZ 85721-0001 E-mail: slackd@u.arizona.edu. *Personal philosophy: Don't take yourself too seriously and don't take anyone else too seriously either.*

SLACK, EDWARD DORSEY, III, financial systems professional, consultant; b. Fairmont, W.Va., June 2, 1942; s. Edward Dorsey Jr. and Margaret Elaine (Higgs) S.; m. Donna Jean Carter, Oct. 19, 1944; children: Ted, Robyn. BS in Indsl. Engring., W.Va. U., 1965, postgrad., 1965-66. Registered profl. engr., W.Va. Assoc. systems and procedures analyst Westinghouse Atomic Power divs., Pitts., 1966-69; systems and procedures analyst Westinghouse Nuclear Energy Systems, 1969-72, sr. systems analyst, 1972-75, mgr. payroll and fin. systems, 1975-77; mgr. standard ledger conversion Westinghouse Energy Systems, 1977, mgr. fin. systems and control, 1978-90, mgr. fin. systems and standard ledger, 1990-91, mgr. payroll, cost and fin. systems control, 1991-94; data processing analyst & decision support coord. Braddock (Pa.) Med. Ctr., 1995-96; systems analyst, decision support coord. U. Pitts. Med. Ctr., Braddock, Pa., 1996—. Developer computer programs; designer and installer computer modules, report writer. Mem. NSPE, W.Va. Soc. Profl. Engrs. Avocations: walking, basketball, spectator sports, sports and other memorabilia. Home: 179 Autumn Dr Trafford PA 15085-1448 Office: U Pitts Med Ctr Braddock 400 Holland Ave Braddock PA 15104-1599

SLACK, LEWIS, organization administrator; b. Phila., Apr. 15, 1924; s. Lewis and Martha (Fitzgerald) S.; m. Sarah Hunt Wyman, Dec. 29, 1948; children— Elizabeth Wyman, Susan Towne, Christopher Morgan. S.B., Harvard U., 1944; PhD, Washington U., St. Louis, 1950. Physicist U.S. Naval Research Lab., 1950-54; assoc. prof. physics George Washington U., Washington, 1954-57, prof. physics, 1957-62, acting head physics dept., 1957-60; asst. exec. sec. div. phys. scis. Nat. Acad. Scis.-NRC, Washington, 1962-67; sec. com. nuclear sci. NRC, 1962-67, mem. commn. human resources, 1974-78; dir. ednl. programs Am. Inst. Physics, N.Y.C., 1967-87. Cons. Gen. Atomics div. Gen. Dynamics Corp., La Jolla, Calif., summers, 1959, 60; chmn. phys. scis. Am. exhibit Internat. Conf. Peaceful Uses Atomic Energy, Geneva, Switzerland, 1958; mem. Sci. Manpower Commn., 1968-87, pres., 1974-75, treas., 1976; mem. U.S. nat. com. Internat. Union for Pure and Applied Physics, 1972-78, sec., 1974-78; Mem. adv. com. Physics Today, 1963-67, chmn., 1967 Mem. Bruce Mus., Greenwich, Conn. (collections com., edn. com., exhbns. com., 1988-95). With USNR, 1943-46. Fellow Washington Acad. Scis., AAAS (mem. council 1971-72, 76-78); mem. Am. Phys. Soc., Am. Assn. Physics Tchrs. Episcopalian. Achievements include research on beta ray and gamma ray spectroscopy. Home: 2104 Tadley Dr Chapel Hill NC 27514-2109

SLACK, MARK ROBERT, lawyer; b. Amherst, Ohio, Aug. 17, 1957; s. Robert James and Lois Jean (Basl) S.; m. Diana Joan Thomas, Sept. 23, 1994. BA in Pub. Adminstrn. & History, Ohio No. U., 1979, JD, 1982. Bar: Ohio 1983, U.S. Dist. Ct. (no. dist.) Ohio 1983, U.S. Tax Ct. 1984, U.S. Ct. Appeals (6th cir.) 1984, U.S. Supreme Ct. 1986; cert. nat. and state Better Bus. Bur. arbitrator. Social worker Columbiana County Welfare Dept., Lisbon, Ohio, 1979-80; criminal intern Allen County Welfare Dept., Lima, 1982; social security intern Blackhoff Area Legal Svcs., 1982; mem. staff for docket indexing sys. juvenile divsn. Columbiana County Common Pleas, 1983; asst. pub. defender Columbiana County Pub. Defender's Office, Lisbon, 1984; pvt. practice law Salem, Ohio, 1983—. Regional counsel Northeast Ohio Legal Svcs., Lisbon, 1984—, Youngstown, Ohio, 1988-89. Active Columbiana County Big Bros., 1985-86; chmn. profl. divsn. No. Columbiana County United Way, 1984-85; ch. elder Holy Trinity Ch., Salem, Ohio, coordinator ch. finances, 1986-89. Recipient 1st place cooking award Salem News, 1986; named Outstanding Young Men Am., 1980-89, 92, 96. Mem. ABA, Ohio Bar Assn., Columbiana County Bar Assn. (grievence com. 1996-97, Recognition for Pro Bono Svc. 1995, 96, 97, 98, 99. 2000), Mahoning Valley Astron. Soc. (legal advisor 1985—), Canal Soc. Ohio (trustee 1996—), Salem Hist. Soc. (v.p., trustee, legal advisor 1985-87, trustee 1997-99), Youngstown Outspoken Wheelman (legal advisor 1985-93, chmn. presdl. sports award 1986-93, Outstanding Svc. award 1986-93), Mayflower Descs. Am., Descs. of the Soldiers of Valley Forge, Descs. of Ohio Civil War Soldiers, Mahoning Valley Civil War Round Table, Sandy and Beaver Canal Assn. (founder 1988), Phi Alpha Delta. Avocations: long distance bicycling, astronomy, regional history, cooking, geneaology. Home: 370 W 9th St Salem OH 44460-1556 Office: PO Box 765 Salem OH 44460-0765

SLADACK, DAVID ROBERT, advertising executive; b. Pitts., Sept. 23, 1967; s. Robert and Helen Sladack; m. Rebecca Sladack, July 3, 1999. BS in Mktg., Gannon U., 1990; MBA, Robert Morris Coll., 1993. Credit exec. Kaufmann's Dept. Store, Pitts., 1990-92; media planner, buyer St. George Group Agy., 1993-94, account exec., 1994-98; sr. account exec. Larson O'Brien Agy., 1998-2000; account supr. St. John & Ptnrs., 2000—. Adj. prof. grad. and undergrad. programs Robert Morris U., 1999—. Bd. dirs. Alumni Assn. Sarah Heinz Ho., Pitts., 1994-99, chmn. adv. bd., 1996-97; mem. mktg. com. Pitts. Pub. Schs., 1999. Home: 114 J and J Ln Belle Vernon PA 15012 Office: St John and Ptnrs Foster Plz 6 681 Andersen Dr Pittsburgh PA 15220 E-mail: davidsladack@sjp.com.

SLADE, BERNARD, playwright; b. St. Catharines, Ont., Can., May 2, 1930; s. Frederick and Bessie (Walbourne) Newbound; m. Jill Florence Hancock, July 25, 1953; children: Laurel, Christopher. Ed., Caernarvon Grammar Sch. Eng. Actor: Garden Ctr. Theatre, Vineland, Ont., Crest Theatre, Toronto, CBC-TV, Citadel Theatre, Edmonton, Alta.; screenwriter of over 20 hour TV plays for CBC, CBS, ABC, NBC, 1957—; writer/creator (TV series) Love on a Rooftop, The Partridge Family, The Flying Nun, The Girl with Something Extra, Bridget Loves Bernie; story editor, writer 15 episodes of TV series Bewitched; writer/creator (plays) A Very Close Family, 1962, Same Time Next Year (Drama Desk award 1975, Tony award nomination 1975), Tribute, 1978, Romantic Comedy, 1979, Special Occasions, 1981, Fatal Attraction, 1984, Return Engagements, 1986, Sweet William, 1987, An Act of the Imagination, 1987, I Remember You, 1991, You Say Tomatoes, 1993, Everytime I See You, 1994, Same Time, Another Year, Fling!, 2000; feature films: Same Time, Next Year, 1977, Tribute, 1978, Romantic Comedy, 1979, Shared Laughter-a memoir, 2000. Recipient Acad. award nomination Motion Picture Arts and Scis., 1978. Mem. Dramatists Guild Am., Writers Guild Am. (award nomination), Acad. Motion Picture Arts and Scis. (Acad. award nomination 1978), Soc. Authors and Artists (France). Avocation: tennis. Address: 3254 Oakdell Rd Studio City CA 91604 *I am a prisoner of a childhood dream: to write for the theatre. The fulfillment of that dream has lived up to all my expectations. I believe the theatre should be a celebration of the human condition and that the artist's job is to remind us of all that is good about ourselves. I feel privileged to be given a platform for my particular vision of life, and, whether my plays succeed or fail, I am always grateful for the use of the hall.*

SLADE, BERNARD NEWTON, electronics company executive; b. Sioux City, Iowa, Dec. 21, 1923; s. William Charles and Katherine Gertrude Slotsky; m. Margot Friedlein, Aug. 18, 1946; children: Steven P., Eric J. BSEE, U. Wis., 1948; MS, Stevens Inst. Tech., 1954. Devel. engr. tube divsn. RCA, Harrison, N.J., 1948-55; devel. engr. RCA Labs., Princeton, 1955-56; mgr. tech. program IBM, Poughkeepsie, N.Y., 1956-60, mgr. product ops. Hopewell Junction, 1960-64; mgr. mfg. tech. IBM World Trade Corp., Armonk, 1964-65; corp. dir. of mfg. tech. IBM Corp., 1965-84; sr. cons. Arthur D. Little, Inc., Cambridge, Mass., 1984-86, Gemini Cons., Morristown, N.J., 1986-93; founder and v.p. Yieldup Internat. Corp., 1993-97, also bd. dirs. Bd. dirs. V3 Semicondr. Corp., Anon, Inc. Co-author: Winning the Productivity Race, 1985; author: Compressing the Product Development Cycle, 1992; contbr. numerous articles to tech. jours.; patentee in field; contbg. author: Transistors, 1956, Handbook of Semiconductor Electronics, 1962. 2nd lt. AUS, 1943-46. Mem. IEEE (sr.), Sigma Xi. Home: 12 Merry Hill Rd Poughkeepsie NY 12603-3214

SLADE, EDWIN WALTER, JR. oral surgeon, lawyer; b. Greenwich, Conn., Dec. 9, 1948; s. Edwin W. and Marie M. Slade; m. Ann M. Showan. BA, U. Conn., 1970; DMD, U. Pa., 1974; JD, Temple U., 1993. Bar: Pa. 1994; diplomate Am. Bd. Oral and Maxillofacial Surgery. Intern dental medicine and surgery Med. Coll. Pa., 1974-75; resident oral and maxillofacial surgery U. Conn. Health Ctr./Hartford Hosp., 1974-77; pres. Oral & Maxillofacial Surgeons, P.C., Doylestown, Pa., 1995—. Advisor AAOMS Nat. Ins. Co., Chgo., 1999-2002. Fellow Am. Assn. Oral and Maxillofacial Surgeons; mem. ADA, ABA, Pa. Soc. Oral and Maxillofacial Surgeons, Del. Valley Soc. Oral and Maxillofacial Surgeons. Office: Oral and Maxillofacial Surgeons PC 101 Progress Dr Doylestown PA 18901-2563

SLADE, HARRY WARREN, neurological surgeon; b. Highland Park, Mich., Nov. 29, 1922; s. Leon Harrison and Clara A. (Nestrom) S.; m. Betty Arlene Hummer, Jan. 28, 1950; children: Theodore Leigh, Cynthia Ann Slade Bennetzen; Steven Lawrence, Christina Louise. BS, Wayne U., 1944; MD, Baylor U., 1946. Diplomate Am. Bd. Neurol. Surgeons. Intern Grace Hosp., Detroit, 1946-47; resident in gen. surgery Meth. Hosp., Houston, 1949—53; resident in neurosurgery Hosp. U. Pa., Phila., 1949-52; resident in neurology Grad. Hosp. U. Pa., 1950-51; resident in pediatric neurosurgery Childrens' Hosp. Phila., 1951; pvt. practice neurosurgery Cleve., 1953-57, Waco, Tex., 1957—. Instr. neurosurgery, U. Pa. Sch. Medicine, Phila., 1949-53; sr. instr. neurosurgery, Western Res. U., Cleve., 1953-57; chief neurosurgery Cleve. City Hosp., 1953-57; med. adviser Waco March of Dimes, 1959-87. Co-editor audio cassettes on neurology, neurosurgery. Fellow ACS; mem. AMA, Tex. Med. Assn., McLennan County Med. Soc., Am. Assn. Neurol. Surgeons, Cong. Neurol. Surgeons, Tex. Assn. Neurol. Surgeons, Rocky Mt. Neurosurg. Soc., So. Clin.-Neurol. Assn., Pan Pacific Surg. Soc., Lions, Masons, Shriners. Baptist. Office: Waco Neurol Assn 5016 Lakeland Cir Ste B Waco TX 76710-2911

SLADE, JOHN DANTON, lobbyist; b. Balt., Apr. 5, 1939; s. Eldon and Marie (Smith) S.; m. Dale Iris Walden, Mar. 14, 1964 (dec. Dec. 1965); 1 child, Kenyatta Conrad; m. Deborah Faye Douglas, Dec. 11, 1987. BA in Sociology, Morgan State U., 1964; MA in Sociology, CUNY, 1966. Mgmt. trainee IBM, N.Y.C., 1966-69; producer, dir. WBAL-TV, Balt., 1969-71, WGBH-TV, Boston, 1971-73, KPIX-TV, San Francisco, 1973-75; announcer KEST Radio, 1975-76; gen. mgr. Channel 8 Access TV, 1975-79; owner Swansbriar Plantation, Cumberland, Va., 1979-85; asst. prof. military sci., dept. chmn. Howard U., Bowie State U., Georgetown U., Washington, 1985-88; acting chief Nat. Guard Bur., 1988-92; exec. dir. Assn. Reserve Minority Svc. Members, Inc., 1992—; founder Iota Phi Theta, Inc. Talk show host WOL Radio, Washington; bd. dirs. Meridian Distributors, St. Thomas, V.I.; guest lectr. Stanford (Calif.) U., Northeastern U., Boston, Morgan State Coll., Balt., Merritt Coll., Oakland, Calif., U. Mass., Amherst; mem. spl. com. San Francisco Chronicle; mem. Balt. Community Rels. Commn.; mem. N.G. Drug Reduction Bd., 1990-91. Author: Last Testament of an American, 1993, Flight of an Angel, 1993, The Founding and Ascendancy of Iota Phi Theta, 1994; Man-Made (Guide to Single Mothers Raising Black Boys Alone), 1994, Iota Phi Theta (Ascending to the Next Millenium), 1999; film producer Breaking the Chains of Bondage, 1972. Lt. col. U.S. Army, 1985-92. Recipient Roy Wilkens Renown Svc. award, 1991, Award of Honor, NAACP, Balt., Community Svc. award Les Hommes Civic and Social Club, Hampton, Va., 1991. Mem. Iota Phi Theta (founding mem., bus. mgr. 1963-64). Republican. Office: ARMS 1401 Madison St NW Washington DC 20011-6805

SLADE, JOHN DOWNEY, physician, educator; b. Atlanta, Feb. 19, 1949; s. John deR. and Helen B. Slade; m. Frances Fowler, Dec. 27, 1972. BA, Oberlin Coll., 1969; MD, Emory U., 1974. Lic. physician internal medicine, rheumatology, addiction medicine. Med. epidemiologist Ctrs. for Disease Control, Atlanta and Trenton, N.J., 1977-80; instr. Robert Wood Johnson Med. Sch. U. Medicine & Dentistry N.J., New Brunswick, 1980-82, from asst. prof. to assoc. prof., 1983-97, prof., from 1997, prof. Sch. Pub. Health, from 2000. Bd. dirs. Stop Teenage Addiction to Tobacco, Springfield, Mass., Marin Inst. for Preventive Alcohol/Drug, San Rafael, Calif., 1989-99; mem. Pub. Health Coun., Trenton, 1987—. Co-editor: Nicotine Addiction-Principle and Management, 1993, Nicotine and Public Health, 2000; co-author: The Cigarette Papers, 1996. Chmn. Commn. Smoking or Health, Trenton, 1985-95, Coalition for a Health N.J., New Brunswick, 1992-93; mem. N.J. Group Against Smoking Pollution, Vestry All Saints Episcopal Ch., Princeton, N.J.[ ]Recipient Redway award N.Y. State Med. Soc., 1987, Pres.'s award N.J. Pub. Health Assn., 1990, Osborne award N.J. Health Officers Assn., 1990, Goethe award German Med. Assn., 1995. Mem. ACP, APHA, AMA, Am. Soc. Addiction Medicine (bd. dirs., annual award 1998). Episcopalian. Home: Skillman, NJ. Died Jan. 29, 2002.

SLADE, LYNN, lawyer; b. Santa Fe, Jan. 29, 1948; m. Susan Zimmerman, 1 child, Benjamin, 1 child from a previous marriage, Jessica. BA in Econs., U. N.Mex., 1973, JD, 1976. Bar: N.Mex. 1976, U.S. Dist. Ct. N.Mex. 1976, U.S. Ct. Appeals (10th cir.) 1978, U.S. Ct. Appeals (D.C. cir.) 1984, U.S. Supreme Ct. 1984. Ptnr. Modrall, Sperling, Roehl, Harris & Sisk, PA, Albuquerque, 1976—. Adj. prof. U. N.Mex. Sch. Law, Albuquerque, 1990. Editor N.Mex. Law Rev., 1975-76; contbr. articles to profl. jours. Trustee-at-large Rocky Mountain Min. L. Found., 1995—97; bd. dirs. N.Mex. First, 1999—, co-chair nominating and membership com., 2001—. Fellow N.Mex. Bar Found.; mem. ABA (sect. of environ., energy and resources, membership officer 1998-2000, chair com. on Native Am. natural resources 1991-94, coun. mem. 1995-98, mem. sects. litigation, dispute resolution, internat. law, pub. utilities and comm., and transp. law), N.Mex. State Bar (chair, bd. dirs. sect. of natural resources 1983-87, bd. dirs. Indian law sect. 1987-90). Home: 143 Olguin Rd Corrales NM 87048-6930 Office: Modrall Sperling Roehl Harris & Sisk PA 500 4th St NW Ste 1000 Albuquerque NM 87102-2186 E-mail: lslade@modrall.com.

SLADE, PAUL GRAHAM, physicist; b. Blackpool, United Kingdom, Dec. 19, 1941; came to the U.S., 1966; s. William Horace and Doris May (Kinnaird) S.; m. Hilary Newton, Aug. 7, 1965; children: Holly Claudia, Peter Grayson. BS in Physics, U. Wales, 1963, PhD in Physics, 1966; MBA, U. Pitts., 1973. Sr. engr. Westinghouse Sci. and Tech. Ctr., Pitts., 1966-72, mgr. power interruption rsch., 1972-75, mgr. power interruption and plasma systems, 1975-83, mgr. plasma and nuclear sci., 1983-90, cons. engr., dir. internat. tech. devel., 1990-93; mgr. vacuum interrupter tech. Cutler Hammer, Horseheads, N.Y., 1993—. Pres., v.p. bd. dirs. CLO Assocs., 1992-93. Author: Circuit Interruption, 1984; contbr. over 45 articles to profl. jours.; editor: IEEE Transactions CHMT, 1987—. Exec. com. Civic Light Opera Assocs., Pitts., 1990-93. Fellow IEEE (adcom 1987—, Ragnar Holm scientific achievement 1985). Achievements include 14 patents; research on the unique behavior of refractory-silver contacts after arc erosion and the effect of surface chemistry on long term stability of contact resistance.

SLADE, REJANE DE OLIVEIRA, Portuguese language educator; b. Santo Antônio do Monte, Minas Gerais, Brazil, Sept. 2, 1938; came to U.S., 1985; d. Alvaro and Erundina Batista (Castro) De Oliveira; m. John Anderson Slade, Jan. 22, 1988. Cert. in elem. edn., Our Lady of Oliveira Coll., Minas Gerais, 1957; degree in sch. adminstrn., Inst. Edn., Belo Horizonte, Minas Gerais, 1967; B in Edn., Philosophy U. Belo Horizonte, 1972; studies in art and art history, Fed. U., Belo Horizonte, 1974, 82-84. Cert. tchr., sch. supr., sch. dir., sch. insp. Tchr. history and Portuguese Our Lady of Fatima Sch., Santo Antônio do Monte, 1960-65; elem. sch. tchr. Minas Gerais State Govt., 1959-61, sch. dir., 1961-65, program supr. Belo Horizonte, 1968-70, tchr. adminstrn. and psychology, 1972-73, insp. schs., 1970-84; instr. Portuguese SUNY/Med. Sch. Columbia U., N.Y.C., 1989-91, NYU, N.Y.C., 1992—, New Sch. for Social Rsch., N.Y.C., 1993—. Gen. ptnr. Braminas, Bklyn., 1989—. Author: Português Básico Para Estrangeiros, 1993; one woman art exhbns. include Varig Airlines, N.Y.C., 1990, Ministry of Comm., Brasilia, Brazil, 1981; group shows in Brazil, U.S., France, Israel. Mem. Am. Assn. Tchrs. Spanish and Portuguese, Nat. Assn. Women Artists, Art Students League, Brazilian-Am. C. of C. Roman Catholic. Avocations: gardening, travel, crafts. Office: Braminas 175 Luquer St Brooklyn NY 11231-4011

SLADE, ROY, artist, college president, museum director; b. Cardiff, U.K., July 14, 1933; came to U.S., 1967, naturalized, 1975; s. David Trevor and Millicent (Stone) S. N.D.D., Cardiff Coll. Art, 1954; A.T.D., U. Wales, 1954; D of Arts, Art Inst. So. Calif., 1994. Tchr. art and crafts Heolgam High Sch., Wales, 1956-60; lectr. art Clarendon Coll., Nottingham, Eng., 1960-64; sr. lectr. fine art Leeds Coll. Art, Eng., 1964-67; prof. painting Corcoran Sch. Art, Washington, 1967-68, assoc. dean, 1969-70, dean, 1970-77; dir. Corcoran Gallery of Art, 1972-77; pres., dir. Cranbrook Acad. Art, Bloomfield Hills, Mich., 1977-94. Sr. lectr. Leeds Coll. Art, England, 1968—69; vis. Boston Mus. Fine Arts, 1970; dir. emeritus Cranbrook Art Mus., 2000—. Exhibited one-man shows Howard Roberts Gallery, Cardiff, Wales, 1958, New Art Ctr., London, 1960, U. Birmingham, 1964, 69, Herbert Art Gallery and Mus., Coventry, 1964, Va. State Art League, 1967, Mus. of Arts and Crafts, Columbus, Ga., 1968, Jefferson Place Gallery, Washington, 1968, 70, 72, 73, Park Sq. Gallery, Leeds, 1969, St. Mary's Coll., Md., 1971, Guelph U., Ont., Can., 1971, Hood Coll., 1974, Pyramid Gallery, Washington, 1976, Robert Kidd Gallery, 1981, 92, Herman Miller, Inc., Mich., 1985; group shows in U.K., Washington, Can.; represented in permanent collections Arts Council Gt. Brit., Contemporary Art Soc., Nuffield Found., Ministry of Works, Eng., Brit. Embassy, Washington, Brit. Overseas Airways Corp., U. Birmingham, Wakefield City Art Gallery, Clarendon Coll., Cadbury Bros., Ltd., Eng., Lord Ogmore, Local Edn. Authorities. Mem. D.C. Commn. on Arts.; bd. dirs. Artists for Environment Found., Nat. Assn. Schs. Art; chmn. Nat. Council Art Adminstrs., 1981. Served with Brit. Army, 1954-56. Decorated knight 1st class Order of White Rose (Finland), Royal Order of Polar Star (Sweden); recipient award Welsh Soc., Phila., 1974, Gov.'s Arts Orgn. award, 1988; Fulbright scholar, 1967-68. Mem. Nat. Soc. Lit. and Arts, AIA (hon. Detroit chpt.), Assn. Art Mus. Dirs. (hon.). Home: #C1009 880 Mandalay Ave Clearwater FL 33767 E-mail: roy.slade@worldnet.att.com.

SLADE, WINTON LEE, forester, consultant; b. Angie, La., Feb. 23, 1927; s. Oscar F. and Maysel (Payton) S.; m. Dorothy A. Prevost, Apr. 2, 1953; 1 child, David Lee. BS in Forestry, La. St. U., 1955. State forester Forestry of La., Baton Rouge, 1955-56; chief forester Clements Bros., Amity, La., 1957; asst. ranger U.S. Forest Svc., Natchitoches, 1957, nursery supr. Pollock, 1958-63, forest genetics so. region, 1963-73; saw mill owner P&S Land Devel., Colfax, La., 1973-78; oil lease owner Winn Parish, 1978—. Owner oil leasing, Winnfield, Nactoches, La., 1978, peach orchard Colfax La., 1973-81. Inventor: method of growing conifers in miniature pots for year 'round planting, 1963 (C.M. award). Vol team mem. Makethian, Edwards & Romer, State of La., 1968—, Nat. Rep. Party, 1989. Petty Officer U.S. Navy, 1944-50, South Pacific, Arctic Oceans. Mem. Masons. Baptist. Avocations: travel, hunting, fishing. Home: 419 Sherwood Dr Dry Prong LA 71423-3558

SLADEK, LYLE VIRGIL, mathematician, educator; b. Pukwana, S.D., Oct. 13, 1923; s. Charles Frank and Emma Margaret (Swanson) S.; m. Patricia Knotts, Sept. 12, 1948; children: Susan, Ann, Laura, Karen. BS, S.D. State U., 1948; MA, U. S.D., 1949, Stanford U., 1963; PhD, UCLA, 1970. Tchr. high sch., Mitchell, S.D., 1950-56; asst. prof. math. Black Hills State Coll., 1957-62; prof. math. Calif. Luth. Univ., Thousand Oaks, 1963-94, prof. emeritus, 1994—. Lectr. history WWII. Contbr. short stories, poems to mags. and newspapers. Pres. congregation Our Savior's Lutheran Ch., Spearfish, S.D., 1961. Served as officer U.S. Army, 1943-46, PTO, ETO. Shell Merit fellow, 1956; NSF fellow, 1956-57, 62-63; recipient Meritorious Achievement award edn. S.D. Mines and Tech., 1957; Fulbright-Hays lectr. Bahamas, 1980-81 Mem. Math. Assn. Am., Blue Key, Pi Kappa Delta, Phi Delta Kappa Home: 3243 Pioneer St Thousand Oaks CA 91360-2730 E-mail: patlyle@hotmail.com. *I learned from my parents during the dust bowl years that adversity often can be overcome through patience and determination, and that problems provide challenges that add spice to life. I have sought to return full measure to society for all the opportunities and joys of life that have come my way.*

SLADEK, RONALD JOHN, physics educator; b. Chgo., Sept. 19, 1926; s. James Joseph and Rose (Vachulka) S.; m. Jeanne T. McFadden, Sept. 19, 1953; children: Linda, James, Frances, Stephen, Rosemarie, Edward. PhB, U. Chgo., 1947, SB, 1949, SM, 1950, PhD, 1954. Rsch. physicist Westinghouse Rsch. Labs., Pitts., 1953-60, fellow scientist, 1960-61; assoc. prof. physics Purdue U., West Lafayette, Ind., 1961-66, prof., 1966-91, prof. physics emeritus, 1992—, acting head dept. physics, 1969-71, assoc. dean sci., 1974-87. Vis. scientist Sci. Center, N.Am. Rockwell Corp., Thousand Oaks, Calif., summer 1967; sabbatical scientist Xerox Rsch. Ctr., Palo Alto, Calif., 1976-77 Contbr. articles to profl. jours. With USNR, 1945-46. AEC fellow U. Chgo., 1952-53. Fellow Am. Phys. Soc. Home: 963 Ridgeview Dr Reno NV 89511-8506

SLADEN, BERNARD JACOB, psychologist; b. Chgo., Mar. 30, 1952; s. Mayer and Anne S. BA, U. Ill., 1974; PhD, Washington U., St. Louis, 1979. Intern U. Minn., Mpls., 1976-77; psychologist Mental Health Ctr., Inc., Ft. Wayne, Ind., 1978-80; psychologist, dir. tng. dept. psychology Hines (Ill.) VA Hosp., 1980—; pvt. practice psychology Chgo., 1982—. Asst. prof. Northwestern U. Med. Sch., Chgo., 1983-92; cons. Assocs. in Adolescent Psychiatry Mental Health Resources, Forest Park, Ill., 1985-95, cons. Inst. Psychodiagnostic Interventions & Svcs., 1995—. VA traineeship, 1974-76; NIMH fellow, 1977-78. Mem. APA, Am. Orthopsychiat. Assn. Home and Office: 421 W Melrose St Apt 12D Chicago IL 60657-3882

SLAFF, ALLAN PAUL, naval officer, university administrator, educator, entrepreneur; b. Mt. Vernon, N.Y., Feb. 2, 1923; s. Frank Alfred and Augusta Raye (Scher) S.; m. Mary Lee Schaeffer; children: Randolph Elliott, Valerie Anne. BS, U.S. Naval Acad., 1944; postgrad., U.S. Naval Post Grad Sch., 1949-50, U.S. Naval War Coll., Newport, R.I., 1959-60, Harvard U., 1967. Commd. ensign USN, 1944, advanced through grades to capt., 1965, WWII Battleship Mass. Fast Carrier TF, 1944-46, personal aide to CNO Adm. Arleigh Burke, 1950-51, spl. security officer commd. in Korean War Navy, comdr. USS Lester, Davis, Luce, Albany, 1957-70, sr. naval advisor to Vietnam Navy, 1967-68, ret., 1970; dean, mem. faculty Bus. Sch. Harvard U., Boston, 1970-80; chmn. Luzerne Co. News Co., Wilkes Barre, Pa., 1980-86, LABSPHERE, Inc., N. Sutton, N.H., 1983-94. Cons. Harvard Bus. Sch., 1980-84. Contbr. numerous articles to profl. jours. Bd. dirs. numerous schs., clubs, civic and polit. orgns. Decorated Legion of Merit, Bronze Star, Nat. Order of Vietnam, numerous other decorations U.S. Navy, 1941-70; recipient Disting. Grad. award Wyoming Sem., Kingston, Pa., 1990. Mem. Port Royal Club (sec. bd. dirs.), The Naples Yacht Club (treas., bd. dirs.), Royal Poinciana Golf Club, Port Royal Property Owners Assn. (bd. dirs.), Lake Sunapee Country Club, Lake Sunapee Yacht Club, Baker Hill Golf Club. Republican. Episcopalian. Avocations: golf, travel, photography, gardening. Home: 4151 Gulf Shore Blvd N # 601 Naples FL 34103-2292 also: PO Box 1836 27 Highland Rdg New London NH 03257-4321 E-mail: allanslaff@aol.com.

SLAGLE, JACOB WINEBRENNER, JR. food products executive; b. Balt., Jan. 18, 1945; s. Jacob Winebrenner and Anne (Vernon-Williams) S.; m. Sharon Carol Muth, Nov. 18, 1973 (div. 1982); children: Alexander, Dylan; m. Nina Kathleen Tou, May 20, 1994. Student, U. Ariz., 1963-65; BA in Sociology, U. Md., 1969; diploma, Broadcasting Inst. Md., Balt., 1975. Claims adjuster Govt. Employees Ins. Co., Towson, Md., 1969-71; exec. Slagle & Slagle, Inc., Balt., 1971-81, pres., 1981-92, Denzer's Food Products, Balt., 1992—. Freelance writer for various newspapers and mags.; monthly columnist Jake About Town, Balt. Chronicle, 1989-93; mem. bd. advisors Broadcasting Inst. Md., 1990-93. Bd. dirs. Hist. Balt. Soc., 1979-96, v.p., 1989-96; bd. dirs. Intervention with Pact, Balt., 1982-89; arbitrator BBB Greater Md., Balt., 1983-91; mem. Greater Balt. Com. Leadership Group, 1996. Mem.: Mid-Atlantic Food Dealers Assn. (bd. dirs. 1997—2001), Balt. Blues Soc. (bd. dirs. 1992—2000, sec. 1995—2000), Md. Splty. Foods Assn. (bd. dirs. 1994—, sec. 1995, pres. 1996), Homebuilders Assn. Md. (bd. dirs. remodelers coun. 1989—96), Herring Run Watershed Assn. (treas. 2001—, 2001—), Rotary Club Balt. (bd. dirs. 1992—94, 1996—98, v.p. 1998—99, pres.-elect 1999—2001, pres. 2000—01, Paul Harris fellow 2000). E-mail: jake@denzer.com.

SLAGLE, JAMES WILLIAM, lawyer; b. Marion, Ohio, Nov. 8, 1955; s. Gene and Emily Frances (Weber) S.; m. Heidi Ann Schweinfurth, Feb. 12, 1983. BA in Polit. Sci., Ohio State U., 1977, JD, 1980. Bar: Ohio 1980, U.S. Dist. Ct. (no. dist.) Ohio 1982. Pvt. practice, Marion, 1980-96. Spl. counsel Ohio Atty. Gen., Cols, 1984-88; pros. atty. Marion County, 1985—. Pres. Hardinge Area coun. Boy Scouts Am., 1991-93, v.p. coun., 1989-91, dist. chmn., 1986-87. Mem. Nat. Dist. Attys. Assn., Ohio Pros. Attys. Assn. (pres. 1995). Methodist. Home: 528 King Ave Marion OH 43302-5320 Office: Marion County Pros Atty 133 1/2 E Center St Marion OH 43302-3801

SLAGLE, LARRY B. human resources specialist; b. Templeton, Pa., Dec. 17, 1934; s. William Harry and Luella (Armstrong) S. AB, Wabash Coll., 1956; postgrad., Am. U., 1967-71. Dep. admistr. for mgmt. and budget USDA Animal & Plant Health Inspection Svc., Washington, 1978-88, assoc. adminstr., 1988-90; dir. pers. USDA, 1990-94; pvt. practice human resources and orgnl. cons., 1994—. With U.S. Army, 1957-59, Korea. Named Meritorious Exec. President Reagan, 1985, President Bush, 1991. Avocation: cycling. Home and Office: 208 6th St SE Washington DC 20003-1134

SLAGLE, ROBERT LEE, II, elementary and secondary education educator; b. Carlisle, Pa., Oct. 16, 1962; s. Robert Lee and Hilda Carolyn (Jones) S.; m. Cynthia Jean Phifer, Feb. 8, 1992; children: Robert Lee III, Theodore Calvin George. BA in Bus. and Acctg., Gettysburg Coll., 1984; MA in Adminstrn., George Washington U., 1988; MA in Edn., Beaver Coll., 1994. Cert. tchr. elem. and secondary social studies, Pa. Engr. officer U.S. Army, Ft. Belvoir, Eustis, Va., 1984-88; ptnr., constrn. mgr. Triple S Quality Builders, Mechanicsburg, Pa., 1988-90; constrn. dir. Rite Aid Corp., Harrisburg, 1989-92; tchr. history, econ., govt. Colonial Sch. Dist., Plymouth Meeting, 1992—. Graduation project dir. Plymouth Whitemarsh H.S., 1998—, student coun. sponsor, 1994—; coach Plymouth Whitemarsh H.S. Football, 1991—, weightlifting, 1991—, baseball, 1995—; coach Whitemarsh (Pa.) Twp. Big League Baseball, 1992-97, Plymouth Whitemarsh H.S. Baseball, 1993—. Lay reader St. Mary's Episcopal Ch., Andorra-Phila., Pa., 1992—. Capt. U.S. Army Corps of Engrs., 1984-88. Decorated Army Commendation medal U.S. Army Dept. Def., 1985, Meritorious Svc. medal U.S. Army Dept. Def., 1988. Mem. ASCD, Colonial Edn. Assn. Republican. Avocations: carpentry, weight training and conditioning, hunting, outdoor recreation, American history and politics. Home: 4033 Center Ave Lafayette Hill PA 19444-1425

SLAIGHT, GARY, broadcasting executive; b. Edmonton, Alta., Can., 1951; married; 2 children. BA in English, U. Western Ont. Media estimator McLaren Advt., 1973; promotion mgr. Quality Records, 1974-75, WEA Records, 1975; account exec. Q107, 1977, program dir., 1978, v.p., gen. mgr., 1982, MIX 99.9, 1987-2000; pres., CEO Std. Radio, Inc., Toronto, 1987—, Std. Broadcasting Corp., Ltd., 2000—; gen. mgr. CFRB, Toronto, 1987-2000. Bd. dirs. Can. Acad. Recording Arts and Scis. Mem. bd. Walk of Fame Bd., Iceberg Media. Recipient ann. music industry awards Gen. Mgr. of Yr., 1986, Program Dir. of Yr., 1987, Broadcast Exec. of Yr., 1992, 93, 96, 98. Office: Standard Radio Inc 2 St Clair Ave W Toronto ON Canada M4V 1L6

SLAKEY, LINDA LOUISE, biochemistry educator; b. Oakland, Calif., Jan. 2, 1939; d. William Henry and Georgia Evelyn Slakey. BS, Siena Heights Coll., 1962; PhD, U. Mich., 1967; postgrad., U. Wis., 1970-73. Elem. sch. tchr. Saint Edmund's Sch., Oak Park, Ill., 1958-61; tchr. Resurrection H.S., Lansing, Mich., 1962-63; instr. in chemistry St. Dominic's Coll., St. Charles, Ill., 1967-69; rsch. assoc. Argonne (Ill.) Nat. Libr., 1969-70; project assoc., dept. physiol. chemistry U. Wis., Madison, 1970-73; asst. prof. dept. biochemistry U. Mass., Amherst, 1973-79, assoc. prof., 1979-87, prof., 1987—, head dept. biochemistry and molecular biology, 1986-91, dean Coll. Natural Scis. and Math., 1993-2000, dean Commonwealth Coll., 2000—. Adv. com. arteriosclerosis and hypertension Nat. Heart & Lung and Blood Inst., Washington, 1978-81, mem. rev. com. B, 1981-87; vis. scientist Clin. Rsch. Ctr, Harrow, Eng., 1984-85. Contbr. articles to profl. jours. NSF predoctoral fellow U. Mich., 1963-67, NIH spl. fellow, 1970-73. Fellow Am. Heart Assn. (established investigator 1977-82), Arteriosclerosis Soc. of Am. Heart Assn.; mem. Am. Soc. Cell Biology, Am. Soc. for Biochemistry and Molecular Biology, Sigma Xi, Sigma Delta Epsilon. Office: U Mass Commonwealth Coll 504 Goodell Amherst MA 01003

SLAKTER, EDMUND LEE, psychiatrist; b. N.Y.C., Sept. 9, 1932; s. Philip Slakter and Jean (Rodstein) Glantz; m. Ruth Goldfarb, Sept. 4, 1955; children: Eve, Paul, Mark, Lynn. BS, Bklyn. Coll., 1953; MD, SUNY, N.Y.C., 1957. Diplomate Am. Bd. Neurology and Psychiatry. Intern Jewish Hosp. Bklyn., 1957-58; resident Bronx Mcpl. Hosp. Albert Einstein Coll. Medicine, 1958-61; fellow in psychosomatic medicine Bronx Mcpl. Hosp., 1961; affiliated staff psychoanalyst N.Y. Psychoanalytic Inst., N.Y.C., 1970—2002; assoc. attending psychiatrist Mt. Sinai Hosp., 1977-95; assoc. prof. Mt. Sinai Sch. Medicine, 1977-95; ret., 1995. Examiner N.Y. Psychoanalytic Inst. Author: Countertransference, 1988; contbr. articles to profl. jours. Mem. Internat. Psychoanalytic Assn., Am. Psychoanalytic Assn., N.Y. Psychoanalytic Soc. Avocations: tennis, travel, music, theatre. E-mail: edmundslakter@aol.com.

SLAMET, YOHAN ROBERTUS, communications executive; b. Bogor, Indonesia, Jan. 9, 1950; s. Budi Jakobus Beng Hoey and Elly Magdalena (Gin Nio) S.; m. Maria Magdalena Sin Lian, Jan. 20, 1993. BA, U. Jayabaya, 1976; MA, Sch. Ministry, San Diego, 1980; M in Orgnl. Communications, Inst. PPM, Jakarta, 1985; M in Mgmt., Prasetia Mulia Inst., 1987. Gen. coord. Cath. Student Assn., Jakarta, 1974-77; cons. Archbishop of Jakarta, 1975-78; store mgr. C.V. Toko Buku Tropen, Jakarta, 1982-85; mgr. Tropen, 1985-88; gen. mgr. Panca Sakti Jaya, 1988-92; vice dir. Persatuan Abadi, 1992—. Cons. Cath. Charismatic Renewal, Jakarta, 1983-88; mng. distbr. Asian Productivity Orgn., Tokyo, 1985-97; bd. dirs. Tropen Groups. Contbr. articles to profl. jours. Chmn. Cath. Student Movement, Jakarta, 1974; chmn. Ecumenical Cath. Commn., Jakarta, 1988. Avocations: reading, writing, photography, painting, recreation. Home: Jalan Harpa II Blok AA # 12 Jakarta Utara 14250 Indonesia Office: Persatuan Abadi Jalan Pasar Baru 113 Jakarta Pusat 10710 Indonesia Fax: (62-21) 3800566. E-mail: tropen@cbn.net.id.

SLANGAL, LOVELLA JOEANN, artist; b. Tonti, Ill., July 29, 1923; d. Lawrence Henry and Ruth LouVisa (Dudley) Smith; m. Neil Richard Hill, Feb. 2, 1940 (div. Nov. 1947); children: Lawrence L. Hill, Victor P. Hill; m. Harold Jones, Nov. 28, 1947 (div. 1954); children: Joan Carole Jones, Bruce Olin Jones; m. Frank Jerry Slangal, Jan. 27, 1968 (div. 1981). Seamstress, 1965. Pres. Sage Brushersart, Bassett, Nebr., 1973-78, Ainsworth (Nebr.) Art Guild, 1980-81; scout leader Boy Scouts Am., St. Charles, Ill., 1957-61; chaplain Profl. Bus. Women, St. Charles, 1959-60; cert. nurses aid Sr. Ctr. Ainsworth, 1981-85. Named Artist of the Mo. Ainsworth (Nebr.) Art Guild, 1983—. Avocations: gardening, auctions.

SLANSKY, JERRY WILLIAM, investment company executive; b. Chgo., Mar. 8, 1947; s. Elmer Edward and Florence Anna (Kosobud) S.; m. Marlene Jean Cannella, Jan. 29, 1950; children: Brett Matthew, Blake Adam. BA, Elmhurst Coll., 1969; MA, No. Ill. U., 1971. Mktg. rep. Bantam Book Co., Chgo., 1972-73, Charles Levy Circulating Co., Chgo., 1973-76; account exec. Merrill Lynch, 1976-77, CIBC-Oppenheimer & Co., Inc., Chgo., 1977—, asst. v.p., 1978, v.p., 1979, sr. v.p., 1981, mng. dir., 1986, ptnr., 1986—. Bd. dirs. Lake Geneva (Wis.) Beach Assn., 1987—, Glen Ellyn Youth Ctr., Glenbard West H.S., pres., 1998-99; mem. bus. affairs com. Presbytery of Chgo., 1999—. Mem. Nat. Assn. Securities Dealers (arbitrator 1988—), N.Y. Stock Exch., Chgo. Bd. Options, Am. Arbitration. Assn, Omaha C. of C. Presbyterian. Avocations: swimming, water skiing, golf, snow skiing. Office: CIBC-Oppenheimer 311 S Wacker Dr Chicago IL 60606-6627

SLAP, JOSEPH WILLIAM, psychiatrist; b. N.Y.C., Aug. 27, 1927; s. Leonard and Elizabeth (Goodman) S.; m. Elizabeth Draper Sagle, Oct. 23, 1954; children: Laura, Robert, Leonard, Edward. BS, CCNY, 1948; MD,

Hahnemann Med. Coll., 1952. Diplomate Am. Bd. Psychiatry and Neurology. Intern Phila. Gen. Hosp., 1952-53, resident in psychiatry, 1953-54, Hillside Hosp., Glen Oaks, N.Y., 1954-56; pvt. practice Phila., 1956—. Tng. analyst Inst. of Phila. Assn. for Psychoanalysis, Bala Cynwyd, Pa., 1976—; clin. prof. psychiatry Hahnemann Med. Coll., Phila., 1974-90, Jefferson Med. Coll., Phila., 1990—. Author: (with L. Slap-Shelton) The Schema in Clinical Psychoanalysis, 1991; contbr. articles to profl. jours. With U.S. Army, 1946-47. Mem. AMA, Am. Psychiatric Assn., Am. Psychoanalytic Assn., Phila. Assn. for Psychoanalysis, Phi Beta Kappa, Alpha Omega Alpha. Home: 553 Heath Rd Merion Station PA 19066-1422 Office: Psychiatric Assocs 1601 Walnut St Ste 1312 Philadelphia PA 19102-2908 E-mail: joslap@aol.com.

SLATE, FLOYD OWEN, chemist, materials scientist, civil engineer, educator, researcher; b. Carroll County, Ind., July 26, 1920; s. Ora George and Gladys Marie (Miller) S.; m. Margaret Mary Magley, Oct. 14, 1939; children: Sally Lee Slate McEnteer, Sandra Kay Slate Miller, Rex Owen. BS, Purdue U., 1941, MS, 1942, PhD, 1944. Chemist Manhattan Project, Columbia U., N.Y.C. and Decatur, Ill., 1944-46; asst. prof. civil engring. Purdue U., Lafayette, Ind., 1946-49; v.p., dir. Geotechnics & Resources Inc., White Plains, N.Y., 1959-63; prof. engring. materials Cornell U., Ithaca, 1949-87; prof. emeritus, 1987. Internat. lectr., cons. concrete, low-cost housing. Author books, research papers on concrete, low-cost housing, soil stabilization, 1944—. Recipient Excellence in Teaching award Cornell U., 1976, sr. fellow East-West Center, 1976, NSF research grantee, 1960-86 Fellow Am. Concrete Inst. (hon., Wason Research medal 1957, 65, 74, 86, Anderson award 1983), Am. Inst. Chemists; mem. ASCE, ASTM, Am. Chem. Soc. Achievements include research on internal structure of concrete vs. properties, chemistry applied to engring. problems, and low-cost housing for developing countries. Home: 255 The Esplanade N Apt 306 Venice FL 34285-1518 Office: Hollister Hall Cornell U Ithaca NY 14853 *Think positively and be optimistic. Be considerate of others, try to help others, and enjoy life.*

SLATE, JOE HUTSON, psychologist, educator; b. Hartselle, Ala., Sept. 21, 1930; s. Murphy Edmund and Marie (Hutson) S.; m. Rachel Holladay, July 1, 1950; children: Marc Allan, John David, James Daryl. BS, Athens Coll., 1960; MA, U. Ala., 1965, PhD, 1970. Mem. faculty Athens (Ala.) State Coll., 1965-92, prof. psychology, 1974-92, chmn. behavioral scis., 1974-92; pvt. practice psychology Athens, 1970-92, Hartselle, 1992—; v.p. Slate Security Systems, Ala., 1984—. Author: Psychic Phenomena, 1988, Self-Empowerment, 1991, Psychic Empowerment, 1995, Psychic Empowerment for Health and Fitness, 1996, Astral Projection, 1998, Aura Energy for Health Healing, and Balance, 1999, Rejevenation: Strategies for Living Younger, Longer and Better, 2001, Psychic Vampires, 2002. Named hon. prof. U. Montevallo, 1973, prof. emeritus Athens State U., 1992. Mem. APA, Am. Soc. Clin. Hypnosis, Inst. Parapsychol. Rsch. (founder), Coun. for Nat. Register Health Svc. Providers in Psychology, NEA, Ala. Edn. Assn., Delta Tau Delta, Phi Delta Kappa, Kappa Delta Pi. Home: 1807 Highway 31 NW Hartselle AL 35640-4442 Office: 310 E Main St Hartselle AL 35640

SLATE, JOHN BUTLER, biomedical engineer; b. Schenectady, N.Y., Sept. 27, 1953; s. Herbert Butler and Violet (Perugi) S. BSEE, U. Wis., 1975, MEE, 1977, PhDEE, 1980. Spl. fellow of cardiovascular surgery U. Ala., Birmingham, 1980-81, dept. biomed. research engr., 1981-82; microbiology fellow, 1981-82; sr. research engr. IMED Corp., San Diego, 1982-83, sr. research scientist, 1983-86; sci. dir. Pacesetter Infusion Ltd. (dba MiniMed Technologies), Sylmar, 1986-87; v.p. tech. MiniMed Technologies, 1987-91; v.p. R & D Siemens Infusion Systems, 1991-93; v.p. tech. devel. Via Med., San Diego, 1993-94; pres. Slate Engring., 1997—2002, Avant Drug Delivery Systems, Inc., San Diego, 1997—; sr. v.p. ops. Slate Engring., 2002—. Mem. IEEE (IEE Ayrton award), Sigma Xi. Office: Slate Engring 3914 Kendall St San Diego CA 92109-6129 E-mail: jslate@san.rr.com.

SLATER, BRIAN, writer; b. Arlington Heights, Ill., June 19, 1973; s. Robert Vincent and Kathe Lynn Slater; m. Debra Renee Staudt (div. Feb. 27, 2002). Author Slate Raven Novels, Ill., 1993—. Author: (novels) Civilized War 2023, 2000, Fresh Start, 2001. Mem.: Knights in Shining Leather (life; swordfighting trainer 1991—2002). Avocations: swimming, martial arts, sword collecting.

SLATER, CHARLES JAMES, construction company executive; b. Munich, Feb. 16, 1949; s. Robert Marsh and Mary Elizabeth (James) S.; m. Pamela S. Senning, Sept. 17, 1974 (div. Apr. 1992); children: Mary Katherine, Robert Charles; m. Kristie J. Alexander, May 11, 1992. BA in Polit. Sci., U. Tenn., 1974. Cert. safety and health mgr. Safety mgr. Daniel Internat. Co., Kingsport, Tenn., 1981-83, safety and med. mgr. Georgetown, S.C., 1983-84; risk mgmt. mgr. Yeargin Inc., Kingsport, 1985-88, Omaha, 1990, resident engr. Frankfort, Ind., 1991, Florence, S.C., 1991; safety and risk mgmt. dir. Harbert-Yeargin Inc., Greenville, 1992-96; safety and health mgr. Fluor-Daniel Inc., Seaford, Del., 1996—. Bd. advisors Assoc. Bldrs. and Contractors/Nat. Safety Coun., Washington, 1993—. Pres. Tenn. Vol. Firefighters Assn., Sullivan County, 1987-89, Kingsport Area Safety Coun., 1989. Mem. Am. Inst. Constructors (chpt. pres. 1993-94), Am. Soc. Safety Engrs., Nat. Safety Mgmt. Soc., Constrn. Industry Coop. Alliance (instr. 1992), Safety Dirs. League (charter), Constrn. Specifications Inst. Episcopalian. Avocations: golf, chess, reading, cinematography. Home: PO Box 361 Seaford DE 19973-0361 Office: Fluor-Daniel Inc 500 Woodland Rd Seaford DE 19973-4398

SLATER, DORIS ERNESTINE WILKE, business executive; b. Oakes, N.D.; d. Arthur Waldemar and Anna Mary (Dill) Wilke; m. Lawrence Bert Slater, June 4, 1930 (dec., 1960). Grad. high sch. Sec. to circulation mgr. Mpls. Daily Star, 1928-30; promotion activities Lions Internat. in U.S., Can., Cuba, 1930-48; exec. sec. parade and spl. events com. Inaugural Com., 1948-49; exec. sec. Nat. Capital Sesquicentennial Commn., 1949-50, Capitol Hill Assos., Inc., 1951, Pres.'s Cup Regatta, 1951; adminstrv. asst. Nat. Assn. Food Chains, 1951-60; v.p., sec.-treas. John A. Logan Assos., Inc., Washington, 1960— ; v.p., sec.-treas. Logan, Seaman, Slater, Inc., 1962— ; mng. dir. Western Hemisphere, Internat. Assn. Chain Stores, 1964— . With pub. relations div. Boston Met. chpt. ARC, 1941-42; mem. Nat. Cherry Blossom Festival Com., 1949— ; mem. Inaugural Ball Com., 1953, 57, 65. Methodist. Lion. Home and Office: 2500 Wisconsin Ave NW Washington DC 20007-4504

SLATER, EVE, federal agency administrator; 2 children. Grad., Vassar Coll. Cert. internal medicine and cardiology. Intern and resident Mass. Gen. Hosp., chief resident medicine; chief hypertension unit, asst. prof. medicine Harvard Med. Sch., 1977—82; sr. dir. biochem. endocrinology Merck Rsch. Labs., 1983—88, sr. v.p. external policy, v.p. corp. pub. affairs; asst. sec. for health Dept. HHS, Washington, 2002—. Chmn. Internat. Conf. on Harmonization Com. on the Structure and Content of Clin. Studies Reports; chmn. regulations adv. bd. Ctr. for Medicine Rsch.; mem. Keystone Nat. Policy Dialogue on HIV; founder Forum for HIV Rsch. Mem.: Phi Beta Kappa. Avocation: flute. Office: Dept HHS Pub Health and Sci 200 Independence Ave SW Washington DC 20201*

SLATER, GARY, retail executive; Pres., CEO BW Techs., Calgary, Canada. Office: BW Tech 2840 2d Ave SE Calgary AB Canada T2A 6T7

SLATER, JAMES ALEXANDER, entomologist, educator; b. Belvidere, Ill., Jan. 10, 1920; s. Ray Alvin and Gladys (Banks) S.; m. Elizabeth Thackston, Feb. 20, 1943; children: James Alexander, Jacquelyn, Samuel, Lydia. BA, U. Ill., 1942, MS, 1947; PhD, Iowa State U., 1950. Asst. prof. Iowa State U., Ames, 1950-53, U. Conn., Storrs, 1953-55, assoc. prof., 1955-60, prof., 1960-87, head dept zoology and entomology, 1961-67, emeritus prof., 1987—, head sect. systematics, evolutionary biology, 1970-82. State ornithologist, Conn., 1955-80; commr. Conn. Geol. and Natural History Survey, 1960s; mem. Conn. Accrediting Bd. Higher Edn., 1960s. Contbr. articles to profl. jours., chpts. to books. Served to lt. USNR, 1943-46. Recipient Faculty Rsch. award, U. Conn. Alumni Assn., 1972, Founder's Meml. ESA award, 1996, Thomas Say award, ESA, 1996, citation of merit, Conn. State Assembly, 2001. Fellow Entomol. soc. Am. (L.O. Howard Disting. Rsch. award 1986); mem. Royal Entomol. Soc. London, Entomol. Soc. South Africa, Assn. Gravestone Studies (Harriet Forbes Meml. award 1981), Nat. Milk Glass Collectors Soc. (pres. 1987-91), Soc. Systematic Zoology (pres. 1983-85). Democrat. Avocations: antique glass collecting. Home: 373 Bassetts Bridge Rd Mansfield Center CT 06250-1305 Office: U Conn Life Sci U 43 Storrs Mansfield CT 06269-0001

SLATER, JAMES MUNRO, radiation oncologist; b. Salt Lake City, Jan. 7, 1929; s. Donald Munro and Leone Forestine (Fehr) S.; m. JoAnn Strout, Dec. 28, 1948; children: James, Julie, Jan, Jerry, Jon. BS in Physics, U. Utah, Utah State U., 1954; MD, Loma Linda U., 1963; PhD (hon.), Andrews U., Berrien Springs, Mich., 1996. Diplomate Am. Bd. Radiology. Intern Latter Day Saints Hosp., Salt Lake City, 1963-64, resident in radiology, 1964-65; resident in radiotherapy Loma Linda U. Med. Ctr., White Meml. Med. Center, L.A., fellow in radiotherapy, 1967-68, U. Tex.-M.D. Anderson Hosp. and Tumor Inst., Houston, 1968-69; from faculty to dir. Loma Linda U., Calif., 1975—93; dir. Cancer Inst. Loma Linda (Calif.) U., 1993—; treas. Med. Ctr., 1995-96; founder, dir. Loma Linda U./NASA Radiation Biology Lab., Calif., 1997—. Co-dir. cmty. radiology oncology program L.A. County-U. So. Calif. Comprehensive Cancer Ctr., 1978-83; mem. cancer adv. coun. State of Calif., 1980-85; clin. prof. U. So. Calif., 1982—; founding mem. Proton Therapy Coop. Group, 1985—, chmn. 1987-91; cons. charged particle therapy program Lawrence Berkeley Lab., 1986-94; cons. R&D monoclonal antibodies Hybritech Inc., 1985-94, bd. dirs., 1985-94; cons. Berkeley lab., 1986-94; mem. panel cons. Internat. Atomic Energy Agy. UN, 1994—; cons. Sci. Applications Internat. Corp., 1979, 89-91. Bd. dirs. Am. Cancer Soc., San Bernardino/Riverside, 1976—, exec. com., 1976—; pres. Inland Empire chpt., 1981-83. NIH fellow, 1968-69; recipient exhbn. awards Radiol. Soc. N.Am., 1973, exhbn. awards European Assn. Radiology, 1975, exhbn. awards Am. Soc. Therapeutic Radiologists, 1978, Alumnus of Yr. award, 1993-94. Fellow Am. Coll. Radiology; mem. AAAS, AMA, ACS (liaison mem. to commn. on cancer 1976-84), Am. Radium Soc., Am. Soc. Clin. Oncology, Am. Soc. Therapeutics Radiologists, Assn. Univ. Radiologists, Soc. for Clinical Trials, N.Y. Acad. Scis., Calif. Med. Assn., Calif. Radiol. Soc., Gilbert H. Fletcher Soc. (pres. 1981-82), Loma Linda U. Med. Sch. Alumni Assn., Radiol. Soc. N.Am., Bernardino County Med Soc., Soc. Chairmen Of Acad. Radiation Oncology Programs, Alpha Omega Alpha. Achievements include development of world's first proton accelerator system for treating patients with cancer and some benign diseases in a hospital environment; development of world's first computer assisted radiation treatment planning system utilizing patient's digitized anatomic images with overlying radiation distribution images. Home: 181 White Horse Trl Palm Desert CA 92211-8937 Office: Loma Linda U Med Ctr Radiation Medicine 11234 Anderson St Loma Linda CA 92354-2804 E-mail: jmslater@dominion.llumc.edu.

SLATER, JESS EVERETT, artist; b. Westfield, Mass., Dec. 31, 1910; s. Jess G. and Eva M. (Warman) S.; m. Helen E. Kozlowski, Sept. 1956. Grad. H.S., Westfield, Mass.; studied with Marco Zim, N.Y.C. Indsl. artist Hamilton Std., Windsor Locks, Conn., 1954-68. Group shows include Nat. Exhbn., Old Forge, N.Y., 1987, 89, 93, 97, New Eng. Water Color Soc. (Merit award), Water Color USA, Nat. Soc. Acrylic Painters; represented in numerous permanent collections. Mem. Midwest Water Color Soc. (Members award 1989). Democrat. Home: 42 Pomeroy Meadow Rd Southampton MA 01073-9410 E-mail: bracreto@javanet.com.

SLATER, JOSEPH ELLIOTT, educational institute administrator; b. Salt Lake City, Aug. 17, 1922; m. Annelore Kremser, Dec. 20, 1947; children: Bonnie Karen Hurst, Sandra Marian Slater BA with honors, postgrad., U. Calif., Berkeley, 1943; LLB with honors, Colo. Coll.; PhD (hon.), U. Denver, U. N.H., Kung Hee, Korea. Teaching asst., reader U. Calif.-Berkeley, 1942-43; dep. U.S. sec. Allied Control Council, Berlin, Germany, 1945-48; UN planning staff Dept. State, Washington, 1949; sec.-gen. Allied High Commn. for Germany, Bonn, 1949-52; exec. sec., U.S. spl. rep. in Europe, U.S. sec. to U.S. del. to NATO and OEEC, Paris, France, 1952-53; chief economist Creole Petroleum Corp. (Standard Oil Co. N.J.), Caracas, Venezuela, 1954-57; mem. and dir. internat. affairs program Ford Found., 1957-68, study dir. spl. com. to establish policies and programs, 1961-62; asst. mng. dir. Devel. Loan Fund, Washington, 1960-61; dep. asst. sec. state for edn. and cultural affairs, 1961-62; pres. Salk Inst., LaJolla, Calif., 1967-72, hon. trustee, pres. emeritus; pres., CEO trustee Aspen Inst. for Humanistic Studies, 1969-86, pres. emeritus, trustee, sr. fellow, 1986—; chmn. John J. McCloy Internat. Ctr., 1986—. Pres. Anderson Found., N.Y.C., 1969-72; adv. bd. Volvo Internat.; dir. Volvo N.Am. Sec. Pres.'s Com. on Fgn. Assistance (Draper Com.), 1959; del. Atlantic Conf., 1959; mem. devel. assistance panel Pres.'s Sci. Adv. Com., 1960-61; cons. Dept. State, 1961-68; founder, dir., bd. dirs. Creole Found., 1956-57; trustee Carnegie Hall Corp., 1960-86, Asia Soc., 1971-86, Am. Coun. on Germany, 1971—; mem. vis. com., dept. philosophy MIT, 1971-83; trustee Acad. for Ednl. Devel., Internat. Council Ednl. Devel., John J. McCloy Fund; bd. dirs. Eisenhower Exchange Fellowships, Internat. Inst. Environ. Devel., Ctr. for Pub. Resources. Served to lt. USNR, 1943-46; mil. govt. planning officer London, Paris, Berlin; trustee Lovelace Med. Found., 1993—. Decorated Order of Merit Fed. Republic Germany). Mem. NAS (mem. pres.'s cir.), Century Assn., Coun. Fgn. Rels., Phi Beta Kappa. Clubs: Century Assn. (N.Y.C.), Mid-Atlantic (N.Y.C.). Home: 870 United Nations Plz New York NY 10017-1807 Home (Summer): Apt 11G 870 United Nations Plz New York NY 10017-1818

SLATER, KRISTIE, small business owner; b. Rock Springs, Wyo., Nov. 14, 1957; d. Fredrick Earl and Shirley Joan (McWilliams) Alexander; m. C. James Slater, May 11, 1992. A in Bus. Adminstrn., Salt Lake City Coll., 1978. EMT, Wyo. Cost engr., material coord. Project Constrn. Corp., LaBarge, Wyo., 1985; cost engr., scheduler Flour Daniel Constrn. Co., Salt Lake City, 1985-86, Bibby Edible Oils, Liverpool, Eng., 1986-87; cost engr., safety technician Sunvic, Inc./I.S.T.S., Inc., Augusta, Ga., 1987-88; cost engr. Brown & Root, Inc., Ashdown, Ark., 1988-89, Wickliffe, Ky., 1989, sr. cost engr. Pasadena, Tex., 1989-90, LaPorte, 1990-91; project controls mgr. Yeargin Inc., Thousand Oaks, Calif., 1991-92; corp. controls mgr. Suitt Constrn. Co., Greenville, S.C., 1993-95; assoc. fin. analyst Fluor Daniel Constrn. Co., Seaford, Del., 1996-2000; freelance bus., 2000—. Pres. 4-H State Coun., Laramie, Wyo., 1976; mem. Houston Livestock Show and Rodeo. Avocations: horseback riding, reading. E-mail: kristie82941@earthlink.net.

SLATER, MICHAEL DAVID, communication educator; b. Mpls., May 11, 1953; s. Paul and Lillian Irene (Pollack) S.; m. Diane Borrman, Nov. 5, 1983; children: Megan Claire, Jesse Paul. BA, Columbia U., 1974; MPA, NYU, 1983; PhD, Stanford U., 1988. Cmty. coord. Ctr. for Ind. Living, N.Y.C., 1974-75; assoc. Roslyn Willett Assoc., 1976-78; acct. supr. M.L. Schneider Assoc., 1979-84; prof. Colo. State U., Ft. Collins, 1988—. Presenter in field. Contbr. chpts. to books and articles to profl. jours. Recipient First award NIH-Nat. Inst. on Alcohol Abuse and Alcoholism, 1992-96; grantee NIH-Nat. Inst. on Alcohol Abuse and Alcoholism, Nat. Inst. Drug Abuse, 1995—. Mem. Assn. for Edn. in Journalism and Comm., Internat. Comm. Assn. (chmn. elect health com. divsn.). Office: Colo State Univ Dept Journalism & Tech Comm Fort Collins CO 80523-1785 E-mail: slatermike@aol.com.

SLATER, PAUL BERNARD, physicist; b. Bklyn., Feb. 23, 1940; s. Irwin Slater and Elsa Wrubel; m. Martha Lou Pollock, June 10, 1968 (div. Apr. 1975); children: Matthew Alan, Daniel Alexander. BS in Math., MIT, 1961; postgrad., Harvard Law Sch., 1961-63; MA, PhD in Regional Sci., U. Pa., 1972. Computer programmer NIH, Bethesda, Md., 1963-64; legal rsch. asst. Rothblatt & Rothblatt, N.Y.C., 1965-66; rsch. assoc. U. Pa., Phila., 1972-73; rsch. assoc., asst. prof. W.Va. U., Morgantown, 1973-79; sr. regional scientist HDR Ecoscis., Santa Barbara, Calif., 1980-82; rsch. assoc. U. Calif., 1982—. Cons. Fed. Res. Bank, Phila., 1986; Russian-English transl. Plenum Press, N.Y.C., 1987-95, Springer-Verlag, Heidelberg, Germany, 1990-91; rsch. affiliate Inst. for Theoretical Physics, Santa Barbara, Calif., 1986—. Author: (monographs) Tree Representations of Internal Migration Flows, 1982, Migration Regions of the U.S., 1983; contbr. articles to sci. jours. Asst. health svc. officer USPHS, 1963-64. Recipient Fulbright award, 1985-86; Charles Hayden scholar MIT, 1957-58; rsch. grantee NSF, 1975, NIH, 1982-84. Avocations: ocean swimming, gardening, general sciences, opera. Home: 522 N Alisos St Santa Barbara CA 93103-2505 Office: Inst for Social Behavioral and Econ Rsch University of Calif Santa Barbara CA 93106-2150 E-mail: slater@itp.ucsb.edu.

SLATER, STEWART EUGENE, theatre producer; b. San Antonio, Jan. 18, 1943; s. Oliver Eugene and EvaB (Richardson) S. BFA, Southwestern U., Georgetown, Tex., 1965; postgrad., U. Tex., 1971. Mem. faculty Gladewater (Tex.) Ind. Sch. Dist., 1965-67, Alamo Heights Ind. Sch. Dist., San Antonio, 1967-69; instr. Baylor U., Waco, 1971-72; tech. dir. Everyman Players, Pineville, Ky., 1973-75; asst. adminstrv. dir. Actors' Theatre of Louisville, 1973-76; bus. mgr. Ind. Repertory Theatre, Indpls., 1976-78; gen. mgr. Am. Conservatory Theatre, San Francisco, 1978-79, San Jose (Calif.) Civic Light Opera, 1980-84, exec. prodr., 1984-95, Am. Mus. Theatre San Jose, 1995-99, pres., exec. prodr., 1999—. Actor Everyman Players, New Orleans, 1973; adj. faculty San Joaquin Delta Coll., Stockton, Calif., 1980; dir. Nat. Alliance Mus. Theatre, N.Y.C., 1985-98, pres., 94-96; bd. dirs. Arts Coun. Silicon Valley, San Jose, 1987-97; founding mem. San Jose Arts Round Table, 1983—, chmn, 1985-87. Exec. prodr. over 80 live musical prodns. Bd. dirs. San Jose Convention and Visitors Bur., 1991—, Jt. Agencies Trust, Los Altos, Calif., 1998—. Named one of Outstanding Young Men in Am., 1970. Mem. Rotary. Office: Am Mus Theatre San Jose 1717 Technology Dr San Jose CA 95110 Fax: 408-453-7123. E-mail: sslater@amtsj.org.

SLATER, THOMAS GLASCOCK, JR. lawyer; b. Washington, Mar. 15, 1944; s. Thomas G. and Hylton R. S.; m. Scott Newell Brent, Aug. 31, 1996; children: Thomas Glascock, Tacie Holden, Andrew Fletcher. BA, Va. Mil. Inst., 1966; LLB, U. Va., 1969. Bar: Va. 1969, U.S. Dist. Ct. (ea. dist.) Va. 1970, U.S. Dist Ct. (we. dist.) Va. 1979, U.S. Ct. Appeals (4th cir.) 1975, U.S. Ct. Appeals D.C. 1980, U.S. Supreme Ct. 1981. Assoc. Hunton & Williams, Richmond, Va., 1969-76, ptnr., 1976—. Bd. dirs. Tredegar Industries. Pres. VMI Found., 1995-97. Fellow ABA, Am. Coll. Trial Lawyers; mem. Va. Law Found.; mem. 4th Cir. Jud. Conf., Va. Bar Assn., Va. State Bar Coun. (exec. com.), D.C. Bar Assn., Richmond Bar Assn. (pres. 1989-90), Va. Mil. Inst. Alumni Assn. (past pres.). Office: Hunton & Williams Riverfrnt Plaza East Tower 951 E Byrd St Richmond VA 23219-4074

SLATER, WANDA MARIE WORTH, property manager; b. Thurston, Ohio, Feb. 18, 1927; d. Daniel Harrison and Grace Marie (Neel) Worth; m. Charles Edwin Slater; children: Margaret Grace(dec.) , Daniel Worthington(dec.) , Donald Edwin. Student, Denison U., 1941-45, Bethany Coll., 1945-46. Recipient certs. Ohio Ho. Reps. and Senate, 116th Ohio Assembly, Creative Living, Columbus. Sub. tchr. Licking County Schs., Union Twp., Ohio, 1946; clerical typist Farm Bur. Ins. Co., Columbus, 1947-49; salesperson Avon Co., Clyde, 1954-63; dep. registrar Sandusky County, 1960-64; notary pub. State of Ohio, Clyde, 1965-78, Hebron-Buckeye Lake, Ohio, 1978-98. Owner, mgr. rental property. Editor OFWC Buckeye mag., 1970-74, 88-98. Pres. Welcome Wagon, Clyde, 1957, Clyde Jr. League of Women, 1966, Leads-Licking County Cmty. Action Com., 1988, 94, 2000-01. Recipient Disting. Leadership award 1992, certificate of appreciation CARE. Mem.: Twentieth Century Club (pres. 1976—77), Order Eastern Star (worthy matron Clyde chpt. 1965, 1978, Hebron Eagon chpt. 1988, 1994, 2001), Mut. and Civic Improvement Club (pres. 1994—), Ohio Fedn. Women's Clubs (pres. 1986—88), Gen. Fedn. Women's Clubs. Republican. Avocations: monologues, flower arranging, travel, crafts. Home and Office: 36 Worth Dr Hebron OH 43025-9760

SLATKES, LEONARD JOSEPH, art history educator; b. Hartford, Conn., Jan. 11, 1930; s. Max Slatkes and Ann Goldin. BFA cum laude, Syracuse U., 1952; MA, Oberlin (Ohio) Coll., 1954; PhD, U. Utrecht, 1962. Asst. prof. U. Chgo., 1962-64, U. Pitts., 1964-66; from asst. to assoc. to prof., also Disting. prof. Queens Coll., CUNY, 1966—. Discipline adv. com. for sr. fulbright awards in art history Coun. for the Internat. Exch. of Scholars, Washington, 1989-92, 93-94; exhbn. cons. Ctrl. Mus., Utrecht, 1984-86, N.C. Mus. of Art, Raleigh, N.C., 1997-98; cons. in field. Author: Dirck Van Baburen, 1965, Vermeer, 1981, Rembrandt and Persia, 1983, Rembrandt, 1992; contbg. editor Jour. of Art, 1989-91; contbr. numerous articles to profl. jours. European travel rsch. awards Rsch. Found. of CUNY, 2000, 1999, 98, 96-97, 95-96, 93-94-92-93, 88, 87, 86, 85, 82, 91, 78, 69, Western Europe Area Fulbright grant, 1988-89, rsch. grant Nat. Endowment for the Humanities, 1983-84, U. Pitts.; sr. rsch. scholar Fulbright-Hays, U. Utrecht, 1979-80; Ohio fellowship Inst. of Fine Arts, NYU, 1956-57. Mem. Coll. Art Assn., Historians of Netherlandish Art. E-mail: ljslatkes@hotmail.com.

SLATKIN, DANIEL NATHAN, pathologist; b. Montreal, Que., Can., Aug. 5, 1934; BSc, McGill U., Montreal, 1955, MD, 1959. Licentiate Med. Coun. Can., 1961; diplomate Am. Bd. Med. Examiners, 1962, Am. Bd. Pathology, 1965. Intern Mt. Sinai Hosp., N.Y.C., 1959-60; assoc. medicine Hosp. Med. Rsch. Ctr., Brookhaven Nat. Lab., 1960-61; resident gen. pathology then neuropathology Montefiore Hosp., Bronx, N.Y., 1961-64; resident pediatric pathology Presbyn. Hosp., N.Y.C., 1964-65; registrar morbid anatomy Hammersmith Hosp., London, 1965-66; biochemistry fellow Anna Fuller Fund Centre de Recherches Scientifiques sur le Cancer, Villejuif, France, 1966-67; assoc. pathologist McKellar Gen. Hosp., Ft. William, Ont., Can., 1968-69; asst. prof. SUNY, Stony Brook, 1970-83. Cons. VA Med. Ctr., Northport, N.Y., 1972-89; attending pathologist Med. Rsch. Ctr., 1973-85; scientist med. dept. Brookhaven Nat. Lab., Upton, N.Y., 1972-96; rsch. cons. Inst. Pathology U. Bern, Switzerland, 1996-, pharmacology dept. U. Conn. Health Ctr., Farmington, 1996-; med. dept. Brookhaven Nat. Lab., Upton, N.Y., 1996-, Nanoprobes, Inc., Yaphank, N.Y., 1996-.

SLATON, JOSEPH GUILFORD, social worker; b. N.Y.C., Sept. 29, 1951; s. Joseph Slachta and Hilda Elizabeth (Sims) S.; 1 child, Nicholas Michael. BS, E. Carolina U., 1974; MSW, U. N.C., 1977. Cert. pub. mgr. Cottage parent supr. N.C. Div. Youth Svcs., Rocky Mount, 1974-75, juvenile evaluation counselor Rocky Mount and Butner, N.C., 1975-77; social worker Murdoch Ctr., N.C. Dept. Human Resources, Butner, 1977-78; facility survey cons., mental retardation profl. N.C. Div. Facility Svcs., Raleigh, 1978-81, facility survey cons. long-term care programs, 1981-83, program mgr. health care facilities br., 1983-87, human svcs. planner cert. of need program, 1987-94; sr. analyst, 1994-98; planning coord. divsn. budget planning and analysis N.C. Dept. Health and Human Svcs., Raleigh, 1998—. Pres. Triangle Rsch. & Planning, Ltd., 1999—; spkr. in field. Author: Guide for the Newly Active Democrat, 1996. Asst. scoutmaster troop 300 Boy Scouts Am.; mem. N.C. Rehab. Task Force, Raleigh, 1988-90; chmn. subcom. N.C. Mental Retardation Task Force, Raleigh, 1982-83; active N.C. Regional Strategic Planning Task Force, Raleigh, 1982-83; active N.C. Regional Strategic Planning Task Force on Mental Retardation, 1982; mem. allocations panel Wake County United Way, Raleigh, 1984-95, Health Issues Panel, 2000—; mem. planning com. Wake County Ptnrs. Program Sta. WRAL-TV, Raleigh, 1980, coord. Auction Day, 1981, mem. exec. planning com., 1982; campaign mgr., vol. coord., treas. rep. for N.C. Ho. Reps.; treas. Wake County Dem. Party, 1997—; charter pres. Cary Civitan Club, 1997-98, bd. dirs. 2000-02, lt. gov. N.C. dist. East Area V, 1998-99; field officer State Emergency Response Team, 1999—. Mem. NASW (legis. policy com.), Acad. Cert. Social Workers, Triangle Health Execs.' Forum, Am. Health Planning Assn. Episcopalian. Avocations: sailing, woodworking, golf. Office: 2002 Mail Service Ctr Raleigh NC 27699-2002 E-mail: joseph.slaton@ncmail.net.

SLATTENGREN, LINN, retired judge; b. Frankfort, Ky., Aug. 24, 1938; BA in Physics and Math., U. Minn., 1960, JD, 1964. Dir. rsch. Senate Minority, Minn., 1963; law clerk Atty. Gen. Walter Mondale, 1963; atty. pvt. practice, Minneapolis, 1964-68; co. atty. Chisago Co., Minn., 1968-76; judge dist. ct., 1976—. Writer: (newspaper column) The Law. Mem. dist. com., Boy Scouts Am. Avocations: running, kayaking, skiing, flying. E-mail: lslattengren@hotmail.com.

SLATTER, JOHN GREGORY, research scientist; b. Guelph, Ont., Can., Feb. 7, 1955; came to U.S., 1988; s. Wallace Osborne Conway and Nancy Dalzel (Hanna) S.; m. Vandana Khare, July 23, 1988. BSc in Biology and Chemistry with honors, Lakehead U., Thunder Bay, Ont., 1977; MSc in Pharm. Scis., U. B.C., Vancouver, Can., 1983, BSc in Pharm. Scis., PhD in Pharm. Scis., U. B.C., Vancouver, Can., 1988. Lic. pharmacist, B.C. Postdoctoral fellow U. Wash., Seattle, 1988-90; rsch. scientist Upjohn Co., Kalamazoo, 1990-94, sr. rsch. scientist, 1994-99; sr. scientist Pharmacia Corp., 1991—2001, assoc. dir., 2001—. Contbr. articles to profl. jours. including Drug Metabolism and Disposition, Chem. Rsch. in Toxicology, Xenobiotica. U. B.C. grad. fellow, 1983. Mem. Am. Chem. Soc., Internat. Soc. for Study Xenobiotics, Am. Assn. Pharml. Scis. Achievements include research in toxic symptoms of survivors of the Bhopal Industrial Accident, team mem. for devel. of Zyvox(TM) and Comptosar(TM). Office: Pharmacia Co Product Life Cycle Mgmt 100 Rte 206N Peapack NJ 07977 Home: 18 Chesterbrook Rd Chester NJ 07930-2016 E-mail: j.greg.slatter@pharmacia.com.

SLATTERY, CHARLES WILBUR, biochemistry educator; b. La Junta, Colo., Nov. 18, 1937; s. Robert Ernest Slattery and Virgie Belle (Chamberlain) Tobin; m. Arline Sylvia Reile, June 15, 1958; children: Scott Charles, Coleen

Kay. BA, Union Coll., 1959; MS, U. Nebr., 1961; PhD, 1965. Instr. chemistry Union Coll., Lincoln, Nebr., 1961-63; asst. prof., assoc. prof. chemistry Atlantic Union Coll., South Lancaster, Mass., 1963-68; rsch. assoc. biophysics MIT, Cambridge, 1967-70; asst. prof., then prof. biochemistry Loma Linda U., Calif., 1970-80; prof. biochemistry-pediatrics, 1980—; chmn. dept., 1983-99. Vis. prof. U. So. Calif., L.A., 1978-79. Contbr. articles to profl. jours. NIH grantee, 1979-82, 86-89, AHA (Calif.), 1981-83, 83-84. Mem. AAAS, Am. Chem. Soc. (biochemistry divsn.), Am. Dairy Sci. Assn., N.Y. Acad. Scis., The Protein Soc., Am. Soc. Biochemistry and Molecular Biology, Internat. Soc. Rsch. on Human Milk and Lactation, Sigma Xi. Office: Loma Linda U Sch Medicine Dept Biochemistry Loma Linda CA 92350-0001

SLATTERY, JAMES JOSEPH (JOE SLATTERY), actor; b. Memphis, Feb. 7, 1922; s. James Joseph and Katie May (Carlin) S.; m. Mary Margaret Costello, May 23, 1944 (dec. Aug. 1987); children: James Joseph, John P., Ann, Mary, Nancy; m. Marilyn Daus, Sept. 16, 1989. AB, Hendrix Coll., Conway, Ark., 1947. Pres. Am. Fedn. TV and Radio Artists, 1976-79. Actor. Served with USAAF, 1942-46; to lt. col. USAF (ret.) Recipient Disting. Grad. award Hendrix Coll., 1986. Mem. Screen Actors Guild. Roman Catholic. Address: 5 The Court Of Bayview Northbrook IL 60062-3201 E-mail: jslatt@aol.com.

SLATTERY, JEFFREY, finance educator, consultant; b. Nebr., 1956; s. P. Coryell and H. Slattery; m. S. A. Slattery, 1989; children: J. E., J. P. PhD, U. Ark., 1993. MBA dir. Northeastern State U., Muskogee, Okla., 2001—, assoc. prof. Tahlequah, 1994—. Cons. Slattery Engring. and Mgmt., Broken Arrow, 1996—. Mem.: Decision Scis. Inst. Episcopalian. Avocation: travel. Office: Northeastern State U 2400 W Shawnee Muskogee OK Office Fax: 918-458-2106. Business E-Mail: slattery@nsuok.edu.

SLAUCITAJS, ANDREW PAUL, videographer, video producer; b. Denver, Nov. 10, 1959; s. Andis Slaucitajs and Shirley Ann Jordan; 1 child, Matthew Lurz. TV instr. Rogers State Coll., Claremore, Okla., 1981-83; ind. videographer Strata Prodns., Tulsa, 1983-85; TV prodr. Okla. Ednl. TV Authority, 1985-86; broadcast sales staff Tulsa Electronic Sys., 1986-87; ind. videographer Mediamax, Tulsa, 1987-89; ind. videographer, video cons., lectr., rschr. Slaucitajs Media, 1989—. Prodr. numerous shows; sculptor outdoor steel sculpture Earth and Sky, 1981. Mem. Okla. Anthropology Soc. Republican. Avocations: archeology, sports car racing, photography, art. Home and Office: 4525 E 33rd St Tulsa OK 74135-2061 E-mail: andys@amsiweb.com.

SLAUGHTER, ALEXANDER HOKE, lawyer; b. Charlottesville, Va., Nov. 24, 1937; s. Edward Ratliff and Mary (Hoke) S.; m. Virginia Borah, 1964 (div.); 1 child, David A.; m. Mary Peeples, 1971. BA, Yale U., 1960; LLB, U. Va., 1963. Ptnr. McGuire, Woods, Richmond, Va., 1969—. Episcopalian. Home: 3016 Rugby Rd Richmond VA 23221-3936 Office: McGuire Woods One James Ctr 901 E Cary St Richmond VA 23219-4030 E-mail: aslaughter@mcguirewoods.com.

SLAUGHTER, DJUANIQUE NATÉ, healthcare analyst, consultant; BS in Criminal Justice, Grambling State U., 1993; MPA, Calif. State U., Dominguez Hills, 1998. Med. clinic asst. Green Clinic, Ruston, La., 1993; pub. health intern Dept. Health and Human Svcs., Long Beach, Calif., 1997; project mgmt. specialist Scan Health Plan, 1998; adminstrv. asst. Salick Health Care, L.A., 1998-99; managed care report analyst Health Care Ptnrs., Torrance, Calif., 1999-2000; project mgr. Ops. Health Care Ptnrs., 2000—. HIV/AIDS peer counselor Campus Awareness Prevention, Grambling, La., 1993. Mem. Reach 2010, Reach 2010 Project, 2001—. Am. scholar Grambling State U. Mem.: ASPA, Nat. Assn. Health Svcs. Execs., Women in Health Adminstrn., Am. Coll. Healthcare Execs., Pi Alpha Alpha, Gamma Beta Phi. E-mail: dee-dee@pacbell.net.

SLAUGHTER, EDWARD RATLIFF, JR. lawyer; b. Raleigh, N.C., Sept. 15, 1931; s. Edward Ratliff and Mary McBee (Hoke) S.; m. Anne Limbosch, July 25, 1957; children: Anne-Marie, Hoke, Bryan. AB, Princeton U., 1953; postgrad. (Rotary Found. fellow), U. Brussels, 1955-56; LLB, U. Va., 1959. Bar: Va. 1959, D.C. 1981. Assoc. firm McGuire, Woods & Battle (now McGuire Woods) and predecessors, Charlottesville, Va., 1959-64; ptnr. McGuire, Woods & Battle and predecessors, 1964-79, head dept. litigation, 1964-79, spl. asst. for litigation to atty. gen. U.S., 1979-81; ptnr. firm Whitman & Ransom, Washington, 1981-84; prin. Slaughter & Redinger, P.C., Charlottesville, 1984-95, Slaughter, Izakowitz, Clarke & Nunley, P.C., 1995-96, Woods, Rogers & Hazlegrove, P.L.C., 1996—2002, of counsel, 2002—. Vis. lectr. trial advocacy U. Va., 1970-77, Va. procedure, 1986-91; disting. lectr. U. Tunis, 1996; mem. standing com. on commrs. of accounts Jud. Coun. of Va., 1993—, chmn., 1995-2001. Chmn. Albemarle County (Va.) Dem. Com., 1969-73; pres. Charlottesville-Albemarle United Way, 1972; commr. accounts Albemarle County, 1986—; trustee Lime Kiln Arts, Inc., 1992-98. Served with USNR, 1953-55. Recipient William J. Brennan award U. Va. Trial Advocacy Inst., 1996. Fellow Am. Bar Found., Am. Coll. Trial Lawyers; mem. Am. Bar Assn., D.C. Bar, Charlottesville-Albemarle Bar Assn. (pres. 1976-77), Va. Bar Assn. (pres. 1978), Va. State Bar (bd. govs. internat. practice sect. 1992-2000), Va. Trial Lawyers Assn., Thomas Jefferson Inn Ct. (pres. 1995-96), Farmington Country. Home: 200 Tuckahoe Farm Ln Charlottesville VA 22901-5531 Office: Woods Rogers & Hazlegrove PLC PO Box 2964 250 W Main St Ste 300 Charlottesville VA 22902 E-mail: eslaught@woodsrogers.com.

SLAUGHTER, FREEMAN CLUFF, retired dentist; b. Estes, Miss., Dec. 30, 1926; s. William Cluff and Vay (Fox) S.; m. Genevieve Anne Parks, July 30, 1948; children: Mary Anne, Thomas Freeman, James Hugh. Student, Wake Forest U., 1944, Emory U., 1946-47; DDS, Emory U. Sch. of Dentistry, 1951. Lic. real estate broker. Practice gen. dentistry, Kannapolis, N.C., 1951-89; ret. Mem. N.C. State Bd. Dental Examiners, 1966-75, pres., 1968-69, sec.-treas., 1971-74; chief dental staff Cabarrus Meml. Hosp. (now N.E. Med. Ctr.), Concord, N.C., 1965-66, 75; mem. N.C. Adv. Com. for Edn. Dental Aux. Pers.-N.C. State Bd. Edn., 1967-70; advisor dental asst. program Rowan Cabarrus C.C., 1974-76; Duke Med. Ctr. Davison Century Club. Trustee N.C. Symphony Soc., 1962-68, pres. Kannapolis chpt., 1961; mem. Cabarrus County Bd. Health, 1977-83, chmn., 1981-83, acting health dir., 1981; vice chmn. Kannapolis Charter Commn., 1983-84; mem. City Coun. Kannapolis, 1984-85; Mayor protem, Kannapolis, 1984-85; past active Boy Scouts Am., Eagle scout with silver palm. Served with USN, 1944-46, WW II, ETO, MTO. Recipient Kannapolis Citizen of Yr. award, 1982. Fellow Am. Coll. Dentists (life); mem. ADA (life), Am. Legion, Kannapolis Jr. C. of C. (v.p. 1952), Toastmasters Internat. (pres. Kannapolis chpt. 1963-64), Am. Assn. Dental Examiners (Dentist Citizen of Yr. 1975, v.p. 1977-79), So. Conf. Dental Deans and Examiners (v.p. 1969), N.C. Dental Soc. (resolution of commendation 1975), N.C. Dental Soc. Anesthesiology (pres. 1964), Southeastern Acad. Prosthodontics, So. Acad. Oral Surgery, Am. Soc. Dentistry for Children (pres. N.C. unit 1957), Internat. Assn. Dental Rsch., Cabarrus County Dental Soc. (pres. 1953-54, 63-64, 69), N.C. Assn. Professions (dir. 1976-80), Kannapolis Music Club (pres. 1962-63), Masons, Shriners, Rotary (dir. 1977-80), Omicron Kappa Upsilon, Alpha Epsilon Upsilon.

SLAUGHTER, RICHARD ARTHUR, economist, consultant; b. Twin Falls, Idaho, Nov. 20, 1943; s. Walter Arthur and Mary Viola Slaughter; m. Susan Kay Clark, Aug. 11, 1966; children: Scott, Ryan. BA in Polit. Sci., U. Idaho, 1966; MA in Internat. Rels., U. Denver, 1968, PhD in Internat. Politics, 1974. Asst. prof. polit. sci. West Ga. Coll., Carrollton, 1972-76; economist divsn. fin. mgmt. State of Idaho, Boise, 1976-80, chief economist, 1980-84; pres. Richard Slaughter Assocs., 1984—; dir. Martin Inst. for Peace Studies, mem. adv. bd. U. Idaho, 1996—2000, sr. rsch. economist Ctr. Bus. R&D, 1996—; internat. economist Cen. Asia, 1998—2001. Dir., sec. Boise Com. on Fgn. Rels., 1989—; co-founder Am. Coun. in fgn. Rels., treas. 1995-2000. Editor Idaho Econ. Forecast jour., 1977-84. Bd. dirs. Capitol Youth Soccer Assn., Boise, 1980-89, soccer commr., 1983-86. Mem. Coun. Fgn. Rels. Avocation: tennis.

SLAUGHTER, ROCHELLE DENISE, elementary school educator; b. Kansas City, Kans., Jan. 3, 1956; d. Theodore and Barbara Jean (Williams) Hall; m. Eddie Slaughter, Nov. 1, 1997. AA, Penn Valley C.C., Kansas City, Mo., 1976; BA, U. Mo., Kansas City, 1978, MA, 1985; Edn. Specialist Degree, U. Mo., 1992. Cert. specialist in reading, Mo. Tchr. Kansas City Sch. Dist., 1979-85, reading resource tchr., 1985-95, tchr. grade 1, 1995—. Del. Literacy and Lang. Arts Instrn. Delegation to Peoples Republic of China, 1995. Supt. Sunday sch. Emmanuel Bapt. Ch., 1992—; del. lang. arts & literacy delegation People to People Citizen Amb. Progra, China, 1995; vol. for adult basic edn. program; tutor Laubach Literacy Coun. Kansas City, 1996-97. Recipient IMPACT Reading award Kansas City Reading dept., 1990. Mem. ASCD, NAACP, Internat. Reading Assn. (chpt. v.p. 1994-95, pres.-elect 1995-97, pres. 1997—), Phi Delta Kappa (youth advisor 1993—). Democrat. Baptist. Avocations: reading, computer work, sewing. Office: E F Swinney Applied Skills 1106 W 47th St Kansas City MO 64112-1215

SLAUGHTER-DEFOE, DIANA TRESA, education educator; b. Chgo., Oct. 28, 1941; d. John Ison and Gwendolyn Malva (Armstead) S.; m. Michael Defoe (div.). BA, U. Chgo., 1962, MA, 1964, PhD, 1968. Instr. dept. psychiatry Howard U., Washington, 1967-68; rsch. assoc., asst. prof. Yale U. Child Study Ctr., New Haven, 1968-70; asst. prof. dept. behavioral scis. and edn. U. Chgo., 1970-77; asst. to assoc. prof. edn. and African Am. studies and Ctr. for Urban Affairs and Policy Rsch. (now Inst. for Policy Rsch.) Northwestern U., Evanston, Ill., 1977-90, prof., 1990-97; Constance E. Clayton prof. urban edn. Grad. Sch. Edn. U. Pa., 1998—. Mem. nat. adv. bd. Fed. Ctr. for Child Abuse & Neglect, 1979-82, coord. Human Devel. and Social Policy Program, 1994-97; mem. nat. adv. bd. Learning Rsch. and Devel. Ctr. U. Pitts., Ednl. Rsch. & Devel. Ctr., U. Tex., Austin; formerly chmn., dir. public policy program com. Chgo. Black Child Devel. Inst., 1982-84; dir. Ill. Infant Mental Health Com., 1982-83; mem. res. adv. bd. Chgo. Urban League, 1986-97. Contbr. articles to profl. jours. Fellow APA (mem. divsn. ethnic and minority affairs, com. on children, youth and families, devel. psychology, sch. psychology, bd. sci. affairs 1995-97, mem. editl. bd. Child Devel. 1995-98, Disting. Contbn. to Rsch. in Pub. Policy award 1993); mem. Soc. for Rsch. in Child Devel. (governing coun. 1981-87), Am. Ednl. Rsch. Assn. (editl. bd. Rev. Ednl. Rsch.), Assn. Black Psychologists, Nat. head Start (past mem. R & E adv. bd.), Nat. Acad. Scis. (com. on child devel. and publ. policy 1987-93), Delta Sigma Theta. Office: U Pa Grad Sch Edn 3700 Walnut St Philadelphia PA 19104-6216 E-mail: dianasd@qse.upenn.edu.

SLAVENS, THOMAS PAUL, library science educator; b. Cincinnati, Iowa, Nov. 12, 1928; s. William Blaine and Rhoda (Bowen) S.; m. Cora Pearl Hart, July 9, 1950; 1 son, Mark Thomas. BA, Phillips U., 1951; MDiv, Union Theol. Sem., 1954; MA, U. Minn., 1962; PhD, U. Mich., 1965. Ordained to ministry Christian Ch., 1953. Pastor First Christian Ch., Sac City, Iowa, 1953-56, Sioux Falls, S.D., 1956-60; librarian Divinity Sch., Drake U., Des Moines, 1960-64; teaching fellow Sch. Info., U. Mich., Ann Arbor, 1964-65; instr. U. Mich., 1965-66, asst. prof., 1966-69, assoc. prof., 1969-77, prof., 1977—. Vis. prof. U. Minn., 1967, U. Coll. of Wales, 1978, 80, 93; vis. scholar U. Oxford, Eng., 1980; adv. bd. Marcel Dekker Inc., N.Y.C., 1982—; cons. Nutrition Planning Abstracts-UN, N.Y.C., 1977-79. Author-editor: Library Problems in the Humanities, 1981, (with John F. Wilson) Research Guide to Religious Studies, 1982, (with W. Eugene Kleinbaur) Research Guide to History of Western Art, 1982, (with Terrence Tice) Research Guide to Philosophy, 1983, Theological Libraries at Oxford, 1984, (with James Pruett) Research Guide to Musicology, 1985, The Literary Adviser, 1985, A Great Library through Gifts, 1986, The Retrieval of Information, 1989, Number One in the U.S.A.: Records and Wins in Sports, Entertainment, Business, and Science, 1988, 2d edit., 1990, Doors to God, 1990, Sources of Information for Historical Research, 1994, Introduction to Systematic Theology, 1992, Reference Interviews Questions and Materials, 3d edit., 1994. Served with U.S. Army, 1946-48. Recipient Warner Rice Faculty award U. Mich., 1975; H.W. Wilson fellow, 1960; Lilly Endowment fellow Am. Theol. Library Assn., 1963. Mem. ALA (chmn. coms. 1964—), Assn. Libr. and Info. Sci. Edn. (pres. 1972), Beta Phi Mu. Office: University of Michigan School of Information 550 E University Ave Ann Arbor MI 48109-1092 E-mail: tslavens@umich.edu.

SLAVICK, ANN LILLIAN, retired art educator; b. Chgo., Sept. 29, 1933; d. Irving and Goldie (Bernstein) Friedman; m. Lester Irwin Slavick, Nov. 21, 1954 (div. Mar. 1987); children: Jack, Rachel. BFA, Sch. of Art Inst. of Chgo., 1973, MA in Art History, Theory, Criticism, 1991. Dir. art gallery South Shore Commn., Chgo., 1963-67; tchr. painting, drawing, crafts Halfway House, 1972-73; tchr. studio art Conant H.S., Hoffman Estates, Ill., 1973-74; tchr. art history and studio arts New Trier H.S., Winnetka and Northfield, 1974-80; tchr. 20th century art history New Trier Adult Edn. Program, Winnetka, 1980-81; tchr. art adult edn. program H.S. Dist. 113, Highland Park, Ill., 1980-81; rschr., writer Art History Notes McDougall-Littel Pub., Evanston, 1984-85; tchr. art and art history Highland Park and Deerfield (Ill.) H.S., 1980-2000; tchr. art history Coll. of Lake County, Grayslake, Ill., 1986-88; ret., 2000. Faculty chair for visual arts Focus on the Arts, Highland Park H.S., 1981-85, faculty coord. Focus on the Arts, 1987—; panelist Ill. Arts Coun. Arts Tour, 1999, Evanston Arts Coun., 2000-2002, Ill. Arts Coun. Multidisciplinary Grant Awards, 2001-2002. One woman show Bernal Gallery, 1979, U. Ill., Chgo., 1983, Ann Brierly Gallery, Winnetka, 1984; exhibited paintings, drawings, prints and constrns. throughout Chgo. area; work represented by Art Rental and Sales Gallery, Art Inst. Chgo., 1960-87, Bernal Gallery, 1978-82; group shows at Bernal Gallery; work in pvt. collections in Ill., N.Y., Calif., Ariz., Ohio. Recipient Outstanding Svc. in Art Edn. award Ea. Ill. U., 1992, Mayors award for contbn. to the arts, Highland Park, 1995. Mem. Nat. Art Edn. Assn., Ill. Art Edn. Assn. Avocations: cooking, reading, theatre. Home: 5057 N Sheridan Rd Chicago IL 60640-3127 Office: Highland Park High Sch 433 Vine Ave Highland Park IL 60035-2099

SLAVIK, DONALD HARLAN, lawyer; b. Milw., June 17, 1956; s. Donald Jean and Sally Ann (Croy) S.; m. Cynthia Sue Barfknecht, Jan 5, 1980. BS in Nuclear Engring., U. Wis., 1978, JD, 1981. Bar: Wis. 1981, U.S. Dist. Ct. (ea. and we. dists.) Wis. 1981, Tex. 2002, Colo. 2002. Mem. Habush, Habush & Rottier, Milw., 1981—. Lectr. engring. extension U. Wis., Madison, 1985-95. Author: (with others) Anatomy of a Roof Crush Case, 1985, Seat Belt Handbook, 1987, Crashworthiness, 1989, 98; contbr. articles to profl. jours. Mem. Assn. Trial Lawyers Am. (co-chair exch. com. 1986-87, 91-93, chmn. computer law office tech. 1993-97, 2000—), Wis. Bar Assn., Attys. Info. Exch. Group (bd. dirs., exec. com. 1987—, lectr. 1987—, pres. 2001-2003), Assn. for Advancement of Automotive Medicine (sci. program com. 1996-2001). Office: Habush Habush Davis & Rottier Ste 2300 777 E Wisconsin Ave Milwaukee WI 53202-5381

SLAVIN, ARLENE, artist; b. N.Y.C. , Oct. 26, 1942; d. Louis and Sally (Bryck) Eisenberg; m. Neal Slavin, May 24, 1964 (div. 1979); m. Eric Bregman, Sept. 21, 1980; 1 child, Ethan. BFA, Cooper Union for the Advancement of Sci. and Art, 1964; MFA, Pratt Inst., 1967. One-woman shows include Fischbach Gallery, N.Y., 1973, 1974, Brooke Alexander Gallery, 1976, Alexander Milliken Gallery, N.Y.C., 1979, 1980, 1981, 1983, U. Colo., 1981, Pratt Inst., N.Y.C., 1981, Am. Embassy, Belgrad, Yugoslavia, 1984, Heckscher Mus., Huntington, N.Y., 1987, Katherine Rich Perlow Gallery, 1988, Chauncey Gallery, Princeton, N.J., 1990, The Gallery Benjamin N. Cardoza Sch. Law, 1991, Norton Ctr. for Arts, Danville, Ky., 1992, Kavesh Gallery , Ketchum, Idaho, 1993, exhibited in group shows at Bass Mus. Art, Fla., Whitney Museum of Art, 1973, The Contempory Arts Center, Cin., 1974, Indpls. Mus. Art, 1974, Madison (Wis.) Art Ctr., Santa Barbara (Calif.) Mus., Winnipeg (Can.) Art Gallery, Gensler Assocs., San Francisco, 1986, Eliane Benson Gallery, Bridgehampton, N.Y., 1987, 1989, 1991, 1993, City of N.Y. Parks and Recreation Central Park, N.Y.C., 1989, Benton Gallery, Southampton, N.Y., 1991, Parish Mus., Southampton, 1991, Michele Miller Fine Art, 1993, Dillon Gallery, N.Y.C., 1998, Hebrew Union Coll., 2000—01, Represented in permanent collections Met. Mus. of Art, Bklyn. Mus., Fogg Art Mus., Cambridge, Mass., Hudson River Mus., Yonkers, N.Y., Heckscher Mus., Huntington, N.Y., Cin. Art Mus., Readers' Digest, Pleasantville, N.Y., pub. commns., ; artist mem. design team Hillsborough Area Regional Transit, Tampa, Fla., 2001—03; subject: bibliography Arlene Slavin: Mediating Public Space, 2001. Grantee Nat. Endowment for Arts, 1977-78, Threshold Found., 1991. Home: 119 E 18th St New York NY 10003-2107 E-mail: aslavin@bellatlantic.net.

SLAVIN, KONSTANTIN VLADIMIROVICH, neurosurgeon; b. Baku, Azerbaijan, USSR, Aug. 20, 1969; s. Vladimir Leonidovich and Frangiz Mirzoevna (Gull) S.; m. Ekaterina Yurievna Shashina, Aug. 3, 1990; children: Mikhail Konstantinovich, Svetlana Konstantinovna. MD, Azerbaijan State Med. Inst., Baku, 1988. Nurse Rep. Neurosurg. Hosp., Baku, 1985-88; clin. coord. Postgrad. Inst., Moscow, 1988-90, aspirant neurosurgeon, 1990-92; rsch. fellow U. Ill., Chgo., 1992-94, resident in neurosurgery, 1994-2001, instr. dept. neurosurgery, 2000-01, asst. prof. dept. neurosurgery, 2001—; fellow in sterotactic and functional neurosurgery OHSU, 1998-99. Asst. to editor Surg. Neurology jour., 1993—; contbr. articles to profl. jours., chpts. to books. Recipient Lenin scholarship Azerbaijan Med. Inst., 1987, 88. Mem. AMA, Am. Assn. Neurol. Surgeons, Congress Neurol. Surgeons, Am. Pain Soc. Avocations: computers, collecting stamps. Office: U Ill Chgo 912 S Wood St Chicago IL 60612-7325 E-mail: kslavin@uic.edu.

SLAVIN, MICHAEL J. nephrologist; b. Phila., Apr. 30, 1948; s. Harold Stanley and Anne Rhea Slavin. BS in Biology, Fairleigh Dickinson U., Madison, N.J., 1969; DO, Phila. Coll. Osteo. Medicine, 1973; MBA, Widener U., Chester, Pa., 1997. Diplomate Am. Osteo. Bd. Internal Medicine, An. Bd. Nephrology, Am. Bd. Quality Assurance and Utilization Rev. Physicians, Nat. Bd. Examiners Osteo. Physicians and Surgeons; lic. physician Pa., N.J., Del., Iowa. Intern Meml. Osteo. Hosp., York, Pa., 1973-74; resident in internal medicine Metro. Hosp., Phila., 1974-76, fellow in nephrology and hypertension, 1976-78; clin. asst. prof. medicine U. Medicine and Dentistry of N.J., 1979-89, clin. assoc. prof. medicine, 1989-94; clin. asst. prof. medicine Thomas Jefferson U., 1993-99, U. Iowa Coll. Medicine, 2000—; attending staff, dir. renal and dialysis svcs. Covenant Med. Ctr., Waterloo, Iowa, 1998—, chief medicine, 2002—. Attending staff Metro. Hosp., Phila., 1978-90, West Jersey Hosp., Marlton, N.J., 1983-91, chief subsection of nephrology, 1986-91, John F. Kennedy Meml. Hosp., Cherry Hill, N.J., 1978-91, head divsn. nephrology, 1983-91, instnl. med. exec. bd., 1985-91, clin. mng. editor Clin. Rev., 1979-81; attending staff Cooper Hosp./Univ. Med. Ctr., Camden, N.J., 1983-91, Albert Einstein Med. Ctr., Phila., 1990-98, St. Agnes Med. Ctr., Phila., 1991-98, Meth. Hosp. divsn. Thomas Jefferson U. Hosp., Phila., 1991—, exec. com., 1996-98; attending staff Thomas Jefferson U. Hosp., Phila., 1993-98, courtesy staff, 1998—; mem. peer rev. com. nephrology Iowa Bd. Med. Examiners, 1999—; mem. quality improvement coun. profl. rev. com. Wellmark Health Plan of Iowa, 1999—; mem. continuing med. edn. com., a subcom. N.E. Iowa Med. Edn. Found. Bd. Dirs., 1999—; program chmn. Ea. Regional Osteo. Conv., Atlantic City, 1988; coord. counsel End Stage Renal Disease Network 24, 1979-82, facility planning com., 1979-82. Cons. editor nephrology Jour. Am. Osteo. Assn., 1980-90, Jour. N.J. Assn. Osteo. Physicians and Surgeons, 1981-91; med. specialty adv. bd. nephrology Med. Malpractice Prevention Jour., 1984-86; contbr. numerous articles to profl. jours. Recipient Sophia Freiter Barth award PCOM, 1973, Oncology award, 1973. Fellow ACP, Coll. Physicians Phila., Am. Coll. Osteo. Internists; mem. AMA, Am. Osteo. Assn., Am. Soc. Nephrology, Internat. Soc. Nephrology, Am. Coll. Physician Execs., Pa. Osteo. Med. Assn., Pa. Med. Soc., Iowa Med. Soc., Iowa Osteo. Med. Assn., Blackhawk County Med. Soc. (exec. com., treas. 1999—), Beta Beta Beta. Office: 2710 Saint Francis Dr Ste 510 Waterloo IA 50702-5620 Fax: (319) 272-8695.

SLAVIN, MORRIS, historian, educator; b. Kiev, Ukraine, Russia, July 11, 1913; s. Lazar and Vera (Hansburg) S.; m. Sophie Shirley Lockshin, May 28, 1913; 1 child, Jeanne Slavin Kaplan. BS, Ohio State U., 1938; MA, U. Pitts., 1952; PhD in History, Western Res. U., 1961; DHL (hon.), Youngstown State U., 1989. Tchr. Wilson H.S., Youngstown, Ohio, 1941-42, 44-61; asst. prof. Youngstown State (Ohio) U., 1961-63, assoc. prof., 1963-68, prof., 1969-81, prof. emeritus, 1981—. Adj. prof. Youngstown Coll., 1948-61. Author: The French Revolution in Miniature, 1984 (award Ohio Acad. of History 1985), The Making of an Insurrection, 1986, The Hébertistes to the Guillotine, 1995, The Left and the French Revolution, 1995; contbr. articles and revs. to profl. jours. Sgt. U.S. Army, 1942-43. Fellow Inst. for Advanced Study; mem. ACLU, Am. Hist. Assn., Am. Soc. for French Hist. Studies, Amnesty Internat. Avocations: golf, theater, chess, hiking. Home: 262 Outlook Ave Youngstown OH 44504-1847 Office: Youngstown State U Dept History Youngstown OH 44555-0001 E-mail: mslavin@cc.ysu.edu.

SLAVIN, PETER L. hospital administrator, medical association administrator; AB Harvard U., 1979, MD Harvard U., 1984, MBA Harvard U., 1990. Chief med. officer Mass. Gen. Hosp.; med. dir. Mass. Gen. Physicians Orgn.; pres. Barnes-Jewish Hosp., St. Louis, 1997-99; chair., CEO Mass. Gen. Physicians Orgn., Boston, 1999—. Address: Mass Gen Hosp BUL 208 55 Fruit St Boston MA 02114-2622

SLAVIN, RAYMOND GRANAM, allergist, immunologist; b. Cleve., June 29, 1930; s. Philip and Dinah (Baskind) S.; m. Alberta Cohrt, June 10, 1953; children: Philip, Stuart, David, Linda. AB, U. Mich., 1952; MD, St. Louis U., 1956; MS, Northwestern U., 1963. Diplomate: Am. Bd. Internal Medicine, Am. Bd. Allergy and Immunology (treas.). Intern U. Mich. Hosp., Ann Arbor, 1956-57; resident St. Louis U. Hosp., 1959-61; fellow in allergy and immunology Northwestern U. Med. Sch., 1961-64; asst. prof. internal medicine and microbiology St. Louis U., 1965-70, assoc., 1970-73, prof., 1973—, dir. div. allergy and immunology, 1965—. Mem. NIH study sect., 1985-89; cons. U.S. Army M.C. Contbr. numerous articles to med. publs.; editorial bd.: Jour. Allergy and Clin. Immunology, 1975-81, Tice Practice Medicine, 1973-84, Jour. Club of Allergy, 1978-80. Chmn. bd. Asthma and Allergy Found. Am., 1985-88. With M.C., U.S. Army, 1957-59. Grantee NIH, 1967-70, 84—, Nat. Inst. Occpl. Safety and Health, 1974-80. Master: ACP; fellow: Am. Acad. Allergy and Immunology (exec. bd., historian, pres. 1983—84); mem.: AAAS, Central Soc. Clin. Research, Am. Assn. Immunologists. Democrat. Jewish. Home: 631 E Polo Dr Saint Louis MO 63105-2629 Office: 1402 S Grand Blvd Saint Louis MO 63104-1004 E-mail: slavinrg@slu.edu.

SLAVIN, ROSANNE SINGER, textile converter; b. N.Y.C., Mar. 24, 1930; d. Lee H. and Rose (Winkler) Singer; divorced; children: Laurie Jo, Sharon Lee. Student, U. Ill. Prodn. converter Doucet Fabrics, silk prints, N.Y.C., 1953-57; sales mgr., mdse. mgr. print divsn. Crown Fabrics, 1957-65; owner Matisse Fabrics, Inc. printed fabrics (now Hottmomma Inc.), 1965—. Recipient Tommy award Am. Printed Fabrics Coun., 1978, 93; designated ofcl. printed fabric supplier for U.S. Olympic swimteam, 1984. Office: 1071 Avenue Of The Americas New York NY 10018-3704

SLAVIT, DAVID HAL, otolaryngologist; b. N.Y.C., Sept. 5, 1960; s. Leonard S. and Barbara H. (Levine) S.; m. Robin E. Feldman, July 31, 1983; children: Danielle, Evan, Roni. BS, Cornell U., 1982; MD, Mt. Sinai U., 1986. Cert. in otolaryngology. Intern Mayo Clinic, Rochester, Minn., 1986-87, resident in otolaryngology, 1987-91; with Lenox Hill Hosp., N.Y.C. Asst. prof. Health Sci. Ctr.-SUNY Downstate; cons. Juilliard Sch. Music, N.Y.C., 1994-99; dir. Ames Vocal Dynamics Lab., N.Y.C., 1998-2001. Author, editor: (book) Essentials of Otolaryngology, 1993; author: (books) Voice Disorders, 1995, Rhinologic Diagnosis and Treatment, 1996, Systemic Disease of the Nasal Airway, 1993; contbr. articles to profl. jours. Mem. AMA, Am. Acad. Otolaryngology-Head and Neck Surgery, Am. Acad. Facial Plastic and Reconstructive Surgery, Am. Rhinologic Soc.

SLAVITT, BEN J. lawyer; b. Newark, Dec. 31, 1934; s. Arthur and Berdie (Goodman) S.; children: Lauri, Julie, Donna, John. BA, Bucknell U., 1956; LLB, U. Va., 1959. Bar: N.J. 1959, U.S. Dist. Ct. N.J. 1959, U.S. Supreme Ct. 1973. Ptnr. Slavitt & Cowen PA, and predecessors, Newark, 1959—. Served with U.S. Army, 1959-60. Mem. N.J. Bar Assn. Democrat. Jewish. Office: Slavitt & Cowen 17 Academy St Ste 415 Newark NJ 07102-2905

SLAVITT, DAVID WALTON, retired lawyer; b. Chgo., Mar. 15, 1931; s. Isaac and Fay (Goldstein) S.; m. Roberta Chelnek, July 26, 1953; children: Steven, Denise, Howard. BS, UCLA, 1952, JD, 1955. Bar: Calif. 1956; C.P.A., Calif. Since practiced in Los Angeles; pres. Slavitt & Borofsky (P.C.), 1969-87. Moderator continuing edn. programs. Author articles in field. Served with USNR, 1955. Mem. Am. Assn. Atty.-C.P.A.s (pres. 1964), ABA, State Bar Calif., Calif. Assn. Atty.-C.P.A.s (pres. 1963), Beverly Hills Bar Assn. (vice chmn. continuing edn. of bar 1970, asst. chmn. law practice mgmt. com. 1973). E-mail: d.slavitt@adelphia.net.

SLAVITT, EARL BENTON, lawyer; b. Chgo., Sept. 12, 1939; s. Harold Hal and Rose (Hoffman) S.; m. Amy Lerner, July 12, 1987; 1 child, Gabriel Harrel; children from previous marriage: Andrew Miller, Lesley Deborah. BS in Econs., U. Pa., 1961, JD, 1964. Bar: Ill. 1964, U.S. Dist. Ct. (no. dist.) Ill. 1964, U.S. Supreme Ct. 1971. Assoc. Wisch, Crane & Kravets, Chgo., 1964-67, Ressman & Tishler, Chgo., 1967-69; assoc., then ptnr. Levy & Erens, 1969-78; ptnr. Tash & Slavitt, 1978-81, Katten Muchin & Zavis, Chgo., 1981—. Contbr. articles to profl. jours.; author poems and plays. Vol. Hospice of Ill. Masonic Med. Ctr., Chgo., 1987-89, Pro bono Advocates, 1989, Chgo.

Ho., 1991 (recipient Outstanding Vol. award), Lawyers for the Creative Arts, Bus. Vols. for the Arts, 1992—; bd. dirs. Playwrights Ctr., Chgo., 1987, Jewish Reconstructionist Congregation, Chgo., 1978, 91, 92, Legal Clinic for the Disabled, 1993-96, pres., 1995-96, Sarah's Circle, 1994-96. Mem. Ill. State Bar Assn. (mem. real estate com. 1976, recipient Pro Bono Cert. Accomplishment 1994), Chgo. Bar Assn. (mem. real estate com. 1976, real estate fin. com. 1982), Chgo. Coun. Lawyers (mem. jud. selection com. 1969), Lawyers in Mensa (bd. govs. 1983). Democrat. Jewish. Office: Katten Muchin Zavis 2029 Century Park E Ste 2600 Los Angeles CA 90067 E-mail: earl.slavitt@kmz.com.

SLAVITT, HOWARD ALAN, lawyer; b. L.A., Aug. 20, 1961; BA summa cum laude, U. Calif., Berkeley, 1985; MA, U. So. Calif., 1989; JD magna cum laude, Harvard U., 1994. Litigation ptnr. Coblentz, Patch, Duffy & Bass, San Francisco, 1996—. Exec. editor: Harvard Civil Right Civil Liberties Law Rev. 1993-94; contbr. articles to profl. jours. Avocations: photography, hiking, travel. Office: Coblentz Patch Duffy & Bass LLP 222 Kearny St Fl 7 San Francisco CA 94108-4510

SLAVKIN, HAROLD CHARLES, biologist; b. Chgo., Mar. 20, 1938; m. Lois S. Slavkin; children: Mark D., Todd P. BA (hon.), U. So. Calif., 1961, DDS (hon.), 1965; Doctorate (hon.), Georgetown U., 1990, U. Paris, 1996, U. Md., 1997. Mem. faculty grad. program in cellular and molecular biology U. So. Calif., L.A., 1968—, mem. faculty gerontology inst., 1969, prof. sch. dentistry, 1974—, chmn. grad. program in craniofacial molecular biology, 1975-85; dir. Ctr. for Craniofacial Molecular Biology, 1989-95; George & Mary Lou Boone prof. craniofacial molecular biology U. So. Calif. Sch. Dentistry, 1989-95, dean, 2000—; dir. Nat. Inst. Dental Rsch., NIH, Bethesda, Md., 1995—2000. Vis. prof. Israel Inst. Tech., Haifa, 1987-88; cons. U.S. News and World Report, 1985-95, L.A. Edn. Partnership, 1983-95, Torstar Books, Inc., 1985-95. Contbr. articles to profl. jours. Mem. sci. adv. bd. Calif. Mus. Sci. and Tech., 1985-95. Rsch. scholar U. Coll. London, 1980. Mem. AAAS, Am. Assn. Anatomists, Am. Inst. Biol. Scis., Am. Soc. for Cell Biology, Am. Assn. for Dental Rsch. (pres. 1993-94), N.Y. Acad. Scis., Inst. Medicine of NAS, Internat. Coll. Dentistry, Am. Coll. Dentistry, Los Angeles County Art Mus. Assocs. Office: 925 W 34th St Los Angeles CA 90089*

SLAVNEY, PHILLIP RICHARD, psychiatrist; b. Madison, Wis., Sept. 13, 1940; s. Coleman Mordecai and Ann Sarah Slavney; m. Jacqueline Lillian Smith, Apr. 15, 1966. BA, U. Wis., 1962; MD, Albert Einstein Coll. Medicine, 1966. Diplomate Am. Bd. Psychiatry and Neurology. Asst. prof. psychiatry U. Oreg. Sch. Medicine, Portland, 1973-76; attending psychiatrist Johns Hopkins Hosp., Balt., 1976—; asst. prof. psychiatry Johns Hopkins U. Sch. Medicine, 1976-80, dir. psychiat. residency edn., 1977-93, assoc. prof. psychiatry, 1980-93, prof. psychiatry, 1993—; dir. gen. hosp. psychiatry Johns Hopkins Hosp., 1993—; Eugene Meyer III prof. psychiatry and medicine Johns Hopkins U. Sch. Medicine, 1993—. Cons. psychiatrist Johns Hopkins Oncology Ctr., Balt., 1994—. Author: Psychiatric Polarities: Methodology and Practice, 1987, Perspectives on "Hysteria", 1990, Psychiatric Dimensions of Medical Practice: What Primary-Care Physicians Should Know About Delirium, Demoralization, Suicidal Thinking, and Competence to Refuse Medical Advice, 1998; co-author: The Perspectives of Psychiatry, 1983, 98. Sr. asst. surgeon USPHS, 1967-69. Avocations: art history, travel. Office: Johns Hopkins Hosp Osler 320 600 N Wolfe St Baltimore MD 21287-5371 E-mail: slavney@mail.jhmi.edu.

SLAVUTIN, LEE JACOB, estate planning life insurance executive; b. Melbourne, Victoria, Australia, Mar. 10, 1951; came to U.S., 1978; s. Nathan Jacob and Irene (Fishman) S.; m. Debra C. Schwartz, Nov. 11, 1979; children: Aaron, Lydia. BSc in Medicine with honors, Monash U., Melbourne, 1972, MB, BS with honors, 1974. Diplomate Am. Bd. Pathology; CLU; cert. pension cons. Pathologist Lenox Hill Hosp., N.Y.C., 1978-82; life ins. and estate planning specialist Stern Slavutin-2, Inc. and predecessor firm, 1983—. Mem. tax hotline adv. bd. Am. Law Inst. Estate Planning Faculty; spkr. in field. Author 2 books; contbr. over 100 articles to profl. jours. Mem. Am. Soc. Pension Actuaries, Tax Action Panel Practitioners Pub. Co., Am. Assn. Advanced Life Underwriters, Million Dollar Round Table, Top of Table. Avocations: walking, reading. Home: 46 W 83rd St Apt 6B New York NY 10024-5253 Office: 530 Fifth Ave New York NY 10036-5101

SLAWIATYNSKY, MARION MICHAEL, biomedical electronics engineer, software consultant; b. Phila., Nov. 21, 1958; s. Walter Wasyl and Maria Margaret (Sauer) S. BA in Biology, LaSalle U., 1980; MS in Biomed. Engring., Drexel U., 1984, BS in Electronics Engring. (hon.), 1982. Sr. systems engr. Innovative Med. Systems, Ivyland, Pa., 1983-95; sr. software engr. Advanced Tech. Labs., Bothell, Wash., 1995-99; sr. DSP software engr. ATL Ultrasound, 1999—. Soloist Male Chorus Prometheus, 1976-95; mem. Steuben Soc. Am., Phila., 1990—; condr., music min. St. Brendan Ch., Bothell, 2000—. Mem. IEEE. Republican. Roman Catholic. Achievements include patent for electro-optical lock-in amplifier detector for coagulation instrument; development of medical quality control for FDA certification of electronic medical instruments, of high precision peristaltic pump with electronic autocalibration, of software quality control guidelines for FDA certification; design of electro-optical curcuitry for medical coagulation analyzer and fluorescence polarization instrument, of system qualification test procedures as well as front end control, signal processing and system software and software architecture for medical diagnostic ultrasound. Home: 20129 Hollyhills Dr NE Bothell WA 98011-7603 Office: ATL Ultrasound 22100 Bothell Everett Hwy PO Box 3003 MS 264 Bothell WA 98041-3003

SLAWSKY, DONNA SUSAN, librarian, singer; b. N.Y.C., Jan. 18, 1956; d. Samuel Slawsky and Lillian (Freizer) Alexander. BA, City Coll. N.Y., 1977; M of Infor. Libr. Sci., Pratt Inst., 1998. Coord. NYNEX Market Info. Ctr., White Plains, N.Y., 1985-87; libr. asst. NYNEX Info. Access Ctr., 1987-88; dir. Info. Ctr./Archives, exhbns. curator HarperCollins Pubs., N.Y.C., 1988-99; singer, 1987—; dir. content devel. BuyerWeb, Inc., 1999-2000; founder Info Diva, 2001—02; mgr. indexing for digital archive Scholastic, Inc., 2002—. Contbr. articles to profl. jours.; co-founder (quartet women's voices) Rose Ensemble debut Weill Recital Hall, Carnegie Hall, 1997. Pres. Assn. HarperCollins Employees, N.Y.C., 1990-94; dir. Tenants Assn., N.Y.C., 1994. Recipient Schubertiade Lieder Competition award 92d St. Y, N.Y.C., 1990. Mem.: Assn. Ind. Info. Profls., Profl. Women Singers Assn. (treas. 1992—96, mem.-at-large 1997—, webmaster 2001—), Spl. Librs. Assn., Beta Phi Mu. Avocations: bicycling, art, reading. Office: Scholastic Inc 557 Broadway Rm 266 New York NY 10012- E-mail: dslawsky@scholastic.com.

SLAWTER, JOHN DAVID, JR. oil company and manufacturing executive; b. Winston-Salem, N.C., May 11, 1917; s. John David and Carrie Wess (Linville) S.; m. Josephine McCloone, June 15, 1943 (div. Oct. 1959); children: Suzanne Marie, Sheila Margaret; m. Joan Margaret Pirek, July 7, 1966. Student, U. N.C., 1935-37, 38-40. V.p. B&B Gas and Petroleum, Corpus Christi, Tex., 1950-59; exec. v.p. Cal-O-Tex Oil, Columbus, Ohio, 1959-65; pres. Atlantic Internat. Oil, Charleston, W.Va., 1966-73; CEO Interstate Hotels, Inc., 1975, Pacific Internat. Prodn. Holding Co. for Activated Carbon Corp. Am., Dallas, 1989, Mid-Continent Oil, 1974—, OFG Corp., 1995—, EMTEC, 1997—, HTS, 1999—. Chmn. adv. bd. Cal-O-Tex, 1966—, Atlantic Internat. Oil, 1974—, Pacific Internat., 1974—, Black Diamond Coal Co., 1978—, Southwest Interstate Support Sys., 1985—, Activated Carbon Corp., 1989—; vice chair AIOC Trust, Slawter Trust (lifetime). Author: (patents and copyrights) purification and desalination sys., 1991, pumping unit tech., 1995, oil field gen., 1996, oil field mobile remote control unit, 1998, heat transfer sys., 1999. Mem. Rep. Nat. Nom. Com., Washington, 1994-2000. Maj. Engrs. 1941-45, WWII, PTO. Decorated Purple Heart, Silver Star, Bronze Star with oak leaf cluster, Presdl. Citation, 4 Battle Stars. Mem. internat. petroleum clubs, Geneva Exec. Club (v.p. 1970-78), Chi Phi. Avocations: aviation, golf. Office: Pacific Internat Prodn/Subs Ste 8108 4350 Trinity Mills Rd Dallas TX 75287-7037 also: PO Box 795273 Dallas TX 75379-5273 E-mail: joslawter2@earthlink.com.

SLAWTER, MARK, golfer; b. Winston-Salem, NC, Dec. 12, 1973; married. Student, NC State U. Profl. golfer Can. Profl. Golf Tour, 1996—. Named winner, Eagle Creek Classic, 2001. Mem.: Heritage Country Club. Office: Canadian Tour 212 King St W Ste 203 Toronto ON Canada M5H 1K5

SLAY, FRANCIS G. mayor; b. St. Louis; s. Francis R. and Anna Slay; m. Kim Slay; children: Francis Jr., Katherine. Law degree, Saint Louis U. Sch. Law, 1980; postgrad in political sci., Quincy Coll., Ill., 1977. Mayor City of St. Louis, 2001—; pvt. lawyer 20 yrs.; law clerk Judge Paul J. Simon, Mo. Court Appeals , 1981; ptnr. Guilfoil, Petzall & Shoemake. Mem. St. Louis Bd. Alderman, 1995, elected pres. Office: City Hall Rm 200 1200 Mrk St Saint Louis MO 63103*

SLAY-BARBER, DORIS A. educational administrator; b. San Antonio, Sept. 22, 1952; d. Harold and Lottie (Pieniazek) Brietzke; m. H. Gene Barber, June 26, 1987; children: G. L. Slay, Gary, Mike. BA, St. Mary's U., 1974; MEd, Trinity U., 1983. Cert. elem. tchr., Tex. Cons. computer software Edn. Svc. Ctr.; tchr., coord. gifted/talented program East Central Ind. Sch. Dist., San Antonio; coord. grade reporting and scheduling Northside Ind. Sch. Dist. Mem. ASCD, Bus. and Profl. Womens Club Inc. of San Antonio, Phi Delta Kappa. Office: 5900 Evers San Antonio TX 78238 E-mail: slaybarb22@hotmail.com.

SLAYBAUGH, JANET LOUISE, social worker; b. Gettysburg, Pa., Oct. 29, 1942; d. Robert Paul and Ruth Bell (Cook) S. BS, U. Ala., 1963; cert. social work, La. State U., 1966, MSW, 1967; PhD, Union Inst., Cin., 1990. Cert social worker Acad. Cert. Social Workers, bd. cert. social workers, cert. info. systems auditor, CPA. Mem. NASW, AICPA, La. Assn. Cert. Pub. Accts., Cert. Info. Sys. Auditors Assn. Lutheran. Home: 620 Chippenham Dr Baton Rouge LA 70808-5611 Office: La Dept Social Svcs 333 Laurel St Ste 571 Baton Rouge LA 70801-1807

SLAYDEN, JAMES BRAGDON, retired department store executive; b. Seattle, Sept. 28, 1924; s. Philip Lee and Ruth Alwin (Bragdon) S.; m. Barbara Marie McBride, May 7, 1955; children: Tracy Anne, James Bragdon. BA, U. Wash., 1948; MBA, U. So. Calif., 1949. Buyer Frederick & Nelson (dept. store), Seattle, 1949-59, div. mdse. mgr., 1959-65; gen. mgr. Bullocks Westwood, Los Angeles, 1965-69. Exec. v.p., gen. mdse. mgr. May D&F Co. dept. store, Denver, 1969-72; pres., CEO J. W. Robinson dept. store, L.A., 1972-78; exec. v.p. ops. Marshall Field & Co., Chgo., 1978-80; gen. mgr. Bullocks Del Amo, 1980-85; lectr. mktg. U. So. Calif., 1985-93. Active United Crusade United Way, L.A., 1973-78, Chgo. Heart Assn., 1978-79; chmn. Pvt. Industry Coun., 1982-95; cons. Internat. Exec. Svc. Corps., 1987—, traffic comm. Rancho Palos Verdes, 1994-97, planning commn., 1997-2000, view restoration com., 2000—. With U.S. Army, 1943-45. Mem. Phi Kappa Psi. Republican. Christian Scientist. Home: 37 Mela Ln Palos Verdes Peninsula CA 90275-5086

SLAYDON-WOLBERT, JEANNE MILLER, secondary school educator; b. Kansas City, Mo. d. Sanderson Staley and Bea Amelia (Hoeger) Miller; m. George Smith Wolbert; children: Kathleen Amelia Slaydon, Dianne Louise Slaydon Springer. BA, Tex. Christian U.; MEd, U. Houston. Pvt. tutor, Midland and Houston, Tex.; elem. tchr. Midland Ind. Sch. Dist.; tchr. sec. social studies Spring Branch Ind. Sch. Dist., Houston, chmn. Social Studies dept., dist. Social Studies coord., 1977-91; social studies cons., 1991—. Cons. So. Assn. Colls. and Univs., 1978—; mem. Tex. State Task Force on Restructuring Social Studies, Grade 1 to 12, 1991-92. Author: (econs. curriculum) Confluent Economic Education, 1979; cons. (textbook) World History, 1982. Mem. Tex. Citizen Bee, Local Close Up, 1985-91; coord. Congl. Dist. 7 Citizenship Edn. Program; spkr. Inst. Internat. Edn., Network for the Population Connection. Mem. AAUW, Social Studies Suprs. Assn., Inst. for Internat. Edn., Spring Br. Coun. for Social Studies (treas. 1970-73, pres. 1983-84), Tex. Coun. for Social Studies (v.p. 1986, pres. 1988), Tex. Social Studies Suprs. Assn., Tex. Assn. Advancement of History (bd. dirs. 1988-92), Tex. Alliance Geog. Edn., Nat. Coun. Social Studies, Phi Delta Kappa (chpt. sec. 1991-93). Congregationalist.

SLAYMAKER, ADRIANNE LEE E. accountant, educator; b. Arlington, Va., May 28, 1945; d. Laurence Brandon and Grace (Cooper) Einfeldt; m. William Earl Slaymaker, Apr. 27, 1965 (div. Feb. 1986); children: Sorell Brandau, Weselley Earl. BA, Ind. State U., Terre Haute, 1970; MBA, Ind. U., 1976; DBA, U. Ky., 1984. CPA, Ind., Mich. Asst. prof. acctg. Hanover (Ind.) Coll., 1977-78; bus. adminstrn. coord. Midway (Ky.) Coll., 1978-80; asst. prof. acctg. Morehead (Ky.) State U., 1980-82; assoc. prof. acctg. Bellarmine Coll., Loisville, 1982-85; asst. prof. acctg. Wayne State U., Detroit, 1985-93; vis. prof. acctg. U. Windsor, Ont., Can., 1994-97; assoc. prof. acctg. Ky. State U., Frankfort, 1997—2000; assoc. prof. Ferris State U. , 2001—. Author in field. Precinct del. Rep. Party, Grosse Pointe Farms, Mich., 1994—; treas. Grosse Pointe Power Squadron, 1994-97, Greater Detroit FreeNet, 1993-96, Rotary Club of Grosse Pointe-Sunrise, 1996-98; rep. senate com. Mich., 2001-. Recipient Outstanding Cmty. Svc. award, Acctg. Aid Soc., 1988—94, Vol. Svc. award, IRS, 1998—99. Mem. AICPA, Am. Acctg. Assn., Am. Taxation Assn., Acad. Acctg. Historians, Nat. Tax Assn, Mich. Assn. CPAs. Episcopalian. Avocations: sailing, biking, hiking, needlework, cooking. Home: 245 Moross Rd Grosse Pointe Farms MI 48236-2948 Office: Ferris State U 352 Business Bldg Big Rapids MI 49307 E-mail: slaymaka@ferris.edu., aslay@ix.neteom.com..

SLAYMAKER, GENE ARTHUR, public relations executive; b. Kenton, Ohio, Sept. 15, 1928; s. Edwin Paul and Anna Elizabeth (Grable) S.; divorced; children: Jill Brook, Scott Wood, Leslie Beth; m. Julie Ann Graff, Feb. 3, 1979; 1 adopted child, Peter Fredric Bannon II; stepchildren: Jennifer Elizabeth Nash, David Frank Nash. BA in Radio Journalism, Ohio State U. Announcer, reporter WLWC-TV, Columbus, Ohio, 1951-52; anchor, reporter WKBN-AM-FM-TV, Youngstown, 1952-56, KYW-TV, Cleve., 1956-60; editor news Sta. WFBM-AM-FM-TV, Indpls., 1960-68; pres., founder Slaymaker & Assocs. Pub. Rels., 1969—; dir. news, sports, pub. affairs WTLC-FM and WTUX-AM, Indpls., 1976-92; community rels. liaison Marion County Pros. Atty. Office, 1993. Pres., founder Slaymaker and Assocs., Indpls., 1969—. Mambo dancer (movie) Going All the Way, 1996. Past bd. dirs. Park-Tudor Father's Assn.; mem. Meridian Kessler Neighborhood Assn., pres., 1968-69. Recipient Disting. Service award (2). Mem. Ind. AP Broadcasters Assn. (awards), UPI (awards), Nat. Fedn. Press Women, Soc. Profl. Journalists (awards Ind. chpt., bd. dirs., chpt. pres. 1991-92, Radio-TV News Dirs. Assn. (region bd. dirs. 1987-91), Indpls. Press Club, Woman's Press Club Ind., Players Club, Lambs Club (pres. 2000—). Clubs: Nat. Headliners, Unity. Democrat. Avocations: writing, painting, singing, gardening, tennis. Home: 5161 N Washington Blvd Indianapolis IN 46205-1071 Office: Slaymaker Assoc 5161 N Washington Blvd Indianapolis IN 46205-1071

SLAYMAKER, OLAV, geography educator; b. Swansea, Wales, Jan. 31, 1939; came to Can., 1968; s. Arthur J. and Astri H. (Breen) S.; m. Margaret A. Rapson, Apr. 8, 1967; children— Karen M., Paul O., Sarah J., Heidi R. BA, King's Coll., Cambridge, Eng., 1961; AM, Harvard U., 1963; PhD, Cambridge U., 1968. Asst. lectr. U. Coll. Wales, Aberystwyth, 1964-66, lectr., 1966-68; asst. prof. geography U.B.C., Vancouver, Can., 1968-70, assoc. prof. Can., 1970-81, prof. Can., 1981—, head dept. Can., 1982-91, assoc. v.p. rsch. Can., 1991-95, prof. geography Can. Cons. water quality br. Inland Waters, Vancouver, 1976—; dir. Liu Ctr. Study of Global Issues. Editor: Mountain Geomorphology, 1972, Field Experiments, 1978, High Mountains, 1981, Extreme Landforming Events, 1983, Geomorphology and Land Managment, 1986, Erosion Budgets and Their Hydrologic Basis, 1986, Canada's Cold Environments, 1993, Steepland Geomorphology, 1995, Geomorphic Hazards, 1996, Physical Geography and Global Environmental Change, 1998, Geomorphology, Human Activity and Global Environmental Change. Senate mem. Vancouver Sch. Theology, 1973-75; bd. dirs. Regent Coll., Vancouver, 1975-78, U. B.C., 1984-87; gov. Internat. Devel. Rsch. Ctr., Ottawa, 1994—. Research grantee Natural Sci. and Engring. Research Council, Ottawa, Ont., Can., 1968-98. Mem. Can. Assn. Geographers (pres. 1991-92), Am. Geophys. Union, Internat. Geog. Union (commn. chmn., sec., chmn. Can. nat. com. 1984-88), Internat. Assn. Geomorphologists (v.p. 1993-97, pres. 1997-2001), Faculty Club (Vancouver). Anglican. Avocations: mountain hiking, philately. Office: Univ BC Dept Geography 6476 NW Marine Dr Vancouver BC Canada V6T 1Z2 E-mail: olav@geog.ubc.ca.

SLAYMAN, CLIFFORD LEROY, biophysicist, educator; b. Mt. Vernon, Ohio, July 7, 1936; s. Clifford Leroy and Ethel May (Stantz) S.; m. Carolyn Ruth Walch, Dec. 26, 1959; children: Andrew Lowell, Rachel Whitehouse. AB, Kenyon Coll., 1958; PhD, Rockefeller Inst., 1963; DSc (hon.), Kenyon Coll, 1991. NSF fellow Cambridge (Eng.) U., 1963-64; asst. prof. Western Res. U., Cleve., 1964-67; from asst. prof. to prof. physiology Yale U., New Haven, 1967—. Mem panel on pre-doctoral fellowships NSF, Washington, 1969-71; DOE-DOA-NSF panel on Plant Sci. Ctrs., Washington, 1988. Editor: Electrogenic Ion Pumps, 1982; contbr. articles to profl. jours. and revs.; editorial bd. Bio Sci. Jour., 1985-88, Jour. Membrane Biology, 1982—. Mem. Hamden (Conn.) Neighborhood Preservation Com., 1980-82. Grantee NIH, 1964-91, NSF, 1979-82, DOE, 1985—. Mem. AAAS, Am. Physiol. Soc., Am. Soc. Plant Physiologists, N.Y. Acad. Scis., Soc. Gen. Physiologists, Conn. Acad. Arts and Scis. Avocations: antique house restoration, conservation, nature watching. Office: Yale Sch Medicine 333 Cedar St New Haven CT 06510-3289 E-mail: clifford.slayman@yale.edu.

SLAYTON, GUS, foundation administrator; b. Pocahontas, Ark., Jan. 20, 1937; s. Alvin M. and Eula Inis (Milam) S.; m. Ruth Virginia Furr, May 27, 1961 (dec. Nov. 1989). BA, U. Md., College Park, 1973. Enslited U.S. Army, 1957, commd. 2nd lt., 1963, advanced through grades to lt. col., 1978; various operational and research and devel. assignments, including The Pentagon, 1974-78; ret., 1980; exec. dir. Assn. of Old Crows, Alexandria, Va., 1980-92, AOC Ednl. Found., 1992—. Decorated Legion of Merit (2), Bronze Star (2) Republican. Avocation: real estate investment. Home: 152 Mill Cove Ln Ponte Vedra Beach FL 32082-4135 E-mail: slaytonag@earthlink.net.

SLAYTON, JOHN ARTHUR, electric motor manufacturing executive; b. St. Joseph, Mo., Aug. 12, 1918; s. Ernest Roy and Cora Belle (Hutchison) S.; m. Elizabeth Van Horn Duerr, Aug. 15, 1942; children: Richard, Elizabeth, Jane, James, Robert, Sarah, Mary. BS, U. Mo., 1940. Salesman Burroughs Co., Chgo., 1940-42; acct. Standard Brands, Green Bay, Wis., 1945-48; exec. v.p. Marathon Electric, Wausau, 1948-88, pres., vice chmn., 1988-97, ret., 1997. Pres. C. of C. Found., Wausau, 1981-89, Woodson YMCA Found., 1977—; bd. dirs. Wausau Hosp. Ctr., 1976-82, North Ctrl. Mental Health Found., 1980-85, Wausau Area Vol. Exch., 1983-89, Wasau Health Found., 1975—; pres., bd. dirs. Grant Theatre Found., 1985—; bd. dirs., treas., pres. Lehigh Yawkey Woodson Art Mus., 1985—, pres., 1996—; trstuee, elder 1st Presbyn. Ch., 1960-65. Served in USN, 1942-44. Recipient Citation of Merit U. Mo., Columbia, 1976, Wausau Disting. Cmty. Service award, 1983, Wis. Gov.'s award, 1986; Paul Harris fellow, 1977; Legacy award established in his honor Wausau Hosp., 1999. Mem. Wausau Area C. of C. (pres., dir. 1977-81) Clubs: Wausau Country (pres., dir. 1958-61), Wausau, YMCA (pres., dir. 1961-67). Lodges: Rotary (pres., dir. 1960-63). Republican. Home: 1115 Wildwood Ln Naples FL 34105-3236

SLAYTON, JOHN HOWARD, lawyer, trust company executive; b. Sparta, Wis., July 6, 1955; s. Rex Gordon and Elizabeth (Ward) S.; m. Judith Hughes. BA in Polit. Sci. cum laude, Marquette U., 1977; JD cum laude, George Washington U., 1980, MBA in Fin., 1982; LLM in Taxation, Georgetown U., 1986. Bar: D.C. 1981, U.S. Ct. Appeals (D.C. cir.) 1981, U.S. Dist. Ct. (D.C. dist.) 1981, Va. 1993. Assoc. Metzger, Shadyac & Schwarz, Washington, 1980-83, Pillsbury, Madison & Sutro, Washington, 1983-87, Leland & Assocs., Inc., Washington, 1987-95, Gordon Getty Family trust; pres., CEO The Trust Co. of the South, Burlington, N.C., 1996—. Instr. real estate syndication, Arlington (Va.) County Continuing Edn./Realty Bd., 1982; mem. Joint Commn. N.C. Bankers Assn. and N.C. Bar Assn.; cons., Washington, 1995-96. Contbr. articles to profl. jours. Mem.: N.C. Bar Assn., D.C. Bar Assn., Va. Bar Assn., ABA (chmn. trusts and investments subcom. of banking com., com. fed. regulation of securities). Roman Catholic. Office: The Trust Co of the South 3041 S Church St Burlington NC 27215-5154 E-mail: jslayton@tcts.com.

SLEDGE, JAMES SCOTT, judge; b. Gadsden, Ala., July 20, 1947; s. L. Lee and Kathryn (Privott) S.; m. Joan Nichols, Dec. 27, 1969; children: Joanna Scott, Dorothy Privott. BA, Auburn U., 1969; JD, U. Ala., 1974, postgrad., 1989. Bar: Ala. 1974, U.S. Ct. Appeals (5th cir.) 1975, U.S. Ct. Appeals (11th cir.) 1981. Ptnr. Inzer, Suttle, Swann & Stivender, P.A., Gadsden, 1975-91; judge U.S. Bankruptcy Ct. No. Dist. Ala., 1991—; chair Nat. Conf. Fed. Judges, 2000—. Instr. U. Ala., Gadsden, 1975-77, Gadsden State C.C., 1989-90. Lay min., vestryman Holy Comforter Episc. Ch., Gadsden, 1976—, sr. warden, 2000; exec. com. Ala. Coun. on the Arts, 1994—, chmn. 2002-; incorporator Episc. Day Sch., Gadsden, 1976, Kyle Home for Devel. Disadvantaged, Gadsden, 1979; bd. dirs. Salvation Army, 1984-91, Etowah County Health Dept., 1975-91, Episc. Day Sch., 1992-96, Gadsden Symphony, 1993-96; active Ala. Dem. Exec. Com., 1990-91, Etowah County Dem. Exec. Com., 1984-91; founder Gadsden Cultural Arts Found., 1983, chmn., 1986-91. Capt. U.S. Army, 1969-71, Vietnam. Decorated Legion of Honor (Vietnam); recipient Gov.'s award for art Ala. Coun. of Arts, 1993. Mem. ABA (publs. chair 1997-98, chair jud. divsn. 2002), Gadsden-Etowah C. of C. (gen. counsel, v.p., bd. dirs. 1986-93), Kiwanis (bd. dirs. 1981-84), Phi Kappa Phi, Phi Eta Sigma. Home: 435 Turrentine Ave Gadsden AL 35901-4059

SLEDGE, REGINALD LEON, planner and consultant; b. Balt., July 8, 1954; s. Herbert Clifton and Juanita (Brantley) S. Grad., Lawrence Acad., 1972; student, Dartmouth Coll., 1968; BS, Boston U., 1976; MBA, Columbia U., 1984. Fin. analyst West Point-Pepperell, Inc., N.Y.C., 1976-77; fin. futures trader European Am. Bank, 1978-82; corp. bond analyst Salomon Bros., 1983—84; fin. cons. Control Assocs., N.Y.C., 1986-87; acct., fin. analyst Spicer & Oppenheim, 1987-88; v.p. bus. continuity planner Bank of Am., San Diego, 1988—. Co-chair pub. outreach subcom. San Diego Planning Dept. Mem. La Jolla Town Coun.; mem. San Diego Mayor's Environ. Adv. Bd.; mem. environ. working group San Diego Found. Mem.: Del Mar TV Found., Ivy League Assn. San Diego (bd. dirs.), Del Mar TV Prodrs. Group, Columbia Univ. Alumni Club San Diego (pres.). Republican. Roman Catholic. Home: 1040 Coast Blvd S Unit 303 La Jolla CA 92037-4165 Office: 450 B St San Diego CA 92101-8001 E-mail: rlsledge84@aol.com.

SLEE, VERGIL N. healthcare informatics executive, physician, author; b. Eaton Rapids, Mich., Sept. 24, 1917; s. William Willey and Matilda Elizabeth Slee; m. Beth Stoke, June 10, 1941; children: Dan, Sara Slee Brown, David, Debora. BA, Albion Coll., 1937; MD, Washington U., St. Louis, 1941; MPH, U. Mich., 1947. Diplomate in pub. health Am. Bd. Preventive Medicine. Dir. Barry County Health Ctr., Hastings, Mich., 1947-56; dir., founder Commn. on Profl. and Hosp. Activities, Ann Arbor, 1956-71, pres., until 1980, pres. emeritus, 1980—; dir., mem. faculty Estes Park Inst., Englewood, Colo., 1981—; CEO The Tringa Group, Brevard, N.C., 1982—. Non-resident lectr. U. Mich. Sch. Pub. Health, Ann Arbor, 1947-78; dir., founder profl. activity study Southwestern Mich. Hosp. Coun., Hastings, 1953-55; chmn. Health Commons Inst., Portland, Maine, 1992—; pres. Coun. on Clin. Classifications, Ann Arbor, 1976-80. Author: Slee's Health Care Terms, 1986, 4th edit., 2001, The Endangered Medical Record: Ensuring Its Integrity in the Age of Informatics, 2000; editor: International Classification of Diseases, 9th revision, Clinical Modification, 1978. Trustee Transylvania Cmty. Hosp., Brevard, 1988—. Flight surgeon USAAC, 1942-46. Recipient Key award Mich. Hosp. Assn., 1968, spl. citation, 1980; resolution of commendation Southwestern Mich. Hosp. Assn., 1978, Am. Hosp. Assn., 1980; award of merit Am. Assn. Healthcare Cons., 1988, Disting. Svc. award Am. Health Info. Mgmt. Assn., 1993; Vergil N. Slee disting. professorship healthcare quality mgmt. established by U.N.C., Chapel Hill, 1998; Jackson Johnson scholar Washington U. Sch. Medicine, 1937-41; Edwin L. Crosby fellow Am. Hosp. Assn., 1980. Mem. ACP (Richard and Hinds Rosenthal award 1982), APHA, AMA, Alpha Omega Alpha, Phi Kappa Phi, Delta Omega, Phi Gamma. E-mail: vslee@juno.com.

SLEED, JOEL, columnist; b. N.Y.C., Jan. 29, 1929; m. MaryLou Kalwara, Nov. 15, 1983; children: Jodie, Jill, Jeffrey, Kristin Kalwara, Karen Hepler. Former travel editor The Star-Ledger and Newhouse News Svc., Newark; columnist travel sect. Sunday Rep., Springfield, Mass.; travel editor Palm Beach Soc. mag. Office: Newhouse Newspapers 711 Third Ave New York NY 10017 E-mail: joelsleed@msn.com.

SLEEPER, THOMAS F. journalist, insurance agent, consultant; b. Worcester, Mass., Feb. 23, 1939; s. Wesley O. and Florence A. Sleeper; m. Patricia E. Dobson, Sept. 23, 1961; children: Neill, Coleman, Diane, Alison. BA, Framingham State Coll., 1989. Polit. reporter Fitchburg (Mass.) Sentinel, 1961—64; exec. editor Town Crier, Sudbury, 1964—71; copy editor, editorialist Evening Gazette, Worcester, 1971—73; editor Boston Ledger, Brookline, 1973—76, The Times, Webster, 1976—79; ind. contractor Dana Assocs., Framingham, 1979—92, SBSI, Inc., Kansas City, Mo., 1992—. Substitute tchr. Natick (Mass.) Pub. Schs., 1997—. Author: (novels) Soldiers Civilized, 1978, poetry. With U.S. Army, 1957—60, ETO. Named Outstanding Young Men of Am., U.S. Jaycees, 1970; recipient Brotherhood award, Nat. Com. Christians and Jews, 1967, Good Neighbor award, Natick Comets, 1968. Mem.: DAVO (volleyball ofcl.), ASA (softball ofcl.), Nat. Fedn. H.S. (sports ofcl.). Avocations: golf, reading, writing. Home: 19 Cherry Rd Framingham MA 01701

SLEETER, JOHN WILLIAM HIGGS, retired physician, health service administrator; b. Toledo, Feb. 16, 1917; s. Charles Elmer and Meta DeLad (Higgs) S.; m. Betti Deming, Aug. 28, 1943 (div. Mar. 1963); m. Patricia C. Parker, July 1963 (dec. Oct. 1986); m. Patricia Catherine Parrillo, July 8, 1989; children: John William, Marilee Ann, Thomas David. BA, Cornell Coll., Mt. Vernon, Iowa, 1942; MD, U. Iowa, 1945. Pres. San Gabriel Primary Care, Arcadia, Calif., 1952-62, L.A. County Acad. GP, 1965-66; inst. paramedic care St. Terisita Hosp., Duarte, 1970-75; pres., chief operating officer Profsnl. Rev. Area 21, 1970-75; 1st pres. L.A. County Paramedic Commn., 1974-75; pres., CEO, dir. pvt. practice assn., Arcadia, 1984-2000; ret., 2000. Capt, AUS, 1945-49. Mem. Balboa Bay Club, Masons (32d degree). Republican. Avocation: golf.

SLEICHER, CHARLES ALBERT, chemical engineer; b. Albany, N.Y., Aug. 15, 1924; s. Charles Albert and Beatrice Eugena (Cole) S.; m. Janis Jorgensen, Sept. 5, 1953; children— Jeffrey Mark, Gretchen Gail. BS, Brown U., 1946; MS, M.I.T., 1949; PhD, U. Mich., 1955. Asst. dir. M.I.T. Sch. Chem. Engring.; Practice Bangor, Maine, 1949-51; research engr. Shell Devel. Co., Emeryville, Calif., 1955-59; assoc. prof. chem. engring. U. Wash., Seattle, 1960-66, prof., 1966-92, prof. emeritus, 1993—, dept. chmn., 1977-89. Cons. Westinghouse-Hanford Co.; profl. photographer, 1994—. Contbr. articles on extraction, heat transfer, fluid mechanics, pesticide transport to profl. jours.; contbr. photos to mags., books & calendars. Served with USN, 1943-47. NSF postdoctoral fellow, 1959-60; SEED grantee, 1973-74; research grantee NSF; research grantee Chevron Research Corp.; research grantee Am. Chem. Soc. Fellow AIChE (program and awards coms.), AAAS; mem. Am. Chem. Soc., N.Am. Nature Photography Assn., Photographic Soc. Am., Sigma Xi. Achievements include chem. reactor design patents, nat. photography awards, co-founder Columbia Winery. Home: 5002 Harold Pl NE Seattle WA 98105-2809 Office: U Wash Dept Chem Engring PO Box 351750 Seattle WA 98195-1750

SLEIGH, SYLVIA, artist, educator; b. Llandudno, North Wales; came to U.S., 1961; d. John Harold and Katherine Amy (Miller) S.; m. Lawrence Alloway, June 28, 1954. Student, Sch. Art, Brighton, Sussex, Eng., 1932-36; diploma, U. London Extra-Mural Dept., 1947. Vis. asst. prof. SUNY-Stony Brook, 1978; instr. New Sch. Social Research, N.Y.C., 1974-77, 78-80; Edith Kreeger Wolf disting. prof. Northwestern U., Evanston, Ill., 1977; vis. artist Baldwin Seminar Oberlin Coll., Ohio, 1982, New Sch. Social Rsch., N.Y.C. One person shows include Bennington (Vt.) Coll., 1963, Soho 20 Art Gallery, N.Y.C., 1974, 76, 80, 82, A.I.R. Gallery, N.Y.C., 1974, 76, 78, Ohio State U., Columbus, 1976, Matrix, Wadsworth Atheneum, Hartford, Conn., 1976, Marianne Deson Gallery, Chgo., 1990, G.W. Einstein, Inc., N.Y.C., 1980, 83, 85, U. Mo., Saint Louis, 1981, Zaks Gallery, Chgo., 1985, 95, Milw. Art Mus., Butler Inst., Youngstown, Ohio, 1990, Stiebel Modern, N.Y.C., 1992, 94, Gallery 609, Denver, Canton (Ohio) Art Inst., Soho 20 Gallery, 1999, Deven Golden Fine Arts, N.Y., 1999, The Art of Sylvia Sleigh and Lawrence Allway Phila. Art Alliance, Phila., 2001; exhibited in group shows Newhouse Gallery, S.I., N.Y., Stamford (Conn.) Mus., 1985, Albany (N.Y.) Inst. Art, Cin. Art Mus., New Orleans Mus. Art, Denver Art Mus., Pa. Acad. Fine Arts, 1989, Carlsten Art Gallery, Stevens Point, Wis., 1993, Stiebel Modern, N.Y.C., 1994, Soho 20, N.Y.C., 1993, 96, Katzen Brown Gallery, N.Y.C., 1989, Zaks Gallery, Chgo., 1986, Steinbaum Krauss Gallery, 1997, Deven Golden Fine Arts, Ltd., N.Y.C., 1997, Rutgers U., New Brunswick, N.J., 1984, 86, RioArriba Gallery, Abiquiu, N.Mex., 1996, Milw. Art Mus., 1996, Steinbaum Krauss Gallery, 1997, N.Y. Mus. exhbn. traveling until 2001, David and Alfred Smart Mus., Chgo., Broome St. Gallery, N.Y.C., Deven Golden Fine Arts, N.Y.C., A.I.R. Gallery, N.Y.C., Apex Art Co., N.Y.C., 1998, McKee Gallery, N.Y.C., 1998, Royal Coll. Art, London, 1998, Heckscher Mus. Art, Huntington, N.Y., 1999, Printworks Gallery, 2000, others. Panelist Creative Artists Pub. Service Program, N.Y.C., 1976. Nat. Endowment for Arts grantee, 1982, Pollock-Krasner Found. grantee, 1985. Home: 330 W 20th St New York NY 10011-3302 Fax: 212-691-3312. E-mail: ssleigh@mindspring.com.

SLEIGHT, ARTHUR WILLIAM, chemist, educator; b. Ballston Spa, NY, Apr. 1, 1939; s. Hollis Decker and Elizabeth (Smith) S.; m. Betty F. Hilberg, Apr. 19, 1963; children: Jeffrey William, Jeannette Anne, Jason Arthur. AB, Hamilton Coll., 1960; PhD, U. Conn., 1963. Faculty U. Stockholm, Sweden, 1963-64; with E.I. du Pont de Nemours & Co., Inc., Wilmington, Del., 1965-89, rsch. mgr. solid. state/catalytic chemistry, 1981-89; Harris Chair prof. materials sci. Oreg. State U., Corvallis, 1989—; dir. Ctr. for Advanced Materials Rsch., 1995—. Adj. prof. U. Del., 1978-89. Editor: Materials Rsch. Bull., 1994—; editorial bd. Inorganic Chemistry Rev., 1979—, Jour. Catalysis, 1986—, Applied Catalysis, 1987—, Solid State Scis., 1987—, Chemistry of Materials, 1988—, Materials Chemistry and Physics, 1988—, Jour. of Solid State Chemistry, 1988—; patentee in field; contbr. articles to profl. jours. Mem. Presdl. Commn. Superconductivity, 1989. Recipient Phila. chpt. Am. Inst. Chemists award, 1988, Gold Medal award Nat. Assn. Sci. Tech. and Soc., 1994. Mem. Am. Chem. Soc. (award Del. sect. 1978, Chemistry of Materials award 1997). Home: PO Box 907 Philomath OR 97370-0907 Office: Oreg State U Dept Chemistry 153 Gilbert Hall Corvallis OR 97331-8546 E-mail: arthur.sleight@orst.edu.

SLEIGHT, VIRGINIA MAE, lawyer; b. Queensbury, N.Y., Mar. 10, 1932; d. Henry Jay and Helen Adelaide (Bennett) S. BA in Polit. Sci., Russell Sage Coll., 1962. Bar: N.Y. 1964, U.S. Dist. Ct. (no. dist.) N.Y. 1966, U.S. Surpeme Ct. 1981. Clk. of ct. & hearing reporter Warren County Family Ct., Queensbury, N.Y., 1954-71; law asst., reporter Warren County Ct., 1971-75, 1st asst. dist. atty., 1975-94, coord. asst. dist. atty., 1994-96; atty. pvt. practice, 1996—. Adminstrv. v.p. Mohican Coun., Boy Scouts Am., Glens Falls, N.Y., 1994-98, mem. exec. bd. Twin Rivers Coun., Albany, 1998-2000. Mem. AAUW, N.Y. Bar Assn., Warren County Bar Assn., Bus. & Profl. Women, Soc. Prevention Cruelty to Animals Upstate N.Y., Chapman Hist. Mus., Hyde Mus. Republican. Avocations: swimming, skiing. Home and Office: 369 Aviation Rd Queensbury NY 12804-2915

SLEIK, THOMAS SCOTT, lawyer; b. La Crosse, Wis., Feb. 24, 1947; s. John Thomas and Marion Gladys (Johnson) S.; m. Judith Mattson, Aug. 24, 1968; children: Jennifer, Julia, Joanna. BS, Marquette U., 1969, JD, 1971. Bar: Wis. 1971, U.S. Dist. Ct. (we. dist.) Wis. 1971. Assoc. Hale Skemp Hanson Skemp & Sleik, La Crosse, 1971-74, ptnr., 1975—. State pres. Boy Scouts Am., 1981-83, bd. dirs. Gateway Area Coun., 1973-99, pres., 1980-81; trustee La Crosse Pub. Libr., 1981—; bd. dirs. Children's Mus. of LaCrosse, Greater La Crosse Area United Way, 1985-92, campaign chmn., 1986, pres., 1987; mem. Sch. Dist. La Crosse Bd. Edn., 1973-77, v.p., 1977; Festmaster, Oktoberfest (LaCross Festivals Inc.), 2001, trustee, 2001--. Fellow Am. Acad. Matrimonial Lawyers (pres. Wis. chpt. 1999-2000); mem. ABA, State Bar Wis. (bd. govs. 1987-94, pres. 1992-93, spkr. litigation sect. and family law seminars), La Crosse County Bar Assn. Roman Catholic. Home: 4082 Glenhaven Dr La Crosse WI 54601-7503 Office: Hale Skemp Hanson Skemp & Sleik 505 King St Ste 300 La Crosse WI 54602-1927 E-mail: tss@halestemp.com.

SLEMMER, CARL WEBER, JR. retired lawyer; b. Camden, N.J., Mar. 28, 1923; s. Carl and Annetta (Donner) S.; m. Renée Jeannette Kinsey, Oct. 11, 1952; children: Michael, John, Sandra. BS, Muhlenberg Coll., 1948; JD, Temple U., 1963. Bar: N.J. 1972, Pa. 1972, U.S. Dist. Ct. N.J. 1972, Fla. 1974. Various pers. positions RCA, Camden, 1950-55; mgr. labor rels. Allied Chem. Corp., Morristown, N.J., 1955-67; dir. employee rels. Exide Corp., Phila., 1967-82; pvt. practice Cherry Hill, N.J., 1982-83; dir. labor rels. Columbia U., N.Y.C., 1983-89; mgr. tax office H & R Block, Marlton, N.J., 1991-93; ret., 1993. Mem. labor coun. U. Pa., Phila., 1967-82. Lt. (j.g.) USN, 1943-46, PTO. Republican. Presbyterian. Avocations: tennis, reading, travel, legal research. Home: 888 Heritage Rd Moorestown NJ 08057-1330 E-mail: carlslemmer@cs.com.

SLEMMONS, ROBERT SHELDON, architect; b. Mitchell, Nebr., Mar. 12, 1922; s. Matthew Garvin and K. Fern (Borland) S.; m. Dorothy Virginia Herrick, Dec. 16, 1945; children: David (dec.), Claire, Jennifer, Robert, Timothy. AB, U. Nebr., 1947, BArch, 1948. Draftsman Davis & Wilson, Archs., Lincoln, Nebr., 1947-48; chief designer, project arch. Office of Kans. State Arch., Topeka, 1948-54; assoc. John A. Brown, Arch., 1954-56; ptnr. Brown & Slemmons, Arch., 1956-69; v.p. Brown-Slemmons-Krueger, Archs., 1969-73; owner Robert S. Slemmons, A.I.A. & Assocs., Archs., 1973—. Cons. Kans. State Office Bldg. Commn., 1956-57; lectr. in design U. Kans., 1961; bd. dirs. Kaw Valley State Bank & Trust Co., Topeka, 1978-92. Prin. archtl. works include Kans. State Office Bldg., 1954, Topeka Presbyn. Manor, 1960-74, Meadowlark Hills Ret. Cmty., 1979, Shawnee County Adult Detention Facility, 1985. Bd. dirs. Topeka Civic Symphony Soc., 1950-60, Midstates Ret. Cmtys., Inc., 1986-92, Topeka Festival Singers; cons. Ministries for Aging, Inc., Topeka, 1984-97; mem. Topeka Bd. Bldg. and Fire Appeals, Kans., 1977-97, Com. for Employer Support of the Guard and Res. With USNR, 1942-48. Mem. AIA (Topeka pres. 1955-56, Kans. dir. 1957-58, com. on housing, com. for hist. resources), Internat. Conf. Bldg. Ofcls., Topeka Art Guild (pres. 1950), Am. Corrections Assn., Kans. Coun. Chs. (dir. 1961-62), Shawnee County Hist. Soc., Greater Topeka C. of C. (sr. coun.), Downtown Topeka Inc. (v.p. 1992-99), Topeka, Shawnee County Libr. (dir. friends of the libr.), St. Andrews Soc. (pres.), SAR (pres. state soc., pres. chpt.), Soc. of Antiquaries of Scotland (fellow), U. Nebr. Alumni Assn. (life), Band Alumni Assn., Kiwanis (pres. 1966-67), Topeka Knife and Fork Club. Presbyterian (elder, deacon, chmn. trustees). Office: Slemmons Assocs Archs 534 S Kansas Ave Ste 140 Topeka KS 66603-3473 E-mail: bpresource@webtv.net.

SLEMON, GORDON RICHARD, electrical engineering educator; b. Bowmanville, Ont., Can., Aug. 15, 1924; s. Milton Everitt and Selena (Johns) S.; m. Margaret Jean Matheson, July 9, 1949; children: Sally, Stephen, Mark, Jane. BASc., U. Toronto, 1946, MASc., 1948; D.I.C., Imperial Coll. Sci., London (Eng.) U., 1951, PhD, 1952; D of Engring. (hon.), Meml. U. Nfld., 1994. Asst. prof. elec. engring. N.S. Tech. Coll., Can., 1953-55; assoc. prof. U. Toronto, Ont., Can., 1955-63, prof. Can., 1964-90, chmn. dept. elec. engring. Can., 1966-76, dean of faculty of applied sci. and engring. Can., 1979-86, prof. emeritus Can., 1990—. Colombo plan adviser, India, 1963-64; pres. Elec. Engring. Consociates, 1976-79; bd. dirs. Inverpower Controls Ltd., Innovations Found. Author: (with J.M. Ham) Scientific Basis of Electrical Engineering, Magnetoelectric Devices, (with A. Straughen) Electric Machinery; (with S.B. Dewan, A. Straughen) Power Semiconductor Drives, Electric Machines and Drives; contbr. articles to profl. jours. Chmn. Innovations Found., 1980-93, vice chmn., 1993—97; chmn. Microelectronics Devel. Ctr., 1983-88. Decorated officer Order of Can.; recipient excellence in tchg. award Western Electric, 1965, Can. Centennial medal, 1967, Ross medal, 1978, 83, Gold medal Jugoslav Union of Nikola Tesla Socs., Engring. Alumni medal, Educator of Yr. award Can. Engrs., 1992, Hall of Distinction award U. Toronto, 1992, Achievement award IEEE Magnetics Soc., 1997, Arbor award U. Toronto, 1997. Fellow Can. Acad. Engring. (pres. 1998-99), Engring. Inst. Can., Instn. Elec. Engrs. (hon. fellow 1995), IEEE (Centennial medal 1984, Nikola Tesla award, Millennium medal 2000); mem. Am. Soc. Engring. Edn., others. Achievements include patents in field. Home: 40 Chatfield Dr Don Mills ON Canada M3B 1K5 Office: U Toronto Fac Applied Sci and Engring Toronto ON M5S 3G4 Canada E-mail: g.slemon@utoronto.com.

SLENCZYNSKA, RUTH, concert pianist, author, educator; b. Sacramento, Jan. 15, 1925; d. Josef and Dorothy (Goldstein) S.; m. George Anderw Born, June 17, 1944 (div. 1955); m. James Richard Kerr, Aug. 12, 1967 (dec. Mar. 2001). Student, Egon Petri, Artur Schnabel, Alfred Cortot, S. Rachmoninoff; MusD (hon.), Lebanon Valley Coll., 1977; D of Art, So. Ill. U., 2000. Instr. piano Coll. of Our Lady of Mercy, 1945-49, San Francisco Cmty. Music Sch., 1949-52; prof. music, artist-in-residence So. Ill. U., Edwardsville, 1966—2002, Soochow U., Taipei, Taiwan, 2002—. Vis. lectr. U. R.I., summers 1961-67; condr. over 400 workshops at univs. in N.Am., S.Am., Europe; adjudicator local, nat. and internat. competitions, including Internat. Liszt Competition, Utrecht, The Netherlands, 1999, Busoni Internat. Piano Competition, Italy, 1999, Chopin Nat. Competition, Miami, Fla., 2000. Author: (with Louis Biancolli) Forbidden Childhood, 1958, (with Ann Lingg) Music at Your Fingertips, 1962; contbr. articles to mus. mags.; rec. artist for Music Libr., RCA Victor, Deca, Mus. Heritage Soc., ACA Digital, Ivory Classic, also others; over 3000 solo and orchestral appearances in N.Am., S.Am., Europe, Africa, Asia, New Zealand. Mem. Delta Omicron, Phi Beta Chi. Avocations: collecting fine art, gourmet cooking. Home: 180 West End Ave Apt 27A New York NY 10023-5543

SLENKER, RICHARD DREYER, JR. broadcast executive; b. New Rochelle, N.Y., June 2, 1957; s. Richard D. and Ellen (Mullins) S.; m. Maria Pope, July 10, 1982; children: Scarlett Anne, Jessica Martha, Elizabeth Ellen, Martha Maria, Richard III. BA in Communications, Colgate U., 1979; MS in Tech. Mgmt., N.Y. Poly. U., 1986. Engr. WPIX, Inc., N.Y.C., 1979-82, engring. supr., 1982-86, dir. tech. ops., 1986-91; v.p. ops. and engring. Sta. WTTG-TV, Fox TV, Washington, 1991-96; v.p. engring. & ops. Fox TV Stas., Inc., 1995-96; exec. v.p., 1997—; sr. v.p., chief tech. officer Am. Sky Broadcasting, 1996-97; exec. v.p. Fox TV Sta. Inc., 1997—. Office: Fox TV Stas Inc 5151 Wisconsin Ave NW Washington DC 20016-4124

SLEPCHENKO, BORIS MOYSEYEVICH, mathematical physicist, educator; b. Chelyabinsk, Russia, Dec. 4, 1954; s. Moysey Abramovich and Mariya Davydovna Slepchenko. BEd with honors, Chelyabinsk Tchrs. Tng. Coll., 1977; PhD, Ural State U., Ekaterinburg, Russia, 1988. Instr. Vologda (Russia) State Tchrs. Tng. Coll., 1982-83; rsch. fellow State U. Edn., Chelyabinsk, 1983-88, asst. prof., 1989-94, assoc. prof., 1995-96; instr. U. Conn. Health Ctr., Farmington, 1998-2000, asst. prof., 2000—. Cons. Bd. Edn., Chelyabinsk, 1983-96. Contbr. articles to profl. jours., including Soviet Jour. Physics, Low Temperature Physics, Biophys. Jour., Jour. Cell Biology, Jour. Computational Physics, Sci., others. Soros Found. award, 1994. Mem. Biophys. Soc. Avocation: playing piano. Office: U Conn Health Ctr 263 Farmington Ave Farmington CT 06030-1507 Fax: 860-679-1039. E-mail: boris@neuron.uchc.edu.

SLEPIAN, DAVID, mathematician, communications engineer; b. Pitts., June 30, 1923; s. Joseph and Rose Grace (Myerson) S.; m. Janice Dorothea Berek, Apr. 18, 1950; children: Steven Louis, Don Joseph, Anne Maria. Student, U. Mich., 1941-43; MA, Harvard U., 1947, PhD, 1949; postdoctoral studies, Cambridge U., Eng., 1949, Sorbonne, Paris, 1950. With AT&T Bell Labs., Murray Hill, N.J., 1950-82, head math. studies dept., 1970-82. Prof. elec. engring. U. Hawaii, Honolulu, 1970-81; McKay prof. elec. engring. U. Calif., Berkeley, 1957-58, Regents lectr., 1977. Editor, author: Development of Information Theory, 1973; contbr. articles to profl. jours.; patentee in field. Served with U.S. Army, 1943-46, ETO. Von Neumann lectr. Soc. for Indsl. and Applied Math., 1982; Parker fellow in physics Harvard U., 1949-50. Fellow IEEE (editor Procs. 1969-70, Alexander Graham Bell award 1981), AAAS, Inst. Math. Stats.; mem. NAS, NAE, Am. Acad. Arts and Scis. Avocations: music, travel, languages. Home: 7 Sunningdale Ct Maplewood NJ 07040 E-mail: dslepian@comcast.net.

SLEPIAN, JACOB ZEIGER, otolaryngologist; b. McKeesport, Pa., June 9, 1938; s. Philip and Violet Frances (Zeiger) S.; m. Carole Ruth Gallancy, Mar. 23, 1968; children: Danielle, Elizabeth. BA, Harvard Coll., 1961; MD, U. Bologna, Italy, 1968; MS, U. Fla., 1969; MBA, U. Conn., 1995. Diplomate Am. Bd. Otolaryngology. Intern N.Y. Polyclinic Hosp., 1969-70; resident in gen. surgery Suburban Hosp., Bethesda, Md., 1970-71; resident in otolaryngology Columbia-Presbyn. Med. Ctr., N.Y.C., 1971-74; practice medicine specializing in otolaryngology Derby, Conn., 1974-84, Bridgeport, 1976—, Ansonia, 1984-95. Active staff Griffin Hosp., 1974-95, courtesy staff, 1995-; active staff Park City Hosp., Bridgeport, 1976-90; cons. physician Southbury (Conn.) Tng. Sch., also nursing homes and army hosps. Col. Med. Corps USAR, 1984—. Mem. ENT Soc. Conn., Conn. State Med. Soc., New Haven County Med. Soc., Lower Naugatuck Valley Med. Soc., Assn. Mil. Surgeons U.S., Soc. Med. Cons. to Armed Forces U.S. Avocation: distance running. Home: 387 Haystack Hill Rd Orange CT 06477-1018 Office: 881 Lafayette Blvd Bridgeport CT 06604-4705 E-mail: jzslep@aol.com.

SLEPIAN, PAUL, mathematician, educator; b. Boston, Mar. 26, 1923; s. Philip and Ida (Goldstein) S.; children— Laura, Jean. S.B., Mass. Inst. Tech., 1950; PhD, Brown U., 1956. Mathematician Hughes Aircraft Co., 1956-60; assoc. prof. math. U. Ariz., 1960-62; assoc. prof. Rensselaer Poly. Inst., Troy, N.Y., 1962-65, prof. math., 1965-69; prof., chmn. dept. math. Bucknell U., Lewisburg, Pa., 1969-70; prof. math. Howard U., Washington, 1970—. Summer vis. staff mem. Los Alamos Sci. Lab., 1976, 78, 79 Mem. Am. Math. Soc., Soc. Indsl. and Applied Math., Math. Assn. Am. Home: 1331 W 40th St Baltimore MD 21211-1728

SLEPOWITZ, GARY A. pediatrician; b. Bklyn., Nov. 28, 1950; s. Hyman and Lillian (Friedlander) S.; m. Robin Gelfand; children: Melissa, Samantha. BS, MD, CUNY, 1972. Intern in pediats. Med. Ctr. Montefiore Hosp., Bronx, N.Y., 1975-76, resident in pediats. Med. Ctr., 1976-78. Mem. Am. Acad. Pediat.

SLESINGER, DORIS PEYSER, sociology educator; b. N.Y.C., Dec. 26, 1927; d. Harold L. and Helene (Fantel) Peyser; m. Jonathan Avery Slesinger, Feb. 2, 1950 (div. 1976); children: Jeffrey, David, Paul Avery; m. Edward Wellin, Aug. 6, 1976. AB, Vassar Coll., 1949; MA, U. Mich., 1960; Phd, U. Wis., 1973. Various rsch. and editl. positions U. Wis.-Milw., U. Mich., Ann Arbor, 1951-69; co-dir. Applied Population Lab., dept. rural sociology U. Wis., Madison, 1975-87; co-dir. Wis. State Data Ctr. U. Wis.-Extension, 1979-87; asst. prof. dept. rural sociology U. Wis., Madison, 1974-80, assoc. prof., 1980-84, prof., 1984-98, chair dept., 1987-91, emerita prof., 1998—. Mem. com. on health and safety implications of child labor Nat. Rsch. Coun., 1997-98; mem. health svcs. devel. grants rev. com., agy. for health care policy and rsch. U.S. Dept. HHS, 1991-94. Author: Mothercraft and Infant Health: A Sociodemographic and Sociocultural Approach, 1981; author software; contbr. chpts. to books, articles to profl. jours. Bd. dirs. Group Health Coop. of South Ctrl. Wis., Inc., 1984-87, Wis. Coun. Hum;n Concerns, 1984-88, 88-92; mem. Wis. Gov.'s Adv. Cou. on Migrant Labor, 1998—. Recipient numerous grants and fellowships. Mem. APHA, Nat. Rural Health Assn., Population Assn. Am., Am. Sociol. Assn. (com. on regulation of rsch. 1980-83), Rural Sociol. Soc. (v.p. 1989-90, chair endowment com. 1992-93, Disting. Rural Sociol. award 2002). Office: U Wis Dept Rural Sociology 1450 Linden Dr Madison WI 53706-1522 E-mail: slesinger@ssc.wisc.edu.

SLESNICK, NATASHA, psychologist, researcher; b. Ajmer, Rajasthan, India, Dec. 19, 1966; , U.S., 1969; d. Irwin Leonard and Donna May Slesnick; m. Eric C. Jaderlund, Aug. 1, 1992 (div. Mar. 10, 1997); children: Dain Slesnick-Jaderlund, Soren Slesnick-Jaderlund; life ptnr. Daniel Henry Segelken (dec.); children: Tatiana; m. Richard J. Gozur, July 8, 2002. BS Psychology, U. Washington, 1985; PhD, U. N.Mex., 1996. Lic. clin. psychologist. Postdoctoral fellow U. N.Mex., Albuquerque, 1996—98, rsch. asst. prof. psychology, 1998—. Director runaway and homeless youth program U. N.Mex. Ctr. Alcoholism Substance Abuse and Addictions, Albuquerque, 1998—. Author: (treatment manual) Ecologically-Based Family Therapy for Runaway Youth, 2002. Active Albuquerque Partnership, 1999. Grantee, Nat. Inst. on Drug Abuse, 1998—, Nat. Inst. on Alcohol Abuse and Alcoholism and Ctr. for Substance Abuse Treatment, 1998—, Nat. Inst. on Drug Abuse, 2001—, Ctr. for Substance Abuse Treatment, 2001—. Mem.: APHA, APA, Assn. Advancement Behavior Therapies. Avocations: homeless advocacy, jogging, writing. Office: U NMex CASAA 2650 Yale Se Albuquerque NM 87106 Office Fax: 505-768-0278. Personal E-mail: tash@unm.edu. Business E-Mail: tash@unm.edu.

SLETTEN, JOHN ROBERT, construction company executive; b. Gt. Falls, Mont., Sept. 19, 1932; s. John and Hedvig Marie (Finstad) S.; m. Patricia Gail Thomas, Dec. 16, 1962; children: Leighanne, Kristen Gail, Erik John. BS in Archtl. Engring., Mont. State U., 1956, PhD (hon.), 1993. Estimator Sletten Constrn. Co., Gt. Falls, 1956-63, v.p., area mgr. Las Vegas, Nev., 1963-65, pres., chief exec. officer Gt. Falls, 1969—. Bd. dirs. 1st Banks, Gt. Falls, Blue Cross-Blue Shield, Helena, Mont. Chmn. Gt. Falls Mil. Affairs Com., 1985; pres. President's Cir., Mont. State U., Bozeman, 1986; trustee Mont. Hist. Soc., Helena, 1987. with USMC, 1950-52. Mem. Mont. Contractors Assn. (bd. dirs. 1969-75, pres. 1974), Mont. C. of C. (chmn. 1984), Pachyderm Club, Rotary (bd. dirs. Gt. Falls), Elks. Republican. Lutheran. Avocations: skiing, fishing, hunting. Office: Sletten Inc 1000 25th St N PO Box 2467 Great Falls MT 59403-2467

SLEVIN, JOHN A. lawyer; b. Peoria, Ill., Sept. 26, 1935; s. J. Spalding and Lucille (Wagner) S.; m. Mary M. Hurst, July 6, 1957; children: Kathleen, John, Maureen, Kevin, Bridget, Brian, Meaghan, Moira. PhB, U. Notre Dame, 1957, JD, 1960. Bar: Ill. 1960, U.S. Dist. Ct. (no. dist., cent. dist. and so. dist.) Ill., U.S. Ct. Appeals (7th cir.) 1966. Assoc. Hershey & Bliss, Taylorville, Ill., 1960-62; ptnr. Koos & Slevin, Peoria, 1962-63; pvt. practice, 1963-66; ptnr. Vonachen, Lawless, Trager & Slevin, 1966—. Bd. dirs. Notre Dame (Ind.) Alumni Assn., 1983-86; bd. dirs., treas. Peoria Cursillo, 1991-95; pres. Vis. Nurses Assn., Peoria, 1984-90. Mem. ABA, ATLA, Ill. Bar Assn., Ill. Trial Lawyers Assn., Nat. Bd. Trial Advocacy (cert. civil trial advocate), Abraham Lincoln Inns of Ct. (bd. dirs. 1990—, pres. 1999-2000). Avocations: golf, cooking. Office: Vonachen Lawless Trager & Slevin 456 Fulton St Ste 425 Peoria IL 61602-1240 E-mail: jslevin@vltslaw.com.

SLEVIN, PATRICK JEREMIAH, media relations consultant; b. White Plains, N.Y., Dec. 25, 1968; s. Jeremiah James Slevin and Frances Maria Fuller; m. Eileen Patricia Barrett, Jan. 25, 1992; children: Brendan Liam, Mary Catherine, Kathleen Joan. Paralegal cert., Inst. for Paralegal Studies, 1994; BA, Eckerd Coll., 1999; postgrad., Fla. State U., 2001—. Mayor City of Safety Harbor, Fla., 1996-99; paralegal Eckerd Corp., Clearwater, 1999—2001; with Nat. Fedn. Ind. Bus., 2001—. Mem. Cmty. Devel. Citizen Adv. Com., Safety Harbor, 1994-96; cons. in field. Fla. state coord. Conservative Polit. Action Conf., Washington, 1997-98; fundraiser Big Bros./Sisters, Tampa, 1996; hon. chmn. Young Ams. for Dole, 1996. With USAF 1988-91. Featured as govt. leader in Tampa Bay mag., 1997. Republican. Roman Catholic. Avocations: weightlifting, running, reading, movies, golfing. Home: 1706 Copperfield Cir Tallahassee FL 32312-3754

SLEWETT, ROBERT DAVID, lawyer; b. N.Y.C., June 4, 1945; s. Nathan and Evelyn (Miller) S.; m. Sheila Faith Winkler, Jan. 27, 1973; children: Gregory, Danielle. BA in Pub. Affairs, George Washington U., 1967; JD, Cornell U., 1970. Bar: Fla. 1970. Mem. Smith and Mandler, Miami Beach, Fla., 1970-73; with Robert D. Slewett, Atty. at Law, 1973-87; ptnr. Steinberg, Slewett & Yaffe, 1987-98, Robert D. Slewett, P.A., Miami Beach, 1998—. Lectr. in probate and medicaid field. Exec. v.p., gen. counsel Nat. Parkinson Found., Miami, Fla., 1993—; bd. dirs., legal counsel Boystown of Jerusalem Found. Am., N.Y.C., 1993—; mem. Dade County Estate Planning Coun., Heritage Soc. Miami Jewish Home and Hosp. Named One of Leading Fla. Attys. in Field of Trusts and Estates. Mem. Nat. Acad. Elder Lawyers, Fla. Bar Assn. (probate litigation com., probate rules com. 2000—), Dade County Bar Assn. (chmn. spl. needs trust com.), Estate Planning Coun. Dade County. Home: 2235 NE 204th St Miami FL 33180-1311 Office: 801 NE 167 St Fl 2 North Miami Beach FL 33162 Fax: 305-455-2049. E-mail: slewlaw@msn.com.

SLEWITZKE, CONNIE LEE, retired career officer; b. Mosinee, Wis., Apr. 15, 1931; d. Leo Thomas and Amelia Marie (Hoffman) S. BSN, U. Md., Balt., 1971; MA in Counseling and Guidance, St. Mary's U., San Antonio, 1976. Commd. 1st lt. U.S. Army, 1957, advanced through grades to brig. gen., 1987; ret., 1987; chief dept. nursing Letterman Army Med. Ctr. U.S. Army, San Francisco, 1978-80; asst. chief nurse Army Nurse Corps U.S. Army, Washington, 1980-83; chief brigadier gen. U.S. Army, 1983-87. V.p. Walter Reed Soc. Contbr. articles to profl. jours. Decorated D.S.M., Legion of Merit, Bronze Star medal. Mem.: Am. Assn. for History of Nursing, Women in Mil. Svc. for Am. Found. (v.p.), Assn. U.S. Army, Alumni Assn. U.S. Army War Coll. Avocations: photography, travel, music.

SLICHTER, CHARLES PENCE, physicist, educator; b. Ithaca, N.Y., Jan. 21, 1924; s. Sumner Huber and Ada (Pence) S.; m. Gertrude Thayer Almy, Aug. 23, 1952 (div. Sept. 1977); children: Sumner Pence, William Almy, Jacob Huber, Ann Thayer; m. Anne FitzGerald, June 7, 1980; children: Daniel Huber, David Pence AB, Harvard U., 1946, MA, 1947, PhD, 1949; DSc (hon.), U. Waterloo, 1993; LLD (hon.), Harvard U., 1996. Rsch. asst. Underwater Explosives Rsch. Lab., Woods Hole, Mass., 1943-46; faculty U.

Ill., Urbana, 1949—, prof. physics, 1955-97, prof. Ctr. for Advanced Study, 1968-97, prof. chemistry, 1986-97, rsch. prof. physics, 1997—, prof. emeritus, 1997—. Morris Loeb lectr. Harvard U., 1961; mem. Pres.'s Sci. Adv. Com., 1964-69, Com. on Nat. Medal Sci., 1969-74, Nat. Sci. Bd., 1975-84, Pres.'s Com. Sci. and Tech., 1976 Author: Principles of Magnetic Resonance, 1963, 3d edit., 1989; Contbr. articles to profl. jours. Former trustee, mem. corp. Woods Hole Oceanog. Instn.; mem. Harvard Corp., 1970-95. Recipient Langmuir award Am. Phys. Soc., 1969, Buckley prize, 1996; Alfred P. Sloan fellow, 1955-61. Fellow AAAS, Am. Phys. Soc., Internat. Electron Paramagnetic Resonance Soc.; mem. NAS (Comstock prize 1993), Am. Acad. Arts and Scis., Am. Philos. Soc., Internat. Soc. Magnetic Resonance (pres. 1987-90, Trienniel prize 1986). Home: 61 Chestnut Ct Champaign IL 61822-7121

SLICKER, FREDERICK KENT, lawyer; b. Tulsa, Aug. 21, 1943; s. James Floyd and Lucille Geneva (Nordling) S.; children: Laura, Kipp. BA, U. Kans., 1965, JD with highest distinction, 1968; LLM, Harvard U., 1973. Bar: Kans. 1968, U.S. Ct. Mil. Appeals 1968, U.S. Supreme Ct. 1972, Tex. 1973, Okla. 1980. Prin. founder Slicker Law Firm, P.C., 2000—. Gen. counsel Image Analysis, Inc., Centrex, Inc., NUBAR, Inc. Author: A Practical Guide to Church Bond Financing, 1985, Angels All Around, 1999. With Promise Keepers. Capt. U.S. Army, 1965—72. Mem. ABA, Okla. Bar Assn., Order of Coif. Democrat. Methodist. Avocation: Christian men's ministries. Office: 4444 E 66th Ste #201 Tulsa OK 74136-4206 E-mail: fslicker@swbell.com.

SLIDER, DORLA DEAN (DORLA FREEMAN), artist; b. Tampa, Fla., Sept. 9, 1929; d. Samuel Manning and Ida Caroline (Heller) Weeks; m. James Harold Slider, July 8, 1951; 1 child, Cindi Darnel Slider Dvornicky. Studied with Dr. Walter Emerson Baum, Allentown, Pa., 1940-48. Profl. advisor Pottstown (Pa.) Area Artists Guild, 1967-94; mem. jury of selection Nat. Soc. Painters in casein and acrylic, N.Y.C., 1992, 95, 99, 2001; juror selection and awards Fla. Keys Watercolor Soc., Key West, 1987-90; nat. art judge and juror nat. and regional art shows; juror selection and awards Bethlehem Pallette Club, Moravian Coll., Bethlehem, Pa., 2002. Exhibited in group shows at Am. Watercolor Soc., The Nat. Acad. of Design, Allied Artists, Audubon Artists, KnickerbockerArtists, Nat. Arts Club, Nat. Soc. Painters in Casein and Acrylic, N.Y.C., Pa. Acad. Fine Arts, Phila. Mus. Art, William Penn Mus., Pa., Butler Inst. Am. Art, Ohio, Watercolor U.S.A., Mainstreams Nat., Ohio, The Salt Palace, Utah, others; represented in permanent collections Brandywine River Mus., Chadds Ford, Pa., Berman Art Mus., Collegeville, Pa., Lenfest Group West Chester Pa.; included in The Collected Best of Watercolor, 2002. Recipient Doris Kennedy Meml. award, Audubon Artists N.Y., 1979, C.L. Wolfe Art Club Gold medal, N.Y.C., 1970; Best of Show award Miami Water Color Soc., 1984, Arjomari/Arches/Rives award Nat. Soc. Painters Acrylic, 1991, award of excellence Nat. League Am. Pen Women, Washington, 1996, top awards Mainstream Internat., Allentown Art Mus., Internat. Soc. Artists, Salmagundi Club, Nat. Soc Painters in Casein and Acrylic, Marion F. Gourville award Bianco Gallery, 1996, Artists Equity Bd. Dirs. award Villanova Coll., 1998, Thomas Moran Meml. award Watercolor, Salmagundi Club, N.Y., 2000, Old Forge Hardware Co. award Adirondacks 19th Ann. Nt. Am. Watercolors, N.Y., 2000, others; featured in Rockport Pubs. Painting Light and Shadow; Best of Watercolor Series, 1997, Best of Watercolor Series III, 1999. Mem. Am. Watercolor Soc. (Herb Olsen award 1972), Nat. Soc. Painters in Casein and Acrylic, Knickerbocker Artists (gold medal 1977), Audubon Artists (Savoir Faire award 1993, Yarka award 1995, David and Elsie Ject-Key Meml. award 1997), Am. Artist Profl. League N.Y., Artists Equity, Phila. Watercolor Soc. (bd. dirs. 1996—, Dawson Meml. award 1994, Judges award 1998, Watercolor U.S.A. cash award, Springfield Art Mus., 1999, Newman Gallery award for excellence in watercolor 2000), Watercolor USA Hon. Soc. (elected). Home: 268 Estate Rd Boyertown PA 19512-1922 E-mail: art99@ptd.net.

SLIEFERT, PAULA RHEA, manufacturing company executive; b. Storm Lake, Iowa, Aug. 30, 1968; d. Gary Lee Sliefert and Sharon Elizabeth (Hansen) Brugger. BA in German and Internat. Mgmt., Simpson Coll., 1990; MA in German, Bowling Green State U., 1993. Regional sales mgr. Dee Zee Mfg., Des Moines, 1994-97; product mgr. Deflecta-Shield Corp., Indianola, Iowa, 1997-99; mktg. mgr. Lund Internat., Anoka, Minn., 1999-2001, dir. mktg. comms., 2001—. Avocations: international and domestic travel, sports, avid book reader. Home: 18948 96th Pl N Maple Grove MN 55311-1225 Office: Lund Internat 911 Lund Blvd Anoka MN 55303-1090 E-mail: psliefert@lundlook.com.

SLIFE, BRENT DONALD, psychologist, educator, author; b. Ames, Iowa, Dec. 7, 1953; s. Leo Nathan and Phyllis (Bryant) S.; m. Karen Somerville, May 22, 1976; children: Conor Merchant, Nathan Matthew, Jacob Tristan. BA, William Jewell Coll., Liberty, Mo., 1976; MS, Purdue U., 1977, PhD, 1981. Lic. clin. psychologist and psychotherapist. Intern Palo Alto (Calif.) VA Med. Ctr., 1980-81; asst. prof. Santa Clara (Calif.) U., 1981-84, Baylor U., Waco, Tex., 1984-87, assoc. prof., 1987-93, prof. psychology, 1993-94, Brigham Young U., Provo, Utah, 1994—, chmn. theoretical program, 1998—. Author: Taking Sides: Clashing Views on Controversial Psychological Issues, 1980, 2002, Time and Psychological Explanation, 1993, What's Behind the Research, 1995, Critical Issues in Psychotherapy, 2001; editor: Jour. Theoretical and Philos. Psychology, 1989—98; assoc. editor Jour. Theoretical and Philos. Psychology, 1998—, mem. edit. bd., assoc. editor Jour. of Mind and Behavior, 1990—, Theory and Psychology, 1990—94, Methods, 1999—. Bd. dirs., treas. Sunny View Manor Retirement Facility, 1982-84; psychol. counselor Caritas Food and Care Coalition, Waco, 1990-94; chmn. com., asst. scoutmaster Boy Scouts Am., Waco, Tex., 1984-93; Lindon, Utah, 1994-98; elder Presbyn. Ch., American Fork, Utah, 1996—. Recipient Circle of Achievement award Baylor U., 1992, Karl G. Maesar award for outstanding rsch., 2002—; named Outstanding Rsch. Prof., Baylor U., 1991, Tchr. of Yr., Brigham Young U., 1997, Most Outstanding Prof., Brigham Young U. Psi Chi, 2000; Elisa R. Snow fellow, 2000-2002. Fellow APA (pres. divsn. 24, 1999-2000, Disting. Contbn. award 1998). Avocations: banjo, piano, organ. Office: Brigham Young U 1072 SWKT Dept Psychology Provo UT 84602

SLIFKIN, LAWRENCE MYER, physics educator; b. Bluefield, W.Va., Sept. 29, 1925; s. Isaac L. and Eva (Baden) S.; m. Miriam Kresses, July 4, 1948; children: Anne, Rebecca, Merle, Naomi. BA, NYU, 1947; PhD, Princeton U., 1950. Rsch. assoc., rsch. asst. prof. U. Ill., Urbana, 1950-54; asst prof. U. Minn., Mpls., 1954-55; asst. prof., then prof. physics U. N.C., Chapel Hill, 1955-91, Bowman Gray prof., 1979-82, Alumni Disting. prof., 1983-91, prof. emeritus, 1991—. Rsch. fellow Oxford U., 1962-63; liaison sci. U.S. Office Naval Rsch., London, 1969-70; collaborateur étranger, CEN-Saclay, France, 1975-76. Editor: (with J. H. Crawford): Point Defects in Solids, vol. I, 1972, vol. II, 1975; contbr. more than 125 articles to profl. jours. and books. With U.S. Army, 1944-46, PTO. Fellow Am. Phys. Soc. (exec. com. div. condensed matter physics 1978-80, Jesse Beams award rsch. excellence S.E. Sect. 1977), Soc. Photographic Scientists and Engrs.; mem. Am. Assn. Physics Tchrs. Democrat. Jewish. Avocations: music, travel, reading, grandfathering. Home: 313 Burlage Cir Chapel Hill NC 27514-2703 Office: U NC Cb 3255 Phillips Hall Chapel Hill NC 27599-3255 E-mail: slifkin@physics.unc.edu.

SLIGER, HERBERT JACQUEMIN, JR. lawyer; b. Urbana, Ill., Nov. 21, 1948; s. Herbert Jacquemin and Marina (Mantia) S.; m. Sandra Ann Ratti, May 3, 1996; children: Lauren Christine, Matthew Ryan, Nicholas Adam, Claire Nicole, Adam Gregory. BS in Fin., U. Ill., 1970; JD, U. Ariz., 1974. Bar: Ariz. 1974, Ill. 1975, U.S. Supreme Ct. 1983, Okla. 1984, U.S. Ct. Appeals (7th cir.) 1980, U.S. Tax Ct. 1980; CPA, Okla. Lawyer Charles W. Phillips Law Offices, Harrisburg, Ill., 1974-75; trust counsel Magna Trust Co., F/K/A Millikin Nat. Bank, Decatur, 1976-80, First of America Trust Co., Springfield, 1980-83; trust counsel personal fin. svcs. group First Interstate Bank Okla. NA, Oklahoma City, 1983-86; mgr. employee benefits trust dept. First Interstate Bank of Okla., NA, 1986-89; v.p., pension counsel Star Bank, NA, Cin., Cin., 1989-90; asst. gen. counsel Bank One Ariz. Corp., Phoenix, 1990-95; asst. gen. counsel, nat. practice group head Banc One Corp., Columbus, Ohio, 1995-98, state gen. counsel Phoenix, 1996-97; sec. of bd. and cashier Bank One, Ariz. NA, 1996-97; sec. of bd. and statutory agt. Banc One Ariz. Corp., 1996-97; sec. bd. Bank One Trust Co. N.A., Columbus, 1996—; asst. gen. counsel, trust counsel practice group head law dept. Bank One Corp., Chgo., 1999—. Co-chmn. Nat. Conf. Lawyers and Corp. Fiduciaries, 1992-94; instr. Chaminade U. Hawaii, Hawaii Tax Inst., 1999. Contbr. articles to profl. jours. Mem. ABA (sect. bus. law, banking law com., trust and investment svcs. subcom. 1991-99, sect. real property, probate and trust law 1974—, fiduciary income taxation subcom. 1994—, fiduciary environ. problems com. 1993-99, sect. of taxation, employee benefits com. 1991-2001), State Bar of Ariz., Okla. Bar Assn., Am. Bankers Assn. (chmn. trust counsel com. 1992-94, mem. and head of fiduciary law dept. Nat./Grad. Trust Sch. Bd. of Faculty Advisors 1994-95, faculty mem. teaching "fiduciary duties under ERISA" Nat. Employee Benefit Trust Sch. 1994-96, spokesman Environ. Risk Task Force 1994-95, mem. trust and investment divsn. exec. com. 1992-94, mini-adv. bd. chairperson trusts and estates 1995-99), Nat. Conf. Lawyers and Corp. Fiduciaries (co-chmn. 1992-94). Roman Catholic. Avocations: phys. fitness, original print collecting.

SLIGH, GARY LEE, English educator; b. Roanoke, Va., May 9, 1958; s. Kinzie Lee and Joyce Berlie (Cawley) S.; m. Julie Simpson, May 5, 1990; children: Carter Lee, Mary Cawley, Graham Simpson. BA in English, U. Va., 1980; MA in Lit., Am. U., Washington, 1984; MDiv, Wesley Theol. Seminary, 1984; PhD in Lit. and Criticism, Indiana (Pa.) U., 1998. Ordained Meth. min., 1983. Mem. clergy United Meth. Ch., Lynchburg and Portsmouth, Va., 1984-92; adj. instr. Old Dominion U., Averett Coll., Tidewater C.C., Norfolk, 1992-99; instr. English Lake-Sumter C.C., Leesburg, Fla., 1999—. Author: Community College Research: An Ivory Tower, 2002. Democrat. Avocation: needlework. Home: 267 E Lady Lake Blvd Lady Lake FL 32159-3898

SLIM, MICHEL S. surgeon, educator, health facility administrator; b. Nov. 18, 1929; s. Saliba and Julia Slim; m. Norma Gebara, Sept. 4, 1958; children: Julie, Lina, Nayla. MD, Am. U., Beirut, Lebanon, 1954. Diplomate Am. Bd. Surgery, Am. Bd. Pediatric Surgery, Am. Bd. Thoracic Surgery. Chief pediatric surgery, prof. surgery Am. U., Beirut, 1963-86; prof. N.Y. Med. Coll., N.Y.C., 1986—; attending Westchester Med. Ctr., Valhalla, N.Y., 1986—, chief pediatric trauma, 1991—, chief pediatric surgery, 1994—. Editl. cons. Pediatric Surg. Internat., 1985—; reviewer Ann. Thoracic Surgery, Jordan Med. Jour.; contbr. articles to profl. jours. Evarts Graham Traveling fellow Am. Assn. Thoracic Surgery, 1970-71. Fellow ACS, Am. Acad. Pediat., Am. Coll. Chest Physicians; mem. Am. Pediatric Surgery Assn., Brit. Assn. Pediatric Surgery, Internat. Soc. Surgery. Office: NY Med Coll Munger Pavilion Valhalla NY 10595 E-mail: mslimpedsurg@hotmail.com.

SLINEY, DAVID HAMMOND, medical physicist; b. Washington, Feb. 21, 1941; s. David Xavier and Ida Lee (Echols) S.; m. Carol Ann Scott, Feb. 19, 1966 (div.); children: Sean S., D. Scott, Stephen P.; m. Judith Sarkany, Sept. 22, 2002. BS in Physics, Va. Poly. Inst., 1963; MS in Physics, Emory U., 1965; PhD in Biophysics, U. London, 1991. Pres. David H. Sliney, Consulting Physicist, Fallston, Md., 1972—; chief laser branch U.S. Army Environ. Hygiene Agy., Aberdeen Proving Ground, 1965-94; program mgr. laser/optical radiation program U.S. Army Ctr. for Health Promotion and Preventive Medicine, 1994—. Chmn. Gordon Research conf. on Lasers in Medicine and Biology, Meriden, N.H., 1976, 84; mem. com. on physical agent TLVs, Am. Conf. Govtl. Indsl. Hygienists, 1966-97, chmn., 1986-96; cons. div. environ. health WHO, Geneva, 1976—; vis. lectr. UNESCO, Beijing, 1987. Author: Safety with Lasers and Other Optical Sources, 1980, Medical Lasers: Their Safe Use, 1992; editor Health Physics Jour., 1976-86, Lasers in the Life Scis.; mem. editorial bd. Lasers in Surgery and Medicine, Lasers and Light in Ophthalmology, Ophthalmic Laser Therapy; contbr. articles to profl. jours. Mem. (apptd.) tech. electronic product radiation safety com. FDA, Rockville, Md., 1982-85; mem. panel on impact of video viewing Nat. Rsch. Coun., Washington, 1981-83; Internat. Electrotech. Commn., Geneva, 1976—; dir. Div. 6, Photobiology, Commn. Internat. de l'Eclairage, 1991—. Capt. U.S. Army, 1965-67. Fulbright fellow U.S. Govt., Herceg-Novi, Yugoslavia, 1976. Fellow Am. Soc. for Lasers in Medicine and Surgery (com. chair 1981-82, bd. dirs. 1989—), Laser Inst. Am. (bd. dirs. 1974-88, 94—, pres. 1997), Soc. Photo-Optical Instrumentation Engrs. (symposia chair); mem. Nat. Coun. Radiation Protection and Measurements, Internat. Radiation Protection Assn. (internat. non-ionizing radiation com.), Internat. Commn. on Non-Ionizing Radiation Protection, Internat. Commn. on Occupational Health, Am. Acad. Ophthalmology (laser safety com.), Optical Soc. Am., Assn. Rsch. in Vision and Ophthalmology. Unitarian Universalist. Avocation: photography. Home: 406 Streamside Dr Fallston MD 21047-2806 Office: Laser/Optical Radiation Pgm USACHPPM Bldg E-1950 Aberdeen Proving Ground MD 21010-5403 E-mail: david.sliney@att.net.

SLINGER, MICHAEL JEFFERY, law library director; b. Pitts., Apr. 12, 1956; s. Maurice and Mary Helen (Kengerski) S.; m. Cheryl Blaney, Apr. 19, 1980; children: Rebecca, Sarah. BA, U. Pitts., 1978; M Librianship, U. S.C., 1979; JD, Duquesne U., 1984. Reference libr. Duquesne U. Sch. Law, Pitts., 1983-84; rsch. libr. U. Notre Dame (Ind.) Sch. Law, 1984-85, head rsch. svcs., 1985-86, assoc. dir. pub. svcs., 1986-90; law libr. dir., assoc. prof. law Suffolk U. Sch. Law, Boston, 1990-93, law libr. dir., prof. law, 1994-95; law libr. dir., prof. law, assoc. dean Cleve. State U., 1995—. Contbr. articles to profl. jours., chpt. to book. Mem. ABA, ALA, Am. Assn. Law Librs., Am. Assn. Law Schs. (exec. bd. sect. on law librs. 1993-94), New Eng. Law Libr. Consortium (treas. 1992-95), Ohio Regional Assn. Law Librs. (v.p. 1987-88, pres. 1988-89, Pres. award 1989). Avocations: reading, sports, family. Office: Cleveland-Marshall Coll Law Law Libr 1801 Euclid Ave Cleveland OH 44115-2223

SLIPMAN, RONALD (SAMUEL SLIPMAN), hospital administrator; b. New Orleans, Aug. 24, 1939; s. Jake and Esther (Steinman) S.; m. Carole Marie Green, July 1, 1961 (div. Feb. 1982); children: Susan Rachel, Lawrence Jay; m. Marilyn Morais, Feb. 5, 1983 (dec. June 1985); m. Lelia Ruth Foster, Jan. 12, 1986; children: Ronald Andrew, Brian Edward. BS, Tulane U., 1961; cert. in supervision techniques, La. State U., 1984; postgrad., NE La. U., 1978-79, 80-81. Design progress estimator Boeing Co., New Orleans, 1964-66; interviewer Tex. Employment Commn., Tyler and Lufkin, 1977-78; pers. technician State of La., Baton Rouge, 1961-62, 63-64, 73-75, 81; rsch. statistician La. Ins. Commn., 1967-68; labor market analyst La. Dept. Labor, 1969-70, 77; pers. dir. Royal Orleans Hotel, New Orleans, 1966-67; mgmt. analyst for quality assurance Earl K. Long Hosp., Baton Rouge, 1981-84, dir. ancillary svcs., 1984-86; mgmt. analyst, spl. asst. to dir. for total quality mgmt. Dept. Vets. Affairs Med. Ctr., Alexandria, La., 1987-88, 89-90; mgmt. cons., 1990-91. Mem. adminstrv. bd. 1st United Meth. Ch., chmn. presch. bd.; cubmaster pack 10 Boy Scouts Am., 1993-94, 96-98, asst. cubmaster, 1994-96, chmn. pack com., 1998-99, mem. pack com., 1999—; trustee Kent Plantation House, Inc., 2000—. Mem. La. Soc. Hosp. Pharmacists, Ctrl. La. Soc. for Human Resource Mgmt., S.W. La. Bridge Assn. (pres., bd. dirs.). Republican. Methodist. Avocations: duplicate bridge, tennis. Home and Office: 105 Foxfire Ln Alexandria LA 71302-8638 E-mail: Rancher200@aol.com.

SLIVE, SEYMOUR, museum director, fine arts educator; b. Chgo., Sept. 15, 1920; s. Daniel and Sonia (Rapoport) S.; m. Zoya Gregorevna Sandomirsky, June 29, 1946; children: Katherine, Alexander, Sarah. AB, U. Chgo., 1943, PhD, 1952; MA (hon.), Harvard U., 1958, Oxford (Eng.) U., 1972. Instr. fine arts Oberlin (Ohio) Coll., 1950-51; chmn. art dept. Pomona (Calif.) Coll., 1952-54; mem. faculty Harvard U., Cambridge, Mass., 1954—, prof. fine arts, 1961—, Gleason prof. fine arts, 1973-91, Gleason prof. fine arts emeritus, 1991—, chmn. dept. fine arts, 1968-71, dir. Fogg Art Mus., 1975-82; Elizabeth and John Moors Cabot dir. emeritus Harvard art museums, 1982. Exchange prof. Leningrad (USSR) U., 1961; Ryerson lectr. Yale U., 1962; Slade prof. Oxford (Eng.) U., 1972-73 Author: Rembrandt and His Critics, 1630-1730, 1953, The Rembrandt Bible, 1959, Catalogue of the Paintings of Frans Hals, 1962, Drawings of Rembrandt, 1965, (with Jakob Rosenberg and E.H. ter Kuile) Dutch Art and Architecture 1600-1800, 2nd edit., 1978, Rembrandt's Drawings, 1965, Frans Hals, 3 vols., 1970-74, Jacob van Ruisdael, 1981, Frans Hals, 1989, Dutch Painting: 1600-1800, 1995, 2d edit., 1998, Jacob van Ruisdael: A Complete Catalogue of His Paintings, Drawings and Etchings, 2001. Trustee Solomon R. Guggenheim Found., 1978—, Norton Simon Mus., 1989-91; bd. dirs. Burlington mag. Found., 1987—. Lt. (j.g.) USNR, 1943-46, PTO. Decorated officer Order Orange Nassau Netherlands, 1962; Fulbright fellow Netherlands, 1951-52; Guggenheim fellow, 1956-57, 78-79; Fulbright research scholar Utrecht (Netherlands) U., 1959-60 Fellow Am. Acad. Arts and Scis.; mem. Karel van Mander Soc. (hon.), Coll. Art Assn. (dir. 1958-62, 65-69), Renaissance Soc., Dutch Soc. Scis. (fgn. mem.), Brit. Acad. (corr. fellow). Office: Harvard U Sackler Art Museum Cambridge MA 02138

SLIVKA, ANDREW PAUL, JR. neurologist, physician; b. Cleve., May 1, 1955; s. Andrew Paul and Yolanda Marie (Casini) S. BS, Bowling Green State U., 1976; MD, Ohio State U., 1980. Intern in internal medicine Montefiore Hosp., Pitts., 1980-81; resident in neurology Ohio State U., Columbus, 1981-84; fellow in cerebral vascular disease Cornell Med. Ctr., N.Y.C., 1984-87; asst. prof. neurology Ohio State U., Columbus, 1987-93, assoc. prof. neurology, 1993—, dir. cerebrovascular divsn. dept. neurology, 1987—, mem. neurology quality assurance com., 1992—, mem. neurology promotion and tenure com., 1993—. Lectr. local cmty. groups. Author: (with others) Diagnosis and Management of Renal Disease and Hypertension, 1994; contbr. articles to profl. jours. including Stroke, Jour. Stroke Cerebrobasc. Diseases. Grantee Am. Heart Assn., 1988, 90, Ohio State U., 1991. Mem. AMA, Am. Acad. Neurology, N.Y. Acad. Scis., Stroke Coun. Am. Heart Assn. Avocations: reading, music, movies, karate. Office: Ohio State U 1654 Upham Dr Columbus OH 43210-1250

SLIVKA, MICHAEL ANDREW, lawyer; b. Ambridge, Pa., Jan. 14, 1955; s. Andrew and Veronica (Yanko) S. AB in Psychology, Cornell U., 1977; JD, U. Miami, 1980. Bar: Fla. 1980, U.S. Dist. Ct. (so. dist.) Fla. 1981, U.S. Ct. Appeals (5th cir.) 1981, U.S. Ct. Appeals (11th cir.) 1981, Colo. 1997, U.S. Dist. Ct. Colo. 1999, U.S. Tax Ct. 2001, cert.: (arbitrator). Pvt. practice, Ft. Lauderdale, Fla., 1990-99; pvt. prac. Colorado Spgs., CO, 1999—. Bd. dirs. Peak Venture Group. Precinct capt., exec. com. Broward County Rep. Party, 1991-92; v.p. West Broward Rep. Club, 1991-92; sec. North Dade/South Broward Estate Planning Coun., 1991-92. Albert C. Murphy scholar Cornell U., 1973. Mem. Fla. Bar Assn. (young lawyers sect., mem. collection forms com. 1983-85, bicentennial com. 1987), Bankruptcy Bar Assn., Assn. for Objective Law, El Paso County Bar Assn., Weston Area Jaycees (past sec.). Republican. Avocations: Objectivist philosophy, weightlifting, motorcycling, gardening. Home and Office: 225 Thames Dr Colorado Springs CO 80906-5952 Fax: 719-576-6963. E-mail: michael@qwest.net.

SLOAME, STUART C. lawyer; b. N.Y.C., Dec. 17, 1939; s. Milton L. and Harriet (Cohen) S.; m. Ellen J. Seeherman, Apr. 5, 1981; 1 child, Joanna Lynn. AB, Columbia Coll., 1961, LLB, 1964; LLM, Bklyn. Law Sch., 1966. Bar: N.Y., D.C. Atty. Fried Frank Harris Shriver & Jacobson, N.Y.C., 1965-66, Kronish Lieb Shainswit Weiner & Hellman, N.Y.C., 1968-69; law asst. to bd. justices 1st dept. N.Y. State Supreme Ct., 1966-68; pvt. practice N.Y.C., 1968-76; ptnr. Hershcopf Sloame and Stevenson, 1977-81; dep. asst. sec. HUD, 1981-85, dep. gen. counsel, 1985-89; pvt. practice Washington, 1990—. Contbr. articles to profl. jours. Bd. dirs. Jewish Social Svcs. Agy. Met. Washington, 1990-93, Am. Jewish Com., 1998—; chmn. Met. Rep. Club, 1972-74. Mem.: ABA (past chmn. sub. com. cmty. reinvestment forum on affordable housing, bd. editors Jour. Affordable Housing and Cmty. Devel. Law), Assn. Bar of City of N.Y. (com. civil ct. 1977—80, com. on state ct. 1972—75, mcpl. affairs com. 1965—68), D.C. Bar Assn., Columbia Law Sch. Alumni Assn. Washington (v.p. 1990—, pres. 1985—89). Avocations: golf, tennis, skiing, sailing, domestic and foreign policy. Office: 4508 28th St NW Washington DC 20008-1034 E-mail: s.sloame@starpower.net.

SLOAN, ALBERT, college president; b. Atlanta, Sept. 24, 1942; s. Albert John Hicks and Addie Cannon S.; m. Emma Lillian Lee, Aug. 29, 1970; children: Ashaki Nicole, Ashante Denise, Alescia Alexandria. BA, Albany State U., 1965; MDiv, Interdenominational Theol., Ctr., Atlanta, 1968; JD, Miles Law Sch., 1982; DDiv, Faith Grant Coll., 1998; LLD, Tex. Coll., 1999. Counselor Upward Bound Program/Ala. State U., Montgomery, 1969-71; team tchr. Huntsville (Ala.) Space Ctr., 1974-75; prof. religion and philosophy Miles Coll., Fairfield, 1972-89, asst. to the pres., 1972-73, dean of chapel, 1971-89, dean of students, 1987-89, pres. Ala., 1989—. Pres. Fairfield Bd. Edn., 1978-93, Birmingham Civil Rights Inst.; mem. Jud. Coun. C.M.E. Ch., Birmingham; assoc. justice C.M.E. Ch. Religious editor: Atlanta Enquirer, 1969-70; contbr. articles to religious publs. Mem. Birmingham Personnel Bd., Leadership Birmingham, 1992—, Fairfield C. of C., 1992—. Recipient Nat. Hist. Preservation award Ala. Hist. Commn., 1994. Mem. Nat. Bar Assn., Omega Psi Phi, Phi Delta Kappa, Delta Theta Pi. Avocations: swimming, singing, public speaking. Office: Miles Coll PO Box 3800 Birmingham AL 35208-0800

SLOAN, ALLAN HERBERT, journalist; b. Bklyn., Nov. 27, 1944; s. Samuel and Doris (Shanblott) S.; m. Nancy Nolan, June 29, 1969; children: Sharon R., Susan M., Dena A. BA, Bklyn. Coll., 1966; MS, Columbia U., 1967. Reporter Charlotte (N.C.) Observer, 1968-72, Detroit Free Press, 1972-79; assoc. editor, staff writer Forbes Mag., N.Y.C., 1979-81; staff writer Money Mag., 1982-84; sr. editor Forbes Mag., 1984-88; columnist N.Y. Newsday, 1989-95; Wall St. editor Newsweek Mag., 1995—. Author: Three Plus One Equals Billions: The Bendix-Martin Marietta War, 1982. Recipient Loeb award for fin. journalism Loeb Found., 1974, 84, 91, 93, 98, Hancock award for fin. journalism Hancock Found., 1992, Loeb Lifetime Achievement award, 2001, Disting. Achievement award Am. Bus. Editors and Writers, 2001. Office: Newsweek 251 W 57th St New York NY 10019-1802

SLOAN, ANDREW EDWARD, neurosurgeon; b. Detroit; BS in Biology, Yale U., 1985; MD, Harvard U., 1990. Resident in surgery UCLA, 1990-91, resident in neurosurgery, 1991-96, chief resident in neurosurgery, 1996-97; fellow in neurosurgery M.D. Anderson Cancer Inst., Houston, 1997-98; asst. prof. neurosurgery, neuro-oncology Wayne State U., Detroit, 1998—; assoc. prof. Karmanos Cancer Ctr., 1998—. Recipient Clinician Investigator award Am. Brain Tumor Assn., 1999. Fellow ACS; mem. Am. Soc. Clin. Oncology (Clin. Rsch. Career Devel. award 2000), Am. Assn. Neurosurgery, Congress of Neurosurgery (sgt.-at-arms), Calif. Assn. Neurol. Surgeons. Avocations: photography, running, swimming. Office: Wayne State U Sch Medicine Dept Neurosurgery Ste 930 4160 John Rst Dept Detroit MI 48201-2020 Fax: (313) 966-0368. E-mail: asloan@neurosurgery.wayne.edu.

SLOAN, DANIEL KAY, electrical engineer; b. Walla Walla, Wash., Oct. 20, 1944; s. James Lester and Bertha Louise (Ulstrup) S.; m. Janice Kay Christensen, Jan. 31, 1965 (dec.). BSEE, Wash. State U., 1967. Product line controls engr. Beloit (Wis.) Corp., 1967-72, product line mgr.-controls, 1972-79; elec. engr. U & I Inc., Kennewick, Wash., 1979-81; elec. project engr. Boise-Cascade, Wallula, 1981-86; sr. elec. project engr. Simpson Tacoma (Wash.) Kraft Co., 1986—. Staff sgt. U.S. Air Guard, 1967-73. Mem. IEEE, Instrumentation, Systems and Automation Soc., Elks. Office: Simpson Tacoma Kraft Co 801 Portland Ave Tacoma WA 98421-3098

SLOAN, DAVID EDWARD, retired corporate executive; b. Winnipeg, Man., Can., Mar. 29, 1922; s. David and Annie Maud (Gorvin) S.; m. Kathleen Lowry Craig, Dec. 26, 1947; children: Pamela Jane, John David, Kathleen Anne. B.Commerce, U. Man., 1942. With Monarch Life Assurance Co., Winnipeg, 1946-47, Can. Pacific Ltd., 1947-88, treas., 1969-88; pres. and chief exec. officer Can. Pacific Securities Ltd., 1985-88. Mem. adv. com. Can. Pension Plan, Can. Govt., 1967-76, chmn., 1974-76. Lt. Royal Can. Army Service Corps, 1942-45. Mem. Fin. Exec. Inst. Can. (past pres. Montreal chpt.), Toronto Soc. Fin. Analysts, Soc. Internat. Treas. (internat. chmn. 1985-86, mem. coun. advisors 1978-87), Assn. Investment Mgmt. and Rsch., U. Man. Alumni Assn., The Toronto Hunt Club. Mem. United Ch. Can. Home: 316 Rosemary Rd Toronto ON Canada M5P 3E3

SLOAN, DONNIE ROBERT, JR. lawyer; b. Nashville, July 24, 1946; s. Donnie R. Sr. and Mary Catharine (Willis) S. BS in Indsl. Engring., Ga. Inst. Tech, 1968; JD cum laude, U. Ga., 1971; LLM, Harvard U., 1975. Bar: Ga. 1971, U.S. Dist. Ct. (no. dist.) Ga. 1971, U.S. Ct. Appeals (11th cir.). Atty. Southwire Co., Carrollton, Ga., 1971-74; assoc., ptnr. Hyatt & Rhoads, P.C., Atlanta, 1975-89; pvt. practice, 1989-96; ptnr. Davidson, Fuller & Sloan, LLP, 1996—. Instr. legal rsch. U. Ga., Athens, 1970-71; instr. music law Ga. State U., Atlanta, 1976. Mem. editl. bd. Ga. Law Rev., 1969-71. Treas. Ga. Wheelchair Athletic Assn., Atlanta, 1981-84; pres., treas. Dixie Wheelchair Athletic Assn., Atlanta, 1984-87. Recipient Appreciation award Ga. Wheelchair Sports and Recreation Assn., 1979; named one of Outstanding Young Men of Am., 1981; named to Dixie Wheelchair Athletic Assn. Hall of Fame, 1990. Mem. Am. Judicature Soc., Phi Kappa Phi, Alpha Phi Mu, Ga. Tech. Club, Harvard Club. Presbyterian. Avocations: skiing, jogging, swimming. Home: 820 Saddlehill Rd Roswell GA 30075 Office: 11330 Lakefield Dr Ste 250 Duluth GA 30097-1578 E-mail: drsloan@dfslaw.com.

SLOAN, EARLE DENDY, JR. chemical engineering educator; b. Seneca, S.C., Apr. 23, 1944; s. Earle Dendy and Sarah (Bellotte) S.; m. Marjorie Nilson, Sept. 7, 1968; children: Earle Dendy III, John Mark. BSChemE, Clemson U., 1965, MSChemE, 1972, PhD in Chem. Engring., 1974. Engr. Du Pont, Chattanooga, 1965-66, Seaford, Del., 1966-67, cons. Parkersburg, W.Va., 1967-68, sr. engr. Camden, S.C., 1968-70; postdoctoral fellow Rice U., 1975; prof. chem. engring. Colo. Sch. Mines, Golden, 1976—, dir. Ctr. for Rsch. on Hydrates and Other Solids, 1990—, Gaylord and Phyllis Weaver dist. prof. chem. engring., 1992—. Inaugural pres. faculty senate Colo. Sch. Mines, 1989-90, disting. lectr., 1997-98, appointed senator, 1998; Tokyo Electric Power Co. chair Keio U., Japan, 1996. Author: Clathrate Hydrates of Natural Gases, 1990, 2d edit., 1998, Hydrate Engineering, 2000; chmn. pub. bd. Chem. Engring. Edn., 1990—. Scoutmaster local Cub Scouts, 1978-81; elder Presbyn. Ch., Golden, Colo., 1977-79, 92-94; elder Ctrl. Presbyn. Ch., Denver, 1999—. Recipient Donald L. Katz award for rsch. Gas Processors Assn. Fellow AIChE (chmn. area Ia thermodynamics and transport 1990-93); mem. Am. Soc. for Engring. Edn. (chmn. ednl. rsch. methods divsn. 1983-85, chmn. chem. engring. divsn. 1984), Am. Chem. Soc., Soc. Petroleum Engrs. (Disting. Lectr. 1996-97). Avocations: cycling, piano, philosophy. Office: Colo Sch of Mines Ctr for Hydrate Rsch Golden CO 80401 E-mail: esloan@mines.edu., edendysloan@home.com.

SLOAN, F(RANK) BLAINE, law educator; b. Geneva, Jan. 3, 1920; s. Charles Porter and Lillian Josephine (Stiefer) S.; m. Patricia Sand, Sept. 2, 1944; children: DeAnne Sloan Riddle, Michael Blaine, Charles Porter. AB with high distinction, U. Nebr., 1942, LLB cum laude, 1946; LLM in Internat. Law, Columbia U., 1947. Bar: Nebr. 1946, N.Y. 1947. Asst. to spl. counsel Intergovtl. Com. for Refugees, 1947; mem. Office Legal Affairs UN Secretariat, N.Y.C., 1948-78; gen. counsel Relief and Works Agy. Palestine Refugees, Beirut, 1958-60; dir. gen. legal divsn., dep. to the legal counsel UN Legal Office, N.Y.C., 1966-78, rep. of Sec. Gen. to UN Commn. Internat. Trade Law, 1969-78, rep. to Legal Sub-com. on Outer Space, 1966-78; rep. UN Del. Vietnam Conf., Paris, 1973; rep. UN Conf. on Carriage of Goods by Sea Hamburg, 1978; prof. internat. law orgn. and water law Pace U., 1978-87, prof. emeritus, 1987—. Law lectr. Blaine Sloan Internat., 1988—. Author: United Nations General Assembly Resolutions in Our Changing World, 1991; contbr. articles to legal jours. Cons. UN Office of Legal Affairs, 1983-84, UN Water Resources Br., 1983; supervisory com., Pace Peace Ctr.; legal advisor Korean Missions, 1951, 53, UNTSO, Jerusalem, 1952, UNEF I, Gaza, 1957-58; prin. sec.UN Commn. to investigate Sec.-Gen. Hammarskjold's crash, 1961-62. Navigator AC, U.S. Army, 1943-46 Decorated Air medal. Mem. Am. Soc. Internat. Law, Am. Acad. Polit. and Social Sci., Am. Arbitration Assn. (panel of arbitrators), Order of Coif, Phi Beta Kappa, Phi Alpha Delta (hon.). Republican. Roman Catholic. Home: HCR-68 Box 72 Foxwind-Forbes Park Fort Garland CO 81133 Office: 78 N Broadway White Plains NY 10603-3710 also: 375 Soubry Pl Forbes Park Fort Garland CO 81133

SLOAN, HUGH WALTER, JR. automotive executive; b. Princeton, N.J., Nov. 1, 1940; s. Hugh Walter and Elizabeth (Johnson) Sloan; m. Deborah Louise Murray, Feb. 20, 1971; children: Melissa, Peter, Jennifer, William. AB in History with honors, Princeton U., 1963. Staff asst. to Pres. U.S. White Ho., Washington, 1969-71; treas. Pres. Nixon's Re-election Campaign, 1971; spl. asst. to pres. Budd Co., Troy, Mich., 1973-74, exec. asst. internat., 1974-77, mgr. corp. mktg., 1977-79; pres., gen. mgr. Budd Can. Inc., Kitchener, Canada, 1979-85; pres. automotive Woodbridge Group, Troy, 1985-98, dep. chmn., 1998—. Bd. dirs. Woodbridge Foam Corp., Mfrs. Life Ins. Co., Wescast Industries, Virtek Vision Internat. Inc. Gov. Jr. Achievement of Can.; bd. govs. Cranbrook Schs.; bd. dirs. Cmty. Ho.; chmn. bd. dirs. Deerwood Found.; dir. Beaumont Found. Lt. USNR, 1963—65. Recipient Outstanding Bus. Leader award, Wilfrid Laurier U., 1987. Mem.: Automotive Market Rsch. Coun. (past pres.), Originial Equipment Suppliers Assn. (dir.), Am. Soc. Employers (dir., past chmn., pres.), Automotive Parts Mfrs. Assn. (past chmn.), World Pres. Orgn., Bloomfield Hills (Mich.) Country Club. Republican. Office: Woodbridge Group 2500 Meijer Dr Troy MI 48084-7146

SLOAN, JAMES PARK, novelist, biographer, educator; b. Greenwood, S.C., Sept. 22, 1944; s. James Park and Alice Catherine (Gaines) S.; m. Jeanette Carol Pasin, July 25, 1968 (div. 1987); ; children: Eugene Blakely, Anna Jeanette; m. Athena Dadjou Uslander, June 2, 2001. BA, Harvard U., 1968. Mem. faculty U. Ill., Chgo., 1972—, assoc. prof. English, 1976-94, prof., 1994—, chmn. program for writers, 1976-79, 89-93. Lectr. in field, 1972—. Author: War Games, 1971 (Best First Novel award Gt. Lakes Colls. Assn. 1971), (Peggy McPhaul award Midwestern Writers Assn. 1971), The Case History of Comrade V, 1972 (Friends of Lit. award 1972), The Last Cold-War Cowboy, 1987, Jerzy Kosinski: A Biography, 1996 (biography award Soc. Midland Authors 1996); also book revs.; contbg. editor: Am. Pen Quar., 1974—. Served with USAR, 1964-67, Vietnam. Decorated Army Commendation medal; recipient Cliff Dwellers award Chgo., 1977 Mem. PEN Midwest (bd. dirs. 1987—, chmn. 1993—). Office: U Ill Dept English 601 S Morgan St Chicago IL 60607 E-mail: jimsloan@uic.edu.

SLOAN, JASON GERARD, aerospace engineer; b. Pa., Apr. 11, 1974; s. Dwight A. and Michele Wadsworth S. BS in Aerospace Engring., U. Fla., 1996, MS in Aerospace Engring., 1998. Grad. rsch. asst. U. Fla., Gainesville, 1997-98; structural design engr. CDI, United Engrs., West Palm Beach, Fla., 1999-2000; analytical engr. United Space Alliance, Cape Canaveral, 2000—. Mem. Am. Inst. Aeronautics and Astronautics.

SLOAN, JEANETTE PASIN, artist; b. Chgo., Mar. 18, 1946; d. Antonio and Anna (Baggio) Pasin; children: Eugene Blakely, Anna Jeanette. BFA, Marymount Coll., Tarrytown, N.Y., 1967; MFA, U. Chgo., 1969. Exhibited in one-woman shows G.W. Einstein Gallery, N.Y.C., 1977-85, Landfall Press Gallery, Chgo., N.Y.C., 1978, 87, Roger Ramsay Gallery, Chgo., 1987, 89, 92, Tatischeff Gallery, Santa Monica, Calif., 1989, Steven Scott Gallery, Balt., 1989, Butters Gallery, Portland, Oreg., 1989, 91, 94, 96, 99, Tatistcheff & Co. Inc., 1995, 97, 99, Ouartet Editions, N.Y.C., 1995, Elliot Smith Gallery, St. Louis, 1994, Peltz Gallery, Milw., 1994-95, 99, Gerhard Wurzer Gallery, Houston, 1997, 2001, Cline Fine Arts Gallery, Santa Fe, N.M., 1998, 2001; represented in permanent collections Art Mus. Chgo., Cleve. Mus. Art, Ill. State Mus., Indpls. Mus. Art, Canton (Ohio) Art Inst., Ball State Bus., Mpls., Inst. Art, Fogg Mus. Harvard U., Yale U. Art Gallery, Snite Mus. U. Notre Dame, Met. Mus. Art, N.Y.C., Herbert F. Johnson Mus. Cornell U., Ithaca, N.Y., Valpariaso (Ind.) Mus. Art, Nat. Gallery Art, Washington; exhibited in group shows; subject of book by Gerritt Henry, Jeanette Pasin Sloan, 2000. Studio: 535 Keystone Ave River Forest IL 60305-1611 E-mail: jeanettesloan@aol.com.

SLOAN, JOHN JOSEPH, III, sociology educator; b. Detroit, May 3, 1956; s. John Joseph Jr. and Christine Anne S. BS in Criminal Justice, Ea. Mich. U., 1980, MS in Sociology, 1982; PhD in Sociology, Purdue U., 1987. Rsch. assoc. dept. sociology Ea. Mich. U., 1980-82, rsch. asst. Inst. for Study of Children and Families, 1982-84; grad. instr. dept. sociology/anthropology Purdue U., West Lafayette, Ind., 1985-87, vis. asst. prof., 1987-88; asst. to assoc. prof. dept. criminal justice U. Ala., Birmingham, 1988—, acting dir. grad. program dept. criminal justice, 1989-90, dir. grad. program, 1994—, adj. asst. to assoc. prof. dept. criminal justice Tuscaloosa, 1990—. Lectr. in field. Co-editor: Campus Crime: Legal, Social, and Policy Perspectives, 1995; contbr. articles to profl. jours.; editorial bd. Criminal Justice and Behavior, 1992—; jour. referee Am. Jour. of Police, 1991—, Justice Quar., 1992—, Jour. Criminal Justice, 1991—, Criminal Justice and Behavior, 1992—; manuscript reviewer Prentice Hall, Coll. Textbook Div., 1991—. Fellow Mich. State Supreme Ct. Adminstrs. Office, 1980, Nat. Inst. Justice, 1986, Chgo. Housing Authority Police, 1992. Mem. Acad. Criminal Justice Scis. (police sect. election com. 1992), Am. Soc. Criminology, Am. Sociol. Assn., Law and Soc. Assn., So. Criminal Justice Assn. Office: Univ of Ala Dept Criminal Justice 901 15th St S Birmingham AL 35205-3406

SLOAN, MARK HAMILTON, art gallery director, educator, author; b. Durham, N.C., Nov. 16, 1957; s. William Lee and Ruth (Hamilton) S.; m. Elise Labe, 1982 (div. 1986); 1 child, Mara Daile; m. Michelle Van Parys, Mar. 10, 1990; 1 child, Andre. BA, U. Richmond, 1980; MFA, Va. Commonwealth U., 1984. Exec. dir. The Light Factory, Charlotte, N.C., 1985-86; assoc. dir. San Francisco Camerawork, 1986-89; ind. curator META Mus., Brasher Falls, N.Y., 1989-92; dir. Roland Gibson Gallery, Potsdam, 1992-94, William Halsey Gallery, Charleston, S.C., 1994—. Adj. prof. SUNY, Potsdam, 1992-94; assoc. prof. Coll. Charleston, 1994—; mem. adv. bd. Office of Cultural Affairs City of Charleston, 1994—; mem. collections com. Gibbes Mus. Art, Charleston, 1997—. Author: Hoaxes, Humbugs and Spectacles, 1990, Wild, Weird and Wonderful, 2002; co-author: Dear Mr. Ripley, 1993, Self-Made Worlds, 1997. Grantee S.C. Arts Commn., 1996-2000. Mem. Soc. Photographic Edn., Coll. Art Assn. Office: William Halsey Gallery Coll of Charleston 66 George St Charleston SC 29424 E-mail: sloanm@cofc.edu.

SLOAN, MARY JEAN, retired media specialist; b. Lakeland, Fla., Nov. 29, 1927; d. Marion Wilder and Elba (Jinks) Sloan. BS, Peabody Coll., Nashville, 1949; MLS, Atlanta U., 1978, SLS, 1980. Cert. libr. media specialist. Music dir. Pinecrest Sch., Tampa, Fla., 1949-50, Polk County Schs., Bartow, 1950-54; pvt. music tchr. Lakeland, 1954-58; tchr. Clayton County Schs., Jonesboro, Ga., 1958-59; media specialist Eastualley Sch., Marietta, 1959-89; ret., 1988. Coord. conf. Ga. Libr. Media Dept., Jekyll Island, 1982-83, sec., Atlanta, 1982-83, com. chmn. ethnic conf., Atlanta, 1978, pres., 1984-85, state pres., 1985-86; program chmn. Ga. Media Orgns. Conf, Jekyll Island, 1988. Contbr. to bibliographies. Recipient Walter Bell award Ga. Assn. Instrnl. Tech., 1988, Disting. Svc. award, 1991. Mem. ALA (del. 1984, 85, 90), NEA, Southeastern Libr. Assn., Am. Assn. Sch. Librs., Soc. for Sch. Librs., Internat., Ga. Assn. Educators (polit. action com. 1983), Beta Phi Mu, Phi Delta Kappa. Republican. Methodist. Home: 797 Yorkshire Rd NE Atlanta GA 30306-3264

SLOAN, MARY LOVE STRINGFIELD, interior designer; b. Waynesville, N.C., Aug. 7, 1947; d. Thomas and Harriet (Coburn) Stringfield; m. Hugh Johnston Sloan, III, Feb. 12, 1982; 1 stepchild, Kathleen Sloan Gebhart. B.S., U. Tenn., 1973. Staff designer Omnia Design, Inc., Charlotte, 1973-79; dir. planning and design Counterpoint, Inc., Knoxville, 1979-81; coordinator interior design Ohio State U. Hosps., Columbus, 1981— ; instr. Central Piedmont Community Coll., Charlotte, 1978, U. Tenn., Knoxville, 1980, trustee Coalition for Interior Design Licensing Ohio, 1987—; mem. bd. visitors Found. for Interior Design Edn. Research, 1988—; trustee Coalition for Interior Design Licensing in Ohio, 1987—. Bd. dirs., pres. ECO, Inc., Charlotte, 1977, 79; sec. Young Democrats Club, Charlotte, 1978; rep. to state bd. Women's Polit. Caucus, Knoxville, 1980; mem. Columbus Com. for UNICEF, 1982— ; mem. centennial com. King Ave. United Meth. Ch., 1985— . Recipient Assn. of Univ. Interior Designers Interior Design Competition award; IBD/Steelcase Design Ptnrship fellow, 1988. Mem. Inst. Bus. Designers (nat. trustee 1978-79, v.p. Tenn. chpt. 1980, edn. chair Ohio regional chpt. 1985-86, Cert. of Appreciation 1980), Assn. Univ. Interior Designers (sec. 1983-85, v.p. 1985—), U. Tenn. Alumni Assn. (sec. 1984-86). Republican. Methodist. Clubs: Women's Guild Opera/Columbus, World Future Soc., Sierra, Nat. Trust Hist. Preservation, Ohio Preservation Alliance. Avocations: travel; gardening; opera; theatre; philately. Home: 607 Manor Dr Oxford MS 38655-2411 Office: Ohio State U Hosps 410 W 10th Ave Columbus OH 43210-1240

SLOAN, MICHAEL DANA, information systems specialist; b. Santa Monica, Calif., Sept. 30, 1960; s. Avery and Beverly Rae (Krantz) S.; m. Barbara Rogers; 1 child, Ashley Harrison. BS in Bus. Adminstrn., Calif. State U., Northridge, 1983; MBA, Pepperdine U., 1987. Programmer/analyst TICOR, Inc., L.A., 1979-80; data processing analyst Deluxe Check Printers, Inc., Chatsworth, Calif., 1980-83; fin. systems analyst Wismer & Assocs., Inc., Canoga Park, 1983-84; sr. systems analyst Coast Savs. & Loan, Granada Hills, 1984-86; microcomputer systems specialist Litton Industries, Woodland Hills, 1986-87; systems mgr., info. resources mgr. TRW, Inc.- Space and Def., Redondo Beach, 1987-93; project mgr. Health Net, Woodland Hills, 1993-95; mgr. fin. and sales systems Merisel Ams. Inc., El Segundo, Calif., 1995-97; sr. mgr. web tech. & devel. Ingram Micro Inc., Santa Ana, 2000—01; with Ptnrs. Cons. Svcs., Inc., Laguna Beach, 2001—02, Consulting Solutions, Inc., Laguna Beach, 2002—. Cons. Data Most, Inc., Chatsworth, 1982—83, Home Savs. & Loan, North Hollywood, Calif., 1987, Micro Tech., L.A., 1987, TRW, Inc.-Space and Def., Redondo Beach, Calif., 1993—2000, Pacificare Health Systems, Inc., 1997, Nissan North America (formerly Nissan Motor Corp., USA), 1998—99, Prosum Info. Techs., Inc., 2000—, Am. Honda Motors, Inc., 1999—2000, Toyota Fin. Svcs., 2001—02, Warner Bros. Studios, 2002—. Mem. IEEE Computer Soc., Salle Gascon Fencing Club, U.S. Fencing Assn., Delta Sigma Pi. Republican. Avocations: fencing, softball, tennis, volleyball, travel, sailing. Office: Consulting Solutions Inc Ste 732 23679 Calabasas Rd Calabasas CA 91302

SLOAN, MICHAEL LEE, secondary education educator; b. Chgo., Jan. 24, 1944; s. Robert Earl Sloan and Cyril (Lewis) Glass; m. Claudia Ann Schultz, Sept. 27, 1969. BS in Physics, Roosevelt U., 1966, MS, 1971. Tchr. physics Glenbard West H.S., Glen Ellyn, Ill., 1966-79; computer cons. Midwest Visual, Chgo., 1979-82; sr. engr. Apple Computer, Rolling Meadows, Ill., 1982-85; tchr. math. and physics Ill. Math. and Sci. Acad., Aurora, 1987—. Asst. prof. Roosevelt U., 1971-73; instr. Harper Coll., Palatine, Ill., 1984. Author: AppleWorks: The Program for the Rest of Us, 1985, 2d edit., 1988, Working with Works, 1987, Word Power, 1989, Working with PC Works, 1989, Working with Works 2.0, 1990. Bd. dirs. Youth Symphony Orch., Chgo., 1977-78, Friends of Fermilab, Batavia, Ill., 1998—; trustee Body Politic Theatre, Chgo., 1981-82. Home: ON008 Evans Ave Wheaton IL 60187 Office: Ill Math and Sci Acad 1500 Sullivan Rd Aurora IL 60506-1000 E-mail: msloan@imsa.edu.

SLOAN, O. TEMPLE, JR. automotive equipment executive; b. Sanford, N.C., Feb. 21, 1939; s. Orris Temple and Thelma (Hamilton) S.; m. Carol Carson; children: C. Carson Henline, O. Temple Sloan III, Mark H. Sloan. BA in Bus. Adminstrn., Duke U., 1961. Founder, pres. Gen. Parts Inc., Raleigh, N.C., 1961—, now chmn. Chmn. bd. dirs. Highwoods Properties Inc., Raleigh; bd. dirs. So. Equipment Co., Raleigh, CARQUEST Corp., Denver, Al Smith Buick Inc., Bank of Am., Charlotte, Acktion Corp. Toronto. Trustee Boys and Girls Homes N.C., Lake Waccamaw, 1973—; mem. adv. bd. Salvation Army, Raleigh, 1973-87, chmn., 1976-77; exec. bd., v.p., treas. Occoneechee council Boy Scouts Am., 1967—; bd. visitors Peace Coll., Raleigh, 1985-87, trustee, 1987-97, vice chmn.; trustee St. Andrew's Presbyn. Coll., 1990—; bd. dirs. Rex Hosp. Found., 1989-90; campaign chmn. Wake County United Way, 2001; elder Presbyn. Ch.; mem. Centennial Authority, Raleigh, 1995—. Recipient Silver Beaver award Boy Scouts Am., Eagle award Boy Scouts Am., Disting. Svc. citation Automotive Hall of Fame, 1997; named Northwood U. Outstanding Bus. Leader, 1999. Mem. Automotive Warehouse Distbrs. Assn. Inc. (dir. 1969—, chmn. 1976-77, scholarship award 1977, Automotive Man of Yr. award 1989), The Fifty Group (bd. dirs. 1983-88, pres. 1986-87), Greater Raleigh C. of C. (bd. dirs. 1989-91), Carolina Country Club (Raleigh). Avocations: fishing, hunting, ranching. Home: 3026 Randolph Dr Raleigh NC 27609-6942 Office: Gen Parts Inc PO Box 26006 Raleigh NC 27611 E-mail: licanipe@gpi.com.

SLOAN, PATRICE S. artist; b. Banner Elk, N.C., Jan. 14, 1955; d. George Wallace and Edna Earle (Heaton) Shook; m. Michael L. Sloan, July 1, 1988; 1 child, George Walter Shook. BA in History, BA in English, U. S.C., 1977. Artist, Myrtle Beach, S.C., 1980-88, Juneau, Alaska, 1988-94; artist, gallery owner Dutch Harbor, 1994—. Graphic cons. Aleutian-Pribilof Islands Assn., Unalaska, Alaska, 1996. Contbg. artist Dutch Harbor Fisherman, 1996; prin. works include pastels Still Water, 1996, The Law, 1996, acrylic Arctic Squirrel, 1996, oil Life in the Arctic, 1996. Mem. Nat. Assn. Fine Arts, Arts for Healthy Alaska, Bering Sea Exch. Home: PO Box 1543 Nome AK 99762-1543

SLOAN, REBA FAYE, dietitian, consultant; b. South Bend, Ind., Feb. 5, 1955; d. Kenneth and Ruby Faye (Long) Lewis; m. Gilbert Kevin Sloan, May 22, 1976. BS, Harding U., 1976; MPH, Loma Linda U., 1989; Cert. Tng. in Child/Adolescent Obesity, U. Calif., San Francisco. Registered dietitian; lic. dietitian and nutritionist; cert. advanced clin. tng. adolescent obesity. Dietetic intern Vanderbilt U. Med. Ctr., Nashville, 1978, rsch. dietitian, 1979-80; therapeutic dietitian Bapt. Hosp., 1981-85; staff dietitian Nautilus Total Fitness Ctrs., 1983-86; cons. dietitian Nashville Met. Govt., 1986-95, Bapt. Hosp. Ctr. for Health Promotion, Nashville, 1987-91, Parkwest Eating Disorder Clinic, Nashville, 1989-91; nutrition therapist, pvt. practice, 1992—. Adj. prof. Vanderbilt U., 1995—; nutrition cons. The Nashville Striders, 1979-81; cons. nutritionist; mem. Vanderbilt U. Eating Disorder Com. Vol. Belmont Ch. Ministries, Nashville, 1981-97; spkr. Am. Heart Assn., Nashvile 1990—; founder Dietetic Scholarship Fund, Harding U. Recipient cert. of appreciation Am. Heart Assn., 1990, Disting. Lectr. cert. Harding U.; Leaders fellow YMCA. Mem. Am. Dietetic Assn., Sports and Cardiovascular Nutritionists, Cons. Nutritionists, Am. Coll. Sports Medicine, Am. Running and Fitness Assn., Nashville Dist. Dietetic Assn. (contbr. diet manual 1984), Nat. Assn. for Chrisian Recovery, Alpha Chi. Avocations: travel, running, fitness, reading. Home: 1817 Shackleford Rd Nashville TN 37215-3525 Office: 121 21st Ave N Ste 208 Nashville TN 37203-6402

SLOAN, RICHARD, artist; b. Chgo., Dec. 11, 1935; s. Samuel Theodore and Lelia (Beach) S.; m. Arlene Florence Miller, Aug. 11, 1962 (dec. June 1994). Attended, Am. Acad. Art, 1951-53. Advt. illustrator; staff artist Lincoln Park Zoo., Chgo.; master wildlife artist Leigh Yawkey Woodson Art Mus., 1994. Exhbns. include Explorer's Hall Nat. Geographic Soc., Brit. Mus. Natural History, Royal Scottish Acad., Carnegie Mus., Calif. Acad. Scis., Boston Mus. Sci., Am. Mus. Natural History, Nat. Collection Fine Art Smithsonian Inst., Washington, 1979, Leigh Yawkey Woodson Art Mus. (20 exhbns., 1979—), Beijing Mus. Natural History, 1987; Roger Tory Peterson Inst. Natural History nat. mus. tour, 1993, James Ford Bell Mus. Nat. History, U. Minn., 1994; spl. guest artist 1st Vancouver Internat. Wildlife Art Show, 1994; permanent collections Smithsonian Inst., Leigh Yawkey Woodson Art Mus., Ill. State Mus.; pvt. collections throughout world; contbr. Nat. Wildlife Stamp Program, World Wildlife Fund, international stamps; paintings featured Nat. and Internat. Wildlife Mag., U.S. Art, Wildlife Art News, Ariz. Wildlife Mag., numerous others; artist, illustrator Encyc. Brit., 1963, (book) Raptors of Arizona, 1998. Recipient Award of Excellence Cin. Mus. Nat. History, 1984, Award of Merit Anchorage Audubon Soc., 1985, Southwest Book award Border Regional Libr. Assn., 1998. Mem.: Soc. Animal Artists (award of excellence 1988—90, People's Choice award 2002). Home: 1623 SW Pineland Way Palm City FL 34990-2779 E-mail: amazonart@msn.com.

SLOAN, SAUNDRA JENNINGS, real estate company executive; b. Prosperity, S.C., June 30, 1961; d. Denny Jennings and Kay Hyler Green; m. Lowell Evan Sloan, Mar. 14, 1998. Student, Midlands Tech. Coll., Airport Location/Columbia, 1979—82. Lic. real estate. Pres. Southpark Svcs., Inc., Columbia, SC, 1990—95; mgr. sales and leasing Foster, Saad & Co., 1995—. Pres. BNI Midlands Chpt., Columbia, SC, 1999—2000. Recipient Gold Club award, Bus. Network Internat., 2001. Avocations: dancing, travel, sewing. Office: Foster Saad & Co Ste 2A 1201 Hampton St Columbia SC 29201 Home Fax: 803-748-7335; Office Fax: 803-254-3795. Business E-Mail: SaunJenSloan@aol.com.*

SLOAN, W(ILSON) KEITH, actuary; b. Red Oak, Iowa, Mar. 11, 1924; s. Francis Asbury and Inez Claire (Snyder) S.; m. Mary Kay Kirby, July 9, 1945; children: Karen Osborne, Kirby Bartlett-Sloan. BS, U. Mich., 1949. Underwriter Commonwealth Life Ins. Co., Louisville, 1951-55; asst. sec. Bankers Security Life Ins. Co., Washington, 1955-57; agt. Penn Mut. Life Ins. Co., Louisville, 1957; chief underwriter, agy. sec. Consumers Nat. Life Ins. Co., Evansville, Ind., 1957-60; gen. mgr. Early Am. Life Ins. Co., 1960-61; actuary, asst. sec., dir. Pioneer Ins. Co., Lincoln, Nebr., 1961-63; group acturial adminstr. Life & Casualty Ins. Co. Tenn., Nashville, 1963-67; chief actuary Tenn. Dept. Ins. & Banking, 1967-71; v.p., acutary Am. Family Life Ins. Co. Columbus (Ga.), 1971-74; life & health actuary Ark. Ins. Dept., Little Rock, 1974-78; asst. actuary Kemper Group, Long Grove, Ill., 1978-81; chief life & health actuary Ky. Dept. Ins., Frankfort, 1981-82; v.p. actuary Citizens Security Life Ins. Co., 1982-88; cons. actuary Bryan, Pendleton, Swats & McAllister, Nashville, 1989-97; retired. Lectr. fin. U. Ark., Little Rock, 1977-78; cons. in field. Co-author: Patchwork: An Uncommon Quilt of Words; contbr. articles to profl. jours. With U.S. Army, 1942-46. Fellow Conf. Cons. Actuaries; mem. Am. Acad. Actuaries, Southeastern Actuaries Club, Nashville Acturial Club (past pres.), Faculty Actuaries Students Soc. (life). Avocation: writing. Home: 1506 Teil Dr Franklin TN 37064-6832 E-mail: wks37064@earthlink.net.

SLOAND, JAMES ANTHONY, physician; b. Rochester, N.Y., Mar. 3, 1954; s. Anthony Sylvester and Muriel Ann (Kieffer) S.; m. Mary Ann Liebman, May 15, 1982; children: David, Colin, Meaghan. BA summa cum laude, Canisius Coll., Bufflo, 1976; MD, St. Louis U., 1980. Diplomate in internal medicine and nephrology Am. Bd. Internal Medicine, cert. specialist in clin. hypertension. Intern, resident in internal medicine St. Luke's/St. Louis City (Washington U.), St. Louis, 1980-83; sr. instr. medicine U. Rochester, 1985-86, asst. prof., 1986-92, assoc. prof., 1992—; mem. staff Highland Hosp., Rochester, Strong Meml. Hosp., Rochester. Mem. med. adv. bd. Lupus Found. Am., Rochester, 1994—; bd. dirs. Upstate Kidney Found.; chmn. med. adv. bd. Reviewer Am. Jour. Kidney Disease, Kidney Internat., Archives of Internal Medicine, 1991—; contbr. articles to profl. jours. Fellow ACP; mem. Am. Soc. Nephrology, Internat. Soc. Nephrology, Nat. Kidney Found., Am. Soc. Hypertension, Beta Beta Beta. Avocations: fishing, skiing, woodworking. Office: Highland Hosp 1000 South Ave Rochester NY 14620-2782

SLOANE, BEVERLY LEBOV, writer, consultant; b. N.Y.C., May 26, 1936; d. Benjamin S. and Annw (Weinberg) LeBov; m. Robert Malcolm Sloane, Sept. 27, 1959 (dec. May 16, 2002); 1 child Alison Lori Slone Gaylin. AB, Vassar Coll., 1958; MA, Claremont Grad. U., 1975, doctoral study, 1975-76; cert. in exec. mgmt. program, UCLA Grad. Sch. Mgmt., 1982; grad. intensive bioethics course Kennedy Inst. Ethics, Georgetown U., 1987, advanced bioethics course, 1988; grad. sem. in Health Care Ethics, U. Wash. Sch. Medicine, Seattle, summer 1988-90, 94; grad. Summer Bioethics Inst., Loyola Marymount U., summer 1990; grad. Annual Summer Inst. on Teaching of Writing, Columbia U. Tchrs. Coll., summer 1990; grad. Annual Summer Inst. on Advanced Teaching of Writing, Columbia Tchrs. Coll., summer 1993; grad. Annual Inst. Pub. Health and Human Rights, Harvard U. Sch. Pub. Health, 1994; grad. pub. course profl. pub., Stanford U., 1982; cert. clin. intensive biomedical ethics, Ethics Fellow, cert. clin. intensive biomedical ethics, Loma Linda U. Med. Ctr., 1989; grad. exec. refresher course profl. pub., Stanford U., 1994; cert Exec. Mgmt. Inst. in Health Care, U. So. Calif., 1995; cert. in ethics corps tng. program, Josephson Inst. of Ethics, 1991; cert. advanced exec. program Grad. Sch. Mgmt., UCLA, 1995; grad. Women's Campaign Sch., Yale U., 1998. Circulation libr. Harvard Med. Libr., Boston, 1958-59; social worker Conn. State Welfare, New Haven, 1960-61; tchr. English Hebrew Day Sch., 1961-64; instr. creative writing and English lit. Monmouth Coll., West Long Branch, NJ, 1967-69; writer, cons., 1970—. V.p. council grad. students, Claremont Grad. U., 1971-72, adj. dir. Writing Ctr. Speaker Series, 1993-2000, spkr., 1996, 97, 98; bd. visitors Claremont Grad. U. Ctrs. for Arts and Humanities, 2001—; mem. adv. coun. tech. and profl. writing Dept. English, Calif. State U., Long Beach, 1980-82; mem. adv. bd. Calif. Health Rev., 1982-83; mem. Foothill Health Dist. Adv. Coun. L.A. County Dept. Health Svcs., 1987-93, pres., 1989-91; vis. scholar Hastings Ctr., 1996; spkr. N.Y. State Task Force on Life and the Law, 1996; panel spkr. ann. conf. Am. Assn. Suicidology, 1998. Author: From Vassar to Kitchen, 1967, A Guide to Health Facilities: Personnel and Management, 1971, 2nd edit., 1977, 3d edit., 1992, Introduction to Healthcare Delivery Organization: Functions and Management, 4th edit., 1999. Mem. pub. rels. bd. Monmouth County Mental Health Assn., 1968—69; chmn. creative writing group Calif. Inst. Tech. Woman's Club, 1975—79; mem. task force edn. and cultural activities City of Duarte, 1987—88; chmn. creative writing group Yale U. Newcomers, 1965—66; dir. creative writing group Yale U. Women's Orgn., 1966—67; grad. AMA Ann. Health Reporting Conf., 1992, 1993; mem. Exec. Program Network UCLA Grad. Sch. Mgmt., 1987—2000; trustee Ctr. Improvement Child Caring, 1981—83; mem. League Crippled Children, 1982—, treas. for gen. meetings, 1990—91, chmn. hostesses com., 1988—89, pub. rels. com., 1990—91; del. Task Force on Minorities in Newspaper Bus., 1987—89; rep. cmty. County Health Cents. County Network Tobacco Control Program, 1991; mem. NY citizens Com. Health Care Decisions; chmn. 1st ann. Rabbi Camillus Angel Interfaith Svc. Temple Beth David, 1978, v.p., 1983—86, spkr., 1997; mem. cmty. rels. com. Jewish Fedn. Coun. Greater L.A., 1985—87; bd. dirs. League Crippled Children, 1988—91; mem. ethics com., human subjects protection com. Jewish Home for Aging, Reseda, Calif., 1994—97; mem. strategic planning task force com., campaign com., preeminence Claremont Grad. U., 1986—87, mem. alumni coun., bd. dirs. alumni assn., 1993—96, mem. vol. devel. com., 1994—96, alumnae awards com., 1993—96; bd. visitors Glaremont Grad. U. Ctr. Arts and Humanities, 2001—; bd. dirs. Coro Nat. Alumni Assn., 1999—, L.A. Commn. Assaults Against

Women, 1983—84; Vassar Coll. class rep. Alumnae Assn. Fall Coun. Meeting, 1965—66, 1989; co-chmn. Vassar Christmas Showcase New Haven Vassar Club, 1965—66; class corr. Vassar Coll. Quar. Alumnae Mag., 1993—98; mem. gift com. class of 1958 Vassar Coll., class of 1958 pres. 40th reunion, 1998, class v.p., 1998—2000, class co-pres., 2000—01, class pres., 2001—; co-chmn. Vassar Club So. Calif. Ann. Book Fair, 1970—71. Recipient cert. of appreciation City of Duarte, 1988, County of L.A., 1988, Ann. Key Mem. award L.A. Dept. Health Svcs., 1990, cert. of appreciation Alumni Coun. Claremont Grad Sch., 1996; Coro Found. fellow, 1979, Ethics fellow Loma Linda U. Med. Ctr., 1989; named Calif. Communicator of Achievement, Woman of Yr. Calif. Press Women, 1992. Fellow: Am. Med. Writers Asn. (Pacific S.W. del. to nat. bd. 1980—87, dir. 1980—93, chmn. nat. book awards trade category 1982—83, chmn. Nat. Networking Luncheon 1983—, 1984, nat. chmn. freelance sect. 1984—85, workshop leader Nat. Annual Conf. 1984—89, gen. chmn. Asilomar Western Regional Conf. 1985, spkr. 1985, workshop leader 1985, nat. exec. bd. dirs. 1985—86, nat. adminr. sects. 1985—86, pres.-elect Pacific Southwest chap. 1985—87, chmn. gen. session nat. conf. 1986—87, chmn. Walter C. Alvarez Mem. Found award 1986—87, program co-chmn. 1987, moderator gen. session nat. conf. 1987, pres. Pacific S.W. chap. 1987—89, pres. Pacific S.W. chpt. 1987—89, spkr. 1988—89, program co-chmn. 1989, Pacific Southwest deleg. to nat. bd. 1989—91, immediate past pres. 1989—91, workshop leader Nat. Annual Conf. 1990—92, bd. dirs. 1991—93, workshop leader Nat. Annual Conf. 1995, chmn. various conv. coms., appreciation award outstanding leadership 1989, named to Workshop Leaders Honor Roll 1991); mem.: AAUP, APHA, AAUW (creative writing chmn. 1969—70, books and plays chmn. Arcadia Br. 1973—74, 1st v.p. program dir. 1975—76, legis. chmn. Arcadia Br. 1976—77, networking chmn. 1981—82, spkr. 1987, chmn. task force promoting individual liberties 1987—88, pres.-elect 1998—99, educ. equity chmn. 1998—99, chmn. deleg. to national conv. 1999, chmn. Technical Trek Sci. Camp Scholarship for Girls 1999, Career Day 1999, pres. Arcadia br. 1999—2000, writer in res Calif. State Comm. Comt. 1999—2000, diversity chmn. Arcadia br. 2000—01, Interbr. Coun. Arcadia br. repr. 2000—02, Calif. State diversity comt. 2000—02, steering com. L.A. County Interbr. Coun. 2001—02, Woman of Achievement Arcadia br. 1986, cert. of appreciation 1987, Woman of Yr.), AAUW Calif. State Diversity Comt. (program co-v.p. 2002—), Town Hall Calif. (vice chmn. cmty. affairs sect. 1982—87, faculty-instr. Exec. Breakfast Inst. 1985—86, spkr. 1986), Pasadena Athletic, Claremont Cols. Faculty House, Women's City (Pasadena), Nat. Writer's Union, Authors Guild, Assn. Writing Programs, NY Acad. Medicine (met. NY Ethics Network), Soc. Health and Human Values, Kennedy Inst. Ethics, Soc. Technical Comt., Nat. Fedn. Press Women (chmn. state women of achievement comt. 1986—87, nat. co-chmn. task force recruitment minorities 1987—89, del. 1987—89, bd. dirs. 1987—93, nat. dir. of spkrs. bur. 1989—93, Plenary Past Pres. state 1989—, workshop leader-speaker ann. national conf. 1990, editor speakers bur. directory 1991, editor Speakers Bur. Dir. 1991, editor Speakers Bur. Addendum Dir. 1992, editor Speakers Bur. Dir. 1992, cert. of appreciation 1991, named 1st runner up Nat. Communicator Achievement 1992, cert. of appreciation 1993), Hastings Cent. (vis. scholar 1996), Ind. Writers So. Calif. (bd. dirs. corp. 1988—89, bd. dirs. 1989—90, dir. at large 1989—90, dir. Specialized Groups 1989—90, dir. Speech Writing Group 1991—92), NY Acad. Scis., Calif. Press Women (v.p. programs L.A. chpt. 1982—85, pres. 1985—87, state pres. 1987—89, immediate past state pres. 1989—91, chmn. state speakers bur. 1989—95, deleg. nat. bd. 1989—95, moderator ann. spring conv. 1990, dir. family literacy day Calif. 1990, chmn. nominating comt. 1990—91, Calif. literacy dir. 1990—92, dir. state literacy com. 1990—92, moderator ann. spring conv. 1992, Cert. of Appreciation 1991, Calif. Communicator of Achievement 1992), Am. Soc. Law, Medicine, Ethics, Clol. English Assn. (program vice chmn. L.A. County Interbr. Coun. 2000—02), AAUW Calif. State Comns. Comt. (writer in residence 1999—), Coro Nat. Alumni Assn. (bd. dirs. 1999—), Am. Assn. Higher Edn., Women in Comm. Inc. (N.E. area rep. 1980—81, dir. 1980—82, v.p. cmty. affairs 1981—82, chmn. awards banquet 1982, chmn. LA chpt. 1st ann. Agnes Underwood Freedom Info. Awards banquet 1982, nominating com. 1982, 1983, sprk. ann. nat. prof. conf. 1985, program adv. com. L.A. chpt. 1987, com. Women of the Press Awards luncheon 1988, Women in com. awards luncheon 1988, dir. 1989—90, v.p. activities 1989—90, sem. leader, Recognition award 1983), Duarte Rotary Club. Home and Office: 1301 N Santa Anita Ave Arcadia CA 91006-2419

SLOANE, CARL STUART, educator and management consultant; b. N.Y.C., Feb. 9, 1937; s. George and Dorothy (Cohen) S.; m. Toby Tattlebaum, Dec. 27, 1958; children: Lisa Beth, Amy Rachel, Todd Cowan. BA, Harvard U., 1958, MBA, 1960. Asst. to pres. Revlon, Inc., N.Y.C., 1960-62; mgmt. cons. Harbridge House, Inc., Boston, 1962-69; exec. v.p., treas. Temple, Barker & Sloane, Inc., Lexington, 1970—91, pres., CEO, 1978-90, chmn., CEO, 1990-91; prof. bus. adminstrn. Harvard Grad. Sch. Bus. Adminstrn., 1991—2001. Mem. policyholders' examining com. N.W. Mut. Life Ins. Co.; mem. bus. adv. com. Transp. Ctr., Northwestern U., 1984-91; mem. adv. com. Ctr. for Sci. and Internat. Affairs, Kennedy Sch. Govt., Harvard U., 1984-94; bd. dirs. Am. Pres. Co.'s Ltd., Oakland, Calif., 1983-90, Moore McCormack Resources Inc., Stamford, Conn., 1976-88, Leaseway Transp., Inc., 1993-95, MedSource Techs., 2002—, Ionics, Inc., 1995—, Sapient Corp., 1995-02, Rayonier, Inc., 1997—, Pittston Co., 1998—, NeedSource Techs., 2002--. Bd. dirs. Harvard-Radcliffe Hillel, Cambridge, Mass., 1987-98, chmn., 1994-98; bd. dirs., trustee Beth Israel Deaconess Med. Ctr., Boston, 1993—, vice chmn., 1996—; nat. fund chmn. Harvard . Bus. Sch., 1987-89, also vis. com. Mem. Assn. Mgmt. Cons. Firms (chmn. 1984-86), Harvard U. Bus. Sch. Alumni Assn. (v.p. 1989, pres. 1989-91), Boston Yacht Club (Marblehead), Kernwood County Club (Salem), Harvard Club N.Y.C. Home: 9 Sargent Rd Marblehead MA 01945-3744 Office: Harvard Bus Sch Soldiers Fld Boston MA 02163-1317

SLOANE, JAMES ROBERT, chemical engineer; b. Pitts., June 14, 1942; s. Paul Guyer Sloan and Mildred Catherine Reuter; m. Susan Richards, Sept. 18, 1995 (div. May 1992); children: Michelle Karin, James Robert Jr., Jonathan Westby; m. Judy Southerland, Dec. 6, 1997. BSChemE, Pa. State U., 1994; postgrad., U. Ctrl. Fla. Registered profl. engr., Fla. Engr. Westinghouse Electric Corp., 1964, Graver Water Cond. Co., 1967; sales engr. Datum Co., Houston, 1971; charter pilot, aircraft sales mgr. W. Houston Airport, 1972; flight supr. Embry-Riddle Aero. U., Daytona Beach, Fla., 1973; project mgr. Russell and Axon Engrs., 1974; sr. project mgr. Briley, Wild and Assocs. Inc., Ormond Beach, Fla., 1986, McKim and Creed Engrs., Daytona Beach, 1994; dep. pub. works dir., city engr. City Daytona Beach, 1998. Mem. AOPA, ASPA, Am. Pub. Works Assn., Fla. Engr. Soc. Methodist. Avocations: flying, aircraft, water skiing. Home: 635 Lake Winnemissett Dr Deland FL 32724-4817 Office: The City Daytona Beach PO Box 2451 Daytona Beach FL 32115-2451 E-mail: JRSloane@aol.com.

SLOANE, J.P. television producer, writer, entertainer, theologian; b. Hollywood, Calif., Sept. 6, 1942; s. Jimmy Jackson and Anita (Thibodeaux) Barrios. Grad., Oral Roberts U., Inst. Charismatic Studies, Moody Bible Inst., Chgo.; diploma, Inst. Jewish-Christian Studies, Dallas; cert. in TV prodn., Purdue U., 1981; BA summa cum laude, Masters Coll., 2003; student, IBEX Campus, Abu Ghosh, Israel, 2001. Biblical scholar and lectr.; appeared on all major Christian networks worldwide. Guest Art Linkletter's House Party (age 5), CBS Radio Network; played Billy Kettle in Ma and Pa Kettle movie series; appeared on Memory Lane TV show, Hollywood; recorded High on a Mountain, 1960, Linda Darling, 1960; lead singer The Brothers Grim, 1965-68; featured act with Charlie Rich; mem. J.P. Sloane & Co. group, 1973-78; albums include Solid Gold; tv and radio prodr. Recipient Excellence in Media Angel awards for Outstanding TV Prodr., Outstanding Male Vocalist and Outstanding Music Video, Medal of Merit, Pres. Ronald Reagan; named Hon. Sheriff, L.A. County, Hon. Ky. Col., Hon. Lt. Gov. State of Ind., Hon. Citizen, Tulsa, Met. Nashville, 22d Internat. Angel award best multiple character voices, 1999, numerous others; nominee Cleo award, 1980; key to cities Nashville and New Orleans, others. Office: Angeles Crest Productions Ste 407 2219 E Thousand Oaks Blvd Thousand Oaks CA 91362-2930

SLOANE, NEIL JAMES ALEXANDER, mathematician, researcher; b. Beaumaris, Wales, Oct. 10, 1939; came to U.S., 1961; s. Charles Ronald and Jessie (Robinson) S.; m. Susanna Stevens Cuyler, Mar. 8, 1980. BA with honors, U. Melbourne, Australia, 1959, BEE, 1960; MS, Cornell U., 1964, PhD, 1967. Asst. prof. Cornell U., Ithaca, N.Y., 1967-69; mem. tech. staff AT&T Bell Labs., Murray Hill, N.J., 1969-96; prin. mem. tech. staff AT&T Rsch. Labs, 1996—, fellow, 1998. Author: Handbook of Integer Sequences, 1973; co-author: (with F.J. MacWilliams) Theory of Error-Correcting Codes, 1977, (with J.H. Conway) Sphere-Packings, Lattices and Groups, 1988, 32d edit., 1998, (with A.D. Wyner) Claude Elwood Shannon:Collected Papers, 1993, (with S. Plouffe) Encyclopedia of Integer Sequences, 1995, (with A.S. Hedayat and J. Stufken) Orthogonal Arrays, 1999, (with P. Nick) Rock Climbing New Jersey, 2000. Fellow IEEE (editor in chief Trans. Info. Theory jour. 1978-80); mem. NAE, Math. Assn. Am. (Chauvenet prize 1979, Earle Raymond Hedrick lectr. 1984), Am. Math. Soc., Am. Stat. Assn. Avocation: rock climbing. E-mail: njas@research.att.com.

SLOANE, ROBERT MALCOLM, university administrator; b. Boston, Feb. 11, 1933; s. Alvin and Florence (Goldberg) S.; m. Beverly LeBov, Sept. 27, 1959; 1 child, Alison Sloane Gaylin. AB, Brown U., 1954; MS, Columbia U., 1958. Adminstrv. resident Mt. Auburn Hosp., Cambridge, Mass., 1957-58; med. adminstr. AT&T, N.Y.C., 1959-60; asst. dir. Yale New Haven Hosp., 1961-67; assoc. adminstr. Monmouth Med. Center, Long Branch, N.J., 1967-69; adminstr. City of Hope Nat. Med. Center, Duarte, Calif., 1969-80; pres. Los Angeles Orthopedic Hosp., Los Angeles Orthopedic Found., 1980-86; pres., CEO Anaheim (Calif.) Meml. Hosp., 1986-94; pres. Vol. Hosp. Am. West, Inc., L.A., 1995; healthcare cons. Monrovia, Calif., 1996-98; v.p. Rudolph Dew and Assocs., Torrance, 1997-98; dir. health adminstrn. program U. So. Calif., L.A., 1998—2001. Mem. faculty Columbia U. Sch. Medicine, 1958—59, Yale U. Sch. Medicine, 1963—67, 1963—67, Pasadena City Coll., 1972—73, Calif. Inst. Tech., 1973—85, U. So. Calif., 1976—96, clin. prof., 1987—95, 1998—, UCLA, 1985—87; chmn. bd. Health Data Net, 1971—73; bd. dirs. Intervalley Health Plan, 1995—2001; pres. Anaheim Meml. Devel. Found., 1986—94; pres., CEO InTech Health Sys., Inc., 1996—2001; sr. cons. APM, Inc., 1996—97. Author: (with B. L. Sloane) An Introduction to Health Care Delivery Organization: Functions and Management, 1971, 2d edit., 1977, 3d edit., 1992, (with Richard Harder) 4th edit., 1999; mem. editl. and adv. bd. Health Devices, 1972-90; contbr. articles to hosp. jours. Bd. dirs. Health Systems Agy. Los Angeles County, 1977-78, Vol. Hosps. of Am., 1986-95, chmn., 1993-94, pres., 1995; bd. dirs. Calif. Hosp. Polit. Action Com., 1979-87, vice chmn., 1980-83, chmn., 1983-85. Served to lt. (j.g.) USNR, 1954-56. Fellow Am. Coll. Healthcare Execs. (regent 1989-93, nominations com. 1994-97); mem. Am. Hosp. Assn., Healthcare Assn. So. Calif. (bd. dirs. , sec. 1982, treas. 1983, chmn. elect 1984, chmn. 1985, past chmn. 1986, 89), Calif. Healthcare Assn. (bd. dirs. exec. com. 1984-86, 89), Anaheim C. of C. (bd. dirs. 1994). Home: 1301 N Santa Anita Ave Arcadia CA 91006-2419 Office: U So Calif Rgl 230 University Park Los Angeles CA 90089-0001

SLOANE, SARAH JANE, English educator; b. Tappan, N.Y., Oct. 5, 1957; d. Thomas Charles and Virginia Louise (French) S. BA in English cum laude, Middlebury Coll., 1979; MFA in English, U. Mass., 1987; MA in English, Carnegie-Mellon U., 1988; PhD in English, Ohio State U., 1991. Dir. women studies U. Puget Sound, Tacoma, 1993-94, 96-98, asst. prof. English, 1991-97, assoc. prof. English, 1996-2000, Colo. State U., 2000—. Vis. scholar U. Wash. HIT-Lab, Seattle, 1996-2000; lectr. in field. Author: Digital Fictions: Storytelling in a Material World, 2000; contbr. numerous articles to profl. jours., chpts. to books, poetry to lit. pubs.; editl. bd. Computers and Composition Jour., 1991—; reviewer Written Comm., 1991-93, Postmodern Culture, 1994—. Recipient Mary Dunning Thwing Poetry award Middlebury Coll., 1979, Henry V. Larom 1st Prize Writing award Rockland C.C., 1982, Grad. Student Rsch. award Ohio State U., 1990, Hugh Burns Dissertation award Computers and Composition Jour., 1992, Enrichment Com. Rsch. award U. Puget Sound, summers 1993, 95, 96, 98, 99, Martin Nelson Summer Rsch. award, 1994, 97; Thomas J. Watson fellow, 1979-80, Carnegie-Mellon U. fellow, 1987-88; N.Y. State Regents scholar, 1975. Mem.: MLA (com. on computers and emerging techs. 1998—2000), Coll. Composition and Comm. (exec. com. 1999—2001, com. on status of women in the profession 2001—), 18th Century Scottish Studies Soc., Nat. Coun. Tchrs. English, Internat. Soc. History of Rhetoric. Office: Colo State U Dept English 359 Eddy Hall Fort Collins CO 80523 E-mail: sjsloane@lamar.colostate.edu.

SLOANE, THOMAS O. speech educator; b. West Frankfort, Ill., July 12, 1929; s. Thomas Orville and Blanche (Morris) S.; m. Barbara Lee Lewis, Nov. 1, 1952; children— Elizabeth Alison, David Lewis, Emily. BA, So. Ill. U., 1951, MA, 1952; PhD, Northwestern U., 1960. Instr. English, Washington and Lee U., 1958-60; asst. prof. speech U. Ill., 1960-65, assoc. prof., 1965-70, assoc. head dept., 1967-68, asst. dean liberal arts and scis., 1966-67; prof. rhetoric, chmn. rhetoric dept. U. Calif., Berkeley, 1970-92, pres.'s chair, 1987-90. Dir. Nat. Endowment Humanities Summer Seminar for Coll. Tchrs., 1979 Editor: The Oral Study of Literature, 1966, The Passions of the Minde in Generall (Thomas Wright), 1971, (with Raymond B. Waddington) The Rhetoric of Renaissance Poetry, 1974, (with Joanna H. Maclay) Interpretation, 1972; Donne, Milton and the End of Humanist Rhetoric, 1985, On the Contrary, 1997, (with Peter Oesterreich) Rhetorica Movet, 1999; editor in chief: Encyclopedia of Rhetoric, 2001; contbr. articles to profl. jours. Served to lt. USNR, 1952-55. Faculty research fellow, 1964; U. Ill. instructional devel. awardee, 1965; Henry H. Huntington Library research awardee, 1967; U. Calif. humanities research fellow, 1974; Guggenheim fellow, 1981-82 Office: U Calif Berkeley CA 94720-0001 E-mail: tos@uclink.berkeley.edu.

SLOAT, BARBARA FURIN, cell biologist, educator; b. Youngstown, Ohio, Jan. 20, 1942; d. Walter and Mary Helen (Maceyko) Furin; m. John Barry Sloat, Nov. 2, 1968; children: John Andrew, Eric Furin. BS, Denison U., 1963; MS, U. Mich., 1966, PhD, 1968. Lic. and cert. emergency med. technician, paramedic. Lab. asst. U. Ghent, Belgium, 1964; teaching fellow, lectr. U. Mich., Ann Arbor, 1964-66, 68-70, asst. rsch. biologist Mental Health Rsch. Inst., 1972-74, vis. asst. prof., lectr. Ann Arbor and Dearborn, 1974-76, dir. women in sci. Ann Arbor, 1980-84, assoc. dir. honors, 1986-87, rsch. scientist, 1976—, lectr. Residential Coll., 1984—; assoc. Inst. Humanities U. Mich., 1991—. Author: Laboratory Guide for Zoology, 1979, Summer Internships in the Sciences for High School Women (CASE Silver medal, 1985, Excellence in Edn. award, U. Mich., 1993). Recipient Acad. Women's Caucus award, U. Mich., 1984, Grace Lyon Alumnae Award, Denison U., 1988; grantee NSF, U.S. Dept. Edcn., Warner Lambert Found., others. Mem. AAAS, Am. Soc. Cell Biology, N.Y. Acad. Scis., Nat. Assn. Women Deans, Adminstrs. and Counselors, Assn. for Women in Sci. (councilor 1988-90, pres. elect 1990, mentor of yr. award Detroit area chpt. 1994), Phi Beta Kappa, Sigma Xi. Avocations: hiking, yoga, Tibetology. Home: 240 Indian River Pl Ann Arbor MI 48104-1825 Office: U Mich Residential Coll 216 Tyler East Quad Ann Arbor MI 48109-1245 E-mail: bsloat@umich.edu.

SLOAT, JANE ROBERTS DEGRAFF, government official, civic worker, consultant; b. N.Y.C., Dec. 31, 1939; d. John Wayne and Agnes (Murton) Roberts; m. Elliott Dodd DeGraff, June 28, 1959 (div.); children: Pamela DeGraff Porter, Jill Katherine; m. Jonathan Welsh Sloat, June 19, 1983. Active Hospitality Info. Svc., Washington, 1964-70, sec. bd., 1971-73; spl. asst. to ambassador-at-large for cultural affairs Dept. State, Washington, 1981; spl. asst. to U.S. coord. refugee affairs Washington, 1982-85; coord. conf. on Ethical Issues and Moral Principles in U.S. Refugee Policy, 1983; real estate broker Samuel P. Padoe Real Estate, Washington, 1986—. Tour lectr. Corcoran Gallery Art, Washington, 1965-70. Vice chmn. UN Concert, Washington, 1971, 50th Jubilee Nat. English Speaking Union, 1971; spl. asst. to chmn. United Givers fund, Washington. 1971-72; chmn. ball Opera Soc., Washington, 1972; bd. dirs. Jr. League, 1970-71, Nat. Ballet Soc., 1972-74, Washington Performing Arts Soc., 1972-75, The Washington Opera, The Nat. Arboretum; mem. D.C. Mayor's Com. on Internat. Visitors, 1972-77; trustee Hosp. for Sick Children, Washington, 1973-76; editor Washington Antiques Show Catalogue, 1972-75; mem. D.C. Rep. Fin. Com., 1972-75; trustee Meridian House Internat. Ctr., founder, chmn. Meridian House Ball, Washington, 1964-82, sec. 1974-75, vice chmn. bd., 1976-82, adv. bd.; mem. bd. advisers D.C. Lung Assn., 1975—; mem. fund-raising drive for Washington Cathedral, 1976; chair assocs. bd. IONA Sr. Svcs.; bd. dirs. Washington Home for Incurables, 1976-89, Nat. Eye Found., 1976-78, Childrens Hosp. Nat. Rsch. Found., 1978-81, D.C. chpt. ARC, 1976-84, Travelers Aid Soc., 1976-90; chmn. Washington Antiques Show, 1976-78, Washington Cathedral Flower Mart; dir. fin. devel. YWCA of Nat. Capital Area, 1979; vice chmn. Reagan Bush Inaugural, Washington, 1981; mem. transition team for Reagan Bush for NEA, 1981; bd. dirs. Family Stress Services, 1981-84; founde, chmn. Entertaining People, 1982-91; bd. dirs. All Hallows Guild, Washington br. English Speaking Union, 1987-90, brd. Washington Opera, 1997—, Nat. Arbonetum; bd. dirs., chair Woodrow Wilson House, 1990-02, Washington; chrm. adv. brd. Iona Senior Services; chmn. Bush-Quayle Inaugural Ball, 1989, Am. Franklin Friends Com., 1992-95; fundraiser Ann. Fund Kennedy Ctr. Performing Arts, 1987, 90; v.p. bd. Washington Home, 1990-92; apptd. mem. Pres.'s Commn. Arts & Humanities, 1990-94; chmn. Am. Friends Fund-Inst. for U.S. Studies, U. London, bd. The Washington Opera 1996—; chair, protocol Rep. Couselor, Phila., 2002. Mem. Million Dollar Club, Sulgrave Club, Chevy Chase Club. Episcopalian. Avocations: art, design, tennis, opera, fly fishing. E-mail: JaneSloat@aol.com.

SLOBODA, BRIAN WILLIAM, economist; b. Morristown, N.J., July 3, 1968; BA, Rowan Coll. N.J., 1990; MS, So. Ill. U., 1992, PhD in Econs., 1997. Instr. dept. econs. So. Ill. U., Carbondale, 1993-94, 95-96; rsch. analyst Planning and Mgmt. Cons., 1996; staff acct. Robert Half Internat., Parsippany, NJ, 1997-98; economist Bur. Econ. Analysis U.S. Dept. Commerce, Washington, 1998-2000; economist/math. statis. Bur. Transp. Stats. U.S. Dept. Transp., 2000—. Part time faculty U. Phoenix, content area chair econs., 2001—; mem. com. Fed. Forecasters Conf., 2001—. Contbr. articles to profl. jours. Mem.: Internat. Inst. Forecasting, Eastern Econs. Assn., Midwest Econs. Assn., Am. Statis. Assn., Mo. Valley Econs. Assn., Soc. Govt. Economists, Soc. Labor Economists, Am. Econs. Assn. Home: 8715 1st Ave Apt 704D Silver Spring MD 20910-3537 Office: US Dept Transp Bur Transp 400 7th St SW Rm 3430 Washington DC 20590-0001 E-mail: brian.sloboda@bts.gov.

SLOBODIEN, HOWARD DAVID, surgeon, educator; b. Perth Amboy, N.J., July 25, 1923; s. Albert Leo and Anna Frances (Sontag) S.; m. Sally Doris Yerkes, May 9, 1950; children: David, Donald, Daniel, Douglas. Diplomate Am. Bd. Surgery. Intern Morrisania City Hosp., N.Y.C., 1947-48, resident, 1948-52; practice medicine specializing in surgery Perth Amboy, 1955-96; pres. John F. Kennedy Med. Ctr., Edison, N.J., 1967-70, dir. surgery, 1975-79, dir. Breast Ctr., 1997—. Attending surgeon Gen. Hosp., Perth Amboy, dir. surgery, 1970-74; chief gen. surgery, past pres. med. staff Roosevelt Hosp., Edison; cons. surgery Meml. Hosp., South Amboy; clin. asst. prof. surgery Rutgers U. Med. Sch., 1971-84, mem. adv. council Office Consumer Health Edn., 1973-81; mem. adv. council Middlesex County Coll., 1968-78; v.p. Regional Health Facilities Planning Council, 1970-73. Editor N.J. Medicine, 1988-99. Pack committeman Cub Scouts, 1960-64; active steering com. Metuchen YMCA, 1962. With USNR, 1943-45, USAF, 1952-54. Fellow ACS; mem. AMA, World, Pan-Am. med. assns., N.J. (trustee 1972-84, chmn. pub. rels. coun. 1973-76, pres. 1982-83), Middlesex County (pres. 1970-71) med. socs., Pan-Pacific Surg. Assn., Royal Soc. Health, Am. Acad. Med. Adminstrs., Royal Soc. Medicine, N.J. Acad. Medicine (trustee 1974-78), Middlesex County Med. Assts. Assn. (county med. advisor 1973-80), N.J. Soc. Surgeons, Phi Beta Kappa, Metuchen Country Club. Home: 34 Linden Ave Metuchen NJ 08840-1418 E-mail: howdmet34@aol.com.

SLOBOZHANIN, LEV ARKADIEVICH, fluid mechanics researcher; b. Nylga, Russia, Sept. 1, 1941; s. Arkadii Alexandrovich and Iraida Stepanovna (Vlasova) S.; divorced; children: Andrei L., Darya L. Degree in mech. engring. with honors, Kharkov (Ukraine) Aviation Inst., 1963; PhD in Physics and Math., Inst. for Low Temperature Physics and Engring., Kharkov, 1968; cert. sr. rsch. scientist, Acad. of Scis. of Ukraine, 1975; DSc in Physics and Math., Lavrentyev Inst. Hydrodynamics, Novosibirsk, Russia, 1989. Engr. B. Verkin Inst. Low Temperature Physics and Engring. Nat. Acad. Scis. of Ukraine, Kharkov, 1963-66, sr. engr., 1966-69, jr. scientist, 1969-71, sr. scientist, 1971-89, leading scientist, 1989-98. Sr. tchr. Kharkov Aviation Inst., 1969—71, prof., 1989—90; vis. prof. Madrid Poly. U., 1993—94; vis. scholar U. Ala., Huntsville, 1995—2002; vis. rschr. Case Western Res. U., Cleve., 1999—2002, prin. rschr., 2002—. Co-author: Fluid Mechanics of Weightlessness, 1976, Low-Gravity Fluid Mechanics, 1987, Solution Methods for Fluid Mechanics Problems Under Weightlessness Conditions, 1992; contbr. articles to profl. jours. Chmn. trade union com. B. Verkin Inst. for Low Temperature Physics and Engring., 1986-89. Mem. Am. Phys. Soc. Office: Case Western Res U 414 Glennan Bldg 10900 Euclid Ave Cleveland OH 44106-7222 E-mail: lion@mae.cwru.edu.

SLOCUM, DONALD HILLMAN, product development executive; b. Flushing, N.Y., Jan. 6, 1930; s. John G. and Frances H. S.; m. June Manning, Sept. 22, 1952 (dec. 1976); children: Richard, Mark, Carol; m. Barbara M. Ruane, Nov. 1, 1985. BS, Davis and Elkins Coll., 1951; MS, U. Vt., 1956; PhD, Ohio State U., 1958; LLD, Fla. Tech. Inst., 1968; MBA, Rider Coll., 1971; ScD, Norton U., 1972; Dr. Profl. Studies, Pace U., 1974; ScD, Davis and Elkins Coll., 2000. Rsch. chem. Charles Pfizer, Inc., Bklyn., 1954; rsch. scientist Procter & Gamble, Cin., 1958-68; mgr. product devel. E.I. DuPont de Nemours & Co., Wilmington, Del., 1960-68; dir. new ventures N.L. Industries, N.Y.C., 1968-71; dir. fin. planning Hoffmann LaRoche, Nutley, N.J., 1971-74; v.p. Curtiss-Wright Corp., Woodridge, 1974-78; sr. v.p. Masonite-USG/Internat. Paper, Chgo., 1978-85; pres. Doner-Viking Corp., Madison, N.J., 1985-87, Woodtec, Inc. subs. Masco, Taylor, Mich., 1987-96, Versitec Industries, 1996—. Author: New Venture Methodology, 1974; contbr. articles to tech. and bus. publs.; patentee in field. Lt. U.S. Army, 1951-54, Korea, Col. Res., ret. Achievements include first to in solid surface industry; invention of of DuPont Corian. Home: 61 Chimney Ridge Dr Morristown NJ 07960-4722 Office: SRA 3400 Bee Ridge Rd Sarasota FL 34239-7223

SLOCUM, DONALD WARREN, chemist; m. Laurel Hopper, 1990 (dec. May 1997); children from previous marriage: Warren, Matthew. BS in Chemistry, BA in English, U. Rochester; PhD in Chemistry, NYU, 1963. Postdoctoral rsch. assoc. Duke U., Durham, N.C., 1963-64; asst. prof. chemistry Carnegie Inst. Tech., Pitts., 1964-65; from asst. to assoc. prof. chemistry So. Ill. U., Carbondale, 1965-72, prof., 1972-81, adj. prof., 1981-84; program dir. chem. dynamics sect., chemistry div. NSF, Washington, 1984-85; program leader div. ednl. programs, sr. scientist chem. tech. div. Argonne (Ill.) Nat. Lab., 1985-90; head dept. chemistry Western Ky. U., Bowling Green, 1990-95, prof. chemistry, 1995—. Sr. scientist Gulf Rsch. and Devel. Co., Pitts., 1980-82; vis. prof. U. Ill., 1970, U. Bristol, Eng., 1973, U. Cin., 1976; vis. fellow U. Bristol, 1972; vis. lectr. Carnegie-Mellon U., 1983-84, U. Pitts., 1983-84; organizer symposia on organometallic chemistry and catalysis; bd. dirs. Ctrl. States Univs., Inc., 1986-88, Arts at Argonne, 1988-90; cons. in field; mem. nat. organizing com. XVth Internat. Conf. on Organometallic Chemistry Wayne State U., Detroit, 1990; mem. internat. adv. bd. XVith Internat. Conf. on Organometallic Chemistry, Warsaw, 1992; mem. NSF/EPSCoR subcom., Ky., 1993-94; mem. coun. on undergrad. rsch. Instnl. Liaison Rep. to Western Ky. U., 1995—. Co-editor: Advances in Chemistry Series of Am. Chem. Soc., Vol. 230, 1992, Methane and Alkane Activation (Plenum), 1995; contbr. over 70 articles to profl. jours., chpts. to books. Recipient Rsch./Creativity award Ogden Coll. of Sci., Technology and Health, Western Ky. U., 1996, Sci. award honoring Brian Andreen, Cottrell Coll. Sci., 1999. Mem. Am. Chem. Soc. (sec. gen. elect catalysis and surface sci. secretariat 1992, sec. gen. 1993, organic divsn. rep. to catalysis and surface sci. secretariat, 1993-98, co-chmn. symposium, San Diego, 1994), Chem. Soc. Gt. Britain, Catalysis Soc., Sigma Xi. Avocations: music, literature, sports. Office: Western Ky U Dept Chemistry Bowling Green KY 42101 E-mail: Donald.Slocum@wku.edu.

SLOCUM, FRED, political science educator; b. Va. BA in Polit. Sci., U. N.C., 1989; MA in Polit. Sci., U. Iowa, 1991, PhD in Polit. Sci., 1997. Asst. prof. polit. sci. Benedictine U., Lisle, Ill., 1997-98, Minn. State U., Mankato, 1998—. Contbg. author: Politics in Action, 2001, Politics and Policy, 2001. Bd. dirs., singer Musicorum, choir, Mankato, 1998—. Mem. Internat. Soc. Polit. Psychology, Am. Polit. Sci. Assn., So. Polit. Sci. Assn. Office: Minn State U Dept Polit Sci 109 Morris Hall Mankato MN 56001 E-mail: frederick.slocum@mnsu.edu.

SLOCUM, RICHARD COPELAND (R.C. SLOCUM), university athletic coach; b. Oakdale, LA, Nov. 7, 1944; Asst. football coach Tex. A&M U. Aggies, 1972-80, 82-89, U. So. Calif., 1981; head football coach Tex. A&M U. Aggies, 1989—. Office: Texas A&M Univ Dept Athletics PO Box 30017 College Station TX 77843-3017

SLOCUM, ROBERT BIGNEY, retired librarian; b. Brockton, Mass., Apr. 6, 1922; s. George Wheaton and Florence Alice (Heustis) S.; m. Christine Stanfield, Aug. 23, 1953; children: Robert Stanfield, Kathryn Slocum Goodwin. BA, Boston U., 1946; MA, Columbia U., 1947; BSLS, Simmons Coll., 1949. Libr. intern Libr. of Congress, Washington, 1949-50; asst. to dir. librs. Simmons Coll., Boston, 1950-51; libr. cataloger, instr. U. Ill. Libr., Urbana, 1951-54; assoc. catalog libr. Cornell U. Libr., Ithaca, N.Y., 1954-88. Author: Sample Catalog Cards, 1962, Biographical Dictionaries and Related Works, 1967-78, 2d edit., 1986, Sample Cataloging Forms, 1968, rev. edit., 1980; editor Manual of Cataloging Procedures, 1959, rev. edit., 1969, New England in Fiction, 1994; contbr. articles to profl. jours. Active Am. for Dem. Action, Pub. Citizen, Am. Farmland Trust, steering bd. Cornell U. Retirees Vols. in Svc.; co-chmn. Dryden Bicentennial Com. With U.S. Army, 1942-45, ETO. Mem. AAUP, ALA, AARP, Am. Hist. Assn., Common Cause, Smithsonian Assocs., Dryden Hist. Soc., Sane/Freeze, Libr. Congress Assocs., Newark Valley Hist. Soc., Cornell Assn. Profs. Emeriti, Cornell U. Libr. Assocs., Drake Group. Presbyterian. Avocations: hiking, movie research, Victorian literature, early Americana. Home: 92 W Main St Dryden NY 13053-9706 E-mail: rbs8@cornell.edu.

SLOCUM, ROBERT BOAK, minister, educator; b. Macon, Ga., May 21, 1952; s. James Robert and Sara Lila (Bell) S.; m. Sheryl Stephanie Walter, May 15, 1982; children: Claire Marie, Rebecca Bell, Jacob Robert. BA, Vanderbilt U., 1974, JD, 1977; MDiv, Nashotah House Sem., 1986; DMin, U. of the South, 1992; PhD, Marquette U., 1997. Ordained priest Episcopal Ch., 1987; bar: Tenn. 1978; cert. trial counsel, cert. def. counsel. USAF. Deacon-in-tng. Trinity Episcopal Ch., New Orleans, 1986-87; vicar St. Patrick's Episcopal Ch., Zachary, La., 1987-91, St. Andrew's Episcopal Ch., Clinton, 1987-91; rector St. Philip's Episcopal Ch., Waukesha, Wis., 1991-92; priest-in-charge Ch. of the Holy Communion, Lake Geneva, 1993, rector, 1994—. Chaplain VA, Milw., 1993-98; lectr. theology Marquette U., Milw., 1997—; chair convention planning com. Episcopal Diocese of Milw., 1996-97. Editor: Prophet of Justice, Prophet of Life, Essays on William Stringfellow, 1997, A New Conversation, Essays on the Future of Theology and the Episcopal Church, 1999, Engaging the Spirit, Essays on the Life and Theology of the Holy Spirit, 2001; author: The Theology of William Porcher DuBose, Life, Movement, and Being, 2000; co-editor: Documents of Witness, A History of the Episcopal Church, 1782-1985, 1994, An Episcopal Dictionary of the Church, A User-Friendly Reference for Episcopalians, 2000, To Hear Celestial Harmonies, Essays on the Witness of James DeKoven and The DeKoven Center , 2002; rev. article editor Anglican Theol. Rev., 2001—. Pres. Lake Geneva Libr. Bd., 1995—, Geneva Lakes Area United Way, 1998-2000. Capt. USAF, 1978-83. Decorated Meritorious Svc. medal. Mem. Am. Acad. Religion, Soc. for Study Christian Spirituality, Soc. Anglican and Luth. Theologians. Avocations: distance running, martial arts. Home: 1325 Madison St Lake Geneva WI 53147-1136 Office: PO Box 1265 Lake Geneva WI 53147-6265

SLOCUM, ROSEMARIE, physician, search and development consultant; b. Port Arthur, Tex., Dec. 19, 1948; d. Edly and Ella (McNeely) Raccard; m. James Rubenstein; 1 child from previous marriage BlairAshton. BS, La. State U., Baton Rouge, 1971; MA in Bus. Comm., Jones Internat. U., 1999. Cert. tchr., La. Edn. specialist La. Dept. Occupl. Stds., Baton Rouge, 1971-74; account exec. Uarco, Inc., 1974-77; owner, broker Rosemarie Slocum Real Estate, 1977—85; physician recruiter MSI, New Orleans, 1985-86; assoc. dir. physician recruitment Physician Search, Inc., Fairfax, Va., 1986-88; spl. cons. Caswell/Winters Physician Search Cons., Milw., 1988-89; v.p. U.S. Med. Search, Inc. subs. of Caswell/Winters, 1988-89; dir. physician recruitment/mktg. East Range Clinics, Ltd., Virginia, Minn., 1989-91; pres. RSI Physician Search, Mpls., 1991—. Office: RSI 3622 W 44th St Minneapolis MN 55410-1366 E-mail: rsi@scc.net.

SLOGOFF, STEPHEN, dean, anesthesiologist, educator; b. Phila., July 7, 1942; s. Israel and Lillian (Rittenberg) S.; m. Barbara Anita Gershman, June 2, 1963; children: Michele, Deborah. AB in Biology, Franklin and Marshall Coll., 1964; MD, Jefferson Med. Coll., 1967. Diplomate Am. Bd. Med. Examiners, Am. Bd. Anesthesiology (jr. assoc. examiner 1977-80, sr. assoc. examiner 1980-81, bd. dirs. 1981-93, pres. 1989-90, joint coun. on in-tng. exams, vice chmn. 1983-86, chmn. 1986-92). Intern Harrisburg (Pa.) Hosp., 1967-68; resident in anesthesiology Jefferson Med. Coll. Hosp., 1968-71; chief anesthesia sect. U.S. Army, Brooke Army Med. Ctr., Fort Sam Houston, Tex., 1971-74; staff anesthesiologist Baylor Coll. Medicne, Houston, 1974-75; attending cardiovascular anesthesiologist U. Tex. Health Sci. Ctr., 1974-93, clin. asst. prof., 1977-81, clin. assoc. prof., 1981-85, clin. prof., 1985-93; prof., chmn. dept. anesthesiology Loyola U., Chgo., 1993—; sr. v.p. for clin. affairs Loyola U. Health Sys., 1999—; dean, Strich Sch. Medicine Loyola U., Chgo., 1999—. Chmn. rsch com., co-dir. rsch. labs Tex. Heart Inst., Houston, 1990-93. Contbr. articles to profl. jours. Trustee Loyola U. Health Sys., Chgo., 1996—; chmn. Loyola U. Physicians Found., 1995-99. Mem. Am. Soc. Anesthesiologists, Alpha Omega Alpha. Avocations: tennis, jogging. Office: Loyola U Med Ctr Office of Dean 2160 S 1st Ave Maywood IL 60153-3304*

SLOMAN, MARVIN SHERK, lawyer; b. Fort Worth, Apr. 17, 1925; s. Richard Jack and Lucy Janette (Sherk) S.; m. Margaret Jane Dinwiddie, Apr. 11, 1953; children: Lucy Carter, Richard Dinwiddie. BA, U. Tex., 1948; LLB with honors, 1950. Bar: Tex. 1950, N.Y. 1951. Assoc. Sullivan & Cromwell, N.Y.C., 1950-56, Carrington, Coleman, Sloman & Blumenthal LLP and predecessor, Dallas, 1956-60, ptnr., 1960-97; sr. counsel, 1998—. Office: Carrington Coleman Sloman & Blumenthal LLP 200 Crescent Ct Ste 1500 Dallas TX 75201-1848

SLOMANSON, LLOYD HOWARD, architect, musician, photographer; b. N.Y.C., July 31, 1928; s. Albert Jerome and Dorothea (Jacobson) S.; m. Joan Barbara Kanel; children: Peter, Eric. BArch, Syracuse U., 1949. Registered architect, 18 states including N.Y. and N.J.; NCARB; registered profl. planner, N.J. Archtl. draftsman Rich & Conn Architects, Bklyn., 1949-50; project architect Fordyce & Hamby/Raymond Loewy, N.Y.C., 1951-53; project architect, assoc. ptnr. Serge P. Petroff, Architect, 1953-58; project dir. Robert W. Hegardt, Architect, 1959-60; project architect, ptnr. Fordyce & Hamby Assocs., 1960-67; ptnr. Fordyce, Hamby & Kennerly, 1967-69, Hamby, Kennerly & Slomanson, N.Y.C., 1969-72, Kennerly, Slomanson & Smith, N.Y.C., 1972-81; mng. ptnr. Slomanson, Smith & Barresi, 1981-99; pvt. practice, 1999—. Arbitrator Am. Arbitration Assn., N.Y.C. Author articles. Served with U.S. Army, 1950-51. Recipient 1st prize for design S.I. C. of C., 1967, 84. Mem. AIA, N.Y. Soc. Architects (Store of Yr. award 1985, Design award 1993), N.Y. State Assn. Architects, Bldg. Ofcls. Conf. Am., Univ. Club, The Players. Avocations: playing music with a big band, photography. Office: 137 W 78th St New York NY 10024-6702 E-mail: woodpics@aol.com.

SLONAKER, DENA MECKLER, occupational therapist, rehabilitation consultant; b. Cleveland Heights, Ohio, May 17, 1946; d. Sam and Esther Ida (Lubovich) M.; m. Barry Alan Shapiro, June 9, 1968 (div. July 1981); m. Rolland Dean Slonaker, Jan. 1, 1982; 1 child, Charles Yong. Student, Cuyahoga C.C., Cleve., 1964-65; BS in Occupl. Therapy, Ohio State U., 1969; MSEd, U. So. Calif., L.A., 1982. Cert. hand therapist; registered occupl. therapist; cert. kinesiotape instr. Staff occupl. therapist, student supr. pediat. Rancho Los Amigos Hosp., Downey, Calif., 1969-70, staff occupl. therapist stroke svc., 1970-71, sr. occupl. therapist arthritis svc., 1971-72; occupl. therapist cons. Greater L.A. Orthop. Specialties Group, L.A., 1973-77; dir. occupl. therapy dept. rehab. ctr. White Meml. Med. Ctr., 1974-78; sr. occupl. therapy rheumatology rehab. unit U.C.L.A., 1978-81, occupl. therapist outpatient divsn. rehab. ctr., 1981-83; occupl. therapy specialist, cons. rheumatology and hand therapy Cedars Sinai Med. Ctr., L.A., 1983-84, Dr. Martin Berry, Bakersfield, Calif., 1983-85; developer, med. distbr. Sani-Fem Corp., 1984—; occupl. specialist, cons. rheumatology and hand therapy Dr. Robert Roth, Mission Hills, Calif., 1985-90; occupl. specialist in hand and rheumatology rehab. Conejo Valley Rehab. Svcs., Thousand Oaks, 1988-93; dir. occupl. therapy Consortium Rehab. and Fitness Therapy, Reseda, 1987-88; co-founder, dir. Profl. Therapeutic Assocs., 1988; dir. occupl. therapy dept. Arthritis Ctr. and Phys. Therapy Svcs., Tarzana, Calif., 1989-93; supr., clin. coord. hand therapy clinic HealthSouth Rehab. Ctr., Van Nuys, 1993-94, coord. hand therapy program and product line devel. HealthSouth Hand Therapy Clinic, 1994—. Occupl. therapy specialist, cons. rheumatology, Simi Valley, Tarzana, Van Nuys, Pasadena, Calif., 1985-87; occupl. therapy cons. hand therapy FACEY Med. Group, Mission Hills, 1986-90; cons. orthop. and sports medicine distbrs. Body Glove, 1993-94; cons., instr., lectr. Sports Clinic Ctr., Florence, Italy, 1998; lectr. in field. Author: (book) Guide to Independent Living for People with Arthritis, 1988; (pamphlets) Taking Care-Protecting Your Joints and Saving Your Energy, 1986, Using oYour Joints Wisely, 1992, Managing Your Activities, 1992; Arthritis Community Resource Guide of the San Fernando Valley, 1990; author: (with others) Rheumatic Diseases, Rehabilitation and Management, 1984, Straight-Talk on Ankylosing Spondylitis, 1985, Straight Talk on Spondylitis, 1993; (manual) Fibromyalgia Self Help Course Leaders' Manual, 1990, Participant's Manual, 1990; co-author: Rheumatologic Rehabilitation Series, Vol. II, 2000; contbr., cons. Rheumatic Disease Occupl. Therapy and Rehab., 1977; chmn. revision Arthritis Cmty. Resource Guide, 1990; editl. rev. bd. Nat. Arthritis Found., 1984—; chair revision Guide to Independent Living for People with Arthritis, 1987-88; med. adv. bd. Arthritis Today mag., 1995-97, Prime Time project, 1997; cons. Consumer Health Pubs., 1995—; contbr. chpt. to book, articles to profl. jours., newsletters, and mags. Mem. So. Calif. Schs. Coun., 1971-72, So. Calif. Patient Svcs. com. Multiple Sclerosis Soc., 1976-78, Congregation B'nai Emet, Simi Valley, Calif., 1986—; founder, chmn. Hand Therapy Study Group, L.A., 1976-79; adv. bd. United Scleroderma Found., 1985; mem. program com. Arthritis Found. So. Calif. chpt., 1972-74, mem. fellowship subcom., 1982-96, project telecare instr., 1987, fibromyalgia subcom., 1988-98, coord. art of practice workshop, 1991; adv. bd. Arthritis Found. San Fernando Valley br.m 1985-94, med. edn. com., 1985-98, co-founder, fibromyalgia support group, 1988; elected nominating com. chmn. Arthritis Found. We. Region, 1989-90; mem. Nat. Arthritis Health Profls. Assn., 1972—, mem. task force, 1977-80, membership com., 1978-79, program subcom. Pan Am. Internat. Meeting, 1981-82, program subcom. nat. meeting, 1982-83, nominating com., 1984-85. Recipient Nat. Arthritis Found. Outstanding Profl. Edn. award, 1991, So. Calif. Chpt. Marilyn Magaram award, 1991; Olympic Torch Bearer, 1996. Mem. Am. Occupl. Therapy Assn., Occupl. Therapy Assn. Calif., So. Calif. Hand Therapy Special Interest Group (founder and chmn. 1977). Jewish. Avocations: photography, Tai Chi, mountain dulcimer, writing, gardening. Home: 1554 Agnew St Simi Valley CA 93065-2028 Office: Ste 237 5363 Balboa Ave Encino CA 91316 E-mail: denaslonaker@therapist.net.

SLONAKER, MARY JOANNA KING, columnist; b. Richmond, Ind., July 18, 1930; d. Claiborn F. and Carlyle (Diffendenfer) King; divorced; children: Mary Sue Hosey, Steven, Allis Ann Fox. Student, Earlham Coll., 1948-49; BS, Ball State U., 1969; MA in Teaching, Ind. U., 1974. Cert. residential child care worker. Home econs. tchr. Lewisville (Ind.) Sch., 1978-79, Morton Meml. Sch., Knightstown, Ind., 1970-83; town coun. mem. Cambridge City, 1991-2001. Mem. Ind. U. Chancellor's Medallion Dinner Com., 2001. Recipient Kiwanis Cmty. award, 1983-84, 95, Appreciation award Am. Bus. Women, 1985, Appreciation award Waseda U. Japanese Exch. Program, 1986-88. Mem. AAUW, Soc. Profl. Journalists, Ind. U. Alumni Club, Ind. U. Varsity Club, The Woman's Club, Psi Iota Xi, Alpha Delta Kappa, Pi Beta Phi. Democrat. Presbyterian. Avocations: basketball, football, harness racing, walking, gardening. Home: 36 W Church St Cambridge City IN 47327-1615 Office: 127 N Foote St Cambridge City IN 47327-1144

SLONAKER, NORMAN DALE, lawyer; b. Havre, Mont., Sept. 16, 1940; s. Frederick and Agnes (Monson) S.; m. Helen Bogumil, Aug. 29, 1964. BS, U. Wash., Seattle, 1962; LLM, Harvard U., 1965. Bar: N.Y. 1966. Assoc. Brown & Wood, LLP, N.Y.C., 1965-72, ptnr., 1973—.

SLONAKER, THOMAS N. federal agency administrator; BA, Williams Coll.; MBA, harvard U. Joined Mellon Bank, 1960, sr. v.p., 1983, Federated Rsch. Corp., 1983—84, First Interstate Bancorp, 1993, exec. v.p., chief investment officer, 1994—96; spl. trustee for Am. Indians U.S. Dept. Interior, Washington, 2000—. Bd. dirs. Fed. Farm Credit Funding Corp. Trustee Allegheny Coll. Mem.: Pub. Securities Assn., The Asset/Liability Mgmt. Assn. (co-founder), Assn. for Investment Mgmt. and Rsch. Office: 1849 C St NW Washington DC 20240*

SLONE, SANDI, artist; b. Boston, Oct. 1, 1939; d. Louis and Ida (Spind) Sudikoff; children: Eric Solomon, Jon Solomon. Student, Boston Mus. Fine Arts Sch., 1970-73; BA magna cum laude, Wellesley Coll., 1974. Sr., grad. painting faculty Boston Mus. Fine Arts Sch./Tufts U., 1975—; instr. grad. program Sch. Visual Art, N.Y.C., 1989-90; lectr. painting Harvard U., Cambridge, Mass., 1982. Vis. artist Triangle Artists Workshop, N.Y., 1982, 87, 90; co-founder, dir. Art/Omi Internat. Artists Found., N.Y.C., 1992—. One-woman shows include ICA, Boston, 1977, Harcus Krakow Gallery, Boston, 1978, 79, 80, 82, 84, 86, Acquavella Contemporary Art, N.Y., 1977, 79, 80, 82, 84, Stephen Rosenberg Gallery, N.Y., 1988, Levinson Kane Gallery, Boston, 1989, Smith Jariwala Gallery, London, 1990, Jersey City Mus., 1996, The Artists Mus., Lodz, Poland, 1997, Cristinerose Gallery, N.Y.C., 1999, Savage Gallery, Portland, Oreg., 2001; exhibited in group shows at Mus. Fine Arts, Boston, 1977, Corcoran Gallery of Art 35th Biennial, Washington, 1977, Edmonton Art Mus., 1977, 85, Hayden Gallery MIT, Cambridge, Mass., 1978, New Generation Andre Emmerich Gallery, N.Y., 1980-81, Am. Ctr., Paris, 1980-81, Amerika Haus, Berlin, 1980-81, Carpenter Ctr., Harvard U., Ctr. de la Cultura Contemporania, Barcelona, 1987, Federated Union of Black Artists, Johannesburg, South Africa, 1989, Jan Weiss Gallery, N.Y., 1990, Olympia Internat. Art Fairs, London, 1991, Gallery Korea, N.Y., 1992, Klarfeld Perry Gallery, N.Y., 1994, Out of the Blue Gallery, Edinburgh, Scotland, 1994, Gallery One, Toronto, 1996, Fine Arts Ctr., U. R.I., Kingston, 1996, Crieger Dane Gallery, Boston, 1996, Visual Arts Gallery, N.Y., 1997, TransHudson Gallery, N.Y., 1997, Butler Inst. of Am. Art, Youngstown, Ohio, 1998, 45th Biennial Corcoran Mus. Art, Washington, 1998, Lombard-Freid Fine Arts, N.Y., 1999, others; represented in permanent collections Mus. Modern Art, N.Y.C., Mus. Contemporary Art, Barcelona, Mus. Fine Arts, Boston, Hirshhorn Mus., Washington, Corcoran Gallery & Mus. Art, Washington; artist-in-residence City Hall, Barcelona, 1987, 89. Mus. Fine Arts Boston fellow, 1977, 81; Ford Found. grantee, 1979; internat. artists residency East-South Project, Poland, 1997. Studio: 13 Worth St New York NY 10013-2922

SLONEM, HUNT, artist; b. Kittery, Maine, July 18, 1951; s. Charles and Louise W. Slonem. Student, Skowhegan Sch. Painting and Sculpture, 1972; BA, Tulane U., 1973. Represented by Marlborough Gallery. Numerous one-man shows, 1977—, including Tilden-Foley Gallery, New Orleans, 1991, Charlotte Milburn Fine Art Mus., Oslo, 1991, Pulitzer Gallery, Amsterdam, 1991, Witteveen Gallery, Amsterdam, 1991, numerous others; exhibited in numerous group shows, 1977—, including Laguna Gloria Mus., Austin, Tex., 1990, Bergen Mus. Art & Sci., Paramus, N.J., 1990, Meredith Long Gallery, Houston, 1990, Marlborough Gallery, N.Y.C., Solomon R. Guggenheim Mus., N.Y.C., Centro Cultural Recoleta, Buenos Aires, 2000, Heriard Cimino Gallery, New Orleans, 2000, Vanier Gallery, Scottsdale, Ariz., 2000, Harmon Meek Gallery, Naples, Fla., numerous others; represented in numerous permanent collections including Met. Mus. Art, N.Y.C., Contemporary Mus., Honolulu, Guggenheim Mus., N.Y.C., Miro Found., Spain, Chrysler Mus., Norfolk, Va., Columbus (Ohio) Mus. Art, Oklahoma Art Ctr., Oklahoma City, Portland (Maine) Mus. Art, Wichita (Kans.) Art Mus., many others; exclusively represented by Marlborough Gallery, N.Y.C. McDowell fellow, 1983, 84, 86, Ragsdale Found. fellow, 1983; Elizabeth T. Greenshields Found. grantee, 1976, NEA grantee, 1991; recipient award Millay Colony, 1982. Avocation: aviculture. Home: 601 W 26th St New York NY 10001-1101

SLOSBERG, MIKE, advertising executive; b. Phila., Aug. 29, 1934; s. Sam. M. and Florence (Frank) S.; m. Joan Shidler, Aug. 29, 1957 (div. 1984); children: Sydney Ellen, Robert Morton; m. Janet Cohn, June 10, 1987. BSBA, U. Denver, 1960. With Young & Rubican, Inc., N.Y.C., 1960-78; pres. Wunderman, Rocotta & Kline, 1978-83; exec. v.p., exec. creative dir. Marsteller, Inc., 1983-84, Bozell Jacobs, Kenyon & Eckhardt, N.Y.C., 1984-86, pres. direct mktg. div., 1986-87; exec. creative dir. Bronner Slosberg Humphrey, Boston, 1987-96; vice chmn., chief creative officer Digitas (formerly Bronner Slosberg Humphrey), 1996-2000; co-founder Digitas, Inc. Author: The August Strangers, 1978. Mem. Friars Club. Avocation: writing novels. Office: Digitas 355 Park Ave S New York NY 10010

SLOSBURG-ACKERMAN, JILL ROSE, artist, educator; b. Omaha, Aug. 28, 1948; d. Harold Walter and Marion (Gill) Slosburg; m. James Sloss Ackerman, Aug. 8, 1987; 1 child, Jesse August. Diploma, Boston Mus. Sch., 1971; BFA, Tufts U., 1971, MFA, 1983. Prof. art Mass. Coll. of Art, Boston, 1973—; vis. artist Cranbrook Acad. of Art, Bloomfield, Mich., Spring 1993. One-person shows include Harcus-Krakow Gallery, Boston, 1978, 80, Helen Shlien Gallery, Boston, 1980, 82, Cohen Arts Ctr., Tufts U., Medford, Mass., 1982, Van Buren/Brazelton/Cutting Gallery, Cambridge, Mass., 1985, Genovese Gallery, Boston, 1995, Manwaring Gallery Cumings Art Ctr., Conn. Coll., New London, 1995, Rose Art Mus., Brandeis U., Waltham, Mass., 1996, Atrium Gallery/U. Mass., Dartmouth, 1999, Judy Ann Goldman Fine Art, Boston, 1999; exhibited in group shows including Naga Gallery, Boston, Boston, 1980, DeCordova Mus., Lincoln, Mass., 1980, Jewett Art Ctr., Wellesley, Mass., 1982, Helen Shlien Gallery, Boston, 1982, Cherry Stone Gallery, Wellfleet, Mass., 1984, Quadrum Gallery, Chestnut Hill, Mass., 1985, Fed. Res. Gallery, Boston, 1986, Danforth Mus., 1986, Conseil de la Sculpture, Montreal, 1986, North Hall Gallery, Boston, 1987, Artists Found. Gallery, Boston, 1990, Mus. Decorative Arts, Prague, 1991, Nancy Margolis Gallery, N.Y.C., 1991, Bellevue (Wash.) Art Mus., 1992, Artwear, N.Y., 1992, Genovese Gallery, Albany, N.Y., 1992, Judy Ann Goldman Fine Art, Boston, 1997, Mills Gallery, Boston, 1997, 98, Traveling Scholars/Boston Mus. Fine Arts, 1999, DeCordova Mus. Ann. Exhbn., Lincoln, Mass., 2000, Judy Ann Goldman Fine Art, Boston, 2002, Forest Hills Cemetary, Boston, 2002; represented in permanent collections J.L. Brandeis & Sons, Omaha, Mass. Coll. Art, Boston, Boston Pub. Libr., also pvt. collections; contbr. articles to profl. jours. Founder, mem. Boston Women's Action Coalition; bd. dirs. Cambridge (Mass.) Multi-Cultural Ctr., 1993. Recipient Patricia Jellinek Hallowell prize for jewelry, 1984, Disting. Svc. award Mass. Coll. of Art, 1980, 4th prize sterling silver design competition Nat. Guild of Sterling Silversmiths, 1970; fellow Haystack Mountain Sch. Crafts, Deer Isle, Maine, 1972, 76, Nat. Endowment Arts, 1974, 86, The Artists Found., Boston, 1984, Mary Ingraham Bunting Inst., 1985-86; Mass. Coll. Art profl. devel. grantee, 1987, Polaroid Corp. photography grantee, 1988, Sch. Boston Mus. Fine Arts traveling scholar, 1998, New Eng. Found. for the Arts fellow, 1998; Mass. Cultural Coun. Artist's grantee, 1999, grantee Artist's Resource Trust, 2001. Jewish. Home: 12 Coolidge Hill Rd Cambridge MA 02138-5510 Studio: C415 1 Fitchburg St Apt C415 Somerville MA 02143-2128 E-mail: jsackerm@fas.harvard.edu.

SLOSSER, JEFFREY ERIC, research entomologist; b. Winslow, Az., Dec. 1, 1943; s. Ernest Clair and Geneva Lee Slosser; m. Harolyn Christine Ellis, July 27, 1968; children: Tamara Joanne, Tracy Suzanne. BS, Arizona State U., 1966; MS, U. Arizona, 1968, PhD, 1971. Postdoctoral rsch. assoc. U. Ark., Fayetteville, 1972-75; asst. prof. Tex. Agrl. Expt. Sta., Vernon, 1975-79, assoc. prof., 1979-86, prof., 1986—. Editor Southwestern Entomologist, Southwestern Entomol. Soc., College Station, Tex., 1986-90. Contbr. articles to profl. jours. Grantee boll weevil and bollworm rsch. Cotton Inc., 1977-82, 94-97, greenbug rsch. Tex. Wheat Prodrs. Bd., 1985-88, cotton aphid rsch. Nat. Cotton Coun., Cotton, Inc., 1992-2002, boll weevil rsch. Plains Cotton Growers, 1989-95, horse fly rsch. Waggoner Found., 1996-97, bruchids affecting mesquite seeds USDA, NRI, 1998-2001, others; recipient award in excellence for rsch. Tex. A&M Univ. Sys., 1990. Mem. Entomol. Soc. Am. (CIBA Crop Protection Agrl. Recognition award 1994), Southwestern Entomol. Soc. (pres.-elect 1991, pres. 1992), Sigma Xi. Avocation: astronomy. Office: Tex Agrl Expt Sta PO Box 1658 Vernon TX 76385-1658 E-mail: j-slosser@tamu.edu.

SLOTKIN, HERMAN, psychologist; b. Bklyn., Jan. 25, 1917; s. Harry and Rose S.; m. Roselyn, July 2, 1939; children: Richard, Theodore. BA, Bklyn. Coll., 1937; MA, NYU, 1954, PhD, 1958. Tchr. English Bd. Edn., N.Y.C., 1938-52, supr., 1952-72; assoc. prof. Fordham U., 1974-81. Cons. in field. Author of poems. Mem. APA, N.Y. Acad. Scis. Avocation: writing poetry.

SLOTKIN, TODD, holding company executive; b. Detroit, Mar. 19, 1953; s. Hugo and Babette Slotkin; m. Judy Scavone, Jan. 30, 1988; children: Matthew, William, Thomas, Peter. BS, Cornell U., 1974, MBA, 1975. With Citicorp, 1975-92, sr. credit officer, 1984-92, head divsn. corp. fin., 1988-90, sr. mng. dir., 1990-92; with MacAndrews & Forbes Holdings, Inc., N.Y.C., 1992—, sr. v.p., 1992-98, exec. v.p., 1998—, CFO, 1999—. Bd. dirs. Trans Tech. Pharma, Cal Fed Bank. Dir. Food Allergy Initiative, 1999—. Home: 876 Park Ave Apt 11 N New York NY 10021-1832 Office: MacAndrews & Forbes Holding 35 E 62nd St New York NY 10021-8032

SLOTNICK, MORTIMER H. artist; b. N.Y.C., Nov. 7, 1920; s. Max S. and Sarah B. S.; m. Phyllis June Gluckin, July 26, 1953; children: Debra Jan, Mark Stuart. BSS, CCNY, 1942; MA, Tchrs. Coll., Columbia U., 1942. Tchr. visual arts, public schs., New Rochelle, N.Y., 1946-64; supr. arts and humanities City Sch. Dist., 1964-72; prin. Davis Elem. Sch., 1972-84. Adj. prof. art CCNY, 1964-72; prof. art Coll. New Rochelle, N.Y., 1972-78; adj. prof. edn. Pace U., 1988-93. One-man shows include Ada Ahrtz Galleries, N.Y.C., 1959, Westport (Conn.) Art Gallery, 1986, New Rochelle Coun. on the Arts, 1989; exhibited in group shows Nat. Acad. N.Y., World Trade Ctr., N.Y.C., Lever House, N.Y.C., Am. Artists Profl. League, Nat. Arts Club, Salmagundi Club; represented in permanent collections Nat. Mus. Am. Art, Smithsonian Instn., New Britain Mus. Am. Art, Johnson Mus. Art Cornell U., Nat. Archives, Washington, Truman Home, Independence, Mo., F.D.R. Mus., Hyde Park, N.Y.; also pvt. and corp. collections; works published in Artists of Am. Calendar. Mem. City Art Comm. New Rochelle, 1977-80. Served with AUS, 1942-46, ETO, PTO. Mem. N.Y. Artists Equity Assn., Allied Artists Am., Am. Artists Profl. League, Coll. Art Assn., Nat. Assn. Humanities Edn., Art. Pub., Am. Artists Group, Bernard Picture Co., McLeery-Cumming Co., Donald Art. Co., Scafa-Tornabene Art Publ., A. B. Franklin Gallery, Internet, Masons. Home and Office: 43 Amherst Dr New Rochelle NY 10804-1814 E-mail: Phyllmor@gateway.net. *An artist must respect the totality of his art. His work must express his integrity, his honesty and his wish to communicate with the viewer. It must strive toward the sublime. Anything less is unworthy of being called art.*

SLOTTERBACK, JOHN W. biologist; b. Ashland, Pa., June 23, 1966; s. Richard and Ruth Ann (Yost) S. BS in Environ. Biology, U. Pa., 1991; MS in Entomology, U. Del., 1999. Wildlife technician U.S. Fish & Wildlife Svc., Hawaii Nat. Park, 1991-93; wildlife biotechnician U.S. Forest Svc., Missoula, Mont., 1995; rsch. asst. Hawk Mt. Sanctuary Assn., Kempton, Pa., 1996; wildlife biologist Wash. Dept. Fish & Wildlife, Olympia, 1997; tchg. asst. U. Del., Newark, 1997-99; entomologist, ornithologist biol. resource divsn. USGS, Hawaii Nat. Park, 1999—. Mem. Cooper Ornithol. Soc., Wilson Ornithol. Soc., Assn. Field Ornithologists, Entomol. Soc. Am., Am. Ornithologists Union, Pacific Seabird Group. Avocations: backpacking, photography, scuba, canoeing, mountain biking. Office: USGS Biol Resources Divsn PO Box 44 Bldg 344 Hawaii National Park HI 96718 Home: PO Box 10361 Hilo HI 96721 E-mail: john_w_slotterback@usgs.gov.

SLOTTERBECK-BAKER, OBERTA A. computer scientist, educator; b. Cincinnati, Ohio, July 3, 1936; d. Ober Carter and Lealia Eliza Slotterbeck; m. Johnnie Warren Baker, June 13, 1970; children: Jonobie Dale Ford. BS, Ohio State Univ., Columbus, OH, 1958; MA, Univ. Tex., Austin, TX, 1966, PhD, 1969. Educator Columbus Pub. Schools, Columbus, Ohio, 1958—60, Union County HS #1, Springfield, 1960—64; asst. prof. Hiram Coll., Hiram, 1974—81, prof., computer sci., 1982—2001, prof./chair comp. sci. dept., 2002—; asst. prof. Univ. Fla., Gainesville, 1969—73. Contbr. articles to profl. jours. Recipient CCLI-AI Software Engring., NSF, 2000-2002. Mem.: Spl. Interest Group in Computer Sci. Edn., Assn. for Computing Machinery. D-Liberal. Avocations: photography, genealogy research, genealogy research. Home: 5525 Allyn Road Mantua OH 44255-9606 Office: Hiram College Dept Computer Science Hiram OH 44234

SLOVES, ROBERT B. obstetrician-gynecologist; b. N.Y.C., Dec. 23, 1934; Student, Columbia Coll., 1956; MD, U. Health Scis., 1960. Diplomate Am. Bd. Ob-Gyn. Intern L.A. County Gen. Hosp., 1960-61, resident, 1964-68; pvt. practice, ptnr. Tormed Women's Med. Group, Inc., Torrance, Calif., 1968—. Office: Tormed Women's Med Group Inc 3400 Lomita Blvd Ste 602 Torrance CA 90505-4984

SLOVIK, SANDRA LEE, art educator, retired; b. Elizabeth, N.J., Mar. 22, 1943; d. Edward Stanley and Frances (Garbus) S. BA, Newark State Coll., 1965, MA, 1970. Cert. art tchr. Art tchr. Holmdel (N.J.) Twp. Bd. Edn., 1965-99, ret., 1999. Computer art in-sv. tng. Holmdel Bd. Edn., 1990; computer art workshop Madison (N.J.) Bd. Edn., 1991; presenter Nat. Edn. Computer Conv., 1999. Charter supporter, mem. Statue of Liberty/Ellis Island Found., 1976—; charter supporter Sheriffs' Assn. N.J., 1993—; mem. PTA, Holmdel, 1965—. Recipient Curriculum award N.J. ASCD, 1992; grantee Holmdel Bd. Edn., 1989, 90, N.J. Bus., Industry, Sci., Edn. Consortium, 1990.

Mem. NEA, Nat. Art Edn., Assn., N.J. Art Educators Assn., N.J. Edn. Assn., Monmouth County Edn. Assn., Holmdel Twp. Edn. Assn. (sr. bldg. rep. 1977-79). Avocations: travel, sports. Office: Village Sch 67 Mccampbell Rd Holmdel NJ 07733-2299 E-mail: sslovik@hotmail.com.

SLOVIS, THOMAS LAURENCE, radiologist; b. Passaic, N.J., June 16, 1941; BA, Hobart Coll., 1963; MD, U. Pa., 1967. Diplomate Am. Bd. Pediats., Am. Bd. Radiology; cert. added qualification in pediat. radiology. Pediat. resident U. Colo. Med. Ctr., Denver, 1967-70; radiology resident Columbia Presbyn. Hosp. Babies Hosp., N.Y.C., 1972-75; prof. radiology and pediats. Wayne State U. Sch. Medicine, Detroit, 1984—; chief pediat. imaging Children's Hosp. Mich., 1987—. Author: Imaging of Pediatric Urinary Tract, 1989, Pediatric Radiology, 1995; contbr. 150 articles to profl. jours. Maj. USAF, 1970-72. Mem. Soc. Pediat. Radiology (pres. 1999-2000, chmn. bd. 2000-2001). Office: Children's Hosp Mich 3901 Beaubien Detroit MI 48201

SLOVITER, DOLORES KORMAN, federal judge; b. Phila., Sept. 5, 1932; d. David and Tillie Korman; m. Henry A. Sloviter, Apr. 3, 1969; 1 child Vikki Amanda. AB in Econs. with distinction, Temple U., 1953, LHD (hon.) , 1986; LLB magna cum laude, U. Pa., 1956; LLD (hon.) , Dickinson Sch. Law, 1984, U. Richmond, 1992, Widener U., 1994. Bar: Pa. 1957. From assoc. to ptnr. Dilworth, Paxson, Kalish, Kohn & Levy, Phila., 1956—69; mem. Harold E. Kohn PA, 1969—72; from assoc. prof. to prof. Temple U. Law Sch., 1972—79; judge U.S. Ct. Appeals (3rd cir.), 1979—, chief judge, 1991—98. Bd. overseers U. Pa. Law Sch., 1993—99; bd. dirs. Nat. Constitution Ctr.; mem. Jud. Conf. of U.S., 1991—98. Active S.E. region Pa. Gov.'s Conf. on Aging, 1976—79, Com. of 70, 1976—79; U.S. com. Bicentennial Constn., 1987—90; com. on Rules of Practice and Procedure, 1990—93; trustee Jewish Publ. Soc. Am., 1983—89. Recipient Juliette Low medal, Girl Scouts Greater Phila., Inc., 1990, Honor award, Girls High Alumnae Assn., 1991, Jud. award, Pa. Bar Assn., 1994, James Wilson award, U. Pa., 1996, Cert. of Honor award, Temple U., 1996; fellow Disting. Fulbright scholar, Chile, 1990. Mem.: ABA, Phila. Bar Assn. (gov. 1976—78, Sandra Day O'Connor award 1997), Am. Judicature Soc. (bd. dirs. 1990—95), Nat. Assn. Women Judges, Am. Law Inst., Fed. Judges Assn., Fed. Bar Assn., Order of Coif (pres. U. Pa. chpt. 1975—77), Phi Beta Kappa. Office: US Ct Appeals 18614 US Courthouse 601 Market St Philadelphia PA 19106-1713

SLOWIK, RICHARD ANDREW, air force officer; b. Detroit, Sept. 9, 1939; s. Louis Stanley ad Mary Jean (Zaucha) S.; 1 stepchild, Amber Dawn Evans. BS, U.S. Air Force Acad., 1963; BS in Bus. Adminstrn., No. Mich. U., 1967; LLB, LaSalle Extension U., 1969; MBA, Fla. Tech. U., 1972; MS in Adminstrn., Ga. Coll., 1979; MA, Georgetown U., 1983; postgrad. cert., Va. Poly. Inst. and State U., 1986. Commd. 1st lt. U.S. Air Force, 1963, advanced through grades to lt. col; pilot Craig AFB, Ala., 1963-64, Sawyer AFB, Mich., 1964-68; forward air contr. Pacific Air Forces, South Vietnam, 1968-69; pilot SAC, McCoy AFB, Fla., 1969-71; asst. prof. aerospace studies Va. Poly. Inst. and State U., Blacksburg, 1972-76; br. chief current ops. br. Robins AFB, Ga., 1976-80; asst. dep. chief ops. group Hdqrs Air Force, Pentagon, Washington, 1980-82; Western Hemisphere and Pacific Area desk officer Nat. Mi. Command Ctr., Pentagon, 1982-83; mil. rep Ops. Ctr., Dept. State, 1983-85; ops. officer 97th Bombardment Wing, Blytheville AFB, Ark., 1985-87; chief base ops. and tng. divsn. 97th Combat Support Group, 1987-88; chief airfield mgmt. divsn. Eaker AFB, 1988-91; freelance writer, 1991—. Contbr. articles to profl. jours. Group ops. officer CAP, Marquette, Mich., 1967-67, Orlando, Fla., 1970-72, sr. programs officer, Blacksburg, 1972-76, Warner Robins, Ga., 1976-80, wing plans and programs officer, Washington, 1980—. Decorated Def. Meritorious Svc. medal, 10 Air medals, 3 Air Force Meritorious Svc. medals, 2 Commendation medals, Corss of Gallantry with palm, Presdl. Legion of Merit, Presdl. Medal of Merit (3), Presdl. Achievement award (3), others; recipient Bill Baker Short Story award Miss. County Writers Guild, 1995. Mem. Acad. of Mgmt., Air Force Assn., Cato Inst., Heritage Found., Mil. Order World Wars, Am. Def. Preparedness Assn., Am. Security Coun., Order of Daedalians. Roman Catholic. Home and Office: 1708 N Broadway St Blytheville AR 72315-1320 E-mail: slowik@blyonline.com., ras6@georgetown.edu.

SLOWINSKI, THOMAS FRANK, priest; b. Detroit, Nov. 23, 1955; s. John Walter and Pauline (Januszczak) S. BA in History, Sacred Heart Sem. Coll., 1977; MDiv, St. John Provincial Sem., 1981. Ordained priest, Roman Cath. Ch., 1981. Deacon intern St. Agatha Ch., Redford, Mich., 1981-82; assoc. pastor St. Sylvester Ch., Warren, 1982-85, St. Edith Ch., Livonia, 1985-88, St. Anastasia Ch., Troy, 1988-90; pastor St. Agatha Ch., Redford, 1990—. Seminary prof. Sacred Heart Sem., Detroit, 1985, 90, St. John Provincial Sem., Plymouth, Mich., 1984-85; advocate and defender of the bond Met. Tribunal, Detroit, 1981-86. Pres., bd. dirs. Living Concepts, Inc., Livonia, 1988—. Lt. USNR, 1988—. Mem. Mil. Chaplains Assn., Priests Conf. for Polish Affairs, Founders Soc. Detroit Inst. of Arts, Redford C. of C., Assn. Death Educators and Counselors. Avocations: golf, reading, hockey, racquetball, downhill skiing. Home and Office: 581 E 14 Mile Rd Clawson MI 48017-2175

SLOYAN, GERARD STEPHEN, religious studies educator, priest; b. N.Y.C., Dec. 13, 1919; s. Jerome James and Marie (Kelley) S. AB, Seton Hall U., 1940; S.T.L., Cath. U. Am., 1944, PhD, 1948; DLitt, Seton Hall U., 1984; HHD, St. Ambrose U., 1995. Ordained priest Roman Cath. Ch., 1944. Asst. pastor in, Trenton, Maple Shade, N.J., 1947-50; mem. faculty Cath. U. Am., Washington, 1950-67, chmn. dept. religion, 1957-67; prof. N.T. studies Temple U., Phila., 1967-90, chmn. dept. religion, 1970-74, 84-86. Disting. lectr. Georgetown U., 1997—; vis. prof. Cath. U. Am., Washington, 1992—, Iowa State U., 1995. English editor: N.T., The New American Bible, 1970; author: Jesus on Trial: Development of the Passion Narratives, 1973, Commentary on the New Lectionary, 1975, Is Christ the End of the Law?, 1978, Jesus in Focus, 1983, 2d edit., 1993, The Jesus Tradition, 1986, John: "Interpretation" Commentary, 1988, Jesus, Redeemer and Divine Word, 1989, What Are They Saying About John?, 1991, Walking in the Truth: 1, 2, and 3 John, 1995, The Crucifixion of Jesus, History, Myth, Faith, 1995, Open Catholicism, The Tradition at Its Best, 1997, Holy Week and Easter, 1999, What Men Owe to Women, Men's Voices from World Religions, 2001. Recipient Pro Ecclesia et Pontifice medal, 1970, Johannes Quasten medal Cath U. Am., 1985, Michael Mathis award Notre Dame Ctr. Pastoral Liturgy, 1994. Mem. AAUP, Cath. Bibl. Assn., Soc. Bibl. Lit., Cath. Theol. Soc. Am. (John Courtney Murray award 1981, pres. 1993-94), Coll. Theology Soc. (pres. 1964-66), Liturg. Conf. (pres. 1962-64, v.p. 1970-71, 75-88, chmn. bd. dirs. 1980-88), N.Am. Acad. Liturgy (Berakah award 1986). Democrat. E-mail: cua-religed@cua.edu.

SLOYAN, PATRICK JOSEPH, journalist; b. Stamford, Conn., Jan. 11, 1937; s. James Joseph and Annamae (O'Brien) S.; m. Phyllis Hampton, Nov. 19, 1960; children: Nora, Amy, Patrick, John. BS, U. Md., 1963. Reporter Albany (N.Y.) Times-Union, 1957-58, Balt. News Post, 1958-60, United Press Internat., Washington, 1960-69, Hearst News Svc., Washington, 1969-74, Newsday, Washington, 1974-81, bur. chief, 1986-88, sr. corr., 1988—, bur. chief London, 1981-86. Dir. Fund for Investigative Journalism, Washington, 1987—. With U.S. Army, 1955-57. Recipient Best Writing award Am. Soc. Newspaper Editors, 1982, War Reporting award George Polk Awards, 1992, Pulitzer Prize for internat. reporting, 1992, Raymond Clapper award, 1996; Alicia Patterson Found. fellow, 2000. Mem. Gridiron Club. Roman Catholic. Avocations: swimming, tennis, gardening. Home: 17115 Simpson Cir Paeonian Springs VA 20129-1735 Office: Newsday 1730 Pennsylvania Ave NW Washington DC 20006-4706

SLUBERSKI, THOMAS RICHARD, international educator, journalist, theologian; b. Jersey City, Dec. 7, 1939; s. Walter and Anna Louise (Gall) S. BA with honors, Concordia U., 1962; MDiv with high honors, Concordia Sem., 1966; postgrad., U. Vienna, Austria, 1966, U. Erlangen-Nuremberg, Fed. Republic Germany, 1966-68; MA in English Lit., Washington U., 1970; ThD with honors, U. Heidelberg, Fed. Republic Germany, 1973, NYU, 1978. Ordained to ministry Luth. Ch.-Mo. Synod, 1969. Vicar Zion Luth. Ch., Wausau, Wis., 1964-65; asst. to dean chapel., lectr. dept. theology Valparaiso (Ind.) U., 1969-70; prof. English, religion, humanities Concordia Univ. Sys., Bronxville, N.Y., 1972—, Duda chair in religion, 2000—; pastor St. Matthew's Luth. Ch., Hastings-on-Hudson, 1977-87; exec. dir. Am. Luth. Publicity Bur., 1987-89. Rsch. asst., editor Luth. World Fedn., Geneva, 1968—69; judge Nat. Physique com., 1983—87, Russian Fedn. Body Builders, 1992—94; coord. 9th and 10th Inter-Luth. forums, 1988—90; bd. dirs. Luth. Soc. Worship, Music and Arts, 1971—73; lectr. U. St. Petersburg, U. Omsk, Merchant Marine Acad., Vladivostok, Russia, U. Khabarovwk, U. Vladivostok, Alexander von Herzen U., Russia; staff Russian-Am. Press Ctr.; warden U.S. Consulate at St. Petersburg; coord. vols. St. Petersburg Goodwill Games, 1994; tchr. sports mktg. Sports Couns. of Singapore, Hong Kong and Kuala Lumpur, Malaysia, 1995; prof. Russian Luth. Sem., 1992—94, Deacon's Tng. Sch., 1992—94; instr., bd. mem. Ben Weider Coll. Bodybldg., St. Petersburg, 1993—94; advisor Internat. Shaping Fedn., 1992—94; mem. exec. bd. 15th Ann. Workshop on Jewish Christian Rels., Stanford, Conn.; bd. dirs. Peterschule, St. Petersburg, 1993—94. Asst. editor Seminarian jour., 1965-66; lit. survey editor, rsch. asst. Luth. World Fedn., Geneva, Switzerland, 1968-69; judge (TV) Emmy's, 1995—; contbr. articles to profl. jours. Juror Am. Film Festival, N.Y.C., 1976-87; mem. nat. faculty of U.S. Sports Acad., Daphne, Ala., 1995—. Austrian State scholar, 1966, Bavarian State scholar, 1966-67; World Coun. Chs. fellow, 1967, Nat. Merit scholar, 1958, Luth. World Fedn. scholar, 1967, Deutscher Akademischer Austauschdienst fellow, 1970-72, Ctr. for Creative Persons fellow, 1975, 76; Aid Assn. for Luths. Faculty Study grantee, 1972. Fellow Christian Writers Inst.; mem. Nat. Acad. TV Arts and Scis., Polish Inst. Arts and Scis., Am. Film Inst., Soc. Arts, Religion and Culture. Home: 26 Dusenberry Rd Bronxville NY 10708-2421 Office: Concordia Univ Sys Bronxville NY 10708 E-mail: sluberski@aol.com.

SLUDIKOFF, STANLEY ROBERT, publisher, writer; b. Bronx, N.Y., July 17, 1935; s. Harry and Lillie (Elberger) S.; m. Ann Paula Blumberg, June 30, 1972; children: Lisa Beth, Jaime Dawn, Bonnie Joy. B.Arch., Pratt Inst., 1957; grad. student, U. So. Calif., 1960-62. Cert. planner Am. Inst. Cert. Planners. Project planner Robert E. Alexander, F.A.I.A. & Assos., Los Angeles, 1965-66, Daniel, Mann, Johnson & Mendenhall (City and Regional Planning Cons.), Los Angeles, 1967-70; pres., editor, pub. Gambling Times Inc., also Two Worlds Mgmt., Inc., 1971—; v.p. Prima Quality Farms, Inc., P.R.; chmn. Creative Games, Inc., 1992—. Pres. Las Vegas TV Weekly, also Postal West, Las Vegas, 1975-79; founder Stanley Roberts Sch. Winning Blackjack, 1976; instr. city and regional planning program U. So. Calif., 1960-63; founding mem. Mfrs. Direct, 1996. Author: (under pen name Stanley Roberts) Winning Blackjack, 1971, How to Win at Weekend Blackjack, 1973, Gambling Times Guide to Blackjack, 1983; author: The Beginner's Guide to Winning Blackjack, 1983, Begin to Win at Blackjack, 1997, Begin to Win at Video Poker, 1997, Begin to Win at Craps, 1997; also monthly column, 1977—; creator & tournament dir. The World Casino Games; inventor Daily Digit lottery game; patentee in field. Mem. Destination 90 Forum, Citizens Planning Group, San Fernando Valley, Calif., 1966-67, Rebuild L.A. land use com., 1992—. Served to lt. col. U.S. Army, now Res. ret. Recipient commendation from mayor Los Angeles for work on model cities funding, 1968 Mem. AIA, Am. Planning Assn., Am. Inst. Cert. Planners, Internat. Casino Assn. (sec. 1980—), Res. Officers Assn. (life), Mensa (life) Achievements include invention of Straight Out gambling game. Home: 10035 Laramie Ave Chatsworth CA 91311-3912 Office: 3883 W Century Blvd Inglewood CA 90303-1003 E-mail: srs@gamblingtimes.com. *The challenge of being alive lies in the development of one's maximum potential. To do less is to fly in the face of the gifts of creation, to shorten the aspect of one's life and to deny the fullness of existence. "The weakness of the flesh" prevents anyone's full development from reaching fruition but the personal and societal loss lies in giving up too soon, before we have fully tested our limits.*

SLUSHER, KIMBERLY GOODE, researcher; b. Benham, Ky., Oct. 4, 1960; d. Herschel James and Nevelyn Faye (Hayes) Goode; m. Joe Allan Slusher, May 1, 1985; children: Tarah Rena, Preston Cole. BS in Agr., Ea. Ky. U., 1982; MS in Agr., U. Tenn., 1989. Rsch. asst. U. Tenn., Knoxville, 1983-89; info. analyst Oak Ridge (Tenn.) Nat. Lab., 1989—, tchr., cons. sci. honors program, 1993. Author: (army study) Drinking Water Contamination Study, 1995; contbr. chpt.: Teratogens: Chemicals Which Cause Birth Defects, 1993. Methodist. Avocations: gardening, piano. Office: Human Gene Info Analysis Sect 1060 Commerce Park Dr # Ms6480 Oak Ridge TN 37830-8043 E-mail: Kfg@ornl.gov.

SLUSSER, EUGENE ALVIN, electronics manufacturing executive; b. Denver, Mar. 13, 1922; s. Jesse Alvin and Grace (Carter) S.; m. Anne L. Longley, Oct. 2, 1943; children: Robert, Jon, Carolyn. BS in Physics, U. Denver, 1947. Registered profl. engr., N.H. Mem. staff MIT Radiation Lab., Cambridge, 1942-45; project engr. Heiland Rsch. Co., Denver, 1945-47; cons. Gen. Telephone Sys., N.Y.C., 1947-51; project engr. Airborne Inst. Lab., Mineola, N.Y., 1951-53; v.p. N.E. Electronics Corp., Concord, N.H., 1953-58; pres. Aerotronic Assocs., Inc., Contoocook, 1958-84, N.H. Automatic Equipment Corp., Concord, 1962-90, N.H. Realty Corp., Concord, 1990-96, E.A. Slusser & Assocs., Concord. Patentee electronics field. Chmn. Hopkinton (N.H.) Water Bd., 1962-69, Hopkinton Planning Bd., 1971-77, Hopkinton Precinct Bd. Adjustment, 1977. Mem. Aircraft Owners and Pilots Assn., Captiva Island (Fla.) Yacht Club (past commodore), Wharf Rat Club, Anglers Club, Pacific Club (Nantucket, Mass.), Masons (32 degree). Office: 232 Putney Hill Rd Concord NH 03301 E-mail: easlusser@aol.com.

SLUSSER, ROBERT WYMAN, aerospace company executive; b. Mineola, Minn., May 10, 1938; s. John Leonard and Margaret McKenzie (Wyman) S.; m. Linda Killeas, Aug. 3, 1968. *Linda Killeas Slusser, originally from Le Mars, Iowa, graduated from Creighton (BS), UCLA (MBA), and completed her Doctorate course work at USC in 1969. They have 4 children. Jonathan Killeas (born 1971) graduated from USC (1994) and is co-founder and General Manager of a Graphics Animation business; Hornet, Inc. Adam Wyman (1975) graduated from the University of Arizona (1998) and is in Real Estate. Robert Killeas (1975) is an actor and is in retailing. Mariah (1977) attended UC Davis (2000) and is a financial adviser. She holds an "A" Pony club rating.* BS, MIT, 1960; MBA, U. Pa., 1962; ERC, Ft. Belvior Def. Sys. Mgmt. Sch., 1977; AMP, Claremont, 1982. Assoc. adminstr.'s staff NASA Hdqrs., Washington, 1962-65; with Northrop Corp., Hawthorne, Calif., 1965-96; adminstr. Space Labs., 1965-68; mgr. bus. and fin. Warnecke Electron Tubes Co. divsn., Chgo., 1968-71; mgr. bus. adminstrn. YF-17 Program Aircraft Divsn., 1971-75, mgr. adminstrn. F-18/Cobra programs, also mgr. F-18 design to cost program, 1975-79, mgr. engring. adminstrn., 1980-82, acting v.p. engring., 1982, v.p. info. resources, 1983-91, mgr. long range planning, 1991-93, program mgr.-bus. F/A-18E/F program, 1994-96, cons., 1996—. Bd. dirs., CFO So. Calif. Hist. Aviation Found., 1987-90, chmn. of bd., pres., 1990-97; treas. Flight Path Learning Ctr. of So. Calif., 1996-2001; bd. dirs., contracting officer, PDES, 1988-91; mem. dirs. adv. bd. S.C. Rsch. Authority, 1991-95. *As Northrop Vice President, Information Resource Management, Mr. Slusser provided Data Processing Technical, Business, and Network Services for 16,000 people. He led a department of 850 people in Strategic Business Process Development, Corporate Business Systems Architecture, Strategic Planning, design and applications programming of technical & business systems, Mainframe & Distributed Computing, Corporate Computing Standards, and Network Management. As Northrop Deputy Program Manager-Business, F/A-18, he managed all business aspects of these Navy programs. Currently a consultant, he has provided Business Process Redesign for Lockheed and Northrop, managed ISO 9000 implementation for Northrop, and participated on the AIA Standards Committee which developed the ISO 9000 Aerospace version.* Grumman Aircraft Engring. scholar, 1956-60. Fellow AIAA (assoc., membership chmn. L.A. sect. 1996-98); mem. So. Calif. Soc. Info. Mgmt. (mem. exec. com. 1987-91), Northrop Mgmt. Club (bd. dirs. 1992-93, Man of Yr. 1991-92). Avocation: private pilot. Home: 7270 Berry Hill Dr Palos Verdes Peninsula CA 90275-4402

SLUSSER, WILLIAM PETER, investment banker; b. June 20, 1929; s. Eugene and Thelma (Donovan) S.; m. Joanne Eleanor Briggs, June 20, 1953; children: Kathleen E., Martin E., Wendelin M., Caroline E., Sarah A. BA cum laude, Stanford U., 1951; MBA, Harvard U., 1953. Mgr. spl. situations dept. Dean Witter & Co., N.Y.C., 1955-60; ptnr., sr. v.p. in charge corp. fin. dept. Shields & Co., 1960-75; co-mgr., investment banking divsn., sr. v.p. Paine Webber, Inc., 1975-80; mng. dir., head merger and acquisitions dept. Blyth Eastman Paine Webber, Inc., 1980-88; pres. Slusser Assocs., Inc., 1988—. Underwriter or fin. cons. Square D Co., Times Mirror co., Ashland Oil, Inc., Ga. Pacific, TRW, Inc., Avon Products, TransAm, Realty Investors, Atex, Inc. subsidiary of Eastman Kodak Co., Perini Corp., Downey Savs. & Loan, Booth Newspapers, Inc., Holly Hill Lumber Co., Stanhome, Inc., Santee Portland Cement Co., Grow Group, Orion Rsch., Inc., Crown Cork & Seal Co., Dr. Pepper Co. of So. Calif., Houghton Mifflin Co., Sparton Corp., Mission West Properties, Inc., San Jose Water Co., Cap Gemini Ernst & Young, Ltd., London, De La Rue, PLC, London, VNU Inc., Haarlem, The Netherlands, Bertlesmann Pub. Co., Fed. Republic Germany, ADT Ltd., London, Bank of Guam, Pacific Holding co., vice chmn., 1969-73. Contbr. to fin. jours. including Handbook of Mergers, Acquisitions and Buyouts, The Mergers & Acquisitions Handbook. Bd. dirs. Ampex Corp., Sparton Corp., Tyco Internat. Ltd., ADT Ltd., Magellan Group Ltd.; founding. stockholder Assoc. Mortgage Cos.; bd. fin. advisors Columbia U. Bus. Sch., Calif. Senate Commn. on Local Govt. Investments; mem. Calif. Senate Commn. on Corp. Governance. Served to 1st lt. USAF, 1953-55. Mem. Investment Assn. N.Y., Soc. Calif. Pioneers, Knickerbocker Club, Downtown Assn., Stanford Assocs., Harvard (N.Y.C.) Club, Lawrence Beach Club, Stanford of N.Y. Club, Alpha Delta Phi (exec. coun. 1956-62, treas. 1961). Home: 901 Lexington Ave New York NY 10021-5924 also: Slusser Ranch Windsor CA 95492 Office: Slusser Assocs Inc 1 Citicorp Ctr Ste 5100 153 E 53d St New York NY 10022-4611

SLUTSKY, LEONARD ALAN, finance executive, consultant; b. N.Y.C., July 25, 1945; s. Hyman and Ruth (Neuman) S.; m. Sharlene Alexis Farber, Oct. 20, 1968; children: Jacquelyn Anne, Jason Ian, Adam Jeffrey. Student, U. Ariz., 1963-66. Chmn., pres., chief exec. officer Republic Pension Svc. Inc., Melville, N.Y., 1981-83; pres., chief exec. officer Am. Money Svc. Corp., Huntington, 1977-97; chmn. bd. Peoples Nat. Bank of Rockland, 1983-85, Millbrook Equity Corp., N.Y.C., 1985-86; chmn., chief exec. officer Republic Advisors, Inc., Lake Success, N.Y., 1981-95; chmn. Am. Money Co., Inc., Huntington, 1982-90; pres. Windsor Funding Corp., West Hills, N.Y., 1987-90. Bd. dirs. Triad Temporary Agy., Inc., Triad Employee Leasing LLC. Sgt. N.Y. N.G., 1966-71. Recipient Disting. Service award Rockland County, 1984, Com. Service award Dist. Atty. Rockland, 1984, Distinguished Service award 6th Congl. Dist., Washington, 1984, Yeshiva U., N.Y.C., 1984. Mem. Am. Soc. C.L.U., KP. Republican. Jewish. Avocations: swimming, fishing, camping, golf. Home: 20 Equestrian Ct Huntington NY 11743-6636 Office: Mktg Motivation Assocs 790 Management Co 790 New York Ave Huntington NY 11743-4499

SLUTSKY, LORIE ANN, foundation executive; b. N.Y.C., Jan. 5, 1953; d. Edward and Adele (Moskowitz) S. BA, Colgate U, 1975; MA in Urban Policy and Analysis, New Sch. for Social Rsch., N.Y.C., 1977. Program officer N.Y. Cmty. Trust, N.Y.C., 1977-83, v.p., 1983-87, exec. v.p., 1987-89, pres., CEO, 1990—. Former mem. and chmn. bd. Coun. on Founds., Inc., Washington, 1986-95. Trustee emerita, former chmn. budget com. Colgate U., Hamilton, N.Y., 1989-98; former mem. bd. dirs. Found. Ctr., Inc., N.Y.C., L.A. Wallace Fund for Met. Mus. Art, N.Y.C., D. Wallace Fund for Meml. Sloan Kettering; bd. dirs. United Way of N.Y.C., Bd. Source; trustee New Sch. U. Office: NY Community Trust 2 Park Ave Fl 24 New York NY 10016-9301

SLY, RIDGE MICHAEL, physician, educator; b. Seattle, Nov. 3, 1933; s. Ridge Joseph and Eva Jean (Ruddell) S.; m. Ann Turner Jennings, June 12, 1957; children: Teresa Ann Perper, Cynthia Marie Schattenfield. AB, Kenyon Coll., 1956; MD, Washington U., St. Louis, 1960. Diplomate Am. Bd. Pediat., Am. Sub-Bd. Pediat. Allergy, Am. Bd. Allergy and Immunology. Intern, resident in pediat. St. Louis Children's Hosp, 1960-62; chief resident in pediat. U. Ky. Med. Ctr., Lexington, 1962-63; fellow in allergy and immunology UCLA Med. Ctr., 1965-67; from asst. prof. to prof. pediat. La. State U. Med. Ctr., New Orleans, 1967-78; head sect. allergy and immunology Children's Nat. Med. Ctr., Washington, 1978—; prof. pediat. George Washington U., 1978—. Author: Textbook of Pediatric Allergy, 1985; mem. editl. bd. Annals of Allergy, Asthma, & Immunology, 1982-98, 99—, Jour. Asthma, 1982-93, Clin. Revs. in Allergy, 1982—, Pediat. Asthma, Allergy, & Immunology, 1987—; assoc. editor Annals of Allergy, Asthma, & Immunology, 1989-90, editor, 1990-98; contbr. articles to profl. jours. Served to capt. USAF, 1963-65 Recipient La. plaque Am. Lung Assn. of La., 1978 Fellow Am. Acad. Allergy, Asthma & Immunology (chmn. com. on drugs 1981-87), Am. Acad. Pediats. (sect. on allergy com. 1972-75), Am. Coll. Allergy, Asthma, and Immunology (Disting. Fellow award 1993, Bela Schick award 1997, chmn. ethics com. 1997-99); mem. Am. Thoracic Soc., Assn. for Care of Asthma (pres. 1980-81, dir. postgrad. courses 1980—, Peshkin Meml. award 1983), Am. Med. Writer's Assn., Phi Beta Kappa. Republican. Baptist. Avocations: music (organ, piano). Office: Children's Nat Med Ctr 111 Michigan Ave NW Washington DC 20010-2970

SMAGORINSKY, PETER, education educator; b. Princeton, N.J., Oct. 24, 1952; s. Joseph and Margaret (Knoepfel) S.; m. Anne O'Gorman, July 10, 1982 (dec. Aug. 1982); m. Jane E. Farrell, Oct. 12, 1985; children: Alysha, David. BA, Kenyon Coll., 1974; MA in Tchg., U. Chgo., 1977, PhD, 1989. English tchr. Westmont (Ill.) H.S., 1977-78, Barrington (Ill.) H.S., 1978-85, Oak Park (Ill.) and River Forest H.S., 1985-90; asst. prof. U. Okla., Norman, 1990-95, assoc. prof., 1995-98, U. Ga., Athens, 1998-2001, prof., 2001—. Author: Standards in Practice, 1996; co-author: How English Teachers Get Taught, 1995, The Language of Interpretation, 1995; co-editor Rsch. in the Tchg. of English, 1996—; mem. editl. bd. Rev. Ednl. Rsch., Am. Jour. Edn., Written Comm., Reading and Writing Quarterly. Recipient Steve Cahir award for rsch. in writing Am. Ednl. Rsch. Assn., 1991, Raymond B. Cattell award for disting. programmatic rsch. Am. Ednl. Rsch. Assn., 1999, Edwin M. Hopkins Jour. award, 2000. Mem. Nat. Coun. Tchrs. English (chair standing com. on rsch. 1995-96, co-chair assembly for rsch. 1996, trustee rsch. found. 1997—, chair 2000—, pres. nat. conf. rsch. in lang. and literacy, 2001, English Jour. Writing award 1989, Edwin M. Hopkins award 2000). Home: 175 Emerald Dr Athens GA 30605-4106 Office: U Ga 125 Aderhold Hall Athens GA 30602 E-mail: smago@coe.uga.edu.

SMAIL, LESLIE ANNE, librarian; b. Pitts., July 25, 1958; d. Laurence Mitchell and Nancy (Fried) S.; m. Eric D. Hunley, July 10, 1998. BA, Christopher Newport Coll., 1980; MSLS, Cath. U., 1982. Libr. intern Tng. and Doctrine Command, Ft. Monroe, Va., 1982-84; libr. Ft. Story (Va.) Libr., 1985-2000; libr. dir. Bryant & Stratton Coll. Libr., Virginia Beach, Va., 2000; libr. Gwinnett County Pub. Libr., Lawrenceville, Ga., 2000—; contractor retrospective conversion project Tortolita Vet. Svcs., PC, Tucson, 2002—. Active Diamond Springs Civic League, Virginia Beach, Va., 1989-2000. Recipient Exceptional Performance award U.S. Army, Ft. Eustis, Va., 1985-99, Comdr.'s award for civilian svc., 1995, 2000; Outstanding Program Mgr. TRADOC, Ft. Monroe, 1988-89. Mem. Sigma Tau Delta. Avocations: arts and crafts, antiques, gardening. Office: Tortolita Vet Svcs PC 14175 N Hawkeye Dr Tucson AZ 85742 E-mail: lesliesmail@yahoo.com.

SMAISTRLA, JEAN ANN, family therapist; b. South Gate, Calif., Oct. 12, 1936; d. Benjamin J. and Janet (Pollock) Craig; m. Charles J. Smaistrla, July 12, 1958; children: Amy Jean, Ben, John. BBA in Mktg., Lamra U., 1958; Elec. Edn. cert., Tex. Wesleyan Coll., 1963; MEd in Counseling, Tex. Christian U., 1975. Lic. profl. cousnelor. Tchr. Houston Ind. Schs., 1958-61, Arlington (Tex.) Ind. Schs., 1961-72; counselor, therapist Arlington Counseling and Cons. Ctr., 1983-85; family therapist Willow Creek Adolescent Ctr., Arlington, 1985-86, dir. edn., 1986-90; therapist Bob Carpenter PhD and Assocs., 1987-89; pvt. practice, triage therapist Kaiser Permanente, Ft. Worth, 1989—; owner, founder, chmn. bd. Adolescnet Svcs. Arlington, 1981—; founder, owner Mindtime, 1988-90; triage counselor Kaiser Permanente, Ft. Worth, 1991-99; cons. Charles J. Smaistrla, DDS, Arlington, 1978-85. Bd. dirs. Bruce Wood Dance Co.; vice chmn. bd. Arlington Cmty. Hosp., 1981—85, Willow Creek Adolescent Ctr., 1984—90; owner, founder Busyfingers, 1999—; co-owner Staje. Life mem. PTA; bd. dirs. Arlington Art Assn., 1981-85, South Arlington Med. Ctr., 1987, Ctr. for Well-being, 1985, Bruce Wood Dance Co., Ft. Worth, 2002--; chmn. clin. svcs. Parenting Ctr. for Tarrant County, Ft. Worth, 1992—, v.p., 1994-95, pres. bd., 1996—; mem. vestry St. Deborah's Guild, St. Anne's Episcopal Ch. Mem.: Cancer Rsch. Found. Woman's Aux., Jr. League Arlington, Arlington Women's Club, Alpha Delta Pi. Avocations: sailing, sewing, doll collecting. Home: 8960 Dickson Rd Fort Worth TX 76179-4403

SMALDONE, EDWARD MICHAEL, composer; b. Wantagh, N.Y., Nov. 19, 1956; m. Karen Ajamian, Aug. 5, 1979; children: Laura, Gregory, Julia. BA in Music, Queens Coll., 1978, MA in Music, 1980; PhD in Music, CUNY, 1986. Lectr. SUNY, Purchase, 1986-90; adj. asst. prof. Hofstra U., Hempstead, N.Y., 1988-90; vis. asst. prof. New Sch. for Social Rsch., N.Y.C., 1988; adminstrv.

dir. Speculum Musicae, 1988-89; artistic dir. Sounds for the Left Bank, Rego Park, N.Y., 1985-92; asst. prof. Copland Sch. of Music, CUNY, Flushing, 1990-99; assoc. prof., 1999—. Composer in residence N.Y.C. Pub. Schs., 1994, 95; Carlisle Project Choreographer and Composer Collaboration Commn., 1994; assoc. composer Atlantic Ctr. Arts, 1999, vis. fac., Univ. Coll. Chichester, Eng., 1999. Composer: Two String Quartets, 1980, 86, Dialogue for orch., 1987, Double Duo (flute, clarinet, violin, cello), 1987, Transformational Etudes (solo piano), 1990, Rhapsody for piano and orch., 1992, Suite for violin and piano, 1993, Three Scenes from "The Heartland" for solo piano, 1994, Saxophone Quartet, 1995, Rituals: Sacred and Profane for flute, cello and piano, 1996, American Spiritual Fantasy for string orch., 1997, Psalm of the Phoenix for Shakuhachi and cello, 1998, Suite for violin and 12 instruments, 2000, Letters from Home, mezzo soprano, flute, clarinet, and piano, 2000, String Quartet No. 2, 2001, Life Imagined, Life Engaged for piccolo and chamber orch., 2001; dance compositions: The Chair, The Table and Tatyana's Letter (choreography by Yin Mei), 1999; albums include Scenes from the Heartland Recipient Standard award ASCAP, 1986—, Creative Incentive award CUNY Rsch. Found., 1992, 95, 97; residency fellow Yaddo Corp., 1986, 87, Composer's fellow Charles Ives Ctr. for Am. Music, 1990, residency fellow MacDowell Colony, 1994, Goddard Lieberson fellow Am. Acad. Arts and Letters, 1993; prize winner Percussive Arts Soc., 1994. Home: 228 Manhasset Ave Manhasset NY 11030-2220 Office: Copland Sch of Music Queens College Flushing NY 11030

SMALE, JOHN GRAY, diversified industry executive; b. Listowel, Ont., Can., Aug. 1, 1927; s. Peter John and Vera Gladys (Gray) S.; m. Phyllis Anne Weaver, Sept. 2, 1950; children: John Gray, Jr., Catherine Anne, Lisa Beth, Peter McKee. BS, Miami U., Oxford, Ohio, 1949; LLD (hon.), Kenyon Coll., Gambier, Ohio, 1974, Miami U., Oxford, Ohio, 1979; DSc (hon.), DePauw U., 1983; DCL (hon.), St. Augustine's Coll., 1985; LLD (hon.), Xavier U., 1986. With Vick Chem. Co., N.Y.C., 1949-50, Bio-Rsch., Inc., N.Y.C., 1950-52; asst. brand mgr. Procter & Gamble Co., 1952-54, brand mgr., 1954-58, assoc. advt. mgr., 1958-63, mgr. advt. dept. toilet goods divsn., 1963-66, mgr. toilet goods divsn., 1966-67, v.p. toilet goods divsn., 1967-68, v.p. bar soap and household cleaning products divsn., 1968-69, v.p. packaged soap and detergent divsn., 1969-70, v.p. group exec., 1970-72, mem. bd. dirs., 1972, exec. v.p., 1973-74, pres., 1974-81, pres., chief exec., 1981-86, chmn. of bd., chief exec., 1986-90, chmn. exec. com. of bd. of dirs., 1990-95; chmn. GM, 1992-95, chmn. exec. com., 1995-2000, chmn. bd. dirs., 1996-2000, chmn. exec. com., 1996-2000, also bd. dirs.; ret., 2000. Bd. dirs. Rand McNally. Emeritus trustee Kenyon Coll. With USNR, 1945-46. Mem. Comml. Club, Queen City Club, Cin. Country Club. Office: Procter & Gamble PO Box 599 Cincinnati OH 45201-0599

SMALES, FRED BENSON, corporate executive; b. Keokuk, Iowa, Oct. 7, 1914; s. Fred B. and Mary Alice (Warwick) S.; m. Constance Brennan, Dec. 11, 1965; children: Fred Benson III, Catherine (Mrs. Jonathan Christensen); children by previous marriage: Nancy (Mrs. Bruce Clark). Student public schs., Los Angeles. With Champion Internat., Inc., 1933-68, successively San Francisco mgr., 1938-44, Los Angeles, Western div. mgr., 1944-55, v.p. Western sales div., 1955-65, v.p., regional dir., 1965-68, pres. Lewers & Cooke, Inc. div., 1966-68; chmn. Securities of Am., Inc., 1968-70; chmn., pres., dir. Hawaiian Cement Co., 1970-84; pres. Transpacific Cons., 1984-94; owner Plywood Hawaii, 1995—. Trustee Hawaii-Pacific U., Hawaii Maritime Ctr. Recipient Disting. Citizen award Nat. Govs. Assn., 1986. Mem. C. of C. Hawaii (past chmn.), So. Calif. Yachting Assn. (sr. staff commodore), Balboa Yacht Club (Corona del Mar, Calif, sr. staff commodore), Transpacific Yacht, Waikiki Yacht (staff commodore), Pacific Club (past pres.), Royal Hawaiian Ocean Racing (dir.), Sequoia Yacht Club (Redwood City, Calif., sr. staff commodore). Home: 46-422 Hulupala Pl Kaneohe HI 96744-4243 Office: 1062 Kikowaena Pl Honolulu HI 96819-4413

SMALKIN, FREDERIC N. federal judge; BA, Johns Hopkins U., 1968; JD, U. Maryland, 1971. Atty. office of judge advocate gen. Dept. Army, 1972-74, asst. to gen. counsel, 1974-76; pvt. practice Monkton, Md., 1976; magistrate U.S. Dist. Ct. Md., Balt., 1976-86, judge, 1986—. Lectr. comml. law U. Md., Balt., 1978—, SMH bar rev., Balt., 1985-86, 93-95, BRI/Modern Bar Rev. Course, Inc., Balt., 1980-81; panel spkr. on Utilization of Magistrates at the 1985 fourth cir., Jud. Conf. Capt. U.S. Army, 1968-76, lt. col. CAP (USAF Auxiliary). Mem. Fed. Bar Assn., Order of Coif, Phi Beta Kappa. Office: US Dist Ct 101 W Lombard St Ste 3A Baltimore MD 21201-2605

SMALL, ALDEN THOMAS, judge; b. Columbia, S.C., Oct. 4, 1943; s. Alden Killin and Shirley Edna (Eldridge) Small; m. Judy Jo Worley, June 25, 1966; children: Benjamin, Jane. AB, Duke U., 1965; JD, Wake Forest U., 1969. Bar: N.C. 1969. Asst. v.p. First Union Corp., Greensboro, N.C., 1969-72; assoc. dir., gen. counsel Cmty. Enterprise Devel. Corp. Alaska, Anchorage, 1972-73; v.p., assoc. gen. counsel First Union Corp., Raleigh, N.C., 1973-82; judge U.S. Bankruptcy Ct., 1982—, chief judge, 1992-99. Bd. govs. Nat. Conf. Bankruptcy Judges, 1987—90; adj. prof. law Campbell U. Sch. Law, 1980—82; bd. dirs. Am. Bankruptcy Inst., 1989—95, Fed. Jud. Ctr., 1997—2001, Am. Coll. Bankruptcy; sec. Nat. Conf. Bankruptcy Judges, 1998—, pres.-elect, 1999, pres., 2000—01; chmn. Nat. Conf. Bankruptcy Judges Ednl. Endowment, 1993—94; mem. long range planning com. U.S. Jud. Conf., 1991—95, adv. com. bankruptcy rules, 1996—99, chair adv. com. on bankruptcy rules, 2000—; faculty mem. Nat. Comml. Lending Sch., 1981—82; cons. Nat. Coalition for Bankruptcy Reform, 1981—82. Contbg. editor: Norton Bankruptcy Law and Practice. Mem.: ABA, N.C. Bar Assn. (bankruptcy coun.), N.C. Bankers Assn. (bank counsel com. 1980—82), Am. Bankers Assn. (bankruptcy task force 1980—82), Am. Coll. Bankruptcy, Phi Alpha Delta, Kappa Sigma. Republican. Office: US Bankruptcy Ct PO Box 2747 Raleigh NC 27602-2747

SMALL, BERTRICE W. writer; b. N.Y.C., Dec. 9, 1937; d. David Roger Williams, Doris Melissa (Maud) Steen; m. George Sumner Small, Oct. 5, 1963; 1 child Thomas David. Student, Western Coll. for Women, Oxford, Ohio, Katherine Gibbs Sectl. Sch., N.Y.C., 1959. With Young & Rubicon, N.Y.C., 1959—60, Weed Radio & TV, N.Y.C., 1960—61, Edward Petry & Co., N.Y.C., 1961—63. Author: The Kadin, 1978—, Sky O'Malley, 1980—, All The Sweet Tomorrows, 1984—, Amount In Time, 1991—, Betrayal, 1998—, The Innocent, 1999—, Rosamund, 2002—, many others, —. Vestrywoman Redeemer Episc. Ch., Mattituck, NY, 1998—2001. Recipient Career Achievement Reviewers Choice award, Romantic Times Mag., 1983, 1988, 1995, 2001. Mem.: L.I. Romance Writers (bd. dirs. 1999—2001), Romance Writers of Am., Authors Guild. Episcopalian. Avocation: gardening. Mailing: PO Box 765 Southold NY 11971

SMALL, BRUCE MICHAEL, health facility administrator; b. Buffalo, June 27, 1947; s. Alvin Sanford and Sylvia Ruth (Lutwack) S.; m. Teresa Chen-Ling Jen, June 20, 1976; children: Louis, Joseph, Daniel. BS in Physics, Yale U., 1969; MS in Physics, Stanford U., 1971; MD, Albert Einstein Coll. Medicine, 1975. Diplomate Am. Bd. Internal Medicine; cert. long-term care med. dir. Asst. dir. hematology Erie County Med. Ctr., Buffalo, 1979-84, dir. hematology, 1984-88; assoc. clin. dir., chief medicine Buffalo Psychiat. Ctr., 1988-91; staff hematologist Buffalo VA Med. Ctr., 1991-95; dir. med. svcs. N.Y. State Vets. Home, Batavia, 1995—. Mem. adv. com. MediShare Internat., 1997—; cons in field. Fellow: ACP; mem.: Am. Soc. Hematology, Am. Med. Dirs. Assn., Am. Radio Relay League (RF safety com. 2002—), Radio Assn. Western N.Y. (dir. 1982—, pres. 1984), Med. Amateur Radio Coun. (dir. 1996—, pres. 2000—02). Avocations: amateur radio, computing, skiing. Office: NY State Vets Home 220 Richmond Ave Batavia NY 14020-1227

SMALL, DANIEL PRIESTLEY, lawyer, educator; b. Washington, Jan. 16, 1943; s. Priestley J. and Genevieve (Clayton) S.; m. Katherine Goudie, June 18, 1966 (div. 1988); children: John D., Karl G., Ross C. BS, Va. Commonwealth U., 1965; JD, Coll. William & Mary, 1975, M Laws & Taxation, 1996. Bar: Va. 1975, U.S. Dist. Ct. (ea. dist.) Va. 1975, U.S. Ct. Appeals (4th cir.) 1978, U.S. Ct. Claims 1978, U.S. Tax Ct. 1975. Assoc. McNamara & Smith, Hampton, Va., 1975-76, Eliades, Nye, Gregory & Papcun, Hopewell, 1976-78, Harris, Tuck, Freasier & Johnson, Richmond, Va., 1977-78; trust tax officer Bank of Va. Trust Co., 1979-80; pvt. practice Daniel P. Small P.C., 1980—; prof. J. Sargeant Reynolds C.C., 1980—. Adminstrv. hearing officer, Supreme Ct. Va., Richmond, 1985—, pres., 1992-94. Author: Additional Problems Manual, 1993. Asst. scoutmaster Boy Scouts Am., Richmond, Va., 1989-92. With U.S. Army, 1966-67. Democrat. Presbyterian. Avocations: running, camping, hunting. Office: PO Box 31474 Richmond VA 23294-1474

SMALL, DONALD MACFARLAND, biophysics educator, gastroenterologist; b. Newton, Mass., Sept. 15, 1931; s. Grace (MacFarland) S.; m. Elisabeth Chan, July 8, 1957 (div. 1979); children: Geoffrey, Philip; m. Kathryn Ross, July 26, 1986 (div. 1999); 1 child, Samuel. BA, Occidental Coll., 1954; MA (hon.), Oxford (Eng.) U., 1964; MD, UCLA, 1960. Intern, asst. resident in medicine Mass. Meml. Hosps., Boston, 1960-62; sr. resident Boston City Hosp., 1962-63, vis. physician med. svcs., 1965—90; asst. prof. medicine Boston U. Sch. Medicine, 1968-69, assoc. prof. medicine and biochemistry, 1969-73, prof., 1973—, prof. biophysics, chmn. dept., 1989-2000, dir. Biophysics Inst., 1972—, prof. chmn. dept. physiology and biophysics, 2000—. Spl. tng. in phys. chemistry of lipids Inst. Pasteur, Paris, 1963-65; mem. adv. bd. Gladstone Found Labs., San Francisco, 1980—; George Lyman Duff Meml. lectr. Coun. Arteriosclerosis, Am. Heart Assn., 1986; cons. Nat. Inst. Arthritis and Metabolic Diseases, NIH, 1968-72, mem. task force Nat. Heart, Lung and Blood Inst., 1990; also others. Author, editor: Physical Chemistry of Lipids, 1986; mem. editl. bd. Gastroenterology, 1967-74, Arteriosclerosis, Thrombosis and Vascular Biology, 1980-2002, Jour. Biol. Chemistry, Current Opinions in Structural Biology, 1990—, Structure, 1992-98; sub-editor: Jour. Lipid Rsch., 1974-78, editor, 1979-83; editor: (with R. Havel) Advances in Lipid Rsch., 1989-99; mem. internat. bd. editors Jour. Nutritional Biochemistry, 1989—; contbr. articles and revs. to profl. jours.; author: (with A. Adams) The Healthy Meateaters Cookbook, 1991. Recipient Eppinger prize IV Internat. Congress on Liver Disease, 1976, Disting. Achievment award Modern Medicine, 1978, Disting. Alumni award UCLA Sch. Medicine Alumni Assn., 1988; Marshall scholar Magdalen Coll., Oxford, 1956-58, Aesculapian scholar UCLA, 1958-60, Markle scholar, 1966-70; others. Mem. AAAS, Am. Heart Assn. (fellow coun. arteriosclerosis, chmn. program com. 1988-90, chmn. coun. 1992-94), Am. Assn. Physicians, Am. Soc. Biol. Chemists, Biophys. Soc., Am. Soc. Clin. Investigation, Am. Gastroent. Assn. (Am. Disting. Achievement award 1972, Beaumont prize 2000), Am. Oil Chemists Soc. (Alton E. Bailey award 1998), Am. Fedn. Clin. Rsch., Am. Chem. Soc., Mass. Med. Soc., Suffolk Dist. Med. Soc., Phi Beta Kappa, Alpha Omega Alpha, Sigma Xi. Achievements include patents for on method for making meat products having a reduced saturated fat and cholesterol content. Office: Boston U Sch Medicine Dept Biophysics 715 Albany St W302 Boston MA 02118-2526 Fax: 617-638-4041. E-mail: dmsmall@bu.edu.

SMALL, ERWIN, veterinarian, educator; b. Boston, Nov. 28, 1924; Cert., Vt. State Sch. Agr., 1943; BS, U. Ill., 1955, DVM, 1957, MS, 1965. Diplomate: Am. Coll. Vet. Internal Medicine, Am. Coll. Vet. Dermatology. Intern Angell Meml. Animal Hosp., Boston, 1957-58; with U. Ill. Coll. Vet. Medicine, Urbana, 1958-92, prof. vet. clin. medicine, 1968-92, assoc. dean alumni and public affairs, chief of medicine, 1970-84, asst. dept. chmn., 1989-92, prof. emeritus, assoc. dean alumni and pub. affairs, 1992—. Contbr. articles to profl. jours. Served with USMC, 1944-46, 50-51, PTO. Recipient Nat. Gamma award Ohio State U., 1971, Ill. State VMA Svc. award, 1973, Nat. Zeta award Auburn U., 1974, Bustad Companion Animal Veterinarian award, 1993, Disting. Svc. award U. Ill. Alumni Assn., 1995; named Outstanding Tchr., Nordens Labs., 1967, Outstanding Educator, 1973, Outstanding Faculty Mem., Dad's Assn. U. Ill., 1990, Veterinarian of Yr., Mass. Soc. for Prevention Cruelty to Animals, 1993; recipient recognition for svc. with USMC War Dog Platoon, War Dog Meml., Quantico, Va., 2001, ISUMA Pres. award, 2002. Fellow Am. Coll. Vet. Pharmacology and Therapeutics; mem. AVMA (chmn. coun. edn. 1981-82, chmn. program com. 1983-87, Pres.'s award 1992, AVMA award 1998), Am. Animal Hosp. Assn. (award 1983, Midwest Region Svc. award 1989), Am. Coll. Vet. Dermatology (pres.), Internat. Vet. Symposia (pres.), Am. Assn. Vet. Clinics (pres., Faculty Achievement award 1992), Ill. Vet. Med. Polit. Action Com. (past chmn.), Chgo. Vet. Med. Assn. (lifetime achievement award 1997), Am. Coll. Vet. Internal Medicine (Robert W. Kirk award 1997), Coll. of Vet. Med. Alumni Assn. (Vet. Med. Achievement award 1997), Am. Legion, VFW, Moose, Omega Tau Sigma (pres. 1971-79), Phi Zeta, Gamma Sigma Delta. Republican. Jewish. Office: Vet Med Adminstrn U Ill Coll Vet Medicine Urbana IL 61802 Home: # A 1815 W Kirby Ave Champaign IL 61821-5410 E-mail: esmall@cvm.uiuc.edu.

SMALL, GARY W. academic administrator, psychiatrist, educator; b. L.A., July 28, 1951; s. Max Sidney and Gertrude (Axelrod) S.; m. Giselle Vorgan, May 28, 1989; children: Rachel, Harrison. BA summa cum laude, U. Calif., L.A., 1973; MD, U. So. Calif. Sch. Medicine, L.A., 1977; resident, clinical fellow psychiatry, Mass. Gen. Hosp., Harvard Med., Boston, 1981. Lic. Calif.; diplomate Am. Bd. Psychiatry & Neurology. Chief Geriatric Psychiatry Program West L.A. VA Med. Ctr., 1990-96; assoc. investigator UCLA Dept. Energy Lab. of Structural Biology & Molecular Med, L.A., 1997—; dir. Imaging & Genetics Core UCLA Alzheimer's Disease Ctr., 1997—; prof. Dept. Psychiatry & Behavioral Scis. UCLA, 1995—; attending psychiatrist UCLA Neuropsychiatric Hosp., L.A., 1993—; assoc. prof. Dept. Psychiatry & Behavioral Scis. UCLA, 1990-95; dir. UCLA Ctr. on Aging, 1997—. Mem. Mental Disorders of Aging Review NIMH, 1993-97; mem. editl. bd. Alzheimer Disease & Associated Disorders, 1985—. Co-author: Parentcare, 1988. Recipient Parlow-Solomon Professorship on Aging UCLA Sch. Medicine, 1998, Zenith award Alzheimer's Assn. 1998. Fellow Gerontological Soc. Am.; mem. APA (Jack Weinberg award Geriatric Psychiatry 2000), Am. Assn. Geriatric Psychiatry (bd. dirs. 1991-96, Sr. Investigator award 2000), Am. Coll. Neuropsychopharmacology, Internat. Psychogeriatric Assn. (Rsch. award 1987), Phi Beta Kappa, Alpha Omega Alpha. Avocations: crossword puzzles, classical music, cinema. Office: UCLA Neuropsychiatric Inst 760 Westwood Plz Los Angeles CA 90095-8353

SMALL, GEORGE LEROY, geographer, educator; b. Malden, Mass., Mar. 27, 1924; s. George Arthur and Alice Mildred (Weston) S.; m. Geraldine H. Koepke, July 4, 1970; 1 dau., Elizabeth Mary. BA, Brown U., 1950; M.I.A., Columbia U., 1952, PhD, 1968. French tchr. pvt. schs., Ariz., 1955-62; instr. geography Hunter Coll., 1964-68; asso. prof. geography Coll. S.I., CUNY, 1968—. Cons. problems of whaling to environ. groups. Author: The Blue Whale, 1971. Served with U.S. Army, 1942-46. Recipient Nat. Book award, 1972; Rotary Found. fellow, 1952-53 Mem. Assn. Am. Geographers. Office: CUNY Coll Staten Is New York NY 10314

SMALL, HAMISH, chemist; b. Newtown Crommelin, No. Ireland, Oct. 5, 1929; s. Johnston and Jean (Wilson) S.; m. Beryl Maureen Burley, Mar. 27, 1954; children: Deborah Jane, Claire Leslie. BS, Queens U., Belfast, Northern Ireland, 1949, MS, 1953. Chemist U.S. Atomic Energy Authority, Harwell, England, 1949-55; rsch. scientist Dow Chem. Co., Midland, Mich., 1955-83; chemist ind. rsch. and consulting, 1983—. Author: Ion Chromatography, 1990; holder 39 U.S. patents; contbr. articles to profl. jours. Recipient Albert F. Sperry award Instrument Soc. Am., 1978, A.O. Beckman award, 1983, Herbert H. Dow Gold Medal Dow Chem. Co., 1983, Stephen Dal Nogare award, 1984, Am. Chem. Soc. award in Chromatography, 1991. Mem. Am. Chem. Soc. Avocations: painting, sketching. Home: 4176 Oxford Dr Leland MI 49654-9716 E-mail: montalto29@aol.com.

SMALL, JONATHAN ANDREW, lawyer; b. N.Y.C., Dec. 26, 1942; s. Milton and Teresa Markell (Joseph) S.; m. Cornelia Mendenhall, June 8, 1969; children: Anne, Katherine. BA, Brown U., 1964; student, U. Paris, 1962-63; LLB, Harvard U., 1967; MA, Fletcher Sch. of Law and Diplomacy, 1968; LLM, NYU, 1974. Bar: N.Y. 1967. VISTA vol., Washington and Cambridge, Mass., 1968; law clk. to judge U.S. Ct. Appeals (2d cir.), 1968-69; assoc. Debevoise & Plimpton, N.Y.C., 1969-75, ptnr., 1976-99; pres. Nonprofit Coord. Com. N.Y., 2000—. Cons. Spl. Task Force of N.Y. State Taxation, 1976 Trustee Brearley Sch., 1985-95; bd. dirs. Nonprofit Coordinating Com. of N.Y., 1985—, Muscular Dystrophy Assn., 1986-88, Human Svcs. Coun. N.Y.C., Inc., 2000—, Investor Responsibility Rsch. Ctr., Inc., 2000—, Lawyers Alliance for N.Y., 2000—, U.S. Com. fo the UN Population Fund, 2000—. Mem. ABA, N.Y. State Bar Assn. (chmn. tax sect. com. exempt orgns. 1980-82, co-chmn., 1995), Assn. Bar City N.Y., Nonprofit Forum, Phi Beta Kappa. Home: 60 E End Ave New York NY 10028-7907 Office: Nonprofit Coord Com of NY 1350 Broadway Rm 1801 New York NY 10018-7718

SMALL, JONATHAN ANDREW, lawyer; b. Balt., June 30, 1959; s. Marvin Myron and Suzanne (Bierstock) S. AA, Foothill Jr. Coll., 1980; BS in Math. with honors, Calif. Poly. State U., 1983; JD, U. Santa Clara, 1986. Bar: Calif. 1987, U.S. Dist. Ct. (no. and so. dists.) Calif. 1987, U.S. Patent Office 1987, U.S. Ct. Appeals (fed. cir.) 1987. Patent atty. Townsend & Townsend, San Francisco, 1986-89; counsel Xerox Corp., Palo Alto, Calif., 1989-92, 97-00, assoc. gen. patent counsel, 1999-2000; assoc. Weil, Gotshal & Manges, Menlo Park, 1992-93; gen. counsel Komag Inc., Milpitas, 1993-97, Calient Networks, Inc. (formerly Chromisys, Inc.), San Jose, 2000—. Editor-in-chief Santa Clara Computer and High-Tech. Law Jour., 1985-86; contbr. articles to legal jours. Mem. ABA (chair intellectual property sect., elect. filing), Am. Intellectual Property Law Assn. Avocations: bicycle touring, kayaking. Office: Calient Networks Inc 5853 Rue Ferrari San Jose CA 95138

SMALL, KENNETH ALAN, economics educator; b. Sodus, N.Y., Feb. 9, 1945; s. Cyril Galloway and Gertrude Estelle (Andrews) S.; m. Adair Bowman, June 8, 1968; 1 child, Gretchen Lenore. BA, BS, U. Rochester, 1968; MA, U. Calif., Berkeley, 1972, PhD, 1976. Asst. prof. Princeton (N.J.) U., 1976-83; rsch. assoc. Brookings Inst., Washington, 1978-79; assoc. prof. U. Calif., Irvine, 1983-86, prof. econs., 1986—, assoc. dean social sci., 1986-92, chmn. econs., 1992-95. Vis. prof. Harvard U., Cambridge, Mass., 1991-92; cons. N.Y. State Legislature, Albany, 1982-83, Rand Corp., Santa Monica, Calif., 1985-86, ECO N.W., Eugene, Oreg., 1987—, World Bank, Washington, 1990—, Port Authority of N.Y. and N.J., 1994, Nat. Coop. Highway Rsch. Program, 1992-94, U. Newcastle, 2000-01, Govt. Inst. for Econ. Rsch., Finland, 2000—; mem. study com. on urban transp. congestion pricing NRC, 1992-94, mem. highway cost allocation rev. com., 1995-96, mem. com. for evaluation of CMAQ program, 1999—. Co-author: Futures for a Declining City, 1981, Urban Decline, 1982, Road Work, 1989; author: Urban Transportation Economics, 1992; co-editor: Urban Studies, Glasgow, Scotland, 1992-97, Kluwer Acad. Publs. book series, Dordrecht, The Netherlands, 1993—, Transport Economics: Selected Readings, 1995, Environment and Transport in Economic Modelling, 1998; assoc. editor Regional Sci. and Urban Econs., Amsterdam, The Netherlands, 1987—; editl. bd. mem. Jour. Urban Econs., San Diego, 1989—, Urban Studies, Glasgow, 1992—, Transportation, Dordrecht, 1993—, Jour. Transport Econs. and Policy, Bath, U.K., 1995—, Jour. Econ. Geography, 1999—; guest editor Regional Sci. and Urban Econs., 1992, Transp., 1992, Jour. Transp. Econs. and Policy, 2000. Grantee NSF, 1977-87, Inst. Transp. Studies U. Calif., 1984-89, Haynes Found., 1987-88, U.S. and Calif. Depts. Transp., 1988-94, 97—, Nat. Coop. Highway Rsch. Program, 1995-96, Daimler-Benz, 1996-99, U. Calif. Energy Inst., 2000—; Gilbert White fellow Resources for the Future, Washington, 1999-2000. Mem. Am. Econ. Assn. (com. on status of women in econs. profession 1995-97, Disting. Mem. award, transp. and pub. utilities group 1999), Econometric Soc., Transp. Rsch. Bd., Royal Econ. Soc., Regional Sci. Assn., Am. Real Estate and Urban Econs. Assn., Assn. Environ. and Resource Economists. Office: Dept Econs Univ Calif Irvine CA 92697-5100 E-mail: ksmall@uci.edu.

SMALL, LINDA H. social worker; b. Mobile, Ala., Sept. 16, 1939; d. Thomas Rix and Verda E. (Dowdle) Horne; m. Constock Small, Aug. 22, 1964; children: Elissa, Antonia. BA, Bennington Coll., 1962; MEd, Antioch U., 1978. Lic. clin. social worker, Mass. Exec. dir. Childrens Health Program Inc., Great Barrington, MA. Co-dir. Cmty. Health Ctr. of the Berkshires. Corporator Legacy Banks, Berkshire Mus. Recipient various awards. Address: PO Box 449 Housatonic MA 01236-0449

SMALL, MARSHALL LEE, lawyer; b. Kansas City, Mo., Sept. 8, 1927; s. Phillip and Lillian Small; m. Mary Rogell, June 27, 1954; children: Daniel, Elizabeth. BA, Stanford U., 1949, JD, 1951. Bar: Mo. 1951, Calif. 1955, N.Y. 1990. Law clk. to Justice William O. Douglas U.S. Supreme Ct., Washington, 1951-52; assoc. Morrison & Foerster, San Francisco, 1954-60, ptnr., 1961-92, sr. of counsel, 1993—. Reporter corp. governance project Am. Law Inst., 1982-92. 1st lt. U.S. Army, 1952-54. Mem. ABA (com. corp. laws 1975-82), Phi Beta Kappa, Order of Coif Office: Morrison & Foerster LLP 425 Market St San Francisco CA 94105-2482 E-mail: msmall@mofo.com.

SMALL, MELVIN, history educator; b. N.Y.C., Mar. 14, 1939; s. Herman Z. and Ann (Ashkinazy) S.; m. Sarajane Miller, Oct. 23, 1958; children: Michael, Mark. BA, Dartmouth Coll., 1960; MA, U. Mich., 1961, PhD, 1965. Asst. prof. history Wayne State U., Detroit, 1965-68, assoc. prof., 1968-76, prof., 1976—, chmn. dept. history, 1979-86. Vis. prof. U. Mich., Ann Arbor, 1968, Marygrove Coll., Detroit, 1971, Aarhus (Denmark) U., 1972-74, 83, Windsor (Ont., Can.) U., 1977-78. Author: Was War Necessary, 1980, Johnson, Nixon and the Doves, 1988, Covering Dissent, 1994, Democracy and Diplomacy, 1996, The Presidency of Richard Nixon, 1999, Antiwarriors, 2002; co-author: Wages of War, 1972, Resort to Arms, 1982; editor: Public Opinion and Historians, 1970; co-editor: International War, 1986, Appeasing Fascism, 1991, Give Peace a Chance, 1992; mem. editl. bd. Internat. Interactions, 1987-91, Peace and Change, 1989—; restaurant critic Detroit Metro Times, 1982-95; history book reviewer Detroit Free Press, 1988-95. Mem. hon. bd. Swords into Plowshares Mus., 1992—, mem. bd. Abraham Lincoln Brigade Archives, 1998—. Recipient Disting. Faculty award Mich. Assn. Governing Bds., 1993; Am. Coun. Learned Socs. fellow, 1969; Stanford Ctr. for Advanced Study fellow, 1969-70; grantee Am. Coun. Learned Socs., 1983, Johnson Libr., 1982, 88, Can. Govt., 1987; NATO rsch. fellow, 1996. Mem. Coun. on Peace Rsch. in History (nat. coun. 1986-90, pres. 1990-92), Am. Hist. Assn., Atlantic Coun. (acad. assoc.), Orgn. Am. Historians, Soc. for Historians of Am. Fgn. Rels. (Warren Kuehl prize 1989). Home: 1815 Northwood Blvd Royal Oak MI 48073-3919 Office: Wayne State U Dept History 3119 Fab Detroit MI 48202 E-mail: M.Small@Wayne.edu.

SMALL, MELVIN D. physician, educator; b. Somerville, Mass., May 22, 1925; s. Sidney J. and Ida (Gelbsman) S.; m. Judith Nogee, Dec. 23, 1962; children: Michael Dorian, Michele. AB, U. Wis., 1953; MD, Duke U., 1959; studied under Dr. Gregory Pincus, Worcester Found. Exptl. Biol. and Medicine, 1950-53; studied under Prof. Brian Abel-Smith, London Sch. Econs, 1986-90, MPhil, 1988. Lic. physician, Fla., Md., D.C., Va. Intern Georgetown U. Med. Ctr., Washington, 1959-60, resident, 1960-61, chief gastrointestinal rsch., 1961-64, instr. medicine, 1961-66, asst. prof. medicine, 1966-67, asst. clin. prof. medicine, 1967-81, 93—; chief gastroenterology sect. Georgetown divsn. D.C. Gen. Hosp., 1964-68. Lectr. on hygiene and preventive medicine Peace Corps groups, Ethiopia, Turkey, Brazil and Columbia, Georgetown U., 1961-62; cons. Children's Hosp., Washington, 1962-66; active staff Fairfax (Va.) Hosp., 1961-73, Commonwealth Drs. Hosp., Fairfax, 1969-74, Arlington (Va.) Hosp., 1961-85, Circle Terr. Hosp., Alexandria, 1965-85, Mt. Vernon Hosp., Alexandria, 1976-85; hon. staff mem. Alexandria Hosp., 1985-89, 92—; attending physician D.C. Gen. Hosp., 1961-68, Georgetown U. Hosp., 1961-81, 93—, Mt. Sinai Hosp., Miami Beach, Fla., 1992—; chief animal experimentation Cancer rsch. under Dr. Sidney Farber Children's Med. Ctr., Boston, 1948-50; rsch. asst. Boston U. Sch. Medicine, 1956-57; chmn. dept. medicine Alexandria Hosp., 1964-85; founder, chmn., No. Va. Consortium for Continuing Med. Edn., 1974-86, chmn. emeritus, 1986; lectr. in field; witness subcom. on small bus. U.S. Senate, 1967; founder, chmn. Nat. Coun. State Coms. on Continuing Med. Edn., 1977-79. Author publs. in field. Trustee Jefferson Meml. Hosp., 1965-74, mem. founding group, 1965, chmn. pharmacy com., 1965-76, co-chmn. tissue com., 1965-74; nominated candidate for Palm Beach (Fla.) Town Coun., 1995-96. Rsch. fellow under Norman Zamcheck Mallory Inst. Pathology, Boston, 1953-59, Gastroenterology rsch. under Franz Ingelfinger, Evans Meml. Hosp., Boston, AEC, 1951-53. Mem. AMA, Am. Coll. Gastroenterology, ACP, Am. Gastroent. Assn., Am. Inst. Nutrition, Am. Physiol. Soc., Am. Soc. Gastrointestinal Endoscopy, D.C. Med. Soc., Med. Soc. Va. (chmn. commn. on continuing med. edn. 1978-81), Alexandria Med. Soc. (v.p. 1979-80), Royal Soc. Medicine, Fla. Med. Soc., Palm Beach County Med. Soc. Home: 47 Saint George Pl Palm Beach Gardens FL 33418 E-mail: drmel25@stis.net.

SMALL, NATALIE SETTIMELLI, pediatric mental health counselor; b. Quincy, Mass., June 2, 1933; d. Joseph Peter and Edmea Natalie (Bagnaschi) Settimelli; m. Parker Adams Small, Jr., Aug. 26, 1956; children: Parker Adams III, Peter McMichael, Carla Edmea. BA, Tufts U., 1955; MA, EdS, U. Fla., 1976, PhD, 1987. Cert. child life specialist. Pediatric counselor U. Fla. Coll. Medicine, Gainesville, 1976-80, Shands Hosp.-U. Fla., Gainesville, 1980-87, supr. child life dept. patient and family resources, 1987—. Adminstrv. liaison for self-dir. work teams, mem. faculty Ctr. for Coop. Learning for Health and Sci. Edn., Gainesville, 1988—, assoc. dir., 1996, supr. pastoral svcs., 1998—; cons. and lectr. in field. Author: Parents Know Best, 1991; co-author team packs series for teaching at risk adolescent health edn. Building Strong Families, 1998. Bd. dirs. Ronald McDonald House, Gainesville, 1980—, mem. exec. com., 1991—; bd. dirs. Gainesville Assn. Creative Arts, 1994—; mem. health profl. adv. com. March of Dimes, Gainesville, 1986-96, HIV prevention planning partnership, 1995-96; mem. Teen Pregnancy Prevention Action Com., 1998-2000, exec. com. Children's Hosp., 1998—. Boston Stewart Club scholar, Florence, Italy, 1955; grantee Jessie Ball Du Pont Fund, 1978, Children's Miracle Network, 1990, 92-95, 97, 2000; recipient Caring and Sharing award Ronald McDonald House, 1995, Appreciation award March of Dimes, 1996. Mem. ACA, Nat. Bd. Cert. Counselors, Child Life Coun., Fla. Assn. Child Life Profls. Roman Catholic. Avocations: travel, reading, swimming. Home: 3454 NW 12th Ave Gainesville FL 32605-4811 Office: Shands Hosp Patient and Family Resources PO Box 100306 Gainesville FL 32610-0306 E-mail: smallns@shands.ufl.edu.

SMALL, NORMAN MORTON, speech and humanities educator, theatre producer, director; b. Phila., Sept. 11, 1944; s. Harry and Rose (Malschick) S.; m. Linda Carol Hill, Feb. 22, 1964; children: Denise H., Kevin P. BA, U. Fla., 1966, MEd, 1967. Prof. humanities Polk C.C., Winter Haven, Fla., 1967—, founder Polk C.C. Players, 1968; founder, producing dir. Theatre Winter Haven, 1970—. Endowed tchg. chair Polk C.C., 2000. Author: (tchg. transparencies) Intro to Drama, 1973; editor: The Making of Drama, 1971; dir., prodr. 225 plays. Bd. dirs. Ritz 100, Winter Haven, 1997—. Recipient 1st place award Fla. Non-Fiction C.C. mag., 1972, Citizen of Yr. award City of Winter Haven, 1977, Dir. Best Play award 27th Internat. Play Festival, Ireland, 1987, lifetime achievement award Fla. Assn. Cmty. Theatre, 1989. Fellow Am. Assn. Cmty. Theatre (1st pl. play competition 1980, 84, 86, 94); mem. Alliance for Mentally Ill (v.p. 1992-93, pres. 2001—, Outstanding Mem. award 1997), Fla. Assn. Cmty. Theatre (bd. dirs. 1984—, Outstanding Mem. award 1989, pres. 2001-). Democrat. Jewish. Home: 20 Casarena Ct Winter Haven FL 33881-3820 Office: Theatre Winter Haven 210 Cypress Gardens Blvd SW Winter Haven FL 33880-4310 E-mail: jnimrod11@aol.com.

SMALL, PARKER ADAMS, JR. pediatrician, educator; b. Cin., July 5, 1932; s. Parker Adams and Grace (McMichael) S.; m. Natalie Settimelli, Aug. 26, 1956; children: Parker Adams, Peter McMichael, Carla Edmea. Student, Tufts U., 1950-53; MD, U. Cin., 1957; BS extraordinem, 1986. Med. intern Pa. Hosp., Phila., 1957-58; research assoc. Nat. Heart Inst. NIH, Washington, 1958-60; research fellow St. Mary's Hosp., London, Eng., 1960-61; sr. surgeon NIMH, Washington, 1961-66; prof. immunology and med. microbiology U. Fla., 1966-95, chmn. dept., 1966-75, prof. pediatrics, 1979—, prof. pathology, 1995—, adj. clin. prof. large animal sci., 1999—; pres. PigVax Inc., 2000—01. Dir. Ctr. for Coop. Learning for Health Sci. Edn., U. Fla., 1988—; vis. prof. U. Lausanne, Switzerland, 1972, U. Lagos, Nigeria, 1982, Al Hada Hosp., Saudi Arabia, 1983; vis. scholar Assn. Am. Med. Colls., Washington, 1973; assoc. life scis. panel Nat. Acad. Scis., 1981-88, co-chmn., 1982-83; bd. dirs. Biol. Sci. Curriculum Study, 1984-90, exec. bd., 1987-90; mem. edn. adv. com. Nat. Fund Med. Edn., 1984-87; mem. study com. Nat. Bd. Med. Examiners, 1983-85, mem. nat. vaccine adv. com., 1987-91, chmn. subcom. on new vaccines, 1987-91; cons. in field. Creator patient oriented problem solving system/POPS, for teaching immunology and coop. learning to med. students and Team Packs for teaching K-12 & college students health edn. and coop. learning; co-dir. Fla. Ptnrs. in Prevention of Substance Abuse, 1997—; editor: The Secretory Immunologic System, 1971; mem. editorial bd. Infection and Immunity, 1974-76, Jour. Med. Edn., 1978-80; cons. editor Microbios, Cytobios; patentee in field; contbr. more than 150 articles to profl. jours. Sec., treas. Oakmont, Md., 1964-65, mayor, 1965-66; chmn. Citizens for Pub. Schs. Gainesville, Fla., 1969-70; mem. Teen Pregnancy Prevention Action Com., 1998-2000. With USPHS, 1958-60, 61-66. Named Tchr. of Yr. U. Fla. Coll. Medicine, 1978-79, Disting. Lectr. AMA, 1986; recipient Presdl. medallion U. Fla., 1987, Nat. Basic Sci. Disting. Teaching award Alpha Omega Alpha, 1993, Jacob Ehrenzeller award, 1995, Pres.'s Faculty Humanitarian award U. Fla., 1996, Pep award U. Fla., 1998; NIH spl. fellow, 1960-61, rsch. grantee, 1966—, U. Fla. Tchr./Scholar and commencement spkr., 1987; invited lectr. Assn. Am. Med. Colls., 1992. Mem. AAAS, Am. Assn. Immunologists (edn. com. 1983-86), Physicians for Social Responsibility, Fla. Med. Assn., Phi Beta Kappa, Sigma Xi, Alpha Omega Alpha, Theta Delta Chi. Home: 3454 NW 12th Ave Gainesville FL 32605-4811 Office: U Fla Coll Med PO Box 100275 Gainesville FL 32610-0275 E-mail: small@pathology.ufl.edu.

SMALL, PARKER ADAMS, III, investment banker; b. Phila., Feb. 1, 1958; s. Parker Adams Jr. and Natalie (Settimelli) S.; m. Katherine Currier, Aug. 24, 1985; children: Margaret Edmea, Elizabeth Parker. BA, Dartmouth Coll., 1980; MBA, Harvard U., 1985. Account exec. Leo Burnett Advt., Chgo., 1980-83; assoc. Merrill Lynch-Becker Paribas, N.Y.C., 1984; product mgmt. The Gillette Co., Boston, 1985-86; mgmt. cons. Arthur D. Little Inc., Cambridge, Mass., 1986-89; v.p. Butler Capital Corp., N.Y.C., 1989-92. Pres. S.R.S. Sera Co., Gainesville, Fla., 1976-91; bd. dirs. Julius Koch USA Inc., Strine Printing Co., Lancaster Press Inc. Author: Understanding Immunology, 1976; producer Dartmouth Coll. video, 1980. Reunion chmn. Dartmouth Coll., 1990, mem. alumni coun., 1999; bd. dirs. Wellesley Edn. Found. Avocations: skiing, tennis, scuba diving. Home: 11 Westwood Rd Wellesley MA 02482-7015

SMALL, RAY, university administrator; b. Winters, Tex., Aug. 2, 1915; s. George Norman Small and Etta Thompson; m. Dollee Georgia Meyer, Aug. 6, 1938 (div. Jan. 1981); children: Marilynn, Andra; m. Maria Victoria De Leon, Aug. 14, 1998. BA, West Tex. A&M, 1937; MA, U. Tex., 1941, PhD, 1958. Prin. Quail (Tex.) Pub. Sch., 1937-38; tchr. Wayside (Tex.) Sch., 1938-40, prin., 1940-41; tchr. Horace Mann Sch., Amarillo, Tex., 1946-81; prof., asst. to pres. Tex. Western Coll., El Paso, 1961-63; prof., dean U. Tex., 1963-79, acting dir. student publication, 1985-90, editl. advisor-student publs., 1990-95, acad. advisor-comms., 1995—. Emeritus dean liberal arts U. Tex., 1979, emeritus prof. English, 1981, emeritus prof. comm., 1995. Presbyterian. Home: 603 E Baltimore Dr El Paso TX 79902 Office: U Tex at El Paso 500 W University El Paso TX 79968

SMALL, RICHARD DONALD, travel company executive; b. West Orange, N.J., May 24, 1929; s. Joseph George and Elizabeth (McGarry) S.; m. Arlene P. Small; children: Colleen P., Richard Donald, Joseph W., Mark G., Brian P. AB cum laude, U. Notre Dame, 1951. With Union-Camp Corp., N.Y.C., Chgo., 1952-62; chmn. Alumni Holidays, Inc., 1962—, AHI Internat. Corp., 1962—; pres. All Horizons, Inc., 1982—. Chmn. AHI, Inc., 1982-89; bd. dirs. French Cruise Lines, Des Plaines, Ill., Russian Cruise Lines, Alumni Campus Abroad, 1994—. Recipient Munich Ptnr. award, 1989. Mem.: Carlton Club (Chgo.), Univ. Club Chgo. Home: Water Tower Pl 180 E Pearson St # 3306 Chicago IL 60611-6730 also: Wailea Golf Estates 3954 Waakaula Pl Kihei HI 96753 Office: 6400 Shafer Ct Rosemont IL 60018 Business E-Mail: royals@Hawaii.rncom ., rds@AHITravel.com.

SMALL, SARAH MAE, volunteer; b. Salisbury, N.C., Nov. 16, 1923; d. Clint and Lillie Mae (Wilbourn) Evans; m. Jesse Small Sr., May 4, 1941; children: Jesse Jr., Jean Carol Small Bell. Cert., Cortez Bus. Sch., 1948. File clk. gen. acctg. office Fed. Govt., Washington, 1941-47; sec., stenographer CIA, 1948-52, adminstrv. asst. McLean, Va., 1952-65, ret., 1965. Elected pres. Energetic Crusaders, Inc., 1993—. Pres. Energetic Crusaders, Inc., 1993; bd. dirs. ARC, Washington, 1986-87, Children's Edn. Found., Inc., 1989—; mem. adv. bd. D.C. Gen. Hosp., 1985-86. Recipient Outstanding and Dedicated Vol. Svc. award Kiwanis Club of Capital Centre, 1985, Plaque in Recognition of Dedicated and Outstanding Vol. Svc. to the Corps and Washington D.C., Cmty. Jr. Citizen's Corps., 1989, Appreciation award for Outstanding and Dedicated Vol. Svc. to Corps, Jr. Citizens Corps., Inc., 1990, Appreciation award Jr. Citizens Corp., Inc., 1990, Cmty. Svc. award for leadership and youth advocacy Bus. and Profl. Women's League, Inc., 1991, Vol. award achievement excellence svc. youths of Jr. Citizens Corps., Inc., 1992, others. Mem. Jr. Citizens Corps (life, pres. 1985—, Dedicated Cmty. Svc. award 1983, Bus. and Cmty. Svc. award 1986), Bus. and Profl. Women's League (treas. 1982-86), Women in Arts (chartered, pres. 1984—), Nat. Coun. Negro Women, World Affairs Coun. Washington, Agrl. Coun. Am. Democrat. Baptist. Avocations: travel, photography, walking, swimming. Home: 2010 Upshur St NE Washington DC 20018-3244

SMALL, THOMAS MILTON, lawyer; b. Sullivan, Ind., Mar. 4, 1933; s. Marion Creston and Ruby Bernice (Thomas) S.; m. Tanya Loy, May 12, 1979; children: Sheree Lynne, Angela Rae. BS in Engring. Law, Purdue U., 1957; JD, Ind. U., 1957. Bar: Ind. 1957, Ill. 1960, Calif. 1970. Assoc. ptnr. Wolf Hubbard Voit and Osann, Rockford, Ill., 1960-68, Fulwider Patton Rieber Lee & Utecht, L.A., 1968-87; ptnr. Baker & McKenzie, 1987-92, Small Larkin, LLP, L.A., 1992—2002, Birch, Stewart, Kolasch & Birch, L.A., 2002—. 1st Lt. U.S. Army, 1957-59. Mem. L.A. Patent Law Assn. (pres. 1975-76), Calif. Bar Assn. (pres. intellectual property section 1979-80), Licensing Execs. Soc. (pres. 1997-98). Avocations: tennis, flyfishing, ballroom dance. Office: Birch Stewart Kolasch & Birch 10940 Wilshire Blvd Los Angeles CA 90024-3915 E-mail: tms@sbskb.com.

SMALL, WILLIAM EDWIN, JR. association and recreation executive; b. Jackson, Mich., Jan. 18, 1937; s. William Edwin and Lena Louisa (Hunt) S.; m. Ruth Ann Toombs, Mar. 28, 1959; children: Suzanne Marie, William Edwin III, Bryan Anthony. AS, Jackson C.C., 1959; BS in Geology, Mich. State U., 1961, MA in Journalism, 1964. Reporter Sci. Svc., Washington, 1961-62; writer sci. U. Chgo., 1963-64; sci. info. officer Pa. State U., State College, 1964-66; corr. McGraw-Hill, Washington, 1966-69; staff com. pub. works U.S. Senate, 1969; founding editor Biomed. News, 1969-71; dir. pub. info. Nat. Bur. Standards, Washington, 1972-76; editor Am. Pharmacy Jour., 1979-82; dir. media and info. svcs. AMA, Washington, 1982-86; exec. dir. Nat. Found. Infectious Diseases, 1986-91, Assn. Biotech. Cos., 1991-93; CEO, Bioconfs. Internat., Bethesda, Md., 1993-95, WESmall & Assocs., Assn. Execs., Louisa, Va., 1976—. Owner recreation resort Small Country, Louisa, 1976—; exec. dir. Va. Biotech. Assn., 1996-2000; exec. dir. Va. Campground Assn., 2001-. Author: Third Pollution, 1971. Exec. dir. Va. Campground Assn., 2001—. With Security Agy., AUS, 1955-59. Recipient Superior Accomplishment award U.S. Dept. Commerce, 1974. Fellow AAAS; life mem. Nat. Assn. Sci. Writers. Office: PO Box 343 Louisa VA 23093-0343

SMALLEY, CHRISTOPHER JOSEPH, pharmaceutical company professional; b. Phila., June 26, 1953; s. Charles Wilfred and Verna May (Coulter) S.; m. Maria Visniskie, Aug. 9, 1974; children: Christa Maria, Mark Charles, Lora Loray. BS, Phila. Coll. Pharmacy and Sci., 1976; MBA, Temple U., 1982; PhD, LaSalle U., 1991. Ordained elder, Presbyn. ch., 1992. Mfg. pharmacist supr. McNeil Labs., Fort Washington, Pa., 1976-77; mfg. pharmacist group supr. McNeil Consumer Products Co., 1978-79, mfg. pharmacist mgr., 1980-85; tech. svcs. mgr. Janssen Pharmaceutica, 1985-88, plant mgr., 1988-94; quality assurance dir. Sanofi rsch. divsn. Sanofi Pharms., Inc., Malvern, Pa., 1994-98; dir. validation compliance Wyeth-Ayerst Pharms., St. Davids, 1998—. Mem. Rep. Nat. Com., 1979—. With USNR Med. Corps., 1986-95, with USAF, 1995—. Mem. Am. Pharm. Assn., Assn. Mil. Surgeons of U.S., Am. Assn. Pharm. Scientists, Internat. Soc. Pharm. Engrs., Aerospace Med. Assn., Am. Acad. Med. Adminstrs., Assn. Med. Svc. Corps Officers, Pa. Pharm. Assn., Inst. Enivron. Scis., Eastern Assn. GMP Trainers, Parenteral Drug Assn. (chmn. tng. com.), Pharm. Mfrs. Assn. (prodn. sect.), Phila. Pharm. Forum, USN Inst., NRA, Kappa Psi. Presbyterian. Home: 816 Kenmara Dr West Chester PA 19380-2022 Office: 240 N Radnor Chester Rd Saint Davids PA 19087-5106

SMALLEY, DAVID VINCENT, lawyer; b. N.Y.C., Mar. 27, 1935; s. Vincent R. and Ethel A. (Sullivan) S.; m. Patricia Doyle Tolles, Nov. 28, 1964; children: Brian W., Gregory T. BA, Hamilton Coll.; LLB, Harvard U. Bar: N.Y. 1960. Assoc. Debevoise & Plimpton, N.Y.C., 1959-67, ptnr., 1968-99. Mem. Assn. Bar City N.Y. Home: 10 Wildwood Cir Larchmont NY 10538-3427 Office: Debevoise & Plimpton 919 Third Ave New York NY 10022

SMALLEY, PENNY JUDITH, healthcare technology consultant; b. Chgo., Feb. 20, 1947; d. Ernest Rich and Muriel L. (Touff) Brown; m. Ivan H. Smalley, Jan. 11, 1972; children: Cherie Ann, Michael John, Geoffry Paul. Grad., Evanston Hosp. Sch. Nursing, Ill., 1980. Cert. Am. Bd. Laser Surgery, 1989. Staff nurse Evanston Hosp., 1979-81, laser coord., 1981-83; office mgr. Women's Health Group, 1981; laser nurse specialist Cooper Lasersonics, various, 1983-86; pres., CEO Technology Concepts Internat., Inc., Chgo., 1986—. Lectr., writer Sino Fgn. Laser Conf., People's Republic of China, 1987; bd. dirs. Laser Inst. Am.; rep. Assn. Perioperative RN's. Contbg. author: Nursing Clinics of North America, 1990; editorial bd. Clin. Laser Monthly, Laser Nursing mag., 1989—. Minimally Invasive Surg. Nursing; contbr. articles to profl. jours. Mem. Am. Soc. Laser Medicine and Surgery (chmn. edn. com. 1987-90, standards of practice com. 1990, quality assurance com., nursing sect. chmn. 1992-94, chair safety com.), award for Excellence in Laser Nursing 1993), Laser Inst. Am. (bd. dirs.), Am. Nat. Standards Com., Inst. Com. Lasers in Health Care, Brit. Med. Laser Assn. (course dir. first laser nursing conf. in U.K., 1990), Assn. Oper. Rm. Nurses (tchr. nat. seminars, spl. com. on internat. issues, liaison to ANSI Z136, Australian/N.Z. 4173 laser safety stds.), Internat. Soc. Laser Surgery and Medicine (chmn. nursing 1988—. chmn. safety com. 2002), Internat. Electrotech. Commn. (Am. delegation). Democrat. Avocations: music, community theater, travel, photography. Home and Office: 1444 W Farwell Ave Chicago IL 60626-3410 E-mail: pennyjs@aol.com.

SMALLEY, RICHARD ERRETT, chemistry and physics educator, researcher; b. Akron, Ohio, June 6, 1943; s. Frank Dudley and Virginia (Rhoads) Smalley; m. Judith Grace Sampieri, May 4, 1968 (div. July 1979); 1 child Chad ; m. Mary Lynn Chapieski, July 10, 1980 (div. Nov. 1994); m. JoNell Marie Chauvin, Mar. 1, 1997 (div. June 1998); 1 child Preston. BS in Chemistry, U. Mich., 1965; MA in Chemistry, Princeton U., 1971, PhD in Chemistry, 1973; PhD (hon.), U. Liege, Belgium, 1991; DSc (hon.), U. Chgo., 1995. Assoc. The James Franck Inst., Chgo., 1973—76; from asst. prof. to prof. William Marsh Rice U., Houston, 1976—82, Gene & Norman Hackerman prof. chemistry, 1982—; prof. Rice U., 1990—. Chmn. Rice Quantum Inst., Houston, 1986—96; dir. Rice Ctr. for Nanoscale Sci. and Tech., 1996—2002. Contbr. numerous articles to profl. jours. Recipient Franklin medal, Franklin Inst., Phila., 1996, Nobel Prize in chemistry, 1996. Fellow: Am. Phys. Soc. (divsn. chem. physics, Irving Langmuir prize 1991, Internat. New Materials prize 1992); mem.: Am. Acad. Arts and Scis., Materials Rsch. Soc., Am. Chem. Soc. (divsn. phys. chemistry, William H. Nichols medal 1993, S.W. regional award 1992, Harrison Howe award Rochester sect. 1994, Madison Marshall award North Ala. sect. 1995), NAS, AAAS, Sigma Xi. Office: Rice Univ Ctr Nanoscale Sci and Tech 6100 Main St # Ms100 Houston TX 77005-1892

SMALLEY, ROBERT MANNING, government official; b. Los Angeles, Nov. 14, 1925; s. William Denny and Helen (McConnell) S.; m. Lois Louisa Williamson, Nov. 28, 1948 (div.) m. Rosemary Sumner, Jan. 4, 1957; children— Leslie Estelle, David Christian. Student, UCLA, 1946-48. Radio news editor Mut. Radio Broadcasting System, Los Angeles, 1950-55; mgr. Agrl. Info. Inc., Sacramento, 1957-59; with Whitaker & Baxter, San Francisco, 1956-57, 59-61; sec. Mayor, 1961-63; asst. dir. pub. relations Republican Nat. Com., 1964; press sec. Republican vice presdl. candidate William E. Miller, 1964; dir. pub. relations Republican Nat. Com., 1965; v.p. Whitaker & Baxter, San Francisco, 1966-68; asst. press sec. Republican vice presdl. candidate Spiro Agnew, 1968; spl. asst. Sec. Commerce, Washington, 1969-72; adminstrv. asst. U.S. Senator Robert P. Griffin, 1972-73; dir. corp. affairs Potomac Electric Power Co., 1973-75; U.S. rep. devel. assistance com. O.E.C.D., Paris, 1975-77; spl. asst. U.S. Senator Robert P. Griffin, Washington, 1977-78; asst. to campaign mgr. Reagan for Pres. Com., 1979; sr. advisor mgmt. communications IBM, 1979-82; dep. asst. sec. of state pub. affairs Dept. of State, Washington, 1982-87, U.S. amb. to Kingdom of Lesotho, 1987-89; lectr. in U.S. politics and pub. policy. Served with USN, 1944-46, PTO Episcopalian. Home: Breton Bay Landing 40439 Breton View Dr Leonardtown MD 20650 E-mail: rsmalley@starpower.net.

SMALLMAN, BEVERLEY N. biology educator; b. Port Perry, Ont., Can., Dec. 11, 1913; s. Richard Benjamin and Ethel May (Doubt) S.; m. Hazel Mayne, Dec. 11, 1937 (dec. 1962); 1 child, Sylvia Gail; m. Florence Hazel Cook, July 27, 1965 BA, Queens U., Kingston, Ont., 1936; M.Sc., Western U. Ont., Can., 1938; PhD, U. Edinburgh, Scotland, 1941; LL.D.(hon.), Trent U., Ont., 1982. Mem. staff Stored Grain Insect Investigations Bd. of Grain Commnrs., Winnipeg, 1941-45; officer-in-charge Stored Products Lab., Agrl. Can., 1945-50; head entomol. sect. rsch. inst. Agrl. Can., London, 1950-57, chief entomol., rsch. dir. entomology, plant pathology Ottawa, 1957-63; prof., head dept. biology Queens U., Kingston, Ont., Can., 1963-73, prof. biology Can., 1973-78, prof. emeritus biology Can., 1979—. Vis. scientist Nat. Inst. Med. Rsch., London, Eng., 1954-56, CSIRO Labs., Brisbane, Australia, 1970-71, 76; apiary insp. Province of Ont., 1981-91; cons., lectr. in field. Prin. author: Agricultural Science in Canada, 1970, Queen's Biology, 1992; co-author: Good Bye Bugs, 1983. Contbr. articles to profl. jours. Fellow Royal Soc. Can.; mem. Entomol. Soc. Can., Zool. Soc. Can., Entomol. Soc. Man. (founding pres. 1945), Entomol. Soc. Ont. Avocations: Mini-farming; beekeeping; writing popular science reviews. Home: 364 Emerald St Kingston ON Canada K7P 3EY

SMALLMAN, GAIL ELIZABETH, entrepreneur; b. Buffalo, Mar. 24, 1953; d. Lemuel James and Beverly Ann (Waldron) S.; m. Ronald Hugh Strasser, 1974 (div. 1975). Student, Oreg. State U., 1971-72, Portland State, 1972-74, City U., Seattle, 1979. Word processor Atty. Gen.'s Consumer Protection, Portland, Oreg., 1974-75, Lane Powell Moss & Miller, Seattle, 1978-79; sec. Carney, Probst & Levak, Portland, 1975-76, Jones, Lang, Klein, et al., Portland, 1978; office mgr. Corl & Willis, Corvallis, Oreg., 1976-77; adminstrv. asst. Reed McClure Moceri et al., Seattle, 1978-80; systems mgr. Lane Powell Spears et al., 1980-94; owner Sunrise Place Bed & Breakfast, Bainbridge Island, Wash., 1994—. V.p. Wang/Informatics special interest group VS Legal Users' Group, Sacramento, 1990-91. Active Residents Opposed to Aircraft ReRouting, 1991. Scholar Oregon State U., 1971. Mem. Am. Mgmt. Assn., LawNet Inc. (v.p., bd. dirs. 1991-93), Bainbridge Island C. of C., Bainbridge Island Bed & Breakfast Assn., Bremerton/Kitsap County Visitors & Conv. Bur. Democrat. Episcopalian. Avocations: sailing, gardening, scuba diving. Address: 16565 Touraco Ln NE Poulsbo WA 98370-8772

SMALLRIDGE, ROBERT CHRISTIAN, endocrinologist; b. Charleston, W.Va., Dec. 28, 1944; s. Horace Hamilton Jr. and Isabel White Smallridge; m. Elizabeth Cone; children: Amy Brewster, Laura Fontaine. BA, Yale Coll., 1966; MD, Med. Coll. Va., 1970. Chief dept. clin. physiology Walter Reed Army Inst. Rsch., Washington, 1978-91, dir. divsn. medicine, 1991-95; chair endocrinology divsn. Mayo Clinic Jacksonville, Fla., 1996—. Mem. endocrinology study sect. NIH, Bethesda, Md.; cons. Assessment Techs., Inc., Lexington, Ky., 1998—; dir. rsch. Mayo Clinic, Jacksonville, 2000—. Author book chpts.; contbr. numerous articles to profl. jours. Col. U.S. Army, 1973-96. Recipient Peter Forsham Endocrinology award Soc. Uniformed Endocrinologists. Fellow ACP, Am. Coll. Endocrinology; mem. Endocrine Soc., Am. Thyroid Assn. (treas. 1988-93, chair fin./audit com. 1993-99). Avocations: golf, family, travel. Office: Mayo Clinic Jacksonville 4500 San Pablo Rd S Jacksonville FL 32224-1865

SMALLWOOD, CAROL, librarian, writer; b. Cheboygan, Mich., May 3, 1939; d. Lloyd Gouine and Lucille Drozdowska; m. T.M. Smallwood, 1963 (div. 1976); 2 children. BS, Ea. Mich. U., 1961, M in History, 1963; MLS, We. Mich. U., 1976. Tchr. Redford Union High Sch., Livonia, Mich., 1961-62, Flat Rock (Mich.) Jr. High Sch., 1963-64; grad. asst. Western Mich. U., Kalamazoo, 1975-76; Title I libr. cons. Northland (Mich.), Grand Traverse (Mich.) Library Systems, 1976-77; head media dir. Pellston (Mich.) Pub. Schs., 1977—. Asst. dir. Northland Libr. System, Alpena, Mich., 1977; developer, operator ednl. materials clearinghouse, 1981-83; adult edn. tchr. Cheboygan Area Schs., 1985-86. Author: Free Michigan Materials for Educator, 1980, Exceptional Free Library Resource Materials, 1994, Free Resource Builder, 1985, 2d edit., 1992, A Guide to Selected Federal Agency Programs and Publications for Librarians and Teachers, 1986, Health Resource Builder, 1988, An Educational Guide to the National Park System, 1989, Current Issues Builder, 1989, Library Puzzles and Word Games, for Grades 7-12, 1990, Reference Puzzles and Word Games for Grades 7-12, 1991, Michigan Authors, 1993, Helpful Hints for the School Library, 1993, Recycling Tips for Teachers and Librarians, 1995; columnist Detroit News, 1983-85, Catch: The Entertainment News, 1988-89, Libr. PR News, 1990—, Ednl. Oasis, 1990—. Charter bd. mem., publicity chmn. Cheboygan Area Arts Coun.; founder, pres. Cheboygan County Humane Soc. Mem. NEA, Mich. Fedn. Humane Socs., Environ. Def. Fund, Pellston Edn. Assn., Mich. Edn. Assn., No. Mich. Edn. Assn., Mich. Assn. Media Edn., Nat. Humane Edn. Soc. Home: 543 S Whiteville Rd Mount Pleasant MI 48858-9761 Office: Pellston High Sch Libr PO Box 16 Pellston MI 49769-0016

SMALLWOOD, FRANKLIN, political science educator; b. Ridgewood, N.J., June 24, 1927; s. J. William and Carolyn (Linkroum) S.; m. Ann Logie, Sept. 8, 1951; children: Susan, Sandra, David, Donald. AB, Dartmouth Coll., 1951, A.M. (hon.), 1968; M.P.A., Harvard U., 1953, PhD, 1958. With AEC, 1953-57; asst. to pres. Dartmouth Coll., 1957-59, mem. faculty, 1959-92, prof. govt., 1967-92, Nelson A. Rockefeller prof. govt. emeritus, 1992—; U. Vt., Burlington, 1989—; chmn. city planning and urban studies program Dartmouth Coll., 1965-72, chmn. social sci. div., 1968-72, asso. dean faculty, 1968-72, acting dean, 1972, v.p. student affairs, 1975-77, chmn. policy studies program, 1977-83, dir. Nelson A. Rockefeller Center for Social Scis., 1983-86. Chmn. Vt. Gov.'s Commn. Higher Edn., 1973-80, Vt. Adv. Commn. on Intergovtl. Relations, 1985-86, Vt. Legis Apportionment Bd., 1990—; fenceviewer Norwich, Vt., 1976-90. Author: Metro Toronto: A Decade Later, 1963, Greater London: The Politics of Metropolitan Reform, 1965, Free and Independent, 1976, The Politics of Policy Implementation, 1980, The Other Candidates, 1983, Thomas Chittenden, Vermont's First Statesman, 1997, The UVM Presidents, 1997. Mem. Vt. Senate, 1973-75; trustee Vt. State Colls., 1967-73, chmn., 1973. Served with AUS, 1945-46. Recipient Superior Achievement award AEC, 1957, Dartmouth Presdl. Leadership medal, 1991; fellow Inst. Pub. Adminstrn., 1960; Dartmouth Coll. Faculty fellow, 1962-63; Nuffield Coll. (Oxford U.), vis. fellow, 1981, 86-87. Mem. Phi Beta Kappa. Office: 804 Wake Robin Dr Shelburne VT 05482

SMALLWOOD, GLENN WALTER, JR. utility marketing management executive; b. Jeffersonville, Ind., Oct. 12, 1956; s. Glenn Walter and Darlene Ruth (Zeller) S. BSBA, S.E. Mo. State U., 1978; MA in Bus., Webster U., 1992, MBA, 1993. Cert. counselor; cert. energy mgr. Customer svc. advisor Union Electric Co., Mexico, Mo., 1979-95, Cape Girardeau, 1995-97; cmty. devel. exec. Ameren Svcs., 1997-98, bus. devel. exec., 1998—. Instr. Mexico Vo-Tech Sch., 1981; panelist on home design Mo. Extension Svc., 1984; co. advisor Mo. Bus. Week. Coord. local United Way, 1984; mem., chair Gt. Rivers coun. Boy Scouts Am., chair Shawnee dist. Eagle Scout advancement com., 1999-2001, chair Shawnee Dist. com., 2002--; panelist Mo. Freedmon Forum, 1990; charter mem. class Mo. Leadership; chmn. Leadership Mexico Program; coordinating advisor Jr. Achievement, Mexico H.S.; committeeman, chmn. Republican Party of Audrain County; bd. dirs. Mo. Rep. Grassroots Caucus, S.E. Mo. Univ. Found., 1998—. Named among Ten Outstanding Young Missourians, Mo. Jaycees, 1993; recipient Disting. Svc. award Mexico, Mo. Jaycees, 1993. Mem. Am. Mktg. Assn. (profl.), Nat. Eagle Scout Assn., Cooper Dome Soc., Boy Scouts Am. Alumni Family, Mexico Area C. of C. (bd. dirs. 1993-95), Cape Girardeau C. of C. (chair govtl. affairs com.), S.E. Mo. U. Alumni Assn., Inst. Cert. Profl. Mgrs. (cert. mgr.), Assn. Energy Engrs. (cert. energy mgr.), Adminstrv. Mgmt. Soc., Optimists (youth appreciation award 1974), Kiwanis (cert. appreciation 1984), Mexico Noon (bd. dirs. 1990, treas. 1990-91, v.p. 1991-92, pres. 1993-94), Audrain County Pachyderm Club (bd. dirs., 2d v.p. 1990-92, pres. 1993), S.E. Mo. Univ. Found. (bd. dirs.), S.E. Mo. Pachyderm Club (founder, pres. 1997-98), Mo. Fedn. Pachyderm Clubs (bd. dirs.), Honorable Order Ky. Cols. (commd. Ky. col. 1995), Sons of Confederate Vets., Disting. Hoosier Com. (State of Ind. 1999), Rotary. Republican. Avocations: music, spectator sports, baseball, basketball, tennis. Office: Ameren Svcs 340 Silver Springs Rd Cape Girardeau MO 63703 E-mail: gsmallwood@ameren.com.

SMALLWOOD, ROBERT ALBIAN, JR. secondary education educator; b. Phila., Oct. 3, 1946; s. Robert Albian and Mildred May (Miller) S.; m. Geraldine Ann Boozan, May 27, 1972; children: Amy Lynn, Daniel James. BSC, Rider Coll., 1969, MA, 1976; EdS, Rutgers U., 1986. Cert. social studies tchr., secondary sch. prin., supr. curriculum and instrn., Pa.; cert. social studies and gen. bus. tchr., prin., supr., sch. bus. adminstr., asst. supt. bus., sch. adminstr. (supt.) N.J. Tchr. social studies Trenton Bd. Edn., 1973-76, tchr. bus. edn., 1975-76, sch. disciplinearian, 1976-84, 94-97; acting asst. prin. Jr. High Sch. 2, 1980-83, tchr. U.S. history, 1983-87, chmn. social studies dept., 1984-85; acting asst. prin. Carroll Robbins Elem. Sch., Jr. High Schs. #1 and #5, 1987-88; tchr. gifted and talented social studies Dunn Jr. High Sch., 1989-93, social studies tchr., 1997-99, whole sch. reform site facilitator,

1999—. Mem. Dist.'s Affirmative Action Adv. Council; mem. Nat. Tchr. Corps Project, Trenton Area; fin. advisor M.S. Prin., 1998—. Asst. ops. officer Trenton CD Unit, 1974-76, asst. disaster analysis officer, 1976, disaster analysis officer, 1976-79; trustee N.J. Coun. for Alcohol/Drug Edn., 1983-99, mem. exec. com., 1985-95, 96-99, chmn. nominating com., 1985, 86, treas., 1987-95, acting exec. dir., 1994-95, v.p., 1996-98, pres. 1998-99. With U.S. Army, 1969-72. Decorated Bronze Star, Army Commendation medal with oak leaf cluster, Joint Svc. Commendation medal. Mem. NEA, Vietnam Vets. Am., Va. Geneal. Soc., Md. Geneal. Soc., Md. Hist. Soc., Geneal. Soc. Pa., Nat. Geneal. Soc., Assn. Profl. Genealogists, Phi Delta Kappa. Home: 2 Leese Ave Trenton NJ 08609-1828

SMALLY, DONALD JAY, consulting engineering executive; b. Cleve., 1922; s. Daniel James and Alice (Rohrheimer) S.; m. Ruth Janet Glasser, July 8, 1944; children: Alan Jon, Leonard Arthur. BME, U. Cin., 1949. Prodn. engr. N. Ransohoff, Inc., Cin., 1949-50; chief engr. Mosby Engring. Assocs., Sarasota, Fla., 1952-55; prin. Smally, Wellford & Nalven, Inc., 1956-91. Mem. tech. adv. com. Manatee Community Coll., Sarasota, 1965-90; mem. adv. com. Vocat.-Tech. High Sch., Sarasota, 1968-80 V.p. Sarasota YMCA, 1968-71, Sarasota Opera Assn., 1975-88, pres., 1988-89; chmn. Sarasota Vol. Talent Pool, 1973-76; sec.-treas. Civitan Found., 1965-79; bd. dirs. Suncoast Heart Assn., 1976; mem. Fla. Coordinating Coun. for Vocat. and Adult Edn., 1984-95, chmn., 1987-88; chmn. Sarasota Hist. Preservation Bd., 1988-91; pres. Sarasota County Rd. Improvement Task Force, 1990-93; mem. Sarasota County Pub. Sch. Found., 1990-95, chmn., 1990-91; v.p. Hist. Soc. Sarasota, 1990-91, Children's Haven and Adult Cmty. Svcs., 1983-99, pres., 1991-94; pres. John Ringling Ctr. Found., 1991-98; mem. Plymouth Harbor Bd., 1994-99. Recipient Good Citizenship award SAR, 1975, Disting. Alumni award U. Cin. Engring. Coll., 1985, Outstanding Svc. award Myakna Chpt. Fla. Engring. Soc., 1993; named Citizen of Yr. Sarasota Civitan Club, 1975, Engr. of Yr. Sarasota-Manatee Engrs. Soc., 1976. Fellow Am. Coun. Engring. Cos. (treas. 1980-82), Fla. Engring. Soc. (pres. Sarasota-Manatee chpt. 1956-58); mem. Sarasota County C. of C. (past dir., v.p. 1983), Cons. Engrs. Council Fla. (pres. 1968), Fla. Soc. Profl. Land Surveyors (chpt. pres. 1973), Am. Water Works Resources Assn. (pres. Fla. Soc. 1981), Sarasota-Manatee Engring. Soc.

SMARANDACHE, FLORENTIN, mathematics researcher, writer; b. Balcesti-Vilcea, Romania, Dec. 10, 1954; came to U.S., 1990; s. Gheorghe and Maria (Mitroiescu) S.; m. Eleonora Niculescu; children: Mihai-Liviu, Silviu-Gabriel. MS in Computer Sci., U. Craiova, 1979; postgrad., Ariz. State U., 1991, U. Phoenix, 1996; PhD in Math., Kishinev U., 1997. Mathematician I.U.G., Craiova, Romania, 1979-81; math. prof. Romanian Coll., 1981-82, 1984-86, 1988; math. tchr. Coop. Ministry, Morocco, 1982-84; French tutor pvt. practice, Turkey, 1988-90; software engr. Honeywell, Phoenix, 1990-95; prof. math. Pima C.C., Tucson, 1995-97; asst. prof. U. N.Mex., 1997—. Author: Nonpoems, 1990, Only Problems, Not Solutions, 1991, numerous other books; contbr. articles to profl. jours. Mem. U.S. Math. Assn., Romania Math. Assn., Zentralblatt fur Math. (reviewer). Achievements include development of Smarandache function, numbers, quotients, double factorials, consecutive sequence, reverse sequence, mirror sequence, destructive sequence, symmetric sequence, permutable sequence, consecutive sieve, prime base, cubic base, square base, class of paradoxes, multi-structure and multi-space, paradoxist geometry, anti-geometry, inconsistent systems of axioms, neutrosophic logic/set/probability. Office: U NMex Dept Math Gallup NM 87301

SMARDON, RICHARD CLAY, landscape architecture and environmental studies educator; b. Burlington, Vt., May 13, 1948; s. Philip Albert and Louise Gertrude (Peters) S.; m. Anne Marie Graveline, Aug. 19, 1973; children: Regina Elizabeth, Andrea May. BS cum laude, U. Mass., 1970, MLA, 1973; PhD in Environ. Planning, U. Calif., Berkeley, 1982. Environ. planner, landscape architect Wallace, Floyd, Ellenzweig, Inc., Cambridge, Mass., 1972-73; assoc. planner Exec. Office Environ. Affairs, State of Mass., Boston, 1973-75; environ. impact assessment specialist USDA extension svc. Oreg. State U., Corvallis, 1975-76; landscape architect USDA Pacific S.W. Forest and Range Expt. Sta., Berkeley, 1977; rsch. landscape architect U. Calif., 1977-79; prof. landscape architecture, sr. rsch. assoc. SUNY Coll. Environ. Sci. and Forestry, Syracuse, 1979-86, prof. environ. studies, 1987—, dir. Inst. for Environ. Policy and Planning, 1987-95, chair faculty of environ. studies, 1996—. Co-dir. Gt. Lakes Rsch. Consortium, Syracuse, 1986—; guest lectr. numerous univs.; adj. asst. prof. U. Mass., Amherst, 1974-75, chair faculty Environment Studies, 1996, dir. R.G. Pack Environment Inst., 1996; Sea Grant trainee Inst. for Urban and Regional Devel., Berkeley, 1976; condr., presenter numerous seminars and workshops; cons. to numerous orgns.; mem. com. on environ. design and landscape Transp. Rsch. Bd.-NAS, 1985-95; mem. tech. adv. bd. Wetlands Rsch., Inc., Chgo., 1985; mem. adv. bd. Wetlands Fund, N.Y., 1985; v.p. Integrated Site, Syracuse, 1990-2002. Co-editor: Our National Landscape, 1979, spl. issue Coastal Zone Mgmt. Jour., 1982, The Future of Wetlands, 1983, Foundations for Visual Project Analysis, 1986, The Legal Landscape, 1993, Protecting Floodplain Resources, 1995, Adirondacks and Beyond, 1998, Environmental Knowledge, 2001; mem. editl. bd. Northeastern Environ. Sci. Jour., 1981-85, Landscape and Urban Planning, 1991—, Environ. Sci. and Policy, 1999—, The Sci. World, 2001—; contbr. over 100 articles to profl. jours. Bd. dirs. Sackets Harbor Area Hist. Preservation Found., Watertown, N.Y., 1984-90; pres. Save the County, Inc., Fayetteville, N.Y., 1986-88; apptd. to Great Lakes (N.Y.) Adv. Commn., chmn., 1993-98, Great Lakes Legal Found., 1999, NY State Wetlands Forum Bd., 2000. Recipient Beatrice Farrand award U. Calif., 1979, Am. Soc. Landscape Architects award, 1972, Pub. Svc. award in edn., 1990, Progressive Architecture mag. award 1992, Pres.'s Pub. Svc. award 1994. Mem. AAAS, N.Y. Acad. of Sci., Am. Land Resource Assn. (charter), Internat. Assn. for Impact Assessment, Coastal Soc., Alpha Zeta (life), Sigma Lambda Alpha. Avocations: folk guitar, hiking, skiing, travel. Office: SUNY Faculty Environ Studies Syracuse NY 13210

SMARELLI, DAVID JOHN, music educator, musician; b. Springfield, Ohio, Sept. 7, 1959; s. John and Margaret Ann Smarelli; m. Brenda Faye Widmark, Aug. 10, 1985; children: Laura, Marissa, Julia. MusB in Performance and Edn., Bowling Green State U., 1982; MusM in Edn., Miami U., Oxford, Ohio, 1996. Profl. tchg. cert. Ohio Dept. Edn. Orch. tchr. Lima (Ohio) City Schs., 1982—89, Sycamore Cmty. Schs., Cin., 1989—. Lectr. Ohio No. U., Ada, Ohio, 1984—85. Musician (violinist): Springfield Symphony Orch., 1975—, Blue Ash (Ohio) Symphony Orch., 1997; co-concertmaster: Lima (Ohio) Symphony Orch., 1982—89, concertmaster: Clermont Philharm. Orch., 1999—. Mem.: NEA, Am. Fedn. Musicians, Ohio Orch. String Tchrs. Assn. (S.W. regional rep. 1998—2000, summer camp mid. sch. orch. dir. 1994—, camp orch. dir. 1994—), Ohio Music Edn. Assn. (S.W. region chair 1993—94). Avocations: computers, coin collecting, gardening. Home: 1522 Laval Dr Cincinnati OH 45255 Office: Sycamore HS 7400 Cornell Rd Cincinnati OH 45242

SMART, ALLEN RICH, II, lawyer; b. Chgo., July 3, 1934; s. Jackson W. Smart and Dorothy (Byrnes) Bowles. Student, Deerfield Acad., 1949-52; AB magna cum laude, Princeton U., 1956; LLB, Harvard U., 1961. Bar: Ill. 1961. Assoc. Bell Boyd & Lloyd, Chgo., 1961-69, ptnr., 1970-91, of counsel, 1992—. Bd. dirs. Rec. for Blind, Inc., Chgo., 1984-95, vice-chmn., 1987-90; co-chmn. zoning com. Old Town Triangle Assn., Chgo., 1987-94; bd. dirs. Lawrence Hall Sch. for Boys, 1965-70, Old Masters Soc., Art Inst., 1987—; governing mem. Orchestral Assn. Lt. USNR, 1956-58. Mem. ABA, Ill. Bar Assn., Chgo. Bar Assn., Infant Welfare Soc. Chgo. (bd. dirs. 1971-95, pres. 1982-86), Friends of the Parks Chgo. (bd. dirs. 1986—), Renaissance Soc. Chgo. (bd. dirs. 1988—), University (bd. dirs. 1986-89), Arts, Legal, Law, Economic clubs of Chgo. Home: 1732 N North Park Ave Chicago IL 60614-5710 Office: Bell Boyd & Lloyd 3200 Three First Nat Pl Chicago IL 60602

SMART, EDITH MERRILL, civic worker; b. N.Y.C., Sept. 10, 1929; d. Edwin Katte and Helen Phelps (Stokes) Merrill; student Smith Coll., 1947-49, Barnard Coll., 1949-50; m. S. Bruce Smart, Jr., Sept. 10, 1949; children—Edith Minturn Smart Moore, William Candler, Charlotte Merrill Smart Rogan, Priscilla Smart Schwarzenbach. Tchr. elem. schs., Gibson Island, Md., 1959-60; guide, instr. Mill River Wetlands Com., Fairfield, Conn., 1967-85; treas. Near and Far Aid Assn., Fairfield, 1970-75, v.p., 1975-77, pres., 1977-79; pres. Nature Ctr. of Environ. Activities, Westport, Conn., chmn., 1981-85; trustee Fairfield Univ., 1987-93; leader No. Cook County council Girl Scouts U.S.A., Kenilworth, Ill., 1962-64; chmn. Southport-Westport Antiques Show, 1974-76; trustee Conn. chpt. Nature Conservancy, 1981-91, trustee, sec. Va. chpt., 1992—, co-chmn. S.E. regional com. campaign for conservation; guide Nat. Acquarium, 1985-90; dir. Piedmont Child Devel. Ctr., 1991-97; vestryman St. Timothy's Ch., Fairfield, 1976-79. Republican. Episcopalian. Clubs: Upperville Garden, MFH The Fairfax Hunt. Home: 20561 Trappe Rd Upperville VA 20184-3021

SMART, FRANK WILSON, physician; b. New Orleans, Apr. 12, 1956; s. Foch Mahlon and Laura Gladys Smart; m. Jaclyn Cutrone, Nov. 16, 1996; children: Daniel, Katherine, Michael. BS in Zoology, So. La. U., 1978; MD, La. State U., New Orleans, 1985. Diplomate Am. Bd. Internal Medicine, Am. Bd. Cardiovascular Disease. Intern Ochsner Found. Hosp., New Orleans, 1985-86, resident, 1986-88; fellow Baylor Coll. Medicine, Houston, 1988-90, fellow in transplant rsch., 1990-91; co-sect. head heart failure and cardiac transplantation Ochsner Med. Instn., New Orleans, 1991-97, dir. med. transplant svcs., multi-organ transplant ctr., 1994-97; dir. transplant Ochsner Clinic, 1991-97; prof. medicine, co-dir. to dir. cardiac transplant program Tulane U. Med. Ctr., 1997—. V.p., co-founder Rsch. Congestive Heart Failure, New Orleans, 1998—; rep. region 3 United Network Organ Sharing, Richmond, Va., 1999—; mem. adv. bd. Action Heart Failure, Parsippany, N.Y. Mem. editl. bd. Cardiology Today, 1996; author: The Transplantation & Replacement of Thoracic Organs, 1997, Primer on Transplantation, 1998; reviewer Am. Jour. Cardiology. Recipient Richard Van Reet award Baylor Coll. Medicine, Houston, 1991. Fellow ACP, Am. Coll. Cardiology (Syntex award 1990); mem. AMA, Internat. Soc. Heart or Lung Transplantation, Am. Soc. Transplantation, So. Med. Assn., Alpha Omega Alpha. Home: 5339 Coliseum St New Orleans LA 70115-3052 Office: Tulane U Med Ctr 1415 Tulane Ave New Orleans LA 70112-2605 E-mail: fsmart@tulane.edu.

SMART, MARY-LEIGH CALL (MRS. J. SCOTT SMART), civic worker; b. Springfield , Ill., Feb. 27, 1917; d. S(amuel) Leigh and Mary (Bradish) Call; m. J. Scott Smart, Sept. 11, 1951 (dec. 1960). Diploma, Monticello Coll., 1934; student, Oxford U., 1935; BA, Wellesley Coll., 1937; MA, Columbia U., 1939, postgrad., 1940-41, NYU, 1940-41; painting student, with Bernard Karfiol, 1937-38. Dir. mgmt. Cen. Ill. Grain Farms, Logan County, 1939—; owner Lowtrek Kennel, Ogunquit, Maine, 1957-73, Cove Studio Art Gallery, Ogunquit, 1961-68; art collector, patron, publicist, 1954—. Cons. in field. Editor: Hamilton Easter Field Art Found. Collection Catalog, 1966; originator, dir. show, compiler of catalog Art: Ogunquit, 1967; Peggy Bacon-A Celebration, Barn Gallery, Ogunquit, 1979. Program dir., sec. bd. Barn Gallery Assocs., Inc., 1958-69, pres., 1969-70, 82-87, asst. treas., 1987-92, hon. dir., 1970-78, adv. trustee, 1992-94, v.p., 1994—; curator Hamilton Easter Field Art Found. Collection, 1978-79, curator exhbns., 1979-86, chair exhbn. com., 1987-94; mem. acquisition com. DeCordova Mus., Lincoln, Mass., 1966-78; mem. chancellor's coun. U. Tex., 1972—; mem. pres.'s coun. U. N.H., 1978—; bd. dirs. Ogunquit C. of C., 1966, treas., 1966-67, hon. life mem., 1968—; bd. overseers Strawbery Banke, Inc., Portsmouth, N.H., 1972-75, 3d vice chmn., 1973, 2d vice chmn., 1974; bd. advisors U. Art Galleries, U. N.H., 1973-89; pres., 1981-89; bd. dirs. Old York Hist. and Improvement Soc., York, Maine, 1979-81, v.p., 1981-82; adv. com. Bowdoin Coll. Mus. Art Invitational exhibit, 1975, '76 Maine Artists Invitational Exhbn., Maine State Mus., Maine Coast Artists, Rockport, 1975-78, All Maine Biennial '79, Bowdoin Coll. Mus. Art juried exhbn.; mem. jury for scholarship awards Maine com. Skowhegan Sch. Painting & Sculpture, 1982-84; nat. com. Wellesley Coll. Friends of Art, 1983—; adv. trustee Portland Mus. Art, 1983-85, fellow, 1985—; mem. mus. panel Maine State Commn. on Arts and Humanities, 1983-86; adv. com. Maine Biennial, Colby Coll. Mus. Art, 1983; coun. advisors Farnsworth Art Mus., Rockland, Maine, 1986-98; collections com. Payson Gallery, Westbrook Coll., Portland, 1987-91; dir. Greater Piscataqua Cmty. Found., N.H. Charitable Fund, 1991-97; mem. com. to establish an artist's fellow, 2001; mem. corp. Ogunquit Mus. Am. Art, 1988-90, 95-2000; mem. Maine Women's Forum, 1993—. Lt. (j.g.) WAVES, 1942-45. Recipient Deborah Morton award Westbrook Coll., 1988, Friend of the Arts award Maine Art Dealers Assn., 1993. Mem. Springfield Art Assn., Jr. League Springfield Ill., Western Maine Wellesley Club. Episcopalian. Address: 30 Surf Point Rd York ME 03909-5053

SMART, STEPHEN BRUCE, JR. business and government executive; b. N.Y.C., Feb. 7, 1923; s. Stephen Bruce and Beatrice (Cobb) S.; m. Edith Minturn Merrill, Sept. 10, 1949; children: Edith Minturn Smart Moore, William Candler, Charlotte Merrill Smart Rogan, Priscilla Smart Schwarzenbach. Student, Milton Acad.; AB cum laude, Harvard U., 1945; SM, MIT, 1947. Sales engr. Permutit Co., N.Y., 1947-51; various sales, gen. mgmt. positions Continental Group, Inc. (formerly Continental Can Co.), N.Y.C., 1953-85, v.p. Central metal divsn., 1962-65, v.p. marketing and corporate planning, 1965-67, v.p., asst. gen. mgr. paper ops., 1967-69, group v.p. paper ops., 1969-71, exec. v.p. paper ops., 1971-73, vice chmn. bd. dirs., 1973-75, pres., 1975-85, chmn., CEO, 1981-85; undersec. for internat. trade U.S. Dept. Commerce, Washington, 1985-88; cons. U.S. Dept. State, 1988-89; sr. fellow World Resources Inst., 1989-95, bd. dirs., 1992-2001. Editor: Beyond Compliance: A New Industry View of the Environment, 1992, Indian Summer--A Memoir, 1999. Trustee, vice chmn. Smith Coll., 1976-86; gov., vice chmn. The Nature Conservancy, 1979-85; bd. dirs. League of Conservation Voters, Va. Thoroughbred Assn., 2001—; chmn. bd. dirs. Notre Dame Acad., Middleburg, Va., 1996-98. Mem. Coun. Fgn. Rels. Home and Office: 20561 Trappe Rd Upperville VA 20184-3021

SMART, SUZANNE D. social worker; b. Youngstown, Ohio, Aug. 19, 1949; BA, Ohio State U., 1971; MSW, U. Mich., 1977. Program coord. Cope-O'Brien Ctr., Ann Arbor, Mich., 1977-79; exec. dir. W.Va. Nat. Assn. Social Workers, Morgantown, 1980-82; parent educator Shack Neighborhood House, Parsglove, W.Va., 1982-96; tng. specialist Vis. Homemakers, Morgantown, 1987-94; cmty. liaison Early Head Start, 1996—. Pres. Morgantown Day Sch., 1986-87; chair Monongalia County Adolescent Task Force, Morgantown, 1990—, Family Connections, Morgantown, 1999—; chair Monogalia County Family Resource Network, 1997-99, treas., 1999; ct. apptd. spl. advocate; presenter in field. Mem. NASW. Home: 50 Smokey Drain Rd Morgantown WV 26501-2147

SMARTSCHAN, GLENN FRED, school system administrator; b. Allentown, Pa., Dec. 11, 1946; s. Fred Gotfred and Joyce Isabel (Hensinger) S.; m. Linda Susan Bastinelli, Mar. 18, 1972; children: Erin Joy, Lauren Nicole. BS in Edn., Kutztown State Coll., 1968; MS in Edn., Temple U., 1972; EdD in Ednl. Adminstrn., Lehigh U., 1979. Cert. tchr. history and comprehensive social studies, secondary prin., supt., Pa. Tchr. 8th grade social studies South Mountain Jr. H.S., 1968-76; adminstrv. asst. to prin. to prin. Raub Jr. H.S., 1976-80, dist. dir. curriculum, 1980-84, asst. to supt. for curriculum and cmty. svcs., 1984-86; supt. schs. Brandywine Hts. Area Sch. Dist., Topton, Pa., 1986-90, Mt. Lebanon Sch. Dist., Pitts., 1990—. Adj. prof. Cedar Crest Coll., 1986-88, Duquesne U., 1997, U. Pitts., 2001; CEO Ednl. Dynamics Cons.; assoc. The Cambridge Group, 1993—; spkr. and cons. Multiple Client Feedback (MCF). Pay for Performance Plans, match of written, taught and tested curriculum, criterion referenced testing, strategic planning. Bd. dirs. Alternative House, Inc., Bethlehem, Pa., 1976-81, chmn. program com., 1977-78, v.p., 1979, pres., 1980; adv. com. Lehigh County (Pa.) Hist. Mus., 1980-86; bd. dirs. Girls Club Allentown, 1983-86, v.p., 1985. Mem. ASCD, Pa. Assn. Supervision and Curriculum Devel. (exec. com., registrar ea. regional meeting, v.p. Ea. region, pres. 1988), Am. Assn. Sch. Adminstrs. (Pa. State Supt. of Yr. 1999), Pa. Assn. Sch. Adminstrs. (pres. 1996), Pa. Sch. Bds. Assn., Juvenile Diabetes Assn. (bd. dirs.), Alumni Coun. Lehigh U. (pres. 1986), Phi Delta Kappa, Fleetwood Club, Rotary (charter mem. Allentown club, exec. com. 1985). Roman Catholic. Home: One Spalding Cir Pittsburgh PA 15228 Office: Mt Lebanon Sch Dist 7 Horsman Dr Pittsburgh PA 15228-1107

SMATHERS, JAMES BURTON, medical physicist, educator; b. Prairie du Chien, Wis., Aug. 26, 1935; s. James Levi and Irma Marie (Stindt) S.; m. Sylvia Lee Rath, Apr. 20, 1957; children— Kristine Kay, Kathryn Ann, James Scott, Ernest Kent. B.Nuclear Enging., N.C. State Coll., 1957, MS, 1959; PhD, U. Md., 1967. Diplomate Am. Bd. Radiology, Am. Bd. Health Physics, Am. Bd. Medical Physics; cert. in radiation oncology physics; registered profl. engr., D.C., Tex., Calif. Research engr. Atomics Internat., Canoga Park, Calif., 1959, Walter Reed Army Inst. Research, Washington, 1961-67; prof. nuclear engring. Tex. A. and M. U., College Station, 1967-80, prof., head bioengring., 1976-80; prof., head med. physics, dept. radiation oncology UCLA, 1980-2001, prof. emeritus, 2001—. Cons. U.S. Army, Dept. Energy, also pvt.; industry. Served with U.S. Army, 1959-61. Recipient Excellence in Teaching award Gen. Dynamics, 1971; Excellence in Research award Tex. A. and M. U. Former Students Assn., 1976 Mem. Health Physics Soc., Am. Assn. Physcists in Medicine, Am. Soc. Engring. Edn. (Outstanding Tchr. award in nuclear engring. div. 1972), Sigma Xi, Sigma Pi Sigma, Phi Kappa Phi. Home: 18229 Minnehaha St Northridge CA 91326-3427 E-mail: smathers@ucla.edu.

SMATRESK, NEAL JOSEPH, physiologist, biology educator, science education consultant; b. Worcester, Mass., July 9, 1951; s. Edwin C. and Dorothy (Lincoln) S.; m. Deborah Hoddick, Aug. 12, 1978; children: Erik Neal, Kristen Elise. BA, Gettysburg Coll., 1973; MA, SUNY, Buffalo, 1978; PhD, U. Tex., 1980. Rsch. expedition NSF, Alpha Helix, Micronesia, 1979; NIH trainee U. Pa. Med. Sch., Phila., 1980-82; asst. prof. biology U. Tex., Arlington, 1982-88, assoc. prof. biology, 1988-94, prof., chmn. biology, 1994-98, dean of sci., 1998—. Sci. edn. cons. local schs. Ad hoc reviewer numerous profl. jours.; contbr. articles, revs., and book chpt. to profl. pubIs. Dir. Tex. Sci. Careers Consortium; dir. Tex. State Sci. and Engring. Fair. Recipient Outstanding Tchr. award, U. Tex. Chancellor, 1988; grantee NSF (3), 1989—, NIH, 1991—, Tex. Sch. to Careers. Mem. Soc. for Integrative and Comparative Biology (program officer), Am. Physiol. Soc., Am. Zool. Soc., Neurobiology Soc., Sci. and Tech. Collaborative, Kiwanis Internat. Avocations: sports, painting. Office: U Tex Coll Sci PO Box 19047 Arlington TX 76019-0001 E-mail: smatresk@uta.edu.

SMEAD, BURTON ARMSTRONG, JR. retired lawyer; b. Denver, July 29, 1913; s. Burton Armstrong and Lola (Lewis) S.; m. Josephine McKittrick, Mar. 27, 1943 children: Amanda Armstrong, Sydney Hall. BA, U. Denver, 1934, JD, 1950; grad., Pacific Coast Bank Trust Sch., 1955. With Wells Fargo Denver (formerly Denver Nat. Bank), 1934-78, trust officer, 1955-70; v.p., trust officer Norwest Bank Denver (now Wells Fargo), 1970-78; of counsel Buchanan Neville & Stouffer, Lakewood, Colo., 1985-99. Author: History of the Twelfth Field Artillery Battalion in the European Theater of Operations, 1944-45, Captain Smead's Letters to Home, 1944-45; editor: Colorado Wills and Estates, 1965. Pres., trustee Stebbins Orphans Home Assn., resigned, 1998; chmn. bd. dirs. Colo. divsn. Am. Cancer Soc., 1961-68. Maj. U.S. Army, 1941-45, ETO. Decorated Bronze Star; Croix de Guerre (France). Mem. Colo. Bar Assn. (treas. 1970-88, chmn. probate and trust law sect. 1967-68, exec. coun., bd. govs. 1970-88, coun. bd. govs. 1970-88, hon. 1989—, award of merit 1979), Denver Bar Assn., Denver Estate Planning Coun. (co-founder, pres. 1971-72), Univ. Club (Denver). Republican. Episcopalian. Home and Office: 111 Emerson St Apt 1143 Denver CO 80218-3790

SMECK, WILLIAM HARRY, computer scientist; b. Chester, Pa., Sept. 1, 1945; s. William H. and Dolores M. S.; m. Barbara Nunan, Aug. 1, 1970; 1 child, Gregory. BA in English Lit., Widener U., 1977; MEd in Tech., Edn., Rosemont Coll., 1995. Computer ops. shift supervisor Certain-Teed Products Co., Valley Forge, Pa., 1969-73; asst. computer ops. mgr. Wawa (Pa.) Food Markets, 1973-77; computer programmer Clement Pub., Concordville, Pa., 1977-79; sr. programmer, analyst Scott Paper Co., Phila., 1979-93; project adminstr. Computer Sci. Corp., Ft. Worth, 1993-95; project leader Lockheed Martin Aircraft Corp., Valley Forge, Pa., 1995-97; project mgr. CAI, Inc., Wilmington, Del., 1997—. Referee coll. and h.s. track and cross country meets. Sgt., U.S. Army, 1963-66. Mem. Project Mgmt. Inst., Rosemont Coll. Alumnae (bd. dirs., grad. sch. rep. 1997—), St. James Cath. H.S. Boys Alumni Assn. Roman Catholic. Avocations: loong distance running, history. Home: 514 Wheatsheaf Rd Springfield PA 19064 Office: Computer Aid Inc 901 Market St Wilmington DE 19801

SMEDLEY, CHARLES VINCENT, sociology educator; b. Washington, Sept. 1, 1955; s. Frederick Joseph Smedley and Ruth (Bouknight) McGee; m. Sue Marie Prosser, Aug. 28, 1976; 1 child, Sarah Jane. BS cum laude, U. S.C., 1978; MA, U. Ill., 1980, PhD, 1986. Asst. prof. U. Charleston, W.Va., 1986-88, Charleston (S.C.) So. U., 1988—. Mem. editorial adv. bd. Roxbury Pub. Co., 1989—, Collegiate Press, 1991—; editor Behavioral Sci. update Charleston So. U., 1989—. Mem. 1st Scots Presbyn. Ch., Charleston, 1990—. Fellowship U. Ill., 1978-79, 85 Fellow Soc. Applied Anthropology; mem. AAAS, Am. Sociol. Assn., Am. Anthropol. Assn., N.Y. Acad. Scis., Am. Acad. Polit. and Social Sci., Soc. for Advancement of Socio-econs., Soc. Psychol. Study Social Issues, Soc. Southeastern Social Psychologists, Archaeol. Inst. Am., S.C. Social Assn., Soc. Applied Anthropology, Mo. Archaeol. Soc., Nat. Trust for Historic Preservation, U.S.C. Alumni Assn., U. Ill. Alumni Assn., U. S.C. Gamecock Club, Berkeley County Soc. for Prevention of Cruelty to Animals, Phi Beta Kappa, Phi Kappa Phi, Pi Gamma Mu, Alpha Kappa Delta. Republican. Home: 111 Dominion Cir Goose Creek SC 29445-5512 Office: Charleston So U PO Box 118087 Charleston SC 29423-8087

SMEDLEY, ELIZABETH, researcher, codifier, consultant, historian, writer; b. Phila., Jan. 5, 1915; d. Elwood Quimby and Hazel deRemer (Ward) S. BA cum laude, Bryn Mawr Coll., 1936. Editor, rechr., writer Hist. Records Survey, Phila., 1939-43; rechr., writer U.S. Army Chief of Ordnance, 1943-45; local govt. specialist Bur. Mcpl. Affairs, Harrisburg, Pa., 1945-51; local govt. codifier, writer Penns Valley Pubs., State College, 1951-75; rschr., writer Pa. State Assn. Boroughs, Harrisburg, 1975-82; dir. codification, co-owner Century IV Codes, Inc., Hershey, Pa., 1982-95, owner, rechr. Hummelstown, 1995—. Cons., writer Pa. State Assn. Boroughs, Harrisburg, 1962-65, Pa. Dept. Transp., Harrisburg, 1979-81. Author: Zion's Path of History, 1987, 1936: A 50 Year Perspective, 1986. Chmn. State College Govt. Study Commn., 1971-73. Mem. DAR, Daus. Am. Colonists. Republican. Mem. Lds Ch. Avocations: collecting postcards and books, gardening, cooking, cats. Home and Office: 54 Ridgeview Rd Hummelstown PA 17036-9721

SMEDLEY, KEYUE MA, engineering educator, researcher; m. Greg Smedley, June 19, 1989; children: Aurora, Orion. BSEE, Zhejiang U., Hangzhou, China, 1982; MSEE, Zhejiang U., 1985, Calif. Inst. Tech., Pasadena, 1987; PhD in Elec. Engring., Calif. Inst. Tech., 1991. Engr. III Superconducting Super Collider, Dallas, 1990—92; asst. prof. dept. elec. and computer engring. U. Calif., Irvine, 1992—98, assoc. prof., 1998—. Contbr. Recipient Golden Lectureship, Tel Aviv U., 1996; fellow Powell fellow, Calif. Inst. Tech., 1988. Mem.: IEEE (sr.; ad com. mem. 1997—, assoc. editor Electronics Engring. 1996—, chmn. constitution and bylaws com. 1995—, Supreme Presentation award Nuclear Sci. Symposium 1991), IEEE Power Electronics Soc., Power Sources Mfrs. Assn., Eta Kappa Nu. Achievements include patents for in field. Avocations: travel, snorkeling. Mailing: Univ of Calif Dept Elec and Computer Engring Irvine CA 92697

SMEDLEY, LAWRENCE THOMAS, retired organization executive; b. Lorain, Ohio, Sept. 2, 1929; s. Robert E. and Gerda Sofia (Johnson) S.; m. Carmen Nancy Suarez, June 29, 1962; children: Lorraine, Robert, Lawrence, Richard. BA, Bowling Green State U., 1952; MA, U. Mich., 1957; PhD, Am. U., 1972. Analyst Social Security dept. AFL-CIO, Washington, 1962-65, asst. dir. dept., 1965-73, assoc. dir. dept. occupation safety-health-social security, 1973-88; exec. dir. Nat. Coun. Sr. Citizens, Inc., 1988-96. Former mem. numerous presdl. task forces and coms. on older Ams. and disabled; mem. planning and adv. coms. White House Conf. on Aging, 1971, 81; former mem. adv. coun. on employee welfare and pension plans Dept. Labor, also former mem. spl. task force examining policies relating to asset reversions from over-funded pension plans; bd. dirs. Nat. Coun. Sr. Citizens. Co-chmn. Leadership Coun. Aging Orgns., Washington, 1988-95; mem. exec. bd. Com. for Nat. Health Ins., WAshington, 1989—; mem. policy conv. White House Conf. on Aging, 1995; chair Montgomery County Com. Aging. With M.I., U.S. Army, 1952-55, Korea. Recipient Svc. award Commn. on Accreditation of Facilities of Rehab., 1975, Dedicated Svc. award White House Conf. on Handicapped, 1977, award of honor Industry-Labor Coun., 1981, Outstanding Svc. award Pres.'s Com. on Employment of Handicapped, 1987. Democrat. Lutheran. Home: 1616 Winding Waye Ln Silver Spring MD 20902-1456 Fax: 301 949-9794. E-mail: ltsmed@aol.com.

SMEDS, EDWARD WILLIAM, retired food company executive; b. Chgo., Feb. 15, 1936; s. Sigvard A. and Ida S.; m. Alice J. Lawler, Jan. 26, 1957; children— Ellen R., Brad W. BS, Carthage Coll., 1957; MS, U. Ill., 1959; grad. advanced mgmt. program, Harvard U., 1977. With Borg Warner Corp.,

1958-61, Kraft Foods div. Kraft Inc., 1961-75, v.p., dir. personnel, ops. group, 1976-78, v.p. human resources, 1978-79, sr. v.p. human resources, 1979-80, sr. v.p. fin. and adminstrn., 1980-84; pres. Kraft Asia Pacific, 1984-88; chmn. Kraft Foods Ltd., Australia, 1984-88; pres. Kraft Ltd. Can., 1988-89; sr. v.p. ops. and logistics Kraft Gen. Foods, Glenview, Ill., 1990-94; pres. customer svc. and ops. Kraft, Northfield, 1993-94, ret., 1994. Dir. Aid Assn. Lutherans Mut. Funds, Appleton, Wis., 1998—. Chmn. bd. trustees Carthage Coll., Cornerstone Found. Mem. Econ. Club of Chgo., Sunset Ridge Country Club, Club at Pelican Bay, Olde Fla. Home: 10 Regentwood Rd Northfield IL 60093-2728 also: 6814 Pelican Bay Blvd Naples FL 34108-8218 E-mail: esmeds@comcast.net.

SMEETON, THOMAS ROONEY, governmental affairs consultant; b. Evanston, Ill., Sept. 26, 1934; s. Cecil Brooks, Jr. and Florence Mary (Rooney).; m. Susan Diane Tollefson, Feb. 23, 1963; children: Sean, Timothy, Shannon, Brendan, Colin. BS in History, Marquette U., 1958; postgrad., U. Notre Dame, 1958-59; grad., Armed Forces Staff Coll., 1972. Intelligence officer U.S. CIA, Langley, Va., 1962-73; vp., gen. mgr. Nowicki Fla. Devel. Corp., Ft. Lauderdale, 1973-75; cons. spl. projects com. on fgn. affairs U.S. House Reps., Washington, 1975-86, minority counsel permanent select com. on intelligence, 1986-92, minority staff dir. Iran/Contra com., 1987-88, exec. dir. Rep. policy com., 1993-94; adminstr., chief investigator House Judiciary Com., 1995-96; govtl. affairs cons., 1996—. Contbg. author: (with Hyde) For Every Idle Silence, 1985. Bd. dirs. Sylvan Beach Found. With U.S. Army, 1959-62. Recipient Agy. Seal medallion CIA, 1993. Mem. Assn. Former Intelligence Officers, Ctrl. Intelligence Retirees Assn., Am. Legion, Notre Dame Club Washington (vice chmn. 1982-84), Amelia Island Club. Republican. Roman Catholic. Avocation: golf. Home and Office: PO Box 8029 Fernandina Beach FL 32035-8029

SMEGAL, THOMAS FRANK, JR. lawyer; b. Eveleth, Minn., June 15, 1935; s. Thomas Frank and Genevieve (Andreachi) S.; m. Susan Jane Stanton, May 28, 1966; children: Thomas Frank, Elizabeth Jane. BS in Chem. Engring., Mich. Technol. U., 1957; JD, George Washington U., 1961. Bar: Va. 1961, D.C. 1961, Calif. 1964, U.S. Supreme Ct. 1976. Patent examiner U.S. Patent Office, Washington, 1957-61; staff patent atty. Shell Devel. Co., San Francisco, 1962-65; patent atty. Townsend and Townsend, 1965-91, mng. ptnr., 1974-89; sr. ptnr. Graham and James, 1992-97; pres., ptnr. Knobbe, Martens, Olson & Bear, 1997—. Mem. U.S. del. to Paris Conv. for Protection of Indsl. Property; mem. adv. com. Ct. of Appeals for Fed. Cir., 1992-96. Contbr. articles to profl. jours. Pres. bd. dirs. Legal Aid Soc. San Francisco, 1982-84, Youth Law Ctr., 1973-84; bd. dirs. Nat. Ctr. for Youth Law, 1978-84, San Francisco Lawyers Com. for Urban Affairs, 1972—, Legal Svcs. for Children, 1980-88; bd. dirs., presdl. nominee Legal Svcs. Corp., 1984-90, 93—. Capt. Chem. Corps, U.S. Army, 1961-62. Recipient St. Thomas More award, 1982. Mem. ABA (chmn. PTC sect. 1990-91, ho. of dels. 1988-2000, mem. standing com. Legal Aid and Indigent Defendants 1991-94, chair sect. officer conf. 1992-94, bd. govs. 1994-97, standing com. on Pro Bono and Pub. Svc. 1997-2001, standing com. on Gavel awards 2001—), Intellectual Property Law Assn. (chmn. nat. coun. 1989), Nat. Inventors Hall of Fame (pres. 1988), Calif. Bar Assn. (v.p. bd. dirs. 1986-87), Am. Patent Law Assn. (pres. 1986), Internat. Assn. Intellectual Property Lawyers (pres. 1995-2001), Bar Assn. San Francisco (pres. 1979), Patent Law Assn. San Francisco (pres. 1974), World Trade Club, Olympic Club, Golden Gate Breakfast Club, Claremont Club (Berkeley). Republican. Roman Catholic. Office: Knobbe Martens Olson & Bear 201 California St Ste 1150 San Francisco CA 94111-5002 Home: 107 King Ave Piedmont CA 94610 E-mail: tsmegal@kmob.com.

SMELT, RONALD, retired aircraft company executive; b. Houghtonle Spring, Durham, Eng., Dec. 4, 1913; came to U.S., 1948, naturalized, 1955; s. Henry Wilson and Florence (Bradburn) S.; m. Marie Anita Collings, Nov. 2, 1940 (dec. May 1964); 1 son, David; m. Jean Stuart, Jan. 15, 1965. BA, King's Coll., Cambridge (Eng.) U., 1935, MA, 1939; PhD, Stanford, 1961. With Royal Aircraft Establishment, 1935-48, chief high speed flight, 1940-45, chief guided weapons dept., 1945-48; dep. chief aeroballistic research dept. USN Ordnance Lab., 1948-50; chief gas dynamics facility ARO, Inc., Tullahoma, Tenn., 1950-57; dir. research and devel. Lockheed Aircraft Corp. (missile systems div.), Sunnyvale, Calif., 1958-59; mgr. Lockheed Aircraft Corp. (Discoverer Satellite system), 1959-60, chief scientist, 1960-62, v.p., gen. mgr. space programs div., 1962-63, v.p., chief scientist, 1963-78. Guggenheim lectr. Internat. Congress Aero. Sci., 1978; Mem. com. on space vehicle aerodynamics NASA, 1965-66, chmn. research adv. com. on space vehicles, 1966-73, chmn. research and tech. adv. council, 1973-77; chmn. tech. adv. bd. Dept. Transp., 1970-74; mem. engring. adv. com. Stanford U., 1988-89; adv. com. NASA-Stanford Ctr. for Turbulence Rsch. Fellow Cambridge Philos. Soc., Royal Aero. Soc. (London), Am. Astronautical Soc., AIAA (hon.; dir.-at-large 1966-68, pres. 1969, 70); mem. Nat. Acad. Engring., Home: PO Box 149 Oakland OR 97462-0149

SMELTZER, MARY SUSAN, pianist, composer; b. Sapulpa, Okla., Sept. 13, 1941; d. Frank Cecil and Mary Margaret (Robertson) S.; MusB (scholar), Oklahoma City U., 1964, MusM magna cum laude, U. So. Calif., 1969; postgrad. (Fulbright scholar) Akademie fur Musik, Vienna, 1969-70; master class with Gregor Piatigorsky, Los Angeles, Rosina Lhevinne, Los Angeles; m. Philip S. Snyder, June 14, 1973. Pvt. tchr. music, Sapulpa, Okla., 1956-62, Los Angeles, 1964-72; instr. piano Oklahoma City U., 1961-64, Holy Name Convent, Los Angeles, 1964-65, Valley Conservatory Music, Studio City, Calif., 1965-66, First Congl. Ch., Los Angeles, 1966-67, Mt. St. Mary's Coll., Los Angeles, 1966-69, 70-72; vis. piano faculty mem. Rice U., Houston, 1972-73; profl. accompanist U. Houston, 1972-73; artist-in-residence, instr. humanities Coll. of Mainland, Texas City, Tex., 1972-79; organist various chs., Okla., Calif., 1957-71; profl. accompanist throughout midwest, 1961-64, Los Angeles area, 1964-72, Houston, 1972—; performed with chamber groups, Los Angeles area, 1964-69, 70-72; Carnegie Recital Hall debut, 1975, European debut Brahmssaal, Vienna; numerous orchestral appearances; composer: Reverie, 1962, Kaleidescope, 1968, Twelve Mood Pictures (variations for piano on theme of Yankee Doodle and the interval sets 1-9-7-6:1-7-7-6), 1975, The Bald Eagle March, 1979, Psalm 121 (for choir and orch.), 1979, An American Tribue For A Royal Marriage, 1982; author: Selected Orchestrations of Poetic Expressions, 1981. Recipient numerous awards including Bloch Young Artist award Ladies Music Club, 1962, award Nat. Fedn. Music Clubs, 1962, Okla. Music Tchrs. Assn., 1962. Fellow Internat. Biog. Assn., Internat. Acad. Poets, Sigma Alpha Iota; mem. Internat. League Women Composers, Am. Women Composers, Nat. Guild Piano Tchrs. (judging staff), Chamber Music Am., Broadcast Music Inc., Pi Kappa Lambda. Democrat. Baptist. Club: Tuesday Musica. Avocations: art, poetry, geneology, medicine. Home: 8102 Tavenor Ln Houston TX 77075-2154

SMERDON, ERNEST THOMAS, engineering educator; b. Ritchey, Mo., Jan. 19, 1930; s. John Erle and Ada (Davidson) S.; m. Joanne Duck, June 9, 1951; children: Thomas, Katherine, Gary. BS in Engring., U. Mo., 1951, MS in Engring., 1956, PhD in Engring., 1959. Registered profl. engr., Ariz. Chmn. dept. agrl. engring. U. Fla., Gainesville, 1968-74, asst. dean for rsch., 1974-76; vice chancellor for acad. affairs U. Tex. System, Austin, 1976-82; dir. Ctr. for Rsch. in Water Resources U. Tex., 1982-88; dean Coll. Engring. and Mines U. Ariz., Tucson, 1988-92, vice provost, dean Engring, 1992-97; sr. edn. assoc. NSF, Arlington, Va., 1997-00; prof. civil engring. and hydrology U. Ariz., Tucson, 2000—01, dean emeritus, 2001—. -mem. bd. sci. and tech. for internat. devel. NRC, 1990-94, mem. com. on plannin and remediation for irrigation-induced water quality problems, 1990-96, chair com. Yucca Mountain peer rev., 1995, mem. com. study of rsch.-doctorate programs in U.S., 1991-95, com. on Missouri River Ecosystem Sci., 1999=2001; others. Editor: Managing Water Related Conflicts: The Engineer's Role, 1989. Mem. Ariz. Gov.'s Sci. and Tech. Coun., Tucson, 1989-98; bd. dirs. Greater Tucson Econ. Coun., Tucson, 1990-95. Recipient Disting. Svc. in Engring. award U. Mo., 1982. Fellow: NAE (peer com. 1986—90, acad. adv. bd. 1989—95, tech. policy options com. 1990—91, chair com. on career-long edn. for engrs. 1997—2000, acad. adv. bd. 1998—99, steering com. on engr. of 2020, policy com. on Engr. of 2020), AAAS, ASCE (hon. Outstanding Svc. award irrigation and drainage divsn. 1988, Royce Tipton award 1989); mem.: Ariz. Soc. Profl. Engrs. (Engr. of Yr. award 1990), Univ. Coun. on Water Resources, Am. Geophys. Union, Am. Soc. Engring. Edn. (chmn., bd. dirs. engring. dean's coun. 1995—97, pres. 1998—99), Am. Water Resources Assn. (Icko Iben award 1989), Am. Soc. Agrl. Engrs., Pi Mu Epsilon, Tau Beta Pi, Phi Kappa Phi, Sigma Xi. Avocations: hiking, golf, scuba diving, painting. Office: U Ariz Rm N521 Tucson AZ 85721-0001

SMEREK, GAY, pharmacist; b. Yonkers, N.Y. d. Samuel and Joy Christine (Wayne) S. BA in Theater Arts, SUNY, Fredonia, 1983; BS in Pharmacy, Albany Coll. Pharmacy, 1995. Registered pharmacist, N.Y., Vt. Pharmacist VA Hosp., Albany, N.Y. Mem. Am. Soc. Health Sys. Pharmacists, Am. Pharm. Assn. Home: 1 Manor Dr Cornwall NY 12518 Office: VA Hosp 43 Holland Ave Albany NY 12208 E-mail: gsmax22@cs.com.

SMERLING, THOMAS ROBERT, think-tank executive; b. Sept. 11, 1949; s. Louis Robert and Beverly Fisher Smerling; m. Reena Miriam Bernards, Aug. 12, 1990 (div.). BA, U. Minn., 1982, postgrad., 1983—84. Adminstrv. asst. Office of Mayor Donald Fraser, Mpls., 1983—85; Bush leadership fellow Am. Enterprise Inst., Washington, 1985—86; sr. cons. Nat. Dem. Inst. for Internat. Affairs, 1987—88; exec. dir. Project Nishma, 1988—97; v.p. Israel Policy Forum, 1997—; dir. Israel Policy Forum Washington Policy Ctr., 1997—. Mem.: Jewish Funders Network (bd. mem. 1999—). Jewish. Avocations: windsurfing, hiking, guitar, piano. Office: Israel Policy Forum Ste 850 1030 15th St NW Washington DC 20005

SMETHERAM, HERBERT EDWIN, management consultant; b. Seattle, Sept. 9, 1934; s. Francis Edwin and Grace Elizabeth (Warner) S.; m. Beverly Joan Heckert, Sept. 7, 1963; children: Alice, Helen, Charles. BA, U. Wash., 1956; diploma, Naval Intelligence Sch., 1962; MA, U. Md., 1971; diploma in Swedish, U.S. Fgn. Svc. Inst., 1978; MBA, Rollins Coll., 1991. Ensign USN, 1956, advanced through grades to capt., 1976; comdr. USS Lind (DD-703), 1971-73; attache to Sweden USN, Stockholm, 1978-81; comdr. Naval Adminstrn. Command, Orlando, Fla., 1981-84; ret. USN, 1984; strategic planner electronics, info. and missiles group Martin Marietta Corp., Orlando, 1985-93; exec. dir. re-use com. Naval Tng. Ctr., 1993-97, mil. base closure cons., 1991-98. Mgmt. cons., ZHA, Inc., 1998—. Mem. ARC Ctrl. Fla.; mem. Ctrl. Fla. coun. USO, Orlando, 1981—93, pres., 1991—93; mem. steering com. U.S. Congressman McCollum for Re-election, 1992—96; mem. U.S. Senator Hawkins Naval Acad. Nominating Com., Orlando, 1982—86, Fla. Gov.'s Def. Reinvestment Task Force, 1992—93; treas. St. Mathews Episcopal Parish, Orlando, 2000—; bd. dirs. Episcopal Diocese Ctrl. Fla., 2002—. Decorated Royal Order of North Star (Sweden). Mem. SAR, Electronics Industry Assn. (requirements com. 1985-93), Nat. Assn. Installation Developers (southeast regional dir. 1996-97, treas. 1996-2000, bd. dirs. 1996-2000), Fla. Def. Alliance, Ret. Officers Assn., Fla. Econ. Devel. Coun., Navy League, Univ. Club of Winter Park, Fla., U.S. Tennis Assn., Fla. Tennis Assn., Army Navy Country Club, Orlando Tennis Ctr., Royal Lawn Tennis Club Stockholm, Winter Park (Fla.) Tennis Ctr., Delta Kappa Epsilon. Republican. Episcopalian. Avocation: tennis. Home: 3985 Lake Mira Dr Orlando FL 32817-1643 E-mail: hesmetheram@msn.com.

SMETHURST, E(DWARD) WILLIAM, JR. brokerage house executive; b. Newark, Apr. 15, 1930; s. Edward William and Helen Lea (Wiener) S.; m. Ludlow Bixby, June 30, 953; children: James, Andrew, Katherine. AB, Amherst Coll., 1952; MBA, Harvard U., 1958. Credit analyst Chase Manhattan Bank, N.Y.C., 1958-60; mgr. securities Irwin Mgmt. Co., Columbus, Ind., 1961-64; ptnr. Wertheim & Co., N.Y.C., 1965-79; sr. v.p. Cyrus J. Lawrence Inc., 1980-87; mng. dir. Wertheim Schroder & Co. Inc., 1988-95; pres., chief investment officer Schroder Wertheim Investment Svcs., 1990-96; chmn., trustee Wertheim Series Trust; retired, 1996; mng. dir. Byram Capital Mgmt., Greenwich, Conn., 2002—. Trustee Mount Holyoke Coll., South Hadley, Mass., 1982—98. Lt. USN, 1952—55. Episcopalian. Home: 861 Bingham Rd Ridgewood NJ 07450-2111 Office: Byram Capital Mgmt 41 West Pitnam Ave Greenwich NY 06830

SMEYAK, GERALD PAUL, telecommunication educator; b. Lakewood, Ohio, Nov. 7, 1940; s. Paul and Mary (Gresko) S.; m. Sylvia Paula Powers, Dec. 16, 1968; 1 child, Stephen Milan. BFA, Ohio U., 1965; MA in Mass Communication, Ohio State U., 1969, PhD in Mass Communication, 1973. Announcer Sta. WHOK FM, Lancaster, Ohio, 1963-64; news reporter/announcer Sta. WCOL AM/FM, Columbus, 1964-65; news reporter/editor Sta. WSEE TV, Erie, Pa., 1965-66; news mgr./producer Sta. WBNS TV, Columbus, Ohio, 1966-70; asst. prof. Eastern Ky. U., Richmond, 1970-73, N. Tex. State U., Denton, 1973-74; assoc. prof. U. Kans., Lawrence, 1974-78; prof. dept. chair U. Fla., Gainesville, 1978-96; dir. Okla. State U. Sch. Journalism and Broadcasting, 1996—; pub. The Daily O'Collegian. Cons. Manhattan, Kans. govt., U. Kans. Med. Tng., Project MAP for Dept. Health, Edn. and Welfare, Fed. U. Maranao, Brazil, Inst. Europeo De Derecho Y Economia, Barcelona, Spain; pub. The Daily O'Collegian, 1996—; workshop presenter Soc. for profl. Journalists. Author: Professional Interviewing, 1980, Broadcast News Writing, 1983, Mass Media Writing: An Introduction, 1997; contbg. author: Guyana, 1982. Served to pvt. U.S. Army, 1959-61, Korea. Mem. Assn. for Edn. in Journalism and Mass Comm., Assn. Schs. Journalism and Mass Comm., Soc. Profl. Journalists. Avocations: sailing, scuba diving. Office: Okla State U Journalism & Broadcasting 206 Paul Miller Stillwater OK 74078-4052 E-mail: smeyak@okstate.edu.

SMIACH, DEBORAH, accountant, educator, consultant; b. Johnstown, Pa., Mar. 10, 1960; d. Frank Raymond and Pearl Lillian (Rudeck) S. BA in Acctg., U. Pitts., Johnstown, 1982; MBA, Katz Grad. Sch. Bus., Pitts., 1989, M of Info. Systems, 1991. CPA Pa., CGFM Va. Staff acct. C.E. Wessel & Co., Johnstown, Pa., 1982-84; sr. acct. Sickler, Reilly & Co., Altoona, 1984-86; assoc. prof. acctg. U. Pitts., Johnstown, 1986—, chmn. dept. bus., 1995—. Cons. Cambria-Somerset Coun. for Health Profls., Johnstown, 1986—; internal inspector Walter Hopkins & Co., Clearfield, Pa., 1995, Wessel & Co., Johnstown, 1992—. Mem. bd. dirs. Bottleworks Ethnic Arts Ctr., Johnstown, Pa., 1993—, Am. Red Cross-Keystone chpt., 1995—; coun. mem. Our Lady of Mount Carmel, South Fork, Pa., 1993-95. Mem. AICPA, Pa. Inst. Cert. Pub. Accts., Pa. Bus. and Profl. Women (dist. 5 chair public relations com. 1993-95, chair woman of the yr. com. 1995-96, chair issues mgmt. 1996-97), Johnstown Bus. and Profl. Women (pres., pres-elect, v.p., treas.) Democrat. Roman Catholic. Avocations: exercising, baking, reading, crafts. Office: U Pitts Johnstown 104 Krebs Hall Johnstown PA 15904

SMICK, SUSAN SCHNEE, tile designer and manufacturer, airline strategic, marketing planner; b. Bklyn., July 12, 1947; d. Henry and Rhoda (Noskin) Schnee; m. Edward Lewis Smick, Feb. 5, 1972 (separated 1994); 1 child, Joshua Henry. BA with honors, C.W. Post Coll., 1970; postgrad., NYU, 1970-71. Cert. tchr., N.Y. Customer svc. and campus rep. Trans World Airlines, N.Y.C., 1966-71, strategic airline mktg. planner, 1971-72, fleet planning analyst, 1972-73; propr. Sailor's Valentine, Chatham, Mass., 1974-76; ednl. and corp. tour developer Crimson Travel, Cambridge, 1977-80; propr., tile designer, mfr. Cape Cod Tile Co., 1986-97; founding ptnr. TileGraphics, Weston, Mass., 1994-97; founding ptnr., tile designer, mfr. Great Am. Tile Works, 1997—. Cons. U.S. Dept. Transp., 1975. Author (ednl. tours) The Flying Classroom, 1977-80; ceramic artist; author mktg. software. Friends of McLean, McLean Hosp., Belmont, Mass., 1997; mem. Mass. Horticulture Soc., 1995—; bd. dirs. Women's Cmty. League of Weston, 1999, chmn. ways and means com., 2000; chmn. of events Pub. Action for the Arts, 1999, adv. bd. mem., 2000. Recipient Howard Gold Polit. Sci. scholarship Howard Gold Meml. Fund, 1965, acad. scholarship C.W. Post Coll., 1967-70, Nat. Profl. Devel. Act fellowship NYU Grad. Sch. Edn. and History, 1970. Mem. Soc. Glass and Ceramic Decorators, Pi Gamma Mu, Phi Beta Kappa. Avocations: fundraising, Am. folk art, interior design, fashion design, horticulture. Home: 89 Ash St Weston MA 02493-1940 Office: Great Am Tile Works PO Box 363 Weston MA 02493-0002 E-mail: ssmick@mediaone.net.

SMIDDY, JOSEPH CHARLES, retired college chancellor; b. Jellico, Tenn., June 20, 1920; s. Joseph F. and Sara Nan (Tye) S.; m. Reba Graham, Sept. 6, 1985; children— Joseph F., Elizabeth Lee. BA, Lincoln Meml. U., 1948, LHD, 1970; MA, Peabody Coll., 1952; LLD, U. Richmond, 1975; LHD, Coll. William and Mary, 1986; DAm, Cumberland Coll., 1993. Tchr. Jonesville High Sch., 1948-51, prin., 1951-52; sec.-treas. Powell Valley Oil Co., Big Stone Gap, Va., 1952-53; prof. biology Clinch Valley Coll., U. Va., Wise, 1953-56, dean, 1956-57, dir., 1957-68, chancellor, 1968-85, chancellor emeritus, 1985—. Mem. Charter Day Award Emory and Henry Coll., 1980, Commonwealth Day awrd James Madison U., 1985. Folk music performer, collector and composer. Trustee Cumberland Coll., Lincoln Meml. U. Served with U.S. Army, 1942—45, PTO. Recipient Laurel Leaves award Appalachian Consortium, 1995, Kanto Ednl. award Wise County, 1995. Mem. Baptist Gen. Assn. Va. (pres. 1974—). Clubs: Masons, Shriners, Kiwanis. Home: Ridgefield Acres Wise VA 24293 Office: PO Box 3160 Wise VA 24293-3160

SMIDT, SEYMOUR, economics educator; b. Chgo., Nov. 2, 1928; s. Joseph and Harriet (Morrison) S.; m. Rita Barbara Liss, Jan. 28, 1951; children— Tamar Rachelle, Stanley Adam. AB, U. Chgo., 1948; MA, 1952, PhD, 1954. Asst. prof. econs. and fin. Cornell U. Johnson Grad. Sch. Mgmt., Ithaca, N.Y., 1956-59, assoc. prof., 1959-65, prof., 1965-78, Nicholas H. Noyes prof., 1978—. Assoc. dir. Instl. Investor Study, SEC, 1969-70; dean faculty of adminstrv. scis. Koç U., Istanbul, Turkey, 1993-95. Author: (with Harold Bierman, Jr.) The Capital Budgeting Decision, 1960, 66, 71, 75, 80, 84, 88, 92 (with others) Management Decision-Making Under Uncertainty, 1969; contbr. articles to profl. jours. Mayor Village of Lansing, N.Y., 1975-81. Served with U.S. Army, 1954-56. Mem. Am. Econ. Assn., Am. Fin. Assn., Fin. Mgmt. Assn. Home: 120 Oakcrest Rd Ithaca NY 14850-1037 Office: Cornell U Johnson Grad Sch Mgmt Ithaca NY 14853-4201

SMIECINSKI-SALKOWSKI, ALICIA, genetic counselor; b. Detroit, Sept. 1, 1961; d. Theodore Benedict and Marian (Stefanka) S.; m. Daniel Joseph Salkowski, Dec. 30, 1988. Assoc. of gen. studies, Macomb Cmty. Coll., Warren, Mich., 1991; BS, Wayne State Univ., 1994, MS in genetic counseling, 1999. Student rsch. asst. dept. physiology Wayne State Univ., Detroit, 1993, student rsch. asst. dept. radiation oncology and cancer, 1993-94; rsch. asst. dept. pathology Detroit Medical Ctr. Univ. Labs., 1996-97; clinical cancer genetic counseling asst. Karmanos Cancer Inst., 1997-98; genetic counselor/study coord. Wayne State Univ., Karmanos Cancer Inst., 1997—, adj. faculty, 1999—. Adj. faculty Wayne State U. Sch. Medicine and March of Dimes Genetics. Contbr. articles to profl. jours. Recipient Presdl. Scholarship award Wayne State UNiv., 1992-94. Mem. Nat. Soc. Genetic Counselors, Am. Soc. Human Genetics, Phi Beta Kappa, Golden Key Honor Soc. Office: Karmanos Cancer Inst Wayne St U Sch of Med-Epidemiol Dept 110 E Warren Ave Detroit MI 48201-1379 Office Fax: 313-831-7806. E-mail: salkowsk@wayne.med.edu.

SMIETANA, WALTER, educational research director; b. New Bedford, Mass., Nov. 8, 1922; s. Stanislaw and Frances (Wojtal) S. AB in Edn., U. Mich., 1948; MS, Boston U., 1956, EdD, 1965; ScD (hon.), U. Mass., Dartmouth, 1975. Cert. tchr., Mich. Tchr. sci. and math. Somerset (Mass.) Pub. Schs., 1948-65; prof. edn. Elmhurst (Ill.) Coll., 1965-69, Alliance Coll., Cambridge Springs, Pa., 1969-87, chmn. divsn. social sci., pres., 1971-72; dir. rsch. SYLLAGENES, New Bedford, 1987—. Liaison Study of Undergrad. Experience in Am., Carnegie Found. for Advancement of Teaching, Alliance Coll., 1984; participant Pa. Dept. Edn. ETS, Tchr. Cert. Test Devel., 1986-87; develop and accredite new tchr. edn. programs, state, regional and nat. levels, 1965-87; develop and evaluate year abroad and exch. programs Alliance Coll./Jagiellonian U., Cracow, Poland in coop. with U.S. Office Edn., 1969-85. Chmn. city com. Rep. Party, New Bedford, 1953-58; mem. citizens adv. com. Heritage State Park, New Bedford, 1989-93; chmn. bd. trustees Inst. Tech., New Bedford, 1963-64; chmn. adv. com. The Rsch. Found., New Bedford, 1962-64. Recipient Cert. of Merit for non-English Lang. Resources Rsch., Yeshiva U., 1981; U.S. Office Edn./ERIC grantee, 1969. Mem. World Future Soc., Inst. for Global Ethics, Nat. Space Soc., Inst. Noetic Scis., Libr. of Congress Assocs. (charter mem.). Republican. Roman Catholic. Avocations: astronomy, photography. Home and Office: 84 Ellen St New Bedford MA 02744-1521

SMIKLE, SHERYL T. manager legal compliance, consultant; b. N.Y.C., Oct. 7, 1959; d. Aubrey Frederick and Harriet Mae (Pondicchello) S. AB in Hispanic Studies, Vassar Coll., 1981; MA in ESL, Hunter Coll., 1984. Trainer Marsh & McClennan, Inc., N.Y.C., 1986-88; tng. cons. Shearson Lehman Hutton, 1988-91; sr. tng. specialist Am. Express TRS Co., Inc., 1991-93, lead tng. cons., 1993-94, mgr. U.S. compliance, 1994—. Bd. mem. Cmty. Vols., Bklyn.; vol. trainer S.H.A.R.E., N.Y.C., 1995, Acad. Fin., N.Y.C., 1991-94. Recipient Mentor of Yr. award Ctrl. Harlem Partnership, Inc., 1993, Ednl. Leadership award Acad. Fin., 1991. Mem. Nat. Soc. for Performance and Instrn. Avocations: reading, theatre-going, travel. Office: Am Express 200 Vesey St New York NY 10285-1000

SMILACK, JERRY D. infectious diseases specialist; b. Mt. Vernon, Ohio, Sept. 7, 1943; BA, Johns Hopkins U., 1965, MD, 1968. Diplomate Am. Bd. Infectious Diseases, Am. Bd. Internal Medicine. Cons. Mayo Clinic Scottsdale, Ariz., 1987—; asst. prof. of internal medicine Mayo Med. Sch., Rochester, Minn., 1987-2001, assoc. prof. medicine, 2001—. Mem. Coccidioidomycosis Study Group; dir. numerous continuing med. edn. courses; spkr. in field. Editor: Medical Extremes: A Book of Records; book reviewer Jour. AMA; contbr. articles to profl. jours. Fellow ACP, Infectious Diseases Soc. of Am.; mem. Ariz. Infectious Diseases Soc. Office: Mayo Clinc Hosp 5E 5777 E Mayo Blvd Phoenix AZ 85054-4502

SMILDE, DAVID ALLEN, sociologist, consultant; b. Bellflower, Calif., Sept. 23, 1966; s. Edward Henry Smilde and Carole Ann Gaiser; m. Maria Natalie Romero, Aug. 15, 1995; children: Yara Bari, Annelies. Ph.D, U. of Chgo., Chicago, IL, 1990—2000. Rsch. assoc. Universidad Ctrl. de Venezeula, Caracas, Venezuela, 1999—2001; us dept. of edn. title vi vis. prof. of latin am. studies U. of Notre Dame, Notre Dame, 2001—01; asst. prof. of sociology U. of Ga., Athens, Ga., 2001—. Consulting Oxford Analytica, Oxford, England, 2000—00. Author (c0-author): (book) Protesta y Cultura en Venezuela: Los Marcos de Acción Colectiva en 1999.; author: (chapter in book) Latin American Religion in Motion, Religious Freedom and Evangelization in Latin America: The Challenge of Religious Pluralism, (journal article) Sociology of Religion, Religion. Fellow Residential Fellowship, Kellogg Inst. for Internat. Studies, U. of Notre Dame, 2001, Internat. Predissertation Fellowship, Social Sci. Rsch. Coun., 1993-94, Fulbright-Hays Doctoral Dissertation Rsch. Abroad Fellowship, US Dept. of Edn., 1995-96; grantee Democracy at Century's End Grant, Consejo Latinoamericano de Ciecias Sociales, 1999-2001. Mem.: Am. Sociol. Assn. (newsletter editor-section on the sociology of religion 2002—). Achievements include research in Dissertation research on Pentecostalism in Caracas; Ethnographic study of street protest in Caracas. Office: University of Georgia Sociology Dept Baldwin Hall Athens GA 30602-1611

SMILES, RONALD, management educator; b. Sunderland, Eng., June 15, 1933; s. Andrew and Margaret (Turns) S.; m. Evelyn Lorraine Webster, Apr. 12, 1959 (div. June 1981); children: Tracy Lynn, Scott Webster, Wendy Louise; m. Linda Janet Miller, June 23, 1990. Assoc. in Bus. Adminstrn., U. Pa., 1968; BSBA, Phila. Coll. Textiles & Sci., 1969; PhD, Calif. Western U., 1977; MA, U. Tex., Arlington, 1985, PhD, 1987. V.p. Liquid Dynamics Corp., Southampton, Pa., 1968-71; pres., gen. mgr. Internat. Election Systems Corp., Burlington, N.J., 1971-76; plant mgr. Rack Engring. Co., Connellsville, Pa., 1977-80; v.p. Ft. Worth (Tex.) Houdaille, 1980-85; chmn. grad. sch. bus. Dallas Bapt. U., 1987-92, prof., 1987—, assoc. dean Coll. Bus., 1996-97. Author: Impact on Legislation of Competition in the Voting Machine Industry, 1978, A Study of Japanese Targeting Practices and U.S. Machine Tool Industry Responses, 1985, Occupational Accident Statistics: An Evaluation of Injury and Illness Incidence Rates, 1987. Mem. Burlington County (N.J.) Selective Svc. Bd., 1974-76. Served with Royal Arty., 1951-53. Mem. Greater Connellsville C. of C. (v.p. 1979-80), Night Watch Honor Soc., Sigma Kappa Phi, Alpha Delta Epsilon (award 1968). Office: Dallas Bapt Univ Dallas TX 75211

SMILEY, ALBERT KEITH, economist, resort executive; b. Mohonk Lake, N.Y., June 30, 1944; s. Keith and Ruth (Happel) S.; m. Nina Sue Feldman, June 29, 1974. BA in Math. magna cum laude, Syracuse U., 1966; PhD in Econs., Princeton U., 1978. Mem. rsch. staff Courant Inst. Math. Scis., N.Y.C., 1967-71; systems analyst Shared Ednl. Computer System, Poughkeepsie, N.Y., 1971-73; rsch. assoc. Ctr. for Energy and Environ. Studies, Princeton (N.J.) U., 1978-80; economist econ. analysis group antitrust div. U.S. Dept. Justice, Washington, 1980-85, dir. rsch., 1986-90; pres., chief exec. officer Smiley Bros., Inc., New Paltz, N.Y., 1990—. Bd. dirs. Smiley Bros., Inc., New Paltz, N.Y., chmn. exec. com., 1987—; trustee Mohonk Mountain House, New Paltz, 1986—; cons. sec.'s outer continental shelf adv. bd. U.S. Dept. Interior, Washington, 1976-77; bus. adv. coun. SUNY; adv. bd. M&T Bank Hudson Vly. Divsn. Author: Competitive Bidding under Uncertainty, 1979. Bd. dirs.

Mohonk Preserve, New Paltz, 1988—, Hudson River Valley Greenway Conservancy, 1993-2000. Sloan Found. grantee, 1976-78; Harold W. Dodds fellow, 1977; award of Merit Antitrust Div., 1985. Mem. Am. Hotel and Motel Assn. (resort com.), Soc. Family Hoteliers, N.Y. State Hospitality and Tourism Assn. (bd. dirs.), Phi Beta Kappa. Mem. Soc. Of Friends. Avocations: hiking, mountain climbing, scuba diving, classical music. Home and Office: Lake Mohonk New Paltz NY 12561

SMILEY, CAROL ANNE, home health administrator, sculptor; b. Cedar Rapids, Iowa, Sept. 11, 1937; d. Ralph Derold and Mary C. Miller; m. Donald Victor Smiley, June 29, 1956 (div. Aug. 1970); children: Donald Victor Jr., Julie Ann, Joseph Charles, Thomas Wayne; m. Douglas Brewster Reed, Aug. 6, 1976 (div. Jan. 1988); 1 child, Brook (dec.). Co-founder, v.p., sec., treas. Anvic Enterprise, Cedar Rapids, Iowa, 1963-70; co-founder, dir. Yankee Horse Trader, Bennington, Vt., 1984-86; organic farmer Solon, Iowa, Argyle, N.Y., 1970-86; fiber sculptor, 1970-86; tchr. Solon (Iowa) H.S., 1973-74; caregiver, coord. Home Health Care and Hospice, Brattleboro, Vt., 1986—. Sculpture shows include Green Mt. Collaborative, Bennington, 1974-78, Woman Art Gallery, N.Y.C., 1977-78, Lincoln Ctr. Group Show, N.Y.C., 1978; exhbns. various group shows. Mem. GOP cen. com. for Johnson County, Iowa, 1971-72. Office: Home Health Care Hospice 80 Clark St Brattleboro VT 05301-6436

SMILEY, DAVID BRUCE, administrative director; b. Pitts., Aug. 6, 1942; s. Alan Gary and Sarah Marie (Frank) S.; m. Eleanor Gayle Houk, Feb. 10, 1966 (dec.); children: Linda Marie, Jonathan David; m. Peggy N. Dannar, June 24, 1995. BS in Edn., Ind. State Coll., 1964; MBA, St. Louis U., 1975. Commd. 2d lt. U.S. Army, 1964, advanced through grades to lt. col., 1981, ret., 1984; dir. adminstrn. Sherman, Wickens, Lysaught & Speck, P.C., Kansas City, Mo., 1984-86, Armstrong Teasdale LLP, Kansas City, 1986—. Decorated Bronze Star medal. Mem. Assn. Legal Adminstrs. (pres. Kansas City chpt. 1990, 99—). Republican. Methodist. Avocations: philately, reading, jogging. Office: Armstrong Teasdale LLP 2345 Grand Blvd Ste 2000 Kansas City MO 64108-2617

SMILEY, FREDERICK MELVIN, education educator, consultant; b. Yuba City, Calif., Apr. 13, 1943; s. Lester Boomer and Claire Leone (DeChesne) S. AA, Yuba Coll., 1963; BA, Chico State U., 1966; MA in Edn., Chapman Coll., 1973, MA in English, 1978, MA in Spl. Edn., 1982; PhD, U. Santa Barbara, 1982; EdD, Okla. State U., 1992. Tchr., coach, v.p. McDermitt (Nev.) High Sch., 1978-80; resource specialist Eagle Mt. (Calif.) High Sch., 1980-81; instr. spl. edn. Mary Stone Sch., San Mateo, Calif., 1981-86; dept. leader Quaezar Corp., Bridgeport, Conn., 1986-87; cons., researcher Multi-functional Resource Ctr., Stillwater and Norman, Okla., 1988-91; prof. edn. Cameron U., Lawton, 1991—. Contbr. articles to profl. jours.; contbg. editor Think!, The Writing Teacher, Okla. Assn. Tchr. Eductors Jour., ATE Jour. Mem. AAUP, Am. Assn. for Teaching and Curriculum, Am. Soc. Curriculum Devel., Am. Coun. Rural Spl. Edn., Am. Assn. Colls. for Tchr. Edn., Coun. for Exceptional Children, Okla. Assn. Tchr. Educators (pres. 2001—), Soc. Educators and Scholars, Kappa Delta Pi, Phi Delta Kappa, Phi Kappa Phi. Democrat. Lutheran. Avocations: reading, writing, racing, tennis, golf. Office: Cameron U 2800 W Gore Blvd Lawton OK 73505-6377 E-mail: freds@cameron.edu.

SMILEY, JANE GRAVES, author, educator; b. L.A., Sept. 26, 1949; d. James La Verne and Frances Nuelle (Graves) S.; m. John Whiston, Sept. 4, 1970 (div.); m. William Silag, May 1, 1978 (div.); children: Phoebe Silag, Lucy Silag; m. Stephen Mark Mortensen, July 25, 1987; 1 child, Axel James Mortensen. BA, Vassar Coll., 1971; MFA, U. Iowa, 1976, MA, PhD, U. Iowa, 1978. Asst. prof. Iowa State U., Ames, 1981-84, assoc. prof., 1984-89, prof., 1989-90, Disting. prof., 1992-96. Vis. asst. prof. U. Iowa, Iowa City, 1981, 87. Author: (fiction) Barn Blind, 1980, At Paradise Gate, 1981 (Friends of American Writers prize 1981), Duplicate Keys, 1984, The Age of Grief, 1987 (Nat. Book Critics Cirle award nomination 1987), The Greenlanders, 1988, Ordinary Love and Goodwill, 1989, A Thousand Acres, 1991 (Pulitzer Prize for fiction 1992, Nat. Book Critics Cirle award 1992, Midland Authors award 1992, Amb. award 1992, Heartland prize 1992), Moo: A Novel, 1995; (non-fiction) Catskill Crafts: Artisans of the Catskill Mountains, 1987, The All-True Travels and Adventures of Lidie Newton, 1998. Grantee Fulbright U.S. Govt., Iceland, 1976-77, NEA, 1978, 87; recipient O. Henry award, 1982, 85, 88. Mem. Author's Guild, Screenwriters Guild. Avocations: cooking, swimming, playing piano, quilting. Office: c/o Molly Friedrich Dept English 708 3rd Ave Fl 23 New York NY 10017-4201*

SMILEY, MARILYNN JEAN, musicologist; b. Columbia City, Ind., June 5, 1932; d. Orla Raymond and Mary Jane (Bailey) S. BS (State scholar), Ball State U., 1954; MusM, Northwestern U., 1958; cert., Ecoles d'Art Americaines, Fontainebleau, France, 1959; PhD (Grad. scholar, Delta Kampa Gamma scholar), U. Ill., 1970. Public sch. music tchr., Logansport, Ind., 1954-61; faculty music dept. SUNY-Oswego, 1961—, Disting. Teaching prof., 1974—, chmn. dept., 1976-81. Presenter papers at confs. Contbr. articles to profl. jours. Bd. dirs. Oswego Opera Theatre, 1978— , Oswego Orch. Soc., 1978— , Penfield Libr. Assocs., 1985—. Recipient Chancellor's award for Excellence in Tchg., 1973; fellow SUNY Rsch. Found. fellow, summers, 1971, 1972, 1974; grantee NEH grantee, 1990—91. Mem.: AAUW (br. coun. rep. dist. III, N.Y. State divsn. 1986—88, br. coun. coord. N.Y. State divsn. 1988—90, pres. Oswego br. 1984—86, N.Y. divsn. area intererst rep. cultural interests 1990—92, grantee 1984, N.Y. divsn. diversity dir. 1993—96, Oswego br. diversity chair 1995—, N.Y. divsn. historian/archivist 2000—), NOW, Oswego County Hist. Soc., Early Music Am., Am. Recorder Soc., Soc. Am. Music (membership chair 1998—), Renaissance Soc. Am., Coll. Music Soc., Music Libr. Assn., Medieval Acad. Am., Am. Musicol. Soc. (chmn. N.Y. chpt. 1975—77, chpt. rep. to AMS coun. 1993—96, bd. dirs. N.Y. State-St. Lawrence chpt. 1993—96, mem. status of women com. 1997—2000), Heritage Found. of Oswego, Phi Kappa Phi, Kappa Delta Pi, Sigma Tau Delta, Sigma Alpha Iota, Pi Kappa Lambda, Delta Phi Alpha, Phi Delta Kappa, Delta Kappa Gamma. Methodist. Office: SUNY Dept Music Oswego NY 13126 E-mail: smiley@oswego.edu.

SMILEY, RICHARD WAYNE, researcher; b. Paso Robles, Calif., Aug. 17, 1943; s. Cecil Wallace and Elenore Louise (Hamm) S.; m. Marilyn Lois Wenning, June 24, 1967; 1 child, Shawn Elizabeth. BSc in Soil Sci., Calif. State Poly. U., San Luis Obispo, 1965; MSc in Soils, Wash. State U., 1969, PhD in Plant Pathology, 1972. Asst. soil scientist Agri. Rsch. Svc., USDA, Pullman, Wash., 1966-69; rsch. asst. dept. plant pathology Wash. State U., 1969-72; soil microbiologist Commonwealth Sci. and Indsl. Rsch. Orgn., Adelaide, Australia, 1972-73; rsch. assoc. dept. plant pathology Cornell U., Ithaca, N.Y., 1973-74, asst. prof., 1975-80, assoc. prof., 1980-85; supt. Columbia Basin Agr. Rsch. Ctr., 1985-2000; prof. Oreg. State U., 1985—. Vis. scientist Plant Rsch. Inst., Victoria Dept. Agr., Melbourne, Australia, 1982-83. Author: Compendium of Turfgrass Diseases, 1983, 2d edit., 1992; contbr. more than 200 articles to profl. jours.; author slide set illustrating diseases of turfgrasses. Postdoctoral fellow NATO, 1972. Fellow Am. Phytopath. Soc. (sr. editor APS Press 1984-87, editor-in-chief 1987-91); mem. Am. Soc. Agronomy, Internat. Turfgrass Soc., Am. Sod Producers Assn. (hon. life), Coun. Agrl. Sci. and Tech., Rotary (pres. Pendleton chpt. 1991-92, Paul Harris fellow 1993). Achievements include discovery of the etiology of a serious disease of turfgrasses, which led to a redefinition of studies and disease processes in turfgrasses. Office: Oreg State U Columbia Basin Agr Rsch Ctr PO Box 370 Pendleton OR 97801-0370 E-mail: richard.smiley@oregonstate.edu.

SMILEY, ROBERT WILLIAM, JR. investment banker; b. Lansing, Mich., Nov. 17, 1943; s. Robert William Sr. and Rebecca Lee (Flint) S. AB in Econs., Stanford U., 1970; postgrad., San Fernando Valley Coll. Law, 1973-75; MBA in Corp. Fin., City U. Los Angeles, 1979; LLB, LaSalle U., 1982. Bar: Calif. 1984. Sr. v.p. mktg. Actuarial Systems Inc., San Jose, Calif., 1972-73; founder, chmn. Benefit Systems Inc., L.A., and SE Nev., 1973-84, Brentwood Square Savs. and Loan, Los Angeles, 1982-84; chmn., CEO The Benefit Capital Cos. Inc., L.A. and S.E. Nev., 1984—. Lectr. U. Calif. Extension, Los Angeles and Berkeley, 1977—; instr. Am. Coll. Life Underwriters. Editor, contbg. author: Employee Stock Ownership Plans: Business Planning, Implementation, Law and Taxation, 1989, 2d edit. 1998; contbg. author: The Handbook of Employee Benefits, 1984, 6th edit., 2000; contbr. articles to profl. jours. Mem. nat. adv. coun., trustee Reason Found., L.A., 1983-91; bd. dirs. Nat. Ctr. for Employee Ownership, Oakland, Calif.; trustee The Employee Ownership Found., Washington. With USN, 1961-64, Vietnam. Recipient Spl. Achievement award Pres.' Commn. on Pension Policy, 1984. Fellow Life Mgmt. Inst.; mem. Employee Stock Ownership Plan Assn. (founder, pres., bd. dirs., lifetime dir.), Assn. for Corp. Growth, Western and SW Pension Confs., Nat. Assn. Bus. Economists, ABA, Calif. Bar Assn. Office: The Benefit Capital Cos Inc PO Box 542 Logandale NV 89021-0542

SMILEY, RONALD MICHAEL, communications executive; b. Phila., Mar. 12, 1949; s. Frank Edward and Regina Ellen (Maquire) S.; m. Kathryn Augusta Giemza, Sept. 16, 1978. BS in Communication, Temple U., 1974. Studio dir. Delaware County Community Coll., Media, Pa., 1974-78; sports producer Sta. WQIQ, Aston, 1978-80; co-founder, v.p. Videosmith, Phila., 1980-83; founder, pres., chief exec. officer RSVP, Inc., 1983-93; pres. Good Day Sunshine Co., Inc., Avalon, N.J., 1988-92; pres., founder Ron Smiley's Visuals in Paradise V, Captiva Island, Fla., 1993-96. Cameraman for CBS Nightly News, CBS Sunday Morning, Entertainment Tonight, Lifestyles of the Rich and Famous, Fox Broadcasting, Walt Disney's Epcot mag.; dir. photography AM Phila., 1982-92; columnist Captiva (Fla.) Current, 1994-96; contbg. writer Sanibel Island Reporter, 1994-96. Mem. NATAS, Internat. TV Assn. (v.p. Phila. chpt. 1985-86). Avocations: sailing, golfing, horticulture, politics, environmental issues.

SMILEY, WYNN RAY, nonprofit corporation executive; b. Danville, Ill., May 18, 1961; s. Arthur Glen and Lois Jean (Lawrence) S. BS in Agriculture Comms., U. Ill., 1983. Asst. prodr. Sta. WCIA-TV, Champaign, Ill., 1982-83, news prodr., 1983-87, gen. assignments reporter, 1987-91, host, anchor news show, 1988-99; founder, owner, pres. Advisory Inc., Indpls., 1989—, CEO, 1997—; dir. communications Alpha Tau Omega Nat. Hqrs., 1991-98. Facilitator Leadershape Inc., Champaign, 1990—. Editor: The Positive Experience, 1992, 96, 2000; pub. Live Life Intentionally!, 1996; prodr. (CD-ROM) Live Life Intentionally!, 1996. Chmn. bd. Am. Cancer Soc., Champaign, 1991-93; bd. dirs., sec. Meadowbrook Cmty. Ch., 1994-98; bd. fraternity affairs, U. Ill., 1993-2002; mem. Grace Cmty. Ch. Mem. Assembly of God. Avocations: running, outdoor ropes course guide. Office: ATO 12th Fl One N Pennsylvania St Indianapolis IN 46204

SMILGIES, DETLEF-MATTHIAS FRIEDRICH, physicist; b. Celle, Germany, May 28, 1960; s. Arno and Edith (Stottmeister) Z.; m. Melanie Stein; 1 child, Maximilian. D in Physics, U. Göttingen and Max-Planck-Inst. für Strömungsforschung, Germany, 1986, Dr.rer.nat, 1991. Postdoctoral AT&T Bell Labs., Brookhaven, 1991-92, Rutgers Univ., New Brunswick, 1992-94, Riso Nat. Lab., Roskilde, Denmark, 1994-96; scientist European Synchrotron Radiation Facility, 1996-2000; with Cornell High Energy Synchrotron Source, 2000—. Recipient Otto Hahn medal Max Planck Gesellschaft, 1991, Feodor Lynen fellowship Alexander von Humboldt Stiftung, 1992. Mem. Deutsche Physikalische Gesellschaft, Am. Physical Soc. Office: Cornell High Energy Synchrotron Source Cornell U Ithaca NY 14853

SMILLIE, DOUGLAS JAMES, lawyer; b. Glen Ridge, N.J., Aug. 16, 1956; s. James and Nancy (Albright) S.; m. Nancy Marie McKenna, Jan. 27, 1990; children: Sara Grace, Jeffrey Douglas, Heather Patricia. BA in Polit. Sci. cum laude, Muhlenberg Coll., 1978; JD, Villanova U., 1982. Bar: Pa. 1982, U.S. Dist. Ct. (ea. dist.) Pa. 1982, U.S. Ct. Appeals (3d cir.) 1983, N.J. 1984, U.S. Dist. Ct. N.J. 1984, U.S. Dist. Ct. (mid. dist.) Pa. 1995. Assoc. Clark, Ladner, Fortenbaugh & Young, Phila., 1982-90, ptnr., 1991-96; dir., shareholder, v.p., chair litigation sect. Fitzpatrick Lentz & Bubba, P.C., Center Valley, 1996—. Lectr. bus. bankruptcy Lehigh-Carbon C.C., 1999. Author: When Worlds Collide: The Impact of the Bankruptcy Stay on Environmental Clean-Up Litigation, 1989, The Absolute Priority Rule: Catch 22 for Reorganizing Closely-Held Businesses, 1992; editor (newsletter) Environ. Impact, 1985—96, Villanova Law Rev.; contbr. articles to profl. jours. Recipient Rev. Joseph Ullman award. Mem. ABA (litigation sect.), Nat. Bus. Inst. (seminar spkr. 1991, 99, 2002), Am. Bankruptcy Inst. (seminar spkr. 1986), Turnaround Mgmt. Assn., Comml. Law League Am. (bankruptcy and insolvency sect., creditors rights sect.), Assn. Comml. Fin. Attys., Robert Morris Assocs. (seminar spkr. 1995), N.J. Bar Assn. (bankruptcy sect., environ. law sect.), Phila. Bar Assn. (Ea. Dist. Bankruptcy Conf.), Lehigh County Bar Assn. Avocation: Second City Troop Rugby Football Club Alumni. Office: Fitzpatrick Lentz & Bubba PO Box 219 Stabler Corp Ctr 4001 Schoolhouse Ln Center Valley PA 18034-0219 also: 301 North Church St Ste 220 Moorestown NJ 08057 Fax: 610-797-6663. E-mail: dsmillie@flblaw.com.

SMINK, MARY JANE, graphic communications technology educator; b. Charlotte, N.C., Feb. 19, 1939; d. Arthur Elmore and Louise (Belue) Moore; m. George Thomas Smink Jr.; children: George Thomas III, Karl Frederich. BS, Winthrop Coll., 1959; MA in Indsl. Arts, Appalachian State U., 1970; EdD in Indsl. Arts, N.C. State U., 1983. Cert. technology edn., N.C. Tchr. Columbia (S.C.) City Schs., 1959-61, Mars City/Adams Twp. Schs., Mars, Pa., 1962-63, Cleveland County Schs., Shelby, N.C., 1964-65, dir. audio visual, 1966-67; coord. adult edn. Wilkes C.C., Wilkesboro, 1967-70; dir. career exploration Wilkes County Schs., 1970-71; tchr. Wake County Schs., Raleigh, 1971-79; cons. N.C. Dept. Pub. Instrn., 1980-90; asst. prof. N.C. A&T State U., Greensboro, 1990—. Articulation adv. com. Guilford Tech. C.C., Greensboro, 1990—. Contbr. articles to profl. jours. Organist Milner Meml. Presbyn. Ch., Raleigh, 1971—; leader Boy Scouts Am., Raleigh, 1973-78. Edn. Profl. Devel. Act fellow, 1980; recipient William Warner Rsch. award Epsilon Pi Tau, 1983, Epsilon Pi Tau Laureate citation N.C. State U., 1987, Award of Distinction, Tech. Student Assn., Inc., 1988, Hall of Fame citation Ednl. Exhibitors Assn. and SHIP, 1995; named State Supr. of Yr., Internat. Tech. Edn. Assn. Coun. of Suprs., 1986. Mem. S.E. Tech. Edn. Assn., N.C. Tech. Edn. Assn. (pres.-elect 1994-95), Internat. Tech. Edn Assn. (Disting. Tech. Educator award 1991, Meritorious Svc. award 1992, pres. bd. 1988), Tech. Student Assn., Inc. (bd. dirs., pres. bd. 1986-87), Nat. Assn. Indsl. Tech. (jour. rev. bd. 1993—), Phi Delta Kappa (capital area chpt.), Phi Kappa Phi. Avocation: model railroading. Home: 5907 S Sharon Dr Raleigh NC 27603-4665 Office: NC A&T State Univ Sch Of Technology Greensboro NC 27411-0001

SMIRAGLIA, RICHARD PAUL, library and information science educator; b. N.Y.C., Mar. 18, 1952; s. Sylvio Carl Smiraglia and Marcia Jane (Hinds) Jacob. BA, Lewis and Clark Coll., 1973; MLS, Ind. U., 1974; PhD, U. Chgo., 1992; MDiv, The Gen. Theol. Sem., 1997. Ordained deacon, 1997, as priest, 1998, Episcopal Ch. Asst. music catalog libr. U. Ill., Urbana, 1974-77, music catalog libr., 1977-86; asst. prof. Columbia U., N.Y.C., 1986-93; assoc. prof. L.I. U., Brookville, N.Y., 1993-98, prof., 1998—; asst. priest Trinity Meml. Episcopal Ch., Phila., 1997-99, St. Mary's Ch. Hamilton Village, Phila., 1999-2000; priest in charge St. Mark's Ch., Frankford, Phila., 2000—. Panelist NEH, Washington, 1989; cons. Smithsonian Instn., Washington, 1988, N.Y. Hist. Soc., N.Y.C., 1991, Kurt Weill Found., N.Y.C., 1993-94. Author: Music Cataloging, 1989, Nature of the Work, 2001; editor: Describing Archival Materials, 1990, Origin, Content and Future of AACR2, 1992, Describing Music Materials, 1997, (jour.) Libr. Resources and Tech. Svcs., 1991-96. Libr. & Info. Sci. rsch. grantee Online Computer Libr. Ctr., 1993. Mem. ALA, Am. Soc. for Info. Sci., Assn. for Libr. and Info. Sci. Edn. Democrat. Office: L I U Palmer Sch Libr & Info Sci Greenvale NY 11548 E-mail: Richard.Smiraglia@liu.edu.

SMIRNOV, ALEXEI VLADIMIROVICH, research scientist, consultant; s. Vladimir Fedorovich Smirnov and Iraida Izmailovna Smirnova; m. Svetlana Georgievna Kadysheva; children: Ivan, Anna Smirnova, Ilya, Sergey, Anastasia Smirnova. Masters cum laude(hon.) , Moscow Engring. Physics Inst., 1982, postgrad., 1985; PhD, Supreme Certifying Com., 1986. Tchr., lectr. math. Moscow Inst. Radio-Electronics and Automatics, 1990—91; reviewer dissertations and projects Russian Rsch. Ctr. Kurchatov Inst., 1992—98; IBM network product mgr. UNIT Group Internat., 1995—96; cons. head analytical dept. GI Cons., 1996—99; patent expert Patent Inst., 1998—99; tech. reviewer manuscripts DULY Rsch. Inc., Rancho Palos Verdes, Calif., 2001—02. Contbr. over 100 articles to profl. jours. Trade union mgr. dept. Russian Rsch. Ctr. Kurchatov Inst., Moscow, 1986—90. Named Winner contest Young Scientists and Engrs.-Rschrs., I.V. Kurchatov Inst. Atomic Energy, 1990; recipient prize Best Engring. Devel., Sci. Coun. Russian Rsch. Ctr., Kurchatov Inst., 1995; grantee, Internat. Sci. Found., Soros Found., 1993, 1994, 1995. Mem.: 1.United Inventors Association UIAUSA, American Physical Society APS. Achievements include invention of section of resonant accelerator of charged particles, system for waveguide cooling, method for determination of radio-frequency parameters of accelerating structures; linear electron accelerator with RF-energy compression, planar electromagnetic undulator, linear accelerator of electrons with RF energy compression and an RF device. Home: 1934 Trudie Dr Rancho Palos Verdes CA 90275 Home Fax: 775-248-4757.

SMISKO, NICHOLAS RICHARD, bishop, educator; b. Perth Amboy, N.J., Feb. 23, 1936; s. Andrew and Anna (Totin) S. BTh, Christ the Saviour Sem., 1959; BA, U. Youngstown, 1961; Lic. in Theology, Halki (Greece) Sch. Theology, 1965. Ordained priest Carpatho-Russian Orthodox Greek Cath. Ch., 1959; elevated to rank of met. bishop, 1997. Pastorate Sts. Peter and Paul Ch., Windber, Pa., 1959-62; prefect of discipline Christ the Saviour Sem., Johnstown, 1963-65; pastor Sts. Peter and Paul Ch., Homer City, 1965-71, St. Michael's Ch., Clymer, 1971-72; pastorate St. Nicholas Ch., N.Y.C., 1972-77; abbot Monastery of the Annunciation, Tuxedo Park, N.Y., 1978-83; bishop of Amissos Carpatho-Russian Orthodox Diocese, 1983—. Mem. del. Ecumenical Patriarchate World Coun. Chs. 6th Gen. Assembly, Vancouver, B.C., Can.; mem. standing conf. Canonical Orthodox Bishops in Ams.; active Orthodox-Cath. Consultation of Hierarchs. Mem. Halki Alumni Assn. Am., Christ the Saviour Sem. Alumni Assn., Am. Soc. Constantinople. Home and Office: 312 Garfield St Johnstown PA 15906-2122

SMISKO, RICHARD G. See NICHOLAS

SMIST, JULIANNE MARIE, chemist, educator; b. Springfield, Mass., Aug. 14, 1950; d. Abel Alves and Mary Gloria DaSilva; m. Stephen Francis Smist, June 29, 1974; 1 child, Jennifer. BA, Elms Coll., 1972; MS, Boston Coll., 1974; PhD, U. Conn., 1996. Cert. tchr. chemistry, math., Mass. Tchr. chemistry Cathedral H.S., Springfield, 1975-77; instr. chemistry Am. Internat. Coll., 1977-79, Springfield Coll., Springfield, 1981-88, asst. prof. to assoc. prof., 1988—. Author: Experiments for Chemistry Survey, 2000. Mem. parish coun. Sacred Heart Ch., Feeding Hills, Mass., 1998—. Gelbrich fellow U. Conn., 1996. Mem. Am. Chem. Soc., Nat. Sci. Tchrs. Assn., Am. Ednl. Rsch. Found., Beta Beta Beta. Avocation: singing. Office: Springfield Coll Bemis Hall Springfield MA 01109 E-mail: jsmist@spfldcol.edu.

SMIT, EILEEN MARQUARDT, nursing educator; b. Clintonville, Wis., May 26, 1947; d. Lester and Elaine Marquardt; m. James R. Smit; children: Michael, Timothy, Soo-Hyung. BSN, U. Wis., 1969, MSN, 1977. RN, Mich. Vol. VISTA, Galveston, Tex., 1969-70; staff nurse Univ. Wis. Hosp., 1971-73, 79-80, Forsyth Co. Mental Health Clinic, Winston-Salem, N.C., 1973-74; prof. nursing No. Mich. U., Marquette, 1980—. Contbr. articles to nursing jours., including Am. Jour. Maternal Child Nursing, Jour. Psychosocial Nursing and Mental Health Svcs. Recipient Disting. Faculty award Mich. Assn. Governing Bds., 2000. Mem. AAUP, Sigma Theta Tau. Mem. Soc. Of Friends. Office: No Mich U Dept Nursing 1401 Presque Isle Ave Marquette MI 49855 Fax: 906-227-1658. E-mail: esmit@nmu.edu.

SMIT, PAULA FRANCINE, research scientist; d. Paul Houhoulis and Frances Theres Belyea; m. Leonard Peter Smit Jr., Nov. 18, 2000. BS, Eckerd Coll., 1989; MA, U. Ga., 1994. Remote sensing specialist JW Jones Ecol. Rsch. Ctr., Newton, Ga., 1993—98; assoc. rsch. scientist Fla. Marine Rsch. Inst., Saint Petersburg, 1998—2000; sci. data specialist USGS EROS Data Ctr., Sioux Falls, SD, 2000—. Contbr. articles to profl. jours. Grantee monitoring Fla. Everglades Restoration Lands, U.S. Fish and Wildlife Service, 1999—2000. Mem.: Am. Soc. Photogrammetry and Remote Sensing (Best Sci. Paper in Remote Sensing award 1998), Phi Kappa Phi. Avocations: art, jewelry making, reading, boating, nature. Office: L-3 Comm Analytics Corp USGS EROS Data Ctr SSB Sioux Falls SD 57198 Business E-Mail: smit@usgs.gov.

SMITH, A. ROBERT, editor, author; b. York, Pa., Feb. 13, 1925; s. Arthur R. and Inez (Dunnick) S.; m. Yvonne Franklin, 1945 (div. 1965); 1 child, Dana C.; m. Elizabeth McDowell Morgan, 1967 (div. 1988); children: Philip S. Morgan IV, Edward A. M. Morgan, Elizabeth A. Morgan; m. Jane Dreifus, 1993 (dec. 1999). BS, Juniata Coll., 1950; postgrad., George Washington U., 1950. Reporter Huntingdon (Pa.) Daily News, 1947, Evening Star, Washington, 1950; Washington corr. Eugene (Oreg.) Register-Guard, 1951-78, Portland Oregonian, 1952-72, King Broadcasting, 1976-78; assoc. editor Virginian-Pilot, Norfolk, 1978-83; editor Venture Inward, Assn. Rsch. and Enlightenment mag., Virginia Beach, Va., 1984—. Author: The Tiger in the Senate, 1962, Hugh Lynn Cayce: About My Father's Business, 1988, The Lost Memoirs of Edgar Cayce, 1997, Misdiagnosed: Was My Wife a Casualty of America's Medical Cold War?, 2001; co-author: (with Eric Sevareid and Fred J. Maroon) Washington: Magnificent Capital, 1965; (with James V. Giles) An American Rape, 1975. With USNR, 1943-46, PTO. Office: ARE 67th And Atlantic Ave Virginia Beach VA 23451 E-mail: abob@infi.net.

SMITH, AARON, retired research director, clinical psychologist; b. Boston, Nov. 3, 1930; s. Harry and Anne (Gilgoff) S.; m. Sept. 7, 1952 (div.); children: Naomi E., Jeffrey O., David G., Andrew H.; m. D. Sharon Casey, Jan. 7, 1972. AB, Brown U., 1952; PhD, U. Ill., 1958. Co-dir. N.E. Psychol. Clinic, Phila., 1959-75; dir. rsch. Haverford State Hosp., Pa., 1962-73, asst. hosp. dir., 1973-75; assoc. rsch. prof. U. Nev., Reno, 1975-2001; dir. rsch. VA Med. Ctr., 1975-2001; exec. dir. Sierra Biomed. Rsch. Corp., 1989-2001. Chmn. Nev. Legislature Mental Health Task Force, Carson City, 1978; sci. adviser Gov.'s Com. on Radiation Effects, Carson City, 1979-82. Co-author: Anti-depressant Drug Studies 1956-66, 1969, Medications and Emotional Illness, 1976; co-editor: Goal Attainment Scaling: Application, Theory, and Measurement, 1994; contbr. chpts. to books and articles to profl. jours. Grantee Squibb Inst. med. Rsch., 1965-69, NIMH, 1965-69, Smith Kline & French Labs., 1968-69, VA Health Svcs. Rsch., 1976-93. Mem. APA, We. Psychol. Assn., Gerontol. Soc. Am., Assn. Health Svcs. Rsch. Home: 1516 Diamond Country Dr Reno NV 89521-6149

SMITH, ABBIE OLIVER, college administrator, educator; b. Augusta, Ga., Jan. 31, 1931; d. Rowland Sheppard and Abigail Seabrook (Hanahan) Oliver; m. William Parkhurst Smith, Jr., July 2, 1953; children: William Parkhurst Smith, III, Oliver Hamilton. BS, George Washington U., 1953, MEd, 1958, EdDin Higher Edn., 1986. Tchr. St. Mary's Acad., Monroe, Mich., 1954-55; tchr., coach Washington-Lee H.S., Arlington, Va., 1955-58; homemaker, cmty. vol. Bethesda, Md., 1959-64; asst. professorial lectr. George Washington U., Washington, 1965-69, adminstr. continuing edn., 1969-80, asst. dean, dir., 1981-89, acting dean divsn. continuing edn., 1989-93, asst. v.p., asst. to dean institutional advancement, 1993—. Panelist TV series WETA, Washington; mem. exec. bd., newsletter editor Tng. Officers Conf., 1989—, chair charter expansion 1992—. Co-author: (workbook) Developing New Horizons for Women, 1975, Manual for Counselors for Developing New Horizons for Women, 1975. Mem. adv. bd. Washington Bd. Trade, 1975-77, women's branch adv. bd. State Nat. Bank, Bethesda, Md., 1978-81; collegiate adv. bd. Episcopal Diocese of Washington, 1977-79. Recipient Leadership in Adult Edn. award, 1976, GW award for outstanding contbn. to univ. life Office of GW Pres., 1991, Washington Women of Achievement, Washington Edn. TV Assn., 1980. Mem. Nat. U. Continuing Edn. Assn. (awards chair divsn. women's edn. 1977-78, nat. chair 1977-78, chair-elect divsn. part-time students program 1984-86, nat. chair 1984-86, chair coun. human resources 1985-86, nat. spl. com. on couns. and divsn. 1984-86, nat. exec. bd. 1984-86, nat. bd. dirs. 1984-98, nat. charters and bylaws coms. 1987-89, sec.-elect divsn. cert. and nontraditional degree programs 1987-89, chair-elect 1989-90, nat. chair 1990-91, nat. ann. planning coms. 1987, 92, sec. region II 1989-90, chair-elect, ann. conf. chair, single host instn. ann. conf. region II 1990-91, chair region II 1991-92, awards com. chair 1992, Walton S. Bittner Svc. Citation 1994, hon. mention for program catalog nat. divsn. mktg. 1988, Floyd B. Fisher Leadership award 1996), Phi Delta Kappa Internat. (G.W. chpt., v.p. for programs 1995-96, pres. 1996-97, newsletter editor 1977—, Newsletter Award Merit 1998-99, Outstanding Newsletter award 1999-2000, 2000-01). Democrat. Episcopalian. Avocations: writing, painting, swimming, dancing, traveling. Home: 3751 Jocelyn St NW Washington DC 20015-1836 Office: George Washington U 2134 G St NW Washington DC 20037-2797 E-mail: asmith@gwu.edu.

SMITH, ADAM See GOODMAN, GEORGE JEROME WALDO

SMITH, ADELINE MERCER, retired librarian; b. Saratoga Springs, N.Y., May 28, 1915; d. Thomas Elwood and Hazel Belle (Farrington) Mercer; m. Jack Monroe Smith, Mar. 3, 1946; 1 child, Jeffrey Monroe. BS in Libr. Sci., N.Y. State Coll. Tchrs., 1937; MS in Libr. Sci., SUNY, Albany, 1968. Designer, sample maker Van Raalte Co., Ladies Lingerie, Saratoga Springs, 1939-63; high sch. libr. Hoosic Valley Ctrl. Sch., Schaghticoke, N.Y., 1964-78; dir. dist. libr. svcs. Hoosic Valley Ctrl. Sch. Dist., 1975-78; practicing retired libr., cataloger James L. Hamner Pub. Libr., Amelia, Va., 1989—. Mem. adv. bd. Index to Free Periodicals, Ann Arbor, Mich., 1977—. Author: Free Magazines for Libraries, 1980, 2nd edit., 1985; co-author: Free Magazines for Libraries, 3d edit., 1989, 4th edit., 1994; contbr. articles to libr. jours., mags. Mem. ALA, Nat. Ret. Tchrs. Assn., N.Y. State United Tchrs., Va. Ret. Tchrs. Assn., Beta Phi Mu. Baptist. Avocations: library volunteer, genealogy, gardening, needlework. Home: 8581 Greenes Rd Amelia Court House VA 23002-3522

SMITH, ADRIAN DEVAUN, architect; b. Chgo., Aug. 19, 1944; s. Alfred D. and Hazel (Davis) S.; m. Nancy L. Smith, Aug. 17, 1968; children: Katherine, Jason. Student, Tex. A&M U., 1962-66; BArch, U. Ill., Chgo., 1969. Registered architect, Ill., Ohio, N.J., N.Y., Mass., Iowa, Md., Conn., D.C., Fla., Ind., Mo., R.I., Tex. Design ptnr. Skidmore, Owings, & Merrill, Chgo., 1967—, ptnr., 1980—, CEO, 1994-96. Vis. faculty Sch. Architecture, U. Ill., Chgo., 1984; chmn. U. Ill. Sch. Archtl. Alumni Assn., AIA Jury on Inst. Honors; adv. jury AIA gold metal and architecture firm award, 2000; chmn. Skidmore Owings Merrill Found., 1990-95; pres. Chgo. Ctrl. Area, 1998-99; bd. dirs. Greater State Street Coun.. trustee; bd. govs. Sch. Art Inst. Chgo., 1999—; cons. and lectr. in field. Designer numerous projects including Jin Mao Tower (World's Tallest Mixed-Use Project), Shanghai, China (Nat. AIA award for interiors 2000), Banco de Occidente, Guatemala City (CCAIA Interior Architecture award 1981, NAIA Honor award 1982), United Gulf Bank, Manama, Bahrain (Progressive Architecture award 1984, CCAIA Disting. Bldg. award 1988, NAIA Honor award 1988, CCAIA Disting. Detail Honor award 1989), 222 N. LaSalle, Chgo., (Disting. Bldg. award CCAIA 1988), Art Inst. Chgo. 2d Fl. Galleries (CCAIA Disting. Bldg. award 1987), Rowes Wharf, Boston (Build Am. award 1988, Build Mass. award 1989, ULI award 1989, PCI Profl. Design award 1989, CCAIA Hon. award 1998, Nat. AIA Honor award 1994), AT&T Corp. Ctr., Chgo. (recipient Gold Metal Ill. Ind. Masonry award), NBC Tower (Chgo. Sun Times Bldg. of Yr. award 1989, CCAIA Disting. Bldg. award 1990, PCI Design award 1989), 75 State St. Boston (Archtl. Woodwork Inst. award 1989, Nat. Comml. Builder's Coun. Merit award 1990, Bldg. Stone Inst. Tucker Archtl. award 1990), Arthur Anderson Tng. Ctr. (Masonry award 1988), St. Charles, Ill., USG Hdqs., Chgo., Heller Internat. Tower, Chgo., State St. Renovation (spl. achievement award 1997, AIA honor award urban design 1998) designer numerous other fgn. projects including: Monterey Cultural Ctr., Mex., 1978; hdqurs. Banco de Occidente, Guatemala City, 1978 (AIA Nat. Honor award Bus. Interior Design award Guatemala 1981, CCAIA Interior Architecture award 1982, NAI A Honor award), Canary Wharf Fin. Ctr., London, Eng., 1988, 10 Ludgate (CCAIA 1994 Honor award), 100 Ludgate, London, 1992, Aramco Hdqs. Dharan Saudi Arabia, Tower Palace III, Seoul, Korea, 7 South Dearborn Tower, Chgo. (world's tallest), McGraw Hill European Headquarters, Canary Wharf (DS4), CSFB European Headquarters, Canary Wharf (DSI), Morgan Stanley Headquarters for Europe (HQI), Canary Wharf; contbr. articles to profl. jours.; subject numerous pubs. in architecture. Mem. com. Task Force for New City Plan, Chgo., Light Up Chgo., Cen. Area Com. Task Force Chgo.; chmn. Senator Richard A. Newhouse Bldg. Competition Jury, 1982, Progressive Architecture Design Jury, 1985; bd. dirs. State St. Coun. Recipient U. Ill. Alumni Achievement award. Fellow AIA (mem. Young Architects Award Design July, 1987, Mich. Jury 1988, Disting. Bldg. award 1990), Royal Inst. Brit. Architects, Archtl. Registration Coun., U.K., Nat. Coun. Archtl. Registration Bds., Architecture Soc. of Art Inst. Chgo., Chgo. Arch. Found. (bd. dirs.), Chgo. Archtl. Club, Urban Land Found. (bd. trustees) University Club, Arts Club. Home: 1100 W Summerfield Dr Lake Forest IL 60045-1545 Office: Skidmore Owings & Merrill LLP 224 S Michigan Ave Ste 1000 Chicago IL 60604-2592

SMITH, AGNES MONROE, history educator; b. Hiram, Ohio, Aug. 8, 1920; d. Bernie Alfred and Joyce (Messenger) Monroe; m. Stanley Blair Smith; children: David, Doris, Darl, Diane. BA, Hiram Coll., 1940; MA, W.Va. U., 1945; PhD, Western Res. U., 1966. Social sci. tchr. Freedom (Ohio) High Sch., 1940-44; instr. of history W.Va. U., Morgantown, 1945; instr. of social sci. Hiram Coll., 1946; inst. history and social sci. Youngstown (Ohio) State U., 1964-66, asst. prof. to prof. of history, 1966-84, prof. history emeritus, 1984—; vis. prof. history Hiram Coll., 1988-90. Co-editor: Bourgeois, Sans Culottes and other Frenchmen, 1981; contbr. articles to profl. jours. Mem. Ohio Acad. History, Delta Kappa Gamma, Phi Alpha Theta, Pi Gamma Mu. Mem. Christian Ch. (Disciples Of Christ). Home: 16759 Main Market Rd West Farmington OH 44491-9608

SMITH, AKILI, professional football player; b. Aug. 21, 1975; Student, U. Oreg. Football player Cin. Bengals, 1999—. Avocations: weightlifting, Bible reading. Office: Cin Bengals 1 Paul Brown Stadium Cincinnati OH 45202*

SMITH, AL, JR. air traffic controller, retired; b. Quakertown, Pa., July 21, 1934; s. Albert L. and Anna H. Smith; m. Miriam A. Smith, June 17, 1961; children: Scott N., Sean A., Susan J. Draftsman U.S. Gauge Co., Sellersville, Pa., 1952-55; baggage handler Capitol Airlines, Phila., 1958-61; air traffic trainee FAA, Oberlin, Ohio, 1961-68, 70-74, tower air traffic contr. Morristown, N.J., 1968-70, Richmond Heights, Ohio, 1974-81, tower air traffic mgr., 1981, ctr. air traffic contr. Oberlin, 1981-84, tower air traffic mgr. Cleve., 1984-89; trainer air traffic control Sys. Requirements and Svc. Agy., Oberlin, 1989-92; owner, operator Duraclean Carpet & Upholstery Cleaning, Vermilion, Ohio, 1974-86; ret., 1992. Laymin. UCC Congrl., Vermilion, 1979—; mentor to boys at risk Cleve. Pub. Sch., 1998—; mem. essay com. VFW, Vermilion, 1999-2000; developer tng. program for Acolyte Tng. Program Recipient Scoutmaster Key Boy Scouts Am., 1980, Dist. award of Merit, 1988, Silver Beaver, 1999. Avocations: fly fishing, camping, collecting postcards. Home: 4719 Colonial Ct Vermilion OH 44089-3143 E-mail: almsmith@bright.net.

SMITH, AL JACKSON, JR. environmental engineer, lawyer; b. Meridian, Miss., Aug. 26, 1935; s. Al Jackson and Katherine (Felker) S.; m. Patricia Scruggs, Dec. 20, 1957; children: Johnny, Vicki, Katherine. BSCE, Miss. State U., 1958; MS in Environ. Engring., Vanderbilt U., 1969; JD, Atlanta Coll. Law, 1977; LLM, Woodrow Wilson Coll., 1980. Bar: Ga. 1979, U.S. Dist. Ct. (no. dist.) Ga. 1979, U.S. Ct. Appeals (11th cir.). Engr. City of Vicksburg, Miss., 1964-66; dir. br. emergency Region IV EPA, Atlanta, 1966-86, dep. dir. div. water, 1986-90; counsel Hurt, Richardson, Todd, Garner and Caddenhead, 1990-93, McRae Secrest & Fox, Atlanta, 1993; pvt. cons., 1994-95; dir. engring. Kiber Environ. Svcs., Inc., Atlanta, 1995—. Solicitor City of Stockbridge, Ga., 1984-87; lectr. Nat. Emergency Tng. Ctr., Emmitsburg, Md. 1980—; city judge Locust Grove, Ga., 1988—. Author: Managing Hazardous Substance Accidents, 1981; Oil Pollution Control, 1973; contbg. author: Hazardous Materials Handbook, 1982; contbr. articles to profl. jours. Served to capt. USAR, 1958-70. Mem. Internat. Assn. Chiefs Police, Ga. Bar Assn., N.C. Assn. Fire Chiefs. Baptist. Home: 1550 S Ola Rd Locust Grove GA 30248-2239

SMITH, ALAN EDWARD, genetic research facility administrator; b. Fareham, Eng., Sept. 9, 1945; came to U.S., 1984; s. William George and Hilda Annie (Fidler) S.; m. Eva Ursula Paucha, Nov. 30, 1979 (dec. 1988); children: Stephen Edward, Alexandera Hannah. BA, U. Cambridge, 1967, PhD, 1970. Mem. sci. staff Imperial Cancer Rsch. Found., London, 1972-80; head biochemistry div. Nat. Inst. Med. Rsch. Mill Hill, 1980-84; v.p., sci. dir. Integrated Genetics, Inc., Farmington, Mass., 1984—. Home: 1 Mill St Dover MA 02030-2241 Office: Genzyme Corp One Kendall Square Cambridge MA 02139-1562

SMITH, ALAN JAY, computer science educator, consultant; b. N.Y.C., Apr. 10, 1949; s. Harry and Elsie Smith. SB, MIT, 1971; MS, Stanford (Calif.) U., 1973, PhD in Computer Sci., 1974. From asst. prof. to full prof. U. Calif., Berkeley, 1974—; assoc. editor ACM Trans. on Computers Systems, 1982-93. Vice-chmn. elec. engring. & computer sci. dept. U. Calif., Berkeley, 1982-84; nat. lectr. ACM, 1985-86; mem. editorial bd. Jour. Microprocessors and Microsystems, 1988—; subject area editor Jour. Parallel and Distbn. Computing, 1989—; mem. IFIP working group 7.3.; program chmn. Sigmetrics 89, Performance 1989, Hot Chips Symposium, 1990, 94, 97. Fellow: AAAS, IEEE (disting. visitor 1986—87), Assn. for Computing Machinery (chmn. spl. interest group on computer architecture 1991—93, chmn. spl. interest group on ops. sys. 1983—87, bd. dirs. spl. interest group on performance evaluation 1989—89, bd. dirs. spl. interest group on computer architecture 1993—, nat. lectr. 1985—86); mem.: Computer Measurement Group. Office: U Calif Dept Computer Sci Berkeley CA 94720-1776

SMITH, ALBERT ALOYSIUS, JR. electrical engineer, consultant; b. Yonkers, N.Y., Dec. 2, 1935; s. Albert Aloysius and Jean Mary (Misiewicz) S.; m. Rosemarie Torricelli, Apr. 4, 1964 (dec. 1982); children: Denise, Matthew. BSEE, Milw. Sch. Engring., 1961; MSEE, NYU, 1964. Staff engr. Adler/Westrex, New Rochelle, N.Y., 1961-64; adv. engr. IBM, Kingston, 1964-78, sr. engr. Poughkeepsie, 1978-85, Kingston, 1985-91; cons., 1991—. Author: Coupling of External Electromagnetic Fields to Transmission Lines, 1977, Measuring the Radio Frequency Environment, 1985, Radio Frequency Principles and Applications, 1998. Com. chmn. Woodstock Boy Scout Troop 34, 1978-79; com. chmn. Woodtwock Cub Pack 34, 1976-78. Served with USN, 1953-56. Recipient Outstanding Alumnus award Milw. Sch. Engring., 1981; Invention Achievement awards IBM, 1979, 90, Div. award, 1981. Fellow IEEE (tech. com. on electromagnetic environments, assoc. editor Trans. on EMC); mem. Am. Nat. Standards Com. Roman Catholic. Home: 11 Streamside Ter Woodstock NY 12498-1521

SMITH, ALBERT CARL, physician, scientist; b. L.A., Sept. 13, 1934; s. Salmon and Sadie (Lewis) S.; m. Mary Ellen Reeley Dec. 31, 1997; children: Connie Powell, Shana Smith, John Reeley, Christopher Reeley, Chelsea Smith. BA in Zoology, UCLA, 1956; PhD Biol. Scis., U. Calif., Irvine, 1967; MD, U. Hawaii, 1975. Diplomate Nat. Bd. Med. Examiners, Am. Bd. Pathology. Rsch. assoc., instr. dept. population and environ. biology U. Calif., Irvine, 1966-67; assoc. prof. biology U. Hawaii, Hilo, 1967-73, rsch. fellow, 1975-76, resident in clin. pathology, 1975-79; sr. scientist Oceanic Inst., Waimanalo, Hawaii, 1977-79; chief clin. lab. VA Med. Ctr., Gainesville, Fla., 1980-85, chief clin. pathology Bay Pines, 1985-91; asst. prof. pathology Coll. of Medicine U. Fla., Gainesville, 1980-85, adj. prof. divsn. comparative medicine Coll. Vet. Medicine, 1982-2001; pvt. practice Panama City, Fla., 1993—; courtesy prof. dept. oceanography Fla. State U., Tallahassee, 1998—; prof. dept. sci. Barry U., Tallahassee Ctr., Panama City, 2001—. Chief cons. Hawaii Biomarine, Honolulu, 1973-80; sr. scientist Oceanic Inst., Waimanalo, Hawaii, 1977-79; dir. Med. Labs. Hawaii, Honolulu, 1979-80; clin. pathology cons. Sunland Ctr., Gainesville, Fla., 1981-85; adj. prof. Vet. Coll., U. Fla., Gainesville, 1987—; courtesy prof. dept. marine sci. U. South Fla., St. Petersburg, 1987—; dean of sci. Saba U. Sch. Medicine, Dutch Netherland Antilles, 1999-2000, dir. Ocean Therapy Inst., Biophilia Found., Brussels, 2000-01; site team mem. NIH. Author: Treasures From the Sea for Medicine, 2000, The Aquatic Roots of Human Pathology; contbr. chpts. to books, more than 90 articles to profl. jours. Fellow Coll. Am. Pathologists; mem. Internat. Soc. Aquatic Medicine (hon.), Soc. for Invertebrate Pathology (charter), Am. Longevity Soc. (hon.), AAAS, Internat. Soc. Devel. and Comparative Immunology, Fla. Med. Assn., Bays Med. Soc., Saba Marine Biol. Rsch. Found., Island Saba (chmn. bd. 1999-2000). Avocations: scuba diving, saxaphone player. Fax: 850-233-9683.

SMITH, ALBERT CROMWELL, JR. investments consultant; b. Norfolk, Va., Dec. 6, 1925; s. Albert Cromwell and Georgie (Foreman) S.; m. Laura Thaxton, Oct. 25, 1952; children: Albert, Elizabeth, Laura. BSCE, Va. Mil. Inst., 1949; MS in Govtl. Adminstrn., George Washington U., 1965; MBA, Pepperdine U., 1975; PhD in Bus. Adminstrn., LaSalle U., 1994. Enlisted man USMC, 1944, advanced through grades to col., 1970, comdr. inf. platoons, cos., landing force; assigned to staffs, U.K. Joint Force, U.S. Sec. Navy, Brit. Staff Coll., Marine Staff Coll., U.K. Staff Coll. and Latimer Staff Coll.; advisor, analyst amphibious sys. USMC; ret., 1974; pres. A. Cromwell-Smith, Ltd., Charlottesville, Va., 1973; head broker, cons. A. Cromwell Smith, Investments, La Jolla and Coronado, Calif., 1975—. Author: The Individual Investor in Tomorrow's Stock Market, 1977, The Little Guy's Stock Market Survival Guide, 1979, Wake Up Detroit: The EVs Are Coming, 1982, The Little Guy's Tax Survival Guide, 1984, Little Guy's Real Estate Success Guide, 1990, Little Guy's Stock Market Success Guide, 1992, Little Guy's Stock Market Future Effectiveness, 1994, The Little Guy's Sailboat Success, 1996, The Little Guy's Business Success, 1997, Business Success, 1997, Stock Market Success, 1998, Semper Fidelis in Peace and War, 1999, Sailboat Success, 1999, Tax Survival Guide, 1999, The EV's Are Coming, 1999, Real Estate Success, 2000, Little Guy's Stock Market Survival, rev. edit., 2000; contbr. articles to civilian and mil. publs. Bd. dirs. La Jolla Reps., 1975-76; vestryman St. Martin's Episcopal Ch., 1971-73. Decorated Legion of Merit with oak leaf cluster with V device, Bronze Star with V device with oak leaf cluster, Air medal with two oak leaf clusters, Purple Heart; Vietnamese Galantry Cross with gold star. Mem. ASCE, SAR, Nat. Assn. Realtors, Calif. Assn. Realtors, San Diego Bd. Realtors, Coronado Bd. Realtors, Stockbrokers Soc., So. Calif. Options Soc., Mil. Order Purple Heart. Office: PO Box 180192 Coronado CA 92178-0192

SMITH, ALDO RALSTON, JR. brokerage house executive; b. Yonkers, N.Y., Mar. 19, 1947; s. Aldo Ralston Sr. and Maggie (Allen) S.; m. Linda McKenney Davila, Oct. 15, 1983; children: Damian Allen, Caitlin Victoria McKenney. BA in Psychology summa cum laude, Talladega Coll., 1973; postgrad., CUNY, 1973-76. Account exec. trainee Advest Inc., N.Y.C., 1978-79; account exec. Merrill, Lynch, Pierce, Fenner & Smith, 1979-80, Lehman Brothers Kuhn Loeb, N.Y.C., 1980-82; fin. cons. Shearson Am. Express, 1982-84; v.p. instl. mcpl. bond sales A.L. Haven Securities, 1984; v.p. Prescott Ball & Turben, Inc., 1984-85; v.p. instl. sales Baird Patrick & Co Inc., 1985-91, Lincoln Pvt. Bank, 1991—; account exec. North Fork Bank Corp., 1995. Bd. dirs. Hale House for Human Potential, N.Y.C., 1978-80; dist. leader Yonkers Rep. Party, 1985—; mem. Mayor's Citizens Adv. Budget Com., 1993; chmn. Yonkers Police Citizens Profl. Standards Adv. Com., 1992. With U.S. Army, 1967-70. Named Outstanding Young Men of Am. Nat. Jr. C. of C., 1981. Mem. Yonkers Lions Club (bd. dirs. 1985—, pres. 1991-92, zone chmn. 1992-93), Masons (dist. dep. grand master 4th Manhattan dist.), Alpha Chi. Republican. Episcopalian. Avocations: scuba diving, photography, horticulture, cooking. Home: 96 Edgecliff Ter Yonkers NY 10705-1609

SMITH, ALEXANDER JOHN COURT, former insurance executive; b. Glasgow, Scotland, Apr. 13, 1934; s. John Court and Mary Walker (Anderson) S.; m. Margaret Gillespie, Oct. 15, 1968. Student, Scottish schs. Actuarial trainee Scottish Mut. Ins. Co., Glasgow, 1957; asst. actuary Zurich Life Ins. Co., Toronto, Can., 1958-61; from actuary to exec. v.p. William M. Mercer Ltd., 1961-74; pres. William M. Mercer, Inc., 1974-82; sr. v.p., dir. Marsh & McLennan, Inc., N.Y.C., 1974-78; group v.p. Marsh & McLennan Cos. Cons. and Fin. Svcs. Group, 1982-84, pres., 1984-85; vice chmn. Marsh & McLennan Cos., 1984-86, pres., 1986-92, chmn., CEO, 1992-99; chmn. The Ctrl. Park Conservancy, 1999—. Trustee The Putnam Funds, 1986—, Cen. Park Conservancy, 1988—, Carnegie Hall Soc., 1992—. Fellow Faculty Actuaries Edinburgh, Can. Inst. Actuaries, Conf. Cons. Actuaries; mem. Soc. Actuaries (assoc.), Am. Acad. Actuaries, Internat. Congress Actuaries, Internat. Assn. Cons. Actuaries, Racquet and Tennis Club, Royal Can. Yacht Club, Apawamis Club, Caledonian Club, Blind Brook Club Inc. Home: 630 Park Ave New York NY 10021-6544 Office: Marsh & McLennan Cos 1166 Ave of the Americas New York NY 10036

SMITH, ALEXANDER GOUDY, physics and astronomy educator; b. Clarksburg, W.Va., Aug. 12, 1919; s. Edgell Ohr and Helen (Reitz) S.; m. Mary Elizabeth Ellsworth, Apr. 19, 1942; children: Alexander G. III, Sally Jean. BS, Mass. Inst. Tech., 1943; PhD, Duke U., 1949. Physicist Mass. Inst. Tech., Radiation Lab., Cambridge, 1943-46; research asst. Duke U., Durham, 1946-48; asst. prof. to prof. physics U. Fla., Gainesville, 1948-61, asst. dean grad. sch., 1961-69, acting dean grad. sch., 1971-73, chmn. dept. astronomy, 1962-71, prof. physics and astronomy, 1956—, Disting. prof., 1981—. Dir. U. Fla. Radio Obs., 1956-85, Rosemary Hill Obs., 1989—. Author: (with others) Microwave Magnetrons, 1958, (with T.D. Carr) Radio Exploration of the Planetary System, 1964 (also Swedish, Spanish and Polish edits), Radio Exploration of the Sun, 1966; also numerous articles in field. Fellow AAAS, Optical Soc. Am., Am. Phys. Soc., Royal Micros. Soc.; mem. Am. Astron. Soc. (editor Photo-Bull. 1975-87), Astron. Soc. Pacific, Internat. Astron. Union, Internat. Sci. Radio Union, Fla. Acad. Scis. (treas. 1957-62, pres. 1963-64, medal 1965), Assn. Univs. for Rsch. in Astronomy (dir., cons.), S.E. Univs. Rsch. Assn. (trustee 1981-91), Soc. Photog. Scientists and Engrs., Athenaeum Club (past pres.), Db Racquet Club, Gainesville Country Club, Sigma Xi (nat. lectr. 1968, past pres. Fla. chpt.), Phi Kappa Phi, Sigma Pi Sigma. Republican. Christian Scientist. Office: U Fla Dept Astronomy 211 Space Scis Bldg Gainesville FL 32611 Home: 605 Dows Rd Cedar Rapids IA 52403-7007 E-mail: asmith@astro.ufl.edu.

SMITH, ALEXANDER WYLY, JR. lawyer; b. Atlanta, June 9, 1923; s. Alexander Wyly and Laura (Payne) S.; m. Betty Rawson Haverty, Aug. 31, 1946; children— Elizabeth Smith Crew, Clarence Haverty, Laura Smith Brown, James Haverty, Edward Kendrick, Anthony Marion, William Rawson. Grad., Marist Sch., 1941; student, Holy Cross Coll., 1941-42; BBA, U. Ga., 1947, LL.B. cum laude, 1949. Bar: Ga. 1948. Practiced in, Atlanta, 1948-98; ret. ptnr. Smith, Gambrell & Russell and predecessor, 1994—. Bd. dirs. Our Lady of Perpetual Help Free Cancer Home; bd. dirs., planning and devel. coun. Cath. Archdiocese Atlanta, Marist Sch., Atlanta, John and Mary Franklin Found. Served with USAAF, 1943-46. Mem. Ga. Bar Assn., Atlanta Bar Assn., Phi Delta Phi, Chi Phi, Piedmont Driving Club Atlanta, Peachtree Golf Club Atlanta (pres. 1989-91). Home: 2771 Peachtree Rd #5 Atlanta GA 30305-3523 Office: 3100 Promenade II Atlanta GA 30309-3574

SMITH, ALFRED GOUD, anthropologist, educator; b. The Hague, Netherlands, Aug. 20, 1921; s. William G. and Joan (Wraslouski) S.; m. Britta Helen Bonazzi, May 30, 1946. AB (Simon Mandlebaum scholar, Am. Council Learned Socs. fellow in Oriental Langs.), U. Mich., 1943; postgrad., Princeton U., Yale U., 1943; MA, U. Wis., 1947, PhD, 1956. Far East analyst OSS and Dept. State, Washington, 1944-46; asst., instr. philosophy and anthropology U. Wis., 1946-50; supr. linguistics, Pacific area specialist Trust Ter. Pacific Islands and Dept. Interior, Micronesia and Washington, 1950-53; asst. prof. anthropology Antioch Coll., Yellow Springs, Ohio, 1953-56; asst. prof., asso. prof. anthropology Emory U., Atlanta, 1956-62; asso. prof., prof. anthropology, community service and pub. affairs. U. Oreg., Eugene, 1962-73; dir. Center for Communication Research, U. Tex., Austin, 1973-78; prof. anthropology and comm. studies Sch. Communication, U. Tex., 1973—. Cons. Ga. Dept. Pub. Health, 1956-60, Peace Corps, 1965-69, Job Corps, 1968-70, USIA, 1972-79, 82; U.S. State Dept. specialist, Mex., 1978; cons. on problems of comm. and anthropology to state and fed. agys., industry, museums, instns. of higher learning; staff mem. AID Comm. Seminars, 1966-81; lectr. in field, Eng., Mex., Venezuela, Germany, and Can. Author: Communication and Culture, 1966, Cognitive Styles in Law Schools, 1979; mem. editl. bd. Communication and Info. Scis., Info. and Behavior, Progress in Communication Scis.; contbr. articles to profl. jours., chpts. to books; further reprintings and revs. Served to 1st lt. AUS, 1942-45. Fellow Am. Anthrop. Assn., AAAS; mem. Internat. Communication Assn. (pres. 1973-74, dir.), Sigma Xi, Alpha Kappa Delta, Phi Kappa Phi Clubs: Town and Gown. Home: 1801 Lavaca St Austin TX 78701-1341 Office: U Tex Coll Communication Austin TX 78712 E-mail: mcdagsbbs@mail.utexas.edu.

SMITH, ALLEN LEONARD, physician; b. Woburn, Mass., Nov. 7, 1959; s. Warner L. and Amely (Baer) S.; m. Denise DuChainey, June 10, 1984; children: Caroline, Connor, Ian, Timothy. BA magna cum laude, Dartmouth Coll., 1981; MD, U. Mass., 1985; MS, U. Wis., 2002. Diplomate Am. Bd. Internal Medicine. Intern and resident Pa. Hosp., Phila., 1985-88; internist Lynnfield Med. Assn., Peabody, Mass., 1988-97, med. dir., 1991, 93-97, Peabody Glen Nursing Home, 1989-98, Employee Health, Salem (Mass) Hosp., 1989-94, Tufts Associated Health Plan, 1998; med. dir. for Secure Horizons Tufts Health Plan for Seniors, 1999—2001; asst. v.p. for strategy and bus. planning Tufts Health Plan, 2001—, chmn. med. trend com., 2002—. Chmn. credentialing com. North Shore Health Sys., Salem, 1996-97, chmn. quality assurance, 1997; chmn. task force on mission statement goals, practice efficiency, Charter Profl. Svc. Corp., Salem, 1996, chmn. pharmacy task force, 1997; bd. dirs. North Shore Hospice, 1999—; faculty Bayer Inst., 1998—. Chmn. Town of Topsfield Emergency Med. Svcs. Delivery Team, 2001—. Recipient Hewlett Packard Excellence in Medicine award U. Mass. Med. Sch., 1985, Ptnrs. in Excellence award Ptnrs., Inc., 1996. Avocation: running. Home: 65 Alderbrook Dr Topsfield MA 01983-2312 Office: 333 Wyman St Waltham MA 02451-1209

SMITH, ALLIE MAITLAND, engineering educator; b. Lumberton, N.C., June 9, 1934; s. Allie McCoy and Emma Hattie (Wright) S.; m. Sarah Louise Whitlock, June 16, 1957; children: Sara Leianne, Hollis Duval, Meredith Lorren. BME with honors, N.C. State U., Raleigh, 1956, MS, 1961, PhD, 1966. Assoc. engr. Martin Co., Balt., 1956-57; devel. engr. Western Electric Co., 1957-60; mem. tech. staff Bell Tel. Labs., Burlington, N.C., 1960-62; instr., then asst. prof. extension N.C. State U., 1958-62; rsch. project engr. Rsch. Triangle Inst., Durham, N.C., 1962-66; rsch. supr. Sverdrup/ARO, Inc., Arnold Air Force Sta., Tenn., 1966-79; adj. prof. U. Tenn., Tullahoma, 1967-79; prof. mech. engring., dean Sch. Engring. U. Miss., 1979—, dean, 1979-2000. Bd. dirs., mem. scholarship bd. Miss. Mineral Resources Inst.; exec. chmn. 14th conf. Southeastern Conf. on Theoretical and Applied Mechanics, mem. exec. com. 13th through 16th confs., mem. ops. com. and policy com., 1990-99, session chair, 1994; mem. organizing com., internat. sci. adv. bd., plenary session presiding officer Internat. Conf. on Hydrosci. and Engring., 1993, 95; mem. organizing com., plenary session chair Conf. on Mgmt. of Landscapes Disturbed by Channel Incision, 1997; keynote lecture and plenary sessions chair, Third Internat. Conf. on Hydrosci. and Engring., Berlin, 1998. Author: Fundamentals of Silicon Integrated Device Technology, Vol. I: Oxidation, Diffusion and Epitaxy, 1967, also articles, revs.; editor: Radiative Transfer and Thermal Control, 1976, Thermophysics of Spacecraft and Outer Planet Entry Probes, 1977, Fundamentals and Applications of Radiation Heat Transfer, 1987, Developments in Theoretical and Applied Mechanics, Vol. XIV, 1988, Radiation Heat Transfer: Fundamentals and Applications, 1990, Fundamentals of Radiation Heat Transfer, 1991, Radiative Heat Transfer: Theory and Applications, 1993, Solution Methods for Radiative Heat Transfer in Participating Media, 1996, Radiative Heat Transfer, 1997. Fellow ASME (mem. aerospace heat transfer com. 1975—; chmn. radiative heat transfer I and II sessions, Pitts. 2000), AIAA (chmn. thermophysics tech. com. 1975-77, chmn. terrestrial energy sys. tech. com. 1979-81, chmn. confs. 1975, 79, assoc. editor jour. 1975-77, 86—, mem. nat. publ. com. 1979-83, Nat. Thermophysics award 1978, Hermann Oberth award 1984-85, Space Shuttle Flag Challenger plaque 1984, supernumerary dir. Ala.-Miss. sect. 1994—); mem. AAUP, NSPE (pres. N.E. Miss. chpt. 1990-91), Am. Soc. Engring. Edn. (host Nat. Engring. Deans' Inst. 1991), N.Y. Acad. Scis., Sigma Xi, Phi Kappa Phi, Tau Beta Pi, Pi Tau Sigma, Upsilon Pi Epsilon, Sigma Pi (scholar 1955), Order of the Engr., Rotary Club. Achievements include discovery of anomalous refraction maxima phenomenon. Home: PO Box 1857 University MS 38677-1857 Office: U Miss 205 Carrier Hall University MS 38677 E-mail: enas@olemiss.edu.

SMITH, ALMA DAVIS, elementary education educator; b. Washington, June 27, 1951; d. Wyatt Deeble and Martha Elizabeth (Lingenfelter) Davis; m. Perry James Smith, Jan. 1, 1979; children: Lauren, Hunter. BS, James Madison U., 1973; MEd, U. Va., 1978. Cert. elem. tchr. and prin., Va. Tchr. Robert E. Lee Elem. Sch., Spotsylvania, Va., 1973-79, Conehurst Elem. Sch., Salem, 1979, Hopkins Rd. Elem. Sch., Richmond, 1980-87, Reams Rd. Elem. Sch., Richmond, 1987-95, asst. prin. summer sch., 1990; tchr. Crestwood Elem. Sch., 1995—. Bd. mem. PTA, 1994-95, life mem., 1995; ambassador Chesterfield County Pub. Schs. Chesterfield Co. ambassador, 1998-2000. Mem. NEA, Spotsylvania Edn. Assn. (numerous chair positions), Chesterfield Edn. Assn. Home: 2811 Ellesmere Dr Midlothian VA 23113-3800

SMITH, ANDREW ALFRED, JR. urban planner; b. Lynchburg, Va., Oct. 3, 1947; s. Andrew Alfred and Josephine (Vaughan) S. BArch (cum laude), Howard U., 1972; M in City Planning, MIT, 1980. Archtl. designer The Architects Collaborative Inc., Cambridge, Mass., 1972-76; archtl. coordinator Fay, Spofford & Thorndike Inc., Boston, 1977-79; assoc. city planner N.Y.C. Planning Commn., 1980—. Active Briarwood (N.Y.) Community Assn., 1985—, Jamaica YMCA, Queens, N.Y.; Newark Area Planning Assn., 1968, Peoples Involvement Corp., Washington, 1971-72, Mission Hill Planning Commn., Boston, 1978-80. HUD grantee, 1978-80; recipient Hallmark medal, 1989. Mem. Am. Planning Assn., Inst. Urban Design, Nat. Assn. Housing and Redevel. Ofcls. (exec. v.p. N.Y. Met. chpt. 1996—), Urban Land Inst. (assoc.), Howard U. Alumni Assn. (regional rep. 1978-79, 82-86, pres. L.I. chpt.

1983-85), Sierra Club, Nat. Travel Club, Mpcl. Art Soc. Democrat. Avocations: scuba diving, horseback riding, travel photographing, fundraising, arts and crafts collecting. Home: 84-55 Daniels St Apt 6L Briarwood NY 11435-2014 Office: NYC Planning Commn 22 Reade St New York NY 10007-1216 E-mail: asmith1@planning.nyc.gov.

SMITH, ANDREW JOSEF, historian, publishing executive, naturalist, writer; b. Suffern, N.Y., June 3, 1954; s. Andrew and Anna May (Gannon) S. BA in Integrated Social Scis., Empire State Coll., 1988, BS in Earth and Life Scis., 1995; MS in Environ. Sci., Columbia Pacific U., 1991, MA in History, 1994; student German, Berlitz Lang. Sch., 1988; postgrad., Leicester (Eng.) U., 1999. Ordained to min. Universal Life Ch., 1979; lic. Nat. Assn. Underwater Instrs., 1980; lic. FCC technician class amateur radio. Assoc. breeder shetland sheepdogs Mary Dell Kennels, Pearl River, N.Y., 1973-77; sr. dist. forester Palisades Interstate Park Commn., Bear Mountain, 1978-92; founder, dir. rsch., curator rsch. libr. Ctr. for Study Natural and Historical Anomalies, Tomkins Cove, 1993—; curator of history and mycology Trailside Mus., Bear Mountain, 1992—; publisher Dutch-Way Publ. and Rustic Resources Newsletter, Stony Point, 1995—; pastoral counselor in pvt. practice, 1990—; exec. dir. Alternatives in Edn. Ctr., 1998—; coord. Palisades Region Myological Survey, 2000—. Instr. history and sci. North Rockland Sch. Dist., Thiells, N.Y., 1989—; adj. prof. history and sci. Rockland C.C., Suffern, 1990-91; adj. prof. environ. sci. The Nature Pl. Kennedy-Western U., 1992-93; adj. prof. sci. Empire State Coll., Nyack, N.Y., 1995—; conservation cons. Town of Stony Point, N.Y., 1990-92; vis. scientist North Rockland Sch. Dist., 1992—; vis. historian Rockland C.C., 1991; lectr., leader historic and natural sci. symposiums, hikes, horseback field excursions, 1996—;dir. horticultural survey Dewindt House, Washington's Hdqs., 2002; dir. Nat. Pub. Employees Info. Ctr., 1996—; bot. cons., tech. advisor Talasago Rsch. Inst. divsn. Takasago Flavors & Fragrances Internat., 2000—; investor Nuveen & Putnam Groups; tech. and geographic advisor U.S. Marshals Posse southern dist. N.Y., Palisades Horse Coun. Author: The Way It Was Up Home, 1995, Exploring the Edible Landscape, 1997; editor: Safe on the Mountain, 1996; monthly column pub. in Beartracks newsletter Trailside Mus., Bear Mountain; sci. columnist Home and Store News, 1993-94; hist. columnist Rockland Rev., 1996—; contbr. articles to profl. jours. and newspapers; photographs exhibited at shows, 1987—; appeared as guest naturalist and historian CBS Today, C-Span, and local cable TV networks; profl. witness in archaeology and environ. sci. Kornfeld, Rew, New Man, Ellworth Law Form, 2000—. Active preserving historic and natural landmarks, Rockland County, N.Y., 1989—, preserving landmarks in Hudson Valley and Highlands; founder, chmn. Bear Mountain Historic Preservation Alliance; co-founder N.Y. State Park Police underwater search and recovery unit, 1980-92; sci. and history home instructor Mahwah Sch. Dist., 1996—; mem. Orange County Directory of Environ. Educators, Pace Univ. Directory of Environ. Educators, N.Y. 20th Congl. Dist.'s Adv. Coun. on Sci. and Tech., N.Y. 20th Congl. Dist.'s Adv. Coun. on the Environment and Labor, Sci. and Tech., Vet.'s Affairs Com.; founder, curator Mus. of the Hamlets, Stony Point, N.Y.; coord. rsch. regionwide mycol. survey Trailside Mus., 2000—. Recipient Commn. award Palisades Interstate Park Commn., 1986, Cert. of Merit and Appreciation, County of Rockland and N.Y. State Dept. VA, 1996, Cert. Honor, Palisades Horse Coun., 2001; named to Gallery of Disting. Alumni SUNY Empire State Coll., 1997; Beethoven-Solomon Masonic scholar grad. studies, 1999. Mem. Am. Soc. Contrarian Writers Spkrs. (founding), Mensa, Rural Culture Heritage Soc. (founder, dir. 1995—, curator Rsch. Libr. 1995—, pub., editor newsletter), Rockland County Hist. Soc., Masons, N.J. Assn. Rifle and Pistol Clubs, German Am. Soc., Rockland County Repeater Assn., Moose (jr. deacon Stony Point 2001). Avocations: mycophagy, edible and medicinal plants, hiking, target shooting, raising collies and Shetland collies. Home: PO Box 77 Thiells NY 10984-0077 Office: Trailsides Mus Interstate Park Commn Bear Mountain NY 10911 E-mail: dutchwaypubs@aol.com.

SMITH, ANDREW MACLELLAN, business administration educator; b. Livonia, Mich., Aug. 18, 1960; BS, Purdue U., 1983; MBA, Butler U., 1989. Grad. teaching asst. Butler U., Indpls., 1986-89; asst. prof. bus. adminstrn. Marian Coll., 1989—. Cons. to small bus., Indpls., 1988—. Author: An Introduction to DOS, 1992. Founding sponsor Challenger Ctr., Alexandria, Va., 1988. Mem. Assn. Computing Machinery, Soc. Advancement of Mgmt. Avocations: music, golf. Office: Marian Coll 3200 Cold Spring Rd Indianapolis IN 46222-1960

SMITH, ANN HAMILL, retired religion educator; b. Lumberton, N.C., Oct. 12, 1929; d. Walter Franklin and Mabel Willey (Braswell) Hamill; (div.); children: Leslie Wade Smith Hodeen, Courtney Drake Smith Johnson. BSEE, Old Dominion U., 1973; Edn. for Ministry degree, U. South, 1986; postgrad., Loyola U., New Orleans, 1986-89. Sunday sch. tchr. Christ Ch., Poughkeepsie, N.Y., 1957-60, E.C.W. pres., 1958-59; asst. Christ Ch. Nursery, 1959-60; asst. parish sec. Christ and St. Luke's Ch., Norfolk, Va., 1970; mgr. Picnic in the Yard St. Paul's Ch., 1982-83; min. Christian edn. St. Andrew's Ch., Newport News, Va., 1985-90; spiritual dir. Virginia Beach, 1990—. Author: (meditations) Our Church Times, 1988-91. Bd. dirs. Christ Ch. Day Sch., Poughkeepsie, 1960-65; mentor Edn. for Ministry, Virginia Beach, 1994—. Democrat.

SMITH, ANN HESS, guidance counselor; b. Balt., Nov. 10, 1948; d. Arthur Emil and Ann McKeown (Davis) Hess; m. Randall Curtis Smith, Dec. 16, 1972 (div. Nov. 1992); children: Randall Arthur, Daniel Hess, Michael Davis, Ann Davis. BA in Edn., U. Md., 1970; MA in Guidance, George Washington U., 1981. Nat. cert. counselor. Tchr. of French Prince George's County Bd. of Edn., Md., 1971-81, Montgomery County Pub. Schs., 1983-86, guidance counselor, 1989—. Mem. Seneca Valley Cmty. Action Team, Germantown, Md., 1991-92. Democrat. Methodist. Avocations: art, antiques, cooking, gardening, Tai Chi. Home: 21020 Goshen Rd Gaithersburg MD 20882-4227 Office: Ronald McNair Elem 13881 Hopkins Rd Germantown MD 20874-6111

SMITH, ANN MARIE, rehabilitation nurse; b. Columbus, Ohio, Sept. 23, 1965; d. Jerome Spangler and Josephine Anna (Wizemann) Smith; m. Stephen Kenneth Smith, Oct. 22, 1988; children: Joseph Stephen, Katherine Ann. BS, Ohio State U., 1987, MS, 1988, PhD, 1995. RN, Ohio; CRRN; cert. adult nurse practitioner ANCC; CPR instr., ACLS. Staff nurse, weekend supr. Columbus Quality Care Nursing Ctr., 1987-88; staff nurse head injury rehab. Ohio State U. Med. Ctr., Columbus, 1988-95; patient care resource mgr. Ohio State U, Med. Ctr., 1995-99, sr. rsch. assoc., nurse practitioner, 1999—. Presenter in field. Mem. editl. bd. SCI Nursing; contbr. articles to profl. pubis., chpt. to book. Recipient Staff Nurse award Health South Corp., 1994, Malcom Maloof scholar 1995 nurse in Washington Internship, Mid Ohio Dist. Nursing Scholarship, 1995, Advanced Practice Nurse Role award, 1999. Mem. ANA, Ohio Nurses Assn., Ohio Brain Injury Assn., Assn. Rehab. Nurses (founding bd. Ctrl. Ohio chpt., pres. 1993-94), Assn. Spinal Cord Injury Nurses, Mortar Bd., Sigma Theta Tau. Office: 2114F Dodd Hall 480 W 9th Ave Columbus OH 43210-1254 E-mail: Smith.270@osu.edu.

SMITH, ANNE ORSI, lawyer; b. Upper Darby, Pa., July 2, 1962; d. John Francis Jr. and Anne Robinson (Nichols) O.; m. Fletcher Bodky Smith Jr., June 3, 1988; 1 child, Fletcher Bodky Smith III. BA, Colgate U., 1984; JD, U. Ark., 1988. Bar: Ark. 1988, U.S. Dist. Ct. Ark. (ea. and we. dists.) 1990. Law clk. Ark. Supreme Ct., Little Rock, 1988-89; staff atty. Office of the Prosecutor Coord., 1989-91; hearing officer Ark. Appeal Tribunal, 1991-93; pvt. practice, 1993—. Mem. ABA, Ark. Trial Lawyers Assn. (chmn. domestic rels.com. 1997-98), Ark. Bar Assn. (mem. com. juvenile justice), Pulaski County Bar Assn., Ark. Assn. of Women Lawyers (pres. 1995-96, v.p. 1994-95, paliamentarian 1993-94). Avocations: genealogy, herbs. Office: PO Box 17087 Little Rock AR 72222-7087

SMITH, ANTHONY YOUNGER, urologist, surgeon; b. Rochester, Minn., June 11, 1955; s. William George and Georgia Lee (Carter) S.; m. Sheila Jean Pym, July 4, 1982; children: Cameron Younger, Sheldon Laverick. BSChemE, N.Mex. State U., 1977; MD, U. Tex., Dallas, 1981. Diplomate Am. Bd. Urology. Intern then resident in gen. surgery U. Louisville, 1981-83; resident in urology U. N.Mex., Albuquerque, 1983-86, assoc. prof. surgery, 1987—; fellow in transplantation U. Tex., Houston, 1986-87. Dir. urologic oncology U. N.Mex. Sch. Medicine, Albuquerque, 1987—. Author several chpts. in books; contbr. articles to profl. jours. Fellow Am. Coll. Surgeons; mem. Am. Soc. Transplant Surgery, Am. Soc. Transplant Physicians, Am. Urologic Assn., Urologic Soc. Transplantation & Vascular Surgery, S.W. Oncology Group (com. mem.), Western Assn. Transplant Surgeons. Republican. Methodist. Avocations: guitar, skiing. Office: Univ N Mex Med Sch Div Urology Lomas Blvd # 2211 Albuquerque NM 87101

SMITH, A(RLETTA) RENEE, agent; b. Columbus, Ohio, Apr. 19, 1945; d. Clem and Sarah Hairston. Student, Howard U., Montgomery Coll. Pres., CEO Affiliated Entertainment Industries, Silver Spring, Md., 1967—; pres. Info. Svcs. Unlimited, 1995—; profl. beauty advisor Viviane Woodward Cosmetics, 1967—, 1967—; exec. asst. to adminstr. mgr. Member Benefits Office NEA, 2001. Exec. dir. New Approaches to Reduce the Use of Drugs (NARUD), 1996; notary public; voter registrant; election judge. January 8 named A. Renee Day by Washington D.C. Mayor Marion Barry. Mem. NAACP, NAFE, Nat. Urban League, Nat. Assn. Women Bus. Owners. Office: Affiliated Entertainment Industries PO Box 7545 Silver Spring MD 20907-7545 E-mail: rene4real@aol.com.

SMITH, ARTHUR B., JR. lawyer; b. Abilene, Tex., Sept. 11, 1944; s. Arthur B. and Florence B. (Baker) S.; m. Tracey L. Truesdale, 1999; children: Arthur C., Sarah R. BS, Cornell U., 1966; JD, U. Chgo., 1969. Bar: Ill. 1969, N.Y. 1976. Assoc. Vedder, Price, Kaufman & Kammholz, Chgo., 1969-74; asst. prof. labor law N.Y. State Sch. Indls. and Labor Rels., Cornell U., 1975-77; ptnr. Vedder, Price, Kaufman & Kammholz, Chgo., 1977-86; founding mem. Murphy, Smith & Polk, 1986-98; shareholder Ogletree, Deakins, 1999—. Guest. lectr. Northwestern U. Grad. Sch. Mgmt., 1979, Sch. Law, spring 1980; mem. hearing bd. Ill. Atty. Registration and Disciplinary Commn. Author: Employment Discrimination Law Cases and Materials, 5th edit., 2000, supplement, 2002, Construction Labor Relations, 1984, supplement, 1993; co-editor-in-chief: 1976 Annual Supplement to Morris, The Developing Labor Law, 1977; chpt. editor: The Developing Labor Law, 4th edit., 2000, supplement, 2002; contbr. articles to profl. jours. Recipient award for highest degree of dedication and excellence in tchg. N.Y. State Sch. Indsl. and Labor Rels., Cornell U., 1977. Fellow Coll. Labor and Employment Lawyers; mem. ABA (co-chmn. com. on devel. law under Nat. Labor Rels. Act, Sect. Labor Rels. Law 1976-77), N.Y. State Bar Assn., Phi Eta Sigma, Phi Kappa Phi, Chgo. Athletic Assn., Mid-Day Club. Presbyterian. Office: Ogletree Deakins et al 2 First National Plz Fl 25 Chicago IL 60603 E-mail: Arthur.Smith@odnss.com.

SMITH, ARTHUR JOHN STEWART, physicist, educator; b. Victoria, B.C., Can., June 28, 1938; s. James Stewart and Lillian May (Geernaert) S.; m. Norma Ruth Askeland, May 20, 1966; children: Peter James, Ian Alexander. BA, U. B.C., 1959, M.Sc., 1961; PhD, Princeton U., 1966. Postdoctoral fellow Deutsches Electronen-Synchrotron, Hamburg, W. Germany, 1966-67; mem. faculty dept. physics Princeton U., 1967—, prof., 1978—, Class of 1909 prof., 1992—, assoc. chmn. dept., 1979-83, chmn. dept. physics, 1990—. Vis. scientist Brookhaven Nat. Lab., 1967—, Fermilab, 1974—, Stanford Linear Accelerator Ctr., 1996—; chair sci. and technology steering com. Brookhaven Sci. Assocs. Brookhaven Nat. Lab.; vis. prof. Stanford Linear Accelerator Ctr., 2000—, spokesperson BaBar experiment, 2000—. Assoc. editor Phys. Rev. Letters, 1986-89; contbr. articles to profl. jours. Fellow Am. Phys. Soc. (chmn. divsn. of particles and fields 1991). Achievements include research on experimental high-energy particle physics; kaon decays, physics of the B particles and quark structure of hadrons. Home: 4 Ober Rd Princeton NJ 08540-4918 Office: PO Box 708 Princeton NJ 08544-0001

SMITH, ARTHUR KITTREDGE, JR. academic administrator, political science educator; b. Derry, N.H., Aug. 15, 1937; s. Arthur Kittredge and Rena Belle (Roberts) S.; m. June Mary Dahar, Nov. 28, 1959; children: Arthur, Valerie, Meredith. BS, U.S. Naval Acad., 1959; MA, U. N.H., 1966; PhD, Cornell U., 1970. Vis. prof. El Colegio de Mexico, Mexico City, 1968-69; asst. prof. polit. sci. SUNY-Binghamton, 1970-74, assoc. prof., 1974-84, prof., 1984-88, provost for grad. studies and research, 1976-83, v.p. for adminstrn., 1982-88; prof. govt. and internat. studies U. S.C., Columbia, 1988-91, exec. v.p. for acad. affairs, provost, 1988-90, 91, interim pres., 1990-91; pres., prof. polit. sci. U. Utah, Salt Lake City, 1991-97; chancellor U. Houston Sys., 1997—; pres., prof. polit. sci. U. Houston Main Campus, 1997—. Author: (with Claude E. Welch, Jr.) Military Role and Rule: Perspectives on Civil-Military Relations, 1975; contbr. articles to profl. jours. With USN, 1959-65. Lehman fellow, 1966-69, NDEA fellow, 1969-70 Mem. Am. Polit. Sci. Assn., L.Am. Studies Assn., Inter-Univ. Sem. on Armed Forces and Soc., Am. Coun. on Edn., World Affairs Coun. (pres. Binghamton chpt. 1976-76), Bus.-Higher Edn. Forum, Phi Beta Kappa, Pi Sigma Alpha, Omicron Delta Kappa, Phi Delta Kappa, Beta Gamma Sigma, Phi Kappa Phi. Home: 1505 South Blvd Houston TX 77006-6335 Office: U Houston Sys Office Of The Chancellor Houston TX 77204-0001 E-mail: aksmith@uh.edu.

SMITH, ARTHUR LEE, lawyer; b. Davenport, Iowa, Dec. 19, 1941; s. Harry Arthur Smith and Ethel (Hoffman) Duerre; m. Georgia Mills, June 12, 1965 (dec. Jan. 1984); m. Jean Bowler, Aug. 4, 1984; children: Juliana, Christopher, Andrew. BA, Augustana Coll., Rock Island, Ill., 1964; MA, Am. U., 1968; JD, Washington U., St. Louis, 1971. Bar: Mo 1971, DC 1983. Telegraph editor Davenport Morning Democrat, 1962-64; ptnr. Peper Martin Jensen Maichel & Hetlage, 1971-95, Husch & Eppenberger, St. Louis, 1995—. Arbitrator Nat Asn Security Dealers, 1980—, Am Arbit Asn, 1980—. Columnist: St Louis Lawyer, columnist: Technolawyer.com. Dir. P. Buckley Moss Found. for Children's Edn., 2001—. Lt USN, 1964—68. Mem.: ABA, Bar Asn Metropolitan St Louis (chmn law mgt comt 1993—96, chair technology comt 1996—99, Pres's award Exceptional Serv 1995), P. Buckley Moss Soc (dir 1994—, v.p. 1998—2000, exec vpres 2001—), Mo Bar Asn (vice-chair ins programs comt 1981—83, vice-chair antitrust comt 1981—83, chair admin law comt 1995—97), DC Bar Asn (chmn law practice mgt 1990—91), Order Coif. Home: 1320 Chesterfield Estate Dr Chesterfield MO 63005-4400 Office: Husch & Eppenberger Ste 600 190 Carondelet Plz Saint Louis MO 63105-3441 E-mail: arthur.smith@husch.com.

SMITH, BAKER ARMSTRONG, management executive, lawyer; b. Oct. 3, 1947; s. William Armstrong and Priscilla (Baker) S.; m. Deborah Elizabeth Ellis, Nov. 13, 1982; children: Ellis Armstrong, Elizabeth Anne, Everett Baker, Emery Manning. BS, U.S. Naval Acad., 1969; MBA, Northeastern U., 1975; JD cum laude, Suffolk U., 1977; LLM in Labor, Georgetown U., 1981. Bar: Ga. 1977, D.C. 1978, U.S. Supreme Ct. 1980; cert. turnaround profl., 1994; fellow Family Firm Inst. Commd. ensign USN, 1969, advanced through grades to lt., 1974; exec. dir., founder Ctr. on Nat. Labor Policy, Inc., North Springfield, Va., 1977-81; asst. to sec., dir. labor rels. U.S. Dept. HUD, Washington, 1981-83; exec. v.p. U.S. Bus. and Indsl. Coun., Nashville, 1983-84; pres. Am. Quality Builders, Inc., 1984-86; v.p. Hopeman Bros., Inc., Waynesboro, Va., 1986-88; pres. Morris, Anderson, Atlanta, 1988—. Sec., founder U.S. Constnl. Rights Legal Def. Fund, Inc., Atlanta, 1983—; trustee Leadership Inst., Springfield, Va., 1978—; v.p., 1998—; dir. Turnaround Mgmt. Assn., Chgo., 1994-2002, v.p., 1998-99; pres. Assn. Cert. Turnaround Profls., Boston, 1997-98; mem. Coun. for Nat. Policy, Washington, 1981—, Civil Rights Reviewing Authority U.S. Dept. Edn., Washington, 1984-88; transition team leader Office of the Pres.-Elect of the U.S., NLRB, Occupl. Safety and Health Rev. Commn., Fed. Mediation and Conciliation Svc., Nat. Mediation Bd., Fed. Labor Rels. Authority, Washington, 1980-81; instr. law, faculty sec. No. Va. Law Sch., Alexandria, Va., 1980-83; instr. law D.C. Law Sch., Washington, 1978-80. Contbg. author: Mandate for Leadership, 1981; contbr. articles to profl. jours. Recipient Outstanding Contbn. to the Turnaround Profession award, 1999. Fellow Family Firm Inst.; mem. ABA (Nat. Law Day chmn. 1976-77, Silver Key award 1977), St. George's House, Windsor Castle (assoc.), Phila. Soc., U.S. Supreme Ct. Hist. Soc., Federalist Soc., Joseph Story Soc., Beta Gamma Sigma, Phi Delta Phi (pres. 1989-91), Capitol Hill Club (Washington), Piedmont Club (Winston-Salem). Republican. Presbyterian. Home: 3360 E Terrell Branch Ct Marietta GA 30067-5164

SMITH, BARBARA ANN, gifted education coordinator; b. Oak Park, Ill., Mar. 20, 1950; d. William J. and Mary T. (Barlow) S. BS in Edn., No. Ill. U., 1971, MS in Edn., 1974, cert. advanced study in edn., 1977, EdD, EdD, No. Ill. U., 1994. Cert. tchr., adminstr. gifted edn., verification, Ill.; lic. counselor, Ill. Coord. gifted edn. Dist. 45 Elem. Schs., Villa Park, Ill., 1986—, counselor to group on leadership devel., tchr. Author numerous articles on gifted edn., self-esteem enhancers, sch.-bus. partnerships. Mem. AACD, ASCD, NEA (chpt. sec., treas.), ACA, Ill. West Suburban Reading Coun., AAUW (coord. families facing change group), Delta Kappa Gamma (chpt. pres.), Phi Delta Kappa. Office: Sch Dist 45 255 W Vermont St Villa Park IL 60181-1943

SMITH, BARBARA ANNE, healthcare management company consultant; b. N.Y.C., Oct. 10, 1946; d. John Allen and Lelia Maria (De Silva) Santoro; m. Joseph Newton Smith, Feb. 5, 1966 (div. Sept. 1984); children: J. Michael, Robert Lawrence. Student, Oceanside/Carlsbad Coll. Real estate agt. Routh Robbins, Inc., Washington, 1973-75; gen. mgr. Mall Shops, Inc., Kansas City, Kans., 1975-80; regional mgr. FAO Schwarz, N.Y.C., 1980-84; clin. adminstr. North Denver Med. Ctr., Thornton, Colo., 1984-88; adminstrv. dir. Country Side Ambulatory Surgery Ctr., Leesburg, Va., 1989-91; pres. SCS Healthcare Mgmt. Inc., Washington, 1991—. Bd. dirs. Franz Carl Weber Internat., Geneva, 1982-84; mng. dir. Nat. Healthcare Consortium, 1997—; mng. assoc. Monarch Assocs. in Healthcare. Pres. Am. Women Chile, 1968; v.p. Oak Park Assn., Kansas City, 1977-78, pres., 1978-79; vol. Visitor Info. and Assn. Reception Ctr. program Smithsonian Instn., Washington. Mem. NAFE, Network Colo., Profl. Bus. Women Assn., Med. Group Mgmt. Assn., Federated Ambulatory Surgery Assn.

SMITH, BARBARA ATKESON, writer, editor; b. Milw., Mar. 21, 1929; d. Arthur Alonzo and Gladys Campbell Atkeson; m. Donald Albert Smith, Dec. 28, 1957; children: Jean, Carolyn, David. BA, Carroll Coll., 1951; MA, U. Wis., 1952. Dir. Bapt. Student Movement Ill. Bapt. Conv., Springfield, 1954-56, Am. Bapt. Chs. USA, Valley Forge, Pa., 1956-60; prof. lit. and writing Alderson-Broaddus Coll., Philippi, W.Va., 1960-96, chair divsn. humanities, 1976-96. Mem. W.Va. Writers, Inc., Charleston, 1960—; workshop leader Appalachian Writers Workshop, Hindman, Ky., 1977—. Author: (book) Images of America: Barbour County, 2000, Six Miles Out, 1981, Coming Together, 1994, Weeping with Those Who Weep, 1998, Wild Sweet Notes, 2000, The Circumstance of Death, 2001. Moderator, tchr., choir mem. Philippi Bapt. Ch., 1960—; founder, pres. Mountain Hospice, Inc., Belington, W.Va., 1992—; bd. dirs. Heart and Hand Ministries, Philippi, 1960—; spkr. W.Va. Network of Ethics Coms., Morgantown, 1991—; mem. Amnesty Internat., 1990—, Planned Parenthood, Fellowship of Reconciliation. Named Outstanding Educator Delta Kappa Gamma, Hometown Hero, Barbour Pub. Co., 2000; recipient Plattner award for fiction Appalachian Heritage, 1993, Editor's Choice award Penwood Rev., 1999. Mem. Appalachian Writers' Assn. (bd. dirs. 1964—), W.Va. Writers Inc. (advisor, 1st prize for poetry, fiction, others). Democrat. Avocations: sports, arts, crafts. Home and Office: 16 Willis Ln Philippi WV 26416

SMITH, BARBARA BARNARD, music educator; b. Ventura, Calif., June 10, 1920; d. Fred W. and Grace (Hobson) S. BA, Pomona Coll., 1942; Mus.M., U. Rochester, 1943, performer's cert., 1945; DMus (hon.), Pomona Coll., 2001. Mem. faculty piano and theory Eastman Sch. Music, U. Rochester, 1943-49; mem. faculty U. Hawaii, Honolulu, 1949—, assoc. prof. music, 1953-62, prof., 1962-82, prof. emeritus, 1982—; sr. fellow East-West Center, 1973. Lectr., recitals in Hawaiian and Asian music, U.S., Europe and Asia, 1956—; field researcher Asia, 1956, 60, 66, 71, 80, Micronesia, 1963, 70, 87, 88, 90, 91, Solomon Islands, 1976. Author publs. on ethnomusicology. Mem. Internat. Soc. Music Edn., Internat. Musicol. Soc., Am. Musicol. Soc., Soc. Ethnomusicology, Internat. Coun. for Traditional Music, Am. Mus. Instrument Soc., Coll. Music Soc., Soc. for Asian Music, Music Educators Nat. Conf., Pacific Sci. Assn., Assn. for Chinese Music Rsch., Phi Beta Kappa, Mu Phi Epsilon. Home: 1314 Kalakaua Ave Apt 1403 Honolulu HI 96826-1929

SMITH, BARBARA DAIL, school nurse; b. Oklahoma City, July 15, 1949; d. James E. and Juanita E. (Butler) Berryhill; m. William Ben Smith, May 23, 1975; children: Rebecca Sue, James Ben. BS in Biology, Oklahoma City U., 1975, BS in Health Edn., 1984; MPH, U. Okla., 1990, postgrad., 1999—, M in Edn., 2000. RN, Okla. Mgmt. nurse St. Anthony Hosp., Oklahoma City, 1979-83, cons. family help group cancer patients, 1981-83; nurse Oklahoma City Bd. Edn., 1983—, Early, Periodic, Screening, Diagnosis & Treatment case mgr., 1994-96, supr. health svcs., 1996-99, adminstr. health and med. svcs., 1999—. Nurse Bapt. Hosp., 1991-99; mem. sick bank com. Oklahoma City Pub. Schs., 1998—, chairperson employee wellness com., 1999-2000. Author: (with others) Chemotherapy Cert. Program, 1981-82. Leader Camp Firee Orgn. Am., Oklahoma City, 1982-84; mem. Ctrl. Okla. Task Force Com. for Children With Spl. Needs; mem. Oklahoma County Task Force Com. on Child Abuse; mem. spl. edn. task force com. Oklahoma City Pub. Schs., 1986-87; mem. gov.'s task force on child abuse, 1985-86; mem. Oklahoma County Task force on Children With Spl. Needs; mem. Oklahoma County Immunization Coalition, Oklahoma City Eye Care Task Force; mem. exec. bd. Oklahoma City Fedn. Tchrs. Local 2309 of the Am. Fedn. Tchrs.; sec., co-coord. Children with Attention Deficit Disorder of Ctrl. Okla., 1992; sec. Cmty. Eye Care, Inc., 1997—; mem. Okla. Commn. on Children and Youth. Mem. Nat. Assn. Sch. Nurses (bd. dirs. 1997—), Nat. Oncology. Nursing Soc., Okla. Oncology Nursing Soc., Okla. Nurses Assn. (governance com. 1998), Oklahoma City Sch. Nurses Soc. (pres. 1985-87), Oklahoma City Pub. Sch. Nurses (procedures com., sec. 1986-87), Sch. Nurse Orgn. Okla. (chair continuing edn./workshop com. 1985—, legis. lobby com. 1988-90, bd. dirs. 1985—, pres.-elect 1990, pres. 1992-94), Children With Attention Deficit Disorder (sec. Okla. chpt. 1992, assoc. chair 1993-95), YWCA, Fraternal Order of Police Aux., Beta Beta Beta, Phi Delta Kappa. Democrat.

SMITH, BARBARA JEAN, real estate broker; b. Miami, Fla., Aug. 13, 1950; d. Hyman and Rose (Braun) Katz; m. David Thomas Smith, Mar. 15, 1975; children: Lindsey Rose, Wesley Harris. BA in Tchg., U. Fla., 1972; MEd in Guidance and Counseling, U. Miami, 1974. Registered real estate broker, Fla. Prof. U. Marietta, Ga., 1975-80; psychologist Cmty. Mental Health Ctr., Rome, 1980-85; pvt. practice psychology, 1980-85; broker assoc. Smith and Assocs. Investment Co., Realtors, Tampa, Fla., 1985—. Real estate instr. Greater Tampa Assn. Realtors, 1985—. Vol. Children's Aux., Tampa., 1980; gardener Stoney Point Garden Club, Tampa, 1982; mem. booster club St. Mary's Episcopal Day Sch. PTA, Tampa, 1984—; mem. booster club, and PTA, Plant H.S., Tampa, 1993—. Recipient Sales Achievement award Riverhills Arvida Cmty., 1993. Mem. Nat. Assn. Realtors, Fla. Assn. Realtors. Republican. Methodist. Avocations: running Gasparilla distance classic, gardening, tennis, piano. Home: 4808 W Estrella St Tampa FL 33629-5409 Office: Smith and Assocs 3801 W Bay To Bay Blvd Tampa FL 33629-6825

SMITH, BARBARA JEANNE, retired librarian; b. Jersey Shore, Pa., Apr. 14, 1939; d. Moyer Emmerson and Mary Kathryn (Ebner) S. BS in Edn. (Biology), Pa. State U., 1961, DEd in Higher Edn., 1981; MS in Edn. (English), SUNY, Oswego, N.Y., 1967; MLS, U. Pitts., 1970. Reference libr. Pa. State U. Librs., University Park, 1970-75, commonwealth campus coord., 1975-82, asst. dean librs., head commonwealth campus librs. divsn., 1982-89; dir. Smithsonian Instn. Librs., Washington, 1989-98. Gen. sci. tchr., Binghampton (N.Y.) City Schs., 1961-62; English tchr., North Syracuse (N.Y.) Ctrl. Schs., 1970-75; mem. Smithsonian Instn. Rsch. Info. Svc. (chair 1993-95), Planning Adv. Group, 1989-93; chair Internet Implementation Com., Smithsonian Instn. Librs. User Adv. Com., 1989-97; founding dir. Chesapeake Info. and Rsch. Libr. Alliance, 1996-98. Contbr. articles to profl. jours.; speaker in field. UCLA Grad. Sch. of Libr. and Info. Sci. Sr. fellow, 1982. Mem. AAUW, ALA (mem. coun. 1987-91), Cosmos Club (Washington), Centre County (Pa.) Hist. Soc. (life), U. Pitts. Alumni Assn. (bd. dirs. 1991-94), Gen. Fedn. Women's Clubs, Beta Phi Mu. E-mail: bsmith5598@pennswoods.net.

SMITH, BARNARD ELLIOT, management educator; b. Mpls., May 6, 1926; s. Sheldon Strong and Jessie (Gould) S.; m. Betty Lou Strohschein, Aug. 28, 1949; children: Carolyn Louise, Eileen Elizabeth. BS in Mech. Engring. with distinction, U. Minn., 1949, MS, 1950; PhD, Stanford U., 1961; MA (hon.), Dartmouth Coll., 1971. Asst. prof. mech. engring. U. N.D., 1950-51; mfg. specialist A.O. Smith Co., Milw., 1951-54; asst. prof. indsl. engring. Oreg. State Coll., 1954-58, Stanford U., 1958-61; asso. prof. mgmt. Sloan Sch. Mgmt., MIT, 1961-68; prof. mgmt. Indian Inst. Mgmt., Calcutta, 1965-68; prof. engring. Thayer Sch. Engring. Dartmouth Coll., 1968-71; dean Stuart Sch. Mgmt. and Finance, Ill. Inst. Tech., 1971-75, prof. mgmt., 1975-80; David M. French disting. prof. mgmt. U. Mich., Flint, 1980-89, emeritus, 1989; pres. Vineyards of the Acad., 1989, The Acad. of Wine of Oreg. Inc., 1993—. Cons. in field. Served with USNR, 1944-46. Mem. Phi Tau Sigma, Beta Gamma Sigma. Home: 18200 Highway 238 Grants Pass OR 97527-8631 E-mail: academy@internetcds.com.

SMITH, BARRY, philosopher, researcher; b. Bury, Lancashire, Eng., June 4, 1952; s. Reginald and Jean Smith. BA, MA, Oxford (Eng.) U., 1973; PhD, U. Manchester, Eng., 1976. Rsch. fellow in philosophy U. Sheffield, England, 1976—79; lectr. philosophy U. Manchester, 1979—89; prof. Internat. Acad. Philosophy, Schaan, Liechtenstein, 1989—93; Julian Park prof. philosophy U. Buffalo, NY, 1993—; dir. Inst. for Formal Ontology and Med. Info. Sci. U. Leipzig, Germany, 2002—. Rsch. scientist Nat. Ctr. for Geographic Info. and Analysis, Buffalo, 1996—. Author: Austrian Philosophy, 1995; editor: The Monist, 1988—, Handbook of Metaphysics and Ontology, 1991. Recipient Wolfgang Paul award, Alexander von Humboldt Found., 2002—05; fellow, 1983—84; grantee rsch. grantee, Fonds Nat. de la Recherche Scientifique, Switzerland, 1991—94, Fonds zur Förderung der wissenschaftlichen Forschung, Austria, 1992—95, NSF, 1999—2002. Mem.: Am. Philos. Assn. Office: SUNY Dept Philosophy 130 Park Hall Buffalo NY 14260 Business E-Mail: phismith@buffalo.edu.

SMITH, BARRY ALAN, hotel executive, real estate broker; b. L.A., Sept. 1, 1945; s. Joel Herman and Daphne Peggy (Wigsten) S.; m. Gayle Swift, Feb. 21, 1970. BBA, U. Houston, 1968. Cert. hotel adminstr., mgr. cmty. assn.; lic. real estate broker. Front office mgr. Warwick Hotel, Houston, 1966-73; asst. mgr. Hyatt Regency Hotel, 1973-75; exec. asst. mgr. Whitehall Hotel, 1975-77; resident mgr. Stouffer's Greenway Plaza Hotel, 1977-79, Registry Hotel, Dallas, 1979-81; mng. dir. NortPark Inn and Conv. Ctr., 1981-84; dir. ops. Bradford Hotels, Austin, Tex., 1984; v.p. ops. Landmark Hotels, Inc., Dallas, 1984-86; gen. mgr. Midland (Tex.) Hilton, 1986-91; pres. 117 Wall St. Corp., 1989-91; gen. mgr. Austin (Tex.) Crest Hotel, 1991-92, Austin Cambridge Tower, 1992—; pres., CEO, Uptown Condos, Inc., Austin, 2000—. Mem. Nat. Assn. Realtors, Tex. Hotel/Motel Assn. (bd. dirs. 1987-91), Tex. Assn. Realtors, Cmty. Assn. Inst., Mobile Hotel Assn. (pres. 1985-86), Midland Hotel Assn. (pres., v.p. 1986-88), Mobile C. of C. (bd. dirs. 1985), Midland C. of C. (adv. bd. 1987-91), Austin Conv. and Visitors Bur. (adv. bd. 1991-92), Rotary. Republican. Methodist. Avocations: photography, real estate, historic renovations. Home: 8001 Spandera Cove Austin TX 78759-8722

SMITH, BARRY DAVID, obstetrician-gynecologist, educator; b. Suffern, N.Y., July 3, 1938; s. Alexander N. and Beatrice (Morris) S.; m. Maryann Blair, Oct. 11, 1963; children: Gillian, Adam. AB, Dartmouth Coll., 1959; MD, Cornell U., 1962. Diplomate Am. Bd. Ob-Gyn. Resident in ob-gyn N.Y. Hosp. Cornell U. Med. Ctr., N.Y.C., 1963-67, chief resident, instr., 1967-68; staff obstetrician/gynecologist Mary Hitchcock Meml. Hosp., Hanover, N.H., 1970—; asst. prof. Dartmouth Coll., 1970-78, assoc. prof., 1979—. Chief sect. ob-gyn. Hitchcock Clinic, 1977-95, bd. govs., 1975-85, bd. dirs., 1980-86; chief sect. ob-gyn. Dartmouth Med. Ctr., 1977—, chmn. dept. ob-gyn., 1992-95, vice chair dept., 1995-97, chair dept., 1997—. Treas., pres. Norwich (Vt.) Recreation and Conservation Council, 1975-77. Served to comdr. USNR. Fellow Am. Coll. Ob-gyn. (v.p. N.H. sect. 1991-94, chair N.H. sect. 1994-97, sec. dist. 1 1997—), Am. Fertility Soc., Am. Soc. Colposcopy. Avocations: skiing, tennis, sailing. Office: Dartmouth Hitchcock Clinic 1 Medical Center Dr Lebanon NH 03756-0001 E-mail: barry.d.smith@hitchcock.org.

SMITH, BARRY HAMILTON, foundation administrator, physician; b. Orange, N.J., Oct. 6, 1943; s. Kenneth Wright and Harriet (Barr) S.; m. Carley Eldredge, Dec. 13, 1969; children: Christopher, Sara. BA, Harvard U., 1965; PhD, MIT, 1968; MD, Cornell U., 1972. Intern, resident N.Y. Hosp., N.Y.C., 1971-75; resident Mass. Gen. Hosp., Boston, 1975-78; program dir. Neuroscis. Rsch. Program MIT, 1975-78; dep. dir. Surg. Neurology Br. NIH, Bethesda, Md., 1978-83; sci. & med. dir. Dreyfus Med. Found., N.Y.C., 1983-88; dir. Dreyfus Health Found., 1988—. Sr. v.p. Rogosin Inst. Bd., 1998—; prof. surgery Cornell U.. Editor Ency. Neurosci.; contbr. articles to profl. jours. Bd. dirs. Desmond Tutu Peace Found., 1999—, Kornfeld Found., 2002—, N.Y.C. Rescue Mission, 1995—. Comdr. USPHS, 1978-83. Recipient Commendation Medal award, USPHS, 1982, EEO award, 1983. Mem. AMA, AAAS, Soc. Neurosci., Am. Pain Soc. (audit com. 1983-85), Nat. Coun. Internat. Health (governing bd. 1990-95, chair 1993-95), Phi Beta Kappa, Sigma Xi, Alpha Omega Alpha. Avocations: sailing, writing. Home: 1192 Park Ave Apt 10B New York NY 10128-1314 Office: Dreyfus Health Found 205 E 64th St Rm 404 New York NY 10021-6635 E-mail: bsmith@thf.org.

SMITH, BARRY SAMUEL, physiatrist; b. Windber, Pa., Jan. 15, 1947; MD, Jefferson Med. Coll., 1969. Diplomate Am. Bd. Phys. Medicine and Rehab. Intern Reading (Pa.) Hosp., 1969-70; resident in phys. medicine and rehab. Inst. Phys. Med. Rehab., Louisville, 1970-73; now with Baylor U. Med. Ctr., Dallas, chief in phys. medicine and rehab. Mem. AMA, Am. Acad. Phys. Medicine and Rehab., Am. Congress Rehab. Medicine, Assn. Acad. Physiatrists, Am. Assn. Electrodiagnostic Medicine, Nat. Bd. Med. Examiners (diplomate). Office: Baylor U Med Ctr Dept Phys Medicine and Rehab 3500 Gaston Ave Dallas TX 75246-2096

SMITH, BERNALD STEPHEN, retired airline pilot, aviation consultant; b. Long Beach, Calif., Dec. 24, 1926; s. Donald Albert and Bernice Merrill (Stephens) S.; m. Marilyn Mae Spence, July 22, 1949; children: Lorraine Ann Smith Foute, Evelyn Donice Smith DeRoos, Mark Stephen, Diane April (dec.). Student, U. Calif., Berkeley, 1944-45, 50-51. Cert. airline transport pilot, flight engr., FAA. Capt. Transocean Air Lines, Oakland (Calif.) and Tokyo, 1951-53, Hartford, Conn., 1954-55; 1st officer United Air Lines, Seattle, 1955, San Francisco, 1956-68, tng. capt. Denver and San Francisco, 1961-68, capt. San Francisco, 1968-86, 2d officer, 1986-93, ret., 1993. Founder, v.p. AviaAm., Palo Alto, Calif., 1970-72, AviaInternat., Palo Alto, 1972-74; cons. Caproni Vizzola, Milan, 1972-84; prin., cons. Internat. Aviation Cons. and Investments, Fremont, Calif., 1985—; instr. aviation Ohlone Coll., Fremont, 1976; founder Pacific Soaring Coun.; founder, trustee AirSailing, Inc., 1970—, Soaring Safety Found., 1985—. Author/editor: American Soaring Handbook, 1975, 80; contbr. articles to profl. jours. Trustee Nat. Soaring Mus., 1975-2001, pres. 1975-78; active RTCA, SSA del., 1992—, FAI del., 1996-. Comdr. USNR. Fellow Internat. GPS Svc. for Geodynamics; mem. AIAA (pub. bd. 1977-94), Soaring Soc. Am. (pres. 1969-70, chmn. pub. bd. 1971-84, ins. com. 1975-93, bd. dirs. 1963-97, Warren Eaton Meml. trophy, 1977, 97, Exceptional Svc. award 1970, 75, 82, 88, 91, Exceptional Achievement award 1996, named to Hall of Fame 1984, hon. vice-chmn. bd. dirs. 2000—), Nat. Aero. Assn., Exptl. Aircraft Assn., Aircraft Owners and Pilots Assn., Airline Pilots Assn., Seaplane Pilots Assn., Orgn. Scientifique et Technique Internat. du Vol a Voile (hon., bd. dirs., U.S. del. 1981-97), Fedn. Aeronatique Internat. (environ. commn. v.p. and U.S. del. 1995—, airspace mgmt. group 1998—, Paul Tissandier diploma 1992, Lilienthal medal 1993), Commn. de Vol A Voile (U.S. del. 1970-71, 78, 85-97, v.p. 1988-96), U. Calif. Alumni Assn. (life), Inst. Navigation, Civil GPS Svc. Interface Com. Democrat. Methodist. Office: Internat Aviation Cons Investments PO Box 3075 Fremont CA 94539-0307

SMITH, BERT KRUGER, retired mental health services professional; b. Wichita Falls, Tex., Nov. 18, 1915; d. Sam and Fania (Feldman) Kruger; m. Sidney Stewart Smith, Jan. 19, 1936; children: Sheldon Stuart, Jared Burt (dec.), Randy Smith Huke. BJ, U. Mo., 1936; MA, U. Tex., 1949; DHL (hon.), U. Mo., 1985. Soc. and entertainment editor Wichita Falls Post, 1936-37; freelance writer Juneau, Alaska, 1937; assoc. pub. Coleman Daily Dem. Voice, 1950-51; assoc. editor Jr. Coll. Jour., Austin, Tex., 1952-55; spl. cons., exec. Hogg Found. for Mental Health, 1952—2001, ret., 2001. Chmn. bd. Austin Groups for the Elderly, 1985—; mem. ethics com. St. David's Hosp.; panelist Nat. Assn. Southwest Conf. Mental Health and Aging; instr. mental health info., special edn., gerontology U. Tex., Austin; mem. com.. Geriatric Rsch., Edn. Clin. Ctr. and Aging Rsch. and Edn. Ctr., U. Tex. Health Sci. Ctr., San Antonio. Author: No Language But A Cry, 1964, Your Non-Learning Child, 1968, A Teaspoon of Honey, 1970, Insights for Uptights, 1973, Aging in America, 1973, The Pursuit of Dignity, 1977, Looking Forward, 1983; contbr. numerous articles to profl. jours. Bert Kruger Smith professorship Sch. Social Work U. Tex., 1982; recipient Disting. Svc. award City of Austin, 1988, Cert. of Appreciation, Tex. Dept. Human Svcs., 1989, Ann Bert Smith award Sr.'s Respite Svc., 1989, S.W. Found. Founders' Spirit award, 1990, Tex. Leadership award Ann. Tex. Joint Conf. on Aging, 1992, Tex. Leadership award Tex. Dept. on Aging, 1992, Tex. Long-Term Care Vol. award, Women in Comm. Lifetime Achievement award, Mental Health Assn. Cmty. Svc. award, Internat. Tng. in Comm. Founder's Day Woman of Yr. award, Most Worthy Citizen award, Golden Rule award Memento, J.C. Penney, Inc., Disting. Svc. award City of Austin, Amazing Aging award Jewish Family Svcs., U. Tex. Sch. Social Work, Founder's award Holt House, 1998; named Woman of Distinction, Girl Scouts U.S., 2002; named to Tex. Women's Hall of Fame, 1988. Mem. Conf. Southwest Founds. (founder's spirit award, archives, film, & video com.), Adult Svcs. Coun. and Family Eldercare (bd. dirs.), Found. Religious Studies Tex. (bd. trustees), Timely Solutions (adv. bd.). Jewish. Avocations: walking, reading. Home: 5818 Westslope Dr Austin TX 78731-3633 Fax: 512-453-8400.

SMITH, BETSY KEISER, telecommunications company executive; b. Washington, July 31, 1960; d. Henry Bruce and Jessie (Weeks) Keiser; m. Patrick C. Smith, June 2, 1984; children: Alexander Keiser, Nicholas Henry. BA in Fine Arts and Art History, U. Mich., 1984. Account rep. Adam A. Weschler Galleries, Inc., Washington, 1984-85; mgr. customer service Presdl. Airways, Inc., 1986; merchandise mgr. Burdines Inc., Boynton Beach, Fla., 1986-87; sr. account exec. AT&T, West Palm Beach, 1987—. Cons. Fed. Publs. Inc., Washington, 1981-83, U.S. Telemktg. Inc., Atlanta, 1986—, Lion Internat., London, 1985—, Inst. Paralegal Tng., Phila., 1986—. Mem. DAR (chaplain), U. Mich. Alumni Assn. (sec.-bd. dirs. Palm Beach chpt.), U. Mich. Alumni Club, Palm Beach Sailing Club. Avocations: art research, sailing, skiing, cooking. Home: 709 Harbour Point Dr # A47 West Palm Beach FL 33410-3416 Office: AT&T 250 S Australian Ave West Palm Beach FL 33401-5018

SMITH, BETTY, writer, nonprofit foundation executive; b. Bonham, Tex., Sept. 16; d. Sim and Gertrude (Dearing) S. Student, Stephens Coll.; BJ, U. Tex. Women's editor Daily Texan; pres. Hope Assocs. Corp., N.Y.C.; pres., owner Betty Smith Assocs. Author: A Matter of Heart, 1969. Bd. dirs. Melchior Heldentenor Found., N.Y.C., 1968—, pres., 1987-97; pres. Gerda Lissner Found., 1994—; v.p. Herman Lissner Found., 1990—. Mem. Author's Guild. Home: 322 E 55th St New York NY 10022-4157 Office: care Lissner Found 135 E 55th St 8th Fl New York NY 10022-4049

SMITH, BETTY DENNY, county official, administrator, fashion executive; b. Centralia, Ill., Nov. 12, 1932; d. Otto and Ferne Elizabeth (Beier) Hasenfuss; m. Peter S. Smith, Dec. 5, 1964; children: Carla Kip, Bruce Kimball. Student, U. Ill., 1950-52; student, L.A. City Coll., 1953-57, UCLA, 1965, U. San Francisco, 1982-84. Freelance fashion coordinator, L.A., N.Y.C., 1953-58; tchr. fashion Rita LeRoy Internat. Studios, 1959-60; mgr. Mo Nadler Fashion, L.A., 1961-64; showroom dir. Jean of Calif. Fashions, 1965—. Freelance polit. book reviewer for community newspapers, 1961-62; staff writer Valley Citizen News, 1963. Bd. dirs. Pet Assistance Found., 1969-76; founder, pres., dir. Vol. Services to Animals L.A., 1972-76; mem. County Com. To Discuss Animals in Rsch., 1973-74; mem. blue ribbon com. on animal control L.A. County, 1973-74; dir. L.A. County Animal Care and Control, 1976-82; mem. Calif. Animal Health Technician Exam. Com., 1975-82, chmn., 1979; bd. dirs. L.A. Soc. for Prevention Cruelty to Animals, 1984-94, Calif. Coun. Companion Animal Advocates, 1993-97; dir. West Coast Regional Office, Am. Humane Assn., 1988-97; CFO Coalition for Pet Population Control, 1987-92; trustee Gladys W. Sargent Found., 1997—, Coalition to End Pet Overpopulation, 1998—; cons. Jungle Book II, Disney Studios, 1997; mem. Coalition to Protect Calif. Wildlife, 1996-97, Spl. Commn. Spay/Neuter City L.A., 1998-99; adv. com. La. Dept. of Animal Reg. 2000; mem. Calif. Rep. Cen. Com., 1964-72, mem. exec. com., 1971-73; mem. L.A. County Rep. Cen. Com., 1964-70, mem. exec. com., 1966-70; chmn. 29th Congl. Cen. Com., 1969-70; sec. 28th Senatorial Cen. Com., 1967-68, 45th Assembly Dist. Cen. Com., 1965-68; mem. speakers bur. George Murphy for U.S. Senate, 1970; campaign mgr. Los Angeles County for Spencer Williams for Atty. Gen., 1966; mem. adv. com. Moorpark Coll., 1988-97; mem. adv. bd. Wishbone Prodn., 1995-97; mem. L.A. County Art Mus., L.A. Libr. Assn. Mem. Internat. Platform Assn., Mannequins Assn. (bd. dirs. 1967-68), Motion Picture and TV Industry Assn. (govt. rels. and pub. affairs com. 1992-97), Lawyer's Wives San Gabriel Valley (bd. dirs. 1971-74, pres. 1972-73), L.A. Athletic Club, Town Hall. Home: 1766 Bluffhill Dr Monterey Park CA 91754-4533

SMITH, BETTY L. results coach, seminar leader; b. Trinidad, Colo., Oct. 17, 1932; d. Howard Melvin and Annabelle (Eastwood) Wade; m. Earl Gilbert Smith, Nov. 26, 1950; children: Wayne David, Christine E. Thomann, Clifford Todd. Student, Santa Rosa (Calif.) Coll., 1961-63. Owner, founder Gilbert's Gallery Frame Shop, Santa Rosa, 1964-84; ind. rep., regional sales dir. Simplex, 1984-91; owner, personal life coach Betty Smith Results Coaching, 1992—. Author: Secrets of Living Life Abundantly, 1995, (poetry biography) Here I Am, There I Went, 1968; contbr. articles to profl. jours. Art commr. City of Santa Rosa, 1967-68; mem. steering coun. Earth Elders, treas., 1999-2001; mem. Sustainable Sonoma County. Democrat. Avocation: environmental education. Home and Office: 2319 Olympia Dr Santa Rosa CA 95405-8119

SMITH, BETTY PAULINE, television producer; b. Benton, Ill., Nov. 27, 1926; d. Roy Herman and Goldie Ada (Rodgers) Keen; m. Richard Caldwell Smith, Jan. 11, 1946; children: Constance Raelene, Elana Gayle, Jill Christina. AA in Mgmt., U. Nev., 1982; cert., Ikenbo Sch. Floral Art, 1985; student, Hawaii Pacific U., 1994. Lic. real estate broker, Nev.; cert. real estate salesperson, Hawaii. TV producer Old Plantation Prodns., Inc. Active Coalition of Women-Legis., Domestic Violence Divsn., State of Hawaii, 1994-96; pres. NaKupuna U. Hawaii, 1999. Exec. prodr. Hawaii Music, 1985; prodr. (TV) The Open Door, 1992, 95, 96, Health Issues: Issues for Women over 55 Years Old, 1992, Honolulu Police Dept., 1995, There's No Excuse for Abuse, 1995, Gang Violence in the Schools, 1995, Women Against Violence, 1996; poem carried by 2002 Olympic Torchbearers who were firefighters at World Trade Center, Sept. 11, 2001; contbr. poetry to lit. books, also on Poetry.com. Recipient Comm. Svc. award Aloha State Assn. of the Deaf, 1993, scholarship Americorps, 1996, cert. Hope Domestic Violence Counselor, 1996, Oahu Unsung Angel award, 1998, Internat. Poet merit Internat. Soc. Poets, 1999, Mayor's Proclomation award City of Honolulu, 1999, seal City and County Honolulu, 1999, Pres. award Nat. Authors Registry, 1999, Powers of Expression Through Poetry commendation Gov. of Hawaii, 2000 Prometheus Trophy award The Famous Soc. Poets, 2000; named Poet of Merit The Famous Soc. Poets, 2000, Muse of Fire, 2000, Internat. Poet of Merit Internat. Soc. Poets, 2002. Mem. Ind. TV Producers Assn., Hometown Media Alliance TV Producers, Elks, LWV, OES, Mason/White Shrine of Jerusalem, Toastmasters (Hall of Fame), others. Avocations: swimming, bicycling, walking, kayaking, Hawaiian music. Home: PO Box 15853-5853 Honolulu HI 96830

SMITH, BETTY W. librarian; b. Lincoln, Nebr., June 29, 1919; d. Clem and Edith Margaret (Stanley) Wilder; m. Dulaney Dale Smith, Mar. 20, 1946; children: Douglas D., Diane E., Richard W. BA, Wayne U., 1940; BS, U. Minn., 1941; MA, Mich. State U., 1955. Cert. libr. Br. libr. Pub. Libr., Park Ridge, Ill., 1941-42, reference libr. Dearborn, Mich., 1942-44; U.S.C.G. SPAR, libr. asst. U.S.C.G. Acad., New London, Conn., 1945-46; reference libr. Libr. Hawaii, Honolulu, 1946-47; libr. Hawaiian Econ. Found., 1947-49; reference libr. Lansing Pub. Libr., Mich., 1967-86, substitute libr., 1986-98. Mem. Citizens for Actions in Mental Health, 1980—86; steering com. Long-Range Planning Mich. Dept. Mental Health, 1986—90; bd. dirs. Tri-Co. Cmty. Mental Health, Lansing, 1992—98; founding and exec. com. mem. Alliance for Mentally Ill, 1985—2002, now v.p.; adv. coun. Mich. Forensic Ctr., 1988—2001, Lafayette Clinic, Detroit, 1986—92. Mem. LWV, Mental Health Assn., Mich. Assn. Emotionally Disturbed Children (bd. dirs. 1963-68), Mich. Mental Health (adv. coun. 1986-90), Phi Alpha Theta. Home: 1782 Eifert Rd Holt MI 48842-1976

SMITH, BEULAH MAE, music educator; b. Okmulgee, Okla., Aug. 14, 1920; d. Willie Arthur Geller and Pearl Oretha Miears; m. Judie C. Smith, May 16, 1943; 1 child, Joni Smith Levinson. BA in Music Edn., Ctrl. State U., 1942; MA in Music Edn., Okla. U., 1948. Cert. piano specialist. H.S. music tchr., Lindsay, Okla., Newkirk; jr. high music tchr. Guthrie; H.S. music tchr. Purcell; elem. music tchr. Norman; tchr. North Ea. U., Tahlequah; jr. high music tchr. Hobbs, N.Mex.; piano specialist Norman. Piano cons. Warner (Okla.) State Coll., 1980. Recipient Cert. of Achievement, Howell-Aretta Conservatory Music, 1955; Beulah Mae Smith Day named in honor Town of Hobbs, 1978. Democrat. Methodist. Avocations: traveling, fishing, musicals, interior decorating. Home: 2007 Creighton Dr Norman OK 73071-7338

SMITH, BEVERLY ANN EVANS, management consultant, small business owner; b. Massillon, Ohio, Apr. 12, 1948; d. Louie Edward and Willa (Dumas) Evans; m. Stephen John Smith, Aug. 1971; children: Brian Stephen, Stacy Nicole. MEd, Kent State U., 1973; BS in Edn., Bowling Green State U., 1970; diploma exch. edn. program, Babson Coll., 1987. Tchr. Garfield High Sch., Akron, Ohio, 1971-72; fin. aids officer, Upward Bound dir. Kent (Ohio) State U., 1971-76; dean student affairs Ga. State U., Atlanta, 1971-76; varied mgmt. positions So. Bell, 1976-84; dist. mgr. AT&T, 1984-96. Cons. in field; bd. advisors Riverside Bank, 1998-99. Bd. dirs., chmn. United Way, Cobb County, Ga., 1991; bd. dirs. Girls Inc., Cobb County; appointee Ga. Clean and Beautiful Commn., Atlanta, 1984-88; mem. Leadership Cobb, 1988—, mem. governing bd., 1993—, co-chair, 1997-98; cert. Stephen (lay) min. Episc. Ch., 1991—; mem. alumni bd. dirs. Bowling Green State U., 1999. Named Cobb County Ga. Woman of Yr. in Bus., Marietta (Ga.) Girls Club, 1984, Outstanding Young Profl., Washington, D.C. Bus. Exch., Outstanding Sr. Woman, Bowling Green State U., 1970, Outstanding Freshman Woman, 1967, recipient Disting. Svc. award, 1970; named one of Outstanding Young Women of Am., 1971, 80. Mem. Omicron Delta Kappa, Delta Sigma Theta (1st v.p. local chpt. 1986-88, nat. exec. dir. 1988-90, exec. bd. 2000--). Avocations: classical piano, writing non-fiction. Home: 1152 Clarendon Dr Marietta GA 30068-2161 E-mail: thehrgroup@mindspring.com.

SMITH, BILL, city manager; b. N.Y.C., June 24, 1940; s. Harry John and Catharine Marie (Wheeler) S.; m. Judith Ann Carroll, Mar. 18, 1961; children: Shawn, Kevin, Susan, Kurt, Eric. BA, Iona Coll., 1962; MS, USN Postgrad. Sch., 1971; MPA, Golden Gate U., 1982. Adminstrv. analyst City of Monterey (Calif.), 1982-84; city adminstr. City of Sonora (Calif.), 1984-86; asst. city mgr. City of Monterey, 1986-90; city mgr. City of Manhattan Beach (Calif.), 1990-94, City of Westminster, Calif., 1994-97; gen. mgr. Ventura (Calif.) Regional Sanitation Dist., 1997—. Instr. USN Postgrad. Sch., Monterey, 1979-82; adj. prof. Golden Gate U., San Francisco, 1984-90. Contbr. articles to profl. jours. Bd. dirs. Monterey County AIDS Project, 1987-90. Lt. col. USMC, 1962-82. Decorated Silver Star, Bronze Star, PurpleHeart, Joint Svc. Commendation medal. Mem. Am. Soc. Pub. Adminstrn. (chpt. pres. 1983-84),Internat. City Mgrs. Assn., Retired Officers Assn., Disabled Am. Vets., VFW, Am. Legion. E-mail: judy. Home: 261 Cherry Hills Ct Thousand Oaks CA 91320-4171 Office: Ventura Regional Sanitation Dist 1001 Partridge Dr Ste 150 Ventura CA 93003-0704 E-mail: billy@msn.com.

SMITH, BOB, lawyer, state senator, educator; b. Scranton, Pa., Mar. 25, 1947; s. Philip and Ruth (Delmar) S.; m. Ellen Theresa Foster, 1968; children: Karen Elizabeth, Lisa. BA in History, U. Scranton, 1969, MS in Chemistry, 1970; MS in Environ. Sci., Rutgers U., 1973; JD, Seton Hall U., 1981. Bar: N.J. 1981. Sci. tchr. Lourdesmont H.S., Clark Summit, Pa., 1968-70; environ. health sci. curriculum coord. Middlesex County Coll., Edison, N.J., 1972-73, adminstrv. asst. to dean sci., 1974-77, instr., 1970-74, asst. prof., 1974-76, assoc. prof., 1976-79, prof. chemistry and environ. sci., 1979-86; law clk. N.J. Dept. Environ. Protection, Trenton, 1980; prin., pvt. practice law Bob Smith and Assocs., Piscataway, N.J., 1981—. Prosecutor East Brunswick, 1997—, South Brunswick, 1998—. Contbg. author Jour. Air Pollution Control Assn., 1976, Environ. Health Sci., 1975; co-editor: New Jersey State Wastewater Treatment Operations Manual, 1979. Mayor of Piscataway Twp., 1981-86; N.J. assemblyman N.J. 17th Legis. Dist., 1986-2001, mem. appropriations com. and environ. quality com., assembly select com. on ocean pollution, 1988, assembly energy and hazardous waste com. policy and rules, 1994; mem. N.J. Satte Senate, 2002—, mem. jud. com. and environment com.; parliamentarian Assembly Dem. Caucus, 1988-90, chmn. task force on environment, 1987; chmn. Piscataway Dem. Orgn., 1981-90; counsel N.J. State Dem. Platform Com., 1987, 89; chmn. Middlesex County Dem. Orgn., 1991-92; Assembly Dem. Dept. Minority Leader, 1993-95; councilman-at-large Piscataway Twp., 1977-80, pres. coun., 1979, v.p., 1978; mem. Middlesex County Transp. Coordinating Com., 1980-86; chmn. Piscataway Planning Bd, 1981-86, sec., 1975, chmn., 1976; bd. dirs. N.J. Conf. Mayors, 1984-86; mem. tech. adv. com. air pollution Middlesex County Planning Bd., 1973-74; mem. Greenbrook Basin com. Area 208 Mgmt. Planning Program, 1975-76; mem. commr.'s adv. com. N.J. Dept. Environ. Protection, 1972-86; N.J. senator 17th legis. dist., 2001—; mem. judiciary com., 2001—, mem. environ. com., 2001—. Recipient Disting. Citizen award Piscataway Jewish Congregation B'nai Shalom, 1982; named Legis. of Yr. Eden Inst., N.J. State VFW, 1998, Environ. Legislator of Yr., N.J. Environ. Fedn., 1990; U. Scranton Presdl. scholar, 1965-69. Mem. Middlesex County Bar Assn. Roman Catholic. Office: 216 Stelton Rd B-1 Piscataway NJ 08854-3284 also: 216 Stelton Rd E-5 Piscataway NJ 08854-2600

SMITH, BONNIE GENE, historian, educator; b. Bridgeport, Conn. d. William Wallace and Harriet Amanda (Howard) Sullivan; m. Donald R. Kelley, June 30, 1979; children: Patrick W., Patience H.; 1 stepchild, John R. Kelley. AB, Smith Coll., 1962; PhD, U. Rochester, 1976. Asst. prof. history U. Wis.-Parkside, Racine, 1977-81; from asst. to full prof. U. Rochester, 1981-90; prof. history Rutgers U., New Brunswick, NJ, 1990—, dir. Inst. Rsch. Women, 1998—2001, bd. govs., disting. prof., 2002—. Dir. Susan B. Anthony Ctr. U. Rochester, 1988-90; chair advanced placement com. Coll. Bd./Educational Testing Service, N.Y.C. and Princeton, 1988-94; vis. prof. history U. Calif., Irvine, 1984, Ecole des Hautes Etudes, Paris, 1993-94, U. Bielefeld, Germany, 1993, Princeton U., 1995, 98. Author: Ladies of the Leisure Class, 1981, Confessions of a Concierge, 1985, Changing Lives: Women in European History, 1989, Gender of History, 1998, Imperialism, 2000, Women in Postwar Europe, 2000, Global Feminisms Since 1945, 2000; co-author: What is Property, 1994, Challenge of the West, 1995, Making of the West: Peoples and Cultures, 2001; co-editor: History and the Texture of Modern Life, 2001; gen. editor (book series) Women's and Gender History in Global Perspective, Am. Hist. Assn., 1996—, Oxford World History; contbr. articles to profl. jours. Fellow Am. Coun. Learned Socs., N.Y., 1979-80, 84-85, Nat. Humanities Ctr., N.C., 1984, Shelby Cullom Davis Ctr., Princeton U., 1992-93, John Simon Guggenheim Found., N.Y., 1992-93. Mem. Am. Hist. Assn., Soc. for French Hist. Studies (bd. editors 1986-89, William Koren Jr. award 1997). Office: Rutgers Univ Dept History 16 Seminary Pl New Brunswick NJ 08901-1108

SMITH, BRADFORD LEE, information technology executive; AB. summa cum laude, Princeton U., 1981; JD, Columbia U., 1985; student, Grad. Inst. Internat. Studies, Geneva, Switzerland. Former ptnr. Covington & Burling, Washington; dep. gen. counsel for worldwide sales Microsoft, Redmond, Wash., 1996—2001, sr. v.p., gen. counsel for law and corp. affairs, 2001—. Contbr. articles. Office: Microsoft One Microsoft Way Redmond WA 98052-6399

SMITH, BRADLEY E. anesthesiologist; b. Cedar Vale, Kans., Jan. 4, 1933; MD, U. Okla., 1957. Diplomate Am. Bd. Anesthesia, 1964. Resident U.S. Naval Hosp., N.Y.C., 1957-60; faculty Yale U., 1962-63, U. Miami, 1963-69; chmn., prof. dept. anesthesiology Vanderbilt U., Nashville, 1969-93, prof., 1993—. Fellow Am. Coll. Chest Physicians, ACOG (assoc.); mem. AMA, Am. Urol. Assn., Am. Soc. Anesthesiologists. Office: Vandy Med Ctr 504 Oxford Nashville TN 37232-0001

SMITH, BRADLEY YOULE, lawyer; b. N.Y.C., Feb. 11, 1948; s. Bradley and Christine (Brown) S.; m. Anne Barre, Dec. 31, 1986; children: Bradley McLaren, Andrew Robert, Lauren Barre, Timothy James, Lynden Eleanor, Christina McLaren. BA in History cum laude, Yale U., 1970; JD, NYU, 1974. Bar: N.Y. 1975, U.S. Dist. Ct. (so. dist.) N.Y. 1975, U.S. Ct. Appeals (2d cir.) 1975. With Davis Polk & Wardwell, N.Y.C., 1974—, ptnr., 1980—. Trustee Royal Coll. Surgeons Found., Inc. Mem. ABA (chmn. subcom. secured transactions 1983-87, moderator and panelist com. banking law and uniform comml. code), Am. Law Inst., N.Y. State Bar Assn. (mem. banking law com.). Office: Davis Polk & Wardwell 450 Lexington Ave New York NY 10017-3982 E-mail: bradley.smith@dpw.com.

SMITH, BRENDA JOYCE, author, editor, social studies educator; b. Washington, Jan. 2, 1946; d. William Eugene and Marjorie (Williams) Young; m. Duane Milton Smith, Aug. 4, 1978. BA in History and Govt. cum laude, Ohio U., 1968, postgrad. in Am. and European History, 1972. Tchr. Jr. High Sch., Lancaster, Ohio, 1968-69, Reynoldsburg (Ohio) Mid. Sch. and High Sch., 1970-71; grad. teaching asst. Ohio U., Athens, 1969-70, 71-72; polit. speech writer Legis. Reference Bur., Columbus, Ohio, 1972-74; pub. rels. writer Josephinum Coll., 1976-78; social studies editor Merrill Pub. Co.,

1979-91; freelance author/editor social studies, 1991—. Project editor: Human Heritage: A World History, 1985, 89, World History: The Human Experience, 1992; author: The Collapse of the Soviet Union, 1994, Egypt of the Pharaohs, 1995; writer-editor on African Am. history series, 5th grade; writer of 3 Am. history books; writer on state histories of N.Y. and Ind. Del. 1st U.S.-Russia Joint Conf. on Edn., 1994. Mem. Nat. Coun. Social Studies, Ohio Coun. Social Studies, Freelance Editl. Assn. Office: 3710 Harborough Dr Gahanna OH 43230-4037

SMITH, BRIAN, business consultant, educator; b. Williamston, S.C., June 30, 1956; s. W. Aaron and Sybil L. (Griffith) S.; m. Miriam Emma Lourdes Atienza Sison, Mar. 28, 1981; children: Theodore Anthony, Caitlin Elizabeth, Hannah Colleen. BA, U. S.C., 1978. Cert. grantsman U. North Fla.; cmty. devel. cert. Penn Ctr., S.C.; cert. assessment facilitator Peter F. Drucker Found. Vol U.S. Peace Corps, The Philippines, 1979-81; regional dir. Muscular Dystrophy Assn., Greenville, S.C., 1982; ESL instr. Luth. Social Svcs., Jacksonville, Fla., 1982-84; pub. rels. dir. N.E. Fla. Builders Assn., 1984-89; pres. Wordsmith Comm., 1989-93; dir. devel. and comm. Cath. Charities, 1993-95; dir. devel. Vol. Jacksonville, 1995-99; owner, CEO Gonzo Cons., Jacksonville, 1999—; CEO, founder Gurus Unltd., Inc. Bd. dirs. Jacksonville Econ. Devel. Co.; instr. Jacksonville U.; facilitator, instr. Fast Trac for Entrepreneurs. Editor: Communities, 1984-89 (Best in Country award 1984-89), Bildor News, 1984-89 (Best in U.S. award 1984-89); assoc. editor Fla. Grove and Vegetable Mgmt. Mag., Jacksonville, 1992-94; author screenplays Die Hard 4: Terrorists Holiday, Paladin 2000, Iceberg Strategy, A Piece of Dirt; author of essays, poems and short stories. Active Enterprise Zone Commn., Jacksonville, 1993—, Cmty. Devel. Adv. Coun., Jacksonville, 1995—, Summit for Jacksonville's Future, 1997, JCCI Study, Jacksonville, 1997; mgr. Historic Seminole Club. Recipient Image award Fla. Pub. Rels. Assn., Jacksonville, 1993. Mem. CDAC, Nat. Soc. Fund Raising Execs. (bd. com. chmn. 1996—, bd. mem. 1993—), U.S. Peace Corps Assn., Peter F. Drucker Found. (facilitator), Alpha Sigma Phi. Avocations: writing, camping, photography, reading. E-mail: GurusUnlimited@juno.com.

SMITH, BRIAN DAVID, lawyer, educator; b. Fayetteville, Ark., Oct. 29, 1953; s. Samuel Charles and Janelle (McCaskill) S.; children: Garrett Walker, Brian Austin, Marshall David; m. Teri Hill Smith. JD, La. State U., 1977. Bar: La. 1978, U.S. Dist. Ct. (we. dist.) La. 1979, U.S. Tax Ct. 1980, U.S. Ct. Appeals (5th cir.) 1980, U.S. Supreme Ct. 1990, Tex. 1993. Law clk. to presiding justice 1st Jud. Cir. Ct. La., Shreveport, La., 1978—79; assoc. Nelson, Hammons & Johnson, 1979—84, Lunn, Irion, Johnson, Salley & Carlisle, Shreveport, 1984—90, Ungarino & Eckert, Shreveport, 1990—. Instr. legal asst. cirriculum La. State U., Shreveport, 1984-87. Bd. dirs. YMCA of Shreveport-Bossier City, 1996-98. Mem. La. Bar Assn., La. Assn. Def. Counsel, State Bar Tex., Mensa, Shreveport Country Club. Methodist. Avocations: golf, running, shooting. Home: 5706 Lake Side Dr Bossier City LA 71111-5508 Office: Ungarino & Eckert 831 Kings Highway Ste 201 Shreveport LA 71104

SMITH, BRUCE DAVID, archaeologist; b. Iowa City, Mar. 24, 1946; s. Goldwin Albert and Emily C. (Bateman) S.; children: David Vernon, Jonathan Oliver. BA, U. Mich., 1968, MA, 1971, PhD, 1973. Mem. faculty Loyola U., Chgo., 1973-74, U. Ga., Athens, 1974-77; curator N.Am. archaeology Nat. Mus. Natural History, Smithsonian Instn., Washington, 1977—, sr. scientist, dir. archaeobiology program, 1991—, spl. asst. to dir., 1983, asst. dir., 1986. Mem. anthropology rev. panel NSF, 1982-83. Author: Mississippian Patterns of Animal Exploitation, 1975, Prehistoric Patterns of Human Behavior, 1978, Mississippian Settlement Patterns, 1978, Mississippian Emergence, 1990, Rivers of Change, 1992, paperback edit., 2002, Emergence of Agriculture, 1995, paperback edit., 1998, Mississippian Households and Communities, 1995. Horace H. Rackham prize fellow, 1971-73, Smithsonian Instn. Regents Pub. fellow, 1987; recipient James Henry Breasted prize Am. Hist. Assn., 1995. Fellow AAAS; mem. Soc. Am. Archaeology (sec. 1985-89, pres. 1993-95, Book award 1997), Southeastern Archaeol. Conf. (pres. 1982-84). Office: Smithsonian Inst Nat Mus Natural History MRC112 Anthropology Washington DC 20560-0001

SMITH, BRUCE DAVID, economics educator, consultant; b. St. Paul, Sept. 21, 1954; s. Samuel and Marian Smith; m. Valerie R. Bencivenga, Oct. 27, 1987. BS, U. Minn., 1977; PhD, MIT, 1981. Asst. prof. Boston Coll., 1981-82; economist Fed. Res. Bank, Mpls., 1982-86; asst. prof. Carnegie-Mellon U., Pitts., 1986-87; assoc. prof. U. Western Ont., London, Can., 1987-90; prof. Cornell U., Ithaca, N.Y., 1990-96, U. Tex., Austin, 1996—. Cons. Fed. Res. Bank, Kansas City, 1997—, Mpls., 1986—96, Cleve., 1996—, Atlanta, 1994—; adv. World Bank. Contbr. articles to profl. jours. Mem. Am. Econs. Assn., Econometric Soc. Office: U Tex at Austin Dept Econs Austin TX 78712

SMITH, BRUCE I. state legislator; b. Harrisburg, Pa., Feb. 19, 1934; s. Bruce I. and Margaret M. (Zerbe) S.; m. Patricia A. Ninkovich; children: Rhonda J., Renee N. BA, Elizabethtown Coll., 1956; MEd, Pa. State U., 1961. Chmn. Newberry Twp. Recreation Bd., Pa., 1971-77, Newberry Twp. Bd. Supr., 1978-83; me. Pa. Ho. of Reps., Harrisburg, 1980—. Chmn. game and fisheries com., 1995—, agrl. and rural affairs com., 1993-94; chmn. Ctrl. Pa. Rep. Caucus, 1995—. Rep. committeeman, 1976-80; active Newberry Twp. Planning Commn., 1978-80; tchr. Cedar Cliff H.S., West Shore. Sgt. USAR, 1958-62. Named Conservation Legislator of Yr., York County, Pa., 1987, 1994—98, Conservationist of Yr., York County, 1999, Pa., 2001, Legislator of Yr., 2001, Sportmens Legislator of Yr., 2002. Mem. Shrine Club, Pinchot Par Isaac Walton League (charter). Address: Fairview Indsl Pk 540B Industrial Dr Lewisberry PA 17339-9534

SMITH, BRUCE R. English language educator; b. Jackson, Miss., Mar. 21, 1946; Student, U. Birmingham, England, 1966-67; BA magna cum laude in English with honors, Tulane U., 1968; MA, U. Rochester, 1971, PhD with distinction, 1973. From asst. prof. to assoc. prof. English Georgetown U., Washington, 1972-87, prof., 1987—; faculty Bread Loaf Sch. English, Middlebury Coll., 1994—. Seminar dir. Folger Inst., 1994, 98-99. Author: Ancient Scripts and Modern Experience on the English Stage 1500-1700, 1988, Homosexual Desire in Shakespeare's England: A Cultural Poetics, 1991, Roasting the Swan of Avon: Shakespeare's Redoubtable Enemies and Dubious Friends, 1994, The Acoustic World of Early Modern England, 1999, Shakespeare and Masculinity, 2000; editor: Shakespeare, Twelfth Night: Text and Contexts, 2001; edit. bd. Shakespeare Quar., 1995—, PMLA, 2000-02; contbr. chpts. to books, articles to profl. jours. Summer grantee Georgetown U. Acad. Rsch., 1976, 84, 87, 89, 91, 92, 99; grantee Intercultural Curriculum Devel., 1982, Agecroft Assn., 1991; Mellon fellow Huntington Libr., 1996, jr. fellow Folger Inst., 1979, 85, fellow, 1990, 96, ACLS fellow, 1979-80, NEH fellow, 1987-88, 99, Va. Found. Humanites fellow, 1989, Internat. Globe fellow Shakespeare's Globe, London, 1997, Guggenheim fellow, 2001-02; recipient Roland Bainton prize for lit. 16th Century Studies Assn., 2000. Mem. MLA (com. gay and lesbian history), Soc. Study Early Modern Women, Ren. Soc. Am., Shakespeare Assn. Am. (pres. 1994-95). Office: Georgetown U Dept English Washington DC 20057-0001

SMITH, BRUCE WILLIAM, safety engineer; b. Louisville, July 23, 1932; s. Roy Sylvester and Anna Lois (Levine) S.; m. Barbara Ruth Lischin, Oct. 13, 1951; children: Carl Wayne, Joyce Leslie, Nancy Florence. Student, U. Cin., 1953-58, Miami U., Oxford, Ohio, 1950-52. Registered profl. engr., Ohio. Materials testing spec. Gen. Electric AE, Cin., 1952-56, systems engr., 1956-79, facitities engr., 1979-83, safety engr., 1983-91, ret., 1991; consulting engr. Exec. Resource Assocs., Inc., Cape Coral, Fla., 1991—. Paramedic, Community Medic Res., No. Hamilton County, 1975-84; asst. fire chief Springdale (Ohio) Vol. Fire Dept., 1956-84; councilman, Springdale, 1960-62; mem. Springdale Charter Comm., 1962. Recipient physics scholarship, Ohio Acad. Sci., 1950. Mem. Am. Soc. Safety Engrs., Nat. Fire Protection Assn. Avocations: sailing, photography. Home: 919 SE 26th Ter Cape Coral FL 33904-2919 E-mail: bsmith@iline.com.

SMITH, C. LEMOYNE, publishing company executive; b. Atkins, Ark., Sept. 15, 1934; s. Cecil Garland and Salena Bell (Wilson) S.; m. Selma Jean Tucker, May 23, 1964; 1 child, Jennifer Lee BS, Ark. Tech. U., 1956; M.Ed., U. Ark., 1958. Tchr. pub. schs., Little Rock, 1956-58; instr. bus. adminstrn. Ark. Tech. U., Russellville, 1958-60; sales rep. South-Western Pub. Co., Cin., 1960-67, editorial staff, 1967-82, pres., chief exec. officer, 1982-90, chmn., 1990-91, ret., 1991. Bd. dirs. Cin. Council on World Affairs, 1983-95. Mem. Nat. Bus. Edn. Assn., Delta Pi Epsilon Republican. Presbyterian. Avocations: bridge, travel, golf. Office: South-Western Pub Co 5191 Natorp Blvd Mason OH 45040-7980 E-mail: lemselm@aol.com.

SMITH, CALVIN DOUGLAS, music educator, musician; b. Lebanon, Ind., Dec. 6, 1961; s. Cletus Calvin Smith and Shirley Alice Carroll; m. Valorie Anne Uptegraff-Smith, Feb. 14, 1987; 1 child Dakota Ryan. B of Music Edn., Butler U., 1984; M of Instructional Tech., U. South Fla., 2002. Cert. tchr. Fla. Music tchr. Ruskin (Fla.) Elem., 1985—91, Cypress Creek Elem., Ruskin, 1991—95; band/chorus tchr. Burns Mid. Sch., Brandon, Fla., 1995—99; band tchr. Eisenhower Mid. Sch., Gibsonton, 1999—. Mem.: Fla. Bandmasters Assn., Music Educators Nat. Conf., Phi Kappa Phi. Avocations: reading, camping, singing. Home: 513 Fox Run Tr Ruskin FL 33572

SMITH, CAREY DANIEL, acoustician, undersea warfare technologist; b. Kenedy, Tex., July 10, 1932; s. Ernest Edwin and Nancy Margaret (Willoughby) S.; m. Fannie Belle Walker, Sept. 18, 1954; children: Daniel Carey, Bryan Owen, Ernest Price, Sara Elizabeth Babyak. BS in Math. and Physics, U. Tex., 1959. Rsch. physicist Def. Rsch. Lab./U. Tex., Austin, 1958-64; electro-acoustic engr. Bur. Ships, Washington, 1964-66; dir. sonar tech. office Naval Sea Sys. Command, 1966-79, dir. Undersea Warfare Tech. Office, 1979-86; sr. cons. U.S. Navy/Sec. of Def., 1987—. Fgn. liaison specialist in undersea warfare as collatoral duty USN, 1966-86; chmn. sonar tech. panel Tech. Coop. Program of multiple allied nations, 1972-86; tech. advisor undersea warfare div. Am. Def. Preparedness Assn., 1976-86. Chair deacons McLean (Va.) Bapt. Ch., 1987-88, 88-89, 96-97; chair Band Parents, McLean H.S., 1979-80, chair Sports Boosters, 1977-78. With USN, 1951-56. Decorated Legion of Honor (France); recipient Disting. Civilian Svc. award Sec. Navy, 1979, also Brit., Can., French, Japanese, and New Zealand navies commendations, 1985-86. Fellow Acoustical Soc. Am. Achievements include development of numerous advanced, innovative techniques incorporated in fleet sonar, torpedo, mine, countermeasure, acoustic communications, underwater combat control/ocean environmental acoustic systems; color display for high resolution sonars. Home and Office: 1638 Dinneen Dr Mc Lean VA 22101-4646

SMITH, CARL BERNARD, education educator; b. Feb. 29, 1932; s. Carl R. and Elizabeth Ann (Lefeld) S.; m. Virginia Lee Cope, Aug. 30, 1958; children: Madonna, Anthony, Regina, Marla. BA, U. Dayton, 1954; MA, Miami U., Oxford, Ohio, 1961; PhD, Case Western Res. U., 1967. Tchr. Cathedral Latin H.S., Cleve., 1954-57; customer corr. E.F. MacDonald Co., Dayton, 1958-59; tchr. Kettering (Ohio) H.S., 1959-61; editor Reardon Baer Pub. Co., Cleve., 1961-62; tchr., rschr. Case Western Res. U., 1962-65, Cleve. Pub. Schs., 1966-67; asst. prof. edn. Ind. U., Bloomington, 1967-69, assoc. prof., 1970-72, prof., 1973—99, prof. emeritus, 1999—. Dir. ERIC Ctr., 1988—, Family Literacy Ctr., 1990—; pres. Grayson Bernard Pub. Co., 1988—, Am. Family Learning Corp., 1996—. Author: Reading Instruction through Diagnostic Teaching (Pi Lambda Theta Best Book in Edn. award 1972), Getting People to Read, 1978; sr. author: Series r, 1983, New View, 1993, Teaching Reading and Writing Together, 1984, Connect! Getting Your Kids to Talk to You, 1994, World History A Resource Book, 1995, Self-Directed Learner Curriculum, 1998, (videotape) Make a Difference, 1996, Improving Your Child's Writing Skills, 1999, Gotcha Grandpa, 2000, Talk to Your Children About Books, 2001, Teaching Children to Learn, 2002. Pres. Bd. Edn., St. Charles Sch., Bloomington, 1976-80. Recipient Sch. Bell award NEA, 1967, Literacy award Ind. State Reading Assn., 1997. Mem. ASCD, Internat. Reading Assn., Nat. Coun. Tchrs. of English, Am. Ednl. Rsch. Assn., Phi Delta Kappa. Republican. Roman Catholic. Home: 401 Serena Ln Bloomington IN 47401-9226 Office: ERIC Clearinghouse Smith Rsch Ctr Bloomington IN 47405 E-mail: smith2@indiana.edu.

SMITH, CARL DEAN, JR. counselor, young adult advocate; b. Denver, Sept. 12, 1949; m. Patricia Ann O'Donnell; Aug. 18, 1973; children: Amanda Paige, Grant Carlton. BA, Springfield Coll., 1972; postgrad., Goethe Inst., Munich, 1972-73, Gordon Conwell Theol. Sem., Hamilton, Mass., 1986-88; MEd, Cambridge Coll., 1993. Bus. analyst Dun & Bradstreet, Inc., Boston, 1974-77; Western U.S. credit mgr. Salomon/N.Am., Inc., Peabody, Mass., 1977-81; regional credit mgr. Stride Rite Corp., Cambridge, 1981-82; sales mgr., franchisee V.R. Bus. Brokers of Chestnut Hill, 1982-85; pres. C.D. Smith Assocs., Wakefield, 1985-90; cons. Swampscott, 1990-94; crisis clinician Ctr. for Mental Health, Lexington, Mass., 1994-97; Christian counselor HRI Counseling, Woburn, 1994-97; counselor The Salvation Army Boston Adult Rehab. Ctr., Saugus, 1997—. Class agt. Brewster Acad., 1968-96; asst. basketball coach Nth Shore C.C., Danvers, Mass., 1997—; mem. Park St. Ch., Boston Common, Mass. Avocation: basketball coaching. Home and Office: 314 Forest Ave Swampscott MA 01907-2109

SMITH, CARL MICHAEL, federal agency administrator, lawyer; b. Oklahoma City, Oct. 11, 1944; s. Carl W. Jr. and Nina (Furr) S.; m. Sharon Kay Lewis, June 5, 1971. BA, U. Okla., 1966, JD, 1969. Bar: Okla. 1969, U.S. Dist. Ct. (we., no. and ea. dists.) Okla. 1971, U.S. Ct. Appeals (10th cir.) 1976, U.S. Supreme Ct. 1976. Mem. firm Lawrence, Smith & Harmon, Oklahoma City, 1977-80; pres. Red Rock Exploration, Inc., 1980-83; mem. firm Lawrence & Ellis, P.A., 1983—; asst. secy. fossil energy U.S. Dept. Energy, Washington, 2002—. Mem. Blue Ribbon Commn. on Natural Gas, Oklahoma City, 1982; chmn. Okla. Polit. Action Com., Oklahoma City, 1986-90; mem. Okla. Legis. Interim Task Force on Environ. Regulation, Oklahoma City, 1991-92; sec. Okla. Energy Resources Bd., 1992-94; mem. Okla. Sec. of Energy, 1995—. Capt. U.S. Army, 1969-71, Vietnam. Mem. Okla. Ind. Petroleum Assn. (pres. 1994-95). Office: US Dept Energy Fossil Energy 1000 Independence Ave SW Washington DC 20585-0301*

SMITH, CAROL ESTES, retired city councilman; b. Phoenix, Nov. 13, 1934; d. John William and Kathleen (Poynter) Estes; m. David Liles Smith, Jan. 8, 1954 (div. Oct. 1981); children: Kelly Liles, Kevin Estes, Kathleen Marie. BS in Edn., Tex. Christian U., 1957. Ptnr. Waste Control of Ariz., N.Mex., Tex., variouslocations, 1964-81; mem. city coun. City of Tempe, Ariz., 1986-98; ret. Bd. dirs., chmn. Ariz. Recycling Bd., State of Ariz., Phoenix, 1991-96; bd. dirs., pres. S.W. Ctr. for Edn. and Environment, Tempe, 1988—, Papago/Salado Assocs., Tempe, 1990—. Pres. Gen. Fedn. Women's Clubs of Ariz., 1986-88; Tempe Gov.'s past pres. Recipient Silver medallion Boys and Girls Clubs Am., 1991; named Woman of Distinction, Tempe St. Lukes Aux., 1985, Jr. Advisor of Yr., 1984. Mem. Zonta of East Valley (pres. 1998-2000, Don Carlos Humanitarian award 1999), Tempe Rotary. Republican. Presbyterian. Avocations: reading, theatre. Home: 6411 S River Dr Unit 60 Tempe AZ 85283-3336

SMITH, CAROLE DIANNE, lawyer, editor, writer, product developer; b. Seattle, June 12, 1945; d. Glaude Francis and Elaine Claire (Finkenstein) S.; m. Stephen Bruce Presser, June 18, 1968 (div. June 1987); children: David Carter, Elisabeth Catherine. AB cum laude, Harvard U., Radcliffe Coll., 1968; JD, Georgetown U., 1974. Bar: Pa. 1974. Law clk. Hon. Judith Jamison, Phila., 1974—75; assoc. Gratz, Tate, Spiegel, Ervin & Ruthrouff, 1975—76; freelance editor, writer Evanston, Ill., 1983—87; editor Ill. Inst. Tech., Chgo., 1987—88; mng. editor LawLetters, Inc., 1988—89; editor ABA, 1989—95; product devel. dir. Gt. Lakes divsn. Lawyers Coop. Pub., Deerfield, 1995—96; product devel. mgr. Midwest Market Ctr. West Group, 1996—97; mgr acquisitions, bus. and fin. group CCH, Inc., Riverwoods, 1997—2002. Author Jour. of Legal Medicine, 1975, Selling and the Law: Advertising and Promotion, 1987; (under pseudonym Sarah Toast) 77 children's books and stories, 1994-2002; editor The Brief, 1990-95, Criminal Justice, 1989-90, 92-95 (Gen. Excellence award Soc. Nat. Assn. Pubs. 1990, Feature Article award-bronze Soc. Nat. Assn. Pubs. 1994), Franchise Law Jour., 1995; editor-in-chief The Brief, ABA Tort and Ins. Practice Sect., 1998-2000; mem. editl. bd. The Brief, ABA Tort and Ins. Practice Sect., 1995-2000. Dir. Radcliffe Club of Chgo., 1990-93; mem. parents council Latin Sch. Chgo., 1995-96. Mem. ABA. E-mail: smithca@cch.com.

SMITH, CARSON CLAY, business executive; b. Rushville, Ind., June 12, 1955; s. Merritt W. and Sally Smith; m. Patricia Jane Dice, Mar. 31, 2001; children: Sara Kathryn, Alexander, Elizabeth. BA in Religious Studies, Ind. U., 1977. Indsl. sales rep. Exotic Automation & Supply, Indpls., 1995—. Account mgr. Daimler Chrysler, Ford, GM, Subaru Isuzu, Delco Remy Am., Delphi Delco, Delphi Energy, Guide Corporation, Visteon Electronics. Contbr. to USA Today, Human Events, The Indpls. Star and News, The Christian Advocate, Citizen Mag.; author: History of the Scottish Society of Indianapolis, Biography of Thomas H. (Tommy) Thompson, the History of the Kirkin' O' the Tartan, The Table Grace of the Scottish Society of Indianapolis; participant in creation and revision Constn. and Bylaws; ofcl. Insignia and Flag Scottish Soc. Ind.; contbr. to AM radio programs. Pres. Kingsway Christian Sch. Bd. Dirs., 1990. Fellow: Soc. Antiquaries of Scotland; mem.: Soc. Colonial Wars (Ind. treas. 2001—), Scotch-Irish Soc. U.S.A., Ind. Soc. SAR (pres. 1993—95), Ind. U. Alumni Assn. (life), Scottish Soc. Indpls. (life; editor The Thistle newsletter 1985—86, 1990—92, pres. 1992—93, 2000—02, charter), Internat. Assn. Plastics Distbrs., SAR (pres. Indpls. chpt. 1991, Patriot medal 1994, Meritorious Svc. medal 1994, Good Citizenship medal 1994), Scottish Soc. of Louisville, Caledonian Soc. of Cincinnati, Scottish Am. Club of Ind., Sigma Chi (life; chpt. editor Lambda Larynx newsletter 1974, Outstanding Pledge 1974). Avocations: running, browsing bookstores, attending concerts. Home: 2207 Van Ness Pl Indianapolis IN 46240-4703 Office: Exotic Automation & Supply 8227 Northwest Blvd Ste 270 Indianapolis IN 46278-1386 Home Fax: 317-253-5624; Office Fax: 317-871-5750. E-mail: carsonsmith@aol.com.

SMITH, CATHERINE LOUISE, library administrator, consultant; b. Pitts., Sept. 29, 1945; d. ARthur Herman and Catherine Mary (Steigerwald) Kalin. BA in Psychology, Carlow Coll., 1967; MLS, U. Pitts., 1969, PhD in Libr., Info. Sci., 1986; MA in Psychology, Cleve. State U., 1975. Cert. pub. libr., N.C.; title IIB higher edn. act U.S. Dept. Edn., 1983-84. Counselor West Side Cmty. Mental Health Ctr., Cleve., 1975-76; libr. ref., adult svc. Cuyahoga County Libr., North Olmsted, Ohio, 1976-79, br. mgr. Olmsted Falls, 1979-81, head dept. materials selection Cleve., 1981-82; libr. cons. State Libr. N.C., Raleigh, 1985-87, chief libr. devel., 1987-89; asst. prof. libr., info. studies U. N.C., Greensboro, 1989-95; libr. adminstr. Gulfport (Fla.) Libr., 1995—. Prin. Pathways Cons., 1982—; pres. Cont. Libr. Edn. and Exch. Round Table, 1995-96. Author: Serving the Difficult Customer, 1994; contbr. articles to profl. jours. Mem. ALA. Avocations: reading, computers, photography. Home: 1847 Bonita Way S Saint Petersburg FL 33712-4211 Office: Gulfport Pub Libr 5501 28th Ave S Gulfport FL 33707-5555

SMITH, CATHY, academic administrator; b. Richlands, Va., May 18, 1954; d. James Alvin and Doris Janet (Wilson) Smith; 1 child, Erin Amanda; m. John G. Cox. AS, S.W. Va. Community Coll., 1974; BS, Clinch Valley Coll., 1978; MS, Radford U., 1983. Cert. elem. grades 4-7, reading specialist grades K-12, devel. edn. specialist. Chpt. I reading tchr. Russell County Schs., Lebanon, Va., 1978-90; adj. faculty, reading S.W. Va. C.C., Richlands, 1983-87; elem. tchr. Russell County Schs., Lebanon; instr. devel. and basic reading and study skills NE State Tech. C.C., Blountville, Tenn., 1990-93; reading faculty Heartland C.C., Bloomington, Ill., 1993-96, open learning coord., 1996—. Dir. transitional studies, title III coord. Lake Mich. Coll., 1999-2000. Mem. Nat. Assn. Devel. Edn., Nat. Assn. Devel. Educators, Kellogg Inst., Coll. Reading and Learning Assn. (mem. Mich. devel. edn. consortium). Office: 2755 E Napier Ave Benton Harbor MI 49022-1881 Address: 7622 Red Arrow Hwy Stevensville MI 49127-9250 E-mail: smithk@lmc.cc.mi.us.

SMITH, CECE, venture capitalist; b. Washington, Nov. 16, 1944; d. Linn Charles and Grace Inez (Walker) S.; m. John Ford Lacy, Apr. 22, 1978. BBA, U. Mich., 1966; MLA, So. Meth. U., 1974. CPA, Tex. Staff acct. Arthur Young & Co. (CPAs), Boston, 1966-68; staff acct., then asst. to contr. Wyly Corp., Dallas, 1969-72; contr., treas. subs. Univ. Computing Co., 1972-74; contr. Steak and Ale Restaurants Am., Inc., 1974-76, v.p. fin., 1976-80, exec. v.p., 1980-81, Pearle Health Services, Inc., 1981-84, pres. Primacare div., 1984-86; gen. ptnr. Phillips-Smith-Machens Venture Ptnrs., 1986—; pres. Le Sportsac Dallas, Inc., 1981-87. Bd. dirs. Brinker Internat. Inc., Beautyco, Inc., Fed. Res. Bank of Dallas, 1992—97, chmn., 1994—96; past v.p., dir. IWF-Dallas. Former co-chmn. pres.'s rsch. coun. U. Tex. S.W. Med. Ctr. Dallas; former mem. vis. com. U. Mich. Grad. Sch. Bus.; exec. bd. So. Meth. U. Cox Sch. Bus.; former v.p., bd. dirs. Jr. Achievement Dallas; past pres. Charter 100; past treas. Dallas Assembly. Mem. Tex. Soc. CPAs, Com. of 200. Home: 3710 Shenandoah St Dallas TX 75205-2121 Office: 5080 Spectrum Dr Ste 805 W Addison TX 75001-4648

SMITH, CHARLES CARTER, JR. publishing executive; b. Mobile, Ala., Jan. 14, 1930; s. Charles Carter Sr. and Sidney Taylor (Adair) S.; m. Elizabeth Covington, July 4, 1959; children: Adair, Carter, Adam. BA with high honors, U. South, 1951; postgrad., Northwestern U., 1954-55. Asst. to nat. housewares sales mgr. Sears-Roebuck & Co., Chgo., 1954-57; acct. supr. McAnn-Erickson Advt., 1957-60; dir. mktg. Ency. Britannica Press, 1960-63; pub. Systems for Edn., Inc., 1963-67; asst. pub. Time-Life Books, N.Y.C., 1967-70; pres. Media Projects, Inc., 1970—. Adj. lectr. NYU, 1992-93; bd. dirs. Sharon (Conn.) Hist. Dist. Com., Sharon Hist. Soc., Sickness Prevention Achieved Through Regional Collaboration. Author: Mobile: 1864, 3 vols., 1964, Images of Healing, 1980, Country Antiques and Collectibles, 1981, Decorating with Americana, 1985, A Day in the Life of a Medical Detective, 1985, Turning Points in American History: The Korean War, 1990, A Day in the Life of an FBI Agent in Training, 1991, Turning Points in American History: The Jamestown Colony, 1991; editor: American Heritage Illustrated History of the U.S., 18 vols., 1988, Images on File: The Faces of America, 1988, Images on File: Key Issues in Constitutional History, 1988, Images on File: The Civil War, 1989, Images on File: Colonial and Revolutionary America, 1990, Images on File: The Faces of America 2, 1990, American Albums from the Library of Congress: Colonial America, 6 vols., 1991, American Albums from the Library of Congress: The American West, 6 vols., 1991, American Albums from the Library of Congress: The Civil War, 6 vols., 1992, American Albums from the Library of Congress: The U.S. Presidency, 6 vols., 1993, Journeys Into the Past: Daily Life in Colonial America, 1993; contbr. articles to Saturday Rev., So. Accents. Trustee Day Sch., N.Y.C., 1980-82. Decorated Army Commendation medal, 1953; recipient VISTA Achievement cert. U.S. Office Econ. Opportunity, 1969. Mem. Am. Book Prodrs. Assn. (founder, pres. 1980-82), Century Assn., Madison Coun. Libr. Congress, Sharon Country Club. Episcopalian. Avocations: tennis, gardening, collecting hist. American prints. Office: Media Projects Inc 245 Palisade St Ste 359 Dobbs Ferry NY 10522 E-mail: ccartersmith@aol.com.

SMITH, CHARLES ANTHONY, business executive; b. Santa Fe, Sept. 16, 1939; s. Frances (Mier) Vigil; m. Paula Ann Thomas, June 26, 1965; 1 child, Charlene Danielle. Student various adminstrv. & law courses. Circulation mgr. Daily Alaska Empire, 1960-63; agt. Mut. of N.Y. Life Ins. Co., Juneau, Alaska, 1964-65; mng. ptnr. Future Investors in Alaska and Cinema Alaska, 1961-62; SE Alaska rep. K & L Distbrs., 1966-68; mgr. SE Alaska Alaska Airlines Newspapers, 1969; dep. Alaska Retirement Sys., Juneau, 1970-71; apptd. dir. hwy. safety, gov.'s hwy. safety rep., 1971-83; pres. Valley Svc. Ctr., I Nc., 1984-94; chmn. S.E. Alaska Employee Support of the Guard and Reserve, 1992—; pres. 3-S Corp., 1995—. Apptd. chmn. S.E. Alaska for ESGR, 1995; apptd. Alaska state dir. Selective Svc., 1996—. Author various hwy. safety manuals and plans. Alaska pres. Muscular Dystrophy Assn. Am.; pres. SE Alaska Emergency Med. Svcs. Coun., 1965-72; state dir. Selective Svc., 1996. Served to maj. Army N.G., 1964-88. Named Alaska Safety Man of Yr., 1977. Mem. Am. Assn. Motor Vehicle Adminstrs., Alaska Peace Officers Assn., Nat. Assn. Gov.'s Hwy. Safety Reps., N.G. Assn., Internat. Platform Assn., Elks (Juneau). Roman Catholic. Home: PO Box 32856 Juneau AK 99803-2856

SMITH, CHARLES EDWIN, computer science educator; b. Columbia, Mo., Apr. 15, 1950; s. William Walter and Nelletha Pearl (Lavendar) S.; m. Mary L. Davis, July 27, 1991. AA, Edison C.C., Ft. Myers, Fla., 1971; BS, Troy State U., 1979; MA, Webster U., St. Louis, 1989. Adj. instr. Manatee C.C., Venice, Fla., 1989-90, Edison C.C., Punta Gorda, 1989-92, prof. computer sci., 1992—, Charles O'Neill endowed chair astronomy, 1997-2001. Cons. Charles E. Smith Consulting, North Port, Fla., 1989-91; owner SmithTech Dental Handpiece Repair. Served to maj. USAF, 1975-79, USAFR, 1979-96. Mem. Air Force Assn. Mem. Fla. Assn. C.C.s, Air Force Assn., Am. Legion. Avocations: reading, fishing, boating, astronomy, woodworking. Office: Edison C C 26300 Airport Rd Punta Gorda FL 33950-5748

SMITH, CHARLES HADDON, geoscientist, consultant; b. Dartmouth, N.S., Can., Sept. 3, 1926; s. Albion Benson and Dora Pauline (McGill) S.; m. Mary Gertrude Saint, Sept. 5, 1949; children: Charles Douglas, Richard David, Alan Michael, Timothy McGill. B.Sc. and Diploma in Engring, Dalhousie U., Can., 1946, M.Sc. in Geology, 1948; MS, Yale U., 1951, PhD in Econ. Geology, 1952. Instr. Dalhousie U., Halifax, N.S., 1946-48; geologist Cerro de Pasco Copper Corp., Morococha, Peru, 1949, Geol. Survey of Can., Ottawa, Ont., 1952-64, chief petrological scis. div., 1964-67, chief crustal geology div., 1967-68; sci. adviser Sci. Council Can., Ottawa, 1968-70; dir. planning Dept. Energy Mines and Resources, 1970-71, asst. dep. minister sci. and tech., 1971-75, sr. asst. dep. minister, 1975-81; pres. Charles H. Smith Cons., 1982-94. Mem. adv. coun. dept. geology and geophysics Princeton U., 1967-76; sci. advisor Can. Commn. for UNESCO, 1983-89; exec. dir. Can. Nat. Com./World Energy Conf., 1983-90; bd. govs. Can. Inst. Radiation Safety, 1983-86; hon. mem. Energy Coun. Can., 1991—; coord. 150th anniversary Geol. Survey Can., 1990-93. Mem. editl. bd. Am. Jour. Sci., 1967-72, Mineralium Deposita, 1968-83, Jour. Petrology, 1966-70, Econ. Geology, 1966-70; contbr. articles to profl. jours. Fellow Royal Soc. Can. (fgn. sec. 1986-90), Mineral. Soc. Am., Soc. Econ. Geologists (v.p. N.Am. 1968-70), Canadian Acad. Engring.; mem. Can. Inst. Mining and Metallurgy (life mem., v.p. 1982-84), Assn. Profl. Engrs. Ont., Geol. Assn. Can., Can. Geosci. Coun. (pres. 1984), Rotary.

SMITH, CHARLES ISAAC, geology educator; b. Hearne, Tex., Feb. 9, 1931; s. Walter Lee and Nellie Lucille (Clearwater) S.; m. Anita Lou Howell, Aug. 22, 1961; children: Lanita Maylene, James Emmett, Timothy Stephen, Sheila Nell. BS, Baylor U., 1952; MA, La. State U., 1955; PhD, U. Mich., 1966. Geologist Shell Devel. Co., Houston, 1955-60, 62-65; prof. geology U. Mich., Ann Arbor, 1965-77, chmn. dept., 1970-77; prof. geology U. Tex., Arlington, 1977-93, prof. emeritus, 1994—, chmn. dept., 1977-89, cons. geologist, 1993—. Contbr. articles to profl. jours. Home: 110 Reservoir Rd Ruidoso NM 88345-9307 Office: Univ Tex Dept Geology Arlington TX 76019-0001

SMITH, CHARLES JOE, SR. music educator; b. Tuskegee, Ala., Aug. 24, 1951; s. Jim Smith and Mattie (Burrell) Wilson; m. Susie Marie Jones, May 9, 1970; children: Charles J., Jr., Yashica C. Profl. diploma, Am. Sch. Photography, Chgo., 1972; B in Music Edn., Jackson (Miss.) State U., 1973; M in Music Edn., Vandercook Coll. Music, 1982; PhD, Kennedy-Western U., Augoura Hills, Calif., 1988. Cert. music educator, Ga. Dir. bands D.C. Wolfe High Sch., Shorter, Ala., 1973-77, T.W. Josey Comprehensive High Sch., Augusta, Ga., 1977—; adminstrv. asst. Richmond County Band Programs, 1977. Guest condr. Amos Alonzo Stagg Bowl, 1979-81; coord. Cen. Savannah River Area Jazz Fest, 1980-85; adjudicator Alcorn State U. Jazz Fest, 1982-85; asst. dir. John Phillip Sousa Nat. High Sch. Hon. Band, 1985; cons. Ga. Dept. Edn. Tchr. Cert. Test Revision; chmn. Richmond County Bd. Edn. Spring Fling; other activities. Recipient award Augusta Black History Com., badge of merit John Phillip Sousa Found., 1985; named with D.C. Wolfe High Sch. Band as Ala.'s Bicentennial Band State of Ala., 1976, Hon. Lt. Col. Aide-de-Camp, 1976, one of Outstanding Young Men of Am., 1977, 83, 85, 87, 88, 90, Tchr. of Yr. Augusta, Ga.-Richmond County, 1988-89, Educator of Yr. Augusta Jaycees, 1989, State Citizen of Yr. Omega Psi Phi, 1989, Local Citizen of Yr., 7th Dist. Citizen of Yr. Mem. NAACP, Nat. Assn. Jazz Educators (chmn. jazz 10th dist. Ga. 1985—, cert. 1986—), Nat. Band Assn., Music Educators Nat. Conf., Richmond County Band Dirs. Assn. (chmn. budget, all-county coms. 1985—), Inst. Cert. Photographers, Inc. (life), Profl. Photographers Am., Ga. Music Educators Assn., 100 Black Men Am., Inc., 100 Black Men Augusta, Omega Psi Phi (chmn. talent hunt, scholarship coms. 1985— Local Citizen of Yr. 1989, State Citizen of Yr. 1989, 7th Dist. Citizen of Yr. Ala., Ga., Fla., Miss., 1989). Clubs: Band Boosters (Augusta) (chmn. budget com. 1977—). Democrat. Baptist. Avocations: music, basketball, tennis, football, golf. Home: 2910 Inwood Dr Hephzibah GA 30815-4158

SMITH, CHARLES LEWIS, retired career officer and association executive; b. Clarkston, Ga., Oct. 27, 1920; s. Robert Clyde and Emelyn (Bloodworth) S.; m. Mildred Lee Stilley, Sept. 5, 1947; children: Jan, Robert Eugene. Student, Ga. Sch. Tech., 1938-39. Enlisted USN, 1937, advanced through grades to comdr., 1968; various assignments including comdg. officer USS Chickasaw (ATF 83), 1962-64; leadership devel. officer Amphibious Force U.S. Pacific Fleet, 1964-66; comdg. officer USS Tioga County (LST 1158), 1966-68; dept. head Amphibious Sch. U.S. Naval Amhibious Base, Coronado, Calif., 1968-70, ret., 1970; dir. pub. rels. and fin. San Diego County Coun. Boy Scouts Am., 1971-80, dir. pub. rels., 1980-82, dir. planned giving, 1982-85, ret., 1985. Mem. nat. adv. bd. Am. Security Coun., 1994-97. Trustee God Bless Am. Week, Inc., 1972-80, pres., 1977-78, co-chmn. San Diego Bicentennial Pageant, 1976; mem. adv. bd. Commd. Officers Mess (Open) U.S. Naval Sta., 1973-89; bd. dirs. Boys Club Chula Vista, Calif., 1985-87; devel. com. Alvarado Health Found., Alvarado Hosp. Med. Ctr., 1986-87; charter rev. com. City of Chula Vista, 1986-88; mem. accolades com. City of San Diego, 1988-90; rsch. bd. advisors Am. Biog. Inst., 1988-2001; vol. Boy Scouts Am. 1935-71, 85—; scout commr. San Diego County coun. 1969-71, mem. internat. rels. com. 1985-92, bd. dirs., 1995-97, scoutmaster 7th Nat. Jamboree, Farragut State park, Idaho, 1969, 13th World Jamboree, Japan, 1971, mem. local staff Nat. Jamboree, Ft. A.P. Hill, Va., 1986, mem. nat. staff, 1997. Recipient svc. award Civitan Internat., 1968, Cmty. Svc. resolution Calif. Senate, 1970, Southwestern Coll., 1973, Silver Beaver award Boy Scouts Am., 1965, Svc. to Youth resolution Calif. Senate, 1985, award Armed Forces YMCA Century Club, 1988, Appreciation award United Way San Diego, 1974-82, citation for heroism Sheriff of San Diego, 1991, Recognition award San Diego Rotary Club, 1991, citation for svc. City of San Diego Accolades Com., 1992, Disting. Svc. award U.S.S. Chickasaw (ATF-83) Assn., 1993, Svc. award U.S.S. Wickes (DD578), 1995, Cert. of Appreciation, USN Meml. Found., 1997, 99, Cert. of Appreciation, Warrant Officers Assn., 1998, Nat. Comdr. Heroes of '76, Patriots of '76 award, 1999, 2000, Cert. of Appreciation, Nat. Sojourners, 2000, Vets. of the Vietnam War, 2001, 65 Year Verts. award Boy Scouts of Am. Youth, 2000, Certificate of Appriciation, Veterans of Foreign Wars, 2001; Scouter Chuck Smith Day proclaimed by City of San Diego, 1985; flagpole dedicated to Scouter Chuck Smith San Diego County Coun. Boy Scouts Am., 1992; named Vet. of Yr., Centurion Info. Assn., 2001; named to Hon. Order Ky. Cols., 1985, bd. dirs., 1987—, pres., 1996. Mem. VFW (Certs. of Appreciation 1995-97, 99-2002), Nat. Soc. Fund Raising Execs. (bd. dirs. San Diego chpt. 1975-80, 84-85, hosp. com. 1984-85), UN Assn. (bd. dirs. San Diego chpt. 1972-85), Ret. Officers Assn. (life, bd. dirs. Sweetwater chpt. 1972-92, pres. 1975, 81), Navy League U.S. (bd. dirs. 1984—, greeters 1983—, Appreciation award 1985, Cert. of Merit 1991), Mil. Order World Wars (comdr. 1989-90, nat. citations 1987, 91, 92, Outstanding Chpt. Comdr. award Dept. So. Calif. 1990, Patrick Henry medallion and medal 1996), Am. Legion, Crazy Horse Meml. Found., Clarkston Civitan Club (founding bd. dirs.), Eagle Scout Alumni Assn. (life; founder 1973, bd. dirs. 1986-88, 98), Hammer Club San Diego, Kiwanis (bd. dirs. 1984-88, chmn. fellowship com. 1983-84, boys and girls com. 1984-85, planned giving com. 1988-89), Order of the Arrow (vigil, Cross Feathers award 1968), Masons, Shriners, Order of Ea. Star (life), Nat. Sojourners (life, Cert. of Appreciation 1999). Methodist.

SMITH, CHARLES NATHANIEL, academic administrator; b. Nov. 17, 1953; BS in Psychology, Va. Commonwealth U.; EdD, Va. Polytech. & State U. Dis. spl. svcs., asst. prof. St. Paul's Coll.; dir. spl. svcs., assoc. prof. psychology Gulf Coast C.C.; dir. minority student affairs, spl. asst. to provost George Mason U.; asst. vice provost, dean student devel. Chgo. State U.; v.p. enrollment mgmt. & student affairs Del. State U. Office: Del State U Grossley Hall #109 Dover DE 19901 Home: 102 Gardengate Rd Camden Wyoming DE 19934-9648

SMITH, CHARLES OLIVER, engineer; b. Clinton, Mass., May 28, 1920; s. Oliver E. and Flora (Small) S.; m. Mary J. Boyle, Feb. 9, 1946; children: Mary J., Charles M., John P., Susan M., Peter G., Robert A., Katherine M. BS in Mech. Engring., Worcester Poly. Inst., 1941; SM, MIT, 1947, ScD in Metallurgy, 1951. Instr. mech. engring. Worcester Poly. Inst., 1941-43; instr., then asst. prof. Mass. Inst. Tech., 1946-51; research engr. Alcoa Research Lab., 1951-55, Oak Ridge Nat. Lab, 1955-65; prof. engring. U. Detroit, 1965-76, U. Nebr., 1976-81, Rose-Hulman Inst. Tech., 1981-86. Author: Product Liability: Are You Vulnerable?, Nuclear Reactor Materials, Science of Engineering Materials, Introduction to Reliability in Design; also numerous papers on materials, design, product liability, engring. edn. Served with USNR, 1943-46. Recipient St. George award Boy Scouts Am. Fellow ASME (Triodyne Safety award 1992, Machine Design award, 1993), Am. Soc. Engring. Edn. (Fred Merryfield award 1981); mem. AIME, Am. Soc. Metals, Sigma Xi, Tau Beta Pi, Pi Tau Sigma, Phi Kappa Theta. Home: 1717 Homewood Blvd Apt 156 Delray Beach FL 33445-6899

SMITH, CHARLES WILLIAM, social sciences educator, sociologist; b. Providence; s. Joseph and Clara (Loitman) S.; m. Rita Cope Saguy, Sept. 3, 1963; children: Abigail Cope, Jonathan Cope. AB, Wesleyan U., 1960; MA, PhD in Sociology, Brandeis U., 1966. Instr. sociology Simmons Coll., Boston, 1964-65; from lectr. to assoc. prof. Queens Coll., Flushing, N.Y., 1965-71, from assoc. to prof. sociology, 1979—; grad. faculty Grad. Ctr. CUNY, 1986—. Vis. scholar Nuffield Coll., Oxford, Eng., 1979-80, Wesleyan U., Middletown, Conn., 1987-88; chair dept. sociology Queens Coll., Flushing, 1988-91, 97-00, acting dean of faculty social sci., 1991-92, dean faculty social sci., 1992-97; cons. auctions, 1986—. Author: Critique of Sociological Reasoning: An Essay in Philosophic Sociology, 1979, Auctions: The Social Construction of Values, 1989, Success and Survival on Wall Street: Understanding the Mind of the Market, 1999, Market Values Im American Higher Education, 2000; editor Jour. for Theory of Social Behavior, 1983—. Bd. dirs., pres. Cmty. Action Program of White Plains, N.Y., 1974-79; bd. trustees, v.p. Temple Israel Ctr. of White Plains, 1975-94; class agt., alumni activities Wesleyan U., Middletown, Conn., 1960—. Recipient FIPSE award Dept. Edn., 1993-96, Ford Found. Diversity grant, 1990-93, 96-98. Office: Queens Coll CUNY 65-30 Kissena Blvd Flushing NY 11367-1575 E-mail: charles_smith@qc.edu.

SMITH, CHARLES Z. state supreme court justice; b. Lakeland, Fla., Feb. 23, 1927; s. John R. and Eva (Love) S.; m. Eleanor Jane Martinez, Aug. 20, 1955; children: Carlos M., Michael O., Stephen P., Felica L. BS, Temple U., 1952; JD, U. Wash., 1955. Bar: Wash. 1955. Law clk. Wash. Supreme Ct., Olympia, 1955-56; dep. pros. atty., asst. chief criminal div. King County, Seattle, 1956-60; ptnr. Bianchi, Smith & Tobin, 1960-61; spl. asst. to atty. gen. criminal div. U.S. Dept. Justice, Washington, 1961-64; judge criminal dept. Seattle Mcpl. Ct., 1965-66; judge Superior Ct. King County, 1966-73; former assoc. dean, prof. law U. Wash., 1973; now justice Wash. Supreme Ct., Olympia. Mem. adv. bd. NAACP, Seattle Urban League, Wash. State Literacy Coun., Boys Club, Wash. Citizens for Migrant Affairs, Medina Children's Svc., Children's Home Soc. Wash., Seattle Better Bus. Bur., Seattle Foundation, Seattle Symphony Orch., Seattle Opera Assn., Community Svc. Ctr. for Deaf and Hard of Hearing, Seattle U., Seattle Sexual Assault Ctr., Seattle Psychoanalytic Inst., The Little Sch., Linfield Coll., Japanese Am. Citizens League, Kawabe Meml. Hous, Puget Counseling Ctr, Am. Cancer Soc., Hutchinson Cancer Rsch. Ctr., Robert Chinn Found.; pres. Am. Bapt. Chs. U.S.A., 1976-77, U.S. Commn. on Internat. Religious Freedom, 1999-2000. lt. col. ret. USMCR Mem. ABA, Am. Judicature Soc., Washington Bar Assn., Seattle-King County Bar Assn., Order of Coif., Phi Alpha Delta, Alpha Phi Alpha. Office: Wash Supreme Ct Temple of Justice PO Box 40929 Olympia WA 98504-0929

SMITH, CHESTER, broadcasting executive; b. Mar. 29, 1930; s. Louis L. and Effie (Brown) S.; m. Naomi L. Crenshaw, July 19, 1959; children: Lauri, Lorna, Roxanne. Country western performer Capitol Records, TV, Radio, 1947-61, Sta. KLOC, Ceres-Modesto, Calif., 1963-81, Sta. KCBA-TV, Salinas-Monterey, 1963-81; owner, gen. ptnr. Sta. KCSO-TV, Modesto-Stockton-Sacramen, 1966-97, Sta. KCVU-TV, Paradise-Chico-Redding, 1986—, Sta. KBVU-TV, Eureka, 1990—, KNSO-TV, Merced-Fresno, 1996—, KCSO-TV, Sacramento, 1996—, KRVU-TV, Redding, 1997—, Univision 28, Chico, K23EW, Monterey-Salinas. Original rec. Wait A Little Longer Please Jesus in Country Music Hall of Fame, Nashville, 1955, album California Blend (with Merle Haggard), 2001. Inductee Western Swing Hall of Fame, Sacramento, 1988; recipient cert. of recognition for 50 years of cmty. svc. Calif. Assembly, 1997. Mem. Calif. Broadcasters Assn. Republican. Mem. Christian Ch. Address: Sainte Partners II L P PO Box 4159 Modesto CA 95352-4159 E-mail: saint@thevision.net.

SMITH, CHRISTINE CHEW, artist, educator; b. Bryn Mawr, Pa. d. David Sands Brown and Eileen T. (Petchell) Chew; m. Christopher A. Smith, Jan. 23, 1960 (dec. 1994); children; Jeffrey, Bradford, Randolph. BA, U. Colo., 1958; postgrad., NYU, 1977—78, Columbia U., 1961-62. Tchr. adult edn. Guild Hall Mus., East Hampton, N.Y., 1992-93. One-woman shows include South Street Seaport Mus., N.Y.C., 1975, New Eng. Ctr. for Arts, Brooklyn, Conn., 1980, Water Mill Mus., L.I., N.Y., 1980, Ashawagh Hall, East Hampton, 1984, 85, 87, Gallery 84, N.Y.C., 1988, Elaine Benson Gallery, Bridgehampton, N.Y., 1985, 87, 92, Bologna Landi Gallery, East Hampton, 1992, Union League Club, N.Y.C., 1993, Architrove Gallery, East Hampton, 1994, Nat. Arts Club, N.Y.C., 1995, numerous others; exhibited in group shows Avery Fisher Hall, 1979, 80, Pace U. Gallery, N.Y.C., 1983, Gail Chase Galllery, Bellevue, Wash., 1983, County Art Gallery, Locust Valley, N.Y., 1988, Clayton-Liberatore Galleries, Bridgehampton, 1989, 90, 92, Gallery East, East Hampton, 1989, Graphic Eye Gallery, Port Washington, 1992, Pastel Soc. Am., N.Y.C., 1993, Ashawagh Hall, 1993, Vanderbilt Mus., Centerport, N.Y., 1993, Lizan-Tops Gallery, East Hampton, 1994, St. Joseph's Coll., Patchogue, N.Y., 1993, 95, Guild Hall, East Hampton, 1981-2001, Hampton Art Ctr., 1995, Firehouse Gallery, Nassau C.C., Garden City, N.Y., 1996, numerous others; represented in permanent collections Colo. Sch. Mines, Golden, also corp. and numerous pvt. collections. Recipient hon. mention Heckscher Mus., 1990, Northport-BJ Spoke Gallery, 1991, Bellport Lane Art Gallery, 1995; S.O.S. grantee N.Y. Found. for Arts, 1993. Mem. LWV, Jimmy Ernst Artists Alliance (bd. dirs. 1993-95), Southampton Artists, Inc. (bd. dirs. 1998-2002), Hampton Art Ctr., Artists Equity N.Y. Democrat. Episcopalian. Avocations: yoga, swimming. Studio: Heron Studios PO Box 247 Bridgehampton NY 11932

SMITH, CHRISTOPHER ALLEN, technology company executive, finance professional; b. Rockford, Ill., Nov. 16, 1961; s. Robert Lee and Martha Ann (Moody) S.; m. Mary G. Meany, Apr. 13, 1991. BA, postgrad., Ind. U., 1983, Golden Gate U., 1986-87, U. Phoenix, 2001—02. Rates analyst North American Van Lines, Ft. Wayne, Ind., 1984-85; mgr., investor rels. BRAE Corp., San Francisco, 1985-87; fin. analyst CIS Corp., 1987-89; dir., corp. devel. Affiliated Computer Systems, Inc., 1989-96; v.p. Sci. Applications Internat. Corp., 1996—. Contbr. articles to profl. jours. Vol. Rep. Party, Foster City, Calif., 1988; apptd. dir. Pvt. Industry Coun. Contra Costa County. With USMCR, 1982-83. Mem. Equipment Leasing Assn. Am. (Jour. award 1991), Ind. U. Alumni Assn. Republican. Roman Catholic. Avocations: freelance writing, photography, gardening. Office: Sci Applications Internat Corp 2000 Powell St Ste 1090 Emeryville CA 94608-1895 E-mail: christopher.a.smith-2@saic.com.

SMITH, CHRISTOPHER HENRY, congressman; b. Rahway, N.J., Mar. 4, 1953; s. Bernard Henry and Katherine Joan (Hall) S.; m. Marie Hahn, July 2, 1977; children: Melissa, Christopher, Michael, Elyse. Student, Worcester Coll., Eng., 1973-74; BA in Bus. Adminstrn., Trenton State Coll., 1975. Exec. dir. N.J. Right to Life Com., 1976-78; dir. instl. sales Leisure Unltd. Inc., Woodbridge, N.J., 1978-80; mem. U.S. Congress from 4th N.J. dist., Washington, 1981—; vice chmn. internat. rels. com., mem. internat. ops. and human rights subcom.; sr. mem. subcom health, chmn. vets. affairs com.; co-chmn. Helsinki com., 1995. U.S. rep. to UN internat. conf. immunizing world's children. Active human rights movements Romania, China, former Soviet Union, Vietnam; co-chmn. House Pro-Life Caucus, 2002; mem. Alzheimer's Task Force and Autism Caucus. Named Legislator of Yr. VFW, Legislator of Yr. Internat. Assn. Chiropractors, Legislator of Yr. KC, 1989, Legislator of Yr. JWV of Am., 1996, Leader of the Yr., N.J. State Postal Workers Union, 2002, William Wilberforce award, 2002; recipient Leader for Peace award Peace Corps. Mem. Nat. Fedn. Ind. Bus. Republican. Roman Catholic. Office: 2373 Rayburn Ho Office Bldg Washington DC 20515-0001

SMITH, CINDY THOMPSON, special education educator; b. Raleigh, N.C., Nov. 6, 1957; d. Donald Wayne and Alice (Dupree) T.; m. Paul Neil Smith, Jan. 2, 1982; 1 child, Paul Cody Ryan. BS, Appalachian State U., Boone, N.C., 1980, MA, 1981. Ednl. specialist Western Carolina Ctr., Morganton, N.C., 1981; day camp dir. Ft. Sill (Okla.) Moral Support Div., 1982; spl. edn. tchr. Carroll High/East Gate Middle Sch., Ozark, Ala., 1982-83; resource specialist Del Rey Woods/Foothill Elem. Sch., Monterey, Calif., 1983-84; spl. day class tchr. Del Rey Woods Elem. Summer Sch., 1984; resource specialist Del Rey Woods/Stilwell Elem. Sch., 1984-85, 85-86; resource spl. day class tchr. Highland Elem. Summer Sch., 1985; spl. edn. resource tchr. East Gate Middle Sch., Ozark, Ala., 1986-89; spl. edn. tchr. Harding Middle Sch., Cedar Rapids, Iowa, 1989—. Named Tchr. of Yr., Ozark City Schs., 1988. Avocations: volleyball, tennis, softball, aerobics. Home: 4501 Pineview Dr NE Cedar Rapids IA 52402-1715 Office: Harding Mid Sch 4801 Golf St NE Cedar Rapids IA 52402-5799

SMITH, CLAIRE, chef; Grad. , Calif. Culinary Acad., San Francisco; grad. in art and art history, Rice U. Chef Green, Oliveto, San Francisco Bay area, The Daily Review Cafe, Houston, 1994—. Office: 3412 W Lamar Houston TX 77019*

SMITH, CLARA JEAN, retired nursing home administrator; b. Berwick, Pa., Aug. 31, 1932; d. Barton Fredrick and Evelyn Miriam (Bomboy) Hough; m. Robert W. Smith, June 7, 1958. BS in Nursing Edn., Wilkes Coll., Wilkes-Barre, Pa., 1960; MS in Edn., Temple U., Phila., 1968. RN, Pa. From staff nurse to DON Retreat State Hosp., Hunlock Creek, Pa., 1953-80; dir. long term care facility Danville (Pa.) State Hosp., 1980-82; ret., 1982. Dir. accreditation coordination and quality assurance, 1980—; spkr., instr. in field. Author tng. and ednl. programs. Mem. Pa. State Employees Retirement Assn. (pres. Luzerne/Columbia County chpt., regional v.p. northeastern Pa.), Pa. Assn. Ret. State Employees Assn., Williamsport Hosp. Sch. Nursing Alumni, Sunshine Club, Town Hill Hobby Group, Town Hill Over 50 Group. Methodist. Home: PO Box 999 Berwick PA 18603-0699 also: 1006 Roslyn Dr Berwick PA 18603

SMITH, CLARK ROBINSON, lawyer; b. Chgo., Feb. 17, 1938; s. Carlton Robinson and Theda Clark (Peters) S.; m. Trina Helen Hendershot, Jan. 20, 1962; children: Clark Carlton, Luke Owen. BS in Econs., U. Pa., 1961; LLB, U. Wis., 1965. Bar: Mass. 1966, U.S. Surpeme Ct. 1976, U.S. Dist. Ct. Mass. 1976, U.S. Tax Ct. 1976. From law clk. to assoc. Johnson Clapp Ives & King, Boston, 1965-67; pvt. practice, 1972—. Bd. dirs., acting chair Zoning Bd. Appeals, Wenham, Mass., 1982-94; bd. dirs. Menasha Corp., Neenah, Wis., Beverly (Mass.) Nat. Bank. Trustee Beverly Regional YMCA, 1984—; bd. dirs. North Country Sch., Lake Placid, N.Y., 1988-95, Menasha Corp. Found., Neenah, 1994; chmn. bd. Theda C. Smith Found., Neenah, 1980—, United Way Cen. North Shore, Beverly, 1993-94. Fellow Mass. Bar Found. (mem. com., county advisor 1990—); mem. ABA, Mass. Bar Assn., Boston Bar Assn. (coms., vol. civil case appts. 1976—), Boston Bar Found. (life, endowment advisor 1990—). Republican. Episcopalian. Avocations: golfing, tennis, skiing. Home: 11 Dodges Row Wenham MA 01984-1601 Office: 101 Federal St Ste 1900 Boston MA 02110-1804

SMITH, CLIFFORD, military association administrator; s. Thomas Smith; 2 children. BA in Polit. Sci, Bus., Ariz. State U., SUNY Binghamto. Mem. Sharon Squadron Sons of Am. Legion, Norfolk County, Mass.; Detachment Mass. Sons of Am. Legion; Registered rep. West Roxbury (Mass.) VA; mem.. Citizens Flag Alliance; cert. field svc. vol.; vol. Boys State; past v.p. Sharon (Mass.) Combined Vets. Coun. Recipient Arthur D. Houghton Meml. award (leader of Mass. Detachment), Nat. Orgn. Sons of Am. Legion, 1992, 1995. Office: The Sons of the Am Legion PO Box 1055 Indianapolis IN 46206

SMITH, CLINTON W. civil engineer, consultant; b. Paducah, Tex., Dec. 9, 1952; s. Arnold T. and V. Pauline (Ramsom) S.; m. Mona B. Robinson, Apr. 10, 1971 (div. Jan. 1982); children: Matthew W., Christina N.; m. J. Renee Howell, Sept. 3, 1982; children: Michael Barrett, Latrece Barrett, Danny Barrett. BSCE, N.Mex. State U., 1974. Registered profl. engr., Tex., N.Mex., Okla., Kans., Colo., Ill., Fla., Minn., Oreg., Ark. Structural engr. Southwestern Pub. Svc., Amarillo, Tex., 1974-79, supervisory structural engr., 1979-82, sr. structural engr., 1982-87; project mgr. Utility Engring., 1987-92, project dir., 1992-93; v.p., COO S.A. Garza Engrs., Austin, Tex., 1993—97; project dir. Utility Engring., Amarillo, 1997—. Adv. bd. mem. West Tex. State U. Engring. Program, Canyon, 1992—. Mem. Tex. Soc. Profl. Engrs. (Young Engr. of Yr. 1987, Engr. of Yr. 2001). Republican. Baptist. Home: 9 Hogan Dr Amarillo TX 79124-1712 Office: SA Garza Engrs 5601 W Interstate 40 Amarillo TX 79106-4605

SMITH, CLYDE RAY, dean; b. Bassett, Va., Apr. 21, 1935; s. William Henry and Ava I. (Roberson) S.; m. Phyllis Jane Watkins, Mar. 25, 1959; children: Anthony William, Cheryl Ann, Theresa Jane. BA, Bridgewater Coll., 1956; MBA, U. Va., 1958. Instr. U. Va. - Darden, Charlottesville, 1961-64, asst. prof., 1964-67, assoc. prof., 1967-72, prof., 1972—, assoc. dean MBA program, 1972-94, assoc. dean exec. edn., 1994-97, interim dean, 1997-98; exec. dir. Darden Sch. Found., 1998—. Adminstrv. dir. Inst. Chartered Fin. Analysts, Charlottesville, 1962-69; bd. dirs. Piccadilly Cafeterias, Inc., Baton Rouge, La., trustee, Bridgewater Coll. Co-author: (books) Executive's Guide to Management Accounting and Control Systems, 1998, Financial Accounting for Management, 1981. Capt. (res.) U.S. Army, 1958-68. Named Disting. Alumnus Bridgewater Coll., Va., 1991. Mem. AICPA, Am. Real Estate Soc., Colonade Club, Farmington Country Club, Raven Soc., Beta Gamma Sigma, Omicron Delta Kappa. Home: 39 Canterbury Rd Charlottesville VA 22903-4700 Office: Univ Va - Darden Sch PO Box 6550 Charlottesville VA 22906-6550 E-mail: crs6n@virginia.edu.

SMITH, CORINNE HOSFELD, librarian; b. Lancaster, Pa., Nov. 22, 1957; d. Lewis Kohler Hosfeld and Myrtle Jeanette Banzhoff; m. Calvin R. Smith Jr., Apr. 10, 1983 (div. Oct. 1991). BS in Edn., Clarion State Coll., 1979; MEd in Comm. Media, Indiana U. Pa., 1982; MEd in Curriculum and Instrn., No. Ill. U., 2000. Sch. libr. Bellwood (Pa.)-Antis Sch. Dist., 1979-88; media resources coord. Pa. State U., University Park, 1988-94; sch. libr. Sch. Dist. U-46, Elgin, Ill., 1995—. Bd. mem. Blair County Geneal. Soc., Altoona, Pa., 1990-93; part-time libr. New Trier Twp. H.S., Winnetka, Ill., 1995-96. Video reviewer Video Rating Guide for Librs., 1990-95; book reviewer The Book Report, 1998--. Vol. docent Volo Bog State Natural Area, Ingleside, Ill., 1997-2000, Tekakwitha Woods Forest Preserve, St. Charles, Ill., 1999—. McHenry County Conservation Dist., 2000—. Mem. Ill. Sch. Libr. Media Assn., Western Pa. Conservancy, Windstar Found., The Nature Conservancy, Thoreau Soc. Avocations: writing, traveling. Office: Elgin HS 1200 Maroon Dr Elgin IL 60120-8145 E-mail: corinne@mc.net.

SMITH, CORLIES MORGAN, publishing executive; b. Phila., Mar. 31, 1929; s. Charles Ross and Mary Howard (Stewart) S.; m. Sheila de Peyster Carey, June 17, 1950; children: Mark, Nicholas, Peter, Baylies, Timothy. BA, Yale U., 1951. Assoc. editor J.B. Lippincott Co., Phila., 1955-62; sr. editor The Viking Press, N.Y.C., 1962-83; editorial dir. Ticknor & Fields, 1984-89; editor in chief Harcourt Brace & Co., 1990-94, editorial con., 1995—. Home and Office: 1435 Lexington Ave New York NY 10128-1625

SMITH, CRAIG MALCOLM, architect, consultant; b. Bloomington, Ind., Nov. 4, 1952; s. Ned Myron and Virginia (Reuter) S.; children: Natalie Fern, Julia. BArch, U. Ill., 1974, MArch, 1976. Registered architect, Ill., Mich., Fla., Ind., Ohio. Design instr. U. Ill., Urbana, 1974-76; intern Piano & Rogers, Paris, 1974; designer Bertrand Golberg, Chgo., 1976-77; architect Schipporeit Inc., 1977-83; prin. Smith-Smith, 1983; dir. architecture Bevins Cons. Inc., 1983-88, Griskelis and Smith, Ltd., Chgo., 1988-2000, pres., 1996-2000; prin., COO Pratt Design Studio, 2000—. Planner City of Hammond and Ind. Arts Coun., 1977; mem. Friends of Downtown, Chgo., 1981-85. Mem. AIA (grantee 1977, chmn. office practice commn. 1985-86, chmn. exhibit Chgo. chpt. housing trends, 1986), Nat. Coun. Archtl. Accreditation Bds. (cert.), Chgo. Archtl. Found. Aux. Bd. (v.p. 1994-95, Newhouse com. 1995—), Phi Kappa Phi. Democrat. Avocations: painting, photography, hist. restoration, skiing, tennis. Office: Pratt Design Studio Ltd 4619 N Ravenswood Chicago IL 60640 E-mail: Craig.Smith@prattdesign.com.

SMITH, CULLEN, lawyer; b. Waco, Tex., May 31, 1925; s. Curtis Cullen and Elizabeth (Brient) S.; m. Laura Risher Dossett, Mar. 6, 1948; children: Sallie Smith Wright, Alethea Risher Smith Gilbert, Elizabeth Brient Smith. Student, Emory U., 1943-44, Duke U., 1944; BBA, Baylor U., 1948, JD, 1950. Bar: Tex. 1950. Ptnr. firm Smith, McIlheran & Smith, Weslaco, Tex., 1950-53, Naman, Howell, Smith & Lee (P.C.), Waco, 1953—. Lectr. law Baylor U. Sch. Law, 1964-72 Contbr. articles to legal publs. Mem. standing com. Episcopal Diocese of Tex., 1960-63, 74-75; trustee Episcopal Theol. Sem. of S.W., 1962-67; mem. Waco City Coun., 1983-86; chmn. bd. Vanguard Sch., 1975; bd. dirs. G.H. Pape Found., 1993-94; bd. dirs., vice chmn. Tex. Ctr. for Legal Ethics and Professionalism, 1994-99; mem. adv. coun. Baylor U. Coll. Arts and Scis., 1998-2001. 1st lt. USMCR, 1943-46. Named One of 5 Outstanding Young Texans Tex. Jr. C. of C., 1957, Baylor Lawyer of Yr., 1980; recipient Disting. Alumnus award Waco Ind. Sch. Dist. Edn. Found., 2002. Fellow Am. Bar Found., Tex. Bar Found. (chmn. bd. 1973-74, 50 Yr. Lawyer award 2000), fellow Coll. of Law Practice Mgmt.; mem. ABA (chmn. standing com. econs. law practice 1965-69, chmn. spl. com. on law book pub. practices 1970-72, chmn. gen. practice sect. 1973-74, mem. house of dels. 1974-81), Am. Law Firm Assn. (chmn. 1989-90), Waco-McLennan County Bar Assn. (pres. 1956-57), Mont. Bar Assn. (hon.), State Bar Tex. (pres. jr. bar 1957-58, chmn. profl. econs. com. 1959-61, chmn. spl. com. on revision Tex. Canons Ethics 1969-71, dir. 1971-74, pres. 1978-79), Baylor U. Law Alumni Assn. (pres. 1962-63), Order of Coif, Delta Sigma Phi, Phi Delta Phi, Am. Inns Ct. (master). Clubs: Ridgewood Country (pres. 1965), Hedonia (pres. 1957). Lodges: Rotary. Avocation: photography. Home: Oak Grove Farm 447 Meandering Way China Spring TX 76633-2905 Office: Naman Howell Smith & Lee PC Tex Ctr PO Box 1470 Waco TX 76703-1470

SMITH, CYNTHIA S. writer; b. N.Y.C., Dec. 29, 1934; d. Harry and Sarah (Cohen) Sharfin; m. David Smith, May 21, 1953 (dec. May 1985); 1 child, Hillary Smith Pannier. BA, Hunter Coll., 1954. Advt. dir. Joshua Meier Co., Inc., N.Y.C., 1955-65; pres. C/D Smith Advt., Inc., Rye, N.Y., 1966-01; assoc. adj. prof. Mgmt. Inst. NYU, 1992—. Author: How to Get Big Results from a Small Advertising Budget, 1978, Doctors' Wives, 1981, Step by Step Advertising, 1985, Seven Levels of Marriage, 1988, Why Women Shouldn't Marry, 1990, What Has She Got?, 1995, Woman's Guide to Starting Business, 1996, Noblesse Oblige, 1996, Misleading Ladies, 1997, Impolite Society, 1997, Silver and Guilt, 1998, Royals and Rogues, 1998. Mem. Authors' Guild, Mystery Writers of Am., Sisters in Crime, Internat. Assn. Crime Writers. Avocations: tennis, chorale singing. E-mail: cssmith@attglobal.com.

SMITH, D. BROOKS, federal judge; b. 1951; BA, Franklin and Marshall Coll., 1973; JD, Dickinson Sch. Law, 1976. Pvt. practice Jubelirer, Carothers, Krier, Halpern & Smith, Altoona, Pa., 1976-84; judge Ct. Common Pleas of Blair County, 1984-88, U.S. Dist. Ct. (we. dist.) Pa., 1988—2002, chief judge, 2001—02. Asst. dist. atty. Blair County, part-time, 1977-79, spl. prosecutor, 1981-83, dist. atty. part-time, 1983-84; instr. Pa. State U., Altoona campus, 1977—, St. Francis Coll., 1986—; adv. com. on criminal rules U.S. Jud. Conf., 1993-99. Trustee St. Francis Coll. vice chmn. of bd. of trustees U. Mem. Am. Law Inst., Pa. Bar Assn., Am. Judicature Soc., Pa. Soc., Amen Corner, Blair County Game, Fish and Forestry Assn., Fed. Judges Assn. (bd. dirs. 1993-97, 2002—), Inns of Ct., Allegheny County Bar Assn., Pi Gamma Mu. Office: US Courthouse 319 Washington St Ste 104 Johnstown PA 15901-1624

SMITH, D. ADAM, congressman; b. Washington, June 15, 1965; m. Sara Bickle-Eldridge, 1993. BA, Fordham U., 1987; JD, U. Wash., 1990. Driver United Parcel Svc., 1985-87; mem. Wash. State Senate, 1990-96; atty. Cromwell Mendoza Belur, 1992-93; asst. prosecuting atty. City of Seattle, 1993-96; mem. 106th Congress from 9th dist. Wash., 1997—. Democrat. Office: 116 Canon Ho Office Bldg Washington DC 20515-0001

SMITH, D. EDWARDS, physician; b. Balt., Aug. 1, 1938; s. Dallas Harold Smith and Eugenia Pursley (Edwards) Fleet; m. Margaret Ann Dennis Smith Ferguson, May 30, 1968 (div. June 1986); children: Todd D. Smith, Sarah P. Smith, Ann M. Smith; m. Janet Pedersen Krag, Mar. 12, 1988. BA in English, Va. Mil. Inst., 1960; MD, Johns Hopkins U., 1964. Diplomate Am. Bd. Internal Medicine, Am. Bd. Rheumatology. Chief rheumatology dept. U.S. Army/Letterman Army Hosp., San Francisco, 1968-70; pvt. practice internal medicine Newport News, Va., 1970-85; asst. prof. medicine Ea. Va. Med. Sch., Norfolk, 1977-85; asst. to assoc. prof. physiology Maharishi U. of Mgmt., Fairfield, Iowa, 1985-93; dir. Maharishi Ayur-Veda U., Columbus and Cleve., Ohio, 1993-96; pres. Maharishi Coll. of Medicine, Albuquerque, 1996—; med. dir. N.Mex. Ctr. for Chronic Disorders, 1997—2001. Contbr. articles to profl. jours. Grantee McCormick, Balt., 1988, Ohio State Rsch. Found., Columbus, 1992. Fellow ACP; mem. Physicians Assn. for Eradicating Chronic Diseases (exec. bd. 1997—), Am. Assn. Physicians for Maharishi Med. Colls. Avocations: woodworking, timber growing. Home: 1537 Bull Lea Rd Lexington KY 40511 Office: Maharishi Coll Vedic Medicine 2721 Arizona St NE Albuquerque NM 87110-3330 E-mail: desmithmd38@earthlink.net.

SMITH, D(AISY) MULLETT, publisher; b. Washington, Aug. 17, 1948; d. Gordon Hunt and Suzanne Myrick (Mullett) Smith. BA, Am. U., 1970; cert. computer programming, U. So. Calif., Arlington, Va., 1986; cert. in records mgmt., Assn. Records Mgrs. Am., Prairie Village, Kans., 1987. Christian Sci. practitioner The First Ch. of Christ, Scientist, Boston, 1970-86; clk. Fifth Ch. of Christ, Scientist, Washington, 1971-74; Christian Sci. campus counsellor The Am. U., 1976-81; editor, computer specialist, desktop pub. Mullett-Smith Press, 1984-89, owner, pub., author, 1989—, music copyist, pub. on computer, 1990—, web weaver, 1996—. Computer cons. and pub. spkr. in field; guest participant divsn. children in trouble White House Conf. on Children, 1970. Author, editor, pub.: AB Mullett, His Relevance in American Architecture, 1990 (Printers award 1990); editor: AB Mullett, Architect Engineer 1862-90, 1985; contbr. articles to profl. jours.; desktop pub. musical scores by Richard Henry Lee, 1991—; art pamphlets by Suzanne M. Smith, 1999—. Participant White House Conf. on Children, 1970; active Save Pioneer Post Office, Portland, Oreg., 1996—; fund raiser com. U.S. Treasury Bill Restoration Fund, 1998-2000; libr. Christian Sci. Reading Rm., 1999-2002. Recipient Key to the City, Mayor Lincoln, Nebr., 1989. Mem. Nat. Soc. Arts and Letters (editor/pub. directory 1971-88, 89-91, 92—, treas. 1988-90, web weaver 1996—), Nat. Trust for Hist. Preservation, Assn. Records Mgrs. and Adminstrs., Assn. for Info. and Image Mgmt. Internat., U.S. Treasury Hist. Assn. (spkr. 1992-96), U.S. Capitol Hist. Soc. Avocations: art, design, teaching and playing classical guitar, windsurfing, computers. Office: Mullett-Smith Press 4450 Dexter St NW Washington DC 20007-1113 E-mail: mspress@mullett-smithpress.com.

SMITH, DALE CARY, medical historian, educator; b. Orlando, Fla., July 2, 1951; s. D. Carl and Margaret Lee; m. Margaret Gatlin Smith, Aug. 18, 1973; 1 child, Darion Christopher. BA, Duke U., 1973; PhD, U. Minn., 1979. Asst. prof. U. Minn., Mpls., 1979-82; with dept. med. history Uniformed Svcs. U., Bethesda, Md., 1982-97, prof., chmn. dept. med. history, 1997—. Historian Mil. Medicine, Bethesda, 1999—; hist. cons. Am. Gastroenterol. Assn., Bethesda, 1995-99. Author: Am. Gastroenterological Assn. (1987-1997) a Centennial History, 1999; editor: William Budd's Essay on Fever, 1984; book rev. editor Jour. History of Medicine, 1979-82, assoc. editor, 1982-87, editl. bd., 1988-91; mem. editl. bd. Bull. History of Medicine, 1996-99. Moderator Redland Bapt. Ch., Rockville, 1997-2001. Recipient The Laurance D Redway award N.Y. State Med. Soc., 1987. Mem. Am. Assn. for History of Medicine (coun. mem. 1985-87, newsletter editor 1998—). Baptist. Office: Uniformed Svcs U Dept Med History 4301 Jones Bridge Rd Bethesda MD 20814-4712 E-mail: dcsmith@usuhs.mil.

SMITH, DANI ALLRED, sociologist, educator; b. Natchez, Miss., Dec. 12, 1955; d. Paul Hollis and Mary Frances (Byrd) Allred; m. Ronald Bassel Smith, Aug. 9, 1980. BS in Social Sci., Lee Coll., 1977; MA in Sociology, U. Miss., 1980; PhD in Sociology, U. Tenn., 2001. Staff writer Natchez Dem., 1977; secondary tchr. Natchez Pub. Schs., 1977-78; instr. sociology U. Miss., 1980-81, 82, rsch. assoc., instr. mgmt. info. systems, 1982-87; secondary tchr. Coffeeville (Miss.) Schs., 1981-82; asst. prof. sociology Lee Coll., Cleveland, Tenn., 1988-96, Fisk U., Nashville, 1996—. Advisor socilogy club Lee Coll., Cleveland, Tenn., 1988—96, advisor Lee Collegian (campus newspaper), 1988—93, advisor Epsilon Lambda Phi, 1989—90, advisor Alpha Kappa Delta, 1992—96, Fisk U., Nashville, 2000—, advisor sr. class, 1997—98, 2001—02. Contbr. articles to profl. jours. and newspapers. Mellon Appalachian fellow, 1993-94; named one of Outstanding Young Women Am., 1981. Mem. Am. Sociol. Assn., So. Sociol. Assn., Christian Sociol. Assn., Gt. Smoky Mountains Natural History Assn., Am. Hiking Soc., Habitat for Humanity Ptnrs. Coun., Phi Kappa Phi, Alpha Chi, Alpha Kappa Delta. Avocations: reading, hiking, camping, plate collecting, cross-stitching. Home: 430 20th St NE Cleveland TN 37311-3949 Office: Fisk Univ Dept Sociology 1000 17th Ave N Nashville TN 37208-3045 E-mail: dasmith@fisk.edu.

SMITH, DANIEL CLIFFORD, lawyer; b. Cin., Aug. 9, 1936; s. Clifford John and Vivian Aileen (Stone) S.; m. Carroll Cunningham; children: Edward, Andrew, Scott. BS, Ariz. State U., 1960; postgrad., George Washington U., 1961-62; JD, Am. U., 1965. Bar: D.C. 1965, U.S. Ct. Appeals (D.C. cir.) 1966, U.S. Ct. Appeals (Fed. cir.), U.S. Dist. Ct. D.C. 1966, Va. 1967, U.S. Supreme Ct. 1969, U.S. Ct. Appeals (4th cir., 5th cir., 6th cir., 7th cir., 9th cir., 11th cir.), U.S. Ct. Claims, U.S. Ct. Customs and Patent Appeals, U.S. Tax Ct. Assoc. Alpern & Feissner, Washington, 1963-66; atty. FTC, 1966-70; ptnr. Arent, Fox, Kintner, Plotkin & Kahn, 1970-93, Canfield & Smith, Washington, 1993—. Pres., dir. Country Pl. Citizens Assn., Inc., 1974-77; bd. dirs. Sea Watch Condominium, Ocean City, Md., 1978—, treas., 1982-86, pres. 1986—; active Supreme Ct. Hist. Soc., The Federalist Soc., Smithsonian Inst. Assocs., Ariz. State Soc. Served with USMC. Mem. D.C. Bar Assn. (bd. dirs. 1974-76, chmn. consumer protection com. 1972-74, chmn. D.C. affairs sect. 1975-76), Va. State Bar Assn., Fed. Bar Assn., Assn. Trial Lawyers Am., Nat. Field Selling Assn. (gen. counsel), Ariz. State U. Alumni Assn., Rotary Club (pres. 1987-88, 96-97), Optimist (pres. 1972-73), Internat. Town and Country Club (dir. 1969-73), Masons, Delta Theta Phi. Office: Canfield & Smith Fed Bar Bldg 1815 H St NW Ste 1001 Washington DC 20006-3604

SMITH, DANIEL EVAN, political science educator, consultant; b. Big Spring, Tex., Feb. 21, 1963; s. Matthew Norris and Sandee (Chernow) S.; m. Susan Elizabeth Marshall, Jan. 11, 1965; children: Benjamin, Sarah. BA, Coll. William and Mary, 1985; JD, U. Va., 1988. Bar: Va. 1985, D.C. 2000. Assoc. atty. Gurman, Kurtis, Blask & Freedman, Washington, 1988-92; grad. fellow/tchg. asst. Rutgers, State U. N.J., New Brunswick, 1992-95; atty. Gurman, Blask & Freedman, Chartered, Washington, 1995-99; asst. prof. polit. sci. N.W. Mo. State U., Maryville, 1999—. Recipient W. Warner Moss prize Coll. William and Mary Dept. Govt., 1985, grad. fellowship Rutgers U., 1992-95. Mem. Am. Polit. Sci. Assn., Pi Sigma Alpha (sec. 1984-85), Phi Delta Phi (Minor Inn chpt. magister 1987-88). Office: NW Mo State Univ 800 University Dr Maryville MO 64468 E-mail: dsbsh_x@hotmail.com., desmith@mail.nwmissouri.edu.

SMITH, DANIEL LYNN, lawyer; b. Ottawa, Kans., June 22, 1952; s. Daniel H. and Mary K. (Lynn) S.; m. Alana A. Windhorst, Aug. 15, 1981; children: Tricia, Lauran, Alexa. BA, U. Kans., 1973; JD, Duke U., 1976. Bar: Kans. 1976, U.S. Dist. Ct. Kans. 1976, U.S. Ct. Appeals (10th cir.) 1977, U.S. Tax Ct. 1977. Assoc. Bronston Law Offices, Overland Park, Kans., 1976-78; ptnr. Oliver, Smith & Oliver, 1978-80, Bronston and Smith, Overland Park, 1981-92, Ankerholz & Smith, Overland Park, Kans., 1992—; pvt. practice Westwood, 1980-81. Mem. Kans. Bar Assn., Kans. Trial Lawyers Assn. (bd. govs. 1981—), Civil War Roundtable Kansas City, Phi Beta Kappa. Home: 10075 Goodman Dr Shawnee Mission KS 66212-3432 Office: Ankerholz & Smith 6900 College Blvd Overland Park KS 66211-1547

SMITH, DANIEL MONTAGUE, engineer; b. Gainesville, Tex., Oct. 17, 1932; s. Alex Morton and Mary Louise (Shriver) S.; married, Oct. 15, 1953; children: Gregory M., Timothy D., Christopher E. BA, North Tex. State Coll., 1952, MS, 1953; PhD, U. Tex., 1959. Mem. tech. staff Oak Ridge (Tenn.) Nat. Lab., 1958-61, Tex. Instruments Inc., Dallas, 1961-75; sr. engr. Nitron div. McDonnell Douglas, Cupertino, Calif., 1975-77; mgr. product engring. Nat. Semiconductor Corp., Santa Clara, 1977-79, Motorola Semiconductor Sector, Austin, Tex., 1979—. Cpl. U.S. Army, 1953-55. Mem. Am. Phys. Soc. Home: 10301 Parkfield Dr Austin TX 78758-5638 Office: Motorola SPS 3591 Ed Bluestein Blvd # Md-f12 Austin TX 78721-2903

SMITH, DANIEL RAY, protective services official; b. Talledega, Ala., Nov. 5, 1962; s. Joseph Clifton and Shirley Christine Smith; m. Amanda Darlene Smith; children: Beth, Jennifer, Joseph, Kyle. BSci in Criminal Justice, Faulkner U., 2000. Cert. Ala. Peace Officer Std. & Tng. Commn., 1990. Fuel specialist, lab. technician USAF, Valdosta, Ga., 1981—84, master fuel specialist instr. Chanute AFB, Ill., 1984—87; fuel storage specialist Crawford Tech. Services, Fort Campbell, Ky., 1987—90; police officer Homewood Police, Homewood, Ala., 1990—97, narcotics detective, 1997—2001, police sgt., 2001—. With USAF, 1981—87. Mem.: Nat. Tech. Investigators Assn., Ala. Narcotics Officers Assn. (Outstanding Achievement award 1999), Alpha Phi Sigma. Conservative. Avocations: online gaming, travel, basketball, reading. Office: Homewood Police Department 1833 29th Avenue South Homewood AL 35209 Personal E-mail: drstinger1@yahoo.com.

SMITH, DANIEL TIMOTHY, lawyer; b. Denver, July 20, 1948; s. Harold Kennedy and Dorothy (Gannon) S. BA, Duke U., 1970; JD, U. Denver, 1973. Bar: Colo. 1973, U.S. Dist. Ct. Colo. 1973, U.S. Ct. Appeals (10th cir.), U.S. Supreme Ct. 1979, U.S. Ct. Claims 1979. Dep. dist. atty. Denver Dist. Atty. Office, 1973-74; spl. asst. atty. gen. Colo. Atty. Gen.'s Office, Denver, 1973-74; asst. U.S. atty. Dist. of Colo., 1974-76; ptnr. Wiggins & Smith P.C., 1977-87; pvt. practice, 1987—. Chmn. fundraising Am. Cancer Soc., Denver., 1992-93; mem. golf com. Am. Heart Assn., Denver, 1988—. Mem. ABA, Colo. Criminal Def. Bar (sec. 1979-81). Avocation: golf. Office: 1900 Grant St Ste 580 Denver CO 80203-4346

SMITH, DAVID JOHN, physicist, educator; b. Melbourne, Australia, Oct. 10, 1948; arrived in U.S., 1984; s. Arthur and Agnes Frances S.; m. Gwenneth Paula Bland, Sept. 18, 1971 (div. 1992); children: Heather F., Marion J. BSc with honors, U. Melbourne, Australia, 1970, PhD, 1978, DSc, 1988. Postdoctoral rsch. asst. Cavendish Lab. U. Cambridge, Eng., 1976-78, sr. rsch. assoc. Eng., 1979-84; assoc. prof. Ariz. State U., Tempe, 1984-87, prof., 1987—, regents prof., 2000—, dir. Ctr. for Solid State Sci., 2001—. Dir. Cambridge U. High Resolution Electron Microscope, 1979-84, NSF Ctr. for High Resolution Electron Microscopy, Tempe, 1991-96. Author 11 chpts. in books; editor 15 conf. procs.; contbr. over 340 articles to profl. jours. Recipient Faculty Achievement award Burlington Resources Found., 1990. Fellow Inst. Physics (U.K., Charles Vernon Boys prize 1985); mem. Am. Phys. Soc., Material Rsch. Soc., Microscopy Soc. Am. Office: Ariz State U Ctr Solid State Sci Tempe AZ 85287 E-mail: david.smith@asu.edu.

SMITH, DAVID A. medical services executive; Public acctg., 1983—87; regional mgr., gen. mgr., sales mgr. and opers. mgr. PSS/World Medical Inc., Jacksonville, Fla., 1987—93, v.p., 1992—96, bd. dirs., 1993—, exec. v.p., 1996—2000, pres., 2000—, CFO, 1992—2002, CEO, 2002—. Office: PSS World Med Inc 4345 Southpoint Blvd Jacksonville FL 32216*

SMITH, DAVID BRUCE, lawyer; b. Moline, Ill., May 9, 1948; s. Neal Schriever and Barbara Jean (Harris) S.; children: Neal, Stephanie. BSME, U. Iowa, 1970; JD, U. Tex., 1973. Bar: Tex. 1973, Wis. 1975. Patent examiner U.S. Patent and Trademark Office, Washington, 1973-74; atty. Nilles & Kirby S.C., Milw., 1974-76, Globe-Union, Inc., Milw., 1976-77; atty., intellectual property practice coord. Michael Best & Friedrich, 1978—. Co-chair Intellectual Property Com. of Lex Mundi. Pres. Milw. County coun. Boy Scouts Am., Milw., 1994-95. Mem. ABA, Am. Intellectual Property Law Assn., State Bar Wis., Wis. Intellectual Property Law Assn., Ozaukee Country Club, Milw. Club. Office: Michael Best & Friedrich 100 E Wisconsin Ave Ste 3300 Milwaukee WI 53202-4108 E-mail: dbsmith@mbf-law.com.

SMITH, DAVID CARR, organic chemist; b. Ft. Wayne, Ind., Aug. 9, 1944; s. James Nolan and Kathryn Ellen (Mefford) S.; m. Dolores Joan Kurz, July 9, 1966; children: David James, Daniel Paul. BS in Chemistry, Clarkson Coll., 1969, PhD in Chemistry, 1975. Postdoctoral fellow Utah State U., Logan, 1974-75, U. S.C., Columbia, 1975-77; sr. rsch. chemist Ash Stevens Inc., Detroit, 1977-80; group leader Sterling Organics, Rensselaer, N.Y., 1980-84, mgr. bus. devel. N.Y.C., 1984-85; mgr. pharm. technology John Brown Inc., Stamford, Conn., 1985-93; sr. project mgr. Lockwood Greene Engrs., Inc., Atlanta, 1993-97; compliance and regulatory affairs cons. David C. Smith, Inc., Norcross, Ga., 1997—. Contbr. articles to profl. jours. Mem. Regulatory Affairs Profls. Soc. (cert). Office: 5675 Sugar Creek Ct Norcross GA 30093-4183 E-mail: d_c_smith_inc@email.msn.com.

SMITH, DAVID CLAIBORNE, construction company executive; b. Burlington, N.C., Sept. 23, 1953; s. Claiborne Pendleton and Betty Jane (Hancock) S.; m. Elizabeth Marjorie Collins, Aug. 19, 1954. Student, Va. Polytech. Inst., 1972-74, student, 1977-78. Sail cons. Bacon and Assocs., Annapolis, Md., 1974-77; project acct. Hardin Constrn. Group, Wilmington, N.C., 1978-79, field engr. Tulsa, 1979-83, asst. supt. Stamford, Conn., 1983-84, Charlottesville, Va., 1984-85, Ft. Wayne, Ind., 1985, Charlotte, N.C., 1985-86, Myrtle Beach, S.C., 1986-87, San Antonio, 1987-88, Stone Mountain, Ga., 1988-89, supt. St. Croix, V.I., U.S.V.I., 1989-90, Atlanta, 1990-95, dir. quality enhancement, 1995-98, corp. svcs. officer, 1998—, dir. ops. support svcs. Elder Chestnut Mountain Presbyn. Ch. Presbyterian. Avocation: sailing. Home: 5609 Monk Dr Oakwood GA 30566-3026 E-mail: DSmith@hardinconstruction.com.

SMITH, DAVID CLARK, research scientist; b. Owensboro, Ky., Feb. 8, 1937; s. Robert Emmitt and Mary Margaret (Flaherty) S.; m. Kathleen Sue Kohne, June 27, 1964; children: Christine, Jennifer, Paula. BSME, U. Dayton, 1959; MS, Northwestern U., 1961, PHD, postgrad., Northwestern U., 1964. Rsch. scientist United Techs. Rsch. Ctr., East Hartford, Conn., 1965-67, sr. rsch. scientist, 1967-68, prin. scientist, 1968-80, mgr. exptl. optics, 1980-82, mgr. optical physics, 1982-91; cons. DCS Assoc., Inc., 1992-99, Conn. Tech. Assocs., 1992—, DCS Lasers/Optics LLC, 1997—. Author: (with G. Bekefi) Principles of Laser Plasmas, 1976; contbr. articles to profl. jours. Chmn. Youth and Family Resource Ctr. Commn., 1979-84; bd. dirs. Glastonbury A Better Chance, Conn., 1970-78; mem. Glastonbury Energy Com., 1979-83; tutor YMCA Read to Succeed Literacy; vol. Habitat for Humanity. Recipient Outstanding Svc. award, 1985, Glastonbury, Conn., United Techs. Outstanding Svc. award, 1987; named Man of Yr., Friends of Glastonbury Youth, 1984. Mem.: IEEE, AIAA, AAAS, Am. Soc. Laser Medicine and Surgery, Am. Phys. Soc., Sigma Xi. Democrat. Roman Catholic. Achievements include patentee in field. Avocations: tennis, sailing. Home: 44 Candlelight Dr Glastonbury CT 06033-2537 Office: DCS Lasers & Optics LLC PO Box 167 East Glastonbury CT 06025-0167 E-mail: kohne@aol.com.

SMITH, DAVID DOYLE, international management consultant, consulting engineer; b. Newport, Tenn., 1956; s. Doyle E. and Maude (Clements) S.; m. Judith Ann Craig, Nov. 1, 1991; children: Adam, Christine, James. BSEE, U. Tenn., 1981. Registered profl. engr., Tenn., Ga. Field engr. IBM Corp., Knoxville, Tenn., 1977-79; rsch. asst. Office of Naval Rsch. U. Tenn., 1980-81; systems test engr. Tex. Instruments, Inc., Johnson City, Tenn., 1981-82, product engr., 1982-83, product mgr., 1983-87, missile design engr., supr. Lewisville, Tex., 1987-89; sr. systems engr. U.S. Data Corp., Richardson, 1989-90; systems cons. Keane, Inc., Atlanta, 1991-94; mgr., mgmt. cons. Ernst & Young LLP, 1994-97, KPMG Consulting, Inc., 1997—; bd. mem. Optimal E-Commerce Tech., Inc. Lectr. Tech. Inst., 1983-86; developer RTU Sys. for oil and gas, water, and electric utilities, 1990-92. Co-author profl. papers. Mem. IEEE, NSPE. Avocations: archaeology, writing. Home: 9201 Stoney Mountain Dr Chattanooga TN 37421 Office: KPMG Cons Inc 303 Peachtree St Atlanta GA 30308 E-mail: delrosa@mindspring.com., ddsmith@kpmg.com.

SMITH, DAVID EDWARD, business executive; b. Battle Creek, Mich., Sept. 16, 1939; s. Hebdin Leslie and Dureatha Rosella (Stephens) S.; m. Margaret Eugenia Clark, June 13, 1964; 1 child, Wendy Leigh. Student, Kellogg Community Coll., 1957-58; BS in Mech. Engring., Mich State U., 1962; MS in Real Estate Investing (hon.), Meta U., Salt Lake City, 1992. Engr., scientist Douglas Aircraft Co., Santa Monica, Calif., 1962-63, McDonnell Douglas Astronautics Co., Cape Kennedy, Fla., 1963-78; broker salesman Cape Kennedy Realty, Inc., Cape Canaveral, 1978-87; pres., founder Cash Flow Seminars, Merritt Island, 1979—, Cash Flow Systems, Inc., Merritt Island, 1983—; prof. fin. Meta U., Salt Lake City, 1992-94. Lectr. fin. convs. and orgns. including Fed. GSA, Pub. Bldg. Svc., Am. League of Savs., Fin. Instns. Mktg. Assn., Acad. Real Estate, Am. Congress Real Estate; prof. fin. Meta U., Salt Lake City, 1992-94; distbr. Hewlett Packard Corp., 1985-88; dir. comml. investment divsn. CKBOR, Merritt Island, 1978-79; adv. bd., lectr. Fin. Freedom Report, Nat. Inst. Fin. Planning, both Salt Lake City, 1985-92; instr. Fla. Real Estate Commn., La. Real Estate Commn., Fla. Bd. Accountancy, Am. Inst. Real Estate Appraisers. Author: Turbo-Diesel, The Time Value of Money, Creative Financing Techniques; contbr. numerous fin. articles to jours. and motorcycle touring mags. Mem.: Gold Wing Rd. Riders Assn., Internat. Platform Assn., Fla. Real Estate Exchangors. Republican. Avocations: flying, transcontinental bicycling, motorcycle touring. Office: Cash Flow Seminars PO Box 540634 Merritt Island FL 32954-0634

SMITH, DAVID ELVIN, physician; b. Bakersfield, Calif., Feb. 7, 1939; s. Elvin W. and Dorothy (McGinnis) S.; m. Millicent Buxton; children: Julia, Suzanne, Christopher Buxton-Smith, Sabree Hill-Smith. Intern San Francisco Gen. Hosp., 1965; fellow pharmacology and toxicology U. Calif., San Francisco, 1965-67; clin. prof. U. Calif., San Francisco Med. Ctr., 1967—, dir. psychopharmacology study group, dir. Inst. of Health, 1966-70, assoc. clin. prof., rsch. physician Med. Sch.; clin. prof. U. Calif., San Francisco; practice specializing in toxicology/addiction medicine San Francisco, 1965—. Physician Presbyn. Alcoholic Clinic, 1965—67, Contra Cost Alcoholic Clinic, 1965—67; dir. alcohol and drug abuse screening unit San Francisco Gen. Hosp., 1967—68; co-dir. Calif. drug abuse info. project U. Calif. Med. Ctr., 1967—72; founder, pres., med. dir. Haight-Ashbury Free Med. Clinic, San Francisco, 1967—; rsch. dir. Merritt Peralta Chem. Dependency Hosp., Oakland, Calif., 1984—; med. dir., bd. dirs. Drug Abuse Scis., 1999; med. dir. Calif. Alcohol and Drug Programs, U. Calif. San Francisco Substance Abuse Policy Ctr., 1999; assoc. med. dir., med. rev. officer Betty Ford Ctr. Profl. Recovery Program; chmn. Nat. Drug Abuse Conf., 1977, Calif. Gov.'s Commn. on Narcotics and Drug Abuse, 1977—; nat. health adviser to former U.S. Pres. Jimmy Carter; mem. Pres. Clinton's Health Care Task Force on Addiction and Nat. Health Reform, 1993; with Office Drug Abuse Policy, White House Task Force Physicians for Drug Abuse Prevention; dir. Benzodiazepine Rsch. and Tng. Project, Substance Abuse and Sexual Concerns Project, PCP Rsch. and Tng. Project; med. editor AlcoholMD.com; vis. assoc. prof. U. Nev. Med. Sch., 1975—; cons. numerous fed. drug abuse agys.; clin. prof. U. Calif. San Francisco Med. Ctr. Author: Love Needs Care, 1970, The New Social Drug: Cultural, Medical and Legal Perspectives on Marijuana, 1971, The Free Clnic: Community Approaches to Health Care and Drug Abuse, 1971, Treating the Cocaine Abuser, 1985, The Benzodiazepines: Current Standard Medical Practice, 1986, Physicians' Guide to Drug Abuse, 1987; co-author: It's So Good, Don't Even Try it Once: Heroin in Perspective, 1972, Uppers and Downers, 1973, Drugs in the Classroom, 1973, Barbiturate Use and Abuse, 1977, A Multicultural View of Drug Abuse, 1978, Amphetamine Use, Misuse and Abuse, 1979, PCP: Problems and Prevention, 1981, Sexological Aspects of Substance Use and Abuse, Treatment of the Cocaine Abuser, 1985, The Haight Ashbury Free Medical Clinic: Still Free After All These Years, Drug Free: Alternatives to Drug Abuse, 1987, Treatment of Opiate Dependence, Designer Drugs, 1988, Treatment of Cocaine Dependence, 1988, Treatment of Opiate Dependence, 1988, The New Drugs, 1989, Crack and Ice in the Era of Smokeable Drugs, 1992, Clinical Guide to Substance Abuse, 2001, others; also drug edn. films; founder, editor Jour. Psychedelic Drugs (now Jour. Psychoactive Drugs), 1967—; co-author: Clinical Guide to Substance Abuse; contbr. over 300 articles to profl. jours.; med. editor Alcohol MD CD-ROM and Web site. Mem. Physicians for Prevention White House Office Drug Abuse Policy, 1995; pres. Youth Projects, Inc.; founder, chmn. bd., pres. Nat. Free Clin. Coun., 1968-72; med. dir. Calif. Alcohol and Drug Programs, 1998, U. Calif. Drug Policy Ctr., San Francisco, 1998—, Drug Abuse Scis., 1998—. Named one of Best Doctors in U.S., 1995, 1996, 1997, 2002; recipient Rsch. award, Borden Found., 1964, AMA Rsch. award, 1977, Cmty. Svc. award U. Calif., San Francisco, 1974, Calif. State Drug Abuse Treatment award, 1984, Vernelle Fox Drug Abuse Treatment award, 1985, UCLA Sidney Cohen Addiction Medicine award, 1989, U. Calif. San Francisco medal of honor, 1995, 1995. Mem. AMA (alt. del.), CMA (alt. del.), Am. Soc. on Addiction Medicine (bd. dirs., pres. 1995), San Francisco Med. Soc., Am. Pub. Health Assn., Calif. Soc. on Addiction Medicine (pres., bd. dirs.), Am. Soc. Addiction Medicine, Sigma Xi, Phi Beta Kappa. Methodist. Home: 289 Frederick St San Francisco CA 94117-4051 Office: Haight Ashbury Free Clinics 612 Clayton St San Francisco CA 94117-2927

SMITH, DAVID ENGLISH, physician, educator; b. San Francisco, June 9, 1920; s. David English and Myrtle (Goodin) S.; m. Margaret Elizabeth Bronson, June 9, 1948; children: Ann English Smith Elbert, David Bronson, Mary Margaret. AB, Central Coll. Mo., 1941; MD cum laude, Washington U., St. Louis, 1944. Intern, resident pathology Barnes Hosp., St. Louis, 1944-46; instr. pathology Washington U. Med. Sch., 1948-51, asst. prof., 1951-54, asst. head dept., 1953-54, assoc. prof., 1954-55; prof. pathology U. Va. Sch. Medicine, 1955-73, chmn. dept., 1958-73; dir. div. U. Va. Sch. Medicine (Cancer Studies), 1972-73; prof. pathology Northwestern U. Sch. Medicine, 1974-75, U. Pa. Sch. Medicine, 1976-80, Tulane U. Sch. Medicine, 1980-85, assoc. dean, 1980-85; prof. pathology U. Tex. Med. Br., 1986—. Assoc. dir.

Am. Bd. Med. Spltys., 1974-75; v.p., sec., dir. undergrad. evaluation Nat. Bd. Med. Examiners, 1975-80; trustee Am. Bd. Pathology, 1966-73, v.p., 1973; mem. Nat. Bd. Med. Examiners, chmn. pathology test com., 1966-72; chmn. test com. Ednl. Commn. for Fgn. Med. Grads., 1979-91; eligibility & due process com. Nat. Commn. Cert. Physician Assts., 1990—. Editor: Survey of Pathology in Medicine and Surgery, 1966-70; contbr. articles to profl. publs. Pres. Va. div. Am. Cancer Soc., 1967-69. Served from 1st lt. to capt. M.C. AUS, 1946-48. Paul Brindley Disting. scholar U. Tex. Med. Br., 1997, Preclin. Tchr. award, 1999. Mem. Va. Soc. Pathology (pres. 1960), Am. Assn. Pathologists, Internat. Acad. Pathology (council 1956-59, pres. 1964-65), Am. Soc. Clin. Pathologists (co-dir. self assessment program 1970-75, Path Educator award 2000), AMA, Am. Assn. Neuropathologists, AAAS, Sigma Xi, Alpha Omega Alpha, Phi Beta Pi, Alpha Epsilon Delta. Home: 59 Colony Park Cir Galveston TX 77551-1737 E-mail: descolpkga@aol.com.

SMITH, DAVID EUGENE, business administration educator; b. Boise, Idaho, Dec. 14, 1941; s. Roy Arthur and Anna Margaret (Fries) S.; m. Patricia Stroy, Aug. 4, 1973; 1 child, Zachary Adam. BS in Applied Stats., San Francisco State Coll., 1964, MS in Mgmt. Sci., 1966; MBA, PhD in Bus. Adminstrn., U. Santa Clara, 1969. Asst. to dir. mgmt ctr. Grad. Sch. Bus., U. Santa Clara, Calif., 1966-69, lectr. mktg., 1968; asst. prof. bus. adminstrn. Mktg./Quantitative Studies Dept., San Jose State U., 1969-71, assoc. prof. bus. adminstrn., 1971-76, prof. bus. adminstrn., 1976—, chmn. dept., 1986-89. Author: Quantitative Business Analysis, 1977, Internat. Edit., 1979, 1982; contbr. articles to profl. jours. Mem.: DSI, INFORMS, Beta Gamma Sigma, Phi Kappa Phi. Republican. Avocations: tennis, fishing, skiing. Home: 22448 Tim Tam Ct Los Gatos CA 95033-8521 Office: San Jose State U Mktg/Decision Scis One Washington Sq San Jose CA 95192

SMITH, DAVID GILBERT, political science educator; b. Norman, Okla., Oct. 10, 1926; s. Gilbert Harmer and Virginia (Haizlip) S.; m. Eleanor Cowan; children: Alison Claire, Joel Anthony; stepchildren: Laura Gergen, Stan Gergen. BA, U. Okla., 1948, MA, 1950; PhD, Johns Hopkins U., 1953. Instr. polit. sci. Swarthmore (Pa.) Coll., 1953-55, asst. prof. polit. sci., 1957, prof., 1967—, Centennial prof., 1977-87, Richter prof. polit. sci., 1987-92, chmn., 1970-87, prof. emeritus, 1992—; asst. prof. polit. sci. Stanford U., Palo Alto, Calif., 1956-57. Cons. HEW, NAS-NRC, Ford Found., NASI. Author: (with J. Roland Pennock) Political Science: An Introduction, 1965, The Convention and the Constitution, 1965, 2d edit., 1987, Paying for Medicare, 1992, Entitlement Politics, 2002; contbr. articles to profl. jours. Chmn. ACLU, Delaware County, Pa., 1965-70, Health and Welfare Coun., Delaware County, 1970-73; v.p. Delaware Valley HMO, Concordville, Pa., 1978-81; pres. Media (Pa.) Child Guidance, 1980-82; bd. dirs. Friends Life Care at Home, 1992—. Sgt. U.S. Army, 1945-46. Mem. Am. Soc. for Polit. and Legal Philosophy, Phi Beta Kappa. Democrat. Presbyterian. Home: 448 S Jackson St Media PA 19063-3716 E-mail: dsmith1@swarthmore.edu.

SMITH, DAVID HAROLD, communication educator; b. Wooster, Ohio, Dec. 2, 1936; s. Harold Alexander and Edna Mae (Snyder) S.; m. Sarah Jeanne Ware; children: Catherine, Karen, Kevin, Colleen, Andrew. BS, Ohio State U., 1957, PhD, 1966; MA, Northwestern U., 1963. Assoc. prof. speech communication U. Minn., 1966-72; assoc. dean social and behavioral scis., prof. communication Ohio State U., 1972-76; dean arts and letters, prof. communication U. South Fla., 1976-81, prof. internal medicine and communication, 1981-94; chair prof. applied communication studies Hong Kong Bapt. U., 1994-97, fellow ctr. for applied ethics, 1994-97; vis. fellow The East West Ctr., 1998. Co-author: The Silicone Breast Implant Story, 1996; editor: Health Communication and China, 1997; contbr. articles to profl. jours. Mem. Nat. Communication Assn., Internat. Communication Assn. (chair orgn. communication divsn. 1970-71), Chinese Communication Assn., Pacific and Asian Communication. Avocation: choral singing. Home: 1 Beach Dr #1908 Saint Petersburg FL 33701 E-mail: waresmit@earthlink.net.

SMITH, DAVID HORTON, social sciences educator; b. L.A., May 2, 1939; s. Paul Roosevelt Smith and Helen Ethel (Frechem) Mitchell; divorced; children: Gregory David, Laura Ghislaine. AB magna cum laude, U. So. Calif., 1960; MA, Harvard U., 1962, PhD, 1965. Asst. prof. U. So. Calif., L.A., 1966-68; assoc. prof. Boston Coll., Chestnut Hill, Mass., 1968-76, prof., 1976—. Rsch. fellow, lectr. Harvard U., 1965-66; cons. to govt. agys. and nonprofit orgns., including Nat. Ctr. for Voluntary Action, Brit. Nat. Vol. Ctr., Ctr. for Voluntary Soc., Filer Commn. on Pvt. Philanthropy and Pub. Needs, Union of Internat. Assns. Author: Latin American Student Activism, 1973, Grassroots Associations, 2000; co-author: Becoming Modern, 1974 (award 1975), Voluntary Sector Policy Research Needs, 1974, Participation in Social and Political Activities, 1980, Why People Recreate, 1987; editor: Voluntary Action Research, 1972, 73, 74, Volunteerism, Voluntary Assns. and Devel., 1981, Internat. Perspectives on Voluntary Action Rsch., 1983; contbr. numerous articles to profl. jours., chpts. to books; founding editor-in-chief Jour. Voluntary Action Rsch. (now Nonprofit and Voluntary Sector Quar.), 1971-76. Founding bd. dirs. Nat. Com. for Responsive Philanthropy, 1976-78, Alliance for Volunteerism; dir. rsch. Ctr. for Voluntary Soc., Washington, 1970-74. NSF grad. fellow, 1960-63; Woodrow Wilson Hon. fellow, 1960. Mem. Assn. Rsch. on Non-Profit Orgns. and Voluntary Action (founder, pres. 1971-73, Lifetime Achievement award 1993), Nat. Assn. Pub. Svc. Orgn. Execs. (co-founder, past bd. dirs.), Authors Guild, Sarasota Fiction Writers, Phi Beta Kappa, Phi Kappa Phi. Avocations: reading, photography, fiction writing, jazz, foreign travel. Office: Boston Coll Sociol Dept 140 Commonwealth Ave Chestnut Hill MA 02467-3800 E-mail: dhortonsmith@hotmail.com.

SMITH, DAVID JAMES, corporate lawyer; Asst. sec. Archer Daniels Midland, Decatur, Ill., 1988-97, asst. gen. counsel, 1995-97, v.p., sec., gen. counsel, 1997—2001, sr. v.p., sec., gen. counsel, 2002—. Office: Archer Daniels Midland Co 4666 E Faries Pkwy Decatur IL 62526-5666

SMITH, DAVID JAMES, literature educator; b. Fresno, Calif., June 6, 1955; s. Donald L. Smith and Teresina Leonardo; m. Kimberly M. Roe, Nov. 13, 1991. BA in Drama, Calif. State U., Fresno, 1979, MA in Counseling, 1989, MA in English, 1993. Cert. tchr. Calif., pupil personal credential. Author: (poetry book) Prayers for the Dead Ventriloquist, 1995, (novels) Fast Company, 1999. Fellow, Nat. Endowment for Arts, 1999. Mem.: Calif. Tchrs. Assn., Fresno Poets Assn.

SMITH, DAVID JOHN, JR. plastic surgeon; b. Indpls., Feb. 20, 1947; s. David John and Carolyn (Culp) S.; m. Nancy Loonsten, June 7, 1975; children: Matthew, Peter, Hadley. BA, Wesleyan U., 1969; MD, Ind. U., 1973. Diplomate Am. Bd. Plastic Surgery. Resident Emory U.-Grady Hosp., Atlanta, 1973-78; resident Ind. U. Med. Ctr., Indpls., 1978-80; Christine Kleinert fellow in hand surgery, 1979; asst. prof. surgery Ind. U. Sch. Medicine, 1980-84; assoc. prof. of surgery Wayne State U. Sch. Medicine, 1984-87; assoc. prof. plastic surgery, surgery sect. head U. Mich. Med. Ctr., Ann Arbor, 1987-92, prof. surgery sect. head, 1992—2001. Mem. Residency Rev. Com. for Plastic Surgery, 1992-2000, vice chmn., 1994, chmn. 1996-99. Mem. editl. bd. Jour. of Surg. Rsch., 1989-95, Annals of Plastic Surgery, 1992—, assoc. editor, 1994—, Yearbook of Hand Surgery, 1989—; guest reviewer Surgery, 1988—, Plastic and Reconstructive Surgery, 1988—; contbr. articles to profl. jours. Recipient numerous grants. Fellow ACS (many coms.), Soc. Univ. Surgeons, Am. Assn. Plastic Surgeons, Am. Surg. Assn., Am. Bd. Plastic Surgeons (vice chmn. 1997-98, chair-elect 1998-99, chmn. oral exam 1995-97, chmn. 1999-2000), Assn. for Acad. Surgery, Western Surg. Assn., Ctrl. Surg. Assn., Am. Soc. for Surgery of the Hand, Am. Soc. Plastic Surgeons, Plastic Surgery Ednl. Found. (bd. dirs. 1988-99, treas. 1994, v.p., pres.-elec., pres., chair nominating com. 1997-98), Plastic Surgery Rsch. Coun., Am. Burn Assn. (chmn. com. on organization and delivery of burn care 1995-98), Am. Burn Life Support Nat. Faculty, Am. Assn. for Hand Surgeons (pres. 1994), Assn. Acad. Chmn. Plastic Surgery (pres.-elect 1997, pres. 1998-99, chmn. nominating com. 1999-2000). Home: 769 Heatherway St Ann Arbor MI 48104-2731 Office: U Mich Med Ctr 2130 Taubman Health Ctr 1500 E Medical Center Dr Ann Arbor MI 48109-0005

SMITH, DAVID KINGMAN, retired oil company executive, consultant; b. Malone, N.Y., June 5, 1928; s. Ernest DeAlton and Louisa Kingman (Bolster) S.; m. Lois Louise Wing, June 13, 1959; children: Mara Louise, David Andrew. BS in Engring., Princeton U., 1952. Registered profl. engr., Tex. Civil engr., supt. Raymont Internat. Inc., N.Y.C., 1952-55, asst. v.p., 1970-71, v.p., 1971-74, group v.p. Houston, 1974-80; mgr. Raymond-Brown and Root, Maracaibo, Venezuela, 1955-70; sr. engring. assoc. Exxon Prodn. Rsch. Co., Houston, 1980-81, supr., 1982-95; cons. project mgmt., 1995—. Pres. Yorkshire Civic Assn., Houston, 1979-80, trustee, 1985-97. With U.S. Army, 1946-48, PTO. Mem. ASCE, NSPE, Soc. Petroleum Engrs. (continuing edn. com. Gulf Coast chmn. 1989-93, treas. 1987-88, nat. continuing edn. com. 1991-93, dir. Gulf Coast sect. 1994-95), Tex. Soc. Profl. Engrs., Men's Garden Club Houston, Am. Legion, Princeton Alumni Assn. (dir. Houston sect.), Cen Ners In Square Dance Club (pres. 1996-97). Republican. Methodist. Avocations: photography, gardening, tennis, golf, square dancing. Home: 611 W Forest Dr Houston TX 77079-6915 E-mail: smithdktx@aol.com.

SMITH, DAVID LEE, newspaper editor; b. Shelby, Ohio, Apr. 4, 1939; s. Ferris Francis and Rita Ann (Metzger) S.; m. Betty Stewart Walker, Sept. 10, 1960; children: Stacie Lynn, Stefanie Linn, David Lee, II (dec.). Student, Pontifical Coll. Josephinum, Worthington, Ohio, 1953-56, Ohio State U., Mansfield, 1961. Sports writer Mansfield News-Jour., 1960-61; sports editor Ashland (Ohio) Times-Gazette, 1961-63, Miami (Fla.) News, 1963-67, Ft. Lauderdale (Fla.) News, 1967-70, Boston Globe, 1970-78, Washington Star, 1978-81; dep. mng. editor, exec. sports editor Dallas Morning News, 1981—, sports dir. AH Belo pub. and new media divsns., 1998—. Condr. seminars. Mem. adv. bd. Dallas Stars Found., Dallas Alliance for the Mentally Ill, SMU Athletics, Jesuit Sch. Found.; bd. dirs. Field Scovell Scholarship Found., Doak Walker Nat. Running Back Award, GTE-SMU Athletic Forum. With USMC, 1957—60. Mem. AP Sports Editors Assn. (1st pres. 1974-75), Baseball Writers Assn. (Red Smith award for major contbns. to sports journalism 1990), Football Writers Assn., Golf Writers Assn., SMU Athletic Forum (bd. dirs.), Bent Tree Country Club, Salesmanship Club of Dallas. Roman Catholic. Home: 12312 Marbrook Dr Dallas TX 75230-2244 Office: Dallas Morning News Communications Center Dallas TX 75265

SMITH, DAVID MARTYN, forestry educator; b. Bryan, Tex., Mar. 10, 1921; s. John Blackmer and Doris (Clark) S.; m. Catherine Van Aken, June 16, 1951; children: Ellen, Nancy. BS, U. R.I., 1941; postgrad., NYU, 1942; MF, Yale U., 1946, PhD, 1950; DSc (hon.), Bates Coll., 1986, U. R.I., 1993. From instr. to prof. Sch. Forestry and Environ. Studies, Yale U., 1946-90, asst. dean, 1953-58; Morris K. Jesup prof. silviculture Yale U., 1967-90, Morris K. Jesup prof. emeritus, 1990—. Vis. prof. U. Munich, 1981; mem. Conn. Forestry Practices Bd., 1991—; bd. dirs. Connwood Foresters, Inc. Author: Practice of Silviculture, 1954, 4th edit., 1997. Capt. Weather Svc., USAAF, 1942-45. Fellow Soc. Am. Foresters (Disting. Svc. New Eng. sect. award 1969, 93); mem. Am. Forests (Disting. Svc. award 1990), Nat. Acad. Forest Scis. Mex. (corr.), Ecol. Soc. Am., Conn. Forest and Park Assn. (dir.), Sigma Xi, Phi Kappa Phi. Mem. United Ch. of Christ. Home: 55 Woodlawn St Hamden CT 06517-1338 Office: 360 Prospect St New Haven CT 06511-2104 E-mail: david.m.smith@yale.edu.

SMITH, DAVID MATTHEW, economist, educator; b. Lansing, Mich., Sept. 5, 1966; s. Roger Grant and Mary Elg (Blair) S.; m. Jennifer Capra, Aug. 7, 1993; children: Karagan Lu, Sinclare Capra. BA, Wheaton Coll., 1988; MA, Mich. State U., 1995, PhD, 1997. Fin. mgr. David Chapman Agy., Inc., Lansing, 1988-95; adj. prof. East Coll., St. Davids, Pa., 1996; asst. prof. econs. Pepperdine U., Malibu, Calif., 1997—. Contbr. articles to profl. jours. Mem. Am. Econ. Assn., Western Econ. Assn., Midwest Econ. Assn., Soc. Labor Economists. Avocations: golf, computers, reading. Office: Pepperdine U Grad Sch Bus Dept Econs 24255 Pacific Coast Hwy Malibu CA 90263 Fax: 310-506-4126. E-mail: dmsmith@pepperdine.edu.

SMITH, DAVID MCMULLEN, retired medical educator; b. Hokuchin, Korea, Jan. 10, 1936; M. Ann Elizabeth, Aug. 23, 1958; children: Laura Elizabeth, Linda Sue. BA, Ind. U., 1958, MD, 1961. Asst. prof. medicine Ind. U. Sch. Medicine, Indpls., 1968-73, assoc. prof. medicine, 1973-77, prof. medicine, 1977—2001; sr. assoc. Regenstrief Inst. Health Care, 1977—2001; ret., 2001. Contbr. articles to profl. jours. Fellow Am. Coll. Physicians; mem. Am. Fedn. Clin. Rsch., Am. Geriatrics Soc., Gerontological Soc. Am., Ctrl. Soc. Clin. Rsch., Soc. Gen. Internal Medicine, Physicians for Social Responsibility. Home: 7608 Newport Bay Dr Indianapolis IN 46240-3300

SMITH, DAVID MITCHELL, fire and explosion consultant; b. San Bernardino, Calif., Feb. 2, 1947; s. Harry Arnold and Norma Deanne (Miles) S.; m. Linda Sue McCormick, Apr. 9, 1994; children: Sean David Kimble, Jennifer Laura Thacker. Cert. fire investigator Internat. Assn. of Arson Investigators. Patrolman Tucson (Ariz.) Police Dept., 1968-70, detective, 1970-81; president Associated Fire Consultants, Tucson, 1981—. Co-author: (manual) National Fire Protection Association 921, 1995; contbr. articles to profl. jours. Chair Catalina Village Coun., Tucson, 1995—; bd. dirs. Catalina Family Med. Ctr., Tucson, 1996—, Pima Youth Partnership, 1996—. Sgt E-5, USMCR, 1966-72. Recipient Appreciation award Bur. Alcohol, Tobbaco and Fireamrs, Dearborn, Mich., 1990. Mem. Internat. Assn. Arson Investigators (life, bd. dirs. St. Louis sect. 1982-87, pres. 1989-90, Disting. Svc. award 1993), Nat. Fire Protection Assn. (com. mem. 1991—), Congl. Fire Svcs. Inst. (bd. dirs. 1989-90), Internat. Fire Svc. Tng. Assn. (com. mem. 1989-). Office: Associated Fire Cons Inc 4257 W Ina Rd Ste 101 Tucson AZ 85741-2233 E-mail: dmsmith@assocfire.com.

SMITH, DAVID SHIVERICK, lawyer, former ambassador; b. Omaha, Jan. 25, 1918; s. Floyd Monroe and Anna (Shiverick) S.; m. June Noble, Dec. 8, 1945 (div. 1968); children:Noble, David Shiverick, Jeremy T., Bradford D.; m. Mary Edson, Feb. 14, 1972. Degre Superieur, Sorbonne, Paris, 1938; BA magna cum laude, Dartmouth Coll., 1939; JD, Columbia U., 1942. Bar: N.Y. 1942, Conn. 1950, D.C. 1954. Asso. Breed, Abbott & Morgan, N.Y.C., 1946-48; legal dept. ABC, 1948-50; partner Chapman, Bryson, Walsh & O'Connell, N.Y.C. and Washington, 1950-54; spl. asst. to undersec. Dept. State, Washington, 1954; asst. sec. Air Force, 1954-59; founder, dir. internat. fellows program Columbia U., 1959-75, coordinator internat. studies, 1960-75, asso. dean sch. internat. affairs, 1960-74; cons. AEC, 1959-60; ptnr. Baker & McKenzie (and predecessor), N.Y.C. and Washington, 1960-75, Martin & Smith (and predecessors), Washington, 1975-76, 77-88, cons., 1988—; ambassador to Sweden, 1976-77. Dir. United Svcs. Life Ins. Corp., Internat. Bank, USLICO Corp., Liberian Svcs., Inc.; mem. Coun. Fgn. Rels.; dir. Fgn. Policy Assn.; mem. adv. coun. Sch. Advanced Internat. Studies, Johns Hopkins U., 1962—; pres., dir. Ctr. for Inter-Am. Rels., N.Y.C., 1969-74. Adv. and contbg. editor: Jour. Internat. Affairs, 1960-74; editor: The Next Asia, 1969, Prospects for Latin America, 1970, Concerns in World Affairs, 1973, From War to Peace, 1974. Chmn. bd. George Olmsted Found., 1977-2001; advisor emeritus Nat. Trust Hist. Preservation; active in past various charitable orgns. Lt. USNR, 1942-54; PTO; col. USAFR, 1955-75. Decorated Purple Heart Mem. ABA, Am. Soc. Internat. Law, Am. Fgn. Law Assn., N.Y. State Bar Assn., Conn. Bar Assn., Fed. Bar Assn. (v.p. for N.Y., N.J. and Conn.), Pilgrims of U.S., France-Am. Soc., English Speaking Union, Asia Soc., Coun. on Foreign Rels., Hudson Inst., Washington Inst. Fgn. Affairs, Coun. Fgn. Rels., Coun. Am. Ambs. (founder, bd. dirs., sec.), Soc. Mayflower Descs., Soc. Cin. (hon. mem.), Brook Club (N.Y.C.), Met. Club (Washington), Chevy Chase Club, Bathing Corp. of Southampton (N.Y.), Meadow Club (Southampton), Soc. Four Arts, Bath and Tennis Club, Everglades Club (Palm Beach), The Crocodiles, Old Guard Soc. Palm Beach Golfers, Phi Beta Kappa. Home: 525 S Flagler Dr Apt 20C West Palm Beach FL 33401-5925

SMITH, DAVID STUART, anesthesiology educator, physician; b. Detroit, May 29, 1946; s. Philip and Eleanor (Bishop) S.; m. Suzanne Wanda Zeleznik, Aug. 17, 1969; children: Katherine Michele, Lisa Anne. BA, Oakland U.; MD, PhD, Med. Coll. Wis., 1975. Intern dept. medicine Med. Coll. Wis., Milw., 1975-76; resident dept. anesthesia U. Pa., Phila., 1976-78, fellow dept. anesthesia, 1978-80; dir. divsn. neuroanesthesia Hosp. U. Pa., 1982-2001, attending anesthesiologist, 1980—; asst. prof. U. Pa., 1980-89, assoc. prof., 1989—. Co-editor: Anesthesia and Neurosurgery, 3d edit., 1994, 4th edit., 2001; mem. editl. bd. Jour. Neurosurg. Anesthesia, N.Y.C., 1987-97; author and co-author of numerous sci. papers, revs., and book chpts. Sr. fellow, Nat. Rsch. Svc. award, Phila., 1985-87. Fellow Coll. Physicians Phila.; mem. Am. Soc. Anesthesiologists, Soc. Neurosurg. Anesthesia and Critical Care (sec., treas. 1987-89, v.p. 1989-90, pres. elect 1990-91, pres. 1991-92), Assn. U. Anesthesiologists, Internat. Soc. Cerebral Blood Flow and Metabolism. Jewish. Office: Hosp U Pa Dept Anesthesia 3400 Spruce St Philadelphia PA 19104-4206

SMITH, DAVID THORNTON, lawyer, educator; b. Pawtucket, R.I., Dec. 11, 1935; s. Herbert Jeffers and Harriet Amelia (Thornton) S.; m. Sandra June Gustavson, Dec. 20, 1958; children: David T., Douglas A., Daniel H. BA, Yale U., 1957; JD cum laude, Boston U., 1960. Bar: Mass. 1961, U.S. Supreme Ct. 1964. Instr. law Ind. U., Bloomington, 1960-62; asst. prof. law Duquesne U., Pitts., 1962-63, Case Western Res. U., Cleve., 1963-65, asso. prof., 1965-68; asso. prof. law U. Fla., Gainesville, 1968-69, prof., 1969—. Lectr. Fla. Bankers Assn., Fla. Trust Sch., 1973— Author: (with M. Sussman and J. Cates) The Family and Inheritance, 1970, Florida Probate Code Manual, 1975. Mem. Am. Bar Assn., Mass. Bar Assn., Am. Law Inst., Am. Judicature Soc., AAUP (past pres. U. Fla. chpt.), Fla. Blue Key, Selden Soc., Omicron Delta Kappa, Phi Alpha Delta. Lutheran. Home: 6405 NW 18th Ave Gainesville FL 32605-3209 Office: Univ Fla Coll Law Gainesville FL 32611

SMITH, DAVID WAYNE, psychologist, educator; b. Ind., Apr. 16, 1927; s. Lowell Wayne and Ruth Elizabeth (Westphal) S.; m. Marcene B. Leever, Oct. 20, 1948; children: David Wayne, Laurreen Lea. BS, Purdue U., 1949; MS, Ind. U., 1953, PhD, 1955. Diplomate Am. Bd. Psychol. Specialities. Prof. rehab., dir. Rehab. Center; asso. dean, later asst. v.p. acad. affairs Ariz. Health Scis. Center, U. Ariz., Tucson, 1955-80; research prof. rehab., adj. prof. medicine, cons. in research S.W. Arthritis Center, Coll. Medicine, 1980-87; prof. rehab. and rheumatology, dept. medicine U. Ariz., 1987—, also dir. disability assessment program. Pres. allied health professions sect. Nat. Arthritis Found.; bd. dirs. Nat. Arthritis Found. (S.W. chpt.); nat. vice chmn. bd. dirs.; mem. NIH Nat. Arthritis Adv. Bd., 1977-84; also chmn. subcom. community programs and rehab.; mem. staff Ariz. Legislature Health Welfare, 1972-73; Mem. Gov.'s Council Dept. Econ. Security, 1978-85; pres., bd. dirs. Tucson Assn. for Blind, 1974-86; chmn. Gov.'s Council on Blind and Visually Impaired, 1987—; active Gov.'s Coun. on Arthritis and Musculoskeletal Disease, 1987—, Gov.'s State wide Coun. on Rehab., 1998—, Am. Bd. Forensic Examiners, 1997—. Author: Worksamples; contbr. chpts. to books and articles to profl. jours. Mem. Gov.'s State Rehab. Coun., 1998—, commr. Commn. on Civil Rights, Az., 2002. Recipient Gov.'s awards for leadership in rehab., 1966, 69, 72, 73; awards for sci. and vol. services Nat. Arthritis Found., 1973, 75; 1st nat. Addie Thomas award Nat. Arthritis Found., 1983, Benson award, 1989, Govt. Affairs award, 1989; Arthritis Found. fellow, 1983. Mem. Am. Psychol. Assn. (div. 17 counseling psychology), Am. Coll. Forensics, Assn. Schs. Allied Health Professions, Nat. Rehab. Assn., Ariz. Psychol. Assn. Home: 5765 N Camino Real Tucson AZ 85718-4213 Office: U Ariz Arizona Health Scis Ctr Tucson AZ 85724-0001

SMITH, DEAN, communications advisor, arbitrator; b. N.Y.C., Aug. 10, 1925; s. Franklin Grant and Anna Lucille (Kranebell) S.; m. Andree Marie Praileur, Aug. 9, 1947; children: David F., Christopher P. Student, NYU, 1945-46, Columbia U., 1946-47, N.Y. Sch. Printing, 1946-47. Editor ShowBill Mag., N.Y.C., 1945-47; news editor Boulder City (Nev.) Daily News, 1947-49; owner, pub., editor Tucson Sun-News, N.Y.C., 1949-51; dir. radio and TV news Sta. WBEN/WBEN-TV, Buffalo, 1951-53; dir. pub. svc. and promotion Indpls. Times, 1953-56; v.p., gen. mgr Kendall Assocs., Inc., N.Y.C., 1956-60; dir. Office Publs. and Info., Commerce Dept., Washington, 1961-70, dir. publs. div., 1970; asst. dir. Nat. Tech. Info. Svc., Springfield, Va., 1971-81, dir. office of market devel., 1982-83; assoc. dir. NTIS, 1984-85, self-employed communications advisor, 1986—. Chmn. for fed. mail list policy Vice Pres.'s Com. on Right of Privacy; chmn. presdl. domestic policy rev. work group on fed. acquisition of fgn. tech., 1979; bd. dirs. Commerce Fed. Credit Union. Served with AUS, 1943-45 Decorated Silver Star with oak leaf cluster, Bronze Star, Purple Heart with oak leaf cluster; recipient award Ariz. Newspaper Assn., 1950, Ind. Photo Journalism award, 1954 Mem. Am. Arbitration Assn. (panelist), Washington Book Pubs., Soc. Mayflower Descs., Sons of Revolution (treas.), Flagon and Trencher, Soc. for the Descs.of the Colonial Clergy, Soc. Descs. of Founders of Hartford, Oldest Inhabitants of DC. Democrat. Home and Office: 2325 49th St NW Washington DC 20007-1002 E-mail: smithdeansmith@cs.com.

SMITH, DEAN EDWARDS, university basketball coach; b. Emporia, Kans., Feb. 28, 1931; s. Alfred Dillon and Vesta Marie (Edwards) S.; m. Linnea Weblemoe, May 21, 1976; children: Sharon, Sandy, Scott, Kristen, Kelly. BS in Math. and Phys. Edn., U. Kans., 1953. Asst. basketball coach USAF Acad., 1955-58; asst. basketball coach U. N.C., 1958-61, head basketball coach, 1961-97. Mem. U.S. and Canadian Basketball Rules Com., 1967-73; U.S. basketball coach Olympics, Montreal, Que., Can., 1976; lectr. basketball clinics, Germany, Italy. With USAF, 1954-58. Named Coach of Year, Atlantic Coast Conf., 1967, 1968, 1971, 1976, 1977, 79, Nat. Basketball Coach of Year, 1977, Nat. Coach of Yr., U.S. Basketball Writers, 1979, one of Top 5 Coaches of the 20th Century, ABC-TV and ESPN; named to Naismith Basketball Hall of Fame, 1982 Mem. Nat. Assn. Basketball Coaches (Nat. Basketball Coach of Yr. 1976, dir. 1972— , pres. 1981-82), Fellowship Christian Athletes (dir. 1965-70) Baptist. Office: U NC Office Basketball Coach PO Box 2126 Chapel Hill NC 27515-2126

SMITH, DEBRA GOLDSTEIN, social worker; b. New Orleans, Sept. 14, 1954; d. David L. and Evelyn Mae (Gottesman) Goldstein; m. Gary Michael Smith, Nov. 16, 1986; 1 child, Justin Lee. BA, Rutgers U., 1976; MSW, Tulane U., 1979. Cert. ACSW, BCSW. Foster care worker Associated Cath. Charities, New Orleans, 1980-81; recruitment specialist State of La., 1981-84; outreach coord. Cath. Charities of Richmond, Va., 1985-89; info. specialist CSR, Inc., Washington, 1989-90; project dir. Cygnus Corp., Nat. Adoption Info. Clearinghouse, Rockville, Md., 1990—. Sec. Adoption Therapy Coalition, Rockville, 1991-92, No. Va. Youth Svcs. Coalition, Fairfax, 1988-89. Co-producer TV program Focus on Youth, 1988-89; contbr. articles to profl. jours. Pub. rels. coord. Fairfax Symphony Orch., 1987-88; bd. dirs. Reston (Va.) Children's Ctr., 1991—. Recipient Lemann Stern Young Leader award Jewish Fedn., 1982. Mem. NASW, Nat. Coun. Jewish Women (life, No. Va. sect. pres. 1988-89, Angel award 1988), Jewish Folk Arts Soc., Families Adopting Children Everywhere. Democrat. Avocations: piano, guitar, swimming, tennis. Office: Nat Adoption Info Clearinghouse 11426 Rockville Pike Ste 410 Rockville MD 20852-3007

SMITH, DEBRA MARIE, special education educator; b. Columbia, S.C., May 15, 1964; d. Charles Perry and Margaret Judith (Grookett) S. BS, Coll. Charleston, 1986; MEd, U. S.C., 1989. Tchr. spl. edn. Richland Sch. Dist. #1 Gadsden (S.C.) Elem. Sch., 1987; tchr. elem. spl. edn. Richland Sch. Dist. #1 Carver Elem. Sch., Columbia, S.C., 1987-91, Richland Sch. Dist. #1 W.G. Sanders Mid. Sch., Columbia, 1991-97, Richland Sch. Dist. #1, Lower Richland H.S., Hopkins, 1998-99; spl. edn. cons. Richland Sch. Dist. #1, Columbia, 1999—. E-mail: debrsmith@richlandone.org.

SMITH, DEIRDRE O'MEARA, lawyer; b. N.Y.C., June 2, 1946; d. Thomas Francis and Mary Veronica (Meehan) O'Meara; children: Thomas Brady Ahr, Andrew Travers Ahr; m. Gerald Monroe Smith, Aug. 15, 1992. BA cum laude, Trinity Coll., 1968; MEd, Va. Commonwealth U., 1976; JD, U. Mo., 1982. Bar: Mo. 1982, U.S. Dist. Ct. (we. dist.) Mo. 1982. Tchr. Prince George's County Schs., Md., 1968-70, St. Michael's Sch., Richmond, Va., 1976-78; staff lawyer Mo. Supreme Ct., Jefferson City, 1982-83; gen. counsel State of Mo. Detention Facilities Commn., 1983, State of Mo. Jud. Fin. Commn., Jefferson City, 1983-85; clk. of the ct. Mo. Ct. Appeals Eastern Dist., St. Louis, 1985-98. Bd. dirs. Downtown St. Louis, 1994-95. Recipient Acad. Excellence award in environ. law U. Mo. Sch. Law, 1981; disting. fellow St. Louis Bar Found. Fellow Am. Bar Found., Mo. Bar Found.; mem. ABA (jud. divsn. lawyers conf., exec. com. 1997-2000), Nat. Conf. Bar Pres., Nat. Conf. Bar Founds., Mo. Bar Assn. (Mo. Client Security Security Trust Fund bd. dirs. 1991-95, chmn. 1995-96), St. Louis County Bar Assn., Lawyers Assn. St. Louis (Outstanding Svc. award 1998), Met. St. Louis Bar Assn. (exec. com. 1988-96, pres. 1994-95), Beafort, S.C. Art Assn. (bd. dirs. 1999-2002), Dataw Island Owners Assn. (sec. 2001-02, v.p. 2002—), St. Louis Bar Found. (bd. dirs. 1989-96, pres. 1995-96), St. Louis Women Lawyers Assn. (bd. dirs. 1989-94, pres. 1992-93), Am. Judicature Soc. (bd. dirs. 1990-94, bd. exec. com. 1993—, v.p. 1995-97, sec. 1997-99, treas. 1999-2001, pres. 2001—), Nat. Conf. Appellate Ct. Clks. (exec. com. 1990-92), Media Club St. Louis (bd. dirs.), Phi Delta Phi. Roman Catholic.

SMITH, DENIS JOSEPH, mathematics educator; b. Boston, Mar. 19, 1949; s. Joseph P. and Margaret L. (Stapleton) S.; m. Mary P. MacDougall, Aug. 26, 1972; children: Brandon Edward, Shane F. AB in math. edn., Boston Coll.,

1971; MEd, Cambridge Coll., 1990. Tchr. Xaverian Bros. High Sch., Westwood, Mass., 1971—; math. instr. Dean Coll., 2000—. Advisor Xaverian Math. Team/New Eng. Math. League, Westwood, Mass.1980—, chmn. Math. Dept. Xaverian Bros High Sch., Westwood, 1982-84, 86-88, 95—; math instr. Dean Coll., 2000—; bd. dirs. Greater Boston Math. League, Canton, Mass., 1989—, advisor, 1980—; ednl. cons. St. Catherine of Sienna, Norwood, Mass., 1990-92; in house coord. Nat. High Sch. Math. Exam., 1980—, supr. Math Olympiad Level I Exam. Eucharistic min. St. Mary's Ch., 1984—; coach Dedham Youth Soccer, 1985-92; pres. St. Catherine's Homes and Sch. Assn., 1989-91; vice chmn. Cardinal Parish Planning Coun., 1990—. Grantee NSF, 1993. Mem. Nat. Coun. Tchrs., Nat. Cath. Ednl. Assn. Democrat. Roman Catholic. Home: 23 Charles St Dedham MA 02026-3049 Office: Xaverian Bros High Sch 800 Clapboardtree St Westwood MA 02090-1718 E-mail: dsmith@xbhs.com.

SMITH, DENISE GROLEAU, data processing professional; b. Worcester, Mass., Feb. 7, 1951; d. Edmond Laurence and Audrey Mildred (Paquin) Groleau; m. Wayne Marshall Smith, Apr. 17, 1976; 1 child, Andrew. BSBA, Fitchburg State U., 1983. Bindery worker Atlantic Bus. Forms, Hudson, Mass., 1969-73; proofreader New Eng. Bus., Townsend, 1974-75, computer operator Groton, 1975-80, adminstrv. asst. bus. systems, 1980-82, adminstrv. asst. info. ctr., 1982-85; info. ctr. analyst Wright Line Inc., Worcester, 1985-88; personal computer coord. Thom McAn Shoe Co., 1988-91. Cons. personal computer Buckingham Transp., Groton, 1987—, Software Mgr. Moppet Sch., 1993—; cons. personal computer Maple Dene Elem. Sch., 1993—, elem. sch. software mgr. Avocations: reading, sewing, quilting. Home: 14 Cedar Cir Townsend MA 01469-1336

SMITH, DENNIS (EDWARD SMITH), author, publisher; b. N.Y.C., Sept. 9, 1940; s. John and Mary (Hogan) S.; m. Patricia Ann Kearney, Aug. 24, 1963 (div. May 1988); children: Brendan, Dennis, Sean, Deirdre and Aislinn (twins); m. Katina Arts Meyer, Dec. 25, 1997. BA, NYU, 1970, MA, 1972. Adj. asst. prof. Coll. New Rochelle, 1973-74; fireman City of N.Y., 1963-80; founder, pub., editor in chief Firehouse Mag., N.Y.C., 1976-89. Author: Report from Engine Co. 82, 1972, Final Fire, 1975, Firehouse, 1977, Dennis Smith's History of American Firefighting, 1978, Glitter and Ash, 1980, The Aran Islands—A Personal Journey, 1980, Steely Blue, 1985, Firefighters, Their Lives in Their Own Words, 1988, The Little Fire Engine That Saved the City, 1990, A Song for Mary, 1999, Report For Ground Zero, 2002. Mem. bd. advisors Boys and Girls Clubs Am., N.Y.C., The New York Fire Safety Found.; bd. dirs. Kips Bay Boys and Girls Club, N.Y.C.; bd. dirs., chmn. emeritus N.Y. Acad. Art; bd. dirs., pres. Found. for Am. Firefighters. With USAF, 1957-60. Recipient Christopher award for non-fiction, 1973. Mem. Century Assn. Club, Irish Georgian Soc. (bd. dirs.). Democrat. Roman Catholic. Home and Office: 71 E 77th St # 9C New York NY 10021-1849

SMITH, DENNIS BRUCE, software engineer; b. N.Y.C., June 4, 1946; s. Bruce E. an Ruth (Solomon) S.; m. Barbara Burnham, Aug. 8, 1970; children: Brian, Amy, Karen, Mark. BA, Columbia U., 1968; MA, Princeton (N.J.) U., 1972, PhD, 1979. Dir. MIS and instl. rsch. Edison Coll., Trenton, N.J., 1973-83; tech. dir. Sycomm Systems Corp., Greenbrook, 1983-88; sr. mgmt. cons. Trecom Bus. Systems, Edison, 1988-89; mgr. CASE Environs. Carnegie Mellon U., Pitts., 1989-93, mgr. Software Engring. Inst., 1989—; mgr. Reengring. Ctr., 1994—. Case adoption project co-editor ISO Geneva, Switzerland, 1993—, Piscataway, N.J., 1993—. Co-author: Understanding CASE Tool Integration, 1994, Principles of CASE Integration, 1994, (tech. report) Guide to CASE Adoption, 1993; contbr. articles to profl. jours. Mem. IEEE (assoc., conf. organizer 1994), Assn. for Computing Machinery. Roman Catholic. Office: CMU SEI 5000 Forbes Ave Pittsburgh PA 15213-3815

SMITH, DENNIS JAY, lawyer; b. Newark, Sept. 2, 1943; s. Sidney H. and Theresa K. Smith; m. Sandra Kotzen Smith, Jan. 25, 1944; children: Sheryl, Lori. BA, Brandeis U., 1961; JD, Boston Coll., 1968. Bar: N.J. 1968, U.S. Ct. Appeals (3d cir.) 1986. Sole proprietor, East Orange, N.J., 1968-77, Millburn, 1977-83; ptnr. Clancy Callahan & Smith, Newark, 1983-87, Roseland, 1987—. Mem. Am. Bar Assn., N.J. State Bar Assn. (ethics com. 1998—), Essex County Bar Assn. (chmn. gen. practice com. 1995-96), Mental Health Assn. Essex County (bd. dirs. 1977, pres. 1980-82, v.p. 2000—). Office: Clancy Callahan & Smith 103 Eisenhower Pkwy Ste 10 Roseland NJ 07068-1090

SMITH, DENYSE LYNNE, journalist, writer; b. Bay City, Mich., Mar. 3, 1962; d. Terrance Joseph Loree and Lynne Marie Gillman; m. Wayne William Smith, Aug. 12, 1989; children: Whitney Marie, Joseph John, Emily Carol-Lyn. BFAA in Journalism, Ctrl. Mich. U., 1990; postgrad., Mich. State U., 2000—. Clk.-typist VA, Houston, 1981—83, Saginaw, Mich., 1983—87; unit sec. Ctrl. Mich. Cmty. Hosp., Mt. Pleasant, 1988—92, cmty. rels. specialist, 1995; freelance journalist, 1991—. Author: (novels) Unearthed Sins, 2001. Leader, pub. rels. specialist Girl Scouts USA, 1998—; sec. Coun. of Cath. Women, 1999—. Recipient Nick Kerbeway Rsch. award, Kerbeway Found., 2001. Republican. Roman Catholic. Avocations: camping, bicycling, swimming, sewing, reading.

SMITH, DEREK ARMAND, information technology executive; b. Hamilton, Ont., Can., Sept. 2, 1953; came to U.S., 1981; s. Alastair A.G. and Jessie Mead (Maben) S.; m. Rebecca Oldfield, Oct. 10, 1981; 1 child, Alastair Maben Oldfield. BCom., U. Toronto, 1976. Chartered acct.; CPA, Mass. Staff acct. Office of Auditor Gen., Ottawa, 1976-78; chartered acct. Peat Marwick Thorne, 1978-79; v.p. fin. adminstrn. Can. Dry Bottling Ltd., Kingston, Ont., 1979-81; supervising sr. Peat Marwick, Boston, 1981-82; mgr. corp. reporting Warren, Gorham & Lamont, Inc., 1981-82, asst. contr. N.Y.C., 1982-84, sr. v.p., CFO, 1988-90, Penguin Books USA Inc., N.Y.C., 1990-96; exec. v.p., 1995-96; exec. v.p., CFO Addison Wesley Longman Inc., Reading, Mass., 1996-98; v.p., chief adminstrv. officer Orgnl. Dynamics, Inc., Burlington, 1998-2000; CFO First Knowledge Ptnrs. Inc., Boston, 2000—01; CFO, v.p. adminstrn. Castel, Inc., Beverly, 2002—. Pres. Trinity Coll. Sch. Fund, Beverly, Mass., 1992; gov. Trinity Coll. Sch., Port Hope, Ont., 1992. Trustee John Hart Hunter Ednl. Found., N.Y.C., 1992. Mem. AICPA (bd. examiners 1998—), Assn. Chartered Accts. U.S. Ltd. (treas. 1990-93, dir. 1989-94, hon. dir. 1994—), Kappa Alpha Soc. (exec. com., v.p. 1991-93, pres. 1993-95, past pres. 1995-97). Episcopalian. Avocations: skiing, sailing, tennis, paddle tennis, golf. Office: Castel Inc 100 Cummings Ctr Ste 157H Beverly MA 01915

SMITH, DIANA MARIE, business educator; b. Des Moines, Oct. 25, 1940; d. Nathan Henry and Helen (Hall) Kitchen; m. Robert Nelson Smith, Jan. 26, 1971; 1 child, Stephen. BA, Drake U., 1968, MA, 1971. Cert. tchr., Iowa. Stenographer Polk County Welfare Dept., Des Moines, 1960-67; typist Polk County Auditor, 1968, Cen. Life Assurance Co., Des Moines, 1976-79; computer oper. IRS, 1988; lead specialist II Norwest Bank, 1978—; sec. Shive-Hattery Engrs., 1976-90; adult edn. instr. Des Moines Ind. Dist., 1969—; tchr. bus., computers Des Moines Pub. Schs., 1968—. Ind. computer cons.; instr.-authorized tng. assoc. program for Word Perfect, 1994; Mary Kay beauty cons., 1993—. Chair meml. com. Burns United Meth. Ch., Des Moines, 1988—, Sunday sch. tchr., 1961-83, 92—, sec. adminstrv. bd. Mem. NEA, Nat. Bus. Edn. Assn., Iowa Bus. Edn. Assn., Des Moines Bus. Edn. Assn., Iowa State Edn. Assn., Des Moines Edn. Assn. Democrat. Avocations: reading, computers. Office: Cen Campus 1800 Grand Ave Des Moines IA 50309-3310

SMITH, DON, communications executive; BS in Engring., Imperial Coll., London. Engr. BT Rsch. Labs., Canada; exec. v.p. Mitel, 1981; pres. AIT Corp.; founder, pres., CEO Cambrian Sys. Corp., 1996; CEO Mitel Networks Corp., Kanata, Canada, 2001—. Office: Mitel Networks Corp 350 Leggett Dr PO Box 13089 Kanata ON Canada K2K 2W7

SMITH, DON ALAN, educator; b. Athens, Tenn., Feb. 7, 1936; s. Maurice Clifton S. and Frances Ellen Higgins. BA, Vanderbilt U., 1957, Oxford U., England, 1959, MA, 1968; PhD, Yale U., 1965. Instr. history Yale U., New Haven, 1963-66, asst. prof. history, 1966-70; assoc. prof. history Grinnell (Iowa) Coll., 1970-75, prof. history, 1975—, L.F. Parker prof. history, 2000—. Vis. prof. history Nanjing U., China, 1993—. Presdl. elector State of Iowa, 1992. Rhodes scholar, 1957-59. Mem. N.Am. Conf. Brit. Studies, Fortnightly Club (pres. 1988-89). Democrat. Avocations: politics, music, contract bridge. Home: 1420 Summer St Grinnell IA 50112-1256 Office: Grinnell Coll 1210 Park St Grinnell IA 50112-1670 E-mail: smithd@grinnell.edu.

SMITH, DONALD ARCHIE, religion business executive, consultant; b. Dayton, Ohio, Feb. 23, 1934; s. Archie Ford and Catherine Rosella (Rabold) S.; m. Joan Sandra Speedie, May 18, 1955; children: Douglas Alan, Keith Cameron, Deirdre Lynn, Neal Ramsey. BA in Sci. and Math., Harvard U., 1956; cert., Indsl. Coll. of Armed Forces, 1971. Mgmt. Acct., 1977, Enrolled Agt., 1996. Nuclear rsch. and project engr. N.Am. Aviation Co., 1956-62; fin. software specialist Nat. Cash Register, 1962-63; mgr. sys. engring. N.Am. Aviation, 1963-67; mgr. bus. planning, mktg. svcs. and pub. rels. N.Am. Rockwell, Columbus, Ohio, 1967-72, mgr. internat. sales and mktg., 1968-73; mgr. strategic planning Rockwell Internat. Corp., 1973-76, program mgr. Condor weapons sys., 1976-77, dir. guided bomb programs, 1977-78, dir. bus. devel. and legis. liaison, 1978-80; v.p. fin. applied tech. group Arvin Industries, Ind., 1980-84; v.p. fin. Calspan Corp., 1980-82, v.p. fin. and adminstrn., 1982-84, CFO, treas., dir., 1983-84; bus. dir. Franklin United Meth. Home, 1984-86; dir. fin. and adminstrn. North Ind. Conf. of the United Meth. Ch., 1986-92; sr. assoc. gen. sec. health benefits/gen. bd. of pensions United Meth. Ch., 1992-96; staff devel. cons. logal ednl. software, 1996-2000; pres. Kid Solve, Inc., 1999—. Ops. rsch. cons., 1962-64; instr. math. Sinclair Coll., Dayton, Ohio, 1961-63; mem. U.S.-U.K. Bipartite Com. on Nuclear Weapons, 1958-61; industry chmn. Mil. Specifications and Stds. Rev. Com,. 1972-79; mgmt. cons., 1984—. Author: Financial Recordkeeping Handbook for Local Churches. Pres., trustee Columbus Arts Guild, 1980-83; treas., dir. Franklin United Meth. Home, 1982-84; auditor First United Meth. Ch,. 1981-84; past pres., treas., trustee Players Theatre of Columbus, 1975-80; v.p. Ohio Assn. of U.S. Army, 1979-80; dist. commr. Boy Scouts Am., 1970-73, cubmaster, 1965-70; mem. audit and rev. com. Gen. Coun. on Fin. and Adminstrn., 1988-92; mem. Denominational Health Task Force, Gen. Bd. Pensions, 1989-92; squadron comdr. CAP, 1976; chmn. Commn. on Racism in Columbus Pub. Schs., 1972. Recipient Nat. award Jr. Achievement, Inc., 1954; Letters of Commendation govt. agys., Am. Def. Preparedness Assn., Boy Scouts Am., 1958-78; Leadership award Nat. Mgmt. Assn., 1979. Mem. AIAA (nat. chmn. soc. and aerospace tech. com. 1980-83, nat. pub. policy com.), AARP (state chmn. Ill. 1993-95, state adminstr. Ind. 1996—, mem. nat. tech. com. 1996-98), Nat. Tng. Com. (chmn. 1998—), SAR, NRA, NAA, NAEA, Royal Inst. Nav., Nat. Mgmt. Assn. (v.p., trustee), Palatines to Am., Harvard Club (Ind.), Army and Navy Club, Masons, Shriners. Home and Office: 7 E Hill Valley Dr Indianapolis IN 46227-2624 E-mail: don@kidsolve.com.

SMITH, DONALD ARTHUR, mechanical engineer, researcher; b. Hartford, Conn., Apr. 9, 1945; s. Winfred Arthur and Marguerite Elisabeth (Johnson) S.; m. Marianne Carol Taverna, June 17, 1967; 1 child, Adam James. BSME, U. Hartford, 1968. Rsch. engr. Combustion Engring. Inc., Windsor, Conn., 1968-71, supr. fluid rsch., 1971-77, mgr. combustion rsch., 1977-84; dir. R&D Hartford Steam Boiler Inspection & Ins. Co., 1984—. Co. rep. Indsl. Rsch. Inst., Washington, 1989—; treas. Am. Flame Rsch. Com., 1983—. Tech. editor: HSB Locomotive, 1990-91. Haddam (Conn.) Planning and Zoning Commn., 1991-95; pres. Sherwood Camp Assn., Haddam, 1971-81. Named Engr. Yr. ASME (Hartford sect.), 1989. Mem. Lions. Republican. Roman Catholic. Achievements include patents in spray atomizers, burners, ignitors and flame scanning systems for indsl. application. Established Combustion Engring.'s fluid mechanics and combustion rsch. facilities, Hartford Steam Boiler's corp. R&D program. Home: PO Box 95-42 Smith Hill Rd Haddam CT 06438 Office: Hartford Steam Boiler One State St Hartford CT 06102

SMITH, DONALD CAMERON, physician, educator; b. Peterborough, Ont., Can., Feb. 2, 1922; came to U.S., 1952, naturalized, 1960; s. James Cameron and Clarice (Leighton) S.; m. Jean Ida Morningstar, Sept. 11, 1946; children: Douglas Frazer, Scot Earle, Donald Ian. MD, Queen's U., 1945; MSc in Medicine, U. Toronto, Ont., 1948, DPH, 1949. Diplomate Am. Bd. Preventive Medicine, Am. Bd. Pediat. Intern Victoria Hosp., London, 1945-46; fellow in physiology U. Toronto, 1947-48; med. officer health Kent County (Ont.) Health Unit, 1950-51; Commonwealth Fund fellow in pediat. U. Mich. Hosp., 1952-55; prof. maternal and child health U. Mich. (Sch. Pub. Health); prof. pediat. U. Mich. (Med. Sch.), 1961-79, chmn. dept. health and human devel., 1961-79; prof. psychiatry and behavioral scis. Northwestern U. Med. Sch., Chgo., 1979-85. Chmn. Medicaid Adv. Coun., 1969-72; prin. advisor on health and med. affairs to gov. Mich., 1972-78; dir. Mich. Dept. Mental Health, 1974-78; chmn. health care policy bd. Mich. Dept. Corrections, 1986-91; chmn. State Pub. Health Adv. Coun., 1982-90; chmn. Expert Com. on AIDS, 1985-88; sr. v.p. Joint Commn. on Accreditation Hosps., Chgo., 1979-81; sr. med. adviser Sisters of Mercy Health Corp., 1981-91; pres. Mental Health Assn. Mich., 1992-94; chmn., cross-nat. study of health care svcs. HEW, 1971; vis. prof. maternal and child health Harvard U., 1969-72; med. dir. Physician's Rev. Orgn. Mich., 1992—. Surgeon lt. Royal Canadian Navy, 1946-47. Address: # 408 807 Asa Gray Dr Ann Arbor MI 48105 Home: # 408 807 Asa Gray Dr Ann Arbor MI 48105-2566 E-mail: leele48105@yahoo.com.

SMITH, DONALD E. broadcast engineer, manager; b. Salt Lake City, Sept. 10, 1930; s. Thurman A. and Louise (Cardall) S.; m. Helen B. Lacy, 1978. BA, Columbia U., 1955; BS, U. Utah, 1970; postgrad., U. So. Calif., U. Utah, Harvard U.; PhD (hon.), Columbia U., 1985. Engr. Iowa State U. (WOI-TV), 1955-56; asst. chief engr. KLRJ-TV, Las Vegas, 1956-60; studio field engr. ABC, Hollywood, Calif., 1960; chief engr. Teletape, Inc., Salt Lake City, 1961; engring. supr. KUER, U. Utah, 1962-74, gen. mgr., 1975-85. Freelance cinematographer, 1950—; cons. radio TV (mgmt. engr. and prodn.), 1965—. Mem. Soc. Motion Pictures and TV Engrs., Lambda Chi Alpha. Home: 963 Hollywood Ave Salt Lake City UT 84105-3347 E-mail: donesmith@attbi.com.

SMITH, DONALD E. banker; b. Terre Haute, Ind., Nov. 4, 1926; s. Henry P. and Ruth I. (Bius) S.; m. Mary F. Ryan, June 25, 1947; children: Virginia Lee, Sarah Jane. Student, Ind. U., 1945-47, Ind. State U., 1947-48. Chmn. Deep Vein Coal Co., Terre Haute, Ind., 1947—; with R.J. Oil Co., Inc., 1948—; chmn. Princeton Mining Co., Terre Haute, 1947—; pres. Terre Haute Oil Corp., 1947—; chmn. of bd. Terre Haute 1st Nat. Bank, 1969—; pres., CEO 1st Fin. Corp., Terre Haute, 1969—. Trustee Ind. State U.; bd. mgrs. Rose-Hulman Inst. Tech., 1978—; treas. Terre Haute Econ. Devel. Commn., 1981—; mem. Ind. Econ. Devel. Coun. Mem. Terre Haute C. of C. (bd. dirs. 1982—), Elks, Country Club of Terre Haute. Home: 94 Allendale Terre Haute IN 47802-4751 Office: Terre Haute First Nat Bank One First Financial Pla PO Box 540 Terre Haute IN 47808-0540

SMITH, DONALD EDWARD HAROLD, research animal specialist; b. Belleville, Ont., Can., Feb. 17, 1952; came to U.S., 1978; s. Donald Edward Smith and Caroline Patience (Johnstone) Porter; m. Monique Marie-Therese Dumesnil, Nov. 29, 1975; children: Ryan Gregory, Michelle Elise, Ian. BS, U. Alberta, 1972, MS, 1974; PhD, Hokkaido U. Registered laboratory animal technologist. From lectr. to dir. animal care Northeastern U., Boston, 1978-86; chief comparative biology & medicine Human Nutrition Rsch. Ctr. on Aging, 1985—. Exec. bd. dirs. Parents of the Handicapped, Natick, Mass., 1987-90, Spl. Olympics, Framingham, 1990-92; adv. com. Learning Ctr. for Deaf Children, Framingham, 1987-90. Mem. Am. Assn. Lab. Animal Sci. (bd. dirs. New England br. 1983-88, chair region examining bd. 1979-82, chair edn. com. 1979-82). Avocations: Special Olympics coach in skiing, soccer, track & field. Office: US Dept Agriculture Human Nutrition Ctr Aging 711 Washington St Boston MA 02111-1524

SMITH, DONALD EUGENE, healthcare facility management administrator owner; b. Mishawaka, Ind., Oct. 15, 1936; s. Ernest Hartmann and Lucile Emma (Krumanaker) S.; m. Nancy Mae Jaffke, Sept. 2, 1961; children: Adam, Reid, Lynn. AB, Wabash Coll., 1959; MBA, U. Chgo., 1963. Adminstrv. resident Ind. U. Med. Ctr., 1960-61; assoc. dir. Ind. U. Hosps., 1966-72; pres. Henderson & Smith Corp., Indpls., 1978—. Lectr. in health adminstrn. Ind. U., 1965-66, adj. asst. prof. in health adminstrn., 1966-78; ptnr. Carmel (Ind.) Care Ctr., Countryside Manor, Anderson, Ind., Dearborn Enterprises, Lawrenceburg, Ind., Rawlins House, Pendleton, Ind., Manor House of Carmel, Ind.; chmn. Ind. State Bd. Registration and Edn. Health Facility Adminstrs., 1969-82. Bd. dirs. Ind. U. Med. Ctr. Fed. Credit Union, 1965-68, Ind. Blue Cross, 1966-71; med. ctr. chmn. United Fund Drive, 1962-65; sec. Carmel (Ind.) Classic, 1979, v.p., 1981, pres., 1982-83; bd. trustees Wabash Coll., 1986—, mem. exec. com., 1986—, chmn. capital campaign drive, 1987-91, mem. long range planning com., 1985; active Hamilton County Rep. Fin. Com., 1990—. Fellow ACHS; mem. Am. Health Care Assn., Ind. Health Care Assn., Wabash Coll. Alumni Assn., U. Chgo. Hosp. Adminstrn. Alumni Assn., Woodland Country Club, Vero Beach Country Club. Office: Henderson & Smith Corp 10333 N Meridian St Ste 250 Indianapolis IN 46290-1144

SMITH, DONALD RAY, magazine dealer; b. Louisville, Dec. 12, 1934; s. Henry Bland and Margaret Frances (Corbett) S. Ed. pvt. schs., Louisville. Clerk Huber & Huber Motor Express, Louisville, 1951-52, Retail Credit Co., Louisville, 1952-53, Louisville & Nashville R.R., Louisville, 1953-65; owner, appraiser, cons. Don Smith's Nat. Geog. Mags., 1969—. Author: Nat. Geog. Mag. for Collectors, 1975, 2d edit., 1978, 3d rev. edit., 1985, 4th rev. edit., 1988, 5th rev. edit., 1992, 6th rev. edit., 1996, Gone With the Wagons, 1980; composer song My Dreams Desire Another Way, 1968, poem Calico Waltz, 1986, Beyond Repast, 1986, The Essence of Darkness, 1986, The Dominant Submissive, 1987, Agony's Prelude, 1987, The Unmoving Distance, 1988, Exercise, 1997, Doris Jean, 1998, Cranfling's Release, 1998, Mr. Gally, 1999, Every Time I Hear My Favorite Song, 1999; price guide booklet for collectors of Nat. Geog. Mag., 2000, Nat. Geog. Collector's Newsletter, 2000, Torell's First Love, 2001; also numerous pamphlets and articles on colecting mags. Author: Purt Your Dreams In a Cup, 2001. Democrat. Roman Catholic. Avocations: finger syle guitar, drawing, painting, auto restoration. Home and Office: 3930 Rankin St Louisville KY 40214-1748

SMITH, DONALD RAYMOND, librarian; b. Highland, Ill., Sept. 25, 1946; s. Raymond Stanley and Gladys Loraine (Martin) S.; m. Elaine Marie Neudecker, Apr. 12, 1969; 1 child, Benjamin Christopher. BA, So. Ill. U., 1968, MA, 1972, MS, 1978; MLS, U. Mo., 1976. Acad. adv. So. Ill. U., Edwardsville, 1970-73, libr. instr., 1973-78, edn. libr., 1978-82; assoc. dir. pub. svc. and collection devel. U. Tulsa, 1982-88, assoc. dir. gen. svcs., 1988-93; dir. libr. N.E. La. U., Monroe, La., 1993-96; dean info. svcs. U. La., 1996—. Cons. Hayner Pub. Libr., Alton, Ill., 1977-82, Tulsa City County Libr., 1984; cons. facilitator Tulsa Area Libr. Coop., 1987-88, 90; collection evaluator Okla. Jr. Coll., Tulsa, 1984. Author: Newspaper Indexing Handbook, 1981; editor and compiler newspaper index, 1976-77. Cataloger Our Lady Queen of Peace Sch., Belleville, Ill., 1979-82; campaign worker Dem. Party, Belleville, 1972; chair bd. dirs. Tulsa Area Libr. Coop., 1991-93. With U.S. Army, 1969-70. Recipient Millicent C. Palmer award Friends of Lovejoy Library, So. Ill. U., 1974, H.W. Wilson scholar, 1974, Higher Edn. Coordinating Act grantee Ill. State Library, 1980-81, Workshop award U. Okla. Sch. Library Sci., 1984. Mem.: La. Libr. Network Commn., Tech. Consortium Tchr. Edn., Trailblazer Libr. Dirs. Bd. and Commn., La. Acad. Libr. Info. Network Consortium (at-large exec. bd. dirs. 1994—96, chmn. rsch. and devel. com. 2001—), La. Assn. Coll. and Rsch. Librs. (automation and tech. com. 2000—), La. Libr. Assn. (sec. scholarship trust 1994—), Okla. Libr. Assn. (chmn. contg. edn. com. 1985—86, chmn. adminstrn. roundtable 1989—90, chair automation roundtable 1991—92), Assn. Coll. and Rsch. Librs., ALA, NOTIS Users Group. Roman Catholic. Avocations: travel, history, reading. Office: U La Univ Libr 700 University Ave Monroe LA 71209-0720

SMITH, DONALD RICHARD, editor, publisher; b. Stockton, Calif., Aug. 20, 1932; s. Robert Gordon and Gertrude (Schweitzer) S.; m. Darlene Ruth Thomas, May 7, 1961; children: Douglas Robert, Deborah Renae. Student, Coll. Pacific, 1951, Delta Coll., 1951-52. Editor, pub. Calif. Odd Fellow & Rebekah, Linden, 1950—; editor Elk Grove (Calif.) Citizen, 1953-55; asst. dir. U.N. Pilgrimage for Youth, N.Y.C., 1956-59; editor, pub. Linden (Calif.) Herald, 1959-86, Lockeford (Calif.)-Clements Post, 1960-62, Internat. Rebekah News, Linden, 1963-86, Internat. Odd Fellow & Rebekah, Linden, 1986-97; dir. communications Sovereign Grand Lodge, 1990-92. Author: From Stagestop to Friendly Community, 1976, Leadership Manual, 1980, The Three Link Fraternity, 1993, Six Links of Fellowship, 1995. Bd. dirs. Odd Fellow-Rebekah Youth Camp, Inc., Long Barn, Calif., 1959-61, Odd Fellows Homes of Calif. Inc., 2002—; bd. dirs. The Meadows of Napa Valley, 1995-2002, pres. bd., 1998-99; bd. dirs., chmn., S.J. County 4-H Found., 1986—; chmn. Linden Rep. Com., 1962-66, Linden Centennial Observance, 1963, Linden Mcpl. Coun., 1981-90, sec., 1981-88, pres., 1988-90. Recipient Legion of Honor Order of Demolay, 1961, John Williams award S.J. Tchrs. Assn., 1963, 87, Golden Key award Stockton Tchrs. Assn., 1971, Achievement award County Bd. Suprs., 1970, Grand Decoration of Chivalry, 1969, Citizen of Yr. award Lions Internat., 1982, Meritorious Svc. Jewel, Ind. Order of Odd Fellows, 1992. Mem. IOOF Internat. Press Assn. (pres. 1962-63), Desktop Pub. Assn., Linden Peters C. of C. (pres. 1968-69), S.J. Hist. Soc. (trustee 1986-90), Lions, Odd Fellows Internat. (sovereign grand master 1969-70), Odd Fellows Calif. (grand master 1958-59), Internat. Coun. Ind. Order Odd Fellows (sec. 1990-96). Avocations: collecting Lionel trains, stamps, coins, historical books, research. Home: 5350 Harrison St Linden CA 95236-9523 Office: Linden Publ PO Box 129 Linden CA 95236-0129 E-mail: donsioof@hotmail.com.

SMITH, DONALD VAUGHAN, artist, educator; b. Pascagoula, Miss., Dec. 4, 1954; s. Arthur V. and Doris (Megehee) S. B in Engring., U. Miss., 1978; BFA in Sculpture, William Carey Coll., 1997, MEd, 2000. Art tchr. Pascagoula H.S. Works represented in pub. and pvt. collections, galleries; prin. works include busts displayed at Trent Lott Mid. Sch., William Carey Coll.; actor in 6 feature films. Home: 906 Sarrazin Ave Pascagoula MS 39567-4955 E-mail: donzart@hotmail.com.

SMITH, DONNA NADINE, army noncommissioned officer; b. Loma Linda, Calif., Feb. 12, 1956; d. Walter Eugene Sr. and Peggy Pauline (Linton) S. BS, SUNY, Syracuse, 1990; MPA, U. Okla., 1997. Enlisted U.S. Army, 1974, advanced through grades to chief warrant officer 4, 1993; all-source analyst Combined Field Army, Camp Red Cloud, Korea, 1982-83, 4th Mech. Infantry Divsn., Ft. Carson, Colo., 1983-85, U.S. Atlantic Fleet, Norfolk, Va., 1985-86; team chief 1st Calvalry Divsn., Ft. Hood, Tex., 1986-88; team chief, Latin Am. U.S. Army Intelligence Threat Ctr., Washington, 1988-91; team chief Joint Intelligence Ctr., 1990-91, U.S. Army Japan, Camp Zama, 1991-93; warrant officer recruiter U.S. Army Recruiting Command, Ft. Knox, Ky., 1993-95; database team chief Joint Intelligence Ctr., MacDill AFB, Fla., 1995—. Bd. dirs. Little League Baseball, MacDill AFB, 1996-97; umpire-in-chief MacDill Little League, 1996-97. Recipient Meritorious Svc. medal, 1993, 95. Mem. ASPA, Mil. Intelligence Corps, Order of Ea. Star. Avocations: reading, counted cross stitching, cake decorating. Address: PO Box 1162 Sierra Vista AZ 85636-1162 E-mail: dsmith2184@aol.com.

SMITH, DONNA YUVONNE, writer, educator; b. Urich, Mo., Jan. 15, 1934; d. Rufus Edgar Rombold and Eddie May Downer; m. William E. Walker Jr., Dec. 24, 1950 (dec. Apr. 10, 1981); children: Christie Walker, Misty Walker, Bill David Walker, Dayna Walker; m. Archie Kenneth Smith, Oct. 28, 1983 (dec. Oct. 13, 2000); children: Dale. Assoc. Arts, Western Okla. State Coll., Altus, OK, 1971; BA, Cameron U., Lawton, OK, 1973; Masters Edn., Southwestern Okla. State U., Weatherford, OK, 1976. Tchr. Altus H.S., Altus, Okla., 1973—97; newsletter editor Assoc. Professors Okla. Educators, Norman, 1995—; area corr. Wichita Falls Times Record News, Wichita Falls, Tex., 2002—; freelance writer Okla., 1993—. Bd. of directors Assoc. Professors Okla. Educators, Norman, Okla., 1995—. Contbr. articles to profl. jours. Recipient Entre Nous Award English, Cameron U., 1973. Mem.: Assoc. Professors Okla. Educators (bd. of directors 1995—2002). R-Conservative. Southern Baptist. Avocations: reading, writing, crocheting. Home: 113 Fairview Tipton OK 73570

SMITH, DORIS CORINNE KEMP, retired nurse; b. Bogalusa, La., Nov. 22, 1919; d. Milton Jones and Maude Maria (Fortenberry) Kemp; m. Joseph William Smith, Oct. 13, 1940 (dec.). BSN, U. Colo., 1957, MS in Nursing Adminstrn., 1958. RN, Colo. Head nurse Chgo. Bridge & Iron Co., Morgan City, La., 1941-45, Shannon Hosp., San Angelo, Tex., 1945-50; dir. nursing Yoakum County Hosp., Denver City, 1951-52; hosp. supr. Med. Arts Hosp., Odessa, 1952-55; dir. insvc. edn. St. Anthony Hosp., Denver, 1961-66; coord. Kiamichi Area Vocat.-Tech. Nursing Sch., Wilburton, Okla., 1969-77; supr. non-ambulatory unit Lubbock (Tex.) State Sch., 1978-85, ret., 1985. Steering com. Western Interstate Commn. on Higher Edn. for Nurses, Denver, 1963-65; curriculum and materials com. Okla. Bd. Vocat.-Tech. Edn., Stillwater, 1971-76; mem. Invitational Conf. To Plan Nursing for Future, Oklahoma City, 1976-77; survey team to appraise Sch. of Vocat.-Tech. Edn. Schs. for Okla. Dept. Vocat.-Tech. Edn., 1975-76. Author, editor: Survey of Functions Expected of the General Duty Nurse, State of Colorado, 1958; co-editor: Curriculum Guides; contbr. articles to profl. jours. Recipient citation of merit

Okla. State U., 1976. Mem. AAAS, ANA, AAUW (life), Nat. League for Nursing, Tex. League for Nursing, Tex. Nurses Assn., Dist. 18 Nurses Assn., Tex. Employees Assn. (v.p. 1984-85), U. Colo. Alumni Assn., Am. Bus. Women's Assn. (pres. Lubbock chpt. 1986-87, rec. sec. 1989-90, edn. chair 1994-95, hospitality chair 1995-96), Am. Bus. Women's Assn. (program co-chair 1996-97, co-chair Am. Bus. Women's Assn. Day, 1997-98, membership com. 1999-2000, 2001-02, fin. com. 1997-98, Woman of Yr. Sunrise chpt. 1994-95), Bus. and Profl. Women's Assn. (sec. 1992-95), Chancellor's Club U. Colo., Pi Lambda Theta (sec. local chpt. 1957-58). Republican. Avocations: gardening, swimming, walking, travel, reading. Home: 2103 55th St Lubbock TX 79412-2612

SMITH, DOROTHY BRAND, retired librarian; b. Beaumont, Tex., Oct. 4, 1922; d. Robert and Lula (Jones) Brand; m. William E. Smith, June 15, 1941; children: Wilson B., Lurinda. BS in Social Sci., Lamar U., 1954; MLS, U. Tex., 1971. Tchr. Beaumont Ind. Sch. Dist., 1954-62, Austin (Tex.) Ind. Sch. Dist., 1962-66; libr. Galindo Elem. Sch., Austin, 1966-94; ret., 1994. Cons. Edn. Svc. Ctr., Austin, 1974, 83; workshop leader Austin Ind. Schs., 1980; China del. Citizen Amb. Program People Internat., 1993. Author: Texas in Children's Books, a Bibliography, 1974. Recipient Siddie Joe Johnson award, Children's Roundtable of Tex. Libr. Assn., 1984. Mem. ALA, AAUW, Tex. Libr. Assn. (life), Tex. State Tchrs. Assn. (life), Delta Kappa Gamma, Phi Delta Kappa. Presbyterian. Home: 6108 Mountainclimb Dr Austin TX 78731-3824 E-mail: dorries@aol.com.

SMITH, DOROTHY LOUISE, pharmacy consultant, author; b. Regina, Sask., Can., Apr. 29, 1946; d. William Edward and Edna Irene (Libby) S. BS in Pharmacy, U. Saskatchewan, 1968; PharmD, U. Cin., 1972. Asst. prof. pharmacy U. B.C., Can., 1972-74; assoc. prof. clin. pharmacy U. Toronto, Ont., Can., 1974-80; coord. ambulatory pharmacy care Sunnybrook Med. Ctr., Toronto, 1974-79; dir. clin. affairs Am. Pharm. Assn., Washington, 1980-83; pres., CEO, Consumer Health Info. Corp., McLean, Va., 1983—. Assoc. clin. prof. Sch. Pharmacy, Med. Coll. Va., 1991—; adj. assoc. prof. community and family medicine Georgetown U., Washington, 1983—. Author several books in field; contbr. articles to profl. jours. Mem. nat. bd. advisors Coll. Pharmacy, Ariz., 1987—; mem. dean's coun. U. Cin., 2000--. Fellow Am. Coll. Clin. Pharmacy, Am. Coll. Apothecaries; mem. Am. Soc. Hosp. Pharmacists, Am. Pharm. Assn. (chmn. policy com. on pub. affairs), Internat. Order Job's Daughters, Rotary. Presbyterian. Avocations: athletics, china painting, organ music, sewing, cooking. Office: Consumer Health Info Corp 8300 Greensboro Dr Ste 1220 Mc Lean VA 22102-3661

SMITH, DOROTHY OTTINGER, jewelry designer, civic worker; b. Indpls., 1922; d. Albert Ellsworth and Leona Aurelia (Waller) Ottinger; m. James Emory Smith, June 25, 1943 (div. 1984); children: Michael Ottinger, Sarah Anne, Theodore Arnold, Lisa Marie. Student, Herron Art Sch. of Purdue U. and Ind. U., 1941-42. Comml. artist William H. Block Co., Indpls., 1942-43, H.P. Wasson Co., 1943-44; dir. Riverside (Calif.) Art Ctr., 1963-64; jewelry designer Riverside, 1970—; numerous design commns. Adviser Riverside chpt. Freedom's Found. of Valley Forge; co-chmn. fund raising com. Riverside Art Ctr. and Mus., 1966-67, bd. dirs. Art Alliance, 1980-81; mem. Riverside City Hall sculpture selection panel Nat. Endowment for the Arts, 1974-75; chmn. fundraising benefit Riverside Art Ctr. and Mus., 1973-74, trustee, 1980-84, chmn. permanent collection, 1981-84, co-chmn. fund drive, 1982-84, trustee, 1998—; chmn. Riverside Mcpl. Arts Commn., 1974-76, Silver Anniversary Gala, 1992; juror Riverside Civic Ctr. Purchase Prize Art Show, 1975; mem. pub. bldgs. and grounds subcom., gen. plan citizens com. City of Riverside, 1965-66; mem. Mayor's Commn. on Civic Beauty, Mayor's Commn. on Sister City Sendai, 1965-66; bd. dirs., chmn. spl. events Children's League of Riverside Community Hosp., 1952-53; bd. dirs. Crippled Children's Soc. of Riverside, spl. events. chmn., 1952-53; bd. dirs. Nat. Charity League, pres. Riverside chpt., 1965-66; mem. exec. com. bd. trustees Riverside Arts Found., 1977-91, fund drive chmn., 1978-79, project rev. chmn., 1978-79, advisor Eveing for the Arts, 1998, juror Gemco Charitable and Scholarship Found., 1977-85; mem. bd. women deacons Calvary Presbyn. Ch., 1978-80, elder, 1989-92; mem. incorporating bd. Inland Empire United Fund for the Arts, 1980-81; bd dirs. Hospice Orgn. Riverside County, 1982-84; trustee Riverside Art Mus., 1998—; mem. Calif. Coun. Humanities, 1982-86. Recipient cert. Riverside City Coun., 1977, plaque Mayor of Riverside, 1977, Spl. Recognition Riverside Cultural Arts Coun., 1981, Disting. Svc. plaque Riverside Art Ctr. and Mus., Jr. League Silver Raincross Community Svc. award, 1989, Cert Appreciation Outstanding Svc. to the Arts Community Riverside Arts Found., 1990, Top Dog award Riverside Art Mus., 1999. Mem. Riverside Art Assn. (pres. 1961-63, 1st. v.p. 1964-65, 67-68, trustee 1959-70, 80-84, 87-92), Art Alliance of Riverside Art Ctr. and Museum (founder 1964, pres. 1969-70). Address: 3979 Chapman Pl Riverside CA 92506-1150

SMITH, DOUGLAS DEAN, lawyer; b. Idaho Falls, Idaho, Apr. 16, 1952; s. Dean C. and Evelyn (Haws) S.; m. Rhonda Lee Rasmussen, June 20, 1974; children: Ryan Douglas, Bradley Dean, Rochelle Lee, Brittany Kaylyn, Jeffery Scott, Michael Douglas. AA, Ricks Coll., 1974; BA, Brigham Young U., 1976, JD, 1978. Bar: Oreg. 1979, U.S. Dist. Ct. Oreg. 1979, U.S. Ct. Appeals (9th cir.) 1982, U.S. Supreme Ct. 1990. Assoc. Lindsay, Hart, Neil & Weigler, Portland, Oreg., 1979-83, ptnr., 1984—88; pvt. practice, Tigard, 1988—. Contbr. articles to legal publs. Mem. ABA (antitrust sect., mem. forum com. of franchising, bus. sect.), Oreg. State Bar Assn. (continuing legal edn. author 1985-2002). Republican. Mem. Lds Ch. Home and Office: 15751 SW Pleasant Hill Rd Portland OR 97140-8437 E-mail: dsmith1212@aol.com.

SMITH, DOUGLAS GEORGE, orthopaedic surgeon, educator; b. Toledo, July 16, 1958; m. Kathryn Ponto Smith; children: Christina Louise, Aliena Marie, Kevin Matthew. BS, U. Notre Dame, 1980; MD, U. Chgo., 1984. Diplomate Am. Bd. Orthopaedic Surgeons. Intern, resident Loyola U. Med. Ctr., Maywood, Ill., 1984-89; fellow U. Wash. Med. Ctr., Seattle, 1989-90, asst. prof., 1990-96, assoc. prof., 1996—. Mem. trauma coun. Harborview Med. Ctr., Seattle, 1990—, quality assurance officer, 1991—; mem. spl. planning com. NIH, 1992. Patentee Gait Activity Monitor, 1996. Mem. Am. Acad. Orthopaedic Surgeons, Orthopaedic Trauma Assn., Am. Orthopaedic Foot and Ankle Soc., Orthopaedic Rehab. Assn., Western Orthopaedic Assn., Wash. State Med. Assn., Phi Beta Kappa. Office: Harborview Med Ctr 325 9th Ave # 359798 Seattle WA 98104-2420

SMITH, DOUGLAS GERALD, health care consultant; b. Passaic, N.J., Feb. 21, 1947; s. Frederick Gerald and Yvonne Virginia (d'Ablemont) S.; m. Martha Engquist, May 23, 1970; children: Matthew Cary, Nicholas Sinclair. BSC, Ohio U., 1969; grad., Crosby Quality Coll., Orlando, Fla., 1985. Mgr. ops. Concord Comm., Chgo., 1969-70; dir. comm. A.B. Dick Co., 1970-72; dir. bus. devel. Martin Marietta Corp., Orlando, Fla., 1972-87; v.p. bus. devel. ROI, Barrington, Ill., 1987-93; cons., pres. FERS Health Care Group, Chgo., 1993—. Mem. adv. bd. Imaging Svcs., Inc., Chgo., 1995—; cons. various health systems, hosps., physician orgns., health plans, 1993—; faculty guest, spkr. lectr. N.C. State Med. Soc., 1995, Conn. State Med. Soc., 1995, AMA Fn. & Practice Mgmt., 1995, Nat. Ctr. Advanced Med. Edn., 1995, 96. Mem. Med. Group Mgmt. Assn., Healthcare Fin. Mgmt. Assn., Assn. U.S. Army (pres. 1985-87). Republican. Avocations: golf, tennis, music, coaching youth soccer. Office: FERS Health Care Group 401 N Michigan Ave Chicago IL 60611-4255

SMITH, DUANE ALLAN, history educator, researcher; b. San Diego, Apr. 20, 1937; s. Stanley W. and Ila B. (Bark) S.; m. Gay Woodruff, Aug. 20, 1960; 1 child, Laralee Ellen. BA, U. Colo., 1959, MA, 1961, PhD, 1964. Prof. history Ft. Lewis Coll., Durango, Colo., 1964—. Author: Horace Tabor, 1973 (Cert. of Commendation 1974), Mining America, 1987, Mesa Verde National Park, 1988, The Birth of Colorado, 1989, Rocky Mountain West, 1992, They Came to Play, 1997, A Tale of Two Towns, 1997, Colorado: Our Colorful State, 1999, No One Ailing Except a Physician, 2001, The Ballad of Baby Dog, 2002. Chmn. La Plata County Dem. Com., Durango, 1984-85; mem. Colo. Centennial Commn., 1974-76, Durango Hist. Preservation Commn., 1989-91, Durango Hist. Preservation Bd., 1991—, Gary Hart Campaign La Plata County, 1974, 80, 84. Huntington (Calif.) Libr. fellow, 1968, 73, 78; recipient Fred H. Rosenstock award Denver Westerners, 1987; named Colo. Humanist of the Yr., Colo. Endowment for the Humanities, 1989, Colo. Prof. of the Yr. 1990, Rodman Paul award, 1992. Mem. Soc. for Am. Baseball Rsch., Mining History Assn. (presiding chmn. 1989-90, pres. 1994-95), Western History Assn. (coun. 1985-88), Colo. Hist. Soc. Methodist. Avocations: writing, jogging, gardening, jeeps. Home: 2911 Cedar Ave Durango CO 81301-4481 E-mail: smith_d@fortlewis.edu.

SMITH, DUDLEY RENWICK, retired insurance company executive; b. N.Y.C., June 10, 1937; s. Crosby Tuttle and Vernon (Siems) S.; m. Juliana Buros, Nov. 17, 1962; children: Clayton Tuttle, Bradley Renwick, Gregory Dudley. AB, Dartmouth Coll., 1960. V.p. Fed. Ins. Co., Warren, N.J.; sr. v.p. Chubb & Son Inc., 1961-96. Trustee Chubb Found. Home: PO Box 1335 12 Sandy Brae Grantham NH 03753-1335 E-mail: djsmith@adelphia.net.

SMITH, DWIGHT CHICHESTER, III, lawyer; b. Ft. Meade, Md., June 24, 1955; s. Dwight Chichester Jr. and Rachel (Stryker) S.; m. Mindy L. Kotler, Aug. 18, 1985; children: Dwight C. IV, Cornelia R. BA, Yale U., 1977, JD, 1981. Bar: D.C. 1982, N.Y. 1982. Para-legal House Ethics Com., Washington, 1977-78; law clk. to Hon. Hugh Bownes U.S. Ct. Appeals (1st cir.), Concord, N.H., 1981-82; assoc. Kaye, Scholer, Fierman, Hays & Handler, Washington, 1982-84, Covington & Burling, Washington, 1984-90; dep. chief counsel for legal policy Office of Thrift Supervision, Dept. of Treasury, 1990-94, dep. chief counsel for bus. transactions, 1995-99; counsel Alston & Bird LLP, 1999—2001; ptnr. Alston & Bird, LLP, 2002—. Article and book rev. editor Yale Law jour., 1980-81; contbr. articles to profl. jours. Mem. Potomac Boat Club, City Tavern Club. Presbyterian. Avocation: rowing. Home: 1606 32nd St NW Washington DC 20007-2930 Office: Alston & Bird LLP North Bldg 11th Fl 601 Pennsylvania Ave NW Washington DC 20004-2601 E-mail: dcsmith@alston.com.

SMITH, DWIGHT L., III, academic administrator; b. St. Louis, Aug. 18, 1955; s. Dwight L. and Charlotte (Gerlach) S.; m. Janna K. Homann, June 18, 1977; children: Corey, Chelsea. BA, Blackburn Coll., 1977; MS, So. Ill. U., 1979; EdD, Rutgers U., 1990. Program advisor Tex. A&M U., College Station, 1979-81; dir. campus programs S.W. Tex. State U., San Marcos, 1981-83; assoc. dean students Rutgers Coll., New Brunswick, N.J., 1984-90; dir. admissions Blackburn Coll., Carlinville, Ill., 1990-91; asst. for acad. programs So. Ill. U., Edwardsville, 1991-98, asst. provost for planning, 1998—, adj. asst. prof., 1999—. Mem. AQIP evaluation team Higher Edn. Learning Commn. of North Cen. Assn. Chair curriculum/staffing com. O'Fallon (Ill.) Econ. Devel. Coun., 1994; chair student achievement com. O'Fallon (Ill.) Elem. Dist., 1994; team evaluator Middle States Comm. Higher Edn., 2000—; mem. Ill. Bd. Higher Edn. Academic Program (Approval and Redesign team), 1998—. Mem. Am. Assn. for Higher Edn., Am. Ednl. Rsch. Assn. E-mail: dwsmith@siue.edu.

SMITH, DWIGHT MORRELL, chemistry educator; b. Hudson, N.Y., Oct. 10, 1931; s. Elliott Monroe and Edith Helen (Hall) S.; m. Alice Beverly Bond, Aug. 27, 1955 (dec. 1990); children— Karen Elizabeth, Susan Allison, Jonathan Aaron; m. Elfi Nelson, Dec. 28, 1991. BA, Ctrl. Coll., Pella, Iowa, 1953; PhD, Pa. State U., 1957; ScD (hon.), Cen. Coll., 1986; LittD (hon.), U. Denver, 1990. Postdoctoral fellow, instr. Calif. Inst. Tech., 1957-59; sr. chemist Texaco Rsch. Ctr., Beacon, N.Y., 1959-61; asst. prof. chemistry Wesleyan U., Middletown, Conn., 1961-66; assoc. prof. Hope Coll., Holland, Mich., 1966-69, prof., 1969-72; prof. chemistry U. Denver, 1972—, chmn. dept., 1972-83, 99-01, vice chancellor for acad. affairs, 1983-84, chancellor, 1984-89; pres., bd. trustees Hawaii Loa Coll., Kaneohe, 1990-92. Mem. Registry for Interim Coll. and Univ. Pres.; mem. adv. bd. Solar Energy Rsch. Inst., 1989—91; mem. vis. com. Zettlemoyer Ctr. for Surface Studies Lehigh U., 1990—96; dept. chemistry and geochemistry Colo. Sch. Mines; mem. sci. adv. bd. Denver Rsch. Inst. Editor Revs. on Petroleum Chemistry, 1975-78; editl. adv. bd. Recent Rsch. Devels. in Applied Spectroscopy, 1998—; contbr. articles to profl. jours.; patentee selective hydrogenation. Chmn. Chs. United for Social Action, Holland, 1968-69; mem. adv. com. Holland Sch. Bd., 1969-70; bd. commrs. Colo. Adv. Tech. Inst., 1984-88, Univ. Senate, United Meth. Ch., Nashville, 1987-88, 91-93; mem. adv. bd. United Way, Inst. Internat. Edn., Japan Am. Soc. Colo., Denver Winter Games Olympics Com.; mem. ch. bds. or consistories Ref. Ch. Am., N.Y., Conn., Mich., United Meth. Ch., Colo. DuPont fellow, 1956-57, NSF fellow Scripps Inst., 1971-72; recipient grants Research Corp., Petroleum Research Fund, NSF, Solar Energy Research Inst. Mem. AAAS, Am. Assn. Aerosol Rsch., Am. Chem. Soc. (chmn. Colo. 1976, sec. western Mich. 1970-71, joint coun. and bd. com. on sci. 1997-98, award Colo. sect. 1986), Soc. Applied Spectroscopy, Mile High Club, Sigma Xi. Home: 1931 W Sanibel Ct Littleton CO 80120-8133 Office: U Denver Dept Chem & Biochem Denver CO 80208-0001

SMITH, DWIGHT RAYMOND, ecology and wildlife educator, writer; b. Sanders, Idaho, July 28, 1921; s. Andrew Leonard and Effie Elizabeth (Simons) S.; m. Carol Elizabeth Breclaw (dec. 1983); children Alan Dwight (dec.), Sharon Lee Smith Dequine, Gary Robert, Mark Jonathan (dec.). BS in Forestry, U. Idaho, 1949, MS in Wildlife Mgmt., 1951; PhD in Ecology, Utah State U., 1971. Rsch. biologist Idaho Fish and Game Dept., Salmon, 1950-52, area game mgr., 1953-56; range scientist U.S. Forest Svc., Ft. Collins, Colo., 1957-61, wildlife rsch. biologist, 1962-65; asst. prof. Colo. State U., 1965-70, assoc. prof., 1971-75, prof., 1975-83, prof. emeritus, 1983—. Nature photographer Alan Landsburg Prodns., Hollywood, Calif., 1971; energy cons. CF&I Steel, Pueblo, Colo., 1981. Author: Above Timberline: A Wildlife Biologist's Rocky Mountain Journal, 1981; writer/photographer (film) Research in the Rockies: A Scientist Explores the Alpine, 1973; contbr. articles to profl. jours. Served to 2d lt. (via battlefield comm.) inf. U.S. Army, 1942-45, PTO, ETO. Decorated Bronze Star; rsch. grantee, fellow U.S. Fish and Wildlife Svc., 1949-50, Wildlife Mgmt. Inst., 1950, Nat. Wildlife Fedn., 1954-55. Fellow Explorers Club; mem. Toastmasters (ednl. v.p. local chpt. 1960-62, pres. 1963), Xi Sigma Pi, Sigma Xi, Gamma Sigma Delta, Phi Kappa Phi. Democrat. Roman Catholic. Avocations: photography, bicycling, skiing. Home: 1916 Harmony Dr Fort Collins CO 80525-3442 E-mail: drsmithy@lamar.colostate.edu. *Do not be afraid of enthusiasm. You can do nothing effectively without it.*

SMITH, DWYANE, university administrator; b. St. Louis, Feb. 16, 1961; s. Magnolia Smith. BS in Psychology, N.E. Mo. State U., 1983, MA in Edn. Adminstrn., 1991; postgrad., Harvard U., 1995; PhD, U. Mo., Columbia, 2000; postgrad., Harvard U., 1995. Intern IRS, St. Louis, 1983; minority counselor N.E. Mo. State U., Kirksville, 1983-88, dir. minority svcs., 1988-91, asst. dir. admissions, asst. dean multicultural affairs, 1991—, assoc. dean multicultural affairs; clin. assoc. U. Mo., Columbia; assoc. v.p. for enrollment mgmt. Park U., Parkville, Mo. Mem. Alpha Phi Alpha (chair statewide conv. 1990, Mo. Man of Yr. 1985), Alpha Phi Omega, Phi Kappa Phi, Habitat for Humanity. Avocations: reading, writing. Home: 837 SE 11th Ter Lees Summit MO 64081-2153 E-mail: dsmith@mail.park.edu.

SMITH, E. BERRY, television and radio consultant; b. Daytona Beach, Fla., Feb. 21, 1926; s. Samuel Rogers and Rosemary (Berry) S.; m. Mary Terese Hoffman, Apr. 3, 1948 (dec.); children: Kevin B., Martin J. BS, Butler U., 1949. Account exec. Sta. WIRE Radio, Indpls., 1949-54; dir. advt. and pub. relations Franklin Fin. Co., Hartford City, Ind., 1954-56; account exec. CBS Radio Network, Detroit, 1956-57; v.p. Sta. WFIE-TV, Evansville, 1957-61, Sta. WFRV-TV, Green Bay, Wis., 1961-62; exec. v.p. Sta. WLKY-TV, Louisville, 1962-64; pres. Sta. WTVW-TV, Evansville, 1964-80, Sta. WSBT, South Bend, Ind., 1981-89; sr. v.p. Schurz Comm. Inc., 1989-2001, cons., 2001—. Dir. adv. bd. CBS-TV Affiliates Assn., 1984-87, sec., treas., 1988-90, chmn., 1990-91. Dir. Goodwill Industries, South Bend, 1984-85, Jr. Achievement Michiana, South Bend, 1984-91. Served to 1st lt. U.S. Army, 1944-46, PTO. Recipient Silver medal Am. Advt. Fedn., Evansville, Ind., 1973; named to Ind. Broadcasters Assn. Hall of Fame, 1989; appointed Sagamore of the Wabash, 1993. Mem. South Bend C. of C. (bd. dirs. 1988-92), Ind. Soc. Chgo., Nat. Press Club, Mensa, Notre Dame U. Club, Elks. Roman Catholic. Home: 5182 Finch Dr South Bend IN 46614-5491 Office: Schurz Comm Inc 5182 Finch Dr South Bend IN 46614-5491 Office Fax: 574-299-1793.

SMITH, EARL CHARLES, nephrologist, educator; b. Pitts., Mar. 1, 1936; s. Mose and Irene (Surloff) S. BS, Tufts U., 1957; MD, U. Pitts., 1961. Diplomate in internal medicine and nephrology Am. Bd. Internal Medicine. Intern Montefiore Hosp., Pitts., 1961-62; resident, fellow Cleve. Clinic, 1964-68; physician Cook County Hosp., Chgo., 1968-71; chief nephrology divsn. Mt. Sinai Hosp., 1971—, pres. med. staff, 1985-87, vice chair medicine, 1987—; chief nephrology divsn. Chgo. Med. Sch., 1994—, prof. medicine, 1995—. Cons. Internat. Jour. Artificial Organs, Milan, 1986—; med. adv. bd. Kidney Found. Ill., Chgo., 1980—. Co-author: Medical Exam Book-Nephrology, 1976, Self Assessment in Internal Medicine, 1980; assoc. editor Kidney jour., 1991—; contbr. articles to profl. jours. Chair hypertension com. Chgo. Heart Assn., 1973-75. Capt. USAF, 1962-64. Recipient Meritorious Svc. award Chgo. Heart Assn., 1975. Fellow Am. Coll. Physicians; mem. Am. Soc. Artificial Internal Organs, Am. Soc. Nephrology, Am. Soc. Hypertension Specialist in Clin. Hypertension, Internat. Soc. Nephrology, Phi Beta Kappa, Alpha Omega Alpha, Sigma Xi. Achievements include research in described cause and pathophysiology of dialysis dementia; hematological problems in patients with renal disease. Office: Mount Sinai Hosp 15th and California Ave Chicago IL 60608

SMITH, EDGAR BENTON, dermatologist; b. Houston, June 2, 1932; s. Burt Benton and Lela Elizabeth (Grant) S.; m. Francis Elaine Newton, Aug. 1, 1953; children— Sheri Elaine Smith Dinehart, Robin Marie Smith Fredrickson. Student, Rice U., 1950-53; BA, U. Houston, 1956; MD, Baylor U., 1957; diploma clin. medicine of the tropics, U. London, 1967. Intern Walter Reed Gen. Hosp., Washington, 1957-58; resident Brooke Gen. Hosp., Ft. Sam Houston, Tex., 1960-63; asst. prof. dermatology U. Miami Sch. Medicine, 1967-68, Baylor Coll. Medicine, Houston, 1968-71; assoc. prof. medicine (dermatology) U. N.Mex. Sch. Medicine, Albuquerque, 1971-75, prof., 1975-78; prof., chmn. dept. dermatology U. Tex. Med. Br., Galveston, 1978-99; prof. dermatology U. N. Mex., Albuquerque, 1999—. Contbr. articles in field to profl. jours. Served with U.S. Army, 1956-66. Recipient Khatali award U. N.Mex. Sch. Medicine, 1976; Fulbright scholar London Sch. Hygiene and Tropical Medicine, 1966-67; Alfred Stengel travelling scholar ACP, 1967 Mem. AMA, Am. Acad. Dermatology (bd. dirs. 1978-82, pres.-elect 1988, pres. 1989, Sulzberger internat. lectr. 1992), Assn. Profs. Dermatology (sec.-treas. 1979-82), Am. Dermatol. Assn. (bd. dirs. 1994—), Southwestern Dermatol. Soc. (sec. 1974-77, pres. 1978), South Ctrl. Dermatol. Congress (sec.-gen. 1973-76, pres. 1976-81), Tex. Dermatol. Soc. (trustee 1986), So. Med. Assn. (chmn. dermatology sect. 1988), Baker Street Irregulars, Alpha Omega Alpha. Democrat. Methodist. Home: 3918 Solano Pl NE Albuquerque NM 87110-5636 Office: U NMex Dept Dermatology 1021 Medical Arts Ave NE Albuquerque NM 87131-5231 E-mail: esmith@salud.unm.edu.

SMITH, EDGAR EUGENE, biochemist, university administrator; b. Hollandale, Miss., Aug. 6, 1934; s. Sam and Augusta Lillie (McCoy) S.; m. Inez Oree Wiley, May 27, 1955; children— E. Donald, Anthony R., Stephen S., Gregory S. BS, Tougaloo Coll., 1955; MS, Purdue U., 1957, PhD, 1960; degree (hon.), U. Mass., 2000. Rsch. fellow in surgery (biochemistry) Harvard Med. Sch., Boston, 1959-61, rsch. assoc., 1961-68; assoc. in surg. rsch. Beth Israel Hosp., Boston, 1959-68; asst. prof. surgery (chemistry) Boston U. Sch. Medicine, 1968-70, assoc. prof. biochemistry, 1970-74, U. Mass. Med. Sch., Worcester, 1974-80, prof. emeritus biochemistry and molecular biology, 1991—, assoc. dean acad. affairs, 1974-77, provost, 1975-83; asst. dean minority affairs, prin. investigator Bur. Health Manpower Spl. Project grant Boston U. Sch. Medicine, 1972-74; v.p. acad. affairs U. Mass. System, 1983-91; v.p. Nellie Mae, 1990-93; acting pres. Tougaloo Coll., 1995, edn. cons., 1996-98; dir. AHEC program U. Miss. Med. Ctr., 1998-2000. Mem. governing bd. Robert Wood Johnson Health Policy Fellowship Program, Inst. Medicine, NAS, 1978-85. Contbr. writings to sci. publs. Chmn. bd. overseers Sch. Medicine Morehouse Coll.; trustee Tougaloo Coll., Metco Scholarship Fund, Lexington, Mass.; bd. dirs. Dimock Community Health Center, Boston, New Urban League of Greater Boston, So. Edn. Found., 1976-79; chmn. Boston Com. for Nat. Med. Fellowships, Inc. Recipient research career devel. award Nat. Cancer Inst., 1969-74, award for outstanding achievement in biochemistry Nat. Consortium for Black Profl. Devel., 1976, human relations award Mass. Teachers Assn., 1977, health award NAACP, 1977; Robert Wood Johnson Health Policy fellow Inst. Medicine, Nat. Acad. Scis., 1977-78; named Alumnus of Yr. Tougaloo Coll., 1969, Disting. Alumnus Nat. Assn. for Equal Opportunities in Higher Edn., 1979, 92, Old Master Purdue U., 1978 Fellow Am. Inst. Chemists; mem. Am. Soc. Biol. Chemists, Am. Chem. Soc. (div. biol. chemists), AAAS, N.Y. Acad. Scis., Am. Assn. for Cancer Research, Boston Cancer Research Assn., Am. Polit. Sci. Assn., Am. Soc. Biol. Chemists (com. on minorities 1980-83), Josiah Macy, Jr. Found. Scholarship Com. Marine Biol. Lab., Woods Hole, Mass., Sigma Xi, Phi Lambda Upsilon, Alpha Phi Alpha. Home: 5934 Paddock Pl Jackson MS 39206-2135 E-mail: Esmithahec@aol.com.

SMITH, EDITH L'ENGLE GRAHAM, accountant; b. Marietta, Ga., Oct. 23, 1950; d. Camillus L'Engle and Susan (Darlington) Graham; m. Kenneth William Finch (div. Feb. 1987); children: Kenneth William Jr. Finch, Carrie Madeleine Finch; m. Paul Alan Smith, Mar. 2001. AS in Acctg., Wake Tech. Coll., Raleigh, N.C., 1983; BA in Bus. summa cum laude, N.C. Wesleyan Coll., Rocky Mount, 1985; MBA with distinction, Pfeiffer U., Charlotte, N.C., 1999. Gen. mgr. acctg. Adams Products, Morrisville, N.C., 1985-89; mgr. accounts payable Cooper Hand Tools, Apex, NC, 2000—. Mem. appearance commn. Town of Garner, NC, 1989—92, mem. bd. adjustments, 1987—89; treas. Wake County Rep. Women, Raleigh, 1999—2000; treas., elder First Presbyn. Ch., Garner. Mem.: Inst. Mgmt. Accts. (bd. dirs., dir. employment 1997—2000), NC Wesleyan Alumni Assn. (bd. dirs. 1997—). Avocations: power walking, reading. Home: 437 Roberson Creek Rd Pittsboro NC 27312

SMITH, EDITH JOAN, librarian, writer; b. Charlotte, N.C., Oct. 17, 1955; d. John Forsythe and Edith Joan (Rodgers) Kurie; m. Lunsford Richardson Smith, Dec. 29, 1976 (div. July 1982); 1 child, William Richardson. BA in English, Guilford Coll., 1978; postgrad. MLIS, U. N.C. Dir. pub. rels. The Webb Sch., Bell Buckle, Tenn., 1979; co-pub. The Mecklenburg Times, Charlotte, 1982-87; legal asst. Law Offices of M.S. Shulimson, 1986; travel agt., tour wholesaler CCI Travel/GoGo Tours, 1987-89; vet. asst. Pineville Animal Hosp., 1989; substitute tchr. Charlotte Mecklenburg Schs., 1990-91; test evaluator Measurements, Inc., Charlotte, 1996; libr. assoc. Pub. Libr. Charlotte and Mecklenburg County, 1996, libr. asst. level I, 1996-98, libr. asst. level III, 1998—. Contbg. poet: Songs on the Wind, 1994, Celebrating Excellence, 1995 (Pres.'s award 1995). Pres. Women's Rep. Club, Bedford County, Tenn., 1981; mem. Queen City Civitan, Charlotte, 1983. Recipient Blue Ribbon award So. Poetry Assn., Pass Christian, Miss., 1994. Mem. Legal and Bus. Pubs. (bd. dirs. 1985X), N.C. Libr. Assn. Republican. Presbyterian. Avocations: reading, tennis, walking, needlework. Home: 271 Palaside Dr NE Concord NC 28025-3041 Office: Pub Libr of Charlotte and Mecklenburg County 310 N Tryon St Charlotte NC 28202-2139

SMITH, EDITH MACNAMARA, artist; b. San Francisco, Apr. 3, 1925; d. Arthur Kingsley and Ann Harriet (Walling) MacN.; m. Leland Clayton, Feb. 26, 1946; children: Stefanie, Clement, Teresa. BA, U. Calif., Berkeley, 1946, MA in Art, 1947. Lectr. art U. Calif., Berkeley, 1947-48; instr. art Y.M.H.A., N.Y.C., 1950, Faulkner Sch., Chgo., 1953-56, Art Inst. Chgo., 1954-57; lectr. dept. humanities U. Chgo., 1955-57; instr. art Foothill Coll., Los Altos Hills, Calif., 1972-96, Pacific Art League, Palo Alto, 1961-64, 67-71, 81—. Vol. with schoolchildren Palo Alto Donkey Project, 1997—2002. One-woman shows include Daliel's Gallery, Berkeley, 1948, Galerie Colette Allendy, Paris, 1949, Oakland (Calif.) art Mus., 1952, Artists' Gallery, N.Y.C., 1954, 1957, Baldwin Kingrey, Chgo., 1955, Gump's Gallery, San Francisco, 1956, Gallery House, Palo Alto, 1968, 1971, Jason Aver Gallery, San Francisco, 1971, Richard Sumner Gallery, Palo Alto, 1974, Dominican Coll., San Rafael, Calif., 1976, Pence Gallery, Davis, Calif., 1976, Palo Alto Civic Ctr., 1977, Galerie Dautzenberg 76, Brussels, 1978, CCRMA, Stanford U., 1980, Ohio State U. Gallery Fine Art, 1980, Colgate U., NY, 1982, Bechtel Internat. Ctr., 1984, Foothill Coll., Calif., 1989, Stanford U. Inst. Rsch. Women & Gender, 1993, Koret Gallery, Palo Alto, 1996, 1999, Coyote Point Mus., San Mateo, Calif., 1997, Norton Gallery, Palo Alto, 2000, Inst. for the Future, Menlo Park, Calif, 2001, exhibited in group shows at Galerie St. Placide, Paris, 1949, Calif. Palace Legion Hon., 1980, Kootz Gallery, N.Y.C., 1950, San Francisco Mus. Modern Art, 1953, Landau Gallery, LA, 1954, Denver Art Mus., 1955, Art Inst. Chgo., 1956, U. Ill., 1957, De Young Mus., 1976, Palo Alto Cultural Ctr., 1977, 1978, 1979, Gallery Show, Tokyo, 1985, Lawson Gallery, San Francisco, 1987, U. Ind. Gallery Art, 1989, N.Mex. State U., Las Cruces, 1991, Napa Art Ctr., 1991, 1992, U. Idaho, Boise, 1992, 1993, Syntex Gallery, Palo Alto, 1993, Trition Mus., Santa Clara, Calif., 1994, Rehoboth Art League, Del., 1995, Agnes Scott Coll., Decatur, Ga., 1997, Somar Gallery, San Francisco, 1998, 551 Gallery, 1997, 1998, Robert William Mus. Papermaking, Atlanta, 1998, Coyote Point Mus., Calif., 1997, Galleria Tonantzin, 1999, U.

Hawaii, 1999, Brigham Young U., Provo, Utah, 1999, Inst. for the Future, Menlo Park, Calif., 2001, Triton Mus., Santa Clara, Calif., 2001, Yerba Buena Arts Ctr., San Francisco, 2002, others. Recipient Artists Coun. award San Francisco Mus. Art, 1950, ARtist-Writer Mag. Critics award, 1994; Taussig fellow U. Calif., 1946-47. Mem. Calif. Soc. Printmakers, L.A. Soc. Printmakers, Pacific Art League (hon.), San Francisco Women Artists, Women Caucus Art (Lifetime Achievement award 1996). E-mail: ems@ems-art.com.

SMITH, EDWARD PAUL, JR. lawyer; b. Westbury, N.Y., Jan. 13, 1939; s. Edward Paul Sr. and Margaret (Eisenhauer) S.; m. Mary Elizabeth Neagle, Mar. 29, 1980; children: Nora, Edward, Brian, Thomas, Brendan. BA, Coll. of the Holy Cross, 1960; LLB, Columbia U., 1963. Bar: N.Y. 1964, Fla. 1966. Assoc. Chadbourne & Parke, N.Y.C., 1964-75, prin., 1975—. Corp. sec. Am. Bur. Metal Statis., N.Y.C., 1978—. Author: Regulation of Employee Benefit Plans, Under Erisa, 1990. Capt. USAF, 1964-67. Mem. N.Y. State Bar Assn., Fla. Bar Assn. Roman Catholic. Home: 36 Avon Rd Bronxville NY 10708-1614 Office: Chadbourne & Parke 30 Rockefeller Plz Fl 31 New York NY 10112-0129 E-mail: esmith@chadbourne.com.

SMITH, EDWARD REAUGH, retired lawyer, cemetery and funeral home consultant; b. Flora, Ill., Sept. 23, 1932; m. Jo Anne Myers, Sept. 10, 1954; children: Mark and Michael (twins), Jillian. BS, Midwestern U., 1953; LLB, So. Meth. U., 1957. Bar: Tex. 1957, U.S. Dist. Ct. (so. dist.) Tex. 1957, U.S. Dist. Ct. (no. dist.) Tex. 1961, U.S. Tax Ct. 1961, U.S. Ct. Appeals (5th cir.) 1971, U.S. Ct. Claims 1971, U.S. Supreme Ct. 1982; CPA, Tex. Atty. Vinson, Elkins, Weems & Searls, Houston, 1957-59, Nelson, McCleskey & Harringer, Lubbock, Tex., 1959-61; pvt. practice, 1961-62; ptnr. Smith, Baker, Field & Clifford Inc. (formerly Smith & Baker Inc.), 1962-84; chmn., CEO Resthaven Funeral Home and Cemetery, 1979-93; cons. Svc. Corp. Internat., 1993—. Bd. dirs. Briercroft Savs. Assn., 1962-84, Tex. Cemetery Assn., 1986-87, 90-91; pres., bd. chmn. Resthaven Funeral Home, 1965-69, Resthaven of Lubbock, Inc., 1979-93, Lakeview Meml. Gardens, 1978-86; lectr. profl. meetings on taxes and estate planning; bd. visitors So. Meth. U. Law Sch., 1968-71; chmn. estate planning seminar for women Tex. Tech. Found., 1971; pres. South Plains Trust and Estate Coun., 1963-64, others. Author: The Burning Bush, 1997, The Incredible Births of Jesus, 1998, The Disciple Whom Jesus Loved, 2000, David's Question "What is man?", 2001; contbr. articles to profl. jours. Mem. Lubbock Planning and Zoning Commn., 1964-65, chmn., 1966, budget divsn. United Fund; co-chmn. profl. divsn. United Way, 1981; tchr., bd. dirs. First Meth. Ch., Lubbock, 1963-88; pres. Haynes Elem. Sch. PTA, 1968-69; past mem. pres.'s adv. bd. Lubbock Christian Coll.; bd. dirs. Tex. Tech. U. Found., 1968-89, sec., 1969-76, vice-chmn., 1976-78, chmn., 1978-81, chmn. fund raising com., 1979-81; bd. dirs. Tex. Tech. U. Med. Sch. Found., 1970-78, vice-chmn., 1972-73, chmn., 1973-74; mem. chancellor's coun. Tex. Tech. U., 1978—; mem. adv. bd. Sophia Found. of N.Am., 2000—; spkr. ann. banquet Flora Acad. Found., Flora H.S., 1991, N.Y. Open Ctr., 1999, Anthrop. Soc. Conf., 2000; bd. dirs. Lubbock Symphony Orch., 1996—. Mem. Am. Acad. Religion/Soc. Biblical Lit., Am. Anthroposophical Soc., Tex. Cemeteries Assn. (hon. life), Alpha Chi. Avocations: mountain trails, research, writing.

SMITH, EDWARD ROBERT, law librarian; b. Newark, Dec. 23, 1952; BA, William Paterson Coll., 1975; paralegal cert., Upsala Coll., 1979; MLS, Rutgers U., 1992. Supr. libr. Rutgers U., 1981-88; law libr. Hudson County Law Libr., 1988, Morris County Law Libr., Morristown, N.J., 1989-91; libr. dir. Fairfield (N.J.) Pub. Libr., 1991—. Mem. ALA, Am. Assn. Law Librs., N.J. Law Librs. Assn., N.J. Libr. Assn., Documents Assn. N.J., Spl. Librs. Assn. Roman Catholic. Office: Fairfield Free Pub Libr 261 Hollywood Ave Fairfield NJ 07004-1360

SMITH, EDWIN DUDLEY, lawyer; b. N.Y.C., Oct. 4, 1936; s. Edwin Dudley Jr. and Mary Jane (Bannigan) S.; m. Joan Joyce Mortenson, June 29, 1963; children: Edwin Dudley V, Patrick Townshend. BA, U. Kans., 1960, JD, 1963. Bar: Kans. 1963, Mo. 1992, U.S. Dist. Ct. Kans. 1963, U.S. Ct. Appeals (10th cir.) 1967, U.S. Supreme Ct. 1972, U.S. Dist. Ct. (we. dist.) Mo., 1998. Assoc. Fisher Patterson Sayler & Summers, Topeka, 1963-66; ptnr. Fisher Patterson Sayler & Smith, L.L.P., Topeka, Overland Park, 1966—. Contbg. author: Pharmacy Law Annual, 1991. Chpt. advisor Tau Kappa Epsilon Frat., 1988-93; mem. adv. bd. Florence Crittenton Svcs., Topeka, 1988-91; chmn. legis. com. U.S. Swimming, 1986-90; chmn. Missouri Valley Swimming, 1987-89. Fellow Kans. Bar Found.; mem. ABA, Kans. Bar Assn. (bd. govs. 1986-92, Outstanding Svc. award 1978), Topeka Bar Assn., Johnson County Bar Assn., Kansas City Met. Bar Assn., Internat. Assn. Def. Counsel, Am. Judicature Soc. (bd. dirs. 1984-89), Am. Bd. Trial Adv. (pres. Kans. chpt. 1989-90), Kans. Assn. Def. Counsel, Def. Rsch. Inst., Am. Soc. Pharmacy Law. Avocation: photography. Home: 4344 W 124th Ter Leawood KS 66209-2277 Office: Fisher Patterson Sayler & Smith LLP 51 Corporate Woods Ste 300 9393 W 110th St Shawnee Mission KS 66210 also: Fisher Patterson Sayler & Smith LLP 3550 SW 5th St Topeka KS 66606-1998 E-mail: dsmith@fisherpatterson.com.

SMITH, EDWIN ERIC, lawyer; b. Louisville, Sept. 29, 1946; s. Lester Henry and Nancy Joy (Heyman) S.; m. Katharine Case Thomson, Aug. 16, 1969; children: Benjamin Clark, George Lewis, Andrew Laurence. BA, Yale U., 1968; JD, Harvard Law Sch., 1974. Bar: Mass. 1974, U.S. Dist. Ct. Mass. 1974. Assoc. Bingham Dana LLP, Boston, 1974-81, ptnr., 1981—. Lectr. in field; Mass. commr. on uniform state laws; mem. uniform comml. code articles 5 and 9 drafting com.; chmn. uniform comml. code payments article divsn. drafting com.; U.S. del. to receivables assignment working group UN Commn. on Internat. Trade Law. Lt. USNR, 1969-71. Recipient Achievement Medal USN, 1971. Mem. ABA (chmn. uniform comml. code com. bus. law sect. 1995-99, advisor to the permanent editl. bd. uniform comml. code 1999—), Am. Law Inst. (Uniform Comml. Code article 9 study com.), Am. Coll. Comml. Fin. Lawyers (pres.), Assn. Comml. Fin. Attys. Home: 4 Chiltern Rd Weston MA 02493-2714 Office: Bingham Dana LLP 150 Federal St Boston MA 02110-1713 E-mail: eesmith@bingham.com.

SMITH, ELAINE DIANA, foreign service officer; b. Glencoe, Ill., Sept. 15, 1924; d. John Raymond and Elsie (Gelbard) S. BA, Grinnell Coll., 1946; MA, Johns Hopkins U., 1947; PhD, Am. U., 1959. Commd. fgn. service officer U.S. Dept. State, 1947; assigned to Brussels, 1947-50, Tehran, Iran, 1951-53, Wellington, N.Z., 1954-56, Dept. State, Washington, 1956-60, Ankara, Turkey, 1960-69, Istanbul, Turkey, 1969-72, Dept. Commerce Exchange, 1972-73; dep. examiner Fgn. Service Bd. Examiners, 1974-75; Turkish desk officer (Dept. State), Washington, 1975-78. Consul gen., Izmir, Turkey, 1978— Author: Origins of the Kemalist Movement, 1919-1923, 1959. Recipient Alumni award Grinnell Coll., 1957 Mem. U.S. Fgn. Svc. Assn., Phi Beta Kappa. Home: The Plaza 800 25th St NW Apt 306 Washington DC 20037-2207

SMITH, ELBERT BENJAMIN, historian, educator; b. Benham, Ky., May 1, 1920; s. Elbert Benjamin and Margaret Gladys (Huffaker) S.; m. Jean Frances Smith, Dec. 26, 1944; children: Randall, Stephen, Amy, Scott, Robert. AB, Maryville Coll., 1940; AM, U. Chgo., 1947, PhD, 1949. Assoc. prof. Youngstown (Ohio) U., 1949-57; assoc. prof., then prof. Iowa State U., Ames, 1957-67; prof. U. Md., College Park, 1968-90, prof. emeritus, 1990—. Vis. prof. U. Wis., Madison, 1967-68; vis. Fulbright prof. U. Tokyo, 1954-55, Moscow State U., 1976, 82, Leningrad (USSR) U., 1991; exch. prof. Beijing U., 1983, 88. Author: Magnificent Missourian: Life of Thomas Hart Benton, 1958, 71, The Death of Slavery, 1967, 71, 73, The Presidency of James Buchanan, 1975 (Phi Alpha Theta award), Francis Preston Blair, 1980 (Phi Alpha Theta award), The Presidencies of Zachary Taylor and Millard Fillmore, 1988; contbr. articles to profl. jours. Dem. candidate U.S. Senate, 1962, 66; mem. U.S. Bd. Fgn. Scholarships, Washington, 1979-81; founding pres. D.C. chpt. Fulbright Assn., 1984, nat. pres., 1989-90. Lt. (j.g.) USNR, 1942-45. Recipient Disting. Alumni citation Maryville Coll., 1981. Mem. Am. Assn. UN (chmn. Iowa Spkr. Bur. 1961-65), Am. Hist. Assn., Orgn. Am. Historians. Presbyterian. Avocations: sailing, travel, athletics. Home: 6647 Chesapeake Ter Tracys Landing MD 20779-2521 E-mail: ebs@wam.umd.edu.

SMITH, ELDON, cardiologist, physiologist, educator, biophysicist, educator; MD, Dalhousie U., Halifax, N.S. From asst. prof. to assoc. prof. medicine and physiology Dalhousie U., Halifax, Canada, 1973—80; prof. medicine and physiology and biophysics U. Calgary, 1980—, chief divsn. cardiology, 1980—86, chair dept. medicine, 1985—90, assoc. dean, clin., 1990—92, dean faculty of medicine, 1992—97. Corp. dir. Biomax, Inc., Vasogen, Inc., Can. Natural Resources, Ltd., Pheromone Scis. Corp. Editor-in-chief: Can. Jour. Cardiology, 1997—. Fellow: Am. Coll. Cardiology, Royal Coll. Physicians and Surgeons Can. Office: U Calgary Faculty Medicine 3330 Hosp Dr Calgary AB Canada T2N 4N1 E-mail: esmith@ucalgary.ca.

SMITH, ELDRED GEE, church leader; b. Lehi, Utah, Jan. 9, 1907; s. Hyrum Gibbs and Martha E. (Gee) S.; m. Jeanne A. Ness, Aug. 17, 1932 (dec. June 1977); children: Miriam Smith Skeen, Eldred Gary, Audrey Gay Smith Vance, Gordon Raynor, Sylvia Dawn Smith Isom; m. Hortense H. Child, May 18, 1978; stepchildren: Carol Jane Child Burdette (dec.), Thomas Robert Child. Employed with sales div. Bennett Glass & Paint Co., Salt Lake City, 6 years; mech. design engr. Remington Arms Co., 2 years; design engr., prodn. equipment design Tenn. Eastman Corp., Oak Ridge, Tenn., 3 years; now presiding patriarch Ch. Jesus Christ of Latter-day Saints. Home: 2942 Devonshire Cir Salt Lake City UT 84108-2526 Office: 47 E South Temple Salt Lake City UT 84150-9701

SMITH, ELDRED REID, library educator; b. Payette, Idaho, June 30, 1931; s. Lawrence E. and Jennie (Reid) S.; m. Judith Ausubel, June 25, 1953; children: Steven, Janet. BA, U. Calif.-Berkeley, 1956, MA, 1962; M.L.S., U. So. Calif., 1957. Aquisition reference librarian Long Beach State Coll. Library, 1957-59; reference librarian San Francisco State Coll. Library, 1959-60; bibliographer U. Calif.-Berkeley Library, 1960-65, head search div. acquisition dept., 1966-69, head loan dept., 1969-70, asso. univ. librarian, 1970-72, acting univ. librarian, 1971-72; dir. libraries, also prof. SUNY, Buffalo, 1973-76; univ. librarian U. Minn., 1976-87, prof., 1976-96. Lectr. Sch. Library Sci., U. Wash., 1972; bd. dirs. Center for Research Libraries, 1975-77 Author: The Librarian, The Scholar, and the Future of the Research Library, 1990; contbr. articles to libr. jours. Council on Library Resources fellow, 1970 Mem. ALA, Assn. Research Libraries (dir. 1979-85, pres. 1983-84), Assn. Coll. and Research Libraries (pres. 1977-78, dir. 1976-79, com. on academic status 1969-74, chmn. univ. libraries sect. 1974-75) Home: 847 Gelston Pl El Cerrito CA 94530-3046

SMITH, ELEANOR JANE, university chancellor, retired, consultant; b. Circleville, Ohio, Jan. 10, 1933; d. John Allen and Eleanor Jane (Dade) Lewis; m. James L. Banner, Aug. 10, 1957 (div. 1972); 1 child, Teresa M. Banner Watters; m. Paul M. Smith Jr. BS, Capital U., 1955; PhD, The Union Inst., Cin., 1972. Tchr. Columbus (Ohio) Pub. Schs., 1956-64, Worthington (Ohio) Pub. Schs., 1964-72; from faculty to administrator U. Cin., 1972-88; dean Smith Coll., Northampton, Mass., 1988-90; v.p. acad. affairs, provost William Paterson Coll., Wayne, N.J., 1990-94; chancellor U. Wis.-Parkside, Kenosha, 1994-97, ret., 1997; ind. cons. in higher edn. Dir. Afrikan Am. Inst., Cin., 1977-84; adv. bd. Edwina Bookwalter Gantz Undergrad. Studies Ctr., Cin.; mem. Gov.'s Tobacco Tax adv. coun. Performances include (concert) Black Heritage: History, Music and Dance, 1972—. Spl. Arts Night Com., Northampton, 1988-89; bd. dirs. Planned Parenthood No. and Ctrl. Ariz., Am. Lung Assn. Ariz./N.Mex. Named career woman of achievement YWCA, Cin., 1983. Mem. AAUW, Nat. Assn. Women in Higher Edn., Am. Assn. for Higher Edn., Leadership Am. (bd. dirs., treas. 1993-95), Nat. Assn. Black Women Historians (co-founder, co-dir. 1979-82), Am. Coun. on Edn. (mem. com. on internat. edn. 1994-97, bd. dirs. 1995-97), Am. Assn. State Colls. and Univs. (mem. com. on policies and purposes 1994-97). Avocations: music, pen and ink drawing, travel, reading. Home: 24823 S Lakestar Dr Sun Lakes AZ 85248-7465

SMITH, ELISE FIBER, international non-profit development agency administrator; b. Detroit, June 14, 1932; d. Guy and Mildred Geneva (Johnson) Fiber; m. James Frederick Smith, Aug. 11, 1956 (div. 1983); children: Gregory Douglas, Guy Charles; life ptnr. Jac Smit, 1990. BA, U. Mich., 1954; postgrad., U. Strasbourg, France, 1954-55; MA, Case Western Res. U., 1956. Tchr. U.S. Binat. Ctr., Caracas, Venezuela, 1964-66; instr. English Am. U., 1966-68; prof. lang. faculty Catholic U., Lima, Peru, 1968-70; coord. English lang. and culture program, lang. faculty El Rosario U., Bogota, Colombia, 1971-73; lang. specialist, mem. faculty Am. U., English Lang. Inst., 1975-78; exec. dir. OEF Internat. (name formerly Overseas Edn. Fund), Washington, 1978-89, bd. dirs.; dir. Leadership Program Winrock Internat. Inst. for Agrl. Devel., 1989-98, sr. policy advisor on gender, 1998—. Founder, pres. Women's EDGE, 1997—; v.p., bd. dirs. Pvt. Agys. Collaborating Together, N.Y.C., 1983-89; trustee Internat. Devel. Conf., Washington, 1983-2001, mem. exec. com., 1985-90; mem. hon. com. for Global Crossroads Nat. Assembly, Global Perspectives in Edn., Inc., N.Y.C., 1984, Washington, 1984-92, mem. gen. assembly, 1992; mem. nat. com. Focus on Hunger '84, L.A.; bd. dirs. U.S. Binat. Sch., Bogota, Colombia, 1971-73; ofcl. observer UN Conf. on Status Women, 1980, UN 3rd World Conf. on Women, 1985, del. NGO Forum, UN 4th World Conf. on Women, del. NGO Forum, 1995; mem. mental health adv. com. Dept. State, 1974-76; U.S. del. planning seminar integration women in devel. OAS, 1978; participant Women, Law and Devel. Forum; mem. exec. com., chair commn. advancement women Interaction (Am. Coun. for Vol. Internat. Action), 1994-97, co-founder, 1985-88, chair commn. advancement of women, 1994-97; bd. dirs. Sudan-Am. Found.; mem. adv. bd. Global Links Devel. Edn., Washington, 1985-86; adv. coun. Global Fund for Women, 1988-93; U.S. del. Vital Voices Conf. Women and Democracy, Iceland, 1999; U.S. del. Women in Democracy Conf., Lithuania, 2000. Co-editor: Toward Internationalism: Readings in Cross-cultural Communication, 1979, 2d edit. 1986. Bd. dirs. Internat. Ctr. Rsch. on Women, 1992-2001; mem. adv. com. on vol. fgn. aid U.S. AID, 1994—; mem. women and conservation adv. com. World Wildlife Fund, 1998—; mem. State Dept. Adv. Com. on Internat. Econ. Policy, 2000—. Rotary Internat. ambassadorial scholar Strasbourg, France, 1954-55; grantee Dept. State, 1975. Mem. Soc. Internat. Devel., Assn. Women in Devel., UNIFEM, Coalition Women in Internat. Devel. (co-founder 1979, chair 1993-96),pvt. Agys. in Internat. Devel. (co-chmn. 1980-82, pres. 1982-85), Nat. Assn. Fgn. Student Affairs (grantee 1975), U. Mich. Alumni Assn., Women's Fgn. Policy Group, Rotary Internat. (mem. global com. Women in Future Soc. 1996). Unitarian Universalist. Home: 4701 Connecticut Ave NW Apt 304 Washington DC 20008-5617 Office: Winrock Internat 1621 N Kent St Ste 1200 Arlington VA 22209-2131 Office Fax: 703-525-9430 605.

SMITH, ELIZABETH, artist; b. New Britain, Conn., Aug. 13, 1943; BS, Cen. Conn. State U., 1969, MS, 1974; student, U. Vt., U. Hartford. Exhibited in group shows at Nat. Acad. Design, N.Y.C., 1988, Mus. Fine Arts, Springfield, Mass., 1988, 90, 92, Bergen Mus. Art and Sci., Paramus, N.J., 1990, Allied Artists Am., N.Y.C., 1988-89, 91, 99, Pastel Soc. Am., N.Y.C., 1990, 91, 92, Silvermine Guild Arts Ctr., Wash. and Lee U., 1991, New Canaan, Conn., 1992, Butler Inst. Am. Art, 2001. Included in book The Best of Pastel II--Collected by the Pastel Soc. of Am.; finalist Artists Mag. Painting Competition, 1991-92. Mem. Am. Artists Profl. League (Coun. Am. Artists Socs. award 1988), Audubon Artists, Acad. Artists Assn. (award 1991), Nat. Assn. Women Artists (Nydia Preede award 1987, C.L. Mason and A.V. Mason Meml. award 1989), Conn. Acad. Fine Arts (bd. dirs. 1991-92, pres. 1992-93), Knickerbocker Artists N.Y. (Silver medal of Honor 1986, 91), Katharine Lorillard Wolfe Art Club (medal of honor 1986, IBM award 1987, Ida Becker Meml. award 1989). Home: PO Box 493 Mendham NJ 07945-0493

SMITH, ELIZABETH HEGEMAN, mental health therapist, hypnotherapist; b. Mineola, N.Y., Oct. 5, 1942; d. Andrew Burt and Ruth Eliza (Velsor) Hegeman; m. Lloyd W. Smith, June 11, 1966; children: Warren Willits, Lisa Velsor. BA, Adelphi U., 1964; MEd, Temple U., 1969. Cert. tchr., Pa.; registered hypnotherapist. Tchr. health, phys. edn. Friends Acad., Locust Valley, N.Y., 1964-66, Darby (Pa.)-Colwyn Schs., 1966-70; pvt. practice mental health therapy Wallingford, Pa., 1980-85, Charlotte, N.C., 1985—. Cons. Dynamic Health Systems, Charlotte, 1989—. Mem. LWV, Wallingford, 1976-85; pres., editor Taxpayers for Quality Edn., Wallingford, 1976-85; chmn. Raintree Archtl. Rev. Com., Charlotte, 1989-91, com. mem., 1987-88; treas. Raintree Homeowners Assn. Mem. Am. Guild Hypnotherapists, Raintree Homeowners Assn. (treas. 1993-95, pres. 1995-96); Village of Raintree and the Southeast Coalition of Neighborhoods (pres. 1996—2001).general manager, village of Raintree, 2001-, Mem. Soc. Of Friends. Avocations: horseback riding, tennis, skiing, photography, gardening. Home and Office: 3609 Windbluff Dr Charlotte NC 28277-9897

SMITH, ELIZABETH MACKEY, financial advisor, consultant; b. Phila., Mar. 23, 1941; d. William Norman and Celeste (Parvin) Mackey; m. George Van Riper Smith, Aug. 15, 1964; children: Douglas George, Todd Mackey. BA, Gettysburg Coll., 1963; MAT in French, Ga. State U., 1978. Tchr. fgn. lang. Haverford (Pa.) High Sch., 1963-65; registered rep. Am. Express Fin. Advisors, Inc., Macon and Savannah, Ga., 1979-2000, br. mgr. Tybee Island, 2000—. Reader Atlanta Serv for the Blind, 1968; hostess Atlanta Coun Int Visitors, 1972—74; foreign exchange student coord Loisirs Culturels a l'Etranger, 1990; staff protocol vol sailing venue Olympic Games, Savannah, 1996. Mem.: Million Dollar Round Table, Delta Gamma, Delta Phi Alpha, Phi Sigma Iota. Avocations: tennis, swimming. Home: 59 Fiddlers Ct Savannah GA 31419 Office: Am Express 303 3d St PO Box 2926 Tybee Island GA 31328-2926 E-mail: elizabeth.m.smith@aexp.com.

SMITH, ELOUISE BEARD, restaurant owner; b. Richmond, Tex., Jan. 8, 1920; d. Lee Roy and Ruby Myrtle (Foy) Beard; m. Omar Smith, Nov. 27, 1940 (dec. July 1981); children: Mary Jean Smith Cherry, Terry Omar, Don Alan. Student, Tex. Womens U., 1937-39. Sec. First Nat. Bank, Rosenberg, Tex., 1939-41; owner Smith Dairy Queen chains, Bryan, 1947—. Author: The Haunted House, 1986; editor The College Widow, 1986. Omar and Elouise Beard Smith chair named in her honor Tex. A&M U., College Station, 1983, Elouise Beard Smith Human Performance Labs. named in her honor Tex. A&M U., 1984, Elouise Beard Smith Girls H.S. Viking Girls Softball Field named in her honor, Bryan, Tex., 1989. Charter Mem. AAUW. Republican. Baptist. Avocations: genealogist, restoring old cemeteries, exploring England. Home: 411 Crescent Dr Bryan TX 77801-3712 Office: Metro Ctr 3833 S Texas Ave Bryan TX 77802-4039

SMITH, EMIL L. biochemist, consultant; b. N.Y.C., July 5, 1911; s. Abraham and Esther (Lubart) S.; m. Esther Press, Mar. 29, 1934; children— Joseph Donald, Jeffrey Bernard BS, Columbia U., 1931, PhD, 1936. Instr. biophysics Columbia U., N.Y.C., 1936-38; John Simon Guggenheim fellow Cambridge U., Eng., 1938-39, Yale U., New Haven, 1939-40; fellow Rockefeller Inst., N.Y.C., 1940-42; biophysicist, biochemist E. R. Squibb & Sons, New Brunswick, N.J., 1942-46; assoc. prof. to prof. biochemistry U. Utah, Salt Lake City, 1946-63; prof. biol. chemistry Sch. Medicine UCLA, 1963-79, prof. emeritus, 1979—. Cons. NIH, Am. Cancer Soc., Office Naval Research Author: (with others) Principles of Biochemistry, 7th edit., 1983; also numerous articles Recipient Stein-Moore award Protein Soc., 1987. Mem. NAS, Am. Acad. Arts and Scis., Am. Philos. Soc., Am. Soc. Biochemistry and Molecular Biology, Am. Chem. Soc., Protein Soc., Acad. Scis. Russia (fgn.). Office: UCLA Sch Medicine Los Angeles CA 90095-1737

SMITH, EMORY CLARK, lawyer, financial advisor; b. Denton, Tex., Nov. 2, 1910; s. James Willis and Julia (Miller) S.; 1 child, Cynthia Smith O'Brien. BA, U. North Tex., 1929; MA, U. Tex., 1933; JD, So. Meth. U., 1937; SJD, George Washington U., 1954. Bar: Tex. 1937, Okla. 1937, U.S. Supreme Ct. 1954, U.S. Ct. Mil. Appeals 1955, U.S. Ct. Claims 1956, U.S. Ct. Customs and Patent Appeals 1956. Pvt. practice, Oklahoma City, 1937-42; commd. USN, 1942-72, advanced through grades to capt., chief U.S. pros. atty., staff Gen. Douglas MacArthur, 1946—48; chief counsel USN Oceanographic Office U.S. Civil Svc., Washington, 1972-73; cons. antitrust atty. Foster Assocs., 1973-84; pvt. practice, 1994; ret., 1995. Adj. prof. internat. law Am. U., Washington, 1977-84; energy cons. Foster Assocs., 1973-84; fin. advisor Friday Music Found., Washington, 1988-94; lectr. in field. Author: Law of the Sea, 1954; contbr. articles to profl. jours. Vestryman St. Alban's Ch., Washington, 1957-59, St. Paul's Within the Walls, Rome, 1967-68. Named Disting. Alumnus U. North Tex., 1972. Fellow N.Y. Explorers Club, Fed. Bar Assn., Inter-Am. Bar Assn. (natural resources com. chmn. 1973-76), Masons. Republican. Episcopalian. Avocation: farming. also: PO Box 3032 Gettysburg PA 17325-0032 Office: 2118 49th St NW Washington DC 20007-1524

SMITH, EPHRAIM PHILIP, academic administrator, former university dean, educator; b. Fall River, Mass., Sept. 19, 1942; s. Jacob Max and Bertha (Horvitz) S.; m. Linda Sue Katz, Sept. 3, 1967; children: Benjamin, Rachel, Leah. BS, Providence Coll., 1964; MS, U. Mass., 1965; PhD, U. Ill., 1968. Chmn. dept. acctg. U. R.I., Kingston, 1972-73; dean Sch. Bus. Shippensburg State Coll., Pa., 1973-75; dean Coll. Bus. Adminstrn. Cleve. State U., 1975-90; dean Sch. Bus. Adminstrn. and Econ. Calif. State U., Fullerton, 1990-98, v.p. acad. affairs, 1998—. Co-author: Principles of Supervision: First and Second Level Management, 1984, Federal Taxation-Advanced Topics, 1995, Federal Taxation-Basic Principles, 2002, Federal Taxation Comprehensive Topics, 2002; contbr. articles to profl. jours. Mem. Am. Acctg. Assn., Am. Taxation Assn., Am. Inst. for Decision Scis., Fin. Execs. Inst., Beta Gamma Sigma, Beta Alpha Psi. Office: Calif State Univ VPAA Office MH-133 800 N State College Blvd Fullerton CA 92831-3599 E-mail: esmith@fullerton.edu.

SMITH, ERIC PARKMAN, retired railroad executive; b. Cambridge, Mass., Mar. 23, 1910; s. B. Farnham and Helen T. (Blanchard) S. AB, Harvard U., 1932, MBA, 1934. Staff fed. coord. transp., Washington, 1934; with traffic and oper. dept.s N.Y. New Haven & Hartford R.R., Boston and New Haven, 1934-53; with Maine Ctrl. R.R., Portland, 1953-82, sec. adv. bd. retirement trust plan, 1958-82, asst. treas., dir. cost analysis, 1970-82, bd. dirs., 1981-82. Author: Verses on an Icelandic Vacation, 1965, The Church in Concord and its Ministers, 1971, In All That Dwell Below the Skies, 1972; contbr. The Meeting House on the Green, 1985. Trustee parish donations 1st Parish in Concord, Unitarian-Universalist Ch., 1960-96, trustee emeritus, 1996—. Mem. New Eng. R.R. Club (hon.; pres. 1973-74), Louisa May Alcott Meml. Assn. (dir. 1984-99, treas. 1987-99), The Thoreau Soc. (dir. 1987-95, treas. 1987-95). Home and Office: 35 Academy Ln Concord MA 01742-2431

SMITH, ERNEST KETCHAM, electrical engineer; b. Peking, China, May 31, 1922; (parents Am. citizens); s. Ernest Ketcham and Grace (Goodrich) S.; m. Mary Louise Standish, June 23, 1950; children: Priscilla Varland, Nancy Smith Johnson, Cynthia Jackson. BA in Physics, Swarthmore Coll., 1944; MSEE, Cornell U., 1951, PhD, 1956. With Mut. Broadcasting Sys., 1946-49, chief plans and allocations engr., 1949; with radio propagation lab. Nat. Bur. Stds., Boulder, 1951-65, chief ionosphere rsch. sect. Colo., 1957-60, divsn. chief, 1960-65; dir. aeronomy lab. Environ. Sci. Svcs. Adminstrn., 1965-67; dir. Inst. Telecom. Scis., 1968, dir. univ. rels., 1968-70; assoc. dir. Inst. Telecom. Scis. Office of Telecom., Boulder, 1970-72, cons., 1972-76; tech. staff Jet Propulsion Lab. Calif. Inst. Tech., Pasadena, 1976-87; adj. prof. dept. elec. and computer engring. U. Colo., Boulder, 1987—. Vis. fellow Coop. Inst. Rsch. on Environ. Scis., 1968; assoc. Harvard Coll. Obs., 1965-75; adj. prof. U. Colo., 1969-78; internat. vice-chmn. study group 6, Internat. Radio Consultative Com., 1958-70, chmn. U.S. study group, 1970-76; mem. U.S. nat. com. Internat. Sci. Radio Union, mem.-at-large U.S. nat. com., 1985-88; convenor Boulder Gatekeepers to the Future, 1990—. Author: Worldwide Occurrence of Sporadic E, 1957; (with S. Matsushita) Ionospheric Sporadic E, 1962. Contbr. numerous articles to profl. jours. Editor: Electromagnetic Probing of the Upper Atmosphere, 1969; assoc. editor for propagation IEEE Antennas and Propagation Mag., 1989—. Mem. 1st Congl. Ch., moderator, 1995-97. Recipient Diplôme d'honneur, Internat. Radio Consultative Com., Internat. Telecom. Union, 1978. Fellow IEEE (fellow com. 1993, 94, 95), AAAS; mem. Am. Geophys. Union, Electromagnetics Acad., Svc. Club, Kiwanis, Univ. Club, Athenaeum (Pasadena), Boulder Country Club, UN Assn. of Am. (convenor Boulder chpt. 1994), Sigma Xi (pres. U. Colo. chpt. 1994-95, v.p. 95-98). Home: 5159 Idylwild Trl Boulder CO 80301-3667 Office: U Colo Dept Elec & Computer Engring Campus Box 425 Boulder CO 80309-0425 E-mail: ernest.smith@colorado.edu., n6hqkek@aol.com. *A weakness of many large organizations is that it is difficult for senior administrators to step down after peaking in their 40s. I'm grateful for a crisis at age 50 which resulted in my taking early retirement at age 54 and then accepting a more modest job until age 65.*

SMITH, ESTHER THOMAS, communications executive; b. Jesup, Ga., Mar. 13, 1939; d. Joseph H. and Leslie (McCarthy) Thomas; m. James D. Smith, June 2, 1962; children: Leslie, Amy, James Thomas. BA, Agnes Scott Coll., 1962. Staff writer Sunday women's editor Atlanta Jour.-Constn., 1961-62; mng. editor Bull. of U. Miami Sch. Medicine, 1965-66; corr. Atlanta Jour.-Constn. and Fla. Times-Union, 1964, 67-68; founding editor Bus. Rev. of Washington, 1978-81; founding editor, gen. mgr. Washington Bus. Jour., 1982; pres., bd. dirs. TechNews, Inc., 1986-96, CEO, 1995-96; founder, editor-at-large Washington Tech., 1986-97, Tech. Transfer Bus. Mag., 1992-95; co-chair editl. bd. TechCapital Mag., 1997-99; prin. Poretz Group Investor Rels., McLean, Va., 1998—2000; ptnr. Qorvis Comm. LLC (successor to Poretz Group), 2000—. Bd. dirs. Provant, Inc., Create Hope.com Inc., telezoo inc.; mem. The Atlantic Coun.; mem. adv. Netpreneur Program Morino Inst., 1996—2002; mem. internat. adv. bd. Kilby Awards Found.; mem. MIT Enterprise Forum of Washington/Balt., 1981—82, Internat. Women's Forum, 1981, No. Va. Bus. Round Table , exec. com. , 1993—98; mem. adv. bd. Va. Math Coalition, 1991—94; commr. NACD Blue Ribbon Commn.; trustee Ctr. for Excellence in Edn., 1993—96; bd. dirs., trustee Capital Region Technology Investors Conf.; bd. advisors George Washington U., Va., 1996—99. Mem.: Md. High Tech. Coun., No. Va. Tech. Coun. (exec. com., bd. dirs., sr. adv. bd. 1998—), Assn. Tech. Bus. Couns. (chmn. bd. advisors 1989—94). Office: 8484 Westpark Dr 8th Fl Mc Lean VA 22102 E-mail: esthersmith@aol.com.

SMITH, ETHEL FARRINGTON, retired social worker, genealogist, writer; b. Arlington, Mass., Mar. 26, 1910; d. Leander Morton and Blanche Emeline (Clough) Farrington; m. Harland Willard Hawes, Mar. 27, 1951 (dec. 1958); m. John Eldredge Smith, 1959 (dec. 1973); four stepchildren. AB, Smith Coll., 1931; MS, Columbia U., 1942. Cert. genealogist. Case worker N.H. State Dept. Pub. Welfare, Manchester, 1934-35; welfare worker City Dept. Welfare, Rochester, N.Y., 1935-36; placement interviewer N.H. State Employment Svc., Nashua, 1936-37; med. social worker Columbia Presbyn. Med. Ctr., N.Y.C., 1938-47, March of Dimes, Asheville, N.C., 1948-49, Boise, Idaho, 1948-49, Easter Seal Soc., Billings, Mont., 1949-50. Author: Adam Hawkes, 1980; rschr.: Colonial Doctors and Doctresses 1975-2001; editor: Colonial Tavernkeepers, Vols. 10-12; editor Hawkes Talks, 1969-93; contbr. articles to New Eng. Historic and Genealog. Register vol. 142, 143, 149, 150. Active Girl Scouts U.S., past vol. tng. dir. Palm Glades coun., bd. dirs.; nat. bd. dirs. Daus. of Founders and Patriots of Am., 1973-90, past pres. Fla. chpt. Mem. Nat. League Am. Pen Women, Nat. Soc. Genealogists, New England Hist. Geneal. Soc. (trustee 1986-89, life, named trustees room the Ethel Farrington Smith Trustees Room 1993), Smith Coll. Club (past pres.), Ancient and Hon. Artillery Co. of Mass. (past state officer women's divsn.), Soc. Mayflower Descendants (past state officer Fla.), Hull Mass. Hist. Soc. (hon. life). Avocations: travel, writing, lecturing, photography, music.

SMITH, EUGENE WILSON, retired university president and educator; b. Forrest City, Ark., June 10, 1930; s. Milton Saumel and Frank Leslie (Wilson) S.; m. Rebecca Ann Slaughter, May 27, 1956; children: Lucinda Anne, Bradley Eugene. BA, Ark. State U., 1952; M.Ed., U. Miss., 1955, Ed.D., 1958. Mem. faculty Ark. State U., State University, 1958-92, prof. edn., 1971-92, v.p. adminstrn., 1968-71, dean Grad. Sch., 1971-84, interim pres., 1980, sr. v.p., 1980-84, pres., 1984-92, 94-95; pres. emeritus Ark. State U., State University, 1992—, interim pres., 1994-95. Pres. Jonesboro Indsl. Devel. Corp., 1983-94; mem. exec. com. Conf. So. Grad. Schs., 1973-74, Ark. State Coun. on Econ. Edn., 1987-90; pres. Am. South Athletic Conf., 1987-89; dir. Mercantile Bank of Jonesboro, Union Planters Bank of Northeast Ark. Alderman, City of Jonesboro, 1982-84. Served to 1st lt. AUS, 1952-54, Korea. W.K. Kellogg Found. rsch. fellow, 1954-58 Mem. Ark. Adv. Council Elem. and Secondary Edn., Jonesboro C. of C. (dir. 1967-69, 80-85, v.p. 1981-82, pres. 1982-83), Phi Kappa Phi, Phi Delta Kappa, Kappa Delta Pi. Clubs: Rotary (pres. 1974-75). Home: 407 Lynne Ct Jonesboro AR 72401-8807

SMITH, EVELYN ELAINE, language educator; b. Waco, Tex., July 25, 1952; d. Walstein Bennett and Evelyn Dougherty (Box) S. BA, Baylor U., 1974, MA, 1979; PhD, Tex. Christian U., 1995. Cert. secondary tchr., Tex. Grad. asst. Baylor U., Waco, Tex., 1975, proofreader, 1980, rsch. assoc., 1981-86; reporter Killeen (Tex.) Daily Herald, 1981; writing tchr. Waco (Tex.) Ind. Sch. Dist., 1989-90; grad. asst. Tex. Christian U., Ft. Worth, 1992-93; adj. prof. English McLennan C.C., Waco, Tex., 1993-94; adj. instr. English Tex. State Tech. Coll., 1993-94, 97; instr. English Hill Coll., Hillsboro, Tex., 1997, Ctrl. Tex. Coll., Killeen, 1997, So. Meth. U., Dallas, 1997, El Centro Coll., Dallas, 1998, North Ctrl. Tex. Coll., Lewisville, 1998. Adj. lectr. Ctrl. Tex. Coll., Killeen, 1997, So. Meth. U., Dallas, 1997; adj. instr. El Centro Coll., Dallas, 1998, North Ctrl. Tex. Coll., Lewisville, 1998; vis. asst. prof. Idaho State U., Pocatello, 1998—. Contbr. articles to profl. jours. Bd. dirs., newsletter editor Historic Waco Found., 1981-85, sec., exec., mem. nominating coms., 1994-96. Mem. MLA, South Ctrl. MLA, S.W./Tex. PGA/ACA, Nat. Conf. Tchrs. English, Conf. Coll. Composition and Comm. Democrat. Mem. So. Bapt. Ch. Avocation: historical preservation. Office: Idaho State U Dept English & Philosophy PO Box 8056 Pocatello ID 83209-0001

SMITH, FAYE L. educator; b. Cherokee, IA, Mar. 25; PhD, University of Iowa, Iowa City, Iowa, 1981—89. Associate Professor Emporia State University, Emporia, KS, 1998—2002, Department Chairperson, 2000—01; Visiting Assistant Professor University of Wisconsin - Milwaukee, Milwaukee, WI, 1997—98; Assistant Professor Oklahoma State University, Stillwater, OK, 1989—95; Department Supervisor Federal Reserve Bank, Kansas City, MO, 1977—81; Product Line Planner Hallmark Cards, Inc., 1967—75. Office: Emporia State University 1200 Commercial Emporia KS 66801 Office Fax: 620-341-6345. Business E-Mail: smitfaye@emporia.edu.

SMITH, FLOYD LESLIE, insurance company executive; b. Silver Creek, N.Y., Nov. 12, 1931; s. Harry Lee and Fanny Diem (Arnold) S.; m. Jane Kathryn Elters, Feb. 18, 1956; children: Keith Arnold, Bruce Erik. AB, Oberlin Coll., (Ohio), 1953; MBA, NYU, 1962. Investment analyst Mut. of N.Y., N.Y.C., 1953-64, dir. investments, 1964-66; asst. v.p. securities investment Mut. of. N.Y., 1966-69; 2d v.p. securities investment Mut. of N.Y., 1969-74, v.p. securities investment, 1974-78, sr. v.p., 1978-81, chief investment officer, 1981-83, exec. v.p., chief investment officer, 1983-89, vice chmn., chief investment officer, 1989-91; trustee The Mut. Life Ins. Co. of N.Y., 1988-91; dir. MONY Series Fund, 1983—, Empire Fidelity Investments Life Ins. Co., 1994—. Trustee MONY Real Estate Investors, N.Y.C., 1981-90; bd. dirs., chmn. exec. com. Ins. Systems Am., Atlanta, 1974-82. Trustee Friends Sem., N.Y.C., 1975-84, Village of Saltaire, 1984-87; dir. St. Maarten Condo. Assn., Naples, Fla., 1993—; mem. Saltaire (N.Y.) Zoning Bd. Appeals, 1982-84. With Signal Corps, U.S. Army, 1954-56. Mem. Ft. Worth Boat Club, Edgewater Club.

SMITH, FLOYD RODENBACK, retired utilities executive; b. San Francisco, June 25, 1913; s. Floyd M. and Elizabeth (Rodenback) S.; m. Marion LaFrae Blythe, Oct. 5, 1935; children: Marion Katherine Smith White, Virginia Helene. Student, Long Beach (Calif.) Jr. Coll., 1931-33; BS, N.Mex. State U., 1935; postgrad., Harvard Bus. School, 1962. Registered profl. engr., Tex. With Gulf States Utilities Co., Beaumont, Tex., 1935-78, dir., 1965-78, v.p. Baton Rouge div., 1965-67, v.p. div. ops., 1967-69, exec. v.p., 1969, pres., 1970-73, prin. exec. officer, 1970-78, chmn. bd., prin. exec. officer, 1973-78. Pres. S.W. Atomic Energy Assocs., 1971-77; mgmt. cons., 1978-85. Bd. dirs., past chmn. Beaumont chpt. ARC; bd. dirs. Central City Devel. Corp., 1971-81, YMCA, 1980-83; trustee United Appeals, pres., 1975; pres. Tex. Atomic Energy Research Found., 1976-78. Named Disting. Alumnus Engring. Sch., N.Mex. State U., 1977 Mem. Tex. Atomic Energy Rsch. Found. (bd. dirs. 1970-78, pres. 1976-78), Southeastern Elec. Exch. (pres. 1975-76, bd. dirs. 1970-78), Tex. Rsch. League (bd. dirs. 1970-78), Assn. Electric Cos. of Tex. (chmn. 1978-79), Utility Shareholders Assn. of Tex. (chmn. 1986-93), Beaumont C. of C. (bd. dirs. 1970-76), Beaumont Country Club, Beaumont Club (bd. dirs. 1974-76), Pompano Club. Presbyterian. Home: 21 Cheska Holw Beaumont TX 77706-2750

SMITH, FRANCIS XAVIER, nurse; b. Towanda, Pa., Nov. 22, 1936; s. Theodore Franklin and Lillian Caroline (Goldbruch) S. Nursing diploma, Essex Vocat. Tech. Inst., Practical Nursing Sch., 1968. Cert. in gerontology nursing. Surg. nurse Salem (Mass.) Gen. Hosp., 1969; nurse emergency rm. Cable Meml. Hosp., Ipswich, Mass., 1969-71; med. nurse Greenwood Convalescent Home, Hartford, Conn., 1971-72; supr. 11-7 shift St. Martin de Porres Infirmary, 1972-78; pvt. duty nurse Nashua, N.H., 1979-88; nursing staff Hartford (Conn.) Dispensary Methadone Treatment Program, 1988-91; nursing staff AIDS unit Project Mercy, Hartford, 1991-96; clin. instr. CNA's E.C. Goodwin RVTS, New Britain, Conn., 1996—2000; nursing supr. 7-3 shift La Salette Missionaries, 2000—. Bd. dirs. Nashua (N.H.) Symphony, 1986-88; mem. adv. bd. for religious Archdiocese of Hartford, 1995—. Recipient Bronze Pelican award Boy Scouts Am., Hartford, 1980, Dist. award of merit, 1983, St. George award Boy Scouts Am., Nashua, 1985, Dist. award of merit, 1986, Cath. Youth Orgn. award St. Benedict the Moor Soc., Washington, 1983. Mem.: Conn. LPN Assn. Inc. (1st v.p. 1991—93, pres. 1993—2001), So. New Eng. AIDS Assn. (treas. 1991—93), Conn. League of Nurses, Assn. Nurses in AIDS Care (sec. 1995—96, pres.-elect 1997—98, pres. 1998—99, treas. 1999—), Nat. Cath. AIDS Network. Republican. Avocations: classical music, reading, hook latching, cross country skiing, camping. Home: Missionaries of La Salette 85 New Park Ave Hartford CT 06106-2124

SMITH, FRANCIS XAVIER, accountant; b. Jenkintown, Pa., Oct. 11, 1960; s. William Joseph and Patricia Josephine (Leeper) S. BBA, U. Pa., 1986. CPA, Pa. Pvt. practice, Jenkintown, 1990—. Mem. AICPA, Pa. Inst. of CPAs, Wharton Club of Phila., Faculty Club of U. of Pa. Republican. Roman Catholic. Office: # 24 615 Paxson Ave Wyncote PA 19095-1339

SMITH, FRANK EARL, retired association executive; b. Fremont Center, N.Y., Feb. 4, 1931; s. Earl A. and Hazel (Knack) S.; m. Caroline R. Gillin, Aug. 14, 1954; children— Stephen F., David S., Daniel E. BS, Syracuse U., 1952. With Mellor Advt. Agy., Elmira, N.Y., 1954-55; asst. mgr. Elmire Assn. of Commerce, 1955-56; retail dept. mgr. C. of C., Binghamton, N.Y.; mgr. Better Bus. Bur., Broome County, 1956-60; exec. v.p. C. of C., Chemung County, Elmira, 1960-65, Schenectady County (N.Y.) C. of C., 1965-69, Greater Cin. C. of C., 1969-78; pres. Greater Detroit C. of C., 1978-95. Dir. Presbyn. Devel. Corp. Detroit, Inc. 1995—. Served to 1st lt. USAF, 1952-54. Named Young Man of Yr. Jr. C. of C. Elmira, 1964 Mem. C. of C. Execs. Mich., Am. C. of C. Execs. (past chmn.), N.Y. State C. of C. Execs. (past pres.), Ohio C. of C. Execs. (past pres.), C. of C. of U.S. (past bd. dirs., past chmn. nat. bd. regents, Inst. for Orgn. Mgmt.). Presbyterian. Home: 173 Windwood Pointe Dr Saint Clair Shores MI 48080

SMITH, FRANK NEALE, materials and corrosion engineer; b. Newcastle-upon-Tyne, Eng., July 6, 1943; arrived in Can., 1970; s. James Wilson and Georgina (Maw) S. BSc, Durham (Eng.) U., 1964; MSc, Newcastle (Eng.) U., 1965; PhD, Queen's U., Kingston, Ont., Can., 1973. Registered profl. engr., Ont. Rsch. chemist Albright & Wilson, Harrogate, Eng., 1966-69; sr. metall. engr. DuPont Can., Maitland, Ont., 1973-78; mgr. product devel. Granges Nyby, Brockville, 1979-81; project leader Alcan Internat. Ltd., Kingston, 1981-87; assoc. J.H. Parker & Assocs., 1987-88; materials engring. specialist Saudi Aramco, Dhahran, Saudi Arabia, 1988-95; tech. dir. Nickel Devel. Inst., Toronto, Ont., Can., 1995-97, cons. materials and corrosion engring. Can., 1998—. Assoc. prof. dept. materials and metall. engring. Queen's U., Kingston, Ont., 1999—; presenter in field. Editor: Nickel-Cobalt 97, Applications and Materials Performance, 1997; contbr. articles to profl. jours.; patentee in Europe and U.S. Noranda Mines fellow Noranda Inc., 1970-73. Mem. ASTM, Am. Soc. Metals Internat., Nat. Assn. Corrosion Engrs., Profl. Engrs. Ont., Royal Soc. Chemistry (U.K.) (chartered chemist). Anglican. Avocations: tennis, racquetball, skiing, sailing, reading.

SMITH, FRANK TUPPER, lawyer; b. May 21, 1929; s. Frank T. and Mary Elizabeth Smith; m. Jill A. Jacobsen, Mar. 9, 1957; children: Delia, Lisa Noel, Kathryn. BA, Columbia Coll., 1951; JD, Columbia U., 1954; MBA, NYU, 1963. Bar: N.Y. 1956, Calif. 1966, Tex. 1974, U.S. Supreme Ct. 1963; cert. estate planning and probate law specialist, Tex. Assoc. Vaughn & Lyons, N.Y.C., 1956-60, Edward R. Peckerman, N.Y.C., 1960-63; v.p. Bank of Calif., San Francisco, 1963-69; assoc. Paul Hastings Janofsky & Walker, L.A., 1969-72; v.p., trust officer Republic Nat. Bank, Dallas, 1972-74; ptnr. Smith, Miller & Carlton, 1975-87; sr. ptnr. Frank Tupper Smith & Assocs. PC, 1987—. Lectr. estate and tax planning U. Tex., Dallas, Dallas Community Coll. Dist. Bd. dirs. Am. Heart Assn., 1979-82, Tex. chmn. planned giving com., 1980-82, nat. chmn. planned giving com., 1983-86; bd. dirs., v.p. fund raising Brain/Behavior Ctr., 1992-98; bd. dirs. Planned Living Assistance Network North Tex., Inc., 1996-2000. With AUS, 1954-56. Mem. ABA, Calif. State Bar Assn., Tex. State Bar Assn., Dallas Bar Assn., Columbia U. North Tex. Club (pres. 1980-86), Univ. Club, Rush Creek Yacht Club. Home: 3975 High Summit Dr Dallas TX 75244-6623 Office: 3860 W Northwest Hwy Dallas TX 75220-5183 E-mail: tuppers@swbell.net.

SMITH, FRANKLIN, music educator; b. Portales, N.Mex., 1973; s. Frank and Diana Smith; m. Marea Thompson Smith, Dec. 31, 1999; children: Bailey, Emma. BS in Music Edn., Ea. N.Mex. U., 1996. Lic. tchr. grades K-12 music N.Mex. Choral dir. Portales Mcpl. Schs., 1999—. Pianist First Spanish Bapt. Ch., Portales, 1988—. Mem.: N.Mex. Music Educators Assn. Avocations: composition, recording, performing. Office: Portales HS 501 S Abilene Portales NM 88130

SMITH, FREDERICK COE, retired manufacturing executive; b. Ridgewood, N.J., June 3, 1916; s. Frederick Coe and Mary (Steffee) S.; m. Ruth Pfeiffer, Oct. 5, 1940; children: Frederick Coe, Geoffrey, Roger, William, Bart. BS, Cornell U., 1938; MBA, Harvard U., 1940. With Armstrong Cork Co., Lancaster, Pa., 1940-41; with Huffy Corp., Dayton, Ohio, 1946-86, pres., chief exec. officer, 1961-72, chmn., chief exec. officer, 1972-76, chmn., 1976-78, chmn. exec. com., 1979-86. Former chmn. Sinclair C.C. Found.; past chmn. nat. bd. dirs. Planned Parenthoo Fedn.;former dir. Internat. Parenthood Fedn.; past chmn. Dayton Found.; trustee emeritus Alan Gutmacher Inst., Ohio United Way; past chmn. employment and tng. com. Gov.'s Human Investment Coun. Lt. col. USAAF, 1941-46. Decorated Legion of Merit. Fax: 937-225-9932.

SMITH, FREDERICK JAMES, JR. web site designer, educator; b. Euclid, Ohio, Mar. 23, 1956; s. Frederick James Smith and Helen May Savchak; m. Judith Ann Matjasic, Oct. 10, 1987; 1 child Lillian Ann. MA, Miami U., Oxford, Ohio, 1986. Graphic artist Katzan Studios, Cleve., 1978—84; media coord. Aquinas Coll., Grand Rapids, Mich., 1987—89; asst. dir., media svcs. Ea. Conn. State U., Willimantic, Conn., 1990—94; web designer/document imaging technician NCD Corp., Eastlake, Ohio, 1997—2002; curriculum design specialist Myers U., Cleve., 2002—. Recipient Eastman/Scholastic Gold Key award for photography, Eastman Kodak Co.-Scholastic Art Awards, 1974. Office: Myers U Rm 618 112 Prospect Ave Cleveland OH 44115 Business E-Mail: fsmith3@dnmyers.edu.

SMITH, FREDERICK ORVILLE, II, wood products manufacturer, retired naval officer; b. Cambridge, Mass., July 17, 1934; s. Harry Francis and Dorothy Spaulding (Zeller) S.; m. Mabel Roxy Moore, June 6, 1965; children: Sarah Zeller, Jennifer Joy, Erika Hildred. BA, Bowdoin Coll., 1956; MA in Polit. Sci., U. Vt., 2000. Deck officer, 1st lt. USN, 1957-59; officer US Naval Sta., Adak, Alaska, 1959-60; clk. & exec. Fred O. Smith Mfg. Co., New Vineyard, Maine, 1960-71, pres., treas., 1971—; res. officer Naval Res. Tng. Ctr., Augusta, 1960-69, Bangor, 1970-79 (ret.). Owner Sugarwood Gallery, Inc. Editor: New Vineyard, Maine 1802-2002, Its Settlement, Its People, Its History, A New Vineyard Historical Society Document, 2002. Notary pub., 1978—; chair, mem. nat. com. Young Reps., Maine, 1960—68, pres. New Eng. coun., 1962—64; chmn. Franklin County (Maine) Rep. Com., 1976—80, v.p. state conv., 1994; mem. Maine Rep. State Com., 1980—86, 1992—94, 1998—2002; mem. state com. ASCO, 1998—2002; town chmn. Rep. Com., New Vineyard, 1972—86, Farmington, 1992—. Paul Harris fellow Farmington Rotary Club, 1996. Master: AF&AM, Davis Lodge; mem.: Up Country Artists (bd. dirs. 1996—, v.p. 1997, pres. 1998—2000, bd. dirs. 2000—), Kora Temple Shrine, Am. Legion. Congregationalist. Avocations: photography, cabinet making & design, skiing, hiking, writing. Home: 127 Anson St Farmington ME 04938-5734 Office: Fred O Smith Mfg Co PO Box 248 New Vineyard ME 04956-0248 Fax: 207-779-0716. E-mail: fosmith@somtel.com.

SMITH, FREDERICK ROBERT, JR. social studies educator, educator; b. Lynn, Mass., Sept. 19, 1929; s. Frederick Robert and Margaret Theresa (Donovan) S. m. Mary Patricia Barry, Aug. 28, 1954; children: Brian Patrick, Barry Frederick, Brendan Edmund. AB, Duke U., 1951; M.Ed., Boston U., 1954; PhD, U. Mich., 1960. Tchr. social studies public, Jackson, Mich., 1954-58; instr. Eastern Mich. U., 1959, U. Mich., 1959-60; mem. faculty Sch. Edn., Ind. U., Bloomington, 1960-94, prof., 1969-94, chmn. social studies edn., 1965-69, chmn. secondary edn. dept., 1969-72, chmn. dept. curriculum and instrn., 1983-84, assoc. dean adminstrn. and devel., 1975-78, dir. external rels., 1991-94; dir. devel. Bloomington campus and annual giving Ind. U. Found., 1984-90; prof. emeritus retired, 1994. Vis. prof. U. Wis., summer 1967, U. Hawaii, summer 1972 Co-author: New Strategies and Curriculum in Social Studies, 1969, Secondary Schools in a Changing Society, 1976; co-editor 2 books. Bd. overseers St. Meinrad Coll. and Sem., 1991-98, trustee, 1995-97; treas. Bloomington Pk. and Recreation Found., 1996-98; bd. dirs. Monroe County YMCA, 1995-2002. With USAF, 1951-53. Recipient Booklist award Phi Lambda Theta, 1965, 69 Mem. Ind. Coun. Social Studies (pres. 1968-69), Phi Delta Kappa, Kappa Sigma, Phi Kappa Phi. Roman Catholic. Home: 2306 E Edgehill Ct Bloomington IN 47401-6839 Office: Indiana Univ Sch of Edu Rm 3032 Bloomington IN 47405

SMITH, FREDERICK WALLACE, delivery service executive; b. Marks, Miss., Aug. 11, 1944; s. Frederick Smith; m. Diane Avis. Grad., Yale U., 1966. Cert. comml. pilot. Owner Ark Aviation, 1969-71; founder, pres. Fed. Express Corp., Memphis, 1971—; chmn. bd., pres, CEO FedEx Corp., 1975—. Served with USMC, 1966-70. Office: 942 S Shady Grove Rd Memphis TN 38120-4117*

SMITH, FREDRIC CHARLES, electrical engineer, consultant; b. Chgo., May 30, 1947; s. Fredric Louis and Beverly Jean (Bito) Smith; m. Kim Nio Song, Aug. 5, 1985 (div.); children: Tracy Lynn, Frederick Dylan, David Sean; m. Cheng Fang Wang, May 30, 2002; m. Marylou Yanowsky, Feb. 5, 1965 (div. Sept. 1978). AAS in Electronic Engring., Middlesex County C.C., 1991. Indsl. electrician Bristol-Meyers Squibb, New Brunswick, N.J., 1985—, electronic technician Lawrenceville, 1990-91. Mgr. cons., David & Smith Engring., Princeton Junction, N.J., 1993—. With U.S. Army, 1966-68. Mem. IEEE, Internat. Soc. Electronic Technicians. Avocations: programming-amateur radio, poetry, creative writing. Home: 3 Marsh Ct Lawrenceville NJ 08648-2664 Office: Bristol-Meyers Squibb PO Box 191 New Brunswick NJ 08903-0191

SMITH, FREDRICA EMRICH, rheumatologist, internist; b. Princeton, N.J., Apr. 28, 1945; d. Raymond Jay and Carolyn Sarah (Schleicher) Emrich; m. Paul David Smith, June 10, 1967. AB, Bryn Mawr Coll., 1967; MD, Duke U., 1971. Intern, resident U. N.Mex. Affiliated Hosps., 1971-73; fellow U. Va. Hosp., Charlottesville, 1974-75; pvt. practice, Los Alamos, N.Mex., 1975—. Chmn. credentials com. Los Alamos Med. Ctr., 1983—, chief staff, 1990; bd. dirs. N.Mex. Physicians Mut. Liability Ins. Co., Albuquerque. Contbr. articles to med. jours. Mem. bass sect. Los Alamos Symphony, 1975—; mem. Los Alamos County Parks and Recreation Bd., 1984-88, 92-96, Los Alamos County Med. Indigent Health Care Task Force, 1989—; mem. ops. subcom. Aquatic Ctr., Los Alamos County, 1988—. Fellow ACP, Am. Coll. Rheumatology; mem. N.Mex. Soc. Internal Medicine (pres. 1993-96), Friends of Bandelier. Democrat. Avocations: swimming, music, reading, hiking. Office: Los Alamos Med Ctr 3917 West Rd Los Alamos NM 87544-2275

SMITH, GAIL HUNTER, artist; b. Nashville, Mar. 18, 1948; d. Walter Gray Smith and Eleanor Theresa (Cregar) Egan. Student, Memphis State U., 1966-67; BFA in Advt. Design, Memphis Acad. Arts, 1971. Prodn. asst. Visual Studios, Phila., 1970; asst. art dir. Eric Ericson and Assocs. and Ken White Design, Inc., Nashville, 1971-72; art dir. Contemporary Mktg., Inc., Ivan Stiles Advt., Bala Cynwyd (Pa.), Phila., 1972-74; specialist publs. design Temple U., Phila., 1974-75. Graphic designer pvt. practice, 1969-85; judge Haddonfield (N.J.) Artists' Exhbn., 1976; tchr. in field. Editor: Artists' USA, 7th edit., Yacht Portraits, 1987, The Art of the Sea, 1990; one woman show Dow Jones Co., Inc., Princeton, N.J., 1987, Johnson & Johnson, Inc., New Brunswick, N.Y.,1990; exhibited in group shows at 12 and 17th Tenn. All-State Artist Exhbn., Nashville, 1972, 77, Arnold Art Gallery, Newport, 1986, 87, 88, 89, 90. 91, Wildfowl Festival, Easton, Md., 1987, Mystic Maritime Gallery, 1984-86. 88-90, Capricorn Gallery, 1986-92, Quester Gallery, 1992, 93, 94; represented by Mystic (Conn.) Maritime Gallery, 1984-90, Capricorn Gallery, Bethesda, Md., 1986-92, Cumberland Gallery, Nashville, 1982-83, The Studio L'Atelier, Nashville, 1983-85, Ambiance Fine Arts, Nashville, 1985, Arnold Art Gallery, Newport, R.I., 1986-92, Quester Gallery, 1992-94. Recipient awards Nashville Ad Fedn., 1973. Mem. NAFE, Am. Inst. Graphic Arts, Am. Soc. Marine Artists, Met. Mus. N.Y.C., Artists Equity Assn., Soc. Illustrators, Soc. Scribes, Mus. Women in Arts. Avocations: bicycling, boating, fishing, hiking, swimming. Address: PO Box 79 Barnegat Light NJ 08006-0079

SMITH, GARDNER WATKINS, physician; b. Boston, July 2, 1931; s. George Van Siclen and Olive (Watkins) S.; m. Susan Elizabeth Whiteford, Sept. 6, 1958; children: Elizabeth Whiteford, Rebecca Tremain, George Van Siclen II. Grad., Phillips Acad., 1949; MD, Harvard U., 1956; AB, Princeton U., 1969. Diplomate: Am. Bd. Surgery, Am. Bd. Thoracic Surgery. Intern Johns Hopkins Hosp., Balt., 1956-57, asst. resident, 1958-59, fellow, 1957-58, asst. in surgery, 1957-59, prof. surgery, 1970-96, emeritus prof. surgery, 1996—, dep. dir. dept. surgery, 1978-85. Asst. resident U. Va., Charlottesville, 1959-61, resident, 1961-62, asst. in surgery, 1959-63, cardiovascular resident, 1962-63, instr., 1963-65, asst. prof., 1965-68, assoc. prof., 1968-70, surgeon, 1963-70; chief surgery Balt. City Hosp., 1970-79, vis. surgeon, 1979-85; chmn. sect. surg. scis. Johns Hopkins Bayview Med. Ctr., 1985-96; bd. dirs. Blue Hill Meml. Hosp. Found., 1998--, chair, 1999-2000; bd. dirs. Blue Hill Meml. Hosp., 1998--, chair, 2000--; cons. Greater Balt. Med. Ctr., 1970-91, Loch Raven VA Hosp., Balt., 1971-92, Walter Reed Army Med. Ctr., 1976-90, Nat. Naval Med. Ctr., 1984-90. Contbr. articles to med. jours. Mem. Soc. U. Surgeons, Am., So. surg. assns., A.C.S., Am. Gastroenterol. Assn., Assn. for Acad. Surgery, Balt. City Med. Soc., Halsted Soc., Med. and Chirurgical Faculty of Md., Soc. Surgery Alimentary Tract, Soc. Vascular Surgery, Internat. Cardiovascular Soc., So. Soc. Clin. Surgeons, Southeastern Surg Congress, So. Assn. Vasular Surgery, Va. Surg. Assn., Cum Laude Soc., Alpha Omega Alpha, Nu Sigma Nu. Home and Office: PO Box 565 Deer Isle ME 04627-0565

SMITH, GARY ALLEN, financial executive, foundation administrator; b. Battle Creek, Mich., Sept. 24, 1932; s. Frederick Almanzo and Adah Aliene (Mastin) S.; m. Joyce Marilyn Shepherd, Feb. 7, 1953; children: Cheryl Marie Smith Wetzstein, Brian Marshall. BS in Bus. Mgmt., Western Mich. U.; postgrad., Ea. Mich. U., U. Minn. Jr. exec. trainee, prodn. foreman Ford Motor Co., 1957-58; market analyst, asst. to nat. aerospace sales mgr. Minn. Mining & Mfg. Co., 1958-65; Mich. divisional mgr. Fin. Programs, Inc., 1965-66; part-owner, bd. dirs. Keener Securities, Inc., 1966-72; chmn., pres., treas., bd. dirs. Handy Corp., 1970-80, Money's Income Fund, Inc., 1970-88; chmn., CEO, bd. dirs. Money $ervice$, Inc., 1981-87; v.p., bd. dirs. Golden Enterprises Unltd., Inc., Fla., 1986-88; bd. dirs., sec. Freeway Truck Svcs., Inc., Dundee, 1988—; pres., treas., bd. dirs. Portfolio Mgmt. Co., Ann Arbor, Mich., 1990—; chmn., CEO, dir. Goods and Svcs. Internat., Inc., 1993—. Field sales mgr., salesman Ednl. Enterprises, Inc., 1958; gen. mgr., bus. devel. mgr. Employment Enterprises Devel. Corp., 1966-67; mktg. mgr., prodn. mgr. Kent Industries, Inc., 1967-69, past asst. to pres.; chmn., v.p., sec., treas. Am. Jetway Corp.; v.p. Fishking Resort de Panama, S.A.; trustee Gary A. Smith Living Trust, 1988—. Exec. trustee of co-trustee over 130 founds and pvt. trusts; investment counselor dist. bd. missions and ch. ext. fund United Meth. Ch., Ann Arbor, 1979—; dir., v.p. Endowment Fund, Inc., Detroit Conf., 1976-80. With U.S. Army, 1954-57, capt Res. ret. Mem. Internat. Assn. Fin. Planners, Nat. Mgmt. Assn., Am. Assn. Ret. Persons, Masons (32d degree), Shriners. Avocations: reading, soft music, gardening, tennis, fishing. Office: 317 S Division St Ste 105 Ann Arbor MI 48104-2203

SMITH, GARY NANCE, economics educator; b. L.A., Nov. 11, 1945; s. William Davis and Bette (Nance) S.; m. Margaret Hwang, Feb. 1, 2002; children: Joshua Barrett, Joanna Rachel, Cory Michael. BS Math., Harvey Mudd Coll., 1967; PhD Econ., Yale U., 1971. Asst. prof. Yale U., New Haven, 1971-78; assoc. prof. U. Houston, 1978-81; Fletcher Jones prof. econ. Pomona Coll., Claremont, Calif., 1981—. Author: Investments, 1990, Money, Banking and Financial Intermediation, 1991, Financial Assets, Markets and Institutions, 1993, Introduction to Statistics Reasoning, 1998. Fellow Woodrow Wilson Found., 1967; grantee NSF, 1995-98, Irving Found., 1996-97. Avocations: squash, aerobics, gardening. Office: Pomona Coll 425 N College Ave Claremont CA 91711-4409 E-mail: gsmith@ppomona.edu.

SMITH, GARY SCOTT, historian, educator, clergyman; b. Franklin, Pa., Oct. 12, 1950; s. Roger Gary and Arlene (Boardman) S.; m. Jane Marie Gilliland, Jan. 4, 1997; children: Gregory Scott, Joel Andrew. BA, Grove City Coll., 1972; MDiv, Gordon-Conwell Theol. Sem., 1977; MA in History, Johns Hopkins U., 1979, PhD in History, 1981. Ordained to ministry Presbyn. Ch. (U.S.A.), 1982. Campus missioner Coalition for Christian Outreach, Edinboro (Pa.) State Coll., 1972-74; guest lectr. religion and philosophy Grove City (Pa.) Coll., 1978-80, instr. sociology, 1980-81, asst. prof., co-dir. Christian ministries program, 1981-85, assoc. prof., 1985-90, prof., 1990-99, prof.

history, 1999—; coord. Humanities Core, 1999—. Interim pastor Clen-Moore United Presbyn. Ch., New Castle, Pa., 1983; stated supply pastor Bethlehem Presbyn. Ch., 1996—. Author: The Seeds of Secularization: Calvinism, Culture and Pluralism in America, 1870-1915, 1985, The Search for Social Salvation: Social Christianity and America, 1880-1925, 2000; editor: Building a Christian World View, Vol. 1, God, Man and Knowledge, 1986, Vol. 2, The Universe, Society and Ethics, 1988, God and Politics. Four Views on the Reformation of Civil Government, 1989, Worldviews, Society, and Ethics: A Reader, 1999. Named Pa. Prof. of Yr., Carnegie Found. for Advancement of Tchg. and CASE, 2001. Mem. Conf. Faith and History. Republican. Home: 13 Westminster Pl Grove City PA 16127-1307 E-mail: gssmith@gcc.edu.

SMITH, GAYNL BEVERLY, hospital director of pastoral care, nurse; b. San Francisco, Nov. 19, 1940; d. Charles Homer and Gladys L. (Harvey) Smith; m. J. Vincent McCann, June 8, 1962 (div. May 1981); children: Kathleen Patricia, Kevin Patrick; m. Paul W. Bachman, Nov. 24, 1989. RN, Johns Hopkins Hosp., 1962; BS, Johns Hopkins U., 1970; MDiv, San Francisco Theol. Sem., 1986. RN, Calif., Md.; cert. bereavement facilitator; ordained by Christian Ch., July 16, 2000. Asst. dir. nursing Washington Home for Incurables, 1971-73; staff nurse coronary care unit Doctors Hosp., Washington, 1973-74; dir. nursing Washington Home for Incurables, 1974; critical care float Sibley Meml. Hosp., Washington, 1975-82; RN, supr. Hillhaven Victorian Convalescent Hosp., San Francisco, 1984-87; chaplain Hospice, Contra Costa County Health Svcs., Martinez, 1984-85; nursing dir. and adminstr. Sisters of the Presentation Convent Infirmary, San Francisco, 1987-88; dir. pastoral care, coord. pain mgmt. Contra Costa Regional Med. Ctr. and Clinics, Martinez, 1988—. Mem. Choice in Dying, Washington, 1985—, AIDS Planning Com., Contra Costa County, Martinez, 1988-89, Bereavement Coalition, Contra Costa County, Concord, Calif., 1988—; nursing cons. Sisters of the Presentation Convent Infirmary, San Francisco, 1988—. Vice moderator Golden Gate Assn., United Ch. of Christ, San Francisco, 1986-87, Lafyette Christian Ch. (DOC), convenor of elders, mem. pastoral rels. com., bd. dirs.; life mem. Girl Scouts U.S., San Francisco, 1947—; bd. dirs. Rhodesian Ridgeback Rescue of No. Calif., 2000—. Mem. Oncology Nursing Soc., Soc. Pain Practice Mgmt. Democrat. Avocations: reading, knitting. Office: Contra Costa Regl Med Ctr Pastoral Care 2500 Alhambra Ave Martinez CA 94553-3156

SMITH, GEORGE ARTELL, chemical engineer; b. Bklyn., Dec. 17, 1938; s. Franklin Artell Smith and Elfriede Gertrude Eppelscheimer; m. Louise Randall Schoonover, Nov. 21, 1964; children: Allison Smith Amezcua, Andrew, Daniel, Eric. BChemE, Newark Coll. Engring., 1961; MChemE, U. Del., 1964. Planning engr. Exxon Rsch. and Engring. Co., Florham Park, N.J., 1963-73, sec. rsch. planning com., 1975-77, engring. assoc. planning, 1981-85, 86-94, licensing mgr., 1994-2000; sr. engr., group leader Esso Eastern, Houston, 1973-75; engring. assoc. Esso Europe, London, 1977-80, 85; ret., 2000. Ch. leadership positions LDS Ch., N.J., Tex. and Eng., 1963—, 2d counselor stake presidency, Staines, Eng., 1979-80, Bishop Short Hills (N.J.) ward, 1987-92, patriarch, 2001—. Mem. AIChE. Avocations: tennis, home repair, music, walking, reading. Home: 99 Crest Rd New Providence NJ 07974-2513 E-mail: georgeandlouise@cs.com.

SMITH, GEORGE BUNDY, state supreme court justice; b. New Orleans, Apr. 7, 1937; m. Alene L. Smith; children: George, Jr., Beth Beatrice. Cert. Polit. Studies, Institut d'Etudes Politiques, Paris, 1958; BA, Yale U., 1959, JD, 1962; MA in Polit. Sci., NYU, 1967, PhD, 1974; M of Jud. Process, U. Va., 2001. Staff atty. NAACP, 1962-64; law sec. to Hon. Jawn Sandifer, 1964-67; law sec. to Hon., Edward Dudley, 1967-71; law sect. to Hon. Harold Stevens, 1972-74; adminstr. model cities City of N.Y., 1974-75; interim judge Civil Ct. N.Y.C., 1975-76, judge, 1976-79, N.Y. State Supreme Ct., 1980-86, assoc. justice appellate divsn., 1st dept., 1987-92; assoc. judge N.Y. State Ct. Appeals, 1992—. Apptd. mem. N.Y. State Ethics Commn. Unified Ct. System, 1989-90; adj. prof. law Fordham U., 1981—. Author: (with Alene L. Smith) You Decide: Applying the Bill of Rights to Real Cases; contbr. articles to profl. jours. Trustee Grace Congl. Ch., Harlem, N.Y., Horace Mann-Barnard Sch., Bronx, N.Y., 1977-99; bd. dirs. Harlem-Dowling Westside Ctr. for Children and Family Svcs., N.Y.C.; former alumni trustee Phillips Acad., Andover, Mass. Mem. Met. Black Bar Assn. (founding, former pres. Harlem Lawyers Assn., bd. dirs., chmn. 1984-88), Assn. of Bar of City of N.Y. (v.p. 1988-89), Judicial Friends. Office: NY Court Appeals 29th Fl 61 Broadway Rm 2900 New York NY 10006-2802 also: Ct of Appeals Hall 20 Eagle St Albany NY 12207-1009

SMITH, GEORGE CURTIS, judge; b. Columbus, Ohio, Aug. 8, 1935; s. George B. and Dorothy R. Smith; m. Barbara Jean Wood, July 10, 1963; children: Curtis, Geoffrey, Elizabeth Ann. BA, Ohio State U., 1957, JD, 1959. Bar: Ohio 1959, U.S. Dist. Ct. (so. dist.) Ohio 1987. Asst. city atty. City of Columbus, 1959-62; exec. asst. to Mayor of Columbus, 1962-63; asst. atty. gen. State of Ohio, 1964; chief counsel to pros. atty. Franklin County, Ohio, 1965-70; pros. atty., 1971-80; judge Franklin County Mcpl. Ct., Columbus, 1980-85, Franklin County Common Pleas Ct., 1985-87. Mem. 2003 Ohio Bicentennial Com.; mem. Historical Marker com., 2003; mem. Ohio Supreme Ct. Coun. on Victims Rights; judge in residence Law Sch. U. Cin.; chair Fed. Ct. Case Settlement Svc.; faculty Ohio Jud. Coll., Litig. Practice Inst.; chmn., Fed. Bench-Bar Conf.; lectr. ABA Anti-Trust Sec.; alumni spkr. law graduation Ohio State U.; pres. Young Rep. Club; chmn. Perry Group, 2003; exec. com. Franklin County Rep. Party, 1971-80. Elder Presbyn. Ch. Recipient Superior Jud. Svc. award Supreme Ct. Ohio; recipient Outstanding Pub. Svc. award Fr. Co. Rep. Orgn., 2001. Mem. Ohio Pros. Attys. Assn. (pres., Ohio Pros. of Yr. Award of Hon. Leadership award), Columbus Bar Assn., Columbus Bar Found., Columbus Athletic Club (pres., dir.), Lawyers Club of Columbus (pres.), Masons (33d degree), Shriners. Office: 85 Marconi Blvd Columbus OH 43215-2823

SMITH, GEORGE DRURY, publisher, editor, collagist, writer; b. Dayton, Ohio, Mar. 10, 1927; s. Martin Jefferson and Viola (Haas) S.; m. Anne Liard Jennings, Apr. 1967 (div. 1975). AB cum laude, Marietta Coll., 1953; Diplome de Phonetique, U. Grenoble, 1950; student, U. Madrid, 1950-51, Heidelberg U., 1951-52, U. Minn., 1953-55, U. Calif.-Berkeley, 1965, UCLA, 1968. CFO Argonaut newspaper, 1972—. Editor: Beyond Baroque, 1968-80, NewLetters, 1969-75, (book series) NewBooks, 1976-78. Founder Beyond Baroque Found., Venice, Calif., 1968, chmn., 1968-80, chmn. emeritus, 1980—; mem. Mcpl. Arts Adv. Bd., L.A., 1980-82; chmn. Save Westminster Auditorium Com., Venice, 1977-80. With U.S. Army, 1945-47. Grantee Nat. Endowment for Arts, 1973-80, Calif. Arts Coun., 1977-80, Mcpl. Arts Commn., 1977-80, Coordinating Coun. Lit. Mags., 1974-80. Mem. Rosicrucians. Democrat. E-mail: georgedrurysmith@yahoo.com. *I believe that if we have faith we can live without fear; that the universe is benevolent if we can love unconditionally; that we can live righteously and prosper if we are honest and seek divine guidance; and that our mission is to enjoy life and strive for beauty.*

SMITH, GEORGE FOSTER, retired aerospace company executive; b. Franklin, Ind., May 9, 1922; s. John Earl and Ruth (Foster) S.; m. Jean Arthur Farnsworth, June 3, 1950; children— David Foster, Craig Farnsworth, Sharon Windsor. BS in Physics, Calif. Inst. Tech., 1944, MS, 1948, PhD magna cum laude (Standard Oil fellow 1949-50), 1952. Founding staff mem. Engring. Research Assos., St. Paul, 1946-48; teaching fellow, resident asso. Calif. Inst. Tech., 1948-52; staff Hughes Research Labs., Malibu, Calif., 1952-87, assoc. dir., 1962-69, dir., 1969-87; v.p. Hughes Aircraft Co., 1965-81, sr. v.p., 1981-87, policy bd., 1966-87. Adj. asso. prof. elec. engring. U. So. Calif., 1959-62; cons. Army Sci. Adv. Panel, 1975-78 Contbr. numerous articles to profl. jours. Adv. local Explorer post Boy Scouts Am., 1965-70; bd. mgrs. Westchester YMCA, 1974— , chmn., 1979-81; chmn. trustees Pacific Presbyn. Ch., Los Angeles, 1959-62. Served to lt. (j.g.) USNR, 1944-46. Recipient Disting. Alumnus award Calif. Inst. Tech., 1991. Fellow IEEE (pres. Sorenson fellows 1972-73, Frederick Philips award 1988), Am. Phys. Soc.; mem. AAAS, Caltech Assocs. (bd. dirs. 1990—, pres. 1993-94), Sierra Club, Sigma Xi (chpt. pres. 1957-58), Tau Beta Pi. Achievements include 6 patents in field; directed leading industrial research in electronics, lasers, and electro-optics; conducted first laser range finder experiments.

SMITH, GEORGE LARRY, analytical and environmental chemist; b. Beloit, Kans., Oct. 11, 1951; s. Richard Bailey and Vonda Ellene (Cox) S.; m. Charlene Janell Musgrove, Sept. 4, 1973; 1 child, Brian Lawrence. BA, Augustana Coll., 1973. Cert. grade 3 water treatment operator, Calif. Lab. technician Sanitary Dist. of Hammond, Ind., 1973; chemist Federated Metals Corp., Whiting, 1973-77; rsch. technician Air Pollution Technology, Inc., San Diego, 1978-80, environ. chemist, 1980-81, sr. tech. asst., 1981; staff chemist I Occidental Research Corp., Irvine, Calif., 1981-82, receiving chemist, 1982-84; processing chemist Chem. Waste Mgmt., Inc., Kettleman City, 1984-87, analytical chemist, 1987-89, wet analytical chemistry group leader, 1989-90, inorganic lab. supr., 1990-94, quality assurance/quality control specialist, 1994-96; lab. mgr. Bolsa Rsch. Assocs., Inc., Hollister, 1996—; lab. mgr., chemist Tri Cal-Bolsa Rsch. Assocs., Inc., 1999—. Lab. analyst for published article in environ. sci. and tech., 1981. Bd. dirs. Apostolic Christian Missions, Inc., San Diego, 1978-82. Mem. Am. Chem. Soc., Nat. Geog. Soc., Assn. Ofcl. Analytical Chemists Internat., Planetary Soc., Sierra Club. Avocations: coin collecting, drawing, photography, reading about science, history and religion. Home: 991 Meridian St Hollister CA 95023-4130 Office: Bolsa Rsch Assocs Inc 8770 Hwy 25 Hollister CA 95024 E-mail: gsmith@trical.com.

SMITH, GEORGE PATRICK, II, lawyer, educator; b. Wabash, Ind., Sept. 1, 1939; s. George Patrick and Marie Louise (Barrett) S. BS, Ind. U., 1961, JD, 1964; certificate, Hague Acad. Internat. Law, 1965; LLM, Columbia U., 1975; LLD, Ind. U., 1998. Bar: Ind. 1964, U.S. Supreme Ct. 1968. Kannert teaching fellow Ind. U. Sch. Law, 1964-65; instr. law U. Mich. Sch. Law, 1965-66; practiced in Ind. and Washington, 1965—; legal adviser Fgn. Claims Settlement Commn., Dept. State, Washington, 1966; asst. prof., asst. dean State U. N.Y. at Buffalo Law Sch., 1967-69; vis. asst. prof. law George Washington U., Nat. Law Center, summer 1968; assoc. prof. law U. Ark., 1969-71; spl. counsel EPA, Washington, 1971-74; adj. prof. law Cath. U. Law Sch., 1973-74, prof., 1977—. Adj. prof. law Georgetown U. Law Ctr., 1971-75; assoc. prof. law U. Pitts. Sch. Law, 1975-78; Commonwealth fellow in law, sci. and medicine Yale U., New Haven, 1976-77; vis. prof. law U. Conn., 1977; disting. vis. scholar Kennedy Bioethics Inst., Georgetown U., 1977-81; vis. scholar Cambridge (Eng.) U., summer 1975, spring 1978-79, Hoover Inst. on War, Revolution and Peace Stanford (Calif.) U., summer 1983, Inst. Soc., Ethics and Life Scis., Hastings Ctr., N.Y., 1981, Lilly Rare Books Libr., Ind. U., July 1981, The Kinsey Inst. for Rsch. in Sex, Gender and Reproduction, U. Ind., July 1981, Am. Bar Found., Chgo., 1986, 87, Vatican Libr., Rome, July, 1989; Rockefeller Found. resdl. scholar, Bellagio, Italy, 1980; lectr. Sch. Medicine, Uniformed Svcs. U. Health Scis., Bethesda, Md., 1979-87; cons. environ. legislation Govt. of Greece, 1977; spl. counsel to Gov. Ark. for environ. affairs, 1969-71; cons. Ark. Planning Commn., 1970-71; mem. Ark. Waterway Commn., 1970-71; chmn. Ark. Com. on Environ. Control, 1970-71; mem. com. on hwy. rsch. NRC, NAS, 1971-81; life mem. Ind. U. Found.; univ. fellow Columbia U. Law Sch., 1974-75; fellow Max Planck Inst., Heidelberg, Fed. Republic of Germany, summer 1983; mem. Pres. Reagan's Pvt. Sector Survey on Cost Control, 1982; vis. fellow Clare Hall Cambridge U., 1983-84, summer 87, law, sci. and medicine Hughes Hall, Cambridge (Eng.) U., 1989, also vis. mem. law faculty, Apr.-Aug., 1989; Fulbright vis. prof. U. New South Wales, Syndey, Australia, 1984, vis. prof., vis. fellow Ctr. for Law and Tech., 1987; vis. fellow Inst. Advanced Study, Ind. U., 1985; vis. prof. law U. Notre Dame, 1986; vis. scholar Am. Bar Found., Chgo., 1986, 87; sr. vis. fellow U. Singapore, 1987; vis. fellow McGill U. Ctr. for Medicine, Ethics and Law, Montreal, 1988, Ctr. for Biomed. Ethics U. Va. Health Scis. Ctr., Charlottesville, 1990, Ctr. for Bioethics Monash U., Melbourne, Australia, 1990, Working Ctr. Studies in German and Internat. Med. Malpractice Law Free U. Berlin, 1992; vis. rsch. fellow Ctr. for Advanced Study of Ethics Georgetown U., Washington, 1990-91; rsch. fellow Divinity Sch. Yale U., New Haven, 1991; assoc. Med. Inst. for Law Faculty, Cleve. Clinic Ctr. Creative Thinking in Medicine Cleve. State U., 1991; vis. prof. rsch. U. Auckland Law Faculty, 1991, U. Sydney Law Faculty, 1991, U. Victoria Law Faculty, B.C., Can., 1992, Trinity Coll., 1992, Dublin U., Ireland, 1992, Wolfson Coll. Cambridge U., 1992, Ind. U. Sch. Public and Environ. Affairs, 1992, Queensland U. Faculty Law, Australia, 1993; vis. scholar Ctr. Biomed. Ethics U. Minn. Med. Sch., Mpls., 1991, Ctr. for Socio-Legal Studies Oxford U., July 1992, Princeton (N.J.) Theol. Sem., 1993, Ctr. Med. Ethics Pritzker Sch. Medicine U. Chgo., 1993; vis. fellow Ctr. for Internat. Malpractice Law Free U. Berlin, Jan. 1992, King's Coll. Ctr. for Med. Law and Ethics U. London, June 1992; vis. sr. fellow Ctr. for Study Aging and Human Devel. Duke U. Med. Ctr., 1994; vis. prof. Rsch. U. Otiago, 1994; faculty of law, vis. fellow U. Bioethics Rsch. Ctr., Dunedin, New Zealand, 1994; vis. scholar Poynter Ctr. for Study of Ethics Am. Instns., Ind. U., Bloomington, 1994, law, medicine and ethics Schs. Medicine and Pub. Health Boston U., 1995, Ctr. Law and Health Ind. U., Indpls., 1995; vis. fellow U. Pa. Sch. Medicine, Phila., 1996, Inst. Study Applied & Profl. Ethics, Dartmouth Coll., Hanover, N.H., 1996, Cambridge (Eng.) U. Rsch. Ctr. Internat. Law, 1996; vis. scholar Vanderbilt U. Divinity Sch., Nashville, 1996, Northwestern U. Med. Sch., Med. Ethics & Humanities Program, Chgo., 1997, Hoover Instn., Stanford U., Palo Alto, Calif., 1997, Sch. Medicine U. Wash., 1997; vis. prof. Ind. U. Sch. Medicine Program Med. Ethics, Indpls., 1997; vis. prof. law Ind. U. Law Sch., Bloomington, 1997; Parson vis. prof. faculty law U. Sydney, 1998; vis. rsch. scholar Ctr. Clin. Bioethics, Georgetown U. Med. Sch., Washington, 1998-99, Ctr. Theology and Natural Scis. U. Calif., Berkeley, 1999; Quarter Century fellow Emmanual Coll., Cambridge U., Eng., 1999, fellow Crowley Program in Human Rights, Fordham U. Law Sch., 1999; vis. fellow faculty divinity U. Cambridge, 2001; vis. prof. law U. New South Wales, Australia, 2001. Author: Restricting the Concept of Free Seas, 1980, Legal, Ethical and Social Issues of the Brave New World, 1980, Genetics, Ethics and the Law, 1981, Medical-Legal Aspects of Cryonics, 1983, The New Biology, 1989, Final Choices: Autonomy in Health Care Decisions, 1989, Bioethics and the Law, 1993, Legal and Healthcare Ethics for the Elderly, 1996, Family Values and the New Society: Dilemmas of the 21st Century, 1998; Human Rights and BioMedicine, 2000; contbr. articles to profl. jours. U. Ark. del. Pacem In Maribus Conf., Malta, 1970. Recipient Disting. Alumni award Ind. U. Bd. Trustees, 1985, citation for Path-Breaking Work; establishment of George P. Smith II Disting. Professorship of Law, Ind. U., Bloomington, 1986. Mem. ABA (rep. UN Conf. on Human Environ., Stockholm 1972, rep. Law of Sea Conf., UN, N.Y.C. 1976, Switzerland 1979, cons. UNESCO Declaration on the Production of the Protection of the Human Genome, Paris 1995-97), Am. Law Inst., Soc. Ind. Pioneers, Am. Friends of Cambridge U., Order of St. John Hospitaller, Alpha Kappa Psi, Phi Alpha Delta, Sigma Alpha Epsilon, Order of Omega. Clubs: Cosmos (Washington). Republican. *Think big, work hard and, above all, have a dream: these are the simple guideposts for a fulfilling life.*

SMITH, GEORGE THOMAS, producer, broadcast executive; b. N.Y.C., Apr. 21, 1947; s. George Thomas and Margaret Teresa (McDonald) S.; m. Caroline Alden Vose, July 28, 1973; children: Sean Alden, Margaret Suzanne. BBA, Nichols Coll., 1968; MA, Ctrl. Mich. U., 1974; EdD, Calif. Coast U., 1985; MDiv, Minn. Grad. Sch. Theology, 1995; DD, St. Mattais Sem., 1992. Musical dir., producer Up With People, Broomfield, Colo., 1968-71; dir. recreation Randolph (N.J.) Twp., 1974-77; prof., chmn. County Coll. Morris, Randolph, 1977-92; producer, dir. Syndicable, Inc., 1986—; prof., chmn. Sussex County C.C., Newton, N.J., 1992—; mgr. Sussex County Ednl. TV, 1993—. Mng. dir. George Town Villas, Grand Cayman, West Indies, 1992-96; theme park cons. Glynn Barclay & Assocs., San Antonio, 1992—. Producer (television spl.) Time for the Music, 1987 (Telly award 1988), Face to Face, 1989, Rhythm of the World, 1991 (Telly award 1991), North American Championship Racing, 1988. Pres. West Morris YMCA, Randolph, 1991; scoutmaster Boy Scouts Am. Troop 166, Randolph, 1992; sec. Up With People Alumni Assn., Broomfield, 1993. Capt. USAF, 1973-81. Recipient Telly awards, 1988, 91, 94, 95, Best Broadcast & Video award Ea. Motorsports Press Assn., 1988, 93. Fellow Acad. Sports Television; mem. Nat. Acad. Television, World Waterpark Asn., Internat. Assn. Amusement Parks & Attractions, Producers Guild Am., Rotary (pres. 1978). Avocations: music, drag racing, religion. Office: Syndi Cable Prodns PO Box 1000 Mount Freedom NJ 07970-1000

SMITH, GEORGE THORNEWELL, retired state supreme court justice; b. Camilla, Ga., Oct. 15, 1916; s. George C. and Rosa (Gray) S.; m. Eloise Taylor, Sept. 1, 1943 (dec.). Grad., Abraham Baldwin Agrl. Coll., 1940; LLB, U. Ga., 1948. Bar: Ga. 1947. Assoc. Cain & Smith, Cairo, 1947-71; city atty. Cairo, 1949-58; atty. Grady County, 1950-59; solicitor Cairo City Ct., 1951-59; mem. Ga. Ho. of Reps., 1959-67, speaker of the house, 1963-67; lt. gov. State of Ga., 1967-71; city atty. East Point, Ga., 1973-76; judge Ga. Ct. Appeals, 1976-81; justice Ga. Supreme Ct., Atlanta, 1981-91, presiding justice, 1990-91; of counsel Barnes, Browning Tanksley and Casurella, Marietta, Ga., 1992—. Past mem. exec. com. Nat. Conf. Appellate Judges; vice chmn. Nat. Conf. Lt. Govs. Trustee Nat. Arthritis Found. Lt. comdr. USN, 1940-45. Only person in the state's history to serve in an elective capacity in all 3 brs. of govt. Mem. State Bar Ga., Cobb County Bar Assn., Lawyers Club Atlanta, Am. Legion, VFW, Moose, Kiwanis. Avocations: hunting, golf. Office: Browning & Tanksley 166 Anderson St SW Ste 225 Marietta GA 30060-1984

SMITH, GEORGE WOLFRAM, physicist, educator; b. Des Plaines, Ill., Sept. 19, 1932; s. Murray Sawyer and Alice Lucile (Wolfram) S.; m. Mary Lee Sackett, Sept. 7, 1956; children— Dean, Grant BA, Knox Coll., 1954; MA, Rice U., 1956, PhD, 1958. Welch Found. fellow Rice U., 1958-59; sr. rsch. physicist GM, Warren, Mich., 1959-76, dept. rsch. scientist, 1976-81, sr. staff rsch. scientist, 1981-87, prin. rsch. scientist, 1987-99; retired, 1999. Lectr. physics and astronomy Cranbrook Inst. Sci., Bloomfield Hills, Mich., 1963-87, mem. sci. adv. com., 1989—; instr. Lawrence Inst. Tech., 1963-65; vice chmn. Gordon Rsch. Conf. on Orientational Disorder in Crystals, 1976, chmn., 1978; co-chmn. Internat. Symposium on Particulate Carbon, 1980; mem. rev. com. Liquid Crystal Inst., Kent (Ohio) State U., 1984-85; mem. adv. com. Conf. on Electrorheological Fluids, 1991, 93; mem. adv. bd. NSF Sci. and Tech. Ctr. for Advanced Liquid Crystalline Optical Materials, 1996-2000; physics co-chair Internat. Sci. and Engring. Fair, 2000. Co-editor: Particulate Carbon: Formation During Combustion, 1981; editl. cons. Ency. Applied Physics, 1988-2000; contbr. Handbook of Chemistry and Physics; contbr. articles to sci. and tech. jours.; patentee on temperature measuring device, liquid crystal device tech., dielectric heating, graphite fiber growth, polymer-dispersed liquid crystals. Mem. Mich. Regtl. Civil War Roundtable, 1965—, pres., 1971-72. Recipient Knox Coll. Achievement award 1977, John M. Campbell Research award, 1980, Charles L. McCuen Achievement award, Gen. Motors, 1985 Fellow Am. Phys. Soc. (com. on applications of physics 1988-91, chmn. 1991, chmn. com. on tutorials 1991, mem. Pake Prize Com. 1993-94); mem. Soc. Info. Display (program com. 1990-93), Detroit Zoological Inst. (docent 2001-), Phi Beta Kappa, Sigma Xi (chpt. pres. 1980-81), Phi Delta Theta, Alpha Delta. Home: 1882 Melbourne St Birmingham MI 48009-1163

SMITH, GERARD PETER, neuroscientist; b. Phila., Mar. 24, 1935; s. Stanley Alward and Agnes Marie (McLarney) S.; m. Barbara McInnis, May 12, 1962; children: Christopher, Mark, Hilary, Maura. BS, St. Joseph's U., Phila., 1956; MD, U. Pa., 1960, U. Camerino, Italy. Intern, resident N.Y. Hosp., 1960-62; asst. prof. physiology U. Pa. Sch. Medicine, Phila., 1964-68; from asst. to assoc. prof. Cornell U., N.Y.C., 1968—, prof. psychiatry (behavioral neurosci.), 1973—. Vis. prof. MIT, 1973—74, Rockefeller U., 1979—80, adj. prof., 1982—86; cons. NIH; Curt Richter lectr. Johns Hopkins U., 1976; Leon lectr. U. Pa., 1990, Stellar lectr., 93; Rushton lectr. Fla. State U., 1992; Merck, Sharpe, and Dohm prof. neurosci. U. Flinder, Australia, 1992; Loucks lectr. U. Wash., 1995; dir. Eating Disorders Inst. N.Y. Hosp.-Cornell Med. Ctr., 1984—88. Recipient Rsch. Scientist, USPHS, 1982, Myers Lifetime Achievement award, Internat. Behavioral Neurosci. Soc.; grantee, NIH. Mem. AAAS, Am. Physiol. Soc., Soc. for Neurosci., Soc. for Study Ingestive Behavior (pres.), Internat. Behavioral Neurosci. Soc. (pres.), Alpha Omega Alpha, Alpha Sigma Nu. Office: NY Presbyn Hosp Westchester Divsn EW Bourne Behavioral Rsch Lab 21 Bloomingdale Rd White Plains NY 10605-1504 E-mail: gpsmith@mail.med.cornell.edu.

SMITH, GERRIT BRUCE, foreign language educator; b. Munich, Germany, Oct. 17, 1971; came to the U.S., 1988; s. Bruce Alan Smith and Gerlinde Karolina Ward. AA magna cum laude, Coll. William and Mary, 1993, BA magna cum laude, 1995; MA in German, U. Hawaii, 1999; MPA, U. Okla., 2000. Cert. sales assoc. Army Air Force Exch. Svc., Ft. Lee, Va., 1991-96; tchg. asst. German U. Hawaii at Manoa, Honolulu, 1997-99; German tchr. Kaimuki Cmty. Sch. for Adults, 2000—. Substitute tchr. City of Colonial Heights Pub. Schs., Va., 2002—. Campaign/poll worker Re-election Campaign Stacy Stafford Clk. of Cir. Ct., Colonial Heights, Va., 1990; part-time vol. adminstrv. and rsch. asst. Judiciary of the State of Hawaii, Honolulu, 1997-99. Presdl. scholar Richard Bland Coll., Petersburg, Va., 1992-93. Mem. ASPA, Dem. Nat. Com., Hawaii Kai Opera Guild, German Nat. Honor Soc. (U. Hawaii chpt. treas. 1997-99), Phi Theta Kappa. Avocations: chess, stamp collecting, opera, reading, weight training. E-mail: gerrit@hawaii.edu.

SMITH, GLADYS ANN, counselor, military medic; b. Leland, Miss., July 19, 1960; d. Gladys Rose. B in Healthcare Mgmt., So. Ill. U., 1993; M in Health Sci., Washington U., St. Louis, MO, 1997; MEd, U. Mo., 2001. Lic. substance abuse counselor, advanced substance abuse counselor, provisional lic. counselor. Mental health counselor Webster U., St. Louis, 2001—, petty officer, 1984—. Counselor, educator St. Louis County Corrections. Recipient Navy Achievement awards, 1992, 1997, 2001. Mem.: Nat. Counselors Assn., Nat. Assn. Drug Abuse Counselors (none), Coalition of 100 Black Women. Democrat. Mem. A.M.E. Ch. Avocations: dancing, running, reading. Home: 7006 Stanford Saint Louis MO 63130 Office: Webster U 470 E Lockwood Saint Louis MO 63119 Personal E-mail: GSmith2222@aol.com. Business E-Mail: gasmith@webster.edu.

SMITH, GLEE SIDNEY, JR. lawyer; b. Rozel, Kans., Apr. 29, 1921; s. Glee S. and Bernice M. (Augustine) S.; m. Geraldine B. Buhler, Dec. 14, 1943; children: Glee S., Stephen B., Susan K. AB, U. Kans., 1943, JD, 1947. Bar: Kans. 1947, U.S. Dist. Ct. 1951, U.S. Supreme Ct. 1973, U.S. Ct. Mil. Appeals 1988. Ptnr. Smith Burnett & Larson, Lanred, Kans., 1947—. Of counsel Barber, Emerson et. al., Lawrence, Kans., 1992—, Kans. state senator, 1957-73, pres. Senate, 1965-73; mem. Kans. Bd. Regents, 1975-83, pres., 1976; bd. govs. Kans. U. Law Soc., 1967—; mem. Kans. Jud. Coun., 1963-65; county atty. Pawnee County, 1949-53; mem. bd. edn. Larned, 1951-63; Kans. commr. Nat. Conf. Commn. on Uniform State Laws, 1963—; bd. dirs. Nat. Legal Svcs. Corp., 1975-79. Served to 1st lt. U.S. Army Air Corps, 1943-45. Recipient disting. svc. award U. Kans. Law Sch., 1976; disting. svc. citation U. Kans., 1984. Fellow Am. Coll. Probate Counsel, Am. Bar Found.; mem. ABA (bd. of govs. 1987-90, chmn. ops. com. 1989-90, exec. com. 1989-90, chmn. task force on solo and small firm practitioners 1990-91, chmn. com. on solo and small firm practitioners 1992-94, chmn. task force on applying fed. legis. to congress 1994-96), Kans. Bar Assn. (del. to ABA ho. of dels. 1982-92, bd. govs. 1982-92, leadership award 1973, medal of distinction 1993), Southwest Kans. Bar Assn., Am. Jud. Soc., Kiwanis, Masons, Rotary. Republican. Presbyterian. Home: 4313 Quail Pointe Rd Lawrence KS 66047-1966

SMITH, GLENN A. lawyer; b. Oakland, Calif., July 11, 1946; BA, Pomona Coll., 1968; JD, U. Calif., Berkeley, 1971; LLM in Taxation, NYU, 1973. Bar: Calif. 1972, D.C. 1975. Law clerk to Hon. William M. Drennen U.S. Tax Ct., 1973-75; ptnr. Heller, Ehrman, White & McAuliffe, Palo Alto, San Francisco, Calif., 1977—. Office: Heller Ehrman White & McAuliffe 525 University Ave Ste 900 Palo Alto CA 94301-1907

SMITH, GLORIA S. local commissioner, educator; b. Midland, SD, July 25, 1924; d. John and Hattie Leora Saucerman; m. Albert Francis Smith, July 21, 1945; children: Gregory, Bradley, Karen. Grad., Dakota Wesleyan U., 1942, U. Minn., 1945. Cert. elem. edn. Elem. tchr. Sansarc (S.D.) Sch. Dist., 1943-44; ins. underwriter Firemans Fund Ins. Co., San Francisco, 1945-46; supr. disability ins. General Electric Co., Schenectady, NY, 1947-49; v.p., then pres. bd. edn. Upper St. Clair (Pa.) Sch. Dist., 1964-77; bd. dir. then pres. South Hills Area Coun. of Govs., Pitts., 1994—; commr., v.p. Upper St. Clair (Pa.) Twp., 1994—. Mem. Upper St. Clair Bd. Commrs., Pa., 1994—; bd. dir. special edn. Allegheny County Intermediate Unit, Pitts., 1974-77; bd. dir. Outreach Teen and Family Svcs., Mt. Lebanon, Pa., 1979—, treas. 1990—. Americans Abroad selection com. Am. Field Svc. Upper St. Clair, Pa., 1970-77; ch. sch. tchr. United Methodist Ch., Bethel Park, Pa., 1960—; mem. Advisory Com. to Establish Home Rule Charter dists., Allegheny Cty., Pa., 1998. Recipient Outstanding Citizen award Upper St. Clair Repub. Com., Pa., 1967. Republican. Methodist. Avocations: family, travel, home decorating, community block parties. Home: 529 Long Dr Upper Saint Clair PA 15241 Office: Twp Bd of Commissioners 1820 Mclaughlin Run Rd Upper Saint Clair PA 15241

SMITH, GLORIA YOUNG, artist, retired graphic artist; b. N.Y.C., Jan. 15, 1926; d. Frederick William and Anastasia Margaret (Regan) Young; m. Henry George Smith, Oct. 1, 1949; children: Stephanie, Kevin, Brian, Robert, Sean. Student, Art Students League, N.Y.C., 1944, 45, Nat. Acad. Design, 1946, 47, 48, Nassau C.C., Uniondale, N.Y., 1971, 72. Artist Lynn Mfg. Co., Astoria, N.Y., 1947-50; forms designer, graphic artist Mercy Hosp., Rockville Centre, 1972-81; art tchr. Art Inst. & Gallery, Salisbury, Md., 1992-98, Art League of Ocean City, 1995—. Mem. com. Nat. Juried Art Show, Salisbury, 1996-2000. Artist numerous paintings. Pres. Artists Co-op, Salisbury, 1998—; bd. dirs. Art League of Ocean City, Md., 1997–; sec., bd. dirs. Art Inst. & Gallery, Salisbury, 1991-95; hdqrs. mgr. congl. campaign Rep. Orgn., Baldwin, N.Y., 1968; treas. Conservative Women, L.I., 1971; judge Nat. Seashore Poster Art Contest, Assateague Island, Md., 1992. Recipient Best in Category award Ann. Arts and Crafts Show, Indian Harbour Beach, Fla., 1987, 2d pl. award Arts Atlantica-Worcester County Heritage, 1996, 1st pl. award Art League Ocean City, 1992, Mem.'s award Fells Point Art Gallery, 1993. Mem. Nat. League Am. Pen Women, Portrait Soc. Am., Inc., Art Students League N.Y. (life), Miniature Art Soc. Fla. Republican. Roman Catholic. Avocations: reading, music, foreign travel, walking. Home: 260 Ocean Pkwy Berlin MD 21811-1525

SMITH, G(ODFREY) T(AYLOR), retired academic administrator; b. Newton, Miss., Nov. 12, 1935; s. Taylor and Edna (Blanton) S.; m. Joni Eaton, Sept. 1, 1956; children: Paul Brian, Sherry Lynn. BA, Coll. of Wooster, 1956; MPA with distinction, Cornell U., 1960; LLD (hon.), Bethany Coll., 1979. Assoc. dir. devel. Cornell U., Ithaca, N.Y., 1960-62; dir. devel. Coll. Wooster, 1962-66, v.p., 1966-77; pres. Chapman U., Orange, Calif., 1977-88, pres. emeritus, 1988—; exec. dir. Talaris Rsch. Inst., Seattle, 2001—. Lectr. in field. Contbr. numerous articles on coll. mgmt. to profl. publs. Bd. dirs. Wayne County (Ohio) Indsl. Devel. Corp., 1966-72, World Affairs Coun. Orange Coun., Calif., 1978-89, Orange County chpt. NCCJ, 1979-86, Orange County coun. Boy Scouts Am., 1980-85, Coun. Ind. Colls., 1985-87; bd. dirs. div. higher edn. Christian Ch. (Disciples of Christ), 1980-86, chmn., 1984-86; bd. dirs., mem. exec. com. Ind. Colls. So. Calif., 1979-88, pres., 1981-82; mem. exec. com. Assn. Ind. Calif. Colls. and Univs., 1980-88, treas., 1982-87. Recipient Steuben Apple award for tchg. excellence Coun. for Advancement and Support Edn., 1984, Disting. Alumnus award Coll. of Wooster, 1991, Faith and Reason award Christian Ch. (Disciples of Christ), 1993, Laureate award for Lifetime Achievement Inst. for Charitable Giving, 1997; Smith Hall dedicated at Chapman U., 1988; Alfred P. Sloan fellow Cornell U., 1960. Presbyterian. Home: 20703 Pelton Pl Leavenworth WA 98826 *If we treat people as they are, they will stay as they are. But if we treat them for what they might be and might become, they will become those better selves.*

SMITH, GOFF, industrial equipment manufacturing executive; b. Jackson, Tenn., Oct. 7, 1916; s. Fred Thomas and Mabel (Goff) S.; m. Nancy Dall, Nov. 28, 1942 (dec. 1972); children: Goff Thomas, Susan Knight; m. Harriet Schneider Oliver, June 23, 1973 (dec. 1998). BSE, U. Mich., 1938, MBA, 1939; MS, MIT, 1953. Trainee Bucyrus Erie, South Milwaukee, Wis., 1939-40; mem. sales staff Amsted Industries, Chgo. and N.Y.C., 1946-55, subsidiary pres. Chgo., 1955-60, v.p., 1960-69, pres., dir., 1969-74, pres., CEO, dir., 1974-80, chmn., 1980-82. Pres. Village of Winnetka, Ill., 1967-69; pres., bd. dirs. United Way Chgo., 1976-85; bd. dirs. Rehab. Inst., Chgo., 1979-99, Chgo. Theol. Sem., 1979-99, Presbyn. Home, Evanston, Ill., 1979—; trustee Sigma Chi Found., 1977-99. Maj. U.S. Army, 1940-46. Sloan Fellow MIT, 1952-53. Republican. Avocations: hunting, fishing, golf.

SMITH, GORDON DEE, corporate intelligence consultant; b. Fort Worth, Tex., Nov. 20, 1956; s. Gordon William and Beverley (Taylor) S.; m. Susan Keating, June 13, 1987; children: William Dee II, Blaine Keating. BA, Tex. Christian U., 1977. Pres., founder InterCultura, Inc., Ft. Worth, 1981—92; prin. Cima Internat., 1992—95; pres. Devel. Group, 1995—2001; chair Corp. Positioning, Inc., 1998—2000; CEO Strategic Insight Group, Ft. Worth, 2001—. Dir. Servicios Cinematograficos, Mexicanos, Mex., 1994— Contbr. articles to mags. and newspapers. Bd. visitors Internat. Fine Arts Sch. Tex. Christian U., Ft. Worth, 1995— Recipient Internat. award Dallas-Ft. Worth Internat. Trade Assn., 1991; named Hot Shot, Ultra Mag., Tex., 1992, to 40 under 40 (list) Bus. Press, Ft. Worth, Tex., 1994. Avocations: music, composing, philosopy, cooking, martial arts. Office: Ste 100 6777 Camp Bowie Blvd Fort Worth TX 76116-7156

SMITH, GORDON EUGENE, pilot; b. Corpus Christi, Tex., Nov. 22, 1953; s. Orvis Alvin and Helen Lucille (Lockhart) A.; m. Crisanta Lacson Queriza, Jan. 5, 1979; children: Pia Marie, Helena Irita. AAS in Electronics, Riverside City Coll., 1985; BSEE, Calif. Polytech., 1987. Electronics technician Lear Siegler, Inc., Ontario, Calif., 1981-86, Rockwell Internat., Palmdale, 1986-87; pilot Orion Air Inc., Raleigh, N.C., 1987-90; pilot, dir. maintenance, asst. dir. ops. Nat. Air, Riverside, Calif., 1990-93; pilot MGM Grand Air, 1993-96, Sun Pacific Internat., Tucson, 1996-99, Sunworld Internat., Cin., 1999—. With USAF, 1972-79, with Res. 1979—. Mem. Aircraft Owners and Pilots Assn., Team One (v.p. 1980—). Republican. Dunkard Brethren. Avocations: flying, golf, bowling, baseball, computers. Office: Sunworld Internat 207 Grandview Dr Fort Mitchell KY 41017-2758

SMITH, GORDON H. civil engineer, consultant, forensic engineer consultant; b. N.Y.C., Mar. 17, 1936; s. Henry and Theodora (Augenstern) S.; m. Norma Kaplan, Feb. 28, 1960; children: Randy Smith Aberg, Robin Smith Kolstad. B in Engring., Yale U., 1957. Registered profl. engr., Mich., N.Y. V.p., chief engr. Albro Metal Products Corp., N.Y.C., 1957-69, pres., 1969-75, Gordon H. Smith Corp., N.Y.C., 1975—, Gordon H. Smith PE, PC, N.Y.C., 1998—. Guest lectr. Yale U. Sch. Arch., Am. Inst. Architects, Construction Specification Inst., Nat. Glass Assn., Glass Assn. N.Am., N.Y. Inst. Tech. Contbr. articles to Archtl. Record, Progressive Arch., ASTM, Chgo. High Rise Com. Mem. NSPE, ASTM, ASCE, AIA (Inst. Honors 1994), Nat. Assn. Archtl. Metal Mfrs. (v.p., prs., bd. dirs.), Archtl. Aluminum Mfrs. Assn. (v.p., bd. dirs.), Nat. Assn. Miscellaneous, Ornamental and Archtl. Metal Mfrs. (bd. dirs.), Constrn. Specifications Inst. Office: Gordon H Smith Corp 200 Madison Ave New York NY 10016-3903

SMITH, GORDON HAROLD, senator; b. Pendleton, Oreg., May 25, 1952; s. Milan Dale and Jessica (Udall) S.; m. Sharon Lankford; children: Brittany, Garrett, Morgan. BA in History, Brigham Young U., 1976; JD, Southwestern U., 1979. Law clk. to Justice H. Vern Payne N.Mex. Supreme Ct.; pvt. practice Ariz.; owner Smith Frozen Foods; mem. Oreg. State Senate, 1992-95, pres., 1995-96; senator from Oreg. U.S. Senate, 1997—. Mem. budget com., chair subcom. water and power, mem. subcom. forests and pub. land mgmt., mem. subcom. energy rsch., devel., prodn. and regulation, mem. energy and natural resources com., chair subcom. European affairs, mem. subcom. Near Eastern and South Asian affairs, mem. fgn. rels. com., mem. subcom. on East Asian and Pacific affairs. Office: US Senate 404 Russell Senate Ofc Bldg Washington DC 20510-0001*

SMITH, GORDON HOWELL, lawyer; b. Syracuse, N.Y., Oct. 26, 1915; s. Lewis P. and Maud (Mixer) S.; m. Eunice Hale, June 28,1947; children: Lewis Peter, Susan S. Rizk, Catherine S. Maxson, Maud S. Daudon. BA, Princeton U., 1932-36; LL.B., Yale U., 1939. Bar: N.Y. 1939, Ill. 1946. Asso. Lord, Day & Lord, N.Y.C., 1939-41, Gardner, Carton & Douglas, Chgo., 1946-51; partner Mackenzie, Smith & Michell, Syracuse, 1951-53, Gardner, Carton & Douglas, 1954-57, 60-85, of counsel, 1986-96, retired ptnr., 1996—. Sec., dir. Smith-Corona, Inc., 1951-54, v.p., Syracuse, 1957-60 Bd. dirs. Rehab. Inst. Chgo., chmn., 1974-78, 83-86; bd. dirs. United Way Met. Chgo., 1962-85. Served to lt. comdr. USNR, 1941-46. Mem. Am. Soc. Corporate Secs., Am., Ill., Chgo. bar assns. Clubs: Comml., Law, Econ., Legal, Chgo., Old Elm (Chgo.). Home: 1302 N Green Bay Rd Lake Forest IL 60045-1108 Office: 321 N Clark St Ste 3400 Chicago IL 60610-4717 E-mail: gsmith1302@aol.com.

SMITH, GORDON PAUL, management consulting company executive; b. Salem, Mass., Dec. 25, 1916; s. Gordon and May (Vaughan) S.; m. Daphne Miller, Nov. 23, 1943 (div. 1968); m. Ramona Chamberlain, Sept. 27, 1969; children: Randall B., Roderick F. BS in Econs, U. Mass., 1947; MS in Govt. Mgmt, U. Denver (Sloan fellow), 1948; postgrad. in polit. sci, NYU, 1948-50; DHL (hon.), Monterey Inst. Internat. Studies, 1994. Economist Tax Found., Inc., N.Y.C., 1948-50; with Booz, Allen & Hamilton, 1951-70, partner, 1959-62, v.p., 1962-67, mng. pntr. Western U.S., 1968-70; partner Harrod, Williams and Smith (real estate devel.), 1962-69; state dir. fin. State of Calif., 1967-68; pres. Gordon Paul Smith & Co., Mgmt. Cons., 1968—; pres., chief exec. officer Golconda Corp., 1972-74, chmn. bd., 1974-85. Pres. Cermetek Corp., 1978-80; bd. dirs., exec. com. First Calif. Co., 1970-72, Groman Corp., 1976-85; bd. dirs. Madison Venture Capital Corp.; adviser task force def. procurement and contracting Hoover Commn., 1954-55; spl. asst. to pres. Republic Aviation Corp., 1954-55; cons., Hawaii, 1960-61, Alaska, 1963; cons. Wash. Hwy. Adminstrn., 1964, also 10 states and fed. agys., 1951-70, Am. Baseball League and Calif. Angels, 1960-62; bd. dirs. Monterey Coll. Law; chmn. Ft. Ord Econ. Devel. Adv. Group, 1991; chmn. Coalition on Rsch. and Edn., 1993—; bd. dirs. Monterey Bay Futures Project; adv. bd. Ctr. for Non-Proliferation Studies, 1997—; over 750 TV, radio and speaking appearances on econs., mgmt. and public issues. Author articles on govt., econs. and edn. Mem. Calif. Select Com. on Master Plan for Edn., 1971—73; mem. alumni coun. U. Mass., 1950—54, bd. dirs. alumni ass., 1964—70; chmn. West Coast Cancer Found., 1976—87, Coalition Rsch. and Edn., 1993—, Jim Tunney Youth Found., 1994—; trustee, chmn. Monterey Inst. Internat. Studies, 1978—92, trustee emeritus, 1995—; trustee Northfield Mt. Hermon Sch., 1983—93, Robert Louis Stevenson Sch., 1993—; mem. devel. coun. Cmty. Hosp. of Monterey Peninsula, 1983—84; sr. advisor to Pres., 1998—; mem. 24 bds. and commns. State of Calif., 1967—72; bd. dirs. Alumni Assn. Mt. Hermon Prep. Sch., 1963; bd. dirs. Stanford Med. Ctr., 1960—62, pres., chmn., 1962—66; bd. dirs. Friends of the Performing Arts, 1985—, Monterey County Symphony Orch., 1991—96, Monterey Bay Futures Project, 1992—, Ctr. for Nonproliferation of Weapons of Mass Destruction, 1998—, Calif. Inst. for Local Self Govt., 2000—. Recipient spl. commendation Hoover Commn., 1955, Alumni of Yr. award U. Mass., 1963, Trustee of Yr. award Monterey-Peninsula, 1991, Monterey-Peninsula Outstanding Citizen of Yr. award, 1992, Laura Bride Powers Heritage award, 1991, U.S. Congl. award, 1992, Calif. Senate and Assembly Outstanding Citizen award, 1992, Wisdom award of honor Wisdom Soc., 1992; permanent Gordon Paul Smith Disting. Chair for Internat. Studies established at Monterey Inst. Internat. Studies; Gordon Paul Smith Scholarship Fund named in his honor Northfield Mt. Hermon Sch.; named to Honorable Order of Ky. Cols. Mem. Monterey History and Art Assn. (bd. dirs. 1987-92, pres. 1985-87, chmn. 1987-92, hon. lifetime dir. 1992—), The Stanton Heritage Ctr. (chmn. 1987-92, chmn. emeritus 1992—), Salvation Army (bd. dirs., chmn. hon. cabinet), Monterey Peninsula Mus. Art, Carmel Valley (Calif.) Country Club, Monterey Peninsula Country Club, Old Capitol Club. Home: 253 Del Mesa Carmel CA 93923 *If the quest for personal success is only for an accumulation of prestige, power or wealth, then personal failure will be assured. Genuine personal success can surely be found, however, through a significant and lasting contribution toward helping the progress of others and raising the human worth. This is the true mark of leadership.*

SMITH, GRANT WARREN, II, university administrator, physical sciences educator; b. Kansas City, Mo., Jan. 21, 1941; m. Constance M. Krambeer, 1962; 1 child, Grant Warren III. BA, Grinnell Coll., 1962; PhD, Cornell U., 1966, postgrad., 1967. Asst. prof. chemistry Cornell U., Ithaca, N.Y., 1966-68, vis. prof. Am. Coun. on Edn. fellow, 1973-74; assoc. prof. U. Alaska, Fairbanks, 1968-77, prof., 1977-78, head dept. chemistry and chem. engring., 1968-73, acting head dept. gen. sci., 1972-73; pres. univ. assembly U. Alaska Sys., 1976-77; prof. physics. scis., dean Sch. Scis. and Tech., U. Houston, Clear Lake, 1979-84; prof. chemistry Southeastern La. U., Hammond, 1984-95, honors prof. arts and scis., 1995-97, v.p. acad. affairs, 1984-86, pres., 1986-95, Slippery Rock U., 1997—. Bd. dirs. Houston Area Rsch. Ctr., 1982-83, Penn-Northwest Devel. Corp., 1998—, Cmty. Devel. Corp. Butler County, 1998—, 3 Rivers Connect, 2000—; violinist, pres. exec. bd. Clear Lake Symphony, 1980-84. NIH fellow, 1963-66, DuPont fellow, 1967. Fellow Royal Soc. Chemistry (London, chartered chemist), Explorers Club; mem. Am. Assn. Higher Edn., Am. Assn. Univ. Adminstrs. (bd. dirs. 1982-88, 99—, v.p. 1988-90), AAAS, The Coll. Bd., Am. Chem. Soc., Internat. Assn. Univ. Pres., Internat. Soc. Ethnopharmacology, Am. Soc. Pharmacognosy, Internat. Soc. of Ethnobiology, Nat. Speleological Soc., Am. Spelean History Assn., Am. Bot. Coun., Arctic Inst. N.Am., soc. for the History of Discoveries, Leadership Pitts. XV, Hammond C. of C. (bd. dirs. 1988-90), World Future Soc., Rotary, Sigma Xi, Phi Kappa Phi, Beta Gamma Sigma, Phi Eta Sigma. Office: Slippery Rock U Office of Pres Old Main Slippery Rock PA 16057-1326 E-mail: gwsmith@sru.edu.

SMITH, GRANT WILLIAM, English language educator, civic fundraiser; b. Bellingham, Wash., July 26, 1937; s. George Whitfield and Hazel (Speirs) S.; m. Lelia Dickinson, June 9, 1961; children: Kathryn, Gavin. BA, Reed Coll., 1964; MA, U. Nev., 1966; PhD, U. Del., 1975. Asst. prof. Eastern Wash. U., Cheney, 1968-76, assoc. prof., 1976-79, prof., 1979—. Faculty pres. Eastern Wash. U., Cheney, 1976-77, chair English dept., 1978-84, acting vice provost, 1987-88, coord. humanities, 1979—, dir. cultural outreach, 1995-97; host Pub. TV, Here's Shakespeare, 1980, 81. Editor Proceedings of the Am. Name Soc., 1997, 98, 99; contbr. articles to profl. jours. and conf. procs. Moderator Cheney United Ch. Christ, 1982-84; trustee Spokane Symphony, 1996—, chair devel. 2000—; program chair Coun. Geo. Names Authorities, 1999. With U.S. Army, 1957-60. Grantee U.S. Geol. Survey, State Humanities Commn., NEH, others. Mem. MLA, AAUP, Placename Survey U.S. (chair 1990—), Connoisseur Concerts Assn. (pres. 1992-95), Am. Dialect Soc. (regional sec. 1982-98), Rocky Mountain MLA (program chair 1987, 95), Internat. Coun. Onomastic Scientists (exec. bd. dirs. 1999—, editl. bd. ONOMA 2000—, v.p. 2002—), Internat. Soc. Dialectology and Geolinguistics, Am. Name Soc. (v.p. 1996-98, pres. 1999-2001), Wash. Bd. Geo. Names, others. Avocations: jogging, reading, singing. Home: 905 Gary St Cheney WA 99004-1341 Address: Eastern Wash Univ 250 Patterson Hall Dept of English Cheney WA 99004-2430 E-mail: gsmith@ewu.edu.

SMITH, GREGORY ALLGIRE, college administrator; b. Washington, Mar. 31, 1951; s. Donald Eugene and Mary Elizabeth (Reichert) Smith; m. Susan Elizabeth Watts, Oct. 31, 1980; 1 child David Joseph Smith-Watts. BA, The Johns Hopkins U., 1972; MA, Williams Coll., Williamstown, Mass., 1974. Adminstrv. asst. Washington Project for the Arts, 1975; intern Walker Art Ctr., Mpls., 1975—76; asst. devel. officer The Sci. Mus. of Minn., St. Paul, 1977; asst. dir. Akron (Ohio) Art Inst., 1977—80; asst. to dir. Toledo Mus. Art, 1980—82, asst. dir. adminstrn., 1982—86; exec. v.p. Internat. Exhbns. Found., Washington, 1986—87; dir. The Telfair Mus. Art, Savannah, Ga., 1987—94, Art Acad. of Cin., 1994—98, pres., 1998—. Trustee Greater Cin. Consortium of Colls. and Univs., vice chmn., 2001—; trustee Assn. Ind. Colls. of Art and Design. Mem.: Coll. Art Assn., Ohio Found. on the Arts (v.p. 1981—83, trustee 1981—84), Assn. Art Mus. Adminstrs. (founder 1984—85), Am. Assn. Mus. (surveyor mus. assessment program 1988—), Rotary (dir. Cin. club 2000—01, sec.-treas. 2001—02, pres. 2002—03), Univ. Club. Avocation: collecting arts and crafts movement objects, landscape design, gardening.. Home: 8380 Springvalley Dr Cincinnati OH 45236-1356 Office: Art Acad of Cin 1125 Saint Gregory St Cincinnati OH 45202-1799 E-mail: gasmith@artacademy.edu.

SMITH, GREGORY DALE, lawyer, judge; b. Knoxville, Feb. 1, 1963; s. James C. and Essie Pearl (Norman) S.; m. Cynthia Luckett, Oct. 15, 1988; children: Leora, Philip. BS, Middle Tenn. State U., 1985; JD, Cumberland Law Sch., 1988. Bar: Tenn., U.S. Supreme Ct., U.S. Ct. Appeals (fed. crct.), U.S. Ct. Mil. Appeals, U.S. Dist. Ct. (mid., ea. and we. dists.) Tenn., Army Ct. of Mil. Rev., U.S. Ct. Vet. Appeals. Mcpl. magistrate City of Birmingham, Ala., 1987-88; assoc. Marks, Marks & Shell, Clarksville, Tenn., 1988-89; juvenile referee Montgomery County Juvenile Ct., 1992-95; assoc. Richardson & Richardson, 1989-93; pvt. practice, 1993—. Adj. prof. Austin Peay State U., Clarksville, 1989—; lectr. in field; hearing officer Tenn. Bd. Profl., 1993—; mcpl. judge, Pleasant View, Tenn., 1997—. Author: The TACDL Guide to Defending Juvenile Cases in Tennessee, 1993; co-author: Juvenile Courts in Tennessee, 1998; contbr. articles to profl. jours. Bd. dirs. United Way of Clarksville and Montgomery County, 1992—, Treehouse Daycare Ctr., 1991-95, sec., 1992, v.p., 1993, pres. 1994; Leadership Clarksville; participant UN conf. juvenile drug prevention, 1994. Named Internat. Man of the Yr. Internat. Biog. Ctr., Cambridge, Eng., 1992, Outstanding Young Alumnus, Middle Tenn. State U., 1999. Mem. ABA (juvenile justice com. nat. chmn. 1990-92, nat. vice chmn. litigation 1992-93), Tenn. Assn. Criminal Def. Lawyers (chmn. juvenile justice com. 1991-95, chmn. ethics com. 1995-97—), Montgomery County Young Lawyers (pres. 1991—), Tenn.Bar Assn. (assoc. gen. counsel 1995-2001, Pro Bono Atty. of Yr. 2001), Tenn. Young Lawyers Conf. (bd. dirs. 1992-94). Democrat. Office: 331 Franklin St Ste 1 Clarksville TN 37040-3448 E-mail: gregorydsmith@prodigy.net.

SMITH, GREGORY ROBERT, engineer, educator, marketing consultant; b. Detroit, May 31, 1956; s. Robert Freeman and Constance Fay (Lewis) S.; m. Lori A. Anglewicz, Sept. 22, 1976; 1 child, Timothy T. BS in Liberal Arts, SUNY, Albany, 1987; MS in Adminstrn., Ctrl. Mich. U., 1990; BS in Engring. Tech., Lawrence Tech. U., 1992; MA in Edn., U. Phoenix, Ariz., 1998. Layout designer Wicks Inc., Ferndale, Mich., 1977-82; tech. coord. Colombo Sales & Engring., 1982-83; designer Modern Engring., Warren, Mich., 1983-85; project engr. TRW Inc., Sterling Heights, 1985—. Owner, mgr. Sterling Gems, Sterling Heights, 1984—; owner Classic Emporium, Sterling Heights, 2000—; v.p. mktg. Applied Controls Tech., Dearborn Heights, Mich., 1996—, bus. cons., 1996-97; mem. faculty U. Phoenix, Southfield, Mich., 1997—, Davenport U.; profl. musician One Beat Back band; instr. Rochester Coll.; asst. dir. student devel. Davenport U., 1999. Author: Technical Promotion: Is the Dual Ladder a Solution to Promotion Professionals, 1992, The Simple Guide for Starting Your Own Business, 1997. Reading tutor Macomb Literacy Project; mem. bd. determination Macomb County Pub. Works Dept., Clinton Twp., Mich., 1996; asst. den leader Boy Scouts Am., Sterling Heights, 1997; mem. alumni com. Lawrence Tech. U., 1997. Mem. Toastmasters (adminstrv. v.p. 1990, Competent Toastmaster award 1988). Achievements include patent pending on automotive component. Avocations: reading tutoring, model building, bicycling. Home: 39534 Farnum Ct Sterling Heights MI 48310-2701 E-mail: gsgem@prodigy.net.

SMITH, GREGORY WHITE, writer; b. Ithaca, N.Y., Oct. 4, 1951; s. William R. and Kathryn (White) S. BA, Colby Coll., 1973; JD, Harvard U., 1977, MEd, 1980. Bar: Mass., 1980. Fellow Thomas J. Watson, 1973-74; pres. Woodward/White, Inc. Author: (with Steven Naifeh) Moving Up in Style, 1980, Gene Davis, 1981, How to Make Love to a Woman, 1982, What Every Client Needs to Know About Using a Lawyer, 1982, The Bargain Hunter's Guide to Art Collecting, 1982, Why Can't Men Open Up?: Overcoming Men's Fear of Intimacy, 1984, The Mormon Murders: A True Story of Greed, Forgery, Deceit, and Death, 1988, Jackson Pollock: An American Saga, 1989 (Nat. Book award nomination for nonfiction 1990, Pulitzer Prize for biography 1991), Final Justice: The True Story of the Richest Man Ever Tried for Murder, 1993, A Stranger in the Family: A True Story of Murder, Madness, and Unconditional Love, 1995, On a Street Called Easy, In a Cottage Called Joye: A Restoration Comedy, 1996, Making Miracles Happen, 1997; editor: (with Naifeh) The Best Lawyers in America, The Best Doctors in America. Chmn. Aiken Historic Preservation Commn. Office: Woodward/White 129 First Ave SW Aiken SC 29801 E-mail: gsmith@bestlawyers.com.

SMITH, GRIFFIN, editor; b. Fayetteville, Ark., June 29, 1941; s. Griffin and Mildred Smith; m. Mary Elizabeth Routh, Sept. 1, 1979. BA in History, Rice U., 1963; MA in Polit. Sci., Columbia U., 1965; postgrad. in philosophy, Oxford U., 1966; JD, U. Tex., 1969. Bar: Tex. 1969, U.S. Dist. Ct. (ea., we., no. and so. dists.) Tex. 1969, Ark. 1981, U.S. Dist. Ct. (ea. and we. dists.) Ark. 1981. Spl. asst. to Senator Fulbright U.S. Senate, Washington, 1968-69; atty. estate and gift tax div. IRS, Houston, 1970; rsch. dir. Tex. gubernatorial campaign Paul Eggers, 1970; chief counsel constl. amendments com. Tex. Senate, 1971, chief counsel drug law reform com., 1971-73; editor natural areas survey Lyndon B. Johnson Sch. Pub. Affairs U. Tex., Austin, 1973-77; speech writer Pres. of U.S., 1977-78; ptnr. Smith & Nixon (formerly Smith, Smith, Nixon & Duke), Little Rock, 1984-92. Author: (book) A Consumer Viewpoint on Taxation, 1971, Marijuana in Texas, 1972, The Best of Texas Monthly, 1978, Texas Monthly's Political Reader, 1978, 1980, Journey into China, 1982, Forgotten Texas: A Wilderness Portfolio, 1983, The Great State of Texas, 1985; sr. editor: Tex. Monthly Mag., 1973—77, exec. editor: Ark. Dem. Gazette Newspaper, 1992—. Fellow Woodrow Wilson, 1964. Mem.: Tex. Inst. Letters (award for best work of journalism in Tex. 1974, 1976), State Bar Tex. Episcopalian-Reformed. Office: Ark Dem Gazette 121 E Capitol Ave Little Rock AR 72201-3819

SMITH, GROVER C(LEVELAND), English language educator; b. Atlanta, Sept. 6, 1923; s. Grover C. and Lillian Julia (McDaniel) S.; m. Phyllis Jean Snyder, June 19, 1948 (div. 1965); children: Alice Elizabeth, Charles Grover; m. Dulcie Barbara Soper, Dec. 29, 1965; children: Stephen Kenneth, Julia Margaret. BA with honors, Columbia U., 1944, MA, 1945, PhD (Alexander M. Proudfit fellow), 1950. Instr. English Rutgers U., 1946-48, Yale U., 1948-52; instr. English Duke U., 1952-55, asst. prof., 1955-61, asso. prof., 1961-66, prof., 1966-93; prof. emeritus, 1993—. Mem. summer faculty CUNY, 1946, 47, 48, Columbia U., 1963, 64, NYU, 1963, Wake Forest U., 1966, vis. lectr., 1963, 64 Author: T.S. Eliot's Poetry and Plays: A Study in Sources and Meaning, 1956 (Poetry Chapbook award) rev. 1974, Archibald MacLeish, 1971, Ford Madox Ford, 1972, The Waste Land, 1983, T.S. Eliot and the Use of Memory, 1996; editor: Josiah Royce's Seminar, 1913-1914: As Recorded in the Notebooks of Harry T. Costello, 1963, Letters of Aldous Huxley, 1969. Mem. Christian Gauss Award com., 1973-75; mem. com. of sponsors Sir Julian Huxley Tribute, N.Y. Soc. for Ethical Culture, 1975. With U.S. Army, 1943. Guggenheim fellow, 1958; Am. Philos. Soc. grantee, 1965; Am. Learned Socs. grantee, 1965; Nat. Endowment Humanities grantee, 1979; fellow, 1980 Mem. T.S. Eliot Soc. (hon., Eliot Meml. Lectr. 1986, bd. dirs. 1986-94, 96-99, v.p. 1986-88, editor News and Notes, 1987-88, 90-91, pres. 1989-91, supr. elections 1992-94, sec. 1996-99), Am. Lit. Assn. (rep. to coun.of Am. Author Socs. 1990-91), Nat. Assn. Scholars. Office: Duke U Dept English PO Box 90015 Durham NC 27708-0015

SMITH, HAMILTON OTHANEL, molecular biologist, educator; b. N.Y.C., N.Y., Aug. 23, 1931; s. Bunnie Othanel and Tommie Harkey S.; m. Elizabeth Anne Bolton, May 25, 1957; children: Joel, Barry, Dirk, Bryan, Kirsten. Student, U. Ill., 1948-50; AB in Math, U. Calif., Berkeley, 1952; MD, Johns Hopkins U., 1956. Intern Barnes Hosp., St. Louis, 1956-57; resident in medicine Henry Ford Hosp., Detroit, 1959-62; USPHS fellow dept. human genetics U. Mich., Ann Arbor, 1962-64, rsch. assoc., 1964-67; asst. prof. molecular biology and genetics Sch. Medicine Johns Hopkins U., Balt., 1967-69, assoc. prof., 1969-73, prof., 1973—, emeritus prof. molecular biology and genetics; scientist Celera Genomics. Asso. Inst. für Molekularbologie der U. Zurich, Switzerland, 1975-76; assoc. Rsch. Inst. Molecular Pathology, Vienna, 1990-91; trustee The Inst. for Genomic Rsch. Contbr. articles to profl. jours. Served to lt. M.C. USNR, 1957-59. Recipient Nobel Prize in medicine, 1978; Guggenheim fellow, 1975-76 Mem. Am. Soc. Microbiology, AAAS, Am. Soc. Biol. Chemists, Nat. Acad. Sci.*

SMITH, HARMON LEE, JR. clergyman, moral theology educator; b. Ellisville, Miss., Aug. 23, 1930; s. Harmon Lee Sr. and Mary (O'Donnell) S.; children: Pamela Lee, Amy Joanna, Harmon Lee III. AB, Millsaps Coll., 1952; BD, Duke U., 1955, PhD, 1962. Ordain to priest Episcopal Ch., 1972. Asst. dean Duke U. Divinity Sch., Durham, N.C., 1959-65, asst. prof. Christian ethics, 1962-68, assoc. prof. moral theology, 1968-73, prof. moral theology, 1973-99, prof. community and family medicine, 1974-99, ret., 1999, prof. emeritus moral theology and cmty. family medicine. Cons. med. ethics; vis. prof. U. N.C., 1964, 70, 72, U. Edinburgh, Scotland, 1969, U. Windsor, Ont., 1974 Author books on Christian theology, ethics and med. ethics; sr. editor Social Science and Medicine, 1973-89; contbr. articles on Christian ethics to various publs. Lilly Found. fellow, 1960; Gurney Harris Kearns Found. fellow, 1961; Nat. Humanities Ctr. fellow, 1982-83 Mem. Am. Assn. Theol. Schs., Am. Soc. Christian Ethics, Am. Acad. Religion, Soc. for Religion in Higher Edn., Soc. Health and Human Values. Home: 3510 Randolph Rd Durham NC 27705-5347 E-mail: orare@aol.com.

SMITH, HAROLD CHARLES, private pension fund executive; b. N.Y.C., Jan. 11, 1934; s. Harold Elmore and Hedwig Agnes (Gronke) S. BA cum laude with honors, Ursinus Coll., 1955; MBA, NYU, 1958; M in Div., Union Theol. Sem., N.Y.C., 1958; DD (hon.), 1993; DD (hon.), Ursinus Coll., 1997; DHum (hon.), Springfield Coll., 1998. CFA; ordained minister United Ch. Christ, 1959. V.p. YMCA Retirement Fund, Inc., N.Y.C., 1958-69, portfolio mgr., 1960—, assoc. sec., 1969-77, v.p., 1977-80, exec. v.p., 1980-82, pres. elect, 1982-83, pres., 1983-2000; assoc. prof. bus. and fin. L.I. U., 1969-71. Trustee Bank Mart, Bridgeport, Conn., 1983-91; bd. dirs. Y Mut. Ins. Co., treas. 1988—. Author: Getting It All Together in Retirement, 1977. Trustee YWCA

Greater Bridgeport, 1975—79, Pension Funds United Ch. of Christ, 1968—, Springfield Coll., Mass., 1983—, United Ch. Found., 1968—, vice chmn., 1995—98, chmn., 1998—99; pastor 1st E&R Ch., Bridgeport, Conn., 1958—88, Unity Hill United Ch. of Christ, 1988—2000, treas., 1988—; pastor 1st Congl. Ch., Union, NJ, 2001—; bd. dirs. United Ch. Residencies, 1962—65; bd. dirs. YMCA Greater N.Y., 1983—97, Bridgeport Area Found., 1989—2000, Ursinus Coll., Pa., 1994—. Coun. of Chs. Greater Bridgeport, 1995—96, Silver Bay Christian Conf. Ctr., 1997. Mem. Am. Econs. Assn., N.Y. Soc. Security Analysts, Fin. Analysts Fedn., World and Trade Club, Masons, Order Ea. Star. E-mail: hcsmith1@email.msn.com.

SMITH, HAROLD RAYMOND, neurologist, sleep medicine specialist, educator; b. Detroit, Dec. 15, 1953; s. Raymond Harold Smith and Veronica Bernice Zawacki; m. Margaret Mary Demaria, May 20, 1977. BS, U. Mich., 1975, MD, 1979. Diplomate Am. Bd. Neurology, Am. Bd. Sleep Medicine. Intern in internal medicine Henry Ford Hosp., Detroit, 1979-80; resident, chief resident U. Calif.-Irvine, Orange, 1980-83, attending faculty mem., 1983—, fellow in sleep medicine, 1984-85, mem. clin. faculty, 1983-86, asst. clin. prof., 1986-94, assoc. clin. prof., 1994-99, clin. prof., 1999—; pvt. practice neurology Irvine, 1983—. Cln. polysomnographer Hoag Hosp. Sleep Ctr., Newport Beach, Calif., 1986—, exec. com. U. Calif. Irvine clin. faculty assn. Contbr. chpts. to textbooks, articles to profl.jours. Fellow Am. Acad. Sleep Medicine, Am. Acad. Neurology (founding mem. sleep sect., chmn. edn. com. 1999, mem. exec. com. 1999—); mem. Am. Assn. Electrodiagnostic Medicine, Am. Coll. Sports Medicine, Clin. Faculty Assn. U. Calif. Irvine (exec. com. adminstrv. coun. 2000—, pres.-elect 2002--), Irvine C. of C. Avocation: competitive long distance running. Office: U Calif-Irvine 4199 Campus Dr Ste 350 Irvine CA 92612-8603

SMITH, HAROLD ALLEN, education administrator, researcher, educator; b. Franklin, La., Nov. 28, 1944; s. Bernie Lloyd and Lily Madge (Thompson) S.; m. Pheny Shang Fen Zhou, May 27, 1985. MusB in Edn., Delta State U., 1966; MDiv, New Orleans Bapt. Theol. Sem., 1977; MEd, Ariz. State U., 1984; EdD, Miss. State U., 1989. Educator Matthews/Doniphan (Mo.) Schs., 1966-70, Phoenix Pub. Schs., 1970-71; pvt. sch. educator John Curtis Schs., New Orleans, 1974-77; founder, dir. Chattanooga Assn. for Resettlement, 1977-83; adult educator Phoenix Union High Sch. Dist., 1983-84; vis. prof. Cen. Fgn. Expert Bur., Beijing, People's Republic of China, 1984-86; dir. China study program Miss. State U., 1986-90, editor Internat. Newsletter, 1987-89, program coord. Asian Studies Ctr., 1990-92; editor Miss. Meets Asia, 1990-92; program coord. ESL Ctr., 1991-92; prof., divsn. chair Shenandoah U., 1993-2000; pres. Shenandoah Enterprises Editing, Writing & Pub. Svcs., Alexandria, Va., 2000—. Cons. AMG Internat., Chattanooga, 1977-79, Chattanooga Area Literacy Movement, 1979-83; vis. prof. Georgetown U., 1992—, Notre Dame Seishin Coll. (Japan), 1993. Author: Education and Culture in China, 1988, Mississippi Agriculture and World Hunger, 1988; editor: International Experience and Relationships, 1988, International Student Handbook, 1991, AMTESOL Newsletter, 1991-92, AMTESOL Jour., 1991-92, WATESOL News, 1997—, TESLEJ, 1999—, BRIEFME, 1999—, TESOL Matters, 1998-99; contbr. numerous articles to profl. jours. Bd. dirs. Chattanooga Area Literacy Movement, 1979-83, Maricopa Refugee Com., Phoenix, 1983-84. With U.S. Army, 1971-74. Mem. NAFSA: Assn. Internat. Educators, Tchrs. of English to Speakers of Other Langs., Japan Assn. Of Lang. Tchrs., Washington Area Tchrs. of English to Speakers of Other Langs., Ala.-Miss. Tchrs. of English to Speakers of Other Langs., Assn. Tchr. Educators, Mid-South Edn. Rsch. Assn., Assn. Multicultural Counseling and Devel., Assn. Comparative and Internat. Edn. (also So. and Western orgns.), Ea. Ednl. Rsch. Assn., Kiwanis (bd. dirs. breakfast club Starkville, Miss. chpt. 1988-89), Phi Delta Kappa. Republican. Baptist. Avocations: travel, tennis, running, reading. Office: Shenandoah Enterprises Box U501 8 S Van Dorn St Dr Alexandria VA 22304-4228 E-mail: hsmith_44@onebox.com.

SMITH, HAROLD B. manufacturing executive; b. Chgo., Apr. 7, 1933; s. Harold Byron and Pauline (Hart) S. Grad., Choate Sch., 1951; BS, Princeton U., 1955; MBA, Northwestern U., 1957. With Ill. Tool Works, Inc., Chgo., 1954—, exec. v.p., 1968-72, pres., 1972-81, vice chmn., 1981, chmn. exec. com., 1982—, also bd. dirs. Bd. dirs. W.W. Grainger, Inc., No. Trust Corp.; trustee Northwestern Mut. Life Ins. Co. Mem. Rep. Nat. Com., 1976-99; chmn. Ill. Rep. Com., 1993-99; del. Rep. Nat. Conv., 1964, 76, 88, 92, 96, 2000; bd. dirs. Adler Planetarium, Boys and Girls Clubs Am., Northwestern U., Rush-Presbyn.-St. Luke's Med. Ctr., Newberry Libr. Mem.: Chicago, Commercial, Commonwealth, Economic, Northwestern, Princeton (Chgo.). Office: Ill Tool Works Inc 3600 W Lake Ave Glenview IL 60025-5811

SMITH, HARRIET GWENDOLYN GURLEY, secondary school educator, writer; b. Goldsboro, N.C., Nov. 14, 1927; d. Charles Harvey and Sadye Reid (Morris) Gurley; m. Albert Goodin Smith, Aug. 29, 1953; children: Susan Reid Smith Erba, Alan English Smith. Grad., St. Mary's Coll., Raleigh, N.C., 1946; BA, U. N.C., 1948; MEd, La. State U., Shreveport, 1982. Cert. tchr., N.C., La. Tchr. English, Journalism, Social Studies Goldsboro City Schs., 1948-49, Rocky Mount (N.C.) City Schs., 1949-51, Durham (N.C.) City Schs., 1951-53, Durham County Schs., 1954-56; realtor assoc. Sam Fullilove and Assocs., Shreveport, 1984-87; contbg. editor, columnist The New Front Gallery Mag., 1988. Bridge tchr. Caddo Magnet High Sch., La. State U., Woman's Dept. Club, pvt. groups, 1978—. Pres. Shreveport Med. Soc. Aux., 1985-86, chmn. various coms., 1970—; pres. Faculty Women's Club La. State U. Med. Ctr., 1990; mem. women's bd. dirs. Centenary Coll.; active United Meth. Women, Symphony Guild, Opera Guild, Rep. Women. Mem. Am. Contract Bridge League (life master, cert. tchr.), Am. Bridge Tchrs. Assn. (master tchr., tchg. del. to Russia 1994), La. Real Estate Commn., Bull and Bear Stock Club (sec. 1973-74, pres. 1975-76), Kappa Delta Pi. Avocations: travel, cultural activities, tennis, health and fitness, volunteer work. Home: 8502 Rampart Pl Shreveport LA 71106-6226 E-mail: hsmith39@msn.com.

SMITH, HARRISON HARVEY, journalism consultant; b. Wilkes-Barre, Pa., Oct. 24, 1915; s. Ernest Gray and Marjorie (Harvey) S.; m. Joanne Christopher, June 7, 1940 (div.); children: Barbara DeWitt, Marjorie Harvey, Susan C. (dec. 1999); m. Margaret Simons, July 18, 1947 (dec. May 1978); children: Rosanne Jameson, Elizabeth Simons; m. Dorothy Wright Welborn, June 22, 1989. Diploma in lit., Wyoming (Pa.) Sem., 1936; postgrad., Northwestern U., 1937-38. Asst. to pub. Wilkes-Barre Times-Leader, 1938-39, v.p., asst. sec., 1939-46, pres., 1946-79; editor Wilkes-Barre Record, 1962-72; newspaper cons. Key Biscayne, Fla., 1979—. Dir. emeritus 1st Ea. Bank Wilkes-Barre; pres. Pa. AP, 1953. Chmn. Wyoming Valley ARC, 1954-55; v.p. bd. dirs. Wilkes-Barre Gen. Hosp., 1954-76. With U.S. Army, 1945-46, Korea. Mem. Am. Soc. Newspaper Editors, Nat. Conf. Editl. Writers, Soc. Profl. Journalists, Pa. Newspaper Pubs. Assn. (mem. exec. com. 1954-62), Wyoming Valley Hist. Soc. (pres. 1971-74), Newcomen Soc., Am. Legion, VFW, Poor Richard Club (Phila.), Mirador Club (Geneva), Westmoreland Club, Sankaty Head Golf and Beach Club (Nantucket Island, Mass.), Country Club Coral Gables, Key Biscayne Yacht Club, Masons (33 degree). Republican. Presbyterian. Home and Office: 177 Ocean Lane Dr Apt 811 Key Biscayne FL 33149-1427 also: 10 Lyons Ln PO Box 180 Siasconset MA 02564-0180

SMITH, HARRY BUCHANAN, JR. graphic designer, painter, photographer, writer; b. Springfield, Ill., Aug. 30, 1924; s. Harry Buchanan and Cordelia Warren (Birchall) S.; divorced; 1 child, Mark Savolainen. B of Design, U. Mich., 1947; MS, ITT Inst. Design, 1948. Designer Chgo. Plan Commn., 1948-49, Warren Wetheral & Assocs., Chgo., 1949-50; dir. design Dekovic-Smith Design Orgn., 1951-58; prin. H.B. Smith & Assocs., 1959-87. Author: Contemporary Fables, 1988; works include graphic design (with Mortimer Adler) Encyclopaedia Britannica, 15th edit., 1975, 176 exhibitions, 1951-87; redesigned YMCA internat. symbol, numerous corporate identity programs, publs.; photographer Objects in Crisis (series); artist numerous mixed media. Lt. (j.g.) USNR, 1943-47, PTO. Mem. Am. Inst. Graphic Arts, Am. Ctr. for Design (steering com.). Home and Office: 2417 N Burling St Chicago IL 60614-2615 E-mail: aristotl@runchicago.com.

SMITH, HARRY LEROY, securities firm executive; b. Waukegan, Ill., Nov. 7, 1909; s. Thomas William and Louise (Krantz) S.; m. Laura Sloo Johnson, Apr. 21, 1938; children: Harry Leroy, William Bridges. Student diplomatic studies, Ecole libre des scis. polit., Paris, 1930-31; BS, Georgetown U., 1933; MA, George Washington U., 1933, postgrad., 1939; LLB, Southeastern U., 1936. Bar: D.C. 1936. With Dist. Nat. Bank, Washington, 1928-29, U.S. Dept. Treasury, Washington, 1929-30, FBI, Washington, 1930, Dept. State, Washington, 1931-32; chief editl. sect. procurement divsn. U.S. Dept. Treasury, 1934-36, planning officer, 1936-40, chief surplus property divsn., 1940-41, chief econ. analysis divsn., 1941; gen. staff officer, chief G-2 dissemination and functional intelligence Army Gen. Staff, 1941—44, cons., 1947-48; asst., acting mil. attache Am. Embassy, Chile, 1944-46; exec. asst., dir. materials supply program Housing Expeditor's Office, 1946-47; commd. fgn. svc. officer Dept. State, 1948; consul Shanghai, 1948-49, Hong Kong, 1949-51; first sect., consul, comml. attache Am. Embassy, Baghdad, Iraq, 1951-53, first sect., consul Athens, Greece, 1953-56; internat. economist Dept. of State, Washington, 1956-58. Bd. chmn., CEO Halaro Products, Inc., Silver Spring, 1982-85, H.L. Smith Co., Silver Spring, 1959-84, investment securities, 1985—; chmn. bd. Smith & Lawrence Co., Arlington, Va., 1984-85; prof. econs. Southeastern U., Washington, 1956-64, asst. dean jr. coll., 1960-64; gen. agt. Std. Life of Ind., Silver Spring, 1960-70; mem. various presdl. commns. and joint Army-Navy coms. Contbr. articles to various publs. With USMC, 1929—32. Mem. Pi Gamma Mu (pres. 1931-33), Delta Phi Epsilon. Libertarian. Episcopalian. Home and Office: 3708 Scenic Dr Cibolo TX 78108-2229

SMITH, HARRY MENDELL, JR. science educator; b. Wichita, Kans., Aug. 19, 1943; s. H. Mendell and Sevilla Mae (Cooper) S.; m. Cecile Marie Adams, Sept. 19, 1964; children: Jeff, Shauna, Noelle. AA, Pasadena Coll., 1966; BA, Calif. State U., L.A., 1970; Vocat. Credential, UCLA, 1979. Tchr. Glendora (Calif.) Unified Schs., 1970-80; instr. Citrus Coll., Azusa, Calif., 1978-82; mgr. Christian Chapel, Walnut, 1980-82; pres. Whitmore Printing, Inc., La Puente, 1982-85; mgr. Evang. Free Ch., Fullerton, 1985-87; prof. Mt. San Antonio Coll., Walnut, 1985—, chair divsn. applied sci. and tech., 1993-2000; prof. physics Biola U., La Mirada, Calif., 1998-2000; instr. sci. Biola Star program. Dir. Faculty Senate, Mt. San Antonio Coll., 1989-91; assoc. dean applied tech. and health sci., Mt. San Antonio Coll., summer 2000. Author: Electronic Devices and Circuits Lab Book, 1994, Experiments in DC/AC Circuits, 1998, Technical Applications in Microcomputers Using Microsoft Office, 2000. Treas. Sojourner Evangelical Free Ch., Fullerton, 1996-98. Chancellor's Office Electronic Tech. grantee, 1990. Mem. Nat. Assn. Radio and Telecommunications Engrs., Home Bldrs. Fellowship (pres. 1990-92), Skills USA-VICA (nat. advisor 2001—), Vocat. Indsl. Clubs Am. (region 3 coord. post secondary 1997—), Calif. Coun. Electronics Instrs. (sec. to bd. dirs. 1997-2000). Republican. Avocations: music, numismatics, electronics, physical fitness, solar energy. Home: 6373 Carter St Chino CA 91710-5390 Office: Mt San Antonio Coll 1100 N Grand Ave Walnut CA 91789 E-mail: hsmith@mtsac.edu.

SMITH, HARVEY ALVIN, mathematics educator, consultant; b. Easton, Pa., Jan. 30, 1932; s. William Augustus and Ruth Carolyn (Krauth) S.; m. Ruth Wismer Kolb, Aug. 27, 1955; children: Deirdre Lynn, Kirsten Nadine, Brinton Averil. BS, Lehigh U., 1952; MS, U. Pa., 1955, AM, 1958, PhD, 1964. Asst. prof. math Drexel U., 1960-65; mem. tech. staff Inst. Def. Analyses, Arlington, Va., 1965-66; assoc. prof. math Oakland U., 1966-68; ops. research scientist Exec. Office of Pres., Washington, 1968-70; prof. math. Oakland U., 1970-77; prof. Ariz. State U., Tempe, 1977—; cons. Inst. Def. Analyses, 1967-69, Exec. Office Pres., 1967-73, U.S. Arms Control and Disarmament Agy, 1973-79, Los Alamos Nat. Lab., 1980-93. Author: Mathematical Foundations of Systems Analysis, 1969. NSF fellow, 1964-65; recipient Meritorious Service award Exec. Office of Pres., 1970 Mem. Soc. Indsl. and Applied Math., Am. Math. Soc., AAAS, Sigma Xi Home: 18 E Concorda Dr Tempe AZ 85282-3517 Office: Ariz State U Dept Math Tempe AZ 85287-1804 E-mail: hsmith@math.la.asu.edu.

SMITH, HEATHER LYNN, psychotherapist, recreational therapist; b. Modesto, Calif., May 31, 1956; d. Gary Fremont and Marilyn Rae (Brown) S. BS, Calif. State U., Fresno, 1979; MA, U. San Francisco, 1989. Lic. marriage, family and child counselor, Calif. Recreational therapist Casa Colina Rehab. Hops., Pomona, Calif., 1979-82; evaluator developmentally delayed, coord. family edn. Cath. Charities, Modesto, 1982-87; bereavement counselor Hospice, 1983-87; high risk youth counselor Ctr. Human Svcs., 1987—; pvt. practice, family therapist, 1988—. Program dir. chemically dependent treatment program Stanislaus County Juvenile Hall, 1990—; program adminstr. First Step, 1999—. Named Outstanding Young Woman of Stanislaus County, 1986, Citizen of Yr., Civitan, 1986, Outstanding Individual award Stanislaus County, 1992. Mem. Calif. Assn. Marriage and Family Therapists, Kappa Kappa Gamma. Republican. Episcopalian. Avocations: skiing, running, backpacking, tennis. Home: 806 Claratina Ave Modesto CA 95356-9610 Office: PO Box 577456 Modesto CA 95357-7456 E-mail: serenity.mft@aol.com.

SMITH, HEDRICK LAURENCE, journalist, television producer, correspondent, author, lecturer; b. Kilmacolm, Scotland, July 9, 1933; s. Sterling L. and Phebe (Hedrick) S.; m. Ann Bickford, June 29, 1957 (div. Dec. 1985); children: Laurel Ann, Jennifer Laurence, Sterling Scott, Lesley Roberts; m. Susan Zox, Mar. 7, 1987. BA, Williams Coll., 1955, LittD (hon.), 1975; postgrad. (Fulbright scholar), Balliol Coll., Oxford, Eng., 1955-56; LittD (hon.), Wittenburg U., 1985, N.H. Coll., 1991; LHD (hon.), Columbia Coll., 1992; LittD (hon.), Amherst Coll., 1992; LHD (hon.), U. S.C., 1992; LittD (hon.), Furman U., 1996. With U.P.I., Memphis, Nashville, Atlanta, 1959-62; with N.Y. Times, 1962-88, Washington and S.E., 1962-63, Vietnam, 1963-64; Middle East corr. N.Y. Times, Cairo, U.A.R., 1964-66, diplomatic news corr. Washington, 1962-64, 66-71, Moscow Bur. chief, 1971-74, dep. nat. editor, 1975-76, Washington Bur. chief, 1976-79, chief Washington corr., 1980-85; Washington correspondent N.Y. Times mag., 1987-88. Vis. journalist Am. Enterprise Inst., 1985-87; fellow Fgn. Policy Inst., Johns Hopkins U. Sch Advanced Internat. Studies, 1989-97; panelist Washington Week in Rev., PBS, 1969-95. Author: The Russians, 1975 (Overseas Press Club award, 1976), The Power Game: How Washington Works, 1988, The New Russians, 1990 (Overseas Press Club citation, 1991), Rethinking America, 1995; co-author: The Pentagon Papers, 1972, Reagan the Man, the President, 1981, Beyond Reagan: The Politics of Upheaval, 1986, Seven Days That Shook the World, 1991, (TV documentaries) Star Wars, 1985, Moscow Jews, 1986, Space Bridge, Chernobyl: Three Mile Island, 1987, 4-part Power Game series, PBS, 1989, Countdown to White House: The Bush Transition, 1989, 4-part series Inside Gorbachev's USSR, 1990 (George Polk award, Gold Baton award Columbia-DuPont), Guns, Tanks and Gorbachev, 1991, Soviets, 1991 (George Peabody award), 4-part series PBS, Challenge to America, 1994 (Cine Golden Eagle award, Rias award), Across the River pub. TV program, 1995 (Hillman award), The People and the Power Game, 1996 (Silver award Houston Film Festival), Surviving the Bottom Line, 1998 (Cine Golden Eagle award, Flagstaff Film Festival Bronze award), Seeking Solutions, 1999 (nat. award for pub. svc. Sigma Delta Chi, spl. gold medal Houston Film Festival), Duke Ellington's Washington, 2000 (N.Y. Film Festival Bronze prize), Critical Condition, 2000 (Emmy nomination), Dr. Solomon's Ontemma, 2000 (Chris award), Juggling Work and Family, 2001, Rediscovering Dave Brubeck, 2001, Inside the Terror Network (Frontline), 2002, Why Didn't the Watchdogs Bark? (Frontline), 2002. Trustee Williams Coll., 1982-97; mem. Aspen Inst. Domestic Strategy Group, 1997-2002. With USAF, 1956-59. Recipient Pulitzer prize for pub. svc. Pentagon Papers Series, 1972, for internat. reporting from Soviet Union and Ea. Europe, 1974, William Allen White award U. Kans., 1996; Nieman fellow Harvard U., 1969-70. Mem. Gridiron Club, Phi Beta Kappa. E-mail: hsmithprod@aol.com.

SMITH, HELEN ELIZABETH, retired career officer; b. San Rafael, Calif., Aug. 11, 1946; d. Jack Dillard and Marian Elizabeth (Miller) S. BA in Geography, Calif. State U., Northridge, 1968; MA in Internat. Rels., Salve Regina, Newport, R.I., 1983; MS in Tech. Comm., Rensselaer Poly. Inst., 1988; postgrad., Naval War Coll., 1982-83. Commd. ensign USN, 1968, advanced through grades to capt., 1989; adminstrv. asst. USN Fighter Squadron 101, Key West, Fla., 1969-70; adminstrv. officer Fleet Operational Tng. Group, Mountain View, Calif., 1970-72; leader human resource team Human Resource Ctr., Rota, Spain, 1977-79; adminstrv. officer Pearl Harbor (Hawaii) Naval Sta., 1979-80; dir. Family Svc. Ctr., Pearl Harbor, 1980-82; officer-in-charge R&D lab. Naval Ocean Systems Ctr., Kaneohe, Hawaii, 1983-85; exec. officer Naval ROTC, assoc. prof. Rensselaer Poly. Inst., Troy, N.Y., 1985-88; comdg. officer Navy Alcohol Rehab. Ctr., Norfolk, Va., 1988-90; faculty mem., commanding officer Naval Adminstrv. Command, dean adminstrv. support, comptr. Armed Forces Staff Coll., 1990-93; ret., 1993; exec. dir. Calif. for Drug-Free Youth, 1995-96. Author: (walking tour) Albany's Historic Pastures, 1987; composer (cantata) Night of Wonder, 1983. Chair Hawaii State Childcare Com., Honolulu, 1981-82; coun. mem. Hist. Pastures Neighborhood Assn., Albany, N.Y., 1985-88; mem. working group Mayors Task Force on Drugs, Norfolk, 1989-90; chair, bd. dirs. Va. Coun. on Alcoholism, 1989-92, Calif. for Drug Free Youth, 1995-96; singer North County Baroque Ensemble; assoc. Westar Inst. Avocation: writing. Home: 952 Frederico Blvd Belen NM 87002-7027 E-mail: capthelen@webeworld.com.

SMITH, HELEN MARIE, social worker, hospital administrator; b. Atlanta, Nov. 9, 1946; d. Walter James Ervin and Maxine (Whitehill) S.; m. Charles Alan Smith, Aug. 17, 1968. BA in Sociology, Miami U., Ohio, 1977; M in Social Work, U. Cin., 1984. Acting dir. ARC, Lawrenceburg, Ind., 1977; children's protective svc. worker Butler County Welfare Dept., Hamilton, Ohio, 1978-80; psychiatric social worker Fort Hamilton Hughes Meml. Hosp., 1980-82, dir. social svcs., 1982—. Pres., bd. trustees Hospice of Miami Valley, Inc., Hamilton, Ohio, 1990—. Mem. NASW, Soc. for Hosp. Social Work Dirs. Am. Hosp. Assn. (nominee for Social Work Dir. of Yr.). Avocations: sailing, music, reading, walking. Office: Ft Hamilton Hughes Hosp 630 Eaton Ave Hamilton OH 45013-2767

SMITH, HELENA ROBINSON, event planner, fund raiser; b. L.A., Apr. 13, 1939; d. James Clarence and Clara Alice Robinson; m. Steven E. Smith, Nov. 17, 1962 (dec. Oct. 1998); children: Steven E. Jr., Jennifer A., Catherine K., James R. Student, De Montfort U., 1957-58. Stewardess West Airlines, Calif., 1960-61; first v.p. Anne Banning Assistance League of So. Calif., 1977, chmn. Christmas benefit, 1977, chmn. operation sch. bell, 1978; chmn. cmty. project Nat. Charity League, Calif., 1981-82; assisted in founding West Valley Food Bank, 1980-81; asst. mgr. Law Offices of Steven Smith, L.A., 1985-91; realtor assoc. Coldwell Banker, Sherman Oaks, Calif., 1992-93; Rabin dinner planner Reagan Libr., Simi Valley, 1994; asst. developer Walt Disney Concert Hall, L.A., 1995-97; event planner Girls and Boys Town USA, 1998—.

SMITH, HENRY CHARLES, III, symphony orchestra conductor; b. Phila., Jan. 31, 1931; s. Henry Charles Jr. and Gertrude Ruth (Downs) S.; m. Mary Jane Dressner, Sept. 3, 1955; children— Katherine Anne, Pamela Jane, Henry Charles IV. BA, U. Pa., 1952; artist diploma, Curtis Inst. Music, Phila., 1955. Solo trombonist Phila. Orch., 1955-67; condr. Rochester (Minn.) Symphony Orch., 1967-68; assoc. prof. music Ind. U., Bloomington, 1968-71; resident condr., ednl. dir. Minn. Orch., Mpls., 1971-88; prof. music U. Tex., Austin, 1988-89, Frank C. Erwin Centennial Prof. of Opera, 1988-89; music dir. S.D. Symphony, Sioux Falls, 1989-2001; prof. Ariz. State U., Tempe, 1989-93, prof. emeritus, 1993—. Vis. prof. U. Tex., Austin, 1987-88; founding mem. Phila. Brass Ensemble, 1956—; music dir. World Youth Symphony Orch., Interlochen, Mich., 1981-96. Composer 5 books of solos for trombone including Solos for the Trombone Player, 1963, Hear Us As We Pray, 1963, First Solos for the Trombone Player, 1972, Easy Duets for Winds, 1972; editor 14 books 20th century symphonies lit. Served to 1st lt. AUS, 1952-54. Recipient 3 Grammy nominations, 1967, 76, 1 Grammy award for best chamber music rec. with Phila. Brass Ensemble, 1969. Mem. Internat. Trombone Assn. (dir.), Am. Symphony Orch. League, Music Educators Nat. Conf., Am. Guild Organists, Am. Fedn. Musicians, Tubist Universal Brotherhood Assn., Acacia Fraternity. Republican. Congregationalist. Home: 8032 Pennsylvania Rd S Bloomington MN 55438-1135

SMITH, HENRY IGNATIUS, engineering educator; b. Jersey City, May 26, 1937; BS, Holy Cross Coll.; PhD, Boston Coll., 1966. Engr. Lincoln Lab., 1968-77, engrng. mgr., 1977-80; prof. elec. engrng. MIT, Cambridge, Mass., 1980—. Vis. scientist U. Coll., London, 1972, Thompson CSF, Paris, Norwegian Inst. Tech., Trondheim, 1976, Nippon Telephone and Telegraph Corp., Atsugi, Japan, 1990, U. Glasgow, Scotland, 1990, U. Goettingen, Germany, 1999; adj. prof. Submicoron Structure Lab., MIT, 1977-80. Recipient Cledo Brunetti award, 1995, Alexander von Humboldt award, 1999. Fellow IEEE; mem. Nat. Acad. Engrng., Am. Phys. Soc., Am. Vacuum Soc., Materials Rsch. Soc., Sigma Xi. Achievements include research to bring new knowledge of submicron structures, nanofabrication, methods for preparing semiconductor-on-insulator films, electronic devices and quantum effects in sub-100 nm structures. Office: MIT 77 Massachusetts Ave Rm 39-427 Cambridge MA 02139-4307

SMITH, HILARY CRANWELL BOWEN, investment banker; b. Balt., Nov. 1, 1937; s. Henry Bowen and Clayton (Cranwell) S.; m. Janet Simmons, June 9, 1962. BA, Colgate U., 1960; MBA, U. Va., 1967. V.p. Goldman, Sachs & Co., N.Y.C., 1969-74, E. F. Hutton & Co., N.Y.C., 1974-77; sr. v.p. Blyth Eastman Dillon, 1977-79; mng. dir. Salomon Bros., 1979-90, Warburg Dillon Read Inc., N.Y.C., 1990—. Trustee Wheaton Coll. Lt. USN, 1960-63. Office: Warburg Dillon Read Inc 299 Park Ave Fl 36 New York NY 10171-0002

SMITH, HOKE LAFOLLETTE, university president; b. Galesburg, Ill., May 7, 1931; s. Claude Hoke and Bernice (LaFollette) S.; m. Barbara E. Walvoord, June 30, 1979 (div. 2001); children by previous marriage: Kevin, Kerry, Amy, Glen. BA (Harold fellow), Knox Coll., 1953; MA, U. Va., 1954; PhD (fellow 1958), Emory U., 1958; hon. degree, Sung Kyun Kwan U., Korea, 1993, Knox Coll., 1995. Asst. prof. polit. sci. Hiram Coll., Ohio, 1958-64, assoc. prof. polit. sci., 1964-67; asst. to pres., prof. polit. sci. Drake U., Des Moines, 1967-70, chmn. interim governing com., 1971-72, v.p. acad. adminstrn., 1970-79; pres. Towson (Md.) U., 1979—2001, pres. emeritus, 2001—. Vis. prof. U. Md., College Park, 2001—; hon. prof. St. Petersburg Electrotech. U., 2001; mem. univ. adv. council Life Ins. Council Am., 1969-71; mem. task force to study the governance, structure and funding U. Sys. Md., 1998-99. Chmn. exec. com. Coun. Econ. Edn., Md., Towson, 1979—; bd. dirs. Balt. Coun. on Fgn. Rels.; chmn. Very Spl. Arts of Md. With U.S. Army, 1954-56. Recipient Eileen Tosney award Am. Assn. Univ Administrs., 1991; Congl. fellow Am. Polit. Sci. Assn., 1964-65; hon. prof. Electrotech. U., Russia, 2001. Mem. Am. Assn. State Colls. and Univs. (bd. dirs. 1984-88, bd. dirs. found., 1985-87, chmn. elect. 1985-86, chmn. 1986-87), Am. Coun. Edn. (bd. dirs., exec. com. 1988-94, chmn. elect 1991-92, chmn. 1992-93, past chmn. 1993-94), Am. Assn. Higher Edn., Soc. for Coll. and Univ. Planning (bd. dirs. 1986-88), Balt. C. of C. (adv. coun.), Renaissance Group (exec. com.), Met. and Urban Colls. and Univs. (co-chair 1996—), St. Petersburg Internat. Consortium of Colls. and Univs. (co-chair 1997), Phi Beta Kappa, Phi Kappa Phi, Omicron Delta Kappa, Delta Sigma Rho, Gamma Gamma, Pi Sigma Alpha. E-mail: hsmith@towson.edu.

SMITH, H(OWARD) DUANE, zoology educator; b. Fillmore, Utah, June 25, 1941; s. Howard Martell and Mary Ellen (Mitchell) S.; m.. Dahnelle Bower, Dec. 18, 1961; children: Cory, Neichol. BS, Brigham Young U., 1963, MS, 1966; PhD, U. Ill., 1969. From asst. prof. to prof. Brigham Young U., Provo, Utah, 1969—; pvt. practice Orem, 1973—; dir. Monte L. Bean Life Sci. Mus., Provo. Dir. Life Sci. Mus. Co-author: Special Publications-Mammalogy, 1994; contbr. articles to profl. jours. Mem. Am. Soc. Mammalogists (sec.-treas. 1987—), Wildlife Soc., Rocky Mountain Elk Found., Mule Deer Found., Safari Club Internat., Sigma Xi (pres. 1996-97). Republican. Mem. Lds Ch. Avocations: hunting, fishing. Office: Brigham Young Univ 290 MLBM Provo UT 84602-1049 E-mail: Duane@Museum.BYU.EDU.

SMITH, HOWARD RUSSELL, manufacturing company executive; b. Clark County, Ohio, Aug. 15, 1914; s. Lewis Hoskins and Eula (Elder) S.; m. Jeanne Rogers, June 27, 1942; children: Stewart Russell, Douglas Howard, Jeanne Ellen Smith James. AB, Pomona Coll., 1936. Security analyst Kidder, Peabody & Co., N.Y.C., 1936-37; economist ILO, Geneva, 1937-40; asst. to pres. Blue Diamond Corp., Los Angeles, 1940—; v.p., gen. mgr., dir. Avery Dennison Corp., Pasadena, Calif., 1946-56, pres., 1956-75, chmn. bd., 1975-84, chmn. exec. com., 1984-95; dir. emeritus, 1995—; chmn. bd. Kinsmith Fin. Corp., San Marino, Calif., 1979—. Bd. dirs., past pres., chmn. Los Angeles Philharm. Assn.; chmn. emeritus, bd. trustees Pomona Coll., Claremont, Calif.; past chmn. bd. Children's Hosp. Los Angeles, Community TV of So. Calif. (Sta. KCET), Los Angeles. Lt. USNR, 1943-46. Home: 1458 Hillcrest Ave Pasadena CA 91106-4503 Office: Avery Dennison Corp 150 N Orange Grove Blvd Pasadena CA 91103-3534

SMITH, HOWARD THOMPSON, business executive; b. Camden, Ark., Apr. 30, 1937; s. Howard Thompson and Pauline Virginia (Rogers) S.; m. Ann Monroe; children: Paul R., Elizabeth M. BS, Tulane U., 1960; postgrad. studies, La. State U., 1961-63; EPBA, Columbia U., 1978. Dir. planning Ethyl Corp., Baton Rouge, 1970-76; exec. v.p., gen. mgr. William Bonnell Co. subs.

Ethyl Corp., Newman, Ga., 1976-81; pres. Steelcraft, Cin., 1981-84; v.p., group exec. Am. Standard, 1984-89, sr. v.p. N.Y.C., 1989-94, also bd. dirs., 1989—; pres., CEO The Trane Co., 1989-94; mng. ptnr. Septa Assocs., 1994—; gen. ptnr. Rutledge Capital, 2000—. Pres. Thompson Smith Found., 1993—; chmn. bd. dirs. Trinity Mother Francis Health Sys., 1996—, Adobe, 2000—, Framed Picture Enterprises, 1999-,; bd. dirs. CROM Corp. Bd. dirs. Salvation Army, 1988—, Tex. Rsch. League, Austin, 1989, U. Tex., Tyler, 1990—, Mother Francis Hosp. Found., 1991—; chmn. bd. dirs. East Tex. Communities Found., 1993—; elder, trustee 1st Presbyn. Ch.; trustee U. Tex., Tyler, East Tex. Pres. Found., Union Theol. Sem., 1994— Mem. Tex. Assn. Taxpayers (dir.), Smith County C. of C. (bd. dirs. 1988-91), Tyler Petroleum Club, Hollytree Country Club, Willowbrook Country Club, Sawgrass Country Club. Republican. Presbyterian. Avocations: golf, tennis. Home: 6110 Covey Ln Tyler TX 75703-4507 Office: The Trane Co PO Box 9010 Tyler TX 75711-9010 also: 819 Spinnakers Reach Dr Ponte Vedra Beach FL 32082-3408

SMITH, HOWARD WELLINGTON, education educator, dean emeritus; b. Granby, Mo., Jan. 19, 1929; s. Howard W. and Margaret L. (Sanderson) S.; m. Margaret E. Bell, Mar. 1, 1953; 1 child, Christopher Alan. BS, S.W. Mo. State U., 1954; MEd, U. Mo., 1955, EdD, 1959. Tchr. Newton County (Mo.) Pub. Schs., 1948-51; instr. U. Mo., Columbia, 1955-59; asst. prof. So. Meth. U., Dallas, 1959-61; from asst. to full prof. U. North Tex., Denton, 1961-97, dean emeritus. Assoc. dean Coll. Edn. U. North Tex., 1972-76, assoc. v.p. acad. affairs, 1976-79, v.p. acad. affairs, 1979-82, interim dean, 1994-97; interim chancellor U. North Tex. Coll. Osteo. Medicine, Denton and Ft. Worth, 1981; sr. cons. Am. Assn. State Colls. and Univs., Washington, 1982; cons. Srinakharinwirot U., Thailand, 1986, Tex. Internat. Edn. Consortium, Austin, 1992, sr. author Operation Manual Al Akhawayn U., 1993; vis. prof. Shanxi Ednl. Coll. Taiyuan, China, 1993. Contbr. articles to ednl. jours. Prin. investigator Micro Tchg. Lab., 1967—69; chair Ret. Instrs., Pers. and Spouses U. North Tex., 2001; accreditation cons. Art Inst. Dallas, 2001—; chair Denton County Hist. Soc., 1999—; mem. adv. bd. Coll. Edn. U. North Tex., 1997—; mem. adv. bd. Bill J. Priest Ctr. for C.C. Edn., 1999—; pres. bd. dirs. Tex. Lakes Trail, 2002. With USAF, 1951—53. Democrat. Presbyterian. Avocations: travel, reading. Office: U North Tex Coll Edn PO Box 311337 Denton TX 76203-1337

SMITH, HOWELL JACKSON, III, physician assistant; b. Mar. 22, 1956; BS, U. Okla., 1988; M Med. Sci., St. Francis Coll., Loretto, Pa., 1994. Enlisted U.S. Army, 1976, physician asst. various assignments, 1988-96, resigned, 1996; adminstr., mem. faculty Nova Southeastern U., Ft. Lauderdale, Fla., 1996-99; physician asst. VA Med. Ctr., Tampa, 1999—. Contbr. Address: 11271 Grandview Dr Dade City FL 33525-2544

SMITH, HUGH ELMORE, retired obstetrician and gynecologist; b. Mullins, S.C., Jan. 27, 1925; s. Howard Buchanan and Ruth (Bethea) S.; m. Martha Elizabeth Meares, June 21, 1947; children: Bonnie Raney, Hugh E. Jr., Jeff H., Brian B. Student, The Citadel, U. Miss.; MD, Med. Coll. S.C., 1950. Diplomate Am. Bd. Ob-Gyn. Intern Roper Hosp., Charleston, S.C., 1950-51, resident in ob-gyn., 1951-54; pvt. practice Orangeburg, 1954-83; ret., 1983. With USN, 1943-46. Fellow ACOG, Am. Fertility Soc.; mem. South Atlantic Assn. Ob-Gyn., South Central Ob-Gyn. Soc. (pres. 1982), S.C. Ob-Gyn. Soc. Methodist.

SMITH, IAN CORMACK PALMER, biophysicist; b. Winnipeg, Man., Can., Sept. 23, 1939; s. Cormack and Grace Mary S.; m. Eva Gunilla Landvik, Mar. 27, 1965; children: Brittmarie, Cormack, Duncan, Roderick. BS, U. Man., 1961, MS, 1962; PhD, Cambridge U., England, 1965; Filosophie Doktor (hon.), U. Stockholm, 1986; DSc (hon.), U. Winnipeg, 1990; Diploma Tech. (hon.), Red River Coll., 1996; DSc (hon.), Brandon U., 2001. Fellow Stanford U., 1965-66; mem. rsch. staff Bell Tel. Labs., Murray Hill, N.J., 1966-67; rsch. officer divsn. biol. scis. NRC, Ottawa, 1967-87, dir. gen., 1987-91; dir.-gen. Inst. Biodiagnostics, Winnipeg, 1992—; adj. prof. chemistry and biochemistry Carleton U., 1973-90, U. Ottawa, 1976-92; adj. prof. chemistry, physics and anatomy U. Man., 1992—; adj. prof. biophysics U. Ill., Chgo., 1974-80. Allied scientist Ottawa Civic Hosp., 1985—, Ottawa Gen. Hosp., 1989-98, Ont. Cancer Found., 1989-91, St. Boniface Hosp., 1992—, Health Scis. Ctr., 1993—, Econ. Tech. Innovation Coun., Man., 1994-98, mem. exec. com., 1995-98, Man. Health Rsch. Coun., 1995—, mem. exec. com. 1996-98, chmn. 1998—; bd. dirs. ENSIS Growth Fund, DIASPEC Holdings, IMRIS Inc., Magnetic Resonance for Vets., Novadaq, Inc., Spectex PTY; mem. adv. bd. Loeb Inst., Ottawa, 1999—, Keystone Ventures, 1999-2002, Western Life Scis. Fund, 2002--. Contbr. 400 chpts. in books, articles in field to profl. jours. Bd. govs. U. Man., 2000—; mem. Premier's Econ. Adv. Bd., Man., 2001--; mem. adv. bd. Can. Inst. for Cancer Rsch., 2001—, Smart Winnipeg, 2000—, Can. Inst. Cancer Rsch., 2001—, Western Life Scis. Growth Fund, 2002—; premier Manitoba Adv. Coun., 2002—. Recipient Barringer award Can. Spectroscopy Soc., 1979, Herzberg award, 1986, Organon Teknika award Can. Soc. Clin. Chemists, 1987, Sr. Scientist award Sigma Xi, 1995. Fellow Chem. Inst. Can. (Merck award 1978, Labatt award 1984), Royal Soc. Can. (Flavelle medal 1996), Soc. Magnetic Resonance Medicine (exec. com. 1989-94); mem. Internat. Coun. Sci. Unions (gen. com. 1993-98), Chem. Inst. Can., Biophys. Soc., Can. Biochem. Soc. (Ayerst award 1978), Biophys. Soc. Can. (pres. 1992-94), Internat. Union Pure and Applied Biophysics (coun. 1993—, v.p. 1996-99, 2002--), U. Man. Alumni Assn. (bd. dirs. 1994-2000, v.p. 1997-98, pres. 1998-99). Office: Inst Biodiagnostics Winnipeg MB Canada R3B 1Y6 E-mail: ian.smith@nrc.ca.

SMITH, IRMHILD WREDE, public health nurse coordinator; b. Uelzen, Germany, July 14, 1948; came to the U.S., 1955; d. Karl Robert and Auguste (Garbe) Wrede; m. Allen Lloyd Smith, Sept. 9, 1972; 1 child, Elissa Katherine. Diploma, Mt. Sinai Hosp. Sch. Nursing, 1969; BSN, Kean Coll. N.J., 1989; MA, Columbia U., 1992, EdD, 1996. RNC. Staff RN Mt. Sinai Hosp., N.Y.C., 1969-70, Overlook Hosp., Summit, N.J., 1970-72, charge RN, 1973-76; staff RN St. Joseph's Hosp., Fort Worth, 1972-73; staff RN psychiatry Lyons (N.J.) VA Med. Ctr., 1977-86, head nurse, 1986-89, clin. instr. nursing edn., 1989-97; pub. health nurse coord. VA N.J. Healthcare Sys., East Orange, 1997—. Adj. prof. Kean U., 1996—. Coord. parish nurse ministry Millington Bapt. Ch. Mem.: ANA, Sigma Theta Tau (treas. Lambda Iota chpt. 1991—93). Avocations: reading, photography. Home: 76 Manchester Dr Basking Ridge NJ 07920-1210

SMITH, IRVING, gerontologist; b. Washington, June 4, 1948; s. Alfonso Marcellus and Nannie (Hunter) S.; children: Bryan, Rashard, Irving, Nevada, Ryan. M Human Svcs., grad. cert. advanced gerontology, Lincoln U., Pa., 1995; PhD in Health and Human Behavior, Walden U., 2002. Lic. profl. counselor, Washington. Dir. Sr. Ctr. Md.-Nat. Capital Park & Planning Commn., Prince George's County, Md., 1969-71, 89—. Internat., nat. forum spkr. on leisure and aging issues; sport sci. instr. Am. Sports Edn. Program; CPR, first aid instr. ARC; defensive driving instr. Nat. Safety Coun.; founder Prince George's County Centenarian Celebration; prin. investigator Prince George's County, Md. Centenarian Rsch. Study; bd. dirs., regional dir. Leisure and Aging. Fellow Washington Area Geriatric Edn. Ctr. Consortium; mem. Nat. Recreation and Park Assn. (state rep. leisure and aging, bd. dirs. leisure and aging sect., dir. Mid-Atlantic region), Pi Gamma Mu. Democrat. Baptist. Home: Apt 404 4815 Texas Ave SE Washington DC 20019-4182 E-mail: lsmith@starpower.net.

SMITH, ISAAC DANIAL, artist; b. Anchorage, Apr. 2, 1970; s. Dannie Lee and Lilas Ann Smith; m. Mina Aoki Smith, Sept. 16, 1995. BA in Art, U. Alaska, Anchorage, 1993. Apprentice Sunlit Glass Works, Anchorage, 1991—95; claims adjustor State Farm Ins., 1993—94; grounds keeper Angelus Meml. Pk., 1995; bellman Best Western Barratt Inn, 1995—99; owner, artist Glass Creations, 1999—. Avocations: reading, bicycling, movies. Office: Glass Creations 344 Krane Dr Anchorage AK 99504

SMITH, ISABEL FRANCIS, financial planner; b. Detroit, May 21, 1935; d. Edward Hugh and Isabel Francis (Winegar); m. Lawrence Smith, June 7, 1958; children: Mark, Hugh, Claire. Student, Newton Coll., 1953-54; BA, U. Mich., 1957, MA, 1958, postgrad., 1975-76. Registered investment adviser SEC. Tchr. Edison Sch., Hazel Park, Mich., 1958-61, Warren Valley Sch., Dearborn Heights, 1958-61; counselor Riverside H.S., 1961-62; pres. Isabel Francis Smith Ltd., Farmington Hills, Mich., 1980—, Integrated Fin. Strategies Ltd., Farmington Hills, 1980—. Registered rep., dist. mgr. Investors Diversified Svcs., Oak Park, Mich., 1978-80; instr. Oakland C.C., 1979—; cons. to womens orgns., 1977—; dir., pres. Oakland County Fin. and Estate Planning Coun., 1988-94; writer, profl. radio and TV personality. Lectr., trustee Bloomfield Twp. Libr., 1978-99, Interlochen Ctr. for Arts, 1989—; founder Interlochen Friends, Vol. Network for Women. Recipient Heart of Gold award United Found., 1976, Outstanding New Rep. award Investors Diversified Svcs., 1979, Outstanding Rep. award Mut. Svcs. Corp., 1981-90. Mem. AAUW, MSC (pres. club 1992-2001), Nat. Assn. Women Bus. Owners, Internat. Assn. Fin. Planners (past pres. S.E. Mich. chpt.), Inst. Cert. Fin. Planners (cert. FP, past regional dir., nat. dir. 198-86, dean retreat 1987, 89, leadership devel. com.), Interlochen Alumni Founder Assn. (past pres., award), U. Mich. Alumni Assn., Women's Econ. Club, Village Club, Phi Beta Kappa (nat. cmn., past pres., mem. exec. com. Pres. award Detroit assn.). Home: 7110 Paterese Dr Bloomfield Hills MI 48301-3764 Office: 31884 Northwestern Hwy Farmington Hills MI 48334-1628 Fax: (248) 932-9345. E-mail: isabel@ifs-ltd.com.

SMITH, J. CLARKE, telecommunications industry executive; b. Detroit, Nov. 9, 1942; s. Bernard Patrick and Irene Frances (Toth) Smith; m. Patricia Jayne Creed, June 26, 1956; children: Jennie, Colleen. BS, U. Detroit, 1964, MBA, 1966. Fin. analyst Chrysler Corp., Highland Park, Mich., 1964-67; bus. mgr., treas. U. Detroit, 1967-74; exec. v.p. Computer Communications Am., Detroit, 1974-86; v.p. Sears Consumer Fin., Lincolnshire, Ill., 1986-87; sr. v.p. corp. planning Sears Mortgage Corp., 1987-88, Riverwoods, Ill., 1988-89, exec. v.p. adminstrn., CFO, 1988-91; pres. Sears Savs. Bank, Chgo., 1989-93; v.p. fin. and adminstrn., CFO, chief adminstrv. officer Aerial Comm., 1995—2000. Bd. dirs. Pinnacle Towers Inc. Mem. Fin. Execs. Inst. (chmn. com. on info. mgmt. 1984—, pres. bd. dirs. Chgo. chpt.). Roman Catholic. Avocation: golf. E-mail: clarke_smith@ameritech.net.

SMITH, J. KELLUM, JR. foundation executive, lawyer; b. N.Y.C., June 18, 1927; s. James Kellum and Elizabeth Dexter (Walker) S.; m. Sarah Tod Lohmann, July 22, 1950 (div. 1993); children: Alison Andrews, Timothy Kellum, Jennifer Harlow, Christopher Lohmann; m. Angela Marina Brown, Feb. 3, 1995. Grad., Phillips Exeter Acad., 1945; AB magna cum laude, Amherst Coll., 1950; LL.B., Harvard, 1953. Bar: N.Y. 1955. Assoc. Lord, Day & Lord, N.Y.C., 1953-59; asst. sec. John Simon Guggenheim Meml. Found., 1960-62; mem. staff Rockefeller Found., 1962-74, asst. sec., 1963-64, sec., 1964-74; v.p., sec. Andrew W. Mellon Found., N.Y.C., 1974-89, sr. fellow, 1989-92; sr. advisor, 1992-98; pvt. practice cons. and writer. Trustee Nat. Sculpture Soc., 1955-71, Nat. Ins. Archtl. Edn., 1961-69, St. Bernard's Sch., N.Y.C., 1968-78, Found. for Child Devel., 1968-74; trustee Brearley Sch., N.Y.C., 1964-80, pres., 1973-78; trustee Am. Acad. in Rome, 1964-95, treas., 1965-66, 2d v.p., 1968-72, 84-88, sec., 1973-84, 89-95. With USAAF, 1945-46. Mem. Phi Beta Kappa. Clubs: Century Association (N.Y.C.). Home: 550 Number 37 Rd Saranac NY 12981-2956

SMITH, J. THOMAS, mental health consultant; b. Detroit, Feb. 19, 1947; s. Louis Edward and Marjorie Ursula Smith. BS, Windsor U., 1974; JD, City U., L.A., 1983; MA, Norwich U., 1988; BS, U. State of N.Y., 1988; PhD, U. San Jose (Costa Rica), 1995; JD, Tex. Southern Univ., 1999. Lic. profl. counselor, Ga., Tex.; lic. marriage and family therapist, Tex.; alcohol and drug counselor III diplomate, Tex.; registered hypnotherapist; lic. chem. dependency counselor, Tex.; cert. clin. mental health counselor. Air personality Sta. KDAY Radio, L.A., 1975-77, KPVU Radio, Houston, 1993-97, Sta. KMJQ Radio, Houston, 1977-87, 94—; assoc. campus dir., instr. Houston Community Coll., 1982-87; program dir. Cultural Health Network, Inc., Houston, 1986-89; dean City U. Sch. of Law, L.A., 1989-90; program dir. Urban Health Network, Inc., Atlanta, 1990-91; minister 1st Ch. of Religious Sci., 1990-91; instr. Altanta Met. Coll., 1990-91; broadcaster Sta. WSTR Radio, Atlanta, 1990-91; dir. clin. svcs. Make-Ready, Inc., Houston, 1997—. Program dir. HCA/Spring Br. Med. Ctr. John Lucas Treatment and Recovery Ctr., Houston, 1991-93; dir. counseling and multicultural svcs. Prairie View (Tex.), A&M U., 1993-97; instr. Tex. So. U. Sch. of Continuing Edn., 1993-97. Author: Mind Science Primer, 1986; columnist Houston Defender, 1982-86; advice columnist Majic the Mag. and KMJQ.com., 1999—. Com mem. March of Dimes, Houston, 1985-87; vol. Lukemia Soc., Houston, 1983; life mem. NAACP, Houston, 1988; min. All-Faiths Ch. Religious Sci., Houston, 1985-89; mem. Hope IV Cmty. Task Force, Housing Authority of the City Houston, 1999—. Mem. Am. Counseling Assn., Am. Mental Health Counselors Assn., Tex. Assn. of Alcoholism and Drug Abuse Counselors, Nat. Assn. Alcohol and Drug Abuse Counselors, United Clergy of Religious Sci., SAG, AFTRA, Internat. New Thought Alliance (life), Nat. Bd. Cert. Counselors (mem. exam. com. 1994-99), Nat. Com. Mental Health (bd. govs. 1995-96), Nat. Assn. Athletes Against Drugs (bd. dirs. 1994-96, 98—), State Bar Tex. (dir. law student divsn. 1999-2000), Phi Alpha Delta. Avocations: syndicated broadcaster. Home: PO Box 681113 Houston TX 77268-1113 Office: J Thomas Smith & Assocs Mental Health Cons 8226 Antoine Dr Houston TX 77088 E-mail: drjsmith@abanet.org.

SMITH, JACK C. supermarket executive; b. Aug. 21, 1925; Ptnr. Smith Realty, Grundy, Va., 1955—; chmn. K-VA-T Food Stores, Abington. Office: 201 Trigg St Abingdon VA 24210-3470

SMITH, JACK CARL, foreign trade consultant; b. Cleve., Sept. 11, 1928; s. John Carl and Florence Agnes (O'Rourke) S.; m. Nannette June Boyd, Dec. 1, 1962; 1 dau., Colleen Wentworth. Student, Baldwin Wallace Coll., 1948-51, postgrad., 1958; BA, Ohio U., 1954. Rep. Flying Tiger Line, Inc., Los Angeles, 1958-61; prin. Pub. Rep. bus., Cleve., 1961-64; pub. Penton Pub., 1964-90; spl. advisor Am. Fgn. Policy Coun., Washington, 1990—. Dir. Central Cleve. Corp., Nat. Distbn. Terminals; graduated Air Tng. Command Intelligence Officer Sch., served from 1958-62 AFR. Trustee Presdl. task force, Rep. Senatorial Inner Circle, Coun. of Logistics Mgmt., U.S. Bus. and Indsl. Coun. With USAF, 1954-58. Mem. Am. Mgmt. Assn., Material Handling Inst., Am. Trucking Assn., Nat. Council Phys. Distbn. Mgmt., Family Motor Coach Assn., Recreation Vehicle Industry Assn., Am. Bus. Press, Mag. Pubs. Assn., Sci. Research Soc., Internat. Platform Assn., Sigma Xi, Sigma Chi Clubs: Wings (N.Y.C.). Home: 457 Devonshire Ct Bay Village OH 44140-3009 Office: Am Fgn Policy Coun 1521 16th St NW Washington DC 20036-1463 *Do your best and God will forgive you the rest.*

SMITH, JACK LEE, bank executive; b. Yale, Okla., Feb. 2, 1948; s. George W. and Alta E. (Tilley) S.; m. Rose Mary Cantrell, Feb. 3, 1968 (div. Feb. 1980); children: Anissa Kay, Melany Elaine; m. Janice A. Houston, Aug. 2, 1981). BS, Okla. State U., 1972. Asst. v.p. Production Credit Assn., 1972-76; v.p., office mgr. Mountain Plains Prodn. Credit Assn., Ft. Collins, 1976-81; dist. mgr. Ralston Purina, St. Louis, 1981-83; 2d v.p. Omaha Nat. Bank, 1983-85; v.p., office mgr. FirsTier Bank, N.A., Omaha, Ft. Collins, 1985-93, mgr. western area agrl. lending Omaha, 1993-96; sr. v.p. agribus. fin. group Farm Credit Svcs., Greeley, Colo., 1996—. Bd. dirs. Colo. Cattle Feeders Assn.; chmn. Allied Industry Coun. for Agr. Mem. Am. Bankers Assn., Colo. Bankers Assn., Nat. Cattlemen's Assn., Kans. Livestock Assn., Colo. Cattlemen's Assn., Elks. Republican. Avocations: photography, hiking, fishing, camping. Home: 2613 Jewelstone Ct Fort Collins CO 80525-6118 Office: AgriBusiness Finance Group Farm Credit Svcs 4505 29th St Greeley CO 80634-8763

SMITH, JAMES BARRY, lawyer; b. N.Y.C., Feb. 28, 1947; s. Irving and Vera (Donaghy) S.; m. Kathleen O'Connor, May 28, 1977; childen: Jennifer, Kelly. BA in Econs., Colgate U., 1968; JD, Boston U., 1974. Assoc. McDermott, Will & Emery, Chgo., 1974-78, Ungaretti & Harris, Chgo., 1978-80, ptnr., 1980. Lt. U.S. Navy, 1968-70. Mem. Chgo. Mortgage Atty. Assn. Avocations: sports, reading, travel. Office: Ungaretti & Harris 3500 Three First Nat Pla Chicago IL 60602 E-mail: jbsmith@uhlaw.com.

SMITH, JAMES MICHEAL, operations executive; b. Ft. Carson, Colo., July 14, 1951; s. Richard Allen Smith and Cathrine Clare (Kehl) Ryan; m. Amelia Joann Carr, June 7, 1973; children: Peter Micheal, Lisa Danielle. BS in Basic Scis., USAF Acad., 1973; MA in Bus. Mgmt., Ctrl. Mich. U., 1977. Sr. cons. Strategic Mktg. Group, Inc., Denver, 1986-87; dir. ops. U.S.A. Direct, Inc., Englewood, 1987; mktg. rep. Martin Marietta Corp., Denver, 1988-90, sr. mktg. rep., 1990-92, mgr. bus. devel., 1992-95; dir. mktg. Hughes Info. Tech. Corp., Aurora, 1995-97; dir. bus. devel. Electronic Data Systems, Plano, Tex., 1997-2000; fed. acct. mgr. Network Appliance, Sunnyvale, Calif., 2000—02; dir. info. tech. dector bd Systems, Inc., Torrance, 2002—. Patroller Nat. Ski Patrol, 1985—; cub scout leader Boy Scouts Am., 1993—. Maj. USAF, 1973-86, col. USAFR, ret. Recipient Purple Merit Star for life saving Nat. Ski Patrol, 1990. Mem. AIAA, Air Force Assn. (life), Res. Officer Assn. (life). Republican. Mem. Lds Ch. Avocations: skiing, racquetball, biking, hiking. Home: 1362 Meadow Trl Franktown CO 80116-7912 Office: bd Sys Inc 1915 Aerotech Dr Ste 100 Colorado Springs CO 80916-4222 E-mail: mike.smith@cos.bdsys.com.

SMITH, JAMES A. lawyer; b. Akron, Ohio, June 11, 1930; s. Barton H. and Myrna S. (Young) S.; m. Melda I. Perry, Jan. 17, 1959; children: Hugh, Sarah Louise. AB, Western Res. U., 1952; postgrad., Columbia U., 1954-56, LLB, 1961; postgrad., Yale U., 1956-58. Bar: Ohio 1961, U.S. Dist. Ct. (no. dist.) Ohio 1963, U.S. Ct. Appeals (6th cir.) 1973, U.S. Supreme Ct. 1974, U.S. Ct. Appeals (11th cir.) 1983, U.S. Ct. Appeals (D.C. cir.) 1984. Assoc. Squire, Sanders and Dempsey, Cleve., 1961-70, ptnr., 1970-91, counsel, 1991-96; adj. prof. Case Western Res. U. Sch. Law, 1997-98, ret. Mem. spl. adv. com. Nat. Conf. Commrs. on Uniform State Laws, 1972-74. Trustee Chagrin Falls Park Cmty. Ctr., 1968-78, Greater Cleve. Neighborhood Ctrs. Assn., 1973-78, Legal Aid Soc. Cleve., 1977-80, Cleve. Inst. Music, 1994—; mem. Charter Rev. Commn., Chagrin Falls, 1966. Lt. (j.g.) USNR, 1952-54. Fellow Am. Coll. Trial Lawyers; mem. ABA, Ohio Bar Assn., Cleve. Bar Assn. (trustee 1988-92), U.S. Ct. Appeals for 6th Cir. Jud. Conf. (life), Ohio Ct. Appeals for 8th Jud. Dist. Conf. (life), Ct. of Nisi Prius (clk. 1975-76, judge 1994-95), Phi Beta Kappa, Omicron Delta Kappa, Delta Sigma Rho. Democrat.

SMITH, JAMES AARON, JR. civil engineer; b. Sellersville, Pa., May 27, 1952; s. James Aaron and Grace Viola (Scheonley) S.; m. Charlene Anna Cesare, Sept. 18, 1976; children: Matthew Aaron, Nathan Andrew. BSCE, Drexel U., 1975. Registered profl. engr., Pa., N.J., Va., Md. Project engr. Norfolk dist. U.S. Army C.E., Ft. Lee, Va., 1975-77, chief project engr. Norfolk dist. Gathright Dam, 1977-79, area engr. Phila. dist. Chambersburg, Pa., 1979-85, supervisory civil engr. Phila. dist. Pitts., 1982-85; asst. dir. constrn. mgmt. Buchart-Horn, Inc., York, 1985-89, dir. constrn. mgmt., 1989—98, regional v.p., 1999—. Project mgmt. instr.; mem. York County Air Transp. Authority. Author procedural manuals. Coach York Youth Soccer, 1986-90, York United Soccer, 1991—; deacon Providence Presbyn. Ch. Mem. ASCE, Am. Soc. Hwy. Engrs., Profl. Engrs. Constrn. (Pa. State Sec./treas. practice div.), Nat. Inst. Cert. Engring. Techs. (exec. com.), Nat. Ry. Hist. Soc. (chpt. pres. 1981-84), Airports Cons. Coun., Am. Assn. Airport Execs., Am. Td. and Transp. Bulders Assn., Am. Rwy. Devel. Assn. Republican. Office: Buchart-Horn Inc 445 W Philadelphia St York PA 17404-3340 E-mail: jsmith@bh-ba.com.

SMITH, JAMES ALMER, JR. psychiatrist; b. Montclair, N.J., May 30, 1923; s. James Almer and Carrie Elizabeth (Moten) S.; m. Elsie Mae Brooks; children: James III, Roger, Margo, Melanie. BS, Howard U., 1947, MD, 1948. Diplomate Am. Bd. Psychiatry and Neurology. Staff psychiatrist Hartley Salmon Child Guidance Ctr., Hartford, Conn., 1955-60; assoc. psychiatrist Child Guidance Clinic Springfield (Mass.), 1960-83; cons. psychiatrist Gandara Mental Health Ctr., Springfield, 1984—; med. dir. Kolburne Sch., New Marlborough, Mass., 1969—. Bd. dirs. Hampden Mental Health Dist., Springfield, 1968—; cons. psychiatrist Childrens' Services Hartford, 1956-60, Childrens' Study Ctr., Springfield, 1960—, W.W. Johnson Ctr., Springfield, 1979—. Bd. dirs. Springfield Commn. on Human Relations, 1961-62, Negro Cath. Scholarship Fund of Springfield, 1976—. Served to capt. M.C., U.S. Army, 1953-55. Recipient Dr. Anthony Brown award W. W. Johnson Ctr., 1987. Fellow Am. Orthopsychiat. Assn., Am. Assn. Psychoanalytic Physicians (pres. 1979-81), Soc. Psychoanalytic Physicians; mem. Am. Psychiat. Assn., Am. Soc. Psychoanalytic Physicians, Sigma Pi Phi. Clubs: Squires of Springfield (pres. 1980-81). Baptist. Home and Office: 96 Dartmouth St Springfield MA 01109-3909

SMITH, J(AMES) BRIAN, education specialist and researcher, writer; b. Camden, Maine, Dec. 13, 1943; s. Clifford Russell and Ruth Melvina (Alexander) S.; m. Cynthia V. Cashman, Aug. 5, 1967 (div. 1971); m. Negar Paydar, Nov. 19, 1978; children: Negin, Vahid, Tristan, James. Student, Coll. Wooster, 1962-63, U. Hawaii, 1963-64; BA in English, U. Maine, 1967; postgrad., Va. Poly. and State U., 1977-78; MS in Ednl. Adminstrn., U. So. Maine, 1982; DEd, Boston Coll., 1993. Cert. sch. supt., Maine. Owner, dir., operator pvt. summer boys camp, 1962-65; asst. sailing instr. Camden Yacht Club, 1966-67; jr. high sch. English & social studies tchr. Bath, Maine, 1967; sr. high sch. English and U.S. history tchr. Old Town (Maine) Schs., 1967-68; jr. high sch. English and U.S. history tchr. Union (Maine) Schs., 1968-71; entrepreneur, broker, fin. planner, 1971-75; tchr. English Wishaw (Scotland) Sr. Secondary Sch., 1975-77; tchr. high sch. English, U.S. history, govt., econs. Iran Electronics Industries Sch., Shiraz, 1977-78; tchr. English Portland (Maine) High Sch., 1977-78; tchr. English and world history Falmouth (Maine) High Sch., 1979-82; teaching prin. Palermo (Maine) Consol. Sch., 1982-84; supt. schs. Maine Sch. Union # 104, 1984-86, Maine Indian Edn., Indian Island, Indian Twp. and Pleasant Point Reservations, 1986-94; consulting rschr. Maine Assistance Ctr., Camden, Maine, 1994—; supt's outreach specialist Edn. Alliance Brown U., Providence. Invited keynote speaker Maine Dept. Edn., 1991; apptd. del. to White House Conf. on Indian Edn., 1992; chmn. edn. com. United South and Ea. Tribes, Nashville; writer The Camden Herald, 1994—; supt.'s outreach specialist Edn. Alliance of Brown U., Providence, R.I.; artistic agt. for Eveline Henner, Zurich, Switzerland and Rockport, Maine, 2000—. Mem. drug and alcohol and exec. coms. Maine Sch. Supts. Assn.; mem. program rev. and comment com. div. alcohol and drug ednl svcs Maine Dept. Edn.; sch. bd. mem. South and Eastern Tribes Agy. Sch. Bd., Bur. Indian Affairs, Dept. Interior. Mem. ASCD, Am. Assn. Sch. Adminstrs. (past mem. resolutions com.), New Eng. Assn. Supts. Schs., Maine Sch. Supts. Assn. (chmn. ad hoc com. on Maine ednl. assessment program). New Eng. Supts. Leadership Coun. (mem. adv. bd.), Washington County Supts. Assn., Am. Evaluation Assn., The Grange, Phi Delta Kappa. Avocations: Alpine skiing, sailing, gourmet cooking, reading, family gardening, internat. travel. Office: The Maine Assistance Ctr 345 Turnpike Dr Apt A Camden ME 04843-4436 E-mail: jbsbrian@midcoast.com.

SMITH, JAMES BROWN, JR. secondary school educator; b. Greenville, N.C., Apr. 6, 1943; s. James Brown Sr. and Clara Lucille (Avery) S.; m. Donna Drake, Aug. 12, 1967; children: Caryn Frances, James Brown III, Sarah Elizabeth. BS, East Carolina U., 1966; MEd, Va. State U., 1976. Cert. tchr., postgrad. prof., Va. Tchr. Great Bridge Jr. High Sch., Chesapeake, Va., 1966-68, Queen's Lake Sch., York County, 1968-76; tchr., chmn. career tech. edn. dept. Bruton High Sch., 1976—. Cons. Acad. Tech, Hampton, Va., 1992-93; tchr. intern Va. Peninsula C. of C., Hampton, 1992. Mem. York County Edn. Assn., Va. Edn. Assn., NEA, Va. Vocat. Assn., Va. Tech. Edn. Assn., Assn. Career and Tech. Edn., Kiwanis (bd. dirs. 1984-92). Methodist. Avocations: photography, gardening, auto repair, fishing. Home: 135 John Pott Dr Williamsburg VA 23188-6328 Office: Bruton High Sch 185 E Rochambeau Dr Williamsburg VA 23188-2121 E-mail: jbsmithjr@hotmail.com.

SMITH, JAMES C. entrepreneur; B, Northeastern U. , 1963. Sales exec. Tex. Instruments; founder ARC Mgmt.; pres., CEO First Health; chmn. Concentra, 2000—. Mem.: Northeastern U. Gov. Bd., Internat. Found. Employee Benefit Plans (chmn. strat. planning and devel. com., adv. dir., mem. edn. com.), Health Ins. Assn. Am. (mem. bd. dirs.), Healthcare Leadership Coun. (treas., mem. exec. com.). Office: 3200 Highland Grove Downers Grove IL 60515-1282 Office Fax: 630-719-0076.*

SMITH, JAMES CLOUDIS, secretary of state, former state attorney general; b. Jacksonville, Fla., May 25, 1940; s. John Albert and Elizabeth F. (West) S.; m. Carole Ann Clark, Dec. 29, 1962; children: Kathryn Elizabeth, Robert Scott, James Clark. BA, Fla. State U., 1962; JD, Stetson U., 1967, LLD (hon.), 1987. Bar: Fla. 1967. Exec. asst. to Fla. Sec. of State, Tallahassee, 1969-71; exec. asst. to lt. gov. Fla., 1971; dep. to Sec. of Commerce State of Fla., Tallahassee, 1971, sr. staff asst. to Gov., 1971-72, atty. gen., 1979-87, chief of staff Office of Gov., 1987, sec. of state of Fla., 1987—. Chmn. Gov.'s Adv. Com. on Corrections; mem. Article V Rev. Commn., Fla. Coun. on Criminal Justice, Sentencing Guidelines Study Commn., Commn. on Bail Bond Reform, Fla. Law Revision Commn. Mem. bd. overseers Stetson Coll. Law; trustee Univ. Found., Fla. State U.; mem. adv. bd. Nat. Fedn. Parents for Drug-Free Youth. Served to capt. U.S. Army, 1962-64. Named Conservationist of Yr. Fla. Audubon Soc.; recipient Disting. Alumnus award Stetson U., award for effectiveness in drug enforcement Dept. Justice. Mem. ABA (criminal law com.), Fla. Bar Assn., Tallahassee Bar Assn., Am. Judicature Soc. Republican. Methodist. Office: Office Sec of State 2 The Capitol Tallahassee FL 32399-6507*

SMITH, JAMES DAVID, food service executive, controller; b. Fond du Lac, Wis., Mar. 15, 1943; s. James R. and Evelyn (Bebow) S.; m. Karen Thomas, July 10, 1966; children: Kristin, Brad. BS, U. Wis., 1965; MBA, Coll. St. Thomas, St. Paul, 1978. Gen. mgr. Cen. West Europe region Control Data Corp., Mpls., 1982; v.p. corp. reporting Gen. Mills Corp., 1982-88; sr. v.p., contr. Gen. Mills Restaurants, Orlando, Fla., 1988—. Co-chmn. membership com. Fin. Execs. Inst., Mpls., 1987-88. Mem. Bay Hill Club. Avocations: golf, tennis. Office: Darden Restaurants Inc 5900 Lake Ellenor Dr Orlando FL 32809-4634

SMITH, JAMES EARL, astronautical engineer; b. Aurora, Colo., Jan. 10, 1973; s. James Raymond and Gaylene Joy (Green) S.; m. Kristine Cromar, May 31, 1997; children: James Nathan, Wesley Raymond. BS in Astronautical Engring., USAF Acad., 1997; SM in Aeronautics and Astronautics, MIT, 1999. Draper fellow Charles Stark Draper Lab., Cambridge, Mass., 1997-99; chief, spacecraft systems analysis 2d Space Ops. Squadron, Schriever AFB, Colo., 1999—2002; intern air force The Pentagon, Washington, 2002—. Capt. USAF, 1997—. Mem. AIAA, Sigma Xi (assoc.), Tau Beta Pi (chpt. pres. 1996-97), Sigma Gamma Tau. Mem. Lds Ch. Avocations: computers, playing piano, family. Home: 7124 Bonnie Brae Ln Colorado Springs CO 80922-3141 Office: 2SOPS/DOAS 300 Omalley Ave Ste 41 Falcon AFB CO 80912-3001 Fax: 208-246-6344. E-mail: smithje@alum.mit.edu.

SMITH, JAMES FINLEY, economist, educator; b. Dallas, Nov. 4, 1938; s. Emerson Russell and Achsah Elizabeth (Foster) S.; m. Susan Schreiber, Aug. 18, 1962; children: Carter Emerson, Jamie, Curtis Noel, Marshall Edward. BA, So. Meth. U., 1961, MA, 1964, PhD, 1971. Math. analyst Sears, Roebuck & Co., Oak Brook, Ill., 1965-68, adminstrv. asst. to v.p. and treas. Chgo., 1968-69, dir. econometric rsch., 1969-75; sr. economist Bd. Govs. FRS, Washington, 1975-77; dir. credit rsch. Sears, Roebuck & Co., Chgo., 1977-80; chief economist Union Carbide Corp., Danbury, Conn., 1980-85; dir. regional svcs. and U.S. cons. Wharton Econometric Forecasting Assocs., Phila., 1986; dir., chief economist Bur. Bus. Rsch. U. Tex., Austin, 1987-88; prof. fin. U. N.C., Chapel Hill, 1988—. Mem. econ. adv. bd. U.S. Dept. Commerce, 1977-80, 83—; cons. Pres.'s Coun. of Econ. Advisers, Washington, 1978-83; pres. Nat. Bus. Econ. Issues Coun., N.Y.C., 1981-83; dir. Nat. Bur. Econ. Rsch., Cambridge, Mass., 1992—; mem. bd. advisors Thurston Arthritis Rsch. Ctr., Chapel Hill, N.C., 1994—. Author: (annual) UNC Business Forecast, 1988—, (with others) Economic Growth and Investment in Higher Education, 1987, The Chemical Industry in America, 1988, The New Texas Economy, 1988, (with Elsie Echeverri-Carroll) The Economic Impact of Travel on Texas Counties: 1986, 1988; contbr. articles to profl. jours. Served to lt. U.S. Army, 1961-62. NDEA fellow, 1962-65 Fellow Nat. Assn. Bus. Economists (v.p. 1988-89, pres. 1989-90, dir. 1980-84, 85-92); mem. Nat. Economists Club (bd. govs. 1984-87), Am. Econ. Assn., Economists Group Switzerland, Fin. Mgmt. Assn., Soc. Bus. Economists U.K. Mem. United Ch. of Christ. Home: 318 11th Ave # 3 Seattle WA 98122-5309 Office: U NC Kenan-Flagler Bus Sch Dept Fin Carroll Hall PO Box 3490 Chapel Hill NC 27515-3490

SMITH, JAMES FREDERICK, securities executive; b. N.Y.C., Jan. 6, 1944; s. James Arthur and Agnes Rose (Kollenz) S.; m. Joan Ann Kelly, June 18, 1966; children: James Patrick, John Michael. BBA in Accountancy Practice, Pace U., 1970. CPA, N.Y.; registered fin. & operational prin., registered rep. Mgmt. trainee Chase Manhattan Bank, N.Y.C., 1965-67; internal auditor MW Kellogg & Co., 1967-69; sr. acct. Price Waterhouse, 1969-72; asst. treas. and contr. Henderson Bros. Inc., 1972-80; pvt. practice Clearwater, Fla., 1980-82; sr. audit mgr. Price Waterhouse, N.Y.C., 1982-84; v.p. & contr. Integrated Resources, 1984-86; pres., CFO, Freeman Securities, Jersey City, 1986—; pres., dir. First Summit Capital Mgmt., 1994—; dir. Summit High Yield Bond Fund. Bd. dirs. Summit Emerging Markets Bond Fund. With USN, 1961-65. Mem. AICPA, Internat. Soc. CEBS (charter mem.), N.Y. State Soc. CPA, Securities Industry Assn., The Bond Market Assn., Wall St. Tax Assn. Avocation: carpentry. Home: 328 Oaklake Ln Niceville FL 32578 Office: Freeman Securities 30 Montgomery St Ste 1300 Jersey City NJ 07302-3893 also: 1st Summit Capital Mgmt 8044 Montgomery Rd Cincinnati OH 45236-2919

SMITH, JAMES LAWRENCE, research physicist; b. Detroit, Sept. 3, 1943; s. William Leo and Marjorie Marie (Underwood) S.; m. Carol Ann Adam, Mar. 27, 1965; children: David Adam, William Leo. BS, Wayne State U., 1965; PhD, Brown U., 1974. Mem. staff Los Alamos (N.Mex.) Nat. Lab., 1973-82, fellow, 1982-86, dir. ctr. materials sci., 1986-87, fellow, 1987—; chief scientist Superconductivity Tech. Ctr., 1988-99; N.Am. editor Philos. Mag., 1990-95; editor Philos. Mag. B., 1995—. Contbr. articles to profl. jours. Recipient E.O. Lawrence award, 1986, Disting. Alumni award Wayne State U., 1993. Fellow Am. Phys. Soc. (internat. prize for new materials 1990); mem. AAAS, Materials Rsch. Soc., Minerals Metals Materials Soc., Am. Crystallographic Assn., Brown Alumni Assn. (bd. govs. 1998-2000), Phi Beta Kappa. Achievements include patents for design of magnetic field and high-strength conductors. Office: Los Alamos Nat Lab Mail Stop G770 Los Alamos NM 87545-0001

SMITH, JAMES PARKER, accountant; b. N.Y.C., July 5, 1959; s. John Paterson and Georgina (Budd) S.; m. Karen Ann Ahrens, June 3, 1989. AS in acctg., Suffolk County Community Coll., Riverhead, N.Y., 1979; BS in acctg., SUNY, Plattsburgh, 1981. Acct. Fink Rainer and Nickl, Lindenhurst, N.Y., 1983-84, Fenelon Crowley and Tutino, East Hampton, 1984-86, Markowitz Preishe and Stevens, East Hampton, 1987-89; sr. acct. Advanced Healthcare Resources, Inc., Hauppauge, 1989-92, Lewis H. Fink, CPA, MBA, Commack, 1992-2000, Chicanos Por La Causa, Inc., Phoenix, 2001; project acct. Ctrl Ariz. Shelter Svcs., Inc., 2001; project tax assoc. trust tax dept. KPMG LLP, Phoenix, 2001—02; mortgage loan cons. Am. Residential Funding, Inc., Tempe, 2002—. Tax preparer, 1982—. Min. Universal Life Ch., 2000—. Mem. Alpha Sigma. Methodist. Avocation: car racing. Office: Am Residential Funding Inc 9280 S Kyrene Rd #107 Tempe AZ 85284 E-mail: smithtax81@aol.com.

SMITH, JAMES PATRICK, economist; b. Aug. 3, 1943; s. James P. and Winefred (Harrison) S.; m. Sandra Berry, Oct. 25, 1983; children: Gillian Clare, Lauren Theresa. BS, Fordham U., 1965; PhD, U. Chgo., 1972. Rsch. assoc. Nat. Bur. Econ. Rsch., N.Y.C., 1972-74; sr. economist Rand Corp., Santa Monica, Calif., 1974—, dir. of rsch. labor and population, 1977-93. Bd. mem. Occupl. Safety and Health Standards State Calif. Editor: Female Labor Supply, 1980, The New Americans, 1997, The Immigration Debate, 1998, Wealth, Work, and Health, 1999; bd. editors: Am. Econ. Rev., 1980-83; author articles in field. Recipient Merit award NIH, 1995—. Mem. NIA (monitoring com., health and retirement survey, chair NAS panel on immigration, prin. investigator New Immigrant Survey), Am. Econ. Assn., Phi Beta Kappa. Office: RAND PO Box 2138 Santa Monica CA 90407-2138

SMITH, JAMES SCOTT, music educator; b. Anniston, Ala., June 16, 1977; s. James Brent and Candy Violet Smith; m. Jessie Odilla Teixeira, Feb. 22, 1997; children: Smantha Kouryn Teixeira, Aaron James. BA, Jacksonville State U., Jacksonville, AL, 1996—2000. Teaching Certificate Ala., Ga. Mgr. McDonalds, Anniston, Ala., 1995—2000; music educator Roopville Elem. Sch., Roopville, Ga., 2000—, 2000—. Dir. Roopville Elem. Chorus, Roopville, Ga., 2000—. Recipient Dedicated Tchr., Roopville Elem. Sch., 2002. Mem.: Music Educators Nat. Conf., Ga. Assn. of Educators, Ga. Music Educators Assn. Episcopalian. Avocations: singing, piano playing, reading. Home: 25 Lovvorn Lane Roopville GA 30170 Office: Roopville Elementary School 60 Old Carrollton Road Roopville GA 30170 Home Fax: 770-854-3001. Personal E-mail: ssmithres@yahoo.com.

SMITH, JAMES W., JR. state supreme court justice; b. Louisville, Oct. 28, 1943; BS, U. So. Miss., 1965; JD, Jackson Sch. Law, 1972; MEd with honors, Miss. Coll., 1973. Bar: Miss. 1972, U.S. Dist. Ct. (no. and so. dists.) Miss. 1973, U.S. Ct. Appeals (5th cir.) 1974. Pvt. practice, Pearl, 1972-78, Brandon, 1979-80; prosecuting atty. City of Pearl, 1973-80; prosecutor Rankin County, 1976; dist. atty. 20th Jud. Dist., 1977-82; judge Rankin County, 1982-92; Supreme Ct. justice Cen. Dist., 1993—. Instr. courtroom procedure and testifying Miss. Law Enforcement Tng. Acad., 1980-91. With U.S. Army, 1966-69. Named Wildlife Conservationist of Yr. Rankin County, 1988; recipient Outstanding Positive Role Model for Today's Youth award, 1991, Child Forever award Miss. Voices of Children and Youth, 1992, You've Made a Difference award, 1995, Alumnus of Yr. award Hinds C.C., 1996. Fellow Miss. Bar Found. (bd. dirs. 1998); mem. Miss. State Bar Assn., Rankin County Bar Assn., Nat. Wildlife Fedn., Nat. Wild Turkey Fedn., Am. Legion, Rotary. Office: Carroll Gartin Justice Bldg PO Box 117 Jackson MS 39205-0117

SMITH, JAMES WALKER, lawyer; b. S.I., N.Y., May 11, 1957; s. James Patrick and Ann Catherine (Sullivan) S.; m. Erin Patricia Murphy, Aug. 15, 1982; children: Patrick James, Daniel Timothy, Meghan Kathleen, James John. BA magna cum laude, Fordham U., 1979, JD, 1982; LLM, NYU, 1988. BAr: N.Y. 1983, N.J. 1984, Pa. 1993, U.S. Supreme Ct. 1994. Assoc. Mendes & Mount, N.Y.C., 1982, Costello Shea & Gaffney, N.Y.C., 1982-86; ptnr. Anderson Kill Olick & Oshinsky P.C., 1986-96, Smith Abbot, LLP, N.Y.C., 1996—. Arbitrator N.Y.C. (N.Y.) Civil Ct., 1987-89; faculty chairperson hosp. law Fordham Law Sch., N.Y.C., 1989-93; mediator U.S. Dist. Ct. (so. dist.) N.Y., N.Y.C., 1992-96. Author: Hospital Liability, 1985—; editor-in-chief: New York Practice Guide, 1993-97; contbg. editor: Medical Malpractice Law and Strategy, 1993—; bd. editors Fordham Urban Law Jour., 1981-82. Mem. N.Y. County Lawyer's Assn. (com. on tort law 1993-95), Assn. of the Bar of the City of N.Y. (com. on tort law 1990-92, com. on state cts. 1994—). Roman Catholic. Avocations: golf, coaching youth basketball. Home: 15 Flagg Ct Staten Island NY 10304-1157 Office: Smith Abbot LLP 100 Maiden Ln New York NY 10038-4818

SMITH, JAMES WARREN, pathologist, microbiologist, parasitologist; b. Logan, Utah, July 5, 1934; s. Kenneth Warren and Nina Lou (Sykes) S.; m. Nancy Chesterman, July 19, 1958; children: Warren, Scott. BS, U. Iowa, 1956, MD, 1959. Diplomate Am. Bd. Pathology. Intern Colo. Gen. Hosp., Denver, 1959-60; resident U. Iowa Hosps., Iowa City, 1960-65; asst. prof. pathology U. Vt., Burlington, 1967-70; prof. pathology Ind. U., Indpls., 1970-98, chmn. dept. pathology and lab. medicine, 1992-98, Nordshow prof. of lab. medicine, 1997-98, prof. emeritus, 1998—. Contbr. articles to profl. jours. Served to lt. comdr. USN, 1965-67. Recipient Outstanding Contbn. to Clin. Microbiology award South Ctrl. Assn. Clin. Microbiology, 1977. Fellow Coll. Am. Pathologists (chmn. mcirobiology resource com. 1981-85); mem. AMA, Infectious Disease Soc. Am., Am. Soc. Investigative Pathology, Royal Soc. Tropical Medicine and Hygiene, Am. Soc. Clin. Pathology, Am. Soc. Microbiology, Am. Soc. Tropical Medicine and Hygiene, U.S.-Can. Acad. Pathology, Assn. Pathology Chairs, Binford Dammin Soc. Infectious Disease Pathologists, Soc. Protozoologists. Home: 4375 Cold Spring Rd Indianapolis IN 46228-3327 Office: Ind U Med Ctr 635 Barnhill Dr Rm A128 Indianapolis IN 46202-5126

SMITH, JAMESETTA DELORISE, author; b. Chgo., Jan. 26, 1942; d. James Gilbert and Ora Mae (Roberts) Howell; m. Leroy Smith, June 2, 1962; children: Leroy, Darryll Keith. Student, Oxford Bus. Coll., Chgo., 1961-62. Office clerk Justice of the Peace, Gary, Ind., 1966-69; bookkeeper, office mgr. Jones Electric, 1971-85. Author: How Strong is Strong, 1988; contbr. articles to profl. jours., newspapers. Treas., bd. dirs. N.W. Ind. Lupus Found., Gary, 1988-92; co-founder, pres. Ark. chpt. Lupus Found., 1993—, mem., race organizer, 1995; facilitator Gary Meth. Hosp. for Lupus Found., 1991-92; pastor's aide Bible study leader Greater St. Paul Bapt. Ch., 1995, sec. ch. food com., 1994-2000, ch. trustee, 1994, hostess and announcing clk., 1997—, spl. recognition trustee, 1998, Sunday sch. tchr., 1998; Bible enrichment instr., 1996—; pastor's aide sec. Clark Rd. M.B. Ch., 1990-92. Named Vol. of Yr., Ark. chpt. Lupus Found., 1995; recipient Legacy award pin AARP, 1998, Growth award, Lupus Found. Am., 1995-96, 98-99, Nat. Fleur-De-Lis award for outstanding svc., 2001, award for fin. support Ark. chpt., 2001. Mem. Jones Electric Gary Ind. (Sec. 1986). Democratic. Baptist. Avocations: writing, cooking, numbers, crafts. E-mail: lupusarkhs@cs.com.

SMITH, JANE MARILYN DAVIS (JANE MAXWELL), writer; b. La Porte, Ind., May 18, 1939; d. Edward Moffett and Katherine Frances (Foutz) Davis; m. Donald Lee Smith, Apr. 15, 1967; children: Heidi Joanne, Allison Reneé, Steven Michael, Scott Edward Moffett Davis Smith. Cert. dental asst., Elkhart U. Med.-Dental Tech., 1964; student, Inst. Children's Lit., 1979, Nat. Writers Club, 1981, Writers Digest Sch., Cin., 1983, 84, Rocky Mountain Writers Inst., Denver, 1985, 86. Transcriptionist U. Notre Dame, Ind., 1966, clk.-typist, 1966-71. Author: Syndee the Chipmunk, 1992, Adventure on White High Island, 2000, Chang Phoouk, 2001; contbr. articles to newspapers and mags., including N.Y. Daily News, Parentguide Mag. and Ctrl. Coast Parent. Recipient hon. mention prose essay contest Byline mag., 1985. Avocations: dancing, bowling, writing, travel.

SMITH, JANE SCHNEBERGER, retired city administrator; b. Chgo., Aug. 9, 1928; d. Frank R. and Marion (Durante) Schneberger; m. Z. Erol Smith Jr., Oct. 28, 1950 (div. 1974); children: Suzan Mac Kenzie Smith, Tracy Smith Cawley, Cameron Farley, Z. Erol III, Kimberly Van Den Elzen, Scott. BA in Chemistry, U. Colo., 1950; MA in Comm., Mich. State U., 1978, PhD in Ednl. Adminstrn., 1987. Chemist Kellogg Switchboard, Chgo., 1950-51; v.p. South Cook County Girl Scouts, Harvey, Ill., 1967-69, staff advisor, 1970-72; tchr. Crab Orchard Sch., Palos Heights, Ill., 1969-70; program and tng. dir. Mich. Capitol. Coun. Girl Scouts, Lansing, Mich., 1972-75; dir. svc. learning ctr. Mich. State U., East Lansing, 1975-81; city clk. City of Ashland, Wis., 1981-89, interim city adminstr., 1989-90; ret., 1990. Cons. vol. adminstrn., Mich., Wis., 1975—. Co-editor: Looking Backward Moving Forward; contbr. articles to profl. jours. V.p. Mich. Capitol Girl Scout Coun., Lansing, 1976-78; bd. dirs. Lansing RSVP, 1976-81, Ashland Mus., 1985-87, Ptnrs. in Recovery, 1985-87; v.p. Friends of the Libr., 1992-97, pres., 1997-99; sec. New Horizons, 1985-90, New Day Shelter, 1990-99, v.p., 1993-95, pres., 1995-97, sec., 1997-99; pres. LWV of Ashland Bayfield County, 1992-93, 96-98; sec. No. Wis. History Ctr., 1992-94; commr. Ashland Water and Wastewater Utility, 1993-96; mem. Ashland Beautification Com., 1993—, Big Top Chautauqua, 1996—, vice chair Alliance for Sustainability, 1994-99; v.p. GFWC/Ashland Monday Club, 1994-98, pres., 1998-2000, 1st v.p. 10th Dist. GFWC-W1, 2000-02; mem. Ashland County Human Svcs. Bd., 1998—, Restore the Depot Com., 2001—; co-chair City of Ashland Comprehensive Plan Com., 2002—. Recipient cert. appreciation Mich. Capitol Girl Scout Coun., 1975, Thanks Badge, 1972, Tribute to Excellence award LWV of Wis., 1999. Mem. Internat. Assn. Mcpl. Clks., Wis. Mcpl. Clks. Assn. (dist. dir. 1984-86), Am. Bus. Women's Assn. (scholarship chmn. 1985), Zonta (pres. 1979-81), Ashland Hist. Soc. (bd. dirs. 2001—). Roman Catholic. Avocations: stained glass, gardening, stamp collecting, genealogy. Home: 700 Macarthur Ave Ashland WI 54806-2903 E-mail: snowmont@cheqnet.net.

SMITH, JANET ELAINE, writer; b. St. Peter, Minn., Oct. 20, 1942; d. Howard Earl Hallett, Edythe Evelyn (Bowen) Hallett; m. Ivan Howard Smith; children: Wilbert Howard, Raquel Lynette, Kevin Joel. A in Christian Edn., Bethany Coll., 1963; postgrad., Moody Bible Inst., 1963, Temple U., 1963. Missionary Worldwide Evang. Crusade, Ft. Washington, Pa., 1963—71; writer East Grand Forks, Minn., 1974—. Dir. mktg. Page Free Pub., Inc., Otsego, Mich., 2001—; tchr. genealogy Adult Edn., Grand Forks, ND, 1993—, tchr. Fiction Writing, 2001—. Author: Dunnottar, Marylebone, A Christmas Dream, In St. Patrick's Custody, Recipe for Murder, My Dear Phebe, Monday Knight, House Call to the Past; contbr. Avocations: genealogy, writing, music.

SMITH, JANET SUE, systems specialist; b. Chgo., Jan. 15, 1945; d. Curtis Edwin and Margaret Louise (Yost) Smith. BA, Ind. U., 1967. Sales mgr. Marshall Field & Co., Chgo., 1968-70, programmer, 1970-72; sr. programmer, analyst Trailer Train Co., 1972-75; mgr. data base and systems devel. Railinc-Assn. Am. R.R., Washington, 1975-85, asst. v.p., corp. sec., 1985-93, asst. v.p. strategic systems, 1994-98; exec. dir. Interline Svcs., 1998-99, asst. v.p. bus. svcs., 1999—2001; self-employed, 2002—. Nat. student v.p. YWCA, 1966-67; bd. dirs., v.p. planning and fin. Guide Internat.; advisor Jr. Achievement. Mem.: Woodburn Guild, Am. Coun. R.R. Women, Ind. U. Alumni Assn. (life). Home and Office: 903 N Columbia St Chapel Hill NC 27516-1824

SMITH, JARED RUSSELL WILLIAM, research executive, research scientist, consultant; b. Cleve., Mar. 24, 1950; s. Russell Floyd William Smith and Mary Wiltrude Lee; m. Deborah Jane Parriott; children: Russell Jared Webster, Heather Frances. BA cum laude, NYU, 1973, MA, 1976. V.p. The Energy Bur., Inc., N.Y.C., 1976-86; assoc. dir. Inst. Gas Tech., Des Plaines, Ill., 1986-99; spl. appointee Argonee (Ill.) Nat. Lab., 1999—2000; cons., 2001—. Adj. faculty NYU, N.Y.C., 1974-76; mem. adv. bd. La. State U., Baton Rouge, 1999—; adviser to Pres.'s Commn. on Critical Infrastructure Protection, Washington, 1997—; bd. dirs., adviser N.Y. Quar. Literary Found., N.Y.C., 1986. Author: (poetry books) Song of the Blood, 1983, Dark Wing, 1986, Keeping the Outlaw Alive, 1988, Walking the Perimeter of the Plate Glass Window Factory, 2000; editor: (books) Integrating Microelectronics into Gas Distribution, 1987, Gas, Oil and Coal Biotechnology, 1990. Election dist. leader Dem. Party, White Plains, N.Y., 1972; chmn. nominating com. Sch. Dist. 181, Hinsdale, Ill., 1993. Mem. Chgo. Poets Club, Poets and Patrons, Ill. State Poetry Soc. Democrat. Avocations: literature, fishing, hiking, painting, music. Home: 2630 Longview Dr Lisle IL 60532 E-mail: smithjrw@aol.com.

SMITH, JEAN, interior design firm executive; b. Oklahoma City; d. A. H. and Goldy K. (Engle) Hearn; m. W. D. Smith; children: Kaye Smith Hunt, Sidney P. Student Chgo. Sch. Interior Design, 1970. v.p. Billco-Aladdin Wholesale, Albuquerque, 1950-92, v.p. Billco Carpet One of Am, 1970. Pres. Opera Southwest, 1979-83, advisor to bd. dirs.; active Civic Chorus, 1st Meth. Ch.; pres. Inez PTA, 1954-55, life mem.; hon. life mem. Albuquerque Little Theater, bd. dirs. Republican. Clubs: Albuquerque County, Four Hills Country, Daus. of the Nile (soloist Yucca Temple). Home: 1417 Wagon Train Dr SE Albuquerque NM 87123-4295 Office: 1417 Wagon Train Dr SE Albuquerque NM 87123-4295

SMITH, JEAN WEBB (MRS. WILLIAM FRENCH SMITH), civic worker; b. L.A.; d. James Ellwood and Violet (Hughes) Webb; B.A. summa cum laude, Stanford U., 1940; m. George William Vaughan, Mar. 14, 1942 (dec. Sept. 1963); children: George William, Merry; m. William French Smith, Nov. 6, 1964. Mem. Nat. Vol. Svc. Adv. Coun. (ACTION), 1973-76, vice chmn., 1974-76; dir. Beneficial Standard Corp., 1976-85. bd. dirs. Cmty. TV So. Calif., 1979-93; mem. Calif. Arts Commn., 1971-74, vice chmn., 1973-74; bd. dirs. The Founders, Music Ctr., L.A., 1971-74; bd. dirs. costume coun. L.A. County Mus. Art, 1971-73; bd. dirs. United Way, Inc., 1973-80, Hosp. Good Samaritan, 1973-80, L.A. chpt. NCCJ, 1977-80, Nat. Symphony Orch., 1980-85, L.A. World Affairs Coun., 1990, L.A. chpt. ARC, 1994-95; bd. fellows Claremont Univ. Ctr. and Grad. Sch., 1987—; bd. dirs. Hosp. Good Samaritan, 1973-80; mem. exec. com., 1975-80; mem. nat. bd. dirs. Boys' Clubs Am., 1977-80; mem. adv. bd. Salvation Army, 1979—; bd. overseers The Hoover Instn. on War, Revolution and Peace, 1989-94; mem. President's Commn. on White House Fellowships, 1980-90, Nat. Coun. on the Humanities, 1987-90; bd. govs. Calif. Cmty. Found., 1990—; bd. regents Children's Hosp. L.A., 1993—. Named Woman of Yr. for cmty. svc. L.A. Times, 1958; recipient Citizens of Yr. award Boys Clubs Greater L.A., 1982, Life Achievement award Boy Scouts Am., L.A. coun., 1985. Mem. Jr. League of L.A. (pres. 1954-55, Spirit of Volunteerism award 1996), Assn. Jr. Leagues of Am. (dir. Region XII, 1956-58, pres. 1958-60), Phi Beta Kappa, Kappa Kappa Gamma. Home: 11718 Wetherby Ln Los Angeles CA 90077-1348

SMITH, JEANETTE ELIZABETH, lawyer; b. Pitts., Sept. 23, 1965; d. Suellen Dell. Internat. rels studies, Univ. de las Americas, Puebla, Mex., 1985, Long Island U., Urbina, Italy, 1986, Athens (Greece) Ctr., 1987; BA in Internat. Rels., Fla. Internat. U., 1989; legal studies, U. Singapore, 1991; JD, U. Miami, 1992; Cert. Legal Edn., U. West Indies, Kingston, 1998-99. Bar: Pa. 1992, Fla. 1993. Asst. dir. NASA So. Tech. Applications Ctr., Miami, Fla., 1987-88; exec. asst. Trade Fin. Corp., Coral Gables, 1989; legal intern Khattar Wong & Ptnrs., Singapore; dir. overseas ops. Trans World Trade and Mktg., Miami, 1991-95; atty., counselor-at-law Law Firm of Jeanette E. Smith, Coral Gables, 1993—; cons. Centricity, Inc., Miami, 1997; mng. ptnr. Jeanette E. Smith & Assocs., P.A., 1996-99; gen. mgr. Meditation Records, Bahamas and Miami, 1998-99; promotions and mktg. Jet Star Records, U.K. and Miami, 2001—; CEO. Stone and Tiger Entertainment Group, Miami, , 2001—; mediator Creative Dispute Resolution, Miami, 2002—. Recipient Women's Inner Circle of Achievement award. Mem. ABA, Internat. Bar Assn., Am. Immigration Lawyer's Assn., Greater Miami C. of C., Haiti Com., Caribbean C. of C. and Industry (bd. dirs. 1995-98), Asian-Am. C. of C., Phi Alpha Delta. Avocations: foreign languages, travel.

SMITH, JEANNE HAWKINS, critical care nurse; b. Atlanta, Dec. 6, 1956; d. Frank Edward Hawkins and Marcelle Cox Watkins; m. Michael G. Smith, Apr. 19, 1986; children: Cristen Michelle, Michael Shane, Lindsay Nicole, Mathew Austin. BSN, Emory U., 1978. RN, Ga.; CCRN. Staff nurse, then head nurse urology unit Emory U. Hosp., Atlanta, 1978-82; staff nurse, asst. nurse mgr. surg ICU, cardiovasc. ICU, CCU Ga. Bapt. Med. Ctr., 1985-96; case mgr. Healthfield, Inc., 1999—2001; staff nurse post anesthesia care unit Kennestone Hosp., 2001—. Home: 703 Rockingham Ct Woodstock GA 30189-2300

SMITH, JEFFREY CARLIN, lawyer; b. Chgo., Aug. 1, 1951; s. Robert Frederick and Marjorie (Carlin) S.; m. Phyllis Stagias, Oct. 7, 1978; children: Alex, Carlin. BS, Lewis and Clark Coll., 1974; JD, U. Calif., San Francisco, 1978; MBA, Pepperdine U., 1989. Bar: Calif. 1979, Md. 1989, D.C. 1989. Assoc. Gibbons, Stoddard & Lepper, Walnut Creek, Calif., 1978-81, Hyde & Drath, San Francisco, 1981-85; sr. staff counsel Times Mirror Co., L.A., 1985-88, assoc. gen. counsel, 1993-94, v.p. planning and devel., 1994-97; gen. counsel Balt. Sun, 1988-93; sr. v.p. gen. counsel IXC Comm., Austin, Tex., 1997-99; chief legal and adminstrv. officer Broadwing Inc., 1999-2001, chief human resources officer, gen. counsel, corp. sec., 2001—. Dir. Md., Del., D.C. Press Assn., Balt., 1990-93. Author: (with others) Fair Housing Advertising, 1992, Handbook Fair Housing Compliance, 1993. Dir. Pre-Columbian Art Rsch. Inst., San Francisco, 1983—; trustee Robert Louis Stevenson Sch., 1982-85, 87-90; mem. cmty. adv. bd. Helping Hand Home for Children. Mem. St. Francis Yacht Club, Austin Country Club, Bohemian Club. Office: Broadwing Inc 1122 S Capital Of Texas Hwy Austin TX 78746-6426

SMITH, JEFFREY CHIPPS, art educator; MA, Columbia U., 1975, MPhil, 1977, PhD, 1979. Kay Fortson chair in European art U. Tex., Austin, 1979—. Bd. dirs. Coll. Art Assn., 1996-2000. Author: Nuremberg, A Renaissance City, 1500-1618, 1983, German Sculpture of the Later Renaissance, c. 1520-1580: Art in an Age of Uncertainty, 1994; editor: New Perspectives on the Art of Renaissance Nuremberg: Five Essays, 1985; assoc. editor Renaissance Quarterly, 2000—; contbr. articles to profl. jours.; reviewer in field. Fellow Alexander von Humboldt-Stiftung of Bonn, Germany; ACLS grantee NEH, Getty, Guggenheim, Kimbell Art Found.; fellow Zentralinstitut Kunstgeschicht. Office: U Tex Dept Art and Art History Austin TX 78712 E-mail: chipps@mail.utexas.edu.

SMITH, JEFFREY GREENWOOD, industry executive, retired army officer; b. Ft. Sam Houston, Tex., Oct. 14, 1921; s. Henry Joseph Moody and Gladys Adrienne (Haile) S.; m. Dorothy Jane Holland, June 2, 1948; children: Meredith B. Exnicios, Jennifer H. Meyer, Jeffrey Greenwood, Tracy E. McDonald, Melissa A. Deutsch, Ashley A. Pollock. BS in Civil Engring, Va. Mil. Inst., 1943; MS in Mech. Engring, Johns Hopkins U., 1949; MA in Internat. Affairs, George Washington U., 1964. Commd. 2d lt. U.S. Army, 1944, advanced through grades to lt. gen., 1975; service in CBI, Korea, Germany and Vietnam; comdr. 2d Inf. Div., Korea, 1971-73; dep. chief staff ops. Hdqrs. Army Forces Command, Ft. McPherson, Ga., 1973-74, chief staff, 1974-75; comdr. 1st U.S. Army, Ft. Meade, Md., 1975-79; ret., 1979; dir. govt. rels. Ethyl Corp., Washington, 1980—, v.p. govt. rels., 1992—, ret., 1994. Decorated D.S.M., Silver Star, Legion of Merit with 3 oak leaf clusters, D.F.C., Bronze Star with V device and 2 oak leaf clusters, Air medal with 12 oak leaf clusters, Army Commendation medal with oak leaf cluster, Purple Heart with oak leaf cluster, Combat Inf. badge (2); breast Order Yun Hui Republic China; Order Security Merit Korea; Gallantry Cross with silver and gold stars (Vietnam) Army Distinguished Service Order Mem. Assn. U.S. Army, Mil. Order Carabao, U.S. Cavalry Assn., Kappa Alpha, Tau Beta Pi. Clubs: Army and Navy. Home: 3000 Sevor Ln Alexandria VA 22309-2221 E-mail: genjeffrey@aol.com.

SMITH, JEFFREY J. pediatric pulmonologist; b. Winona, Minn., Feb. 17, 1950; s. Leo Reginald and Jean Elizabeth (Leverson) S.; m. Heather Joy Ohrt, June 30, 1979; children: Ruxton, Spencer. BA in Chemistry, St. Mary's Coll., Winona, 1972; MD, Mayo Med. Sch., 1976. Diplomate Am. Bd. Pediatrics Pulmonology. Pediatric intern U. Minn. Hosp., Mpls., 1976-77, pediatric resident, 1976-79; practice medicine specializing in pediatrics Park Nicollet Med. Ctr., 1979-84; clin. instr. Pediatric Dept. U. Minn., 1981-83, clin. asst. prof., 1983-84; clin. asst. Pediatric Dept. U. Ariz., Tucson, 1985-88; rsch. asst.

prof. Physiology Dept. U. Ariz., 1987-88; assoc. Pediatric Dept. U. Iowa, Iowa City, 1988-89, asst. prof., 1989-95; assoc. prof. U. Iowa, 1995—. Chmn. Dept. Pediatrics Nicollet Clinic, Mpls., 1981-82. Recipient Clin. Fellowship award Am. Lung Assn., N.Y.C., 1985-87, Abstract Travel award, Am. Fed. for Clin. Rsch., Thorofare, N.J., 1987, Rsch. Fellowship award Cystic Fibrosis Found., 1987-88, Basil O'Connor Scholar Rsch. award March of Dimes, 1988-91, Gold Coast award for excellence in cystic fibrosis rsch., 1996; fellow in Pulmonary rsch. Parker B. Francis Found., 1989-91. Mem. AAAS, Am. Thoracic Soc., Am. Acad. Pediat., Soc. Pediat. Rsch., Am. Fed. for Clin. Rsch., N.Y. Acad. Scis. Avocations: flying, gardening, rug weaving. Office: U Iowa Hosp & Clinics Iowa City IA 52242

SMITH, JEFFREY MICHAEL, lawyer; b. Mpls., July 9, 1947; s. Philip and Gertrude E. (Miller) S.; 1 son, Brandon Michael. Student, U. Malaya, 1967-68; BA cum laude, U. Minn., 1970, JD magna cum laude, 1973. Bar: Ga. 1973. Assoc. Powell, Goldstein, Frazier & Murphy, 1973-76; ptnr. Rogers & Hardin, 1976-79, Bondurant, Stephenson & Smith, 1979-85, Arnall, Golden & Gregory, 1985-92, Katz, Smith & Cohen, 1992-98; shareholder Greenberg Traurig, 1998—. Vis. lectr. Duke U., 1976-77, 79-80, 89-93; adj. prof. Emory U., 1976-79, 81-82; lectr. Vanderbilt U., 1977-82. Co-author: Preventing Legal Malpractice, 1999, Legal Malpractice, 1999. Bd. visitors Law Sch. U. Minn., 1976-82. Mem. ABA (vice-chmn. com. profl. liability 1980-82, mem. standing com. lawyer's profl. liability 1981-85, chmn. 1985-87, standing com. lawyer competency 1993-95), State Bar Ga. (chmn. profl. liability and ins. com. 1978-89, trustee Inst. Cont. Legal Edn. in Ga. 1979-80), Order of the Coif, Phi Beta Kappa. Home: 145 15th St NE Apt 811 Atlanta GA 30309-3559 Office: 3290 Northside Dr NW Ste 400 Atlanta GA 30305-1910

SMITH, JEFFREY ROBERT, historian, educator; b. New London, Conn., Dec. 12, 1966; s. L. Glenn and Joan Karen Smith BA, Rice U., 1989; MA, U. Ill., 1991, PhD, 1997. Prof. history Northwestern State U., Natchitoches, La., 1998—. Author: World War I and the Cultures of Modernity, 2000. German Acad. Exchange Svc. rsch. grantee, 1993-94; U. Ill. history fellow, 1994-95. Mem. Am. Hist. Assn., Phi Alpha Theta, Phi Kappa Phi. Avocation: golf. Office: Dept Social Scis Northwestern State U Natchitoches LA 71497 E-mail: smithj@nsula.edu.

SMITH, JEFFREY S. music educator; b. Stamford, Conn., Nov. 19, 1952; s. John C. and Jane S. Smith; m. Diane S. Smith, June 23, 1975; children: Alan D., Peter C., Jonathan W. BS in Music Edn., Western Conn. State U., 1975, MS in Music Edn., 1982. Cert. tchr. Conn. Band dir. Ponus Ridge Middle Sch., Norwalk, Conn., 1975—77, Brien McMahon H.S., Norwalk, 1977—82, Norwalk H.S., Norwalk, 1982—. Hawthorne Caballeros designer Sr. Drum and Bugle Corps, Hawthorne, NJ, 1998—2001, Com. Hurricanes show coord., NJ, 1998—2001; Brien McMahon H.S. show designer Brien McMahon Band Parts, Norwalk, 2001—. Mem. parent com. Boy Scouts Am., Norwalk, 1982—. Named Music Educators of Yr., Conn. Music Edn. Assn., 1998, Band Dir. of Yr., Ea. Marching Bd. Assn., 1999; recipient Alumnus award of Yr., West Conn. State U., 2001. Mem.: Am. Sch. Band Dirs. Assn., Music Educators Nat. Conf., Phi Beta Mu. Avocations: fishing, dog obedience training. Home: 12 Suburban Dr Norwalk CT 06851 Office: Norwalk HS 23 Calvin Murphy Dr Norwalk CT 06851

SMITH, JEFFRY ALAN, health administrator, physician, consultant; b. L.A., Dec. 8, 1943; s. Stanley W. and Marjorie E. S.; m. Jo Anne Hague. BA in Philosophy, UCLA, 1967, MPH, 1972; BA in Biology, Calif. State U., Northridge, 1971; MD, UACJ, 1977. Diplomate Am. Bd. Family Practice. Resident in family practice WAH, Takoma Park, Md., NIH, Bethesda, Walter Reed Army Hosp., Washington, Children's Hosp. Nat. Med. Ctr., Washington, 1977-80; occupational physician Nev. Test Site, U.S. Dept. Energy, Las Vegas, 1981-82; dir. occupational medicine and environ. health Pacific Missile Test Ctr., Point Mugu, Calif., 1982-84; dist. health officer State Hawaii Dept. Health, Kauai, 1984-86; asst. dir. health County of Riverside (Calif.) Dept. Health, 1986-87; regional med. dir. Calif. Forensic Med. Group, Monterey, Calif., 1987-94; med. dir. Cmty. Human Svcs., 1987-94, Colstrip (Mont.) Med. Ctr., 1994-97; cons. San Bernadino County, Riverside County, Riverside, Calif., 1998—; regional med. dir. Point Loma Healthcare Med. Group, Inc., San Diego, 1997-99; med. dir., CEO So. Calif. Mobile Physician Svcs., Riverside, Calif., 1997—. Fellow Am. Acad. Family Physicians; mem. AMA, Am. Occupational Medicine Assn., Flying Physicians, Am. Pub. Health Assn. Avocations: pvt. pilot. Office: Ste 71-448 5225 Canyon Crest Dr Riverside CA 92507-6301

SMITH, JERRALYN RENÉE, marketing professional, consultant; b. Houston, Oct. 8, 1957; d. Gerald Harris and Rita Faye (Minsky) S. BS with honors, U. Tex., 1979. Lic. interior designer, Tex., 1992-99. Design assoc./urban planner J.T. Dunkin & Assocs., Dallas, 1980-83; interior designer/store planner Sanger Harris/Federated Stores, 1983-85; project designer/space planner Crescent Interior Planning Group divsn. Rosewood, 1985-86; prin., designer and cons. J.R. Smith & Assocs., 1986-92; dir. comm. and mktg. Internat. Assn. Elec. Insps., Richardson, 1992-98, with, 1992—98, also mng. editor IAEI News; mktg. comm. cons. Electronic Data Sys. Corp., Plano, 1998—2002, global mktg and portfolio mgmt., 2002—. Mng. editor IAEI News, 1992—. Vol. Habitat for Humanity, Dallas., 1995-96; race dir. Kidsport Triathlon, Am. Red Cross Dallas, 1989, chair, 1990-91, exec. com. for youth svcs., 1990-92; newsletter editor, vol. trainer Inner City outings Sierra Club, Dallas., 1992-94. Recipient Vol. Appreciation award Am. Red Cross, Dallas, 1991. Mem. Internat. Assn. Bus. Communicators (media coord. Dallas 1995-96). Avocations: running, snow skiing. Office: Electronic Data Systems Corp 5400 Legacy Dr Plano TX 75024-3199 E-mail: jerri.smith@eds.com.

SMITH, JERRY EDWIN, federal judge; b. Del Rio, Tex., Nov. 7, 1946; s. Lemuel Edwin and Ruth Irene (Henderson) Smith; m. Mary Jane Blackburn, June 4, 1977; children: Clark, Ruth Ann, J.J. BA, Yale U., 1969, JD, 1972. Bar: Tex. 1972. Law clk. to judge U.S. Dist. Ct. (no. dist.) Tex., Lubbock, 1972—73; assoc. then ptnr. Fulbright & Jaworski, Houston, 1973—84; dir. Harris County housing auth., 1978—80; special asst. office of atty. gen., 1981—82; Chmn. Houston Civ. Svc. Comm., 1982—84; city atty. City of Houston, 1984—87; cir. judge U.S. Ct. Appeals (5th cir.), Houston, 1988—. Chmn. Harris County Rep. Party, Houston, 1977—78; committeeman State Rep. Exec. Com., 1976—88. Mem.: Houston Bar Assn., State Bar Tex. Methodist. Office: US Ct Appeals Bob Casey US Courthouse 515 Rusk St Rm 12621 Houston TX 77002-2698*

SMITH, JESSE GRAHAM, JR. dermatologist, educator; b. Winston-Salem, N.C., Nov. 22, 1928; s. Jesse Graham and Pauline Field (Griffith) S.; m. Dorothy Jean Butler, Dec. 28, 1950; children: Jesse Graham, Cynthia Lynn, Grant Butler. BS, Duke U., 1962, MD, 1951. Diplomate: Am. Bd. Dermatology (dir. 1974-83, pres. 1980-81). Intern VA Hosp., Chamblee, Ga., 1951-52; resident in dermatology Duke U., 1954-56, assoc. prof. dermatology, 1960-62, prof., 1962-67; resident U. Miami, 1956-57, asst. prof., 1957-60; prof. dermatology Med. Coll. Ga., 1967-91, chmn. dept. dermatology, 1967-91, acting chmn. dept. pathology, 1973-75, acting v.p. devel., 1984-85; chief staff Talmadge Meml. Hosp., Augusta, Ga., 1970-72; prof. dermatology, chief divsn. of dermatology U. South Ala., Mobile, 1991-98, prof. emeritus, 1999—. Mem. advisory council Nat. Inst. Arthritis, 1975-79 Editorial bd. Archives of Dermatology, 1963-72, Jour. Investigative Dermatology, 1966-67, Jour. AMA, 1974-80; editorial bd. So. Med. Jour., 1976-2000, assoc. editor, 1991-92, editor, 1992-2000; editor Jour. Am. Acad. Dermatology, 1978-88; contbr. chpts. to books, articles to profl. jours. Served with USPHS, 1952-54. Recipient Disting. Alumnus award Duke U. 1981 Fellow ACP, Royal Soc. Medicine; mem. Am. Acad. Dermatology (hon., dir. 1971-74, 78-88, pres.-elect 1988-89, pres. 1989-90), Can. Dermatol. Assn. (hon.), Am. Dermatol. Assn. (hon. sec. 1976-81, pres. 1981-82), Soc. Investigative Dermatology (dir. 1964-69, pres. 1979-80), S.E. Dermatol. Assn. (sec. 1970-71, pres. 1975-76), Ga. Soc. Dermatology (pres. 1979-80), So. Med. Assn. (chmn. sect. dermatology 1973-74), Assn. Profs. Dermatology (dir. 1976-77, 80-82, pres. 1984-86), Med. Rsch. Found. Ga. (bd. dirs. 1967-91, pres. 1974-75), Alpha Omega Alpha. Home: 4272 Bitand Spur # 4 Mobile AL 36608 Office: Diagnostic and Med Clinic Ste 100 1700 Spring Hill Ave Mobile AL 36604-1407 E-mail: skeesmith@mindspring.com.

SMITH, JILL GALBREATH, lawyer; b. Kansas City, Mo., Nov. 1, 1963; d. William Lawrence and Joyce (Webb) Galbreath; m. Tracy Neil Smith, Apr. 28, 1990; children: Collin Blakely, William Connor, Cooper Whitney. BA in Polit. Sci., U. Kans., 1986, JD, 1989. Bar: Mo. 1989, Kans. 1990, U.S. Dist. Ct. (we. dist.) Mo. 1989, U.S. Dist. Ct. Kans. 1990. Assoc. Brown, James & Rabbitt, Kansas City, 1989-90, Perry, Hamill & Fillmore, Overland Park, Kans., 1990-95; of counsel Spencer, Fane, Britt & Browne, LLP, 1995—2002; ptnr. Holman, Hansen, Colvile & Coates, P.C., 2002—. Sec., bd. dirs. Johnson County CASA, Olathe, Kans., 1995-2001; mem. Jr. League of Wyandotte and Johnson Counties, Kansas, 1992—. Recipient 1st place award for svc. to pub. ABA, 1995. Mem. Kans. Bar Assn., Mo. Bar Assn., Johnson County Bar Assn. (sec., pres.-elect, pres. young lawyers sect. 1992-95, bd. dirs. 1994-95, 96-2000), Kansas City Met. Bar Assn. Office: Holman Hansen Colvile & Coates PC 10724 Nall Ste 200 Overland Park KS 66212

SMITH, JIM, professional sports team executive; m. Marlene Smith; 1 child Melissa. Team owner Ultra Motorsports, Mooresville, NC, 1993—. Founder Ultra Wheel Co. Active several charities. Office: Ultra Motorsports 222 Raceway Dr Mooresville NC 28115

SMITH, JIMMY, JR. football player; b. Detroit, Feb. 9, 1969; m. Sandra; 1 child, Jimmy Lee III. BS in Bus. Mgmt., Jackson State, 1992. Wide receiver Dallas Cowboys, 1992-94, Philadelphia Eagles, 1994, Jacksonville Jaguars, 1995—. Active Wolfson Children's Hosp., Jimmy Smith Scholarship Fund; personalized and signed child-sized chair to raise funds for re-design of Neonatal Intensive Care Unit, critical rsch. in asthma, and expansion of Bone Marrow Transplant Unit, hon. chmn. Chairs that Care fundraiser; Jaguars' 1999 NFL-United Way co-spokesman; ptnr. with Am. Lung Assn. Fla. for asthma awareness campaign; pub. svc. announcement with Jacksonville Mayor John Delaney; anti-tobacco pub. svc. announcement Jaguars Found. Named to Pro Bowl, 1997, 98, 99; named second-team All-Pro, AP, 1998, 99, Football News, Coll. and Pro Football Newsweekly, 1999, All-AFC, Pro Football Weekly, Football News, 1999; recipient Mackey award, 1996. Office: One ALLTEL Stadium Pl Jacksonville FL 32202*

SMITH, JO ANN COSTA, retired comptroller; b. Houston, Dec. 19, 1937; d. Joseph Anthony and Anna Lois (Grice) Costa; m. Alton Paul Smith, Mar. 3, 1957; children: Robert Carlton, Rex Alan. Grad. high sch., Navasota, Tex. Bookkeeper Our Lady of Victory Ch., Paris, 1968-69; asst. office mgr. Ayres Dept. Store, 1969-71; cashier, clk. Mid South Electric Co-op, Navasota, 1971-77; owner, mgr. The Gift Shop, 1977-97; v.p., comptroller Smith Bros. Impl. Co. Inc., Tex., 1998—2001; ret., 2001. Pack mother Cub Scouts, Paris, 1965-67; v.p. Grimes County United Way, 1988-89, pres., 1989-90, bd. dirs., 1987—. Mem. Grimes County C. of C. (2d v.p. 1986, pres. 1987-88), Ciara Study Club (pres. 1969-70), Brazos Valley Bus. and Profl. Womens Club (charter, chmn. pub. rels. com. 1989-90). Democrat. Roman Catholic. Home: PO Box 70 Navasota TX 77868-0070 Office: Smith Bros Impl Co Inc PO Box 112 Navasota TX 77868-0112

SMITH, JO ANNE, writer, retired educator; b. Mpls., Mar. 18, 1930; d. Robert Bradburn and Virginia Mae S. BA, U. Minn., 1951, MA, 1957. Wire and sports editor Rhinelander (Wis.) Daily News, 1951-52; staff corr., night mgr. UPI, Mpls., 1952-56; interim instr. U. N.C., Chapel Hill, 1957-58; instr. U. Fla., Gainesville, 1959-65, asst. prof. journalism, communications, 1965-68, assoc. prof., 1968-76, prof., 1976-88, disting. lectr., 1977. Author: JM409 Casebook and Study Guide, 1976, Mass Communications Law Casebook, 1979, 3d edit., 1985. Active, Friends of Libr., Alachua County Humane Soc. Recipient outstanding Prof. award Fla. Blue Key, 1976; Danforth assoc., 1976-85. Mem. Women in Communications, Assn. Edn. in Journalism, Phi Beta Kappa, Kappa Tau Alpha. Democrat. Unitarian Universalist. Home: 208 NW 21st Ter Gainesville FL 32603-1732

SMITH, JOAN H. retired women's health nurse, educator; b. Akron, Ohio; d. Joseph A. and Troynette M. (Lower) McDonald; m. William G. Smith; children: Sue Ann, Priscilla, Timothy. Diploma, Akron City Hosp., 1948; BSN in Edn., U. Akron, 1972, MA in Family Devel., 1980. Cert. in inpatient obstetric nursing. Mem. faculty Akron Gen. Med. Ctr. Sch. Nursing, 1964; former dir. obstet. spl. procedures Speakers Bur., Women's Health Ctrs. Akron Gen. Med. Ctr., 1988; ret., 1990. Cons., speaker women's health care. Mem. Assn. Women's Health, Obstet. and Neonatal Nursing (charter, past sec.-treas., past vice chmn. Ohio sect., chmn. program various confs.). Home: 873 Kirkwall Dr Copley OH 44321-1751

SMITH, JOAN LOWELL, syndicated columnist, feature writer; b. Orange, N.J., June 20, 1933; d. William Jr. and Katherine Margaret (Macpherson) Lowell; m. John A. Nave, Dec. 14, 1957 (div. May 1961); children: Deborah Lowell Kelly, Nancy Nave Ferguson; m. Warren W. Smith, July 19, 1969. Student, Lasell Coll., 1951-52, Drake Bus. Sch., N.Y.C., 1952-53. Exec. sec. Amb. Ernest A. Gross, N.Y.C., 1954-57; adminstrv. asst./v.p. J.B. Williams Co. (Geritol), Clark, N.J., 1966-74; pub. rels. dir. N.J. State Opera, Newark, 1974-78; weekly talk show host-radio WJDM (AM) WFME (AM-FM), Elizabeth and West Orange, N.J., 1974-82; weekly talk show host Sta. WCTV, Wometco, 1975-79; exec. dir. Chamber of Commerce, Westfield, N.J., 1976-79; legis. aide Assemblyman C. Hardwick, 1980-82; exec. dir. Alzheimer's Disease Fund, Westfield, 1986-87; pub. rels. dir. Children's Specialized Hosp., Mountainside, 1993-94; pres./owner Media Mgmt., Westfield, 1974-95; feature writer, weekly columnist on animals The Star-Ledger, Newark, 1996—. Named one of 40 Women of Achievement, N.J. State Assembly, 2001; recipient 39 awards, N.J. Press Woman, 1991—, Humane Edn. award, Jersey Animal Coalition, 2001. Mem.: DAR (regent 1987—89), Westfield Day Care Ctr. (bd. dirs.), Nat. Fedn. Press Women (2d pl. award 1997, 1st pl. columnist award 1998), Assn. Children with Learning Disabilities (chmn. bd. dirs. 1980—82), Cat Writers Assn. Am. (2d pl. columnist 1999), Dog Writers Assn. Am. (top features writer 1998, top columnist award 2001), Daus. of Cin., Geneal. Soc. of West Fields (bd. dirs. 1984—88). Republican. Presbyterian. Avocations: Bible studies, swimming, bridge, geneology. Office: PO Box 302 Garwood NJ 07027-0302

SMITH, JOBAN JONATHAN, security consultant; b. Albuquerque, Mar. 7, 1962; s. William Oswalt and Lou Ella (Agan) Hernandez; 1 child, Connor Nigel Smith. Student, Pensacola Christian Coll., 1980-81, Bradley U., 1981-82; BA in Psychology, Fellowship U., 1985; AA in Alcohol and Drug Counseling, SIPI, Albuquerque, 1990. Underwater demolitions trainer Dept. Defense, Pensacola, Fla., 1980-81, courier, escort Peoria, Ill., 1982-86, U.S. Consulate, N.Y.C., 1987-88; security cons. Atlantic Record Co., L.A., 1988; recreation therapist Indian Health Svc., Iselta, New Mex., 1990-91, Manor Care Nursing Home, Albuquerque, 1991—; owner, CEO Med. Security Corp., 1999—. Owner Joban Smith & Assocs., Albuquerque, 1990—; cons. S.W. Fun & Lesiure, Albuquerque, 1991—, McGartland & Assocs., 1991—. Mem. NRA, Nat. Assn. Security Cons., New Mex. Activities Assn. Avocations: scuba diving, fishing, track and field.

SMITH, JOE DORSEY, JR. retired newspaper executive; b. Selma, La., Apr. 6, 1922; s. Joe Dorsey and Louise (Lindsay) S.; 1 child, Lawrence Dorsey. BA, La. Coll. Pineville, 1939-43. Gen. mgr. Alexandria Daily Town Talk, La., 1958—, pub., 1965—; pres. McCormick & Co., Inc., 1968—, chmn., 1990-96. Served with USAF, 1942-45. Mem. Alexandria Golf and Country Club, Boston Club, New Orleans Club. Democrat. Episcopalian. Home: 2804 Georges Ln Alexandria LA 71301-4723 Office: Ste 1003 Hibernia Bldg 934 3rd St Alexandria LA 71301-8383 E-mail: smith7462@aol.com.

SMITH, JOEY SPAULS, mental health nurse, home health nurse, biofeedback therapist, consultant, educator; b. Washington, Oct. 9, 1944; d. Walter Jr. and Marian (Och) Spauls; children: Kelly, Sean. BSN, Med. Coll. Va., 1966; MA in Edn., U. Nebr., Lincoln, 1975. RNC, ANCC; cert. psychiat. and mental health nurse; cert. zero balancer, cert. hypnotist, cert. biofeedback therapist; cert. perineometry cons.; ANCC cert. home health nurse. 1st lt. U.S. Army Nurse Corps, 1965-67; staff nurse Booth Meml. Hosp., Omaha, 1969-71; asst. house supr. Nebr. Meth. Hosp., 1971-72; head nurse, clin. instr. U. Calif., Davis, 1976-78; staff nurse Atascadero State Hosp., Calif. Dept. Mental Health, 1978-79; nurse instr. psychiat. technician Atascadero State Hosp., 1979-84, insvc. tng. coord., 1984-86; nursing coord. chem. dependency recovery program French Hosp. Med. Ctr., San Luis Obispo, Calif., 1986-87; relief house supr. San Luis Obispo County Gen. Hosp., 1982-88; regional program assoc. statewide nursing program Consortium Calif. Sate U., 1986-88; nurse instr., health svcs. staff devel. coord. Calif. Men's Colony, Dept. Corrections, San Luis Obispo, 1987-92; pvt. practice Calif., 1990—; clin. instr. nursing divsn. Cuesta Coll., 1988—. Fellow Biofeedback Certification Inst. of Am.; mem. Assn. Applied Psychophysiology and Biofeedback, Biofeedback Soc. of Calif., Zero Balancing Assn. (cert.), Esalen Massage and Bodyworkers Assn., Soc. Urol. Nurses and Assocs., Ctrl. Coast Nurses Coop. Coun., Biofeedback Cert. Inst. Am., Alpha Sigma Chi, Phi Delta Kappa. Office: PO Box 4823 San Luis Obispo CA 93403-4823

SMITH, JOHN ANDREW, veterinarian; b. Atlanta, Jan. 19, 1951; s. John Edwin and Ruby Hazel (Andrews) S.; m. Emily Ann Meriwether, July 10, 1982. DVM, U. Ga., 1975, MS in Med. Microbiology, 1983, M in Avian Medicine, 1991. Lic. veterinarian, Ala., Ga., N.C., S.C.; diplomate Am. Coll. Vet. Internal Medicine, Am. Coll. Poultry Veterinarians. Veterinarian Highland Park Animal Clinic, Dallas, 1976-77; intern, instr. Auburn (Ala.) U., 1977-79, asst. prof., 1982-83; resident U. Ga., Athens, 1979-82, grad. asst., 1989-91; asst. prof. Colo. State U., Ft. Collins, 1983-89, assoc. prof., 1989; dir. health svcs. Fieldale Farms Corp., Baldwin, Ga., 1991—. Contbr. chpts. to books. Capt. U.S. Army, 1975-77. Mem. AVMA, Am. Assn. Avian Pathologists, Poultry Sci. Assn., Assn. Veterinarians in Broiler Prodn. (pres. 1995-96), Nat. Broiler Coun. (chmn. com. 1996), Nat. Chicken Coun., U.S. Animal Health Assn., Am. Coll. Vet. Internal Medicine, Poultry Vets., Phi Eta Sigma, Phi Kappa Phi, Phi Zeta, Gamma Sigma Delta. Avocations: upland game bird hunting, skeet shooting, sporting clays. Home: 395 Ridge Cir Baldwin GA 30511-2409 Office: Fieldale Farms Corp PO Box 558 Baldwin GA 30511-0558 E-mail: johnsmith@fieldale.com.

SMITH, JOHN BREWSTER, library administrator; b. Bryan, Tex., June 26, 1937; s. Elmer Gillam and Sara Roland (Lull) S.; m. Ida Hawa, Dec. 28, 1963; children: Susan Helen, Rona Esther. BA, Tex. A & M U., 1960; MS, Columbia U., 1963, cert. advanced librarianship, 1984, DLS, 1991. Asst. law librarian Columbia U., N.Y.C., 1963-66; asst. library dir. for pub. services Tex. A & M U., College Station, 1966-69, dir. libraries, 1969-74; dir. libraries, dean library scis. SUNY, Stony Brook, 1974-96, dir. library and info. sci. tchg. program, 1996-97; chief libr. Bronx Cmty. Coll., CUNY, 1997-2000, cons. on libr. mgmt., 2000—. Named Librarian of Year Tex. Library Assn., 1972 Mem. ALA. Home and Office: 108 Inverness Dr Montgomery TX 77356-5877

SMITH, JOHN EDWIN, philosophy educator; b. Bklyn., May 27, 1921; s. Joseph Robert and Florence Grace (Dunn) S.; m. Marilyn Blanche Schulhof, Aug. 25, 1951; children: Robin Dunn, Diana Edwards. AB, Columbia U., 1942, PhD, 1948; BD, Union Theol. Sem., N.Y.C., 1945; MA, Yale U., 1959; LL.D., U. Notre Dame, 1964. Instr. religion and philosophy Vassar Coll., 1945-46; instr., then asst. prof. Barnard Coll., 1946-52; mem. faculty Yale U., 1952—, prof. philosophy, 1959—, chmn. dept., 1961—, Clark prof. philosophy, 1972-91, Clark prof. philosophy emeritus, 1991—. Vis. prof. Union Theol. Sem., 1959, U. Mich., 1958; guest prof. U. Heidelberg, Germany, 1955-56; Fagothey chair of philosophy U. Santa Clara, 1984, vis. prof. Boston Coll., 1992; Dudleian lectr. Harvard, 1960; lectr. Am. Week, U. Munich, Germany, 1961; Suarez lectr. Fordham U., 1963; pub. lectr. King's College, Univ. London, 1965; Aquinas lectr. Marquette U., 1967; Warfield lectr. Princeton Theol. Sem., 1970; Fulbright lectr. Kyoto U., Japan, 1971; Sprunt lectr. Union Theol. Sem., Va., 1973; Mead-Swing lectr. Oberlin Coll., 1975; H. Richard Niebuhr lectr. Elmhurst Coll., Ill., 1977; Merrick lectr. Ohio Wesleyan U., 1977; Roy Wood Sellars lectr. Bucknell U., 1978; O'Hara lectr. U. Notre Dame, 1984; Hooker disting. vis. prof. Mc Master U., 1985; mem. adv. com. Nat. Humanities Inst., New Haven, 1974, dir., 1977-80. Author: Royce's Social Infinite, 1950, Value Convictions and Higher Education, 1958, Reason and God, 1961, The Spirit of American Philosophy, 1963, 2d edit., 1983, The Philosophy of Religion, 1965, Religion and Empiricism, 1967, Experience and God, 1968, revised edit., 1995, Themes in American Philosophy, 1970, Contemporary American Philosophy, 1970, The Analogy of Experience, 1973, Purpose and Thought: The Meaning of Pragmatism, 1978, America's Philosophical Vision, 1992, Jonathan Edwards, Puritan, Preacher, Philosopher, 1992, Quasi-Religions: Humanism, Marxism, Nationalism, 1994, Reason, Experience, and God, 1997; translator: (R. Kroner): Kant's Weltanschauung, 1956; editor: (Jonathan Edwards): Religious Affections, Vol. 2, 1959, An Edwards Reader, 1995; gen. editor, Yale edit.: Works of Jonathan Edwards, 1965-91, gen. editor emeritus, 1992—; Editorial bd.: Monist, 1962—, Jour. Religious Studies, Philosophy East and West, Jour. Chinese Philosophy, The Personalist Forum, Jour. Faith and Philosophy, Jour. Speculative Philosophy. Named Hon. Alumnus, Harvard Div. Sch., 1960; recipient Herbert W. Schneider award Soc. for Advancement of Am. Philosophy, 1990, Founder's medal Metaphys. Soc. Am., 1996; Am. Coun. Learned Socs. fellow, 1964-65. Mem. Culinary Inst. Am. (dir. New Haven affiliate), Am. Philos. Assn. (v.p. 1980, pres. 1981), Am. Theol. Soc. (pres. 1967-68), Metaphys. Soc. Am. (pres. 1970-71, founder's medal, 1996), Hegel Soc. Am. (pres. 1971), Charles S. Peirce Soc. (pres. 1992). Home: 300 Ridgewood Ave Hamden CT 06517-1428 Office: PO Box 201562 New Haven CT 06520-1562 E-mail: john.smith@yale.edu.

SMITH, JOHN FRANCIS, materials science educator; b. Kansas City, Kans., May 9, 1923; s. Peter Francis and Johanna Teresa (Spandle) S.; m. Evelyn Ann Ross, Sept. 1, 1947 (dec. July 1994); children— Mark Francis, Letitia Ann Smith Harder; m. Eileen R. Ross, Apr. 12, 1997. BA with distinction, U. Mo.-Kansas City, 1948; PhD, Iowa State U., 1953. Grad. asst. Iowa State U., Ames, 1948-53, faculty and research scientist 1953-88, dept. chmn., div. chief Ames Lab., 1966-70. Cons. Tex. Instruments, Inc., Dallas and Attleboro, Mass., 1958-63, Argonne Nat. Lab., Ill., 1964-70, Iowa Hwy. Commn., Ames, Los Alamos Nat. Lab., N.Mex., 1984-88, bur. standards Nat. Inst. Standards and Tech., Gaithersburg, Md., 1988-91, Sandia Nat. Lab., Albuquerque, N.M., 1991-92, ASM Internat., Cleve., 1992—. Patentee ultrasonic determination of texture in metal sheet and plate, lead-free solder; author: Phase Diagrams of Binary Vanadium Alloys; Hellcats Over the Philippine Deep; co-author: Thorium: Preparation and Properties, 1975; editor: Calculation of Phase Diagrams and Thermochemistry of Alloy Phases, 1978; editor Jour. Phase Equilibria; contbr. articles to profl. pubs. Mem. former comdr. Ames-Boone Squadron CAP, 1970-75. With USN, 1942-46, PTO, comdr. USNR, 1946-64. Decorated Air medal with star; recipient Disting. Svc. award CAP, Maxwell AFB, Ala., 1979, faculty citation Iowa State U. Alumni Assn., Ames, 1977. Fellow Am. Inst. Chemists, ASM (chmn. Des Moines chpt. 1966); mem. AIME, Materials Rsch. Soc., Am. Legion, Silent Knights, Inc. (trustee 1980-96), Exptl. Aircraft Assn., Alpha Sigma Mu (trustee 1984-86). Roman Catholic. Avocation: flying. Home: 2919 S Riverside RR 5 Box 343 Ames IA 50010-9520 Office: Iowa State U Ames Lab 136F Wilhelm Hall Ames IA 50010

SMITH, JOHN JOSEPH, JR. textile company executive, educator; b. Fall River, Mass., Feb. 11, 1913; s. John J. and Mabel E. (Reid) S.; m. Mary C. Moson, Aug. 8, 1936; children— Nancy S. (Mrs. John Lee Lesher, Jr.), Robert J. BS in Chem. Engring., Tufts U., 1935. With Johnson & Johnson subsidiary Chicopee Mfg. Corp., New Brunswick, N.J., 1935—; pres. Chicopee Mfg. Corp., 1959—, chmn., 1971-74; with Chicopee Mills, Inc., N.Y.C., 1959—, pres., 1960—, chmn., 1971-75. Dir. Johnson & Johnson, New Brunswick, 1961-74, mem. exec. com., 1966-74; chmn. Chicopee Cuyk Holland, Devro Moodiesburn Scotland; adj. prof. Fla. Atlantic U., Boca Raton, 1976-82. Mem. Am. Assn. Tech. Colorists and Chemists, Am. Chem. Soc., Tau Beta Pi, Gulf Stream Golf Club, The Little Club, Delray Beach (Fla.) Club, The Misquamicut Club, Watch Hill (R.I.) Yacht Club. Home: 1225 S Ocean Blvd Delray Beach FL 33483-6534 also: Rock Ridge 7 Everett Ave Westerly RI 02891-5737

SMITH, JOHN JOSEPH, JR. financial management executive; b. Binghamton, N.Y., Mar. 1, 1942; s. John J. and Rosina C. Smith; m. Yvonne Foley; children: John, Maura, Jennifer. BS in Bus. Adminstrn., King's Coll., 1965. CPA, N.C., N.Y.; CFP; registered investment advisor. Supervising acct. Touche Ross & Co., N.Y.C., 1966-71; asst. to contr. Akzona, Asheville, N.C., 1971-78; divisional planning mgr. BASF, Wyandotte, Mich., 1978-79; CPA, audit mgr. Crawley, Johnson, Price & Sprinkle, Asheville, 1978-79; pvt. practice, 1979-86; ptnr., principal Parsec Fin. Mgmt., 1986—. Bd. fin. advisors Charles Schwab & Co., San Francisco, 1992; mem. bd. examiners Cert. Fin. Planners, 1999-2002. Bd. dirs. WCQS Pub. Radio, Asheville, 1982-89; dir. St. Joseph's Hosp. Found., Asheville, 1987-91; bd. chmn., treas. Asheville YMCA, 1992-93. Mem. AICPA, N.C. Assn. CPAs, Nat. Assn. Fin. Planners (bd. dirs., former pres., so. region), Internat. Assn. Fin. Planners.

SMITH, JOHN KERWIN, lawyer; b. Oct. 18, 1926; 1 child, Cynthia. BA, Stanford U.; LLB, Hastings Coll. Law. Ptnr. Haley, Purchio, Sakai & Smith, Hayward, Calif. Bd. dirs. Berkeley Asphalt, Mission Valley Ready-Mix, Coliseum Found., Mission Valley Rock, Rowell Ranch Rodeo, Hastings Coll. Law (alumnus of yr. award 1989). Gen. ptnr. Oak Hills Apts., City Ctr. Commercial, Creekwood I and II Apts.; Road Parks commn. 1957; city coun. 1959-66, mayor 1966-70; chmn. Alameda County Mayors conf. 1968, revenue taxation com. League Calif. Cities, 1968; vice chmn. Oakland-Alameda County Coliseum; vol. Hastings 1066 Found. (pres., vol. svc. award 1990), Martin Kauffman 100 Club; bd. dirs. Hastings Coll. of Law, 1999—. Mem. ABA, Calif. Bar Assn., Alameda County Bar Assn., Am. Judicature Soc., Rotary. Office: Haley Purchio Sakai & Smith 22320 Foothill Blvd Ste 620 Hayward CA 94541-2700 E-mail: hpssckb@aol.com.

SMITH, JOHN LEROY, mathematics educator; b. Cooper, Tex., July 15, 1944; s. John Jr. and Annie (West) Smith; m. Barbara Ann Frazier, Dec. 27, 1965 (div. Apr. 1972); m. Mary Anne Anthony, June 17, 1978; children: Alexander Anthony, Anastasia Marie, Jeannette Joy. BS in Math., U. Wash., 1966; MA in Math., San Diego State U., 1971; BS in Info. & Computer Sci., U. Calif., Irvine, 1986. Computer operator U. Wash., Seattle, 1964-66; tchr. math., sci., English Highline (Wash.) Sch. Dist., Highline, 1966-70; tchr. math. & computer scis. Kwajalein (Marshall Islands) Jr./Sr. H.S., 1973-75; instr. scuba diving Santa Ana (Calif.) Coll., 1978-91; prof. math., computer sci. Rancho Santiago C.C. Dist., Santa Ana, 1975—; math dept. chair Santiago Canyon Coll., Orange, Calif., 1998—2002. Mem. adv. bd. govs. Faculty Assn. Calif. C.C., Sacramento, 1991—99; treas. faculty assn. Rancho Santiago C.C., 1988—, FARSCCD PAC, 1990—2001, v.p., 2001—, mem. or-co-log task force, 2001—02; pres. Santiago Canyon Coll. Acad. Senate, 1999—; spkr. Internat. Conv. Underwater Edn., 1978, 86, 87. Editor (newsletter) FAR-SIGHT, 1989—; editor Dive Boat Calender, 1987-91. Choir mem. St. Paul's Greek Orthodox Ch., Irvine, 1993—, mem. parish coun., 1987-89, 98-2000, choir pres., 1999—; asst. scoutmaster Boy Scouts Am., Irvine, 1994-2002. Recipient Tchr. of Yr. award Santa Ana C. of C., 1997, NISOD Excellence award U. Tex., 1998. Mem.: NEA, Calif. Math Coun. C.C. (faculty assn. CCC), Profl. Assn. Diving Instrs., Am. Math. Assn. Two Yr. Colls., Nat. Coun. Tchrs. Math., Nat. Assn. Underwater Instrs. Avocations: scuba diving, camping, hiking, running. Home: 1 Caraway Irvine CA 92604-3217 Office: Santiago Canyon Coll 8045 E Chapman Ave Orange CA 92869

SMITH, JOHN MARVIN, III, surgeon, educator; b. San Antonio, July 31, 1947; s. John M. and Jane (Jordan) S.; m. Jill Jones, Aug. 1, 1981. MD, Tulane U., 1972. Diplomate Am. Bd. Surgery, Am. Bd. Thoracic Surgery. Intern U. Tex. Southwest Med. Sch., Dallas, 1972-73; resident in surgery U. Tex., San Antonio, 1973-77; resident in thoracic and cardiovascular surger Tex. Heart Inst., Houston, 1977-79; practice medicine specializing in cardiovasc. surgery San Antonio, 1979—. Mem. Staff Bapt. Med. Ctr., S.W. Tex. Meth. Hosp., Santa Rosa Med. Center, Met. Hosp., Nix Meml. Hosp.; clin. prof. surgery U. Tex. Health Sci. Ctr., San Antonio, 1979—; bd. mgrs. Bexar County Hosp. Dist.; chmn. bd. dirs. Tex. Ranger Assn., San Antonio Med. Found., Internat. Affairs Coun. Served to maj. USAF, 1979-81. Fellow Am. Coll. Cardiology, Am. Coll. Surgery; mem. AMA, Tex. Med. Assn., Bexar County Med. Soc. (pres. 1998—), Denton A. Cooley Cardiovascular Surg. Soc. (pres. 1988-90), Cooley Hands, J. Bradley Aust. Surg. Soc., Soc. Air Force Clin. Surgeons, San Antonio Surg. Soc., San Antonio Cardiology Soc., Soc. Thoracic Surgeons, Tex. Surg. Soc., Tulane Med. Alumni Assn. (bd. dirs.), Tex. Hist. Soc., Sigma Alpha Epsilon, Nu Sigma Nu, Tex. Cavaliers, San Antonio Country Club, The Argyle Club, Giraud Club, Order Alamo, German Club, Christmas Cotillion, Rolling Rock Club, Sons Rep. Tex., San Antonio Gun Club, The Pilon Club. Episcopalian. Home: 204 Zambrano Rd San Antonio TX 78209-5459 Office: 4330 Medical Dr Ste 300 San Antonio TX 78229-3380 Fax: 210-616-0231. E-mail: jmsiii204@pol.net.

SMITH, JOHN RICHARD, analytical chemist; b. Balt., Jan. 26, 1954; s. William Wallace Smith and Barbara Ann Larson; m. Rosalie Elizabeth Parker, Aug. 1, 1987; children: Jeremy Richard, Emily Elizabeth. BA in Biology, U. Md., 1977. Lab. scientist Md. Inst. Emergency Medicine, Balt., 1980-83; analytical chemist U.S. Army Med. Rsch. Inst. Chem. Def., Aberdeen Proving Ground, Md., 1984—. Contbr. articles to sci. jours. Mem. Arbutus (Md.) Edn. Enrichment Com., 1997—. Mem. Am. Soc. for Mass Spectrometry, Md. Geol. Soc., Sigma Xi. (Chesapeake chpt., pres. 1999-00, Edn. award 1998). Avocation: paleontology. Home: 1253 Brewster St Arbutus MD 21227-2719 Office: US Army Med Rsch Inst Chem Def 3100 Ricketts Point Rd Aberdeen Proving Ground MD 21010-5400 E-mail: john.smith@amedd.army.mil.

SMITH, JOHN STANLEY, lawyer, mediator; b. Albany, N.Y., Nov. 15, 1946; s. Robert Stanley Smith and Sylvia Rose Murgia Neary; m. Lourdes Umandap; children from previous marriage: Jon Jeffrey, James Michael, Brian Matthew, Melissa Marie. BA, St. Bernardine of Siena Coll., Loudonville, N.Y., 1968; JD, U. Balt., 1986. Bar: Md. 1986, U.S. Dist. Ct. Md. 1987, D.C. 1988. Commd. U.S. Army, 1968, advanced through grades to lt. col., comdr. assault helicopter platoon Vietnam, 1970-71, comdr. A Btry 3d Bn. 38th Field Artillery Okla., 1972-74, comdr. 132 Assault Support Helicopter Co. Hunter Airfield, 1975, ops. officer 145th Aviation Bn., 1976-78, divsn. artillery aviation officer 25th Divsn. Artillery Schofield Barracks, 1979-80; dep. dir. Directorate of Res. Forces, Ft. Meade, Md., 1981-82; dep. chief Unit Tng. Br. First U.S. Army, 1982-84; divsn. chief Concepts Analysis Agy., Bethesda, Md., 1984-87; exec. officer war plans Dept. of Army, Washington, 1987-90; ptnr. Dziennik & Smith, Glen Burnie, Balt., 1990-92; v.p., gen. counsel Academy Title Group, Glen Burnie, 1992-93; pvt. practice, 1992—; owner Smith Mediation Svcs., 1992—. Pres. Lorimar Title Corp., Glen Bunnie, 1995—. Author: Mid Range Forces Study 88-92, 1985, Mid Range Forces Study 90-94, 1986, Mid Range Forces Study 90-97, 1987. Bd. dirs. No. Anne Arundel County Rep. Club, 1994-95. Decorated Legion of Merit, Bronze Star, Air Medal, Purple Heart. Mem. ABA, Md. Bar Assn., Anne Arundel County Bar Assn., Balt. City Bar Assn., Acad. Family Mediators, No. Anne Arundel County C. of C. (pres. 1996), K.C. Roman Catholic. Avocations: running, bowling, basketball, hiking, camping. Office: 5 Crain Hwy N Glen Burnie MD 21061-2803

SMITH, JOHN WALLACE, retired surgeon, educator; b. Hutchinson, Kans., Feb. 18, 1931; s. W. Donald and Claramary S.; m. Margaret Lee, Dec. 26, 1959; children: John Wallace Jr., Frances, George MacDonell. AB, Harvard U., 1952; MD, U. Nebr., 1956. Diplomate Am. Bd. Surgery, Am. Bd. Gen. Vascular Surgery. Intern San Francisco Hosp., 1956-57; resident Stanford U. Hosps., San Francisco, 1957-60, U. Calif. Hosps., San Francisco, 1960-62; pvt. practice in gen. surgery Omaha, 1964-70; practice specializing in vascular surgery, pres. Vascular Surgery, P.C., 1970-96; ret. Clin. prof. surgery Coll. Medicine U. Nebr., Omaha, 1966-2001; pres. med. staff Meth. Hosp., Omaha, 1986-87 Author fiction and nonfiction; contbr. articles to profl. jours. Bd. dirs. Omaha Symphony Assn., 1974-96. Served to capt. Med. Corps U.S. Army, 1962-64. Fellow ACS (gov. 1987-92); mem. Midwestern Vascular Surg. Soc. (chmn. membership com. 1982), Internat. Soc. Cardiovascular Surgery, Western Surg. Assn. (chmn. membership com. 1995, 1st v.p. 1997), Alpha Omega Alpha (pres. 1982-83).

SMITH, JOHN W(ESLEY), JR. data processing executive, consultant; b. Bklyn., Jan. 6, 1946; s. John Wesley and Eunice (Davis) S.; m. Carolyn Ferrebbee, Aug. 19, 1971 (div. 1980); children: John Wesley III, Janine Carol. Student, NYU, 1989—. Computer ops. supr. Shearson Lehman Stone, Inc., N.Y.C., 1967-70; sr. ops. analyst Fin. Data Svcs., Inc., 1970-77; tng. program coord. Chem. Bank, 1977-78; sr. hardware analyst ADP, Clifton, N.J., 1978-79; data base adminstr. Depository Trust Co., N.Y.C., 1979-81; mgr. data ctr. ops. Leviton Mfg. Co., Littleneck, N.Y., 1981-83; dir. corp. info. svcs. Reed Robers Assocs., Inc., Uniondale, 1983-86; dir. prodn. planning and control Human Resource Adminstrn., N.Y.C., 1986-87; mgmt. cons. Asbach/Sci., Inc., 1987—. Mem. Data Processing Mgmt. Assn., Am. Soc. Notaries, Am. Mgmt. Assn., Am. Arbitration Assn. (comml. panel 1983—), Inst. Certification Computer Profls. (cert systems profl.). Avocation: real estate. Office: Smith Wesley Assocs Inc 1072 Barbey St Brooklyn NY 11207-9202

SMITH, JOHN WILLIAM HUGH, civil engineer; b. Port Arthur, Ont., Can., Oct. 16, 1937; s. George Edward and Nina Edith Smith; m. Anne Patten; children: Scott, Steven, Richard. AA with honors, Lakehead U., Thunder Bay, Ont., 1959; BSCE with honors, Mich. Tech. U., 1962. Proposal engr. surface combustion div. Midland-Ross Corp., Toledo, 1962-65, sr. project engr. Toronto, Ont., 1965-70; div. mgr. Holcroft & Co. (Can.) Ltd., London, 1970-76; mgr. engring. Holcroft, Livonia, Mich., 1976-81, tech. dir., mgr., sales and mktg., v.p., tech. dir., 1981-93; pres. Sterling Systems, Royal Oak, 1993—. Contbr. chpts. to books; patentee in field. Mem. Assn. Profl. Engrs. of Province Ont., Am. Soc. Metals Internat. Office: 5060 Delemere Ave Royal Oak MI 48073-1005

SMITH, JOSEF RILEY, internist; b. Council Bluffs, Iowa, Oct. 1, 1926; s. George William Smith and Margaret (Wood) Hill; divorced; children: Sarah L. Kratz, David L., Mary E. Loeb, John R., Ruthann P. Sherrier, Mark A.; m. Susan Frances Irwin, Feb. 9, 1973; 1 child, Christopher I. Student, Tulane U., 1944-46; BM, Northwestern U., 1950, MD, 1951; MSEE, Marquette U., 1964. Diplomate Am. Bd. Internal Medicine. Instr. internal medicine U. Miss. Med. Sch., Jackson, 1956-59; asst. prof. Marquette U. Med. Sch., Milw., 1959-63; from assoc. prof. to full prof. U. Mich. Med. Sch., Ann Arbor, 1963-72; physician Youngstown (Ohio) Hosp., 1972-79, Group Health Med. Assn., Tucson, 1979-84, Assocs. in Internal Medicine, Tucson, 1985-87; pvt. practice, 1987—. Co-author: Clinical Cardiopulmonary Physiology, 1960, Textbook of Pulmonary Disease, 1965, 2d rev. edit., 1974; contbr. articles to profl. jours. Controller Mahoning County TB Clinic, Youngstown, 1973-79. Served to lt. USNR, 1952-54. Fellow ACP, Sigma Xi; mem. Ariz. Med. Assn., Pima County Med. Assn., Am. Thoracic Soc., Ariz. Thoracic Soc., Bioengring. Med. Soc. (founder). Avocations: photography, computer programming. Office: 2224 N Craycroft Rd Ste 109 Tucson AZ 85712-2811

SMITH, JOSEPH PHELAN, film company executive; b. N.Y.C., 1911; s. John William and Margaret Mary (Phelan) S.; m. Madelyn Eleanor Davis, Jan. 17, 1942; children: Kevin, Karen, Margaret, Lisa. BS, Columbia U. Former salesman Van Alstyne Noel & Co., N.Y.C., RKO Radio Pictures, Inc., Boston, Omaha, div. mgr., Los Angeles, Portland, Oreg., San Francisco, 1938-47; former exec. v.p. Lippert Prodns., Hollywood, Calif.; former v.p., gen. mgr. sales Telepictures, N.Y.C.; founding pres. Cinema Vue Corp.; now chmn. Pathe News Inc., N.Y.C., 1995—, Pathe Pictures Inc., N.Y.C., 1995—. Served with U.S. Army. Mem. Motion Picture Pioneers, Am. Film Inst., Elks. Republican. Office: Pathe News Inc 630 9th Ave Ste 305 New York NY 10036-3708

SMITH, JOYCE ANN, secondary school educator; b. Baton Rouge, Dec. 27, 1976; d. Elizabeth and Otis Smith; children: Kailya. BS in Secondary Edn., So. U. A&M Coll., 1998; postgrad., Xavier U. Tchr. North Forest ISD, Houston, 1998—99, Colleton County Sch., Walterboro, SC, 1999—2000; english tchr. Orleans Parish Sch., New Orleans, 2000—. Mem.: Delta Sigma Theta. Avocations: reading, poetry, piano, writing novels and screenplays. Personal E-mail: smithja76@yahoo.com.

SMITH, JULES LOUIS, lawyer; b. N.Y.C., Oct. 7, 1947; s. Henry Newman and Leonora (Fuerth) S.; m. Alexandra Remington Northrop, Feb. 15, 1986. BS, Syracuse U., 1969, JD, 1971. Bar: N.Y. 1972, U.S. Dist. Ct. (no. dist.) N.Y. 1972, U.S. Dist. Ct. (we. dist.) N.Y. 1973, U.S. Ct. Appeals (2d cir.) 1975, U.S. Supreme Ct. 1982. Assoc. Blitman and King LLP, Syracuse, N.Y., 1971-77, ptnr., 1977-88, resident ptnr., 1988—. Lectr. to legal and profl. assns., confs., colls., 1980—, including AFL-CIO Union Lawyers Conf., 1991, ABA Labor and Employment Law, 1992, 25th Pacific Coast Labor Law Conf., 1992, ABA Satellite Seminar, 1992, N.Y. State Bar Assn. Labor and Employment Law Sect. Ann. Meeting, 1993; lectr. Inst. Indsl. Labor Rels.; mem. N.Y. State Bar Assn. Task Force on Adminstrv. Hearings, Albany, 1986—; bd. advisors LeMoyne Inst. Labor Rels., LeMoyne Coll., Syracuse Inst. Labor Rels.; mem. exec. bd. Greater Mem. editl. bd. Syracuse Law Rev., 1970-71; contbr. articles to legal publs. Sec. Onondaga Neighborhood Legal Svcs., 1978, pres., 1979, v.p. bd. dirs., 1983-87; chair Prevention Ptnrs., 1994-97, pres. 1994-96; co-chair legal divsn. fund raising activities Syracuse Symphony Orch., 1985-86; bd. dirs. fundraising activities Am. Heart Assn., 1985-86; bd. dirs. Greater Rochester Fights Back, 1990-92, vice chair, 1992-93, chair, 1994; pres. Prevention Ptnrs., 1994-96, bd. dirs., 1999—; bd. dirs. United Way Greater Rochester, Cmty. Legal Intake Project, 1998—; v.p. Rochester Com. on Fgn. Rels., 1990-94. Fellow N.Y. Bar Found.; mem. ABA (union chmn. EEO com. labor and employment law sect. 1985-88, co-chairperson labor and employment law sect., mem. ad hoc com. to comment on EEO com. Ams. with Disabilities Act regulations, Coll. of Labor and Employment Lawyers award 1996), FBA, N.Y. State Bar Assn. (chmn. membership and fin. com. 1980-83, mem. spl. com. on specialization 1983-85, chmn. labor and employment law sect. 1984-85, mem. ho. dels. 1989-92), Onondaga County Bar Assn., Monroe County Bar Assn., N.Y. State Trial Lawyers Assn., Am. Trial Lawyers Assn., Fed. Bar Coun., Indsl. Rels. Rsch. Assn., Assn. Ctrl. N.Y. (co-founder, v.p. 1981), Justinian Honor Soc., Order of Coif. Democrat. Jewish. Avocations: skiing, running, cooking, reading. Office: Blitman and King LLP 16 Main St W Ste 207 Rochester NY 14614-1601

SMITH, JULIA A. internist, oncologist, educator; b. N.Y.C., July 18, 1951; d. Carl A. and Ruth G. Smith; children: Matthew Smith Ryan, Rachel Smith Ryan. BA, NYU, 1974, MS in Cell Biology, 1979, PhD in Cell Biology, MD, 1980. Diplomate Am. Bd. Internal Medicine, Am. Bd. Oncology, Am. Bd. Hematology; lic. physician, N.Y., Mass. Intern, resident dept. internal medicine Peter Bent Brigham Hosp., Boston, 1980-83; fellow divsn. hematology-oncology dept. internal medicine Meml. Hosp. Sloan-Kettering Cancer Ctr., N.Y.C., 1983-86; postdoctoral fellow molecular genetics Rockefeller U., 1984-86; rsch. fellow Sloan-Kettering Inst. for Cancer Rsch., 1984-86; clin. fellow dept. internal medicine Harvard U. Med. Sch., 1980-83; acting fellow blood banking N.Y. Blood Ctr., N.Y.C., 1983; clin. fellow dept. internal medicine N.Y. Hosp.-Cornell Med. Ctr., 1983-86; asst. attending Bellevue Hosp. Ctr., 1986—; asst. prof. medicine NYU Med. Ctr., 1986-88, clin. asst. prof. medicine, 1988—; pvt. practice, 1986-95, 98—. Acting fellow blood banking N.Y. Blood Ctr., N.Y.C., 1983; clin. fellow dept. internal medicine Harvard U. Med. Sch., 1980-83. Contbr. articles to profl. jours. Mem. adv. bd. Laurie Straus Leukemia Found., Nabco Cancer Rsch. Grants. Recipient Citation for outstanding acad. achievement Am. Med. Women's Assn.; Am. Cancer Soc. clin. rsch. fellow, NIH Med. Scientist Tng. Program fellow Mem. Alpha Omega Alpha. Office: NYU Med Ctr Faculty Practice Office 530 1st Ave Ste 4G New York NY 10016-6402

SMITH, JUNE SYLVIA KOLBE, artist, educator; b. Chgo., June 8, 1926; d. Clarence William and Marie Wilma Colby; m. Harold Eugene Reed, Sept. 23, 1947 (div. June 1948); m. Joseph Patric Smith, June 7, 1951; children: Donna Kaye, Craig Douglas. AA, UCLA, 1948; student, Occidental Coll., 1961, Am. Inst. Fine Arts, 1962. Artist Biltmore Hotel, L.A., 1966-78; docent, instr. pub. rels. San Gabriel (Calif.) Fine Arts Assn., 1997—; instr. Michael's Arts & Crafts, Pasadena, Glendale, Monrovia, Calif., 1998—99, 2001—02. Represented in permanent collections Millard Sheets Gallery, one-woman shows include San Gabriel Fine Arts, 1991; contbr. Public rels. St. James Ch., S. Pasadena, 1991-99. Recipient 2d pl. Santa Paula Art C.C., 1963, 2d pl. Highland Park Art Assn., 1968. Mem. Calif. Art Club. Democrat. Episcopalian. Avocations: rollerskating, gardening. Home: 3129 Chadwick Dr Los Angeles CA 90032 Office: San Gabriel Fine Arts Assn Mission and Santa Anita San Gabriel CA 90032

SMITH, K. CLAY, machinery transport company executive; b. New Orleans, Aug. 29, 1937; s. Kenneth Eugene and Yvonne Smith; children: Elizabeth, K. Clay, Andrew. BBA, U. Notre Dame, 1960; JD, Georgetown U., 1964; DBA (hon.), Marian Coll., Indpls., 1988. Bar: Ind. 1964. Spl. agt. FBI, Los Angeles, 1964-68; assoc. Kightlinger, Gray, Indpls., 1968-71; pres., chief exec. officer Underwood Machinery Transport, 1971—. Bd. dirs. Marsh Supermarkets, Inc., Specialized Carriers; former vice chmn. Ind. Horse Racing Commn. Chmn. lic. rev. bd., City of Indpls., 1974; mem. reciprocity com., State of Ind., 1988. Mem. Ind. Bar Assn., Indpls. Bar Assn., Indpls. Athletic Club (bd. dirs. 1986-92, pres. 1992), Highland Country Club. Republican. Roman Catholic. Avocations: reading, music, golf, tennis. Home: PO Box 977 Indianapolis IN 46206-0977 Office: Underwood Cos 940 W Troy Ave Indianapolis IN 46225-2244

SMITH, KAREN ANN, visual artist; b. Trenton, N.J., May 25, 1964; d. James Roy and Clara Patricia (Walton) S. A in Comml. Art, Art Inst. Phila., 1984; BFA in Graphic Design and Art Therapy, U. Arts, Phila., 1989; grad. in graphic design, Basel Sch. for Design, 1991; MA in Expressive Therapies, Lesley Coll., 1993. Graphic designer Mercer County C.C., Trenton, 1984-86; mural painter, supr. Anti-Graffiti Network, Phila., 1988; tchr. drawing and set design Chestnut Hill (Mass.) Sch., 1995, 96; freelance graphic designer Swiss Fed. Rys., Bern, 1993-95; tchr. drawing Wentworth Inst. Tech., Boston, 1996, 97; tchr. design Northeastern U., 1997. Fireworks crew mem. Pyrotech. Inc., Boston, 1997; apprentice Johnson Atelier Tech. Inst. of Sculpture, Trenton, 1997-99; artist Airtex Interiors, Fallsington, 2000-. One-woman shows include , Contempo Galerie, Bern, Switzerland, 1994, Boston Archtl. Ctr. Atelier, 1997, George Sch., Newtown, Pa., 1997, exhibited in group shows, Howard Yezerski Gallery, Boston, 1994, Kingston Gallery, Boston, 1995, Phillips' Mill, New Hope, Pa., 1997, 1998, Woodmere Art Mus., Chestnut Hill, Pa., 1998, Princeton (N.J.) Day Sch., 1999, Trenton City Mus., 1999, Vorpal Gallery, N.Y.C., 2000—02, Artsbridge, Prallsville Mills, N.J., 2000, Riverbank Arts, Stockton, N.J., 2000—, iTheo.com, San Francisco, 2000—01, Nat. Bottle Mus., Ballston Spa, N.Y., 2001; contbr. poetry to anthologies. Scholar Women in Graphic Arts, 1987-89; grantee Mystic Studios Trust, 1994-97. Mem. Coll. Art Assn., Boston Athenaeum, Origami USA.

SMITH, KAREN B. educational consultant; b. Monahans, Tex., Oct. 15, 1946; d. Ralph J. and Christine W. Barnes; m. Jack W. Smith, July 19, 1997. BS, No. Tex. State U., Denton, 1965—68; postgrad., Angelo State U., San Angelo, Tex., 1970—73. Provisional Tchg. Cert. 1968. Tchr. Fort Worth ind. sch. dist., Tex., 1968—70; tchr. and vocat. adjustment coord. San Angelo ind. sch. dist., 1973—91; site base com. mem. Ctrl. H.S., 1990—91; vocat. adjustment coord. San Angelo ind. sch. dist., 1997—. Instr. displaced workers Concho Valley Coun. Govts., San Angelo, Tex., 1994—97; v.p. of bd. dirs. Candlelight Apts., Inc. Past pres. C. of C. Concho Cadre, San Angelo, Tex., 1992—; exhibits com. mem. San Angelo Stock Show and Rodeo, 1990—; com. mem. Concho Valley Alliance for Transition, 1999—, Concho Valley Social and Health Resources Coalition, San Angelo, 2000—; transition task force mem. Mental Svcs. for Concho Valley, 2001—; vice chair Make a Wish Found., 1983—84; mem. Tom Green County Rep. Women, 1982—90; hon. mem. Goodfellow AFB Officers' Wives Club, 1982—86, 1995—96; mem. Order of Eastern Star, 1965—2002; chair membership Mayor's Com. for Persons with Disabilites, 1984—86; GROW com. Glen Meadows Baptist Ch., 2001—; mem. San Angelo Mus. Fine Arts, 2000—01, Tex. Assn. Profl. Educators, San Angelo, 1997—2001; vol. Fort Concho Nat. Hist. Landmark and Miss Hattie's Mus., 1991—. Named Pub. Employee of Yr., Mayor's Com. for Disabled Persons, 1988, Cadre Person of Yr., San Angelo C. of C., 1996. Mem.: Guardianship Alliance (nomination com. mem. and bd. dirs. 2001—), Ctrl. H.S. PTA, Tex. Assn. Vocat. Adjustment Coords., Tex. Classroom Tchrs. Assn. Baptist. Home: 219 Dellwood San Angelo TX 76903 Office: San Angelo Ctrl HS 100 Cottonwood San Angelo TX 76901

SMITH, KATHERINE ELLINGER, artist, art educator; b. Crookston, Minn., Dec. 5, 1951; d. Melvin Walter and Ruth Nanette (Ross) Ellinger; m. David Kingsbury Smith, Jr., Mar. 12, 1978; children: Sarah Elizabeth, Kristin Kingsbury. BA, St. Cloud State U., 1975; MFA, Mich. State U., 1988. Copywriter Modern Merchandising, Mpls., 1977-78; advt. layout and corp. designer Maurices, Inc., Duluth, Minn., 1978-81; graphic designer Awardcraft, Mpls., 1981-84; asst. prof. art Sterling Coll. Extension, Cape Girardeau, Mo., 1995; instr. art Lansing (Mich.) C.C., 1989-91; adj. asst. prof. art S.E. Mo. State U., Cape Girardeau, 1991—, dir. Art Acad. Jackson, 1996—. Exhibited in shows at Faust Gallery, St. Louis, 1993, Design Ctr., St. Louis, 1993, Yeiser Art Ctr., Paducah, Ky., 1994, Hunter Mus. Art, Chattanooga, 1996, Margaret Harwell Art Mus., Poplar Bluff, Mo., 1996, Nat. Women's Art Caucus, N.Y.C., 1997, Brady Commons Gallery/U. Mo., Columbia, 1998, Chatahoochee Valley Art Mus., Lagrange, Ga., 1998, N.J. Ctr. for Visual Arts, Summit, 1999, John Jay Coll., N.Y.C., 1999, Viridian Artists, Inc., N.Y.C., 1999, others. Mem. Coll. Art Assn., Viridian Artists, Inc. (N.Y.C.), Phi Kappa Phi. Lutheran. Avocation: hiking. Home: 258 Edgewood Rd Jackson MO 63755-8116 Office: SE Mo State U 1 University Plz Cape Girardeau MO 63701-4799

SMITH, KATHERINE TERESA, history educator; b. New Orleans, Apr. 30, 1946; d. Gerald Alfred and Margaret Mary (Murphy) S. BA in History, Nazareth Coll., 1967, BS in Elem. Edn., 1970; MA in History, SUNY, Genesco, 1975. Cert. Elem. Educator. Tchr. Rochester (N.Y.) Cath. Schs., 1969-70, Rush-Henrietta (N.Y.) Schs., 1970—. Mem. Henrietta Planning bd., 1975-82; membership com. Rochester Orchestra, 1982-85; treas., sec. Henrietta Dem. com., 1969-2000; bd. dirs. Riverton, sec., treas., 1973-74, 82-85; sec., treas. PTA R-H, 1970-2000. Recipient Citizenship award Henrietta Planning bd., 1982, Svc. award Riverton Cmty. Assn., Henrietta, 1985. Mem. Rush-Henrietta Educators Assn. (v.p. 1974-84, gold apple award 1984, delegate NEX, AFT, NYSUT). Democrat. Roman Cath. Home: 292 Countess Dr West Henrietta NY 14586-9416 Office: Rush Henrietta Schs 5509 E Henrietta Rd Rush NY 14543-9755

SMITH, KATHERYN JEANETTE, music educator; b. Siloam Springs, Ark., July 6, 1944; d. Charlie H. and Victoria Virginia (Jameson) Porter; m. Curtis Barth Smith, Jan. 10, 1975; 1 child, Melody Jeanette. B in Music Edn., So. Nazarene U., 1966; M in Music Edn., Kent (Ohio) State U., 1970. Gen. music tchr. Duncan (Okla.) Jr. H.S., 1966-68; elem. music tchr. Akron (Ohio) Pub. Schs., 1971-72; music prof. MidAm. Nazarene U., Olathe, Kans., 1972—. Clinician Lillenas Music Confs., Olathe, Kans., 1994, 96, 97. Keyboard accompanist Coll. Ch. of the Nazarene, 1973—. Mem. Music Educators Nat. Conf., Music Tchrs. Nat. Assn., MidAm. Nazarene Univ. Women's Aux. (chairperson 1973-74, 94-98). Avocation: whale collection. Office: MidAm Nazarene Univ 2030 E College Way Olathe KS 66062-1831 E-mail: ksmith@mnu.edu.

SMITH, KATHLEEN ANN, mathematics educator; BA in Math., U. Dallas, 1970; MS in Math., U. Ctrl. Ark., 1975. Cert. secondary prin., elem. prin. and tchr., secondary math., phys. sci. tchr., Ark. Tchr. math. and sci. Sacred Heart H.S., Morrilton, Ark., 1970-73, West Jr. H.S., West Memphis, 1973, Mt. St. Mary Acad., Little Rock, 1974, 75-76, St. Joseph Sch., Conway, Ark., 1976-90, asst. prin., 1981-84, prin., 1986-90; instr. math. U. Ctrl. Ark., 1990-2000; tchr. math. Sacred Heart Cath. Sch., Morrilton, 2000—. Adj. prof. math. Hendrix Coll., Conway, 1990-93. Named Tchr. of Yr., St. Joseph Sch., 1979. Mem. Nat. Coun. Tchrs. Math., Math. Assn. Am., Ark. Coun. Tchrs, Math. Roman Catholic. Avocations: needlework, camping.

SMITH, KATHLEEN TENER, bank executive; b. Pitts., Oct. 19, 1943; d. Edward Harrison Tener Jr. and Barbara Elizabeth (McCormick) Tener; m. Roger Davis Smith, May 30, 1970 (dec.); children: Silas Wheelock, Jocelyn Tener, Luke Ewing Taft. BA summa cum laude, Vassar Coll., 1965; MA in Econs., Harvard U., 1968. Rsch. assoc. Harvard U. Grad. Sch. Bus., Cambridge, Mass., 1967-69; assoc. economist Chase Manhattan Bank, N.Y.C., 1969-70, asst. treas., 1971, 2d v.p., 1972, v.p., 1973—, sec. asset liability mgmt. com., 1985-90, treas. Global Bank, 1990-91, divsn. exec. structured investment products, 1991-93, global mktg. and comms. exec. Global Risk Mgmt. Sect., 1993-94, global mktg. and comms. product devel. exec., 1994-96, global asset mgmt. and pvt. bank mktg., 1996-98; network ptnr. The Sullivan Group, Salomon Smith Barney, 1999—. Editor: Commodity Derivatives and Finance, 1996. Trustee Eleanor Roosevelt Ctr. Val-Kill, 2000—, chmn. fin. com., 2001—; mem. subcom. on edn. Chase Manhattan Found., N.Y.C., 1985—90; trustee Huguenot Hist. Soc. New Paltz, 1999—, chair fin. com., 1999—; mem. working com. Huguenot Heritage, 1999—; chair Pyramid Soc. Former Trustees Vassar Coll., Poughkeepsie, 2001—, trustee NY, 1979—91, mem. exec. com., 1987—91, class pres., 2000—. Fellow, NSF, 1965—67. Mem.: Am. Fin. Assn., Yale Club, Phi Beta Kappa. Republican. Episcopalian. Address: PO Box 129 New Paltz NY 12561-0129

SMITH, KATHY ANN, music educator; b. Syracuse, N.Y., July 2, 1953; d. Clifford Wayne Hirsh and Helen Erdine (Schlie) Warner; m. Kevin Joseph Smith, July 31, 1993. MusB magna cum laude, Crane Sch. of Music, Potsdam, N.Y., 1975; MS in Edn., Elmira Coll., 1980; Cert. of Advanced Study, SUNY-Cortland, 1993. Cert. music educator, sch. dist. adminstr., N.Y. Music tchr. Vernon Verona (N.Y.) Sherrill Ctrl. Sch., 1975—, music dept. chairperson, 1986-98. Pvt. instr. studio lessons, Oneida, N.Y., 1975—, jazzband dir., 2000—; facilitator for music boosters club and middle sch. panel tchrs. orgn., Vernon, 1991—; mem. Colgate Symphony Orch., 1992; chairperson Sch. Improvement Project, Verona, 1992-94. Recipient Profl. Recognition award Vernon Verona Sherrill Ctrl. Schs., 1990, 92. Mem. ASCD, N.Y. State Sch. of Music Assn., N.Y. State Coun. Adminstrs. in Music Edn., Music Educators

Nat. Conf., N.Y. State Band Dirs. Assn., Madison County Music Educators Assn. (v.p., pres. 1998—). Democrat. Roman Catholic. Avocations: reading, art, music, camping, baseball. Office: Vernon Verona Sherril Ctrl Schs Rte 31 Verona NY 13478 E-mail: katsmith@america.net., ksmith@vvs-csd-high.moric.org.

SMITH, KATO DEL, architect; b. Anderson, Ind., Oct. 25, 1963; s. Everett Lamar and Lela Mae Smith; m. Melisa Lynn, July 6, 1985; children: Kato Del Jr., Heather Monique. BS, BArch, Ball State U., Muncie, Ind, 1994. Registered Ill., Ind., Mich., Ohio. Draftsman Anderson (Ind.) City Engrs. Office, 1981—83; abstractor Record Data, Inc., Indpls., 1983-86; draftsman J S K Architects, Anderson, 1986—91, intern, 1991—94, grad. architect, 1994—95; pres. Kato Design Studio, 1994—. Archtl. cons. Cmty. Partnership, Inc., Muncie, 1994-98. Pres. Historic 8th St Neighborhood Assn., Anderson, 1997—; bd. dirs. Christian Ctr. Rescue Ministries, Anderson, 1996—. Recipient outstanding svc. award Rotary Internat., Anderson, 1994, Paul Harris fellowship, 1997. Mem. AIA, Historic Landmarks Found. Ind., Nat. Trust Historic Preservation, Western Pa. Conservancy, Ind. Soc. Architects, Anderson C. of C. (chmn. cmty. image coun. 1994—). Office: Kato Design Studio 7 E 12th St Anderson IN 46016-1704 E-mail: info@katodesignstudio.com.

SMITH, KATRINA DIANE, writer; b. Oakland, Calif., Dec. 23, 1957; d. Mack Edward and Mary Jean Smith; children: Rose, Jason Larenzo. Student, Alameda Coll., Calif., Laney Coll., Oakland, Calif., Careercom Bus. Coll., Oakland, 1998. Author: The Founders Guide of Girl Scouting, 1994, The Floral Factor of the Cotton Mill, 1998, The History of the War in Theatrical Genology, 1997. Vol. So. Poverty Law Ctr., Montgomery, Ala., 1996, Sr. Citizens League, Washington, 1996, Notch Reform Campaign, Washington, 1996; adv. bd. Missing Persons, Oakland, Calif., 1999, Consular Search Statistics, Dept. State, 2001; mem. U.S. Olympic Com., 1996. Named to Internat. Poetry Hall of Fam, Internat. Poetry Hall of Fame Mus.; recipient Colgate Youth for Am. award, Colgate Palmolive Co., 1993—94, Editor's Choice award, Internat. Libr. Poetry. Mem.: AARP (bd. dirs. 2001—02), Nat. Geog. Soc. (bd. dirs. 1989), TWA Club (SFO bd. 1991). Avocation: reading. Home: 1699 70th Ave Oakland CA 94621 Office: Internat Library of Poetry 1 Poetry Plz Owings Mills MD 21117

SMITH, KELLY COULSON, health services administrator; b. Dearborn, Mich. m. Roger Douglas Smith. BS, Ohio State U., 1993, MHA, 1995. Adminstrv. fellow Oakwood Healthcare Sys., Dearborn, 1995—96, dir. women and children, 1997—99, corp. dir. strategy, 1999—2001, adminstr. clin. svcs., 2001—. Mem. NAFE, Am. Coll. Healthcare Profls. (assoc.), Southeastern Mich. Health Care Execs. Forum. Office: Oakwood Healthcare Sys PO Box 2500 18101 Oakwood Blvd Dearborn MI 48123-2500 E-mail: smithk@oakwood.org.

SMITH, KELLY COX, philosophy educator; b. Jan. 18, 1964; BA in Philosophy magna cum laude, Ga. State U., 1986; MS in Zoology, Duke U., 1992, PhD in Philosophy, 1994. Instr. philosophy and zoology Duke U., 1989-93, Bernard Peach instr. zoology and philosophy, 1991-92; vis. asst. prof. philosophy Ga. State U., 1993-94; asst. prof. philosophy The Coll. of N.J., Ewing, 1994-98, Clemson (S.C.) U., 1998—; asst. prof. Clemson U., 1998—2001, assoc. prof., 2002—. Referee: Perspectives on Sci., Philos. Psychology, Philosophy of Biology, Philosophy of Sci., Synthese; contbr. numerous papers to profl. publs., including Critical Revs. in Biomed. Engring., Philosophy of Sci., Biology and Philosophy. Mem. AAAS, Am. Assn. for Bioethics and Humanities, Am. Philos. Assn., Internat. Soc. for the History, Philosophy and Social Studies of Biology, Nat. Ctr. for Sci. Edn., Philosophy of Sci. Assn. Office: Clemson U Dept Philosophy & Religion 113 Holtzendorff Hall Clemson SC 29634-0001 E-mail: kcs@clemson.edu.

SMITH, KENNETH ALAN, chemical engineer, educator; b. Winthrop, Mass., Nov. 28, 1936; s. James Edward and Alice Gertrude (Walters) S.; m. Ambia Marie Olsson, Oct. 14, 1961; children: Kirsten Heather, Edward Eric, Andrew Ian Beaumont, Thurston Garrett. S.B., MIT, 1958, S.M., 1959, Sc.D., 1962; postgrad., Cambridge (Eng.) U., 1964-65. Asst. prof. chem. engring. MIT, 1961-67, assoc. prof., 1967-71, prof., 1971—. Edwin R. Gilliland prof. chem. engring., 1989—, acting head dept., 1976-77, assoc. provost, 1980-81, assoc. provost, v.p. rsch., 1981-91, dir. Whitaker Coll. Health Sci. and Tech., 1989-91. Cons. chem. and oil cos. NSF fellow, 1964-65, Overseas fellow, Churchill Coll., (Eng.), 1993, 01. Mem. Am. Inst. Chem. Engrs., Nat. Acad. Engring., Am. Chem. Soc., AAAS, Sigma Xi, Phi Lambda Upsilon, Tau Beta Pi. Episcopalian. Home: 32 School St Manchester MA 01944-1336 Office: MIT Bldg 66-540 Cambridge MA 02139

SMITH, KENNETH DAVID, performance technologist, musician; b. Newark, Mar. 25, 1963; s. David Morgan and Mary (Peperato) S. BA in Music, Psychology, Rutgers U., 1985; MA in Indsl./Orgnl. Psychology, Montclair State U., 1992. Tng. specialist KPMG Peat Marwick, Montvale, N.J., 1990-92, sr. instrnl. designer, 1992—. Recipient Windows World Open award Microsoft and Computer World, 1995, Outstanding Instructional Product award Internat. Soc. Performance Improvement, 1996. Mem. ASTD, Nat. Soc. for Performance and Instrn. (co-presenter 1995), Phi Beta Kappa. Avocations: photography, gardening. Office: KPMG Peat Marwick 3 Chestnut Ridge Rd Montvale NJ 07645-1842

SMITH, KENNETH JUDSON, JR. chemist, theoretician, educator; b. Raleigh, N.C., Sept. 4, 1930; s. Kenneth Judson and Irene (Strickland) S.; m. Dorothy Margaret Ratcliffe, Mar. 6, 1953; children: Patricia Lynne Smith Pittman, Pamela Jean. AB, East Carolina U., 1957; MA, Duke U., 1959, PhD, 1961. Research chemist Chemstrand Research Center, Durham, N.C., 1961-65, sr. research chemist, 1965-68; asst. prof. polymer research SUNY Coll. Environ. Sci. and Forestry, Syracuse, 1968-70, assoc. prof., 1970-73, prof., 1973-95, emeritus prof., 1995—, asst. dir. Polymer Research Center, 1971-79, acting dir., 1979-83, dir. Organic Materials Sci. Program, 1971-75, chmn. dept. chemistry, 1972-84. Vis. prof. Instituto di Chimica Industriale, U. Genoa, Italy, 1979; cons. U.S. Army Materials and Mechanics Rsch. Ctr., Watertown, Mass., 1973-75, cert. of appreciation 1973, NRC, Washington, 1980-87; mem. adv. coun. Syracuse Met. Transp. Coun., 1975-84; mem. adv. bd. confs. in polymer sci. and tech. SUNY, New Paltz, 1977-85; mem. rsch. found. joint com. on procedures SUNY, Albany, 1974-81; cons. Hong Kong Rsch. Coun., 1995—. Contbr. articles to profl. jours. Served with USMC, 1951-54. Recipient cert. Appreciation U.S. Army Materials and Mechanics Rsch. Ctr., 1973. Mem. AAAS, Am. Chem. Soc. (dir. Syracuse sect. 1977-79, chmn. 1978, councilor 1979-82), Am. Phys. Soc. (com. on internat. freedom of scientists, small coms.), Am. Inst. Chemists, Soc. Plastics Engrs., Math. Assn. Am., N.Y. Acad. Scis., Sigma Xi, Phi Lambda Upsilon, Kappa Delta Pi. Achievements include research on statistical mechanics, mechanical properties and theoretical studies of polymers; rubber elasticity and thermoelasticity; crystallization of networks; structure-property relationships; ultimate properties of fibers; thermodynamic theory of polymer fiber properties; thermodynamic theory of fiber strength. Home: 108 Scottholm Blvd Syracuse NY 13224-1728 Office: Coll Environ Sci and Forestry Suny Syracuse NY 13210

SMITH, KENNETH RUPERT, JR. neurosurgeon, educator; b. St. Louis, Sept. 23, 1932; s. Kenneth R. and Jocelyn (Ulmet) S.; m. Marjorie R. Sandin, 1956; children: Susan, Sally, Kenneth III, Nancy, Carol, Joanne, Patricia. Student, Greenville (Ill.) Coll., 1950-53; MD, Washington U., St. Louis, 1957. Diplomate Am. Bd. Neurol. Surgery. Intern in medicine Johns Hopkins Hosp., Balt., 1957-58; asst. resident surgery Washington U., St. Louis, 1958-59, resident neurosurgery, 1960-63, instr. neurosurgery and anatomy, 1964-66; asst. prof. surgery St. Louis U., 1966-67, assoc. prof., 1967-71, prof., 1971—. Contbr. articles to profl. jours. Cons. Bd. Police Commrs., St. Louis, 1967; chmn. Mayor's Health Task Force, St. Louis, 1977-81; mem. bd. commrs. St. Louis Mus. Sci. and Natural History, 1979-85. Named Disting. Alumnus Greenville (Ill.) Coll., 1983. Mem. AAAS, Am. Assn. Anatomists, Soc. Neurosci., Am. Assn. Neurol. Surgeons (nominating com. 1992-94), Soc. Univ. Neurosurgeons (pres. 1986), Soc. Neurol. Neurosurgeons (pres. 1986), Soc. Neurol. Surgeons (pres. 1995-96), St. Louis Med. Soc. (pres. 1983), St. Louis Soc. Neurol. Scis. (pres. 1975-77), Alpha Omega Alpha. Democrat. Avocations: hunting, music. Office: St Louis U Sch Medicine 3635 Vista Ave Saint Louis MO 63110-2539

SMITH, KENT ASHTON, scientific and technical information executive; b. Boston, Sept. 3, 1938; s. Kent Wooliscroft and Dorothy Patten Smith; m. Mary Margaret Gaffney; children: Holly L. Smith, Kent W. BA, Hobart Coll., 1960; MBA, Cornell U., 1962; postgrad., Am. U., 1978-79. Mgmt. analyst Office of Sec., HEW, Washington, 1962-65; adminstrv. officer divsn. rsch. facilities and resources NIH, Bethesda, Md., 1965-67, asst. exec. officer divsn. rsch. facilities and resources, 1967-68, exec. officer divsn. rsch. resources, 1968-71, asst. dir. adminstrn. Nat. Libr. Medicine, 1971-78, dep. dir., 1978—, PHS spl. expert-info. scientist, 2000—. Mem. exec. bd. and bureau Internat. Coun. Sci. and Tech. Info., Paris, 1983—2001, treas., 1986—88, Paris, 1989, pres., 1990—94; treas. Nat. Fed. Abstracting and Info. Sci., Phila., 1986—88, exec. bd., 1985—90, pres. elect, 1989, pres., 90; v.p. U.S. Nat. Com. of UNESCO-PGI, Washington, 1983—85; mem. exec. adv. bd. Fed. Libr. and Info. Ctr. Com., Washington, 1984—89; chmn. Info. Policy Com., 1988—89; exec. com. CENDI-Info. Consortia, Washington, 1985—, chmn., 2001—02; mem. U.S. Nat. Commn. for CODATA, 1990—; mem. panel on Dept. Energy Info. Infrastructure NAS, 2000; reviewer study digital strategy for Libr. Congress NRC, 2000; mem. panel on Nat. Tech. Info. Svc. Nat. Commn. Libr. and Info. Sci., 2000. Contbr. articles to profl. jours., chpt. to book: Management of Federally Sponsored Libraries, 1995. Mem. Citizens Com. for Pub. Libr. Montgomery County, Bethesda, 1981-82; fin. dir. Christ Ch., Rockville, Md., 1990-91. Recipient Asst. Sec. for Health Exceptional Achievement award USPHS, 1978, Sr. Exec. Svc. award, 1996, 97, 98, 99, HEW Superior Svc. medal 1974, Nat. Fedn. Abstracting Info. Sci., 1998, Miles Conrad hon. lectureship, Hammer award V.P. U.S., 1999. Mem. ASPA (vice chmn. 1971-72), AAAS, Int. Assn. Sci. Tech. and Med. Pubs., Am. Mgmt. Assn., Am. Soc. Info. Svcs., Med. Libr. Assn. (Pres. award 1997, ICSTI Disting. Svc. award 2001, chair Alfred Zipf fellowship com. 2001-02), Assn. Rsch. Librs., Cosmos Club. Episcopalian. Avocations: theater, golf, baseball, bird watching, genealogy. Home: 17903 Gainford Pl Olney MD 20832-1657 Office: Nat Libr Medicine 8600 Rockville Pike Bethesda MD 20894-0002

SMITH, KENT ERNEST, non-profit organization executive; b. Oak Park, Ill., May 21, 1939; s. James Paul and Jane Louise (Gardner) S.; m. Pamela Ann Streich, Sept. 11, 1965; children: Julie Ellen, Stephen Paul. BS in Journalism, U. Ill., 1961. Prodr., writer pub. svc. programming Sta. WLW-TV, Cin., 1965-67; radio/TV news writer prodr. Sta. WGN, Chgo., 1967-69; TV news prodr., writer, project planner Sta. WLS-TV, 1969-78; exec. dir. Spina Bifida Assn., 1978-86, Cmty. Counseling Svc. Co. Inc., Chgo., 1986-89, Ill. Spina Bifida Assn. Am., Chgo., 1989-91; v.p. resource devel. Lifelink/Bensenville (Ill.) Home Soc., 1991-95; dir. devel. Luth. Child & Family Svcs. Ill., River Forest, 1995-2000, Am. Diabetic Assn., Chgo., 2000—. Chmn. bd. Coun. Disability Rights, Chgo. Served in U.S. Army, 1961-65. Mem. Am. Soc. Assn. Execs., Nat. Soc. Fund Raisers, Chgo. Soc. Assn. Execs., Chgo. Headline Club, Rotary (Elmhurst). Mem. United Ch. Christ. Home: 472 Prairie Ave Elmhurst IL 60126-4022 Office: 715 S Wells St Chicago IL 60607-4507

SMITH, K(ERMIT) WAYNE, computer company executive; b. Newton, N.C., Sept. 15, 1938; s. Harold Robert and Hazel K. (Smith) S.; m. Audrey M. Kennedy, Dec. 19, 1958; 1 son, Stuart W. BA, Wake Forest U., 1960; MA, Princeton U., 1962, PhD, 1964; postgrad., U. So. Calif., 1965; LLD (hon.), Ohio U., 1992; LHD (hon.), Ohio State U., 1998. Instr. Princeton U., 1963; asst. prof. econs. and polit. sci. U.S. Mil. Acad., 1963-66; spl. asst. to asst. sec. def. for sys. analysis Washington, 1966-69; program mgr. def. studies RAND Corp., Santa Monica, Calif., 1969-70; dir. program analysis NSC, Washington, 1970-72; group v.p. planning Dart Industries, L.A., 1972-73, group pres. resort devel. group, 1973-76; exec. v.p. Washington Group, Inc., 1976-77; mng. ptnr. Coopers & Lybrand, Washington, 1977-80, group mng. ptnr., 1980-83; chmn., CEO World Book, Inc., 1983-86; prof. Wake Forest U., 1986-88, 2000—; CEO OCLC Online Computer Libr. Ctr., Inc., Dublin, 1989-98, pres. emeritus, 1998—. Sr. cons. Dept. Def., Dept. State, NSC, NASA, Dept. Energy, OMB, GAO; bd. dirs. Nat. City Bank, K. Wayne Smith and Assocs., OCLC Info Dimensions, Inc.; con. prof. (hon.) Tsinghua U., Beijing, 1996; chmn. Rainbow Care For Kids Found., 1999-2000. Author: How Much is Enough? Shaping the Defense Program, 1961-69, 1971; editor: OCLC 1967-97: Thirty Years of Furthering Access to the World's Information, 1998; contbr. articles to profl. jours. Mem. vis. com. Brookings Instn., Washington, 1971-79; mem. bd. visitors Wake Forest U., 1974-78, 82-90, chmn. bd. visitors, 1976-78, trustee, 1991-95, 96-2000, 2001—; mem. bd. visitors Def. Sys. Mgmt. Coll., 1982-85, Lenoir Rhyne Coll., 1988-94, Mershon Ctr. Ohio State U., 1990-92, Columbus Assn. for Performing Arts, 1991-95, U. Pitts. Sch. Libr. and Info. Sci., 1992-95; mem. bd. visitors Bowman Gray Bapt. Hosp. Med. Ctr., 1992-95, chmn. bd. visitors, 1993-95. Danforth fellow, Woodrow Wilson fellow Princeton U., 1962. Mem. ALA (hon., life), Coun. Fgn. Rels., Internat. Inst. Strategic Studies, Inst. Internat. Edn., Coun. Higher Edn., Am. Assn. Higher Edn., Am. Soc. Info. Sci., Chgo. Club, Lakes Golf and Country Club, Capital Club, Phi Beta Kappa, Omicron Delta Kappa, Kappa Sigma. Methodist. Home: 2606 Sigmon Dairy Rd Newton NC 28658-8607 Office: Online Computer Libr Ctr Inc 6565 Frantz Rd Dublin OH 43017-5308

SMITH, KERRY CLARK, lawyer; b. Phoenix, July 12, 1935; s. Clark and Fay (Jackson) S.; m. Michael Waterman, 1958; children: Kevin, Ian. AB, Stanford U., 1957, JD, 1962. Bar: Calif. 1963, U.S. Supreme Ct. 1980. Assoc. Chickering & Gregory, San Francisco, 1962-70, ptnr., 1970-81, Pettit & Martin, San Francisco, 1981-95, Hovis, Smith, San Francisco, 1995-99; pvt. practice, 1999—. Mem. editl. bd. Stanford Law Rev., 1961-62. Lt. USN, 1957-60. Mem. ABA (bus. law sect.), Calif. Bar Assn., San Francisco Bar Assn., Orinda County Club, Palms Golf Club, La Quinta Citrus Golf Club, San Francisco World Trade Club. Office: Smith Law Offices 601 California St Ste 1600 San Francisco CA 94108-2821 E-mail: kerrysmith50965@msn.com.

SMITH, KEVIN HARVEY, video producer; b. Schenectady, N.Y., Sept. 14, 1948; s. Harvey Crawford and Teresa (Archambeault) S.; m. Barbara A. Virgone, Dec. 22, 2000; 1 stepchild, James M. Miller. BS in Radio, TV and Film, U. Tex., 1970. Asst. program dir. Sta. WHMA-TV, Anniston, Ala., 1970-71; broadcast producer Luckie & Forney, Inc. Advt., Birmingham, 1971-75, Steiner-Bressler Advt., Birmingham, 1975; producer, dir. Birmingham Pub. Schs. Ednl. TV, 1975-82; media coord. Blue Cross & Blue Shield of Ala., Birmingham, 1982-90; coord. curriculum devel. and prodn. Multi-Media Programs So. Med. Assn., 1991-93; dir. Media Svcs. Alacare Home Health Agy., Birmingham, 1993-95; instr. TV prodn. Phillips H.S., 1995-2000, G.W. Carver H.S., Birmingham, 2000—. Telephone counselor Crisis Ctr. Phone Line, Birmingham, 1979-81; media producer United Way's Camp Fire, Inc., Birmingham, 1985-88; bd. dirs. Birmingham Internat. Ednl. Film Festival, 1981-88. Recipient Laurel award United Way Birmingham, 1985, Award of Distinction Internat. Assn. Bus. Communicators, 1986, Award of Excellence, 1984, Shield of Excellence award Nat. Mgmt. Assn., 1989; named Med. Reporter of Yr., Med. Assn. Ala., 1980, one of Outstanding Young Men of Am., U.S. Jaycees, 1983. Mem. Internat. TV Assn. (pres. local chpt. 1985-87, regional v.p. 1988-90), Am. Soc. Tng. and Devel. (chmn. media com. 1985-86, Mem. of Yr. Birmingham chpt. 1988), Assn. Career and Tech. Edn. Avocations: reading, writing, films. Home: 977 Egret Dr Birmingham AL 35214 Office: GW Carver HS 3900 24th St No Birmingham AL 35207 E-mail: ksmith914@aol.com.

SMITH, KEVIN S. civil engineer; b. New Castle, Pa. BSCE, Youngstown State U., 1993; MBA, Bloomsburg U., 2001. Constrn. insp. Ohio Dept. Transp., Ravenna, summers 1992-93; quality assurance supr. CSR Hydro Conduit, Diamond, Ohio, 1994; civil engr. Zeff Zell Cons., Coraopolis, Pa., 1994-95; transp. technician Pa. Dept. Transp., Montoursville, 1995, civil engr. trainee, 1995-96, civil engr. supr., 1996-99, sr. civil engr. supr., 1999—. Zoning hearing officer Fairfield Twp., 1999—. Recipient Cert., Portland Cement Assn., 1994, Dale Carnegie Tng., 1998, Cert./Legis. citation Pa. Ho. of Reps., 1998. Mem. Youngstown State U. Alumni Assn., Rule Alumni Assn.

SMITH, KRISTY SADONA, accountant; b. Louisville, Aug. 21, 1976; d. Van Mitchell and Janith Ann Smith. AA, N.E. Miss. C.C., Booneville, 1996; BA, U. Miss., 1998. Office asst. Underground Pipelines, Inc., Plantersville, Miss., 1994—; acct. Harold Hodges & Co., PA, Tupelo, 1998—. Contbr. poetry. Vol. United Way Walk A Mile In My Shoes, Tupelo, 2001. Named Poet of the Yr., Internat. Poets Soc., 1999, 2000. Mem.: Tau Beta Sigma (sec. 1997, v.p. 1997—98). Baptist. Avocations: swimming, reading, cooking. Office: Harold Hodges & Co PA 1041 Cliff Gookin Blvd Tupelo MS 38801

SMITH, L. MONTGOMERY, electrical engineering educator; b. Chattanooga, Mar. 28, 1956; s. Nap M. and Mary (Stone) S. BS, Rhodes Coll., 1978, U. Tenn., 1982, MS, 1984, PhD, 1988. Asst. physicist So. Rsch. Inst., Birmingham, Ala., 1978-79; radiol. physicist Tenn. Dept. Pub. Health, Nashville, 1980-81; rsch. engr. U. Tenn. Space Inst., Tullahoma, 1984-89, asst. prof. elec. engring., 1989-95, assoc. prof. elec. engring., 1995—. Author: (with others) The Electrical Engineering Handbook, 1993, The Circuits and Filters Handbook, 1995. Mem. IEEE (sr.), Sigma Xi. Achievements include patent in field; devel. of weighted least-squares design technique for two-dimensional finite impulse response digital filters; rsch. (with other) in accelerating execution of the integrated TIGER series Monte Carlo radiation transport code; in refractive surface flow visualization using image processing; in a sys. for sequential step detection with application to video image processing; in determining railgun plasma current distbn. using Jansson's method to deconvolve B-Dot probe signals; (with others) in floating-point roundoff noise analysis of second-order state-space digital filter structures; in solidification studies using a confocal optical signal processor. Office: Univ Tenn Space Inst B H Goethert Pkwy Tullahoma TN 37388

SMITH, LAMAR SEELIGSON, congressman; b. San Antonio, Nov. 19, 1947; s. Campbell and Eloise Keith (Seeligson) S.; m. Elizabeth Schaefer, Mar. 20, 1992; children: Nell Seligson, Tobin Wells. BA, Yale U., 1969; JD, So. Meth. U., 1975. Mgmt. intern SBA, Washington, 1969-70; bus. writer The Christian Sci. Monitor, Boston, 1970-72; assoc. Maebius & Duncan, Inc., San Antonio, 1975-76; chmn. Rep. Party of Bexar County, 1978—82; state rep. Dist. 57-F, 1981-82; county commr. Precinct 3 Bexar County, 1983—85; mem. U.S. Congress from 21st Tex. dist., 1987—; mem. jud. com.; mem. joint econ. com.; mem. sci. com. Ptnr. Lamar Seeligson Ranch, Premont, Tex., 1975—. Christian Scientist. Office: US Ho of Reps 2231 Rayburn Ho Office Bldg Washington DC 20515-0001*

SMITH, LANTY L(LOYD), lawyer, business executive; b. Sherrodsville, Ohio, Dec. 11, 1942; s. Lloyd H. and Ellen Ruth (Newell) S.; m. Margaret Hays Chandler, June 11, 1966; children: Abigail Lamoreaux Presson, Margaret Ellen, Amanda Prescott. BS in Math. with honors, Wittenberg U., Springfield, Ohio, 1964; LLB with honors, Duke U., 1967. Bar: Ohio 1967. Assoc. Jones, Day, Cockley & Reavis, Cleve., 1967-73; ptnr. Jones, Day, Reavis & Pogue, 1974-77; exec. v.p., sr. gen. counsel Burlington Industries, Inc., Greensboro, N.C., 1977-86, pres., 1986-88; chmn. Precision Fabrics Group Inc., 1988—, The Greenwood Group, Inc., Raleigh, N.C., 1992—, Soles Brower Smith & Co., 1998—, Incellico, Inc., 2001—. Bd. dirs., chmn. exec. com. Wachovia Corp.; bd. dirs. Wikoff Color, Renfro Corp., Image Logistics Corp.; pres., CEO MediWave Star Tech. Inc., 1999—. Mem. exec. com. Greensboro Devel. Corp.; bd. visitors Duke U. Sch. Law; bd. trustees, exec. com. Duke U.; mem. exec. com. The Ridge YMCA Retreat. Mem. ABA, N.C. Inst. Medicine, N.C. Textile Found. Episcopalian. Home: 1401 Westridge Rd Greensboro NC 27410-2912 Office: Sales Brower Smith & Co First Union Tower Ste 925 Greensboro NC 27401-2167 E-mail: lsmith@solesbrower.com.

SMITH, LARRY DENNIS, paper mill stores executive; b. Altoona, Pa., Dec. 12, 1954; s. Bernard Robert and Dollie Edith (Nofsker) S. BS in Art Edn., Ind. U. Pa., 1977. Audio artist, 1974—; artist Mail Art Network, 1980—. Organizer, curator Manifesto Shnn Archives, East Freedom, Pa., 1982-86; established Patriots of the Am. Revolution Heraldic Register, 1993. Author: Manifesto Shnnalchemy, 1981, In the Wake of the Disaster Machine, 1981, Mother Bedford and the American Revolutionary War, 1999; editor: Artcomnet, 1981-87; artist The Labours of Grimnlaek, 1984; one-man shows in Rome, Stockholm, Zurich, Brusque and Helsinki; group show Seoul Internat. Bienale, 1984; editor 150th Anniversary History of Blair County, 1993-96; website creator: motherbedford.com. Mem. SAR. Republican. Avocations: genealogical research, rare book collector, gardening. Home: RR 1 Box 704-a East Freedom PA 16637-9770 Office: Appleton Papers Inc 100 Paper Mill Rd Roaring Spring PA 16673-1488 E-mail: ldshnn@motherbedford.com., larrysmith@appletonpapers.com.

SMITH, LARRY GLENN, retired state judge; b. Montgomery, Ala., Aug. 6, 1924; s. Alonzo Nathan and Louise (Norman) S.; m. Mary Emmalyn Murphree, Feb. 28, 1948; children: Cynthia Lynn Smith, Larry Glenn Jr., Celia Dell Smith Rudolph. Student, U. Ala., Tuscaloosa, 1942-43, 46-48; LLB, U. Fla., 1949. Bar: Fla. 1949. Pvt. practice, Panama City, Fla., 1949-53; assoc. Mathis & Mathis, 1953-57; asst. state's atty. Office State's Atty. for 14th Cir., 1953-57; rsch. asst. Fla. Supreme Ct., Tallahassee, 1958-60; ptnr. Baker, Baker & Smith, Orlando, Fla., 1960-64, Isler, Welch, Smith, Higby & Brown, Panama City, 1964-72; judge cir. ct. Fla. 14th Jud. Cir., 1973-79; judge Fla. 1st Dist. Ct. Appeal, Tallahassee, 1979-94; ret., 1994; chief judge Fla. 1st Dist. Ct. Appeal, Tallahassee, 1987-89; ret., 1994; sr. judge State of Fla. Mem. Fla. Bd. Bar Examiners, Tallahassee, 1967-72, Fla. Ct. Edn. Coun., Tallahassee, 1979-81, 86-91, Fla. Bench and Bar Commn., Tallahassee, 1990-91; pres. Fla. Conf. of Dist. Ct. Appeals Judges, Tallahassee, 1986-87. Mem. Panama City Airport Authority, 1952-55; past pres. Bay County Libr. Assn., Panama City. Lt. (j.g.) USNR, 1943-45. Mem. ABA, Fla. Bar, Tallahassee Bar Assn., Am. Judicature Soc., Bay County Bar Assn., St. Andrews Bay Am. Inn of Ct. (pres. 2001-2002). Avocations: hiking, biking, skiing, photography, reading. Home: 4115 W 17th St Panama City FL 32401-1122 E-mail: s.larry1@worldnet.att.net.

SMITH, LARRY STEVEN, financial analyst, farmer, accountant; b. Jasper, Tenn., Sept. 30, 1950; s. Samuel Lester and Stella Mae (Barnes) S. BA in Econs., U. Ala., Tuscaloosa, 1972, MBA, 1975. Laborer Lester Smith Farms, Scottsboro, Ala., 1975-76; acct. Ala. Hwy. Dept., Montgomery, 1976-77, Ala. State Agy. for Social Security, Montgomery, 1977-78; acct., analyst Ala. Pub. Svc. Commn., 1978-79, utilities analyst II, 1980-81, supr., 1981-89, chmn. computer oversight com., 1988-91, supr. Telecommunications div., 1989—; sales assoc. Jack Hendrix Real Estate, 1979-80. Interim dir. telecomm. divsn. Ala. Pub. Svc. Commn., 1993, mem. Telecomm. Task Force, 1996-99. Mem. Montgomery Jaycees, 1978-81, bd. dirs., 1979, 80; bd. dirs. Ala. Jr. Miss. , Montgomery, 1979-81; mem. Ala. Reps., 1983—. Nat. Grad. Coun. Fellowship grantee, 1973. Mem. N.Am. Limousin Found., Nat. Audubon Soc., Wilderness Soc., Environ. Def. Fund, Am. Assn. of Ind. Investors, Amnesty Internat., Nat. Wildlife Fedn, Sierra Club. Baptist. Avocations: photography, snow skiing, hunting, hiking, fly fishing, backpacking. Home: 1600 Cobblestone Ct Montgomery AL 36117-1702 Office: Ala Pub Svc Commn PO Box 991 Montgomery AL 36101-0991

SMITH, LARRY WAYNE, medical/surgical nurse; b. Washington, Jan. 2, 1962; s. Larry Grey and Norma D. Wilson. Grad. lic. practical nurse, Craven Community Coll., 1984, AAS, 1989. RN; cert. BCLS, ACLS, PALS. Patient care asst. Craven Regional Med. Ctr., New Bern, N.C., 1980-84, lic. practical nurse surg. unit, 1984-89, nurse in surg. unit, 1989, nurse in hosp. homecare, 1989, neurology nurse, 1989-90, staff nurse ICU, 1990-94, Naval Hosp., Camp Lejeune, 1991—. Home: 336 Cedar St Emerald Isle NC 28594-2803 Office: Craven Regional Med Ctr 2000 Neuse Blvd New Bern NC 28560-3499

SMITH, LAUREN, interior designer, writer; b. N.Y.C. d. Joseph and Rosemary (Griffin) Martin; m. Robert Zane Smith (dec. 1999), June 17, 1967. Student, N.Y. Sch. Interior Design, 1968-70. Pres. Lauren Smith, Inc., N.Y.C., 1973—. Product design Imperial Wallcoverings, Pillowtex, Ex. Cell; cons. Decorating with Wallcovering, 1987; spokesperson (TV show) Taste of New York, 1992. Author: Your Colors at Home, 1985, Colors for Brides, 1989, What Goes with What: Home Decorating Made Easy, 2001; editor: Discover Your Decorating Colors, 1987, Discover Your Colors at Home, 1988. Mem. Am. Soc. Interior Designers (allied). Roman Catholic. Avocations: art, music, antiques, photography, travel.

SMITH, LAUREN ASHLEY, lawyer, journalist, clergyman, physicist; b. Clinton, Iowa, Nov. 30, 1924; s. William Thomas Roy and Ethel (Cook) S.; m. Barbara Ann Mills, Aug. 22, 1947; children: Christopher A., Laura Nan Smith Pringle, William Thomas Roy II. BS, U. Minn., 1946, JD, 1949; postgrad., U. Chgo., 1943-49; MDiv, McCormick Theol. Sem., 1950; postgrad., U. Iowa, 1992. Bar: Colo. 1957, Iowa 1959, Ill. 1963, Minn. 1983, U.S. Supreme Ct. 1967; ordained to ministry Presbyn. Ch., 1950. Pastor Presbyn. Ch., Fredonia, Kans., 1950-52, Lamar, Colo., 1952-57, Congl. Ch., Clinton, 1975-80; editor The Comml., Pine Bluff, Ark., 1957-58; ptnr. Schoenauer Smith & Fullerton ASP, Clinton, 1995—. CEO LASCO Pub. Group, Clinton, 1995—; CEO, founder Interlink for the Internet Generation; internat. conferee Stanley

Found., Warrenton, Va., 1963—72; legal observer, USSR, 1978; co-sponsor All India Renewable Energy Conf., Bangalore, 1981; law sch. conferee U. Minn., China, 1983; lectr. law, religion, physics, nat. policy U. Wis., 2001, Spl. lectr. contemporary physics and religion, 01. Author: (jurisprudence treatise) Forma Dat Esse Rel, 1975, (monograph) First Strike Option, 1983; co-author: India On to New Horizons, 1989; columnist Crow Call, 1968—; co-editor Press and News of India, 1978-82; pub. Crow Call; pseudonym Christopher Crow, 1981—; writer BBC World Svc., London; editor Asian Econ. Cmty. Jour.; contbr. articles to religious publs. Minister-at-large Presbyn. Ch. U.S.A., Iowa, 1987—; bd. dirs. Iowa divsn. UN Assn. U.S.A., Iowa City, 1970-85; fellow Molecular Nanotechnology Foresight Inst., Palo Alto, Calif.; Franciscans United Nations Non Govt. Orgn.; assoc. Westar Inst. (The Jesus Seminar), Santa Rosa, Calif., 1997; active Quad City Estate Planning Coun.; founder, CEO Interlink relating quantum mechanics and religion. Mem. Iowa Bar Assn., Ill. Bar Assn., St. Andrews Soc., Clinton County Bar Assn. (pres. 1968, Best in Iowa citation), Clinton Ministerial Assn., Samaritan Health Systems Chaplain Corps. (pres.), European Soc. for Study of Sci. and Religion, Quad City Estate Planning Coun., Quaker Internat. Yokefellow, Nat. Network for New Spiritual Formation Presbyn. Ch. USA, Franciscans Internat., City Club of Quad Cities (bd. dirs.).

SMITH, LAURENCE ROGER, journal editor; b. N.Y.C., Sept. 30, 1939; s. John and Edith (Haabestad) S.; m. Betty Ann Larsen, Oct. 9, 1965; children: Erik Lars, Alesa Ann. AAS, Staten Island Community Coll., 1962; BS, SUNY, Oswego, 1965; MBA, St. John's U., 1975. Dir. cmty. devel. S.I. (N.Y.) C. of C., 1965-77; exec. v.p., CEO, Yonkers (N.Y.) C. of C., 1977-78; chief exec. officer Greater Lawrence (Mass.) C. of C., 1978-91; pres. The LeaderShip, North Andover, Mass., 1991-94; editor Jour. Innovative Mgmt., Methuen, 1994—. Dir., clk. Lawrence Downtown Parking Assocs., 1979-91; dir., asst. treas. Greater Lawrence Revolving Loan Fund, 1979-91; mem. U.S. C. of C. Com. on Edn. and Tng., 1990-91; dir. Mgmt. Innovations Group, GOAL/QPC, 1997—. Author: Godfidence, 1991. Chmn. Lower Merrimack Valley Pvt. Industry Coun., Lawrence, 1981; treas. Lawrence YMCA, 1985; vice-chmn. literacy com. Mass. Regional Employment Bd., 1989-90; bd. dirs. Greater Lawrence Red Cross; apptd. to Mass. Dept. Edn. Sch.-Bus. Partnership Com., 1990-91. With USCG, 1958-60. Recipient Pvt. Sector award Presdl. Commn., 1985, Flood Relief award ARC, 1987; named to U. Notre Dame Acad. Orgn. Mgmt., 1989, CUNY Hall of Fame. 1990. Mem. Am. C. of C. Execs., New Eng. Assn. C. of C. Execs. (pres., 1986), Mass. Assn. C. of C. Execs. (pres. 1984). Democrat. Episcopalian. Avocations: writing, golf. Home: The LeaderShip 233 Osgood St North Andover MA 01845-4025 Office: Jour Innovative Mgmt Two Manor Pkwy Salem NH 03079-1900

SMITH, LAVENSKI R. (VENCE SMITH), federal judge; m. Trendle Smith; 2 children. JD, U. Ark., 1987. Pvt. practice, Springdale, 1991-94; staff lawyer Ozark Legal Svcs., 1987-91; asst. prof. John Brown U., 1994-96; interim assoc. justice Ark. State Supreme Ct., 1999—2000; commr. Ark. Pub. Serv. Commn., 2001—. Bd. dirs. N.W. Ark. Christian Justice Ctr.; trainer Ptnrs. for Family Tng., 1993-96; chmn. Ark. Pub. Svc. Commn., 1996-98. Republican. Office: Ark. Pub. Serv. Commn. 1000 Center St. Little Rock AR 72201*

SMITH, LAWRENCE BERK, economics educator, consultant; b. Toronto, Ont., Can., Nov. 10, 1939; s. Isadore E. and Ruth (Berk) S.; separated; children— Cynthia Joy, Ilyse Jan, Natalie Jill. B.Com., U. Toronto, 1962; A.M., Harvard U., 1964, Ph.D., 1966. Teaching fellow Harvard U., Cambridge, Mass., 1964-66, instr. econs., 1966; asst. prof. econs. U. Toronto, Ont., Can., 1966-69, assoc. prof., 1969-72, prof., 1972— , dir. econs., assoc. chair dept. polit. economy, 1975-79; vis. scholar Grad. Sch. Mgmt., UCLA, 1973-74, Grad. Sch. Bus Adminstrn., U. Calif.-Berkeley, 1981-82; cons. Bank of Can., Ministry of Urban Affairs, Salomon Bros., Inc., others. Mem. editorial adv. bd. Fraser Inst., 1975— ; editorial rev. bd. Jour. Am. Real Estate and Urban Econs. Assn., 1980— ; editorial bd. Jour. Real Estate Fin. and Econs., 1988—. Author: The Postwar Canadian Housing and Residential Mortgage Markets and the Role of Government, 1974; Anatomy of a Crisis: Canadian Housing Policy in the Seventies, 1977; (co-author) Government in Canadian Capital Markets: Selected Cases, 1978. Co-editor: Canadian Economic Problems and Policies, 1970; Issues in Canadian Economics, 1974; Public Property: The Habitat Debate Continued, 1977. Contbr. articles to profl. jours. Mem. policy and govt. relations com. United Way Greater Toronto, 1983-85, mem. social services planning com., 1985. Woodrow Wilson fellow, 1962-63; Harvard grad. scholar, 1963-64; Can. Council fellow, 1963-64; Ford Motor Co. Internat. fellow, 1964-65; others. Mem. Can. Econs. Assn. (exec. 1977-80), Am. Real Estate and Urban Econs. Assn. (exec. 1980-83), Am. Econs. Assn., Am. Fin. Assn. Avocations: tennis; sailing; yoga; bridge. Office: U Toronto Dept Econs 150 St George St Toronto ON Canada M5S 1A1

SMITH, LEE LLAKE, hotel executive; b. Long Beach, Calif., Oct. 15, 1936; s. Lowell Llake and Violet Margaret (Chrissman) S.; m. Sharon McLanahan, (div. 1977). AA, Long Beach City Coll., 1958; BA in Music, Chapman Coll., 1965; postgrad., Calif. State U., Long Beach, 1966-67, U. Calif., Santa Barbara, 1974. Cert. tchr. Calif.; lic. ins. agt., Calif. Owner, mgr. Lee's Land Cattle Ranch, Cuyama Valley, Calif., 1960—; tchr. Cuyama Valley Schs., New Cuyama, 1967-79; owner, mgr. Cuyama Buckhorn Restaurant & Motel, 1979-83; owner Allstate Ins. Agy., Desert Hot Springs, Calif., 1987-91; owner, mgr. Caravan Resort Spa, 1983-91; prof. music Taft Coll., 2002—. Owner S & S Printing, 1990—, Lee's Land Bed & Breakfast, 1992—. Violinist Bakersfield (Calif.) Symphony, 1967—, Brook String Quartet, Palm Springs, Calif., 1984-91; dir. Planning Commn., Desert Hot Springs, 1985-87; chmn. Environ. Rev., Desert Hot Springs, 1986-88; mem. Redevel. Com., Desert Hot Springs, 1983-88; mem. exec. bd. growth and devel. Boys and Girls Club; bd. dirs. Food Now Program, 1988-91. Mem. Am. Fedn. Musicians, Desert Hot Springs C. of C. (Bus. Person Yr. 1987), Taft C. of C. (pres. 1997), Breakfast Rotary (pres. 1987-88), Taft Rotary, Elks. Republican. Avocations: hiking, flying. Home: 9409 Carvalho Ct Bakersfield CA 93311 Office: S & S Printing 606 Center St Taft CA 93268-3125 E-mail: ssprint@gte.net.

SMITH, LEE ELTON, surgery educator, retired military officer; b. Ventura, Calif., July 19, 1937; s. Raymond Elroy and Edith Irene (Jordan) S.; m. Carole Sue Smith; children: Justine Diane, Alexander Loren. BS, U. Calif., Berkeley, 1959; MD, U. Calif., San Francisco, 1962. Diplomate Am. Bd. Surgery, Am. Bd. Colon and Rectal Surgery (pres. 1992-93). Commd. ens. USN, 1960, advanced through grades to capt., 1977; intern U. Utah, Salt Lake City, 1962-63; resident USN, San Diego, 1966-70, staff surgeon Bremerton, Wash., 1970-72; resident colorectal surgery U. Minn., Mpls., 1972-73; dir. colorectal surgery Nat. Naval Med. Ctr. USN, Bethesda, Md., 1973-82, ret., 1983, Seattle, 1982; clin. prof. surgery Uniformed Svcs. U., Bethesda, 1976—; prof. surgery George Washington U., Washington, 1983-96, prof. surgery, 1996—; clin. prof. surgery Georgetown U., 2001—; dir. sect. of colon and rectal surgery Washington Hosp. Ctr., 1996—. Pres. Am. Bd. Colon and Rectal Surgery, 1993-94. Editor: Practical Guide to Anorectal Physiology, 1990, 2d edit., 1995; assoc. editor Diseases of the Colon & Rectum, 1984-96, Perspectives in Colon and Rectal Surgery, 1989—. Mem. ACS (pres. Met. Washington chpt. 1993-94), Soc. Am. Gastrointestinal Endoscopic Surgeons (pres. 1989-90), Am. Cancer Soc. (v.p. D.C. chpt. 1985-93), Am. Soc. Colon & Rectal Surgeons (pres. 1998-99). Home: 1200 N Nash St Apt 1134 Arlington VA 22209-3682 Office: Washington Hosp Ctr 106 Irving St NW Washington DC 20010-2975

SMITH, LEILA HENTZEN, artist; b. Milw., May 20, 1932; d. Erwin Albert and Marian Leila (Austin) Hentzen; m. Richard Howard Smith, Sept. 12, 1959; 1 child, Jennie. BFA, Miami U., 1955; cert., Famous Artists Schs., 1959. Quilting tchr. Milw. Pub. Schs., 1975-79. One-woman shows include Boerner Bot. Gardens, Whitnall Park, Wis., 1995, exhibited in group shows at Milw. Art Ctr., 1961, West Bend (Wis.) Gallery Fine Arts, 1963, Wustum Mus. Art, Racine, Wis., 1966, Mapledale Sch. Gallery, Bayside, Wis., 1977, 1981, Mount Mary Coll., Milw., 1969—77, 1979—2001, Artist's World Gallery, Cedarburg, Wis., 1975, Ozaukee Art Ctr, 1982—86, 1993, John Michael Kohler Arts Ctr., Sheboygan, Wis., 1984, 1987, 1989—2001, Cedarburg Cultural Ctr., 1988—2001, West Bend Gallery Fine Arts, 1993, 1996, 1999, 2002, Rahr-West Art Mus., Manitowoc, Wis., 1994, 1997, Gallery 110 North, Plymouth, Wis., 1996, Cardinal Stritch U., 1998—2001, Represented in permanent collections Milw. County Art Commn. Women's aux. vol. Salvation Army, Milw.; mem. dean's adv. coun. U. Wis. Milw. Sch. Arts. Recipient Honorable Mention for painting Bayshore Merchants Assn, 1969, Delta Gamma Art Fair, 1981, Best of Show for painting John Michael Kohler Arts Ctr., 1988. Mem. AAUW, Cedarburg Artists Guild, Wis. Watercolor Soc., Seven Arts Soc. Milw. (pres. 1967-68, painters group chmn. 1962-63), DAR (Milw. chpt. Holiday Folk Fair chmn. 1965-76, libr. historian 1974-77, corr. sec. 1977-80, dir. 1983-86, rec. sec. 1992-95, regent 1995-98, Outstanding Jr. Mem. 1966), Wis. Soc. Daus. of Founders and Patriots of Am. (pres. 1964-66, 2d v.p. 1966-68, 70-73, corr. sec. 1976-79), Wis. Ct. Assts., Nat. Soc. Women Descendants Ancient and Hon. Arty. Co. Boston, Wis. Soc. Mayflower Descendants (sec. 1999-02), Delta Zeta. Congregationalist. Avocations: quilting, needlework, swimming.

SMITH, LEONARD BINGLEY, musician; b. Poughkeepsie, N.Y., Sept. 5, 1915; s. Frank Roderick and Ethel (Schubert) S.; m. Helen Gladys Rowe, Apr. 20, 1940 (dec. 1993); 1 dau., Sandra Victoria. Student, N.Y. Mil. Acad., 1930-33, Ernest Williams Sch. Music, 1933-36, NYU, 1936-37, Curtis Inst. Music, 1943-45; H.H.D., Detroit Inst. Tech., 1965. Pres. Accompaniments Unltd., Inc., 1952—. Cornet soloist, Ernest Williams Band, 1933-36, The Goldman Band, summers 1936-42; 1st trumpet, Barrere Little Symphony, 1935-37, Detroit Symphony Orch., 1937-42, Ford Sunday Evening Hour, 1937-42; condr., The Leonard Smith Concert Band, 1945—, Detroit Concert Band, 1945—, U. Detroit Bands, 1949-50, Moslem AAONMS Band, 1945-57, Scandinavian Symphony Orch. of Detroit, 1959-61, guest condr., Indpls. Symphony Orch., 1967; guest condr., soloist, clinician numerous concerts, U.S., Can.; mus. dir. John Philip Sousa documentary for BBC, 1970; Sousa Am. Bicentennial Recorded Collection; record series Gems concert band, Blossom Festival Band; condr. Blossom Festival Concert Band, 1972—; The Indomitable Teddy Roosevelt; producer: Our Am. Heritage in Music, 1970; pres., Bandland, Inc., 1951-61; Author: Treasury of Scales; over 350 pub. compositions; mem. bd. advisors Instrumentalist mag. Chmn. music com. Mich. Civil War Centennial Commn., 1961-64; gov. bd. Mac Award. With USNR, 1942-45. Recipient spl. medal Mich. Polish Legion Am. Vets., Distinguished Service medal Kappa Kappa Psi; Mich. Minuteman Gov.'s award, 1973; Freedom Found. award, 1975; Gen. William Booth award, 1976, Embassy Mich. Tourism award, 1979; named Alumnus of Distinction N.Y. Mil. Acad., 1976 Mem. ASCAP, Philippine Bandsmen's Assn. (hon.), Am. Fedn. Musicians, Internat. Platform Assn., Assn. Concert Bands (pres. 1982-83). Clubs: Masons (33 deg.), Shriners, K.T, Jesters. Office: c/o Detroit Concert Band Inc 7443 E Butherus Dr Ste 100 Scottsdale AZ 85260-2459

SMITH, LEONORE RAE, artist; b. Chgo. d. Leon and Rose (Hershfield) Goodman; m. Paul Carl Smith, Apr. 17, 1943; children: Jill Henderson, Laurie Christman. Student, Chgo. Art Inst., 1935-40, U. Chgo., 1939—. Performer in many Broadway shows, with Met. Opera Quartet, Carnegie Hall, nat. concerts; portrait, landscape painter; signature artist Oil Painters of Am., Chgo., 1992-2000, Am. Acad. of Women Artists, 1997-98; ofcl. artist U.S. Coast Guard, Washington, 1989-2000; cert. artist Am. Portrait Soc., Huntington Harbor, Calif., 1985; nat. adv. bd. The Portrait Club, N.Y.C., 1983. Pres. Pacific Palisades Rep. Women, Calif. Recipient Best of Show awards Salamagundi U.S. Coast Guard, N.Y.C., 1989, Pacific Palisades Art Assn., 1987, 1st prize in oils Greater L.A. Art Competition, Santa Monica, Calif., 1995, prize The Artist's Mag., 1995, Internat. Soc. Artists, 1977, 1st pl. award Dream Studio competition, 1996, 1st pl. in portrait O.P.A. Nat. Show, 2001; named One of Master Artists of World Internat. Artists Mag., 1996, several awards Calif. Art Club, shown at Nat. Mus. of Naval Aviation, Carnesie Mus., Frederick Weisman Mus., Malibu, Calif., Internat. Artist award Still Life Competition, 2002, cover contest award Northlight mag., 2002. Mem. Am. Acad. Women Artists (signature mem.), Salmagundi Club, Pacific Palisades Art Assn. (past pres.), Calif. Art Club, Oil Painters of Am. (signature mem.), Am. Portrait Soc. (cert.). Avocations: singing, acting, poetry.

SMITH, LEROY HARRINGTON, JR. mechanical engineer, aerodynamics consultant; b. Balt., Nov. 3, 1928; s. Leroy Harrington and Edna (Marsh) S.; m. Barbara Ann Williams, July 7, 1951; children: Glenn Harrington, Bruce Lyttleton, Cynthia Ann. BS in Engring., Johns Hopkins U., 1949, MS, 1951, Dr. Engring., 1954. Compressor aerodynamacist Gen. Electric Co., Cin., 1954-61, mgr. turbomachinery devel., 1961-68, mgr. compressor & fan design tech., 1968-75, mgr. turbomachinery aerodynamics tech., 1975-92, cons. technologist Turbomachinery Aerodynamics, 1992-94, cons., 1994—. Contbr. articles to ASME Trans. Recipient Perry T. Egbert Jr. awards, 1969, 83, Charles P. Steinmetz award, 1987 Gen. Electric Co. Fellow ASME (Gas Turbine award 1981, 87, R. Tom Sawyer award 1987, Aircraft Engine Tech. award 1993, ISABE award 2001); mem. NAE, Ohio River Launch Club. Achievements include patents for 12 in field. Office: GE Aircraft Eng Mail Drop A411 1 Neumann Way Cincinnati OH 45215-1915 E-mail: leroy.smith@ae.ge.com.

SMITH, LESLIE ROPER, hospital and healthcare administrator; b. Stockton, Calif., June 20, 1928; s. Austin J. and Helen (Roper) S.; m. Edith Sue Fincher, June 22, 1952; children: Melinda Sue, Leslie Erin, Timothy Brian. AB, U. Pacific, 1951; MS in Pub. Adminstrn, U. So. Calif., 1956. Adminstrv. asst. Ranchos Los Amigos Hosp., Downey, Calif., 1953-57; asst. adminstr. Harbor Gen. Hosp., Torrance, 1957-65; adminstr. Harbor UCLA Med. Ctr., 1966-71; acting regional dir. Los Angeles County Coastal Health Services Region, 1973; pres. San Pedro Peninsula Hosp., San Pedro, Cal., 1974-86; exec. dir. Los Angeles County/U. So. Calif. Med. Center, 1971-73; adminstr. Long Beach (Calif.) Hosp., 1965-66; asso. clin. prof. community medicine and pub. health, also emergency medicine U. So. Calif., 1968-78; instr. U. So. Calif. (Sch. Pub. Adminstrn.), 1968; preceptor hosp. adminstrn. UCLA Sch. Pub. Health, 1964—; chief exec. officer French Hosp. Med. Ctr. and Health Plan, 1986-87; dir. health care services McCormack & Farrow, 1987—. Lectr. in field, 1963— ; cons. emergency health services HEW, 1970-73; chmn. com. disaster preparedness Hosp. Council So. Calif., 1966-72, sec., 1971— , pres., 1973; mem. Calif. Assembly Com. on Emergency Med. Services, 1970, Calif. Emergency Med. Adv. Com., 1972-75, Los Angeles County Commn. on Emergency Med. Services, 1975-83, Los Angeles Health Planning and Devel. Agy. Commn., 1980-83; bd. dirs. Blue Cross of So. Calif.; mem. hosp. relations com. Blue Cross of Calif.; mem. adv. com. on emergency health services Calif. Dept. Health, 1974-75; bd. dirs., mem. exec. com. Truck Ins. Exchange of Farmers Ins. Group, 1977-82; bd. dirs. Hosp. Council of So. Calif., 1966-76, 81-86, Health Resources Inst., 1985-86; chmn. Preferred Health Network, 1983-86 Mem. goals com., Torrance, 1968— ; pres. Silver Spur Little League, Palos Verdes, 1969-70. Served with AUS, 1946-48. Recipient Silver Knight and Gold Knight award Nat. Mgmt. Assn., 1970, 85, Walker Fellowship award, 1976 Fellow Am. Coll. Health Care Execs. (life); mem. Am., Nat. mgmt. assns., Am. Hosp. Assn. (chmn. com. on community emergency health services 1973), Calif. Hosp. Assn. (chmn. com. emergency services 1965-70, trustee 1973-76, bd. dirs. Calif. Ins. Service Group 1980-82), County Suprs. Assn. Calif. (chmn. joint subcom. on emergency care 1970) Presbyn. (elder, trustee). Home: 27 Marseille Laguna Niguel CA 92677-5400 E-mail: lrs_essmith1@msn.com.

SMITH, LEWIS DENNIS, academic administrator, educator; b. Muncie, Ind., Jan. 18, 1938; s. Thurman Lewis and Dorothy Ann (Dennis) S.; m. Suzanne F. Metcalfe; children: Lauren Kay, Raymond Bradley. AB, Ind. U., 1959, PhD, 1964. Asst. embryologist Argonne (Ill.) Nat. Lab., 1964-67, assoc. biologist, 1967-69; assoc. prof. Purdue U., West Lafayette, Ind., 1969-73, prof. biology, 1973-87, assoc. head dept. biol. scis., 1979-80, head dept., 1980-87; prof. dept. devel. and cell. U. Calif., Irvine, 1987-94, dean Sch. Biol. Scis., 1987-90, exec. vice chancellor, 1990-94; pres. U. of Nebr., 1994—. Instr. embryology Woods Hole (Mass.) Marine Biology Lab., summers 1972, 73, 74, mem. Space Sci. Bd., Washington, 1984-91; chmn. Space Biology and Medicine, Space Sci. Bd., 1986-91; mem. cell biology study sect. NIH, Bethesda, Md., 1971-75; chmn., 1977-79, bd. sci. counselors Nat. Inst. Child Health and Human Devel., 1990-95, chmn. 1992-95; mem. space biology peer rev. bd. AIBS, 1980-85. Guggenheim fellow, 1987. Mem. Am. Soc. Biochemistry and Molecular Biology, AAAS, Internat. Soc. for Devel. Biology, Soc. for Devel. Biology, Am. Soc. Cell Biology, Am. Soc. for Microbiology. Home: 2524 Wilderness Ridge Rd Lincoln NE 68516 Office: 3835 Holdrege St Lincoln NE 68503-1435

SMITH, LEWIS MOTTER, JR. retired advertising and direct marketing executive; b. Kansas City, Mo., Nov. 4, 1932; s. Lewis Motter and Virginia (Smith) S.; m. Alice Allen, June 28, 1975; children: Katherine Allen, Patience Allen. Student, Kenyon Coll., 1951-53, Columbia U., 1956-58. Copywriter mail order divsn. Grolier Soc., Inc., N.Y.C., 1957-59; free lance copywriter Santa Fe, 1960-61; v.p. creative svcs. Grolier Enterprises Inc., N.Y.C., 1962-67; v.p., creative planning dir. Wunderman, Ricotta & Kline, Inc., 1968-72; exec. v.p., creative dir., 1972-79; exec. v.p. Young & Rubicam Direct Mktg. Group, 1980; sr. v.p., dir. mktg. Book-of-the-Month Club, Inc., 1980-84, dir., 1981-84; exec. v.p., creative dir. SSC&B: Vos Direct Inc., N.Y.C., 1985-87; pres., dir. creative services Lintas: Direct Inc. (formerly SSC&B: Vos Direct Inc.), 1987-89; pres. Lew Smith & Assocs., Inc., Hyde Park, NY, 1989—2001. Bd. dirs. Young Concert Artists, Inc., N.Y.C., 1966-67, Harlem Sch. Arts, 1967-68. Served with U.S. Army, 1953-56. Mem. Delta Phi. Episcopalian. Home: 17 Beadart Pl Hyde Park NY 12538-1217

SMITH, LINDA ANN GLIDEWELL, accountant; b. Birmingham, Ala., Aug. 11, 1944; d. Emmett O'Neal and Iola Florence (Harris) Glidewell; m. Lindsey Stribling Smith, Nov. 5, 1966 (div. Dec. 1990); 1 child, Lindsey Nelson; m. Charles G. Espey, Sept. 11, 1997; 1 stepchild, Heidi Espey Holladay. BA cum laude, Birmingham-So. Coll., 1984. Stenographer Cook's Pest Control, Decatur, Ala., 1962, Nelson-Weaver Cos., Birmingham, 1963-69; resident mgr. Twin Homes of Mt. Brook, 1966-69; bookkeeper, sect. to v.p. Molton, Allen & Williams, 1969-72; sec. quality assurance dept. So. Co. Svc., Birmingham, 1972-74, sec. sys. constrn. budget, 1974-82, sr. sec. treasury dept., 1982-83; jr. acct. major projects-acctg. Ala. Power Co., 1983-87, sr. acct. fuel dept., 1987-90, sr. acct. stats. dept., 1990-92; fin. adminstr., comptr. Ala. Bapt., Inc., 1992-99; bus. revenue tax compliance officer Shelby County, 1999—. Asst. treas. So. Co. Svcs. State and Fed. PAC,, Ala. PowerCo. State and Fed. PAC. Mem. Am. Soc. Women Accts., The Club, Inc., Alpha Lambda Delta, Birmingham So. Alumni Assn. (coun. mem.). Baptist. Avocations: travel, culinary art, walking, fishing.

SMITH, LINDA ZIMBALIST, investment research executive; b. St. Louis, Jan. 27, 1953; d. Sidney Eli and Blanka M. (Wassermann) Zimbalist; m. William Martin Smith, May 27, 1979; children: Brian Alexander, Tyler Scott. BA, Pitzer Coll., Claremont, Calif., 1975; MBA, U. Chgo., 1978. Research asst. Stein Roe & Farnham, Chgo., 1975-76, Chgo. Bd. Options Exchange, 1976-79; arbitrage analyst First Boston, N.Y.C., 1980-82; gen. ptnr. Zimbalist Smith Investments, Bend, Oreg., 1982—. Avocation: tennis. Office: Zimbalist Smith 3052 NW Merchant Way Ste107 Bend OR 97701-7509 E-mail: zims@bendcable.com.

SMITH, LIZ (MARY ELIZABETH SMITH), newspaper columnist, broadcast journalist; b. Ft. Worth, Feb. 2, 1923; d. Sloan and Sarah Elizabeth (McCall) S. B.J., U. Tex., 1948. Editor Dell Publns., N.Y.C., 1950-53; assoc. producer CBS Radio, 1953-55, NBC-TV, 1955-59; assoc. Cholly Knickerbocker newspaper column, N.Y.C., 1959-64; film critic Cosmpolitan mag., 1966; columnist Chgo. Tribune-N.Y. Daily News Syndicate (now Tribune Media Services), 1976-91; TV commentator WNBC-TV, N.Y.C., 1978-91; commentator Fox-TV, 1991—; columnist Newsday, L.A. Times Syndicate, 1991—, Family Circle mag., 1993—; freelance mag. writer; commentator Gossip Show E! Entertainment, 1993—; columnist N.Y. Post, N.Y.C., 1995—, 1995—. Author: The Mother Book, 1978. Home and Office: 160 E 38th St New York NY 10016-2651 *A career in Journalism? Any career at all? I say learn to type. Read a lot. Keep on keeping on. Work is its own reward and success is loving your work. And remember, never give up. After the Middle Ages comes the Renaissance.*

SMITH, LLOYD, musician; b. Cleve., Dec. 1, 1941; s. Thomas George Russell and Anita May (Speer) S.; m. Rheta R. Naylor, Mar. 30, 1967 (div. Nov. 1994); 1 child, Peter Eldon; m. Nancy R. Bean, June 6, 1995. MusB, Curtis Inst. Music, 1965. Tchr. Settlement Music Sch., 1970-72, 92—. Cellist Pitts. Symphony, 1965-67, Phila. Orch., 1967—, asst. prin. cello, 1988—; soloist Indpls. Symphony, 1958, 68, Garden State Philharmonic, 1964, Lansdowne Symphony, 1965, West Jersey Chamber Orch., 1991, Haverford-Bryn Mawr Symphony, 1992, The Phila. Orch., 1994, Ocean City Symphony, 2001; mem. Huntingdon Trio, 1974-93, Wister quartet, 1988—; composer Sonata for cello and piano, Op. 1, 1997, Quintet, Op. 2 for Saratoga Chamber Music Festival, 1998, duet for cello Four Hands, 1999, "You're Invited" for string quartet and violin, 1999, Suite for accordion and strings, Op. 4, 2000, String Quartet Op. 3, 2000. Alumni rep. Curtis Inst. Music Bd. Trustees, chmn. Parents' Com., 1989-90; bd. dirs. Phila. Youth Orch., 1987-91, Community Out Reach Partnership, 1988-90. Mem. Am. Soc. Ancient Instruments (asst. artistic dir. 1975-77, music dir. 1977-80), Curtis Inst. Music Nat. Alumni Assn. (treas., bd. dirs. 1989-90), 1807 & Friends (bd. dirs. 1994—). Home and Office: 5639 E Wister St Philadelphia PA 19144-1522 E-mail: frnd1807@bellatlantic.net.

SMITH, LLOYD DAVID, community activist; b. Chgo., Apr. 27, 1933; s. Lloyd Francis and Frances Maria (Alexander) Smith; m. Esther Snead Smith, 1952 (div. 1978); children: Anthony, Patrice, Robyn, Cheryl, Angela; m. Mary Ann Huff, 1979. Various positions USMC Hdqs., Washington, 1954—67; dep. dir. Planning Office, 1967—80; pres., CEO Marshall Heights Cmty. Devel. Orgn., 1980—98; chmn. City First Bank, 1997—2001, Nat. Capital Revitalization Corp., Washington, 2000—01. Guest lectr. urban pub. policy George Washington U., Washington, 1995, Washington, 97. Trustee St. Mary's Coll., Md., 1998—; mem. D.C. Zoning Commn., Washington, 1988—93; bd. dirs. Strategies Com. to Reduce Chronic Poverty, Cmty. Partnership for Prevention of Homelessness, D.C. Bldg. Industry Assn.; chmn. bd. dirs. C.O.G. Growth Policy Com. Sgt. U.S. Army, 1950—52, Korean War. Recipient Local Minority Bus. Adv. award, 1993, Cmty. Leadership award, Points of Light Found., 1994, Cmty. Svc. award, D.C. Bldg. Industry Assn., 1994. Democrat. Roman Catholic. Avocations: fishing, travel, genealogy. Home: 3642 Highwood Dr SE Washington DC 20020-2349 Personal E-mail: kvet715@aol.com.

SMITH, LLOYD HOLLINGSWORTH, physician; b. Easley, S.C., Mar. 27, 1924; s. Lloyd H. and Phyllis (Page) S.; m. Margaret Constance Avery, Feb. 27, 1954; children— Virginia Constance, Christopher Avery, Rebecca Anne, Charlotte Page, Elizabeth Hollingsworth, Jeffrey Hollingsworth. AB, Washington and Lee U., 1944, D.Sc., 1969; MD, Harvard, 1948. Intern, then resident Mass. Gen. Hosp., Boston, 1948-50, chief resident physician, 1955-56; mem. Harvard Soc. Fellows, 1952-54; asst. prof. Harvard Soc. Fellows (Med. Sch.), 1956-63; vis. investigator Karolinska Inst., Stockholm, 1954-55, Oxford (Eng.) U., 1963-64; prof. medicine, chmn. dept. U. Calif. Med. Sch., San Francisco, 1964-85, assoc dean, 1985-2000. Mem. Pres.'s Sci. Adv. Com., 1970-73 Bd. overseers Harvard, 1974-80. Served to capt., M.C. AUS, 1950-52. Mem. Am. Acad. Arts and Scis., Am. Soc. Clin. Investigation (pres. 1969-70), Western Soc. Clin. Rsch. (pres. 1969-70), Assn. Am. Physicians (pres. 1974-75), Am. Fedn. Clin. Rsch. Achievements include special research genetic and metabolic diseases. Home: 309 Evergreen Dr Kentfield CA 94904-2709 Office: U Calif San Francisco Med Ctr San Francisco CA 94143-0001 E-mail: lloydhsmith@aol.com.

SMITH, LOIS ANN (L.A. SMITH), foundation administrator, consultant; b. Chattanooga, Nov. 30, 1944; d. W. and Rose C. (Tucker) Hicks; divorced; 1 child, Tony A. Student, Lemoyne-Owen Coll., 1962-64; BA in Sociology and Bus. Adminstrn., Howard U., 1976, postgrad., 1977-78. Cert. notary pub., Md., Ga. Field underwriter, sales trainer N.Y. Life Ins. Co., Franklin Life Ins. Co., 1979-82; pres., gen. mgr. Lotona Enterprises, Inc., Washington, 1979-85; mktg. coord. Montgomery County Dept. Transp., Md., 1985-87; fund raising and tng. cons. Princess Ann & Co., Washington, 1987-91; grant/contract adminstr. cell. medicine Howard U., NIH, 1991-92; founder, exec. dir. Good News & Give Aways, Inc., Tucker, Ga., 1989—. Pub. speaker Princess Ann & Co., Md., Ga., 1970-94, seminar presenter, 1985-94; radio host Managing Your Income & Personal Budget; freelance writer, 1975—; counselor in various fields, 1977—. Author: The Most Precious Moments, 1973, Let's Consider, A Sociological View of Employment, 1976, (play) A Reversible Oreo, 1974; pub., editor newsletter Good News & Give Aways, Inc., 1989-93; author, speaker (audio cassette tapes) I Care . . . , 1989, 90. Speaker, soloist various ednl., religious and civic orgns., 1960—; coord. Up the Hill Gang, 1979—; treas. Faith Cmty. Bapt. Ch., 1986-87; pub. speaker, vol. Dekalb Responds/Dekalb Econ. Opportunity Authority, Decatur, Ga., 1993-94. Recipient Disting. Svc. award Sta. WNOO, 1979. Mem. Ga. Coll. Counselors

Assn., Bus. & Profl. Women's Club (charter, editor newsletter 1980-82, Woman of Yr. honoree 1980), Kappa Delta Pi, Phi Beta Lambda. Avocations: singing, fund raising. Office: Good News & Give Aways Inc PO Box 1495 Suitland MD 20752-1495

SMITH, LOIS ARLENE, actress, writer; b. Topeka, Nov. 3, 1930; d. William Oren and Carrie D. (Gottshalk) Humbert; m. Wesley Dale Smith, Nov. 5, 1948 (div. 1973); 1 child, Moon Elizabeth. Student, U. Wash., 1948-50; studied with Lee Strasberg, Actor's Studio, N.Y.C., 1955—. Guest dir. Juilliard Sch., 1987; Clarence Ross fellow Am. Theater Wing at Eugene O'Neill Theater Ctr., 1983; mem. adv. panel program fund Pub. Broadcasting Service, 1981-82; hon. founder Harold Clurman Theatre Artists Fund, Ctr. for Arts, SUNY-Purchase, 1981 Author: play All There Is, 1982; debut in Time Out for Ginger, 1952; actress Broadway and off-Broadway prodns., 1952—; stage appearances include Theater of the Living Arts, Mark Taper Forum, Long Wharf Theater, Balt. Centerstage and Steppenwolf Theater Co.; appears on network and pub. TV programs; stage appearances include, The Young and the Beautiful, 1955, The Glass Menagerie, 1956, Blues for Mr. Charlie, 1964, Orpheus Descending, 1957, Miss Julie, 1966, Uncle Vanya, 1965, 69, The Iceman Cometh, 1973, Harry Outside, 1975, Hillbilly Women, 1979, 81, the Vienna Notes, 1985, The Stick Wife, April Snow, 1987, The Grapes of Wrath, 1988-89, 90, Measure for Measure, Beside Herself, 1989, Escape from Happiness, 1993, Buried Child, 1995-96, Defying Gravity, 1997, Impossible Marriage, 1998, Mrs. Warren's Profession, 1999, Give Me Your Answer, Do, 1999, Mother Courage, 2001; films include East of Eden, 1955, Five Easy Pieces, 1970, Next Stop Greenwich Village, 1975, Resurrection, 1980, Green Card, 1990, Fried Green Tomatoes, 1991, Falling Down, 1993, How to Make an American Quilt, 1995, Dead Man Walking, 1995, Larger than Life, 1996, Twister, 1996, Tumbleweeds, 1998, Minority Report, 2002, The Laramie Project, 2002. Named Best Supporting Actress for Five Easy Pieces, Nat. Soc. Film Critics, 1971; recipient Tony nominations for Grapes of Wrath, 1990, Buried Child, 1996; named to Filmdom's Famous Fives for East of Eden, Failm Daily mag., 1955, Steppenwolf Ensemble Nat. Medal of Arts, 1998. Mem. SAG, AFTRA, Actors Equity Assn., Dramatists Guild, Actors Studio, Ensemble Studio Theater, Steppenwolf Theatre Co. Ensemble, Acad. Motion Picture Arts and Scis.

SMITH, LORAN BRADFORD, educator; b. Medford, Mass., July 23, 1946; s. Gordon T. and Edith A. S. BA, Salem State Coll., 1968; MA, Okla. State U., 1971; PhD, U. Nebr., 1980. Instr. Black Hills State Coll., Spearfish, S.D., 1971-74, Augustana Coll., Sioux Falls, 1974-77; asst. prof. Mo. So. State Coll., Joplin, 1980-82, Washburn U., Topeka, 1982-86, assoc. prof., 1988-92; grad. faculty U. Kans., Lawrence, 1988-89; prof. Washburn U., 1992—. Election analyst KSNT-TV, Topeka, 1984-92. Contbr. articles to profl. jours. Chair pilot task force City of Topeka, 1983-84, mem. charter rev. com., 1999. Mem. Am. Polit. Sci. Assn., Am. Soc. Pub. Adminstrs. (Kans. chpt. v.p. 1985-87, pres. 1987-88), Urban Affairs Assn., Kansas Delta Alumni Corp., Sigma Phi Epsilon (Disting. Alumnus award 1997). Home: 4301 SW 15th St Apt 309 Topeka KS 66604-4311 Office: Washburn U 1700 SW College Ave Topeka KS 66621-0001

SMITH, LOREN ALLAN, federal judge; b. Chgo., Dec. 22, 1944; m. Catherine Yore; children: Loren Jr., Adam (dec.). BA in Polit. Sci., Northwestern U., 1966, JD, 1969; LLD (hon.), John Marshall Law Sch., 1995, Capital U. Law Sch., 1996, Campbell U., 1997. Bar: Ill. 1970, U.S. Ct. Mil. Appeals 1973, U.S. Ct. Appeals (D.C. cir.) 1974, U.S. Supreme Ct. 1974, U.S. Ct. Claims, 1985, U.S. Ct. Appeals (fed. cir.) 1986, U.S. Ct. Fed. Claims. Host nightly radio talk show What's Best for America?, 1972; cons. Sidney & Austin, Chgo., 1972-73; gen. atty. FCC, 1973; asst. to spl. counsel to the pres. White House, Washington, 1973-74; spl. asst. U.S. Atty., D.C., 1974-75; chief counsel Reagan for Pres. campaigns, 1976, 80; prof. Del. Law Sch., 1976-84; dep. dir. Office Exec. Br. Mgmt. Presdl. Transition, 1980-81; chmn. Adminstrv. Conf. U.S., 1981-85; appointed judge U.S. Ct. Fed. Claims, Washington, 1985, designated chief judge, 1986-2000; sr. judge, 2000—. Prof. law Del. Law Sch., 1976-84; adj. prof. Internat. Law Sch., 1973-74, Georgetown U. Law Ctr., 1992—, Washing Coll. Law, Am. U., 1996, Columbus Sch. Law, Cath. U. Am., 1996—, George Mason U. Sch. Law, 1998—; past mem. Pres.'s Cabinet Coun. on Legal Policy, Pres.' Cabinet Coun. on Mgmt. and Adminstrn.; chmn. Coun. Ind. Regulatory Agys.; served as disting. jurist in residence U. Denver; Allen chair U. Richmond Sch. Law, 1995. Co-author: Black America and Organized Labor: A Fair Deal?, 1979; contbr. articles to profl. jours. Adv. bd. mem. WETA Pub. Radio Cmty. Adv. Bd. Recipient Presdl. medal Cath. U. Am. Law Sch., 1993, Romanian medal of justice Romanian Min. of Justice, 1995, Ronald Reagan Pub. Svc. award Nat. Property Rights Conf., 1997. Mem. Bar Assn. D.C. (hon. mem., judicial honoree award 1997), Univ. Club (Washington, named club mem. of the yr. 1991, chmn. entertainment com., centennial com.). Republican. Jewish. Office: US Ct of Fed Claims 717 Madison Pl NW Suite 328 Washington DC 20005

SMITH, LORETTA MAE, civilian military officer; b. Washington Twp., Pa., May 25, 1939; d. Irvin Calvin and Viola Mary (Deibler) Shambaugh; 1 child, Miriam Estella Smith. B in Humanities, Pa. State U., 1984. Bookkeeper Harrisburg (Pa.) Nat. Bank, 1957-62; contract specialist USN, Mechanicsburg, Pa., 1987—. Founder Telecare, Harrisburg, Pa., 1972-82. Active ARC, instr. CPR, 1982—; active Girl Scouts U.S., trainer, 1972—. Recipient Hemlock award Hemlock coun. Girl Scouts U.S., Harrisburg, 1981; Merit scholar Hall Found., 1982. Mem. Nat. Contract Mgmt. Assn., Mensa. Avocations: walking in woods, birding, swimming, making music.

SMITH, LOUIS, sports association administrator; m. Sharon Smith; 4 children. BSEE, U. Mo., Rolla; MBA, Rockhurst Coll.; postgrad., U. Kans. Assoc. engr. to asst. gen. mgr. AlliedSignal Inc., Kansas City, Mo., 1966-86, v.p. prodn. ops. Bendix Aerospace Sector Arlington, Va., 1986-88; v.p. mfg. AlliedSignal Aerospace Co., Torrance, Calif., 1988-89; asst. gen. mgr., adminstrn. AlliedSignal Inc., Kansas City, 1989-90, pres., 1990-95; pres., COO, bd. dirs. Ewing Marion Kauffman Found., 1995—. Bd. dirs. Western Resources, Commerce Bank Kansas City. Bd. dirs. Kansas City Royals, Greater Kansas City C. of C., Midwest Rsch. Inst., Civic Coun. Greater Kansas City, The Learning Exch.; mem. exec. com. Kansas City Area Devel. Coun., Rockhurst Coll. Bd. Trustees; mem. numerous coms. U. Mo.-Rolla, U. Kans.; ;past chmn. corp. devel. coun., mem. Acad. Elec. Engring. U. Mo.-Rolla; adv. bd. U. Kans. Sch. Engring. On Board of Directors of KC Royals since 1992. Office: Kansas City Royals Kauffman Stadium PO Box 419969 Kansas City MO 64141-6969

SMITH, LOWELL SCOTT, physicist; b. Akron, Ohio, July 20, 1950; s. Wilson Newton and Anne Lu Smith. BS, U. Rochester, N.Y., 1972; PhD, U. Pa., Phila., 1976. Physicist R&D GE, Schenectady, 1976—. Named Inventor of Yr., Ea. N.Y. Patent Law Assn., Albany, 1986, Disting. Alumni Cuyahoga Falls (Ohio) Schs. Found., 1989. Mem. IEEE (sr.; mem. tech. program com. ultrasonics symposium 1999—, vice-chair, 2002), Am. Phys. Soc., Phi Beta Kappa. Office: GE Global Rsch KWC 1309 PO Box 8 Schenectady NY 12301-0008 E-mail: smithls@crd.ge.com.

SMITH, LYNDA I. social worker; b. Raton, N.Mex., Feb. 5, 1953; d. Hignio and Manuela (Pacheco) Touar; children: Kathy Moore, Ronald Smith. BA in Sociology, N.Mex. Highlands U., 1985, MA in Sociology, 1987. Counselor Rio Grande Longterm Treatment, Mora, N.Mex., 1987-88, Sangre de Cristo, Raton, 1988-89; social worker III N.Mex. Human Svcs. Dept., Santa Fe, 1989—. Home: 701 Kay Lynn Dr Las Vegas NM 87701-5117 Office: New Mexico Human Svcs Dept 604 W San Mateo Rd Santa Fe NM 87505-4143

SMITH, MAGGIE CARROLL See SMITH, MARGARET A.

SMITH, M(AHLON) BREWSTER, psychologist, educator; b. Syracuse, N.Y., June 26, 1919; s. Mahlon Ellwood and Blanche Alice (Hinman) S.; m. Jean Dresden Schwartz, June 1942 (div. 1945); m. Deborah Anderson, June, 1947; children: Joshua H., T. Daniel, Rebecca M., J. Torquil. Student, Reed Coll., Portland, Oreg., 1935- 38; AB, Stanford U., 1939, AM, 1940; PhD, Harvard U., 1947. Rantoul scholar Harvard U., 1940-41; jr. analyst Office Coordinator of Information, U.S. Govt., 1941; Social Sci. Research Council fellow Harvard U., 1946-47; asst. prof. social psychology Harvard U. (Dept. Social Relations), 1947-49; prof. psychology, chmn. dept. Vassar Coll., 1949-52; staff Social Sci. Research Council, 1952-56; prof. psychology NYU, 1956-59, U. Calif. at Berkeley, 1959-68, dir. Inst. Human Devel., 1965-68; prof., chmn. dept. psychology U. Chgo., 1968-70; prof. psychology U. Calif. at Santa Cruz, 1970-88, prof. emeritus, 1988—, vice chancellor social scis., 1970-75. Fellow Center Advanced Studies Behavioral Scis., 1964-65; Vice pres. Joint Commn. Mental Illness and Health, 1955-61 Author: Social Psychology and Human Values, 1969, Humanizing Social Psychology, 1974, Values, Self and Society, 1991; co-author: The American Soldier, 1949, Opinions and Personality, 1956; editor: Jour. Social Issues, 1951-55, Jour. Abnormal Soc. Psychology, 1956-61; contbr. articles to profl. jours. Served from pvt. to maj. Adj. Gen. Div. AUS, 1942-46; research officer Information and Edn. div. War Dept., 1943-46; research asso. spl. com. on soldier attitudes Social Sci. Research Council 1946. Decorated Bronze Star medal.; NIMH fellow, 1964-65, NEH fellow, 1975-76; Belding scholar Found. for Child Devel., 1982-83; Gold medal award lifetime contbn. to psychology in pub. interest Am. Psychol. Found., 1992. Fellow AAAS, APA (pres. 1978, Disting. Contbn. to Pub. Interest award 1988, Henry A. Murray award in personality psychology 1993); mem. Soc. Psychol. Study Social Issues (pres. 1959, Kurt Lewin Meml. award 1986), Western Psychol. Assn. (pres. 1986, Lifetime Contbn. award 1996), Psychologists for Social Responsibility (pres. 1987-90), Internat. Soc. Polit. Psychology (Harold Lasswell award 1993), Internat. Assn. Applied Psychology (pres. divsn. polit. psychology 1994-98), Cosmos Club (Washington), Soc. for Study of Peace, Conflict and Violence (Lifetime Contbn. to Peace Psychology award 1999), Phi Beta Kappa, Sigma Xi. Democrat. Home: 316 Escalona Dr Santa Cruz CA 95060-2607 E-mail: brsmith@cats.ucsc.edu.

SMITH, MALCOLM BARRY ESTES, philosophy educator, lawyer; b. Houston, Oct. 24, 1939; s. Fairleigh Estes and Norna Barry (McNab) S.; m. Patricia Sweetser; children: Malcolm, Eric. BA, Va. Mil. Inst., 1961; PhD, Cornell U., 1969; JD, U. Calif., Berkeley, 1984. BarL Mass. 1985, U.S. Supreme Ct. 1992. Instr. philosophy Smith Coll., Northampton, Mass., 1967-69, asst. prof. philosophy, 1969-74, assoc. prof., 1974-79, prof., 1979—. Served to capt. USAR, 1964-66. Mem. Mass. Bar Assn., Am. Philos. Assn. Home: 9 Park St Northampton MA 01062-1236 Office: Smith Coll Dept Philosophy PO Box 839 Northampton MA 01061-0839

SMITH, MALCOLM BERNARD, investment company executive; b. Lynn, Mass., May 27, 1923; s. Philip and Ida (Zenis) S.; m. Betty Booth, June 20, 1948; children: Eric, Daniel. BA summa cum laude, Dartmouth Coll., 1944; MA in Econs., Harvard U., 1948; hon. degree, New Sch. for Social Rsch., 1995. Sec. Gen. Am. Investors Co., N.Y.C., 1956-57, treas., 1957-59, v.p., 1958-61, pres., 1961-89, vice chmn., 1989-97; sr. cons., 1997—. Chmn. fin. com. N.Y. Found. , 1973—82, treas., 1979—82, trustee, 1973—89, N.Y. Found. , 1991—99, chmn., 1982—85; chmn. New Sch. for Social Rsch., N.Y.C., 1985—95, trustee, 1982—, treas., 1982—84, chmn. ednl. policy com., 1984—85, chmn. exec. com., 1985—95; mem. investment com. Phi Beta Kappa Found., 1987—96; bd. dirs. Learning Smith, Inc., 1992—93, Cybersmith, Inc., 1994—97; mem. investment com. Fedn. Jewish Philantrophies, NY, 1975—96; trustee John Simon Guggenheim Meml. Found., 1982—95, chmn. fin. com., 1985—95, Human Rights Watch, 1993—2001, dir. emeritus, 2001—; mng. trustee Permanent Fund of MLA, 1987—. With U.S. Army, 1943—46. Mem. AAAS (chmn. investment and fin. com. 1975—), Investment Co. Inst. (bd. govs. 1987-95), Assn. Publicly Traded Investment Funds (bd. dirs. 1970-87, chmn. 1971-79, Coun. on Fgn. Rels., N.Y. Soc. Security Analysts, Harvard Club (bd. mgrs. 1984-86), Century Assn. N.Y.c. (treas., bd. mgrs. 1999—), Phi Beta Kappa Assocs. (adv. com. 1984-93, bd. dirs. 1993—), Phi Beta Kappa. Home: PO Box 358 Pound Ridge NY 10576-0358 Office: 1150 Park Ave New York NY 10128-1244

SMITH, MALCOLM SOMMERVILLE, bass; b. Rockville Centre, N.Y., June 22, 1933; s. Carlton Newell and Margaret (Sommerville) S.; m. Margaret Yauger, Oct. 4, 1975. B.Music Edn., Oberlin Coll., 1957, B.Mus., 1960; MA in Ednl. Adminstrn, Columbia Tchrs. Coll., 1958; student, Ind. U. Sch. Music, 1960-62. Dir. choral music Ramapo Regional H.S., Wyckoff, NJ, 1958—60. Bass: Lyric Opera, bass soloist: Russian tour, Robert Shaw Choral, 1962; leading bass N.Y.C. Opera, 1965—70, Deutsche Oper Am Rhein, Dusseldorf, Germany, 1971—, Vienna State Opea, 1973—74, 86 Met. Opera, Japan tour, 1975, Met. Opera, N.Y.C., 1975—77, Paris Opera, 1978, Barcelona Opera, 1978, Sao Paulo, Brazil, 1978, Mexico City, 1979, 80, Berlin Opera, 1979, 80, Montreal Symphony, 1979, 80, 81, 82, Hamburg Opera, 1981, Koln Opera, 1980, Stuttgart Opera, 1980, Frankfurt Opera, 1980, Rome Opera, 1980, Trieste (Italy) Opera, 1981, Berlin Staatsoper, 1982, 85, Lyric Opera Phila., 1982, L.A. Philharm. at Hollywood Bowl, 1984, Mannheim Opera, Germany, 1986, Turin Opera, Italy, 1986, 88, Bordeaux, France, 1987, Dresden Opera, Germany, 1987, Staats Opera Berlin Japan tour, 1987, Polish TV, 1989, Oslo Opera, 1987, Paris Radio, 1988-89, Orange Festival, France, 1988, Penderecki Festival, Krakow, Poland, 1988, maj. soloist Schleswig Holstein Festival, Germany, 1989, Krakow Philharmonic, Poland, 1988, Maggio Musicale, Florence, Italy, 1988, Boston Symphony, Minn., Cin., Houston, Utah, Seattle, Chgo., Phila., Balt. Symphony, 1993, Mex. Nat. Symphony, 1993, nat. symphonies, also Cin. Summer Opera, Central City (Colo.), Summer Opera, Festival of Two Worlds, Spoleto, Italy, Saratoga Festival, 1985, debut La Scala, Milan, Italy, 1982, Salzburg Festival, 1986, Athens Festival, 1987, Bordeaux (France) Opera, 1987, Ft. Worth Opera, 1988, Orange Festival, France, 1988, Staatsoper Munich, 1990, Bastille Opera, Paris, 1991, Heidelberg Summer Festival, 1991, 92, Brussels Opera, 1992, 93, 94, 97, Opera Nice, France, 1992, Opera Montpelier, France, 1992, Cin. Opera, 1994, Dusseldorf Opera, 1994, Japan tour, 1994, Bregenz (Austria) Festival, 1996, Honolulu Opera, 1996, 98, Balt. Opera, 1996, Prague Autumn Festival, 1997, Cin. Opera, 1998, 2000, Grand Rapids Opera, 2000, Dusseldorf Opera, 2001, 2002, Portland Opera, 2001, Portland Symphony, 2002, recorded War and Peace, 1986, Penderecki Requiem, 1990, Aspen Music Festival, 1997. Served with AUS, 1954-56. Recipient Kämmersanger title Dusseldorf (Germany) Opera, 1996. Congregationalist. Office: care Thea Dispeker Artists Rep 59 E 54th St New York NY 10022-4211 *Hard work and a sense of humor.*

SMITH, MARA A. small business owner, artist; b. Houston, July 31, 1945; d. Charles Parker and Mary Lee (Langford) S. BS, Tex. Woman's U., 1969, MFA, 1980. Owner, pres. Archtl. Murals in Brick, Seattle, 1977—. Lectr. in field. Executed murals in brick Loew's Anatole Hotel, Dallas, 1978, 83, Am. Bank and Trust Co. Bldg., Reading, Pa., 1983, Pacific N.W. Bell Ctr., Seattle, 1985, One Bethesda Ctr., Bethesda, Md., 1986, Dragon Hill Hotel, U.S. Army, Seoul, Republic of Korea, 1989, Tarleton State U. (Tex. A&M U.), Stephenville, Tex., 1994, Small Mammal Reptile Pavilion Lincoln Park Zoo, Chgo., 1996, Milken Cmty. H.S. Stephen S. Wise Temple, Los Angeles, 1998, others; contbr. articles to profl. jours. Mem. NOW (co-director). Named one of Outstanding Young Women of Am., 1978, Disting. Alumna, Tex. Woman's U. Avocations: vedic astrology. Office: 339 NW 82nd St Seattle WA 98117-4033

SMITH, MARCIA JEAN, accountant, tax specialist, financial consultant; b. Kansas City, Mo., Oct. 19, 1947; d. Eugene Hubert and Marcella Juanita (Greene) S. Student, U. Nebr., 1965-67; BA, Jersey City State Coll., 1971; MBA in Taxation, Golden Gate U., 1976, postgrad., 1976-77; MS in Acctg., Pace U., 1982; cert. of completion, Cours Commerciaux de Geneve, 1985-86. Cert. practitioner in taxation; cert. govt. fin. mgr.; accredited tax advisor. Legal intern Port Authority, N.Y., N.J., N.Y.C., 1972; legis. aide to Senator Harrison A. Williams Washington, 1973; tax accountant Bechtel Corp., San Francisco, 1974-77; sr. tax accountant Equitable Life Assurance Soc. U.S., N.Y.C., 1977, sec., 1977-79; tax sr. Arthur Andersen & Co., 1979-82; pres. M.J. Smith Co., 1983-85; prin. owner MJS Cons. Svcs. Internat. Tax Cons., Boston, 1988-93; gen. auditor dept. fin. Fulton County Govt., Atlanta, 1993-95; auditor State of Georgia, Dept. Med. Assistance, 1995-97; pres. ExecuTax, Inc., Chgo., 1997—. Cons. U.N., specialized agys., Geneva, 1985-87, CNA Fin. Corp., Chgo., 1998-99, CNA Ins. (Corp. Tax), 2000—; asst. sec. Equico Lessors, Inc., Mpls., 1977-78, Equitable Gen. Ins. Group, Ft. Worth, 1977-79, Heritage Life Infield Assurance Co., Toronto, Ont., Can., 1978-79, Informatics, Inc., L.A., 1978-79; sec. Equico Capital Corp., N.Y.C. 1977-79, Equico Personal Credit, Inc., Colorado Springs, Colo., 1978-79, Equico Securites, Inc., N.Y.C., 1977-79, Equitable Environ. Health, Inc., Woodbury, N.Y., 1977-79; tax cons., real estate salesperson. Spl. advisor U.S. Congl. Adv. Bd.; human rights chmn. YWCA, Lincoln, Nebr., 1966-67; mem. Atlanta Women's Network. Spl. advisor U.S. Congl. Adv. Bd.; human rights chmn. YWCA, Lincoln, Nebr., 1966-67; mem. Atlanta Women's Network. Mem. AAAS, AAUW, NAA (Swiss Romande chpt.), ACLU, Am. Mgmt. Assn., Nat. Soc. Pub. Accts., Am. Econs. Assn., Inst. Mgmt. Accts., Am. Acctg. Assn., Internat. Assn. Fin. Planners, Internat. Fin. Mgmt. Assn., Am. Women's Club of Geneva, Nat. Assn. Women Bus. Owners, Am. Assn. Individual Investors, Inst. Internal Auditors, N.Y. Acad. Scis., Nat. Hist. Soc., Nat. Assn. Tax Practitioners, Assn. Managerial Economists, Postal Commemorative Soc., Am. Mus. Natural History, Nat. Trust Historic Preservation, Ga. Govt. Fin. Officers Assn., Internat. Tax Inst., Calif. Soc. CPAs, Fla. Inst. CPAs, N.Y. State Soc. CPAs, Ga. Soc. CPAs, Ill. CPA Soc., Assn. Cert. Fraud Examiners, Assn. Govt. Accts., UN Assn. USA, Chgo. Coun. Fgn. Rels., EDP Auditors Assn., Mass. Soc. Ind. Accts., Acad. Legal Studies in Bus., Internat. Platform Assn., Nat. Assn. Cert. Valuation Analysts, U.S. Senatorial Club. Office: 151 N Michigan Ave Ste 1908 Chicago IL 60601-7566 Address: EXECU-Tax Incorporated Amoco Finance Facility PO Box 81049 Chicago IL 60681-0049 E-mail: executax@juno.com.

SMITH, MARCIA JEANNE, secondary school educator; b. Carthage, N.Y., Apr. 27, 1935; d. Herman Leon and Vera Magdelena (Weir) Zahn; div.; 1 child, Patrick Brian. BA, Syracuse U., 1958; MA, Middlebury Coll., 1962. Cert. in secondary edn./English. Tchr. English, South Jefferson Ctrl. H.S., Adams, N.Y., 1958-98; asst. prof. extension and evening div. Jefferson C.C., Watertown, 1967-69; ret., 1998. Adj. instr. project advance Syracuse U., 1984-91, mem. cabinet, 1989-91. Vol. Samaritan Med. Ctr., Watertown, NY. Mem. N.Y. State English Council (named High Sch. Tchr. of Excellence 1989), Nat. Council Tchrs. English, AAUW, Coll. Women's Club of Jefferson County (corr. sec. 1989-90), Jefferson County Hist. Soc., Pi Lambda Theta, Alpha Delta Kappa. Avocations: gardening (flowers), ceramics, travel, reading. Home: 26836 Ridge Rd Watertown NY 13601-5401

SMITH, MARGARET A. (MAGGIE CARROLL SMITH), community volunteer; b. Akron, Ohio, Nov. 2, 1928; d. John Raymond Seiler and Helen Joseph Roach; m. Richard C. Carroll, Feb. 1, 1958 (div.); children: Stephan, Christopher, Daniel, John, Michael; m. Wiley Smith, Jr., May 3, 1985. Grad., St. Vincent H.S., Akron, Ohio, 1947. Interviewer Ohio Bur. of Employees Svcs., Akron, 1949-53; sales agt. Boebinger Realtors, 1979-86; lectr. on mental health, Akron U., Kent State U., Summit County Paramedics, Akron Police Dept., others; developer spl. mental health crisis intervention tng. program for Akron Police and Fire Dept., Ohio, 2000. Editor: (newsletter) National Alliance for the Mentally Ill of Summit County, 1987-99. Founding pres. Nat. Alliance/Mentally Ill of Summit County, Akron, 1986; pres. Nat. Alliance/Mentally Ill of Ohio, Columbus, 1988; steering com. for redesigning cmty. mental health system, 1986. Recipient Heart of Gold award Mental Health Assn. of Summit County, 1989, Recognition for Advocacy, Alcohol, Drug, and Mental Health, Summit County, 1996, Vol. of Yr. award We. Res. Psychiat. Hosp., Summit County, 1988, Solid Gold Mem. award Alliance for the Monthly Ill of Ohio, Columbus, 1991; Maggie C Smith House Residential Facility named in her honor, Ohio, 2000. Avocation: gardening. Office: Nat Alliance/Mentally Ill PO Box 462 Cuyahoga Falls OH 44222-0462

SMITH, MARGARET TAYLOR, volunteer; b. Roanoke Rapids, N.C., May 31, 1925; d. George Napoleon and Sarah Luella (Waller) T.; m. Sidney William Smith Jr., Aug. 15, 1947; children: Sarah Smith, Sidney William Smith III, Susan Smith, Amy Smith. BA in Sociology, Duke U., 1947. Chair emeritus bd. trustees Kresge Found., Troy, Mich., 1985—; chmn. Nat. Coun. for Women's Studies Duke U., N.C., 1986—, chmn. Trinity Bd. Visitors, 1988-98; chair emeritus. Chmn. bd. visitors Wayne State U. Med. Sch., 1993; bd. dirs., mem. exec. com. Detroit Med. Ctr.; mem. bd. govs. Detroit Med. Ctr. Recipient the Merrill-Palmer award Wayne State U., Detroit, 1987, Zimmerman award Gtr. Detroit Health Coun., Athena award C. of C., 1998, Women of Achievement award Mich. Women's Fedn., 1999, disting. svc. award Wayne State U., 1999; named disting. alumna award Duke U. Mem. The Village Club, Internat. Women's Forum, Pi Beta Phi, Phi Beta Kappa. Methodist. E-mail: sidmyth@aol.com.

SMITH, MARGERY W. family practice physician; b. Port Washington, N.Y., Jan. 23, 1926; d. Frank and Margery (Weyrauch) S.; m. Harry Garry, Nov. 28, 1953; children: Charles J. Garry, Frank B. Garry, Johanna M. Halsey, Elizabeth A. Garry. AB, Syracuse U., 1946, MD, 1950. Diplomate Am. Bd. Family Practice. Resident Albany (N.Y.) Med. Ctr., 1950-53, St. Peter's Hosp., Albany, 1953-54; from preceptor to clin. assoc. prof. family practice Albany Med. Coll., 1973—. Preceptor residency program St. Clare's Hosp., Schenectady, NY, 1979—; clin. asst. prof. SUNY, Syracuse, 1989—99, clin. assoc. faculty grad. program nursing Sage Grad. Sch., 1995—99. Mem. coun. St. Bernadette's Ch., Berne, N.Y., 1978-79, chair com. Christian svc., 1978-79, music coord. liturgy com., 1980-81, organist, 1975-86. Fellow Am. Acad. Family Physicians; mem. AMA, Med. Soc. State N.Y., Med. Soc. County Albany, N.Y. State Acad. Family Practice. Home: 339 Helderberg Trl East Berne NY 12059-2805 E-mail: msmithmd@worldnet.att.net.

SMITH, MARGHERITA, writer, editor; b. Chgo., May 24, 1922; d. Henry Christian and Alicia (Koke) Steinhoff; m. Rufus Zartman Smith, June 26, 1943; children: Matthew Benjamin, Timothy Rufus. AB, Ill. Coll., 1943. Proofreader Editorial Experts, Inc., Alexandria, Va., 1974, mgr. proofreading div., 1978-79, mgr. publs. div., 1979-81, asst. to pres., 1980-81; freelance editor, cons. Annandale, Va., 1981-97. Instr. proofreading and copy editing, George Washington U., Washington, 1978-82; presenter workshops on proofreading for various prof. orgns., 1981-95. Author: (as Peggy Smith) Simplified Proofreading, 1980, Proofreading Manual and Reference Guide, 1981, Proofreading Workbook, 1981, The Proof Is In the Reading: A Comprehensive Guide to Staffing and Management of Typographic Proofreading, 1986, Mark My Words: Instructions and Practice in Proofreading, 1987, rev. edit., 1993, 98, Letter Perfect: A Guide to Practical Proofreading, 1995; contbr. articles to revs. to various publs. Recipient Best Instrnl. Reporting award Newsletter Assn. Am., 1980, Disting. Achievement award for excellence in ednl. journalism Ednl. Press Assn. Am., 1981, Disting. Citizen award Ill. Coll., 1992. Avocation: writing verse. Home and Office: 9120 Belvoir Woods Pkwy Apt 110 Fort Belvoir VA 22060-2722 E-mail: mssmss@pobox.com.

SMITH, MARIE EDMONDS, real estate agent, property manager; b. Quapaw, Okla., Oct. 5, 1927; d. Thomas Joseph and Maud Ethel Edmonds; m. Robert Lee Smith, Aug. 14, 1966 (dec. 1983). Grad. vocat. nurse, Hoag Hosp., Costa Mesa, Calif., 1953; BA, Vanguard U., 1955; MS, U. Alaska, 1963. Lic. vocat. nurse, Calif.; cert. sci. tchr., Alaska. Nurse Calif. Dept. Nurses, Costa Mesa, 1952-60; tchr. Alaska Dept. Edn., Aniak and Anchorage, 1955-60; tchr. sci. Garden Grove (Calif.) Sch. Dist., 1960-87; property mgr. Huntington Beach, Calif., 1970—; agent Sterling Realtors, 1988—. Author: Ocean Biology, 1969. Bd. dirs., tchr. Newport Mesa Christian Ctr., Costa Mesa, 1983-2001; com. chmn. Garden Grove Unified Sch. Dist. PTA, 1977. NSF grantee, 1960-62. Mem. AAUW, Vanguard U. Alumnae Assn. Republican. Avocations: skin diving, travel. Home: 83ll Reilly Dr Huntington Beach CA 92646 Office: L8153 Brookhurst St Fountain Valley CA 92708

SMITH, MARILYN NOELTNER, science educator, consultant; b. Los Angeles, Feb. 14, 1933; d. Clarence Frederick and Gertrude Bertha (Smith) Noeltner; m. Edward Christopher Smith, Sept. 11, 1971 (dec. Oct. 1999). BA, Marymount Coll., 1957; MA, U. Notre Dame, 1966; MS, Boston Coll., 1969. Cert. tchr.; cert. community coll. tchr., Calif.; cert. adminstr., Calif. Tchr., chmn. sci. dept. Marymount High Sch., Santa Barbara, Calif., 1954-57, Los Angeles, 1957-58, 69-79, tchr., chmn. sci. and math. depts. Palos Verdes, Calif., 1959-69; tchr., chmn. math. dept. Corvallis High Sch., Studio City, 1958-59; instr. tchr. tng. Marymount-Loyola U., Los Angeles, 1965-71, instr. freshman interdisciplinary program, 1970-71; tchr. math. Santa Monica (Calif.) High Sch., 1971-72; instr. math., chemistry, physics Santa Monica Coll., 1971—; tchr. sci. Beverly Vista Sch., Beverly Hills, Calif., 1972—. Cons. Calif. State Sci. Framework Revision Com., Los Angeles, 1975; chmn. NASA Youth Sci. Congress, Pasadena, Calif., 1968-69, Hawaii, 1969-70; participant NASA Educators Conf. Jupiter Mission, Ames Research, San Francisco, 1973, NASA Educators Conf. Viking-Mars Ames Project, San Francisco, 1976-77, NASA Landsat Conf., Edward's AFB, Calif., 1978, NASA Uranus Mission, Pasadena, Calif., 1986, NASA Uranus-Voyager Mission, Pasadena, 1989, NASA Neptune-Voyager Mission, Pasadena, 1989; mem. test scoring com. Calif. Learning Assessment System, U. Santa Barbara, 1993, writing com. Trainers Manual, 1993. Author articles, books and computer progs. on space and physics including NASA Voyager-Uranus Sci. Symposium for Educators, 1989, NASA Voyager 2 Neptune Encounter Conf., 1989, others. Sponsor Social Svc. Club, Palos Verdes, 1959-69, moderator, sponsor ARC Youth Svc. Chmn., Beverly Hills, 1974-77, judge L.A. County Sci. Fair, 1969—, mem. blue ribbon com. NATAS, 1971—; bd. dirs. Children First, Beverly Hills, 1990-91; vol. sch. initiative, Beverly Hills, 1989-90; mem. steering com. on tech. Beverly Vista Sch., 1994-95; del. Congress of Am. Women Scientists to Cuba, People to People Amb. Program, 2001; mem. U. Notre Dame Badin Guild, 1989—. Recipient Commendation in Teaching cert. Am. Soc. Microbiology, 1962, Salute to Edn. award So. Calif. Industry Edn. Council, 1962, Outstanding Teaching citation Cons. Engrs. Assn. Calif., 1967, Cert. Honor, Silver Plaque Westinghouse Sci. Talent Search, 1963-68, Tchr. award Ford-Future Scientists of Am., 1968, Biomed. award Com. Advance Sci. Tng., 1971, Outstanding Tchr. award Los Angeles County Sci. Fair Com., 1975-76, Contbns. to Youth Service citation ARC, 1976-77, Outstanding Tchr. award Kiwanis Club Beverly Hills, 1987, NAST Pres'. award, 1990, Woman of Yr. award, 1990, cert. appreciation Profl. Leadership and Support for Advancing Sci. Edn. Calif. Dept. Edn., 1992, 93, Outstanding Tchr. Gifted Students award Johns Hopkins U., 1999-2000. Mem. We. Assn. Schs. and Colls. (vis. com. 1968, writing com. 1969—), Assn. Advancement Biomed. Edn. (pres. 1970-71), 1st Internat. Sci. Tchrs. Conf. (presider, evaluator 1977), Nat. Sci. Tchrs. Assn. (presider, evaluator 1976, chmn. contributed papers com. 1977-78, presenter 1990), Beverly Hills Edn. Assn. (pres. faculty coun. 1980-81, 85-86, sch. rep. 1990—, Ann. WHO award 1995, 96), Chemist's Club, Calif. Statewide Math. Adv. Com., So. Calif. Industry Edn. Council, Calif. Assn. Chemistry Tchrs. (program chmn. 1960), Calif. Sci. Tchrs. Assn., Am. Chem. Soc., AAAS, South Bay Math. League (sec. 1967-68, pres. 1968-69, 72, 1969-70), Calif. Math. Council, Nat. Assn. Biology Tchrs., U. Notre Dame Sorin Soc. Republican. Roman Catholic. Avocations: stone age architecture, Gaelic, Irish fisheries population samplings and contributions to data bank. Home: 3934 Sapphire Dr Encino CA 91436-3635 Office: Beverly Vista Sch 200 S Elm Dr Beverly Hills CA 90212-4011

SMITH, MARILYN PATRICIA, city government official, management consultant and facilitator; b. Jamaica, N.Y., July 5, 1942; d. Raymond Lionel and Katherine Marie (Doepp) Cowan; m. Adrian Roy Smith, Dec. 7, 1991 (dec. July 2001); 1 child, Paul William Hibner. Student various aviation schs., St. Joseph's Coll., N.Y. cert. in Leadership and Human Resources Devel., Goldratt Inst., Conn., JONAH cert. Inst. Elected Ofcls., Advanced Inst. for Elected Ofcls., Leadership Charlotte Class of 97-98, Local Govt. Leadership Fla., Class IV-99. Exec. sec. to chief design Wiedersum Assocs., Archs. and Engrs., Valley Stream, N.Y., 1960-61; office mgr., arch. apprentice, interior designer Keith I. Hibner, Archs., Hicksville, Garden City, 1961-73; owner, pres. Hibner Atelier, Ltd., Garden City, 1968-75; interior design and gen. constrn., 1968-76; office mgr., tech. planning, manual writer Ward Assocs./Planning Assocs., Archs. and Engrs., Bohemia, N.Y., 1975-76; chief pilot, flight/ground aviation instr. Islip (N.Y.) Aviation Ltd., 1974-77; exec. asst. to pres. Arkay Packaging Corp., Hauppauge, N.Y., 1977-86; in-house constrn. mgr., 1980-82; adminstrn. and human resources mgr. Arkay Packaging Corp., Hauppauge, 1986-89, dir. corp. devel., 1989, dir. materials mgmt., 1989-90. Cert. assoc. Goldratt Inst. for L.I./Metro N.Y. area, 1990-92; owner Concepts for Constructive Change, Educators and Facilitators for Continuous Improvement, Lake Grove, N.Y., 1990-92; ind. aviation flight/ground instr. airplane and instrument, 1977—; safety counselor FAA, 1974-92, Ea. region counselor coord., 1985-86; mem. city charter rev. com. City Punta Gorda, Fla., 1996; mem. city coun. City of Punta Gorda, Fla., 1996—, vice mayor, 1998-99, 2000-2001, first woman mayor, 2001—; past bd. dirs., officer Aviation Coun. L.I.; founder Seminar on Air Travel for Everyone (S.A.F.E.), 1975, Fly-C-Cure/We Air Condition People, 1979; city coun. appointee to S.W. Fla. Regional Planning Coun., 1999—, Charlotte County tourist devel. coun., 1998—, Charlotte County Assembly, 1998, 2001, Punta Gorda Historic Mural Soc., past mem. bd. dirs.; county appointee Enterprise Charlotte Econ. Devel. team. Author articles, seminar syllabus. Past mem. nat. panel Consumer Arbitrators, Nat. Consumer Arbitration Program, Better Bus. Bur.; lic. comml. pilot, flight and ground instr.; Charlotte Symphony League; chmn. bd. Charlotte Skatepark, Inc.; Bd. mem., past officer Punta Gorda Elko Lodge 2606. Mem. NAFE, Ninety-Nines (past chmn. L.I. chpt., founding internat. chmn. safety edn., Amelia Earhart Bronze medal 1975), Aircraft Owners and Pilots Assn., NAt. Assn. Flight Instrs., Silver Wings, Exptl. Aircraft Assn., Old Punta Gorda, Inc. (past mem. bd. dirs.), Punta Gorda Bus. Alliance, Kiwanis. Home: 654 Andros Ct Punta Gorda FL 33950-5809

SMITH, MARION PAFFORD, avionics company executive, retired; b. Waycross, Ga., Dec. 12, 1925; s. Rossa Elbert and Lillian Solee (Pafford) S.; m. Esther Pat Davis, Nov. 23, 1952; children: Bryan P., Danton D., Patricia Anne. Student, Okla. State U., 1944, Yale U., 1945; BS in EE, La. State U., 1949; postgrad., U. So. Fla., 1966-70. Engr. Bell Telephone Co., Baton Rouge, 1949-51; mgr. engring. Vitro Labs., Silver Spring, Md., 1952-57; design engring. mgr. dept. design and constrn. flight hand contrs. Space Shuttle and Space Sta. Honeywell Avionics Div., Clearwater, Fla., 1957-98. Vice chmn., bd. dirs. First Union, Largo, Fla., 1985-93; cons. U.S. Army Mgmt. Engring. Tng. Agy., 1975-79; U.S. Del. Internat. Elec. Tech. Commn., 1965-85, chmn. chief U.S. tech. adviser com. on reliability and maintainability, 1975-85, v.p., exec. com. U.S. nat. com., 1975-84; U.S. del. NATO Quality Conf., 1973; mem. White House Summit Conf. on Inflation, 1975; del. White House Conf. on Handicapped, 1977; mem. nat. adv. coun. on devel. disabilities HEW, 1974-78, Fla. Devel. Disabilities Coun., 1974-78; pres. Fla. Advocacy Ctr. for Persons with Disabilities, Inc., 1997-2000; commr. State of Fla. Occupl. Access Commn., 2000-2002; mem. devel. coun. Morton Plant Hosp., Clearwater, 1971-74. 1st lt. Signal Corps, AUS, 1944-45, 51-52. Served to 1st lt. Signal Corps AUS, 1944-45, 51-52. Recipient McDonald award Fla. Rehab. Assn., 1968; Bilgore award Citizen of Year Clearwater, Fla., 1969; Outstanding Service award Am. Soc. Quality Control, 1968-69; United Comml. Travelers award Most Outstanding Service Retarded Fla., 1970; named Engr. of Year Fla. W. Coast, 1970; Service to Mankind award Sertoma Clubs, 1977 Fellow IEEE (dir., Nat. Reliability award 1979); mem. Assn. Retarded Citizens USA (pres. 1973-75, nat. govt. affairs chmn. 1975-83), Am. Assn. Mental Deficiency, Nat. Symposium Reliability Quality Control (gen. chmn.), Sigma Chi. Presbyterian elder. Club: Kiwanis (Marion P. Smith award established in his honor). Home: 1884 Oakdale Ln N Clearwater FL 33764-6441 E-mail: mpaff@gte.net. *True turning points in life are sometimes difficult to recognize, but for those who have become parents of a handicapped child, particularly a mentally retarded child, then that turning point is easy to recognize. After the difficult period of adjustment, one becomes aware of a realization that all persons have human dignity and worth and can make a contribution to humanity and to society.*

SMITH, MARJORIE AILEEN MATTHEWS, museum director; b. Richmond, Va., Aug. 19, 1918; d. Harry Anderson and Adelia Charlotte (Howland) Matthews; m. Robert Woodrow Smith, July 23, 1945 (dec. Mar. 1992). Pilot lic., Taneytown (Md.) Aviation Svc., 1944, cert. CAA navigation ground sch. instr., 1945. Founder, editor, pub. Spinning Wheel, Taneytown, 1945-63; v.p. Antiques Publs., Inc., 1960-68; pres. Prism Inc., 1968-78; mus. dir. Trapshooting Hall of Fame, Vandalia, Ohio, 1976-2000, mus. dir. emeritus, 2001—, sec., 1993-99. Co-author: Handbook of Tomorrow's Antiques, 1954; contbr. articles to profl. publs. Sec. Balt. area coun. Girl Scouts USA, 1950. Named to All-Am. Trapshooting team Sports Afield mag., 1960, 61; inductee Trapshooting Hall of Fame, 1998. Mem. Nat. League Am. Pen Women, Amateur Trapshooting Assn. (life), Internat. Assn. Sports Mus. and Halls of Fame (bd. dirs. 1993-94, W.R. Schroeder Disting. Svc. award 1999). Lutheran. Avocations: duplicate bridge, trapshooting, antiques collecting.

SMITH, MARK LEE, architect; b. L.A., Nov. 16, 1957; s. Selma (Moidel) Smith. BA in History of Architecture, UCLA, 1978, MA in Architecture, 1980. Registered architect Calif., Nev., Oreg., Wash., Tenn., Colo., N.Y., Ohio. Designer, drafter John B. Ferguson and Assocs., L.A., 1976-83, architect, 1983; pvt. practice architecture, 1984—. Mem. Los Angeles County Archtl. Evaluation Bd., 1990—; spkr. Western Pool and Spa Show, 1997—. Essay columnist AIA/SFV monthly, 1997—; contbr. articles to profl. jours. Bd. govs. UCLA John Wooden Ctr., 1978-80; judge Bank Am. Achievement Awards, 1998—, chair, 1999-2000. Regents scholar, U. Calif., Berkeley, UCLA, 1975-78; UCLA Grad. Sch. Architecture Rsch. fellow, 1979-80. Mem. AIA (treas. San Fernando Valley chpt. 1986, bd. dirs. 1986—, v.p. 1987, pres. 1988, Design award 1988, 89, 90, 91, 99, chmn. Design awards 1994, bd. dirs. Calif. coun. 1989-94, v.p. 1991-94, chmn. continuing edn. 1991-93, chmn. 1992 conf.), Phi Beta Kappa. Office: 18340 Ventura Blvd Ste 225 Tarzana CA 91356-4278

SMITH, MARK ALAN, management consultant; b. Lafayette, Ind., May 15, 1934; s. Mark Andrew and Sarah Fredissa (Palin) S.; children by previous marriages: Michelle Renee, Janene Marie. BA in Mus. Edn., BS in French, Ind. State U., 1957; MS in Adminstrn., George Washington U., 1976; postgrad., U. Pa. Wharton Sch., U. Denver Coll Law, U. Md. Coll. Law. Tech. writer Douglas Aircraft Co., Santa Monica, Calif., 1961-62; editor Copyright Law Office, Library Congress, Washington, 1963-64; asst. dir. pers. Holy Cross Hosp., Silver Spring, Md., 1964-65, dir. pers. adminstrn., 1965-80, dir. human resources adminstrn., 1980-82, asst. v.p., 1982-88; pres. HRM Assocs., Rockville, 1989—. Instr. pers. mgmt. and labor rels. Strayer U., Washington, 1970-73, bus. adminstrn. Ctrl. Mich. U. Grad. Sch., Washington extension, 1975-80; vis. lectr. George Washington U. Grad. Sch. Bus. Adminstrn., Washington, 1969, 70, 76; cons. to various hosps. in Md., Va. and Washington, Am. Hosp. Assn. and other nat. profl. assns., 1975—; bd. dirs. Potomac Employers' Roundtable, 1991—, dir. membership, 1992—. Contbr. articles on orgn. devel. to profl. jours. Served with CIC, U.S. Army, 1957-60. Mem. Am. Hosp. Assn., Am. Soc. for Hosp. Pers. Dirs. (mem. labor rels. com. 1970), Soc. for Human Resource Mgmt. (cert., sr. prof. in human resources, mem. pub. affairs com. 1975), Am. Mgmt. Assn., Washington Pers. Assn., Hosp. Coun. of Nat. Capital Area (pres. pers. dirs. divsn. 1969, 71), Md. Hosp. Pers. Adminstrn. Assn., Am. Soc. Law and Medicine, Phi Delta Kappa, Phi Mu Alpha Sinfonia, Blue Key. Home and Office: 872 New Mark Esplanade Rockville MD 20850-2750 Fax: 301 340-2889. E-mail: HRMPROS@hotmail.com.

SMITH, MARK EDWARD, music educator; b. Farmington, N.Mex, May 26, 1955; s. Merle Emerson and Marjorie (Powell) S. B in Music Edn., Eastern N.Mex. U., 1978; MMus, U. N.Mex., 1994. Cert. music educator, N.Mex., Ariz. Music tchr. Ctrl. Consolidated Schs., Shiprock, N.Mex., 1979-80; dist. wide music tchr. Mesa Vista Consolidated Schs., El Rito, 1984-85; music tchr. Window Rock (Ariz.) Elem. Sch., 1985-86, Many Farms (Ariz.) High Sch., 1986-89, Navajo Preparatory Sch., Farmington, N.Mex., 1991-93, Santa Fe Pub. Schs., 1993-94, Red Mesa Unified Schs., Teec Nos Pos, Ariz., 1994-99, Ctrl. Consolidated Schs. Dist. 22, Kirtland, N.M., 1999-2001, Bloomfield Schs., 2001—02. Founding mem. Reservation Music Educators, Keyenta, Ariz., 1986-89; lectr. Title I Parent Workshops, Chinle, Ganado, Red Mesa, Ariz., 1994-96. Performer (opening act) B.W. Stevenson, 1982, Paul Carrack and Nick Lowe, 1982, Willie Dixon, 1983, Marshal Tucker Band, 1984. Performer Dan Quayle Visit to Farmington, 1992, Vietnam Vets. Benefit, Farmington, 1993, Wild Rose, 1993, Clay Walker, 1995, John Anderson, 1995, Aaron Tippin, 1997, Eddy Money, 1998. Mem. Music Educators Nat. Conf., Kappa Kappa Psi. Democrat. Episcopalian. Avocations: swimming, bicycle riding. Home: 903 Hallett Cir Farmington NM 87401-9113

SMITH, MARK EUGENE, architectural engineering service company executive; b. Wareham, Mass., Apr. 1, 1951; s. Mark Alvin and Evelyn Marie (Somers) S.; m. Brigid Ann Murray, Oct. 17, 1979; children: Hugh Talmidge, Patrick Morgan. AS, New England Inst. Tech., 1981. Owner Marks Motor Co., Wareham, 1965-69; chief designer HF Scientific Instrument, Ft. Myers, Fla., 1981-83; chief designer HVE Keltron Corp., Waltham, Mass., 1984-85; CEO Home Svcs., Ft. Myers, 1985-90, Gen. Capitol, Mocksville, N.C., 1990—. Cons. Underwood & Assocs., Cape Coral, Fla., 1981-89, Shaban Mfg. Co., Ft. Myers, 1982-83; chief designer Keltron Corp., Waltham, 1984-85; sr. designer Proctor & Schwartz, Lexington, N.C., 1990-99. Co-author: The Art of Custom Painting, 1978. With USMC, 1969-72. Named Advanced Designer, Metalflake Design Group, Springfield, Mass., 1977. Mem. Soc. Mech. Engrs., Soc. Automotive Engrs., Am. Inst. for Design and Drafting (nat. drafting award 1981). Republican. Avocations: numismatics, antiquarian. Office: Gen Capitol 202 Mason Dr Mocksville NC 27028-7318 E-mail: markussmithium@email.com.

SMITH, MARK JOSEPH, cartographer; b. Page, AZ, Sept. 29, 1974; s. Joseph W Smith, Doris T Smith. B. S. Geography, Appalachian State University, Boone, NC, 1993—97; MS Instructional Technology, East Carolina University, Greenville, NC, 2000—02; Diploma, Squadron Officer School, Maxwell AFB, AL, 1999—99. GIS Specialist NC Emergency Management, Raleigh, NC, 1997—2002; GIS, Computer Mapping Staff Global Mapping International, Colorado Springs, CO, 1996—96. Aerospace Education Officer Civil Air Patrol, NC, 1998—2000. Author: (Article) Aerospace History, 1999. Mem.: Air and Space Society (Member 2000—02), Gamma Theta Upsilon Honor Society (Chapter President 1995—96), Kappa Delta Pi Honor Society (Member 2001). Christian. Avocation: Wood carving, photography.

SMITH, MARSHALL SAVIDGE, foundation administrator; b. East Orange, N.J., Sept. 16, 1937; s. Marshall Parsons and Ann Eileen (Zulauf) S.; m. Carol Goodspeed, June 25, 1960 (div. Aug. 1962); m. Louise Nixon Claiborn, Aug. 1964; children: Adam, Jennifer, Matthew, Megan. AB, Harvard U., 1960, EdM, 1963, EdD, 1970. Systems analyst and computer programmer Raytheon Corp., Andover, Mass., 1959-62; instr., assoc. prof. Harvard U., Cambridge, 1966-76; asst., assoc. dir. Nat. Inst. Edn., Washington, 1973-76; asst. commr. edn. HEW, 1976-79, chief of staff to U.S. Dept. Edn. sec., 1980; prof. U. Wis., Madison, 1980-86, Stanford (Calif.) U., 1986—, dean Sch. Edn., 1986-94; under-sec. edn. U.S. Dept. Edn., 1993-2000, acting dep. sec. edn., 1996-2000; program dir. Hewlett Found., 2001—. Task force, chmn. Clinton Presdl. Transition Team, 1992-93; chmn. PEW Forum on Ednl. Reform; chmn. bd. internat. com. studies in edn. NAS, 1992-93. Author: The General Inquirer, 1967, Inequality, 1972; contbr. several articles to profl. jours, chpts. to books. Pres. Madison West Hockey Assn., 1982-84. Mem. Am. Ednl. Rsch. Assn. (chmn. orgn. instl. affiliates 1985-86), Nat. Acad. Edn. Democrat. Avocations: environmental issues, philanthropy. Home: 1256 Forest Ave Palo Alto CA 94301 Office: Wm & Flora Hewlett Found Menlo Park CA

SMITH, MARTHA VIRGINIA BARNES, retired elementary school educator; b. Camden, Ark., Oct. 12, 1940; d. William Victor and Lillian Louise (Givens) Barnes; m. Basil Loren Smith, Oct. 11, 1975; children: Jennifer Frost, Sean Barnes. BS in Edn., Ouachita Bapt. U., 1963; postgrad., Auburn U., 1974, Henderson State U., 1975. Cert. tchr., Mo. 2d and 1st grade tchr. Brevard County Schs., Titusville and Cocoa, Fla., 1963-65, 69-70; 1st grade tchr. Lakeside Sch. Dist., Hot Springs, Ark., 1965-66, Harmony Grove Sch., Camden, 1972-76; 1st and 5th grade tchr. Cumberland County Schs., Fayetteville, N.C., 1966-69; kindergarten tchr. Pulaski County Schs., Ft. Leonard Wood, Mo., 1970-72; 3d grade tchr. Mountain Grove (Mo.) Schs., 1976-99; ret., 1999. Chmn. career ladder com. Mountain Grove Dist., 1991-99. Children's pastor 1st Bapt. Ch., Vanzant, Mo., 1984-88. Mem. NEA (pres.-elect Mountain Grove chpt. 1995-97, pres. Mountain Grove chpt. 1997-99), Kappa Kappa Iota. Avocation: antique and classic cars.

SMITH, MARTIN BERNHARD, journalist; b. San Francisco, Apr. 20, 1930; s. John Edgar and Anna Sophie (Thorsen) S.; m. Joan Lovat Muller, Apr. 25, 1953; children: Catherine Joan, Karen Anne. AB, U. Calif., Berkeley, 1952, M Journalism, 1968. Reporter, city editor Modesto (Calif.) Bee, 1957-64; reporter, mng. editor Sacramento Bee, 1964-75; polit. editor, columnist McClatchy Newspapers, Sacramento, 1975-92; ret., 1992. Episcopalian.

SMITH, MARTIN HENRY, retired pediatrician; b. Gainesville, Ga., Nov. 3, 1921; s. Charles E. and Mamie Mae (Emmett) S.; m. Mary Gillis, Feb. 25, 1950; children: Susan, Margaret, Mary MD, Emory U., 1945. Diplomate Am. Bd. Pediatrics. Intern City Hosp. System, Winston-Salem, N.C., 1945-46; fellow in infectious diseases Grady Meml. Hosp., Atlanta, 1948-49; resident Henrietta Egleston Hosp., 1949-50, Children's Hosp., Washington, 1950-51; practice medicine, specializing in pediatrics Gainesville, Ga.; ret., 1988; clin. asst. prof. Emory U. Hosp., Atlanta; chief of staff Hall County Hosp., Gainesville, 1965-66. Mem. Nat. Vaccine Adv. Commn., 1990—, chmn., 1991. Contbr. articles to profl. jours. Chmn. Nat. Vaccine Adv. Com., 1991—. Capt. M.C., U.S. Army, 1946-48 Fellow Am. Acad. Pediatrics (chpt. chmn. 1966-69, dist. chmn. 1977-83, pres.-elect 1984-85, pres. 1985-86); mem. Hall County Med. Soc. (pres. 1960), Ga. Pediatric Soc. (pres. 1965-66), Med. Assn. Ga., AMA, Alpha Omega Alpha Clubs: Chattahoochee Country (Gainesville); Piedmont Driving (Atlanta). Episcopalian.

SMITH, MARTIN JAY, advertising and marketing executive; b. N.Y.C., Feb. 1, 1942; s. Nathan and Helen (Schwartz) S.; m. Ellen Susan Chadakoff, Dec. 20, 1964; children: Hilary, Nancy. BA, U. Pitts., 1963. With sta. clearance dept. ABC Radio Network, N.Y.C., 1965-66; asst. account exec. Norman Craig & Kummel, 1966-67, account exec., 1967-68, Gotham, Inc., N.Y.C., 1968-72, account supr., 1972-74, v.p., 1974-78, sr. v.p., 1978-80, exec. v.p., 1980-84, vice chmn., 1984—. Sgt. USAR, 1963-69. Mem. Am. Advt. Assn. Am. (mem. mgmt. com. 1987). Avocations: flying, tennis, golf. Home: 920 Park Ave New York NY 10028-0208 Office: Gotham Inc 100 5th Ave Fl 16 New York NY 10011-6996

SMITH, MARTIN JAY, physician, biomedical research scientist; b. Bklyn., May 21, 1934; s. I. Richard and Marilyn (Bernard) S.; m. Joyce Ellen Gleason, June 26, 1960 (div. Nov. 1968); children: Danielle, Robert, Alexander; m. Ruby Helen Rhodes, Apr. 7, 1972. BA, Hofstra Coll., 1955; MD, Columbia U., 1959. Diplomate Am. Bd. Internal Medicine, Am. Bd. Internal Medicine in Hematology, Am. Bd. Pathology in Clin. Pathology, Am. Bd. Pathology in Immunopathology. Intern Meth. Hosp., N.Y.C., 1959-60, resident in medicine, 1960-61, Montefiore Hosp., N.Y.C., 1963-64; rsch. fellow in medicine Harvard Coll., Cambridge, Mass., 1964-66; clin. and rsch. fellow in medicine Mass. Gen. Hosp., Boston, 1964-66; physician Gundersen Clinic and Luth. Hosp., La Crosse, Wis., 1966-99, chmn. dept. internal medicine, 1971-73; dir. spl. hematology lab. Gundersen Clinic, 1967-99, chmn. dept. lab. medicine, 1973-96; dir. lab. medicine Luth. Hosp., 1973-96. Dir. rsch. Gundersen Med. Found., 1975-88; med. dir. Med. Lab. Tech. Program Western Wis. Tech. Inst., 1978-99. Contbr. articles to New Eng. Jour Medicine, Jour. Lab. Clin. Medicine, Blood, Ann. Internal Medicine, Biochim, Biophys. Acta, Jour. Infectious Diseases, Clin. Chemistry. Capt. USNR, ret. Fellow ACP, Coll. Am. Pathologists (inspector labs. 1983-99); mem. Am. Assn. for Cancer Rsch., Am. Soc. Hematology, Internat. Soc. Hematology, Assn. Med. Lab. Immunologists, Phi Beta Kappa. Home: 1428 Main St La Crosse WI 54601-4225 Office: Gundersen Clinic Ltd 1836 South Ave La Crosse WI 54601-5494

SMITH, MARTIN LANE, biomedical researcher; b. Seattle, Mar. 15, 1959; s. Melvin Dale and Rosemary (Nations) Smith. BA, Austin Coll., 1981; PhD, Emory U., 1990. Assoc. U. Pitts. Sch. Medicine, 1990-93, NIH, Bethesda, Md., 1993-98; asst. prof. Ind. U. Sch. Medicine, 1998—. Instr. biology Emory U., Atlanta, 1985—89. Contbr. articles to profl. jours. Recipient Am. Cancer Soc. award, 1992, 1998, 2002; grantee NIH, 1991—93. Mem.: AAAS, Radiation Rsch. Soc., Am. Assn. Cancer Rsch., Sigma Xi. Avocations: coin collecting, hiking, travel.

SMITH, MARVIN FREDERICK, JR. chemical engineer, consultant; b. Newark, Oct. 22, 1932; s. Marvin F. and Helen (Marsh) S.; m. Jacqueline Pettit, June 20, 1959; 1 child, Scott C. BSChE, Newark (N.J.) Coll. Engring., 1954. Field engr. E.I. DuPont, Newark, 1954-55, Newport, 1957-59; dir. mfg. and rsch. Bon Ami Co., N.Y.C., 1959-63; sr. rsch. engr. Exxon Rsch. & Engring. Co., Linden, N.J., 1964-68; project head, engring. assoc. Exxon Chem. Co., 1968-89; engring. assoc. Exxon Rsch. & Engring. Co., 1989-92; cons., expert witness Paul, Weiss, Rifkind, Wharton & Garrison, N.Y.C., 1992-94. Author/co-author: 18 tech. papers Transactions of Soc. Automotive Engrs. ASTM, Nat. Petroleum Refiners Assn. Mgr. baseball team Aberdeen Little League, 1978-83; team mgr., dir. basketball league Aberdeen Recreation League, 1978; chmn. tennis com. Strathmore Bath and Tennis Club, Aberdeen, 1980-82. With U.S. Army, 1955-57. Fellow ASTM (chmn. high temperature rheology 1978-91, Appreciation award 1988, Excellence in Symposium Mgmt. award 1990, Merit award 1993, George V. Dyroff award Hon. Mem. 2001, hon. mem.); mem. ASTM, U.S. Tennis Assn., Exptl. Aircraft Assn. Achievements include patents for Petroleum Additives and a Shear-Stability Test Device; key innovations in high temperature and low temperature viscometers used by petroleum industry; concept and devel. of novel multigrade motor oils for autos and trucks. Avocation: senior singles competition in national and regional tennis tournaments. Home and Office: 81 Avondale Ln Matawan NJ 07747-1239

SMITH, MARY ELIZABETH, retired art historian; b. Three Rivers, Mich., Aug. 2, 1932; d. Emery C. Smith and Margaret L. Anderson. BA, U. Mich., 1954; MA, Columbia U., 1960; PhD, Yale U., 1966. Asst. prof. U. N.Mex., Albuquerque, 1966-71, assoc. prof., 1971-77, prof., 1977-87; guest prof. U. Hamburg, Germany, 1981; prof. Tulane U., New Orleans, 1987-94, ret., 1994. Sr. fellow Dumbarton Oaks Pre-Columbian Collection, Washington, 1982-88. Author: Picture Writing From Ancient Southern Mexico: Mixtec Place Signs and Maps, 1973, The Codex Lopez Ruiz: A Lost Mixtec Pictorial Manuscript, 1998; co-author: The Codex Colombino, 1966, The Codex Tulane, 1991; contbr. articles to profl. jours. Recipient fellowship Doherty Found., 1962-63, fellowship Pan Am. Union, 1963-64, fellowship John Simon Guggenheim Meml. Found., 1978; Rsch. grant Am. Philosophical Soc. Phillips Fund, 1974. Mem. Am. Soc. Ethnohistory (pres. 1980-81). Avocations: fun fiction reader, baseball fan.

SMITH, MARY FRANCES, social worker, educator; b. Albany, N.Y., Aug. 24, 1943; d. Egon and Hildegard (Weyrauch) Plager; m. Francis N. Smith, June 24, 1967; 1 child, Christopher Francis. BS in Biology, Nazareth Coll., Rochester, N.Y., 1965; MSW, Syracuse U., 1967; PhD, SUNY, Albany, 1990. Cert. social worker. Psychiat. social worker St. Anne Inst., Albany, 1967-71; supervising social worker Albany County Mental Health Clinic, 1971-74; prof. dept. family practice Albany Med. Coll., 1979—. Grantee N.Y. State Acad. Family Physicians Rsch. and Edn. Found., 1990-91. Mem. NASW, Soc. Tchrs. Family Medicine, Gerontol. Soc. Am., Acad. Cert. Social Workers. Roman Catholic. Avocations: travel, tennis, needlepoint. Home: 3 Westlyn Ct Albany NY 12203-3415 Office: Albany Med Coll Dept Family Practice 1 Clara Barton Dr Albany NY 12208-3401 E-mail: smithmf@mail.amc.edu.

SMITH, MARY HILL, volunteer; b. Dallas, Jan. 14, 1943; d. Wendell Tennyson and Laura Leta (Massey) Hill; m. Andrew Jeptha Kincannon Smith, July 10, 1965; children: Emily Catherine Smith McGrath, Andrew III, Bradley Tennyson. BA with Volunteer Adminstrn. Cert., Metro. State U., 1987. Pres., mem. Raggedy Ann chpt. Children's Health Ctr. Assn., Mpls., 1972-83; pres. exec. com. Jr. League Mpls., 1973-84; dir. 75th Anniversary bd. Minn. Orchestral Assn., Mpls., 1977-78; dir. Guthrie Theater Bd., 1979-83; bd. dirs. YWCA, 1981-82; pres. Wayzata (Minn.) Cmty. Edn. Bd., 1981-83; mem. adv. bd. N. Hennepin C. C., Brooklyn Center, Minn., 1982-84; chair, sec. Wayzata Sch. Bd., 1984-92; chair Minn. Women's Polit. Caucus, St. Paul, 1984-92; bd. dirs. Hennepin Tech. Coll., Plymouth, Minn., 1985-92; chair, bd. dirs. Art Ctr. Minn., Orono, 1985-92; mem. Metro. Coun., St. Paul, 1993—. Chmn. transp. com. Twin West Chamber Leadership com., Minnetonka, Minn., 1992; mem. State Ethical Practice Bd., St. Paul, 1986-91, Gov. Carlson's Re-election com., 1994-95, State Adv. Coun. on Metro Airports, St. Paul, 1995; del. Orono (Minn.) Rep. Party, 1992; active Hennepin County Libr. Found., 1996-99; active Sheltering Arms Found., 1996-2002, pres., 1999-2000; bd. dirs. Minn. Women's Campaign Fund, 1996—, pres., 2000-2002; mem. exec. com. U. Minn. Ctr. for Transp. Studies, 1995-2001; bd. dirs. Met. State U. Found., St. Paul, 2000—; chair Met. Airports Commn. Joint Airport Zoning Bd., 2001-02. Named Woman of the Yr., Women's Transp. Seminar, Minn., 2001; recipient Disting. Pub. Leadership award, U. Minn. Ctr. Transp. Studies, 2002. Republican. Episcopalian. Avocations: reading, gardening, cooking. Home: 515 Ferndale Rd N Wayzata MN 55391-1008 Office: Metro Coun 230 5th St E Saint Paul MN 55101-1672 E-mail: smith199@gold.tc.umn.edu., mary.smith@metc.state.mn.us.

SMITH, MARYA JEAN, writer; b. Youngstown, Ohio, Nov. 12, 1945; d. Cameron Reynolds and Jean Rose (Sause) Argetsinger; m. Arthur Beverly Smith Jr., Dec. 30, 1968 (div. 1996); children: Arthur Cameron, Sarah Reynolds. BA, Cornell U., 1967. Editorial asst. Seventeen Mag., N.Y.C., 1967-68; promotion writer U. Chgo. Press, 1968-70; asst. account exec. Drucilla Handy Co., Chgo., 1970-72; feature writer various mags., 1972-74; freelance writer Cornell U., Ithaca, N.Y., 1975-76, lectr., 1976-77; playwright Playwrights' Ctr. Prodn., Chgo., 1978; humor columnist various jours., 1979-81; freelance writer, 1982—. Author: Across the Creek, 1989, Winter-Broken, 1990, Danish edit., 1991, (play) Hire Power, 1998; contbr. poetry Primavera, Ariel VI and VIII, 1974, 87, 89; contbr. articles and essays to mags.

and papers, 1984—. Vol. reading tutor Literacy Vols. Western Cook County, Oak Park, Ill., 1988-89, Oak Park Pub. Libr. Reading Program, 1990-94. Recipient 1st place for news writing Assoc. Ch. Press, 1986, poetry award Poets and Patrons, 1986, Triton Coll. Salute to Arts, 1987, 89. Mem. Nat. Writers Union, Authors Guild, Soc. Midland Authors. Roman Catholic.

SMITH, MAURA ABELN, lawyer; b. Reading, Pa., Oct. 3, 1955; d. Henry Joseph and Lynn (Blashe) Abeln; children: Gwendolyn Casebeer, Karl Casebeer; m. Steven A. Smith, Dec. 18, 1999. AB, Vassar Coll., 1977; M Philosophy, Oxford U., 1979; JD, U. Miami, 1982. Bar: Fla. 1982, Ohio 1999. Assoc. Steel, Hector & Davis, Miami, 1982—87; ptnr. Baker & McKenzie, 1987-91; v.p., gen. counsel GE Co./Plastics, Pittsfield, Mass., 1991-98; sr. v.p., gen. counsel, sec. Owens Corning, Toledo, 1998-2000, chief restructuring officer, sr. v.p., gen. counsel, sec., 2000—, also bd. dirs. Rhodes scholar, Oxford, Eng., 1977-79; John M. Olin fellow in law and econs., Olin Found., 1979-82. Mem. Elfun, Phi Beta Kappa. Avocations: skiing, horseback riding, tennis, golf. E-mail: maura.abelnsmith@owenscorning.com.

SMITH, MAUREEN MCBRIDE, laboratory administrator; b. Santa Monica, Calif., Mar. 4, 1952; d. Clayton Laird McBride and Luella (Sullivan) Boudreau; step-father Henry A Boudreau; m. Gary Howard Cothran, July 27, 1974 (div. Apr. 1982); m. Guy Gordon Smith, Feb. 12, 1983; stepchildren: Keri Lynn, Scott Allen. BS magna cum laude, Calif. State Coll., San Bernardino, 1978, MS, 1993. Analytical chemist Chalco Engring., Edwards AFB, Calif., 1978-79, 82; microbiol. lab. tech. AVEK Water Agy., Quartz Hill, 1979-81, chemist, lab. mgr., 1982—. Instr. Antelope Valley Coll., Lancaster Calif., 1980-82. Mem. AAAS, Am. Chem. Soc. Avocations: skiing, photography, training and showing golden retrievers. Address: 6500 W Avenue N Palmdale CA 93551-2855 E-mail: msavekwa@aol.com.

SMITH, MAURY DRANE, lawyer; b. Samson, Ala., Feb. 2, 1927; s. Abb Jackson and Rose Drane (Sellers) S.; m. Lucile West Martin, Aug. 15, 1953; children: Martha Smith Vandervoort, Sally Smith Legg, Maury D. Smith, Jr. BS, U. Ala., 1950, LLB, JD, 1952. Bar: Ala., 1952; U.S. Dist. Ct. (mid., no. and so. dists.) Ala. 1953; U.S. Ct. Appeals, 1957, U.S. Supreme Ct., 1957. Asst. atty. gen. State of Ala., Montgomery, 1952-55; asst. dist. atty. Montgomery County, 1955-63; ptnr. Balch & Bingham LLP, Montgomery, 1955—. Chmn. lawyers adv. com. Mid. Dist. Ala., Montgomery, 1990—; mem. U.S. Ct. of Appeals 11th cir. adv. com. on rules, Montgomery, 1990—, U.S. Dist. Ct. Mid. Dist. civil justice reform act adv. com., Montgomery, 1991—. Pres. Montgomery Area United Way, Ala., 1987; mem. Leadership Montgomery, 1994. Fellow Am. Coll. Trial Lawyers, Am. Bar Found.; mem. Univ. Ala. System (bd. trustees 1991-97, trustee emeritus 1997—), Ala. Law Inst. (mem. coun.), ABA (mem. litigation sect.), Montgomery County Bar Assn. (pres. 1976), Montgomery Area C. of C. (pres. 1984), Ala. State Bar (chmn. jud. bldg. task force 1987-94). Avocations: farming, tennis. Home: 2426 Midfield Dr Montgomery AL 36111-1529 Office: Balch & Bingham LLP PO Box 78 Montgomery AL 36101-0078

SMITH, MELISSA CHRISTINE-MARY, flight nurse; b. Denver, Sept. 30, 1956; d. Harry William and Briony Jane (Travers) Herter; m. Marlin M. Smith Jr., Sept. 20, 1980; children: Thomas J., Alexander J., Levi J. ADN, San Jacinto Jr. Coll., Pasadena, Tex., 1985; BSN, U. Tex. Med. Br., Galveston, 1989. Staff nurse Sun Belt Regional Med. Ctr. East, Channelview, Tex., 1986-87; nursing supr. MacGregor Med. Clinic, Houston, 1987-88; charge nurse Baywood Hosp., Webster, Tex., 1988-93; office nurse Bay Area Pediat., Houston, 1990-96, Sanus Health Plan, Houston, 1993-97. With U.S. Army, 1974-80; with nurse corps USAF, 1995—. Mem. Assn. Military Surgeons U.S., Sigma Theta Tau.

SMITH, MERELYN ELIZABETH, elementary and middle school educator; b. Providence, June 30, 1957; d. Arnold Hobson and Frances Louise (Carpenter) S. BS, Gordon Coll., 1979; postgrad., U. N.H., 1990-93. Cert. elem., mid., and secondary tchr., Mass. 5th and 6th grade tchr. Glen Urquhart Sch., Beverly Farms, Mass., 1979-80, 4th and 5th grade tchr., 1980-81, 5th grade tchr., 1981-87, 6th to 9th grade math. and computer tchr., 1987—, math. specialist and tchr., 1996—. Diagnostician, edn1. therapist Inst. for Learning and Devel., 1996; adj. prof. Gordon Coll., Mass., 1996—, U. N.H., Durham, 1996; presenter workshops in field. Leader Beverly (Mass.) Group Home Fellowship, 1982—; vacation Bible sch. tchr. North Shore Community Bapt. Ch., Beverly Farms, 1982-85. Recipient Vol. Svc. award Assn. Retarded Citizens, 1987, 95. Mem. Nat. Coun. Tchrs. Math., Assn. Tchrs. Math. in Mass., Assn. Tchrs. Math. in New Eng. Avocations: piano, hiking, cross country skiing, building furniture, reading. Office: Glen Urquhart Sch 74 Hart St Beverly MA 01915-2195

SMITH, MERILYN ROBERTA, art educator; b. Tolley, N.D., July 24, 1933; d. Robert Coleman and Mathilda Marie (Staael) S. BA, Concordia Coll., Minn., 1953; MA, State U. of Iowa, Iowa City, 1956, MFA, 1966. Tchr. Badger (Minn.) High Sch., 1954; instr. in art Valley City (N.D.) State Tchrs. Coll., 1957, 58, U. Wis., Oshkosh, 1967, asst. prof. art, 1969, assoc. prof., 1977-91, prof., 1991-93, prof. emeritus, 1993—; represented by Miriam Perlman Gallery, Chgo. Counselor Luth. Student Ctr., U. Iowa, 1959-65, rsch. asst. in printmaking, 1960-65; owner, dir. James House Gallery, Oshkosh, 1972-77; dir. Allen Priebe Gallery, U. Wis., Oshkosh, 1975. Exhibited in group shows at N.W. Printmakers Internat., Seattle and Portland, Oreg., 1964, Ultimate Concerns 6th Nat. Exhbn., Athens, Ohio, 1965, 55th Nat. Exhbn., Springfield, Mass., 1974, 11th An. So. Tier Arts and Crafts, Corning, N.Y., 1974, Soc. of the Four Arts, Palm Beach, Fla., 1974, Appalachian Nat. Drawing Competition, Boone, N.C., 1975, Rutgers Nat. Drawing Exhbn., Camden, N.J., 1975, 8th and 9th Biennial Nat. Art Exhibit, Valley City, N.D., 1973, 75, Clary-Miner Gallery, Buffalo, 1988, Nat. Art Show, Redding, Calif., 1989, Internat. Printmaker, Buffalo, 1990, Westmoreland Nat. Juried Competition, Youngwood, Pa., 1990, Ariel Gallery, Soho, N.Y., 1990, Grand Prix de Paris Internat., Chapelle De La Sorbonne, Paris, 1990, Nat. Juried Exhbn., Rockford, Ill., 1991, Nat. Invitational Exhbn., Buffalo, 1991, East Coast Artists Nat. Invitational Art Exhbn., Havre de Grace, Md., 1991, Ariel Gallery, Soho, N.Y., 1991, N.Y. Art Expo, 1991, Milw. Art for AIDS Auction, 1991, 92, 94. Mem. Winnebago Hist. Soc., Oshkosh, 1987—. Lutheran. Avocation: gardening. Home: 226 High Ave Oshkosh WI 54901-4734

SMITH, MERRITT ROE, history educator; b. Waverly, N.Y., Nov. 14, 1940; s. Wilson Niles and Mary Eleanor (Fitzgerald) S.; m. Bronwyn M. Mellquist, Aug. 24, 1974. AB, Georgetown U., 1963; MA, Pa. State U., 1965, PhD, 1971; LHD (hon.), Rensselaer Poly. Inst., 1997. Asst. prof. history Ohio State U., Columbus, 1970-74, assoc. prof., 1974-78; vis. prof. history and sociology of sci. U. Pa., Phila., 1976; prof. history tech. program in sci., tech. and society M.I.T., Cambridge, 1978—, Metcalfe prof. engring. and liberal arts, 1989-92, dir. progam in sci., tech. and society, 1992-96, 2000—, Leverett and William King Cutten prof., 1993—. Author: Harpers Ferry Armory and the New Technology, 1977, Military Enterprise and Technological Change, 1985, Science, Technology and the Military, 2 vols., 1988, Does Technology Drive History?, 1994, Major Problems in the History of American Technology, 1998, Inventing America, 2002; mem. editorial bd. Tech. and Culture, 1973-91, Bus. History Rev., 1978-85, MIT Press, 1986-91, Archimedes, 1995—. Mem. Mass. Hist. Soc.; bd. advisors MIT Mus. Recipient Cert. of Commendation Am. Assn. State and Local History, 1978, Disting. Tchg. award Ohio State U., 1978; grantee Ohio State U., 1972, Am. Philos. Soc., 1974, Harvard Bus. Sch., 1974-75, Eleutherian Mills-Hagley Found., 1978-79, Alfred P. Sloan Found., 1994-2002; Guggenheim fellow, 1983-84, Regents fellow Smithsonian Instn., 1984-85. Mem. AAAS, Am. Acad. Arts and Scis., Soc. History Tech. (mem. exec. council, Dexter Prize com., Da Vinci medal 1994, mus. com., v.p., pres. 1989-91), Orgn. Am. Historians (Frederick Jackson Turner award 1977), Bus. History Conf., Am. Antiquarian Soc., Newcomen Soc. N. Am., Soc. Indsl. Archeology, History Sci. Soc. (Pfizer award 1978), Phi Kappa Phi, Phi Alpha Theta. Home: 17 Longfellow Rd Newton MA 02462-1505 Office: MIT Rm E51-185 Cambridge MA 02139

SMITH, MICHAEL ALAN, insurance industry analyst; b. Schenectady, N.Y., Mar. 5, 1947; s. Norman Leslie and Margaret (Gleeson) S.; m. Denise Pagliaro, July 27, 1972 (separated Dec. 1989); children: James Michael, Dawn Susan. BS in Agrl. Econs., Cornell U., 1970; MBA in Fin., Fairleigh Dickinson U., 1978. Methods analyst Liberty Mut. Ins. Co., Boston, 1970-71; mktg. rep. Texaco Inc., Washington, 1972-74; sec. underwriting div. Palisades Life Ins. Co., Orangeburg, N.Y., 1974-76; sr. planning officer Home Ins. Group, N.Y.C., 1976-83; v.p. planning Ideal Mut. Ins. Co., 1983-85; sr. v.p., ins. industry analyst Lehman Bros. Inc., 1985-96; dir., sr. ins. analyst Salomon Bros., 1996-97; mng. dir. Bear Stearns & Co., 1998—. Contbr. articles to profl. jours. Mem. Assn. Ins. and Fin. Analysts. Avocations: youth coach, skiing, go-kart racing. Office: Bear Stearns & Co Inc 245 Park Ave New York NY 10167-0002

SMITH, MICHAEL ALLEN, mechanical engineer; b. Chgo., Mar. 22, 1948; s. Warren H. and Joan M. Smith; m. Mary N. Sjolund, Sept. 8, 1973; children: Diana, David, Mariel. BSME, U. South Fla., 1972; MS in Bus. Mgmt., SUNY, Utica, 1992. Lic. profl. engr., N.Y. Devel. engr. photo products equipment divsn. DuPont, Wilmington, Del., 1972-75; mech. engr. Remington Arms Co., Ilion, N.Y., 1975-86; sr. facilities engr. GE Co., Utica, 1987-91; with Buckbee-Mears, Cortland, N.Y., 1993-98, Bergman Assocs., Rochester, 1999, St. John Engrs., Binghampton, 2000—. Mem. ASME, ASHRAE, NSPE, Mohawk Valley Personal Computer Soc. (pres. 1990-91). Home: 273 S 3rd Ave Ilion NY 13357-2401 Office: St John Engrs 1115 Front St Binghamton NY 13905-1115

SMITH, MICHAEL DAVID, music educator; s. Vernon and Virginia Smith; m. Joann C. Smith, May 24, 1957; children: Jeane' Wilkinson, Jonna Hawkins. MA in Music Edn., U. of Ala., Tuscaloosa, Alabama, 1978—80; MusB in Music Edn., U. of Miss., Oxford, MS, 1973—77. Teaching Tenn. Dept. of Edn. Asst. band dir. Haleyville Bd. of Edn., Haleyvillle, Ala., 1977—81; band dir. Poplarville H.S., Poplarville, Miss., 1981—82, Hamilton H.S., Hamilton, Ala., 1982—97; dir. of bands David Crockett H.S., Jonesborough, Tenn., 1997—. Instr. Spirit of Atlanta Drum & Bugle Corps, Atlanta, 1991—92; cons. Pygraphics, Grapevine, Tex.; assoc. condr. Johnson City Cmty. Band, Johnson City, Tenn., 2000—02, condr., Tenn. Musician (none): (editing music) Peace Maker. Music dir. Pleasant Grove Bapt. Ch., Hamilton, Ala., 1983—97, North Johnson City Bapt. Ch., Johnson City, Tenn., 1998—2002; pres. Johnson City Cmty. Band, 2000—01, v.p., 1999—2000; upper area representitive East TN Sch. Band & Orch. Assn., 2002—. Mem.: Ala. Bandmasters Assn., East TN Sch. Band & Orch. Assn. (upper area rep 2002—), Johnson City Cmty. Band (condr. 2002—02). Baptist. Avocations: performing music (trumpet player), performing music (trumpet player), computer. Office: David Crockett High School 684 Old State Route 34 Jonesborough TN 37659

SMITH, MICHAEL EDWARD, academic administrator; b. Providence, Sept. 16, 1956; s. Ralph Edward and Ursula Renate (Herzig) S.; m. Eileen Elizabeth Lennon, Sept. 10, 1989; children: Bryan Patrick, Christina Ann. BA in Polit. Sci., R.I. Coll., 1979; MPA, Harvard U., 1984. Program adminstr. R.I. Dept. Edn., Providence, 1978-83; chief of staff R.I. Senate Minority Office, 1984-86; sr. asst. to gov. Gov's. Office, 1986-90; asst. to commr. R.I. Office Higher Edn., 1990-95; asst. to pres. R.I. Coll., 1995—. Cons. Close Up Found., Alexandria, Va., 1980-83; lectr. R.I. Coll., Providence, 1985-92, U. R.I., Kingston, 1991-94, Providence Coll., 1992-97. Editor: The Rhode Island Book, 1980. Active Common Cause of R.I., 1990—, v.p., 1992-95; chmn. Johnston (R.I.) Home Rule Charter Rev. Commn., 1983; chmn. Johnston Rep. Party, 1977-79; mem. Johnston Sch. Com., 1977-81. Republican. Avocations: skiing, travel, gardening, reading, writing. Home: 24 Moccasin Trl Cranston RI 02921-2537 Office: Pres's Office RI Coll Providence RI 02908 E-mail: msmith@ric.edu.

SMITH, MICHAEL ERNEST, archaeologist, educator; b. Olongapo Zambales, The Philippines, Sept. 12, 1953; came to U.S., 1954; s. Dudley Burcham and Esther Lucille (Oyler) S.; m. Cynthia M. Heath, Jan. 19, 1979; children: April Nicole, Heather Colleen. BA in Anthropology, Brandeis U., 1975; MA in Anthropology, U. Ill., 1978, PhD of Anthropology, 1983. Prof. Loyola U., Chgo., 1982-90, SUNY, Albany, 1991—. Dir. Inst. Mesoam. Studies, Albany, 1994-99, Archaeol. Excavations, Cuernavaca, Mex., 1985—; cons. U.S. Libr. Congress, 1997-2001. Author: The Aztecs, 1996, Aztec Imperial Strategies, 1996, Archaeological Excavations at Aztec Sites, 1992, Tlahuica Ceramics, 2002; editor: Economies and Politics in Aztec Realm, 1994, Ancient Civilizations of Mesoamerica: A Reader, 1999, The Postclassic Mesoamerican World, 2002; editl. bd. mem. Ancient Mesoam., 1990—; book rev. editor Latin American Antiquity, 1998-2002. Rsch. grantee NSF, 1995, 86, 89, 92, 2002, Nat. Geog. Soc., 1994, Nat. Endowment Humanities, 1992. Mem. Soc. Am. Archaeology, Am. Anthropol. Assn., Sigma Xi. Office: Dept Anthropology State Univ Ny Albany NY 12222-0001 E-mail: mesmith@csc.albany.edu.

SMITH, MICHAEL JONATHAN, treasury analyst; b. Newark, Mar. 8, 1974; s. James and Merilyn (Hawkins) S. BA Econ., U. Pa., 1996. Jr. analyst Best Foods Fin., Englewood Cliffs, N.J., summer 1994; jr. tax assoc. Best Foods, summer 1995, cash mgmr. analyst, 1996-97, treasury analyst, 1997—. Mem. Treasury Mgmt. Assn., Inroads Alumni Assn. N.J. (vice-chmn. 1997—). Roman Catholic. Avocations: exercise, tutoring. Home: 19 Van Ness Pl Newark NJ 07108-1411

SMITH, MICHAEL PETER, social science educator, researcher; b. Dunkirk, N.Y., Aug. 2, 1942; s. Peter Joseph and Rosalie Barbara (Lipka) S.; m. Patricia Anne Lendway, Aug. 21, 1965. BA magna cum laude, St. Michael's Coll., 1964; MA in Polit. Sci., U. Mass., 1966, PhD in Polit. Sci., 1971. Instr., asst. prof. dept. govt. Dartmouth Coll., Hanover, N.H., 1968-71; asst. prof. dept. polit. sci. Boston U., 1971-74; assoc. prof., prof. dept. polit. sci. Tulane U., New Orleans, 1974-86; prof. community studies U. Calif., Davis, 1986—, chmn. dept. applied behavioral scis., 1986-91. Vis. prof. pub. policy U. Calif., Berkeley, 1981, city planning U. N.C., Chapel Hill, 1982, city planning U. Calif., Berkeley, 1985; vis. scholar in govt. U. Essex, Eng., 1979; vis. scholar polit. and social sci. U. Cambridge, Eng., 1982; vis. scholar Inst. Urban and Regional Devel., U. Calif., Berkeley, 1990, 94 Internat. Ctr. for Advanced Studies, NYU, 1998. Author: The City & Social Theory, 1979, City, State and Market, 1988, Transnational Urbanism, 2001; co-author: Restructuring the City, 1983, California's Changing Faces, 1993; editor: Cities in Transformation, 1984, Breaking Chains, 1991, After Modernism, 1992, Marginal Spaces, 1995, Comparative Urban & Community Research, 1986—; co-editor: The Capitalist City, 1987—, The Bubbling Cauldron, 1995, Transnationalism from Below, 1998, City and Nation: Rethinking Place and Identity, 2001; mem. editl. bd. U. Press Am., 1976—. Mem. Internat. Polit. Sci. Assn., Am. Polit. Sci. Assn., Internat. Sociol. Assn. Rsch. Coms. on Urban & Regional Devel. and Comparative Cmty. Rsch. Office: Dept Human & Cmty Devel Univ Calif Davis CA 95616 E-mail: mpsmith@ucdavis.edu.

SMITH, MICHAEL ROBERT, electro-optical engineer, physicist; b. Tela, Honduras, Aug. 24, 1937; s. Ike Morgan and Edith Helen (Hudson) S.; m., div., remarried Lorraine L. Smith, Apr. 26, 2002; children: Stephen, Monica, Meryl. BME, Ga. Inst. Tech., 1959, MS in Nuclear Engring., 1961; PhD, Case Inst. Tech., 1965. Mem. tech. staff Hughes Rsch. Labs., Malibu, Calif., 1965-68; v.p., dir. rsch. Britt Corp., L.A., 1968-73; sr. staff engr. Singer/Librascope divsn., Glendale, Calif., 1973-78; pres. Exocor Tech., Newbury Park, 1978-95; asst. prof., head physics program Calif. Luth. U., Thousand Oaks, 1990-96; design leader LIGO project Calif. Inst. Tech., Pasadena, 1996—. Contbr. articles to profl. jours.; inventor emergency vehicle warning and traffic control sys., emergency vehicle warning sign, flat electro-optic display panel, high power mirror, laser recording film with opaque coating, pulsed gas laser with radiation cooling, infrared laser photocautery device; 8 U.S. patents; 9 fgn. patents. Greek folk dance tchr. Arts Coun., Thousand Oaks, Calif., 1991-97. Mem. IEEE, Laser Electro-Optic Soc. (chair 1995-97), Sigma Xi, Pi Tau Sigma. Republican. Home: 1611 N Roosevelt Ave Pasadena CA 91104-1927 E-mail: smith@ligo.caltech.edu.

SMITH, MICHAEL VINCENT, surgeon; b. Athens, Ga., Mar. 30, 1957; s. Thomas Allen and Lucile Vivian (Jackson) S.; m. Jeralyn Demetria Scott, July 28, 1979; 1 child, Demetria Joy. BS in Agr., U. Ga., 1979; MD, Med. Coll. of Ga., 1983. Diplomate Nat. Bd. Med. Examiners, Diplomate Am. Bd. Surgery, Am. Bd. Thoracic Surgery. Intern in surgery U. Ky. Med. Ctr., Lexington, 1983-84, resident in surgery, 1984-89, chief resident in gen. surgery, 1988-89; clin. asst. prof. surgery Sch. Medicine Morehouse Coll., Atlanta, 1989-90; assoc. vascular surgeon Midtown Vascular Surgery, 1989-90; attending surgeon Ga. Bapt. Med. Ctr., 1989-90, 96, Crawford Long Hosp. of Emory U., Atlanta, 1989-90, 96, Northlake Regional Med. Ctr./S.W. Cmty. Hosp. and Med., Atlanta, 1989-90, 96; assoc. cardiothoracic surgeon Atlanta Cardiac and Thoracic Surgery Assocs., 1995—; fellow in cardiothoracic surgery Coll. of Medicine Mt. Sinai Med. Ctr., N.Y.C., 1990-91; fellow cardiovascular rsch. U. Mass. Med. Ctr., Worcester, 1991-92, resident cardiothoracic, 1992-95; attending surgeon St. Joseph Hosp., Atlanta, 1996, cardiothoracic surgery chief resident, 1994-95; attending surgeon Piedmont Hosp., 1996, Dunwoody Med. Ctr., Atlanta, 1996, South Fulton Med. Ctr., Atlanta, 1989-90, 96, Southern Regional Med. Ctr., Riverdale, 1996. Mem. ICU S.W. Cmty. Hosp., Atlanta, 1989—90; mem. clin. pathway coms. St. Joseph Hosp., 1996, Atlanta Med. Ctr., 1996, head multidisciplinary lung cancer task force, chief cardiothoracic surgery, dir. thoracic oncology; assoc. med. dir. Premier Healthcare Network, LLC; pres. Ga. Inst. for Lung Cancer Rsch. Sunday sch. tchr. First African Meth. Episcopal Ch., Athens, Ga., 1975-79, Bethel African Meth. Episcopal Ch., Augusta, Ga., 1980-83, St. Paul A.M.E. Ch., Lexington, Ky., 1985-89, St. Philip A.M.E. Ch., 1996; trustee Lovett Sch., 1999, Fernbank Mus. Natural History. Nat. Achievement scholar, 1974; named one of Outstanding Young Men of the Yr., Jaycees, 1983. Fellow ACS; mem. Atlanta Med. Assn., Soc. Thoracic Surgeons, Nat. Med. Assn., Am. Coll. Cardiology, Am. Coll. Physician Execs., Internat. Soc. Minimally Invasive Cardiac Surgery, Med. Assn. Atlanta (bd. dirs. 2000), Alpha Phi Alpha. Avocations: computers, photography, music, reading. Office: 345 Boulevard NE Ste 101 Atlanta GA 31312 E-mail: cardsurg@bellsouth.net.

SMITH, MICHAEL WILLIAM, construction executive, consultant; b. Chgo., Aug. 1, 1944; s. John Joseph and Maryann (Poczatko) Smith; m. June Dolores Wieciech, Sept. 9, 1967; 1 child Michael William II. Student, Wright Coll., 1962-63, Amondsen Coll., 1963-65. Comm. engr. Automatic Elec. Co., Northlake, Ill., 1968-70; asst. engr. elec. design Pioneer Svc. & Engring., Chgo., 1970-72, start-up engr. Kewaunee Nuc. Power Plant, 1972-73; design leader Fluor Power, 1973-75; project mgr. Fluor Nederland BV, Harlem, Netherlands, 1975-77; project leader Fluor Engrs., Houston, 1977-79; project engr. Texamation, LaPorte, 1980-82; cons., project mgr. Shell Devel. Co., Houston, 1985—; pres. ASCI-All Side Constrn. Inc., 1978—. Instr. Houston C.C., 1978; presenter 25th Ann. Honeywell Internat. User Group Symposium, Phoenix, 1998. Recipient Outstanding Paper award, ISA Internat. Program ICC-Computer, 1991. Mem.: NRA (life), Coun. Energy Advisors, Aircraft Owners and Pilots Assn., Am. Radio Relay League (life), Instrumental Soc. Am. (sr.), W. Houston Squadron, W. Tex. Wing, Confederat Air Force (col.).

SMITH, MICHELE, lawyer; b. Ogden, Utah, Feb. 12, 1955; d. Max S. and Grace B. (Gerstman) Smith. BA, SUNY, Buffalo, 1976; JD, U. Chgo., 1979. Law clk. U.S. Ct. Appeals (7th cir.), Chgo., 1979-81; asst. atty. no. dist. U.S. Atty's Office, 1981-89; assoc. gen. counsel Internat. Truck and Engine Corp., 1989-2001, gen. counsel engine group, 2001—. Mem. Am. Corp. Counsel Assn., Phi Beta Kappa. Office: Internat Truck and Engine Corp 4201 N Winfield Rd Warrenville IL 60555 E-mail: michele.smith@nav-international.com.

SMITH, MIEKO KOTAKE, education educator; b. Osaka, Japan, Sept. 19, 1941; arrived in U.S., 1968; d. Kohei and Toshiko Kotake; m. James Allen Smith; children: Sunday Scarbrough, Darius, Stacy, Dorian Blake, Denia Lane, Damon. BA, Tsuda Coll., Tokyo, Japan, 1964; MA, Ednl. Specialist Degree, Kent State U., 1972; PhD, Case Western Res. U., 1980. LCSW ind. social worker Ohio. Student activities coord., internat. student advisor Cleve. State U., 1972—78; rsch. assoc. Case Western Res. U., 1978—81; dir. aftercare Murtis H. Taylor Multi-Svcs. Ctr., 1981—82; dir. rsch. and tng. Hill House Mental Health Rehab. and Rsch., Inc., 1982—87; ind. cons. Beachwood, 1987—90; asst. prof. Cleve. State U., 1990—93, assoc. prof., 1993—2000, prof., 2000—. Cons. Summit County Children Svcs. Bd., Akron, Ohio, 1988—90. Contbr. chapters to books, articles to profl. jours. Bd. dirs., v.p., pers. com. chair Cleve. YWCA, 1975—87; bd. dirs., edn. chair Women's City Club of the Greater Cleve., 1991—96; trustee Help Found., 1994—96; chairperson Women Celebrating the Bicentennial, 1994—97; trustee, com. chair Women's Cmty. Found., 1991—97; bd. governance, chair Multi-Cultural Tng. Inst., 1993—98; trustee Phoenix Soc., 1996—98; bd. govs., first vice chair, program planning and policy com. chair Cuyahoga County Cmty. Mental Health Bd., 1998; bd. dirs. Univ. Christian Movement, 1992—94. Recipient Rsch. Recognition award, Ohio Program Evaluators' Group, 1992; grantee, Ohio Dept. Mental Health, 1985, 1990, 1999, U.S. Dept. Edn., 1999, City of Cleve., 1999, 2000, 2001, U.S. Dept. Health and Human Svcs., 2000. Mem.: AAUP, NASW, Am. Evaluation Assn. D-Liberal. Presbyterian. Avocation: reading. Home: 3766 Concord Dr Beachwood OH 44122 Office: Cleve State Univ 1212 Euclid Ave CB321 Cleveland OH 44115

SMITH, MIRANDA CONSTANCE, writer, educator; b. Denver, June 19, 1944; d. Duncan Campbell and Mabel Elsie (Roller) Clark; m. Charles Ellsworth Smith, May 3, 1963 (div. 1967); m. Armand Cecil Lepage, July 9, 1979 (div. 1982); children: Tagore Duncan Smith, Simone Michelle Lepage. BA in Writing and Lit., Burlington (Vt.) Coll., 1992. Employment counselor San Jose (Calif.) Employment Agy., 1966-68; adminstrv. asst. to pres. Rochdale Coll., Toronto, Ont., Can., 1968-70; tchr. Mylora Farms, Richmond, B.C., Can., 1972; asst. dir. campaign save whales Greenpeace East, Montreal, Can., 1973-74; tchr., grower Rooftop Gardens, 1974-76; dir. urban agrl. Inst. Local Self Reliance, Washington, 1976-78; group leader agrl., waste and recycling Nat. Ctr. Appropriate Tech., Butte, Mont., 1978-79; horticultural dir. Coolidge Farms, Topsfield, Mass., 1981-82; farmer, tchr. Hardwick (Vt.) Organic, 1985-86; cons. Memphremagog Group, Newport, Vt., and Can., 1979-88; writer, tchr. Vt., Mass., 1989-97; tchr. horticulturalist Sullivan Diagnostic Treatment, Harris, N.Y., 1997-99; sr. editor, gardening Creative Home Press, Upper Saddle River, N.J., 1999—. Author: Advanced Home Gardening, 2001, Your Backyard Herb Garden, 1996, 200 Tips for Growing Vegetables in the Northeast, 1995, 200 Tips for Growing Flowers in the Northeast, 1995, Rodale's Pest and Disease Problem Solver, 1995, Backyard Fruits and Berries, 1994, The Real Dirt, Farmers Tell about Organic and Low-Input Farming in the Northeast, 1994, The Expert's Book of Garden Hints, 1993, Rodale's All-New Encyclopedia of Organic Gardening, 1992, The Chemical Free Yard and Garden, 1991, Rodale's Garden Insect, Disease and Weed Identification Guide, 1988, Greenhouse Gardening, 1985. Organizer Lampson Brook Food Group, Belchertown, 1996-97. Mem. New Eng. Small Farm Inst. (bd. dirs. 1976-97, 2001—). Office: 24 Park Way Upper Saddle River NJ 07458

SMITH, MORTON ALAN, lawyer; b. N.Y.C., Mar. 13, 1931; s. David and Augusta S.; m. Nancy, July 2, 1954 (div. July 1974); children: Robynn, Jeffrey, Richard; m. Jane Saffir, June 10, 1979; children: Michael, Richard. BA, U. Fla., 1953; LLD with honors, U. N.C., 1956. Bar: N.Y. 1957, D.C. 1957. Spl. trial atty. Office Chief Counsel IRS, Phila., 1956-58; spl. asst. U.S. Atty. Dist. N.J., 1957; law clk. to judge U.S. Tax Ct., Washington, 1958-60; assoc. Kaye Scholer, N.Y.C., 1960-62, Saul Silverman, N.Y.C., 1962-67; sr. ptnr. Hall, Dickler, Lawler, Kent & Friedman, 1967—. Bd. dirs. Eden Park Health Corp., Albany, N.Y. Contbr. articles to profl. jours. V.p. Rye Brook (N.Y.) Bd. Edn., 1968-73; organizer of incorporation of Village of Rye Brook, 1982, now spl. counsel; bd. dirs. Herbert Birch Sch. for Exceptional Children, N.Y.C., Westchester County United Way, 1991; leadership chmn. United Way Campaign, Rye Brook, 1989-91; mem. Westchester County Housing Implementation Commn.; bd. dirs. Eden Park Health Svcs., Albany, N.Y.; pres. Bocaire Home Owners Assn., Boca Raton, Fla. Mem. ABA (tax sec.). Avocations: golf, skiing, tennis, gardening, reading. Office: Hall Dickler Lawler Kent & Friedman 909 3rd Ave New York NY 10022-4731 E-mail: msmith@halldickler.com.

SMITH, MORTON EDWARD, ophthalmology educator, dean; b. Balt., Oct. 17, 1934; BS, U. Md., 1956, MD, 1960. Bd. cert. Ophthalmology Bd.; lic. physician Mo., Md., Wis. Rotating intern Denver Gen. Hosp., 1960-61; resident, nat. inst. of neorol. diseases and blindness fellow in opthalmology Washington U. Sch. Medicine-Barnes Hosp., 1961-63; NIH spl. fellow in ophthalmic pathology Armed Forces Inst. of Pathology, Washington, 1964; chief resident, instr. ophthalmology Washington U. Sch. Medicine, St. Louis, 1965-66, instr. ophthalmology, 1966-67, asst. prof. ophthalmology and pathology, 1967-69, assoc. prof. ophthalmology and pathology, 1969-75, prof. ophthalmology and pathology, 1975—, asst. dean, 1978-91, assoc. dean, 1991-96, prof. emeritus, assoc. dean emeritus, 1996—; prof. ophthalmology U. Wis., Madison, 1995-2001. Vis. scholar Eye Inst., Columbia Presbyn. Med. Ctr., N.Y.C., 1966; prof./lectr. Montefiore Hosp., Pitts., 1969, U. Ark., 1970, 77, 80, 82, 84, 86, 88, U. Fla., 1972, 81, U. Tex. and Lackland AFB, San Antonio, 1973, U. Colo., 1974, 82, U. Mo., 1974, 79, 80, 88, So. Ill. U., Springfield, 1974, U. Md., 1975, Montreal (Can.) Gen. Hosp., 1975, U. Wis., 1976, 87, 93, U. Pitts., 1977, 83, 87, U. Iowa, 1977, 87, Cleve. Clinic, 1978, Colo. Ophthalmol. Soc., 1978, Brooke Army Hosp., San Antonio, 1979, Wills

Eye Hosp., Phila., 1980, USPHS Hosp., San Francisco, 1981, U. Calif., Davis, 1981, Sinai Hosp., Balt., 1985, 89, 94, U. Calif., San Diego, 1985, Tufts U., Boston, 1985, Cornell U., N.Y.C., 1988, U. Wash., Seattle, 1990, Brown U., Providence, 1990, Vanderbilt U., Nashville, 1991, Duke U., Durham, N.C., 1992; Chandler lectr. Harvard U., 1988; The Lois A. Young-Thomas Meml. lectr. U. Md., 1991; Braley lectr. U. Iowa, 1993; Havener Meml. lectr. Ohio State, 1994. Editor pathology sect.: Perspectives in Ophthalmology, 1977; mem. editl. bd. Ophthalmic Plastic & Reconstructive Surgery, 1986-90; contbr. articles to profl. jours. With USAR M.C., 1958-66. Scholar U. Md., 1958, 59. Fellow Am. Acad. Ophthalmology (ophthalmic pathology com. 1977-83, chmn. ophthalmic com. 1979-83, Honor award for svc. 1981, Sr. Honor award 1992); mem. AMA, Am. Bd. Ophthalmology (diplomate, bd. dirs. 1992—), Assn. for Rsch. in Vision and Ophthalmology (chmn. sect. pathology ann. meeting 1971), Am. Assn. Ophthalmic Pathologists (pres. 1977-80), Assn. Am. Med. Colls. (group med. edn. 1985—), Mo. Med. Assn., Mo. Ophthalmol. Soc., Verhoeff Soc., Theobald Soc., St. Louis Med. Soc., St. Louis Ophthalmol. Soc., Soc. Med. Coll. Dirs. for Continuing Med. Edn., Alpha Omega Alpha (sec.-treas. Wash. U. chpt. 1993-95). Office: PO Box 8096 Saint Louis MO 63156-8096 E-mail: smithm@vision.wustl.edu.

SMITH, MORTON HOWISON, religious organization administrator, educator; b. Roanoke, Va., Dec. 11, 1923; s. James Brookes and Margaret Morton (Howison) S.; m. Lois Virginia Knopf, July 7, 1925; children: Samuel Warfield, Susanne Rochet Margaret. BA, U. Mich., 1947; BD, Columbia Theol. Sem., 1953; ThM, ThD, Free U., Amsterdam, The Netherlands, 1962. Ordained to ministry Presbyn. Ch., 1954. Pastor Springfield-Roller Presbyn. Chs., Carroll County, Md., 1954; prof. bible Belhaven Coll., Jackson, Miss., 1954-63; guest lectr. Westminster Theol. Sem., Phila., 1963-64; prof. Reformed Theol. Sem., Jackson, 1964-79; stated clk. gen. assembly Presbyn. Ch. in Am., Decatur, Ga., 1973-88; prof. systematic theology Greenville Presbyn. Theol. Sem., 1987—, dean faculty, 1987-98. Moderator gen. assembly Presbyn. Ch. Am., 2000-01; advisor to bd. dirs. Greenville (S.C.) Presbyn. Theol. Sem., 1986-98, bd. dirs.; mem. bd. dirs. Presbyn. Jour., Asheville, N.C., 1965-87; lectr. on theology Republic of So. Africa, June-July, 1988, Riga, Latvia, 1992, Budapest, Hungary, 1994, Prague, Czech Republic, 1994, 95, Trinidad and Tobago, 1995, Zlin, Czech Republic, 1998, 99, on missions, Republic of Korea, June-July, 1989, Munkton, Can., 1998, 99, Recife, Brazil, 1998, Reformed Sem., St. Petersburg, Russia. Author: Studies in Southern Presbyterian Theology, 1962, 2d edit. 1987, How Is the Gold Become Dim, 1973, republished 1998, (pamphlet) Reformed Evangelism, 1970, Testimony, 1986, Commentary on the Book of Church Order, 1990, Harmony of the Westminster Confession and Catechisms, 1990, Systematic Theology, 1994; contbr. articles to Reformed Theology in Am., 1985, Did God Create in Six Days?, Written for our Instruction: The Sufficiency of Scripture for All of Life. Trustee Covenant Coll., Lookout Mountain, Tenn., 1982-90. 1st lt. USAAF, 1942-45. Fulbright fellow U.S. Govt., 1958. Mem. N.Am. Presbyn. and Reformed Coun. of Chs. (sec. 1977-92). Avocations: flying, traveling, genealogy. Office: Greenville Presbyn Theol Sem PO Box 690 Taylors SC 29687-0014

SMITH, MURRAY THOMAS, transportation company executive; b. Hudson, S.D., 1939; s. Rex D. and Frances M. Smith; m. Diane R. Cramer, Dec. 4, 1959 (div. June 1994); children: Lisa B., Thomas M., Amy R.; m. Donna Thomas Kjonaas, Jan. 1995. V.p. Overland Express Inc., Indpls., 1978-82; v.p. ops. R.T.C. Transp. Inc., Forest Pk., Ga., 1982-83; with Midwest Coast Transport L.P., Sioux Falls, S.D., 1983—, sr. v.p., 1983-84; pres. Midwest Coast Transport L.P., 1984-89, prin., pres., chief exec. officer, 1989—, also bd. dirs.; pres. Willis Shaw Express, Elm Springs, Ark., 1999—. Bd. dirs. Interstate Carrier Conf., Nat. Perishable Logistics Assn. Bd. dirs. Sioux Valley Hosp., 1991-2000, United Way, Sioux Falls, 1991-2000. Office: Midwest Coast Transport LP 1600 E Benson Rd Sioux Falls SD 57104-0822 E-mail: smithm@mct-comcar.com.

SMITH, MYRON GEORGE, former government official, consultant; b. Terrebonne, Minn., June 9, 1920; s. Adrian G. and Marie E. (Crompe) S.; m. Louise J. Hennessey, May 22, 1944 (div. 1973); children: Michael, Thomas, John, Patricia, Dennis; m. Nguyen Anh My, Aug. 30, 1975; children: Yvette, Bryan. BS in Agrl. Econs. and Soil Sci., U. Minn., 1946. Soil scientist USDA, 1946-50, agrl. ext. advisor, 1950-58; owner No. Ill. Agrl. Svc., 1958-62; with USAID, Dept. State, 1962-84, agrl. sales advisor India, 1962-66, asst. dir. crop prodn. Vietnam, 1966-70, chief agrl. divsn. Indonesia, 1970-73, assoc. dir. Vietnam, 1974-75, chief agrl. divsn. Mali, 1976-81, chief agrl. project mgr. West Africa, 1981-84, agrl. cons. Zaire, 1988-90, Indonesia, 1993-94. Assoc. prof. U. Ark., 1985. 1st lt. USAAF, 1941-45. Decorated Purple Heart, Air medal with 6 oak leaf clusters, DFC; Agr. medal 2d class, Vietnam, 1969, Agr. medal 1st class, Vietnam, 1970, Labor medal 1st class, Vietnam, 1970, Economy medal 2d class, Vietnam, 1970. Mem. Am. Fgn. Service Assn. Home and Office: 309 N Manchester St Arlington VA 22203-1118 E-mail: msmith1051@comcast.net. *Life's many paths selected and ultimate goals achieved can rarely be forseen in the early career years. Life's many, peripatetic journeys are most interesting and rewarding when professional and social self-improvement is pursued continuously and sincerely.*

SMITH, MYRON JOHN, JR. librarian, author; b. Toledo, May 3, 1944; s. Myron John and Marion Oliva (Herbert) S.; 1 son, Myron John III. Student, Coll. Steubenville, 1962; AB, Ashland Coll., 1966; MLS, Western Mich. U., 1967; MA, Shippensburg U., 1969; postgrad., U. Wis., Purdue U.; LittD, Cardinal Newman Coll., 1982. Rsch. librarian G.W. Blunt White Libr., Mystic Seaport, Conn., 1967-68; asst. librarian Western Md. Coll., Westminster, 1969-72; libr. dir. Huntington (Ind.) Pub. Libr., 1972-76; prof. history and libr. sci., dir. librs. Benedum Libr. Salem-Teikyo U.; dir., then assoc. dir. aviation program Salem (W.Va.) Coll., 1976-90; prof. history and libr. sci., libr. dir. Tusculum Coll., Greeneville, Tenn., 1990—. Mem. Am. Com. on History 2d World War, Assn. for Bibliography of History Author: American Naval Bibliography Series, 1972-74, Huntington Centennial Handbook, 1973, The Sophisticated Lady: The Battleship Indiana in World War II, 1973, World War II at Sea: A Bibliography of Sources in English, 1976, (with Robert Webber) Sea Fiction Guide, 1976, The Cloak and Dagger Bibliography, 1976, World War I in the Air, 1977, Air War Chronology 1939-45, 1977, Air War Bibliography Series, 1977—, The Mountain State Battleship: USS West Virginia, 1979, Air War Southeast Asia, 1979, The Soviet Navy, 1941-1978, 1979, The Secret Wars Series, 1980-81, The Soviet Air and Strategic Rocket Forces, 1941-1980, 1981, The Soviet Army, 1941-1980, 1981, Equestrian Studies: The Salem College Guide, 1981, The Cloak and Dagger Fiction Guide: An Annotated Guide to Spy Thrillers, 1981, (with Terry White) 3d edit., 1994, The Mountaineer Battlewagon: USS West Virginia, 1982, The Keystone Battlewagon: USS Pennsylvania, 1983, The Golden State Battlewagon: USS California, 1983, Watergate: A Bibliography, 1983 World War II: Mediterranean and European Theaters, 1984, The United States Navy and Coast Guard, 1946-1983: A Bibliography of English Language Works and 16mm Films, 1984, U.S. Television Network News: A Guide to Sources in English, 1984, Battleships and Battlecruisers, 1884-1984: A Bibliography and Chronology, 1985, Baseball: A Comprehensive Bibliography, 1986, 99th Infantry Division Bibliography, 1986, The Airline Bibliography: The Salem College Guide to Sources on Commercial Aviation, Vol. I, The United States, 1986, Vol. II, Airliners and Foreign Carriers, 1987, Passenger Airliners of the United States, 1926-86: A Pictorial Guide, 1987, rev. edit. through 1991, 1991, 3d rev. edit. through 1995, 4th revised edit., 2002, Brooklyn/Los Angeles Dodgers: A Bibliography, 1987, American Warplane Bibliography, 1989, Volunteer Battlewagon: The U.S.S. Tennessee (BB-43), 1989; editor: Sports Teams and Players Bibliography Series, 1987, Battle and Leaders Bibliography Series, 1988, 100 Years of Opportunity: A Pictorial History of Salem College, 1888-1988, 1988, Pro Football Bio-Bibliography, 1920-1988, 1989, Pearl Harbor, December 7, 1941: An Annotated Bibliography, 1991, Battles of the Coral Sea and Midway, 1942: A Bibliography, 1991, World War II at Sea, 1974-1989: A Bibliography, 1990, Professional Football: The Official Pro Football Hall of Fame Bibliography, 1993, Baseball: A Comprehensive Bibliography-1st Supplement: 1985-1991, 93, The College Football Bibliography, 1994, Glimpses of Tusculum College: A Pictorial History, 1794-1994, 1994, Baseball: A Comprehensive Bibliography-2d Supplement: 1992-1997, 1998, The Airline Encyclopedia, 1909-2000, 2002, The Airline Bibliography, 2002; contbr. articles to various jours. Recipient Nelson Ross award Profl. Football Rsch. Assn., 1993; 1st Am. recipient Richard Franck Gold medal Bibliothek für Zeitgeschichte, Stuttgart, Fed. Rep. Germany, 1981. Mem. ALA, U.S. Naval Inst., U.S. Mil. Inst., U.S. Air Force Found., Assn. Bibliog. of History (pres. 1981-82), Alliance of Librs. in Northeast Tenn. (pres. 1997—), Beta Phi Mu, Phi Alpha Theta. Clubs: Optimist. Office: Tusculum Coll PO Box 5005 Greeneville TN 37743-0001

SMITH, NANCY ANGELYNN, federal agency administrator; b. Nashville, Mar. 28, 1950; d. Russell Monroe and Louise (Stephenson) Smith; m. Richard Christian Egan, Jan. 1, 1999. Student, Blair Acad. Music, 1966, Am. Internat. Acad. Europe, 1970; BA in Psychology with distinction, Rhodes Coll., 1972; MS with honors, U. Tenn., 1974; cert. in acctg., U. New Orleans, 1985; degree in acctg. with honors, U. S.C., 1987. Contract adminstr. State of Tex. Dept. Health and Human Svcs., Houston, 1976-78; dept. Head Coop. Edn. Program No. Va. C.C., Annandale, 1978-81; revenue agt. IRS Dept. of Treasury, Nashville, 1988-99. Faculty rep. Faculty Senate No. Va. C.C., Annandale, 1979—81. Contbr. articles to profl. jours. Vol. Voter Registration program, Denver, 1981—84, Adopt-a-Sch., Nashville, 1993—97, Tenn. State Guard; disaster relief coord. Ky. and Tenn., 1998—99, Red Cross Inst., 1976—78, VITA, 1990—95; vol. Congresswoman Pat Shroeder, Denver, 1981—84, Al Gore for Senate, Nashville, 1987—88, Federica Pena for Mayor, Denver, 1981—; bd. dirs. No. Va. C.C., Annandale, 1978—81; vol. DAR. Mem.: Profl. Mayors Assn., Cert. Fraud Examiners Assn., Gamma Beta Phi, Alpha Omicron Pi (chmn. bd. dirs. Colo. chpt.), Omicron Nu (hon.), Phi Kappa Phi (hon.). Avocations: painting, skeet shooting, camping, historical battlefields.

SMITH, NANCY HOHENDORF, sales and marketing executive; b. Detroit, Jan. 30, 1943; d. Donald Gerald and Lucille Marie (Kopp) Hohendorf; m. Richard Harold Smith, Aug. 21, 1978 (div. Jan. 1984). BA, U. Detroit, 1965; MA, Wayne State U., 1969. Customer rep. Xerox Corp., Detroit, 1965-67, mktg. rep. Univ. Microfilms subs. Ann Arbor, Mich., 1967-73, mktg. coord., 1973-74, mgr. dir. mktg., 1975-76, mgr. mktg. Can., 1976-77, major account mktg. exec. Conn., 1978-79, New Haven, 1979-80, account exec. State of N.Y. N.Y.C., 1981, N.Y. region mgr. customer support Greenwich, Conn., 1982, N.Y. region sales ops. mgr., 1982, State of Ohio account exec. Columbus, 1983, new bus. sales mgr. Dayton, Ohio, 1983, major accounts sales mgr., 1984, info. systems sales and support mgr., quality specialist Detroit, 1985-87, new product launch mgr., ops. quality mgr., 1988, dist. mktg. mgr., 1989-92, major accounts sales mgr., 1992—; graphics arts industry sales mgr., 1998—. Reg. graphic arts industry cons. mgr., 1999. Named to Outstanding Young Women of Am., 1968, Outstanding Bus. Woman, Dayton C. of C., 1984, Women's Inner Circle of Achievement, 1990. Mem. NAFE, Am. Mgmt. Assn., Women's Econ. Club Detroit, Detroit Inst. Arts Founders' Soc., Detroit Hist. Soc., Detroit Hist. Soc. Republican. Roman Catholic. Avocations: interior decorating, reading, music, art. Home: 6462 West Oaks Dr West Bloomfield MI 48324-3269 Office: Xerox Corp 300 Galleria Officentre Southfield MI 48034-4700

SMITH, NANCY LEE, communications official; b. Junction City, Kans., May 10, 1953; d. James Emerson and Donna Lee (Cousins) Smith. BA with hons., Stephens Coll., Columbia, Mo., 1975; MPA with hons., Am. U., 1990. Appt. sec. to chief of staff The White House, Washington, 1975; appt. sec. to sec. of def. Dept. Def., 1975-77; sec., office mgr. to various congressmen U.S. Ho. of Reps., 1977-83; Congl. specialist U.S. Geol. Survey, 1983-84; staff asst. to sec. of land and mineral mgmt. U.S. Dept. Interior, 1984-85; Congl. liaison officer Office of Surface Mining, Reclamation and Enforcement, 1985-95, comms. officer, 1995-2000; group mgr. legis. affairs Bur. of Land Mgmt., 2000—. Mem.: Pi Alpha Alpha, Alpha Lambda Delta. Avocations: white-water rafting, photography, reading, origami, fitness. Office: Bur of Land Mgmt 1849 C St NW # 4015 Washington DC 20240-0001

SMITH, NATHAN MCKAY, library and information sciences educator; b. Wendell, Idaho, Apr. 22, 1935; s. M. Blair and Vaunda H. (Hawkes) S.; m. Joyce A. Carman, July 5, 1953; children: Nathan M., Jeffrey M., Pamela J., Russell A., Kristen E. BS in Secondary Edn., Eastern Oreg. Coll., 1961; MS in Gen. Sci., Oreg. State U., 1965; MLS, Brigham Young U., 1969, PhD in Zoology, 1972. Tchr. sci. Dalles Jr. High Sch., The Dalles, Oreg., 1961-64; asst. sci. libr. Brigham Young U., Provo, Utah, 1968, life sci. libr., 1970-73, prof. Sch. Libr. and Info. Sci., 1973-82, dir. Sch. Libr. and Info. Sci., 1982-93, life sci. libr. Sch. Libr. and Info. Sci., 1993-97. Cons. Weber County Library, Ogden, Utah, 1980— ; back issues sec. Herpetologists League, 1976-81 Served to sgt. USAF, 1953-57. Yr. scholar NSF Acad., 1964; fellow NDEA Title IV, 1969; recipient research award Assn. Library and Info. Sci. Edn., 1983 Mem. ALA (councilor legis. council), Assn. Library Info. Sci. Edn., Mountain Plains Library Assn., Utah Library Assn. (exec. bd., pres.), N. Am. Soc. Adlerian Psychology, Phi Kappa Phi, Sigma Xi, Beta Phi Mu Mem. Lds Ch. Home: 1606 Locust Ln Provo UT 84604-2806 E-mail: nsmith@networld.com.

SMITH, NEAL EDWARD, congressman; b. Hedrick, Iowa, Mar. 23, 1920; s. James N. and Margaret M. (Walling) S.; m. Beatrix Havens, Mar. 23, 1946; children— Douglas, Sharon. Student, U. Mo., 1945-46, Syracuse U., 1946-47; JD, Drake U., 1950. Bar: Iowa 1950. Farmer, Iowa, 1937—; sole practice Des Moines, 1950-58; atty. 50 sch. bds. in Iowa, 1951-58; asst. county atty. Polk County, Iowa, 1951; mem. 86th-103rd Congresses from 4th Dist., 1959—. Chmn. Polk County Bd. Social Welfare, 1954-56; pres. Young Democratic Clubs Am., 1953-55. Served with AUS, World War II. Decorated Air medal with 4 oak leaf clusters, Purple Heart, nine battle stars. Mem. Am. Bar Assn., Farm Bur., Farmers Union, DAV. Clubs: Masons. Home: Plaza Box 90 300 Walnut Des Moines IA 50309 Office: Davis Brown Koehn Shors The Financial Ctr 666 Walnut St Ste 2500 Des Moines IA 50309-3904

SMITH, NEALE DAINE, physician; b. Seattle, July 30, 1947; MD, U. Wash., 1973. Diplomate Am. Bd. Internal Medicine, Am. Bd. Cardiovascular Disease. Intern Swedish Hosp. Med. Ctr., Seattle, 1973-74; resident in medicine U. N.Mex. Affil. Hosp., Albuquerque, 1974-76; fellow cardiovasc. disease U. Oreg., Portland, 1976-78; chief divsn. cardiovasc. disease Providence Med. Ctr. Everett, Wash. Fellow Am. Coll. Cardiology. Office: 1330 Rockefeller Ave Ste 540 Everett WA 98201-1677 E-mail: elaen@aol.com.

SMITH, NEIL, geography educator; b. Leith, Scotland, July 18, 1954; came to U.S., 1974; s. Ronald Alexander and Nancy (Williamson) S. Student, U. Pa., 1974-75; BSc with honours, U. St. Andrews, Scotland, 1977; PhD, Johns Hopkins U., 1982. Asst. prof. Columbia U., N.Y.C., 1982-86, Rutgers U., New Brunswick, N.J., 1986-88, assoc. prof., 1988-90, prof. geography, 1990-99, acting dir. Ctr. Critical Analysis of Contemporary Culture; dist. prof. CUNY Grad. Ctr., 2000—, dir. Ctr. for Place Culture and Politics. Vis. rsch. fellow Australian Nat. U., 1986; adj. asst. prof. Princeton U., 1988; vis. rsch. prof. U. Queensland, 1988; vis. prof. U. Utrecht, 1990. Author: Uneven Development. Nature, Capital and the Production of Space, 1984, Geography, Social Welfare and Underdevelopment, 1977, New Urban Frontier: Gentrification and the R. City, 1996, Gentrification of the City, 1986, (with Anne Godleweba) Geography and Empire, 1994; mem. editorial bds. of several jours.; contbr. numerous articles to profl. jours. and newspapers. Recipient J.S. Guggenheim fellow, 1995-96. Mem. Am. Authors Assn., Assn. Am. Geographers, Soc. Historians of Am. Fgn. Rels. Home: 103 Lawrence Ave Highland Park NJ 08904-1850

SMITH, NELSON DAVID, artist educator; b. Detroit, Apr. 29, 1955; s. Curtis E. and Mary D. Smith. BFA, Coll. Wooster, 1977; MFA in Painting, Cranbrook Acad. Art, 1980. Artist, designer Nelson Smith, Oak Park, Mich., 1977—; pres., co-dir. Contemporary Art Inst. Detroit, 1990-94. Adj. prof. Lawrence Tech. U., Southfield, Mich., 1991—, Mary Grove Coll., Detroit, 1992—; bd. pres. Contemporary Art Inst. Detroit, 1990-94; com. mem. Detroit Focus Gallery, 1994-97. Author, designer: (book) Victims of Circumstance, 1987, (multi-media work) Psychological Gravity, 1993, (performance/installation work) Electricity, 1995, Human Radiation, 1996, Forced Air, 1999; one-man show Bunting Gallery, Royal Oak, Mich., 1997; exhibiting artist at various galleries, mus., and in Creative Contact on Internet. Panelist Mich. Coun. for Art & Cultural Affairs, Detroit, 1993; design editor Detroit Focus Quar., 1989-93; co-producer Ear Whacks! New Music Festival, Contemporary Art Inst., Detroit, 1993, 94; curator, producer "Short & Sweet", Detroit Focus, 1996, 97—. Recipient Creative artist grant Mich. Coun. for Arts, 1987, Prodn. grant Art Matters Inc., 1989, Creative Artist grant Mich. Coun. for Art/Cultural Arts, 1993, 94, Mich. Coun. for Art/Artserve Mich., 2000, Sound residency Harvest Works, 1996. Mem. Detroit Artists Market, Coll. Art Assn., Performance Network. Home: 8100 W Nine Mile Rd Oak Park MI 48237-2341 E-mail: ndsmith1@ix.netcom.com.

SMITH, NEWMAN DONALD, retired financial executive; b. Chesterville, Ont., Can., Dec. 26, 1936; s. Clarke Harold and Ethelwyn Irene (Cross) S.; chartered acct., 1961; certified mgmt. acct., 1966; chartered Inst. of Secretaries, 1967; m. Mary Elizabeth Murdoch, June 27, 1964; children: Clarke Murdoch, Brian Newman. With Coopers & Lybrand Inc., Ottawa, Ont., 1955-62; sec.-treas. Deloro Smelting & Refining Co. Ltd., Ottawa, 1963-69, M.J. O'Brien Ltd., Ottawa, 1963-69; exec. sec. Andres Wines Ltd. and subs., Winona, Ont., 1969-94 , CFO, 1980-94, sr. exec. v.p. ops., 1978-94, ret.; dir. Les Vins Andres du Quebec Ltee., Peller Wines of Calif., Watleys Ltd., Superior Wines Ltd., Andres Wines (B.C.) Ltd., Andres Wines (Alta.) Ltd., Andres Wines Atlantic Ltd.; bd. dirs., chmn. Strewn Estate Winery. Fellow Chartered Inst. Secs.; mem. Fin. Execs. Inst., Chartered Accts., Hamilton Golf and Country Club, Hamilton Club. Home: 463 Ontario St Ancaster ON Canada L9G 3E1

SMITH, NICK, congressman, farmer; b. Addison, Mich., Nov. 5, 1934; s. LeGrand John and Blanche (Nichols) S.; m. Bonnalyn Belle Atwood, Jan. 1, 1960; children: Julianna, Bradley, Elizabeth, Stacia. BA, Mich. State U., 1957; MS, U. Del., 1959. Radio & TV farm editor Sta. WDEL, Wilmington, Del., 1957-59; radio editor Sta. KSWD, Wichita Falls, Tex., 1959-60; capt. intelligence USAF, 1959-61; mem. twp. bd. Somerset Twp., Addison, 1962-68; asst. dep. adminstr. USDA, Washington, 1972-74; state rep. Mich. Ho. of Reps., Lansing, 1978-82; state senator Mich. State Senate, 1982-92; mem. U.S. Congress from 7th Mich. dist, 1993—, mem. agr., sci., and internat. rels. coms. Chmn. Mich. Senate Agrl. Com., 1982-92, Mich. Senate Corrections Appropriation Com., 1984-90, Mich. Senate Mil. Affairs Com., 1984-90, Mich.Senate Fin. Com., 1990-92 Del. Am. Assembly on World Population & Hunger, Washington, 1973; nat. del. on U.S.-Soviet Cooperation and Trade, 1991; former trustee Somerset Congl. Ch. Capt. USAF, 1959-61. Fellow Kellogg Found., 1965; named Hon. FFA State Star Farmer, 1987, SCF Conservator of Yr. Hillsdale County, 1988. Mem. Mich. Farm Bur. (bd. dirs.), Jackson C. of C., Mich. State U. Alumni Club, Masons. Republican. Office: US House of Reps 2305 Rayburn House Office Bldg Washington DC 20515-2207 also: 110 First St Ste A Jackson MI 49201*

SMITH, NINA, economics educator; b. Sdr Broby, Denmark, Oct. 17, 1955; d. Laurits and Birte Rasmussen; m. Valdemar Smith, Aug. 17, 1978; children: Hans Martin, Christian, Anne Marie, Frederik. Candidate Econs., U. Aarhus, Denmark, 1981. Asst. prof. Inst. Econs. U. Aarhus, 1981-82, Sonderborg (Denmark) Sch. Econs. and Bus. Adminstrn., 1982-86; assoc. prof. econs. Inst. Polit. Sci. U. Aarhus, 1986-90, Econ. Inst., U. Aarhus, 1990-93, prof., 1993—. Contbr. articles to profl. jours. Office: Aarhus Sch Bus Fuglesangs Alle 20 DK 8210 Aarhus V Denmark E-mail: nina@asb.dk.

SMITH, NINA MARIA, mental health nurse, administrator, consultant; b. Bethesda, Md., July 15, 1950; d. Albert Henry and Magdalena (Portusach) Geiken; m. Robert John Smith, Nov. 18, 1972; children: Cara Anne, Rachel Marie. ADN, Tarrant County Jr. Coll., 1984; BA in Psychology, U. Md., 1972; MEd, Tex. Christian U., 1990. Charge nurse Psychiat. Inst. Ft. Worth; adolescent program coord. Community Psychiat. Ctr. Oak Bend, Ft. Worth; adminstr. Life Ctrs.; dir. nursing Community Psychiat. Ctr. Oak Bend; adminstr. Total Home Health Care; dir. clin. svcs. Mountain Crest Hosp., Ft. Collins, Colo., 1992-94; nat. dir. psychiat. home svcs. Western Med. Svcs., 1994-96; owner, cons. Integrated Behavioral Health Cons., 1996—; nat. assoc. dir. Behavioral Health Staff Builders, 1998—; divsnl. dir. ops. West/Ctrl. Staff Builders, 2000—. Mem. psychiat. symposium planning com. U. Tex., Arlington, 1988-91; presenter in field. Guest editor, reviewer Continum: Devel. in Ambulatory Mental Health Care, 1996; co-author: Behavior Management Guide for Home Care, 1997; contbr. to Handbook of Home Healthcare Administration, 2d edit., 1997, Mental Health Nursing: The Nurse Pt Journey, 2nd edit., 1998, Behavioral Health Services Delivery: Models & Methods, 1998, Home Care Nursing Handbook, 3rd edit., 1998, Orientation to Home Care, 2nd edit., 1998; mem. editl. bd.: Home Healthcare Nurse, 1998—. Mem. Am. Psychiat. Nurses Assn., Am. Assn. Partial Hosps., Partial Hosp. Assn. Colo. (pres. 1994-95), Assn. Ambulatory Behavioral Healthcare (nat. bd. dirs. 1995—), Home Healthcare Nurses Assn. Home: 7701 Park Ridge Cir Fort Collins CO 80528-8909

SMITH, NOEL WILSON, psychology educator; b. Marion, Ind., Nov. 2, 1933; s. Anthony and Mary Louise (Wilson) S.; m. Marilyn C. Coleman, June 17, 1954; children: Thor and Lance (twins). AB, Ind. U., 1955, PhD, 1962; MA, U. Colo., 1958. Asst. prof. psychology Wis. State U., Platteville, 1962-63, SUNY, Plattsburgh, 1963-66, assoc. prof., 1966-71, prof., 1971-95, prof. emeritus, 1995—; courtesy prof. U. Fla., 1997—. Author: Greek and Interbehavioral Psychology, 1990, rev. edit., 1993, An Analysis of Ice Age Art: Its Psychology and Belief, 1992, Current Systems in Psychology: History, Theory, Research, and Application, 2001; co-author: The Science of Psychology: Interbehavioral Survey, 1975; sr. editor: Reassessment in Psychology, 1983; editor: Interbehavioral Psychology newsletter, 1970-77; contbr. articles to profl. jours. Fellow APA; mem. AAUP (pres. SUNY coun. 1980-82), Am. Psychol. Soc., Cheiron Internat. Soc. History of Behavior Sci., Sigma Xi. Home: 3027 Willow Green Sarasota FL 34235 Office: SUNY Dept Psychology Beaumont Hall Plattsburgh NY 12901

SMITH, NONA COATES, academic administrator; b. West Grove, Pa., Apr. 1, 1942; d. John Truman and Elizabeth Zane (Trumbo) Coates; m. David Smith, Oct. 12, 1968 (div. May 1986); children: Kirth Ayrl, Del Kerry, Michael Sargent, Sherri Lee. BA, West Chester (Pa.) U., 1988; PhD, Temple U., 1998. Legal sec. Gawthrop & Greenwood, West Chester, 1968-73, MacElree, Gallagher, O'Donnell, West Chester, 1981-84; social sec. Mrs. John B. Hannum, Unionville, Pa., 1975-81; rsch. asst. West Chester U., 1984-88, cons., 1988; dir. sponsored rsch. Bryn Mawr (Pa.) Coll., 1989—, chair rsch./tchg. evaluation, 1993-95. Treas. Kennett Vol. Fire Co., Kennett Square, Pa., 1984-86; founding mem. Colls. of Liberal Arts-Sponsored Programs. Recipient Scholastic All-Am. award U.S. Achievement Acad., 1988, Rsch. award Truman Libr., 1992, Goldsmith Rsch. award Harvard U., 1993; fellow Truman Dissertation, 1997—. Fellow Phi Alpha Theta; mem. AAUW, Am. Hist. Assn., Soc. Historians of Am. Fgn. Rels., Nat. Coun. Univ. Rsch. Adminstrs. (mem. nat. conf. com. 1995-96). Republican. Presbyterian. Avocations: reading, gardening, travel, cultural events. Home: PO Box 239 Unionville PA 19375-0239 Office: Bryn Mawr Coll 101 N Merion Ave Bryn Mawr PA 19010-2859

SMITH, NORMAN CLARK, fund raising and non-profit management consultant; b. Hartford, Conn., Jan. 2, 1917; s. Raymond W. and Elinor (Smith) S. AB, Middlebury Coll., 1939; postgrad., Hartford Coll. Law, Trinity Coll. Tchr. Loomis Sch., 1945-50, adminstr., tchr., 1952-53, asst. bus. mgr., 1953-55, bus. mgr., 1955-58, controller, 1958-63; treas. Vassar Coll., 1963-64; v.p. devel., planning Emory U., Atlanta, 1964-76; v.p. univ. devel. U. Del., 1976-79. Bd. dirs., past chmn. bd. Nat. Soc. Fund Raising Execs.; past trustee LoomisInst., Watkinson Sch.; past chmn. Ga. Conservancy; past pres. Mashantucket Land Trust of Southeastern Conn.; trustee emeritus, pas pres. Conn. River Mus., Essex; mem. Conn. State Coun. on Environ. Quality, Naval War Coll. Found. (mem. The Navy League); mem. citizens adv. coun. Project Oceanology; trustee Conn. Antiquarian and Landmarks Soc.; former mem. Nat. Exec. Svc. Corps.; past pres. Groton Edn. Found. Capt. USNR, 1941-45, 50-52; commanding officer Conn. State Naval Militia, 1946-50. Decorated Navy Cross. Mem. Chi Psi, Omicron Delta Kappa. Clubs: Rotary. Home and Office: 161 Pequot Ave Mystic CT 06355-1728 E-mail: nsmith6010@aol.com.

SMITH, NORMAN OBED, physical chemist, educator; b. Winnipeg, Man., Can., Jan. 23, 1914; came to U.S., 1950, naturalized, 1958; s. Ernest and Ruth (Kilpatrick) S.; m. Anna Marie O'Connor, July 1, 1944; children: Richard Obed, Graham Michael, Stephen Housley. B.Sc., U. Man., 1935, M.Sc., 1936; PhD, NYU, 1939. Teaching fellow NYU, 1936-39; mem. faculty dept. chemistry U. Man., Winnipeg, 1939-50, asst. prof., 1946-49, assoc. prof., 1949-50, Fordham U., N.Y.C., 1950-65, prof. chemistry, 1965-84, prof. emeritus, 1984—, chmn. dept., 1974-78. Sr. phys. chemist Arthur D. Little, Inc., Cambridge, Mass., 1957; indsl. cons. Author: (with others) The Phase Rule and Its Applications, 1951, Chemical Thermodynamics, A Problems Approach, 1967, Elementary Statistical Thermodynamics, A Problems Approach, 1982; contbr. to: Ency. Brit, 1974. Fellow Chem. Inst. Can.; mem. Am. Chem. Soc., Asso. Can. Coll. Organists, Am. Guild Organists (dir. chpt. 1964-66, 79-82, 91-92), Sigma Xi, Phi Lambda Upsilon. Home: 811 E Central Rd Apt 112 Arlington Heights IL 60005-3293

SMITH, NORMAN RAYMOND, university president; b. Toronto, Ont., Can., Oct. 24, 1946; s. William Raymond and Jeanne (Malin) S.; m. Susan Robinson, Dec. 26, 1981; 1 child, Caroline Robinson. BS, Drexel U., 1969, MBA, 1971; EdD, Harvard U., 1984; HLD (hon.) (hon.) , Phila. U., 2001, Wagner Coll., 2002. Assoc. dean students Drexel U., Phila., 1971-73; dean of students, professor Phila. Univ., 1973-78; asst. dean Harvard Grad. Sch. Edn., Cambridge, Mass., 1978-80, John F. Kennedy Sch. Govt., Harvard U., Cambridge, 1980-84; exec. v.p. Moore Coll. Art, Phila., 1984-87; pres. Wagner Coll., S.I., NY, 1988—2002, pres. emeritus, 2002—; pres. Richmond, The Am. Internat. Univ. in London, 2002—. Dir. Dime Bancorp; assoc. Harvard U. Philosophy of Edn. Rsch. Ctr., Cambridge, 1987—. Author: Selecting the Right College, 6th edit., 2000. Chair mayor's cabinet transition search City of Boston, 1983-84; trustee N.Y. Coun. of Ind. Colls. and Univs., 1994-97. Lt. U.S. Army, 1969-73. Recipient U. medal Drexel U., 1993, Pres.'s medal NYU, 1994. Mem. Ind. Coll. Fund N.Y. (sec.-treas.), Harvard Club of N.Y.C., Richmond County Country Club. Home: Orchard House Queens Rd Richmond-upon-Thames TW10 6JP England Office: Richmond U Queens Rd Richmond-upon-Thames TW10 6JP England

SMITH, NUMA LAMAR, JR. lawyer; b. Rock Hill, S.C., Nov. 22, 1915; s. Numa Lamar and Grace (Hanes) S.; m. Mary Catherine Gray, Mar. 24, 1941; children: Patricia Gray (dec.), Elizabeth Hanes, Lamar Douglas. AB, Furman U., 1938; LL.B. with distinction, Duke U., 1941. Bar: N.Y. 1942, D.C. 1946. Assoc. firm White & Case, N.Y.C., 1941-42, Miller & Chevalier, Washington, 1946-49, partner, 1949-83, counsel, 1983—; bd. visitors, 1973-83. Sr. fellow Duke U. Law Sch., 1979-80 Assoc. editor: Duke Law Jour, 1940-41. Served with U.S. Army, 1942-46; with Judge Adv. Gen. Corps 1944-46. Recipient Gen. Excellence award Furman U., 1938 Fellow Am. Bar Found.; mem. ABA, D.C. Bar Assn., Am. Law Inst., Duke Law Alumni Assn. (pres. 1967-69), Order of Coif, Met. Club (Washington), Burning Tree Club (Bethesda, Md.), Washington Golf Club (Arlington, Va.), The Club at Pelican Bay, Sigma Alpha Epsilon. Baptist. Home: 7515 Pelican Bay Blvd Naples FL 34108-6518

SMITH, OLLEN BRUTON, sports association executive; divorced; 4 children. Founder, exec. officer, dir. Lowe's Motor Speedway , Concord, NC, 1959—61, CEO, dir., 1975—; CEO, pres., dir. Atlanta Motor Speedway, 1990—; CEO, chmn. Speedway Motorsports, 1994—; chmn., pres. Bristol Motor Speedway, 1996—. Sears Point Raceway, 1996—. Tex. Motor Speedway, 1996—; owner, operator Town & County Ford, Inc. Office: Speedway Motorsports 5555 Concorde Pkwy S Concord NC 28027

SMITH, ORIN ROBERT, chemical company executive; b. Newark, Aug. 13, 1935; s. Sydney R. and Gladys Emmett (DeGroff) S.; m. Stephanie M. Bennett-Smith; children: Lindsay, Robin; 1 stepchild, Brendan. BA in Econometrics, Brown U., 1957; MBA in Mgmt., Seton Hall U., 1964; PhD in Econs. (hon.), Centenary Coll., 1991; LLD (hon.), Monmouth Coll., 1994. Various sales and mktg. mgmt. positions Allied Chem. Corp., Morristown, N.J., 1959-69; dir. sales and mktg. Richardson-Merrell Co., Phillipsburg, 1969-72; with M&T Chems., Greenwich, Conn., 1972-77, pres., 1975-77; with Engelhard Minerals & Chems. Corp., Menlo Park, Edison, N.J., 1977-81, corp. sr. v.p., 1978-81, pres. div. minerals and chems., 1978-81, also bd. dirs., 1979-81, pres., dir. various U.S. subs., 1979-81; exec. v.p., pres. div. minerals and chems. Engelhard Corp., 1981-84, bd. dirs., 1981—, pres., CEO, Iselin, N.J., 1984-95, chmn., CEO, 1995—; also bd. dirs. Bd. dirs. Summit Bank Co., The Summit Bancorp, Vulcan Materials Co., PE Corp., Ingersoll-Rand Corp., Engelhard Corp., Mfrs. Alliance. Trustee N.J. State C. of C., Inst. for Tech. Advancement; mem. bd. overseers N.J. Inst. Tech.; trustee Plimoth Plantation; 1st vice chmn. bd. trustees Centenary Coll.; past dir. Minorco, La. Land and Exploration Co.; past trustee Henry R. Kessler Found., Inc.; past chmn. Ind. Coll. Fund N.J.; past dir.-at-large U. Maine Pulp and Paper Found. Lt. (j.g.) USN, 1957-59. Mem. Chem. Mfrs. Assn. (past bd. dirs.), Econ. Club (N.Y.C.), Union League Club (N.Y.C.), Duxbury Yacht Club, New Bedford Yacht Club, N.Y. Yacht Club. Office: Engelhard Corp 101 Wood Ave S Iselin NJ 08830-2703

SMITH, ORVILLE AUVERNE, physiology educator; b. Nogales, Ariz., June 16, 1927; s. Orville Auverne and Bess (Gill) S.; m. Clara Jean Smith; children— Nanette, Marcella. BA in Psychology, U. Ariz., 1949; MA, Mich. State U., 1950, PhD, 1953. Instr. psychology Mich. State U., East Lansing, 1953-54; fellow U. Pa., Phila., 1954-56; trainee dept. physiology and biophysics U. Wash., Seattle, 1956-58, instr. physiology and biophysics, 1958-59, asst. prof., 1959-61, 62-63; asst. dir. Regional Primate Research Ctr., 1962-69, assoc. prof., 1963-67, prof., 1967-97; assoc. dir. Regional Primate Research Center, 1969-71, dir., 1971-88, prof. emeritus, 1997—. Contbr. articles to profl. jours. Mem. Am. Physiol. Soc., Am. Soc. Primatologists (pres. 1977-79), Internat. Congress Physiol. Scis., Am. Assn. Anatomists, AAAS, Pavlovian Soc. N.Am. (pres. 1977-78), Internat. Primatological Soc., AAUP, Neurosci. Soc. Home: 30311 201st Ct SE Kent WA 98042-5920 Office: U Wash Nat Primate Rsch Ctr PO Box 357330 Seattle WA 98195-7330

SMITH, OSCAR WILLIAM, nursing home administrator; b. Odem, Tex., Sept. 21, 1933; s. Christopher Columbus, Jr. and Myrtle (Younts) Smith; m. Peggy June Hoefar, June 2, 1962 (wid. Mar. 1994); children: Rhonda, Mike, Billy (dec.). Student, Del Mar Coll., 1970-71, San Jacinto Coll., 1974-75. Lic. nursing home administr., Tex. Enlisted U.S. Army, 1950, advanced through grades to sgt., 1952-62; artillery assignment Tex. Army Nat. Guard, 1978-80; office mgr. Manhattan Constrn. Co., Houston, 1975-80; adminstr. Houston Water Purification Plant and Tranquillity Park, 1975-80. Patentee in field; poet, country music songwriter: (poetry transcribed to country music recordings) Loving Memories, 1995, The Key to My Heart, 1996, Eternity, 1996, An Angel in Heaven, 1996, I Won't Forget You, 1996, Visions of Him, 1996, Two-Timing Woman, 1996, I Can't Get You Off of My Mind, 1996, I'll Take the Chains from Your Heart, 2000, others. Master sgt. U.S. Army res., ret., 1993. Mem. Disabled Am. Vets. (life; comdr. Pasadena chpt. 1994-2001, adjutant, treas. 2001—), Am. Security Coun. (nat. adv. bd. 1984-97), N.Y. Acad. Scis., Internat. Soc. of Poets (disting. mem.), Internat. Platform Assn., N.G. Assn. Tex. (life). Democrat. Baptist. Avocations: writing poetry and country music, assisting the blind/disabled and sr. citizens of Tex., Mex. Home: 2716 Sweetgum St Pasadena TX 77502-5754 E-mail: June334@aol.com.

SMITH, OZZIE (OSBORNE EARL SMITH), retired professional baseball player; b. Mobile, Ala., Dec. 26, 1954; m. Denise Jackson, Nov. 1, 1980; children: Osborne Earl Jr., Dustin Cameron. Grad., Calif. State Poly. U., San Luis Obispo. Shortstop San Diego Padres Baseball Club, Nat. League, 1977-82, St. Louis Cardinals Baseball Club, Nat. League, 1982-96; baseball analyst St. Louis Cardinals Sta. KPLR, St. Louis, 1997—. Player Nat. League All-Star Team, 1981-92, 94, All-Star Team Sporting News, 1982, 84-87, World Series Championship Team, 1982; recipient Most Valuable Player award Nat. League Championship Series, 1985, Gold Glove award, 1980-92, Silver Slugger award, 1987; named to Baseball Hall of Fame, 2002 Avocations: jazz, word puzzles, backgammon. Office: KPLR-TV/WB-11 Station 4935 Lindell Blvd Saint Louis MO 63108-1587*

SMITH, PAMELA RODGERS, elementary education educator; b. Hartselle, Ala., Feb. 21, 1961; d. Jesse Gene and Zella Lurline (Brown) Rodgers; m. Jeffrey Neal Smith, July 21, 1990. Student, Calhoun C.C., Decatur, Ala., 1979-82; BS in Early Childhood and Elem. Edn., Athens (Ala.) State Coll., 1984; M in Early Childhood Edn., U. Ala., Birmingham, 1990, AA cert. early childhood specialist, 1992. Day care tchr. Little Red Schoolhouse, Hartselle, 1977-84; tchr. kindergarten Neel (Ala.) Elem. Sch., 1985-86, Crestline Elem. Sch., Hartselle, 1987-95, Barkley Bridge Elem. Sch., Hartselle, 1995—. Cons. whole lang. workshop No. Ala. Tchr. Exch., 1991—. Mem. NEA, Ala. Edn. Assn., Hartselle Edn. Assn., Internat. Reading Assn., Ala. Reading Assn., Tenn. Valley Reading Assn. (v.p. 1998-99), Constructivist Math. Network, Whole Lang. Network, Kappa Kappa Iota (pres. 1998-99, 99-00). Democrat. Baptist. Home: 210 Wayward Ave NW Hartselle AL 35640-7794 E-mail: pamesmith@hcs.k12.al.us.

SMITH, PATRICIA ANNE, special education educator; b. West Chester, Pa., Aug. 19, 1967; d. William Richard and Carol Anne (Benn) S. BS in Spl. Edn. cum laude, West Chester U., 1989; postgrad., Immaculata Coll., 1993-98. Cert. mentally and physically handicapped tchr., Pa. Learning support tchr. Chester County Intermediate Unit, Downington, Pa., 1989-90, early intervention tchr., 1990-92; autistic support tchr. Coatesville (Pa.) Area Sch. Dist., 1992—, event coord. WOYC workshops, 1993-2000, event coord. WOYC ext. workshops, 1999-2000, event coord. WOYC childrens workshops, 1999-2000. Presenter ann. conf. Pa. Assn. of Resources for People with Mental Retardation, Hershey, 1994; co-presenter ARC, 1996, Paoli Meml. Hosp., 1997; presenter info. sessions ann. conf. Del. Valley Assn. for Edn. of Young Children, Phila., 1994, Lions, Downingtown, Pa., 1992, early childhood conf. Capital Area Assn. for Edn. of Young Children, Harrisburg, Pa., 1995, vols. Caln Athletic Assn. Challenger League, 1995-96, Chester County MH/MR Consultation and Edn. Adv. Bd. Com., 1997-2000; mentor West Chester U., 1995-98. Mem. recreation adv. bd. dirs. Assn. for Retarded Citizens, Exton, Pa., 1993-98, Daisy Girl Scout Leader, 1995-96; vol. tutor Chester County Libr. Adult Literacy Program, 1995-98. Recipient Outstanding Svc. award Coatesville Area Parent Coun., 1994, 96, Vol. award Friendship PTA, 1993, 96, 99, Pa. Early Childhood Edn. Assn. Workshop presenter award, 1993; grantee Pa.Dept. Edn., 1993, Coatesville Area Sch. Dist., 1990, Pa. Bur. Spl. Edn., 2001. Mem. ASCD, Nat. Assn. for the Edn. of Young Children, Autism Soc. Am., Kappa Delta Pi. Republican. Roman Catholic. Home: 501 Clover Mill Rd Exton PA 19341-2505 Office: Friendship Elem Sch 296 Reeceville Rd Coatesville PA 19320-1520

SMITH, PATRICK JOHN, editor, writer; b. N.Y.C., Dec. 11, 1932; s. H. Ben and Geraldine (Wilson) S.; m. Elisabeth Munro, Nov. 27, 1964; children: Douglass Munro, Matthew Wilson. Student, Phillips Exeter, 1951; AB, Princeton U., 1955. Freelance writer and critic, 1958-70; editor, pub. The Mus. Newsletter, N.Y.C., 1970-77; pres. Music Critics Assn., Washington, 1977-81; dir. opera mus. theater program NEA, 1985-89; editor Opera News, N.Y.C., 1989-98, editor-at large, 1998—. Author: The Tenth Muse: A History of the Opera Libretto, 1970, A Year at the Met, 1983. Office: Opera News 70 Lincoln Center Plz New York NY 10023-6548

SMITH, PAUL COLLIER, systems hardware and software engineer; b. San Francisco, Jan. 18, 1955; s. Paul Burton and Betty Jane (Olthoff) S.; m. Elizabeth A. Deering, June 27, 1981; children: Matthew, Eric, Emily, Adam. BS in Engring., Wash. State U., 1977; MSEE, Calif. State U., Long Beach, 1982. Staff engr. Hughes Aircraft Co., Fullerton, Calif., 1978-84; sr. engr. CAST, Los Alamitos, 1984-85; systems engr. for program devel. Infotec Devel. Inc., Costa Mesa, 1985-93; cons., developer Tetra Info. Tech., Huntington Beach, 1994—; systems engr. Douglas Aircraft, 1996-97; v.p. softwar PDA solutions Ctr. of Excellence for Web Applications Boeing, 1998—. Libertarian. Presbyterian. Achievementas include patent for signal processing for ILS. Home: 9431 Gulstrand Cir Huntington Beach CA 92646-7903 Office: Tetra Info Tech 21551 Brookhurst St Apt 122 Huntington Beach CA 92646-8070

SMITH, PAUL DAVID, electrical engineer, administrator; b. Omaha, Sept. 30, 1936; s. James Posley and Dorothy (Rosicky) S.; m. Martha Anne MacDonald, Sept. 12, 1964; children: Kara Anne, Samantha Anne, Todd David. BSEE, U. Nebr., 1959; SMEE, MIT, 1961. Mem. staff Lincoln Lab. MIT, Lexington, 1961-69; regional mgr. PERTEC Peripheral Equipment Co., Chatsworth, Calif., 1969-76; pres., owner Cape Cod Electronics, Chatham, Mass., 1976-78; v.p. product devel. ITT Courier, Tempe, Ariz., 1978-84; sr. v.p., chief tech. officer Summagraphics, Seymour, Conn., 1984-92; pres. NBS Card Tech. Corp., Paramus, N.J., 1992-97, Norcom Electronics Corp., Trumbull, Conn., 1998-99. Contbr. articles to profl. jours. Mem. IEEE, Sigma Xi, Eta Kappa Nu, Tau Beta Pi, Pi Mu Epsilon, Sigma Tau. Home: 7 Full Sweep Hilton Head Island SC 29928-5229 E-mail: pds61@alum.mit.edu.

SMITH, PAUL EDWARD, biologist; b. Emmetsburg, Iowa, May 24, 1933; s. James H. and Naomi James Smith; m. Loretta Lee Middleton, June 1, 1957; 1 child Scott Grant 1 child Stuart 1 child Marcia 1 child Ryan 1 child Amy Parks. PhD, U. Iowa, 1962; BS, U. No. Iowa. Rsch. fishery biologist NOAA Fisheries SW Fish. Sci. Ctr., La Jolla, Calif., 1963—96; supervisory fisheries biologist Fishery Rsch. Div. SWFSC, 1996—. Pres. Leucadia Town Coun., Leucadia, Calif., 1975—78. Cpl. U.S. Army, 1953—55. Recipient Postdoctoral fellowship, NSF, 1962, Sverdrup Postdoctoral fellowship, Scripps Instn. of Oceanography, 1962—63. Mem.: Ecol. Soc. of Am. Office: NOAA Fisheries Southwest FisheriesSciCtr 8604 La Jolla Shores Drive La Jolla CA 92038 Office Fax: 858-546-5656. E-mail: pesmith@ucsd.edu.

SMITH, PAUL FREDERICK, economist, former educator; b. Mansfield, Ohio, Dec. 21, 1919; s. Phillip Fred and Myrtle Grace (Robinson) S.; m. Margaret Alice Peacock, Oct. 30, 1942; children: Terence James, Barbara Jo Smith Moren. AB, U. Chgo., 1941; A.M., Northwestern U., 1946; PhD, Am. U., 1955. Economist bd. govs. Fed. Res. System, 1947-59; prof. fin. U. Pa., Phila., 1959-85, chmn. fin. dept., 1963-67, 72-75; vice-dean, dir. doctoral programs Wharton Sch. Bus., 1976-85. Assoc. staff mem. Nat. Bur. Econ. Research, 1960-70 Author: Consumer Credit Costs, 1949-59, 1964, Economics of Financial Institutions and Markets, 1971, Money and Financial Intermediation, 1977, Comparative Financial Systems. Served with USNR, 1941-46. Decorated Bronze Star, Purple Heart. Mem. Am. Econs. Assn., Am. Fin. Assn. Home: 1429 Dubonnet Ct Fort Myers FL 33919-2711

SMITH, PAUL LOWELL, realtor, minister; b. Fairfield, Ala., July 5, 1940; m. Janet E. Lindsay, Jan. 23, 1964; children: Janine Smith Shelby, Paul L. Jr., Scott Lyndsay, Andrew Hamilton. BA, Samford U., 1962; ThM, New Orleans Bapt. Sem., 1965, ThD, 1972. Pastor Fulton (Ala.) Bapt. Ch., 1962-66, Ruth (Miss.) Bapt. Ch., 1968-70, Ethel (Miss.) Bapt. Ch., 1970-72, First Bapt. Ch., Citronelle, Ala., 1972-74; pres. Paul Lowell Smith Evangelistic Ministries, 1974-91, Smitty Realty, Inc., Saraland, Ala., 1975—, MTS Investment Corp., Saraland, 1989-91, 95—, Foley Plantation, Inc., 1994—; pastor Romar Beach Bapt. Ch., Orange Beach, Ala., 1995—. Cons. land devel. Mcht.'s Nat. Bank, Mobile, Ala., 1985-86. Author: Greek Mystery Religions, 1971; contbr. articles on real estate investments and devels. Pres. Citronelle Youth Football League, 1982; master ceremonies Citronelle Oil Bowl Pageant, 1982; auctioneer various charities, Mobile, 1980-94; fgn. mission bd. So. Bapt. Conv.; evangelist for crusades in Ecuador, Antigua, Guyana. Avocations: hunting, fishing. Home: 10801 Celeste Rd Saraland AL 36571-9705 Office: Smitty Realty Inc PO Box 683 Saraland AL 36571-0683 E-mail: psmithsr@bellsouth.net.

SMITH, PAUL THOMAS, financial services company executive; b. Garden City, N.Y., May 17, 1938; s. Leo Joseph and Martha Duncan (Perine) S.; m. Carole A. Dlugolenski, Sept. 1, 1962; children— Laura Jane, Paul Thomas, Elizabeth Ann, Kathryn Celinda. BBA, U. Notre Dame, 1960; MBA, Harvard U., 1964. CPA, N.Y. chartered fin. analyst. In charge acct. Deloitte & Touche, N.Y.C., 1964-67; from investment analyst to 2d v.p. N.Y. Life Ins. Co., 1967-78, v.p. investments, 1978-83, v.p., chief equity investment officer, 1983-88, sr. v.p. corp. planning and devel., 1988-91, sr. v.p. venture capital, chief equity investment officer, 1991-96. Lt. USN, 1960-62. Mem. Inst. Chartered Fin. Analysts, N.Y. Soc. Security Analysts, Cherry Valley Club. Clubs: Cherry Valley. Office: PO Box 362 Center Harbor NH 03226-0362

SMITH, PAUL VERGON, JR. corporate executive, retired oil company executive; b. Lima, Ohio, Apr. 25, 1921; s. Paul Vergon and Aleta Rose (Bowers) S.; m. Alta Fern Chipps, Mar. 2, 1945; children: Douglas, Marsha, Jeffrey, Alison. AB, Miami U., Oxford, Ohio, 1942; MS, U. Ill., 1943, PhD, 1945. With Exxon Research & Engring. Co., 1946-66, 72-86, mgr. pub. affairs, 1972—86, mgr. ednl. and profl. soc. relations, Florham Park, N.J., 1981-86; asst. dir. chem. research Esso Petroleum Co., Abingdon, Eng., 1966-67; dir. chem. research Esso Research S.A., Brussels, 1967-71; mem. adv. bd. Cache, Inc., Austin, Tex., 1979-86; pres. APS Assocs., Westfield, N.J., 1986-90. Bd. dirs., treas. Jets, Inc., Alexandria, Va.; dir. CENTCOM, Ltd.; mem. exec. bd. N.J. Bus./Industry/Sci. Edn. Consortium. Patentee in field; contbr. numerous articles to profl. jours., chpts. to books. Bd. dirs. United Way of Union County, N.J., 1980-86; chmn. research adv. council Miami U., 1980-84. Recipient Pres.'s award Am. Assn. Petroleum Geologists, 1955; Spl. award N.J. Sci. Tchrs. Assn., 1985. Mem. AAAS, Am. Chem. Soc. (dir. 1978-86, chmn. bd. 1984-86; Belden award 1984), Am. Soc. Engring. Edn. (dir. 1980-86, v.p. 1980-86), Country Club Naples, Phi Beta Kappa, Sigma Xi, Omicron Delta Kappa, Phi Eta Sigma, Alpha Chi Sigma, Pi Mu Epsilon, Sigma Pi Sigma, Phi Lambda Upsilon. Republican. Methodist.

SMITH, PAULA MARION, urology and medical/surgical nurse; b. Provincetown, Mass., Apr. 2, 1930; d. Manuel V. and Marion V. (Cabral) Raymond; m. George A. Smith, July 2, 1952; children: Steven, Michael, Elizabeth. Diploma in nursing, Quincy (Mass.) City Hosp., 1951; student, Boston Coll., U. S.C. RN, Tex., Kans., Mass., Fla. Operating room nurse Richland County Hosp., El Paso, Tex., 1958-62, Hotel Dieu, El Paso, 1962-64, U.S. Army Hosp., Ft. Riley, Kans., 1967-68; splty. head nurse urology unit Cape Cod Hosp., Hyannis, Mass., 1972-1994, Health Ctrl., Orlando, Fla., 1995—. Cons. Urologic Nursing Jour. Past editor Uro-Gram. Recipient H. Harrison Hartwell award. Mem. ANA, Assn. Operating Rm. Nurses, Internat. Acad. Nurse Editors, Am. Urologic Assn. Allied (editor Uro-Gram, award New Eng. chpt. 1988).

SMITH, PEGGY O'DONIEL, physicist, educator; b. Lakeland, Fla., Nov. 27, 1920; d. John Arthur and Carrie Mattie (Jackson) O'Doniel; m. Fenton Frederick Smith, Oct. 11, 1943; children: James Scott, Stephen Arthur, Melody Ann, Candy Lou. Aviation Pilot Lic., Stetson U., Deland, Fla., 1941; BS in Sci. and Math., Fla. So. Coll., 1942; MA in Edn., U.S. Internat. U., San Diego, 1968. Physicist degausser U.S. Navy, Key West, Fla., 1942, physicist compass compensator Charleston, S.C., 1943, physicist magnetic signature analyst Washington, 1944; tchr. Chula Vista (Calif.) Sch. Dist., 1963-73, math specialist, 1974-77; owner Mineral Store, Chula Vista, 1977-82; ret. Leader math. workshops for girls, 1992-96. Author: Laz Goes to New Zealand; contbr. articles to profl. jours. Del. White House Conf. on Edn., 1956; sec. Chula Vista Rep. Women, 1995-97; chmn. Orphans of Italy, 1957-58. Recipient Kazanjian award, Joint Coun. Econ. Edn., Chula Vista, 1972, Fla. So. Coll. Alumni Achievement citation, 1999, 21st Century Achievement award, 2002; Chula Vista Sch. Dist. math grantee, 1975. Mem. AAUW (v.p. 1989), Inner Circle, Calif. Ret. Tchrs. Assn. (v.p. 1998-00), San Diego Gem and Mineral Soc. Avocations: golf, mineral collecting, coin collecting, bridge, travel. Home: 87 K St Chula Vista CA 91911-1409

SMITH, PETER, chemist, educator, consultant; b. Ashton-Upon-Mersey, Cheshire, Eng., Sept. 7, 1924; came to U.S., 1951; s. Peter and Winifred Emma (Jenkins) S.; m. Hilary Joan Hewitt Roe, 1951; children: Helen Andrews Winifred, Eric Peter, Richard Harry, Gillian Carol. BA Queens' Coll., Cambridge U., 1946, MA, 1949, PhD, 1953. Jr. sci. officer Royal Aircraft Establishment, Farnborough, Hampshire, Eng., 1943-46; demonstrator chemistry dept. Leeds U., Yorkshire, England, 1950-51; postdoctoral research fellow in chemistry Harvard U., Cambridge, Mass., 1951-54; asst. prof. chemistry Purdue U., West Lafayette, Ind., 1954-59, Duke U., Durham, N.C., 1959-61, assoc. prof., 1961-70, prof., 1970-95, prof. emeritus chemistry, 1995—. Contbg. author: chem. research jours. Fulbright post-doctoral scholar Fulbright Commn., Harvard U., 1951-53 Mem. Am. Chem. Soc., Royal Soc. Chemistry, Am. Phys. Soc., Sigma Xi, Phi Lambda Upsilon, Alpha Chi Sigma Office: Duke U Dept Chemistry Paul M Gross Chem Lab PO Box 90346 Durham NC 27708-0346 Home: Apt A237 2600 Croasdaile Farm Pkwy Durham NC 27705-1336 E-mail: psmith@chem.duke.edu.

SMITH, PETER EDWARD, sculptor, artist; b. Yonkers, N.Y., Jan. 1, 1946; s. Elwin Earl Smith and Mary Ellen Kirchmaier; m. Maria M. Smith, May 23, 1968. BA, Hobart Coll., 1967; MBA, Rutgers U., 1971. Light weapons infantryman U.S. Army, Ft. Carson, Colo., 1968-69; 2d v.p. investment dept. N.Y. Life Ins. Co., N.Y.C., 1971-86; sculptor, painter Pietro Designs Studio, Princeton Junction, N.J., 1986—. Designer, sculptor West Windsor (N.J.) Vets.' Monument, 1986-89 (citation Am. Legion 1990); designer, sculptor, painter Altar, Ambo, Baptistery, Tabernacle, Tympanum, St. David the King Ch., Princeton Junction, 1990-92 (Visual Art award 1992); designer, mosaicist Stations of the Cross, 1995-96; sculptor limestone stele U.S. Forest Svc., Fredericksburg, Va., 1993; designer triptych, altars and font Prince of Peace Ch., Taylors, S.C., 2000-02; author: Cherubim of Gold, 1993; contbr. Art and Environment Letter, 1994—. With U.S. Army, 1967—69. Recipient artistic contbns. to cmty. award Nat. Art Honor Soc., Princeton Junction, 1993. Office: Pietro Designs Studio 962 Alexander Rd Princeton Junction NJ 08550-1024 E-mail: pietro@pietrodesigns.com.

SMITH, PETER LEONARD, diversified financial services company executive; b. N.Y.C., Feb. 6, 1932; s. Purcell Leonard and Elizabeth (Wright) S.; m. Janet Andrews, May 3, 1964; children: Sarah, Andrew. BA, Yale Coll., 1955; cert. in advanced cryptology, Nat. Security Agy., 1965; MS, Southeastern U., 1977. Cashier Paine Webber, Washington, 1972-74; sr. examiner SEC, 1974-97; spl. investigator NASDR, Inc., N.Y.C., 1997-98; sr. v.p. Monument Funds Group, Inc., 1998—2001; v.p. Monument Series Fund, Inc., Bethesda, Md., 1998—2001; registered rep. Intersecurities, Inc., McLean, Va., 2001—. Served to lt. (s.g.) USNR, 1956-67. Home: 4834 Langdrum Ln Chevy Chase MD 20815-5413

SMITH, PETER RUSSELL, physician; b. N.Y.C., May 21, 1942; s. Harold S. and Jeanette Geller; divorced. BS magna cum laude, CCNY, 1964; MD, Columbia U., 1968. Diplomate Am. Bd. Internal Medicine, Am. Bd. Pulmonary Disease, Am. Bd. Critical Care. Intern SUNY Health Sci. Ctr., Bklyn., 1968-69, resident, 1969-70, 71-72, Bronx Mcpl. Hosp., 1970-71; attending physician Univ. Hosp., Bklyn., 1974-92, Kings County Hosp., Bklyn., 1974-96, dir. chest clinic, 1976-92; acting chief pulmonary SUNY Health Sci. Ctr., 1983-86; attending physician pulmonary medicine L.I. Coll. Hosp., Bklyn., 1992—, chief divsn. pulmonary medicine, 1993—. Clin. instr. dept. medicine, SUNY Health Sci. Ctr., 1974-76, asst. prof., 1976-89, clin. assoc. prof., 1989-97, assoc. prof. clin. medicine, 1997-2000, prof. clin. medicine, 2000—; presenter in field. Co-author: (chpts.) Internal Medicine Review and Assessment, 1982, Questions: Patients Most often Ask Their Doctors, 1983, Hurst's Medicine for the Practicing Physician, 1996; contbr. articles to profl. jours. Pulmonary fellow SUNY Health Sci. Ctr., 1972-74; Salk scholar, 1964. Fellow Am. Coll. Chest Physicians, Am. Coll. Physicians; mem. Am. Thoracic Soc., Am. Soc. Internal Medicine, N.Y. State Thoracic Soc., N.Y. Acad. Sci., Soc. Critical Care Medicine. Avocations: collecting art and antiques, tennis. Home: 2 Montague Ter Brooklyn NY 11201-4105 Office: LI Coll Hosp 339 Hicks St Brooklyn NY 11201-5509 E-mail: psmith@dnamail.com.

SMITH, PETER THOMAS, lawyer; b. Red Wing, Minn., Feb. 9, 1946; s. Everell Adrian and Mary Ann (Tondl) S.; m. Sandra Jeanne Konieczny, Aug. 31, 1968; children: Alexander John, Nicole Marie. BS with honors, Loyola U., 1968; JD with honors, George Washington U., 1971. Bar: D.C. 1971, Ill. 1977; U.S. Ct. Appeals (D.C. cir.) 1974; U.S. Ct. Mil. Appeals 1972; U.S. Supreme Ct., 1980. Judge advocate USMC, Washington, 1971-74; assoc. atty. Keller & Heckman, 1974-77; pvt. practice Sycamore, Ill., 1977-79; ptnr. Minnihan & Smith, 1980-84; pvt. practice, 1985-90; ptnr. Smith & Strauss, 1990-2000, Smith Tucker & Brown, 2000—. City atty. City of Sycamore, 1990—. Treas. DeKalb County Reps., 1980; pres. Sycamore Kiwanis Club, 1990; chmn. Sycamore United Givers Fund, 1985; chmn. DeKalb County Unit, Am. Cancer Soc., 1992-96, St. Mary's Sch. Found., 1997—. Capt. USMCR, 1968-75. Mem. ABA, Ill. State Bar Assn., DeKalb County Bar Assn., Kane County Bar Assn. Republican. Roman Catholic. Avocations: golf, fishing, hunting, travel. Office: Smith Tucker & Brown 207 W State St Sycamore IL 60178-1493

SMITH, PETER WALKER, finance executive; b. Syracuse, N.Y., May 19, 1923; s. Stanley Sherwood and Elizabeth Wilkins (Young) S.; m. Lucile Elizabeth Edson, June 22, 1946; children: Andrew E., Laurie Smith-Frailey, Pamela C. (Mrs. Denison W. Schweppe, Jr.), Stanley E. B.Chem. Engring., Rensselaer Poly. Inst., 1947; MBA, Harvard U., 1948; LL.B., Cleve. Marshall Law Sch., 1955. Bar: Ohio 1955; Registered profl. engr., Ohio. Div. controller Raytheon Co., Lexington, Mass., 1958-66; v.p. finance, indsl. systems and equipment group Litton Industries Inc., Stamford, Conn., 1966-70; v.p. finance, treas. Copeland Corp., Sidney, Ohio, 1970-74; v.p. fin., treas., dir. Instrumentation Lab. Inc., Lexington, Mass., 1974-78; chief fin. officer, treas. Ionics, Inc., Watertown, 1978-80; v.p. fin., treas. Data Printer Corp., Malden, 1980-84, Orion Research Inc., Boston, 1984-87; pvt. practice cons. Concord, Mass., 1987—. Mem. fin. adv. bd., Northeastern U., Boston. Lt. AUS, 1943-46, 50-52. Mem. Fin. Execs. Inst., Am. Prodn. and Inventory Control Soc. (founding), Rensselaer Soc. Engrs., Sigma Xi, Tau Beta Pi. Home and Office: 155 Monument St Concord MA 01742-1808

SMITH, PETER WILLIAM EBBLEWHITE, electrical engineering educator, scientist, physicist; b. London, Nov. 3, 1937; m. Jacqueline Marie Mankiewicz, June 18, 1966; children: Christal, Dawn N. BSc, McGill U., Montreal, Que., Can., 1958, MSc, 1961, PhD, 1964. Mem. of staff Can. Marconi Co., Mont., 1958-59; mem. tech. staff Bell Labs., Holmdel, N.J., 1963-83; dist. mgr. Bellcore, Red Bank, 1984-88, div. mgr., 1988-92; prof. elec. and computer engring. U. Toronto, 1992—; exec. dir. Ont. Laser and Lightwave Rsch. Ctr., 1992-95; dir. Nortel Inst. for Telecomms., 1999—. Editor-in-chief IEEE Press Progress in Lasers and Electro-Optics Series, 1987—92, Optics Letters, 1989—95; contbr. Board dirs. Monmouth Arts Found., Red Bank, 1965-82. Recipient Sr. Scientist award NATO, 1979. Fellow IEEE (Quantum Electronics award 1986, Third Millennium medal 2000), Optical Soc. Am. (bd. dirs., chmn. bd. editors); mem. IEEE Lasers and Electro-Optics Soc. (pres. 1984), Am. Phys. Soc., Can. Assn. Physicists. Achievements include first demonstration of waveguide gas laser, non-linear optical interface; development of hybrid bistable optical devices; 33 patents in field and 2 patents pending. Office: U Toronto Dept Elec & Computer Engring Toronto ON Canada M5S 3G4

SMITH, PETER WOLFGANG, physicist, artist; b. Rostock, Germany, May 16, 1929; U.S. citizen, 1983; s. Hans Schmidt-Isserstedt and Gertrude Calo; m. Marie Smith, Sept. 8, 1954; children: Nicholas, Lydia, Caroline. Scholar, King's Coll. Choir Sch., Cambridge, Eng., 1940-43, Felsted Sch., Essex, Eng., 1943-48; student, Cambridge Art Coll., 1950; BS with 1st honors in natural philosophy, St. Andrews (Scotland) U., 1952; postgrad., Edinburgh U., 1952-54. Sci. officer Admiralty Signal and Radar Establishment, Portsmouth, Eng., 1954-60; scientist Plessey Co., Hampshire, Eng., 1960-67; supr. Norden Systems, Norwalk, Conn., 1967-89; cons. Peter Smith, Westport, 1989—; artist Pierre Cochon, 1993—. Patentee in field; contbr. articles to profl. jours.; artist exhibiting in Wessex shows, U.K., 1956-60, various Conn. shows, 1996—. Mem. Inst. of Physics of London. Avocations: music, art history, golf. Home and Office: 7 Darbrook Rd Westport CT 06880-3611

SMITH, PHILIP MEEK, science policy consultant, writer; b. Springfield, Ohio, May 18, 1932; s. Clarence Mitchell S. and Lois Ellen (Meek) Dudley. BS, Ohio State U., 1954, MA, 1955; DSc (hon.), N.C. State U., 1986. Mem. staff U.S. Nat. Com. for Internat. Geophys. Yr., Nat. Acad. Scis., 1957-58; program dir. NSF, 1958-63, dir. ops. U.S. Antarctic Research program, 1964-69, dep. head div. polar programs, 1970-73; chief gen. sci. br. Office Mgmt. and Budget Exec. Office of Pres., 1973-74; exec. asst. to dir. and sci. advisor to pres. NSF, 1974-76; assoc. dir. Office Sci. and Tech. Policy, Exec. Office of Pres., 1976-81; exec. officer NRC-Nat. Acad. Scis., Washington, 1981-94; ptnr. McGeary and Smith, 1995—; chmn. external adv. com. Nat. Computational Sci. Alliance, 1997—2001, mem., 2002—. Bd. dirs. Aurora Flight Scis. Corp.; adv. cons. bd. U. Ala. Geophys. Inst., 1994—98; adv. bd. Sci.'s Next Wave, 1998—; advisor Com. for Econ. Devel., 1997; com. on sci., tech. & health aspects fgn. policy agenda U.S. NRC, 1998—2000, com. on sci. and tech. for counterism, 2001—; chair com. orgn. & strategy Sci. Com. Antarctic Rsch., 1999—2000; co-chair adv. bd. Calif. Inst. Telecomms. & Info. Tech., 2000—; prin. Coun. for Excellence in Govt.; mem. NRC Com. on Sci. Basis for Decision Making in Internat. Sustainable Devel. Orgns., 2002. Author: (with others) Defrosting Antarctic Secrets, 1962; The Frozen Future, a Prophetic Report from Antarctica, 1973; contbr. numerous articles to profl. jours. Bd. dirs. Washington Project for Arts, 1983-84, Washington Sculptors Group, 1983-84. 1st lt. U.S. Army, 1955-57. Mem. AAAS, Antarctican Soc., Cosmos Club (Washington), Am. Alpine Club (Golden, Colo.), Sigma Xi. Office: McGeary and Smith 464 M St SW Washington DC 20024-2603 E-mail: pmsmith@mcgearyandsmith.com.

SMITH, PHILIP A. academic administrator; b. Prince Edward Is., Can. Grad., Providence Coll., 1963; M, St. Stephen's Coll.; D in Philosophy and Religion, Drew U. Mem. philosophy dept. Providence Coll., R.I., 1981-91, pres., 1994—. Office: Providence Coll Harkins Hall 103 549 River Ave Providence RI 02918-0002*

SMITH, PHILIP DANIEL, academic administrator, education educator; b. Dayton, Ohio, Dec. 25, 1933; s. Hubert Edgar and Edith (Parker) S.; m. Marilyn Brown, Nov. 25, 1953; children: Carolyn Smith Valentine, Norman Daniel, Stanley Nathan. BS cum laude, Bob Jones U., 1955; MEd, Miami U., Oxford, Ohio, 1956; EdD, Pa. State U., 1964. Dean coll. arts and sci. Bob Jones U., Greenville, S.C., 1961-65, registrar, 1965-81, prof. edn., 1956—, provost, 1981—. Mem. edn. adv. bd. One Touch Systems, Inc., 1995-96. Cons. for BJ Help Network, BJ Linc, and BJU Press books Beginnings for Christian Schools, English Skills for Christian Schools, Handwriting for Christian Schools. Pres. Bob Jones U. Alumni Assn., Greenville, 1970-71; mem. coll. parallel adv. com. Tri-County Tech. Coll., Pendleton, S.C., 1973-86. Mem. Assn. Ednl. Communications and Tech. (life mem.; membership coordinator for profl. assns. 1969-72, vice chair nat. membership com. 1972-73, chair nat. membership com. 1973-75, council del. S.C. chpt. 1972-73, audiovisual instrn. editorial adv. com. 1974-75, del. to Lake Okoboji ednl. media leadership conf. 1972, 74), Assn. Ednl. Communications and Tech. of S.C. (bd. dirs. 1970-75, pres. 1972-73, award for outstanding contbns. and service 1971), Am. Assn. Collegiate Registrars and Admissions Officers, Phi Delta Kappa. Republican. Baptist. Office: Bob Jones U Office Provost Greenville SC 29614-0001

SMITH, PHILIP JOHN, industrial and systems engineering educator; b. Bradenton, Fla., July 11, 1953; s. John Fredrick and Valerie Eline (Polk) S. BA in Psychology, U. Mich., 1975, MS in Indsl. and Ops. Engring., 1976, PhD in Psychology and Indsl. Engring., 1979. Lectr. dept. indsl. engring. U. Mich., Ann Arbor, 1979-80, rsch. scientist Ctr. for Ergonomics, 1979-80; asst. prof. dept. indsl. engring. Ohio State U., Columbus, 1980-86, assoc. prof., 1986-92, prof. indsl. and sys. engring., 1992—, dir. Inst. for Ergonomics, 1998—. Cons. Ford, Dearborn, Mich., 1986—, Metron, Washington, 1998—, PPG, Columbus, Ohio, 1999-2000, Booze Allen Hamilton, 2001-02. Co-editor: Challenges in Indexing Electronic Text and Images, 1994; contbr. articles, paper to profl. publs. Mem. IEEE Sys., Man and Cybernetics, Am. Soc. for Info. Sci., Assn. Computing Machinery (spl. interest group for info. retrieval 1992-93), Human Factors Soc. Avocation: dressage. E-mail: phil+@osu.edu. Home: 7197 Calhoun Rd Ostrander OH 43061-9335 Office: Ohio State U Engring Dept 1971 Neil Ave Columbus OH 43210-1210 Business E-Mail: Smith.131@osu.edu.

SMITH, PHILIP JONES, lawyer; b. York, Pa., May 14, 1941; s. Clark S. and Margaret Ann (Jones) S.; m. Ann F. Johnson, Apr. 21, 1973; 1 child, James M. BA cum laude, Williams Coll., 1963; LLB, U. Va., 1966. Bar: Mass. 1967. Assoc. Ropes & Gray, Boston, 1967-76, ptnr., 1976—. Lectr. Boston U. Sch. of Law, Boston, 1984-98. Contbr. chpts. to books, articles to profl. jours. Bd. dirs., pres. Greater Boston Youth Symphony Orch., Boston, 1978-2000; bd. dirs., v.p. The Keewaydin Found., Salisbury, Vt., 1980—; bd. dirs., past treas. Project STEP, Boston, 1987-95; overseer, chair facilities com. New Eng. Conservatory, Boston, 1989-95. Fulbright scholar U. Madrid, 1966-67. Mem.: ABA, Essex County Club, N.Y. Yacht Club, Eastern Yacht Club (sec. 1977—83, bd. dirs. 2001—), Order of Coif. Home: 35 Harbor Ave Marblehead MA 01945-3636 Office: Ropes & Gray One Internat Pl Boston MA 02110-2624 E-mail: Psmith@Ropesgray.com.

SMITH, PHILIP LUTHER, scientist; b. Milan, Dec. 23, 1956; s. Donald Walter and Evelyn Emma (Vornheder) S.; m. Mary Ann Radike, Feb. 9, 1985; children: Martha Jesse, Philip Benjamin. BS, Purdue U., 1980. Rsch. asst. U. Cin. Coll. of Medicine, Cin., 1981-84; sr. phys. biochemist Med. Coll. of Ohio, Toledo, 1985-89; sr. rsch. molecular geneticist Marion Merrell Dow Rsch. Inst., Cin., 1990-95; patent info. scientist Hoechst Marion Roussel, Inc., 1996-98; sr. scientist Procter and Gamble Co., 1999—. Contbr. articles to profl. jours. Mem. Am. Chem. Soc., Patent Info. Users Group, Am. Radio Relay League (life), Soc. of Competitive Intelligence Profls., Am. Chem. Soc. (divsn. of chem. info., divsn. of chemistry and the law, divsn. med. chemistry), Purdue U. Alumni Assn. (life). Roman Catholic. Achievements include rsch. in synthesis, purification and characterization of DNA/RNA oligonucleotides, peptides, proteins and synthetic compounds with a pharmaceutical significance; rsch. in protein chemistry with an emphasis on protein structure and function; rsch. info. sci.; competitive technical intelligence Avocations: amateur radio, electronics, volunteer instructor, FCC/ARRL accredited volunteer examiner and ofcl. observer. Office: The Procter & Gamble Co Winton Hill Tech Ctr 6300 Center Hill Ave Cincinnati OH 45224

SMITH, PHILIP W. epidemiologist; b. Chgo., Dec. 4, 1946; s. James J. and Mary E. Smith; m. Sharon W. Smith, May 28, 1982; children: Nathan, Alexander, Matthew. BS in Chemistry, U. Wis., 1968; MD, U. Chgo., 1972. Diplomate Am. Bd. Internal Medicine with subspecialty in infectious disease. Intern U. Iowa, 1972-73, resident in internal medicine, 1973-75, fellow in infectious diseases, 1975-77; epidemiologist Clarkson Hosp., Omaha, 1977-98; chief sect. of infectious diseases U. Nebr. Med. Ctr., 1998—. Editor: Infection Control in Long Term Care Facilities, 1984, 2d edit., 1994. Recipient Sir William Osler Tchg. award U. Nebr. Dept. Internal Medicine, 1983. Fellow ACP, Infectious Diseases Soc. of Am. Avocations: philosophy, poetry. Office: 985400 Nebraska Med Ctr Omaha NE 68198-0001

SMITH, PHILLIP THURMOND, historian, educator; b. Van Nuys, Calif., Dec. 11, 1942; s. John Thomas McElroy and Eloise (Coggin) Smith; m. Ellen Laurie Walker, June 27, 1970; children: Roger Stephen, Kristen Susan. BA, U. Tex., El Paso, 1964; postgrad., Westfield Coll., U. London, 1967-68; MA, Ind. U., 1969; MPhil, Columbia U., 1975, PhD with distinction, 1976. Asst. dir. grad. admissions Columbia U., N.Y.C., 1969-70; lectr. U. Mass., Boston, summer 1976, Endicott Coll., Beverly, 1976-78; asst., assoc. prof. history St. Joseph's U., Phila., 1978-96, prof. history, 1996—, chmn. dept. history, 1988-94, 2001—. Author: (book) Policing Victorian London, 1985, Mafeking Memories, 1996. Capt. U.S. Army, 1964—66. Fellow NEH, 1978, 1988, 1991; grantee Cooper-Woods Study, English-Speaking Union, 1979. Mem.: Phila. Conf. Modern European History, Anglo-Am. Assocs., Mid. Atlantic Conf. Brit. Studies, NE Victorial Studies Assn., N.Am. Conf. Brit. Studies, Am. Hist. Assn., Delaware Valley Amateur Astronomers, Columbia U. Club. Democrat. Avocations: classical guitar, tennis, bicycling, astronomy. Home: 1310 Delmont Ave Havertown PA 19083-2626 E-mail: psmith@sju.edu.

SMITH, PHILLIPS ALAN VARS, investment company executive; b. Richland, Wash., June 21, 1949; s. Phillips Perry Smith and Joyce Katherine Kunz. BA in Econs., Cornell U., 1971. Cert. fin. planner. Ins. & securities sales exec. Money Mgmt. Agy., Cortland, N.Y., 1977-81; securities sales exec. Marsan Securities, 1981-84; registered rep. First Albany Corp., Syracuse, N.Y., 1984-88; investment exec. Janney Montgomery Scott, Inc., 1988-93, v.p. investments divsn., 1993-95, 1st v.p. investments divsn., 1995—. Active fin. com. Bellevue Heights United Meth. Ch., 1995—. Capt. U.S. Army, 1971-75. Mem. Internat. Assn. Fin. Planning, Sports Car Vintage Racing Assn., U.S. Fencing Assn., Onondaga Fencing Club. Republican. Methodist. Avocations: vintage sports car racing, vintage car collecting, fencing, travel. Home: 111 Garnet Dr Camillus NY 13031-2011 Office: Janney Montgomery Scott Inc 101 S Salina St Ste 502 Syracuse NY 13202-1348

SMITH, PHILLIPS GUY, banker; b. Orange, N.J., Sept. 15, 1946; s. Phillips Upham and Helen Ottilie (Voderberg) S.; m. Ann Dixon Schickhaus, Dec. 29, 1973; children: Guy Dixon, William Schickhaus, Louisa Upham. B in Engring., Stevens Inst. Tech., Hoboken, N.J.; MBA, U. Pa., 1975. Comml. banking rep. The Bank of N.Y., N.Y.C., 1976-78, asst. treas., 1978-79, asst. v.p., 1979-80, v.p., 1980-85, sr. v.p., 1985-93; mng. dir. Internat. Strategy Svcs., Inc., 1993-2000; prin. Sippican Group LLC, Greenwich, Conn., 2000—. Vestryman Ch. of The Heavenly Rest, N.Y.C., 1983-88, treas., 1985-87; trustee Tabor Acad., Marion, Mass., 1987—, treas., 1991—. Lt. USN, 1970-74, Vietnam. Mem. Racquet and Tennis Club, Down Town Assn., Rockaway Hunting Club, Nantucket Yacht Club. Episcopalian. Home: 9 E 94th St New York NY 10128-0611 Office: Sippican Group LLC 15 E Putnam Ave Ste 3280 Greenwich CT 06830-5424 E-mail: psmith@sippicangroup.com.

SMITH, PHYLLIS MAE, healthcare consultant, educator; b. Coeur d'Alene, Idaho, May 2, 1935; d. Elmer Lee Smith and Kathryn Alice (Newell) Wilson. Diploma, Luth. Bible Inst., Seattle, 1956, Emanuel Hosp. Sch. Nursing, Portland, Oreg., 1959, Coll. San Mateo, Calif., 1971. Staff nurse in surgery Emanuel Hosp., Portland, 1962-63; head nurse ctrl. svc. Sacred Heart Hosp., Eugene, Oreg., 1964-69; dir. ctrl. svcs. Peninsula Hosp., Burlingame, Calif., 1969-74; pres. Phyllis Smith Assocs., Inc., Lewiston, Idaho, 1975-88; sr. tech. advisor, dir. ednl. programs Parkside Material Mgmt. Svcs., Park Ridge, Ill., 1988-90; AIDS coord. Asotin County Health Dist., 1989-2000. Lectr., cons. in field in over 14 countries. Contbr. to manuals and profl. jours. Mem. NAFE, Internat. Assn. Hosp. Ctrl. Svc. Mgmt. (dir. edn. 1973-88, chmn. technician edn. and affairs com. 1978-88, John Perkins award 1977, Cheshire award 1977), Assn. for Advancement Med. Instrumentation. Lutheran. Avocations: fishing, walking, photography, chess, reading. Home and Office: 1415 Chestnut St Clarkston WA 99403-2429

SMITH, R. GORDON, lawyer; b. Roanoke, Va., May 28, 1938; BA with highest honors, U. Va., 1960; LLB magna cum laude, Harvard U., 1964. Bar: Va. 1964. Law clk. to judge U.S. Ct. Appeals (5th cir.), 1964-65; ptnr. McGuire, Woods, Battle & Boothe, Richmond, Va., 1969—. Exec., legislation editor Harvard Law Rev., 1963-64; bd. dirs. Scott & Stringfellow Fin., Inc., Trigon Healthcare, Inc., Va. C. of C. Fellow Am. Bar Found.; mem. Va. Bar Assn. (pres. 1987-88), Am. Law Inst., Phi Beta Kappa, Omicron Delta Kappa. Office: McGuire Woods 901 E Cary St Richmond VA 23219-4057

SMITH, R. J., JR. oil company executive; b. Big Spring, Tex., Sept. 9, 1930; s. R. J. and Myrtle (O'Quinn) S.; m. Sarah Sue Holmes, Sept. 8, 1950 (div. 1962); children: Molly Smith Frank, Cassie Smith Roop; m. Sandra Ann Schroeder, Jan. 21, 1971. Student, Abilene Christian U., 1948-50, So. Meth. U., 1951-52, Goethe U., Frankfurt, Germany, 1953-55; LLD, Northwood U., 1983. Aero. engr. Chance-Vought Aircraft, Dallas, 1951-52; ind. oil operator, 1960-62; ops. chief Leland Fikes, 1963-66; owner, operator Texon Petroleum Corp. (sold to Exxon USA 1983), 1967-83; owner, pres. Cheyenne Petroleum Corp., 1967—, Texan Petroleum Corp., Dallas, 1985—; pres., CEO Lehndorff Minerals, 1989—. Bd. dirs. Aztec Energy Corp. Bd. dirs., then chmn. bd. dirs. Effie and Wofford Cain Found., Dallas, 1979—, Friends Dallas Police, U. Tex. Southwestern Med. Ctr. Fund, So. Meth. U. John Tower Ctr. Polit. Studies; chmn. bd. govs. Northwood U., Tex., trustee, West Palm Beach, Fla., Midland, Mich. and Dallas, 1968—; Tex. del. at large Rep. Nat. Conv., 1996; dir. Bob Dole for Pres. Com., Tex. Mem. Ind. Prodrs. Assn. Am., Tex. Ind. Prodrs. and Royalty Owners, Mid-Continent Prodrs. Assn., N.Mex. Ind. Prodrs. Assn., Preston Trail Golf Club, Dallas Gun Club, Crescent Club, Montaigne Club, Bent Tree Country Club (alt. Tex.), Del Mar Turf Club (Calif.). Republican. Office: Texan Petroleum Corp 2626 Cole Ave Ste 603 Dallas TX 75204-0823

SMITH, RALPH, artist; b. San Francisco, July 12, 1919; s. Joseph Jacob and Anna (Holecek) S.; m. Francis Ferne Sierth, Aug. 15, 1942; children: Peter Joseph, Beverly Christine. Student, Art Ctr. L.A., 1940, Oakland Arts/Crafts, 1946, Am. U., 1962-67. Aircraft mechanic Naval Repair Stas., Alameda, Calif., 1945-56; aircraft engring. technician Dept. Navy, Washington, 1956-74; artist, tchr. Ralph Smith Workshops, Annandale, Va., 1974—. Juror awards 100th Ann. Art Exhbn., Nat. League of Am. Pen Women, Washington, 1996. With USN, 1941-43. Mem. Am. Soc. Marine Artists (elected artist mem. 1999), Midwest Watercolor Soc., Va. Watercolor Soc. Republican. Roman Catholic. Avocations: fishing, travel, visiting museums and galleries. Home and Office: 7114 Cindy Ln Annandale VA 22003-5812

SMITH, RALPH ALEXANDER, cultural and educational policy educator; b. Ellwood City, Pa., June 12, 1929; s. J.V. and B. V. S.; m. Christiana M. Kolbe, Nov. 16, 1955. AB, Columbia Coll., 1954; MA, Teachers Coll., Columbia U., 1959, Ed.D., 1962. Faculty, art history and arts edn. Kent (Ohio) State U., 1959-61, Wis. State U., Oshkosh, 1961-63, SUNY, New Paltz, 1963-64; faculty edn. and art edn. U. Ill., Urbana-Champaign, 1964—, also prof. cultural and ednl. policy & aesthetic edn., prof. emeritus, 1996—. First Italo DeFrancesca Meml. lectr. Kutztown State U., 1974, Leon Jackman Meml. lectr., Perth, Australia, 1985, Dean's lectr. Coll. Fine Arts and Comm., Brigham Young U., 1985, Dunbar lectr. Millsaps Coll., 1993; John Landrum Bryant lectr. Harvard U., 1999; disting. vis. prof. Ohio State U., 1987; sr. scholar Coll. Edn. U. Ill., 1991. Author: (with Albert William Levi) Art Education: A Critical Necessity, 1991; founder, editor Jour. Aesthetic Edn., 1966-2000; editor: Aesthetics and Criticism in Art Education, 1966, Aesthetic Concepts and Education, 1970, Aesthetics and Problems of Education, 1971, Regaining Educational Leadership, 1975, Cultural Literacy and Arts Education, 1991; contbg. editor: Arts Edn. Policy Rev., 2001—; co-author: Research in the Arts and Aesthetic Education: A Directory of Investigators and Their Fields of Inquiry, 1978, Excellence in Art Education: Ideas and Initiatives, 1987, The Sense of Art: A Study in Aesthetic Education, 1989; editor: Discipline-Based Art Education, 1989, (with Alan Simpson) Aesthetics and Arts Education, 1991, (with Bennett Reimer) The Arts, Education and Aesthetic Knowing, 1992, (with Ronald Berman) Public Policy and the Aesthetic Interest, 1992, General Knowledge and Arts Education, 1994, Excellence II: The Continuing Quest Art Education, 1995, Online Bibliography: Discipline Based Art Education, 1997, Readings in Discipline-Based Art Education: A Literature of Educational Reform, 2000. With Med. Svc. U.S. Army, 1954—57. Recipient spl. merit recognition Coll. Edn., U. Ill., 1975, Disting. lectr. Studies in Art Edn. award, 1991. Fellow Nat. Art Edn. Assn. (Disting., Manuel Barkan Meml. award 1973, Nat. Educator award 2000); mem. Coun. Policy Studies in Art Edn. (first exec. sec. 1978-82), Ill. Art Edn. Assn. (Disting.). Home: 2909 Heathwood Ct Champaign IL 61822-7659 Office: 361 Education 1310 S 6th St Champaign IL 61820-6925

SMITH, RALPH EARL, virologist; b. Yuma, Colo., May 10, 1940; s. Robert C. and Esther C. (Schwarz) S.; m. Sheila L. Kondy, Aug. 29, 1961 (div. 1986); 1 child, Andrea Denise; m. Janet M. Keller, 1988. BS, Colo. State U., 1961; PhD, U. Colo., 1968. Registered microbiologist Am. Soc. Clin. Pathologists. Fellow Duke U. Med. Ctr., Durham, N.C., 1968-70, asst. prof., 1970-74, assoc. prof., 1974-80, prof. virology, 1980-82; prof., head dept. microbiology Colo. State U., Ft. Collins, 1983-88, prof. microbiology, assoc. v.p. rsch., 1989-99, interim v.p. rsch., 1990-91, prof. microbiology, assoc. v.p. rsch., 1991-99, interim head dept. microbiology, 1999—2002, prof. microbiology, immunology and pathology, 2002—. Cons. Bellco Glass Co., Vineland, N.J., 1976-80, Proctor & Gamble Co., Cin., 1985-86, Schering Plough Corp., Bloomfield, N.J., 1987-89. Contbr. articles to profl. jours.; patentee in field. Bd. dirs. Colo. Ctr. for Environ. Mgmt., v.p. for rsch.; mem. pollution prevention adv. bd. Colo. Dept. Pub. Health and Environment; mem. Rocky Mountain U. Consortium on Environ. Restoration, Environ. Inst. Rocky Flats; asst. scoutmaster Boy Scouts Am., Durham, 1972-82, com. mem., Ft. Collins, 1986-91; mem. adminstrv. bd. 1st United Meth. Ch., Ft. Collins. Eleanor Roosevelt fellow Internat. Union Against Cancer 1978-79. Mem. AAAS, Am. Soc. Microbiology, N.Y. Acad. Scis., Am. Soc. Virology, Gamma Sigma Delta. Democrat. Methodist. Avocations: photography, hiking. Home: 2406 Creekwood Dr Fort Collins CO 80525-2034 Office: Colo State U Dept Microbiology Fort Collins CO 80523-0001 Business E-Mail: ralph.smith@colostate.edu.

SMITH, RALPH EDWARD, psychology assistant; b. Bellfountaine, Ohio, May 19, 1953; s. Ralph Raymond and Virginia (Picklesimer) S.; m. Melody Lee Welbaum Smith, Sept. 3, 1988. B of Gen. Studies, Ohio U., 1980; MS in Edn., U. Dayton, 1987. Houseparent Roweton Boys Ranch, Chillicothe, Ohio, 1974-86, social worker, 1981-82; employment counselor Ross County Community Action, 1980-81, 83; social worker Roweton Residential Ctr., 1986-87; psychology asst. Ross Correctional Inst., 1988-89, 97—, Chillicothe Correctional Inst., State of Ohio, 1989-97. Pres. H.Y.S. Fed. Credit Union, Chillicothe, 1981-86. Vol. Ross County Community Action, Inc., Chillicothe, 1983-87, commodity distbn. vol. Mem. Sons of Union Veterans, Sons and Daughters of Pioneer Rivermen. Avocations: music, film, books. Office: Ross Correctional Institution PO Box 7010 Chillicothe OH 45601-7010

SMITH, RALPH LEE, author, musician; b. Phila., Nov. 6, 1927; s. Hugh Harold and Barbara (Schatkin) S.; m. Betty H. Smith, Sept. 1954 (div. Jan. 1963); children: David Bruce, Robert Hugh; m. Mary Louise Hollowell, 1971 (div. 1977); m. Shizuko Maruyama, 1977; 1 child, Lisa Koyuki. BA, Swarthmore Coll., 1951; MEd, U. Va., 1987. Folk musician on Appalachian dulcimer; recs. include Dulcimer: Old Time and Traditional Music, 1973, Tunes of the Blue Ridge and Great Smoky Mountains, 1983; author: The Story of the Dulcimer, 1986, Appalachian Dulcimer Traditions, 1997, Songs and Tunes of the Wilderness Road, 1999. Recipient writing awards Columbia U. Grad. Sch. Journalism, U. Mo. Grad. Sch. Journalism, AMA. Home: 1662 Chimney House Rd Reston VA 20190-4302 E-mail: rls2@erols.com.

SMITH, RALPH WESLEY, JR. retired federal judge; b. Ghent, N.Y., July 16, 1936; s. Ralph Wesley and Kathleen S. (Callahan) S.; m. Nancy Ann Fetzer, Dec. 30, 1961 (div. 1981); children: Mark Owen, Tara Denise, Todd Kendall; m. Barbara Anne Milian, Nov. 8, 1982; stepchildren: Kim Highter, Jeffrey Highter, Eric Highter. Student, Sorbonne, U. Paris, Paris, 1954-55; BA, Yale U., 1956; LLB, Albany Law Sch., 1966. Bar: N.Y. 1966, U.S. Dist. Ct. (no. dist.) N.Y. 1966. Assoc. Hinman, Straub Law Firm, Albany, N.Y., 1966-69; chief asst. dist. atty. Albany County, 1969-73, dist. atty., 1974; regional dir. state nursing home investigation Asst. Atty. Gen., Albany, 1975-77; dir. State Organized Crime Task Force, 1978-82; U.S. magistrate judge U.S. Dist. Ct. (no. dist.) N.Y., Albany, 1982-2001. Judge moot ct. Albany Law Sch., 1983-2001; lectr. N.Y. State Bar Assn., 1985—, Am. Inns of Ct., 1994-99. Capt. (ret.) USNR, 1957-82. Mem. Fed. Magistrate Judges Assn. (dir. 2d cir. 1992-99), Columbia County Magistrates Assn. Republican. Roman Catholic. Avocations: fishing, bicycling, skiing, sailing, camping. Home: 40 Wequasset Rd Harwich Port MA 02646

SMITH, RANDALL EUGENE, construction executive; b. Warsaw, May 7, 1955; s. Robert Joseph and Joan Marilyn (Snyder) S.; m. Barbara Ann Stoddard, Sept. 22, 1980; children: Travis Lockwood, Brooke Ann. BA in Constrn., U. Fla., 1978. Asst. project mgr. Frank J. Rooney Co., Ft. Lauderdale, Fla., 1979; supt., expeditor Robert F. Wilson Constrn., Oakland Park, 1980-81, project mgr., 1981-84, Tuttle Bldg. Contractors, Inc., Longwood, 1984—. Drafted plans for residential development Ft. Lauderdale, 1979. Mem. Am. Concrete Inst., Delta Tau Delta. Republican. Presbyterian. Avocations: fishing, woodworking, scuba diving. Home: 1800 Atlantic Suite B-318 Key West FL 33040

SMITH, RANDALL NORMAN, orthopedist; b. Hicksville, N.Y., Mar. 1, 1948; s. Lester I. and Meta (Moskowitz) S.; m. Marcia Hope Bluestein, Jan. 23, 1949; children: Todd Adam, Taryn Leigh. BS, Ohio U., 1969; MD, Temple U., 1973. Diplomate Am. Bd. Orthopedics. Intern Einstein Med. Ctr., Phila., 1973-74, orthopedic resident, 1974-78, chief resident, 1976-78, staff physician, 1978—; pvt. practice, 1978—. Dir. emergency rm. JFK Hosp., Phila., 1975-79; spkr. in field. Contbr. articles to profl. jours. Bd. dirs. Plymouth Soccer League, Plymouth Twp., Pa., 1986-90; coach Plymouth Baseball and Basketball League, Plymouth Twp., 1982-89; referee Whitemarsh Soccer and Basketball, Lafayette Hill, Pa., 1985-91; mem. golf com. Meadowlands Country Club, Blue Bell, Pa., 1986-93. Recipient Pharmacy Family of Yr., Nat. Assn. Retail Druggists, 1972. Fellow Am. Acad. Orthopedics; mem. Am. Coll. Sports Medicine, Am. Coll. Occupl. Medicine, Ea. Orthopedic Assn., Am. Running and Fitness Assn., Brotherhood of Ami. Jewish. Avocations: golf, health club activities, children's sports, reading, chess. Office: Palmaccio Smith Assoc 12000 Bustleton Ave Philadelphia PA 19116-2151 E-mail: rmtt21@aol.com.

SMITH, RANDOLPH RELIHAN, plastic surgeon; b. Augusta, Ga., Aug. 13, 1944; s. Lester Vernon and Maxine (Relihan) S.; m. Becky Jo Hardy; children: Katherine, Randolph, Rebecca, Michael. BS, Clemson U., 1966; MD, Coll. Ga., 1970; LLD (hon.), Clemson U., 1997. Diplomate Am. Bd. Otolaryngology, Am. Bd. Plastic Surgery. Intern Bowman Gray Sch. Medicine Wake Forest U., Winston-Salem, N.C., 1970-71; resident in surgery and otolaryngology Duke U., Durham, 1971-75; resident in plastic and reconstructive surgery Med. Coll. Ga., 1975-77; Christine Kleinert fellow in hand surg. U. Louisville, 1977; attending physician U. Hosp., Augusta, Ga., 1977—. Asst. clin. prof. plastic surgery Med. Coll. Ga., 1978—; pres. med. staff Univ. Hosp., Augusta, mem. exec. coun. health care sys.; vol. surgeon in developing countries, 1982—. Contbr. articles to profl. jours. Trustee, chmn. bd. Univ. Health, Inc.; trustee Clemson U. Found.; mem. bd. visitors Clemson U.; vestryman, sr. warden St. Paul's Episc. Ch.; bd. dirs. United Way, Ga. Bank and Trust Co. of Augusta, Richmond County Hosp. Authority. Maj. med. corps USAR, 1971—78. Recipient Book of Golden Deeds award, Exch. Club of Augusta, 1997, Civic Endeavor award, Richmond County Med. Soc., 1998, Jack A. Raines Humanitarian award, Med. Assn. Ga., 1999, Pride in Profession award, AMA, 2001, award for yrs. ov svc. to Polish patients and edn. of Polish surgeons, City Coun. Nowy Sacz, Poland, 2001. Fellow ACS, Am. Acad. Otolaryngology; mem. Am. Soc. Plastic and Reconstructive Surgeons, Am. Soc. Aesthetic Plastic Surgery, Ga. Soc. Plastic and Reconstructive Surgeons, Southeastern Soc. Plastic and Reconstructive Surgeons,

Exch. Club of Augusta (bd. dirs., pres. 2001), Augusta Symphony League, Beech Island Agrl. Club, Rotary (Paul Harris fellow 1998), Alpha Omega Alpha. Office: Univ Hosp Med Ctr 811 13th St Ste 28 Augusta GA 30901-2772

SMITH, RAOUL NORMAND, computer science educator; b. West Warwick, R.I., May 15, 1938; s. Luke Joseph and Lucienne (Anchambault) S.; m. Mary Frances Hand, Nov. 12, 1966; children: Stephen Edward, Timothy Luke. AB, Brown U., 1963, AM, 1964, PhD, 1968. Instr. Northwestern U., Evanston, Ill., 1967-68, asst. prof., 1968-73, assoc. prof., 1973-80; sr. mem. of tech. staff GTE Labs., Waltham, Mass., 1981-83, prin. mem. of tech. staff, 1983; prof. Northeastern U., Boston, 1983—, dir. grad. schs., 1984-85, dir. rsch., 1985-86, prof. emeritus, 2000—; vis. prof. Jilin U. of Tech., Changchun, People's Republic of China, summer 1985; v.p. China Edn. Corp., 2000—. Chmn. bd. dirs. Cognitive Computers, Newton, Mass., 1985-87; prin. Raoul N. Smith and Assocs., Cons. Author: Dictionary of Artificial Intelligence, 1989, The Language of Jonathan Fisher, 1985, Probabilistic Performance Models of Language, 1973; co-author: Lexical-Semantic Relations, 1980. Trustee Acton (Mass.) Hist. Soc., 1988-90; mem. AIDS action com., 1985-88. With USAF, 1957-61. Grantee NSF, 1966, 66-67, 71, Am. Philos. Soc., 1974, Am. Coun. of Learned Socs., 1974, Nat. Endowment for the Humanities, 1975, 76-79. Mem. Assn. for Computing Machinery (co-chair spl. interest group on computer and human interaction 1981-85), Union Club. Avocations: antique porcelain, silver and jewelry. Home: 206 Nagog Hill Rd Acton MA 01720-3228 E-mail: raoulS500@aol.com.

SMITH, RAYMOND LEIGH, plastic surgeon; b. Norristown, Pa., Sept. 27, 1940; s. Walter Joseph and Pauline C. (Wolfskill) S.; m. Coralynn Elder, Jan. 8, 1966; children: Susan, Elizabeth, Christine. BS, Ursinus Coll., 1962; MD, Temple U., 1966. Diplomate Nat. Bd. Med. Examiners, Am. Bd. Plastic Surgery. Active staff Reading Hosp., Pa., 1976—, chief sect. of plastic surgery, 1994-2000. Mem. ACS, AMA, Republican Majority Found., Washington Legal Found. Mem. Am. Soc. Plastic Surgeons, Robert H. Ivy Soc., Am. Assn. Hand Surgery, Northeastern Soc. Plastic Surgeons, Pa. Med. Soc., Lipoplasty Soc. N.Am., Berks County Med. Soc. Lutheran. Office: 926 Penn Ave Wyomissing PA 19610-3017

SMITH, RAYMOND EDWARD, retired health care administrator; b. Freeport, N.Y., June 17, 1932; s. Jerry Edward and Madelyn Holman (Jones) S.; m. Lena Kathryn Jernigan Hughes, Oct. 28, 1983; children: Douglas, Ronald, Kevin, Doris Jean, Raymond. BS in Edn., Temple U., 1953; MHA, Baylor U., 1966. Commd. 2d lt. U.S. Army, 1953, advanced through grades to lt. col., 1973, helicopter ambulance pilot, 1953-63; comdr. helicopter ambulance units Korea, 1955, Fed. Republic of Germany, 1961; various hosp. adminstrv. assignments, 1963-73; pers. dir. Valley Forge (Pa.) Gen. Hosp., 1966; adminstr. evacuation hosp. Vietnam, 1967; dep. insp. Walter Reed Gen. Hosp., Washington, 1970; dir. personnel divsn. Office of Army Surgeon Gen., 1971-73, ret., 1973; adminstr. Health Care Ctrs., Phila., Phila. Coll. Osteo. Medicine, 1974-76; dir. bur. hosps. Pa. Dept. Health, Harrisburg, 1976-79; contract mgr. Blue Cross of Calif., San Diego, 1979-88, Cmty. Care Network, San Diego, 1989—95; ret., 1995. Decorated Bronze Star, Legion of Merit. Mem. Am. Hosp. Assn., Am. Legion, Ret. Officers Assn., Kappa Alpha Psi, Sigma Pi Phi. Episcopalian. Home: 7630 Lake Adlon Dr San Diego CA 92119-2518

SMITH, RAYMOND LLOYD, former university president, consultant; b. Vanceboro, Maine, Jan. 25, 1917; s. Ivan and Genevieve (Gatcomb) S.; m. Beatrice Bennett, Dec. 4, 1943; children: Bennett Charles, Martin Lloyd. BS in Mining Engring. cum laude, U. Alaska, 1943; MS in Metall. Engring, U. Pa., 1951, PhD in Metall. Engring, 1953; D.Sc. (hon.), Western Mich. U.; LL.D., No. Mich. U.; D.Eng. (hon.), Mich. Technol. U., S.D. Sch. Mines and Tech. Instr. math. U. Alaska, 1946-47, asst. prof. metallurgy, 1948-49; rsch. assoc. dept. metallurgy U. Pa., 1949-53; sr. rsch. metallurgist Franklin Inst. Labs., Phila., 1953, sect. chief metallurgy, 1954-56, assoc. dir., 1957, tech. dir., 1958-59; prof., head metall. dept. Mich. Technol. U., Houghton, 1959-64, coord. rsch., 1960-64, pres., 1965-79, Am. Soc. Metals, 1979-80, Houghton (Mich.) Daily Mining Gazette, 1979-81, R. L. Smith, Inc. Am. Soc. Metals/The Metallurgical Soc. joint disting. lectr. in materials; lectr. in field. Contbr. numerous articles to metall. sci. jours.; patentee in field. Chmn. bd. dirs. Community Water Co., Green Valley. With AUS, 1943-46. Recipient Distinguished Alumnus award U. Alaska, Clair M. Donovan award Mich. Tech. U., D. Robert Yarnall award U. Pa. Engring. Sch.; Outstanding Service award Air Force ROTC; Rotary Paul Harris fellow. Fellow Metall. Soc., AIME (Henry Krumb meml. lectr. 1981), Am. Soc. for Metals (hon.); mem. Scabbard and Blade, Blue Key, Tau Beta Pi, Alpha Sigma Mu (hon. lectr. 1982), Alpha Phi Omega, Phi Kappa Phi, Theta Tau. Home: PO Box 726 Green Valley AZ 85622-0726 *A sense of humor is one of the important building blocks for that firm sense of balance so necessary to meet the challenges of life. It's like the seasoning of a chef's masterpiece.*

SMITH, RAYMOND THOMAS, anthropology educator; b. Oldham, Lancashire, Eng., Jan. 12, 1925; s. Harry and Margaret (Mulchrone) S.; m. Flora Alexandrina Tong, June 30, 1954; children: Fenela, Colin, Anthony. BA, Cambridge (Eng.) U., 1950, MA, 1951, PhD, 1954. Sociol. research officer govt., Brit. Guiana, 1951-54; research fellow U. W.I., 1954-59; prof. sociology U. Ghana, 1959-62; sr. lectr. sociology, prof. anthropology U. West Indies, 1962-66; prof. anthropology U. Chgo., 1966-95, prof. emeritus, 1995—, chmn. dept. anthropology, 1975-81, 84-85, 94-95. Vis. prof. U. Calif.-Berkeley, 1957-58, McGill U., Montreal, 1964-65; mem. com. on child devel. rsch. and pub. policy NRC, 1977-80; dir. Caribbean Consortium Grad. Sch., 1985-86. Author: The Negro Family in British Guiana, 1956, British Guiana, 1962, 2d edit., 1980, Kinship and Class In The West Indies, 1988, The Matrifocal Family, 1996; co-author: Class Differences in American Kinship, 1978; editor: Kinship Ideology and Practice in Latin America, 1984; contbr. articles to profl. jours. Co-investigator urban family life project U. Chgo., 1986-90. Served with RAF, 1943-48. Guggenheim fellow, 1983-84 Fellow Am. Anthrop. Assn.; mem. Assn. Social Anthropologists. Office: Univ Chicago Dept Anthropology 1126 E 59th St Chicago IL 60637-1580 E-mail: r-smith@uchicago.edu.

SMITH, REBECCA SUE, music educator; b. Mishawaka, Ind., Sept. 14, 1950; d. James Edwin and Mary Alice (Schrader) S. BA, Ind. State U., 1972; M. Music, So. Meth. U., 1976; elem. edn. cert., Ind. U., South Bend, 1983; Orff cert. level I, Memphis State U., 1986. Elem. music tchr. Kouts (Ind.) Pub. Sch., 1973-74; piano tchr., accompanist Samford U., Birmingham, Ala., 1976-77; founder, tchr. Bethel Coll. Prep. Dept. Music, Mishawaka, 1977-82; elem. music tchr. South Bend Pub. Sch. Corp., 1977-82; class piano tchr. Ind. U. Prep. Dept. Music, South Bend, 1987-89; elem. music tchr. Penn-Harris-Madison Sch. Corp., Osceola, Ind., 1983—; pvt. piano tchr., 1966—. Practice supr. Nat. Music Camp, Interlochen, Mich., summers, 1975-80; presenter Mus. Tchrs.' Nat. Conf., 1983. Mem. South Bend Symphonic Choir, v.p., 1985-87; vol. Romanian Orphanage, 1991, 92; active with sr. citizens; handbell choir dir. and player, Carillon ringer, choir mem., chmn. shepherd's coun., mem. missions com., mem. new seekers class, vol. Bible sch., adminstrv. bd. disciple class II, accompanist 1st United Meth. Ch., Mishawaka, Ind. Mem. Am.-Orff Schulwerk Assn., PEO (chaplain 1987-92). Methodist. Avocations: handwork, raising rabbits, travel. Home: 2616 Wildflower Cv Mishawaka IN 46545-3940

SMITH, REGINALD BRIAN FURNESS, retired anesthesiologist, educator; b. Warrington, Eng., Feb. 7, 1931; s. Reginald and Betty (Bell) S.; m. Margarete Groppe, July 18, 1963; children: Corinne, Malcolm. MB, BS, U. London, 1955; DTM and H, Liverpool Sch. Tropical Medicine, 1959. Intern Poole Gen. Hosp., Dorset, Eng., 1955-56, Wilson Meml. Hosp., Johnson City, N.Y., 1962-63; resident in anesthesiology Med. Coll. Va., Richmond, 1963-64, U. Pitts., 1964-65, from clin. instr. to prof., 1965-78; acting chmn. dept. anesthesiology, 1977-78; prof., chmn. dept. U. Tex. Health Sci. Center, San Antonio, 1978-98; anesthesiologist in chief hosps. U. Tex. Health Sci. Ctr., 1978-98, med. dir. hyperbaric medicine and woundcare unit Univ. Hosp., 1993-2000; dir. anesthesiology Eye and Ear Hosp., Pitts., 1971-76; Univ. Hosp.; anesthesiologist in chief Presbyn. Univ. Hosp., Pitts., 1976-78; ret., 2000. Contbg. editor: Internat. Ophthalmology Clinics, 1973, Internat. Anesthesiology Clinics, 1983; contbr. articles to profl. jours. Served to capt. Brit. Army, 1957-59. Fellow ACP, Am. Coll. Anesthesiologists, Am. Coll. Chest Physicians; mem. AMA, Internat. Anesthesia Rsch. Soc., Am. Soc. Anesthesiologists (pres. Western Pa. 1974-75), Tex. Soc. Anesthesiologists, San Antonio Soc. Anesthesiologists (pres. 1990), Tex. Med. Assn., Bexar County Med. Soc. Home: 213 Canada Verde St San Antonio TX 78232-1104

SMITH, REX, information technology executive; BSEE, Oreg. State U.; MSEE, Stanford U. Dir. ops. Sun Microsystems Inc.; head hardware product developer Apple 2 Products; lead hardware product developer Newton; designer, program mgr. calculator devel. group Hewlett-Packard Co.; v.p. product devel. FutureTel; chmn. bd., COO Hotmail; gen. mgr. MSN Hotmail, 1998, MSN Ops.; corp. v.p. MSN Ops. Microsoft, Redmond, Wash. Office: Microsoft One Microsoft Way Redmond WA 98052-6399*

SMITH, RHONDA LAVONNE, food scientist, researcher; b. Madison Heights, Mich., May 15, 1971; d. Charlie Thomas Jr. and Yevonne Rita (Shelton) S. BA in Biochemistry, Oberlin Coll., 1993; MS in Food Sci. and Tech., Cornell U., 1998. Rsch. asst. Ohio Wesleyan U., Delaware, Ohio, 1992, Oberlin Coll., Oberlin, 1991, 93, Henry Ford Hosp., Detroit, 1993, Cornell U., Geneva, 1993-98, Internat. Flavors and Fragrances, Union Beach, N.J., 1997—. Tchg. asst. Oberlin Coll., 1991-93, Cornell U., 1995. Contbr. articles and presentations to profl. jours. Concord Grape Hort. Rsch. grant Viticulture Consortium East, 1996; fellow Cornell U., 1993-96. Mem. Inst. Food Technologists, Am. Chem. Soc., Soc. Cosmetic Chemists, Sigma Xi. Achievements include research in flavor and sensory profile of N.Y. state Concord grape juices. Office: Cornell Univ Food Rsch Lab PO Box 15 Geneva NY 14456-0015

SMITH, RICHARD ALTON, mechanical contracting company executive; b. Florence, S.C., Nov. 12, 1955; s. Lemuel Alton and Mary (Ham) S.; m. Sandra Adell Bruorton, Feb. 26, 1977; children: Amy Colleen Smith, Ernest Alton Smith. AA in Bus., Trident Tech. Coll., Charleston, S.C., 1982; BS in Trades and Indsl. Edn., U. Ga., 1992. Cert. assoc. welding insp. Welding foreman General Dynamics, Goose Creek, S.C., 1975-78; maint. mechanic Exxon Co. USA, Charleston, 1978-80, Alumax of S.C., Mt. Holly, 1980-83; mech. trainer Kendall Co., Bethune, S.C., 1983-86; maint. supr. Hercules Inc., Covington, Ga., 1986-88; v.p. Indsl. Mech. Inc., Watkinsville, 1988—; tng. cons. pvt. practice, Conyers, 1988—; v.p. Reinicke Corp., Athens, 1992—. Tng. cons. Lanier Tech. Inst., Gainesville, Ga., 1992—, Athens (Ga.) Tech., 1984—. Served with U.S. Army N.G., Operation Desert Storm, 1991. Decorated Army Commednation medal. Mem. Am. Welding Soc., Fluid Power Soc. Am., Am. Vocat. Assn., Ga. Vocat. Assn., Nat. Guard Assn. Am., Nat. Guard Assn. Ga., Ga. Military Inst. Avocations: camping, boating. Home: 102 Wappoo Creek Dr Ste 8C Charleston SC 29412-2144 Office: Reinicke Corp 180 Hanover Pl Athens GA 30606-7114

SMITH, RICHARD BOWEN, retired national park superintendent; b. Grandville, Mich., Mar. 8, 1938; s. William Jr. and Mary Elizabeth (Bowen) S.; m. Katherine Theresa Short, Sept. 21, 1980. BA in History, Albion Coll., 1960; MA in English, Mich. State U., 1967. Tchr. Grand Rapids (Mich.) Jr. H.S., 1960-66; vol. Peace Corps, Asuncion, Paraguay, 1968-70; ranger Nat. Pk. Svc., Yosemite, Calif., 1971-76, ranger. instr. Grand Canyon, Ariz., 1976-78, ranger, legis. specialist Washington, 1978-80, asst. supt. Everglades, Fla., 1980-83, assoc. regional dir. ops. Phila., 1984-86, supt. Carlsbad Caverns, N.Mex., 1986-88, assoc. regional dir. ops. Santa Fe, 1988-89; assoc. regional dir. resources mgmt. Nat. Park Service, 1990-94; cons. on protected area mgmt. in L.Am., 1994—; temp. supt. Yellowstone Nat. Pk., 1994—; owner R & K Internat., 1994—2000; assoc. Orgnl. Quality Assocs., , 2000—. Pres. Assn. Nat. Park Rangers, 1977-78; coord. Congress of Internat. Ranger Fedn., San Jose, Costa Rica, 1997, v.p., 1998-2000, pres., 2000—. Bd. dirs. Yellowstone Assn., 1995-97, Ptnrs. in Parks, 1998-2000. Recipient Meritorious Svc. award Dept. Interior, 1992. Mem. Assn. Nat. Park Rangers (chmn. internat. com. 1997-2000), George Wright Soc. (bd. dirs. 1998—). Home: 2 Roadrunner Trl Placitas NM 87043-9424 E-mail: rsmith0921@aol.com.

SMITH, RICHARD C., JR. public relations executive, quality assurance professional; BEE, Vanderbilt U.; M, PhD, Yale U. Pres. ISACOMM (acquired by Sprint 1981), 1979-81; numerous mktg. positions, pres. divsn. nat. accts., pres. divsn. nat. mkts. Sprint, Washington, 1981-91, sr. v.p. quality devel. and pub. rels., 1991-98; CEO Telcordia Techs., Morristown, 1998—. Office: Telcordia Techs 445 South St Morristown NJ 07960-6454

SMITH, RICHARD CHARLES, not-for-profit developer, educator; b. St. Paul, July 30, 1947; s. Arthur George Smith, Edna Alma Smith; m. Joan Rita Oxendine. BA, Calif. State U., San Bernardino, 1976; MBA, U. Calif., Riverside, 1981. Dir. mktg. SCW and Assoc., Riverside, Calif., 1981—84; dir. mktg. and ops. Thomas and Assoc., 1984—85; v.p. br. adminstrn. First Fed. Savings and Loan, Ridgecrest, 1985—90; gen. mgr. KLOA Radio, 1990—92; dir. mktg. Ridgecrest Auto Ctr., 1992—94; exec. dir. Partnership to Preserve Indep. Living for Srs. and Persons with Disabilities, Riverside, 1994—. Mem. Riverside County Integrated Home and Cmty. Based Long Term Care Task Force, Riverside, 1998—, Riverside County Disability Adv. Com., Calif., 2000—, Riverside County C.A.R.E. Team, 2001—. Contbr. articles; prodr., prodr.: Health Education Program Series. E5 Army, 1966—69, Vietnam. Office: Partnership for Independent Living 6296 Rivercrest Dr Ste K Riverside CA Personal E-mail: rsmith@vitalco.net. Business E-Mail: rsmith@vitalco.net.

SMITH, RICHARD DAVID, economics educator; b. Derby, Eng., July 15, 1968; s. David Rees and Vera (Wheeldon) S.; m. Jane Rebecca Powell, Mar. 16, 1996. BA in Econs., U. York, 1990, MSc in Econs., 1991. Health economist U. Sydney, Australia, 1991-93; cons. Cambridge (Eng.) Pharma-Consultancy, 1993-94; rsch. assoc. U. Bristol, Eng. 1995-96; sr. lectr. Monash U., Melbourne, Australia, 1996-99, U. E. Anglia, Eng., 1999—. Contbr. articles to profl. jours. including: Health Econs., Health Policy, Social Sci. and Medicine, Med. Jour. of Australia. Preacher Wesleyan Meth. Ch. of Australia, Melbourne, 1997-99; lay preacher Meth. Ch. Eng., 2001—. Mem. Internat. Health Econs. Assn., Health Econs. Soc. Australia, Health Economist Study Group, Pub. Health Assn. Australia. Avocation: photography. Office: U East Anglia Sch Medicine Health Policy Norwich NR4 7TJ England E-mail: richard.smith@uea.ac.uk.

SMITH, RICHARD EMERSON (DICK SMITH), make-up artist; b. Larchmont, N.Y., June 26, 1922; s. Richard Roy and Coral (Brown) S.; m. Jocelyn De Rosa, Jan. 10, 1949; children: Douglas Todd, David Emerson. BA, Yale U., 1944. Pioneer dir. first TV make-up dept. NBC-TV, N.Y.C., 1945-59; make-up dir. David Susskind Prodns., 1959-61; freelance make-up artist, cons., 1961—. Lectr. Yoyogi Animation Sch., Tokyo, 1992—, Polytek Devel. seminar, 1996; key spkr. Internat. Make-up and Effects Trade Show, 1997-99; featured make-up expert in Movie Magic tv documentaries, Monster Effects, 1994, Aging Effects, 1995; lectr. on spl. make-up effects. Credits include Requiem for a Heavyweight, 1962, The World of Henry Orient, 1963, Mark Twain, Tonight!, 1967 (Emmy award 1967), Midnight Cowboy, 1968, Little Big Man, 1969, The Godfather, 1971, The Exorcist, 1973, The Godfather, Part II, 1974, The Sunshine Boys, 1975, Taxi Driver, 1975, Altered States, 1979, Scanners, 1980, Ghost Story, 1981, The Hunger, 1982, Amadeus, 1983 (U.S. Acad. award 1984, Brit. Acad. award 1985), Starman, 1984, Poltergeist III, 1987, Everybody's All-American, 1988, Sweet Home (Japanese film), 1988, Dad, 1989, Death Becomes Her, 1991, Forever Young, 1992; author: The Advanced Professional Make-Up Course, The Basic 3-D Make-up Course, 2002; permanent exhbn. of make-up work from Little Big Man, The Exorcist, Amadeus, others, at N.Y. Mus. of the Moving Image, 1992—; columnist Makeup Artist Mag., 1997. Honored on his 50th ann. in make-up by Am. Film Inst., Visionary Cinema, Cinefex mag., 1995. Home and Office: 27 Wilford Ave Branford CT 06405-3822 E-mail: pros355@aol.com.

SMITH, RICHARD ERNEST, retired insurance company executive; b. Adrian, Mich., Oct. 29, 1935; s. Albert Forrest and Thelma (Brock) S.; m. Joanne Piplow, Oct. 11, 1955; children: Kathryn, Albert, Sharon, Richard, Heidi. Student, Spring Arbor Coll., 1955. CLU. Mgr. White Hardware, Adrian, 1950-59; dist. mgr. Met. Life, Adrian and Lafayette, Ind., 1959-75; dir. regional Ohio Nat. Life, Cin., 1975-78; agy. v.p. Provident Life, Bismarck, N.D., 1978-86, pres., 1986-90. Bd. dirs. Provident Life Ins. Co. Commr. City of Adrian, 1966-71; trustee Medctr. One, Bismarck, 1986—, Bismarck State Coll. Found., 1987-91; bd. dirs., v. chmn. Mackinac Straits Hosp., St. Ignace, Mich., 1995—, Bismarck Devel. Assn., 1987-91, Greater Adrian Devel. Assn., 1966-70. Mem.: Apple Creek Country (Bismarck), Elks. Republican. Avocation: travel. Home: N5072 Epoufette Bay Rd Naubinway MI 49762-9722

SMITH, RICHARD HEWLETT, II, senior analyst; b. Richmond, Va., Nov. 21, 1950; s. Sydney Strother and Elizabeth Peale (Oglesby) S.; m. Sara Margaret Larch, June 16, 1993; children: Richard H. Smith III, Leigh Smith Danby. BSBA, Thomas Edison Coll., 1995; MS, Va. Poly. Inst. and State U., 1997. Cert. med. practice adminstr. Pres. Miners & Mfr.'s Ins., Bristol, Va., 1975-78; dir., govt. liaison AT&T, Morristown, N.J., 1978-86; mgr. tactical programs Sys. Devel. Corp., Paoli, Pa., 1986-88; dir. systems mktg. SONY Corp. Am., Park Ridge, N.J., 1988-90; pres. Consol. Systems Group Inc., Alexandria, Va., 1990-92; dir. planning and rsch. Georgetown U., Washington, 1993-95; sr. analyst Coates and Jarratt, Inc., 1999—. Contbr. articles to profl. jours. Mem. MHSS 2020 Nanotech. Task Force; mem. bd. advisors No. Va. Grad. Ctr. Recipient Arnold Fletcher award for exceptional achievement, 1996. Mem. Nat. Coun. Rsch. Adminstrs., Med. Group Mgmt. Assn., World Future Soc., Foresight Inst. (sr. assoc.), Am. Coll. Med. Practice Execs. Democrat. Home: 2121 Jamieson Ave Unit 505 Alexandria VA 22314-5709 Office: Coates and Jarratt Inc 4455 Connecticut Ave NW Washington DC 20008-2328

SMITH, RICHARD HOWARD, banker; b. Tulare, Calif., Aug. 27, 1927; s. Howard Charles and Sue Elizabeth (Cheyne) S.; B.A., Principia Coll, 1958; LL.B., LaSalle U., 1975; postgrad. Sch. Banking U. Wash., 1970-72; m. Patricia Ann Howery, Mar. 12, 1950; children— Jeffrey Howard, Holly Lee, Gregory Scott, Deborah Elaine. Prin., Aurora Elementary Sch., Tulare, 1951-53; prin. Desert Sun Sch., Idyllwild, Calif., 1953-55; trust adminstr. trainee Bank of Am., San Diego, 1955-58, asst. trust officer, Ventura, Redlands, Riverside and L.A., 1958-65; asst. trust officer Security Pacific Bank, Fresno, Calif., 1965-68; trust officer, 1968-72, v.p., mgr., 1972-88, Pasadena, 1988-94; v.p. Bank of Am., L.A., 1994-95; ret., 1995; pres. Fiduciary Svcs., Fresno, 1995—; instr. San Bernardino Valley Coll., 1962— , Fresno City Coll., 1977— . With USN, 1945-46. Home: 3222 W Dovewood Ln Fresno CA 93711-2125 Office: 1 City Blvd W Orange CA 92868-3621

SMITH, RICHARD JACKSON, elementary education educator; b. Mt. Airy, N.C., Feb. 17, 1947; s. Robert Wayne and Ruth (Jackson) S.; m. Sue Monday, Sept. 10, 1971 (dec. Nov. 21, 1981); 1 child, Richard Jackson Jr. BA, U. N.C., 1972; MA, Appalachian State U., 1975; EdD, U. N.C., 1994. Elem. tchr. Surry County Schs., Dobson, N.C., 1967-96, Title I parent coord., 1992-96, K-5 instnl. specialist, 1996—; project coord. Reading Is Fundamental, 1996-2000. Part-time instr. grad. equivalency diploma/adult basic edn. and effective tchr. tng. classes Surry C.C., Dobson, 1988-92, tchr. literacy class, 1999-2000; cons. Eckerd Family Youth Alternatives, Inc., 1994-96. Local and dist. chmn., state treas. N.C. Polit. Action Com. for Edn., Raleigh, 1976-81; state exec. com. N.C. Dem. Party, Raleigh, 1981-83; trustee, deacon First Bapt. Ch. of Pilot Mountain, 1988—, Sunday sch. dir. 1991—, mem. nominating com., 1991—, sec. bd. deacons 1990-91, vice chmn. 1996-97, chmn. 1997-99; trustee Charles M. Stone Meml. Libr., 1997-2000, vice chmn., 1998-99, chmn., 1999-2000; chaplain Pilot Mountain Camp, 2000—; bd. dirs. Surry County chpt. ARC, 2000—, chair nominating com., 2000—. Mem. ASCD, NEA (congressional lobbying 1976-80), Internat. Reading Assn. (local unit chair 1986-90), N.C. Assn. Educators (local, dist. pres. 1979-81, local, dist., state chmn. legis. commn. 1980-81), Pilot Mountain Jaycees (life, charter mem., pres. 1979-80, Officer of Yr. 1978, 79), Geneal. Soc. Rockingham & Stokes Counties, Stokes County Hist. Soc., Sons Confederate Vets. (Stokes County camp 1994—), Masons (32 degree, Scottish Rite Winston-Salem consistory 1988—, amb. 1990—, lodge master 1990, edn. chmn. 1986—, scholarship chmn. 1986—, Cert. of Meritorious Svc. 1988). Home: PO Box 127 517 E Main St Pilot Mountain NC 27041-8519 Office: Surry County Schs PO Box 364 Dobson NC 27017-0364 E-mail: drrichardsmith@yahoo.com., SmithR@SurryCountyk12.nc.us.

SMITH, RICHARD JAY, anthropologist, orthodontist, educator; b. Bklyn., Aug. 10, 1948; s. Benjamin and Miriam S.; m. Linda Sharon Harris, Aug. 22, 1970; children: Jason Andrew, Owen Harris, Hilary Rachele. BA, Bklyn. Coll., CUNY, 1969; MS in Anatomy, Tufts U., 1973, DMD, 1973; PhD in Anthropology, Yale U., 1980. Asst. clin. prof. orthodontics U. Conn., Farmington, 1976-79; asst. prof. U. Md., Balt., 1979-81, assoc. prof., 1981-84; prof. orthodontics, biomed. sci., chmn. dept. orthodontics, adj. prof. anthropology Washington U., St. Louis, 1984-91, assoc. dean, 1987-89, dean sch. dental medicine, 1989-91, cons. orthodontics Cleft Palate and Craniofacial Anomalies Team, 1984-91, prof. anthropology, 1991-2001, disting. prof. Ralph E. Morrow U., 2001—, chmn. dept. anthropology, 1993—; vis. assoc. prof. cell biology Sch. Medicine, Johns Hopkins U., Balt., 1980-84; orthodontic cons. St. Louis VA Med. Ctr., 1986-91; staff Barnes Hosp., 1986-91, St. Louis Children's Hosp., 1985-91. Editor-in-chief Jour. Balt. Coll. Dental surgery, 1981-84. Contbr. numerous articles in orthodontics, anthropology, comparative biology to profl. jours. Am. Fund for Dental Health dental tchr. tng. fellow, 1977-78; NIH postdoctoral fellow, 1978-79. Fellow Internat. Coll. Dentists, Am. Coll. Dentists ; mem. ADA, Alumni Assn. Student Clinicians (bd. govs. 1984-90, pres. 1988-89, Alan J. Davis award 1983), Am. Assn. Orthodontists, Am. Assn. Phys. Anthropologists, Internat. Primatological Soc. Home: 816 S Bemiston Ave Saint Louis MO 63105-2602 Office: Washington U Dept Anthropology One Brookings Dr Saint Louis MO 63130 E-mail: rjsmith@artsci.wustl.edu.

SMITH, RICHARD SCOTT, network support manager; b. Chgo., Apr. 28, 1953; s. Arthur Martin and Jeanne Riemenschneider Smith; m. Gayl Dasher, Mar. 30, 1954; children: Erik, Rebecca. AS in Computer Sci., So. Ill. U.; BA in Computer Sci., North Ctrl. Coll., Naperville, Ill. Network support mgmt. cons., Chgo., 1990—. Stress meditation and judo instr. Naperville Pk. Dist., Ill., 1985—. Author: The Tao of Healing, 2001. Avocation: writing. Home: 1905 Stanford Naperville IL 60565 Personal E-mail: rsmith0428@aol.com.

SMITH, RICHARD THOMAS, electrical engineer, consultant; b. Allentown, Pa., June 15, 1925; s. Raymond Willard and Mary (Rau) S.; m. Naomi Elsie Anthony, May 26, 1956; children: Cynthia Louise, Carol Ann. BS with high honors, Lehigh U., 1946, MS, 1947; PhD, Ill. Inst. Tech., 1955. Registered profl. engr., Mass., Okla., Tex., Gt. Britain. Instr., Lehigh U., Bethlehem, Pa., 1947-50; analytical and design engr. Gen. Electric Co., Schenectady, 1952-58; asso. prof. U. Tex., Austin, 1958-61; George Westinghouse prof. elec. engring. Va. Poly. Inst., Blacksburg, 1961-62; project dir. Tracor, Inc., Austin, 1962-64; sr. engr., asst. dir., dir., v.p. Southwest Research Inst., San Antonio, 1964-66; Okla. Gas and Electric prof. elec. engring. U. Okla., Norman, 1966-68; prof. elec. machinery Rensselaer Poly. Inst., Troy, N.Y., 1968-70; NSF fellow U. Colo., 1970; Alcoa&UMR Disting. prof. elec. engring. U. Mo., Rolla, 1970-73; inst. engr., dir. Nondestructive Testing Info. Analysis Center, Southwest Research Inst., San Antonio, 1973-83; cons., 1983—. Adj. prof. U. Tex., 1974-83, prof., 1983-87; cons., reviewer numerous cos. Author: Analysis of Electrical Machines, 1982; patentee in field. Recipient Excellence Fund U. Tex., 1959, DuPont Meml. prize Lehigh U., 1946 Fellow AIAA (assoc.), Instn. Elec. Engrs. (Eng.); mem. Am. Soc. Engring. Edn., I.E.E.E. (1st paper prize 1960, 63, sr.), N.Y. Acad. Scis., I.E.E.E. (numerous coms.), Internat. Electrotech. Commn. (adv. group 1971-74), Sigma Xi, Tau Beta Pi, Pi Mu Epsilon, Phi Eta Sigma, Eta Kappa Nu, Phi Kappa Phi. Office: 402 Yosemite Dr Hollywood Park TX 78232-1251 E-mail: snar@idworld.net.

SMITH, RICHEY, chemical company executive; b. Akron, Ohio, Nov. 11, 1933; s. Thomas William and Martha (Richey) S.; m. Sandra Cosgrave Roe, Nov. 25, 1961; children: Mason Roe, Parker Richey. Grad. The Hotchkiss Sch.; BS, U. Va., 1956. Asst. to pres. Sun Products Corp., Barberton, Ohio, 1960-64, v.p., 1964-67, gen. mgr., dir., 1967-69, chmn., CEO, 1969-76; prin. A.T. Kearney Co., Cleve., 1977-87; chmn., CEO Richey Industries, Inc., Medina, Ohio, 1987—. Bd. dirs. Jaite Packaging, Inc. Exec. com. Gt. Trail coun. Boy Scouts Am.; chmn. capital funds dr. Summit County Planned Parenthood; trustee, found. pres. Old Trail Sch., Barberton Citizens Hosp., Medina County Arts Coun., Akron Regional Devel. Bd.; treas. Friends of Metro Park; found. trustee, vestryman St. Paul's Episcopal Ch.; corp. bd. Cleve. Mus. of Art; bd. govs. The Hotchkiss Sch. Lt. USNR, 1957—67. Mem. Bluecoats, Navy League (pres. Akron coun. 1972-73), Young Pres. Orgn., Portage Country Club (bd. dirs.), Mayflower Club, Sawgrass Club (Fla.)

Farmington Club (Charlottesville, Va.), Rotary (trustee Akron 1974-75), Chi Psi (pres.). Home: 721 Delaware Ave Akron OH 44303-1303 Office: PO Box 928 910 Lake Rd Medina OH 44256-2453 E-mail: rsmith@richeyind.com.

SMITH, RICK A. mechanical engineer, consultant; b. Shelby, Ohio, Sept. 10, 1948; s. Reginald A. and Ella Mae (Bolin) S.; m. Rhea Dawn Wilcox, Dec. 15, 1973. BSME, Purdue U., 1976; M of Engring., Ohio State U., 1988. Registered profl. engr., Ohio. Project engr. Armour-Dial, Inc., Montgomery, Ill., 1976-77, Purdue U., West Lafayette, Ind., 1977-79; plant energy engr. ALCOA, Lafayette, 1979-81; facility project mgr. Cummins Engine Co., Columbus, 1981-83; project mgr., sr. engr. Ohio State U., 1983-88; pres., cons. mech. engr. Applied Thermal Engring., Ostrander, Ohio, 1988—. Mem. Mayor's Dist. Heating Task Force, Columbus, Ohio, 1984-86. 1st lt. USMC, 1968-72, Vietnam. Mem. ASME, Am. Pub. Power Assn., Am. Legion, Pi Tau Sigma. Republican. Avocations: flying, shooting, motorcycling, Dalmatians, physical fitness. Office: Applied Thermal Engring Inc 7400 Brown Rd Ste 200 Ostrander OH 43061-9326 E-mail: rasmith2@gte.net.

SMITH, ROBERT MICHAEL, lawyer, mediator, arbitrator; b. Boston, Nov. 4, 1940; s. Sydney and Minnie (Appel) S.; m. Catherine Kersey, Apr. 14, 1981 (dec. 1983); m. Clarissa Redmond, Feb. 11, 1999 (dec. 2001). AB cum laude, Harvard Coll., 1962; diploma, Centro de Estudos de Espanol, Barcelona, 1963; MA in Internat. Affairs, Columbia U., 1964, MS in Journalism with high honors, 1965; JD, Yale U., 1975. Bar: Calif., N.Y., D.C., U.S. Supreme Ct.; solicitor Supreme Ct. of Eng. and Wales; accredited mediator Hong Kong Internat. Arbitration Ctr.; chartered arbitrator, Eng. Intern in econ. devel. UN, Geneva, 1964; corr. Time Mag., N.Y.C., 1965-66, The N.Y. Times, Washington, 1968-72, 75-76; atty. Heller, Ehrman, White & McAuliffe, San Francisco, 1976-78; spl. asst. Office of Atty. Gen. of U.S., Washington, 1979-80; dir. Office Pub. Affairs U.S. Dept. Justice, 1979-80; mem. U.S. delegation U.S. v. Iran Internat. Ct. of Justice, The Hague, 1980; asst. U.S. atty. No. Dist. Calif., San Francisco, 1981-82; counsel, sr. counsel to sr. litigation counsel Bank of Am. NT & SA, 1982-86. Lectr. FBI Acad., Quantico, Va., 1980, Internat. Bankers Assn. Calif., 1994, Calif. Bankers Assn., 1994, Cmty. Bankers No. Calif., 1994, 95; judge Golden Medallion Broadcast Media awards State Bar of Calif., 1985; judge pro tem Mcpl. Ct. City and County of San Francisco, 1989—; conciliator Peninsula Conflict Resolution Ctr.; panelist World Intellectual Property Orgn., Geneva; arbitrator internat. Commercial arbitration ctrs., Vancouver, Cairo, Singapore, Kuala Lumpur, India; CPR Panel of Disting. Neutrals; mem. panel Nat. Assn. for Dispute Resolution. Author: Alternative Dispute Resolution for Financial Institutions, 1995, revised, 1996, 97, 98; bd. editors Yale Law Jour., 1974-75; editor Litigation, jour. ABA litigation sect., 1978-81; mem. editl. adv. bd. Bancroft-Whitney, 1991-94; contbr. articles to profl. jours. Bd. dirs. Neighborhood Legal Assistance Found., San Francisco, 1985-87, Nob Hill Assn., San Francisco, 1985-93; bd. dirs., fin. com. St. Francis Found., San Francisco, 1993-94. 1st lt. inf., USAR, 1965-71. Recipient UPI Award for Newswriting, 1958; Harvard Coll. scholar, 1958-62, Fulbright scholar, 1962-63; Columbia U. Internat. fellow, 1964-65. Fellow Internat. Acad. Mediators, Am. Coll. Civil Trial Mediators, Hong Kong Inst. Arbitrators, Chartered Inst. Arbitrators (London); mem. ABA (corp. counsel com. 1986-96, alternative dispute resolution sect. 1994-98), Assn. Atty. Mediators (v.p. No. Calif. chpt. 1995), State Bar of Calif. (pub. affairs com. 1982-85, litigation sect. 1990-96), Bar Assn. of San Francisco (bench-bar media com. 1985-96, alternative dispute resolution com. 1994-98), Assn. Bus. Trial Lawyers No. Calif., Assn. of Former U.S. Attys. No. Dist. Calif., Am. Arbitration Assn. (mem. comml. arbitration panel, No. Calif. adv. coun., mediator Am. Arbitration Ctr. for Mediation), Nat. Assn. Dispute Resolution, The Mediation Soc. (chmn. bd., pres.), Profl. Atty. Mediators, Cmty. Bds. of San Francisco (conciliator), French-Am. C. of C., German-Am. C. of C. West U.S., Harvard Club of San Francisco (bd. dirs. 1986-94, pres. 1992-94), Yale Club of San Francisco (bd. dirs. 1989-94), Soc. Profls. in Dispute Resolution, Columbia U. Alumni Club of No. Calif. (exec. com. 1978-92). Office: 120 Montgomery St Ste 1790 San Francisco CA 94104-4320 E-mail: rms@robertmsmith.com.

SMITH, ROBERT VICTOR, university administrator; b. Glendale, N.Y., Feb. 16, 1942; s. Robert Arthur and Marie Marlene (Florence) S. BS in Pharm. Sci., St. John's U., Jamaica, N.Y., 1963; MS in Pharm. Chemistry, U. Mich., 1964, PhD in Pharm. Chemistry, 1968. Asst. prof., then assoc. prof. U. Iowa, Iowa City, 1968-74; assoc. prof., asst. dir. U. Tex., Austin, 1974-77, area coordinator basic pharmaceutics, 1975-76, assoc. dir. Drug Dynamics Inst., 1977-78, dir. Drug Dynamics Inst., Coll. Pharmacy, 1979-85, James E. Bauerle Centennial prof. Coll. Pharmacy, 1983-85; prof., dean Coll. Pharmacy, Wash. State U., Pullman, 1985-86, vice provost for rsch., dean Grad. Sch., 1987-97; vice provost for rsch. and grad. edn., dean Grad. Sch., U. Conn., Storrs, 1997-2000; provost, vice chancellor acad. affairs U. Ark., Fayetteville, 2000—. Cons. E. R. Squibb, New Brunswick, N.J., 1979-82, Upjohn Co., Kalamazoo, Mich., 1982-85; external examiner U. Malaysia, Penang, 1981-82; mem. sci. adv. bd. Biodecision Labs., Pitts., 1985-86; Wash. Exposition Sci. Tech. Found., 1989-90; mem. noms. com. Coun. Grad. Schs., Washington, 1990-91, 96-97; accreditation evaluator Northwest Assn. Schs. and Colls., Seattle, 1991-97; mem. exec. com. grad. deans African-Am. Inst., N.Y., 1992-2000; bd. dirs. Coun. Grad. Schs., 1998. Author: Textbook of Biopharmaceutic Analysis, 1981, Graduate Research: A Guide for Students in the Sciences, 1998, Development and Management of University Research Groups, 1986. Bd. dirs. Wash. Tech. Ctr., 1990-92. Grantee NIH, 1974-83; fellow Acad. Pharm. Scis., 1981, Am. Assn. Pharm. Scientists, 1987; recipient Disting. Alumnus award Coll. Pharmacy U. Mich., 1990, Outstanding Svc. award Wash. State U., Grad. and Profl. Student Assn., 1993, 95. Mem. Am. Assn. Colls. Pharmacy (chmn. research and grad. affairs com. 1983-84), U.S. Pharmacopeia (revision com. 1985-90), Acad. Pharm. Scis. (chmn., vice chmn. 1983-85, 90, Presdl. citation 1985), Wash. Rsch. Found. (bd. dirs. 1989-97). Unitarian Universalist. Home: 665 Samara Cir Fayetteville AR 72701-3035 Office: U Ark Adminstrn Bldg Fayetteville AR 72701

SMITH, ROBERT BOULWARE, III, vascular surgeon, educator; b. Atlanta, June 15, 1933; s. Robert Boulware Jr. Smith and Mary Eva (Black) Fanning; m. Florence Chance Limehouse, Aug. 22, 1953; children: Victoria Joanne Smith Harkins, Robert Boulware IV, Brian Scott. MD, Emory U., 1957. Diplomate Am. Bd. Surgery, Am. Bd. Vascular Surgery. Intern in surgery Columbia Presbyn. Hosp., N.Y.C., 1957-58, resident in surgery, 1960-65; asst. prof. surgery Emory U. Sch. Medicine, Atlanta, 1966-69, assoc. prof., 1969-77, prof., 1977—, head gen. vascular surgery, 1984-98. Chief surg. svc. VA Med. Ctr., Atlanta, 1969-88; assoc. med. dir. Emory U. Hosp., 1993-95, med. dir., 1995—. Contbr. numerous articles, book chpts. to profl. publs.; co-editor: Trauma to the Thorax and Abdomen, 1969, Medical Management of the Surgical Patient, 1982, 3d edit., 1995. Capt. M.C., U.S. Army, 1958-60. Mem. ACS, Am. Surg. Assn., So. Assn. Vascular Surgery (sec. 1986-91, pres. 1992-93), Soc. Vascular Surgery, Assn. VA Surgeons (pres. 1983-84, Disting. Svc. award 1988), Ga. Surg. Soc. (pres. 1992-93), Atlanta Vascular Soc. (pres. 1986-88), Internat. Soc. for Cardiovasc. Surg. (pres. 1996-97). Phi Beta Kappa, Alpha Omega Alpha. Republican. United Methodist. Avocation: music, travel. Home: 2701 Coldwater Canyon Dr Tucker GA 30084-2358 Office: The Emory Clinic 1365 Clifton Rd NE Atlanta GA 30322-1013 E-mail: robert_smith@emoryhealthcare.org.

SMITH, ROBERT BRUCE, former security consultant, retired career officer; b. De Quincy, La., Apr. 22, 1920; s. Malcolm Monard and Jewell (Perkins) S.; m. Gladys Opal Borel, Feb. 22, 1941; children: Susan, Richard, Bruce. B.J., La. State U., 1941; grad., Command and Gen. Staff Coll., 1951-52, Army War Coll., 1958-59. Commd. 2d lt. U.S. Army, 1941, advanced through grades to maj. gen., 1969; plans and ops. officer 83d Div. Arty., Europe, 1943-45; personnel officer Philippine-Ryukyus Command, Manila, 1947-49; prof. mil. sci. and tactics ROTC, Lanier High Sch., Macon, Ga., 1949-51; chief res. officers sect., procurement br. Dept. Army, 1952-55; chief troop info. Office Chief Info., Dept. Army, 1962-63, dep. chief info., 1968-69; comdg. officer 8th F.A. Bn., 25th Inf. Div., Hawaii, 1955-56; G-1 25th Inf. Div. and U.S. Army Hawaii, 1956-58; mem. staff, faculty Command and Gen. Staff Coll., Fort Leavenworth, Kans., 1959-62; chief Alt. Nat. Mil. Command Center, Fort Ritchie, Md., 1963-64; dep. dir. ops. Office Joint Chiefs of Staff, 1964-65; asst. div. comdr. 7th Inf. Div., Korea, 1965-66; dep. comdt. Army War Coll., Carlisle, Pa., 1966-68; dep. comdg. gen. Ryukyus Islands, 1969-72, 6th U.S. Army, Presidio of San Francisco, 1972-73; ret. active duty, 1973; reporter, news editor Lake Charles (La.), 1946-47; region adminstrv. mgr. Burns Security Service, Oakland, Calif., 1974-76; ptnr. constrn. co. Napa, 1976-77, Burns Security Service, 1978-81; now ret.; dir. 1st Am. Title Co., Napa, Calif., 1988-92. Trustee Queen of Valley Hosp. Found., 1987-89; mem. Nat. coun. Boy Scouts Am., 1969-70; pres. Silverado Property Owners Assn., Inc., 1990-95. Decorated D.S.M. with oak leaf cluster, Legion of Merit with 2 oak leaf clusters, Bronze Star with oak leaf cluster; inducted into La. State U.'s Manship Sch. of Mass Communication Hall of Fame, 1996, Disting. Leadership Cadets Ole War Skule Hall of Honor, 1998. Mem.: Silverado Country (Napa, Calif.). Home: 350 St Andrews Dr Napa CA 94558-1544 E-mail: robtsmith@juno.com.

SMITH, ROBERT BRUCE, college administrator; b. Phila., July 8, 1937; s. Graeme Conlee and Margaret Edith (Moote) S.; m. Eileen Adele Petznick, Aug. 21, 1959; children: Monica, Sara, Douglas. BS, Wheaton (Ill.) Coll., 1958; PhD, U. Calif., Berkeley, 1962. Asst. prof. chemistry U. Nev., Las Vegas, 1961-66, assoc. prof., chmn. dept., 1966-68, prof., dean Coll. Sci., Engring. and Math., 1968-81; v.p. acad. affairs Weber State U., Ogden, Utah, 1981-93, provost, 1993-96, asst. to pres., 1996-98, provost emeritus, 1998—; ind. cons., 1995—. Mem. Nev. Bd. Examiners Basic Scis., 1970-75, Nev. Bd. Pharmacy, 1972-77; mem. Commn. on Colls., N.W. Assn. Schs. and Colls., 1985-94, chmn. Commn. on Colls., 1989-94; dir. Am. Assn. State Colls. and Univs. Acad. Leadership Inst., 1986-96. NSF fellow, 1959-61 Mem. AAAS, Sigma Xi, Phi Kappa Phi. Home: PO Box 3203 Idyllwild CA 92549-3203

SMITH, ROBERT CARLISLE, department administrator, welding educator; b. St. Albans, W.Va., Sept. 2, 1939; s. Clarence Mack (stepfather) and Artimitia (Blake) Smith Fowler; m. Janet Lee Koehn, Dec. 28, 1958; children: Teresa Lynn, Stephen Carlisle. BA, Glenville State U., 1984; MSc, Marshall U., 1994. Cert. welding inspector, non-destructive tester. Br. mgr. Va. Welding, Charleston, W.Va., 1963-76; prin. Weld Inspection and Cons., St. Albans, 1976-94; quality assurance mgr. Kanawha Mfg., Charleston, 1988-99; dept. head, welding instr. W.Va. U., Parkersburg, 1981-94. Lt. ROTC 1957-71; committeeman Rep. Party, Kanawha County, 1968-69; former Sun. sch. tchr. Highlawn Baptist Ch.; presenter Nat. Educators Workshop NASA, Langley Space Flight Ctr., 1993. Recipient Disting. West Virginian award Gov. W.Va., 1968. Mem. Am. Welding Soc. (chmn. 1971-72, program chairperson 1989-90, educator of yr. 1990, 92), Am. Soc. Non-Destructive Testing (membership recruiter 1988), W.Va. Edn. Assn., W.Va. C.C. Assn. Protestant. Avocations: autos, trucks, writing, fishing, banjo. Home: 2302 S Walnut Dr Saint Albans WV 25177-3947

SMITH, ROBERT CHARLES, political science educator, researcher; b. Benton, La., Feb. 12, 1947; s. Martin and Blanch (Tharpe) S.; m. Scottie Bess Gibson, May 6, 1952; children: Blanch, Jessica, Scottus-Charles. BA, U. Calif., Berkeley, 1970, MA, UCLA, 1972; PhD, Howard U., 1976. Asst. prof. Coll. at Purchase SUNY, 1976-80; assoc. prof. Howard U., Washington, 1980-88; prof. Prairie View (Tex.) Agrl. Mech., 1988-89, San Francisco State U., 1989—. Rsch. assoc. Columbia U., N.Y.C., 1972-73, 78-80; guest scholar Joint Ctr. Polit. Studies, Washington, 1985-86. Author: Racism in the Post Civil Rights Era, 1995, We Have No Leader: African Americans, 1996; co-author: Race, Class and Culture, 1992; co-editor: Urban Black Politics, 1978. Co-founder Congress of Black Faculty, Washington, 1987; founding fellow Open Mind: Cultural Diversity, 1988; co-chair Bay Area Malcum 25th Anniversary Com., 1990. Mem. Am. Polit. Sci. Assn., Nat. Conf. Black Polit. Scientists, Ctr. for Study Presidency, Acad. Polit. Sci. Baptist. Avocations: reading, walking. Home: 5044 Santa Rita Rd Richmond CA 94803-3236 Office: San Francisco State U 1600 Holloway Ave San Francisco CA 94132-1722 Address: 5044 Santa Rita Rd Richmond CA 94803-3236 E-mail: rcs@sfsu.edu.

SMITH, ROBERT CLINTON, senator; b. Trenton, N.J., Mar. 30, 1941; s. Donald and Margaret (Eldridge) S.; m. Mary Jo Hutchinson, July 2, 1966; children: Jennifer L., Robert Clinton, Jason H. AA, Trenton Jr. Coll., 1963; BA, Lafayette Coll., 1965; postgrad., Long Beach State U., 1968-69. Tchr., realtor, Wolfeboro, N.H., 1970-85; chmn. Gov. Wentworth Dist. Sch. Bd., 1978-84; mem. 99th-101st Congresses from 1st N.H. dist., Washington, 1985-90, U.S. Senate from N.H., Washington, 1990—. Mem. armed svcs., environ. and pub. works, chmn. ethic com., chmn. and sen. judiciary com. With USN, 1962-69, Vietnam. Mem. Am. Legion, Theta Xi. Republican. Roman Catholic. Office: US Senate 307 Dirksen Senate Ofc Washington DC 20510-0001*

SMITH, ROBERT EARL, space scientist; b. Indpls., Sept. 13, 1923; s. Harold Bennett and Bernice (McCaslin) S.; m. Elizabeth Lee Usak, Jan. 3, 1947 (dec. 1984); children: Stephanie Lee, Robert Michael, Cynthia Ann, Kelly Andrew; m. Lyla Lee Lewellen, July 1, 1988. BS, Fla. State U., 1959, MS, 1960, U. Mich., 1969, PhD, 1974. Enlisted U.S. Army Air Force, 1943-44; advanced through grades to maj. U.S. Air Force, 1955; airway traffic controller Berlin, Germany, 1945; staff weather reconnaissance officer 9th Air Force, 1956; ret., 1963; project scientist Atmospheric Cloud Physics Lab.; dep. chief atmospheric scis. div. NASA/Marshall Space Flight Ctr., Ala., 1963-86; sr. scientific cons. Univs. Space Rsch. Assn., Huntsville, 1986-87; sr. computer cons. Computer Scis. Corp., 1987-89; chief space sci. and applications div. FWG Assocs., Inc., 1989-92; NASA program mgr. Physitron, Inc., 1992-96; sr. computer scientist Computer Scis. Corp., 1996—. Mem. AIAA, Pi Mu Epsilon, Sigma Phi Epsilon. Home: 125 Westbury Dr SW Huntsville AL 35802-1619 Office: NASA/MSFC Huntsville AL 35812

SMITH, ROBERT ELLIS, lawyer, journalist; b. Providence, Sept. 6, 1940; s. Ronald Bancroft and Clarice (Evans) S.; m. Kathryn Ritter, Aug. 4, 1984; children: Mark O., David E., Benjamin E., Gregor E. BA, Harvard U., 1962; JD, Georgetown U., 1975. Bar: D.C. 1976, R.I. 1987. News reporter Detroit Free Press, 1962-65, Newsday, Garden City, N.Y., 1966-70; asst. dir. Office for Civil Rights HEW, Washington, 1970-73; pub. Privacy Jour., Washington and Providence, 1974—; pvt. practice Washington and Block Island, R.I., 1978—; spl. asst. atty. gen. State of R.I., Providence, 1991-92; vice-chmn. R.I. Coastal Resources Mgmt. Coun., 1996—2002. Mem. D.C. Commn. Human Rights, 1983-85. Author: Privacy: How to Protect What's Left of It, 1979, Compilation of State and Federal Privacy Laws, 1976, 78, 81, 84, 88, 92, 97, 2002, Workrights, 1983, Celebrities and Privacy, 1985, The Law of Privacy Explained, 1993, Our Vanishing Privacy, 1993, Ben Franklin's Web Site, 2000. Pres. Block Island Conservancy, 1990-94; arbitrator R.I. Superior Ct.; chair Harvard Crimson Grad. Bd., 1999-2002. With U.S. Army, 1963-65. Mem. ABA, R.I. Bar Assn., Harvard Club. Avocation: writer, arbitrator, expert witness. Office: Privacy Jour PO Box 28577 Providence RI 02908-0577 also: PO Box 984 Block Island RI 02807-0984 E-mail: privacyjournal@prodigy.net.

SMITH, ROBERT EVERETT, lawyer; b. N.Y.C., Mar. 15, 1936; s. Arthur L. and Augusta (Cohen) S.; m. Emily Lucille Lehman, July 17, 1960; children: Amy, Karen, Victoria. BA, Dartmouth Coll., 1957; LLB, Harvard U., 1960. Bar: N.Y. 1960, U.S. Dist. Ct. (so. dist.) N.Y. 1962, U.S. Ct. Appeals (2d cir.) 1963, U.S. Supreme Ct. 1967, U.S. Dist. Ct. (ea. dist.) N.Y. 1969, U.S. Ct. Appeals (3d cir.) 1982, U.S. Ct. Appeals (9th cir.) 1988. Assoc. Paul, Weiss, Rifkind, Wharton & Garrison, N.Y.C., 1960-65; from assoc. to ptnr. Baar, Bennett & Fullen, 1965-74; ptnr. Guggenheimer & Untermyer, 1974-85, Rosenman & Colin LLP, N.Y.C., 1985-98, chmn., 1994-97, counsel, 1998—2002, KMZ Rosenman, N.Y.C., 2002—. With U.S. Army, 1961-64. Mem. ABA, N.Y. State Bar Assn., Assn. of Bar of City of N.Y., Fed. Bar Coun., N.Y. County Lawyers Assn., Am. Arbitration Assn. (nat. panel arbitrators), The Am. Law Inst. Office: KMZ Rosenman 575 Madison Ave Fl 26 New York NY 10022-2585 E-mail: Robert.Smith@kmzr.com..

SMITH, ROBERT F., JR. civil engineer; b. Oneida, N.Y., Apr. 17, 1949; s. Robert F. and Lucy (Rice) S.; m. Lane K. McDonald, Nov. 21, 1984 (div. 1989); children: Sean Michael, Kevin Robert. BCE, Clarkson U., 1971. Registered profl. engr., N.Y., Ky. Asst. city engr. City of Oneida, 1971—78; chief stormwater mgmt. engr. Met. Sewer Dist., Louisville, 1978—99; water resources dir. Gresham Smith & Ptnrs., 1999—2001; pres. Robert Smith Engring. Svcs., Inc., 2002—. V.p. United Way, Oneida, 1976-77. Named Ky. Col., 1982. Mem. Nat. Soc. Profl. Engrs. (southeast region v.p. 1996-98, chmn. profl. engrs. in govt., 1993-94), Ky. Soc. Profl. Engrs. (v.p. 1989-91, D.V. Terrell award 1990, Disting. Engr. 1983, 88), ASCE (chpt. pres. 1984, Zone II Govt. Civil Engr. of Yr. 1989), Am. Pub. Works Assn. Democrat. Roman Catholic. Achievements include development of stormwater utility for city of Louisville and Jefferson County, Kentucky. Office: Robert Smith Engring Svcs Inc 816 Washburn Ave #13 Louisville KY 40222 E-mail: bobsmith49@earthlinnk.net.

SMITH, ROBERT FRANCIS, psychologist, consultant; b. Independence, Mo., May 4, 1943; s. Ernest L. and Grace Evelyn (Buck) S.; m. Susan Marie Quanty, Sept. 3, 1976; children: Justin Quanty, Natalie Christine. BA, U. Mo., Kans. City, 1973, MA, 1976; PhD, U. Kans., 1984. Registered investment advisor. Assoc. field svc. engr. Diamond Power Speciality Corp., Lancaster, Ohio, 1968-71; rsch. assoc. Kans. U. Med. Ctr. Otolaryn. Dept., Kansas City, Kans., 1973-78; rsch. psychologist VA Behavioral Radiology Labs., Kans. City, Mo., 1978-95. Chmn. subcom. working group on biorhythms for C95-1-IV, Am. Nat. Stds. Inst., Washington, 1983-91; cons. Midwest Rsch. Inst., Kansas City, Mo., 1982—, West Assocs. Energy Task Force, Rosemead, Calif., 1984-86; guest speaker NAS Workshop, Washington, 1985. Contbr. articles to profl. jours. Served in USN, 1962-68. Mem. Psi Chi. Avocation: tennis. Home and Office: 9351 E 60th Ter Raytown MO 64133-3803 E-mail: bob@resourceful.com.

SMITH, ROBERT FREEMAN, history educator; b. Little Rock, May 13, 1930; s. Robert Freeman and Emma Martha Gottlieb (Buerkle) S.; m. Alberta Vester, Feb. 1, 1951 (dec. 1985); children: Robin Ann, Robert Freeman III; m. Charlotte Ann Coleman, Sept. 9, 1985. BA, U. Ark., 1951, MA, 1952; PhD, U. Wis., Madison, 1958. Instr. U. Ark., Fayetteville, 1953; asst. prof. Tex. Luth. Coll., Seguin, 1958-62; assoc. prof. U. R.I., Kingston, 1962-66, U. Conn., Storrs, 1966-69; prof. history U. Toledo, 1969-86, disting. univ. prof., 1986—. Vis. prof. U. Wis., Madison, 1966-67. Author: The United States and Cuba: Business and Diplomacy 1917-1960, 1961 (Tex. Writers' Roundup award 1961), What Happened in Cuba: A Documentary History of U.S.-Cuban Relations, 1963, The United States and Revolutionary Nationalism in Mexico, 1916-1932, 1973 (Ohio Acad. History award 1973), The Era of Caribbean Intervention, 1890-1930, 1981, The Era of Good Neighbors, Cold Warriors, and Hairshirts, 1930-82, 1983, The Caribbean World and the United States: Mixing Rum & Coca-Cola, 1994; contbr. to numerous publs. Retired Col. 7th Hist. Detachment, Ohio Mil. Res. 1st lt. U.S. Army, 1953-55. Knapp fellow in history U. Wis., 1957; Tom L. Evans rsch. fellow Harry S. Truman Libr., Independence, Mo., 1976-77, Mexican Ministry Fgn. Rels. fellow, 1991-92. Mem. Soc. Historians of Am. Fgn. Rels., Soc. Mil. History, U.S. Naval Inst., Ohio Acad. History, So. Hist. Assn., Orgn. Am. Historians, Assn. U.S. Army, State Guard Assn. of U.S., Am. Legion, Masons, Scottish Rite, Shriners, Army Hist. Found., Inst. Land Warfare, Sons of Confederate Vets., Phi Beta Kappa, Phi Alpha Theta. Episcopalian. Avocation: photography. Home: 4110 Dunkirk Rd Toledo OH 43606-2217 Office: U Toledo Dept History Toledo OH 43606

SMITH, ROBERT GILLEN, political science consultant; b. Dover, N.J., Oct. 16, 1913; s. John Wesley and Elizabeth Wolfe (Gillen) S.; m. Lois S. Squier, Dec. 23, 1942; children: Robert Logan, Donald Paul. AB summa cum laude, Drew U., 1936, LLD (hon.), 1977; MA in History and Govt., Columbia U., 1939, PhD in History and Govt., 1950. From instr. to Pfeiffer prof., chair Drew U., Madison, N.J., 1940-71, prof. emeritus, 1977—; pvt. cons. intergovernmental policy implementation Arnold, Md., 1977—. Adj. prof. polit. sci. Hunter Coll., 1965-67; vis. prof. NYU, 1966-67; lectr. in field. Author: Public Authorities, Special Districts and Local Government, 1964, Public Authorities in Urban Areas, 1969, Ad Hoc Governments, 1974; contbr. chpt. to (Jerry Mitchell) Public Authorities and Public Policy, 1992; co-author, editor: Military Medical Manual, 1945; contbg. editor: Dictionary of Political Science, 1966; also evaluation teams Mid. States Commn. Higher Edn., 1962-70; bd. dirs. Coll.-Fed. Agy. Coun., N.Y., 1969-72. With U.S. Army, 1942-46. Decorated Bronze Star; Robert G. Smith scholar established by Drew U. Alumni Assn., 1979; grantee 20th Century Fund, 1967, Eagleton Found., Danforth Found., Ford Found, NSF, Coun. Internat. Urban Liaison, Washington; inducted into Drew U. Athletic Hall of Fame, 1999. Mem. Phi Beta Kappa, Pi Sigma Alpha. Home and Office: 250 Rugby Rd Arnold MD 21012-2136

SMITH, ROBERT HAMIL, writer, fund raiser; b. Oak Park, Ill., Nov. 8, 1927; s. Henry Garfield and Mary Ellen (Hamil) S.; m. Mary Helen Kingsley, Dec. 29, 1948; children: David H., Mark K., Steven H., Rebecca Anne. Student, U. Denver, 1946-48; LLB, 1953, JD, 1960. Dep. clk. County Ct. City and county of Denver, 1948-53; with Colo. Ins. Group, 1953-59; mgr. claims dept. R.H. Smith & Assocs., 1959-64; cons. Am. BApt. Home Mission Soc., 1964-68; assoc. dir. devel. Ill. Wesleyan U., 1968-69; asst. to chancellor U. Calif., San Diego, 1969-77; exec. dir. devel. Scripps Clinic and Rsch. Found., La Jolla, Calif., 1977-82; v.p. devel., 1982-88; pres. Cartographic Enterprises, 1981—. Owner C Books, 1981. Author: Guide to Harbors, Anchorages and Marinas So. and No. California edits., 1983, The Physician as a Fundraiser, 1984, Naval Inst. Guide to Maritime Museums in U.S./Canada, 1991, Smith's Guide to Maritime Museums U.S./Canada, 1993; pub.: Maritime Museums of North America Including Canada, 1998. Bd. dirs. Nat. Com. on Planned Giving, 1990-94; fund raising cons. deferred giving. Served with USNR, 1945. Mem. Nat. Soc. Fund Raising Execs., Internat. Yachting Fellowship of Roatrians (San Diego fleet comdr. 1979-81). Baptist. Home and Office: PO Box 176 Del Mar CA 92014-0176 E-mail: rhs2@ix.netcom.com.

SMITH, ROBERT JAMES, structural engineer, consultant; b. Bainville, Mont., June 14, 1935; s. Charles Edward and Ruth Hattie (Leeson) S.; m. Ramona Garnet Woolsey, Mar. 31, 1967; 1 child, Bradley Robert. BSCE, Mont. State U., 1958; MS in Geol. Engring., U. Minn., 1970. Registered profl. engr., Nebr. Structural engr. U.S. Army Corps Engrs., Omaha, 1958, 60-68, Washington, 1968-78, chief structural engring. sect., 1978-84, chief structural engring. br., 1984-89; pvt. practice cons. in structural engring. Tempe, Ariz., 1989—. Contbr. articles to ASCE Conf., Am. Concrete Inst. Internat., Inst. Civil Engrs., London, ASTM Standardization News, other profl. publs. With U.S. Army, 1958-60. Recipient Decoration for Meritorious Civilian Svc., 1989. Fellow Am. Concrete Inst. (mem. bldg. code com. 1984-91); mem. ASTM (std. for steel sheet piling task group, chmn. std. for high strength steel bars task group, sec. subcom. on structural steel 1985-89), Reinforced Concrete Rsch. Coun. (chmn. com. on reinforced concrete durability 1985-89). Achievements include research in structural steel and concrete durability. Home and Office: 1630 W Hackberry Dr Chandler AZ 85248-3665

SMITH, ROBERT JOHN, anthropology educator; b. Essex, Mo., June 27, 1927; s. Will Dan and Fern (Jones) S.; m. Kazuko Sasaki, Aug. 22, 1955. BA summa cum laude, U. Minn., 1949; MA, Cornell U., 1951, PhD, 1953. Engaged in cultural anthrop. field research, N.S., Can., 1950, Japan, 1951-52, 55, 57-58, Brazil, 1966-67; mem. faculty Cornell U., 1953—, prof. anthropology, 1963-74, Goldwin Smith prof. anthropology, 1974-97, prof. emeritus, 1997—, chmn. dept. Asian studies, 1961-66, chmn. dept. anthropology, 1967-71, 76-82, prof. emeritus, 1997—. Vis. prof. anthropology U. Ariz., 1971, U. Hawaii, 1978, Nat. Mus. Ethnology, Osaka, Japan, 1982 Author: (with Cornell) Two Japanese Villages, 1956, (with Cornell, Saito and Maeyama) Japanese and Their Descendants in Brazil, 1967; editor: (with Beardsley) Japanese Culture: Its Development and Characteristics, 1962, Social Organization and the Applications of Anthropology, 1974, Ancestor Worship in Contemporary Japan, 1974, Kurusu: The Price of Progress in a Japanese Village, 1951-75, 1978, (with Wiswell) Women of Suye Mura, 1982, Japanese Society: Tradition, Self and the Social Order, 1983, (with K. Smith) Diary of a Japanese Innkeeper's Daughter, 1984 Served with AUS, 1944-46. Tng. grantee Social Sci. Rsch. Coun., Japan, 1951-52; recipient Individual Exch. award to Japan Inst. Internat. Edn., 1957-58; Fulbright lectr. Tokyo Met. U., 1962-63; NSF rsch. grantee, 1965-67; Japan Found. grantee, 1979; awarded Order of the Rising Sun, Govt. of Japan, 1993. Fellow Am. Anthrop. Assn., Assn. for Asian Studies (v.p. 1987-88, pres. 1988-89), Soc. Applied Anthropology (editor jour. Human Orgn. 1961-66). Home: 107 Northview Rd Ithaca NY 14850-6039 Office: Cornell U Dept Anthropology Ithaca NY 14853 E-mail: rjs6@cornell.edu.

SMITH, ROBERT JOHN, JR. real estate executive; b. Rochester, N.Y., June 1, 1951; s. Robert and Irene (Frisbie) S.; m. Sherry L. Silberman, July 5, 1981; 1 child, Jordan. Student, Ohio U., 1969-73. CPA, Ohio. Gen. mgr. Televac, Inc., Athens, 1975—; CFO Practice Mgmt., Inc. (PMI), Cleve., 1988—. Bd. dirs. Cleve. Sports Stars Found., 1992—. Mem. AICPA. E-mail: televac@aol.com.

SMITH, ROBERT LEE, agriculturalist; b. Ottawa, Ill., Apr. 2, 1921; s. Charles Emanuel and Helen Beatrice (Cray) S.; m. Lillian Pearl Francisco, 1947 (div. 1969); children: Charles, Jerome (dec.), Rodger, Lawrence, Eileen, Arlene. PhD in Humane Sci. (hon.), Cleo U., 1990. Elder, tchr. Meth. Ch., El Paso, Ill., 1955-67; dir. rsch. Ill. Farmers Union, Springfield, 1963-68. Radio officer, pilot search and rescue unit Civil Air Patrol, Woodford County, 1964-69; lectr. U. Ill., Champaign, 1989-90. Contbr. articles to profl. jours. Dir. Ill. Youth Corps, No. Ill., 1965-68; Dem. candidate for state rep. Capt. USAF, 1944-46; with USAFR, 1955-68. Mem. Mensa (life, pres. cen. Ill. chpt. 1980-85, editor 1981-84), Moose. Avocations: writing, bridge, dancing, hiking, reading. Home: 1120 Northwood Dr N Champaign IL 61821-2116 E-mail: bellyla@juno.com.

SMITH, ROBERT LOUIS, construction company executive; b. Parkersburg, W.Va., Apr. 19, 1922; s. Everett Clerc and Janet (Morrison) S.; m. June Irene Odbert, Oct. 25, 1948; children: Peter Clerc, Morrison James, Edna Louise. BS in Civil Engring., Lehigh U., 1944. Design engr. Chrysler Corp., 1944-46; engr. Harrison Constrn. Co., Charleston, W.Va., 1946-47; sr. engr. Creole Petroleum Co., Las Piedras, Venezuela, 1947-55; v.p. Rea Constrn. Co., Charlotte, N.C., 1955-64; exec. v.p. Warren Bros. Co., Cambridge, Mass., 1964-68, pres., 1968-79; also dir.; sr. v.p. Ashland Oil, Inc., Ky., 1974-79; pres. Robert L. Smith & Assos., Lexington, 1979—; pres., dir. Tree Farm Devel. Corp., Cambridge, 1979—. Dir. Panastalto (S.A.), Wilder Constrn. Co., Inc., J.H. Shears Sons, Inc. Fellow ASCE; mem. Nat. Asphalt Pavement Assn. (dir.), Phi Beta Kappa, Tau Beta Pi, Sigma Chi. Republican. Unitarian Universalist. Home and Office: 1010 Waltham St Apt A412 Lexington MA 02421-8065 E-mail: 103710.3552@compuserve.

SMITH, ROBERT MASON, academic administrator; b. Sill, Okla., May 8, 1945; s. Arnold Mason and Lillyan (Scott) S.; m. Ramona Lynne Stukey, June 15, 1968; children: David, Angela. BA, Wichita State U., 1967; MA, Ohio U., 1968; PhD, Temple U., 1976. Debate coach Princeton (N.J.) U., 1971-73; debate coach Wichita (Kans.) State U., 1973-87; assoc. dean Coll. Liberal Arts and Scis., 1977-87; dean coll. arts and scis. U. Tenn., Martin, 1987-99; provost and vice pres. for academic affairs Slippery Rock Univ., 1999—. Dir. Govt. Sch. for Humanities, 1996-99; spl. asst. U.S. Dept. Health Human Svcs., Washington, 1980-81. Mem. State Behavioral Sci. Regulatory Bd., Topeka, 1984-87; trustee Leadership Kans., topeka, 1986-87; founder, bd. dirs. WestStar Regional Tenn. Leadership program, 1989-99. Recipient Excellence in Tchg. award Coun. for Advancement and Support of Edn., 1994, Crystal Apple award for outstanding tchg., 1995, Nat. Assn. for Cmty. Leadership award for disting. leadership, 1995; named Health Human Svc. fellow 1980, Governors Awd. for Outstanding Achievement, 1999, Preceptor Awd., 1999. Mem. Kans. Speech Comm. Assn. (pres. 1977, Outstanding Coll. Speech Tchr. award 1977), Assn. for Comm. Adminstrn. (pres 1988), Tenn. Coun. Colls. Arts & Scis. (pres. 1989-90), Tenn. Speech. Comm. Assn. (pres. 1993-94), Rotary Club, Phi Kappa Phi, Phi Eta Sigma, Beta Theta Pi, Phi Theta Kappa. Baptist. Home: 106 Ojibwa Dr Butler PA 16001-0528 Office: Slippery Rock Univ Acad Affairs 308 Old Main Slippery Rock PA 16057

SMITH, R(OBERT) MICHAEL, lawyer; b. Cin., Nov. 25, 1951; s. Barney and Jean (Maloney) S.; m. Leslie Y. Straub. BA in Polit. Sci., U. Cin., 1982; JD, Ohio State U., 1985. Bar: Ohio 1985, U.S. Dist. Ct. (so. dist.) Ohio 1992, U.S. Supreme Ct. 1992. Law clk. to Justice Holmes Ohio Supreme Ct., Columbus, 1985-89; sr. staff atty., referee, editor Ohio Ct. Claims, 1989-94. Instr. law Ohio State U., 1985—, instr. continuing edn. courses, 1990—. Incorporator, trustee various non-profit orgns., Cin. and Columbus; pres. So. Bapt. Messianic Fellowship, 1994-97; 2d v.p. Ohio So. Bapt. Conv. Republican. Avocations: target shooting, writing, running. Home: 4325 Kinloch Rd Louisville KY 40207-2853 Office: 4325 Kinloch Rd Louisville KY 40207-2853

SMITH, ROBERT MYRON, investment company executive; b. Hartford, Conn., Jan. 10, 1930; s. Sterling Bishop and Harriet (Chamberlain) S.; m. Ellen Prouty, March 31, 1956 (div. 1982); m. Mary Peterson, Dec. 26, 1982; children: Catherine, Allison, Deborah, Elizabeth, Melissa. BA, Wesleyan U., Middletown, Conn., 1951; MBA, U. Pa., 1957. Underwriter Travelers Ins. Co., Hartford, 1951-56; asst. sec. Investors Mgmt. Co., Elizabeth, N.J., 1957-62; asst. v.p. Security Trust Co., Rochester, N.Y., 1962-64; exec. v.p. Keystone Custodian Funds, Inc., Boston, 1964-74; sr. v.p. Reliance Ins. Co., Phila., 1974-80; pres. Intervest Capital Mgmt., N.Y.C., 1980-81, J. Rothschild Capital Mgmt. Corp., N.Y.C., 1981-83, Ansbacher (Dublin) Asset Mgmt. Ltd., N.Y.C., 1983-95, Smith Adv. Ltd., Annapolis, MD, 1995—, also bd. dirs. Bd. dirs. Gabelli Comstock Strategy Fund, Gabelli Comstock Capital Value Fund, Rye., N.Y. Mem. fin. com. Town of Cohasset, Mass., 1973-74; treas. First Parish in Cohasset, 1969-73, trustee, Severn Sch., Severna Park, MD. Served to 1st lt. USAF, 1951-53. Mem. Inst. CFA's, Balt. Security Analysts Soc., Assn. for Investment Mgmt. and Rsch., Annapolis Yacht Club, Ocean Reef Club. Avocations: sailing, gardening, bridge. Home: 812 Coach Way Annapolis MD 21401-6417 E-mail: smithadvisors@compuserve.com.

SMITH, ROBERT NELSON, former government official, anesthesiologist; b. Toledo, Apr. 2, 1920; s. Robert Frederick and Amy Laura (Nelson) S.; children: Sandralyn, Sharon, Robert Nelson, Marilyn Anne, Marcia, Elizabeth. Student, U. Mich., 1938-39; BS, U.S. Mil. Acad., 1943; MS, MIT, 1945; MD, U. Nebr., 1952. Diplomate Am. Bd. Anesthesiologists. Commd. capt. USAAF, 1943, resigned, 1948; intern Toledo Hosp., Ohio, 1952-53, resident, 1954-57; anesthesiologist KFC Med. Corp., Toledo, 1954-76; asst. sec. def. for health affairs Washington, 1976-78; bd. dirs. Ohio Med. Indemnity Corp., Columbus., 1968-78. Mem. anesthetic and life support drugs adv. com. FDA, Dept. HHS, 1986-90; mem. disability adv. coun. SSA, Dept. HHS, 1986-89; mem. Ohio Pub. Health Coun., 1976—. Chmn. State Health Planning Council, 1974-76; mem. Statewide Health Coordinating Council, until 1976; gov. apptd. mem. Ohio Pub. Health Council, 1997-2002. Recipient Sec. Def. medal for outstanding pub. service, 1977 Mem. AMA (Ho. of Dels. Resolution of Commendation), Ohio Med. Assn. (pres. 1970, commendation 1977), Am. Soc. Anesthesiology, Inverness Club, Rotary, The Toledo Club. Clubs: Inverness (Toledo). Home: 3424 Gallatin Rd Toledo OH 43606-2442

SMITH, ROBERT P. physician; b. Pontiac, Ill., Aug. 5, 1953; s. Oscar William and Anna Merle (Robertson) S.; m. Maureen Ann McCaffrey, Dec. 27, 1975; children: Jenny, Emily, Paul, Stephen. MD, Northwestern U., Chgo., 1976. Diplomate Am. Bd. Family Practice with added qualifications in geriatrics. Cert. med. dir. Am. Med. Dirs. Assn., 1994—. Mem. KC. Roman Catholic. E-mail: roberts@richlandmedctr.com.

SMITH, ROBERT PEASE, JR. physician; b. Burlington, Vt., Feb. 24, 1949; s. Robert Pease and Carol (Wheelock) S.; m. Margaret Scott Creighton, Aug. 12, 1976. BA magna cum laude, Harvard Col., 1971; BMS, Dartmouth Col., 1973; MD, Johns Hopkins, 1975; MPH, Harvard U., 1979. Infectious disease fellow Beth Israel Hosp., Dana Farber Cancer Inst., Boston, 1979-80; asst. prof., clinician Dartmouth Hitchcock Med. Ctr., Hanover, N.H., 1980-86, assoc. prof., clinician, 1986-88; physician Maine Med. Ctr., Portland, 1987—. Prog. dir. Infectious Disease Fellowship, Maine Med. Ctr., Portland, 1991—; med. dir. AIDS Consultation Svc., Portland, 1992—; program com. mem. VII Internat. Conference on Lyme, San Francisco, 1996; cons. NIH, 1994, 95; clin. prof. U. Vt. Coll. of Medicine. Contbr. articles to profl. jours. including Jour AMA, Jour. Infectious Diseases, Am. Jour. Pub. Health, Annals of Internal Medicine. Trustee Maine Audubon Soc., 1992-97. Fellow Infectious Disease Soc. Am., Am. Col. Physicians, Am. Soc. Tropical Medicine, Northern New England Infectious Disease Soc. (pres.). Office: Intermed 238 Western Ave Portland ME 04106

SMITH, ROBERT PHILLIP, poet; b. L.A., Oct. 22, 1946; s. Claudt Leslie and Toni Helena (Schmidt) S.; m. Febronia de los Reyes, May 17, 1977 (div.). BA in Philosophy, Ohio State U., 1968. Libr. asst. Clinton Heights Luth. Ch., Columbus, Ohio, 1999. Libr. vol. Cornerstone, Columbus, 1999—, Columbus Pub. Libr., 1994. Author: Old Norse Practicion, 1995, Byzantine Greek Practicion, 2d edit., 1996, The Goblin in the Ruins, 1997, (calligrapher) Selected Writings of Hildegard of Bingen, 1999, The Amos Tetraglot, 1999, (original poem) Chrysatos and Melissa; translator: Koukoules: Food and Drink during Byzantine Times, 2002; contbr. poetry, articles to collections and jours.; artist numerous paintings. Active Ohio Valley Film Festival, 1997—. Mem. Soc. for Creative Anachronism (min. arts and scis. 1990-98, Purple Fret award 1994, Order of Willow 1994). Democrat. Lutheran. Avocations: painting, drawing, linguistics, calligraphy, illumination, music. Home: 4115 Commodore St Columbus OH 43224-1821

SMITH, ROBERT POWELL, former ambassador, former foundation executive; b. Joplin, Mo., Mar. 5, 1929; s. Powell Augusta and Estella (Farris) S.; m. Alice Irene Rountree, Aug. 22, 1953; children: Michael Bryan, Steven Powell, Karen Louise, David Robert. BA, Tex. Christian U., 1954, MA, 1955. Fgn. svc. officer Dept. State, 1955-81; press officer Washington, 1955; vice-consul Lahore, West Pakistan, 1956-58; 2d sec. Beirut, Lebanon, 1959-61; consul and prin. officer Enugu, Nigeria, 1962-65; officer-in-charge Ghanaian Affairs, 1966; officer-in-charge Nigerian Affairs, dep. dir. Office West African Affairs, 1967-69; dep. chief of mission, counselor of embassy Pretoria, South Africa, 1970-74; ambassador to Malta, 1974-76, Ghana, 1976-79, Liberia, 1979-81. Pres. Africa Wildlife Leadership Found., 1981-85. Served with USMCR, 1946-49, 50-52. Decorated Air medal.; recipient Meritorious Honor award State Dept., 1967 Mem. Am. Fgn. Service Assn. Baptist.

SMITH, ROBERT RUTHERFORD, university dean, communication educator; b. Buffalo, Nov. 18, 1933; s. Thomas Newlands and Mary Jane (Rutherford) S.; m. Suzanne Louise Stines, June 7, 1958; children: Eric Anthony, Gwendolyn Anne. BA cum laude, U. Buffalo, 1955; MA, Ohio State U., 1956, PhD, 1963. Prof. communication, chmn. div. broadcasting and film Sch. Pub. Communication, Boston U., 1961-78; prof., dean. Sch. Communication and Theater Temple U., Phila., 1978-95. Author: poems Participations, 1972; criticism Beyond the Wasteland, 1980, (with G. Ingram and R. Marler) Fishing the Delaware Valley, 1997; editorTV Quar., 1971, Feedback, 1973-76; contbr. articles to profl. jours. Mem. communication com. Mass. Council Chs., 1971-76. Served with USAR, 1959-64. Mem. Broadcast Edn. Assn. (pres. 1984-85), Broadcast Pioneers (pres. Phila. 1985-86), Soc. Profl. Journalists (pres. 1983-85), Appalachian Mountain Club (Boston), Delmont Club (pres. 1992-94), Genesis Club, Choral Art Soc. (chmn. 1997). com. Home: 6 Trout Farm Ln Plympton MA 02367-1617 E-mail: surob@compuserve.

SMITH, ROBERT SAMUEL, banker, former agricultural finance educator; b. Laconia, N.H., June 16, 1920; s. Samuel W. and Winnifred (Page) S.; m. Mary Morgan, June 20, 1942; children: Patricia, Peggy, Morgan Scott, Sharon, Starlee. BS, Cornell U., 1942, MS, 1950, PhD, 1952. County agrl. agt. Livingston County, Mt. Morris, N.Y., 1942-44, Lewis County, Lowville, 1944, Belknap County, Laconia, 1947-49; assoc. prof. edn. Cornell U., Ithaca, N.Y., 1952-54, assoc. prof. farm mgmt., 1954-58, prof. agrl. fin., 1958-77, W.T. Myers prof. agrl. fin., 1977-81; chmn. Tompkins County Trust Co., 1978-92, chmn. emeritus, 1992—. Trustee Mut. of N.Y./MONY Fin. Svcs., N.Y.C., 1981—93, emeritus, 1993—99; bd. dirs. Challenge Industries, Ithaca, NY; advisor Ministry of Agr., Israel, 1960—61, Agrl. Devel. Bank of Iran, 1968. Contbr. numerous articles to profl. jours. Elder First Presbyn. Ch., Ithaca, NY, 1970; bd. dirs. Am. Agriculturist Found., 1980, East Lawn Cemetery Assn., Ithaca, 1987; bd. dirs. emeritus Hospicare Found. 1st lt. U.S. Army, 1944—47, ETO. Recipient Tax Edn. award IRS, Buffalo, 1973, Disting. Svc. citation N.Y. State Agrl. Soc., 1982. Mem. Country Club of Ithaca, City Club Ithaca, Phi Kappa Phi, Epsilon Sigma Phi. Republican. Avocations: golf, bridge. Home: 60 Wedgewood Dr Ithaca NY 14850-1063 Office: Tompkins County Trust Co The Commons Ithaca NY 14850

SMITH, ROBERT WILLIAM, state official, educator; b. May 10, 1956; s. William Robert and Ann (Kalytyn) S.; m. Kathleen Cecilia Gallagher, June 27, 1987; children: Keegan, Nolan. BA magna cum laude, Coll. St. Rose, Albany, N.Y., 1980; MPA, U. Albany, Albany, 1984; PhD in Pub. Adminstrn., SUNY, Albany, 1998. Regional dir. Office of U.S. Senator Daniel P. Moynihan, Oneonta, N.Y., 1984-86; asst. dir. fin. aid Siena Coll., Loudonville, 1986-87; sr. examiner budget divsn. State of N.Y., Albany, 1987—, 1987-99. Asst. dir. fin. aide SUNY, Cobleskill, 1980-84, adj. prof. SUNY, Albany, 1993; adj. lectr. Hudson Valley C.C., Troy, N.Y., 1991; adj. prof. Coll. St. Rose, 1993; adj. prof. grad. program in pub. adminstrn. Marist Coll., 1996-99, Drucker Found. Grant, 1998; asst. prof. Clemson U., 1999—; mem. Clemson Acad. Grievance Comm. Treas. Schoharie County chpt. ARC, 1983-84; mem. mil. affairs coun. Griffiss AFB, 1985-86; land claims Gov.'s Task Force on Ft. Drum, 1985-86; past offical Gov.'s Task Force on St. Regis Mohawk; candidate Schenectady Coutny Legis., 1989, 91; planning commr. Town of Rotterdam Planning Commn., 1993-98; chmn. Mohonasen Found. for Excellence, Inc., 1997-98. Faculty SUNY grantee, 1992. Mem. ASPA (sec. Empire State Capital area 1988-90, exec. coun. 1990-92, co-chair pub. rels. com. 1992), Delta Epsilon Sigma. Democrat. Roman Catholic. Avocations: athletics, reading, music.

SMITH, ROD, football player; b. May 15, 1970; postgrad in econ. & fin., postgrad in gen. bus., postgrad in mktg. & mgmt. , Mo. So. State Coll. Wide receiver Denver Broncos, 1994—. Office: Denver Broncos Football Club 13655 Broncos Pky Englewood CO 80112*

SMITH, RODGER FIELD, financial executive; b. Milw., Jan. 23, 1941; s. Millard Beale and Alice Catherine (Field) S.; m. Sarah Godfrey, June 19, 1964 (dec. Dec. 1999); children: Rodger F. Jr., Scott G., Reid W. BSChemE, U. Wis., 1964, MBA in Fin. with distinction, 1965. V.p. Allis Chalmers, Milw., 1966-76; mng. dir. Greenwich (Conn.) Assocs., 1976—. Trustee Harbor Funds, Toledo, 1987—; bd. dirs. Arlington Capital, London, 1992—. Author articles and spkr. on investing pension funds. Fund raiser United Way, Milw., 1966-76. Mem.: Bascom Hill Soc., U. Wis. Alumni Assn. (nat. bd. dirs. 1994—2000), Wee Burn Country Club (fin. com.), Beta Gamma Sigma, Tau Beta Pi (chmn. trust adv. com. 1986—). Avocations: travel, golf, tennis, coin collecting. Office: Greenwich Assocs Office Park Eight Greenwich CT 06831-5195 E-mail: rodger@greenwich.com.

SMITH, RODNEY, electronics executive; b. 1941; BSEE, Southampton Coll. Advanced Tech., Eng. Various positions to v.p., gen. mgr. Fairchild Semiconductor Corp., Mountain View, Calif., 1969-83; pres., CEO Altera Corp., San Jose, 1983—2000, chmn., 1983—. Office: Altera Corp 101 Innovation Dr San Jose CA 95134-1941*

SMITH, RODNEY RUSSELL, operations executive; b. Flint, Mich., July 30, 1946; s. Walter Joseph and Patricia Frances (Dellow) S.; m. Deborah Ann Braunstein, Nov. 25, 1967; children: Gregory Ryan, Candece Deeann. BA, U. Md., 1972. Mgr. planning AAI Corp.-United Ind., Cockeysville, Md., 1967-81; dir. ops. Applied Communications-Amstar, Frederick, 1981-86, Becton Dickinson, Diagnostic Instrument Systems, Sparks, 1986-92, Becton Dickinson Primary Care Diagnostics, Sparks, 1992-96, gen. mgr., 1996-97; dir. IT bus. syss. Becton Dickinson Bioscis., 1997. Col. Med. Svcs. Corp. USAR, 1966-97, ret. 1997. Mem. Am. Prodn. and Inventory Control Soc. (treas. 1983-85), Am. Mgmt. Assn., Res. Officers Assn. Republican. Roman Catholic. Home: 1901 Pine Knob Rd Eldersburg MD 21784-7042 Office: Becton Dickinson PO Box 370 7 Loveton Cir Sparks MD 21152 E-mail: rodsmith@annapolis.net.

SMITH, RODNEY SHANNON, public administrator; b. Kettering, Ohio, Oct. 4, 1968; s. James Roger and Sharon Francis (Shoemaker) S.; m. J. Susan Smith, Mar. 20, 1996; children: Katherine Elizabeth, Cameron Alexander. BA in Polit. Sci., Wright State U., 1997. Coop. advt. coord. Books & Co., Kettering, Ohio, 1991-93; legis. intern U.S. Senate, Washington, 1986; intern Ohio Rep. Party, Columbus, 1995, Congressman Frank Cremeans, Hillsboro, 1995; intern Rep. J. Donald Mottley Ohio Ho. of Reps., Columbus, 1996; econ. devel. specialist Warren County, Lebanon, Ohio, 1997-98; dir. econ. devel. City of Moraine, 1999-2000; exec. dir. Waynesville (Ohio) Cmty. Improvement Corp., 2000—01; dir. econ. devel. City of Dayton, 2001—02. Mem. coun. Village of Waynesville, 1996-98, pres., 1997; mem. Waynesville Athletic Boosters, Waynesville Friends of the Park, Inc.; chmn. Waynesville Red Carnation Cmty.; mem. Big Bend Park planning com. Centerville-Washington Twp. Parks Dist.; mem. Ashbrook Place Homeowners Assn. Recipient Bus. News 40 under 40 award, 1998. Mem. Ohio Devel. Assn. (legis. affairs com., mktg. and pub. rels. com), Dayton Area C. of C. (econ. devel., edn. and tax. com., govt. affairs com.), Waynesville Area C. of C. (second v.p. 2001), Internat. City/County Mgmt. Assn., Am. Polit. Sci. Assn., ASPA (Greater Cin. chpt., Miami Valley chpt.), Ohio Mcpl. League (resolutions com. 1996, annexation com.), Acad. Polit. Sci., Ohio Environ. Protection Agy. (Ohio environ. edn. fund grant peer reviewer), Am. Econ. Devel. Coun., Nat. Ctr. for Small Cmtys., Mid.-Am. Econ. Devel. Coun., Dayton Tooling and Machining Assn. (govt. rels. team), Ohio City Mgmt. Assn. Republican. Roman Catholic. Avocations: family, civic activities, golf, tennis, church. Home: 10650 Summer Park Way Centerville OH 45458-4758 Office: City of Moraine 4200 Dryden Rd Moraine OH 45439 Office Fax: 937-535-1284. E-mail: rodsmith@donet.com.

SMITH, RODNEY WIKE, engineering executive; b. Havre de Grace, Md., July 29, 1944; s. Marshall Thomas and Ellen Nora (Wike) S.; m. Mary Katherine Trent, Dec. 20, 1967; children: Scott Walker, Craig Duncan. BS, Va. Poly. Inst. and State U., 1972. Registered profl. engr., Va., W.Va., N.C. Project engr. Hercules Inc., Radford, Va., 1967-72; planning engr. Va. state Water Control Bd., Richmond, 1972; project mgr. Cen. Shenandoah Planning Dist. Commn., Staunton, 1972-76; v.p., br. office mgr. Patton, Harris, Rust & Assocs., Bridgewater, Va., 1976-82, prin. in charge office Buchanan, W.Va., 1980-82; sr. v.p. Copper & Smith, PC, Harrisonburg, Va., 1982-88; pres. R.W. Smith & Assocs. PC, Verona, 1988-95, Va. Sports Tech., Verona, 1995—, Intellectual Properties Inc., Hampton, 1996—; sr. project mgr. Olver, Inc., Blacksburg. Contbr. articles to profl. jours.; 4 patents in field. Apptd. to Va. Resources Authority Citizens Adv. Commn., 1987-91. Named Exec. of Yr. Profl. Secs. Internat.; Copper and Smith listed among fastest growing pvt. cos. by Inc. mag., 1987. Mem. Nat. Soc. Profl. Engrs., Water Polllution Control Fedn. Republican. Lutheran. Home: 227 Lebanon Church Rd Staunton VA 24401-6405

SMITH, ROGER WINSTON, political theorist, educator; b. Birmingham, Ala., July 9, 1936; s. Buford Houston and Sarah Louise (Trucks) S.; m. Martha Christin Daniels, Jan. 16, 1960; children— Louisa, David AB magna cum laude, Harvard U., 1958, postgrad. in law, 1958-59; MA in Polit. Sci., U. Calif.-Berkeley, 1963, PhD in Polit. Sci., 1971. Teaching assoc. U. Calif.-Berkeley, 1965-66; asst. prof. govt. Coll. William and Mary, Williamsburg, Va., 1967-72, assoc. prof., 1972-80, prof, 1980-2001, prof. emeritus, 2001—. Sr. lectr. politics Glasgow (Scotland) U., 1977-78; lectr. N.E.H., 1988; cons. Nelson-Hall Pubs., Chgo.; mem. coun. Inst. Internat. Conf. on the Holocaust and Genocide, Jerusalem; co-founder, v.p., pres. Assn. Genocide Scholars; film cons. Armenian Heritage Project. Co-author, editor: Guilt: Man and Society, 1971; co-author: Genocide and the Modern Age, 1987, Genocide, vol. 2, 1991, Bearing Witness to the Holocaust, 1939-89, 1987, The Coming Age of Scarcity, 1998, Genocide, 1999; editor: Genocide, 1999; contbg. editor Internet on the Holocaust and Genocide; contbr. articles to profl. jours. Served to 1st lt. U.S. Army, 1960-62, Japan Fellow NSF, 1966, College of William and Mary, 1977 Mem. AAUP, Am. Polit. Sci. Assn., Assn. Genocide Scholars (past pres.), Human Rights Watch. Democrat. Baptist. Avocations: gardening, walking, opera. Home: 102 Lake Dr Williamsburg VA 23185-3113 Office: Coll William and Mary Dept Govt Williamsburg VA 23187

SMITH, ROGER KEITH, investment executive; b. Hazard, Ky., Mar. 31, 1962; s. Homer and Ruth (Hampton) S.; m. Carla Slone, June 5, 1982. AA in Bus. Mgmt., U. Ky., Hazard, 1981. CLU; ChFC; LUTCF; lic. life, health, property, casualty, Ky.; NASD lic. series 7, 6, 63, 65. Heavy equipment operator Golden Oak Mining Co., Isom, Ky., 1981-84; debit agt. Commonwealth Life Ins. Co., Louisville, 1984-90, spl. agent, then account rep., 1990-96; agt. Blair Ins. Agy., Whitesburg, Ky., 1997-98; investment rep. Trust Co. of Ky., 1998—. Guest spkr. Southeast C.C., Whitesburg, Ky., 1990-92. Mem. exec. com. Letcher County Dems., 1996-2000. Recipient Guest Speaker award Big Sandy Assn. Life Underwriters, Prestonburg, Ky., 1992. Fellow Life Underwriters Tng. Coun.; mem. Nat. Assn. Life Underwriters (Nat. Quality award 1989-92, Nat. Sales Achievement award 1992), Big Sandy Assn. Life Underwriters (chmn. comty. svc. 1994-96, bd. dirs. 1994-98, sec., treas. 1996-97), U.S. Jr. C. of C. (mgmt. devel. v.p. 1992-93, Key Man award, Most Outstanding Mgmt. Devel. v.p. 1992-93), Jaycees (pres. Letcher area 1993-94, regional dir. Ky. 1994-95), Letcher County C. of C. (v.p., chmn. tourism com., pres. 1995-96, past pres. 1996-97, pres. 1997-98), Ky. Assn. of Life Underwriters (sec., treas. 1997-98, v.p. 1998-99, Letcher County Relay for Life chmn. 2001), Alpha Beta Gamma. Avocations: golf, fishing, walking. Home: 201 Sycamore Loop Jeremiah KY 41826-8921 Office: Community Trust Financial Svcs Compulife Investor Svcs Inc 155 Main St Whitesburg KY 41858-7314 E-mail: rogerk@kih.net.

SMITH, ROLAND BLAIR, JR. university administrator; b. Washington, Mar. 21, 1946; s. Roland Blair and Annie Louise S.; m. Valerie Peyton, June 16, 1969; children: Rovelle Louise, Roland Blair III. BA, Bowie State U., 1969; MPA, Ind. U., 1976; EdD, Harvard U., 1988. Dir. upward bound Notre Dame (Ind.) U., 1973-83, 86-88, dir. Ctr. for Edn. Opportunity, 1980-83, assoc. prof., 1991-96, dir. urban inst., 1992-96; assoc. provost Rice U., Houston, 1996—. Tchg. fellow and grad. asst. Harvard U., 1983-86; exec. asst. to pres. U. Notre Dame, Notre Dame, Ind., 1988-96; 1st v.p., treas. Pvt. Industry Coun., St. Joseph Coun., Ind., 1987-91; cons. Lilly Endowment, Indpls., 1990-91; outside reviewer Nat. Ctr. Ednl. Stats, Washington, 1991-92; chmn. bd. dirs. Nat. Assn. Presidential Assts. in Higher Edn., Washington, 1993-94. Contbg. author: (ency.) African- American Education, 1996. Commr. Martin Luther King Fed. Holiday Commn., Washington, 1993-94; trustee YMCA of Michiana, St. Joseph County, Ind.; bd. dirs. NRTS Corp., City of South Bend, Ind., 1993-96, Harvard Alumni Assn. Bd., Cambridge, Mass., 1995—, LifeGift Organ Donation Ctr., 2000—; bd. visitors Bowie State U., 1998—; mem. South Bend Elkhart camp United Negro Coll. Fund. Recipient Outstanding Achievement award Bowie (Md.) State U., 1985; Named Disting. Alumnus Ind. U., South Bend, Ind., 1983, Nat. Assn. for Equal Opportunity in Higher Edn. (Bowie State U.), 1998. Mem. Am. Assn. Higher Edn. (Black caucus vice chair 1995-97, chair 1997-99, Service award 1998), Phi Delta Kappa, Kappa Alpha Psi (Achievement award 1986). Democrat. Methodist. Office: Rice U PO Box 1892 Houston TX 77251-1892 E-mail: rbsmith@rice.edu.

SMITH, RONALD CHARLES, lawyer, educator; b. Chgo., Dec. 9, 1933; s. Riley C. Smith and Rita Elizabeth (Thompson) De Vito; m. Mary Ann Scherer, June 27, 1971; children: Michael Charles, Matthew James. BS, Loyola U., 1955, JD, 1965. Bar: Ill. 1965, U.S. Dist. Ct. (no. dist.) Ill., 1967, U.S. Ct. Appeals (7th cir.) 1977, U.S. Supreme Ct. 1992. Lectr. Loyola U., Chgo., 1955-56; clk. Justice John McCormick Ill. Appellate Ct. Cook County, 1965-66; atty. law dept. Santa Fe R.R., 1966-68; mem. faculty John Marshall Law Sch., 1966-68, prof., 1968—. Mem. Ill. Constitutional Conv., Springfield, 1969-70; asst. state's atty. Cook County, 1975-76, 1979-80; spl. hearing officer Ill. Civil Svc. Commn., 1977-78 Author: (trial books) ABA National Criminal Justice Trial Advocacy Competition, 1990—; contbr. articles on Ill. Constitution to profl. jours. Bd. dirs. Com. on Ill. Govt., Chgo., 1971-78, Ill. Bd. Ethics, 1974-77; chmn. Ind. Precinct Orgn., Chgo., 1973-74; mem. Gov.'s Transition Task Force, Ill., 1972-73; mem. Ill. Supreme Ct. Criminal Rules Com., 1992—; mem. Cook County Criminal Justice Coord. Com., 1992-96; chair edn. com. Chgo. Sisters Internat. Program, Galway, Ireland. Lt. comdr. USNAF Res., 1956-77. Recipient Alumni scholarship Loyola Law Sch., Chgo., 1962-65./ Mem. ABA (criminal justic sect., dir. Nat. Criminal Justice Trial Advocacy Competition 1990—, vice chair publs. 1996-98, vice chair planning 1999-2000, chair elect 2000-01, chair 2001-02), Internat. Bar Assn., Internat. Assn. Prosecutors, Blue Key, Pi Gamma Mu, Alpha Sigma Rho. Home: 5400 N Wayne Ave Chicago IL 60640-1305 Office: John Marshall Law Sch 315 S Plymouth Ct Chicago IL 60604-3968 E-mail: 7smith@jmls.edu.

SMITH, RONALD EHLBERT, lawyer, educator, referral-based distributor, public speaker, writer and motivator, real estate developer; b. Atlanta, Apr. 30, 1947; s. Frank Marion and Frances Jane (Canida) S.; m. Annemarie Krumholz, Dec. 26, 1969; children: Michele, Erika, Damian. BME, Stetson U., 1970; postgrad., Hochschule Fuer Musik, Frankfurt, Fed. Republic Germany, 1971-74; Masters in German Lit., Germany & Middlebury Coll., 1975; JD, Nova U., 1981; postgrad., Gammon Sem. Sch., 2000—. Bar: Fla. 1982, U.S. Dist. Ct. (mid. dist.) Fla. 1983, U.S. Ct. Appeals (11th cir.) 1990, Ga. 1994, U.S. Dist. Ct. (no. dist.) Ga. 1994; cert. ednl. leader, Ga. Asst. state atty. 10th Jud. Cir. Ct., Bartow, Fla., 1982-85; pvt. practice Lakeland, Fla., 1985-94, Atlanta, 1994—; of counsel Mark Boychuk & Assocs., 1998—. Asst. 10th Jud. Cir. Ct., Bartow, 1981-82; instr. Broward County C.C., Ft. Lauderdale, Fla., 1976-79, 91-94, pub. and pvt. schs., Broward County, Atlanta Schs., 1998—, Offenbach, Germany, 1971-78; instr. Polk C.C. and Police Acad., Winter Haven, Fla., 1981-94; adj. prof. English, Ga. State U., 1996—; adj. prof. law DeKalb Coll., 1997—; part-time police instr. Police Acad., Forsyth, Ga., 1996—; music instr.

Atlanta Pub. Schs., 1999—. Tchr., drama dir. Disciples I and II, United Meth. Ch., Lakeland, 1980-94, Glenn Meml. United Meth. Ch., Atlanta, 1994—, cand. to ministry, 2000—; Billy Graham counseling supr., 1994—;promoter Promise Keepers, 1995—; spkr., promoter ProNet, 1996—; min. music Scott Blvd. Bapt. Ch., Decatur, Ga., 1998. Gideon Internat., 1999—; candidate Ordained Ministry United Meth. Ch. Freedom Bridge fellow German Acad. Exch. Svc., Mainz, 1974-75. Mem. ABA, Christian Legal Soc., Lakeland Bar Assn., Am. Immigration Lawyers Assn. E-mail: smith321@bellsouth.net.

SMITH, RONALD EMORY, financial executive; b. Shelburne, N.S., Can., May 26, 1950; s. Edgar Earle and Ida Mae (Porter) S.; children: Stephen, Sarah, Susan. BBA, Acadia U., Wolfville, N.S., 1971. Chartered acct., N.S. Staff acct., mgr. Clarkson Gordon (now Ernst & Young), Halifax, N.S., 1971-78, Toronto, Ont., Can., 1978-80; prin., ptnr. Woods Gordon (now Ernst & Young), 1980-87; CFO Maritime Tel. & Tel., Halifax, 1987-99, Emera Inc., Halifax, 2000—. Bd. dirs. Crossoff Inc., Halifax, Bangor (Maine) Hydro-Electric Co. Dir. Can. Unity Coun., 1994—; bd. govs. Acadia U., 1994—; chmn. Atlantic Provinces Econ. Coun., Halifax, 1993-95, Roeher Inst., 1997-2000; pres. Can. Assn. for Cmty. Living, 1989-93, chmn. Min.'s Task Force on Physician Policy Devel., N.S., 1991-93; mem. coun. fin. execs. Conf. Bd. Mem. Fin. Execs. Inst., Can. Inst. Chartered Accts., Inst. Chartered Accts. N.S., Ashburn Golf Club. Roman Catholic. Avocations: golf, hiking, travel, genealogy.

SMITH, R(ONALD) SCOTT, lawyer; b. Washington, June 30, 1947; s. Joseph Peter Smith and Roberta Ann (Bailey) George; m. Cheryle Rae Coffman, Nov. 15, 1974 (div. July 1977); m. Gloria Jean Haralson, Nov. 30, 1985. BJ, U. Mo., 1970, JD, 1973. Bar: Mo. 1973, U.S. Dist. Ct. (we. dist.) Mo. 1973, U.S. Ct. Appeals (10th cir.) 1990, U.S. Ct. Appeals (8th cir.) 1992, U.S. Dist. Ct. (ea. dist.) Mo. 1996. Field dir. The Mo. Bar, Jefferson City, 1973-75; law clk. to judge Mo. Ct. Appeals (we. dist.), 1975-76; ptnr. Shirkey, Norton & Smith, Kansas City, 1976-77, Jackson & Sherman, P.C. and predecessors, Kansas City, 1977-84, Birmingham & Furry, Kansas City, 1984, Birmingham, Furry & Smith, 1985-92, Birmingham, Furry, Smith & Stubbs, 1992-95, Furry & Smith, P.C., Kansas City, 1996—. Author: (with others) Automobile Accident Handbook, 1984, rev., 1986, Vexatious Refusal and Bad Faith, 1990, Insurance Claims, 1993; editor: The Rights & Responsibilies of Citizenship in a Free Society, 1974, Due Process of Law, 1974, News Headnotes, 1976-84, Young Lawyer, 1977-80; mem. editorial bd. Mo. Bar Jour., 1978-81; (TV series) legal script advisor Lex Singularis, 1973-75; (multimedia) producer, author Freedoms Lost, 1976; producer, playwright (musical-comedy play) Silly in Philly, 1987. Mem. ABA (mem. various coms.), Mo. Bar Assn. (dist. 12 chmn. 1979—, mem. various coms., Disting. Svc. award young lawyers sect. 1978, 79, 80), West Mo. Def. Lawyers Assn., Kansas City Met. Bar Assn. (pres. young lawyers sect. 1981-82, mem. various coms., Disting. Svc. award young lawyers sect. 1982, Leadership award sr. sect. 1985, First Ann. Pres. award sr. sect. 1987), Kansas City Claim Assn., Phi Delta Phi. Democrat. Roman Catholic. Home: 3411 Shady Bend Dr Independence MO 64052-2816 Office: 200 Noland Plz Office Bldg 3675 S Noland Rd Independence MO 64055-6505 Fax: 816-252-5319. E-mail: scottsmith@furrysmithlaw.com.

SMITH, RONALD THOMAS, environmental scientist; b. Palmerton, Pa., Feb. 17, 1952; s. Albert Hubert and Jeanne Alice (Kemmerle) S.; m. Jeri Lee Hammond, June 21, 1997; 1 child, Clara Lucy. BA in English, U. Notre Dame, 1974; MS in Environ. Sci., Ind. U., 1983. Chemist City of Bloomington (Ind.), 1984-91; rsch. sci. Ind. Geol. Survey, Bloomington, Ind., 1994—. Sci. advisor and activist McRae & McRae Attys., Bloomington, 1987, People Against the Incinerator, 1988-92, Thousands of People, 1983-87. Author: The Blind Eagle Blues: Power and Poison in the Heartland, 2002. Environ. activist Citizens Clearinghouse on Hazardous Waste, Arlington, Va., 1987; founder Ind. Voters Party, 1991; pro se litigant Schalk & Smith vs. Lee Thomas, U.S. Ct. Appeals (7th cir.), 1990. Notre Dame scholar, 1970-74; Pi Alpha Alpha Hon. Soc., 1982; recipient Giraffe Award for Pub. Svc., Giraffe Soc. Am., Everett, Wash., 1992. Mem. Nat. Coalition Against Mass Burn Incineration. Independent. Avocations: writing, music, politics, outdoors activities. Office: Ind U Ind Geol Survey 611 N Walnut Grv # S427 Bloomington IN 47405-2208

SMITH, ROWLAND JAMES, educational administrator; b. Johannesburg, Aug. 19, 1938; s. John James and Gladys Spencer (Coldrey) S.; m. Catherine Anne Lane, Sept. 22, 1962; children: Russell Claude, Belinda Claire. BA, U. Natal, 1959, PhD, 1967; MA, Oxford U., Eng., 1967. Lectr. English U. Witwatersrand, Johannesburg, S. Africa, 1963-67; asst. prof. Dalhousie U., Halifax, N.S., Can., 1967-70, assoc. prof. English Can., 1970-77, prof. Can., 1977-88, McCulloch prof. Can., 1988-94, chmn. English dept. Can., 1977-83, 85-86, dir. Centre for African Studies Can., 1976-77, asst. dean arts and scis. Can., 1972-74, dean arts and social scis. Can., 1988-93, provost Coll. Arts and Scis. Can., 1988-89, 90-91, 92-93; vis. prof., rsch. assoc. Multidisciplinary Ctr. Can. Studies, U. Rouen, 1994; prof. Wilfrid Laurier U., Waterloo, Ontario, 1994—, v.p. acad., 1994—. Author: Lyric and Polemic: The Literary Personality of Roy Campbell, 1972; editor: Exile and Tradition: Studies in African and Caribbean Literature, 1976, Critical Essays on Nadine Gordimer, 1990, Postcolonizing the Commonwealth: Essays in Literature and Culture, 2000. Bd. govs. Halifax Grammar Sch., 1972-74, Neptune Theatre Found., 1977-78; selection com. IODE Meml. Scholarships for N.S., 1969-71, Rhodes Scholarships N.S., 1972-74; edn. com. Victoria Gen. Hosp., 1986-90; dir. publicity and promotion N.S. Rugby Football Union, 1987-89; chair liaison com. edn. dept. N.S. U., 1990-93; book prize jury Can. Fedn. for Humanities, 1990, regional judge (Can. and the Caribbean) Commonwealth Writers Prize, 1991; chair com. on employment and ednl. equity Coun. Ont. Univs., 1996-99, chair working group on post-diploma degrees, 1999-2001; bd. dirs. Opera Ontario, 2001-; active Coll. Univ. Consortium Coun., 2000—; chmn. Ontario Coun. Acad. V.P. Recipient Transvaal Rhodes scholar, 1960; vis. fellow Dalhousie U., 1965-66, vis. scholar Ctr. Canadian Studies U. Western Sydney, Macarthur, New South Wales, 1996; Can. Council leave fellow, 1974-75, research grantee, 1977; grantee Social Scis. and Humanities Research Council of Can., 1978, internat. grantee, 1985, grantee Cultural Personalities Exchange program Assn. Canadian Studies in Australia and New Zealand, 1996, grantee Cultural Personalities Exch. Program, Assn. in Can. Studies in German Speaking Countries, 1997. Mem. Assn. Can. Univ. Tchrs. English (sec.-treas. 1968-70, profl. concern com. 1979-81), Can. Assn. for Commonwealth Lit. and Lang. Studies (exec. mem. 1989-92, pres. 1995-99), Can. Assn. Chmn. English (v.p. 1981-82, pres. 1982-83, exec. mem.-at-large 1985-86), Can. Fedn. Humanities (aid to scholarly publs. com. 1979-85, bd. dirs. 1992-94), MLA (div. chmn. 1984, mem.), Social Scis. and Humanities Rsch. Coun., Can. (chair rsch. grants adjudication com. 1994-96), Can. Rsch. Chairs Program (Coll. Reviewers 2000—). Office: Wilfrid Laurier U Office of VP Acad Waterloo ON Canada N2L 3C5

SMITH, ROY HILTON, science educator; b. Knoxville, Tenn., Mar. 22, 1945; s. Hilton Albert and Elizabeth Zorbaugh Smith; m. Stephanie Sue Boyer, May 20, 1978; children: Lindsay Van Wyck, Elizabeth Leeman. BS in Zoology, U. Tenn., 1965; PhD in Psychology, U. Pa., 1970. Disting. prof. Mary Washington Coll., Fredericksburg, Va., 1999—. Author: A Curriculum for Alcohol Education, 1980, Cognitive Neuroscience: An Introduction, 2001; contbr. articles to profl. jours. Sponsor Best Buddies, Fredericksburg, Va., 1995—; founding mem. Mary Washington Coll. Orch., Fredericksburg, 1971—, Chamber Chorale of Fredericksburg, 1989— Fellow Va. Psychol. Found.; mem. Am. Psychol. Soc., Va. Psychol. Assn. (pres. 1996, editor Va. Psychologist), Va. Assn. Acad. Psychologists (pres. 1994), Behavior Genetics Assn. Episcopalian. Avocations: music, horticulture, motorcycling. Office: Mary Washington Coll 1301 College Ave Fredericksburg VA 22401 E-mail: rhsmith@mwc.edu.

SMITH, ROY PHILIP, judge; b. S.I., N.Y., Dec. 29, 1933; s. Philip Aloysius and Virginia (Collins) S.; m. Elizabeth Helen Wink, Jan. 23, 1965; children: Matthew P., Jean E. BA, St. Joseph's Coll., Yonkers, N.Y., 1956; JD, Fordham U., 1965. Bar: N.Y. Asst. reg. counsel FAA, N.Y.C., 1966-79; adminstrv. law judge U.S. Dept. Labor, Washington, 1979-83; adminstrv. appeals judge Benefits Rev. Bd., 1983—, chmn., chief adminstrv. appeals judge, 1988-90. Adj. prof. aviation law Dowling Coll., Oakdale, N.Y., 1972-79; adj. prof. transp. law Adelphi U., Garden City, N.Y., 1975-79; vis. prof. Georgetown U. Law Sch., 1989—. With U.S. Army, 1957-59. Mem. Assn. of Bar of City of N.Y. (sec.-treas. aeronautics com. 1978-79), Fed. Adminstrv. Law Judges Conf. (treas. 1983-84, mem. exec. com. 1982-83), Internat. Platform Assn., Friendly Sons of St. Patrick, Edgemoor Club, Georgetown U. Libr. Assocs. Avocation: tennis. Home: 6700 Pawtucket Rd Bethesda MD 20817-4836 Office: Benefits Rev Bd 200 Constitution Ave NW Washington DC 20210-0001 E-mail: smith-roy@DOL.gov.

SMITH, RUBY LUCILLE, retired librarian; b. Nobob, Ky., Sept. 19, 1917; d. James Ira and Myrtie Olive (Crabtree) Jones; m. Kenneth Cornelius Smith, Dec. 25, 1946; children: Kenneth Cornelius, Corma Ann. AB, Western Ky. State Tchrs. Coll., 1943, MA, 1966. Tchr. rural schs., Barren County, Ky., 1941-42; tchr. secondary sch. English, libr. Temple Hill Consol. Sch., Glasgow, 1943-47, 49-51, 53-56, sch. libr., 1956-83. Sec. Barren County Cancer Soc., 1968—70, Barren County Fair Bd., 1969—70; leader 4-H Club, 1957—72; coord. tax-aide program AARP, 1985—88, dist. dir., 1988—2000, local chpt. v.p., 1996—98, pres., 1999—2000, instr. 55 Alive Mature Driving, 1993—; sec. Oak Grove Bapt. Ch., 1979—; coun. mem. Barren County; bd. dirs. Barren County Hist. Found., Inc., 1997—; trustee Mary Wood Weldon Meml. Libr., 1964—, Barren County Pub. Libr. Bd., 1969—2001; sec. Barren County Pub. Libr., 1969—2001; trustee Barren County Hist. Found., 1996—. Mem. NEA (life), Ky. Edn. Assn., Ky. Sch. Media Assn. (sec. 1970-71), 3d Dist. Libr. Assn. (pres. 1944, 66), Barren County Edn. Assn. (pres. 1960-62, treas. 1979-80), 3d Dist. Ret. Tchrs. Assn. (pres. 1991-92), Ky. Ret. Tchrs. Assn. (v.p. 1992-93, pres.-elect 1993-94, pres. 1994-95), Glasgow-Barren County Ret. Tchrs. Assn. (pres. 1984-86, 96-98, sec. 1989, treas. 1990), Ky. Libr. Trustee Assn. (bd. dirs. 1985-98, pres. 1986-88, 93-95, dir. Barren River region 1985-97), Barren County Rep. Women's Club, Monroe Assn. Woman's Missionary Union (dir. 1968-72, 79-83, sec. 1985-98), Monroe Assn. Bapts. (libr. dir. 1972-88), Ky. Libr. Assn., South Ctrl. Hist. Soc. (v.p. 1997-98, pres. 1998-2000), DAR (chaplain Edmund Rogers chpt. 1998—), Delta Kappa Gamma (pres. Delta chpt. 1996-98). Home: 54 E Nobob Rd Summer Shade KY 42166-8405

SMITH, RUSSELL FRANCIS, transportation executive; b. Washington, Mar. 26, 1944; s. Raymond Francis and Elma Gloria (Daugherty) S.. Student East Carolina U., 1964, N.C. State U., 1964-65; BS with honors, U. Md.-Coll. Park, 1969, MBA, 1975. Exec. asst. mgr. Hotel Corp. Am. Internat. Inn and Mayflower Hotel, Washington, 1966-68; sr. venture capital cons. Initiative Investing Corp., Washington, 1968-69; pres., gen. mgr. Associated Trades Corp., Washington, 1970-74; cons. in fin., Greenbelt, Md., 1974-76; mng. cons. Bradford Nat. Corp., Washington, 1976-79; v.p. OAO Corp., Washington, 1979-81; ptnr. for fin. evaluation and ops. analysis Blake, Brunell, Lehmann & Co., Washington, 1981-86; v.p. mgmt. services adminstrn. United Airlines Svcs. Corp., Lakewood, Colo., 1986-91, cons. Venture Fund of Washington, 1991—. Chmn. com. on wildlife Prince George Humane Soc., Hyattsville, Md., 1968-71, Soc. for Prevention Cruelty to Animals, Hyattsville. 1971-75. Served with U.S. Army, 1963-66. Decorated Silver Star medal, Bronze Star medal with V device, Purple Heart. Mem. Am. Fin. Assn., Ops. Research Soc. Am., Am. Acctg. Assn., N.Am. Soc. Corp. Planners, Internat. Assn. Math. Modeling, Assn. MBA Execs. (registered investment advisor), Beta Gamma Sigma, Beta Alpha Psi. Libertarian.

SMITH, RUSSELL JACK, former intelligence official; b. Jackson, Mich., July 4, 1913; s. Lee C. and Georgia L. (Weed) S.; m. Rosemary Thomson, Sept. 5, 1938; children: Stephen M., Scott T., Christopher G. AB, Miami U., Oxford, Ohio, 1937; PhD, Cornell U., 1941. Asst. instr. English Cornell U., 1937-41; instr. English Williams Coll., 1941-45; with OSS, 1945; asst. prof. English Wells Coll., 1946-47; with CIA, 1947-74, mem. bd. nat. estimates, 1957-62, dir. current intelligence, 1962-66, dep. dir. for intelligence, 1966-71; spl. asst. U.S. Embassy, New Delhi, 1971-74; rsch. cons., 1975—. Assigned Nat. War Coll., 1951-52, U.S. rep. Brit. Joint Intelligence Com., Far East, Singapore, 1954-56. Author: John Dryden, A Study in Controversy, 1941, The Unknown CIA: My Three Decades with the Agency, 1989, The Little Red House that Jack Built, 2002, (novels) The Secret War, 1986, The Singapore Chance, 1991, Lodestone, 1993, Whirligig, 1994, Always Afternoon, 1997, Time's Prism, 2000, Downriver, 2001, The Listener, 2002. Recipient Nat. Civil Svc. League award, 1971, Disting. Intelligence medal CIA, 1974. Mem. Phi Beta Kappa, Phi Delta Theta, Omicron Delta Kappa. Home: 1138 Bellview Rd Mc Lean VA 22102-1104

SMITH, RUSSELL WESLEY, management and computer applications consultant, organizational development trainer; b. Penn Yan, N.Y., Jan. 23, 1947; s. Wesley Sanford and Gladys Klothe Smith; m. Janice Larzelere, June 16, 1984; stepchildren: Gerald Allen, Christopher Michael. AAS, SUNY, 1973; BS cum laude, N.H. Coll., 1976; BS in Computer Sci., SUNY, Rochester, 1993. Cert. prodn. and inventory control mgr., cert. Novell adminstr. Evaluator SUNY Empire State Coll., Rochester, 1992-94; cons. Naus & Newlyn, Inc., Paoli, Pa., 1977-78, C. Todd, Inc., Haddonfield, N.J., 1978-79; assoc. Resource Assocs., Inc., Newmarket, N.H., 1979-84; pres. Smith Klothe Assocs., Warsaw, 1983-95; processing supt. Champion Products, Inc., Perry, 1988-91; prin. Watkins Concepts Co., Lusby, Md., 1991-95; mgr. functional tech. Oracle Corp., Redwood City, Calif., 1995—. Cons. Resource Mgmt. Group, Boston, 1984-85, Bus. Planning Group, Westport, Conn., 1985-88, project mgr. Robert Bell & Co., Balt., 1976-77. With Signal Corps, U.S. Army, 1966-68. Home: 3308 Forest Gale Dr Forest Grove OR 97116-1074 Office: 1000 SW Broadway Ste 1200 Portland OR 97205-3064

SMITH, RUTH HODGES, city clerk; b. Roanoke, Va., Jan. 15, 1931; d. James Elpherson and Ruth Elizabeth (Morgan) Hodges; m. Leon Menaclus Smith, June 18, 1978; children: Dorothy Ruth Smith Swift, Marvis Frances Smith Mills. Student, Potomac State Coll., 1949-51. Cert. mcpl. clk. Va. Legal sec. Commonwealth Atty., Woodstock, Va., 1952-54; adminstrv. asst. Nelson Oil Corp., Mt. Jackson, 1954-56; exec. sec., office mgr. Tidewater Va. Devel. Co., Norfolk, 1956-72; from corp. sec. to purchasing agt. Nepratex Industries, Virginia Beach, 1972-77; realtor, life agt. Real Estate/Ins., 1977—; city clk. City of Virginia Beach, 1978—. Sec.-treas. Hospice Virginia Beach, 1981-86; liaison, coord. Mayor's Sister City Commn., 1993—; mem. IIMC Acad. Advanced Edn., 1984-87, 87— (Quill award 1991); founder Z House shelter for battered spouses. Mem. Internat. Mcpl. Clks. (bd. dirs. 1986-89, chair internat. com. 1989-91, chair year 2000 planning com. 1998—), Va. Mcpl. Clks. Assn. (pres. 1982-84, master mcpl. clk. 2000—), Lifelong Acad. Advanced Edn., 1996—. Club: Pilot (officer 1960-72). Lodges: Zonta Internat. (dir. 1983-90), Order Eastern Star (worthy grand matron grand chpt. Va. 1993-94, worthy matron Westminster chpt. #99 2000—), Daus. of Nile, Shriners. Avocations: crafts, bicycling, skating, traveling. Home: 1153 Belvoir Ln Virginia Beach VA 23464-6766 Office: City of Virginia Beach Room 281 City Hall Virginia Beach VA 23456

SMITH, S. DOUGLAS, investment company executive, venture capitalist; BSBA, Abilene (Tex.) Christian U., 1960; M in Healthcare Adminstrn., Duke U., 1966; PhD in Adminstrn., U. Ala., 1999. Adminstrv. resident The Watts Hosp., Durham, NC, 1966; asst. to v.p. for health affairs Duke U. Sch. Medicine, 1966—69; asst. dir. Duke U. Med. Ctr., 1969—71; assoc. adminstr. Greenville (S.C.) Hosp. Sys., 1971—72; asst. regional mgr. Humana, Inc., Dallas, 1972—73, Southwestern regional mgr., 1973—77; assoc. adminstrv. dir. Duke Univ. Hosps., Durham, 1977; adminstr. Duke North Hosp., 1977; v.p. HCA Mgmt. Co. Hosp. Corp. of Am., Nashville, 1977—80, divsn. v.p. Tenn. ea. ops., 1980—83, pres. The Ctr. for Health Studies, 1983—85, pres. HCA Mgmt. Co., 1985—89; vice chmn. Quorum Health Group, Inc., Brentwood, 1989—93; pres. Zoe Properties, LLC, Nashville, 1993—; mng. mem. Z Bar Z Ranch, LLC, View, Tex., 1995—; chmn. Passport Health Comm., Brentwood, 1997—; prin. Evergreen Investments and Mgmt., LLC, 1997—; chmn. Healthcare Mgmt. Directions, Inc., 2001—. Spl. cons. Quorum Health Group, Inc., Brentwood, 1993—95; adj. prof. healthcare mgmt. Owen Grad. Sch. Mgmt. Vanderbilt U., Nashville, 1995—99; vis. lectr., preceptor Duke U., Durham, 1982—87; instr. U. Ala., Birmingham, 1994, Lipscomb U., Nashville, 2000. Author (with M.M. Blanks and W.E. Corley): Ray E. Brown: Lectures, Messages and Memoirs, 1991; contbr. articles to profl. jours., chapters to books. Commr. Joint Commn. on Accreditation of Healthcare Orgns., 1985—90; trustee Abilene Christian U., 1985—; chmn. bd. trustees Zoe Found., Nashville, 1995—; co-chmn. Gov.'s Commn. on the Future of TennCare, 2000; bd. dirs. Fedn. Am. Healthcare Systems, 1983—85, mem. com. on quality care, mem. com. on indigent care; examiner Malcolm Baldridge Nat. Quality Award, 2001—. Fellow Price-Babson entrepreneurship, 2001. Fellow: Am. Coll. Healthcare Execs. (com. on comm. 1996—97, com. on evaluating the CEO 1985, com. on ethics 1982, com. on awards and testimonials 1984, task force on governance and constituencies 1986, Disting. Svc. award 1990); mem.: Tenn. Hosp. Assn., Am. Hosp. Assn., Strategic Mgmt. Soc., Acad. Mgmt. Address: 874 S Curtiswood Ln Nashville TN 37204

SMITH, SALLY LYON, portrait artist; b. Pitts., Oct. 31, 1919; d. Prescott Langworthy and Mary Louise (Steele) Lyon; m. Robert E. Smith, Jan. 5, 1942 (dec. 1992); children: Prescott Lyon, Robert E., Samuel Thayer. Grad. h.s., Phila. Cert. Am. Portrait Soc. Portrait artist, Old Sacramento, Calif., 1974-77, Sacramento, 1977-80, Folsom, Calif., 1980-95, Carmichael, 1995—. One woman shows Casa de Los Ninos, 1985, 88, 89, 92, Midtown Gallery-Sacramento, 1995, 96, Dr. Patrick McMenamin-Sacramento Office Complex, 1995; groups exhibitions include Calif. Arts League, 1980-96, Soc. of Western Artists, 1980, 91, 95, Pastels Soc. of the West Coast, 1987, 88, 89, 91, 93, 95; represented in permanent collections. Bd. dirs. Gateway Ho., Sacramento, 1965-75, guild mem. 1975-85, founder 1965. Recipient numerous awards. Mem. Pastel Soc. of West Coast (sec. 1986-87), Soc. of Western Artists, Calif. Arts League. Republican. Episcopalian. Avocations: painting, sketching. Home: Apt 115 2750 Sierra Sunrise Ter Chico CA 95928-3993

SMITH, SALLYE WRYE, librarian; b. Birmingham, Ala., Nov. 11, 1923; d. William Florin and Margaret (Howard) Wrye; m. Stuart Werner Smith, Sept. 20, 1947 (dec. June 1981); children: Carol Ann, Susan Patricia, Michael Christopher, Julie Lynn, Lori Kathleen. BA, U. Ala., 1945; MA, U. Denver, 1969. Psychometrician U.S. Army, Deshon Gen. Hosp., Butler, Pa., 1945-46, U.S. Vet. Adminstrn. Vocat. Guidance, U. Ala., Tuscaloosa, 1946; clin. psychologist U.S. Army, Walter Reed Gen. Hosp., Washington, 1946-47, U.S. Army, Fitzsimons Gen. Hosp., Denver, 1948, U.S. Vets. Adminstrn., Ft. Logan, Colo., 1948-50; head sci.-engring. libr. U. Denver, 1969-72; instr., reference libr. Penrose Libr., U. Denver, 1972-80, asst. prof., reference libr., 1980-90, interim dir., 1990-92, asst. prof. emerita, 1992—. Vis. prof. U. Denver Grad. Sch. Libr. Info. Mgmt., 1975-77, 83; info. broker Colo. Rschrs., Denver, 1979—; cons., presenter The Indsl. Info. Workshop Inst. de Investigaciones Tecnologicas, Bogota, Colombia, 1979, LIPI-DRI-PDIN workshop on R&D mgmt., Jakarta, Indonesia, 1982; mem. BRS User Adv. Bd., Latham, N.Y., 1983-86. Indexer: Statistical Abstract of Colorado 1976-77, 1977. Recipient Cert. of Recognition, Sigma Xi, U. Denver chpt., 1983. Mem. ALA, Am. Soc. Indexers, Spl. Libr. Assn., Colo. Libr. Assn., Phi Beta Kappa, Beta Phi Mu. Office: Colo Researchers PO Box 22779 Denver CO 80222-0779

SMITH, SAM, columnist, author; b. Bklyn., Jan. 24, 1948; s. Leon and Betty (Pritzker) S.; m. Kathleen Ellen Rood, Jan. 24, 1976; 1 child, Connor. BBA in Acctg., Pace U., N.Y.C., 1970; MA in Journalism, Ball State U., Muncie, Ind., 1974. Acct. Arthur Young & Co., N.Y.C., 1970-72; reporter Ft. Wayne (Ind.) News Sentinal, Ft. Wayne, 1973-76, States News Svc., Washington, 1976-79; press sec. U.S. Senator Lowell Weicker Jr., 1979; writer/reporter Chgo. Tribune, 1979-90, columnist, 1991—. Commentator ESBN Radio. Author: The Jordan Rules, 1991, Second Coming, 1995; contbg. writer (magazine) ESPN Mag.; contbr. articles. With USAR, 1970-76. Named Ball State U. Journalism Alumnus of Yr.; named to Ball State U. Journalism Hall of Fame, 2002; recipient Journalism awards, AP, UPI, Sigma Delta Chi, Sports Local Emmy award, WGN-TV. Mem.: Basketball Writers Assn. (pres. 1998—). Office: Chicago Tribune 435 N Michigan Ave Chicago IL 60611-4066

SMITH, SAM CORRY, retired foundation executive, consultant; b. Enid, Okla., July 3, 1922; s. Chester Hubbert and Nelle Kate (Corry) S.; m. Dorothy Jean Bank, Sept. 21, 1945; children: Linda Jean, Nancy Kay, Susan Diane. Student, Phillips U., 1940-43; BS in Chemistry, U. Okla., 1947, MS in Chemistry, 1948; PhD in Biochemistry, U. Wis., 1951. Asst. and assoc. prof. Med. Sch. U. Okla. Med. Sch., Oklahoma City, 1951-55; assoc. dir. grants Research Corp., N.Y.C., 1957-65, dir., 1965-68, v.p. grants, 1968-75; exec. dir. M.J. Murdock Charitable Trust, Vancouver, Wash., 1975-88. Foundation cons., 1988—; pres. Pacific Northwest Grantmakers Forum, 1983-84. Contbr. sci. articles to profl. jours. Trustee Nutrition Found., Washington, 1976-84, Internat. Life Scis. Inst., Washington, 1984-86; bd. councilors U. So. Calif. Med. Sch., L.A., 1977-82; mem. adv. com. Coll. Natural Scis. Colo. State U., 1977-80; pres. Cardiopulmonary Rehab. Programs Oreg., 1990-91; bd. dirs. Clark Coll. Found., 1992-98. Named Boss of Yr., Am. Bus. Women's Assn., 1982, Bus. Assoc. of Yr., 1983. Fellow AAAS; mem. Am. Chem. Soc. Avocations: tennis, photography, gardening. Home: 5204 Dubois Dr Vancouver WA 98661-6617 *Personal philosophy: "There is no limit to what a man can do or where he can go if he doesn't mind who gets the credit." Author unknown.*

SMITH, SAMUEL BOYD, history educator; b. Adams, Tenn., Oct. 23, 1929; s. Carl S. and Annie (Tolleson) S.; m. Martha Sue Fitzsimmons, Dec. 23, 1956; children— David Fitzsimmons, Mark Tolleson, Stephen Boyd. Student, Milligan Coll., 1947-48, U. Tenn., 1948-49, Syracuse U., 1951-52; BS, Peabody Coll., 1956; MA, Vanderbilt U., 1960, PhD, 1962. Asst. prof. history U. South Fla., 1961-64; state librarian and archivist, chmn. Tenn. Hist. Commn., 1964-69; lectr. history Peabody Coll., 1965-66; assoc. prof. history U. Tenn., 1969-72, prof., editor Andrew Jackson Presdl. Papers, 1972-79; prof. Tenn. State U., Nashville, 1979-97. Co-author: This is Tennessee, 1973; Editor and compiler: Tennessee History: A Bibliography, 1974; co-editor: The Papers of Andrew Jackson, vol. I, 1980. Served with USAF, 1951-54. Mem. Tenn. Hist. Soc., Shakespeare Club, Univ. Club. Democrat. Methodist. Home: 1135 Sewanee Rd Nashville TN 37220-1017 E-mail: smith1135@juno.com.

SMITH, SARAH JEANNE, retired gerontologist; b. Marshalltown, Iowa, Aug. 29, 1936; d. Cecil Edward and Sarah C. (Wardman) Ware; m. David H. Smith, 1956; children: Catherine, Karen, Kevin, Colleen, Andrew. BA cum laude, U. Minn., 1971; MA in Gerontology, U. South Fla., 1977. From project mgr. dept. aging svcs. to cmty. svc. mgr. Hillsborough County, Tampa, 1983-94; instr. Hong Kong Bapt. U., 1994-96; gerontology specialist U. Hawaii, Honolulu, 1997-99. Adj. instr. Hillsborough C.C., 1980-86, U. South Fla., 1979-84. Mem.: NAFE, Fla. Coun. Aging, Assn. Pacific Gerontology Soc. (bd. dirs. 1998—2000), Sigma Phi Omega. Democrat. Avocations: photography, travel, musical performance, fiction writing. Home: 1 Beach Dr #1908 Saint Petersburg FL 33701 E-mail: waresmit@earthlink.com.

SMITH, SARAH LINDSAY, real estate developer, investor executive, consultant; b. Wilmington, Del., Mar. 29, 1951; d. Penn Rueben and Gertrude Mary (Prout) Lindsay; m. Ernest Ridley Smith, Sept. 17, 1977; children: Lindsay, Elizabeth, Zachary. BA in Math., Cornell U., 1973, MBA, 1976. CPA, R.I., Ala., Tex. Staff acct. Peat, Marwick, Mitchell, Providence, 1976-77, mgr. Singapore, 1982-83; sr. acct. Deloitte, Haskins & Sells, Mobile, Ala., 1977-79; contr. David S. Wolff Cos., Inc., Houston, 1979-82, contr., treas., 1984-87, v.p., treas., 1987—; pvt. practice Sarah L. Smith, Inc., 1991—. Home: PO Box 260888 Plano TX 75026-0888 Office: David S Wolff Cos Inc 20 Briar Hollow Ln Houston TX 77027-2802

SMITH, SCOTT CLYBOURN, media company executive; b. Evanston, Ill., Sept. 13, 1950; s. E. Sawyer and Jerolanne (Jones) S.; m. Martha Reilly, June 22, 1974; children— Carolyn Baldwin, Thomas Clybourn BA, Yale U., 1973; M.Mgmt., Northwestern U., 1976. Comml. banking officer No. Trust Co., Chgo., 1973-77; fin. planning mgr. Tribune Co., 1977-79, asst. treas., 1979-81, treas., 1981-82, v.p., treas., 1982-84, v.p. fin., 1984-89, sr. v.p., chief fin. officer, 1989-91, sr. v.p. for devel., 1991-93; pres., CEO, pub. Sun Sentinel Co., Ft. Lauderdale, Fla., 1993-97; pres., pub., CEO Chgo. Tribune Co., 1997—. Mem.: Glen View (Golf, Ill.), Lauderdale Yacht Club, Fort Lauderdale Country Club. Episcopalian. Office: Chgo Tribune Co 435 N Michigan Ave Chicago IL 60611-4066*

SMITH, SELMA MOIDEL, lawyer, composer; b. Warren, Ohio, Apr. 3, 1919; d. Louis and Mary (Oyer) Moidel; 1 child Mark Lee. Student, UCLA, 1936-39, U. So. Calif. Law School, 1939-41; JD, Pacific Coast U., 1942. Bar: Calif. 1943, U.S. Dist. Ct. 1943, U.S. Supreme Ct. 1958. Gen. practice law; mem. firm Moidel, Moidel, Moidel & Smith, 1943—. Field dir. civilian adv. com. WAC, 1943—45; mem. nat. bd. Med. Coll. Pa. (formerly Woman's Med. Coll. Pa.), 1953—, mem. exec. bd., 1976—80, pres., 1980—82, chmn, past pres. com., 1990—92. Author: A Century of Achievement: The National Association of Women Lawyers, 1998, The First Women Members of the ABA, 1999; composer: Espressivo-Four Piano Pieces (orchestral premiere, 1987, performance Nat. Mus. Women in the Arts, 1989), numerous works. Decorated La Orden del Merito Juan Pablo Duarte (Dominican Republic),

1956. Fellow: Am. Bar Found. (life); mem.: ASCAP, ABA (jr. bar conf. 1946—52, activities com. 1948—49), Calif. Supreme Ct. Hist. Soc. (bd. dirs. 2001—), Assn. Learning in Retirement Orgns. in West (pres. 1993—94, exec. com. 1994—95, Disting. Svc. award 1995), Plato Soc. UCLA (discussion leader UCLA Constitution Bicetennial Project 1985—87, moderator UCLA extension lecture series 1990, Toga editor 1990—93, sec. 1991—92, chmn. colloquium com. 1992—93, Exceptional Leadership award 1994), Euterpe Opera Club (chair auditions 1972, chair awards 1973—75, v.p. 1974—75), Docents L.A. Philharm. (press and pub. rels. 1972—75, cons. coord. 1973—75, v.p. 1973—83, chair Latin Am. cmty. rels.), Calif. Fedn. Music Clubs (chair Am. music 1971—75, conv. chair 1972), Nat. Fedn. Music Clubs (vice-chair Western region 1973—78), Nat. Assn. Composers U.S.A. (dir. 1974—79, luncheon chair 1975), ABA Sr. Lawyers Divsn. (vice-chair editl. bd. Experience mag. 1997—99, chair arts com. 1998—99, chair editl. bd. Experience mag. 1999—2001, exec. coun. 1999—, Experience mag. adv. bd. 2001—), Calif. Pres. Coun. (1st v.p.), L.A. Bus. Women's Coun. (pres. 1952), Calif. Bus. Women's Coun. (dir. 1951), Coun. Bar Assns. L.A. County (charter sec. 1950), So. Calif. Women Lawyers Assn. (pres. 1947, 1948), Inter-Am. Bar Assn., League of Ams. (dir.), Nat. Assn. Women Lawyers (regional dir. western states, Hawaii 1949—51, jud. adminstrn. com. 1960, nat. chair world peace through law com. 1966—67, liaison to ABA Sr. Lawyers Divsn. 1996—, chair bd. elections 1997—98, centennial com. 1997—99, chair com. unauthorized practice of law, social commn. UN, Lifetime Svc. award 1999), L.A. Lawyers Club (pub. defenders com. 1951), L.A. Bar Assn. (servicemen's legal aid com. 1944—45, psychopathic ct. com. 1948—53, Outstanding Svc. award 1993), State Bar Calif. (conf. com. on unauthorized practice of medicine 1964, Disting. Svc. award 1993), Women Lawyers Assn. L.A. (life; chair Law Day com. 1966, subject of oral hist. project 1986, hon. life mem. 1998), Iota Tau Tau Legal Scholastic Soc. (dean L.A. 1947, supreme treas. 1959—62, 1st prize 1942). Home: 5272 Lindley Ave Encino CA 91316-3518

SMITH, SHARMAN BRIDGES, state librarian; b. Lambert, Miss. BS, Miss. U. for Women, Columbus, 1972; MLS, George Peabody Coll., Nashville, 1975. Head libr. Clinton (Miss.) Pub. Libr., 1972-74; asst. dir. Lincoln-Lawrence-Franklin Regional Libr., Brookhaven, Miss., 1975-77, dir., 1977-78; info. svcs. mgr. Miss. Libr. Commn., Jackson, 1978-87, asst. dir. libr. ops., 1987-89, dir. libr. svcs. div., 1989-92; state libr. State Libr. Iowa, Des Moines, 1992—2001; exec. dir. Miss. Libr. Commn., Jackson, Miss., 2001—. Recipient Iowa Computer Using Educators Friend of Edn. award, 1995, Iowa Libr. Assn. Mem. of Yr. award, 1996. Office: Miss Libr Commn 1221 Ellis Ave Jackson MS 39209

SMITH, SHARON LOUISE, lawyer, consultant; b. Williamsport, Pa., Apr. 21, 1949; d. Stuart Mallory and Phyllis Virginia (Hartzell) S. Student, Schiller Coll., Heidelberg, Fed. Republic Germany, 1969-70; AB, Grove City Coll., 1971; MA, Kent State U., 1973; JD, Temple U., 1978. Bar: Pa. 1978, U.S. Dist. Ct. (we. dist.) Pa. 1980, U.S. Ct. Appeals (3rd cir.) 1992. Assoc. Laurel Legal Services, Brookville, Pa., 1980-82; pvt. practice, 1982—. Cons. Prothonotary, Brookville, 1984-86. Mem. multidisciplinary team for child abuse Jefferson County Child Welfare Dept., Brookville, 1985; bd. dirs. Clarion-Jefferson Community Action, Brookville, 1982, Clearfield-Jefferson Drug and Alcohol Commn., DuBois, Pa., 1983-84. Mem. Pa. Bar Assn., Law Alumnae Assn. Temple U. Presbyterian. Avocations: swimming, reading. Home: 172 Franklin Ave Brookville PA 15825-1164 Office: 197 Main St Brookville PA 15825

SMITH, SHARRON WILLIAMS, chemistry educator; b. Ashland, Ky., Apr. 3, 1941; d. James Archie and May (Waggoner) Williams; m. William Owen Smith, Jr., Aug. 16, 1964; children: Leslie Dyan, Kevin Andrew. BA, Transylvania U., 1963; PhD, U. Ky., 1975. Chemist Proctor & Gamble, Cin., 1963-64, NIH, Bethesda, Md., 1974-75; tchr. sci. Lexington (Ky.) Pub. Schs., 1964-67; asst. prof. chemistry Hood Coll., Frederick, 1975-81, assoc. prof., 1981-87, prof., 1987—, chair dept. chemistry and physics, 1982-86, 95-99, acting dean grad. sch., 1989-91, Whitaker prof. chemistry, 1993—. NDEA fellow, 1967-70, Beneficial-Hodson faculty fellow Hood Coll., 1984, 92; grantee Hood Coll. Bd. Assocs., 1981, 85, 91, NSF, 1986, 2001. Mem. AAAS, Am. Chem. Soc. (E. Emmet Reid award 2001), Mid.-Atlantic Assn. Liberal Arts and Chemistry Tchrs. (pres. 1984-85). Democrat. Office: Hood Coll Dept Chemistry Frederick MD 21701 E-mail: ssmith@hood.edu.

SMITH, SHEILA ANNE, nursing administrator, lecturer; b. La Jolla, Calif. d. Rex Hoe and Ola Vivian (Baxter) S. BA in Health Sci. and Environ. Health, Calif. State U., Fresno, 1974; diploma in nursing, U. So. Calif., 1980; M Health Adminstrn., U. La Verne, 1996. RN, Calif.; cert. perioperative nurse. Staff nurse LAC/U. So. Calif. Med. Ctr., L.A., 1980-81, Huntington Meml. Hosp., Pasadena, Calif., 1981—; ENT specialty coord. Hungington Outpatient Surgery Ctr., 1989-97, insvc. edn. coord., 1990-96; clin. supr. operating rm. perioperative svcs. Friendly Hills Health Care Network, La Habra, Calif., 1996-97; asst. dept. adminstr. perioperative svcs. Kaiser Permanente, West L.A., 1997-99, dept. adminstr. proeperative svcs. L.A., 1999—. Contbr. articles to profl. jours; award winning poet. Religious restoration worker Ch. of Ascension, Sierra Madre, 1982—. Mem. Am. Assn. Managed Care Nurses, Assn. Oper. Rm. Nurses (bd. dirs. 1987-90, 96-97, edn. chairperson 1996-98, bd. dirs. 1998-00), Soc. Otorhinolaryngology and Head-Neck Nurses, Inc. (v.p. So. Calif. region 1992-96), Nat. Assn. Managed Care Physicians, Inc., Operating Rm. Nursing Coun. Calif., Sierra Madre Woman's Club (nurse cons., healthcare lectr. 1988—), Delta Zeta (pres. Alumni chpt. 1974-75). Avocations: painting, writing, sewing, hiking, religious restoration work. Home: PMB 611 4195 Chino Hills Pkwy Chino Hills CA 91709-2618 Office: Kaiser Permanente Nursing Adminstrn 6041 Cadillac Ave Los Angeles CA 90034-1702

SMITH, SHEILA DIANE, medical transcriptionist; b. Caribou, Maine, Aug. 20, 1965; d. Melvin and Flora Jane (Michaud) Kennard; m. John Philip Smith, Aug. 25, 1984; children: Daniel Craig, Janelle Marie. Cert. legal asst., Hillcrest Inst., Portland, Maine, 1993; cert med. transcriptionist, At-Home Professions, Ft. Collins, Colo., 1993; cert. in fin. statement analysis, payroll I & collections, Am. Inst. Profl. Bookkeepers, 1995; AA in Bus. Mgmt., So. Calif. U., 1998. Lic. occupl. sec., Fla. Sec., data entry processor Aroostook County Courthouse, Caribou, Maine, 1983; typist, adminstrv. asst. Continental Contracting Co., Mascoutah, Ill., Houston, 1986-87; sales assoc. AAFES Main Exch., Torrejon AB, Spain, 1990-91; family daycare provider MWR (USAF), Spain, 1991; med. clk., adminstrv. asst. 401st Hosp. (USAF), Spain, 1991-92; med. transcriptionist, sec. Bridgeway Ctr., Inc., Ft. Walton Beach, Fla., 1993-94; owner, med. transcriptionist, billing specialist Smith's Bus. Svcs., Eglin AFB, 1994—2001; office mgr. J.P. Smith's Dental Handpiece Repair, 1996—99. Vol. Girl Scouts Am., Eglin AFB, 1994-95; mem. nat. steering com. Clinton/Gore '96 Campaign, Washington, 1995-96. Mem. AAUW, NAFE, Am. Inst. Profl. Bookkeepers, Smithsonian Inst. (assoc.). Roman Catholic. Avocations: snorkeling, travel, reading, cooking, gardening. Office: Smith's Bus Svcs 102 Fir St Eglin AFB FL 32542-1216

SMITH, SHEILA MARIE, lawyer; b. Chgo. d. Donald Thomas and Catherine Ellen (Mariga) Morrison; m. Melvin Smith, Nov. 11, 1989. BSEE, Purdue U., 1981; JD, U. Cin., 1995. Bar: Ohio 1995, U.S. Dist. Ct. (so. dist.) Ohio 1996, U.S. Ct. Appeals (6th cir.) 1996, U.S. Supreme Ct., 1999. Mfg. engr., 1981-92; assoc. Freking & Betz, Cin., 1995-99, ptnr., 2000—. Spkr. in field. Named to Order of Coif U. Cin., 1995. Mem. ABA, Am. Trial Lawyers Assn., Nat. Employment Lawyers Assn., Ohio Employment Lawyers Assn., Cin. Employment Lawyers Assn., Ohio Bar Assn., Cin. Bar Assn. Avocations: golf, traveling, cooking. Home: 3345 Legendary Trails Dr Cincinnati OH 45245-3074 Office: Freking & Betz 215 E 9th St Fl 5 Cincinnati OH 45202-2139 E-mail: ssmith@frekingandbetz.com.

SMITH, SHELAGH ALISON, public health educator; b. Oak Ridge, Tenn., June 3, 1949; d. Nicholas Monroe and Elizabeth (Kimbrough) S.; m. Milton John Axley, 1991; 1 child, Elizabeth Claire. BS in Edn., U. Tenn., 1971, AS in Dental Hygiene, 1974; MPH in Health Svcs. Adminstrn., Johns Hopkins, 1979. Lic., cert. health edn. specialist, 1989. Social sci. rsch. analyst Dept. Health and Human Svcs., Health Care Fin. Adminstrn., Balt., 1980-85; pub. health educator, evaluator Nat. Cancer Inst.-NIH, Bethesda, 1985-90; sr. policy analyst NIMH, Rockville, 1990-92; pub. health advisor Ctr. Mental Health Svcs., 1992-96, sr. pub. health advisor orgn. and financing, 1997—. Recipient Adminstr.'s Citation, Health Care Fin. Adminstrn., 1981, Dir.'s award, Nat. Cancer Inst., 1989, Spl. Act Svc. award, 1997, 1999, 2000, 2001, Quality Step Increase, 2001. Mem. APHA (pub. health edn. sect., governing coun. 1996-98, chmn. fin. and reimbursement for prevention svcs. com. 1987-89, 96, resolutions chair 1999, del. coalition nat. health edn. orgn. 1999-2001, advocacy chair 2001), Soc. of Pub. Health Edn. (governing bd. and ho. of dels. 1993-95, legis. co-chmn. 1990-91, nat. capital area exec. bd., profl. devel. chair 1996, chpt. pres. 1996-97, treas. 1998-00, honor award 1999), Washington Ethical Soc. (family coun.), Phi Kappa Phi. Democrat. Avocations: swimming, cooking, reading, animal activist, sailing. Home: 14106 Heathfield Ct Rockville MD 20853-2760 Office: SAMHSA Ctr Mental Health Svc Office of Orgn and Financing 5600 Fishers Ln Rockville MD 20857-0001 E-mail: ssmith@samhsa.gov.

SMITH, SHERWOOD HUBBARD, JR. retired electric utilities executive; b. Jacksonville, Fla., Sept. 1, 1934; s. Sherwood Hubbard and Catherine Gertrude (Milliken) S.; m. Eva Hackney Hargrave, July 20, 1957; children: Marlin Hamilton Dohlman, Cameron Hargrave Callaway, Eva Hackney Davis. AB, U. N.C., 1956, JD, 1960; D civil laws, St. Augustine's Coll., 1988; LDD, Campbell U., 1990; HHD, Francis Marion Coll., 1990. Bar: N.C. 1960. Assoc. Lassiter, Moore & Van Allen, Charlotte, 1960-62; ptnr. Joyner & Howison, Raleigh, 1962-65; assoc. gen. counsel Carolina Power & Light Co., 1965-70, sr. v.p., gen. counsel, 1971-74, exec. v.p., 1974-76, pres., 1976-92, CEO N.C., 1979-96, chmn. bd., 1980-99, chmn. emeritus, 1999—. Dir. No. Tel Network, Northwestern Mut. Life Inst. Co. Trustee Z Smith Reynolds Found., 1978-96, Nat. Humanities Ctr., 1990-93; bd. dirs. N.C. Citizens for Bus. and Industry, chmn., 1985-86; bd. dirs. Rsch. Triangle Found. of N.C., N.C. Inst. Medicine; mem. bd. govs. Ctr. for Creative Leadership; mem., chmn. Triangle Univs. Ctr. Advanced Studies, 1986—; mem. Kenan Inst. Pvt. Enterprise; former chmn. bd. trustees, chmn. Rex Hosp; gov. Boys and Girls Clubs of Am. Recipient Nat. Humanitarian award Am. Lung Assn., 1993, Outstanding Leadership award in Mgmt. scis. Am. Soc. Mech. Engrs., 1983, A.E. Finley Disting. Svc. award Greater Raleigh C. of C., 1985, Disting. Citizenship award N.C. Citizens Bus. and Industry, 1997; named to N.C. Bus. Hall of Fame, 1999. Mem.: Greater Raleigh C. of C. (pres. 1979), Phi Beta Kappa. Home: 408 Drummond Dr Raleigh NC 27609-7006 Office: Carolina Power & Light Co PO Box 1551 One Hanover Square Bldg Raleigh NC 27602-1551

SMITH, SHERYL VELTING, organization administrator; b. Grand Rapids, Mich., Apr. 5, 1946; d. Louis and Martha (Kamminga) Velting; children: Laura, Paul. BA in Elem. Edn., Western Mich. U., Kalamazoo, 1968; MA in Adminstrn. and Supr./Edn., Akron U., 1980. Cert. edn. adminstr. and supr. Elem. tchr. Northview Pub. Schs., Grand Rapids, Mich., 1968-69, Ft. Knox (Ky.) Dependent Schs., 1969-70, Dept. of Def., Okinawa, 1970-71, Jefferson County Schs., Louisville, 1971-76, Hudson (Ohio) Local Schs., 1976-80; dir., presch. tchr. The Treehouse Presch., 1981-83; exec. dir. High Meadows Sch., Roswell, Ga., 1993-96; exec. v.p. Rivers of World, Inc., Alpharetta, 1997-99; dir. ind. programs Eaton Acad., Inc., Roswell, 1997—; pres. S.S. Internat. Cons., Alpharetta, 2001—. Mem. regional conf. bd. Assn. Gifted Children, Akron, Ohio, 1979; chmn. bd. dirs. Friends of High Meadows, Roswell, 1990-94;; mem. adv. bd. Mt. Pisgah Christian Sch., Alpharetta, 1991-92, mem. headmaster search com., 1998—; bd. dirs. North Fulton Cmty. Found., 1996—, Howling Wolf Ranch Found., Whitefish, Mont.; mem. adv. bd. Peer Learning. Avocations: sports, gardening, travel, reading.

SMITH, SHIRLEY, artist; b. Wichita, Kans., Apr. 17, 1929; d. Harold Marvin and Blanche Carrie (Alexander) S. BFA, Kans. State U., 1951; postgrad., Provincetown (Mass.) Workshop, 1962-66. One-woman shows include 55 Mercer St. Gallery, N.Y.C., 1973, Wichita Art Mus., Kanas, 1978, Stamford Mus. and Nature Ctr., Conn., 1987, Aaron Gallery, Washington, 1987, 1988, Joan Hodgell Gallery, Sarasota, Fla., 1987, Marianna Kistler Beach Mus., Kans. State U., 1999, John Jay Gallery, N.Y.C., 2000, Represented in permanent collections Whitney Mus. Am. Art, Phoenix Art Mus., The Aldrich Mus. Contemporary Art, Ridgefield, Conn., Ulrich Mus., Wichita State U., Everson Mus., Syracuse, N.Y., U. Calif. Berkeley Art Mus., Marianna Kistler Beach Mus., Manhattan, Kans. Recipient Grumbacher Cash award for mixed media New Eng. Exhibition, Silvermine, Conn., 1967, Acad. Inst. award Am. Acad. Arts and Letters, N.Y.C., 1991, Richard Florsheim Art Funds grantee, 1998, Retrospective Opening grantee, 1999. Mem. Artist Equity. Democrat. Presbyterian. Avocation: bike riding. Home: 141 Wooster St New York NY 10012-3163

SMITH, SHIRLEY ANN NABORS, secondary school educator; b. Lake Creek, Tex., Dec. 9, 1938; d. Herbert Lee and Golden Ann (George) Nabors; m. Don G. Smith, Mar. 31, 1962. BS, East Tex. State U., 1960, MEd, 1962. Jr. high sch. English tchr. Mesquite (Tex.) Ind. Sch. Dist., 1960-61, 65-66; tchr. English, drama Chisum High Sch., Paris, 1966—. Bd. mem. Delta County pub. Libr.; chmn. Delta County Hist. Commn. Mem. DAR, Tex. State Tchrs. Assn., Nat. Coun. Tchrs. English, Delta Kappa Gamma. Democrat. Methodist. Avocation: genealogy. Home: 9687FR895 Lake Creek TX 75450-3422

SMITH, SIBLEY JUDSON, JR. historic site administrator, educator; b. Alexandria, La., June 26, 1955; s. Sibley Judson and Eunice Lee (Raulins) S.; children: Jacob Lee, Casey Raulins. Student, N.E. La. U., 1973-76; BA in History magna cum laude, Christopher Newport Coll., 1985; MA in Am. Studies, Coll. of William and Mary, 1992. Mus. interpreter Colonial Williamsburg (Va.) Found., 1979-87; coord. of interpretation Hist. Hudson Valley, Inc., Tarrytown, N.Y., 1987-88; historic site mgr. Philipse Manor Hall State Hist. Site, Yonkers, 1988-91; exec. dir. Hist. Allaire (N.J.) Village, Inc., 1991-97; dir. edn. Vietnam Era Ednl. Ctr., N.J. Vietnam Vets. Meml. N.J. Dept. Mil. and Vet. Affairs, Holmdel, 1997—. Mem. Alpha Chi, Alpha Psi Omega. Avocations: gardening, theater, movies, mus. Office: Vietnam Era Ednl Ctr 1 Memorial Ln PO Box 648 Holmdel NJ 07733-0648 E-mail: sjsmith@njvvmf.org.

SMITH, SIDNEY OSLIN, JR. lawyer; b. Gainesville, Ga., Dec. 30, 1923; s. Sidney Oslin and Isabelle Caroline (Charters) S.; m. Patricia Irwin Horkan, Aug. 4, 1944 (dec. Oct. 19, 2001); children— Charters Smith Wilson, Ellen Smith Andersen, Sidney Oslin III AB cum laude, Harvard Coll., 1947; LL.B. summa cum laude, U. Ga., 1949. Bar: Ga. 1948. Ptnr. Telford, Wayne & Smith, Gainesville, Ga., 1949-62; asst. solicitor Superior Cts., Northeastern Jud. Cir. Ga., 1951-61, judge, 1962-65, U.S. Dist. Ct. (no. dist.) Ga., 1965-68, chief judge, 1968-74; ptnr. Alston, Miller & Gaines, Atlanta, 1974-82, Alston & Bird, Atlanta, 1982-94, of counsel, 1994—. Chmn. Gainesville Bd. Edn., 1959-62; trustee Brenau Coll., Gainesville, 1974— , chmn., 1976-84; mem. state bd. regents Univ. System of Ga., 1980-87, chmn., 1984-85. Served to capt. U.S. Army, 1943-46, ETO. Fellow ABA, Am. Coll. Trial Lawyers; mem. Am. Law Inst., Am. Judicature Soc., Commerce Club, Chattahoochee Club, Phi Beta Kappa, Phi Kappa Phi, Phi Delta Phi, Phi Delta Theta. Democrat. Episcopalian. Home: 3206 Club Pointe Way Gainesville GA 30506-1638 Office: Alston & Bird 1 Atlantic Ctr Atlanta GA 30309-3400 E-mail: sosjr@bellsouth.net.

SMITH, SIDNEY RUFUS, JR. linguist, educator; b. Greensboro, N.C., Sept. 18, 1931; s. Sidney Rufus and Page (Johnston) S.; m. Vera Pautzsch, Apr. 19, 1969 (div. 1975); children: Stephanie Alice, Eric Brian. BA, Duke U., 1953; PhD, U. N.C., 1965. Asst. prof. U. Conn., Storrs, 1965-66, U. N.C., Chapel Hill, 1966-71, assoc. prof., 1971-79, prof., 1979—, chmn. Germanic langs., 1979-89, 94-97, chmn. linguistics, 1981-84, prof. emeritus, 1997—. Author numerous articles for profl. publs. Local troop leader Girl Scouts U.S.A. Served to sgt. AUS, 1953-56. Recipient Stephen Freeman award N.E. Conf. Teaching Langs., 1969, cert. of merit Goethe Inst., 1997. Mem.: Internat. Brotherhood Magicians, Am. Assn. Tchrs. German, Soc. Advancement Scandinavian Study, Linguistic Soc. Am. Democrat. Office: U NC Dept Germanic Langs Chapel Hill NC 27599-0001

SMITH, SIDONIE, literature educator; Student, U. Sheffield, Eng., 1965; BA, MA, U. Mich., 1966; PhD, Case Western Res. U., 1971. Tchg. asst. Case Western Res. U., 1968—70; instr. Cuyahoga C.C., 1969—71; asst. dean Coll. Continuing Edn. Roosevelt U., 1971—72; asst. prof. U. Ariz., 1973—78, assoc. prof., 1978—83; assoc. prof. Eng. and women's studies Binghamton U., 1983—89, prof. Eng., comparative lit., and women's studies, 1989—96; prof. women's studies and Eng. U. Mich., Ann Arbor, 1996—. Program officer instl. grants edn. divsn. NEA, Washington, 1981—82; assoc. dean acad. affairs, arts and sci. and Harpur Coll. SUNY, Binghamton, assoc. dean adminstrn., arts and sci., and Harpur Coll., acting dean arts and sci. and Harpur Coll., interim dean arts and sci. and Harpur Coll.; dir. grad. studies dept. Eng. Binghamton U., NY, 1991—93; dir. women's studies U. Mich., Ann Arbor, 1996—. Author: Where I'm Bound: Patterns of Slavery and Freedom in Black American Autobiography., 1974, A Poetics of Women's Autobiography: Marginality and the Fictions of Self-Representation, 1987, Subjectivity, Identity, and the Body: Women's Autobiographical Practices in the Twentieth Century., 1993; co-editor: De/Colonizing the Subject: Gender and the Politics of Women's Autobiography, 1992, Getting a Life: Everyday Uses of Autobiography, 1996, Writing New Identities: Gender, Nation, and Immigration in Contemporary Europe, 1997, Indigenous Australian Voices: A Reader, 1998, Women, Autobiography, Theory: A Reader, 1998; contbr. articles. Fellow Canterbury fellow, 1993; grantee Ford grant, 1971, Travel grant, U. Ariz. Found., 1978; scholar Sr. Fulbight scholar, 1994. Mem.: Comparative Lit. Assn., Soc. Study of Narrative Lit., Midwest Modern Lang. Assn., Modern Lang. Assn. Am. (exec. coun. 2000—, exec. bd. divsn. life writing 1989—94, exec. bd. divsn. women's studies lit. 1994—99). Office: Univ Mich 234 West Hall Ann Arbor MI 48109-1092 E-mail: sidsmith@umich.edu.*

SMITH, SIMEON CHRISTIE, III, lawyer, judge; b. Alexandria, La., Feb. 4, 1941; s. Simeon Christie II and Margaret Ford (Ferguson) S.; m. Shirley Mae Pearce, Jan. 28, 1967; children: Simeon Christie IV, E. Pearce Smith. BA, La. State U., 1964; JD, Loyola U., New Orleans, 1967. Bar: La. 1967, U.S. Dist. Ct. (we. dist.) La. 1972, U.S. Ct. Appeals (5th cir.) 1972, U.S. Dist. Ct. (mid. dist.) La. 1973, U.S. Dist. Ct. (ea. dist.) La. 1976, U.S. Supreme Ct. 1976, U.S. Ct. Appeals (11th cir.) 1981. Assoc. Wood & Jackson, Leesville, La., 1967-69; ptnr. Jackson Smith, 1969-75; sr. ptnr. Smith, Ford & Clark, 1975-95, The Smith Law Firm, L.L.P., Leesville, 1996—. Ward judge, Leesville, 1978—. Mem. ATLA, Am. Judicature Soc., La. Trial Lawyers Assn. (mem. bd. govs. 1976-90), La. State Bar Assn. (mem. ho. of dels. 1975-79), 30th Jud. Dist. Bar Assn. (pres. 1974-76). Democrat. Methodist. Office: PO Drawer 1528 300 Courthouse St Leesville LA 71496-1528

SMITH, SIMEON CHRISTIE, IV, lawyer; b. Lake Charles, La., Oct. 21, 1969; s. Simeon Christie III and Shirley Mae (Pearce) S.; m. Christina A. Lord. BA, La. State U., 1992, JD, 1996. Bar: La. 1997, U.S. Dist. Ct. (we., ea. and mid. dists.) La. 1997, U.S. Ct. Appeals (5th cir.) 1997, U.S. Supreme Ct. 2001. Ptnr. The Smith Law Firm, L.L.P., Leesville, La., 1997—. Fellow Roscoe Pound Found.; mem. ATLA, Fed. Bar Assn., La. State Bar Assn., La. Trial Lawyers Assn. (bd. gos. 1997—), 30th Jud. Cir. Bar Assn. (pres. 2000). Roman Catholic. Office: 300 Courthouse PO Box 1528 Leesville LA 71496-1528

SMITH, SPENCER BAILEY, engineering and business educator; b. Ottawa, Ont., Can., Jan. 31, 1927; s. Sidney B. and Etta (Bailey) S.; m. Mildred E. Spidell, Dec. 31, 1954 B in Engring., McGill U., 1949; MS, Columbia U., 1950, DSc in Engring., 1958. Adminstrv. engr. Mergenthaler Linotype Co., N.Y.C., 1953-58; ops. research mgr. Raytheon Co., Newton, Mass., 1958-61; ops research mgr. Montgomery Ward & Co., Chgo., 1961-66; assoc. prof., then prof. Ill. Inst. Tech., 1966-96, prof. emeritus, 1996—, chmn. dept. indsl. and systems engring., 1971-77, dir. Stuart Sch. Office of Research, 1977-82. Tchr. TV courses Nat. Tech. U. Author: Computer-Based Production and Inventory Control, 1989; contbr. articles to profl. jours.; patentee on order quantity calculator, 1964. Vol. cons. on sch. redistricting Elem. Sch. Dist., Evanston, Ill., 1972-74 Research grantee Harris Trust and Savs. Bank, 1968-70, Ill. Law Enforcement Commn., 1972-74, U.S. Army C.E., 1981, Am. Prodn. and Inventory Control Soc., 1980 Mem. INFORMS, Inst. Indsl. Engrs., ASME, Am. Prodn. and Inventory Control Soc. Clubs: University (Chgo.). Presbyterian. Home: 2530 Lawndale Ave Evanston IL 60201-1158 E-mail: montrosemillennium@attbi.com.

SMITH, STACEY LEE, psychiatrist; b. Delaware, Ohio, Apr. 3, 1954; d. James D. and Nancy Smith; m. Richard Katz, Sept. 20, 1985; children: Rachel, Julian. BA, Northwestern U., 1986, MD, 1991. Clin. instr. in psychiatry Wash. U. Med. Sch. Forensic examiner Probate Ct., City of St. Louis, 1996—. Mem. U.S. Olympic Team, 1980. Named 3 Time U.S. Nat. Ice Dance Champion, 1978, 79, 80. Avocations: gardening, music. Office: 4660 Maryland Ave Ste 250 Saint Louis MO 63108-1968

SMITH, STAN VLADIMIR, economist, financial service company executive; b. Rhinelander, Wis., Nov. 16, 1946; s. Valy Zdenek and Sylvia Smith; children: Cara, David. BS in Ops. Research, Cornell U., 1968; MBA, U. Chgo., 1972, PhD in Econs., 1997. Diplomate Am. Bd. Disability Analysts. Lectr. U. Chgo., 1973; economist bd. govs. Fed. Res. System, Washington, 1973-74; staff economist First Nat. Bank of Chgo., 1974; assoc. December Group, Chgo., 1974-77; founding pres. Seaquest Internat., 1977-85; mgr., ptnr. Ibbotson Assocs., 1981-85; pres. Corp. Fin. Group, Ltd., 1985—. Expert econ. witness in field; adj. prof. Coll. Law DePaul U., Chgo. Author: Economic/Hedonic Damages, 1990; founding editor Stocks, Bonds, Bills and Inflation yearbook, 1983-2001; bd. editors Jour. Forensic Economics, 1990-2001; also contbr. articles in field. Founder, exec. dir. Inst. for Value of Life, 1996. Fellow Allied Chem., 1967, John McMullen Trust, 1969; grantee Ford Found., 1972, U.S. Fed. Res., 1973. Fellow Am. Coll. Forensic Examiners (bd. cert.); mem. Am. Econ. Assn., Am. Fin. Assn., Nat. Assn. Forensic Econs. (v.p. 2000—), Nat. Acad. Econ. Arbitrators (founder 1989—), Am. Arbitration Assn. (arbitrator 1994-96), Nat. Future Assn. (arbitrator), Am. Bd. Forensic Examiners, Am. Acad. Econ. and Fin. Experts, Soc. Litigation Economists (bd. govs. 1999--), Alpha Delta Phi. Office: Corp Fin Group Ste 600 1165 N Clark St Chicago IL 60610-7861 E-mail: stan@CFG-Economics.com.

SMITH, STANDISH HARSHAW, non-profit company executive; b. Germantown, Pa., Dec. 28, 1931; s. Standish Oscar and Kathryn Jeanette (Harshaw) S.; m. Joan H. Lallou, Dec. 29, 1956; children: Hamilton, Robertson. BA, Kenyon Coll., 1956; postgrad., State U. Iowa, 1956-58, Villanova U., 1959-61, U. Pa., 1963, Temple U., 1967. Rsch. analyst Rowland and Lo., Haddonfield, N.J., 1961, Franklin Inst., Phila., 1961-63, RCA Svc. Co., Moorestown, N.J., 1963-64, Fed. Aviation Agy., Pomona, 1964-66, Gen. Elec., Phila., 1966-70; founder, treas. Aqua Systems, Inc., Villanova, Pa., 1970-72; founder, owner Auto. Bus., Phila., 1970-84; ret., 1984-91; founder Heirs, Inc., Villanova, 1991-92. Human factors engr. Burroughs Corp., Paoli, Pa., 1959-61; lectr. Burroughs Night Sch., Paoli, 1960; founder Heirs, Inc., Villanova, Pa. Inventor Marine pipelaying system, 1973; contbr. articles to profl. jours. Mem. Mayflower Soc., Merion Cricket Club. Avocation: piano. Office: 1744 Cedar Ln Villanova PA 19085-2018 E-mail: stancedar@home.com.

SMITH, STANFORD SIDNEY, former state treasurer; b. Denver, Oct. 20, 1923; s. Frank Jay and Lelah (Beamer) S.; m. Harriet Holdrege, Feb. 7, 1947; children: Monta Smith Ramirez, Franklin Stanley. Student, Calif. Inst. Tech., 1941-42, Stanford U., 1942-43; BS, U.S. Naval Acad., 1946. Pres. Vebar Livestock Co., Thermopolis, Wyo., 1961—; mem. Wyo. Senate, 1974-76; pres. Wyo. Wool GrowersAssn., 1976-78; mem. Wyo. Ho. of Reps., Cheyenne, 1978-82; treas. State Wyo., 1983-99; ret., 1999. Dir. Coun. of State Govts., 1990-92; v.p. Wyo. Wool Growers, dir., 1976-82. County commr. Hot Springs County, Wyo., 1966-74. Lt. USN, 1943-54. Decorated Bronze Star Mem. Nat. Assn. State Treas. (pres. 1990-91). Republican. Methodist.

SMITH, STANLEY BERTRAM, clinical pathologist, allergist, immunologist, anatomic pathologist; b. Phila., 1929; MD, Washington U., St. Louis, 1956. Diplomate Am. Bd. Clin. Pathology, Am. Bd. Allergy and Immunology, Am. Bd. Anatomic Pathology. Intern Barnes Hosp., St. Louis, 1956-57; resident in pathology Jackson Meml. Hosp., 1957-62; fellow in immunology Sch. Medicine Yale U., New Haven, 1963-65; pathologist Miami (Fla.) Children's Hosp. Mem. AAAS, AMA, Internat. Acad. Pathology, Am. Soc. Clin. Pathology, Coll. Am. Pathologists, Am. Soc. Hematology, Am. Assn. Pathol. Biology. Office: Miami Children's Hosp 3100 SW 62nd Ave Miami FL 33155-3009 E-mail: Stanley.Smith@mch.com.

SMITH, STANTON KINNIE, JR. utility executive; b. Rockford, Ill., Feb. 14, 1931; s. Stanton Kinnie and Elizabeth (Brown) S.; m. Mary Beth Sanders, July 11, 1953; children: Stanton E., Kathryn A., Dana. BA, Yale U., 1953; JD, U. Wis., 1956. Bar: Ill. 1956, Mich. 1976. Ptnr. Sidley & Austin, Chgo., 1964-84; vice chmn., gen. counsel Am. Natural Resources Co., Detroit, 1984-87; sr. v.p. Costal Corp., Houston, 1985-87, also bd. dirs.; vice chmn., gen. counsel CMS Energy Corp., 1987-88, pres., 1988-92, vice chmn., 1992-96, also bd. dirs.; sr. spl. counsel Skadden, Arps, Slate, Meagher & Flom,

N.Y.C., 1996—2002; vice chmn., bd. dirs. Trans-Elect Inc. Bd. dirs. Clarcor Corp., Mich. Natural Corp., Mich. Nat. Bank. Trustee Founders Soc., Detroit Inst. Arts, Rockford Coll., Devel. Bd. Yale U., Mich. Opera Theater; bd. advisors U. Wis. Law Sch., Mich. State U., Pub. Utility Inst. Office: 3 Cameron Pl Grosse Pointe MI 48230

SMITH, STEPHANIE ZAHAROUDIS, producer; b. Washington, May 12, 1958; d. Angelo Constantine and Sally (Laliotis) Zaharoudis; m. John Dorrance Smith, Sept. 15, 1990. BS, U. Md., 1980. Asst. editor Bus. Aviation Weekly, Washington, 1980-81; copy aide, free-lance writer Washington Post, 1980-83; assoc. producer Satellite News Channel, Washington, 1982-83; assignment editor, assoc. producer Sta. WJLA-TV, 1983-84; assoc. producer weekend news Sta. ABC-TV, 1984-86, producer weekend news, 1986-89, producer Pentagon, 1989-93, producer World News Tonight, 1993-97, sr. White House prpducer, 1997—. Recipient Joan Barone award House Radio-TV Gallery, Washington, 1988, George Foster Peabody award, 2001. Office: ABC News 1717 Desales St NW Washington DC 20036-4407

SMITH, STEPHEN ALLEN, mathematician, educator; s. William Francis and Gertrude Elizabeth Smith; m. Karen Ann Jensen, Apr. 27, 2002; children: Gregory, Daniel. BS in Math., U. Cin., 1965; MS in Math., Stevens Inst. Tech., 1967; PhD in Engring.-Econ. Sys., Stanford U., 1972. Rsch. scientist Xerox Rsch. Ctr., Palo Alto, Calif., 1972—82; J.C. Penney prof. Leavey Sch. Bus. Santa Clara U., 1982—. Prin. Pricing Strategy Assocs., Berkeley, Calif., 1984—95; adv. bd. Spotlight Solutions, Inc., Cin., 1998—, StoreSight Sys., Palo Alto, 2000—. Author: (book) New Service Opportunities for Electric Utilities, 1993; contbr. articles to profl. jours.; mem. editl. bd.: Ops. Rsch. Jour., 1984—2000, mem. editl. bd.: Mfg. and Svc. Ops. Mgmt., 1996—2002, mem. editl. bd.: Inst. Indsl. Engring., 1997—2002. Recipient award for best pub. paper, Jour. Retailing, 1991. Mem.: Inst. Ops. Rsch. and Mgmt. Sci. (chmn. bus. applications 1986—90). Office: Santa Clara Univ Dept OMIS 500 El Camino Real Santa Clara CA 95053 E-mail: ssmith@scu.edu.

SMITH, STEPHEN AUSTIN, communications educator; b. Fayetteville, Ark., May 15, 1949; s. Austin Clell and Margaret (King) S.; m. Lindsley Farrar Armstrong, Aug. 6, 1994; children: Caleb Jefferson, Margaret Baldridge. BA in Comm., U. Ark., 1972, MA in Comm., 1974; PhD in Comm. Studies, Northwestern U., 1983. Chief staff Atty. Gen. Ark., Little Rock, 1977-78; exec. asst. Gov. Ark., 1979-80; prof. comm. U. Ark., Fayetteville, 1982—. Author: Myth, Media and the Southern Mind, 1985; author, editor: Clinton on Stump, State, and Stage, 1994. State legislator Ark. Ho. of Reps., Little Rock, 1971-75; v.p. Ark. Constl. Conv., Little Rock, 1979-80. Recipient Madison prize So. States Comm. Assn., 1991. Fellow Am. Comms. Assn.; mem. Speech Comm. Assn. (chair, vice-chair Commn. on Freedom of Expression 1987—, Golden Anniversary Monograph award 1992, Haiman award 1989, Wichelns award 1978). Democrat. Unitarian Universalist. Office: U Ark Dept Comm 417 Kimpel Hall Fayetteville AR 72701 E-mail: Libertas@uark.edu.

SMITH, STEPHEN DEWITT, finance educator; b. Jacksonville, Fla., Apr. 30, 1956; s. Lawrence DeWitt and Ruth Virginia (Miller) S. BA in Bus. Adminstrn., U. South Fla., 1977; PhD in Fin., U. Fla., 1980. Asst. prof. U. Tex., Austin, 1981-85; assoc. prof. Ga. Inst. Tech., Atlanta, 1986-90, Mills B. Lane prof. banking and fin., 1990-91; H. Talmage Dobbs Jr. prof. fin. Ga. State U., 1992—. Vis. scholar 4th dist. Fed. Home Loan Bank Atlanta, 1988-90, 6th dist. Fed. Res. Bank Atlanta, 1991—. Author: Principles of Interest Rates, 1993; contbr. articles to profl. jours. Mem. Am. Fin. Assn., Fin. Mgmt. Assn., Commerce Club. Democrat. Avocations: squash, whitewater rafting, fishing. Office: Ga State U 35 Broad St Fl 12 Atlanta GA 30303-2302

SMITH, STEPHEN EDWARD, lawyer; b. Boston, Aug. 5, 1950; s. Sydney and Minnie (Appel) S.; m. Eileen Beth O'Farrell, June 15, 1986; children: Nora, Bennett, Liliana. AB in Polit. Sci., Boston U., 1972; JD, Washington U., St. Louis, 1976. Bar: Ill. 1976, Mass. 1985, U.S. Dist. Ct. (no. dist.) Ill. 1977, U.S. Dist. Ct. (no. dist.) Ind. 1986, U.S. Dist. Ct. Mass. 1987, U.S. Dist. Ct. (ea. dist.) Wis. 1987, U.S. Ct. Appeals (7th cir.) 1981, U.S. Supreme Ct. 1998. Assoc., ptnr. Brown & Blumberg, Chgo., 1976-80; founding ptnr. Cantwell, Smith & Van Daele, 1980-84; ptnr. Gottlieb & Schwartz, 1984-85; of counsel Siemon, Larsen & Prudy, 1985-90; solo pracittioner, 1990-94; assoc. prof. clin. practice Ill. Inst. Tech. Chgo.-Kent Coll. law, 1994-95; of counsel Field & Golan, 1995—2001, Stephen Edward Smith & Assocs., Chgo., 2001—. Mediator Ctr. for Conflict Resolution, Chgo., 1992—; cmty. adv. coun. WBEZ, Chgo., 1985-2000; arbitrator NASD, Chgo., 1994—, Nat. Futures Assn.; mediator, arbitrator Duke U. Pvt. Adjudication Ctr.; mem. adj. faculty Northwestern U. Sch. Law, 2000—. Author: Update, ADR for Financial Institutions, 1996, 97. Past. bd. dirs., past pres. Jane Addams Ctr., Hull House Assn., Chgo. Fellow Chartered Inst. Arbitrators; mem. Am. Arbitration Assn. (comml. panel), Maritime Law Assn. U.S., Chgo. Internat. Dispute Resolution Assn. (dir.), Internat. Ct. Arbitration (panel of neutrals), London Ct. Arbitration (panel of neutrals), Univ. Club Chgo., The Lawyer's Club Chgo. (sec.-treas. 1999-2000), Chgo. Lincoln Am. Inn. Ct., Internat. C. of C. (panel of neutrals). Office: 55 E Monroe St Ste 3910 Chicago IL 60603-5831

SMITH, STEPHEN GRANT, journalist; b. N.Y.C., Mar. 6, 1949; s. John J. and Nora O.S.; m. Sarah Rowbotham Bedell, May 22, 1982; children: R. Kirk Bedell, Elisabeth DeCou Bedell, David Branson Smith. Student, Deerfield Acad.; BA, U. Pa., 1971. City Hall reporter Daily Hampshire Gazette, Northampton, Mass., 1971-73; spl. assignment reporter Albany Times-Union, 1973-74; dep. regional editor Phila. Inquirer, 1974-76; asst. met. editor Boston Globe, 1976-78; sr. editor Horizon Mag., 1978; staff writer Time Mag., 1978-80, sr. editor, 1980-82, Nation editor, 1982-85, acting asst. mng. editor, 1985-86; exec. editor Newsweek Mag., 1986-91; Washington news editor Knight-Ridder newspapers, 1991-94; founding editor Civilization Mag., Washington, 1994-96; editor Nat. Jour., 1996-98, U.S. News and World Report, 1998-2001. Mem. athletic adv. bd. U. Pa., 2001—. Mem. Coun. on Fgn. Rels., World Affairs Coun. Washington,U. Pa. Alumni Soc. (exec. com. 1994-2000), Fourth Estate Golf Soc. Clubs: Nat. Press, Brook, Century, Met., Beefsteak, White's, Overseas Press, Sakonnet Golf. Home: PO Box 183 Little Compton RI 02837-0183 E-mail: sgrasmith@aol.com.

SMITH, STEPHEN RANDOLPH, aerospace executive; b. Des Moines, Apr. 17, 1928; s. Norvin Ellis and Helen (Heberling) S.; m. Margaret Anne Graves, Dec. 20, 1950; children: Stephen Randolph Jr., Susan Canning, Sara Kutler, Anne Barrette, Julia Carroll. BSME, Stanford U., 1951, MSME, 1952; MBA Advanced Mgmt. Program, Harvard U., 1974. Registered profl. engr., Calif. Sr. analyst, preliminary design engr. Northrop & Garrett Corps., L.A. and Hawthorne, Calif., 1952-55; propulsion lead design engr. Northrop Corp., Hawthorne, 1955-59, engring. rep. ea. dist. Washington, 1959-60, T-38/F-5/F-5X program mgr. Hawthorne, 1960-75, v.p. Iran ops. Tehran, 1975-78, v.p. advanced stealth projects Hawthorne, 1978-83, v.p. engring. and advanced devel., 1983-86, v.p., program mgr. F-20/YF-23A, 1986-88, corp. v.p., gen. mgr. aircraft divsn., 1988-92; cons. tech. mgmt. Palos Verdes, Calif., 1992—. Bd. mem. Quarterdeck Ptnrs., Inc., L.A. and Washington, 1992—; NASA Advanced Aeronautics Com., 1984-86; invited lectr. aircraft design USAF Acad., 1983. Author, designer, patentee in field. Bd. dirs. Boy Scouts Am., L.A. coun., 1986—, explorer exec. com., 1943—; pres. Penn Srs., Palos Verdes, Calif., 1996; trustee Western Mus. Flight; jr. warden St. Francis Ch. Sgt. U.S. Army, 1946-48. Recipient Disting. Civilian Svc. medal for Tacit Blue, U.S. Dept. Def., Washington, 1983. Fellow AIAA (chmn. L.A. sect. 1985-86, adv. bd. 1988—, Spl. Citation 1994), Inst. Advancement Engring.; mem. Soc. Automotive Engrs. (chmn. aerotech. 1986-87, honors 1987), Sierra Club, Trailfinders Conservation Coun. (life, coun. chief 1940), Redondo Beach Yacht Club (charter), King Harbor Yacht Club (charter). Republican. Episcopalian. Avocations: competitive sailing, tennis, backpacking, skiing, running. Home and Office: 2249 Via Guadalana Palos Verdes Estates CA 90274

SMITH, STEPHEN ROSS, endocrinologist; b. Iowa City, Mar. 5, 1938; s. Wendell Ross and Ruth Anne (Frudenfeld) S.; m. Elaine Cashman Frazier, July 4, 1964 (div. Dec. 1990); children: Julia Helene, Stuart Ross; m. Regina Alilada Clarito, Dec. 26, 1990; 1 child, Alexander Ross. AB, Princeton U., 1959; MD, Harvard U., 1963. Instr. medicine Johns Hopkins U. Sch. Medicine, Balt., 1970-72, asst. prof. medicine, 1972-73, 82—; chief endocrinology Kern County Hosp., Bakersfield, Calif., 1973-76; assoc. prof. medicine Tex. Tech. U. Sch. Medicine, El Paso, 1977-80; chief medicine Thomason Gen. Hosp., 1977-80, Bon Secours Hosp., Balt., 1980-83, Security Forces Hosp., Riyadh, Saudi Arabia, 1984-88; pvt. practice Balt., 1988—; med. dir. Nat. Clin. Rsch. Ctrs., Bethesda, 1988-93. Rsch. assoc. Johns Hopkins Ctr. Med. Rsch. and Tng., Calcutta, India, 1970-72; bd. dirs. El Paso Diabetes Assn., 1978-80; cons. Liberty Med. Ctr. Diabetes Mgmt. Ctr., Balt., 1991-98, pharm. industry, 1993—; pres. med. staff Deaton Hosp., Balt., 1996—. Contbr. articles to profl. jours. Capt. USAF, 1965-67. Fellow Am. Coll. Physicians; mem. Am. Diabetes Assn., Am. Fedn. Clin. Rsch., Princeton Club Md., Hampton Swim Club, Bodie Island Beach Club (pres. bd. dirs. 2002--). Republican. Avocations: swimming, internat. travel, history. Home: 1104 Temfield Rd Baltimore MD 21286 Office: 8709 Harford Rd Baltimore MD 21234-4607

SMITH, STEVEN THOMAS, signal processing engineer; b. LaJolla, Calif., Apr. 1, 1963; s. Thomas Jay and Mary Jill Smith; m. Laura Teresa Bortolin, Sept. 2, 1989 (div. 2001). BASc, U. B.C., Vancouver, Can., 1986; PhD, Harvard U., 1993. Rsch. staff Environtl. Rsch. Inst. of Mich., Ann Arbor, 1986-88; lectr. Harvard U., Cambridge, Mass., 1996; tech. staff Lincoln Lab., MIT, Lexington, 1993—. Mem. IEEE (assoc. editor Transaction on Signal Processing, 2000-02), SIAM (Outstanding Paper prize 2001). Office: MIT Lincoln Lab 244 Wood St Lexington MA 02421-6426

SMITH, STEVEN LEE, judge; b. San Antonio, Apr. 19, 1952; s. Bill Lee and Maxine Rose (Williams) S.; m. Rebecca Ann Brimmer, Aug. 5, 1978; children: William Christopher, Laura Charlotte. B in Music Edn. magna cum laude, Abilene Christian U., 1974; JD, U. Tex., 1977. Bar: Tex. 1977. U.S. Dist. Ct. (so. dist.) Tex. 1979, U.S. Dist. Ct. (we. dist.) Tex. 1980; cert. civil trial lawyer, Tex. Bd. Legal Specialization. Assoc. Dillon & Giesenschlag, Bryan, Tex., 1977-80, ptnr., 1980-84, Dillon, Lewis, Elmore & Smith, Bryan, 1985-88, Hoelscher, Lipsey, Elmore and Smith, College Station, Tex., 1988-94; asst. mcpl. judge City of College Station, 1988-91, presiding mcpl. judge, 1992-95; judge Brazos County Ct. at Law # 1, Bryan, 1995-98, 361st Dist. Ct., Bryan, 1999—. Chair Nat. Conf. Spl. Ct. Judges, 2001—02. Chmn. Brazos Valley chpt. March of Dimes, 1983-84; Leadership Brazos Devel. Program, Bryan/Coll. Sta. C. of C., 1984-85; pres. Meml. Student Ctr. Opera and Performing Arts Soc., College Station, 1985-86; trustee Abilene Christian U., 2001—. Recipient Charles Plum Disting. Svc. award Tex. A&M U., 1986. Mem. ABA, Abilene Christian U. Alumni Bd., U. Tex. Law Sch. Alumni Assn. (dist. dir. 1986-89), U. Tex. Ex-Students Assn. Exec. Coun. (club rep. 1987-88), Optimists (pres. 1982-83). Mem. Ch. of Christ. Avocations: golf, flying. Home: 3840 Cedar Ridge Dr College Station TX 77845-6275 Office: 361st Dist Ct 300 E 26th St Ste 305 Bryan TX 77803-5361 E-mail: ssmith@co.brazos.tx.us.

SMITH, STEVEN RAY, law educator; b. Spirit Lake, Iowa, July 8, 1946; s. Byrnard L. and Dorothy V. (Fischbeck) S.; m. Lera Baker, June 15, 1975. BA, Buena Vista Coll., 1968; JD, U. Iowa, 1971, MA, 1971. Bar: Iowa 1971, Ky. 1987, Ohio 1992. From asst. to assoc. dean Sch. Law U. Louisville, 1974-81, acting dean, 1974-75, 76, prof. law, 1971-88, assoc. in medicine Med. Sch., 1983-88; dep. dir/ Assn. Am. Law Schs., 1987-88; dean, prof. law Cleve. State U., 1988-96; pres., dean and prof. Calif. Western Sch. of Law, 1996—. Author: Law, Behavior and Mental Health: Policy and Practice, 1987; contbr. chpts. to books, articles to profl. jours. Trustee U. Louisville, 1980-82, SCRIBES, 1993—; pres. Ky. Congress of Senate Faculty Leaders, 1982-84; bd. trustees Am. Bd. Profl. Psychology, 1994-2001; bd. dirs. Nat. Register of Health Svc. Providers in Psychology, 2002—, San Diego Vol. Lawyers Program, 1998—; sec., bd. dirs. Assn. for Accreditation of Human Rsch. Protection Programs, 2001—. Recipient Grawemeyer award Innovative Teaching. Metroversity Consortium, 1983. Fellow Ohio State Bar Found.; mem. ABA (stds. rev. com. 1991-95, govt. rels. com. 1993-95, joint commn. ABA/Assn. Am. Law Schs. financing of legal edn. 1993-94, 97-98, coun. sect. legal edn. and admission to the bar 1997—), APA (pub. mem. ethics com.), Am. Econs. Assn., Assn. Am. Law Schs. (chmn. librs. com., dep. dir. 1987-88, mem. accreditation com. 1993-96, chair accreditation com. 1994-96), Ohio State Bar Assn. (coun. of dels. 1992-96), Order of Coif, City Club of Cleve. (pres. 1994-95). Office: Calif Western Sch Law Office of Pres 225 Cedar St San Diego CA 92101-3046

SMITH, S(TEWART) GREGORY, ophthalmologist, inventor, product developer, consultant, author; b. Wyandotte, Mich., Jan. 24, 1953; s. Stewart Gene and Veronica (Latta) S. BA in Econs. with distinction, U. Mich., 1974; MD, Wayne State U., 1978. Diplomate Am. Bd. Ophthalmology, Nat. Bd. Med. Examiners. Intern, Sacred Heart Med. Ctr., Spokane, Wash.,1978; resident in ophthalmology U. Minn., Mpls., 1979-82, fellow cornea and anterior segment surgery, 1982-83; practice medicine specializing in cornea and anterior segment surgery, and ophthalmology Wilmington, Del., 1983—; clin. prof. ophthalmology U. Pa., Hershey Med. Ctr., 1984—; clin. asst. prof. Thomas Jefferson U.; attending surgeon Wills Eye Hosp., Phila., 1995—; mem. sr. faculty 3M Vision Care Dept., Mpls., 1984-90, rsch. cons., 1984, lectr., 1983—, cons. Am. Cyanamid Opthalmic Divsn., 1990-94, Am. Home Product, 1995—; lectr. in field, Korea, Hong Kong, Thailand, Malaysia, Phillipines, France, Spain, Ireland, Portugal, Holland, Denmark, England, Sweden; cons. Am. Home Products, 1995—, cons. Alcon, 1999—; Author: Complications ofIntraocular Lenses and Their Management, 1988, Can You Really See Perfectly Again Without Glasses?, 1996; co-author: Vision Without Glasses, 1990, Sight for Life, 1990; contbr. articles to Fly Fisherman Mag. and other profl. publs. Patentee investigational devices and pharmaceutical, tilt control for automotive vehicles. Recipient award for Best Sci. Poster, Contact Lens Assn. of Ophthalmologists, 1980; Best Film award Internat. Congress of Cataract Surgeons, 1985; Grand Prize Am. Soc. Cataract and Refractive Surgeons Film Festival, 1986. Fellow Am. Intraocular Implant Soc., Castroviejo Soc. (Best Paper award 1984), AMA, Eye Bank Assn. Am., Am. Soc. Cataract and Refractive Surgery Internat. Soc. Refractive Surgery, Am. Acad. Ophthalmology (Honor award 1996), Assn. for Rsch. and Vision in Ophthalmology, Internat. Intraocular Implant Club, Wills Eye Hosp. Alumni Soc., European Soc. Cataract & Refracture Soc. Avocations: fly fishing, hunting, saxophone, tennis, skiing. Home: Nine Gates Rd Yorklyn DE 19736 Office: 1100 N Grant Ave Wilmington DE 19805-2671

SMITH, STUART SEABORNE, writer, government official, union official; b. N.Y.C., Jan. 27, 1930; s. Purcell Leonard and Elizabeth (Wright) S.; m. Birte Moeller Jacobsen, Apr. 27, 1956 (div. 1972); children: Stuart Seaborne, Bjarne Moeller; m. Editha Maria Fuchs, Jan. 3, 1973; children: Cornelia Gerda, Melanie Carla. Grad., Lawrenceville (N.J.) Sch., 1948; student, Princeton U., 1948-51, U. Heidelberg, Germany, 1953-54, U. Madrid, Spain, 1954-55, U. Copenhagen, Denmark, 1955-56. Reporter Balt. Sun, 1957-65, fgn. corr. chief Bonn (Germany) bur., 1965-69, corr. Washington Bur., 1969-70; with ABA, 1970-71, Dept. Justice, Washington, 1971—; exec. dir. Capitol Employees Organizing Group, 1979—; pub. Balt. Banner, 1965. Served with AUS, 1951-53. Recipient Spl. award for meritorious svc. Washington-Balt. Newspaper Guild, 1965, Meritorious Svc. award Dept. Justice, 1985, 87, Sustained Superior Performance award Dept. Justice, 1992, 93. Mem. Am. Fedn. State, County and Mcpl. Employees (pres. coun. 26 1977-80, 87-95, chief steward Local 2830 1975-80, 81-82, pres. 1982—, Meritorious Svc. award Local 2830, 1980). Home: 10522 Tyler Ter Potomac MD 20854-4059 Office: Office Of Justice Programs Washington DC 20531-0001 E-mail: stu@ojp.usdoj.gov., stuart.smith20@verizon.net. *I believe in honor and democracy and social justice. I further believe that for the most part we are the ignorant slaves of political and philosophical superstitions, but in the end the truth shall set us free.*

SMITH, STUART LYON, psychiatrist, corporate executive; b. Montreal, Que., Can., May 7, 1938; s. Moe Samuel and Nettie (Krainer) S.; m. Patricia Ann Springate, Jan. 2, 1964; children: Tanya, Craig. BSc, McGill U., 1958, MD, CM, 1962, diploma in psychiatry, 1967; LLD (hon.), Mt. Allison U., 1992, Royal Rds. U., 2000. Intern. Montreal Gen. Hosp., 1962-63, resident in psychiatry, 1963-67; from asst. prof. to assoc. prof. medicine McMaster U., Hamilton, Ont., Can., 1967-75; leader Ont. Liberal Party Ont. Legislature, 1976-82, leader of the opposition, 1977-82; chmn. Sci. Coun. Can., Ottawa, 1982-87; pres. RockCliffe Rsch. and Tech., Inc., 1987—, Philip Utilities Mgmt. Corp., Toronto, Ont., 1994-97. Chmn. com. inquiry Can. U. Edn., 1989—91; chmn. Ensyn Tech. Inc., 1990—; sr. adv. ICF Cons., 2002—; chmn. Nat. Round Table on Environment and Economy, Ottawa, 1995—; bd. dirs. Humber Coll. Decorated knight Nat. Order of Merit (France); McLaughlin travel fellow, 1964-65. Fellow Royal Coll. Physicians and Surgeons of Can. E-mail: smithstuart@rogers.com.

SMITH, SUE FRANCES, newspaper editor; b. Lockhart, Tex., July 4, 1940; d. Monroe John Baylor and Myrtle (Krause) Mueck; m. Michael Vogtel Smith, Apr. 20, 1963 (div. July 1977); 1 child, Jordan Meredith; m. Kirkland Gideon Smith, Apr. 17, 1999. B of Journalism, U. Tex., 1962. Feature writer, photographer Corpus Christi Caller Times, 1962-64; feature writer, editor Chgo. Tribune, 1964-76; features editor Dallas Times Herald, 1976-82; sales assoc. Bumpas Assocs., Dallas, 1982-83; asst. mng. editor for features Denver Post, 1983-84, assoc. editor, 1984-91; asst. mng. editor in charge of Sunday paper Dallas Morning News, 1991-94, asst. mng. editor Lifestyles, 1994-96, dep. mng. editor Lifestyles, 1996—2001, dep. mng. editor recruiting/devel., 2001—. Active Coun. Pres., 1993. Mem. Am. Assn. Sunday and Feature Editors (pres. 1993), Newspaper Features Coun. (pres. 2002), Tex. Associated Press Mng. Editors (pres. 1999-2000), Delta Gamma. Home: 6241 Park Meadow Ln Plano TX 75093-8863 Office: 508 Young St Dallas TX 75202-4893 E-mail: ssmith@dallasnews.com.

SMITH, SURVILLA MARIE, outreach worker; b. Chattanooga, Oct. 17, 1933; d. Charlie and LeGusta (Robinson) Prater; children: Charles, Calvin, Robin. Student, Mass. Bay Community Coll., Boston, 1965-66, Northeastern U., 1967-79, Mus. Sch. of Fine Arts, 1989-90, U. Mass., 1989-95. Exec. sec. The Ecumenical Ctr., Roxbury, Mass., 1965-67, Roxbury Fedn. of Neighborhoods, 1965-68; bus. mgr. Coun. of Elders, Inc., Boston, 1969-72; exec. sec., asst. bookkeeper Edn. Renewal, Inc., 1972-73; asst. dir. METCO Inter-Dist. Transfer Inc., Roxbury, 1973-75; pupil pers. coord. Met. Coun. for Ednl. Opportunity, 1975-78; with Vis. Nurse Assn. of Boston, 1978-79; sec. Bay State Banner Newspaper, Roxbury, 1980; sr. outreach coord. Mattahunt Community Sch Sr. Outreach, Mattapan, Mass., 1989-95. Founder, chmn., CEO S.P.A.C.E. Artistic Cmty., Inc Active Mass. Sr. Action, Boston, 1990—, Women's Caucus Art, Boston chpt., Coalition Black Women, Women Boston; chmn. health campaign Grove Hall/Franklin Park AARP, Boston, 1990—. Mem.: PEN N.E., NAACP, Am. for the Arts, Nat. Writer's Assn., Poetry Soc. Am. Avocations: writing, painting, reading. Home: 4 Wentworth St Dorchester MA 02124-3517 E-mail: ispace@gte.net.

SMITH, SUSAN ELIZABETH, guidance director; b. Phila., Mar. 24, 1950; d. E. Burke Hogue and Janet Coffin Hogue Ebert; m. J. Russell Smith, June 17, 1972 (div. June 1989); 1 child, Drew Russell. BS in Elem. Edn., E. Stroudsburg Coll., 1972; MEd in Counseling, U. Okla., 1974, postgrad., 1976-77, Trenton State Coll., 1989-90; EdM in Devel. Disabilities, Rutgers U., 1992, postgrad., 1994—. Cert. elem. tchr., N.C.; cert. elem. tchr., early childhood edn. tchr., guidance and counseling, Okla.; cert. elem. tchr., guidance and counseling, tchr. of handicapped, psychology tchr., supr. instrn., dir. student pers. svcs., N.J. Elem. tchr. Morton Elem. Sch. Onslow County Schs., Jacksonville, N.C., 1971-72; instr. U. Isfahan, Iran, 1974-76; guidance counselor Moore (Okla.) Pub. Schs., 1976-77; counselor Johnstone Tng. Ctr. N.J. Divsn. Devel. Disabilities, Bordentown, 1988-90; spl. edn. tchr. Willingboro (N.J.) Schs., 1990-91; guidance counselor Haledon (N.J.) Pub. Schs., 1991-92; spl. edn. adj. tchr. Gateway Sch., Carteret, N.J., 1991-93; guidance counselor Bloomfield (N.J.) Pub. Schs., 1992-94; dir. guidance Somerville (N.J.) Pub. Schs., 1994-95. Adj. prof. in spl. edn. Essex County (N.J.) Coll., 1994; guidance Ft. Lee (N.J.) Schs., 1995-2001; guidance dir. Bogota Schs., N.J., 2001-02, Closter Schs., Closter, N.J.; cons., seminar and workshop presenter on behavior mgmt., parenting skills, and behavior modification techniques; cons. N.J. Fragile X Assn. Author: Motivational Awards for ESL Students, 1993, Parent Contracts to Improve School Behaviors, 1996; contbr. articles to profl. jours. Leader Boy Scouts Am., Oklahoma City, 1983-87, com. chmn., Redmond, Wash., 1987-88. Recipient Rsch. award ERIC/CAPS, 1992, Svc. award N.J. Fragile X Assn., 1993. Mem. ACA, Am. Sch. Counselor Assn. (grantee 1992), N.J. Counseling Assn., N.J. Sch. Counseling Assn., Assn. for Multicultural Counseling and Devel., AAUW, Assn. for Counselor Edn. and Supervision, N.J. Assn. for Counselor Edn. and Supervision, N.J. Prins. and Suprs. Assn., Nat. Assn. Coll. Admissions Counselors (grantee 1995), Alpha Omicron Pi. Episcopalian. Home: 916 Lincoln Pl Teaneck NJ 07666-2572

SMITH, SUSAN PORTER, artist, environmentalist; b. Weston, W.Va., Aug. 11, 1934; d. Edward Conrad and Eugenia Porter (Arnold) S. BA, Vassar Coll., 1956; postgrad., Inst. Allende, San Miguel de Allende, Mex., 1975-76, Bellas Artes, 1977-79, Nat. Acad. Design, N.Y.C., 1981. Editorial asst. Spl. Libraries Jour., N.Y.C., 1958-59; edn. advisor Sci. Am., 1962-63; sci. rsch. editor Readers Digest, 1964-74; freelance artist, painter, photographer East Quogue, NY, 1978—98. Exhibited in group shows at Bellas Artes, Mex., 1981, San Miguel de Allende, 1987, East End Arts Coun., Riverhead, N.Y., 1988, 93; contbr. to book: Rooms with No View, 1974. Adviser, supporter Ctr. for Adolescents, San Miguel de Allende, 1986—; organizer San Miguel Artists for the Environment; assoc. dir. for environ. Letitia Echlin Meml. Fund, 1997-99; v.p. San Miguel Audubon Soc., 1984-93; pres. Sociedad Audubon de Mex., 1993-96; assoc. dir. Rio Laja project Fundacion Ecologica de Guanajuato, 1997-99; pres., founder Salvemos el Rio Laja, A.C., 1999—, Save the Laja, Inc., 2000—.

SMITH, SUZANNE RENEE, science educator, researcher; b. Atlanta, Mar. 6, 1968; d. Kenneth Altman and Linda Johnson Smith. BA, Erskine Coll., Due West, S.C., 1990; MS, Va. Tech., 1992; PhD in Child and Family Devel., U. Ga., Athens, 1996. Instr. sociology Erskine Coll., Due West, 1992—93; instr. U. Ga., Athens, Ala., 1993—97; asst. prof. Wash. State U., Vancouver, 1997—. Author: (book) Introduction to Family Theories, 2002; contbr. Mem. Family and Consumer Sci. Edn. Adv. Com., Battle Ground, 1999—2002. Grantee rsch. grantee, Carcinoid Found., 2001—02, Am. Diversity mini-grant, Wash. State U., 2001—02, rsch. grantee, 2001, Am. Diversity mini-grant, 1998—99. Mem.: Nat. Assn. for Edn. of Young Children, Am. Assn. Family and Consumer Scis., Nat. Coun. Family Rels. (pres. N.W. coun. 2000—02). Methodist. Avocations: travel, tennis, reading. Home: 13013 NE 38th St Vancouver WA 98682 Office: Wash State U 14204 NE Salmon Creek Ave Vancouver WA 98686-9600 Office Fax: 360-546-9040. Business E-Mail: smithsu@vancouver.wsu.edu.

SMITH, SYDNEY DAVID, data processing executive; b. San Antonio, Nov. 25, 1947; s. Sydney Philip and Doris Annette (King) S.; m. Helen Louise Smith; 1 child, Anne. BBA, Baylor U., 1969; MBA, Northwestern U., 1973. CPA, Ill. Sr. cons. Arthur Andersen & Co., Chgo., 1973-76; sr. systems engr. Bd. Edn., 1976-77; applications mgr. Estech, Inc., 1977-84; info. ctr. mgr. GATX Corp., 1984-85; N.Am. support mgr. Trinzic Corp., 1986-95; dir. adminstrv. svcs. McKesson Corp., 1995—. Served with U.S. Army, 1969-71. Mem. AICPA, Ill. CPA Soc. Office: McKesson Corp 650 Warrenville Rd Ste 301 Lisle IL 60532-4317

SMITH, TAD RANDOLPH, lawyer; b. El Paso, Tex., July 20, 1928; s. Eugene Rufus and Dorothy (Derrick) S.; m. JoAnn Wilson, Aug. 24, 1949; children: Laura Borsch, Derrick, Cameron Ann Compton. LLB, U. Tex., 1951, BBA, 1952. Bar: Tex. 1951. Assoc. firm Kemp, Smith Duncan & Hammond P.C., El Paso, Tex., 1951-52, ptnr., 1952-81, CEO, 1975-97, shareholder, 1981-88; of counsel Kemp Smith, P.C., 1999—. Active United Way of El Paso; chmn. El Paso County Reps., 1958-61, Tex. Rep. State Exec. Com., 1961-62; alt. del. Rep. Nat. Conv., 1952, 62, del. 1964, dir. El Paso Elec. Co. , 1961-90, State Nat. Bank of El Paso, 1969-90, The Leavell Co., 1970-94; trustee Robert E. and Evelyn McKee Found., 1970-90, Property Trust of Am., 1971-91; mem. devel. bd. U. Tex., El Paso, 1973-81, v.p., 1975, chmn. 1976; dinner treas. Nat. Jewish Hosp. and Rsch. Ctr., 1977, chmn. 1978, presenter of honoree, 1985; bd. dirs. NCCJ 1965-76, chmn. 1965-78; bd. dirs. Southwestern Children's Home, El Paso, 1959-78; trustee Hervey Found., 1990-99, Lydia Patterson Inst., 1994-99. Named Outstanding Young Man, El Paso Jaycees; named to Bd. of Fellows, U. Tex., El Paso, 1997—2001; recipient Humanitarian award, El Paso chpt. NCCJ, 1983. Fellow Am. Bar Found., Tex. Bar Found.; mem. ABA, Tex. Bar Assn., El Paso Bar Assn. (pres. 1971-72), El Paso C. of C. (dir. 1979-82), Sigma Chi. Republican. Methodist. Home: 5716 Mira Grande Dr El Paso TX 79912-2006 Office: Kemp Smith PC Norwest Plz 221 N Kansas St Ste 1700 El Paso TX 79901-1401

SMITH, TED JAY, III, mass communications educator; b. Dobbs Ferry, N.Y., Sept. 14, 1945; s. Ted Jay Jr. and Marie Glencora (Hershey) S.; m. Rosemary Tibbe, June 12, 1971. Student, U. Pitts., 1963-64; Student, U. So. Miss., 1968-69; BA with high honors, Mich. State U., 1971, MA, 1972, PhD, 1978. Commd. 2nd lt. USAF, 1971, advanced through grades to 1st lt., 1973, from electronics technician to electronics instr., 1965-70, airman edn. &

commissioning program student Mich., 1970-71, info officer, 1971-74, resigned, 1974; grad. teaching/rsch. asst. Mich. State U., E. Lansing, 1974-77; asst. prof. SUNY, Albany, 1977-79; lectr. I, Warrnambool Inst. Advanced Edn., Warrnambool, Australia, 1979-82; asst. prof. U. Va., Charlottesville, 1982-87, dir. grad. studies, 1984-87; assoc. prof. Va. Commonwealth U., Richmond, 1987—, dir. grad. studies, 1990-94; sr. rsch. fellow Ctr. for Media & Pub. Affairs, 1996—. Bradley resident scholar Heritage Found., Washington, 1992-93; pres. Applied Analytics, Inc., Richmond, Va., 1986—; sr. analyst Rowan & Blewitt, Inc., Washington, 1986-90; co-founder, sr. rsch. fellow Ctr. for Comm. Rsch., Warrnambool, 1982—; mem. policy adv. coun. VA Inst. for Pub. Policy, 1996—; mem. nat. adv. bd. Comm. Rsch. Corp., Washington, 1986-95, nat. adv. coun. The Media Inst., Washington, 1987—; faculty adviser FBI Nat. Acad., Quantico, Va., 1983-87; bd. dirs. Nat. Assn. Scholars, 1990—; mem. Main St. Commn., Rockford Inst., 1992—; educators adv. bd. Inst. for Pub. Rels. Rsch. & Edn., 1992—; co-founder Statis. Assessment Svc., 1993. Author: The Vanishing Economy, 1988, Moscow Meets Main Street, 1988; co-author: What Do the People Want From the Press?, 1997; editor: Communication in Australia, 1983, Propaganda: A Pluralistic Perspective, 1989, Steps Toward the Restoration of Our World, 1998, In Defense of Tradition, 2000; co-editor: Communication and Government, 1986; co-editor human communication book series SUNY Press, Albany, 1987—; contbr. articles to profl. jours. Mem. The Nature Conservancy, Albany, 1977-79, Charlottesville, 1982—, Accuracy in Media, Washington, 1982—; contbg. mem. Va. Mus. Fine Arts, Richmond, 1987—. Grantee FBI, U. Va., Warrnambool Inst., Bradley Found., Raldolph Found., Scaife Found., Earhart Found. Mem. Am. Assn. for Pub. Opinion Rsch., Assn. for Edn. in Journalism and Mass Communication, Australian Communication Assn. (founding), Internat. Communication Assn., Anglican Guild of Scholars, Nat. Assn. Scholars (bd. dirs. 1990—), Pub. Rels. Soc. Am., Phila. Soc., Va. Assn. Scholars (founding bd. dirs., pres. 1990—), So. Speech Communication Assn., St. George Tucker Soc., Southern League, Va. Speech Communication Assn. (chair theory divsn. 1986-91, 1st v.p. 1991-94), Phi Kappa Phi, Kappa Tau Alpha. Republican. Anglican Catholic. Avocations: nature study, fine arts and crafts, classical music. Home: 4010 Sherbrook Rd Richmond VA 23235-1643 Office: Va Commonwealth U Sch Mass Communications 901 W Main St Richmond VA 23284-9014

SMITH, TEFFT WELDON, lawyer; b. Evanston, Ill., Nov. 18, 1946; s. Edward W. and Margery T. (Weldon) S.; m. Nancy Jo Smith, Feb. 25, 1967; children: Lara Andrea, Tefft Weldon II. BA, Brown U., 1968; JD, U. Chgo., 1971. Bar: Ill. 1971, U.S. Supreme Ct. 1977. Sr. litigation ptnr. Kirkland & Ellis, Chgo., 1971—, ptnr.-in-charge competition and antitrust practice group. Mem. adv. bd. Bur. Nat. Affairs Antitrust and Trade Regulation Reporter; instr. trial advocacy. Contbr. numerous articles on trial practice and antitrust issues to law jours. Mem. ABA (litigation sect., antitrust law sect.), Econ. Club., Univ. Club, Mid-Am. Club, Sea Pines Country Club (Hilton Head, S.C.). Avocations: squash, Ferraris, sculpture. Office: Kirkland & Ellis 200 E Randolph St Fl 54 Chicago IL 60601-6636 also: 655 15th St NW Washington DC 20005-5701

SMITH, TERRY LYNN, information scientist; b. La Porte, Ind., Dec. 8, 1944; s. Paul F. and Ferne R. (Eplett) S.; m. Mary Jo Hartley, Jan. 31, 1970; children: Todd Alan, Timothy Eric. BS, Butler U., 1968. Programmer LTV Steel Co., East Chicago, Ind., 1971-74; systems analyst Allis Chalmers Co., Harvey, Ill., 1974-76; mgr. finished inventory La Salle Steel Co., Hammond, Ind., 1976-80; internal cons. Wheelabrater-Frye Co., Harvey, 1980-82; dir. mgmt. info. systems Trailmobile, Inc., Chgo., 1982-83; prin., cons. Ernst and Young, 1983-86; sr. mgr. KPMG Peat Marwick, 1986-88; prin. Ernst and Young, 1988—, CSC Cons., 1988-90, Mfg. Mgmt. Assocs., Oakbrook, Ill., 1992-96; sr. prin. Tech. Solutions Co., Chgo., 1996—. Mem. client strategy com., Ernst and Young, Chgo., 1986, peer rev. team, Orange County, Calif., 1986. Mem. Com. for Strategic Ednl. Planning Lake Cen. Ind. Sch., 1987, 88. Served as sgt. U.S. Army, 1968-71. Mem. Am. Prodn. and Inventory Control Soc. (edn. com. 1981, cert.), Data Processing Mgmt. Assn., Spl. Interest Group for Cert. Data Processors, Assn. Inst. Cert. Group Computer Profls. (cert.). Clubs: East Bank (Chgo.). Republican. Methodist. Avocations: tennis, basketball, softball, reading autobiographies. Home: 8752 Lantern Dr Saint John IN 46373-9316 Office: TSC 205 N Michigan Ave Chicago IL 60601-5927 E-mail: mjhtostm@jorsm.com.

SMITH, THELMA TINA HARRIETTE, gallery owner, artist; b. Folkston, Ga., May 5, 1938; d. Harry Charles and Malinda Estelle (Kennison) Causey; m. Billy Wayne Smith, July 23, 1955; children: Sherry Yvonne, Susan Marie, Dennis Wayne, Chris Michael. Student, U. Tex., Arlington, 1968-70; studies with various art instrs. Gen. office worker Superior Ins. Corp., Dallas, 1956-57, Zanes-Ewalt Warehouse, Dallas, 1957-67; bookkeeper Atlas Match Co., Arlington, 1967-68; sr. acct. Automated Refrigerated Air Conditioner Mfg. Corp., 1968-70; acct. Conn. Gen. Life Ins. Corp., Dallas, 1972-74; freelance artist Denton, Tex., 1974—; gallery owner, custom framer Tina Smith Studio-Gallery, Mabank, 1983—. Painting in pub. and pvt. collections in numerous states including N.Y., Fla., Ga. and N.D.; editor Cedar Creek Art Soc. Yearbook, 1983—. Treas. Cedar Creek Art Soc., 1987-88, 89—; mem. com. to establish state endorsed Arts Coun. for Cedar Creek Lake Area, Gun Barrel City, Tex. Recipient numerous watercolor and pastel awards Henderson County Art League, Cedar Creek Art Soc., Cmty. Svc. award Mayor Wilson Tippit, Gun Barrel City, Tex., 1986. Mem. Southwestern Watercolor Soc. (Dallas), Soc. Outdoor Painters, Pastel Soc. of the S.W. (Dallas), Cedar Creek Art Soc. (Gun Barrel City)(v.p. 1983-86, treas.), Profl. Picture Framers Assn. Baptist. Avocations: water activities, gardening. Studio: Tina Smith Studio-Gallery 251 Shady Shores Dr Mabank TX 75156-

SMITH, THOMAS CLAIR, retired manufacturing company executive; b. Indiana, Pa., Mar. 14, 1925; s. William Bryan and Edna Louise (Thomas) S.; m. Marilyn Louise Globisch, May 29, 1948; children: Claudia Lynn Smith Holtry, Craig Randall. BSME, Pa. State U., 1946; A, Alexander Hamilton Bus. Inst., 1949. Registered profl. engr., Pa., N.J., Del. Structural test engr. Chance Vought Aircraft Co., Bridgeport, Conn., 1946-48; test engr. Fed. Mogul Bearings Co., Lancaster, Pa., 1949-51; fuse engr. to mgr. materials Hamilton Watch Co. (name now Hamilton Tech.), 1952-70; plant mgr. Woodstream Corp., Lititz, 1970-79, v.p. mktg., 1980-96, ret., 1996. Faculty, coach Lacrosse Franklin and Marshall Coll., Lancaster, 1950-53. Pub. Smith, Bryan, Allison & Morris Geneal. Chart, 1989; author and pub. of 1600 person geneal. chart in Libr. of Congress, 1989; patentee electric watch, 1957, swivel snap, 1975; author Penna Law 110 of 1992 and Pa. Law 22 of 1994/saving ancestral cemetaries. Pres. bd. dirs. Lancaster County Mental Health Assn., 1952-60, Lancaster County Cmty. Svc. Ctr., 1968-78; pres., bd. dirs. Am. Cancer Soc., 1970-72, bd. dirs., 1965-97, life bd. dirs., 1998—; bd. dirs. Hearing Conservation Assn., Lancaster, 1955-60, ARC, Lancaster, 1967-86, United Way, Lancaster, 1968-72, Ephrata (Pa.) Area Rehab. Ctr., 1986—, Grave Concern, Inc., 1994—; pres. Ephrata (Pa.) Area Rehab. Found., 1997—; mem. All-Am. Lacrosse Team, 1945, Heritage Ctr. Lancaster, 1980—, Ind. County Hist. Soc., 1984—, Greene County Hist. Soc., Waynesburg, Pa., 1985—, Selective Svc. Bd., 1992—; trustee Lancaster County Hist. Soc., 1992-98, mem., 1983—; judge elections, Lancaster County, 1994-2001. Named Boss of Yr., Am. Bus. Women's Assn., 1978, Vol. of Yr., Am. Cancer Soc., 1998, Tennis Family of Yr. Pa. N.J., Del., 1970; named to Lancaster County Tennis Hall of Fame, 2001; recipient Outstanding Svc. award, Mental Health Assn. Lancaster, 1961, Edward D. Eshelman award as Humanitarian of Yr., Am. Cancer Soc., 1991. Mem. Order of Crown of Charlemagne in U.S.A. (life), Pa. State U. Alumni Club (life), Pa. Sons of Revolution (bd. dirs., sec. 1990—), Phi Delta Theta (pres. Pa. State U. chpt. 1945), Wheatland Tennis Club (v.p. 1990-94, pres. 1995-96). Clubs: Lancaster Country (chmn. tennis com. 1960-75). Republican. Presbyterian. Avocations: genealogy, tennis, skiing. Home: 1420 Quarry Ln Lancaster PA 17603-2426 *You only go through this life on earth once. Don't waste that time. Put it to use in helping to make the earth a better place.*

SMITH, THOMAS EUGENE, investment company executive, financial consultant; b. Brown's Summit, N.C., Aug. 23, 1930; s. Howard Cleveland and Annie May (Warren) S.; m. Joan Cretcher Hopkins, Sept. 22, 1948; 1 dau., Vicki Joan. Student, George Washington U., 1948-50, Am. U., 1950-55 (intermittently). Pres., dir. T. Eugene Smith, Inc. investment co. and real estate and fin. cons. co., Falls Church, Va., 1950—; pres. The Potomac Corp., 1960-74; pres., dir. Nat. Bank of Fairfax, 1975-81, dir.; exec. v.p. First & Mchts. Nat. Bank, Richmond, 1981-83; chmn., dir. Decisions and Designs, Inc., McLean, 1983-86; ptnr. Braddock-Ravensworth Ltd. Partnership, 1964—; sec., dir. Port Royal, Inc., 1965—; ptnr. Lee Graham Shopping Ctr., 1969—; chmn., pres., dir. Am. Mobile Home Towns, Inc., holding co., 1969-85; dir., pres. Topsail, Inc., 1983-89; ptnr. Potomac Greens Assn., 1986—. Bd. dirs. Growth Fund of Washington, Am. Funds Tax Exempt Series I, Washington Mut. Investors, M.G. Thalheimer Realty Advisors, Inc.; chmn., bd. dirs. River Capital Corp., Alexandria, Va., 1986-89, J. Webb, Inc., 1986—; acting dir., mem. mgmt. com. Alexandria 20/20, 1988-91, acting dir., 1988-89; pres., dir. Pender Marina Holdings, Inc., 1988—, Pender Land Holdings, Inc., 1990—; mem. CSX Realty Adv. Bd., 1992—. Bd. dirs. Wolftrap Found., Washington, 1974-84; trustee Sta. WETA-TV, 1978-86; mem. Nat. Capital Planning Commn., Washington, 1980-83, vice chmn., 1981-83; mem. Va. Hwys. and Transp. Commn., Richmond, 1982-86; trustee Ch. Schs., Diocese of Va., 1983-88; mem. Va. Gov.'s Coun. Econ. Advisors, 1985-94, Met. Washington Airports Authority, 1986-94; chmn. Fairfax County Transp. Commn. for the Future, 1988-89; dir. Air and Space Heritage Coun., 1987-90. Mem.: Nat. Assn. Small Bus. Investment Cos. (treas. and bd. dirs. 1962—66), Met. Club (Washington). Democrat. Episcopalian. Home: 666 Tintagel Ln Mc Lean VA 22101-1835

SMITH, THOMAS GORDON, architect; b. Oakland, Calif., Apr. 23, 1948; s. Sheldon Wagers and Margaret (Prendergast) S.; m. Marika Wilson, Dec. 19, 1970; children— Alan, Stuart, Demetra, Andrew, Philip, Duncan. A.B., U. Calif.-Berkeley, 1970, M.Arch., 1975. Lic. architect, Calif. Prin. Thomas Gordon Smith, Architect, Chgo., 1980-86; instr. archtl. history Coll. of Marin, Kentfield, Calif., 1976-77; guest instr. archtl. design So. Calif. Inst. Architecture, Santa Monica, 1983; guest lectr., seminar leader Kunstegeschichtlieches Institut der Philipps Universitat, Marburg, W.Ger., 1983; guest tchr. U. Ill., Chgo., UCLA, 1984; assoc. prof. U. Ill., Chgo.; chmn. Sch. Architecture U. Notre Dame, Ind., 1989. Exhibited art in shows at Santa Barbara Mus. Art, 1977, Cooper-Hewitt Mus., Chgo. Art Inst., 1980, Louisiana Mus. Modern Art, Copenhagen, 1981, Venice Biennale, 1980, Smith Coll. Mus. Art, 1981, La Jolla Mus. Modern Art, Calif., 1982, Deutsches Architekturmuseum, Frankfurt, W.Ger., 1984; revision of Modern IBM Gallery, N.Y., 1987; author: Classical Architecture: Rule and Invention, 1987. AIA Grad. fellow, 1973, U. Calif. grad. fellow, 1974, John K. Branner fellow, 1975, Rome Prize fellow, 1979; grantee Graham Found. Advanced Study in Fine Arts, 1984, 87, Am. Philos. Soc., 1987. Mem. Soc. Archtl. Historians, AIA. Home: 1903 Dorwood Dr South Bend IN 46617-1818 Office: U Notre Dame Sch Architecture Notre Dame IN 46556

SMITH, THOMAS H. priest; b. Hanover, Pa., May 19, 1931; s. Mark Stanislaus Smith and Anna Mabel Keaqy. BA, St. Charles Sem., 1957; DD (hon.) , Lebanon Valley Coll., 1993. Ordained 1957, hon. prelate (monsignor) 1989. Asst. pastor St. Catherine Labocac Ch., Harrisburg, Pa., 1957—61, St. Anne's Ch., Lancaster, 1961—63; chaplain Holy Spirit Hosp., Camp Hill, 1963—67; asst. pastor St. Peter Ch., Mt. Carmel, 1967—70, St. Joseph Ch., Mechanicsburg, 1970—72; pastor St. Columbz Parish, Bloomsburg, 1972—73, St. Paul the Apostle Ch., Annville, 1973—92, St. Joseph Ch., Lancaster, 1992—. Chaplain Lebanon Valley Coll., Annville, Pa., 1973—92, Ft. Indiantown Gap, Annville, 1973—92; pres. Lebanon Cath. H.S. Bd., O.L. of the Valley of Lebanon. Chaplain Am. Guild and Organist, Harrisburg, Pa., 1985—2001; mem. bd. dir. Lebanon YMCA, 1985—92. Recipient Pa Commendation Medal, Dept. Mil. Affairs, 1992. Mem.: Organ Hist. Soc. Republican. Roman Cath. Avocations: travel, music, art, theological study. Office: St Joseph Ch 440 St Joseph St Lancaster PA 17603 Office Fax: 717-397-2120.

SMITH, THOMAS HAROLD, III, instrumental music educator, musician, writer; b. Greenville, N.C., May 10, 1957; s. Thomas Harold Jr. and Julia Anne (Tracy) S.; m. Sarah Ann Anderson, Jan. 18, 1987; 1 child, Matthew Tracy Smith. B in Music Edn., U. So. Miss., 1979; M in Music, U. N.C., Greensboro, 1990. Cert. secondary music tchr., N.C. Band dir. Fayetteville (N.C.) Pub. Schs., 1981-82, Rockingham County Schs., Eden, N.C., 1996-97, Wake County Pub. Schs., Raleigh, 1982-84; dir. instrumental music Caldwell C.C., Lenoir, 1984-88; artist-in-residence Rowan-Cabarrus C.C., Salisbury, 1988-90, Blue Ridge C.C., Hendersonville, 1990-92; feasability study coord. Baron Ross Corp., 1992-94; solo trombonist Glenn Miller Orch., Maitland, Fla., 1994; bandmaster Norwegian Cruise Lines, Miami, 1995; dir. instrumental music Rockingham County Schs., Eden, N.C., 1996, Pfeiffer U., Misenheimer, 1997—. Founder So. Miss. Ednl. Jazz Fest., Hattiesburg, 1977; founder, pres., fellow mem. Unifour Jazz Soc., Newton, N.C., 1986—; bd. dirs. N.C. Jazz Network, Carrboro, N.C., 1989-91. Prodr., dir. (recording) First Steps, 1986, Roadwork, 1988; founder, editor Foothills Jazz Jour., 1988-89; writer: The Tahchee Chronicles Triad Publs., 2001; contbr. ITA Jour., 1998—. Pres. pro-tem Student Govt. Assn., U. So. Miss., Hattiesburg, 1977-78. Downbeat auditions recipient Down Beat Mag., 1986; recipient Cmty. Jazz Ensemble Gold award, 1987, fifth place world trombone, Downbeat Reader's Poll, 1988, seventh place world big band, 1988; Fulbright scholar Bucharest Acad. Music, Romania, 2002—. Fellow Internat. Assn. Jazz Educators (chairperson N.C. State 1998-99); mem. Internat. Trombone Assn., Nat. Assn. Jazz Educators, (founder Miss. chpt., pres. 1977—, outstanding musician award 1978, outstanding svc. to jazz edn. award 1998, 2000, 01, 02). Methodist. Avocations: traveling, historical investigation. Office: Pfeiffer Univ Hwy 52 Misenheimer NC 28109 Home: 315B W Council St Salisbury NC 28144-4209 E-mail: thsmith@pfeiffer.edu.

SMITH, THOMAS HUNTER, ophthalmologist, ophthalmic plastic and orbital surgeon; b. Silver Creek, Miss., Aug. 10, 1939; s. Hunter and Wincil (Barr) S.; m. Michele Ann Campbell, Feb. 27, 1982; 1 child, Thomas Hunter IV. BA, U. So. Miss., 1961; MD, Tulane U., 1967; BA in Latin Am. Studies, Tex. Christian U., 1987, MA in History, 1995, PhD in L.Am. History, 1999. Diplomate Am. Bd. Ophthalmology (bd. examiners 1983-90). Intern Charity Hosp., New Orleans, 1967-68; resident in ophthalmology Tulane U., 1968-71; dir., sec. bd. dirs. Ophthalmology Assocs., Ft. Worth, 1971-99; adj. prof. history of medicine and L.Am. history Tex. Christian U., 2000—01; adj. instr. history of medicine and pub. health, L.Am. history Tulane U., 2001—02. Clin. prof. Tex. Tech U. Med. Sch., Lubbock, 1979-99; guest lectr., invited speaker numerous schs., confs., symposia throughout N.Am., Ctrl. Am., South Am., Europe and India; hon. mem. ophthalmology dept. Santa Casa de São Paulo Med. Sch. Contbr. articles to profl. jours. Cons. ophthalmologist Helen Keller Internat.; deacon South Hills Christian Ch.; mem. Rocky Mountain Coun. Latin Am. Studies. Recipient Tex. Chpt. award Am. Assn. Workers for the Blind, 1978, Recognition award Lions Club Sight & Tissue Found., Cen. Am., 1977-79; named to Alumni Hall of Fame U. So. Miss., 1989. Fellow ACS, Am. Acad. Ophthalmology (bd. counsellors 1995-98), Am. Acad. Facial Plastic and Reconstructive Surgery; mem. Tex. Med. Assn. (com. socio-econs.), Pan-Am. Assn. Ophthalmology (adminstr. 1988-93, bd. dirs. 1993-99), Internat. Cos. Cryosurgery, Royal Soc. Medicine (affiliate), Tex. Soc. Ophthalmology and Otolaryngology, Peruvian Ophthalmol. Soc. (hon.), Santa Casa De São Paulo (hon. assoc.), Tex. Ophthalmol. Assn. (past mem. exec. coun., treas.), Tex. Med. Assn., Tarrant County Med. Soc., Byron Smith Ex Fellows Assn., Tarrant County Multiple Sclerosis Soc. (past pres.), Tarrant County Assn. for Blind, Tulane Med. Alumni Assn. (bd. dirs.), S.Am. Explorers Club, Colonial Country Club, Petroleum Club Ft. Worth, Sigma Xi, Omicron Delta Kappa. Mem. Christian Ch. (Disciples Of Christ). Avocations: hunting, fishing, flying, world travel.

SMITH, THOMAS J. surgeon, educator; BA cum laude, Amherst Coll., 1967; MD, Tufts U. Sch. Medicine, 1971. Diplomate Am. Bd. Surgery, Nat. Bd. Med. Examiners. Intern, resident in surgery Tufts New England Med. Ctr., Boston, 1971-73, chief resident in surgery, 1975-78; clin. assoc. surgery br. Nat. Cancer Inst., Bethesda, Md., 1978-80; from asst. prof. to assoc. prof. surgery Tufts U. Sch. Medicine, 1980-94; assoc. prof. U. South Fla., 1994; asst. prof. clin. surgery Columbia U., N.Y.C., 1995—. Clin. prof. surgery UMDNJ Med. Sch., 1997—. Editl. bd. Internat. Jour. Cancer Rsch. & Treatment, Oncology; contbr. articles, abstracts to profl. jours. Mem. Am. Coll. Physician Execs., Am. Soc. Clin. Oncology, Soc. Surg. Oncology (edn. com. 1988—), Am. Cancer Soc. (sword of hope award com.). Office: Everett Clinic 3927 Rucker ve Everett WA 98201 E-mail: tsmith@everettclinic.com.

SMITH, THOMAS KENT, retired radiologist, viticulturist; b. Bowling Green, Ohio, Aug. 21, 1934; s. Robert O. and Roslyn Smith; m. Jaleh Saidi, Feb. 1, 1974; children: Jeffrey, Todd, Mark, Blake, Tyler. BS with high honors, U. Cin., 1957; MD, Case Western Res. U., 1961. Intern Nat. Naval Med. Ctr., Bethesda, Md., 1961-62; resident in radiology VA Med. Ctr., Long Beach, Calif., 1965-69; fellow in radiologic pathology Armed Forces Inst. Pathology, Washington, 1968; dir. radiology Harriman Jones Med. Group, Long Beach, 1969-88; fellow in MRI/CT U. Calif., San Francisco, 1988-89; dir. MRI Orange County MRI, Fountain Valley, 1989-90; chmn. dept. diagnostic imaging Kaiser Permanente Med. Ctr., Honolulu, 1990-2000, dir. MRI, 1994-2000; ret. Mem. adv. bd. Hawaii Permanente Med. Group, Honolulu, 1990—2000; assoc. clin. prof. radiology U. Hawaii, Honolulu, 1990—2000; asst. clin. prof. U. Calif., Irvine, Calif., 1970—88, clin. instr., San Francisco, 1988—89, asst. clin. prof., 1989—99; cons. in radiologic devel. Kaiser Permanente Internat., 1996—98; owner Rubaiyat Vineyard, Sonoma County, Calif. Lt. M.C. nuclear submarine svcs. USN, 1961-65. Fellow Am. Coll. Radiology; mem. Hawaii Radiol. Soc. (pres. 1992-93), Radiol. Soc. N.Am., Internat. Soc. Magnetic Resonance in Medicine, Margulis Soc., Alpha Omega Alpha. Avocations: fishing, travel, viticulture. Home: Rubaiyat Vineyard 5409 Sonoma Mountain Rd Santa Rosa CA 95404-8884 Fax: 707-544-4117. E-mail: rubaiyatvineyard@aol.com.

SMITH, THOMAS RAYMOND, III, software engineer; b. Phila., Dec. 6, 1946; s. Thomas Raymond and Naomi (Hart) S.; m. Marguerite Anne LeMoyne de Martigny, Sept. 6, 1969; children: Michelle Renée, Heather Anne, Thomas Raymond IV. Student, MIT, 1964-68. Sr. analyst Dabcovich and Co., Lexington, Mass., 1969-71; sr. analyst, prin. Multi-Logic Corp., Burlington, 1970-73; cons. engr. Digital Equipment Corp. (now Hewlett-Packard Co.), Palo Alto, Calif., 1974—. Co-editor: IEEE Dictionary, 1993; author, co-editor numerous stds. books for Internat. Electrotech. Commn. and IEEE, 1984-93. Mem. IEEE (chmn. various stds. coms., 1980—). Home: 36 Toppans Ln Newburyport MA 01950-3843 Office: Hewlett-Packard Co ZK01-3/H42 110 Spit Brook Rd Nashua NH 03062-2711 E-mail: smith@alum.mit.edu.

SMITH, THOMAS SHORE, lawyer; b. Rock Springs, Wyo., Dec. 7, 1924; s. Thomas and Anne E. (McTee) S.; m. Jacqueline Emily Krueger, May 25, 1952; children: Carolyn Jane, Karl Thomas, David Shore. BSBA, U. Wyo., 1950, JD, 1959. Bar: U.S. Dist. Ct. Wyo. 1960, U.S. Ct. Appeals (10th cir.) 1960, U.S. Tax Ct. 1969, U.S. Supreme Ct. 1971. Of counsel Smith, Stanfield & Scott, LLC, Laramie, Wyo., 1963-94, Brown, Nagel, Waters & Hiser, LLC, Laramie, 1994—. Atty. City of Laramie, 1963-86; instr. mcpl. law U. Wyo., 1987; dir. budget and fin. Govt. of Am. Samoa, 1954-56. Bd. dirs. Bur. Land Mgmt., Rawlins, Wyo., 1984-89, chmn. bd. dirs., 1991-95; bd. dirs. Ivinson Hosp. Found., 1994-95; bd. dirs. U. Wyo. Found., 1991-99, pres., 1994-95, bd. dirs. Bank of Laramie, 1998—. Francis Warren scholar, 1958. Mem Wyo. Bar Assn. (pres. 1984-85), Albany County Bar Assn., Western States Bar Conf. (pres. 1985-86), Elks. Republican. Episcopalian. Avocation: golf. Office: Brown Nagel Waters & Hiser LLC PO Box 971 515 E Ivinson Ave Laramie WY 82070-3157

SMITH, THOMAS SULLIVAN, humanities educator; b. Natchez, Miss., June 18, 1949; s. James Thomas Smith, Bessie Mildred Smith; m. Ginger Sue Herrington; children: Thomas Smith II, Susan Paige. BA, Northeast La. U., 1971; MEd, La. State U., 1977, MA, 1994. Cert. tchr. La. Tchr., asst. prin. Hessmer H.S., La.; asst. prin. Bunkie H.S., Riverside Elem. Sch.; prin. Lafargue H.S., Bunkie Mid. Sch.; English, social studies resource tchr., grants coord. Avoyelles Parish Sch. Bd., Marksville, 1999—. Adj. instr. Northwestern State U. La., La. State U., Alexandria, Ctrl. Tex. Coll. Author short stories, poetry. Various positions United Meth. Ch., Marksville. Recipient Outstanding H.S. Educator award, La. Coll., Pineville, 1985, Outstanding Young Man of Am., 1985; fellow Independent Study in the Humanities fellow, Coun. Basic Edn., 1995; grantee Rsch. Grant, Gerald R. Ford Found., 1996. Mem.: NEA, ASCD, La. Mid. Sch. Assn. (bd. dirs. 1995—2001), Avoyelles Assn. Educators, Nat. Coun. History Edn., North La. Hist. Assn., La. Hist. Assn., La. Assn. Educators, Nat. Coun. for the Social Studies, Orgn. Am. Historians, Nat. Coun. Tchrs. English, Avoyelles Administators Assn., La. Preservation Alliance. Office: Avoyelles Parish Sch B 221 Tunica Dr W Marksville LA

SMITH, THOMAS WILLIAM, neuropathologist; b. Columbus, Ohio, Sept. 22, 1946; BS, Ohio State U., 1968; MD, Cornell U., 1972. Diplomate Am. Bd. Pathology. Resident in pathology N.Y. Hosp., N.Y.C., 1972-73; resident in neuropathology Peter Bent Brigham Hosp., Boston, 1973-76, resident in pathology, 1977-78; resident in radiology Mass. Gen. Hosp., 1976-77; staff pathologist, prof. pathology and neurology U. Mass. Med. Sch., Worcester, 1978—, dir. neuropathology and diagnostic electron microscopy, —. Contbr. over 112 articles to profl. jours., chpts. to books. Mem. Am. Assn. Neuropathologists, Am. Acad. Neurology, Soc. of Exptl. Neuropathology, Internat. Acad. Pathology. Office: Univ of Massachusetts Med Sch Dept Pathology 55 Lake Ave N Worcester MA 01655-0002 E-mail: smitht@ummhc.org.

SMITH, THOMAS WINSTON, cotton marketing executive; b. Crosbyton, Tex., Mar. 16, 1935; s. Lance L. and Willie Mae (Little) S.; m. Patricia Mae Zachary, Dec. 13, 1958; children— Janna Olean, Thomas Mark. B.S., Tex. A&M U., 1957; P.M.D., Harvard U., 1964. Various positions Calcot Ltd., Bakersfield, Calif., 1957-77, exec. v.p., pres., 1977—; v.p. Amcot, Inc., Amcot Internat., Inc., Bakersfield, 1977—, also bd. dirs.; bd. mgrs. N.Y. Cotton Exchange, N.Y.C., v.p., Memphis. Bd. dir. Greater Bakersfield Meml. Hosp.; mem. pres.'s adv. commn. Calif. State Coll., Bakersfield; v.p. Nat. Cotton Coun., Memphis. Mem. Rotary. Business E-Mail: twsmith@calcot.com.

SMITH, THOMAS Y. protective services official; b. Daytona Beach, Fla., Feb. 3, 1954; s. Johnny H. and Irene Isabel (Young) S.; m. Charlene Kaylor, Dec. 7, 1996. Assoc. Fire Sci., Daytona Beach C.C., 1984; B Orgnl. Mgmt., Warner So. Coll., 1996. Cert. fire instr. Fla. State Fire Marshal's Office. Dispatcher Daytona Beach News Jour., 1972; fingerprint examiner FBI, Washington, 1973-76; paramedic Beacon Ambulance, Daytona Beach, 1976-79; firefighter, paramedic City of Port Orange, Fla., 1979-86; firefighter Volusia County Fire Svcs., Deland, 1986-87, fire/emergency med. svcs. officer, instr., 1987-92, fire capt., 1992—, pub., writer, 1992—. Adj. faculty mem. Daytona Beach C.C., 1992—, Flagler County Vocat. Tech., Flagler Beach, Fla., 1994—. Author: Florida Firefighting - Minimum Standards Exam, 1992, Florida Paramedic - A Study Guide, 1994, Florida Fire Officer I - A Study Guide, 1994, Florida Basic Fire Instructor, 1995. Dist. grant evaluator Fla. Dept. Health, Tallahassee, 1994; instr. ARC, 1969—, Am. Heart Assn., 1972—; instr. trainer Fla. State Fire Coll., 1986—. Recipient Grant Com. Recognition award Fla. Dept. H.R.S., 1995, cert. for life saved Volusia County Govt., 1996, cert. of appreciation Volusia County Govt., 1997, Length of Svc. award Am. Heart Assn., 1994. Mem. Am. Radio Relay League (life). Democrat. Roman Catholic. Avocations: amateur radio, satellite communications, fishing, teaching, travel. Home: PO Box 404 Daytona Beach FL 32115-0404 Office: Volusia County Dept Fire Svcs 123 W Indiana Ave Deland FL 32720-4615

SMITH, THOMASINA DENISE, computer programmer analyst, accountant; b. Columbia, S.C., Mar. 20, 1954; d. Tom Smith and Tecora Claratine (Shaw) Drake; m. Jerry Williams, Mar. 15, 1982 (div. Jan. 1983). BS, Winthrop Coll., Rock Hill, S.C., 1974. Computer programmer trainee Blue Cross/Blue Shield, Columbia, S.C., 1974-75; computer operator Kline Iron & Steel Co., 1976-78; jr. computer programmer NCR Corp., Dayton, Ohio, 1978-80; systems analyst Bank One, 1980-83; programmer analyst Elder Beerman, 1984-85, Def. Contract Adminstrn., Columbus, Ohio, 1985-86, U.S. Army, Atlanta, 1986—. Owner, operator TDS Enterprises, Atlanta, 1988-91, Columbia, S.C.; seller Safety Plus fire extinguisher, flame retardant and smoke alarms; pub. rels., talent scout Sharp Records; installer computer software and hardware for chs.; tax preparer H&R Block, Columbia; bd. dirs. Shaper Bros., Inc., Atlanta. Vol. Adopt a Sister/Adopt a Brother, Atlanta, 1989, Ben Hill United Meth. Ch. Missionary Soc., Atlanta. Mem. Data Processing Mgmt. Assn., The Phoenix Soc. for Burn Survivors, Endometriosis Assn., Nat. Found. of Ileitis and Colitis. Zeta Phi Beta. Avocation: fixing up old houses for resale. Home and Office: 7011 Gavilan Ave Columbia SC 29203-5231

SMITH, TIMOTHY W. musician; b. Louisville, Feb. 3, 1969; s. Glendol Lewis and Linda Kay Smith. B Music Edn., Murray State U., 1995. Cert. State of Ohio Dept. of Edn. Tchg. Cert. 2001, State of Ky. Dept. of Edn. Tchg. Cert. 1995. Music tchr./band dir. Calloway County Schs., Murray, 1995—2001; instrumental music tchr. Princeton City Schs., Cin., 2001—02. Recipient Mid. Sch. Music Educator of The Yr., First Dist. Ky. Music Educators Assn.,

2000—01. Mem.: NEA, Ohio Music Edn. Assn., Ky. Music Educators Assn., Music Educators Nat. Conf., Internat. Assn. of Jazz Educators, Internat. Trumpet Guild, Phi Mu Alpha Sinfonia. Avocation: music, travel, golf, fishing.

SMITH, TODD MALCOLM, political consultant; b. Hallettsville, Tex., Aug. 7, 1961; s. Jerome Malcolm and Mary Eugenia (Devall) S. BS in Criminal Justice, S.W. Tex. State U., 1983; postgrad. in Criminal Justice Adminstrn., Sam Houston State U., 1988—; cert., Fed. Law Enforce. Tng. Acad., 1987. Juvenile probation officer 25th Jud. Dist. Tex., 1983-84; field coord. Mac Sweeney for Congress, Victoria, Tex., 1984; dist. coord. U.S. Congress-14th Congl. Dist. Tex., 1984-85; chief dep. sheriff Lavaca County Sheriff's Dept. Tex., 1985-88; dir. ops. Clayton Williams for Gov. Com., Austin, Tex., 1988-90; pres. Property Valuation Advisors, San Marcos, 1991-93; gen. ptnr. Wm. A. Tryon and Todd M. Smith Polit. Cons. Group, Austin, 1991-93; prin. Todd Smith & Assoc., Inc., 1993—. Coord. Lavaca County Crime Stoppers, Hallettsville, 1985-88; apptd. by Tex. Gov. to Tex. Crime Stoppers Commn. Regulatory Agy., 1986-90; mem., appointee Golden Crescent Regional Planning Commn., Victoria, 1986-88; exec. v.p. E-Comm. Advantage, Inc., Austin, 2000—; pres. Demografx, Inc., Austin, 2000—. Candidate selection com. Assoc. Reps. Tex., Austin, 1991—, rep. senatorial dist. 18 State Rep. Exec. Com., 1992-94; pres. Tex. Citizens United; chmn. Taxpayers Def. Fund. 2d lt. Tex. State N.G., 1990-92. Recipient Outstanding Svc. award Tex. Crime Stoppers Adv. Coun., 1990, Outstanding Coord. award Lavaca County Crime Stoppers, 1988. Mem. Am. Assn. Polit. Cons., Masons. Republican. Episcopalian. Avocation: politics. Home: 2204 Hazeltine Ln Austin TX 78723 Office: 7020 E US Hwy 290 Bldg II Ste C Austin TX 78701

SMITH, TOM, poet, educator, retired; b. Schenectady, N.Y., Mar. 19, 1933; s. Thomas Alfred and Julia (Zaleskiewycz) S.; m. Virginia Thelma DeAngelis, Jan. 24, 1965; children: Julian David, Benjamin Thomas. BA, SUNY, Albany, 1956; MA, Rutgers U., 1958, postgrad., 1959-62. Tchg. asst. Rutgers U., New Brunswick, NJ., 1956-59; lectr. Douglass Coll., 1959-62; instr. Union Coll., Schenectady, 1963-64; prof., then prof. emeritus Castleton (Vt.) State Coll., 1964-95, ret., 1995. Actor in cmty. and college theater, Killington, Vt., Rutland and Castleton. Author: Some Traffic, 1976, Singing the Middle Ages, 1982, Traffic, 1983, The Broken Iris, 1991, A Well-Behaved Little Boy, 1993, Cow'sleap: A Nightbook, Waiting on Pentecost, Trash: The Dahmer Sonnets, 2000; contbr. to numerous anthologies.

SMITH, TROY ALVIN, aerospace research engineer; b. Sylvatus, Va., July 4, 1922; s. Wade Hampton and Augusta Mabel (Lindsey) S.; m. Grace Marie Peacock, Nov. 24, 1990. BCE, U. Va., 1948; MS in Engring., U. Mich., 1952, PhD, 1970. Registered profl. engr., Va., Ala. Structural engr. U.S. Army C.E., Norfolk, Va., Wilmington, N.C., Washington, 1948-59; chief structural engr. Brown Engring. Co., Inc., Huntsville, Ala., 1959-60; structural rsch. engr. U.S. Army Missile Command, Redstone Arsenal, 1960-63, aerospace engr., 1963-80, aerospace rsch. engr., 1980-96, ind. profl. engr., 1996—. Contbr. articles to AIAA Jour., Jour. Sound and Vibration. With USNR, 1942-46, PTO. Fellow Dept. Army, 1969. Mem. N.Y. Acad. Scis., Assn. U.S. Army, Elks, Sigma Xi. Achievements include research on procedures for analysis of structures. Home: 2202 Yorkshire SE Decatur AL 35601-3470

SMITH, TROY FRANCIS, protective services official; b. Murfreesboro, Tenn., Nov. 10, 1967; s. Harold Francis Donahue and Dorothy Charlene Smith; m. Dawn May Elizabeth Valentine, May 15, 1994; children: Josh Russell, Trevor. Student social sci., Treveca Nazarene U., Nashville, 1986—91. Host, waiter Spinnakers, Nashville, 1986—89; waiter, cook, bartender, host Applebees, 1990; patrolman Met. Nashville Police Dept., 1991—99, domestic violence detective, 1999—. Mem.: Nashville Police Benefit Assn. (bd. dirs. 1996—), Fraternal Order Police. Republican. Avocations: computer games, dungeons and dragons. Home: 2823 Twin Lane Dr Nashville TN 37214 Office: Met Nashville Police Dept 60 Peabody St Nashville TN 37210 E-mail: troyfsmith@myexcel.com.

SMITH, V. KERRY, economics educator; b. Jersey City, Mar. 11, 1945; s. Vincent C. and Dorothy E. (Linehan) S.; m. Pauline Anne Taylor, May 10, 1969; children: Timothy, Shelley. AB, Rutgers U., 1966, PhD, 1970. Asst. prof., then assoc. prof. Bowling Green State U., Ohio, 1969-72; rsch. assoc. Resources for Future, Washington, 1971-73; assoc. prof. SUNY, Binghamton, 1973-75, prof., 1975-78; sr. fellow Resources for Future, Washington, 1976-79; prof. U. N.C., Chapel Hill, 1979-83; Centennial prof. Vanderbilt U., Nashville, 1983-87; Univ. Disting. prof. N.C. State U., 1987-94, univ. disting. prof., dir. Ctr. Environ. and Resource Econ. Policy, 1999—; Arts and Scis. prof. environ. econs. Duke U., 1994-99. Adviser energy div. Oak Ridge Nat. Lab., 1978-80, U. N.C. Inst. Environ. Studies, 1980-83; mem. panel NSF, 1981-83, sci. adv. bd. EPA. Author: Monte Carlo Methods, 1973, Technical Change, Relative Prices and Environmental Resource Evaluation, 1974, The costs of Congestion: An Econometric Analysis of Wilderness Recreation, 1976, Structure and Properties of a Wilderness Travel Simulator: An Application to the Spanish Peaks Area, 1976, The Economic Consequences of Air Pollution, 1976, Scarcity and Growth Reconsidered, 1979, (with others) Explorations in Natural Resource Economics, 1982, (with others) Environmental Policy Under Reagan's executive Order, 1984, (with W.H. Desvousges) Measuring Water Quality Benefits, 1986, (with others) Environmental Resources and Applied Welfare Economics, 1988, (with R.J. Kopp) Valuing Natural Assets: The Economics of Natural Resource Damage Assessment, Resources for the Future, 1993, Estimating Economic Values for Nature, 1996; editor Advances in Applied Micro Econs. series; contbr. numerous articles to profl. jours. Guggenheim fellow, 1976; grantee Resources for Future, 1970, 73, 74, 86, Fed. Energy Adminstrn. 1975, N.Y. Sea Grant Inst., 1975, Ford Found., 1976, NSF, 1977, 79, 83, Electric Power Rsch. Inst., 1978, Nat. Oceanic and Atmospheric Adminstrn., 1980, Sloan Found., 1981, 86, EPA, 1983-88, N.C. Sea Grant Program, 1987-93. Russell Sage Found., 1989-91; recipient Frederick V. Waugh medal Am. Agrl. Econ. Assn., 1992. Mem. Am. Econ. Assn., Am. Statis. Assn., Econometric Soc., So. Econ. Assn. (exec. com. 1981-83, 1st v.p. 1987, pres. elect 1988, pres. 1989), Assn. Environ. and Resource Economists (bd. dirs. 1975-79, v.p. 1979-80, chmn. com. 1982-83, pres. 1985-86, Disting. Svc. award 1989). E-mail: kerry. E-mail: smith@ncsu.edu.

SMITH, V. ROY, neurosurgeon; b. N.Y.C., Feb. 12, 1943; s. Leslie Ewart and Vera (Dhlosh) S.; m. Elizabeth Kay Bartlett, June 12, 1971; children: Rebecca L., Adam L., Andrew R. BA, Ohio State U., 1964, MD, 1967. Diplomate Am. Bd. Neurol. Surgeons. Ptnr. Fresno Neurol. Med. Group, Calif., 1975—. Pres. med. staff St. Agnes Hosp., Fresno, Calif., 1987-89, chief of surgery, 1983-85, chmn. div. neurosurgery, 1993-95. Lt. U.S. Navy, 1969-71, Vietnam. Fellow Am. Coll. Surgeons; mem. AMA, Am. Coll. Surgeons, Am. Assn. Neurol. Surgeons. Home: 2627 E Birch Ave Clovis CA 93611-9167 Office: Fresno Neurosurg Med Group 6167 N Fresno St Ste 101 Fresno CA 93710-5207

SMITH, VALERIE GAY, school counselor; b. Austin, Tex., Oct. 31, 1947; d. James Griffin and Ida Mae (Routon) Black; m. James David Smith, July 20, 1993. BA in English, McMurry Coll., 1969; MEd in Counseling, U. North Tex., 1974. Lic. profl. counselor, Tex.; cert. sch. counselor, Tex. Tchr. Nimitz H.S., Irving, Tex., 1969-71, MacArthur H.S., Irving, 1971-74, counselor, 1974-89, Ditto Elem. Sch., Arlington, 1989-94, Withers Elem. Sch., Dallas, 1994—. Mem. ACA, Am. Sch. Counselor Assn., Tex. Sch. Counselor Assn. (elem. v.p. 1990-92, senator 1988-90, sec. 1986-88, Rhosine Fleming Outstanding Counselor award 1987, pres.-elect 1992-93, pres. 1993-94), Tex. PTA (life), Tex. Counseling Assn. (region 4 dir. 1990-93, pres.-elect 1995-96, pres. 1996-97, past pres. 1997-98), Phi Delta Kappa. Home: 2120 Nob Hl Carrollton TX 75006-2817 Office: Withers Elem Sch 3959 Northaven Rd Dallas TX 75229-2758

SMITH, VAN P. holding company executive; b. Oneida, N.Y., Sept. 8, 1928; m. Margaret Ann Kennedy, Nov. 19, 1960; children: Lynn Ann Smith Walters, Mark Charles, Paul Gregory, Susan Colleen Smith Newell, Victor Patrick. AB in Pub. Adminstrn. and Econs., Colgate U., 1950; JD, Georgetown U., 1955; LLD (hon.), Ball State U., 1980; D of Bus. (hon.), Vincennes U., 1985; LLD (hon.), Ind. State U., 1986. Bar: D.C., Ind. Assoc. Warner, Clark & Warner, Muncie, Ind., 1955-56; co-founder, dir. Ontario Corp. of Muncie, 1956-63, sec. then v.p. sales, 1956-63, pres., CEO, 1963-97, also chmn. bd., 1978—. Chmn. bd. Ontario Corp. Found., all in Muncie, and other subs. Ontario Corp.; chmn. bd. Hoosier Motor Club, Indpls.; ptnr. Smittie's Men's Store, Village Developers, all in Muncie. Rep. mem. Ind. Ho. of Reps., 1960-62; del. Ind. and Nat. Rep. Conv.; pres. Muncie Police & Fire Commn., 1963-66; mem. parochial sch. bd. St. Mary's Sch., Muncie, 1968-70; mem. Ind. Employment Security Bd., 1969-71, Ind. Commn. Higher Edn., 1971-93, Nat. Adv. Council SBA, 1982-87, Gov.'s Fiscal Policy Adv. Council, 1982-87, Ind. Labor & Mgmt. Council, 1983-90, Ind. Econ. Devel. Council, 1985-90, Presdl. Observation Team Phillipine Nat. election, 1986, Presdl. Trade Mission to several Far Eastern countries, 1984; bd. dirs. Bus.-Industry Polit. Action Com., 1984-98; trustee Colgate U., 1985-96, La Lumiere Sch., 1983-87, Acad. for Community Leadership, 1975—; bd. dirs. Muncie Symphony Assn., 1980-88, pres. 1986-87; pres. Del. County United Way, 1969-70; bd. dirs. Newman Found. Ind., 1969—, Religious Heritage Am. 1986-88; active St. Mary's Cath. Parish, Muncie; mem. Diocese of Lafayette Bishop's Com. 100, 1969-80, pres. 1969-70; bd. regents Cath. U. Am., Washington, 1986-90, trustee 1990—; trustee Interlochen (Mich.) Ctr. for Arts, 1991—. Served 1st lt. USAF, 1951-53. Named one of Outstanding Young Men of Am., Jaycees, 1960; recipient Bus. and Layman award, Religious Heritage Am., 1984, Ind. Cath. Layman award, Faith, Family & Football of Ind., Inc. 1985, Civic Service award, Ind. Assn. Cities and Towns, 1985; invested Knight of Equestrian Order of Holy Sepulchre of Jerusalem, 1986. Mem. ABA, Ind. Bar Assn., Ind. Mfrs. Assn. (chmn. 1978-80, bd. dirs. 1978—), Forging Industry Assn. (pres. 1976-77), Alliance of Metalworking Industries (chmn. 1978-80), U.S. C. of C. (chmn. numerous coms., active panels and councils 1977—), Ind. State C. of C. (exec. com. 1982—), Rotary (past pres.), Elks, K.C., Meridian Hills Country Club, Theta Chi (pres. Iota chpt. 1950), Delta Theta Phi, Beta Gamma Sigma (hon.), Delta Sigma Pi (hon.). Clubs: Columbia, Skyline (Indpls.); Ind. Soc. of Chgo. Office: 123 E Adams St Muncie IN 47305-2402

SMITH, VANGY EDITH, accountant, consultant, writer, artist; b. Saskatoon, Sask., Can., Dec. 17, 1937; d. Wilhelm and Anne Ellen (Hartshorne) Gogel: m. Clifford Wilson, May 12, 1958 (dec. Dec. 1978); children: Kenneth, Koral, Kevin, Korey, Kyle; m. Terrence Raymond Smith, Dec. 14, 1979. Student, Saskatoon Tech. Collegiate Inst., 1956, BBA, 1958, MBA, 1987, PhD in English with honors, 1988. Prin. Vangy Enterprises, Springfield, Oreg., 1960—; accounts payable clk. Maxwell Labs., Inc., San Diego, 1978; invoice clk. Davies Electric, Saskatoon, 1980-81; office mgr. Ladee Bug Ceramics, 1981-87, Lazars Investments Corp., Eugene, Oreg., 1987; bookkeeper accounts payable Pop Geer, 1987; office mgr., bookkeeper Willamette Sports Ctr., Inc., 1985-89; clk. I Lane C.C., Springfield, 1992-96, adv. chair Ctr. for Leisure and Learning, 1999—. Self-employed Vangy Enterprises, 1992—; circulation mgr. Nat. WCTU, 1990-92, UN rep. for World WCTUm 1989-91; appointed mem. Parliament for the U. for Peace, Holland, 1991; adv. chair Lane C.C. Ctr. for Leisure and Learning, 1999-2001. Contbr. articles to scholarly jours. (recipient doctoral award 1987). Counselor Drug and Rehab. Ctr., Eugene, 1970—88; trustee Children's Farm Home, Corvallis, Oreg., 1989—91, 3d v.p., 1989—90; co-pres. Lane County UN Assn., 1989—90; mem. artist Nat. Bd. Edn., 1989, 1990; mem. adv. com. Dept. Pub. Safety for City of Eugene, 1989—90; exec. dir. H.E.L.P., 1993—; pres. Lane County Coun. of Orgns., 1994—96; treas. Cascade/Coast chpt. Alzheimers Assn., 1994; mem. UN Devel. Fund for Women, mem. exec. com., 1999; chair adv. com. Ctr. for Leisure and Learning, Lane C.C., 1999—2001; mem. Found. Christian Living; pres. Oreg. State Christian Temperance Union, 1989—90. Recipient 3d and 4th place artists' awards Lane County Fair, 1987, 1st and 2d place awards Nat. Writing Contest, 1987, 88, 89, 90, 91, Oasis Vol. Model award, 1998; named City of Eugene Hometown Hero, 1998, named Woman of Yr., Am. Bus. Women's Assn., 1999-00. Mem. WCTU (life, pres., state bd. dirs. projection methods circulation 1987-90, Appreciation award 1982, Presdl. award 1985, Lane County Eugene Woman of Yr. 1990), UNIFEM (chpt. pres. 1997—, exec. bd. 1999—, Women in Leadership award 1997), Am. Soc. Writers, Alzheimers Assn. (treas. Cascade/Coast chpt. 1994), Rebekah Lodge (Noble Grand 1995-99), Lions (sec. 1994), Oasis (adv. coun. chair 1993-98), Am. Bus. Women's Assn. (pres. 2000—). Democrat. Avocations: needlework, rug hooking, reading, writing, oil painting. Home and Office: 4531 Franklin Blvd # 100 Eugene OR 97403 E-mail: vsmith3237@aol.com.

SMITH, VERNA MAE, sociology educator, freelance writer, photographer; b. Marshfield, Wis., June 19, 1929; d. Clifton Cedric and Vilia Clarissa (Patefield) Edom; children: Teri Smith Freas, Anthony Thomas. AB in Sociology, U. Mo., 1951; MA in Sociology, George Washington, 1965; PhD in Human Devel., U. Md., 1981. Tchr. Alcohol Safety Action Program Fairfax County, Va., 1973-75; instr. sociology No. Va. C.C., Manassas, 1975-77, asst. prof., 1977-81, assoc. prof., 1981-84, prof., 1984-94, prof. emerita, 1995, coord. coop. edn., 1983-89, Chancellor's Commonwealth prof., 1991-93; adj. faculty Tidewater C.C., 1996—; freelance writer, editor and photographer, 1965—; dir. Clifton C. Edom Truth With a Camera (photography workshops), 1994—. Asst. prodr. history of photography program Sta. WETA-TV, Washington, 1965; rsch. and prodn. asst., photographer, publs. editor No. Va. Ednl. TV, Sta. WNVT, 1970—71; cons. migrant divsn. Md. Dept. Edn., Balt., 1977; rschr. photographer Roundabout presch. high sch. series Am. Values Sta. WNVT, 1970—71; documentary photographer Portsmouth (Va.) Redevel. and Housing Authority, 1998—2000. Author, photographer: Middleburg and Nearby, 1986; co-author: Small Town America, 1993; contbr. photography to various works including Visual Impact in Print (Hurley and McDougall), 1971, Looking Forward to a Career in Education (Moses), 1976, Child Growth and Development (Terry, Sorrentino and Flatter), 1979, Photojournalism (Edom), 1976, 80, Migrant Child Welfare, 1977, (Cavenaugh), Caring for Children, 1973 (5 publs. by L.B. Murphy), Dept. Health, Edn. and Welfare, Nat. Geog., 1961, Head Start Newsletter, 1973-74, Women in Photojournalism, Nat. Press Photographers Assn., Nat. Fedn. Press Women, Photographic Soc. Am., Va. Found. for Humanities and Pub. Policy exhibits. Mem. ednl. adv. com. Head Start, Warrenton, Va. Recipient Emmy, Ohio State Children's Programming award; Fulbright-Hays rsch. grantee, 1993, Va. Found. for Humanities and Pub. Policy grantee, 1997-99. Mem. Va. Assn. Coop. Edn. (com. mem.). Democrat. E-mail: vme@macs.net.

SMITH, VERNON G. education educator, state representative; b. Gary, Ind. BS, Ind. U., 1966, MS, 1969, EdD, 1978; postgrad., Ind.U.-Purdue U., 1986-90. Tchr. Gary Pub. Schs. Systems, 1966-71, resource tchr., 1971-72; asst. prin. Ivanhoe Sch., Gary, 1972-78; prin. Nobel Sch., 1978-85, Williams Sch., Gary, 1985-92; part-time counselor edn. div. Ind. U. N.W., 1967-69, adj. lectr., 1987-92, asst. prof., 1992—; mem. Ind. Ho. of Reps., Indpls., 1990—. Columnist Gary Crusader, 1969-71; speaker Devel. Tng. Inst., 1986—. Author: (with D. McClam) Building Bridges Instead of Walls—History of I.U. Dons, Inc., 1979; also articles. Mem. Gary City Coun., 1972-90; precinct committeeman Gary Dem. Com., 1972-92; founder, chmn. Gary City-wide Festival Com.; bd. dirs. N.W. Ind. Urban League; founder, pres. I.U. Dons, Inc.; past pres. Gary Cmty. Mental Health Bd.; v.p. Gary Common Coun., 1982, 85-87, pres., 1976, 83-84, 88; past mem. bd. dirs. Little League World series; founder, past sponsor Youth Ensuring Solidarity, Young Citizens' League; chmn. Ind. Commn. on Status of Black Males, 1992—; mem. Gov.'s Commn. for Drug-Free Ind., 1990—. Recipient citation in edn. Gary NAACP, 1970, Good Govt. award Gary Jaycees, 1977, Outstanding Svc. award Gary Young Dems., 1979, Businessman of Yr. award Gary Downtown Mchts., 1979, Bd. Dirs. Svcs. award Gary Cmty. Health Ctr., 1982, G.O.I.C. Dr. Leon H. Sullivan award, 1982, Gary Jaycees Youth award, 1983, Info Newspaper Outstanding Citizen of N.W. Ind. and Info. Newspaper's Outstanding Educator award, 1984, Post Tribune Blaine Marz Tap award, 1984, Gary Cmty. Sch. Corp. Speech Dept. Recognition award, 1984, Gary Cmty. Mental Health Ctr.'s 10th Yr. Svc. award, 1985, Roosevelt H.S. Exemplary Svc. award, 1985, Gary Crusader 25th Anniversary award, 1986, Purdue U. Ednl. Opportunity Programs Black History Svc. award, 1986, Educator Par Excellence award Williams Sch., 1987, Black Woman Hall of Fame Found. Success award, 1987, Black Women Hall of Fame Bethune-Tubman-Truth award, 1987, Our Lady of Perpetual Help Ch. Hon. Mem. award, 1987, Gary Educator of Christ Adminstr. Leadership award, 1988, NBC-LEO Appreciation award, 1988, Omega Psi Phi Citizen of Yr., 1989, Omicron Rho chpt. Appreciation award, 1991, Gary Cmty. Schs. Presenters award, 1991, Mr. G.'s Svc. award, 1991, Appreciation award Ind. Assn. Chiefs Police, 1992, Meth. Hosp., 1992, Bros. Keeper, 1992, Svc. award Ind. Assn. Elem. and Mid. Sch. Prins., 1992, I.U. N.W. Alumni Assn. Divsn. of Edn. Disting. Educator award, 1992, N.W. Ind. Black Expo's Sen. Carolyn Mosby Above and Beyond award, 1995, In the Bethune Tradition award Nat. Coun. Negro Women, 1996, Citizen of Yr. award NASW, 1997, Appreciation award Ind. chpt., 1997. Mem. NAACP (life), Ind. Assn. Sch. Prins., No. Ind. Assn. Black School Educators (founder), Ind. U. N.W. Alumni Assn. (life, Disting. Educator award 1992), Phi Delta Kappa (25 Yr. award), Omega Psi Phi (life, Omega Man of Yr. award 1974, Citizen of Yr. award 10th dist. 1989, appreciation award Omicron Rho chpt. 1991). Baptist. Home: PO Box M622 Gary IN 46401-0622 Office: Ind U NW 3400 Broadway # 339 Gary IN 46408-1101

SMITH, VERNON LOMAX, economist, researcher; b. Wichita, Kans., Jan. 1, 1927; s. Vernon Chessman and Lula Belle (Lomax) S.; m. Joyce Harkleroad, June 6, 1950 (div. Aug. 1975); m. Carol Breckner, Jan. 1, 1980. BSEE, Calif. Inst. Tech., 1949; MA in Econs., U. Kans., 1952; PhD in Econs., Harvard U., 1955; D of Mgmt. (hon.), Purdue U., 1990. Asst. prof. econs. Purdue U., West Lafayette, Ind., 1955-58, assoc. prof., 1958-61, prof., 1961-65, Krannert prof., 1965-67; prof. Brown U., Providence, 1967-68, U. Mass., Amherst, 1968-75, U. Ariz., Tucson, 1975—2001, Regents' prof., 1988—2001; prof. econs. & law George Mason U., 2001—. Contbr. articles to profl. jours. Fellow Ctr. for Advanced Study in Behavioral Scis., Stanford, Calif., 1972-73; Sherman Fairchild Disting. Scholar Calif. Inst. Tech., Pasadena, 1973-74; adj. scholar CATO Inst., Washington, 1983—; recipient Nobel prize in econs., 2002. Fellow AAAS, Am. Acad. Arts and Scis., Econometric Soc., Am. Econ. Assn. (Disting. fellow); mem. Pvt. Enterprise Edn. Assn. (Adam Smith award), Nat. Acad. Sci. Office: George Mason U. Interdisc. Ctr. for Econ. Sci. 4400 University Blvd., MSN 1B2 Fairfax VA 22030*

SMITH, VERONICA LATTA, real estate corporation officer; b. Wyandotte, Mich., Jan. 13, 1925; d. Jan August and Helena (Hulak) Latta; m. Stewart Gene Smith, Apr. 12, 1952; children: Stewart Gregory, Patrick Allen, Paul Donald, Alison Veronica, Alisa Margaret Lyons, Glenn Laurence. BA in Sociology, postgrad., U. Mich., 1948. Tchr. Coral Gables (Fla.) Pub. Sch. System, 1949-50; COO Latta Ins. Agy, Wyandotte, 1950-62; treas. L & S Devel. Co., Grosse Ile, Mich., 1963-84; v.p. Regency Devel., Riverview, 1984—. Active U. Mich. Bd. Regents, 1985-92, regent emeritus, 1993—; mem. Martha Cook Bd. Govs., U. Mich., pres., 1976-78; del. Rep. County Conv., Grand Rapids, Mich., 1985, 87, 89, 91, 92, 94, 96, Lansing, Mich., 1996, Detroit, 1986, 88, 90, 92, 97; mem. pres. adv. com. Campaign for Mich., 1992-97, mem. campaign steering com., 1992-97. Mem. Mich. Lawyers Aux. (treas. 1975, chmn. 1976, 77, 78, 79), Nat. Assn. Ins. Women (cert.), Faculty Women's Club U. Mich. (hon.), Radrick Farms Golf Club (Ann Arbor), Pres.'s Club U. Mich., Investment Club (pres. 1976, sec. 1974-75, treas. 1975-76), Alpha Kappa Delta. Home: 22225 Balmoral Dr Grosse Ile MI 48138-1403

SMITH, VESTAL BEECHER, SR. physician; b. Hot Springs, Ark., June 12, 1925; s. Virgil Ezra and Georgia Ella (Rhodes) S.; m. Melodean Fisher, July 1, 1948 (dec. Apr. 1960); children: James R., Michael G., Stephen D.; m. Mary O. Capooth, Oct. 21, 1960; 1 child, Vestal Beecher Jr. Student, O.B.U. of Arkadelphia, Ark., Ark., 1943, 46, NYU, 1944-45; MD, U. Ark., 1950. Lic. physician, Ark. Intern Beaumont Gen. Hosp., El Paso, Tex., 1950-51; pvt. practice Marked Tree, Ark., 1954—. Part-time county health officer Marked Tree, 1983—. Pres., mem. Marked Tree Sch. Bd., 1964-80. Col. U.S. Army, 1943-85. Mem. Lions (pres. Marked Tree chpt. 1954-90). Republican. Methodist. Avocations: golf.

SMITH, VIN, sports editor, business owner, novelist; b. Whittier, Calif., May 19, 1944; s. M. Clifford and Anna Eugenia (Hill) S.; m. Marthea Karen Callaham, May 15, 1969 (div. 1979); children: Jayare Smith, Eric Smith; m. Ginger Hammon, Oct. 20, 1984; children: Amy Michelle, Stacey Erin, Kellie Rae. Student, Columbia Sch. Broadcasting, San Francisco, 1967; AA, Cuesta Coll., 1974; grad., Am. Sch. of Piano Tuning, 1978. Sales mgr. Sta. KTAT, Frederick, Okla., 1967-69; announcer KOCY, Oklahoma City, 1969; owner Melmart Markets, San Luis Obispo, Calif., 1971-73, Am. Direct Sales, Grover City, 1973-79; instr. piano Valley View Acad., Arroyo Grande, 1977-78, Long Piano Co., San Luis Obispo, 1977-79, piano technician, 1978-79; owner Chocolate Piano, Yreka, Calif., 1979—; instr. piano Makah Indian Tribe, Neah Bay, Wash., 1981-82; sports editor New Words Digest, Bakersfield, Calif., 1988—. Cons., stress evaluator seminar Yreka Stress Therapy Clinic, 1986-87; founder Vinco Distbrs. (formerly Vinco Enhancement Sys.), 1998; chair piano dept. Bogus Sch., 1999—, internat. relationship counselor Ask Me com., 2000—, askdrpiano.com., 2000. Author: (novel) Neon Streets, 2002; sports columnist New Words Digest, 1987-91; guest columnist Siskiyou Daily News, 1991-94; nat publicist chamber music concerts So. Oreg. State Coll., 1993—; contbr. articles to profl. jours. Chmn. heart fund Tillman County Okla., 1968; pub. co-chmn. Siskiyou County No-Prop 174, 1994; campaign worker Ken Jourdan for sheriff, Yreka, 1986; publicity dir. Gene Breceda for supr., 1993-94. Recipient Cert. of Appreciation, Siskiyou County, 1988, Achievement award, 1988; winner Golden Poet award World of Poetry, 1989. Mem. Nat. Writers Club (chmn. student com. Yreka chpt. 1988), Author's Guild, Inc., Author's League of Am., Mystery Writers Am., Soc. Children's Book Writers, Jr. C. of C. (sgt.-at-arms Frederick chpt. 1967-69), Kiwanis, Moose. Avocations: horse shoe pitching, photography, reading. Home: 710 Knapp St Yreka CA 96097-2343 Office: Chocolate Piano Svcs PO Box 447 Yreka CA 96097-0447 E-mail: drpiano@snowcrest.net.

SMITH, VINCENT MILTON, lawyer, designer, Feng Shui lecturer, consultant, writer; b. Barbourville, Ky., Nov. 21, 1940; s. Virgil Milton and Louis (McGalliard) Smith; children: Jessica Todd, Duncan. BA, Harvard U., 1962; LLB, Yale U., 1965. Bar: N.Y. 1966. Assoc. Breed, Abbott & Morgan, N.Y.C., 1965-70, Debevoise & Plimpton, N.Y.C., 1970-75, ptnr., 1975-95; CEO Lang, Winslow & Smith Co., Chatham, N.J., 1995-98; owner The VMS Feng Shui Design Co., 1998—. Mem. adv. bd. Chgo. Title Ins. Co., N.Y.C., 1979—2002; vis. Feng Shui prof. Berea (Ky.) Coll., 1999, Williams Coll., Williamstown, Mass., 2001—02; Feng Shui lectr. N.Y. Open Ctr., 1999—; co-founder, chmn. bd. Keen Co., 2000—. Trustee Chatham Players, N.J., 1967-77, 87-91, Summit Friends Meeting, Chatham, 1973-99, N.J. Shakespeare Festival, Madison, 1975-80, Playwrights Theatre N.J., 1989-91. Mem.: Harvard, N.Y. Athletic. Mem. Soc. Of Friends. Office: Debevoise & Plimpton 875 3rd Ave Fl 23 New York NY 10022-6225 E-mail: vmsdesign@aol.com.

SMITH, VINCENT C. information technology executive; married; 2 children. Bachelor, U. Del. Sales mgr. Oracle Corp., 1987—92; co-founder, v.p. Worldwide Sales and Mktg., Patrol Software N.Am., 1992—94; dir. open systems BMC Software, 1994; dir. Quest Software, Irvine, Calif., 1995—, CEO, 1997—, chmn. bd., 1998—. Dir. Emergent Info. Techs., Inc. Office: Quest Software 8001 Irvine Center Dr Irvine CA 92618*

SMITH, VINCENT DACOSTA, artist; b. Bklyn., Dec. 12, 1929; s. Beresford Leopold and Louise S.; m. Cynthia I. Linton, July 15, 1972. Student, Art Students League, N.Y.C., 1953, Bklyn. Mus. Sch., 1955-56; B. Profl. Services, Empire State Coll., 1980. Instr. painting and graphics Whitney Mus. Art, N.Y.C., 1967-76; instr. painting Ceda Project, 1978-80. Artist in residence Smithsonian Conf. Center, Elkridge, Md., 1967, Cite des Arts Internat., Paris, 1978, 1999; participant 2d World Black and African Festival Arts and Culture, Lagos, Nigeria, 1977; commns. include Impressions: Our World Portfolio of Prints, 1974, mural at Boys and Girls High Sch., Bklyn., 1976, mural for Tremont/Crotona Social Svc. Ctr. Human Resources Adminstrn. and CETA Project, N.Y.C., 1980, mural for Oberia D. Dempsey Multi-Svc. Ctr. for Cen. Harlem, Dept. Cultural Affairs, N.Y.C., 1988, 2 murals for 116 St. Sta., N.Y.C. Met. Transit Authority, Portrait of Reginald F. Lewis, Harvard U., Cambridge; film tapes and videos include Bernie Casey: Black Dimensions in Contemporary Am. Art, Carnation Co., Los Angeles, 1971, Tee Collins, Barbara Cobb: The First Water, Theatre Eleven, 1977, Robert Fassbinder: The Creative Pulse of Afro-Am. Culture, WTVG, N.J., 1978, Bearden Plays Bearden, Third World Cinema, 1980, Works on Paper, Storefront Mus./Paul Robeson Theatre, Jamaica, N.Y., 1981; host bi-weekly program, discussions with 45 activists WBAI-FM Radio. Illustrator: Folklore Stories from Africa, 1974; exhbns. include Hall of Springs Mus., Saratoga, N.Y., 1970, Contemporary Black Am. Artists, Whitney Mus. Am. Art, N.Y.C., 1971, Two Generations, Newark Mus., 1971, Mus. of Sci. and Industry, Chgo., 1975, Bronx Mus. Art, 1977, Bklyn. Mus., 1979; one-man exhbns. include Lacarda Gallery, N.Y.C., 1967, 68, 70, 73, 75, 77, Paa Ya Paa Gallery, Nairobi, Kenya, 1973, Chemchemi Creative Arts Center, Arusha, Tanzania, 1973, Kibo Art Gallery, Mt. Kilimanjaro, Tanzania, 1973, Portland (Maine) Art Mus., 1974, Reading (Pa.) Public Mus., 1974, Erie (Pa.) Art Center, 1977, Gallery 7, Detroit, 1977; represented in permanent collections, Mus. Modern Art, N.Y.C., Newark Mus., Bklyn. Mus., U. Va. Art Mus.; also subject of TV film; host Vincent Smith Dialogues with

Contemporary Artists, Radio Sta. WPAI-FM, 1986-88. Served with U.S. Army, 1948-49. Recipient Thomas B. Clark prize N.A.D., 1974; Winslow and Newton prize Nat. Soc. Painters in Casein and Acrylic, 1978; John Hay Whitney fellow, 1959; Nat. Endowment Arts grantee, 1973; Nat. Inst. Arts and Letters grantee, 1968; Cultural Council Found. grantee, 1971 Mem. Nat. Conf. Artists. Home: 264 E Broadway New York NY 10002-5670 *I have tried to develop three things which I feel are necessary to achieving some success in one's chosen field: a philosophy in which one keeps physically fit, mentally aware and consistent in one's work. Through a belief in the importance of the work one can constantly strive to grow and reach new heights.*

SMITH, VIRGIL BAKER, retired electrical engineer; b. Bastrop, La., Oct. 13, 1916; s. George and Virginia (Mallette) S.; m. Phyllis Patterson, Nov. 10, 1945; children: Nancy E., Patricia A., Randall T.. BSEE, La. State U., Baton Rouge, 1935-39. Supr., elec. engr. USN, Washington, 1941-77, ret., 1977; sr. elec. engr. George G. Sharp Inc., Arlington, Va., 1981-82, Systems & Applied Sci. Corp., Arlington, 1982-85, Designers & Planners, Arlington, 1985-91; ret., 1991. Contbr. article to profl. jour. Com. chmn. Boy Scouts Am. Indian guides, Four Corners, Md., 1949; trustee elem. sch., Four Corners, Md., 1950. Recipient Superior Civilian Svc. award USN, 1978, Spl. Achievement award USN, 1975.

SMITH, VIRGINIA A. marketing communications professional; b. Washington, Oct. 23, 1962; d. Kenneth Ross and Patricia Marcella (Maher) S. BBA, Va. Commonwealth U., 1986; postgrad., George Washington U., 1994—. Pub. rels. coord. Richmond Comedy Club, Va., 1987-90; media coord. Medalist Sports, Richmond, 1991; event coord. ProServ, Washington, 1992; paralegal Law Resources, 1993-94; cons. internat. mktg. MCI, McLean, Va., 1994-96, mktg. comm. mgr. global alliance products, 1996—. Cons., media rels. Va. Internat. Gold Cup, Middleburg, Va., 1993-94, Project Life Animal Rescue, Washington, 1994, media chairperson; cons., media rels. The President's Golf Cup, Washington, 1994, 96. Editor: Tour DuPont Mag., 1991. Vol. Octagon Club, Winchester, Va., 1980-81, Senatorial Campaigns, Richmond, 1988, Washington, 1994. Mem. Smithsonian, Nat. Assn. Female Execs. Republican. Roman Catholic. Avocations: writing, golfing, reading. Home: 14 Bridle Ct Somerset NJ 08873-5354

SMITH, VIRGINIA BROWN, classical musician; b. Nashville, July 24, 1954; d. Jordan Stokes and Annie Frances (Sory) Brown; m. Mark Brampton Smith, Feb. 28, 1976 (div. 1986); 1 child, Evelyn Anne. MusB, Eastman Sch. Music, 1976; MusM, U. Mich., 1979. Dir. music Good Shepherd United Meth. Ch., Dearborn, Mich., 1977-81, Westminster Presby. Ch., Ann Arbor, 1981-84; instr. voice Schoolcraft Coll., Livonia, 1986-89; pvt. practice voice and piano instrn. Ann Arbor, 1976—. Adj. instr. Albion (Mich.) Coll., 1991-95; solo recitals, performances Ann Arbor, Detroit, Mpls., Nashville, Washington, 1977—. Soprano soloist Christ Ch. Cranbrook, Bloomfield Hills, Mich., 1984—, U. Mich. Early Music Ensemble, 1977-89, 1994-96, Ann Arbor Cantata Singers, 1981-89, Ars Musica Choir, Ann Arbor, 1984-85, Vocal Arts Ensemble, 1995-96. Mem. Nat. Assn. Tchrs. Singing (bd. dirs. Mich. chpt.), Music Tchrs. Nat. Assn. (nat. profl. cert. 1989), Acad. for Study and Performance Early Mus. (bd. dirs. and sec. 1994), Early Mus. Am., Mich. Music Tchrs. Assn. (bd. dirs., cert. 1988, state voice chairperson 1989-95), Nat. Guild Piano Tchrs. (cert. piano tchr.), Ann Arbor Piano Tchrs. Guild (treas. 1983-85), Livonia Area Piano Tchrs. Forum (pres. 1991-93), Detroit Musicians League, Pi Kappa Lambda, Sigma Alpha Iota. Democrat. Episcopalian. Avocations: cultural events, travel, movies, dogs. Home: 3730 Burns Ct Ann Arbor MI 48105-3037

SMITH, W. JAMES, health facility administrator; b. Shenandoah, Iowa, Mar. 26, 1942; s. Willis C. and Lois M. (Hurst) S.; m. Sharon E. Hogue, May 4, 1940; children: Sharon Wendy, W. James II, Stacey E. BA in Psychology, Nat. Coll. Kansas City, 1960; MA in Psychology, Gerontology, John F. Kennedy U., 1969. Lic. nursing home adminstr., Fla., Iowa, Nebr., Calif. Pres. Retirement Svcs., Oakland, Calif., 1966-77; adminstr. Good Samaritan Soc., Sioux Falls, S.D., 1977-80; pres. Good Shepherd Ctrs., Palm Harbor, Fla., 1980-84; program coord. Hospice of Fla. Suncoast, Inc., Largo, 1984-91; founder, pres., CEO, Alzheimer's Ctrs., Inc., Palm Harbor, 1991—; pres., founder The House of Friends, Inc., 1997—, Fundación La Casa de Amigos, Guatemala, 1997—. Home: 10 Plum Ct Homosassa FL 34446 E-mail: wjs19422@yahoo.com.

SMITH, W. PRESTON, publishing executive, educator, real estate broker; b. Little Rock, Oct. 30, 1938; s. Arthur W. (dec.) and Syble M. (Love) S. (dec.); children: Cynthia Ann Smith Jones, Carey R. BS, Little Rock U., 1959; postgrad., Henderson State U., Arkadelphia, Ark., 1968-69, Ark. State U., 1969, Texarkana Coll., 1981-82, U. Ark., Pine Bluff, 1983, Tulane U., Miss. County Community Coll., 1985; MEd, U. Ark., 1984. Cert. sch. adminstr., social studies tchr., Laubach reading instr. Tchr. math. and social studies 4th St. Jr. H.S., North Little Rock, 1959-61; owner Walker Enterprises, Hot Springs Village, Ark., 1964—; tchr. Malvern (Ark.) Pub. Schs., 1967-68, Prattsville (Ark.) H.S., 1968-69, Poyen (Ark.) H.S., 1969-70, Horatio (Ark.) H.S., 1981-82, Bingham Rd. Acad., Little Rock, 1982-83, Luxora (Ark.) H.S., 1985, Stanton Rd. Sch., Little Rock, 1986; tchr., prin. Dept. Correction Sch. Dist., Tucker Penitentiary Unit, Ark., 1989-95; ret., 1995. Mem. sci. textbook selection com., Prattsville H.S., 1968-69; mem. math. stds. com. Ark. Coun. Tchrs. Math., Little Rock, 1983; lectr. Zero Down seminars on creative real estate financing; owner Silver Dollar Press. Author, pub.: Jokebook of the Century, 1989; author: Jokebook of the Century, vol. II, 1990, vol. III, 1991, How To Start Your Own Business, 1992, Forms For Business, vol. I and II, 1995, Consumers Should Know, vol. I-vol. IV, 1996, vol. V-vol. IX, 1997, How to Adjust and Repair Your Sewing Machine, Jokebook of the Century, Vol 4. Past pres., song leader Sunday Sch. class; former mem. Ch. choir. Mem. AARP (immediate past pres. England, Ark. chpt., chpt. specialist), Ark. Assn. Ednl. Adminstrn. (assoc.), Ark. Ret. Tchr. Assn. (state membership chmn. 1998—), Lonoke County Ret. Tchr. Assn. (pres. 1997-2000). Lodges: Order of DeMolay (master councillor). Avocations: candlemaking, refinishing furniture, tape recording classical music. Home and Office: Po Box 8394 Hot Springs Village AR 71910-8394

SMITH, W. THOMAS, JR. writer; b. Columbia, S.C., Apr. 30, 1959; s. William Thomas and Alba Antoinette (Jones) S. BA in History, U. S.C., 1982. SWAT team officer, 1987-88; with ins. sales, 1988-95; freelance writer and editor, 1995—; assoc. editor Greater Columbia Bus. Monthly, 1998-99; adj. prof. U. S.C., 2002—. Writer, lectr., 1995—; corr. George mag., 1998, Charlotte (N.C.) Observer, 1999, Atlanta Jour. Constn., 1999, U.S. News & World Report, 1999—, USA Today, 2000—, Bus. Week, 2000—, Orlando Sentinel, 2001, N.Y. Post, 2001, Natl. Review, 2001. Bd. dirs. S.C. Athletic Hall of Fame, 1997-2000. With USMC, 1982-87. Mem. Am. Soc. Journalists and Authors, World Affairs Coun., Nat. Press Club. Home: PO Box 8783 Columbia SC 29202

SMITH, WANN GRAHAM, writer; b. Tulsa, Okla., May 16, 1949; s. Wann Edwin and Betty Jo Smith; m. Iris Martina Freidel; children: Greta, Erin, Madeline. Home: 818 Windsor Gardens Ct Ballwin MO 63021 Personal E-mail: wigem@earthlink.net.

SMITH, WARREN ALLEN, writer; b. Minburn, Iowa, Oct. 27, 1921; s. Harry Clark and Ruth Marion (Miles) S. BA, U. No. Iowa, 1948; MA, Columbia U., 1949. Chmn. dept. Eng. Bentley Sch., N.Y.C., 1949-54, New Canaan (Conn.) H.S., 1954-86; founder, pres., chmn. bd. Variety Sound Corp., N.Y.C., 1961-90; pres. Afro-Carib Records, 1971-90, Talent Mgmt., 1982-90, AAA Rec. Studio, 1985-90; founder, pres. Variety Rec. Studio, 1961-96. Instr. Columbia U., 1961-62. Author: Who's Who in Hell, 2000, Celebrities in Hell, 2002; book rev. editor: The Humanist, 1953—58; editor: (jour.) Taking Stock, 1967—93, Pique, 1990—93, Van Rijn's Pad, 1991, Janestreeter, 1997—98; contbr. book revs.; editl. assoc.: Free Inquiry, 1992—2000; contbg. editor: GALHA, 1996—; syndicated columnist: Manhattan Scene in W.I. newspapers, —, syndicated columnist: Humanist Potpourri in Free Inquiry, 1994—98, drama critic: Brontë Newsletter, 1995—2000, book reviewer: New Humanist, 1997—2000, CD prodr.: Manuel Salazar: Costa Rica's Forgotten Tenor. Pres. Taursa Fund, 1971-73; bd. dirs. Jane Street Corp. Treas. Secular Humanist Soc. N.Y., 1988-93; sec. Jane St. Corp., 1995-97, 98-99. With ACT UP, Hume Soc.; founding mem. Voltaire Soc. Am. With AUS, 1942-46. Recipient Leavey award Freedoms Found. at Valley Forge, 1985. Mem.: ASCAP, N.Y. Soc. Ethical Culture, Bertrand Russell Soc. (bd. dirs. 1973—, v.p. 1977—80), Brit. Humanist Assn., Conn. Edn. Assn., Rationalist Press Assn., Am. Unitarian Assn., Internat. Press Inst., N.Y. Skeptics Soc. (bd. dirs. 1990—94), Asociación Iberoamericana Ético Humanista (hon.), Stonewall Vets. Orgn. (treas. 1998—99), Omaha Beach Vets. Assn., Mensa, Mensa Investment Club (chmn. 1967—2001), Humanist Book Club (pres. 1957—62). Avocation: teratology. Home and Office: 31 Jane St Apt 10 D New York NY 10014-1980 E-mail: wasm@nyc.rr.com.

SMITH, WARREN DANIEL, surgeon, retired; b. Rochester, N.Y., Mar. 18, 1931; s. Chester James and Marguerite Elanor (Leary) S.; m. Ann Steger, Aug. 26, 1959; children: Jeffrey, Kristian, Andrew, Matthew, Mark. AB, Hamilton Coll., 1953; MD, Boston U., 1956. Diplomate Am. Bd. Surgery. Surg. intern Genesee Hosp., Rochester, 1956-57; surg. resident U. Rochester, 1957-58, 60-63; pvt. practice in gen. surgery Rochester, 1963-96; ret., 1996. Clin. asst. prof. surgery U. Rochester Sch. Medicine and Dentistry, 1963—; assoc. surgeon Strong Meml. Hosp., 1963-96; sr. attending surgeon Genesee Hosp., 1963-96, pres. med. staff, 1975; cons. Office Profl. Misconduct, N.Y. State, 1982—; med. dir. Westfall Surg. Ctr., Rochester, 1993-99. Pres. Rochester Surg. Soc., 1968. With U.S. Army, 1958-60; col. USAR, 1980-85. Fellow ACS; mem. AMA, N.Y. State Med. Soc., Monroe County Med. Soc. E-mail: wdsmith@bluehog.net.

SMITH, WARREN JAMES, optical scientist, consultant, lecturer; b. Rochester, N.Y., Aug. 17, 1922; s. Warren Abrams and Jessica Madelyn (Forshay) S.; m. Mary Helen Geddes, May 18, 1944 (dec. 1999); children: David Whitney, Barbara Jamie; m. Dung My Luong, Dec. 24, 2000. BS, U. Rochester, 1944; postgrad., U. Calif., Santa Barbara, 1960. Physicist Clinton Engr. Works, Tenn. Eastman Co., Oak Ridge, 1944-46; chief optical engr. Simpson Optical Mfg. Co., Chgo., 1946-59; mgr. optical sect. Raytheon Corp., Santa Barbara, 1959-62; v.p. R & D, Infrared Industries, 1962-87; chief scientist Kaiser Electro-Optics, Inc., Carlsbad, Calif., 1987—. Lectr. U. Wis., Madison, 1972—, Genesee Computer Ctr., Rochester, 1982—93, U. Rochester, 1988—; . Sinclair Optics, 1994—2000; cons. in field; expert witness. Author: Modern Optical Engineering, 1966, 3d edit., 2000, Modern Lens Design, 1992, Practical Optical System Layout, 1997; editor McGraw-Hill series Optical and Electro-Optical Engineering; also articles. Fellow: Optical Soc. Am. (pres. 1980, organizer, chmn. tech. confs., Fraunhofer medal 2001), Internat. Soc. Optical Engring. (life; pres. 1983, organizer, chmn. tech. confs., Gold medal 1985, Dirs. award 1992), Soc. Photo-Optical Instrumentation Engrs. (life), Sigma Chi. Avocations: tennis, sailing. Home: 1165 Countrywood Ln Vista CA 92083-5334 Office: Kaiser Electro Optics Inc 2752 Loker Ave W Carlsbad CA 92008-6603 E-mail: wsmith@keo.com.

SMITH, WAYNE CALVIN, chemical engineer, consultant; b. Beaver, Okla., Mar. 19, 1935; s. Dean C. and Loraine S.; m. Suellyn Joyce Canon, Aug. 18, 1984. BS, Okla. U., 1958, MSChemE, 1964; PhDChemE, Colo. U., 1974. Registered profl. engr., Tex., Okla., Colo.; cert. emergency response specialist. Process engr. Shell Oil Co., Deer Park, Tex., 1958-59; sr. devel. engr. Monsanto, Pensacola, Fla., 1965-66; project leader Phillips Petroleum Co., Bartlesville, Okla., 1967-69; acting chief process control EPA Nat. Enforcement Investigations Ctr., Denver, 1971-78; firm wide mgr. pollution control Dames & Moore, Golden, Colo., 1978-81; regional mgr. Hittman Assocs., Englewood, 1981-82; pres. Encon Environs Control Svcs., Golden, 1982-83; chief hazardous waste mgmt. Woodword-Clyde Cons., Englewood, 1983-84; exec. cons. Kellogg Corp., Littleton, Colo., 1984-86; program mgr. Radian Corp., Austin, Tex., 1986-93; prin. engr., office mgr. Tetra Tech, Inc., Oklahoma City, 1993—. Contbr. over 30 articles to profl. jours. Capt. USMC, 1959-62. Scholar Magnolia Petroleum Co., 1956-58; fellow Phillips Petroleum Co., 1962-64, Marathon Oil Co., 1966-67, Gulf Oil Co., 1969-71. Mem. AIChE, Am. Arbitration Assn., The Greens Country Club, Sigma Xi. Baptist. Avocations: golf, woodworking. Office: Tetra Tech Inc 806 W Curtis Dr Ste I Midwest City OK 73110-3041 E-mail: wcsttokc@swbell.net.

SMITH, WAYNE LARUE, lawyer, consultant; b. Marietta, Ohio, June 15, 1955; s. Benjamin LeCompte and Bettigene (Jerman) S. BS, Ariz. State U., 1980, MBA, 1987; JD, U. Ariz., 1986. Bar: Fla. 1994, D.C. 1998, U.S. Dist. Ct. (so. dist.) Fla. 1995. Pres. D,B&H Staffing Svcs., Phoenix, 1984-87; v.p. Alan LaRue & Assocs., 1987-88; pres. The Proview Group, Boca Raton, Fla., 1988-93; lawyer Morgan & Hendrick, Key West, 1993-99, The Smith Law Firm, Key West, 1999—. Bd. dirs. Fla. Lawyers Assistance, Inc., Ft. Lauderdale. Pres. Stop AIDS Project of South Fla., Inc., West Palm Beach, 1988-91; bd. dirs., treas. Comprehensive AIDS Program of Palm Beach County, 1989-93; mem. adv. bd. The Red Barn Theatre, Key West, 1995—, The Met. Musical Theatre Co., Phoenix, 1996-99; pres. The Experience, Inc., Santa Fe, 1990-95. Recipient New Mem. award, Excellence award Fla. Atlantic Builders Assn., 1989; Up and Comer awards Price Waterhouse/South Fla. Bus. Jour., 1991-92. Mem. ABA, Fla. Bar Assn. (computer law com. 1998-99), Monroe County Bar Assn. (pres. 1995-96), D.C. Bar Assn. Democrat. Office: The Smith Law Firm 330 Whitehead St Key West FL 33040-6543 E-mail: wsmith@thesmithlawfirm.com.

SMITH, WAYNE RICHARD, lawyer; b. Petoskey, Mich., Apr. 30, 1934; s. Wayne Anson and Frances Lynetta (Cooper) S.; m. Carrie J. Swanson, June 18, 1959; children: Stephen, Douglas (dec.), Rebecca. AB, U. Mich., 1956, JD, 1959. Bar: Mich. 1959. Asst. atty. gen. State of Mich., 1960-62; pros. atty. Emmet County (Mich.), 1963-68; dist. judge 90th Jud. Dist., Mich., 1969-72; city atty. City of Petoskey, 1976-98. Trustee North Central Mich. Coll., 1981-98, chmn., 1992-97; trustee/chmn. N. Ctrl. Mich. Coll. Found., 1999—; mem. No. Mich. Community Mental Health Bd., 1972-92, chmn., 1979-81. Mem. Emmet-Charlevoix Bar Assn. (pres. 1967), State Bar Mich., Mich. State Bar Found. Presbyterian. Home: PO Box 4677 Harbor Springs MI 49740-4677 Address: 365 E Main St PO Box 4677 Harbor Springs MI 49740-4677

SMITH, WAYNE THOMAS, healthcare company executive; b. Jan. 29, 1946; BS, Auburn Univ, 1968, MS, 1969; M in hosp. adminstrn., Trinity U.; postgrad., King's Fund Coll. Hosp. Adminstrn. With Trinity Univ, 1971-73, Humana Inc, Louisville, 1973-96, v.p. ctrl. hosp. region, 1978-80, sr. v.p., 1980-85, exec. v.p., 1985-86, pres., COO group health divsn., 1986-96, also bd. dirs.; exec. v.p. Humana Health Care Ops., 1991-96; ret. Humana Inc., 1996; pres., CEO, Cmty. Health Sys., Brentwood, Tenn., 1996—, chmn. bd., 2001—. Exec. v.p. health plan ops., bd. dirs. Humana Health Plan, Inc., Louisville; pres. Humana Health Ins. Nev., Inc., Humana Health Plan Fla., Inc., Humana Health Plan Ohio, Inc., Humana Health Chgo. Ins. Co., Humana Kansas City, Inc.; pres., COO Humana Health Plan Tex., Prime Health Mgmt. Svcs.; pres., bd. dirs. HMPK, Inc. Bd. dirs. Gov.'s Scholars Program, Ky., Actors Theatre of Louisville, Ky. Ctr. for the Arts, The Louisville Orchestra; bd. overseers U. Louisville; mem. exec. com. Greater Louisville Fund for the Arts; past chair bd. dirs. Louisville Collegiate Sch. With U.S. Army, 1969-73, capt., 1973. Mem. Group Health Assn. Am. (bd. dirs.), Health Ins. Assn. Am. (bd. dirs.). Office: Community Health Systems 155 Franklin Rd Ste 400 Brentwood TN 37027-4646

SMITH, WENDY HAIMES, federal agency administrator; b. Tex. m. Jay L. Smith. BA in Econs., U. Mich.; postgrad., Ohio State U., Am. U., Washington Studio Sch., Aspen Inst., Wye, Md., 1997. Cert. real estate agt. Office mgr. Haimes Travel Agy., Ohio, 1972-73; mgmt. intern U.S. Dept. Commerce, 1973-75, country specialist for Korea, 1973, spl. asst. to dep. asst. sec. for internat. commerce, 1973-74, project officer, maj. projects divsn., 1974-75, project mgr. indsl. sys., maj. projects divsn., 1975-77, country specialist for Brazil, 1978, project mgr., hydrocarbons and chem. process plants, maj. export projects divsn., 1977-79, exec. asst. to dep. asst. sec. of commerce for export devel. and staff dir. Pres. Export Coun., 1979-81, dir. Pres. Export Coun., 1981-92, acting dir. Office Planning and Coordination, 1988-89, dir. adv. coms. and pvt. sector programs Internat. Trade Adminstrn., 1992-97; dir. Trade Info. Ctr., 1997—, acting dir. office of export promotion, 1999, 2000-01. Exhibited in group shows at Courtyard Gallery, Brian Logan Artspace, Washington, Designer's Art Gallery, Bethesda, Md., Artists Mus., one-woman shows include Courtyard Gallery, Washington, 2001; author, editor: U.S. Trade in Transition: Maintaining the Gains, 1988; co-author, editor: The Export Imperative, 1980, Coping with the Dynamics of World Trade in the 1980s, 1984. Active Art League, Smithsonian Instn., Washington Opera Guild; bd. dirs. Washington Studio Sch; one man show Courtyard Gallery, 2001. Mem. Washington Internat. Trade Assn.

SMITH, WENDY HOPE, lawyer; b. N.Y.C., Jan. 19, 1957; d. Morton and Doris Smith. AB, Smith Coll., 1978; JD, Boston U., 1981. Bar: N.J. 1981, U.S. Dist. Ct. 1981, U.S. Ct. Appeals (3d cir.), Supreme Ct. U.S. Law sec. to judge Superior Ct. N.J., Bergen County, 1981-82; assoc. firm Sellar, Richardson, Stuart & Chisholm, Roseland, N.J., 1982-89, ptnr., 1989-97, Sellar Richardson, P.C., 1997-2000, Marshall, Dennehey, Warner, Coleman & Goggin, Roseland, N.J., 2000—. Mem. adv. com. Inst. CLE, 1983-91. Mem. ABA, N.J. Bar Assn., Bergen County Bar Assn., Essex County Bar Assn., Trial Attys. N.J., Mensa, Smith Coll. Alumnae Assn. (fund rep. 1978-83). Home: 401 Hancock Ct Edgewater NJ 07020-1627 Office: Marshall Dennehey Warner Coleman & Goggin 425 Eagle Rock Ave Ste 302 Roseland NJ 07068

SMITH, WENDY L. foundation executive; b. Chgo., Sept. 12, 1950; d. John Arthur and Dolores Mae (Webb) Rothenberger; m. Alan Richard Smith; children: Angela Fuhs, Erica Smith. Ed., Oakton C.C., Des Plaines, Ill., 1986, Mundelein Coll., 1990. Purchasing clk. AIT Industries, Skokie, Ill., 1975-76; purchasing agt. MCC Powers, 1976-78; office mgr. Spartan Engring., 1978-80, Brunswick Corp., Skokie, 1980—; successively sr. sec., coord. indsl. rels., dir. Brunswick Found., Lake Forest, Ill., 1982-89, pres., 1989—. Asst. sec. Brunswick Pub. Charitable Found., Lake Forest, 1989—; mem. adv. com. Found. for Ind. Higher Edn., Stamford, Conn., 1989—. Coun. Better Bus. Burs., Arlington, Va., 1988-90; bd. dirs. Associated Colls. of Ill., 1991—; bd. dirs., mem. trustees com., mem. compensation and benefits com. Donors Forum of Chgo., 1988-93. Bd. dirs. INROADS/Chgo., Inc., 1994—; mem. steering com. Dist. 57 Edn. Found., Mt. Prospect, Ill., 1996—. Recipient Pvt. Sector Initiative Commendation, U.S. Pres., 1987-89. Mem. Donors Forum Chgo. (treas. 1988-91, bd. dirs., mem. exec. com., chairperson audit and fin. com., mem. trustees com. 1992—), Coun. on Founds., Ind. Sector Suburban Contbns. Network (chairperson 1987-89), Women in Philanthropy Corp. Founds. (mem. cmty. rels. com. 1985-87), Chgo. Women in Philanthropy. Avocations: antique restoration, pleasure reading, bowling, golf.

SMITH, WILBUR LAZEAR, radiologist, educator; b. Warwick, N.Y., Oct. 11, 1943; s. Wilbur and Betty (Norris) S.; m. Rebecca Rowlands, June 19, 1965; children: Jason, Daniel, Joanna, Noah, Ethan, Jacob. BA, SUNY, Buffalo, 1965, MD, 1969. Diplomate Am. Bd. Radiology, Am. Bd. Pediatrics, Am. Bd. Pediatric Radiology. Intern, then resident Buffalo Children's Hosp., 1969-71; resident in pediatric radiology Cin. Gen. and Children's Hosp., 1971-74; asst. prof. pediatrics and radiology Ind. U., Indpls., 1975-78, assoc. prof., 1978-80, acting dir. pediatric radiology, 1979-80; assoc. prof. U. Iowa, Iowa City, 1980-82, prof., 1982—, dir. med. edn. in radiology, 1980-86, vice chmn. dept. radiology, 1986-94, interim head, 1994-96, dir. pediatric radiology, 1980-92; chmn. dept. radiology Henry Ford Health Sys., Detroit, 1998-99; prof. radiology Wayne State U., 2000—; staff radiologist Mich. Children's Hosp., 2000—. Vice chmn. radiology for academics Wayne State U., 2001; radiology residency dir. Wayne State U. Radiology, 2001. Assoc. editor Gastrointestinal Imaging in Pediatrics, Acad. Radiology, 1992—; exec. assoc. editor Acad. Radiology, 1997-2000, assoc. editor, 2000—; contbr. articles to profl. jours. Mem. equity adv. com. Iowa City Sch. Bd., 1983-87. Served with USAR, 1969-77. Fellow Am. Acad. Pediatrics, Am. Coll. Radiology; mem. AMA, Radiol. Soc. N.Am., Iowa Radiol. Soc. (pres. 1987-88), Assn. Univ. Radiologists (pres. 1995-96), Soc. Pediat. Radiology (treas. 1995-98, rep. coun. Acad. Socs. of AAMC 1996—). Mem. Soc. Of Friends. Avocation: photography. Home: 10124 Lasalle Blvd Huntington Woods MI 48070-1162 Office: Children's Hosp of Mich Dept Pediat Imaging 3901 Beaubien St Detroit MI 48201-2119 E-mail: wsmith@dmc.org.

SMITH, WILBURN JACKSON, JR. retired bank executive; b. Charlotte, N.C., June 13, 1921; s. Wilburn Jackson and Banna (Oswalt) S.; m. Terry Mosteller, Jan. 4, 1944; children: Kenneth M., M. Scott (dec.), Wilburn Jackson III, Curtis Todd. BS in Acctg., U. N.C., 1943; postgrad. in comml. banking, Rutgers U. Sch. Banking, 1953, postgrad. in investment banking, 1956. With First Union Nat. Bank, Charlotte, 1946-74, exec. v.p., 1960-67, 1st exec. v.p., 1967-74; pres., mng. trustee Cameron-Brown Investment Group, Raleigh, N.C., 1974-78; chmn. loan policy com. N.C. Nat. Bank, Charlotte, 1979-88. Cons. in field. Served with USN, 1943-46. Recipient Citizenship award Charlotte Civitan, 1972. Mem. Robert Morris Assocs., Myers Park Country Club (Charlotte). Baptist.

SMITH, WILLARD GRANT, psychologist, educator; b. Sidney, N.Y., June 29, 1934; s. Frank Charles and Myrtle Belle (Empet) S.; m. Ruth Ann Dissly, Sept. 14, 1957; children: Deborah Sue Henri, Cynthia Lynn Koster, Andrea Kay Richards, John Charles. BS, U. Md., 1976; MS, U. Utah, 1978, PhD, 1981. Diplomate Am. Bd. Forensic Examiners, Am. Bd. Psychol. Specialities, Am. Bd. Disability Analysts; lic. psychologist Utah, cert. sch. psychologist nat. . Tchg. asst. dept. ednl. psychology U. Utah; rsch. asst. U. Utah Med. Ctr., 1976-78; rsch. cons. Utah Dept. Edn., 1977; program evaluator Salt Lake City Sch. Dist.; program evaluator, auditor Utah State Bd. Edn., 1978; sch. psychologist Jordan Sch. Dist., Sandy, Utah, 1978-82, tchr., 1979-80; exec. dir. Utah Ind. Living Ctr., Salt Lake City, 1982-83; spl. edn. cons. Southeastern Edn. Svc. Ctr., 1983-85; sch. psychologist Jordan Sch. Dist., Sandy, 1985-96; assoc. psychologist Don W. McBride & Assocs., Bountiful, Utah, 1989-91; pvt. practice Sandy, 1991—. Master sgt. USAF, 1953-76. Decorated Air Force Commendation medal with 2 clusters. Fellow Am. Coll. Forensic Examiners; mem. APA, Nat. Assn. Sch. Psychologists, Air Force Sgts. Assn., Ret. Enlisted Assn., , Am. Legion, Vets. of Fgn. Wars, Phi Kappa Phi, Alpha Sigma Lambda. Home: 8955 Quail Hollow Dr Sandy UT 84093-1903

SMITH, WILLIAM CHARLES, lawyer; b. Batavia, N.Y., June 9, 1930; s. William F. and Verna B. (Busmire) S.; m. Lucia P. Pierce, July 10, 1954; children: William Charles, Leonard P., Victoria J. BA, U. Buffalo, 1952; LLB, Harvard U., 1955. Bar: Maine 1955, D.C. 1962, Fla. 1995, U.S. Dist. Ct. Maine, 1956, U.S. Tax Ct. 1960, U.S. Ct. Appeals (1st cir.) 1977, U.S. Ct. Claims 1985, U.S. Supreme Ct. 1960. Assoc., Portland, Maine, 1955-57; ptnr. Hutchinson, Pierce, Atwood & Allen, 1957-59; counsel Office Tax Legis. Counsel, U.S. Treasury Dept., Washington, 1959-61; ptnr. Pierce, Atwood, Scribner, Allen, Smith and Lancaster, Portland, 1961-96, of counsel, 1996—. Exec. com. Fed. Tax Inst., New Eng. Vice chmn. budget com. United Community Services, 1966-68, chmn., 1968-70, nat. budget and consultation com., 1969-71; bd. dirs. Portland Goodwill, Inc., 1967-69, United Way, Inc., 1968-74, 75-80, Portland Widow's Wood Soc., 1962— ; trustee Portland Regional Opportunity Program, 1967-68, Freyburg Acad., 1976-96 , Found. Blood Research, 1979-85. Mem. ABA, Maine Bar Assn., D.C. Bar, Fla. Bar, Cumberland County Bar Assn., Am. Law Inst., Am. Coll. Trust and Estate Counsel, Am. Coll. Tax Counsel, Portland Country Club, Mid-Ocean Club (Bermuda), Meadows Country Club (Fla.), Cumerland Club (Maine). Republican. Unitarian Universalist. Home: 392 Spring St Portland ME 04102-3642 Office: Pierce Atwood One Monument Sq Portland ME 04101-1110 E-mail: wsmith@pierceatwood.com.

SMITH, WILLIAM EDWARD, sales executive, telecommunications executive; b. Port Washington, N.Y., Mar. 24, 1940; s. William Edward and Elizabeth Ann (Willis) S.; m. Kathleen Ann Guy, Nov. 4, 1972 (div. June 1979). AAS, Broome Tech. C.C., Binghamton, N.Y., 1960. Various sales mgmt. positions Contel, Sherburne, N.Y., 1973-84; br. sales mgr. NYNEX (BISC), Syracuse, 1984-94; region sales mgr. ACC Local Svc., 1994-95; sr. acct. mgr. Nortel Networks, Richardson, Tex., 1995-98; region mgr. Triton Network Sys., Orlando, Fla., 1998-2001; prin. assoc. W.E. Smith Assoc., Sherburne, 2001—. Founding mem. Tri Valley Aviation Assn., Norwich, N.Y., 1974-78; committeeman Rep. County Com., Sherburne, 1976-80; pres. Sherburne Rotary Club, 1981-82, Upper Chenango Valley Assn., 1983-85. Splst. 4 U.S. Army, 1963-65. Republican. Roman Catholic. Avocations: woodworking, flying, clay shooting, golf. Home: 168 Webb Rd Sherburne NY 13460-3732 E-mail: williame@citilink.com.

SMITH, WILLIAM FRENCH, safety engineer, special projects administrator; b. Bay City, Tex., Nov. 30, 1941; s. William and Willie Mae (Perry) S.; m. Sylvia Knight, Feb. 4, 1977; children: William III, Maurice. BS, Tuskegee U., 1964; postgrad., Washington U., 1968-70. Equipment engr. Boeing Co., Huntsville, Ala., 1964-67; plant design engr. McDonnell Douglas Corp., St. Louis, 1967-69; project engr. St. Louis County Govt., 1969-72; divsn. engr. E.I. duPont de Nemours &Co., Inc., Wilmington, Del., 1972-74, Victoria, Tex., 1972-74; engring. mgr. Westinghouse Corp., Millburn, N.J., 1974-76; bldg. safety engr. Denver Pub. Schs., 1976—, project adminstr., 1977—, energy conservationist, 1978—. Dir. hazardous materials Tuskegee U., Denver, 1985-88, environ. safety dir., 1988—; reservist Fed. Emergency Mgmt. Agy. Bd. dirs. Denver Opportunities Industrialization Ctr., 1979-80, Nat. Commn. on Future of Regis Coll.; mem. Mayor's Citizens Adv. Com. on Energy, 1980—, City of Lakewood Sr. Citizens Adv. Coun., Lakewood Bd. Appeals, Lakewood Code Enforcement Com.; past bd. dirs. Colo. Alliance Environ. Edn., Colo. Emergency Planning Commn. Served with USNR, 1979—. Recipient Pres.'s Nat. award for energy conservation, 1980. Mem. Am. Soc. Safety Engrs., Colo. Assn. Sch. Energy Coords., Am. Assn. Blacks in Energy, Denver Pub. Schs. Black Adminstrs. and Suprs. Assn. (treas.), Colo. Environ. Health Assn., Nat. Asbestos Coun., Colo. Hazardous Waste Mgmt. Soc., Colo. Hazardous Materials Assn. (past treas.), Denver Emergency Planning Commn., Civil Air Patrol, Colo. Renewable Energy Soc., Colo. Energy Network, Nat. Assn. Minority Contractors, Internat. Hazardous Materials Assn., Tuskegee U. Alumni Assn. Republican. Home: 102 S Balsam St Lakewood CO 80226-1344 Office: Denver Public Schs 900 Grant St Denver CO 80203-2907

SMITH, WILLIAM G. transportation executive; Chmn., pres., CEO Smithway Motor Xpress Corp., Ft. Dodge, Iowa, 1993—. Office: Smithway Motor Xpress Corp 2031 Quail Ave Fort Dodge IA 50501-8511 Fax: 515-576-8794.

SMITH, WILLIAM HENRY PRESTON, writer, editor, former corporate executive; b. Pleasanton, Tex., Sept. 8, 1924; s. Sidney Newton and Willie Gertrude (Cloyd) S.; m. Frances Dixon, July 1, 1950; children: Juliet, Dixon, David. B.J., U. Tex., 1949. Reporter Dallas Morning News, 1949-52; advt. asst. Dallas Power & Light Co., 1952-55; dir. pub. relations Greater Boston C. of C., 1955-58; with New Eng. Telephone and Telegraph Co., Boston, 1958-86, asst. v.p., 1966-75, corp. sec., 1975-83, dir. pub. relations, 1983-86; free-lance writer Dover, Mass., 1986—. Editor: Bus. Ethics Resource Newsletter. Bd. dirs., v.p. Mass. Soc. for Prevention Cruelty to Children; bd. dirs. Bus. Ethics Found., Urban Dynamics Adv. Coun.; mem. support policies com. United Way Mass; bd. advisors to pres. Andover Newton Theol. Sch. With paratroopers U.S. Army, 1943-46. Decorated Purple Heart. Mem. Am. Soc. Corp. Secs., Friars, Dedham Country and Polo Club, Down Town Club, Wellesley Coll. Club, Sigma Delta Chi, Delta Kappa Epsilon. Republican. Home and Office: 10 Turtle Ln Dover MA 02030-2053

SMITH, WILLIAM HULSE, forestry and environmental studies educator; b. Trenton, N.J., May 9, 1939; s. Philip Andrews and Marion (Hulse) S.; m. Judith Chapin Pease, July 6, 1963 (div. 1982); children— Scott William, Philip Chapin; m. Deborah Banks Coit, June 17, 1983; 1 child, Tyler Banks. BS, Rutgers U., 1961, PhD, 1965; M.F., Yale U., 1963. Asst. prof. forestry Rutgers U., 1965-66; asst. prof. Yale U., 1966-72, assoc. prof., 1972-75, prof., 1975—, dean, 1981-83, 98-99, Clifton R. Musser prof. forest biology, 1985—, dean, 1998-99; emeritus, 2001. Mem. sci. adv. bd. U.S. EPA, 1990—. Author: Tree Pathology, 1970, Air Pollution and Forest Ecosystems, 1981, 2d edit., 1990. Mem. Conn. Siting Coun., 1985—2001. NSF grantee, U.S. Dept. Agr. Forest Service grantee. Mem. Soc. Am. Foresters, Am. Phytopath. Soc., Ecol. Soc. Am. Home: PO Box 585 Center Harbor NH 03226-0585 E-mail: whulsesmith@aol.com.

SMITH, WILLIAM JAY, author; b. Winnfield, La., Apr. 22, 1918; s. Jay and Georgia (Campster) S.; m. Barbara Howes, Oct. 1, 1947 (div. June 1965); children: David Emerson, Gregory Jay; m. Sonja Haussmann, Sept. 3, 1966. Student, Institut de Touraine, Tours, France, 1938; BA, Washington U., St. Louis, 1939, MA, 1941; postgrad., Columbia U., 1946-47; postgrad. Rhodes scholar, Oxford U., 1947-48; postgrad., U. Florence, Italy, 1948-50; Litt.D., New Eng. Coll., 1973. Asst. in French Washington U., 1939-41; instr. English and French Columbia U., 1946-47; lectr. English Williams Coll., 1951, poet in residence, lectr. English, 1959-64, 66-67; Ford Found. fellow Arena Stage, Washington, 1964-65; writer in residence Hollins Coll., 1965-66, prof. English, 1967, 70-80, prof. emeritus, 1980. Poet laureate Libr. of Congress, Washington, 1968-70, hon. cons. in Am. letters, 1970-76; vis. prof., acting chmn., writing divsn. Sch. Arts, Columbia U., 1973, 74-75; mem. staff Salzburg (Austria) Seminar, 1975; mem. jury Nat. Book award, 1962, 70, 75, Neustadt Internat. prize for lit., 1978, Com. of Pegasus Prize for Lit., 1979-98; poet in residence Cathedral St. John the Divine, N.Y., 1985-88. Author: Poems, 1947, Celebration at Dark, 1950, Laughing Time, 1955, Poems, 1947-57, Boy Blue's Book of Beasts, 1957, Puptents and Pebbles: A Nonsense ABC, 1959, Typewriter Town, 1960, The Spectra Hoax, 1961, What Did I See, 1962, Ho for a Hat, 1964, (with Louise Bogan) The Golden Journey; Poems for Young People, 1965, The Tin Can and Other Poems, 1966, If I Had a Boat, 1966, Poems from France, 1967, Mr. Smith and Other Nonsense, 1968, New and Selected Poems, 1970, The Streaks of the Tulip, selected criticism, 1972, Poems from Italy, 1973, Venice in the Fog, 1975, The Telephone, 1977, Laughing Time, 1980, The Traveler's Tree, New and Selected Poems, 1980, Army Brat, a Memoir, 1980, A Green Place: Modern Poems, 1982, Plain Talk: Epigrams, Epitaphs, Satires, Nonsense, Occasional Concrete and Quotidian Poems, 1988, Ho for a Hat (rev.), 1989, Collected Poems 1939-1989, 1990, Laughing Time: Collected Nonsense, 1990, Birds and Beasts, 1990, Big and Little, 1992 (with Carol Ra) Behind the King's Kitchen: A Roster of Rhyming Riddles, 1992, The Cyclist, 1995 (with Carol Ra) The Sun is Up: A Child's Year of Poems, 1996, The World Below the Window: Poems 1937-1997, 1998, Here is My Heart: Love Poems, 1999, The Cherokee Lottery: A Sequence of Poems, 2000, Around My Room, 2000, The Spectra Hoax (paperback reissue), 2000, The World Below the Window: Poems, 1937-1997, 2002, The Girl in the Glas: Love Poems, 2002; translator: (with Emanuel Brasil) Brazilian Poetry 1950-80, 1984, (with Ingvar Schousboe) The Pact: My Friendship with Isak Dinesen by Thorkild Bjørnvig, 1983, (with J.S. Holmes) Dutch Interior: Post-War Poetry of the Netherlands and Flanders, 1984, Scirocco by Romualdo Romano, 1951; Poems of a Multimillionaire by Valery Larbaud, 1955, Selected Writings of Jules Laforgue, 1956, Children of the Forest by Elsa Beskow, 1969, Two Plays by Charles Bertin: Christopher Columbus and Don Juan, 1970, The Pirate Book by Lennart Hellsing, 1972, (with Leif Sjöberg) Agadir by Artur Lundkvist, 1979, Moral Tales of Jules Laforgue, 1985, Collected Translations: Italian, French, Spanish, Portuguese, 1985, (with Dana Gioia) Poems from Italy, 1985, (with Leif Sjöberg) Wild Bouquet: Nature Poems by Harry Martinson, 1985, (with Sonja Haussmann Smith) The Madman and the Medusa by Tchicaya U Tam'Si, 1989, Songs of Childhood by Federico Garcia Lorca, 1994, Berlin: The City and the Court, 1995, (with Leif Sjöberg) The Forest of Childhood: Poems from Sweden, 1996, Gyula Illyés: Selected Poems, 1999; editor: Herrick, 1962, Light Verse and Satires by Witter Bynner, 1978, (with F.D. Reeve) An Arrow in the Wall: Selected Poetry and Prose by Andrei Voznesensky, 1986 (one of 16 Best Books of 1986, N.Y. Times), Life Sentence: Selected Poems of Nina Cassian, 1990. Mem. Vt. Ho. of Reps., 1960-62. Served to lt. USNR, 1941-45. Recipient Alumni citation Washington U., 1963; prize Poetry mag., 1945, 64; Henry Bellamann Major award, 1970; Russell Loines award Nat. Inst. Arts and Letters, 1972; Gold medal Labor Hungary 1978; Golden Rose award New Eng. Poetry Club, 1979, médaille de vermeil French Acad., 1991, Pro Cultura Hungarica medal, Hungary, 1993; Nat. Endowment for Arts fellow, 1972, 95; NEH fellow, 1975, 89; Ingram Merrill fellow, 1982; Camargo Found. fellow, 1986, René Vásquez Díaz prize Swedish Acad., 1997. Mem. Am. Acad. Arts and Letters (v.p. for literature 1986-89), Am. Assn. Rhodes Scholars, Acad. Am. Poets, Authors Guild, P.E.N. Clubs: Century. Home: 63 Luther Shaw Rd Cummington MA 01026-9787 also: 52-56 rue d'Alleray 75015 Paris France

SMITH, WILLIAM RANDOLPH (RANDY SMITH), health care management executive; b. Spartanburg, S.C., July 23, 1948; s. Jesse Edward and Helen (Knox) S.; m. Donna Marie HAwthorne, July 18, 1970; children: Kirstin Leigh, Andrea Marie. BA, Furman U., 1970; MHA, Duke U., 1972. Exec. dir. Riverside Hosp., Wilmington, Del., 1974-79; assoc. exec. dir. Brookwood Med. Ctr., Brimingham, Ala., 1979-81, exec. dir., 1983-85; v.p. ops. Am. Med. Internat., Atlanta, 1981-89, interim chief fin. officer Beverly Hills, Calif., 1989-90, chief adminstrv. officer Dallas, 1990, exec. v.p. ops., 1990-95; exec. v.p. Tenet Health Corp, 1995—. Bd. dirs. EPIC Healthcare Group, Dallas, 1989-92. Bd. dirs. Ala. Symphony Assn., Birmingham, 1985, State of Ala. Ballet, Birmingham, 1983-85, Esoterix, Inc., 1997—. Lt. U.S. Army, 1972-74. Mem. Fedn. Am. Health Systems (bd. dirs. 1989-99, pres. 1993, chmn. 1994). Epsicopalian. Avocations: skiing, tennis, automobiles. Office: Tenet Healthcare Inc 14001 Dallas Pkwy Ste 200 Dallas TX 75240-4346

SMITH, WILLIAM RAY, former biophysicist, former engineer; b. Lyman, Okla., June 26, 1925; s. Harry Wait and Daisy Belle (Hull) S. *The Smith family is of English descent, coming to America with early settlers of the Virginia Colony. William Smith's grandfather, James William Francis Smith, served in the Union Army during the Civil War. His father, Harry Wait Smith, attended Vennard College at University Park, Iowa. William's mother and father became ordained ministers in the church of the Nazarene and held pastorates in Kansas and Oklahoma. They also did mission work in El Dorado, Kansas where they had a "Helping Hand Mission." They organized a church of the Nazarene in Potwin, Kansas and assisted in the organization of the El Dorado Church of the Nazarene in September of 1917.* BA, Bethany Nazarene Coll., 1948; MA, Wichita State U., 1950; PhD, UCLA, 1967. Engr. Beech Aircraft Corp., Wichita, Kans., 1951-53; sr. group engr. McDonnell Aircraft Corp., St. Louis, 1953-60; sr. engr. Lockheed Aircraft Corp., Burbank, Calif., 1961-63; sr. engr. scientist McDonnell Douglas Corp., Long Beach, 1966-71; mem. tech. staff Rockwell Internat., L.A., 1973-86, CDI Corp.-West, Costa Mesa, Calif., 1986-88, McDonnell Douglas Aircraft Corp., Long Beach, 1988-93; ret., 1993. Tchr. math. Pasadena Nazarene Coll. (now Point Loma Nazarene Coll., San Diego), 1960-62, Glendale Coll., Calif., 1972; asst. prof. math. Mt. St. Mary's Coll., L.A., 1972-73; math. cons. L.A. Union Rescue Mission Bank of Am. Learning Ctr., 1995—, Wayfarer's Ministry 1997—, Heart of L.A. Youth, 2001--. Vol. Heart of LA Youth; Deacon Presbyn. Ch. Recipient Recognition cert. NASA, 1982. Mem. Town Hall Calif., Yosemite Assocs., UCLA Faculty Club, Sigma Xi, Pi Mu Epsilon. Republican. Avocations: sailing, photography, teaching Sunday school first grade. Home: 2405 Roscomare Rd Los Angeles CA 90077-1839 E-mail: billsmitcom@webtv.net.

SMITH, WILLIAM RAYMOND, farmer, thoroughbred owner, breeder and trainer, retired history educator, philosophy educator; b. Bowling Green, Ky., June 5, 1932; s. William Raymond and Rose Velta (Biggerstaff) S.; m. Robin Sommers, July 12, 1954 (div. Sept. 1977); children: Dana Leslie Henning, Lauren Reneé Imgrund; m. Lee Ann McClathchey, Dec. 31, 1994. BA in Liberal Arts, U. Chgo., 1953, MA in English, 1959, PhD in History of Culture, 1961. Lic. thoroughbred trainer. Asst. prof. English Pa. State U., Univ. Park, 1961-63, Haverford (Pa.) Coll., 1963-66, Scripps Coll., Claremont, Calif., 1966-67, exec. officer literature divsn., 1966-67; chmn. integrative studies Shimer Coll., Mt. Carroll, Ill., 1967-70; asst. prof. humanities Reed Coll., Portland, 1970-71; prof. history and philosophy U. Pitts., Johnstown, Pa., 1971-98, acad. dean, 1971-72; ret., 1998. Fulbright prof. Am. studies U. Utrecht, Netherlands, 1969-70. Author: History as Argument, 1966, The Rhetoric of American Politics, 1969; contbr. chpts. to books The Colonial Legacy, 1971, Nineteenth Century Literary Criticism, 1986. Cpl. U.S. Army, 1955-57. Recipient fellow Union for Rsch. in Higher Edn., Kenneybunkport, Maine, 1968. Mem. Va. Thoroughbred Assn., Va. Horseman's Assn., Va. Racing Commn. (com. Va. Breeders Fund). Avocation: fox hunting rider. Home: Paradigm Farm 8699 Green Rd Warrenton VA 20187-7732 E-mail: paradigmfarm2@aol.com.

SMITH, WILLIAM ROBERT, utility company executive; b. Mt. Clemens, Mich., Nov. 11, 1916; s. Robert L. and Elsie (Chamberlain) S.; m. Sandra Martha Philips; children from previous marriage: William R. (dec.), Laura A. (dec.). BS, Detroit Inst. Tech., 1947; postgrad., Detroit Coll. Law, U. Mich. Grad. Sch. Bus. Adminstrn. Registered profl. engr., Mich., Ohio. Indsl. engr. Detroit Edison Co., 1934-60; mgr. econ. devel. East Ohio Gas Co., Cleve., 1960-80; mgr. nat. accounts Consol. Natural Gas Co., 1980-85; dir. mktg. Edison Polymer Innovation Corp., 1985-88; exec. dir. Western Res. Econ. Devel. Coun., 1988-97; pres. T.S.T. Corp.; ret. Bd. dirs. Animal Protective League and Humane Soc. Served with USAAF, 1942-45. Fellow Am. Indsl. Devel. Coun.; mem. Indsl. Devel. Rsch. Coun., Assn. Ohio Commodores, Shaker Heights (Ohio) Country Club, Delta Theta Tau. Presbyterian. Home: 99 Gillette St Painesville OH 44077-2931

SMITH, WILLIE TESREAU, JR. retired judge, lawyer; b. Sumter, S.C., Jan. 17, 1920; s. Willie T. and Mary (Moore) S. ; student Benedict Coll., 1937-40; AB, Johnson C. Smith U., 1947; LLB, S.C. State Coll., 1954, JD, 1976; m. Anna Marie Clark, June 9, 1955; 1 son, Willie Tesreau, III. Admitted to S.C. bar, 1954; began gen. practice, Greenville, 1954; past exec. dir. Legal Svcs. Agy. Greenville County, Inc.; state family ct. judge 13th Jud. Circuit S.C., 1977-91; ret. 1991. Past mem. adv. bd. Greenville Tech. Edn. Ctr. Adult Edn. Program and Para-Legal Program; mem. adv. bd. Greenville Tech. Coll. Found. Bd.; mem., past bd. visitors Presbyn. Coll., Clinton, S.C.; past bd. dirs. Greenville Urban League; past trustee Greenville County Sch. Dist.; past v.p. Peace Ctr. for Performing Arts. With AUS, 1942-45, USAF, 1949-52. Represented in Bell South African Am. History Calendar. Mem. Am., Nat. (jud. coun.), S.C., Greenville County bar assns., Southeastern Lawyers Assn., Nat. Coun. Juvenile and Family Ct. Judges, Am. Legion, Greater Greenville C. of C. (past dir.), Phillis Wheatley Assn. (dir.), NAACP, Omega Psi Phi, Delta Beta Boule, Sigma Pi Phi. Presbyterian (past chmn. bd. trustees Fairfield-McClelland Presbytery, past moderator Foothills Presbytery). Clubs: Masons, Shriners, Rotary. Home: 601 Jacobs Rd Greenville SC 29605-3318

SMITH, WOOLLCOTT, statistician, educator; b. Balt., June 9, 1941; s. Henry Clay and Nancy Woollcott S.; m. Leah Johnson, Feb. 3, 1968; children: Amelia, Keston. BS, Mich. State U., 1962, MS, 1964; PhD, Johns Hopkins U., 1969. Asst. prof. U. N.C., Chapel Hill, 1969-72; sr. statis. Woods Hole (Mass.) Oceanographic Instn., 1972-81; prof. Temple U., Phila., 1981—. Dir. Data Analysis Lab., Temple U., 1982-89; sr. rsch. fellow Woods Hole Oceanographic Instn., 1996-98. Author: (book) The Cartoon Guide to Statistics, 1993; editor: (book) Ecological Diversity in Theory and Practice, 1979. Mem. Am. Statis. Assn. (pres. Phila. chpt. 1988-89). Office: Stats Dept/Temple Univ N Broad & Cecil D Moore Philadelphia PA 19122

SMITH, YOUNG MERRITT, JR. lawyer; b. Hickory, N.C., July 25, 1944; s. Young Merritt and Christine Ellen (White) S.; m. Louise Garner Price, Sept. 6, 1966 (div. Aug. 1974); 1 child, Patrick Adam; m. Charlie Mae Early, Nov. 19, 1977 (div. May 1985); m. Mary Gayle Jones, June 8, 1985; children: Mary Gaither, Jennifer Gayle. AB, U. N.C., 1966; JD, Duke U., 1969. Bar: N.C. 1969. Pres. The Litchfield Plantation Co., Pawleys Island, S.C., 1969-74, The Figure Eight Island Co., Wilmington, N.C., 1971-74; ptnr. Smith and Smith, Hickory, 1974-87; lawyer in pvt. practice, 1987—. Trustee Fund for Peace, N.Y.C., 1970-79, United Health Services N.C., Durham, 1971-73, N.C. Design Found., Raleigh, 1973-76. Mem. N.C. Bar Assn., Delta Kappa Epsilon. Democrat. Episcopalian. Office: Young M Smith Jr Atty PO Drawer 1948 225 4th St NW Ste 200 Hickory NC 28603 E-mail: ysmith@youngsmithlaw.com.

SMITH, YVONNE SMART, advertising executive; b. Asheville, N.C. BFA, Auburn U. Asst. art dir. Mademoiselle mag., N.Y.C.; art dir. Cargill, Wilson & Acree Advt. divsn. Doyle Dane Bernbach; v.p., assoc. creative dir., exec. art dir. Chiat/Day Advt., L.A., sr. v.p., assoc. creative dir. Venice, Venice, N.Y.C., London, mng. ptnr., creative dir. L.A.; prin. Yvonne Smith, Inc. Guest lectr. UCLA, Art Ctr. Coll. Design, L.A., U. So. Calif., L.A., Art Dirs. Club, Paris; co-chair Internat. Clio Awards, 1999. Subject profl. articles. Recipient One Show awards, N.Y. Art Dirs. Club, Andy awards, Belding awards, award, Art Dirs. Club, Steven Kelly awards, Clio awards, Emmy award, 1998, Silver and Bronze Lions, Cannes Film Festival, 1998. Office: 21344 Rambla Vista Malibu CA 90265-5348

SMITH, ZACHARY ALDEN, political science and public administration educator; b. Stanford, Calif., Aug. 8, 1953; s. Alden Wallace and Lelia (Anderson) S. BA, Calif. State U., Fullerton, 1975; MA, U. Calif., Santa Barbara, 1979, PhD, 1984. Adj. lectr. polit. sci. U. Calif., Santa Barbara, 1981-82; asst. prof., dir. Ctr. for Island and Ocean Resources Mgmt. U. Hawaii, Hilo, 1982-87, assoc. prof., 1987-89, No. Ariz. U., Flagstaff, 1989-93, prof., 1993—. Author: Groundwater and the Future of the Southwest, 1984, Groundwater Policy in the Southwest, 1985, Groundwater in the West, 1989, The Environmental Policy Paradox, 3rd edit., 2000, Hawaii State and Local Government, 1992, Politics and Public Policy in Arizona, 1993, 3d edit., 2001, Environmental Politics and Policy in the West, 1993, Groundwater Management in the West, 1999, Hawaii Politics and Government, 2000, The National Environmental Policy Act: Promise Unfilled, 2001. Active campaign for various state propositions, 1970, 74, 76; elected to Orange County (Calif.) Dem. Cen. Com., 1976-78; councilman City of Flagstaff, 1996-98. Rsch. grantee U. Calif., Los Alamos (N.Mex.) Sci. Lab., Water Resources Ctr., Davis, Calif., U.S. Dept. HUD. Mem. ASPA, Am. Water Resources Assn., Am. Polit. Sci. Assn., Southwestern Social Sci. Assn., Western Polit. Sci. Assn., Western Social Scis. Assn. (exec. coun. 1995-99). Office: No Ariz U Dept Polit Sci PO Box 15036 Flagstaff AZ 86011-0001

SMITH-ALNIMER, MARIE MARGARET CELLA, mental health nurse; b. Nyack, N.Y., Oct. 23, 1942; d. Joseph E. and Carmela L. (Renella) Cella; children: Kevin M., Brian C. Diploma, Rockland State Hosp., Orangeburg, N.Y., 1963; BSN, Fairleigh Dickinson U., 1971; MA, NYU, 1974. Edn. coord. N.Y. Hosp., White Plains, 1978-82; asst. prof. Hostos C.C., N.Y.C., Dominican Coll., Blauvelt, N.Y., 1974-76; clin. specialist N.Y. State Psychiat. Inst., N.Y.C., 1988-90; asst. prof. Bronx (N.Y.) C.C., 1992-95, assoc. prof., 1995—. Instr. Herbert H. Lehman Coll., 1981-92; editorial rev. bd. Perspectives in Psychiat. Care, 1978-82; expert witenss, N.Y., N.J. Reviewer Am. Jour. Nursing; contbr. chpts. to books. Mem. ANA, N.Y. State Nurses Assn., Rockland County Mental Health Assn., Sigma Theta Tau. Home: 9 S Edsall Ave Nanuet NY 10954-3102 Office: Bronx Community Coll Nursing Program 181st and Univ Ave Bronx NY 10453 E-mail: mriesmit@optonline.net.

SMITH-ALSTON, TONI COLETTE, government official, social worker; b. Columbus, Ohio, Oct. 31, 1952; BA, Ohio State U., Columbus, 1974, postgrad., 1975-76, postgrad., 1978-90; MS in Edn., U. Dayton, 1993. Lic. social worker, Ohio. Cons. Ohio Dept. Human Svc., Columbus, 1974-75; mgr. Fisher Body Div., 1977-78; with Franklin County Human Svc., 1975—, supr., 1979-86, adminstr., 1986-91, asst. dep. dir., 1991-95, dep. dir., 1996—; v.p. Best Inc., Westerville, Ohio, 1998-2000; CEO TLC/Best, Inc., 2001—. Pub. speaker human svcs. program Franklin County Human Svc., 1988—; instr., human svc. devel. Columbus State C.C., 1990—; grad. United Way Project Diversity Leadership Program; adj. faculty Columbus State C.C., 1998—, Marion Tech. Coll., 1998—. Mem. adv. bd. Columbus City Comprehensive Plan, 1989—, pres. Syntaxis Group Home, Columbus, 1989—; Informed Neighbors Com., 1989—, Berwick Civic Assn., Columbus (v.p. 1990-92, pres. 1992—); trustee Mental Health Assn., Columbus. Mem. AAUW (corr. sec. Columbus Chpt. 1988—), NAFE, LWV, Columbus Women's Network, Berwick Civic Assn. (pres. 1992-94). Democrat. Roman Catholic. Avocations: boating, reading, travel, golf. Home: 6740 Temperance Point St Westerville OH 43082-8747 Office: Franklin County Dept Human Svc 80 E Fulton St Columbus OH 43215-5128 also: TLC/Best Inc 6740 Temperance Pt St Westerville OH 43082 E-mail: tonismith@att.net.

SMITH-CARROLL, MYRTLE, civic worker, former journalist; b. N.Y.C., July 16, 1926; d. John Leo and Violet Jane (Robertson) Reilly; m. Charles Jackson Smith Jr., Sept. 21, 1946 (div. Aug. 1962); children: Charles Jackson III, Lynda Maureen Smith Necker (dec.), Robert William, Raymond Gerard, Rosemary Rita, Walter Alfred, Virginia Anne Werly; m. Charles F. Carroll, Mar. 17, 1979. BA in English, Hunter Coll., 1947. Columnist Midland News, S.I., N.Y., 1960-63, Amsterdam News, N.Y.C., 1963-66; editor religious sect. St. Petersburg (Fla.) Times, St. Petersburg, Fla., 1972-73; diocesan reporter, photographer Fla. Cath., 1973-76; columnist, photographer Pinellas Dem., 1974-76; reporter Sta. WTSP-TV, 1975-76; talk show host Sta. WTSP, 1977-90; media specialist St. Petersburg Fire Dept., 1983-88. Cons. Pinellas County Emergency Med. Svc., Clearwater, Fla., 1987-88, St. Petersburg Jr. Coll., 1992. Asst. prodr.: (TV show) Link to a Lifeline, 1986; prodr.: (child's puppet show) Fire Station 911, 1989; author, prodr.: (theatrical prodn.) Book of Neweronomy, 1995. St. Petersburg rep. on trip to China, 1983; cons. Juvenile Welfare Bd., St. Petersburg, 1992, bd. dirs., 1994—, sec., 1997—; bd. dirs. Brookwood, St. Petersburg, 1992-94, ACLU, Pinellas County, 1994—; state committeewoman Fla. Dem. Party, 1992—; sec. Women's Caucus, Dem. Nat. Com., 1994—; coord. women's network Fla. Dem. Party, 1995—; del. Dem. Nat. Conv., 1992, 96, 2000; del. Women's Initiative on Race, 1998. Recipient Susan B. Anthony award NOW, Pinellas County, 1980. Mem. Suncoast Tiger Bay Club (bd. dirs.). Democrat. Avocations: gardening, creative writing, domestic violence victims' advocate, community redevelopment. Home: 330 Belleair Dr NE Saint Petersburg FL 33704-2437

SMITH-COX, ELIZABETH SHELTON, art educator; b. Washington, Feb. 12, 1924; d. Benjamin Warren and Sarah Priscilla (Harrell) Shelton; m. John Edwin Smith, Aug. 16, 1947 (dec. July 1992); children: Shelley Hobson, Dale Henslee, John Edwin Jr.; m. Headley Morris Cox Jr., Dec. 30, 1994. BA in Art, Meredith Coll., 1946; MEd in Supervision and Adminstrn., Clemson U., 1974. Youth dir. St. John's Bapt. Ch., Charlotte, N.C., 1946-47; art tchr. Raleigh (N.C.) Pub. Schs., 1947-49, East Mecklenberg H.S., Charlotte, 1968-69, D. W. Daniel H.S., Central, S.C., 1970-86; art instr. U. S.C., Columbia, 1966-68; adj. prof. Clemson (S.C.) U., 1991-93; artist-in-residence edn. program S.C. Arts Commn., Columbia, 1991-2001. Exhibited in numerous one and two person shows and in group exhibits; solo show at Meredith Coll. Rotunda Gallery, Raleigh, 2002; invitational alumnae exhibit Meredith Coll., 2000; exhibited in 2-person show Pickeus County (S.C.) Mus., 2000. Vol. worker, editor newsletter Pickens County Habitat for Humanity, Clemson, 1981—; vol. art tchr. St. Andrew's Elem. Sch., Columbia, 1962-68; vol. Habitat for Humanity Mission to Honduras, summers 1996—. Recipient Svc. to Mankind award Clemson Sertoma Club, 1997, Disting. Alumni award Meredith Coll., 1996; named S.C. Tchr. of Yr., S.C. Dept. Edn. and Ency. Britannica, 1976, Citizen of Yr., Clemson Rotary Club, 1979. Mem. S.C. Art Edn. Assn. (pres. 1978, Lifetime Svc. award 1990, Lifetime Achievement in Art Edn. award 1995), Nat. Art Edn. Assn. (ret. art educator affiliate, pres. 1994-97, Disting. Svc. award 1995, Electronic Gallery 1999, 2000, 01, 02, Ret. Art Educator of Yr. award 2000), Nat. Art Edn. Found. (trustee 1996-2002), S.C. Watercolor Soc. (Mem. with Excellence 1993), Upstate Visual Artists (Best in Show award). Baptist. Avocations: travel, reading, writing, music. Home: 1604 Six Mile Hwy Central SC 29630-9483 E-mail: lizhmcox@innova.net.

SMITHEE, JOHN TRUE, lawyer, state legislator; b. Amarillo, Tex., Sept. 7, 1951; s. John J. and Mildred B. (True) S.; m. Becky Collins, Aug. 18, 1979; children: Jennifer, Rebecca, John True. BBA, West Tex. State U., Canyon, 1973; JD, Tex. Tech U., 1976. Bar: Tex. 1976, U.S. Supreme Ct., 1983. Atty. Templeton, Smithee, Hayes, Heinrich & Russell, Amarillo, Tex., 1976—; mem. Tex. Ho. of Reps., Austin, 1985—, chmn. ins. com., 1993—. Mem. State Bar Tex., Amarillo Bar Assn. Republican. Home: 2808 Parker St Amarillo TX 79109-3546 Office: Templeton Smithee Hayes Fields Young & Heinrich PO Box 15010 Amarillo TX 79105-5010

SMITH-EPSTEIN, MARY KATHLEEN, dancer; b. Austin, Tex., Sept. 12, 1940; d. Walter Bentley Jr. and Kathleen Beatrice (Lancaster) Smith; m. Witaly Osins, June 6, 1967 (div. 1975); m. Howard Irwin Epstein, June 20, 1987. Grad. high sch., Dallas. Demi soloist Am. Festival Ballet, European Tour, 1961; prin. dancer HET Nat. Ballet, Amsterdam, Holland, 1962-67; guest artist Berliner Ballet, Berlin, 1964, Ballet De L'Atlantique, Nantes, France, 1967-68, Cologne, Fed. Republic Germany, 1968-70, Ballet Spectacular, Miami, Fla., 1973-74; prin. dancer Opernhaus, Hannover, Fed. Republic Germany, 1968-70, Musiktheater, Gelsenkirchen, Fed. Republic Germany, 1968-71, Ballet Van Vlaanderen, Antwerp, Belgium, 1971-73, Ballet De Wallonie, Charleroi, Belgium, 1973-74, Irish Nat. Ballet, Cork, Ireland, 1975-85, Chgo. Ballet, 1977-78, Ballet Met., Columbus, Ohio, 1978-79; founder, co-dir. Conservatory Classical Dance, Eugene, Oreg., 1989—. Founder N.W. Chamber Ballet, 1988—; artistic dir. 8 Dance Ensemble; guest tchr. Imperial Eleven Ballet, 2000-01, Internat. Ballet Sch., 2000. Choreographer: (ballet) Opus 1, 1978, For Him From Her, 1982, The Catalyst, 1983 (Bursary Irish Arts Council award 1985), Pas De Deux, 1985 (Bursary Irish Arts Council 1985), Logic of the Heart, 1988, Masquerade Suite, 1988, Tango, 1999, Nocturne, 1998, Pro-Fun-Ditties, 1997, No One Knew, 1997; choreographer Ballet N.W., Performing Ensemble Conservatory Classical Dance, 1989—. Treas. Neighborhood Watch, Vida, Oreg., 1988-89, bd. mem. (sec. to pres.) of Lane Arts Coun., 1993-96; dir. bldg. fund, pres. bd. dirs. Kaygu Dakshang Chuling, 1995—. Alexandra Danilova scholar, Dallas, 1958. Buddhist. E-mail: hepsteinor@earthlink.net.

SMITHER, EDWARD MURRAY, art consultant, appraiser; b. Huntsville, Tex., July 23, 1937; s. Douglas Laverne and Cova Estella (Galloway) S. BS in Journalism, Sam Houston State Coll., Huntsville, 1955-58. Asst. editor Middleton Press, Dallas, 1958-60; prodn. editor Tex. Instruments, 1960-64; asst. dir. Atelier Chapman Kelley, 1964-70; co-owner Cranfill Gallery, 1970-72, Delahunty Gallery, Dallas, 1974-83; owner Smither Gallery, 1972-74, Murray Smither Inc., Dallas, 1983—. Mem. art in public places adv. com., Dallas City Coun., 1982-89; advisor artist's eye program, Kimbell Art Mus.,

Ft. Worth, 1987-89. Co-founder Art & Antiques ann. auction Housing Crisis Ctr., Dallas, 1993—; mem. art com. Dart Art Design program Hampton Sta., Dallas, 1992-94. Recipient Legend award Dallas Visual Arts Ctr., 1998. Avocation: collecting art of self-taught artists. Home and Office: 1934 Kessler Pkwy Dallas TX 75208-2727 E-mail: emsart@altinet.net.

SMITHER, HOWARD ELBERT, musicologist, educator; b. Pittsburg, Kans., Nov. 15, 1925; s. Elbert S. and Ethel (Schwab) S.; m. Doris J. Arvin (div. 1976); children: Thomas A., Jesse N. Woodsmith; m. Ann M. Woodward. AB magna cum laude, spl. honors in music, Hamline U., 1950; MA in musicology, Cornell U., 1952; postgrad., U. Munich, 1953-54; PhD in musicology, Cornell U., 1960. Instr. Oberlin Coll. and Conservatory of Music, Oberlin, Ohio, 1955-57, asst. prof., 1957-60, U. Kans., Lawrence, 1960-63; assoc. prof. Tulane U., New Orleans, 1963-68, U. N.C., Chapel Hill, 1968-71, prof., 1971-79, dir. grad. studies in music, 1977-79, 83-84, 86-88, James Gordon Hanes prof. humanities in music, 1979-92, James Gordon Hanes prof. emeritus humanities in music, 1992—; John Bird prof. of music U. Wales, Cardiff, 1993-95. Lectr., chmn. panels regional, nat. and internat. meetings, confs., symposiums, 1964-90. Author: A History of the Oratorio, Vol. 1, The Oratorio in the Baroque Era: Italy, Vienna, Paris, 1977 (transl. Italian), Vol. 2, The Oratorio in the Baroque Era: Protestant Germany and England, 1977 (Deems Taylor award ASCAP 1978), Vol. 3 The Oratorio in the Classical Era, 1987, Vol. 4, Oratorio in the 19th and 20th Centuries, 2000; editor The Italian Oratorio 1650-1800, Vols. 1-3, 6, 8, 11, 12, 13, 16, 18, 19, 20, 24, 25, 27, 1986-87; editor, translator poems in Alfred Einstein's The Italian Madrigal, 1971; author publs. in periodicals, dictionaries, encys., congress reports, record-jacket notes, abstracts, revs.; music rev. editor Notes, 1967-69; mem. editorial bd. Detroit Monographs in Musicology, 1971-87; chmn. editorial bd. Early Musical Masterworks: Editions and Commentaries, 1978-83; mem. editorial bd. Videodisc Music Series, NEH, 1982-86; editor Oratorios of the Italian Baroque, 1983—. Fellow Cornell U., 1953-54, NEH, Italy, 1972-73, England, 1979-80, Guggenheim, 1984-85; Fulbright sr. rsch. grant in Italy, 1965-66, sr. Fulbright lectr. Moscow State Conservatory, 1990. Mem. Am. Mus. Soc. (chmn. S.E. chpt. 1969-71, mem. coun. 1969-71, 75-77, bd. dirs. 1977-79, pres. 1980-82, del. to Am. Coun. Learned Socs. 1984-88, to Internat. Congress Strasbourg 1982), Music Libr. Assn. (bd. dirs. 1968-70), Soc. for Am. Music, Internat. Assn. Jazz Educators, Internat. Trumpet Guild. Avocations: hiking, jazz trumpet performance.

SMITHER-KOPPERL, MARGARET LYDIA, plant pathologist; b. Woking, England, July 8, 1955; d. Derry C. and Lydia (Grugeon) Smither; m. H. Benjamin Kopperl, Sept. 30, 1980; children: Aaron D., Hannah L. BSc in Botany, Royal Holloway U., London, 1976; MSc in Plant Scis., Wye London U., Wye, Kent, London, 1977; PhD in Plant Pathology, Mich. State U., 1988. Rsch. asst. Mich. State U., East Lansing, 1981-88, rsch. assoc., 1988-90; plant physiologist Inst. of Offshore Engring., Orkney, Edinburgh, Scotland, 1991-94; postdoctoral U. Fla., Gainesville, 1995-98; sr. scientist Predation Inc., 1998-99; v.p. rsch. Entomos LLC, 1999—2002. Contbr. articles to profl. jours. Mem. AAAS, Am. Phytopathological Soc. (com. women 1997-2000, soil 1998—). Achievements include research in biocontrol of soilborne pathogens, weeds, and insect pests. Avocations: cooking, swimming, reading. E-mail: mlsk55@aol.com.

SMITHERMAN, DAVID CONRAD, medical marketing professional; b. Tuscaloosa, Ala., July 27, 1953; s. Lowell Conrad and Ruth (Patton) S.; m. Anne Torrey Van Antwerp, Oct. 13, 1979; children: David Van Antwerp, Garet Patton. BA, U. Ala., 1976; MA, Birmingham-So. Coll., 2001. Adminstrv. dir. U. Ala. Mgmt. Inst., Tuscaloosa, 1976-80; mktg. mgr. Gulf States Paper Corp., 1980-86, Advantage Med. Inc., Birmingham, Ala., 1986-90; dir. mktg. Carraway Meth. Health Sys., 1990-99; exec dir. Carraway Hosps. Found., 1993-97; asst. adminstr. for corp. comm. and devel. Carraway Meth. Med. Ctr., 1999—. Advisor Jr. League Birmingham, 1999—. Editor: Culture of Excellence: A History of Carraway Methodist Medical Center Vols. 1-2, 1995. Team capt. Boy Scouts Am., Birmingham, 1993-96, Met. Devel. Bd., Birmingham, 1994-95; mem. comm. com. United Way of Ctrl. Ala., Birmingham, 1996; bd. dirs. Jefferson County Task Force on Infant Immunization, Birmingham, 1996—; bd. dirs., trustee Episcopal Found. of Jefferson County, 1995-2001; trustee Birmingham Broadway Series, Inc., 2001—. Mem. Am. Heart Assn. (bd. dirs. Ala. chpt. 1998—), Am. Cancer Soc. (bd. dirs. Ala. chpt. 1992-96, 98—), Am. Hosp. Assn., Am. Coll. Healthcare Execs., Soc. Healthcare Strategy and Devel., Assn. for Healthcare Philanthropy (bd. dirs., treas. Ala. chpt. 1992—), Ala. Hosp. Assn. Mktg. Soc. (bd. dirs., treas. 1991-98, pres-elect 1998-99, pres. 1999-2000, chmn. bd. 2000—), Mountain Brook Swim and Tennis Club, Pi Kappa Phi Episcopalian. Avocations: tennis, travel, skiing. Home: 752 Montgomery Dr Birmingham AL 35213-2504 Office: Carraway Meth Health Sys 1600 Carraway Blvd Birmingham AL 35234-1913

SMITHERS, DONALD LEE, telecommunication consultant; b. Oklahoma City, Mar. 7, 1937; s. Elmer Horace and Grace Lee (Cothern) S.; m. Ola Merle Sechrist, Apr. 13, 1955; children: Nancy Grace, Donna Merle, Glenda Joyce, Donald Eugene. Student, U. Okla., 1964-70; AAS, Community Coll. of USAF, 1982. Unit tester Western Electric Co., Inc., Oklahoma City, 1958-65, with quality assurance, 1965-66, engring. assoc., 1966-69, mfg. supr., 1969-71, installation supr. Houston, 1971-81; engring. mgr. Southwestern Bell Telephone, 1981-91; sr. project mgr. telecommunication engring. Wiesser Engring. Co., 1991-94; telecom. cons., Sugar Land, Tex., 1994—; project mgr. telecom. engring. Cobb, Fendley & Assocs., Houston, 1994—. Mem. City Coun., Sugar Land, 1997—; mayor pro tem City of Sugar Land, 2001-02. With USAF, 1954-57. Mem. Enlisted Assn. Nat. Guard of U.S. (life), Nat. Guard Assn. Tex. (life, com. chmn. 1976—), Air Force Assn. (Tex. Air Nat. Guard Man of Yr. 1985), Air Force Sgts. Assn., Houston Soc. Telephone Engrs., Telephone Pioneers (pres. 1984-85), Rotary (pres. 1989-90), Masons (32d degree, master Sugar Land 1982-83), Shriners. Republican. Baptist. Avocations: golfing, fishing, hunting. Home and Office: 1327 Bramblebury Dr Sugar Land TX 77478-2442 E-mail: cmsret@swbell.net., smithedl@swbell.net.

SMITHEY, PAMELA, consultant, organist, freelance accompanist; b. Greensboro, N.C., Apr. 6, 1956; d. Calvin Loyd and Mary Lou (Wiles) Smithey. BMusic, Mars Hill (N.C.) Coll., 1978; MMusic, u. S.C., 1981. Organist, music instr. First Bapt. Ch., Kannapolis, N.C., 1992-96; music dir. theater dept. Gardner-Webb U., Boiling Springs, SC, 1996—99, staff accompanist, 1996—2000; music dir., organist Ascension Luth. Ch., Shelby, NC, 1996—2001; organist Trinity Luth .Ch., Greenville, SC, 2002—; freelance accompanist, 2001—; cons. Case Bros. of Spartanburg, N.C., 1999—. Founder, coach Piano Plus Ensemble, Shelby, 1997-2001; organizer benefit concert, cons. Abuse Prevention Coun., Shelby, 1997; piano tchr. Converse Coll., 2002-. Mem.: Choristers Guild, Music Tchrs. Nat. Assn. (profl. tchg. cert 1982), Am. Guild Organists. Avocations: conducting and accompanying, making greeting cards, flower gardening. Office: Case Bros of Spartanburg 906 S Pine St Spartanburg SC 29302-3311

SMITH-HUNTER, ANDREA ELAINE, finance educator, management consultant; b. Apr. 1, 1969; d. Daphne Evadne Smith; m. Andrew Hunter, Aug. 29, 1992; children: Jared Meshak, Gabrielle Elizabeth, Jacob Asiah. B in Acctg., U. West Indies, Mona, 1990, MBA in Fin., 1995; PhD, SUNY, Albany, 2000. Fin. analyst Exxon Corp., Kingston, Jamaica, 1990—92; grad. asst. SUNY, Albany, 1995—99; asst. prof. Siena Coll., Londonville, NY, 1999—. Grantee Harvey Summer grant, 2000; scholar Exxon scholarship, Exxon Corp., 1997. Mem.: PhD Project, Acad. Mgmt., Acad. Mgmt.

SMITHIES, OLIVER, geneticist, educator; b. Halifax, Eng., June 23, 1925; , naturalized; PhD in Biochemistry, Oxford U., Eng., 1951. Postdoctoral fellow phys. chemistry U. Wis., Madison, 1951—53, from asst. prof. to prof. genetics and med. genetics, 1960—63, Leon J. Cole prof., 1971—80, Hilldale prof., 1980—88; rsch. asst., assoc. Connaught Med. Rsch. Lab., Toronto, Canada, 1953—60; Excellence prof. dept. pathology and lab. medicine U. N.C., Chapel Hill, 1988—. Mem. nat. adv. med. sci. coun. NIH, 1985. Contbr. Recipient William Allen Meml. award, Am. Soc. Human Genetics, 1964, Karl Landsteiner Meml. award, Am. Assn. Blood Banks, 1984, Internat. award, Gairdner Found., 1990, 1993, State of N.C. award, 1994, Alfred P. Sloan Jr. prize, 1994; scholar Markle, 1961. Fellow: AAAS; mem.: Genetics Soc. Am. (v.p. 1974, pres. 1975), Am. Acad. Arts & Sci., NAS. Achievements include research in on targeted modification of specific genes in living animals. Office: Univ of N C Dept Pathology & Lab Med Chapel Hill NC 27599-0001

SMITH-JONES, MARY EMILY, elementary school physical education educator; b. Ducktown, Tenn., Jan. 9, 1949; d. Oscar Clinton and Mary Myrtice (Hayes) S. Student, Kennesaw (Ga.) Jr. Coll., 1967-69; BS in Edn., Ga. So. Coll., 1971; MEd, Delta State U., 1974; EdS, West Ga. Coll., 1991. Cert. tchr., Ga. Tchr. phys. edn. East Hall High Sch., Gainesville, Ga., 1971-73, Morrow (Ga.) Elem. Sch., 1974—. Mem. com. to write phys. edn. curriculum for grades kindergarten through 4 State of Ga.; mem. com. to write elem. phys. edn. curriculum Clayton County, Ga. Mem. AAHPERD (mem. conv. hospitality com. 1991), Ga. Assn. Health, Phys. Edn., Recreation and Dance (exhibits chairperson 1992, 93). Home: 180 Falling Waters Dr Jonesboro GA 30236-5485 Office: Morrow Elem Sch 6115 Reynolds Rd Morrow GA 30260-1151

SMITH-LEINS, TERRI L. mathematics educator; b. Salina, Kans., Sept. 19, 1950; d. John W. and Myldred M. (Hays) Smith; m. Larry L. Leins, May 26, 1984. BS, Ft. Hays (Kans.) U., 1973, MS, 1976; AA, Stephen Coll., Columbia, Mo., 1970. Math tchr. Scott City (Kans.) Jr. H.S., Howard (Kans.) Schs.; instr. math. U. Ark., Ft. Smith. Contbr. articles to profl. jours., chpts. to books. Mem. AADE, ASCD, Nat. Assn. Devel. Edn. (state sec. 1986-88, computer access com. 1980-85), Phi Delta Kappa (Kappan of Yr. 1985), Delta Kappa Gamma (state chairperson women in art 1993-95, Kappa state area one leader 1999—). Home: PO Box 3446 Fort Smith AR 72913-3446 E-mail: tleins@uafortsmith.edu.

SMITH MCKEE, MAUREEN JACQUELENE, marketing professional; b. Chgo., Jan. 1, 1967; d. Robert William and Josephine Anne (Trusner) S. BS, Butler U., 1989; MS, Northwestern U., 1996. Public rels. intern Ind. Health Care Assn., Indpls., 1988, Melvin Simon & Assocs., Inc., Indpls., 1988; prodn. designer Inst. Real Estate Mgmt., Chgo., 1989-90, program coord., 1990-95; dir. mktg. and pub. rels. Am. Warehouse Assn., 1995-97; dir. mktg. comm. Logix, 1997-98; dir. mktg. Stanard & Assocs., Inc., Chgo., 1998-99; dir. mktg. and pub. rels. Universal Tng., Northbrook, Ill., 1999—. Mem. Pub. Rels. Soc. Am., Am. Mktg. Assn. Democrat. Roman Catholic. Home: 586 Farina Ct Mundelein IL 60060-2649 E-mail: msmckee@universaltraining.com.

SMITH-SANDERS, CAROL ANN, music therapist, psychologist; b. Montgomery County, Tenn., Apr. 19, 1951; d. Carl and Ruth (Gettinger) S. BME in Music Therapy, U. Kans., 1974; MA in Clin. Psychology, Mid. Tenn. State U., 1977; EdS in Human Svc. Mgmt., Vanderbilt U., 1979; EdD in Ednl. Adminstrn., Auburn U., 1997. Gen. therapeutic recreation specialist VA Med. Ctr., Murfreesboro, Tenn., 1973-79, music therapist Marion, Ind., 1979, chief recreation therapy service Tucson, 1979-84, chief recreation therapy Northport, N.Y., 1984-87, health systems specialist Dir.'s Office Cleve., 1987-88, adminstrv. asst. to assoc. dir., 1988-91, adminstrv. asst. to chief of staff Tuskegee, Ala., 1991-97; sr. health sys. specialist, med. dir. clin. programs Ctrl. Ala. Vets. Health Care sys., 1997—. Adj. instr. Mid. Tenn. State U., part-time 1978—; guest speaker, 1975—; facilitator AchieveGlobal. Contbr. articles to profl. jours. Mem. Am. Psychol. Assn. (assoc.), Nat. Assn. Music Therapy (cert.), NAFE, Pi Lambda Theta, Phi Kappa Phi. Home: 1003 Wallace Ave Opelika AL 36801-6958

SMITHSON, CHARLES WAYNE, economist, consultant; b. Dallas, Sept. 29, 1946; s. Charles Winston and LaVerne (Putman) S.; m. Cynthia Ann Thomas, May 18, 1973; children: Nathan Thomas, Charles Matthew. BA in Econs., U. Tex., Arlington, 1969, MA, 1973; PhD, Tulane U., 1976. Instr. econs. U. New Orleans, 1975-76; asst. prof. Tex. A&M U., College Station, 1976-82, assoc. prof., 1983-85; sr. economist FTC, CPSC, 1982-83; v.p. Chase Manhattan Bank, N.Y.C., 1985-87, mng. dir. risk mgmt. rsch., 1990—94, sr. v.p., 1994—95; AT&T resident mgmt. fellow Simon Grad. Sch. Bus. U. Rochester, 1987; prof. fin. dir. PhD program U. North Tex., Denton, 1987-88; v.p. product devel., risk mgmt. products Continental Bank, Chgo., 1988-89, mng. dir. rsch., product devel. global trading, distbn., 1989-90; mng. dir. sch. fin. products CIBC World Markets, N.Y.C., 1995—99; mng. ptnr. Rutter Assocs., 1999—. Mem. working group Group of 30 Derivatives Project. Author: (with others) The Economics of Mineral Extraction, 1980, (with S.C. Maurice) Managerial Economics, 1981, (with S.C. Maurice) The Doomsday Myth: 10,000 Years of Economic Crisis, 1984, (with others) Managing Financial Risk, 1990, 94, (edited collection with C.W.Smith) Handbook of Financial Engineering, 1990; assoc. editor Financial Management; author (with others) of numerous monographs; adv. bd. Jour. Applied Corp. Fin.; contbr. articles to profl. jours. and other publs. 1st lt. USAF, 1969-73. 1st lt. USAF, 1969—73. Mem. Fin. Mgmt. Assn., Am. Econ. Assn., Internat. Assn. Fin. Engrs. (bd. dirs.). Avocations: golf, sailing, snorkeling. Home: 190 Shelter Ln Jupiter FL 33469 Office: Ste 2110 275 Madison Ave New York NY 10016-1101

SMITHSON, DAVID MATTHEW, lawyer; b. Chgo., Jan. 14, 1957; s. Paul Stanley and Barbara Jane (Sherman) S.; m. Susan Marie Bletcher, Aug. 11, 1984; 1 child, Rachel Carmella. BS, U. Oreg., 1980; JD, Boston Coll., 1984. Bar: Calif. 1985, Conn. 1997, U.S. Dist. Ct. (ctrl. dist.) Calif. 1985, U.S. Dist. Ct. (so. dist.) Calif. 1987. Atty. Parker & Stanbury, L.A., 1984-89, Shield & Smith, L.A., 1989-91, Hornberger & Criswell, L.A., 1991-93, Chapman & Glucksman, L.A., 1993-95, Cummins & White, L.A., 1995—. Avocations: tennis, golf, travel, museums. Home: 624 S Grand Ave Ste 1900 Los Angeles CA 90017-3320

SMITH TARCHALSKI, HELEN MARIE, piano educator; b. Washington, Dec. 24, 1957; d. Albert John and Marie Ethel (Wellens) Smith; m. Stanislaw Edward Tarchalski, Sept. 26, 1981. MusB in Applied Piano, Peabody Conservatory Md., 1979. Master cert. music tchr. Ind. piano instr., accompanist, various cities, 1978—; edn. rep., clinician Baldwin Piano and Organ Co., 1982-94. Clinician various univs., 1984—; com. mem., seminar leader Nat. Conf. on Piano Pedagogy, Chgo., 1990-94; mem. adv. bd. Pacific Music Alliance, Pasadena, Calif., 1994-97; mem. organizing com. World Piano Pedagogy Conf., 1996—. Editor (periodical) Soundboard, 1989-94, (textbook) Teaching Toward Tomorrow, 1994; contbg. author Encyclopedia of Keyboard Instruments, 1994, various jours.; author (computer software) Symbol Simon, 1995. Mem. Am. Liszt Soc. (bd. dirs. 1996—), Music Tchrs. Nat. Assn., Md. State Music Tchrs. Assn. (tech. chair 1996—), Montgomery County Music Tchrs. Assn. (pres. 1999—), Anapolis Sch. Music, 1998—. Avocations: scuba diving, water skiing, sailing, biking, rollerblading. Home: 1802 River Watch Ln Annapolis MD 21401-2009

SMITH-THOMPSON, PATRICIA ANN, public relations consultant, educator; b. Chgo., June 7, 1933; d. Clarence Richard and Ruth Margaret (Jacobson) Nowack; children: Deborah, Kurt, Nancy, Janna, Gail, Lori; m. Tyler Thompson, Aug. 1, 1992. Student, Cornell U., 1951-52; BA, Centenary Coll., Hackettstown, N.J., 1983. Prodn. asst. Your Hit Parade Batten, Barton, Durstine & Osborne, 1953-54; pvt. practice polit. cons., 1954-66; legal sec., asst. Atty. John C. Cushman, 1966-68; field dep. L.A. County Assessor Office, 1968-69; pub. info. officer L.A. County Probation Dept., 1969-73; dir. consumer rels. Fireman's Fund, San Francisco, 1973-76; spl. projects officer L.A. County Transp. Commn., 1977-78; tchr. Calif. State U., Dominguez Hills, 1979-86. Editor, writer Jet Propulsion Lab., 1979-80; pub. info. dir. L.A. Bd. Pub. Works, 1980-82; pub. info. cons. City of Pasadena, Calif., 1982-84; pub. rels. cons., 1983-90; cmty. affairs cons. Worldport L.A., 1990-92; substitute tchr. Tehachapi Unified Schs., 2002. Contbr. articles to profl. jours. Active First United Meth. Ch. Commn. on Missions and Social Concerns, 1983-89; bd. dirs. Depot, 1983-87; devel. com. Pasadena Guidance Clinics, 1984-85; pres. Cultural Arts Assn., Bear Valley Springs, 1999-2000. Calif Press Women, Bay Area, 1975. Recipient Pro award L.A. Publicity Club, 1978, Outstanding Achievement award Soc. Consumer Affairs Profls. in Bus., 1976, Disting. Alumni award Centenary Coll., 1992. Mem. Pub. Rels. Soc. Am. (accredited mem., award for consumer program, 1977, 2 awards, 1984, Joseph Roos Cmty. Svc. award 1985), Nat. Press Women (pub. rels. award 1986), Calif. Press Women (pres. Bay area 1975-76, awards 1974, 78, 83, 84, 85, cmty. rels. 1st place winner 1986, 87, 88, 89), Nat. Assn. Mental Health Info. Officers (3 regional awards 1986). Republican. Home and Office: 24145 Jacaranda Dr Tehachapi CA 93561-8309

SMITH-YOUNG, ANNE VICTORIA, health services coordinator; b. Long Beach, Calif., Aug. 25, 1947; d. James Warren and Jeanne Anne (Cooney) Wright; m. Lynn Walker Smith, Aug. 11, 1968 (div. Feb. 1980); children: Amy Lyanne and Caroline Walker (twins); m. Stephen Nicholas Young, May 29, 1982. AS, Long Beach City Coll., 1967; BS, Marymount Coll., 1984. Diplomate Certification Bd. for Urologic Nurses and Assocs. Mgr. office Williams-Brinton Med. Corp., Huntington Beach, Calif., 1975-80; adminstr. Westchester Urol. Assocs., White Plains, N.Y., 1980-82; adminstr. Pediatric Urol. Assocs. Westchester Med. Ctr., Valhalla, 1982-86, clin. coord. urodynamics lab. cystoscopy ste. dept. urology, 1986-2000, chairperson exec. com. employee adv. coun., 1987-2000. Cons. Office Career Svcs., Marymount (N.Y.) Coll., 1984—, Cert. Bd. Urologic Nurses & Assocs., 1980-87, sec., 1987-93; pres., co-dir. Continence Restored Inc., 1984—; cons. to mfrs., individuals and healthcare providers on urinary incontinence and urodynamics; pres. Y&Y Interactives, 1996—; editl. adv. bd. The Incontinence Product Sourcebook, 1999-2001, clin. editor, 2001—. Mem. editorial bd. Sex Over Forty; contbr. articles to profl. jours. Bd. dirs. Women's Healthcare Network, 1999—; charter mem. Nat. Mus. of Women in Art, Women's Health Resource Network. Mem.: NAFE, Am. Assn. Med. Assts., Assn. Urinary Continence Control (bd. dirs. 1988—92), Soc. Urology Nurses and Assocs. (nat. fundraiser 1980—86, bd. dirs. N.Y. chpt. 1988—95, Recognition award 1984), Nat. Mus. Women in the Arts (charter mem.), Nat. Trust for Historic Preservation, Lions (pres. 1991—93, dist. 20-R2, zone chmn. 1993—94, region chmn. 1994—95, cabinet sec. 1995—96, cabinet treas. 1996—97, vice dist. gov. 1997—98, dist. gov. 1998—99, editor Lions Roar newsletter, bd. dirs. White Plains 1989—91, 1997—, Lion of Month award 1990, Officer of Yr. award 1991, Melvin Jones fellow 1996, Robert J. Uplinger Svc. award 1999, Westchester County Disting. Svc. award 1999), Mothers of Twins Club (pres. Long Beach 1974—75). Democrat. Avocations: fitness, travel, reading, sewing, swimming. Home: 407 Strawberry Hill Ave Stamford CT 06902-2513 E-mail: as4young@optonline.net.

SMITKA, MICHAEL JOHN, economics educator; b. Ft. Knox, Ky., Nov. 16, 1953; m. Gloria Amayun, July 1980; children: Mayumi Beth, John Morgan. AB cum laude, Harvard U., 1975; PhD in Econs., Yale U., 1989. Staff Internat. Fin. Ctr. Bank of Tokyo, N.Y.C., 1977-80; Intern Small and Medium Bus. Agy., Tokyo, 1982; Fulbright researcher Hitotsubashi U., 1983-85; asst. prof. Washington and Lee U., Lexington, Va., 1986-91, assoc. prof., 1991—. Rsch. fellow Japan Found., vis. scholar Faculty of Law Rikkyo U., Tokyo, 1991-92; vis. prof. Internat. U. Japan, 1997; rschr. Internat. Motor Vehicle program MIT, Cambridge; judge automotive supplier of yr. PACE award. Author: Competitive Ties, 1991; editor Japanese Econ. History, 7 vols., 1998. Mem. Good Shepher Luth. Ch., Lexington, 1987—; sec.-treas. The EMBA Found., Inc., 1987—. Grantee Econ. Housing grantee, NEH, 1997, Short-Term Rsch. grantee, Japan Found., 2002. Mem. Am. Econ. Assn., Assn. Christian Economists, Assn. Japanese Bus. Studies. Democrat. Evangelical Christian. Office: Washington and Lee U Williams Sch Commerce Lexington VA 24450

SMITS, EDWARD JOHN, museum consultant; b. Freeport, N.Y., Dec. 11, 1933; s. Karl M. and Jennie (Spring) S.; m. Ruth K. Hall; children: E. John, Robert K., Theodore R. BA, Hofstra U., 1955; MA, NYU, 1959. Curator Nassau County Hist. Mus., East Meadow, N.Y., 1956-70; dir. mus. svcs. Div. Mus. Svcs. Nassau County, Syosset, 1971-92. Nassau County historian, 1985—; planning coord. Mus. at Mitchel Ctr., 1994-2001; chmn. Nassau County Centennial Com.; CEO Nassau Heritage, 2002-. Author: Long Island Landmarks, 1970, Creation of Nassau County, 1959, Nassau, Suburbia U.S.A., 1974. Trustee Friends for L.I.'s Heritage, Nassau County Hist. Soc.; trustee, past pres. Levittown Libr. Bd. 1st lt. U.S. Army, 1955-56. Fulbright grantee, 1965; recipient Nassau County disting. svc. award, 1970, alumni disting. svc. award Hofstra U., 1970, H. Sherwood Historic Preservation on L.I. award Soc. for the Preservation of L.I. Antiquities, 1975. Mem. Am. Assn. Mus. Avocations: book collecting, antique toys, golf. Home: 14 Wavy Ln Wantagh NY 11793-1202

SMITS, HELEN LIDA, physician, administrator, educator; b. Long Beach, Calif., Dec. 3, 1936; d. Theodore Richard Smits and Anna Mary Wells; m. Roger LeCompte, Aug. 28, 1976; 1 child, Theodore. BA with honors, Swarthmore Coll., 1958; MA, Yale U., 1961, MD cum laude, 1967. Intern, asst. resident Hosp. U. Pa., 1967-68; fellow Beth Israel Hosp., Boston, 1969-70; chief resident Hosp. U. Pa., 1970-71; chief med. clinic U. Pa., 1971-75; assoc. adminstr. for patient care svcs. U. Pa. Hosp., 1975-77; v.p. med. affairs Community Health Plan Georgetown U., Washington, 1977; dir. health standards and quality bur. Health Care Financing Adminstrn., HHS, 1977-80; sr. rsch. assoc. The Urban Inst., 1980-81; assoc. prof. Yale U. Med. Sch., New Haven, 1981-85; assoc. v.p. for health affairs U. Conn. Health Ctr., Farmington, 1985-87; prof. community medicine U. Conn. Sch. Medicine, 1985-93; hosp. dir. John Dempsey Hosp., 1987-93; dep. adminstr. Health Care Financing Adminstrn., Washington, 1993-96; pres., chmn. Health Right, Inc., Meriden, Conn., 1996-99; vis. prof. Robert F. Wagner Grad. Sch. Pub. Svc., NYU, 1999—. Commr. Joint Com. on Accreditation Hosps., Chgo., 1989-93, chair, 1991-92; mem., co-chair strategic framework bd. Nat. Forum on Health Care Quality Measurement and Reporting, 2000—. Contbr. numerous articles to profl. jours. Bd. dirs. The Ivoryton Playhouse Fedn., Inc., 1990-92, The Connecticut River Mus., 1990-93, Hartford Stage, 1990-93; mem. Dem. Town Com., Essex, Conn., 1982-89. Recipient Superior Svc. award HHS, Washington, 1982; Royal Soc. Medicine Found. fellow, London, 1973; Fulbright scholar, 1959-60. Mem. ACP (master, regent 1984-90), Inst. Medicine, Nat. Acad. Scis., Phi Beta Kappa, Alpha Omega Alpha. Episcopalian. Avocations: sailing, cooking, gardening. Office: 4 Washington Sq N Rm 23 New York NY 10003-6671

SMITS, KATHLEEN CURRAN, artist, educator; b. Urbana, Ill., Oct. 14, 1958; d. David James and Ruth Nancy (Judson) Curran; m. Allan Wayne Smits, May 28, 1988; 1 child, Samuel. BS in Plant and Soil Scis., U. Mass., 1981. Greenhouse mgr. Conn. Valley Biol. Supply Co., Southampton, Mass., 1982-85; bus. owner Mass., Tex., Conn., 1986-97; artist, tchr. Cheshire, Conn., 1996—; exhibit dir. Cheshire Acad., 2001—. Tchr., cons. Housatonic Children's Ctr., Ansonia, Conn., 1997-98; art edn. dir. Wallinford (Conn.) Parks and Recreation, 1997-2000; tchr. Stratford (Conn.) Childs Ctr., 1999-2000; dir. art exhibit Cheshire Pub. Libr., 1999—; mem. faculty fine arts dept. Cheshire (Conn.) Acad. Exhibited paintings at Salmagundi Club, N.Y.C., West Hartford Art League (award), Housatonic Art League (award), Arts & Crafts Assn., Meriden (award), others. Chair environ. com. Mansfield (Tex.) C. of C., 1990—93; chair Mansfield Area Fund, 1990—95; v.p. Mansfield C. of C., 1990—91; bd. dirs., ann. show chair Cheshire (Conn.) Art League, 1998, 2000, 2001, v.p. in charge of programs, 1998—2000; chair adult edn. com. First Congl. Ch. of Cheshire. Recipient Citizen of Yr. award Mansfield C. of C., 1991, Unsung Hero award Trust for Pub. Land, 1992, Citizen's Excellence award City of Mansfield, 1996 Mem.: West Hartford Art League, New Britain Mus. Am. Art, Assn. Ctrl. Conn. Artists (founding pres. 1998), Arts and Crafts Assn. Meriden (bd. dirs. 1997), Kent Art Assn., Oil Painters Am., Am. Artists Profl. League. Avocations: gardening, environmental activist, cross country skiing, hiking, bird watching. E-mail: Kathycsmits@cs.com.

SMITS, RONALD FRANCIS, English educator, poet; b. Bayonne, N.J., Dec. 22, 1943; s. Edwin Joseph and Florence Ann Smits; m. Bonnie Lee Brown, June 10, 1970 (div. Mar. 1976); 1 child, Ronald Thomas. AB, Rutgers U., 1966; MS, Ind. State U., 1969; PhD, Ball State U., 1978. Instr. English, Kaskaskia Coll., Centralia, Ill., 1969-74; instr. Ball State U., Muncie, Ind., 1976-78; asst. prof. English, Indiana U. Pa., 1979-92, assoc. prof., 1992-96, prof., 1996—. Dir. faculty forum br. campus Indiana U. Pa., Kittanning, 1998—. Contbr. poetry to various publs., including So. Rev., Wildsong, Poetry East, Jour. AMA, Pa. English, The Tex. Observer, Appalachia, Coll. English, Nat. Forum, Tar River Poetry, Jour. of Poetry Therapy. 1st lt. U.S. Army, 1966-68, Vietnam. Doctoral fellow Ball State U., 1974-78. Avocations: walking, nature hikes, walks through city neighborhoods, nature study, reading. Home: PO Box 466 Ford City PA 16226-0466 Office: Ind U of Pa Armstrong County Campus Kittanning PA 16201

SMITTLE, NELSON DEAN, military analyst, artist; b. Peebles, Ohio, Sept. 19, 1934; s. Nelson John and Alma Katherine (Green) S.; m. Claire Wiggins, May 5, 1973. BS, BFA, U. Cin., 1962, MA, 1971. Commd. 2d lt. U.S. Army, 1962; staff officer U.S. Army Photo Agy. Pentagon, Washington, 1966; detachment comdr. tactical comms. Republic South Vietnam, 1967-68; commn. transferred to USAF, 1970; instr. art U. Cin., 1972; comdr. 907th communications squadron Rickenbacker AFB, Ohio, 1972; dir. ops. fixed communications Air Combat Command Langley AFB, Va., 1982; dir. info. systems AWACS Saudi Arabia, 1984-85; dep. chief of staff standard systems Air Material Command Wright-Patterson AFB, Ohio, 1985; comdr. engring.

installation divsn. Tinker AFB, Okla., 1988; commd. col., ret. USAF, Cin., 1988, 91, ret., 1991; pres. Falcon Techs., 1991-98; tchr. Princeton City Sch. Dist., 1992-94; pres. Thumbs Up Aerospace Art, 1998—; instr. art history Cin. State Tech. & Cmty. Coll., 2000—; mil. analyst Fox 19 TV, WLW AM Radio, Cin., 2001—; lectr. Thumbs Up Am., Ams. at War, 2001—; asst. prof. drawing and painting Clermont Coll., U. Cin., 2002—. Cons. Air War Coll., Air Univ., Maxwell AFB, Ala., 1987—, Defense Systems Mgmt. Coll., Ft. Belvior, Va., 1988—; lectr. spl. ops. Warrior Found., 2002—. Author: Army Visual Presentation, 1966 (medal 1966), Famous Moments in Aerospace History, 1997; exhibited in group shows Mus. of Flight, Seattle, 1997, Midland (Mich.) Arts Ctr., 1997, Wichita Ctr Arts, 1998, Ralice Studio, Cin., 1998, Master Works Exhibit, Cin., 1999, Cin. Mus. Ctr., 1998, Mus. Aviation, Warner Robbins, Ga., 1999, Pub. Libr. Cin., Hamilton County, Ohio, 1999, Cin. Art Club, 2001; author cover art Jour of League of World War I Aviation Historians, Jour. WWI Aviation Historians, 1999 Mem. Batavia (Ohio) City Coun., 1972; pres. Ohio Buckeye Wing Assn., Columbus, 1973; mem. Air Force Policy Coun., Washington, 1978; congl. campaign mgr., 1993; bd. dirs. Cin. Art Club, 1995-96. Decorated Commendation medal; recipient Meritorious Svc. medal Dept. Def., 1986, 91. Mem. DAV, VFW, Air Force Assn., Res. Officers Assn., Am. Soc. Aviation Artists, Aircraft Owners and Pilots Assn. Avocations: freelance writer, walking, science fiction, lecturer, military analyst. Home and Office: Thumbs Up Aerospace Art 198 Palisades Pointe Cincinnati OH 45238-5653

SMOAK, EVAN L. lawyer; b. Columbia, S.C., Jan. 30, 1967; s. Lewis E. and Phyllis Anderson. BAS cum laude, U. S.C., 1989; JD, U. Va., 1992. Bar: Conn. 1992, N.Y. 1993, U.S. Dist. Ct. (so. and ea. dists.) N.Y. 1993, U.S. Ct. Appeals (2d cir.) 2000. Actor S.C. Ednl. Television, Columbia, 1977-86; atty. Werner & Kennedy, N.Y.C., 1992-97; assoc., ptnr. Barger & Wolen, 1997—. Art auction co-chair Empire State Pride Agenda, N.Y.C., 1996-98, devel. com., 1999—, bd. dirs., 2000—, N100 fundraiser co-chair, 2001-02, exec. com. 2002—, bd. counsel, 2002; vice-chair fall dinner fundraiser, 2002—. Recipient Thomas Moore Craig award U. S.C., 1988; Carolina scholar, 1985-89, Nat. Merit scholar, 1985-89. Mem. ABA, Assn. Bar of City of N.Y., Phi Beta Kappa, Omicron Delta Kappa. Democrat. Home: 445 W 23d St New York NY 10011 Office: Barger & Wolen 500 5th Ave Fl 46 New York NY 10110-4699 E-mail: esmoak@barwol.com.

SMOAK, RANDOLPH DUNCAN, JR. surgeon; b. Bamberg, S.C., May 5, 1933; MD, Med. Coll. S.C., 1959. Diplomate Am. Bd. Surgery. Intern Grady Meml. Hosp., Atlanta, 1959-60; resident surgery Med. U. S.C.-Teaching Hosps., 1962-65, resident, tchg. fellow, 1965-66; fellow surgery MD Anderson Cancer Ctr., Houston, 1966-67; surg. staff Orangeburg (S.C.) Calhoun Regional Hosp., 1967-87, emeritus staff, 1987; clin. prof. surgery Med. U. S.C., Charleston, 1987—, U.S.C. Sch. Medicine, Columbia, 86—. Fellow ACS; mem. AMA (pres. 2000-01), So. Med. Assn., Soc. Head and Neck Surgeons, So. Soc. Clin. Surgeons, Soc. Clin. Oncology. E-mail: randy. Office: 275 Mason Rd Orangeburg SC 29118-8201 E-mail: smoak@ama-assn.org.

SMOCK, DONALD JOE, governmental liaison, political consultant; b. Ponca City, Okla., Sept. 24, 1964; s. Joe Clellan and Ruth Esther Smock. BA in Polit. Sci., U. Ctrl. Okla., 1991, MA in Urban Affairs, 1993. Rschr. The Nigh Inst. State Govt., Edmond, 1993-94. U. Ctrl. Okla. del. to Ctr. Study of Pres. Symposium, Washington, 1993; govt. liaison Elizey Electric Motor Co., 1994-96; govt. affairs dir. Oklahoma City Met. Assn. Realtors, 1997—. Charter founder Ronald Reagan Rep. Ctr., 1989; del. State of Okla. Rep. Presdl. Task Force, 1996; mem. Rep. Presdl. Trust, 1996. Recipient Okla. Rep. Blue Key award, 1984, Presdl. Commn., 1992, Merit cert. Rep. Nat. Com., 1990; named to Ronald Reagon Rep. Ctr. Presdl. Commemorative Honor Roll, 1991; by order of President George Bush flag dedicated in name Rotunda of U.S. Capitol, 1990. Mem. Tau Kappa Epsilon (Delta Nu colony inductee, chpt. advisor 1990-92, Fraternity for Life iniductee, David Crain Leadership award 1986, Ed Howell Leadership award 1988-89, Red Carnation Ball dedicated in name 1989-90, 94, Top Alumnus 1990-91), Pi Sigma Alpha. Republican. Mem. Ch. of Christ. Home: PO Box 6323 Edmond OK 73083-6323

SMOCK, RAYMOND WILLIAM, historian; b. Jeffersonville, Ind., Feb. 8, 1941; s. Richard and Lottie (Paciorek) S.; m. Phyllis Lee Chadwick, Feb. 12, 1961 BA, Roosevelt U., Chgo., 1966; PhD, U. Md., College Park, 1974. Rsch. asst. Md. Constl. Conv., Annapolis, 1967-68; lectr. in history U. Md., College Park, 1968-72; co-editor The Booker T. Washington Papers, 14 vols., 1972-83; pres. Instructional Resources Corp., Lanham, Md., 1976-83, Rsch. Materials Corp., College Park, 1982-83, dir., 1982-85; historian, dir. Office for Bicentennial, U.S. Ho. of Reps., Washington, 1983-89, Office of Historian, U.S. Ho. of Reps., Washington, 1989-95. Mem. bd. editorial advisers Md. Historian, College Park, 1971-95; hist. cons., 1995-2002; dir. Ctr. for Legis. Studies, Shepherd Coll., Shepherdstown, W.Va., 2002—; sr. hist. cons. Biography of Am. telecourse, WGBH, Boston, 2000-2001. Author: A Talent for Detail: The Photographs of Miss Frances Benjamin Johnston 1889-1910, 1974; co-editor: A Guide to Manuscripts in the Presidential Libraries, 1985, Masters of the House, 1998; editor:Booker T. Washington in Perspective: The Essays of Louis R. Harlan, 1988; author, editor: Landmark Documents on the U.S. Congress, 1998. Ford Found. fellow, 1970; recipient Philip M. Hamer award Soc. Am. Archivists, 1979 Mem. Nat. Coun. Pub. History, Assn. for Documentary Editing (pres. 1983-84), Orgn. Am. Historians, So. Hist. Assn., Soc. History in Fed. Govt. (v.p./pres.-elect 2000— Avocations: photography; astronomy. E-mail: RaySmock@aol.com.

SMOCK, TIMOTHY ROBERT, lawyer; b. Richmond, Ind., June 24, 1951; s. Robert Martin and Thelma Elizabeth (Cozad) S.; m. Martha Carolene Middleton, Apr. 4, 1992; children: Andrew Zoller, Alison Pierce. BA, Wittenberg U., 1973; JD cum laude, Ind. U., 1977. Bar: Ind. 1977, Ariz. 1979, U.S. Dist. Ct. (so. dist.) Ind. 1977, U.S. Dist. Ct. Ariz. 1979, U.S. Ct. Apeals (7th cir.) 1977, U.S. Ct. Appeals (9th cir.) 1979. Jud. clk. Ct. of Appeals of Ind., Indpls., 1977-79; assoc. Lewis and Roca, Phoenix, 1979-82; assoc./shareholder Gallagher & Kennedy, 1982-89; ptnr. Scult, French, Zwillinger & Smock, 1989-94, Smock and Weinberger, Phoenix, 1994-99, Richards and Smock, Phoenix, 1999—. Judge, pro tempore Maricopa County Superior Ct., Phoenix, 1989—; faculty, State Bar Course on Professionalism, Ariz. Supreme Ct./State Bar, Phoenix, 1992—; speaker, Continuing Legal Edn., Maricopa County and Ariz. State Bar, 1988—. Mem. ABA, Ariz. Bar Assn., Maricopa Bar Assn., Def. Rsch. Inst. Office: Richards and Smock 1202 E Missouri Ave Ste 150 Phoenix AZ 85014-2900 E-mail: Timothy.Smock@azbar.org.

SMOKE, RICHARD EDWIN, lawyer, investment adviser; b. Detroit, Sept. 16, 1945; s. Bruno Donald and Else Marie (Reinvaldt) S. BA, Kalamazoo (Mich.) Coll., 1967; JD, Wayne State U., 1970. Bar: Mich. 1970, Calif. 1975, U.S. Supreme Ct. 1980. Gen. counsel Grosse Ile (Mich.) Bridge Co., 1975-78, pres., 1980-83, v.p., 1983—88; gen. counsel Campbell-Ewald Co., Warren, Mich., 1978-80; pvt. practice law, investment adviser Grand Rapids, 1985—2002. Dir. Kent County Cmty. Mental Health, 1996; adj. faculty Davenport Coll., 1993-95; trustee Grand Rapids Charter Twp., 1991-96; commr. County of Kent, 1996-2002. Bd. dirs. World Affairs Coun. Western Mich., Grand Rapids, 1988-93, pres., 1991-92; mem. exec. com. Kent County Rep. Party, Grand Rapids, 1989-92, 1995-2002; trustee Kalamazoo Coll., 1970-79. London-Sloan fellow, 1983. Mem.: Investment Analysts Chgo., State Bar Calif., State Bar Mich. Home: PMB 428 588 Sutter St San Francisco CA 94102-1102 E-mail: RESMOKE@CS.COM.

SMOKER, ROY ELLIS, military officer; b. Richmond, Ind., Dec. 7, 1943; s. Vernon Willard and Emma May (Creager) S.; m. Linda Carol Kensinger, Sept. 7, 1969; children: Cheryl Lynn, Deborah June; m. Jo Ann Bratcher, May, 2001. BA in Econs. and Math., Blackburn Coll., 1965; MA in Econs., U. N.D., 1967; PhD, U. Mo., 1984. Commd. 2d lt. USAF, 1971, advanced through grades to col., 1992, chief rsch. integration Office Productivity and Rsch., 1980-82, sr. mil. estate program analyst Office Sec. Def., 1982-84, sr. logistics analyst, 1984-85, dep. dir., dir. program control Milstar Joint Program Office, 1985-89, chief econ. analysis asst. sec. USAF for fin. mgmt., 1989-90, chief space and strategic def., 1990-91; dir. bus. ops. Titan Sys. Program Office, 1991-93; comptroller Arnold (Tenn.) Engring. Devel. Ctr., 1993-95, Air Force Devel. TestCtr., 1995-97, Air Force Space and Missile System Ctr., 1997-2000; dir. program mgmt. MCR Fed., Inc., 2001—. Bd. dirs. Aerospace Fed. Credit Union, 1998—2000. Bd. dirs. Aerospace Fed. Credit Union, 1998-2000; fin. advisor Alzheimer's Assn., Tullahoma, Tenn., 1993-95; chmn. bd. trustees 1st United Meth. Ch., Huntington Beach, Calif., 1987-89. Decorated Joint Svc. Achievement medals, Air Orgnl. Excellence award, and numerous others. Mem. Mo. U. Alumni Assn., Air Force Assn., Soc. Cost Estimating and Analysis, Am. Soc. Mil. Comptrollers (pres. L.A. chpt. 1998), Franklin County C. of C. (bd. dirs. 1993-95).

SMOKER, WENDY RUE KARTINOS, neuroradiologist, consultant, educator; b. Evanston, Ill., Feb. 28, 1948; d. Nicholas John and Marjorie (Smith) Kartinos; 1 child, Andrew Jason Smoker. BS, U. Iowa, 1971, MS, 1972, MD, 1977. Diplomate Am. Bd. Radiology. Asst. prof. radiology U. Iowa Hosps., Iowa City, 1982-86; assoc. prof. radiology U. Utah, Salt Lake City, 1986-90, acting dir. neuroradiology, 1989-90; prof. radiology Med. Coll. of Va., Richmond, 1990—2001, dir. neuroradiology, 1990-2000, prof. neurosurgery, 1997—2001, prof. otolaryngology, 1998—2001; prof. radiology U. Iowa Hosps., Iowa City, 2002—. Contbr. chpts. to books; dep. editor Radiology, 1997-01; mem. editl. adv. bd. Am. Jour. Neuroradiology, 1989-97, The Radiologist, 1993-96, Stroke, 1996-97. Fellow Am. Coll. Radiology; mem. Am. Soc. Head and Neck Radiology (pres. 1998-99, first past pres. 1999-2000, councilor 1999—), Am. Assn. Women Radiologists (treas. 1993-99), Am. Soc. Neuroradiology (sec. 1996-98), Radiol. Soc. N.Am. (program com. 1992-97), Am. Roentgen Ray Soc. (com. 1998—, Silver medal 1992, Gold medal 1993). Avocations: scuba diving, river rafting, jazz singing. Office: U Iowa Hosps Dept Radiology 200 Hawkins Dr 0436 JCP Iowa City IA 52242- E-mail: wendy-smoker@uiowa.edu.

SMOKOROWSKI, PETER, retired artist; b. Kolosova, Kremenets, Ukraine, Mar. 1, 1938; s. Vasil (Wasyli) and Tatjana Smokorowski; m. Eunice Darlene Caldwell, Jan. 31, 1960; children: Melva Huston, Michelle Brauer, Peter Jr. BFA, Kansas City (Mo.) Art Inst., 1961. Artist Hallmark Cards, Kansas City, 1961-99; ret. Alt. commr. of Ukraine, Ethnic Enrichment Commn., Kansas City, 1993—. Mem. Watercolor Soc. US (Purchase award 1988). Republican. Baptist. Avocations: painting, tennis, scuba. Home: 14015 W 47th Ter Shawnee KS 66216-1149 E-mail: psmok62@yahoo.com.

SMOLANSKY, BETTIE MORETZ, sociology educator; b. Columbia, S.C., June 04; d. Walter Jennings Sr. and Opal (Ledford) Moretz; m. Oles M. Smolansky, Dec. 29, 1966; children: Alexandra Smolansky Zentmeyer, Nicholas Jennings. AB in Sociology, Lenoir-Rhyne Coll., 1962; MA in Sociology, Duke U., 1964; PhD in Sociology, Pa. State U., 1984. Instr. sociology Moravian Coll., Bethlehem, Pa., 1964-68, asst. prof., 1968-82, asst. dean, 1980-82, assoc. prof., 1982-88, prof., 1988—, chair dept. sociology, 1991-97, interim dean faculty, 1998-99, dean acad. affairs, 2000—01. Trustee Moravian Coll., 1977-81, 91-95, NEH visitor core curriculum workshop, 1985, sec. presdl. search com., 1996-97; mem. curriculum evaluation conf. Bklyn. Coll., 1988. Co-author: The USSR and Iraq, 1991 (AAAS Marshall Schulman prize 1992). Bd. dirs. Northampton County Area on Aging, Bethlehem, 1984-90; vice chair United Way Allocations Panel, Bethlehem, 1984-90; chair YWCA Commn. on Status of Women, Bethlehem, 1992-94; bd. dirs. YWCA of Bethlehem, 1993-97, 98-2002, 1st v.p., 1998-2000, pres., 2001-02. Recipient NDEA fellow, 1962-64, Disting. Alumnus award Lenoir-Rhyne Coll., 1995. Mem. Am. Sociol. Assn., Ea. Sociol. Assn., Lehigh Valley Assn. Acad. Women (pres. 1988-89, Woman of Yr. 1995-96), ODK (advisor 1987-90), AKD (advisor 1991-97). Home: 3665 Walt Whitman Ln Bethlehem PA 18017-1553 Office: Moravian Coll Dept Sociology 1200 Main St Bethlehem PA 18018-6614 Fax: 610-861-3980. E-mail: mebms01@moravian.edu.

SMOLEK, ROCHELLE THÉRÈSE, interior designer; b. Stamford, Conn., Jan. 31, 1948; d. Joseph Peter and Gladys Therese Bruno; m. Howard Thomas Uhal, Oct. 19, 1972 (div. July 1995); 1 child, Geoffrey Thomas; m. Frank D. Smolek, Jr., Aug. 30, 1995; stepchildren: Jason David, Kevin Kent. Designer Celange, Inc., N.Y.C., 1976-79, Len Coleman Designs, Charleston, S.C., 1980-83; cons. Rochelle T. Uhal Interiors, Cleve., 1983-86; owner Heritage Interiors, Ledyard, Conn., 1988-94; designer Jane Mabry Interior Design, Alpharetta, Ga., 1994-95; owner Fine Room Design, Inc., Roswell, 1995—. Chair 1999 Magnolia Ball, Bullock Hall, Roswell, 1999; chair encore ASA Atlanta Symphony Assoc., 1996, asst. membership chair, 1998-99, showhouse opening night party, 1996, 97, chmn. ensemble unit, 2001-, designer for decoration show house, 2000, 01. Mem. Am. Soc. Interior Design, Interior Design Soc. Republican. Roman Catholic. Avocation: travel.

SMOLEN, CHERYL HOSAKA, special education educator; b. Fairview, Ohio, Dec. 17, 1959; d. James Yukio and Midori (Osaki) Hosaka; m. Alan Smolen; children: Tyler, Dylan. BA, Ohio U., 1983; M in Curriculum and Instrn., Cleve. State U., 1992. Tchr. devel. handicapped Scioto Valley Sch. Dist., Piketon, Ohio, 1983-85; tchr. learning disabled Darlington County Sch. Dist., Darlington, S.C., 1985-88; small group instrn. tchr. Upper Arlington (Ohio) Sch. Dist., 1988-89; tchr. handicapped presch. Euclid (Ohio) Sch. Dist., 1989-91, Cuyahoga County Bd. Edn., North Olmsted, Ohio, 1991—; tutor learning disabled Avon Lake City Schs., 1991-92; presch. spl. needs tchr. Spl. Horizon, North Olmsted, 2000—02, Lakewood (Ohio) Sch. Dist., 2002—. Coord. Spl. Olympics, Darlington County, 1987-88; counselor Snoopy Camp, Hartsville, S.C., 1987; tchr. Spl. Horizon, North Olmsted, Ohio, summer, 1992; tutor Project LEARN, Cleve., 1990-92; mem. spl. edn. curriculum devel. com., handicapped presch. curriculum devel. com., coord. spl. edn. newsletter; ESL tutor, 1992—; mem. adv. bd. Spl. Horizon. Asst. Cub Scout leader, 2000—01; mem. Avon East PTA. Mem. Coun. for Exceptional Children. Avocations: aerobics, playing flute, cross-stitching, spectator sports, jogging. Home: 4298 S Fall Lake Dr Avon OH 44011

SMOLENSKI, LISABETH ANN, family practice physician; b. Pitts., Oct. 1, 1950; d. Anthony Edward and Betty Jean (Gross) S.; m. William Ward Daniels, May 24, 1980; 1 child, Kathryn Elizabeth. BA, Carlow Coll., 1972; MD, Hahnemann U., 1982. Diplomate Am. Bd. Family Practice. Resident in family practice West Jersey Health Sys., Voorhees, N.J., 1982-85; pvt. practice, Somerville, Tenn., 1985-90, Memphis, 1990—. Sec. exec. com. med. staff Meth. Hosp. Somerville, 1988-90. Fellow Am. Acad. Family Physicians. Republican. Avocation: reading. Office: Health First Med Group 1588 Union Ave Memphis TN 38104

SMOLENSKY, EUGENE, economics educator; b. Bklyn., Mar. 4, 1932; s. Abraham and Jennie (Miller) S.; m. Natalie Joan Rabinowitz, Aug. 16, 1952; children: Paul, Beth. BA, Bklyn. Coll., 1952; MA, Am. U., 1956; PhD, U. Pa., 1961. Prof. econs. U. Wis., Madison, 1968-88, chmn. dept., 1978-80, 86-88; dir. Inst. for Research on Poverty, U. Wis., 1980-83; dean Grad. Sch. Pub. Policy, U. Calif., Berkeley, 1988-97, prof. pub. policy, 1997—. Author: Public Expenditures, Taxation and the Distribution of Income: The U.S., 1950, 61, 70, 77. Mem. Nat. Acad. Pub. Adminstrn., 1994; mem. com. on child devel. rsch. and pub. policy NAS, Washington, 1982-87, mem. com. on status of women in labor market, 1985-87. With USN, 1952-56. Mem. Am. Econs. Assn. Democrat. Jewish. Avocation: collecting old master etchings and lithographs. E-mial. Home: 669 Woodmont Ave Berkeley CA 94708-1233 Office: U Calif Dept Pub Policy 2607 Hearst Ave Berkeley CA 94720-7305 E-mail: geno@socrates.berkeley.edu.

SMOLEV, TERENCE ELLIOT, lawyer, educator; b. Bklyn., Oct. 5, 1944; s. Lawrence and Shirley (Lebowitz) S.; m. Sherry Gale Rosen, Nov. 24, 1968 (div.); children: Cindy, Scott; m. Phyllis C. Rudko, Oct. 8, 1995. BBA, Hofstra U., 1966; JD, American U., 1969; LLM, NYU, 1974. Bar: N.Y. 1970. Acct. Peat Marwick & Mitchell, N.Y.C., 1969-70; dir. deferred giving Hofstra U., Hempstead, N.Y., 1971-74; editor Panel Publishers, Greenvale, 1970-71; ptnr. Naidich & Smolev, P.C., Bellmore, 1972-92; pvt. practice Terence E. Smolev, P.C., Mineola, 1992-2000; ptnr. Forchelli, Curto, Schwartz, Mineo, Carlino & Cohn LLP, 2000—, ptnr. in charge tax, trusts and estates, 2001—. Bd. trustees Hofstra U., 1992—; adj. prof. Hofstra U., Hempstead, N.Y., 1971—; dist. counsel North Merrick (N.Y.) UFSD, 1975-99. Author of book chpt. Mem. Nassau County, N.Y. Dem. Com., 1972-80, mem. judicial screening com., 1992—; mem. IRS Small Bus. Adv. Com., Washington D.C., 1975-77; bd. dirs. Arthritis Found. L.I., 1995-97, mem Israeli Bond Cabinet Long Island, 1996—; bd. dirs. L.I. chpt. Anti-Defamation League. Recipient George M. Estabrook award Hofstra U., 1991, Alumni Achievement award Hofstra U., 1993, Cmty. Svc. award Hebrew Acad. Nassau County, 1997; named Senator of Yr., Hofstra U., 1985, Alumnus of Yr., 1996. Mem. ABA, N.Y. State Bar Assn., Nassau County Bar Assn., N.Y. State Assn. Sch. Attys. (pres. 1984), Hofstra U. Alumni Senate (pres. 1987-89), Hofstra U. Club (bd. dirs. 1981-95). Avocations: photography, golf. Office: PO Box 31 330 Old Country Rd Ste 301 Mineola NY 11501 E-mail: tsmolev@fcsmcc.com.

SMOLIN, LEE, physicist, educator; b. N.Y.C., June 6, 1955; s. Michael and Pauline (Selman) S. BA, Hampshire Coll., Amherst, Mass., 1975; MA, Harvard U., 1978, PhD, 1979; postgrad., U. Chgo., 1983-85. Mem. Inst. for Advanced Study, Princeton, N.J., 1979, 81-83; postdoctoral physicist Inst. for Theoretical Physics, Santa Barbara, Calif., 1980-81; asst. prof. Yale U., New Haven, 1985-88; assoc. prof. Syracuse (N.Y.) U., 1988-91, prof., 1991—. Contbr. articles to profl. jours. Active Clamshell Alliance, 1978; organizer Star Wars Pledge Campaign, 1984-86. Recipient 1st award essay Gravity Rsch. Found., 1985, 2d award, 1983, 81. Mem. Internat. Soc. for Gen. Relativity and Gravitation. Avocations: jazz guitar, sailing, philosophy. Office: Syracuse U Dept Physics Syracuse NY 13244-0001

SMOLINSKI, EDWARD ALBERT, holding company executive, lawyer, accountant, deacon; b. N.Y.C., Jan. 6, 1928; s. Albert John and Adele (Weber) S.; m. Joan E. Winslow, Nov. 12, 1955; children: Albert, Edward, Linda, Donna. BS in Acctg., L.I. U., 1948; MBA, NYU, 1950, JD, 1956. Bar: N.Y. 1957; C.P.A., N.Y.; ordained deacon Roman Cath. Ch., 1977. Acct. various cert. pub. acctg. firms., N.Y.C., 1948-53; acctg. supr. Curtiss Wright Co., Woodridge, N.J., 1953-60; mem. treasury staff Sperry-Rand Corp., Great Neck, N.Y., 1960-62; contr. PRD electronics Harris Corp., Hicksville, NY, 1962-68; corp. controller Fairchild Camera and Instrument Co., Syosset, N.Y., 1968-69; v.p., treas., chief fin. officer Grow Group, Inc., N.Y.C., 1969-89; asst. treas./sec. United Indsl. Corp., 1989—. Adj. asst. prof. Hunter Coll., 1989 Bd. dirs. Long Island U.-Bus. Game, N.Y.C., 1977-83, NYU Mgmt. Decision Lab., 1983-88; deacon Diocese of Bklyn., Roman Cath. Ch., 1977—. Mem. AICPA (com. on nat. def. 1963), N.Y. Bar, Fin. Execs. Inst. Lodges: Elks. Roman Catholic. Home: 70-19 Juno St Forest Hills NY 11375-5839 Office: United Indsl Corp 570 Lexington Ave New York NY 10022-6837

SMOLKA, JAMES WILLIAM, aerospace research pilot; b. Mt. Clemens, Mich., July 31, 1950; s. Joseph William and Patricia Joan (Righetti) S. BS in Astronautics, USAF Acad., 1972; MS in Aero., Astronautics, MIT, 1980; engineers degree in aero. & astronautics, Stanford U., 1994. Commd. 2d lt. USAF, 1972, advanced through grades to col., 1996; served as pilot 3d Tactical Fighter Squadron, Korat RT AFB, Thailand, 1974, 21 Tactical Air Support Squadron, Shaw AFB SC, 1975-77; test pilot 6510 Test Wing, Edwards AFB CA, 1980-83; exptl. test pilot Ft. Worth div. Gen. Dynamics, Edwards AFB, 1984-85; aerospace rsch. pilot N.A.S.A. Dryden FRC, 1985—; officer USAF, 1972-83, USAFR, 1983-99, ret. as col., 1999. Adj. prof. Calif. State U., Fresno, 1984—. Author: Analysis and Testing of Aircraft Flight Control Systems, 1982. Mem. Soc. Exptl. Test Pilots. Home: PO Box 2123 Lancaster CA 93539-2123 Office: NASA Dryden Flight Rsch Ctr PO Box 273 Edwards CA 93523-0273

SMOLKER, GARY STEVEN, lawyer; b. L.A., Nov. 5, 1945; s. Paul and Shayndy Charolette (Sirott) S.; m. Alice Graham; children: Terra, Judy, Leah. BS, U. Calif., Berkeley, 1967; MS, Cornell U., 1968; JD cum laude, Loyola U., L.A., 1973. Bar: Calif. 1973, U.S. Dist. Ct. (ctrl. dist.) Calif. 1973, U.S. Tax Ct. 1973, U.S. Ct. Appeals (9th cir.) 1973, U.S. Supreme Ct. 1978, U.S. Dist. Ct. (so., ea. and no. dists.) Calif. 1981. Guest rschr. Lawrence Radiation Lab., U. Calif., 1967; tchg. fellow Sch. Chem. Engring., Cornell U.; mem. tech. staff Hughes Aircraft Co., Culver City, Calif., 1968-70; in advanced mktg. and tech. TRW, Redondo Beach, 1970-72; sole practice Beverly Hills, 1973-89, L.A., 1989—. Guest lectr. UCLA Extension, 1973-74, Loyola U. Law Sch., 1979; speaker, panelist in field; adv. Loyola U. Law Sch., 1973—. Columnist Heating Piping Air Conditioning Engring. Mag., 1999—; contbr. articles to profl. jours. Mem. Nat. Assn. Real Estate Editors, Calif. State Bar Assn., L.A. County Bar Assn., Beverly Hills Bar Assn. (sr. editor jour. 1978-79, contbg. editor jour. 1980-82, 86-90, editor-in-chief 1984-86, pub. Smolker Letter 1985—), B'nai B'rith (anti-defamation league). Jewish. Achievements include inventor self-destruct aluminium tungstic oxide films, electrolytic anticompromise process. Office: 4720 Lincoln Blvd Ste 280 Marina Del Rey CA 90292

SMOLLA, RODNEY ALAN, lawyer, educator; b. Pueblo, Colo., Mar. 13, 1953; s. Richard Paul and Harriet (Waskowiak) S. BA, Yale U., 1975; JD, Duke U., 1978. Bar: Ill. 1979, U.S. Supreme Ct. 1987. Law clk. to presiding judge U.S. Ct. Appeals, Jackson, Miss., 1978-79; assoc. Mayer, Brown & Pratt, Chgo., 1979-80; asst. prof. De Paul U. Sch. Law, 1980-81, U. Ill. Coll. Law, 1981-83; prof. U. Ark. Sch. Law, 1983-87; vis. prof. U. Denver Coll. Law, 1987-88; Arthur B. Hanson prof. constl. law Coll. of William and Mary, Williamsburg, Va., 1988-98, dir. Inst. Bill of Rights Law, 1988-96; George E. Allen prof. law U. Richmond (Va.) Sch. Law, 1998—. Author: Suing the Press: Libel, The Media & Power, 1986 (cert. of merit ABA 1987), Law of Defamation, 1986, Jerry Falwell V. Larry Flynt: The First Amendment on Trial, 1988; (with Banks and Braveman) Constitutional Law: Structure and Rights in Our Federal System, 1991, 3rd edit., 1996, Free Speech in an Open Society, 1992 (William O. Douglas award 1993), Smolla and Nimmer on Freedom of Speech, 1994, 3rd edit., 1996, Federal Civil Rights Acts, 1994; editor: A Year in the Life of the Supreme Court, 1995 (ABA Silver Gavel award), Deliberate Intent: A Lawyer Tells the True Story of Murder by the Book, 1999. Fellow, cons. Annenberg Washington Program in Communications, 1987-96; project dir. Annenberg Libel Reform Task Force, 1988-89; reporter Bill of Rights Adv. Com. to the Commn. on the Bicentennial of U.S. Constitution, 1989—. Recipient Recipient Disting. Prof. of Yr. award, U. Ark., 1986, Outstanding Faculty award, Va. State Coun. Higher Edn., 2002. Mem. ABA, Ill. Bar Assn., AAUP (mem. litigation com. 1988—). Home: 2423 Lake Loreine Ln Richmond VA 23233-2523 Office: U Richmond TC Williams Sch of Law Richmond VA 23173 E-mail: rsmolla@richmond.edu.

SMOLLER, BRUCE MELVYN, psychiatrist; b. Chgo., Sept. 19, 1944; s. Norman and Beatrice Betty (Janows) S.; m. Cosette Nieporent, Aug. 20, 1967; children: Jamie, Lauren. AB, Cornell U., 1965; MD, Tulane U., 1969. Diplomate Am. Bd. Psychiatry and Neurology. Intern Maimonides Med. Ctr., N.Y.C., 1969-70; resident in orthopedic surgery Einstein Med. Ctr., 1970-73; resident in psychiatry Cornell Med. Ctr., 1973-76; pvt. practice medicine specializing in psychiatry with spl. emphasis on clin. and rsch. aspects of pain Bethesda, Md., 1976—; chmn. dept. psychiatry Holy Cross Hosp., Silver Spring, 1980-83; assoc. clin. prof. psychiatry George Washington U., 1977-91, clin. prof. psychiatry, 1991—. Cons. NIH. Co-author: Pain Control: The Bethesda Program; editor: Md. Medicine, The State Med. Jour. With MC, USAR, 1970-78. Mem.: Montgomery County Med. Soc. (v.p.). Office: 5530 Wisconsin Ave Bethesda MD 20815-4404 E-mail: bsmoller@radix.net.

SMOLLER, IRENE MILDRED, artist, educator; b. Chgo., July 28, 1919; d. Frank and Martha (Rothwell) Volkert; m. Louis Ben Smoller (dec.); 1 child, William. Student, N.Y. Acad., 1937-40, Art Inst. Chgo., 1950-51. One-man shows include Chgo. Pub. Libr., Merchants and Mfrs. Club, Chgo., Bernheim and Jeune Galerie, Paris, O'Hanna Gallery, London, Broadway Galleries, Ltd., Milw., LeBow Gallery, Evanston, Ill., Thor Gallery, Louisville, Palm Beach (Fla.) Gallery, Price Gallery, Chgo.; exhibited in groups shows including St. Paul Gallery and Sch. Arts, Russell Gallery, Bloomington, Ill., Adele Rosenberg Gallery, Chgo., Harper Gallery, Chgo., Butler Inst., Youngstown, Ohio, N.Y. Acad., Evanston (Ill.) Art Ctr., Denver Mus., Art Inst. Chgo., Krannert Mus., Springfield, Ill., McKerrie Galleries, Pitts., Biennale Internationale France, Paris, Rual Askew Gallery, Dallas, Ft. Wayne (Ind.) Mus., Societe des Artistes Independants Annuelle, Paris, Berheim-Jeune Gallery, Paris, Memmel Gallery, Milw., Downtown Gallery, New Orleans, Thor Gallery, Louisville, Internat. Exhbn., Lucca, Italy, Palm Beach (Fla.) Gallery, others; represented in permanent collection sGalerie Bernheim and Jeune, Paris, Vincent Price collection, Cedar Rapids (Mich.) Mus. Art; pvt. instr., Chgo., 1960—. Midwest regional dir. Nat. Arts Coun. Recipient Maxwell Pearl purchase award, London, 1960, 2d prize Solomon Art purchase award, Phila., 1960, 2d prize Lincolnwood (Ill.) Art Festival, 1967, 1st prize Suburban Art Ctr. Ann., Highland Park, Ill., 1965, 1st prize Midwest Regional Representational, Chgo., 1964, Silver medal Internat. Italian Exbn., Rome; diplome d'honneur Laureate la France, 1964. Mem. Artist Equity Am., Renaissance Soc. U. Chgo., Royal Acad. (London). Home: 5555 N Sheridan Rd Chicago IL 60640-1601

SMOLYAR, ADAM J. business executive; b. Baku, Azerbaijan; s. Alex and Jane Smolyar. MBA, Harvard U., 2000; BA, Boston U. Mgr. KPMG Consulting, Boston, 1994-2001; dir. corp. strategy devel. Pitney Bowes, Stamford, Conn., 2001—. Mem. Acad. Polit. Sci., Mensa. Republican. Office: Pitney Bowes MSC 44-63 1 Elmcroft Rd Stamford CT 06926-0700 Fax: 203-351-6553. E-mail: adam.smolyar@pb.com.

SMOOK, MALCOLM ANDREW, chemist, chemical company executive; b. Seattle, Aug. 22, 1924; s. Joseph Murray and Bonnie (Hanson) S.; m. Mary Louise Nominee, Dec. 19, 1945; children— Frances Lynn Fenton, Valerie Dale Martin. BS, U. Calif., Berkeley, 1945; PhD in Organic Chemistry, Ohio State U., 1949. With E. I. duPont de Nemours & Co., Wilmington, Del., 1949—, research supr., 1952-53, div. head, 1953-57, asst. lab. dir., 1957-60, lab. dir., 1960-63, asst. research dir., 1963-75, gen. lab. dir., 1975-80, mgr. patents and regulatory affairs, 1980-84; cons. Malcolm A. Smook, Inc., 1985—. Mem. adv. com. NASA, 1971-76 Contbr. articles to profl. jours.; holder 9 patents. Served to lt. (j.g.) USN, 1943-46. Socony Vacuum fellow, 1948-49 Mem. Am. Chem. Soc., Sigma Xi. Home and Office: 59 Rockford Rd Wilmington DE 19806-1003 E-mail: mal.smook@verizon.net.

SMOOT, BURGESS HOWARD, federal official; b. Washington, Mar. 28, 1947; s. James Elias and Frances Galdinia (Hawkins) S.; m. Ann Louise Gordon, Aug. 9, 1982; children: Frederick Hawkins, Chanel Gordon, Ervine Gholston, Shemerrian. Cook Freedmans Hosp., Washington, 1968-70; mail & file clk. Asst. Chief of Staff Intelligence, 1970-74; adminstrv. asst. logistics Office Joint Chiefs of Staff, Pentagon, 1974-77, adminstrv. asst. policy & plans, 1977-80. Author: (poetry) Lost in the Beginning. Capt. Neighborhood Watch Group, Fort Washington, Md., 1995-97; presdl. election official, 2000—. With U.S. Army, 1965-68, Civil Air Patrol, 1964-65. Decorated Army Commendation medal, Combat Infantry badge, Good Conduct medal, Nat. Def. medal, Vietnam Svc. medal, Vietnam Campaign ribbon. Mem. Disabled Am. Vets. (comdr., svc. officer, sgt. at arms, hon. guard), Masons. Democrat. Mem. Lds Ch. Avocations: baseball, football, wrestling, bowling, pool. Home: 10103 Kathleen Dr Fort Washington MD 20744-2530

SMOOT, DAVID PAUL, finance company executive; b. Guthrie, Okla., Jan. 9, 1947; s. Jerry Edward and Katherine Ann (Doyle) S.; m. Marie Kathleen Stokes, Aug. 6, 1971; children: Aimee, Melissa. Student, Cumberland Coll., 1965-67, Glassboro State Coll., 1967, U. Cin., 1968-69. Regional mgr. Dennison Mfg., Chgo., 1969-77, Wordstream, Chgo., 1978-79; dist. mgr. AM Jacquard, San Francisco, 1979-82; co-founder, v.p. sales Phaser Systems Pub. Co., 1980-82; dir. cen. ops. Digital Research, Schaumburg, Ill., 1982-85; founder, chmn. bd., chief exec. officer Software Funding Internat., Deerfield, 1985-89; Software Funding Internat. (acquired by The Meridian Group), 1989; pres. Meridian Software Funding, 1989-92, Am. Indian Svcs. Inc., 1992-95; pres., founder Airborne Remote Mapping, 1995-98, Am. Indian Fin. Svcs. LLC, 1998—. Mem. Native Vision program Johns Hopkins U. Hosp., NFL Players Assn. and Nick Lowery Found. Bd. of Consult Little City Home for Retarded, Palatine, Ill., 1986. Served with U.S. Army, 1969-75. Mem. Assn. Data Processing Services Orgns., Software Pubs. Assn., Syntopicaon XII, IBM PC User's Group (speaker). Avocations: basketball, sailing, camping, fishing, tennis. Home and Office: 6831 E Sunset Sky Cir Scottsdale AZ 85262-7161 also: 111 S Pfingsten Rd Ste 115 Deerfield IL 60015-4994

SMOOT, JOSEPH GRADY, university administrator; b. Winter Haven, Fla., May 7, 1932; s. Robert Malcolm and Vera (Eaton) S.; m. Florence Rozell, May 30, 1955 (dec.); m. Irma Jean Kopitzke, June 4, 1959; 1 child, Andrew Christopher. BA, So. Coll., 1955; MA, U. Ky., 1958, PhD, 1964. Tchr., Ky. Secondary Schs., 1955-57; from instr. to assoc. prof. history Columbia Union Coll., Takoma Park, Md., 1960-68, acad. dean, 1965-68; prof. history Andrews U., Berrien Springs, Mich., 1968-84, dean Sch. Grad. Studies, 1968-69, v.p. acad. adminstrn., 1969-76, pres., 1976-84; v.p. for devel. Pittsburg State U., Kans., 1984—; exec. dir. Pitts. State U. Found., 1985—; bd. dirs. 1st State Bank and Trust Co., Pitts., 1994—; founder Pitts. State U. Radio Sta.-KRPS-FM, 1988; commr. North Cen. Assn., 1987-91, cons., evaluator, 1978—; cons. internat. edn; trustee Loma Linda U., 1976-84, U. Ea. Africa, Baraton, Kenya, 1979-84, Hindsdale Hosp., Ill., 1973-84; chmn., bd. trustees Andrews Broadcasting Corp., 1976-84; bd. dirs. Internat. U. Thailand Found., 1987-95, trustee, 1994-95. Contbr. articles to profl. jours; editor: Spottiswoode Soc. Record, 1990—. Active Pitts. Area Festival Assn., 1984-86, bd. dirs. Pitts. United Way, 1987-92, Pitts. C. of C. Found., 1990-93; bd. advisors Pitts. Salvation Army, 1987-92, vice-chmn., 1990-91, chmn., 1991-92; bd. trustees Mt. Carmel Med. Ctr. Found., 1991-95; bd. dirs. S.E. Kans. Symphony Orch., 1995—. Recipient Disting. Pres. award Mich. Coll. Found., 1984. Mem. Inst. Early Am. History and Culture (assoc.), Am. Hist. Assn., So. Hist. Assn., Orgn. Am. Historians, Soc. for Historians of Early Am. Rep., Soc. History of Authorship, Reading & Pub., Phi Alpha Theta. Club: Crestwood Country. Lodge: Rotary (dist. chmn. scholarship com. 1986-88, Paul Harris Fellow) Home: 1805 Heritage Rd Pittsburg KS 66762-3556 Office: Office of V P for Development Pittsburg State U Pittsburg KS 66762

SMOOT, OLIVER REED, JR. lawyer, trade association executive; b. San Antonio, Aug. 24, 1940; s. Oliver Reed and Angie Frances (Watters) S.; m. Sandra Lee Curry, July 25, 1964; children: Stephen Reed, Sheryl Anne. BS, MIT, 1962; JD, Georgetown U., 1966. Bar: D.C. 1966, Va. 1967. Computer systems mgr. Inst. for Def. Analyses, Arlington, Va., 1962-69; program mgr., v.p., then exec. v.p. and treas. Info. Tech. Industry Coun. (previous Computer & Bus Equipment Mfrs. Assn.), Washington, 1969-2000; v.p. extrnal vol. standards rels. Info Tech Industry Coun., 2000—. Author: (with others) Computers and the Law, 3d edit., 1981; chpt. editor: Toward a Law of Global Communications Networks, 2001. Vice chmn. Am. Nat. Stds. Inst.; chmn. Info. Infrastructures Stds. Panel, 1998—, pres. elect Internat. Organization for Standardization 2001-2002. Mem. ABA (chmn. sci. and tech. sect. 1989-90), Computer Law Assn. (pres. 1990-91), Assn. for Computing Machinery. Methodist. Avocations: alpine skiing, gardening. Office: Info Tech Industry Coun 1250 I St NW Ste 200 Washington DC 20005-3922

SMOOT, RAYMOND D., JR. academic administrator; b. Lynchburg, Va., Jan. 21, 1947; s. Raymond Dillard and Gladys Masencup Smoot; m. Jean Newlon Smoot; children: Amanda, Ben. BA, Va. Tech., Blacksburg, 1969; M Edn., Va. Tech., 1971; PhD, Ohio State U., Columbus, 1976. Dir. Carilion Health Sys., Roanoke, Va., 1997—, New River Valley Med. Ctr., 2002—; v.p. adminstrn., treas. Va. Tech., Blacksburg. Bd. dirs. First Nat. Bank, Christiansburg; chmn. bd. Va. Tech. Corp. Rsch., 1995--; mem. investment com. Va. Retirement Sys. Mem. Sanitation Authority, Blacksburg, 1993--; bd. dirs. Roanoke C. of C., 1995—, Warm Hearth Retirement Ctr., 1988—, Smithfield/Preston Found., 1996—; commr. Hotel Roanoke Conf. Ctr., 1993—. Staff Sgt. US Army, 1969-75. Episcopalian. Office: Va Tech 312 Burruss Hall 0142 Blacksburg VA 24061

SMORAL, VINCENT J. electrical engineer; b. Syracuse, N.Y., May 13, 1946; s. Anthony Vincent and Stephanie (Koutin) S.; m. Theresa W. Gut, Aug. 5, 1967; children: Jennifer, Laura, Anne. BSEE, Syracuse U., 1967. Jr. engr. Fed. Systems Div. IBM, Owego, N.Y., 1967-68, adv. engr. logic design, 1968-80, sr. engr./systems, 1980-90, sr. engr./program mgr., 1990-93; sr. engr. Lockheed Martin Fed. Systems Co., 1994—2000; program mgr. Eastman Kodak C&GS, Rochester, 2000—. Designer 688 Class Sonar, An/UYS-1 Signal Processor, AWACS Computer, 3838 Array Processor, 1968-80; mgr. AN/UYK-43 Computer, AWACS Computer, Rugged Processor, F117 Processor, 1980-93; patentee in field. Fellow AIAA (assoc.; mem. nat. computer systems tech. com. 1990-95); mem. IEEE, KC. Democrat. Roman Catholic. Avocations: swimming, sailing, fishing, skiing. Home: 12 Founders Grn Pittsford NY 14534-2165 Office: Eastman Kodak Co Commerical & Govt Sys 1447 Paul St Rochester NY 14653-7214

SMOTHERMON, PEGGI STERLING, middle school educator; b. Dallas, Nov. 11, 1948; d. Kiel Sterling and Ann C. (Wolfe) Sterling; m. William C. Smothermon Jr., June 20, 1981; children: Kirsten, Melinda, William III. BA, So. Meth. U., Dallas, 1973; MLA, So. Meth. U., 1978. Tchr. Richardson (Tex.) Ind. Sch. Dist., 1973-90, Coppell (Tex.) Ind. Sch. Dist., 1990-96, 2002—. J.J. Pearce scholar. Mem. Nat. Coun. Tchrs. Math., NSTA, NEA (faculty rep., membership chmn., sec.), Tex. Tchrs. Assn., Assn. Coppell Educators, Tex. Computer Edn. Assn., Tex. Coun. Tchrs. Math., Kappa Delta Pi. Home: 408 Greenridge Dr Coppell TX 75019-5714

SMOTHERS, JIMMY, editor, sportswriter; b. Geraldine, Ala., Jan. 4, 1933; s. John Ezra and Lois Olga (Taylor) S.; m. Mary Kay Brock, July 7, 1954; 1 child Jim Jr. Grad., Jacksonville State U., 1954. Sports editor Gadsden (Ala.) Times, 1960—. Contbr. articles to popular mags. With USNG, 1951-65. Recipient Helms award, more than 66 AP awards including Sweepstake award for writing, 1996, Lifetime Achievement award All-Am. Football Found., 1997, Ala. Sports Writer of Yr. award, 1999, Media of Yr. award Ala. Jr. Coll., 2001; nominated for Pulitzer prizes, 1963; inductee Etowah County (Ala.), Ala. Sport Writers Halls of Fame, 1997, DeKalb County (Ala.) Sports Hall of Fame, 1998, Ala. H.S. Hall of Fame, 2001. Mem. Ala. Sports Writers Assn. (sec.-treas. 1971—), Baseball Writers Assn., Coll. Football Writers Assn., Jacksonville State U. Alumni Assn. (past. Alumnus of Yr.). Avocations: fishing, studying Civil War. Office: Gadsden Times PO Box 188 Gadsden AL 35902-0188

SMOTHERS, TOM, actor, singer; b. Feb. 2, 1937; s. Thomas B. and Ruth Smothers; children: Tom, Bo, Riley Rose; m. Marcy Carriker, Sept. 9, 1990. Student, San Jose State Coll. Owner winery, Kenwood, Calif. Nightclub appearances in Reno, Lake Tahoe, Las Vegas, Nev., and various venues in the U.S.; co-star TV situation comedy Smothers Brothers Show, 1965-66, Smothers Brothers Comedy Hour, CBS-TV, 1967-69, 70, weekly variety show The Smothers Brothers Show, NBC-TV, 1975; starred in films The Silver Bears, Get To Know Your Rabbit, A Pleasure Doing Business, Serial, There Goes the Bride, Pandemonium, Speed Zone; starred on Broadway in I Love My Wife, 1978-79; appeared in TV movie Terror at Alcatraz, 1982; starred in Smothers Brothers Spl. and Series, 1988-89. Office: Knave Prodns Ste 107B 6442 Coldwater Canyon Ave North Hollywood CA 91606-1137 E-mail: SMOBRO1@AOL.COM.

SMOTHERS, WILLIAM EDGAR, JR. geophysical exploration company executive; b. Shawnee, Okla., July 9, 1928; s. William Edgar and Lena Rivers (Randolph) S.; m. Marilyn Myrtle Cales, Sept. 6, 1952; children: Bill, Susan. BS in Commerce, Okla. State U., 1950. Staff acct. Amoco Prodn. Co., Tulsa, 1953-56; chief internal auditor Seismography Svc. Corp., 1956-63, mgr. tax and auditing, 1964-77, v.p., treas., 1978—. Vice chmn. Tulsa United Way Drive, 1976, chmn., 1977. Capt. U.S. Army, 1951-53. Mem. Am. Mgmt. Assn., Tax Execs. Inst., Nat. Assn. Accts., Systems Mgmt. Assn., Petroleum Club, Tulsa Country Club. Democrat. Presbyterian. Home: 9103 E 38th Pl Tulsa OK 74145-3437 Office: Seismograph Svc Corp PO Box 1590 Tulsa OK 74102

SMOTRICH, DAVID ISADORE, architect; b. Norwich, Conn., Oct. 6, 1933; s. Max Z. and Ida (Babinsky) S.; m. Bernice D. Strachman, Mar. 25, 1956; children— Ross Lawrence, Maura Faye, Hannah. AB, Harvard Coll., 1955, MArch, 1960. Master planning team, Town of Arad, State of Israel, 1961-62; assoc. Platt Assocs., N.Y.C., 1963-65; gen. ptnr. Smotrich & Platt, 1965-74, Smotrich Platt & Buttrick, N.Y.C., 1975-76, Smotrich & Platt, N.Y.C., 1976-85, David Smotrich & Ptnrs., N.Y.C., 1985—. Cons. to Jerusalem Master Plan Office, Israel Ministry of Housing, 1967. Planning bd. Town of New Castle, N.Y., 1974-81; exec. bd. Road Rev. League, Bedford, N.Y., 1966-70. With AUS, 1955-57. Recipient Bard award, 1969, 85, Archtl. Record award, 1971, 73-75, 78, Design award HUD, 1980. Mem. AIA (Nat. Honor award 1969, N.Y. State Honor awards 1984, 94, Cmty. Design awards 1991, 93, AIA Coll. of Fellows 1993), Assn. Engrs. and Archs. in Israel, Phi Beta Kappa, Harvard Club (N.Y.C.). Home: 7 Mayberry Close Chappaqua NY 10514-1113 Office: David Smotrich & Ptnrs 443 Park Ave S New York NY 10016-7322

SMOUSE, H(ERVEY) RUSSELL, lawyer; b. Oakland, Md., Aug. 13, 1932; s. Hervey Reed and Vernie (Rush) S.; m. Creta M. Staley, June 15, 1955; children: Kristin Anne, Randall Forsyth, Gregory Russell. AB, Princeton U., 1955; LLB, U. Md., 1958. Bar: Md. 1958, U.S. Tax Ct. 1979, U.S. Ct. Appeals (4th cir.) 1960, U.S. Supreme Ct. 1974. Atty., Atty. Gen.'s Honors Program, Dept. Justice, Washington, 1958-60, asst. U.S. atty. Dist. Md., 1960-62; assoc. Pierson and Pierson, Balt., 1962-64; atty. B.&O. R.R., Balt., 1964-66; mem. Pierson and Pierson, 1966-69; mem. Clapp, Somerville, Black & Honemann, Balt., 1969-74; Law Offices H. Russell Smouse, 1974-81; mem. Melnicove, Kaufman, Weiner & Smouse, P.A., Balt., 1981-89, chair litigation, 1985-89, Whiteford, Taylor & Preston, Balt., 1989-93, chair, litigation dept., 1989-93; head gen. litigation Law Offices Peter G. Angelos, 1993—; gen. counsel Balt. Orioles, 1993—; permanent mem. judicial conf. U.S. Ct. Appeals (4th cir.); v.p. Legal Aid Bur. Balt. City, 1972-73; bd. dirs. Md. Legal Svcs. Corp., 1987-93. Fellow Am. Coll. Trial Lawyers; mem. ABA, Md. State Bar Assn. (gov. 1981-83), Bar Assn. Balt. City (chmn. grievance com. 1969-70, chmn. judiciary com. and nominating com. 1980, mem. exec. com. 1969-70, 80, chmn. exec. com. lawyers' com. for ind. judiciary 1989-96), Nat. Assn. R.R. Trial Counsel (exec. com., v.p. ea. region 1986-92). Republican. Presbyterian.

SMREKAR, KARL GEORGE, JR. financial planner; b. Houston, Aug. 5, 1954; BA, Indiana U. of Pa., 1975; cert., Inst. Paralegal Tng., Phila., 1978, Inst. Cert. Fin. Planners, Denver, 1986, student, 1988. CFP. Asst. fin. planner AYCO Corp, Pitts., 1981-84; fin. planner Allegheny Fin. Group, 1984—, sr. v.p., 1994—; dir. Allegheny Fin. Group and Allegheny Investments, 1997—. Mem. MADD, Allegheny County and nat., 1987—, Alzheimer's Assn., Allegheny County and nat., 1990—, Nat. Coun. on Aging, Inc., 1992-96. Mem. Internat. Assn. Fin. Planners, Inc. CFPs (practitioner, bd. dirs. Greater Pitts. Soc. 1989-96, pres. 1994-95, chmn. 1995-96), Pa. Assn. Inst. CFP's (govt. liaison 1989-91, chmn. 1991-99, govt. rels. com. 1995-96), Fin. Planning Assn. Office: Allegheny Fin Group Ltd 3000 Mcknight East Dr Pittsburgh PA 15237-6439

SMUCKLER, RALPH HERBERT, dean, political scientist, educator; b. Milw., Apr. 10, 1926; s. Robert H. and Celia (Berliand) Smuckler; m. Lillian Zembrosky, July 6, 1946; children: Gary, Sandra, Harold. BA, U. Wis., 1948, MA, 1949, PhD, 1952. Mem. faculty Mich. State U., East Lansing, 1951-93, prof. polit. sci., 1963-93, dean internat. studies and programs, 1968-90, asst. to pres., 1987-91, emeritus prof., dean, 1993—. Chief advisor tech. assistance team in Siagon Mich. State U., 1955—56, 1958—59; v.p. Edn. and World Affairs, N.Y.C., 1963—64; rep. Ford Found., Pakistan, 1967—69; dir. U.S. Internat. Sci. and Tech. Coop. Planning Office, Washington, 1978—79; mem. rsch. adv. com. AID, 1972—82, chmn., 1973—82, dep. asst. adminstr., 1991—92. Author (with Leroy Ferguson): (book) Politics in the Press, 1953; author: (with George Belknap) Leadership and Participation in Urban Political Affairs, 1956; author: (with R. Berg) New Challenges New Opportunities: U.S. Cooperation for Interantional Growth and Development in the 1990s, 1988; author: A University Opens to the World, 2002; contbr. articles to profl. jours. Mem. adv. com. Kellog Found. Nat. Fellowship Program, 1980—84; mem. bd. sci. and tech. for internat. devel. Nat. Acad. Sci., 1982—88, chmn., 1984—88; v.p. Mich. UN Assn., 1972—76; State of Mich. chmn. UN Day, 1960; bd. dirs. Midwest Univs. Consortium Internat. Activities, 1965—67, 1969—90; trustee Inst. Internat. Edn., 1974—91. With inf. AUS, 1944—46. Decorated Bronze Star; recipient Disting. Citizen award, Stueben Jr. H.S., Milw., 1965, John Gilbert Winant Humanitarian award, Marine City, Mich., 1976, Outstanding Faculty award, 1990; scholar Phi Beta Delta Internat., 1990. Mem.: Nat. Assn. Fgn. Student Affairs (governing bd. 1986, M. Houlihan award 1990), Nat. Assn. State Univs and Land-Grant Colls. (chmn. internat. acad. affairs com. 1986—90), Assn. Internat. Edn. Adminstrs. (pres. 1986—87), Soc. Internat. Devel., Am. Polit. Sci. Assn., Mich. State U. Club, Phi Kappa Phi (named Disting. Mem. 1990). Jewish. Home: 4201 Cathedral Ave NW Apt 814W Washington DC 20016-4965 E-mail: ralphhs@aol.com.

SMUIN, MICHAEL, choreographer, director, dancer; b. Missoula, Mont., Oct. 13, 1938; m. Paula Tracy; 1 child, Shane. Studied with Christensen Bros.; studied, San Francisco Ballet Sch.; DFA, U. Mont., 1984. Dancer U. Utah Ballet, Salt Lake City, 1955-57; dancer, choreographer, dir. San Francisco Ballet, 1957-62, 73-85; dancer Am. Ballet Theatre, N.Y. State Theatre, N.Y.C., 1967; prin. dancer, choreographer Am. Ballet Theatre, 1969-73, resident choreographer, 1992—; founder, dir. Smuin Ballets/SF, 1994—. Worked as free-lance dancer with wife Paula Tracy, ind. choreographer; co-chmn. dance adv. panel Nat. Endowment for the Arts, Washington; mem. U.S. dance study team, People's Republic of China, 1983. Dir., musical stager, choreographer: (with Donald McKayle) Sophisticated Ladies, 1981 (Tony award nomination best direction of musical 1981, Outer Critics Circle award 1981); dir., choreographer: Chaplin, 1983, Shogun, 1990; choreographer: Anything Goes, 1987 (Tony award best choreography 1988, Drama Desk award best choreography 1988), Pulcinella Variations, Private Lives, 1991; staged dance works for Leslie Caron, Mikhail Baryshnikov, Rudolf Nureyev with Am. Ballet Theatre/Paris Opera Ballet, 1986; prodr. for San Francisco Ballet: Cinderella, Romeo and Juliet, The Tempest, A Song for Dead Warriors; dir.: Faustus in Hell, Peter and the Wolf, Very Merrily, Verdi, To The Beatles, Revisited, 2001, Stabat Mater, 2001; choreographer: (films) Rumble Fish, 1983, The Cotton Club, 1984, Fletch Lives, 1989, Bram Stoker's Dracula, 1992, So I Married an Axe Murderer, 1993, Angie, 1994, The Fantasticks, 1995; tech. adviser: (film) The Golden Child, 1986, Star Wars Trilogy, 1997; choreographer: (TV) The Tempest, 1981 (Emmy award nomination outstanding achievement in choreography, 1981), A Song for Dead Warriors, 1984 (Emmy award outstanding achievement in choreography 1984), Cinderella, 1985, Romeo and Juliet; dir. Suites by Smuin, Nutcracker on Ice; (TV spls.) Jinx, 1985, Voice/Dance: Bobby McFerrin and the Tandy Beal Dance Company, 1987; choreographer: (TV episode) Corridos! Tales of Passion and Revolution, 1987; creator: (TV show) The Omo, 1987; dir., choreographer: (TV spl.) Linda Ronstadt's Canciones de Mi Padre, 1989, Aid and Comfort. Recipient Dance Magazine award, 1983. Office: Smuin Ballets/SF 1314 34th Ave San Francisco CA 94122-1309*

SMUKALL, CARL FRANKLIN, accountant; b. Rochester, N.Y., Nov. 2, 1967; s. Franklin J. Smukall and Mary M. (Laber) Schiller. BS in Acctg. cum laude, SUNY Oswego, 1989; MBA with distinction, SUNY Buffalo, 1997. CPA, Wash.; cert. fin. mgr. Acct. Battaglia, Moag & Co., P.C., LeRoy, NY, 1989—90; asst. contr. WOKR TV-13, Rochester, N.Y., 1991-94; sr. acct. LeRoy Industries Inc., 1994-97, supr. fin. acctg., 1997-99; contr. Pratt & Huth Assocs., Buffalo, 2000—. Soccer historian Nat. Soccer Hall of Fame, Oneonta, 1996—. Mem. Inst. Mgmt. Accts. (cert.), Soc. Am. Soccer Historians, Beta Gamma Sigma. Roman Catholic. Avocations: soccer, music. Home: 41 Walden Creek Dr Batavia NY 14020-1628 Office: Pratt & Huth Assocs LLP 4950 Genesee St Ste 165 Buffalo NY 14225

SMULLENS, STANTON NOEL, radiologist, surgeon, medical educator; b. Phila., Mar. 13, 1936; m. SaraKay Cohen; children: Elizabeth R., Douglas R., Elisabeth J., Kathyanne S. BA, Harvard U., 1957; MD, Jefferson Med. Coll., 1961. Diplomate Am. Bd. Surgery, Am. Bd. Thoracic Surgery, Am. Bd. Gen. Vasc. Surgery; lic. Pa., N.J. Intern Presbyn./U. Pa. Med. Ctr., Phila., 1961-62; resident in gen. and thoracic surgery Jefferson Med. Coll. Hosp., 1964-65; instr. surgery Jefferson Med. Coll., 1969-72, asst. prof. surgery, 1972-79, assoc. prof. surgery, 1979—, clin. prof. surgery, 1991—; coord. Surg. Residents Rsch. Day, 1983-88; resident in gen. and thoracic surgery Pa. Hosp., Phila., 1965-68; trainee in cardiovascular surgery Nat. Heart Inst. Thomas Jefferson U. Hosp., 1968-69, attending physician, 1970—; chmn., dir. numerous coms., 1985—; chief outpatient svcs. U.S. Army Hosp., Mineral Wells, Tex., 1962-64; asst. attending physician Jefferson Divsn. dept. surgery Phila. Gen. Hosp., 1969-71; asst. physician surgery Our Lady of Lourdes Hosp., 1973-76. Pres., med. dir. Jefferson Health Network Jefferson Health Sys., 1997—, chmn. quality coun., 1998—, care mgmt. com., 1998—, staff support clin. affairs and quality com., 1998—; co-investigator NIH, 1981-86, mem. rev. bd. evaln. for grants, 1985, 87; clin. investigator Upjohn, 1980-82, Bristol Myers, 1985-86; lectr., presenter in field. Contbr. numerous articles to profl. jours., chpts. to books. Bd. trustees Walnut St. Theatre, Phila., 1993-98. Capt. USAR; gen. med. officer U.S. Army, 1962-64. Named Top Doc Phila. Mag., 1990-98, recipient, Leon A. Peris Awd. of Class of 1992, Jefferson Med. Coll. Fellow Am. Cancer Soc.; mem. Am. Coll. Physician Execs., ACS, AHA, AMA, Am. Pain Soc., AAAS, Internat. Cardiovascular Soc., Pa. Lung Assn., Pa. Med. Soc., Pa. Soc. Thoracic Surgery, Phila. Coll. Physicians, Phila. Acad. Surgery, Phila. County Med. Soc., Soc. Clin. Vascular Surgery, Del. Valley Vascular Surgery (founding), Ea. Vascular Surgery Soc., N.Y. Acad. Scis., State Soc. (alt. del. 1974-76), Alumni Assn. Jefferson Med. Coll. (exec. com. 1976—, chmn. pubs. com. 1986-96, v.p. 1993-95, pres. 1996-97), Vol. Faculty Assn. Jefferson Med. Coll. (pres. 1989-91), Sigma Xi, Alpha Omega Alpha. Office: Jefferson Health System 259 N Radnor Chester Rd Radnor PA 19087-5240 Fax: 610-225-6279.

SMUNT, MARSHA LYNN HAEFLINGER, financial executive; b. Chgo., July 9, 1955; m. Timothy Lawrence Smunt, Aug. 17, 1974. BS in Acctg., Purdue U., 1976; MBA in Finance and Investments, Ind. U., 1980. CPA, cert. mgmt. acct., fin. mgmt.; CFA level I. Auditor Deloitte & Touche, St. Louis, 1977-78; analyst corp. diversification McDonnell Douglas Corp., 1979; sr. fin. analyst Cummins Engine Co., Columbus, Ind., 1980-81, capital investments mgr., 1981-82; corp. capital analysis mgr. Gen. Dynamics Corp., St. Louis, 1982-84, corp. mgr. fin. planning, 1984-87; sr. capital investments Anheuser-Busch Cos., Inc., 1987-88, mgr. treasury ops., 1988-91, exec. asst. to treas., 1991-92, mgr. investor rels., 1992-94; dir. fin. planning and forecasting R.J. Reynolds Internat. Inc., Winston-Salem, N.C., 1995-96; sr. v.p. corp. analysis Wachovia Corp., 1997-99, sr. v.p. investor rels., 1999—. Mentor, career symposium spkr. MBA program Wake Forest U., 1995-96; bd. dirs. Sawtooth Ctr. for Visual Art; with Jr. League, Habitat for Humanity. Mem. AICPA, Inst. Mgmt. Accts. (treas., bd. dirs. Piedmont-Winston-Salem chpt.), Profl. Women of Winston-Salem (pres. 1999-2000, bd. dirs.), Nat. Investor Rels. Inst. (pres. St. Louis chpt. 1993-94), Beta Gamma Sigma. Home: 1061 W Kent Rd Winston Salem NC 27104-1131

SMUNT, TIMOTHY LAWRENCE, management educator, business researcher, consultant; m. Marsha Smunt. BS in Indsl. Mgmt., Purdue U., 1976; MBA, U. Mo., 1978; DBA, Ind. U., 1981. Assoc. instr. Ind. U., Bloomington, 1978-81, vis. asst. prof., 1981-82; asst. prof. Wash. U., St. Louis, 1982-86, assoc. prof., 1986-90, U. Ill., Urbana-Champaign, 1990-95; Babcock Rsch. prof., assoc. prof. Wake Forest U., Winston-Salem, N.C., 1995-99, prof. mgmt., 1999—. Cost estimator, price analyst McDonnell Douglas Astronautics Co., St. Louis, 1976-81; vis. assoc. prof. Purdue U., 1991; spkr. in field. Mem. editl. bd. Prodn. Ops. Mgmt., Jour. Ops. Mgmt.; referee Mgmt. Sci., Decision Scis., Jour. Ops. Mgmt., others; contbr. numerous articles to profl. jours. Fellow APICS; mem. Inst. Indsl. Engrs. (sr.), Decision Scis. Inst. (v.p. planning devel. 1992-94, treas. 1994-96), Inst. Ops. Rsch. Mgmt. Sci., Prond. Ops. Mgmt. Soc. Home: 1061 W Kent Rd Winston Salem NC 27104-1131 Office: Babcock Grad Sch Mgmt Wake Forest U Winston Salem NC 27109 Fax: 336-758-4514.

SMUTNY, JOAN FRANKLIN, academic director, educator; b. Chgo. d. Eugene and Mabel (Lind) Franklin; m. Herbert Paul Smutny; 1 child, Cheryl Anne. BS, MA, Northwestern U. Tchr. New Trier H.S., Winnetka, Ill.; mem. faculty, founder, dir. Nat. H.S. Inst. Northwestern U. Sch. Edn., Chgo.; faculty, founder, dir. h.s. workshop critical thinking/edn. Nat. Coll. Edn., Evanston, Ill., exec. dir. h.s. workshops, 1970-75; founder, dir. Woman Power Through Edn. Seminar, 1969-74; dir. Right to Read Seminar in critical reading, 1973-74; dir. seminar gifted h.s. students, 1973; dir. gifted programs for 6th, 7th, 8th graders Evanston pub. schs., 1978-79; dir. gifted programs 1st-8th grade Glenview (Ill.) pub. schs., 1979—. Dir. gifted programs Nat.-Louis U., Evanston, 1980-82, dir. Ctr. for Gifted, 1982—; dir. Bright and Talented Project, 1986—, North Shore Country Day Sch., Winnetka, 1982—; dir. Job Creation Project, 1980-82; dir. New Dimensions for Women, 1973; dir. Thinking for Action in Career Edn. Program 1976-79; dir. TACE, dir. Humanities Program for Verbally Precocious Youth, 1978-79; co-dir., instr. seminars in critical thinking Ill. Family Svc., 1972-75; writer edml. filmstrips in lang. arts and lit. Soc. Visual Edn., 1970-74; spkrs. bur. Coun. Fgn. Rels., 1968-69; adv. com. edn. professions devel. act U.S. Office Edn., 1969—; state team for gifted, Ill. Office Edn., Office of Gifted, Springfield, Ill., 1977; writer, cons. Radiant Ednl. Corp., 1969-71; cons. ALA, 1969-71, workshop leader and spkr. gifted edn., 1971—; coord. career edn. Nat. Coll.Edn., 1976-78, dir. Project 1987—, dir. Summer Wonders, 1986—, Creative Children's Acad., bd. dirs., Worlds of Wisdom and Wonder, 1978—; dir. Future Tchrs. Am. Seminar in Coll. and Career, 1970-72; cons. rsch. & devel. Ill. Dept. Vocat. Edn., 1973—; evaluation cons. DAVTE, IOE, Springfield, Ill., 1977, mem. Leadership Tng. Inst. Gifted, U.S. Office Edn., 1973-74; dir. workshops for h.s. students; cons., spkr. in field; dir. Gifted Young Writers and Young Writers confs., 1978, 79; dir. Project '92 The White House Conf. on Children and Youth; mem. adv. bd. Educating Able Learners, 1991—; chmn. bd. dirs. Barbereux Sch., Evanston, 1992—; asst. editor, editl. bd. Understanding our Gifted, 1994—. Author: (with others) Job Creation: Creative Materials, Activities and Strategies for the Classroom, 1982, A Thoughful Overview of Gifted Education, 1990, Your Gifted Child—How to Recognize and Develop the Special Talents in Your Child from Birth to Age Seven, 1987, paperback, 1991, Education of the Gifted: Programs and Perspectives, 1990, The Young Gifted Child: Potential and Promise: An Anthology, 1998, The Gifted Young Child in the Regular Classroom, 1997, Gifted Girls, 1998, Perspectives in Gifted Education: Young Gifted Children, 1999, Stand Up For Your Gifted Child, 2001, Understand Gifted Population, 2002; contbg. editor Roper Rev., 1994—; asst. editor Understanding Our Gifted, 1995—; editor, contbr. Maturity in Teching; writer ednl. filmstrips The Brothers Grimm, How the West Was Won, Mutiny on the Bounty, Dr. Zhivago, Space Odyssey 2001, Christmas Around the World; editor IAGC Jour. for Gifted, 1994—; adv. bd. Gifted Edn. Press Quar., 1995—; contbr. editor numerous books in field; contbr. articles to profl. jours. including Chgo. Parent Mag.; reviewer programs for Gifted and Talented, U.S. Office Edn., 1976-78; editor Creativity Series Ablex, 1998—. Mem. AAUP, Nat. Assn. Gifted Child (nat. membership chmn. 1991—, co-chmn. schs. and programs, co-editor newsletter early childhood divsn.), Nat. Soc. Arts & Letters (nat. bd., 1st and 3d v.p. Evanston chpt. 1990-92), Mortar Bd., Outstanding Educators of Am. 1974, Pi Lambda Theta, Phi Delta Kappa (v.p. Evanston chpt. rsch. chmn. 1990-92). Home: 633 Forest Ave Wilmette IL 60091-1713 *Commitment to education is defined as contribution. We who are privileged to work in education know that the focus is the educant-the learner. Gifted education is particularly vital in that it discerns the needs of bright, talented children who have an immense amount to contribute to our country and our world. Gifted children are our country's most neglected resource--and most needed. It is my privilege to work in this area, to work with children, parents and teachers. The community of mankind is needed to support the talent and growth of the gifted. Then we are really contributing to the educant.*

SMYER, MYRNA RUTH, drama educator; b. Albuquerque, June 10, 1946; d. Paul Anthony and Ruth Kelly (Klein) S.; m. Carlton Weaver Canaday, July 5, 1980. BFA, U. N.Mex., 1969; MA, Northwestern U., 1971. Pvt. practice drama instr., Albuquerque, 1974-78; dir. drama Sandia Preparatory Sch., 1977-98, chmn. dept. fine arts, 1980-98; exec./artistic dir. touring theater co. Once Upon A Theatre, 1998—. Dialect coach, dir. Chgo. Acting Ensemble, 1969-71; lectr., workshop instr., performer Albuquerque Pub. Schs. and various civic orgns., Albuquerque, 1974—; writer, dir., performer Arts in the Pks., Albuquerque, 1977-80; performer, crew various indsl. videos, 1981-86; instr. workshops and continuing edn. U. N.Mex. 1977-80. Writer, dir., designer children's plays including May The Best Mammal (Or Whatever) Win, 1977, A Holiday Celebration, 1977, Puppets on Parade, 1978, A Witch's Historical Switches, 1979, Once Upon a Rhyme Series, 1987—, Little Red Riding Hood, 1987, 2001, Goldilocks and The Three Bears, 1988, 2000, Cinderella, 1989, Hansel and Gretel, 1990, Rumpelstiltskin, 1991, 2002, The Dancing Princesses, 1992, The Three Pigs, 1994, Sleeping Beauty, 1996, A Governess Wronged or He Betrayed Her Trust, 2001; The Magic of Shakespear, 2002, dir. numerous other children and adult plays. Instr., writer, dir. various cmty. theatres including Albuquerque Little Theatre, Corrales Adobe Theatre, Kimo Theatre, Albuquerque Civic Light Opera, Now We Are Theatre; N.Mex. arts commr., 1999—; mem. task force City of Albuquerque Cultural Plan, 2001; mem. City of Albuquerque Cultural Plan Adv. Com. , 2002—, Albuquerque Arts in Edn. Task Force, 2000—. Recipient Helen and Doug Bridges award for Outstanding Instr., 1990, 1st Place award for Quality in Edn. N.Mex. Rsch. and Study Coun. and U. N.Mex., 1990, Albuquerque Acad. grant (children theatre), 1993, 95, 97, Neighborhood Appreciation award Four Hills, 1993, Albuquerque Arts Alliance Bravo award for Outstanding Contribution to Arts in Edn., 1995, Zia award, U. N.Mex. Disting. Alumni, 1999. Mem.: Albuquerque Performing Arts Mgrs., Albuquerque Arts Alliance. Avocations: reading, hiking, dancing. Office: Once Upon a Theatre 13170B Central Ave SE # 130 Albuquerque NM 87123-3032

SMYNTEK, JOHN EUGENE, JR. editor; b. Buffalo, Aug. 24, 1950; BA, U. Detroit, 1972. Asst. instr. Mich. State U., East Lansing, 1981; features editor Free Press, Detroit, 1985-92; dir. online svcs. and dir. libr. Free Press Plus, 1992-95, spl. features and syndicate editor, 1995—; asst. instr. U. Detroit Mercy, 2000—. Vis. fellow in journalism Duke U., 1988; profl. student publs. advisor U. Detroit Mercy, 1992—94; bd. visitors Wayne State U. Coll. Fine, Performing and Comm. Arts, 2001—. Recipient Fine Arts Reporting award, Detroit Press Club, 1985. Roman Catholic. Office: Detroit Free Press 600 W Fort St Detroit MI 48226-2706 E-mail: smyntek@freepress.com.

SMYRE, CALVIN, political organization worker, state legislator; div.; 1 child. BS in Bus. Adminstrn., Fort Valley State U. Mem. Ga. Ho. of Reps., Atlanta, 1974—, asst. adminstrn. floor leader, 1983; mem. Dem. Nat. Com., 1984, adminstrn. floor leader. Chmn. univ. sys. Ga. com.; mem. appropriations com., rules com.; banker; exec. v.p. corp. affairs Synovus Fin. Corp. Nat. sec. Nat. Black Caucus State Legislators; bd. trustees Med. Coll. Ga. Found., Morehouse Sch. Med., Jack D. Hughston Found.; chmn. bd. trustees Fort Valley State U. Found.; former nat. pres. Fort Valley State U. Nat. Alumni Assn.; bd. advisors Atlanta U. Sch. Social Work. With U.S. Army. Democrat. Office: Georgia House of Representivies 415 State Capitol Atlanta GA 30334 also: Georgia Democratic Party 1100 Spring Street, Suite 710 Atlanta GA 30309*

SMYRNIOS, NICHOLAS A. physician, educator; b. Saugus, Mass., Sept. 2, 1959; s. Philip Nicholas and Mary Eunice Smyrnios; m. Roxanne Kim, Sept. 2, 1995; chiildren: Alexandra Kim, Philip Nicholas. BS, Tufts U., 1981; MD, Albany Med. Coll., 1985. Diplomate in internal medicine, pulmonary diseases and critical care medicine Am. Bd. Internal Medicine. Asst. prof. medicine U. Mass. Med. Sch., Worcester, 1991-98, assoc. prof. medicine, 1998—, dir. fellowship in critical care medicine, 1996—; dir. med. ICU, U. Mass. Meml. Med. Ctr., 1992—. Spkr. in field. Editor: Review of Intensive Care Medicine, 1999; contbr. articles to profl. jours. Vol., St. Spyridon Cathedral, Worcester, 1996—. Will Rogers Pulmonary fellow, 1988-90. Fellow Am. Coll. Chest Physicians (gov. for Mass. 1999—); mem. ACP, AMA, Am. Thoracic Soc., Soc. Critical Care Medicine. Greek Orthodox. Avocations: music, sports. Office: U Mass Meml Healthcare Pulmonary Divsn 55 Lake Ave N Worcester MA 01655-0002

SMYTH, CORNELIUS EDMONSTON, retired hotel executive; b. N.Y.C., Aug. 20, 1926; s. Cornelius Joseph and Roberta Ernestine (Anderson) S.; m. Jeanne Laura Dillingham, Nov. 25, 1950 (dec. Oct. 1996); m. Jeanette M. Hubbard, Apr. 18, 1998; children: Cornelius E. Jr., Loretta M., William D., James B., Laura I., Robert B. BS in Econs., U. Pa., Phila., 1946. Cert. Hospitality Acct. Exec. Contr. Caesars Palace Hotel and Casino, Las Vegas, Nev., 1970-73, fin. v.p., 1974, adminstrv. v.p., 1975-77, exec. v.p., 1977-81; pres. Sands Hotel and Casino, 1981-83; exec. v.p. Latin Am. ops. Caesars World Internat., L.A., 1983-89, pres. Mexican ops., 1989-90; bd. dirs. Venture Catalyst, Inc., San Diego, 1994—. Cons., Coronado, Calif., 1994—2002. Co-author: A Uniform System of Accounts for Hotels, 7th rev. edit., 1977. Comdr. USNR, 1944-70. Named to U.S. Table Tennis Hall of Fame, 1996. Mem. Pi Gamma Mu, Sigma Chi. Republican. Roman Catholic. Avocations: table tennis, body surfing.

SMYTH, CRAIG HUGH, fine arts educator; b. N.Y.C., July 28, 1915; s. George Hugh and Lucy Salome (Humeston) S.; m. Barbara Linforth, June 24, 1941; children: Alexandra, Edward Linforth (Ned). BA, Princeton U., 1938, MFA, 1941, PhD, 1956; MA (hon.), Harvard U., 1975. Sr. mus. aid, rsch. asst. Nat. Gallery Art, Washington, 1941-42; officer-in-charge, dir. Cen. Art Collecting Point, Munich, 1945-46; lectr. Frick Collection, N.Y.C., 1946-50; asst. prof. Inst. Fine Arts NYU, 1950-53, assoc. prof. Inst. Fine Arts, 1953-57, prof. Inst. Fine Arts, 1957-73, acting dir. Inst. Fine Arts, acting head dept. fine arts Grad. Sch. Arts and Scis., 1951-53, dir. inst., head dept. fine arts Grad. Sch., 1953-73; prof. fine arts Harvard U., 1973-85, prof. emeritus, 1985—; Samuel Kress prof. Ctr. for Advanced Study in Visual Arts Nat. Gallery Art, Washington, 1987-88; dir. Villa I Tatti Harvard U. Ctr. Italian Renaissance Studies, Florence, 1973-85. Art historian in residence Am. Acad. in Rome, 1959-60; mem. U.S. Nat. Com. History Art, 1955-85; alt. U.S. mem. Comité Internat. d'Histoire de l'Art, 1970-83, U.S. mem., 1983-85; chmn. adv. com. J. Paul Getty Rsch. Inst. History of Art and Humanities, 1982-99; mem. architect selection com. J. Paul Getty Trust, 1983-84; mem. organizing com., keynote speaker 400th Anniversary of Uffizi Gallery, 1981-82; vis. scholar Inst. Advanced Study, Princeton, N.J., 1971, mem., 1978, visitor, 1983, 85-86; vis. scholar Bibliotheca Hertziana, Max Planck Soc., Rome, 1972, 73; mem. vis. com. dept. art and archaeology Princeton U., 1956-73, 85-89; mem. adv. com. Villa I Tatti, 1985-92; trustee Hyde Collection, Glens Falls, N.Y., 1985-87, The Burlington mag., 1987—; mem. commn. Ednl. & Cultural Exch. between Italy and U.S., 1979-83. Author: Mannerism and Maniera, 1963, rev. edit. with introduction by E. Cropper, 1992, Bronzino as Draughtsman, 1971, Michelangelo Architetto (with H.M. Millon), 1988, English edit., 1988, Repatriation of Art from the Collecting Point in Munich After World War II, 1988; editor: Michelangelo Drawings (Nat. Gallery of Art), 1992; editor (with Peter M. Lukehart), contbr.: The Early Years of Art History in the United States, 1993; founding chmn. (periodical) I Tatti Studies: Essays in the Renaissance, 1984-85; contbr. to profl. jours. Hon. trustee Met. Mus. Art, N.Y.C., 1968— ; trustee Inst. Fine Arts, NYU, 1973—; mem. mayor's com. Piazza Della Signoria, Florence, 1975-78. Lt. USNR, 1942-46. Decorated Chevalier Legion of Honor France, U.S. Army Commendation medal, Netherlands Medal for Svc. to the State; sr. Fulbright Rsch. fellow, 1949-50, honored by establishment of CHS professorship, Inst. of Fine Arts NYU, 1999. Mem. Am. Acad. Arts and Scis., Am. Philos. Soc., Coll. Art Assn. Am. (bd. dirs. 1953-57, sec. 1956), Accademia Fiorentina delle Arti del Disegno (academician, assoc.), Accademia di San Luca (hon. 1995), Harvard Club (N.Y.C.), Century Assn. (N.Y.C.), Phi Beta Kappa. Address: PO Box 539 Cresskill NJ 07626-0039

SMYTH, DAVID, editor, author; b. Buenos Aires, Feb. 7, 1929; came to U.S. 1962, naturalized 1970; s. Currell Hutchinson and Jessie Rodger (Dodds) S.; m. Elli Helene Dusterhoft, Nov. 9, 1968; 1 child, Clifford Dieter. BA, Cambridge (Eng.) U., 1951, MA, 1967. Tech. writer, copywriter, 1953-55; movie promotion writer, 1956; owner Ace Translation Agy., Buenos Aires, 1957-58; sec. Found. Econ. Edn., 1959; cables editor Buenos Aires Herald, 1960; lexicographer Simon & Schuster English-Spanish Dictionary, 1961; Latin Am. desk editor UPI, N.Y.C., 1962-63, AP, N.Y.C., 1963-73, world svcs. fin. editor, 1973-96; freelance writer, translator, editor, 1997—. Author: You Can Survive Any Financial Disaster, 1977, Worldly Wise Investor, 1988; co-author: The Speculator's Handbook, 1974, Unusual Investments That could Make You Rich, 1978, No Cost/Low Cost Investing, 1987. Served with Argentine Army, 1952. Mem. N.Y. Fin. Writers Assn. Home: 8 Beechwood Ave Metuchen NJ 08840-2107 E-mail: Currell@aol.com.

SMYTH, DAVID JOHN, economist; b. Twickenham, Eng., Apr. 19, 1936; came to U.S., 1967; s. John Richard and Ena Caryle (Stuart) S.; m. Jane Mair, July 19, 1969; children: Seamus John, Alexander David. B.Econs., U. Queensland, Australia, 1957, M.Econs., 1960; PhD, U. Birmingham, Eng., 1968. Lectr. econs. U. Queensland, 1957-60; univ. research scholar London Sch. Econs., 1960-63; lectr. econs., then sr. lectr. math. econs. U. Birmingham, 1963-67; prof. SUNY, Buffalo, 1967-70; prof. econs. Claremont (Calif.) Grad. Sch., 1971-76, chmn. dept., 1973-76; prof. econs. Wayne State U., Detroit, 1976-86, chmn. dept., 1976-85; LSU Found. Disting. prof. econs. La. State U., Baton Rouge, 1987—. Mem. internat. adv. bd. Jour. Econ. Surveys, 1985—; mem. adv. bd. N.Am. Econ. and Fin. Assn., 1989—; mem. interdisciplinary adv. bd. Policy Studies Orgn., 1991—; visitor Ctr. for Econ. Rsch., Tilburg U., The Netherlands, 1993. Author: The Demand for Farm Machinery, 1970, Forecasting the United Kingdom Economy, 1973, Size, Growth, Profits and Executive Compensation in the Large Corporation, 1975; editor: Jour. Macroeconomics, 1977— ; contbr. articles to profl. jours. Recipient award Bd. Govs. Wayne State U., 1980; Erskine fellow U. Canterbury, New Zealand, summer 1990. Mem. Am. Econ. Assn., Econometric Soc., Royal Econ. Soc., So. Econ. Assn., Am. Fin. Assn., Western Econ. Assn., Am. Agrl. Econ. Assn., AAUP (chpt. pres. 1975-76), Acad. of Scholars of Wayne State U. Home: 12812 Woodshire Pl Baton Rouge LA 70816-2547 Office: La State U Dept Econs 2107 Ceba Baton Rouge LA 70803-0001

SMYTH, DONALD MORGAN, chemical educator, researcher; b. Bangor, Maine, Mar. 20, 1930; s. John Robert and Selma (Eubanks) S.; m. Elisabeth Luce, Aug. 1, 1951; children: Carolyn, Joanne. BS in Chemistry, U. Maine, 1951; PhD in Inorganic Chemistry, MIT, 1954. Sr. chemist Sprague Electric Co., North Adams, Mass., 1954-58, sect. head, 1958-61, dept. head, 1961-71; assoc. prof. Lehigh U., Bethlehem, Pa., 1971-73, prof., 1973-95, dir. Materials Rsch. Ctr., 1971-92, Paul B. Reinhold prof. materials sci., engrng. and chemistry, 1988-95; emeritus, 1995—. Mem. various coms. Lehigh U., 1973-95; mem. materials rsch. adv. com. NSF, 1984-88, chmn., 1985-86, co-chair ad-hoc com. to brief dir., 1986; mem. coun. materials sci. Dept. Energy, 1986-90; presenter in field. Contbr. articles to profl. jours. Recipient Libsch Rsch. award Lehigh U., 1990, Buessem award Dielectrics Rsch. Ctr., Pa. State U., 1991; grantee in field. Fellow Am. Inst. Chemists, Am. Ceramic Soc. (com. edn. electronics divsn. 1974-78, chmn. Lehigh Valley sect. 1978-79, counselor 1982-00, assoc. editor jour. 1988-92, best paper award 1987, 95, Kraner award Lehigh Valley sect. 1990, Sosman lectr. 1996); mem. Am. Chem. Soc., Nat. Acad. Engrng., Materials Rsch. Soc., Electrochem. Soc. (various coms., sec. dielectrics and insulation divsn. 1967-69, vice chmn. 1969-70, chmn. 1970-71, rsch. award battery divsn. 1960). Achievements include patents (with others) for Solid-State Battery Cell with Complex Organic Electrolyte Material, Capacitor with Dielectric Film Having Phosphorous-Containing Component Therein, Solid Barrier Electrolyte Incorporating Additive, others; research in defect chemistry and electrical properties of complex oxides. Home: 3429 Mountainview Cir Bethlehem PA 18017-1807 Office: Lehigh U Materials Rsch Ctr 5 E Packer Ave Bethlehem PA 18015-3102 Business E-Mail: dms4@lehigh.edu.

SMYTH, GERARD A. lawyer, administrator; b. N.Y.C., June 29, 1945; s. Eugene J. and Theresa Smyth; m. Janice Anderson, Aug. 1, 1987; children: Gregg Smyth, Tricia Smyth, Lindsey Hall, Thomas Hall. BA, Fairfield U., 1967; JD, U. Conn., 1975. Bar: Conn. 1975. Asst. atty. gen. State of Conn., Hartford, 1975-76; asst. pub. defender Divsn. Pub. Defender Svcs., State of Conn., 1976-85, chief of capital def. and trial svcs., 1985-91, dep. chief pub. defender, 1991-94, chief pub. defender, 1994—. Mem. Conn. Alcohol and Drug Policy Coun., Hartford, 1996—, Gov.'s Task Force on Justice for Abused Children, Hartford, 1997—, Ct. Prison and Jail Overcrowding Commn., 1994—, Ct. Commn. on the Death Penalty, 2001--, Ct. Criminal Justice Info. Sys. Governing Bd., 2000--. Bd. dirs. Ct. Justice Edn. Ctr., Ct. Correctional Ombudsman, Cmty. Ptnrs. in Action; mem. Zoning Bd. Appeals, Town of Granby, Conn., chmn. charter revision com. Capt. USAF, 1968-73. Mem. Nat. Assn. Criminal Def. Lawyers, Conn. Criminal Def. Lawyers Assn., Conn. Bar Assn. (exec. com. criminal justice 1994—), Hartford County Bar ASsn., Nat. Legal Aid and Defender Assn. (defender policy group 2000), Am. Coun. Chief Defenders. Office: Office of Chief Pub Defender 30 Trinity St Fl 4 Hartford CT 06106-1629 E-mail: g.smyth@po.state.ct.us.

SMYTH, GLEN MILLER, management consultant; b. Abingdon, Va., July 26, 1929; s. Glen Miller and Kathleen (Dunn) S.; m. Cynthia Olson, Aug. 25, 1954 (div. 1967); children: Catherine Ellen, Glen Miller, III, Cynthia Allison; m. Lilian Castel Edgar, Oct. 31, 1968; children: Stephanie Castel, Kimberley Forsyth, Lindsay Dunn. BA, Yale U., 1951; MS in Psychology, Rutgers U., 1958. Mktg. rep. Wheeling Stamping Co., N.Y.C., 1953-56; personnel dir. Celanese Internat., 1958-71; mgr. orgn. and Manpower Internat. and Can. group Gen. Electric Co., 1971-73; sr. v.p. human resources Northwest Bancorp., Mpls., 1973-82; sr. v.p. Calif. Fed. Savs., L.A., 1983-85; v.p. Career Transition Group, 1985-87; pres. Fuchs, Cuthrell & Co., Inc., 1987-93, Fuchs & Co., L.A., 1993-94; pres., CEO Smyth, Fuchs & Co., Inc., 1995-99; v.p. Spherion, 1998—. Leader seminars. Co-author: International Career Pathing, 1971; Contbr. articles to profl. jours. Served with AUS, 1951-53. Mem. Am. Psychol. Assn., Nat. Fgn. Trade Coun. (founder, past chmn. human resources, orgn. com. 1966—), Human Resources Planning Soc., Employment Mgmt. Assn., Jonathan Club, Yale Club of N.Y., North Ranch Country Club, Phi Gamma Delta. Home: 1115 Westcreek Ln Westlake Village CA 91362-5467 E-mail: smythla@aol.com.

SMYTH, JAMES J. civilian military employee; B in Civil Engrng., Villanova U. Registered profl. engr., Pa. From mem. staff to dep. asst. sec. U.S. Army Corps of Engrs., Washington, 1965, dep. asst. sec. project planning & rev. Mem.: ASCE. Office: Office of Secretary of Army for Civil Engineers Army Pentagon Washington DC 20310-1500*

SMYTH, JOEL DOUGLAS, newspaper executive; b. Renovo, Pa., Nov. 8, 1941; s. Bernard John and Eva Mae (Stone) S.; m. Madonna Robertson, Nov. 29, 1959; children: Deborah Sue, Susan Kelly, Michael Robertson, Patricia Ann, Rebecca Lee, Jennifer Neilia. Student, Lycoming Coll., 1959. Reporter Del. State News, Dover, 1960-62, news editor, 1962-65, mng. editor, 1965-70, editor, pres., 1970-78; editor Del. Sunday News, 1964-65; pres. Ind. Newspapers, Inc., Dover, 1970-89, chmn., CEO, 1989—. Founding pres. Valley Citizen's League, 1987-90. Recipient writing awards. Mem. AP Mng. Editors Assn. (dir.), Am. Soc. Newspaper Editors, Young Pres.'s Orgn., Sigma Delta Chi. Home: 39833 N 100th St Scottsdale AZ 85262-2975 Office: Independent Newspaper Inc PO Box 70001 Dover DE 19903 Home: 39833 N 100th St Scottsdale AZ 85262-2975

SMYTH, JOSEPH PATRICK, retired naval officer, physician; b. Norwalk, Conn., Mar. 2, 1933; s. Patrick and Helen (Heffernan) S.; m. Ursula Marie (Kirwin), Dec. 28, 1960; children: Donna, Jennifer, Joseph. BA, Fairfield U., 1960; MD, Creighton U., 1964. Diplomate Am. Bd. Med. Examiners. Commd. ensign USN, 1963, advanced through grades to rear adm., 1988; intern Phila. Naval Hosp., 1964-65, internal medicine resident, 1965-68, staff physician, 1968-69; internist, chief of medicine U.S. Naval Hosp., DaNang, Vietnam, 1969-70, Orlando, Fla., 1970-76, chief of medicine, exec. officer Yokosuka, Japan, 1976-80, exec. officer Oakland, Calif., 1980-82, comdg. officer, 1984-86, Okinawa, Japan, 1982-84, Naval Med. Command European Region, London, 1986-90; dep. dir. for med. readiness The Joint Staff, Pentagon, Washington, 1990-92; retired US Navy, 1992; med. dir. Volusia County (Fla.) Dept. of Corrections, 1994—. Instr. medicine Jefferson Med. Coll., 1966-69; preceptor USN Physician Asst. Program, Orlando, 1971-76; inst. mgmt. course Navy Med. Dept., Washington, 1986; Joint Staff med. coord. for entire Gulf War build-up reporting to JCS chmn. Gen. Colin Powell Operation Desert Shield/Storm, Saudi Arabia, 1990-91. Physician Orange County, Fla. Alcohol Ctr., Orlando, 1974-76. Decorated Def. Superior Svc. medal, Legion of Merit, Meritorious Svc. medals with 2 oak leaf clusters, Navy Commendation medal with combat V. Mem. AMA, Assn. Mil. Surgeons of U.S., Am. Acad. Med. Adminstrs. (Levandowski award 1991), Fla. Med. Assn., Am. Acad. Physician Execs., Orange County Med. Soc. Republican. Roman Catholic. Home: 400 Sweetwater Blvd S Longwood FL 32779-3422

SMYTH, JOSEPH PHILIP, travel industry executive; b. N.Y.C., Aug. 16, 1939; s. Joseph P. and Virginia S. (Gibbs) S.; m. Janet Hughes; 1 child, Philip. BA, Hamilton U., 1961; MBA, Harvard U., 1967; student, Naval Intelligence Sch., 1961-62. Dir. planning N.E. Airlines, Boston, 1967-70; acct. supr. Wells, Rich, Greene, N.Y.C., 1970-72; sr. v.p. mktg. Inter-Continental, 1972-86, Hilton Hotels, Beverly Hills, Calif., 1986-88; head of ops. Cunard, N.Y.C., 1988-94; sr. v.p. fleet ops. Holland Am., Seattle, 1994; chmn Gibbs Bros., Huntsville, Tx., 1995—. Bd. mem. First Nat. Bank Huntsville, Tex. Lt. USN, 1961-65, ETO. Mem. Harvard Club. Avocation: running. Home: 1088 Park Ave New York NY 10128-1132 Office: Gibbs Bros PO Box 711 Huntsville TX 77342-0711

SMYTH, JOSEPH VINCENT, manufacturing company executive; b. Belfast, Ireland, July 18, 1919; s. Joseph Leo and Margaret M. (Murray) S.; m. Marie E. Cripe, Mar. 22, 1941; children: Kevin W., Brian J., Ellen M., Vincent P. BS cum laude, U. Notre Dame, 1941. With Arnolt Corp., Warsaw, 1946-63, exec. v.p., gen. mgr., until 1963; pres., gen. mgr. Hills-McCanna Co., Carpentersville, Ill., 1963-72; pres. Lunkenheimer Co., Cin., 1972-79; v.p. Condec Flow Control Group, Chgo., 1979-82; cons., 1982—. Mem.: K.C. Address: 7656 Spring Bay Cove Orlando FL 32819-7208

SMYTH, MARY ELLEN, management consultant; b. Lander, Wyo., July 2, 1935; BA with honors, U. Wyo., 1956, MA, 1969. Instr. Pa. State U., State College, 1960-63; tchr. Lyons Twp. H.S., LaGrange, Ill., 1964-70; dir. adminstrn. Reconstructive Orthops., Ltd., River Forest; pres., owner Smyth Orgn., Chgo., 1985—. Mem. governing bd. Chgo. Symphony Orch., 1978—, Chgo. Zool. Soc., Brookfield, Ill., 1985-2001; mem. nat. adv. bd. U. Wyo. Art Mus., Laramie, 1980-2000, pres., 1996-98; sec. AAUW Edn. Found., Washington, 1993-97, devel. v.p., 1999-2001, pres., 2001—; bd. dirs. Leadership Ill., 1993-2000, Leadership Am., 1994. Ford Found. grantee, 1958. Mem. Phi Beta Kappa, Phi Kappa Phi. Democrat. Roman Catholic. Home and Office: 1550 N Lake Shore Dr # 26G Chicago IL 60610-6608 Fax: 312-943-4806. E-mail: smyth5@aol.com.

SMYTH, NICHOLAS PATRICK DILLON, surgeon; b. Dublin, Ireland, Apr. 1, 1924; came to U.S., 1951; s. Patrick Joseph and Nano Elizabeth (Dillon) S.; m. Elizabeth Stavely Long; children: Sheila, Brian, Nicholas, Augustine, Patrick. BSc, Univ. Coll. Dublin, 1946, MSc, 1948, MB, BCh, 1949; MS, U. Mich., 1954. Diplomate Am. Bd. Surgery, Am. Bd. Thoracic Surgery. Intern Mater Misericordiae Hosp., Dublin, 1949-50, Norfolk and Norwich Hosp., Eng., 1950-51; resident in gen. surgery Henry Ford Hosp., Detroit, 1951-55; resident in thoracic surgery George Washington U. Hosp., Washington, 1957-59; pvt. practice, 1959-86; clin. prof. surgery emeritus George Washington U. Sch. Medicine. Mem. staff Washington Hosp. Ctr., George Washington U. Med. Ctr. Contbr. articles to profl. jours.; patentee in field. Capt. M.C., U.S. Army, 1955-57 Fellow: ACS, Am. Coll. Cardiology; mem.: N.Am. Soc. Pacing and Electrophysiology, So. Thoracic Surg. Assn., Soc. Thoracic Surgery, Am. Assn. Thoracic Surgery. Republican. Roman Catholic. Avocation: writing.

SMYTH, PAUL BURTON, lawyer; b. Phila., Aug. 15, 1949; s. Benjamin Burton and Florence Elizabeth (Tomlinson) S.; m. Denise Elaine Freeland, May 31, 1975. BA, Trinity Coll., 1971; JD, Boston Coll., 1974. Bar: Conn. 1974, D.C. 1975, U.S. Dist. Ct. D.C., 1980, U.S. Supreme Ct., 1985. With Dept. Interior, 1974—. Atty. Office of Hearings and Appeals, Arlington, Va., 1974—76, Office of Solicitor, Washington, 1976—82; asst. solicitor for land use and realty, Washington, 1982—87; deputy assoc. solicitor for energy and resources, Washington, 1987—95; acting dir. Office of Hearings and Appeals, Arlington, Va., 1993—94; deputy assoc. solicitor for land and water uses, 1995—; lectr. environ. law George Wash. U. Law Sch., Washington, 1997—. Editor: Federal Reclamation and Related Laws Annotated, Reclamation Reform Act Compilation, 1982—88; contbr. articles to legal pubs. Bd. dirs. EcoVoce, 1998—; trustee Rocky Mtn. Mineral Law Found., 1999—2001. Mem. ABA (coun. 1991-94, budget officer 1994-98, sec. natural resources, energy and environ. law, exec. editor Nat. Resources and the Environ. 1989-91). Office: Office of Solicitor Dept Interior 18th And C Sts NW Washington DC 20240-0001 E-mail: paul_smyth@ios.doi.gov.

SMYTH, STUART J. history educator; b. Mar. 11, 1939; MA, U. Albany, 1990; PhD, SUNY Albany, 1998. Vis. asst. prof. Marist Coll., Poughkeepsie, N.Y., 1997; asst. prof. Fordham U., Bronx, NY, 1998—99, SUNY, New Paltz, 1998—2001, SUNY , Albany, 2000—, Berkshire County Coll., 2000—. Contbr. articles to profl. publs. Home: 35 Harlemville Rd Hillsdale NY 12529-6104 Office: SUNY Albany 2 Ten Breck Hall 1400 Washington Ave Albany NY 12222 E-mail: taiping@csc.albany.edu., smyth@taconic.net.

SMYTH, THEODORE HILTON, real estate developer; b. New London, Conn., Apr. 3, 1915; s. Joseph H. and Ida Mae (Towson) S.; m. Elizabeth Norton McBride, Apr. 2, 1949; children: Elizabeth Towson, Theodore Hilton Jr. BA, Bard Coll., 1937, PhD, 1973; D of Bus. Adminstrn. (hon.), Hillsdale Coll., 1997. Shoe buyer Melville Shoe Corp., 1937-40; commercial aviator Am. Overseas Airlines, N.Y., 1946-50; investment counselor Lakeside Co., Seattle, 1950-52; real estate developer Hawaii, 1952—; ltd. ptnr. Conversion Project, Atlanta, 1980. Pres. Santa Barbara (Calif.) Symphony, 1960-62, dir., 1958-68; dir. United Way, Santa Barbara, 1970-74, Calif. Tech. Assocs., Pasadena, 1980-85; chmn. Info Genesis, Santa Barbara, 1985—; former trustee Bard Coll.; mem. bd. vistors and govs. St. John's Coll., 1990-96. Lt. Comdr. USNR, 1940-45. Republican. Avocations: tennis umpiring, swimming, tennis. Home: 4234 Cresta Ave Santa Barbara CA 93110-2410

SMYTH, WALTER G. real estate broker; b. Oakland, Calif., June 22, 1937; s. Howard McGaw and Hertha (Kainrath) S.; m. Nadine Mezentsoff, June 1964 (div. 1984); children: Scott, Robert, Susan; m. Madeline Griffith, Mar. 20, 1984; children: Douglas, Andrew. AB, Princeton U., 1960. From metallurgist to gen. mgr. corp. responsibility Armco Steel Corp., Balt., Middletown, Ohio, 1960-85; comml. real estate agt. St. Petersburg, Tampa, Fla., 1987-93; mgr. comml. investment Coldwell Banker Hashem Realty, St. Petersburg, 1993-98, Premier Group Realty, Inc., St. Petersburg, 1998—. Commr. St. Petersburg Housing Auth., 1995—, chmn. 2001; 33 gallon vol. blood donor. Capt. USMC, 1961-64. Mem.: NRA, City of St. Petersburg Housing Roundtable, Pub. Housing Authority Dirs. Assn., Nat. Assn. Housing and Redevel. Ofcls., Pinellas Suncoast Assn. Realtors (chmn.-elect 2002), Fla. Gulf Coast

Assn. Realtors, St. Petersburg Suncoast Assn. Realtors (sec., dir. 1998—, pres. 2001—), Fla. Assn. Realtors (dir. 1998—), Nat. Assn. Realtors, Am. Legion. Republican. Presbyterian. Avocations: fishing, reading, collecting beer cans, military history, fish & wildlife. Home: 4853 Venetian Pl NE Saint Petersburg FL 33703-4223 Office: Premier Group Realty Inc 2201 4th St N Saint Petersburg FL 33704-4300 E-mail: wsmyth@tampabay.rr.com., walt6B34@aol.com.

SMYTH, WARD ALAN, retired food products executive; b. Sherbrooke, Que., Can., Aug. 9, 1951; came to U.S., 1958; naturalized, 1964; s. Ward Awald and Gwendolyn Muriel (Lawrence) S.; m. Carolyn Schaefer (div.); m. Katherine Kendall Fisher, Aug. 11, 1979 (dec. Jan. 1998); children: Logan Falconer, Katherine Lawrence. BS in Liberal Studies, SUNY, 1990; postgrad., U. Vt., 1994—. Ski instr., ski supr. Ski Sundown Ski Area, New Hartford, Conn., 1971-73; from engr., estimator to project supt. Pine Constrn. Inc., Farmington, 1973-74, project mgr., 1974-77, asst. corp. sec., 1976-77; pres., owner Salmon Creek Co., Salisbury, 1977-82, Beaver Creek/Thermal Wall, Inc., Salisbury, 1987-90, Salmon Creek Builders, Ltd., Salisbury, 1982-90; bus. cons. Sun/Shelter Design Group, Warren, Vt., 1987-93, ind. rep., 1987-92; COO, Three Bears Company, Waitsfield, 1993-97; ret., 1997; exec. dir. Vt. Subcontractors Assn., 1994—2002; mng. dir. Peregrine Mgmt. Group, Ocala, Fla., 1998-99; owner Turtle Creek Builders, Warren, Vt., 2000—. Tchr., seminar presenter Mind Your Own Bus., Sturbridge, Mass., 1989, Tng. and Keeping Crews, Sturbridge, 1989, Computers in Constrn., Cromwell, Conn., 1988, Cost Estimating by Computer, Monticello, N.Y., 1987, Small Bus. Forum, Sturbridge, 1986, The Optimized Wall System, Hartford, Conn., 1986, various industry forums and panels; speaker Conn. Audubon Soc., 1991, Conn. Pub. Interest Rsch. Group, Trinity Coll., 1991, Berkshire-Litchfield Environ. Coun., 1990, N.E. Environ. Def. Coun., 1990. Contbr. articles to profl. jours. Pres. Salisbury Glen Condominium Owners' Assn., Conn., 1984-86; chair candidate recruitment com. Rep. Town Com., Salisbury, 1984-88, mem., 1984-88, 90-91; chair Young Reps. Salisbury, 1983-84, mem. 1983-85, mem. state exec. com., 1983-84; mem. vestry St. Dunstan's Episcopal Ch., Waitsfield, Vt., 1994-99; trustee Berkshire-Litchfield Environ. Coun., Lakeville, Conn., 1991-93; bd. dirs., chair grounds and maintenance com. The Holley Williams Mus., Lakeville, 1991; mem. N.E. Sustainable Energy Assn., 1983-92, bd. dirs., 1986-92, chair and exec. com., 1991-92, treas. and exec. com., 1987-91, chair outreach/advocacy com., 1990-91, chair quality bldg. coun., 1989-90; mem. builder's adv. bd. dirs. Energy-Crafted Home Program, 1989-90; pres. Valley Clergy Coun., Waitsfield, Vt., 1996-99. Mem. Associated Builders and Contractors (bd. dirs. Middletown, Conn. chpt. 1984-86, legis. com. 1985-86, chair bus. devel. com. 1985-86), Contractors Against Inflation (charter dir. 1973-75), Lions (bd. dirs. Sharon, Conn. chpt. 1980-81). Episcopalian. Avocations: skiing, reading. Home: PO Box 383 Warren VT 05674-0383

SMYTHE, CHEVES MCCORD, dean, medical educator; b. May 25, 1924; Student, Yale Coll., 1942—43; MD cum laude, Harvard, 1947. Diplomate Am. Bd. Internal Medicine, Am. Bd. Geriatrics. Intern, asst. resident Harvard Med. Svc., Boston City Hosp., 1947—49, chief resident, 1954—55; resident chest svc. Bellevue, 1949—50; rsch. fellow Presbyn. Hosp., N.Y.C., 1950—52; assoc. medicine Med. Coll. S.C. Sch. Medicine, 1956—58, asst. prof. medicine, 1958—60, assoc. prof. medicine, 1960—66, dean, 1963—65; attending physician Wesley Meml., Cook County North Side VA Hosps., Chgo., 1967—70; with Aga Khan U. Hosp., Karachi, Pakistan, 1990—91; dean faculty health scis., prof. medicine Aga Khan U., Pakistan, 1982—85, prof., chmn. dept. medicine Pakistan, 1990—91; chief Med. Svcs. at LBJ Hosp., Houston, 1991—95; prof. divsn. gen. medicine dept. internal medicine U. Tex. Med. Sch., 1970—, dean, 1970—75, dean pro tem, 1995—96. Assoc. med. dir. Hermann Hosp., 1996—. Bd. dirs. Assn. Am. Assoc. Med. Colls., Office: Univ Tex Med Sch 6431 Fannin St # 1.108 Houston TX 77030-1501

SMYTHE, STEVEN JOHN, microbiologist, researcher; b. Orangeburg, N.Y., Apr. 10, 1945; s. George Jeffrey and Stephanie Anne Smythe; m. Jennifer Joyce Burns, Aug. 10, 1975; children: Brian, James, Stacy, Anne. PhD in Microbiology, MIT, 1969. Rsch. asst. Bio Corp., Metuchen, NJ, 1970—75; chief scientist Microbiology Tech. Industries, N.Y.C., 1975—. Rschr. Am. Biol. Rsch. Ctr., N.Y.C., 1990—2001. Author: The Inside Look, 1995. Capt. U.S. Army, 1962—64. Mem.: Microbiologists Am.

SMYTHE, THOMAS IRA, JR. finance educator, researcher; b. Biloxi, Miss., Aug. 16, 1963; s. Thomas Ira and Mary Elizabeth S.; m. Sally Scarbrough, Aug. 16, 1986; children: Meagan Elizabeth, Erica Suzanne. BS in Math., Furman U., 1985; MBA, George Mason U., 1993; PhD, U. S. C., 1999. 1st lt. U.S. Army, Fort Benning, Ga., 1985-89; analyst Mobil Oil Corp., Fairfax, Va., 1989-95; graduate asst. U. S.C., Columbia, S.C., 1996-99; mem. staff U.S. Army, Fort Benning, Ga., 1985-89; asst. prof. fin. U. Tenn., Chattanooga, 1999—2001; asst. prof. econ. and bus. adminstrn. Furman U., Greenville, SC, 2001—. Mem. Financial Mgmt. Assn., So. Finance Assn., Am. Finance Assn. Methodist. Home: 3 Dunwoody Ct Travelers Rest SC 29690 Office: Furman U 3300 Poinsett Hwy Greenville SC 29613 E-mail: thomas.smythe@furman.edu.

SMYTHE ZAJC, M. CATHERINE, library administrator, development officer; b. Washington, Jan. 5, 1956; d. William Sterling Jr. and Anna Rosamund (Johnson) S.; m. John M. Zajc, Jr., May 27, 1995. BA in History, Westminster Coll., 1976; MLS, Syracuse U., 1982. Rsch. libr. White House Libr., Washington, 1982-86; dep. dir., rsch. libr. Time, Inc. Sports Libr., N.Y.C., 1986-89; dir. libr. svcs. Nat. Sports Daily, 1989-90; rsch. assoc. Jury Verdict Rsch., Solon, Ohio, 1990-91; cons., owner Sports Source, Inc., Painesville, 1990-92; dir. prospect devel. Baldwin-Wallace Coll., Berea, 1992-2000; prospect R&D dir. WVIZ/PBS and 90.3 WCPN Ideastream, Cleve., 2000—. Cons. Bowman Gray Sch. Medicine at Wake Forest U./N.C. Bapt. Hosp. Med. Ctr., Winston-Salem, 1990-93. Author: Geothesaurus, 1982. Former trustee, sec. bd. Global Issues Resource Ctr.; mem. Adoption Network Cleve., WCPN-Cleve. Pub. Radio; WVIZ/PBS vol. Cleve. Sight Ctr., Radio Reading Svc. Mem.: Soc. for Am. Baseball Rsch., Ohio Prospect Rschrs. Network, Assn. Fundraising Profls., Assn. of Profl. Rschrs. for Advancement. Presbyterian. Avocations: reading, collecting Shelley china and Poole pottery, physical fitness, music, crossword puzzles. Office: WVIZ/PBS 4300 Brookpark Rd Cleveland OH 44134-1124 E-mail: czajc@wviz.org.

SNADER, JACK ROSS, publishing company executive; b. Athens, Ohio, Feb. 25, 1938; s. Daniel Webster and Mae Estella (Miller) S.; m. Sharon Perschnick, Apr. 4, 1959; children: Susan Mae, Brian Ross. BS, U. Ill., 1959. Cert. mgmt. cons. With mktg. Richardson-Merrell, Cin., 1959-65, Xerox Corp., N.Y.C., 1965-67, Sieber & McIntyre, Chgo., 1967-69; pres. Systema Corp., Northbrook, Ill., 1969—. Author Systematic Selling, 1987, The Sales Relationship, 1988. Mem. ASTD, Instrnl. Sys. Assn., Inst. of Mgmt. Cons., Am. Mgmt. Assn. Office: Systema Corporation Ste 240 633 Skokie Blvd Northbrook IL 60062-2824 E-mail: jrsnader@systema.com.

SNAID, LEON JEFFREY, lawyer; b. Johannesburg, Republic of South Africa, Dec. 24, 1946; came to U.S., 1981; s. Mannie and Hene (Blume) S.; children: Jedd, Nicole. Diploma in Law, U. Witwatersrand, Johannesburg, 1969. Bar: Supreme Ct. Republic South Africa 1971, High Ct. of the Kingdom of Lesotho 1976, Calif. 1982, U.S. Dist. Ct. (so. and ctrl. dists.) Calif. 1982, U.S. Supreme Ct. 1999; cert. immigration law specialist, State Bar Calif. Bd. Legal Specialization. Assoc. Reeders, Teeger & Rosettenstein, Johannesburg, 1972; sole practice, 1973-76; ptnr. Snaid & Snaid, 1976-81; sole practice San Diego, 1982—. Lectr. legal edn. seminars, San Diego, 1984—. Author, pub. quar. newsletter Immigration and Internat. Law, The Newcomers Guide to Living in the U.S.A. Mem. ABA, Am. Immigration Lawyers Assn. (past chmn. continuing legal edn. San Diego chpt.), San Diego County Bar Assn. (past chmn. immigration com.). Lodges: Rotary. Home: 5060 Via Papel San Diego CA 92122-3923 Office: Ste # 211 2727 Camino Del Rio S San Diego CA 92108

SNAKENBERG, SHARON ANN, special education educator; b. Plum City, Wis., Feb. 6, 1952; d. Warren Adolf and Renee Ann (Thibodeau) Meyer; m. William John Hetherington, May 6, 1972 (div. Dec. 1976); 1 child William John Hetherington II; m. David F. Snakenberg, July 6, 1985; children: Elizabeth Emma, Reneé Jessica, Helen Elba, David Cesar, Ardee José. BA, Dominquez Hills, 1984. Substitute tchr. Templeton (Calif.) Sch. Dist., 1987-88; tchr. Calif. Youth Authority, Paso Robles, 1991-92, St. Rose Sch., Paso Robles, 1988-92; spl. edn. tchr. L.A. Unified Sch. Dist., 1992-98, tech. coord., 1992-99, assistive tech. specialist, 1998—. Part-time faculty Calif. U., Northridge. Mem.: Computer Using Educators (ATP cert. 2000), Coun. Exceptional Children (treas. 1998—2001), Calif. Assn. Phys. Health Impairmnets (treas. 1996—99). Roman Catholic. Avocations: quilting, horseback riding, archery. Home: 260 Juniper Ridge Ln Palmdale CA 93550-9709 Office: 2302 S Gramercy Pl Los Angeles CA 90018-1323

SNAPER, ALVIN ALLYN, engineer; b. Hudson City, N.J., Sept. 9, 1929; m. Kathleen M. Scovel, Apr. 17, 1964; children: Sheryl, Curtis. BS, McGill U., Montreal, Can., 1949. Registered profl. engr., Calif. Sr. chemist Bakelite/Union Carbide, Bound Brook, N.J., 1949-52; chief chemist McGraw Colorgraph Co., Burbank, Calif., 1952-56; chief engr. Houston Fearless Corp., L.A., 1958-62; sr. engr. Marquardt Corp., Van Nuys, Calif., 1962-65; v.p. Advanced Patent Tech., Las Vegas, Nev., 1968-73; pres. Neo-Dyne Rsch., Inc., 1979—. Cons. Sumitomo/JCC, Kanagawa, Japan, 1991—, Multi-Arc Vacuum Sys., Inc., St. Paul, 1981-85, SGC Internat., St. Petersburg, Russia, 1992, Govt. Kazakstan, 1992—, Govt. Peru, 1992—; dir. Advanced Patent Tech., Inc., Las Vegas, 1968-79. Recipient Patent of Yr. award Design News Mag., 1968, 70, 73. Achievements include over 600 U.S. and foreign patents. Home: 2800 Cameo Cir Las Vegas NV 89107-3213 Office: Neo-Dyne Rsch Inc 1000 W Bonanza Rd Las Vegas NV 89106-3529

SNAPP, HARRY FRANKLIN, historian, educator; b. Bryan, Tex., Oct. 15, 1930; s. H.F. and Ethel (Manning) Snapp; m. Elizabeth Mitchell, June 1, 1956 (div. Dec. 20, 2001). BA, Baylor U., 1952, MA, 1953; PhD, Tulane U., 1963. Instr. U. Coll. Tulane U., 1960—62; asst. prof. history Wofford Coll., 1963—64, U. North Tex. (formerly North Tex. State U.), Denton, 1964—69, assoc. prof., 1969—94; dir. Tex. Rsch. Ctr. Biog. Study of Women, 1995—; pres., dir. Read All About Her Tex. Women's Biographic Ctr., Inc., 1995—. Editor: Brit. Studies Mercury, 1970—84, Tex. Acad., 1973—76; co-editor: Read All About Her! Texas Women's History: A Working Bibliography, 1995, enlarged edit., 1997; author (with others): West Texas Historical Assn. Year Book, 1994, 1996; contbr. articles. Mem. Bridwell Assocs. of So. Meth. U., Friends of Southwestern Art, Am. Com. Irish Studies; mem. adv. com. on acad. freedom and tenure policy, coord. bd. Tex. Coll. and Univ. System. Recipient North Tex. State U. Faculty Rsch. award, 1966, 1967. Mem.: AAUP (pres. North Tex. chpt. 1968—69, pres. Southwestern regional conf. 1971—72, pres. Tex. conf. 1974—76, nat. coun. 1976—86), Butler Soc. (Ireland), Northamptonshire Record Soc., Libr. History Round Table, Libr. Rsch. Round Table, Hist. Assn. (London), Tex. State Hist. Assn., Panhandle-Plains Hist. Soc., West Tex. Hist. Assn. (bd. dirs. 1997—), Am. Hist. Assn., So. Conf. Brit. Studies (sec.-treas. 1969—84), Tulane U. Alumni Assn., Lambda Chi Alpha, Alpha Chi. Methodist. Home: 1904 N Lake Trl Denton TX 76201-0602 Office: Read All About Her Tex Women's Biographic Ctr Inc PO Box 424053 Denton TX 76204-4053

SNARE, CARL LAWRENCE, JR. business executive; b. Oct. 25, 1936; s. Carl Lawrence and Lillian Marie (Luoma) S. BBA, Northwestern U., 1968; postgrad. in econs., San Francisco State U., 1976-77; BS, SUNY, 1995; postgrad., Roosevelt U. CPA, cert. fin. planner, Calif. Asst. sec., controller Bache Halsey Stuart & Shields Inc. (now Prudential Securities), Chgo., 1968-73; controller Innisfree Corp. div. Hyatt Corp., Burlingame, Calif., 1973-76; cash mgr. Portland (Oreg.) Gen. Electric Co., 1976-79; chief fin. officer, controller Vistar Fin. Inc., Marina del Rey, 1979-82; pres. Snare Properties Co., Long Beach, 1984-96, Snare Fin. Svcs. Corp., Rialto, 1985-89, Carl Snare & Assocs., Long Beach; v.p., treas. Carson Estate Co., Rancho Dominguez, Calif., 1988-96; pres., ceo Glenshire Homes, Inc., Phoenix, 1996-98, Glenshire Tech., Boulder, Colo., 1997-99; acct., fin. planner Calif. Mem. AICPA. Founder Cash Mgmt. Assn., Portland, Oreg. Home: PMB 2495 PO Box 2430 Pensacola FL 32513

SNAREY, JOHN ROBERT, psychologist, researcher, educator; b. 1948; s. John Herbert and Esther Snarey; m. Carol Dunn Snarey, 1970; children: Johnny, Elizabeth. BS, Geneva Coll., 1969; MA, Wheaton (Ill.) Coll., 1973; EdD, Harvard U., 1982. Postdoctoral rsch. fellow dept. psychiatry Harvard U., Cambridge, Mass., 1982-84; assoc. rsch. psychologist Wellesley (Mass.) Coll., 1984-85; asst. prof. human devel. Northwestern U., Evanston, Ill., 1985-87; prof. human devel. Emory U., Atlanta, 1987—. Author: How Fathers Care for the Next Generation, 1993; mem. editl. bd. Harvard Ednl. Rev., 1979-81, Jour. Psychology and Theology, 1986-90, Jour. Moral Edn., 1998—, Am. Ednl. Rsch. Jour., 2001—; mem. editl. adv. bd. Lawrence Erlbaum Assocs., 1988-90; editor: Conflict and Continuity: A History of Ideas on Social Equality and Human Development, 1981; contbr. numerous articles to profl. jours. Recipient Exemplary Dissertation award Nat. Coun. for the Social Studies, 1982, Kuhmerker Dissertation award Assn. for Moral Edn., 1983, Outstanding Human Devel. Rsch. award Am. Ednl. Rsch., 1988, James D. Moran Book award Assn. Family and Consumer Scis., 1994. Mem. APA, Am. Ednl. Rsch. Assn. (E exec. bd. 1990-2000, sec. div. E 1997-99, moral devel. and edn. spl. interest group co-chair 1994-96), Assn. for Moral Edn. (exec. bd. 1986—, treas. 2001—, program chair 1997), Soc. for Rsch. in Child Devel., Nat. Coun. on Family Rels. Home: 2165 Pine Forest Dr NE Atlanta GA 30345-4184 Office: Emory U Pitts Libr # 3 Atlanta GA 30322-0001 E-mail: jsnarey@emory.edu.

SNAVELY, SHARON MARTIN, interior designer, general contractor; b. Columbus, Ohio, July 31, 1946; d. John William and Patricia Mary (Mantel) Martin; m. Charles William Isaly, Nov. 5, 1966 (div. May 1989); children: Jeffrey Isaly, Bradley Isaly; m. Donald Snavely, 1994. BA in Liberal Arts, No. Ariz. U., 1967. Interior designer John Martin Construction, Phoenix, 1967-73; v.p., owner Martin Constrn., Missoula, Mont., 1973-80; pres., owner SMS & Assocs., Ariz., Mont., and Calif., 1980—; constrn. adminstr. Trittipo & Assoc., Carlsbad, Calif., 1989-91; owner, ptnr. Design Group, Missoula, 1992-96. Mem. adv. bd. Florence Crittendon, Helena, Mont., 1994-96, Missoula Symphony Bd., 1990-92; pres. Symphony Guild; mem. action bd. Young Reps., Mont., 1994; bd. dirs. Extended Families, Missoula, 1994-99, Camp-Make-A-Dream. Mem. Am. Soc. Interior Designers, Am. Inst. Archs., Gen. Contractors Assn., Art Assocs. (pres.), Women in Art San Francisco, Missoula C. of C. Redcoats, Rotary. Avocations: skiing, golf, painting, horticulture. Home: 8 Moon Mountain Trail Phoenix AZ 85023 Fax: (602) 993-1012. E-mail: snavely@qwest.net.

SNAVELY, WILLIAM BRANT, management educator and consultant; b. Balt., June 18, 1951; s. Charles Albert and Helen (Morris) S.; m. Bretta Kay Smith, Aug. 16, 1974; children: Michael David, Sarah Anne. BS, Ill. State U., 1973; MA, W.Va. U., 1974; PhD, U. Nebr., 1977. Vis. asst. prof. Miami U., Oxford, Ohio, 1977-80, from asst. prof. to assoc. prof. mgmt., 1980—2002, chair mgmt. dept., 2000—, prof. mgmt., 2002—. Pres. Talawanda Band Boosters, 1995-97; chmn. Univ. Senate Exec. Com., 2000-01; cons. in field. Author: Interpersonal Communication Experiences, 1980; contbr. articles to profl. jours. Active Oxford Planning Commn., 1987-88, 90-91, 2002-, Oxford City Coun., 1987-95, 97-2001, Firefighters Dependents Bd., 1989-93, 97-2001, Retirement Cmty. Adv. Com., 1992-96, bd. dirs., 2002-, Ohio-Ky.-Ind. regional Coun. Govts., 1993-95, Butler County Regional Transit Auth., 1996-97, Oxford Hist. Preservation Commn., 2001-; vice-mayor City of Oxford, 1989-91, mayor, 1991-93, 97-2001, Hist. Preservation Commn., 2001-; bd. dirs. Oxford Sr. Citizens, Inc., 1988-90, 99-2001, Woodside Cemetery, Oxford, 1988-90, 99-2001, Cmty. Improvement Corp., 1990-91, 93-99, Oxford Area Cmty. Theatre, 1990-92, Knolls of Oxford, 2002—; exec. com. Butler County Land Use Coordinating Com., 1993-95, chmn., 1995; pres., founder Oxford Conservancy, Inc., 2002—. Mem. Acad. Mgmt. (divsn. program chmn. 1988-89, divsn. chmn 1989-91, local chmn. 1995-96, conf. coord. 1998-2001), Midwest Acad. Mgmt. (bd. dirs., procs. editor 1997-2000), Kiwanis (pres. Oxford chpt. 1997-98). Avocations: golf, community theatre, Russian and European business. Office: Miami U Dept Mgmt Oxford OH 45056

SNEAD, GEORGE MURRELL , JR. army officer, scientist, consultant; b. San Diego, Nov. 6, 1922; s. George Murrell and Helen (Olsen) S.; m. Kathleen Hill Dawson, Apr. 26, 1947; children: George Murrell III, James M., William M., John P., Edward W. BS, Va. Mil. Inst., 1943; MS, U. Ill., 1948; PhD, U. Va., 1953. Commd. 2d lt. U.S. Army, 1943, advanced through grades to brig. gen., 1969; with Central Germany campaign 805th Signal Co., Europe, 1945-46; Aleutian sector comdr. Alaska Communication System, 1948-50; sta. at Electronic Warfare Center Ft. Monmouth, N.J. and Ft. Huachuca, Ariz., 1953-56; student U.S. Army Command and Gen. Staff Coll., 1956-57; signal adviser MAAG Vietnam, 1957-58; signal officer Dept. Army, 1958-60; acting dir. research ballistic missile def. Advanced Research Projects Agy., 1960; with U.S. Army Satellite Communications Agy. Ft. Monmouth, 1960-63; student Nat. War Coll., 1963-64; div. signal officer 24th Inf. Div., 1964-65; comdg. officer 7th Signal Group, 1965; dir. Communication /ADP Lab. Ft. Monmouth, 1966-68; exec. asst. chief of staff Communications Electronics, Dept. Army, 1968; dir. army research Dept. Army Washington, 1968-71; dep. comdr. Army Strategic Communications Command, 1971-73; prin. scientist Gen. Research Corp. McLean, Va., 1973-82; pres. Nat. Sci. Ctr. Found., Burke, 1982-84. Chmn. bd. Am. Fed. Savs. & Loan Assn., Lynchburg, Va., 1985-86; sci./bus. cons., 1986—. Active Boy Scouts Am., 1958-68; bd. dirs. Ctrl. Youth Summer Activities, Ft. Monmouth, 1960-63, Arthritis Found., Washington, 1981-84, Lynchburg Symphony, 1990-95; pres. Acad. Music Theatre, Lynchburg, 1985-95; trustee, vice chmn. bd. dirs. Westminster-Canterbury, Lynchburg, 1991-99; trustee Sci. Mus. Va., 1995—; elder Presbyn. Ch., 1986—. Decorated D.S.M., Legion of Merit with two oak leaf clusters, Bronze Star, Air medal, Army Commendation medal with 4 oak leaf clusters. Mem. Assn. U.S. Army, Armed Forces Communications and Electronics Assn. (sec. Washington chpt. 1968-69), Sigma Xi, Kappa Alpha. Office: PO Box 3306 Lynchburg VA 24503-0306

SNEAD, KATHLEEN MARIE, lawyer; b. Steubenville, Ohio, July 1, 1948; d. Donald Lee and Mary Alice (Hobright) O'Dell; m. John Jones Snead, Oct. 14, 1972; 1 child, Megan Marie. BA, Pa. State U., 1970; JD, U. Denver, 1979. Bar: Colo. 1979, U.S. Ct. Appeals (10th cir.) 1980, U.S. Supreme Ct. 1986. Field examiner NLRB, Pitts., 1970-72; freelance photographer Charleston, W.Va., 1973-74; labor relations examiner U.S. Dept. Labor, Denver, 1974-77, labor relations officer, 1978-79; staff atty. Denver & Rio Grande Western R.R., 1979-81, asst. gen. atty., 1981-84, gen. atty., 1984-92, Southern Pacific Lines, 1992-96, Union Pacific R.R., Denver, 1996-97; pvt. practice Golden, Colo., 1997—. Mem. ABA, Colo. Bar Assn. (adv. coun. environ. law sect.), Colo. Women's Bar Assn., Colo. R.R. Assn. (dir. 1982-84). Avocations: reading, swimming, biking, skating. Home: 233 S Devinney St Golden CO 80401-5316 E-mail: skaterlaw@aol.com.

SNEDDEN, JAMES DOUGLAS, retired health service management consultant; b. Toronto, Ont., Can., Mar. 4, 1925; s. David Morrison and Sarah Hayton (Monteith) S.; m. Elizabeth Ann McCauley, Dec. 20, 1953. B.Comm., U. Toronto, 1948; C.A., Inst. Chartered Accts. Ont., 1951. With Hosp. for Sick Children, Toronto, 1952-86, asst. dir., 1961-67, adminstr., 1967-70, chief exec. officer, 1970-86; nat. dir. health and social service cons. Peat, Marwick & Ptnrs., 1986-87; pres. J. Douglas Snedden and Assocs., 1987-97. Bd. dirs. Mallinckrodt Can., Cyberfluor Can. Hon. dir. Woodgreen Community Centre, Toronto, 1963-65, v.p., 1965-67, pres., 1967-69, hon. mem. bd. dirs., 1973—; past bd. dirs. Hosp. Coun. Met. Toronto; mem. Bd. Trade Met. Toronto, 1965-97; bd. dirs. United Way Met. Toronto, 1986-89; bd. dirs. Wedgewood at Bonita Bay, Bonita Springs, 1990-94, pres., 1992-94. Served with RCAF, 1943-45. Decorated Can. Centennial medal. Fellow Can. Coll. Health Svc. Execs. (founding mem. 1970, bd. dirs. 1972-83, treas. 1978-81, chmn. 1981-82, past chmn. 1982-83), Inst. Chartered Accts. Ont. (life), Acad. of Medicine, Toronto; mem. Am. Coll. Healthcare Execs. Clubs: University, Bd. of Trade. Presbyterian. Home: 26550 Clarkston Dr Bonita Springs FL 34135-2315 E-mail: jdsnedden@juno.com.

SNEDEKER, JOHN HAGGNER, university president; b. Plainfield, N.J., May 30, 1925; s. Alfred H. and Anna Marie (Ward) S.; m. Noreen I. Davey, Dec. 30, 1950; children— John D., Philip A., Patrick W. BS cum laude, MA, N.Y. U., 1951; Ed.D., Ind. U., 1959. Dir. lab. human devel. U. Mont., 1952-56; cons. psychologist research Purdue U., 1955; assoc. prof., dir. bur. research Ball State U., 1956-61; prof. higher edn., research asso. Ind. U., 1958; prof., dean Western Wash. State U., Bellingham, 1961-62; pres. Western N.Mex. U., Silver City, 1962—. Mem. exec. bd. Internat. Coun. Spl. Edn., 1952-56; Rocky Mountain regional rep. APA, 1953-56; mem. Gov. Wash. Com. Licensing Tchr. Edn., 1961, Wash. State Legislature Rsch. Tech. Com., 1961. Author or co-author rating scales, attitude and opinion measurement devices; contbr. jours. Bd. dirs. Nat. Sci. Fair; trustee N.Mex. Health Found. Served with U.S. Army, 1943-48. Fellow AAAS; mem. Midwest Psychol. Assn., Inter-Am. Soc. Psychology, Am. Ednl. Research Assn., Holland Soc. N.Y. Address: 2200 Pinon St Silver City NM 88061-7735

SNEDEKER, RICHARD STOCKTON, research engineer; b. Bklyn., Apr. 14, 1927; s. Leonard Nicholson and Annis Dunbar (Jenkins) S.; m. Mary Ellen Burroughs, Sept. 27, 1952; children: Mary Jenkins, James Peter, Amy Elisabeth. BS in Aero. Engring., Princeton U., 1951, MS in Aero. Engring., 1961. Editor, illustrator Princeton (N.J.) Univ. Press, 1951-57; instrn. asst. Princeton U., 1955-57; rsch. engr. Aero. Rsch. Assocs. Princeton, Inc., 1957-86; sr. cons. Titan Corp., Princeton, 1986-97; consulting engr. West Windsor, N.J., 1997—. Illustrator maps and ink drawings for various books, mags. and other publs.; assoc. editor (reference books) High Speed Aerodynamics and Jet Propulsion, 12 vols., 1951-59; patentee in thermal control and ballistic armor; contbr. articles to profl. jours. Chmn. numerous bds. and study coms., West Windsor Twp., N.J., 1966—; mem. West Windsor-Plainsboro Bd. Edn., 1968-80, pres., 1974-79; mem. Planning Bd., West Windsor, 1999-2001. Mem. AIAA (sr.), Sigma Xi. Democrat. Episcopalian. Avocations: wood working, model building, most creative media, competitive running. Home: 10 Bolfmar Ave Princeton Junction NJ 08550-2819 E-mail: Diksne@aol.com.

SNEED, ELLOUISE BRUCE, nursing educator emeritus; b. Monroe, La., June 21, 1945; d. Wesley Newton Bruce and Oza Celeste Parker; m. Gary Arnold, Aug. 10, 1978. RN, Mather Sch. Nursing, New Orleans, 1966; BS in Nursing, William Carey Coll., Hattiesburg, Miss., 1975; MS in Nursing, Med. Coll. Ga., Augusta, 1978; EdD, U. So. Miss., Hattiesburg, 1981. Instr. community-psychiat. nursing Charity Hosp. Sch. Nursing, New Orleans, 1975-77; family nurse cons. Drs. R. Gregory and G. Keller, Mandeville, La., 1978-83; assoc. prof. Sch. Nursing William Carey Coll., New Orleans, 1980-88; employee well health and health fair cons. St. Tammany Parish Hosp., Covington, La., 1987-88; prof., Holder Coughlin Sanders chair nursing La. Coll., Pineville, 1988-95, prof. emeritus, 1999. Ednl. program cons., 1984-85; speaker-presenter for profl. orgns. and instns. throughout La. Contbg. author: Crisis Intervention Theory and Practice: A Clinical Handbook, 1980, Mosby's 1988, 92 Secured Assess Test: A Practice Test Exam for RN Licensure, 1988, 92. Deacon Emmanuel Bapt. Ch. Alexandria. Named A Great One Hundred Nurse, New Orleans Dist. Nurses Assn., 1987. Mem. ARC, Friend of Nursing of La. (coll. divsn. of nursing 1997), Sigma Theta Tau (mem. com. Nu Tau chpt.). Home: 4703 Warwick Blvd Alexandria LA 71303-2610 E-mail: ellouise@cox-internet.com.

SNEED, JIMMY, chef, restaurant owner; married; 3 children. Studied with Guenther Seeger; student with Jean-Louis Palladin, Le Cordon Bleu. Exec. chef Windows on Urbana Creek; chef with Jeff Buben The Four Seasons; sous-chef Capital Hill Club, 1980; chef, owner The Frog and the Redneck, Richmond, Va., 1993—. Translator to Am. students Le Cordon Bleu cooking sch. Appearance America's Greatest Chef. Named 1 of Am.'s finest chefs, Esquire mag., 2000. Office: 1423 E Cary St Richmond VA 23219*

SNEED, JOSEPH TYREE, III, federal judge; b. Calvert, Tex., July 21, 1920; s. Harold Marvin and Cara (Weber) Sneed; m. Madelon Juergens, Mar. 15, 1944 (dec. Dec. 1998); children: Clara Hall, Cara Carleton, Joseph Tyree IV. BBA, Southwestern U., 1941; LLB, U. Tex., Austin, 1947; SJD, Harvard, 1958. Bar: Tex. 1948. From instr. bus. law to prof. U. Tex., Austin, 1947—57, asst. dean, 1949—50; counsel Graves, Dougherty & Greenhill, Austin, 1954—56; prof. law Cornell U., 1957—62; prof. Stanford Law Sch., 1962—71; dean, prof. of law Duke Law Sch., 1971—73; dep. atty. gen. U.S. Justice Dept., 1973; judge U.S. Ct. Appeals (9th cir.), San Francisco, 1973—, now sr. judge. Author: The Configurations of Gross Income, 1967, Footprints on the Rocks of the Mountain, 1997; contbr. articles to profl. jours. With USAAF, 1942—46. Mem.: ABA, Am. Law Inst. (cons. estate and gift tax project 1960—69), State Bar Tex., Order of Coif. Office: US Ct Appeals PO Box 193939 San Francisco CA 94119-3939 also: US Ct Appeals 9th Cir 95 Seventh St San Francisco CA 94103-1526*

SNEED, JOSEPH DONALD, philosophy educator, writer; b. Durant, Okla., Sept. 23, 1938; s. Dabney Whitfield and Sallybelle (Atkinson) S. BS, Rice U., 1960; MS, U Ill., 1962; PhD, Stanford U., 1964. Prof. Stanford U., Palo Alto, Calif., 1966-73; policy analyst SRI Internat., Menlo Park, 1973-74; prof. U. Munich, 1974-75, U. Eindhoven, Holland, 1976-77, SUNY, Albany, 1977-79; prof. philosophy Colo. Sch. Mines, Golden, 1980—. Author: The Logical Structure of Mathematical Physics, 1971, (with W. Balzer and C. Moulines) An Architectonic for Science, 1987; editor: (with S. Waldhorn) Restructuring the Federal System, 1974. Mem. Am. Philos. Assn. Office: Colo Sch Mines Golden CO 80401 E-mail: jsneed@mines.edu.

SNEED, MARIE ELEANOR WILKEY, retired secondary education educator; b. Dahlgren, Ill., June 12, 1915; d. Charles N. and Hazel (Miller) Wilkey; m. John Sneed, Jr., Sept. 18, 1937; children: Suzanne (Mrs. Geoffrey B. Newton), John Corwin. Student, U. Ill., 1933-35; BS, Northwestern U., 1937; postgrad., Wayne State U., 1954-60, U. Mich., 1967. Tchr. English, drama, creative writing Berkley (Mich.) Sch. Dist., 1952-76. Mem. Mich. Statewide Tchr. Edn. Preparation, 1968-72, regional sec., 1969-70; mem. Pleasant Ridge Arts Coun., 1982—; mem. Pleasant Ridge Parks and Recreation Commn., 1982-88, sr. citizen cons., 1989—; chmn. Student Tchr. Planning Com. Berkley, 1971-72. Mem. NEA, Mich. Edn. Assn., Berkley Edn. Assn. (pres. 1961-62, 82-87), Oakland Tchr. Edn. Coun. (exec. bd. 1973-76), Farm Bur. Ill., Founder's Soc., Phi Alpha Chi, Pi Lambda Theta, Alpha Delta Kappa, Alpha Omicron Pi. Clubs: Pleasant Ridge Woman's (pres. 1980-83), Royal Oak Rep. Woman's, Nomad's. Home: 21 Norwich Rd Pleasant Ridge MI 48069-1027 also: Miller Heritage Farm LLC Dahlgren IL 62828

SNEED, RAPHAEL CORCORAN, physiatrist, pediatrician; b. Selma, Ala., 1942; MD, U. Ala., 1968. Diplomate Am. Bd. Pediat., Am. Bd. Phys. Medicine and Rehab. Intern U. Ala. Hosp. Clinic, Birmingham, 1968-69, resident in pediat., 1969-71, resident in phys. medicine and rehab., 1981-83, fellow in phys. medicine and rehab., 1983-84; with Children's Rehab. Ctr. Miss. Med. Ctr., Jackson. Mem. Am. Acad. Pediat., Am. Acad. Phys. Medicine and Rehab. Office: U Miss Med Ctr Children's Rehab Ctr 2500 N State St Jackson MS 39216-4500

SNEED, RONALD ERNEST, engineering educator emeritus; b. Oxford, N.C., Nov. 23, 1936; s. Henry Ernest and Jewel Leigh (Hughes) S.; m. Shelba Jean Walters, June 8, 1958; children: Kathy Geneva Grosvenor, Jennie Leigh Berrier. BS in Agrl. Engring., N.C. State U., 1959, PhD in Biol. and Agrl. Engring., 1971. Registered profl. engr., N.C.; cert. irrigation designer. Sales trainee John Deere Co., 1959-60; ext. specialist N.C. State U., 1960-62, ext. instr., 1962-69, 70, ext. asst. prof., 1971-75, ext. assoc. prof., 1971-80, prof., 1980-92, prof. emeritus, 1993—; project engr. Agri-Waste Tech., Inc., 1993-2000, Irrigation Consulting, Inc., 1995—; project engr. Divsn. Soil and Water N.C. Dept. Environ. and Nat. Resources, 1997-99. Cons. Lexington (N.C.) Swine Breeders, 1973, 1st Colongy Farms, Creswell, N.C., 1977-78, Greek Tobacco Co. Uruguay, 1973-84, Internat. Potato Ctr., Lima, Peru, 1981-85, Philip Morris Tobacco Co., Richmond, Va., 1992-94, Stowe's Nursery, Inc., Belmont, N.C., 1993-94, Floyd Harrell Farms, Inc., Conetoe, N.C., 1994, Gilliam & Mason, Inc., Harrellsville, N.C., 1994, Craven County Com. of 100, Ltd., 1995, Murphy Family Farms, 1997—, Larry Eason Farms, 1998, Panoramic Farm, Inc., 1997—, Latham's Nursery, Inc., 1998— and numerous others. Active Civitan, Raleigh, 1994—. Maj. Gen. retired, U.S. Army, 1960-95. Recipient Outstanding Paper award So. region Am. Soc. Horticultural Sci., 1986, 91; Ronald E. Sneed Irrigation Soc., Inc. scholarship established in his honor, 1991. Fellow Am. Soc. Agrl. Engrs. (ednl. aids competition Blue Ribbon 1963-64, 68, 78-79, 85, 89, 91-92, Gunlogson Countryside Engring. award 1992, Outstanding Paper award 1984), The Irrigation Assn. (life tech. mem., Man of Yr. 1981), N.C. Irrigation Soc., Inc. (Outstanding Contbn. to Irrigation award 1973, former tech. advisor), Soil and Water Conservation Soc., N.C. Land Improvement Contractors Assn. (former tech. advisor), Carolinas Irrigation Assn. (hon.), Res. Officers Assn. (life). Democrat. Baptist. Office: 3405 Malibu Dr Raleigh NC 27607-6505 E-mail: rsneed@intrex.net.

SNEERINGER, STEPHEN GEDDES, lawyer; b. Lancaster, Ohio, Mar. 27, 1949; s, Stanley Carlylle and Mary Eleanor (Fry) S.; m. Kristine Karen Serfling, Oct. 6, 1974; children: Mary Rhonda, Robyn Kathleen. BA magna cum laude, Denison U., 1971; JD, Washington U., 1974. Bar: Mo. 1974. Sr. v.p. A.G. Edwards & Sons Inc., St. Louis, 1974—. Arbitrator N.Y. Stock Exch., NASD Dispute Resolution, Inc., Nat. Futures Assn., Am. Arbitration Assn. Editor: Urban Law Ann., 1973-74; bd. editors Securities Arbitration Commentator. Am. Jurisprudence scholar, 1974. Mem. ABA (dispute resolution sect., arbitration com.), Mo. Bar Assn., Securities Industries Assn. (arbitration com.), Futures Industries Assn., Nat. Assn. Securities Dealers (mem. nat. arbitration and mediation com. 1992-94, 2001—), Securities Industry Conf. on Arbitration. Office: AG Edwards & Sons Inc 1 N Jefferson Ave Saint Louis MO 63103-2205

SNEEUWJAGT, FREDERIK AUGUST, JR. technology management consultant; b. Washington, Aug. 30, 1963; s. Frederik August Sr. and Juanita (Edwards) S.; m. Deborah Sue Horton, Nov. 21, 1987; children: Brooke Elizabeth, Heather Marie. BA in Human Devel., St. Mary's Coll. Md., 1987; MS in Mgmt., Fla. Inst. Tech., 1993. With tech. assessment engring. Booz-Allen & Hamilton, Lexington Park, 1987—, sys. integration and test cons., 1987-88, mgr. shipboard comms. integration site, 1989-91, mgr. tech. transfer program, 1992-93, mgr. tech. assessment and strategic bus. planning practice, 1994-95, bus. process reengr., change mgmt. workflow process analysis, 1995—. Intern. program dir. St. Mary's Coll. Md., 1994—. Mem. Am. Def. Preparedness Assn., Nat. Contracts Mgmt. Assn., Armed Forces Comms. and Electronics Assn. Republican. Roman Catholic. Avocations: tennis, golfing, sailing. Home: 28 Waterview Dr Saint Inigoes MD 20684 Office: Booz-Allen & Hamilton 350 Bradley Blvd Lexington Park MD 20653-2233

SNEIDER, JOYCE PAPPACHRISTOU, dietitian, educator; b. Springfield, Mass., May 15, 1932; d. Hector and Henrietta (Hemerling) Flores; m. Stanley Sneider; children: Dianne, Donna, Paul Jr., Gary. AA, Nassau Community Coll., 1970; BA in Math., Sci. and Home Econs. with honors, Queens Coll., 1973; MA, MS in dietetics/nutrition, NYU, 1976; postgrad., Nova U., 1989—. Cert. tchr., N.Y.C., N.Y., tchr. home econs., health edn., sci., Fla.; lic. dietitian, nutritionist Fla. Tchr. Roslyn High Sch., Elmont Meml. High Sch.; dietitian L.I. (N.Y.) Jewish Hosp.; dietician St. Mary's Hosp.; instr. nutrition Cath. Med. Ctr. Nursing, 1974-76; chief dietician Jamaica (N.Y.) Hosp., 1976-80; tchr. Broward Coutny (Fla.) Bd. Educators, 1981—. Adj. prof. Nassau Community Coll., Fla. Internat. U., 1980-81. Contbr. articles to profl. jours. Mem. Am. Dietetics Assn., Am. Home Econs. Assn. (cert.), Fla. Dietetics Assn., Fla. Assn. Computer Educators, Fla. Correctional Edn. Assn., Fla. Assn. Alternative Educators, Phi Beta Kappa, Kappa Delta Pi. E-mail: Joysta@Atlantic.net.

SNELL, ALMA HOGAN, artist; b. Crow Agency, Mont., Jan. 10, 1923; d. George Washington and Helen (Goes Ahead) Hogan; m. William Frederick Snell, Sept. 20, 1947; children: Ted, Faith Lynn, Pearl Jean, William Frederick, Jr. Student, Flandreau High Sch., S.D., Mont. Advisor Mus. Am. Indian Art, Washington, 1997-98; presenter in field. Author: Grandmothers Grand Child, 1999. Ethnobotanis Taste of Heritage, Yellowtail, Mont., 2001; v.p. Pretty Shield Found., Billings, Mont., 2000-2001. Recipient Mont. Plaque of Honor Mont. Indian Edn. Assn., 1989, Folk and Traditional Art Apprenticeship award Mont. Arts Coun., 2000-2001, Key to City of Mpls. award Mayor of Minn. Avocations: writing, cooking, beading, field work, reading. Home: PO Box 7548 Yellowtail MT 59035 Office: 2906 2nd Ave N Billings MT 59101-2026

SNELL, CHARLES MURRELL, physicist, astrophysicist; b. Johnson City, Tenn., Aug. 19, 1946; s. Murrell Watkins and Ruth Snell. BS, Vanderbilt Univ., 1967; MS, Univ. Ariz., 1969. Physicist U.S. Army Corps. Engrs., Livermore, Calif., 1971-73, Lawrence Livermore Lab., Livermore, 1973-78, Los Alamos (N.M.) Nat. Lab., 1978—. Contbr. over 100 articles to profl. publs.; patentee in field. With U.S. Army, 1969-71. Mem. Phi Beta Kappa. Avocations: astronomy, hiking, walking. Office: Los Alamos Nat Lab Los Alamos NM 87545-0001 E-mail: cms@lanl.gov.

SNELL, ESMOND EMERSON, biochemist; b. Salt Lake City, Sept. 22, 1914; s. Heber Cyrus and Hedwig Emma (Ludwig) S.; m. Mary Caroline Terrill, Mar. 15, 1941; children: Esmond Emerson (dec.), Richard T., Allan G., Margaret Ann. BA, Brigham Young U., 1935; MA, U. Wis., 1936, PhD, 1938, D.Sc. (hon.), 1982. Rsch. assoc. chemistry U. Tex., 1939-41, asst. prof. chemistry, 1941-43, assoc. prof., 1943-45, prof. chemistry, 1951-56; assoc. prof. biochemistry U. Wis., 1945-47, prof., 1947-53, on leave 1951-53; prof. biochemistry U. Calif., 1956-76, chmn. dept., 1956-62; prof. microbiology and chemistry U. Tex., Austin, 1976-90, Ashbel Smith prof., 1981-90, prof. emeritus, 1990—, chmn. dept. microbiology, 1976-80. Guggenheim Meml. Found. fellow U. Cambridge, 1954-55, Max-Planck Institut für Zellchemie, München, 1962-63, U. Wash., Seattle, Rockefeller U., N.Y.C., Hebrew U., Jerusalem, 1969; Walker-Ames prof. biochemistry U. Wash., Seattle, spring 1953. Author numerous research articles in sci. jours.; Editor: Volume III Biochemical Preparations, 1963-64, Chemical and Biological Aspects of Pyridoxal Catalysis, 1963, Pyridoxal Catalysis, Enzymes and Model Systems, 1968; Mem. editorial bd. Jour. Am. Chem. Soc, 1948-58, Jour. Biol. Chemistry, 1949-59, Biochemistry, 1961-70, Biochem. and Biophys. Research Communication, 1970-85, Biofactors, 1988-91; editor: Ann. Rev. Biochemistry, 1969-83. Recipient U.S. Sr. Scientist award Alexander von Humboldt Found., 1977 Fellow AAAS, Am. Inst. Nutrition (Meade-Johnson B-Complex award 1946, Osborne-Mendel award 1951); mem. Nat. Acad. Scis., Am. Acad. Arts and Scis., Japanese Biochem. Soc. (hon.), Am. Chem. Soc. (chmn. div. biol. chemistry 1954, Kenneth A. Spencer award 1974, Nebr. Lectureship award 1983), Am. Soc. Biol. Chemists (pres. 1961-62, William Rose award 1985), Soc. Am. Bacteriologists (Eli Lilly award in bacteriology and immunology 1945), Am. Acad. Microbiology. Home: 5001 Greystone Dr Austin TX 78731-1118 E-mail: esnell@aol.com.

SNELL, JOHN RAYMOND, civil engineer; b. Suzhou, China, Dec. 9, 1912; (parents Am. citizens); s. John A. and Grace (Birkett) S.; m. Florence Moffett, Dec. 8, 1939; children: Chica Dorothea, Karen Snell Dailey, Martha E. Snell Rood, John Raymond Jr., David Moffett. BE, Vanderbilt U., 1934; MS, U. Ill., 1936; DSc, Harvard U., 1939. Registered profl. engr., Mass., Mich., Ohio, Ill., Ind., La. Wis., N.Y., Tex. Fla., Idaho, Oreg., Ont., Can.; cert. san. engr.; diplomate Am. Acad. Environ. Engrs. Instr. civil engring. Hangchow U., 1934-35; with Water Supply Fed. Pub. Works Dept., Venezuela, 1939-40; design engr. Metcalf & Eddy, also Fay Spofford and Thorndyke, Stone & Webster, Boston, 1941-42; san. engr., head water and sewage sect. 1st Svc. Command, 1946; assigned UNRA restoration water, sewage, solid wastes 5 no. provinces China San. Engring. Services Inc., 1945-46; project engr. Burns & Kenerson, Boston, 1947; pres., chief engr. Engring. Svcs. Inc., 1948-51; lectr. MIT, 1949-51; prof., head dept. civil and san. engring. Mich. State U., 1951-55; owner John R. Snell & Assocs., 1956; sr. prin. Mich. Assocs., cons. engrs., 1956-60; pres. John R. Snell Engrs. Inc., 1960-75, Snell Environ. Group, 1975-80, hon. chmn. bd., spl. cons., 1980-88; joint venturer Snell-Republic Assocs. Ltd., Lahore, West Pakistan, 1961-80; with Assoc. Architects & Engrs., Dacca, Bangladesh, 1965-80; pres. Caribbean Devel. Corp. and subs. Gen. Shrimp Ltd., Belize, 1984-92. Sr. adj. scientist Mich. Biotech. Inst., 1990—; 1994 guest of China-Suzhou Hosp. 110 Aniv.; solid waste cons. Xiaogan Recycling Treatment Utilization of Organics, Peoples Republic of China, 1995—; founder Trans Mich. Waterway Inc., S.W. Waterway (Ont.) Ltd., N.Y.; spl. cons. on ast high rate compost plant to Govt. of Japan, 1955-56; cons. in Orient, WHO, 1956; chmn. bd. Bootstrap Internat. Inc., 1972; chmn. bd. Save Our Spaceship/nc.NFP 2001 (to abate pollution, sustainability and population control); expert witness on over 50 ct. cases. Author: Toward a Better World, 1997, trans. into Chinese, 1999, 12 sects. Environment Engineering Handbook; co-author: Municipal Solid Waste Disposal; contbr. articles to profl. jours.; patentee in composting field. Maj. USPHS, 1945-47. Recipient Prescott Eddy award, 1944. Mem. Nat., Mich. (life) socs. profl. engrs., Am. Water Works Assn., Hwy. Rsch. Bd., ASTM, ASCE, Am. Pub. Works Assn., Water Pollution Control Fedn. (life), Mich. Engring. Soc. (life), Cons. Engrs. Coun. (past dir.), Cons. Engrs. Assn. Mich. (past pres.), Inter-Am. Assn. San. Engrs., World Aquaculture Soc., Composters Inc. (pres. Worldwide Techs. Inc. East Lansing 1980—), Rotary, Tau Beta Pi, Chi Epsilon. Home and Office: 918 Rosewood Ave East Lansing MI 48823-3127 Fax: 517-351-3929. E-mail: snelljo@pilot.msu.edu.

SNELL, JOHN RAYMOND, industrial trainer; b. Boston, Nov. 13, 1948; s. John Raymond and Florence Crawford (Moffett) S.; m. Lizabeth Ann Parr, May 28, 1972; children: Andrew Clayton, Suzannah Kate. Student, Mich. State U., 1976. Trainer Ctrl. Vt. Cmty. Action, Barre, 1978-80, Resdl. Energy Commn., Montpelier, Vt., 1980-82, Infraspection Inst., Shelburne, 1982-94, Montpelier, 1994—; ptnr., trainer Snell Infrared, 1994—. Chmn. bd. Thermosense-SPIE, Bellingham, Wash., 1994—, Theraml Solutions-ASNT, Columbus, Ohio, 1997. Contbr. articles to profl. jours. Bd. dirs. Vt. Hist. Soc., Montpelier, 1994-97; chmn. Montpelier Tree Bd., 1994—. Avocations: photography, gardening, hiking, travel, writing. Office: PO Box 6 Montpelier VT 05601-0006

SNELL, NED COLWELL, financial planner; b. Cowley, Wyo., May 16, 1944; s. Jay Hatton and Freda Hope (Colwell) S.; m. Barbara Anne Frandsen, Apr. 24, 1969; children: Taylor Anthony, Trevor Cameron. BA, U. Utah, 1969; CLU, Am. Coll., 1983, ChFC, 1985. English tchr. Granite Sch. Dist., Salt Lake City, 1969-71; ins. agt. Prudential Ins. Co., 1971-76; pres. Snell Fin. Corp., 1976—. Bd. dirs. Utah chpt. Arthritis Found., Salt Lake City, 1980-82, pres. 1982-83; missionary Mormon Ch. 1963-66; chmn. voting dist. 2604 Rep. Nominating Convs., 1986, 90. Recipient Golden Key Soc. Devel. award, 1990; named Poet Laureate/Jessee Poet, Poets at Work, 2000. Mem. NALU (Nat. Sales Achievement award 1971-89, Nat. Quality award), Am. Soc. CLU and ChFC (bd. dirs. Utah chpt. 1990-93, treas. 1993-94, v.p. 1994-96, pres. 1996-97, com. chmn. Grant Taggart symposium 1996—), Million Dollar Round Table (knight 1988—), Salt Lake Assn. Life Underwriters (bd. dirs. 1974-76, 80-82). Republican. Avocations: creative writing, fly tying, fishing, basketball, tennis. Home: 1101 S 2000 E Salt Lake City UT 84108-1971 Office: 1800 S West Temple Ste 416 Salt Lake City UT 84115-5854 E-mail: sbsenior@aol.com.

SNELL, PATRICIA POLDERVAART, librarian, consultant; b. Santa Fe, Apr. 11, 1943; d. Arie and Edna Beryl (Kerchmar) Poldervaart; m. Charles Eliot Snell, June 7, 1966. BA in Edn., U. N.M., 1965; MSLS, U. So. Calif., 1966. Asst. edn. libr. U. So. Calif., L.A., 1966—68; med. libr. Bedford (Mass.) VA Hosp., 1968—69; asst. law libr. U. Miami, Coral Gables, Fla., 1970—71; acquistions libr. U. N.Mex. Law Sch. Libr., Albuquerque, 1971—72; order libr. Los Angeles County Law Libr., 1972—76, cataloguer, 1976—90; libr. Parks Coll., Albuquerque, 1990—92; records technician Technadyne Engring. Cons. to Sandia Nat. Labs., 1992—93; libr. Tireman Learning Materials Ctr. U. N.Mex., Albuquerque, 1993—96, instr. libr. sci. program Coll. Edn., 1991—; rsch. technician City of Albuquerque, 1996—. Ch. libr.. Beverly Hills Presbyn. Ch., 1974-90, ch. choir libr., 1976-90. Southwestern Library Assn. scholar 1965. Mem.: ALA, N.Mex. Libr. Assn., Pi Lambda Theta. Avocations: travel, reading.

SNELL, RICHARD, holding company executive; b. Phoenix, Nov. 26, 1930; s. Frank L. and Elizabeth (Berlin) S.; m. Alice Cosette Wiley, Aug. 1, 1954. BA, Stanford U., 1952, JD, 1954. Bar: Ariz. Ptnr. firm Snell & Wilmer, Phoenix, 1956-81; pres., chmn., chief exec. officer Ramada Inc., 1981-89; chmn., chief exec. officer Aztar Corp., 1989-90, chmn., bd. dirs., 1990-92; chmn. bd. dirs. Pinnacle West Capital Corp., Phoenix, 1990—2001; chmn. Ariz. Pub. Svc., 1990—2001; bd. dirs. Pinnacle West Capital Corp., Phoenix. Adv. bd. Bank One Ariz. NA; bd. dirs. Aztar Corp., Ctrl. Newspapers Inc.; bd. dirs., chmn. Ariz. Pub. Svc. Co. Trustee Am. Grad. Sch. Internat. Mgmt., Phoenix; past pres. YMCA Met. Phoenix and Valley of Sun. With U.S. Army, 1954-56. Mem. ABA, Ariz. Bar Assn., Paradise Valley Country Club, Phoenix Country Club. Republican. Lutheran. Office: Pinnacle West Capital Corp 400 N 5th St Phoenix AZ 85004 also: Pinnacle West PO Box 53999 Phoenix AZ 85072-3999

SNELL, RICHARD SAXON, anatomist; b. Richmond, Surrey, Eng., May 3, 1925; came to U.S., 1963; s. Claude Saxon and Daisy Lilian S.; m. Maureen Cashin, June 4, 1949; children: Georgina Sara, Nicola Ann, Melanie Jane, Richard Robin, Charles Edward. MB, BS, Kings Coll., U. London, 1949, PhD, 1955, MD, 1961. House surgeon Sir Cecil P.G. Wakeley, Kings Coll. Hosp. and Belgrave Hosp. for Children, London, 1948-49; lectr. anatomy Kings Coll., U. London, 1949-59, U. Durham, Eng., 1959-63; asst. prof. anatomy and medicine Yale U., 1963-65, assoc. prof., 1965-67, vis. prof. anatomy, 1969; prof., chmn. dept. anatomy N.J. Coll. Medicine and Dentistry, Jersey City, 1967-69; vis. prof. anatomy Harvard U., 1970, 71, 80, 86; prof. anatomy Coll. Medicine, U. Ariz., Tucson, 1970; prof., chmn. dept. anatomy George Washington U. Med. Ctr., Washington, 1972-88, prof. emeritus, 1988—. Author: Clinical Embryology for Medical Students, 1972, 3d edit., 1983, Clinical Anatomy for Medical Students, 1973, 6th edit., 2000, Atlas of Normal Radiographic Anatomy, 1976, Atlas of Clinical Anatomy, 1978, Gross Anatomy Dissector, 1978, Clinical Neuroanatomy for Medical Students, 1980, 5th edit., 2001, Student's Aid to Gross Anatomy, 1986, Clinical Anatomy for Anesthesiologists, 1988, Clinical Anatomy of the Eye, 1989, 2d edit., 1997, Gross Anatomy: A Review with Questions and Explanations, 1990, Neuroanatomy: A Review with questions and Explanations, 1992, Clinical Anatomy for Emergency Medicine, 1993, Clinical Anatomy: An Illustrated Review with Questions and Explanations, 3d edit., 2000, Clinical Neuroanatomy: An Illustrated Review with Questions and Explanations, 3d edit., 2001, Clinical Anatomy: An Illustrated Review, 2000; contbr. articles to med. jours. Med. Research Council grantee, 1959; NIH grantee, 1963-65 Mem. Anat. Soc. Gt. Britain, Am. Soc. Anatomists, Alpha Omega Alpha. Home: 518 Boston Post Rd Madison CT 06443-2930

SNELLEN, DEBORAH SUE, training consulting company executive; b. Columbia, Mo., Oct. 23, 1956; d. Howard Earl and Jessie Jewel (Johnson) Durk; m. Steven Wayne Snellen, Jan. 17, 1987; 1 child, Ashlen Dolores. BS in Edn. cum laude, U. Mo., 1979, MA in Speech Communication, 1980. Provider rels. rep. EDS Fed., Columbia, 1981-83; dir. human resources MBS Textbook Exch., Inc., 1983-88; pres., owner Business Class, 1988—. Chmn. adv. bd. for bus. edn. Columbia Adult Edn., 1990-92. Bd. dirs. U. Mo. Arts and Sci. Alumni Exec. Bd., Advent Enterprises, Inc., Columbia, 1990-92; inaugural participant Greater Mo. Focus on Leadership Program, 1990; participant Tiger Scholarship Fund, Jr. League of Springfield, 1994-97; cert. Herrmann Brain Dominance Instrument Adminstr. and Interpretation, 1994; treasurer U. Mo. Alumni Assoc., 2000—. Honors scholar U. Mo. Mem. ASTD (past pres. Cen. Mo. chpt.), Columbia C. of C. (bd. dirs. 1991-92), Leawood C. of C. (charter, bd. dirs. 1997), Women's Network (pres. 1988-89, amb. 1989-92), U. Mo. Alumni Assn. (treas. 2000—). Republican. Presbyterian. Avocations: tailoring, snow skiing, horseback riding. E-mail: dsnellen@attglobal.net.

SNELLING, BARBARA W. state legislator; b. Fall River, Mass., Mar. 22, 1928; d. Frank Taylor and Hazel (Mitchell) Weil; m. Richard Arkwright Snelling, June 14, 1947 (dec. Aug. 1991); children: Jacqueline, Mark, Diane, Andrew. AB magna cum laude, Radcliffe Coll., 1950; D of Pub. Svc. (hon.), Norwich U., 1981; LLD (hon.), Middlebury Coll., 1997; LLD (hon.) , St. Michaels Coll., 2002. Pres. Snelling and Kolb, Inc., 1982-95; lieut. gov. State of Vt., 1993-97; mem., Chittenden County Vt. Senate, Montpelier, Vt., 1997—99, 2001—02, ret., 2002. Bd. dir. U.S. Inst. Peace. Trustee Radcliffe Coll., 1990-95; bd. dirs. Vt. Cmty. Found., 1986-94, Shelburne Mus., 1988-98; mem. Vt. Ednl. Partnerships, 1992—; v.p. for devel. and external affairs U. Vt., 1974-82; mem. Vt. State Bd. Edn., 1971-77; trustee Champlain Coll., 1971-74; mem. Vt. Alcohol and Drug Rehab. Commn., 1970-73, Shelburne Sch. Bd., 1958-73, chmn. 1965-73; mem. Vt. Edn. Adv. Coun., 1968-71, Vt. Tchr. Edn. Adv. Com., 1968-70, Bd. of Sch. Dirs., Champlain Valley Union H.S., 1962-69, chmn. 1962-68, others; mem. New Eng. Bd. Dollars for Scholars, 1997—; bd. dirs. Vt. Program for Quality, 1997—; mem. Champlain Valley Area Health Edn. Coun., 1997—. Recipient Fanny G. Shaw award for Disting. Community Svc., Burlington Community Coun., 1972, Laymen's award Vt. Edn. Assn., 1965.

SNELLING, GEORGE ARTHUR, banker; b. St. Petersburg, Fla., June 27, 1929; s. William Henry and Eula Hall S.; m. Carolyn Shiver, Mar. 3, 1963; children— George, John S. BSBA, U. Fla., 1951. Partner Smoak, Davis, Nixon & Snelling, C.P.A.s, Jacksonville, Orlando, Fla., 1956-66; v.p. planning Barnett Banks of Fla., Jacksonville, 1966-76; exec. v.p. 1st Bancshares of Fla., Boca Raton, 1976-78; exec. v.p. Fla. Nat. Banks of Fla., Jacksonville, 1978-80; exec. v.p. corp. devel., chief fin. officer Sun Banks of Fla., Orlando, 1981-85; exec. v.p. corp. devel. SunTrust Banks, Inc., Atlanta, 1986-90; pres. Unicoy, Inc., 1991—. Trustee Fla. So. U. Served with USAF, 1951-55. Mem. AICPA. Democrat. Methodist. Home and Office: Unicoy Inc 2682 Varner Dr Atlanta GA 30345-1559 E-mail: gsnellingsr@msn.com.

SNELLING, ROBERT ORREN, SR. franchising and employment executive; b. Aug. 16, 1932; s. Louis Raymond and Gwendolyn Anne (Preble) S.; m. Joan E., 1951 (dec. 1979); children: Robert, Krista; m. Anne Morris, June 30, 1979; children: Rick Spragins, Leigh Crews, Linda Paulk. Student, Pa. State U., 1951-52; Dr. Lit. (hon.), Albright Coll., 1968. Profl. employment counselor Snelling & Snelling, Phila., 1952-53, gen. mgr., 1954—62, pres., 1962—96, chmn. bd. dirs., 1969—2000, CEO, 1997—2000; bus. and franchising cons., 2000—. Spkr., lectr. in field. Author: The Opportunity Explosion, 1969, Jobs—What They Are-Where They Are-What They Pay, 1985, rev. edit., 1992, The Right Job, 1987, rev. edit., 1992; contbr. articles to profl. jours. Mem. long-range planning Sarasota 2000, 1976; mem. pvt. sector employment svcs. com. Dept. Labor, 1982; mem. Com. on Skilled Employment Brokering Svcs., 1984; mem. White Ho. Com. on Small Bus., 1986; mem. adv. com. to U.S. Sec. William Brock, 1986; mem. Gov.'s Select Com. on Workforce 2000, 1988—89, chmn. govtl. regulations and benefits subcom., 1989; apptd. to Nat. Com. for Employment Policy, 1994—97; trustee Regent U., 1988—, Found. for Thought and Ethics, 1990—, Acts 29, 1998—. With U.S. Army, 1953—54. Recipient Golden Plate award, 1964, W.O. Blanchet award, Pa. Assn. Pers. Svc., 1976, Outstanding Citizen award, Assn. Pers. N.Y., 1977, award for excellence, Am. Acad. Achievement, 1964, Harold B. Nelson award, 1985. Mem. Internat. Franchise Assn., Nat. Assn. Pers. Cons., Nat. Assn. Temp. Svcs., U.S. C. of C. Republican.

SNELLINGS, DANIEL BREARD, lawyer; b. New Orleans, Jan. 11, 1960; s. Breard and Emilie (Locascio) S.; m. Lisa Snellings, Oct. 14, 1989; children: Cody, Brooke, Kali, Daniel Jr. BS, Trinity U., 1983; MBA, Loyola U., 1985; JD, Tulane U., 1989. Bar: La. 1990, Miss. 1991, U.S. Supreme Ct. 1996, U.S. Fed. Claims Ct. 1995. Pvt. practice, New Orleans. Mem. ATLA, Miss. Trial Lawyers Assn., La. Trial Lawyers Assn., Miss. Bar Assn., La. Bar Assn., Pearl River County Bar Assn., St. Tammany Parish Bar Assn. Roman Catholic. Office: James Minge & Assocs 2600 Energy Ctr New Orleans LA 70163-2600 also: 503 W Canal St Picayune MS 39466-3914

SNELLINGS, ELEANOR CRAIG, economics educator; b. Laurinburg, N.C., Nov. 3, 1926; d. Carl Brackett and Eleanor (Johnston) Craig; m. Henry L. Snellings Jr., Oct. 1, 1960 (dec. 1970); 1 child, Hill. B.A., U. N.C., 1947, M.A., 1950; Ph.D., Duke U., 1959. Instr. U. Ark., Fayetteville, 1948-49, U. N.C.-Greensboro, 1949-56; research assoc. Fed. Res. Bank of Richmond, Va., 1956-58, assoc. economist, 1959-60, economist, 1960-62; adj. faculty Va. Commonwealth U., Richmond, 1962-68, assoc. prof. econs., 1968-92; econ. dir. South River Assn., Greensboro, 1974-77. Grantee So. Fellowships Fund, 1954, So. Bus. Adminstrn. Assn., 1981-82. Mem. Am. Econ. Assn., Va. Assn. Economists (v.p. 1980-81). Presbyterian. Home: Apt 833 1600 Westbrook Ave Richmond VA 23227-3322

SNELSON, KENNETH DUANE, sculptor; b. Pendleton, Oreg., June 29, 1927; s. John Tavner and Mildred F. (Unger) S.; m. Katherine Eve Kaufmann, May 2, 1972; 1 child, Andrea Nicole. Numerous. Student, U. Oreg., 1946-47, Black Mountain Coll., 1948-49, Chgo. Inst. Design, 1950-51, Academie Montmartre, Paris, 1951-52; D of Arts and Humane Letters (honoris causa), Rensselaer Poly. Inst., 1985. Subject of articles in art publs.; one-man shows U.S. and Germany, Holland, including Portrait of an Atom, Balt., 1979-80, De Cordova and Dana Mus. and Park, Lincoln, Mass., 1984, Zabriskie Gallery, 1984, Yoh Art Gallery, Osaka, Japan, 1991, Contemporary Sculpture Ctr., Tokyo, 1995, Maxwell Davidson Gallery, N.Y.C., 1994, Marlborough Gallery, N.Y.C., 1999; major retrospective, Hirshhorn Mus. and Sculpture Garden of Smithsonian Instn., 1981, Albright-Knox Art Gallery, Buffalo, 1981, N.Y. Acad. Scis., 1989; group shows include Mus. Modern Art, N.Y.C., 1967, Whitney Mus., N.Y.C., 1966, 69, 70, Albright Knox Gallery, 1968, Prospect '68, Dusseldorf, Germany, 1968, Salon International de Galeries Pilotes, Lausanne, Switzerland, 1970, Sammlun Etzold, Kolnischer Kunstverein, Cologne, Germany, 1970, Expo '70, Osaka, Japan, 1970, Fondation Maeght, St. Paul de Vence, France, 1970, Art Inst. Chgo., 1972; represented in permanent collections including, Mus. Modern Art, Whitney Mus. Am. Art, cities of Hannover and Hamburg, Germany, Rijksmuseum Kroller Muller, Otterlo, Holland, Rijksmuseum, Amsterdam, Holland, Japan Iron, Steel Fedn., Osaka, City of Balt., Hirshhorn Mus., Milw. Art Center, City of Buffalo, Mus. Modern Art, Shiga, Japan; author: Full Circle: Panoramas of Paris, Venice, Rome, Siena and Kyoto, 1990; patentee discontinuous compression structures, model for atomic forms. Served with USNR, 1945-46. DAAD fellow Berlin Kunstlerprogram, 1976; recipient AIA Artist's medal, 1981, Art award Am. Inst. Arts and Letters, 1987, Prix Ars Electronica Siemens AG for Computer Graphics, Linz, Austria, 1989, Lifetime Achievement award Internat. Sculpture Ctr., 1999. Mem. Am. Acad. Arts and Letters. E-mail: k_snelson@mindspring.com. *My art is concerned with nature in its most fundamental aspect, the patterns of physical forces in space.*

SNIBBE, PATRICIA MISCALL, advertising executive; b. Hackensack, N.J., June 1, 1932; d. Jack and Margaret Lois (Drake) Miscall; m. Richard Wilson Snibbe, Sept. 8, 1962; stepchildren: John Robinson, Paul Clor. BFA, R.I. Sch. Design, 1954; postgrad., New Sch. for Social Rsch., 1975-80, U. London, 1989. Art dir., film prodr. Peckham Prodns., N.Y.C., 1960-64; dir. art, ptnr. Stallman and Snibbe, 1964-66; dir. art Shevlo Advt., 1966-72, Bernard Hodes Advt., N.Y.C., 1972-77; owner, creative dir. Archtl. Film Libr., 1978-88, creative dir., 1980—; pres. Crommelin and Bliss, Parfumier, 1988—. Author and artist: Feminist Funnies, 181—; author: (with Richard W. Snibbe) The New Modernist in World Architecture, 1999. Recipient Golden Cir. award Affiliated Advt. Agys. Internat., 1975-77, Creativity award of distinction, 1978. Mem. NOW (bd. dirs. N.Y.C. 1983-84), Graphic Artists Guild (steering com. Cartoonists Guild divsn. 1984-85), NATAS, Archeol. Inst. Am. Avocation: abstract modern painting. Home: 139 E 18th St New York NY 10003-2470

SNIBBE, RICHARD W. architect; b. Balt., Oct. 31, 1916; s. George W. and Mildred (Robinson) S.; m. Miriam Bergman, Jan. 3, 1942 (dec.); children: John Robinson, Paul Clor; m. Patricia Lois Miscall, Sept. 8, 1962. BA, St. Johns Coll., 1939; postgrad., Harvard Grad. Sch. Design, 1939-41. Registered profl. architect, lic. architect N.Y. Asso. Edward D. Stone (architect), N.Y.C., 1951-56; partner Ballard, Todd & Snibbe, 1957-61; individual practice architecture, 1962; partner Myller, Snibbe, Tafel, 1962-67, Snibbe, Tafel, Lindholm, 1967-73, Wilson & Snibbe (architects, planners, engrs.), N.Y.C., from 1970; formed Snibbes Inc. (producers archtl. films), 1981. Instr. Cooper Union, N.Y.C., 1949; vis. critic Columbia, N.Y.C., 1956, Pratt Inst., N.Y.C., 1962; founder Archtl. Film Library, 1982. Author: Small Commercial Buildings, 1956, Snibbe, Selected Works and Essays, 1983, (with Patricia M. Snibbe) The New Modernist in World Architecture, 1999; important works include U.S. embassy, New Delhi, India (as assoc.), 1955, Tennis Pavilion, Princeton, 1960 (AIA honor award 1962), grad. student apts. Princeton U., 1961, comprehensive campus plan and bldgs. State U. Coll, Geneseo, N.Y., 1962-72, grad. dormitories Princeton U., 1970, Handloser Project, Future Town, 1973, entry to Paris Opera Competition, 1983; pub. L'Arca, 1990; exhibited in Mus. Modern Art, N.Y.C., Transformations in Modern Architecture, 1979; producer: (film) Maison La Roche-Jeanneret by Le Corbusier, 1983, (TV film) Great Modern Architecture of the Last 25 Years, 1994; patentee for suspended structure, Landspan. Chmn. aesthetics com. Gramercy Neighborhood Assn. Inc.; bd. dirs.; founder Architects Com. N.Y., 1992, Congress of Internat. Modern Archs., N.Y.C., 2000; active Bill Clinton for Pres., 1992. Brunner scholar N.Y. chpt. AIA, 1957 Fellow AIA (founder, chmn. nat. com. on aesthetics 1963, mem. emeritus 1990—); mem. Harvard Grad. Sch. Design Assn., Am. Arbitration Assn., Players Club, Nat. Arts Club. Address: 3 Baltimore St Providence RI 02909 E-mail: miscallshibbe@aol.com.

SNIDER, CLIFTON MARK, English educator, writer, poet; b. Duluth, Minn., Mar. 3, 1947; s. Allan George and Rhoda Marion (Tout) S. BA, Calif. State U., Long Beach, 1969, MA, 1971; PhD, U. N.Mex., 1974. Lectr. English, Calif. State U., 1974—; instr. English, Long Beach City Coll., 1975—. Author: (poetry) Jesse Comes Back, 1976, Bad Smoke Good Body, 1980, Jesse and His Son, 1982, Edwin: A Character in Poems, 1984, The Stuff That Dreams Are Made On: A Jungian Interpretation of Literature, 1991, (poetry) Blood & Bones, 1988, Impervious to Piranhas, 1989, The Age of the Mother, 1992, The Alchemy of Opposites, 2000, (novels) Loud Whisper, 2000, Bare Roots, 2001, Wrestling with Angels: A Tale of Two Brothers, 2001. Former officer steering com. Long Beach Lambda Dem. Club. Resident fellow Yaddo, Saratoga Springs, N.Y., 1978, 82, Helene Wurlitzer Found. N.M., Taos, 1984,, 90, 98, Karolyi Found., Vence, France, 1986, 87. Home: 2719 Eucalyptus Ave Long Beach CA 90806-2515 Office: Calif State U 1250 Bellflower Blvd Long Beach CA 90840-0001 E-mail: csnider@csulb.edu.

SNIDER, EDWARD MALCOLM, professional hockey club executive; b. Washington, Jan. 6, 1933; s. Sol C. and Lillian (Bonas) S.; children: Craig Alan, Jay Thomas, Lindy Lou, Tina Suzanne, Sarena Lynn, Samuel Everett. BS, U. Md., 1955. CPA, Md. Maj. stockholder, exec. v.p. Edge Ltd., Washington, 1957-63; v.p. Phila. Eagles Football Club, 1964-67; owner Phila. Flyers Hockey Club, 1967—; chmn. bd. Spectrum Arena, Phila., 1967—; bd. govs. NHL, 1967—. Established Spectacor (now Comcast-Spectacor), chmn. bd. 1996; adv. bd. Sol C. Snider Entrepreneurial Ctr. U Pa.; bd. overseers Wharton Sch. U. Pa.; bd. dirs. Inst. for Cancer and Blood Diseases Hahnemann U., Simon Weisenthal Ctr.; bd. trustees Inst. for Objectivist Studies. Office: Phila Flyers Phila 76ers First Union Center, 3601 S Broad St Philadelphia PA 19148-5250*

SNIDER, GEORGE RUNYON, JR. franchising company executive; b. Huntington, W.Va., Jan. 25, 1941; s. George R. and Marjorie Steuart S.; m. Nora C. Jacobs, Aug. 26, 1988; children: George R. III, Jeremy W. BA, Yale U., 1962. Assoc. dir. pub. affairs Procter & Gamble Co., Cin., 1972-76; dir. pub. rels. BF Goodrich Co., Akron, Ohio, 1977-82; dir. mktg. BF Goodrich Chem. Group, Cleve., 1982-88; dir. mktg. and comms. Walter & Haverfield, 1988-92; pres., CEO SRA Internat., Inc., Akron, 1992—. Trustee Old Trail Sch., Bath, Ohio, 1982-88, trustee emeritus, 1989—. Mem. Nat. Assn. Pers. Svcs. (dir., chmn. govt. affairs com. 1997-2000, chmn. pub. rels. 2000-2001), Soc. Cin., Akron City Club, The Club at Key Ctr. (Cleve.). Office: SRA Internat Inc 3737 Embassy Pkwy Ste 200 Akron OH 44333-8369

SNIDER, GORDON LLOYD, physician; b. Toronto, Apr. 11, 1922; came to U.S., 1946, naturalized, 1956; s. Isadore Leonard and Rebecca (Freeman) S.; m. Ruth Charlotte Tobias, May 18, 1945; children: Barry Bernard, Martin David, Rebecca Eve. MD, U. Toronto, 1944. Intern Toronto Gen. Hosp., 1944-45; resident in medicine Bronx Hosp., N.Y.C., 1946-47; resident in pathology Mass. Meml. Hosps., Boston, 1947-48; fellow in medicine Lahey Clinic, 1948-49; fellow in pulmonary medicine Trudeau San., Trudeau, N.Y., 1949-50; asst. dir. chest dept. Michael Reese Hosp., Chgo., 1950-61; attending physician Winfield (Ill.) Hosp., 1950-61; cons. physician, dir. pulmonary function lab. Mcpl. Tb San., Chgo., 1954-68; chief div. thoracic medicine Mt. Sinai Hosp., 1961-66; acting chmn. depts. medicine Chgo. Med. Sch. and Mt. Sinai Hosp., 1965-66; chief pulmonary disease sect. Wood VA Hosp.; attending physician Milwaukee County Gen. Hosp., Wood, Wis., 1966-68. Asst. prof. Chgo. Med. Sch., 1958-61, assoc. prof., 1961-64, prof., 1964-66; prof. Marquette U. Sch. Medicine, 1966-68; prof. medicine, head pulmonary medicine sect. Boston U. Sch. Medicine, 1968-87; chief pulmonary medicine sect., Boston VA Med. Ctr., 1968-88, chief med. svc., 1986-2000, physician med. svc. VA Boston Healthcare Sys., 2000-2001; pulmonary sect. mem. Evans Dept. Clin. Rsch., Univ. Hosp., Boston, 1968—; Maurice B. Strauss prof. medicine, Boston U. and Tufts U. Schs. Medicine, 1986-93, Boston U. Sch. Medicine, 1993—; Presdl. lectr. Soc. European Pulmonologists, 4th Ann. Congress, Stressa-Milan, Italy, 1986, Blankenhorn lectr. Cin. Soc. Ind. Medicine, 1989; Parker B. Francis lectr. 6th Thomas L. Petty Aspen Lung Conf., 1991, Theodore Badger Meml. lectr. Mass. Thoracic Soc., 1995; vis. prof. U. Cin. Sch. Medicine, 1989; Frank T. Fulton vis. physician-in-chief pro tempore R.I. Hosp. and Brown U., Providence, 1988; med. adv. bd. Puritan-Bennett Corp.; chmn. sci. adv. com. Norman B. Salvesen Emphysema Trust, U. Edinburgh, 1981-93; Theodore Badger Meml. lecture Mass. Thoracic Soc., 1995, Irving Kass lectr. U. Nebr., 1992. Chair sci. adv. com. Am. Lung Assn., 2002. Served to capt. M.C. Royal Can. Army, 1945-46. Co-recipient Alton Ochsner award relating smoking and health, 1990; NIH grantee, 1962-91; Francis S. North travel fellow, 1978; 6th Robert K. Match Disting. scholar L.I. Jewish Hosp., 1991; recipient David M. Worthen for academic excellence award Dept. Vets. Affairs, 1998; Gordon and Ruth Snider Professorship in Pulmonary Medicine established at Boston U. Sch. Medicine, 2000. Fellow Am. Coll. Chest Physicians (Simon Rodbard lectr. 1985), ACP; mem. Am. Fedn. Clin. Research, Am. Thoracic Soc. (pres. 1986, Amberson lectr. 1992), Central Soc. Clin. Research, Sigma Xi, Alpha Omega Alpha. Jewish. Home: 24 Holly Rd Newton MA 02468-1449 Office: VA Med Center 150 S Huntington Ave Jamaica Plain MA 02130-4817 E-mail: gordon.snider@med.va.gov.

SNIDER, HARLAN TANNER, former manufacturing company executive; b. Owensboro, Ky., July 20, 1926; s. George William and Lydia (Tanner) S.; m. Helen Boswell, Mar. 7, 1953; children— William Jeffrey, Katherine Snider. BA, Transylvania U., 1949. Territory salesman Sunray DX Corp., Owensboro, 1950-57, dist. sales mgr. Ind., 1958-63, div. mgr. Iowa, 1963-65, dir. mktg. services, 1965-67; pres. Red Barn Chems., 1967-69; dir. petrochems. Sun Oil Co., Phila., 1969-71, v.p. mktg., 1973-75; pres. Sunmark Industries, Phila., 1975-79; sr. v.p., external affairs Sun Co., Inc., Radnor, Pa., 1980-84, sr. v.p. planning pub. affairs, 1984-88; ret., 1988. Served with USAF, 1944-46. Mem. Am. Petroleum Industry, 25 Yr. Club Petroleum Industry. Clubs: Union League (Phila.), Aronimink Golf (Newtown Square, Pa.), Mariner Sands Golf Club (Stuart, Fla.). Home (Winter): 7013 Pacific Dr SE Stuart FL 34997 E-mail: hbhtsnid@aol.com.

SNIDER, JAMES RHODES, radiologist; b. Pawnee, Okla., May 16, 1931; s. John Henry and Gladys Opal (Rhodes) S.; B.S., U. Okla., 1953, M.D., 1956; m. Lynadell Vivion, Dec. 27, 1954; children— Jon, Jan. Intern, Edward Meyer Meml. Hosp., Buffalo, 1956-57; resident radiology U. Okla. Med. Center, 1959-62; radiologist Holt-Krock Clinic and Sparks Regional Med. Center, Ft. Smith, Ark., 1962-66, dir. Fairfield Community Land Co., Little Rock, 1968-87, Fairfield Communities, Inc., 1968-87. Mem. Ark. Bd. Pub. Welfare, 1969-71. Bd. dirs. U. Okla. Assn., 1967-70, U. Okla. Alumni Devel. Fund, 1970-74; bd. visitors U. Okla. Served to lt. comdr. USNR, 1957-62. Mem. Am. Coll. Radiology, Radiol. Soc. N.Am., Am. Roentgen Ray Soc., AMA, Phi Beta Kappa, Beta Theta Pi, Alpha Epsilon Delta. Assoc. editor Computerized Tomography, 1976-88. Home: 5814 Cliff Dr Fort Smith AR 72903-3845 Office: 1500 Dodson Ave Fort Smith AR 72901-5128

SNIDER, JANE ANN, elementary school educator; b. Inglewood, Calif., Nov. 18, 1939; d. Percy E. and Mamie D. (Gorman) S. MusB, U. So. Calif., 1962; MS, Azusa Pacific U., 1987. Cert. gen. elem. and spl. secondary music tchr. Tchr. 6th grade Centralia Sch. Dist., Buena Park, Calif., 1963—, mentor, tchr. computer tech., 1983-97. Home: 1433 Royer Ave Fullerton CA 92833-4719 E-mail: jsnider7@earthlink.net.

SNIDER, L. BRITT, government executive; b. Rocky Mount, N.C., Jan. 12, 1945; s. Arnold Holmes and Kate Mills (Suiter) S.; m. Virginia Lansford, Aug. 24, 1974; 1 child, Britt Arnold. BA, Davidson (N.C.) Coll., 1966; JD, U. Va., 1969. Counsel judiciary subcom. on constl. rights U.S. Senate, Washington, 1971-75, counsel select com. on intelligence, 1975-76; ptnr. Ketner & Snider, Salisbury, N.C., 1976-77; counsel govt. ops. subcom. on govt. info. U.S. Ho. Reps., Washington, 1977; asst. dep. undersec. counterintelligence and security Dept. Def., 1977-87; minority counsel U.S. Senate Intelligence Com., 1987-89, gen. counsel, 1989-95, staff dir. commn. on roles and capabilities of U.S. Intelligence Cmty., 1995-96; sr. fellow Ctr. for Study of Intelligence, 1996-97; spl. counsel to dir. CIA, 1997-98, inspector gen., 1998-2001. Staff dir. Commn. to Rev. Security Practices and Procedures Dept. Def., Washington, 1985. Served to capt. U.S. Army, 1969-71, Vietnam. Mem. Va. Bar Assn., D.C. Bar Assn. Democrat. Episcopalian. Avocations: golf, jogging, reading.

SNIDER, LAWRENCE K. lawyer; b. Detroit, Dec. 28, 1938; s. Ben and Ida (Hertz) S.; m. Maxine Bobman, Aug. 12, 1962; children: Stephanie, Suzanne. BA, U. Mich., 1960, JD, 1963. Bar: Mich. 1964, Ill. 1991. Ptnr. Jaffe, Snider, Raitt & Heuer, Detroit, 1968-91, Mayer, Brown & Platt, Chgo., 1991—. Mem. Nat. Bankruptcy Conf., Am. Coll. Bankruptcy, 1991—. Contbr. articles to profl. jours. Mem. Mich. Coun. for the Arts, 1990-91. Avocations: photography, collections. Office: Mayer Brown & Platt 190 S La Salle St Ste 3100 Chicago IL 60603-3441

SNIDER, MARIE ANNA, syndicated columnist; b. Croghan, N.Y., Aug. 9, 1927; d. Nicholas and Dorothy (Moser) Gingerich; m. Howard Mervin, Nov. 27, 1954; children: Vada Marie, Conrad Howard. BS, Goshen Coll., 1949; M in Religious Edn., Mennonite Bibl. Sem., 1957; MS, Kans. State U., 1980. High sch. tchr. Rockway Collegiate, Kitchener, Ont., Can., 1949-53; free-lance writer, 1953-54; pub. rels. Goshen Coll., Ind., 1955-57; free-lance writer, homemaker, 1957-67; info. editor Prairie View, Inc., Newton, Kans., 1967-76, dir., pub. info. & edn., 1976-85, dir. communications, 1985-91; freelance writer, columnist North Newton, 1991—; syndicated columnist "This Side of 60", 1992—. Bd. dirs. Health Systems Agy. of S.E. Kans., 1981-86, v.p., 1986-87; workshop presenter Nat. Coun. of Community Mental Health Ctrs., Atlanta, 1980, N.Y., 1982, 89, Miami, 1987. Editor: Media and Terrorism--The Psychological Impact, 1976; columnist: This Side of 60. Pres. City Council, N Newton, 1977-79, pres. 1980. Recipient 1st Pl. MacEachern award Assn. of Hosp. Pub. Rels., 1981, 1st Pl. Media award Nat. Coun. Community Mental Health Ctrs., 1977, 84, runner-up Pub. Rels. award Nat. Assn. Pvt. Psychiat. Hosps., 1980. Mem. Nat. Soc. Newspaper Columnists. Democrat. Avocations: research on role of women in American comics (speaker and media interviews on this topic), empowerment in aging. Home and Office: PO Box 332 North Newton KS 67117-0332

SNIDER, ROBERT F. chemistry educator, researcher; b. Calgary, Alta., Can., Nov. 22, 1931; s. Edward C. and Agnes S. (Klaeson) S.; children: Wendy A., Timothy J., Terry E., Geoffrey Y, Eric A. M. Burrough. BS, U. Alta., 1953; PhD, U. Wis., 1958. Postdoctoral fellow Nat. Research Council Can., Ottawa, 1958; instr. II U. B.C., Vancouver, 1958-60, asst. prof., 1960-65, assoc. prof., 1965-69, prof., 1969-96, prof. emeritus, 1997—; vis. research prof. U. Leiden, Netherlands, 1973-74. Recipient gov. gen. gold medal U. Alta., 1953; U. Wis. WARF unassigned fellow, 1953-55; Izaac Walton Killam Meml. fellowship, 1985-86. Fellow Chem. Inst. Can., Royal Soc. Can.; mem. Am. Phys. Soc., Can. Assn. Physicists Home: 3952 W 29th St Vancouver BC Canada V6S 1T9 Office: U BC 2036 Main Mall Vancouver BC Canada V6T 1Z1 E-mail: snider@chem.ubc.ca.

SNIDER, ROBERT LARRY, management consultant; b. Muskogee, Okla., Aug. 10, 1932; s. George Robert and Kathryn (Smiser) S.; m. Gerlene Rose Tipton, Nov. 26, 1953; children: Melody Kathryn Porter, Rebecca Lee. BS in Indsl. Engring., U. Houston, 1955, postgrad., 1956, Pomona Coll., 1960. Cert. mgmt. cons. Instr. U. Houston Coll. Engring., 1955-56; sr. indsl. engr. Sheffield Steel Corp., Houston, 1955-59, Kaiser Steel Co., Fontana, Calif., 1959-60; cons. Arthur Young & Co., L.A., 1960-61; mgmt. analyst Iranian Oil Exploration & Producing Co., Masjidi-Suliman, Iran, 1961-62; cons., 1962-65; v.p. operating methods divsn. Booz, Allen & Hamilton, Inc., Dallas, 1965-69; mngr., ptnr. RLS Profl. Svcs., LiLic, Houston, 1995—; prin., gen. cons. practice Peat Marwick Mitchell, CPAs, 1969-71; exec. v.p. mfg. Sterling Electronics Corp., 1971-72, COO, pres., 1972-77; CEO, pres. Rapoca Energy Corp., Cin., 1977-79; mng. ptnr., cons. Coopers & Lybrand, Southwest, Houston, 1979-81; mng. dir. S.W. region Korn Ferry Internat., 1981-86; ptnr.-in-charge Houston Mgmt. Cons. Practice, 1986-91; ptnr. cons. Southwest Enterprise Coopers & Lybrand, Houston, 1991-92, ptnr. S.W. Mfg. Cons. Process Improvement Group Pakistan/Mid. Asia, 1992-93, internat. cons. ptnr., 1993-95; mng. ptnr. RLS Profl. Svcs. LLC, 1995—; chmn., dir. L&G Snacks, 1997-2000. Chmn. L&G Snacks. Past chmn. bd. mem. found. bd. and adminstrv. bd. Chapel Wood Meth.Ch.; former mem. adminstrv. bd. Meml. Drive Meth. Ch., Willis, Tex., 1995—99; past bd. dirs. Houston Jr. Achievement, exec. com.; ret. exec. com. Houston Grand Opera, bd. dirs.; former trustee Gene Craig Caring Forever Fund, 1995—99; sr. trustee Titon-Snider Minister Edn. Fund., 1999—. With C.E. AUS, 1956. Recipient Outstandng Mil. Engr. award Soc. Mil Engrs., 1955; named Disting. Alumni, Cullen Coll. Engring., U. Houston, 1991. Mem.: Soc. Mining Engrs., U. Houston Alumni Assn. (past bd. dirs., exec. com. 1987—94, pres. and chmn. bd. 1990—93), Phi Kappa Phi, Phi Theta Kappa. Home and Office: 9387 Escondido Dr Willis TX 77318-6621 E-mail: rlarry32@hotmail.com.

SNIDER, STACEY, film company executive; b. Phila., Apr. 29, 1961; BA, U. of Penn., 1982; JD, U. of Calif. at Los Angeles, Sch. of Law, 1985. Dir. of development Guber-Peters Entertainment Co., 1986—90, exec. v.p., 1990—92; pres. prodn. TriStar Pictures, 1992-96; co-pres. prodn. Universal Pictures, Universal City, Calif., 1996-98, head prodn., 1998, pres., 1998—, chmn., CEO, 1999—. Office: Universal Pictures 100 Universal City Plz Universal City CA 91608-1002*

SNIDER, STEPHEN WILLIAM, art director, graphic designer; b. Boston, July 21, 1943; s. Louis Oscar and Etta Zelda (Rosenberg) S.; m. Marlene Sandra Shuman, Sept. 2, 1973; children: Emily Allison, Jill Tracy. Grad., Sch. Mus. Fine Arts, Boston, 1961-65. Asst. art dir. Arthur D. Little, Inc., Cambridge, Mass., 1965-70; creative dir. Snider Design, Boston, 1970-78; art dir. The Atlantic Monthly, 1978-81; design dir. Arnold & Co. Advt., 1981-85; creative dir. Snider Design, Wellesley, Mass., 1985-87; art dir. Little, Brown & Co., Boston, 1987-96; creative dir., v.p. St. Martin's Press, N.Y.C., 1996—. Recipient 1st place and Silver medal New Eng. Hatch awards, Boston, 1974, Gold medal N.Y. Art Dirs. Club, 1984, Best of Category Design, New Eng. Book Show, Boston, 1994, N.Y. Art Dirs. Club, 1997, Lit. Market Pl. award, named Graphic Design Person of Yr. Lit. Market Pl., 1998. Mem. Am. Inst. Graphic Artists. Avocations: tennis, theatre, film, photography, antique collecting. Home: 99 Brook St Wellesley MA 02482-6644 also: 226 E 25th St New York NY 10010-3150 Office: St Martin's Press 175 5th Ave Frnt 4 New York NY 10010-7703 E-mail: steve.snider@stmartins.com.

SNIDER, VIRGINIA L. antitrust consultant; b. Chgo., July 17, 1946; d. Edwin Gaines and Sue (Kemmer) Lansford; m. L. Britt Snider, Aug. 24, 1974; 1 child, Britt Arnold. BA, Wash. State U., Pullman, 1971. Merger analyst U.S. Fed. Trade Commn., Washington, 1973-89, spl. projects dir., 1989-94; antitrust cons. Clifford Chance Rogers & Wells, N.Y.C. and Washington, 1994—. Co-author of U.S. merger guidelines for U.S. Govt., 1992; contbr. articles to profl. jours. Mem. bd. visitors Washington Episcopal Sch., 1988—, founding trustee, 1986. Recipient Disting. Svc. award U.S. Govt., 1994. Episcopalian. Office: Clifford Chance Rogers & Wells 2001 K St NW Washington DC 20006

SNIERSON, LYNNE WENDY, communications executive; b. Laconia, N.H., Feb. 28, 1952; d. Bernard Irwin and Muriel Stella (Goldberg) S. BA, Duke U., 1973. Reporter, prodr. WMUR-TV, Manchester, N.H., 1981-83; sportswriter Boston Herald, 1983-87, Miami (Fla.) News, 1987-89, St. Louis Sun, 1989-90; contbg. reporter KMOX Radio, St. Louis, 1990-93; sportswriter The Racing Times, N.Y.C., 1991-92; dir. comm. Arlington Internat. Racecourse, Arlington Heights, Ill., 1992-95; dir. comm. and mktg. Rockingham Park, Salem, N.H., 1995—. Reporter (tv show) Arlington Weekend, 1993-94; contbr. articles to publs. Recipient Best Sports Story award New Eng. Womens Press Assn., 1986, award of excellence New Eng. Womens Press Assn., 1986; named one of 10 most powerful women in NFL, Coll. and Pro Football Weekly, 1988. Mem.: NOW, Turf Publicists Am. (v.p. 1997—98, 2000—01), Assn. for Women in Sports Media, New Eng. Turf Writers Assn. (sec.-treas. 1995—2000, v.p. 1996—98, pres. 2001—02), Nat. Turf Writers Assn., Profl. Football Writers Am., Nat. Abortion Rights Action League (N.H. bd. dir. 2002—). Democrat. Avocations: reading, traveling, fitness training, gardening. Office: Rockingham Park Rockingham Park Blvd Salem NH 03079

SNITCH, THOMAS HAROLD, science educator, consultant; b. Cleve., July 14, 1954; s. Harold and Betty (Siek) S.; m. Mary Leslie Lassiter, Oct. 13, 1990. BA in Asian Studies, Bowling Green State U., 1975; MA in Internat. Econs., The Am. U., 1977, PhD in Internat. Econs., 1981. Dir. fgn. policy programs The Am. U., Washington, 1977-82; sr. polit. advisor U.S. Arms Control and Disarmament Agy., 1982-87; dir. strategic studies The Applied Scis. Corp., Arlington, Va., 1987-89; dir. study NAS, Washington, 1989-91; dir. internat. programs Applied Rsch. Lab., Arlington, 1991; CEO Little Falls Assocs. Inc., Bethesda, Md., 1992—. Guest scholar The Brookings Instn., Washington, 1976. Author: International Terrorism, 1982, (study) Finding Common Ground, 1991. Internat. scholar NASA, 1977; doctoral scholar The Am. U., 1979. Mem. AIAA (sr. mem.), Nat. Space Club (sr. mem.), Asia Soc. (sr. mem.), Japan Soc. Republican. Episcopalian. Home: 5202 Little Falls Dr Bethesda MD 20816-2813 Office: Little Falls Assocs Inc 5205 Little Falls Dr Bethesda MD 20816-2814 E-mail: thsnitch@erols.com.

SNITZER, ELIAS, physicist; b. Lynn, Mass., Feb. 27, 1925; s. Isaac and Jenny (Sussman) Snitzer; m. Shirley Ann Wood, Nov. 22, 1950; children: Sandra, Barbara, Peter, Helen, Louis. BSEE, Tufts U., 1946; MS in Physics, U. Chgo., 1950, PhD, 1953. Rsch. physicist Honeywell Corp., Phila., 1954-56; assoc. prof. Lowell Technol. Inst., Mass., 1956-58; dir. rsch. Am. Optical Co., Southbridge, 1959-76; mgr. applied physics United Technologies Rsch., East Hartford, Conn., 1977-84; mgr. fiber optics Polaroid, Cambridge, Mass., 1984-88; prof. Rutgers U., 1989-97, prof. emeritus, 1997—. Contbr. articles to profl. jours. With USN, 1943—46. Fellow: Ceramic Soc., Optical Soc. Am. (John Tyndall award 1994); mem.: IEEE (George Morey award 1971, Quantum Electronics award 1979, Charles Townes award 1991, Otto Schott award 1999, Opto-Electronic Rank prize 2000, LEOS Millenium award 2001), NAE, Am. Phys. Soc. Democrat. Jewish. Achievements include invention of glass laser; fiber laser amplifier. Home: 8 Smoke Tree Close Piscataway NJ 08854-5109 Office: Rutgers U Dept Ceramic & Materials Engring 607 Taylor Rd Piscataway NJ 08854-8065 Fax: 732-463-1675. E-mail: snitzer@rci.rutgers.edu.

SNIVELY, PAMELA ANNETTE, county official; b. Columbus, Ind., Nov. 10, 1951; d. Ronald Lee and Helen Carol (Higgins) S. BFA, William Woods Coll., Fulton, Mo., 1974. Cert. peace officer, Calif. Paralegal Legal Aid Soc. Lincoln, Nebr., 1974-75; family counselor Kaleidoscope, Inc., Chgo., 1975-79; office mgr. John B. Coleman & Co., Chgo., 1979-80; tchr. Peace Corps, Kenya, 1980-82; office mgr. Data Resources, Inc., Los Angeles, 1983-84; dep. sheriff Los Angeles County Sheriff's Dept., Los Angeles, 1984—; mem. Summit Orgn. Inc. Mem. Assn. Los Angeles County Dep. Sheriffs. Avocations: needlecrafts, scuba diving, snow skiing, reading, singing, pub. speaking. Office: Los Angeles County Sheriffs Dept 211 W Temole St Los Angeles CA 90012

SNIVELY, STEPHEN WAYNE, lawyer; b. Danville, Ill., Apr. 27, 1949; s. Roberts Eyster and Margaret Louise Snively; m. Heather Lea Patten, Mar. 19, 1988; children: Toby, Ben, Madeline, Taylor. BA, U. Ill., 1971, JD, 1975. Bar: Ill. 1975, Fla. 1980. Assoc. Kavanagh, Scully, Sudow, White & Frederick, Peoria, Ill., 1975-80, Maguire, Voorhis & Wells, P.A., Orlando, Fla., 1980—; merged with Holland & Knight LLP, 1998—. Seminar speaker, 1987. Contbr. articles to profl. jours. Bd. dirs. Found. for Orange County Pub. Schs., Orlando, 1987-96, officer, 1987-96, pres., 1993-94, chmn., 1994-96; bd. dirs. Found. for Hospice of Ctrl. Fla., Inc., 1995-96; treas., bd. dirs. HCF Found., Inc., 1996—, pres., 1998—. Mem. ABA (retail leasing com.), Fla. Bar (liaison to land surveyor com. 1982—), Orange County Bar Assn., Internat. Coun. Shopping Ctrs., Fla. C. of C. (Leadership Fla. 1991-92), Fla. Zool. Soc. (sec., bd. dirs. 1991-96), Tiger Bay Club, Phi Beta Kappa. Republican. Presbyterian. Avocations: running, writing, computers, photography. Office: Holland & Knight LLP 200 S Orange Ave Ste 2600 Orlando FL 32801-3453 E-mail: ssnively@hklaw.com.

SNODDY, JAMES ERNEST, education educator; b. Perrysville, Ind., Oct. 6, 1932; s. James Elmer and Edna May (Hayworth) S.; m. Alice Joanne Crowder, Aug. 15, 1954; children: Ryan Anthony, Elise Suzanne. BS, Ind. State U., 1954; MEd, U. Ill., 1961, EdD, 1967. Tchr. Danville (Ill.) Pub. Schs., 1954-57, prin., 1961-64; instr. U. Ill., Champaign, 1965-67; prof. edn. Mich. State U., East Lansing, 1967-72, 78-96, chmn. dept. elem. and spl. edn., 1972-78, ret., 1996, prof. emeritus, 1997—; dir. Program CORK, 1978-82. With U.S. Army, 1955-57. Mem. Am. Assn. for Adult and Continuing Edn., Commn. of Profs. of Adult and Continuing Edn. Methodist. Home: 1926 Creek Lndg Haslett MI 48840-8704 Office: Mich State U 419 Erickson Hall East Lansing MI 48824-1034 E-mail: jsnoddy@pilot.msu.edu.

SNODGRASS, KLYNE RYLAND, seminary educator; b. Kingsport, Tenn., Dec. 28, 1944; s. Charles Sidney and Wanda Virginia (Lauderback) S.; m. Phyllis Parks, Aug. 28, 1966; children: Nathan, Valerie. BA, Columbia Bible Coll., 1966; MDiv magna cum laude, Trinity Evang. Div. Sch., 1969; PhD, St. Andrews U., 1973. Instr. N.T. Georgetown (Ky.) Coll., 1973-74; asst. prof. bibl. lit. North Park Sem., Chgo., 1974-78, assoc. prof., 1978-84, prof., 1984-89, Paul Brandel prof. N.T. studies, 1989—, dean of faculty, 1988-93. Author: The Parable of the Wicked Tenants, 1983, Between Two Truths, 1990, Ephesians: The NIV Application Commentary, 1996; contbr. articles to profl.

jours. Assn. Theol. Schs. grantee, 1981, PEW Evang. Scholars Program grantee, 1995. Fellow Inst. Bible Rsch. (exec. sec. 1989-93, pres. 1993-95); mem. Chgo. Soc. Bibl. Rsch. (pres. 1990-91), Soc. Bibl. Lit., Studiorum Novi Testamenti Societas. Office: North Park Theol Sem 3225 W Foster Ave Chicago IL 60625-4823 E-mail: ksnodgrass@northpark.edu.

SNODGRASS, LYNN, small business owner, former state legislator; married; children: Jenne, Megan. BS in Elem. Edn., Oreg. State U., 1973; degree, Portland State U., 1975. Owner Drake's 7 Dees Nursery & Landscape Co., Oreg.; mem. Oreg. Ho. of Reps., 1995—2000; dep. majority leader, 1995-97; majority leader, 1997—2000; speaker of the house Oregon House of Reps, Salem, 1998—2000. Mem. Damascus (Oreg.) Sch. Dist. Budget Com., 1985-88, Damascus Sch. Bd., 1991-94; mem. Oreg. Ho. of Reps. Human Resources and Edn. Com. (Edn. sub-com.), 1995-97, Labor Com., 1995-97, Commerce Com. (Bus. sub-com.), 1995-97, Children and Families Com., 1995-97, Emergency Bd. Com. (Edn. sub-com.), 1995-97, Interim Edn. Com., 1995-97, Legis. Administrn. Com., 1995—, Rules and Election Com., 1997—. Mem., past pres. Mt. Hood Med. Ctr. Found.; bd. dirs. Specialized Housing, Inc., Metro Home Builder; mem. Good Shepherd Cmty. Ch.; tchr. Jr. Achievement; classroom vol. Avocations: racquetball, reading, singing, camping, cooking. Fax: 503-986-1347.*

SNODGRASS, ROBERT EUGENE, psychiatrist; b. Indpls., Feb. 27, 1930; s. William Howard and Della Gladys (Satterly) S.; m. Constance Fusco, Mar. 1, 1958; 1 child, Robert Brent. AB in Anatomy and Physiology, Ind. U., 1952, MD, 1955. Diplomate Am. Bd. Psychiatry and Neurology. Intern Marion County Gen. Hosp., Indpls., 1955-56; resident in psychiatry Ind. U. Med. Ctr., 1964-67; pvt. gen. practice Greenwood, Ind., 1958-64; pvt. practice Indpls., 1967-90; staff psychiatrist Madison (Ind.) State Hosp., 1991—. Author: Beloved Madison, 1990; contbr. articles to profl. jours. Mem. Hist. Dist. Bd. Rev., Madison, 1991—. Capt. U.S. Army, 1956-58. Decorated Meritorious Svc. Commendation medal. Fellow Am. Psychiatric Assn.; mem. AMA, Ind. Psychiatric Soc. (past pres.), Jefferson County Hist. Soc. (bd. dirs. 1989—), Elks. Avocation: foreign languages. Home: 707 E Main St Madison IN 47250-3650 Office: Life Spring Mental Health Ctr 606 E Main St Madison IN 47250

SNOOK, PAUL, real estate company executive; b. Swindon, Wilt, Eng., Dec. 31, 1949; came to U.S., 1979; s. Eric Arthur and Eira Glynis Snook; m. June Chambers, Apr. 17, 1971 (div. Sept. 1977); m. Elizabeth Keefe, June 25, 1999; children: Sarah, Erica. Student, Northamton (Eng.) Coll. Exec. property mgr. Zaremba Mgmt. Svcs. Inc., Cleve., 1979-85, dir. mktg. ops., 1985-88; sr. v.p. Riverview Mgmt. Co., Akron, Ohio, 1988-96; pres. Strategic Property Mgmt., Cleve., 1999—, Paul Snook & Assocs., Cleve. Contbr.: Professional Apartment Rental Techniques, 1999. Recipient Cmty. Improvement award City of Mayfield Heights, 1986. Mem. No. Ohio Apt. Assn. (trustee 1985—, Mgr. of Yr. 1994, Pres. award 1987, 88, 89, 90), Inst. of Real Estate Mgmt. (Pres. award 1987, 88, 89, 90, cert. property mgr.), Cleve. Area Bd. of Realtors. Avocation: sailing.

SNOOK, QUINTON, construction company executive; b. Atlanta, July 15, 1925; s. John Wilson and Charlotte Louise (Clayson) S.; m. Louis Mullen, Jan. 19, 1947; children: Louis Ann Snook Matteson, Quinton A., Edward M., Clayson S., Charlotte T. Student, U. Idaho, 1949-51. Rancher, Lemhi Valley, Idaho, 1942—; owner, mgr. Snook Constrn., Salmon, 1952—; owner Snook Trucking, 1967—, Lemhi Posts and Poles, Salmon, 1980—. Construction company executive; b. Atlanta, July 15, 1925; s. John Wilson and Charlotte Louise (Clayson) S.; student U. Idaho, 1949-51; m. Lois Mullen, Jan. 19, 1947; children: Lois Ann Snook Matteson, Quinton A., Edward M., Clayson S., Charlotte T. Rancher Lemhi Valley, Idaho, 1942—; owner, mgr. Snook Constrn., Salmon, Idaho, 1952—; owner Snook Trucking, 1967—, Lemhi Posts and Poles, 1980—. Mem. Lemhi County Commn., Dist. 2, 1980-93. Named to Idaho Agrl. Hall of Fame, 1996. Mem. Am. Quarter Horse Assn., Farm Bur., Nat. Rifleman's Assn., Idaho Assn. Commrs. and Clerks (sec. 1986, v.p. 1987, pres. 1988), Am. Hereford Assn., Idaho Cattlemen's Assn., Elks. Republican. Episcopalian. Active Lemhi County Commn., Dist. 2, 1980-93. Named to Idaho Agrl. Hall of Fame, 1996. Mem. Am. Quarter Horse Assn., Farm Bur., Nat. Riflemens Assn., Idaho Assn. Commrs. and Clerks (sec. 1986, v.p. 1987, pres. 1988), Am. Hereford Assn., Idaho Cattlemens Assn., Elks. Republican. Episcopalian. Home: 9 Quinton Ln Salmon ID 83467

SNOOKS, GRAEME DONALD, political economist, stratologist; b. Perth, Australia, July 22, 1944; s. William Donald and Eleanor Violet (Williams) S.; m. Loma Rae Graham, Jan. 24, 1970; children: Adrian Graham, Roland William. BS in Econs., U. Western Australia, 1966, MS in Econs., 1968; PhD, Australian Nat. U., 1972. Tutor U. Western Australia, 1966—68; lectr. U. Queensland, Australia, 1971—72, Flinders U., Australia, 1972—74, sr. lectr., 1975—83, reader, 1984—89; Coghlan rsch. prof. Inst. Advanced Studies Australian Nat. U., Canberra, 1989—. Cons. visual arts bd. Australia Council Sydney, 1974, S. Australian Premiers Dept., Adelaide, 1974-77, Arts Council Great Brit., London, 1978, British Pub. Record Office, London, 1984-86, BBC, London, 1986. Author: Depression and Recovery, 1974, Domesday Economy, 1986, Exploring S.E. Asia's Economic Past, 1991, Land and Sea, 1992, Economic Policy in Australia since the Great Depression, 1993, Historical Analysis in Economics, 1993, Economics Without Time, 1993, Portrait of the Family within the Total Economy, 1994, Chinese edit., 2001, Was the Industrial Revolution Necessary?, 1994, Wealth and Wellbeing in Australasia, 1996, The Dynamic Society, 1996, The Ephemeral Civilization, 1997, The Laws of History, 1998, Longrun Dynamics, 1998, Global Transition, 1999, The Global Crisis Makers, 2000; editor: Australian Econ. History Rev., 1988-96; gen. editor Macmillan Econ. History of S.E. Asia, 1989—; cons. editor Cambridge Econ. History of Australia, 1990-96; contbr. articles to profl. jours. Australia Coun. grantee, 1974, Australian Rsch. Coun. grantee, 1974-89. Fellow Royal Hist. Soc., Acad. Social Scis. in Australia; mem. Econ. History Assn., Econ. History Soc., Econ. History Soc. Australia and New Zealand, Cliometric Soc. Avocations: bonsai, literature, art, fly-fishing. Office: Australian Nat U Inst Advanced Studies Canberra ACT 0200 Australia E-mail: gds301@coombs.anu.edu.au.

SNORTLAND, HOWARD JEROME, education financial consultant; b. Sharon, N.D., June 22, 1912; s. Thomas and Aline (Vig) S.; m. Anna Adeline Anderson, Sept. 1, 1940; children— Jan Signe, Kristi Jo, Howard Jay. BA, U. N.D., 1937, MS, 1958. Cashier N.D. Workmen's Compensation Bur., 1937-42, N.D. State Treas.'s Office, 1945-48; with N.D. Dept. Pub. Instrn., Bismarck, 1948-81, supt. pub. instrn., 1977-81; edn. fin. cons., 1981—. Pres. State Econ. Council, 1978; nat. pres. Com. Ednl. Data Systems, 1965-67 Chmn. Burleigh ARC, 1963-67, bd. dirs., 1946— , vice chmn., 1964— ; bd. dirs. Burleigh County Tb Assn., 1950— ; stated clk. United Presbyterian Ch., 1942— ; pres. N.D. United Christian Campus Fellowship, 1964-67, N.D. Westminster Found., 1963-70; mem. N.D. Synod Council, 1970— ; chmn. United Way Fund, 1983. Served with USAAF, 1942-45. Recipient Summit Conf. award for outstanding pub. service, 1976 Mem. NEA, N.D. Edn. Assn., N.D. Sch. Bus. Ofcls., N.D. Assn. Adminstrs., Nat. Assn. Adminstrs., N.D. Assn. Ret. Employees (pres. 1987—), Am. Assn. Ret. Persons (vice chmn. N.D. legis. com. 1992-94, chmn. 1994—), Kiwanis, Phi Beta Kappa, Phi Delta Kappa (dir. emeritus).

SNOUFFER, CHET ALAN, gymnastics club owner, coach; b. Columbus, Ohio, Sept. 22, 1956; s. Richard Kendall and Patti Janice S.; m. Maria del Carmen Foster, Oct. 19, 1985; children: Cody Alan, Lydia Rae. BS, Wheaton Coll., 1979. Cert. phys. edn. tchr., Ohio; cert. safety U.S. Gymnastics Fedn. Tchr. phys. edn. Delaware (Ohio) Joint Vocat. Schs., 1979-80; coach men's gymnastics Hayes High Sch., Delaware, 1979-86, coach women's gymnastics, 1987—; supr. gymnastics Delaware Parks and recreation dept., 1979-93; owner, boomerang mfr., editor newsletter Leading Edge Boomerangs, Delaware, 1979—; co-owner C & C Sch. Gymnastics, 1993-99. Ednl. & motivational spkr., 1985—. Bd. dirs. Ohio H.S. Gymnastics, Columbus. Recipient Sportsmanship, Ethics and Integrity award Ohio H.S. Athletic Assn., 1999. Mem. U.S. Boomerang Assn. (v.p. 1983-85, 88-94, 96-97, pres. 1994-96), World Boomerang Assn. (v.p. 1991—), Free Throwers Boomerang Soc. (founder), U.S. Boomerang Team (U.S. Nat. champion 1983, 87-96, U.S. Open champion 1992-96, Internat. Team champion 1981, 87, 88, 91, 94, World champion overall 1985, 89, 94, World champion fastcatch & trick catch 1996). Avocations: kayaking, mountain biking, kite flying, holder world record in juggling event, 1989, 92, 93, 94. Office: Leading Edge Boomerangs 1868 Panhandle Rd Delaware OH 43015-9080

SNOUFFER, NANCY KENDALL, English and reading educator; b. Long Branch, N.J., Aug. 22, 1941; d. Percival Wallace and Ruby Mae (Braswell) Kendall; m. Eugene Joseph Snouffer, Aug. 27, 1966; 1 child, Kendall Ann. BA in English, Gettysburg (Pa.) Coll., 1962; MA in English and Journalism, U. N.C., 1964; MS in Edn. and Reading, Western Ill. U., 1974; postgrad., U. Mo., 1976-78. Instr. English U. N.C., Wilmington, 1963-65, Shaw U., Raleigh, N.C., 1965-66; from instr. to asst. prof. English Wright Coll. and Chgo. City Colls., 1967-74; from instr. to asst. prof. reading Western Ill. U., Macomb, 1974-81; prof. comm., lang. and reading Del Mar Coll., Corpus Christi, Tex., 1982—, reading coord., 2001—. Mem. adv. bd. Tex. A&M U., Corpus Chrisit, 1993—; cons. in field. Author: College Reading Power, 5th edit., 1976-82; assoc. editor jour. Epistle, 1980-83, mem. editoral bd., 1983-85; contbr. articles to profl. jours. Master Tchr. Del Mar, 1986. Grantee Western Ill. U., 1974-81, Del Mar Coll., 1982—, NISSOD Teaching Excellence award, 1993 Mem. Tex. Assn. Developmental Educators, Tex. Coll. Reading Learning Assn. (chair So. membership 1994—, state sec. 1995-97, pres.-elect 1997-98, pres. 1998-99, past pres. 1999-2000), Nat. Assn. Developmental Educators (co-chair nat. com., profl. liaison), Internat. Reading Assn., Corpus Christi Literacy Coun. (bd. dirs. 1986—, sec. 1988-93, vice-chair 1991-92, v.p.-elect 2000-02, chair 2001—), Harbor Playhouse (bd. dirs. 1988, 91-93), Alliance Francaise. Republican. Episcopalian. Avocations: tennis, travel, reading. Home: 4206 Acushnet Dr Corpus Christi TX 78413-2004 Office: Del Mar Coll 101 Baldwin Blvd Corpus Christi TX 78404-3805

SNOW, ALICE BETTY MAUNEY, artist; b. Brevard, N.C., Aug. 20, 1924; d. Paul and Lillian Ramsaur Mauney; m. Richard Maynard Snow, Nov. 12, 1944 (dec. Aug. 1993); children: Linda Hofacker, Richard M. Jr., Jerre Dean. BS in Sec. Adminstrn., U. N.C., Greensboro, 1945. Outreach com. mem. Dundee Presbyn. Ch., Omaha, 1960-66; promotional staff Mt. Airy (N.C.) Arts Coun., 1968-80; founder So. Arts Soc., Inc., Kings Mountain, N.C., 1981—. One-person show Art I Gallery, Gastonia, N.C., 2001; group shows include Puebla, Mex., 2000, Lincolnton (N.C.) Culture Ctr., 2001, Cleve. Cmty. Coll., Shelby, N.C., 2002; exhbns. include Mt. Airy (N.C.) Libr., High Point (N.C.) Conv. Hall, Eden (N.C.) Libr., U. Mich, Ann Arbor, Cleveland County Arts Coun., Shelby, N.C., others. Mem. So. Arts Soc., Inc. (founder, newsletter and scholarship com. 1986-99), Cleveland County Working Artist Guild (treas. 1995-99), Charlotte Art League, Guild Charlotte Artists (v.p. 1995-96), Gaston County Art Guild (newsletter 1996-97). Presbyterian. Home and Office: AB Snow Originals 3600 Margrace Rd Kings Mountain NC 28086-3907 E-mail: ABSnow@carolina.rr.com.

SNOW, CHARLES, lawyer, director; b. Bklyn., May 3, 1932; s. Irving S. and Bessie S.; m. Deanna Friedman, Jan. 15, 1961; children: Lisa C., Amy M. BA, U. Vt., 1954; LLB, Bklyn. Law Sch., 1959. Bar: N.Y. 1959, U.S. Dist. Ct. (ea. and so. dists.) N.Y. 1961, U.S. Ct. Appeals (2d cir.) 1961, U.S. Supreme Ct. 1965. Dep. asst. atty. gen. N.Y. Dept. Law, N.Y.C., 1959-60; asst. U.S. atty. U.S. Dist. Ct. (ea. dist.) N.Y., Bklyn., 1960-61; asst. regional adminstr. SEC, N.Y.C., 1961-68; ptnr. Wofsey Certilman Habt Snow & Becker, PC, 1968077, Snow Becker Krauss, P.C., N.Y.C., 1977—. Gen. counsel Securities Traders' Assn. N.Y. Chmn. Harrison (N.Y.) Planning Bd., 1977-88. Mem. N.Y. State Bar Assn. (mem. bus. sect., com. on securities regulation), Securities Traders Assn. N.Y. (hon.). Republican. Jewish. Office: 605 3rd Ave New York NY 10158-0180 E-mail: csnow@sbklaw.com.

SNOW, CLAUDE HENRY, JR. information services executive, consultant; b. Lumberton, N.C., Feb. 25, 1954; s. Claude Henry and Vada Isabelle (Simpson) S.; m. Theresa Lee Gibson, Dec. 17, 1976 (div. Aug. 1981); m. Sarah Catherine Turnbull, Sept. 26, 1981. BA, U. N.C., 1976, MA, 1978. Communications systems rep. So. Bell Tel. & Tel., Charlotte, N.C., 1978-82; systems mgr. Sykes Datatronics, Atlanta, 1982-83; strategic planning mgr. Lockheed-Ga. Co., Marietta, 1983-86; regional mgr. communications Wang Labs., Atlanta, 1986-88, regional mgr. mktg., mfg., 1989; mgr. Deloitte & Touche, 1989-94; mng. dir. IBM Healthcare Consulting divsn., 1994-2000; exec. dir. IBM Pub. Sector Divsn. Global Svcs., 2000—. Mem. U. N.C. Libr. Bd., 1995—; bd. dirs. Ctrs. Disease Control Found., 1999—; bd. visitors U. N.C., Chapel Hill, 2001--. Mem. SAR, U. N.C. Alumni Assn. (pres. Atlanta chpt. 1985, mem. adv. bd. 1986-89), United Sons of Confederacy, Old Guard Atlanta, Chancellors Club of N.C. Democrat. Episcopalian. Avocations: golf, Scottish games, historic preservation. E-mail: chsnow@us.ibm.com.

SNOW, DEAN RICHARD, anthropology educator, archaeologist; b. New Ulm, Minn., Oct. 18, 1940; s. Roger Pershing and Gloria Jane Snow; m. Janet Charlene Keller, Dec. 21, 1963; children: Katherine, Barbara, Joshua. BA, U. Minn., 1962; PhD, U. Oreg., 1966. Asst. prof. anthropology U. Maine, Orono, 1966-69; asst. prof. SUNY, Albany, 1969-74, assoc. prof., chmn., 1974-80, prof., assoc. dean, 1980-83, prof., 1983-89, prof., dept. chmn., 1989-91, prof., 1991-95; prof., head Penn State, 1995—. Author: Archaeology of New England, 1980, Archaeology of North American Indians, 1989; editor: Foundations of Northeast Archaeology, The Iroquois, 1994; co-author: (with Michael Coe and Elizabeth Benson) Atlas of Ancient America. Pres. N.Y. Archaeol. Coun., 1987-89; active N.Y. State Bd. for Hist. Preservation, vice chair, 1985-95. Grantee Nat. Geog. Soc., 1983, 85, NEH, 1984-85, 85-86, 87-89, 91-93, NSF, 1991-92. Fellow AAAS (chair sect. H 1999-2000), Am. Anthrop. Assn., N.Y. State Archaeol. Assn.; mem. Am. Soc. Ethnohistory (pres. 1978-79), N.E. Anthrop. Assn. (pres. 1984-86). Office: 409 Carpenter University Park PA 16802

SNOW, GEORGE BARTLETT, city official, accountant; b. Feb. 23, 1943; s. Frank Batchelder and Corinne Althea (Fuller) Snow; m. Tuula Anita Kahila, Feb. 6, 1965; children: Frank Edwin II, James Hooper. BS in Acctg., Babson Coll., 1964. Acct. Morgan & Morgan, Boston, 1965—70; town acct. Town of Marblehead, 1970—, data processing coord., 1986—, fin. dir., 1994—. Treas., bd. dirs. Employees Fed. Credit Union, Marblehead, 1979—; mem. com. to rewrite Uniform Mcpl. Acctg. Sys. Manual, 1983—94; acctg. tchr. Mass. Mcpl. Auditors and Accts. Assn., Amherst, 1981—. Clk. Town of Marblehead Bd. Selectmen, 1970—75; mem. Marblehead Retirement Bd., 1970—; trustee Abbot Fund, Town of Marblehead, 1970—90; mem., clk. sch. bldg. com. Town of Marblehead, 1971—72; mem. Marblehead Harbor Study Com., 1997—98. Mem.: Sugarloaf Condo. Pres.' Assn. (pres. 1995—2001), Sugarloaf Phase VII Condo. Assn. (pres. 1988—), Govtl. Fin. Officers Assn., Mass. Govtl. Fin. Officers Assn. (v.p. 1986—87, pres. 1987—88), Mass. Mcpl. Auditors and Accts. Assn. (pres. 1981—82, chmn. legis. com. 1983—88), North Shore Auditors and Accts. Assn. (pres. 1981—82), Onamor Hills Neighborhood Assn. (treas. 1988—94), Pleon Yacht Club (dir. 1979—82), Boston Yacht Club (treas. 1974—78). Home: 242 W Shore Dr Marblehead MA 01945-1324 Office: Town of Marblehead Mary A Alley Bldg 7 Widger Rd Marblehead MA 01945 E-mail: snowb@town.marblehead.ma.us.

SNOW, JAMES BYRON, JR. physician, research administrator; b. Oklahoma City, Mar. 12, 1932; s. James B. and Charlotte Louise (Andersen) S.; m. Sallie Lee Ricker, July 16, 1954; children: James B., John Andrew, Sallie Lee Louise. BS, U. Okla., 1953; MD cum laude, Harvard U., 1956; MA (hon.), U. Pa., 1973. Diplomate Am. Bd. Otolaryngology (dir. 1972-90). Intern Johns Hopkins Hosp., Balt., 1956-57; resident Mass. Eye and Ear Infirmary, Boston, 1957-60; prof., head dept. otorhinolaryngology Sch. Medicine U. Okla., Oklahoma City, 1962-72; prof., chmn. dept. otorhinolaryngology and human communication U. Pa., 1972-90; dir. Nat. Inst. on Deafness and Other Comm. Disorders, NIH, Bethesda, Md., 1990-97. Mem. nat. adv. coun. neurol. and communicative disorders and stroke NIH, 1972-76, 82-86; chmn. Nat. Com. Rsch. Neurol. and Communicative Disorders, 1979-80. Editor: Am. Jour. Otolaryngology, 1979-83; Contbr. articles to sci. and profl. jours. Officer, M.C., U.S. Army, 1960-62. Recipient Regents award for superior tchg. U. Okla., 1970, Golden award Internat. Fedn. Otorhinolaryngological Socs., 1989, Disting. Achievement award Deafness Rsch. Found., 1993, Presdl. Meritorious Exec. Rank award, 1994; named to Soc. Scholars Johns Hopkins U., 1991. Fellow Japan Broncho-Esophagological Soc. (hon.), Am. Laryngological Assn. (hon.); mem. ACS (regent 1982-90), AMA (coun. on sci. affairs 1975-86), Soc. Univ. Otolaryngologists (pres. 1975), Am. Acad. Otolaryngology-Head and Neck Surgery, Assn. Acad. Depts. Otolaryngology (pres. 1981-82), Am. Laryngol., Rhinol. and Otol. Soc., Am. Otol. Soc., Am. Laryngol. Assn. (editor 1983-89, pres. 1990-91), Am. Broncho-Esophagol. Assn. (editor trans. 1973-77, pres. 1979), Collegium Otorhinolaryngologicum (pres. 2000-02), Phi Beta Kappa, Alpha Omega Alpha. Home: 33506 Tuckahoe River Rd Easton MD 21601-6752 E-mail: jsnow@crosslinks.net.

SNOW, JOEL ALAN, research director; b. Brockton, Mass., Apr. 1, 1937; s. George H. Jr. and Mary W. (Sproul) S.; m. Laetitia Harrer, June 29, 1957 (div. 1983); children: Jonathan E., Nicholas H.; m. Barbara Kashian, Feb. 7, 1992; stepchildren: James, Alexander. BS in Physics, U. N.C., 1958; MA in Physics, Washington U., St. Louis, 1963, PhD in Physics, 1967. Fellow Ctr. Advanced Study U. Ill., Champaign, 1967-68; program dir. for theoretical physics NSF, Washington, 1968-70, head office of interdisciplinary rsch., 1969-71, dep. asst. dir. for sci. and tech., rsch. applications, 1971-74, dir. office of planning and resources mgmt., 1974-76, dir. div. of policy rsch. and analysis, 1976; sr. policy analyst, office of sci. and tech. policy Exec. Office of the Pres., 1976-77; assoc. dir. for rsch. policy U.S. Dept. Energy, 1977-81, dir. sci. and tech. affairs, 1981-88; assoc. v.p. for rsch. Argonne Nat. Lab., U. Chgo., 1988-92; dir. Inst. for Phys. Rsch. and Tech. Iowa State U., Ames, 1993-98, prof. elec. and computer engring., 1993—, prof. polit. sci., 1998-2000, exec. assoc. dir. Internat. Inst. Theoret./Applied Physics, 1998—. Rsch. assoc. dept. physics U. Ill., Urbana, 1967-68; instr. physics and electronics U.S. Navy Nulcear Power Shc., New London, Conn., 1958-61; sci. tech. organizer Pres.'s Conf. on Superconductivity, 1987, NSF program rsch. applied to nat. needs, 1971, designer, mgr., founder NSF program interdisciplinary rsch. relevant to problems of society, 1969. Contbr. over 130 articles to mags. and profl. jours. Lt. (j.g.) USN, 1958-61. Recipient Meritorious Svc. award NSF, 1972, Meritorious award William A. Jump Found., 1973, Arthur S. Fleming award Downtown Jaycees, 1974; NSF postdoctoral fellow Ctr. for Advanced Study U. Ill., 1967-68; NSF fellow, 1963-65. Fellow AAAS, Am. Phys. Soc.; mem. IEEE, Am. Chem. Soc., Am. Nuc. Soc., World Future Soc., Sigma Xi, Phi Beta Kappa, Phi Kappa Phi. Achievements include pioneering devel. of federal programs in environment, solar and geothermal energy and energy conservation, sustainable development; fed. programs in technology transfer to industry; developed collaborations between univ., govt. and industry; fostering internat. collaboration in sci., engring. and edn. Office: IITAP/Iowa State U 2318 Howe Hall Ames IA 50011-0001 E-mail: jasnow@iastate.edu.

SNOW, JOHN WILLIAM, railroad executive; b. Toledo, Aug. 2, 1939; s. William Dean and Catharine (Howard) S.; m. Fredrica Wheeler, June 11, 1964 (div. 1973); children: Bradley, Ian; m. Carolyn Kalk, Aug. 31, 1973; 1 child, Christopher BA, Kenyon Coll./U. Toledo, 1962; PhD, U. Va., 1965; LLB, George Washington U., 1967. Asst. prof. econs. U. Md., College Park, 1965-67; assoc. Wheeler & Wheeler, Washington, 1967-72; asst. gen. counsel Dept. Transp., 1972-73, dep. asst. sec. for policy, plans and internat. affairs, 1973-74, asst. sec. for govtl. affairs, 1974-75, dep. under sec., 1975-76; adminstr. Nat. Hwy. Traffic Safety Adminstrn., 1976-77; v.p. govt. affairs Chessie System Inc., 1977-80; sr. v.p. corp. services CSX Corp., Richmond, Va., 1980-84, exec. v.p., 1984-85; pres., CEO Chessie System R.R.s, Balt., 1985-86, CSX Rail Transport, Jacksonville, Fla., 1986-87, CSX Transp., Jacksonville, Va., 1987-88; pres., COO CSX Corp., Richmond, 1988-89, pres., CEO, 1989-91, chmn., pres., CEO, 1991—, also bd. dirs. Adj. prof. law George Washington U., 1972-75; vis. prof. econs. U. Va., Charlottesville, spring 1977; vis. fellow Am. Enterprises Inst., Washington, spring 1977; bd. dirs. USX Corp., Circuit City Stores, Inc., Johnson & Johnson, Verizon. Bd. trustees Johns Hopkins U. Mem. Va. State Bar. Clubs: Chevy Chase, Metropolitan (Washington); Commonwealth, Country of Va. (Richmond). Episcopalian.*

SNOW, KARL NELSON, JR. public management educator, university administrator, former state senator; b. St. George, Utah, July 1, 1930; s. Karl Nelson and Wanda (McGregor) S.; m. Donna Jean Dain, Jan. 29, 1960; children: Karl Nelson, III, Melissa, Daniel D., Jeanmarie, Elisabeth, Howard H. BS, Brigham Young U., Provo, Utah, 1956; MA, U. Minn., 1958; MPA, U. So. Calif., 1965, DPA, 1972. Budget examiner Minn. Dept. Adminstrn., 1956-59; staff asst., instr. Sch. Pub. Adminstrn. U. So. Calif., 1959-62; mem. faculty Brigham Young U., Provo, Utah, 1962-96, dir. Inst. Govt., 1969-79, prof. pub. mgmt., 1979—, asst. exec. v.p., 1987-91; state legis. fiscal analyst, 1966-70; mem. Utah Senate from 16th Dist., 1972-85, majority leader, 1981-85. Chmn. Utah State House Fellowship Commn., 1973-79, Utah Constl. Revision Commn., 1977-89; bd. dirs. Legis. Leaders Found., 1981-85; chmn. bd. trustees Utah Tech. Fin. Corp., 1983-94; pres., trustee Utah Tech. Equity Found., 1994-96; chmn. Conf. of State Sponsored Seed and Venture Funds, 1993-96; internat. affairs rep. LDS Ch., N.Y.C., 1997-2000. Bd. editors Public Adminstrn. Rev, 1969-70, State and Local Govt. Rev, 1977-83; contbr. articles to profl. jours. Missionary Mormon Ch., 1950-52, mem. stake high council, 1975-85, 93-97, bishop, 1985-90, dir. ch. internat. affairs, N.Y.C., 1997—; mem. Warren Burger Prison Task Force, 1983-87; bd. dirs. Utah Innovation Found., 1984-88. Adminstrv. fellow State of Minn., U. Minn., 1956-57; Univ. fellow U. So. Calif., 1959-61. Mem. Am. Soc. Pub. Adminstrn. (chpt. pres. 1968-69), dir. nat. council (1969-72), Sons Utah Pioneers. Home: 1847 N Oak Ln Provo UT 84604-2140

SNOW, MARCELLUS SCOWCROFT, economics educator; b. Ogden, Utah, Apr. 2, 1942; s. Marcellus Keyting and Charlene (Scowcroft) S.; m. Edwina Jo Burton, Mar. 27, 1967; children: David Burton, Jonathan Marcellus, Matthew Stephen. BA magna cum laude, U. Utah, 1965; MS, MIT, 1967; MA, Johns Hopkins U., 1969; PhD, U. Calif., Berkeley, 1974. Rsch. asst. World Bank, Washington, 1969; fin., polit. analyst Communications Satellite Corp., Washington, 1969-71, summer 1972; instr. econs. Calif. State U., San Francisco, 1972; rsch. asst. dept. econs. U. Calif., Berkeley, 1971-74; asst. prof. econs. U. Hawaii, Honolulu, 1974-79, assoc. prof., 1979-86, prof., 1986—; Fulbright rsch. prof. U. Bonn, 1980-81; vis. scholar Stanford U., summer 1983; cons. ITT, 1978, Dept. Commerce, 1979, Max Planck Inst., 1986-87. Author: International Commercial Satellite Communications, 1976, The International Telecommunications Satellite Orgn. (INTELSAT), 1987, INTELSAT: An Economic Assessment, 1988; co-editor: Economic and Policy Problems in Satellite Communications, 1977; editor: Marketplace for Telecommunications: Regulation and Deregulation in Industrialized Democracies, 1986; co-author: Telecommunication Economics and Internet Regulatory Policy, 1986; book review editor Information Economics and Policy, 1993—; contbr. articles to profl. jours. Scoutmaster, Boy Scouts Am., Honolulu, 1984-90, scouting unit commnr., 1990-93. NSF fellow, 1965-68, NSF grantee, 1984; Harvard U. fellow, 1988-89. Mem. Am. Econ. Assn., Pacific Telecommunications Council, Internat. Inst. Communications, Econometric Soc., Hawaii Coun. Econ. Edn. Home: 4774 Aukai Ave Honolulu HI 96816-5242 Office: U Hawaii Dept Econs 2424 Maile Way Honolulu HI 96822-2223

SNOW, MARINA SEXTON, writer; b. Boston, Apr. 9, 1937; d. Charles Ernest Snow and Katherine Alice Townsend; m. Richard DeVere Horton, 1958 (div. 1968); children: Heather Kertchem, James Horton; m. Charles A. Washburn, 1978 (div. 1979). BA, U. Iowa, 1958; MA in Speech Pathology, N.Mex. State U., 1967; MA in Librarianship, San Jose State U., 1976; MA in Theatre Arts, Calif. State U., Sacramento, 1979. Cert. clin. competence Am. Speech and Hearing Assn. Tchr. ESL Inst. Colombo-Americano, Cali, Colombia, 1958-59; tchr. Las Cruces (N.Mex.) Pub. Schs., 1964-66; speech therapist Sutter County Schs., Yuba City, Calif., 1967-72; reference libr. Calif. State U. Libr., Sacramento, 1976-95. Author: (novels) (1999) The Black Iris, The Walking Wounded, 2001; contbr. articles to profl. jours.; author: (plays) Apricot Coffee, Alkali Flat; contbr. book. Pres. Alkali Flat Neighborhood Assn., Sacramento, 1987—94. Mem.: Calif. Writer's Club, Sacramento Old City Assn. Avocations: theater , historic preservation, gardening.

SNOW, MARLON O. trucking executive, state agency administrator; m. Ann; children. Gen. mgr. spl. commadities Milne Truck Lines, Phoenix, L.A., 1970-81; gen. mgr. spl. commodities, sales Motor Cargo, Salt Lake City, 1981-82; owner MST Trucking, Inc., 1982—. V.p. Utah Motor Carriers for State of Utah, 1997-98; bd. dirs. Zions Bank. Mem. State Bd. Edn., 1994-97, chair, 1995-97; trustee Utah Valley State Coll., 1998; mem. Ho. of Reps., Utah, 1999-2001; bd. regents Bd. Higher Edn. State of Utah, 2001—; bd. dirs. Children's Justice Ctr., State of Utah, 2002--. Mem. Utah Valley State Coll. Found. (bd. dirs. 1991—), Alpine Sch. Dist. Found. (bd. dirs. 1990-94). Office: 1247 E 430 N Orem UT 84097-5400

SNOW, MARYLY ANN, librarian, artist; b. Oakland, Calif., Dec. 1, 1944; d. John Condit Snow and Mary Aileen (Lawler) Cauchois. BA in Social Welfare, U. Calif., Berkeley, 1966, M in Libr. and Info. Studies, 1974. Libr. asst. reference and interlibr. loan depts. McHenry Libr., U. Calif., Santa Cruz, 1970-72; libr. asst. Ctr. for Libr. Rsch. U. Calif., Berkeley, 1972-74, ctr. libr. Ctr. for Study of Law and Soc., 1973-75, asst. libr. map rom., 1974-75, lectr. Sch. Libr. and Info. Studies, 1974-76, 78, head arch. slide and photograph libr., 1979—. Cons. Calif. State U., Long Beach, 1976, N.J. Inst. Tech., 1994, Harold Stump Archtl. Found., 1995—, Denver Pub. Libr., 1993, 97; presenter in field. One-person shows include Sun Gallery, Hayward, Calif., 1977, Van Doren Gallery, San Francisco, 1977, Nathan Hart Gallery, San Francisco, 1985; exhibited in group shows Concourse Gallery, Bank of Am. World Hdqs., San Francisco, 1976, Crown Zellerbach Exhbn., San Francisco, 1981, Creative Growth Gallery, Oakland, Calif., 1984, Los Medanos Coll., Martinez, Calif., 1987, Kala Inst., Berkeley, 1990, Internat. Print Biennial, Sapporo, Japan, 1991, Sebastopol (Calif.) Art Ctr., 1995, Tex. Art Assn. traveling exhbn., 1996-98, Inst. Franco-Am., Renne, France, 1997; represented in collections 3M Corp., Minn., ITEL Corp., San Francisco, Claire Carlevaro, El Cerrito, Calif., Wells Fargo Bank, San Francisco, others; represented in permanent collections Achenbach Found. Prints and Drawings, Fine Arts Mus. San Francisco; author: (book chpts.) Beyond the Book, 1991; contbr. articles to profl. jours. Libr. fellow Townsend Ctr. for the Humanities, U. Calif., Berkeley, 1997-98; grantee Librs.'s Assn. of U. of Calif., 1997-98, Librs.'s Assembly, U. of Calif., Berkeley, 1988, U. Calif., Berkeley, Office of Ednl. Devel., 1989, 96. Mem. Art Librs. Soc. N.Am. (visual resources divsn. task force on authorities 1986-90, art and arch. adv. com. 1989-92, liaison to Visual Resources Assn. data stds. com. 1995-96, sec. 1995-97, mem. awards com. 1997-98, mem. visual resources adv. com. 1997-98), Visual Resources Assn. (MARC format com. 1989-93, data stds. com. 1993-95, intellectual property rights com. 1995-2000), Calif. Soc. Printmakers. Office: U Calif Berkeley Arch Slide Libr 232 Wurster Hall Berkeley CA 94720-1805 E-mail: slides@socrates.berkeley.edu.

SNOW, ROBERT ANTHONY, journalist; b. Berea, Ky., June 1, 1955; s. James Allen and Betty Jo (Threlkeld) S.; m. Jill Ellen Walker, Sept. 26, 1987; children: Kendall Elizabeth, Robert Walker, Kristin Anna. BA, Davidson Coll., 1977; postgrad. in Philosophy and Econs., U. Chgo., 1978-79. Editl. writer The Greensboro (N.C.) Record, 1979-81, The Virginian Pilot, Norfolk, 1981-82; editl. page editor The Daily Press, Newport News, Va., 1982-84; dep. editl. page editor The Detroit News, 1984-87, columnist, 1993—; editl. page editor The Washington Times, 1987-91; dep. asst. to pres. comm., dir. speechwriting The White House, Washington, 1991-92, dep. asst. for media affairs to Pres., 1992-93; columnist USA Today, Arlington, 1993—; syndicated columnist Creators Syndicate, 1993-2001. Substitute host Rush Limbaugh Radio Program, 1994—; polit. analyst Good Morning America, 1995; host Fox News Sunday, 1996—. Active Leadership Washington. Mem. Coun. Fgn. Rels. Avocations: sports, music, traveling, writing. Office: Fox News Sunday 400 N Capitol St NW Ste 550 Washington DC 20001-1502

SNOW, THEODORE PECK, astrophysics educator; b. Seattle, Jan. 30, 1947; s. Theodore P. and Louise (Wertz) S.; s. Constance M. Snow, Aug. 23, 1969; children: McGregor A., Tyler M., Reilly A. BA, Yale U., 1969; MS, U. Wash., 1970, PhD, 1973. Mem. rsch. staff Princeton (N.J.) U., 1973-77; prof. U. Colo., Boulder, 1977—, dir. Ctr. for Astrophysics and Space Astronomy, 1986-96, dir. Fiske Planetarium, 2000—. Mem. instrument devel. teams for far Ultraviolet Spectroscopic Explorer, 1999—, Cosmic Origins Spectrograph to be installed in Hubble Space Telescope. Author: (textbook) The Dynamic Universe, 1983, 4th edit., 1991, Essentials of the Dynamic Universe 4th edit., 1993 (textbook excellence award Text and Academic Authors Assn. 1994), Physics, 1986, Universe: Origins and Evolution, 1997; contbr. over 200 articles to profl. jours. Fellow Royal Astron. Soc.; mem. Am. Astron. Soc., Astron. Soc. Pacific, Sigma Xi. Achievements include discovery, through observations in ultraviolet visible, and infrared wavelengths, and through laboratory measurement of chemical reactions, of several important processes involving interstellar gas and dust, and their roles in star formation and late stages of stellar evolution. Office: U Colo Ctr Astrophysics Space Astronomy Campus Box 389 Boulder CO 80309-0389 E-mail: tsnow@casa.colorado.edu.

SNOW, TOWER CHARLES, JR. lawyer; b. Boston, Oct. 28, 1947; s. Tower Charles and Margaret (Harper) S.; m. Belinda L. Snow. AB cum laude English, Dartmouth Coll., 1969; JD, U. Calif., Berkeley, 1973. Bar: Calif. 1973, U.S. Dist. Ct. (no. dist.) Calif. 1973, U.S. Ct. Appeals (9th cir.) 1973, U.S. Supreme Ct. 1976, U.S. Dist. Ct. (ea. dist.) Calif. 1979, U.S. Ct. Appeals (fed. cir.) 1980, U.S. Ct. Claims 1980, U.S. Ct. Appeals (2d cir.) 1987, N.Y. 1988, U.S. Dist. Ct. (ea. and so. dists.) N.Y. 1988, U.S. Dist. Ct. (ctrl. dist.) Calif. 1989, U.S. Dist. Ct. (no. dist.) Tex. 1995, U.S. Dist. Ct. (so. dist.) Calif. 1996, U.S. Dist. Ct. Ariz. 1996. Ptnr., chmn. litigation dept. Orrick, Herrington & Sutcliffe, San Francisco, 1973-89; ptnr. Shearman & Sterling, 1989-94; ptnr., chmn. securities litigation group, mem. policy com. Brobeck, Phleger & Harrison, LLP, 1995-97; chmn., CEO Brobeck, Phleger & Harrison, 1998—2002; ptnr. Clifford Chance LLP, 2002. Arbitrator Nat. Assn. Securities Dealers, Am. Stock Exch., N.Y. Stock Exch., Pacific Coast Stock Exch., Superior Ct. City and County San Francisco, Am. Arbitration Assn.; lectr. in field. Author numerous law handbooks and articles to prof. jours. Mem. San Francisco Mus. Soc., San Francisco Symphony, San Francisco Ballet, San Francisco Opera, Am. Conservatory Theatre. Named Best Lawyer in the U.S. in his Field, Corp. Bd. Member Mag., 2001; named one of 100 Most Influential Lawyers in Am., Nat. Law Jour., 2000, 100 Most Influential Lawyers in Calif., Calif. Law and Bus., 2000. Mem. ABA (chmn. subcom. pub. offering litig. 1984-88, co-chair task force on securities arbitration 1988-89, vice chair securities litig. com. 1986-88), Continuing Edn. Bar (bus. law inst. planning com. 1986), Securities Industry Assn., Nat. Inst. Trial Advocacy, San Francisco Bar Assn. (pres. securities litig. sect. 1995). Democrat. Avocations: internat. travel, skiing, running, scuba diving, photography. Home: 177 Ridge Dr Napa CA 94558-9777 E-mail: tower.snow@cliffordchance.com.

SNOWBARGER, VINCE, former congressman; b. Kankakee, Ill., Sept. 16, 1949; s. Willis Edward and Wahnona Ruth (Horger) S.; m. Carolyn Ruth McMahon, Mar. 25, 1972; children: Jeffrey Edward, Matthew David. BA in History, So. Nazarene U., 1971; MA in Polit. Sci., U. Ill., 1974; JD, U. Kans., 1977. Bar: Kans. 1977, U.S. Dist. Ct. Kans. 1977, Mo. 1987. Instr. Mid-Am. Nazarene Coll., Olathe, Kans., 1973—76; ptnr. Haskin, Hinkle, Slater & Snowbarger, 1977—84, Dietrich, Davis, Dicus et al, 1984—88, Armstrong, Teasdale, Schafly & Davis, Overland Park, 1989—92, Holbrook, Heaven & Fay, P.C., Merriam, 1992—94, Snowbarger & Veatch LLP, Olathe, 1994—96; mem. 105th Congress from 3rd Kans. dist., 1997—99; exec. dir. Kans. Assn. Am. Educators, 2000—01; asst. exec. dir. legis. affairs Pension Benefit Guaranty Corps., Washington, 2002—. Mem. Kans. Legislature, Topeka, 1985-96; majority leader Ho. of Reps., 1993-96; mem. Olathe Planning Commn., 1982-84, Leadership Olalthe; divsn. chmn. United Way, Olathe, 1985-88, chmn. citizen rev. com., 1991-95. Mem. Olathe Area C. of C. (bd. dirs. 1984). Republican. Nazarene. Avocation: politics. Home: 7902 Oak St Dunn Loring VA 22027-1017 Office: 1200 K St NW Washington DC E-mail: vincesnowbarger@netscape.net.

SNOWDEN, BARRY HOWARD, lawyer; b. Freer, Tex., Feb. 22, 1945; s. Arthur Ray and Ambanez (Paris) S.; children: Philip, Stephen, Mitch, Haley, Amber.; m. Bobbie J. Snowden. BA, Baylor U., 1967, JD, 1970. Bar: Tex. 1970, U.S. Dist. Ct. (so. dist.) Tex. 1970. Asst. dist. atty. 79th Jud. Dist., Tex., 1970-73; pvt. practice, 1970—; shareholder Morris, Lendais, Hollrah & Snowden, Houston, 1977—. With USNG, 1968-69. Republican. Baptist. Avocations: wine collector, travel. Home: 5436 Fm 723 Rd Richmond TX 77469-8706 Office: Morris Lendai Hollrah & Snowden 1980 Post Oak Blvd Ste 700 Houston TX 77056-3881 E-mail: bsnowden@mlhs.net.

SNOWDEN, BERNICE RIVES, former construction company executive; b. Houston, Mar. 21, 1923; d. Charles Samuel and Annie Pearl (Rorex) Rives; m. Walter G. Snowden; 1 child. Grad., Smalley Comml. Coll., 1941; student, U. Houston, 1965. With Houston Pipe Line Co., 1944-45; clk.-typist Charles G. Heyne & Co., Inc., Houston, 1951-53, payroll asst., 1953-56, sec. to pres., also office mgr., 1956-62, sec. to pres., also controller, 1962-70, sec.-treas., 1970-77, CFO, also dir. Mem. Women in Constrn., Nat. Assn. Women in Constrn. (past pres.), San Leon C. of C., Lord and Ladies Dance Club. Methodist. Home: 6611 Kury Ln Houston TX 77008-5101

SNOWDEN, B(ERTHA) J(EANNE), composer; b. Lowell, Mass., Aug. 26, 1948; d. Donald Latimer and Virginia Ruth (Finnagan) Snowden; m. Alan Lee Wilson, Aug. 4, 1973 (div. Oct. 1992); 1 child, Andres Donald. MusB, Berklee Coll. of Music, 1973. Music tchr. Phila. Sch. Bd., 1977-82, Immaculate Conception Sch., Lowell, 1988-89; substitute music tchr. various schs., Woburn/Lexington, others, Mass., 1990-93; music composer, pub. Gingercake Pub. Co., Billerica, 1989—; tchr. Gen. Elem. Sch., Narragansett Regional Sch. Dist., Templeton, Phillipston, 1994-95, Boston Public Sch., 1995-98; tchr. music Sommerville Pub. Sch., 1999—2001. Music dir. Middlesex Sch. Summer Arts, Concord, Mass., 1994. Pub./composer rec., 1990; composer CD A Life in the U.S.A. and Canada, 1996. Mem. 1st Cong. Ch., Billerica, 1989—. Mem. NAFE, BMI, Merrimac Valley Musicians Assn. Democrat. Congregationalist. Avocations: bowling, swimming, dancing, playing keyboards. Office: Gingercake Publishers PO Box 285 Billerica MA 01821-0285

SNOWDEN, LAWRENCE FONTAINE, retired aircraft company executive, retired marine corps general officer; b. Charlottesville, Va., Apr. 14, 1921; s. Lawrence Fontaine Snoddy and Beatrice M. (Huffman) S.; m. Martha Roselyn Ham, Nov. 17, 1942; children: John Stephen, Brian Fontaine. Student, Stetson U., 1938-39; BS, U. Va., 1942; MA, Northwestern U., 1950; postgrad., Harvard U., 1968; grad., Indsl. Coll. Armed Forces, 1967. Commd. 2d lt. USMC, 1942, advanced through grades to lt. gen., 1975; comdr. 7th Marine Regt., Vietnam, 1966; ops. officer III Marine Amphibious Force, Vietnam, 1967; asst. dir. personnel Hdqrs. Marine Corps, Washington, 1968-69, dir. systems support group, 1969-70; dir. Marine Corps Devel. Ctr., Quantico, Va., 1970-72; chief of staff U.S. Forces, Japan, 1972-75; U.S. chmn. UN Bd., Japan, 1973-75; chief of staff Hdqrs. U.S. Marine Corps, 1977-79; ret., 1979; v.p. Far East Internat. Service Co. Hughes Aircraft Co., 1979-86, group v.p. Internat. Ground Systems Group Calif., 1986-88; pres. Snowden Internat. Assocs., Tallahassee, 1988—. Recipient Silver Beaver award Boy Scouts Am.; decorated Disting. Svc. medals (2), Legion of Merit (5), Army Commendation medal, Navy Commendation medal, Purple Heart (2), Cross of Gallantry (3) Vietnam, Second Order of Sacred Treasure Japan). Mem. Marine Corps League, U.S. Navy League, Am. C. of C. in Japan, Am.-Japan Soc., Marine Corps Assn., Econ. Club Fla., Sigma Nu. Clubs: Tokyo.

SNOWDEN, RUTH O'DELL GILLESPIE, artist; b. Gary, W.Va., Apr. 16, 1926; d. Haynes Thornton and Blanche Beaula (Boling) Gillespie; m. Eugene Louis Snowden, Dec. 21, 1946; children: Wanda Snowden Ballard, Eugene III, Ronald, Marian Snowden Warren, Jeffry. RN, Nathanith Coll., 1946; student Sch. Art, Transylvania U., 1983-84, U. Ky., 1985-89. RN. Painter, publicity chmn. Artists's Attic Inc., Lexington, Ky., 1988-89. Exhibited in group shows at U. Ky. Art Mus., Lexington, 1988, 5th Internat. Juried Exhibition Pastels, Nyack, N.Y., 1988, Small Paintings Nat., Ky. Highlands Mus., Ashland, 1988, The Appalachian Cen., U. Ky., 1988, Ft. Wayne (Ind.) Mus. Art, 1986, John Howard Sanden Nat. Artists Seminar, Washington, Nat. Artists' Seminar, Chgo., Huntington (W.Va.) Galleries, Nat. Nursing Art Exhibit, Meth. Med. Cen., Peoria, Ill., Chautauqua Art Assn. Galleries, N.Y., 1990, Central Bank gallery, Chatauqua, 1990, Pastel & Chisel Acad. Fine Arts, 1990, Opera House Gallery, 1990, Sacramento Fine Arts Ctr., 1990, Ariel Gallery, Soho, N.Y., 1990, 91, Sumi-e Soc. Am., Inc., 1993, Watercolor Soc. Ala., 1994; represented in the Director of American Portrait Artists, Am. Portrait Soc., Huntington Harbour, Calif.; numerous local and nat. shows; in pvt. collections. Recipient Assn. Alliance award Am. Frame Co., 1993, also various watercolor and oil painting awards. Mem. Oil Pastel Assn., Nyack, N.Y., Winchester Art Guild, Lexington Art League, Ky. Watercolor Assn. (Bluegrass regional dir. 1988, 89, 90, 91, 92), Ky. Guild Artists and Craftsmen, Inc., Berea, Northwest Pastel Soc., Seattle, Degas Pastel Soc., New Orleans. Avocations: golfing, bowling. Home: 2800 Old Boonesboro Rd Winchester KY 40391-8805 Office: Artists Attic Inc Victorian Square 401 W Main St Lexington KY 40507-1640

SNOWE, ALAN MARTIN, lawyer; b. Bklyn., May 24, 1935; s. Nat and Lillian Rose (Anixter) S.; m. Susan Goldman, May 30, 1958; children: Karen J., Linda. B Commerce, NYU, 1957; LLB, Bklyn. Law Sch., 1962. Bar: N.Y. 1962, U.S. Dist. Ct. (so. and ea. dists.) N.Y. 1965, U.S. Tax Ct. 1974, U.S. Supreme Ct. 1976. Ptnr. Wachtel & Snowe, Hicksville, N.Y., 1967-94; pvt. practice, 1994-96; ptnr. Snowe & Goldman, Esq., 1996—. Lectr. NYU Sch. Continuing Edn., N.Y.C., 1975-82, Hofstra U. Sch. Continuing Edn., Uniondale, N.Y., 1994-96; arbitrator Dist. Ct. Nassau County, Hempstead, N.Y., 1985—. Mem. N.Y. State Bar Assn., Nassau County Bar Assn. (chair lawyer referral com. 1991-93). Avocations: sports, reading. Office: 382 S Oyster Bay Rd Hicksville NY 11801-3529

SNOWE, OLYMPIA J. senator; b. Augusta, Maine, Feb. 21, 1947; d. George John and Georgia G. Bouchles; m. John McKernan. BA, U. Maine, 1969; LLD (hon.), U. Maine, Machias, 1982, U. Maine, Orono, 1981, Nasson Coll., 1981, Bowdoin Coll., 1982, Colby Coll., 1985; LHD (hon.), Thomas Coll., 1987; LLD (hon.), Suffolk U., 1994; DSc (hon.), Maine Maritime Acad., 1995; LLD (hon.), Colby Coll., 1996, U. New England, 1996; hon. degree, John F. Kennedy Sch. Govt. Harvard U., 1997; LLD (hon.), Bates Coll., 1998. Businesswoman; mem. Maine Ho. of Reps., 1973-76, Maine Senate, 1976-78, 96th-103d Congresses from 2d Maine Dist., 1979-94, mem. budget com., foreign affairs com., com. on aging, 1979-94; co-chair Congl. Caucus for Women's Issues, 1983-94; U.S. senator from Maine, 1995—. Mem. Senate com. armed svcs., 1997-2001, chair, seapower subcom., Senate com. on commerce, sci. and transp., 1995—, chair, oceans and fisheries subcom., Senate Budget com., 1995—, Senate com. small business, 1995—, Senate com. Fgn. Rels., 1995-97; counsel to asst. majority leader, 1997—, House Budget com., 1991-95, House Fgn. Affairs com., 1979-95, House Aging com. 1979-95, Congl. Caucus on Women's Issues 1979-84, co-chair 1983-95; dep. Repub. Whip, 1984-95; dep. Whip, 1996-97; corporator Mechanics Savs. Bank. Recipient Homeric award for adv. of human rights Chian Fedn., 1999, award for "Excelling in Standing up for Choice" Women's Campaign Fund, 1999, Spirit of Enterprise award U.S. Chamber of Commerce, 1997, 99, Woman of Yr. award Glamour Mag., 1998, David and Sherry Huber award for leadership on family planning, women's health issues, Family Planning Assn. of ME, 1998, Golden Bulldog award Watchdogs of the Treasury, Inc., Wash., 1994, 96, 98, Guardian of Small Business award Nat. Fedn. Indep. Bus., Wash., 1994, 96, 98, Responsible Choices award Planned Parenthood of Am., 1998, Spl. honor Nat. Assn. Devel. Orgns., 1998, Disting. Pub. Svc. award Am. Legion, Wash., 1998, Neil W. Allen award Greater Portland Chamber of Commerce, 1997, Legis. award for outstanding svc. to schs. and pub. librs., White Ho. Conf. on Libr. and Info. Svcs. Task Force, Wash., 1997, Pub. Leadership award, Nat. Breast Cancer Coalition, 1997, Magnificent Seven award Bus. & Profl. Women/USA, Wash., 1997, Deborah Morton award Westbrook Coll., Portland, ME, 1997, Golden Gavel award U.S. Senate Leadership, Wash., 1996, Nat. Osteoporosis Assn. award for leadership, Wash., 1996, award for leadership U.S. Distance Learning Assn., Crystal City, Va., 1996, award for leadership United Hellenic Am. Cong., 1995, William H. Natcher Disting. Svc. award Com. for Edn. Funding, 1995, Pub. Svc. award Am. Coll. Obstetricians and Gynecologists, 1995, Nat. Security Leadership award Am. Security Coun., Wash., 1994, Thomas Jefferson award Nat. Am. Wholesale Grocers Assn./Internat. Foodsvc. Distbrs. Assn., 1994, Grace Caucus award Citizens Against Govt. Waste, 1994, Sound Dollar award Free Cong. Found., 1994, Appreciation award Agrl. Stblzn. and Conservation Com. Somerset County chpt., Lifetime Achievement award Am. Hellenic Inst., 1994, Golden Heart award Assn. for Children for Enforcement of Support, ME chpt., 1993, Am. Social Health Assn. award on behalf of women's health issues, 1993, Medal of St. Andrew presented by His All Holiness Dimitrios Ecumenical Patriarch of Constantinople, Wash., 1990, Congrl. Waste Watchers award Coalition to Reform the Davis-Bacon Act, 1990; named to "CQ 50" Congrl. Quarterly Mag., Wash., 1999, Maine Women's Hall of Fame, 1999, Washingtonian Mag. 100 Most Powerful Women, 1997, All Maine Women Honor Soc. U. Maine, 1996, Deficit Reduction Honor Roll Concord Coalition, 1994, Honor Roll for dairy farmer support Associated Milk Prodrs., 1993; named Taxpayer's Hero for preventing govt. waste Citizens Against Govt. Waste, 1997, No Nonsense Am. Women, No Nonsense Coun. on Women's Issues, 1995, Congresswoman of Yr. Nat. Assn. for Transp. Alternatives, 1986; honored by Nat. Coalition for Osteoporosis and Related Bone Diseases, 1999, Edn. and Libr. Networks Coalition, 1997, Am. Assn. Univ. Pres., 1996, Pub. Policy Com. for Hellenic-Am. Women, 1995, Nat. Vietnam Vet. Coalition, 1994. Mem.: Philoptochos Soc. Republican. Greek Orthodox. Office: US Senate 154 Russell Senate Bldg Washington DC 20510-1903 E-mail: olympia@snowe.senate.gov.*

SNOWISS, ALVIN L. lawyer; b. Lock Haven, Pa., June 16, 1930; s. Benjamin and Lillian (Kalin) S.; m. Jean Yarnell, Mar. 16, 1973. BA, U. Pa., Phila., 1952, JD, 1955; hon. alumnus, Pa. State U., 1998. Bar: Pa. 1956, U.S. Dist. Ct. (mid. dist.) Pa. 1958, U.S. Supreme Ct. 1972. Pvt. practice, Lock Haven, 1955-61; ptnr. Lugg & Snowiss, 1961-74, Lugg, Snowiss, Steinberg & Faulkner, Lock Haven, 1974-86, Snowiss, Steinberg Faulkner, and Hall LLP, Lock Haven, 1987—. Solicitor Clinton County, Lock Haven, 1964-72. Chmn. bd. Lock Haven Hosp. Found., 1986-92; pres. Lock Haven Hosp., 1982-86; bd. govs. Clinton County Cmty. Found., Lock Haven, 1970-97; chmn. adv. bd. Palmer Mus. Art, State College; v.p. bd. trustees Ross Libr., Lock Haven, 1963-86; mem. exec. com. Pa. Rep. Com., Harrisburg, 1974-80; state committeeman Clinton County Rep. Com., 1967-80. Fellow Am. Coll. Trust and Estate Counsel, Am. Bar Found., Pa. Bar Found. (founding, bd. dirs. 1984-95); mem. Pa. Bar Assn. (zone del. 1976-82, zone gov. 1983-86, treas. 1987-90), Clinton County Bar Assn. (pres. 1975-76), Kiwanis (pres. Lock Haven 1966-67). Republican. Avocations: art history, golf, historical research. E-makl. Home: 414 W Main St Lock Haven PA 17745-1107 Office: 333 N Vesper St Lock Haven PA 17745-1342 E-mail: ajsnow16@aol.com.

SNOW-SMITH, JOANNE INLOES, art history educator; b. Balt. d. Henry Williams and Elsie Orrick (Bagley) Snow; m. Robert Porter Smith (dec.); children: Joanne Tyndale Darby, Henry Webster Smith, III (dec.), Constance Elizabeth Bagley, Cynthia Porter Bloom, Robert Porter Smith, Jr., Christoph Bagley; m. Robert Edward Willstadter. BA, Goucher Coll.; MA, U. Ariz., 1968; PhD, UCLA, 1976. Prof. Italian Renaissance art history U. Wash., Seattle, 1981—. Program dir. of art history U. Wash. Rome Ctr. in Palazzo Pio, Rome, 1998, 2000, 2002. Author: (book) The Salvator Mundi of Leonardo da Vinci, 1982 (Internat. award 1983), The Primavera of Sandro Botticelli: A Neoplatonic Interpretaion, 1993; contbr. numerous articles to profl. jours. Recipient Rsch. Professorship to study in Oxford and London, U. Wash. Grad. Sch., 1986. Mem. Nat. Soc. Colonial Dames of Am., Renaissance Soc. of Am., Leonardo Soc./U. London, Coll. Art Assn., Seattle Art Mus., Met. Mus. Art, Ashmolean Mus. (Oxford, Eng.). Home: 1414 Shenandoah Dr E Seattle WA 98112-3730 Office: Univ Wash PO Box 353440 Seattle WA 98195-3440 E-mail: jsnowsmi@u.washington.edu.

SNYDER, ANDREA, performing arts association administrator; BS, The Am. U.; MA in Arts Mgmt., NYU. Asst. to dir. Dance Notation Bureau; assoc. adminstr. Cunningham Dance Found.; adminstr. of arts dance dept. NYU Tisch Sch.; booking agent Sheldon Soffer Mgmt.; exec. dir. Laura Dean Dancers & Musicians; asst. dir. Nat. Endowment for Arts Dance Program, 1987—93; dir. Nat. Initiative to Preserve Am.'s Dance, 1993—2000; pres., exec. dir. Dance/USA, Washington, 2000—. Adj. prof. The Am. U. Office: Dance USA 1156 15th St NW Washington DC 20005*

SNYDER, ARLEN DEAN, actor; b. Rice, Kans., Mar. 5, 1933; s. Glenn Arlen and Sylvia Thelma (Guiot) S.; m. Angela Thornton, Jan. 7, 1970 (div. July 1976); m. Joanne Elizabeth Burke, May 8, 1983; 1 child, Kimble Burke. BA in Theater, U. Tulsa, 1957; MA in Theater, U. Iowa, 1959. Facilities designer Diamond Circle Theatre, Durango, Colo., 1961, ptnr., mgr., actor, 1961-63. Instr. dept. cinema Hunter Coll., N.Y.C., 1975-76. Dir.: (plays) Under Milkwood, 1974, Miss Pete, 1975; appeared in motion pictures including Yanks, 1978, Heartbreak Ridge, 1986, Bird, 1987, Internal Affairs, 1989, Marked For Death, 1990, Mommy's Day, 1996; recurring roles (TV series) Dallas, TV 101, Eisenhower & Lutz, Designing Women; guest appearances (TV series) Hart to Hart, M*A*S*H, Murder She Wrote, Benson, Dynasty, Private Benjamin, St. Elsewhere, Quantum Leap, Trial By Jury, others; appeared in theatrical plays including The Candy Apple, 1970, Trial of the Catonsville Nine, 1972, Big Broadcast on E. 53rd, 1973, One World at a Time, 1973, The Poison Tree, 1974, 75, Streamers, 1976, The Trip Back Down, 1977, Curse of the Starving Class, 1978, Better Living, 1989, Mr Rickey Calls A Meeting, 1992; starred in TV series including Secret Storm, 1966-68, As The World Turns, 1968-69, Dear Detective, 1979, The Texas Rangers/Pilot, 1981, Trauma Center, 1983, One Life to Live, 1984, Macgruder and Loud/Pilot, 1984; starred in movies for TV viewing including Young Love, First Love, 1979, Attica, 1979, Red Flag, 1980, RFK, 1981, Bus Stop, 1982, Night Partners, 1983, North & South Book II, 1986, The Oliver North Story, 1989, Frog Girl, 1989, Terror in Copper Valley, 1989, The Beach Boys' Story, 1990, Willing To Kill: The Texas Cheerleader Story, 1992, Cora Unashamed, PBS, 1999; recs. for Iowa's Books for the Blind and Handicapped. Bd. dirs. San Fernando Valley (Calif.) Arts Coun., 1987-88, mem. bd. advisors, 1989-90, pres., 1991. With U.S. Army, 1953-55. Named Leading Male Performer, L.A. Weekly, Matrix Theatre, 1989. Mem. AFTRA, SAG (bd. dirs. 1991), Actors' Equity Assn., The Players' Club (bd. dirs. 1974-76), Theta Alpha Phi. Democrat. Avocations: set design, political history, farming, cabinet making. Office: 4580 Broadway Ste 4D New York NY 10040 E-mail: arlen@adsturtlehouse.com.

SNYDER, ARNOLD LEE, JR. retired air force officer, research director; b. Washington, Oct. 12, 1937; s. Arnold Lee and Frances May (Humbert) S; m. Patricia Dorine Ward, July 6, 1963; children: Heinrick Jason, Sonya Doreen, Ross Nansen. BCE, George Washington U., 1960; MS, U. Colo., 1966; PhD, U. Alaska, 1972. Commd. 2d lt. USAF, 1960; advanced through grades to col., 1981; chief space environ. support sys. devel. sect. Air Force Global Weather Central, Offutt AFB, Nebr., 1972-76; chief ionospheric dynamics br. Geophysics Lab., Hanscom AFB, Mass., 1976-80; test dir. CONUS OTH-B radar system, Columbia Falls AFB, Maine, 1980-81, program dir. Hanscom AFB, 1981-85; dir. Office of Tech. Support, 1985-87; tech. dir. U. Lowell Ctr. Atmospheric Rsch., 1987-89; with The Mitre Corp., 1989-96; pvt. practice, 1996—. Adj. prof. U. Lowell, 1987-89. Contbr. articles to sci. jours. Recipient Legion of Merit, Meritorious Svc. medal with one oak leaf cluster, Commendation medal USAF, R&D award, 1981; Def. Value Engrng. award, 1984; Henry Harding scholar, 1955-56. Mem. Am. Geophys. Union, Am. Meteorol. Soc., Air Force Assn., Sigma Xi. Home and Office: 22 Blake Rd Orrington ME 04474-3637

SNYDER, ARTHUR, publishing executive; b. Valley Stream, N.Y., Feb. 6, 1925; s. Arthur and Kathryn (Staubitzer) Snyder; m. Betty Lain Harper, July 8, 1950; children: Susan, Arthur, Betsy, Jack, Heidi, Bonnie. B in Metall. Engrng., Cornell U., 1950, MBA, 1952. Mfg. engr. Norton Co., Worcester, Mass., 1952-56, chief acct., 1956-58, asst. contr., 1958-59, mgr. data processing, 1959-61, contr., 1961-65; exec. v.p. A.M. Best Co., Oldwick, NJ, 1965-67, pres., 1968—, chmn., 1971—. Author: (book) Principles of Inventory Control and Managing Capital Expenditures. 1st lt. AUS, 1942—45. Decorated Battlefield Commn., Bronze Star with oak leaf cluster, Purple Heart. Mem.: U.S. Srs. Gofl Assn., Cornell Soc. Engrs., Fin. Execs. Inst., Loch Lomond Golf Club (Scotland), Lyford Cay Club (Nassau, Bahamas), Baltusrol Golf Club (Springfield, N.J.). Presbyterian. Home: Lloyd Rd Bernardsville NJ 07924-1710 Office: A M Best Company Inc Ambest Rd Oldwick NJ 08858

SNYDER, ARTHUR KRESS, lawyer; b. L.A., Nov. 10, 1932; s. Arthur and Ella Ruth (Keck) S.; m. Mary Frances Neely, Mar. 5, 1953; children: Neely Arthur, Miles John; m. Michele Maggie Noval, May 14, 1973; 1 child, Erin-Marisol Michele; m. Delia Wu, Apr. 18, 1981. BA, Pepperdine U., 1953; JD, U. So. Calif., 1958; LLD, Union U., 1980. Bar: Calif. 1960, U.S. Supreme Ct. 1982. Sole practice, L.A., 1960-67; founder, pres. Arthur K. Snyder Law Corp., 1981-94; pres. Snyder & Assocs., Attys., 1994—. Pres. Marisol Corp., real estate and fgn. trade, 1978—; pres. real estate holdings Keck Investment Properties, 1990—; CFO Royal Star of Nev., Restaurateurs, 1999—; past instr. L.A. City Schs.; CEO Marisol of Nev., LLC Restaurateurs , 2002—. Mem. City Coun. L.A., 1967-85. Served to capt. USMC. Decorated La Tizona de El Cid Compeador (Spain), medal Legion of Honor (Mex.), Hwa Chao Zee You medal (Republic of China), numerous other commendations, medals, awards. Mem. ABA, ATLA, Los Angeles County Bar Assn., Calif. Bar Assn., World Film Inst. (chmn. bd. dirs. 1997--), Masons. Baptist. Office: 1000 W Sunset Blvd Ste 200 Los Angeles CA 90012-2105 E-mail: artsnyder@alumni.usc.edu.

SNYDER, BARBARA ROYALTY, pharmaceutical executive; b. Kokomo, Ind., May 20, 1958; d. Donald Edgar and Alma Frances Snyder; life ptnr. Yvon Lauren. MA in Am. Lit., Conn. State U., 1986; BA in Brit. Lit. & Composition,

U. Evansville, 1980. Med. writer Bristol-Myers Co., Evansville, Ind., 1980—88; mgr., med. writing Lorex Pharms., Skokie, Ill., 1988—94; sect. head med. writing Proctor & Gamble Pharms., Mason, Ohio, 1994—. Treas. Tri-State Alliance, Evansville, 1984—86. Mem.: Drug Info. Assn., Am. Med. Writers Assn. (bd. of directors 2001—, pres. Ohio Valley chpt. 2001—02). Democrat. Avocations: fishing, gardening, painting. Office: Procter & Gamble Pharms 8700 Mason Montgomery Rd Mason OH 45040-9462 Office Fax: 513-622-5365. E-mail: snyder.br@pg.com.

SNYDER, CAROLYN ANN, education educator, librarian; b. Elgin, Nebr., Nov. 5, 1942; d. Ralph and Florence Wagner. Student, Nebr. Wesleyan U., 1960-61; BS cum laude, Kearney State Coll., 1964; MS in Librarianship, U. Denver, 1965. Asst. libr. sci. and tech. U. Nebr., Lincoln, 1965-67, asst. pub. svc. libr., 1967-68, 70-73; pers. libr. Ind. U. Librs., Bloomington, 1973-76, acting dean of univ. librs., 1980, 88-89, assoc. dean for pub. svcs., 1977-88, 89-91, interim devel. officer, 1989-91; adminstrv. army libr. Spl. Svcs. Agy., Europe, 1968-70; dean libr. affairs So. Ill. U., Carbondale, 1991-2000, prof., 2000—. Team leader Midwest Univs. Consortium for Internat. Activities-World Bank IX project to develop libr. system and implement automation U. Indonesia, Jakarta, 1984-86; libr. devel. cons. Inst. Tech. MARA/Midwest Univs. Consortium for Internat. Activities Program in Malaysia, 1985; ofcl. rep. EDUCAUSE, 1996-2000; mem. working group on scholarly comm. Nat. Commn. on Librs. and Info. Sci., 1998-2000; dir. found. rels. So. Ill. U., Carbondale, 2002-. Editor Library and Other Academic Support Services for Distance Learning, 1997; contbr. chpt. to book and articles to profl. jours. Active Humane Assn. Jackson County, 1991—, Carbondale Pub. Libr. Friends, 1991—. Cooperative Rsch. grant Coun. on Libr. Resources, Washington, 1984. Mem. ALA (councilor 1985-89, Bogle Internat. Travel award 1988, H.W. Wilson Libr. Staff devel. grant 1981), Libr. Adminstrn./Mgmt. Assn. (pres. 1981-82), Com. on Instnl. Coop./Resource Sharing (chair 1987-91), Coalition for Networked Info. (So. Ill. U. at Carbondale rep. 1991-2000), Coun. Dirs. State Univ. Librs. in Ill. (chair 1992-93, 99-2000), Coun. on Libr. and Info. Resources Digital Leadership Inst. Steering Com. (Assn. Rsch. Librs. rep. 1998-2000), Ill. Assn. Coll. and Rsch. Librs. (chair Ill. Bd. Higher Edn. liaison com. 1993-94), Ill. Network (bd. dirs.), Ind. Libr. Assn. (chair coll./univ. divsn. 1982-83), U.S. Grant Assn. (bd. dirs. 1992—), Ill. Libr. Computer Sys. Orgn. (policy coun. 1992-95, 96-2000), Nat. Assn. State Univs. and Land-Grant Colls. (commn. on info. tech. and its distance learning and libr. bds. 1994-96), NetIllinois (bd. dirs. 1994-96), OCLC Users Coun. (elected rep. 1995-98), Big 12 Plus Libr. Consortium (chair 1997-98), Nat. Commn. on Librs. and Info. Sci. Working Group on Scholarly Comms., Assn. Rsch. Libr. (vis. program officer 2000—01). Avocations: antiques, theater, movies, reading. Office: So Ill U Morris Libr Carbondale IL 62901-6632

SNYDER, CHARLES AUBREY, lawyer, director; b. Bastrop, La., June 19, 1941; s. David and Shirley Blossom (Haas) S.; m. Sharon Rae Veta, Aug. 29, 1963; children: David Veta, Shelby Haas, Claire Frances. BBA, Tulane U., 1963; JD, La. State U., 1966. Bar: La. 1966. Assoc. firm. Milling Benson Woodward, LLP and predecessors, New Orleans, 1966-69, ptnr., 1969—. Bd. dirs. Delta Petroleum Co., La. Motel and Investment Corp., Terre aux Boeufs Land Corp., Kemper and Leila Williams Found. Bd. dirs. New Orleans Speech and Hearing Ctr., pres., 1978-80; bd. dirs. City Pk. Commn., 1991-98, pres., 1995, dir. emeritus, 1999—; bd. dirs. New Orleans Mus. Art, 1996—, v.p., 1998-99, sec., 1999-2000; fellow La. Coll. Securities Counsel. Mem. ABA, La. Bar Assn. (chmn. sect. on corp. and bus. law 1982-83), New Orleans Bar Assn., Am. Law Inst., La. Law Inst. (coun. 2000—, coms. on mineral code and revision of partnership law, property law tutorship), Covington Country Club, City Energy Club, Plimsoll Club, Bienville Club, Beta Gamma Sigma. Home: 74724 River Rd Covington LA 70435-2222 Office: Milling Benson Woodward LLP 909 Poydras St Ste 2300 New Orleans LA 70112-1010 E-mail: csnyder@millinglaw.com.

SNYDER, CHARLES ROYCE, sociologist, educator; b. Haverford, Pa., Dec. 28, 1924; BA, Yale U., 1945W, MA, 1949, PhD, 1954. Mem. staff Ctr. Alcohol Studies Yale U., 1950-60, asst. prof. sociology, 1956-60; prof. sociology So. Ill. U., Carbondale, 1960-85, chmn. dept., 1964-75, 81-85, prof. emeritus, 1985—. Vis. prof. human genetics Sackler Sch. Medicine, Tel Aviv U., 1980; cons. behavioral scis. tng. com. Nat. Inst. Gen. Med. Scis., NIH, 1962-64; mem. planning com., chmn. program 28th Internat. Congress Alcohol and Alcoholism, 1964. Author: Alcohol and the Jews, 1958; editor: (with D.J. Pittman) Society, Culture and Drinking Patterns, 1962; editorial bd. Quar. Jour. Studies on Alcohol, 1957-83; assoc. editor Sociol. Quar., 1960-63. Mem. theol. commn. United Ch. of Christ, 1964-71; bd. dirs. Ill. Stewardship Alliance, 1990-95. With USNR, WWII. Fellow Am. Sociol. Assn.; mem. Soc. Study Social Problems (v.p. 1963-64, rep. to council Am. Sociol. Assn. 1964-66), Midwest Sociol. Soc. (bd. dirs. 1970-71), AAUP. Home: Apt 1606 8680 E Alameda Ave Denver CO 80231

SNYDER, DANIEL, professional sports team executive, communications executive; CEO Snyder Comm.; chmn. bd., owner Washington Redskins. Office: c/o Washington Redskins 21300 Redskin Park Rd Ashburn VA 20147*

SNYDER, DAVID RICHARD, lawyer; b. Kalamazoo, Oct. 9, 1949; s. Richard E. and Margaret L. (Vanderplough) S.; m. Phyllis Alford, Aug. 14, 1971; children: Jason Richard, Carrie Lynn. BA with high honors, Mich. State U., 1971; JD with distinction, Cornell U., 1974. Bar: Calif. 1974. Assoc. Jenkins & Perry, San Diego, 1974-77, ptnr., 1978-83, Aylward, Kintz & Stiska, San Diego, 1983-86, Luce, Forward, Hamilton & Scripps, San Diego, 1986-93, Pillsbury Madison & Sutro LLP, San Diego, 1993—; mng. bd. Pillsbury Winthrop LLP, 1999—. V.p., dir. San Diego Venture Group, 1989-91; adj. prof. Calif. Western Sch. Law, San Diego, 1982-84; lectr. Calif. Continuing Edn. of Bar, 1983—. Co-author: Drafting Legal Instruments, 1982; editor Cornell Law Rev., 1973-74. Bd. dirs. Boys Club Chula Vista, Calif., 1979-83; pres. Corpus Christi Parish Coun., Bonita, Calif., 1988-90; trustee Children's Hosp. Found., San Diego, 1988—, chmn., 1990-92. Mem.: ABA (fed. securities law com. 1987—, chmn. subcom. on ann. rev. fed. securities regulation, dir. corp. dirs. forum), Corp. Dirs. Forum (bd. dirs. 2001—), San Diego County Bar Assn., State Bar Calif., Am. Electronics Assn. (bd. dirs., mem. exec. com. San Diego chpt. 1991—93), Order of Coif, Phi Beta Kappa. Republican. Roman Catholic. Office: Pillsbury Winthrop 101 W Broadway Ste 1800 San Diego CA 92101-8298

SNYDER, DONALD BENJAMIN, biology educator; b. N. Manchester, Ind., Oct. 6, 1935; s. Benjamin Franklin and Eva Katherine (Speicher) S.; m. Wilma Frankie Simpson, Aug. 8, 1965; children: Douglas, Jonn. BS, Manchester Coll., Ind., 1957; MS, Ohio State U., 1959, PhD, 1963; postgrad., U. Puerto Rico, 1966. Cert. wildlife biologist. From grad. asst. in zoology to rsch. fellow in wildlife Ohio State U., 1957-63; biology instr. Houghton (N.Y.) Coll., 1963; asst. prof. biology So. (S.C.) Wesleyan U., 1963-64, Geneva Coll., Beaver Falls, Pa., 1964-69; prof. biology Edinboro (Pa.) U., 1969-96, Pymatuning Lab. of Ecology U. Pitts., Pitts., 1982, 88, 89. Bird records com. Presque Isle Audubon Soc., Erie, Pa., 1975—; vol. for wildlife Pa. Game Commn., Harrisburg, 1990-96; ornithol. tech. com. Pa. Biol. Survey, Harrisburg, 1991—. Contbr. numerous articles to profl. jours. Committeeman Boy Scouts Am., Laketon, Ind., 1965-70; elder Christian & Missionary Alliance Ch., Erie, 1987-90, 98—; trustee Purple Martin Conservation Assn., Edinboro, Pa., 1988—. Equipment grantee Atomic Energy Commn., Oak Ridge, Tenn., 1966; recipient Meritorious Svc. award Edinboro U. Pa., 1974. Mem. Wildlife Soc., Assn. Field Ornithologists, Commonwealth of Pa. Univ. Biologists, Beta Beta Beta. Avocations: hiking, biking, canoeing. Home: 13190 Cambridge Rd Edinboro PA 16412-2837 E-mail: dbswfs@lycos.com.

SNYDER, DONALD EDWARD, corporate executive; b. Rochester, N.Y., Nov. 10, 1928; s. Benjamin Orman and Arlien Henrietta (Wing) S.; m. Dorothy Edna Stanke, Oct. 16, 1954; children— Donald Edward, Anne Arlien Snyder Marone, Barbara Lynn Snyder Mitchell, Richard John Snyder. AB, Cornell U., 1950, JD, 1952; postgrad., Ind. U., 1962. Bar: N.Y. 1953. Pvt. practice law, 1953-56; with Eastman Savs. and Loan Assn., 1956-68, pres., 1970-75, chmn. bd., 1979-88; asst. to treas. Eastman Kodak Co., Rochester, 1968-70, gen. credit mgr., 1975-77, with Comptroller's div., 1977-78, asst. treas., 1978-79, treas., 1979-88; chmn. Eastman Kodak Credit Corp., 1985-88; chief exec. officer, chmn. bd., pres. Corp. Officers and Dirs. Assurance Ltd., Hamilton, Bermuda, 1990-93. Bd. dirs. Greater Rochester chpt. Epilepsy Found. Am., 1979-85, Allendale Mut. Ins. Co., 1983-92; bd. dirs. Luth. Ch.-Mo. Synod, 1983-95; vice chmn. bd., chmn. fin. com., mem., chmn. audit com., 1989-95; bd. dirs., mem. exec. com. ACE Ltd., 1985-90, EXEL Ltd., 1985-90, CODA Ltd., 1986-93; mem. investment rev. com. United Way of Greater Rochester, 1979-2000; trustee Seneca Zool. Soc., 1983-90. With USNR, 1946-48. Mem. N.Y. State Bar Assn., Monroe County Bar Assn., Rochester C. of C. (trustee 1980-86), Cornell Club (Rochester), Phi Kappa Tau (nat. fin. advisor, mem. nat. coun. 1988-95, treas., mem. exec. com. Phi Kappa Tau Found. 1991-2002). Home and Office: 14 Hidden Springs Dr Pittsford NY 14534-2897 also: 2700 N AIA Ste 705 Fort Pierce FL 34949

SNYDER, DOROTHY Z. social worker; b. Detroit, June 26, 1952; d. William Edward and Ann Mildred Zynda; m. Edward William Snyder, Sept. 4,1 976; children: Julie Ann, Janey Lee. BA, Mich. State U., 1974; MSW, U. Mich., 1981. Cert. social worker. Foster care worker Cath. Social Svcs., Detroit, 1974-81, pregnancy counselor, 1984-87, psychotherapist Livonia, Mich., 1987-99; mem. staff devel. com., 1997-99; psychotherapist, dir. Bridgewood Clinic, Livonia, 1999—. Chair yearbook com. PTA, Farmington, Mich., 1986-95; mem. Cheerleader Backers, Farmington, 1999—; mem. Booster Club, Farmington, 1995—. Fellow Nat. Assn. Social Workers; mem. Farmington Glen Aquatic Club, Our Money Making Investment Club (sec. 1998-99). Republican. Roman Catholic. Avocations: gardening, fitness, walking, restaurants.

SNYDER, EDWARD ADAMS, dean, economics educator; b. Danville, Pa., July 3, 1953; s. Harry Coolidge and Fay (Adams) S.; m. Kimberly Marie Snyder; children: Alison Marie, Jeffrey Adams, Kevin James. Ba in Econs. and Govt., Colby Coll., 1975; M of Pub. Policy, U. Chgo., 1978, PhD in Econs., 1984. Staff economist Antitrust div. U.S. Dept. Justice, Washington, 1979-82; asst. prof. bus. econs. and pub. policy Sch. Bus. Adminstrn. U. Mich., Ann Arbor, 1983-90, assoc. prof. Sch. Bus. Adminstrn., 1990-94, prof., chmn. bus. econs., 1994-98; dean Darden Bus. Sch. U. Va., Charlottesville, 1998—2001; dean U. Chgo. Grad. Sch. Bus., 2001—, prof., 2001—02, George Pratt Schultz prof., 2002—. Rsch. fellow Office for Study of Pub. and Pvt. Instns., U. Mich.; cons. Antitrust div. U.S. Dept. Justice, Chgo., 1982-84, Fed. Home Loan Bank Bd., Washington, 1989; antitrust expert, 1985—; John M. Olin vis. assoc. prof. U. Chgo., 1991-92; dir. William Davidson Inst. Mich. Bus. Sch. Author: Crisis Resolution in the Thrift Industry, 1989; contbr. articles to econ. jours. and law revs., 1985-91. Avocations: foreign policy, sports, sailing. Home: 5622 S Woodlawn Ave Chicago IL 60637- Office: U Chgo Grad Sch of Bus 1101 E 58th St Chicago IL 60637- E-mail: tsnyder@uchicago.edu.

SNYDER, FRANKLIN FARISON, hydrologic engineering consultant; b. Holgate, Ohio, Nov. 11, 1910; s. Samuel Lewis and Nettie May (Farison) S.; m. Mary Elizabeth Bruton, Oct. 1, 1938; children: Marilyn Kay Snyder Lutz, Carol Lamb Snyder Garnett, Gregory Lewis(dec.). Student, U. Toledo, 1928-30; B.C.E., Ohio State U., 1932, C.E., 1942; postgrad., Dept. Agr. Grad. Sch., 1940-42, 62. Registered profl. engr., Ohio. Hydraulic engr. U.S. Geol. Survey, Washington, 1934-35; hydraulic engr. TVA, Knoxville, 1936-37, Pa. Dept. Forests and Waters, Harrisburg, 1938-39, U.S. Weather Bur., Pitts. and Washington, 1940-42, Office Chief Engrs., Washington, 1942-66; ptnr. Nunn, Snyder & Assocs., Fairfax, Va., 1972-78. Hydrologic engrng. cons., McLean, Va., Can., Mex., Sudan, Greece, Bangladesh, Pakistan, Colombia, Jamaica, 1954-90; mem. Internat. St. Lawrence River Bd. Control., 1961-74, U.S. Nat. Com. for Internat. Hydrol. Decade, 1964-67, mem. commn. for Hydrology, World Meteorol. Orgn., 1960-72. Contbr. articles to profl. publs. Supr. Citizens Assn. Security Patrol, Chesterbrook Woods, McLean, 1978-94. Recipient exceptional civilian service award War Dept., 1946, Outstanding Civil Engrng. Alumnus award Ohio State U. Civil Engrng. Alumni Assn., 1989, Disting. Alumnus award Ohio State U., 1990; named to Gallery of Disting. Civilian Employees, C.E., 1983 Fellow ASCE (Cross medal); mem. Am. Geophys. Union, Am. Meteorol. Soc., Nat. Acad. Engrng., Cosmos Club Washington, Sigma Xi, Tau Beta Pi. Republican. Presbyterian. Avocations: genealogy; golf; travel. Home: 1128 Astoria Ln Peachtree City GA 30269 E-mail: fsny007@aol.com.

SNYDER, GARY MICHAEL, music educator; b. Pittsburgh, Pa., Aug. 6, 1970; s. Edward Paul and Mary Louise Snyder; m. Cara Joy Myers, June 21, 1997. BA, Duquesne Univ., Pittsburgh, PA, 1994. Cert. Maryland Dept. of Education 1994, Virginia Dept. of Education 1994, Pennsylvania Dept. of Education 1995, Florida Dept. of Education 1999. Music educator k-12 No. Sub-Service, Pittsburgh, Pa., 1995—96; band tchr. Shaler Area Sch. Dist., Glenshaw, 1996, St. Theresa Sch., Pittsburgh, 1996—98, St. Ann Hist. Sch., West Palm Beach, 1998—. Pvt. music instr., West Palm Beach, Fla., 1998—. Scholar Minardi scholarship, Minardi Found., 1994. Mem.: Internat. Assn. of Jazz Educators, Fla. Band Masters Assn., Music Educators Nat. Conf. R-Liberal. Roman Catholic. Home: 117 Belmont Drive Royal Palm Beach FL 33411 Office: St Ann School 324 North Olive Ave West Palm Beach FL 33401

SNYDER, GEORGE EDWARD, lawyer; b. Battle Creek, Mich., Feb. 7, 1934; s. Leon R. and Edith (Dullabahn) S.; m. Mary Jane Belt, July 27, 1957 (div. Sept. 23, 1982); children: Sara Lynn, Elizabeth Jane; m. Claudia Gage Brooks, Feb. 25, 1984 BS, Mich. State U., 1957; JD, U. Mich., 1960. Bar: Mich. 1961, U.S. Dist. Ct. (we. and ea. dists.) Mich. 1961. With Gen. Electric Co., 1957-58; asso. firm Miller, Johnson, Snell & Commisky, Grand Rapids, 1960-62, Goodenough & Buesser, Detroit, 1962-66; partner firm Buesser, Buesser, Snyder & Blank, Detroit and Bloomfield Hills, 1966-85, Meyer, Kirk, Snyder & Lynch PLLC, Bloomfield Hills, 1985—. Chmn. bd. dirs. Bill Knapps Mich., Inc., 1998-2000. Chmn. E. Mich. Environ. Action Council, 1974-78; pub. mem. inland lakes and streams rev. com. Mich. Dept. Natural Resources, 1975-76. Served as 2d lt. AUS, 1957. Fellow Am. Acad. Matrimonial Lawyers (pres. Mich. chpt. 1991-92), Am. Coll. Family Trial Lawyers, Am. Bar Found., Internat. Acad. Matrimonial Lawyers, Mich. Bar Found; mem. ABA, Am. Judicature Soc., Am. Arbitration Assn. (panel arbitrators), State Bar Mich. (chmn. family law com. 1968-72, mem. rep. assembly 1972-78, chmn. rules and calendar com. 1977-78, mem. family law sect. coun. 1973-76, environ. law sect. coun. 1980-85, prepaid legal svcs. com. 1973-82, com. on judicial selection 1974, com. on specialization 1976-82), Detroit Bar Assn. (chmn. family law com. 1966-68), Oakland County Bar Assn., Delta Upsilon (chmn. trustees, alumni chpt. dep. 1965-70), Tau Beta Pi, Pi Tau Sigma, Phi Eta Sigma. Clubs: Detroit Athletic, Birmingham (Mich.) Athletic. Episcopalian. Home: 32965 Outland Trl Bingham Farms MI 48025-2555 Office: Meyer Kirk Snyder & Lynch PLLC Ste 100 100 W Long Lake Rd Bloomfield Hills MI 48304-2773 E-mail: gsnyder@meyerkirk.com.

SNYDER, GLENN HERALD, political science educator, writer; b. Superior, Wis., Oct. 8, 1924; s. Herald Arthur and Alma Pauline (Hillestad) S.; m. Otty Verhoogh, Jan. 21, 1951; children: Abigail, Jared, Adam. BS, U. Oreg., 1948; MA, Columbia U., 1953, PhD, 1956. Reporter Wall St. Jour., N.Y.C., 1949-51; tchg. fellow Wesleyan U., Middletown, Conn., 1953-55; rsch. assoc., lectr. Columbia U., N.Y.C., 1955-58; rsch. assoc. Princeton (N.J.) U., 1958-60; from asst. to assoc. prof. Univ. Denver, 1960-62; vis. assoc. prof. U. Calif., Berkeley, 1962-1964; from assoc. prof. to prof. SUNY, Buffalo, 1964-84; prof. U. N.C., Chapel Hill, 1984-1991, prof. emeritus, 1991—. Chmn. bd. Ctr. for Internat. Conflict Studies, Buffalo, 1965-82. Author: Deterrence and Defense, 1961, Stockpiling Strategic Materials, 1967, Alliance Politics, 1997; co-author: Strategy, Politics, and Defense Budgets, 1962, Conflict Among Nations, 1977. 2d lt. U.S. Army, 1943-45. Grantee NSF, 1969-76; fellow The Wilson Ctr., 1981-82, Guggenheim Found., 1990-91. Mem. Internat. Inst. Strategic Studies, Am. Polit. Sci. Assn., Triangle Inst. Security Studies. Avocations: music (piano), golf. Home: 750 Weaver Dairy Rd Apt 163 Chapel Hill NC 27514-1482 E-mail: gsnyder1@email.unc.edu.

SNYDER, GRAYDON F. religion educator; b. Peru, Ind., Apr. 30, 1930; s. Clayton Fisher and Irene Elizabeth (Fisher) S.; m. Lois Hannah Horning, June 13, 1953; children: Jonathan Edvard, Anna Christine, Stephen Daniel. BA, Manchester Coll., North Manchester, Ind., 1951; MDiv, Bethany Theol. Sem., Chgo., 1954; ThD, Princeton Theol. Sem., 1961. Asst. prof. Bibl. studies Bethany Theol. Sem., Chgo., 1959-65, prof. Oak Brook, Ill., 1965-79, dean, 1975-86, Wieand prof. N.T. studies, 1979-86; acad. dean, prof. N.T. Chgo. Theol. Sem., 1986-90, prof. N.T., 1990-96, adj. prof. N.T., 1996-99. Mem. accrediting commn. Assn. Theol. Schs., 1976-82. Author: Ante Pacem, 1985, First Corinthians, 1992, Health and Medicine in the Anabaptist Tradition, 1995, Inculturation of the Jesus Tradition, 1999, Irish Jesus, Roman Jesus, 2002; mem. editl. bd. Bibl. Rsch., 1965-95, Brethren Life and Thought, 1962-94. Mem. Bd. Edn. # 88, Elmhurst, Ill., 1970-73; chmn. bd. trustees Bethany Hosp., Chgo., 1979-92; del. governing bd. Nat. Coun. Chs., 1986-91. Fellow Westar Inst.; mem. Soc. Bibl. Lit., Chgo. Soc. Bibl. Rsch. (pres. 1969), Studiorum Novi Testamenti Societas. Mem. Ch. of The Brethren. Avocation: early Christian art. Home: 5475 S Ridgewood Ct Chicago IL 60615-5314 E-mail: graydonsny@aol.com.

SNYDER, HENRY LEONARD, history educator, bibliographer; b. Hayward, Calif., Nov. 3, 1929; s. Henry Runyon and Mary (Rosenberg) S.; m. Janette Marie Hannus, July 21, 1961; children: Michael Jesse, Christopher Henry, David Lyle. BA, U. Calif., Berkeley, 1951, MA, 1960, PhD, 1963. Sr. buyer Dohrmann Comml. Co., San Francisco, 1951-59; instr. to prof. U. Kans., Lawrence, 1963-78, assoc. dean to dean research adminstrn., 1967-78; prof. history, dean arts and scis. La. State U., Baton Rouge, 1979-86; prof. history U. Calif., Riverside, 1986—; dir. Ctr. for Bibliog. Studies, 1989—; dean humanities and social scis. U. Calif., Riverside, 1986; vis. lectr. Bedford Coll., U. London, 1965-66; Fulbright lectr., research scholar U. Hamburg, Fed. Republic Germany, 1974; dir. English Short Title Catalogue for N.Am., 1978—. Editor: The Marlborough Godolphin Correspondence, 1975; co-editor: The Scottish Heritage, 1981. Pres. Baton Rouge Opera, 1981-83, Riverside Opera, 1987-90; pres. United Way, Lawrence, 1977; bd. dirs. Arts and Humanities Com., Baton Rouge, 1981-85; Sigmund, Martin, Heller Traveling fellow U. Calif.-Berkeley, 1962-63. Am. Council Learned Soc. sr. fellow, 1969-70 Fellow Royal Hist. Soc. Gt. Brit. Bibliog. Soc. London; mem. Am. Soc. 18th Century Studies (pres. 1980-81), Conf. Brit. Studies (exec. com. 1978-83), Am. Hist. Assn., Internat. Fed. Librs. (chair rarebooks and ms. sect. 1995—). Republican. Congregationalist. Home: 220 Trinity Ave Kensington CA 94708-1139 Office: U Calif Ctr For Bibliog Studies Riverside CA 92521-0001 E-mail: hlsnyder@earthlink.net.

SNYDER, HOWARD ALBERT, educator, author; b. Santo Domingo, Dominican Republic, Feb. 9, 1940; s. Edmund Campbell and Clara Alberta S.; m. Janice Marian Lucas, Aug. 18, 1962; children: Mark, Jerilyn Winstead. PhD, U. Notre Dame, 1983. Prof. United Theol. Sem., Dayton, Ohio, 1988—96; prof. history and theology of mission Asbury Theol. Sem., Wilmore, Ky., 1996—. Author: The Problem of Wineskins, 1975, 12 other books; contbg. editor: Christianity Today. Bd. trustees Spring Arbor Coll., 1991—. Methodist. Home: 168 Seamands Dr Wilmore KY 40390 Office: Asbury Theol Sem 204 N Lexington Ave Wilmore KY 40390 E-mail: HASnyder1@prodigy.net., Howard_Snyder@asburyseminary.edu.

SNYDER, HOWARD MCCRUM, III, pediatrician, educator; b. Carlisle, Pa., Aug. 25, 1943; s. Howard McCrum Jr. and Loaine (McLaughlin) S.; m. Mary Woodville, June 29, 1974; children: Emily curtis, Lawrence Curtis, Jonathan Colt. BA, Princeton U., 1965; MD, Harvard Med. Sch., 1969. Diplomate Am. Bd. Surgery, adult gen. surgery, pediat. gen. surgery, Am. Bd. Urology. Intern surgery, asst. resident Peter Bent Brigham Hosp., Boston, 1969-73; resident pediat. surgery Children's Hosp. Med. Ctr., 1973-74; resident surgery Tufts U.-New Eng. Med. Ctr., 1974-75; pediat. urologic and gen. surgery Mass. Gen. Hosp., 1975; clin. asst. Hosp. for Sick Children, London, 1975-76; sr. houseman Alder Hey Children's Hosp., Liverpool, Eng., 1976; resident urology Harvard Program in Urology Peter Bent Brigham Hosp., Boston, 1978-80; instr. surgery Harvard Med. Sch., 1978-80; from asst. prof. to prof. U. Pa., Phila., 1980—. Asst. surgeon, assoc. dir. Children's Hosp. Phila., 1980-89, sr. surgeon divsn. urology, 1989—; med./surg. staff mem. Hosp. U. Pa., Phila., 1980—, Presbyn.-U. Pa. Med. Ctr., Phila., 1981—, A.I. duPont Inst., Wilmington, Del., 1987—, Bryn Mawr (Pa.) Hosp., 1996, Chester County Hosp., West Chester, Pa., 1997-99, A.I. duPont Hosp. for Children, Wilmington, 1999; prof. staff mem. Pa. Hosp., Phila., 1999; vis. prof. Seoul (Korea) Nat. U., 2000, St. Justine Children's Hosp., Montreal, Can., 1999, Montreal Children's Hosp., 1999, Shriner's Hosp. for Children, Montreal, 1999, Jewish Gen. Hosp., Montreal, 1999, U. Chgo., 1999, Maimonides Med. Ctr., Bklyn., 1999, L.I. Jewish Med. Ctr., 1996, 99, Westchester County Med. Ctr., Valhalla, N.Y., 1999, R.I. Hosp., Providence, 1998, Rainbow Babies Hosp., Cleve., 1997, SUNY, Stony Brook, 1997, Syracuse, 1996, Walter Reed Army Med. Ctr., Washington, 1994, 96, Emory U., Atlanta, 1994, U. Calif. San Francisco, 1993, Boston Children's Hosp., 1993, U. Pitts., 1993, U. Iowa, Iowa City, 1993, Children's Hosp., Columbus, Ohio, 1993. Contbr. numerous chpts. in books and articles to profl. jours. Surgeon U.S. Army, 1976-78, active res., 1984—. Recipient Disting. Svc. award Nat. Kidney Found., Inc., 1993, Barry Goldwater Svc. award, 1997. Fellow Royal Soc. Medicine London, ACS; mem. AMA, NIH, Brit. Assn. Urol. Surgeons (affiliate, recipient St. Paul's medal 2002), European Soc. Pediat. Urology, Soc. Internat. d'Urologe (U.S. sect.), Confederacion Americana De Urologia, Am. Bd. Urology (trustee 2002-), Am. Urol. Assn., Soc. Pediat. Urology (pres. 1998), Am. Acad. Pediat. (surg. and urology sects.), Am. Pediat. Surg. Assn., Soc. Genitourinary Reconstructive Surgeons, Nat. Kidney Found. (Disting. Svc. award 1993), Am. Assn. Clin. Urologists, Boyleston Med. Soc., Mass. Med. Soc., Soc. Univ. Urologists, Ea. Pediat. Urol. Soc., Coll. Physicians of Phila. (trustee 2000), Phila. County Med. Soc., Phila. Urologic Soc. (pres.), John Morgan Soc., Phila. Acad. Surgery, Brookline Country Club, Merion Cricket Club, Phila. Club. Republican. Episcopalian. Avocations: fishing, jogging, antiques, gardening. Office: Children's Hosp Phila Divsn Pediat Urology 34th St & Civic Ctr Blvd Philadelphia PA 19104 Fax: 215 590-3985. E-mail: snyderh@email.chop.edu.

SNYDER, JACK L. social sciences administrator; Past dir. Inst. War & Peace Studies Columbia U., chmn. dept. polit. scis., 1997-2000, prof., 2000—. Office: Columbia Univ Dept of Polit Scis 420 W 118th St New York NY 10027-7213

SNYDER, JAMES P. audio and digital television engineer, videographer, editor; b. Oct. 20, 1964; s. John Henry Jr. and Anne Snyder. Student, George Washington U., 1982-84; cert. AM broadcast tech., No. Va. Community Coll., 1986; BA in Comm. and Visual Media, Am. U., 1993; BA in CLEG, 1993. Prodn. asst. Sta. WIPB-TV, Muncie, Ind., 1980-84; prodn./engrng. asst., bd. operator Sta. WBST-FM, 1982-83; chief engr. Sta. WRGW, Washington, 1982-84; technician George Washington U., Marvin Ctr., 1982-87; engrng. asst. Sta. WPFW-FM, 1984-85; ops. dir. Stas. WAMU/WVAU-FM, 1985-86; founder, dir. Sta. WRGW Radio/TV, 1984-87; mng. dir. Sta. WRGW-AM-FM, 1986-87; news/tech. dir. Sta. WVAU-AM/FM, 1990; adminstrv. asst. Sullivan & Cromwell, 1985-92; libr. asst. Paul, Weiss, Rifkind, Wharton & Garrison, 1989; asst. to the acad. counselor Sch. Communication, Am. U., 1990-91, sr. asst. to the acad. counselor, 1991; technician, projectionist CAS Media Ctr., 1989-96; chief engr. Am. TV & WVAU Radio, 1990-98; ops. coord. internat. program sales Discovery Channel Inc., 1994; engr. and HDTV editor Advanced Television Test Ctr., 1995-96; engr. Fox News Washington Bureau, 1996-98; ops. dir. Unity Motion High Definition System, 1998; Digital TV engrng. specialist, studio course lectr. Harris/PBS DTV Express, 1998-99. Freelance engr., TV/HDTV prodn. specialist, ops. specialist, videographer, editor, 1991—; founding mem. Am. U. CATV/Fiber Optic Systems Com., 1991; engrng. cons. digital and high definition TV David Sarnoff Rsch. Ctr., Model HDTV Sta. WHD TV Inc., PBS Adv. TV Field Test Project, Turner Engrng., Unity Motion HDTV Satellite Svc., PBS Digital TV Strategies Svcs. Group, Advanced TV Tech. Ctr., FedNet-Fed. Network, Inc., ABC Radio Network, Caribiner Internat, News Corp., 1995—; freelance engr. Reuters Television, 1996—. Audio-visual dir. Planned Parenthood of East-Cen. Ind., Muncie, 1982-83; George Washington U. coord. D.C. Spl. Olympics Superdance, 1984-85; bd. dirs. Vol. Clearinghouse of D.C. Student Network, Rosslyn, Va., 1985. Recipient Cert. Appreciation Planned Parenthood of East-Cen. Ind., 1982, Cert. Appreciation D.C. Spl. Olympics, 1984, Cert. Appreciation Ea. Ind. Community Television, 1980. Mem. IEEE, Soc. Motion Picture and TV Engrs., Soc. Broadcast Engrs., Audio Engrng. Soc. Avocations: historical research, educational advancement, collecting stamps and coins, bicycling, electronics. Office: Apt 210 2700 Wisconsin Ave NW Washington DC 20007-4605

SNYDER, JAMES ROBERT, protective services official, educator; b. Atchinson, Kans., Nov. 11, 1952; s. Don Q. and Waunita D. Snyder; m. Catherine Lefholz, July 10, 1982; children: James Matthew, Cara Nichole. BBA, Ctrl. Mo. State U., 1975; MPA, Park Coll., 2002. Cert. EMT, Mo. Supr. Blue Springs (Mo.) Police Dept., 1981—; instr. Western Mo. Regional Police Acad., Independence, 1994—. Field investigator Jackson County Coroner,

Kansas City, Mo., 1982—; homicide investigator Kansas City Met. Squad, 1989—; nat. instr. Talking Hands-Non Verbal Comm., 1991—. Recipient 74 disting. svc. awards including excellence in performance awards. Mem. ASPA, FBI Nat. Acad. Assn., Fraternal Order Police, Mo. Police Officers Assn., Lambda Chi Alpha. Avocations: sports, home repair, golf. Office: Blue Springs Police 1100 SW Smith St Blue Springs MO 64015-3649 E-mail: jrsnyder@bluesprings.gov.us.

SNYDER, JAN LOUISE, administrative aide; b. Warrington Twp., Pa., Sept. 15, 1935; d. Wilbert Adam and Alice (Myers) March; divorced; children: Steven Michael Krone, David Sylvan Snyder. Grad. H.S., Dover, Pa. With McCrory Stores Divsn. McCrory Corp., York, 1966-97, receptionist exec. buying divsn.; receptionist, switchboard operator human resources Healthsouth Rehab. Hosp., Pa., 1997-99, ret., 2000. Active Northwestern region York Hosp. Aux., 1979—, mem. membership com. and administer II, 2002; active York Symphony Assn., 1990—, membership com., 1992—; active York chpt. Am. Cancer Soc. Am., 1990—, York Chorus, 1988-90; mem. Ch. of the Open Door of Shiloh, 1956—2002, Dover Twp. Fire Co. Aux. for Women, 1975—, Harrisburg Jr. League Lectr. Series, 1980-95, York Jr. League Lectr. series, 1989-96; womens aux. Johns Hopkins Hosp., 1999—. Mem. Am. Bus. Women's Assn. (pres. Colonial York charter chpt. 1980, mem. adv. bd. 1980-89), nat. Trust for Historic Preservation. Democrat. Avocations: traveling, music, educational lecturing series, church activities, flower and vegetable gardening. Home: 2823 Grandview Ave York PA 17404-3905

SNYDER, JED C. foreign affairs specialist; b. Phila., Mar. 24, 1955; s. David and Lynn S. BA, Colby Coll., 1976; MA, U. Chgo., 1978, postgrad., 1978-79. Rsch. asst. U. Chgo., 1979; asst. rschr. Pan Heuristics div. R&D Assocs., Marina del Rey, Calif., 1979-80, assoc. rschr., asst. div. mgr., 1980-81, cons., 1982-83, Sci. Applications, Inc., 1979-81, Rand Corp., Santa Monica, Calif., 1979-81, Los Alamos Nat. Lab., 1984; sr. spl. asst. to dir. Bur. of Politico-Mil. Affairs, Dept. State, Washington, 1981-82; rsch. assoc. Internat. Security Studies Program, Woodrow Wilson Internat. Ctr. for Scholars, Smithsonian Instn., 1982-84; founder, chmn. Washington Strategy Seminar, 1984-90, pres., 1984-93, corp. dir., 1984-93; dep. dir. nat. security studies Hudson Inst., 1984-87; sr. rsch. fellow Nat. Strategy Info. Ctr., 1988-90; mgr. internat. strategic planing MPRI, Inc., 1997-2000; sr. nat. security advisor Dyncorp, 2001; sr. analyst CNA Corp., 2001; cons. in strategic planning and internat. affairs, 2001—. Appointee v.p. Bush's Adv. Task Force on Mid. East, 1987-88; appointee sr. fellow Inst. for Nat. Strategic Studies, Nat. Def. U., 1992-97, supr. rsch. prof., team leader; cons. Office of Sec. of Def., 1988-92, Rand Corp., 1983-88. Contbr. articles on U.S. fgn. policy and mil. def. to profl. publs. Trustee Kents Hill (Maine) Sch., 1987-92. Guest scholar Sch. Advanced Internat. Studies, Johns Hopkins U., 1982-83; fellow U. Chgo., 1979, Inter-Univ. Seminar on Armed Forces and Soc., 1980, MacArthur Sr., 1985-86, Herman Kahn, 1985-86, Smith Richardson, 1987-88, John M. Olin, 1987-88; selected as a Young Am. Leader, Am. Coun. on Fed. Republic of Germany, 1984. Mem. Internat. Inst. for Strategic Studies, Royal United Svcs. Inst., U.S. Naval Inst., Fgn. Policy Rsch. Inst., Coun. on Fgn. Rels. Mailing: 1718 M St NW # 197 Washington DC 20036-4504 E-mail: snyder7@attglobal.net.

SNYDER, JOEL BENNETT, engineering executive, educator; b. N.Y.C., Feb. 4, 1936; s. Sol and Anne (Bernstein) S.; m. Harriet Brenda Polinsky, Aug. 11, 1957; children: Eileen Schneyman, Jeffrey, Sharon Jones. BEE, Poly. Inst. Bklyn., 1956, MSEE, 1964. Registered profl. engr., N.Y.; charter engr., U.K. Mathematician and programmer IBM, N.Y.C., 1956-58; engr. Airborne Instruments Lab., Melville, N.Y., 1958-60; sr. project engr. Harman Kardon, Plainview, 1960-63; ptnr. Snyder Assocs., 1963—. Sr. industry prof. Poly. U., Bklyn., 1984-99; spkr. in field; bd. dirs. Motiontronics for Sci., N.Y.C., 1990—, Multimedia for Sports, N.Y.C., 1995—, Internet Golf Multimedia, N.Y.C., United Engring. Found., N.Y.C., 2002—. Editor: Data Systems Engineering Magazine, 1970; patentee video play counting techniques, 1986; contbr. numerous articles to profl. jours. Recipient George Gronner award Mid-Island Y, Plainview, N.Y., 1987, Achievement award Engrs. Joint Coun., 1998. Mem. IEEE (citation of honor, 1979, Centennial medal, 1984, Gruenwal award, 1994, Millennium medal 2000, Larry K. Wilson Transnat. award 1999, pres. elect 2000, pres. 2001, v.p. prof. activities 1995-96, region 1 dir. 1992-93), Alumni Assn. Poly. U., Bklyn. (dedicated alumnus award 1989, disting. alumnus award, 2002, life. dir.). Office: Snyder Assocs 58 Diamond Dr Plainview NY 11803-2120 E-mail: jsnyder@snyderassoc.com., j.snyder@ieee.org.

SNYDER, JOHN MICHAEL, lobbyist, public relations director; b. Kingston, N.Y., Dec. 18, 1939; s. John Ignace and Agatha (Flick) S.; m. Ling-Ling Woo, Jan. 1, 1996. BA, Georgetown U., 1961, MA, 1968. Legis. sec. U.S. Ho. of Reps., Washington, 1964-65; assoc. editor The Am. Rifleman, 1966-74; chief lobbyist, dir. publs. and pub. affairs Citizens Com. for Right to Keep and Bear Arms, 1975—. Editor (newsletter) Point Blank, 1974—; Capitol Hill editor (newspaper) Gun Week, 1986—. Active Arlington County Rep. Com., 1994-2002. Recipient Grand Knighthood award Order of Michael the Archangel, 1988, Cicero award Nat. Assn. Federally Licensed Firearms Dealers, 1996. Mem. Am. Fedn. Police (nat. v.p. pub. rels. 1989—), Nat. Assn. Chiefs of Police (v.p. pub. affairs 1995—, v.p. Washington Liaison 2000—), Second Amendment Found. (treas. 1986—), St. Gabriel Possenti Soc. Inc. (pres. 1989—), Sr. Power Campaign Com. (treas. 2001-), Coun. for Am. (dir. 2001-), The Asia Soc., Internat. Platform Assn., Kiwanis Internat., Coun. for Am. (bd. dirs. 2001-), Nat. Press Club, Capitol Hill Club. Republican. Roman Catholic. Avocations: swimming, cycling, reading, movies, theater. Home: 401 12th St S Apt 2218 Arlington VA 22202-4240 Office: Citizens Com Right to Keep and Bear Arms 1090 Vermont Ave NW Ste 800 Washington DC 20005-4961 E-mail: gundean@aol.com., john0849@aol.com.

SNYDER, JOHN EVAN, physicist; b. Norristown, Pa., Mar. 3, 1955; s. Evan Samuel and Virginia (Boyer) S. BS with honors in Physics summa cum laude, Moravian Coll., 1980; MSEE, Carnegie Mellon U., 1985, PhD in Physics, 1994, postgrad. Tchr. aide, substitute tchr. Md. Sch. for the Deaf, Frederick, 1975-77; sign lang. instr. Lehigh County C.C., Allentown, Pa., 1977-78; lab. instr. Moravian Coll., Bethlehem, 1978-80; rsch. asst. elect. engring. dept. Carnegie Mellon U., Pitts., 1980-85, rsch. asst. physics dept. data storage sys. ctr., 1985-94; NRC rsch. assoc. materials sci. and tech. divsn. Naval Rsch. Lab, Washington, 1994-96; process devel. cons. Commonwealth Sci. Corp., Alexandria, Va., 1996-97; postdoctoral rsch. fellow U.S. Dept. Energy Ames (Iowa) Lab., 1997-98, assoc. scientist, 1998—. Rsch. engr. IBM Corp., San Jose, Calif., summer 1982; adj. asst. prof. materials sci. and engring dept. Iowa State U., 1999—. Contbr. articles to Phys. Rev. Letters, Jour. Applied Physics, Rev. of Sci. Instruments, IEEE Transactions on Magnetics, Jour. Magnetism and Magnetic Materials, Phys. Rev. B., Applied Physics Letters, Low Temperature Physics; patentee in field. NSF rsch. fellow U. Ga., Athens, 1979, IBM grad. fellow Carnegie Mellon U., 1982-83. Mem. AAAS, IEEE (sr. mem.), Am. Phys. Soc. (session chmn. 1996, 98, 99, 2000, 02), Materials Rsch. Soc., IEEE Magnetics Soc. (session chair ann. conf. on magnetism and magnetic materials 1998, 99, session chair joint MMM-intermag conf. 1998, organizing com. M4-2000 symposium), Iowa Acad. Sci., Moravian Coll. Triangle Honor Soc., Sigma Pi Sigma, Sigma Xi. Achievements include observation of anomalous phase separation in CoCr films by high temperature thermomagnetic analysis, local structure in the amorphous precursor to Ba-hexaferrite thin films, and how it causes the crystallization texture; research on thermodynamic model calculations of grain boundary segregation in CoCr thin films, local structure of as-prepared and partially-reduced Co,Ti, Sn-substituted Ba-hexaferrite powder using extended x-ray absorption fine strucure, development of a direct ion beam deposition process for amorphous diamond-like carbon (DLC) thin films, process for reactive ion-beam sputtering of aluminum nitride thin films, microstructure-magnetic property relationships in Nb-Fe-B inert gas atomized powders, developed a new composite magnetostrictive material for automotive torque sensing and other sensor and actuator applications, effect of nitrogen on the micro/nanostructure, stress and magnetic properties of rf-sputtered Fe-Si-Al-(N) soft magnetic thin films. Office: Ames Lab Iowa State U 205 Metals Development Ames IA 50011-0001 E-mail: jesnyder@iastate.edu.

SNYDER, JOHN GORVERS, lawyer; b. Boston, June 20, 1960; s. Philip Francis and Sylvia (Gorvers) S.; m. Hinda Mala Simon, July 8, 1984; children: Monica Paige, Kimberly Blaine. BA, Johns Hopkins U., 1982; JD, Cornell U., 1987. Bar: Mass. 1988, U.S. Dist. Ct. Mass. 1989. Assoc. banking law, bus. law and corp. law dept. Craig and Macauley P.C., Boston, 1987—94, ptnr. banking law, bus. law and corp. law dept., 1995—2000; sr. v.p. and gen. coun. Simon Cos., LP, Braintree, 2000—. Lectr. New England Coll. Fin., 1994-2000. Active Combined Jewish Philanthropies, Boston, 1991—, Anti-Defamation League, Boston, 1993-94, Buckingham, Browne & Nichols Sch. Annual Fund, 1999-. Mem. Mass. Bar Assn., Boston Bar Assn., Phillips Exeter Acad. Alumni Assn., Phi Alpha Delta Internat., Omicron Delta Kappa (Johns Hopkins U. chpt., pres. 1981-82), Delta Upsilon (Johns Hopkins U. chpt.). Avocations: golf, tennis. Home: 7 Laurus Ln Newton Center MA 02459-3138 Address: The Simon Cos LP Attn: John G Snyder VP 10 Forbes Rd Braintree MA 02184-2605

SNYDER, JOHN JOSEPH, optometrist; b. Wonewoc, Wis., June 30, 1908; s. Burt Frederick and Alta Lavinia (Hearn) S. AB, UCLA, 1931, postgrad., 1931-32, U. Colo., summers 1935-36, 38, 40, 41, U. So. Calif., 1945-46; BS in Optometry, Los Angeles Coll. Optometry, 1948, O.D., 1949. Tchr. La Plata County (Colo.) Pub. Schs., 1927-28; supt. Marvel (Colo.) Pub. Schs., 1932-33; tchr. Durango (Colo.) High Sch., 1933-41; pvt. practice optometry Los Angeles, 1952-72, Torrance, Calif., 1972-78; now retired. Former bd. dirs. Francia Boys' Club, Los Angeles; former pres. Exchange Club South Los Angeles, also sec. Mem. AAAS, Am. Inst. Biol. Scis., Am., Calif., Optometric Assn., Internat. Biog. Assn. Republican. Home: Apt 231 25585 Van Leuven St Loma Linda CA 92354-2452

SNYDER, JOHN MILLARD, recreation resources executive, educator; b. Chelsea, Mass., Apr. 3, 1946; s. John Henry and Grace (Eby) S.; m. Barbara Ripple, Nov. 8, 1969 (div. 1979); 1 child, Logan; m. Glenda Allene Snyder, Sept. 10, 1983; children: Erika, Kimberly. BA, Franklin & Marshall Coll., 1968; MS, Colo. State U., 1974, PhD, 1982; cert., Harvard Sch. Design, 1987. Econ. rsch. asso. Coll. Natural Resources, Ft. Collins, Colo., 1972-76; econ devel. City Devel. Dept., Kansas City, Mo., 1976-77; v.p. Oblinger Smith Corp., Denver, 1977-79; sr. resource analyst Abt Assocs., 1979-80; dr. devel. analysis URS Engrs., 1980-83; pres. Strategic Studies, Inc., Littleton, Colo., 1983—. Pres. Glacier Bay Outfitters, 1990—; co-founder Ecotourism Internat., 1994—; faculty environ. policy and mgmt. U. Denver, 1990—, dir. environ. policy and mgmt., 1997-2000; econ. faculty Regis U., 1984—; spl. projects dir. Ctr. Sustainable Tourism, U. Colo. Author: (poems) A Far Off Place, 1995, Best Poems of 1995, 1995; contbr. articles to profl. jours. Econ. advisor Treas. and Gov. Colo., Denver, 1979-84; officer YMCA Guides Program, LIttleton, 1984-85; sr. advisor Spl. Family Recreation, Denver, 1985-90; benefactor Le Bal de Ballet, Denver, 1989—. 1st lt. U.S. Army military intelligence, 1968-72. Fellow The Explorers Club, N.Y. Mem. Ctr. for Whale Studies, Stanford Libr. (assoc.), Denver Zoological Found., Nat. Parks and Conservation Assn., several environ. orgns., Phi Kappa Phi, Xi Sigma Pi.

SNYDER, JOSEPH JOHN, editor, historian, author, lecturer, consultant; b. Aug. 27, 1946; s. Joseph John and Amy Josephine (Hamilton) S.; m. Sally Hale Walker, July 4, 1973; children: Lauren Elizabeth, Brian Joseph Seth. BA in Anthropology, George Washington U., 1968; MA in Anthropology, U. N.Mex., 1973. With U.S. CSC, Washington, 1974-77; editor, writer U.S. Nat. Pk. Svc., Harpers Ferry, W.Va., 1977-81; cons. editor Early Man mag., Evanston, Ill., 1978-83; spl. project editor Sea Power Mag., 1986-87, cons. editor, 1987—, Jour. Archaeoastronomy, 1987—. Freelance writer, 1981—; pres. Sta. at Shepherdstown Inc., 1992-2000; pres., chmn. bd. dirs., Atlantic & Pacific High Speed Railway, Inc., 1993—; lectr. Maya archaeology Norwegian-Caribbean Lines, Miami, Fla., 1982; cons. in field. Author: Kenneth Westcott James Transport Menu Collection, 1998, A.D. 2025: Transportation in America, 1995, Musings from a New Manse, 1999, The Phaistos Disc, A Commentary , 1999, Fragments of My Fleece, 2000, 1859: Turning Point of the Modern Era, 2001; editor: The Only Fight the Cops County Not Stop, 1998; book rev. assoc. editor: Athena Rev., 1999—; contbr. articles to popular mags. Chmn. pks. com. Neighborhood Planning Adv. Group, Croydon Park, Rockville, Md., 1980-81; bd. dirs. Agrl. R&D Orgn., 1985—; v.p., bd. dirs. Hagerstown (Md.) Roundhouse Mus., 1989-91; v.p. bd. dirs. Hagerstown-Washington County Conv. and Visitors Bur., 1993-96, sec., 1993-96; pres. Tourism Found., Inc., 1996-99. With U.S. Army, 1969-71, Vietnam. Decorated Bronze Star. Mem.: Nat. Ry. History Soc., Nat. Geog. Soc. (cons. 1987—), Am. Com. to Advance Study of Petroglyphs and Pictographs (editor), Hakluyt Soc., Coun. Md. Archaeology, Internat. Assn. Torch Clubs, James Rumsey Torch Club (pres. 1997—99). Democrat. Home: 2008 Ashley Dr Shepherdstown WV 25443-9767 E-mail: sws@intrepid.net.

SNYDER, JUDITH LYNN, fund development consultant; b. Louisville, Apr. 8, 1950; d. William P. Snyder and Jean Gahlert (Schmidt) Stallings; m. Ivo Ronald Ware, Sr., May 20, 1978 (div. Sept. 1989); m. John Joseph Mason III, Dec. 22, 1991 (div. Aug. 1999). BA, Ind. U., 1972; M in Pub. Svc., Western Ky. U., 1974; postgrad., U. Louisville, 1978, 90-91. Cert. fund raising exec. Dir. fund raising & vol. rels. Big Brothers/Big Sisters of Kentuckiana, Louisville, 1983-85; from alumni rels. adminstrv. officer to dir. res. curriculum U. Louisville, 1985-92; dir. corp./found. rels. Defiance (Ohio) Coll., 1992-94, U. Toledo, 1994-96; cons. JSM Consulting Group, Inc., Canton, Ohio, 1996—. Cons. in field. Bd. dirs. David's House Compassion, Inc., 1995-96, bd. dirs. Women's Network, Ohio Assn. of Nonprofit Orgns. Mem. Nat. Soc. Fund Raising Execs. (bd. dirs., chair program greater Toledo chpt. 1994, treas. 1995-96, sec. bd. dirs. North Ctrl. Ohio chpg. 1996, membership chair, 1999), Ohio Coun. Fund Raising Execs., No. Ohio Planning Giving. Avocations: cross-stitch, flower gardening, basket weaving, photography, beach walking. Home and Office: 4130 Belden Ave SE Canton OH 44707-1663

SNYDER, L. MICHAEL, hospital administrator; b. May 10, 1935; BA, Brown U., 1957; MD, Chgo. Med. Sch., 1962. Dir. hematology-blood bank St. Vincent Hosp., Worcester, Mass., 1968-86, chair dept. lab. medicine, 1986-91; chair dept. hosp. labs. U. Mass. Med. Ctr., 1991-98, U. Mass. Meml. Health Care, Worcester, 1998—. Contbr. numerous articles and abstracts to profl. publs. and confs., including New Eng. Jour. of Medicine, Biochimica et Biophysica Acta, Brit. Jour. Haematology, Am. Soc. Hematology meetings, Internat. Soc. Exptl. Hematology meetings. Office: U Mass Med Ctr H2 502 Worcester MA 01655

SNYDER, LEWIS EMIL, astrophysicist, educator; b. Ft. Wayne, Ind., Nov. 26, 1939; s. Herman Lewis and Bernice (McKee) S.; m. Doris Jean Selma Lautner, June 16, 1962; children: Herman Emil, Catherine Jean. BS, Ind. State U., 1961; MA, So. Ill. U., 1964; PhD, Mich. State U., 1967. Research assoc. Nat. Radio Astronomy Obs., Charlottesville., Va., 1967-69; prof. astronomy dept. U. Va., Charlottesville, 1969-73, 74-75; vis. fellow Joint Inst. for Lab. Astrophysics, U. Colo., Boulder, 1973-74; prof. astronomy dept. U. Ill., Urbana, 1975—. Co-editor: Molecules in the Galactic Environment, 1973; contbr. articles to sci. jours. NASA-Am. Soc. Engring. Edn. summer fellow, 1972, 73; Alexander von Humboldt Found. sr. U.S. scientist award, 1983-84. Mem. AAAS, Astron. Soc. Pacific, Am. Phys. Soc., Am. Astron. Soc., Internat. Astron. Union, Union Radio Scientifique Internationale, Alexander von Humboldt Assn. Am. Lutheran. Office: U Ill 1002 W Green St Urbana IL 61801-3074

SNYDER, LINDA ANN, book editor; b. Pitts., Feb. 24, 1957; d. Arthur Anthony and Patricia Ann (Balzer) Krysinski; m. Christopher Lee Snyder, June 1, 1996. BFA, Carnegie Mellon U., 1979. Systems adminstr. Duncan, Lagnese & Assocs. (now known as Killam Assocs.), Pitts., 1979-86; editorial office supr. Materials Rsch. Soc., 1986-94; monographs editor Air & Waste Mgmt. Assn., 1994-95; mktg. specialist Killam Assocs., Warrendale, Pa., 1995-96; mng. editor Soc. of Automotive Engrs., 1996—. Freelance corr. Pitts. Post-Gazette, 1990-93. Named Jaycee of Quar., North Hills Jaycees, 1990. Republican. Roman Catholic. Avocations: photography, gardening, hiking, writing. Home: 210 Hillendale Rd Pittsburgh PA 15237-1804 Office: Soc of Automotive Engrs 400 Commonwealth Dr Warrendale PA 15096-0001 E-mail: lsnyder@sae.org.

SNYDER, LIZA, actress; Appeared in T.V. movie Race Against Time: The Search for Sarah, 1996; T.V. series Sirens, 1993, Jesse, 1998-2000, Yes, Dear, 2000-; T.V. guest appearance Chgo. Hope, 1996; Film appearance in Pay it Forward, 2000. Office: c/o Yes, Dear CBS Studios 7800 Beverly Blvd Los Angeles CA 90036*

SNYDER, MARK JEFFREY, financial consultant, actuary; b. Bklyn., May 16, 1947; s. Milton A. and June (Freed) S.; m. Gloria Carol Beskin, May 31, 1969; children: Chad Alan, Heather Lynn. B of Engring. Sci., SUNY, Stony Brook, 1969. CLU; chartered fin. cons.; registered fin. planner. Ins. agt. Mass. Mut. Life Ins., Holbrook, N.Y., 1971-79; dist. mgr. Guardian Life Ins. Co., Port Jefferson, 1979-81; v.p. pensions Exec. Planners, Ronkonkoma, 1981-84; pres. CAS Adv. Services, Inc., Patchogue, 1984-93; mng. exec. Integrated Resources Equity Corp., 1986-89, Royal Alliance Assocs., Inc., Patchogue, 1990—; pres. Snyder Fin. Svcs., 1986-91, Snyder Kresh Pension Svcs. Inc., Patchogue, 1989-97, Snyder Kresh Fin. Svcs., Inc., Medford, N.Y., 1990-98, Mark J. Snyder Fin. Svcs., Medford, 1998—. Speaker in field. Moderator, host Moneywise, Brookhaven Cable TV, Port Jefferson Sta., N.Y., 1987-88; host. WLIM Radio program; contbr. articles to profl. jours. Mem. South Setauket (N.Y.) Civic Assn., 1972—, Three Village Dem. Club, Setauket, 1984—; bd. dirs., pres. Suffolk Estate Planning Coun., 1991-92; chmn. planned giving com. Suffolk County coun. Boy Scouts Am., 1985-87, 93—, mem. exec. bd. 1985—, v.p. 94—, mem. trust com., 1989-98, chmn. Boy Scouts Am. endowment devel. trust com., 1985-87, 93—; v.p. Suffolk County Coun.; pres. SUNY at Stony Brook Alumni Assn., 2000—. Named one of top 300 fin. planners in the country, Worth mag., 1998, top 250, 1999, 2001; named to Rsch. Mag. Advisor Hall of Fame; recipient top 250, Worth mag., 2002. Mem. Soc. Fin. Svcs. Profls.Registered Fin. Planners L.I. (bd. dirs., pres. 1986-87), Pension Forum L.I. (bd. dirs., chmn. pub. rels. 1986-88), Rotary Internat., KP. Democrat. Jewish. Avocations: racquetball, swimming. Office: Royal Alliance Assocs Inc 1731 N Ocean Ave Medford NY 11763-2649

SNYDER, MARK ALLEN, lawyer; b. Balt., Nov. 20, 1951; s. Hyman William Snyder and Rhea Belle Thiman; m. Nancy Virginia Salmon, Aug. 18, 1974; children: Erin Hayley, Meredith Ann. JD, U. Baltimore Sch. Law, 1975; BS, U. Md. Coll. Park, 1973. Cert. Md. Ct. Appeals, 1976, U.S. Supreme Ct., 1981—. Pres., mng. ptnr. Cohen, Snyder, Eisenberg & Katzenberg, Balt., 1976—. Bd. trustees Fair Oaks Cmty. Assn., Severna Park, Md., 1995-97, Md. Inst. for Continuing Profl. Edn. of Lawyers, 1995-97. Mem. Md. State Bar Assn. (bd. govs. 1998-00), Md. Trial Lawyers Assn. (bd. govs. 1994-96), Anne Arundel Bar Assn. (bd. dirs. 1994—, pres. 1997-98, Pres. award 1994, trustee's award 1999), Md. Workers Compensation Ednl. Assn. (bd. govs. 1996—), U. Balt. Alumni Assn. (bd. trustees 1980-82). Democrat. Jewish. Avocations: SCUBA, golf, skiing. Office: Cohen Snyder Eisenberg & Katzenberg 347 N Charles St Baltimore MD 21201-4307

SNYDER, MARVIN, neuropsychologist; b. Bklyn., Oct. 14, 1940; s. Samuel and Sarah Snyder; m. Arlyne S. Naphtali, June 23, 1963; 1 dau., Sian Leslie. BA (N.Y. State Regents scholar 1958-62, Meml. award psychology 1962), Bklyn. Coll., 1962; PhD (NDEA fellow 1962-65, USPHS fellow 1965-66, trainee 1966-67), Duke U., 1967. Research psychologist NIMH, 1967-71; Nat. Eye Inst., 1971-72; program dir., neuroscis. Nat. Inst. Drug Abuse, 1974-79, dir. div. research, 1979-90, dir. Office of Sci. Policy, Edn. and Legislation, 1990-94; acting dep. dir. Nat. Inst. on Drug Abuse, 1992-93; dir. life scis. rsch. office Fedn. of Am. Socs. for Exptl. Biology, 1995-97; prs. Snyder Assocs., 1995—; cons. to biosensor devel., 1995. Mem. sr. exec. svc. USPHS exec. com. AIDS, 1983-85; mem. Dept. Health and Human Svcs. Orphan Products Bd., 1982-88; mem. The White House Task Force on Drug Abuse Health Issues; co-chmn. Interagy. Com. on Smoking and Health, Interagy. Com. on New Therapies for Pain and Discomfort; exec. sec. Interagy. com. on Pain and Analgesia, chmn. subcom. on edn. and tng., 1985—; cons. to WHO on drug abuse policy issues, 1985-87, Ctr. Substance Abuse Treatment, 1999-2000; testifier on drug abuse sci. and policy issues to U.S. Congress; mem. Fed. Coordinating Com. for Sci., Engring. and Technology, Com. on Brain and Behavior, 1990-91, Devel. Guidelines for Protection Human Subjects in Drug Abuse Studies, 1991; sci. adv. Dynamac Corp., 1999—; adv. bd. Business-Higher Edn. Forum, Rsch. Collaboration Initiative, 1999—. Author papers and reports on comparative neurology, drug abuse, nutrition, and health policy. Recipient Michael Morrison award for excellence in sci. adminstrn. Com. on Problems of Drug Dependence, 1988, Presdl. Meritorious Rank award 1990.

SNYDER, NATHAN, entrepreneur; b. Hartford, Conn., Oct. 7, 1934; s. Saul and Betsy (Wand) S.; m. Geraldine Wolff, Dec. 27, 1964; children: Hannah Abigail, Alexander Lowell Wolff. AB, Harvard U., 1956; LLB, Columbia U., 1963; postgrad. in bus., NYU, 1967-68. Bar: N.Y. 1963. Assoc. Paul, Weiss, Rifkind, Wharton & Garrison, N.Y.C., 1963-66; v.p., sec. Randolph Computer Corp., Greenwich, Conn., 1966-69, exec. v.p., gen. counsel, bd. dirs., 1969-73; exec. v.p., chief operating officer BanCal Tri-State Corp. (holding co. Bank of Calif.), San Francisco, 1974-76; v.p. acquisitions CBS Inc., N.Y.C., 1976-87; pres. VS & A Communications Ptnrs., 1987-89, The Snyder Co., New Canaan, Conn., 1989—. Lectr. of mgmt. Golden Gate U., San Francisco, 1974-76, Annenberg Sch. Comms., Phila., 1982-87; bd. dirs. First Eagle Sogen Funds, N.Y.C. Editor: Columbia Law Rev., 1962-63. Vol. legal services Office Econ. Opportunity, 1963. Served to lt. USNR, 1956-60. Harlan Fiske Stone scholar, 1964-65 Mem. Econ. Club N.Y., Harvard Club (N.Y.C.), Harvard Club (Fairfield County). E-mail: naterun7@hotmail.com.

SNYDER, RACHEL ANN, manufacturing company specialist; b. Newcomers Town, Ohio, Dec. 17, 1942; d. Russell Edward and Alma Garland (McCormick) Huff; m. Howard Leland Snyder, Dec. 2, 1967 (div. Jan. 1996); children: Philip Wayne, Michelle Marie. AA with distinction, Kent State U., 1994, BA, 1999. Nurse asst. Timken-Mercy Hosp., Canton, Ohio, 1965, 72-73; teller Beneficial Loan Co., 1966-67; sign inspector Assn. Visual Comms., 1995-96, 97—; day and night housekeeper Glenmoor Country Club, 1996-97; dept. organizer Wal-Mart, Massillon, 2000—. Mem. Golden Key Nat. Honor Soc. (Scholastic Achievement and Excellence award 1991, 94), Phi Alpha Theta (scholar 1994). Roman Catholic. Avocations: reading, jogging, baking, cooking, sewing. Home: 2880 Thackeray Ave NW Apt 10 Massillon OH 44646-2674

SNYDER, RICHARD GERALD, research scientist; administrator, educator, consultant; b. Northampton, Mass., Feb. 14, 1928; s. Grant B. and Ruth (Putnam) S.; m. Phoebe Jones, March 2, 1949; children: Dorinda, Sherrill, Paul, Jeff, Jon, David. Student, Amherst Coll., 1946-48; BA, U. Ariz., 1956, MA, 1957, PhD, 1959. Diplomate Am. Bd. Forensic Anthropology. Teaching asst. dept. anthropology U. Ariz., Tucson, 1957-58, assoc. rsch. engr. Applied Rsch. Lab., Coll. Engring., 1958-60, mem. staff Ariz. Transp. and Traffic Inst., 1959-60, assoc. prof. syss. engring., 1960; chief phys. anthropology Civil Aeromed. Rsch. Inst. FAA, Oklahoma City, 1960-66, rsch. pilot, 1962-66, acting chief Protection and Survival Labs., 1963-66; mgr. biomechanics dept. Office Automotive Safety Rsch. Ford Motor Co., Dearborn, Mich., 1966-68, prin. rsch. scientist, 1968; assoc. prof. anthropology U. Mich., Ann Arbor, 1968-73, prof., 1973-85; rsch. scientist Hwy. Safety Rsch. Inst. U. Mich. Trans. Rsch. Inst., 1968—85; head biomed. dept. U. Mich., 1969-84, dir. NASA Ctr. of Excellence in Man-Vehicle Syss., 1984-85, prof. emeritus, 1985—, rsch. scientist emeritus, 1989—; pres. Biodynamics Internat., Tucson, 1986—. Pres., bd. dirs. George Snively Rsch. Found., 1992-98; adj. assoc. prof. U. Okla., 1963; rsch. assoc. Zoller Lab., U. Chgo., 1964-65, rsch. assoc. dept. anthropology, 1965-67; assoc. prof. Mich. State U., East Lansing, 1967-68; cons. USAF Aerospace Med. Rsch. Labs., Nat. Acad. Scis., U.S. Dept. Transp., adv. com. Office Naval Rsch. Dept. Navy, numerous others. Assoc. editor Jour. of Comm., 1961-63; cons. editor Jour. Biomechanics, 1967-81;mem. editl. bd. Product Safety New, 1973—; adv. bd. Aviation Space and Environ. Medicine, 1980-91, 94—; contbr. chpts. to books and numerous articles to profl. jours. Judge Internat. Sci. Fair, Detroit, 1968; mem. coun. Explorer Scouts, Ann Arbor, 1968-70; dir. Am. Bd. Forensic Anthropology, 1978-84, 85-91; dir. Snell Meml. Found., 1990—; bd. dirs. N.Mex. Rsch. Inst., 1996-2000. 1st lt. USAF, 1949-54, Korea. Recipient Met. Life award Nat. Safety Coun., 1970, Admiral Luis de Flores Flight Safety award Flight Safety Found., 1981; named to Safety and Health Hall of Fame Internat., 1993, Ariz. Aviation Hall of Fame, 1998. Fellow AAAS, Aerospace Med. Assn. (Harry G. Moseley award 1975, Profl. Excellence award 1978, John Paul Stapp award in aerospace biomechanics 1994), Royal Anthrop. Inst., Am. Anthrop. Assn., Am. Acad. Forensic Scis. (T. Dale Stewart award 1992), Soc. Automotive Engrs. (Arch T. Colwell Merit award 1973, Aerospace Congress award 1982, Tech. Contbns. to Air Transport Safety), mem. AIAA (assoc. fellow), Am. Assn. Phys. Anthropologists, Ariz.-Nev. Acad. Sci., Internat. Soc. Aircraft Safety Investigators, Aerospace Physiologists Soc., Sigma Xi, Beta Beta Beta.

Republican. Congregationalist. Avocations: aviation, aerospace medicine, forensic anthropology. Home: 3720 N Silver Dr Tucson AZ 85749-9709 Office: Biodynamics Internat Tucson AZ 85749

SNYDER, ROBERT CARL, retired minister; b. Chgo., Dec. 26, 1937; s. Harold Homer and Gertrude Mary (Bischof) Snyder; m. Gwen Ardith Smith, Aug. 15, 1959; 1 child, Melisa Joy Snyder Izzo. BA, Western Mich. U., 1959; MDiv, Hartford Sem. Found., 1963. Ordained to ministry United Ch. of Christ, 1963. Pastor 1st Congl. Ch., Crystal, Mich., 1963-65, Trinity Congl. Ch., Grand Rapids, 1965-72, Park Congl. Ch., Toledo, 1972-78, 1st Congl. Ch., Armada, Mich., 1980-83, South Haven, 1983-92, W. Adrian United Ch. of Christ, Adrian, 1992-95, Kenilworth United Ch. of Christ, Buffalo, 1995-2000. Moderator Grand Rapids Assn., United Ch. of Christ, 1971-72, N.W. Ohio Assn., Tiffin, 1978-79, S.W. Assn., Kalamazoo, Mich., 1988-89, Mich. Conf. United Ch. of Christ, 1990-92; chmn. N.Y. conf. ann. meeting planning com. United Ch. of Christ, 1998; sec. Western N.Y. chs. in covenant United Ch. of Christ/Disciples of Christ, 1999. Mem. Kiwanis (sec. South Haven chpt. 1985-91). *The strongest defense a nation possesses is the contentment and satisfaction of its own people, established in part by the religious establishment serving in the role of national conscience.*

SNYDER, ROBERT JOHN, lawyer; b. Phila., June 2, 1952; s. Robert John and Lilja (Anderson) S. BA cum laude, St. John's U., 1974; JD, U. N.D., 1977. Bar: N.D. 1977, Minn. 1977, U.S. Dist. Ct. N.D. 1977, U.S. Ct. Appeals (8th cir.) 1982, U.S. Supreme Ct. 1982. Ptnr. Coles & Snyder, Chartered, Bismarck, ND, 1977—89, Wheeler, Wolf, Bismarck, 1989—93, Snyder Coles Lawyers, Bismarck, 1993—99, Snyder Law Office, Bismarck, 1999—. Judge, Bismarck Teen Ct., 1999—; alt. bd. dirs. Legal Aid N.D., Bismarck, 1982-84. Vol. Bismarck United Way, 1979; active talking book S.D. State Program for Handicapped, Pierre, 1983-84. Named one of Outstanding Young Men of Am., 1979. Mem. ABA, Assn. Trial Lawyers A., N.D. Bar Assn. (com. revision o pattern jury instrns. 1981, revision code of profl. responsibility 1983-87), Internat. Platform Assn., Mensa, Intertel. Bismarck Jaycees (outstanding officer 1979, Outstanding Young Bismarcker 1985), Apple Creek Country Club, Elks, Ky. Cols. Office: Snyder Law Office PO Box 1321 Bismarck ND 58502-1321 E-mail: snyhunt@btigate.com.

SNYDER, ROBERT LEE, anesthesiologist; b. Midland, Mich., Aug. 26, 1952; s. Robert M. and Kathleen M. Snyder; m. Shelley Ann Marquiss, June 29, 1974; children: Kenneth Robert, Kacie Lee Ann. BS in Zoology, Mich. State U., 1974, D of Osteopathy, 1979. Diplomate Am. Osteopathic Bd. Anesthesiology. Intern Saginaw (Mich.) Osteo. Hosp., 1979-80, cons., 1982—; resident in anesthesia Flint (Mich.) Osteo. Hosp., 1980-82; staff anesthesiologist McPherson Community Health Ctr., Howell, Mich., 1982-88, chief of anesthesia services, 1986-88, chmn. dept. anesthesia, 1986, McPherson Cmty. Health Ctr., 1988; staff anesthesiologist Mid-Mich. Regional Med. Ctr., Midland, Mich., 1988—, cons. privileges anesthesia Clare, 1991-99, med. dir., chmn. dept. anesthesia Midland, 1994-96; pres. Mid-Mich. Anesthesiology Group, P.C., 1998—. Examiner Am. Osteo. Bd. Anesthesiologists, 1990—; assoc. clin. prof. Mich. State U. East Lansing, 1982—; lectr. Mich. Osteo. Med. Ctr., Detroit, 1986; program chmn. Am. Osteo. Coll. Anesthesiologist Ann. Conv. and Sci. Seminar, 1990. Legis. asst. to Thomas Holcomb State Rep., 1974-75; physician liaison United Way, Livingston County, Mich., 1986. Recipient Richard P. Alper Meml. award for Community Service, Mich. State U., 1979. Fellow Am. Osteo. Coll. Anesthesiologists (bd. govs., v.p. 1996-97, pres.-elect 1997-98, pres. 1998-99); mem. Am. Osteo. Assn. (residency insp. 1994—), Mich. Assn. Osteo. Physicians and Surgeons (del. 1985-89, numerous coms.), Livingston County Osteo. Assn. (sec.-treas. 1984-86), Mich. Soc. Osteo. Anesthesiologists (pres. 1988-90, chmn. bd. trustees 1990-92), Mich. Soc. Anesthesiologists (dir. 1999-2001, sec.-treas. 2001—), Am. Soc. Anesthesiologists, Mich. State Med. Soc. (del. 1993-98), Midland County Med. Soc. (sec.-treas. 1993, v.p. 1994, pres. 1995), Mich. State U. Alumni Assn., Jaycees, Sigma Sigma Phi (founding chpt. pres. 1977). Methodist. Avocations: golf, skiing, Corvette restoration, hunting, fishing. Home and Office: 2367 Deer Valley Rd Midland MI 48642-8800

SNYDER, ROGER ALAN, physician, neurologist; b. Phila., Apr. 8, 1939; s. Harry Z. and Ida Snyder; m. Margaret Zemel, June 23, 1962 (div. Apr. 1996); children: Richard Owen, Karen Dana. AB, Harvard Coll., 1961; MD, U. Pa., 1965. Diplomate Am. Bd. Psychiatry and Neurology. Intern , med. resident U. Rochester, 1965-67; rsch. assoc. NIH, 1967-70; neurology resident U. Pa., 1970-73; fellow Mass Eye and Ear Infirmary, 1972; clin. instr. Georgetown U. Med. Ctr., Washington, 1974-76, clin. asst. prof., 1976—. Bd. dirs. N.Va. chpt. Am. Heart Assn., 1979-83. Fellow Am. Acad. Neurology; mem. Harvard Alumni Assn. (dir. 1990-93), Harvard Club (Washington, pres. 1986-88). Avocations: sailing, tennis. Office: 8316 Arlington Blvd Ste 602 Fairfax VA 22031-5216

SNYDER, ROGER B. music educator; b. St. Paul, Dec. 19, 1950; s. Paul E. and Marye R. Snyder; m. Joanne M. Halloran, Aug. 14, 1971; children: Seth, Kirk. BS in Music Edn. with distinction, U. Minn., 1972, MA in Music Edn., 1975. Cert. music tchr. Minn., tchr. K-12 Minn. Band dir. Kenyon Pub. Schs., Minn., 1972—74, 1975—77; dir. instrumental music Golden Valley Luth. Coll., Mpls., 1977—85; band director-h.s. Byron Pub. Schs., 1985—2001; band dir. Byron Mid. Sch., 2001—. Chorus mem. Faribault Chpt. Barbershop Chorus, Minn., 1972—74; orch. mem. Cannon Valley Regional Orch., Northfield, Minn., 1980—85; founding mem. Northfield Brass Quintet, Minn., 1980—85, Dir.'s Brass Quintet, Kenyon, 1985—90; band mem. Rochester Civic Music Concert Band, Minn., 1990—95; quintet mem. Rochester Brassworks, 1992—; head dept. music Byron Schs. , 1985—2002; mem. Mid. Sch. Site Coun., 2001—02, Site Based Team, 1996—2001, Dist. Facilities Com., 2001—02, Dist. Staff Devel. Com., 2001—02. Grantee Sudden Opportunity grantee-concert sponsorship, Southeastern Minn. Arts Coun., 1997. Mem.: Byron Edn. Assn. (v.p. 1989—90, pres. 1990—91), Minn. Music Educator's Assn. (region rep. 2002). Office: Byron Mid Sch 630 1st Ave NW Byron MN 55920 Business E-Mail: roger.snyder@byron.k12.mn.us.

SNYDER, SANDRA M. massage therapist; b. Abington, Pa., Jan. 4, 1955; d. Frederick E. Snyder and Josephine S. Papes; children: Heleana Weber, Christian Weber. Cert. therapeutic massage and bodywork, hypnotherapist Fla. Owner Therapeutic Bodywork, Inc., Port Royal, Pa., 1995. Owner, facilitator Tranquility Retreat Ctr., Port Royal, Pa., 1999. Mem. Am. Massage Therapy Assn., Nat. Psychic Sch. Metaphysics, Internat. Assn. Health Care Practitioners. Home and Office: 624 Washington Ave Mifflintown PA 17059-1414 E-mail: tranquill@acsworld.net.

SNYDER, SHANE ALLEN, chemist, educator; b. York, Pa., Sept. 30, 1969; s. Richard Lee Snyder, Rebecca Ann Snyder. BA, Thiel Coll., 1994; PhD, Mich. State U., 2000. Rsch. asst. Mich. State U., East Lansing, Mich., 1994—2000; sr. scientist Total Environ. Solutions, Inc., Henderson, Nev., 1998—2002; adj. assoc. prof. U. of Nev., Las Vegas, Las Vegas, 2000—02; adj. prof. C.C. of So. Nev., 2000—02; R&D project mgr. So. Nev. Water Authority , Boulder City. Mem. endocrine disruptor methods validation subcom. Environ. Protection Agy., Washington, 2002—. Contbr. author Instrumental and Bioanalytical Measures of Endocrine Disruptors in Water, 2000, Pharmaceuticals and Personal Care Products in the Environment: Methods, Analyses, and Sources, 2001; contbr. articles. Grantee, Chem. Mfrs. Assn., 1998—2000, So. Nev. Water Authority and U.S. Bur. Reclamation, 1998—2000, U.S. Dept. Def., 2000—02, Am. Water Works Assn. Rsch. Found., 2000—. Mem.: AAAS, Soc. Environ. Toxicology and Chemistry, Am. Chem. Soc., Am. Water Works Assn., Sigma Xi. Office: Southern Nev Water Authority 243 Lakeshore Rd Boulder City NV 89014 Office Fax: 702-564-7222. Business E-Mail: shane.snyder@lvvwd.com.

SNYDER, SOLOMON HALBERT, psychiatrist, pharmacologist; b. Washington, Dec. 26, 1938; s. Samuel Simon and Patricia (Yakerson) S.; m. Elaine Borko, June 10, 1962; children: Judith Rhea, Deborah Lynn. MD cum laude, Georgetown U., 1962, DSc (hon.), 1986, Northwestern U., 1981; PhD (hon.), Ben Gurion U., 1990; DSc (hon.) , Technion Inst., 2002. Intern Kaiser Found. Hosp., San Francisco, 1962-63; rsch. assoc. NIMH, Bethesda, Md., 1963-65; resident psychiatry Johns Hopkins Hosp., Balt., 1965-68; assoc. prof. psychiatry and pharmacology Johns Hopkins Med. Sch., 1968-70, prof., 1970-77, disting. svc. prof. psychiatry and pharmacology, 1977-80, disting. svc. prof. neurosci., psychiatry, and pharmacology, 1980—, dir. dept. neurosci., 1980—. NIH lectr., 1979; Nicholas Giarman lectr. Yale U., 1975; Salmon lectr., 77; Harvey lectr., 78; Paul K. Smith Meml. lectr. George Washington U., 1986; Julius Axelrod lectr. CUNY, 1988, 2001; John Flynn Meml. lectr. Yale U., 1988; V. Erspamer lectr. Georgetown U., 1990; Chauncey Leake lectr., 92; William Veatch lectr. Harvard Med. Sch., 1992; Kinrad Bloch lectr. Harvard U., 1992; basic neurochemistry lectr. Am. Soc. Neurochemistry, 1993; Nanine Duke lectr. Duke U., 1993; Salvador Luria lectr. MIT, 1993; Rudin lectr. Columbia U., 1995; Christian Herter lectr. NYU, 1995; Maclean lectr. Baylor Med. Coll., 1995; Nancy Pritzker lectr. Stanford U., 1998; Yahr lectr. Mt. Sinai Med. Sch., 1998; Bidwell lectr. MIT, 1999; O'Donohue Meml. lectr. Howard U., 1999; Wellcome disting. prof. U. Wash., 1999; Stokes lectr. U. Pa., 2001; Kuffler lectr. U. Calif., San Diego, 2002. Author: Uses of Marijuana, 1971, Madness and the Brain, 1973, Opiate Receptor Mechanisms, 1975, The Troubled Mind, 1976, Biologic Aspects of Mental Disorder, 1980, Drugs and the Brain, 1986, Brainstorming, 1989; editor Perspectives in Neuropharmacology, 1971, Frontiers in Catecholamine Research, 1973, Handbook of Psychopharmacology, 1974; contbr. articles to profl. jours. Served with USPHS, 1963-65. Recipient Outstanding Scientist award, Md. Acad. Scis., 1969, John Jacob Abel award, Am. Pharmacology Soc., 1970, A.E. Bennett award, Soc. Biol. Psychiatry, 1970, Gaddum award, Brit. Pharm. Soc., 1974, F.O. Schmitt award in neuroscis., MIT, 1974, Rennebohm award, U. Wis., 1976, Stanley Dean award, Am. Coll. Psychiatrists, 1978, Lasker award, 1978, Wolf prize, 1983, Dickson prize, 1983, Sci. Achievement award, AMA, 1985, Ciba-Giegy-Drew award, 1985, Strecker prize, 1986, Edward Sachar Meml. award, Columbia U., 1986, Sense of Smell award, Fragrance Rsch. Found., 1987, J. Allyn Taylor prize, 1990, Pasarow Found. award, 1991, Bower award, Achievement Sci. Franklin Inst., 1991, Joseph Priestley prize, Dickinson Coll., 1992, Baxter award, Am. Assn. Med. Colls., 1995, Bristol-Myers-Squibb Neurosci. prize, 1996, City of Medicine award, 2000, Gerard prize, Soc. Neurosci., 2000, Salmon medal, 2001, Lieber prize, NARSAD, 2001. Fellow: Am. Philos. Soc., Am. Acad. Arts and Scis., Am. Psychiat. Assn. (Hofheimer award 1972, Disting. Svc. award 1989, Judd Marnor award 2000), Am. Coll. Neuropsychopharmacology (Daniel Efron award 1974); mem.: Inst. Medicine, Am. Pharmacology Soc., Am. Soc. Biol. Chemists, Soc. for Neurosci. (pres. 1979—80, Presdl. lectr. 2000, History of Neurosci. lectr. 2001), Nat. Acad. Scis. (Sarnat prize in mental health 2001). Home: 3801 Canterbury Rd Unit 1001 Baltimore MD 21218-2379 Office: Johns Hopkins U Med Sch Dept Neurosciences 725 N Wolfe St Baltimore MD 21205-2105

SNYDER, SUSAN LEACH, science educator, writer; b. Columbus, Ohio, Nov. 25, 1946; d. Russell and Helen Marie (Sharpe) Leach; m. James Floyd Snyder, June 18, 1988. BS in comprehensive sci. edn., Miami U., 1968; MS in entomology, U. Hawaii, 1970. Gen. and health sci. tchr. Columbus Pub. Schs., 1971-73; life, earth & physical sci. tchr. Upper Arlington (Ohio) Schs., 1975—2000. Author: The Ocean Environment, 1992, 96; co-author: Focus on Earth Science, 1987, 89, Merrill Earth Science, 1993, 95. Glencoe Earth Science, 1997, 99, 2002, The Air Around Us, 2002, The Changing Surface of Earth, 2002, The Water Planet, 2002; mem. author team: Science Interactions, 1993, 95, 98, Science Voyages, 2000, 2001; contbr. articles to profl. jours. Trustee N.Am. Astrophys. Obs., Delaware, Ohio, 1983-97; pres. Consortium of Aquatic and Marine Educators Ohio, 1983-84; sec. Ohio chpt. Nat. Tchrs. of Yr., 1993-95; docent, vol. Conservancy of S.W. Fla. Mus. Natural History. Named Outstanding Earth Sci. Tchr. of State of Ohio and East Cen Sect. Nat. Assn. Geology Tchrs., 1983, Ohio Tchr. of Yr. Ohio State Dept. Edn., 1987, Finalist Nat. Tchr. of Yr. Coun. of Chief State Sch. Officers, 1987; Pres. award for Excellence in Sci. and Math Teaching Nat. Sci. Tchrs. Assn., 1992, Outstanding Tchr. award Geological Soc. Am., 1992. Mem. Nat. Sci. Tchrs. Assn. (Exemplary Earth Sci. Teaching Team 1983, 84, 85, conf. workshop presenter 1985), Nat. Marine Educators Assn. (Nat. Outstanding Marine Sci. Tchr. 1984, bd. mem. 1984, 2000-02, conf. workshop presenter 1983, 84, 86, 92), Great Lakes Educators of Aquatic and Marine Scis. Avocation: photography. Home: 1361 Marlyn Dr Columbus OH 43220-3973

SNYDER, TERESA ANN, medical/surgical nurse; b. Evansville, Ind., Mar. 4, 1946; d. Stephen Michael and Fredricka Otilia (Memmer) Kurtz; m. James Howard Snyder, June 12, 1976; children: Katrina Michelle, Jacqueline Sue. Diploma, Lakewood (Ohio) Sch. Practical Nursing, 1965; BSN, U. Akron, 1989. Emergency room nurse Parma (Ohio) Community Hosp.; cardiac nurse Cleve. Clinic Found.; neuro-sci. and med.-surg. nurse Akron (Ohio) City Hosp. Acting mem., corr. sec., pres. Summa Nursing Senate, Summa Health Care, Akron City Hosp. V.p. Chatham Vol. Fire and Rescue Assn. Mem. Acad. Med. Surg. Nurses (bd. dirs. N.E. chpt.), N.E. Ohio chpt. Acad. Med. Surg. Nursing (gen. bd. mem., exec. bd. dirs., recording sec., pres. elect 2001-2002), Sigma Theta Tau. Home: 10145 Shaw Rd Spencer OH 44275-9306

SNYDER, TERRY, filmmaker, educator; MFA, U. of So. Calif., Los Angeles, CA, 81—84; MA, Fairfield U., Fairfield, CT, 1980—81, BA, 1974—78. Assoc. prof. NY Inst. of Tech., New York, NY. Prodr.: (film development project) Whisper In My Ear. Office: New York Institute of Technology 1855 Broadway New York NY 10023

SNYDER, TRAVIS CARROLL, evangelist; b. Apr. 9, 1942; s. L.B. and Eula Jean Snyder; children: Trevor Arnoult, Syndy Susanne. Student, Bethany Nazarene Coll., Bethany, Okla., 1960-62; BS, U. Ark., 1964; MS, La. State U., Baton Rouge, 1970. Rschr., tchr. La. State U., Baton Rouge, 1965-67; indsl. chemist Dowell, Arco, Union, Tulsa, 1970-82; owner SEE, Inc., 1982-83; quality control mgr. Bama Pie Inc., 1983-84; prophet of God Tahlequah, Okla., 1969—. Patentee in field of chemistry. With USMC, 1967-69, USAR, 1979-91. Avocations: biking, weight lifting, swimming, walking. Home: 325 S College Ave # C Tahlequah OK 74464-4417

SNYDER, VIC, congressman, physician; b. Medford, Oreg., Sept. 27, 1947; BA in Chemistry, Willamette U., 1975; MD, U. Oreg. Health Scis. Ctr., 1979; JD, U. Ark., Little Rock, 1988. Resident family practice U. Ark. Med. Scis., 1979-82; physician family practice Ark., 1982—; mem. Ark. State Senate, 1991-96, U.S. Ho. Reps. from 2d Ark. dist., 1996—. Med. missions to Cambodian regufee camps, Thailand, El Salvadoran regufee camps, Honduras, mission hosp., Sierra Leone, Africa, Ethiopian refugee camp, Sudan. With USMC, 1967-69. Democrat. Office: 1319 Longworth House Office Bl Washington DC 20515-0402 also: 3118 Fed Bldg 700 W Capitol Ave Little Rock AR 72201-3225 E-mail: snyder.congress@mail.house.gov.*

SNYDER, WESLEY WARREN, interior space planner and designer; b. Chgo., June 4, 1935; s. Warren Elmore and Grace Elizabeth (Gray) S. BS in Gen. Speech, Northwestern U., Evanston, Ill., 1958; student, Chgo. Art Inst., 1964. Furniture sales trainee Heywood Wakefield Co., Chgo., 1960-62; med. space planner and designer V. Mueller & Co., 1962-63; mgr. wholesale showroom Charles L. Orr, Inc., 1963-68; owner, pres., prin. designer Cristies of Chgo., Inc., 1968-81; instr. interior design Ringling Sch. of Art and Design, Sarasota, Fla., 1981-82; div. mgr. Comml. Designs by Saba, 1983; sr. designer Lambert Interiors, 1983-84; sales rep. Wagner Office Furniture, Tampa, Fla., 1984-85; v.p. and design dir. Office Design and Supplies, Inc., Sarasota, 1985-87; pres. Cristies Design Group, 1988-98, 2000—, Cristies Collection, Sarasota, 1992-98, Kane's Furniture of Sarasota, 1998-2000. Mem. Landmark Preservation Coun. of Ill., 1972-79, exec. v.p., 1974, mem. city house preservation fair founding com. City of Chgo., 1979; mem. Inst. Bus Designers, Chgo., 1973-84, pres. Chgo. Regional chpt., 1978-79, nat. trustee, 1979-81; vice chmn. Sarasota County Arts Coun., 1986-89; lectr. in field. Designer various bldgs., including Northwestern U., No. Ill. U., DeKalb, Ill. State U., Luth. Gen. Hosp., Des Plaines, Ill., Cen. Maloney, Arcadia, Fla., Sarasota Bank, Nokomis br. trust and ops. depts. 1st Nat. Bank Venice, Cafe Baci, Sarasota, Key West Fish House, Naples, Bermuda Bay Cafe, Osprey, Fla., House of Chang, Bradenton, Fla., 1st of Englewood Bank, Guaranty Bank & Trust Bd. Room, Ops. Ctr., Jacaranda Br., Venice, Fla., Marudianna Estate, Boca Grande, Fla., Sarasota Chamber Office, also residences, Long Boat, Siesta Keys, Anna Maria Island, Bird Key, Venice, Fla., Riverwoods, Ill., Lake Forest, Ill.; author: Building a Home, How to Get It Right the First Time, 2000; contbr. articles to profl. jours. and local press. Mem. adv. bd. Inst. Psychiatry, Northwestern Meml. Hosp., 1975-81, Chrysalis Learning Ctr., 1977-80; active Oak Park Music Theatre, 1967-72, Am. Cancer Soc. Bid for Bachelors, 1987, Jail and Bail, 1991; mem. alumni steering com. Speech Sch., Northwestern U., 1970-81, Chorus of Keys, Soc. for Preservation Barbershop Quartet Singing in Am.; chmn. ann. show, 1984, 85, v.p. membership com., 1985; grad. Leadership Sarasota, 1986, co-chmn. alumni program steering com., 1989, chmn. Arts Day, 1986-90, mem. steering com., 1990. Recipient Pres.'s award Chgo. region Inst. Bus. Designers, 1981. Mem. AIA (affiliate 1983-89), Am. Soc. Interior Designers (mem. steering com. Fla. chpt. 1982-96, v.p. North Fla. chpt. 1985, 89-90, chmn. design resource show 1985-91, local chmn. 1986, 89-90, Presdl. citation 1986, Spl. Recognition award 1989-90, Svc. awards 1991, 92, 93, 94, 95, 96, 98, 99, Fla. West Coast chpt. foradrion com. 1999-2000), Sarasota County C. of C. (chmn. amb. and consul program 1986-88, mem. bd. 1987-91, vice chair membership 1989, chmn. Sarasota AM-Monthly broadcast event), Northwestern Alumni of Chgo. (bd. dirs. 1978-79, newsletter editor), John Evans Club (Chgo.), Kiwanis (v.p. Sarasota Sunrise chpt., bd. dirs., program chmn. 1985-86, newsletter writer 1987-88, Spl. award 1985, Bell award 1986, Editors award 1987), Masons, Northwestern U. Alumni Club (program chmn. 2000-01, pres. Sarasota/Manatee 2001—), Delta Tau Delta (mem. alumni house bd., Spl. Svc. award 1981). Independent. Avocations: singing, entertaining at retirement residences, writing, gardening, reading. Home: 720 47th St Sarasota FL 34234-4524 Office: Cristies Design Group 720 47th St Sarasota FL 34234 Fax: (841) 358-3984. E-mail: wessnyder2@earthlink.net.

SNYDER, WILLARD BREIDENTHAL, lawyer; b. Kansas City, Kans., Dec. 18, 1940; s. N.E. and Ruth (Breidenthal) S.; m. Lieselotte Dieringer, Nov. 10, 1970 (dec. Nov. 1975); 1 child, Rolf; m. T.J. Sewall, May 17, 1996. BA, U. Kans., 1962, JD, 1965; postgrad., Hague Acad. Internat. Law, The Netherlands, 1965-66, U. Dijon, France, 1966; grad., Command and Gen. Staff Coll., Ft. Leavenworth, Kans., 1977. Bar: Kans. 1965, Mo. 1986, U.S. Tax Ct. 1977, U.S. Ct. Mil. Appeals 1981, U.S. Dist. Ct. Kans. 1965, U.S. Supreme Ct. 1977. Atty., Kansas City, 1970-80, 85—; trust officer, corp. trust officer Security Nat. Bank., 1980-83, corp. sec., 1983-85; pres. Real Estate Corp. Inc., Leawood, Kans., 1984—; adv. dir. United Mo. Bank, 1985-90. Bd. dirs. Blue Ridge Bank, mem. trust and investment com., 1991—; German Consul (H) for Kans., Western Mo., 1972—. Mem. Platte Woods (Mo.) City Coun., 1983-84; mem. exec. bd. dirs. regional coun. Boy Scouts Am.; 1st v.p. Liberty Meml. Assn.; mem. nomination com. MacJannett Found., Talloires, France; chmn. Breidenthal-Snyder Found.; mem. nominating and exec. com. Hoover Pres. Libr.; bd. dirs. Unicorn Theatre, KCKs Cmty. Found.; trustee St. Mary Coll., 1998-2001; dir. Wy. Co. Kans. Cmty. Found., Kansas City Metro Crime Com, The Unicorn Theater. Col. ret. USAR & KARNG. Decorated Bundensverdienst Kreuz, 1982, BVK 1KL (Germany), 1992, Bundeswehr Kreuz (silver), 1987, Ge. Abn., Legion of Merit; KARNG medal of excellence; named to Hon. Order Ky. Cols., 1988; recipient Golden Honour badge German Vet. Orgn., Bavaria, 1988, Mil. Order of WW award, OCS Hall of Fame. Mem. Mo. Bar Assn., Kansas City Bar Assn., Kansas City Hosp. Attys., Mil. Order of World Wars (chpt. comdr. 1983-84, regional comdr. 1987-91, Patrick Henry award), Nat. Eagle Scout Assn. Avocations: scuba, hunting, Notgeld collections, cartridge collection. Office: 8014 State Line Rd Ste 203 Shawnee Mission KS 66208-3712

SNYDER, WILLIAM BRANDON, linguistics educator; b. Norfolk, Va., Nov. 27, 1966; s. William Ramsey and Annie Redd Snyder. SB, MIT, 1989, PhD, 1995. Rsch. intern Mass. Gen. Hosp., Boston, 1989-90; asst. prof. linguistics U. Conn., Storrs, 1995—. Rsch. scientist Haskins Labs., New Haven, 1998—. Editor: Formal Approaches to Slavic Linguistics: The Connecticut Meeting, 1998; contbr. articles to profl. jours. NIH co-grantee, 1998-2002. Mem. AAAS, Linguistic Soc. Am., Internat. Assn. for Study of Child Lang., Sigma Xi.

SNYDER, WILLIAM BURTON, insurance company executive; b. Clarksburg, W.Va., July 9, 1929; s. William Burton and Mary Catherine (Cornwell) Snyder; m. Georgie Gaye, Oct. 27, 1951 (dec.); children: William Burton, Melissa Ann. BBA in Acctg. cum laude, Tex. Tech U., 1955. With Travelers Ins. Co., 1955-77, v.p., 1970-77; with Govt. Employees Ins. Co., Washington, 1977-93; chmn., pres., CEO GEICO Corp., 1985-93; gen. ptnr. Merastar Ptnrs. LLP, 1993—. Bd. dirs. CACI, Inc., Doctor's Preferred, Inc., Auto Body Am., Inc.; mem. adv. bd. Riggs Nat. Bank. Past chmn., mem. econ. adv. coun. Montgomery County; bd. dirs. Nat. Capital Area coun. Boy Scouts Am. Capt. USAF, 1950—53. Decorated Air medal. Mem.: Nat. Assn. Ind. Insurers (hon.; past chmn.), Kenwood Country Club (Bethesda, Md.). Republican. Baptist.

SNYDER, WILLIAM IRWIN, secondary school educator, artist; b. Detroit, Sept. 22, 1948; s. William Douglas Snyder and Jane Grace Caroll; m. Mary Louise Case, Aug. 1, 1975; children: Merrill Snyder-Case, Albert Snyder-Case. BA, Ctrl. Mich. U., 1975, MA, 1983. Artist HAMBONES Going Over, Saginaw, Mich., 1976—2002; tchr. Swan Valley H.S., 1979—2002. Mem.: ACLU, NCTE. Home: 1485 North River Rd Saginaw MI 48609-4231 Office: HAMBONES Going Over 314 S Hamilton St Saginaw MI 48602-2015 Home Fax: 989-781-0377; Office Fax: 989-781-0377. E-mail: wsnyder@snyder.net.

SNYDER, PH.D. CAROLYN L. SMITH, pharmaceutical executive; m. Mike Snyder; children: S Snyder, N Snyder. PhD, U. Pa, Phila., 1986. Sr. dir., med. writing Johnson & Johnson Pharm. R&D, Raritan, NJ, 1992—.

SNYDERMAN, RALPH, medical educator, physician; b. Bklyn., Mar. 13, 1940; m. Judith Ann Krebs, Nov. 18, 1967; 1 child, Theodore Benjamin BS, Washington Coll., Chestertown, Md., 1961; MD magna cum laude, SUNY, Bklyn., 1965, DSc (hon.) Health Sci. Ctr., 1996. Diplomate Am. Bd. Internal Medicine, Am. Bd. Allergy and Immunology. Med. intern Duke U. Hosp., Durham, N.C., 1965-66, med. resident, 1966-67; public health officer NIH, 1967-72; Howard Hughes med. investigator, asst. prof. medicine and immunology Duke U. Hosp., Durham, N.C., 1972-74, assoc. prof., 1974-77, chief divsn. rheumatology and immunology, 1975-87, prof. medicine and immunology, 1980-87, Frederic M. Hanes prof. medicine and immunology, 1984-87, adj. prof. medicine, 1987-89; surgeon USPHS, NIH, Bethesda, Md., 1967-69; sr. staff fellow Nat. Inst. Dental Rsch., NIH, 1969-70, sr. investigator immunology sect. lab. microbiology and immunology, 1970-72; chief divsn. rheumatology Durham VA Hosp., 1972-75; v.p. med. rsch. and devel. Genentech, Inc., South San Francisco, Calif., 1987-88, sr. v.p. med. rsch. and devel., 1988-89; chancellor for health affairs, dean Sch. Medicine Duke U., Durham, 1989-99, James B. Duke prof. medicine, 1989—, chancellor for health affairs, exec. dean Sch. Medicine, 1999—; pres., CEO Duke U. Health Sys., 1999—. Howard Hughes med. investigator, Durham, 1972-77; dir. Lab Immune Effector Function, Howard Hughes Med. Inst., Durham, 1977-87; adj. prof. medicine U. Calif., San Francisco, 1987-89; chmn. coun. of deans Assn. Am. Med. Colls., 1999-2000, assn. chmn., 2001-02. Editor: Contemporary Topics in Immunobiology, 1979, Inflammation: Basic Concepts and Clinical Correlates, 1988, 2nd edit., 1992, Medical Clinics of North America, 1997, Journ. Integrated Med., 1997, Proceedings of Amer. Physician, 1997; contbr. articles to profl. jours. Recipient McLaughlin award for inflammation rsch., 1978, Alexander von Humboldt award Fed. Republic Germany, 1985, award for lifetime achievements in inflammation rsch. Ciba-Geigy Morris Ziff, 1992, Bonazinga award for excellence in leukocyte biology rsch. Soc. for Leukocyte Biology, 1993, Disting. Alumni Achievement award SUNY Bklyn., 1995, Disting. Alumni Achievement award Washington Coll., 1995, Disting. Alumni citation, 1996, Lifetime Achievement award Arthritis Found., Eastern Reg., 1997, Lifetime Achievement award Argentine Nat. Acad. Medicine, 1998, others. Mem.: NAS, Soc. for Med. Adminstrs., Assn. Am. for Med. Colls. (chair task force on clin. rsch. 1998, chmn. coun. deans 1999—2000, chmn. 2001—), Am. Coll. Rheumatology, Assn. Acad. Health Ctrs., Am. Soc. for Biochemistry and Molecular Biology, Am. Assn. Pathologists, Am. Fedn. Clin. Rsch., Soc. for Leukocyte Biology, Am. Assn. Cancer Rsch., Am. Acad. Allergy, Am. Soc. Clin. Investigation, Am. Assn. Immunologists, Assn. Am. Physicians, Inst. Medicine, Sigma Xi. Office: Duke U M106 Davison Bldg Box 3701 Med Ctr & Health System Durham NC 27710-0001

SNYDERMAN, SELMA ELEANORE, pediatrician, educator; b. Phila., July 22, 1916; d. Harry Samuel and Rose (Koss) S.; m. Joseph Schein, Aug. 4, 1939; children: Roland M. H., Oliver Douglas. AB, U. Pa., 1937, MD, 1940. Diplomate Am. Bd. of Physician Nutrition Specialists, Am. Bd. Pediatrics. Intern Einstein Med. Ctr., Phila., 1940-42; resident Bellevue Hosp., N.Y.C., 1944-45; fellow NYU Med. Ctr., 1945-46; instr. pediat. NYU Sch. Medicine, 1946-50, asst. prof., 1950-57, assoc. prof., 1957-67, prof., 1967-95; assoc. prof. U. Tex. Med. Br., Galveston, 1952-53; attending physician Bellevue Hosp., 1947—; dir. Pediatric Metabolic Disease Ctr. Bellevue Med. Ctr., 1965-95; attending physician Tisch Hosp., N.Y.C., 1947-95; prof. human genetics and pediat., attending physician Mt. Sinai Med. Ctr., 1995—, dir. Metabolic Disease Ctr., 1995—. Mem. nutrition study sect. NIH, Bethesda,

Md., 1973-77. Contbr. numerous med. articles to profl. jours. Named career scientist Health Rsch. Coun., 1961-75. Fellow Am. Acad. Pediatrics (Borden award 1975); mem. Am. Inst. Nutrition, Am. Pediatric Soc., Soc. for Pediatric Rsch., Am. Soc. Clin. Nutrition, Soc. Inherited Metabolic Disorders (v.p. 1978, pres. 1979, bd. dirs. 1980-83), Soc. Parenteral and Enteral Nutrition, Soc. for Study of Inborn Errors of Metabolism, Phi Beta Kappa. Jewish. Avocations: gardening, orchid growing, reading. Office: Mount Sinai Med Ctr Dept Human Genetics Fifth Ave & 100th St New York NY 10029 E-mail: selma_snyderman@mssm.edu.

SNYDERS, DIRK JOHAN, electrophysiologist, biophysicist, educator; b. Wilrijk, Antwerpen, Belgium, July 18, 1955; came to U.S., 1984; s. Godlief Stefaan and Mariette L. (Dieu) S. BS in Med. Sci., U. Antwerp, Belgium, 1976; MD with great honor, U. Antwerp, 1980. Lic. physician, cert. cardiologist, Belgium. Resident then fellow in internal medicine and cardiology Univ. Hosp. Antwerp, 1980-84; postdoctoral fellow U. Calif., San Francisco, 1984-85; instr. medicine Vanderbilt U., Nashville, 1986-87, asst. prof., 1987-95, assoc. prof. medicine and pharmacology, 1995—. With V.I.B. dept. biophysics and pharmacology Antwerp (Belgium) U., 1998—99; prof. biochemistry U. Antwerp, 1998—, vice-chair dept. biochemistry, 1999—2001, chair dept. biomed. scis., 2001—. Co-author: The Heart and the Cardiovascular System, 1991; mem. editorial bd. Circulation Rsch.; reviewer Jour. Gen. Physiology, Cardiovascular Rsch., Jour. Molecular and Cellular Cardiology, Molecular Pharmacology, European Jour. Pharmacology, Biophys. Jour., Jour. Biol. Chemistry; contbr. articles to profl. jours. Lt. Med. Svc., Belgian Army, 1987-88, Germany. Recipient Specia award Specia NV., Belgium, 1980; hon. fellow Belgian Am. Ednl. Found., NATO rsch. fellow, 1984, med. rsch. fellow Alta. Heritage Found., 1984; rsch. grantee NIH, Am. Heart Assn. Mem. AAAS, Biophys. Soc., Soc. Gen. Physiologists, Am. Heart Assn. (Basic Sci. Coun.). Achievements include research on mechanism of action of "specific bradycardiac agents", use-dependent unblocking and voltage clamp validation of modulated receptor theory (cardiac sodium channels and antiarrhythmic agents), electrophysiology and pharmacology of cloned, molecular localisation of antiarrhythmic drug binding sites, cardiac potassium channels (including human), molecular ion channel structure-function relationships, molecular basis of congenital excitability disorders. Office: Antwerp U Dept Biochemistry Universiteitsplein 1 T4 2160 Antwerp Belgium Address: Fazantenlaan 6 Antwerp B2610 Belgium E-mail: dirk.snyders@ua.ac.be.

SNYDMAN, DAVID RICHARD, infectious diseases specialist, educator; b. Phila., Sept. 23, 1946; m. Diane Canter, June 26, 1971; children: Laura Kate, Alexander Julian. BA, Williams Coll., 1968; MD, U. Pa., 1972. Diplomate Am Bd. Infectious Disease, Am. Bd. Internal Medicine. Intern New Eng. Med. Ctr., Boston, 1972-73, resident in medicine, 1973-74; asst. prof. Sch. Medicine Tufts U., 1979-84, assoc. prof., 1984-90, prof. medicine and pathology, 1990—; hosp. epidemiologist New Eng. Med. Ctr., 1979-89, 1998—, dir. clin. microbiology, 1987-98, chief divsn. infectious diseases, 1998—. Epidemic Intelligence Svc. officer CDC, Atlanta, 1974-76. Assoc. editor: Yearbook of Infectious Diseases, 1986-98; contbr. over 140 articles to profl. jours. Lt. comdr. USPHS, 1974-76. Grantee NIH, 1982-93; recipient U. Pa. A.O.J. Kelly prize, 1972, Tufts U. Sch. Medicine Zucker prize, 1998. Fellow Infectious Disease Soc. (Bristol fellow 1978-79); mem. ACP (Tchng. and Rsch. scholar 1979-82), Soc. Hosp. Epidemiologists, Am. Soc. Transplant Physicians. Achievements include first description of Lyme arthritis; rsch. in hosp. infections, intravenous catheter-associated infections, transplant-related infectious diseases, antibiotic resistance, sepsis, cytomegalovirus prevention; developer of cytomegalovirus immune globulin. Office: New Eng Med Ctr 750 Washington St Boston MA 02111-1526 E-mail: DSnydman@lifespan.org.

SO, YING-HUNG, chemistry researcher; b. Hong Kong, Apr. 8, 1948; came to U.S., 1973; s. Wah and Yuen-Yan (Siu) So; m. Dora Tsui Dang, Apr. 22, 1978; children: Albert J., Lisa M. BS with honors, Chinese U. of Hong Kong, 1971; PhD in Organic Chemistry, Colo. State U., 1977; postdoctoral appointment, U. B.C., 1977-79, U. Minn., 1979-81. Sr. rsch. chemist. Ctrl. Rsch. Polymers Dow Chem. Co., Midland, Mich., 1981-84, project leader Ctrl. Rsch.-Polymeric Materials, 1984-89, rsch. leader CR&D-Advanced Composites Lab., 1989-93, rsch. assoc. CR&D-Advanced Composites Lab., 1993-94, R & D leader CR&D/new bus.-electronics, 1995—. Vis. assoc. prof. U. Hong Kong, 1997—; H.S. sci. tchr. Sacred Heart Cannosian Coll., Hong Kong, 1971-73; sec. Chinese-Am. Chem. Soc., 1990-94. Contbr. more than 40 articles to profl. jours.; holder 16 U.S. and world patents. Mem. Am. Chem. Soc. (com. mem. regional meeting 1990), Materials Rsch. Soc. Avocations: tennis, travel. Home: 1524 Dilloway Dr Midland MI 48640-2786 Office: The Dow Chem Co Bldg 1712 Midland MI 48674-0001

SOARES, CARL LIONEL, quality control engineer, metrologist; b. New Bedford, Mass., Sept. 14, 1944; s. Lionel Francis and Sarah Vincent (Flor) S.; m. Jean Rosalee Bettencourt, Nov. 11, 1965 (div. Oct. 1974); children: Kevin Carl, Keith Christopher, Kenneth Craig. Student in Indsl. Tech., Fitchburg State Coll., 1980—. Quality assurance specialist Cornell-Dubilier Electronics, Inc., New Bedford, Mass., 1965-66; computer controlled test equipment technician Raytheon Co., Waltham, Quincy, North Dighton, 1966-79, quality control supt. Waltham, 1982-85, metrologist, dept. quality dir., 1979-96; pres., treas., mgr. S.&O. Cleaning Corp. d/b/a The MAIDS, New Bedford, 1995—. Choir mem. St. James Ch., chair Booster Club Com.; pres. bd. dirs. New Bedford Coun. on Substance Abuse; sec. New Bedford First Night Com. With USN, 1963-65. Mem. Buttonwood Park Zool. Soc. (bd. dirs., first night com., events chmn.), Friends of Dartmouth Librs., New Bedford C. of C., Am. Legion. Roman Catholic. Avocations: gardening, bicycling, records and CDs, home computing, music. Home: 205 Maple St New Bedford MA 02740-3513

SOARES, GREGORY LOUIS, social services executive, consultant; b. Fall River, Mass., Nov. 14, 1951; s. Louis Massa and Hilda (Enos) S.; m. Maria Fatima Fernandes, July 9, 1977 (div. 1982); m. Deborah Ann Smusz, Apr. 28, 1984 (div. 1997); m. Deborah Nelson, 1997. AA in Pre-profl. Studies, Bristol Community Coll., Fall River, Mass., 1971; BA in Psychology, Roger Williams Coll., 1973; MEd in Integrated Studies, Cambridge (Mass.) Coll., 1989. Nat. bd. cert. clin. hypnotherapist. Spl. edn. tchr. St. Vincent's Home, Fall River, 1973-80, coord. vocat. edn. programs, 1980-83; family therapist Edgehill Newport, Newport, R.I., 1983-88, supr. family dept., 1988-90, dir. inpatient/outpatient rehab. svcs., 1992—. Cons., New Eng. area, 1992—; dir. profl. svcs. Family rsch., Inc., 1993-97; dir. Outpatient Svcs., Marathon, Inc. Address: 604 Rose Hill Rd South Kingstown RI 02879-1726

SOARIES, DEFOREST B., JR. former state official; m. Donna Soaries; 2 children. Ph.D (hon.), Drew U.; BA, Fordham U.; MDiv, Princeton Theol. Sem.; DMin, United Theol. Sem., Dayton, Monmouth U. Ordained minister Bapt. Ch., 1990. Sr. pastor First Bapt. Ch. of Lincoln Gardens, Somerset, NJ, 1990—; sec. of state State of N.J., Trenton, 1999—2002. Internat. lectr. in field.; founder First Bapt. Cmty. Devel. Corp., Renaissance Cmty. Devel. Credit Union, CDC Properties, Renaissance Employment & Tng. Acad.; faculty Princeton Theol. Sem., Drew U. Theol. Sch., Kean U., Mercer County Coll. Contbr. articles to profl. jours. Vol. Urban League, Newark, Operation PUSH, Chgo.; advocate for at-risk youth; addressee Pres.'s Summit for Am.'s Future in Phila. Office: First Baptist Church of Lincoln Gardens 630 Franklin Boulevard Somerset NJ 08873*

SOARIES, RAFIKA C. media relations specialist, writer, computer applications educator; b. Bklyn., Mar. 22, 1960; d. John W. Soaries and Lois E. Dimry-Soaries; life ptnr. James T. Gresham; children: Sadat Rafik Muhammad. BA Mass Media Comm., Bklyn Coll., 1984. Program coord., tchr. Phipps Cmty. Devel. Corp., Bronx, NY, 1995—99; media rels. coord. Internat. Arts Found., New Orleans, 2000—02; writer Everybody's Caribbean Mag., Bklyn., 1992—2002; tchr. N.Y.C. Bd. of Edn., 1990—2000; computer applications tchr. Youth Build USA, 2001—02. Home: 669 Winthrop St Brooklyn NY 11203 Office: Zookeeper Media Rels 669 Winthrop St Brooklyn NY 11203 Home Fax: (718) 467-2265; Office Fax: (718) 467-2265. Personal E-mail: Rafika@zookeeperbc.com. Business E-Mail: Rafika@zookeeperbc.com.

SOAVE, ROSEMARY, internist; b. N.Y.C., Jan. 23, 1949; BS, Fordham U., 1970; MD, Cornell Med. Coll., 1976. Diplomate Am. Bd. Internal Medicine, Subspecialty Bd. in Infectious Diseases. Intern, resident N.Y. Hosp., N.Y.C., 1976-79; chief med. resident Meml.-Sloan Kettering Cancer Ctr., 1979-80; fellow infectious diseases N.Y. Hosp., 1980-82, asst. prof. medicine, 1982-89, assoc. prof. medicine and pub. health, 1989—. Spkr. in field; mem. Nat. Insts. Allergy and Infectious Diseases-AIDS and Related Diseases Study Sect. Contbr. numerous articles to profl. jours., chpts. to books, reviews and abstracts to profl. jours. Recipient Mary Putnam Jacobi fellowship for rsch., 1981-82, Leopold Schepp Rsch. fellowship, 1983-84, Nat. Found. for Infectious Diseases Young Investigator Matching Grant award, 1984-85; NIH grantee, 1986-89, 83-86, 87-90, 99-00. Fellow ACP, Infectious Diseases Soc. Am.; mem. AAAS, Am. Fedn. Med. Rsch., N.Y. Acad. Scis., Am. Soc. for Microbiology, Harvey Soc., Sigma Xi. Office: NY Presbyn Hosp Weill Cornell Med Ctr Box 125 1300 York Ave New York NY 10021-4805

SOBANJO, JOHN OLUSEGUN, civil engineering educator, researcher; BS in Civil Engring., U. Lagos, Nigeria, 1980; MS in Civil Engring., U. Mich., 1984; PhD in Civil Engring., Tex. A&M U., 1991. Profl. engr., Tex., Calif. Lectr. Auchi (Nigeria) Poly. U., 1980-81; project engr. Akintobi, Oyenekan & Assocs., Lagos, 1981-82; civil engr. Tex. Dept. Transp., Lufkin, 1986-88; rsch., tchg. asst. Tex. A&M U., College Station, 1988-91; civil engr. Calif. Dept. Transp., L.A., Sacramento, 1991-95; asst. prof. dept. civil engring. Fla. A&M U.-Fla. State U., Tallahassee, 1995—. Contbr. articles to profl. publs. and conf. procs. Judge sci. fair State of Fla., Tallahassee, 1997. Mem. ASCE. Avocations: soccer, movies, travel. Office: FAMU-FSU Dept Civil Engring 2525 Pottsdamer St Rm 129 Tallahassee FL 32310-6046

SOBCZAK, DARLENE MARIE, police officer; b. Chgo., Nov. 17, 1956; d. Richard and Marilyn (Fuesting) Dvorak; children: Christopher B., Gina K. A of Criminal Justice, Morton Coll., 1991; B in Criminal Justice, U. Ill., Chgo., 1993. Police officer Town of Cicero, Ill., 1984—; field tng. officer Cicero Police Dept., 1989—, detective, 1992-95, sgt., 1995—. Pres. Cicero Police Pension Bd. Active PTA, Cicero, 1984—. Named Police Officer of Yr., 1995. Fellow Ill. Police Assn., Fraternal Order Police; mem. Cicero Police Benevolent Assn. (pres. 1985—), Cicero Police Pension Bd. (bd. dirs. 1992—). Address: 4360 N Sturbridge Dr Hoffman Estates IL 60195-1358

SOBCZAK, JUDY MARIE, clinical psychologist; b. Detroit, Dec. 28, 1949; d. Thaddeus Joseph and Bernice Agnes (Sowinski) Gorski; m. John Nicholas Sobczak, Aug. 17, 1974. BE cum laude, U. Toledo, 1971; postgrad., Ea. Mich. U., 1980-82; PhD, U. Toledo, 1987. Lic. psychologist. Tchr. Ottawa (Ohio)-Glandorf Schs., 1971-73; prin., tchr. St. Mary Sch., Assumption, Ohio, 1973-77; tchr. Our Lady of Perpetual Help Sch., Toledo, 1978-79; staff psychologist Outer Dr. Hosp., Lincoln Park, Mich., 1987-90; psychologist Adult/Youth Devel. Svcs., Farmington, 1991-95, Davis Counseling Ctr., Farmington Hills, 1996—; with Northwestern Cmty. Svcs. (now Lifespan Clin. Svcs.), Livonia, 1996-2000, Orchard Hills Psychiat. Ctr., Plymouth, 1996-98. Adj. asst. prof. Madonna U., Livonia, Mich., 1987-94. Eucharistic minister St. Anthony Cath. Ch., Belleville, Mich., 1991—, parish coun. 1993-96; Cath. Svc. Appeal co-chmn., 1993—; sec. bd. dirs. Children Are Precious Respite Care Ctr., 1995. Fellow Mich. Women Psychologists (charter; newsletter editor 1987-92, treas 1989-93, Plaque of Appreciation 1992-96, sec. 1993—, pres.- elect 1997-98, pres. 1998-99, past pres. 1999-2000, consulting editor 1993—); mem. APA, Mich. Psychol. Assn., Phi Kappa Phi. Home: 41498 Mckinley St Belleville MI 48111-3439 Office: Davis Counseling Ctr 37923 W 12 Mile Rd Farmington MI 48331-3035

SOBEL, ALAN, electrical engineer, physicist; b. N.Y.C., Feb. 23, 1928; s. Edward P. and Rose (Naftalison) S.; m. Marjorie Loebel, June 15, 1952; children: Leslie Ann, Edward Robert. BSEE, Columbia U., 1947, MSEE, 1949; PhD in Physics, Poly. Inst. Bklyn., 1964. Lic. Profl. Engr., N.Y. and Ill. Asst. chief engr. The Electronic Workshop, N.Y.C., 1950-51; head, functional engr. Fairchild Controls Corp., 1951-56; project engr. Skiatron Electronics and TV Corp., 1956-57; sr. rsch. engr. Zenith Radio Corp., Glenview, Ill., 1964-78; v.p. Lucitron inc., Northbrook, 1978-87, pres., 1987; pvt. practice cons. Evanston, 1988—; v.p. Machine Vision and Control Internat. Inc., 1994—, LightWave Technologies Corp., 2000—. Asst., instr. Poly. Inst. Bklyn.,1957-64; mem. program coms. SID Internat. Symposium, Internat. Display Rsch. Conf., 1970—. Inventor: 14 patents on various display and electron devices; author 55 papers on electronics, physics, electronic displays, etc.; editor Jour. Soc. Info. Display, 1991—99; adv. editor Info. Display Mag.; assoc. editor: IEEE Trans. on Electron Devices, N.Y., 1970-77. Mem. Democratic Party of Evanston. NSF fellow, 1959, 60. Fellow Soc. Info. Display; mem. IEEE (sr., life), SPIE, Am. Phys. Soc., Sigma Xi. Democrat. Home and Office: 633 Michigan Ave Evanston IL 60202-2552

SOBEL, BURTON ELIAS, physician, educator; b. N.Y.C., Oct. 21, 1937; s. Lawrence J. and Ruth (Schoen) S.; m. Susan Konheim, June 19, 1958; children: Jonathan, Elizabeth. AB, Cornell U., 1958; MD magna cum laude, Harvard U., 1962. Intern Peter Bent Brigham Hosp., Boston, 1962-63, resident, 1963-64, 66-67; clin. asso., cardiology br. NIH, Bethesda, Md., 1964-66, 67-68; asst. prof. medicine U. Calif. at San Diego, La Jolla, 1968-71; asso. prof. medicine, dir. myocardial infarction research unit, dir. coronary care, 1971-73; asso. prof. medicine Barnes Hosp.-Washington U., St. Louis, 1973-75; adj. prof. chemistry Washington U., 1979-94; prof. medicine Barnes Hosp.-Washington U., 1975—, dir. cardiovascular div., 1973—, program dir. specialized ctr. rsch. ischemic heart disease, 1975-89, program dir. specialized ctr. rsch. in coronary and vascular diseases, 1990-94, program dir. principles in cardiovascular rsch., 1975-94; chmn. and prof. medicine, prof. biochemistry U. Vt., Burlington, 1994—; physician-in-chief Med. Ctr. Hosp. Vt., 1994—; physician-in-chief Fletcher Allen Health Care, 1995—. Mem. steering com. In Time Study, 1997—; program dir. Collaborative Clin. Trial Therapy to Protect Ischemic Myocardium, Washington U., 1977; principle investigator BARI, II, NIH Fibrinalysis and Coagulation Core U. Vt., 2000; chmn. cardio renal drugs U.S. Pharmacopeial Conv., 1990—; bd. dir. Scios Corp. Assoc. med. editor The Heart Bull, 1971-72; editor Clin. Cardiology, 1971-74, Clin. Guides to Med. Mgmt., 1996—; mem. circulation bd., 1971—; editor Circulation, 1983-88; mem. editorial bd. Circulation Research, 1974—, Annals of Internal Medicine, 1976—, Am. Jour. Cardiology, 1976—, Cardiology Digest, 1976-77, Jour. Continuing Edn. in Cardiology, 1978—, Cardiology in the Elderly, 1991—, Jour. Clin. Investigation, 1977—, Am. Jour. Physiology: Heart and Circulatory Physiology, 1978—; Churchill Livingstone editorial advisory bd. Internat. Seminars in Cardiovascular Medicine, 1978—, Cardiology in Review, 1992—; mem. editorial bd. Current Med. Lit., Current Opinion in Cardiology, editor, 1989—, Arteriosclerosis, Thrombosis, and Vascular Biology, 1996—, Clin. Therapeutics, 1996, Heart Disease, 2000, Clin. Insights in Diabetes, 1999, Diabetes Treatment Today, 2000, Am. Jour. Geriatric Cardiology, 2000, Internat. Jour. Cardiology, Fibrinolysis, 1986, assoc. editor, 1990—; cons. editor Circulation, 1988—; editor Coronary Artery Disease, 1989—; mem. editorial bd. Can. Jour. Cardiology, 1995—, Diabetes Care, 2002- Served to lt. comdr. USPHS, 1964-68. Recipient Career Rsch. Devel. award USPHS, 1972, internat. recognition award Heart Rsch. Found., 1981, Disting. Achievement award Am. Heart Assn. Sci. Couns., 1984, award Robert J. and Claire Posatow Found., 1988, award Va. Heart Ctr., 1991, Drake award Maine Heart Assn., 1992. Master ACP/ASIM; fellow ACP, Molecular Medicine Soc., Royal Soc. Medicine, AAAS (councilor 1997—); Am. Fedn. Clin. Rsch. (councilor), Am. Heart Assn. (couns. on basic cardiovasc. scis., clin. coun., circulation, and arteriosclerosis, thrombosis and vascular biology, James B. Herrick award 1992, Spl. Recognition award coun. on arteriosclerosis, thrombosis and vascular biology 1999), Am. Coll. Cardiology (Disting. Scientist award 1987), Assn. Univ. Cardiologists, Am. Soc. Clin. Investigation (councilor), Assn. Am. Physicians, Am. Physiol. Soc., Cardiac Muscle Soc., Western Soc. Clin. Rsch., Internat. Soc. Fibrinolysis and Thrombolysic (councilor), Assn. Profs. Cardiology (pres.-elect 1992), Soc. for Exptl. Biology and Medicine (councilor 1998—), Am. Soc. Clin. Investigation (instnl. rep. 1997—), Internat. Soc. Applied Cardiovasc. Biology, Alpha Omega Alpha. Home: 171 Lost Cove Rd Colchester VT 05446-7473 Office: Fletcher Allen-MCHV Campus Fletcher 311 Burlington VT 05401 E-mail: burton.sobel@btmednet.org.

SOBEL, HOWARD BERNARD, osteopath, educator; b. N.Y.C., May 15, 1929; s. Martin and Ella (Sternberg) S.; m. Ann Louise Silverbush, June 16, 1957 (dec. May 1978); children— Nancy Sobel Schumer, Janet Sobel Medow, Robert; m. Irene S. Miller, June 8, 1980; stepchildren— Avner Saferstein, Daniel Saferstein, Naomi Saferstein AB, Syracuse U., 1951; D.O., Kansas City Coll. Osteopathy and Surgery, 1955. Intern Zieger Osteo. Hosp., Detroit, 1955-56; gen. practice osteo. medicine Redford Twp., Mich., 1956-74, Livonia, 1974—. Chief of staff Botsford Gen. Hosp., Farmington, Mich., 1978; mem. faculty Mich. State U. Coll. Osteo. Medicine, 1969— , clin. assoc. prof. family practice, 1973— ; mem. exec. and med. adv. coms. United Health Orgn. Mich.; mem. Venereal Disease Action Com., Mich.; apptd. to asst. impaired osteo. physicians Mich., 1983 Mem. Am. Osteo. Assn. (ho. of dels. 1981—), Mich. Assn. Osteo. Physicians and Surgeons (ho. of dels.), Am. Coll. Osteo. Rheumatologists, Coll. Am. Osteo. Gen. Practitioners, Osteo. Gen. Practice Mich., Wayne County Osteo. Assn. (pres.) Jewish. Home: 6222 Northfield Rd West Bloomfield MI 48322-2431 Office: 28275 5 Mile Rd Livonia MI 48154-3944

SOBEL, MICHAEL EDWARD, sociologist, educator; b. St. Louis, Oct. 13, 1950; s. Irvin and Peggy Sobel. PhD, U. Wis., 1980. Rsch. analyst Bur. Labor Stats., Washington, 1980-82; asst. prof. U. Ariz., Tucson, 1982-86, assoc. prof., 1986-91, prof., 1992-99; prof. dept. sociology Columbia U., N.Y.C., 1999—. Author: Lifestyle and Social Structure, 1981; editor: Handbook of Statistical Methods, 1995, Sociological Methodology, 1999. Mem. Am. Sociol. Assn., Am. Statis. Assn., Sociol. Rsch. Assn. Avocations: fitness, tennis. Office: Columbia U Sociology Dept New York NY 10027 E-mail: mes105@columbia.edu.

SOBELL, NINA R. artist; b. Patchogue, N.Y., May 4, 1947; d. Jack and Helen Ruth (Rosenberg) S.; m. Christopher Rogers Shearer, Sept. 8, 1982 (div. Mar. 1987); 1 child, Jacqueline Corianne. BFA, Temple U., 1969; MFA, Cornell U., 1971. Cert. educator N.Y. Vis. artist Calif. Inst. of the Arts, Valencia, 1975, Sch. of Architecture, London, 1976; vis. lectr. dept. art Reading (Eng.) U., 1976-77; vis. lectr. dept. design & sculpture UCLA, 1979, assoc. prof. electronic imagery, 1984-85; artist-in-residence interactive telecomm. program NYU, N.Y.C., 1991-92, artist-in-residence Ctr. Digital Multimedia, 1994—; instr. video prodn. Sch. Visual Arts, 1992-93; dir. tech. integration Aux. Svc. High Schs., N.Y.C. Bd. Edn., 1994—. Artist-lectr. Documenta VII, Kassel, Germany, 1977; juror U.S. Film and Video Festival, L.A., 1984; juror media arts divsn. N.Y. State Coun. on the Arts, N.Y.C., 1994; artist-presenter Siggraph, New Orleans, 1996; resident Banff Ctr. for the Arts, 1998-99. Prin. works include installation Interactive Brainwave Drawings, 1974—, interactive installation Videophone Relay, 1977-79; artist/dir. HIV-INFO Interactive Call-In TV Show, Manhattan Pub.-Access Cable, 1992, ParkBench Pub-Access Web Kiosks, 1994—; curriculum designer Online Art Network for At-Risk Youth, N.Y.C. Bd. Edn., 1996; represented in permanent collection Mus. Modern Art, N.Y.C., Whitney Mus. Art Whitney Web Site. Installation/Lecture grantee Found. Art Resources, 1981; Installation grantee N.Y. State Coun. Arts, 1981. Mem. Art and Sci. Collaborations, Inc., Coll. Art Assn., Assn. Ind. Video and Filmmakers, United Fedn. of Tchrs. Democrat. Jewish. Avocations: swimming, cooking, biking, birdwatching, skating. Home: 128 E Broadway # 506 New York NY 10002-6373 Office: NYU Ctr Digital Multimedia 719 Broadway Fl 12 New York NY 10003-6860

SOBELLE, RICHARD E. lawyer; b. Cleve., Mar. 18, 1935; BA, Stanford U., 1956, JD, 1960; LLM, U. So. Calif., 1967. Bar: Calif. 1961, U.S. Supreme Ct. 1969. Exec. Tracinda Corp. Mem. ABA (mem. corp., banking and bus. law sect. 1969-95), State Bar Calif. (del. to conf. state bar dels. 1965-77, mem. exec. com. bus. law sect. 1977-78), L.A. County Bar Assn. (mem. exec. coun., jr. barristers 1965-68, mem. exec. com. bus. and corps. sect. 1973-75). Office: Tracinda Corp 150 S Rodeo Dr Ste 250 Beverly Hills CA 90212-2417

SOBEN, ROBERT SIDNEY, systems scientist; b. Corpus Christi, Tex., Feb. 7, 1947; s. Sydney Robert and Rose Mary S.; 1 child, Dena Dianne. BSEE, La. Tech. U., 1973; MA in Comm., U. Okla., 1982; MS in Mgmt. Scis., Troy (Ala.) State U., 1988; PhD in Engring. Mgmt. Sci., U. Fla. and LaSalle U., 1990. Digital computer sci. USAF Air Training Command, Keesler AFB, Miss., 1966-71; command pilot USAF, worldwide, 1971-82; NATO instr. pilot 80th Fighter Training Wing, Sheppard AFB, Tex., 1978-82; electro-optics br. chief Electronics Sys. Test Divsn., Eglin AFB, Fla., 1982-84; mission ops. officer Deputate for Testing Engring., 1984-85, test support divsn. chief, 1985-93; sr. TQ analyst 46TW/OG-1 TQM in 46 OG, 1993-94; CEO ORCOM, Niceville, Fla., 1984—. Adj. asst. prof. Troy State U., Ft. Walton Beach, Fla., 1987-94, St. Leo's Coll., Eglin AFB, 1988-94; sys. analyst PACE Group, Orlando, Fla., 1994-98, Fidelio Techs., Naples, Fla., 1999-2001, ECI Telecom, Petach Tekva, Israel; CEO Tiger Team Solutions, Inc., 2001—. Author: Digital Computer Basics, 1970, Application of Expert Systems to Scientific and Technical Information Command, Control and Communication Management, 1990, Score Strategic Business Planning Document, 1999; author USAF tech. report Video Augmentation, 1984, tng. manual and system test engring., 1988, POGI for Quality Results, a mil. pub., 1995. Avocations: sailing, scuba diving, writing, racing cars. Home: 260 Lakeview Ct Interlachen FL 32148-6941 E-mail: drsoben@hotmail.com.

SOBER, ARTHUR JOEL, dermatologist, researcher; b. Washington, July 16, 1943; s. William and Yetta Shirley (Schneider) S.; m. Cheryl Winifred Harris, Mar. 28, 1976; children: Felicia Gail, Stephanie Paula. BA with distinction, George Washington U., 1965, MD with distinction, 1968; MA (hon.), Harvard U., 1996. Diplomate Am. Bd. Dermatology, Am. Bd. Internal Medicine. Clin. assoc. NIH, Bethesda, Md., 1970-72; resident in dermatology Mass. Gen. Hosp., Boston, 1972-74, acad. dermatologist, 1974—; from instr. to assoc. prof. Harvard Med. Sch., 1974-96, prof., 1996—. Advisor Nat. Research Council, Washington, 1978-81; cons. Rand Corp., Santa Monica, Calif., 1981-83, U. Calif., Berkeley, 1985-90. Editor: Year Book of Dermatology, 1983-97; co-editor Year Book of Cancer, 1976-88; chief assoc. editor Jour. Investigative Dermatology, 1984-87. Med. v.p. Westend Boston chpt. Am. Cancer Soc., 1983. Lt. comdr. USPHS, 1970-72. Fellow Am. Acad. Dermatology; mem. Am. Fedn. Clin. Research (sr.), Soc. Investigative Dermatology, Internat. Pigment Cell Soc. Jewish. Home: 191 Kirkstall Rd Newton MA 02460-2452 Office: Mass Gen Hosp Fruit Street Boston MA 02114 E-mail: sober.arthur@mgh.harvard.edu.

SOBER, DEBRA EVONNE, environmental services administrator; b. Oklahoma City, May 20, 1953; d. Donald E. and Zona E. (Taylor) Tillman; m. Gary L. Sober, May 24, 1980; children: Kara, Jeffrey, Kimberly, Riley Nicole. BS, Columbia Pacific U. Lic. water and wastewater operator; registered X-ray lab. technician; notary pub. Chmn. bd. PACE Corp., Austin, 1986—; gen. mgr. Envir-O-Spec, Inc., 1972-95; owner, pres. Environ. Tng., Inc., 1980—. Cons. B40-Gon PX-109, 1990—. Author numerous textbooks on water and wastewater treatment and operation. Founder ann. Just Fishin Show, Austin, 1989; bd. dirs. Austin Women's Soccer League, 1991-93; bd. dirs., founder Austin Amateur Soccer Assn., 1991; women's commr. Tex. State Soccer Assn. South, 1994-99, v.p., 1999— (Mem. Soccer Hall of Fame 1999); nat. cup commr. United States Soccer Fedn./U.S. Amateur Soccer Assn., Region III, 1996—. Mem. Nat. Environ. Tng. Assn., Tex. Water Utilities Assn. (chmn. pub. rels. 1981-85, safety chmn. 1987-88), Okla. Water and Pollution Control Assn., Am. Water Works Assn., Water Pollution Control Fedn., Am. Bus. Women's Assn., N.W. Adult Athletic Assn. (founder and dir. 1986), N.W. Austin Women's Basketball Assn. (founder and pres. 1986), N.W. Austin Women's Soccer Assn. (founder and pres. 1986), Beta Sigma Phi. Baptist. Office: PO Box 200815 Austin TX 78720-0815 Home: 3054 Lakeshore Ave Benton Harbor MI 49022-2522

SOBER, SIDNEY, retired diplomat, educator; b. N.Y.C., Nov. 12, 1919; s. Isaac and Mary (Krug) S.; m. Elizabeth Holmes Sober, Apr. 2, 1947; children: Stephen, Elizabeth (dec.). BA magna cum laude, CCNY, 1939; MA, George Washington U., 1964. Fgn. svc. officer Dept. of State, Tananarive, Prague, Reykjavik, Ankara, Bombay, 1947-63; econ. affairs South Asia, dir. regional affairs Bur. Near Ea. and So. Asian Affairs, Dept. of State, Washington, 1964-69; staff dir. Interdepartmental Regional Group for Near East and So. Asia, 1967-69; min. counselor, dep. chief of mission Am. Embassy, Islamabad, Pakistan, 1969-73, chargé d'affaires Pakistan, 1972-73; sr. dep. asst. sec. state N.E. & S. Asia, frequently acting asst. sec. state Dept. of State, 1974-78; chair South Asia Seminar Fgn. Svc. Inst., Dept. of State, Washington, 1982-96. Vis. prof., adj. prof. Am. U., Washington, 1978-87; cons. Sisco Assocs., Washington, 1984-93; declassification specialist Dept. of State, Washington, 1981—. Past pres. Sumner Village Cmty. Assn. Lt. (j.g.) USNR, 1944-46. Mem. Am. Fgn. Svc. Assn., Diplomatic and Consular Officers Ret., Asia Soc., Mid. East Inst., Phi Beta Kappa. Home: 4928 Sentinel Dr Apt 106 Bethesda MD 20816-3543

SOBERON, PRESENTACION ZABLAN, state bar administrator; b. Cabambangan, Bacolor, Pampanga, Philippines, Feb. 23, 1935; came to U.S., 1977; naturalized, 1984; d. Pioquinto Yalung and Lourdes (David) Zabian; m.

Damaso Reyes Soberon, Apr. 2, 1961; children: Shirley, Sherman, Sidney, Sedwin. Office mgmt., stenography, typing cert., East Cen. Colls., Philippines, 1953; profl. sec. diploma, Internat. Corr. Schs., 1971; A in Mgmt. Supervision, Skyline and Diablo Coll., 1979, LaSalle Ext. U., 1980-82; AA, cert. in Mgmt. and Supervision, Diablo Valley Coll. With U.S. Fed. Svc. Naval Base, Subic Bay, Philippines, 22 yrs, clerical, stenography and secretarial postitions, 1955-73, adminstrv. asst., 1973-77; secretarial positions Mt. Zion Hosp. and Med. Ctr., San Francisco, 1977, City Hall, Oakland, Calif., 1978; with State Bar Calif., San Francisco, 1978-79; secretarial positions gen. counsel divsn. and state bar ct. divsn., adminstrv. asst. fin. and ops. divsn., 1979-81; office mgr. sects. and coms. dept., profl. and pub. svcs., 1981-83; appointment adminstr. office of bar rels., 1983-86; adminstr. state bar sects. bus. law sect., estate planning, trust and probate law sect., labor and employment law sect., office of bar rels., 1986-89; adminstr. antitrust and trade regulation law sect., labor and employment law sect., workers' compensation sect., edn. and meeting svcs., 1989-96; adminstr. criminal law sect., 1996—; labor and law employment law sect., 1996—; internat. law sect., 1996—; workers' compensation sect., 1996—; edn. and meeting svcs., 1996-98; ret., 1998. Disc jockey/announcer Philippine radio stas. DZYZ, DZOR and DWHL, 1966-77. Organizer Neighborhood Alert Program, South Catamaran Circle, Pittsburg, Calif., 1979-80. Recipient 13 commendation certs. and outstanding pers. monetary awards U.S. Fed. Svc., 1964-77, 20 Yr. U.S. Fed. Svc. pin and cert., 1975; Nat. 1st prize award for cmty. svc. and achievements Nat. Inner Wheel Clubs Philippines, 1975; several plaques and award certs. for cmty. and sch. activities and contbns. Olongapo City, Philippines. Mem. NAFE, Am. Soc. Assn. Execs., N.Y.C. Olongapo-Subic Bay Assn. No Calif. (Pittsburg rep. 1982-87, bus. mgr. 1988-89, 97-98, 99-2000, 01-02, pub. rels. officer 1993-94), Castillejos Assn. of No. Calif., SRF Tigers No. Calif. Roman Catholic. Home: 207 South Catamaran Circle Pittsburg CA 94565 Office: State Bar of Calif 180 Howard St San Francisco CA 94105-1639

SOBERON KURI, ALEJANDRO, performing company executive; Founder, chmn., CEO Corporacion Interamerica de Entretenimiento, Mexico City, 1990—. Office: CIE Corporativo Paseo de las Palmas No 1005 Col Lomas de Chapultepec Mexico City 11 Mexico

SOBEY, DAVID FRANK, food company executive, retired food products executive; b. Stellarton, N.S., Can., Mar. 22, 1931; s. Frank Hoyse and Irene (MacDonald) S.; m. Faye B. Naugle, June 2, 1953; children: Paul David, Janis Irene Hames. D of Commerce (hon.), St. Mary's U., 1991. With Sobeys Inc., Stellarton, 1949—, store mgr., dir. merchandising and advt., v.p., exec. v.p., pres., dep. chmn., chief exec. officer, dir., 1981-85, chmn., 1985—2001, chmn. emeritus, 2001—, also bd. dirs. Bd. dirs. Empire Co. Ltd., Sobeys Inc., Sobey Leased Properties Ltd., Atlantic Shopping Ctrs. Ltd., Sobeys Land Holdings Ltd.; chmn. The Sobey Found., Frank H. Sobey Fund for Excellence in Bus. Studies. Bd. dirs. Tim Horton Children's Found., The Sobey Art Found., Boy Scouts Can., Atlantic Salmon Fedn.; mem. Halifax Bd. Trade. Mem. Order of Can., 1996. Mem.: Halifax; City (New Glasgow), Abercrombie Golf. Office: Sobeys Inc 115 King St Stellarton NS Canada B0K 1S0

SOBEY, DONALD CREIGHTON RAE, real estate developer; b. New Glasgow, N.S., Can. s. Frank Hoyse and Irene (MacDonald) S.; m. Elizabeth H. Purvis; children: Robert George Creighton, Irene Elizabeth, Kent Richard. B of Commerce, Queen's U.; LLD (hon.), Dalhousie U., 1989. Dir. Alliance Atlantis Corp., 1989—; pres. Empire Co. Ltd., 1969, chmn., 1985—; also bd. dirs. Bd. dirs. Atlantic Shopping Ctrs. Ltd., Toronto-Dominion Bank, Wajax Ltd., Sobeys Inc., Trader.com, World Wildlife Found. Gov. Olympic Trust Can.; patron 1986 World Congress on Edn. and Tech.; mem. Conf. Bd. Can.; found. chmn. Camp Hill Med. Ctr.; mem. Club de Rels. d'Affaires Can.-France; bd. dirs. Nat. Gallery Can. Mem. Internat. Assn. for Students Econs. and Commerce. Avocations: skiing, tennis, music, art, travel. Office: Empire Co Ltd 115 King ST Stellarton NS Canada B0K 1S0

SOBEY, EDWIN J. C. museum director, oceanographer, consultant; b. Apr. 7, 1948; s. Edwin J. and Helen (Chapin) S.; m. Barbara Lee, May 9, 1970; children: Ted Wooddall, Andrew Chapin. BS, U. Richmond, 1969; MS, Oreg. State U., 1974, PhD, 1977. Rsch. scientist Sci. Applications, Inc., Boulder, Colo., 1977-79, divsn. mgr., 1979-81; exec. dir. Sci. Mus., West Palm Beach, Fla., 1981-88, Mus. Sci. and History, Jacksonville, 1988, Nat. Invention Ctr., Akron, Ohio, 1989-92, Fresno (Calif.) Met. Mus., 1993-95; ednl. cons., 1995—. Exec. dir. A.C. Gilbert's Discovery Village, Salem, Oreg., 1997-99; pres. Northwest Invention Ctr., 1999—; founder Nat. Toy Hall of Fame, 1998; instr. mus. mgmt. U. Wash., 1998-2001. Author: Complete Circuit Training Guide, 1980, Strength Training Book, 1981, (with others) Aerobic Weight Training Book, 1982, The Whole Backpacker's Catalog, 1988, Increasing Your Audience, 1989, Inventing Stuff, 1995, Wrapper Rockets and Trombone Straws-Science at Every Meal, 1996, Car Smarts, 1997, Just Plane Smart, 1998, Young Inventors at Work, 1999, How to Enter and Win an Invention Contest, 1999, Fantastic Flying Fun with Science, 2000, Wacky Water Fun with Science, 2000, Inventing Toys: Kids Having Fun Learning Science, 2001, How to Build Your Own Prize-Winning Robot, 2002; mem. editl. adv. bd. Invent Mag., 1989-92; exec. prodr.: (TV show) Idea Factory, Sta. KFSN-30, Fresno, 1995-97; co-host: (ednl. TV show) Blow the Roof Off, 1992. Alumni v.p. Leadership Palm Beach County; expdn. leader Expdn. Tng. Inst., S.E. Alaska, 1980; mem. U.S. Antarctic Rsch. Program, 1974; founder, bd. dirs. Visually Impaired Sports Program, Boulder, 1978-81; fitness instr. YMCA Boulder, 1977-81; convener 1st Nat. Conf. Sports for the Blind, 1979; bd. dirs. Leadership Palm Beach; vice chmn. County Com. on Artificial Reefs; treas. Leadership Akron Alumni Assn., 1990-91, class pres. Leadership Akron; v.p. Ohio Mus. Assn., 1991-92, pres., 1992-93; bd. dirs. Fla. Mus. Assn., 1988-89; mem. adv. bd. Marine Sci. Inst., 1990—. Lt. USN, 1970-73. Fellow Explorers Club (chair Pacific Midwest chpt. 2002—); mem. Marine Tech. Soc. (sect. chmn. 1982-84), Coral Reef Soc. (chpt. pres. 1982-87), Nat. Inventive Thinking Assn. (bd. dirs. 1989—). Home: 2420 178th Ave NE Redmond WA 98052-5820 E-mail: sobey@gte.net.

SOBH, TAREK MAHMOUD, computer science educator, researcher; b. Giza, Egypt, Feb. 16, 1967; came to U.S., 1988; s. Mahmoud Abd-El-Hakeem Sobh and Nagwa Abd-el-Meguid Reda; m. Nihal Samy Kandil, Sept. 16, 1992; children: Omar Tarek, Haya Tarek. BSc in Engring. with honors, Alexandria (Egypt) U., 1988; MS in Engring., U. Pa., 1989, PhD in Computer and Info. Sci., 1991. Registered profl. engr., Utah; cert. mfg. engr. Soc. Mfg. Engrs., profl. mgr. Inst. Cert. Profl. Mgrs. Postdoctoral rsch. fellow dept. computer and info. sci. Gen. Robotics and Active Sensory Perception Lab. U. Pa., Phila., 1991-92; rsch. asst. prof. dept. computer sci. Coll. Engring., U. Utah, Salt Lake City, 1992-95; prof. computer sci. and engring. U. Bridgeport, Conn., 1995—; dir. robotics, intelligence sensing and control lab. dept. computer sci. and engring., 1995—; dean Sch. Engring. U. Bridgeport, 1999—. Dir. external engring. programs, 1998-99. Editor Jour. Robotics and Autonomous Sys., 1994; reviewer for books, jours.; contbr. more than 80 articles to profl. jours., book chpts., and conf. papers. Grantee NSF, 1993, 94, Def. Advanced Rsch. Projects Agy./Office Navy Rsch., 1993—, Def. Advanced Rsch. Projects Agy., 1993—. Mem. NSPE, IEEE (chair session on object recognition 1993 2nd CAD-Based Vision Workshop 1994, session chair internat. conf. robotics and automation 1994), IEEE Computer Soc. (mem. tech. com. on pattern analysis and machine intelligence), IEEE Robotics and Automation Soc. (co-chairperson discrete event dynamic sys. tech. com. 1992-99, chair robot prototyping tech. com. 2000—, Best Paper award 1998), Am. Soc. Engring. Edn., Internat. Soc. Optical Engring., Assn. Computing Machinery, Soc. Indsl. Computing, Am. Soc. Quality, Egyptian Engring. Syndicate, Tau Beta Pi (advisor Utah chpt.), Phi Beta Delta, Sigma Xi, Upsilon Phi Epsilon. Avocations: reading, squash, soccer, scuba diving, photography. Office: U Bridgeport Dept Computer Sci & Engring 169 University Ave Bridgeport CT 06604-5763 E-mail: sobh@bridgeport.edu.

SOBHAN, TANVEER, physician; b. Dec. 12, 1965; MBBS, Dhaka (Bangladesh) Med. Coll., 1992; MPH, U. Tex. Health Sci. Ctr., 1997; MD, Ednl. Commn. Fgn. Med. Grads., Phila., 1998. Grad. rsch. asst. Ctr. for Substance Abuse Prevention, Houston, 1994-99; rsch. asst. phys. medicine U. Tex. Sch. Medicine, 1998, rsch. asst. pediat. infectious disease, 1998; postdoctoral fellow Baylor Coll. Medicine, 1998; resident physician psychiatry U. Ala., Birmingham, 1999—2002, chief resident psychiatry Ala., 2002—. Contbr. articles to profl. jours. Provider healthcare for flood victims Dhaka Med. Coll., 1988, for homeless Search Clinic for Homeless, Houston, 1998. Address: 6910 Tree Crossings Pkwy Hoover AL 35244-5048 E-mail: tsobhanmd@yahoo.com.

SOBIESKI, JAROSLAW, aerospace engineer; b. Wilno, Poland, Mar. 11, 1934; came to U.S., 1966; naturalized, 1971. s. Stanislaw and Sabina Sobieszczanski; m. Wanda Dlugosz, Dec. 31, 1958; children: Margaret Ann, Ian Patrick. BS aeros., Tech. U. Warsaw, 1955, MS aeros., 1957, DEng, 1964. Cons. Polish Aircraft Industries, Warsaw, 1957-64; asst. and adj. prof. Tech. U. Warsaw, 1955-64; rsch. assoc. Tech. U. Norway, Trondheim, 1964-66; assoc. prof. St. Louis U., 1966-71; aerospace engr. NASA Langley Rsch. Ctr., Hampton, Va., 1971-89, head rsch. office, 1979-93, chief scientist, 1993-94, multidisciplinary rsch. coord., 1994—2001, mgr. Computational AeroScis. team, 1996—2001, sr. rsch. scientist, 2001—. Mem. faculty George Washington U., 1972—, U. Va., 1992-99; pres. and cons. engr. Tech. Analysis Optimization, Inc. Hampton, Va., 1982—. Co-editor: Structural Optimization jour., 1989—; contbr. articles to profl. jours. Recipient medal for exceptional achievement in engring. NASA, 1988. Fellow AIAA (mem. tech. com., Nat. Multidisciplinary Design Optimization award 1996). Home: 518 Elizabeth Lake Dr Hampton VA 23669-1724 Office: NASA Langley Rsch Ctr MS 240 Hampton VA 23681-0001 E-mail: j.sobieski@larc.nasa.gov.

SOBIN, ALLAN J. neurologist; b. Bklyn., Oct. 13, 1930; MD, SUNY, Bklyn., 1955. Diplomate Am. Bd. Psychiatry and Neurology. Intern U. Chgo. Clinics, 1955-56; resident Mount Sinai Hosp., N.Y.C., 1959-63; pvt. practice Bklyn., 1963—; attending neurologist Beth Israel Med. Ctr., N.Y.C., 1980—. Office: 3131 Kings Hwy Ste D-1 Brooklyn NY 11234 E-mail: asobin@dnamail.com.

SOBIN, LESLIE HOWARD, pathologist, educator; b. N.Y.C., Feb. 10, 1934; s. Martin L. and Kitty N. Sobin; m. Margareta E.D. Ahlstrom, Dec. 21, 1962; 1 child, Annika D. BS, Union Coll., 1955; MD, SUNY, N.Y.C., 1959. Diplomate Am. Bd. Pathology. Instr. pathology Cornell U. Med. Coll., N.Y.C., 1962-65, asst. prof. pathology, 1965; WHO visiting prof. pathology Univ. Kabul, Afghanistan, 1965-68; assoc. prof. pathology Cornell U. Med. Coll., 1968-70; pathologist WHO, Geneva, 1970-81; prof. pathology Uniformed Svcs. Univ. Health Scis., Bethesda, Md., 1984—; head WHO collaborating ctr. tumor classification Armed Forces Inst. Pathology, Washington, 1983—, dir. sci. publs., 1987—, chief gastrointestinal pathology, 1991—. Adj. prof. pathology Cornell U. Med. Coll., 1980-2001, Georgetown U. Med. Coll., 1992—; expert, panel on cancer WHO, Geneva, 1981—. Author: Pathology Primer in Verse, 1978, 91, Tales of the Ampulla of Vater, 1994, The Last Examination: The Prosecutor's Guide to the Autopsy—In Verse, 1996; editor: International Histological Classification of Tumors, 1970-2002; co-editor: WHO Classification of Tumors, 2000—, TNM Classification of Tumors, 1987, 97, Prognostic Factors in Cancer, 1995, 2001. Recipient Sr. Exec. Svc. award Dept. of Army, 1990, Meritorious Presdl. Rank award, 1991. Fellow Royal Coll. Pathologists; mem. Internat. Acad. Pathology (sec. 1982-88).

SOBIN, RODNEY, technology analyst; b. Paterson, N.J., Apr. 25, 1961; s. Allan J. and Vera (Fedoroff) S.; m. Rebecca B. Bennett, June 1984; children: Ethan B., Amelia B. AB, Cornell Univ., 1983; MA, MS, Washington Univ., 1989. Rsch. analyst World Resources Inst., Washington, 1990-91; analyst Congressional Office Tech. Assessment, 1991-95; sr. tech. transfer analyst Concurrent Tech. Corp., Johnstown, Pa., 1995-99; innovative tech. mgr. Va. Dept. Environ. Quality, Richmond, 1999—. Adj. faculty Cambria County Area C.C., 1997-99. Contbr. articles to profl. jours. Mem. OECD Working Group on Environ. Industry, Paris, 1994-95, UN Environ. Program ENTA adv. group, Paris, 1994-95, Globe 92 Coord. Com., Vancouver, B.C., Can., 1991-92. Mem.: Am. Soc. Agrl. Engring., NY Acad. Scis. Home: 13204 Autumn Chase Pl Richmond VA 23233-1061 Office: Va Dept Environ Quality 629 E Main St Richmond VA 23219-2429 E-mail: rsobin@deq.state.va.us.

SOBKOWICZ, HANNA MARIA, neurology researcher; b. Warsaw, Poland, Jan. 1, 1931; came to U.S., 1963; d. Stanislaw and Jadwiga (Ignaczak) S.; m. Jerzy E. Rose, Mar. 12, 1972. BA, Girls State Lyceum, Gilwice, Poland, 1949; M.D. Med. Acad., Warsaw, 1954, PhD, 1962. Intern. 1st Internal Med. Clinic Med. Acad., Warsaw, 1954-55; resident 1st Internal Med. Clinic, Med. Acad., 1955-59, Neurol. Clinic, Med. Acad., 1959, jr. asst., 1959-61, sr. asst., 1961-63; research fellow neurology Mt. Sinai Hosp., N.Y.C., 1963-65; Nat. Multiple Sclerosis Soc. fellow Columbia U., 1965-66; asst. prof. neurology U. Wis., Madison, 1966-72, assoc. prof., 1972-79, prof., 1979—. Contbr. articles to profl. jours. NIH research grantee, 1968— Mem. Internat. Brain Rsch. Orgn., Assn. Rsch. in Otolaryngology, Soc. Neurosci., Internat. Soc. Devel. Neurosci. (editorial bd. 1984—), Electron Microscopy Soc. Am. Office: U Wis Dept Neurology 1300 University Ave Madison WI 53706-1510

SOBLE, MARK RICHARD, lawyer; b. San Francisco, Dec. 25, 1964; life ptnr. Leslye Soble, Nov. 2000. BA with deptl. honors, Stanford U., 1985; JD, U. Mich., 1988. Bar: Calif. 1988, U.S. Dist. Ct. (cen. dist.) Calif. 1988, U.S. Dist. Ct. (ea. dist.) Calif. 1990. Law clk. to chief judge U.S. Dist. Ct. for S.D., Pierre, 1988-89; assoc. Lewis, D'Amato, Brisbois & Bisgaard, L.A., 1989-90; counsel enforcement div. Fair Polit. Practices Commn., Sacramento, 1990-96, sr. counsel, 1996—2001; dep. atty. gen. civil div. Office of Calif. Atty. Gen., 2001—. *Mark Soble dedicated over eleven and a half years of distinguished service to the State of California Fair Political Practices Commission. He successfully prosecuted or settled over 140 administrative and civil cases, resulting in imposition of enforcement fines totaling approximately $3.15 million, the largest number of cases and the highest fine total for any single staff attorney in the agency's history. He was extremely effective in settling or prosecuting 41 cases involving the serious violation of campaign contribution money laundering, resulting in Fair Political Practices Commissions fines of approximately $2.2 million, including the first and third largest fines for this violation in the Commission's history.* Note editor U. Mich. Jour. Law Reform, 1987-88. Raymond K. Dykema scholar U. Mich. 1987. Mem. State Bar Calif., Sacramento County Bar Assn. (mng. editor Docket 1997, mem.-at-large bar coun. 1998-00).

SOBOL, ELISE SCHWARCZ, music educator; b. Chgo., June 12, 1951; d. Morton and Harriet Jacobsohn Schwarcz; m. Lawrence Paul Sobol, Aug. 21, 1977 (div. Sept. 1989); children: Marlon I., Aaron L. AA, Simon's Rock of Bard Coll., 1971; student, Mannes Coll. Music, 1971—73, Juillard Sch. Music, 1973—74; BA, New Sch. for Social Rsch., 1985; MA, Columbia U., 1987. Staff auditorium events, concerts, lectures Met. Mus. Art, 1972-73; sec. to pres. Harry Beall Mgmt. Inc., N.Y.C., 1973-76; sales rep. M.L. Falcone Pub. Rels., 1976-77; asst. to pres. Jacques Leiser Artist Mgmt., 1977-78; artist rep. Elise Sobol Mgmt. Inc., South Huntington, N.Y., 1978-82; tchr. music Nassau Boces Elem., 1988—; dir. L.I. Music Workshop, 1992—. Adj. prof. NYU Steinhardt Sch. Edn., 2000—; advisor arts and humanities Internat. Biog. Ctr., Cambridge, England; guest lectr. NYU, 1999, Hofstra, 2000; adj. faculty C.W. Post Coll. L.I. U., 2000; instr. SUNY , Farmingdale, 1993—98; music tchr. The Roslyn Middle Sch., 1987—88; dir. Early Musical Devel. Program for Children at Calling All Kids, South Huntington, 1981—86; tchr. young and adult piano students, 1968; piano adj. educator N.Y. State, 1993—. Musician: (piano concerts) Chamber Music series at U.S. Mil. Acad., N.J. met. area, Disting. Artists series, 2002—03; author: An Attitude and Approach for Teaching Music to Special Learners, 2001. Active Nassau Boces Elem. Program PTA, cultural arts coord., 1988—. Recipient Award of Honor, L.I. Very Spl. Arts Festival, 1993, Spl. Citation N.Y. State Assembly Ames Elem. Program, 1998, Spl. Recognition Nassau Music Educators Assn., 1999, 1st prize Dr. Martin Luther King Jr. Performing Arts Competition for Exceptional Students Nassau County, 1999, 2000, 01. Mem. NAFE, ASCD, N.Y. State Sch. Music Assn. (chair music for spl. learners 1993—), Amnesty Internat., Internat. Jazz Educators Assn., Music Educators Nat. Conf., Music Tchrs. Nat. Assn., Nassau Music Educators Assn., Nat. Mus. for Women, Met. Mus. of Art. Home: 21 Saxon St Melville NY 11747

SOBOL, HAROLD, retired dean, manufacturing executive, consultant; b. Bklyn., June 21, 1930; s. Stanley and Minnie S.; m. Marion Gross, Dec. 29, 1957; children— Diane, Neil, Jessica, Martin. BSE.E., CUNY, 1952; MSE.E., U. Mich., 1956, PhD, 1960. Research asst. Willow Run Labs. U. Mich., 1952-55, research assoc., 1956-59; staff mem. IBM Research, Yorktown Heights, N.Y., 1960-62; with RCA Labs., Princeton, N.J., 1962-73, staff engr., 1970-72, head communication tech., 1972-73; sr. mem. tech. staff Collins Radio Rockwell-Internat., Dallas, 1973-74; dir. product devel. Collins Transmission Systems div., 1974-85; dir. engring. Rockwell Telecommunications, 1985-86, v.p. engring., 1986-88, ret., 1988; prof. elec. engring., assoc. dean U. Tex., Arlington, 1988-93. Author: Advances in Microwaves Volume 8, 1974; contbr. in field. Cubmaster Tex.-Okla. council Boy Scouts Am., Dallas, 1978-80. Sperry fellow, 1955-56 Fellow IEEE (pres. microwave theory and techniques soc. 1979); mem. Am. Phys. Soc., Nat. Mgmt. Assn., Sigma Xi, Tau Beta Pi, Eta Kappa Nu. Office: U Tex PO Box 19019 Arlington TX 76019-0001

SOBOL, LAWRENCE RAYMOND, lawyer; b. Kansas City, Mo., May 8, 1950; s. Haskell and Mary (Press) S.; m. Maureen Patricia O'Connell, May 29, 1976; children: David, Kevin. BBA, U. Tex., 1972; JD, U. Mo., 1975. Bar: Mo. 1975, U.S. Dist. Ct. (ea. dist.) Mo. 1975. Gen. counsel, gen. ptnr. Edward D. Jones & Co., Maryland Heights, Mo., 1975—. Allied mem. N.Y.C. Stock Exchange, 1977—; sec. Lake Communications Corp., Conroe, Tex., 1984-86, LHC Inc., EDJ Holding Co. Inc., Unison Capital Corp., 1990—, Cornerstone Mortgage Investment Group, 1987-92; sec., bd. dirs. Cornerstone Mortgage Inc., St. Louis, 1986; v.p., bd. dirs. Tempus Corp., St. Louis, 1984—. Omar Robinson Meml. scholar U. Mo., 1974-75. Mem. ABA (securities law com. 1982—), Met. St. Louis Bar Assn. (securities law sect.), Nat. Assn. Securities Dealers (dist. bus. com., registered prin. officer, nat. arbitration com. 1991—), Securities Industry Assn. (fed. regulation securities com. 1987-88), Persimmon Woods Country Club, Lake Las Vegas South Shore Country Club, Phi Eta Sigma. Avocations: tennis, golf. Office: Edward D Jones & Co 12555 Manchester Rd Saint Louis MO 63131-3729

SOBOLEV, ALEXANDRE ANDREEVICH, physicist; b. Ramenskoye, Russia, June 18, 1952; s. Andrew Puzirev and Anna (Soboleva) Terekhova; m. Yaroslava Stepanovna Schumliakovskaya, Nov. 5, 1975 (div. 1980); 1 child, Yegor; m. Tatiana Arkadievna Silitch, Dec. 19, 1992; 1 child, Maria. MSc, Moscow Inst. Engring. Physics, 1978, PhD, 1990. Rschr. Inst. Physics & Power Engring., Obninsk, Russia. Dep. Obninsk City Coun., 1989-93. Jr. sgr. Soviet Army, 1971-73. Mem. Moscow Phys. Soc., Obninsk Phys. Soc. Mem. Orthodox Ch. E-mail: agor@sprint.ca.

SOBOLEWSKI, JOHN STEPHEN, computer scientist, consultant; b. Krakow, Poland, July 14, 1939; came to U.S., 1966; s. Jan Zygmund and Stefania (Zwolinska) S.; m. Helen Skipper, Dec. 17, 1965 (div. July 1969); m. Carole Straith, Apr. 6, 1974; children: Anne-Marie, Elisa, Martin. BE, U. Adelaide, Adelaide, South Australia, 1962, ME, 1966; PhD in Computer Sci., Wash. State U., 1971. Sci. officer Weapons Research Establishment, Salisbury, South Australia, 1964-66; asst. prof. computer sci. Wash. State U., Pullman, 1966-73; dir. research, assoc. prof. U. Wash., Seattle, 1973-80, dir. computer svcs., 1980-88; assoc. v.p. computing U. N.Mex., Albuquerque, 1988—. Cons. govt. and industry, Seattle, 1973—; mem. bd. trustees Fisher Found., Seattle, 1984—. Author: Computers for the Dental Office, 1986; contbr. articles to profl. jours. Served as engr. with Royal Australian Army, 1957-60. Australian govt. scholar, 1954-60, Elec. Res. Bd. scholar CSIRO, Melbourne, Australia, 1961-64. Mem. IEEE, Computer Soc. Roman Catholic. Avocation: mineral collecting. Home: 8501 Northridge Ave NE Albuquerque NM 87111-2107 Office: U NMex CIRT 2701 Campus Ave NE Albuquerque NM 87131-0001 E-mail: jssob@unm.edu.

SOBOLEWSKI, TIMOTHY RICHARD, marketing executive; b. Buffalo, May 29, 1951; s. Richard Theodore and Gertrude Marie (Chudzik) S.; m. Melissa R. Thorburn, Apr. 13, 1985; 1 child, Richard. AB, Columbia U., 1972. Regional mgr. Universal Communicatons, Roanoke, Va., 1977-80; ptnr. Systems Planning Assocs., Braintree, Mass., 1980-81; v.p. Telecon, Inc., Boston, 1981-83; sr. mktg. cons. Telelogic, Inc., Cambridge, Mass., 1983-84; dist. mgr. Republic Telcom, Braintree, 1985; founder, pres., gen. mgr. Operaworld, Inc., Boston, 1985-89; v.p. Homisco, Inc., Melrose, Mass., 1989-95; dir. sales & mktg. DINE Sys., Amherst, N.Y., 1995-97; pres. One Call Software, 1998—. Cons. Opera Con Brio, Brookline, Mass., 1986-92. Mem. Puritan Club (Braintree). Democrat. Roman Catholic. Office: One Call Software 5540 Porter Rd Niagara Falls NY 14304-1523

SOBONG, LORETO CALIBO, nursing researcher; b. Oroquieta City, The Philippines, Feb. 7, 1931; naturalized U.S. citizen, 1982; d. Jeremias Emilio and Expectacion (Calibo) S. BSE, Misamis Jr. Coll., Oroquieta City, 1954; MA, Philippine Normal Coll., Manila, 1962; postgrad., U. Philippines, Diliman, 1969, 71; PhD, NYU, 1975. Elem. tchr. Bur. Pub. Schs., Molave, The Philippines, 1955-57, Oroquieta, 1958-66, supr. gen. edn., 1966-72; rsch. asst. Pa. State U., University Park, 1974-76; data editor Ill. Office Edn., Springfield, 1977; with So. Ill. U., 1978; rsch. asst. Baylor Coll. Medicine, Houston, 1978-80; dir. sorority house Delta Delta Delta, Morgantown, W.Va., 1982-83; rsch. assoc. W.Va. U. Sch. Nursing, 1982-2001. Instr. Harvardian Colls., Oroquieta City, 1963-71. Contbr. articles to profl. jours. Bd. dirs. Misamis Occidental Pub. Sch. Tchrs. Assn., 1964-66, Misamis Occidental chpt. Boy Scouts of the Philippines, 1966-71, Misamis Occidental chpt. Girl Scouts of the Philippines, 1966-71, Misamis Occidental chpt. Philippine Nat. Red Cross, 1966-71. Philippine Bur. of Pub. Schs. scholar, 1961-62, Philippine Pub. Schs. Tchrs. Assn. scholar, 1971, Than and Luz Porter scholar NYU, 1972-75. Mem. APHA, Am. Ednl. Rsch. Assn. Republican. Presbyterian. Avocations: gardening, travel, swimming, cooking, hiking. Home: 16295 SW 14th St Pembroke Pines FL 33027

SOBRALSKE, BARBARA NILA, educator; b. Wild Rose, Wis., May 10, 1949; d. Kenneth John and Beverly Janice Graydon; m. Michael John Sobralske Jr., Oct. 17, 1970; 1 child, Mark Michael. Cert., Waushara County (Wis.) Tchrs. Coll., 1969; BS, U. Wis., Oshkosh, 1974; MA, Marian Coll., 1991. Cert. elem. tchr., Wis. Tchr. elem. schs. Waupun (Wis.) Sch. Dist., 1969-72; title I aide Wild Rose Sch. Dist., 1975, tchr. elem. schs., 1975-95, elem. prin., 1995—. Mem.: ASCD, Nat. Assn. Elem. Sch. Prins., Assn. of Wis. Sch. Adminstrs., Wis. Assn. Environ. Edn. Bus. Home: N5268 17th Dr Wild Rose WI 54984-6220 Office: Wild Rose Elem Sch PO Box 119 Wild Rose WI 54984-0119 E-mail: barb@staff.wildrose.k12.wi.us., sbralske@vbe.com.

SOBRATO, JOHN A. construction executive; married; 3 children. Real estate agt., Palo Alto, 1957; founder, prin. Sobrato Devel. Cos., Cupertino, Calif. Trustee U. Santa Clara; vice chmn. Nat. Hispanic U. Named Philanthropist of Yr., NSFRE, 1998. Office: Sobrato Devel Cos Ste 200 10600 N De Anza Blvd Cupertino CA 95014-2075

SOBUS, KERSTIN MARYLOUISE, physician, physical therapist; b. Washington, June 16, 1960; d. Earl Francis and Dolores Jane (Gill) G.; m. Paul John Jr., March 10, 1990; children: Darlene Marie, Julieann Marie. BS in Phys. Therapy summa cum laude, U. N.D., 1981, MD, 1987. Clinic instr. pediatric physical therapy U.N.D. Sch. Medicine, Grand Forks, 1981-83; pediat. phys. therapist child evaluation-treatment program Med. Rehab. Ctr., 1981-83, med. dir. program, 1997—; asst. prof. dept. pediatrics, asst. prof. dept. physical medicine and rehab. U. Ark. for Med. Scis., Little Rock, 1992-96; resident in internal medicine Sinai Hosp. Balt., 1987-88; resident in phys. medicine and rehab. Johns Hopkins program Sinai Hosp., Balt., 1988-91; pediatric rehab. clin. and rsch. fellow Alfred I. DuPont Inst., Wilmington, Del., 1991-92; pediatric pysiatrist Altru Health System, Grand Forks, 1997—. Contbr. articles to med. jours. Mem. Am. Acad. Cerebral Palsy and Devel. Medicine, Alpha Omega Alpha Honor Soc. Home: 1548 30th Ave NE Manvel ND 58256-9793 Office: Altru Health Sys PO Box 6002 1300 S Columbia Rd Grand Forks ND 58201-4012

SOCARIDES, CHARLES WILLIAM, psychiatrist, psychoanalyst, educator, writer; b. Brockton, Mass., Jan. 24, 1922; s. James and Theodora (Cokas) S.; m. Veronica Rak (div.); children: Richard, Daphne (dec.); m. Barbara Bonner, Jan. 28, 1973 (div. Apr. 1987); children: Alexandra, Charles Jr.; m. Claire Alford, Oct. 19, 1988; 1 child, Jacqueline Nichole Cert., Harvard Coll., Cambridge, Mass., 1945; MD, N.Y. Med. Coll., 1947; cert., Columbia U., N.Y.C., 1952. Diplomate Am. Bd. Psychiatry and Neurology. Instr. in psychiatry Columbia U., N.Y.C., 1956-60, assoc. in psychiatry, 1960-62; clin. asst. prof. psychiatry SUNY, 1955-58, clin. prof. psychiatry, 1976-78; assoc. attending psychiatrist Vanderbilt Clinic Coll. U., 1960-62; assoc. clin. prof. psychiatry Albert Einstein Coll. Medicine, 1969-76, clin. prof., 1976-97; clin. prof. psychiatry Montefiore Med. Ctr., 1978-97; pvt. practice psychoanalysis and psychiatry, 1997—. Med. cons. Armed Svcs. Dept. Def., Washington, 1978—; tng. psychiat. residents Albert Einstein Coll. Medicine, 1968-90.

Author: The Overt Homosexual, 1968, Homosexuality, 1978, The Preoedipol Origin and Psychoanalytic Treatment of Sexual Perversion, 1988, Beyond Sexual Freedom, On Sexuality: Psychoanalytic Observations, 1979, The Homosexualities and the Therapeutic Process, 1991; co-author: (with V. Volkan) Homosexuality: Reality, Fantasy and the Arts, 1990, (with V. Volkan) Homosexuality: A Freedom Too Far, 1995, (with Abraham Freedman) The Sexual Deviations: Theory and Therapy, 1999; co-author, editor (with Selma Kramer): Work and Its Inhibitions, 1996; contbr. articles to profl. jours.; numerous book reviews. Lt. USNR, 1952-54. Recipient Sigmund Freud award Am. Soc. Psychoanalytic Physicians, 1987, N.Y. Soc. for Psychoanalytic Tng., 1975, Disting. Prof. award Assn. Psychoanalytic Psychologists, Brit. Health Svc., London, 1995. Fellow Am. Psychoanalytic Assn., Am. Psychiat. Assn., Am. Coll. Psychoanalysts, Am. Soc. Psychoanalytic Physicians (hon. fellow); mem. AMA, Nat. Assn. Rsch. and Therapy of Homosexuality (pres. 1992—), N.Y. County Med. Soc., Internat. Psychoanalytic Assn., Nat. Assn. Scholars (Princeton, N.J.), Coral Beach Club. Democrat. Greek Orthodox. Avocations: tennis, writing, professional books. Home and Office: 242 E 94th St New York NY 10128-3706

SOCHACKI, ANDRZEJ, mechanical engineer, researcher, tourism educator; b. Warsaw, Poland, July 26, 1948; came to U.S., 1973; s. Jerzy and Halina (Błażejczyk) S.; married. MS, Warsaw U., 1969; AAS, Maricopa Tech. Coll., Phoenix, 1983; postgrad., Ariz. State U., 1985. Sr. mech. engr. Roger Bus. Products div. Rogers Corp., Mesa, Ariz., 1986-87; sr. mech. design engr. Parker Aerospace Co., Phoenix, 1987-88; sr. project engr. Micro-Rel Inc., Tempe, Ariz., 1988-90; cons., project engr., pres., owner Design & Fabricating Co., Phoenix, 1985-96; founder, pres., chmn. The Vagabond Ctr., 1992; tool engr. Boeing Co., Mesa, Ariz., 1996-98; tchr., lectr. traveling Tourism and Hotels Mgmt. Coll., Warsaw, 1998—. Contbr. ednl. articles to publs. Recipient award Medtronic Corp., Phoenix, 1989. Mem. Soc. Mfg. Engrs. (sr.). Roman Catholic. Avocations: piano, research, 6 times travel around the world by car, plane, sailboat, train, and twice by motorcycle. Home and Office: The Vagabond Ctr 3715 E Taylor St Phoenix AZ 85008-6316 E-mail: asochacki@yahoo.com.

SOCHEN, JUNE, history educator; b. Chgo., Nov. 26, 1937; d. Sam and Ruth (Finkelstein) S. BA, U. Chgo., 1958; MA, Northwestern U., 1960, PhD, 1967. Project editor Chgo. Superior and Talented Student Project, 1959-60; high sch. tchr. English and history North Shore Country Day Sch., Winnetka, Ill., 1961-64; instr. history Northeastern Ill. U., 1964-67, asst. prof., 1967-69, assoc. prof., 1969-72, prof., 1972—. Author: The New Woman, 1971, Movers and Shakers, 1973, Herstory: A Woman's View of American History, 1975, 2d edit., 1981, Consecrate Every Day: The Public Lives of Jewish American Women, 1981, Enduring Values: Women in Popular Culture, 1987, Cafeteria America: New Identities in Contemporary Life, 1988, Mae West: She Who Laughs Lasts, 1992, From Mae to Madonna: Women Entertainers in 20th Century America, 1999; editor: Women's Comic Visions, 1991; contbr. articles to profl. jours. Nat. Endowment for Humanities grantee, 1971-72 Office: Northeastern Ill U 5500 N Saint Louis Ave Chicago IL 60625-4679 E-mail: j-sochen@neiu.edu.

SOCKEY, FELICIA WILLENE, elementary school educator; b. Stigler, Okla., Sept. 17, 1957; d. Jessie Fredrick abd Genevieve Madeline (Garland) Venable; m. Leland L. Sockey. BS, Northeastern State U., Tahlequah, Okla., 1979; AS, Ea. State Coll., Wilburton, Okla., 1977. Cert. tchr., Okla. Elem. tchr. Pocola (Okla.) Pub. Schs.; elem. English tchr. Quinton (Okla.) Pub. Schs., 2001—. Active Pocola PTA. Mem. NEA, Okla. Edn. Assn., Internat. Soc. Poets, Pocola Classroom Tchrs. Assn.

SOCOL, MICHAEL LEE, obstetrician, gynecologist, educator; b. Chgo., Oct. 3, 1949; s. Joseph and Bernice (Bofman) S.; m. Donna Kaner, Dec. 17, 1972. BS, U. Ill., 1970; MD, U. Ill., Chgo., 1974. Diplomate Am. Bd. Ob-Gyn., Am. Bd. Maternal-Fetal Medicine. Resident obstetrics and gynecology U. Ill. Hosp., Chgo., 1974-77; clin. rsch. fellow dept. obstetrics and gynecology L.A. County-U. So. Calif. Med. Ctr., 1977-79; assoc. attending physician Northwestern Meml. Hosp., Chgo., 1980-86, attending physician dept. ob-gyn., 1986—; co-dir. Northwestern Perinatal Ctr., 1987—; head maternal-fetal medicine, chief obstetrics Northwestern U. Med. Sch., 1987—, dir. maternal-fetal medicine fellowship program, 1987-99, asst. prof. obstetrics and gynecology, 1979-84, assoc. prof., 1984-92, prof., 1992—. Vice chmn. dept. ob-gyn Northwestern Meml. Hosp., Chgo., 1992—. Author: (with others) Clinical Obstetrics and Gynecology, 1982, 1984, Diagnostic Ultrasound Applied to Obstetrics and Gynecology, 1987, Principles and Practice of Medical Therapy in Pregnancy, 1992; peer reviewer Am. Jour. Obstetrics and Gynecology, 1980—, Obstetrics and Gynecology, 1984—; contbr. numerous articles to profl. jours. Fellow Am. Coll. Ob-Gyn., Soc. Maternal-Fetal Medicine, Ctrl. Assn. Ob-Gyn., Chgo. Gynecol. Soc., Soc. for Gynecol. Investigation, Am. Gynecol. and Obstetrical Soc.; mem. AMA, Assn. Profs. of Gynecology and Obstetrics, Ill. State Med. Assn., Chgo. Med. Soc. Avocation: marathon running. Office: 333 E Superior St Ste 410 Chicago IL 60611-3015

SOCOL, SHELDON ELEAZER, university official; b. N.Y.C., July 10, 1936; s. Irving and Helen (Tuchman) S.; m. Genia Ruth Prager, Dec. 26, 1959; children: Jeffrey, Steven, Sharon, Robyn, Leslie, Steven Warren. BA, Yeshiva U., 1958; JD, NYU, 1963. From asst. bursar to dir. student fins. Yeshiva U., N.Y.C., 1958-70, sec., 1970—, chief fiscal officer, 1971-72, v.p. bus. affairs, 1972—. Mem. N.Y. State Adv. Coun. on Fin. Assistance to Coll. Students, 1969-76; asst. dir. Tng. Inst. for Fin. Aid Officers, Hunter, Coll., CUNY, 1970-71; mem. presdl. adv. com. Temple U., 1986; mem. regents adv. task force N.Y.C. Regional Plan for Higher Edn., 1971-73; bd. dirs. N.Y. Structural Biology Ctr., 2000; spkr. in field. Pres. Minyon Park Estates, Inc. Mem. NEA, Nat. Assn. Coll. and Univ. Attys., Met. N.Y.C. Fin. Aid Adminstrs. Assn., Ea. Assn. Student Fin. Aid Officers, Am. Mgmt. Assn., Am. Assn. for Higher Edn., Nat. Assn. Coll. and Univ. Bus. Officers, Soc. Coll. and Univ. Planning, Mid. States Assn. Colls. (evaluation team Commn. on Higher Edn., U. Medicine and Dentistry N.J., 1985, Upstate Health Sci. Ctr. 1986, Carnegie-Mellon U. 1988, Albany Med. Ctr. 1989). Office: Yeshiva U 500 W 185th St New York NY 10033-3299 E-mail: dses@ymail.yu.edu.

SOCOLOW, ARTHUR ABRAHAM, geologist; b. Bronx, N.Y., Mar. 23, 1921; s. Samuel and Yetta (Solomon) S.; m. Edith S. Blumenthal, Apr. 10, 1949; children: Carl, Roy. Jeff. BS, Rutgers U., 1942; MA, Columbia U., 1947, PhD, 1955. Reg. profl. geologist, Commonwealth Pa. Photogrammetrist, U.S. Army Air Corps, 1942-46; with Eagle Picher de Mexico, 1947; instr. geology So. Methodist U., 1948-50; dir. geology field camp Colo., 1948-50; asst. prof. Boston U., 1950-55; geologist Def. Minerals Exploration Authority, Alaska, 1952; assoc. prof. U. Mass., 1955-57; econ. geologist Pa. Geol. Survey, 1957-61, dir., state geologist, 1961-86; cons. geologist Gloucester, Mass., 1986—; prof. environ. geology Salem (Mass.) State Coll., 1993-98; dir. New Eng. Govs. Conf. Project on Aggregate Resources New Eng., 1990-97. Mem. Outer Continental Shelf Policy Com., 1974-88, Pa. rep., 1978-88; lectr. mineral conservation Pa. State U., 1959-75; mem. conf. earth sci. source materials NSF, 1959; chmn. ann. field conf. Pa. Geologists, 1961-86; past mem. U.S. Nat. Com. on Tunnelling Tech.; mem. com. on N.Y. State low level waste program Nat. Acad. Sci.; past mem. gov.'s adv. com. Nat. Coun. on Environ. Quality; past chmn. Pa. Water Resources Coordinating Com.; geol. advisor Boston Mus. Sci., 1955-57. Former editor Pa. Geol. Bull.; mem. editorial bd. Northeastern Geol. Jour.; contbr. over 100 publs. and papers on environ. and econ. geology to profl. jours. Served with USAAF, 1942-46. Fellow Geol. Soc. Am. (sec.-treas. N.E. sect., past nat. councilor), Mineral Soc. Am., AAAS (past pres. geography-geology sect.), Soc. Econ. Geologists; mem. AAUP, Am. Geol. Inst., Nat. Assn. Geology Tchrs. (past regional pres., Ralph Digman award for contbns. to geologic edn. 1980), Am. Meteoritical Soc., Assn. Am. State Geologists (past pres., editor, compiler State Geological Surveys-A History 1988), Am. Geophys. Union, Am. Commn. Stratigraphic Nomenclature (past chmn.), Gloucester Conservation Commn. (chmn.), Fgn. Policy Assn. (past chpt. pres.), Sigma Xi. Clubs: Internat. Torch (past pres. chpt.). Home and Office: 26 Salt Island Rd Gloucester MA 01930-1945 E-mail: docsoc@earthlink.net. *I have great respect for the individualism of man in the midst of a society and a world where there is an unavoidable interrelationship and interdependence of man upon man, and of man upon his environment. While we strive to maintain our individualism, we must share our common resources and our common aspirations. This is the challenge that makes our lives worth living.*

SOCOLOW, DANIEL JAMES, foundation administrator; b. N.Y.C., Feb. 3, 1940; s. A. Walter and Edith Gutman S.; m. Susan Migden, Dec. 21, 1965; children: Ari B., Joshua A. AB, U. Wis., 1962; AMT, Harvard U.; PhD, U. Chgo.; LHD, Am. U., Paris, 1988. Program assoc. Ford Found., Buenos Aires, 1965-70; dir. ctr. internat. studies SUNY, Plattsburgh, N.Y., 1971-76; v.p. Spelman Coll., Atlanta, 1978-83; pres. Am. U., Paris, 1983-88; dir. programs Carter Ctr., Atlanta, 1989-93; pres. Socolow Group, N.Y.C., 1993-97; dir. MacArthur Found. Fellows Program, Chgo., 1997—. Cons. in field. Sr. fellow Nat. Inst. Edn., Washington, 1976-78. Jewish. Office: MacArthur Found 140 S Dearborn St Fl 11 Chicago IL 60603-5269

SODAL, INGVAR EDMUND, electrical engineer, scientist; b. Hemne, Norway, Feb. 12, 1934; came to U.S., 1962; s. Ingebrigt L. and Johanna Sodal; m. Sally Rollins; 1 child Silje M. Degree in elec. engring., Trondheim Tech. Coll., Norway, 1959; BSEE, U. Colo., 1964. Engr. Fjeldseth Engring., Trondheim, 1959-61; rsch. engr. U. Norway, 1961-62, U. Colo. Med. Ctr., Denver, 1964-66, rsch. assoc., 1966-75, instr., lectr., 1975-79; vis. rsch. assoc. dept. engring. U. Colo., Boulder, 1974-75, lectr., 1975-76; asst. prof., div. head. Ohio State U., Columbus, 1979-82, mem. grad. faculty, 1982; pres., chief exec. officer Masstron, Inc., Boulder, Colo., 1983-87; chief scientist Paradygm, 1987-89; pres. Pacemark, Inc., 1989-90, Med. Physics Colo., Inc., 1991—. Contbr. articles to profl. jours., chpts. to books; holder 6 patents in field. Instr. and/or program coord. in Scandinavian folklore and folk dancing for numerous groups and instns. throughout U.S., Can., and Norway, 1959—. Grantee NIH and various pvt. orgns. Mem. Village Arts Coalition, Sons of Norway. Office: 1550 Moss Rock Pl Boulder CO 80304-1543 E-mail: sodaling@csd.net.

SODARO, EDWARD RICHARD, psychiatrist; b. Glen Cove, N.Y., Oct. 3, 1947; s. Edward Richard and Mae Florence Sodaro; 2 children. BS, Siena Coll., Loudonville, N.Y., 1969; MD, Georgetown U., 1973; MA, Grad. Faculty of New Sch., N.Y.C., 1976. Diplomate Am. Bd. Psychiatry and Neurology, Am. Bd. Adolescent Psychiatry, Am. Bd. Quality Assurance and Utilization Rev. Physicians, Am. Soc. Addiction Medicine, Am. Forensic Psychiatry, Am. Bd. Geriatric Psychiatry, Am. Bd. Addiction Psychiatry. Resident in psychiatry L.I. Jewish Hosp., New Hyde Park, N.Y., 1973-76; staff psychiatrist N.Y. Hosp./Cornell Med. Ctr., White Plains, 1979-81, faculty, 1979-81; sr. psychiatrist South Oaks Hosp., Amityville, N.Y., 1981—; quality assurance dir. Suffolk Psychiat. Svcs., Stony Brook, 1996—. Clin. asst. prof. SUNY Stony Brook Sch. Medicine. Mem. Am. Psychiat. Assn., Med. Soc. State of N.Y. (com. for physicians, health), Am. Soc. Addiction Medicine, Am. Coll. Physician Execs., Sons Am. Revolution. Roman Catholic. Office: 137 Broadway Ste E Amityville NY 11701

SODEMAN, THOMAS MICHAEL, pathologist, educator, science administrator; b. New Orleans, Mar. 4, 1941; s. William Anthony and Mary Agnes (Wagner) S.; m. Mary Kathryne Hancock, June 20, 1964; children: Jeffrey, Gregory, Julia, Kristen. BS, Coll. of William and Mary, 1962; MD, U. Va., 1966. Asst. prof., then assoc. prof. U. Mich., Ann Arbor, 1972-76; prof. pathology W.Va. U., Morgantown, 1976-77; clin. assoc. prof. E. Carolina U., Greenville, N. Carolina, 1978-80, U. Kans., Lawrence, 1980-85; assoc. dean clin. affairs Health Scis. Ctr. Sch. Medicine, Tex. Tech U., Lubbock, 1986-88, May Owen prof., chmn. pathology, 1985—; assoc. dean Health Scis. Ctr., Sch. Medicine, Tex. Tech U., 1988-90, dir. clin. microbiology univ. med. ctr., 1985—. Fellow ACP, Am. Soc. Clin. Pathologists, Coll. Am. Pathologists; mem. AMA, Tex. Soc. Pathologists. Avocation: fishing. Office: Christ Hosp 2139 Auburn Ave Cincinnati OH 45219-2989

SODEN, RUTH M. geriatrics nurse, educator; b. Tipton, Iowa, Nov. 29, 1940; d. Tony and Clarissa Arlene (Beall) Koreman; m. James D. Soden; children: Shannon, Scott, Suzan, Staci. AA, Highline Community Coll., Midway, Wash. Cert. in intravenous therapy. Charge nurse Wildwood Health Care Ctr., Puyallup, Wash.; admissions coord. Forestglen Nursing Ctr., Seattle, staff devel. dir.; charge nurse Green River Terrace Nursing Ctr., Auburn, Discovery Care Ctr., Hamilton, Mont.; nurse mgr. Tacoma Luth. Home; charge nurse Discovery Care Ctr., Hamilton. Mem. Clover Park Tech. Coll., Tacoma. Mem. Nat. Gerontol. Nursing Assn. (practical nurse program adv. com.), Wash. State Nurses Assn., Assn. for Practitioners in Infection Control, Nat. Coun. on Family Rels., Phi Theta Kappa. Home: 157 West Hills Way Hamilton MT 59840-9316

SODER-ALDERFER, KAY CHRISTIE, counseling administrator; b. Evanston, Ill., Oct. 25, 1949; d. Earl Eugene and Alice Kathryn (Lien) Soder; m. David Luther Alderfer, May 15, 1976. BSE, No. Ill. U., 1972; postgrad., Luth. Sch. Theology, Phila., 1973; MA, Gov.'s State U., University Park, Ill., 1978; PhD, Walden U., 1985. Consecrated deaconess Luth. Ch., 1974. News reporter Suburban Life Newspaper, La Grange Park, Ill., 1972; counselor various orgns. Ill. & Pa., 1973—; parish worker Luth. Ch., De Kalb, Ill., 1973-74; pub. rels. asst. Luth. Ch. Women, Phila., 1974-76; editor Luth. Ch., Chgo., 1979—; spiritual dir. Gentle Pathways, Downers Grove, Ill., 1988—, psychotherapist, 1990—, also bd. dirs. Founder Wordsmith Wizards, 2002; cons. Evang. Luth. Ch. in Am., Chgo., 1988—, Lehigh Valley Hosp. Assn., Allentown, Pa., 1986, Luth. Social Ministry Orgns. of Pa. and N.J., 1997; cons. multinat. corps., 2001—. Author: Gentle Journeys, 1993, With Those Who Grieve, 1995, Help! There's a Monster in My Head, 2000; editor Entree, 1988-93, Multicultural Jour., 1992-99, project mgr., 1996-98; graphic designs exhbn. Franklin Mus., Phila., 1981; photography published in 3 books. Spokeswoman Progressive Epilepsy Network, Phila., 1980-85; chair spiritual life com. Luth. Deaconess Cmty., Gladwyne, Pa., 1990-92; founder Teens with Epilepsy and Motivation, 1995; vol. March of Dimes, Ill., 1991-93, Am. Cancer Soc., 2000—; amb. of goodwill Good Bears of the World, 1993-94; spiritual dir. Evang. Luth. Ch. in Am. Recipient Silver award Delaware Valley Neographics Soc., 1981; 50th anniversary scholar Luth. Deaconess Community, 1983. Mem. AAUW, APA, Webmasters of the World. Avocations: painting, mixed media, story telling, traveling, Native American studies. Office: Gentle Pathways 1207 55th St Downers Grove IL 60515-4810

SODERBERG, BO S. marketing executive; b. Avesta, Sweden, Mar. 22, 1939; came to U.S., 1979; s. John Sigfrid and Elisabet A. (Bjorkvall) S.; m. Kerstin Linnea Nordling; children: Monica, Mikael, Bogge, Margareta. BS in Engring., TGO, Orebro, Sweden, 1960; MBA, Fla. Inst. Tech., 1985. Mng. dir. Scandinavian Computer Systems, Stockholm, 1967-69; pres. Bror Andersson AB (BRA), 1969-78; exec. dir. Cap Gemini Sogeti, Paris, 1978-80, Cap Gemini Inc., Washington, 1980-82; pres. DMA Marketing Inc., Palm Bay, Fla., 1982-86, Prisma Am. Inc., Vero Beach, 1986-87, also bd. dirs.; pres. Scandinavian USA Bus. Ctr., Inc., Clearwater, 1988-92, DMA Mktg. Inc., St. Petersburg, 1993-98, Atlanta, 1998—. Seminar instr. Swedish Computer Soc., Stockholm, 1970-78; instr., lectr. Swedish Soc. for Info. Processing, Stockholm, 1972-78; lectr. Fla. Outdoor Advt. Assn.,Orlando, Fla., 1986-87. Served as specialist Sweden Air Force, 1960-61. Home: 3375 Spring Hill Pkwy # 1034 Smyrna GA 30080 Office: PO Box 420337 Atlanta GA 30342

SODERBERG, DALE LEROY, English language educator, drama director, producer; b. Warren, Pa., Apr. 24, 1929; s. Leroy Wilbur and Olive Hazel (Conboy) S.; m. Marjorie Ann Hamm, Aug. 19, 1951; children: David J., Valli K., W. Mark, Lisa T., Kathi L. BA, Gettysburg Coll., 1951; BD, Luth. Theol. Sem., Gettysburg, Pa., 1954. Cert. secondary English tchr., N.Y.; ordained mins. Luth. Ch., 1954. Pastor Grace Luth. Ch., Clarion, Pa., 1954-57; mission developer, 1st pastor Our Saviour's Luth. Ch., Horseheads, N.Y., 1957-60; dir. Ecclesia Tours (Luth. Fgn. Tours), Horseheads and North Syracuse, 1958-67; mgr. Soderberg Travel Svc., Corning, 1960-62; pastor St. John's Luth. Ch., Syracuse, 1962-66; guest chapel preacher Wittenberg U., Ohio, 1966; tchr. English Ft. Myers (Fla.) High Sch., 1967-68; tchr. English, dir. drama Hamilton (N.Y.) Cen. Sch., 1968-92; retired, 1992; sermon and story writer Ecclesia Svcs., Hamilton, 1984-96. Lay preacher Upstate N.Y. Synod Evang. Luth. Ch. Am., Syracuse, 1968—; advisor student tchrs.at Hamilton Cen. Sch. for Colgate U., Hamilton, 1975-92; clk. Hamilton Stores, Yellowstone Nat. Park, summer 1948, 93. Author: (novels) Pawns, 1980, The Amsterdam Connection, 1999, A Time for Choosing, 2001, My Protestant, 2002 Dir. tours to Europe, Holy Land and Luth. mission fields in Brit. Guiana, East and West Africa, and India; bd. dirs. Luth. Homes Found., 1993-96; vol. missionary religious edn. tchr. U. of Papua New Guinea, Goroka, spring 1996; mem. Global Missions Team, Upstate N.Y. Synod Evang. Luth. Ch. Am., Syracuse, 1999—; organizer and dir. Bishop's tour to Zimbabwe, 2001. Mem. N.Y. State United Tchrs., Hamilton Tchrs. Assn., N.Y. State Ret. Tchrs. Assn. Republican. Avocations: travel, photography, home video, creative writing, Hemingway specialization. Home: 1907 Preston Hill Rd Hamilton NY 13346-9522

SODERBERG, WILLIAM CHARLES, philosophy educator; b. Thorp, Wis. s. Arthur William and Eileen Marie S.; m. Susan Cooke, June 13, 1970; children: Anna, Jenka, Keir. PhD, Georgetown U., 1991. Program coord. philosophy Montgomery Coll., Rockville, Md., 1976-90, dept. chair, 1990-93. Author: The Game of Philosophy, 2000. Mem. citizens adv. bd. County Coun., Rockville, Md., 1986-87. Smithsonian fellow, 1998-99. Mem. Am. Philos. Assn. Office: Montgomery Coll 51 Mannakee St Rockville MD 20850

SODERLAND, DOUGLAS R. lawyer; b. Seattle, Apr. 6, 1960; s. Stanley C. and Mary E. (Sutherland) S.; m. Parcae Lea Morford, Sept. 15, 1984; children: Devin L., Morgan L. BA magna cum laude, Western Wash. U., 1982; JD cum laude, U. Puget Sound, 1986. Bar: Wash. 1986, U.S. Dist. (we. dist.) Wash. 1986, U.S. Dist. (ea. dist.) Wash. 1994. Assoc. Houger, Miller & Stein, Seattle, 1986—90, Wilson, Smith, Cochran & Dickerson, Seattle, 1990—93, Groshong & Thornton, Seattle, 1993—98; ptnr. Soderland Waechter PLLC, 1999—2002, Law Offices of Douglas R. Soderland, Seattle, 2002—. Contbg. author: Washington Motor Vehicle Accident Deskbook, 1994. Office: Law Offices of Douglas R Soderland 2025 First Ave Ste PH-A Seattle WA 98121

SODERLIND, STERLING EUGENE, newspaper industry consultant; b. Rapelje, Mont., Sept. 6, 1926; s. William John and Florence (Longbotham) S.; m. Helen Boyce, Apr. 9, 1955; children: Steven (dec.), Sarah, Lori. BA, U. Mont., 1950; Rhodes Scholar, Oxford U., Eng., 1950-52. Reporter Mpls. Tribune, 1952-55; reporter Wall St. Jour., Chgo., 1955-56, Southeastern bur. chief Jacksonville, Fla., 1956-57, mem. page one editing staff N.Y.C., 1957-65, asst. mng. editor, 1966-70, mng. editor, 1970; econs. editor Dow Jones & Co., Inc., 1970-77, asst. to pres., 1975-77, v.p., 1977-91; newspaper industry cons., 1992—. Served with USNR, 1944-46. Congregationalist. Home: 58 Wellington Ave Short Hills NJ 07078-3308

SODERLUND, JEAN R. historian, educator, historian, researcher; b. Phila., Jan. 17, 1947; d. John and Joyce Ruth; m. Rudolf W. Soderlund, June 3, 1967. BA, Douglas Coll., New Brunswick, N.J., 1968; MA, Glassboro (N.J.) State Coll., 1971; PhD, Temple U., Phila., 1982. Tchr. Deptford Twp. (N.J.) High Sch., 1968—72; instr. Camden County Coll., Camden, NJ, 1972—75; assoc. editor Papers of William Penn, Phila., 1981—83; curator Swarthmore (Pa.) Coll. Peace Collection, 1983—88; asst. then assoc. prof. history U. Md., Catonsville, 1988—94; prof. history Lehigh U., Bethlehem, Pa., 1994—, dept. chair, 1998—. Author: Quakers & Slavery: A Divided Spirit, 1985 (N.J. Hist. Commn., 1984); co-author: Freedom by Degrees, 1991, (textbook) American Passages, 2000. Mem.: Orgn. Am. Historians, Am. Hist. Assn. Office: Lehigh U Dept of History 9 W Packer Ave Bethlehem PA 18015

SODERQUIST, LARRY DEAN, lawyer, educator, consultant, writer; b. Ypsilanti, Mich., July 20, 1944; s. Hugo E. and Emma A. (Johanson) S.; m. Ann Mangelsdorf, June 15, 1968; children: Hans, Lars. BS, Ea. Mich. U., 1966; JD, Harvard U., 1969. Bar: N.Y. 1971, Tenn. 1981. Assoc. Milbank, Tweed, Hadley & McCloy, N.Y.C., 1971-76; assoc. prof. law U. Notre Dame, South Bend, Ind., 1976-80, prof., 1980-81; vis. prof. law Vanderbilt U. Law Sch., Nashville, 1980-81, prof., 1981—. Dir. corp. and securities law inst. 1993—; of counsel Dinsmore & Shohl LLP; spl. master U.S. Dist. Ct. (no. dist.) Ohio, 1977; vis. prof. law Harvard U. Law Sch., Cambridge, Mass., 1999. Author: Corporations, 1979, 5th edit., 2001, Understanding the Securities Laws, 3d edit., 1993, Securities Law, 1998, Securities Regulation, 4th edit., 1999, Corporate Law and Practice, 2d edit., 1999, Law of Federal Estate and Gift Taxation: Code Commentary, 1978, Analysis, 1980, Investor's Rights Handbook, 1993; (novel) The Labcoat, 1998; contbr. articles to profl. jours. Capt. U.S. Army, 1969-71. Decorated Army Commendation medal. Mem. ABA, Am. Law Inst. Presbyterian. Home: 2000 Grand Ave Ste 801 Nashville TN 37212 Office: Vanderbilt U Sch Law 131 21st Ave S Nashville TN 37203-1120

SODERQUIST, RONALD BRUCE, minister, ministry consultant; b. Pine City, Minn., Mar. 16, 1943; s. Russell Eugene and Abigail Mae (Berger) S.; m. Carol Lynn Peterson, Aug. 20, 1966; children: Peter Gustav, Ingrid Ann-Marie, Anna Kristine. BA, Northwestern Coll., 1965; MA, U. Wis., 1967; D in Ministry, Bethel Theol. Sem., 1993. Ordained min. So. Bapt. Conv., 1988. Acad. dean Kings Inst. Coll., Koronodal, Cotabato, The Philippines, 1967-69; asst. prof. English Trinity Coll., Deerfield, Ill., 1969-70; student ministry staff Campus Crusade for Christ, L.A., Mpls., Madison, 1970-77, regional dir. midwest, 1977-80, internat. rep. Sweden, 1980-84; spl. rep. Christian Embassy, Washington, 1984-87, dir. mil. ministry, 1987-98; adj. prof. MS in Orgnl. Leadership Program Geneva Coll., 1998; min., cons. Campus Crusade's U.S. Ministry, 1999—2001; city dir. Priority Assocs., Mpls., 2001—. Recipient Disting. Alumnus award, Northwestern Coll. St. Paul, 1999. Avocations: travel, photography, reading. Home and Office: 5371 S Park Dr Savage MN 55378 Fax: 952-226-4132. E-mail: ron@seruantleadership.com.

SODERVICK, BRUCE WERNER, sculptor, art educator; b. Chgo., Feb. 28, 1939; s. Werner and Bertha Amelia (Lott) S.; m. Judith Zerbe, May 29, 1980. BS, Ind. U., 1962; MFA, So. Ill. U., 1967. Asst. prof. Ohio U., Chillicothi, 1967-71; prof. Rochester (N.Y.) Inst. Tech., 1971—. Artist residency Bemis Found., Omaha, 1985-86; vis. artist Ill. State U., Normal, 1987, Oxbow Art Inst. Chgo., 1991, Artpark, Lewiston, N.Y., 1994; co-dir. Sodervick Studios, Sodus, N.Y., 1977—; artist selection panel Regional N.Y. State Arts Coun., Lyons, 1993-94; moderator creative symposium SUNY, Oswego, 1993. One-man exhibits include SUNY, Oswego, 1992, Coffey Gallery, Rochester, 1994; group exhibts include Kittrell/Riffkind Gallery, Dallas, 1993, John Elder Gallery, N.Y.C.; featured artis Berkshire Ctr. Contemprary Glass, West Stockbridge, Mass., Waterside Gallery , West Stockbridge, Mass., Sculpture Installation Pedvale Open Air Art Mus., Sabile, Latvia, 2000; guest artist Hodgell Gallery, Sarasota, Fla., 1995. Coord. hist. ch. resorations, Episc. Diocese, Rochester, 1992-93; cons. hist. preservation, planning bd. chmn. Village of Sodus, 1992-94. Recipient Sculpture Installation award Rochester Arts Selection Com., 1986, First prize Sculpture Everson Mus., 1990; grantee S.C. Arts Commn., 1987. Mem. AAUP, ABYC, USSA, Coll. Arts Assn. Am., Glass Arts Soc., Sodus Bay Hist. Soc., Wayne County Coun. Arts. Achievements include research in glass casting with copper laden bronze, cast glass into cast iron, photo-emulsions into cold glass surfaces. Avocations: classic wooden boat restoration, sailing, wind surfing. Home: 27 E Main St Sodus NY 14551-1042 Office: Rochester Inst Tech Coll Imaging Arts & Scis/Sch Art 73 Lomb Memorial Dr Bldg 07A Rochester NY 14623-5603 E-mail: bwsodervick@hotmail.com.

SODHI, MANBIR SINGH, manufacturing engineer, researcher; s. Ajit Kaur and Sohan Singh Sodhi; m. Kristin Elizabeth Sodhi, May 27, 1956; children: Hilary Ajit, Kristin Prakash, Brendon Kirk Bjorness-Murano. Ph. D, U. of Ariz., Tucson, 1985—91. Prof. and chair Indsl. and Mfg. Eng., U. of RI, Kingston, RI, 2001—, asst. and assoc. prof., 1991—2000. Pres. Tech. and Scheduling Solutions, Narragansett, RI, 2001; software cons. CMC India, Calcutta, W. Bengal, India, 1984—85; project engr. Dytron India, Calcutta, W. Bengal, India, 1984—84; engring. trainee Larsen and Toubro, Kansbahal, Orissa, India, 1983—84. Author: (study) Glance Analysis of Driver Eye Movements. Recipient Carlotti Award for Faculty Excellence, U. of RI, 1999; fellow Environ. Ecology Fellowship, Lucent/ATT, 1997-1999; grantee Econ. Processing in Modern Mfg. Systems, NSF. Mem.: Inst. of Indsl. Engineers (bd. mem. (local chpt.) 1998—2002), Assn. of Computing Machinery. Independent. Achievements include research in Glance Analysis of Driver Eye Movements; Tool Loading in Modern Manufacturing Systems. Office: University of Rhode Island 103 Gilbreth Hall Kingston RI 02881 Office Fax: 401-874-5540. Personal E-mail: sodhi@uri.edu. E-mail: sodhi@uri.edu.

SODI, MARCO, communications executive; b. Florence, Italy, Oct. 12, 1958; came to U.S., 1975; s. Mario and Diana (Hutchinson) S.; m. Ariane Monica Noel, June 25, 1994; children: Nadia Ariane, Isabella Diana. BS, Cornell U., 1980. Mgmt. trainee Exxon Enterprises, N.Y.C., 1980-81, analyst, 1981-83; br. mgr. Computer Wks., 1984-87; ptnr. Salem Solutions, 1987-89; dir. Veronis, Suhler & Assocs., 1989-91, mng. dir., 1991—. Mem. Mag. Pubs. of Am., Internat. Fedn. of the Periodical Press, Assn. Am. Pubs. Avocations: squash, golf, tennis, running. Office: Veronis Suhler & Associates 350 Park Ave New York NY 10022-6022

SODMAN, CHARLES EDWARD, probation/parole agent, educator, writer; b. Lansing, MI, June 6, 1949; s. William Carl Sodman, Joyce Jean Sodman; m. Sharon Kay Ballenger; children: Charles, Shari. Master of Science(Criminal Justice), Michigan State Unv., East Lansing, 1983—86. Author: (Books) The Satan Ring(1997) Amoung Close Friends and Family, 2001. Member Fraternal Order of Police, Owosso, MI, 1977—2002. Sp 4 Army, 1969—71, For Riley. Office: Probation/Parole Shiawasse Co. 112 E. McArthur St. Corunna MI Personal E-mail: scsodman@aol.com.

SODOLSKI, JOHN, retired association administrator; b. Menasha, Wis., Apr. 11, 1931; s. L.V. and L.W. (Pinkowski) S.; m. C.J. Eppard BS, U. Wis., 1953. Vice pres. Electronic Industries Assn., Washington, 1961-83; pres. U.S. Telephone Assn., 1983-93; ret., 1993. Served to 1st lt. USMC, 1955 Home: PO Box 1014 Middleburg VA 20118-1014

SODUMS, DZINTARS, writer; b. Riga, Latvia, May 13, 1922; came to U.S., 1963; s. Andrejs and Ella Brastins Sodums; m. Skaidrite Kronbergs, Feb. 23, 1946 (dec. May 1999); children: Andris, Marcis. Student, Lynn C.C., 1975-80. Translator Ulysses, 1960, 93, Narziss und Goldmund, 1961, Waste Land, 1990. Mem. Latvian Writers Assn. in Exile. Democrat. Home: 56 Liberty St # 4 Spencer NY 14883-9701

SOEDERSTROM, ELISABETH ANNA, opera singer; b. Stockholm, May 7, 1927; d. Emanuel Albert and Anna (Palasova) S.; m. Sverker Olow, Mar. 29, 1950; children: Malcolm, Peter, Jens. Student, Opera Sch., Stockholm; also pupil of Andrejewa Skilondz. Appearances include Stockholm Opera, 1950, Salzburg Festival, 1955, Glvndebourne Opera, 1957, 59, 61, 63, 64, Met. Opera, 1959, 60, 62, 63, 83, 86-87, 99; sang three leading roles in Rosencavalier within one year, 1959; toured USSR, 1966; others roles include Fiordiligi in Cosi Fan Tutte, Susanna and Countess in Figaro, Countess in Capriccio, Countess in Queen of Spodes; radio, TV and concert appearances in U.S. and Europe; artistic dir., Drottningholm Ct. Theatre, 1993-97; author: I Min Tonart, 1978, Sjung ut, Elisabeth!, 1986. Decorated Order of Vasa, Sweden, 1997, Stelle Della Solidarieta Dell'Italia; recipient King Olav's reward, Norway, prize for best acting Royal Swedish Acad., 1965, Literis et Artibus award, 1969; named comdr. Most Disting. Order Brit. Empire, CBE, comdr. des Arts et des Lettres, Singer of the Ct., Sweden, prof. Swedish Govt. Mem. Royal Acad. Music Gt. Britain (hon.). Office: Drottningholms Theatre Mus Box 15417 S-10465 Stockholm Sweden also: care Columbia Artists Mgmt 165 W 57th St New York NY 10019-2201

SOEJIMA, DAISUKE, international trade engineer, economist; b. Tokyo, Jan. 17, 1959; s. Aritoshi and Hiroko Soejima; m. Kiyomi Soejima, Sept. 26, 1987; children: Sayuri, Taiga, Chiaki. BS in Econs., Tokyo U., 1983; MBA, Georgetown U., 1991. Assoc. cons., mgr. coord. Mitsubishi Corp., Tokyo, 1991-95; mgr. Mitsubishi Internat. Corp., Washington, 1995-97, mgr. project and planning N.Y.C., 1997-98, mgr. chem. groups M&A divestitures, 1998-2001; dir. E-Commerce Devel., 1999—, unit mgr. investment and devel., 2001—. Sr. rschr. Japan Inst. for Econ. Rsch., Tokyo, 1981-83. Grad. adv. bd. Georgetown U.; bd. dirs. Avonite, Inc. Mem. Asian Chem. Mgmt. and Rsch. Assn., Met. Club, Beta Gamma Sigma, Alpha Mu Alpha. Home: 71 Hoyt St Darien CT 06820-3116 Office: Mitsubishi Internat Corp 520 Madison Ave New York NY 10022-4213 E-mail: soejima@boa.georgetown.edu.

SOELBERG, DIANE, music educator; b. Ogden, Utah, July 29, 1960; d. William Lamar and Charlene (Budge) S. MusB, U. Utah, 1982; BS in Music Therapy, Utah State U., 1987; MusM, Brigham Young U., 1993. Registered music therapist, 1987. Music therapist Terrebonne Assn. Retarded Citizens, Houma, La., 1987-88; band dir. Weber H.S., Ogden, 1988-92, Bonneville H.S., Ogden, 1993-94; band dir., dept. chair Fremont H.S., Plain City, Utah, 1994-96, Timpanogos H.S., Orem, 1996—. Mem. staff Utah Ambs. Music, 1995—. Prin. oboist New Am. Symphony, Ogden, 1994-96; assoc. condr. Am. Fork (Utah) Symphony, 1996-2002, condr., 2002-. Recipient Music Educator Yr. award Utah Region I Bd. Mgrs., 1994, 95, Accent on Excellence award Alpine Sch. Dist. Found., 2001. Mem.: Nat. Band Assn., Music Educators Nat. Conv., Utah Educators Assn., Utah Music Educators Assn. (state band com. 1996—, band v.p. 2000—02, all-state band chmn. 2002—, Rookie of Yr. award 1989). Avocation: traveling. Office: Timpanogos HS 1450 N 200 E Orem UT 84057-6270

SOERGEL, KONRAD HERMANN, physician; b. Coburg, Germany, July 27, 1929; came to U.S., 1954, naturalized, 1962; s. Konrad Daniel and Erna Henrietta (Schilling) S.; m. Rosina Klara Rudin, June 24, 1955; children: Elizabeth Ann, Karen Theresa, Marilyn Virginia, Kenneth Thomas. MD, U. Erlangen, Germany, 1954, Dr. med., 1958. Intern Bergen Pines County Hosp., Paramus, N.J., 1954-55; resident in pathology West Pa. Hosp., Pitts., 1955-56; rsch. asst. U. Erlangen, Germany, 1956-57; resident in medicine Mass. Meml. Hosp., Boston, 1957-58; fellow in gastroenterology Boston U. Med. Sch., 1958-60, instr., 1960-61; mem. faculty Med. Coll. Wis., Milw., 1961—2002, prof. medicine, 1969—2002, prof. physiology, 1993—2002, chief sect. gastroenterology, 1961-93. Chmn. gastroenterology and clin. nutrition study sect. NIH, 1979-80 Contbr. articles to profl. jours., chpts. to books. Recipient Research Career Devel. award USPHS, 1963-72; Alexander von Humboldt Found. sr. fellow, 1973-74 Mem. Am. Gastroenterol. Assn., Am. Soc. Clin. Investigation, Am. Assn. Physicians, German Soc. for Digestive and Metabolic Disorders (hon.), Ger. Soc. Internal Medicine (hon.). Home: 14245 Hillside Rd Elm Grove WI 53122-1677 Office: Med Coll Wis 9200 W Wisconsin Ave Milwaukee WI 53226-3522 E-mail: ksoergel@mcw.edu.

SOETEBER, ELLEN, journalist, newspaper editor; b. East St. Louis, Ill., June 14, 1950; d. Lyle Potter and Norma Elizabeth (Osborn) S.; m. Richard M. Martins, Mar. 16, 1974. BJ, Northwestern U., 1972. Edn. writer, copy editor Chgo. Today, 1972-74; reporter Chgo. Tribune, 1974-76, asst. met. editor, 1976-84, assoc. met. editor, 1984-86, TV and media editor, 1986, met. editor, 1987-89, assoc. mng. editor for met. news, 1989-91, dep. editor editorial page, 1991-94; mng. editor South Fla. Sun-Sentinel, Ft. Lauderdale, 1994-2001; editor St. Louis Post-Dispatch, 2001—. Fellow journalism U. Mich., Ann Arbor, 1986-87. Office: The St Louis Post-Dispatch 900 N Tucker Blvd Saint Louis MO 63101 E-mail: esoeteber@post-dispatch.com.

SOETH, JAMES RICHARD, forester; b. Oakland, Calif., Oct. 4, 1946; s. David Peter and Agnes Lilian (Burke) S.; m. Gretchen Mary Zell, Mar. 31, 1979 (div. Dec. 1989). Student, Laney and Merritt Colls., 1964-66; BS in Forestry, U. Idaho, 1969; postgrad., U. Mont., 1971-72, Calif. State U., San Bernardino, 1975; MPA, Calif. State U., Northridge, 1984; PhD, LaSalle U., 2002. Registered profl. forester, Calif. Forest technician, Oreg., Calif., 1972-73; resource forester USDA Forest Svc., Rimforest, 1974-76, asst. adminstrn. forester Somes Bar, 1976-78, dist. recreation officer Flintridge, 1978-85, forest recreation planner Arcadia, 1985-87, dist. ranger Young, Ariz., 1987-99, program mgr. Tech. Design Ctr. Lakewood, Colo., 1999—. Vis. instr. forest tech. Southwestern Oreg. C.C., Coos Bay, 1973-74; sec. so. com. Calif. Forest Pest Control Coun., Sacramento, Calif., 1975-76; instr. in forestry San Bernardino (Calif.) Valley Coll., 1976, Citrus Coll., Glendora, Calif., 1979-87. Co-author (booklet) For the Forest Technology Programs at the Community Colleges in Oregon, 1974. Bd. dirs. Young Pub. Sch. Dist. Bd., 1991-92, 94-97. With U.S. Army, 1969-71. Mem. Soc. Am. Foresters (past chpt. chair 1969—), Benevolent and Protective Order of Elks, 1994-99, K of C (past dep. grand knight of coun. 1990—). Republican. Roman Catholic. Achievements include development of ecosystem management program for restoration of the pinyon/juniper and juniper/savanna habitats on the Pleasant Valley Ranger Dist. Avocations: reading, hunting, golf. Office: PO Box 25485 Lakewood CO 80225-0485 E-mail: jsoeth@fs.fed.us.

SOFAER, ABRAHAM DAVID, lawyer, legal advisor, federal judge, law educator; b. Bombay, India, May 6, 1938; came to U.S., 1948, naturalized, 1959; m. Marian Bea Scheuer, Oct. 23, 1977; children: Daniel E., Michael J., Helen R., Joseph S., Aaron R., Raphael J. BA in History magna cum laude, Yeshiva Coll., 1962; LLB cum laude, NYU, 1965. Bar: N.Y. 1965, D.C. 1988. Law clk. to Hon. J. Skelly Wright, U.S. Ct. Appeals (D.C. cir.), Washington, 1965-66; law clk. to Hon. William J. Brennan Jr. U.S. Supreme Ct., 1966-67; asst. U.S. atty. U.S. Dist Ct. (so. dist.) N.Y., N.Y.C., 1967-69; prof. law Columbia U., 1969-79; judge U.S. Dist. Ct. (so. dist.) N.Y., 1979-85; legal advisor U.S. Dept. State, Washington, 1985-90; ptnr. Hughes Hubbard & Reed, 1991-94; George P. Shultz disting. scholar, sr. fellow Hoover Instn., Stanford U., 1994—; prof. law by courtesy Stanford U., Calif., 1996—. Hearing officer N.Y. Dept. Environ. Conservation, 1975-76. Author: War, Foreign Affairs and Constitutional Power: The Origins, 1976; contbr. articles to legal, polit., fgn. jours.; editor-in-chief: NYU Law Rev, 1964-65. Served with USAF, 1956-59. Root-Tilden scholar NYU, 1965. Mem. ABA, Fed. Bar Assn., N.Y.C. Bar Assn., N.Y. Bar Assn., Am. Law Inst. Jewish. Home: 1200 Bryant St Palo Alto CA 94301-2716 Office: Stanford Univ The Hoover Instn Stanford CA 94305-6010 Fax: 650-723-2103. E-mail: sofaer@hoover.stanford.edu.

SOFFER, GRACE FLOREY, retired elementary educator, artist; b. Jeannette, Pa. d. James Paul Florey and Mary Ann Wlnewski; m. Rubin Soffer, Mar. 16, 1946; 1 child, Jerry Paul. BA, Ohio State U., 1944; MA, Adelphi U., 1975. Tchr. common br. N.Y.C. Bd. of Edn., 1966-85. One women shows include N.Y. Poly. U., Farmingdale, 1995, South Nassau Unitarian Ch., 1989, Parlor Gallery Cmty. Ch., 1989, Malverne Pub. Lib., 1985; exhibited in group shows at Fine Arts Mus. of L.I., Art Circa 2100, 1995, Inter-Media Art Ctr., Huntington, Art Circa 2100, 1995, 97, South Nassau Cmty. Hosp., 1990, TriCounty Arts Invitational Small Group Fine Arts exhibit, N.Y., 1999, N.Y. Tech. U., Wisser Libr., Old Westbury, 1990, Shelter Rock Gallery, Manhasset, 1994, Adelphi Art and Art History Alumni Assn., N.Y.C., 1990, Five Towns Music and Art Found., Woodmere, 1990, others, Village Art Club, 1988, 89, 90, 91 (prizes), Lee Scarfone Gallery, 1998, Guild Hall East Hampton, 1992, Fine Arts Mus. of L.I., 1997 (3d pl. winner 1998), Nassau County Mus. of FIne Art, 1992, Long Beach Art League, 1999, 2002 (prize), South Nassau Unitarian Ch., 1989, 92 (prizes), Village Art Club at Chelsea Ctr., 1991, others. Mem. Nat. Assn. Women Artists, Long Beach Art Leauge, Nat. League Am. Pen Women (exhibits chair 1995-2001), Nat. Mus. Women in the Arts (charter), Village Art Club, Tri County Artists of L.I. (newsletter 1980-95), Art Circa 2100, Adelphi Art Hist. Alumni Assn., Mensa. Home: 56 Dickson St Inwood NY 11096-1004 E-mail: depainter@aol.com.

SOFFER, LOWELL CHARLES, financial executive; b. N.Y.C., Feb. 4, 1954; s. George Jack and Marcia (Black) S.; m. Victoria Ann Bongiorno, June 30, 1984; children: Jonathan, Jeffrey. BS, U. Pitts., 1976; MBA, Columbia U., 1980. Dir. fin. Columbia Pictures, The Coca-Cola Co., N.Y.C., 1983-88; dir. fin. and strategic planning ESPN, Capital Cities/ABC, Inc., Bristol, Conn., 1988-91; chief fin. officer Nat. Geog. TV, Washington, 1991-98; prin. Media and Entertainment, IBM, Bethesda, Md., 1998—. Fellow Assn. for Investment Mgmt. and Rsch.; mem. N.Y. Soc. of Security Analysts. Office: IBM 6710 Rockledge Dr Bethesda MD 20817-1827

SOFFER, MARTIN HARVEY, environmentalist, city planner; b. Phila., Feb. 26, 1945; s. Bernard and Selma (Barrot) S.; m. Kathleen O'Neill, Aug. 24, 1969; children: Nicole, Jonathan, Daniel. AA in Applied Sci., C.C. Phila., 1969; BS in Social Sci., Pa. State U., 1969, M in Urban Planning, 1972; MPA, Temple U., 1979; student, Tyler Sch. Fine Arts. Editl. rschr. Washington Post, 1965-66; assoc. planner Ga. Dept. Industry and Trade, Atlanta, 1972-73; cmty. cons., comprehensive planner Mullin & Lonergan Assocs., Inc., Phila., 1973-75; pvt. cons. in planning and land use, 1975-76; environ. assessment and land use specialist Phila. City Planning Commn., 1976-78, project planning adminstr., 1978-85, chief environ. officer, 1985—. Chmn., asst. scout master Boy Scouts Am., Phila., 1990—. Served with U.S. Army, 1966-68, Vietnam. Decorated Silver Star, Air Medal with bronze oak leaf cluster; recipient Fine Arts award Pa. Acad. Fine Arts, 1970. Mem. Am. Inst. Planners (cert.), Nat. Assn. Local Govt. Environ. Profls. (adv. coun. 1998—), Masons, Scottish Rite. Home: 9124 Diplomat Pl Philadelphia PA 19115-4638 E-mail: martin.soffer@phila.gov.

SOFIA, SABATINO, astronomy educator; b. Episcopia, Italy, May 14, 1939; came to U.S., 1961; married, 1963; 2 children. BS, Yale U., 1963, MS, 1965, PhD in Astrophysics, 1966. Rsch. assoc. astrophysics Goddard Inst. Space Studies NASA, N.Y.C., 1966-67; from assoc. prof. to prof. astronomy U. South Fla., Tampa, 1967-73; vis. fellow Joint Inst. Lab. Astrophysics, Boulder, Colo., 1973-74; sr. rsch. assoc. U. Rochester, N.Y., 1974-75; adj. prof. astronomy U. Fla., 1975-78; staff scientist NASA, 1975-77; sr. rsch. assoc. solar physics Nat. Acad. Sci., Nat. Rsch. Coun., 1977-79; space scientist Goddard Space Flight Ctr., Greenbelt, Md., 1979-85; mem. space and earth sci. adv. com. NASA, 1985-88; prof. astronomy Yale U., New Haven, 1985—, chmn. astronomy dept., 1993-99. Mem. Am. Astron. Soc., Internat. Astron. Union, Am. Geophys. Union. Office: Yale U Dept Astronomy PO Box 208101 260 Whitney Ave New Haven CT 06520-8101 E-mail: sofia@astro.yale.edu.

SOFONIO, MARK VINCENT, plastic and reconstructive surgeon; b. L.A., May 14, 1963; s. Lawrence and Hendrika Sofonio. BS in Biomed. Sci. magna cum laude, U. Calif., Riverside, 1984; MD, UCLA, 1988. Diplomate Am. Bd. Plastic Surgery; lic. physician, Calif., Ohio, Mich., Hawaii, N.Y. Intern gen. surgery integrated surg. residency program U. Hawaii, Honolulu, 1988-89, resident, 1989-91; fellow burn surgery N.Y. Med. Coll., Westchester County Med. Ctr., Valhalla, 1991-92; resident plastic and reconstructive surgery Med. Coll. Ohio, Toledo, 1992-94; fellow cosmetic surgery Bruce Connell, MD, Santa Ana, Calif., 1994-95; pvt. practice plastic and reconstructive surgery Rancho Mirage, 1996—. Author: (with others) Plastic, Maxillofacial and Reconstructive Surgery, 3rd edt., 1997, Grabb and Smith's Plastic Surgery, 5th edt., 1997; contbr. to profl. jours. Named Palm Springs Teenager of the Year 1981; recipient Rsch. Presentation award Am. Coll. Surgeons Ann. Hawaiian Conf., 1990. Mem. ACS, AMA, Am. Soc. Laser Medicine and Surgery, Am. Soc. Plastic and Reconstructive Surgery, Calif. Med. Assn., Am. Burn Assn. Republican. Avocations: exercising, tennis, golf, weight lifting, biking. Office: Kiewit Bldg 39000 Bob Hope Dr Ste 407 Rancho Mirage CA 92270-7040 E-mail: M.Sofonio@aol.com.

SOFTLI, LINDA ELAINE, small business owner; b. Corona, N.Y., Nov. 10, 1944; d. Rudolpho B. and Isi A. (Hinds) S. BA in Psychology and Bus., U. D.C., 1978. Events planner IBM Corp., Washington, 1968-94; pres. Gala Spl. Events & Mtg. Planning, 1994—. Bd. mem. LWV, Washington, 1994; mem. Africare, Washington, 1984—; recruiter Am. Red Cross, 1984—; fin. sec. Draft Colin Powell Pres., Washington, 1994-95; founder, pres. Black Rep. Women Internat. Recipient Pres. award Nat. Recreation Assn. D.C., 1993, Knights Honor, Washington, 1994. Mem. D.C. C.C. Republican. Avocations: sewing, reading, music. Home and Office: 1930 Columbia Rd NW Ste 302 Washington DC 20009-5063

SOFTNESS, DONALD GABRIEL, marketing and manufacturing executive; b. Bklyn. s. Burt H. and Ida (Kaiser) S.; m. Sydell Meyerson; children: Michael, Anita May, Beth. AB, NYU, 1949, MBA, 1959; L.H.D., St. John's U., 1979. Chmn. Softness Group, Inc., N.Y.C., 1960-79; pres. Softness Groupe, 1979—, SecureVue, Inc., N.Y.C., 1984—. V.p., maj. prin. Radio Stas. WVNJ-AM-FM, Newark and N.Y.C.; mem. faculty Advt. Week seminars Advt. Age; prodr., promoter Bklyn. Rollathon (skating marathon). Co-author: Cardiologists' Guide to Health and Fitness Through Exercise, 1979; contbr. articles to bus. and trade jours. Patentee in mech. field. Served with USN. Mem. Public Relations Soc. Am., Internat. Radio TV Soc., Am. Coll. Sports Medicine Clubs: N.Y. Yacht. Home and Office: 28 Trues Dr West Islip NY 11795-5139 Office: SecureVue Inc 251 E 51st St New York NY 10022-6534

SOFTNESS, JOHN, public relations executive; b. Bklyn., Nov. 7, 1930; s. Burt H. and Ida (Kaiser) S.; m. Leona R. Softness (dec.); m. Carol Brady Blades; children: Barney, David, Daniel. BA, U. Miami, 1955. Reporter Miami Herald, 1953; reporter Sta. WTVJ, Miami, Fla., 1954; asso. pub. relations dir. aviation dept. Shell Oil Co., N.Y.C., 1958-60; pres., chief exec. officer The Softness Group, Inc., 1960-91, chmn., 1992-98; spl. asst. to dean Sch. Bus. U. Miami, 1998-2000; pres. Moonstruck, Inc., 1998—. Spl. counselor to Bklyn. Borough pres., 1966-76; adj. prof. comm. arts St. John's U., 1981-98; counselor comms. com. N.Y. Heart Assn.; mem. comm. coun. U. Miami; speechwriter, comm. advisor to Miami-Dade Mayor. Author: (autobiography) Boy Outta Brooklyn. Dir. Alliance for Ethical Govt., Miami. Served to capt. USAF, 1955-58. Mem. Pub. Rels. Soc. Am., Pride and Alarm (chmn.), Counselors' Acad. Home and Office: 2 Grove Isle Dr Apt 210 Coconut Grove FL 33133-4102

SOGABE, AKIKO, artist; b. Mishima, Japan, June 1, 1945; came to the U.S., 1987; d. Kaoru and Miki (Takahashi) Hirata; m. William Sogabe, Jan. 29, 1971; children: Steve, Sandy. Student, Tokyo Flower Acad., 1970; diploma, Japan Art Inst., 1972. Illustrator: Cinnamon, Mint & Mthballs, 1993, Washington Water Weeks, 1994, The Loyal Cat, 1995, Oregon Trout, 1995. Mem. Guild Am. Paper Cutters, Northcoast Collage Soc., Soc. Children's Book Writers and Illustrators. Home: 3319 170th Ave NE Bellevue WA 98008-2038

SOGANI, PRAMOD CHANDRA, surgeon, educator; b. Ajmer, India, July 1, 1938; arrived in U.S., 1966; m. Lalita Sogani. Intermediate sci., Govt. Coll., Ajmer, 1955; MD, Mahatma Gandhi Meml. Med. Coll., Indore, India, 1960, MS, 1964. Lic. physician N.Y., N.J., Calif., cert. bd. cert. Am. Bd. Urology. Intern MGM Med. Coll. Hosp., Indore, 1960—61, resident gen. surgery, 1961—65, Cleve. Met. Gen. Hosp., 1966—68; resident urology NYU Med. Ctr., N.Y.C., 1968—69, George Washington U. Med. Ctr., Washington, 1969—71; spl. fellow urology Meml. Sloan Kettering Cancer Ctr., N.Y.C., 1971—73; instr. surgery Med. Coll., Raipur, India, 1965—66, Cornell U. Med. Coll., N.Y.C., 1974; clin. asst. surgeon urology svc. dept. surgery Meml. Hosp., 1973—78; asst. prof. surgery Cornell U. Med. Coll., 1975—88; asst. attending surgeon urology svc. dept. surgery Meml. Sloan Kettering Cancer Ctr., 1978—82, assoc. attending surgeon. urology svc. dept. surgery, 1982—96, attending surgeon. urology svc. dept. surgery, 1996—; assoc. prof. surgery Cornell U. Med. Coll., 1988—98, prof. clin. urology, 1998—; acting chief urology svc. dept. surgery Meml. Sloan Kettering Cancer Ctr., 1995, 1997—98. Mem. Meml. Sloan Kettering Cancer Ctr., N.Y.C., 1996—; rsch. fellow Sloan-Kettering Inst., N.Y.C., 1971—72; assoc. clin. mem. Meml. Sloan Kettering Cancer Ctr., N.Y.C., 1984—96. Reviewer abstracts: Am. Urol. Assn. Ann. Meetings Sci. Program, 1999—2002. Scholar Rajasthan State Merit scholar, MGM Med. Coll., 1955—60, MGM Med. Coll. Merit scholar, 1958—60. Mem.: ACS, AMA, AAAS, Soc. Internat. D'Urologie, Soc. Urologic Oncology, Am. Endocuritherapy Soc., Soc. Surg. Oncology, Royal Soc. Medicine, Pan-Pacific Surg. Assn., Pan Am. Med. Assn., N.Y. State Urol. Assn., N.Y. State Soc. Surgeons, N.Y. State Med. Soc., N.Y. County Med. Soc., N.Y. Cancer Soc., N.Y. Acad. Scis., N.Y. Acad. Medicine, Indian Am. Urol. Assn. (Susruta Award of Excellence in Urology 1996), Internat. Coll. Surgeons, Can. Urol. Assn., Am. Urol. Assn. (mem. exec. com. N.Y. sect. 1999), Am. Soc. Clin. Oncology, Am. Fertility Soc., Am. Coll. Nuclear Medicine, Am. Assn. Clin. Urologists, Royal Coll. Physicians and Surgeons of Can. Office: Meml Sloan Kettering Cancer Ctr 1275 York Ave New York NY 10021

SOGG, WILTON SHERMAN, lawyer; b. Cleve., May 28, 1935; s. Paul P. and Julia (Cahn) S.; m. Saralee Frances Krow, Aug. 12, 1962 (div. July 1975); 1 child, Stephanie; m. Linda Rocker Lehman, Dec. 22, 1979 (div. Dec. 1990); m. Nancy Rosenfield Walsh, June 2, 1991. AB, Dartmouth Coll., 1956; JD, Harvard U., 1959; postgrad., London Grad. Sch. Bus. Studies, 1974-76. Bar: (Ohio) 1960, (Fla) 1970, (U.S. Tax Ct.) 1961, (U.S. Supreme Ct.) 1969. Assoc. Gottfried, Ginsberg, Guren & Merritt, 1960-63, ptnr., 1963-70, Guren, Merritt, Feibel, Sogg & Cohen, Cleve., 1970-84; of counsel Hahn, Loeser, Freedheim, Dean and Wellman, 1984-85; ptnr. Hahn Loeser & Parks LLP, 1986-2000; of counsel McCarthy, Lebit, Crystal & Liffman Co., 2001—. Trustee, pres. Cleve. Jewish News; adj. prof. Cleve. State Law Sch., 1960—; lectr. Harvard U. Law Sch., 1978-80. Author: (with Howard M. Rossen) new and rev. vols. of Smith's Review Legal Gems series, 1969—; editor: Harvard Law Rev.; contbr. articles to profl. jours. Trustee Jewish Cmty. Fedn. of Cleve., 1966-72; bd. overseers Cleveland Marshall Coll. Law, Cleve. State U., 1969—, vis. com. Coll. Bus. Adminstrn., 1996-00; mem. U.S. and State of Ohio Holocaust commns. Fulbright fellow U. London, 1959-60. Mem. Ohio Bar Assn., Fla. Bar Assn., Germany Philatelic Soc., Oakwood Club, Union Club, Chagrin Valley Hunt, Phi Beta Kappa. Home: PO Box 278 Gates Mills OH 44040-0278 Office: McCarthy Lebit Crystal & Liffman 1800 Midland Bldg 101 W Prospect Ave Cleveland OH 44115-1088 E-mail: wss@mccarthylebit.com.

SOGNIER, JOHN WOODWARD, retired judge; b. Savannah, Ga., Dec. 17, 1919; 03937564s. Joseph W. and Viola (Trott) S.; divorced; children: John Woodward Jr. (dec.), Anne Sognier Murray; m. Loretto Boswell, Nov. 9, 1985. Legal edn., Catholic. U., 1941; LLM in Tax, Emory U., 1994. Bar: Ga. 1946, U.S. Dist. Ct. Ga. 1946, U.S. Ct. Appeals 1964. Ptnr. Kennedy & Sognier, Savannah, 1946-80; judge Ga. Ct. Appeals, Atlanta, 1980-92; ret., 1992. Rep. Gen. Assembly Ga., Atlanta, 1955-56; registrar Chatham County, Savannah, 1957-60, county atty., 1960-68. Sr. warden Christ Ch., Savannah; chmn. Ga. State Bd. Bar Examiners, 1974-79; trustee Continuing Jud. Edn. Com. 1982-88. Lt. col. USAF, 1942-45, ETO, 1951-53. Decorated D.F.C. Fellow Am. Coll. Trial Lawyers, Am. Bar Found.; mem. ABA. Episcopalian.

SOH, CHUNGHEE SARAH, anthropology educator; b. Taegu, Korea, May 1, 1947; came to U.S., 1970; d. Sang Yung and Ock Yun (Choi) S.; m. Jerry Dee Boucher. BA summa cum laude, Sogang U., 1971; postgrad., U. Calif., Berkeley, 1971; MA in Anthropology, U. Hawaii, 1983, PhD in Anthropology, 1987. Staff instr. English Korean Air Lines, Edn. & Tng. Ctr., Seoul, 1978-79; instr. anthropology Ewha Womans U., 1985; asst. prof. U. Hawaii, 1990; asst. prof. anthropology Southwest Tex. State U., San Marcos, 1991-94, San Francisco State U., 1994-96, assoc. prof. anthropology, 1996—. Guest lectr. Chaminade U. Honolulu, 1988; vis. asst. prof. anthropology U. Ariz., 1990-91; adj. prof. Intercultural Inst. Calif., 1996-98; vis. sr. fellow Internat. Inst. for Asian Studies, Leiden U., The Netherlands, 1998; cons. in field. Author: The Chosen Women in Korean Politics: An Anthropological Study; contbr. articles to profl. jours. Bd. dirs. Women Devel. Inst. Internat., 2000—. Grantee East-West Ctr., 1981-87, NSF, 1985-86; fellow Korea Found., 1993, Japan Found., 1997-98, vis. fellow Inst. Social Sci., U. Tokyo, 1997-98; vis. scholar Hoover Inst., 1996-97, affiliated scholar Inst. for Rsch. on Women and Gender, Stanford U., 2000-01; rsch. and writing grantee Program on Global Security and Sustainability, John D. and Catherine T. MacArthur Found., 2000-2001. Fellow Am. Anthrop. Assn. (treas. East Asia sect. 2001-), Inst. for Corean-Am. Studies; mem. Am. Ethnological Soc., Soc. Psychol. Anthropology, Assn. Asian Studies (exec. bd. Com. Women Asian Studies), Korean Assn. Womens Studies, Royal Asiatic Soc. Korean Br. Office: San Francisco State U Dept Anthropology 1600 Holloway Ave San Francisco CA 94132-1722 E-mail: soh@sfsu.edu.

SOH, LIP-KHOON (KENNETH SOH), music educator, musician; b. Klang, Selangor, Malaysia, May 11; s. Boon-Keng Soh and Oon-Sim Khoo; m. Bin Xu. Grade 8(hon.) , Royal Acad. Music, London, 1988; BA (hon.) , N.W. Mo. State U., Maryville, 1996; M in Music (hon.) , U. Nebr., Omaha, 1998. Pres. Music for Wellness, Klang, Malaysia, 1998—, evangelist Omaha, composer; prof. music Grace U., 1999—, pub. spkr., 1999—2002, pianist, 1999—2002. Concert pianist, Omaha. Composer: (albums) First Fruit, 1997 (Best-seller Elim Bookstore, Taipei, 1997), Shines of Glory, 1998 (Best-seller Elim Bookstore, Taipei, 1999), Peace Beyond Measure, 2000; inventor music numerology technique, 1995. Recipient Ada Royston Meml. Instrumental Music award, N.W. Mo. State U., 1993, Alpha Chi hon. award, Nat. Coll. Honor Scholarship Soc., 1995; scholar John Smay Meml. music scholar, N.W. Mo. State U., 1993, Donald and Mary Jane Sandford music scholar, 1994, Fgn. Lang. scholar, Alpha Mu Gamma, 1994, Vernon Barrett Meml. music scholar, N.W. Mo. State U., 1995, U.S. Achievement Acad., 1995, Anna Christensen scholar in piano, U. Nebr., 1996, Martin Bush Meml. keyboard scholar, 1996, Violet Reich music scholar, 1997, Hellman music scholar, 1997. Mem.: Omaha Music Tchr. Assn., Nebr. Music Tchr. Assn., Music Tchr. Nat. Assn. Achievements include knowledge of 7 languages and dialects including Mandarin, English, Malay, Cantonese, Hokkien, Hakka and French. Avocations: reading, evangelism, travel. Office: Grace U 1311 S 9th St Omaha NE 68108 Office Fax: 402 341 9587. Personal E-mail: musicforwellness@hotmail.com. Business E-Mail: ksoh@graceu.edu.

SOHAILI, MONIRA, special education educator, writer; b. Pune, India, Nov. 4, 1933; d. Ispandiar and Keshvar Yaganegi; m. Shahpur Sohaili, Oct. 15, 1953 (dec. Dec. 2000). BA in Edn., Northeastern Ill. U., 1981, MA, 1982. Cert. behavioral therapy Behavioral Therapy Tng. Ctr., L.A., 1996. Tchr. Parramalta Marist H.S., Australia, 1970—71; guide Bahai House of Worship, Chgo., 1973—83; ESL instr. Cuban/Hatian Refugee Program, 1983—84, Chgo. Bd. Edn., 1984—87; ESL and Eng. instr. Santa Monica (Calif.) City Coll., 1987—89; Esl. and reading tchr. Le Conte Mid. Sch., L.A., 1989—96; head dept. Ctr. Mid. Sch., 1994—96; spl. edn. tchr. L.A., 1996—; dept. head, 1996—. Author: (children's book) Monira's Fables, 2000. Coord. childproof medicine vials donation , Papua New Guinea, 1995—97. Recipient Cert. of Achievement, L.A. USD Lang. Acquisition, 1993, I Made a Difference award, L.A. Dept. Edn., 1995. Mem.: NEA (reading and writing program 1990—),

Calif. Tchrs. Assn. (assisted in program 1990—). Avocations: reading, writing, traveling, swimming. Office: John Burroughs HS 600 McCadden Pl Los Angeles CA 90005 Address: PO Box 95 Santa Monica CA 90406-0095

SOHIE, GUY ROSE LOUIS, electrical engineer, researcher; b. Antwerp, Belgium, Nov. 8, 1956; came to U.S., 1978; s. Andre and Lydia (Boussery) S.; m. Angela M. Sloman, Apr. 9, 1987; children: Oliver A., Harry N., Dylan A., Annie R. Ind. Ingenieur, Industriele Hogeschool Antwerpen Mechelen, Antwerp, 1978; PhD, Pa. State U., 1983. Asst. prof. Ariz. State U., Tempe, 1985-87; applications engr. Motorola Inc., Austin, Tex., 1988-89; tech. staff GE, Schenectady, 1989-95; mgr. image detection subsystems Global X-Ray Engring. GE Med Sys. Europe, Buc, France, 1995-97; pres. Global Insite, Austin, 1997—. Co-author: The Elements of System Design, 1993; contbr. articles to profl. jours.; pub. 2 newsletters, 3 spl. reports on globalized tech. Ensign Belgian Navy, 1983-84. Fulbright fellow, Brussels, 1978. Mem. IEEE, Sigma Xi, Phi Kappa Phi, Eta Kappa Nu. Achievements include 3 patents in emergency signal warning systems, patent in image processing system for detection and tracking. Office: Global Insite 701 Brazos St Ste 500 Austin TX 78701-3232 Home: # C-531 17595 Harvard Ave Irvine CA 92614-8516

SOHIGIAN, DIRAN JOHN, humanities educator; b. N.Y.C., Dec. 17, 1951; s. Diran and Loretta Anna (Pazdyka) S. BA, Columbia Coll., 1973; MA, Columbia U., 1978, MPhil, 1984, PhD, 1991. Fgn. expert, vis. asst. prof., ednl. devel. worker Henan Normal U., Xinxiang, China, 1992-94; instr. ELS Lang. Ctr., Riverdale, N.Y., 1995-99, Coll. Mt. St. Vincent, N.Y.C., 1996. Lectr. modern Chinese cultural history, The New Sch. for Social Rsch., N.Y.C., 1995; adj. prof. Chinese History Queens Coll., N.Y.C., 1999; vis. lectr. Asian Studies Elmira Coll., 1999-2000; asst. prof. gen. edn. ctr. Shih Chien U., Kaohsiung, Taiwan, Rep. of China, 2000—. Author: The Life and Times of Lin Yutang, 1991. Mem. MLA, Assn. Asian Studies. Home: 5604 Post Rd Bronx NY 10471-2609 Office: Shih Chien U Gen Edn Ctr 200 University Rd Nei-Men Hsiang Hsiang Taiwan E-mail: diranscu@kh.scc.edu.tw.

SOHL, RAYMOND, JR. video company executive; b. Hammond, Ind., Jan. 8, 1949; s. Raymond Sr. and Flora (Schmidt) S.; m. Nancy Belknap, June 23, 1973. Student, Drake U., 1971-73; BA, North Cen. Coll., Naperville, Ill., 1975. Lic. FCC radiotelephone operator. Announcer Sta. WONC-FM, Naperville, 1974-75; salesperson Block Drug Co., Jersey City, 1975-80; div. mgr. Owen Lab's., Ft. Worth, 1980-84; regional mgr. Embassy Home Entertainment, L.A., 1984-87; nat. sales mgr. Virgin Vision, 1987-89, dir. nat. accounts, 1989; regional mgr. nat. accounts video div. Paramount Pictures, Hollywood, Calif., 1990-96; nat. accounts dir. Paramount Home Video, 1992-97; video sales rep. Universal Studios, Chgo., 1997-99; territory rep. Hallmark Cards, 2000—. With U.S. Army, 1968-71, Viet Nam. Named Most Valuable Staffer Am. Newspaper Pubs. Assn., 1967. Home: 646 59th St Lisle IL 60532-3113

SOHLER, NANCY LYNN, epidemiologist; b. Santa Monica, Calif., Oct. 11, 1964; d. Jerome Francis and Darlene Joyce (Clifton) S. BA, Friends World Coll., 1991; MPH, Columbia U., 1995, PhD with distinction, 2001. Editl. asst. UN Africa Recovery Program, N.Y.C., 1988; migration supr. Hebrew Immigrant Aid Soc., 1989-95; rsch. scientist N.Y. State Psychiat. Inst. & Rsch. Found. Mental Hygiene, 1995—99, Rutgers U., New Brunswick, 2000—01; asst. prof. Montefiore Med. Ctr., Bronx, NY, 2002—. Cons. Physicians for Human Rights, Boston, 2000—. Psychiatric Epidemiology fellow Nat. Inst. Mental Health, 1995-2000, Health Svcs. fellow, 2000—. Mem. APHA, Soc. Epidemiologic Rsch., Acad. for Health Svcs. Rsch. and Health Policy. Office: Montefiore Med Ctr Divsn Epidemiology and Social Medicine 111 E 210th St Bronx NY 10462 E-mail: nsohler@montefiore.org.

SOHMER, BERNARD, mathematics educator, administrator; b. N.Y.C., July 16, 1929; s. Sol and Florence (Schonfeld) S.; m. Margot Rosette, July 27, 1952; children: Emily Sohmer Tai, Olivia Sohmer Rosenbaum. BA, NYU, 1949, MS, 1951, PhD, 1958. Lectr. CCNY, 1952-57, faculty, 1958—, prof. math., 1969—, dean students, 1969-72, v.p. student affairs, 1972-75, chmn. faculty senate, 1977-79, 85-91, ombudsman, 1991-98, chmn. liberal arts and sci. faculty council, 1979-85, pres. Hillel, 1988—. Asst. prof. N.Y. U., 1957-58; trustee PSC-CUNY Welfare Fund, 1982-97. Sec. Univ. Faculty Senate, CUNY, 1992-94, vice chair, 1994-98, chair, 1998-2002, ex-officio bd. trustees, 1998-2002. Mem. AAAS, AAUP (pres. CCNY chpt. 1966-67, sec. 1977-78), Am. Math. Soc., Math. Assn. Am. (pres. elect N.Y. Met. sect. 1989-90, pres. 1992-93, past pres. 1993-94, gov. 1996-98), Profl. Staff Congress (chair CCNY chpt. 1993-96, exec. coun. 1997-2000). Home: 3345 92nd St Jackson Heights NY 11372-1851 Office: 535 E 80th St New York NY 10021 E-mail: bescc@cuny.edu.

SOHN, CATHERINE ANGELL, pharmaceutical executive, pharmacist; b. San Francisco, Mar. 21, 1953; d. Vincent Herbert and Margaret Ann Ware Angell; m. John Edwin Sohn, Aug. 10, 1974; children: Karen Elizabeth, Jennifer Michele. Ed., U. Calif., Davis; PharmD, U. Calif., San Francisco, 1977. Registered pharmacist, Calif., Pa. Pharmacist Kaiser Permanente, San Francisco, 1977-78; asst. prof. pharmacy Phila. Coll. Pharmacy and Sci., 1978-82; mgr. med. affairs Smith Kline & French, Phila., 1982-86; assoc. dir. bus. devel. pharm. divsn. Smith Kline Beecham, 1986-88, product dir., 1988-93, v.p. worldwide strategic product devel., 1994-97; v.p. worldwide bus. devel. Glaxo Smith Kline Consumer Healthcare, 1998—. Lectr. St. Andrew the Apostle, Gibbsboro, NJ, 1989—; adv. bd. Healthcare Bus. Women's Assn., N.Y.C., NY, 1996—; bd. overseers U. Calif. Sch. Pharmacy, San Francisco, 1997—; health adv. bd. Johns Hopkins U. Sch. Pub. Health, Balt., 1998—. Author: (with others) Applied Clinical Therapeutics, 1980, Handbook of Non-Prescription Drugs, 1980, rev. edit., 1982; contbr. chpts. to profl. pubs. Mem. Am. Pharm. Assn., Calif. Pharmacists Assn., Consumer Healthcare Products Assn. (chmn. internat. affairs com. 1998—, bd. dirs. 1999—), Licensing Exec. Soc., Rho Chi. Roman Catholic. Avocations: family activities, swimming, bicycling. Office: GlaxoSmithKline FP1370 200 N 16th St Ste 1800 Philadelphia PA 19102-1282

SOHN, CHANG WOOK, energy systems researcher, educator; b. Seoul, Jan. 10, 1947; parents Kye Taek and Young Bo (Koh) S.; m. Chung Hae Han Sohn, Aug. 24, 1974; children: Douglas Jemin, Sammy Sungmin. BS in Engring., Seoul Nat. U., 1969; MS in Mech. Engring., Tex. Tech. U., 1975; PhD in Mech. Engring., U. Ill., Urbana, 1980. Registered profl. engr., Ill. 1st lt. Korean Army, 1969-71; tchr. KyungGi H.S., Seoul, 1971-72; rsch. asst. Tex. Tech. U., Lubbock, 1973-74, U. Ill., Urbana, 1974-79, rsch. assoc., 1979-80; rsch. engr. U.S. Army Engring. R&D Ctr., Champaign, Ill., 1980-84, acting. team leader, 1992, prin. investigator, 1984—, project leader, 1995—2000. Adj. assoc. prof. U. Ill., Urbana, 1992-97; vis. rsch. fellow Korea Inst. Energy Rsch., 1995-96. Contbr. articles on fluid mechanics, heat transfer to profl. jours, ASHRAE transactions. Recipient Tech. Transfer award U.S. Army Corps of Engrs., Washington, 1991, Spl. Act award U.S. Army Yuma (Ariz.) Proving Ground, 1988; Korea Inst. Energy Rsch. fellow, 1995-96. Mem. ASME (K-19 com. 1993—2000), ASHRAE (com. chair Cool Storage Design Guide 1992, air conditioning rsch. ctr. industry adv. bd. mem. 1991-96). Home: 2910 Robeson Park Dr Champaign IL 61822-7609 Office: US Army ERDC-CERL PO Box 9005 Champaign IL 61826-9005 E-mail: c-sohn@cecer.army.mil.

SOHN, HONG YONG, chemical and metallurgical engineering educator; b. Kaesung, Kyunggi-Do, Korea, Aug. 21, 1941; arrived U.S., 1966; s. Chong Ku and Soon Deuk (Woo) S.; m. Victoria Bee Tuan Ngo, Jan. 8, 1972; children: Berkeley Jihoon, Edward Jihyun. BS in Chem. Engring., Seoul (Korea) Nat. U., 1962; MS in Chem. Engring., U. N.B., Can., 1966; PhD in Chem. Engring., U. Calif., Berkeley, 1970. Engr. Cheil Sugar Co., Busan, Korea, 1962-64; rsch. assoc. SUNY-Buffalo, 1971-73; rsch. engr. DuPont Co., Wilmington, Del., 1973-74; prof. metall. engring., adj. prof. chem. engring. U. Utah, Salt Lake City, 1974—. Cons. Lawrence Livermore Nat. Lab., 1976—, Kennecott Co., Salt Lake City, 1976—, Cabot Corp., 1984—, DuPont Co., 1987—, Utah Power and Light Co., 1987—, H.C. Starck, 1997—. Co-author: Gas-Solid Reactions, 1976; co-editor: Rate Processes of Extractive Metallurgy, 1979, Extractive Metallurgy of Refractory Metals, 1980, Advances in Sulfide Smelting, 2 vols., 1983, Recycle and Secondary Recovery of Metals, 1985, Gas-solid Reactions in Pyrometallurgy, 1986, Flash Rection Processes, 1988, Metallurgical Processes for the Year 2000 and Beyond, 1988, Metallurgical Processes for the Early Twenty-First Century, 2 vols., 1994, Proceedings of the Julian Szekely Memorial Symposium on Materials Processing, 1997, Value-Addition Metallurgy, 1998; patentee process for treating sulfide-bearing ores, continuous solvent extraction with bottom gas injection; contbr. numerous articles to sci., tech. jours. Camille and Henry Dreyfus Found. Tchr. Scholar awardee, 1977; Fulbright Disting. lectr., 1983; Japan Soc. for the Promotion of Sci. fellow, 1990. Mem. AIME (James Douglas Gold medal 2001), The Minerals, Metals and Materials Soc. (past dir., Extractive Metallurgy Lectr. award 1990, Champion H. Mathewson Gold Medal award 1993, Extraction and Processing Sci. award 1990, 94, 99), Korean Acad. Sci. and Tech. (Fellow award 1998), Am. Inst. Chem. Engrs., Korean Inst. Chem. Engrs. Office: U Utah 135 S 1460 E Rm 412 Salt Lake City UT 84112-0114 E-mail: hysohn@mines.utah.edu. *Fortunate are those who earn a living by doing what they would rather be doing even if they do not have to do it to earn a living. Material wealth accumulated by doing what one does not enjoy doing is not worth the effort.*

SOHN, LOUIS BRUNO, lawyer, educator; b. Lwów, Poland, Mar. 1, 1914; came to U.S., 1939, naturalized, 1943; s. Joseph and Fryderyka (Hescheles) S.; m. Elizabeth Mayo. LLM, Diplomatic ScM, John Casimir U., 1935; LLM, Harvard U., 1940, SJD, 1958; LLD (hon.), Free U. Brussels (Flemish sect.), 1990, George Washington U., 2000. Asst. to Judge M. O. Hudson, 1941-48; John Harvey Gregory teaching fellow Harvard Law Sch., 1946-47, lectr. law, 1947-51, asst. prof. law, 1951-53, John Harvey Gregory lectr. in world orgn., 1951-81, prof. law, 1953-61, Bemis prof. internat. law, 1961-81; Woodruff prof. internat. law U. Ga., 1981-91; vis. Congl. prof. George Washington U. Law Sch., 1991-92; Disting. rsch. prof. and dir. rsch. and studies Internat. Rule of Law Ctr., George Washington U. Law Sch., 1992—. Disting. fellow Jennings Randolph program U.S. Inst. Peace, 1991-92; cons. U.S. ACDA, 1960-70, Office Internat. Security Affairs, Dept. Def., 1963-70; rsch. asst. joint project for internat. law of future ABA and Can. Bar Assn., 1943-44; asst. to del. Permanent Ct. Internat. Justice, San Francisco Conf. UN, 1945; exec. sec. legal subcom. on atomic energy Carnegie Endowment for Internat. Peace, 1946; asst. reporter on progressive devel. internat. law Am. and Canadian bar assns., 1947-48; cons. UN secretariat, 1948, 69, legal officer, 1950-51; counselor internat. law Dept. State, 1970-71, cons., 1982—; U.S. counsel Internat. Ct. Justice, 1971, 84; U.S. del. to UN Law of Sea Conf., 1974-82; U.S. del. head Athens Conf. on Settlement Internat. Disputes, 1984. Author: Cases on World Law, 1950, Cases on United Nations Law, 1956, 2d edit., 1967, (with G. Clark) World Peace Through World Law, 1958, 3d edit., 1966, Basic Documents of African Regional Organizations, 4 vols, 1971-72, (with T. Buergenthal) International Protection of Human Rights, 1973, (with K. Gustafson) The Law of the Sea in a Nutshell, 1984, International Organization and Integration: student edit. 1986, (with T. Buergenthal) The Movement of Persons Across Borders, 1992, Rights in Conflict: The United Nations v. South Africa, 1994 ; also articles on internat. legal subjects; editor devel. internat. law: Am. Bar Assn. Jour, 1947-50; editorial bd.: Am. Jour. Internat. Law, 1958— . Recipient World Peace Hero award World Federalists of Can., 1974, Grenville Clark award, 1984, William A. Owens award for creative rsch. in social and behavioral scis. U. Ga., 1985, Harry Leroy Jones award Washington Fgn. Law Soc., 1993, Internat. Human Rights award UN Assn. Nat. Capital Area, 1997. Mem. ABA (hon., co-rapporteur joint working group with Can. Bar Assn. on peaceful settlement of disputes 1976—, vice chmn. internat. law and practice sect. 1983-91, chmn. 1992-93, mem. coun. 1993-97, councillor 1997—, Leonard J. Theberge award 1992), Am. Soc. Internat. Law (mem. exec. coun. 1954-57, v.p. 1965-66, hon. v.p. 1980-87, 90—, pres. 1988-90, Manley O. Hudson medal 1996), World Parliament Assn. (legal advisor 1954-64), Internat. Law Assn. (v.p. Am. br.), Am. Law Inst. (assoc. reporter Fgn. Rels. Law 1978-87), Inst. Internat. Law (Geneva) (reporter on consensus in internat. law 1997-99), Fedn. Am. Scientists (vice chmn. 1963, mem. coun. 1964-65, 68-69), Commn. Study Orgn. Peace (chmn. 1986-98). Home: 801 15th St S Apt 1504 Arlington VA 22202-5023 Office: George Washington U Law Sch 720 20th St NW Washington DC 20052-0001

SOHNEN, HARVEY, lawyer; b. Bklyn., June 20, 1947; s. Nathan M. and Shirley (Strauss) S.; m. Kathleen M. Meagher, Mar. 17, 1978; children: Eleanor, Julia. BA, Columbia U., 1968; MS in Math., MIT, 1969; JD, U. Calif., Berkeley, 1974. Bar: Calif. 1974, U.S. Dist. Ct. (no. dist.) Calif. 1974, U.S. Dist. Ct. (ea. dist.) Calif. 1975, U.S. Supreme Ct. 1981. Staff atty. Stanislaus Co. Legal Assistance, Modesto, Calif., 1975-76, Legal Aid for Alameda County, Oakland, 1977-82; assoc. Lerner & Veit, San Francisco, 1982-85; ptnr. Page & Sohnen, Walnut Creek, Calif., 1986-98; prin., 1998—. Mem. Am. Inns of Ct., Calif. Employment Lawyers Assn., Contra Costa Bar Assn. Office: 1850 Mt Diablo Blvd Ste 650 Walnut Creek CA 94596-4427 E-mail: hs@fairpaycal.com.

SOIBELMAN, YAN SEMENOVICH, mathematician; b. Kiev, Ukrain, USSR, Apr. 15, 1956; s. Semen and Inna (Gokhman) S.; m. Belokopytova Tatyana, Sept. 30, 1983; 1 child, Aleksander. M, Rostov State U., Rostov-on-Don, USSR, 1978, PhD, 1983. Researcher Rostov State U., 1984—. Invited prof. Cambridge (Eng.) U., 1991; vis. scholar Rsch. Inst. Math. Scis., Kyoto, Japan, 1991, MIT, 1991, Inst. des Hautes Etudes des Scientifiques, France, 1992. Contbr. articles to profl. jours. Mem. Am. Math. Soc. Avocations: climbing, football. Home: Zhmailova21/1 apt 14 344104 Rostov-on-Don Russia Office: Rostov U Engelsa 105 344006 Rostov-on-Don Russia also: Harvard U Dept Math Cambridge MA 02138

SOILEAU, KERRY MICHAEL, aerospace technologist, researcher; b. New Orleans, June 8, 1956; s. Donald and Heloise Marie (LeBourgeois) S. BS, U. Cen. Fla., 1976; MS, La. State U., 1980. Aerospace technologist Johnson Space Ctr., NASA, Houston, 1980—. Trajectory officer, flight dynamics officer Space Shuttle Mission Control NASA. Contbr. articles to profl. jours.; presenter sci. papers to confs.; developer (computer program) GradePlus. Newscaster Houston Taping for the Blind, 1984-90. Office: NASA JSC Houston TX 77058 E-mail: ksoileau@yahoo.com.

SOJKA, GARY ALLAN, biologist, educator, university official; b. Cedar Rapids, Iowa, July 15, 1940; s. Marvin F. and Ruth Ann (Waddington) Sojka Green; m. Sandra Kay Smith, Aug 5, 1962; children: Lisa Kay, Dirk Allan. BS, Coe Coll., 1962; MS, Purdue U., 1965, PhD, 1967; DL (hon.) , Lycoming Coll., 1995; Dr. Sci. (hon.) , Purdue U., 2002. Rsch. assoc. Ind. U., Bloomington, 1967-69, asst. prof., 1969-73, assoc. prof., 1973-79, prof., 1979-84, assoc. chmn. biology, 1977-79, chmn. biology, 1979-81, dean arts and scis., 1981-84; pres. Bucknell U., Lewisburg, Pa., 1984-95, prof. biology, 1984—. Mem. higher edn. commn. Mid. States Assn. Colls. and Schs., 1992-96, chmn. task force on instnl. effectiveness, 1999-2000; chmn. tax policy subcom. Nat. Assn. Ind. Colls. and Univs., 1991-93; mem. study group on internat. edn. Am. Coun. Edn., 1992-94. Chmn. bd. dirs. Stone Belt Coun. Ret. Citizens, Bloomington, 1977-78; mem. nominating com. Ind. Assn. Ret. Citizens, Indpls., 1979; mem. So. Ind. Health Sys. Agy., Bedford; bd. dirs. Geisinger Med. Found., Danville, Pa., 1985-97, regional bd., 1997—; gov. Inst. European Studies, 1989-94; trustee St. Mary-of-the-Woods Coll., Ind., 1988-94; chmn. Pa. Commn. Ind. Colls. and Univs., 1989-90; dir. Suncom Industries, Northcumberland, Pa., 1991-93; mem. Pres.'s Commn. NCAA, 1993-95; mem. planning adv. com. Snyder County Pa., 1994—, planning commn., 2001—; bd. dirs. Bethesda Found., Lewisburg, 1996-98, Citizen for the Future of Pa., 1999—; trustee, bd. dirs. Am. Livestock Conservancy, 2001—. Recipient Ind. U. Sr. Class Tchg. award, 1975, Frederick B. Lieber award, 1977, Coe Coll. Alumni award of merit, 1982, Gary A. Sojka award Bucknell U., 1992, Cmty. Leadership award Susquahanna Valley Boy Scouts, 1994; named to Coe Coll. Athletic Hall of Fame, 1988. Mem.: AAAS, Pa. Assn. Coll. and Univs. (interim pres. 1997—98, Sheepskin award 1999), Phila. Soc. Promotion of Agriculture, Am. Coun. Edn. (study group on internat. edn. 1992—94), Nat. Assn. Independent Colls. and Univs. (subcom. chmn. 1991—93), Am. Soc. Biol. Chemists, Am. Acad. Microbiology, Am. Soc. Microbiology, Omicron Delta Kappa, Sigma Nu, Sigma Xi. Baptist. Office: Bucknell U Dept Biology Lewisburg PA 17837

SOJKA, SANDRA KAY, investor, livestock conservator; b. Ames, Iowa, Jan. 22, 1942; d. Clyde Burdette and Helen Rae (Daley) Smith; m. Gary Allan Sojka, Aug. 5, 1962; children: Lisa Kay, Dirk Allan. BS in Bus. Mgmt. with acad. honors, Ind. U., 1968, MS in Counseling-Guidance with honors, MS in Coll. Student Pers. with honors, Ind. U., 1979. Asst. to vet. extension office Purdue U., Lafayette, Ind., 1962-67; CPA asst. Geo. Greene & Co., Bloomington, 1975-76; office mgr., bldg. supr. Univ. Ministries, 1973-75; counselor, adminstrv. asst. dept. athletics Ind. U., Bloomington, 1977-84; first lady Bucknell U., Lewisburg, 1984-95, coord. univ./cmty. activities for pres.'s office, 1984-95, asst. sec. to bd. trustees, 1989-95. Mem. Susquehanna Valley program adv. com. Pub. TV and Radio Sta. WVIA and FM90, 1994-95; mem. steering com. cmty. health assessment Evang. Cmty. Hosp./Sun Home Health Svcs., 1995-99; mem. formation com. Bucknell in Action, 1990-91; mem. leadership adv. group for capital campaign WVIA/TV, 1994. Co-author: Job Readiness Training Guide, 1977, Graduate Course Design and Evaluation Module, 1979. Trustee Coe Coll., Cedar Rapids, Iowa, 1988—95, chmn. nominating com., 1992—95; chmn. nominating com., 2000 Suncom Industries Sheltered Workshop for the Physically and Mentally Challenged, Northumberland, Pa., 2000; adv. bd. Four County Mental Health/Mental Retardation Orgn., Danville, 1986—94, pres., 1991—93; fundraising com. Camp Victory for Disabled Children, Millville, 1988—91; Bd. dirs. Evang. Cmty. Hosp., Lewisburg, 1984—91, Bloomsburg Theatre Ensemble, 1986—89, Weis Ctr. for the Performing Arts, Bucknell U., Lewisburg, Pa., 1995—; bd. dirs. Assn. for Arts Bucknell U., 1984—2000, Suncom Industries Sheltered Workshop for the Physically and Mentally Challenged, Northumberland, Pa., 1997—. Recipient Disting. Svc. award Four County Mental Health/Mental Retardation Orgn., 1993. Mem. AAUW (bd. dirs. 1989-90), Bucknell U. Campus Club (pres. 1985-87), Lewisburg Aux. to Evang. Cmty. Hosp., Union County Hist. Soc., Lewisburg Garden Club (chair social program com. 1987-88, 94-95, chair nominations com. 1990-91, program spkr./presenter 1995-96, 96-97), Civic Club Lewisburg, Lewisburg Federated Womens Club, Alpha Xi Delta, Beta Gamma Sigma. Avocations: historic preservation, interior design, travel, theatre, flower arranging and design.

SOKAL, ROBERT REUVEN, biology educator, author; b. Vienna, Austria, Jan. 13, 1926; came to U.S., 1947, naturalized 1958; s. Siegfried and Klara (Rattner) S.; m. Julie Chen-Chu Yang, Aug. 12, 1948; children: David Jonathan, Hannah Judith. BS in Biology, St. John's U., Shanghai, Republic of China, 1947; PhD in Zoology, U. Chgo., 1952; DSc (hon.), U. Crete (Greece), 1990. From instr. to prof. U. Kans., Lawrence, 1951-69; prof., then leading prof., Disting. prof. SUNY, Stony Brook, 1969-95, dept. chmn., 1980-83, vice provost for rsch. and grad. studies, 1981-82, disting. prof. emeritus, 1995. Fulbright vis. prof. Hebrew/Tel Aviv U., Israel, 1963-64, U. Vienna, Austria, 1977, 78, 84; vis. prof. Inst. Adv. Studies, Oeiras, Portugal, 1971-80; vis. disting. prof. U. Mich., 1975-76; vis. prof. Coll. de France, Paris, 1989. Author: Principles of Numerical Taxonomy, 1963, Biometry, 1969, 3d rev. edit., 1995, Statistical Tables, 1969, 3rd rev. edit. 1995, Introduction to Biostatistics, 1973, 2d rev. edit., 1987, Numerical Taxonomy, 1973; editor Am. Naturalist, 1969-74. Career investigator NIH, 1964-69; sr. fellow NSF, 1959-60, NATO fellow, 1974, Guggenheim fellow, 1975-76, 84; Ctr. Advanced Study in Behavioral Sci. fellow, 1992-93. Fellow AAAS, Am. Acad. Arts and Scis.; mem. Soc. Study Evolution (pres. 1977), Am. Soc. Naturalists (hon. mem., pres. 1984), The Classification Soc. (pres. 1969-71), Internat. Fedn. Classification Socs. (pres. 1988-89), Nat. Acad. Scis., Linnean Soc. London (fgn.), Soc. Systematic Zoology (hon.), Natural History Mus. (Paris, corr. mem.), B'nai Brith (pres. 1966). Democrat. Jewish.

SOKOL, DENNIS ALLEN, hospital administrator; b. Chgo., May 3, 1945; s. Stanley John and Mildred Veronica (Krenslake) S.; m. Gwen Noble, Dec. 19, 1971 (div.); children: Anne, Ellen; m. Jolene K. Buehrer, Jan. 28, 1989. BS in Bus., No. Ill. U., 1968; MBA, U. Nebr., Omaha, 1974; M of Hosp. Adminstrn., U. Minn., 1976. Radio personality various stas., Ill., Iowa and Nebr., 1968-72; pub. rels. officer Children's Meml. Hosp., Omaha, 1972-73, Meth. Hosp., Omaha, 1973-74; v.p. adminstrn. Golden Valley (Minn.) Health Ctr., 1976-82; pres. Sacred Heart Health Svcs., Yankton, S.D., 1982-97; regional pres. Presentation Health Sys., 1996-98; pres., CEO Firelands Regional Health Sys., Sandusky, Ohio, 1998—. Instr. health care mgmt. Mt. Marty Coll., 1986-87, U. Minn., 1986-88. Pres. Valley Health Svcs., Inc., 1984-97, Health Mgmt. Svcs., 1987-97. Fellow Am. Coll. Health Care Execs. (regent 1991-95); mem. S.D. Hosp. Assn. (trustee 1990-97), Missouri Valley Health Network (v.p. 1986-97), Yankton Area C. of C. (pres. 1989-90), Rotary. Republican. Roman Catholic. Office: Firelands Regional Health System 1101 Decatur St Sandusky OH 44870-3335

SOKOL, JOHN MCCUE, artist, writer; b. Canton, Ohio, Aug. 30, 1947; s. John James and Hilda Sokol. MA, Kent State U., 1973. Author: (book) Kissing the Bees, 1999 (1999 Redgreene Press Chapbook award, 1999), In the Summer of Cancer, 2002 (1st Annual Ludlow Press Search award, 2002), A Thousand Years from Nowhere, 2002 (Pudding House Publs. Chapbook award (2nd place & publication), 2002). Home: 115 N Portage Path Akron OH 44303

SOKOL, LARRY NIDES, lawyer, educator; b. Dayton, Ohio, Sept. 28, 1946; s. Boris Franklin and Kathryn (Konowitch) S.; m. Beverly Butler, Aug. 3, 1975; children: Addie Teller, Maxwell Philip. BA, U. Pa., 1968; JD, Case Western Res. U., 1971. Bar: Oreg. 1972, U.S. Dist Ct. Oreg. 1972, U.S. Ct. Appeals (9th cir.) 1973, U.S. Supreme Ct. 1980. Law clk. chief judge Oreg. Ct. Appeals, Salem, 1971-72; pvt. practice Portland, Oreg., 1972—; prof. law Lewis and Clark Law Sch. Adj. prof. law sch. environ. litigation Lewis & Clark U., 1984— Commr. planning City of Lake Oswego, Oreg., 1981-84. Sgt. USAR, 1968-74. Mem. Oreg. State Bar Assn. (chmn. litigation sect. 1983, disciplinary rev. bd. 1982-85), Oreg. Trial Lawyers Assn. Democrat. Jewish. Avocations: running, swimming, squash, model trains, scuba diving. Office: 735 SW 1st Ave Portland OR 97204-3326

SOKOL, ROBERT JAMES, obstetrician, gynecologist, educator; b. Rochester, N.Y., Nov. 18, 1941; s. Eli and Mildred (Levine) S.; m. Roberta Sue Kahn, July 26, 1964; children: Melissa Anne, Eric Russell, Andrew Ian. BA with highest distinction in Philosophy, U. Rochester, 1963, MD with honors, 1966. Diplomate Am. Bd. Ob-Gyn (assoc. examiner 1984-86), Sub-Bd. Maternal-Fetal Medicine. Intern Barnes Hosp., Washington U., St. Louis, 1966-67, resident in ob-gyn., 1967-70, asst. in ob-gyn., 1966-70, rsch. asst., 1967-68, instr. clin. ob-gyn., 1970; Buswell fellow in maternal fetal medicine Strong Meml. Hosp.-U. Rochester, 1972-73; fellow in maternal-fetal medicine Cleve. Met. Gen. Hosp.-Case Western Res. U., Cleve., 1974-75, assoc. obstetrician and gynecologist, 1973-83, asst. prof. ob-gyn., 1973-77; asst. program dir. Perinatal Clin. Rsch. Ctr., 1973-78, co-program dir., 1978-82, program dir., 1982-83, acting dir. obstetrics, 1974-75, co-dir., 1977-83, assoc. prof., 1977-81, prof., 1981-83, assoc. dir. dept. ob-gyn., 1981-83; prof. ob-gyn. Wayne State U., Detroit, 1983-2000, disting. prof., 2000—, chmn. dept. ob-gyn., 1983-89, mem. grad. faculty dept. physiology, 1984—, interim dean Med. Sch., 1988-89, dean, 1989-99, pres. Fund for Med. Rsch. and Edn., 1988—99, disting. prof. ob-gyn, 2000—; chief ob-gyn. Hutzel Hosp., 1983-89; interim chmn. med. bd. Detroit Med. Ctr., 1988-89, chmn. med. bd., 1989-99, sr. v.p. med. affairs, 1992-99, trustee, 1990-99; past pres. med. staff Cuyahoga County Hosps.; mem. profl. adv. bd. Educated Childbirth Inc., 1976-80; dir. C.S. Mott Ctr. for Human Growth and Devel., 1983-89, 99—. Sr. Ob cons. Symposia Medicus; cons. Grant Planning Task Force Robert Wood Johnson Found., Nat. Inst. Child Health and Human Devel., Nat. Inst. Alcohol Abuse and Alcoholism, Ctr. for Disease Control, NIH, Health Resources and Services Adminstrn., Nat. Clearinghouse for Alcohol Info., Am. Psychol. Assn.; mem. alcohol psychosocial research rev. com. Nat. Inst. Alcohol Abuse and Alcoholism, 1982-86; mem. ob/gyn adv. panel U.S. Pharmacopeial Conv., 1985-90, adv. com. on policy Am. Jour. Ob-Gyn., 1999-, internat. adv. bd. Karmanos Cancer Inst., Detroit, Mich., 2002-; mem. clin. rsch. task force Assn. Am. Med. Colls., 1998-2000. Mem. internat. editorial bd. Israel Jour. Obstetrics and Gynecology; reviewer med. jours.; mem. editorial bd. Jour. Perinatal Medicine; editor-in-chief Interactions: Programs in Clinical Decision-Making, 1987-90; researcher computer applications in perinatal medicine, alcohol-related birth defects, perinatal risk and neurobehavioral devel.; contbr. articles to profl. jours. Mem.Pres.'s leadership coun. U. Rochester, 1976—80; mem. exec. com. bd. trustees Oakland Health Edn. Program (OHEP), 1987—2000, permanent trustee, 2000—, U. Rochester, 1986—. Maj. M.C. USAF, 1970—72. Mem.: APHA, ACOG (chmn. steering com. drug and alcohol abuse contract 1986—87, rep. ctr. for disease control & prevention task force 2000—, editor-in-chief ACOG Update 2001—), NAS (Inst. of Medicine, com. to study fetal alcohol syndrome 1994—96), AMA, Soc. Physicians Reproductive Choice and Health, World Assn. Perinatal Medicine, Internat. Soc. Computers in Obstetrics, Neonatology, Gynecology (v.p. 1987—89, pres. 1989—92), Soc. for Neuroscis. (Mich. chpt.), Am. Med. Soc. on Alcoholism and Other Drug Dependencies, Am. Gynecol. and Obstet. Soc., Neurobehavioral Teratology Soc., Soc. Perinatal Obstetricians (pres.-elect 1987—88, pres. 1988—89, v.p., achievement award 1995), Rsch. Soc. Alcoholism, Cen. Assn. Obstetricians-Gynecologists (pres.-elect 1997—99, pres. 1999—2000), Detroit Acad. Medicine (pres.-elect 1999—2001, pres. 2001—02), Wayne County Med. Soc., Mich. Med. Soc., Royal Soc. Medicine, Assn. Profs. Gyn.-Ob, Perinatal Rsch. Soc., Soc. Gynecologic Investigation, Am. Med. Informatics Assn., Chgo. Gyn. Soc. (hon.), Detroit Physiol. Soc. (hon.), Alpha Omega Alpha, Sigma Xi, Phi Beta Kappa. Republican. Jewish. Home: 7921 Danbury Dr West Bloomfield MI 48322-3581 Office: Wayne State U CS Mott Ctr for Human Growth and Devel Detroit MI 48201 E-mail: rsokol@moose.med.wayne.edu. *The drive for academic accomplishment was instilled early in childhood in a home environment which placed value on a multiplicity of interests in science and the arts. My parents taught me what to do. In retrospect, exposure to strong role models-professors of philosophy, pathology, psychiatry and obstetrics-gynecology-takes on increased importance-these individuals showed me how to do it. My family continues to support me in seeking and meeting new challenges. The opportunity to develop and transmit new knowledge sustains a high level of activity. I enjoy what I do.*

SOKOL, STEPHEN M. lawyer; b. Melbourne, Australia, Jan. 14, 1945; came to U.S., 1948; s. George J. and Cynthia E. (Wilson) S.; m. Susan S. Schreiber, Jan. 23, 1973; children: Andrew, Debora. BA magna cum laude, U. Pitts., 1968; JD, Duquesne U., 1971. Bar: Pa. Staff atty. FTC, Washington, 1971-72; atty. gen. Atty.'s Gen. Office, Harrisburg, Pa., 1972-75; pvt. practice Pitts., 1975—. Bd. dirs. Keystone Printing Co., Pitts. Law rev. editor Duquesne U., 1970-71. Mem. Big. Bros. of Pa., Pitts., 1994-95, Dem. Com., Pitts., 1974-80. Fellow Pa. Bar Assn., Allegheny County Bar Assn. (adv. bd. 1978-85); mem. Lions, Rotary. Avocations: oil painting, handball, tennis, hiking, travel. Office: SM Sokol 517 Frick Bldg Pittsburgh PA 15219

SOKOLOFF, LEON, pathology educator; b. Bklyn., May 9, 1919; s. Barnet and Ray (Cohen) S.; m. Barbara Snow, June 1950 (dec. 1960); children—Michael D., Naomi B. Sokoloff Berry; m. Beverly Beinfeld Trachtenberg, July 18, 1971. BA, NYU, 1938, MD, 1944; postgrad. Columbia U., 1938-39. Diplomate Am. Bd. Pathology. Resident, Bellevue Hosp., N.Y.C., 1945-47; asst. prof. NYU, N.Y.C., 1948-52; chief, sect. on rheumatic diseases Lab. Exptl. Pathology, NIH, Bethesda, Md., 1953-73; prof. pathology SUNY-Stony Brook, 1973-91. emeritus, 1991—; vis. prof. Royal Soc. Medicine, Eng., 1985. Author: Biology of Degenerative Joint Disease, 1969. Editor: The Joints and Synovial Tissue, 1978. Contbr. articles to profl. jours. Served to capt. USPHS, 1953-73. Recipient J. van Breemen medal Dutch Rheumatism Assn., 1967, Disting. Alumnus award NYU, 1975; NIH grantee, 1973-87. Mem. Am. Coll. Rheumatol (Master 1987), Am. Soc. Investigative Pathology, Am. Coll. Veterinary Pathologists, 1992, (hon. mem.); Jewish. Avocation: medical history. Office: SUNY Dept Pathology Health Sci Ctr Stony Brook NY 11794-8691 E-mail: leobevsok@aol.com.

SOKOLOFF, LOUIS, physiologist, neurochemist; b. Phila., Oct. 14, 1921; married; 2 children. BA, U. Pa., 1943, MD, 1946; Dr. (hon.), Philipps U. Marburg, Germany, 1990; MD (hon.), U. Rome, 1992; ScD (hon.), Georgetown U., 1992, Mich. State U., 1993, U. Pa., 1997. Intern Phila. Gen. Hosp., 1946-47; rsch. fellow in physiology U. Pa. Grad. Sch. Medicine, 1949-51, instr., then assoc., 1951-56; assoc. chief, then chief sect. cerebral metabolism NIMH, Bethesda, Md., 1953-68, chief lab. cerebral metabolism, 1968—. Chief editor Jour. Neurochemistry, 1974-78. Served to capt. M.C. U.S. Army, 1947-49. Recipient F.O. Schmitt medal in neurosci., 1980, Albert Lasker clin. med. research award, 1981, Karl Spencer Lashley award Am. Philos. Soc., 1987, Disting. Grad. award U. Pa., 1987, Nat. Acad. Scis. award in Neurosci., 1988, George Charles de Hevesy Nuclear Medicine Pioneer award Soc. Nuclear Medicine, 1988, Mihara Cerebrovascular Disorder Rsch. Promotion award, 1988. Mem. NAS, Inst. Medicine (sr.), Am. Physiol. Soc., Assn. Rsch. Nervous and Mental Diseases, Am. Biophys. Soc., Am. Acad. Neurology, Am. Neurol. Assn., Am. Soc. Biol. Chemists, Am. Soc. Neurochemistry. Achievements include development of methods for measurement of cerebral blood flow and metabolism in animals and man. Office: NIMH/NIH Bldg 36 Rm 1A07 9000 Rockville Pike Bethesda MD 20892-4030

SOKOLOFF, TERRI ANN, real estate broker; b. Long Beach, Calif., June 12, 1964; d. Joe and Eileen (Smith) Sawdai; m. Sokoloff, Sept. 7, 1986; 1 child, Sidney. BA, U. Pitts., 1982-86. Cert. real estate broker. Sales rep. Teney, Pitts., 1986-87; account rep. Donnlley Directory, 1987-88; pres. Specialty Tavern & Restaurant Brokers, 1988—. Mem. Internat. Bus. Brokers Assn., Comml. Investment Inst., Pitts. Realtor Com. (author), Realtor Brokerage Mgrs. (designee), Realtor Assn. Pitts. (past bd. dirs.), Pitts. Purveyor Assn. (past bd. dirs.), Women in Comml. Real Estate (bd. dirs.). Avocations: golf, reading, travel. Office: Specialty Group 3205 Mcknight East Dr Pittsburgh PA 15237-6423 E-mail: terri@specialtygroup.com.

SOKOLOV, HOWARD H. psychiatrist; b. Apr. 4, 1940; AB, Columbia Coll., 1961; MD, SUNY, Bklyn., 1965; grad., Cin. Psychoanalytic Inst., 1987. Diplomate Am. Bd. Psychiatry and Neurology, Am. Bd. Forensic Psychiatry. Intern Cin. Gen. Hosp., 1965-66; resident in psychiatry U. Cin., 1966-69; commr. mental health Ohio Dept. Mental Health, Columbus, 1981-83; dir. Netcare Forensic Psychiatry Ctr., 1983-89; med. dir. Harding Hosp., Worthington, Ohio, 1989-94, Office Forensic Svcs., Ohio Dept. Mental Health, Columbus, 1994—; assoc. clin. prof. psychiatry Ohio State U., 1982—. Fellow Am. Psychiat. Assn.; mem. Ohio Psychiat. Assn. (pres. 1989-90). Office: 30 E Broad St Fl 24 Columbus OH 43215 E-mail: sokolovh@mhmail-mh.state.oh.us.

SOKOLOV, RICHARD SAUL, real estate company executive; b. Phila., Dec. 7, 1949; s. Morris and Estelle Rita (Steinberg) S.; m. Susan Barbara Saltzman, Aug. 13, 1972; children: Lisa, Anne, Kate. BA, Pa. State U., 1971; JD, Georgetown U., 1974. Assoc. Weinberg & Green, Balt., 1974-80, ptnr., 1980-82; v.p., gen. counsel The Edward J. DeBartolo Corp., Youngstown, Ohio, 1982-86, sr. v.p. devel., gen. coun., 1986-94; pres., CEO DeBartolo Realty Corp., 1994-96; pres., COO Simon DeBartolo Group, Indpls., 1996-98; pres, COO Simon Property Group, 1998—. Mem. investment com. Jewish Fedn., Youngstown, 1992—; trustee U. Wis.-Madison Ctr. for Urban Land Econs. Rsch., Youngstown/Mahoning Valley United Way. Alumni fellow Pa. State U., 2000. Mem. Internat. Coun. Shopping Ctrs. (trustee 1994—, chmn. 1998-99), Urban Land Inst. (assoc.). Office: Simon Property Group 115 W Washington St Ste 1465 Indianapolis IN 46204-3464

SOKOLOW, ISOBEL FOLB, sculptor; b. Bklyn. d. Henry Folb and Betty Forshaw; m. Gilbert Sokolow; children: Helene, Cheryl. Student, Silvermine Coll. Art, 1965-68, Art Students League, Nat. Acad. Design, Westchester C.C., N.Y., Ednl. Alliance Art Sch. Tchr., art therapist Jewish Guild for the Blind, Yonkers, N.Y., 1974-76; dir. Westchester Art & Culture Assn., Ardsley, NY, 1984—86; coord. sculpture workshops Pietrasanta, Italy, 1984-86; coord. summer workshop Pratt U., Venice, Italy, 1987. Artist in residence Nat. Woman's Com., Brandeis U., 1995; premanent collection Mus. Bozetti, Pietrasanta, Italy; prodr., host cable TV show Art Scene Thru An Artist's Eye, 1995—2000. One-woman shows include Bell Gallery, Greenwich, Conn., 1977, River View Gallery, Dobbs Ferry, N.Y., 1978, North Shore Sculpture Ctr., Great Neck, N.Y., 1980, Harkness House, N.Y.C., 1981, Musavi Art Ctr., N.Y.C., 1984, Atlantic Gallery, N.Y.C., 1988, 90, 92, 94, 96, 98, 2000, 2002, Sara Lawrence Coll., 1995-96, 2002, Shelter Rock Art Gallery, 1997, La Lac Gallery, Lake Lugano, Switzerland, 2001; exhibited in group shows at Monmouth Mus. Art, Red Bank, N.J., 1990, Westbeth Gallery, N.Y.C., 1991, Capital Bldg. Gallery, Tallahassee, 1991, Atlantic Gallery, N.Y.C., 1991, N.Y. Acad. Sci., N.Y.C., 1991, Broome St. Gallery, N.Y.C., 1991, Gallery Stendahl, N.Y.C., 1991, 97, 2002, Raleigh Gallery, Dania, Fla., 1993, Casa d'arte Gadiva Gallery, Forte dei Marmi, Italy, 1993, Bigi Art Gallery, Florence, Italy, 1993, Living Arts Gallery, Milan, Italy, 1994, Steiner Gallery, Bal Harbor, Fla., 1995, 97, Atlantic Gallery, 2000, Galleria Faustini, Florence, Italy, 2000; permanent collections include Museo dei Bozzetti, Pietrasonta, Italy, 1995; selected exhibits include Yonkers Art Assn., 1978, Audubon Artists Guild, 1978-80, N.J. Painters and Sculptors, 1980, Sculptors Alliance, 1982, Nat. Assn. Women Artists, 1984, N.Y. Soc. Women Artists, 1986, Am. Soc. Contemporary Artists, 1992; spl. exhibits include Dancer, GM Bldg., N.Y.C., 1978-79, Torso, Schulman Realty Group, N.Y.C., 1983-85, Dancer I, Westchester C.C., Valhalla, N.Y., 1982-92, Dancer Reborn, Roosevelt H.S., Yonkers, N.Y., 1992-98; prodr./host: (cable TV show) Art Scene Thru and Artist's Eye, 1997—. Recipient Silver medal Audubon Artists, 1978, Sculpture award Mamaroneck (N.Y.) Artists Guild; Tres Jolle des Arts award Nat. Assn. Women Artists, 1984, Best in Show award, 1993, David Perce Meml. prize, 2001. Mem.: Atlantic Gallery, Art Students League, Artists Equity (past bd. dirs., past v.p.), Am. Soc. Contemporary Artists (v.p., Meml. award 2001). Avocations: music, literature, travel. Home: 498 Winding Rd N Ardsley NY 10502-2702 E-mail: isart24184@aol.com.

SOKOLOW, MAURICE, physician, educator; b. N.Y.C., May 19, 1911; s. Alexander and Anna (Spiegelman) S.; m. Ethel Schwabacher, June 30, 1941 (dec. 1970); children: Gail Anne, Jane Carol (dec.), Anne May. AB cum laude, U. Calif., Berkeley, 1932; MD, U. Calif., San Francisco, 1936. Intern San Francisco Gen. Hosp., 1935-36; resident U. Calif., San Francisco, 1936-37, rsch. fellow, 1939-40; resident New Eng. Med. Ctr., Boston, 1937-38; rsch. fellow Michael Reese Hosp., Chgo., 1938-39; gen. practice medicine San Francisco, 1946-62; faculty cardiovascular divsn. Sch. Medicine, U. Calif., 1946—, assoc. prof. medicine, 1952-58, prof., 1958-78, prof. emeritus, 1978—, chief electrocardiograph dept., chief hypertension clinic, 1946-78, chief cardiovascular divsn., 1955-73; program and founding dir. cardiology tng. grant USPHS, 1960-73; sr. and founding mem. Cardiovascular Rsch. Inst., 1957—. Cons. in field. Author: Clinical Cardiology, 1977, 6th edit., 1993; contbr. articles to profl. jours. ; mem. editorial bd. Jour. Cardiovascular Medicine, 1975—, Western Jour. Medicine, 1946-68. Bd. dirs. Fromm Inst Life Long Learning, U. San Francisco. Lt. comdr. M.C. USN, 1942-46. Rsch. fellow U. Calif., 1939-40; Nat. Heart Inst. grant, 1950-78; named U. Calif. San Francisco Alumnus of Yr., 1986. Fellow Am. Coll. Cardiology (hon.); mem. Am. Fedn. Clin. Research (v.p 1948-49), Assn. Univ. Cardiologists, Am. Soc. Clin. Investigation, Brit. Cardiac Soc. (corr.), Am. Heart Assn., San Francisco Heart Assn. (pres. 1950-51), Menlo Circus Club. Clubs: Menlo Circus. Home: 3452 Jackson St San Francisco CA 94118-2021 Office: U Calif Sch Medicine San Francisco CA 94143-0001 E-mail: mssoke@aol.com.

SOKOLSKY, ROBERT LAWRENCE, journalist, entertainment writer; b. Boston, May 18, 1928; s. Henry and Lillian (Gorodetzky) S.; m. Sally-Ann Moss, Aug. 11, 1955; 1 son, Andrew E. AB, Syracuse (N.Y.) U., 1950. Reporter Springfield (Mass.) Union, 1950; asst. dir. pub. info. ARC, Syracuse, 1952-54; entertainment editor Syracuse Herald-Jour., 1954-61, Buffalo Courier Express, 1961-72, Phila. Bull., 1972-82; entertainment writer Riverside (Calif.) Press-Enterprise, 1983-2000; syndicated TV columnist Ottaway News Svc., 1988-96, Scripps Howard, 1996-2000; freelance writer, radio commentator pub. radio, 2000—; columnist San Bernardino Sun, 2001—; entertainment editor Inland Empire News Radio, 2001—. Radio show host; freelance writer; guest lectr. Contbr. columns in newspapers, articles to profl. jours. Bd. dirs. Brush Hollow Civic Assn., Evesham Twp., N.J. Served with U.S. Army, 1950-52. Recipient Sigma Delta Chi award for feature writing, 1950, award for entertainment coverage Twin Counties Press Club, 1984, 87, Lifetime Achievement award Inland Theatre League, 2001. Mem. Am. Newspaper Guild (Page One award for opinion writing), Syracuse Press Club, Greater Buffalo Press Assn., TV Critics Assn., Soc. Profl. Journalists (Excellence in Journalism award 1989, 93), Pen and Pencil Club of Phila., Variety Club. Republican. Jewish. Home: 3080 Saratoga St Riverside CA 92503-5435 Office: 3080 Saratoga St Riverside CA 92503

SOLA, JANET ELAINE, secondary school educator; b. New Britain, Conn., Oct. 23, 1935; d. Walter Andrew and Helen (Mandl) Sinkiewicz; m. Raymond Albert Sola BS, Cen. Conn. State U., 1957; MS, So. Conn. State U., 1962; postgrad., U. Conn, 1969. Tchr. bus. Amity Regional High Sch., Woodbridge, Conn., 1957-60; bus. instr. Stone Coll., New Haven, 1962; instr. Manpower Devel. and Tng. Act, New Britain, 1970-74, So. Ctrl. C.C., New Haven, 1977, lectr., 1987; mgmt. lectr. II, Quinnipiac Coll., Hamden, Conn., 1981-87; mayor's aide Town of Hamden, 1987-89, recycling coord., 1989-92; tchr. bus. edn. Hamden High Sch., 1992—, coord. coop. work experience and diversified occupations, 1992—. Assessor credit for life Quinn Coll., Hamden, 1986-89; advisor Hamden Hub Student Interns, 2000. Author: (poetry) Flights of Fancy, 1991, Recycled Thoughts, 1992; contbr. poetry to Contemporary, The Hamden Chronicle, Treasured Poems of Am., Nat. Arts Soc. Campaigner Sola for Town Clk. Com., Hamden, 1981; community liaison Carusone for Mayor Com., Hamden, 1981-87; v.p., Am. Legion Aux. Unit 88, Hamden, 1985-95; treas. Green Dragon Enterprises, Inc., 2002. Named Tchr. of Yr., Hamden H.S., 2000—01. Mem. ASCD, NAFE, AAUW, Nat. Bus. Educators, Ctrl. Conn. State U. Alumni Assn. (bd. dirs.), Internat. Platform Assn., Internat. Soc. Poetry (disting. mem.), Hamden Lions Internat. Avocations: bowling, swimming. Home: 50 Vernon St Hamden CT 06518-2825 Office: Hamden HS 2040 Dixwell Ave Hamden CT 06514-2404 E-mail: jsola@hamdenschools.org.

SOLA, JURE, electronics executive; BSEE, San Jose State U., 1972. Various mgmt. positions Lika Corp., Stockton, Calif., 1972-80; various mgmt positions Hanmina Corp. and predecessor, 1980—; now pres. & chmn. Sanmina Corp. and predecessor, 1991—2001; chmn. & CEO Sanmina-SCI, 2001—. Office: Sanmina Corp 2700 N 1st St San Jose CA 95134-2015*

SOLAI, LALITHKUMAR KUPPUSAMY, psychiatrist, educator; b. Madurai, Tamil Nadu, India, Apr. 1, 1968; came to U.S., 1992; s. Kuppuswamy Alagarsamy and Jothimani Kuppusamy Solai. MB BS, U. Madras, India, 1991; MD in Psychiatry, Henry Ford Hosp., 1996; MD in Geriatric Psychiatry, U. Pitts., 1997. Bd. cert. Am. Bd. Psychiatry and Neurology. Asst. prof. clin. psychiatry, med. dir. U. Pitts. Med. Ctr., Beaver Valley, Rochester, Pa., 1998—. Cons. psychiatrist Mariner Health Ctr., Westhills, Pa., 1997—, Geriatric Ctr., Beaver, 1997—, St. Joseph Villa, Baden, 1997—. Named Psychiat. Resident of Yr., Pfizer, 1996; recipient New Investigator's award NIMH, 1997. Mem. AAAS, Am. Psychiat. Assn., Indo-Am. Psychiat. Assn. (mem.-in-tng. rep. 1997), Am. Assn. for Geriatric Psychiatry, Pa. Psychiat. Assn. Hindu. Avocations: astronomy, star gazing, listening to music, traveling. Office: WPIC Beaver Valley MHS 176 Virginia Ave Rochester PA 15074-1723

SOLAN, LAWRENCE MICHAEL, lawyer; b. N.Y.C., May 7, 1952; s. Harold Allen and Shirley (Smith) S.; m. Anita Lois Rush, Mar. 27, 1982; children: Renata, David. BA, Brandeis U., 1974; PhD, U. Mass., 1978; JD, Harvard U., 1982. Bar: N.J. 1982, N.Y. 1984. Law clk. to Hon. Pollock Supreme Ct. N.J., Morristown, 1982-83; assoc. Orans, Elsen & Lupert, N.Y.C., 1983-89, ptnr., 1989-96; assoc. prof. law Bklyn. Law Sch., 1996-2000, prof. law, 2000—. Bd. dirs. Internat. Acad. Law and Mental Health; vis. assoc. prof. Princeton U., NJ, 1999—2000, vis. prof., NJ, 2002. Author: The Language of Judges, 1993, Pronominal Reference, 1983. Mem. Assn. of Bar of City of N.Y., Phi Beta Kappa. Home: 163 Ralston Ave South Orange NJ 07079-2344 Office: Bklyn Law Sch 250 Joralemon St Brooklyn NY 11201-3700

SOLAN, STUART MILEY, physician; b. Washington, Aug. 20, 1951; s. George Miley and Marjorie Ann (Sonneman) S.; m. Carol Jean Cummins, Oct. 14, 1952; children: Christopher Miley, Melissa Ann. BA, W.Va. U., 1973; MD, Med. Coll. Va., 1977. Diplomate Am. Bd. Family Practice. Intern, then resident Riverside Hosp., Newport News, Va., 1977-80; pvt. practice McGuire Med. Group (now Va. Physicians, Inc.), Richmond, 1980—; asst. clin. prof. family practice Med. Coll. Va., 1982-2000, assoc. clin. prof. family practice, 2000—. Pres. med. staff St. Lukes Hosp., Richmond, 1986-87, trustee, 1986-87; question writer Am. Bd. Family Practice, 1989-93. Deacon, elder Third Presbyn. Ch., Richmond, 1987—. Fellow Am. Acad. Family Physicians; mem. Va. Acad. Family Physicians (v.p. 1991-92, pres. 1993-94, Va. Family Dr. of Yr. 1991-92), Richmond Acad. Medicine. Avocations: hunting, fishing, pocket billiards, Civil War history. Home: 9001 Chapaqua Ct Richmond VA 23229-7745 Office: Va Physicians Inc 10431 Patterson Ave Richmond VA 23233-5101

SOLANO, CARL ANTHONY, lawyer; b. Pittston, Pa., Mar. 26, 1951; s. Nick D. and Catherine A. (Occhiato) S; m. Nancy M. Solano, 1989; children: Melanie A., Carla Nicole. BS magna cum laude, U. Scranton, 1973; JD cum laude, Villanova U., 1976. Bar: Pa. 1976, U.S. Dist. Ct. (ea. dist.) Pa. 1978, U.S. Ct. Appeals (3rd cir.) 1980, U.S. Ct. Appeals (5th cir.) 1981, U.S. Supreme Ct. 1982, U.S. Ct. Appeals (9th cir.) 1986, U.S. Dist. Ct. (mid. dist.) Pa. 1988, U.S. Ct. Appeals (6th cir.) 1988, U.S. Ct. Appeals (Fed. cir.) 1989, U.S. Ct. Appeals (7th cir.) 1996. Law clerk Hon. Alfred L. Luongo U.S. Dist. Ct., Ea. Dist. Pa., Phila., 1976-78; assoc. Schnader, Harrison, Segal & Lewis, Phila., 1978-84, ptnr., 1985—. adj. prof. Villanova U. Sch. Law, 1999. Mem. ABA, Am. Law Inst., Pa. Bar Assn. (statutory law com. 1980-95), Phila. Bar Assn., St. Thomas More Soc., Justinian Soc., Order of Coif, Pi Gamma Mu. Roman Catholic. Home: 5 Barrister Ct Haverford PA 19041-1137 Office: Schnader Harrison Segal & Lewis LLP 1600 Market St Ste 3600 Philadelphia PA 19103-7287

SOLANO, JANINE T. physician assistant; b. Aurora, Colo., May 31, 1954; d. Thomas R. and Ralphie T. (Ortez) Lutrey; m. Henry L. Solano, Nov. 18, 1972; children: Mateo Antonio, Amalia Maria, Guadalupe Elizabeth. BFA, U. Colo., Boulder, 1976; BS in Med. Sci., U. Colo., Denver, 1980, MS, 1981. Cert. physician asst., Colo., Mass. Physician asst. TriCounty Health Dept., Englewood, Colo., 1981-85; mem. faculty U. Colo. Sch. Medicine, Denver, 1985-88; physician asst. Denver Health and Hosps., 1988-91, South Boston Cmty. Health Ctr., Boston, 1992-94, Denver Health and Hosps., 1995—; clin. coord. North H.S. Based Health Ctr., Denver, 1997—. Bd. dir. Clinica Tepeyac; asst. clin. prof. U. Colo. Sch. Medicine, 2001. Trustee Denver Art Mus., 1990-91; mem. Hispanic Adv. Coun. to Mayor of Denver, 1986-91; bd. dirs. The Colo. Children's Campaign, Denver, 1988-91. Recipient 1st Ann. award as Colo. Outstanding Physician Asst., Denver, 1988, Cert. of Commendation, City Coun., City of Boston, 1994. Mem.: Soc. Adolescent Medicine, Nat. Hispana Leadership Inst. Alumnus, Hispanic Alumni Assn. U. Colo.-Boulder (bd. dirs. 1994—97). Democrat. Roman Catholic. Avocation: art. Home: 4121 Bryant St Denver CO 80211-1735

SOLANO, JULIO RAFAEL, priest, educator; b. Barranquilla, Atlantico, Colombia, Sept. 12, 1946; came to U.S., 1971; s. Domingo Rafael Solano and Christine Balderrama. Degree in acctg., Centro Intensificacion Comml., Bogota, Colombia, 1970; BA, St. John Vianney Coll. Sem., Miami, Fla., 1989; MDiv, St. Vincent de Paul Regl. Sem., Boynton Beach, Fla., 1993. Transitional deacon St. Louis Cath. Ch., Miami, 1992—93; asst. pastor St. Elizabeth Cath. Ch., Pompano Beach, Fla., St. Patrick Cath. Ch., Miami Beach, 1996—98; parochial vicar St. Coleman Cath. Ch., Pompano Beach, 1998—99, St. Elizabeth of Hungary Cath. Ch., Pompano Beach, 1999—2001, St. Vincent Cath. Ch., Margate, 2001—02; pastor Our Lady Queen of Heaven Cath. Ch., North Lauderdale, Fla., 2002—. Tchr. La Salle H.S., Miami, 1996-98; asst. chaplain Serra Club Internat. Pompano Beach, 1994-95. Mem. Assn. Sacerdotes Hispanos. Democrat. Roman Catholic. Avocations: travel, reading, writing, stamps, coins.

SOLANO, PAUL (PAUL LEONARD SOLANO), finance educator; b. Somerville, Mass., Apr. 19, 1943; s. Edmund Joseph and Nora Mary (Di Pietro) S.; m. L. Linn Adams, Sept. 8, 1973; children: Amy, Alexis. BA, Northeasern U., 1966, MA, 1968; postgrad., U. Pa., 1968-70; PhD, U. Md., 1978. Ins. underwriter and rater Kemper Ins. Co., Boston, 1961-64; rsch. analyst Foreign Policy Rsch. Inst., Phila., 1970; rsch. cons. U.S. Agy. for Internat. Devel., Washington, 1972-73; budget analyst dept. budget and progamming Prince George's County, Md., 1974; instr. U. Md., College Park, 1974, 1976-77; asst. prof. U. Del., Newark, 1977-85, assoc. prof., 1985—. Cons. State Agys. Del., 1977—; faculty Inter Univ. Ops. Rsch., U. Del., 1988—; ex officio economist State of Del. Commn. for Local Govt. Financing, 1987-88; mem. Pub. Mgmt. Program, U. Del., Newark, 1990—; mem. City of Wilmington Del. Econ. and Fin. Adv. Coun., 1995—; cons. U.S. Govt., De State Govt. Contbr. articles to profl. jours., chpts. to books. Avocations: oil painting, cabinet making, antique furniture restoration. Home: 49 Shenandoah Dr Newark DE 19711-3772

SOLAR, RICHARD LEON, banker; b. Boston, Aug. 15, 1939; s. Hervey L. and Mildred (Beckerman) S.; m. Stephanie Bennett; children: Andrew, Lisa. BA, Harvard U., 1961; MBA, Columbia U., 1963. Asst. v.p. Bankers Trust Co., N.Y.C., 1963-71; treas. Val D'Or Inds., N.Y.C., 1971-74, Diamondhead Corp., Mountainside, N.J., 1975-76; sr. v.p., mng. dir. Bankers Trust Co., N.Y.C., 1976-96; chmn., dir. Bankers Trust Comml. Corp., 1996—; sr. v.p., dir. Gerber Childrens Wear Inc., N.Y.C., 1996—. Mem. Nat. Comml. Fin. Assn. (chmn., dir.), Wyantenuck Country Club (Great Barrington, Mass.). Office: Gerber Childrenswear Inc 1333 Broadway New York NY 10018-7204

SOLARI, PAUL GREGORY, physician; b. San Francisco, Dec. 1, 1958; s. Rafael Anthony Solari. BA in Neurobiology, U. Calif., Berkeley, 1980; MD, U. So. Calif., L.A., 1984. Diplomate Am. Bd. Internal Medicine, Am. Bd. Geriatrics. Resident in internal medicine St. Mary's Med. Ctr., San Francisco, 1984-87, vice chmn. dept. medicine, 1992-97, dir. clin. clerkship program, 1993-99, chmn. dept. medicine, 1998-99; pvt. practice, 1987-2000; asst. clin. prof. medicine U. Calif., 1995—; regional dir. med. affairs Glaxo Smith Kline, San Ramon, Calif., 2000—. Fellow ACP, AMA (alt. del. young physicians sect. 1993-94); mem. San Francisco Med. Soc. (bd. dirs. 1991-96), Calif. Med. Assn. (del. young physicians sect. 1990-95) Office: 2010 Crow Canyon Pl Ste 200 San Ramon CA 94583

SOLARI VICENTE, ANDRÉS HUMBERTO, economist, educator; b. Lima, Peru, Nov. 30, 1945; arrived in Mex., 1978; s. Humberto and Consuelo (Vicente) Solari; m. Martha Eliana Landa, Nov. 2, 1945; children: Yamila, Melina. BA, U. Agraria, Lima, 1969; MA, Ctr. Investigation and Tchg. Econs., Mexico City, 1980; Dr.Economy, U. Nac. Autonoma de Mex., 2001. Lectr. U. Mayor de San Marcos, Lima, 1969-70, 72, U. de la Cantuta, Lima, 1969; researcher U Federico Villarreal, 1972-76; mgr. Ministry of Industry, Huaráz, Peru, 1972-76; lectr., researcher U. Michoacana, Morelia, Mex., 1980—. Mgr. wholesale computing, 1991-95; mgr. internat. trading co. Naturales Cóndor SA.CV., 1994—. Author: Contemporary Economy, 1986, Latin America in the World Economic Re-structuration, 1987, USA Monopolies and Japanese Conglomerates, 1987, Verticality and Horizontality in Today's Northamerican Industry, 1987, Privatizations for the Transnational Re-estructuration, 1987, Economic Policy and Monopolist Power: The Limits of the Heterodox Economic Policy of Today's Peru, 1988, Privitazations, Fiscal Crisis and Transnational Capital, 1988, Tendencies of the World Economic Environment, 1989, Trail, Foot Paths or Big Avenues? Critique to the Legalistic Conceptions about the Informal Economies, 1990, Economic Crisis and the Reforms of Eastern Europe, 1991, Dictionary of the External Debt: Financial Systems and Transnational Capital, 1992, Intensivity and Extensivity in the United States Agriculture, 1992, Continuous Quality Improvement, 1998, Dynamism and Retraction in the Exporters Companies, 2000, The Economic-Managerial and the Conglomeral Production, 2001; contbr. articles to profl. publs. Mem. Coll. Economists. Avocations: Chinese cooking, playing the cajón. Home: Rusia 39 58060 Morelia Michoachan Mexico Office: Rusia 45 Villa Universidad 58090 Morelia Michoacán Mexico E-mail: asolari@unimedia.net.mx.

SOLARO, ROSS JOHN, physiologist, biophysicist; b. Wadsworth, Ohio, Jan. 9, 1942; s. Ross and Lena (Chuppa) S.; m. Kathleen Marie Cole, Sept. 18, 1965; children: Christopher, Elizabeth. BS, U. Cin., 1965; PhD, U. Pitts., 1971. Asst. prof. Med. Coll. Va., Richmond, 1973-77; assoc. prof. pharmacology and physiology U. Cin., 1977-81, prof. pharmacology and cell biophysics, 1981-85, prof. physiology, 1981-88; prof. physiology, head U. Ill., Chgo., 1988—, disting. univ. prof., 1998—. Sec. gen. Internat. Soc. Heart Rsch., 1989-93, sec./treas., 1995-98, pres., 1999, assoc. chair dept. physiology; chmn. exptl. cardiovasc. study sect. NIH, 1990-92; vice-chmn. physiology U. Cin., 1987-88. Editor: Protein Phosphorylation in Heart Muscle, 1986; contbr. articles to profl. jours. including Nature, Jour. Biol. Chemistry, Circulation Rsch. Chmn. rsch. coun. Am. Heart Assn., Met. Chgo., 1990-92. Grantee NIH, 1977—, Fogarty fellow, 1986; Brit. Am. Heart fellow Am. Heart Assn., 1974-75; Sr. Internat. fellow U. Coll. London, 1987. Mem. Am. Physiol. Soc. (chmn. subgroup), Am. Soc. Pharm. Exptl. Therapeutics, Biophys. Soc. (chmn. subgroup 1983-84). Office: U Ill at Chgo MC901 Physiology & Biophysics 835 S Wolcott Ave Chicago IL 60612-7340

SOLBERG, MARY, federal agency administrator; Grad., Western Mich. U. Dep. dir. Office Nat. Drug Control Policy Exec. Office of Pres., Washington, 2001—; exec. dir. Coalition of Health Comtys., Troy (Mich.) Cmty. Coalition for Prevention of Drug and Alcohol Abuse; various positions Troy Adult and Cmty. Edn., 1977—91. Mem. adv. com. to develop a nat. prevention sys. Nat. Ctr. for Substance Abuse Prevention; mem. adv. com. Nat. Ad Coun.'s Cmty. Anti-Drug Campaign; mem. Pres.'s Commn. on Drug-Free Cmtys., 1998, co-chairperson. Office: Exec Office of Pres Office Nat Drug Control Policy 750 17th St NW Washington DC 20503

SOLBERG, WINTON UDELL, history educator; b. Aberdeen, S.D., Jan. 11, 1922; s. Ole Alexander and Bertha Georgia (Tschappat) S.; m. Ruth Constance Walton, Nov. 8, 1952; children— Gail Elizabeth, Andrew Walton, Kristin

Ruth. AB magna cum laude, U. S.D., 1943, LHD (hon.), 1987; student, Biarritz (France) Am. U., 1946; A.M., Harvard, 1947, PhD, 1954. Instr., then asst. prof. social scis. U.S. Mil. Acad., 1951-54; instr., then asst. prof. history Yale U., 1954-58; fellow Pierson Coll., 1955-58, Morse fellow, 1958; James Wallace prof. history Macalester Coll., 1958-62; vis. prof. U. Ill., 1961-62, assoc. prof. history, 1962, prof., 1967—, chmn. dept. history, 1970-72. Research fellow Ctr. Study History of Liberty in Am., Harvard U., 1962-63; summer research scholar Henry E. Huntington Library, San Marino, Calif., 1959; dir. Coe Found. Am. Studies Inst., summers 1960-62; lectr., cons. Army War Coll., 1959-62; lectr. U.S. Command and Gen. Staff Sch., 1963-64; Fulbright lectr. Johns Hopkins U. Bologna, 1967-68, Moscow (USSR) State U., 1978, U. Calcutta India, 1993; vis. prof. Konan U., Kobe, Japan, 1981; USIA Lectr., Korea and Malaysia, 1985, Korea, 1992. Author: The Federal Convention and the Formation of the Union of the American States, 1958, The Constitutional Convention and the Formation of the Union, 1990, The University of Illinois, 1867-1894, 1968, Redeem the Time: The Puritan Sabbath in Early America, 1977, History of American Thought and Culture, 1983, Cotton Mather, The Christian Philosopher, 1994, The University of Illinois, 1894-1904: The Shaping of the University, 2000; also articles. Mem. Ill. Humanities Council, 1973-75; sec. Council on Study of Religion, 1981-85. Served to maj. inf. AUS, 1943-46, 51-54; lt. col. U.S. Army Res. Recipient Faculty Achievement award Burlington No. Found., 1986, Disting. Teaching award U. Ill. Coll. Liberal Arts and Scis., 1988; NEH sr. fellow, 1974-75; NSF research grantee, 1981-82 Mem. Am. Hist. Assn., So. Hist. Assn., Orgn. Am. Historians, Am. Studies Assn. (pres. Mid-Am. 1985-86), Am. Soc. Ch. History (pres. 1985-86), AAUP (chpt. pres. 1965-66, mem. council 1969-72, 1st v.p. 1974-76), Phi Beta Kappa. Episcopalian. Home: 8 Lake Park Rd Champaign IL 61822-7101 Office: U Ill History Dept Urbana IL 61801 E-mail: wsolberg@uiuc.edu.

SOLBRIG, INGEBORG HILDEGARD, German literature educator, writer; b. Weissenfels, Germany, July 31, 1923; came to U.S., 1961, naturalized, 1966; d. Reinhold J. and Hildegard M.A. (Ferchland) S. Grad. in chemistry, U. Halle, Germany, 1948; BA summa cum laude, San Francisco State U., 1964; postgrad., U. Calif., Berkeley, 1964-65; MA, Stanford U., 1966, PhD in Humanities and German, 1969. Asst. prof. U. R.I., 1969-70, U. Tenn., Chattanooga, 1970-72, U. Ky., Lexington, 1972-75; assoc. prof. German U. Iowa, 1975-81, prof., 1981-93, prof. emerita, 1993—. Domestic and abroad lectr. Author: Hammer-Purgstall und Goethe, 1973, Modulationen von Gold und Licht in Goethes Kunstmärchen, 1997, Momentaufnahmem , 2000, J.G. Herder: Echo of the Cultural Philospher's Ideas in Early African-American Intellectual Writing, 2000, Maria Sibylla Merian..., 2001; main editor: Rilke Heute, Beziehungen und Wirkungen, 1975, translator, editor: bilingual edit. Reinhard Goering: Seeschlacht/Seabattle, 1977, translator, editor: bilingual edit. Orient-Rezeption, 1996, mem. editl. bd.: Kairoer Germanistische Studien, vol. 9 & 10, 1998, mem. editl. bd.: Multiculturalism in Literary Criticism: A German-American Perspective, 1998; contbr. articles to profl. jours., chpts. to books. Mem. Iowa Gov.'s Com. on 300th Anniversary German-Am. Rels. 1683-1983, 1983. Recipient Hammer-Purgstall Gold medal Austria, 1974; named Ky. col., 1975; fellow Austrian Ministry Edn., 1968-69, Stanford U., 1965-66, 68-69; Old Gold fellow Iowa, 1977; Am. Coun. Learned Socs. grantee; German Acad. Exch. Svc. grantee, 1980; sr. faculty rsch. fellow in the humanities, 1983; NEH grantee, 1985; May Brodbeck fellow in the humanities, 1989; numerous summer faculty rsch. grants. Mem.: MLA (life), Soc. for the History of Alchemy and Chemistry (founding mem.), Internat. Herder Soc. (founding mem.), Goethe Soc. N.Am., Inc., Can. Soc. for 18th Century Studies, Am. Soc. for 18th Century Studies, Deutsche Schiller Gesellschaft, Goethe Gesellschaft, Internat. Vereinigung fur Germanische Sprach und Lit. Wiss., Egyptian Soc. Lit. Criticism (hon.). Avocations: horseback riding, photography, writing, travel. Home: 1126 Pine St Iowa City IA 52240-5711 E-mail: isolbrig@blue.weeg.uiowa.edu. *The circumstances of my life took me to many places and cultures. Despite the discord and problems plaguing many parts of this planet, let us not forget that it's the home of the human family, our home. Always remember: Life is, by definition, change.*

SOLDAN, ANGELIKA, philosopher, political scientist, educator; b. Hennigsdorf, Germany, Feb. 10, 1953; d. Hans and Erika Potempa; m. Wolfgang Karl Soldan, May 8, 1987; 1 child, Anja Soldan. MA in Philosophy, Humboldt U., 1975, PhD, 1990, Martin Luther U., Halle-Wittenberg, Germany, 1982. Assoc. prof. philosophy, polit. ethics Humboldt U., Berlin, 1989-91; adj. prof. philosophy, ethics, govt. U. Tex., Brownsville, 1991-98. Sr. lectr. U. Wis. Eau Claire, 1998-99; lectr. social issues, philosophy, 1999-2000, asst. prof., 2000—. Contbr. articles to profl. jours. Mem. Sch.-Parent com. 35th 52nd H.S., Berlin, 1979-90; supporter Sch. Tchr. Exch. Program USA-Germany, 1991—; co-founder Gesellschaft für Solidarische Entwicklungszusammenarbeit, 1990. Scholarship Max Planck Gesellschaft, 1990. Mem. Am. Philos. Assn., Internat. Fromm Soc. Office: U Tex Brownsville 80 Fort Brown St Brownsville TX 78520-4956 E-mail: asoldan@utb.edu.

SOLDAY, ALIDRA (LINDA BROWN), psychotherapist, psychoanalyst, filmmaker; b. Mineola, N.Y., Feb. 18, 1941; d. Charles Harold and Helen (Golbach) Brown. Student, Smith Coll., Northampton, Mass., 1958-60; BA, Barnard Coll., N.Y.C., 1962; MPS in Art Therapy, Pratt Inst., Bklyn., 1973; MSW, Hunter Coll., N.Y.C., 1976. Cert. social worker, psychoanalyst, N.Y.; lic. clin. social worker, Calif.; diplomate clin. social work Am. Bd. Examiners in Clin. Social Work. Singer, actress Broadway theatres, N.Y.C., 1962-65, pub. rels./community rels. specialist, real estate, publicist/editor, pub., edn. cons., 1965-71; art therapist Bronx (N.Y.) Psychiat. Ctr., 1972-74; clin. social worker North Richmond Community Mental Health Ctr., S.I., N.Y., 1977-79; staff therapist Lincoln Inst. Psychotherapy, N.Y.C., 1978-80; sr. staff therapist Ctr. for Study Anorexia and Bulimia, 1983-85; staff therapist Inst. Contemporary Psychotherapy, 1988-95; pvt. practice psychotherapy, 1978—. Prodr., dir. video documentaries for TV on elderly in Am., 2001—; mem. human svc. faculty Tristate Inst. Traditional Chinese Acupuncture, N.Y.C., 1986—89; mem. faculty N.Y. Open Ctr., N.Y.C., 1987—98; adj. faculty Health Choices Ctr. for Healing Arts, Princeton, NJ, 1987—90; clin. cons. Personal Performance Cons., EAP, 1988; human resources cons. industry, N.Y.C., 1988—; workshop leader seminars on stress mgmt., assertiveness tng., comm. and counseling skills, intimate relationships skills, creative expression. Mem. NASW. Office: 211 W 56th St #9H New York NY 10019 E-mail: asolday@aol.com.

SOLDO, JOHN J. educator, writer; b. Bklyn., May 16, 1945; s. Victor and Mildred Carmela (Ferrari) S.; m. Martha Schwink, Aug. 24, 1968 (div. Apr. 1971). BA magna cum laude, Fordham U., 1966; MA, Harvard U., 1968, PhD, 1972. Asst. prof. Wells Coll., Aurora, N.Y., Bronx (N.Y.) C.C., Kingsborough C.C., Bklyn., Columbia U., N.Y.C.; chmn. dept. langs. and lit. Ea. N.Mex. U.; prof. Five Towns Coll., Dix Hills, N.Y. Author: The Tempering of T.S. Eliot, 1983; (poetry) Delano in American, 1972, Odes and Cycles, 1983, In An Arid Clime, 1984, In the Indies, 1991, Sonnets for our Risorgimento, 1992. Bd. advisors N.Y. Poetry Forum, N.Y.C.; chancelor N.Mex. State Poetry Soc. Mem. Internat. Spkrs. Platform. Democrat. Roman Catholic. Home: 1627 81st St Brooklyn NY 11214-2107 E-mail: dr.johnjsoldo@msn.com.

SOLE, MICHAEL JOSEPH, cardiologist; b. Timmins, Ont., Can., Mar. 5, 1940; s. Fred and Lillian Sole; m. Susan Karen Samuels, May 26, 1964; children: David Frederick, Leslie Meredith. BSc, U. Toronto, Ont., Can., 1962, MD, 1966. Cert. Coll. Physicians and Surgeons Ont.; diplomate Am. Bd. Internal Medicine. Rotating intern, jr. asst. resident, sr. asst. resident in internal medicine Toronto Gen. Hosp., 1966-69; cardiology fellow Cardiovasc. Rsch. Inst., U. Calif., San Francisco, 1969-71; cardiology fellow Peter Bent Brigham Hosp., Boston, 1971-73, jr. assoc. medicine, 1973-74; rsch. assoc. MIT, Cambridge, 1973-74; instr. medicine Harvard Med. Sch., 1973-74; from asst. to assoc. prof. medicine U. Toronto, 1974-83, prof. medicine and physiology, 1983—, mem. staff inst. med. sci., 1978—, dir. cardiology rsch., 1987-89, dir. centre cardiovascular rsch., 1989-99, Searle chair cardiovascular rsch., 1998—; staff cardiologist Toronto Hosp., 1974-89, dir. non-invasive cardiology, 1974-79, dir. cardiology rsch., 1979-89, dir. divsn. cardiology, 1989-98, dir. cardiovascular program, 1992-93, dir. Peter Munk Cardiac Ctr., 1992-97. Vis. prof. Harvard U., 1975, NIH, Bethesda, Md., 1981, U. B.C., 1982, 91, 92, Capital Med. Sch. and Beijing Hosp., 1985, U. Tokyo, 1992, others; mem. Can. Govt. Task Force Diagnostic Ultrasound, 1976-78; vice-chmn. econs. com. dept. medicine Toronto Gen. Hosp., 1977, chmn., 1978, 79, chmn. emeritus, 1980, mem. various coms., 1981-98, chmn. cardiology rsch. com., 1988-89, mem. cardiovascular collaborative practice group, 1989-92; rsch. assoc. Ont. Heart Found., 1979-89; assoc. rsch. inst. pediatrics Hosp. Sick Children, Toronto, 1979—; mem. med. staff Mt. Sinai Hosp., Toronto, 1979—; mem. adv. bd. Merck Pharms., 1983—, Boots Pharms., 1992-93; mem. Health Rsch. and Devel. Coun., Province of Ont., 1983-86, mem. exec. com., 1984-86; Levesque lectr. Montreal Heart Inst., 1984; mem. cardiovascular panel Med. Rsch. Coun. Can., 1985-87; mem. heart and blood vessel rsch. adv. com. Toronto Hosp., 1986-89; chmn. cardiovascular rsch. adv. com. faculty medicine U. Toronto, 1986-87, mem. various coms., 1987—, chmn. rsch. com. dept. medicine, 1987-88, mem. rsch. adv. bd., 1989-97, chair life scis. com., 1990-92, chair decanal promotions com. faculty medicine, 1992-94; mem. exec. com. Centre Cardiovascular Rsch., 1988—, chmn. sci. com., 1989-99, mem. exec. com. cardiovascular clin. rsch. lab., 1992-99, chmn. rsch. com., 1992-99; Pfizer vis. fellow Clin. Rsch. Inst., Montreal, 1988; mem. sr. adv. com. Toronto Western Hosp., 1989-90; Katz vis. prof. U. Chgo., 1989; mem. provincial working group cardiovascular svcs. Ministry of Health, 1990-91, mem. ctrl. east region cardiovascular patient care mgmt. group, 1990-91; mem. trial devel. com. diabetes atherosclerosis intervention study WHO and Fournier Pharms., 1991-93, mem. trial exec. com., 1993-2000; mem. Joint Med. Rsch. Coun. Can./Pharm. Mfrs. Assn. Can. Adv. Com. Sci., 1993; mem. organizing coms. various sci. meetings; presenter in field. Mem. editl. bd. Can. Jour. Cardiology, 1988—, Index and Revs. Congestive Heart Failure, 1988-90, Hypertension Can., 1988-90, European Jour. Pharmacology, 1992-96, Cardiosci., 1993, Jour. Heart Failure, 1994—, Circulation, 1996—, Jour. Molecular Medicine, 1996—, Jour. Molecular Cell Cardiology, 1999-2001; mem. internat. editl. bd. Cardiology Digest, 1992—; contbr. chpts. to books and articles to profl. jours.; patentee in field. Recipient Robert Beamish Leadership award, Inst. CV Sci., U. Man., 2001; fellow Ivan Smith Rsch. fellow, U. Toronto, 1964, Hunter fellow, Ont. Heart Found., 1973; grantee Grantee, Heart & Stroke Found. Ont., 1969—, Med. Rsch. Coun. Can., 1982—92, 1994—97; scholar Walter Watkins scholar, U. Toronto, 1962. Fellow Am. Coll. Cardiology (abstract reviewer 1989, 91), Royal Coll. Physicians and Surgeons; mem. Am. Soc. Clin. Investigation, Assn. Am. Physicians, Am. Heart Assn. (fellow couns. clin. cardiology, hypertension, circulation and basic sci., mem. exec., basic sci. coun. 1986-89, mem. Katz prize selection com. 1988-90), Can. Soc. Clin. Investigation, Can. Cardiovascular Soc. (mem. young investigators award panel 1982-84, mem. student presentation award com. 1988-90, mem. nat. task force cardiovascular sci. 1992-93, Ann. Rsch. award 1975, Rsch. Achievement award 1989), Heart and Stroke Found. Can. (mem. sci. rev. bd. 1976-79, vice-chmn. 1980-83, chmn. hypertension and cardiovascular pharmacology panel 1982-83, chmn. molecular biology, biochemistry, pathology panel 1989-90), Can. Med. Assn. (mem. coun. 1982-87), Am. Fedn. Clin. Rsch., Ont. Med. Assn. (alt. del. Toronto Gen. Hosp. bd. 1988-90), Heart and Stroke Found. Ont. (mem. med. rsch. com. 1978-81, bd. dirs. 1986-92, 96—, mem. fin. com. 1986-90, 96-97, mem. corp. rels. com. 1990-92, mem. rsch. policy com. 1991-93, 96-97, chmn. 1997-99, mem. exec. com. 1997-99, nomination com. 1997-99, chmn. 50th anniversary com., mem. audit com., Disting. Rsch. prof. 1989-96, Murray Robertson Meml. lectr. 1989), Internat. Soc. Heart Rsch. (exec. Am. sect. 1979-88, lectr. Latin Am. sect. 1995), Banting Rsch. Found. (hon. sec.-treas. 1979-81), Gairdner Found. (mem. rev. panel 1979-94), Heart Failure Soc. Am. (publs. com. 2000—, nominating com. 2001—), Alpha Omega Alpha. Office: Toronto Gen Hosp Eaton N 13-212 200 Elizabeth St Toronto ON Canada M5G 2C4 E-mail: michael.sole@uhn.on.ca.

SOLÉ, PEDRO, management consultant; b. Guatemala, Guatemala, Sept. 4, 1936; came to U.S., 1974; s. Pedro Solé and Luisa Raquel (Castellanos) de Solé; m. Dorothy Tuteur, Mar. 19, 1961; children: Tania Dolores, Jeanne Marguerite, Pedro Ernesto. Degree chem. engring., San Carlos U., Guatemala, 1958; MChE, Polytech U., N.Y., 1960, PhD in Chem. Engring., 1965. Mgr. Ctrl. Am. Rsch. Inst. Industry, 1963-68; ops. mgr. Alimentos Kern de Guatemala, 1968-72; gen. dir. Riviana España S.A., Seville, Spain, 1972-74; plant mgr. Casera Foods Inc., San Juan, P.R., 1974-78; gen. mgr. processed bananas Tela RR Co., La Lima, Honduras, 1979-82; v.p. bus. devel. Numar Processed Foods Group, San José, Costa Rica, 1982-86; dir. tech. svcs. Chiquita Brands Inc., N.Y.C., 1986-89; v.p. quality assurance/control Chiquita Brands Internat., Inc., Cin., 1989-94, mgmt. cons., 1994-98; v.p. quality assurance and R&D Colo. Greenhouse, LLP, Ft. Lupton, Colo., 1998-2000; mgmt. cons., 2000—. Co-author: Bananas, Processing Fruits, 1996; contbr. articles to profl. jours. Exch. scholar U.S. Dept. State, 1959-60, Food Tech. scholar, Karlsruhe (Germany) U., 1966-67. Mem. AIChE (profl.), Inst. Food Tech. (profl.), Am. Assn. Profl. Consultants. Roman Catholic. Achievements include patents for individual coffee extractor; for recovery of vegetable oil; for banana processing; for banana peel processing; several fgn. patents. Home and Office: 23839 Francone Ct Hayward CA 94541 E-mail: psole1@aol.com.

SOLECKI, R. STEFAN, anthropologist, educator; b. Bklyn., Oct. 15, 1917; s. Kazimierz John and Mary (Tarnawski) S.; m. Rose Muriel Lilien, June 24, 1955; children— John Irwin, William Duncan. B.Sc., City Coll. N.Y., 1941; MA, Columbia, 1950, PhD in Anthropology, 1958. Archaeologist Smithsonian Instn., 1948-54; archaeol. asst. anthropology Columbia U., N.Y.C., 1954-55, mem. faculty, 1959-88, prof. anthropology, 1965-88, prof. emeritus, 1989—, chmn. dept., 1975-78; adj. prof. dept. anthropology Tex. A&M Univ., College Station, 1989—; assoc. curator old world U.S. Nat. Mus., 1957-59. Archael. expdns. to Alaska, 1949, 61, Iraq, 1950-51, 53, 56-57 (field dir.), 60, 78, Sudanese Nubia, 1961, Turkey, 1963, Syria, 1963, 64, 65, 88, 89, Iran, 1968, Lebanon, 1969-73, France, 1975, Ea., Midwestern and Western U.S.; collaborator in archaeology Smithsonian Instn., 1953; cons. UNESCO, 1959. Served with AUS, 1943-45. Fulbright scholar, Iraq, 1952-53; William Bayard Cutting travelling fellow Columbia, 1956-57; Fulbright-Hays faculty research awardee Syria, 1980-81; Fulbright fellow, Iraq, 1988-89. Fellow Am. Anthrop. Assn., Arctic Inst. Am., N.Y. Acad. Scis. (chmn. anthropology sect. 1977-79); mem. N.Y. Archaeol. Assn. (pres. 1960-62), N.Y. Oriental Club (pres. 1965), Profl. Archeologists of N.Y.C. (pres. 1980-81), Soc. Archaeology, Am. Schs. Oriental Research (assoc. trustee 1969-71), Prehistoric Soc., Deutsches Archaeologisches Inst., Soc. Préhistorique Français, Archaeol. Inst. Am. (exec. com. 1968-70), Assn. Field Archaeology (pres. 1972-74). Home: 86 Park Pl South Orange NJ 07079-2303 Office: Columbia U Dept Anthropology New York NY 10027

SOLEIMANI, MASSOUD, internist, rheumatologist; b. Rasht, Iran, Jan. 5, 1955; MD, U. del Salvador, Buenos Aires, 1991. Diplomate Am. Bd. Internal Medicine and Rheumatology. Intern Meml. Med. Ctr., Savannah, Ga., 1992-93; resident Providence Hosp., Southfield, Mich., 1993-95; fellow Wayne State U.-Hutzel Hosp., Detroit, 1995-98; with Health Care Ptnrs., Pasadena, Calif. Office: Healthcare Ptnrs Med Group 55 E California Blvd Pasadena CA 91105-3954

SOLENBERGER, ROBERT I, surgeon, educator; b. Oakland, Calif., 1943; MD, U. Md., 1974. Diplomate Am. Bd. Surgery. Intern Med. Coll. Ga., Augusta, 1974-75, resident in gen. surgery, 1975-79; resident in pediat. surgery Johns Hopkins Hosp., Balt., 1979-80; fellow in pediat. surgery med. br. U. Tex., Galveston, 1980-81; commd. maj. U.S. Army, 1984; mem. staff Brooke Army Med. Ctr., San Antonio; mem. staff Wilford Hall Airforce Med. Ctr.; chief dept. surgery Darnell Hosp., Ft. Hood; advanced through grades to col. U.S. Army, 1994; "a" designator, 1997. Assoc. prof. surgery med. br. U. Tex., San Antonio. Fellow ACS, Am. Acad. Pediat., Childrens Oncology Group, Tex. Pediatric Surgical Soc. (sec., treas.), Soc. Am. Gastrointestinal Endoscopic Surgeons, Am. Acad. Pediatrics. Office: Darnall Meddac Gen Surgery Box 53 157 Fort Hood TX 76544-4752

SOLENDER, ROBERT LAWRENCE, real estate executive, retired newspaper executive; b. Rochester, N.Y., Sept. 1, 1923; s. Samuel S. and Catherine (Goldsmith) S.; m. Ellen Van Raalte Karelsen, Nov. 25, 1948; children: Elizabeth, Jefferson, Katherine. BA, Oberlin Coll., 1943. Asst. to pres. Craven & Hedrick, Inc., N.Y.C., 1946-49; with Dallas Times Herald, 1949-75, v.p., advt. dir., 1964-69, v.p., gen. mgr., 1969—71, v.p. sales, 1971—75; prin. Robert L. Solender & Assocs., Dallas, 1975—; mng. ptnr. The Devonshire Co., 1978-95. Interim chmn., CEO, AccuBanc Mortgage Corp., 1992. Pres. Dallas Child Guidance Clinic, 1956, Dallas Assn. Mental Health, 1958, Hope Cottage Children's Bur., 1973— ; bd. dirs. Dallas Theatre Center, Child Care Assn. Met. Dallas, Friends of the Dallas Pub. Libr.; trustee Southwestern Med. Found.; mem. adv. council Communities Found. of Tex.; assoc. Dallas Mus. Art; bd. dirs., mem. exec. com. Dallas County United Way, 1973. Served to lt. USNR, 1944-46, PTO. Mem.: Masons. Home: 9131 Devonshire Dr Dallas TX 75209-2411

SOLENDER, SANFORD, social worker, consultant; b. Pleasantville, N.Y., Aug. 23, 1914; s. Samuel Solender and Catharine (Goldsmith); m. Ethel Klonick, June 19, 1935; children: Stephen, Peter, Ellen Susan(dec.). BS, NYU, 1935; MS, Columbia U., 1937. Dir. activities Neighborhood House, Bklyn., 1935-36; asst. headworker Bronx House, N.Y., 1936-39; headworker Madison House, N.Y.C., 1939-42; exec. dir. Coun. Ednl. Alliance, Cleve., 1942-48; dir. bur. pers. and tng., also dir. Jewish community ctr. div. Nat. Jewish Welfare Bd., N.Y.C., 1948-60, exec. v.p. bd., 1960-70; exec. v.p. Fedn. Jewish Philanthropies N.Y., 1970-81, exec. cons., 1982-86. Exec. v.p. United Jewish Appeal Fedn. Campaign, 1975-81; past pres. Nat. Conf. Jewish Communal Svc.; past chmn. planning com. Internat. Conf. Jewish Communal Svc.; chmn. Task Force on N.Y.C. Crisis, 1976-81. Contbr. articles to profl. jours., chpts. in books. Chmn. sec. ad hoc. com. to study fed. govt. social welfare programs HEW, 1962, adv. coun. pub. welfare, 1963—65; active Mid East Watch-Human Rights Watch, Jewish Mus., 1982—, bd. dirs.; mem. Gov. Hugh Carey's Task Force on Human Svcs., NY, 1975; bd. dirs. Nat. Jewish Ctr. for Learning and Leadership, 1984—; adv. bd. Brandeis U., Hornstein Program in Jewish Communal Svc.; bd. dirs. Americans for Peace Now, 1995—, Nat. Found. for Jewish Culture, 1985—; mem. Mt. Vernon Bd. Edn., 1953—58, pres., 1957—58; bd. dirs. Herman Muehlstein Found. Named Most Disting. Citizen of Mt. Vernon, 1960; recipient Joseph E. Kappel award Nat. Conf. Jewish Communal Svc., 1968, Florence G. Heller award Nat. Jewish Welfare Bd., 1972. Mem. Nat. Assn. Jewish Ctr. Workers (past pres.), Nat. Conf. Social Welfare (past pres.). Home: 1957 N Honore Ave Apt C414 Sarasota FL 34235-9188 E-mail: ssolender@aol.com.

SOLER, OSCAR LUIS, electrical engineer; b. San Juan, P.R., Dec. 31, 1940; BSEE, U. P.R., Mayaguez, 1963. Profl. engr., P.R. Dep. comptr. armament divsn. USAF, Eglin AFB, Fla., 1977-89, dep. dir. Aero. Sys. Ctr., 1988-93, program dir. Aero. Sys. Ctr., 1993-95, program dir. Air Armament Ctr., 1995-2000, chief assessment & demonstration divsns., 2000—. 1st lt. U.S. Army, 1963-65. Office: Air Force Rsch Lab Bldg 13 101 W Eglin Blvd Eglin AFB FL 32542-6810

SOLES, ADA LEIGH, former state legislator, government advisor; b. Jacksonville, Fla., May 19, 1937; d. Albert Thomas and Dorothy (Winter) Wall; m. James Ralph Soles, 1959; children: Nancy Beth, Catherine. BA, Fla. State U., 1959. Mem. New Castle County Libr. Adv. Bd., 1975-80, 95—, chmn., 1975-77; chmn. Del. State Libr. Adv. Bd., 1975-78; mem. Del. State Ho. Reps., 1980-92; sr. advisor Gov. of Del., 1993-94; mem. U. Del. Libr. Assocs. Bd., 1995—; adminstrv. asst. U. Del. Commn. on Status of Women, 1976-77; acad. advisor U. Del. Coll. Arts and Scis., 1977-92. Mem. LWV (state pres. 1978-80), Phi Beta Kappa, Phi Kappa Phi, Mortar Bd., Alpha Chi Omega. Episcopalian.

SOLES, WILLIAM ROGER, insurance company executive, director; b. Whiteville, N.C., Sept. 16, 1920; s. John William and Margaret (Watts) S.; m. Majelle Marrene Morris, Sept. 22, 1956 (dec. 1993); children: William Roger, Majelle Janette. BS in Commerce, U. N.C., 1947, postgrad., 1956; LLD, Campbell U., 1981; DHL, High Point U., 1996. With Jefferson Standard Life Ins. Co., Greensboro, N.C., 1947—, v.p., mgr. securities dept., 1962-64, asst. to pres., 1964-66, exec. v.p., mgr. securities dept., 1966, pres., also dir., 1967-86; chmn., pres., chief exec. officer Jefferson-Pilot Life Ins. Co.; retired, 1993; chmn., pres. Jefferson-Pilot Corp., retired, 1993. Trustee, past chmn. High Point U.; past chmn. Wesley Long Community Hosp.; trustee, past chmn. Ind. Coll. Fund N.C.; past pres. Bus. Found. of N.C.; bd. dirs., past chmn. N.C. Ins. Edn. Found. Served with USAAF, 1941-45. Mem. N.C. Citizens for Bus. and Industry (past chmn.), Am. Council Life Ins. (past chmn., dir.), Beta Gamma Sigma. Clubs: Greensboro Country. Home: 604 Kimberly Dr Greensboro NC 27408-4914 Office: Jefferson-Pilot Corp PO Box 21008 Greensboro NC 27420-1008

SOLET, MAXWELL DAVID, lawyer; b. Washington, May 15, 1948; s. Leo and Pearl (Rose) S.; m. Joanne Marie Tolksdorf, Sept. 27, 1970; children: David Marc, Paul Jacob. AB, Harvard U., 1970, JD, 1974. Bar: Mass. 1974, U.S. Tax Ct. 1976, U.S. Ct. Claims 1976, U.S. Supreme Ct. 1976. Assoc. Gaston Snow & Ely Bartlett, Boston, 1974-79, Mintz, Levin, Cohn, Ferris, Glovsky & Popeo, P.C., Boston, 1979-82, ptnr., 1982—. Mem. ABA, Mass. Bar Assn., Boston Bar Assn. (chmn. tax sect. 1987-89), Nat. Assn. Bond Lawyers (mem. steering com. bond atty.'s workshop 1992-95). Home: 15 Berkeley St Cambridge MA 02138-3409 Office: Mintz Levin Cohn Ferris Glovsky & Popeo PC One Financial Ctr Boston MA 02111 E-mail: msolet@mintz.com.

SOLEY, ROBERT LAWRENCE, plastic surgeon; b. N.Y.C., Feb. 26, 1935; s. Max and Saide (Leader) S.; m. Judy Wasserman, June 16, 1963; children: John, Jill. BS, Yale U., 1956; MD, NYU, 1959. Diplomate Am. Bd. Surgery, Am. Bd. PLastic Surgery. Intern Bellevue Hosp., N.Y.C., 1959-60; resident in gen. surgery Mt. Sinai Hosp., 1960-65; resident in plastic surgery Hosp. U. Pa., Phila., 1967-69; practice medicine specializing in plastic surgery White Plains, N.Y., 1969—. Mem. staff, mem. med. bd. White Plains Hosp., 1985—88, chief sect. plastic surgery, 1988—94; mem. staff Westchester County Med. Ctr., St. Agnes Hosp. Contbr. articles to profl. jours. Capt. M.C., USAF, 1965-67. Grantee USPHS, 1968-69. Fellow ACS; mem. Am. Soc. Plastic Reconstructive Surgery, Am. Soc. Aesthetic Surgery, N.Y. State Med. Soc. (mem. ho. of dels.), Westchester County Med. Soc. (pres. 1996-97, bd. dirs. 1988—), Rotary (bd. dirs. White Plains chpt. 1982-85). Home: 30 Griffin Ave Scarsdale NY 10583-7661 Office: 170 Maple Ave White Plains NY 10601-4710 E-mail: bob@soley.com.

SOLGANIK, MARVIN, real estate executive; b. Chgo., Nov. 7, 1930; s. Harry and Dora (Fastoff) S.; m. Judith Rosenberg, Sept. 11, 1960; children: Randall, Janet, Robert. BBA, Case Western Res. U., 1952. Real estate broker, Cleve., 1950-65, Herbert Laronge Inc., 1965-68; sr. v.p. real estate Revco D.S., Inc., Twinsburgh, Ohio, 1968—, corp. dir., 1974—; guest lectr. Cleve. State U., Case Western Res. U., Cuyahoga Community Coll., Ohio No. U., Cleve. Real Estate Bd. Adj. prof., Ohio No. U. Vol. jewish Welfare Fund, Shaker heights, Ohio; chmn. capital and budget coms. Jewish Fedn.; chmn. Agnon Sch. Bdlg. Com.; bd. dirs. Bellfair-J.C.B.-Home for Emotionally Disturbed Children, Visconsi Cos. Recipient Appreciation award Am. Soc. Real Estate Appraisers, Akron-Cleve. chpt., 1971 Mem. Nat. Assn. Corp. Real Estate Officers, Internat. Council Shopping Ctrs. Office: D S Revco 22925 Holmwood Rd Shaker Heights OH 44122-3005

SOLIC, JOHN JOSEPH, physician; b. Johnstown, Pa., July 24, 1950; s. John and Margaret Ann (Majer) S.; m. Cynthia Louise Jones, Dec. 20, 1975; children: John, Katie, Tim, Peggy. AB, Princeton U., 1972; MD, U. Pitts., 1976. Diplomate Am. Bd. Internal Medicine, Am. Bd. Pulmonary Medicine, Am. Bd. Critical Care Medicine; cert. NIOSHB reader. From intern to resident internal medicine N.C. Meml. Hosp., Chapel Hill, 1976-79; fellow in pulmonary medicine U. N.C., 1979-81; ptnr., physician Ctr. Med. and Surg. Assocs., State College, Pa., 1981—. Fellow ACP, Am. Coll. Chest Physicians. Home: 552 Melissa Ln State College PA 16803-1221 Office: Ctr Med and Surg Assocs 1850 E Park Ave State College PA 16803-6706 E-mail: jjs25@psu.edu.

SOLIDUM, JAMES, finance and insurance executive; b. Honolulu, Mar. 12, 1925; s. Narciso and Sergia (Yabo) S.; m Vickie Mayo, Aug. 14, 1954; children: Arlin James, Nathan Francis, Tobi John, Kamomi Teresa. Student, U. Hawaii, 1949-50; BA, U. Oreg., 1953. C.L.U. Promotional salesman Tongg Pub. Co., 1953-54; editor Fil-Am. Tribune, 1954-55; master planning technician Fed. Civil Svc., 1955-57; publs. editor Hawaii Sugar Planters Assn., 1957; field agt. Grand Pacific Life Ins. Co., 1957-59, home office asst., 1959-60, supr., 1960-62, asst. v.p., 1962-64; propr. J. Solidum & Assos. Honolulu, 1964—; pres. Fin. Devel. Inst., 1967—. Contbg. writer Paradise of Pacific Mag., 1957-58, Hawaii Agrl. Mag., 1957-58; gen. ptrn. R.Z. Limited Partnership, 1981—; v.p. Grand Pacific Life Ins. Co., 1983-90; bd. dirs. Hawaii Econ. Devel. Corp., 1982-89; mem. adv. com. Honolulu dist. SBA, 1971-77; bd. advisors Phillipine Consulate of Hawaii, 1959. Pres. Keolu Elem. PTA, 1960-62; mem. satisfaction com. Hawaii Visitors Bur., 1963-66; chmn. budget and rev. panel IV, Aloha United Way, 1966-72, bd. dirs., 1971-77,

82-88, chmn. bd., 1984; mem. mgmt. svcs. com., 1977, mem. cen. com., 1977-82, chmn. budget and allocations com., 1982-84; chmn. Kamehameha Dist. fin. com. Aloha coun. Boy Scouts Am., 1966; vice chmn. Businessmen's Cancer Crusade, 1965; chmn. Operation Bayanihan, Hawaii Immigration Task Force, 1970; participant Oahu Housing Workshop, State of Hawaii, Hawaii chpt. HUD, 1970; mem. task force on housing and transp. Alternative Econ. Futures for Hawaii, 1973; chmn. Bicentennial Filipiniana, 1976; campaign chmn. State Rep. Rudolph Pacarro, 1964-68; mem. exec. com. Campaign for Reelection U.S. Senator Hiram L. Fong, 1970, Gov. William Quinn for U.S. Senate, 1976; Rep. candidate for Hawaii Ho. of Reps., 1972; mem. Rep. Citizens Task Force on Housing, 1973; trustee St. Louis Alumni Found., 1970—, Kuakini Med. Ctr., 1984-86, Palama Settlement, 1975-82, v.p., 1976, treas., 1980-82; bd. mgrs. Windward YMCA, 1964-67; bd. advisers St. Louis H.S., 1963-64; bd. govs. Goodwill Industries, 1964; bd. dirs. Children's Ctr., Inc., 1975-77, Hawaii Multi-Cultural Arts Ctr., 1977-81, treas., 1979; fin. chmn. St. Stephen's Parish Coun., 1974—; bd. dirs. St. Louis Fine Arts Ctr., 1985-88. With U.S. Army, 1945-47. Recipient Man of Yr. award Filipino C. of C., 1965, cert. of merit Aloha United Way, 1971, Wisdom mag. honor award, 1974, Outstanding Alumnus honor medal St. Louis High Sch., 1976. Mem. Hawaii State C. of C. (bd. dirs. 1964-67, chmn. legis. com. 1966-67, v.p. 1970, chmn. election judges 1971, mem. ad hoc com. bus.-youth rels. 1970_, Filipino C. of C. (past pres. 1965, com. chmn.), Am. Soc. CLU, Honolulu Assn. Life Underwriters (bd. dirs. 1963-66, del. nat. conv. 1967, chmn. life underwriters tng. coun. 1962-67), Hawaii Estate Planning Coun., Hawaii Plantation Indsl. Editors Assn. (sec.-treas. 1957), St. Louis Alumni Assn. (bd. dirs. 1964—, chmn. fin. 1969-75, pres. 1976, treas. 1977—), Phi Kappa Sigma. Republican. Roman Catholic. Home: 2622 Waolani Ave Honolulu HI 96817-1362 Office: 225 Queen St Apt 12-a Honolulu HI 96813-4603

SOLIMAN, KARAM FARAH ATTIA, pharmacy educator; b. Cairo, Oct. 15, 1944; came to the U.S., 1968; s. Farah Attia and Elaine (Kellini) S.; m. Samia Gorgy Sidhom, Aug. 2, 1973; children: John, Gina, Mark, Mary. BS, Cairo U., 1964; MS, U. Ga., 1971, PhD, 1972. Asst. prof. Sch. Vet. Medicine Tuskegee (Ala.) U., 1972-75; assoc. prof. Fla. A&M U.-Coll. Pharmacy, Tallahassee, 1975-79, prof., 1979—, chmn. divsn. basic pharm. sci., 1981—, asst. dean, 1993—, disting. prof., 1997—. Author: (with others) Practical Clinical Pharmacy, 1977, Chronopharmacology and Chronotherapeutics, 1981; contbr. articles to profl. jours. Rsch. grantee NIH. Mem. Am. Assn. Coll. Pharmacy, Am. Soc. Pharmacology and Exptl. Therapeutics, Am. Physiol. Soc., Neurosci. Soc., Endocrine Soc. Democrat. Avocations: reading, gardening. Home: 5358 Pembridge Pl Tallahassee FL 32309-6800 Office: Coll Pharmacy Fla A&M Univ Tallahassee FL 32307 Fax: 850-599-3667. E-mail: ksoliman@famu.edu.

SOLIMANDO, DOMINIC ANTHONY, JR. pharmacist, educator; b. Bklyn., Apr. 4, 1950; s. Dominic Anthony and Grace Evelyn (Phillips) S. BS, Phila. Coll. Parm. and Sci., 1976; MA, Cen. Mich. U., 1980; postgrad., Purdue U., 1986-89. Bd. cert. oncology pharmacist. Pharmacist Walter Reed Army Med. Ctr. Pharmacy Svc., Washington, 1977; chief pharmacy svc. Andrew Rader USA Health Clinic, Ft. Myer, Va., 1977-79; oncology pharmacist Walter Reed Med. Ctr., Washington, 1979-82; clin. preceptor Sch. Pharmacy, Med. Coll. Va., 1980; chief hem./oncology pharmacy Tripler Army Med. Ctr., Honolulu, 1983-86, Letterman Army Med. Ctr., San Francisco, 1989-90, 91-92; chief pharmacy svc. 28th Combat Support Hosp., Operation Desert Shield/Desert Storm, Saudi Arabia, 1990-91; chief hematology/oncology pharmacy sect. Walter Reed Army Med. Ctr., Washington, 1992-96, dir. hematology-oncology pharmacy residency program, 1992-96; oncology pharmacist Thomas Jefferson U. Hosp., Phila., 1996-98; oncology pharmacy mgr. Lombardi Cancer Ctr./Georgetown U. Med. Ctr., Washington, 1998-99; dir. oncology drug info. CancerEducation.com, 1999-2000; oncology cons., med. writer, 2000—; pres. Oncology Pharmacy Svcs., Inc., 2000—. Adj. prof. Coll. Pharmacy, U. Pacific, Stockton, Calif., 1983-86, 89-91; mem. editorial panel Drug Intelligence and Clin. Pharmacy, Cin., 1984-88; clin. asst. prof. Coll. Pharmacy, U. Md., 1992-96, Coll. Pharmacy, U. Ark., 1995; clin. preceptor Coll. Pharmacy, Howard U., 1992-96; clin. faculty Phila. Coll. Pharmacy and Sci., 1996-98, clin. assoc. prof., 1998-2000; clin. faculty Temple U. Coll. Pharmacy, 1998. Ret. lt. col. U.S. Army, 1996. Recipient Upjohn rsch. grant Am. Coll. Clin. Pharmacy, 1988, Bristol award Phila. Coll. Pharmacy and Sci., 1976, WMSHP-Bayer Recognition award Washington Met. Area Soc. Health Sys. Pharmacists, 2000, Disting. Achievement award in hospl. and instnl. practice Am. Pharm. Assn. Acad. Pharmacy, Practice and Mgmt., 2001. Fellow: Am. Soc. Hosp. Pharmacists, Am. Pharm. Assn. (various coms.); mem.: Am. Med. Writers Assn., Fedn. Internat. de Pharm. (hosp.), Va. Pharmacists Assn. (various coms.), Washington Metro.Area Soc. Health-Sys. Pharmacists, Am. Inst. Hist. Pharmacy, Acad. Pharmacy Practice and Mgmt. (mem.-at-large 1989—90, chair clin./pharm. therapeutic practice sect. 1991—92, chair hosp. and instnl. practice sect. 1998—99, chair-elet adminstrv. practice sect. 2002—, Disting. Achievement award in Hosp. & Instnl. Practice 2001), Am. Coll. Clin. Pharmacy (various coms.), Internat. Soc. Oncology Pharmacy Practioners, Assn. US Army, Kappa Psi, Rho Chi. Avocations: bicycling, chess, history, cooking, travel. Home: 5204 22d St N Arlington VA 22205-3137 Office: # 110-545 4201 Wilson Blvd Arlington VA 22203 E-mail: OncRxSvc@aol.com.

SOLINGER, JANET W. museum executive; b. Cin., Dec. 20, 1921; d. Fred and Dorothy G. (Gross) Weiland; widowed; children: Dorothy, Regina, Martha. BA, U. Cin., 1943; MA, NYU, 1973; DFA (hon.), Corcoran Coll. of Art, 1998. Asst. to pres. Hebrew Union Coll., Cin., 1957-60; adminstr. Jewish Mus., N.Y.C., 1961-65; exec. dir. Finch Coll., 1965-66; dir. pub. info. and spl. events NYU, 1966-72; dir. Smithsonian resident assoc. program Smithsonian Instn., Washington, 1972-93; v.p. Corcoran Gall. of Art, 1994—. Lectr. in field. Author: Museums and Universities: New Paths for Continuing Education, 1990, Marketing the Arts, 1992; contbr. articles to profl. jours. Recipient decorations, Belgium, 1980, The Netherlands, 1981, Germany, 1982, Gold medal Smithsonian Instn., 1990; named Washingtonian of Yr., Washingtonian Mag., 1984, Wash. Woman of the Millenium award Art Table, 2000. Mem. AIA (hon.), Washington Archtl. Found. (bd. dirs. 1996-2001), Art Table (bd. dirs. 1994-2000), Faberge Found. (bd. dirs. 1991—), Cosmos Club, Kenwood Golf and Country Club. Democrat. Jewish. Avocations: golf, bridge, reading, travel. Home: 2801 New Mexico Ave NW Washington DC 20007-3921 Office: Corcoran Gall of Art 500 17th St NW Washington DC 20006-4804 E-mail: jsolinger@corcoran.org.

SOLIS, GILBERTO, JR. county official; b. El Rancho, N.Mex., Sept. 19, 1940; s. Gilberto and Matilda Solis; m. Gloria C. Garcia, Jan. 17, 1975; 1 child, Dennis Ofene. BA, St. Michaels Coll., 1962; MA, U. N.Mex., 1971, U. Autonoma, Guadalajara, Mexico, 1975. Cert. adminstrn./sch., Calif. Tchr. Santa Fe Pub. Schs., 1966-73; supr. U. Autonoma, Guadalajara, 1973-76; resource tchr. Hollister (Calif.) Sch. Dist., 1976-91; program adminstr. Santa Clara County Office Edn., San Jose, Calif., 1991-97, Monterey County Office Edn., Salinas, 1997—. Mem. ARC, Hollister, 1985-2000; clk. of session 1st Presbyn. Ch., Hollister, 1985-2000; bd. dirs. Emmaus House, Hollister, 1996. Recipient award U.S. Dept. Edn., U. of Pacific, 1978. Mem. Adminstr. Sch. Curriculum Devel., Exec. Excellence, Am. Legion. Democrat. Presbyterian. Avocations: watercolors, woodwork, toy collections, story telling. Office: 901 Blanco Cir Salinas CA 93901-4401 E-mail: gsolisjr@monterey.k12.ca.us.

SOLIS, HILDA LUCIA, congresswoman, educational administrator; b. Los Angeles, Oct. 20, 1957; d. Raul and Juana (Sequiera) S.; m. Sam H. Sayyad, June 26, 1982. BA in Polit. Sci., Calif. State Poly U., 1979; MA in Pub. Adminstrn., U. So. Calif., 1981. Interpreter Immigration and Naturalization Service, Los Angeles, 1977-79; editor in chief Office Hispanic Affairs, The White House, Washington, 1980-81; mgmt. analyst Office Mgmt. and Budget, 1981-82; field rep. Office Assemblyman Art Torres, L.A., 1982; dir. Calif. Student Opportunity and Access, Whittier, 1982—; rep. 57th assembly dist. Calif. State Assembly, Sacramento, 1992-94; mem. Calif. Senate from 24th dist., 1994-2000, U.S. Congress from Calif. 31st dist., Washington, 2001—; mem. edn. and workforce com., resources com. Cons. South Coast Consortium, L.A., 1986—; mem. South Coast Ednl. Opportunity Pers. Consortium. Bd. dirs. Calif. Commn. on Status of Women, 1993—; corr. pres. Friendly El Monte (Calif.) Dem. Club, 1986—; mem. credentials com. Calif. Dem. Com., 1987-88; trustee Rio Hondo C.C., 1985-92. Recipient Meritorious Svc. award Dept. Def., 1981, Young Careerist award El Monte Bus. and Profl. Women, 1987; fellow Nat. Edn. Inst., Kellogg Found., 1984-85. Mem. Western Assn. Ednl. Opportunity Pers. (sec. bd. dirs. 1986—), Comision Feminil de Los Angeles (bd. dirs. 1983-84, edn. chmn.), Women of Moose. Roman Catholic. Home: 5250 La Madera Ave El Monte CA 91732-1236 Office: 1641 Longworth House Office Bldg Washington DC 20515 Office Fax: 202-225-5467.*

SOLIS-KLEIN, RUTH ELIZABETH, foreign language educator; b. Oberlin, Ohio, July 28, 1935; d. Bertram James and Ruth Langworthy (Brown) Smyth; m. Guillermo Abel Solis-Bonilla, Sept. 14, 1963; children: Roselia Ruth, Bertram Oliver; m. Charles B. Klein, Jr., Nov. 20, 1993. BA, Coll. of Wooster, 1957; MA, U. Kans., 1960; PhD, U. Akron, 1990. Cert. secondary tchr., Kans. Teaching asst. U. Kans., Lawrence, 1957-60; instr. Hiram (Ohio) Coll., 1960-62; asst. instr. Case Western Res. U., Cleve., 1962-64; from. instr. to prof. fgn. langs. Cuyahoga C.C., 1964-93; ret., 1993. Lectrice Ecole de Commerce, Clermont-ferrand, France, 1958-59; dir. courses Inst.-Guatemalteco, Guatemala City, Guatemala, 1979-80. Author: Curriculum Development, 1990; executed sculpture (1st Place award 1961); editor: (newspaper insert) Canterbury Tales. Deaconess 1st Christian Ch., Hudson, Ohio, 1988—93; bd. dirs. Canterbury Lake Estates, Hernando, Fla., 1998, sec., 1999—2001; bd. dirs. Hernando Heritage Coun., 2000—, sec., 2001. Recipient Innovator of Yr. award, 1991; Cuyahoga Community Coll. grantee, 1968, 88. Mem.: AARP, AAUP (pres. 1965—66), Ohio Fgn. Lang. Assn., Nat. Inst. Staff and Orgnl. Devel., Order Eastern Star, Phi Delta Kappa, Pi Lambda Theta, Phi Sigma Iota (pres. 1956—57). Republican. Avocations: jogging, biking, collecting plates, world travel, writing.

SOLIVAN, BERT, television executive; b. N.Y.C., Aug. 13, 1967; BA in Govt./Law, Lafayette Coll., 1989; MA in Polit. Mgmt., George Washington U., 1991. Reference libr. Cadwalader, Wickersham & Taft, N.Y.C., 1989-91; dir. Rsch. Libr. Continental Ins., 1991-94; chmn. COO Joint Info., Inc., 1994-96; mgr. news info. Fox News Channel, 1996-97, dir. news info., 1997-2000, v.p. news info., gen. mgr. foxnews.com, 2000—. Pres.'s scholar Grad. Sch. Polit. Mgmt., 1990-91. Mem. Spl. Librs. Assn. Office: Fox News Channel 1211 Ave of the Americas New York NY 10036 Office Fax: 212-391-4847. E-mail: bert.solivan@foxnews.com.

SOLKOFF, JEROME IRA, lawyer, consultant, lecturer; b. Rochester, N.Y., Feb. 15, 1939; s. Samuel and Dorothy (Krovetz) S.; m. Doreen Hurwitz, Aug. 11, 1963; children: Scott Michael, Anne Lynn. BS Sch. Indsl. Rels. and Labor Rels., Cornell U., 1961; JD, U. Buffalo, 1964. Bar: N.Y. 1965, Fla. 1974, U.S. Dist. Ct. (we. dist.) N.Y. 1965; cert. specialist Elder Law, Elder Law Found., The Fla. Bar. Assoc. Nusbaum, Tarricone, Weltman, Bilgore & Silver, Rochester, N.Y., 1964-66, Mousaw, Vigdor, Reeves, Heilbronner & Kroll, Rochester, 1966-70; sr. mcpl. atty. Urban Renewal Agy., 1970-73; sole practice, 1970-73; chief legal counsel Arlen Realty Mgmt., Inc., Miami, Fla., 1973-75; assoc. Britton, Cohen, Kaufman, Benson & Schantz, 1975-76; chief legal counsel First Mortgage Investors, Miami Beach, Fla., 1976-79; ptnr. Cassel & Cassel, P.A., Miami, 1979-82; sole practice Deerfield Beach, Fla., 1982—. Lectr. on fgn. investment practices in U.S., Eng., 1981-88, Montreal, Que., Can., 1981, estate planning, 1982—, medicaid law and elder law, 1988—. Author: Fundamentals of Foreign Investing in American Real Estate and Businesses, 1981, Checklist of N.Y. Mortgage Foreclosure Procedures, 1970, History of Municipal Employee Unions, 1964, Practice Guide for Florida Elder Law, 1996, and yearly supplements. Bd. dirs. Broward Homebound Program, 1990—, pres. 1998—; bd. dirs. Jewish Cmty. Ctrs. of South Broward, Fla., 1979-90, NE Alzheimers Daycare Ctr., Inc., 1990-92; mem. exec. bd. dirs. Broward Alzheimers Assn., 1995—; co-chair Fla. Alzheimers Pub. Policy steering com., 1999—. Mem. ABA (mem. sects. real property, trust and probate law), Fla. Bar Assn. (sects. real property, trust and probate law, vice-chmn. com. on the elderly 1987-91, lectr. estate planning for the aging and disabled 1989—, founder, chmn. elder law sect. 1994-95, elder law sect., chmn. ethics com. 1998-2000), Nat. Acad. Elder Law Attys., Elder Law Attys.

SOLL, HERBERT D. attorney general of Northern Mariana Islands; b. 1936; BS, U. Denver, 1958, LLB, 1960. Dir. Peace Corps , Rio de Janeiro, 1967—70; chief pub. defender Alaska, 1971—75; trust territory pub. defender, 1975—79; dir. criminal prosecution Alaska, 1986—90; dir. Peace Corps, Sao Tome, 1990—93; judge Superior Ct., 1979—86; atty. gen. No. Mariana Islands, Saipan, 2000—. Office: Office Atty Gen PO Box 10007 Adminstrn Bldg Saipan MP 96950 E-mail: acsoll@gtepacifica.net.

SOLL, JOSEPH M. psychotherapist; b. New York, N.Y., Nov. 3, 1939; s. Charles R. and Florence Y. S. BS, John Hopkins, 1960; postgrad., Centure U.; MSW, Fordham, 1990. Cert. social worker. Dir. engring. Belmont Electric Co., N.Y.C., 1963-68; pres. Soll, Inc., 1968—, Cat Systems, Inc., N.Y.C., 1981—; dir. support services Alma Soc., 1983-86; dir. Adoption Crossroads. Cons. CBS-FM-TV, N.Y.C., 1968—, TV Network of Brazil, N.Y.C., 1976, Govt. of Guinea, Africa, Conakry, 1981, Office of Pres., Washington, 1986; regional cons. RCA, Camden, N.J., 1968-81; speaker Soc. Motion Picture and TV engrs., Los Angeles, 1983, 85; bd. dirs. Adoption Circle, N.Y.C., 1986—. Producer (play) Fixed, 1981; author: Adoption Healing: A Path to Recovery, 2000. Regional dir. Am. Adoption Congress, Washington, 1987—; pres. Amherst Tenants Assn., N.Y.C., 1987. Lifemaster Am. Contract Bridge League, 1974. Mem. Nat. Assn. Broadcasters (assoc.), IEEE, Soc. Broadcast Engrs., Nat. Assn. Social Workers, AFTRA. Democrat. Jewish. Home and Office: 74 Lakewood Dr Congers NY 10920 E-mail: cera@idt.net.

SOLLARS, CANDIS KAY, social worker, therapist; b. Albany, Oreg., Dec. 25, 1948; d. Max Ai and Loraine Frances Ann (Larios) Warren; m. Steven Lamar Sollars, July 2, 1971; children: Anthony Lamar, Rachelle Marie. BS, Linfield Coll., 1996; M in Social Work, Portland (Oreg.) State U., 1999. Dir. vols. ARC, Stuttgart, Germany, 1977-79; adminstrv. asst. various corps., 1968-82; bookkeeper, tax cons. CKSollars, San Antonio, 1983-88, Tacoma, 1983-88; area devel. dir. Ptnrs. Resource Network, Beaumont, Tex., 1989-92; founder, exec. dir., CEO Parents Outreach for Individual Needs Tng. Inc., Astoria, Oreg., 1992—; grief counselor, 1995—. Co-author: Case Management Record Guide, 1991; author: Hiding Behind the Trees: A Pictorial of One Womans Recovery from Childhood Trauma. Scholarship Oreg. Laurels Scholarship Commn., 1997; recipient Cert. of Appreciation Specialized Tng. of Mil. Parents, 1993, Recognition award Spl. Edn. Dirs. Assn., Cert. of Commendation Ptnrs. Resource Network, Inc., Beaumont, 1992, Disting. Svc. award Tourette Syndrome Assn. South Ctrl. Tex. chpt. 1992, Award of Appreciation Washington State Tourette Syndrome Assn., 1988, Cert. of Appreciation ARC, 1977, Letter of Appreciation 1976. Mem. AAUW, NASW, Oregon Gerontological Assn. Democrat. Avocations: reading, sewing, gardening, walking. E-mail: sollarsc@aone.com.

SOLLENDER, JOEL DAVID, management consultant, financial executive; b. N.Y.C., Nov. 11, 1924; s. Samuel and Flora (Blumenthal) S.; m. Dorothy Leaf, Aug. 6, 1958; children: Jeffrey D., Jonathan L. BS, N.Y. U., 1946. C.P.A., N.Y. Staff auditor Ernst & Young, N.Y.C., 1946-50; with United Mchts. & Mfrs., Inc., 1950-86, corp. contr., 1977—, sr. v.p., 1980—, chief acctg. officer, 1976—, also bd. dirs., officer various subs., mem. mgmt. com. parent co., 1986-88; assoc. dir. N.Y. Hist. Soc., N.Y.C.; mem. adv. coun. to Office of Charities Registration Dept. State, N.Y. State, 1988-89; v.p. fin. Piedmont Industries, N.Y.C., 1989-90; exec. v.p., CFO Earthworm Inc., 1990-95; fin. mgmt. cons.; sr. cons. Internat. Exec. Svc. Corps Agy. for Internat. Devel., Kazakstan, 1996—. Mem. adv. coun. San Diego State U., 1997—, audit com. San Diego Mus. Art, 1997—. Served with U.S. Army, World War II Decorated Combat Infantry Badge, Purple Heart with cluster, Prisoner of War medal, Bronze Star. Mem. AICPA, N.Y. State Soc. CPAs (chief fin. officer com.), Am. Inst. Corp. Contrs., Rancho Bernardo (Calif.) Men's Club, Bailiwick Club (Greenwich, Conn.), Greenhaven Yacht Club (Rye).

SOLLER, R. WILLIAM, association executive, pharmacologist; b. Bronxville, N.Y., Nov. 18, 1946; s. William Henry and Barbara Mildred (Bryde) S.; m. Phyllis Sharon Hess, Jan. 12, 1979 (div. Nov. 1986); children: Adam Kipling, Eric Charles, Kyle William; m. Janet Marie Flanagan, June 11, 1988; children: James Frederick, William Henderson. BS, Colby Coll., 1968; PhD, Cornell Grad. Sch. Med. Scis., 1975. Rsch. assoc. U. Pa. Sch. of Medicine, Phila., 1976-77, asst. prof. pharmacology, 1977-79; scientific assoc. Sterling Drug, Inc., N.Y.C., 1979-80, dir. scientific affairs, 1980-81, v.p. scientific affairs, 1982-85; v.p. product devel. Lederle Labs., Pearl River, N.Y., 1985; v.p., dir. scientific affairs Nonprescription Drug Mfrs. Assn., Washington, 1985-87, sr. v.p., dir. scientific affairs, 1987-90, sr. v.p., dir. of sci. and tech., 1990—. Cons. nonprescription drug and dietary supplement industry, Washington, 1985-92; expert in drug devel., drug safety, dietary supplements and regulatory affairs. Contbr. articles to profl. jours. Adult Leader Boy Scouts Am. Sr. scholar Colby Coll., Waterville, Maine, 1968; NATO fellow, Cornell U. Grad. Sch. Medicine, N.Y.C., 1971, Pharm. Mfrs. Assn. fellow, U. Pa. Sch. Medicine, 1976-77. Republican. Episcopalian. Avocation: mountaineering. Home: 9008 Chickawane Ct Alexandria VA 22309-2908 Office: Consumer Healthcare Products Assn 1150 Connecticut Ave NW Washington DC 20036-4104

SOLLID, FAYE EISING, civic worker; b. Milw., Aug. 31, 1913; d. George Walter and Jessie Belle (Davey) Eising; m. Erik Sollid, Aug. 1, 1936 (dec. Mar. 1977); 1 child, Jon Erik. BA in Journalism, U. Wis., 1936; postgrad., U. Denver, 1947. Asst. in basic communications U. Denver, 1947. Editor Am. Hindi cookbook for Am. Woman's Club New Delhi, 1956; mem. Clearwater (Fla.) Libr. Bd., 1981-89, liaison between Libr. Bd. and Friends of Libr. Bd., 1984-89; mem. Clearwater Beautification Com., 1989-92. Recipient Citation of Sincere Appreciation for pub. svc. as mem. libr. bd. 1981-89 Mayor City of Clearwater, 1989. Mem. AAUW, Smithsonian Inst. Nat. Mus. Am. Indian (charter), Nat. Mus. Women in Arts (charter), Upper Pinellas African Violet Soc. (v.p. 1973-74, pres. 1974-75), Sovereign Colonial Soc. Ams. Royal Descent, Plantagenet Soc., Soc. Descs. Most Noble Order Garter, Order of Crown Charlemagne in U.S.A., Colonial Order of the Crown, Suncoast Magna Charta Dames (rec. sec. 1980-83), Nat. Soc. Colonial Dames XVII Century (v.p. 1983-85, 89-93). Avocations: genealogy, handwriting analysis.

SOLLMAN, GEORGE HENRY, venture capitalist; b. Michigan City, Ind., Nov. 2, 1941; s. Henry Charles and Margaret Elisabeth (Gockel) S.; m. Maureen Tosh, July 12, 1968; children: Jennifer, Erich. Spl. student, MIT, 1965-66; BSEE, Northwestern U., 1964; MSEE, Northeastern U., 1967. Engrng. dir. Honeywell Info. systems, Waltham, Mass., 1964—73; product line mgr. Control Data, Hawthorne, Calif., 1973—76; v.p., gen. mgr. Shugart/Xerox, Sunnyvale, 1976—84; spl. ptnr. Sand Hill Venture Group, Menlo Park, 1984; pres., CEO, Centigram Corp., San Jose, 1985—97; pres., CEO AtMotion Inc. (now OpenWave Corp.), Redwood City, 1997—2000, Arabesque Investments LLC, Atherton, 2000—. Chmn. nat. bd. dirs. Am. Elec. Assn.; presdl. nomination Semicondr. Tech. Coun.; co-chmn. Alexis d'Toqueville Soc.; adv. coun. Joint Venture Silicon Valley. Patentee in field. Co-chmn. United Way of Santa Clara County; mem. steering com. George Lucas Ednl. Found., Marin County. Home: 242 Polhemus Ave Atherton CA 94027-5439 Office: Arabesque Investments LLC 242 Polhemus Ave Atherton CA 94027-5439 E-mail: george_sollman@hotmail.com.

SOLLORS, WERNER, English language, literature and American studies educator; PhD, Freie U., Berlin, 1975. Wissenschaftlicher asst., asst. prof. John F. Kennedy Inst. Freie U., Berlin; from asst. to assoc. prof. English and Comparative Lit. Columbia U.; Henry B. and Anne M. Cabot Prof. English Lit., prof. Afro-Am. studies Harvard U., Cambridge, Mass. Author: Amiri Baraka/LeRoi Joines: The Quest for a Populist Modernism, 1978, Beyond Ethnicity: Consent and Descent in American Culture, 1986, Neither Black Nor White Yet Both: Thematic Explorations of Interracial Literature, 1997; contbr. , , , , , , , , ; editor: A Bibliographic Guide to Afro-American Studies, 1972, A Bibliographic Guide to Afro-American Studies Supplement I, 1974; co-editor: Bibliographie amerikanistischer Veröffentlichungen in der DDR bis, 1968, 1976, Varieties of Black Experience at Harvard, 1986, The Invention of Ethnicity, 1989, The Life Stories of Undistinguished Americans as Told by Themselves, 1990, 1999, The Return of Thematic Criticism, 1993, Cane, 1993, Blacks at Harvard: A Documentary History of African-American Experience at Harvard and Radcliffe, 1993, The Black Columbiad: Defining Moments in African-American Literature and Culture, 1994, Theories of Ethnicity: A Classical Reader, 1996, The Promised Land, 1997, Multilingual America: Transnationalism, Ethnicity and the Languages of American Literature, 1998, The Multilingual Anthology of American Literature, 2000, The Norton Critical Edition of Olaudah Equiano, 2000, Interracialism: Black-White Intermarriage in American History, Literature and Law, 2000; composer: The Adrienne Kennedy Reader, 2001; contbr. articles. Recipient Constance Rourke prize Am. Studies Assn., 1990; John Simon Guggenheim Meml. fellow, Andrew W. Mellon faculty fellow Harvard U., Walter Channing Cabot fellow Harvard U., 1997-98; NEH fellow, 1999-00. Fellow: Am. Acad. of Arts and Scis. Office: Harvard U Barker Center Rm 225 12 Quincy St Cambridge MA 02138-3804

SOLLOTT, TOBY F. health information administrator; b. Camden, N.J., July 26, 1934; d. Max A. and Ruth R. (Goldenberg) Freedman-Rose; m. Gilbert P. Sollott, Oct. 10, 1954; children: Steven J., Michael H. A in Gen. Studies, Montgomery County C.C., Blue Bell, Pa., 1982; BS in Health Records Adminstrn., Temple U., 1984. Registered health info. adminstr. Quality assurance asst., med. records dept. Hosp. U. Pa., Philadelphia, 1984-85; asst. dir. med. records Bryn Mawr (Pa.) Hosp., 1985-91, assoc. dir. med. records, 1991-92, dir. med. records, 1992-95. Mem.: Fla. Health Info. Mgmt. Assn., Am. Health Info. Mgmt. Assn.

SOLMAN, JOSEPH, artist; b. Vitebsk, Russia, Jan. 25, 1909; came to U.S. 1912; s. Nathan and Rose (Peskin) S.; m. Ruth Romanofsky (dec. July 1999); children: Paul, Ronni. , Nat. Acad. of Design, 1927-30. Nat. Academician 1967. Easel painter WPA, N.Y.C., 1935-41; pvt. art instr., 1951-66; art instr. CUNY, 1967-75; artist, 1935—. Exhibitions: Retrospective at Phillips Mem. Mus., Washington, 1949, Retrospective at Wichita (Kansas) Mus. of Art, 1984; author: books, Joseph Solman, Crown Publishers, 1966, Monotypes of Joseph Solman, Da Capo Press, 1977, Joseph Solman, Da Capo Press, 1995; artist: several paintings. Recipient of several awards for paintings and portraits including the Nat. Inst. of Arts & Letters, 1961, and 8 prizes from the Nat. Acad. of Design Annuals, 1967-89. Mem. Nat. Acad. of Design (treas. 1979-85), Fedn. of Modern Painters & Sculptors (exec. bd. 1968-89); fellow (life) Art Student League. Home: 156 2nd Ave New York NY 10003-5716

SOLMSSEN, PETER, academic administrator; b. Berlin, Nov. 1, 1931; AB, Harvard U., 1952; JD, U. Pa., 1959. Atty. Ballard, Spahr, Andrews & Ingersoll, Phila., 1959-60; with U.S. Fgn. Service, 1961; vice consul Singapore, 1962-63; asst. to under sec. of state, 1963-65; 2d sec. Rio de Janeiro, 1965-67; Cultural attache U.S. Dept. State, Sao Paulo, Brazil, 1967-70; adviser on arts Washington, 1974-80; dep. ambassador at large for cultural affairs, 1981-83; pres. Phila. Coll. Art, 1983-87, U. of the Arts, Phila., 1987-2000. One-man photography exhbns. include: Mus. Art, Sao Paulo. Author and illustrator. Mem.: Philadelphia; Century Assn. Office: Univ Arts Office of Pres 320 S Broad St Philadelphia PA 19102-4994

SOLO, JOYCE RUBENSTEIN, volunteer; b. Buffalo, Feb. 14, 1924; d. Jay Harry and Rose (Maisel) Rubenstein; m. Richard D. Solo, Jan. 6, 1946; children: Harry Jay Solo, Eleanor Solo, Sally Solo. BA, Wellesley Coll., 1945. Mem. governing bd. Health Systems Agy. S.E. Pa., 1977—86; mem. S.E. Pa. Health Coord. Coun., 1978—84; chair reach to recovery Phila. divsn. Am. Cancer Soc., 1985—87; sec. Sarasota County Health Care Coord. Adv. Coun., Fla., 1993—95; active Planned Approach to Cmty. Health; chair sr. adv. com. Sarasota Meml. Hosp., 1996—98; vol. Reach to Recovery Breast Cancer Task Force, Manatee County Am. Cancer Soc.; pres. numerous other health and civic orgn. activities, Temple Beth Israel Women Bd., 1996—98, Temple Beth Israel Bd., 1998—2000. Mem.: LWV (v.p. Pa. chpt. 1969—73, pres. Phila. 1975—77, pres. Sarasota County 1990—92, healthcare com. chair 1988—90, 1992—), Phi Beta Kappa. E-mail: rjoysolo1@msn.com.

SOLO, ROBERT ALEXANDER, economist, educator; b. Phila., Aug. 2, 1916; s. Louis C. and Rebecca (Muchnick) S.; m. Roselyn Starr; 1 dau., Tova Maria. BS, Harvard U., 1938; MA, Am. U., 1941; PhD, Cornell U., 1953. Economist fed. and war agys., 1939-41; author, script chief Sta. WCAU-TV, Phila., 1949-50; mem. faculty Rutgers U., New Brunswick, N.J., 1953-55, McGill U., Montreal, Que., Can., 1955-56, CCNY, 1956-58; sr. research economist Princeton U., 1965-66; prof. dept. econs. Mich. State U., East Lansing, 1966-87, prof. emeritus, 1987—; dir. Inst. Internat. Bus. and Devel. Studies, 1966-68. Mem. faculty Johns Hopkins U., Balt., summer 1953, U. Mich., Ann Arbor, summer 1958; lectr. L'Ecole Practique des Hautes Etudes, Sorbonne, Paris, 1964-65; research Institut Recherch Economique et Planification, lectr. U. Grenoble, France, 1972-73; prof. associe U. Paris IV,

Dauphine, 1971, 73; cons. NASA, 1965-67, OECD, 1963-65, Commonwealth of P.R., 1959-61, U.S. Dept. Justice, 1994-96; project chmn. Study on Info. Tech., Nat. Conf. Bd., 1969-72; project dir. Nat. Planning Assn., Washington, 1961-63; U.S. del. Yugoslavian Conf. on Transfer of Tech., Belgrade, 1974; mem. Alan T. Waterman award Com., 1976-77; expert witness Dept. Justice, Washington, L.A., 1995-97. Author: Economics and the Public Interest, 1955, Synthetic Rubber: A Case Study in Technological Development under Public Direction, 1959 (reprinted as Across the High Technology Threshold 1980), Economic Organizations and Social Systems, 1967 (reissued 2001), (with Everett Rogers) Inducing Technological Change for Economic Growth and Development, 1973, The Political Authority and the Market System, 1974, Organizing Science for Technology Transfer in Economic Development, 1975, The Positive State, 1981, (with Charles Anderson) Value Judgement and Income Distribution, 1981, Opportunity Knocks: American Economic Policy after Gorbachev, 1991, The Philosophy of Science and Economics, 1991, The Super Power and the Serb, 1998, The Song of Songs: The Harvard Version, 1998, also other books in field; contbr. chpts. to books, articles to profl. jours. Fulbright fellow, 1972-73 Mem. Council European Studies (steering com., exec. com., chmn. research com. 1974-77). Home: 4609 Chippewa Dr Okemos MI 48864-2009 E-mail: solo@pilot.msu.edu.

SOLOMON, ANDREW WALLACE, author; b. N.Y.C., Oct. 30, 1963; s. Howard and Carolyn Ruth (Bower) S. BA in English magna cum laude, Yale U., 1985; BA, MA in English, Jesus Coll., Cambridge U., Cambridge, Eng., 1987. Editl. intern Met. Mus. Art, N.Y.C., 1981, editl. asst., 1982, asst. editor, 1983, editor, 1986; intern dept. old master paintings Sotheby's N.Y., 1984; galleries corr., contbg. editor Harpers and Queen, London, 1987-91; contbg. editor HG, 1991-93; contbg. writer The N.Y. Times Mag., 1993—. Author: The Irony Tower: Soviet Artists in a Time of Glasnost, 1991, A Stone Boat, 1994, The Noonday Demon: An Atlas of Depression, 2001 (Nat. Book award, finalist Pulitzer Prize); contbr. articles to profl. jours. Bd. dirs. World Monuments Fund Outward Bound, Hurricane Island Sch., CEC Internat. Partnership, Alliance for the Arts, The Shakespeare Project, The Moscow ICA. Jesus Coll. Travel grantee, Cambridge U., 1986; Yale Conservation Project fellow for travel, 1985; Brit.-Am. Project fellow; Bogliasco fellow, 1998; recipient Nat. Book award Books for a Better Life, 2001, New Visions award OPB, Ken award Nat. Alliance for Mentally Ill; finalist Lambda award Am. Libr. Assn. Mem. Groucho Club, Oxford & Cambridge Club, Chelsea Arts Club, Century Assn., Nat. Arts Club, Coun. on Fgn. Rels., Conservators Coun. of N.Y. Pub. Libr. Democrat. Address: 18 W 10th St New York NY 10011-8702 also: 154 Kensington Park Rd London W11 2ER England

SOLOMON, ARTHUR CHARLES, pharmacist; b. Gary, Ind., May 30, 1947; s. Laurence A. and Dorothy B. (Klippel) S.; m. Janet Evelyn Irak, Aug. 23, 1969; children: Thomas, Michael, Mark, Jill. BS in Pharmacy, Purdue U., 1970, MS in Clin. Pharmacy, 1972; PharmD. Registered pharmacist; cert. nuclear pharmacist. Clin. prof. pharmacy U. Tex., Austin, 1972-75; v.p. Nuclear Pharmacy, Inc., Atlanta, 1975-83; exec. v.p., COO Diagnostek, Inc., Albuquerque, 1983-95; pres. Health Care Svcs., Inc., 1990-95; exec. v.p., COO Value Rx, Albuquerque, 1995-96; pres. Solomon and Assocs., 1996-97; pres., CEO, dir. SP Pharmaceuticals LLC, 1997—. Adj. prof. U. N.Mex., 1992—. Contbr. articles to profl. jours. Named Disting. Alumnus Purdue U., 1998. Fellow Am. Soc. Cons. Pharmacists, Parental Drug Assn.; mem. Am. Pharm. Assn., Am. Assn. Pharm. Scis., Am. Soc. Hosp. Pharmacy, Nat. Assn. Retail Druggists, Nat. Coun. Prescription Drug Programs, Am. Managed Care Pharmacy Assn. (pres., dir.), Rho Chi, Pi Kappa Phi. Republican. Roman Catholic. Avocations: golf, woodworking, gardening. Home: 1504 Catron Ave SE Albuquerque NM 87123-4218 Office: SP Pharmaceuticals LLC 4272 Balloon Park Rd NE Albuquerque NM 87109-5801 E-mail: asolomon@sppharma.com.

SOLOMON, ARTHUR KASKEL, biophysics educator; b. Pitts., Nov. 26, 1912; (married); 2 children. AB, Princeton U., 1934; MA, Harvard U., 1935, PhD in Phys. Chemistry, 1937; PhD in Physics, Cambridge U., Eng., 1947, Sc.D., 1964. Research assoc. in physics and chemistry Harvard, 1939-41; officer Brit. Ministry Supply, 1941-43; mem. staff Radiation Lab., Mass. Inst. Tech., 1945; asst. prof. phys. chemistry Med. Sch., Harvard, 1946-57, asso. prof. biophysics, 1957-68, prof., 1968-82, prof. emeritus, 1982—; assoc. in biophysics Peter Bent Brigham Hosp., Boston, 1950-72; dir. Read's Inc., Balt., 1946-77, pres., 1961-77. Mem. U.S. Nat. Com. for Pure and Applied Biophysics, 1965-72, U.S. Nat. Com. for Biology, 1966-71; mem. U.S. Nat. Com. for UNESCO, 1969-74, mem. U.S. del. to gen. assembly, Nairobi, 1976; mem. vis. com. biology dept. Brookhaven Nat. Lab., 1961-65; mem. NRC com. on radiology, 1957-59, com. on growth, 1954-57; sec. Gen. Internat. Union for Pure and Applied Biophysics, 1961-72; mem. NIH radiation study sect., 1960-63, biophys. sci. tng. com., 1963-68, chmn., 1966-68; mem. U.S. del. Gen. Assembly of UNESCO, Paris, 1978; mem. adv. panel on sci., tech. and society UNESCO, 1981-84; mem. bd. internat. orgns. and programs Nat. Acad. Scis., 1973-80, chmn., 1977-79; mem. Commn. on Internat. Relations, 1977-79; mem. exec. com. Internat. Council Sci. Unions, 1966-72; U.S. del. 17th, 18th Gen. Assemblies of Internat. Council Sci. Unions, Athens, 1978, Amsterdam, 1980; chmn. disting. fellowship com. Internat. Council Sci. Unions-UNESCO, 1980-85; chmn. Harvard com. on higher degrees in biophysics, 1959-80; chmn. Harvard Med. Sch. Oral History Com.; chmn. Harvard Council on the Arts, 1973-76 Mem. editorial bds.: Quarterly Revs. of Biophysics, 1972-74, Journal Gen. Physiology, 1958-90. Trustee Inst. Contemporary Art, Boston, 1946-76, pres., 1965-71; bd. overseers Boston Mus. Fine Arts, 1978-84; mem. collectors com. Nat. Gallery Art, Washington, 1985-88. Decorated Order Andres Bello Venezuela). Fellow AAAS, Am. Acad. Arts and Scis.; mem. Am. Chem. Soc., Am. Physiol. Soc., Biophysics Soc., Soc. Gen. Physiology. Clubs: Cosmos (Washington); St. Botolph (Boston); Harvard (N.Y.C. and Boston). Home: 27 Craigie St Cambridge MA 02138-3457

SOLOMON, BARBARA PROBST, writer; b. N.Y.C. d. J. Anthony and Frances Kurke Probst; m. Harold William Solomon, Dec. 21, 1952 (dec. Jan. 1967); children: Carla, Maria. Student, Sorbonne, Paris; BS, Columbia U., 1960. Editor Peninsula Mag., Paris, 1950; with letters dept. Spanish edit. Life Mag., N.Y.C., 1952; corr. Cambio 16, Madrid & N.Y.C., 1982-91, El País, Madrid & N.Y.C., 1991—; prof. grad. writing dept. Sarah Lawrence Coll., 1994—. Pub. The Reading Room; author 6 books. Recipient Barcelona Pablo de Olavide Memoir award, 1979, Lancelot Whyte award 20th Century Archives, Boston U., 1997. Jewish. Office: Sarah Lawrence Coll 1 Meadway Bronxville NY 10708-5931

SOLOMON, BARRY JASON, healthcare administrator; b. Boston, May 16, 1934; s. Samuel and Ethel (Fleishman) Solomon; m. C. Priscilla Fugate, June 29, 1958; children: R. Stephen, Jon, Julie Ellen. BS in Biology and Chemistry, Tufts U., 1955; MBA in Health Care Adminstrn., Xavier U., Cin., 1960; MPH in Health Care Adminstrn., U. N.C., 1989. Chief med. record adminstr. USPHS Hosp., Lexington, Ky., 1956-59; asst. dir. Union Meml. Hosp., Balt., 1960-61; asst. adminstr. James Lawrence Kernan Hosp., 1961-67; asst. to dean, lectr. health edn. and med. care sects. Yale U. Sch. Medicine, New Haven, 1967-70; dir. health svcs., clin. asst. prof. pharmacy adminstrn. U. R.I., Kingston, 1970-76; assoc. dir. for adminstrn. USPHS Hosp., Norfolk, Va., 1976-81; dir., COO, sr. fellow in social medicine Montefiore Hosp., Bronx, N.Y., 1981-84; assoc. v.p. for med. affairs, mem. exec. coun. of Med. Sch. U. South Fla., Tampa, 1984-89; assoc. prof., acting chmn. dept. comprehensive medicine U. So. Fla., 1984-89, assoc. prof. Coll. Pub. Health, 1984-89; cons. in health adminstrn., Columbia, Md., 1989-93; v.p. for acad. affairs North Broward Hosp. Dist., Ft. Lauderdale, Fla., 1993-96; chmn. bd. dirs. Sr. Benefit Ctrs. Am., Inc., 1998-2000. 1st v.p. bd. trustees Count and Countess de Hoernle Alzheimer's Pavillion, 2000—; pres., bd. dirs. Villa D'Este Condominium, Inc., 1999—2001; bd. dirs. Vis. Nurse Corp., 1987—90; bd. dirs., mem. exec. and nominating coms. Vis. Nurse Assn. Tampa Bay, 1987—90; mem. planning com. bd. trustees Hillsborough County Hosp. Authority, 1986—88; mem. profl. affairs com. bd. trustees H. Lee Moffitt Cancer Ctr. and Rsch. Inst., 1986—88; mem. affiliation com. S.W. Fla. Blood Bank, 1988—89; instr. hosp. adminstrn. Xavier U., 1960; course asst., instr. Am. Med. Record Assn., 1962—72; instr. Howard U. Coll. Continuing Edn., Washington, 1993; cons. St. Elizabeth Hosp., Covington, Ky., 1959, City Hosp. Ctr. Elmhurst, 1965, Hall-Brooke Hosp., Westport, Conn., 1968—69, Conn. Mental Health Ctr., New Haven, 1969—70, South County Hosp., Wakefield, RI, 1970—76, Centurion Hosp., Tampa, 1989, Primary Care Svcs., Tampa, 1991, Holland & Knight, Tampa, 1991, NCC Internat., Colchester, England, 1991, F. W. Assocs., Tampa, 1989—92, Decking Design, Norfolk, 1986—93, SMinc., Columbia, 1993, Internat. Flooring & Protective Coatings, Inc., Norfolk, 1993—; sr. cons. Meisel Assocs., Inc., N.Y.C., 1983—. Contbr. articles to profl. jours. Mem. Nat. Com. Religion and Health, 1982—84; mem., vice chmn. Chariho Sch. Bd., Richmond, RI, 1974—76; mem. Broward Econ. Devel. Coun., Inc.; trustee Montefiore-Mosholu Cmty. Ctr., 1981—84. Lt. USPHS, 1956—59, capt. USPHS, 1976—81. Recipient citation, Suncoast chp. Am. Heart Assn., 1988. Fellow: Am. Coll. Healthcare Execs.; mem.: APHA. Avocation: tennis. Home: 2863 Via Venezia Deerfield Beach FL 33442-8633

SOLOMON, BETH CAROL, writer; b. Bklyn., Oct. 8, 1953; d. Howard Sidney and Gloria (Pazer) S. BA in Psychology, Coll. of Staten Island, N.Y., 1975; cert. in bookkeeping, Midtown Bus. Sch., 1980; BA in English, Coll. of Staten Island, 1985, MA in English, 1990, BA in Women's Studies and Sociology/Anthropology, 1994, BA in History, 2002, cert. in bookkeeping and acctg., 1995; cert. in computers, Workers Career Ctr., 1996. Classified advt. agt. Realsvc. Advt. Agy. Inc., N.Y.C., 1984-91; sec. Robert Richarde, Inc., 1991-94; vol. intern Staten Island U. Hosp., 1995—. Author: Always A Woman, 1987, These Three, 1996, Arlene & Rubin: A Love Story, 1999, Collected Works, 2002; contbr. poetry to Spiritual Pathways, 1986, Cath. Singles mag., 1987, Serpentine 17, 1997-98.. Vol. Alzheimer's Found. of Staten Island, Inc., 1987—; vol. for developmentally disabled children Willowbrook State Sch., 1969, Pub. Sch. 16, 1970; vol. sr. citizens Clove Lake Nursing Home, 1970, Silver Lake Nursing Home, 1971; vol. Cmty. Assn. Sr. Citizens, 1988, Snug Harbor Cultural Arts Ctr., 1994-95. Avocations: puzzles, senior citizens, family dramas, traveling, creative visualization.

SOLOMON, CAREN GROSSBARD, internist; b. N.Y.C., Feb. 20, 1963; MD, Harvard U., 1988. Resident Brigham and Women's Hosp., Boston, 1988-90, fellow in endocrinology, 1990-93, assoc. physician, 1993—. Asst. prof. medicine Harvard Med. Sch., 1998—. Mem.: AMA, Endocrine Soc., Mass. Med. Soc., Am. Diabetes Assn. Office: Brigham Womens Hosp Div Womens Health 45 Francis St # St5 Boston MA 02115-6105

SOLOMON, CHARLES FRANCIS, electronics educator; b. Newark, Feb. 1, 1932; s. Milton Casper and Anne Marie (Casgrove) S.; m. Alice Margret Morris, Feb. 5, 1955; children: Charles Michael, Theresa Marie, Elizabeth Ann, Thomas Francis. BS, Okla. State U., 1966; MEd, Tex. A&M U., 1971, PhD, 1984. Aircraft mech. electronics Spartan Sch. Aero., Tulsa, Okla., 1956-62; bldg. maintenance engr. student union Okla. State U., Stillwater, 1962-64, rsch. technician, 1964-66; assoc. prof. Tex. State Tech. Coll., Waco, 1966-69; program chair Tex. State Tech. Inst., 1969-83, master instr. electronics, 1983-90, program chmn., 1990-93, master instr. electronics tech. and elec. electronics core, 1993-99; ret., 1999—. Cons. in field. Author: Audio Circuit Analysis, 1976, (manual) Audio Circuits, 1976; contbr. articles to profl. jours.; reviewer book Introduction Electronic Devices and Circuits, 1989. Music dir. St. Joseph Catholic Ch., Bellmead, Tex., 1966-90. Airman 1st class USAF, 1951-55. Mem. Tex. Tech. Soc., Tex. Jr. Coll. Tchrs. Assn., Campus Colleague Computer Assn. (com. 1985-96, chmn. instnl. effectiveness com. 1992-94), Waco Civic Chorus, KC (trustee 1958-90). Avocations: music, hunting, fishing, camping, hiking, round dancing. Home: 399 Beaver Ln Waco TX 76705-4956 E-mail: cfams@txucom.net.

SOLOMON, DAVID HARRIS, geriatrician, educator; b. Cambridge, Mass., Mar. 7, 1923; s. Frank and Rose (Roud) Solomon; m. Ronda L. Markson, June 23, 1946; children: Patti Jean Sinaiko, Nancy Ellen. AB, Brown U., 1944; MD, Harvard U., 1946. Intern Peter Bent Brigham Hosp., Boston, 1946—47, resident, 1947—48, 1950—51; fellow endocrinology New Eng. Center Hosp., 1951—52; faculty UCLA Sch. Medicine, 1952—, prof. medicine, 1966—93, vice chmn. dept. medicine, 1968—71, chmn. dept., 1971—81, assoc. dir. geriatrics, 1982—89; dir. UCLA Ctr. on Aging, 1991—96; prof. emeritus UCLA, 1993—. Chief med. svc. Harbor Gen. Hosp., Torrance, Calif., 1966—71; cons. Wadsworth VA Hosp., L.A., 1952—93, Sepulveda VA Hosp., 1971—93; cons. metabolism tng. com. USPHS, 1960—64, endocrinology study sect., 1970—73; cons. RAND Corp., 1997—. Editor: Jour. Am. Geriatric Soc., 1988—93; contbr. numerous articles to profl. jours. Master: ACP (John Phillips Meml. award 2002); mem.: AAAS, Gerontol. Soc. Am. (Freeman award 1997), Am. Geriatrics Soc. (bd. dir. 1985—93, Milo Leavitt award 1992, Disting. Svc. award 1993, Edward Henderson award 1999), Am. Fedn. Aging Rsch. (Irving S. Wright award 1990), Western Assn. Physicians (councillor 1972—75, pres. 1983—84), Inst. Medicine Nat. Acad. Sci., Am. Thyroid Assn. (pres. 1973—74, Disting. Svc. award 1986), Endocrine Soc. (Robert H. Williams award 1989), We. Soc. Clin. Rsch. (councillor 1963—65, Mayo Soley award 1986), Am. Soc. Clin. Investigation, Assn. Am. Physicians, Assn. Profs. of Medicine (pres. 1980—81), Alpha Omega Alpha, Sigma Xi, Phi Beta Kappa. Home: 2103 Ridge Dr Los Angeles CA 90049-1153 E-mail: d.solomon4@verizon.net.

SOLOMON, DAVID EUGENE, engineering company executive; b. Milton, Pa., June 22, 1931; s. Oren Benjamin and Bernardine Claire Solomon; m. Joyce Marie Hoffman, June 24, 1950; children: Timothy, Melissa, Daniel. AB, Susquehanna U., 1958; MS, Bucknell U., 1960; MBA, Ea. Mich. U., 1974. Sr. engr. Westinghouse Electric Corp., Balt., 1959-65; rsch. engr. U. Mich., 1965-67; chief engr. Electro-Optics divsn. Bendix Corp., 1967-72; v.p. ops. KMS Fusion, Inc., Ann Arbor, Mich., 1972-85; pres., CEO Solohill Engring. Inc., 1985—. Bd. dirs. Ann Arbor Engring. Inc., SoloHill Labs. Inc. Patentee in field. With USN, 1950-55. Fellow IEEE. Office: 4220 Varsity Dr Ann Arbor MI 48108-2241 E-mail: solomon@ic.net.

SOLOMON, DEBORAH ANTOINNETTE, volunteer; b. N.Y.C., Oct. 25, 1938; d. Robert Benjamin and Helene Catherine (Skaluba) Gross; m. Arthur Paul Solomon, Dec. 20, 1958; children: Melanie Elizabeth, Denise Carol, Russell David, Lauren Jodi. BA, Queens Coll., 1958, MEd, 1960. Profl. TV dancer June Taylor Dancers, Jackie Gleason Show, N.Y.C., 1955-59; high sch. tchr. William H. Maxwell Vocat. High Sch., Bklyn., 1959-61. Vol. Women's Am. Orgn. for Rehab. Through Tng., 1970—, dir. ORT Strolling Players, 1977—, co-convener Women's Pleas for Soviet Jewry through ORT, L.I., N.Y., 1986-87, chmn. exec. 1988-90, programming chmn.; exec. bd. N.Y. dist. Women's Am. ORT; choreographer fund-raising shows Temple Israel Great Neck, 1978-82. Named Woman of Yr. ORT, 1987. Democrat. Jewish. Avocations: tennis, swimming, attending ballet and mus. events. Home: 10 Somerset Dr S Great Neck NY 11020-1822 Office: Women's Am ORT-NY dist 29 W 34th St New York NY 10001-3007

SOLOMON, DIANE HURST, neurologist; b. Albuquerque, Jan. 28, 1956; d. E. Henry and Jonel Tinson Hurst; m. Dale Edward Solomon, Jan. 20, 1979; children: Stuart, Scott, Spencer. BA in Psychology, Biology, U. Tex., 1978; MA in Clin. Psychology, Corpus Christi State U., 1980; MD, U. Tex., Health Sci. Ctr., San Antonio, 1986. Diplomate Am. Bd. Psychiatry and Neurology. Resident neurology U. Tex. Health Sci. Ctr. San Antonio, 1987-91, chief resident neurology, 1990-91, fellow geriatrics, 1991-92, clin. instr., 1991-93, asst. prof., 1993—, clin. assoc. prof. dept. medicine, 1998—; dir. neurology S. Tex. Vets. Health Care Sys., Kerrville, 1997—. Co-author: Behavioral Neurology of Movement Disorders, 1995, Surgical Management of Cerebrovascular Disease, 1995, Textbook of Neuroanesthesia and Neurological Dysfunction, 1997; contbg. author: Clinical Anesthesia Practice, 2000. Mem. med. and sci. com. Am. Heart Assn., Austin, 1996—2001, liaison stroke coun. Tex. affiliate, 1996—2001; co-chmn. Stroke Awareness Task Force, San Antonio, 1996—2001; chmn. pub. awareness com. Tex. Coalition Cardiovascular Disease and Stroke, Austin, 1999—2000; mem. Tex. Dept. Health Cardiovascular Disease and Stroke Coun., 2000—, vice chmn., 2001—; Stephen's minister Univ. United Meth. Ch., 2002—; mem. exec. com. TMA Stroke Project, Austin, 1995—, chmn., 1999—, mem. cardiovascular disease com., 1999—; bd. dirs. Am. Heart Assn., 1997—, affiliate bd. mem., 2001—, nominating com., 2002, pres. San Antonio divsn., 2002—. Named Disting. Alumnus Corpus Christi State U., 1983, Outstanding Young Women Am., 1984, Paul V. Ledbetter Physician Vol. of the Yr. award Tex. affiliate Am. Heart Assn., 1998, Stroke Vol. of Yr., 2000. Fellow: Am. Heart Assn. (Outstanding Achievement award 2001, Disting. Svc. award San Antonio divsn. 2001), Stroke Coun.; mem.: Bexar County Med. Assn., Tex. Med. Assn., Tex. Neurol. Soc., Am. Fedn. Clin. Rsch., Am. Acad. Neurology (mem. profl. and pub. info. com.). Methodist. Avocations: poetry, playing the harp, snow skiing, camping, swimming. Office: U Tex Health Sci Ctr San Antonio Dept Medicine, Neurology 7703 Floyd Curl Dr San Antonio TX 78284-6200 E-mail: solomondd@cs.com.

SOLOMON, DONALD WILLIAM, mathematics and computer science educator, consultant; b. Detroit, Feb. 6, 1944; s. Sidney Caesar and Bertha C. (Chaiken) S.; m. Evelyn Mae Scott, Jan. 29, 1990; 1 child, Emily. B.S. with distinction, Wayne State U., 1961, B.Medicine, 1961, M.S., 1963, Ph.D., 1966, M.D., 1968. Instr. math. Wayne State U., Detroit, 1966; asst. prof. math. U. Wis., Milw., 1966-70, assoc. prof. math., 1970-75, assoc. chmn. dept. math., 1975-78, chmn. div. natural scis., 1976-78, prof. math. scis., 1975—; cons. Lineax Corp., Milw., 1980—. Contbr. articles to profl. jours. NSF fellow, 1962, 63, 64-65; U. Wis. Grad. Sch. research grantee, 1967-68, 73-74; NSF research grantee, 1968-73. Mem. Am. Math. Soc., Math. Assn. Am., N.Y. Acad. Scis. Home: 5436 N Lydell Ave Milwaukee WI 53217-5005 Office: U Wis Dept Dept Math Scis Milwaukee WI 53201

SOLOMON, DOROTHY JEANNE ALLRED, writer, communications executive; b. Salt Lake City, June 24, 1949; d. Rulon Clark and Mabel (Finlayson) Allred; m. Bruce Craig Solomon, Jan. 8, 1968; children: Denise, Layla, Jeffrey, Laurie. BA in Lit., Theater and Speech, U. Utah, 1971, MA in Lit. and Creative Writing, 1981. Cert. secondary edn. educator, Utah. Storyteller, libr. Salt Lake City Libr., 1971; tchr. Salt Lake Sch. Dist., 1971-74; instr. U. Utah/Columbia Coll., Salt Lake City, 1974-80; writer-in-residence Utah Arts Coun., 1980-93; human devel. trainer Lifespring, San Rafael, Calif., 1983-87; media specialist Rivendell Psychiat. Hosps., West Jordan, Utah, 1987-90; curriculum writer Positive Action Pub., Twin Falls, Idaho, 1990-96; co-founder, v.p. Rising Star Comm. and Team Resource Assocs., Salt Lake City, 1994—. Bd. dirs. Rising Star Comm. Author: In My Father's House, 1984 (1st prize Biography, 1981, Pub. prize 1982), Inside Out: Creative Writing, 1989, Of Predators, Prey and Other Kin, 1996 (1st prize Non-fiction 1996); contbr. stories to anthologies Stories That Shape Us, What There Is, The Best of Writers at Work, A New Genesis, Great and Peculiar Beauty, In Our Lovely Deseret, Mormon Fictions, 1998; screenwriter: In My Father's House, 1986-87. Bd. dirs. The Children's Ctr., Salt Lake City, 1982-85, Writers at Work, Park City, Utah, 1986-89, Lifespring Found., San Rafael, Calif., 1985-89; mem. curriculum com. Salt Lake Sch. Dist., 1971-74; coord. (with Bruce Solomon) lit. arts Utah Arts Festival "Performing Word", Salt Lake City, 1982; vol. Big Sisters, Salt Lake City, 1970-71; coord. cmty. edn. Rivendell Conf., West Jordan, Utah, 1987-89. Recipient Disting. Journalism 1st prize Am. Acad. Pediat., San Francisco, 1979, 1st prize feature writing Sigma Delta Chi, Salt Lake City, 1979, 1st prize essay Utah Original Writing Contest, Salt Lake City, 1995, 1st prize Biography, 1981, 96, award of excellence Gov.'s Media Awards, Utah, 1990, Utah State Pub. prize, 1982. Mem. Associated Writing Programs, Acad. Am. Poets. Mem. Lds Ch. Avocations: golf, reading, movies, environmental protection, child/family advocacy projects. Home: 6557 Snowview Dr Park City UT 84098-6167

SOLOMON, ELDRA PEARL BROD, psychologist, educator, biologist, writer; b. Phila., Apr. 9, 1940; d. Theodore and Freda Miriam (Warhaftig) Brod; m. Edwin Marshall Solomon, June 28, 1959 (div. Jan. 1985); children: Mical Kenneth, Amy Lynn, Belicia Efros. BS, U. Tampa, 1961; MS, U. Fla., 1963; MA, U. South Fla., 1987, PhD, 1989. Lic. clin. psychologist; cert. diplomate in clin. hypnotherapy Nat. Bd. Cert. Clin. Hypnotherapy. Adj. biology prof. Hillsborough C.C., Tampa, Fla., 1968-86; biopsychologist Ctr. for Rsch. in Behavioral Medicine, U. South Fla., 1985-89; dir. rsch. Advanced Devel. Sys., 1989-92; pvt. practice, 1990—; clin. dir. Ctr. for Mental Health Edn., Assessment and Therapy, Fla., 1992—. Adj. prof., mem. grad. faculty U. South Fla., 1992—; expert witness, psychol. expert county and cir. cts., 1989—; health edn. cons. Advanced Devel. Sys., Tampa, 1985-92. Author: Human Anatomy and Physiology, 1990, The World of Biology, 5th edit., 1995; author: (book chpt.) Health Psychology: Individual Differences and Stress, 1988; sr. author: Biology, 6th edit., 2002; contbr. Mem. APA, Am. Soc. Criminology, Fla. Psychol. Assn., Internat. Soc. for the Study of Dissociation (chair Tampa chpt., 1994-95, bd. dirs. 1993—), Tampa Bay Assn. Women Psychotherapists (pres. 1998-99, bd. dirs. 1996—). Democrat. Jewish. Avocations: boating, swimming, reading. E-mail: epbsolomon@aol.com.

SOLOMON, ELINOR HARRIS, economics educator; b. Boston, Feb. 26, 1923; d. Ralph and Linna Harris; m. Richard A. Solomon, Mar. 30, 1957; children: Joan S. Griffin, Robert H., Thomas H. AB, Mt. Holyoke Coll., 1944; MA, Radcliffe U., 1945; PhD, Harvard U., 1948. Jr. economist Fed. Res. Bank Boston, 1945-48; economist Fed. Res. Bd. Govs., Washington, 1949-56; internat. economist U.S. State Dept., 1957-58; professorial lectr. Am. U., 1964-66; sr. economist antitrust div. U.S. Dept. Justice, 1966-82; prof. econs. George Washington U., 1982—. Econ. cons., Washington, 1982—; expert witness antitrust, fin. networks, electronic funds transfer cases, Washington, 1988—. Author: Virtual Money, 1997; author, editor: Electronic Funds Transfers and Payments, 1987, Electronic Money Flows, 1991; contbr. articles on econs., banking and law to profl. jours. Mem. Am. Econs. Assn., Nat. Economists Club (bd. govs. 1997-2000), The Cosmos Club (chair Digital Age series 1999—), Frontiers of Sci. Home: 6805 Delaware St Chevy Chase MD 20815-4164 Office: George Washington U Dept Econs Washington DC 20052-0001

SOLOMON, EZRA, economist, educator; b. Rangoon, Burma, Mar. 20, 1920; came to U.S., 1947, naturalized, 1951; s. Ezra and Emily (Rose) S.; m. Janet Lorraine Cameron, May 7, 1949; children— Catherine Shan, Janet Ming, Lorna Cameron. AB (hons.), U. Rangoon, 1940; PhD, U. Chgo., 1950. Instr. U. Chgo., 1948-51, asst. prof. fin., 1951-55, assoc. prof., 1955-57, prof., 1957-61; Dean Witter prof. fin. Stanford U., 1961-71, 73-90; dir. Internat. Ctr. Mgmt. Edn.; mem. Coun. Econ. Advisers, 1971-73. Author: The Theory of Financial Management, 1963, Money and Banking, 5th edit, 1968, The Management of Corporate Capital, 1959, Metropolitan Chicago: An Economic Analysis, 1958, The Anxious Economy, 1975, An Introduction to Financial Management, 2d edit, 1980, Beyond the Turning Point, 1981; editor: International Patterns of Inflation— A Study in Contrasts, 1984, Jour. Bus, 1953-57; bd. editors Jour. of Finance, 1965-66, Jour. Bus. Finance, 1969-73, Jour. Quantitative and Financial Analysis, 1969-71. Served as lt., Burma div. Royal Naval Vol. Res., 1942-47. Mem. Am. Econ. Assn. Home: 775 Santa Ynez St Stanford CA 94305-8478 Office: Stanford U Grad Sch Bus Stanford CA 94305

SOLOMON, GAIL ELLEN, physician; b. Bklyn., May 26, 1938; d. Samuel and Estelle (Suffin) S.; m. Harvey Hecht, Oct. 28, 1962; children: Daniel, Jonathan, Elizabeth. AB, Smith Coll., 1958; MD, Albert Einstein Coll. Medicine, 1962. Diplomate Am. Bd. Pediats., Am. Bd. Psychiatry and Neurology (assoc. examiner), Am. Bd. Electroencephalography, Am. Bd. Electroencephalography and Neurophysiology, Am. Bd. Clin. Neurophysiology. Intern in pediat. Bronx Mcpl. Hosp. Ctr., 1962-63, resident in pediat., 1963-64, N.Y. Hosp.-Cornell U. Med. Coll., N.Y.C., 1964-65; NIH vis. fellow in neurology and child neurology Columbia-Presbyn. Med. Ctr., 1965-68, NIH vis. fellow in clin. neurophysiology and electroenceph.; instr. neurology Columbia U. Coll. of Physicians and Surgeons, 1968-69; instr. in neurology and pediat. Cornell U. Med. Coll., 1969-70, asst. prof. neurology and pediat., 1970-76; asst. attending in neurology and pediat. N.Y. Hosp., N.Y.C., 1969-76, dir. electroencephalography, 1969—; assoc. prof. clin. neurology and pediat. Cornell U. Med. Coll., 1976—, assoc. prof. clin. neurology in psychiatry, 1983; assoc. attending in neurology and pediat. N.Y. Hosp., 1976—, assoc. attending neurologist in psychiatry, 1983—. Mem. joint com. for stroke facilities NIH; mem. FDA Peripheral and CNS Adv. Com., 1979-83, chmn., 1983, cons., 1983-84; mem. med. audit com. N.Y. Hosp., mem. utilization rev. com.; mem. profl. adv. bd. N.Y. State Epilepsy Assn.; adj. attending physician in neurology Meml.-Sloan Kettering Cancer Ctr., 1982-93; assoc. attending pediatrician Hosp. Spl. Surgery, 1987—; neurology cons. Blythedale Children's Hosp., Valhalla, N.Y., 1991—, Meml.-Sloan Kettering Cancer Ctr., 1993—. Author: (with F. Plum) Clinical Management of Seizures: A Guide for the Physician, 1976, (with Plum and Kutt) 2d edit., 1983; editor: (with Kaufman and Pfeffer) Child and Adolescent Neurology for Psychiatrists, 1992, Neurologic Disorders: Developmental and Behavioral Sequelae, 1999; contbr. articles to profl. jours., chpts. to med. books. Fellow Am. Acad. Neurology, Am. Acad. Pediats., Am. Electroencephalographic Soc. mem. AMA (Physician's Recognition award in Continuing Med. Edn.), N.Y. State Med. Soc., N.Y. County Med. Soc., Am. Med. Women's Assn., Am. Epilepsy Soc., Am.

Acad. Clin. Neurophysiology, Eastern EEG Soc., Am. Med. EEG Assn., Child Neurology Soc., Internat. Child Neurology Assn., Tristate Child Neurology Soc., Assn. for Rsch. in Nervous and Mental Diseases, N.Y. Acad. Sci. Avocations: art museums, reading literature, French language, travel. Office: NY Presbyn Hosp Cornell U Med Coll 525 E 68th St New York NY 10021-4870

SOLOMON, GOODY LOVE, journalist, editor; b. N.Y.C., June 1, 1929; d. Frank A.H. and Anna (Caplan) S.; m. Theodore A. Braun, July 1, 1953. BA, Bklyn. Coll., 1950; MA, NYU, 1954. Bus. writer, asst. editor Stores, N.Y.C., 1956-61; contbr. Barrons's, 1961-69; tchr. consumer edn. and journalism George Washington U., Washington, 1966-68; exec. editor Office Consumer Svcs. HEW, 1971-73; syndicated food/consumer columnist Washington Star and other papers, 1974-90; editor Nutrition Policy, Washington, 1985-86, The Food & Drug Letter, Washington, 1986-91; exec. editor Food, Nutrition, Health News Svc., 1991—; tchr. food writing George Washington Ctr. for Profl. Edn., 1999—2001. Speaker in field. Author: The Radical Consumer's Handbook, 1972; editorial cons. Pres.'s Consumer Adv. Coun., Washington, 1966; contbr. articles to profl. jours. Consumer edn. dir. N.Y. State Consumer Protection Bd., 1973. Recipient Spl. Citation award Nat. Press Club, 1980. Mem. Capital Press Woman (Communication award 1991, and other awards), Nat. Fedn. Pres Women, Les Dames d'Escoffier, Am. News Women's Club. Avocations: tennis, sports, music, reading, theater. E-mail: goody.solomon@verizon.net.

SOLOMON, HARVEY DONALD, engineer, educator; BS, NYU, New York, NY, 1963; PhD, U. Pa, Philadelphia, PA, 1968. Staff GE Global Rsch., Schenectady, NY, 1968—; adj. assoc. prof. Union Coll., 1989—. Recipient Vilella award, ASTM, 1979, IEEE-CHMT Transactions Prize Paper award, IEEE-CHMT, 1986, Hudson-Mohawk AIME Disting. Career award, AIME, 2002, AWS James F. Lincoln Gold Medal, AWS, 2002. Achievements include patents for 14 Patents Issued. Office: GE Global Research 1 Research Circle Schenectady NY 12309 Office Fax: 518-387-7495. E-mail: solomon@crd.ge.com.

SOLOMON, HENRY, university dean; b. Bronx, N.Y., Nov. 28, 1926; s. Max and Tillie (Gilerowitz) S.; m. Jacqueline Mona Cohen, May 31, 1953; 1 son, Michael Robert. BA, Bklyn. Coll., 1949; MA, NYU, 1950, PhD, 1960. Research assoc., then sr. staff investigator and dep. prin. investigator, logistics research project George Washington U., 1950-66, prof. econs., chmn. dept., 1962-74, 91-96; dean George Washington U. (Grad. Sch. Arts and Scis.), 1974-90, prof. and dean emeritus, 1996—. Dep. asst. adminstr. econs., acting asst. adminstr. planning, research and analysis SBA, 1966-67; cons. in field. Assoc. editor: Naval Research Logistics Quar, 1957-90 . Served with U.S. Army, 1945-46. Recipient Founder's Day award N.Y. U., 1960 Mem. Am. Econ. Assn., Am. Statis. Assn. Home: # 603 5450 Whitley Park Terr Bethesda MD 20814 Office: George Washington Univ Funger 507 Washington DC 20052-0001 : E-mail: henry20814@aol.com.

SOLOMON, HILDA PEARL, wholesale executive; b. Conway, S.C., Dec. 15, 1948; d. Ezel and Dorothy (Gottlieb) S. BFA, U. S.C., 1968. Buyer Solomon Bros. Dept. Store, Conway, 1969-73; coutourier sales Julius Lewis, Memphis, 1973-75; buyer Helen of Memphis, 1975-78, George M. Muse Clothing Co., Atlanta, 1978-83; sales rep. Whiting & Davis Co. Inc., Plainville, Mass., 1983-84, exec. sales mgr. southeast dist., 1984-92; owner Solomon, Atlanta, 1992—. Sec. bd. dirs. Bur. Wholesale Accessory Reps., Atlanta, 1983-87, Accessories On 6 Atlanta Apparel Mart, 1986-87; dir. trade shows, key accounts, export mgr., 1994-98; nat. key account mgr. Westminster, Inc., 1999—. Prin. works include Posh Petals, Atlanta, 1986—. Mem. Atlanta Hist. Soc., Young Careers High Mus. Art. Jewish. Avocations: design, travel, writing. Home: 2917 Hamilton Sq Decatur GA 30033-1140

SOLOMON, HOWARD, pharmaceutical company executive; b. Aug. 12, 1927; s. David and Faye (Gussow) S.; m. Carolyn Ruth Bower, Dec. 17, 1961; children: Andrew Wallace, David Frederick. BSS, CCNY, 1949; LLB, Yale U., 1952. Bar: N.Y. 1952. Atty. Moses & Singer, N.Y.C., 1952-55, Kay Scholer, Fierman Hays & Handler, N.Y.C., 1956-60; pres. Hildred Mgmt. Corp., 1967-83; dir. Forest Labs., Inc., 1964—. Chmn., CEO Forest Labs., Inc., 1998—; dir. Pharmax Ltd., Bexley, Kent., U.K., 1979—; bd. trustees Cold Spring Harbor Labs. Bd. dirs. Met. Opera, N.Y.C. Ballet, chmn.; bd. dirs. Lincoln Ctr. for Performing Arts. Mem. N.Y. State Bar Assn., Yale Club, Harmonie Club of N.Y. Office: Forest Labs Inc 909 3rd Ave New York NY 10022-4731

SOLOMON, JACK AVRUM, JR. lawyer, automotive distributor, art dealer; b. Omaha, Oct. 25, 1928; s. John A. and Matilda (Bienstok) S.; m. Josephine J. Kleiman, June 1948 (div. Mar. 1971); children: Debra, Alisa, Michael, Rena; m. Carolyn Summers, Dec. 1973. BS, U. Nebr., 1950, LL.B. cum laude, 1952; LL.M. (Cook fellow), U. Mich., 1953. Bar: Nebr. 1950, Ill. 1951. Practice law, Chgo., 1950—; with firm Stiefel, Greenberg, Burns, Baldridge & Solomon, 1953-66, ptnr., 1958-66, Solomon, Rosenfeld, Elliot & Stiefel, and predecessor, 1966—, sr. ptnr., 1966—. Dir. Amco Industries, Inc., Chgo., 1968—, chmn. bd., 1968-69, sec., gen. counsel, 1969—; sec., dir. Mogen David Wine Corp., Chgo., 1964-71; chmn. bd., dir. Arts and Leisure Corp., 1969-76; pres., chmn. bd., dir. Circle Fine Art Corp., 1968-94; chmn. bd. S2 Art Group, Ltd., 1996—, Re Society, 1997—, Art of the Movies.com, 1999—. Mem. Ill., Nebr. bar assns.; mem. Fine Art Pubs. Assn. (pres. 1982—); Mem. Order of Coif. Jewish (pres. temple 1959-61). Club: Nat. Arts (N.Y.C.). Home: 2870 Augusta Las Vegas NV 89109 Office: 1 E Charleston Las Vegas NV 89104 E-mail: jsolomon@s2art.com.

SOLOMON, JAMES EMORY, music educator; b. Jacksonville, Fla., Sept. 16, 1946; s. Crawford and Nancy (Adamson) S.; 1 child, James Tyler. BA in History, Stanford (Calif.) U., 1970; MAT in Music, Jacksonville U., 1980; master level Orff cert., Memphis State U., 1981. Cert. elem. and pre-sch. tchr., music tchr., Calif., Fla. Tchr. Stonewall Jackson Elem. Sch., Jacksonville, 1977-78; tchr. music St. Paul's By-The-Sea Elem. Sch., Jacksonville Beach, Fla., 1978-80; musician Defrates trio, 1981; tchr. music Evelyn Hamblen Elem. Sch., St. Augustine, 1981-91, Osceola Elem. Sch., St. Augustine, 1991-2000, R.B. Hung Elem. Sch., St. Augustine, 2000—. Adj. prof. music Jacksonville U., 1980-92; instr. Orff tchr. Fla. Atlantic U., Boca Raton, Fla., 1984-85, 87-89, Jacksonville U., 1990-96, Eastman Sch. Music, Rochester, N.Y., 1992—; instr. Fla. Music Demonstration Sch., 1993-96. Author: (book) Monkey Business-Progress Lessons, 1987, Village Day, 1989, The Body Rondo Book, 1990, Conga Town, Percussion Ensembles, 1995, D.R.U.M., 1998; co-author: The Tropical Recorder, 1997; prodr.: (video) Congas, Bongos & Other Percussion--A Guide to Technique, 1988. Named Oustanding Fla. Educator, Fla. Dept. Edn., 1991-92, St. Johns County Tchr. of Yr., St. Augustine, 1991. Mem. Am. Orff-Schulwerk Assn. (presenter nat. conf. 1985—, regional rep. nat. bd., 1990-94), Music Educators Nat. Conf. (cert. music educator). Avocations: learning new percussion instruments, following sports, reading. Home: 838 Shoreline Cir Ponte Vedra Beach FL 32082-2740 Office: 125 Magnolia Dr Saint Augustine FL 32080-4684

SOLOMON, JERRY LAWRENCE, sports marketing executive; b. N.Y.C., June 11, 1954; s. Edward David and Roberta Eleanor Madison; m. Kathryn Yanuck, June 15, 1986 (div.); 1 child, B. Clayton; m. Nancy Kerrigan, Sept. 9, 1995; 1 child, Matthew Eric. Liaison men's/women's tennis tour Colgate Palmolive Co., N.Y.C., 1978-79; ProServ, Inc., Washington, 1980-95; dir. tennis tour Volvo Grand Prix, N.Y.C., 1980-82; client mgr. Washington, 1982-84; from v.p., tennis divsn. to sr. v.p. Proserv, Inc., 1984-87, exec. v.p., COO, 1987-90, pres., COO, 1990-95, also bd. dirs.; pres. Proserv Pub. Corp., 1990-92; pres., CEO StarGames LLC, Boston, 1995—; exec. dir., CEO Assn. Volleyball Profls., 1995-97; exec. producer The Heat is On, Walt Disney's Dreams on Ice, 1995, Fairy Tales on Ice, 1996. Bd. dirs. Aquatrend, Inc., TFN; pres., CEO The Football Network, 2001; founder, pub. Kidsports Mag., 1989-92; co-founder Sportsinstruction.com, 2000; chmn. Nancy Kerrigan Pro Celebrity Golf Classic, 2000. Exec. prodr. Spike, 1998 (Telly award), One Enchanted Evening, 1999, A Holiday Celebration on Ice, 1999, An Evening of Country on Ice, 1999, Ice Angel, Halloween on Ice, 1995—, Footloose on Ice, 2001. Founder Karch Kiraly Scholarship Fund to Benefit Jr. Volleyball; founder, pres. Kidsports Found. to Benefit Children Through Sports, 1989-96; donor U.S. Olympic Com.; mem. 2d generation co. Nat. Holocaust Mus.; mem. bd. U.S. Com. Sports for Israel. Named Agt. to Watch World Tennis mag., 1987, One of Top 100 Most Powerful People in Sports The Sporting News, 1992, One of Top 25 Most Influential People in Figure Skating Internat. Figure Skating mag., 1996. Mem. Young Pres. Orgn. Democrat. Jewish. Avocations: tennis, piano, reading, wine collecting, music. Office: StarGames 40 Salem St Ste 7 Lynnfield MA 01940-2659

SOLOMON, JULIUS OSCAR LEE, pharmacist, hypnotherapist; b. N.Y.C., Aug. 14, 1917; s. John and Jeannette (Krieger) S.; student Bklyn. Coll., 1935-36, CCNY, 1936-37; BS in Pharmacy, U. So. Calif., 1949; postgrad. Long Beach State U., 1971-72, Southwestern Colls., 1979, 81-82, San Diego State U., 1994—; PhD, Am. Inst. Hypnotherapy, 1988; postgrad. San Diego State U., 1994—. m. Sylvia Smith, June 26, 1941 (div. Jan. 1975); children: Marc Irwin, Evan Scott, Jeri Lee. Cert. hypnotherapist; cert. hypnoanaesthesia therapist. Dye maker Fred Fear & Co., Bklyn., 1935; apprentice interior decorator Dorothy Draper, 1936; various jobs, N.Y. State Police, 1940-45; rsch. asst. Union Oil Co., 1945; lighting cons. Joe Rosenberg & Co., 1946-49; owner Banner Drug, Lomita, 1949-53, Redondo Beach, Calif., 1953-72, El Prado Pharmacy, Redondo Beach, 1961-65; pres. Banner Drug, Inc., Redondo Beach, 1953-72, Thrifty Drugs, 1972-74, also Guild Drug, Longs Drug, Drug King, 1976-83; pres. Socoma, Inc. doing bus. as Lee & Ana Pharmacy, 1983-86, now Two Hearts Help Clinic, 1986—. Charter commr., founder Redondo Beach Youth Baseball Council; sponsor Little League Baseball, basketball, football, bowling; pres. Redondo Beach Boys Club; v.p. South Bay Children's Health Ctr., 1974, Redondo Beach Coordinating Coun., 1975; bd. dirs. So. Bay Assn. Little Theatres, 1972-75; actor in 8 shows; founder Redondo Beach Community Theater, 1975; actor Man of La Mancha Vangard Theatre, San Diego, 1995; active maj. gift drive YMCA, 1975; mem. SCAG Com. on Criminal Justice, 1974, League Calif. Environ. Quality Com., 1975; mem. Dem. State Cen. Com., Los Angeles County Dem. Cen. Com.; del. Dem. Nat. Conv., 1972; chmn. Redondo Beach Recreation and Parks Commn.; mem. San Diego County Parks Adv. Commn., 1982; mem. San Diego Juvenile Justice Commn., 1986-92; mem. San Diego County Adv. Com. Adult Detention, 1987-92; mem. human resource devel. com., pub. improvement com. Nat. League of Cities; v.p. Redondo Beach Coordinating Coun.; councilman, Redondo Beach, 1961-69, 73-77; treas. 46th Assembly Dist. Coun.; candidate 46 Assembly dist. 1966; nat. chmn. Pharmacists for Humphrey, 1968, 72; pres. bd. dirs. South Bay Exceptional Childrens Soc., Chapel Theatre; bd. dirs. so. div. League Calif. Cities, U.S.-Mex. Sister Cities Assn., Boy's Club Found. San Diego County, Autumn Hills Condominium Assn. (pres.), Calif. Employee Pharmacists Assn. (pres. 1985), Our House, Chula Vista, Calif., 1984-86; mem. South Bay Inter-City Hwy. Com., Redondo Beach Round Table, 1973-77; mem. State Calif. Commn. of Californias (U.S.-Mexico), 1975-78; mem. Chula Vista Safety Commn., 1978, chmn., 1980-81; chmn. San Diego County Juvenile Camp Contract Com., 1982-83; mem. San Diego County Juvenile Delinquency Prevention Commn., 1983-85, 89-91, San Diego County Juvenile Justice Commn., 1986-91, San Diego County Adv. Com. for Adult Detention, 1987-91; spl. participant Calif. Crime and Violence Workshop; mem. Montgomery Planning Commn., 1983-86; mem. Constnl. Observance Com., 1990-93, Troubled Teenagers Hypnosis Treatment Program, 1989—; vol. mentor Palomar H.S. S.D. County Sch. Dist., Chula Vista, 1998, Gang Related Intervention Program/Future Leaders Program, 1998-99. With USCGR, 1942-45. Recipient Pop Warner Youth award, 1960, 1962, award of merit Calif. Pharm. Assn., 1962, award Am. Assn. Blood Banks, 1982. Diplomate Am. Bd. Diplomates Pharmacy Internat., 1977-81; Fellow Am. Coll. Pharmacists (pres. 1949-57); mem. South Bay Pharm. Assn. (pres.), South Bay Councilman Assn. (founder, pres.), Palos Verdes Peninsula Navy League (charter), Am. Legion, U. So. Calif. Alumni Assn. (life), Assn. Former N.Y. State Troopers (life), AFTRA, Am. Pharm. Assn., Nat. Assn. Retail Druggists, Calif. Pharmacists Assn., Calif. Employee Pharmacist Assn. (bd. dirs. 1980-81), Hon. Dep. Sheriff's Assn., San Ysidro C. of C. (bd. dirs. 1985-87), Fraternal Order of Police, San Diego County Fish and Game Assn., Rho Pi Phi (pres. alumni). Club: Trojan (life). Lodges: Elks (life), Masons (32 deg.; life), Lions (charter mem. North Redondo). Established Lee and Ana Solomon award for varsity athlete with highest scholastic average at 10 L.A. South Bay High Schs. in Los Angeles County and 3 San Diego area South Bay High Schs.

SOLOMON, MACK BUSCH, retired newspaper editor; b. Pensacola, Fla., Mar. 14, 1932; s. Sigmund and Fannie (Busch) S. BA in Journalism, La. State U., 1953, MA, 1959. Reporter, editor News Jour., Pensacola, 1956-57; asst. prof. journalism, dir. news bur. N.E. La. State Coll., Monroe, 1959-60; mem. copy desk Wall St. Jour., N.Y.C., 1960-65; writer World-Wide column, 1965-70; Page One rewriteman Wall St. Jour., 1970-75, dep. editor Page One, 1975-89, dep. editor Second Front Page, 1989, dep. editor Wall St. Jour. Reports, 1989-90. Cons. editor SmartMoney mag., N.Y.C., 1991-95. Served with U.S. Army, 1953-55. Mem. Soc. Profl. Journalists. Jewish. Avocations: reading, theater, movies. Home: 2465 John F Kennedy Blvd Apt 5B Jersey City NJ 07304-1955

SOLOMON, MARILYN KAY, educator, consultant; b. Marshall, Mo., Oct. 16, 1947; d. John W. and Della M. (Dille) S. BS, Ctrl. Mo. State U., 1969; MS, Ind. U., 1974. Cert. in early childhood and nursery sch. edn., Mo., Ind. Tchr. Indpls. Pub. Schs., 1969-74; dir. Singer Learning Ctrs., Indpls., 1974-78; v.p. ECLC Learning Ctrs., Inc., 1978-95; pres., CEO, owner Early Learning Ctrs., Inc., 1995—; owner, pres., CEO, Solomon Antique Restoration, Inc., 1996—. Mem. OJT tng. task force Dept. Labor, Washington; mem. nat. task force for parenting edn. HEW, Washington; cons. to numerous corps. on corp. child care; built 29 child care ctrs. for corps., hosps. and govt. Co-author curricula. Founding bd. dirs. Mid City Pioneer, Indpls., 1977; mem. adv. bd. Enterprise Zone Small Bus. Incubator, Indpls., 1995—; founding bd. dirs. Family Support Ctr., Indpls., 1983, pres. bd. dirs., 1985-87; founding mem., co-chair Voices for Children, 1996—; mem. White Rivers Gardens State Park, Indpls. Mus. Art. Recipient Outstanding Leadership award Ind. Conf. on Social Concerns, 1975, 76, 77, Children's Mus. Edn. award, 1974; named to Outstanding Young Women of Am., 1984. Mem. Indpls. Mus. Art, Ind. Lic. Child Care Assn. (v.p. 1992, pres. 1974, 75), State of Ind. Quality and Tng. Coun. (chair 1992), Step Ahead-Marion County (rep. for child care 1992—, co-chair educare com. 1999—), Ind. Alliance for Better Child Care (bd. dirs. 1992, adv. bd. 1990-95), Pub. Broadcasting (tng. com. 1992—, child devel. tng. com. 1996—), Order Ea. Star, Indpls. Zool. Soc. (charter). Office: Early Learning Ctrs Inc 1315 S Sherman Dr Indianapolis IN 46203-2210 E-mail: earlylearn@iquest.net.

SOLOMON, MARK RAYMOND, lawyer, educator; b. Pitts., Aug. 23, 1945; s. Louis Isadore and Fern Rhea (Josselson) S. BA, Ohio State U., 1967; MEd, Cleve. State U., 1971; LLM in Taxation, Georgetown U., 1976. Bar: Ohio, Mich., U.S. Dist. Ct. (ea. dist.) Mich., U.S. Ct. Appeals (6th cir.), U.S. Tax Ct., U.S. Ct. Fed. Claims. Tax law specialist corp. tax br. Nat. Office of IRS, 1973-75; assoc. Butzel, Long, Gust Klein & Van Zile, Detroit, 1976-78; dir., v.p. Shatzman & Solomon, P.C., Southfield, Mich., 1978-81; prof., chmn. tax/bus. law dept., dir. MS in Taxation Program Walsh Coll., Troy, 1981—; of counsel Meyer, Kirk, Snyder & Lynch, PLLC, Bloomfield Hills, 1981—. Adj. prof. law U. Detroit, 1977-81. Editor: Cases and Materials on Consolidated Tax Returns, 1978, Cases and Materials on the Application of Legal Principles and Authorities to Federal Tax Law, 1990. Mem. Mich. Bar Assn., Kiwanis (bd. dirs.), Phi Eta Sigma. Avocation: bridge (life master). Home: 2109 Golfview Dr Apt 102 Troy MI 48084-3926 Office: Meyer Kirk Snyder & Lynch PLLC 100 W Long Lake Rd Ste 100 Bloomfield Hills MI 48304-2773 also: Walsh Coll 3838 Livernois Rd Troy MI 48083-5066 E-mail: msolomon@walshcol.edu.

SOLOMON, MARTIN M. judge; b. Jan. 24, 1950; BA magna cum laude, SUNY, Albany, 1972; JD, N.Y. Law Sch., 1975. Bar: N.Y. 1976. Judge N.Y.C. Civil Ct., Bklyn., 1996—; mem. N.Y. State Senate, 1978-95. Former mem. exec. com. Nat. Conf. Ins. Legislators, ranking mem. sen. ins. com., mem. health, bank, judiciary coms. Mem. Oddfellows, KP. Office: NYC Civil Ct 141 Livingston St Brooklyn NY 11201-5133

SOLOMON, MAYNARD ELLIOTT, music historian, former recording company executive; b. N.Y.C., Jan. 5, 1930; s. Benjamin and Dora (Levine) S.; m. Eva Georgiana Tevan, Jan. 22, 1951; children: Mark Jonathan, Nina Stephanie, Maury David. BA, Bklyn. Coll., 1950; postgrad., Columbia U., 1950-51. Co-founder, co-owner Vanguard Rec. Soc., Inc., N.Y.C., 1950-86; faculty grad. div. CUNY, 1979-81. Vis. prof. SUNY Stony Brook, 1988, Columbia U., N.Y.C., 1990, Harvard U., Cambridge, Mass., 1992, Yale U., New Haven, 1994-95; scholarly advisor Beethoven Archive, Bonn, 1997—; faculty grad. divsn. Juilliard Sch., 1998—. Author: Marxism and Art, 1973, Beethoven, 1977 (translated into German, French, Spanish, Portuguese, Japanese, Italian, Bulgarian), Myth, Creativity and Psychoanalysis, 1978, Beethoven's Tagebuch, 1982, Beethoven's Tagebuch, German translation, 1990, Italian translation, 1992, Beethoven Essays, 1988, Italian translation, 1998; Mozart: A Life, 1995 (translated into Swedish, Italian, Japanese), Late Beethoven, 2003; contbg. editor: Am. Imago; mem. editl. bd. Beethovenhaus edit. Beethoven's Letters; editor: Memories of Beethoven, 1992; contbr. articles to profl. jours. Recipient Deems Taylor award ASCAP, 1978, 89, 96, Disting. Vis. award U. Toronto, 1996. Mem. PEN, Am. Musicol. Soc. (bd. dirs. 1984-86, Otto Kinkeldey award 1989, hon. mem. 1999), Authors Guild, N.Y. Inst. for Humanities, Phi Beta Kappa. Home: 1 W 72nd St New York NY 10023-3486

SOLOMON, NATHAN ANDREW, clinical psychologist; b. San Antonio, June 19, 1946; s. Max and Eva (Rosenthal) S.; m. Esther Klein Solomon, June 1974; children: Avraham, Yehoshua, Moshe Chaim, Chava. Student, U. Tex., 1964-67; BA, Yeshiva U., 1969; postgrad., Bklyn. Coll., 1969-71; PhD in Clin. Psychology, L.I. U., 1976. Cert. psychologist, N.Y. Rsch. asst. sociology Yeshiva Coll., Yeshiva U., 1967, dormitory counselor, 1969-71; student supr. Housing and Devel. Adminstrn., City of N.Y., 1967-70; psychology extern Roosevelt Hosp., rsch. asst. L.I. U., 1972-73; psychology trainee Bklyn. Psychiat. Ctrs., 1973-74; psychology intern Jewish Bd. Guardians, Madeline Borg Child Guidance Inst., N.Y.C., 1974-75; psychotherapist counterforce program Hebrew Day Sch., Bklyn., 1975-76; staff psychologist adult inpatient svc. Kingsboro Psychiat. Ctr., 1975-78, dir. psychology, dir. clin. tng., children and youth svc., 1978-79; family cons. Hebrew Inst. Deaf and Exceptional Children, 1978-79; lectr. NYU Sch. Continuing Edn., 1979-80; dir. Boro Park office Madeline Borg Counseling Svcs. Jewish Bd. Family & Children's Svcs., Bklyn, 1979-86; cons. psychologist Ohel Children's Home and Family Svcs., 1983-96; pvt. practice clin. psychology, 1976—. Mem. profl. panel Jewish Assn. Attention Deficit Disorder, Bklyn., 1992-98—; mem. task force on children & families at risk Orthodox Jewish Cmty.; presenter at various confs. Co-author: (video tapes) Becoming a Group, 1976, Keeping Watch, 1979; contbr. articles to profl. jours. Mem. human svcs. task force Coun. Jewish Orgns. of Boro Park, 1983-86; bd. dirs. Pvt. Sector Resource Ctr., 1984-85, Yitti Leibel Helpline, 1999—. Recipient Clin. Svc. award Jewish Assn. for Attention Deficit Disorder, 1996. Mem. Nat. Assn. Rsch. & Therapy Homosexuality, Children and Adults with Attention Deficit Disorder, Nefesh Internat. (pres. 1995-97, exec. bd. 1997—, chmn. N.E. Region), N.Y. State Psychol. Assn., Assn. Orthodox Jewish Scientists (treas. behavioral sci./mental health sect. 1979-80, chmn. Task Force on Cmty. Svc. 1979-80). Avocations: music, Talmudic study. Home and Office: 1478 E 27th St Brooklyn NY 11210-5309

SOLOMON, NEAL EDWARD, management consultant, executive recruiter, social theorist, entrepreneur, author; b. San Diego, Mar. 9, 1960; s. Donald Jay and Roberta Yvonne (Recht) S. BA in Philosophy, Reed Coll., Portland, Oreg., 1981; AM in Philosophy, U. Chgo, 1982. Founder Calif. Legal Search, 1983—; chmn., CEO Geodesic Dynamics, 2000—. Author: A Turning Point in World History?, 1992, High Performance Venture Characteristics, 1992, Dilemmas of Democracy (3 vols.: A Critique of Liberalism, A Critique of Political Ideology, and The Limits of Social Theory), 1992, The Problem of Modernity, 1993, Theoretical Foundations of Dynamic Macroeconomics, 1993, The Evolution of Philosophy, 1995, Legal Management Theory, 2d edit., 1997, Transformation of the Corporate Law Firm, 1998, others. Democrat. Achievements include inventions regarding electronic commerce. Avocations: fine arts nature photography, high end audio and book and art collecting. Address: 388 Market St Ste 500 San Francisco CA 94111-5313 E-mail: ulysses@well.com.

SOLOMON, NORMAN, author, columnist; b. Washington, July 7, 1951; s. Morris Jacobson and Miriam (Abramowitz) S.; m. Cheryl D. Higgins, May 31, 1996. Freelance journalist, 1974—; syndicated columnist Creators Syndicate, L.A., 1992—; exec. dir. Inst. for Pub. Accuracy, Washington, 1997—. Pub. spkr. and lectr., 1977—; assoc. Fairness and Accuracy In Reporting, N.Y.C., 1989—. Author: The Power of Babble, 1992, False Hope: The Politics of Illusion in the Clinton Era, 1994, The Trouble with Dilbert: How Corporate Culture Gets the Last Laugh, 1997, The Habits of Highly Deceptive Media: Decoding Spin and Lies in Mainstream News, 1999 (George Orwell award for disting. contbn. to honesty and clarity in pub. lang.); co-author: Adventures in Medialand, 1993 (Hugh M. Hefner 1st Amendment award), Wizards of Media Oz, 1997. E-mail: mediabeat@igc.org.

SOLOMON, NORMAN FRANK, finance company executive; b. N.Y.C., May 16, 1923; s. Samuel and Rhoda (Goldstein) S.; m. Arlene D. Gersh, Nov. 7, 1954 (div. Aug. 1979); children: Sharon, Marilyn, Carol. BA, U. Fla., 1947, MA, 1950, JD, 1954. Bar: Fla. 1954. Attys., 1954-79; pres., CEO G.L.R.C. Corp., Miami, Fla., 1979—. Bd. dirs. Nat. Employee Benefits Adminstrs. Inc., Nat. Employee Adminstrs. Inc., Pa., Nat. Employee Adminstrs. Inc., Ohio, Nat. Med. Rev. Inc. Author: Juvenile Courts of Florida, 1950. Mem. Miami-Dade County Downtown Devel. Authority, 1998—. Mem. Woodmen of the World (pres. 1990—, State of Fla. trustee), Masons (32d degree). Jewish. Avocation: stamps. Office: GLRC Corp Ste 111 1720 NE 79th Causeway North Bay Village FL 33141

SOLOMON, PAUL ROBERT, neuropsychologist, educator; b. Bklyn., Aug. 27, 1948; s. Maynard and Norma Harris (Ruben) S.; m. Suellen Zablow, Aug. 16, 1970; children: Todd, Jessica. BA in Psychology, SUNY, New Paltz, 1970, MA in Psychology, 1972; PhD in Psychology, U. Mass., 1972. Diplomate Am. Coll. Forensic Examiners; lic. psychologist, Mass. Prof. psychology and neurosci. Williams Coll, Williamstown, Mass., 1976—, neurosci. program chmn., 1990-95; dir. memory disorders clinic S.W. Vt. Med. Ctr., Bennington, 1990—; pres. Clin. Neurosci. Rsch. Assocs., 1997—. Bd. dirs. No. Berkshire Mental Health Assn., North Adams, Mass. Author: Scientific Writings, 1985, Memory, 1989, Psychology 4th edit., 1993; contbr. articles to profl. jours. Bd. dirs. W. Mass. Alzheimers Assn., 1992—. Recipient Distinguished Teaching award U. Mass., Amherst, 1975; Rsch. grantee EPA, NIH, NSF, 1978—; Rsch. fellowships NIH, 1979, NSF, 1980. Fellow APA, AAAS, Am. Psychol. Soc.; mem. Soc. for Neuroscience. Home: 130 Forest Rd Williamstown MA 01267-2029 Office: Williams Coll Dept Psychology Williamstown MA 01262

SOLOMON, PETER J. investment banker; b. N.Y.C., Sept. 17, 1938; s. Sidney L. and Jeannette (Rabb) S.; m. Linda Newman, Oct. 20, 1963; children— Joshua, Abigail, Kate BA cum laude, Harvard U., 1960, MBA, 1963. Assoc. Lehman Brothers, N.Y.C., 1963-70, mng. dir., 1971-78; dep. mayor econ. policy and devel. City of N.Y., 1978-80; chmn. Health Hosp. Corp., 1979-80; counselor U.S. Treasury Dept., Washington, 1980; mng. dir., dir. Lehman Bros., N.Y.C., 1981-84; chmn. merger acquisition dept. Shearson Lehman Hutton Inc., 1984-87, vice chmn., 1985-88, chmn. mcht. banking div., 1988; now chmn. Peter J. Solomon Co. Bd. dirs. Culbro Corp., N.Y.C., Edison Bros. Stores Inc., St. Louis, Phillips-Van Heusen, N.Y.C., Century Communications, Inc., New Canaan, Conn., Chief Auto Parts, Inc., Dallas, Munro Muffler/Brake, Inc., Rochester, N.Y. Trustee Fedn. Jewish Philanthropies, N.Y.C., 1970-78, 81— ; overseer Harvard U., Cambridge, Mass., 1982-88. Mem.: Harmonie, Grolier, Harvard (N.Y.C.); Century Country (Purchase, N.Y.). Democrat. Jewish. Avocations: bee-keeping; tennis; fishing; skiing. Office: 31 W 52d St 16th Fl New York NY 10019

SOLOMON, PHYLLIS LINDA, social work educator, researcher; b. Hartford, Conn., Dec. 6, 1945; d. Louis Calvin and Annabell Lee (Nitzberg) S. BA in Sociology, Russell Sage Coll., 1968; MA in Sociology, Case Western Res. U., 1970, PhD in Social Welfare, 1978. Lic. social worker, Pa. Rsch. assoc. Inst. Urban Studies Cleve. State U., 1970-71; program evaluator Cleve. State Hosp., 1971-74; project dir. Ohio Mental Health and Mental Retardation Rsch. Ctr., Cleve., 1974-75; rsch. assoc. Psychiat. Rsch. Found. of Cleve., 1975; project dir. Ohio Mental Health and Mental Retardation Rsch. Ctr., 1977-78; rsch. assoc. dirs. rsch. and mental health planning Fedn. for Community Planning, 1978-88; prof. dept. mental health scis., dir. sect. mental health svcs. and systems research Hahnemann U., Phila., 1988-94; prof. Sch. Social Work U. Pa., 1994—. Secondary appointment Prof. Social Work in Psychiatry U. Pa. Sch. Medicine, 1994—; adj. prof. dept. psychiatry Allegheny U., 1994-97. Author: (with others) Community Services to Discharged Psychiatric Patients,

1984; mem. editl. bd. jour. Brief Treatment and Crisis Intervention, 2001; co-editor: New Developments in Psychiatric Rehabilitation, 1990, Psychiatric Rehabilitation in Practice, 1993; editorial adv. bd. Community Mental Health Jour., 1988—; editl. bd. Jour. Rsch. in Social Work, 1997-2000, Social Work Forum, 1997—, Health and Social Work, 1998-2000, Psychiat. Rehab. Jour., 1999—; contbr. articles to profl. jours.; editl. bd. Mental Health Svcs. Rsch. Jour., 2002-. Trustee Cleve. Rape Crisis Ctr., 1981-84, CIT Mental Health Svcs., Cleve., 1985-88; mem. citizen's adv. bd. Sagamore Hills (Ohio) Children's Psychiat. Hosp., 1984-88. Named Evaluator of the Yr., Ohio Program Evaluators Group, 1987; recipient Ann. award Cuyahoga County Cmty. Mental Health Bd., 1988, Armin Loeb award Internat. Assn. Psychosocial Rehab. Svcs., 1999, Outstanding Non-Psychiatrist award Am. Assn. Cmty. Psychiatrists, 2002. Mem. NASW, Internat. Assn. Psychosocial Rehab. Svcs., Soc. for Social Work and Rsch. (1st place award for pub. article 1997). Jewish. Home: 104 Woodside Rd Apt A108 Haverford PA 19041-1831 Office: U Pa Sch Social Work 3701 Locust Walk Philadelphia PA 19104-6214

SOLOMON, RANDALL ADAM, physician; b. Bay Shore, N.Y., Dec. 24, 1957; MD, SUNY, Buffalo, 1984. Diplomate Am. Bd. Psychiatry. Staff psychiatrist VA Med. Ctr., Northport, N.Y., 1988-89, pvt. practice psychiatry Port Jefferson, 1989-92; staff psychiatrist J.T. Mather Hosp., 1989-96, pvt. practice psychiatry South Setauket, 1992—. Cons. N.Y. State Dept. Social Svcs., Child and Adolescent Psychiatry Unit, Hauppage, N.Y., 1989—; adj. faculty SUNY Stonybrook. Mem. Am. Psychiat. Assn. Office: Randall Solomon MD 3771 Nesconset Hwy Ste 103 South Setauket NY 11720

SOLOMON, RANDALL LEE, lawyer; b. Dayton, Ohio, June 8, 1948; BA summa cum laude, Wright State U., 1970; JD, Case Western Res. U., 1973. Bar: Ohio 1973, U.S. Dist. Ct. (no. dist.) Ohio 1973, U.S. Ct. Appeals (6th cir.) 1973, U.S. Ct. Appeals (fed. cir.) 1988. Ptnr. Baker & Hostetler, Cleve. Speaker in field. Fellow Am. Coll. Trial Lawyers; mem. ABA (mem. litigation, tort and ins. practice sects., mem. toxic and hazardous substances and environ. law coms.), Ohio State Bar Assn., Cleve. Bar Assn. (chair litigation sect. 1991-92), Nat. Inst. Trial Advocacy (mem. nat. session 1978), Def. Rsch. Inst., Anthony J. Celebrezze Inn. of Ct. (master). Office: Baker & Hostetler LLP 3200 Nat City Ctr 1900 E 9th St Ste 3200 Cleveland OH 44114-3475 E-mail: rsolomon@bakerlaw.com.

SOLOMON, RHONDA HOPE, school and educational psychologist; b. L.A., Dec. 1, 1962; d. Jerry and Lynn (Cabin) S. BA in Psychology and Child Devel., Calif. State U., Northridge, 1985, MA in Psychology, 1987; PhD in Psychology, Calif. Grad. Inst., 1994. Lic. ednl. psychologist, Calif. Play therapist, children's counselor family stress program San Fernando Valley Child Guidance Clinic, Van Nuys, Calif., 1981-84; sch. psychologist, cons., presenter L.A. Unified Sch. Dist., 1987—. Pvt. practice ednl. psychology, 1987—. Crisis counselor, helpline worker Haven Hills Shelter for Battered Women, 1983-84. Mem. APA (assoc.), Nat. Assn. Sch. Psychologists, Calif. Assn. Sch. Psychologists (Outstanding Psychologist divsn. IV 2002), Calif. Psychol. Assn., L.A. Assn. Sch. Psychologists (past pres., named Psychologist of Yr. 2001), L.A. County Psychol. Assn., Psi Chi. Home: PO Box 260726 Encino CA 91426-0726 Office: LA Unified Sch Dist Valley Infant/Presch Progrs 6621 Balboa Blvd Van Nuys CA 91406 E-mail: DrRHS@prodigy.net.

SOLOMON, RICHARD HARVEY, political scientist; b. Phila., June 19, 1937; s. Bertram Harvey and Ellen (Harris) S.; m. Anne G. Keatley, Dec. 16, 1991. Student, Harvard U., 1959-63, Yale U., 1961, 63-64; SB, MIT, 1960, PhD, 1966. Tech. photographer, lab. worker Photon, Inc., Cambridge, Mass., 1957; rschr. Polaroid Corp., 1959-61; rsch. assoc. Ctr. for Chinese Studies U. Mich., Ann Arbor, Mich., 1966-71, from asst prof. to prof. polit. sci., 1966-71; staff mem. NSC, Washington, 1971-76; head. polit. sci dept. The Rand Corp., Santa Monica, Calif., 1976-86, program dir. Internat. Security Policy Research, 1977-83; mem. Pres.' Commn. on Fgn. Lang. and Internat. Studies Washington, 1978-80; mem. Chief of Naval Ops. exec. panel, 1983—; dir. policy planning staff Dept. of State, 1986-89, asst. sec. of state for East Asian and Pacific affairs, 1989-92; U.S. ambassador to Philippines, 1992-93; pres. U.S. Inst. of Peace, Washington, 1993—. Author: Mao's Revolution and the Chinese Political Culture, 1999, Chinese Political Negotiating Behavior, 1999; contbr. articles to profl. jours. Office: US Inst of Peace 1200 17th St NW Ste 200 Washington DC 20036-3011

SOLOMON, RISA GREENBERG, clinical social worker, child and family therapist, former entertainment industry executive; b. N.Y.C., June 22, 1948; d. Nathan and Frances (Guttman) Greenberg; m. Philip Howard Solomon, June 21, 1970 (dec. 1994); children: Elycia Beth, Cynthia Gayle. BA, NYU, 1969, MA, 1970, MSSW, 1996. Asst. editor Redbook Mag., N.Y.C., 1969-70; assoc. editor Greenwood Press, Westport, Conn., 1970-71; mng. editor Dushkin Pub., Guilford, 1971-72; freelance editor Yale U. Press, New Haven, 1972-75; v.p. ops. Videoland, Inc., Dallas, 1980-82; v.p. Video Software Dealers Assn., Cherry Hill, N.J. and Dallas, 1981-83; pres. Videodome Enterprises, Dallas, 1983-94; clin. social worker, child and family therapist pvt. practice, 1994—. Cons. Home Rec. Rights Coalition, Washington, 1983—84; spkr. in field of child and adolescent therapy. Bd. dirs. Congregation Anshai Emet, Dallas, 1985-86. Mem. Video Software Dealers Assn. (founder, dir. 1981-82). Democrat. Jewish. Avocations: water and snow skiing, world travel, tennis, scuba diving.

SOLOMON, ROBERT, economist; b. N.Y.C., May 2, 1921; s. Sol and Betty (Brownstone) S.; m. Fern Rice, Sept. 11, 1946; children: Carol Ann, Barbara Betty, Anne Eleanor. BA, U. Mich., 1942; MA, Harvard U., 1947, PhD, 1952. With Fed. Res. Bd., 1947-76, assoc. adviser research div., 1963-65, adviser research div., 1965, adviser to bd. govs., 1965-76, dir. div. internat. fin., 1966-72; sr. fellow Brookings Instn., Washington, 1976-80, guest scholar, 1980—. Pres. RS Assos., pub. Internat. Econ. Letter, 1981— ; vice chmn. deps. of com. of 20 IMF, 1972-74; adj. prof. Am. U., 1962-67; sr. staff economist Council Econ. Advisers, 1963-64 Author: The International Monetary System, 1945-81, 1982, Partners in Prosperity, 1991, Money on the Move, 1999, The Transformation of the World Economy, 1999; contbr. articles to profl. jours. Served to 1st lt. USAAF, 1942-45. Decorated D.F.C., Air medal, officier Legion of Honor France; recipient Rockefeller Pub. Service award, 1971 Mem. Am. Econ. Assn., Council on Fgn. Relations. Clubs: Cosmos (Washington). Home and Office: 8502 W Howell Rd Bethesda MD 20817-6827 E-mail: Rsolo52178@aol.com.

SOLOMON, ROBERT CHARLES, philosopher, educator; b. Detroit, Sept. 14, 1942; s. Charles M. and Vita (Petrosky) S. BA, U. Pa., 1963; MA, U. Mich., 1965, PhD, 1967. Teaching fellow U. Mich., Ann Arbor, 1965-66; lectr. Princeton (N.J.) U., 1966-67, 67-68; asst. prof. U. Pitts., 1969-71, CUNY, 1971-72; assoc. prof. philosophy U. Tex., Austin, 1972-77, prof., 1977—, Quincy Lee Centennial prof., 1986-97, disting. tchg. prof., 1997—. Vis. prof. U. Pa., UCLA, U. Auckland, N.Z., La Trobe U., Melbourne, Australia, U. B.C.; chmn. Phi Beta Kappa Emerson Award Com.; cons. in field. Author: From Rationalism to Existentialism, 1972, The Passions, 1976, Introducing Philosophy: Problems and Perspectives, 1977, History and Human Nature: A Philosophical Review of European History and Culture, 1750-1850, 1979, Love: Emotion, Myth and Metaphor, 1981, In the Spirit of Hegel, 1983, (with C. Calhoun) What Is an Emotion?, 1984, It's a Good Business, 1985, (with Kristine Hanson) Above the Bottom Line, 1983, From Hegel to Existentialism, 1987, Continental Philosophy After 1750, 1988, About Love, 1988, A Passion for Justice, 1990, Ethics: A Briefer Introduction, 1991, Ethics and Excellence, 1992, Entertaining Ideas, 1992, (with J. Solomon) Up the University, 1993, (with Kathleen Higgins) A Short History of Philosophy, 1996, A Passion for Wisdom, 1997, A Better Way to Think About Business, 1999, The Joy of Philosophy, 1999, (with Kathleen Higgins) What Nietzsche Really Said, 2000, (with Fernando Flores) Building Trust Spirituality for the Skeptic, 2002, Not Passions Slave, 2002; editor: Phenomenology and Existentialism, 1972, Nietzsche, 1973, Existentialism, 1974, (with Kathleen Higgins) Reading Nietzsche, 1988, From Africa to Zen, 1993, The Age of German Idealism, 1993, (with Mark A. Murphy) What Is Justice?, 1990, Wicked Pleasures: Meditations on the Seven Deadly Sins, 1999, The Joy of Philosophy, 2000, Spirituality for the Skeptic, 2002, Not Passion's Slave, 2002; contbr. articles to profl. jours. Recipient Outstanding Tchr. award Standard Oil Co., 1973, Pres.' Teaching Excellence award, 1985, 96., Chad Oliver Honors Tchg. award, 1998; named to Acad. Disting. Tchrs., 1997. Mem. Am. Philos. Assn., N.Am. Nietzsche Soc. (exec. bd.), Internat. Soc. Rsch. on Emotions (bd. dirs.), Soc. for Bus. Ethics (pres.), Acad. Disting. Tchrs.

SOLOMON, ROBERT DOUGLAS, pathology educator; b. Delavan, Wis., Aug. 28, 1917; s. Lewis Jacob and Sara (Ludgin) S.; m. Helen Fisher, Apr. 4, 1943; children: Susan, Wendy, James, William. Student, MIT, 1934-36; BS in Biochemistry, U. Chgo., 1938; MD, Johns Hopkins U., 1942. Intern John's Hopkins Hosp., 1942-43; resident in pathology Michael Reese Hosp., 1947-49; lectr. U. Ill., Chgo., 1947-50, fellow NIH pathology, 1949-50; asst. prof. U. Md., Balt., 1955-60; assoc. prof. U. So. Calif., L.A., 1960-70; chief of staff City of Hope Nat. Med. Ctr., 1966-67; prof. U. Mo., Kansas City, 1977-78, SUNY, Syracuse, 1968-78; chief of staff The Hosp., Sidney, N.Y., 1985-86; adj. prof. biology U. N.C., Wilmington, 1989—. Cons. VA Hosp., Balt., 1955-60, Med. Svc. Lab., Wilmington, 1989-93; active in field of bariatrics, 1997—. Co-author: Progress in Gerontological Research, 1967; contbr. papers and profl. jours. and rsch. in biochemistry, revascular of heart, carcinogenesis, cancer chemotherapy, atherogenesis, discovery of reversibility of atherosclerosis, chemistry of urochrome pigments. V.p. Rotary, Duarte, Calif., 1967; v.p. and pres. Force for an Informed Electorate. Capt. Med. Corps, AUS, 1943-46, PTO. Grantee NIH, Fleischmann Found., Am. Heart Assn., Nat. Cancer Inst., 1958-70. Fellow ACP (pres. Md. chpt.), Western Geriatrics Soc. (founding); mem. Coll. Am. Pathologists (past pres. Md. chpt.), Am. Soc. Clin. Pathologists, Assn. Clin. Scientists, Am. Chem. Soc., Royal Soc. Medicine (London), Phi Beta Kappa, Sigma Xi. Achievements include development of fiber-optic arterial catheter for visualization and making movies of aortic endothelium in vivo. Avocations: cruising, astronomy, mathematics, fishing, stamps. Home: 113 S Belvedere Dr Hampstead NC 28443-2504 E-mail: Rdsolomon@aol.com.

SOLOMON, ROBERT H. lawyer; b. Bklyn., Aug. 23, 1958; s. Murray and Mildred (Teger) S.; m. Felicia Irene Smith, June 30, 1985; children: Zachary, Alexander. BS in Econ cum laude, U. Pa., 1979; JD, Duke U., 1982. Bar: N.Y. 1983, U.S. Supreme Ct., U.S. Ct. Internat. Trade, U.S. Dist. Ct. (ea. & so. dists.) N.Y. Assoc. LeBeouf Lamb Leiby & MacRae, N.Y.C., 1982-84, Wofsey Certilman Haft et al, N.Y.C., 1984-87, Zimmer Victor Schwartz et al, N.Y.C., 1987-89; prin. Robert H. Solomon P.C., Long Beach, 1989—. Arbitrator N.Y. Dist. Ct., Hempstead, 1989—. Trustee Long Beach Bdn. Edn., 1995, Long Beach Med. Ctr.; pres. Lido Home Civic Assn. David Siegal scholar Duke U., 1980-82, Regents scholar, 1980. Mem. ABA, N.Y. State Bar Assn., Bar Assn. of N.Y.C., Nassau County Bar Assn., Long Beach Lawyers Assn. (pres. 1995-2000), Wharton Club. Avocation: tennis. Office: 24 E Park Ave Long Beach NY 11561-3504 E-mail: Pennduke@aol.com.

SOLOMON, ROBERT S. psychologist; b. Montgomery, Ala., July 25, 1954; s. Seymour and Ethel Solomon; m. Vicki L. Solomon; children: Ryan, Kevin. BA in Psychology, Wayne State U., 1975; MA in Psychology, Pepperdine U., 1977; PhD in Psychology, Calif. Grad. Inst., 1981. Contbr. articles to profl. jours. Mem.: Orange County Psychol. Assn., Inland Psychol. Assn. (Leadership award 1991), Calif. Psychol. Assn., APA. Avocation: running. Office: # 207 802 Magnolia Ave Corona CA 92879

SOLOMON, RODNEY JEFF, lawyer; b. Hamilton, Ohio, Apr. 14, 1949; s. Julius Franklin and Justine Paula (Rodney) S.; m. Nancy Griesemer, Oct. 17, 1976; children: Julia, Justin. BA, Amherst Coll., 1971; MPA, Harvard U., 1976, JD, 1979. Bar: Mass. 1979, D.C. 1979, U.S. Dist. Ct. Mass. 1988. Legis. asst. Office of sen. Robert Taft Jr., Washington, 1971-76; legal asst. Cambridge-Somerville Legal Svcs., Cambridge, Mass., 1977-78; cons. Mayor's Office Cmty. Devel., Chelsea, 1977-78; assoc. Caplar & Bok, Boston, 1978; spl. counsel Mass. Housing Fin. Agy., 1979-80; acting asst. adminstr. planning and redevel. Boston Housing Authority, 1980-81, spl. counsel to receiver, dir. spl. projects, 1980-83, from acting gen. counsel to gen. counsel, 1983-92; from dep. exec. dir. to acting exec. dir. Housing Authority City of Atlanta, 1992-94; dir. spl. actions Office Pub. and Indian Housing/U.S. Dept. HUD, Washingon, 1994-96, sr. dir. policy and legislation, 1996-99; dep. asst. sec. for policy, program and legis. initiatives U.S. Dept. HUD, 1999—. Mem. staff distressed properties com. Coun. Large Pub. Housing Authorities, Washington, 1990-94; mem. Housing Working Group, Pres.'s Commn. on Model State Drug Laws, 1992. Author reports, legislation in field. Bd. dirs. Midnight Basketball League of Atlanta, Inc., 1992-96. Recipient Friend of Coun. of Large Pub. Housing Authorities award (nat. legis.), 1991, Proclamation by Mayor of City of Boston of "Rod Solomon Day", June 18, 1992; citations for svc. to Boston's Pub. Housing Residents, Mass. Senate and Ho. of Reps., 1992; recognition of assistance provided on Housing and Community Devel. Act of 1992, U.S. Senate Banking, Housing and Urban Affairs Com., 1992, Coun. of Large Pub. Housing Authorities, 1999, others. Mem. Mass. Bar Assn., D.C. Bar. Office: US Dept Housing Urban Devel 451 7th St SW Washington DC 20410-0001

SOLOMON, SAMUEL, biochemistry educator, administrator; b. Brest Litovsk, Poland, Dec. 5, 1925; s. Nathan and Rachel (Greenberg) S.; m. Sheila R. Horn, Aug. 11, 1953 (div. 1974); children: David Horn, Peter Horn, Jonathan Simon; m. Augusta M. Vineberg, July 12, 1974. BS with honors, McGill U., 1947, MS, 1951, PhD in Biochemistry, 1953. Rsch. asst. Columbia U., 1953-55, assoc. in biochemistry, 1958-59, asst. prof., 1959-60; assoc. prof. biochemistry and exptl. medicine McGill U., 1960-66, prof., 1967-95, prof. emeritus, 1995—, prof. ob-gyn., 1976-95; dir. endocrine lab. Royal Victoria Hosp., Montreal, Que., 1965-95, dir. research inst., 1982-85; affilate dept. pharmacology U. Sherbrooke, 1995—. Mem. endocrinology and metabolism grants com. Med. Rsch. Coun. Can., 1967-71, regional dir. for Que., 1993-95; vis. prof. endocrinology U. Vt., 1964; cons. in field; Joseph Price orator, 1982, Am. OB-GYN Soc.; mem. steering com. Pharm. Mfg. Assn. Med. Rsch. Coun. Can. Partnership, 1993—; Med. Rsch. Coun. Can. dir. for McGill U., 1993-95. Co-editor: Chemical and Biological Aspects of Steroid Conugation, 1970; mem. editl. bd. Endocrinology, 1962; assoc. editor Can. Jour. Biochemistry, 1967-71, Jour. Med. Primatology, 1971; contbr. articles to profl. jours. Mem. bd. govs. McGill U., 1975-78; mem. steering com. European Study Group on Steroid Hormones, 1974-99, chmn. steering com., 1983-99, chmn. program com., 1990-91; mem. Dubin Commn. on Inquiry Drugs in Athletes, 1988-90. Decorated officer Order of Can. 1997; recipient McLaughlin medal Royal Soc. Can., 1989, Michel Sarrazin prize, 1997. Fellow Chem. Inst. Can., Am. Ob-Gyn. Soc. (hon.), Perinatal Rsch. Soc. Am. (pres. 1976), Soc. Gynecol. Investigation (program chmn. 1980), Endocrine Soc. (publ. com. 1986-89). Home: 239 Kensington Ave 804 Montreal QC Canada H3Z 2H1 Office: Royal Victoria Hosp M315 687 Pine Ave W Montreal QC Canada H3A 1A1 E-mail: samuel.solomon@mcgill.ca., samuel.solomon@muhc.mcgill.ca.

SOLOMON, SEAN CARL, geophysicist, lab administrator; b. L.A., Oct. 24, 1945; BS geophysics, Calif. Inst. Tech., 1966; PhD geophysics, MIT, 1971. From asst. prof. to prof. geophysics MIT, Cambridge, 1972-92; dir. dept. terrestrial magnetism Carnegie Instn. Washington, 1992—. Vis. scientist Lunar Sci. Inst., 1975, Lawrence Livermore Nat. Lab., 1978, Jet Propulsion Lab., 1990—91; guest investigator Woods Hole Oceanographic Inst., 1979—92; vis. faculty Inst. Geophysics and Planetary Physics, dept. earth and space scis. UCLA, 1982—83; Roland and Jane Blumberg vis. prof. planetary scis. U. Tex., Austin, 1988; vis. assoc. divsn. geol. and planetary scis. Calif. Inst. Tech., 1990—91; mem. various groups, teams, coms. NASA, 1974—; earthquake hazards reduction program peer rev. panel U.S. Geol. Survey, 1975, 85; lunar and planetary sci. coun. Univs. Space Rsch. Assn., 1978—80, 1991—93; tech. rev. panel, gephysics rev. panel Dept. Def., 1981—86; chmn. steering com. space sci. working group Assn. Am. Univs., 1987—89; rev. panelist NSF, 1986, 88, 95, 96, 2001; chmn. standing com. global seismic network Inc. Rsch. Instns. Seismology, 1988—90; participant numerous oceanographic expeditions, 1967—88. Editor (assoc. editor): Proceedings of the Lunar and Planetary Sci. Conf., 1976, 1978, Jour. Geophys. Rsch. , 1976—78, Physics Earth and Planetary Interiors, 1977, Eos Transactions of Am. Geophys. Union, 1979—81, Geophys. Rsch. Letters, 1986—88; editor: Tectonophysics, 1981; mem. editl. bd.: Physics and Chemistry of Earth, 1981—85, mem. editl. bd.: Astrobiology, 2001—, mem. editl. bd.: Earth and Planetary Sci. Letters, 2001—, mem. editl. com.: Ann. Rev. Earth and Planetary Scis., 1993—97; contbr. articles to profl. jours. Recipient Arthur L. Day prize, NAS, 1999; fellow Grad., NSF, 1966—68, Postdoctoral, 1971—72, Fannie and John Hertz Found., 1968—71, Alfred P. Sloan Rsch., 1977—81, John Simon Guggenheim Meml., 1982—83. Fellow: AAAS, Geol. Soc. Am. (G.K. Gilbert award 1999), Am. Geophys. Union (pres. elect and pres. 1994—98, pres. planetology sect. 1984—88, chmn. geophys. monograph bd. 1983—84, numerous coms.), Am. Acad. Arts and Scis.; mem.: NAS, European Geophys. Soc., Seismol. Soc. Am., Am. Astron. Soc. (divsn. planetary scis.), Tau Beta Pi. Office: Carnegie Instn Dept Terrestrial Magnetism 5241 Broad Branch Rd NW Washington DC 20015-1305 E-mail: scs@dtm.ciw.edu.

SOLOMON, SOLOMON SIDNEY, endocrinologist, pharmacologist, scientist; b. N.Y.C., Dec. 2, 1936; s. Nathan and Irene (Oransky) S.; m. Linda M. Shaw, June 17, 1962 (div. 1980); children: Joan Geller, Rebecca Karen. AB in Chemistry, Harvard U., 1958; MD, U. Rochester, 1962. Intern in internal medicine New Eng. Med. Ctr., Tufts U., Boston, 1963; resident in internal medicine Boston City Hosp., 1964, 65; fellow in endocrinology and metabolism U. Wash. Sch. Medicine, Seattle, 1965-67; teaching fellow Tufts U. and Boston City Hosp., Boston, 1964-65; asst. prof., assoc. prof. then prof. medicine U. Tenn. Sch. Medicine, Memphis, 1969—, assoc. dean for rsch., 1983-98, prof. pharmacology, 1986—; chief endocrinology and metabolism VA Med. Ctr., 1971—. Cons. in field; mem. merit rev. bd. VA Rsch. Svc., Washington, 1978—81, Washington, 1999—2002. Coeditor: The Lab in Clinical Diagnosis, l98l; contbr. numerous articles and abstracts to profl. jours. Capt. MC, USAF, 1967-69. Harvard Coll. scholar, 1954-58; Whipple scholar, 1959-62; VA and NIH grantee, 1965—. recipient career and devel. award VA Ctrl. Office Rsch. Svc., 1969-71, 1st place for excellence in clin. rsch. Memphis Area Health Industry Couns., 1994. Fellow Am. Coll. Endocrinology; mem. Am. Diabetes Assn. (pres. Tenn. chpt. 1975-76, rsch. com., chmn. metabolism sect. 1982), So. Soc. Clin. Investigation (chmn. metabolism sect. 1975, 88, nominating com. 1989), Endocrine Soc., Am. Fedn. for Clin. Rsch. (counselor south sect. 1976-79), Am. Soc. Clin. Investigation, Cen. Soc. for Clin. Rsch., Am. Soc. Pharmacology and Exptl. Therapy, Fedn. Am. Soc. Exptl. Biology. Jewish. Avocations: antique furniture, history, music, tennis, running. Home: 5196 Longmeadow Dr Memphis TN 38134-4316 Office: VA Med Ctr 1030 Jefferson Ave Memphis TN 38104-2127 E-mail: ssolomon@utmem.edu. *At the risk of being mundane, my philosophy in life has always been to get involved...my motto is "I came to play, not to watch.".*

SOLOMON, SUSAN CAROL, hospital administrator, marketing specialist; b. Glen Cove, N.Y., July 17, 1959; d. Allen L. and Elaine (Miller) S.; m. Joseph M. Ribakoff, Jan. 1, 1989; children: Samuel, Shira. BA, U. Calif., Berkeley, 1981; MA, Calif. State U., Northridge, 1985; MBA, Simmons Coll., 1988. Pub. rels. rep. Hoag Meml. Hosp., Newport Beach, Calif., 1981-83; mktg. mgr. St. Joseph Med. Ctr., Burbank, 1983-87; account exec. Coleman & Christison, Inc., San Francisco, 1988-89; v.p. mktg. St. John's Hosp., Santa Monica, 1990-91; dir mktg. Beverly Hills Med. Ctr., 1992-93; dir. mktg. Las Encinas Hosp., 1993—95, UCI Med. Ctr., 1995—96; v.p. mktg. Meml. Health Svcs., 1996—. Mem. faculty UCI, UCLA. Bd. dirs. Wise Sr. Svcs., Santa Monica, 1991-93. Recipient excellence in editing award Pub. Rels. Soc. Am., 1982, 83, excellence in writing award Internat. Assn. Bus. Communicators, 1985, excellence in feature writing award Women in Communications, 1985. Mem. Women in Health Care Adminstrn., Health Care Pub. Rels. and Mktg., Internat. Assn. Bus. Communicators. Home: 6145 E Pageantry St Long Beach CA 90808-4005 Office: 7677 Center Ave Huntington Beach CA 92647

SOLOMON, WILLIAM TARVER, general construction company executive; b. Dallas, Aug. 11, 1942; s. Marion Bryant and Margaret (Moore) S.; m. Gay Ferguson, Feb. 15, 1964; children— William Tarver Jr., Meredith M. BSCE, So. Meth. U., 1965; MBA, Harvard U., 1967. With Austin Industries, Inc., Dallas, 1967—, chmn., pres., CEO, 1970—; chmn. Austin Comml., Inc., Brit. Am. Ins. Co., Dallas; chmn., CEO Austin Industries, Inc., now chmn. Bd. dirs. A.H. Belo Corp., Nat. Bank Tex. Past chmn. Dallas Citizens Coun. and Greater Dallas C. of C.; bd. dirs. Baylor U. Med. Ctr. Found., Dallas Mus. Art; trustee Southwestern Med. Found., So. Meth. U. Recipient citation of honor Dallas chpt. AIA, 1985, Humanitarian award NCCJ, Dallas, 1982, Champion of Free Enterprise award Associated Builders and Contractors, 1985, Outstanding Alumni award Southern Meth. U., 1988; inductee Tex. Bus. Hall of Fame, 1996. Mem. ASCE, Young Pres.'s Orgn. (past chmn. Dallas chpt.), Dallas Assembly, Salesmanship Club Dallas, Dallas C. of C. (bd. dirs.). Republican. United Methodist Home: 3830 Windsor Ln Dallas TX 75205-1743

SOLOMONOW, MOSHE, biomedical engineer, scientist, educator; b. Tel Aviv, Oct. 24, 1944; came to U.S., 1965; s. Jonathan and Eva (Efraim) S.; m. Susanne Elisbeth Nickerson, May 31, 1981; children: Deborah Leigh, Esther Monique. BSc, Calif. State U., L.A., 1970, MSc, 1972; PhD, UCLA, 1976; MD (hon.), Brussels, 1997. Rsch. engr. UCLA, 1976-80; assoc. prof. La. State U. Med. Ctr., New Orleans, 1980-87, prof., 1987—, dir. bioengring., 1983—; I. Cahen M.D. professor La. State U., 1997; dir. occupational med. Rsch. Ctr. La. State U., 2000—. Assoc. prof. Tulane U., New Orleans, 1980-83; dir. paraplegic clinic Rehab. Inst., New Orleans, 1991—; cons. Nat. Acad. of Scis., 1998, NIH, 1978—, NSF, 1985, VA, 1978—, also others; reviewer 16 sci. jours. Editor-in-chief Jour. EMG and Kinesiology, 1991—; contbr. over 100 articles to sci. jours.; patentee in field. Pres. Lakeshore Day Sch., New Orleans, 1990. Recipient Crump award UCLA, 1977, Mayor's medal City of Rennes, France, 1992, Disting. Merit award Delta 7 Assn., Paris, 1991, Volvo award for low back pain rsch., 1999. Avocation: sailing. Office: Dept Orthopedic Surgery 2025 Gravier St Ste 400 New Orleans LA 70112-2289 E-mail: msolom@lsuhsc.edu.

SOLOMONS, GUS , JR. (GUSTAVE MARTINEZ), choreographer, dancer, writer; b. Boston; s. Gustave Martinez and Olivia Mae. Student, Boston Conservatory of Music, 1956-59; BArch, MIT, 1961; postgrad., Martha Graham Sch., N.Y.C., 1961-66. Dance soloist Martha Graham Co., N.Y.C., 1964-65, Donald McKayle Co., 1961-64, Merce Cunningham Co., N.Y.C., 1965-68; artistic dir. The Solomons Dance Co., 1972—; dean, artistic dir. Calif. Inst. of the Arts, Valencia, 1976-78. Vis. artist-in-residence U. Calif., Santa Cruz, Calif. State U., Long Beach, others; dance panelist Nat. Endowment Arts; various other other state art couns., 1983—; assoc. prof. dance numerous colls., univs., including UCLA, Un. Nev.-Las Vegas, Tex. Christian U., York, Simon Fraser, NYU; mem. faculty Tisch Sch. of Arts, 1994—; USIA cons. to Nat. Dance Co., Tanzania, East Africa, 1988, Argentina, 1994. Appearances maj. TV networks, Sta. WGBH-TV, Boston; choreographr for various univs. and dance cos.; writer dance criticism for Village Voice, Dance Mag., others. Recipient numerous grants Nat. Endowment for Arts, 1983—, N.Y. State Coun. on the Arts, 1972—; fellow Nat. Endowment for Arts, 1978-80; recipient Master Tchr. award NYU/Tisch, 1998, Bessie award for sustained achievement in choreography, 2000, Robert A. Muh award for disting. MIT artist/alumnus, 2001. Studio: 889 Broadway New York NY 10003-1212 E-mail: gus.solomonsjr@nyu.edu. *The content of a good dance is the truth about its maker. Performing it is a confession to the audience. The dancer places himself in the position of ultimate vulnerability each time he performs; it is at once cleansing, fulfilling, and courageous.*

SOLOMONS, MARK ELLIOTT, lawyer, art dealer, entrepreneur; b. Buffalo, Mar. 4, 1946; s. Alvin and Trude (Salant) Solomons; m. Jill E Kent, Aug. 20, 1978. BA, U. Rochester, 1967; JD, U. Pa., 1970; LLM, George Washington U., 1973. Staff atty. U.S. Dept. Labor, Washington, 1970-73, counsel coal miners benefits, 1973-77, legis. counsel, 1977-80; prin. Kilcullen Wilson & Kilcullen, 1980-86; ptnr. Arter and Hadden, 1986-2001, mem. exec. com., 1989-98; shareholder Greenberg Traurig, 2001—. Guest lectr law and hist SUNY, Stony Brook, 1970—76, Univ Mich, 1977—78, Hobart Col, 1972—76; prin Coun for Excellence in Govt, 1991—; co-owner Frogeye Co; chmn Atlantic Threadworks; del Atlantic Treaty Asn Gen Assembly, 2000—. Contbr. articles to profl jours. Trustee, secy China Found, 1997—. Master: Am Inn of Ct (counselor 1996—97); mem.: ABA (chair workers compensation and employers liability comt 1987—88, sr. vice chair 1988—, vice chair appellate advocacy comt), NY Bar Asn, DC Bar Asn, Fed Bar Asn (chair regulatory reform comt 1988—89). Republican. Office: Greenberg Traurig LLP 800 Connecticut Ave NW Washington DC 20006 E-mail: solomonsin@gtlaw.com.

SOLON, DEBORAH EPSTEIN, curator; b. N.Y.C., Apr. 5, 1961; d. Gerson and Lila Epstein; married; children: Alexandra, Gabrielle. BA, Vassar Coll., 1982; MPhil, CUNY, 1990. Adminstr. Sotheby's , N.Y.C., 1982—86; lectr. SUNY, Purchase, 1988—90; dir. rsch. Karge Fine Art, L.A., 1991—96; guest curator Laguna Art Mus., Laguna Beach, 1998—99, adj. curator, 1999—. Acquisitions com., collections com Laguna Art Mus., Laguna Beach, 1999—, hist. collections coun., 2001—. Author: Birds, Boughs and Blossoms, 1995, Cornelis Botke, 1996, Colonies of American Impressionism, 1999, In and Out of California: Travels of American Impressionists, 2002. Avocation: music. Home and Office: 30801 Palmetto Pl Laguna Beach CA 92677 E-mail: deborahsolon@aol.com.

SOLON, LEONARD R(AYMOND), retired physicist, educator, consultant; b. White Plains, N.Y., Sept. 11, 1925; s. Morris and Rebecca (Bobrov) S.; m. Charlotte Rothman, June 30, 1946; children: Miriam Beth Solon Weintraub, Matthew Benjamin, Emily Lynn Solon Bader. *After separation from the army, where he received the Combat Infantryman Badge, Leonard Solon returned to Hamilton College with his wife. Miriam is mother of his two grandchildren, Idan Samuel and Leland Scott. In the first graduating class of Cardozo School of Law, she is an attorney specializing in children's issues. Matthew graduated from Hamilton College and earned a Master of Fine Arts degree from the University of Arizona. He is a prominent artist and his paintings of Vermont structures and Florida wildlife have received important critical notice. Emily attended East Carolina University and Parsons School of Design. She is an active music instructor and cofounder of Musica Dolce, a performance group.* BA, Hamilton Coll., 1947; MSc, Rutgers U., 1949; PhD, NYU, 1960. Cert. Am. Bd. Health Physics. Physicist Nuc. Devel. Assocs., Inc., White Plains, 1950-52; asst. chief, then chief radiation br. AEC, N.Y.C., 1952-60; dir. applied nuc. tech. Tech. Rsch. Group, Inc., Syosset, N.Y., 1960-62; cons. Burns & Roe, N.Y.C., 1962-64, Servo Corp. Am., Hicksville, N.Y., 1962-64; mgr. R&D Del Electronics Corp., Mt. Vernon, 1964-67; founder, exec. v.p., tech. dir. Hadron, Inc., Yonkers, 1967-75; dir. bur. radiation control N.Y.C. Dept. Health, 1975-91; ret., 1991. Lectr., then adj. assoc. prof. N.Y.U. Inst. Environ. Medicine, 1955-93; environ. & radiol. health cons.; prof. health physics U.S. Mcht. Marine Acad., 1963. Contbr.: Dictionary of American Biography, 1995, The Scribner Encyclopedia of American Lives, vol. 1, 2, 3, 4, 5, 1998-2002; contbr. articles to profl. jours. Served with inf. U.S. Army, 1944-46, ETO. Mem. AAAS, Am. Nuc. Soc., Health Physics Soc., Am. Phys. Soc., N.Y. Acad. Scis., Conf. Radiation Control Program Dirs., Radiol. and Med. Physics Soc. N.Y., Phi Beta Kappa, Sigma Xi. Achievements include co-patentee for laser photocauterizer used in treatment of detached retina; powering lasers using nuclear sources. Home and Office: 1756 Lakefront Blvd Fort Pierce FL 34982-8003 E-mail: crsolon@aol.com.

SOLONCHE, JOEL R. English educator, poet; b. N.Y.C., July 16, 1946; s. Abraham and Sally (Karp) S.; m. Joan I. Siegel, Jan. 12, 1992; 1 adopted daughter, Emily Ni Tao. BS, NYU, 1971; MA, SUNY, New Paltz, 1986. Instr., then asst. prof. English Orange County C.C., Middletown, N.Y., 1986—. Contbr. poems to numerous lit. publs., including The Am. Scholar, New Criterion. Office: Orange County CC 115 South St Middletown NY 10940

SOLOSE, JANE MARIE, pianist, educator; b. Niagara Falls, Ont., Can. BMusic, U. Toronto, 1972-76; MM, U. Western Ont., London, Can., 1980; DMA, Eastman Sch. Music, 1990. Instr. Medicine Hat Coll., Brooks, Alta., Can., 1980-84, Brock U., St. Catharines, Ont., Can., 1985-86; grad. asst. Eastman Sch. Music, Rochester, N.Y., 1988-90; from asst. prof. to assoc. prof., coord. keyboard studies U. N.D., Grand Forks, 1990-98; assoc. prof., coord. keyboard studies Bowling Green (Ohio) State U., 1998—. Pianist/lectr., master tchr., concerto soloist, recitalist in Japan, Austria, Can., U.S.; CD rec. Kathleen and Jane Solose, 1994. Named Tchr. of Yr., N.D. Music Tchrs. Assn., 1998. Mem. Music Tchrs. Nat. Assn. (coll. faculty cert., profl. cert.), Ohio State Music Tchrs. Assn. (chair Collegiate Buckeye State Competition), Coll. Music Soc. (campus rep.), Am. Liszt Soc. Office: Bowling Green State U Coll Mus Arts Bowling Green OH 43403-0001

SOLOV, ZACHARY, choreographer, ballet artist; b. Phila., Feb. 15, 1923; s. Carl Nathan and Sima (Silnutzer) S. Student, Littlefield Ballet Sch., 1937-40, U. of the Dance, 1947. Appeared with, Am. Jubilee, N.Y. World's Fair, 1940, tour with, Littlefield Ballet, 1941, Am. Ballet, S.A., 1941; with, Dance Players, summer quarters, New Hope, Pa., 1942, The Lady Comes Across, N.Y. City, 1942, Ballet Theatre, London, 1946; choreographer ballet master, Met. Opera, N.Y. City. Served as staff sgt. A.A.C., 1943-46. Recipient Capezio Dance award, 1952. Office: 200 W 58th St New York NY 10019-1432

SOLOVAY, MARK LIONEL, cardiologist, educator; b. N.Y.C., June 21, 1942; s. Benjamin and Irene (Lerner) S.; m. Alice Faye Rosenbluth, July 4, 1965 (div. Oct. 1994); children: Sondra, Matthew. BA with honors, Clark U., 1963; MD, SUNY, N.Y.C., 1967. Diplomate Am. Bd. Internal Medicine with subspecialty in cardiovascular disease and critical care medicine, 1989. Intern and asst. resident USPHS Hosp., S.I., NY, 1967-69; assoc. resident Bellevue Hosp., N.Y.C., 1970-71; cardiology resident Mt. Sinai Hosp. and Sch. of Medicine, 1972-73; sr. cardiology fellow U. Miami, 1974; pvt. practice Hollywood, Fla., 1974-78, Yuma, Ariz., 1978-85; cardiologist, pres. Yuma Multispecialty Med. Group, 1985-89; pvt. practice Yuma, 1989-94; cardiologist, group dir. Yuma Heart Inst., 1995—; clin. faculty U. Calif.-San Diego Med. Ctr., 1980—; dir. EECP Heart Ctr., Yuma, 2000—; pres. Heart and Lung Vascular Ctr. of Yuma, 2002—. Bd. govs. Yuma Regional Med. Ctr., 1988, 89, 97, 98; chief of staff YRMC, 1988, co-chief 1997, 98. Contbr. articles to profl. jours. Founding v.p./pres. Am. Heart Assn., Yuma, 1986-90. Lt. comdr. USPHS, 1967-70. Fellow Am. Coll. Cardiology (coun. mem., adv. com. 1986-89). Office: Yuma Heart Inst 1773 W 24th St Ste B Yuma AZ 85364-6230 E-mail: yumaheart@yahoo.com.

SOLOVY, JEROLD SHERWIN, lawyer; b. Chgo., Apr. 10, 1930; s. David and Ida (Wilensky) S.; m. Kathleen Hart; children: Stephen, Jonathan. BA, U. Mich., 1952; LLB, Harvard U., 1955. Bar: Ill. 1955. Assoc. Jenner & Block, Chgo., 1955-63, ptnr., 1963—, chmn., 1991—. Chmn. Spl. Commn. on Adminstrn. Justice in Cook County, 1984-91, Ill. Supreme Ct. Spl. Commn. on Adminstrn. of Justice, 1992-93, Criminal Justice Project of Cook County, 1987-91. Mem. Cook County Jud. Adv. Council, Chgo., 1975-77, 82-89, chmn., 1989-91; trustee U.S. Supreme Ct. Hist. Soc., 1993—. Fellow Am. Coll. Trial Lawyers; mem. ABA, Chgo. Bar Assn., Ill. State Bar Assn., Am. Law Inst. Clubs: Standard; Lake Shore Country (Chgo.). Office: Jenner & Block 1 E IBM Plz Ste 4400 Chicago IL 60611-5698 E-mail: jsolovy@jenner.com.

SOLOW, ROBERT MERTON, economist, educator; b. Bklyn., Aug. 23, 1924; s. Milton Henry and Hannah Gertrude (Sarney) Solow; m. Barbara Lewis, Aug. 19, 1945; children: John Lewis, Andrew Robert, Katherine. BA, Harvard U., 1947, MA, 1949, PhD, 1951, DLitt (hon.) , 1976; LLD (hon.) , U. Chgo., 1967; LLD (hon.) , Brown U., 1972, U. Warwick, 1976, Tulane U., 1983, Dartmouth Coll., 1990; DLitt (hon.) , Williams Coll., 1974, Lehigh U., 1977, Wesleyan U., 1982; DLitt (hon.) , Boston Coll., 1986; DLitt (hon.) , Harvard U., 1992, Colgate U., 1990; DSc (hon.) , U. Paris, 1975; DSc (hon.) , U. Geneva, 1982; DSc (hon.) , Bryant Coll., 1988; D of Social Sci. (hon.) , Yale U., 1976, U. Mass., Boston, 1989; D Social Sci. (hon.) , U. Helsinki, 1990, SUNY, Albany, 1991, U. Glasgow, 1992, Rutgers U., 1994; D honoris causa (hon.) , U. Chile, 1992; Conservatoire, Nat. des Arts et Mètiers, Paris, 1994; D in Engring., Colo. Sch. Mines, 1996; postgrad, U. Buenos Aires, 1999; D Lit. Humanities, New York U., 2000. Mem. faculty MIT, 1949—95, prof. econs., 1958—95, inst. prof., 1973—95, prof. emeritus, 1995—; W. Edwards Deming prof. NYU, 1996—97. Sr. economist Coun. Econ. Advisers, 1961—62, cons., 1962—68, RAND Corp., 1952—64; Marshall lectr., fellow commoner Peterhouse Cambridge (Eng.) U., 1963—64; Eastman vis. prof. Oxford U., 1968—69; overseas fellow Churchill Coll., Cambridge; sr. fellow Soc. Fellows, Harvard U., 1975—89; bd. dirs. Boston Fed. Res. Bank, 1975—80, chmn., 1979—80; active President's Commn. on Income Maintenance, 1968—70, President's Com. on Tech., Automation and Econ. Progress, 1964—65, Carnegie Commn. Sci., Tech. and Govts., 1988—93, Nat. Sci. Bd., 1994—2000. Author: Linear Programming and Economic Analysis, 1958; author: (with R. Dortman, P. Samuelson) Capital Theory and the Rate of Return, 1963; author: The Sources of Unemployment in the United States, 1964, Growth Theory, 1970, Price Expectations and the Behavior of the Price Level, 1970; author: (with M. Dertouzos, R. Lester) Made in America, 1989; author: The Labor Market as a Social Institution, 1990; author: (with F. Hahn) A Critical Essay on Modern Macroeconomic Theory, 1995; author: Learning from "Learning by Doing", 1997; author: (with J. Taylor) Inflation, Unemployment and Monetary Policy, 1998; author: Monopolistic Competition and Macroeconomic Theory, 1998, Work and Welfare, 1998; editor (with Alan Krueger): The Roaring Nineties, 2002. Bd. dirs., mem. exec. com. Nat. Bur. Econ. Rsch.; trustee Inst. for Advanced Study, Princeton U., 1972—78, Woods Hole Oceanographic Inst., 1988—, Alfred P. Sloan Found., 1992—, Resources for the Future, 1994—, Urban Inst., 1994—, German Marshall Fund of U.S., 1994—. With U.S. Army, 1942—45. Recipient David A. Wells prize, Harvard U., 1951, Seidman award in polit. economy, 1983, Nobel prize in Econs., 1987, Nat. Medal of Sci., 2000, trustee, Ctr. Advanced Study Behavioral Scis., 1982—95, chmn., 1987—95; fellow, 1957—58, Russell Sage Found., 2000—. Fellow: Am. Acad. Arts and Scis., Brit. Acad. (corr.); mem.: NAS (coun. 1977—80, 1995), AAAS (v.p. 1970), Internat. Econ. Assn. (pres. 1999—), Econometric Soc. (pres. 1964, mem. exec. com.), Am. Econ. Soc. (exec. com. 1964—66, v.p. 1968, pres. 1979, John Bates Clark medal 1961), Royal Irish Acad. (hon.), Order Pour le Merite (Germany), Acad. dei Lincei, Am. Philos. Soc. Home: 528 Lewis Wharf Boston MA 02110-3920 Office: MIT Dept Econs Cambridge MA 02139

SOLOWAY, ALBERT HERMAN, medicinal chemist; b. Worcester, Mass., May 29, 1925; s. Bernard and Mollie (Raphaelson) S.; m. Barbara Berkowicz, Nov. 29, 1953; children: Madeleine Rae, Paul Daniel, Renee Ellen. Student, U.S. Naval Acad., 1945-46; BS, Worcester Poly. Inst., 1948; PhD, U. Rochester, 1951. Postdoctoral fellow Nat. Cancer Inst. at Sloan-Kettering Inst., N.Y.C., 1951-53; research chemist Eastman Kodak Co., Rochester, N.Y., 1953-56; asst. chemist Mass. Gen. Hosp., Boston, 1956-61, asso. chemist, 1961-73; asso. prof. med. chemistry Northeastern U., 1966-68, prof. medicinal chemistry, chmn. dept., 1968-71, prof. medicinal chemistry and chemistry, chmn. dept. medicinal chemistry and pharmacology, 1971-74; dean Coll. Pharmacy and Allied Health Professions, 1975-77; dean Coll. Pharmacy Ohio State U., Columbus, 1977-88, prof. medicinal chemistry, 1977-98, Kimberly prof. pharmacy, 1997-2000, dean, prof. emeritus, 1998—. Author rsch. in medicinal chemistry, boron neutron capture therapy of cancer. Recipient Disting. Achievements in Boron Sci. award Boron USA, 1994. Fellow AAAS, Acad. Pharm. Soc.; mem. AHS, Am. Chem. Soc., Am. Assn. Coll. Pharmacy, Am. Assn. Cancer Rsch. Office: Ohio State U 500 W 12th Ave Columbus OH 43210-1214 E-mail: soloway.1@osu.edu.

SOLOWAY, DANIEL MARK, lawyer; b. Buffalo, Jan. 21, 1959; s. Sol Murray and Shirley (Prashker) S.; m. Natalie Ann-Marie Chin, June 10, 1989; children: Rachel Ann, Rebecca Leigh. BA cum laude, SUNY, Buffalo, 1982; JD with honors, Fla. State U., 1985. Bar: Fla. 1985, U.S. Dist. Ct. (no. dist.) Fla. 1985, (mid. dist.) Fla. 1995, (so. dist.) Ala. 1986, U.S. Ct. Appeals (11th cir.) 1985, U.S. Supreme Ct. 1989; bd. cert. in civil trial law, Fla.; cert. Nat. Bd. Trial Advocacy, 1998, civil ct. mediator, 2000. Law clk. Circuit Judge, Tallahassee, 1983-84, Douglass, Davey, Cooper & Coppins, Tallahassee, 1984-85; ptnr. McKenzie & Soloway, Pensacola, Fla., 1985-98; pvt. practice Daniel M. Soloway, P.A., 1998—. Author: Criminal Justice: An Analysis Toward Reform, 1981; contbr. articles to profl. jours.; editor Escambia-Santa Rosa Bar Assn. newsletter, 1989-90, Dry Shoes, Fla. Bar Jour., 1992. Profl. adv. bd. N.W. Fla. Epilepsy Soc., Pensacola, 1989—; speaker on AIDS, State of Fla. Dept. HRS, 1988—; active Escambia County Human Rels. Commn., 1996-98. Recipient Pro Bono Svc. award Escambia-Santa Rosa Bar, 1989-90, Pro Bono Svc. Pres.'s award Fla. Bar, 1990. Mem. Million Dollar Advocates Forum (diplomat), ABA, Assn. Trial Lawyers Am., Escambia-Santa Rosa Bar Assn. (editor newsletter 1989-90), Acad. Fla. Trial Lawyers (speaker 1993—), Nat. Orgn. Social Security Claimants Reps.. Democrat. Jewish. Avocation: writing. Office: 901 Scenic Hwy Pensacola FL 32503-6866

SOLOWAY, JAY STEPHEN, consulting firm executive; b. Bklyn., Mar. 19, 1956; s. Martin and Joan (Jacobs) S. BA, Columbia U., 1978; MBA, U. Pa., 1980. Buyer Abraham & Straus, Bklyn., 1980-84; divsn. mgr. May Co. Dept. Stores, L.A., 1985; mgr. tng. and devel. Hartmarx Specialty Stores, Western U.S., 1986-90; mgr. mgmt. devel. Thrifty Drug Stores, L.A., 1990-92; cons. DBM, 1992—96; area ops. dir. So. Calif. and Ariz. Drake Beam Morin, Pasadena, Calif., 1996-2000, dir. core svcs., 2000—. Democrat. Jewish. Office: Drake Beam Morin 35 N Lake Ave Pasadena CA 91101-4110

SOLOWAY, ROSE ANN GOULD, clinical toxicologist; b. Plainfield, N.J., Apr. 19, 1949; d. George Spencer Jr. and Rose Emma (Frank) Gould; m. Irving H. Soloway, Dec. 13, 1979. BSN, Villanova U., 1971; MS in Edn., U. Pa., 1976. Diplomate Am. Bd. Applied Toxicology. Staff nurse Hosp. of U. Pa., Phila., 1971-73; asst. clin. instr. Hosp. of U. Pa. Sch. Nursing, 1973-77; staff devel. instr. Hosp. of Med. Coll. Pa., 1977-78; dir. emergency nurse tng. program Ctr. for Study of Emergency Health Svcs., U. Pa., 1979-80; edn./comms. coord. Nat. Capital Poison Ctr. Georgetown U. Hosp., Washington, 1980-94; clin. toxicologist Nat. Capital Poison Ctr. George Washington U. Med. Ctr., 1994—; adminstr. Am. Assn. Poison Control Ctrs., 1994-99, assoc. dir., 1999—. Mem. clin. toxicology and substance abuse adv. panel U.S. Pharmacopeial Conv., Inc., Washington, 1990—2000, mem. expert panel clin. toxicology and substance abuse, 2000—. Contbr. articles to profl. jours. Mem. APHA, Am. Assn. Poison Control Ctrs. (co-chmn. pub. edn. com. 1985-90), Am. Acad. Clin. Toxicology (mem. edn. com. 2000—), Poison Prevention Week Coun. (vice-chair 1988-91, chair 1991-93, vice-chair 2001—). Avocations: reading, cooking, knitting, jewelry making. Office: Am Assn Poison Control Ctrs 3201 New Mexico Ave NW Ste 310 Washington DC 20016-2756

SOLSO, ROBERT L. psychology educator; b. Sioux City, Iowa, June 22, 1933; s. F.I. and Elizabeth (Pressly) S.; children: Anne, Laird, Robert. BA, Hastings Coll., 1957; MA, U. Nebr., 1959; PhD, St. Louis U., 1967. Prof., dept. chmn. Moorhead (Minn.) State U., 1957-68; prof. Loyola U., Chgo., 1968-74; postdoctoral rschr. Stanford (Calif.) U., 1974-75; prof., chmn. U. Idaho, Moscow, 1975-81; prof., chmn. dept. psychology U. Nev., Reno, 1982—. Vis. prof. Stanford (Calif.) U., 1975-81, Oxford (Eng.) U., 1980, Moscow State U., 1980-81; world lectr. tours, 1981, 97. Author: Cognition and the Visual Arts, 1996, Cognitive Psychology, 2001; editor: The Science of the Mind, 1995, Mind and Brain Sciences, 1997, Show, The Nat. Portrait Gallery, London, 1999. Bd. dirs. Nev. Opera Bd., Reno, 1986-92. Mem. Western Psychol. Assn. (pres. 1997, dir. Pan Pacific program 2000). Office: U Nev Dept Psychol Reno NV 89557-0001

SOLSO, THEODORE M. manufacturing executive; m. Denny; 3 children. BA, DePauw U., 1969; MBA, Harvard U., 1971. Asst. to v.p. personnel Cummins Engine Co., Inc., Columbus, Ind., 1971, exec. dir. personnel, 1977-80, v.p. spl. engine markets, 1984-86, v.p. mktg., 1986-88, v.p., gen. mgr. engine bus., 1988-92, exec. v.p. opers., 1992-95, COO, 1994-00, pres., 1995-00, chmn., CEO, 1999—; dir. adminstrn. CAEMI Cummins., Brazil; v.p., mng. dir. Holset Engring. Co., Ltd. (Cummins' U.K. subs.), 1980-84. Bd. dirs. Ashland, Inc., Cyprus Amax Minerals, Inc. Bd. trustees DePauw U.; bd. advisors U. Mich. Sch. Bus.; past bd. dirs. Heritage Fund Bartholomew County, Ind.; chmn. campaign Bartholomew County United Way; bd. dirs. Otter Creek Golf Course, Columbus, Ind. Mem. Mfrs. Alliance (bd. trustees). Office: Cummins Engine Co Inc 500 Jackson St Columbus OH 43206-1353*

SOLT, ROBERT LEE, JR. retired surgeon; b. Bucyrus, Ohio, Dec. 28, 1931; s. Robert Lee and Grace Velma (Rinehart) S.; m. Marilyn J. Smith, June 11, 1955; children: Robert L. III, Timothy S. BS, Ohio State U., 1953, MD, 1957. Diplomate Am. Bd. Surgery. Intern White Cross Hosp., Columbus, Ohio, 1957-58; resident White Cross Hosp. (name now Riverside Meth. Hosp.), 1958-62; pvt. practice Bucyrus, 1962—96. Contbr. articles to profl. jours. Fellow ACS, Am. Acad. of Disability Evaluating Physicians; mem. Ohio State Med. Assn., AMA. Home and Office: 1401 Home Circle Dr Bucyrus OH 44820-3441

SOLTER, MILJENKO, endocrinologist, educator; b. Zagreb, Croatia, Aug. 23, 1947; s. Nevenka Solter; m. Vesna Vargek, Nov. 20, 1976; children: Darko, Ana. MD, Med. Faculty, Zagreb, 1972, PhD, 1982. Resident Sisters of Mercy Hosp., Zagreb, 1974-78; lectr. Med. Faculty, 1978-85, asst. prof., 1985-89, assoc. prof. internal medicine, 1989—. Contbr. articles to Am. Jour. Clin. Nutrition, Hormone Rsch., Hormone Metabolic Rsch., Jour. Clin. Endocrinology Metabolism, others. Roman Catholic. Avocations: do-it-yourself, fishing, cruising. Home: Radnicki Dol 25 HR-10000 Zagreb Croatia Office: Sisters of Mercy Univ Hosp Vinogradska 29 HR-10000 Zagreb Croatia

SOLTERO-HARRINGTON, LUIS RUBÉN, surgeon, educator; b. San Juan, P.R., Sept. 4, 1925; s. Augusto Rafael Soltero and Ana Lila Harrington; m. Alice Joyce Carpenter, Apr. 24, 1958; children: Luis Ruben, Kathleen Ann, Susan Joyce, Robert Richard, Sharon Theresa. BS in Agr., U. P.R., Rio Piedras, 1945; BM, MD, Northwestern U., Chgo., 1949. Diplomate Am. Bd. Surgery, Nat. Be. Med. Examiners, P.R. Rd. Med. Examiners. Intern Michael Reese Hosp., Chgo., 1949-50; resident in gen. surgery Aguadilla (P.R.) Dist. Hosp., 1950-51; resident in gen. surgery, instr. Baylor U. Coll. Medicine and Affiliated Hosps., Houston, 1954-59; resident in gen. surgery Jefferson Davis, VA and M.D. Anderson Hosps., 1954-57; resident in pediatric, thoracic and cardiovasc. surgery St. Luke's-Tex. Children's Hosp., 1957-59; asst. prof. surgery U. P.R. Sch. Medicine, 1960-64, assoc. clin. prof., 1972-73, assoc. clin prof., 1973—, in charge devel. heart surgery program, 1960-64, dir. surgery residency tng. program, 1961-64; pvt. practice, San Juan, P.R., 1959—. Prof. surgery U. del Caribe Sch. Medicine, Cayey, P.R., 1981—; cons. in cardiovasc. and thoracic surgery Med. Examing Bd. P.R., San Juan, 1989; chief thoracic and cardiovasc. surgery Tchrs. Hosp., San Juan, from 1959; dir. surgery residency tng. program Univ. Hosp., Rio Piedras, from 1961; cons. in thoracic and cardiovasc. surgery San Juan City Hosp., 1962—, cons. in surgery, 1964—; cons. in surgery Presbyn. Hosp., 1972—, Mimiya's Hosp., 1987—; cons. in thoracic and cardiovasc. surgery Indsl. Hosp., San Juan, 1975—, Hosp. Met., 1982—, Clinic Fernández García, 1983—; chief surgery Ruiz Arnau Hosp., Bayamon, P.R., 1978—; asst. dir. ICU, Hosp. del Maestro, 1987—; bd. dirs. Rsch. Found. Cardiovasc. Surgery Tex., 1984—, Am. Cancer Soc., 1974; mem. Nat. Adv. Cun. Mended Hearts, Inc., 1969. Contbr. articles to med. jours.; patentee partial occlusion vascular clamp to be used in small blood vessels; inventor respirator for infants based on electronic equipment. Capt., M.C., USAF, 1953-54. Recipient award for outstanding work in cardiovasc. surgery Lions Club, Hato Rey, 1961. Fellow Am. Acad. Pediat., Am. Coll. Legal Medicine (assoc.); mem. AMA (physician recognition award 1986); mem. Denton A. Cooley Cardiovasc. Surg. Soc., Michael E. De Bakey Internat. Cardiovasc. Soc., Pan Am. Med. Assn. (coun. pediatric surgery), P.R. Soc. Cardiology, Am. Heart Assn., P.R. Hear Assn., Phi Chi. Avocations: travel, horticulture, bridge.

SOLTYS, JOHN JOSEPH, lawyer; b. Portsmouth, Va., Feb. 4, 1942; children: John J. III, Amy Elaine. BS, USCG Acad., 1963; JD, Willamette U., 1970. Bar: Wash. 1970, U.S. Dist. Ct. (we. and ea. dists.) Wash. 1970. From assoc. to sr. ptnr. Karr, Tuttle, Seattle, 1970-89; sr. ptnr. Cozen & O'Connor, 1989—. Writer, spkr. in field; editor Wash. State Bar Assn. Motor Vehicle Accident Litigation Deskbook, 2000-01. Lt. (j.g.) USCG, 1963-67. Mem. Wash. Def. Trial Lawyers (pres. 1986-87), Fedn. Def. and Corp. Counsel. Avocations: fishing, hunting, gardening. Office: Cozen O'Connor 1201 3rd Ave Ste 5200 Seattle WA 98101-3071 E-mail: jsoltys@cozen.com.

SOLUM, JOHN HENRY, flutist, educator, author; b. New Richmond, Wis., May 11, 1935; s. Irwin M. and Helen L. (Anderson) S.; m. Millicent Kemp Hunt, July 30, 1960; children: Eric, Andrew. AB, Princeton U., 1957. Concert flutist, 1957—; tchr. Ind. U., Bloomington, 1973, Vassar Coll., Poughkeepsie, N.Y., 1969-71, 77—, Oberlin (Ohio) Conservatory, 1976. Dir. Bath (Eng.) Summer Sch. Baroque Music, 1979-89; artistic dir. Conn. Early Music Festival, New London, 1982-99; pres. N.Y. Flute Club, 1983-86; mem. music adv. panel NEA, 1990-93; arts adv. panel N.H. Arts Coun., 1995-98. *In addition to his activities related to music, in 1994 John Solum began championing the work of the pioneering American modernist artist, James Daugherty (1887-1974). This led to the rediscovery or restoration of many of Daugherty's large public murals, special exhibitions of his art, television documentaries, lectures, articles, and the undertaking by Solum of a complete-works catalog in collaboration with the artist's son, Charles Daugherty.* Composer Cadenzas for Mozart's Flute Concertos, 1964; editor flute music; music critic for Notes, Pro Musica, The Consort; author: The Early Flute, 1992; contbg. author: New Grove Dictionary of Musical Instruments; contbr. articles to Mus. Am., Flutist Quar., Hist. Performance Mag., Woodwind World, Traversieres, Revue de la Société Liégeoise de Musicologie; flutist throughout N.Am., 1957—, Europe, 1962—, Asia, 1969—, S.Am., 1978—, Russia, 1983—; rec. artist Albany, Arabesque, Boston Skyline, Cambridge, Chesky, Columbia, CRI, Decca Gold Label, EMI, Epiphany, Innova, MSR, RCA, Seraphim, Smithsonian, Vanguard, others. Chmn. Hanoverian Found., 2000—. Recipient Phila. Orch. Youth Contest award, 1957. Mem. Nat. Flute Assn. (treas. 1989-94, Disting. Svc. award 1998), Dolmetsch Found. (bd. dirs.), Galpin Soc., Am. Musical Instrument Soc., Century Assn. (N.Y.). Home: 10 Bobwhite Dr Westport CT 06880-1001

SOLVELL, ORJAN OLOF, economist, educator; b. Gothenburg, Sweden, Sept. 23, 1956; s. Lennart Erik Solvell and Inga-Lisa Hammar; m. Ingela Birgitte Jensen, Aug. 1, 1987; children: Frida, Christian. MSc, Stockholm Sch. Econs., 1979, PhD, 1987. Vis. prof. Hitotsubashi U., Tokyo, 1988—89; prof. Stockholm Sch. Econs., 1996—; inst. fellow Sch. Bus. Harvard U., Boston, 2001—. Mem. sci. coun. Swedish Antitrust Authority, Stockholm, 1999—. Author: Advantage Sweden, Norstedts, 1991; editor: The Dynamic Firm, 1998. Judge Swedish Antitrust Ct., Stockholm, 1995—2000; bd. dirs. European Internat. Bus. Acad., Brussels, 1997—. Lt. Swedish Army. Mem.: Internat. House Japan, SVC Exec. Club, Harvard Club of Boston. Office: Harvard Bus Sch Inst for Strategy and Competitiveness Boston MA 02163 E-mail: osolvell@hbs.edu.

SOLYMOSSY, JOSEPH MARTIN, retired nuclear engineer; b. Wegscheid, Fed. Republic Germany, Oct. 11, 1945; came to U.S., 1952; s. Martin Von and Marlie (Mailath) S.; Kathleen Hammond, Aug. 1968 (div. 1977); m. Linda Hatley, Oct. 29, 1977; stepchildren: Lawrence Dale, Michael, Michele, Richard. BSEE, U.S. Naval Acad., 1968. Commd. ensign USN, 1968, advanced through grades to lt. comdr., 1975, resigned, 1978; mgr. field support Newport News (Va.) Indsl., 1978-81; with Inst. Nuc. Power Ops., Atlanta, 1981—, dir. plant ops. divsn., 2000—01; dir. nuc. quality and assessment svcs. N.E. Utilities, Waterford, Conn., 1993-95; plant mgr. Ft. Calhoun Nuclear Sta., Omaha, 1998-2000; ret., 2001. Tech. expert IAEA, Vienna, Austria 1985-87. Vol. March of Dimes, Marietta, Ga., 1983-85, Multiple Sclerosis, 1990—, Spl. Olympics, 1994—. Capt. USNR, 1978-91, ret. Mem. Am. Soc. Nuclear Engrs., Naval Reserve Assn., Naval Acad. Alumni Assn. (treas. 1989-93, sec. 2000-01), Navy League, Garden Club (pres. 1989-91). Republican. Episcopalian. Avocations: skiing, tennis, gardening, golf. Office: Nuc Mgmt Co LLC 700 1st St Hudson WI 54016 E-mail: jmsollymossy@nmcco.com.

SOLYMOSY, EDMOND SIGMOND ALBERT, international marketing executive, retired army officer; b. Budapest, Pest, Hungary, Sept. 3, 1937; came to U.S., 1949; s. Sigmond Ladislas and Gabrielle (Lindelof) S.; m. Mary Ellen Via, Sept. 9, 1961; children: Edmond S.A. Jr., Stephan G., Philip A. BSME, Tex. A&M U., 1960, BBA, 1961, MBA, 1970; postgrad., Mich. U., 1985, Harvard U., 1991. Commd. 2d lt. U.S. Army, 1961, advanced through grades to gen., 1985; student Nat. Def. U., Washington, 1980-81; comdr. 1st Air Def. Arty. Brigade, Ft. Bliss, Tex., 1981-83; chief of staff U.S. Army Air Def. Ctr., 1983; dir. Human Resources Directorate, Hdqrs. Dept. Army, Washington, 1983-85; dep. comdr. U.S. Army Community and Family Support Ctr., Alexandria, Va., 1985-86; chief of staff U.S. Army I Corps, Ft. Lewis, Wash., 1986-88; chief exec. U.S. Office of Def. Coop., Athens, Greece, 1988-91; ret., 1991; pres. Global Project Mgmt., Houston, 1991—, Am. Southwest Properties Inc., 1993-95, Prime Daniel Asset Mgmt. Corp., 1997-2001; sr. ptnr. Solymosy Investment Assocs., 2000—. Advisor Sec. of Army Panel, Washington, 1983-86, Hellenic-Am. C. of C., Athens, 1988-91; bd. dirs. Am. Ikarus Inc., Maxoil Inc., So. Nat. Bank Tex.; hon. consul Republic of Hungary; chmn. Houston Com. on Fgn. Rels. Author: Continental Economic Alliances, 1981. Sponsor Spl. Olympics, Ft. Lewis, 1986; advisor Mil. Mus., Ft. Lewis, 1986-88; regional v.p. Mediterranean coun. Boy Scouts Am., Athens, 1988-91; mem. devel. com. Tex. A&M U., College Station, 1991, advisor Ctr. for Internat. Bus.; mem. bd. advisors Mosher Inst. for Internat. Policy Studies; mem. Mil. Com., Houston.; bd. dirs. Tex. A&M U. Rsch. Found. Decorated D.S.M., Def. D.S.M., Combat Infantryman's Badge, Airborne Parachutist's Badge, Army Ranger, Legion of Merit (3); recipient U.S. and Vietnamese awards for heroism, Greek Disting. Svc. award, 1991. Mem. Assn. U.S. Army (Svc. to Soldiers award 1985), VFW, Armed Forces YMCA (chmn. com. 1982, Nat. Vol. of Yr. award 1983), Internat. Propeller Club (Greece advisor 1989), Kiwanis Club Houston, Hungarian Knights Hospitaller of Order of St. John. Republican. Lutheran. Avocations: sports, jogging, sailing, fishing, hunting. Home: 10150 Dogwood Tr College Station TX 77845-6740 Office: Global Project Mgmt PO Box 27253 Houston TX 77227-7253 E-mail: essglobal@aol.com.

SOLYMOSY, HATTIE MAY, writer, publisher, storyteller, educator; b. Kew Gardens, N.Y., Apr. 1, 1945; d. Julius and Sylvia Becky (Glantz) Fuld; m. Richard Milk, June 30, 1966 (div. Feb. 1974); 1 child, Jared Marc Milk.; m. Abraham Edward Solymosy, Apr. 21, 1974 (div., Sept. 2000). BA, Queens Coll., 1966, MS in Edn., 1973. Cert. tchr., N.Y.C. and N.Y. Actress, model, 1950-60; elem. tchr. N.Y.C. Bd. of Edn., 1966—; owner Ultimate Jewelry, N.Y.C., 1976-80; tutor, 1983-91; children's writer N.Y., 1991—; romance writer, 1993—; owner Hatties' Tales, Cedarhurst, 1993—, Cigar Box Factory, Cedarhurst, 1993—. Bd. dirs. Hamajama Gifts; co-owner Cigar Box Factory, 1996—, Spouse-For-Hire, 1999—; Pen Pal psychic advisor, 1999, Psychic Line, 1999—, ATM Mktg., 1999—, Credit Card Machines, 2000—. Ads-in Motion, Hot Nuts. Author: (sound recs.) Delancy Dolphin, 1993, Thaddius Thoroughbred, 1993, Willie's War, 1993, Noodles-An Autobiography, 1993, (with Jared Marc Milk) Trapped With The Past, 1993, Thick Slick Tangled Webs, 1993, Cinderella Cockroach, 1993, A Christmas Tale, 1993, Chanukah Tale, 1993, Doc Simon, 1995, Mr. Music, 1996, Women on Film, 1996, Buying a Dream, 1996, Rock and Roll, 1996, The Psycho Line, 1999, Legally Raped, 1999; author: Myster of the Old Fishing Shack, 1999, Hot Nuts, 2000. Social sec., fundraiser Children's Med. Ctr., N.Y.C., 1969-79; aux. mem. St. John's Hosp., N.Y., 1987—; storyteller children's stories Oklahoma City Fed. Bldg. bombing victims, Mo. flood victims, children's hosps.; assoc. mem. Mus. Natural History; fundraiser Lung Assn., 1997—, Am. Heart Assn., 1998—. Mem. Romance Writers of Am., Soc. of Children's Writers and Illustrators, Simon Wiesenthal Ctr., World Jewish Congress, del. People to People Internat. Missions in Understanding. Democrat. Jewish. Avocations: music, tennis, movies, gardening, dance. Home: Chatham Sq 326 A Peninsula Blvd Cedarhurst NY 11516 Office: Hatties Tales Cigar Box Factory and Spouse-for-Hire Psychic Line Pen Pal Psych PO Box 24 Cedarhurst NY 11516-0024

SOMACH, S. DENNIS, communications executive; b. Allentown, Pa. s. Lawrence and Lillian Rose Somach. BA in English, Art, Moravian Coll., 1975. Announcer Sta. WSAN, Allentown, 1971-75, program dir., 1975; announcer, music dir. Sta. WYSP-FM, Phila., 1975-81; producer Evening/PM Mag., 1980-82; producer, pres. Denny Somach Prodns., Havertown, Pa., 1979—. Pres. Cinema Records, Phila., 1986—; pres., founder Musicom Internat., 1992—; pres., founder Music Art LLC, 1997—. Prodr.: (radio shows) Psychedelic Psnack, 1985—, Ticket to Ride, 1985—, Legends of Rock, 1985—, Don Kirshner's History of Rock 'n' Roll, 1990, The Rock of the Century, 1999, The Classics, 1999—, (TV shows) Hot Spots, USA Network, 1982-84, Rock 'n' Roll Show CBS-TV, 1983, John Debella Show, 1990; exec. prodr.: (albums) Dave Mason, 1987, Patrick Moraz, 1987, Johnny Winter, 1988, Eric Johnson, 1990, Barbara Mandrell, 1994, Alan Parsons, 1998; author: Ticket to Ride, 1989, Meet the Beatles...Again, 1996. Recipient Grammy award for best rock instrumental Eric Johnson's Cliffs of Dover, 1992. Avocations: traveling, magic, collecting records. Office: 812 W Darby Rd Havertown PA 19083-4607

SOMANI, ARUN KUMAR, electrical engineer, educator; b. Beawar, India, July 16, 1951; came to the U.S., 1985; s. Kanwar Lal and Dulari Devi (Mundra) S.; m. Deepa-Toshniwal, Jan. 21, 1976 (dec. 1985); children: Ashutosh, Paritosh; m. Manju-Kankani, July 6, 1987; 1 child, Anju. BS with honors, B.I.T.S., Pilani, India, 1973; MTech, IIT, Delhi, 1979; MSEE, McGill U., 1983, PhD, 1985. Tech. officer Electronics Corp. India, Hyderabad, 1973-74; scientist Dept. Electronics, Delhi, 1974-82; asst. prof. dept. elec. engring. U. Wash., Seattle, 1985-90, assoc. prof. elec. engring. and computer sci. and engring., 1990-95, prof. elec. engring. and computer sci. engring., 1995-97; Nicholas prof. elec. and computer engring. Iowa State U., Ames, 1997—2002, Jerry R. Jenkins chair prof. elec. and computer engring., 2002—. Designer Proteus multi computer system for automated classification of objects; patentee in field; contbr. over 160 articles to profl. jours., chpts. to books. Fellow IEEE; mem. Assn. for Computing Machinery, Eta Kappa Nu. Hindu. Avocations: squash, tennis, Indian cooking, bridge. Home: 2445 Ridgetop Cir Ames IA 50014-4552 Office: Dept Elec Computer Engring Iowa State U 201 Coover Hl Ames IA 50011-0001

SOMARY, JOHANNES FELIX, conductor; b. Zurich, Switzerland, Apr. 7, 1935; came to U.S., 1940; s. Felix and May (Demblin) S.; m. Anne Voorhees Van Zandt, July 20, 1963; children: Stephen, Geoffrey, Karen. BA magna cum laude, Yale U., 1957, MMus, 1959. Founder, music dir., condr. Amor Artis, N.Y.C., 1962—; chmn. arts and music dept. Horace Mann Sch., 1971—2002; condr. Fairfield County Chorale, Westport, Conn., 1975—, Great Neck (L.I., N.Y.) Choral Soc., 1983-94, Taghkanic Chorale, Peekskill, N.Y., 1992-2000; dir. music St. Patrick's Cathedral, N.Y.C., 2001—. Condr. recs. English Chamber Orch., London, 1968-79; vis. prof. Yale Sch. Music, New Haven, 1983-84; choral dir. Madeira (Portugal) Bach Festival, 1984-86; guest condr. Dubrovnik (Yugoslavia) Music Festival, 1986, Sion (Switzerland) Music Festival, 1990; condr. for recs. Polish Radio Orch., Katowice, 1990; guest lectr., condr. U. Tex., Austin, 1973, U. B.C., Vancouver, 1987, U. Ala., Montevallo, 1985; guest condr. Irish Chamber Orch., 1997; program dir. UN Assn., Riverdale, N.Y., 1970-74. Condr. 61 recordings on CD, casettes, records including Handel oratorios, first recs. Handel's Theodora and Jephthe, Schuetz and Bach passions, music by Vivaldi, Haydn, Mozart, Tschaikowsky, Weill, others, onVanguard, Omega, Vox, Decca, Leonarda, Newport Classic, Polygram, Premier, Lyrichord, Naxas, 1963—; composer liturgical music G.I.A., Galaxy, Collins, 1975—; composer oratorios and smaller works commissioned by various choral orgns.; composer, condr. Jefferson Music Festival, Washington, 1994; guest condr. New Orleans Philharmonic, Milw. Chamber Orch., Royal Philharmonic, London, XXI Sajundi Orchester, Tallinn, Estonia, others; organist solo recitals; composer Blessed Sacrament Fathers in North America, 1999, Te Deum, Rome, 2000. Recipient Record of Yr. awards Stereo-Rev., N.Y.C., 1969, 70, 75, 78; recipient Certs. of Merit Yale Sch. Music Alumni Assn., New Haven, 1982, U. Chgo., 1981, Choirmaster Cert., Am. Guild Organists, N.Y.C., 1959; French Baroque Music study grantee, 1982. Fellow Am. Guild Organists (bds. New Haven and N.Y. chpts.), Am. Symphony Orch. League, Assn. Musiciens Suisses, Yale Club N.Y.C., Riverdale Yacht Club; mem. Friendship Ambassadors, Inc. (bd. dirs. 1985-99), N.Y. Archdiocesan Music Commn. Roman Catholic. Avocations: walking-hiking, gardening, tennis, bicycling, reading books. Home and Office: Amor Artis 620 W 254th St Bronx NY 10471-1252

SOMASEGAR, SIVARAMA KICHENANE, information technology executive; b. 1965; m. Akila Somasegar; children: Sahana, Archana. BSEE, Anna U., India; MS in Computer Engring., La. State U. From software design engr. to v.p. Microsoft, Redmond, Wash., 1989, v.p. windows engring. solutions & svc. group. Office: One Microsoft Way Redmond WA 98052-6399*

SOMASUNDARAN, PONISSERIL, surface and colloid engineer, applied science educator; b. Pazhookara, Kerala, India, June 28, 1939; came to U.S., 1961; s. Kumara Moolayil and Lakshmikutty (Amma) Pillai; m. Usha N., May 25, 1966; 1 child, Tamara. BS, Kerala U., Trivandrum, India, 1958; BE, Indian Inst. Sci., Bangalore, 1961; MS, U. Calif., Berkeley, 1962, PhD, 1964. Rsch. engr. U. Calif., 1964, Internat. Minerals & Chem. Corp., Skokie, Ill., 1965-67; rsch. chemist R.J. Reynolds Industries, Inc., Winston-Salem, N.C., 1967-70; assoc. prof. Columbia U., N.Y.C., 1970-78, prof. mineral engring., 1978-83, La Von Duddleson Krumb prof., 1983-97; dir. NSF Industry U. Coop. Rsch. Ctr. in Novel Surfactants, 1998—; hon. prof. Wuhan Inst. Chem. Tech., 2001—. Chmn. Henry Krumb Sch. Chem. Engring., Materials Sci. and Mining Engring., Columbia U., 1988—97; dir. Langmuir Ctr. for Colloids and Interfaces Columbia U., 1987—; cons. numerous agys., cos., including NIH, B.F. Goodrich, NSF, 1974, Alcan, 1981, UNESCO, 1982, Sohio, 1984—85, IBM, 1984, Am. Cyanamid, Duracell, 1988—89, DuPont, 1989, Canmet, 1990—93, Unilever, 1991—, Engelhard, 1991—94, UOP, Alcoa, 1991—92, Allied Signal, GAF, 1999—2000, INCO, Arch.Chem.; mem. panel NRC; chmn. numerous ianternat. symposia and NSF workshops; mem. adv. panel Bur. Mines Generic Ctr., 1983—91; keynote and plenary lectr. internat. meetings; hon. prof. Ctrl. South U. Tech., China; Brahm Prakash prof. metallurgy and material sci. Indian Inst. Sci., Bangalore, 1990; hon. rsch. advisor Beijing Gen. Rsch. Inst., 1991—; Henry Krumb lectr. AIME, 1988. Editor: (books) Fine Particles Processing, 1980; hon. editor-in-chief Colloids and Surfaces, 1980—, Ency. of Colloids and Interfaces, —; contbr. ; editor-in-chief: Encyclopedia of Colloid and Surface Chemistry. Pres. Keralasamajam of Greater N.Y., N.Y.C., 1974-75; bd. dirs. Fedn. Indian Assocs., N.Y.C., 1974-95, Vols. in Svc. to Edn. in India, Hartford, Conn., 1974—; mem. planning bd. Village of Piermont, N.Y., 1995-2000, mem. zoning bd. appeals, 2000—, mem. citizens adv. com., 2000—. Recipient Disting. Achievement in Engring. award, AINA, 1980, Antoine M. Gaudin award Soc. Mining Engrs.-AIME, 1983, Achievements in Applied Sci. award 2d World Malayalam Conf., 1985, Robert H. Richards award, AIME, 1986, Arthur F. Taggart award Soc. Mining Engrs.-AIME, 1987, honor award Assn. Indian in Am., 1988, VHP award of Excellence, Ellis Island medal of Honor, 1990, Commendations citation State of N.J. Senate, 1991; named Mill Man of Distinction, Soc. Mining Engrs.-AIME, 1983, Disting. Alumnus award Indian Inst. Sci., Bangalore, 1989, Outstanding Contbns. and Achievement award Cultural Festival India, 1991, Recognition award SIAA, 1992, Asian-Am. Heritage award Asian Am. Higher Edn. Coun., 1994. Fellow Russian Acad. Nat. Scis. (fgn.), Chinese Acad. Engring. (fgn.) Indian Nat. Acad. Engring., Instn. Mining and Metallurgy (U.K.); mem. AICE, NAE, Soc. Mining Engrs. (bd. dirs. 1982-85, Disting. mem. award, also others), Engring. Found. (chmn. bd. 1993-95, chmn. conf. com. 1985-88, bd. exec. com. 1985-88, bd. dirs. 1991—, Frank Aplan award 1992), Am. Chem. Soc., N.Y. Acad. Scis., Russian Acad. Natural Scis. (fgn.), Internat. Assn. Colloid and Surface Scientists (councillor 1989-92), Indian Material Rsch. Soc. (hon.), Chinese Acad. Engring., Sigma Xi. Achievements include patents for in field.

SOME, STEVEN EDWARD, lobbyist, public affairs consultant; b. Jersey City, June 3, 1955; s. Marvin Lester and Sondra Gloria S. BA, George Washington U., 1976. Media dir., chief spokesman Am. Conservative Union, Washington, 1977; cons. Shell Oil acct. Ogilvy & Mather Advtsg., Houston, 1979—79; policy analyst Gulf Oil Corp., 1979; mgr. legis. analysis, govtl. affairs The Coastal Corp., 1979—83; spl. asst. to dir. congl. and legis affairs office U.S. Dept. Interior, Washington, 1983; spl. asst. to asst. sec. labor employment and tng. Labor Dept., 1983—85, spl. asst. to U.S. Sec. of Labor; v.p. Hannaford Co., Inc., 1985—88; pres. govt. affairs and pub. rels. Steven E. Some Assocs., 1988—93; pres. Capital Pub. Affairs, Inc., New Brunswick, 1993—. Mem. regional adv. bd. N.J. Anti-Defamation League. Chmn. N.J. Commn. on Holocaust Edn.; mem. U.S. Holocaust Meml. Coun., 1992-95; bd. govs. Rep. Jewish Coalition, co-chair N.J. chpt.; bd. dirs. Jewish Policy Ctr., Washington. Home: 9 Hampstead Ct Princeton NJ 08540-7075 Office: Capital Pub Affairs Inc 5 Mapleton Rd Princeton NJ 08540 Business E-Mail: steven.some@verizon.net. E-mail: ssome@cpanj.com.

SOMEKAWA, MINA C. pianist, educator; b. Dec. 25, 1958; d. Akira and Nobuko Somekawa. BA in English, Sophia U., 1981; postgrad., U. Mo., 1990—92; MusB in Piano Performance, U. Ill., 1993, MusM, postgrad., U. Ill., 1995—. Piano tchg. asst. U. Ill., Urbana-Champaign, 1994—96; keyboardist Civic Orch. of Chgo., 1995—96; prin. keyboardist Sinfonia da Camera, Urbana, 1995—, Champaign-Urbana Symphony, 1996—, Ill. Symphony Orch., Springfield, 1997—, Fresno Philharmonic, Calif., 1998—. Pvt. piano instr., various, Ill., 1996—; piano faculty mem. Blue Lake Fine Arts Camp, Twin Lake, Mich., 1998; audition judge Nat. Fedn. Music Clubs, 1998, Miss. Symphony Orch. Young Artists Competition, 2002; vis. asst. prof. music Millsaps Coll., Jackson, Miss., 2002—. Musician: St. Louis Artist Presentation Soc., 1993, Brahms First Piano Concerto , 1994, Dame Myra Hess Meml. Concert, 1998; musician: (piano/harpsichord solo) Ill. Chamber Orch., 2000. Recipient Phi Beta Kappa Jr. honor, U. Mo., Columbia, 1991, Ruth Melcher Allen Meml. award, Sigma Alpha Iota, 1991, Artist Presentation Soc. award, The St. Louis Artist Presentation Soc., 1992, Simone Belsky Music award, Litchfield, Conn., 1993, Bartók-Kabalevsky Internat. Piano Competition, Radford, Va., 1993, Beethoven Piano Sonata Competition, Memphis, Tenn., 1995; fellow Music fellow, U. Ill., 1993—94. Mem.: Coll. Music Soc., Am. Fedn. Musicians, Pi Kappa Lambda, Golden Key Nat. Honor Soc. Home: Apt 214 1315 N Jefferson St Jackson MS 39202-1764

SOMER, STANLEY JEROME, lawyer; b. N.Y.C., Oct. 29, 1943; s. David Meyer and Rose (Bleifeld) S.; children: Penny Lynn, Andrew Michael; m. Batia Lebhar, Sept. 13, 1987. BBA in Acctg., Hofstra U., 1966; JD, New York Law Sch., 1969. Bar: N.Y. 1970, U.S. Dist. Ct. (ea. and so. dists.) N.Y. 1972, U.S. Tax Ct. 1983. Assoc. Halpin, Keough & St. John, N.Y.C., 1970-71, Bodenstein & Gumson, N.Y.C., 1971-73; counsel Heatherwood Comm., Hauppauge, N.Y., 1973-74; ptnr. Somer & Wand, P.C., Commack and Smithtown, 1974-88, Somer, Wand & Farrell, Commack and Smithtown, 1989-90; sole practice, 1990-98; ptnr. Somer & Heller LLP, Commack, 1999—. Lectr. N.Y. Law Sch., N.Y.C., 1970-73, Income Property Cons., Huntington, N.Y., 1976-85. Commiteeman Suffolk Reps., East Northport, N.Y., 1978. Mem. N.Y. State Bar Assn., Suffolk Bar Assn., Comm. Assoc. Inst., L.I. Builders Inst. Lodges: Lions (pres. East Northport chpt. 1977-78). Office: Somer & Heller LLP 2171 Jericho Tpke Ste 350 Commack NY 11725-2947

SOMERMAN, MARTHA J. academic administrator; DDS, NYU, 1975; PhD, U. Rochester, 1980. Asst. prof., periodontics and pharmacology Balt. Coll. Dental Surgery, 1984—87, assoc. prof., pharmacology, 1987—91, U. Mich., 1991—95, chair, dept. periodontics, prevention and geriatrics, 1991—2001, prof., pharmacology, 1995—2000, assoc. dean rsch., Sch. Dentistry, 2001—02; dean, Sch. Dentistry U. Wash., 2002—. Contbr. articles to profl. jours. Office: RMD 322 Box 356365 Seattle WA 98195*

SOMERS, ANNE RAMSAY, retired medical educator; b. Memphis, Sept. 9, 1913; d. Henry Ashton and Amanda Vick (Woolfolk) Somers; m. Herman Miles Somers, Aug. 31, 1946; children: Sara Ramsay, Margaret Ramsay. BA, Vassar Coll., 1935; postgrad., U. N.C., 1939—40; DSc (hon.), Med. Coll. Wis., 1975. Ednl. dir. Internat. Ladies Garment Workers Union, 1937—42; labor economist U.S. Dept. Labor, 1943—46; rsch. assoc. Haverford Coll., 1957—63; rsch. assoc. indsl. rels. sect. Princeton U., 1964—84; prof. U. Medicine and Dentistry of N.J.-R. Wood Johnson Med. Sch. (formerly Rutgers Med. Sch.), 1971—84, adj. prof., 1984—. Adj. prof. geriat. medicine U. Pa. Sch. Medicine, 1990—; mem. Nat. Bd. Med. Examiners, 1983—86; cons. in health econs., health edn., geriats., gerontology, realted areas. Author: Hospital Regulation: The Dilemma of Public Policy, 1969, Health Care in Transition: Directions for the Future, 1971; author: (with H.M. Somers) Workmen's Compensation: The Prevention, Rehabilitation and Financing of Occupational Disability, 1954; author: Medicare and the Hospitals, 1967, Doctors, Patients and Health Insurance, 1961, Health and Health Care: Policies in Perspective, 1971; author: (with N.L. Spears) The Continuing Care Retirement Community: A Significant Option for Long Care?, 1992; editor (with D.R. Fabian): he Geriatric Imperative: An Introduction to Gerontology and Clinical Geriatrics, 1981. Mem. bd. visitors Duke U. Med. Ctr., 1972—77, U. Tex. Health Scis. Ctr., Houston, 1982—86. Named to Health Care Hall of Fame, 1993; recipient Elizur Wright award, Am. Risk and Ins. Assn., 1962. Fellow: Coll. Physicians Phila. (hon.), Am. Coll. Hosp. Adminstrs. (hon.); mem.: Nat. Acad. Social Ins., Inst. Medicine of NAS, Soc. Tchrs. of Family Medicine (hon.). Home: Pennswood Village # C-202 Newtown PA 18940-2401

SOMERS, HANS PETER, lawyer; b. Berlin, Germany, Nov. 11, 1922; came to U.S., 1938; s. Fritz A. and Karoline E. (Neuert) S.; m. Claudia C. Schuette, May 3, 1947; children: Daniel E., Stephen A., Deborah J., Conrad S. BA, Cornell Coll., 1946; MA, U. Iowa, 1948; LL.B. magna cum laude, Harvard U., 1951. Bar: Mass. 1951, Pa. 1957. Assoc. Hill & Barlow, Boston, 1951-56, Morgan, Lewis & Bockius, Phila., 1956-60, ptnr., 1960-88, counsel, 1988—. Lectr. law Northeastern U., Boston, 1951-53, Boston U. Law Sch., 1953-55; lectr. Villanova U. Law Sch., Phila., 1959-63; research assoc. Am. Law Inst., Cambridge, Mass., 1955-56 Editor: Harvard Law Rev., 1949-51; contbr. articles to legal jours. Served to 2d lt. AUS, 1943-46, ETO. Mem. ABA (chmn. com. tax sect. 1967-69, real property, probate and trust law 1974-77), Nat. Conf. Lawyers and Corp. Fiduciaries (chmn. 1978-81), Am. Coll. Probate Counsel (mem. editorial bd. dirs. 1976-77), Internat. Acad. of Estate and Trust Law (exec. council 1974-78, 81—) Clubs: Radnor Hunt (Malvern, Pa.) (bd. govs.); Union League (Phila.). Home: 8024 Goshen Rd Newtown Square PA 19073-1122 Office: Morgan Lewis & Bockius 1701 Market St Philadelphia PA 19103-2903

SOMERS, JAMES LAVAUGHN, tool manufacturing executive; b. Portland, Ind., Jan. 19, 1944; s. Ralph Lavaughn and Matilda Fay (Van Trees) S.; m. Carol Sue Zorn, Jan. 25, 1964; children: Michael, Jeffrey, Gregory, Daniel. BS, Purdue U., 1967, MS, 1968, PhD, 1972. Registered profl. engr., Wis. Material handling expediter Armstrong Cork Co., Dunkirk, Ind., 1963-65; prodn. control coord., prodn. control supr., sr. staff indsl. engr., mgr. materials mgmt. Collin's Radio Co., Cedar Rapids, Iowa, 1969-73; mgr. inventory mgmt., dir. phys. distbn., dir. mktg. planning, v.p. mktg. services, v.p. corp. quality, v.p. mfg., sr. v.p. mfg. and engring. Snap-on, Inc., Kenosha, Wis., 1973-96. Contbr. articles to profl. jours. Bd. dirs. Gateway Vocat., Tech. and Adult Edn. Dist., 1978-80, Gateway Tech. Inst. Found., 1980-86, Great Lakes Composites Ctr., 1991-95, Kenosha Found.; mem. exec. bd. Southeast Wis. coun. Boy Scouts Am.; mem. environ. working group Wis. Mfrs. and Commerce, 1990-95. Mem. Coun. Logistics Mgmt., Am. Prodn. and Inventory Control Soc., Inst. Indsl. Engrs., Am. Soc. Quality Control, Sigma Xi, Alpha Pi Mu, Tau Beta Pi. Lutheran. Home: 8200 44th Ave Kenosha WI 53142-2042

SOMERS, JOHN ARTHUR, insurance company executive; b. Cin., Feb. 24, 1944; s. Arthur Edward and Margaret Mary (Netschke) S.; m. Ann-Christin Ahlander, Dec. 28, 1968; children— Monica Ann, Christina Elizabeth, Mark Edward BS in Econs., Villanova U., 1966; postgrad., Sch. Law, U. Conn., 1966-67; MBA in Fin., U. Conn., 1972. Asst. town mgr. Town of Newington, Conn., 1970-72; v.p. Prudential Ins. Co. Am., Newark, 1972-81; sr. v.p. Tchrs. Ins. & Annuity Assn., N.Y.C., 1981—, exec. v.p., 1996—. Bd. dirs. Cmty. Preservation Corp., Emigrant Bank, Guardian Life. Roman Catholic. Office: Tchrs Ins & Annuity Assn Am 730 3rd Ave New York NY 10017-3206

SOMERS, LOUIS ROBERT, retired food company executive; b. Pontiac, Mich., Aug. 8, 1926; s. Jay G. and Maggie (Gee) S.; m. Rynda Horinga, July 28, 1950; children: Linda, Laurie. BS, Mich. State U., 1950. With Kellogg Co., Battle Creek, Mich., 1955-88; controller Kellogg Internat., 1967-70, 72-75; fin. dir. Kellogg Gt. Brit. Ltd., 1970-72; v.p. fin., treas. Kellogg Co., 1975-85, sr. v.p. fin., 1985-88. Trustee Alma Coll., 1982—2001; bd. govs. ARC, 1985—92, chmn. audit com.; bd. dirs. Mich. State U. Devel. Fund, 1983—88.

SOMERS, MARION, gerontologist, family counselor; children: Lynne, Randy, Cortney, Jessica, Craig, Matthew. PhD, The Fielding Inst., 1988, M in Neuro Lenguestic Programming, 1999. Lic. nursing home adminstr. N.Y. Adminstr. in tng. Hebrew Home for the Aging, Palisades Nursing Home, Riverdale, N.Y., 1991-92; dir. prof. geriatric care mgrs. Brookdale Ctr. on Aging. Grant reader HHS, Washington, 1980—; observer White House Conf. on Aging, 1982; dir. of profl. geriatric care mgrs. Brookdale Ctr. on Aging Hunter Coll. Author: (novels) The Home: A Brief Moment in Time, 1999. Office: 601 7th St Brooklyn NY 11215-3708

SOMERS, SALLY WEST, librarian; b. Duncan, Okla., July 6, 1939; d. Mahlon Clifford and Lorene (Shore) West; m. Dale Andrew Somers, Oct. 15, 1961 (dec. Mar. 1972); children: Jennifer, Stephen Andrew. BA, Trinity U., 1961; postgrad., East Tex. State U., 1966; MLS, Emory U., 1975; postgrad., Ga. State U., 1976. Adminstrv. asst., bookkeeper Ga. State U. Libr., Atlanta, 1972-74; head serials receiving U. Ga. Librs., Athens, 1976-79, head acquisitions dept. 1979-89; asst. univ. libr. tech. svcs. Tulane U., New Orleans, 1989-99; asst. dir. tech. svcs. Fla. State U., Tallahassee, 2000—. Co-editor: Practical Issues in Collection Development , 1995; author book article; contbr. articles to profl. jours. Scholar Ga. Libr. Assn., 1974, Emory U., 1974. Mem. ALA (com. chair serials sect., 1990, 1994-95), Assn. for Libr. Collections and Tech. Svcs. Avocations: walking, reading. Office: Tulane Univ Libr 7001 Freret St New Orleans LA 70118-5549

SOMERS, SARAH PRUYN, retired elementary school educator; b. Albany, N.Y., Oct. 15, 1936; d. Howard Sewall and Carolyn (Decker) Pruyn; m. Richard Moss Somers Jr., Aug. 15, 1959 (dec. Jan. 1986); children: Sewall Wendy Somers Hautzinger, Sarah Louise. BS in Edn., Wheelock Coll., 1958. Cert. elem. tchr., Mass., N.J. Elem. tchr. Madison (N.J.) Pub. Schs., 1960-63, 76-99; ret., 1999—. Group chmn., student tchr. sponsor Madison Pub. Schs., 1980-99, rep. roundtable, 1988-99. Vol. libr. Torey J. Sabatini Sch., Madison, 1970-76, room mother, 1970-81; room mother Kings Rd. Sch., 1976-77, Madison High Sch., 1976-81, The Gill/St. Bernards Sch., Bernardsville, N.J., 1977-82, The Morristown Beard Sch., 1982-86; chaperone, coach YMCA Nat. Swim Meet, 1979-81; mem. aquatic com. YMCA, Madison, 1973-80; mem. Jr. League Boston, Morristown; mem. Madison Hist. Soc., 1988-99; chaperone Madison Teen Ctr., 1991-99. Recipient Govs. Tchr. Recognition award, 1988. Fellow NEA (ret.); mem. N.J. Edn. Assn. (ret.), Morris County Edn. Assn. (ret.), Madison Edn. Assn. (rep. coun. 1992—), Bucks County Hist. Soc. Republican. Episcopalian. Avocations: reading, active sports, tennis, walking, TV. Home: 5126 Barness Ct Doylestown PA 18901-6240

SOMERS, SUSAN EILEEN, business educator; b. Quincy, Mass., Mar. 28, 1951; d. Donald William and Flora (Andrews) S. BS, Northeastern U., Boston, 1984; MBA, Utah State U., 1985. Adminstr. Stone & Webster Engrs., Boston, 1973-83; prof. Quincy (Mass.) Coll., 1986—. Cons. Quincy 2000, 1995-96, Sml. Bus. Mgmt. Ctr., Logan, Utah, 1985-86. Mem. Internat. Pers. Mgmt. Assn., Phi Delta Kappa, Sigma Epsilon Rho. Avocations: reading, travel, crafts. Office: Quincy College 34 Coddington St Quincy MA 02169 E-mail: ssomers@quincycollege.com.

SOMERS, VIREND KRISTEN, physician, researcher; b. Durban, Natal, South Africa; came to the U.S., 1986; MB, BChir cum laude, U. Natal, Durban, 1980; PhD, Oxford (Eng.) U., 1986. Diplomate Am. Bd. Internal Medicine subspecialty cardiology. Intern U. Natal, Durban, 1981, resident, 1982; Nuffield scholar Oxford U., 1983-86; resident medicine U. Iowa, Iowa City, 1988-91, fellow cardiology, 1991-93, faculty cardiology, 1993-99; prof. medicine Mayo Clinic, Rochester, Minn., 2000—. Cons. Am. Soc. Hypertension, 1999. Mem. editl. bd. Circulation, 1998—, Jour. Hypertension, 1998—; consulting editor: Am. jour. Physiology-Regulatory and Integrative, 2001—. Recipient Demuth Young Investigator prize Internat. Soc. Hypertension, 1988, 94, Malherbe Disting. Alumnus award U. Natal, 1998, Young Scholar award Am. Soc. Hypertension, 2000; Nuffield Dominion scholar Oxford U., 1983-86. Fellow High Blood Pressure Coun., Coun. on Circulation; mem. Am. Soc. Clin. Investigation, Am. Heart Assn. (established investigator, Cournand Comroe award 1993). Office: Mayo Clinic 200 1st St SW Rochester MN 55905-0002

SOMERSET, HAROLD RICHARD, retail executive; b. Woodbury, Conn., Sept. 25, 1935; s. Harold Kitchener and Margaret Mary (Roche) S.; m. Marjory Deborah Ghiselin, June 22, 1957 (dec. Jan. 1984); children: Timothy Craig, Paul Alexander; m. Jean MacAlpine DesMarais, Jan. 2, 1985; stepchildren: Cheryl Lyn DesMarais, James Fenelon DesMarais. BS, U.S. Naval Acad., 1957; B.C.E., Rensselaer Poly. Inst., Troy, N.Y., 1959; LL.B., Harvard U., 1967. Bar: Mass. 1967, Hawaii 1973. Commd. ensign U.S. Navy, 1957, advanced through grades to lt., 1961; service in U.S. and Hawaii; resigned, 1964; with firm Goodwin, Procter & Hoar, Boston, 1967-72; corp. counsel Alexander & Baldwin, Inc., Honolulu, 1972-74, v.p., gen. counsel, 1974-78, group v.p.-sugar, 1978-79, exec. v.p.-agr., 1979-84; with Calif. & Hawaiian Sugar Co., San Francisco, 1984-93, exec. v.p., chief operating officer, 1984-88, pres., chief exec. officer, 1988-93, bus. cons., 1994—2002; pres., CEO Longs Drug Stores Corp., 2002—. Bd. dirs. Longs Drug Stores Corp., Brown and Caldwell. Mem. adv. bd. San Francisco Nat. Maritime Mus. Mem. St. Mary's Coll. Sch. Edn. (adv. coun.). Home: 19 Donald Dr Orinda CA 94563-3646 Office: 141 N Civic Dr Walnut Creek CA 94596

SOMERSON, PAUL, editor-in-chief; Former v.p., editor-in-chief P.C. Computing, San Francisco; v.p., ed. dir. Ziff Davis Develop. Group , 2000—. Office: Ziff Davis Publishing 11766 Wilshire Blvd Los Angeles CA 90025*

SOMERSTEIN-CAMPBELL, JASMINE AURORA ABRERA, preschool administrator, educator; b. Manila, Feb. 17, 1943; d. Bernardo Paez and Rosalia (Sityar) Abrera; m. Jules Leon Somerstein, Dec. 10, 1967 (div. July 1995); children: Joseph, Sandra, Marc (dec. Mar. 2001); m. James Walter Campbell, Jan. 13, 2001. BA in English, U. Philippines, Manila, 1964; MA in English Edn., NYU, 1978, MA in Elem. Edn., 1987; postgrad., U. Pitts., Oxford (Eng.) U., 1964-66, 86. Cert. tchr., N.Y. Instr. U. Pitts., 1965-66, U. of the East, Manila, 1968-69; tchr. Am. Internat. Sch., 1966, Domenec High Sch., Pitts., 1967-68; substitute tchr. Lakeland and Peekskill Sch. Dist., N.Y., 1975-77; exec. dir. Internat. Pre-Sch. Ctr., Inc., N.Y.C., 1977—; instr. Bd. Coop. Ednl. Svcs., 1989-97; exec. dir. Horas Alegres Bilingual Presch., Dallas, 1997—; early childhood coord. Good Shepherd Catholic Ch., Colleyville, 2000—; dir. Good Shepherd Little Lambs Program. Exec. sec. Ctr. Ednl. TV, Manila, 1964; sec. NYU, 1973—74, UN, N.Y.C., 1975; prodr., interviewer Continental Cablevision, N.Y.C., 1984—97; child devel. advisor Westchester

County, N.Y.C., 1989—; cons. Hudson Valley Export-Import, Inc., N.Y.C., 1988—92; adj. instr. Tarrant County Coll., Hurst, 2001—. Vol. Philippine Band of Mercy, Manila, 1963-93. Mem. Nat. Child Care Assn., Nat. Assn. Edn. Young Children, Nat. Coun. Tchrs. English, N.Y. Child Care Assn., Assn. Childhood Edn. Internat., Child Care Coun. Westchester, Manitoga, Peekskill/Cortlandt C. of C. (bd. dirs. 1989-92), Greater Dallas Hispanic C. of C., Hispanic C. of C. Greater Dallas, Hispanic Bus. Alliance. Democrat. Avocations: reading, photography, music, travel, piano. Office: PO Box 93056 Southlake TX 76092-1056 E-mail: Jasminvale@aol.com.

SOMERVILLE, ATWELL WILSON, JR. medical editor; b. Charlottesville, Va., Nov. 24, 1949; s. Atwell Wilson and Anne Carter Somerville. AB in English, U. N.C., 1972, PhD in English, 1992; MA in English, U. Va., 1977. Editor in life scis. Bd. of Editors in the Life Scis., Inc.; instr. Warren Wilson Coll., Ashville, N.C., 1974-76, dir. pub. info., 1982-83, dir. admissions, 1983-87; instr. Va. Episcopal Sch., Lynchburg, 1978-80; comms. coord. So. Highland Handicraft Guild, Asheville, 1980-82; instr. U. N.C.-Chapel Hill, 1988-92, U. N.C.-Greensboro, 1988-92; med. editor dept. anesthesiology Wake Forest U. Sch. Medicine, Winston-Salem, N.C., 1992—. Editl. cons. Regional Anesthesia and Pain Medicine jour., 1996-98; asst. book rev. sect. Anesthesiology jour., Phila., 1997. Author: The Tuesday Club of Annapolis (1745-1756) as Cultural Performance, 1996, A History of the Department of Anesthesiology: 1942-1997, The Wake Forest University School of Medicine, 1998; editor: Appalachia/America: The Proceedings of the 1980 Appalachian Studies Conference, 1981; mem. editl. bd. Anesthesia Patient Safety Newsletter, 2001-; contbr. articles to profl. publs. Coach Optimist Soccer Program, Winston-Salem, 1995—2000; mem. chorale Wake Forest Univ., 2000—. Morehead scholar, 1968-72; Mason fellow, 1976-77; recipient (2) 1st Pl. award Coun. for Advancement and Support of Edn., 1987. Mem.: Soc. Scholarly Publishing, The Am. Assn. for History Medicine, Soc. Early Americanists, N.C. Soc. Anesthesiologists, Am. Med. Writers Assn., Am. Soc. Anesthesiologists, Coun. Sci. Editors, Phi Beta Kappa. Office: Wake Forest U Sch Medicine Dept Anesthesiology Medical Center Blvd Winston Salem NC 27157-0001 E-mail: wsomerv@wfubmc.edu.

SOMERVILLE, DAPHINE HOLMES, retired elementary education educator; b. Clinton, N.C., Jan. 19, 1940; d. George Henry and Mamie Estelle (Streeter) Holmes; m. Kalford Burton Somerville, Dec. 26, 1970 (div. Sept. 1992); 1 child, Daria Lynn. AA, Blackburn Coll., 1959, BA, 1961; MS in Edn., Hofstra U., 1967; postgrad., Columbia U., 1971, SUNY, Farmingdale, 1999-2000. Permanent teaching cert. common br. subjects grades 1-8. Tchr. East Islip (N.Y.) Sch. Dist., 1961-99, ret., 1999; tchr. computer/writing Opportunities Industrialization Ctr., 1998—, cert. webmaster, 2000—. Mem., instr. Outcome Based/Mastery Learning/Excellence in Learning Com., East Islip, 1984—89; mentor East Islip Sch. Dist., 1987—88, mem. sch. improvement team, 1989—91, staff devel. com., 1992—96; chair Ptnrs. in Edn., 1991—2001; instr. AARP's 55/Alive Mature Driver Course, 2001, 02; election inspector, 2001—02. Author: Beaman Family Reunion Journal, 2001, Baptist Training Union Study Guide; founder, co-author: tutoring program Adopt-A-School Child/Family, 1990. Mem. Bay Shore (N.Y.) Civic Assn. and Bay Shore Pub. Schs. Task Force for the Advancement of Equality of Ednl. Opportunity, 1967—69; sec. Islip Town NAACP, Bay Shore, 1965—90; dir. Bapt. Tng. Union, 1974—81; trustee First Bapt. Ch., Bay Shore, 1979—90. Recipient Cmty. Svc. award Town Bd.-Town of Islip, Suffolk County, 1982, Br. Recognition award Islip Town NAACP, 1987, Disting. Svc. award L.I. Region NAACP, 1993, Dedicated Svc. award Ptnrs. in Edn. First Bapt. Ch. of Bayshore, 1995, 98, Proclamation for genuine concern edn. residents Suffolk County Exec. Robert Gaffney, 1997, Cert. Spl. Congl. Recognition, Congressman Rick Lazio, 1997, African-Am. Educators award Martin L. King Commn. of Suffolk County, 1997, Editors Choice award The Nat. Libr. of Poetry, 1999, Citation, Town of Islip, 1999; L.I. Sch. to Career Partnership for Proposed Sch./Bus. Govt. Project grantee, 1998. Mem. Nat. Coun. Negro Women (life, ednl. involvement award 1993), East Islip Tchrs. Assn. (past bldg. rep.), N.Y. State United Tchrs. Democrat. Avocations: theater, writing, tennis, reading, working with children, travel. Home: 130 Carman Rd Dix Hills NY 11746-5648 Fax: 631-423-6418. E-mail: dsomer@optonline.net.

SOMERVILLE, JAMES MIDDLETON, III, retired philosophy educator, writer; b. Sept. 21, 1915; s. James Middleton II and Helen (Hannigan) S.; m. Beatrice Bruteau, Jan. 26, 1971. BA in French, Fordham U., 1937, MA in Psychology, 1939; Licentiate in Philosophy, U. St. Louis, 1944; Licentiate in Sacred Theology, Woodstock Coll., 1951; PhD in Philosophy, Fordham U., 1954. Instr. philosophy Fordham U., Bronx, N.Y., 1954-56, asst. prof. philosophy, 1956-61, assoc. prof. philosophy, 1961-70, chair philosophy dept., 1957-66; prof. philosophy Xavier U., Cin., 1971-82; ret., 1982. Co-founder, exec. editor Internat. Philos. Quar., 1961—; editor, pub. Schola, Quar. Jour. Philosophy, Religion and Scripture in an East-West Context, 1982—. Author: The Mystical Sense of the Gospels, 1997, Total Commitment, 1965; translator: Blondel and Christianity, 1966; contbr. over 30 articles to profl. jours. (Best Scholarly Article 1961 Cath. Press Assn.). Democrat. Roman Catholic. Avocation: contemporary scripture scholarship.

SOMERVILLE, RICHARD CHAPIN JAMES, atmospheric scientist, educator; b. Washington, May 30, 1941; s. James William and Mollie (Dorf) S.; m. Sylvia Francisca Bal, Sept. 17, 1965; children: Anatol Leon, Alexander Chapin. BS in Meteorology, Pa. State U., 1961; PhD in Meteorology, NYU, 1966. Postdoctoral fellow Nat. Ctr. Atmospheric Rsch., Boulder, Colo., 1966-67; rsch. assoc. geophysical fluid dynamics lab. NOAA, Princeton, N.J., 1967-69; rsch. scientist Courant Inst. Math. Scis., N.Y.C., 1969-71; meteorologist Goddard inst. space studies NASA, 1971-74; adj. prof. Columbia U., NYU, 1971-74; head numerical weather prediction sect. Nat. Ctr. Atmospheric Rsch., Boulder, 1974-79; prof. meteorology Scripps Inst. Oceanography, U. Calif.-San Diego, La Jolla, 1979—. Chmn. bd. dirs. Aspen Global Change Inst. Author: The Forgiving Air: Understanding Environmental Change, 1996. Fellow: AAAS, Am. Meteorol. Soc.; mem.: Am. Geophys. Union. Office: U Calif San Diego Scripps Inst Oceanography 9500 Gilman Dr Dept 0224 La Jolla CA 92093-5004

SOMERVILLE, WALTER RALEIGH, JR. government official; b. Macon, N.C., Feb. 17, 1930; s. Walter Raleigh and Bettie Lou (Hunt) S.; m. Jean Renwick Nava, Sept. 12, 1975; 1 child, Thomasine A. Walker-Adams, 1 stepchild, Pamela Nava-Whitter. BA in Bus. Adminstrn., U. Md., 1970. cert. sr. exec. edn. program Fed. Exec. Inst., 1975; diploma program sr. mgr.s in govt. John F. Kennedy Sch. Govt., Harvard U., 1992. Personnel staffing specialist FAA, Washington, 1962-65; personnel mgmt. specialist OEO, 1965-67, Office Sec. Transp., Washington, 1967-70; chief civilian equal opportunity div. USCG Transp. Dept., 1970-83, dir. civil rights, 1983-96, asst. commandant civil rights, 1996—. Trainee Fed. Exec. Devel. Program, 1975-76. Chmn. fin. com. Christ United Meth. Ch., Washington, 1976-85, chmn. adminstrv. coun., 1985-86; mem. human rels. edn. bd. Dept. Def., 1983-85; mem. Dept. Def. Equal Oportunity Coun.; chmn. placement and counseling com. for industry cluster Paul Quinn Coll.; bd. trustees USCG Acad., 1994—. Served in USAF, 1951-60. Recipient Outstanding Performance award, 1981, 82, 83, Proclamation award City Coun. New Orleans, 1987, Key to City of Franklin, Ky., 1992, Sr. Exec. Svc. Cash Performance award, 1993, 2000, Outstanding Contbns. to Higher Edn. Spl. award Nat. Assn. Equal Opportunity in Higher Edn., 1995, nat. role model innovator award Minority Access, Inc., 2000; named to Nat. Assn. Equal Opportunityin Higher Edn. Registry of Disting. Individuals, 1995. Mem. Am. Mgmt. Assn., NAACP (diamond life membership, Roy Wilkins meritorious svc. award, 1987, Benjamin L. Hooks disting. svc. award, 1993), Sr. Execs. Assn., Washington Urban League (life), U. Md. Alumni Assn. (century club), Nat. Urban League (charter mem. Pres.'s Club, mem. black exec. exch. program, vis. prof. historically black colls. and univs.). Home: 1228 4th St SW Washington DC 20024-2302 Office: 2100 2nd St SW Washington DC 20593-0002

SOMERVILLE, WARREN THOMAS, II, management consultant; b. Balt., Oct. 28, 1942; s. Charles Arthur and Ruth Simpson (Bachtell) S.; m. Susan May Wittgrefe, Aug. 5, 1972; children: Stacey Michelle, Warren Thomas III. BBA, Towson U., 1978. Electronics technician Towson Labs., Balt., 1963-64, Electronic Modules, Inc., Timonium, Md., 1964-65; specification writer Western Electric, Cockeysville, 1965-67; bldgs. and support system engr. Lucent Techologies/Western Electric, 1967—; mgmt. cons., hot slide engring. network cons. svcs. Lucent Technologies, 1983—, engr. group/engr. support systems, 1996—. Pres. Jestage Investments, Shrewsbury, Pa., 1973—. Commr. Shrewsbury Water & Sewage Com., 1976-84. Served with USN, 1961-63. Republican. Episcopalian. Avocations: swimming, sailing, target shooting. Home: 47 Crosswind Dr Shrewsbury PA 17361-1842 Office: Lucent Techs 225 Schilling Cir Cockeysville Hunt Valley MD 21031-1102 E-mail: wsomerville@lucent.com.

SOMES, JOAN MARIE, emergency nurse; b. St. Paul, Aug. 17, 1952; d. Richard and Jane (Blaiser) Friesen; m. Michael Somes, Nov. 15, 1975. BA in Nursing, Coll. of St. Catherine, St. Paul, 1974; paramedic cert., Inver Hills C.C., Inver Grove Heights, Minn., 1976; MSN, U. Minn., 1989; postgrad., Columbia So. U., Orange Beach, Ala., 1998—. RN, Minn.; cert. emergency nurse; nat. registered EMT-paramedic; cert. ACLS instr., PALS instr.; cert. TNCC instr.; cert. CATN instr., ENPC instr.; cert. ACLS-EP instr. Paramedic A.L.F. Ambulance, Apple Valley, Minn., 1987-97; charge nurse emergency dept. Divine Redeemer Hosp., South St. Paul, 1974-94; staff nurse emergency dept. St. Joseph's Hosp., St. Paul, 1994—, emergency dept. educator/staff nurse, 1999—. Instr. numerous local cmty. colls., hosps. and ambulance svcs.; item writer CEN exam., 1994-96, 96-98; edn. specialist Regions Emergency Med. Svcs., 1994—; spkr. in field; co-chair Cornerstones Emergency Nursing Conf., 2000. Author nursing home study courses; contbr. articles to profl. jour. Grantee Glaxo Pharm. Co., 1989, Health East Found. 1991, 94, 97, 98, recipient Mary Piner award Minn. Emergency Nurses Assn. State Coun. 1994-98. Mem.: Vision Coun. for Profl. Devel., Nat. Emergency Nurses Assn., Emergency Nurses Assn. (dir./state coun. liaison Greater Twin Cities chpt., sec. 1996—98, chair state trauma com. 1994—95, sec. treas. Minn. state coun. 1994—95, 1997—98, 1999—2000, state coun. rep. 2001—, pres. Greater Twin Cities chpt. 2001—).

SOMIT, ALBERT, political educator; b. Chgo., Oct. 25, 1919; s. Samuel and Mary (Rosenblum) S.; m. Leyla D. Shapiro, Aug. 31, 1947; children: Scott H., Jed L. AB, U. Chgo., 1941, PhD, 1947. Prof. polit. philosophy N.Y. U., 1945-65; chmn. dept. polit. sci. State U. N.Y. at Buffalo, 1966-69, exec. v.p., 1970-80; acting pres. SUNY, Buffalo, 1976-77; pres. So. Ill. U., Carbondale, 1980-87, disting. service prof., 1987—. Fellow Netherlands Inst. Advanced Study, 1978-79; Nimitz prof. polit. philosophy U.S. Naval War Coll., 1961-62 Author: (with Joseph Tanenhaus) The Development of American Political Science: From Burgess to Behavioralism, 1967, expanded edit., 1982, (with Tanenhaus) American Political Science: A Profile of A Discipline, 1964, Political Science and the Study of the Future, 1974, Biology and Politics: Recent Explorations, 1976, (with others) The Literature of Biopolitics 1963-1977, 1978, 1980, 1983, 1986, Biopolitics and Mainstream Political Science A Master Bibliography, 1990, (with Wildenmann) Hierarchy and Democracy, 1991, (with Peterson) The Dynamics of Evolution, 1992, (with Wildenmann) The Victorious Incumbent: A Threat to Democracy?, 1994, (with Peterson) The Political Behavior of Older Americans, 1994, Research in Biopolitics: Human Nature and Politics, 1995, Birth Order and Political Behavior, 1996, Recent Explorations in Biology and Politics, 1997, Darwinism, Dominance, and Democracy: The Biological Basis of Authoritarianism, 1997. Served with AUS, 1950-52. Address: 4971 Cindy Ave Carlsbad CA 92008

SOMLYO, ANDREW PAUL, physiology, biophysics and cardiology educator; b. Budapest, Hungary; s. Anton and Clara Maria (Kiss) S.; m. Avril V. Russell, May 25, 1961; 1 child, Andrew Paul. BS, U. Ill., 1954, MS, MD, U. Ill., 1956; MS, Drexel Inst. Tech., Phila., 1963; MA (hon.), U. Pa., Phila., 1981; hon. D, U. Catholique de Louvain, Belgium, 1997. Asst. physician Columbia-Presbyn. Med. Ctr., N.Y.C., 1960-61; rsch. assoc. Presbyn. Hosp., Phila., 1961-67; asst. prof. pathology U. Pa., 1964-67, assoc. prof., 1967-71, prof., 1971-88, prof. physiology and pathology, 1973-88, dir. Pa. Muscle Inst., 1973-88; Charles Slaughter prof. molecular physiology-biol. physics U. Va., Charlottesville, 1988—, chmn. dept., 1988—, prof. cardiology, 1988—, dir. ctr. structural biology, 1997—. Cons. NIH; Brit. Heart Found. vis. prof. Hammersmith Hosp., London, Shanghai (China) Med. U.. Author: (with others) Vascular Neuroeffector Systems, 1971, The Handbook of Physiology, Vascular Smooth Muscle, 1981, Microprobe Analysis of Biological Systems, 1981, Recent Advances in Light and Optical Imaging in Biology and Medicine, 1986; editor: Jour. Muscle Research and Cell Motility, 1987, FASEB Jour., 1996; contbr. numerous articles to jours. including Biol. Chemistry, Jour. Physiology, Am. Heart Jour., Jour. Pediatrics, Jour. Cell Biology, Cell Calcium, others; mem. editl. bd. Blood Vessels, Am. Jour. Physiology, 1979-83, Magnesium: Experimental and Clinical Rsch., Jour. Structural Biology. Recipient The Louis and Artur Lucian award for rsch. in circulatory diseases, 1996; Biophysical Soc. fellow, 1999. Fellow AAAS; mem. Soc. Gen. Physiologists, Am. Physiol. Soc. Biophys. Soc., Electron Microscopy Soc., Microbeam Analysis Soc. (Presdl. Sci. award 1996), Am. Soc. for Cell Biology, Hungarian Physiol. Soc. (hon.), Microscopy Soc. Am. (Disting. Scientist award for biol. scis. 1994), Alpha Omega Alpha Med. Soc. (CIBA-GEIGY award for Hypertension Rsch. 1991). Office: U Va Sch Medicine Dept Molecular Phys/Biol Physics PO Box 800736 Charlottesville VA 22908-0736

SOMMA, BEVERLY KATHLEEN, medical and marriage educator; b. Bayonne, N.J., June 13, 1938; d. Leroy and Isabelle (Lysaght) Latourette; m. Louis Anthony Somma, Nov. 24, 1973; children: Francis, Keith. AS, Ocean County Coll., 1973; BA, Georgian Ct., 1977; MAT, Monmouth Coll., 1978; postgrad., U. Pa., 1980-85, 88-89. Nurse's aide Community Meml. Hosp., Toms River, N.J., 1971-72; with marriage coun. dept. psychiatry U. Pa. Sch. Medicine, Phila., 1993—; with Helene Fuld Med. Ctr. Edn., 1993—. Ednl. cons. Ctr. for Cognitive Edn., Yardley, Pa., 1990—, tng. program Archdiocese Phila., Penn Found., Inc., 1993; lectr. Marriage Coun. of Phila. dept. psychiatry, sch. medicine U. Pa., 1993—; with Helene Fuld Med. Ctr. Edn., 1993—. Voter svc. chmn. LWV, Toms River, N.J., 1971-72; contact rep. Pro Life Coalition, Phila.; vol. nursing tutor Ocean County Coll., Toms River, 1972; vol. tchr.'s aide St. Michael the Archangel, Levittown, Pa., 1987-88; vol. VITA; counselor Bucks County Coun. Alcoholism and Drug Dependence, Inc., 1984-93; active World Affairs Coun. Phila. All Am. scholar; recipient U.S. Achievement Acad. Nat. award. Mem. Nat. Soc. for Fund Raising Execs., Alumni Assn. Georgian Ct. Coll., Ocean County Coll., Bucks County C.C., Sigma Tau Delta. Republican. Methodist. Avocations: cooking, tennis, golf, jogging, ice-skating. Home: 1506 Kathy Dr Yardley PA 19067-1717

SOMMARUGA, CORNELIO, humanitarian services organization administrator, diplomat; b. Rome, Dec. 29, 1932; s. Carlo and Anna Maria (Valagussa) S.; m. Ornella Marzorati; 6 children. LLD, U. Zurich, Switzerland, 1957; D of Polit. Affairs (hon.), U. Fribourg, Switzerland, 1985; D in Internat. Rels. (hon.), U. Minho, Portugal, 1989; D of Medicine (hon.), U. Bologna, Italy, 1991; D in Law (hon.), U. Nice-Sophia, Antipolis, France, 1992, Seoul Nat. U., Rep. of Korea, 1992; PhD in Law (hon.), Geneva U., 1997; LHD (hon.), Webster U., 1998. Various diplomatic positions Swiss Confedn.'s Svc., 1960-73; dep. sec. gen. European Free Trade Assn., Geneva, 1973-75; minister plenipotentiary Dept. Pub. Economy, Berne, Switzerland, 1976-77, amb. plenipotentiary Switzerland, 1977-80, del. Swiss Govt. for Trade Agreements Switzerland, 1980-83; state sec. external econ. affairs Switzerland, 1984-86; pres. Internat. Com. Red Cross, Geneva, 1987-99, Found. Caux-Initiatives of Change, Caux, Switzerland, 2000—. Chmn. bd. J.P. Morgan (Suisse) Geneva, 2000—; pres. Geneva Internat. Ctr. for Humanitarian Demining, 2000—; chmn. bd. Karl PopperFound., Zug, 2000—. Recipient Presdl. award Tel-Aviv U., 1995, North-South prize Coun. of Europe, 2001. Home: 16 chemin Crets-de-Champnel CF-1206 Geneva Switzerland Office: GICHD BP 1300 CH-1211 Geneva Switzerland E-mail: cornelio.sommaruga@bluewin.ch.

SOMMER, ALFRED, medical educator, scientist, ophthalmologist; b. N.Y.C., Oct. 2, 1942; s. Joseph and Natalie Sommer; m. Jill Abramson Sommer, Sept. 1, 1963; children: Charles Andrew, Marni Jane. BS summa cum laude, Union Coll., 1963; MD, Harvard U., 1967; MHS in Epidemiology, Johns Hopkins U., 1973. Diplomate Am. Bd. Ophthalmology, Nat. Bd. Med. Examiners. Tchg. fellow in medicine Harvard U. Med. Sch., Boston, 1968—69; dir. Nutritional Blindness Prevention Rsch. Program, Bandung, Indonesia, 1976—79; vis. fellow Inst. Ophthalmology U. London, 1979—80; founding dir., Dana Ctr. for Preventive Ophthalmology Johns Hopkins Med. Insts., Balt., 1980—90; assoc. prof. Johns Hopkins U., 1981—85, prof. ophthalmology, epidemiology and internat. health, 1985—, dean Johns Hopkins Sch. Hygiene and Pub. Health, 1990—. Vis. prof. ophthalmology U. Padjadjaran, Indonesia, 1976—79; cons., advisor Helen Keller Internat., N.Y.C., 1973—; cons., chmn. com. NIH, Bethesda, Md., 1981—; bd. dirs. Internat. Agy. for the Prevention of Blindness, Geneva; cons., com. mem. NAS, Washington, 1989; chmn. program adv. group on blindness prevention WHO, Geneva, 1989—90, com. mem., 1978—90, expert com., 1990—; chmn. steering com. Internat. Vitamin A Cons. Group, Washington, 1975—; pres. Internat. Fedn. of Tissue Banks; chmn. sci. adv. bd. Edna McConnell Clark Found.; mem. adv. com. Internat. Coun. Ophthalmology; dir. Becton Dickenson Corp., 1998—, Acad. Ednl. Devel.; lectr. in field. Author: Epidemiology and Statistics for the Ophthalmologist, 1980, Nutritional Blindness: Xerophthalmia and Keratomalacia, 1982, Vitamin A Deficiency: Health, Survival and Vision, 1995, Detection and Control of Vitamin A Deficiency and Xerophthalmia, 1978, 1982, 1995; chmn. bd. overseers Am. Jours. Epidemiology and Epidemiologic Revs., 1990—, also bd. dirs., —; contbr. articles to profl. jours. Recipient Charles A. Dana Found. award for Pioneering Achievement in Health, 1988, Disting. Svc. award for Contbn. to Vision Care, APHA, 1988, E.V. McCollum Internat. Lectureship in Nutrition, Am. Inst. Nutrition, 1988, Second Ann. Am. Coll. Advancement in Medicine Achievement award in Preventative Medicine, 1990, Disting. Contbn. to World Ophthalmology award, Internat. Fedn. Ophthal. Socs., 1990, Smadel award, Infectious Diseases Soc. Am., 1990, Doyne Meml. award, Oxford, 1995, Albert Lasker award Clin. Rsch., 1997, Helmut Horten Rsch. award, 1997, Gold medal, Singapore Ophthalmology Soc., 1997, Duke Elder Gold medal, Internat. Coun. Ophthalmology, 1998, Prince Mahidol award for contbns. to pub. health, 1998, Bristol-Meyers Nutrition Rsch. award, 2001, Danone Internat. award in nutrition rsch., 2001. Mem.: NAS, Chgo. Ophthal. Soc. (Gifford Meml. award 1997), Pa. Coll. Physicians (de Schweinitz award 1996), Assn. Schs. of Pub. Health (pres.), Internat. Assn. to Prevent Blindness (bd. dirs. 1978—), Nat. Soc. to Prevent Blindness (bd. dirs. 1989), Am. Acad. Ophthalmology (chmn. pub. health com. 1982—88, chmn. Quality of Care/Clin. Guidelines 1986—90, Hon. award 1986, Sr. Hon. award 1997, blindness prevention award 1998, Jackson Meml. lectr. award 1999), Inst. Medicine of NAS (Food and Nutrition bd.). Achievements include first to detail and pulish epidemiologic approach disaster assessment; nutritional indices predict subsequent mortality in children, surveillance and containment is effective intervention strategy for controlling smallpox; vitamin A deficiency increases childhood mortality and vitamin A supplementation decreases childhood mortality; nerve fiber layer is valuable diagnostic and prognostic sign of early glaucoma; routine preventive services cost-effective in eye disease; clinical guideline development and importance of outcome assessment; research in epidemiologic and public health approaches to ophthalmology, blindness prevention, and improved health and survival. Office: Johns Hopkins U Bloomburg Sch Pub Health 615 N Wolfe St Rm 1041 Baltimore MD 21205-2103 Fax: 410-955-0121. E-mail: asommer@jhsph.edu.

SOMMER, EMMANUEL, civil engineering consultant; b. Paris, July 1, 1937; arrived in Israel, 1963; s. Hélène Chécinski, Aug. 30, 1959; children: Hillel, Yael, Eldad. Degree in engring., ETP Spl. Sch. of Pub. Works, Paris, 1961. Registered and lic. engr., Israel. Planning engr. Metrikin, Efrony & Schoenberg, Architects, Jerusalem, 1964-68; ind. cons. engr., 1968—. Arbitrator, provider expert testimony various ct. procs., Jerusalem, 1985—. Mem. Internat. Assn. for Bridge and Structural Engring., Assn. Civil Engring. (mem. Jerusalem com. 1993). Jewish. Office: E Sommer Cons Engr Ben-Yehuda St 36 IL-94583 Jerusalem Israel E-mail: emsommer@inter.net.il.

SOMMER, ROBERT GEORG, dermatologist; b. Vienna, Austria, May 14, 1933; came to U.S., 1940; s. Robert and Mathilda Anne (Eberling) Feger S.; m. Barbara Ann Black, Dec. 27, 1958 (dec. Feb. 1981); children: Karen A., Robert W., John W., Jeffrey B.; m. Margaret Ellen Markey Payson, Dec. 29, 1993. BS in Liberal Arts, Tufts U., 1955; MD, U. Rochester, 1959. Pvt. practice dermatology, Portland, Maine, 1967-98; from instr. to asst. prof. dermatology U. Vt. Coll. Medicine at Maine Med. Ctr., 1967-74, dir. divsn. dermatology, 1974-98, retired, 1998. Capt. USAF, 1961-64. Fellow Am. Acad. Dermatology, New Eng. Dermatol. Soc. Avocation: fly fishing. Office: 45 Foreside Common Dr Falmouth ME 04105-2319

SOMMER, ROBERT GEORGE, public relations executive; b. N.Y.C., Feb. 6, 1959; s. Ernest Lorge and Donna Anne (Lapin) S.; m. Marjorie Ann Glaser, Oct. 20, 1985; children: Alexander David, William Ernest. BA, Columbia U., 1983; MA, Rutgers U., 1984. Policy analyst EPA, Washington, 1984-85; profl. staff, speechwriter energy and commerce com. U.S. Ho. of Reps., 1985-87; exec. v.p. MWW/Strategic Communications, East Rutherford, N.J., 1987—. Bd. dirs. Ridgewood Savings Bank of N.J. Contbr. editls. to N.Y. Times. Commr. Environ. Commn. Village of Ridgewood, N.J., 1989—, N.J. Pub. BroadcastingAuthority, 1990-94; chmn. Ridgewood Dem. Com., 1989-93, Eagleton Inst. of Politics Found., 1993-96, Rutgers Univ.; trustee Cmty. Resource Coun., 1990, Gov. Elect Environ. Task Force, Trenton, N.J., Dem. Nat. Com., Washington, 1992—, N.J. Network Found., 1994—; del. Dem. Nat. Conv. 1992; vice chair N.J. Network, Newark, 1992-94; bd. mem. Boy Scouts Am., 1994—, Pub. Affairs Coun., Washington, 1998—; bd. govs. Ramaso Coll., Mahwah, N.J., 1997—. Mem. Pub. Rels. Soc. Am., Nat. Assn. Profl. Environ. Communicators, N.J. Assn. Environ. Commissioners, Trenton, (adv. bd.) 1990—. Jewish. Home: 211 Sunset Ave Ridgewood NJ 07450-2420*

SOMMER, VALERIE KULIS, occupational health nurse; b. Balt., July 1, 1957; d. Melvin R. and Ann (Adamik) Kulis.27546226 AA, Harford Community Coll., 1984; BSN, U. Md., 1990; M in Health Svcs. Adminstrn., Ctrl. Mich. U., 1994. Cert. med./surgical nurse, advanced cardiac life support, basic trauma life support. Staff nurse med./surgical Loch Raven VA Med. Ctr., Balt., 1984-86, Perry Point (Md.) VA Med. Ctr., 1986-90; staff nurse emergency rm. U.S. Kirk Army Health Clinic, APG, Md., 1990-93, occupational health nurse, 1993—; IV therapy nurse Fallston Gen. Hosp., 1997-99; cmty. health nurse Upper Chesapeake Health Sys., 1996—; staff nurse Patient First, 1999—. Contbr. poetry to lit. mag. Mem. Bel Air Vol. Fire Dept. Mem. Md. Nurses Assn., Emergency Nurses Assn., Delta Kappa Gamma Internat. Home: 2600 Long Meadow Dr Abingdon MD 21009 Office: Dept Army Kirk US Army Health Clinic 2501 Oakington St OHC Clin Aberdeen Proving Ground MD 21005 E-mail: vkl357@webtv.net.

SOMMERER, JOHN, accountant; b. Mt. Holly, N.J., Oct. 30, 1947; s. John Price and Barbara Elizabeth (Davis) S.; m. Diane Catherine Kuszaj, Aug. 5, 1967; children: James Peter, John Joseph, Paul Andrew, Matthew Thomas. BS, U. Hartford, 1969; MBA, U. Toronto, 1972; postgrad., Columbia U., 1972-74. CPA, Fla., N.J., N.Y. Sr. cons. Deloitte and Touche, N.Y.C., 1974-78; dir. mgmt. info. systems Pantry Pride Enterprises, Ft. Lauderdale, Fla., 1978-82; mng. ptnr. John Sommerer and Co., P.A., Coral Springs, 1982—; mayor City of Coral Springs, 1994—. Treas. Coral Springs Cmty. Chest, 1988-94. Mem. Coral Springs Kiwanis (bd. dirs. 1990, 92), Coral Springs C. of C. (pres. 1987, treas. 1986, bd. dirs. 1986-88). Roman Catholic. Home: 9501 NW 44th Pl Coral Springs FL 33065-6602 Office: John Sommerer and Co PA 3300 N University Dr Coral Springs FL 33065-6309 E-mail: cpa@accountant.com.

SOMMERFELD, DAVID WILLIAM, lawyer, educator; b. Detroit, Jan. 21, 1942; s. Henry Anthony and Hilda (Diffley) S.; m. Anne Marlaine Toth, June 27, 1964; children: Catherine, David Jr., Michael, Caroline. BS, U. Detroit, 1963; JD, Detroit Coll., 1967. Trust officer Nat. Bank Detroit, 1963-68; tax supr. Ernst & Ernst, Detroit, 1968-73; ptnr. Monaghan, Campbell, LoPrete & McDonald, 1973-77; prof. Detroit Coll., 1977-86; ptnr. Butzel Long, Detroit, 1987—. Lectr. Ind. Soc. CPAs, Indpls., 1980-93, Ohio Soc. CPAs, Columbus, 1987, W.Va. Soc. CPAs, Charleston, 1983-86, 91. Editor Mich. Probate and Trust Law Jour., 1981-83. Named one of Best Lawyers in Am. Woodward/White Inc., 1999-2001. Fellow Am. Coll. of Trust and Estate Counsel; mem. Mich. Bar Assn., Detroit Bar Assn., Am. Inst. CPA's, Mich. Assn. CPA's, Forest Lake Country Club, Detroit Athletic Club. Roman Catholic. Avocations: bowling, spectator sports, gardening. Office: Butzel Long Ste 200 100 Bloomfield Hills Pkwy Bloomfield Hills MI 48304

SOMMERFELD, JUDE THOMAS, chemical engineer, educator; b. Cin., Feb. 4, 1936; s. Henry Anthony and Hilda Catherine (Diffley) S.; m. Rosemary Sniatkowski, May 17, 1958 (div. 1983); children: Loretta, Margaret, Maria, Joanna; m. Elizabeth Ryder, Apr. 18, 1992. B in Chem. Engring., U. Detroit, 1958; MS in Engring., U. Mich., 1960, PhD, 1963. Registered profl. engr., Ga. Systems engr. Monsanto Co., St. Louis, 1963-66; dir. process engring. BASF-Wyandotte (Mich.) Corp., 1966-70; assoc. prof. Ga. Inst. Tech.,

Atlanta, 1970-75, prof., 1975—. Contbr. numerous articles to profl. jours. Fellow AIChE. Roman Catholic. Avocations: tennis, guitar, classical music, whitewater rafting. Home: 2204 Oakawana Dr NE Atlanta GA 30345-3551 Office: Dept Chem Engring Ga Tech U Atlanta GA 30332-0100 E-mail: jude.sommerfeld@che.gatech.edu.

SOMMERFELD, MARIANNA, retired social worker, writer; b. Frankfurt, Germany, Jan. 25, 1920; d. Martin and Helene (Schott) S. BA, Smith Coll., 1940; MA, Radcliffe Coll., 1946; MSW, Simmons Coll., 1957. Lic. ind. social worker. Tchr. Latin, German, English Burnham Sch. Girls, Northampton, Mass., 1940-43; German translator Yale Inst. Human Rels., New Haven, 1943-44; tchr. Northfield (Mass.) Sch. Girls, 1944-45; psychiat. social worker McLean Hosp., Belmont, Mass., 1957-59, Gaebler Children's Unit/Met. State Hosp., Waltham, 1959-62, Boston U./Boston City Hosp., 1962-67, New Eng. Med. Ctr., Boston, 1967-71; pvt. practice Cambridge, Mass., 1962-68; supr. clin. social work Erich Lindeman Health Ctr., Boston, 1971-90; writer, 1976—. Author: Marianna Sommerfeld: Diary of a Single Woman, 1991. Vol. Cambridge Sch., 1993. Mem. NOW, AFL-CIO, Planned Parenthood, Nat. Writers Union, Women's Nat. Book Assn., PEN New Eng. (assoc.).

SOMMERFELDT, JOHN ROBERT, historian, educator; b. Detroit, Feb. 4, 1933; s. Melvin John and Virginia Zita (Gruenheck) S.; m. Patricia Natalie Levinske, Aug. 25, 1956; children: Ann, James, John, Elizabeth. AB, U. Mich., 1954, AM, 1956, PhD, 1960. Instr. history Stanford U., 1958-59; from instr. to prof. Western Mich. U., 1959-78; prof. history U. Dallas, 1978—, chmn. dept. history, 1984-87, univ. pres., 1978-80. Dir. Medieval Inst., Western Mich. U., 1961-76; exec. dir. Inst. Cistercian Studies, 1973-78; dir. Center Contemplative Studies, 1976-78; pres. Cistercian Publs., 1973-79, chmn. bd., 1976-79 Author: The Spiritual Teachings of Bernard of Clairvaux, 1991; editor: Studies in Medieval Culture, 12 vols., 1964-78, Studies in Medieval Cistercian History, II, 1977, Cistercian Ideals and Reality, 1978, Simplicity and Ordinariness, 1980, The Chimaera of His Age: Studies in Bernard of Clairvaux, 1980, Abba: Guides to Wholeness and Holiness, East and West, 1981, Erudition at God's Service, 1987, Bernardus Magister, 1992, Studiosorum Speculum, 1993, Studies in the Theology of St. Thomas Aquinas, 1995. Fulbright scholar, 1954-55; Univ. fellow U. Mich., 1956-57. Mem. Mediaeval Acad. Am., Am. Hist. Assn., Am. Catholic Hist. Assn., Am. Soc. Ch. History, Phi Beta Kappa, Phi Eta Sigma, Phi Kappa Phi. Republican. Roman Catholic. Home: 2809 Warren Cir Irving TX 75062-8938 Office: U Dallas Dept History Irving TX 75062-4736 E-mail: jrsommer@acad.udallas.edu.

SOMMERFELT, SOREN CHRISTIAN, foreign affairs, international trade consultant, former Norwegian diplomat, lawyer; b. Oslo, May 9, 1916; s. Soren Christian and Sigrid (Nicolaysen) S.; m. Frances Bull, June 27, 1947; 1 child, Cathrine. LLD, Oslo U., 1940. Joined Norwegian Fgn. Svc., 1941; pvt. sec. to fgn. minister, UN sec. gen. Trygve Lie, 1941-44; assigned to UN Secretariat, 1946, Div. Refugees' and Displaced Persons, 1st sec. Norwegian Embassy, Copenhagen, 1948-50; counselor Norwegian del. to NATO, 1950-52; dep. head. econ. dept. Norwegian Ministry Fgn. Affairs, 1953-56, head, 1956-60; amb., head Norwegian del. to European Free Trade Assn., Gen. Agreement on Tariffs and Trade (GATT), and UN European Office, 1960-68; chmn. GATT Contracting Parties, 1968; amb. to Fed. Republic Germany, 1968-73, U.S.A., 1973-79, Italy, 1979-81; head Norwegian del. negotiating entry into European Communities, 1970-72; counsel Arent, Fox, Kintner, Plotkin & Kahn, Washington, 1982-84; ptnr. cons. firm Washington Resources, Inc., 1984-91; sr. ptnr. Sommerfelt Assocs., Washington, 1992—. Decorated comdr. Order St. Olav, Norway, grand cross Order of Merit, Fed. Republic Germany, grand cross Order of Merit, Italy, comdr. with star Order of North Star, Sweden, comdr. Order of Leopold II, Belgium, knight Order of Falcon, Iceland, knight Order of Dannebrog, Denmark. Mem. Metropolitan Club (Washington), Chevy Chase Club (Md.), Norske Selskab Club (Oslo). Home: PO Box 1183 Middleburg VA 20118-1183 Office: Sommerfelt Assocs 1250 24th St NW Washington DC 20037-1124

SOMMERLAD, ROBERT EDWARD, environmental research engineer; b. Jersey City, Aug. 27, 1937; s. Herman Francis and Helen Rita (Joyce) S.; m. Margaret Doreen Breen, Sept. 9, 1961; children: Sharon K., Michael E., Ellen J. BSME, N.J. Inst. Tech., 1960, MSME, 1963, postgrad., 1965. Devel. engr., rsch. assoc. Foster Wheeler Energy Corp., Livingston, N.J., 1960-71, head air pollution control sect., 1971-74; v.p. contract ops. Foster Wheeler Devel. Corp., 1974-84; pres. Enviresponse Inc., 1985-86; dir. bus. devel. Energy and Environ. Rsch. Corp., Edison, N.J., 1987-88; cons., 1988-89; dir. environ. bus. devel. Midwest Rsch. Inst., Falls Church, Va., 1989-90; mgr. combustion tech. Rsch.-Cottrell Cos ., 1990-92, cons., 1992-93; mktg. dir. PSI Powerserve, Andover, Mass., 1993-94, cons., program mgr., 1994-95; cons. Gas Rsch. Inst., Chgo., 1995-98, GE Energy and Environ. Rsch. Corp., Gurnee, Ill., 1998—. Mem. coal combustion and applications working group U.S. Dept. Energy U. San Diego, 1981-84. Patentee in field. V.p. Cranford (N.J.) Cmty. Pools Parents Assn., 1975-77, 86-87, pres., 1977-79, 84-89; chmn. N.J. Swimming and Diving Conf., Cranford, 1986-89; v.p. Stonebrook Crossings Homeowners Assn., Gurnee, 1998-2000, pres., 2000—; com. for family awuatic ctr. Gurnee Park Dist., 1996—. Recipient Outstanding Achievement award Westfield YMCA, 1975. Fellow ASME (mem. rsch. com. indsl. and mcpl. waste 1971—, vice chmn. 1972-74, sec. 1987-91, mem. environ. affairs com. 1982-92, mem. dioxin com. 1985-92, mem. bd. performance test codes 1986-97, chmn. boiler-calorimeter com. 1986-89, numerous com. and conf. chairmanships); mem. Air and Waste Mgmt. Assn. (mem. AE-1 com. on particulate and associated acid gases, sec. 1991-94, vice chair 1996), Watchung Amateur Ski Club (mem. exec. bd. 1986-87) (Mountainside, N.J.). Roman Catholic. Home: 1368 Knottingham Dr Gurnee IL 60031-5632

SOMMERS, CONRAD HOYLE, lawyer; b. Dallas, July 5, 1952; s. Conrad John and Latrelle (Dunaway) S.; m. Angela Sue Wells, Sept. 9, 1978; children: Jaime Lynn, Jessica Lee. BA, U. Tex., 1973, JD, 1975, LLM, 1976. Bar: Tex. 1976, U.S. Supreme Ct. 1981, U.S. Ct. Appeals (5th cir.) 1977, U.S. Tax Ct. 1977, U.S. Ct. Mil. Appeals, 1978, U.S. Dist. Ct. (no. dist.) Tex. 1977. Ptnr. Lee & Sommers, Dallas, 1976-77; ptnr., v.p. Lee, Sommers & Parks, P.C., 1977-78; sole practice, 1978—. Mem. Tex. Criminal Def. Lawyers Assn., Dallas County Criminal Bar Assn. Republican. Lutheran. Office: 6440 N Central Expy Ste 302 Dallas TX 75206-4132

SOMMERS, DANA EUGENE, insurance agency executive; b. Marion, Ind., Oct. 15, 1953; s. Darlton L. and Martha F. (Bontrager) S.; m. Judy L. Grotenhuis, Aug. 21, 1976; children: Erin L., Danae N. BA in Social Work, Taylor U., 1976; MA in Student Personnel Adminstrn., Ball State U., 1977. Resident dir., coordinator Calvin Coll., Grand Rapids, Mich., 1977-79; ins. agt. Grotenhuis, 1979—80, ops. mgr., agt., 1980—81, v.p. adminstrn., treas., 1981—82, exec. v.p., treas., 1982—83, pres., treas., 1983—, chmn., 1993, chmn., CEO No. Benefits Network, 2000. Vice chmn. bd. dirs. Grand Rapids Area Youth for Christ, 1986; bd. dirs., exec. com. Marantha Bible Conf., 1995—, chmn. pers. com., 1987, selection com., 1988, bus. com., 1990-91; devel. coun. St. Mary's Hosp., Grand Rapids, 1987—, co-chair corp. campaign, 1991, 93, 97-98, bd. dirs., bd. vice chair 1998-2001, bd. chair, 2002—; exec. bd., chmn. Leader Grand Rapids, 1990—, chmn. program com., 1987-88, selection com. 1988-89, immediate past chair 1991-92; active Greater Grand Rapids Chamber Found. Bd., 1987-88, 90-2000, v.p., 1989, pres., 1992-93; vice chair bd. trustees Mich. Colls. Found., 1996-97, chair, 1997-99; trustee Davenport coll., 1995-98, vice chair, 1998-2001. Mem. Grand Rapids C. of C. (bd. dirs. 1990-98, vice chmn. adminstrn., treas. 1993-94, sr. vice chmn. 1995, chair 1996, past chair 1997, PAC steering com. 1999—, family bus. coun. 1998-2000), Cascade Hills Country Club, Grand Rapids Downtown Rotary (bd. dirs. 1991-94, program chair 1995-96), Econ. Club of Grand Rapids (bd. dirs. 1992-96, vice chair 1996—, chair 1997-98), Grand Rapids Pub. Edn. Fund (bd. dirs. 1995-98, sec. 1996, v.p. 1997, chair 1997-98, secchia millenium commn. chair natural resources com. 1999-2001, Grand Bank bd. dirs.). Republican. Avocations: reading, biking, golf. Office: Grotenhuis 660 Cascade West Pky SE Grand Rapids MI 49546-2147

SOMMERS, DAVID LYNN, architect; b. Salem, Ohio, June 17, 1949; s. Carl Ervin and Jean (Mohr) S. BArch, Kent State U., 1974. Registered architect, Ohio. Designer, draftsman Rice & Stewart, Architects, Painesville, Ohio, 1974-76; assoc. architect Prentiss Brown Assoc., Kent, 1977-81; project architect Edward W. Prusak, Assoc., Ravenna, 1982-83; pvt. practice Kent, 1983—. Mem. archtl. adv. com. Kent Planning Commn., 1985—; mem. Franklin Twp. Bd. Zoning Appeals; bd. bldg. appeals, City of Kent Bldg. Dept.; bd. dirs. Townhall II Drug and Crisis Intervention Ctr., Kent, 1986. Named one of Outstanding Young Men of Am., 1979-81. Mem. AIA (pres. Akron chpt. 1991—), Archs. Soc. Ohio, Jaycees (pres. Kent chpt. 1981-82, Jaycee of Yr. 1980, Keyman of Yr. 1981), Rotary (bd. dirs. 1994-96). Office: 136 N Water St # 208 Kent OH 44240-2450

SOMMERS, GEORGE R. lawyer; b. N.Y.C., Jan. 27, 1955; BA, U. So. Fla., 1975; JD, NYU, 1987. Bar: N.J. 1987, U.S. Dist. Ct. N.J. 1987, N.Y. 1988, U.S. Dist. Ct. (all dists.) N.Y. 1988, U.S. Ct. Appeals (3d cir.) 1988, U.S. Ct. Appeals (2d cir.) 1989, U.S. Supreme Ct. 1992. Assoc. Sullivan & Cromwell, N.Y.C., 1987-90; pvt. practice lawyer, 1990—. Pres. Bill of Rights Found., N.Y.C., 1994—. Seidler scholar NYU Sch. Law, N.Y.C., 1985. Mem. Hoboken Bar Assn. (pres. 1994). Jewish. Avocations: sailing, chess. Office: Ste 2211 67 Wall St New York NY 10005-3101

SOMMERS, MAXINE MARIE BRIDGET, travel writer, author, educator, publisher; b. Crystal Falls, Mich., May 7, 1932; d. Francis Ernest and Irene Catherine (Raher) Munns; m. Clemens Struve, June 10, 1952 (div. 1975); children: Stephen, Joseph; m. Norval Isom Sommers (dec. 1989). Student, Milw. Downer Coll. for Women, 1948-49, U. Tex. Med. Br., Galveston, 1949-51, St. Mary's Hosp., 1950-52. Owner, operator Pound Sterling Publ., 1982—, Pound Sterling Media Svc., 1983—. Author: A Texan on the Road Again to the Far East, 1992; author 30 travel, cuisine, children's and text books. Pres. Corpus Christi Symphony Guild, 1967-69, Tex. Assn. Symphony Orchestras, 1969; bd. dirs. Corpus Christi Symphony Soc., 1975—, South Tex. Health Syss. Agy., 1982-85; bd. dirs., pvt. svc. trainer Tex. divsn. Am. Cancer Soc., 1974-94; pres. Tex. Coastal Bend Mental Health Assn., 1976-78. Recipient cert. of award Byliners Tex. Writers, 1992, Bus. Assoc. Night award Am. Bus. Women's Assn., 1992, cert. merit Corpus Christi Symphony Guild, 1969, cert. recognition Tex. Women's Assn. Symphony Orchestras, 1969, various awards Am. Cancer Soc. Mem.: East West News Bur., N.Am. Travel Journalists Assn. Avocation: travel. Home: 4270 Ocean Dr Corpus Christi TX 78411-1283 E-mail: msommers@interconnect.net.

SOMMERS, PAUL MARTIN, economics educator; b. N.Y.C., May 17, 1948; s. Richard Faust and Gladys Alice (Gans) S. BA, U. Calif., Santa Cruz, l970; MA, U. Mich., 1972; PhD, U. Calif., San Diego, l976. Asst. prof. econs. Middlebury (Vt.) Coll., 1976-80, 81-82, assoc. prof., 1982-87, 88-89, prof., l989—. Vis. asst. prof. U. Calif., San Diego, l980-81; vis. assoc. prof. Va. Poly. Inst. and State U., Blacksburg, 1987-88. Author: Instructor's Manual for Microeconomics (Mansfield), 1979, 4th edit. 1988; editor: Welfare Reform in America, 1982, Diamonds Are Forever: The Business of Baseball, 1992; contbr. articles to profl. jours. Recipient Outstanding Tchr. award U. Calif., San Diego, l98l, lst prize Inst. for Socioecon. Studies, l985. Mem. Am. Econ. Assn., Atlantic Econ. Soc., Am. First Day Cover Soc., Vt. Philatelic Soc. Democrat. Avocation: cover collector.

SOMMERS, ROBERT THOMAS, editor, publisher, author; b. Balt., Aug. 6, 1926; s. Thomas Michael and Pearl Florence (Glendenning) S.; m. Helen Louise Ray, Oct. 19, 1952; children— Thomas Michael II, Patricia Ray. BS, U. Md., College Park, 1950. Reporter Evening Sun, Balt., 1950-62; reporter Evening Star, Washington, 1962-66; editor U.S. Golf Assn. Jour., N.Y.C., 1966-72, Far Hills, N.J., 1972-92. Author: The Oxford Book of Golf Anecdotes, 1995, The U.S. Open: Golf's Ultimate Challenge, 1987, 2nd edit., 1996, Bobby Jones in Chapman's Library of Golf, 1992; co-author: Great Shots, 1989; contbr. articles to profl. jours. Served with U.S. Coast Guard, 1944-46, PTO. Mem. Golf Writers Assn. Am., Assn. Golf Writers Gt. Britain, Authors Guild, Plainfield (N.J.) Country Club, Ballybunion Golf Club (Ireland), Kingston Heath Golf Club (Australia), Royal and Ancient Golf Club of St. Andrews (Scotland), The Legacy Golf and Tennis Club (Fla.). Republican. Episcopalian. Avocations: reading, golf, music. Home and Office: 8083 Spendthrift Ln Port Saint Lucie FL 34986-3122

SOMMERS, STEPHEN, film director; b. Indianapolis, IN; Motion picture dir., writer, prodr. Prodr., dir. films Tom and Huck, 1995; writer, dir. Catch Me If You Can, 1989, The Adventures of Huck and Finn, 1993, The Jungle Book, 1994, Deep Rising, 1998, The Mummy, 1999; The Mummy Returns, 2001; writer, prodr. The Scorpion King, 2002. prodr. T.V. movie Oliver Twist, 1997. Office: c/o DGA 7920 W Sunset Blvd Los Angeles CA 90046-3300*

SOMMERS, WILLIAM PAUL, management consultant, research and development institute executive; b. Detroit, July 22, 1933; s. William August and Mary Elizabeth (Baietto) S.; m. Josephine A. Sommers; children: William F., Clare M., John C. Hughes, Joanna M. Weems, Russell L. Hughes. BSE (scholar), U. Mich., 1955, MSE, 1956, PhD (Riggs fellow, Texaco fellow, Univ. fellow), 1961. Rsch. assoc. U. Mich. Inst. Sci. and Tech., Ann Arbor, 1958-61; chief chem. propulsion space and missile sys. Martin Marietta Corp., Balt., 1956-58, 61-63; v.p. Booz, Allen & Hamilton, Inc., Bethesda, Md., 1963-70, pres. tech. mgmt. group, 1973-79, sr. v.p., 1979-92; exec. v.p. Iameter, Inc., San Mateo, Calif., 1992-94; pres., CEO SRI Internat., Menlo Park, 1994-98, ret., 1998. Bd. dirs. Deutsche Scudder Fin. Svcs., Nuance Comm., Evergreen Solar, Inc., Pressure Sys., Inc., Gugenheimer Enterprises, Zassi Med., H2 Gen. Contbr. articles to profl. jours., also chpt. in book. Pres. Washington chpt. U. Mich. Alumni Club, 1970-71; v.p. Wildwood manor Citizens Assn., 1968-70; chief Adventure Guide program YMCA, 1971-72; bd. visitors Coll. Engring. U. Calif., Davis; mem. nat. adv. bd. Coll. Engring. U. Mich.; mem. conf. bd. Internat. Coun. on Innovation and Tech. Mem.: Met. Club, Ponte Vedra Inn and Country Club, Wianno Yacht Club, Marsh Landing Country Club, Willow Bend Country Club, Columbia Country Club, Pi Tau Sigma, Tau Beta Pi, Sigma Xi. Republican. Roman Catholic. E-mail: wsommers@attbi.com.

SOMMERVILLE, CHARLES JOHN, humanities educator; b. Lawrence, Kans., Aug. 15, 1938; s. William Baker and Katheryn Marie Sommerville; m. Susan Gail Hines, June 12, 1964; children: Eden Elizabeth, Henry Samuel. BA History, U. Kans., Lawrence, KS, 1960; MA History, U. Kans., Lawrence, Kansas, 1963; PhD History, U. Iowa, Iowa City, IA, 1970. Instr. Stanford U., Stanford, Calif., 1968—71; prof. U. Fla., Gainesville, Fla., 1971—. Mem. Inst. for Advanced Study, Princeton, NJ, 1993—94; sr. mentor Pew Younger Scholars Mentoring Program, Notre Dame, Ind., 2000—. Author: (book) The News Revoltution in England, The Secularization of Early Modern Day England, The Discovery of Childhood in Puritan England, The Rise and Fall of Childhood. Fellow: Ctr. the Study World Religions. Protestant. Avocation: opera. Office: History Dept University Florida PO Box 117320 Gainesville FL 32611-7320

SOMMESE, ANDREW JOHN, mathematics educator; b. N.Y.C., May 3, 1948; s. Joseph Anthony and Frances (Lia) S.; m. Rebecca Rooze DeBoer, June 7, 1971; children: Rachel, Ruth. BA in Math., Fordham U., 1969; PhD in Math., Princeton U., 1973. Gibbs instr. Yale U., New Haven, 1973-75; asst. prof. Cornell U., Ithaca, N.Y., 1975-79; assoc. prof. U. Notre Dame, Ind., 1979-83, prof. of math., 1983—, chair dept. math., 1988-92, Vincent J. Duncan and Annamarie Micus Duncan chair math., 1994—. Mem. Inst. for Advanced Study, Princeton, N.J., 1975-76; guest prof. U. Bonn, Germany, 1978-79; guest rschr. Max Planck Inst. for Math., Bonn, 1992-93; cons. GM Rsch., Warren, Mich., 1986-97. Editor: Manuscripta Mathematica jour., 1986-93, Advances in Geometry, 2000;mem. editl. bd. Milan Jour. Math., 2002; contbr. articles to profl. publs. Recipient Rsch. award for Sr. U.S. Scientists Alexander Von Humboldt found., 1993; A.P. Sloan Found. rsch. fellow, 1979. Mem. Am. Math. Soc., Soc. for Indsl. and Applied Math., Phi Beta Kappa. Office: U Notre Dame Dept Math Notre Dame IN 46556 E-mail: sommese@nd.edu.

SOMOGYI, JENNIE, dancer; b. Easton, Pa. Studied with Madame Nina Youshkevitch; student, Sch. Am. Ballet. Apprentice N.Y.C. Ballet, 1993—94, mem. corps de ballet, 1994—98, soloist, 1998—2000, prin., 2000—. Dancer (ballets) The Nutcracker, Allegro Brillante, Apollo, Tschaikovskys Pas De Deux, Glass Pieces, The Sleeping Beauty, Swan Lake, Quartet for Strings, Appalachia Waltz, Urban Dances, Swerve Poems, Polyphonia. Recipient Mae L. Wien award, The Princess Grace Found. award, Martin E. Segal award. Office: NYC Ballet NY State Theatre 20 Lincoln Ctr Plz New York NY 10023-6913*

SOMORJAI, GABOR ARPAD, chemist, educator; b. Budapest, Hungary, May 4, 1935; came to U.S., 1957, naturalized, 1962; s. Charles and Livia (Ormos) S.; m. Judith Kaldor, Sept. 2, 1957; children: Nicole, John. BS, U. Tech. Scis., Budapest, 1956; PhD, U. Calif., Berkeley, 1960; D (hon.), D (hon.), U. Manchester, Eng., 2001. Mem. research staff IBM, Yorktown Heights, N.Y., 1960-64; dir. Surface Sci. and Catalysis Program Lawrence Berkeley Lab., Calif., 1964—; mem. faculty dept. chemistry U. Calif.-Berkeley, 1964—, assoc. prof., 1967-72, prof., 1972—, Miller prof., 1978, Unilever prof. dept. chemistry U. Bristol, Eng., 1972; vis. fellow Emmanuel Coll., Cambridge, Eng., 1989; Baker lectr. Cornell U., Ithaca, N.Y., 1977; mem. editorial bds. Progress in Solid State Chemistry, 1973—, Jour. Solid State Chemistry, 1976-92, Nouveau Jour. de Chemie, 1977—, Colloid and Interface Sci., 1979—, Catalysis Revs., 1981, Jour. Phys. Chemistry, 1981-91, Langmuir, 1985—, Jour. Applied Catalysis, Molecular Physics, 1992—. Author: Principles of Surface Chemistry, 1972, Chemistry in Two Dimensions, 1981, Introduction to Surface Chemistry and Catalysis, 1994; editor-in-chief Catalysis Letters, 1988—; contbr. articles to profl. jours. Recipient Emmett award Am. Catalysis Soc., 1977, Kokes award Johns Hopkins U., 1976, Albert award Precious Metal Inst., 1986, Sr. Disting. Scientist award Alexander von Humboldt Found., 1989, E.W. Mueller award U. Wis., Chemical Pioneer award Am. Inst. of Chemists, 1995, Von Hippel award Materials Rsch. Soc., 1997; Guggenheim fellow, 1969, Wolf prize in chemistry, 1998. Fellow AAAS, Am. Phys. Soc.; mem. NAS, Am. Acad. Arts and Scis., Am. Chem. Soc. (chmn. colloid and surface chemistry 1981, Surface and Colloid Chemistry award 1981, Peter Debye award 1989, Arthur W. Adamson award 1994, award for Creative Rsch. in Homogeneous and Heterogeneous Catalysis 2000), Catalysis Soc. N.Am., Hungarian Acad. Scis. (hon. 1990, Pauling medal 2000). Home: 665 San Luis Rd Berkeley CA 94707-1725 Office: U Calif Dept Chemistry D 58 Hildebrand Hl Berkeley CA 94720-0001 E-mail: somorjai@socrates.berkeley.edu.

SOMSEN, HENRY NORTHROP, retired lawyer; b. New Ulm, Minn., Aug. 12, 1909; s. Henry N. and Meta (Koch) S.; m. Anne Elizabeth Duncan, Sept. 12, 1936 (dec.); children: Pennell Anne, Stephen Duncan. BA, U. Minn., 1932, JD, 1934. Bar: Minn. 1934. Practice law, New Ulm, 1934-85; ptnr. Somsen, Dempsey, Johnson & Somsen, 1934-40, Somen Dempsey & Somsen, 1940-46, Somsen & Somsen, 1946-55; sole practice, 1955-64; ptnr. Somsen & Dempsey, 1965-71, Somsen Dempsey & Schade, 1971-85, of counsel, 1985—. Bd. editors U. Minn. Law Rev., 1932-33. Trustee Minn. State Parks Found., 1967-77; bd. dirs. Minn. Council State Parks, 1956—, pres., 1974-75; bd. dirs., pres. New Ulm Community Concert Assn., 1947-85; bd. dirs. Union Hosp., New Ulm, 1959-77, Highland Homes, Inc., 1970-79, New Ulm Meml. Found., 1958-79; bd. dirs. New Ulm Industries Inc., 1952-85, pres., 1968-77; bd. dirs. New Ulm Industries Found., Inc., 1953-85, pres., 1968-77, bd. dirs. 1953-83, chmn., 1958-83 Farmers and Mchts. Bank, New Ulm, Minn.; bd. dirs. Klossner State Bank, Minn., 1947-84, State Bond and Mortgage Co., 1950-80, Am. Artstoone Co., 1955-84, others; mem. City Charter Commns., 1940, 51, 66, pres., 1966. Served from pvt. to capt. JAGC, AUS, 1943-46. Mem. ABA, Minn. Bar Assn., Am. Judicature Soc., Am. Arbitration Assn. (panel of arbitrators 1967-85), Mpls. Club, Masons, Rotary, Shriners. Episcopalian. Home: 211 2d St NW Apt 1907 Rochester MN 55901-3101

SONBERG, MICHAEL ROBERT, judge; b. Bklyn., Oct. 17, 1947; s. Harold R. and Betty (March) Lifton. AB, CUNY, 1968; JD, Harvard U., 1971. Bar: N.Y. 1972. Assoc. Weiss, Rosenthal, Heller & Schwartzman, N.Y.C., 1971-79, Moore, Berson, Lifflander & Mewhinney, N.Y.C., 1979-82; ptnr. Moore, Berson, Lifflander, Eisenberg & Mewhinney, 1983-90; counsel Serchuk & Zelermyer, 1991; judge N.Y.C. Civil Ct., 1991-95, N.Y.C. Criminal Ct., 1995—. Mem. Overseers' Com. to Visit Harvard Law Sch., 1978-83; bd. Dirs., chmn. com. on legis. Citizens Union of City of N.Y., 1978-91. Mem.: ABA, Internat. Assn. of Lesbian and Gay Judges (sec. 1993—99, pres. 1999—), N.Y. County Lawyers Assn., Bronx County Bar Assn., Assn. of Bar of City of N.Y. (chmn. com. on state cts. of superior jurisdiction 1987—90, co-chmn. coun. on jud. adminstrn. 1993—96, sec., mem. exec. com. 1997—2000), N.Y. State Bar Assn., Harvard Law Sch. Assn. (coun. 1995—99, exec. com. 1996—99, chmn. nominations com. 2001—), Assn. of Lesbian and Gay Judges (pres. 1996—), Lesbian and Gay Law Assn. of Greater N.Y. Office: Criminal Ct City NY 215 E 161st St Bronx NY 10451-3511 E-mail: mrsonberg@abanet.org.

SONDAK, ARTHUR, retired management consultant; b. N.Y.C., Oct. 16, 1929; s. Louis and Eva (Dolin) S.; m. Sylvia Mayran, Jan. 17, 1953 (div. 1975); children: Janet, Steven, Donald; m. Susan Altman, Oct. 17, 1999. BBA, Baruch Coll., 1950, MBA, 1958. Employment mgr. Saks Fifth Ave, N.Y.C., 1954-57; wage and salary adminstr. Royal Typewriter Co., 1957-61; employment mgr. Sperry Rand Corp., 1961-62; compensation dir., region personnel mgr. Royal Typewriter Co., 1962-66; mgr. personnel program planning MAI, 1966-69; personnel dir. ITEl Corp., White Plains, N.Y., 1969-73; dir. personnel and adminstrn. MAI, N.Y.C., 1973-75; instr. Baruch Coll. Grad. Sch., 1969-70; prin. Personnel Mgmt. Svcs., Delray Beach, Fla., 1975-99. Editorial adv. bd. AMACOM, N.Y.C., 1986-96; contbr. articles to profl. jours. Adv. bd. Cmty./Advancement Resource Ctr., Middlesex Coll., Edison, 1985-90; career guidance counselor USAF, 1950-54. Avocations: photography, nostalgia, sports, golf. Home: 6320 Crystal View Ln Boynton Beach FL 33437-4041

SONDE, SUSAN, writer; b. N.Y.C., Nov. 17, 1940; d. John Walter and Elizabeth (Frant) Kolisch; m. Theodore Irwin Sonde, Sept. 12, 1964; children: Andrea Hawthorne, David. MA in German Lit., Johns Hopkins U., 1967; MA in Studio Art, U. Md., 1970. Poetry instr. U. Md., College Park, 1970-72; instr. Writer's Ctr., Glen Echo Park & Bethesda, Md. Author: (poetry) Inland Is Parenthetical, 1979, (fiction) Say It, 1999 (Peregrine prize), My Scout, My River Baby, 1993 (Writer's Digest award); assoc. editor The Crescent Rev. Recipient Capricorn Book award West Side YMCA, Md. State Arts award in Poetry Md. State Arts Coun., 2001; fellow Va. Ctr for Arts. Mem. Acad. Am. Poets, Writer's Voice, Poetry Soc. Am. (Gordon Barber Meml. award 1985). Avocation: pottery. Home: 2011 St Stephens Woods Dr Crownsville MD 21032 E-mail: susansonde@msn.com.

SONDE, THEODORE IRWIN, lawyer; b. N.Y.C., Jan. 7, 1940; s. Martin and Anne (Greenbaum) S.; m. Susan Kolisch, Sept. 10, 1964; children: Andrea Martine, David Ian. BA, CCNY, 1961; LLB, NYU, 1964; LLM, Georgetown U., 1967. Bar: N.Y. 1964, D.C. 1978, U.S. Supreme Ct. With SEC, Washington, 1964-80, asst. gen. counsel Office Gen. Counsel, 1970-74, assoc. dir. divsn. enforcement, 1974-80; dir. Office Enforcement, FERC, 1980-81; mem. firm Cole, Corette & Abrutynn, 1982-90, Dechert, Price & Rhodes, 1990—2002, Crowell & Moring, Washington, 2002—. Adj. prof. Georgetown U. Law Sch. 1977-95, George Washington U. Nat. Law Ctr., 1976-82. Contbr. articles to law jours. Office: Crowell & Moring 1001 Pennsylvania Ave NW Washington DC 20004 E-mail: tsonde@crowell.com.

SONDEL, PAUL MARK, pediatric oncologist, educator; b. Milw., Aug. 14, 1950; s. Robert F. and Audrey J. (Dworkus) S.; m. Sherie Ann Katz, Jan. 1, 1973; children: Jesse Adam, Beth Leah, Elana Rose, Jodi Zipporah. BS with honors, U. Wis., 1971, PhD in Genetics, 1975; MD magna cum laude, Harvard Med. Sch., Boston, 1977. Diplomate Nat. Bd. Med. Examiners, Am. Bd. Pediatrics; lic. physician, Wis. Postdoctoral rsch. fellow Harvard Med. Sch., Boston, 1975-77; intern in pediatrics U. Minn. Hosp., Mpls., 1977-78; resident in pediatris U. Wis. Hosp. and Clinics, Madison, 1978-80; asst. prof. pediatrics, human oncology and genetics U. Wis., 1980-84, assoc. prof., 1984-86, prof. pediatrics, human oncology and genetics, 1987—, head divsn. pediatric hematology/oncology, program leader, 1990—; assoc. dir. U Wisc. Cancer Ctr., 1996-99. Sub-fellow pediatric oncology; Midwest Children's Cancer Ctr., Milw., 1980; vis. scientist dept. cell biology Weizmann Inst. Sci., Rehovot, Israel, 1987; chmn. immunology com. Children's Cancer Group 1990—; mem. cancer ctr. rev. com. Nat. Cancer Inst., 1997—. Sr. editor Clin. Cancer Rsch., 1996-99; mem. editl. bd. Jour. Immunology, 1985-87, Jour. Nat. Cancer Inst., 1987—, Jour. Biol. Response Modifiers, 1990—, BLOOD, 1992—, Natural Immunity, 1992—; contbr. articles to Jour. Exptl. Medicine, Jour. Immunology, Cellular Immunology, Immunol. Revs., Med. Pediatric Oncology, Wis. State Med. Jour., Jour. Biol. Response Modifiers, Jour. Pediatrics, Jour. Clin. Oncology, Jour. Clin. Investigation, and others. State of Wis. Regents scholar, 1968; J.A. and G.L. Hartford Found. fellow, 1981-84. Mem. Am. Assn. Immunologists, Am. Assn. Clin. Histocompatibility Typing, Am. Fedn. Clin. Rsch., Am. Soc. Pediatric Hematology/Oncology, Am. Assn.

Cancer Rsch., Am. Soc. Transplant Physicians, Am. Soc. Clin. Oncology, Am. Acad. Pediatrics, Leukemia Soc. Am. (bd. dirs. Wis. chpt. 1987-90 Achievements include patent for Typing Leukocyte Antigens; research on clinical and immunological effects of human recombinant Interleukin-2 and monoclonal antibodies. Home: 1114 Winston Dr Madison WI 53711-3161 Office: U Wis K4/448 Clin Sci Ctr 600 Highland Ave Madison WI 53792-3284 E-mail: pmsondel@facstaff.wisc.edu.

SONDERBY, SUSAN PIERSON, federal judge; b. Chgo., May 15, 1947; d. George W. and Shirley L. (Eckstrom) Pierson; m. James A. De Witt, June 14, 1975 (dec. 1978); m. Peter R. Sonderby, Apr. 7, 1990. AA, Joliet (Ill.) Jr. Coll., 1967; BA, U. Ill., 1969; JD, John Marshall Law Sch., 1973. Bar: Ill. 1973, U.S. Dist. Ct. (cen. and so. dists.) Ill. 1978, U.S. Dist. Ct. (no. dist.) Ill. 1984, U.S. Ct. Appeals (7th Cir.) 1984. Assoc. O'Brien, Garrison, Berard, Kusta and De Witt, Joliet, 1973-75, ptnr., 1975-77; asst. atty. gen. consumer protection div., litigation sect. Office of the Atty. Gen., Chgo., 1977-78, asst. atty. gen., chief consumer protection divsn. Springfield, 1978-83; U.S. trustee for no. dist. Ill. Chgo., 1983-86; judge U.S. Bankruptcy Ct. (no. dist.) Ill., 1986—, chief fed. bankruptcy judge, 1998—2002. Mem. law faculty Fed. Judicial Tng. Ctr., Practising Law Inst., U.S. Dept. Justice, Nat. Bankruptcy Inst., Ill. Continuing Edn.; adj. faculty De Paul U. Coll. Law, Chgo., 1986; spl. asst. atty. gen., 1972—78; past mem. U.S. Trustee adv. com.; consumer adv. coun. Fed. Res. Bd.; past sec. of State Fraudulent I.D. com. Dept. of Ins. Task Force on Improper Claims Practices; former chair pers. rev. bd., mem. task force race and gender bias U.S. Dist. Ct.; jud. conf. planning com. 7th Cir. Jud. Conf.; former mem. Civil Justice Reform Act Adv. Com., Ct. Security com.; mem. Adminstrv. Office of the U.S. Cts. Bankruptcy Judges Adv. Group. Contbr. articles to profl. jours. Mem. Fourth Presbyn. Ch., Art Inst. Chgo.; past mem. Westminster Presbyn. Ch., Chgo. Coun. of Fgn. Rels.; past bd. dirs. Land of Lincoln Coun. Girl Scouts U.S.; past mem. individual guarantors com. Goodman Theatre, Chgo.; past chair clubs and orgns. Sangamon County United Way Capital campaign; past bd. dirs., chair house rules com. and legal subcom. Lake Point Tower; past mem. Family Svc. Ctr., Aid to Retarded Citizens, Henson Robinson Zoo. Named Young Career Woman, Bus. and Profl. Women; recipient Spl. Achievement award, Dept. Justice, 1984, Disting. Svc. Alumni award, Joliet Jr. Coll., 1987, Disting. Alumni award, John Marshall Law Sch., 1988, Dir.'s award, Exec. Office U.S. Trustee, Leadership award, Internat. Orgn. Women Execs., Outstanding Svc. to Bench, Am. Bankruptcy Inst., 1990. Master: Abraham Lincoln Marovitz Inn of Ct. (former pres., membership com.); fellow: Am. Coll. Bankruptcy (circuit admissions com.); mem.: ATLA, Comml. Law League Am. (former exec. coun. mem., bankruptcy and insolvency sect., coord. with nat. conf. bankruptcy judges com.), Nat. Conf. Bankruptcy Judges (co-chair ednl. program com. conf. 2001, liaison with bankruptcy rev. commn. com.), 7th Cir. Bar Assn. (former treas., judicial conf. planning com.), Am. Bankruptcy Inst. (bd. dirs. Chgo. chpt.), Fed. Bar Assn., Chgo. Archtl. Found., John Marshall Law Sch. Alumni Assn. (bd. dirs.), Nordic Law Club (past legisl. com.), Lawyers Club Chgo. (hon.). Avocations: travel, flying, interior decorating. Office: US Bankruptcy Ct 219 S Dearborn St Ste 638 Chicago IL 60604-1702

SONDEREGGER, THEO BROWN, psychology educator; b. Birmingham, Ala., May 31, 1925; d. Ernest T. and Vera M. (Sillox) Brown; children: Richard Paul, Diane Carol, Douglas Robert. BS, Fla. State U., 1946; MA in Chemistry, U. Nebr., 1948, MA in Exptl. Psychology, 1960; PhD in Clin. Psychology, U. Nebr., 1965. Lic. psychologist, Calif; clin. lic., cert. Nebr. Asst. prof. U. Nebr. Med. Ctr., Omaha, 1965-71, Nebr. Wesleyan U., Lincoln, 1965-68, U. Nebr., Lincoln, 1968-71, assoc. prof., 1971-76, prof., 1976-94; ret., 1994; prof. emeritus, 1995—. Vol. assoc. prof. U. Nebr. Med. Ctr., 1972-77, courtesy prof. med. psychology, 1977-95. Editor: Nebr. Symposium on Motivation, 1974, 84, 91, Problems of Perinatal Drug Dependence: Research and Clinical Implications, 1986, Neurobehavioral Toxicology and Teratology vol. 8, 1988-89, Problems of Perinatal Drug Dependence, 1979, 82, 84, Feminist Therapy Interchange, 1988-89, 91, Perinatal Substance Abuse: Research and Clinical Implications, 1992, Agendas for Aging, 1994-97. Mem. grant rev. coms. Nat. Inst. Drug Abuse, 1983-84, 85, 91-94. Tribute to Women award Lincoln YMCA, 1985, named Outstanding Rsch. Scientist Nebr. Chpt. Sigma Xi, 1991, Outstanding Contbn. to Status of Women, U N-L Chancellors Commn. on Status of Women, 1994, Pound Howard Disting. Career Achievement award, 1996. Fellow: AAS, Am. Psychol. Soc., Am. Psychol. Assn.; mem.: Region V Adv. Coun. on Drugs, Fetal Alcohol (bd. dir. child guidance ctr. 1992—97, bd. dir. UN-L emeriti assoc. 1999—2001), Soc. Neuroscis., Nebr. Psychol. Assn. (pres. 1972), Internat. Soc. Psychoneuroendocrinology, Internat. Soc. Devel. Psychobiology, Midwestern Psychol. Assn., Advanced Feminist Therapy Inst., Altrusa YWCA, Sigma Xi (pres. 1986), Phi Beta Kappa (sec. Nebr. chpt. 1974). Avocations: painting, photography.

SONDHEIM, STEPHEN JOSHUA, composer, lyricist; b. N.Y.C., Mar. 22, 1930; s. Herbert and Janet (Fox) S. BA, Williams Coll., 1950. Composer, lyricist. Vis. prof. contemporary theater Oxford U., England, 1990. Composer, lyrics West Side Story, 1957, Gypsy, 1959, Do I Hear A Waltz?, 1965; music and lyrics A Funny Thing Happened on the Way to The Forum, 1962, Anyone Can Whistle, 1964, Evening Primrose, 1966, Company, 1970 (Tony award 1971), Follies, 1971 (Tony award 1972), A Little Night Music, 1973 (Tony award 1973), The Frogs, 1974, Pacific Overtures, 1976, Sweeney Todd, 1979 (Tony award 1979), Merrily We Roll Along, 1981, Sunday in the Park with George, 1984 (Pulitzer prize 1985), Into the Woods, 1987 (Tony award 1988), Assassins, 1991, Passion, 1994 (Tony award 1994); incidental music Girls of Summer, 1956, Invitation to a March, 1961, Twigs, 1971; additional lyrics Candide, 1973; anthologies Side by Side by Sondheim, 1976, Marry Me a Little, 1981, You're Gonna Love Tomorrow, 1983, Putting It Together, 1993; film scores Stavisky, 1974, Reds, 1981; composer songs for film Dick Tracy, 1990 (Acad. award); co-author film The Last of Sheila, 1973, Birdcage, 1996, Getting Away with Murder, 1996. Recipient Creative Arts medal Brandeis U., 1982, Grammy award, 1970, 73, 75, 79, 84, 88, Kennedy Ctr. Honor for Lifetime Achievement, 1993, Nat. medal of Arts, NEA, 1997, Praemium Imperiale, 2000. Mem. Am. Acad. and Inst. Arts and Letters.*

SONDIK, EDWARD J. health science administrator; BEE, MEE, U. Conn.; PhD in Elec. Engring., Stanford U. Faculty dept. engring econ. sys. Stanford U.; acting dir. Nat. Cancer Inst., acting dept. dir., dept. dir. divsn. cancer prevention and control, assoc. dir. surveillance program; dir. Nat. Ctr. Health Stats., Ctrs. Disease Control Prevention, Hyattsville, Md., 1996—. Sr. adv. health stats. Sec. Health Human Svcs. Office: Dept Health Human Svcs Nat Ctr Health Stats Presidential Bldg 6525 Belcrest Rd Rm 1140 Hyattsville MD 20782-2003*

SONDOCK, RUBY KLESS, retired judge; b. Apr. 26, 1926; d. Herman Lewis and Celia (Juran) Kless; m. Melvin Adolph Sondock, Apr. 22, 1944; children: Marcia Cohen, Sandra Marcus. AA, Cottey Coll., Nevada, Mo., 1944; BS, U. Houston, 1959, LLB, 1961. Bar: Tex. 1961, U.S. Supreme Ct. 1977. Pvt. practice, Houston, 1961-73, 89—; judge Harris County Ct. Domestic Rels. (312th Dist.), 1973-77, 234th Jud. Dist. Ct., Houston, 1977-82, 83-89; justice Tex. Supreme Ct., Austin, 1982; of counsel Weil Gotshal and Manges, 1989-93, Houston Ctr., 1993—. Mem. ABA, Tex. Bar Assn., Houston Bar Assn., Houston Assn. Women Lawyers, Order of Barons, Phi Theta Phi, Kappa Beta Pi, Phi Kappa Phi, Alpha Epsilon Pi. Address: 550 Westcott #220 Houston TX 77007

SONEGO, IAN G. assistant attorney general; b. Louisville, May 27, 1954; s. Angelo and Zella Mae (Causey) S. BA in Polit. Sci. with high honors, U. Louisville, 1976, JD, 1979. Bar: Ky. 1979, U.S. Dist Ct. (ea. dist.) Ky. 1980, U.S. Dist. Ct. (we. dist.) Ky. 1989, U.S. Ct. Appeals (6th cir.) 1989, U.S. Supreme Ct. 1990. Asst. atty. Office Commonwealth's Atty. Pike County, Pikeville, Ky., 1980, sr. asst. atty., 1988-89; assoc. John Paul Runyon Law Firm, 1981-87; asst. atty. gen. Office Atty. Gen., Frankfort, Ky., 1989—. Lectr. criminal law Ky. Bar Assn., Jenny Wiley Park, 1981, Ky. Prosecutors Confs., 1989, 93; mem. Atty. Gen.'s task force child sexual abuse, 1992-94, Nat. Conf. on Domestic Violence, 1996. Contbg. editor Ky. Prosecuter Newsletter, 1991—. Recipient Kesslman award, U. Louisville, 1975, Bd. trustee award, 1979, Outstanding Prosecutor award, Ky. Atty., Award Outstanding Advocacy, Assn. Govt. Attys. in Capital Litigation, 2001. Mem.: Ky. Commonwealth's Attys. Assn. (hon.; lectr. 1987, 90, chmn. com. ethics 1984—86, bd. dirs. 1983—85, Spl. award 1987). Office: Office Atty Gen Criminal Appellate Divsn 1024 Capital Center Dr Frankfort KY 40601-8204 E-mail: isonego@law.state.ky.us.

SONENBERG, SUZY DALTON, foundation administrator; b. N.Y.C., Oct. 3, 1943; d. Ernest Roger Dalton and Edith Ruth (Loebl) Karel; m. Neil Stephen Sonenberg, Dec. 22, 1963 (dec. Oct. 1981); children: Nina Elise, Daniel Matthew. BA in English Lit., Queens Coll., 1965; M in Social Work, Adelphi U., 1976. Cert. social worker Acad. Cert. Social Workers. Resource assoc. Community Coun. Greater N.Y., N.Y.C., 1976, network cons., 1977, dir. info. svcs. project, 1978-79, dir. employment and tng. projects, 1979-81, dir. dept. info. svcs., 1981-82; caterer, 1982-83; program officer The N.Y. Found., 1984-88; exec. dir. The L.I. Community Found., 1988—. V.p., exec. bd. L.I. Coalition for Fair Broadcasting. Mem. L.I. Ctr. for Bus. and Profl. Women (Outstanding Achievement in Community Svc. award 1992), Nat. Soc. Fundraising Execs. (bd. dirs. L.I. chpt. 1989—). Avocations; remodeling houses, swimming. Office: LI Community Found Elias Hicks House 1740 Old Jericho Tpke Jericho NY 11753-1206

SONENSHEIN, ABRAHAM LINCOLN, microbiology educator; b. Paterson, N.J., Jan. 13, 1944; s. Israel Louis and Celia (Rabinowitz) S.; m. Gail Entner, Jan. 28, 1967; children: Dina Miriam, Adam Israel. AB, Princeton U., 1965; PhD, MIT, 1970. Postdoctoral fellow U. Paris, Orsay, France, 1970-72; asst. prof. Tufts U., Boston, 1972-78, assoc. prof., 1978-82; prof. microbiology Tufts U. Sch. Medicine, 1982—. Vis. prof. U. Paris, 1998. Rsch. grantee NIH, 1972—; fellow Am. Cancer Soc., 1970-72. Mem. AAAS, Am. Soc. for Microbiology, Am. Acad. Microbiology, Fedn. Am. Scientists, Sigma Xi. Office: Tufts U Dept Molecular & Microbiol 136 Harrison Ave Dept & Boston MA 02111-1800

SONFIELD, MATTHEW CHARLES, finance educator, writer; b. N.Y.C., Sept. 27, 1942; s. Edwin Charles and Anne Louise (Shulman) Sonfield; m. Judith Jayson, June 20, 1965; children: Brian, Adam. AB, Cornell U., Ithaca, N.Y., 1964; MBA, Harvard U., Cambridge, Mass., 1966; PhD, NYU, N.Y.C., 1976. V.p G. Bruno & Son, Inc., N.Y.C., 1966—71; asst. prof. mgmt. N.Y. Inst. Tech., Old Westbury, 1971—75; Robert F. Ball disting. prof. in bus. Hofstra U., Hempstead, NY, 1975—. Mem editl. bd. Jour. Small Bus. Strategy, 1991—, Jour. Small Bus. Mgmt., 2001—. Contbr. articles over 140 primarily in acad. jours. Mem. Oyster Bay Main St. Assn., 2001—. Mem.: Small Bus. Inst. Dirs. Assn. (bd. dirs. 1980—), Classic Car Club Am. (bd. dirs. 1981—91), Soc. Automotive Historians (bd. dirs. 1993—97). Avocation: automotive historian and writer. Office: Dept of Bus Hofstra U Bus Hempstead NY 11549

SONFIELD, ROBERT LEON, JR. lawyer; b. Houston, Oct. 28, 1931; s. Robert Leon and Dorothy Harriett (Huber) S.; 1 dau., Sheree. BA, U. Houston, 1956, LL.B., JD, 1959; PhD (hon.), U. Eastern Fla., 1962; LL.D. (hon.), London Inst. Applied Research, 1973; certificate fed. taxation, NYU, 1973; certificate securities regulation, Harvard U., 1983. Bar: Tex. 1959, U.S. Supreme Ct. 1959, U.S. Dist. Ct. Tex. 1960, U.S. Tax Ct. 1960, U.S. Ct. Appeals 1960, U.S. Ct. Claims 1974. Mng. dir. Sonfield & Sonfield, Houston, 1959—. Mem. nat. adv. council Nat. Fedn. Ind. Bus. Author: Corporate Financing by Sale of Securities to the Public, 1969, Mergers and Acquisitions, 1970, Student Rights, 1971, The Limited Partnership as a Vehicle for Real Estate Investment, 1971, Integration of Partnership Offerings, 1974, The Grantor Trust Rules After The Tax Reform Act of 1986, Incentive Equity Program, Corporate Name Protection Along With Name Registration, A Guide to SEC Corporate Filing, Organizational Professionals' Residual Litigation and Investment Strategy, Comparing California, Delaware and Nevada: Corporate Laws in Light of California Corporations Code Section 2115 and Offering of Unregistered Securities Only to Accredited Investors, Disclosure Policies, Practices and Procedures For Public Companies, Regulation of Franchises, How to Become a Publicly Held Company Via the Registered Ditribution of a Percentage of Your Company's Stock to Shareholders, numerous others. Recipient St. John Garwood award, 1957, Frio-Finnegan Outstanding Alumnus award, 1970-71, citation for outstanding contbn. to legal profession, 1971 Mem. Am. Tax Lawyers Assn. (pres.), Lawyers Soc. Houson, Am. Judicature Soc., ABA, Tex. Bar Assn. (dist. com. on admission to state bar, chmn. clients security fund com.), Houston Bar Assn. (com. chmn. council, tax sect.), Tex. Equal Access to Justice Found., Houston Bar Found., Real Estate Securities and Syndication Inst., Huguenot Soc. of London, Order Stars and Bars, SAR, Sons Confederate Vets., Mil. Order World Wars, Mil. and Hospitaller Order St. Lazarus of Jerusalem, Knightly Assn. St. George the Martyr, Smithsonian Assocs., Houston Heritage Soc., Houston Mus. Fine Arts, Newcomen Soc. N.Am., Phi Delta Phi, Delta Sigma Phi. Clubs: Metropolitan (N.Y.C.); Argyle (San Antonio); Houston, Houstonian. Office: Sonfield & Sonfield 770 S Post Oak Ln Houston TX 77056-6665 E-mail: robert@sonfeld.com.

SONG, BYEONG-MUN, electrical engineer, researcher; b. Puyeo, Chungnam, Repubic of Korea, Aug. 15, 1962; arrived in U.S., 1994; s. Kum-Tae Kim, Nam-Sik Song; m. Eun-Hee Kim; children: Diana (Ji-Hae), David (In-Bum). BS, Chungnam Nat. U., 1986, MS, 1988; PhD, Va. Tech. U., 2001. Vis. rsch. engr. T.U. Braunschweig, Germany, 1991—91; sr. rschr. Korea Electrotechnology Rsch. Inst., Changwon, Republic of Korea, 1988—94; GRA Va. Tech. U., Blacksburg, 1994—2000; staff engr. Gen. Atomics, San Diego, 2000—. Mem.: IEEE (sr.). Home: 13447 Tiverton Rd San Diego CA 92130 Office: Gen Atomics 4949 Greencraig Ln San Diego CA 92123 Office Fax: 858-522-8424. Personal E-mail: bmsong_vt@hotmail.com. Business E-mail: songb@gat.com.

SONG, CATHY, author, poet; BA in English Lit., Wellesley Coll., 1977; MA in Creative Writing, Boston U., 1981. Author: Picture Bride, 1983, Frameless Windows, Squares of Light, 1988, School Figures, 1994, The Land of Bliss, 2001; contbr. to numerous anthologies, jours., other publs. Recipient award Yale Series of Younger Poets, 1982, Frederick Bock prize for poetry, 1988, Elliot Cades award for lit., 1988, Shelley Meml. award for lit., 1993, Hawaii award for lit., 1993, Pushcart prize, 1999, Best Am. Poetry award, 2000; Nat. Endowment for Arts creative writing fellow, 1997. Address: PO Box 27262 Honolulu HI 96827-0262

SONG, CHUNSHAN, chemist, chemical engineer, educator; b. Shijiazhuang, Hebei, China, Feb. 11, 1961; came to U.S., 1989; s. Jingsheng Song and Fengxian He; m. Lu Sun, Jan. 10, 1985; children: Lucy J., James J. BS in Chem. Engring., Dalian (China) U. Tech., 1982; diploma in Japanese, N.E. Shifan U., Changchun, China, 1983; MS in Applied Chemistry, Osaka (Japan) U., 1986, PhD in Applied Chemistry, 1989. Postdoc. rsch. assoc. Osaka Gas Co., 1989; rsch. assoc. Pa. State U., University Park, 1989-94, asst. prof. fuel sci., 1994-97, assoc. prof., 1997—, assoc. dir. lab. hydrocarbon process chemistry, 1995-98, dir. applied catalysis in energy lab., 1998—. Editor: Catalytic Conversion of Polycyclic Aromatic Hydrocarbons, 1996, Advances in Catalysis and Processes for Heavy Oil Conversion, 1998, Shape-Selective Catalysis, 1999, Catalysis in Fuel Processing and Environmental Protection, 1999, Chemistry of Diesel Fuels, 2000, CO2 Conversion and Utilization, 2002, Environmental Challenges and Greenhouse Gas Control for Fossil Fuel Utilization in the 21st Century, 2002; contbr. Recipient Outstanding Svc. award, Internat. Pitts. Coal Conf., 2001; fellow Agy. Ind. Sci. Tech. fellow, Japan, 1995, NEDO, Japan, 1998. Mem. AAAS, AIChE, Am. Chem. Soc. (co-chair several symposia 1995—, program com. petroleum chemistry divsn. 1996—, exec. com. 1997—, chmn. website com. 1997-2000, chmn. program for fuel chem. divsn., exec. com. of fuel chem. divsn. 2000—). Achievements include development of concept for designing sulfur-resistant noble-metal catalysts, tri-reforming process concept for production of synthesis gas using waste flue gas; discovery of new method for preparing highly active molybdenum sulfide catalysts by using water and Mo precursor; established several new shape-selective catalytic reactions of polycyclic hydrocarons, including ring-shift isomerization, conformational isomerization, shape-selective alkylation, and shape-selective hydrogenation; established the features and reaction pathways of thermal degradation and stabilization of coal-derived and petroleum-derived aviation jet fuels in pyrolytic regime; established a new desulfurization process concept of selective adsorption for removing sulfur (SARS). Office: Pa State U Energy and Geo-Environ Engring Dept[ ]Fuel Sci Program 206 Hosler Bldg University Park PA 16802-5001 E-mail: csong@psu.edu.

SONG, EDWARD, healthcare company executive, physician; b. Seoul, Korea, Jan. 15, 1950; s. Jung Soo Song and C.K. Park; m. In Ja Song, July 4, 1988; children: Andrew, Jessica. BS, Chimese Med., Seoul, Korea, 1974, U. Sciences, Louisiana, 1987, MS, 1989, PhD, 1991; MD, PhD, Internat. U., Sri Lanka, Colombo, 1994. Pres. T. Baduk Assn., Dallas, 2002—02, Nctma / Actma, Dallas, 2002—02, Am. Bd. Ea. Medicine, Dallas, 2002—02, OHTC Martial Arts Assn., Dallas, 2002—, OHTC Health Care Sys., Dallas, 2002—. Office: OHTC Healthcare 3068 Forest Lane #102 Dallas TX 75234 E-mail: doctor@ohtc.com.

SONG, JOSEPH, pathologist, educator; b. Pyong Yang, Korea, May 11, 1927; s. Ha Ju and Hwa Soon (Koh) S.; m. Kumsan Ryu, Apr. 12, 1958; children: Patricia, Michael, Jeff. MD, Seoul (Korea) U. Sch. Medicine, 1950; MS in Pathology, U. Tenn., Memphis, 1956; MD, U. Ark. Med. Sch., Little Rock, 1965. Diplomate Am. Bd. Pathology. Pathologist in charge State Cancer Detection Survey, Providence, 1956-59; assoc. pathologist Providence Lying-In Hosp., 1959-61; assoc. prof. pathology U. Ark. Med. Ctr., Little Rock, 1961-64; dir. lab. Mercy Hosp., Des Moines, 1965-92, cancer rschr., 1993-95; clin. prof. pathology Creighton U. Sch. Medicine, Omaha, 1968-95; med. dir. Corning Clin. Labs., Des Moines, 1995-97; ret. Cons. EPA, Washington, 1975-85; pres. med. staff Mercy Hosp., Des Moines, 1981 Author: (book) The Human Uterus, 1964, Pathology of Sickle Cell Anemia, 1971 (award 1975), Beyond the Horizon, 1995. Elder Winsdor Presbyn. Ch., Des Moines, 1964; com. mem. Aldersgate Meth. Ch., Des Moines, 1995. Major Med. Corps, 1950-52, Korea. Recipient Martin Luther King Med. Achievement award, So. Christian Leadership Conf., Statesmanship award Am. Assn. Med. Adminstrs., Las Vegas, Nev., 1987. Fellow Am. Coll. of Physicians, Coll. of Am. Pathologists, Am. Soc. of Clin. Pathology, Am. Assn. for Cancer Rsch. Methodist. Avocation: classical music. Home: 2345 Park Ave Des Moines IA 50321-1505

SONG, MICHAEL, marketing educator; b. Putian, Fujian, China, Aug. 24, 1961; came to U.S., 1983; s. Qing Jiao and Guang Zha Song; m. Lisa Song, April 18, 1986; children: Roger, Katherine. BS, Jinan U., 1982; MS, Cornell U., 1986; MBA, U. Va., 1990, PhD, 1991. Asst. prof. U. Tenn., Knoxville, 1991-95; prof. Mich. State U., East Lansing, 1996-2000; prof., disting. chair in entrepreneurship, exec. dir. Ctr. for Technology Entrepreneurship, U. Wash., 2000—. Founding dir. Ctr. for Tech. Entrepreneurship; cons. to maj. cos.; keynote spkr. in field. Editl. bd. Advances in Internat. Mktg., 1998—, Jour. Product Innovation, 1999—; contbr. articles to profl. jours. Recipient Wachovia award for Excellence The Darden Found., Va., 1994; Math. Graduate fellow Cornell U., 1984, Consortium fellow The 1991 Acad. Mgmt. TIM Doctoral Consortium, Doctoral Merit fellow The Darden Sch., 1988-91, Doctoral fellow DuPont, 1989-91; grantee Mktg. Sci. Inst., The Darden Found., Citibank Rsch. Funds, The China Nat. Aero-Tech. Import and Export Corp., Hitachi Rsch. Funds, Hewlett Packard Co., NSF, Citicorp Global Scholar Programs, Am. Chem. Mfg. Assn., others. Fellow Acad. Mktg. Sci.; mem. Inst. Mgmt. Sci. (conf. chair 1996), Am. Mktg. Assn. Avocations: music, stamp collecting, travel. Office: Univ Washington Business School PO Box 353200 Seattle WA 98195-3200

SONG, SHUNFENG, economist, researcher; b. Jinhua, China, July 6, 1962; came to U.S., 1986; s. Lin Fu Song and Xiaoying He; m. Jian Ling Feng, July 9, 1985; children: Sisi, Conan A. BS in Mechanics, Beijing U., 1983; MA in Econ., U. Calif., Irvine, 1991, PhD in Econ., 1992. Instr. Xiamen (China) U., 1983-86; asst. prof. dept. econ. U. Nev., Reno, 1992-96, assoc. prof., 1996—. Author, editor: Raising International Competitiveness, 1998; contbr. articles to profl. jours. Mem. Am. Econ. Assn., Am. Real Estate Soc., Chinese Economists Soc. (dir. 1996-98, v.p. 1997-98), Western Regional Sci. Assn., Western Econ. Assn. Internat., Regional Sci. Assn. Internat. Avocations: travel, table tennis, playing cards. Office: U Nev Dept Econ 030 Reno NV 89557-0001

SONG, SIHONG, science educator; b. Chao-Yang-Zhen, Jilin, China, Mar. 29, 1959; came to U.S., 1990; s. Xingbang Song and Qiu Mi; m. Yufei Tang, May 17, 1986; children: Xujia (Annie), Alexander T. BS, Jilin Agrl. U., Changchun, China, 1982, MS, 1990; PhD, U. Fla., 1996. Tchg. and rsch. asst. Jilin Agrl. U., Changchun, 1982-86, lectr., 1987-91; grad. asst. U. Fla., Gainesville, 1992-96, postdoctoral assoc., 1996-99, rsch. asst. prof., 1999—2001, asst. prof., 2001—. Recipient Young Investigaator award Alpha One Found., 1999. Mem. AAAS, Am. Soc. Gene Therapy, Sigma Xi, Gamma Sigma Delta. Avocations: sports, pinting, travel. Office: U Fla Coll Pharmacy Dept Pharmaceutics PO Box 100494 Gainesville FL 32610-0494 Office Fax: 352-392-5280., 352-392-4447. E-mail: shsong@ufl.edu.

SONG, XIAOTONG, physicist, educator; b. Taizhou, Jiangsu, People's Republic of China, Oct. 18, 1934; came to U.S., 1989; s. Hoshu Song and Jingying Wang; m. Chuchu Zhu, 1966; 1 child, Jianyang. BS in Physics, Fudan U., Shanghai, China, 1955, PhD in Physics, 1963. Rsch. fellow Dept Def., China, 1955-58; asst. prof. Hangzhou U., China, 1958-63; lectr., 1963-66, 77-83; assoc. prof., 1983-86; prof., 1986—; rsch. cons. dept. physics Inst. Nuclear and Particle Physics, U. Va., Charlottesville, 1989-90, rsch. prof., cons., 1990—. Adv. com. for professorship exam., Zhejiang, China; dir. theory divsn. dept. physics Hangzhou U., China, 1984-89, prof. Zhejiang Univ., China, 1997—; referee Phys. Rev., High Energy Physics and Nuclear Physics, Nat. Natural Sci. Found., China; vis. scientist Tech. U. Munich, 1986, 88-89, European Lab. for Particle Physics, Geneva, 1986-87, Inst. Nat. Fisica Nuclear Turin Sect., Italy, 1986-88, Internat. Ctr. Theoretical Physics, Italy, 1986-88, Los Alamos Nat. Lab., 1987, Utah State U., 1987, Kans. State U., 1989, Brookhaven Nat. Lab. Contbr. articles to profl. jours. Recipient Prize of Natural Sci., Com. Sci. and Tech., Zhejiang Province, China, 1983, 84; grantee Nat. Natural Sci. Found., 1984-87. Mem. AAAS, Internat. Ctr. Theoretical Physics (sr. assoc.), Am. Phys. Soc., Chinese High Energy Physics Soc., Chinese Phys. Soc., N.Y. Acad. Sci., Sigma Xi. Achievements include research in theoretical nuclear and particle physics. Office: U Va Physics Dept PO Box 400714 Mccormick Rd Charlottesville VA 22904 E-mail: xs3e@virginia.edu.

SONG, YOUNG D. interior designer, artist; b. Seoul, Republic of Korea, Jan. 1, 1947; d. Jae-Hee Song and Che-Moon Choi. BFA, Ewha Woman's U., Seoul, 1969; postgrad., Acad. Art Coll., 1970, U. Calif., Berkeley, 1971, Oakton C.C., 1998-99; BFA, Calif. Coll. Arts and Crafts, 1973. Cert. interior designer Nat. Coun. for Interior Design Qualification. Interior designer/archtl. drafter Applied Design Assocs., Ltd., Mt. Prospect, Ill., 1989-92; archtl. drafter Friedoon Hakimian Arch., Northbrook, 1993-94, James B. Landaker, Arch., Deerfield, 1994-95; project mgr. interior design NuHaus Corp., Highland Park, 1997; archtl. drafter Kemper Cazzetta Archs., Barrington, 1998; interior designer, archtl. drafter Haylock Design, Inc., Gurnee, 1999—. Exam. juror Nat. Coun. Interior Design, 1998-99. Mem. Am. Soc. Interior Designers Office: Haylock Design Inc 135 N Greenleaf Ave Gurnee IL 60031-3393 E-mail: songinc@core.com.

SONGAYLLO, RAYMOND THADDEUS, music educator; b. Chicopee, Mass., Aug. 23, 1930; s. Alexander and Katherine S.; m. Mary Ann Seaman, Sept. 1, 1954; children: Paul Alexander, Ilona Katherine. MusB, Northwestern U., 1951, MusM, 1952. Ast. prof. music Ithaca (N.Y.) Coll., 1957-58; instr. music Ctrl. Mich. U., Mount Pleasant, 1961, Tenn. Tech. U., Cookville, 1961-62; asst. prof. music U. Denver, 1962-67; assoc. prof. music Simpson Coll., Indianola, Iowa, 1967-87. Adjudicator Nat. Guild Piano Tchrs., 1980—. Music dir. Unity Ch. Des Moines, 1998—01. Recipient Keyboard Category First prize Delius Composition Contest, 1976, 92, 93. Mem. Music Tchrs. Nat. Assn. (cert., adjudicator 1993—), Am. Matthay Assn., Am. Liszt Soc., Midwest Hist. Keyboard Soc., Iowa Composers' Forum (founding, bd. dirs. 1986—, Pyle Commn. award 1993), Southeastern Hist. Keyboard Soc.. Office: PO Box 604 Indianola IA 50125

SONGER, DANIEL RICHARD, security firm executive; b. Trenton, Mich., Mar. 27, 1961; s. Richard Bruce and Barbara Jean Songer; m. Cathy Ann Sellers, May 24, 1984 (div. May 1987); children: Christopher D., Nicholas R.; m. Patricia Ann Lynn, Apr. 2, 1991 (div. Dec. 1999); children: Bradley W., Melody D. Student, Schoolcraft C.C., Livonia, Mich., Lawrence Tech. Inst., Southfield, Mich., Prince George C., Largo, Md. With Portland Constrn. Co.,

Springfield, Mich., 1961—73, Greenwood Acres, Jackson, 1973—79; electronic technician Southfield, 1982—84; security installer/technician ADT Security, Washington, 1984—89; security master technician Rollins Protective, Charlotte, NC, 1989—90; pres. Stardate Security Systems, various locations, 1990—. Author: (poetry) I'm a Statue, 2001; composer: (song lyrics) on 6 albums, 2001. With U.S. Army, 1979—82. Roman Catholic. Avocations: walking, singing, sports, swimming, poetry. Home and Office: 88 Maplelake Ct Acworth GA 30101-7749

SONG ONG, ROXANNE KAY, lawyer, judge; b. Phoenix; d. Joe Henry and Sue (Tang) Song; m. Richard H. Ong, Nov. 25, 1978; children: Jocelyn, Bradley. BA, Ariz. State U., 1975; JD, U. Ariz., 1978. Bar: Ariz. 1979, U.S. Dist. Ct. Ariz. 1979, U.S. Ct. Appeals (9th cir.) 1986, U.S. Supreme Ct. 1992. Pvt. practice, Phoenix, 1979, 85—; asst. city prosecutor Phoenix City Prosecutor's Office, 1979-82; asst. city prosecutor, asst. city atty. Scottsdale (Ariz.) City Atty.'s Office, 1982-85; pro tempore judge Scottsdale City Ct., 1986-89; assoc. city judge City of Scottsdale, 1989-91; mcpl. ct. judge City of Phoenix, 1991-2001; asst. presiding judge The Phoenix Mcpl. Ct., 2001—. Mem. Ariz. Supreme Ct.'s Commn. on Minorities, adv. com. on Judicial Ethics; vice chair of Ariz. Supreme Ct. Com. on Judicial Edn. and Tng. Former mem. community adv. bd. Sta. KAET-TV, Tempe, Ariz; mem. First Chinese Bapt. Ch., Scottsdale Leadership Class V, Valley Leadership Class XV; mem. exec. bd. Ariz. So. Bapt. Conv.; co-leader Ariz. Cactus Pine troop Girl Scouts/Brownies; former mem. parent adv. bd. Paradise Valley/Scottsdale YMCA; bd. dirs. Ariz. Bapt. Children's Svcs., Inst. Cultural Diversity; mem. commn. on minorities, adv. com. on jud. ethics, vice chair com. on jud. edn. and tng., Ariz. Supreme Ct. Recipient Law Related to Edn. award Ariz. Bar Found., 1999; named among 100 Outstanding Women and Minorities, Maricopa County Bar Assn. and Ariz. State Bar. Mem. ABA, Maricopa County Bar Assn., Christian Legal Soc., Ariz. Women Lawyers Assn., Am. Judges Assn., Nat. Assn. Women Judges, Ariz. Magistrates Assn., Ariz. Cts. Assn., U. Ariz. Law Coll. Assn., Phi Delta Phi, Phi Kappa Phi, Alpha Lambda Delta, Kappa Delta Phi, Pi Lambda Theta. Republican. Avocations: music, sports. E-mila. Office: Phoenix Mcpl Ct 300 W Washington St # 607 Phoenix AZ 85003-2103 E-mail: roxanne.songong@azbar.org.

SONKOWSKY, ROBERT PAUL, classicist, educator, actor; b. Appleton, Wis., Sept. 16, 1931; s. Paul and Loretta Stella (Nooyen) S.; m. Barbara Lou Zierke, June 8, 1956; children— Paul Victor, Steven Robert, Michael Edward. BA, Lawrence Coll., 1954; postgrad., U. Rome, 1956-57; PhD, U. N.C., 1958. Instr., asst. prof. U. Tex., 1958-61; fellow Inst. Research in Humanities, U. Wis., 1961-62; asso. prof. U. Mo., 1962-63, U. Minn., Mpls., 1963-64, chmn. dept. classics, 1964-78, prof., 1964—. Disting. Marbrook vis. prof. Macalester Coll., 1987-88; actor Attic Theatre, Appleton, Wis., 1950-54, Wilderness Rd. Theater Co., Berea, Ky., The Confederacy Co. Virginia Beach, Va., summers, 1955-58, Pillsbury House and Lyric Theaters, Mpls., 1991, Looking Glass Theater, St. Paul, 1993, Theater on the Park, Mpls., 1994-2000, Guthrie Lab Theater, Mpls., 2000—; guest artist U. Minn. Theatre, 1996. Author books; contbr. articles to profl. jours.; also recitations and recordings of classical Latin lit. in restored pronunciation; lit. recs., ednl. feature and indsl. films, TV commls. Lay reader Episc. Cathedral Ch. of St. Mark; lector Gregorian Singers, 1980-89; mem. St. Paul Sch. Com., 1971-76. Mem. AAUP, AFTRA, Am. Philol. Assn., Soc. for Oral Reading of Greek and Latin Lit., Classical Assn. Mid West and South, Internat. Soc. Chronobiology (nomenclature com.), Fulbright Assn. (pres. Minn. chpt. 1991-92), Phi Beta Kappa (pres. U. Minn. chpt. 1973-74, nat. senator 1976-82, pres. Minn. Assn. 1991-95, books reviewer for Key Reporter).

SONMOR, MARILYN IDELLE, music educator; b. Wilson, Wis., Jan. 18, 1933; d. John Reuben and Mary (Feldhahn) Haglund; m. Stephen Malcom Sonmor, Aug. 3, 1957; children: Tamara Lynn and Terri Lee (twins), Stephen Mark. B in Mus., Northwestern Coll., Roseville, Minn., 1958; postgrad. studies in mus., Ariz. State U., 1985-86; MA, Fuller Theol. Sem., 1992. Tchr. Mesquite (Tex.) High Sch., 1959-60, Dallas Christian Grade Sch., 1960-61; prof. Dallas Bible Coll., 1960-62; missionary Conservative Bapt. Fgn. Mission Soc., Manila, 1965-75; prof. Conservative Bapt. Bible Coll., 1973-75; prof., dean women Southwestern Coll., Phoenix, 1976-95. Dir. mus. and outreach minstry Conservative Bapt. Bible Coll., 1971-75; dir. women's work Campariza Assn. Philippines, Manila, 1973-75; speaker Conservative Bapt. Assn., 1964-75. Named First Place Winner voice Minn. Vocal Tchrs. Assn., 1957. Mem. Am. Assn. Christian Counselors, Southwestern Women's Aux. (pres. 1980-82). Republican. Avocations: vocalist, pianist, needlework, interior decorating. Home: 2305 N 127th Ave Avondale AZ 85323-6583

SONNEBORN, DANIEL ATESH, composer, ethnomusicologist, producer, author; b. Chgo., Oct. 31, 1949; s. Curt Lewis and Annette (Lubove) S.; m. Patrizia Pallaro, Sept. 21, 1986; children: Samuel Clement, Jonas. AB in Music with honors, U. Calif., Santa Cruz, 1982; MA in Music Theory, U. Calif., San Diego, 1984; PhD in Music (Ethnomusicology), UCLA, 1995. Music dir., composer Company Theatre Found., L.A., 1970-72, ProVisional Theatre, L.A., Theater Workshop Boston, 1973-76, James Joyce Meml. Liquid Theatre, Paris, London, 1972; prodn. mgr. Music Ctr. L.A. Forum Lab, Hollywood, Calif., 1972-73; producer Cosmic Mass, World Spiritual Summit Conf., UN, N.Y.C., 1975; freelance composer, producer, artists mgr. L.A., San Francisco, 1976-98; gen. mgr. Whole Earth Access Co., Berkeley, Calif., 1978-79; tchr. asst. U. Calif., La Jolla, 1982-84; tchr. assoc., rschr. music dept. UCLA, 1984-88; project dir. 360 (Degrees) Prodns., San Rafael, Calif., 1988-92; ops. dir. BRG Corp., Mill Valley, 1992-94; exec. producer Available Sound, Salzburg, Austria, 1995-96. Cons. Kuper Advt., Boulder, Colo., 1986, Lotus Records, Salzburg, 1996-98; exec. prodr. Fleischmann's Yeast, San Leandro, Calif., 1993; guest lectr. U. Calif., Davis, San Francisco U., 1997, 98; asst. dir. Smithsonian Folkways Recs., Washington, 1998—. Co-author: Planet Drum, 1991; composer: Dominus Marlowe: A Play on Dr. Faustus, 1972 (Best Show of Yr. award 1972), Class, 1976 (Best Show of Yr. award 1976); contbr. articles and revs. to jours. including Sufism, 1989-90, The Sound, 1988-91, 98, Asian Music, 1998-2000, Garland Encyclopedia of World Music, 1999, 2001, Ethnomusicology, 2001; music dir., arranger: Jumping Over the Fence, 1993. President's fellow U. Calif., Santa Cruz, 1981-82, grad. fellow UCLA, 1984-85, NDEA Title VI fellow UCLA, 1986-87; grantee Nat. Endowment for Arts, 1970-76, also Rockefeller Found., Ford Found., Calif. Council on Arts, Mass. Council on Arts, Bezalel Found. Mem. Nat. Acad. Recording Arts and Scis., Soc. for Ethnomusicology, Internat. Council for Traditional Music, Am. Fedn. Musicians. Democrat. Avocations: hiking, canoeing, photography. Address: Smithsonian Folkways Recs CFCH Smithsonian Instn 750 9th St NW Ste 4100 Washington DC 20560-0953 E-mail: atesh@si.edu.

SONNECKEN, EDWIN HERBERT, management consultant; b. New Haven, July 22, 1916; s. Ewald and Pauline (Halfmann) S.; m. Elizabeth Gregory, June 3, 1939; children: William H., Richard G., Paul D. BS, Northwestern U., 1938; MBA, 1940. With Montgomery Ward & Co., Chgo., 1940-42; price adminstr. OPA, 1943; mgr. sales B.F. Goodrich Co., Akron, Ohio, 1943-53; dir. planning Ford Motor Co., Dearborn, Mich., 1953-57; pres. Market Planning Corp., N.Y.C., 1957-61; from dir. corp. planning and research to v.p. corp. bus. planning Goodyear Tire & Rubber Co., 1961-80; chmn. Mktg. Sci. Inst., Cambridge, Mass., 1980-84, also trustee, chmn. research policy com.; mgmt. cons., Akron, 1985—. Pres. Akron (Ohio) chpt. Am. Mktg. Assn., 1950, v.p. Detroit chpt., 1955, nat. v.p., dir., 1957, nat. pres., 1964-65, mem. global mktg. coun., 1986—. Pres. YMCA, Akron, 1978; chmn. trustees First Congl. Ch., Akron, 1985, chmn. endowment trust, 1987—. Served with AUS, 1945-46. Mem. Am. Statis. Assn., Am. Assn. Pub. Opinion Research, Nat. Assn. Bus. Economists, Am. Mktg. Assn., Internat. Mktg. Fedn. (pres.), European Soc. for Opinion and Market Research, Beta Gamma Sigma, Portage Country (Akron). Avocation: golf. Home and Office: Apt 333 100 Brookmont Rd Akron OH 44333-3094

SONNEDECKER, GLENN ALLEN, pharmaceutical historian, pharmaceutical educator; b. Creston, Ohio, Dec. 11, 1917; s. Ira Elmer and Letia (Linter) S.; m. Cleo Bell, Apr. 3, 1943; 1 child, Stuart Bruce. BS, Ohio State U., 1942; MS, U Wis., 1950, PhD, 1952; Dr. Sci. honoris causa, Ohio State U., 1964, Phila. Coll. Pharmacy and Sci., 1989; PharmD honoris causa, Mass. Coll. Pharmacy, 1974. Lic. pharmacist. Mem. editorial staff Sci. Service, Washington, 1942-43; editor Jour. Am. Pharm. Assn. (practical pharmacy edit.), 1943-48; asst. prof. U. Wis., 1952-56, asso. prof., 1956-60, prof., 1960-81, Edward Kremers prof., 1981-86; sec. Am. Inst. History of Pharmacy, 1949-57, dir., 1957-73, 81-85, hon. dir. life, chmn. bd., 1988-89; editor-in-chief RPh, 1978-80. Sec., bd. dirs. Friends of Hist. Pharmacy, 1945-49; chmn. Joint Com. on Pharmacy Coll. Librs., 1960-61; U.S. del. Internat. Pharm. Fedn., 1953, 55, 62; U.S. rep. to Mid. East Pharm. Congress, Beirut, 1956; sec. sect. history of pharmacy and biochemistry Pan-Am. Congress Pharmacy and Biochemistry, 1957. Co-author books; contbr. to pharm. and hist. publs. Recipient Edward Kremers award (for writings), 1964, Nat. award Rho Chi, 1967, Schelenz plaquette German Soc. for History of Pharmacy, 1971, Remington honor medal Am. Pharm. Assn., 1972, Urdang medal, 1976, Folch Andreu prize, Spain, 1985, Profile award Am. Found. Pharm. Edn., 1994; Am. Found. fellow, 1948-52, Guggenheim fellow, 1955, Fulbright Rsch. scholar, Germany, 1955-56. Mem. Am. Pharm. Assn. (life mem.; sec. sect. history of pharmacy 1949-50, vice chmn. 1950-51, chmn. 1951-52, rsch. assoc. 1964-65, chmn. joint task force with Acad. Pharm Scis. 1985, hon. chmn. bd. trustees 1985), Internat. Acad. History Pharmacy (1st v.p. 1970-81, pres. 1983-91, hon. pres. 1991—), Am. Assn. History of Medicine (exec. coun. 1966-69), Internat. Gesellschaft fur Geschichte der Pharmazie (exec. bd. 1965-89), hon. mem. socs. for history of pharmacy of Italy, Benelux, pan-Arab, Spain; mem. Sigma Xi, Rho Chi (mem. nat. exec. coun. 1957-59), Phi Delta Chi. Unitarian Universalist. Home: 2030 Chadbourne Ave Madison WI 53705-4047 Office: Univ Wis Sch of Pharmacy 777 Highland Ave Madison WI 53705-2222

SONNEMAN, EVE, artist; b. Chgo., 1946; d. Eric O. and Edith S. BFA, U. Ill., 1967; MFA, U. N.Mex., 1969. One-woman shows include Castelli Gallery, N.Y.C., 1976, 78, 80, 82, 84-86, Tex. Gallery, Houston, 1976, 78, 80, 82, 85, Galerie Farideh Cadot, Paris, 1978, 80, 83, François Lambert Gallery, Milan,Italy, 1980, 87, Mpls. Inst. Arts, 1980, La Noveau Musèe, Lyon, France, 1980, Musèe de Toulon (France), 1983, Centre Georges Pompidou, Paris, 1984, Circus Gallery, L.A., 1989, 97, Jones Troyer Fitzpatrick, Washington, 1989, Zabriskie Gallery, N.Y., 1990, Gloria Luria Gallery, Miami, 1990, Grand Central Terminal, N.Y.C., 1991, Charles Cowles Gallery, 1992, Sidney Janis Gallery, N.Y.C., 1996, La Geode Mus., Paris, 1996, Cirrus Gallery, 1997, Bruce Silverstein Gallery, N.Y., 2002, Jadite Gallery, N.Y., 2002, Galeria Turchi, Sienna, Italy, 2002; author: America's Cottage Gardens, 1990, Where Birds Live, 1992; co-author: How To Touch What, 2000; photographs subject of book Real Time, 1976. Grantee Nat. Endowment Arts, 1971, 78, Polaroid Corp., 1978; Cartier fellowship, France, 1989. Address: 446 W 47th St Apt 5C New York NY 10036-2381

SONNEMAN, JOSEPH ABRAM, lawyer, researcher, mediator, photographer; b. Chgo., Apr. 22, 1944; s. Eric O. and Edith A. Sonneman. BS, U. Ill., 1968; MA, Claremont (Calif.) Grad. Sch., 1970, PhD, 1977; JD cum laude, Georgetown U., 1989. Bar: Alaska. Pres., owner Five Star Photos, Juneau, 1989—, Pacific Mediation and Arb, Juneau, 1989—, Alaska Legal Rsch., Juneau, 1989—; pvt. practice, 1990—. Author: the Exxon Valdez Deals, 1992; co-author, co-editor Rights in Data, 1988. Nominee Alaska Dem. Party U.S. Senate, 1998; pres. Juneau World Affairs Coun., 1995-99, Juneau Arts and Humanities Coun., 1973; sec. Juneau Internat. Rels. Adv. Com., 2000—. With U.S. Army, 1963-66. Mem. ATLA, Alaska Bar Assn., Hawaii Bar Assn., Am. Assn. Ret. People (pres. Mt. Juneau chpt. 1999-2001), Pioneers of Alaska. Jewish. Avocations: gardening, target shooting, bicycling, walking. Office: Alaska Legal Rsch 324 Willoughby Ave Juneau AK 99801-1723 E-mail: senator@gci.net.

SONNEMANN, HARRY, electrical engineer, consultant; b. Munich, Germany, Sept. 3, 1924; came to U.S., 1938, naturalized, 1944; s. Leopold and Emmy (Markus) S.; m. Shirley E. Battles, Nov. 25, 1949; children: Carol Jean, Joyce Elaine, Patricia Ann. BS, Poly. Inst. Bklyn., 1954. Research electroencephalography, 1944-47; asst. to dir. electronics dept. AEC contract, Columbia U., 1947-50; supr. electronics shop Columbia Hudson Labs., 1951-53, head electronics dept., 1954-59; asst. dir. Project Artemis, 1959-64, Project Artemis (Hudson labs.), 1961-64; asst. dir. field engrng. Advanced Research Projects Agy., Nuclear Test Detection Office, 1964-67; acting dep. dir. Nuclear Test Detection Office, 1967-68; spl. asst. in electronics to asst. sec. navy for research and devel. Navy Dept., 1968-76, spl. asst. to asst. sec. navy for research and devel., 1976-77; asst. to chief engr. NASA, 1977-78, dep. chief engr., 1978-84, asst. chief engr., 1984-86, cons., 1986—; pres. SBC Assocs., McLean, Va., 1988-95. Chmn. Dept. Def. Tactical Satellite Exec. Steering Group, 1968-69, chmn. Dept. Def. nav. satellite exec. steering group, 1969-70, 72-73 Treas. Art League. No. Va., 1967-68; pres. Rotonda Condominium Unit Owners Assn., 1982-84, 97-98, 99-2000. Mem.: Washington Figure Skating (dir. 1968-73, treas. 1969-72), Ice Club of Washington (pres. 1974-76). Home and Office: 8360 Greensboro Dr Apt 907 Mc Lean VA 22102-3514 E-mail: HSSBC@aol.com.

SONNENBERG, HARDY, data processing company research and development executive, engineer; b. Schoensee, Fed. Republic Germany, Apr. 12, 1939; s. Gustav and Wanda (Neumann) S.; m. Doris Linda Adam, June 20, 1964; children: Kevin, Denise. BS, U. Alta., 1962; MS, Stanford U., 1964, PhD, 1967. Registered profl. engr., Ont. Advanced devel. engr. GTE Sylvania, Mountain View, Calif., 1966-68, engrng. specialist, 1968-70, sect. mgr., 1970-73; dir. rsch. Optical Diodes Inc., Palo Alto, 1973-74; mem. rsch. staff Xerox Rsch. Centre Can., Mississauga, Ont., 1975-78, area mgr., 1978-80, lab. mgr., 1980-86, mgr. rsch. ops., 1986-87, mgr. tech. and engring. systems, 1987-94, v.p. rsch. and tech., 1994-96; pres. Calixo Cons., Freelton, 1997—. Chmn. indsl. adv. coun. McMaster U., Hamilton, Ont., 1990-93, active, 1987-94. Contbr. articles to profl. jours. Patentee in field. Chmn. bd. dirs. local ch., Hamilton, Ont., 1983-85, 89-93, 98-2002; pres. Sheridan Park Assn., Mississauga, 1988-89; chmn. Conf. Bd. Can. Rsch. Mgrs. Forum, 1991-93. Recipient cert. of recognition for invention NASA, 1973, 74, Achievement award Xerox Corp., 1981, Charles E. Ives Engring. award, 1983. Mem. IEEE, Am. Phys. Soc., Assn. Profl. Engrs. Ont., Sigma Xi. Avocations: outdoor activities, singing, church participation. Home and Office: 900 Hwy 97 Box 126 Freelton ON Canada L0R 1K0 Fax: (905) 659-3029. E-mail: HardyS@attcanada.ca.

SONNENBLICK, BERNARD, obstetrician-gynecologist; b. N.Y.C., July 16, 1935; MD, N.Y. Med. Coll., 1959. Diplomate Am. Bd. Ob-Gyn. Intern Beth Israel Hosp., N.Y.C., 1959-60; resident in ob-gyn. N.Y. Med. Ctr., 1960-64. Fellow ACOG. Office: 7101 Francisco Bend Dr Delray Beach FL 33446

SONNENBLICK, EDMUND HIRAM, medical educator, cardiologist; b. New Haven, Oct. 7, 1932; s. Ira J. and Rosalind (Helfand) S.; m. Linda Bland, Dec. 21, 1954; children: Emily Sonnenblick Offit, Charlotte Sonnenblick Van Doren, Annie E. (dec.). BA, Wesleyan U., Middletown, Conn., 1954; MD, Harvard U., 1958. Diplomate Am. Bd. Internal Medicine. Resident in medicine Presbyn. Hosp., N.Y.C., 1958-60, 62-63; sr. investigator Nat. Heart Inst., Bethesda, Md., 1960-62, 63-68; asst. prof. medicine Harvard Med. Sch., Boston, 1968-70, assoc. prof., 1970-75; co-dir. cardiology Peter Bent Brigham Hosp., 1968-75, dir. cardiovasc. rsch., 1970-75; Olson prof. medicine, chief carddiology Albert Einstein Coll. Medicine, Bronx, NY, 1975—96, Edmond J. Safra prof. medicine, 1996—, chief emeritus cardiology, 1996—. Editor Progress in Cardiovasc. Diseaess; contbr. over 600 articles to med. jours. Author 15 books and chpts. in books; editor Progress in Cardiovasc. Diseases; contbr. over 600 articles to med. jours. Trustee Wesleyan U., 1994-97. Sr. surgeon USPHS, 1960-62. Fellow ACP, Am. Coll. Cardiology (Disting. Scientist award 1989); mem. Am. Coll. Physicians, Am. Assn. Physicians, Am. Soc. Clin. Investigation, Am. Physiol. Soc., Interurban Club, N.Y. Yacht Club, Noroton Yacht Club. Avocation: sailing. Home: 138 Goodwives River Rd Darien CT 06820-5807 Office: Albert Einstein Coll Medicine Weiler Hosp 1825 Eastchester Rd Bronx NY 10461-2301 E-mail: esonnenbli@aol.com.

SONNENBLICK, HARVEY IRWIN, psychiatrist; b. N.Y.C., June 3, 1936; s. Paul and Adele (Newman) S.; children: Lissa, Jordan. BA, U. Va., 1958; MD, NYU, 1962. Diplomate Am. Bd. Psychiatry and Neurology. Intern Kings County Hosp., Bklyn., 1962-63, resident, 1963-65; resident, fellow S.I. (N.Y.) Mental Health Soc., 1965-67; staff psychiatrist Seamen's Soc. for Children and Families, S.I., 1978—, Jewish Bd. Family & Children's Svcs., S.I. and Bklyn., 1981—. Vis. psychiatrist Sea View Hosp. Rehab. Ctr. and Home, S.I., 1966—. Maj. U.S. Army, 1968-70. Mem. AMA, Am. Psychiat. Assn., Phi Beta Kappa. Avocation: basketball.

SONNENFELD, JOSEPH, geographer, researcher; b. N.Y.C., Sept. 1, 1929; s. Isaac and Miriam (Goldhirsh) S.; m. Valerie Wilmot, Sept. 1952 (div. Aug. 1968); children: David Allan, Michael Jacob, William Edward; m. Liana Bisiani, June 19, 1982; children: Kristin Selina Cruz, Sondra Nell Robbins. BS, Oreg. State Coll., 1952; PhD, Johns Hopkins U., 1957. Instr. U. Del., Newark, 1955-57, asst. prof., 1957-62, assoc. prof., 1962-68; prof. Tex. A&M U., College Station, 1968-93, prof. emeritus, 1993—, asst. dean for acad. affairs, 1975-79. Contbr. articles to profl. jours. Wenner-Gren Found. for Anthropol. Rsch. fellow, 1954; Rsch. grantee Arctic Inst. N.Am., 1954, 63, Office of Naval Rsch., 1954, 63, Tex. A&M U., 1970, NSF, 1991. Mem. AAAS, Am. Psychol. Soc., Assn. Am. Geographers, Behavioral and Brain Scis. (assoc.), Current Anthropology (assoc.), Internat. Arctic Social Sci. Assn., Sigma Xi. Home: 302 W 11th St Port Angeles WA 98362-7605

SONNENFELD, SANDI, writer; b. Queens, N.Y., May 22, 1963; d. Fred I. and Myra G. (Gever) S.; m. Warren A. Berry, Sept. 6, 1992. BA in English/Dance, Mount Holyoke Coll., 1985; MFA in Creative Writing, U. Wash., Seattle, 1989. Adj. English instr. Seattle Cmty. Coll., 1989-91, Pierce Coll., Puyallup, Wash., 1991-95; devel. coord. Hope Heart Inst., Seattle, 1995-96; dir. devel. Tacoma Actors Guild, 1996-97; media rels. dir. Publicis Dialog, Seattle, 1998—. Freelance writer, Seattle, 1989—; planning com. co-chair Northwest Bookfest, Seattle, 1995-97. Author: Case Study Harvard Bus. Rev., 1994, 95; contbg. author Literary Anthology, 1995, (short story) Sex and the City, 1992, Family: A Celebration; contbr. feature articles to Wall St. Jour., Nat. Bus. Employment Weekly, Animals Mag. Recipient award David Dornstein Nat. Fiction Writing Contest, Coalition for the Advancement of Jewish Edn., 1998. Mem. Pen Ctr. West, Soc. Profl. Journalists, Mount Holyoke Coll. Club Puget Sound (pres. alumnae club 1996-97). Democrat. Jewish. Home: 125 N 105th St Seattle WA 98133-8701 Office: Publicis Dialog 424 2nd Ave W Seattle WA 98119-4140

SONNENFELDT, HELMUT, former government official, educator, consultant, author; b. Berlin, Germany, Sept. 13, 1926; came to U.S., 1944, naturalized, 1945; s. Walter H. and Gertrud (Liebenthal) S.; m. Marjorie Hecht, Oct. 4, 1953; children— Babette Sonnenfeldt Lubben, Walter H., Stewart H. AB, Johns Hopkins, 1950, MA, 1951. With Dept. State, Washington, 1952-77; formerly dir. Office Rsch. and Analysis for USSR and Eastern Europe, 1965-69; lectr. Sch. Advanced Internat. Studies, Johns Hopkins U., 1958-69, vis. scholar, 1977-78; guest scholar Brookings Instn., Washington, 1978—. Sr. mem. Nat. Security Coun., 1969-74; counselor Dept. State, 1974-77. Former gov. UN Assn. of U.S.; dir. Atlantic Coun. of U.S., World Affairs Coun. Washington; trustee Johns Hopkins U. With AUS, 1945-46. Mem. Coun. on Fgn. Rels. N.Y., Pi Delta Epsilon. Home: 5600 Wisconsin Ave Apt 1505 Chevy Chase MD 20815-4412 Office: Brookings Instn 1775 Massachusetts Ave NW Washington DC 20036-2103 E-mail: hsonnenfeldt@brook.edu.

SONNENFELDT, RICHARD WOLFGANG, management consultant; b. Berlin, July 3, 1923; s. Walter H. and Gertrude (Liebenthal) S.; m. Shirley C. Aronoff, Dec. 23, 1949; m. Barbara A. Hausman, Mar. 8, 1981; children: Ann Elizabeth, Lawrence Alan, Michael William. BSEE, Johns Hopkins U., 1949; postgrad., U. Pa., 1953-56. Mgr. engring. and prodn. RCA, 1949-62; gen. mgr. digital systems div. Foxboro Co., 1962-65; chief exec. officer, pres., dir. Digitronics Corp., 1965-70; v.p. RCA Corp., 1970-79; chmn. bd. dirs., CEO Electronic Indsl. Engrng. Corp., 1972-75; exec. v.p. ops. NBC, N.Y.C., 1979-82; dean Sch. Mgmt. Poly Inst. N.Y., Bklyn., 1982-84, prof. mgmt., 1982—; chmn. bd. dirs., CEO NAPP Systems, Inc., 1987-90; CEO Solar Outdoor Lighting, 1997—. Lectr. Harvard U. Bus. Sch., Sloan Sch., MIT; cons. in field; bd. dirs. Tetktronix, Inc., Foxboro Co., Lee Enterprises, Decision Industries Corp., Compuflight Corp., Biospherics Inc., Deerpark Baking Co., Tridex Corp., Internat. Harvest Group, Comm. Satellite Network Corp., Medlife Software Inc., Solar Outdoor Lighting Inc. Contbr. articles to profl. jours.; patentee in field. Fellow IEEE; mem. Am. Coun. Germany, Coun. Fgn. Rels., Tau Beta Pi, Omicron Delta Kappa. Home and Office: 4 Secor Dr Port Washington NY 11050-3418

SONNENSCHEIN, ADAM, lawyer; b. N.Y.C., Oct. 15, 1938; s. Harry D. and Sybil (Reinus) S.; m. Phyllis Cokin, Oct. 25, 1968; children: Andrew, Michael. BA, Amherst Coll., 1960; LLB, Columbia U., 1965. Bar: N.Y. 1965, Mass. 1970. Assoc. Berlack, Israels & Liberman, N.Y.C., 1965-70; ptnr. Sprague Assocs., Boston, 1970-72, Walter & Sonnenschein, Boston, 1972-78, Hausserman, Davison & Shattuck, Boston, 1978-83, Foley, Hoag & Eliot, Boston, 1983—. Mem. ABA, Mass. Bar Assn., Boston Bar Assn., Assn. of Bar of City of N.Y. Office: Foley Hoag & Eliot 1 Post Office Sq Boston MA 02109-2106

SONNENSCHEIN, HUGO FREUND, academic administrator, economics educator; b. N.Y.C., Nov. 14, 1940; s. Leo William and Lillian Silver Sonnenschein; m. Elizabeth Gunn, Aug. 26, 1962; children: Leah, Amy, Rachel. AB, U. Rochester, 1961; MS, Purdue U., 1963, PhD, 1964, PhD (hon.) , 1996; PhD (hon.) , Tel Aviv U., 1993; D (hon.) , U. Autonoma Barcelona, Spain, 1994; PhD (hon.) , Lake Forest Coll., 1995, North Ctrl. Coll., 2001, U. Chgo., 2002. Faculty dept. econs. U. Minn., 1964—70, prof., 1968—70; prof. econs. U. Mass., Amherst, 1970—73, Northwestern U., 1973—76, Princeton (N.J.) U., 1976—87, Class of 1926 prof., 1987—88, provost, 1991—93; dean, Thomas S. Gates prof. U. Pa. Sch. Arts & Scis., Phila., 1988—91; pres. U. Chgo., 1993—2000, Hutchinson disting. prof., pres. emeritus, 2000—. Vis. prof. U. Andes, Columbia, 1965, Tel Aviv U., 1972, Hebrew U., 1973, U. Paris, 1978, U. Aix-en-Provence, France, 1978, Stanford U., 1984—85; bd. dirs. Van Kampen Mutual Funds. Editor: Econometrica, 1977—84; mem. editl. bd.: Jour. Econ. Theory, 1972—75, mem. editl. bd.: Jour. Math. Econs., 1974—, mem. editl. bd.: SIAM Jour., 1976—80; contbr. articles to profl. jours. Trustee U. Rochester, 1992—, U. Chgo., 1993—. Fellow, Social Sci. Rsch. Coun., 1967—68, NSF, 1970—, Ford Found., 1970—71, Guggenheim Found., 1976—77. Fellow: Econometric Soc. (pres. 1988—89), Am. Acad. Arts and Scis.; mem.: NAS, Am. Philos. Soc.

SONNENSCHEIN, RALPH ROBERT, physiologist; b. Chgo., Aug. 14, 1923; s. Robert and Flora (Kieferstein) S.; m. Patricia W. Niddrie, June 21, 1952; children— David, Lisa, Ann. Student, Swarthmore Coll., 1940-42, U. Chgo., 1942-43; BS, Northwestern U., 1943, BM, MS, Northwestern U., 1946, MD, 1947; PhD, U. Ill., 1950. Research asst. in physiology Northwestern U. Med. Sch., 1944-46; intern Michael Reese Hosp., Chgo., 1946-47; successively research fellow clin. sci., research asst. psychiatry, research asso. psychiatry U. Ill. Med. Sch., 1947-51; mem. faculty U. Calif. Med. Sch., Los Angeles, 1951-88, prof. physiology, 1962-88, prof. emeritus, 1988—; liaison scientist Office Naval Research, London, 1971-72. Author papers on pain, innervation of skin, peripheral circulation. Served with AUS, 1943-46. Spl. research fellow USPHS, 1957-58; fellow Swedish Med. Research Council, 1964-65; grantee USAF; grantee Office Naval Research; grantee NIH; grantee NSF. Mem. Am. Physiol. Soc., Microcirculatory Soc., Soc. Exptl. Biology and Medicine, AAAS, Hungarian Physiol. Soc. (hon.). Home: 18212 Kingsport Dr Malibu CA 90265-5636 Office: U Calif Sch Medicine Dept Physiology Los Angeles CA 90095-1751

SONNHALTER, CAROLYN THERESE, physical therapist, consultant; b. Bedford, Ohio, Apr. 26, 1942; d. Gabriel Edward Jr. and Josephine Irene (Kubera) Farkas; m. Donald Joseph Lippert, June 11, 1966 (div. June 1981); 1 child, Kevin Michael; m. Robert Louis Sonnhalter, Aug. 31, 1985. BS, Ohio State U., 1964. Lic. phys. therapist, Ohio. Staff and sr. phys. therapist Akron (Ohio) City Hosp., 1964-69; asst. dir. phys. therapy Akron Gen. Med. Ctr., 1975-82; dir. phys. therapy Litchfield Rehab. Ctr., Akron, 1983-87; phys. therapist HMO Health Ohio, 1987-97, Phoenix-Hudson Corp., Middleburg Heights, Ohio, 1993-98; dir. phys. therapy Tri-County Home Nursing, Mogadore, 1997-99; phys. therapist VNS, Kent, 1999—. Revel. phys. therapy first outpatient Chronic Pain Mgmt. Program, Ohio, 1983; cons. video animation on mechanism of whiplash for use by med. and legal profls., Ohio, 1996. Mem. Am. Phys. Therapy Assn., Alpha Gamma Delta. Avocations: traveling Ohio and nearby states in search of antiques, gardening. Home: 3631 Oak Rd Stow OH 44224-3934 Office: VNS 234 S Water St Kent OH 44240-3526

SONNIER, DAVID JOSEPH, wholesale distributing executive; b. Lafayette, La., Aug. 25, 1939; s. Fernand and Joyce Marie (Lester) S.; m. Ellen Christine Fusselman, July 18, 1964; 1 child, Carole Marie. BS, McNeese State U., 1962. Mgr. tng. program Coburn Supply Co., Lake Charles, La., 1957—62, mgr., v.p. Longview, Tex., 1964—98, regional coord., v.p., 1998—2002, gen. mgr., 2002—. Lt. col. USAR, 1962-90, Tex. N.G., 1966-76. Lt. col. USAR, 1962—90, with Tex. N.G., 1966—76. Mem. Wholesale Distbrs. Assn., Nat.

Assn. Home Builders, Tex. Assn. Builders, East Tex. Builders Assn., East Tex. Plumbing, Heating, Cooling Contractors, Res. Officers Assn. Roman Catholic. Home: 865 Forest Lake PO Box 97 Judson TX 75660-0097 Office: Coburn Supply Co 1010 W Cotton St Longview TX 75604-5510

SONNTAG, STEVEN JOSEPH, humanities educator; b. L.A., Calif., Nov. 28, 1944; s. Lewis Ludwig Sonntag, Natalie Ruth Sonntag; m. Pearl Aida Levin, Aug. 6, 1972 (dec. June 1997); children: Sabrina, Marissa; m. Ruby May Lew, Nov. 3, 2001; 1 child Brenna. AA, Merritt Coll., 1965; BA, Calif. State U. San Francisco, 1967, MA, 1970. Tchr. Middletocon H.S., Middleto-con, Calif., 1970—71, Manteca H.S., Manteca, 1971—. Instr. Delta Coll., Stockton, Calif., 1976—92. Democrat. Jewish. Avocations: movies, travel, plays, cultural events. Home: 3746 W Ben Holt Dr Stockton CA 95219

SONS, LINDA RUTH, mathematics educator; b. Chicago Heights, Ill., Oct. 31, 1939; d. Robert and Ruth (Diekelman) S. AB in Math., Ind. U., 1961; MS in Math., Cornell U., 1963, PhD in Math., 1966. Tchg. asst. Cornell U., Ithaca, N.Y., 1961-63, instr. math., summer 1963, rsch. asst., 1963-65; asst. prof. math. No. Ill. U., De Kalb, 1965-70, assoc. prof., 1970-78, prof., 1978—, presdl. tchg. prof. DeKalb, 1994-98, disting. tchg. prof., 1998—. Vis. assoc. prof. U. London, 1970-71; dir. undergrad. studies math. dept. No. Ill. U., 1971-77, exec. sec. univ. coun., 1978-79; chair faculty fund No. Ill. U. Found., De Kalb, 1982—. Author: (with others) A Study Guide for Introduction to Mathematics, 1976, Mathematical Thinking in a Quantitative World, 1990; contbr. articles to profl. jours. Mem. campus ministry com. No. Ill. Dist. Luth. Ch./Mo. Synod, Hillside, 1977—2001; mem. ch. coun. Immanuel Luth. Ch., DeKalb, 1978—85, 1987—89; pres. Luth. Women's Missionary League, 1974—87; bd. dirs., treas. DeKalb County Migrant Ministry, 1967—78. NSF Rsch. grantee, 1970-72, 74-75; recipient 1988 Award for Disting. Svc. of Ill. Sect. of the Math Assn. Am., 1991 Award for Excellence in Coll. Teaching of Ill. Coun. Tchrs. Math. Mem. Am. Math. Soc., Assn. for Women in Math., Math. Assn. Am. (mem. nat. bd. govs. 1989-92, mem. com. undergrad. program in math. 1990-96, chmn. coun. on awards 1997—, Disting. Svc. to Ill. Sect. award 1988, Disting. Coll. or Univ. Tchg. of Math. Sect. award 1995, Cert. Meritorious Svc. nat. award 1998), Ill. Sect. Math. Assn. (v.p. sect., pres.-elect, pres., then past pres. 1982-87, bd. dirs. 1989-92), London Math. Soc., Phi Beta Kappa (pres. No. Ill. assn. 1981-85), Sigma Xi (past. chpt. pres.). Achievements include research in mathematics education and research in classical complex analysis--especially value distribution for meromorphic functions with unbounded characteristic in the unit disc. Office: No Ill U Dept Math Scis Dekalb IL 60115

SONS, RAYMOND WILLIAM, journalist; b. Harvey, Ill., Aug. 25, 1926; s. William Henry and Gladys Lydia (Steinko) S.; m. Bettina Dieckmann; children: David, Pamela Sons Clarke, Ronald. BA, U. Mich., 1950. Reporter, mng. editor Murphysboro (Ill.) Daily Ind. edit. So. Illinoisan newspaper, 1950-52; assoc. news editor Middletown (Ohio) Jour., 1952-53; reporter, asst. city editor, sportswriter, sports editor Chgo. Daily News, 1953-78; sports editor, columnist Chgo. Sun-Times, 1978-92. Served with USAAF, 1945-46. Recipient Best Sports Story in Ill. award U.P.I., 1970, Marshall Field award for outstanding editorial contbn. to Chgo. Daily News, 1972; Best Sports Column award AP Sports Editor, 1979, Best Sports Column award Ill. AP, 1987, Chgo. Journalism Hall of Fame, 1996. Roman Catholic. Home: 4100 Torrington Ct Fort Collins CO 80525-3419

SONTAG, DAVID B. producer, writer, educator; b. N.Y.C., Aug. 17, 1934; s. Samuel John and Lily (Gumple) S. BS in Textile Engring., N.C. State U., 1955. Dir., cameraman Sta. UNC-TV, 1954-55; program exec. NBC, 1955-59; dir. devel. CBS Films, 1959-61; owner, operator David Sontag Enterprises, 1961-63; exec. prodr., head of spls. ABC, 1963-67; pres. David Sontag Prodns. Inc., 1968-98; sr. v.p. creative affairs 20th Century Fox, 1976-81; pres. Western Slope Comms., Ltd., 1973-87; Wesley Wallace vis. prof. U. N.C., Chapel Hill, 2000-2001, Wesley Wallace prof., 2001—, chair writing for screen and stage program. Lectr. Aspen Inst. Humanistic Study, Action for Children's TV, Washington, Colo. Mountain Coll., U. So. Calif., U. Colo., Coll. Santa Fe, Aspen Film Festival; faculty mem. Am. Film Inst., The Ctr. for Advanced Film and TV Studies, 1987-89; cons. U. Calif., Riverside. Prodr., writer: (feature films) Break A Leg Mr. President, 1979, Mission: MIA, 1981, Outlaws: A Legend, 1982, Changes, 1987, Threat Case, 1993, Dancer in Madrid, 1998; prodr.: (feature films) I'll be Down to Get You in a Taxi, Honey, 1979 (also co-author of original story), Mila 18, 1985; creator: (TV programs) What's A Nice Girl Like You Doing In A Place Like This?, 1964, The Las Vegas Show, 1968 (also exec. prodr.), James At Fifteen, 1976, Central High, 1987, The Knife and Gun Club, 1990, Kennedy for the Defense, 1990; developer (TV show) Shindig, 1963, The Paper Chase, 1979; exec. prodr. In Concert, 1971-72; exec. prodr., writer My Father's House, 1972, Abandoned Child, 1993; co-exec. prodr., writer, creator Southside, 2001. Past trustee, mem. exec. com. Aspen Music Festival; founder Native Ams. Internat. Film Expn., Santa Fe; trustee, past vice chmn., bd. trustees Carolina Theater, Durham; bd. dirs. Documentary Arts, N.C. Jewish Film Festival; past bd. dirs. Inst. Preservation of the Original Lang. of Ams., Ctr. for Contemporary Art, Santa Fe; bd. dirs. Full Focus Documentary Film Festival. Mem. Writers Guild Am. Office: U NC @ Chapel Hill Dept Comm Studies 205 Swain Hall CB #3285 Chapel Hill NC 27599-3285 E-mail: sontag@email.unc.edu.

SONTAG, ED, federal agency administrator; BA in Spl. Edn., MA in Elementary Sch. Adminstrn. and Supervision, SUNY; PhD in Spl. Edn. Adminstrn., Syracuse U. Resident scholar for Wisc. Gov. Tommy G. Thompson; deputy asst. sec. U.S. Dept. Interior, 1989—92; prof. U. Wisc. - Stevens Point Sch. Edn., 1992—99; senior-level positions Ill. State Bd. Edn., U.S. Dept. Edn., Ind. U., Wisc. and N.Y. pub. sch. sys.; asst. sec. adminstrn. and mgmt. U.S. Dept. Health and Human Svcs., 2001—. Recipient U. Wisc.-Steven Point Vice Chancellor Merit award, Dept. Interior Disting. Safety award. Office: US Dept Health and Human Svcs 200 Independence Ave SW Washington DC 20201*

SONTAG, FREDERICK EARL, philosophy educator; b. Long Beach, Calif., Oct. 2, 1924; s. M. Burnett and Cornelia (Nicholson) S.; m. Carol Furth, June 10, 1950; children: Grant Furth, Anne Burnett Karch. BA with great distinction, Stanford U., 1949; MA, Yale U., 1951, PhD, 1952; LLD (hon.), Coll. Idaho, 1971. Instr. Yale U., 1951-52; asst. prof. philosophy Pomona Coll., Claremont, Calif., 1952-55, assoc. prof., 1955-60, prof., 1970—, Robert C. Denison prof. philosophy, 1972—, chmn. dept. philosophy, 1960-67, 76-77, 1980-84; chmn. coord. com. in philosophy Claremont Grad. Sch. and Univ. Ctr., 1962-65. Vis. prof. Union theol. Sem., N.Y.c., 1959-60, Collegio de Sant' Anselmo, Rome, 1966-67, U. Copenhagen, fall 1972; theologian-in-residence Am. Ch. in Paris, fall 1973; fulbright regional vis. prof., India, East Asia, Pacific areas, 1977-78; mem. nat. adv. coun. Kent Fellowship Program of Danforth Found., 1963-66. Author numerous books, the most recent being; Love Beyond Pain: Mysticism Within christianity, 1977, Sun Myung Moon and the Unification Church, 1977, also German, Japanese and Korean transl.; (with John K. Roth) God and America's Future, 1977, What Can God Do?, 1979, A Kierkegaard Handbook, 1979, The Elements of Philosophy, 1984, (with John K. Roth) The Questions of Philosophy, 1988, Emotion, 1989, The Return of the Gods, 1989, Willgenstein and the Mystical, 1995, Uncertain Truth, 1995, The Descent of Women, 1997, The Acts of the Trinity, 1997, Truth and Imagination, 1998, 2001: A Spiritual Odyssey, 2001, The Mysterious Presence, 2002. Pres. bd. dirs. Claremont Family Svc., 1960-64; trustee The Coro Found., L.A. and San Francisco, 1967-71; bd. dirs., chmn. ways and means com. Pilgrim Place, Claremont, 1970-77. With AUS, 1943-46. Vis. scholar Ctr. for Study Japanese Religions, Kyoto, Japan, spring 1974; vis. fellow East-West Ctr., Honolulu, summer 1974; Wig Disting. prof. award, 1970, 76. Mem. Am. Philos. Assn., Metaphys. Soc. Am. Soc. on Religion in Higher Edn. (Kent fellow 1950-52), Am. Acad. Religion, Phi Beta Kappa. Congregationalist. Office: Pomona Coll 551 N College Ave Claremont CA 91711-4410

SONTAG, JAMES MITCHELL, cancer researcher; b. Denver, Dec. 8, 1939; s. Samuel Henry and Rose Hazel (Silverman) S.; m. Elizabeth Crockett Tunis; children: Ariella, Eythan. BS, Lamar State Coll. Tech., Beaumont, Tex.; MS, U. Ill., 1967; PhD, Weizmann Inst. Sci., Rehovot, Israel, 1971; MPH, Harvard U., 1982. Damon Runyon Meml. Fund Cancer Research postdoctoral fellow, 1971-72; guest worker Nat. Cancer Inst., NIH, Bethesda, Md., 1972-73, staff fellow, 1973-74, exptl. oncologist, 1973-76, mgr. carcinogen bioassay program, 1973-76, asst. to divsn. dir. cancer cause and prevention, 1976-80; exec. sec. Clearinghouse on Environ. Carcinogens, 1976-80, asst. dir. for interagy. affairs Office of Dir., 1980-82, spl. asst. epidemiology and biostatistics program, 1982-96; chief office divsn. ops. & analysis divsn. cancer epidemiology and genetics Nat. Cancer Inst., 1996-99; ind. cons., 1999—. Author, editor in field. Served with AUS, 1956-59. Beaumont LWV section, 1963-65 Mem. Beta Beta Beta. Home and Office: 10500 Rockville Pike Apt 610 North Bethesda MD 20852-3341 E-mail: sontagj@hotmail.com.

SONTAG, SUSAN, writer; b. N.Y.C., Jan. 16, 1933; m. Philip Rieff, 1950 (div. 1958); 1 son, David. BA, U. Chgo., 1951; MA in English, Harvard U., 1954, MA in Philosophy, 1955. Instr. English U. Conn., Storrs, 1953-54; editor Commentary, N.Y.C., 1959; lectr. philosophy City Coll., 1959-60, Sarah Lawrence Coll., Bronxville, 1959-60; instr. dept. religion Columbia U., N.Y.C., 1960-64. Writer in residence Rutgers U., 1964-65. Author: (novels) The Benefactor, 1963, Death Kit, 1967, The Volcano Lover: A Romance, 1992; (plays) Alice in Bed: A Play in Eight Scenes, 1993; (stories) I, etcetera, 1978, The Way We Live Now, 1991; (essays) Against Interpretation, 1966 (Mat. Book award nomination 1966), Styles of Radical Will, 1969, Trip to Hanoi, 1969, On Photography, 1977 (Nat. Book Critics Circle award for criticism 1978), Illness as Metaphor, 1978, Under the Sign of Saturn, 1980, AIDS and Its Metaphors, 1989; (anthology) A Susan Sontag Reader, 1982; screenwriter, dir.: (films) Duet for Cannibals, 1969, Brother Carl, 1971; dir.: (films) Promised Lands, 1974, Unguided Tour, 1983; editor, author of introduction: Antonin Artaud: Selected Writings, 1976, A Roland Barthes Reader, 1982, Danilo Kis's Homo Poeticus: Essays & Interviews, 1995. Guggenheim fellow, 1966, 75, Rockefeller Found. fellow, 1965, 74, MacArthur fellow, 1990-95; recipient George Polk Meml. award, 1966, Ingram Merrill Found. award in lit. in field of Am. Letters, 1976, Creative Arts award Brandeis U., 1976, Malaparte prize, 1992; named Officier de l'Ordre des Arts et des Lettres, France, 1984. Mem. Am. Acad. Arts and Scis. (elected 1993), Am. Acad. Arts and Letters (Arts and Letters award 1976), PEN (pres. Am. Ctr. 1987-89). Office: Farrar, Straus & Giroux 19 Union Square West New York NY 10003*

SOOKNE, HERMAN SOLOMON (HANK SOOKNE), retirement services executive; b. Far Rockaway, N.Y., June 30, 1932; s. Harry Martin Sookne and Sarah (Kopolov) Sterenstein; m. Joan Gilman, Apr. 12, 1954 (div. Apr. 9, 1971); children: Charles Michael, David Howard, Susan Frances; m. Polly Henry Johnson, Mar. 1972 (dec. Feb. 2000); m. Trudy Harrelson, Dec. 8, 2000. Student, Georgetown U., 1949-50; BS in Bus. & Econs., NYU, 1953. Pres., owner Gilclan Bldg. Corp., Merrick, N.Y., 1955-68; divsn. mgr. Boise Cascade Bldg. Corp., Freehold, N.J., 1968-70; dir. property mgmt. and engring. Amprop, Inc., Miami, Fla., 1970-73; pres., CEO Bowman Property Investors, Dallas, 1973-79; gen. mgr. Fidinam, Inc., Houston, 1979-82; mktg. cons. Cooper Communities, Inc., Bella Vista, Ark., 1982-88; sr. v.p. Epworth Villa Retirement Ctr., Oklahoma City, 1988—. Scoutmaster Boy Scouts Am., L.I., N.Y., 1955-60; bd. dirs., pres. Copperchase Condo's Inc., Oklahoma City, 1991-95; chmn. trustees United Meth. Ch. of the Servant, 1997. With U.S. Army, 1953-55, Korea. Mem. Ark. Bd. Realtors, Nat. Soc. for Fund Raising Execs., Soc. for Advancement of Mgmt., Nat. Assn. Home Builders, Nat. Soc. Heat, Refrigeration & Air Conditioning Engrs., Rotary (Paul Harris fellow). Republican. Methodist. Avocations: sailing, tennis, ch. affairs, woodworking, reading. Home: 11300 N Pennsylvania Ave Oklahoma City OK 73120-7781 Office: 14901 N Pennsylvania Ave Oklahoma City OK 73134-6069

SOON, BOON YI, engineer; b. Singapore, Oct. 18, 1971; s. Ren Joo Soon and Yoke Lan Lee. MS in Electro-Optics, U. Dayton, 1997, MS in Applied Math., 2000. Rsch. engr. U. Dayton Electro-Optics Program , Dayton, Ohio, 1996—. Contbr. articles to profl. jours. Charles Buckley scholar, 1993-95, Dayton Area Grad. Studies Inst. scholar, 1998-2002. Mem. Tau Beta Pi, Eta Kappa Nu, Phi Kappa Phi, Pi Mu Epsilon, Golden Key. Avocations: running, surfing the net, movies. Office: U Dayton Electro-Optics Program Dayton OH 45469-0245 E-mail: boonyi@yahoo.com.

SOONG, TSU-TEH, engineering science educator; b. Honan, China, Feb. 10, 1934; s. Tung and Yu-Hsieh (Lee) S.; m. Dorothy Yen-Ling Tsai, June 5, 1959; children— Karen, Stephen, Susan. BS, U. Dayton, 1955; postgrad., U. Ill., 1955-56; MS, Purdue U., 1958, PhD, 1962. Instr. engring. sci. Purdue U., 1958-62; sr. research engr. Jet Propulsion Lab., Pasadena, Calif., 1962-63; asst. prof. engring. sci. State U. N.Y. at Buffalo, 1963-66, asso. prof., 1966-68, prof., 1968-89; Samuel P. Capen prof., 1989—. Part-time lectr. engring. UCLA, 1962-63; part-time rsch. mathematician Cornell Aero. Lab., Buffalo, 1964-67, prin. rsch. mathematician, 1967-70 NSF Sci. Faculty fellow Tech. U. Delft, Netherlands, 1966-67; Humboldt Sr. Scientist, U. Hanover, Fed. Republic of Germany, 1987-88. Fellow ASCE (Norman medal 1999, Newmark medal 2002) ; mem. NSPE, Earthquake Engring. Rsch. Inst., Sgma Xi, Tau Beta Pi. Achievements include research in stochastic processes and structural control in engring. Home: 249 Wellingwood Dr East Amherst NY 14051-1750 E-mail: tsoong@eng.buffalo.edu.

SOORIYAARACHCHI, GAMINI SARATHCHANDRA, oncologist, hematologist, educator, researcher; b. Kosgama, Sri Lanka; m. Chandrika Senerath; children: Jasmine, Marcus. MBBS with honors, U. Ceylon, Colombo, Sri Lanka, 1970; diploma in child health, Conjoint Bd. Examiners, London, 1975; diploma in obstetrics, Royal Coll. Ob-Gyn Gt. Britain, 1975; LRCP, MRCS, MRCP, U. London, 1974. Diplomate Am. Bd. Internal Medicine, Am. Bd. Geriatric Medicine, Am. Bd. Med. Oncology, Am. Bd. Hematology. Intern U. Ceylon Tchg. Hosps., 1970-71; sr. house officer Guildford (Eng.) Hosps., 1971-73; registrar St. Helens (Eng.) Hosp., 1974-75; sr. house officer Royal Marsden Hosp. and Inst. Cancer Rsch., Sutton, Eng., 1973-74; fellow in med. oncology and hematology U. Wis. Comprehensive Cancer Ctr., Madison, 1975-77; cons. med. oncologist and hematologist Rockford (Ill.) Clinic and Rockford Meml. Hosp., 1977-83, Oncology Hematology West and Alegent Bergan Mercy Cancer Ctr., Omaha, 1983—; med. dir. Alegent Bergan Mercy Cancer Ctr., 1984—; co-dir. bone marrow transplantation program Oncology Hematology West and Alegent Bergan Mercy Med. Ctr., 1993—. Asst. clin. prof. medicine U. Ill. Sch. Medicine, Rockford, 1977—83; bd. dirs. Cancer Biotherapy Rsch. Group, Franklin, Tenn., 1993—; mem. at-large med. exec. com. Alegent Bergan Mercy Med. Ctr.; bd. dirs. Missouri Valley Cancer Consortium, Omaha, 1994—, pres., 1999—; assoc. clin. prof. medicine Creighton U. Sch. Medicine, Omaha, 1984—96, clin. prof., 1996—; chmn. prof. edn. Am. Cancer Soc., 1986, Nebr. divsn., 87, bd. dirs. Douglas and Sarpy Counties, Neb., 86, Nebr. divsn., 87; med. dir., founding mem. No. Ill. Hospice Assn., Rockford, 1980—83; mem. novel therapeutics com., ethnic diversity com. N. Ctrl. Cancer Treatment Group, Mayo Clin., Rochester, Minn. Contbg. author: Cancer Genetics in Women, 1987; contbr. over 50 articles and astracts to med. jours., including Jour. Clin. Oncology, Blood, Archives Surgery, Jour. Immunotherapy, Cancer Investigation, Annals Pharmacotherapy, Jour. Am. Acad. Dermatology, Jour. Clin. Pathology. Fellow ACP, Royal Coll. Physicians London (cert.), Soc. for Biological Therapy; mem. AMA, Royal Coll. Surgeons (Eng.), Am. Soc. Clin. Oncology, Am. Soc. Hematology, Am. Soc. for Blood and Marrow Transplantation, Nebr. Med. Assn. Office: Alegent Health Bergan Mercy Cancer Ctr 7710 Mercy Rd Ste 122 Omaha NE 68124-2346

SOOS, RICHARD ANTHONY, pastor; b. Passaic, Calif., Apr. 24, 1955; s. Richard A. and Shirley M. (Schneider) S.; m. Beverly J. Dauphinais, Aug. 27, 1987; children: Leann, Erin, Sarah, Richie. Student, San Jose State U., 1982-86; Bachelors Degree, Bethany Bible Coll., 86; Masters Degree, Bethany Bible Sem., 1993. Editor Realities Libr., San Jose, 1969—; pastor Redwood Family Chapel, 1990—. Web programmer Poets Park, San Jose, 1994-98, tchr., 1987—. Author: Why Poetry, 1972 (Poetry Shell award 1972), A Foreign Landscape, 1988, Garden Songs, 1994; editor Poet's Park, 1994 (Yahoo award 1996, Microsoft award 1997, IISME award 1999, MidiMusic award 1999, nat. semicondr. internet innovative award 2000, excellence in edn. award City of San Jose 2000); performer CDs California Breeze, 1997, Darling Dolphins, 1998, Blue Dreams, 1999, Guitars, 2000, Train of Love, 2001. With U.S. Army, 1973-74. Avocations: guitar, music, hiking. Home: 2745 Monterey Hwy Spc 76 San Jose CA 95111-3130 E-mail: soosict@yahoo.com.

SOOY, WILLIAM RAY, electrical engineer, systems analyst; b. Jan. 12, 1951; s. Edward Leinau and Alice Elizabeth (Franklin) S.; m. Jean Marie Sooy, Sept. 17, 1976; children: Jennifer, Karen, Diana, Julia. BSEE, U. Miami, 1973, MS, 1977. Registered profl. engr., Fla. Engr. Fla. Power and Light, Miami, 1973-80, prin. engr. nuc. instrumentation and control, power sys. controls, sys. protection designer, 1981-97; tech. rsch. cons., designer internet svcs., mgr. sys. ops. Energy Mktg. and Trading, Fla. Power and Light, 1998-2000; sr. fin. analyst Energy Mktg. and Trading, 2000—. Engr. Harris Corp., Melbourne, Fla., 1980-81; adj. prof. elec. engring. Palm Beach C.C., 2000—. Mem. IEEE (sr.). Home: 12735 Ellison Wilson Rd North Palm Beach FL 33408-2113 Office: Fla Power and Light PO Box 14000 North Palm Beach FL 33408-0420 E-mail: wsooy@fpl.com.

SOPANEN, JERI RAINER, photography director; b. Helsinki, Finland, Aug. 14, 1929; came to U.S., 1950; s. Rainer and Helvi Raakel (Salminen) S.; m. Carolyn Maier, 1952 (div. 1956); 1 child, Erik; m. Eileen A. Humeston, 1961 (div. 1980); ptnr. Christine Huneke, 1975 (separated 1991); children: Anya Maarit, Mark; m. Marja Roth, 2000. MusB, Lawrence Coll., 1952; BA, U. So. Calif., 1956. Ind. dir. photography Sopanen Films, Inc., N.Y.C., 1966—. Dir. photography: (films) My Dinner With Andre, 1982, The Gig, 1986, The Luckiest Man in the World, 1989; (documentaries) The Brain, 1986, The Ring of Truth, 1987, The Mind (Emmy award 1989); dir. photography Nova programs, 1991—, Gardens of the World with Audrey Hepburn, 1993. With U.S. Army, 1952-54. Mem. Dirs. Guild Am., Internat. Assn. Theatrical Stage Employees. Democrat. Avocation: cross-country skiing. Home and Office: 100 W 89th St Apt 8D New York NY 10024-1936 E-mail: jrsopanen@aol.com.

SOPER, JAMES HERBERT, botanist, curator; b. Hamilton, Ont., Can., Apr. 9, 1916; s. Herbert Armitage and Anna Eliza Gertrude (Cooper) S.; m. Jean Elizabeth Morgan, Aug. 17, 1946; children: Nancy Elizabeth, Mary Florence, Daphne Evans, Ian Morgan. BA, McMaster U., 1938, MA, 1939; PhD (Harris fellow, Austin fellow), Harvard U., 1943. Mem. faculty U. Toronto, 1946-67, curator, 1946-67, prof. botany, 1966-67; chief botanist Can. Mus. Nature, Ottawa, Ont., 1967-81, curator emeritus, 1981—, rsch. assoc., 1993-95. Author: Mt. Revelstoke National Park Wildflowers, 1976, Shrubs of Ontario, 1982; contbr. articles to profl. jours. Served with RCAF, 1943-45. Recipient Royal Jubilee medal, 1978 Mem. Royal Canadian Inst. (life) (pres. 1962-63), Canadian Bot. Assn. (pres. 1982-83), Ottawa Field Naturalists Club, Fedn. Ont. Naturalists (hon.).

SOPER, JOHN TUNNICLIFF, obstetrician-gynecologist, educator; b. Iowa City, Mar. 15, 1952; MD, U. Iowa, 1978. Cert. in ob-gyn. Intern U. Utah Med. Ctr., Salt Lake City, 1978-82, resident in ob-gyn., 1978-82; fellow in gynecol. oncology Duke U., Durham, 1982-85; attending physician Duke U. Med. Ctr., 1982—, Rex Hosp., Raleigh, N.C., 1995—, Womens Hosp., Greensboro, 1995—, Wesley Long Hosp., Greensboro, 1995—; asst. prof. Duke U., 1982-83, 83-89, assoc. prof., 1989-95, prof., 1995—. Mem. ACOG, Am. Soc. Clin. Oncology, Soc. Gynecol. Oncologists, Mid-Atlantic Gynecologic Oncology Soc. Office: Duke U Med Ctr PO Box 3079 Durham NC 27715-3079

SOPER, NATHANIEL JOLAS, surgeon; b. Iowa City, July 10, 1955; MD, U. Iowa Coll. Medicine, 1980. Diplomate Am. Bd. Surgery. Resident in gen. surgery U. Utah Hosps., Salt Lake City, 1980-86, fellow in digestive disease, 1986-88; staff surgeon Barnes Hosp., St. Louis, 1988—, Jewish Hosp., St. Louis, 1988—, VA Med. Ctr., St. Louis, 1988—, St. Louis Regional Med. Ctr., 1988—. Prof. surgery Washington U., St. Louis. Mem. Assn. Acad. Surger, Am. Surg. Assn., Am. Med. Soc., Am. Coll. Surgeons, Soc. Univ. Surgeons, St. Louis Surg. Soc., Soc. Am. Gastrointestinal Endoscopic Surgeons (pres.), Southern Surg. Assn., Soc. for Surgery of the Alimentary Tract. Office: Washington U Sch Med Dept Surgery Campus Box 8109 660 S Euclid Ave Saint Louis MO 63110-1010

SOPKIN, GEORGE, cellist, music educator; b. Chgo., Apr. 3, 1914; s. Isador and Esther (Sopkin) S.; m. Thelma Friedman, July 5, 1936; children— Monica, Paula; m. Carol Borchard Durham, Aug. 30, 1956; children— Edwin, Anthony. Student with, Daniel Saidenberg, Am. Conservatory Music, 1930-32; with, Emmanuel Feurermann, Chgo., Mus. Coll., 1932-34; D.Mus. (hon.), Northland Coll., 1977. Assoc. prof. music U. Wis., 1940-42, artist-in-residence, 1963-79, prof., 1967-77, Disting. prof., 1977-85; prof. Carnegie Mellon U., 1985—, formed trio concert tour of Europe, 1985. Staff ABC, Chgo., 1946-52; artist-in-residence Northwestern U., 1952-55, U. Wisconsin-Milw., Cleve. Inst.; founder New Eng. Piano Quartette, 1980 Mem., Kansas City (Mo.) Philharmonic Orch., 1933-34, Chgo. Symphony Orch., 1934-40, Pro Arte String Quartet, 1940-42, founder, 1946, since mem., Fine Arts Quartet, Chgo., soloist, Kansas City (Mo.) Philharmonic Orch., Chgo. Symphony Orch., Ill. Symphony Orch., Milw. Chamber Orch., Saidenberg Symphonette, frequent TV appearances; artist of film for, Ency. Brit. films, Nat. Ednl. TV films; recording artist for, Mercury, Decca, Concert-disc, Everest, numerous tours, Europe. Bd. dirs. Contemporary Concerts, Inc., Chgo. Served with USAAF, 1943-45. Mem. Lincoln Acad. Address: Newbury Neck Rd Surry ME 04684

SOPPELSA, GEORGE, artist; b. Youngstown, Ohio, July 16, 1939; s. Joseph and Rose (Gaiarsa) S. BFA, Ohio State U., 1961. One-man shows include Mulvane Art Mus., Washburn U., Topeka, 1985, John Szoke Gallery, N.Y.C., 1989, Homer Babbidge Libr., U. Conn., Storrs, 1990, The Gallery, St. Mary's Coll. Md., St. Mary's City, 1991, Inter Art Galerie Reich, Cologne, Germany, 1977, 81, 84, 87, 90, 94, 98, 2001, Randall Tuttle Fine Arts, Woodbury, Conn., 1996, New Britain (Conn.) Mus. Am. Art, 1999; exhibited in group shows at John Szoke Gallery, N.Y.C., 1989, Art at 100 Pearl, Hartford, Conn., 1989, Butler Inst. Am. Art, Youngstown, Ohio, 1985, 90, 98, 2000, 02, Hurlbutt Gallery, Greenwich, Conn., 1993, Mattatuck Mus., Waterbury, Conn., 1995, Aldrich Mus., Ridgefield, Conn., 1995, Chase-Friedman Gallery, Greater Hartford Jewish Cmty. Ctr., West Hartford, Conn., 1999; represented in permanent collections at Mulvane Art Mus., Topeka, Conn. Collection, Hartford. Fellow Nat. Endowment for Arts, 1987, Vt. Studio Ctr., 1988; grantee Conn. Commn. on Arts, 1991, vis. artist Weir Farm Nat. Hist. Site, Wilton, Conn., 1994-95. Office: Brairton & Tubbs Art Agts 135 Central Ave East Hartford CT 06108-3103

SOPPELSA, JOHN JOSEPH, decal manufacturing company executive; b. Cleve., Apr. 23, 1948; s. Anthony Joseph and Elizabeth Ann (McCarthy) S.; m. Nikki Lynn Stevens, Sept. 7, 1968. Student, Cleve. State U., 1966-68, Baldwin-Wallace Coll., Berea, Ohio, 1985. Sales rep. Manning Studios, Inc., Cleve., 1967-70, Pitney-Bowes, Inc., Stamford, Conn., 1970-72, Wampole Chem., Stamford, 1972-75; pres. Sun Art Decals Inc., Cleve., 1975—. Office: Sun Art Decals Inc 885 W Bagley Rd Berea OH 44017-2903

SOPRANOS, ORPHEUS JAVARAS, manufacturing company executive; b. Evanston, Ill., Oct. 4, 1935; s. James Javaras and Marigoula (Papalexatou) S.; m. Angeline Buches, Dec. 31, 1959; children— Andrew, Katherine. AB, MBA, U. Chgo., 1957. Mgmt. trainee Ford Motor Co., Chgo., 1958-59; with Amsted Industries, 1959—, dir. bus. research, 1966-70, treas., 1970-80, v.p., 1980—; pres. Amsted Internat., 1991-93, corp. v.p., 1993-2000, ret. Served with U.S. Army, 1958, 61-62. Mem. Univ. Club (Chgo.), Skokie Country Club.

SORA, SEBASTIAN ANTONY, business machines manufacturing executive, educator; b. N.Y.C., June 29, 1943; s. Joseph Louis and Angelina Maria (Maletta) S.; m. Janet Lee Dietz, Apr. 11, 1970 (dec. July 1972); l child, Joseph Walter; m. Mary Frances Elizabeth Boscketti, Oct. 12, 1974; children: Joseph Walter, Sebastian Nicholas, Frances Ann, Jenny Concetta. BS, Bklyn. Coll., 1964; MBA, Iona Coll., 1974, PMC, 1976; DPS, Pace U., 1989. Math. modeller Assoc. Univs. Inc., 1964-66; with U.S. Coast and Geodetic Survey, Washington, 1967-70; mgr. programming IBM, Yorktown, N.Y., 1966-67, 70-75, programmer, modeller, 1970-72, mgr. program system and design Fishkill, 1971-77, analyst on market models Harrison, 1977-81, sr. programmer Boeblingen, Fed. Republic Germany, 1981-82, mgr. rsch. staff 1st Josephson system Yorktown, 1982-84, program dir. Systems Rsch. Inst. N.Y.C., 1984-87; mgr. edn. program World Trade Corp. IBM, North Tarrytown, N.Y., 1989-90; mgr. promotional-artificial intelligence systems IBM, White Plains, 1990—; assoc. prof. MIS Montclair State Coll., Upper Montclair, N.J., 1992-95; pres. Bus. Edn. Systems Tech., 1992-95. Assoc. prof. info. sci. Pace U., White Plains, N.Y., 1977-96; asst. prof. telecomm. Iona Coll., New Rochelle, N.Y., 1986; asst. prof. mgmt. Manhattan Coll., Bronx, N.Y., 1988; cons. AID,

Washington, 1989; vis. prof. L.I. U., 1997; assoc. prof. computer sci. Marymount Coll., Tarrytown, 1999; spkr. in field. Editor Jour. Value Based Mgmt., 1987—, Jour. Cross Cultural Mgmt., Jour. of Am. Mgmt., 1994-99; pub. Paradegon Shifts in Edn: Paradise Lost or Regained, U. Press of Am.; contbr. articles to profl. jours.; patentee fluxless solder. Mem. IEEE (technol. leadership com. 1986—, info. policy com. 1986-95), Data Processing Mgmt. Assn., Assn. Computing Machinery. Roman Catholic. Home and Office: Internat Bus Edn Sys Techs 1 Christie Ct Somers NY 10589-2430 E-mail: sora@us.ibm.com., sarlou@attglobal.net.

SORBELLO, JOSEPH CHARLES, retired lawyer; b. Redlands, Calif., Apr. 8, 1925; s. Salvatore and Maria (Gallotto) S.; m. Sharon Broome, June 3, 1945, Margaret Pillsbury, June 10, 1969 (dec. June 1995); m. Marguerite Geftakys, Apr. 23, 1997. BS in Pharmacy, Wash. State U., 1951; JD, Lincoln U., 1975. Bar: Calif. 1975; lic. pharmacist Calif., Wash. Owner Community Pharmacy, Edgemont, Calif., 1955-60; pharmacist Owens Pharmacy, Bishop, 1961-69; supervising insp. Calif. State Bd. Pharmacy, San Francisco, L.A., 1969-87; pvt. practice Westminster, Calif., 1987-95; ret., 1996. Lectr. in pharmacy law U. So. Calif., L.A., 1984, 85, 86. Bd. dirs. Moreno Valley Sch. Dist., Sunny Mead, Calif. Staff sgt. USMC, 1942-46, PTO. Mem. Masons, Nu Beta Epsilon, Rho Chi. Democrat. Avocation: amateur radio. Home: 3942 S Mission Rd Fallbrook CA 92028-9455

SORBER, CHARLES ARTHUR, academic administrator; b. Kingston, Pa., Sept. 12, 1939; s. Merritt Walter and Marjory (Roachford) S.; m. Linda Ellen Babcock, Feb. 20, 1972; children: Kimberly Ann, Kingsley Charles. BS in Sanitary Engring., Pa. State U., 1961, MS in Sanitary Engring., 1966; PhD, U. Tex., 1971. Sanitary engr. U.S. Army, France and Fed. Republic Germany, 1961-65; chief gen. engring. br. U.S. Army Environ Hygiene Agy., Edgewood Arsenal, Md., 1966-69; comdr. U.S. Army Med. Environ. Rsch. Unit, 1971-73; dir. environ. quality divsn. U.S. Army Med. Bioengring. R&D Lab., Frederick, Md., 1973-75; asst. dean coll. scis. and math. U. Tex., San Antonio, 1976-77, acting dir. divsn. earth & phys. scis., 1977-80, dir. Ctr. Applied Rsch. & Tech., 1976-80, assoc. dean coll. engring. Austin, 1980-86, L.B. (Preach) Meaders prof., 1985; dean sch. engring. U. Pitts., 1986-93; pres. U. Tex.-Permian Basin, Odessa, 1993-2001; prof. U. Tex., Austin, 2001—. Bd. dirs., adv. coun., cons. various cos. and agys., Midland/Odessa area. Author, co-author more than 140 papers, book chpts., reports on land application of wastewater and sludges, water and wastewater reuse, water and wastewater disinfection, and higher edn. Recipient Disting. Alumnus award Wilkes Coll., 1987, Disting. Grad. award Coll. of Engring., U. Tex., Austin, 1994, Outstanding Engring. Alumnus award Pa. State U., 1994; John A. Focht teach fellow U. Tex.-Austin, 1982. Fellow ASCE; mem. NSPE, Am. Acad. Environ. Engrs. (trustee 1994-97, diplomate, Gordon Maskew Fair award 1993), Water Environ. Fedn. (com. chmn. 1983-85, 86-89, 93-96, bd. control 1988-94, Svc. award 1985, 89, 90, 96, v.p. 1990-91, pres.-elect 1991-92, pres. 1992-93), Am. Soc. Engring. Edn., Am. Water Works Assn., Coun. Pub. Univ. Pres. and Chancellors (exec. com. Tex. 1994-95, sec.-treas. 1999-2001), The Univ. Tex. Club. Office: U Tex Dept Civil Engring ECJ 9.102 G Austin TX 78712

SORBO, ALLEN JON, actuary, consultant; b. Blue Earth, Minn., Aug. 7, 1953; m. Karen Lee Anderson, June 5, 1982; children: Matthew Allen, Sunny Lynn. BA, Gustavus Adolphus Coll., 1975; MS, U. Wis., 1976. Cons. Stennes and Assocs., Mpls., 1976-78, Towers Perrin Forster and Crosby, Mpls., 1978-86, prin., 1986-87; prin.-in-charge health care actuarial svcs. Ernst and Whinney, Chgo., 1987-89; prin. Tillinghast, Towers, Perrin, Mpls., 1989-94; prin. and mgr. Towers Perrin Integrated Health Systems Cons., 1995-98; v.p. actuarial and underwriting svcs. Oxford Health Plans, Inc., Trumbull, Conn., 1998—. Mem. Am. Acad. Actuaries, Soc. Actuaries. Republican. Avocations: golf, skiing, fitness. Office: Oxford Health Plans Inc 48 Monroe Turnpike Trumbull CT 06611 E-mail: asactuary@aol.com.

SORBY, DONALD LLOYD, university dean; b. Fremont, Nebr., Aug. 12, 1933; s. Lloyd A. and Orpha M. (Simmons) S.; m. Jacquelyn J. Burchard, Nov. 7, 1959; children: Thomas, Sharon. BS in Pharmacy, U. Nebr., 1955; MS, U. Wash., 1958, PhD, 1960. Dir. pharm. services U. Calif., San Francisco, 1970-72; chmn. dept. pharmacy practice Sch. Pharmacy, U. Wash., Seattle, 1972-74; dean Sch. of Pharmacy, U. Mo., Kansas City, 1974-84, Sch. of Pharmacy, U. Pacific, Stockton, Calif., 1984-95, dean emeritus, 1995—. Bd. dirs. Longs Drugstores Inc. Contbr. articles in field to profl. jours. Named Disting. Alumnus, U. Nebr. Coll. Pharmacy, 2000. Mem. Am. Pharm. Assn. (Linwood F. Tice award 1995), Am. Assn. Colls. of Pharmacy (pres. 1980-81), Calif. Pharm. Assn., Calif. Soc. Health-Sys. Pharmacists, Sigma Xi, Phi Kappa Phi, Rho Chi. Home: 4362 Yacht Harbor Dr Stockton CA 95204-1126 Office: U Pacific Sch Pharmacy Stockton CA 95211-0001 E-mail: dsorby@att.net.

SOREL, EDWARD, artist; b. N.Y.C., Mar. 26, 1929; s. Morris and Rebecca (Kleinberg) Schwartz; m. Nancy Caldwell, May 29, 1965; children: Jenny, Katherine; children by previous marriage: Madeline, Leo. Diploma, Cooper Union, 1951; DFA (hon.), Art Inst. Boston, 1998. Co-founder Pushpin Studio, 1953; free-lance artist, 1956—; syndicated Sorel's News Service, 1969-70, King Features. Author, illustrator: Making the World Safe for Hypocrisy, 1972; exhibited in Pushpin Studio retrospective at the Louvre, 1970, other European galleries, 1970-71; exhibited one-man show, Graham Galleries, N.Y.C., 1973, 78, Galerie Bartsch & Chariau, Munich, 1986, Retrospective Exhibition Cooper Union, 1987, Susan Conway Galleries, Washington, 1992, Soc. Illustrators Am. Mus. Illustration, N.Y.C., 1993, Davis and Langdale Galleries, N.Y.C., 1994, 97, Nat. Portrait Gallery, Washington, 1999; illustrator: Pablo Paints a Picture, 1961, Gwendolyn the Miracle Hen, 1963 (N.Y. Herald Tribune Book award for illustration 1962), What's Good for a Five-Year-Old, 1969, The Duck in the Gun, 1969, Word People, 1970, Magical Storybook, 1972, Superpen, 1978, The Zillionaire's Daughter, 1990, First Encounters, 1994, Unauthorized Portraits, 1997, Johnny on the Spot, 1998, The Saturday Kid, 2000; contbr. to The Nation, The New Yorker, American Heritage and The Atlantic mags. Recipient awards Soc. Illustrators, Art Dirs. Club N.Y.; Augustus St. Gauden's medal Cooper Union; George Polk award for satiric drawing, 1981; Page One award Newspaper Guild of N.Y. for best editorial cartoon (magazines), 1988, Hamilton King award Soc. Illustrators, 1990, John Singleton Copley medal Smithsonian Instn., 1999, Art Dirs. Hall of Fame, 2001, Karikaturfreis Deutschen Anwaltschaft 2002.

SORELL, KITTY JULIA, public relations executive; b. Vienna, Austria, Apr. 20, 1937; came to U.S. 1938; d. Bruno Alexander and Ilse (Fischl) Singerman. BA, Syracuse U., 1959. Lic. realtor Real Estate Bd. N.Y. Spl. events coord. Gimbel's, N.Y.C., 1966—69; pub. rels./account exec. Hamra Assocs., 1969—71; spl. events/pub. rels. dir. Stern Bros., Paramus, NJ, 1972; pub. rels. account exec. Zachary & Front, N.Y.C., 1972—76; dir. pub. rels. RSM&K Advt., 1976—77; owner Kitty Sorell Pub. Rels., 1977—; realtor Corcoran Group, 1994—. Reporter Wisdom's Child, 1981-84, The Villager, 1986-88; lectr. in field. Contbg. editor Mktg. Maker mag., 1976. Fundraiser WNET-TV, N.Y.C., 1974-75; vol. pub. rels. Sheridan Sq. Triangle Assn., N.Y.C., 1984-89; pres. bd. dirs. Apt. House Coop., 1991—; bd. dirs. Greenwich Village Alliance, 1994—; mem. Greenwich Village Soc. for Hist. Preservation, 1999—. Mem. Am. Soc. Profl. and Exec. Women, Publicity Club. Democrat. Jewish. Avocations: books, theatre. Office: Kitty Sorell Pub Rels 250 W 57th St New York NY 10107 E-mail: kjs@corcoran.com.

SORELLE, RUTH DOYLE, medical writer, journalist; b. Port Arthur, Tex., Oct. 9, 1948; d. Richard Thomas and Ruth Elaine (Droddy) D.; m. Paul Charles SoRelle, Apr. 10, 1970; children: Danielle Amanda, Richard Paul. BJ, U. Tex., 1971; MPH, U. Tex., Houston, 1988. Reporter Port Arthur News, summer 1968, 69, Univ. and Info. Svc., Austin, Tex., 1970-71; med. editor U. Tex. MD Anderson Hosp., Houston, 1973-74; editor Resources Devel. Corp., 1974-76; med. editor Baylor Coll. Medicine, 1977-78; copy editor Houston Chronicle, 1978-79, med. writer, 1979-99; sr. dir. for spl. projects Baylor Coll., Houston, 1999—. Instr. U. Houston, 1986, 87, 89. Leader Presbyn. Youth Fellowship, Houston, 1989. Recipient John P. McGovern award Am. Med. Writers Assn., Community Svc. award Tex. Assoc. Press, 1993, Katie award Dallas Press Club, 1992, 93, Anson Jones award Tex. Med. Assn., 1981, 83, 85, 86, 88, 90, 92, 95, 96, 98, Francis C. Moore award Harris County Med. Assn., 1984-98, Silver Star Tex. award Tex. Hosp. Assn., 1984, 86, 89, 92, Tex. Pub. Health Assn. award, 1981, 89, 90, 91, 94, Houston Area Health Care Coalition's Health Policy Leadership award, 1990, Paul Ellis award Am. Heart Assn., 1988, 95, Nat. Multiple Sclerosis Soc. award for med. writing, 1998, Inernat. Health Reporting award Pan Am Health Orgn., 1998, others. Mem. Am. Med. Writer's Assn. (bd. dirs. southwest chpt. 1994-95), Press Club of Houston (Deadline Coverage award 1984, Investigative Series award 1990, Mag. Feature award 1994). E-mail: dsorelle@bcm.tmc.edu.

SOREN, DAVID, archaeology educator, cinema author; b. Phila., Oct. 7, 1946; s. Harry Friedman and Erma Elizabeth (Salamon) Soren; m. Noelle Louise Schattyn, Dec. 22, 1967. BA, Dartmouth Coll., 1968; MA, Harvard U., 1972, PhD, 1973. Cert. Rome Classics Ctr. Curator of coins Fogg Art Mus., Cambridge, Mass., 1972; asst. prof. U. Mo., Columbia, 1972-76, assoc. prof., dept. head, 1976-81; prof. archaeology U. Ariz., Tucson, 1982-97, Regents prof., 1997—, dept. head, 1984-89. Guest curator Am. Mus. Natural History, N.Y.C., 1983—90, lectr, 1993—; creator, dir. Kourion Excavations, Cyprus, 1982—89, Portugal, 1983—84, Am. Excavations at Lugnano, Italy, 1988—93; pot cons., field dir. Tunisa Excavations, Chgo. Oriental Inst./Smithsonian Instn., 1973—78; dir. excavations Chiaciano, Terme, Italy, 1995—. Author: (book) Unreal Reality, 1978, Rise and Fall of Fantasy Film, 1980, Carthage, 1990, Carthage, French edit., 1994, Vera-Ellen: The Magic and the Mystery, 1999, Excavation of a Roman Villa, 1999, Kourion: Search for a Lost Roman City, 1988, Corpus des Mosaiques de Tunisie, 1972, Corpus des Mosaiques de Tunisie, 3d rev. edit., 1986, Carthage: A Mosaic of Ancient Tunisia, 1987; editor: Excavations at Kourion I, 1987; contbg. editor: Archaeology Mag.; prodr.: (films) Carthage: A Mirage of Antiquity, 1987; creator, guest curator (internt traveling exhbn.) Carhtage: A Mosaic of Ancient Tunisia, 1987—92; editor, founder: Roscius, 1993—95; creative cons. (TV miniseries) Lost Civilizations, 1994; contbr. articles to profl. jours.; prodr.: (documentaries) BBC-TV documentary Malaria and the Fall of Rome, 2002. Named Outstanding Am. Under 40, Esquire Mag., 1985, hon. Italian citizen, Lugnano, Italy, 1989; recipient Cine Golden Eagle, 1980, Angenieux Film award, Indsl. Photography Mag., 1980, Oustanding Am. Under 40 award, C. Johns Hopkins-Britain's Royal Inst. Internat. Affairs, 1985; grantee, NEH, 1979, 1987, Fulbright, Lisbon, 1983. Fellow: Brit. Royal Inst. Internat. Affairs; mem.: Luso-Am. Commn. (citation 1983—84), Archaeol. Inst. Tucson (pres. 1983—86), Am. Sch. Oriental Rsch. (dept. rep. 1981—85), Nat. Geog. Soc. (project dir. 1983—84). Office: U Ariz Dept Classics 371 Mlb Tucson AZ 85721-0001 E-mail: soren@u.arizona.edu.

SORENSEN, ALAN JOHN, county official; b. Oneonta, N.Y., Feb. 15, 1965; s. Harold Peter and Theresa S.; m. Janie Frances Cavallino, Nov. 11, 1963; children: Christopher Alan, Jaclynn Nicole, Sara Jane. B of Geography and Anthropology cum laude, SUNY, Oneonta, 1987; MPA, Pace U., 1996; M of City and Regional Planning, Rutgers U., 1989. Planner City of Palm Bay, Fla., 1989-91; sr. planner Yonkers (N.Y.) Planning Bur., 1991-92; planner Westchester County, White Plains, N.Y., 1992-94, assoc. planner, 1994-96; sr. planner Ferrandina & Assocs., Elmsford, 1996-97; commr. planning & cmty. devel. Sullivan County, Monticello, 1997—. Vol. Sullivan First, Rock Hill, N.Y., 1997; bd. dirs. Hudson Valley Regional Coun., Sullivan County Agrl. Farmland Protection Bd.; regional v.p. N.Y. State Urban Coun. Recipient Heissenbuttel award for planning excellence N.Y. Planning Fedn., Partnership award Upper Del. Coun., Statewide Friend of Extension 2000 Cornell Cooper Extension. Mem. Am. Planning Assn. (Met. N.Y. chpt., Hudson Valley West dir.), N.Y. Urban Coun. (Hudson Valley region v.p.). Avocations: guitar, running, flying, swimming, reading. Office: Sullivan County Divsn Planning 100 North St Monticello NY 12701-1160

SORENSEN, ALLAN CHRESTEN, service company executive; b. Edson, Alta., Can., Apr. 27, 1938; came to U.S., 1962, naturalized, 1965; s. Henry and Vivien A. Sorensen; children: Scott, Jody. BS in Pharmacy, Drake U., 1961. Salesman Hoffman LaRoche Pharm. Co., Kitchener, Ont., Can., 1961-62; salesman Personnel Pool of Am., Inc., Chgo., 1962-63, sales mgr., 1963-67, dir., pres., 1967-89, chief exec. officer, 1978-91, chmn. interim svcs., 1989-97; vice chmn., co-founder Interim Healthcare Inc., Ft. Lauderdale, 1997—; dir. Republic Svcs., Inc., 1998—. Mem. Am. Staffing Assn. (past pres., bd. dirs.), Am. Assn. for Homecare (past chmn., bd. dirs.). Clubs: Rotary. Republican. Home: 920 Indigo Pt Gulf Stream FL 33483-6110 Office: Interim Healthcare Inc 1601 Sawgrass Corporate Pkwy Sunrise FL 33323-2827

SORENSEN, ANDREW AARON, university president; b. Pitts., July 20, 1938; s. Albert Aaron and Margaret (Lindquist) S.; m. Donna Ingemie, Aug. 4, 1968; children: Aaron Ashley, Benjamin Samuel. BA, U. Ill., 1959; BDiv, Yale U., 1962, MPh, 1970, PhD, 1971; MPH, U. Mich., 1966. Asst. prof. Cornell U., Ithaca, N.Y., 1971-73, U. Rochester, 1973-76, assoc. prof., 1976-83; prof., dean U. Mass., Amherst, 1983-86, Johns Hopkins U., Balt., 1986-90, exec. dir. AIDS Inst.; provost, v.p. acad. affairs U. Fla., Gainesville, 1990-96; pres. U. Ala., Tuscaloosa, 1996—. Chmn. administrv. bd. Whitney Marine Biol. Lab., 1990—96; chmn. editl. bd. Univ. Press. Fla., 1990—96; vis. fellow U. Cambridge, 1979—80; pres. So. U. Conf. Author 6 books; contbr. over 100 articles to profl. jours. Vice chmn. bd. dirs. Chautauqua Instn., 1996-98; bd. dirs. Ala. Shakespeare Festival, 1996—, Blount, Inc., 1997-99. U.S. Dept. Edn. fellow Lincoln U., 1966-67, NSF fellow Harvard U., 1975-76. Mem.: Univ. Rsch. Assn. (trustee), So. Univs. Rsch. Assn. (past chmn. coun. presidents). Presbyterian. Office: U Ala Office Pres Box 870100 Tuscaloosa AL 35487-0100

SORENSEN, CARL EDWARD, company executive; b. San Diego, Sept. 21, 1964; s. Carl Edward and Bonnie Jean Sorensen; m. Cynthia Ann Sorensen, June 5, 1987; 1 child, Carl Edward. B Bus. Mgmt., St. Leo Coll., Norfolk, Va., 1995; M Bus. Fin. and Acctg., Mont. State U., Bozeman, 1998. Commd. USN, 1983, advanced through grades to comdr., 1998; owner, pres., CEO Sorensen Enterprises Inc., Virginia Beach, Va., 1998—. Adv. bd. chmn. Rural Bus. Enhancement, Virginia Beach; chmn. Pennys From Heaven, Sunbury, S.C. Mem. DAV, WW II Meml. Fund, Elks. Republican. Methodist. Avocations: buying small companies, improving and selling them, antique collecting. Home and Office: Sorenson Enterprises 5049 Hunt Club Chase Suffolk VA 23435-3203

SORENSEN, DEBRA J. social worker; b. Chanute, Kans., Oct. 15, 1955; BA in Psychology, Wichita State U., Kans., 1980; MSW, U. Kans., 1987. Lic. ind. social worker. Renal and cardiac social worker Med. Coll. Hosp., Toledo, 1987-88; clin. social worker Cummings Zucker Ctr., 1988-91; pvt. practice, Maumee, Ohio, 1991—. Mem. NASW. Avocations: hypnotherapy, rsch. in sexual abuse treatment, metaphysics. Home: 720 Corey St Maumee OH 43537-3610

SORENSEN, ELIZABETH JULIA, retired cultural administrator; b. Kenora, Ont., Can., Nov. 24, 1934; d. John Frederick and Irene Margaret (Dowd) MacKellar; m. O. Leo P. Sorensen, July 7, 1956 (div. 1963); children: Lianne Kim Sorensen Kruger. BA, Lakehead U., 1970; MA, Brigham Young U., 1972; Assoc. Royal Conservatory, U. Toronto, 1978; Assoc., Mt. Royal Coll., Calgary, AB, 1978. Sec. Canadian Med. Assn. Manitoba, Winnipeg, 1956-59; legal sec. Filmore, Riley & Co., 1961-63; tchr. Fort Frances (Ont.) High Sch., 1963-70; instr. drama, speech, English Lethbridge (Alta.) C.C., 1972-77; tchr. bus. edn. Henderson Coll. Bus., Lethbridge, 1978-80; supt. cultural svcs. City Medicine Hat, Alta., 1980-99; ret., 1999. Mem. Stirling Hist. Soc. (sec.). Mem. Lds Ch. Avocations: directing plays, writing, genealogy, storytelling, scrapbooking.

SØRENSEN, ERIK, international company executive; b. Randers, Denmark, July 19, 1944; s. Christen and Erna Sørensen; m. Brigitte Berg; children: Anne Marie, Thomas, Anne Louise, Anne Mette, Anne Sophie. MS in Chemistry, Tech. U. Denmark, 1968; MBA in Internat. Fin., Cph Sch. Econs., 1971. Sr. economist Novo Industri A/S, Bagsvaerd, Denmark, 1970-71, mgr. econs. and planning Denmark, 1972-74, v.p. sales and mktg. Denmark, 1974-80, pres. bioindsl. group Denmark, 1980-88; pres. Health Care Grp Novo Nordisk A/S, Denmark, 1988-1995; pres., CEO Christian Hansen Group, Denmark, 1995—. Bd. dirs., vice chmn. ISS A/S; bd. dirs. Maersk Med. A/S. Lt. Danish Army, 1968-70. Office: Chr Hansen Group Bøge Allé 10 2970 Hoersholm Denmark

SØRENSEN, FLEMMING BRANDT, pathologist; b. Copenhagen, Apr. 12, 1956; s. Vagn and Vibeke Brandt (Lassen) S. MD, U. Aarhus, 1983, pathologist cert., 1994. Resident Aarhus (Denmark) U. Hosp., 1986-87, 94-95, Randers (Denmark) Hosp., 1983-86; tng. resident pathology Aarhus U. Hosp., 1990-92, sr. resident pathology, 1992-95, chief pathologist, 1997—, prof. pathology, 1999—; chief pathologist Odense (Denmark) U. Hosp., 1995-97. Rsch. fellow Aarhus, 1987-90; Rsch. scholar Danish Cancer Soc., 1987-90. Mem. Danish Soc. Pathological Anatomy and Clin. Cytology (sec., bd. dirs. 1993-97, pres. 1997-2000). Avocations: fishing, hunting, travel. E-mail: flemming.soerensen@aas.auh.dk.

SORENSEN, GILLIAN MARTIN, United Nations official; b. Columbus, Ohio, Mar. 4, 1941; d. John Butlin and Helen (Hickam) Martin; m. Theodore C. Sorensen, June 28, 1969; 1 child, Juliet. BA, Smith Coll., 1963. Commr. N.Y.C. Commn. for UN and Consular Corps, 1978-90; pres. Nat. Conf., 1990-93; undersec gen., spl. advisor for pub. policy UN, N.Y.C., 1993-97, UN asst. sec. gen. for external rels., 1997—. Del. Dem. Nat. Conv., 1976, 84, 88. Mem.: Acad. Coun. on the UN, Women's Forum, Coun. on Fgn. Rels. Office: UN Rm S-3840 New York NY 10017

SORENSEN, HARLEY MORAN, columnist; b. St. Paul, Nov. 12, 1931; s. Chester Loraine and Ellen Beatrice Sorensen; 1 child Dominic Ethan. Student, U. Minn., 1953—55. Reporter, sect. editor Mpls. Tribune, 1971—79; columnist San Francisco Examiner.com, 1997—99, San Francisco Chronicle.com, 2001—. Recipient various newspaper reporting awards, 1971—79. Avocations: travel, chess, nature walks.

SORENSEN, HARVEY R. lawyer; b. Chgo., Nov. 3, 1947; s. Harvey T. and Jean Louise (Cline) S.; m. Emily Smith, May 31, 1969 (div. May 1980); children: Abigail, Jeanne, Cornelia; m. Stephanie Sorensen, Dec. 31, 1980; 1 child, Tyler. BA, Beloit Coll., 1969; MSBA, Boston U., 1972; JD cum laude, Northwestern U., 1974. Bar: Wis. 1974, U.S. DISt. Ct. (ea. dist.) Wis. 1974, U.S. Dist. Ct. Kans., U.S. Tax Ct., 1975. Tax acct. Arthur, Young & Co., Chgo., 1974; assoc. Whyte & Hirschboeck, Milw., 1974-75; asst. adj. prof. Wichita (Kans.) State U. Sch. Bus., 1979; ptnr. Foulston & Siefkin, Wichita, 1975—. Trustee, vice chmn. Kans. Pub. Telecom. Svc., 1978—97, chmn., 1997—99, Wichita Downtown Devel. Corp., 1996—; chmn. adv. bd. City of Wichita Self Supporting Mcpl. Improvement Dist., 2001—; project bus. cons. Jr. Achievement, 1978—93; trustee Wichita Symphony Soc., 1986—96, Wichita Collegiate Sch., 1994—, Wichita Sedgewick County Hist. Mus., 1986—89, Wichita Arts Coun., 1979—82, Goodwill Industries/Easter Seals of Kans. Area, 2001—; bd. cmty. adv. KMUW, 1981—82; commr. City of Eastborough, Kans., 1991—93; treas. St. James Episcopal Ch., 1996—99. With U.S. Army, 1970—72. Fellow Am. Coll. Tax Counsel; mem. ABA, Wichita Bar Assn., Kans. Bar Assn. (past sect., v.p., pres. tax. sect. 1984-88), Attys. for Family Held Enterprises, Wichita Area C. of C. (bd. dirs. 2000—), Rotary. Republican. Episcopalian. Home: 13 Colonial Ct Wichita KS 67207-1056 Office: Foulston Siefkin LLP 700 Bank of Am Ctr Wichita KS 67202-2207

SORENSEN, HENRIK VITTRUP, electrical engineering educator; b. Skanderborg, Denmark, Jan. 17, 1959; came to U.S. 1983; s. Evan Anton and Anna Marie (Vittrup) S.; m. Karen Ann Taylor, Mar. 5, 1988; children: Amanda Elisabeth, Christian Henrik, Alexander Evan. MS, Aalborg U. Ctr., 1983; PhD, Rice U., 1988. Asst. prof. Dept. Electrical Engring. U. Pa., Phila., 1988-95; v.p. Ariel Corp., Cranbury, N.J., 1995-97, Lucent Techs., 1997—. Cons. AT&T Bell Labs., Murray Hill, N.J., 1990-95. Author: Handbook for Digital Signal Processing, 1992, The FFT Bibliography, 1995, A Digital Signal Processing Laboratory, 1997; contbr. articles to profl. jours. Fellow Rotary; mem. IEEE (editor 1990-94, vice chmn. Phila. sect. 1991-94), Sigma Xi, Eta Kappa Nu. Lutheran. Achievements include development of fast algorithms for the split radix fast Fourier transform and for the fast Hartley transform. Home: 75 Franklin Dr Plainsboro NJ 08536-2310

SORENSEN, JACKI FAYE, choreographer, aerobic dance company executive; b. Oakland, Calif., Dec. 10, 1942; d. Roy C. and Juanita F. (Bullon) Mills; m. Neil A. Sorensen, Jan. 3, 1965. BA, U. Calif., 1964. Cert. tchr., Calif. Ptnr., Big Spring Sch. Dance, 1965; tchr. Pasadena Ave. Sch., Sacramento, 1968; founder, pres., choreographer Jacki's Inc., DeLand, Fla., 1990—; cons., lectr. on phys. fitness. Author: Aerobic Dancing, 1979, Jacki Sorensen's Aerobic Lifestyle Book, 1983; choreographer numerous dance exercises for records and videocassettes. Trustee Women's Sports Found. Recipient Diamond Pin award Am. Heart Assn., 1979, Individual Contbn. award Am. Assn. Fitness Dirs. in Bus. and Industry, 1981, Spl. Olympics Contbn. award, 1982, Contbn. to Women's Fitness award Pres.'s Coun. Phys. Fitness and Sports, 1982, Healthy Am. Fitness Leader award U.S. Jaycees, 1984, Lifetime Achievement award Internat. Dance Exercise Assn., 1985, New Horizons award Caldwell (N.J.) Coll., 1985, Legend of Aerobics award City Sports mag., 1985; Pres. Coun. award Calif. Womens' Leadership Conf., 1986, Hall of Fame award Club Industry mag., 1986, IDEA, 1992. Mem. AAHPERD, AFTRA, Am. Coll. Sports Medicine, Nat. Intramural and Recreation Assn. Office: care Jacki's Inc 129 1/2 N Woodland Blvd Ste 5 Deland FL 32720-4269

SORENSEN, JANE FORESTER, small business owner, consultant; b. Cleve., Dec. 23, 1942; d. Hazel (Dunn) Sorensen; m. Gordon William Lord, May 27, 1983. Student, Skidmore Coll., 1960-62; BS, Tufts U., 1965; PhD, Ind. No. U., 1974. Lic. occupational therapist, N.Y., real estate salesperson. Pvt. practice in cons., N.Y.C., 1971—; internat. v.p. Soparco, Inc., Drew, Miss., 1978-83; prin. Communications Express East Co., N.Y.C., 1983-87; owner B&B Timber Products Co., 1987—. Guest lectr. various colls., including Harvard U., Tufts U., NYU, Pace U., L.I. U., 1974—. Author: The New Way to Become the Person You'd Like to Be, 1973; bus. columnist OT Advance, 1990—; columnist N.Y. Forest Owner, 1992-99, Am. Tree Farmer, 1999; contbr. articles to profl. jours. ERA lobbyist U.S. Congress, NOW, 1969-70, lobbyist abortion amendment N.Y. Legislature, 1970-72, chair consiousness raising, 1969-71; chair organizing and steering com. Nat. Women's Polit. Caucus, 1971—, edn. com., 1972-73; mem. Gov.'s Com. on Correctional Instns., 1972; mem. adv. com. N.Y. region SBA, 1976-78; chair ad hoc spl. projects com. UN Decade for Women, 1976-79; comms. liaison N.Y. State Tree Farm Com., 1990-95; mem. birthmother adv. com. Spence Chapin, N.Y.C., 2000—; trustee Neversink Valley Mus., 2000—. Republican. Office: 418 E 73rd St Ste 1E New York NY 10021-3856 E-mail: drjane@fcc.net.

SORENSEN, JEAN, artist; b. San Diego, Nov. 18, 1920; d. William James and Hallie (Moran) Hart; m. Ralph James Sorensen, Sept. 1, 1939; children: Ellen Marie Pacchetti, Ann Christine Coons, James Christian. Student, San Jose State U., 1938-39, U. Calif., Santa Cruz, 1972—. Tchr. watercolor workshop DeAnza State Coll., Cupertino, Calif., 1984, Santa Clara Valley Watercolor Soc., Yosemite Nat. Park, 1984; tchr. botany Stanford U., 1985; ptnr. View Points Art Gallery, Los Altos, Calif., 1972-92; pres. View Prints Art Gallery, 1988-90. Exhibitor at Palazzo Veccico, Florence, Italy, 1972, Soc. Western Arts, DeYoung Mus., San Francisco, 1970-75; guest exhibiter biennial Kofu Watercolor Exhibit, Japan, 1983; commd. painting City of Syktyvhear, Russia, 1990, Tait Mus. Art, Los Gatos, Calif., 1997, Rose Shensen Gallery, Triton Mus., Santa Clara, Calif., 2001. Vol. docent Mid-Peninsula Regional Park Open Space Dist., San Mateo and Santa Clara counties, Calif., 1977-91. Mem. Nat. Assn. Women Artists, Soc. Western Artists, Allied Artists West (pres. 1990-92), Santa Clara Valley Watercolor Soc., Monterey County Watercolor Soc., Calif. Native Plant Soc. Avocations: genealogy, botany.

SORENSEN, JIMMY LOUIS, management consultant; b. Chgo., June 11, 1927; s. Soren Johannes and Jensine Elizabeth (Jensen) S.; m. Esther Nancy Sorensen, Nov. 27, 1954; children: Nancy, Mark, Karen, Ruth. BA cum laude, Dana Coll., 1951. CPA, Ill. Asst. dir. data processing Continental Assurance Co., Chgo., 1951-57; spl. rep. UARCO, 1957-59; asst. treas. Signode Steel, Glenview, Ill., 1959-60; ptnr. Arthur Young & Co., Chgo., 1960-84; dir. mgmt. info. services Cotter & Co., 1984-90. Bd. dirs. Luth. Gen. Health Care System, Park Ridge, Ill., 1980-95; chmn. bd. trustees Danish Old People's Home, Chgo., 1976—; chmn. bd. dirs. Pioneer Ministries, Inc., 1968-72. Decorated Order Ridder of Dannebrog (Denmark). Mem. AICPA, Ill. Soc. CPAs, Midwest Danish Am. C. of C. Home and Office: 329 Carter Ave Wood Dale IL 60191-1934 E-mail: jensoren@ameritech.net.

SORENSEN, JOHN NOBLE, mechanical and nuclear engineer; b. Mpls., Jan. 2, 1934; s. Alfred Noble and Helen Viola (Baker) S.; m. Joan Elizabeth Reiche, Sept. 15, 1954; children: Laura Elizabeth, Nancy Helen, Karen Lynn. BSME, U. N.D., 1955; MSME, U. Pitts., 1958. Cert. engr. Sr. engr. Westinghouse Electric, Pitts., 1955-67; v.p., gen. mgr. NUS Corp., Rockville, Md., 1967-86; v.p., dir. Grove Engring., Inc., 1986-93; tech. asst. to commr. NRC, Washington, 1993-97, sr. fellow adv. com. on reactor safeguards,

1997—2001, sr. fellow adv. com. on nuclear waste, 1997—2001, spl. asst. spent fuel project office, 2002—. Mem. ASME, NSPE, Am. Nuclear Soc., Sigma Xi. Home: 629 Crocus Dr Rockville MD 20850-2046 Office: Nuclear Regulatory Commn 11545 Rockville Pike Rockville MD 20852-2747 E-mail: jns@nrc.gov.

SORENSEN, KELD, biochemist; b. Copenhagen, June 5, 1953; came to U.S. 1987; s. Alf and Karin S.; m. Susan Linda Hom, June 3, 1980; 1 child, Kasper. PhD, U. Copenhagen, 1980. Research assoc. U. Bern, Switzerland, 1980-82; postdoctoral researcher Tex. A&M U., Temple, 1982-83; asst. prof. U. Bern, 1983-87; dir. biochemistry and immunology NTD Labs., Carle Place, N.Y., 1987-89; lab. dir. Equichem. Rsch. Inst., 1989-91; sr. rsch. scientist Pierce Chem. Co., Rockford, Ill., 1991-97; asst. prof. Coll. Medicine, U. Ill., 1993-98; mgr. tech. transfer rsch. & devel. Sigma Chem. Co. (now Sigma-Aldrich), St. Louis, 1997-98, dir. R&D, 1998—. Editorial bd. Clinica Chemica Acta, Glasgow, 1987-89; referee several sci. jours.; contbr. articles to profl. jours.; patentee in field. Unitarian Universalist. Avocations: skiing, scuba diving, hiking. Home: PO Box 14508 Saint Louis MO 63178-4508 Office: Sigma Aldrich PO Box 14508 2909 Laclede Ave Saint Louis MO 63101 Fax: 314-286-7617. E-mail: ksorensen@sial.com.

SORENSEN, LEIF BOGE, physician, retired educator; b. Odense, Denmark, Mar. 25, 1928; came to U.S., 1955, naturalized, 1963; s. Henry V. and Mary (Nielsen) S.; m. Janice D. Nolan; 1 child, Heidi. BS, Odense Katedralskole, 1946; MD, U. Copenhagen, Denmark, 1953, PhD in Biochemistry, 1960. Intern Copenhagen County Hosp., Hellerup, Denmark, 1954; resident Copenhagen Municipal Hosp., 1955, U. Chgo. Hosp., 1957-60; faculty, scientist U. Chgo. and Franklin McLean Meml. Research Inst., 1956—; prof. medicine U. Chgo., 1970—2002; attending physician dept. medicine, assoc. chmn. dept. Pritzker Sch. Medicine, U. Chgo., 1976-99. Interim chmn. dept. medicine U. Chgo., 1997-98; cons. FDA, 1972—. Mem. editl. bd. Jour. Lab. and Clin. Medicine, 1964-70, Arthritis and Rheumatism, 1965-72; Contbr. articles to profl. jours. With M.C. Danish Army, 1951. Fulbright scholar, 1955; Ill. Arthritis Found. grantee, 1970-72; NIH Fogarty Internat. Center sr. fellow, 1980 Mem. AAAS, Am. Rheumatism Soc., Am. Soc. Clin. Investigation, Central Soc. Clin. Research, N.Y. Acad. Scis., Danish Med. Assn., Ill. Acad. Gen. Practice., Am. Geriatrics Soc., Gerontologic Soc. Am., Am. Fedn. Aging Research Home: 1700 E 56th St Apt 2801 Chicago IL 60637-5093 E-mail: leif@medicine.bsd.uchicago.edu.

SORENSEN, LISA ELLEN, nurse practitioner; b. San Francisco, Apr. 23, 1949; d. Arnold Irvin Manson and Dasie Sappington Giese; m. Peter Christian Sorensen, Oct. 7, 1978; children: Ashley Mia, Andrea Kristine. BSN, Humboldt State U., 1978; cert. family nurse practitioner, U. Calif., Davis, 1994; MSN, Calif. State U., Sacramento, 1998. RN, Calif. Staff nurse Pioneers Hosp., Meeker, Calif., 1978-80, Mercy Gen. Hosp., Sacramento, 1981-95; family nurse practitioner Ctr. for AIDS Rsch. and Edn., 1996, Dr. Raymond Dann Med. Office, Escondido, Calif., 1997—, Vista (Calif.) Cmty. Clinic, 1998—. Mem. peer rev. bd. Sharp Healthcare, San Diego, 1999—; family nurse practitioner preceptor U. San Diego, 1997-98; family nurse practitioner Haight Ashbury Free Clinic, Rock Medicine, San Francisco, 1995-97. Mem. Calif. Coalition Nurse Practitioners (sec. govt. rels. group 1994-95, continuing edn. coord. 1994-95). Avocations: playing guitar, camping, hiking, travel, bird watching. Home: 527 Hardell Ln Vista CA 92084-6622 Office: Vista Cmty Clinic 1000 Vale Terrace Dr Vista CA 92084-5218

SORENSEN, SHEILA, state legislator; b. Chgo., Sept. 20, 1947; d. Martin Thomas Moloney and Elizabeth (Koehr) Paulus; m. Wayne B. Slaughter, May, 1969 (div. 1976); 1 child, Wayne Benjamin III; m. Dean E. Sorensen, Feb. 14, 1977; (stepchildren) Michael, Debbie, Kevin, Dean C. BS, Loretto Heights Coll., Denver, 1965; postgrad. pediatric nurse practicioner, U. Colo., Denver, 1969-70. Pediatric nurse practicioner Pub. Health Dept., Denver, 1970-71, Boise, Idaho, 1971-72, Boise (Idaho) Pediatric Group, 1972-74, Pediatric Assocs., Boise, 1974-77; mem. Idaho Ho. Reps., 1987-92, Idaho Senate, Dist. 13, Boise, 1992—; chair senate health and welfare com. Idaho Senate, 1992-94, chair senate majority caucus, 1994-96, vice chair state affairs com., 1996-98, chair state affairs, 1998—. State chair Am. Legis. Exchange Coun. Precinct committeeman Ada County Rep. Ctrl. Com., Boise, 1982-86, dist. vice chair, 1985-88; polit. chair Idaho Med. Assn. Aux., 1984-87, Ada County Med. Assocs., 1986-87; bd. dirs. Family Practice Residency Program, 1992-94, Univ./Cmty. Health Sci. Assn., Bishop Kelly Found., 1993—99; chair Senate Majority Caucus, 1995-96, chair state affairs com., 1999—; mem. adv. com. on health care edn. and workforce devel. State Bd. Edn. Recipient AMA Nathan Davis award for Outstanding State Legislator, 1994. Mem. Nat. Conf. State Legislators, Nat. Orgn. Women Legislators (state chair), Am. Legis. Exch. Coun. (Legis of Yr. award 1999). Roman Catholic.

SORENSEN, W. ROBERT, clergy member, church administrator; BA, Concordia Coll., Moorhead, Minn., 1956; MDiv, Luther Theol. Sem., 1959; PhD, U. Iowa, 1978. Exec. dir. Divsn. Higher Edn. and Schs., Evang. Luth. Ch. in Am., Chgo., 1988. Office: Evangelical Lutheran Church Am 8765 W Higgins Rd Chicago IL 60631-4101

SORENSON, GEORGIA LYNN JONES, political scientist, educator; b. Abilene, Tex., Aug. 23, 1947; d. Wyly King and Olive M. (Sorenson) Jones; 1 child, Suzanna Simmonds Strasburg. BA, Am. U., 1974; MA, Hood Coll., 1976; PhD, U. Md., 1992. Social scientist Nat. Inst. Edn., Washington, 1978-79, U.S. Commn. Civil Rights, Washington, 1976-79; sr. policy analyst The White House, 1979-80; founder, sr. scholar James MacGregor Burns Acad. Leadership U. Md., College Park, 1980—. Adv. mem. W.K. Kellogg Found. Nat Fellows, Battle Creek, Mich., 1996-99. Co-author: (with James MacGregor Burns) Dead-Center: Clinton-Gore Leadership and the Perils of Moderation, 1999; contbr. articles to profl. jours. Chair Md. Women's Polit. Caucus, 1991-94; mem. White House Productivity Coun., Washington, 1979; mem. V.P. Youth Employment Task Force, 1979-80. Mem. Am. Polit. Sci. Assn., Internat. Soc. Polit. Psychologists, A.K. Rice Inst. Office: James MacGregor Burns Acad Leadership Univ Md College Park MD 20742-0001 E-mail: gsorenson@academy.umd.edu.

SORENSON, JAMES ROGER, public health educator; b. Yakima, Wash., Feb. 9, 1943; s. Paul Olaf and Helen Leona (Anderson) S.; m. Nancy Ellen O'Neal, May 24, 1968;1 child, Peter Matthew. BA in Sociology, U. Wash., 1965, MA in Sociology, 1966; PhD in Sociology, Cornell U., 1970. Asst. prof. Princeton (N.J.) U., 1969-74; assoc. prof. Boston U. Sch. of Medicine, 1974-84, Boston U. Sch. of Pub. Health, 1979-84; prof. Boston Univ. Schs. of Medicine and Pub. Health, 1984-85; prof. Sch. Pub. Health U. N.C., Chapel Hill, 1985—. Cons. NIMH (Changing Role of Women Com.), 1971, Rutgers U. Ednl. Decision Making Project, 1970-74, Nat. Inst. Child Health and Human Devel., 1977-79, Nat. Heart , Lung and Blood Inst., Sickle Cell Br., 1977-80, 1991-92, Boston Comprehensive Sickle Cell Ctr., 1979-85, Nat. Ctr. for Human Genome Rsch., 1990-91; com. mem. Ea. Sociol. Soc. Papers Com., 1970-73, Genetics Core Group, Inst. for Soc., Ethics and the Life Scis., 1971-76, NYU com. on Med. and Ethical Issues in Treating Spina Bifida, 1973-74, Nat. Found. March of Dimes Clin. Rsch. (Human) adv. com. 1974-75; sci. assoc. Boston City Hosp., 1975-85, N.E. Group on Med. Edn., 1976-77; also many coms. at U. N.C. including Dean's Cabinet Sch. of Pub. Health, 1985—; dir. and chair steering com. Sch. of Pub. Health Promotion/Disease Prevention Program, 1986-89; adv. bd. Injury Prevention Rsch. Ctr., many others. Author: (with others) In Sickness and in Health: Social Dimensions of Medical Care, 1981, Reproductive Pasts, Reproductive Futures: Genetic Counseling and Its Effectiveness, 1981; also numerous articles to profl. jours. and chpts. to books; reviewer Am. Jour. Med. Genetics, Am. Jour. Preventive Medicine, Am. Jour. Pub. Health, Archives of Pathology and Laboratory Medicine, Human Relations, Jour. of Health and Social Behavior, Jour. Am. Geriatrics Soc., Milbank Meml. Fund Quarterly, New Eng. Jour. of Medicine, Patient Edn. and Counseling, Prenatal Diagnosis, Sci., Tech. and Human Values, Social Sci. and Medicine; exec. editor: Health Edn. Rsch., 1996—. Mem. adv. coun. Com. to Combat Huntington's Disease, Mass. chpt., 1979-85, edn. and comty. adv. bd. Am. Heart Assn., N.C. affiliate, 1986-89. Named fellow NIMH, Cornell U., 1967-69, Inst. of Soc., Ethics and Life Scis; named Falk lectr. Ea. Sociol. Soc., 1975-76; recipient Disting. Alumnus award Yakima Valley Coll., 1985; grantee; Mass. Dept. Pub. Health, Nat. Found., March of Dimes, NIDA, Nat. Cancer Inst. and others (19 grants in all). Mem. Am. Pub. Health Assn., Soc. Profl. Health Educators, N.C. Soc. Profl. Health Educators. Coun. on Health Edn. in Higher Edn., N.C. Pub. Health Assn., Phi Beta Kappa, Delta Omega. Avocations: music, theatre. Home: 21 Wysteria Way Chapel Hill NC 27514-1637 Office: U NC Sch Pub Health 326 Rosenau Hall 7400 Chapel Hill NC 27599-0001

SORENSON, JOHN ROBERT JOSEPH, chemistry educator; b. Sturgeon Bay, Wis., June 13, 1934; s. Clarence Wilford and Genevieve (Navarre) S.; children: Michael, Patrick, Paul, Anne, Joseph, Amy, Judith. BS, U. Wis., 1960; PhD, U. Kans., 1965. Sr. rsch. chemist G.D. Searle, Skokie, Ill.; asst. prof. U. Cin.; prof. U. Ark., Little Rock. Cons. J.R.J. Sorenson Corp., Little Rock; corr. mem. UNESCO Internat. Ctr. for Trace Element Study, Lyon, France, 1984. Sponsor Sci. Fair, Little Rock, 1993-98. Served in USN, 1953-57. Recipient medallion U. Catania, 1986. Roman Catholic. Avocations: research, fishing. Office: U Ark Coll Pharmacy Dept Pharm Sci Slot 522 4301 W Markham St Little Rock AR 72205-7122

SORENSON, KATHERINE ANN, elementary school educator; b. Hastings, Minn., Aug. 30, 1947; d. Fredrick William Nearing and Marguerite Lucille Keene-Nearing; m. Michael Alfred Sorenson; children: Brock, Scott. BS in Edn., Black Hills State Coll., 1972; MA in Early Childhood Edn., U. Colo., Denver, 1995. Profl. tchr. lic. Colo., cert. reading recover tchr. Tchr. Maternity Mary Cath. Sch., St. Paul, 1967—68, St. Andrew's Cath. Sch., St. Paul, 1968—70, Hill City Pub. Schs., 1972—73, Groton (S.D.) Pub. Schs., 1973—75; substitute tchr. Billings (Mont.) Pub. Schs., 1975—76; tchr. Livingston (Mont.) Pub. Schs., 1977—85; asst. dir. childcare Children's Creative Encounters, Littleton, Colo., 1986—87; tchr. Cherry Creek Sch. Dist., Eastridge Elem., Aurora, 1985—96, 1996—. Co-author: (book) Blue Ribbon Application, 1998 (Blue Ribbon School, 1999), Reading Recovery Longitudinal Analysis, National Association for Year Round Education Application. Pack leader Boy Scouts Am., Parker, 1988—94, bd. dirs., 1988—94; mem. Cherry Creek Schs. North Area Task Force, Aurora, 2001—02; Sunday sch. tchr. St. Mary's Cath. Ch., Livingston, 1981—84, religious edn. coord., 1981—82; Sunday sch. tchr. Ave Maria Cath. Ch., Parker, 1992—94; mem. team fundraising Parker Baseball, 1990—92; sec. Moorhead Foster Parent Assn., 1976—77. Recipient Exemplory Reading Program, Colo. Coun. Internat. Reading, 1998-1999, Dewitt Wallace Libr. Power, Dewitt Wallace Found., 1997, Tchr. Recognition award, Anti-Defamation League, 2002. Mem.: Cherry Creek Edn. Assn., Reading Recovery Assn., Colo. Coun. Internat. Reading Assn. Avocations: reading, sewing, travel, south west history, baseball. Home: 11182 Cambridge Ct Parker CO 80138 Office: Eastridge Elem Sch 11777 E Wesley Ave Aurora CO 80014

SORENSON, MARY LOUISE, interior design firm executive and owner; b. Wadena, Minn., Mar. 28, 1950; d. Bernard F. and Jeneva S. (Bjondal) Neuerburg; m. Mark E. Sorenson, Dec. 5, 1981; children— Shawn, Chad, Naomi, Seth, Sara. Student, U. Minn., 1974-75. Cert. Nat. Assn. Credit Mgmt., 1971. Credit mgr. Homecrest Co., Wadena, 1971-73, Northland Aluminum, Mpls., 1973-75, Econs. Lab., St. Paul, 1975-77; owner, mgr. dance hall, 1977-78; salesperson Sleep Country, Dallas, 1978-80; designer Jo Mar Furniture, Duncanville, 1980-82; pres. Cedar Hill (Tex.) Design Ctr., Inc., 1983—; owner timber frame and building component rep. orgn. Home on the Hill, 2000—. Mpls.-St. Paul Credit Women's Group, 1978-79, I Am Victorious, Dallas, 1984—. Pastor Straight St. Ministries. Recipient Community Svc. award, 1988; named Woman of Yr., Mpls.-St. Paul chpt. Nat. Assn. Credit Mgmt., 1979, Best of Show various show homes and models, ASSD awaard, 2001 Parad of Homes. Mem. Cedar Hill C. of C. Republican. Avocations: Bible study. Office: Cedar Hill Design Ctr Inc 712 Cedar St Cedar Hill TX 75104-4606

SORENSON, ROGER A. international relations consultant; b. Salina, Utah, May 4, 1928; s. Elmo S. Sorenson and Nellie Jensen; m. Shirley Rae Sorenson, Sept. 15, 1930; children: Erik Roger, David E., Karl W., Laurie. BA, Brigham Young U., 1955, MA, 1958; postgrad., Johns Hopkins U., 1965-66. Internat. economist Dept. State, Washington, 1966-69, mem. policy planning staff, 1975-77; deputy chief of mission U.S. Embassy, Dublin, Ireland, 1969-74; minister U.S. Mission, Geneva, 1977-79; permanent rep. UN Agys., Rome, 1979-82; dir. N.Am. office Food and Agr. Orgn. UN, Washington, 1983-90; internat. rels. cons. Sorenson Consulting Co., Chevy Chase, Md., 1991—. Head of U.S. delegation to renegotiation of Nice Agreement, State Dept. Geneva, 1977; signatory Nice Treaty, 1977. Patentee in field. Recipient Meritorious Svc. award Dept. State, Washington, 1966, Superior Honor award Dept. State, Washington, 1969, 74, 80. Mem. DACOR House. Avocations: music, literature. Home: 806 Northpoint Dr Salt Lake City UT 84103-3346 E-mail: ras28@erols.com.

SORENSON, SANDRA LOUISE, merchandising manager; b. Santa Monica, Calif., Nov. 30, 1948; d. Edward John and Gordon Dudley (Pollock) S. BA in Telecommunications, BS in Mktg., U. So. Calif., 1970. Merchandiser Montgomery Ward Inc., Los Angeles, 1970-82; sr. fin. planner Plums Co., 1982-84; mgr. merchandising systems devel. and tng. Millers Outpost, Ontario, Calif., 1984-89; merchandising systems specialist Oshmans Sporting Goods, Santa Ana, 1989-90; dir. allocations Clothestime, Anaheim, 1990-96; dir. planning and allocation Pacific Sunwear, 1996-97, Clothestime Anaheim, 1997—. Recipient Achievement award Bicentennial Com. Norwalk, Calif., 1976. Mem. Mensa, Commerce Assocs., Assn. Retail Technologies, Mensa, Internat. Platform Soc., Casitas de San Jose, Chi Omega, Phi Chi Theta, Alpha Epsilon Rho. Republican. Mem. Reformed Ch. Am. Club: Players of Orange. Home: 14913 Little Bend Rd Chino Hills CA 91709-3494 Office: Clothestime 5325 E Hunter Ave Anaheim CA 92807-2090 E-mail: ssorenso@ctme.com.

SORESCU, ALINA, marketing professional, educator; b. Bucharest, Romania, Oct. 23, 1970; d. Stefan and Adriana Rodica Bogdan; m. Sorin Sorescu, Aug. 24, 1994; children: Patrick. BS, U. Bucharest, Romania, 1994; Master of Stats., U. Fla., 1997; PhD, U. Houston, 2002. Tchg. fellow U. Houston, College Station, Tex., 1999—2002; asst. prof. Tex. A&M U., 2002—. Contbr. articles to profl. jours. Mem.: AMA, INFORMS. Avocations: travel, literature, music. Office: Mays Sch Business Texas A&M U College Station TX 77843-4112 E-mail: asorescu@cgsb.tamu.edu.

SORESE, DENISE POWERS, reading and language arts consultant, educator; b. N.Y.C., Sept. 11, 1945; d. Daniel Dennis and Frances Louise (Kruft) Powers; m. Vincent James Sorese, Aug. 12, 1967; children: Jaclyn, Lauren. BS in Edn., SUNY, Cortland, 1967; M of Reading, U. Bridgeport, 1970; cert. advanced study in adminstrn., Fairfield U., 1993. Tchr. early childhood N.Y.C. Bd. Edn., 1965-67; tchr. elem. sch. Greenwich (Conn.) Bd. Edn., 1967-72, reading/language arts specialist, 1972-77, 91—, learning facilitator, 1995—, mainstreaming assoc., 1986-91, adminstr. summer sch., 1993—2000; dir., program coord. summer acad. Convent of Sacred Heart Sch., 1994—. Aftersch. adminstr. Hamilton Ave. Sch., Greenwich, 1993-96; state assessor Conn. State Dept. Edn., Hartford, 1993—, tech. advisor, 1993-97; presenter and author in field. Mem. project Charlie, chmn. Jr. League Greenwich, 1989-92; bd. dirs. St. Pauls Day Sch., Riverside, Conn., 1981-92, PTA, Greenwich, 1984-93, St. Catherines Players, Riverside, 1993-94. Reading grantee State of Conn., 1973, 74. Mem. NEA, ASCD, Conn. Edn. Assn., Conn. Reading Assn. (bd. dirs., exemplary reading award, chairperson 1994-96), Conn. Coun. Tchrs. English, Internat. Reading Assn. (Exemplary Reading award for Conn. 2002), Delta Kappa Gamma (pres. chpt. 2002), Phi Delta Kappa. Roman Catholic. Avocations: tennis, reading, theatre. Office: Cos Cob Sch 300 E Putnam Ave Cos Cob CT 06807-2545 E-mail: De-Sorese@greenwich.k12.ct.us.

SOREY, THOMAS LESTER, JR. architect, educator; b. Wichita Falls, Tex., Jan. 26, 1927; s. Thomas Lester and Katherine (Peak) S.; m. Carolyn Drake, Dec. 24, 1959 (div. 1973); 1 child, Drake. Student, U. Okla., 1944-47; BArch, Okla. State U., 1952; MArch, Harvard U., 1954. Registered architect, Okla. Designer McKim Mead & White, Architects, N.Y.C., summer 1954; ptnr. Sorey Hill & Sorey Architects, Oklahoma City, 1958-70; pvt. practice, 1971-95; vis. prof. arch. U. Okla., Norman, 1972-74, prof. arch., 1975-90, prof. emeritus arch., sculptor, 1991—. Work included in books: Oklahoma Landmarks, 1967, Houses Architects Design for Themselves, 1974, Architecture in Oklahoma: Landmark and Vernacular, 1978, Affordable Houses Designed by Architects, 1979, Oklahoma Homes Past and Present, 1980; sculptor in one-man and group exhbns. Oklahoma City, Norman, Tulsa, 1977—. Mem. prof. adv. com. Okla. State U. Sch. Arch., Stillwater, 1967-69, Neighborhood Alliance, Inc., Oklahoma City, 1971-73; founding dir. CAF, Contemporary Arts Found., Oklahoma City, 1965-67; dir. Sunbeam Family Svcs., Oklahoma City, 1967-75; trustee Oklahoma City Art Mus., 1968-77, v.p., 1975; mem. Citizens League of Ctrl. Okla., Interfaith Alliance . With U.S. Army, 1954-56. Recipient Award of Excellence for House Design, Archtl. Record, 1968, Assocs. Disting. Lectr. award U. Okla., 1984-86. Mem. AIA (pres. Oklahoma City sect. 1965, bd. dirs. Okla. chpt. 1968-69, 75-77), Men's Dinner Club. Democrat. Avocations: photography, travel, reading non-fiction, racket sports. Home and Office: 3801 Ives Way Norman OK 73072-4009

SORGE, KAREN LEE, commercial printing company executive, consultant; b. Warwick, N.Y., May 27, 1958; d. Wesley Thomas and Margaret Anne (Storms) Kervatt; m. David W. Farquhar, July 16, 1982 (div. Feb. 1990); 1 child: Lauren Nicole; m. Thomas E. Sorge, May 16, 1997; children: Natalie MaKalen Sorge, Ryan Thomas. AS, Roger Williams Coll., 1978, BS cum laude, 1980. Office mgr. Price-Rite Printing Co., Dover, N.J., summer 1975-76; cons. SBA, Bristol, R.I., 1978-80; account exec. P.M. Press Inc., Dallas, 1980-90, sales trainer, 1984-85; v.p. KDF Bus. Forms Inc., 1984-90; account exec. Jarvis Press, 1990—; pres. Print Trends, 1990—. Printer Tex. Aux. Charity Auction Orgn., Dallas, 1985, Cystic Fibrosis, Dallas, 1989—93, Life Enhancement Assn. Programs Found., 1992—, Dallas Soc. Visual Comm., 1992, AIDS Resources Com., Dallas chpt. Cerebral Palsy, 1994, Lloyd-Paxton AIDS Benefit, 1994, Feast for the Eyes Gala-Benefit to Prevent Blindness, 2001, Genesis Women's Chelter, 2002, others. Recipient various awards Clampitt Paper Co., Dallas., 1982, P.M. Press Inc., 1983-89, Mead Paper Co., 1985-89, award Feast for the Eyes Gala, 2001. Mem. Printing Industry in Am. (recipient Judges Favorite award 1992, Best of Show Hon. Mention award 1994, gold award Best of Tex. 1996), Internat. Assn. Bus. Communicators, Nat. Bus. Forms Assn. Republican. Baptist. Avocations: piano, aerobics. Home: 2600 Raintree Dr Southlake TX 76092-5536

SORGEL, SYLVIA, financial services executive; b. Peoria, Ill., June 3, 1951; d. Robert William and Leona Alberta (Filkins) Peterson; m. John Walter Sorgel, Nov. 28, 1987 Student, U. Ill., Chgo., 1969-70. Sale mngr. Chgo. Financial Collection Agys., Montreal, Can., 1979-82, area sales mgr., 1982-86, v.p. midwest sales mgr., 1986-89, dir. U.S. local sales, 1989-91; v.p. nat. sales Nat. Credit Mgmt. Corp., Hunt Valley, Md., 1991-99; v.p. sales CMD Investment Group, 1999—. Mem. steering com. Coalition of Higher Edn. Orns., Washington, D.C., 1995-99. Vestry mem. Ch. of the Ascension, Chgo., standing, discernment, fin. and worship coms., 1996-2001, sr. warden, 2001-2002. Recipient Ill. State scholarship, 1969; assoc. Order of St. Anne, Chgo., 1995. Mem. Am. Assn. Healthcare Adminstrv. Mgmt., Ill. Bursar Orgns. (sec.), Hosp. Fin. Mgmt. Assn., Med. Group Mgmt. Assn. Office: CMD Investment Group 6425 N Caldwell Ave Chicago IL 60646-2739 E-mail: ssorgel@cmdigi.com.

SORGEN, ELIZABETH ANN, retired educator; b. Ft. Wayne, Ind., Aug. 21, 1931; d. Lee E. and Miriam N. (Bixler) Waller; m. Don DuWayne Sorgen, Mar. 8, 1952; children: Kevin D., Karen Lee Sorgen Hoeppner, Keith Alan. BS in Edn., Ind. U., 1953; MS in Edn., St. Francis Coll., Ft. Wayne, 1967. Tchr., bldg. rep. and math. book adoption rep. East Allen County Schs., Monroeville, Ind., 1953-94, ret., 1994. Founder nursery sch., choir mem. St. Marks Luth. Ch., Monroeville, 1960—; active Allen County Local Edn. Fund; vol. Sci. Ctr.; pres. Heritage Homemakers, 1990-2000; substitute tchr. Recipient Golden Apple award East Allen County Schs., 1976, Monroeville Tchr. of Yr. award, 1993. Mem. AAUW, Ft. Wayne Retired Tchrs. Assn., Ind. Two Steppers, Delta Kappa Gamma. Avocations: square and line dancing, camping, gardening. Home: 25214 Lincoln Hwy E Monroeville IN 46773-9710

SORGEN, HERBERT J. international education educator; b. Bklyn., July 29, 1938; s. Milton Sidney and Frances (Glass) S.; m. Nancy Lee, June 22, 1963; children: David, Laurie. AB, Syracuse U., 1960; MS, SUNY, Oswego, 1964; MLS, U. Mich., 1969. Tchr. English Paul V. Moore Ctrl. Sch., Central Square, N.Y., 1960-65; from asst. prof. to coord. internat. edn. SUNY Coll. Technology, Delhi, 1965—. Libr. cons. Northwest Inst. Light Industry, Xianyang, Shaanxi, China, 1998. Mem. Appalachian Mtn. Club, Rotary. Avocations: hiking, travel, photography, cross-country skiing. Home: 21720 State Hwy 28 Delhi NY 13753-9503 Office: SUNY Coll Technology Bush Hall Delhi NY 13753 E-mail: Sorgenhj@delhi.edu.

SORGI, MERCEDES PRIETO, psychologist; b. Havana, Cuba, Sept. 8, 1953; came to the U.S., 1961; d. Roberto Isaac and Dora Natalia (Fernandez) Prieto; m. John David Sorgi, Sept. 2, 1978; children: James, John, Roberto. BA in Psychology, Vanderbilt U., 1974; MA in Spl. Edn., George Peabody Coll., 1976; EdS in Spl. Edn., U. Miami, 1978; PhD in Sch. Psychology, Kent State U., 1994—. Cert. sch. psychologist, Ohio. Lead tchr. Mailman Ctr. for Child Devel., Miami, Fla., 1976, parent tng. coord., 1976-78; owner, buyer, salesperson The Land of Make Believe Shop, Hudson, Ohio, 1979-87; pre-sch. owner Mother's Day Out, 1984-87; Open Doors program dir. Hattie Larlham Found., Mantau, Ohio, 1986-91, dir. cmty. alternatives, 1988-92; pvt. cons. N.E. Ohio Agys., 1992-93; sch. psychology intern Orange (Ohio) Sch. Dist., 1996-97; sch. psychologist Seton Elem. Sch., Hudson, 1997-98; tchg. fellow Kent State U., 1997-99; bilingual sch. psychologist Cleve. City Schs., 1998—. Bd. mem., chair various coms. Summit County Assn. for Retarded Citizens, Akron, Ohio, 1980—; mem. adv. bd. Pre-Sch. Parents Assn., Hudson, 1982-85, Chem. Abuse Reduction Through Edn., Hudson, 1983-85; founding mem., chair Hattie Larlham League Hudson, 1985—. Mem. Rep. Women's League, Hudson, 1983-94; coun. mem. St. Mary Parish Coun., Hudson, 1985-88. Mem. APA, Nat. Assn. Sch. Psychologists, Ohio Assn. Sch. Psychologists, Cleve. Assn. for Sch. Psychologists, Support Spl. Edn. in Hudson (founder), Grad. Orgn. Sch. Psychology Studies (founder, chair). Roman Catholic. Avocations: gardening, horses, antiques. Home: 333 Aurora St Hudson OH 44236-2917

SORIANO, ALFONSO GUILLEARD, baseball player; b. San Pedro De Macoris, Dominican Republic, Jan. 1, 1978; Profl. baseball player N.Y. Yankees, 1999—. Office: NY Yankees Yankee Stadium 161st St and River Ave Bronx NY 10451*

SORIANO, NANCY MERNIT, editor-in-chief; married; 1 child. Degree in Art History, Bard Coll. Former editor Good Food; former contbg. editor Cosmopolitan, Food & Wine, Brides; joined Country Living, 1982, assoc. decorating editor, home bldg. and arch. editor, exec. editor, 1995-97, editor, 1997-98, editor-in-chief, 1998—. Founder Country Living Restoration Mag., 1996. Design editor: (book series) American Country Design, Time Life Books; editor spl. interest publ. Country Living Dream Homes. Office: Heart Mags 224 W 57th St Fl 7 New York NY 10019-3212

SORIYA, LASHMAN W. neurosurgeon; b. Colombo, Ceylon, June 10, 1936; MD, Royal Coll. Surgeons, Dublin, Ireland, 1963. Diplomate Am. Bd. Neurol. Surgery. Resident, fellow, then chief resident in neurol. surgery, assoc. cons. Mayo Clinic, Rochester, Minn., 1965-73; with Yellowstone Neurosurg. Assocs., P.C., Billings, Mont. Chmn. dept. surgery Deaconess Hosp., Billings, 1984, pres. med. staff, 1995, 96; chmn. sec. neurosurgery St. Vincent Hosp., Billings, 2000. Maj. U.S. Army, 1969-71. Fellow ACS, Internat. Coll. Surgeons; mem. AMA, Am. Assn. Neurol. Surgeons, Congress Neurol. Surgeons, Mont. Med. Assn. Office: Yellowstone Neurosurg Assocs PC 2900 12th Ave N Billings MT 59101-7506

SORKIN, ADAM J. English educator; b. N.Y.C., Aug. 9, 1943; s. Samson Z. and Anna Sorkin; m. Nancy Rosen, June 28, 1964; children: Rachel, Erica. AB with distinction, Cornell U., 1964, MA, 1965; PhD, U. N.C., 1972. Instr. dept. English U. Ill., Chgo., 1965-66, U. N.C., Chapel Hill, 1970-71; instr. lit. faculty arts and humanities Stockton State Coll., Pomona, N.J., 1971-73; asst. prof. English divsn. lang. arts Bluefield (W.Va.) State Coll., 1974-78; disting. prof. English Pa. State Delaware County, Media, 1978—. Adj. instr. dept. lit. and lang. Drexel U., Phila., 1973; adj. instr. dept. English C.C. Phila., 1973. Editor: Politics and the Muse: Studies in the Politics of Recent American Literature, 1989, Conversations with Joseph Heller, 1993; adv. editor Jour. Am. Culture, 1991—; contbg. editor Poetry N.Y., 1999—; contbr. numerous articles to profl. jours.; translator numerous books and poetry. Mem. Am. Culture Assn. (area chair lit. and politics 1985-96, governing bd. 1989-95, recorder 1991-95, Carl Bode awards com. 1990-92, chair Carl Bode awards com. 1991-92), Am. Literary Translators Assn. (bd. dirs., sec. 1999-01). Home: 54 Princeton Rd Havertown PA 19083-3622 Office: Pa State Delaware County 25 Yearsley Mill Rd Media PA 19063-5522 E-mail: ajs2@psu.edu.

SORKIN, DAVID JAMES, lawyer; b. N.Y.C., June 26, 1959; BA, Williams Coll., 1981; JD, Harvard U., 1984. Bar: N.Y. 1985. Law clk. judge Charles M. Merrill U.S. Ct. Appeals 9th Cir., San Francisco, 1984-85; assoc. Simpson Thacher & Bartlett, N.Y.C., 1985-92, ptnr., 1993—. Office: Simpson Thacher & Bartlett 425 Lexington Ave Fl 15 New York NY 10017-3954 E-mail: DSorkin@stblaw.com.

SORKIN, LAURENCE TRUMAN, lawyer; b. Bklyn., Oct. 20, 1942; s. Sidney and Lilly (Kowensky) S.; m. Joan Carol Ross, June 25, 1972; children: Andrew Ross, Suzanne Ross. AB summa cum laude, Brown U., 1964; LLB, Yale U., 1967; LLM, London Sch. Econs./Polit. Sci., 1968. Law clk. to Judge J. Joseph Smith U.S. Ct. Appeals (2d cir.), 1968-69; assoc. Cahill Gordon & Reindel, N.Y.C., 1969-75, ptnr., 1975—. Vis. lectr. Yale U., 1972, 73; lectr. various profl. orgns.; rsch. asst. to Lester and Bindman for book Race and Law in Great Britain, 1972. Contbr. to State Antitrust Law (Lifland), 1984; author: (with Lifland, Sorkin and Van Cise) Understanding the Antitrust Laws, 1986. Bd. dirs. Legal Aid Soc., N.Y.C., 1988-94, N.Y. Lawyers for Pub. Interest, 1990-93. Fulbright scholar, 1967-68. Mem. ABA (antitrust law sect. 1978—), N.Y. State Bar Assn. (antitrust sect., chmn. com. on legislation 1978-79, sect. sec. 1979-80, chmn. com. on mergers 1987-89, chmn. Clayton Act com. 1989-94, exec. com. 1989-94, comml. and fed. litigation sect. chmn. com. antitrust 1996-98), Assn. Bar City N.Y. (mem. com. trade regulation 1974-77, 95-98, com. on electric funds transfer 1979-80), Yale Law Sch. Assn. (exec. com. 2000—), Phi Beta Kappa. Office: Cahill Gordon & Reindel 80 Pine St Fl 17 New York NY 10005-1790 E-mail: lsorkin@cahill.com.

SORLEY, LEWIS, writer; b. West Point, N.Y., Aug. 3, 1934; s. Merrow Egerton Sorley and Louise MaBelle Barnes; m. Virginia Mezey Sorley, Nov. 21, 1970; 1 child from previous marriage, Kathleen Stone; stepchildren: Douglas Becker, Timothy Becker, Susan Becker Pelkey. BS, U.S. Mil. Acad., 1956; MA, U. Pa., 1963; MPA, Pa. State U., 1973; PhD, Johns Hopkins U., 1979; Grad., U.S. Army War Coll., 1973. Officer U.S. Army, 1956-76; intelligence officer CIA, Washington, 1976-83; writer Potomac, Md., 1983—. Exec. dir. Assn. Mil. Colls. and Schs. of U.S., Potomac, 1998—; bd. dirs. Army Hist. Found., Arlington, Va. Author: (books) Arms Transfers Under Nixon: A Policy Analysis, 1983, Thunderbolt: General Creighton Abrams and the Army of His Times, 1992, Honorable Warrior: General Harold K. Johnson and the Ethics of Command, 1998 (recipient Army Hist. Found.'s Disting. Book award 1998), A Better War: The Unexamined Victories and Final Tragedy of America's Last Years in Vietnam, 1999 (nominated for Pulitzer prize). Lt. col. U.S. Army, 1956-76. Recipient Peterson prize Year's Best Scholarly Article on Am. Mil. History, Ea. Parks and Monuments Assn., 1991, George Washington Honor medal Freedoms Found., Valley Forge, Pa., 1966, Gold medallion, Order of St. George U.S. Armor Assn., 1999, others; decorated Legion of Merit (2 oak leaf clusters), Meritorious Svc. medal, Air medal (2 oak leaf clusters) Army Commendation medal. Fellow: Inter-Univ. Sem. on Armed Forces and Soc.; mem.: Army Hist. Found. (dir. 2000—, sec. bd.dirs. 2001—), Soc. Mil. History, Assn. of Grads./U.S. Mil. Acad. (trustee 1983—89), Soc. Cin (bd. dirs. 1980—86), Nat. Eagle Scout Assn., Army Navy Club.

SORMAZ, DUSAN NEDELJKO, industrial engineer, educator, researcher; b. Ilijas, Yugoslavia, Jan. 11, 1956; came to U.S., 1990; s. Nedeljko Milos and Olga (Jovo) S.; m. Stanka Milan, Aug. 4, 1979; children: Branka, Olga. BSc in Indsl. Engring., U. Novi Sad, Yugoslavia, 1979, MSc, 1985; MSc in Computer Sci., U. So. Calif., 1995, PhD in Indsl. Sys. Engring., 1994. Tchg. asst. U. Novi Sad, 1980-90; rsch. asst. U. So. Calif., L.A., 1990-95; cons. Adizes-SEEurope, Novi Sad, 1997-99; asst. prof. Ohio U., Athens, 1995—. Author: (with others) Group Technology and Cellular Manufacturing, 1998; contbr. articles to profl. jours. Fulbright grantee, USIA, 1990-91; recipient grad. scholarship U. So. Calif., 1991-94, Stocker Faculty scholarship Ohio U., 1996, 2000. Mem. IEEE (sr.), Soc. Mfg. Engrs. (sr.), Am. Soc. Engring. Educators, Inst. Indsl. Engrs. (sr.). E-mail: sormaz@ohio.edu.

SOROKIN, ETHEL SILVER, lawyer; b. Hartford, Conn., 1928; d. Jacob M. and Jennie (Klein) Silver; m. Milton Sorokin, June 25, 1950; children: Rachel B., Sharon L., Leo T. BA, Vassar Coll., 1950; LLB with honors, U. Conn., 1953. Bar: Conn. 1953, U.S. Dist. Ct. Conn. 1955, U.S. Ct. Appeals (2d cir.), U.S. Supreme Ct. 1960. Assoc. Levine & Katz, Hartford, Conn., 1953-56; ptnr. Sorokin & Sorokin, 1956-89, Sorokin, Gross & Hyde PC, Hartford, 1989-93, of counsel, 1994—. Lectr. law., advisor law rev. U. Conn., 1955-58, 61-66; sec. Conn. Jud. Rev. Council, 1978-92; spkr. in field. Editor-in-chief U. Conn. Law Rev., 1953; mem. editl. bd. Conn. Bar Jour., 1951-56; contbr. articles to profl. jours. Trustee U. Conn. Law Found., Hartford, 1976-92, pres., 1978-79; dir. treas. Ctr. for First Amendment Rights, Inc., 1993-96, pres., 1996—. Mem. ABA (media law com., 1st amendment com.), Conn. Bar Assn. (family law sect., chmn. legis. com. 1984-87, chmn. UMPA study com. 1986, media-law com. 1992—). Office: Pullman & Conley LLC 90 Statehouse Sq Hartford CT 06103 E-mail: soroke@pullcom.com.

SOROS, GEORGE, fund management executive; b. Budapest, Hungary, Aug. 12, 1930; came to U.S., 1956; s. Tivadar and Elisabeth (Szucs) S.; m. Annaliese Witschak, Sept. 17, 1960 (div. June 1983); children: Robert, Andrea, Jonathan; m. Susan Weber, June 19, 1983; children: Alexander, Gregory. BS, London Sch. Econs., 1952; LLD (hon.), New Sch. for Social Rsch., 1990; D. Civil Law, U. Oxford, Eng., 1990; LHD (hon.), Yale U., 1991. Arbitrage trader F.M. Mayer, N.Y.C., 1956-59; analyst Wertheim & Co., 1959-63; v.p. Arnhold and S. Bleichroeder, 1963-73; sole proprietor Soros Fund Mgmt., 1973—; chmn. Soros Fund Mgmt., LLC, 1996—. Author: The Alchemy of Finance, 1987, 2nd edit., 1994, Opening the Soviet System, 1990, Underwriting Democracy, 1991. Mem. Coun. on Fgn. Rels., N.Y.C., 1988—, Royal Inst. Internat. Affairs, London, 1990—, Bretton Woods Com., Washington, 1989; mem. exec. com. Helsinki Watch, N.Y.C., 1982—; mem. com. Americas Watch, N.Y.C., 1982—; chmn., founding pres. Ctrl. European U., Budapest, 1991; chmn. Open Soc. Fund, 1981, Open Soc. Inst., 1993, founds. in Albania, Belarus, Bosnia and Herzegovina, Bulgaria, Croatia, Czech Republic, Estonia, Georgia, Hungary, Kazakhstan, Kyrgyestan, Latvia, Lithuania, Macedonia, Moldova, Poland, Romania, Russia, Slovakia, Slovenia, South Africa, Rroma, Ukraine, Yugoslavia. Recipient honor Lawyers Co. for Human Rights, N.Y.C., 1990. Avocations: tennis, skiing, chess, backgammon. Office: Soros Fund Mgmt 888 7th Ave Ste 3300 New York NY 10106-0001

SOROSKY, JERI RUTH, academic administrator; b. Chgo. d. Hans S. and Florence J. (Hurwitz) Pakula; m. Gene E. Sorosky; children: Cindi, Dana, Lesli. BA, Roosevelt U., Chgo., 1952; MEd, Fla. Atlantic U., Boca Raton, 1967; EdS, Nova Southeastern U., Ft. Lauderdale, Fla., 1972; EdD, MS, Nova Southeastern U., 1981. Cert. adminstr., supr., media specialist, gifted and elem. educator, Fla. Chairperson Elem. Highland Oaks, North Miami Beach, Fla., 1967-75; mem. faculty gifted program Highland Oaks Gifted Ctr., 1975-85; chairperson gifted program Miami (Fla.) Dade C.C., 1985-2000; site adminstr. grad. tchr. edn. program Nova. Southeastern U., Ft. Lauderdale, 1992—. Adj. prof. Nova Southeastern U., Ft. Lauderdale, 1979-87, adv. doctoral practicums, 1985-2000, cluster coord., 1987—, admissions com. doctoral programs Tech. & Distance Edn. and Child & Youth Studies, 1996—; chairperson gifted edn. Dade County Schs., Miami, 1990-93; mem. com. State Gifted Task Force, Tallahassee, 1992; presenter in field. Author: GEM Major Module in Gifted Education, 1981, Ideas Unlimited, 1985, Guide for Elementary Educators, 1995, Technology in the Curriculum, 1998; editor: Readings: Gifted Education, 1991, Early Childhood Education, 1982. Project chairperson Kids in Distress, Ft. Lauderdale, 1989. Named Woman of Yr. Bus. Profl. Women, 1985. Mem. Fla. Assn. Gifted (charter, v.p. 1975-97), Nova Southeastern U. Alumni (bd. dirs. 1981-97), AAUW, Phi Delta Kappa (chairperson newsletter 1985-97). Avocations: dancing, technology. Office: Nova Southeastern U 1750 NE 167th St North Miami Beach FL 33162-3017

SORREL, WILLIAM EDWIN, psychiatrist, educator, psychoanalyst; b. N.Y.C., May 27, 1913; s. Simon and Lee (Lesenger) S.; m. Rita Marcus, July 1, 1950; children: Ellyn Gail, Joy Shelley, Beth Mara. BS, NYU, 1932; MA, Columbia U., 1934, MD, 1939; PhD, NYU, 1963. Diplomate Am. Bd. Med. Psychotherapists (profl. adv. coun. 1992—); qualified psychiatrist, also cert.examiner N.Y. State Dept. Mental Hygiene. Intern Madison (Tenn.) Sanitarium and Hosp., 1939; resident physician Alexian Bros. Hosp., St. Louis, 1940; officer instrn. St. Louis U. Sch. Medicine, 1940-41; asst. psychiatrist Central State Hosp., Nashville, 1941; assoc. psychiatrist Eastern State Hosp., Knoxville, 1942-44; assoc. attending neuropsychiatrist, chief clin. psychiatry Jewish Meml. Hosp., N.Y.C., 1946-59; assoc. attending neuropsychiatrist, chief clin. child psychiatry Lebanon Hosp., Bronx, N.Y., 1947-65; psychiatrist-in-chief Psychiatry Clinic, Yeshiva U., 1950-66, asst. prof. psychiatry, 1952-54, assoc. prof., 1954-58, prof., 1959-62, psychiatrist-in-chief, assoc. dir. Psychol. Center, 1957-67; prof. emeritus human behavior Touro Coll., 1974—; attending psychiatrist St. Clare's Hosp., N.Y.C., 1983—; asst. prof. clin. psychiatry Albert Einstein Coll. Medicine, 1986—. Psychiat. cons. SSS, 1951, N.Y. State Workmens Compensation Bd., 1951— , Bronx-Lebanon Med. Ctr., 1985— ; vis. psychiatrist Fordham Hosp., N.Y.C., 1951; attending neuropsychiatrist, chief mental hygiene svc. Beth-David Hosp., 1950-60; attending neuropsychiatrist Grand Central Hosp., 1958-66, Morrisania Hosp., 1959-72; psychiatrist-in-chief Beth Abraham Hosp., 1954-60; psychiat. cons. L.I. U. Guidance Ctr., 1955-60, Daytop Village, 1970-71; assoc. psychiatrist Seton City Hosp., 1955; guest lectr. U. London, 1947; vis. prof. Jerusalem, Israel Acad. Med., 1960, Hebrew U., 1960; mem. psychiat. staff Gracie Sq. Hosp., 1960— ; chief psychiatry Trafalgar Hosp., 1962-72; vis. prof. psychiatry Tokyo U. Sch. Medicine, 1964; adj. prof. N.Y. Inst. Tech., 1968; vis. lectr. in psychiatry N.Y. U., 1971-73; Am. del. Internat. Conf. Mental Health, London, 1948; mem. Am. Psychiat. Commn. to USSR, Poland and Finland, 1963, Empire State Med., Sci. and Ednl. Found. Author: (booklets) Neurosis in a Child, 1949, A Psychiatric Viewpoint on Child Adoption, 1954, Shock Therapy in Psychiatric Practice, 1957, The Genesis of Neurosis, 1958, The Prejudiced Personality, 1962, The Schizophrenic Process, 1962, The Prognosis of Electroshock Therapy Success, 1963, Psychodynamic Effects of Abortion, 1967, Violence Towards Self, 1971, Basic Concepts of Transference in Psychoanalysis, 1973, A Study in Suicide, 1972, Masochism, 1973, Emotional Factors Involved in Skeletal Deformities, 1977, Cults and Cult Suicide, 1979, Further Viewpoints on the Genesis of Neurosis, 1996; assoc. editor Jour. Pan Am. Med. Assn., 1992—; contbr. articles on the psychoses. Vice pres. Golden Years Found.; N.Y.C. chmn. Com. Med. Standards in Psychiatry, 1952-54. Recipient Sir William Osler Internat. Honor Med. Soc. Gold Key; 3d prize oil paintings N.Y. State Med. Art Exhibit, 1954; NYU Founders Day award, 1963; Presdl. Achievement award, 1984, medal for med. excellence Pan Am. Med. Assn., 1997, others. Fellow Am. Psychiat. Assn. (life, pres. Bronx dist. 1960-61, other offices, Gold medal 1974, 94), Am. Assn. Psychoanalytic Physicians (pres. 1971-72, bd. govs. 1972—); mem. AMA, Ea. Psychiat. Assn., N.Y. State Soc. Med. Rsch., Am. Med. Writers Assn., N.Y. Med. Soc., N.Y. County Med. Soc., N.Y. Soc. for Clin. Psychiatry, Pan Am. Med. Assn. (various offices including pres. 1989—, assoc. editor jour. 1992—, Disting. Med. Svc. award 1997), Assn. for Advancement Psychotherapy, Bronx Soc. Neurology and Psychotherapy (pres. 1960-61, Silver medal 1970), Mensa. Home: 23 Meadow Rd Scarsdale NY 10583-7642 Office: 263 West End Ave New York NY 10023-2612 *Very meaningful to me is the matter of professionalism in the practice of my discipline. A helping service to individuals is to add and enhance their contentment of living; especially in a world of turmoil. Medical science has added greatly to the art of my training; and I apply it daily.*

SORRELL, MICHAEL E. consulting company executive; b. Pasadena, Calif., Mar. 31, 1945; s. James Hendrick Sorrell and Marie Vivian Bristow. AA, Normandale C.C., Bloomington, Minn.; BA, Concordia Coll., St. Paul. Pres., CEO, owner Daggers/La. Inc., Metairie, 1987-89, Mesa Cons. Svcs./MN/Inc., Mpls., 1989-94, Mesa Cons. Svcs., Inc., Las Vegas, Nev., 1994—99; pres., CEO, majority ptnr. W&S Enterprises Group, Inc., 1999—; chmn., CEO Bristow-Norwich Internat. Corp., 2000—; ptnr., dir. Sr. Owl Inc., 1999—. With USN, 1963-69, 74-89. Mem. VFW, Nat. Assn. Small Bus., Nat. Lic. Beverage Assn., Inst. Mgmt. Cons., Soc. Human Resources Mgmt., Soc. Hospitality Cons., Am. Legion, Fleet Res. Assn., Navy League U.S., U.S. Naval Inst., Amateur Athletic Union of U.S. Roman Catholic. Avocations: golf, hiking, tennis. Office: Mesa Cons Svcs Inc 3888 W Sahara Ave Ste 33 Las Vegas NV 89102-0505

SORRELL, ROZLYN, singer, recording artist, actress, educator, entrepreneur; b. Bklyn. d. Nathaniel Otis and Cupid Viola (Logan) S. BA in Theatre, CUNY, 1976, MS Edn., 1985. Cert. tchr., Calif., N.Y. Tchr. L.A. Unified Sch. Dist., 1997, Sylvan Learning Ctr., L.A., 1998; mem. Albert McNeil Jubilee Singers, 1994—; tchr. Westmark Sch., Encino, Calif., 2000, The Achievement Sch., Raleigh, NC, 2002. Voice tchr., L.A., 1992—; bus. cons., L.A., 1989—. Actress various TV programs, commls., stage prodns. and films, 1986—; soloist Hour of Power, Glory of Christmas, Glory of Easter, Garden Grove, Calif., 1994—, Miyazaki Civic Culture Hall, Japan, 1996, Anaheim Pond, Calif., 1997, Honolulu Symphony, 1998, Hollywood Bowl, Calif., 1998, Gospel Recording Artist, 2000, Temple of Music and Art, Tucson, 1990. Mem. AFTRA, SAG, Actors Equity Assn. Avocations: dancing, walking, working out, theatre. Home and Office: Double E Enterprises Double E Christian Ministries 809 Aversboro Rd Garner NC 27529 E-mail: sorrell@bww.com.

SORRELL, WILLIAM H. state attorney general; b. Burlington, Vt., Mar. 9, 1947; s. Marshal Thomas and Esther Sorrell; m. Mary Alice McKenzie; children: McKenzie, Thomas. AB, U. Notre Dame, 1970; JD, Cornell U., 1974. Dep. state's atty. Chittenden County State of Vt., 1975—77, state's atty. Chittenden County, 1977—78, 1989—92; ptnr. McNeil, Murray & Sorrell, 1978—89, sec. adminstrn., 1992—97; atty. gen. State of Vt., 1997—. Pres. United Cerebral Palsy Vt.; sec. Vt. Coalition Handicapped; bd. dirs. Winooski Valley Pk. Dist. Office: Office Atty Gen 109 State St Montpelier VT 05609-0001

SORRELLS, FRANK DOUGLAS, retired mechanical engineer, consultant; b. Toccoa, Ga., May 14, 1931; s. Ralph Price and Ila B. (Freeman) S.; m. Alma M. West, June 19, 1954; 1 child, Desiree G. BSME, U. Tenn., 1957, MS, 1968. Chief engr. Formex Co., Greeneville, Tenn., 1960-67; exec. v.p. Charles Lee Assoc., Knoxville, 1967-76; pvt. practice consulting engr., 1976-78, 83-88; dir. engring. Cole Nat. Corp., 1978-83; mgr. tech. transfer Valmet Paper Machinery div. Valmet-Enerdry, 1988-93; pres. PEPE Software LLC, 1996-98; ind. cons., 1976—. Cons., Knoxville, 1976—; mem. Advanced Toroidal Facility Design Team, cons. Oak Ridge (Tenn.) Nat. Lab., 1984-85. Inventor, patentee of 8 patents and co-inventor, patentee of 14 patents in fields of filtration, web processing, plastic forming and lens processing; developer and author copyrighted technical software. Staff sgt. USAF, 1950-54. Mem. ASME (Energy Resources Rsch. award 1987), Tenn. Soc. Profl. Engrs. Avocations: fishing, boating. E-mail: sorrells@ntown.com., mrmcdaris@msn.com.

SORRELS, CARRIE L. federal agency administrator; BA in Polit. Sci., Tex. Tech U., 1983; MPA, Tex. Tech. U., 1985. Presdl. mgmt. intern Office Space Sci. and Applications NASA, Washington, 1985, program analyst, 1989—93, dir. policy and bus. mgmt. divsn. Office Space Scis., 1993—. Pub. svc. fellow, 1983. Office: NASA Hdqrs Mail Code S 300 E St SW Washington DC 20546

SORRELS, RANDALL OWEN, lawyer; b. Va., Dec. 11, 1962; s. Charles Vernon and Marjorie Elaine (Jones) S.; m. Cheryl Ann Casas, June 29, 1985; children: Ashley Michelle, Stephanie Leigh, Darby Nicole, Garrett Ryan. BA in Polit. Sci.and Speech Comm. magna cum laude, Houston Bapt. U., 1984; JD magna cum laude, South Tex. Coll. Law, 1987. Bar: Tex. 1987, U.S. Dist. Ct. (so. dist.) Tex.; bd. cert. in civil trial law and personal injury trial law tex. Bd. Legal Specialization. Assoc. Fulbright & Jaworski, Houston, 1987-90; ptnr. Abraham, Watkins, Nichols, Sorrels, Matthews & Friend, 1990—. Contbr. articles to profl. jours. Fellow Tex. Bar Found. (trustee 1997-2000, sustaining life), Houston Bar Found. , Tex. Bar Found. (sustaining life); mem. ABA, Houston Bar Assn. (v.p. 2000-2001, dir. 1998-2000), Houston Trial Lawyers Found. (pres. 2000-2001), Houston Trial Lawyers Assn. (pres. 1999-2000), Houston Lawyer's Referral Svc. (pres. 2000-2001), State Bar Tex. (dir. 1994-97), Tex. Trial Lawyers Assn. (dir. 1994—), Houston Trial Lawyers Found. (dir. 1998—), Houston Trial Lawyers Assn. (v.p. 1996-98, dir. 1993-96), Am. Bd. Trial Advs. (1997—), Nat. Bd. Trial Advs., Coll. State Bar Tex., Coll. State Bar Tex., Houston Trial Lawyers Found., Houston Bar Assn., Tex. Young Lawyers Assn., Houston Young Lawyers Assn., Assn. Civil Trial and Appellate Specialists, Am. Trial Lawyers Assn., Million Dollar Advs. Forum, Tex. Assn. Def. Counsel (former mem.), Am. Inns of Ct. Home: 311 Terrace Dr Houston TX 77007-5046 Office: Abraham Watkins Nichols Sorrels Matthews & Friend 800 Commerce St Houston TX 77002-1776

SORRENTINO, GILBERT, English language educator, novelist, poet; b. Bklyn., Apr. 27, 1929; s. August E. and Ann Marie (Davis) S.; m. Victoria Ortiz; children: Jesse, Delia, Christopher. Student, Bklyn. Coll., 1950—2195, student, 1954—56. In various positions, 1947-70; including reins. clk. Fidelity and Casualty Co., N.Y.C., 1947-48; freight checker Ace Assembly Agy., 1954-56; packer Bennett Bros. Inc., 1956-57; messenger Am. Houses, Inc., 1948-49; shipping-room supr. Thermo-fax Sales, Inc., Queens, N.Y., 1957-60; editor Grove Press, 1965-70; tchr. Columbia U., 1966, Aspen Writers Workshop, 1967, Sarah Lawrence Coll., 1972, The New Sch. for Social Rsch., 1976—; NEH chairperson in lit. U. Scranton, 1979; prof. English Stanford U., Calif., 1982—99, prof. emeritus, 1999—. Editorial cons. Contemporary Lit., 1989-97. Author: The Darkness Surrounds Us, 1960, Black and White, 1964, The Sky Changes, 1966, The Perfect Fiction, 1968, Steelwork, 1970, Imaginative Qualities of Actual Things, 1971, Corrosive Sublimate, 1971, Splendide-Hotel, 1972, Flawless Play Restored, 1974, A Dozen Oranges, 1976, White Sail, 1977, Sulpiciae Elegidia/Elegiacs of Sulpica, 1977, The Orangery, 1978, Mulligan Stew, 1979, Aberration of Starlight, 1980, Selected Poems, 1958-80, 1981, Crystal Vision, 1981, Blue Pastoral, 1983, Something Said: Essays, 1984, Odd Number, 1985, Rose Theatre, 1987, Misterioso, 1989, Under the Shadow, 1991, Red the Fiend, 1995, Pack of Lies: A Trilogy, 1997, Gold Fools, 2001, Little Casino, 2002. With U.S. Army, 1951-53. Recipient Samuel Fels award in fiction Coord. Coun. Lit. Mags., 1974, John Dos Passos prize, 1981, Am. Acad. and Inst. Arts and Letters award in lit., 1985, Lannan Lit. award for fiction, 1992; John Simon Guggenheim Meml. fellow, 1973-74, 87-88; grantee Creative Artists Pub. Svc. Program, 1974-75, Nat. Endowment for Arts, 1974-75, 78-79, 83-84. Mem. PEN Am. Ctr.

SORRENTINO, JOHN PAUL, obstetrician-gynecologist, educator; b. Bayonne, N.J., Oct. 27, 1943; MD, U. Medicine and Dentistry N.J., 1969. Diplomate Am. Bd. Ob-Gyn. Intern St. Vincent Hosp., Worcester, Mass., 1969-70; resident in ob-gyn. SUNY, Syracuse, 1972-75; staff Baystate Med. Ctr., Springfield, Mass. Assoc. clin. prof. Tufts U. Sch. Medicine. Fellow ACOG; mem. Am. Inst. Ultrasound in Medicine, Am. Soc. Clin. Gynecologists, Mass. Med. Soc. Office: Baystate Med Office Bldg 2 Med Ctr Dr Ste 406 Springfield MA 01107-1280

SORRENTINO, JOSEPH NICHOLAS, prosecutor, writer; b. N.Y.C. s. Nicholas A. and Angelina C. (Trezza) S.; 1 child, Joseph Jr. BA, U. Calif., Santa Barbara, 1963; MA, U. Calif., L.A., 1971; JD, Harvard Law Sch., 1967; doctorate, So. Vt. Coll., 1976. Bar: Calif. 1968. Prosecutor intern U.S. Dept. Justice, L.A., 1968; writer Prentice Hall, Englewood Cliffs, N.J., 1968-71; adj. prof. U. So. Calif., UCLA, U. Calif. Irvine, Pepperdine U., 1971-81; juvenile ct. judge (pro tem) L.A., 1974-76; prosecutor Office of Riverside/L.A. Dist. Atty., 1981—. Lectr., nationwide, 1970-84; host, guest numerous TV programs including 60 Minutes, Newsmakers, Good Morning Am., Tonight Show, 1970-84. Author: Up From Never, 1971, 2nd edit., 1976, The Moral Revolution, 1973, The Concrete Cradle, 1975, The Gold Shield, 1980, (poems) People Who Stopped for You, 1995; contbr. numerous articles to profl. jours. and mags. Chmn. United Way mentally disabled com. L.A. Human Rights Commn., 1970-72. With USMC, 1963-64, USMCR, 1964-67. Recipient Notable Book award ALA, 1971; named Outstanding Spkr. of Yr. Nat. Authors and Celebrities Forum, 1977. Mem. Calif. Bar Assn., Calif. Assn. Dist. Attys., Calif. Consumers Activist Group (bd. dirs.), Constl. Rights Found., Sugar Ray Robinson Found. (bd. dirs.). Avocations: amateur archeology, mountain climbing, world travel. Home: 2350 Nichols Canyon Rd Los Angeles CA 90046-1733

SORRENTINO, RENATE MARIA, illustrator; b. Mallnitz, Carinthia, Austria, June 21, 1942; came to the U.S., 1962; d. Johann and Theresia (Kritzer) Weinberger; m. Philip Rosenberg, Nov. 22, 1968 (dec. 1982); m. Francis J. Sorrentino, Sept. 4, 1988. Grad. gold and silversmith artist, Höhere Technische Lehranstalt, Austria, 1961. Draftswoman Elecon Inc., N.Y.C., 1962-65; jr. designer Automatics Metal Prod. Corp., 1965-70; designer, art dir. Autosplice, Inc., Woodside, N.Y., 1970-90; freelance artist Jupiter, Fla., 1990—. Patentee Quick Disconnect from Continuous Wire, 1977. Home: 2301 Marina Isle Way Apt 404 Jupiter FL 33477-9423 Office: Autosplice Inc 10121 Barnes Canyon Rd San Diego CA 92121-5797 Fax: 561-626-2853. E-mail: sorrenate@adelphia.net.

SORRENTINO, ROBERT ANGELO, medical educator; b. Bklyn., Sept. 17, 1955; s. Umberto A. and Theresa (Ercolano) S.; m. Rebecca Lai-Kwan Leung, May 18, 1985; children: Theresa Ann, Katherine Marie, Natalie Rose. BA, NYU, 1977; MS, Wagner Coll., 1978; MD, Albany Med. Coll., 1985. Diplomate Am. Bd. Internal Medicine, Am. Bd. Cardiovascular Diseases, Am. Bd. Clin. Cardiac Electrophysiology. Intern, resident Duke U. Med. Ctr., Durham, N.C., 1985-88, fellow in cardiology, 1988-91, assoc. medicine, 1991-94, asst. prof. medicine, 1994—. Fellow Am. Coll. Cardiology; mem. N.Am. Soc. Pacing and Electrophysiology (exam. testamur 1999), Nat. Bd. Med. Examiners (cert.), Alpha Omega Alpha. Office: Duke U Med Ctr PO Box 3330 Durham NC 27702-3330 E-mail: sorre001@mc.duke.edu.

SORRIN, MARY LOUISE, artist, nurse; b. Woodward, Okla., Mar. 9, 1946; d. Harland Ralph and Mary Elizabeth McCurdy; m. Bruce Michael Sorrin, Oct. 31, 1969; children: Aimee Lynn, Sean David, Keri Leigh. Diploma in nursing, St. John's Hosp., 1967; AA, Ulster County C.C., 1979. Exhbns. include Women Creating-A Celebration of Cape Cod Women, 1996-98, Leo Diehl Exhbn., 1996-98, Midwest Pastel Soc. Nat., 1996, Cape Cod Art Assn., 1997, 99 (1st pl. 1999), Newport Art Mus., 1998, Northwest Pastel Soc., 1998, Creative Arts Ctr., 1998, Internat. Assn. Pastel Soc., 1999, Northern Colo. Artist Assn., 1999, La Fond Galleries, 1999, Conn. Pastel Soc. (Bd. Dirs. award 2000), Pastel Soc. West Coast, Hudson Valley Art Assn., Pastel Soc. No. Fla., Pastel Painters Soc. Cape Cod, Pastel Soc. Southwest (Merit award), Pastel Soc. (Mountain High award 2001). Pres. chpt. Vietnam Veterans Am., 1985; treas. West Hurley (N.Y.) Libr. Assn. 1st lt. Army Nurse Corps, 1967-69. Mem. Pastel Painters Soc. Cape Cod (treas. 1994-98), Pastel Soc. West Coast, Pastel Soc. Southwest, Pastel Soc. Conn. Democrat. Roman Catholic. Avocations: reading, movies, gardening. Home: 2721 N Meridian Pl Oklahoma City OK 73127-1917 E-mail: mlousorr@swbell.net.

SORSCHER, MARVIN LOEB, religious studies educator, rabbi; b. Bklyn., Apr. 29, 1924; s. Abraham and Miriam (Cohen) S.; m. Sylvia London, Feb. 7, 1954; children: Esther S. Rister, Abraham M., Sroya S. BA, Yeshiva Coll., 1946; MA, Hunter Coll., 1950; MHL, Yeshiva U., 1950, MS, 1958, DHL, 1968. Cert. sch. adminstr. and supr., N.Y.; cert. guidance counselor, N.Y. Pres. Yeshiva Haichel Ha Torah, Bklyn., 1969—; guidance counselor John D. Wells Jr. H.S., 1970-74, Franklin D. Roosevelt H.S., Bklyn., 1975-89; chmn. fgn. lang. dept. Washington Irving Evening H.S., 1973-80; rabbi Beth Aaron Synagogue, 1990—; chmn. Hebrew regents testing com. N.Y. State Edn. Dept., 1976—; instr. Yeshiva Tores Emes H.S., Bklyn., 1997—. Mem. edn. adv. bd. Yeshiva Gedolah Acad., Bklyn., 1990—; exam. scorer (in Hebrew and Yiddish) oral and written tchr. cert. lics. Nat. Evaluations Systems, N.Y.; translator Hebrew and Yiddish langs. N.Y.C. Bd. Edn., Hard of Hearing-Visually Impaired Bur., 1997—. Author: Havah Nasocheach, Part I, 1969, Part 2, 1972; Manual of Tape Scripts, 1970, Lashon V'Dibbur, 1971, The Laws of Shabbos Erev Pesach, 1974, Blessings and Prayers for the Sabbath Holidays and Special Occasions, 1974, Hakshaiv Va Anai, 1976, I Can Learn Hebrew, 1986. Recipient 1st prize (trip to Israel) Torah Quiz Contest, Jewish Press, 1989. Mem. Am. Assn. Tchrs. Hebrew (pres. 1970—), Assn. Orthodox Jewish Tchrs. (life mem.; former v.p., mem. exec. bd. 1972—). Home: 1375 57th St Brooklyn NY 11219-4637 Office: Beth Aaron Synagogue 2261 Bragg St Brooklyn NY 11229-5401

SORSTOKKE, SUSAN EILEEN, systems engineer; b. Seattle, May 2, 1955; d. Harold William and Carrol Jean (Russ) Sorstokke. BS in Systems Engring., U. Ariz., 1976; MBA, U. Wash., Richland, 1983. Warehouse team mgr. Procter and Gamble Paper Products, Modesto, Calif., 1976-78; quality assurance engr. Westinghouse Hanford Co., Richland, Wash., 1978-80, supr. engring. document ctr., 1980-81; mgr. data control and adminstrn. Westinghouse Electric Corp., Madison, Pa., 1981-82, mgr. data control and records mgmt., 1982-84; prin. engr. Westinghouse Elevator Co., Morristown, N.J., 1984-87, region adminstrn. mgr. Arleta, Calif., 1987-90; ops. rsch. analyst Am. Honda Motor Co. Inc., Torrance, 1990-95; project leader parts sys. Am. Honda Motor Co., Inc., 1995-96, mgr. parts systems and part number adminstrn., 1996-97, mgr. parts systems, 1997-2000, mgr. process control and regulatory issues, 2002—.

Adj. prof. U. LaVerne, Calif., 1991—92; pres. Fussy Cuts Inc., Torrance, Calif., 2000—. Advisor Jr. Achievement, 1982—83; literacy tutor Westmoreland Literacy Coun., 1983—84; host parent EF Found., Saugus, Calif., 1987—88, Am. Edn. Connection, Saugus, 1988—89, 1991; instr. Excell, L.A., 1991—92; mem. Calif. Acad. Math. and Sci., 1996—97. Mem.: Am. Inst. Indsl. Engrs., Soc. Women Engrs., Optomists Charities Inc. (bd. dirs. Acton, Calif. 1991—94, 2000—). Republican. Methodist. Home: 2567 Plaza Del Amo Unit 205 Torrance CA 90503-8962 Office: Am Honda Motor Co Inc Dept Parts 100 5C 3B 1919 Torrance Blvd Torrance CA 90501-2722

SORTE, JOHN FOLLETT, investment firm executive; b. Boston, June 30, 1947; s. Martin Eugene and Elizabeth Foster (Bradley) S.; m. Colleen Sarah Costello, July 28, 1979; children: Bradley Follett, Laura Elizabeth, Kathryn Clare. BAChemE, Rice U., 1969, M in Chem. Engring., 1970; MBA, Harvard U., 1972. Assoc. Shearson Hammill & Co., Inc., N.Y.C., 1972-74; v.p. Shearson Hayden Stone, Inc., 1974-79; 1st v.p. Shearson Loeb Rhoades, Inc., 1979-80, Drexel Burnham Lambert, Inc., N.Y.C., 1980-82, mng. dir., 1982-88, exec. v.p., 1989-90, pres., CEO, dir., 1990-92; pres., CEO New Street Capital Corp., 1992-94; pres. New Street Advisors L.P., 1994—2001; pres., CEO, dir. Morgan Lewis Githens & Ahn, Inc., 2001—. Chmn. N.Y. Media Group, Inc., 1995-2001; bd. dirs. Vail Resorts, Inc., WestPoint Stevens, Inc. Trustee Rippowam Cisqua Sch. Office: Morgan Lewis Githens & Ahn Inc 600 Fifth Ave 19th Fl New York NY 10020-2302 E-mail: jsorte@MLGA.com.

SORTER, BRUCE WILBUR, federal program administrator, educator, consultant; b. Willoughby, Ohio, Sept. 1, 1931; s. Wilbur David and Margaret Louise (Palmer) S.; m. Martha Ann Weirich, Sept. 2,1960 (div. 1967); 1 child, David Robert. BA, U. Md., 1967; MCP, Howard U., 1969; PhD, U. Md., 1972. Cert. community developer. Commd. USAFR, 1967, advanced through grades to lt. col., 1964; sr. planner, cons. Md. Nat. Capital Park and Planning Com., 1968-71; instr. psychology, sociology Howard and P.G. C.C., Columbia and Largo, Md., 1971-72; cmty. resource devel. dept. Md. Coop. Extension Svc., U. Md., College Park, 1972-92; coord. rural info. ctr. Md. Coop. Ext. Svc., U. Md., 1989-92; affiliate prof. U. Md., 1985-92, ret., 1996. Ext. advisor USDA Internat. Programs, Washington, 1991-96; co-author, co-dir. Dept. Edn. Coun. Effectiveness Tng. Program, 1979-81; author First County Energy Conservation Plan, Prince George's County, 1978-85. Author, co-author 12 books; contbr. articles to profl. publs., chpts. to books. Developer, dir. teamwork tng. programs U.S. Dept. Edn., U.S. Dept. Agriculture, Brazil, Poland, Nat. Grange, 1972-92; cons. Fed. Power Commn. U.S., 1973-75, State Dept. Natural Resources, Md., 1978-79, Dept. Edn., Brazil, 1981-82, Nat. Grange, 1987, Edn. Ext. Svcs., Poland, 1991-92. Urban Planning fellow Howard U., 1968, Human Devel. fellow U. Md., 1970; recipient Meritorious Svc. award Dept. Def., 1983, Disting. Community Svc. award Md. Community Resource Devel. Assn., 1983, Citation for Outstanding Svc., Ptnrs. of Am., 1983, Excellence in Ednl. Programs award Am. Express, 1984, Project of Yr. award Am. Psychol. Assn., 1976, Award of Yr. Am. Vol. Assn., 1976, Achievement award Nat. Assn. of Counties, 1980. Mem. Internat. Cmty. Devel. Soc. (bd. dirs., Achievement award for outstanding contbn. to cmty. devel. 1985, Disting. Svc. award 1990), Md. Cmty. Resource Devel. Assn. (sec.-treas. 1979, pres. 1980, 88-89). Republican. Methodist. Avocations: volunteer work, tennis, sailing, skiing. *Decide where you want to go. Ask yourself, is it worth the cost? If the answer is yes, then go with determination for time is in short supply.*

SORTER, GEORGE HANS, accounting and law educator, consultant; b. Vienna, Austria, Dec. 2, 1927; came to U.S., 1938; s. Alfred and Hertha (Kohn) S.; m. Dorienne Lachman, Aug. 18, 1966; children: David, Ivan, Adrienne. Ph.B., U. Chgo., 1953, MBA, 1955, PhD, 1963. C.P.A., N.Y. Instr. U. Chgo., 1955-58, asst. prof., 1959-63, assoc. prof., 1963-65, prof., 1966-74; Vincent C. Ross prof. acctg., prof. of law NYU, N.Y.C., 1974—. Arthur Young prof. U. Kans., 1969; Coopers & Lybrand prof. Tuck Sch. Dartmouth Coll., 1982; bd. dirs. NYU Credit Union, 1982-85; dir. Greater N.Y. Savs. Bank, N.Y.C., 1983-97; audit com. City of N.Y., 1985-94. Author: Accounting Theory, 1963, Accounting Thoughts of W.W. Werntz, Boundaries of Accounting Universe, 1978, Relevant Financial Statements, 1978, Financial Accounting: An Events and Cash Flow Approach, 1990, The Mix-Max Co., 1990. Mem. Ill. Sch. Bd. Dist. 233, Flossmoor, 1970-74; bd. dirs. Sch. Emotionally Disturbed Children, Chgo., 1960-74, Renaissance Soc., 1956-74, Found. Acctg. Edn., N.Y.C., 1975-79. Erskine fellow U. Canterbury, 1979 Mem. Am. Acctg. Assn. (v.p 1980-81 Outstanding Acctg. Educator), N.Y. State Soc. C.P.A.s (dir. 1980-82), Am. Inst. C.P.A.s, Fin. Acctg. Standard Adv. Com. Home: 37 Washington Sq W New York NY 10011-9181 Office: NYU Tisch Hall 40 W 4th St New York NY 10012-1106

SORTLAND, PAUL ALLAN, lawyer; b. Powers Lake, N.D., July 30, 1953; s. Allan Berdette and Eunice Elizabeth (Nystuen) S.; m. Carolyn Faye Anderson, June 23, 1979; children: Joseph Paul, Martha Marie, Nicholas John, Benjamin David. BA, St. Olaf Coll., 1975; JD, U. Minn., 1978. Bar: Minn. 1978, N.D. 1981, U.S. Dist. Ct. Minn. 1979, U.S. Dist. Ct. N.D. 1980, U.S. Ct. Appeals (8th cir.) 1987, U.S. Supreme Ct. 1991. Assoc. Alderson & Ondov, Austin, Minn., 1978-80, Qualley, Larson & Jones, Fargo, N.D., 1980-83; ptnr. Holand, Lochow & Sortland, 1983-85; pres. Sortland Law Office, 1985-88; ptnr. Messerli & Kramer, Mpls., 1988-92; Sortland Law Office, 1993—. Adj. prof. bus. law Moorhead State U., 1987. Mem. ATLA, N.D. Bar Assn., Minn. Bar Assn. (cert. civil trial specialist), Kiwanis, Million Dollar Advocates Forum, Gamma Eta Gamma. Lutheran. Home: 120 Quebec Ave S Minneapolis MN 55426-1509 Office: 33 S 6th St Ste 4100 Minneapolis MN 55402-3729

SOSA, ERNEST, philosopher, educator; b. Cardenas, Cuba, June 17, 1940; s. Ernesto and Maria (Garriga) S.; m. Sara Mercedes, Dec. 21, 1961; children: E. David, Adrian J. BA, U. Miami, 1961; MA, U. Pitts., 1962, PhD, 1964. Instr. U. Western Ontario, London, Can., 1963-64, U. Pitts., 1964; postdoctoral fellow Brown U., Providence, 1964-66; asst. prof. U. Western Ontario, London, 1966-67; asst. prof. to full prof. Brown U., Providence, 1967-74, chmn. of philosophy, 1970-76, full prof., 1974—, Romeo Elton prof., 1981—. Vis. prof. U. Miami, 1970, Nat. U. Mexico, 1979, 80, 81, Harvard U., Cambridge, Mass., 1982, U. Salamanca, 1995, 98, Oxford U., 1997; disting. vis. prof. Rutgers U., 1998—; co-chair program com. 20th World Congress of Philosophy, 1998. Author: Knowledge in Perspective, 1991; gen. editor book series, Cambridge Univ. Press, 1990—, Blackwell Publishers, 1991—; editor Philosophy and Phenomenol. Rsch.; co-editor: Nous; contbr. numerous articles to profl. jours. Grantee NSF, 1970-72, Exxon Ednl. Found., 1980-82; recipient Sr. fellowship NEH, 1988-89. Mem. Am. Acad. Arts and Scis., Am. Philos. Assn. (sec.-treas. 1974-82, chair internat. coop. com. 1984-89, ea. divsn. rep. 1995—), Am. Coun. Learned Socs./Soviet Acad. Commn., Internat. Fedn. Philos. Soc. (steering com. 1988-98, v.p. 1988-93), Institut Internat. de Philosophie (exec. com. 1993-96). Avocations: running, travel. Office: Brown U Dept Philosophy Providence RI 02912-0001

SOSA, SAMUEL (SAMMY SOSA), professional baseball player; b. San Pedro de Macoris, Dominican Republic, Nov. 12, 1968; With Tex. Rangers, 1989; outfield Chgo. Cubs, 1992—. Selected to N.L All-Star Team, 1995, 98; 66 Homeruns in 1998 2nd only to Mark McGwire all time homeruns; lead major leagues in RBI, runs and total bases (416), 1998; RBI total 4th highest in NL history, 1998; record for new major league baseball record for homeruns in a single month (21), 1998; single season club record of 35 homeruns at Wrigley Field, 1998; named Player of Month of June, 1998; winner Roberto Clemente award for outstanding svc. to cmty. Major League Baseball, 1998. Office: Chgo Cubs 1060 W Addison St Chicago IL 60613-4383*

SOSKEL, NORMAN TERRY, physician; b. Sept. 1, 1948; s. Fred and Ruth (Chapel) S.; m. Judith Anne Barrie, Apr. 9, 1980; children: Daniel Aaron, Shira Anne. BA, U. Va., 1970, MD, 1974. Cert. piano tchr. St. Louis Inst. Music. Intern Hosp. of St. Raphael-Yale U., New Haven, 1974-75; resident in internal medicine Salem (Va.) VA Hosp.-U. Va., 1975-77; pulmonary fellow U. Utah, Salt Lake City, 1977-80, instr. medicine, 1980-82, asst. prof. medicine, 1982-84, U. Tenn., Memphis, 1984-89, assoc. prof. medicine, 1989-92; pvt. practice pulmonary and critical care medicine, 1992—. Adj. instr. pathology U. Utah, Salt Lake City, 1980-83; assoc. chief pulmonary sect. VA Med. Ctr., Memphis, 1989-92; dir. pulmonary medicine Eastwood Hosp., Memphis, 1992-95; clin. assoc. prof. dept. medicine pulmonary divsn. U. Tenn., 1992—; founder, med. dir., chmn. bd. Sarcoidosis Ctr., Memphis, 2000; cons. in field. Contbr. articles to profl. jours. Recipient Paderewski medal Nat. Guild Piano Tchrs., 1967, Pulmonary Acad. award Nat. Heart-Lung-Blood Inst., 1980-84, Career Devel. and Merits awards VA, 1984-87; Am. Lung Assn. fellow; Utah Heart Assn. grantee. Fellow ACP, Am. Coll. Chest Physicians (interstitial lung disease steering com., Govs. Cmty. Svc. award 2000); mem. AAAS, Am. Lung Assn., Am. Thoracic Soc. (respiratory cell and molecular biology sect.), World Assn., Sarcoidosis and Other Granulamatous Disorders, Sarcoidosis Rsch. Inst. (bd. dirs.), Nat. Speleol. Soc., Western Connective Tissue Soc., So. Connective Tissue Soc., N.Y. Acad. Sci., Sigma Chi. Achievements include research in T cell antigen receptor expression in sarcoidosis and other diffuse infiltrative lung diseases, connective tissue metabolism and damage in the lung especially the role of elastin and its destruction and synthesis in emphysema. Address: 6005 Park Ave Ste 501 Memphis TN 38119-5215 E-mail: soskelnt@sarcoidcenter.com.

SOSLOW, ARNOLD, quality consultant; b. Phila., Nov. 13, 1938; s. Samuel and Betty (Goldfine) S.; m. Frances Isen, May 15, 1960; children: Michael Allan, Beverly Ruth Soslow Warner. AS in Bus. Adminstrn., Temple U., 1974, BBA in Ind. Mgmt., 1976. Design draftman Unisys, Blue Bell, Pa., 1959-66; process control/quality specialist Gen. Electric Co., Phila., 1966-69; mgr. ops. B & F Instruments, Cornwells Heights, Pa., 1969-75; quality engr. Ronson Corp., Bridgewater, N.J., 1976-78; quality assurance mgr. Kooltronics Inc., Hopewell, 1978-83; quality mgr. Electro-Sci. Labs., King of Prussia, Pa., 1983-90; pres., quality advisor The Quality Mgmt. Co., Phila., 1988—. Mem. Am. Soc. for Quality Control, Internat. Electronic Package Soc., Internat. Soc. for Hybrid Microelectronics (program chmn. joint symposium 1987-89, pres. Keystone chpt. 1989, gen. chmn. joint symposium 1990-92, gen. chmn. quality workshop 1992-93), Surface Mt. Tech. Assn. Republican. Jewish. Achievements include research in field. Home and Office: The Quality Mgmt Co 8844 Manchester St Philadelphia PA 19152-1515 E-mail: tqmco@att.net.

SOSNICK, FAY MAXINE, retired educator, volunteer; b. N.Y.C., June 25, 1914; d. Philip and Gussie (Cohen) Shapiro; m. Max Sosnick, Dec. 25, 1937 (dec. Sept. 1989); children: Renee Beth Bain, Janet Ruth Hughes. BA in Chemistry, Math. and Sci., Hunter Coll., 1934; MEd in Math., Fairleigh Dickinson U., 1964; AAS in Philosophy, Brookdale C.C., N.J., 1984. Auditor U.S. Fin. Office, 1943-46; acctg., analyst and payroll staff Quindar Electronics, N.J., 1955-68; exec. Inglemoor Nursing Homes, 1969-74. Creator, organizer Home Owners Assn., The Guardian-Newspaper Pub. Condo. Assn., 1973-76; creator, liaison Self-Help Groups in Arthritis, Fitness, Svcs. to Hosp., Freehold Boro Hosp., 1974—, ombudsmen's team; vol. govtl. svc. Sr. Health Ins. N.J. State, 1976-80; with Brookdale C.C. Alumni Assn., N.J., 1983-87; mem. juvenile conf. com. Superior Ct. Chancery Divsn., N.J., 1985-89; creator patient support group St. Peters U. Hosp., Circle of Friends, Cmty. Sr. Ctr.; resident, program chmn. Sr. Homes, Temple. Recipient Svc. award, Bikun Choleem. Avocations: study of voice, choir, sing alongs, retreats, music appreciation groups. Achievements include creator of ombudsmen's team for redress of grievances plans to create a community at own residence; working with governor and legislative bodies to create a community of residents of senior living facilities.

SOSNICK, STEPHEN HOWARD, economics educator; b. Portland, Oreg., Feb. 24, 1930; s. Benjamin and Natalie (Schmulowitz) S.; m. Galya Chernow, July 14, 1951; children— Beryl, Elika, Randall, Tobin. A.B., U. Calif.-Berkeley, 1950, Ph.D., 1954. Inst., Princeton U., N.J., 1954-57; mem. faculty U. Calif., Davis, 1957— , now prof. agrl. econs. Author: Hired Hands, 1978; Budget's New Clothes, 1971; also articles. Office: U Calif-Davis Dept Agrl Econs Davis CA 95616

SOSNOW, ELLEN ROSENTHAL, interior designer; b. N.Y.C., June 12, 1942; d. Laurence Stanley and Clara (Steinhardt) R.; m. Lawrence Ira Sosnow, May 30, 1965; children— Peter, Ivan, Meg W. B.A., Chatham Coll., 1964. Editorial asst. TV Guide Mag., N.Y.C., 1965-67; press. rep. CBS, N.Y.C., 1967; acct. exec. Spade & Archer, N.Y.C., 1968; interior designer Ellen Sosnow Interiors, N.Y.C., 1976— ; tchr. interior design Scarsdale Adult Sch., N.Y., 1987-88. Author (mag.) How to Decorate Your Waiting Room, 1980. Bd. dirs., sec. Camp Isabella Friedman, N.Y.C., 1983— . Democrat. Jewish. Avocations: tennis; skiing.

SOSOKA, JOHN RICHARD, consulting firm executive, engineer; b. L.A., Nov. 30, 1929; s. John and Mary (Kovach) S.; m. Audrey T. Trezona, Apr. 26, 1952; children: John Richard Jr., Cathie Ann, Karen Elizabeth. BS in Gen. Engring., UCLA, 1952; MBA, Calif. State U., 1975. Registered mech., elec., fire protection, metallurgy, control systems and civil engr., Calif. Project engr. Stathem Instrument, L.A., 1954-55; staff engr. Aerojet Gen., Azusa, Calif., 1955-60; tech. dir. Unitek Corp., Monrovia, 1960-65; staff engr. TRW Systems, Redondo Beach, 1965-69; engr. mgr. Allen-Jones Electronics, Gardena, 1969-70; sect. head City of Long Beach, 1970-79; pres. Sosoka & Assoc.s, Los Alamitos, 1979-90; exec. v.p. Sparvan, Inc., Long Beach, 1990-91; pres., CEO P2S Engring., Inc., 1991—. Fellow ASHRAE (dir. and regional chair 1990-93, Disting. Svc. award 1988), Inst. Advancement Engring., L.A. Coun. Engrs. and Scientists (Disting. Engr. award); mem. Assn. Energy Engrs. (v.p. 1980-81, Energy Engr. of Yr. award 1985). Republican. Episcopalian. Achievements include patent in Welding. Home: 848 Roxanne Ave Long Beach CA 90815-5013 Office: P2S Engineering Inc 5000 E Spring St Ste 800 Long Beach CA 90815-5218 E-mail: jrs@p2seng.com.

SOSS, DANIEL LEE, social work educator; b. Spokane, Wash., May 30, 1931; s. Walter Lee and Ethelyn F. (Daniel) S.; m. Dorine C., June 17, 1955; children: Nancy Lee, Mark Daniel, Shari Lee, Michael Wayne. BA, Ea. Wash. U., 1955; MSW, U. Wash., 1963. Asst. prof. emeritus Wash. State U., Pullman; adminstr. juvenile ct. Whitman County Superior Ct., Colfax, Wash.; pub. health adminstr. Thurston-Mason Health Dist., Olympia. Dir. social svcs. Nursing Home and Retirement Ctr. Mem. Nat. Eagle Scout Assn. Home: HC 1 Box 394-C Naples ID 83847-9722

SOSSAMAN, WILLIAM LYNWOOD, lawyer; b. High Point, N.C., May 30, 1947; s. Robert Allison and Elizabeth Bryce (Hethcox) S.; m. Sandra Clare Ward, June 9, 1973; children: Joana Leslie, David Lynwood. AB, Davidson Coll., 1969; JD, Vanderbilt U., 1972. Bar: Fla. 1972, U.S. Ct. Mil. Appeals 1973, U.S. Dist. Ct. (mid. dist.) Fla. 1977, Tenn. 1978, U.S. Dist. Ct. (we. dist.) Tenn. 1979, U.S. Dist. Ct. (no. dist.) Miss. 1979, U.S. Dist. Ct. (ea. and we. dists.) Ark. 1980, U.S. Dist. Ct. (mid. dist.) Tenn. 1985, U.S. Dist. Ct. (ea. dist.) Mich. 1988, U.S. Ct. Appeals (6th and 8th cirs.) 1989, U.S. Ct. Appeals (11th cir.) 1991. Mktg. resch. analyst First Tenn. Bank, Memphis, 1967-70; assoc. Alley, Rock & Dinkel, Tampa, Orlando and Miami, Fla., 1972-73, Rock & Brown, Orlando, 1976-77, Young & Perl, Memphis, 1978-88; ptnr. Allen, Scruggs, Sossaman, & Thompson, 1988—. Asst. county atty. Shelby County Govt., Memphis, 1978-79; asst. city atty. City of Memphis, 1978-79. Author: Preventing Lawsuits for Wrongful Termination, 1995. N.Am. regional sec. Project Ams., Davidson, N.C., 1967-69. Capt. U.S. Army, 1973-76. Named Hon. City Councilman City of Memphis, 1982. Mem. ABA (labor and employment sect., litigation sect., EEO com.), Fla. Bar (labor and employment law sect.), Mgmt. Counsel Roundtable (chmn. 1986-87), Def. Rsch. Inst. (employment law com.), Tenn. Bar Assn. (labor law sect.), Memphis Bar Assn., The Justice Network (bd. dirs. 1990-93), Poplar Pike Arts Guild (bd. dirs. 1998—). Presbyterian. Home: 8411 Beaverwood Dr Germantown TN 38138-7641 Office: Allen Scruggs Sossaman & Thompson Brinkley Plz Ste 650 80 Monroe Ave Memphis TN 38103-2481 E-mail: wls@asstlaw.com.

SOSSI, MARIE FRANCES, elementary education educator; b. Newburgh, N.Y., Jan. 24, 1940; d. Lewis Joseph and Frances Mary Mele; m. Edward Joseph Sossi, Oct. 31, 1959; children: Mark, Beth, Luke, Matthew. BA, Mt. St. Mary's Coll., Newburgh, 1979; MSc in Edn., Coll. New Rochelle, N.Y., 1983; diploma profl. adminstrn., Fordham U., N.Y.C., 1989. Tchr. spl. edn. Newburgh Enlarged City Sch. Dist., 1979-89, tchr. reading, 1989-97, tchr. reading, writing jr. high sch., 1997—. Adj. prof. edn. Mt. St. Mary's Coll., Newburgh, 2000—. Bd. dirs. YWCA, Newburgh, Newburgh Day Nursery. Grantee Newburgh Tchrs. Content, 1995. Mem. Internat. Reading Assn., Nat. Council Tchrs. English, Mt. St. Mary's Coll. Alumni Assn. (former pres.), Delta Kappa Gamma. Roman Catholic. Address: PO Box 4137 New Windsor NY 12553

SOSSIADIS, KATINA, artist, filmmaker; b. Bethlehem, Pa., May 9, 1971; d. Emmanuel and Maria Stephanie (Skoutelas) S. BA, grad. with honors in art, Moravian Coll., 1993; MFA, U. Pa., 1996. One-woman shows include , Payne Gallery, Bethlehem, 1993, pvt. gallery, Tarpon Springs, Fla., 1994, The Artisan, Bethlehem, 1995—96, Connexians, Easton, 1996, Touchstone Theater, Bethlehem, 1994, Java Jack's Cafe, Bethlehem, 1995, exhibited in group shows, Moravian Coll., 1991, 1992, Rotunda Gallery, Bethlehem, 1992, Geometrics Gallery, Bethlehem, 1994—, Open Space Gallery, 1994—95, U. Pa., 1994, 1995, 1996, Art Alliance Phila., 1996, October Show, 1996, Washington Art Assn., 1997; co-dir.: (short film) Lynn's Wake, 1999. Finalist best short film, Austin film Festival, best short film and best actress, Nat. Film Festival, Drama, Greece; recipient Daniel W. Tereshko Meml. prize in studio art, Moravian Coll., 1993, Best Painting award, 1992, Silver Screenplay award, Atlantic City Film Festival, inclusion, Internat. Women's Festival Creteil, France; grantee gen. studies tchg., U. Pa. Democrat. Greek Orthodox. Home and Office: 159 Madison Ave Apt 4K New York NY 10016-5437

SOSTILIO, ROBERT FRANCIS, office equipment marketing consultant; b. Boston, Nov. 17, 1942; s. Natale J. and Louise Sostilio; m. Gail Marie McGuinness, Apr. 17, 1966. Student, U. Maine, 1960-61, Broward Jr. Coll., Ft. Lauderdale, 1967-70, Miami-Dade Jr. Coll., 1979. Product assurance engr. Saxon Copystatics, Miami, Fla., 1970-77; internat. svc. mgr. Saxon Export Corp., 1977-80; nat. svc. mgr. Cybernet Internat., Warren, N.J., 1980-81; mgr. nat. copier svc. Monroe Systems for Bus., Morris Plains, 1981-82; nat. OEM mgr. Panasonic Indsl. Co., Secaucus, 1982-86; assoc. dir. copier rsch. Dataquest, San Jose, Calif., 1987-90; mgr. product program Ricoh Corp., West Caldwell, N.J., 1986-87, dir. copier mktg., 1990-94, dir. strategic planning, 1994-96; group svc. dir. converging digital peripherals Cap Ventures, 1996—2000; pres., CEO Sostilio and Assocs. Internat. Inc., Ocala, Fla., 2002—. Editor: (newsletter) Multifunctionality, 1987, Color Copiers, 1989. Block capt. Meadow Ridge Civic Assn., Basking Ridge, NJ, 1985—87; sgt.-at-arms UNICO Nat., San Jose, 1990. With USN, 1964—67. Roman Catholic. Avocations: woodworking, home remodeling, dog training, travel, cooking. Office: Sostilia & Assocs Internat PO Box 830190 Ocala FL 34483

SOSTOWSKI, RICHARD MARK, physician, forensic psychiatrist, psychoanalyst; b. Peckville, Pa., Oct. 1, 1947; s. Henry and Josephine S.; m. Patricia Duncan, Aug. 27, 1971; children: Kristin, Aimee. MD, Jefferson Med. Coll., 1973. Diplomate Am. Bd. Psychiatry. Resident NYU Bellevue, N.Y.C., 1973-76; analytic tng. William Alanson White Inst., 1977-82; chmn. dept. psychiatry St. Michael's Med. Ctr., Newark, 1979-88, St. Barnabas Med. Ctr., Livingston, N.J., 1992-97; pvt. practice, Millburn, Bernardsville, 1988—. Fellow Am. Psychiat. Assn., Am. Acad. Psychoanalysis. Office: 75 Main St Millburn NJ 07041-1322 also: 250-1 Brook Hollow Ln Bernardsville NJ 07924

SOTER, GEORGE NICHOLAS, advertising executive; b. Chgo., May 16, 1924; s. Nicholas A. and Emily (Damascus) S.; m. Effie Hartocollis, Feb. 7, 1949; children: Nicholas, Thomas, Peter. Student, U. Chgo., 1947-51. Writer McCann-Erickson, Chgo., 1951-53; with Needham, Louis & Brorby, 1954-62, v.p., creative dir. N.Y.C., 1958-62; v.p., assoc. creative dir. Lennen & Newell Inc., 1962-67; v.p., co-dir. creative svcs., mgmt. supr. Kenyon & Eckhardt Inc., 1968-73; exec. v.p., creative dir. Pampuzac-Soter Assocs. Inc., 1974-76; sr. writer Marsteller Inc., 1980-82; v.p., creative Lord, Geller, Federico, Einstein, Inc., 1982-87; sr. v.p., creative dir. Great Scott Advt. Co. Inc., 1987-93; dir. Soter Advt. & Mktg. Consulting Svcs., 1993—. Founder, pres. Greek Island Ltd., N.Y.C., 1963—; dir. Interpub. Product Devel. Workshop, N.Y.C., 1967. With U.S. Army, 1943-47, ETO. Home: 404 Riverside Dr New York NY 10025-1861

SOTER, STEVEN, research scientist; BSc in Astronomy, UCLA, 1965; PhD in Astronomy, Cornell U., 1971. Rsch. asst. radio astronomy project Aerospace Corp., El Segundo, Calif., 1964—66; rsch. asst. Ctr. for Radiophysics and Space Rsch., Ithaca, NY, 1966—71, rsch. assoc., 1973—79, sr. rsch. assoc., 1980—87; fellow Miller Inst. for Basic Rsch. in Sci., Berkeley, Calif., 1971—73; asst. to dir. Smithsonian Instn. Nat. Air and Space Mus., 1988—97; rsch. scientist dept. astrophysics Am. Mus. Natural History, N.Y.C., 1997—. Co-dir. Helike Project, Greece, 1988—. Co-writer, head rsch. (TV series) Cosmos, 1977—80. Office: Am Mus Natural History Dept Astrophysics Central Park West at 81st St New York NY 10024*

SOTIRHOS, MICHAEL, ambassador; b. N.Y.C., Nov. 12, 1928; m. Estelle Manos; 2 children BBA, CCNY, 1950. Ptnr. Ariston Sales Co., Ltd., 1948, founder, chmn., 1958—; chmn. bd. Ariston Interior Designers, Inc., 1973-85; U.S. amb. to Jamaica, 1985-89; U.S. amb. to Greece Athens, 1989-93. Bd. dirs. Atlantic Bank of N.Y., Alexander S. Onassis Found.; cons. various internat. shipping & pharm. firms. Former mem. Nat. Vol. Service Adv. Council; former chmn. Internat. Ops. Com., Peace Corps; mem. nat. adv. council SBA, 1976; former chmn. Nat. Republican Heritage Groups Council Decorated comdr. Order of Distinction (Jamaica); recipient Man of Yr. award Nat. Rep. Heritage Groups Coun.

SOTIRIOS OF TORONTO, **See ATHANASSOULAS, SOTIRIOS**

SOTIRIOU-LEVENTIS, CHARIKLIA, chemist, educator, researcher; b. Nicosia, Cyprus, Jan. 20, 1960; came to U.S., 1982; d. Sotiris and Eleni (Papakyriacou) S.; m. Nicholas Leventis, Nov. 12, 1988; 1 child, Theodora. BS in Chemistry summa cum laude, U. Athens, Greece, 1982; PhD in Organic Chemistry, Mich. State U., 1987. Grad. asst. Mich. State U., East Lansing, 1982-87; rsch. assoc. Northeastern U., Boston, 1987-89, Harvard U., Cambridge, Mass., 1989-92; rsch. scientist Ciba Corning Diagnostics, East Walpole, 1992-93, sr. rsch. scientist, 1993; adj. asst. prof. U. Mo., Rolla, 1994-95, asst. prof., 1995-2001, assoc. prof., 2001—. Contbr. articles to profl. jours. including Jour. Am. Chem. Soc., Jour. Organic Chemistry, Tetrahedron; patentee hydrophilic Acridinium Esters. Fellow SOHIO, 1986; recipient Greek Inst. State scholarship awards, 1978-82, Gustel Giessen Advanced Rsch. award Barnett Inst. Chem. Analysis and Materials Sci., 1988, Outstanding Tchg. award U. Mo., Rolla, 1996-97, 99-2000. Mem. AAAS, Am. Chem. Soc. Office: U Mo-Rolla Dept Chemistry Rolla MO 65409-0001

SOTIROPOULOS, DIMITRIOS A. engineering educator, academic administrator; b. Rhodes, Greece, Apr. 3, 1953; came to U.S., 1971; s. Anastasios D. and Kathryn H. Sotiropoulos; m. Stella Parhas, June 15, 1986; children: Anastasios, Vaggelis, Alexander. BA, Drew U., 1973; MS, U. Calif., San Diego, 1979, PhD, 1983. Asst. prof. U. Ky., Lexington, 1984-85, Northwestern U., Evanston, Ill., 1985-88; prof. Tech. U. Crete, Chania, Greece, 1988-99, dir., 1995-99, pres., 1996-99; v.p. acad. affairs So. Poly. State U., Marietta, Ga., 1999—. Vis. prof. Ill. Inst. Tech., Chgo., 1995-96; invited lectr. Expressions of Culture from Greece in the U.K., London, 1998; mem. adv. bd. Acta Mechanica, Springer-Verlag, 1996—, Ultrasonics, Elsevier, 1998—; chair organizing com. 21st Century Techs., Chania, 1998, Arts in Engring.-Pub. Fora, Marietta, 2000. Contbr. articles to profl. jours.; editor: Mechanical Waves for Composite Structures Characterization, 2000. Mem. Nat. Coun. Edn., Ministry of Edn., Athens, Greece, 1996-99, Supreme Nat. Pers. Coun., 1997-99; bd. dirs. Mediterranean Ctr. Architecture, Chania, 1996-99. Conf. grantee UNESCO, U.S. Army Rsch. Lab., Chani, 2000, rsch. and project grantee European Cmty., 1997, 98, 99. Fellow Am. Acad. Mechanics; mem. ASME (vice chair, mem. chair, AMD com.), Am. Assn. Higher Edn., Coun. for Advancement and Support of Edn., Am. Soc. Engring. Edn. Avocations: playing piano, writing poetry, soccer, politics. E-mail: jsotirop@spsu.edu.

SOTO, RAMONA, training specialist; b. East Chicago, Ind., Apr. 14, 1963; d. Robert Rudy and Antonia (Perez) S. Student, Purdue U., 1982-86, U. Ill., Chgo., 1990, DePaul U., 1992-95. Salesperson The Gap, Inc., Ind., 1979-84, asst. mgr. Ind. and Ill., 1984-88, tng. mgr. Ill., 1988-90; tng. specialist Montgomery Ward & Co., 1990-93; temp. worker The Richard Michael Group, Chgo., 1993, Resort Travel Corp, Oakbrook Terrace, Ill., 1993; ind. tng. cons. Chgo., 1994—. Tutor Cabrini Green Tutoring Program, Chgo., 1991-98, tutor tng. mgr., 1991-94, tutor preparing an attitude for learning, leadership and success, 1991-94, jr. asst. advisor and coord., 1995-96. Mem. ASTD. Avocations: fitness, reading, volunteering, cooking, biking. Home: 1130 W Morse Ave Chicago IL 60626-3507

SOTO, ROBERTO FERNANDO EDUARDO, journalist; b. Oct. 12, 1960; s. Antonio J. and Margarita (Bonachea) S.; children: Natasha, Sabrina. BFA in Speech/Theater, Fla. Internat. U., Miami; MA in Comm./Broadcasting, Paterson State Coll., 1987. News prodr. NBC-TV, 1979-87; exec. prodr. Univision, L.A., 1987-89; News dir. Telemundo, L.A., N.Y.C., 1989-91; divsn. chief USIA, Washington, 1991-92; prodn. mgr. WJAN-TV, Miami, 1992-93; sta.

mgr. KTRG-TV, San Antonio, 1994-95; dir. news svcs. Telemundo, L.A., 1996; sta. mgr. Cablevision, N.Y.C., 1997-98; bur. chief AP Television News, 1999—. Mem. AFTRA, Soc. Broadcast Engrs., Soc. Profl. Journalists. Office: AP Television News 1995 Broadway New York NY 10023-5882 E-mail: robertosoto_ub@yahoo.com.

SOTO-FERNANDEZ, LILIANA, education educator; b. Banes, Oriente, Cuba, Apr. 25, 1954; came to U.S., 1970; d. Juan Antonio and Laudelina Soto; m. Vicente Antonio Fernandez, Aug. 20, 1977. BA magna cum laude, Bklyn. Coll., 1976; MPhil, CUNY, 1986, PhD, 1994. Fellow CUNY, 1994, asst. prof., 1997—. Adj. asst. prof. Bklyn. Coll., 1985-97, St. John's U., Staten Island, N.Y., 1989-97, Wagner Coll., Staten Island, 1996; edn1. cons. St. John Neumann, Staten Island, 2000—. Author: La Autobiografia Ficticia en Miguel de Unamuno, Garmen Martin Gaite y Sereprún, 1996, Grolier, 2000; editor: Voices, 1995 RCIA tchr., edn. cons. St. John Neumann, Staten Island, 2000—. Mem. AATSP (newsletter editor, exec. bd. dirs. 2000—), MLA, Latino Civic Assn. (exec. bd. dirs. 2001), Fgn. Lang. Soc. (co-faculty adv. 1997—), Sigma Delta Pi, Sigma Delta Mu (hon.), Circulo de Cultura Panamericano. Roman Catholic.

SOTOMAYOR, SONIA, judge; b. N.Y.C., June 25, 1954; d. Sonia and Celina (Baez) Sotomayor; m. Kevin Edward Noonan, Aug. 14, 1976 (div. 1983). AB, Princeton U., 1976; JD, Yale U., 1979; LLD honoris causa (hon.) , 1999, JD (hon.) honoris causa, 2001. Bar: N.Y. 1980, U.S. Dist. Ct. (ea. and so. dists.) N.Y. 1984. Asst. dist. atty. Office of Dist. Atty. County of N.Y., N.Y.C., 1979—84; assoc., ptnr. Pavia & Harcourt, 1984—92; fed. judge U.S. Dist. Ct. (so. dist.) N.Y., 1992—98; cir. judge U.S. Ct. Appeals (2d Cir.), 1998—. Adj. prof. NYU Sch. Law, 1998; lectr. law Columbia Law Sch., 1999. Editor: Yale U. Law Rev., 1979. Mem. State Adv. Panel on Inter-Group Rels., N.Y.C., 1990—92, 1990—91; bd. dirs. P.R. Legal Def. and Edn. Fund, 1980—92, State of N.Y. Mortgage Agy., N.Y.C., 1987—92, N.Y.C. Campaign Fin. Bd., 1988—92. Mem.: ABA, Am. Philos. Soc., N.Y. Women's Bar Assn., P.R. Bar Assn., Hispanic Bar Assn., Phi Beta Kappa. Office: US Courthouse 40 Foley SqRm 410 New York NY 10007-1502

SOUDER, MARK EDWARD, congressman; b. Ft. Wayne, Ind., July 18, 1950; s. Edward Getz and Irma (Fahling) S.; m. Diane Kay Zimmer, July 28; children: Brooke Diane, Nathan Elias, Zachary. BS, Ind. U., Ft. Wayne, 1972; MBA, U. Notre Dame, 1974. Mgmt. trainee Crossroads Furniture Co., Houston, 1974; mktg. mgr. Gabberts Furniture & Studio, Mpls., 1974-76; mktg. mgr., exec. v.p. Souder's Furniture & Studio, Grabill, Ind., 1976-80, pres., 1981-84; econ. devel. liaison for U.S. Rep. Dan Coats, from 1983; mem. U.S. Congress from Ind. 4th Dist., 1995—. Mem. edn. and workforce com., govt. reform and oversight com., small bus. com., natural resources com. Publicity chmn. Grabill County Fair, 1977—; advisor Dan Coats for Congress Com., 1980-81; mem. Ind. Area Devel. Coun.; mem. bus. alumni adv. com. Ind. U.-Ft. Wayne. Mem. Midwest Home Furnishings Assn. (dir. 1976-84, past treas., exec. v.p.), Ft. Wayne, Grabill C. of C., Allen County Hist. Soc., Alumni Assn. Ind. U. at Ft. Wayne (dir., past pres.), Alumni Assn. U. Notre Dame. Republican. Mem. Apostolic Christian Ch. Home: 13733 Ridgeview Ct Grabill IN 46741 Office: US House Reps 1227 Longworth House Office Building Washington DC 20515-1404*

SOUDER, SUSAN, lawyer; b. Washington, Sept. 20, 1956; BA, U. Md., 1978; JD, Georgetown U., 1981. Bar: Md. 1981. Trial atty. U.S. Dept. Justice, Washington, 1981-85; spl. asst. U.S. atty. Los Angeles, 1983; ptnr. Gordon, Feinblatt, Rothman, Balt., 1985-94, Ballard Spahr Andrews & Ingersoll, Balt., 1994-97; pvt. practice, Catonsville, Md., 1997—. Mem.: FBA, Women's Bar Assn., Baltimore County Bar Assn., Md. Bar Assn. Office: 300 Frederick Rd Ste 100 Catonsville MD 21228

SOUDERS, BERYL V. medical/surgical and rehabilitation-detox nurse; b. Pottsville, Pa., Mar. 10, 1938; d. Roy Ralph and Susan Leola (Harding) Dohner; m. Thomas Griffith Souders, Sept. 17, 1960; children: Susan Leith Goold, Miriam Irene, Martha Lynn Janczewski. Diploma, Allentown (Pa.) Gen. Hosp., 1959. Cert. port-a-cath care and use. Charge nurse night shift Allentown Hosp.; camp nurse East Pa.Boy Scouts, Girl Scouts and Campfire Girls, Marshalls Creek, Phila., Boyertown, Pottstown, Lancaster; oper. rm. nurse Lancaster (Pa.)-St. Joseph Hosp.; staff nurse on med.-surg. trauma unit, part-time detox nurse and rehab. unit nurse. Med. Coll. Hosp., Bucks County Hosp., Warminster, Pa., Warminster Gen. Hosp., Allegheny Univ. Hosps.; ret., 1997. Camp nurse United Ch. of Christ Camps. Active Girl Scouts USA, 1969-79, Campfire Girls, Inc., 1977-87; assoc. advisor Explorer Post 173, Boy Scouts Am., 1977-85; organist, music dir. St. Mark's Reformed Ch., 1974—; chaplain, past treas. Huntingdon Valley Fire Co. Ladies Aux.; pres., v.p., chmn. pers. com., bd. dirs. Christian Concern, Inc., Collegeville, Pa. Mem.: Huntingdon Valley Women's Club (v.p., exec. bd.). Home: 525 Welsh Rd Philadelphia PA 19115-1817

SOUDERS, JEAN SWEDELL, artist, educator; b. Braham, Minn., July 13, 1922; d. John Almond and Frances Johanna (Alm) Swedell; m. Robert Livingston Souders, Sept. 22, 1945 (dec. 1985). BA, Duluth (Minn.) State Coll., 1944; postgrad., Minn. Sch. of Art, 1944, Walker Sch. of Art, 1948; MA, U. Iowa, 1955, MFA, 1956. Instr. art St. Olaf Coll., Northfield, Minn., 1947-50; instr. craft U. Minn., 1951; prof. art history painting Calif. State U., Chico, Calif., 1957-74, prof. art history, 1959-60, faculty gen. studies Calif., 1971-73. Exhbn. Creative Art Ctr., 1975, Des Moines Art Ctr., Crocker Mus. of Art, Chico State U. and Chico Art Gallery, 1994, and various others; paintings in over 200 collections. Mem.: Women Artists Assn. San Francisco, Mus. of Women in the Arts, Nat. Archives (work and exhibit records). Lutheran. Avocations: photography, hiking, backpacking, classical music.

SOUDERS, NICOLE ELIZABETH, oncological nurse, researcher; b. Wilkinsburg, Pa., June 4, 1943; d. Nicholas and Elizabeth Agnes (Martinac) Kauric; m. Donald Souders (div.); children: Donald, Jr., Audrey L. Student, Warren County C.C., Washington, N.J., 1982-89; BS in Edn., Pa. State U., 1964; postgrad., Marywood Coll., 1985; ADN, Northampton C.C., Bethlehem, Pa., 1991. RN, Pa., N.J. Tchr. Easton (Pa.) Are High Sch., 1964-67; rsch. and adminstr. asst. Warren County C.C., 1984-85; tchr. Am. Bankers Assn., Easton and Phillipsburg, N.J., 1989; tng. instr. Chem. Bank of N.J., Morristown, 1986-89; residential program worker Regional Devel. Corp., Pottsville, Pa., 1985; receptionist Warren Med. Assocs., Phillipsburg, N.J., 1985-87; nursing asst. Care Ctr. of Lopatcong, 1988-89, St. Luke's Hosp., Bethlehem, 1989-91, nurse, 1991-95; home health nurse Easton (Pa.) Hosp. Home Health Svcs., 1995—. Avocations: reading, cooking. Home: 598 John Mitchell Ave Phillipsburg NJ 08865-1441

SOUED, STEVEN MICHAEL, physician; b. Bklyn., Dec. 17, 1960; s. William Anthony and Nadia (Tomeh) S. BA, U. Buffalo, 1982; MD, U. Guadalajara/N.Y. Med. Coll., Mexico and Valhalla, 1989. Diplomate Am. Bd. Internal Medicine. Intern L.I. Coll. Hosp., Bklyn., 1989-90; resident S.I. (N.Y.) U. Hosp., 1991-93; police surgeon N.Y.C. Police Dept., 1994—; physician Univ. Physicians Group, 1994—; pvt. practice N.Y.C., 2002—; mem. staff Lenox Hill Hosp., 2002—. Preceptor S.I. Univ. Hosp., 1995, med. attending, 1994, Luth. Med. Ctr., 1994. Mem. AMA, Am. Coll. Physicians.

SOUHAM, GÉRARD, communications executive; b. Paris, May 30, 1928; s. Lucien and Mary-Françoise (Husson) S.; m. Eliane Meyrat, June 23, 1951; children: Glenn (dec.), Yan, Philip. Diploma, Am. Community Sch., Paris, 1948; cert., Ecole Commerciale de Paris. Chargé de mission State Dept., Europe, 1950-52; pub. info. officer Allied Air Forces NATO, Fontainebleau, 1953-55; chmn. bd., chief exec. officer J. Walter Thompson, Paris, 1955-75, v.p. N.Y.C., 1970-75; prin. S3C Gerard Souham Group Communication Cos., Paris and Lausanne, Switzerland, 1975—, SC3 Gerard Souham Group Communication Cos., N.Y.C., 1979—. Bd. dirs. Am. Overseas Meml., I.T. Fin., AVON, France, Mattel-France; chmn. bd. Turner Prodn. Europe, 1994—98, IT Fin. Corp.; vice chmn. bd. Avon. Author: Général Souham Comte de l'Empire, 1964, Impressions sur..., 1970, Souham, 1989, Sur les Champs de Bataille de la Révolution et de l'Empire, 1990. Mem. pvt. sector internat. and pub. rels. coms. USIA, 1985; mem. world bd. govs. USO, Washington, 1984, chmn. fundraising com., 1989—, pres., Paris, 1995, bd. dirs., 2000—. Decorated officer Legion of Honor (France); officer Order of Leopold, knight Belgian Crown (Belgium). Mem. Internat. Advt. Assn. (v.p. pub. svc., bd. dirs.), Internat. Inst. Strategic Studies London, France, USA (bd. dirs.), Am. Overseas Meml. Assn. (bd. dirs. 1988—). Clubs: HM Guards Polo (Windsor, Eng.) (life); Polo de Bagatelle (Paris); N.Y. Athletic; Yacht of Monaco. Roman Catholic. Avocation: collecting fine bindings. Office: Souham Group Comm 500 5th Ave New York NY 10110-0002

SOUHAMI, LUIS, physician, radiation oncology; b. Vitoria, Brazil, Feb. 22, 1949; arrived in Can., 1987; s. Luis and Carolina R. (Serra) S.; m. Julia Maria Lopes, Oct. 22, 1974; children: Marcelo, Daniel. MD, Escola Medicina Cirurgia, Rio de Janeiro, 1972. Diplomate Am. Bd. Radiology. Chmn. dept. radiotherapy Instituto Nacional Cancer, Rio de Janeiro, 1981-85, chief med. divsn., 1986-87; prof. McGill U., Montreal, Que., Can., 1987-95, Ont., Can., 19955, assoc. dir. dept. radio-oncology Can., 1991—. Advisor WHO, Geneva, Switzerland, 1991; cons. Govt. Que., Montreal, Can., 1994-95; mem. Union Internat. Contre le Cancer, Internat. Sci. Adv. Com., 1995; vis. prof. Instituto Nacional Can cer, Rio de Janeiro, 1992, Queen's U., Kingston, Can., 1993. Editor: Revista Brasileira Cancerologia, 19825; mem. editl. bd. Internat. Jour. Radiation Oncology Biology Physics, Current Oncology; contbr. papers to profl. jours., chpts. to books. Mem. Internat. Stereotactic Radiosurgery Soc. (bd. dirs. 19955), Am. Soc. Therapeutic Radiology and Oncology, Can. Assn. Radiation Oncologists (dir. Que. 1995-97). Avocation: sports. Office: McGill U Radiation Oncology 1650 Cedar Ave Montreal QC Canada H3G 1A4 E-mail: luis.souhami@muhc.mcgill.ca.

SOUJAH, JAKE, investment company executive; b. Beirut, Lebanon, Mar. 11, 1954; came to U.S., 1984; s. Atif M. and Mona Aida (Ashkar) S. BS, Am. U. Beirut, 1976; MBA, George Washington U., 1986. V.p. sales Arapco Internat., Inc., Beirut, 1976-81, Arapco Ltd., Inc., Riyadh, Saudi Arabia, 1981-84; exec. v.p, coo Aramnet Internat., Inc., Washington, 1986-91; chmn., ceo Orca Holdings Inc., San Francisco, 1990—. Ceo Ivan Holdings Co., San Francisco, 1992—; bd. dirs. Personal Image Inc., San Rafael, Calif., Centauri Comms., Inc., San Francisco, K. Lee Internat. Corp., San Francisco. Avocations: birdwatching, skiing, sailing. Home: 41 Sutter St # 1325 San Francisco CA 94104-4903

SOULÉ, CHARLES RAYMOND, JR. psychologist; b. El Paso, Tex., Feb. 9, 1954; s. Charles Raymond Sr. and Carolina (Bencomo) S. BA in History with honors, U. Tex., El Paso, 1975; PhD in Psychology, U. Calif., Berkeley, 1992; cert. in family therapy, Yeshiva U., 1996; candidate postdoctoral program psychoanalysis, NYU, 2000—. Lectr., program coord. Yale Child Study Ctr., New Haven, 1990-93; sr. psychologist North Ctrl. Bronx (N.Y.) Hosp., 1993-95, dir. child and adolescent crisis intervention program, 1995-97; dir. clin. svcs. Roberto Clemente Ctr.-Gouverneur Hosp., N.Y.C., 1997-98; dir. partial hospitalization program North Ctrl. Bronx (N.Y.) Hosp., 1998-99; dir. sch.-based mental health program N.Y. Presbyn. Hosp., 1999—; asst. clin. prof. med. psychology in psychiatry Columbia U. Coll. Physicians and Surgeons, N.Y.C., 1999—; pvt. practice, 1999—. Instr. cont. edn. program Rutgers Sch. Social Work, New Brunswick, N.J., 1993—; co-chair Bronx child and adolescent svcs. com. Bronx Fedn. Mental Health, 1995-97; adj. clin. assoc. clin. psychology program CUNY, 1999—, Ferkauf Grad. Sch. Psychology, Yeshiva U., 1999-2001. Co-author: Advancing Family Preservation Practice, 1993. Mem. bd. dirs. Pacific Ctr. Human Growth, Berkeley, 1987-88. Tng. fellow NIMH, 1983-86. Mem. APA, N.Y. State Psychol. Assn. Roman Catholic. Office: NY Presbyn Hosp Divsn Pediat Psychiatry Babies Hosp Rm 619 N 622 W 168th St New York NY 10032-3720

SOULE, GARDNER BOSWORTH, writer; b. Paris, Dec. 16, 1913; s. Edgar Huckabee and Floy DeVore (Perfect) S.; m. Janie Lee McDowell, Sept. 20, 1940 (dec.); m. Mary Muir Downing, Apr. 23, 1994. BA, Rice Inst., 1933; BS, Columbia U., 1935, MS, 1936. With A.P., N.Y.C., 1936-41, Newspaper PM, 1942; mng. editor Better Homes and Gardens, Des Moines, 1946-50. Free-lance writer articles, books, N.Y.C., 1950— ; Author: The Maybe Monsters, 1963, Tomorrow's World of Science, 1963, Gemini and Apollo, 1964, The Mystery Monsters, 1965, Trail of the Abominable Snowman, 1966, The Ocean Adventure: Science Explores the Depths of the Sea, 1966, Sea Rescue, 1966, UFO's and IFO's, 1967, Undersea Frontiers, 1968, Under the Sea, 1969, Strange Things Animals Do, 1970, Wide Ocean, 1970, The Greatest Depths, 1970, Surprising Facts, 1971, New Discoveries in Oceanography, 1974, Wide Ocean, Brit. edit, 1974, Remarkable Creatures of the Seas, 1975, Men Who Dared The Sea: The Ocean Adventures of the Ancient Mariners, 1976, German edit., 1978, The Long Trail: How Cowboys and Longhorns Opened The West, 1976, Mystery Monsters of the Deep, 1981, Mystery Creatures of the Jungle, 1982, Antarctica, 1985, Christopher Columbus, 1988; Contbr.: articles to mags. including Boys' Life. Served to lt. USNR, 1943-46. Mem. Authors League, Columbia University Club (N.Y.C.), Sigma Delta Chi, Sigma Nu. Died Oct. 26, 2000.

SOULE, GEORGE ALAN, literature educator, writer; b. Fargo, N.D., Mar. 3, 1930; s. George Alan and Ruth Georgia (Knudsen) S.; m. Carolyn Richards, Nov. 24, 1961; 1 child, Katherine. BA, Carleton Coll., 1947; postgrad., Corpus Christi Coll., Cambridge (Eng.) U., 1952-53; MA, Yale U., 1956, PhD, 1960. Instr. English lit. Oberlin (Ohio) Coll., 1958-60; asst. prof. U. Wis., Madison, 1960-62; from asst. prof. to prof. Carleton Coll., Northfield, Minn., 1962-95, prof. emeritus, 1995—, chair English dept., 1980—83; tchr. Cannon Valley Elder Collegium, 1998—; also bd. dirs. Cons. Ednl. Testing Svc., Princeton, N.J., 1967-84, 94-97. Author: Four British Women Novelists: An Annotated and Critical Secondary Biblioigraphy, 1998; editor: Theatre of the Mind, 1974; contbr. articles to profl. jours. Mem. Libr. Bd., City of Northfield, 1997-2000; bd. dirs. Northfield Area Found., 2001-02. With U.S. Army, 1954-55. Internat. fellow Rotary, 1952-53, Sterling pre-doctoral fellow Yale U., 1957-58. Mem.: Anthony Powell Soc., Angela Thirkell Soc., The Iris Murdoch Soc., The Charles Lamb Soc., Friends of Dove Cottge, Boswell Soc. of Auchinleck, Johnson Soc. of Lichfield, Oxford and Cambridge Club, Rotary, Phi Beta Kappa. Episcopalian. Avocations: cooking, traveling, Jeopardy (Champion Sr. Tournament 1990). Home: 313 Nevada St Northfield MN 55057-2346 Office: Carleton Coll 1 N College St Northfield MN 55057-4001 Fax: 507-645-5099. E-mail: gsoule@charter.net.

SOULE, JEFFREY LYN, urban planner, consultant; b. Watertown, N.Y., Apr. 8, 1953; s. Robert William and Melva (Howe) S. BA cum laude, Colgate U., 1975; M in City and Regional Planning, Harvard U., 1978. Sr. resource planner N.Y. State Commn. on Tug Hill, Watertown, 1978-80; rural devel. specialist USDA, 1980-82, policy analyst Office of Rural Devel., 1982-84, policy coord., 1984-87; leadership coord. Nat. Endowment Arts Design Divsn., 1987-92; dir. Ctr. for Rural Pa., 1992-95; policy dir. Am. Planning Assn., Washington, 1995—. Phys. planning coord. Park Heights Community Corp., Balt., 1986-87; leader Planner Cert. Tng. Program, Washington, 1986-92; faculty Mayor's Inst. for City Design, Washington, 1989-90; program dir. Your Town: Designing It's Future, 1990-92; lectr. on urban design; lectr. growth mgmt. U. Md., 1999—. Author: Design Competitions for Public Facilities, 1989; editor; Rural Pennsylvania; contbr. articles to profl. jours. including Planning mag. Mem. Countryside Stewardship Exchange team, 1993; v.p. Pa. Downtown Ctr., 1994-96; trustee Nat. Ctr. for Heritage Devel. 1994—; mem. bd. dirs. Internat. Land Econ. Soc.; leader U.S./China land use planning exch., 1998. N.Y. State Regents scholar, 1971. Fellow AICP; mem. Am. Inst. Cert. Planners, Am. Planning Assn., Beta Theta Pi, Lambda Alpha Internat. (pres. Balt. chpt. 1995-97), Cosmos Club. Office: Am Planning Assn 1776 Massachusetts Ave NW Washington DC 20036-1904

SOULE, LUCILE SNYDER, pianist, music educator; b. Fargo, N.D., Sept. 21, 1922; d. Roy Henry and Gene (McGhee) Snyder; m. Leon Cyprian Soule Jr., Sept. 1, 1954 (dec. Dec. 1994); children: Robert Leon, Anne Lucile. MusB, MusB in Edn., MacPhail Coll. Music, 1943; MA, Smith Coll., Northampton, Mass., 1945; postgrad. diploma, Juilliard Sch. Music, 1948. Organist various chs., Mont., La., and Ohio, 1935-68; instr. Smith Coll., Northampton, 1945-46; freelance pianist, accompanist Juilliard Sch. Music, also pvt. groups and individuals, N.Y.C., 1946-49; from instr. to assoc. prof. Newcomb Coll., Tulane U., New Orleans, 1949-61; staff pianist, soloist New Orleans Symphony, 1954-61; guest artist Contemporary Music Festival La. State U., Baton Rouge, 1953-61; lectr. Lakewood br. Ohio State U., 1964-66; music tchr. East Cleveland (Ohio) Pub. Schs., 1969-85; music dir. East Cleveland Theater, 1985—2001, cons. and mgr. of spl. programs, 2001—; pianist for Zhao Rongchun, Cleve., 1995—2001, William Dempsey, Cleve., 1997—. Pres. New Orleans Music Tchrs. Assn., 1958-59; publicity chair Rocky River (Ohio) Chamber Music Soc., 1963-67; v.p. Cleve. chpt. Am. Orff Schluwerk Assn., 1974-75, presenter in field; mem. The Trio, 1998—. Pianist (compact disc with Zhao) Master of the Erhu, 1996; debut recital with Zhao at Weill Recital Hall, Carnegie Hall, 1999. Mem. Citizens Adv. Group, East Cleveland, 1967-69; vocal coach, composer Serenity Prayer, 1998—, The Crown of Life, 1999. Woolley Found. fellow, 1950-51, Tchg. fellow Case Western Res. U., 1967-68, Smith Coll., 1943-45; Juilliard Sch. Music scholar, 1946-48. Mem. Darius Millhaud Soc. (bd. dirs. 1984—), Fortnightly Mus. Club (corr. sec. 1996-2000), Lecture Recital Club (bd. dirs. 1993-95), Mu Phi Epsilon. Democrat. Christian Scientist. Avocations: church work, gourmet cooking, travel, art. Home and Office: 15617 Hazel Rd East Cleveland OH 44112-2904

SOULE, ROBERT D. safety and health educator, administrator; b. DeTour Village, Mich., July 8, 1941; s. Harold M. and Mildred M. (Abear) S.; m. Mary Ann Kretzschmar, June 13, 1964; children: Dawn Marie, Robert John, Rebecca Ann. BS, Mich. State U., 1963; MS in Chem. Engring., Purdue U., 1965; EdD in Higher Edn. Adminstrn., U. Pitts., 1993. Cert. safety profl. cert in indsl. hygiene; registered profl. engr., Mich., Ind., Tex. Calif. Environ. health engr. Dow Chem. Co., Midland, Mich., 1965-69, sr. indsl. hygienist Freeport, Tex., 1969-70; v.p. Clayton Environ. Cons., Southfield, Mich., 1970-77; prof. safety and health Indiana U. of Pa., 1977—, assoc. dean health & human svcs., 1999-2000. Cons. in pvt. practice, Indiana, Pa., 1977—. Contbr. chpts. to books; mem. editorial bd. Am. Indsl. Hygiene Assn. Jour., 1979-85, Occupational Hazards, 1992-98, Professional Safety, 1998—. Fellow Am. Indsl. Hygiene Assn.; mem. Am. Conf. Govtl. Indsl. Hygienists, Am. Soc. Safety Engrs. (profl.), Am. Acad. Indsl. Hygiene (sec.-treas.). Office: Indiana U Pa Safety Scis Dept 123 Johnson Indiana PA 15705-1087 E-mail: bobsoule@grove.iup.edu.

SOULE, ROBERT GROVE, lawyer; b. Boston, Jan. 12, 1958; s. Augustus W. and Mary R. Soule; m. Maura Kelley, Aug. 21, 1982; children: Courtney K., Katherine W., Zachary A. BA, Harvard U., 1979; JD, Suffolk U., 1983. Bar: Mass. 1983, U.S. Dist. Ct. Mass. 1983. Of counsel First Am. Title Ins. Co., Boston, 1982-85, asst. regional counsel, 1985-87; New Eng. states counsel Minn. Title Ins. Co., 1987-89; N.E. regional counsel Old Republic Title Ins. Co., 1989-93; mgr. nat. divsn. Lawyers Title Ins. Corp. (LandAmerica), 1993—. Contbr. articles to profl. jours., chpts. to books. Mem. Am. Land Title Assn., New Eng. Land Title Assn. (bd. dirs. 1996—, pres. 1999—), Mass. Conveyancers Assn. (title standards com. 1987—, exec. com. 1989-92), Mass. Bar Assn. Office: LandAmerica One Washington Mall Boston MA 02108-2804 Fax: 617-619-4848. E-mail: rsoule@landam.com.

SOULTOUKIS, DONNA ZOCCOLA, library director; b. Princeton, N.J., July 28, 1949; d. Peter Joseph and Josephine (Taraschi) Zoccola; m. Dimitrios Athanasios Soultoukis, July 26, 1980. AB, Georgian Ct. Coll., Lakewood, N.J., 1971; MS, Drexel U., 1976; Cert., Italian U. for Foreigners, Perugia, 1974. Libr. asst. Geology Libr. Princeton U., 1971-73; libr. Friends Hosp., Phila., 1976-86, dir. libr. svcs., 1986-98; head libr. Temple U., Sch. Podiatric, 1998-99; ref. libr. MCP/Hahnemann U., Phila., 1999-2000; sr. info. scientist Bristol-Myers Squibb Pharm. Rsch. Inst., Hopewell, N.J., N.J., 2000; libr. Our Lady of Lourdes Sch. Nursing, Camden, NJ, 2001—. Cons. Lower Bucks Hosp., Bristol, Pa., 1991-95. Vol. outreach program Old St. Joseph's Ch., Phila., 1992-95, sanctuary min., 1993—, mem. pastoral coun., 1995-98, 2001--, bd. ministers 1999-2001, mem. outreach program, bd. dirs., 1997—. Mem. Med. Libr. Assn. (chair mental librs. divsn. 1991-93, chair rsch. com. 1996—), Spl. Librs. Assn. (Phila. chpt. bd. dirs. 1985-88, pres. 1987-84, chmn. long-range planning 1993, mem. adv. bd. 1995—, sec. solo divsn. 2000-01). Avocations: travel, cooking. Home: 290 Cinnabar Ln Yardley PA 19067-5717

SOULTZ, JERRY LEE, small business owner; b. Marion, Ind., July 26, 1949; s. J. Phillip and Wilma Jean (Underwood) S.; divorced; children: Brandley, Brooke; m. Margaret Peg Richards, Mar. 1, 1981; step-children: Andrew Brewer, Betsy Brewer, Aaron Brewer. Student, IU., Kokomo. Owner, mgr. JerPeg Contracting, Inc., Marion, 1985--. Mem. Local 147 Ironworkers Union. Home: 11240 E Noos Marion IN 46952 Office: JerPeg Contracting Inc 1795 E Loew Rd PO Box 991 Marion IN 46952-0991

SOUNEY, PAUL FREDERICK, pharmacist; b. Bristol, Conn., Mar. 29, 1947; s. Frederick Raymond and Julia Yvonne (Weeks) S.; m. Billie Lorraine Petersen, Apr. 7, 1972; children: Jared Paul, Jeremy Christian. BS, Northeastern U., 1971, MS, 1984. Drug info. pharmacist Hartford (Conn.) Hosp., 1971-77; pharmacy supervisor Boston Hosp. for Women, 1977-81; clin. rsch. pharmacist Channing Labs./Harvard Med. Sch., Boston, 1981-92; med. info. scientist Astra Merck Inc., Providence, 1992-97; field sci. ptnr. N.E. Customer Ctr. Astra Pharms., L.P., 1997-99; med. mktg. scientific leader AstraZeneca Pharms., Wayne, Pa., 1999-2000, group dir. med. mktg., 2000, nat. sci. dir. GI, 2000—. Dir. drug info. Brigham and Women's Hosp., Boston, 1981-90, dir. clin. pharmacy, 1985-92; cons. in field. Editor: Comprehensive Pharmacy Review, 4th edit., 2000; contbr. articles to profl. jours.; editl. adv. panelist Internat. Pharm. Abstracts, Pharmacy Practice News, Am. Jour. Gastroenterology. Treas. men's club First Congl. Ch., 1993-2000; vol. Mansfield (Mass.) Animal Shelter, 1990-94. Mem. Am. Coll. Clin. Pharmacy, Am. Soc. Health Sys. Pharmacists, Am. Pharmaceutical Assn., Acad. Managed Case Pharmacy, New Eng. Coun. Hosp. Pharmacists, Northeastern Univ. Alumnae Assn. Office: AstraZeneca Pharms 725 Chesterbrook Blvd Wayne PA 19087-5677 E-mail: paul.souney@astrazeneca.com.

SOURBRINE, RICHARD DON, II, architect; b. Akron, Ohio, Aug. 26, 1965; s. Richard Don and Clara Violet (Garritano) S. BS, Kent State U., 1987, BArch, 1988. Lic. architect, Ariz., Ohio, Calif.; cert. architect Nat. Coun. Archtl. Registration Bds. Intern-architect James Reinbolt Architect, Inc., Akron, Ohio, 1986-88, Reinbolt, Evans & Mann Inc, Akron, 1988-94; architect David Pelligra and Architects, Inc., Cuyahoga Falls, Ohio, 1994-95, Ziska Architects and Assocs., Cleve., 1995-98; project dir. van Dijk Westlake Reed Leskosky Architects, 1998—; project architect van Dijk Pace Westlake Architects, Phoenix. Trustee LeBlond Housing Corp., 1996-98. Mem. Artlink Phoenix. Scholar Kent (Ohio) State U., 1983. Mem. AIA, Nat. Trust for Hist. Preservation, Alfa Romeo Owners Club, Jaguar Clubs of N.Am. Republican. Roman Catholic. Avocations: traveling, automobiles. Home: 3445 W Louise Dr Phoenix AZ 85027 Office: van Dijk Westlake Reed Leskosky Architects 1 E Camelback Rd Ste 690 Phoenix AZ 85012-1651 E-mail: rsour@vpwa.com. *Personal philosophy: Words I have come to live by: Whatever it takes.*

SOURIAL, ALFY SAIF, surgeon; b. Tanta, Egypt, Jan. 10, 1928; s. Saif and Erada Atiah (El-Sanady) S.; m. Elizabeth Ann Siebert, 1960; children: Edward S., Wynn Heather; m. Shirley Ann Maniscalco, Oct. 7, 1971; children: Dean Michael, Jill Soraya. MD, Cairo U., 1950. Diplomate Am. Bd. Surgery. Intern Doctors Hosp., Cleve., 1955-56, resident in surgery, 1956-57, Huron Rd. Hosp., Cleve., 1957-60; fellow in surgery Case Western Res. U., 1960-61; surgeon Valley Hosp., Pomona, Calif., 1962-72; pvt practice Thousand Oaks, 1970-93; active staff Los Robles Hosp., 1968-92, hon. staff Calif., 1992—. Author: Beyond Mathematics, A Standard Physical Particle and the Unified Field of Energy; patentee in field. Lt. col. USAF, 1982-87. Fellow ACS; mem. AMA. E-mail: Asourial@aol.com.

SOURIAN, PETER, writer, English educator; b. Boston, Apr. 7, 1933; s. Zareh Missak and Zabelle (Bayentz) S.; m. Eve Jeanne Pocquet, Sept. 25, 1971; children: Mark, Delphine. BA, Harvard U., 1955. Lectr. ext. divsn. NYU, N.Y.C., 1963-65; instr. English Bard Coll., Annandale-on-Hudson, N.Y., 1965-66, asst. prof., 1966-68, assoc. prof., 1968-75, prof., 1975—, dept. chmn., 1984-86, 90-94. Mem. faculty New Sch. Social Rsch., N.Y.C., 1975—; TV critic The Nation mag., N.Y.C., 1975-81; mem. Anahit Prize Com., 1988—; mem. nat. adv. panel George Polk Awards Com., 1979-92. Author: (novels) Miri, 1957, The Best and Worst of Times, 1961, The Gate, 1965, (essays and criticism) At The French Embassy in Sofia, 1992; mem. editl. bd. Ararat Quar., 1975—; contbr. fiction to mags. and articles to profl. jours. Bd. dirs. Armenian Ctr. Columbia U., N.Y.C., 1988-97; mem. clemente Course Humanities Adv. Bc., 1999—. With U.S. Army, 1957-59. Recipient Bardian award Bard Coll. Alumni, 2000; Lilly Endowment grantee, 1976, Kellogg Found. grantee, 1977. Mem. MLA, PEN, Nat. Book Critics Circle, Century Assn. Home: 30 E 70th St New York NY 10021-4942 Office: Bard Coll Annandale on Hudson New York NY 12504

SOURS, JAMES KINGSLEY, association executive, former college president; b. Corydon, Iowa, Sept. 16, 1925; s. James N. and Virginia (Kantor) S.; m. Alice Hyde, July 11, 1947; children— James W., Mary Jan, David Bryan. Student, Phillips U., 1943; BA, U. Wichita, 1949; MPA, Harvard U., 1951,

PhD, 1954. Adminstrv. aid City Mgr.'s Office, Wichita, 1947-49; mem. faculty Wichita State U., 1951-65; prof. polit. sci.; head dept., 1958-62; dean Fairmount Coll. Arts and Scis., 1962-65; chmn. Fairmount Coll. Arts and Scis. (Center Urban Studies), 1957-63; pres. So. Oreg. State Coll., Ashland, 1969-79; ednl. cons. Dankook U., Seoul, 1979-80, dir. Inst. Asian Studies and Cultures, 1990-97; ednl. cons. Korean Ministry Edn., 1979-80. Exec. v.p. Am. Coll. Testing Program, Iowa City, 1965-68; hon. Fulbright (Dept. of State and U. Iowa), vis. prof. polit. sci. U. Istanbul, Turkey, 1968-69; vis. prof. Dankook U., Seoul, Korea, 1976, 79-80; dir. devel. Oreg. Shakespearean Festival Assn., 1980-85; v.p., bd. dirs. Dankook U. Am., 1990-97; bd. dirs. Rogue Valley Manor Found.; pres. bd. dirs. Internat. Wildlife Recovery Ctr., Eagle Point, Oreg., 1999—; chmn. bd. dirs. Aletheia Psycho-Phys. Found., 1988-96; mem. Jackson County Strategic Planning Adv. Com., 1999—. Author: series Some Observations on the Management of Large Cities, 1957; also numerous articles. V.p. NCAA, 1959-64; founding pres. Urban League Wichita, 1953-56; chmn. Wichita City Commn. Human Rels., 1962; trustee Carpenter Found., 1983-87, v.p., 1984-87; chmn. Sedgwick County, Kans. chpt. ARC, 1964, Jackson County, Oreg. chpt., 1973-75; bd. dirs. So. Oreg. Hist. Soc., 1987-89; mem. Oreg. Am. Revolution Bicentennial Commn., 1972-76; chmn. com. nursing edn. Wesley Med. Ctr., Wichita, 1962-64. Served with USNR, 1943-46. Adminstn. fellow Harvard U., 1949-51. Democrat. Home: 3100 Payne Rd Medford OR 97504-9407

SOUSA, IRENE HELEN, guidance counselor; b. Somerville, Mass., Sept. 29, 1948; d. Clyde Johnson and Helen Mary (Roberts) Frost; m. Frank Ernest Sousa, Feb. 27, 1970; 1 child, Amy Christine. AS in Acctg., Newbury Coll., Boston, 1981; BS in Mgmt., Daniel Webster Coll., 1985; MEd in Counseling, Rivier Coll., 1988; PhD in Edn., Walden U., Mpls., 1991. Nat. cert. counselor; N.H. cert. guidance counselor. Fin. and acctg. staff Army Corp of Engrs., Waltham, Mass., 1968-73; adminstrv. asst. Wang Labs., Lowell, 1974-77; counselor Middlesex Regional Treatment Ctr., Waltham, 1983-84; credit specialist Allied Instrumentation Lab., Andover, 1985-86; guidance counselor Londonderry (N.H.) Sch. Dist., 1986-89; therapist/dir. Positive Pathways Counseling Svcs., Inc., Windham, N.H., 1988-89; guidance counselor Timberlane Sch. Dist., Sandown, 1989—. Mem. ASCD, Assn. for Counselor Edn. and Supervision, N.H. Assn. for Counseling and Devel., N.H. Sch. Counselors Assn. (inter-professions rels. chair 1990-91). Avocations: painting, gardening, reading. Home: 9 Bowman Ln Pelham NH 03076-3002 Office: Sandown Cen Sch 295 Main St Sandown NH 03873-2647

SOUTAS-LITTLE, ROBERT WILLIAM, mechanical engineer, educator; b. Oklahoma City, Feb. 25, 1933; s. Harry Glenn and Mary Evelyn (Miller) Little; m. Patricia Soutas, Sept. 3, 1982; children: Deborah, Catherine, Colleen, Jennifer, Karen. BS in Mech. Engring, Duke U., 1955; MS, U. Wis., 1959, PhD, 1962. Design engr. Allis Chalmers Mfg. Co., Milw., 1955-57; instr. mech. engring. Marquette U., 1957-59; instr. U. Wis., Madison, 1959-62, asst. prof., 1962-63, Okla. State U., 1963-65; prof. Mich. State U., 1965—, chmn. dept. mech. engring., 1972-77, chmn. dept. biomechanics, 1977-90; dir. biomechanics evaluation lab., 1989—. Cons. A. C. Electronics Co., Ford Motor Co., CBS Research Lab., B. F. Goodrich Co.; lectr. AID, India, 1965 Author: Elasticity, 1973, Engineering Mechanics: Statics, 1999, Engineering Mechanics: Dynamics, 1999; contbr. articles to profl. jours. Vice pres. Okemos (Mich.) Sch. Bd., 1967-72; mem. Meridian Twp. (Mich.) Charter Commn., 1969-70, Meridian Twp. Zoning Bd. Appeals, 1969-71. Recipient award for excellence in instrn. engring. students Western Electric Co., 1970-71, Disting. Faculty award, 1996; NSF grantee, 1964-69, 79, NIH grantee, 1973-75, 79—. Fellow ASME; mem. Soc. Engring. Sci., Am. Soc. Biomechanics, Internat. Soc. Biomechanics, N.Am. Soc. Clin. Gait and Movement Analysis, Sigma Xi, Pi Tau Sigma, Ta Beta Pi. Home: 187 S Highland Dr Leland MI 49654-1143 Office: PO Box 1143 Leland MI 49654-1143 E-mail: soutas@egr.msu.edu.

SOUTER, DAVID HACKETT, United States supreme court justice; b. Melrose, Mass., Sept. 17, 1939; s. Joseph Alexander and Helen Adams (Hackett) Souter. BA, Harvard U., 1961, LLB, 1966; Rhodes scholar, Oxford U., 1961—63, MA, 1989. Bar: N.H. Assoc. Orr & Reno, Concord, 1966—68; asst. atty. gen. N.H., 1968—71; dep. atty. gen., 1971—76; atty. gen., 1976—78; assoc. justice Superior Ct. N.H., 1978—83, N.H. Supreme Ct., 1983—90; judge U.S. Ct. Appeals (1st cir.), NH, 1990; assoc. justice U.S. Supreme Ct., Washington, 1990—. Trustee Concord Hosp., 1973—85, pres. bd. trustees, 1978—84; bd. overseers Dartmouth Med. Sch., 1981—87. Mem.: N.H. Bar Assn., N.H. Hist. Soc. (v.p. 1980—85, trustee 1976—85), Phi Beta Kappa. Republican. Episcopalian.*

SOUTER, SYDNEY SCULL, lawyer; b. Trenton, N.J., June 17, 1931; s. Sydney H. and Josephine (Scull) S.; children: Gifford MacLeod, Julia Elizabeth, Matthew Thomas, Jeffrey James, Michael Andrew. BA, Yale U., 1954, JD, 1959. Bar: Conn. 1959, N.J. 1960. Assoc. Minton, Dinsmore & Bohlinger, Trenton, 1960-62, McCarthy, Bascik & Hicks, Princeton, N.J., 1963-64; ptnr. Baggit, Souter & Stonaker, 1965-66; sr. ptnr. Souter, Scozzari & Steffens, 1966-69, Souter & Kettell, Princeton, 1970-75, Souter & Steffens, Princeton, 1977-80, Souter & Selecky, Princeton, 1980-82, Souter & Morrow, Princeton, 1983-91, Souter and Voliva, Princeton, 1991—. Bd. dirs. Ewing Bank & Trust Co. (counsel 1962-70); pres. The Hamilton Bank (counsel 1971-77). Mcpl. Judge Montgomery Twp., Somerset County, N.J., 1966-68, East Windsor Twp., Mercer County, N.J., 1971-73, Princeton Twp., Mercer County, 1981-89; asst. counsel County of Mercer, Trenton, 1990-91, dep. counsel, 1991-96, 2001—; counsel Mercer County Park Commn., 1996—; state committeeman Rep. Party, 2001—. Mem. ABA, N.J. State Bar Assn., Mercer County Bar Assn., Princeton Bar Assn., Rotary Club Princeton (pres. 1990-91), Kiwanis Club (pres. Princeton 1968). Presbyterian. Office: Souter and Voliva 40 Nassau St Princeton NJ 08542-4522

SOUTHALL, FRANCIS GENEVA, retired education educator music; b. New Orlean, Dec. 5, 1925; d. William Talbot and Darthney Pauline (Pleasant) Handy; 1 child, Patricia Camille Jones. BA, Dillard U., 1945; MusM, Am. Conservatory, 1958; PhD, U. Iowa, 1966. Artist diploma, Nat. Guild of Piano Tchrs., 1953. Instr. piano Paul Quinn Coll., Waco, Tex., 1958-59; chair piano dept. Knoxville (Tenn.) Coll., 1959-61; asst. prof. piano/music history S.C. State, Orangeburg, 1962-64; teaching asst. piano U. Iowa, Iowa City, 1964-66; prof. piano/music history Grambline (La.) State U., 1966-70; prof. Afro-Am. music U. Minn., Mpls., 1970-92; ret. Bdd. dirs. Dillard U., New Orleans, 1977— Author: (book) Blind Tom, Book I, 1979, Blind Tom, Book II, 1983; pianist (cassette tape) Piano Music of Blind Tom, 1983, Blind Tom, The Black Pianist-Composer: Continually Enslaved, In Celebration of Black Music, 1984-94. Referee Minn. Humanities Commn., St. Paul, 1983-87; editl. bd. Black Music Rsch. Jour., 1984-94; bd. trustees Camphor United Meth. Ch., St. Paul, 1995—. Recipient Prix de Martell Achievement award Minn. Orch., 1992, MLK Cmty. Svc. award Found. for Social Action, 1992; nmaed Hon. Sterling patron Mu Phi Epsilon Music Frat., 1993, Nat. Women of Yr., Iota Phi Lambda Sorority, 1979. Mem. AAUW (long range planning com., program com. 1994-96), NAACP (coord. music events NAACP conv. 1995), Nat. Assn. Negro Musicians (chair scholarship competition 1989). Methodist. Avocations: travel, reading. Home: 4929 4th Ave S Minneapolis MN 55409-2637

SOUTHALL, VIRGINIA LAWRENCE, retired artist; b. Portsmouth, Va., Aug. 25, 1927; d. Malachi Ashley Lewis and Bessie (Oliver) Lawrence; m. Junius Nathan Southall, Apr. 18, 1959; children: Lawrence Nathan. Student Norfolk divsn., Va. State Coll., 1945-46; student, Prince George's C.C., Largo, Md., 1988—. Sec. to dean sch. engring. Tuskegee (Ala.) Inst., 1949-51; passport clk., ID clk. dept. army The Pentagon, Washington, 1951-62; pers. clk. AID, Dept. State, 1963-67. Exhibited in group shows including U. Md. Coll. Arts Program Gallery, College Park, 1993, Prince Georges C.C., Marlboro Gallery, Largo, Md., 1993-94, Montpelier Cultural Art Ctr., Laurel, Md., 1996, Md. State Ho., Annapolis, 1998, Children's Nat. Med. Ctr. Atrium Gallery 1, Washington, 1999, Mary McCleod Bethune Coun. Ho., Washington, 1999; one-woman shows include Outreach and Devel. Ctr. Ebenezer United Meth. Ch., Lanham, Md., Art Atrium II Gallery, Portsmouth, Va., 1998. Concert choir mem. Prince Georges C.C.; Chancel Choir mem. Ebenezer United Meth. Ch., vol. art tchr. for youth programs. Mem. Nat. Mus. Women in the Arts, Md. Choral Soc. Avocations: arts and crafts, music, singing. Home: 9015 Wallace Rd Lanham Seabrook MD 20706-4211

SOUTHARD, PAUL RAYMOND, financial executive; b. Albany, N.Y., May 15, 1948; s. Harold G. and Frances L. (Shaylor) S. BS, Rochester Inst. Tech., 1970. CPA, N.Y. Staff acct. Haskins & Sells, CPA's, Rochester, N.Y., 1969-70; sr. acct. Maurice F. Sammons & Co., CPAs, 1970-73; fin. mgr. Radionics, Inc., Webster, N.Y., 1973-82, contr., 1982-87, Kitchen Concepts, Co., Fairport, N.Y., 1987-88, Spectra Svcs., Inc., Rochester, 1989-93, Rochester Lino & Carpet, 1993-94, Arena Products Inc., 1994-95, Overland Constrn., Inc., 1996-2000, ICS Telecom, Inc., Rochester, 2000—. Mem. N.Y. State Soc. CPAs. Home: 1096 Everwild Vw Webster NY 14580-8740

SOUTHARD, WILLIAM G. lawyer; b. Toledo, May 6, 1953; s. James Theodore and Dorothy (Fergusson) S.; m. Martha Donelan, Aug. 14, 1976. BA, Williams Coll., 1975; JD, Columbia U., 1978. Bar: Ill. 1978, U.S. Dist. Ct. Ill. 1979, Mass. 1981, U.S. Dist. Ct. Mass. 1981, U.S. Ct. Appeals (1st cir.) 1985. Assoc. Schiff Hardin & Waite, Chgo., 1978-81, Bingham, Dana & Gould LLP, Boston, 1981-85, ptnr., 1985—, dep. chmn. litig., 1994-2000, chmn. litig., 2000—, co-chair litigation, 2002—. Assoc. editor Columbia Jour. Transnat. Law, 1978; contbr. articles to profl. jours. Mem. ABA, ASTM, Boston Bar Assn. Office: Bingham McCutchen LLP 150 Federal St Fl 15 Boston MA 02110-1745 E-mail: southawg@bingham.com.

SOUTHARD-BORNYASZ, MARJORIE, special education educator, consultant; b. Fremont, Mich., Jan. 24, 1939; d. Milo R. Southard and Margaret E. Totten; m. Matthew Bornyasz, Aug. 20, 1960 (div. Oct. 1985); children: Megan Sue, Mitchel Stephen, Mikaela Southard. BA in Edn., Ctrl. Mich. U., 1961; MA in Spl. Edn., Calif. State U., 1985. Cert. resource specialist. High sch. phys. edn. tchr. Carlton (Mich.) Unified, 1961, Southfield (Mich.) Unified, 1961-62; adult edn. tchr. Dearborn (Mich.) Unified, 1963-65; phys. edn. specialist Palos Verdes (Calif.) Unified, 1972-83; spl. edn. tchr. San Pedro (Calif.) High, 1983-89; resource specialist Temecula (Calif.) Mid. Sch., 1989-95; spl. edn. tchr. Temecula Valley High, 1995—. Instr. U. Calif., Riverside Ext., 1997; contbg. mem. monograph Problems Facing Tchr. Edn. in 21st Century, Calif. State U., Long Beach, 2000. Site rep. Temecula Valley Educators Assn., 1994-2000; sch. site coun. Temecula Valley H.S., 1996-2000; mem. Gov.'s Tchg. Fellowship Com., 2001—; charter mem. Nat. Women's History Mus., Washington. Named Outstanding Alumni Tchr., Calif. State U. Dominguez Hills, Carson, 1999; recipient Resolution for Outstanding Tchg., Calif. State Senate, 2000, Calif. House of Reps., 2000. Mem. AAUW (charter, v.p. Temecula Valley chpt. 1992—), Temecula Valley Edn. Assn. (rep.), Alpha Gamma Delta. Methodist. Avocations: traveling, antiquing, skiing, reading, camping. Home: 31520 Corte Pacheco Temecula CA 92592-6401 E-mail: yornyasz@hotmail.com.

SOUTHBY, RICHARD MCKELLAR FAIRFAX, health services educator, consultant; b. Melbourne, Victoria, Australia, Feb. 3, 1940; arrived in U.S., 1979, naturalized, 1985; s. Robert and Marie Heywood (Whyte) Southby; m. Janet Sue Rexrode, June 9, 1979. B.Com., U. Melbourne, 1965; M.P.A. Cornell U., 1967; PhD, Monash U., Clayton, Victoria, Australia, 1973. Rsch. asst. Inst. Applied Econ. Research U. Melbourne, 1965; Sloan scholar in hosp. and med. care adminstrn. Cornell U., Ithaca, NY, 1965—67; tchg. fellow Monash U., 1967—70, sr. tchg. fellow dept. social and preventive medicine Faculty of Medicine, 1970, lectr. in social and preventive medicine, 1971—75, sr. lectr., 1975—78; commr. Australian Hosps. and Health Services Commn., Canberra, 1975; dir. pub. health services research and tchg. Sch. Pub. Health and Tropical Medicine U. Sydney, Australia, 1978—79; assoc. dean health svcs. and Friesen prof. internat. health and health policy and prof. health care scis. The George Washington U. Med. Ctr., Washington, 1979—2001, dean, Ross prof. internat. health, sch. pub. health and health svcs., 2001—. Adj. prof. dept. preventive medicine and biometrics Sch. Medicine Uniformed Services U. Health Scis. Dept. Def., Bethesda, Md., 1979—; dir. Interagy.-Inst. for Fed. Health Care Execs., 1984—; cons. in hosp. adminstrn. Walter Reed Army Med. Ctr., Washington, 1983—. Author (with E. Chesterman): Australia: Health Facts, 1979; editor (with others): Health Care Technology Under Financial Constraints, 1987, Health Care Law and Ethics, 1989, AIDS and Long Term Care: A New Dimension, 1989. Fellow: Royal Soc. Medicine (U.K.), Australian Coll. Health Svc. Execs., Am. Coll. Legal Medicine (hon.); mem.: APHA, Assn. Mil. Surgeons U.S, Internat. Epidemiol. Assn., Cosmos Club (Washington), Army and Navy Club (Washington), Mil. Club (Melbourne), Naval Club, Wallaby Club. Anglican. Avocations: tennis, gardening, hiking. Office: Sch Pub Health and Health Svcs George Washington U Med Ctr Washington DC 20037

SOUTHER, JEAN LORRAINE, accounting and management educator, accountant; b. North Weymouth, Mass. d. Herbert Roy and Ruth Agnes (Perry) S. BBA in Acctg., Northeastern U., 1960, MBA, 1968; EdD, U. Mass., 1986. Lic. pub. acct. From acct. to auditor to div. acctg. mgr. to systems mgr. to asst. to contr. Howard Johnson Co., Quincy, Mass., 1949-74; prof. Cape Cod C.C., Barnstable, 1974-91, prof. emeritus, 1991—. Founding dir. Cape Cod Women's Credit Union, Barnstable; lectr. MBA program Kathmandu U.-Sch. of Mgmt., 1997; fin. contr. United Mission to Nepal, Kathmandu, 2001-2002. Editor: Basic Finance (Gitman), 1987. Chair pers. bd. Town of Eastham, Mass., 1980-84, vice chair fin. bd., 1986-89; pres. Friends of Cape Cod Nat. Sea Shore, bd. dirs., 1991-97; active Nauset Regional H.S. coun., 1993—; vol. Lakeland Coll., Sheboygan, Wis., 1994, Cook Coll. & Theol. Sch., Tempe, Ariz., 1995, Back Bay Mission, Biloxi, Miss., 1996-99, Slumber Falls Camp and Retreat Ctr., New Braunfels, Tex., 2000; vol. for homeland ministries United Ch. of Christ; bd. vol. World Ministries, Kathmandu U., Nepal, 1997, 2000-2001; mem. delegation Witness for Peace, Columbia, 2002. Recipient Merit award Town of Eastham, 1984. Mem. Nat. Soc. Pub. Accts., Am. Soc. Women Accts. (mem. editl. bd. 1980-93), Assn. Sys. Mgmt. Republican. Avocations: aerobics, swimming, gardening, biking, traveling. Home: PO Box 326 50 Van Dale Ave Eastham MA 02642-3310

SOUTHER, JOSEPH CARROLL, family practice physician; b. Jan. 3, 1946; m. Cindy Gay Herrin; children: Chris, Karen, Dan. Diplomate Am. Bd. Family Practice. Gen. practice physician Winder (Ga.) Med. PA. Office: Winder Med PA 251 E Broad St Winder GA 30680-2206

SOUTHERLAND, DERRICK THEODORE, microbiologist; b. Temple Hills, Md. s. Theodore and Vernetta S. BS, N.C. AT&T State U., 1994; MS, Howard U., 1997. Rsch. scientist Lab Support, Rockville, Md., 1997-99; claims examiner U.S. Dept. Labor, Washington, 1999—. Mem. Am. Soc. Microbiology, Am. Inst. Biol. Scis., N.C. AT&T State U. Alumni Assn. Avocations: reading, swimming, photography, classic automobiles. Home: 4304 19th Ave Temple Hills MD 20748-5620 Office: 800 N Capitol St NW Rm 800 Washington DC 20211 E-mail: dsoutherland@hotmail.com.

SOUTHERLAND, S. DUANE, manufacturing company executive; b. Durham, N.C., Apr. 24, 1949; s. Sydney Duane and Beatrice Marie (Carver) S.; m. Linda F. Lewis, Jan. 5, 1974, 1 child, S. Duane III. BSE, Duke U., 1971, MS in Engring., 1973, MBA, 1974. Ops. analyst Cooper Group Div. Cooper Industries, Apex, N.C., 1974-78, planning analyst Houston, 1978-81, dir. fin. Cooper Electronics Div. Nashua, N.H., 1981-83, gen. mgr. Conn. ops. Kirsch Div. Beacon Falls, Conn., 1983-87, pres. Kirsch Div. Sturgis, Mich., 1987-94; pres., CEO Conso Products Co., Union, S.C., 1995-98, Equality Specialties, Inc., N.Y.C., 1999—2001, Conso Products, Union, SC, 2002—. Republican. Baptist.

SOUTHERN, ANN GAYLE, nurse, educator; b. Radford, Va., Oct. 1, 1950; d. William Gale and Harless (Rogers) Farmer. Degree in nursing cum laude, Wytheville (Va.) C.C., 1985; BS, Radford (Va.) U., 1988, MS, 1995. RN. Nurse Pulaski (Va.) Cmty. Hosp., 1985-88, St. Alban's Psychiat. Hosp., Radford, 1988-98; clin. instr. Wytheville RN Program, 1996-98; nurse Sunbridge of New River Valley, Dublin, 1999—, Columbia Pulaski Cmty. Hosp., Pulaski, Va., 1999—. Counselor AIDS/hepatitis disease process cmty. support groups, Radford, 1992—; lectr. breast cancer and self-exam., Radford, 1995. Mem. ANA, Sigma Theta Tau. Methodist. Avocations: old movies, gardening. Home: 6746 Dudley Ferry Rd Radford VA 24141-8876

SOUTHERN, HUGH, retired performing arts manager; b. Newcastle-on-Tyne, Eng., Mar. 20, 1932; came to U.S., 1955; s. Norman and Phyllis Margaret (Hiller) S.; m. Jane Rosemary Llewellyn, Dec. 18, 1954 (div.); children: Hilary, William Norman; m. Kathy Ayers Dwyer, Dec. 10, 1988; 1 child, Jaime Andres. BA, King's Coll., Cambridge, Eng., 1956. Assoc. account exec. Fuller & Smith & Ross, N.Y.C., 1956-58; treas. Westport Country Playhouse Conn., 1958; adminstrv. mgr. Theatre Guild-Am. Theatre Soc., N.Y.C., 1959-62; asst. dir. Repertory Theatre, Lincoln Ctr., 1962-65; gen. mgr. Nat. Repertory Theatre, 1965-67; mgmt. assoc. San Francisco Opera, 1967-68; exec. dir. Theatre Devel. Fund, N.Y.C., 1968-82; dep. chmn. programs Nat. Endowment for Arts, Washington, 1982-89, acting chmn., 1989; gen. mgr. Met. Opera Assn. Inc., N.Y.C., 1989-90; dir. Va. Festival of Am. Film, Charlottesville, Va., 1995-96. Acting dir. performing arts program N.Y. State Council on Arts, N.Y.C., 1974-75, acting exec. dir., 1976; dir. New Dramatists, N.Y.C., 1978-82, Film Forum, N.Y.C., 1978-82; trustee Actor's Fund Am., N.Y.C., 1978-85 Trustee Manhattan Country Sch., N.Y.C., 1970-82, chmn., 1971-74; mem. Mayor's Com. on Cultural Policy, N.Y.C., 1974-75. Home: 3406 18th St N Arlington VA 22207 E-mail: hsouth2@aol.com.

SOUTHERN, JAMES TERRY, secondary education educator; b. Haleyville, Ala., June 1, 1945; s. Floyd Richardson and Linnie (McNutt) S.; m. Brenda Gay Rice, Aug. 23, 1968; children: Craig Alan, Jason Lee. BS in English and History, Florence State Coll., 1967; MA in English, U. Ala., Tuscaloosa, 1970, PhD in English, 1995. Cert. secondary edn. educator, Ala. English tchr. N.W. Ala. State Jr. Coll., Phil Campbell, Ala., 1969-71; writer, editor, intern U.S. Army Missile Command, Redstone Arsenal, 1971-72; writer editor printed media U.S. Army Aviation Systems Command, St. Louis, 1972-74; rsch. assoc., editor Ctr. Bus. and Econ. Rsch. U. Ala., Tuscaloosa, 1975-80; tchr. English and social studies Northside H.S., Northport, Ala., 1980-81; tchr. English Hale County H.S., Moundville, 1981-82, Hillcrest H.S., Tuscaloosa, 1982—. Editor Ala. Bus. periodical, 1975-80. Cubmaster Boy Scouts Am., Northport, 1981-83; deacon Bapt. Ch., 1999—, NEH fellow Emory U., 1995. Mem. NEA, Ala. State Tchr. Forum, Nat. Coun. Tchrs. English, Ala. Coun. Tchrs. English, South Atlantic Modern Lang. Assn., Am. Philatelic Soc., Kappa Delta Pi. Avocations: reading, stamp collecting. Home: 16220 McAllister Rd Buhl AL 35446-9214 Office: Hillcrest HS 300 Patriot Pkwy Tuscaloosa AL 35405-8606

SOUTHERN, NANCY C. utilities executive; Co-chmn., CEO ATCO Ltd. and Can. Utilities, Calgary, Canada, also bd. dirs. Canada. Exec. v.p. Spruce Meadows. Former mem. Can. Equestrian Team. Office: ATCO Ltd 1500/1600 909 11th Ave SW Calgary AB Canada T2R 1N6

SOUTHERN, ROBERT ALLEN, lawyer; b. Independence, Mo., July 17, 1930; s. James Allen and Josephine (Ragland) S.; m. Cynthia Agnes Drews, May 17, 1952; children: David D., William A., James M., Kathryn S. O'Brien. BS in Polit. Sci., Northwestern U., 1952, LL.B., 1954. Bar: Ill. 1955. Assoc. Mayer, Brown & Platt, Chgo., 1954-64, ptnr., 1965-96, mng. ptnr., 1978-91, L.A., 1991-96; CEO So. Assocs., Gurnee, Ill., 1997—. Editor in chief Northwestern U. Law Rev., 1953-54. Trustee, v.p., gen. counsel LaRabida Children's Hosp. and Rsch. Ctr., Chgo., 1974-89; trustee Kenilworth (Ill.) Union Ch., 1980-88; pres. Joseph Sears Sch. Bd., 1977-79; trustee Rush-Presbyn.-St. Luke's Med. Ctr., 1983-91, life trustee, 1991—; bd. dirs. Boys and Girls Clubs Chgo., 1986-91; governing mem. Orchestral Assn. Chgo., 1988-93. With U.S. Army, 1955-57. Mem. ABA, Chgo. Bar Assn., Lawyers Club Chgo., Order of Coif, Indian Hill Club, Chgo. Club. Office: 7600 Bittersweet Dr Gurnee IL 60031-5110 E-mail: rsouthern2@earthlink.net.

SOUTHERN, RONALD D. diversified corporation executive; b. Calgary, Alta., Can., July 25, 1930; s. Samuel Donald and Alexandra (Cuthill) S.; m. Margaret Visser, July 30, 1954; children: Nancy, Linda. BSc, U. Alta., Edmonton, 1953; LLD (hon.), U. Calgary, 1976, U. Alberta, 1991. Chmn., CEO ATCO Ltd. and Can. Utilities Ltd., Calgary, 1994-99, ATCO Ltd., Calgary, 1994-99, Can. Utilities Ltd., Calgary, 1994-99, co-chmn., CEO, 1999—. Chmn. Akita Drilling Ltd.; bd. dirs. Royal & Sun Alliance Ins. Ltd., Atco Ltd., Can. Utilities Ltd.; co-chmn., CEO Spruce Meadows, 1999—; chmn. Spruce Meadows Round Table. Decorated Order of Can., comdr. Brit. Empire; recipient Disting. Entrepreneur award U. Man. Faculty Mgmt., 1990; inducted into Can. Bus. Hall, 1995; named Businessman of Yr. U. Alta., 1986, CEO of the Yr. Fin. Post, 1996. Mem. Ranchmen's Club. Calgary Golf and Country Club. Office: ATCO Ltd & Can Utilities 1600 909-11 Ave SW Calgary AB Canada T2R 1N6

SOUTHERN, VALERIE, transportation consultant; b. Great Lakes, Ill., Nov. 6, 1952; d. William Harry and Mattie Ruth Southern. BA in Journalism, U. R.I., 1975, M in Urban and Regional Planning, 1980; MPA, Harvard U., 1987. Transport planner City of Portland, Oreg., 1979-82, City of Washington, D.C., 1982-84; dep. dir. policy Gov.'s Office, State of R.I., Providence, 1988-91; fed. coord. U.S. Dept. Transp.-FHWA, Cambridge, Mass., 1991-93; dep. sec. transport Commonwealth of Mass., Boston, 1993-94; mgr. transport planning King County Dept. Transp., Seattle, 1996-97; transp. cons. in pvt. practice, Issaquah, Wash., 1997—. Contbr. articles to profl. jours. Congl. candidate Dist. 1, R.I., 1994; mem. Jamestown (R.I.) Town Coun., 1991-93; candidate Sec. of State, State of R.I., 1992; trustee U. R.I., Kingston, 1991-94. Recipient Disting. Pub. Svc. award Washington Mayor's Office, 198,3 84; Kahn fellow Harvard U., 1987. Mem. Issaquah C. of C. (com. chair 1998—), Women Bus. Owners, Black Alumni Assn. Harvard U. (pres. 1988-90). Avocations: guitar, body building, biking, reading. Home and Office: 3849 Klahanie Dr SE Apt 8-201 Issaquah WA 98029-5723

SOUTHWARD, PATRICIA C. volunteer; b. Alexandria, La., Mar. 9, 1942; d. George Emerson and Mary Alice (Boland) Cilley; m. Arnold Lester Greenfield, May 18, 1963 (div. June 1968); m. Ernest Merritt Southward, Mar. 1970; 1 daughter. BA, U. Fla., Gainesville, 1963; MS, Fla. State U., Tallahassee, 1966; postgrad., U. Ctrl. Fla. Office mgr. Southward Gardens, Lake Mary, Fla., 1977-84, Southward Investment and Realty, Lake Mary, 1970—2001. Adj. instr. Caldwell C.C., Boone, NC, 1999—, Seminole C.C., Lake Mary, Fla., 2001—; city commr. Lake Mary, 1977-79, 82. Com. mem. Fla. Govs. Coun. on Housing Goals, 1980; sponsor, vol. and social worker Refugee Resettlement Office, Cath., 1980—; bd. dirs., sec. Cen. Fla. Migrant and Community Health Clinic, Sanford, 1981-89; bd. dirs. LWV Seminole County, 1982-92, 1st v.p. 1990-94; voters' svc. chair, bd. dirs. LWV Fla., 1989-90. Democrat. Avocation: anthropology. Home: 316 Oak Leaf Cir Lake Mary FL 32746-3059 Office: PO Box 950730 Lake Mary FL 32795-0730 also: 161 Meadow Avenue Loop Rd Banner Elk NC 28604-9659 E-mail: psouthward@hotmail.com.

SOUTHWELL, SAMUEL BEALL, English educator; b. Lockhart, Tex., Jan. 15, 1922; s. George Thomas Jr. and Lucile Mariam (Beall) S.; m. Mary Jane Bamford, Dec. 16, 1944; children: Michael Beall, Teresa Bamford. BJ, U. Tex., 1947, MA, 1948, PhD, 1955; D (hon.), U. Autonoma de Guadalajara, Mex., 1965. Assoc. prof. Tex. A&M U., College Station, 1950-58; ednl. exch. officer USIA, Mexico City, 1959-60, U.S. Consul, Guadalajara, 1961-65; assoc. prof. U. Houston, 1965-69, chmn. dept. English, 1969-73, prof., 1970-95, ret., 1995, prof. emeritus, 1996—. Author: (novel) If All the Rebels Die, 1966, Quest for Eros: Browning and "Fifine", 1980, Kenneth Burke and Martin Heidegger: With a Note on Deconstructionism, 1987, Crossing the Wasteland: An Intellectual Quest for God, 2002. Lt. (j.g.) USN, 1944-45, Pacific Fleet. Democrat. Roman Catholic. Avocations: reading, bicycle riding, walking. Home: 1217 W Main St Houston TX 77006-4819 Fax: 713-521-0164. E-mail: samsam77@msn.com.

SOUTHWICK, CHARLES HENRY, zoologist, educator; b. Wooster, Ohio, Aug. 28, 1928; s. Arthur F. and Faye (Motz) S.; m. Heather Milne Beck, July 12, 1952; children: Steven, Karen. BA, Coll. Wooster, 1949; MS, U. Wis., 1951, PhD, 1953. NIH fellow, 1951-53; asst. prof. biology Hamilton Coll., 1953-54; NSF fellow Oxford (Eng.) U., 1954-55; faculty Ohio U., 1955-61; assoc. prof. pathobiology Johns Hopkins Sch. Hygiene and Pub. Health, Balt., 1961-68, prof., 1968-79; assoc. dir. Johns Hopkins Internat. Ctr. for Med. Rsch. and Tng., Calcutta, India, 1964-65; chmn. dept. environ., population and organismic biology U. Colo., Boulder, 1979-82, prof. biology, 1979—, prof. emeritus, 1993—. Researcher and author publs. on animal social behavior and population dynamics, influences animal social behavior on demographic characteristic mammal populations, primate ecology and behavior, estuarine ecology and environmental quality; mem. primate adv. com. Nat. Acad. Sci.-NRC, 1963-75, com. primate conservation, 1974-75; mem. Gov.'s Sci. Adv. Com. State of Md., 1975-78; mem. com. on rsch. and exploration Nat. Geog. Soc., 1979-2000; mem. adv. bd. Caribbean Primate Rsch. Ctr., 1987-99, Wis. Primate Rsch. Ctr., 1990-98; mem. Integrated Conservation Rsch., 1989—. Editor, author: Primate Social Behavior, 1963, Animal Aggression, 1970, Nonhuman Primates in Biomedical Research, 1975, Ecology and the

Quality of Our Environment, 1976, Global Ecology, 1985; Ecology and Behavior of Food-Enhanced Primate Groups, 1988; author: Global Ecology in Human Perspective, 1996. Recipient Fulbright Rsch. award India, 1959-60, Tchg. Excellence award U. Colo., 1993. Fellow AAAS, Acad. Zoology, Animal Behavior Soc.; mem. Am. Soc. Zoologists, Ecol. Soc. Am., Am. Soc. Mammalogists, Am. Soc. Primatology (Disting. Primatologist award 1994), Internat. Primatology Soc., Am. Inst. Biol. Scis.

SOUTHWICK, LAWRENCE, JR. management educator; b. Northampton, Mass., Sept. 5, 1938; s. Lawrence Sr. and Caroline (Ingram) S.; m. Patricia A. Matthews, Oct. 21, 1961; children: Lawrence III, Rebecca A., Catherine A. BS in Math., Case Western Res. U., Cleve., 1960; MBA, Western Mich. U., 1963; MS in Indsl. Adminstrn., Carnegie-Mellon U., 1965, PhD in Econs., 1967. Cert. mgmt. acct., fin. mgmt. Asst. prof. mgmt. SUNY, Buffalo, 1966-70, assoc. prof., 1970—, chmn. dept. mgmt., 1976-81, 91-94, 99-2001; comptr. Town of Amherst (N.Y.), 2000—. Cons. in field. Author: Managerial Economics, 1985. Councilman Town of Amherst, 1972-91, comptroller, 2000—; bd. dirs. Seneca Nation of Indians Econ. Devel. Corp., 1994-97, Restoration Soc., Friendship Found. Mem. NAFE, Am. Econ. Assn., Inst. Mgmt. Accts., Am. Statis. Assn. Republican. Unitarian Universalist. Home: 100 Oakland Rd Williamsville NY 14221-6816 Office: SUNY Sch Mgmt Buffalo NY 14260-0001

SOUTHWICK, MARCIA ANN, poet; b. Boston, Oct. 30, 1949; d. Wayne Orin and Jessie Ann Southwick; m. Larry Patrick Levis, Mar. 8, 1975 (div. May 1982); 1 child Nicholas Southwick Levis ; m. Murray Gell-Mann, June 20, 1992. AA, Pine Manor Jr. Coll., Chestnut Hill, Mass., 1970; BA, Emerson Coll., Boston, 1973; MFA, U. Iowa, 1975. Instr. Stephens Coll., Columbia, Mo., 1979; vis. poet Iowa Writers' Workshop, Iowa City, 1981—83, U. Colo., Boulder, 1984; vis. lectr. Warren Wilson MFA Program, Swannanoa, NC, 1982; assoc. prof. U. Nebr., Lincoln, 1985—91; vis. assoc. prof. U. N.Mex., Albuquerque, 1994—2000. Bd. dirs. Aspen (Colo.) Writers Found., 1994—96; co-founder The Mo. Rev., Columbia, 1976; vis. poet Fla. Internat. U., Miami, 2002. Author: (poetry) The Night Won't Save Anyone, 1980, Why The River Disappears, 1990, Saturday Night at the Flying Dog, 1999 (Field Poetry prize, 1998); contbr. poetry to anthologies. Mem. exhbn. com. SITE Santa Fe, 1999—2001. Recipient Stanley B. Young fellowship, Bread Loaf Writers Conf., Middlebury, Vt., 1980; grantee, NEA, 1984. Mem.: Associated Writing Programs, Poetry Soc. Am. Democrat. Episcopalian. Avocation: study of simplicity, complexity and the arts. Home: 1001 Pinones Santa Fe NM 87505 Fax: 505-989-8770. E-mail: smouthwick@aol.com.

SOUTHWICK, PAUL, retired public relations executive; b. West Newton, Mass., Mar. 27, 1920; s. Alfred and Pauline (Winkler) S.; m. Susan Barbara Heider, Feb. 24, 1947; children: Thomas Paul, Peter Alfred, Linda Susan. AB in Econs. cum laude, Harvard Coll., 1943. Coor. AP, Concord, N.H., 1947-49; UP UPI, Washington, 1949-57; mem. profl. staff govt. info. subcom. U.S. Ho. Reps., 1957-59; legis. asst., adminstrv. asst. U.S. Senator Long of Hawaii, 1959-62; dep. adminstr. charge accelerated pub. works program Area Redevel. Adminstrn., 1962-63; spl. asst. The White House, 1963-65; spl. asst. for congl. rels. Office of U.S. Sec. Commerce, 1965-67; v.p. Newmyer Assocs., Inc., Washington, 1967-87; ind. cons., 1987-93; ret., 1993. With USNR, 1941-45, PTO. Mem. Nat. Press Club (Washington). Democrat. Presbyterian. Home: 4012 Underwood St Bethesda MD 20815-5028

SOUTHWORTH, JAMIE MACINTYRE, retired education educator; b. Ironton, Ohio, Oct. 16, 1931; d. Gaylord and Lydia Marcum (Adkins) MacIntyre; m. Horton C. Southworth; children: Jaye, Brad, Alexandra, Susann, Janet, Jim. BS, Ball State U., 1952, MA, 1961; EdD, U. Pitts., 1981; attended, Oxford (Eng.) U., 1997. Cert. adminstr. and tchr., reading specialist, Pa. Instr. Mich. State U., East Lansing, 1964-67; instr., coord. U. Minn., Mpls., 1967-71; rsch. assoc. Pitts. Pub. Schs., 1971-80; assoc. prof. California U., Pitts., 1988, prof. edn., 1993—, state grants educator, 1990-95, dir. leadership tng. proposal, 1996-00, retired, 2000. Chancellor state adv. com., California U. rep., 1994—, faculty profl. devel. com. state rep., 1991-99; invited participant Oxford (Eng.) U. Leadership Studies, 1995, 97; cons. TITL project Duquesne U.; CEO Learning Tree Corp., 1975-2000; presentor, rsch. conf. 2000, Waikato Univ., New Zealand, rsch. young childrens conf. 2000, San Diego; chair-IRA, internat. conf. nat. scholars, San Francisco, 2000. Contbr. articles to profl. jours. Recipient Seal of St. Peter's Coll., Oxford, 1997; U.S. Office of Edn. title III & IVC grantee; grantee Pa. Vocat. Tech. State, 1990-91, 93, Bibliotherapy Project California Univ. Pa., 1992, Pa. State, 1993, Pa. Campus Compac, 1993. Mem. Am. Assn. Colls. Tchr. Edn., NEA Young Children, Kappa Delta Pi (counselor), Phi Delta Kappa.

SOUTHWORTH, LINDA JEAN, artist, critic, educator, poet; b. Milw., May 11, 1951; d. William Dixon and Violet Elsie (Kuehn) S.; m. David Joseph Roger, Nov. 16, 1985 (div. July 1989). BFA, St. John's U., Queens, N.Y., 1974; MFA, Pratt Inst., Bklyn., 1978. Pvt. practice self-employed, N.Y.C., 1974—; art critic Resident Publs., 1993-95. Adj. prof. art history St. Francis Coll., Bklyn., 1985-94; artist-in-residence Our Saviour's Atonement Luth. Ch., N.Y.C., 1993-95. One-woman shows include Galimaufry, Croton-on-Hudson, N.Y., 1977, Kristen Richard Gallery, N.Y.C., 1982, Gallery 84, 1990, The Bernhardt Collection, Washington, 1991, Netherland Club, N.Y.C., 1992, Chuck Levitan Gallery, Soho, 1996, Seventh and Second Photo Gallery, 1998, Pen & Brush Solo Award Show, 2001, exhibited in group shows at Union St. Graphics, San Francisco, 1974, Nuance Gallery, Tampa, 1987, 1988, Illustrators Ann. Drawing Show, N.Y.C., 1989—90, Salmagundi Club, 1991, 1992, Henry Howells Gallery, 1992—93, Mus. Gallery, 1994, Cavalier Gallery, Greenwich, Conn., 1995, CaribGallery, N.Y.C., 1996, N.Y. State Mus., 1997, Knickerbocker Gallery, 1999, Maison Royale, New Orleans, La., 2002, Represented in permanent collections Peltz,Walker & Dubinsky, Valois of Am. Recipient first prize award annual watercolor exhibit, Pen and Brush, 2000. Mem. Pen and Brush, Poetry Soc. Am. Mem. Collegiate Ch. Avocations: ballroom dancing, old inns and architecture. Home: 106 Cabrini Blvd Apt 5D New York NY 10033-3422 E-mail: linda@lindasouthworth.com.

SOUTHWORTH, ROD BRAND, retired computer science educator; b. Binghampton, N.Y., Aug. 24, 1941; s. William Tanner Southworth and Ruth Evelyn (Brabham) Woods; m. Patrice Marie Gapon, Jan. 10, 1978 (div.); children: Suzi Lynn, Jodi Leigh, Megan Marie, Robin Ashley. BS in Bus., U. Ariz., 1965; MS in Mgmt. Sci. and Info Systems, Colo. State U., 1978. Mktg. rep. IBM, Denver, 1966-69; system analyst Colo. State U., Fort Collins, 1969-73, grad. tchg. asst., 1978-79; project mgr. Systems and Computer Tech., Portland, Oreg., 1973-75, asst. dir. Fairbanks, Alaska, 1975-77; instr. computer info. systems Laramie County C.C., Cheyenne, Wyo., 1979-99; now semi-ret. Author: (software) PC-DOS/MS-DOS Simplified, 1st edit. 1988, 3rd edit. 1992, DOS Complete and Simplified, 1990, DOS Essentials, 1991, DOS 5 Simplified, 1992, DOS 6.2 Simplified, 1994. Mem. Civil Air Patrol, Cheyenne, 1991. Mem. Data Processing Mgmt. Assn. (mem. assoc. level model curriculum 1984-85), Assn. Computing Machinery (mem. assoc. level computer info. processing model curriculum 1991-92). Avocations: boating, water skiing, fishing, stamp collecting, tennis. Home: 1929 Cheyenne Pl Cheyenne WY 82001 Office: Laramie County Comm Coll 1400 E College Dr Cheyenne WY 82007-3204 E-mail: southwor@Lccc.cc.wy.us.edu.

SOUTHWORTH, WILLIAM DIXON, retired education educator; b. Union City, Tenn., Dec. 28, 1918; s. Thomas and Gertrude (Dyer) S.; m. Violet Kuehn, July 22, 1944; children: Geoffrey Scott, Linda Jean. PhB, Marquette U., 1948, MEd, 1950; PhD, NYU, 1961. Tchr., coach La Follette Sch., Milwaukee County, Wis., 1948-51; teaching dist. prin. Grand View Sch., 1951-56; supervising dist. prin. Maple Dale Sch., 1956-58; bldg. prin. Main St. Sch., Port Washington, N.Y., 1958-65; asst. supt. for elem. edn. Huntington (N.Y.) pub. schs., 1965-67; assoc. prof., acting head dept. adminstrn. and supervision St. John's U., Jamaica, N.Y., 1967, chmn. dept., 1968-73, prof., 1968-84. Parliamentarian for 35 internat., nat. regional orgns., expert witness, pub. moderator, and workshop leader. Author: Care and Nurture of the Doctoral Candidate, 1968, 74, Q The Story of Captain Quimby Scott, U.S. Navy WWII, 1997, The Art of Successful Meetings, 1997, Murder on the Flagship, 1998, Corpsman!, 1998; contbr. over 260 articles to ednl. jours., condominium and parliamentary publs. Served with USN, 1938—44. Lutheran. Home: Apt 608 7100 Sunshine Skyway Ln S Saint Petersburg FL 33711-4926 E-mail: vibilfid1@juno.com. *In the conflicting demands of self and society, one must strike a balance by retaining the uniqueness of one's individuality while serving the society that nurtured that uniqueness. It is in the balance thus struck that the complete person evolves self-esteeming, and socially involved.*

SOUTO, CARLOS DIAS, engineer; b. Lisbon, Portugal, Nov. 4, 1938; came to the U.S., 1986; s. Carlos Ernesto and Ilda Alves (Dias) S.; m. Brenda Kay English, Feb. 27, 1971; children: Cristina Lynn, Carlos Roberto. BSc in Naval Sci., Portuguese Naval Acad., 1959; MSc in Geodetic Sci., Ohio State U., 1971. Cert. hydrographic engr. Head of surveys Hydrographic Inst., Lisbon, 1974-78; dir. Sch. of Hydrography and Oceanography, 1981-83; sci. and tech. dir. Hydrographic Inst., 1983-86; naval attaché Embassy of Portugal, Washington, 1986-89, indsl./sci. counselor, 1990-99; dir. Office Indsl. Support-Ministry of Def.-Portugal, 1999—. Mem. Nat. Commn. on Oceanography, Lisbon, 1984-86. Capt. Portuguese Navy, 1959-90. Mem. Profl. Engrs. Assn. Portugal, Soc. Am. Mil. Engrs., N.Y. Acad. Scis. Home: 7020 Tilden Ln Rockville MD 20852-4549 E-mail: cdsouto@capu.net.

SOUTTER, THOMAS DOUGLAS, retired lawyer; b. N.Y.C., Nov. 1, 1934; s. Thomas G. and Hildreth H. (Callanan) S.; m. Virginia Hovenden; children: Alexander D., Christopher A., Hadley H. BA, U. Va., 1955, LL.B., 1962; postgrad., Advanced Mgmt. Program, Harvard U., 1980. Bar: N.Y. 1962, R.I. 1969. Atty. Breed, Abbott & Morgan, N.Y.C., 1962-68; with Textron Inc., Providence, 1968-95, gen. counsel, 1970-95, v.p., 1971-80, sr. v.p., 1980-85, exec. v.p., gen. counsel, 1985-95; cons., 1995-97. Mem. adv. bd. Internat. and Comparative Law Ctr., 1975-95; mem. Assn. Gen. Counsel; bd. dirs. Avco Fin. Svcs., Inc., 1985-95, Paul Revere Corp. 1993-95; trustee New England Legal Found. Nat. chmn. ann. giving campaign U. Va. Law Sch., 1992-94, mem. exec. com. campaign, 1995-2000; former trustee Providence Preservation Soc., Providence Performing Arts Ctr.; mem. U. Va. Arts and Scis. Alumni Coun.; mem. Narragansett coun. Boy Scouts Am. Lt. USNR, 1955-59. Mem. ABA, N.Y. State Bar Assn., R.I. Bar Assn., Internat. Bar Assn. Office: 2 White Birch Ln Barrington RI 02806-4932 E-mail: tdsout@aol.com.

SOUVEROFF, VERNON WILLIAM, JR. business executive; b. L.A., Aug. 12, 1934; s. Vernon William Sr. and Aileen (Young) S.; m. Aileen Patricia Robinson; children— Gail Kathleen, Michael William, Kirk Laron. BS in E.E., Stanford U., 1957; postgrad., Ohio State U., 1958-59. With Litton Industries, Beverly Hills, Calif., 1960-75; with ITT Corp., N.Y.C., 1975-87; prin. Bus. Acquisitions and Investments, 1988—; corp. v.p. ITT Corp., N.Y.C., 1983-84, sr. v.p., 1984-87; pres. ITT Gilfillan, 1979-83; group exec. ITT Def. Space Group, 1983-84; CEO ITT Telecom and Electronics N.Am., 1984-86; pres., chief exec. officer ITT Def. Tech. Corp., 1986-87. Mem. U.S. Def. Policy Adv. Com. on Trade, Washington, 1984-88; bd. advisors, investor Venture Resources, Venture Capital, 1988-92; bd. dirs. Elanix, Inc., Formida Holdings Ltd., Australia; chmn. bd. dirs. Formida Software Corp., San Jose, Calif. Author books on def. downsizing. Served as officer USAF, 1957-60 Recipient Exec. Salute award Los Angeles C. of C., 1981. Mem. IEEE (life), Nat. Contracts Mgmt. Assn., Electronics Industries Assn., Am. Def. Preparedness Assn. (former dir.), Nat. Security Indsl. Assn., Air Force Assn., Navy League, Assn. U.S. Army. Presbyterian.

SOUZA, GILVAN CASTRO, operations and management educator; b. Goiania, Brazil; BS in Aero. Engring., Tech. Inst. Aeronautics, Sao Jose dos Campos, Brazil, 1990; MBA, Clemson U., 1995; PhD, U. of N.C., 1200. Product devel. engr. Volkswagen, Sao Paulo, Brazil, 1991—94; asst. prof. U. of Md., Coll. Pk., Md., 2000—. Contbr. articles to profl. jours. Recipient Outstanding Grad. Student Rsch. award, Kenan Inst., U. of NC, 1998, Summer Rsch. award, U. of Md., 2001; scholar, Technol. Inst. of Aeronautics, Brazil, 1986—90. Mem.: Decision Sciences Inst., Prodn. and Ops. Mgmt. Soc., Inst. for Ops. Rsch. and Mgmt. Sci. Office: University of Maryland Smith School of Business College Park MD 20742 Office Fax: 301-405-8655.

SOUZDALTSEV, IGOR NIKOLAYEVICH, economist; b. Krasnousolsky, Bashkiria, Russia, Nov. 30, 1962; came to U.S., 1995; s. Vladimir Egorovich Baev and Tamara Georgievna Souzdaltseva; m. Elena Alfredovna Ratner, June 22, 1985; 1 child, Svyatoslav. BA in History, Krasnodar (Russia) State U., 1985. Social scis. tchr. H.S., Krasnodar, 1985-90; market analyst E.V.A. Co., 1990-95, Marlin Trading Co., Inc., Ballston Spa, N.Y., 1995-97, Coriander LLC, Ft. Lee, N.J., 1997-2000; chmn. Inst. Natiology, LLC, N.Y.C., N.Y., 2000—. Author: Natiology: Social Science for the Third Millennium, 1999. Mem. AAAS, Am. Polit. Sci. Assn., Fin. Markets Assn., Assn. Study of Nationalities, N.Y. Acad. Scis. Fax: 212-208 3095. E-mail: igor.souzdaltsev@natiology.com.

SOVANI, SANDEEP DINKAR, mechanical engineer, educator, researcher; b. Nagpur, India, Dec. 1, 1971; s. Dinkar Gangadhar and Shailaja Dinkar Sovani; m. Meghana Vijaykumar Divekar, Dec. 10, 1999. B in Engring., U. Pune, 1993; M Tech. in Mech. Engring., Indian Inst. Tech., Madras, 1995; PhD in Mech. Engring., Purdue U., 2001. Sr. rsch. engr. Tata Engring. and Locomotive Co., Ltd., Pune, India, 1995-96; grad. rsch. asst. Purdue U., West Lafayette, Ind., 1996-99, instr., 2000; engr. Fluent, Inc., Ann Arbor, Mich., 2001—. Author rsch. in field. Recipient Nat. Talent Search scholarship Nat. Coun. for Ednl. Rsch. and Tng., Govt. of India, New Delhi, 1987. Mem. ASME, Am. Phys. Soc., Am. Soc. Engring. Edn., Soc. Automotive Engrs. Avocations: travel, photography, painting, writing. Office: Fluent Inc Ste 470 220 Huron St E Ann Arbor MI 48104 E-mail: sandeepsovani@hotmail.com.

SOVDE-PENNELL, BARBARA ANN, sonographer; b. McPherson, Kans., Sept. 27, 1955; d. Benton Ellis and Mary Ann (Ball) Sovde; m. Paul Edwin Pennell, June 5, 1982; 1 child, Eric Louis. AA in Radiologic Tech., Hutchinson Community Jr. Coll., 1977; BS in Radiologic Tech., U. Okla., 1993. Registered diagnostic med. sonographer, radiological technol. Radiographer Hertzler Clinic, Halstead, Kans., 1977-78, Mercy Health Ctr., Okla. City, 1978-81, sonographer, supr. ultrasound dept., 1981-83; mobile sonographer Sun Med. Systems, 1983-84, Diagnostic Radiology, Edmond, Okla., 1984-87; prin., owner, pres. of corp. Ultrasound Unltd., Inc., 1987—. Part-time clin. specialist ultrasound Circadian Can. Ultrasound Equipment Co., 1991—. Active neighborhood recycling, Edmond, 1990—; mem. Greenpeace. Named Outstanding Leader in S.W. Nat. Allied Health Assn., 1981; recipient Outstanding Alumnus award U. Okla. Coll. Allied Health, 1990. Mem. Soc. Diagnostic Med. Sonographers (state rep. 1981-87, regional dir., bd. dirs. 1987-90), Okla. Sonographers Soc. (pres. 1982-84, steering com. 1984—). Democrat. Avocations: reading, biking, camping, environmental issues.

SOVERN, MICHAEL IRA, law educator; b. N.Y.C., Dec. 1, 1931; s. Julius and Lillian (Arnstein) S.; m. Lenore Goodman, Feb. 21, 1952 (div. Apr. 1963); children: Jeffrey Austin, Elizabeth Ann, Douglas Todd; m. Eleanor Leen, Aug. 25, 1963 (div. Feb. 1974); 1 child, Julie Danielle; m. Joan Wit, Mar. 9, 1974 (dec. Sept. 1993); m. Patricia Walsh, Nov. 12, 1995. AB summa cum laude, Columbia U., 1953, LLB (James Ordronaux prize), 1955, LLD (hon.), 1980; PhD (hon.), Tel Aviv U., 1982; LLD (hon.), U. So. Calif., 1989. Bar: N.Y. 1956, U.S. Supreme Ct. 1976. Asst. prof., then assoc. prof. law U. Minn. Law Sch., 1955-58; mem. faculty Columbia Law Sch., 1957—, prof. law, 1960—, Chancellor Kent prof., 1977—, dean Law Sch., 1970-79; chmn. exec. com. faculty Columbia U., 1968-69, provost, exec. v.p., 1979-80, univ. pres., 1980-93, pres. emeritus, 1993. Rsch. dir. Legal Restraints on Racial Discrimination in Employment, Twentieth Century Fund, 1962-66; spl. counsel to gov. N.J., 1974-77; cons. Time Mag., 1965-80; bd. dirs. AT&T, Sequa; mem. panel of arbitrators N.J. Bd. Mediation, Fed. Mediation and Conciliation Svc.; bd. dirs. Asian Cultural Coun., Shubert Orgn., Sta. WNET-TV, NAACP Legal Def. Fund, 1976-97, Freedom Forum Newseum; chmn. N.Y.C. Charter Revision Commn., 1982-83; co-chmn. 2d Cir. Commn. on Reduction of Burdens and Costs in Civil Litigation, 1977-80; chmn. Commn. on Integrity in Govt., 1986; pres. Italian Acad. Advanced Studies in Am., 1991-93, Shubert Found., 1996—; chmn. Japan Soc., 1993—, Am. Acad. Rome, 1993—; chmn. nat. adv. coun. Freedom Forum Media Studies Ctr., 1993-2001; chmn. Sotheby's, 2000—. Author: Legal Restraints on Racial Discrimination in Employment, 1966, Law and Poverty, 1969, Of Boundless Domains, 1994; host Sta. WNET-TV series Leading Questions. Mem. Pulitzer Prize Bd., 1980-93, chmn. pro tem. 1986-87; trustee Kaiser Family Found., 1994-2002, Presdl. Legal Expense Trust, 1994-98; chmn. Sotheby's, 2000. Decorated commendatore Order of Merit (Italy); recipient Alexander Hamilton medal Columbia Coll., 1993, Citizens Union Civic Leadership award, 1993, Town Hall Friend of the Arts award, 2001. Fellow Am. Acad. Arts and Scis.; mem. ABA, Coun. Fgn. Rels., Assn. Bar City N.Y., Am. Philos. Soc., Am. Arbitration Assn. (panel arbitrators), Am. Law Inst., Econ. Club, Nat. Acad. Arbitrators. Office: Columbia U Sch Law 435 W 116th St New York NY 10027-7297

SOVIE, MARGARET DOE, nursing administrator, educator, clinician, researcher; b. Ogdensburg, N.Y., July 7, 1934; d. William Gordon and Mary Rose (Bruyere) Doe; m. Alfred L. Sovie, May 8, 1954; 1 child Scot Marc. Student, U. Rochester, 1950—51; diploma in nursing, St. Lawrence State Hosp. Sch. Nursing, Ogdensburg, 1954; student, St. Lawrence U., 1956—60; BSN summa cum laude, Syracuse U., 1964, MS in Edn., 1968, PhD in Edn., 1972; DSc (hon.) , Health Sci. Ctr. SUNY, Syracuse, 1989; MSN, U. Pa., 1995, adult health nurse practitioner, 1996. Cert. post-masters gerontol. nurse practitioner. Staff nurse, clin. instr. St. Lawrence State Hosp., Ogdensburg, 1954—55, instr. nursing, 1955—62; staff nurse Good Shepherd Hosp., Syracuse, 1962; nursing supr. SUNY Upstate Med. Ctr., 1963—65, insvc. instr., 1965—66, edn. dir. and coord. nursing svc., 1966—71, asst. dean Coll. Health Related Professions, 1972—84, assoc. prof. nursing, 1973—76, dir. continuing edn. in nursing, 1974—76, assoc. dean and dir. div. continuing edn. Coll. Health Related Professions, 1974—76; spl. assignment in pres.'s office SUNY Upstate Med. Ctr. and Syracuse U., 1972—73; assoc. dean for nursing U. Rochester, NY, 1976—88, assoc. prof. nursing, 1976—85, prof., 1985—88; assoc. dir. for nursing Strong Meml. Hosp., U. Rochester Med. Ctr., 1976—88; chief nursing officer Hosp. U. Pa., Phila., 1988—96, assoc. exec. dir., 1988—94, assoc. dean for nursing practice Sch. Nursing, 1988—96; prin. investigator hosp. restructuring NINR U. Pa., 1996—2000, Jane Delano prof. nursing adminstrn. Sch. Nursing, 1988—, sr. fellow Leonard Davis Inst. Health Econs., 1992—; trustee bd. U. Pa. Health Sys., 1993—96; NP PNN Health Annex, 1998—2001. Nursing coord. and project dir. Ctrl. N.Y. Regional Med. Program, Syracuse, 1968—71; mem. edn. dept. State Bd. Nursing, Albany, NY, 1974—84, chmn., NY, 1981—83, chmn. practice com., NY, 1975—80, mem. joint practice com., NY, 1975—80, vice chmn., NY, 1980—81; mem. adv. com. to clin. nurse scholars program Robert Wood Johnson Found., Princeton, NJ, 1982—88; adj. assoc. prof. Syracuse U. Sch. Nursing, 1973—76, chmn. vis. com. Coll. Nursing, 1996—99; mem. Gov.'s Health Adv. Panel N.Y. State Health Planning Commn., 1976—82, task force on health manpower policy, 1978, informal support networks sect. steering com., 80; mem. health manpower tng. and utilization task force State N.Y. Commn. on Health Edn. and Illness Prevention, 1979; mem. task force on nursing pers. N.Y. State Health Adv. Coun., 1980; mem. adv. panel on nursing svcs. U.S. Pharm. Conv., Inc., Washington, 1985—90; cons. Nat. Ctr. for Svcs. Rsch. and Health Care Tech. Assessment, Rockville, Md., 1987; mem. nursing stds. task force Joint Commn. Accreditation Health Care Orgns., 1988—90; mem. various other adv. coms.; lectr. in field. Mem. editl. bd. Health Care Supr., 1982—87, Nursing Econs., 1983—, Best Practices and Benchmarking in Health Care, 1995—98, mem. manuscript rev. panel Nursing Outlook, 1987—91, mem. editl. bd. Seminars for Nurse Mgrs., 1994—; contbr. articles, chapters to books. Bd. visitors Sch. Nursing, U. Md., Balt., 1984—89; mem. bd. mgrs. Strong Meml. Hosp., Rochester, 1983—88; bd. dirs. Monroe County Assn. for Hearing, 1979—82, Vis. Nurse Svc. of Rochester and Monroe County, 1978, Southeastern Pa. chpt. ARC, 1991—97. Recipient Ann. Margaret D. Sovie lectureship inaugurated, Strong Meml. Hosp., U. Rochester, 1989, Dean's Outstanding Alumni award, Coll. of Nursing, Syracuse U., 1994; fellow spl. nurse rsch. fellow, NIH, 1971—72; grantee various orgns. Fellow: Am. Acad. Nursing (program com. 1980—81, task force on hosp. nursing 1981—83, chair expert panel on quality health care 1994—97, mem. panel 1994—); mem.: Inst. Medicine of NAS (com. design strategy for quality rev. and assurance in Medicare 1988—90), N.Y. State Nurses Assn. (med. surg. nursing group, chmn. edn. com. dist. 4 1974—76, chmn. cmty. planning group for nursing dist. 4 1974—75, coun. on regional planning in nursing 1974—76, del. to conv. 1978, Nursing Svc. Adminstrn. award 1985), Am. Orgn. Nurse Execs. (stds. task force 1987, rsch. com. 1997—98), ANA (nat. rev. com. for expanded role programs 1975—78, site visitor to programs requesting accreditation 1976—78, cabinet on nursing svcs. 1986—90, cert. bd. nursing adminstrn. 1983—86, ad hoc com. on advanced practice 1992—95), Sigma Theta Tau. Republican. Roman Catholic. Avocations: golf, cross-country skiing, swimming, dancing. Office: U Pa Sch Nursing 420 Guardian Dr Philadelphia PA 19104-6096 E-mail: msovie@nursing.upenn.edu.

SOVIK, EDWARD ANDERS, architect, consultant; b. Honan, China, June 9, 1918; s. Edward Anderson and Anna (Tenwick) S.; m. Genevieve Elaine Hendrickson, June 29, 1946 (dec.); m. Anne Running, Mar. 25, 2001; children: Rolf, Martin, Peter. BA, St. Olaf Coll., 1939; student, Art Students League N.Y., 1939-40, Luther Theol. Sem., 1940-42; MArch, Yale U., 1949; DFA (hon.), Concordia Coll., 1981. Ret. chmn. SMSQ, Architects and predecessors, Northfield, Minn.; prof. art emeritus St. Olaf Coll. Lectr. on ch. design at various confs., schs., univs.; participant, planner, del. numerous domestic and fgn. confs. on religion and architecture; mem., officer various profl., religious and pub. bds. and commns. Author: Architecture for Worship; Contbr. numerous articles to mags., anthologies.; works include chs., coll. and univ. bldgs., instns. With USMC, 1942-45; maj. Res. Decorated D.F.C., Purple Heart, Air medals. Fellow AIA; mem. AIA Minn. (pres. 1977, Gold medal 1981), Phi Beta Kappa. Democrat. Lutheran. Home: 711 Summit Ave Northfield MN 55057-1568 E-mail: sovik@rconnect.com.

SØVIK, NILS, education educator; b. Os in Hordaland, Norway, June 18, 1928; s. Bertin and Nilsina (Lekven) S.; m. Gerd Margrethe Sørhuus; children: Edmund, Øyvind. MA, U. Oslo, 1960, PhD, 1972. Asst. prof. U. Trondheim, Norway, 1963-67; rsch. scholarship U. Wis., Madison, 1968-70; assoc. prof. U. Trondheim, 1971-77, dir. rsch. social sci., 1977-80, prof. edn., 1981. Author: Developmental Cybernetics of Handwriting and Motor Coordination, 1975. Mem. Royal Norwegian Soc. Scis. and Letters (leader humanities 1988-89, sec. gen. 1990-96). Avocation: music. Home: Tyholtveien 16 N-7052 Trondheim Norway Office: Dept Edn NTNU N-7491 Trondheim Norway E-mail: nils.sovik@ovt.ntnu.no.

SOWA, ARTUR, mathematician, researcher; b. Poland, Oct. 27, 1965; came to U.S., 1992; s. Witold and Lucyna Sowa; m. Jolanta Sowa, Aug. 15, 1987; children: Izaak, Oliver. MS in Math., Warsaw U., 1990; PhD in Math., CUNY, 1995. Postdoctoral asst. CUNY, N.Y.C., 1995-97; postdoctoral rsch. assoc. Yale U., New Haven, 1997-2000, lectr., 2000; scientist Pegasus Imaging Corp., Tampa, Fla., 2000—02. Cons. Fast Mathematical Algorithms and Hardware, Hamden, Conn., 1997-2000. Contbr. articles to profl. jours. Recipient 1st prize, The Marcinkiewicz Competition, Poland, 1990, Rsch. Associateship award, NRC, 2001. Mem.: IEEE, Math. Assn. Am. Avocations: philosophy, hiking, music. Achievements include proposing a field theory for the mesoscopic description of correlated systems of electrons. E-mail: ArturSowa@mesoscopia.com.

SOWA, PAUL EDWARD, research engineer; b. Chgo., Dec. 10, 1952; s. Edward Joseph and Gladys Angela (Bogdas) S.; m. Nanette Elizabeth Raddatz, Dec. 17, 1977; children: Adam, Alexander, Emily. BSME, U. Ill., 1976; MBA, Keller Grad. Sch., 1990. Mech. engr. Commonwealth Edison, Chgo., 1976-79; product specialist Signode Corp., Glenview, Ill., 1979-81, packaging engr., 1981-85, product mgr., 1985-86; sr. packaging engr. ITW/Signode, 1986—. Del. Nat. Safe Transit Assn., Chgo., 1988—. Inst. Packaging Profls. (cert.), ASTM (mem. com. D-10 1990—). Democrat. Roman Catholic. Office: ITW/Signode 3640 W Lake Ave Glenview IL 60025-1215

SOWALSKY, PATTI LURIE, author; b. Hartford, Conn., Oct. 16, 1940; d. Joseph Aaron and Mildred (Weisinger) Lurie; m. Jerome Saul Sowalsky, Oct. 22, 1961; children: Richard, John, Susan. Cert. dental hygiene, U. Pa., 1960. Author, pub. On Exhibit Fine Art Publs., Potomac, Md., 1992-98. Author, publisher: (art travel guide) On Exhibit: The Art Lover's Travel Guide to American Museums, 1992-98. Docent Corcoran Mus., Washington, 1985-90; cert. in Braille, Libr. of Congress, Washington, Golden Circle mem. Kennedy Ctr., Washington, 1988—. Recipient Docent of Yr. award Corcoran Mus., Washington, 1989. Avocations: art collector, rosearian. Home: 8613 Chateau Dr Potomac MD 20854-4528

SOWDER, DONALD DILLARD, pharmaceutical executive; b. Rocky Mt., Va., Mar. 28, 1937; s. Roman Dillard and Virginia (Dowdy) S.; m. Beverly Reid , Nov. 29, 1957; children: Reid Dillard, Susan Allison, Donald Stuart.

BS, Va. Tech., 1959; cert. in sales mgmt., Columbia U., 1976, cert. in fin., 1984; diploma, U.S. Army Command & Gen. Staff Coll., 1978; cert. in mgmt., U. Va., 1993. Sales rep. Sealtest Foods, Norfolk, Va., 1962-64; med. sales rep. Lederle Labs. div. Am. Cyanamid Co., 1964-69, dist. sales mgr. Washington, 1969-74, nat. mgr. sales tng. Pearl River, N.Y., 1974-76, mgr. fed. govt. affairs Washington, 1976-81, nat. sales mgr. hosp. div. Wayne, N.J., 1981-85, nat. sales mgr. oncology div., 1985-88, dir. govt. sales Fairfax, Va., 1988-95; pharmaceutical mktg. cons., 1995-97; v.p. tng. & mng. dir. Peer Perspectives divsn. R.A. Becker, 1998—. Instr. U.S. Army Command & Gen. Staff Coll., Washington, 1977-81; govt. sales advisor Nat. Wholesale Drug Assn., Alexandria, Va., 1991; mem. Health Industry Fed. Adv. Coun., 1994. Editorial reviewer Mil. Medicine, 1992—; contbr. articles to profl. jours. Bd. dirs. Shadow Walk Devel. Assn., 1990—. Col. USAR. Instr. of Yr. USAR, 1979. Mem. Assn. Mil. Surgeons U.S. (chmn. sustaining mems. 1980-81, lectr. 1989), Am. Soc. Hosp. Pharmacists, Res. Officers Assn., Va. Tech. Corps of Cadets Alumni Assn. (bd. dirs.), Mil. Dist. of Washington Officers Club System. Republican. Methodist. Avocations: golf, tennis, water sports. Home: 12701 Knightcross Rd Midlothian VA 23113-9611 Office: 1633 Broadway New York NY 10019-6708

SOWDER, FRED ALLEN, foundation administrator, alphabet specialist; b. Cin., July 17, 1940; s. William Franklin and Lucille (Estes) S.; m. Sandra Ann Siegman, July 15, 1961 (div. Sept. 1963); 1 child, William. Student, Cin. Sch. Ct. Reporting, 1975; diploma Self-Health Insts., Sch. of Med. Masso-Therapy, 1985; diploma, Cin. Sch. Hypnosis, 1989. Founder World Union Universal Alphabet, Cin., 1981—, Internat. Assn. Sch. Massage, Cin., 1988—. Inventor of hundreds of published and unpublished alphabets and writing systems, including light wave, color and musical tone systems and tactile systems for the blind; author: Sowder Shorthand, 1980, Universal Alphabet: What and Why, 1981, Your Intimacy Quotient: The Symptoms, Causes & Consequences of Intimacy Deprivation, 1996; contbr. numerous articles to mags. State dir. Soc. Separationists, Cin., 1967-70; bd. dirs. ACLU of Ohio, ACLU Found., 1984-89, sec., Cin. chpt., 1984-89. Mem. AAAS, Amnesty Internat., Ohio Com. to Abolish Capital Punishment, Assn. for Humanistic Psychology, Internat. Soc. for Gen. Semantics, Am. Sunbathing Assn., The Naturist Soc., Am. Massage Therapy Assn., Urban Appalachian Coun. Democrat. Home: PO Box 252 Cincinnati OH 45201-0252 Office: World Union Universal Alphabet PO Box 252 Cincinnati OH 45201-0252

SOWDER, KATHLEEN ADAMS, marketing executive; b. Person County, N.C., Feb. 9, 1951; d. George W. and Mary W. (Woody) A.; BS, Radford Coll., 1976; MBA, Va. Poly. Inst., 1978; m. Angelo R. LoMascolo, Apr. 11, 1980 (div.); 1 child, Mary Jennifer. Asst. product mgr. GTE Sylvania, Waltham, Mass., 1978-79, product mgr. video products, 1979-80; comml. mktg. mgr. Am. Dist. Telegraph, N.Y.C., 1980-87; v.p. mktg. ESL, Hingham, Mass., 1987-91; exec. v.p. Falcon Detection Techs., Inc., Plymouth, Mass., 1991-94; gen. mgr. Westec Bus. Security, Irvine, Calif., 1995—2002, CEO Nova Security Sys., Fullerton, Calif., 2002-. Mem. Am. Mktg. Assn., Am. Soc. Indsl. Security (past chair standing com. on phys. security). Republican. Office: Nova Security Systems 819 Pueblo Fullerton CA 92835 Home: 10473 La Sombra Ave Fountain Valley CA 92708-5210 E-mail: ksowder@novasecuritysystems.com.

SOWDER, ROBERT ROBERTSON, architect; b. Kansas City, Kans., Dec. 29, 1928; s. James Robert and Agnes (Robertson) S.; m. Joan Goddard, July 26, 1954; 1 dau., Lisa Robertson Lee. BA, U. Wash., 1953; B.Arch., U. Va., 1958; grad. diploma in Architecture, Ecole Des Beaux Arts, Fontainebleau, France, 1952. Designer Architects Collaborative, Boston, 1958-59, Peirce & Pierce (architects), Boston, 1959-63; asso. Fred. Bassetti & Co. (architects), Seattle, 1963-67; partner Naramore, Bain, Brady & Johanson (architects), 1967-81; pres. NBBJ Internat., 1976-81; architect TRA, Seattle, 1981-83; v.p. Daniel, Mann, Johnson & Mendenhall, San Francisco, 1983-93; prin. RRS Consulting, 1993—. Archtl. design critic Boston Archtl. Ctr., 1961-62. Important works include Ridgeway III Dormitories, Bellingham, Wash. (Dept. Housing and Urban Devel. Honor award), Seattle Rapid Transit (HUD Excellence award), Safeco Ins. Co. Home Office Complex, Seattle, King County Stadium, Balt. Conv. Ctr., Oreg. Conv. Ctr., San Francisco (Moscone) Conv. Ctr. Expansion, Honolulu Conv. Ctr., Wilmington (Del.) Conv. Ctr. Mem. Redmond (Wash.) Design Rev. Bd., 1996-2000. Served with CIC U.S. Army, 1954-56. Recipient Premier Prix D'Architecture Ecole Des Beaux Arts, Fontainebleau, 1951, 52, Prix D'Remondet Fontainebleau, 1952 Mem. AIA (emeritus), Internat. Assn. Assembly Mgrs., Seattle Tennis Club, Seattle Rainier Club, Scarab, Sigma Chi. Episcopalian. Home and Office: 17032 NE 135th Ct Redmond WA 98052-1715

SOWELL, LAVEN, retired music educator; b. Wewoka, Okla., Jan. 9, 1933; s. Vestal Laven and Viola Jane Sowell. MusB, U. Okla., 1955, MA, Columbia U., 1964; postgrad., Manhattan Sch. Music, 1956—57, Conservatoire de Musique de Fontainebleau, France, 1966; studied with Clark Snell, Martial Singher, Joseph Benton, John Brownlee, Samuel Margolis, Nadia Boulanger. Choral condr. Edison H.S., Tulsa, 1961—70; chorus master Tulsa Opera, 1962—94; dir. music 1st Presbyn. Ch., Tulsa, 1969—85; prof. music U. Tulsa, 1970—91. Vocal adjudicator various mus. orgns.; tchr. pvt. voice lessons. Co-author: Tulsa Opera Chronicles, 1992; author: My Music Notebook, 2000. Bd. dirs. Tulsa Opera. Recipient Gov.'s Arts award, State of Okla., 1991. Democrat. Presbyterian. Avocations: travel, reading, opera. Home: 3540 S Wheeling Ave Tulsa OK 74105

SOWER, VICTOR EDMUND, management educator; b. Roanoke, Va., Sept. 3, 1946; s. Hammond Edmundson and Daphne Muriel (Dymond) S.; m. Judith Lynn Carroll, June 17, 1967; children: Diane C. Sower Fuller, Christopher Hammond. BS in Chemistry, Va. Poly. Inst. and State U., 1968; MBA, Auburn U., 1980; PhD, U. North Tex., 1990. Process engr. Radford (Va.) Army Ammunition Plant, 1968-69; process devel. engring. mgr. Ampex Corp., Opelika, Ala., 1971-80; gen. mgr. Tandy Magnetics, Ft. Worth, 1980-87; mfg. cons. Tandy Corp., 1987-90; prof. dept. mgmt. and mktg. Sam Houston State U., Huntsville, 1990—. Steering com. Ctr. Bus. and Econ. Rsch., Huntsville, 1990—; cons. various mfg. and svc. orgns. Author: Classic Readings in Operations Management, 1995, An Introduction to Quality Management and Engineering, 1999; mem. editl. rev. bd. Jour. Bus. Strategies, Huntsville, 1990—, Jour. Ops. Mgmt., 1995—; contbr. articles to profl. jours. Dist. com. mem. Bedford (Tex.) area Boy Scouts Am., 1987-90, dist. advancement chmn., 1988-89. 1st lt. U.S. Army, 1969-71. Mem. AIChE, Am. Chem. Soc., Am. Soc. Quality Control (sr. cert.), Am. Prodn. and Inventory Control Soc., Decision Scis. Inst., Acad. Mgmt. Roman Catholic. Office: Sam Houston State U Dept Mgmt and Mktg Huntsville TX 77341

SOWERS, AMELIA BARNET, speech and language pathologist; b. Houston, Mar. 13, 1952; d. Albert Glenn and Helen June (Meador) Barnet; m. George Vernon Sowers Jr., Aug. 23, 1975; children: George Vernon III, Adam Glenn. BA, U. Houston, 1975, MA, 1993. Lic. and cert. speech-lang. pathologist, Tex. Speech-lang. pathologist Aldine Ind. Sch. Dist., Houston, 1976-78, Tomball (Tex.) Ind. Sch. Dist., 1978-83, Conroe (Tex.) Ind. Sch. Dist., 1984-96; pvt. practice, 1996—. Mem. Crighton Players; organizer Crighton Kids, Crighton Players Performing Arts Sch. for Youth; apptd. to City of Conroe Commn. on Arts & Culture; pres. Crighton Theatre Found.; clin. supr. Grad. Sch., Tex. Women's U. Mem. NEA, Am. Speech, Lang. and Hearing Assn., Tex. Speech and Hearing Assn., Tex. Tchrs. Assn., Houston Assn. Comm. Disorders, Montgomery County Performing Arts Soc. (com.), Conroe Svc. League. Methodist. Avocations: reading, crafts, dancing, community theatre. Home and Office: 25 Village Hill Dr Conroe TX 77304-3525

SOWERS, WESLEY HOYT, lawyer, management consultant; b. Whiting, Ind., Aug. 26, 1905; s. Samuel Walter and Bertha E. (Spurrier) S.; m. Gladys Krueger, Jan. 21, 1929; children: Penny (Mrs. David Buxton), Wesley Hoyt Jr. BS, Purdue U., 1926, MS, 1927; JD, DePaul U., 1941; grad., Advanced Mgmt. Program, Harvard, 1960. Bar: Ill. 1940; registered patent atty. and practitioner ICC. Chemist Shell Oil Co., East Chicago, Ind., 1927-29; sales engr. Nat. Lead Co., St. Louis, 1929-31; lab. supr. patent atty. Pure Oil Co., Chgo., 1932-42; v.p. Bay Chem. Co., New Orleans, 1942-50, Frontier Chem. Co., Wichita, Kans., 1950-57; pres. Frontier Chem. div. Vulcan Materials Co., 1957-65; exec. v.p., dir. Vulcan Materials Co., Birmingham, 1958-65; mgmt. counsel, 1965—. Mem. health professions vis. com. Wichita State U. Patentee in field Past chmn. Met. Planning Commn., Wichita and Sedgwick County, 1958; commr. Kans. Econ. Devel. Bd.; chmn. Kansas Com. for Constitutional Revision, Sedgwick County U.S. Savs. Bonds Sales; past chmn. Kans. Radio Free Europe; past mem. adv. com. Kans. Geol. Survey; mem. Kans. Senate, 1970-81; former mem. engring. adv. council Sch. Engring. and Architecture, Kans. State U.; regent, trustee Wichita State U., HCA/Wesley Med. Ctr., Wichita; bd. dirs. Health Systems Agy. of Southeast Kans., Bd. of Health Sedgwick County, Inst. Logopedics, Quivira council Boy Scouts Am., YMCA, Health Systems Agy. S.E. Kans.; past trustee Midwest Research Inst.; mem. adv. bd. Kans. U. Bus. Sch.; vis. com. Coll. Health Profession, Wichita State U.; chmn. Kans. Health Care Providers Malpractice Commn.; mem. Kans. Health Care Costs Commn., Kans. Health Coordinating Council, Wichita/Sedgwick County Bd. Health; mem. gov.'s adv. commn. Kans. Dept. Health and Environment. Mem. AAAS, Kans. C. of C. (past pres., past dir.), Wichita C. of C. (past pres. 1959, past dir., Uncommon Citizen award 1988), Kans. Assn. Commerce and Industry (past pres., dir.), Am. Chem. Soc., AAAS, Smithsonian Assocs., Soc. Chem. Industry, Ill. Bar Assn., Wichita Bar Assn., Phi Delta Theta. Lodges: Rotary. Home and Office: Apt 108 6110 N Pennsylvania Ave Oklahoma City OK 73112-7389

SOWERS, WILLIAM ARMAND, civil engineer; b. Willis, Va., Apr. 23, 1923; s. Harry Cline and Effie Vivian (Slusher) S.; m. Gale Johnson, May 20, 1978; children: Jane Dixon, Jean Marie. Student, Roanoke Coll., 1940-42; BCE, Va. Poly. Inst., 1947, BS in Archtl. Engring., 1948. Registered profl. engr., Va. Assoc. Brown, Wells & Meagher, Roanoke, Va., 1948-50; ptnr. R.L. Brown and Assocs., 1950-53, Sowers, Knowles & Rodes, Roanoke, 1953-59, Sowers, Rodes & Whitescarver, Roanoke, 1959-84, Sowers & Assocs., Roanoke, 1984-94; DJG Sowers, Mann Sowers-Mann, 1994-96; ptnr. McKinney, Sowers-Mann, 1996-97, McKinney & Co., 1997-98, ret., 1998. Trustee ACEC Health Life Ins., St. Louis, 1975-83; commr. city planning City of Roanoke, 1976-92. Mem. Am. Cons. Engrs. (nat. pres. 1970-72), Cons. Engrs. Coun. Va. (svc. award 1972), Va. Soc. Profl. Engrs. (Svc. to Profession award 1972), Illuminating Engring. Soc., Shenandoah Club, Masons. E-mail: gbpiedmont@aol.com.

SOWLE, DONALD EDGAR, management consultant; b. Mt. Pleasant, Mich., May 27, 1915; s. Sidney Edgar and Mary Agnes (West) S.; m. Gretchen Elizabeth MacRae, July 4, 1942 (dec. Feb. 1993); children: Lisa Sowle Cahill, Mary Ann Sowle Messing; m. Catherine Taggart Lewis, Nov. 25, 1995 (dec. Apr. 1999). BS, Central Mich. U., 1940; postgrad., Harvard U., 1942, M.I.T., 1942; MBA, U. Chgo., 1950. Sales rep. Armour & Co., Grand Rapids, Mich., 1940-41; commd. 2d lt. USAF, advanced through grades to col., 1958; asst. dir. Jet Propulsion Lab., Calif. Inst. Tech., Pasadena, 1965-68; group v.p. Gulf & Western Industries, Los Angeles, 1968-69; dir. studies Congl. Commn. on Govt. Procurement, Washington, 1970-73; pres., chmn. bd. dirs. Don Sowle Assocs., Inc., Arlington, Va., 1973-81; adminstr. Fed. Procurement Policy, Exec. Office of The Pres. of The U.S., Washington, 1981-85; mgmt. cons., 1985—. Dir. Procurement Round Table, 1985—; mem. adv. bd. Fed. Contracts Report, Bur. Nat. Affairs, 1965-91; nat. regent Inst. Cost Analysis, 1981; instr. Georgetown U., 1961-65; adj. prof. and mem. adv. council procurement mgmt. program Kogod Coll. Am. U., Washington, 1981—. Mem. adv. coun. Sch. Bus. Marymount U., 1985-94. Recipient Dept. Def. Joint Svc. Commendation medal, 1963, Legion of Merit award Sec. Def., 1964, Pub. Svc. award Los Angeles County, 1969, award Cen. Mich. U., 1968, 92. Fellow Nat. Contract Mgmt. Assn. (cert. profl. contract mgr., bd. advisers emeritus, Herbert Roback Meml. award 1990); mem. U.S. C. of C. (procurement coun. 1985), Nat. Security Indsl. Assn. (hon. life), Nat. Assn. Uniforms Svcs. (life mem., bd. dirs. 1984-88), Ret. Officers Assn. (life), Ronald Regan Alumni Assn., Am. Legion, Capitol Hill Club, Officers Club, NASA Alumni League, Beta Gamma Sigma. Republican. Roman Catholic. Home: 6800 Fleetwood Rd Apt 1205 Mc Lean VA 22101-3611

SOWMAN, HAROLD GENE, ceramic engineer, researcher; b. Murphysboro, Ill., July 21, 1923; s. Harold Thomas and Thelma (Crombar) S.; m. Gladys May Wright, Dec. 8, 1945; children— Letitia Ann, Daniel Patrick BS in Ceramic Engring., U. Ill., 1948, MS in Ceramic Engring., 1949, PhD in Ceramic Engring., 1951. Assoc. ceramist Titanium Alloy, Niagara Falls, N.Y., 1951-52; research assoc. Knolls Atomic Power Lab., Gen. Electric Co., Schenectady, 1952-57; various supervisory and mgmt. positions in nuclear materials research and devel. 3M Co., St. Paul, 1957-65, research specialist, 1965-67, sr. research specialist, 1967-70, corp. scientist, 1970-87. Friedberg Meml. lectr. Nat. Inst. Ceramic Engrs., 1988. Author articles, govt. reports on research and devel. of ceramic and nuclear materials; patentee in field Served to 2d lt. AUS, 1943-46 Recipient Hon. Alumni award for disting. service in engring. U. Ill. Coll. Engring., 1983 Fellow Am. Ceramic Soc. (John Jeppson medal 1985, Samuel Geijsbeek award 1989); mem. Nat. Acad. Engring., Acad. of Ceramics, 3M Carlton Soc., Sigma Xi, Tau Beta Pi (chpt. Eminent Engr. award 1983). Home: 1861 Pondside Ln Naples FL 34109-1409

SOX, HAROLD CARLETON, JR. physician, educator, editor; b. Palo Alto, Calif., Aug. 18, 1939; s. Harold Carleton and Mary (Griffiths) Sox; m. Carol Helen Hill, Aug. 26, 1962; children: Colin Montgomery, Lara Katherine. BS, Stanford U., 1961; MD cum laude, Harvard U., 1966. Diplomate Am. Bd. Internal Medicine. Intern and resident Mass. Gen. Hosp., Boston, 1966—68; clin. assoc. Nat. Cancer Inst., Bethesda, Md., 1968—70; instr. Dartmouth Med. Sch., Hanover, NH, 1970—73; asst. prof. medicine to prof. Stanford U. Sch. Medicine, Calif., 1973—88; Joseph Huber prof., chmn. dept. medicine Dartmouth Med. Sch., 1988—2001; editor Annals of Internal Medicine Am. Coll. Physicians, Am. Soc. Internal Medicine, Phila., 2001—. Pretest writing com. Am. Bd. Internal Medicine, 1992—94; panel mem. Nat. Bd. Med. Examiners, Physician Assts. Nat. Certifying Exam., 1973—76; chair com. on priority-setting for health tech. assessment Inst. Medicine, 1990—91, U.S. preventive svcs. task force chair, 1990—95, mem., 1998—2001; chair Inst. Medicine com. on HIV and U.S. blood supply, 1994—95; chair task force to revise internal medicine residency curriculum Federated Coun. Internal Medicine, 1993—97; chair Inst. Medicine Com. Health Effects Persian Gulf War Svc., 1998—2000; mem. nat. adv. com. Generalist Physician Scholars program Robert Wood Johnson Found., 1992—; physician Leaders on Nat. Drug Policy, 1997—; chair exec. com. Medicare Coverage Adv. Com., 1999—. Author: Medical Decision Making, 1988; editor: Common Diagnostic Tests, 1987, Common Diagnostic Tests, 2d edit., 1990; mem. editl. bd.: Med. Decision Making, 1980—87, mem. editl. bd.: Jour. Gen. Internal Medicine, 1985—87, mem. editl. bd.: New Eng. Jour. Medicine, 1990—97, cons. assoc. editor: Am. Jour. Medicine, 1988—95, assoc. editor: Sci. Am. Medicine, 1995—2001; contbr. chapters to books, articles to profl. jours. Master: ACP-ASIM (clin. efficacy assessment subcom. 1985—92, bd. regents 1991—2000, chmn. editl. policy com. 1994—97, pres. 1998—99); fellow: AAAS, Royal Australasian Coll. Physicians (hon.); mem.: Inst. Medicine of NAS, Assn. Profs. Medicine (bd. dirs. 1996—2000), Assn. Am. Physicians, Am. Fedn. Clin. Rsch., Soc. for Med. Decision Making (trustee 1980—83, pres. 1983—84, 4th Career Achievement award 1998), Soc. for Gen. Internal Medicine (coun. 1980—83, Robert J. Glaser Career Achievement award 2000), Alpha Omega Alpha. Home: 232 Philip Pl Philadelphia PA 19106 Office: Am. Coll Physicians Am Soc Internal Medicine 190 N Independence Mall W Philadelphia PA 19106-1572 E-mail: hsox@mail.acponline.org.

SOX, STEPHEN EDWARD, engineer; b. Palo Alto, Calif., Mar. 17, 1965; s. Edward Ellis and Josephine (Delgado) S. BSME, U. Pacific, 1988. Engr. in training Naval Energy & Environ. Support Activity, Port Hueneme, Calif., 1985-86; asst. engr. Westinghouse Electric Co., Sunnyvale, 1987-88; engr. Huges Aircraft Co., El Segundo, 1988—. Mem. Am. Soc. Mechanical Engrs. (sec. 1987, treas. 1986), Tau Beta Pi, Phi Kappa Phi Honor Soc., Palo Alto Ski. Democrat.

SOYER, DAVID, cellist, music educator; b. Phila., Feb. 24, 1923; s. Samson and Esther (Faggin) S.; m. Janet Putnam, June 23, 1957; children: Daniel, Jeffrey. Student pub. schs., N.Y.C.; D.F.A. (hon.), U. South Fla., 1976, SUNY, 1983. Prof. cello Curtis Inst. Music, 1967; prof. music U. Md. Cellist with, Bach Aria Group, 1948-49, Guilet Quartet, 1949-51, New Music Quartet, 1954-55, Guarneri String Quartet, N.Y.C., 1964— , (Recipient 5 Grammy awards for Guarneri Quartet recs. 1965-74). Served with USNR, 1942-46. Mem. Century Assn. Jewish. Home: 6 W 77th St New York NY 10024-5125 Office: Herbert Barrett Mgmt care H Beall Mgmt 1776 Broadway Ste 1610 New York NY 10019-2083

SOYSTER, MARGARET BLAIR, lawyer; b. Washington, Aug. 5, 1951; d. Peter and Eliza (Shumaker) S. AB magna cum laude, Smith Coll., 1973; JD, U. Va., 1976. Bar: N.Y. 1977, U.S. Dist. Ct. (so. and ea. dists.) N.Y. 1977, U.S. Ct. Appeals (2nd cir.) 1979, U.S. Supreme Ct. 1981, U.S. Ct. Appeals (4th cir.) 1982, U.S. ct. Appeals (11th cir.) 1987, U.S. Ct. Appeals (7th cir.) 1991, U.S. Ct. Appeals (3d cir.) 1992. Assoc. Rogers & Wells, N.Y.C., 1976-84, ptnr., 1984-99, Clifford Chance Rogers & Wells LLP, N.Y.C., 2000—. Mem. ABA, Assn. of Bar of City of N.Y., Nat. Assn. Coll. and Univ. Attys., Phi Beta Kappa. Office: Clifford Chance US LLP 200 Park Ave Ste 5200 New York NY 10166-0005

SPACE, THEODORE MAXWELL, lawyer; b. Binghamton, N.Y., Apr. 3, 1938; s. Maxwell Evans and Dorothy Marie (Boone) S.; m. Susan Shultz, Aug. 18, 1962 (div. Apr. 1979); children: William Schuyler, Susanna; m. Martha Collins, Apr. 6, 1991. AB, Harvard U., 1960; LLB, Yale U., 1966. Bar: Conn., 1966, U.S. Dist. Ct. Conn. 1966, U.S. Supreme Ct. 1970, U.S. Tax Ct. 1989, U.S. Ct. Appeals (2nd cir.) 1967, U.S. Ct. Appeals (6th cir.) 1992, U.S. Ct. Appeals (11th cir.) 1994, U.S. Dist. Ct. (ea. dist.) Mich. 1997. Assoc. Shipman & Goodwin LLP, Hartford, Conn., 1966-71, ptnr., 1971—, mng. ptnr., 1984-87, adminstv. ptnr., 1988-91. Mem. Bloomfield (Conn.) Bd. Edn., 1973-85, chmn., 1975-85; treas. Citizens Scholarship Found., Bloomfield, 1971-73, bd. dirs., 1973-91; mem. Bloomfield Human Rels. Commn., 1973-75; mem. Bloomfield Town Dem. Com., 1976-83; corporator Hartford Pub. Libr., 1976—; trustee Conn. Hist. Soc., 1997—, mem. libr. com., 1990—, chair, 1993-2000; chmn. fin. com., coun. mem. Unitarian Soc. Hartford, 1988-91. Lt. (j.g.) USN, 1960-63. Mem. ABA, Conn. Bar Assn. (mem. exec. com. adminstrv. law sect. 1980—), Hartford County Bar Assn., Am. Law Inst., Am. Health Lawyers Assn., Conn. Health Lawyers Assn., Swift's Inn, Hartford Club. Democrat. Unitarian Universalist. Avocations: reading, classical music. Home: 59 Prospect St Bloomfield CT 06002-3038 Office: Shipman & Goodwin LLP One American Row Hartford CT 06103-2833

SPACEK, SISSY (MARY ELIZABETH SPACEK), actress; b. Quitman, Tex., Dec. 25, 1949; d. Edwin S. and Virginia S.; m. Jack Fisk, 1974; children: Schuyler Elizabeth, Virginia Madison. Student, Lee Strasberg Theatrical Inst. Motion picture appearances include Prime Cut, 1972, Badlands, 1974, Carrie, 1976 (Acad. award nomination for best actress 1976), Three Women, 1977 (Best Supporting Actress 1977), Welcome to L.A., 1977, Heartbeat, 1980, Coal Miner's Daughter, 1980 (Acad. award best actress 1980, Golden Globe best actress 1980, Brit. Acad. award nomination best actress 1980, L.A. Film Critics for best actress 1980, Nat. Soc. Film Critics best actress 1980), Raggedy Man (Golden Globe nomination best actress 1981), 1981, Missing, 1982 (Acad. award nomination best actress, Golden Globe nomination best actress 1982, Brit. Acad. award nomination best actress 1982), The River, 1984 (Acad. award nomination best actress), Marie, 1985, 'Night Mother, 1986, Crimes of the Heart, 1986 (Acad. award nomination best actress, Golden Globe best actress 1986), Violets Are Blue, 1986, JFK, 1991, The Long Walk Home, 1990, Hard Promises, 1992, Trading Mom, 1994, The Grass Harp, 1995, Affliction, 1997, Blast From the Past, 1998, Songs in Ordinary Time, 2000, In the Bedroom, 2001 (Best Actress in Drama Golden Globe 2001, Am. Film Inst. award, Ind. Spirit award, Broadcast Critics award, Chgo. Film Critics award, Fla. Film Critics award, Golden Satellite award, Sundance Film Festival award, Southeastern Film award, N.Y. Film Critics award, L.A. Film Critics award 2001), Midwives, 2001, (TV movie) Last Call, 2002 (nominee Outstanding Supporting Actress in Miniseries or Movie Emmy award); TV movie appearances include Straight Story, 1999, In the Bedroom, 2001 (Acad. award nomination best actress 2001, Brit. Acad. award nomination best actress 2001, Brit. Film Critics Choice award best actress 2001, Sundance Film Festival Spl. prize 2001, Golden Globe best actress 2001, Ind. Spirit award best felmale lead 2001, AFI, Actress of Yr. 2001, L.A. Film Critics best actress 2001, N.Y. Film Critics best actress 2001, SAG nomination best actress 2001, nominee Best Actress Acad. award 2001), The Migrants, 1973, Katherine, 1975, Verna: USO Girl, 1978, A Private Matter, 1992, A Place for Annie, 1994, The Good Old Boys, 1995, Streets of Loredo, 1995, If These Walls Could Talk, 1996, Midwives (SAG nomination best actress 2001), 2001, Beyond the Call (Emmy nomination best actress 2002), 2002; guest host TV show Saturday Night Live, 1977; appeared in episode TV show The Waltons. Office: care Creative Artists Agy LLC c/o Steve Tellez 9830 Wilshire Blvd Beverly Hills CA 90212-1804*

SPACEY, KEVIN, actor; b. South Orange, N.J., July 26, 1959; Student, Juilliard Sch., 1979-81. Stage appearances include Henry IV, part I, 1981, Barbarians, 1982, Hurlyburly, 1985, Long Days Journey into Night, 1986, National Anthems, 1988, Lost in Yonkers, 1991 (Tony award for Best Featured Actor, 1991, Drama Desk award, 1991), Playland, 1993, The Iceman Cometh, 1997 (Tony award Best Male Performance/Drama 1999); TV appearances include (series) Wiseguy, 1987-88, (films) The Murder of Mary Phagan, 1988, Will You Remember Me, 1990, Fall From Grace, 1990, Darrow, 1991; films include Heartburn, 1986, Working Girl, 1988, Rocket Gibraltar, 1988, Dad, 1989, See No Evil, Hear No Evil, 1989, A Show of Force, 1990, Henry and June, 1990, Glengarry Glen Ross, 1991, Consenting Adults, 1992, The Ref, 1994, Outbreak, 1995, Swimming With Sharks, 1995, The Usual Suspects, 1995 (Acad. award for best supporting actor 1996), Seven, 1995, A Time to Kill, 1996, Looking for Richard, 1996, Midnight in the Garden of Good and Evil, 1997, L.A. Confidential, 1997, Hurlyburly, 1998, The Negotiator, 1998, A Bug's Life (voice), 1998, American Beauty, 1999 (Best Actor Oscar)., Pay it Forward, 2000, K-Pax, 2001, The Shipping News. 2001. Office: Altman Greenfield & Salvaje 36th Fl 120 W 45th St Fl 36 New York NY 10036-4041 also: William Morris Agy 151 S El Camino Dr Beverly Hills CA 90212-2704*

SPACH, JULE CHRISTIAN, church executive; b. Winston-Salem, N.C., Dec. 21, 1923; s. Jule Christian and Margaret Stockton (Coyner) S.; m. Nancy Clendenin, Sept. 18, 1948; children: Nancy Lynn Lane, Margaret Cunningham, Ann Thomerson, Cecelia Welborn, Robert. Student, Va. Mil. Inst., 1942-43; BSChemE, Ga. Inst. Tech., 1949; postgrad., Union Theol. Sem., Richmond, Va., 1951-52, Duke U., 1955-56; MA in Ednl. Adminstrn., U. N.C., Greensboro, 1976; LHD (hon.), Stillman Coll., Tuscaloosa, Ala., 1977; LittD (hon.), Belhaven Coll., Jackson, Miss., 1977; LLD, King Coll., Bristol, Tenn., 1977. Salesman Mengle Corp. subs. Internat. Container Corp., Winston-Salem, 1950-52; from prof. scis., athletic dir. to pres. Quinze de Novembro Coll., Garanhuns, Pernanbuco, Brazil, 1952-64; edn. dir. Cruzada ABC-Recife, 1965-70, pres., 1969-70; exec. sec. Parliamentary Christian Leadership, Brasilia, Fed. Dist., Brazil, 1970-73; exec. dir. Presbyn. Mission in Brazil, Campinas, Sao Paulo, 1973-75; moderator Gen. Assembly of Presbyn. Ch. in U.S., Atlanta, 1976-77; exec. dir. Triad United Meth. Home, Inc., Winston-Salem, 1977—. Dir. First Home Fed. Savs. and Loan Author: (biography) Every Road Leads Home, 1997. Bd. dirs. Instituto Gammon, Presbyn. Ch. U.S., Forsyth County Coun. on Aging Forsyth County Sr. Svcs. Forsyth County, Covenent Fellowship of Presbyns., William Black Lodge, Synod of N.C., Presbyn. Ch. U.S.A.; bd. visitors Lee's McRae Coll., Montreat Anderson Coll.; mem. cabinet United Way, 1987; chmn. Winston-Salem Forsyth County Coun. on Svcs. to Homeless; chmn. bd. dirs. Sr. Svcs., Inc., Winston-Salem, Missionary Family Counseling Svc. With USAAF, 1943-45, prisoner of war, Poland. Decorated Purple Heart; recipient Jefferson award, 1991. Mem. Sertoma Club (3 Svc. awards), Lions, Rotary. Republican. Home: Arbor Acres 1244 Arbor Rd Apt 197 Winston Salem NC 27104-1199 Office: 1240 Arbor Rd Winston Salem NC 27104-1106 *The Christian faith teaches us that the greatest of all gifts is love. This gift comes from God, and it is ours through the presence of His spirit dwelling in us. This love gives man peace within and with his fellow man.*

SPACKMAN, DENNIS PAUL, accountant; b. Provo, Utah, Feb. 18, 1946; s. Paul Penrose and Audrey Maurine (Warner) S.; m. Ann Marie Pyne, June 22, 1966; children: Matthew Paul, Annette Marie, Natalie Danielle, Nathan Andrew. BS, Brigham Young U., 1968, M.Accountancy, 1969. CPA, Utah. Staff acct. Peat Marwick Mitchell & Co., L.A., 1969-71; audit mgr. Office of Utah State Auditor, Salt Lake City, 1971-75; contr. Utah Dept. Transp., 1975-79; operational audit mgr. Ch. of Jesus Christ of Latter-day Saints, 1979-81, zone contr., 1984, internat. tax mgr., 1984-88, area contr., 1986-89, chief acct., 1989—. Sec.-treas. Citizens for a Safe Future for Midvale (Utah), 1991—; bd. dirs., treas. South Salt Lake County Recreation dist., Midvale, 1978-86; zone commr. Great Salt Lake Coun. Boy Scouts Am., 1988-91. Named to Outstanding Young Men of Am., 1981, Dising. Svc. award, 2000, named Top 100 Most Influential People in Accounting, Accounting Today,

1999, 2000. Mem. AICPAs, Nat. Assn. of State Bds. of Accountancy (chmn. bd. dirs. 1999-2000), Utah Assn. CPAs (pres. 1983-84, Outstanding Com. Chmn. 1982), Am. acctg. Assn. Mem. Lds Ch. Avocation: photography. Office: The Ch of Jesus Christ of Latter-day Saints 50 E North Temple # 1600 Salt Lake City UT 84150-0002

SPACKMAN, THOMAS JAMES, radiologist; b. Oak Park, Ill., Apr. 24, 1937; s. Thomas Frederick and Louise Mary (Kaiser) S.; m. Donna S. Stewart, June 25, 1960; children— Kirsten, Thomas James, Victoria. BA, DePauw U., 1959; MD, Western Res. U., 1964; Diploma in Bus. Studies, London Sch. Econs., 1987. Intern, then resident in internal medicine Yale-New Haven Med. Center, 1964-66, resident in diagnostic radiology, 1966-68, fellow clin. research tng. unit, 1968-69; instr., then asst. prof. radiology Yale U. Med. Sch., 1969-74; asso. prof. U. Pa. Med. Sch., 1974-78; prof. radiology U. Conn. Med. Sch., Farmington, 1978—, head dept., 1978-90; dir. radiology St. Francis Hosp. and Med. Ctr., Hartford, Conn., 1992-93; pres. Elscint, Inc., Hackensack, N.J., 1993-97; sr. v.p. Elscint, Ltd., Haifa, Israel, 1993-97; pres. The Spackman Assocs., Vero Beach, Fla., 1997—; chmn. Xicon Technologies LLC, 1997-98; v.p. for med. affairs Quorum Health Resources and Cambio Health Solutions, LLA, 2000—; v.p. physician affairs Cambio Health Solutions LLC, 2000—; v.p. med. affairs Quorum Health Resources LLC, 2000—. Mem. Conn. Med. Exam. Bd., 1980-86; bd. dirs. Elscint, Inc. Mem. editorial adv. bd. Diagnostic Imaging, 1989-92; author articles in field, chpts. in books. Fellow Am. Coll. Radiology; mem. AMA, Assn. Univ. Radiologists, Soc. Pediatric Radiology, Radiol. Soc. N.J. E-mail: tspackman@cambiohealth.com.

SPADA, DOMINICK, pharmacist; b. Bklyn., Oct. 21, 1969; s. Vito and Maria A. (Palazzo) S. BS in Pharmacy, L.I. U., 1992; MA in Health Adminstrn. Registered pharmacist, N.Y.; cert. orthotic fitter. Staff pharmacist Cobble Court Pharmacy, Bklyn., 1992-94; dir. pharmacy, corp. bus. officer Ocean Breeze Infusion Care, S.I., 2000—; dir. pharmacy svcs. NYU Hosp., N.Y.C., 1998-2000; dir. pharmacy/supervising pharmacist Ocean Breeze Infusion Care, S.I., 1994-98; cons. pharmacist, 1999—; CEO Ocean Breeze Infusion Care, S.I., 2002. Bd. dirs. Cmty. Bd. #3, Staten Island, 1996-97, 99—; mem. Rocco Laurie Patrolmen's Scholarship Fund, Staten Island, 1995—. Named Drug Topics Pharmacist of Yr., Homecare divsn., 2001; recipient Anderson gold medal, L.I. U. Schwartz Coll. Pharmacy, 1992, PSSNY, Innovative Pharmacist award, 2002. Mem. Nat. Assn. Retail Druggists, Am. Pharm. Assn., Pharm. Soc. State of N.Y., Am. Soc. Health Sys. Pharmacists, Nat. Hospice Orgn. Roman Catholic. Avocations: travel, computers, career-oriented activities, fishing. Home: 193 Connecticut St Staten Island NY 10307-1521 Office: Ocean Breeze Infusion Care 3rd Fl 1817 Hylan Blvd Staten Island NY 10305

SPADA, JAMES, author, photographer, publisher; b. S.I., N.Y., Jan. 23, 1950; s. Joseph Vincent and Mary Ruberto S. Student, Wagner Coll., 1968-71, Calif. State U., 1979-80. Pres. Spada Publs., L.A.; pub. Barbra Quar., 1980-83. Author: Barbra: The First Decade—The Films and Career of Barbra Streisand, 1974, The Films of Robert Redford, 1977, The Spada Report, 1979, Streisand—The Woman and the Legend, 1981, Monroe—Her Life in Pictures, 1982, Judy and Liza, 1983, Hepburn: Her Life in Pictures, 1984, The Divine Bette Midler, 1984, Fonda: Her Life in Pictures, 1985, Shirley and Warren, 1985, Grace: The Secret Lives of a Princess, 1987, Peter Lawford: The Man Who Kept the Secrets, 1991, More Than A Woman: An Intimate Biography of Bette Davis, 1993, Streisand: Her Life, 1995, Jackie: Her Life in Pictures, 2000; photographer: Black & White Men, 2000, Ronald Reagan: HIs Life in Pictures, 2001, John and Caroline: Their Lives in Pictures, 2001; book packager The 1984 Marilyn Monroe Pin-Up Calendar, 1983, The Telephone Book, 1984, Elizabeth Taylor: A Biography in Photographs, 1984, Bette Davis: A Biography in Photographs, 1985, Natalie Wood: A Biography in Photographs, 1986; one-man photography shows at Against the Grain Gallery, Cape Cod, 1998, Gallery One, Boston, 2000, Radiant Light Gallery, Portland, Maine, 2001. Mem. ACLU, Authors Guild. Democrat.

SPADAFORA, DAVID CHARLES, university administrator; b. Hamilton, Ohio, June 4, 1951; s. Samuel Charles and Dorothy (Hardy) S.; m. Carolyn Elizabeth Gaugler, Mar. 24, 1973; children: Andrew, Claire. BA, Williams Coll., 1972; PhD, Yale U., 1981. Instr. Simon's Rock Coll., Great Barrington, Mass., 1977-78; lectr. Univ. Conn., West Hartford, 1978-80; research analyst Conn. Gen. Assembly, Hartford, 1980-81; dean of Morse Coll. Yale U., 1982, lectr. in history, 1982—, dean of Calhoun Coll., 1982-85, assoc. dean of grad. sch., 1985—. Contbr. articles to profl. jours. Bd. dirs. Yale Coop, New Haven, 1987—. Recipient award for meritorious svc., Conn. Gen. Assembly, 1981. Mem. Phi Beta Kappa, Mory's. Avocations: golf, tennis.

SPADE, GEORGE LAWRENCE, scientist; b. Sioux City, Iowa, Dec. 14, 1945; s. Walter Charles and LaVancha May (Green) S.; m. Carol Margaret Deaton, Mar. 14, 1966 (div. June 1985); children: Aaron Michael, Margaret. Mem. earthquake study group for China, U.S. Citizen Amb. Programs, 1989. Contbr. articles to profl. jours. Mem. AAAS, Internat. Soc. Philos. Enquiry, Am. Math. Soc., Math. Assn. Am., N.Y. Acad. Scis., Mensa. Avocations: poetry, painting, music. Home and Office: PO Box 2260 Columbia Falls MT 59912-2260

SPADY, JOANNE SMITH, secondary school educator; b. Phila., Jan. 17, 1935; d. Houston Thomas and Odeas Frances (Ewell) Savage; m. Sydney thomas Smith, June 1, 1963 (dec. July 1989); children: Deborah, Gregory; m. Lester Herbert Spady Sr., Apr. 3, 1994. AS, Norfolk State U., 1954; BA, U. Md., 1956. Choral, band tchr. Worcester County H.S., Snow Hill, Md., 1956-57; tchr. choral, history Acomac County, Mary N. Smith H.S., Accomac, Va., 1957-73; part-time tchr. Montgomerycounty Dept. Edn., Rockville, Md., 1973-76; asst. mgr. csh office Bradlees Inc., 1976-86; tchr. fine arts Northampton County Dept. Edn., Eastville, Va., 1987-97. Vice chmn. planning commn. City of Cape Charles; sec. Arts Coun.; me. AFS BlackCoalition; bd. dirs. Eastern Shore C.C., Melfa, Va., 1989—. Mem. NEA, NAACP, Northampton County Edn. Ass., Edn.Assn. Va., Assn. Am. Choral Dirs., Va. Music Educators Assn., Nat. Music Educators Assn., Nat. Assn. Female Execs. Democrat. Methodist-Episcopalian. Avocations: music teaching, creative needle work. Home: PO Box 170 Capeville VA 23313-0170

SPADY, MARGARET VIDYA, lawyer, nurse; b. Georgetown, Guyana, July 24, 1958; came to U.S., 1974; d. Frank R. and Ena I. (Bissember) Jacob; m. Richard Dean Spady, Feb. 27, 1990; children: Justin D., Conor, D., Rachael N. AS in Nursing, Loma Linda (Calif.) U., 1980; BS in Acctg., Loma Linda U., La Sierra, Calif., 1983; JD, Pepperdine U., 1989. Bar: Calif. 1989, U.S. Dist. Ct. (cen. dist.) Calif. 1989, U.S. Dist. Ct. (ea. dist.) Calif. 1995. Staff nurse, team leader Loma Linda U. Med. Ctr, 1980-89; assoc. Gibson, Dunn & Crutcher, Newport Beach, L.A., Calif., 1988 89-90; staff nurse Plumas Dist. Hosp., Quincy, 1990-92; dep. co. counsel II Co. of Plumas-Office of Co. Counsel, 1992-96. Summer law clk. Marchison & Cumming, L.A., 1987. Co Bd. dirs. Plumas Comm. Clin., Quincy, 1991-94, Town Hall Theatre, Quincy, 1990-92, United Way of Adams County, Decatur, 2000—, Adams County Extension Bd., Decatur, 2000—. Recipient award for Excellence in Preparation for Trial Practice of the Law, Am. Bd. Trial Advocates, L.A., 1989, Am. Jurisprudence awards, Malibu, 1986, 87. Mem. ABA. Republican. Seventh Day Adventist. Avocations: reading, writing, music, skiing, golf. Address: PO Box 327 Decatur IN 46733-0327

SPAEDER, ROGER CAMPBELL, lawyer; b. Cleve., Dec. 20, 1943; s. Fred N. and Luceil (Campbell) S.; m. Frances DeSales Sutherland, Sept. 7, 1968; chidlren: Michael, Matthew. BS, Bowling Green U., 1965; JD with honors, George Washington U., 1970. Bar: D.C. 1971, U.S. Dist. Ct. D.C. 1971, U.S. Ct. Appeals (D.C. cir.) 1971, U.S. Ct. Claims 1979, U.S. Dist. Ct. Md. 1984, U.S. Ct. Appeals (2d and 4th cirs.) 1985, U.S. Supreme Ct. 1976. Asst. U.S. atty. D.C., Washington, 1971-76; ptnr. Zuckerman Spaeder LLP, 1976—. Faculty Atty. Gen. Advocacy Inst., 1974-76, Nat. Inst. Trial Adv., 1978-79; adj. faculty Georgetown U. Law Ctr., 1979-80, Am. U. Ctr. Adminstrn. Justice, 1976-79; lectr. D.C. Bar Continuing Legal Edn. Programs, 1980-90; Cardozo Prize judge Yale Law Sch., 1992; master Edward Bennett Williams Inn of Ct., 1996—; mem. D.C. Cir. Jud. Conf., 1991. Contbr. articles to profl. jours. and chpts. to books. Recipient Spl. Achievement award Dept. Justice, 1971. Mem. ATLA, ABA (co-chair com. on complex crimes litigation 1989-92, divsn. co-dir. sect. litigation 1992-94), Bar Assn. D.C. (lectr. Criminal Practice Inst. 1977-80), D.C. Bar (com. criminal jury instrns. 1972, divsn. cts. lawyers, adminstrn. of justice 1976-78; adv. com. continuing legal edn. 1986), Def. Rsch. Inst., Assn. Plaintiffs' Trial Attys., Nat. Assn. Criminal Def. Lawyers, Omicron Delta Kappa. Home: 7624 Georgetown Pike Mc Lean VA 22102-1412 Office: Zuckerman Spaeder LLP 1201 Connecticut Ave NW Fl 12 Washington DC 20036-2605

SPAEPEN, FRANS AUGUST, applied physics researcher, educator; b. Mechelen, Belgium, Oct. 29, 1948; arrived in U.S., 1971; s. Jozef F. M. and Ursula (Roppe) Spaepen; m. Moniek Steemans, Aug. 21, 1973; children: Geertrul M., Elizabet U., Hendrik J. L. Burgerlijk Metaalkundig Ingenieur, U. Leuven, Belgium, 1971; PhD, Harvard U., 1975. IBM postdoctoral fellow Harvard U., Cambridge, Mass., 1975-77, asst. prof. applied physics, 1977-81, assoc. prof., 1981-83, Gordon McKay prof. applied physics, 1983—. Vis. prof. U. Leuven, 1984, Deutsches Zentrum für Luft-und Raumfahrt-Köln, 2000, Forschungszentrum Jülich, 2001; chmn. Gordon Conf. on Phys. Metallurgy, 1988; dir. Harvard Materials Rsch. Lab., 1990—98; NRC com. on solid state scis., 1990—93; NRC com. on condensed matter and materials physics, 1996—98; Krengel lectr. Technion, Israel, 1994; mem. summer rsch. group Los Alamos Nat. Lab., 1986—99; mem. sci. and tech. steering com. Brookhaven Nat. Lab.; chmn. scientific adv. bd. Netherlands Inst. for Metals Rsch. Co-editor: (book) Solid State Physics; mem. editl. bd.: Jour. Applied Physics, mem. editl. bd.: Applied Physics Letters, 1990—93, mem. editl. bd.: , 1999—2001, mem. editl. bd.: Applied Physics Revs., 1991—97, mem. editl. bd.: Phys. Rev., 1994—99, mem. editl. bd.: Jour. Non-Crystalline Solids, 1990—94; editor (prin. editor): Jour. Materials Rsch., 2001—; contbr. articles to profl. jours., chapters to books. Recipient Best Paper award, Acta Metallurgica, 1994, Humboldt award, 1999, R.F. Mehl award, TMS Inst. Metals, 2002. Fellow: AIME-The Metall. Soc., Am. Phys. Soc. (chmn. divsn. materials physics 1992); mem.: Vlaamse Academie voor Wetenschappen en Kunsten (fgn.), Orde van den Prince, Böhimische Physikalische Gesellschaft, Koninklijke Vlaamse Ingenieurs Vereniging, Materials Rsch. Soc. (councillor 1986—88, 1990—92, co-chmn. fall meeting Boston 1990, chmn. program com. 1993—2000, Woody award 1998), Am. Soc. Metals (lectr.). Office: Harvard U Div Engring and Applied Scis 29 Oxford St Cambridge MA 02138-2901 E-mail: spaepen@deas.harvard.edu.

SPAETH, EDMUND BENJAMIN, JR. lawyer, law educator, former judge; b. Washington, June 10, 1920; s. Edmund B. and Lena (Link) S. AB magna cum laude, Harvard U., 1942, LLB, 1948. Bar: Pa. 1949. Judge Ct. of Common Pleas, Phila., 1964-73, Superior Ct of Pa., 1973-86, pres. judge, 1983-86; of counsel Pepper Hamilton LLP, Phila., 1986—2002. Adj. prof. U. Pa. Law Sch., 1986-97; chair Pennsylvanians for Modern Cts., 1987-2000. Fellow Am. Bar Found. (life); mem. Am. Law Inst. (life), Am. Judicature soc., Order of Coif, Phi Beta Kappa. Home: Cathedral Village Apt L-206 600 E Cathedral Rd Philadelphia PA 19128-1933

SPAETH, GEORGE LINK, physician, ophthalmology educator, writer; b. Phila., Mar. 3, 1932; s. Edmund Benjamin and Lena Marie (Link) S.; m. Ann Ward, May 17, 1955; children: Kristin Lea Crowley, George Link Jr., Eric Edmund. BA magna cum laude, Yale U., 1954; MD cum laude, Harvard U., 1959; postgrad., U. Mich., 1960, U. Pa., 1961. Diplomate Am. Bd. Ophthalmology. Resident surgeon Wills Eye Hosp., Phila., 1961-63, attending surgeon, 1970—, dir. glaucoma svc., 1968—; clin. fellow NIH, Bethesda, Md., 1963-65; instr. U. Pa., Phila., 1965-68; pvt. practice, 1965-68; prof. ophthalmology Temple U. Med. Sch., 1968-75, Jefferson Med. Coll., Phila., 1975—, Louis Esposito glaucoma rsch. prof., 2000—. Ophthalmologist Chestnut Hill Hosp., Phila., 1975—; attending surgeon, Graduate Hosp.; cons., Bryn Mawr Hosp., Wills Eye Hosp., Hosp. Jefferson Med. Coll. Author: 18 books in ophthalmology and surgery, 1970—; contbr. over 500 articles to profl. jours.; editl. editor Ophthalmic Surgery jour., 1985-96; mem. editl. bd. Jour., Ocular Surgery News, Glaucoma Abstracts, Jour. of Glaucoma; manuscript reviewer, New Eng. Jour. Medicine, Med. Letter Drugs and Therapy, others; patentee differometer, tonometer tip cover. Pres. Chestnut Hill Cmty. Assn., Phila., 1970-72; trustee, treas. Thomas Harrison Found., 1975—; trustee, founder, pres. E.B. Spaeth and Glaucoma Svcs. Found., 1978—, Profls. for Nuclear Army Control, 1985-88; interviewer Yale Alumni Schs. Com., Phila., 1965—; Yale Class coun., 1968—, Yale Assn. Alumni Reps., 1996-2002; trustee Recording for the Blind and Dyslexia, 1996—, Internat. Arts-Medicine Assn., Thomas Skelton Harrison Found., Inc., 1984—, Pa. Ballet, 2002—, Bach Festival of Phila., 2002—; curriculum com. Jefferson Med. Coll., 1987-90; institutional review bd. Jefferson Med. Coll., 1990-95; pres. Phila. Glaucoma Inst., 1997—. Lt. comdr. USPHS, 1963-68. Recipient Pub. Svc. award Chestnut Hill Coll., 1972, Sir Stuart Duke Elder Glaucoma award Internat. Glaucoma Soc., 1986, Newberg award Lawyers Alliance for World Security, 1995, Derrick Vail award Ill Soc. Prevention of Blindness, 1996, Trantas award Greek Ophthalmol. Soc., 2000; NIH grantee, 1968—. Fellow Am. Acad. Ophthalmology (chmn. ethics com. San Francisco 1987-95, coun. 1980-93, vice chmn. residency rev. com. Chgo. 1982-88, Sr. honor award 1988, life time achievement award 1999), Am. Assn. Rsch. in Vision and Ophthalmology, Royal Coll. Ophthalmologist, United Kingdom, Danish Ophthalmological Soc., Ind. Soc. of Ophthalmology; mem. Am. Glaucoma Soc. (pres. 1983-85), Coll. Physicians Phila. (sec. 1976-84), Phila. County Med. Soc., Pa. Acad. Ophthalmology (pres. coun.), German Ophthalmological Congress, Physicians for Social Responsibility (pres. emeritus Phila. chpt.), ACS (bd. govs., chmn. adv. coun. for ophthalmology), Phila. Club, Phila. Cricket Club, Phi Beta Kappa, Alpha Omega Alpha. Democrat. Episcopalian. Avocations: composing, playing piano, sports, photography, gardening, poetry writing. Office: Wills Eye Hosp 11th Fl 840 Walnut St Philadelphia PA 19107-5109

SPAETH, KARL HENRY, retired chemical company executive, lawyer; b. Phila., Mar. 12, 1929; s. Edmund Benjamin and Lena Marie (Link) S.; m. Ann Dashiell Wieland, Sept. 14, 1963; children: Karl Henry, Edmund Alexander, Christopher Philip. AB, Haverford Coll., 1951; postgrad., Oxford U., 1955; JD, Harvard U., 1958. Bar: Pa. 1959, U.S. Ct. (ea. dist.) Pa. 1959, U.S. Ct. Appeals (3d cir.) 1959. Assoc. MacCoy, Evans & Lewis, Phila., 1959-62; counsel for fgn. ops. Scott Paper Co., 1962-69; v.p., corp. sec. Quaker Chem. Corp., Conshohocken, Pa., 1969-95, ret. v.p., 1995, ret. corp. sec., 1998. Bd. dirs. Greater Phila. Devel. Corp., 1991-98; bd. dirs., sec.-treas. Edmund B. Spaeth Clin. Rsch. Found., 1982—; chmn. bd. dirs. Pa. Chem. Industry Coun., 1984-86. Chmn. bd. trustees Quaker Chem. Found., 1982—; bd. overseers Univ. Mus., U. Pa., Phila., 1983-89, 90-96; bd. dirs. Opera Co. Phila., 1988—, Anglican Found. of Phila., 1998—, St. James Sch., Phila., 1999—, v.p.; vestry Ch. St. James the Less, Phila., 1992—; bd. dirs. Chestnut Hill Acad., Phila., 1976-83, pres. 1979-83; mem. Whitemarsh Twp. Bd. Suprs. Pa., 1969-75, chmn., 1972-74; mem. Com. of Seventy, Phila., 1984-96; internat. adv. com. Phila. First Partnership Econ. Devel., 1994—. Comdr. USNR, 1952-55, ret. Mem. Pa. Bar Assn. (chmn. sect. on internat. and comparative law 1980-92), Phila. Com. on Fgn. Rels. (exec. com., sec. 1984-94, chmn. 2002—), Phila. Club, Phila. Athenaeum, Libr. Co. of Phila., Phila. Cricket Club, Oxford Union Club, Univ. Barge (sec. 1988-94), Mil. Order Fgn. Wars (registrar 1989-91, vice commdr. 1991-93). Republican. Anglican. Home: 2129 Harts Ln Conshohocken PA 19428-2416 E-mail: kspaeth66@aol.com.

SPAETH, NICHOLAS JOHN, lawyer, former state attorney general; b. Mahnomen, Minn., Jan. 27, 1950; AB, Stanford U., 1972, JD, 1977; BA, Oxford U., Eng., 1974. Bar: Minn. 1979, U.S. Dist. Ct. (Minn.) 1979, U.S. Ct. Appeals (8th cir.) 1979, N.D. 1980, U.S. Dist. Ct. (N.D.) 1980, U.S. Supreme Ct. 1984. Law clk. U.S. Ct. Appeals (8th cir.), Fargo, N.D., 1977-78; law clk. to Justice Byron White U.S. Supreme Ct., Washington, 1978-79; pvt. practice, 1979-84; atty. gen. State of N.D., Bismarck, 1984-93; ptnr. Dorsey & Whitney, Fargo, 1993-99, Oppenheimer, Wolff & Donnelly, Mpls., 1999, Cooley Godward, Palo Alto, 1999—. Adj. prof. law U. Minn., 1980-83. Rhodes scholar, 1972-74. Democrat. Roman Catholic. Office: 5200 Metcalf Ave Overland Park KS 66202-1265

SPAETH, STEVEN MICHAEL, lawyer; b. Janesville, Wis., Oct. 10, 1963; s. Herman Joseph and Lonna Rae (Weeks) S. BS in Econs., Ea. Mich. U., 1986; JD, Northwestern U., 1989. Bar: Wis. 1989. Gen. atty. FCC, Washington, 1989—. Contbr. articles to profl. jours. Mem. Wis. Bar Assn. Republican. Lutheran. Office: FCC 445 12th St SW Washington DC 20554-0001 E-mail: sspaeth@fcc.gov.

SPAETHLING, ROBERT HERBERT, retired German language educator; b. Weissenstadt, Germany, July 30, 1927; s. Adam Zahn and Pauline Spaethling; m. Ellen Louise Sonnenberg, June 20, 1953; children: Christine Louise, Kimberly Ann, Dominic Sonnenberg. BA, U. Calif., Berkeley, 1953, MA, 1957, PhD, 1959; MA (hon.), Harvard U., 1966. Instr., asst. prof. Harvard U., Cambridge, 1959-65, assoc. prof., 1966-68, Williams Coll., Williamstown, Mass., 1965-66; prof. German U. Mass., Boston, 1968-69, provost, vice chancellor, 1974-75, dean of grad. studies, 1976-78, vice chancellor, 1989-90; prof. German U. Calif., San Diego, 1969-71. Author: Mozart and Goethe, 1987, Mozart's Letters, Mozart's Life, 2000; contbr. articles to profl. jours. Fellowship Nat. Endowment Humanities, 1982, grantee, 1991. Avocations: hiking, swimming. Home: 101 Washington Ave Cambridge MA 02140-2716 E-mail: elrobspaeth@earthlink.net.

SPAGHI, STEFANO, economist; b. Milan, July 8, 1964; s. Giuseppe Spaghi and Antonietta Pavesi. BEcon, Cath. U., Milan, 1986. With Comml. Studio, Milan, 1991-99. Avocations: religious studies, social welfare.

SPAGNOLO, SAMUEL VINCENT, internist, pulmonary specialist, educator; b. Pitts., Sept. 3, 1939; s. Vincent Anthony and Mary Grace (Culotta) S.; children: Samuel, Brad, Gregg; m. Dorcas R. Hardy, Sept. 29, 1996. BA, Washington & Jefferson Coll., 1961; MD, Temple U., 1965. Diplomate Am. Bd. Internal Medicine, Bd. Pulmonary Disease, lic. physician Fla., Calif., Md., D.C., Va., Ariz., Pa., Mass. Sr. resident in medicine VA Med. Ctr., Boston, 1969-70, chief resident in medicine, 1970-71; Harvard Clin. and Rsch. fellow in pulmonary diseases Mass. Gen. Hosp., 1971-72; asst. chief med. svc. VA Med. Ctr., Washington, 1972-75, acting chief med. svc., 1975-76, chief pulmonary disease sect., 1976-94, chief of staff, 1998-99, dir. respiratory care & sr. attending in pulmonary diseases, 1999—; instr. in medicine Boston U. Sch. of Medicine, Tufts U. Sch. Medicine, Boston, 1970-71; clin. and rsch. fellow in pulmonary diseases Harvard U. Sch. of Medicine, Mass. Gen. Hosp., 1971-72; clin. asst. prof. medicine Georgetown U., Washington, 1975-77; asst. prof. medicine George Washington U. Sch. of Medicine and Health Scis., 1972-75, assoc. prof., 1975-81, prof. medicine, 1981—, dir. divsn. pulmonary diseases and allergy, 1978-93; assoc. chmn. dept. medicine George Washington U. Med. Ctr., 1986-89. Cons. in pulmonary diseases The Washington Hosp. Ctr., Washington, D.C., 1977—, Will Rogers Inst., White Plains, N.Y., 1980—, U.S. Dept. Labor, Washington, 1980—, Walter Reed Army Med. Ctr., Washington, 1987; rep. Am. Coll. Chest Physicians to Am. Registry Pathology, Washington, 1981-92; numerous radio tv appearances on Health Oriented Programs; invited lectr. in U.S., Russia, Jordan; chmn., mem. many coms. George Washington U. Sch. of Medicine, George Washington Med. Ctr., VA Med. Ctr., Washington; med. chest cons. in attempted assasination of former Pres. Regan. Author: (books): Clinical Assessment of Patients with Pulmonary Disease, 1986; co-author: (with A.E. Medinger) Handbook of Pulmonary Emergencies, 1986, (with others) Handbook of Pulmonary Drug Therapy, 1993, (with Witorsch, P.) Air Pollution and Lung Disease in Adults, 1994; contbr. numerous articles to profl jours. including Med. Clin. N. Am., Chest, So. Med. Jour., Am. Jour. Cardiology, Jour. Am. Med. Assn., Clin. Rsch., Am. Rev. Respiratory Disease, Am. Lung Assn. Bull., Clin. Notes on Respiratory Diseases, Jour. Nuclear Medicine, Drug Therapy; presented abstracts at over 13 profl. meetings; reviewer for Chest, Am. Review Respiratory Diseases. Pres., chmn. Found. Vets. Health Care, 1998—. Lt. cmmdr. U.S. Pub. Health Svc., 1966-68; founder, chmn. bd. Found. Vets. Health Care, 1998—. Decorated Cavaliere in Order of Merit, Republic of Italy, 1983; nominated for Golden Apple award by med. students Geo. Washington Sch. of Medicine, Phila., 1977; recipient cert. appreciation D.C. Lung Assn., 1983. Fellow Am. Coll. Physicians (coun. critical care 1983-85), Am. Coll. Chest Physicians (gov. D.C., coun. of govs. 1989-96); mem. Am. Thoracic Soc. (exec. com. D.C. chpt. 1978, 85, 89, mem. adv. com. tuberculosis control, 1978-84, pres. D.C. chpt. 1981-83), Nat. Assn. VA Physicians (sec. 1987-89, v.p. 1989-91, pres. 1992-98), Internat. Lung Found. (pres. 1991—). Achievements include first major review of patient outcome during early history of intensive care units; an analysis of mechanisms of hypoxemia in patients with chronic liver disease; first report of Pneumocystis Carinii Pneumonitis in patients with lung cancer; first prospective evaluation of short course therapy reported in U.S. using Isoniazid and Rifampin; first American report using laser through fiberoptic bronchoscope to treat lung cancer; first report to evaluate continuous intravenous morphine to control pain in cancer patients; description of a simple technique to measure the total lung volume non-invasively using the routing chest x-ray. Avocations: reading, swimming, stamp collecting, gardening, chess. Office: Geo Washington U 5-411 2150 Pennsylvania Ave NW Washington DC 20037-3201

SPAGNUOLA, FRANCIS MICHAEL, interior designer; b. Phila., Nov. 2, 1940; s. Michael and Marie (Vicchiarelli) S.; m. Janet Adelle Moretti, Nov. 23, 1963; children: Stephen, Carrie. BA, Phila. Coll. Art, 1972. Interior designer Rittenhouse Carpets, Phila., 1972-73, Sears, Roebuck & Co., Moorestown, N.J., 1973-76; pvt. practice interior design Phila., 1976—. Mem. Am. Soc. Interior Designers (bd.dirs. 1982-86), Nat. Trust Hist. Preservation (assoc. design), Sons Italy. Avocations: dancing, tennis, drawing. Home and Office: 2 Ridge Ct Sewell NJ 08080

SPAGNUOLO, PASQUALINA MARIE, rehabilitation nurse; b. Phila., Jan. 21, 1942; d. Charles and Lena (Damiano) Caruolo; children: Louis, Charles, Jason. Lic. practical nurse diploma, Salem (N.J.) Community Coll., 1985; BSN, Widener U., Chester, Pa., 1989. Lic. practical nurse, Del., N.J., Pa.; RN, Del., N.J., Pa. Practical nurse A.I. Dupont Rehab. Hosp., Wilmington, Del.; med. sec. Underwood Meml. Hosp., Woodbury, N.J., nurse's aide; pvt. duty nurse, Mt. Ephraim. Merit scholar Widener U., 1985-86, Charlotte Newcomb scholar, 1986-87; recipient Eleanore O. Dower award, 1988.

SPAHN, GARY JOSEPH, lawyer; b. N.Y.C., July 23, 1949; s. Harry G. and Mary (Hopkins) S.; m. Lois Luttinger, Aug. 9, 1975; children: Gary J. Jr., Lori J. BA, L.I. U., 1971, MA, 1976; JD, U. Richmond, 1975. Bar: Va. 1975, U.S. Ct. Appeals (4th cir.) 1975, U.S. Supreme Ct. 1980. Law clk. to Hon. Judge Dortch U.S. Dist. Ct. (ea. dist.) Va., Richmond, 1975-77; from assoc. to ptnr. Mays & Valentine, 1977—, now ptnr., past chmn. products liability and ins. sect. Lectr. in field, 1980—; mem. judicial conf. U.S. Ct. Appeals (4th cir.). Co-author: Virginia Law of Products Liability, 1990. Pres. Southhampton Citizens Assn., Richmond, 1982-85; bd. dirs. Southhampton Recreation Assn., Richmond. 1983, Chesterfield County Crime Solvers, 1997—; mem. coun. Southside Montessori Sch., Richmond, 1983-85. With USAF, 1967-73. Mem. ABA (litigation and tort and ins. sects.), Internat. Assn. Def. Counsel, Am. Assn. Ins. Attys., Assoc. Def. Trial Attys., Def. Rsch. Inst., Va. Assn. Def. Attys., Va. Mfrs. Assn., Products Liability Adv. Counsel, Va. Power Boat (commodore). Avocations: boating, basketball, racquetball. Office: Troutman Sanders Mays & Valentine PO Box 1122 1111 E Main St Richmond VA 23219-3531

SPAHN, JAMES FRANCIS, marketing professional; b. Dubuque, Iowa, Oct. 4, 1957; s. Ervin Henry and Denise Marie (Shuhert) S.; m. Beverly Joan Burns, Oct. 22, 1983. Grad., Brown Inst. Tech., 1977. Lic. real estate commn.; cert. mktg. dir. Mktg. dir., cert. shopping ctr. mgr. The Cafaro Co., Dubuque, 1979-80; mktg. dir. The Herring Marathon Group, Dallas, 1980-83, Dusco Property Mgmt., Inc., Lancaster, Pa., 1983-87, Jim Wilson and Assocs., Montgomery, Ala., 1987—. Co-author: Operating Shopping Centers, 1984. Mem. Cen. Bus. Dist. Revitalization Task Force, Savannah, Ga., 1984-86, Transit Task Force, Savannah, 1985-86; bd. dirs. Conv. and Vis. Bur., Savannah, 1986-87. Recipient Addy awards Dubuque Advt. Club, 1980. Mem. Internat. Coun. Shopping Ctrs. (Maxi award 1982, Maxi finalist 1987, 89, 90, 94), Savannah Advt. Club (bd. dirs. 1984-87), Birmingham Advt. Club (Addy awards 1983-87, 89). Roman Catholic. Avocations: camping, bicycling. Home: 7375 Thomas Hall Dr Trussville AL 35173-1851 Office: Jim Wilson & Assocs Inc 3000-400 Riverchase Galleria Birmingham AL 35244-2315

SPAHNIE, MICHELLE MARIE, accountant; b. Cleve., June 2, 1966; d. Felix Aloyisius and Clare Ann (Ruzicka) Spittler; m. Brian Morgan Spahnie, Oct. 8, 1994; children: Morgan Michael, Brian Michael. BS, Notre Dame Coll., 1988. Acctg. intern Kopperman & Wolfe Co., Cleve., 1986-88; bus. studies tchr. U.S. Peace Corps, Western Samoa, 1988-90; inventory analyst B.P. Oil Co., Cleve., 1991-95; subs. acct. Am. Greetings, 1995-96, acct., fin. analyst, 1997-99; sr. fin. analyst Americangreetings.com, Brooklyn, Ohio, 1999—. Scholar Am. Soc. Woman Accts., 1987. Mem. Phi Chi Theta, Pi Delta

Chi. Avocations: photography, gardening, horses. Office: Americangreetings-.com 3 American Rd Brooklyn OH 44144-2301 Home: 5294 E 100th St Cleveland OH 44125-2402 E-mail: iamkoalaty@aol.com., sspahnie@ag.com.

SPAHR, CLINTON S., JR. retired elementary education educator; b. Bayshore, N.Y., Feb. 3, 1942; s. Clinton Smith and Averil Witona (Courier) S. BS, Hofstra U., 1967, MA, 1972. Tchr. Brentwood (N.Y.) Pub. Schs., 1966-97. Mem. Am. Philatelic Soc., Brentwood Tchrs. Assn., Internat. Soc. World Stamp Collectors. Avocations: collecting stamps, tapes, cds, books. Home: 62 Clarendon Rd Lake Ronkonkoma NY 11779

SPAHR, ELIZABETH, business executive; b. Warren, Ohio, Nov. 12, 1930; d. Sullivan and Elizabeth (St. Clair) Spahr; children: Gretchen, Carolyn. BS, Case Western Res. U., 1952, MS, 1954, PhD, 1957, MBA, 1973. Sr. rsch. scientist Nat. Aeronautics & Space Adminstrn., Clevel., 1956-71; mgr. internat. ops., mgr. spl. projects The Standard Oil Co., 1973-86; v.p. strategic planning Ameritrust Corp., 1987-92; dir. fin. & adminstrn. AAUW, Washington, 1993-98; CEO Technol. Exec. Inst., 1998—2002; pres. AcromaTech Group, Inc., 1999—2002; asst. dir. U. Md. Ctr. for Environ. Scis. Horn Point Lab., Cambridge, 2002—. Dir. supply emergency team Internat. Energy Agy., Paris, 1984-86; chair fed. women's program Fed. Exec. Bd., Cleve., 1969-71. Trustee Case Western Res. U., Cleve., 1988-92, chair ann. fund, 1989-93; pres. bd. dirs. Cuyahoga City Hosp. Found., Cleve., 1983-85. Grantee USPHS, 1952-56. Mem. Women in Tech., Arlington C. of C., Strategic Alliance Va. Employers, Strategic Alliance Md. Employer. Home: PO Box 216 Secretary MD 21664 Office: Univ Md Ctr Environ Sci Horn Point Lab PO Box 775 Cambridge MD 21613-0775 E-mail: espahr@hpl.umces.edu.

SPAHR, FREDERICK THOMAS, association executive; b. South Bend, Apr. 27, 1939; s. Ervin Leonard and Elizabeth Mary (Layden) S.; m. Patricia Margaret McGraw, Aug. 6, 1966; children— Susan, John, Kathryn, Joseph. BA, Ind. U., Bloomington, 1961; M.Ed., Boston U., 1963; PhD, U. So. Calif., 1968. Asst. prof. Pa. State U., 1968-70; dep. exec. sec. Am. Speech Lang. Hearing Assn., Rockville, Md., 1971-79, exec. dir., 1980—. Treas. Nat. Com. for Rsch. in Neurol. and Communication Disorders, 1983-89. Fellow Am. Speech-Lang.-Hearing Assn, Honors Nat. Student Speech, Lang. and Hearing Assn. Am. Soc. Assn. Execs. (Key award 1987, bd. dirs. 1995-98), Greater Washington Soc. Assn. Execs. (chmn. bd. dirs.), Washington Assn. Rsch. Found. (chmn. bd. trustees), Assn. Coun. of Montgomery Co. (Md.,pres.), World Future Soc., Phi Delta Kappa. Office: Am Speech-Language-Hearing Assn 10801 Rockville Pike Rockville MD 20852-3226

SPAIDE, RICHARD FREDERICK, ophthalmologist; b. Allentown, Pa., Nov. 19, 1955; s. Frederick and Dorothy Spaide; m. Wai Chang Ho, May 25, 1985; children: Theodore, Christopher, Emily. BS, Muhlenberg U., 1977; MD, Jefferson Med. Coll., 1981. Diplomate Am. Bd. Ophthalmology. Resident in ophthalmology St. Vincent's Hosp., N.Y.C., 1982-85; chief ophthalmologist Landstuhl (Germany) Army Regional Med. Ctr., 1986-89; fellow in retina Manhattan Eye, Ear, Throat Hosp., N.Y.C., 1989-90; pvt. practice ophthalmology, 1990—; ophthalmologist Vitreous, Retina, Macula Cons. of N.Y., 1994—. Clin. asst. prof. N.Y. Med. Coll., N.Y.C., 1993—; bd. advisors Macular Degeneration Partnership. Med. advisor Jour. Ophthalmic Photography; mem. editl. bd. Jour. Retina; contbr. chpts. to books and articles to profl. jours.; book editor; mem. editl. bd. various jours.; inventor in field. Recipient Honor award Am. Acad. Opthalmology, 1997, award in visual scis. Richard and Linda Rosenthal Found.; named one of the best ophthalmologist in N.Y. The Best Doctors N.Y. Metro Area, 1994, 96, 98, 99, 2000. Fellow ACS, Am. Acad. Ophthalmology; mem. Am. Uveitis Soc., Macula Soc., Retina Soc., Vitreous Soc., Nat. Assn. for Visually Handicapped (chmn. bd. med. dirs. 1995—), Assn. for Rsch. in Vision and Ophthalmology, Retina Soc., N.Y. Soc. Clin. Ophthalmology, N.Y. Med. Soc., N.Y. Ophthalmol. Soc., Ophthalmic Laser Soc. Avocation: photography. Home: 1365 York Ave New York NY 10021-4035 Office: Vitreous Retina Macula Cons NY 519 E 72nd St Ste 203 New York NY 10021-4028

SPAIN, FREDERICK WILLIAM, secondary school educator, writer; b. Detroit, Jan. 21, 1933; s. Frederick Carl and Leona Marie Spain; m. Elizabeth Jane LaBonte, May 5, 1959 (div. Apr. 20, 1979); children: Raymond Frederick, Susan Mary Spain Klein; m. Gloria Jean Roehm, May 26, 1979; stepchildren: Karl Allen Walz, Vicki Lynn Walz Spain-Brookshear. BA in English, Alma Coll., 1956. Cert. tchr. Mich. English tchr. Alpena (Mich.) Pub. Schs., 1962—75, Waterford (Mich.) Lady of Lakes H.S., 1979—83, St. Clement H.S., Center Line, 1986—89; sci. tchr. St. Benedict Elem. Sch., Pontiac, 1978—79; English tchr., athletic coach Aquinas H.S., Augusta, Ga., 1983—86; driver edn. tchr. Brandon H.S., Ortonville, Mich., 1986—. Pres. Bestway Driving Sch., Clarkeston, Mich., 1989—99. Author: (children's book) Missy the Mutt, Maynerd the Australian, Missy Surprise Birthday Party, 1989, Cockatiel, 1998; contbr. poetry to lit. publs. (Editor's Choice award Disting. Poets Am., 93, Editor's Choice award Best Poems of 1996, 96). Pres. Cath. Sch. Bd., Alpena, 1968—70; bd. dirs. Mich. Driver and Safety Edn., Lansing, 1995—97. With U.S. Army, 1956—58. Mem.: Audubon Soc. Avocations: fishing, horse racing. Home: 7864 S 11/2 Rd Wellston MI 49689 Office: Roehm Pubs 4542 Wildwood Loop Clarkston MI 48348-1466 E-mail: roehm-pub@mindspring.com.

SPAIN, JAMES DORRIS, JR. biochemist, educator; b. Washington, Feb. 3, 1929; s. James Dorris and Frances (Pitkin) S.; m. Patricia Mann, Oct. 3, 1952; children: James Williamson, Caryn Ann, Mary Alisa. Student, Tulane U., 1947-48; BS, Mich. Technol. U., 1951; MS, Med. Coll. Va., 1953; PhD, Stanford, 1956. Research fellow biochemistry U. Tex.-M.D. Anderson Hosp. and Tumor Inst., 1955-56; assoc. prof. dept. chemistry Mich. Technol. U., Houghton, 1956-62, head dept. biol. scis., 1962-68, prof. biochemistry, 1962-84, prof. emeritus, 1985—. Dir. Ctr. for Instrnl. Computing, Ea. Mich. U., Ypsilanti, 1984-85; vis. prof. Clemson U., S.C., 1985-94; pres. Electronic Homework Sys., Inc., 1994—; cons. Computer Applications in Biology and Chemistry; dir. SUMIT Courseware Devel. Project, 1979-82. Author: Some Computer Programs for Biology, 1970, Biological Simulation Techniques, 1972, Lake Superior Basin Bibliography, 1976, BASIC Computer Models in Biology, 1978, BASIC Microcomputer Models in Biology, 1982, Developing Chemical Skills with Computerized Instruction, 1990, Computer Simulation in Biology: A BASIC Introduction, 1992, CHEMI-SKILL-BILDR Electronic Homework System, 1994, ChemSkill Builder for Windows, 1997, ChemSkill Foundations, 1998, Chem Skill Builder/2000, 1999; contbr. articles to profl. jours. Chmn. adv. council St. Josephs Hosp. Sch. Nursing, 1967; Trustee, pres. Portage Twp. Sch. Bd., 1968-76; trustee Copper Country Intermediate Sch. Dist., 1975-78. Recipient Faculty Research award Mich. Technol. U., 1965 Mem. Am. Chem. Soc. (past sect. v.p., chmn.), Rotary, Sigma Xi, Phi Lambda Upsilon. Clubs: Miscowaubik (gov. 1971-74, 79-82), Boscobel Country. Episcopalian. Home: 129 Leslie Ln Pendleton SC 29670 E-mail: jspain.chemskil@prodigy.net.

SPAIN, JAMES WILLIAM, political scientist, writer, investor; b. Chgo., July 22, 1926; s. Patrick Joseph and Mary Ellen (Forristal) S.; m. Edith Burke James, Feb. 21, 1951; children: Patrick, Sikandra, Stephen, William. MA, U. Chgo., 1949; PhD, Columbia U., 1959. Cons. sec. army, 1949-50; with U.S. Fgn. Service, 1951-53; researcher, lectr. Columbia, 1955-62; mem. policy planning council State Dept., 1963-64; dir. Office Research and Analysis for Near East and South Asia, 1964-66; country dir. for Pakistan and Afghanistan, 1966-69; charge d'affaires Am. embassy, Rawapindi, 1969; consul gen. Istanbul, Turkey, 1970-72; minister Am. embassy, Ankara, 1972-74; diplomat-in-residence, vis. prof. history and govt. Fla. State U., Tallahassee, 1974-75; amb. to Tanzania Dar es Salaam, 1975-79; amb., dep. permanent rep. UN, N.Y.C., 1979; amb. to Turkey, Ankara, 1980-81; amb. to Sri Lanka, Colombo, 1985-89; fgn. affairs fellow Carnegie Endowment for Internat. Peace and Rand Corp., Washington, 1982-84; guest resident investor Colombo, Sri Lanka, 1991—. Chmn. Lanka Infrastructure Ltd.; bd. dirs. Hawk Mountain Fed. Express, Ltd.; adj. prof. polit. sci. Am. U., Washington, 1965-67. Author: The Way of the Pathans, 1962, The Pathan Borderland, 1963, American Diplomacy in Turkey, 1984, Pathans of the Latter Day, 1995, Innocents of the Latter Day, 1997, In Those Days: A Diplomat Remembers, 1998, Holding Out in the Eternal City, 2000, The Emperor's Medallion, 2000, The Devils' Mountain, 2000, Digging the Desert, 2000, The Tribsmen's Treasure, 2000, The Monks' Secret, 2000, The Islands' Quota, 2000, Holy Ireland, 2001, Out Beyond, 2002, Innocents, 2002, To Boil a Stew, 2002. Pres. bd. trustees Joseph Frazer Meml. Hosp.; trustee Diyagala Boys Town. With U.S. Army, 1946-47. Fellow Ford Found., 1953-55; recipient Presdl. Exec. award, 1983, Wilbur I. Carr award for Disting. Diplomacy, 1989. Mem. Coun. Fgn. Rels., Washington Inst. Fgn. Affairs, Assn. Diplomatic Studies and Tng., Cosmos Club. Home: Galle Face Ct II # 42 Colombo 3 Sri Lanka E-mail: jwspain@panlanka.net.

SPAIN, JAYNE BAKER, corporate executive, educator; b. San Francisco; d. Lawrence Ian and Marguerite (Buchanan) Baker; student U. Calif. at Berkeley, 1944-47, Music U. Cin., 1947-50; LL.D., Edgecliff Coll., Cin., 1969; Dr. Pub. Service, George Washington U., 1970; LL.D., U. Cin., 1971, Dumbarton Coll., 1972, Springfield (Mass.) Coll., 1973, Gallaudet Coll., Washington, 1973; L.H.D. Bryant Coll., 1972, Russell Sage Coll., Troy, N.Y., 1973, Loyola Coll., Balt., 1975; m. John A. Spain, July 14, 1952; children— Jeffry Alan, Jon Kimberly. Pres., Alvey-Ferguson Co., Cin., 1952-66, pres. Alvey-Ferguson Operations div. Litton Industries, Inc., 1966-70, also dir. parent co., 1970-94; vice chmn. CSC, 1971-75 ; sr. v.p. Gulf Oil Corp., Pitts., from 1975; Disting. vis. prof. and exec.-in-residence George Washington U., Washington, 1979-88; dir. Beatrice Foods, Chgo., Ohio Nat. Life Ins., Cin. Vice chmn. Pres.'s Com. on Employment Handicapped, 1966-82; participant internat. trade fairs U.S. Depts. State, Commerce, Europe, North Africa, 1961-66, mem. trade and investment mission, India, 1965; mem. U.S. com. Internat. Council Social Welfare; mem. Pres.'s Adv. Com. on Productivity; dir. Pvt. Sector Council, Washington, Dean's Adv. com. Coll. of Bus. U. Cin.; mem. Internat. Soc. Rehab. Disabled; mem. adv. com. sheltered workshops U.S. sec. labor; mem. Ohio Gov.'s Commn. on Status of Women; mem. bldg. com. Children's Med. Center, Cin. Bd. dirs., past pres. Convalescent Hosp. Children, Cin., Greater Cin. Hosp. Council, Children's Neuromuscular Diagnostic Center, Cin., Cin. Sci. Center; bd. dirs. President's Commn. on Personnel Interchange; chmn. bd. trustees Fed. Women's Award; mem. dean's adv. council Coll. Bus. Adminstrn. U. Cin.; chmn. Found. of Ams. for the Handicapped; bd. dirs. Recs. for the Blind. Recipient Distinguished Service award for work overseas blind People Com., Washington, 1965; Migel medal Am. Found. Blind, N.Y., 1966; Gold Plate award industry Acad. Achievement, Dallas, 1967; Top Hat award Bus. and Profl. Women's Clubs. Am., N.Y., 1967; named to Cin. Bus. Hall Fame, 1994. Mem. Conveyor Equipment Mfrs. Assn. (sec., treas., dir. 1960-63), Machinery and Allied Products Inst., Am. Mgmt. Assn., Internat. Platform Assn. Episcopalian. Contbr. articles to profl. jours.

SPAIN, RICHARD COLBY, lawyer; b. Evanston, Ill., Nov. 17, 1950; s. Richard Francis and Anne Louise (Brinckerhoff) S.; m. Nancy Lynn Mavec, Aug. 3, 1974; children: Catherine Day, Sarah Colby. BA cum laude, Lawrence U., 1972; JD, Case Western Reserve U., 1975; LLM in taxation, John Marshall Law Sch., 1985. Bar: Ohio 1975, Ill. 1982, U.S. Dist. Ct. (no. dist.) Ohio 1977, U.S. Dist. Ct. (no. dist.) Ill. 1982, Mass. 1996. Ptnr. Spain & Spain, Cleve., 1975-82, Whitted & Spain, PC, Chgo., 1985-89, Spain, Spain & Varnet PC, Chgo., Northborough, Mass., 1989—; assoc. Canel Whitted & Whitted, Chgo., 1982-85. Dir., sec. Stone Perforating Co., Chgo., 1988—, Chgo. EDM, Inc., Chgo., Wheeling, Ill., 1994—. Contbr. articles to profl. jours. Treas. ARC Ill., 1993—; dir. Chgo. Youth Symphony Orch., 1983—. Mem.: Carlton Club (Chgo.), Chikaming Country Club (dir. 1992—94). Home: 1320 N State Pkwy Chicago IL 60610-2118 Office: Spain Spain & Varnet PC 33 N Dearborn St Ste 2220 Chicago IL 60602-3118 E-mail: rspain@spainspainvarnet.com.

SPAINHOWER, JAMES IVAN, retired college president; b. Stanberry, Mo., Aug. 3, 1928; s. Elmer Enoch and Stella Irene (Cox) S.; m. Joanne Steanson, June 10, 1950; children: Janet Dovell, James Jeffrey. BA, Phillips U., Enid, Okla., 1950, LLD (hon.), 1967; BD, Lexington (Ky.) Theol. Sem., 1953; MA in Polit. Sci., U. Mo., Columbia, 1967, PhD, 1971, U. Ark., 1954; diploma, U. Pacific Sch. Religion, Berkeley, Calif., 1958; DPA (hon.), Culver-Stockton Coll., 1973; LL.D. (hon.), Maryville Coll., St. Louis, 1976; Litt.D. (hon.), Kirksville (Mo.) Coll. Osteo. Medicine, 1977; D.H.L. (hon.), Mo. Valley Coll., 1984; LLD (hon.), Eureka Coll., 1989, Lynchburg Coll., 1993. Ordained to ministry Christian Ch. (Disciples of Christ), 1950; pastor chs. in Ark. and Mo., 1953-70; mem. Mo. Ho. of Reps. from, Saline County, 1963-70; pres. Asso. Med. Schs. Mo., Jefferson City, 1970-72; part-time prof. polit. sci. Lincoln U., 1970-72; treas. State of Mo., 1973-80; pres. Sch. of Ozarks, Point Lookout, Mo., 1981-82, Lindenwood Coll., St. Charles, 1983-89; pres. divsn. higher edn. Christian Ch. (Disciples of Christ), 1989-93. Author: Pulpit, Pew and Politics, 1979. Chmn. Mo. del. Dem. Nat. Conv., 1976; elected mem. Acad. Squires, 1981; 1st chmn. Mo. Children's Trust Fund, 1984-86. Recipient Mental Health award Mo. Mental Health Assn., 1967, Meritorious Service award St. Louis Globe Dem., 1968, Harry S. Truman award Saline County Young Democrats, 1970, citation of merit Alumni Assn. U. Mo., 1975; named Mo. Lay Educator of Year Mo. chpt. Phi Delta Kappa, 1968 Home and Office: 8067 Old White River Rd Rogers AR 72756-7662 E-mail: spainj@ipa.net.

SPAKE, DEBORAH FOSTER, marketing professional, educator; b. Mobile, Ala., June 3, 1964; d. Raymond Ernest and Beryl (Kennedy) Foster; m. Randall Dean Spake, Sept. 22, 1990; children: Sean, Ryan. BA, U. of South Ala., Mobile, 1986; MA, U. Ala., Tuscaloosa, 1988, PhD , 1999. Market rsch. dir. Randall Pub. Co., Tuscaloosa, Ala., 1988—90; account exec. Moore & Symons, Inc., Atlanta, 1991—93; sr. project dir. The Winfield Group, 1993—94; instr. U. of Ala. at Birmingham, Birmingham, Ala., 1997—99; asst. prof. Western Mich. U., Kalamazoo, 1999—2001, U. South Ala., Mobile, 2001—. Contbr. articles to profl. jours., sci. papers to confs. Named Outstanding Grad. Student, Am. Mktg. Assn. - Birmingham Chpt., 1997; recipient Prof. of the Yr. - Western Mich. U., Nat. Panhellenic Conf. and Inter-Fraternity Coun., 2000, Watson-Little Award for Excellence in Acad.and Svc. Activities, U. of Ala., 2000, Award for Excellence in Rsch. by a Doctoral Student, Culverhouse Coll. of Commerce and Bus. Adminstrn., 1998; grantee AMA-Sheth Found. Doctoral Consortium Fellow, U. of Ala., 1998. Mem.: Soc. for Mktg. Advances, Beta Gamma Sigma, Alpha Mu Alpha, Alpha Kappa Psi. Office: Univ South Ala Dept Mktg & Transport Mobile AL 36688-0002 Office Fax: 251-460-7909. E-mail: dspake@usouthal.edu.

SPAKE, KLUANE, minister, writer; b. Sarasota, Fla., Jan. 24, 1943; d. H. Austin and M. June Simonds; m. Rodell A Spake; children: Shawn Miller, Rod, David; children: Dyanna. PhD., Vision Christian U., Romana, Calif., 1991. Pastor Jubilee, Dededo, 1984—99, traveling spkr. and author Atlanta, 1999—. Lectr. in field. Author: From Enmity to Equality, 1999, Understanding Headship, 1999, (children's book) "Angel's Friends", 2001, The Happiness of Finding Wisdom, 2000, Whole & Holy, 1999. Mem. governing bd. sr. citizens Govt.of Guam, Agana, 1995—97. Mem.: NCcA, ICFM, FCF. Personal E-mail: spake@mindspring.com.

SPAKE, NED BERNARR, energy company executive; b. Montpelier, Ohio, Sept. 18, 1933; s. Lewis W. and Gertrude E. (Foley) S.; m. Marilyn Rae Faulk, July 14, 1956; children: Julie Ann Spake Scott, Cynthia Ann Spake Lovern B. Indsl. Engring., U. Fla., Gainesville, 1957; MBA, Rollins Coll., Winter Park, Fla., 1967. Mgr. Fla. Power Corp., Winter Park, Fla., 1962-72, dir. St. Petersburg, 1972-76, asst. v.p., 1976-78, v.p., 1978-83, Fla. Progress Corp., St. Petersburg, 1983-86; pres., chief exec. officer, dir. Progress Technologies Corp., Fla., 1985-89; pres., chief exec. officer, chmn. bd. Advanced Separation Technologies, Inc., 1985-89, Rein Energy Corp., Alachua, 1989-92; pres., CEO The Nouveau Group Inc., Winter Park, 1992—, also bd. dirs. Patentee in field Mem. adv. coun. Engring. Sch. U. Fla., Gainesville, 1978-95; bd. dirs. U. Fla. Rsch. Found., Inc., 1986-94; dir. GelTech, Inc., 1986-87. Recipient Disting. Svc. award Coll. Engring. U. Fla., 1988. Lutheran. Home and Office: Apt 5B 633 N Park Ave Winter Park FL 32789-3237

SPAKOSKI, MARCIA, insurance agent; b. Bklyn., Oct. 8, 1936; d. Matthew Dabrowski and Helen Tomaszewski; m. Francis L. Spakoski, Apr. 16, 1955 (div. Feb. 1969); children: Francis L. Jr., Evelyn M., Louise A. A in Bus., Mohegan Coll., 1977. CLU; ChFC; comml. pilot; cert. flight instr. Cert. flight instr. Coastal Airways, Groton, Conn., 1967—76; real estate sales staff Century 21, 1977-80; tax preparer H&R Block, 1977-78; ins. sales staff Allstate Ins., Groton, 1980-99; ret., 1999. Dist. leader Rep. Town Com., Groton, 1973—74; majority leader Rep. Town Meeting, 1974—75; mem. City Planning and Zoning Commn., 1979—87; support group leader Multiple Sclerosis Soc., 1983—91; mem. mystic River Chorale, 1991—99; vol. Spl. Olympics, Groton Food Bank, Mary Elizabeth Nursing Home, Child and Family Agy., Nutmeg Pavilion, Meals on Wheels; bd. dirs. Habitat for Humanity, 1993—96, selection chmn., 1993—96. Shirley Mann Aviation scholar New Eng. Sect. 99s, 1977. Mem. Mensa (area cood. 1980-82). Republican. Congregationalist. Avocations: flying, sailing, volunteering, travel. Home (Summer): 16 Whitehall Pond Mystic CT 06355-1954 Home (Winter): 2960 59th St South #515 Gulfport FL 33707 E-mail: marciactfla@aol.com.

SPALDING, ANDREW FREEMAN, lawyer; b. Toledo, June 24, 1951; s. Dean and Shirley Louise (Maitland) S.; m. Adele Taylor, May 17, 1980; children: Amy Louise, Adam Freeman, Audrey Wade, Abigail Maitland. BA, U. Calif., Berkeley, 1973; JD, So. Meth. U., 1977. Bar: Tex. 1977, U.S. Dist. Ct. (so., ea. and we. dists.) Tex. 1978, U.S. Ct. Appeals (5th cir.) 1978; bd. cert. civil trial law, personal injury trial law. Assoc. Bracewell & Patterson, Houston, 1977-84, ptnr., 1985—. Notes and comments editor Southwestern Law Jour., Dallas, 1976-77. Fellow Tex Bar Found., Houston Bar Found.; mem. State Bar Tex., Houston Bar Assn., Tex. Assn. Def. Counsel, Def. Rsch. Inst., Knights Momus, Krewe Maximilian, Pan Tex. Assembly, Houston Country Club. Office: Bracewell & Patterson 2900 S Tower Pennzoil Pla 711 Louisiana St Ste 2900 Houston TX 77002-2781 E-mail: aspalding@bracepatt.com.

SPALDING, JAMES STUART, retired telecommunications company executive; b. Edinburgh, Scotland, Nov. 23, 1934; arrived in Can., 1957, permanent resident, 1962; Student, Edinburgh U., 1951-52, Glasgow U., 1953. Gen. mgr., dir. United Corps. Ltd., Montreal, Que., Can., 1970-72; from pension fund mgr. to exec. v.p. fin. BCE, Inc., 1972-90. Mem. Inst. Chartered Accts. Scotland, Order Chartered Accounts Que., Fin. Execs. Inst. Can. (past chmn.), Montreal Soc. Fin. Analysts (past pres.). Home: 126 King St E Brockville ON Canada K6V 1B9 E-mail: stuart231134@aol.com.

SPALDING, MARY BRANCH, psychologist, psychotherapist; b. Roanoke, Va. d. Branch and Mary (Hancock) S.; m. John H. Land, June 13, 1964 (div. 1974); m. Hugh C. Welborn, May 25, 1985; 1 child, Catherine. BA in Art History, Vassar Coll., 1964; MA in Psychology in Edn., Columbia U., 1972, MEd in Counseling Psychology, 1974, EdD in Counseling and Applied Human Devel., 1979. Counselor, rsch. asst. Ruth M. Knight Counseling Svc., Manhattan Sch. Music, N.Y.C., 1971-76; psychologist Rockland County Cmty. Mental Health Ctr., Pomona, N.Y., 1975-95, supr. group psychotherapy crisis ctr., 1992-95; pvt. practice psychotherapy, New City, 1979—. Psychologist Eating Disorders Treatment Assocs., Rockland County, N.Y., 1985-87. Contbr. poems to jours., anthologies. Fellow Am. Orthopsychiat. Assn.; mem. ACA, APA, Acad. Am. Poets, Met. Mus. Art, Poetry Soc. Am., Rockland County Psychol Soc. Democrat. Office: 120 N Main St New City NY 10956-3717

SPALDING, RITA LEE, artist; b. Pitts., Nov. 30, 1928; d. Clarence E. and Irene Francis (Israel) McEldowney; m. Willard Perkins Spalding, Sept. 15, 1956; children: Gregory Scott, Laura Lee Dooley. BA, Chatham Coll., 1950. Artist IDL, Inc., Pitts., 1950-56; tchr. West Pa. Sch. for Deaf, 1970-82; dir. family daycare Beulah Presbyn. Ch., 1983-87. Sec. Penn Hills (Pa.) Arts Coun., 1989-91, 98. Exhibited in many one-woman shows and group shows including Three Rivers Arts Festival, West Va. U., Chatham Coll., Pitts. Ctr. for the Arts, Scaife Gallery, Westmoreland Mus. of Art, Studio Z. Vol. Meals on Wheels, Churchill, 1995—2001; judge of elections Penn Hills 5-5, 1993—2001; mem. Penn Hills Arts Coun., 1991—2001, sec., 1991—2001; elder, trustee Beulah Presbyn. Ch. , Churchill, Pa., 1979—82, pres. deacons, 1976—79. Recipient Jean Thoburn award, Aqueous Open, 1979, Jurors award, Pitts. Watercolor Soc., 1988, Merit award, Westmoreland Art Nats., 1993, awards, Wilkins Art Festival, 1991—98, 2000, 1st Place award, Saxonburg Arts Festival, 1996—98, awards, Penn Hills Arts Festival, 1988—, S.W. Regional award of excellence, Westmoreland Mus. Art, 2001, many local awards. Mem.: Pitts. Watercolor Soc. (membership chair 1993—97), Pitts. Print Group, Assoc. Artists Pitts., Pa. Art Assn. (bd. govs. 1994—, pres. 1989—94). Republican. Avocations: reading, crafts, bridge, swimming. Home: 611 Dixie Dr Pittsburgh PA 15235-4529 E-mail: wspald3557@aol.com.

SPALLA, ANNE BUCK, interior designer; b. Chgo., June 16; d. W. Gerald and Rita Bernadine (Maher) Buck; 1 child, Frank Gerald. BEd with honors, Chgo. State U., 1959, postgrad, 1965, Roosevelt U., 1960-61; cert. in interior design with honors, Seminole Coll., 1986. Cert. tchr., Ill. Tchr. Chgo. Pub. Schs., 1959-61, 63-71, Huntsville (Ala.) Pub. Schs., 1961-62, Dallas Pub. Schs., 1971-72; artist Woodstock (Ill.) Gallery, 1975-77; interior designer Joan Carron Interiors, Lake Forest, Ill., 1977-79; pres. Anne Spalla Interiors, Inc., Longwood, Fla., 1980—. Lectr. interior design Seminole Coll., Sanford, Fla., 1986; interior designer Orlando (Fla.) Opera Showhouse, 1985-86, March of Dimes Gourmet Gala, 1987-88; soloist Orlando Opera Edn. Program, 1979-82; mem. Orlando Opera Co., 1979—. Contbr. articles to various publs. Vol. Birth Edn. Tng. Acceptance, Orlando, 1979-82. Mundelein Coll. scholar, 1955-56; recipient Tchr. Certification Exam award, Chgo., 1959, Outstanding Future Tchr. award, 1959, Presdl. citation Am. Soc. Interior Design, 1987. Mem. Am. Soc. Interior Design (assoc., chmn. fund-raising com. Orlando chpt., Presdl. citation. 1987), NAFE, Nat. Trust for Hist. Preservation, Horizon Club (Orlando, founder), Sweetwater Country Club (Longwood, founder). Clubs: Horizon (Orlando) (founder); Sweetwater Country (Longwood) (founder). Republican. Roman Catholic. Avocations: opera, symphony, ballet. Office: 820 W Gore St Orlando FL 32805-3802 also: PO Box 283 Novelty OH 44072-0283

SPALLHOLZ, JULIAN ERNEST, biochemistry educator, consultant; b. Boston, Oct. 8, 1943; s. Ernest Henry Spallholz and Sharah Janice Orton-Spallholz; m. Eleanor Louise Wright-Spallholz, Aug. 24, 1994 (div. Oct. 20, 1993); children: Brian Trevett, Jana Lind; m. L. Mallory Boylan, May 26, 1994. AAS, Adirondack C.C., Glens Falls, N.Y., 1963; BS, Colo. State U., 1965, MS, 1968; PhD, U. Hawaii, 1971. Rsch. asst. Colo. State U., 1966-67, tchg. asst., 1967-68, post-doctoral fellow, 1971-72, rsch. assoc., 1972-73; instr. biochemistry Colo. State U., U. Colo., 1973-74; rsch. chemistry Lab. Exptl. Metabolic Diseases VA Hosp., Long Beach, Calif., 1974-78; assoc. rsch. prof. dept. chemistry SUNY, Albany, 1978; assoc. prof. Ctr. for Food and Nutrition Tex. Tech. U., Lubbock, 1978-84, prof., 1984—; interim dir. Inst. Nutritional Scis. Tex. Tech. U., TEx. Tech. U. Health Scis. Ctr., 1981-84, dir. Inst. Nutritional Scis., 1985-91. Adj. prof. biochemistry dept. chemistry and biochemistry Tex. Tech. U., Lubbock, 1994—2000; lectr. in field. Author: Nutrition: Chemistry and Biology, 1989; co-author: (with J.D. Driskell and L.M. Boylan) Nutrition: Chemistry and Biology, 2nd edit., 1999; co-editor: (with J.L. Martin and H. Ganther) Selenium in Biology and Medicine, 1981, (with G. Combs, O.A. Levander, J. Oldfield) Selenium in Biology and Medicine, 1987; editor-in-chief, founder Jour. Nutritional Immunology, 1989-96; contbr. articles to profl. jours. Mem. Phi Kappa Phi (pres.-elect 1998-99, pres. 1999-2000). Achievements include patents for Selenium Compounds and a Method for Their Preparation, Stable Isotopic Immunoassay Method Employing Non-Radioactive Selenium Label, Method for the Preparation of Free Radical Pharmaceuticals, Diagnostic and Devices Using Selenium Conjugates. Avocations: architecture, painting, collecting, antiques, travel. Home: 4305 96th St Lubbock TX 79423 Office: Tex Tech Univ 19th and University Lubbock TX 79409

SPALTEN, DAVID ELLIOT, lawyer; b. N.Y.C., June 13, 1956; s. Robert and Elinor Ruth (Okie) S.; m. Sharon Lee Seigrist, Aug. 10, 1988; 2 children. BA in Biology, Alfred U., 1978; JD, Emory U., 1983. Bar: Ga. 1983, N.Y. 1986, U.S. Dist. Ct. (no. dist.) Ga. 1983, U.S. Dist. Ct. (mid. dist.) 1985, U.S. Ct. Appeals 1987, U.S. Tax Ct. 1996. Assoc. Merritt & Tenney, LLP, Atlanta, 1986-92, ptnr., 1993—. Vis. faculty Emory U. Trial Techniques Program, Atlanta, 1996—; spkr. civil litig. Emory U. Adult Edn. Program, Atlanta, 1993. Mem. ABA, State Bar Ga. (intellectual property, litigation sect.), N.Y. State Bar Assn. Presbyterian. Avocations: economics, current events, tennis. Office: Merritt & Tenney LLP Ste 500 200 Galleria Pkwy NW Atlanta GA 30339-3183

SPALTER, ANNE MORGAN, artist; b. Cambridge, Mass., Apr. 16, 1965; d. Dane David and Alice Blank Morgan; m. Michael Spalter; children: Amelia. BA, Brown U., 1987; MFA, R.I. Sch. Design, 1992. Adj. lectr. Brown U., Providence, 1992—94; rschr., outreach coord. NSF Sci. and Tech. Ctr. Computer Graphics and Sci. Visualization, 1995—. Artist in residence Brown U., Providence, 1999—; adj. lectr. R.I. Sch. Design, Providence, 1992—94; adv. bd. mem. Digital Learning Interactive, Medford, 2000—. Author: (book) The Computer in the Visual Arts, 1999;Exhibited in group shows at List Bldg.,

Brown U., 1993, DeCordova Mus., 1994, Colville Place Gallery, 1998, David Winton Bell Gallery, 1994. Mem.: Coll. Art Assn., Acm Siggraph. Office: Brown Univ 115 Waterman St Box 1910 Providence RI 02912 Business E-Mail: ams@cs.brown.edu.

SPALTY, EDWARD ROBERT, lawyer; b. New Haven, Oct. 1, 1946; s. Kermit and Elinor (Phelan) Turgeon; m. Suzy Clune; children: Thomas John, Kathlene Tess. AB, Emory U., 1968; JD, Columbia U., 1973. Bar: Mo 1975, US Dist Ct (we dist) Mo 1975, US Ct Claims 1977, US Supreme Ct 1994, Nebr 1997, Kans 1998, US Ct Appeals (8th cir) 1984, US Ct Appeals (10th cir) 1999. Assoc. Webster & Sheffield, N.Y.C., 1973-74; mng. atty. Armstrong Teasdale LLP, Kansas City, Mo., 1991-2001. Contbr. articles to profl jours. Chmn bd dirs Mo Easter Seals, 1990—92; various positions Nat Easter Seal Soc, former chmn rules, agenda and resolutions comt, former chmn membership and orgn structure comt house dels, chmn bylaws comt; founding mem Heartland Franchise Asn. With U.S. Army, 1968—70. Mem.: ABA (litigation sect, franchising forum comt), Am Arbit Asn (nat panel comt arbitrators 1987), Int Relations Coun Kansas City, Def Research Inst, Mo Orgn Def Attys, Lawyers Asn Kansas City, Kansas City Metropolitan Bar Asn (chmn atnitrust and franchise law comt, co-chair 14th and 16h ann Nat Franchise Law Inst), Mo Bar Asn (civil rules and procedures comt), German-Am CofC (vpres Kansas City chpt), Nat Golf Club Kansas City (founder), Phi Delta, Pi Sigma Alpha, Sigma Nu. Home: 13703 NW 73rd St Parkville MO 64152-1120 Office: Armstrong Teasdale LLP 2345 Grand Blvd Ste 2000 Kansas City MO 64108-2617 Business E-Mail: espalty@armstrongteasdale.com.

SPALVINS, JANIS GUNARS, steamship company executive; b. Riga, Latvia, May 26, 1936; arrived in Australia, 1949; s. Peter Spalvins and Hilda (Ditmanis) Blumentals; m. Cecily Westall Rymill, Dec. 16, 1961; children: John Rymill and Richard Rymill. Group sec., dir. Camelec Group of Cos., South Australia, 1955-73; asst. gen. mgr. The Adelaide Steamship Co. Ltd., 1973-77, chief gen. mgr., dir., 1977-81, mng. dir., 1981-90; dir., chief exec. David Jones Ltd., Australia, 1980, Australia, 1988-90. Bd. dirs. Howard Smith Ltd., Adelaide S.S. Co. Ltd. Group, D.J's Properties Ltd. Group, John Martin Retailers Ltd., Macmahon Holdings Ltd., Metro Meat Ltd., Nat. Consol. Ltd. Group, Petersville Sleigh Ltd. Group, Tooth & Co. Ltd. Group, Markheath Securities PLC-UK, Indsl. Equity Ltd., Pioneer Property Group Ltd., AWA Ltd., Queensland Cement Ltd. Group, Coal & Allied Industries Ltd. Fellow Australian Inst. Mgmt., Inst. Dirs. Avocations: sailing, tennis, snow and water skiing. Home: 2 Brookside Rd Springfield SA 5061 Australia

SPAMAN, MORGAN PATRICK, protective services official; b. Springfield, Mass., Feb. 27, 1960; s. Gerald Allen and Marilyn Jean (Rouselle) S.; m. Sherry Anita Jennings, Apr. 10, 1979; children: Michael Wayne, Lisette Amanda. A in Fire Sci., Cmty. Coll. Air Force, Maxwell AFB, Ala., 1985. Cert. fire officer II, fire instr. II.; accredited, Internat. Fire Svc. Accreditation Congress. Fire protection supr. USAF, Anchorage, 1978-94; sr. fire and safety specialist Alyeska Pipline Svc. Co., 1994—. Part-time tchr. U. Alaska, Galena, 1985-86. Sgt. USAF, 1978-94. Avocations: fishing, snowmobile riding, travel. Office: Alyeska Pipeline Svc Co 1835 S Bragaw St Anchorage AK 99512-0099 Home: HC 89 Box 8535 Talkeetna AK 99676-9705

SPANBOCK, MAURICE SAMUEL, lawyer; b. N.Y.C., Jan. 6, 1924; s. Benjamin and Belle (Ward) S.; m. Marion Rita Heyman, Nov. 21, 1954; children: Jonathan H., Betsy W. BA, Columbia U., N.Y.C., 1944; LLB, Harvard U., 1950. Bar: N.Y. 1950. Assoc. Goldstone and Wolff, N.Y.C., 1950-52; ptnr. Carro and Spanbock (name changed to Carro, Spanbock, Kaster et al), 1952-94; of counsel Kleinberg Kaplan Wolff & Cohen, 1994—. Trustee Carnegie Coun. on Ethics and Internat. Affairs, N.Y.C., 1980-86, 93-2000, hon. trustee, 2002--, chmn. bd., 1987-92; hon. pres. Lincoln Square Synagogue, N.Y.C.; sec. Ohr Torah Stone Instns. Israel. Cpl. AUS, 1943-46, ETO. Mem. ABA (chmn. com. on taxation, patent, trademark and copyright law sect. 1979-81), Assn. of Bar of City of N.Y. (com. on copyright 1965-67, art law com. 1977-80, 86-88), Fed. Bar Coun., Nat. Panel Arbitrators, Am. Abitration Assn., Practising Law Inst. (panel on copyrights, 1979). Jewish. Home: 88 Central Park W New York NY 10023-5209 Office: Kleinberg Kaplan Wolff & Cohen 551 5th Ave Fl 18 New York NY 10176-1800

SPANDORFER, MERLE SUE, artist, educator, author; b. Balt., Sept. 4, 1934; d. Simon Louis and Bernice P. (Jacobson) S.; m. Lester M. Spandorfer, June 17, 1956; children: Cathy, John. Student, Syracuse U., 1952-54; BS, U. Md., 1956. Mem. faculty Cheltenham (Pa.) Sch. Fine Arts, 1969—; instr. printmaking Tyler Sch. Art Temple U., Phila., 1980-84; faculty Pratt Graphics Ctr., N.Y.C., 1985-86. One woman shows include Richard Feigen Gallery, N.Y.C., 1970, U. Pa., 1974, Phila. Coll. Textiles and Sci., 1977, Ericson Gallery, N.Y.C., 1978, 79, R.I. Sch. Design, 1980, Syracuse U., 1981, Marian Locks Gallery, Phila., 1973, 78, 82, Temple U., 1984, Tyler Sch. Art, 1985, University City Sci. Ctr., 1987, Gov.'s Residence, 1988, Wenninger Graphics Gallery, Provinceton, Mass., 1989, Widener U. Art Mus., 1995, Gloucester County Coll., 1996, Mangel Gallery, 1992, 97, 2000, Cabrini Coll., 1999, Mangel Gallery, 2000; group shows Bklyn. Mus. Art, 1973, San Francisco Mus. Art, 1973, Balt. Mus. Art, 1970, 71, 74, Phila. Mus. Art, 1972, 77, Fundacio Joan Miro. Barcelona, Spain, 1977, Del. Mus. Art, Wilmington, 1978, Carlsberg Glyptotek Mus., Copenhagen, 1980, Moore Coll. Art, Phila., 1982, Tyler Sch. Art, 1983, William Penn Meml. Mus., Harrisburg, Pa., 1984, Ariz. State U., 1985, Tiajin Fine Arts Coll., China, 1986, Beaver Coll., Phila., 1988, The Port of History Mus., Phils., 1987, Sichuan Fine Arts Inst., Chong Qing, China, 1988, Glynn Vivian Mus., Swansea, Wales, 1989, Phila. Mus. Art, 1990, Fgn. Mus., Riga, Latvia, 1995, Woodmere Art Mus., Phila., 1996, Am. Coll., 1997, Cheltenham Ctr. for the Arts, Phila., 1997, Rowan Coll., 1997, Villanova U., 1998, U. Pa., 1999, U. of the Arts, 2001, others; represented in permanent collections Met. Mus. Art, N.Y.C., Whitney Mus. Am. Art, N.Y.C., Mus. Modern Art, N.Y.C., The Israel Mus., Balt. Mus. (gov.'s prize and purchase award 1970), Phila. Mus. Art (purchase award 1977), Toyoh Bijutsu Gakko, Tokyo, Library of Congress, Temple U.; commd. works represented in U. Pa. Inst. Comtemporary Art, 1991; co-author: Making Art Safely, 1993. Recipient award Balt. Mus. Art/Md. Inst. Art, 1971, Govs. prize and Purchase award Balt. Mus. Art, 1970, Outstanding Art Educators award Pa. Art Edn. Assn., 1982, Purchase award Berman Mus., 1995, Artist Equity award, 1996; grantee Pa. Coun. Arts, 1989. Mem. Am. Color Print Soc., Pa. Art Edn. Assn. Jewish. Office: 307 E Gowen Ave Philadelphia PA 19119-1023 E-mail: lesspand@home.com.

SPANGENBERG, THEODORE S. retired civil engineer; b. Miami, Sept. 22, 1924; s. Carl Henry and Lily May (Pettyjohn) S.; m. Marian A. Hawthorne, June 5, 1950; children: Mary Sandra, Theodore S., Caryl, Diane, Erin. BCE, U. Fla., 1951. Registered profl. engr., Fla., Ala. Engr. technician Fla. State Road Dept., Perry, 1951-53, engr. trainee 2d dist. Lake City, 1953-55, maintenance engr. 3d dist. Panama City, 1955-62, asst. dist. maintenance engr. 3d dist. Chipley, 1962-68; dist. maintenance engr. Fla. State Road Dept./Fla. Dept. Transp., 1968-86; reservist Fed. Emergency Mgmt. Agy., 1986-94; constrn. mgr. bldg. constrn. and disaster relief So. Bapt. and Fla. Bapt. Convs. Active Boy Scouts Am. Served with U.S. Army, 1943-46, ETO. Fellow Fla. Engrng. Soc. (state dir.); mem. NSPE, ASCE, Optimist Club (prs., sec.-treas.). Avocation: wood carving. Home: PO Box 446 Chipley FL 32428-0446

SPANGLER, ARNOLD EUGENE, investment banker; b. Ft. Dodge, Iowa, Aug. 1, 1948; s. Kermit Charles and Cora (Buroos) S.; m. Penelope Angell, Nov. 8, 1980; children: Christopher Paul, Allison Elizabeth. BS, Iowa State U., 1970; MBA, Harvard U., 1972. Assoc. Hornblower & Weeks-Hemphill, Noyes, N.Y.C., 1972-74; product officer Citibank, 1974-76; with Lazard Freres & Co., 1976-89, gen. ptnr., 1983-89; mng. dir. mergers and acquisitions Paine Webber Inc., 1989-91; sr. advisor Bentley Assocs., L.P., 1992-93; mng. dir. Mancuso & Co., 1993—. Bd. dirs. Syncor Internat. Corp., L.A. Home: 1165 Park Ave New York NY 10128-1210

SPANGLER, ARTHUR STEPHENSON, JR. psychologist; b. Boston, June 20, 1949; s. Arthur Stephenson and Barbara Louise (Fellows) Spangler; m. Deborah A. Kauders, Nov. 27, 1971; children: Heather Anita, Rebecca Haley. BS, Hobart Coll., 1971; MEd, Boston Coll., 1974; ScD, Boston U., 1985. Diplomate Am. Acad. Pain Mgmt.; Nat. bd. cert. counselor; lic. psychologist, Mass., clin. social worker, Mass., rehab. counselor, Mass. Mass. counselor Met. State Hosp., Waltham, Mass., 1971-73; rehab. counselor J.T. Berry Rehab. Ctr., North Reading, 1974-75; program coord. Shore Collaborative, Medford, 1975-76; dir. instl. sch. programs South Shore Collaborative, North Weymouth, 1976-79; dir. mental retardation program South Shore Mental Health Ctr., Quincy, 1979-85; coord. outpatient clinic Boston Pain Ctr., Spaulding Rehab. Hosp., 1985-86; v.p., dir. behavioral medicine svcs. Mass. Bay Counseling, Quincy, 1985—; dir. indsl. disability mgmt. svcs., psychologist chronic pain program Miriam Hosp., Providence, 1987-88; psychologist John Graham Headache Ctr. Faulkner Hosp., Boston, 1992-94. Adj. prof. Sargent Coll., Boston U., 1990—99. Vol. counselor Multi-Svc. Ctr., Newton, Mass., 1973-75; bd. dirs. Newton-Wellesley-Weston-Needham Community Mental Health and Mental Retardation Ctr., Newton, 1976-80, pres. 1979-80; mem. Boston Symphony Assn. Vols. Recipient award Nat. Assn. Retarded Citizens, 1974. Mem.: ACA, APA (assoc.), New Eng. Pain Assn., Soc. Behavioral Medicine, Internat. Assn. for Study of Pain, Assn. for Study of Pain. Episcopalian. Home: 151 Tremont St # 11P Boston MA 02111-1110 Office: 36 Weston Ave Quincy MA 02170-1833 E-mail: stevespangler@rcn.com.

SPANGLER, CLEMMIE DIXON, JR. construction company executive; b. Charlotte, N.C., Apr. 5, 1932; s. Clemmie Dixon and Veva C. (Yelton) S.; m. Meredith Jane Riggs, June 25, 1960; children: Anna Wildy, Abigail Riggs. BS, U. N.C., 1954; MBA, Harvard U., 1956; LHD (hon.), Queens Coll., 1985; LLD (hon.), Davidson Coll., 1986, Furman U., 1993. Pres. C.D. Spangler Constrn. Co., Charlotte, 1958-86, Golden Eagle Industries, Inc., 1968-86; chmn. bd. Bank of N.C., Raleigh, 1973-82; dir. NCNB Corp., 1983-86; chmn. N.C. Bd. Edn., 1982-86; pres. U. N.C., Chapel Hill, 1986-97; CEO, chmn. C.D. Spangler Constrn. Co., Charlotte, 1997—. Bd. dirs. BellSouth Corp., Atlanta; chmn. bd. dirs. Nat. Gypsum Co., Charlotte. Past deacon Myers Park Bapt. Ch., vice-chmn. Charlotte-Mecklenburg Bd. Edn., Charlotte, 1972-76; past trustee Charlotte Symphony Orch., Crozer Theol. Sem.; past chmn. Charlotte adv. bd. Salvation Army; past bd. dirs. YMCA, Equitable Life Assurance Soc., Jefferson-Pilot Corp.; pres. bd. trustees Mint Mus. Art; bd. dirs. Union Theol. Sem., 1985-90, Assocs. Harvard Bus. Sch.; mem. bd. overseers Harvard Coll. With U.S. Army, 1956-58. Recipient Liberty Bell award Mecklenburg County Bar Assn., 1985, Alumni Achievement award Harvard Bus. Sch., 1988. Mem. Assn. Am. Univs., Bus. Higher Edn. Forum, Harvard Club (N.Y.C.), Univ. Club (N.Y.C.), Quail Hollow Country Club (Charlotte). Office: CD Spangler Constrn Co Office of Chmn Box 36007 Charlotte NC 28236-6007

SPANGLER, DOROTHY BENITA, artist; b. St. Louis, Mar. 9, 1928; d. Fred and Della (Baker) Reynolds; m. Charles B. Spangler, Feb. 26, 1926; children: Charles Jr., Cathy D. Student, Coll. San Mateo, 1946-48, Henery Henche Sch. Art, Cape Cod, Mass., 1968. Pvt. practice window decorator, Mt. View and Los Altos, Calif. Exhbns. include Winblad Gallery, San Francisco, 1965-68, So. Pacific Gold Spike Centennial, San Francisco and Japan, 1967, Provence Town Charles Hawthorne Mus., 1968, Gallery DeTours, San Francisco and Carmel, Calif., 1968-86, Lawrence Ross Gallery, Beverly Hills and Palm Dessert, Calif., 1986-89, Gage Galleries, Newport Beach and Irvine, Calif., 1989-91, Union Square Galleries, San Francisco, 1991-2000, Christopher Clark Galleries, San Francisco, 2001, Windsor Fine Art, New Orleans, 2002, Hospic Mask Project, 2002; represented in permanent collections Montery Inst. Internat. Studies, San Francisco Hist. Soc. Bd. mem., historian Los Altos Art Club. Recipient 1st place Santa Clara Valley Hist. Landmarks, 1963, 2nd place oil award Cupertino Fine Arts Exhibit, 1964, Best of Show award West Valley Hist. Soc. Art Show, 1967, 1st annual prize Provincetown Art Assn., 1983; guest of hon. Acad. Jacques Boitiat, Barbizon, France, 1992. Mem. Musée de la Grenovillere-Croissy sur Seine, Nat. Mus. Women in the Arts. Avocations: travel, family, reading, gardening, crafts. Home: 1285 Portland Ave Los Altos CA 94024

SPANGLER, EDRA MILDRED, clinical psychologist; b. Webbville, Ky., Sept. 6, 1941; d. Chester A. and Laura B. (Webb) Sawyer; m. Robert Noel Spangler, Sept. 6, 1959; children: Robert Mark Spangler, Kendra Lynn Lovett. AS in Bus. Adminstrn., Franklin U., 1975; BA in Social Psychology, Park Coll., 1979; MA in Mgmt. and Supervision, Ctrl. Mich. U., 1980; D in Psychology, Wright State U., 1989. Lic. psychologist Ohio, Fla.; diplomate clin. hypnotherapy; diplomate Am. Bd. Psychol. Specialties in Med. Psychology, Forensic Clin. Psychology and Neuropsychology. With adminstrn., mgmt., fin. and computer sys. design various pvt. and govt. orgns., 1958-85; psychology assoc. Stonegate Psychol. Assocs., Columbus, Ohio, 1989-91; dir. pain & stress program The Rehab. Ctr., 1991-94; pvt. practice, 1991—; mem. med. staff Riverside Meth. Hosps., Columbus, 1992—, health psychologist, 1993-95, Mind/Body Med. Inst., 1993-95; mem. med. staff Grady Meml. Hosp., Delaware, Ohio, 1997—. Fellow Biofeedback Cert. Inst. of Am.; mem. Am. Pain Soc., Am. Coll. Forensic Examiners, Ohio Psychol. Assn., Fla. Psychol. Assn., Assn. Applied Psychophysiology and Biofeedback. Avocations: reading, travel, hiking, family, research in mind/body. Office: Wedgewood Behavioral Health 4141 N Hampton Dr Powell OH 43065-7550

SPANGLER, JOHN THOMAS, lawyer; b. Superior, Mont., Mar. 28, 1953; s. Thomas G. and Catherine (Strasser) S.; m. Cynthia Marie Muller, Aug. 3, 1985; 1 child, Nicholas. BBA, U. Mont., 1977; JD, UCLA, 1983. Bar: Mont. 1984, U.S. Dist. Ct. Mont. 1984. Acct. Maier & Carney, Portland, Oreg., 1977-80; assoc. Worden, Thane & Haines, P.C., Missoula, Mont., 1984, Cummings Law Firm, Missoula, 1985-92; pvt. practice, 1984-85, 92—. Mem. ABA, State Bar Mont., Western Mont. Bar Assn. Roman Catholic. Office: PO Box 8925 Missoula MT 59807-8925

SPANGLER, LORNA CARRIE, pharmacy technician; b. San Jose, Calif., Feb. 4, 1938; d. Earl Albert and Elsie Carol (Lincoln) LaPorte; children: Kirk Earl, Eric Clair, David Paul, Linda Jean Spangler-Porter. AA, Monterey Peninsula Coll., 1958; AS in Pharmacy Tech., Santa Ana (Calif.) Coll., 1982; BSBA, Calif. State U., Long Beach, 1986, MS in Vocat. Edn., 1992. Registered pharmacy technician, Calif.; cert. Pharmacy Technician Certification Bd., 1995; cert. C.C. instr., Calif. Pharmacy technician Meml. Med. Ctr., Long Beach, Calif., 1976-78, technician coord., 1979-87; pharmacy technician Hoag Meml. Hosp., Newport Beach, 1987-92, Sharp Health Care, Murrieta, 1992-98, name changed to Rancho Springs Med. Ctr., Tenet Healthcare, 1998—; preceptor Pharmacy Technician Interns, 1992—. Accreditation team Am. Bur. Health Edn. Schs., 1987-91; adv. com. Cerritos (Calif.) Coll., 1982-90, Calif. Paramed. Tech. Coll., 1996-2001; spkr. in field. Ctrl. com. Libertarian Party, Riverside County, 1996-2001, treas., 1997-99; team stream Santa Rosa Plateau Nature Conservancy, 2000—; leader AWANA, 1998—. Mem. Assn. of Pharmacy Technicians (founder, treas. 1989-91), Valley Computer Soc. (founder 1991), So. Calif. Assn. Pharmacy Technicians (treas. 1990-92, sec. 1992-96, pres. 1996-98, sec. 1998-99), Am. Vocat. Assn., Calif. Soc. of Hosp. Pharmacy (task force mem. 1982, nominating com. technician div., 1988, mem. ho. of dels. technician divsn. 1997-98, mem.-at-large 1998-99), Omicron Tau Theta. Avocations: hiking, reading, gardening. Office: Rancho Springs Med Ctr 25500 Medical Center Dr Murrieta CA 92562-5965

SPANGLER, NITA REIFSCHNEIDER, volunteer; b. Ukiah, Calif., Apr. 17, 1923; d. John Charles and Olga Augusta (Wuertz) Reifschneider; m. Raymond Luper Spangler, Sept. 22, 1946 (dec.); children: Jon Martin, Mary Raymond, Thor Raymond. BA, Univ. Nev., 1944. News reporter Redwood (Calif.) City Tribune, 1944-46, Country Almanac, Woodside, Calif., 1969-77. Mem. bd. dirs. San Mateo (Calif.) County Hist. Assn., 1961-68, pres., 1964-66; founder, 1st pres. Portolá Expedition Bicentennial Found., 1966-70; chmn. San Mateo County Scenic Rds. Com., 1967-76; mem. San Mateo County Hist. Resource Adv.; mem. comm. San Mateo County Parks and Recreation, 1983-97, past chmn.; cons. hwy. aesthetics Cal Trans., 1981-83; mem. sch. coms. Recipient Commendation, County Bd. Suprs., 1968, 1977, 92. Mem. Sierra Club, Western History Assn., Mormon History Assn., Nev. State Hist. Soc. (life), San Mateo County Hist. Assn. (life, Resolution of Thanks 1968, 76, 94), Friends Redwood City, Kappa Alpha Theta. Democrat. Episcopalian. Avocations: historic preservation. Home: 970 Edgewood Rd Redwood City CA 94062-1818

SPANGLER, RICHARD CARL, mathematics educator; b. Seattle, Apr. 7, 1931; s. Carl William and Julia (Wittkowski) S.; m. Margaret Eleanor Wubbena, June 10, 1955; children: Michael, David, Carol. BA in Edn., Seattle Pacific U., 1956, MEd, 1960; MA in Teaching, Reed Coll., 1965. Tchr. Kelso (Wash.) Pub. Schs., 1956-66; instr. Lower Columbia Coll., Longview, Wash., 1966-71, Tacoma Community Coll., 1971-78, div. chair, 1978-91, ret., 1991. Free-lance editor in field, 1969—. Author: Student's Solution Books, 1974, 1976, 1977, 1982, 1988, 1989, 1994, textbooks, 1994, 1995, 1996, 2000, 2001. With USN, 1948. Mem. Destroyer Escort Assn., USS Benham Assn., Kiwanis (pres. Tacoma 1990-91), Elks. Republican. Avocations: flying, sailing, gardening.

SPANGLER, RONALD LEROY, retired television executive, aircraft executive, automobile collector; b. York, Pa., Mar. 5, 1937; s. Ivan L. and Sevilla (Senft) S.; m. Svetlana Spangler; children: Kathleen, Ronald Jr., Beth Anne, Pavel. Student, U. Miami (Fla.), 1955-59. Radio announcer Sta. WSBA, York, 1955-59; TV prodr. Sta. WBAL-TV, Balt. and NBC TV, 1958-65; pres., chmn. bd. LewRon Television, N.Y.C., Hollywood, Calif., 1965-78, Spanair Inc.; distbr. Rockwell bus. aircraft, 1975-85. Owner Prancing Horse Farm; collector, dealer, racer vintage and modern Ferrari automobiles; racer numerous courses including LeMans, Dayton, Sebring; Ferrari cons. (PBS show) Motorweek. Mem. Video Tape Producers Assn. N.Y.C., Rolls Royce Owners Club, Ferrari Clubs Am. and Italia, Mercedes Benz Club Am., Porsche Club Am. Home: Prancing Horse Farm 3710 Ady Rd Street MD 21154-1432

SPANGLER, STANLEY EUGENE, international relations educator; b. Billings, Mont., Apr. 7, 1929; s. John Harold Spangler and Winifred Watt; m. Addie Belle Moore, Sept. 21, 1968; children: John Wayland Spangler, Julia Watt Spangler Garlatz. BA, U. Mont., 1952; MA, Columbia U., 1958; PhD, U. N.C., 1978. Program officer Asia Found., San Francisco, 1960-65; assoc. regional dir. Fgn. Policy Assn., Atlanta, 1965-69; dir. Office Pub. and Internat. Affairs U. N.C. Extension Divsn., Chapel Hill, 1969-73; exec. dir. World Affairs Coun. Boston, 1973-81; internat. program advisor Fletcher Sch. Law and Diplomacy, Medford, Mass., 1983-84; sr. fellow Air Univ. USAF, 1984-89; Sec. of Navy sr. fellow U.S. Naval War Coll., Newport, R.I., 1989-92, sr. fellow, prof. strategy, 1993—. Prof. govt. and fgn. affairs Bentley Coll., Waltham, Mass., 1995—; commr. U.S. Nat. Commn. for UNESCO, Washington, 1976-81; pres. Nat. Coun. World Affairs Orgns., Washington, 1977-80; mem. editl. adv. bd. Fgn. Policy Assn., N.Y.c., 1975-78; exec. mem. Nat. Def. Exec. Res., Washington, 1980-97. Author: Force and Accommodation in World Politics, 1991; contbr. articles to profl. jours. Dir. Curtis-Saval Internat. Ctr., Boston, 1976-81; mem. exec. com., bd. dirs. Ala. World Affairs Coun., Montgomery, 1986-89; bd. dirs. Ctr. for Internat. Visitors, Boston, 1978-81; mem. African studies adv. com. Boston U., 1978-80. Capt. USAF, 1954-56. Johns Hopkins U. fellow, 1952-53; Columbia U. scholar, 1957-58. Mem. AAUP, Am. Polit. Sci. Assn., Boston Com. on Fgn. Rels. Democrat. Methodist. Avocations: hiking, writing fiction, travel, reading. Home: 17 Kings Way Scituate MA 02066-2609 E-mail: sspangler@attbi.com.

SPANIER, GRAHAM BASIL, academic administrator, family sociologist, demographer, marriage and family therapist; b. Capetown, South Africa, July 18, 1948; s. Fred and Rosadele (Lurie) Spanier; m. Sandra Kay Whipple, Sept. 11, 1971; children: Brian Lockwood, Hadley Alison. BS, Iowa State U., 1969, MS, 1971; PhD, Northwestern U., 1973. Assoc. dean, prof. in charge Pa. State U., University Park, 1973—82, pres., 1995—; vice-provost, prof. SUNY, Stony Brook, 1982—86; provost, v.p. for acad. affairs Oreg. State U., 1986—91; chancellor U. Nebr., Lincoln, 1991—95. Chmn. Presdl. Adv. Group on Info. Tech., 1997—99, Kellogg Commn. on Future of State and Land-Grant Univs., 1997—2000; nat. adv. bd. The Ctr. for Study of Sport in Soc., 1996—; host TV and radio programs, 1973—2001. Founding editor : Jour. Family Issues; contbr. articles to profl. jours. Del. White House Conf. on Families, Washington, 1980; Pres., chmn. bd. dirs. Christian Children's Fund, Richmond, Va., 1985—94; bd. dirs. Nat. 4H Coun., 1997—2000. Named Named Outstanding Young Alumnus, Iowa State U., 1982. Fellow: Nat. Coun. Family Rels. (pres. 1987—88, Outstanding Grad. Student award 1972), Am. Assn. for Marriage and Family Therapy (Woodrow Wilson fellow 1972); mem.: Assn. Am. Univs. (com. intellectual property 1997—), Acad. Health Ctrs. (commn. on future of acad. health ctrs. 1996—98), Am. Assn. State Colls. and Univs. (joint commn. on accountability report 1993—95), Nat. Collegiate Athletic Assn. (pres. commn. 1995—97, bd. dirs., exec. com. 1997—2001, divsn. I bd. dirs., chmn. 1998—2001), Am. Coun. on Edn. (commn. on women 1992—95), Nat. Assn. State Univs. and Land Grant Colls. (exec. com. coun. on acad. affairs 1990—91, bd. pres. commn. on info. technologies 1993—99, chmn. 1996—99, bd. dirs. 1997—, chmn. coun. of pres. 1999—2000, bd. chair 2000—02), Am. Assn. Family and Consumer Scis. (Moran award 1972), Am. Assn. Higher Edn., Am. Sociol. Assn. (family sect. chmn. 1983—84), Population Assn. Am. Democrat. Avocations: aviation, magic, sports. Office: Pa State Univ Office of Pres 201 Old Main University Park PA 16802-1503

SPANIER, SANDRA WHIPPLE, English language educator; b. Des Moines, Oct. 17, 1951; d. Richard A. and Maxine J. (Lockwood) Whipple; m. Graham B. Spanier, Sept. 11, 1971; children: Brian, Hadley. BA, U. Ill., Chgo., 1972; MA, Pa. State U., 1976, PhD, 1981. Lectr. SUNY, Stony Brook, 1982-86; from asst. to assoc. prof. Oreg. State U., Corvallis, 1986-92; assoc. prof. U. Nebr., Lincoln, 1992-95, Pa. State U., University Pk., 1995—. Author: Kay Boyle: Artist and Activist, 1986; editor: Life Being the Best and Other Stories (Kay Boyle), 1988, Love Goes to Press (Martha Gellhorn and Virginia Cowles), 1995, Process: A Novel (Kay Boyle), 2001; co-editor: American Fiction, American Myth (essays by Philip Young), 2000; gen. editor Hemingway Letters Project. Fellow NEH, 1993-94. Mem. MLA (del. assembly 1986-88), Am. Lit. Assn., Pacific N.W. Am. Studies Assn. (v.p. 1991-92, pres. 1993-94), Hemingway Soc. (editl. bd. Hemingway Rev. 1992—), Modernist Studies Assn., Soc. for Study Am. Women Writers, Assn. for Documentary Editing. Home: One Schreyer House University Park PA 16802 Office: Dept English Pa State U 103 Burrowes Bldg University Park PA 16802-6200 E-mail: sxs74@psu.edu.

SPANN, EDWARD K. historian, educator; b. Fairlawn, N.J., Apr. 12, 1931; s. Hans R. and Gladys K. Spann; m. Joanne E. Spann, Aug. 5, 1961; children: Laura, Suzan, Bryant, Jason. BA, Iona Coll., 1952; MA, NYU, 1953, PhD, 1957. Lectr. NYU, N.Y.C., 1957, 61; instr. CUNY, 1958-60; asst. editor Albert Gallatin Papers NYU, 1960-61; asst. prof. Ind. State U., Terre Haute, 1961-65, prof., 1965—98, disting. prof., 1998—. Author: Ideals & Politics, 1972, The New Metropolis, 1981, Brotherly Tomorrows, 1990, Hopedale, 1992, Designing Modern America, 1996, Gotham at War, 2002. Avocations: bicycling, tennis. Office: Ind State U History Dept Terre Haute IN 47809-0001 E-mail: hispann@ruby.indstate.edu.

SPANN, EVA ANN, laboratory technologist; b. Bogalusa, La., Apr. 15, 1940; d. Jasper and Christine Virginia (Davis) Margiotta; m. James Douglas Spann, July 29, 1961; children: Gina Christine Jones, Maria Emily, James Nicholas. Lab. Technologist, Tex. Coll. Med. Technology, 1960; AS in Med. Technology, City Univ., Renton, Wash., 1995. Am. registry radiologic technologist, Am. med. technologist. Lab. technologist Rockglenn Hosp., Houston, 1960-61, DeSoto Gen. Hosp., Mansfield, La., 1961-63, Panola Gen. Hosp., Carthage, Tex., 1963-64, Huntsville (Tex.) Meml. Hosp., 1972-75; hematologist supr. Doctors Ctr. Profl. Labs., Houston, 1978-80; hematology supr. Twelve Oaks Ctr., 1980-82; lab. supr. Pleasant Hill (La.) Gen. Hosp., 1982-87; lab. technologist Sabine Med. Ctr., Many, La., 1987-91; evening lab. supr. Meml. Hosp. of Ctr., Tex., 1991—. Sec. Quality Assurance of Pleasant Hill Gen. Hosp., 1983-85; mem. MHC Employee Comm. Coun., 1995-96. Mem. Battle of Pleasant Hill (La.) Com., 1985-87. Recipient Svc. award Battle of Pleasant Hill Com., 1987. Mem. Tex. State Soc. of Am. Med. Technologist, La. State Soc. of Am. Med. Technologist, The Am. Registry of Radiologic Technologist. Roman Catholic. Avocations: reading, writing poetry. Home: PO Box 218 Joaquin TX 75954-0218 Office: Meml Hosp of Center 602 Hurst St Center TX 75935-3414

SPANN, GEORGE WILLIAM, management consultant; b. Cuthbert, Ga., July 21, 1946; s. Glinn Linwood and Mary Grace (Hiller) S.; m. Laura Jeanne Nason, June 10, 1967; children: Tanya Lynne, Stephen William. BS in Physics with honors, Ga. Inst. Tech., 1968, MS, 1970, MS in Indsl. Mgmt., 1973. Engr. Martin Marietta Corp., Orlando, Fla., 1968-70; rsch. scientist Engrng. Expt. Sta., Ga. Inst. Tech., 1970-75; v.p., dir. Metrics, Inc., mgmt. and engrng. cons., Atlanta, 1973-78, pres., dir., 1978—; v.p., dir. Exec. Data Sys., Inc., 1981—. Mem. Ga. Energy Policy Coun., Ga. Metrication Coun., NASA applications survey group for Landsat follow-on; mem. com. on practical applications of remote sensing from Space Applications Bd. NRC; market rsch. cons. NOAA, NASA, pvt. cos. Author papers, reports. Regents scholar, 1964. Mem. Am. Soc. Photogrammetry, Urban and Regional Info.

Sys. Assn., Atlanta Jaycees, Tau Beta Pi, Phi Kappa Phi, Sigma Pi Sigma. Home: 3475 Clubland Dr Marietta GA 30068-2509 Office: Bldg 14 1640 Powers Ferry Rd SE Marietta GA 30067-5491

SPANN, KATHARINE DOYLE, marketing and communications executive; b. Holton, Kans. d. Edward James and Josephine (Hurla) Doyle; m. Hugh J. Spann; 1 child, Susan Katharine. BS, Emporia State Coll. V.p. Bozell & Jacobs Advt. (formerly L.C. Cole Co.), San Francisco, 1951-76; pres. Katharine Doyle Spann Assocs., 1977—. Propr. Kate's Vineyard, Napa Valley, Calif. Bd. dirs. No. Calif. Am. Inst. Wine and Food, Napa Valley Opera House; trustee, bd. dirs., mem. exhbn. com., audience devel. com. Fine Arts Mus. San Francisco. Named Advt. Woman of Yr., 1962; recipient El Capitan award Peninsula chpt. Pub. Rels. Soc. Am., 1962, 66, Am. Silver Anvil award, 1962, 66, Excellence award Publicity Club of Bay Area, 1966. Mem. Am. Soc. Enology, Am. Inst. Wine and Food, Napa Valley Women in Wine, Calif. Vintage Wine Soc. (wine com.), Officier Commandeur, Conferie des Chevaliers du Tastevin (events com.), Metropolitan Club (San Francisco) Delta Sigma Epsilon. Home: 1447 Whitehall Ln Saint Helena CA 94574-9684

SPANN, LAURA NASON, data processing executive; b. Columbus, Ga., Aug. 5, 1947; d. Albert Dewey and Edith Maureen (Miller) Nason; m. George William Spann, June 10,1967; children: Tanya Lynne, Stephen William. BA in Math., Ga. State Coll., Atlanta, 1969. Programmer, analyst Coastal States Life Insur. Co., Atlanta, 1969-71, Rollins, Inc., Atlanta, 1972-73, Computech. Systems, Inc., Atlanta, 1975-77; private practice systems programming cons., 1977-81; pres., prin. Exec. Data Systems, Inc., 1981—. Troop leader Girl Scouts U.S., Atlanta, 1982-90; den leader Boy Scouts Am., Atlanta, 1987-92. Mem. Alpha Lambda Delta. Office: Exec Data Systems Inc Bldg 14 1640 Powers Ferry Rd SE Ste 300 Marietta GA 30067-5491

SPANN, LAWRENCE HENRY (CHIP SPANN), physician associate; b. Buffalo, Jan. 23, 1951; s. Lawrence Henry and Mildred Mary (Dotterweich) S.; m. Elizabeth Robinson, Oct. 4, 1996. BA in English, U. Miami, Coral Gables, Fla., 1974; BS in Health Scis., Duke Univ., 1982; MS in Health Scis., Duke U., 1992; postgrad., Union Inst. and Univ., 2001—. Cert. exercise program dir. Am. Coll. Sports Medicine, physician asst. Nat. Commn. Cert. Physician Assts. Physician assoc. coagulation svcs. Duke U. Med. Ctr., Durham, NC, 1996—2000, sr. physician assoc. N.C., 1982-88, 96-00; sr. physician assoc., program dir. Heart Disease Reversal Clinic, 1993-96; program dir. St. Francis Hosp., Greenville, S.C., 1988-91; exec. dir. Preventive Med. Rsch. Inst., Sausalito, Calif., 1991-93. Co-Author: (chpt.) Interventional Cardiology, 1994; contbr. articles to profl. jours. Fellow Am. Assn. Cardiovasc. Pulmonary Rehab., Am. Acad. Physician Asst.; mem. Am. Heart Assn. Avocations: poetry, reflective writing, creative expression. Office: 2522 E St Sacramento CA 95816 E-mail: lifebard@aol.com.

SPANN, MONICA FELICE, environmental health scientist; b. Washington, Oct. 18, 1968; d. Melvin Leon and Gloria (Taylor). S. BS, 1991; MPH, George Washington U., 1997; postgrad., George Mason U., 1998—; BS, Howard U., 1991. Cultural diversity coord. Nat. Wildlife Fedn., Washington, 1991-92, membership action coord., 1992-94; analyst ICF Inc., Fairfax, Va., 1994; environ. health scientist EPA, Washington, 1995. Asst. coach Silver Spring (Md.) Track Club, summer 2000, 01, dir. pub. rels., summer 2001—. Avocations: skiing, reading, exercising. Office: EPA 7509 C 1200 Pennsylvania Ave NW Washington DC 20460 E-mail: spann.monica@epa.gov

SPANNAGEL, ALAN WAYNE, physiologist; b. Harlingen, Tex., May 9, 1958; s. Billy Wayne and Ersel Lou (Jones) S.; m. Kathy Lynn Lang, 1980 (div. 1982); m. Maristella Partin, 1987 (div. 1988). BS in Marine Biology, Tex. A&M U., 1980; MS in Biology, U. Houston, Clear Lake City, 1985; PhD in Physiology, U. Tex. Health Sci. Ctr., San Antonio, 1999. Rsch. technician dept. surgery U. Tex. Med. Br., Galveston, 1981-85, rsch. assoc., 1985-87; grad. rsch. asst. dept. physiology U. Tex. Health Sci. Ctr., San Antonio, 1987-99. Instr., lectr. Physiology for Occupl. Therapy Students, 1990-93; reviewer and cons. on Physiol. Studies. Contbr. articles to profl. sci. jours. Mem. Am. Pancreatic Assn. Achievements include isolation, purification and physiological studies on a novel gastrointestinal peptide, the luminal CCK-releasing factor; demonstration that adapted changes in pancreatic juice composition have physiological effects on gastrointestinal hormone secretion and gastrointestinal function; showed that dietary peptides, not intact protein, stimulated pancreatic secretion during a meal. Home: 154 Barbara Bnd Universal City TX 78148-3602 Office: Univ Tex Health Sci Ctr Dept of Physiology 7703 Floyd Curl Dr San Antonio TX 78284-6200

SPANNINGER, BETH ANNE, lawyer; b. Bucks County, Pa., July 3, 1950; d. Feryl Louis and Nancy Elizabeth (Hendricks) S. AB magna cum laude, Muhlenberg Coll., 1972; MA, MEd, Lehigh U., 1975; JD, Temple U., 1979. Bar: Pa. 1979. Asst. dist. atty. Phila. Dist. Atty.'s Office, 1979-81; assoc. Bolger, Picker, Hankin & Tannenbaum, Phila., 1981-86, ptnr., 1986-88; sr. counsel SmithKline Beecham Corp., 1988-96; v.p., assoc. gen. counsel Glaxosmithkline, 1996—. Mem. ABA, Pa. Bar Assn., Phila. Bar Assn. (law com. 1992—), Phi Beta Kappa. Avocations: literature, jogging, theater, piano. E-mail: beth.a.spanninger@gsk.com.

SPANO, JOSEPH, actor; b. San Francisco, July 7, 1946; s. Vincent D. and Virginia Jean Spano; m. Joan Zerrien; 2 children. BA, U. Calif., Berkeley, 1967. Actor stage, founding mem. Berkeley (Calif.) Repertory, 1968-78, The Wing, San Francisco, 1968-78, Magic Theatre, L.A. Actor's Theatre, South Coast Repertory Theatre. Star TV series Hill Street Blues, 1981-87 (Emmy award nomination 1983), Amazing Grace, 1995, Murder One, 1995-96, Mercy Point, 1998; appeared in films American Graffiti, 1973, The Enforcer, Roadie, The Incredible Shrinking Woman, Northern Lights, Appollo 13, Primal Fear, Blessed Art Thou, Texas Rangers; plays American Buffalo, 1989 (LADCC award 1989), School for Scandal, 1988, Chorus of Disapproval, 1989, Speed the Plow, 1990, The Price, 1992; numerous TV films and TV series guest appearances including Midnight Caller, 1988 (Emmy award 1989); producer, actor (stage prodn.) Dracula, A Musical Nightmare, Los Angeles, N.C., San Francisco; rec. Ed McBain novels for Simon Schuster. Office: care Gilbertson/Kincaid 73 Market St Venice CA 90291-3603

SPANO, KENNETH ANDREW, surgeon, educator; b. N.Y.C., Nov. 4, 1944; MD, George Washington U., 1968. Diplomate Am. Bd. Surgery. Intern Meml. Hosp., Worcester, Mass., 1968-69, surg. resident, 1969-70, St. Francis Hosp., Hartford, Conn., 1970-73; attending staff Univ. Hosps., Cleve., 1994—; courtesy staff Lake Hosp. Systems, 1980—. Clin. instr. surgery Case Western Res. U., Cleve., 1990—; chmn. bd. trustees U. Mednet. Fellow ACS; mem. AMA, Am. Soc. Gen. Surgeons (charter), Ohio State Med. Soc., Cleve. Acad. Medicine, Cleve. Surg. Soc. Office: Univ Mednet Euclid Clinic Fedn 18599 Lake Shore Blvd Cleveland OH 44119-1054

SPANO, ROBERT, conductor; b. Conneaut, Ohio, May 7, 1961; Grad., Oberlin Conservatory Music; student, Curtis Inst. Music. Asst. condr. Boston Symphony Orch., 1990-93; faculty Oberlin (Ohio) Conservatory of Music, 1989—; music dir. Bklyn. Philharm. Orch., 1996—; musical dir. Atlanta Symphony Orch., Atlanta, 2000—. Faculty Tanglewood Music Ctr., head conducting fellowship program, 1998—; guest condr. Boston Symphony Orch., Chgo. Symphony Orch., Cleve. Orch., L.A. Philharmonic, Nat. Symphony Orch., Phila. Orch., Royal Opera Covent Garden, Welsh Nat. Opera, Orchestra Filharmonica della Scala, City of Birmingham Symphony, others. Office: Atlanta Symphony Orch 1293 Peachtree St NE Ste 300 Atlanta GA 30309-3552

SPANOS, ALEXANDER GUS, construction executive, professional sports team executive; b. Stockton, Calif., Sept. 28, 1923; m. Faye Spanos; children: Dean, Dea Spanos Berberian, Alexis Spanos Ruhl, Michael. LLD (hon.), U. Pacific, 1984. Chmn. bd. dirs. A.G. Spanos Constrn. Inc., Stockton, Calif., 1960—; chmn. bd. dirs. A.G. Spanos Mgmt. Inc., 1967—, A.G. Spanos Enterprises Inc., Stockton, 1971—, A.G. Spanos Devel. Inc., Stockton, 1973—, A.G. Spanos Realty Inc., Stockton, 1978—, A.G.S. Fin. Corp., Stockton, 1980—, A.G. Spanos Securities Corp., Stockton, 1981—, San Diego Chargers, 1984—. Former trustee Children's Hosp., San Francisco, San Francisco Fine Arts Mus.; trustee Eisenhower Med. Ctr., Rancho Mirage, Calif.; hon. regent U. Pacific, Stockton, 1972-82; gov. USO, Washington, 1982—; former gov. Ronald Reagan Presdl. Found.; chmn. U.S. chpt. U.S. Greece bus. coun. Served with USAF, 1942-46. Recipient Albert Gallatin award Zurich-Am. Ins. Co., 1973, Horatio Alger award Horatio Alger Found., 1982, medal of Honor Statue of Liberty-Ellis Islan Found., 1982. Mem. Am. Hellenic Ednl. Progressive Assn., Calif. C. of C. (bd. dirs. 1980-85). Republican. Greek Orthodox. Avocation: golfing. Office: San Diego Chargers Qualcomm Stadium PO Box 609609 San Diego CA 92160-9609 also: A G Spanos Cos Ste 1A 1341 West Robinhood Dr Stockton CA 95207 E-mail: agspr@agspanos.com.

SPANOS, CHRISTINE LOUISE, interior designer, consultant; b. Wheeling, W. Va., Apr. 2, 1950; d. Louis John and Bernardine J. (Sweener) Yahn; m. Richard Paul Spanos, Nov. 2, 1979. Student, Art Inst. of Pitts., 1970-71. Designer Metro Decorators, Allentown, Pa., 1971-76; Designer Morris Black & Sons, Bethlehem, 1976-82; owner, designer Interiors by Christine, Inc., Allentown, 1989—. Pres. Jr. Aides of the Allentown Hosp., 1987, bd. dirs. 1985-86. Mem. SBA (bd. dirs. 1989—), Nat. Assn. Profl. Saleswomen, Allentown/Lehigh County C. of C. (bd. dirs. 1988), Exec. Women's Council (bd. dirs. 1988), Small Bus. Coun. Republican. Avocations: sailing, skiing, hiking, golf, horseback riding. Office: 403 E 10th St # 2 Northampton PA 18067-1734

SPANOS, DEAN A. professional sports team executive, business executive; b. Stockton, Calif., May 26, 1950; s. Alex G. Spanos; m. Susan Spanos; children: Alexander Gus, John Dean. BBA, U. Pacific, 1972. Pres., vice-chmn. San Diego Chargers, 1984—; pres. Spanos corp. entities; vice-chmn. AGS Fin. Corp. Past bd. regents U. Pacific. Co-winner Bing Crosby Nat. Pro-Am. Golf Tournament, 1985; winner Bob Hope Chrysler Classic, 1990, 91, AT&T Nat. Pro-Am. Golf Tournament, 1990; recipient Most Valuable Amateur trophy; mem. winning team in Sr.'s Reunion Tournament, Dallas, 1985. Avocation: golf. Office: San Diego Chargers 4020 Murphy Canyon Rd San Diego CA 92123-4407*

SPANOS, POL DIMITRIOS, engineering educator; b. Messini, Peloponnesus, Greece, Feb. 27, 1950; came to U.S., 1973; s. Dimitrios Constandin Spanos and Aicaterine Polychronis Bonaros; children: Demetri, Eudokia. Diploma in mech. engring., Nat. Tech. U., Athens, 1973; MSCE, Calif. Inst. Tech., 1974, PhD in Applied Mechanics, 1976. Registered profl. engr., Tex., Greece. Rsch. asst. Calif. Inst. Tech., Pasadena, 1973-76, rsch. fellow, 1976-77; from asst. prof. to assoc. prof. U. Tex.-Austin, 1981-84, P.D. Henderson assoc. prof. engring., 1983-84; prof. mech. engring. and civil engring. Rice U., Houston, 1984-88, L.B. Ryon endowed chair in engring., 1988—. Cons. on analytical and numerical applications of theory of dynamics and vibrations, worldwide. Author: Random Vibrations, Probabilistic Offshore Mechanics, Probabilistic Methods in Civil Engineering, Random Vibration and Statistical Linearization, Dynamic Analysis of Non-Linear Structures by the Method of Statistical Quadratization, Stochastic Finite Elements: A Spectral Approach, Computational Stochastic Mechanics, Probabilistic Structural Mechanics: Advances in Structural Reliability Methods, Random Vibrations: A Broad Perspective; contbr. to profl. jour. issues devoted to dynamics and vibrations; mem. editl. bd. 8 jours.; editor-in chief or co-editor 2 primary jours. on mechanics. Recipient European award of sci. N.V. Phillipps Co., Eindhoven, Netherlands, 1969, Presdl. Young Investigator award in earthquake engring. NSF, 1984-89, Cert. merit McDonnell Douglas Astronautics Co., Houston, 1987, G.R. Brown award for superior tchg. Rice U., 1995, 96, Newmark medal for lifetime contbns. to dynamics and vibrations ASCE, 1999. Fellow ASCE, AAM, ASME (participant tech. confs. and coms., Pi Tau Sigma Gold medal 1982, W.L. Huber Civil Engring. Rsch. prize 1989, G.L. Larson Meml. award 1991, Alfred M. Freudenthal medal 1992, Humboldt Rsch. award 1995, Disting. Lectr. 1997—, Newmark Medal, 1999); mem. Am. Acad. Mechanics, Earthquake Engring. Rsch. Inst., Internat. Assn. for Structural Safety and Reliability (rsch. prize in the area of stochastic dynamics 1997), Hellenic Profl. Soc. (sponsor scholarship com.), A. von Humboldt Assn. Am. (life). Office: Rice U Dept Mech Engring MS 321 PO Box 1892 Houston TX 77251-1892 Fax: (713) 348-5191. E-mail: spanos@rice.edu.

SPANOVICH, MILAN, retired civil engineer; b. Steubenville, Ohio, Feb. 19, 1929; s. Stanley and Katherine (Komazec) S.; m. Sylvia J. Tomko, Apr. 16, 1971. BS Civil Engring. Carnegie-Mellon U., 1956, MS Civil Engring., 1957. Registered profl. engr., Pa., Ohio, Va., W.Va., Mich., Ky., N.J. Instr. Carnegie-Mellon U., 1957-60; charter assoc., v.p. E. D'Appolonia Assocs., 1957-61; mem. civil engring. staff U. N.Mex., 1961-63; founder, sr. cons. Engring. Mechs., Inc., Pitts., 1963-96. Contbr. articles on soil mechs. to tech. jours.; patentee found. systems. Bd. dirs. Carnegie Mellon U. Andrew Carnegie Soc. Recipient Pitts. Young Civil Engr. of Yr. award, 1969 Fellow ASCE (Pitts. Civl Engr. of the Yr. 1987, chmn. numerous coms.), Am. Cons. Engrs. Council; mem. Cons. Engrs. Council Greater Pitts. (pres. 1972-74), Engring. Soc. Western Pa. (dir. 1972, 77-83), Nat. Soc. Profl. Engrs., Pa. Soc. Profl. Engrs. (pres. Pitts. chpt. 1971, Hornfeck award Pitts. chpt. 1979, state dir. 1976-79, Disting. Service award Pitts. chpt. 1985, Pa. Engr. of the Yr. 1988, Profl. Devel. award 1989, Outstanding Svc. award Pitts. chpt. 1993), ASTM (chmn. task com. on relative density of granular soils 1959-63), Am. Concrete Inst., Hwy. Research Bd., Internat. Soc. Soil Mechs. and Found. Engring., Pitts. Geol. Soc., Am. Arbitration Assn., Profl. Engrs. in Pvt. Practice (chmn. 1970-71), Pitts. Builders Exchange, Soc. Explosives Engrs., Am. Soc. Hwy. Engrs., Carnegie-Mellon U. Alumni Assn. (mem. planning com.), Chi Epsilon Nat. Civil Engring. Honor Soc. Home: 216 Eton Rd Pittsburgh PA 15205-1733

SPANSKY, ROBERT ALAN, computer systems analyst, retired; b. Hamtramck, Mich., July 29, 1942; s. Harry Joseph and Alicia Eileen (Kossak) S. BS, U. Detroit, 1964, MBA, 1967. Asst. br. mgr. Nat. Bank Detroit, 1965-67, sr. asst. br. mgr., 1969-71; computer programmer Ford Motor Co., Dearborn, Mich., 1972-76, sys. analyst, project leader, 1976-99; ret., 1999. Active in food delivery to elderly Focus Hope, Detroit, 1990—2001; chmn. 75th anniversary reunion dinner dance St. Matthew Parish, 2002. Sgt. U.S. Army, 1967—69, Vietnam. Recipient Disting. Svc. award Alpha Kappa Psi, 1967, 83, 90—91, 25-Yr. Svc. award Alpha Kappa Psi/Ford Motor Co., 1987, 97. Mem. Assn. MBAs, Econ. Club Detroit Roman Catholic. Avocations: coin collecting, stamp collecting, landscaping. Home: 5574 Haverhill St Detroit MI 48224-3245 E-mail: rspansky@msn.com.

SPARBER, DALE PAUL, banker; b. Erie, Pa., Aug. 21, 1948; s. John Russel and Wilma Jean (Grettler) S. BSBA, Thiel Coll., Greenville, Pa., 1971. Supr. Cleve. Trust Co., 1972-73, ops. officer, 1973-75; exec. dir. MidAm. Automated Payments System, Cleve., 1975-77; asst. v.p. AmeriTrust Co. of Franklin County, Columbus, 1977-79; v.p. AmeriTrust Co., Cleve., 1980-85, Security Pacific Mcht. Bank, Chgo., 1985-88, Barclays Bank Pub. Ltd. Corp., Cleve., 1988-93; v.p. new bus. devel. Provident Bank, 1996—2002; sr. v.p. BankOne, 2002—. Arbitrator Nat. Future Assn., Chgo.; bd. dirs. Cheboygan (Mich) Tap & Tool; pres. Shorn Enterprises Inc., 1995—; bd. dirs. Millcreek Cmty. Hosp., Erie, Pa., The EM Square Group, Cleve., Ohio. Fundraiser Chgo. area March of Dimes, 1987, Sta. WQLN Ednl. TV, Erie, 1990. Mem. Cleve. Art Mus., Hunting and Fishing Club of Crawford County (sec.-treas. 1980-87, bd. dirs. 1980-87), Cleve. Athletic Club, Iroquois Boat Club of Conneaut Lake, Hillbrook Club (Chagrin Falls, Ohio), Sawbridge Golf Club (Chardon, Ohio). Republican. Methodist. Avocations: downhill and water skiing, hunting, fishing. Home: 3020 Woodbury Rd Cleveland OH 44120-2441

SPARBERG, MARSHALL STUART, gastroenterologist, educator; b. Chgo., May 20, 1936; s. Max Shane and Mildred Rose (Haffron) S.; m. Eve Gaymont Enda, Mar. 15, 1987. BA, Northwestern U., 1957, MD, 1960. Intern Evanston Hosp., Ill., 1960-61; resident in internal medicine Barnes Hosp., St. Louis, 1961-63; fellow U. Chgo., 1963-65; practice medicine specializing in gastroenterolgy Chgo., 1967—; asst. prof. medicine Northwestern U., 1967-72, assoc. prof., 1972-80, prof. medicine, 1980—; instr. Wash. U., St. Louis, 1961-63, U. Chgo., 1963-65. Author: Ileostomy Care, 1969, Primer of Clinical Diagnosis, 1972, Ulcerative Colitis, 1978, Inflammatory Bowel Disease, 1982; contbr. numerous articles to profl. jours. Pres. Fine Arts Music Found., 1974-76, Crohn's Disease and Colitis Found. of Am., pres. Ill. chpt., 1994-97; bd. dirs. Lyric Opera Guild, 1974-94, Chamber Music Soc. North Shore Chgo., 1984—; physician to Chgo. Symphony Orch., 1981-97. With USAF, 1965-67. Named Outstanding Tchr. Northwestern U. Med. Sch., 1972 Mem. AMA, ACP, Am. Gastroent. Assn., Am. Coll. Gastroent. (bd. govs.), Chgo. Med. Soc., Chgo. Soc. Internal Medicine, Chgo. Soc. Gastroenterology (pres.), Chgo. Soc. Gastrointestinal Endoscopy (pres.) Office: 676 N Saint Clair St Ste 1525 Chicago IL 60611-2862

SPARER, MALCOLM MARTIN, rabbi; b. N.Y.C. m. Erna Reichl (dec. Sept. 1990); children: Ruth, Arthur (dec.), Jennifer, Shoshana. AB, M in Hebrew Lit., Yeshiva U.; MA in Sociology, CCNY; cert. in pastoral counseling, Des Moines Coll. Osteopathic Medicine; PhD in Sociology, NYU. Ordained rabbi, 1953. Pres. Menorah Inst., San Francisco, 1981—; exec. dir. Rabbinical Coun. Calif., L.A., 1957-66; chaplain VA; adminstr. Tchr's. Coll. of West Coast, Torah U. (now Yeshiva U.), 1957-66; rabbi Beth El Jacob, Des Moines, 1966-69, Chevra Thilim, San Francisco, 1969-72. Pres. No. Calif. Bd. Rabbis, 1977-96, pres. emeritus, 1996—; sr. lectr. San Francisco C.C.; liason Union of Orthodox Jewish Congregations Am., 1957-66, moderator radio series Lest We Forget, 1962, moderator TV spls. Sta. KNXT, L.A., 1964-65, Des Moines, 1967-69; instr. dept. philosophy Drake U., 1966-69; pres. San Francisco dist. Zionist Orgn. Am., 1969-82, also bd. dirs.; chmn., mem. nat. bd. San Francisco Bay Area Zionist Fedn., 1971-84; co-chmn. Jerusalem Fair, 25th Ann. State of Israel, 1973; chmn. Commn. on Soviet Jewry, Jewish Cmty. Rels. Coun., 1974-81; cons. internat. leaders, founder Menorah Inst.; cons. Commn. on Christian-Jewish and Moslem Rels. to European Parliament Nations; cons. in field; writer, lectr. colls., ch. groups on Judaica and world affairs; chmn. dept. world affairs/internat. politics C.C. San Francisco; former chaplain Letterman Army VA Hosp., San Francisco Presidio; co-founder Black and Jewish Clergy; mem. San Francisco Coun. Chs., bd. dirs. food bank program, United Jewish Appeal, chmn. rabbinic cabinet of western region; invited mem. del. bishops and ch. leaders various denominations conducting meml. svc. at Dachau on 50th ann. Reich's Kristallnacht, Fed. Republic Germany, 1988. Hon. chmn. Mayor's Commn. on Holocaust Meml., San Francisco; mem. Mayor's Task Force for Homeless; co-chmn. Gov.'s Family Task Force, San Francisco. With USN, WWII, Korean War, chaplain USAF. Annual Jerusalem Lectr. Series named in his honor, 1998. Address: PO Box 15055 San Francisco CA 94115-0055

SPARGO, BENJAMIN H. educator, renal pathologist; b. Six Mile Run, Pa., Aug. 11, 1919; s. Benjamin H. and Lillian (Rankin) S.; m. Barbara Scollard, Mar. 12, 1942; children— Janet, Patricia. BS in Biol. Scis, U. Chgo., 1948, MS in Pathology, MD with honors, U. Chgo., 1952. Intern Univ. Hosp., Ann Arbor, Mich., 1953-54; resident pathology U. Chgo. Med. Sch., 1954-55, mem. faculty, 1954—, prof. renal pathology, 1964-95; prof. pathology emeritus, 1995—; assoc. chmn. dept., 1974-80. Cons. Armed Forces Inst. Pathology, 1975-79, Midwest Regional Organ Bank of Ill., 1989-94. Served with USAAF, 1941-46. Recipient Rsch. Career award Nat. Heart Inst., 1964-99, Disting. Svc. award Kidney Found. Ill., 1991, Disting. Lifetime Achievement award The Renal Pathology Soc., 1996. Mem. U.S.-Can. Acad. Pathology (chmn. edn. com. 1975-77) Home: 5550 S South Shore Dr Chicago IL 60637-5051

SPARKMAN, BRANDON BUSTER, educator, writer, consultant; b. Hartselle, Ala., Aug. 2, 1929; s. George Olan and Mary Louise (Jones) S.; m. Wanda Phillips, Sept. 13, 1952; children— Ricky Brandon, Rita Sharon, Robert Lee. BS, U. North Ala., 1952; MA, U. Ala., 1958, EdS, 1961; EdD, Auburn (Ala.) U., 1970. Tchr., asst. prin. Phllips High Sch., Bear Creek, Ala., 1954-57; prin. Tuscumbia, 1957-65; asst. supt., 1965-69; ednl. cons. Auburn Center, 1969-70; mem. faculty dept. sch. adminstrn. Auburn U., 1970; asst. supt. for staff personnel devel. Jackson (Miss.) Pub. Schs., 1970-71, supt., 1971-73; sch. supt. Richland County Sch. Dist. 1, Columbia, S.C., 1973-75; asst. supt. instruction Hartselle (Ala.) City Schs., 1975-80; supt. Guntersville (Ala.) City Schs., 1980-88; CEO The Right Combination Pub. & Ednl. Svcs. Corp., Guntersville, Ala., 1984-93. Adj. prof. U. Ala., Birmingham, 1998-2000; writer, cons. in field. Sr. author: Blueprint for a Brighter Child, 1973, STEPS (System for Teacher Evaluation of Pre-reading Skills), 1974; co-author: Preparing Your Preschooler for Reading, 1977, Competency Tests for Basic Reading Skills, 1978, Soaring High with Science, 1985, Soaring High with Social Studies, 1985; author: How Well Does Your Child Read, 1979, Writing Composition Made Easy, 1991, Blueprint for Expository Writing, 1993, Reading Skills Competency Tests, 1999; editor: The In-Between Years, 1979; creator: CORE (Program Management Through Computer Systems), 1975; editor, contbg. author: The Advantaged, A Preschool Program for the Disadvantaged, 1969; contbr. articles to profl. jours. Bd. dirs. Morgan County chpt. ARC, United Givers Fund, Colbert-Lauderdale Child Study Center, Sheffield-Tuscumbia Credit Union; bd. govs. Jackson Symphony Orch.; adv. bd. Jackson Mental Health Center. Served with AUS, 1952-54. Recipient Human Relations award Jackson. Mem. Am., Ala assns. sch. adminstrs. (past pres.), Ala. Council Sch. Adminstrn. and Supervision (past pres.), Assn. Supervision and Curriculum Devel., Ala. Assn. Supervision and Curriculum Devel. (past pres.), Florence State U. Alumni Assn. (past pres.) Methodist (ch. sch. tchr., supt., vice chmn. ofcl. bd., chmn. commn. edn.). Home and Office: PO Box 961 Guntersville AL 35976-0961

SPARKMAN, STEVEN LEONARD, lawyer; b. Sarasota, Fla., May 30, 1947; s. Simeon Clarence and Ursula (Wahlstrom) S.; m. Terry Jeanne Gibbs, Aug. 23, 1969; children: Joanna Jeanne, Kevin Leonard. BA, Fla. State U., 1969, JD, 1972. Bar: Fla. 1972, U.S. Dist. Ct. (mid. dist.) Fla. 1974, U.S. Ct. Appeals (5th cir.) 1975. Legal rsch. asst. Office Gen. Counsel, Fla. Dept. Revenue, Tallahassee, 1971; legis. intern com. on community affairs Fla. Ho. of Reps., 1971-72; jud. rsch. aide Fla. 2d Dist. Ct. Appeals, Lakeland, 1972-73; asst. county atty. Hillsborough County, Tampa, Fla., 1973-75; assoc. Carlton, Fields, Ward, Emmanuel, Smith & Cutler, P.A., 1975-80, sr. atty., 1980-2001; pvt. practice Plant City, Fla., 2001—. Mem. bd. visitors Fla. State U. Coll. Law, 1994-00. Sec., bd. dirs. Bapt. Towers Plant City, Inc., 1981-84; deacon 1st Bapt. Ch., Plant City, 1980—. 1st lt. USAFR, 1973. Mem. Fla. Bar Assn. (exec. coun. local govt. law sect. 1978-79), Hillsborough County Bar Assn., Plant City Bar Assn., Tampa Kiwanis (bd. dirs. 1980-82, 96-98, Layman of Yr. 1984, 89), Tampa Kiwanis Found. (bd. dirs. 1997-2000). Democrat. Office: Steven L Sparkman PA 212 N Collins St Ste 1 Plant City FL 33563 E-mail: sls@sparklaw.com.

SPARKS, BENNETT SHER, retired military officer; b. Pitts., Oct. 10, 1925; s. Julius and Anna K. Sparks; m. Elizabeth Regina Sparks, May 8, 1943; children: Bennett Sher Jr., James Robert, Richard T. (dec.), John N., Julieann, Donna Beth. Diploma, Navy War Coll., 1973, Army War Coll., 1988, Nat. War Coll., 1978; PhD in Philosophy (hon.), Sampson U., Oxford, Eng., 1986. Lic. aircraft pilot. Commd. ensign USCG, 1957, advanced through grades to rear admiral, 1985, reserve inspector 11th Coast Guard Dist., sr. res. officer Pacific Area, sr. res. officer Atlantic Area N.Y.C., comdr. Navy's No. Calif. Maritime Def. Zone San Francisco; comdr. Navy's Maritime Def. Zone USCG, sector 6, Charleston, S.C.; ret. USCG, 1993; nat. dep. exec. dir. Res. Officers assn. U.S., Washington, 1987-91, dir. adminstrn. and dir. fin., 1987-91. Civilian aviator Geodetic Survey, Alaska; bd. dirs. Bank of Hollywood; chief U.S. Delegation to CIOR, NATO Hdqrs., Belgium, 1985-86; internat. sec.-gen. Inter-Allied Confedn. of Res. Officers, Brussels, 1992-94. Chmn. bd. trustees ROA/US, Washington; mem. Calif. Vets. Bd., 1995—, chmn., 1998-99. Decorated Legion of Merit, Coast Guad Commendation medals (2), Coast Guard Achievement medal, Humanitarian Svc. medal, Arctic Svc. medal, Coast Guard Combat Air Crew Wings, others; recipient Navy Disting. Pub. Svc. medal Sec. of Navy, 1983, Coast Guard Disting. Pub. Svc. medal Commandant of Coast Guard, 1983, 93. Mem. Res. Officers Assn. U.S. (pres. 1982-83). Home: 573 Pistachio Pl Windsor CA 95492-8168

SPARKS, BILLY SCHLEY, lawyer; b. Marshall, Mo., Mar. 1, 1923; s. John and Clarinda (Schley) S.; m. Dorothy O. Stone, May 14, 1946; children: Stephen Stone, Susan Lee Sparks Raben Taylor, John David. AB, Harvard U., 1945, LLB, 1949. Bar: Mo. 1949. Ptnr. Langworthy, Matz & Linde, Kansas City, Mo., 1949-62, Linde, Thomason, Fairchild, Langworthy, Kohn & Van Dyke, Kansas City, 1962-91; ret., 1991. Mem. Mission (Kans.) Planning Coun., 1954-63; treas. Johnson County (Kans.) Dem. Ctrl. Com., 1958-64; candidate for rep. 10th Dist., Kans., 1956, 3d Dist., 1962; mem. Dist. 100 Sch. Bd., 1964-68, pres., 1967-69; mem. Dist. 512 Sch. Bd., 1969-73, pres., 1971-72; del. Dem. Nat. Conv., 1964; ; mem. Kans. Civil Svc. Commn., 1975-90. Lt. USAAF, 1944-46. Mem. ABA, Mo. Bar Assn., Kansas City Bar Assn., Law Assn. Kansas City, Harvard Law Sch. Assn. Mo. (past dir.), Nat. Assn. Sch. Bds. (mem. legis. com. 1968-73), St. Andrews Soc., Harvard Club (v.p. 1953-54), The Kansas City (Mo.) Club, Milburn Golf and Country Club, Am. Legion, Kansas City C. of C. (legis. com. 1956-82), Mem. Christian Ch. Home and Office: 8517 W 90th Ter Shawnee Mission KS 66212-3053

SPARKS, CHARLES EDWARD, pathologist, educator; b. Peoria, Ill., July 29, 1940; s. William Joseph and Meredith (Pleasants) S.; m. Janet Lindsay Dehoff, Aug. 18, 1977; children: William, Debra, Robert. BS in Biology, MIT, 1963; MD, Thomas Jefferson U., 1968. Diplomate Am. Bd. Pathology, Am. Bd. Clin. Chemistry. Rsch. asst. Mass. Gen. Hosp., Boston, 1963; intern N.Y. Hosp., Cornell Naval Hosp., St. Albans, 1968-69; resident in clin. pathology Hosp. of U. Pa., 1972-75; fellow in cardiopulmonary medicine U. Pa., Phila., 1975-76; fellow in biochemistry Med. Coll. Pa., 1976-77; asst. instr. U. Pa., 1972-75; instr. Med. Coll. Pa., 1976-77, asst. to assoc. prof. biochemistry and physiology, 1977-82; assoc. prof. pathology U. Rochester (N.Y.), 1982-88, prof. pathology, 1988—. Advisor med. scientist tng. program U. Rochester (N.Y.), 1984-92; attending pathologist, dir. clin. chemistry unit Strong Meml. Hosp., 1982—, chair rsc. adv. com., assoc. chair pathology, 1994—, dir. grad. studies in Integrative Biomed. Scis., 1998—. Contbr. articles to profl. jours.; patentee in field. Lt. comdr. USN, 1969-72. Postdoctoral fellow NIH, 1975-77. Mem. AAAS, Am. Diabetes Assn. (co-chmn. nat. symposium meeting 1988), The Acad. Clin. lab. Physicians and Scientists, Am. heart Assn. (fellow coun. on arteriosclerosis, mem. nominating com.). Office: Dept Pathology U Rochester 601 Elmwood Ave Rochester NY 14642-0001

SPARKS, DAVID STANLEY, university administrator; b. Phila., Dec. 8, 1922; s. Richard Frederick and Grace Dorothy (Tuttle) S.; m. Phyllis Ann Bate, June 12, 1949; children: Robert F., E. Anne. AB, Grinnell (Iowa) Coll., 1944; MA, U. Chgo., 1945, PhD, 1951. Instr., asst. prof., asso. prof. U. Md., College Park, 1947-65, prof. history, 1965—, assoc. dean grad. studies and research, 1967-70, dean, 1970-77, acting vice chancellor for acad. affairs, 1976-77, acting v.p. grad. studies and research, 1978-79, v.p. grad. studies and research, 1979-87, acting v.p. for acad. affairs, 1982-83, v.p. acad. affairs, grad. studies and research, 1987-88, vice chancellor for acad. affairs, 1988-91, vice chancellor emeritus, 1991. Vis. professorial lectr. dept. history Johns Hopkins, 1965; mem., chair Grad. Record Examinations Bd., 1979-85. Co-editor, author: American Civilization: A History of the United States, 1960, The Making of American Democracy, Readings and Documents, 2 vols, 1962; Editor: Inside Lincoln's Army: The Diary of General Marsena Rudolph Patrick, 1964. Recipient research awards Am. Philos. Soc., 1958, Social Sci. Research Council, 1957 Mem. Am., So. hist. assns., Orgn. Am. Historians, Am. Assn. U. Profs. (pres. U. Md. chpt.), Nat. Acad. Univ. Research Adminstrs., Phi Kappa Phi. Clubs: Cosmos (Washington). Home: 10500 Rockville Pike Apt 1309 Rockville MD 20852-3350

SPARKS, DAVID THOMAS, lawyer; b. Bowling Green, Ky., Dec. 17, 1968; s. Lee Thomas and Ann Louis S. BS, We. Ky., 1992; JD, U. Ky., 1995. Bar: Ky. 1995, U.S. Dist. Ct. (we. dist.) Ky. 1995, U.S. Dist. Ct. (ea. dist.) Ky. 1996. Assoc. atty. Bell, Orr, Ayers & Moore, Bowling Green, 1995—2000; atty. Mike Bran Attys. at Law, PSC and David T. Sparks Law Office, 2000—. Deacon First Christian Ch., Bowling Green, 1988-98, elder, 1998, mem. personnel com., 1998. Mem. ABA, Ky. Bar Assn., Bowling Green Warren County Bar Assn., Future Bus. Leaders Am., Phi Beta Lambda. Republican. Mem. Christian Ch. Avocations: basketball, softball, model railroading, marine aquarium, reading. Home: 2512 Thompson Dr Bowling Green KY 42104-4375 Office: Bell Orr Ayers & Moore 1700 Destiny Ln Bowling Green KY 42104

SPARKS, DONALD LEWIS, soil chemistry educator; b. Paris, June 26, 1953; s. Elmer Johnston and Christine (McKenzie) S.; m. Joy Lynn Gooden, Sept. 14, 1984. BS, U. Ky., 1975, MS, 1976; PhD, Va. Poly. Inst. and State U., Blacksburg, 1979. Asst. prof. soil chemistry U. Del., Newark, 1979-83, assoc. prof., 1983-87, prof., 1987—, chmn. dept. plant and soil scis., 1989—, disting. prof., 1994—, Francis Alison prof., 1996—, T.A. Baker prof., 2001—02, S. Hallock duPont chair, 2002—. Cons. DuPont Corp., Wilmington, Del., 1981—. Author: Kinetics of Soil Chemical Processes, 1989, Environmental Soil Chemistry, 1995; editor: Soil Physical Chemistry, 1986, rev. 2d edit. 1998, Rates of Soil Chemical Processes, 1991, Method of Soil Analysis: Chemical Methods, 1996; mem. editl. bd. Am. Jour. Soil Sci. Soc., 1984-93, Geoderma, 1986—, Soil Sci., 1987—, Pedosphere, 1999—, Geochimica Cosmochimica Acta, 1999—, Vadose Zone Jour., 2002--; editor: Advances in Agronomy, 1990—; contbr. over 120 articles and 26 book chpts. to profl. publs. Pres. Torch Club of Del., Newark, 1989—. Fellow AAAS, Soil Sci. Soc. of Am. (pres.-elect 1998-99, pres. 1999-2000, Soil Sci. Rsch. award 1994, M.L. and Chrystie M. Jackson Soil Sci. award), Am. Soc. of Agronomy (N.E. br. rsch. award 1986); mem. Internat. Union Soil Sci. (pres-elect 2000-02, pres. 2002—), Am. Chem. Soc., Clay Minerals Soc., Geochemical Soc. Mem. Christian Ch. (Disciples Of Christ). Achievements include pioneering application of chemical kinetics to soil systems. Office: U Del Dept Plant and Soil Scis Newark DE 19717-1303 E-mail: dlsparks@udel.edu.

SPARKS, JACK NORMAN, college dean; b. Lebanon, Ind., Dec. 3, 1928; s. Oakley and Geraldine Ruth (Edrington) S.; m. Esther Lois Bowen, Apr. 11, 1953; children: Stephen Michael, Robert Norman, Ruth Ann, Jonathan Russell. BS, Purdue U., 1950; MA, U. Iowa, 1951, PhD, 1960. Tchr. math. Leyden Community High Sch., Franklin Park, Ill., 1954-58; rsch. asst. U. Iowa, Iowa City, 1958-60; assoc. prof. applied stats., dir. bur. of rsch. U. No. Colo., Greeley, 1960-65; assoc. prof. ednl. psychology Pa. State U., State Coll., 1965-68; dir. corr. Campus Crusade for Christ, San Bernardino, Calif., 1968-69; dir. Christian World Liberation Front, Berkeley, 1969-75; pastor, ch. overseer New Covenant Apostolic Order, 1975-77; dean St. Athanasius Acad. Orthodox Theology, Santa Barbara, Calif., 1977-87, St. Athanasius Coll., Santa Barbara, 1987-93, St. Athanasius Acad. of Orthodox Theology, Elk Grove, Calif., 1996—. Cons. Measurement Rsch. Ctr., Iowa City, 1959-60, Western States Small Schs. Project, Greeley, 1962-65, Colo. Coun. on Edn. Rsch., Denver, 1963-65; project dir. Orthodox Study Bible Old Testament Project, 1998—. Author: Letters to Street Christians, 1971, The Mind Benders, 1977, 79, The Resurrection Letters, 1978, The Preaching of the Apostles, 1987, Victory in the Unseen Warfare, 1993; editor: Apostolic Fathers, 1978, 88; gen. editor: The Orthodox Study Bible, 1993, Virtue in the Unseen Warfare, 1995, Prayer in the Unseen Warfare, 1996, Christ Is Our Holiness, 1996, The Coming of the Prince, 1997, Tradition in the Early Church, 1997, The Letters of St. Ignatius, 1998, Faith and Godlines, 1999, Pentecost: A Homily of St. John Chrysostom, 2000, No Graven Image, 2000, The Valley of the Shadow of Death, 2000, Death, Fear of Death, Hope of Resurrection, 2000, Kindling the Fire Within, 2000, How Can Jesus Be Both God and Man, 2001, The Annunciation, 2001, The Bride of Christ, 2001, The Boundless Beauty, 2001, Walking Through the Night, 2001. Trustee Rock Mont Coll., Denver, 1962-77, Thomas Nelson Co., Nashville, 1977-78. 1st lt. U.S. Army, 1952-54. Mem. Am. Sci. Affiliation, Assn. Orthodox Theologians, Conf. on Faith and History, Phi Delta Kappa (pres. Epsilon chpt. 1959-60). Republican. Orthodox Christian. Home: 8758 Williamson Dr Elk Grove CA 95624-1829 Office: St Athanasius Acad Orthodox Theology 10519 E Stockton Blvd Ste 170 Elk Grove CA 95624-9704 E-mail: frjack@saaot.edu.

SPARKS, JANET LINDSAY DEHOFF, pathology educator; b. Lawrence, Mass., Sept. 13, 1950; d. Ronald Lee and Barbara Isabelle (Platt) DeHoff; m. Charles Edward Sparks, Aug. 18, 1977; 1 child, Robert. BA in Biology, BS in Med. Tech., U. Pa., 1972, PhD in Pathology, 1980. Cert. med. technologist Am. Soc. Clin. Pathologists. Instr. clin. chemistry U. Pa., Phila., 1974-76; fellow Wistar Inst. Anatomy and Biology, 1975-80; postdoctoral fellow U. Rochester (N.Y.), 1983-85, scientist, 1985-94, asst. prof. pathology and lab. medicine, 1994-96, assoc. prof. pathology and lab. medicine, 1996—. Cons. NIH, Indpls., 1994-96. Contbr. numerous articles to profl. jours.; patentee in field. Nat. NIDDK RO1 grantee, 1995—. Fellow Coun. on Arteriosclerosis Thrombosis and Vascular Biology; mem. AAAS, Am. Soc. Clin. Pathologists, Am. Diabetes Assn., Am. Heart Assn. (coun. on arteriosclerosis, coun. on clin. cardiology), N.Y. Lipid Club, N.Y. Acad. Scis. Office: U Rochester Dept Pathology 601 Elmwood Ave # 626 Rochester NY 14642-0001 E-mail: janet_sparks@ume.rochester.edu.

SPARKS, JARED J. social worker, educator; b. Fort Smith, Ark., July 11, 1968; s. Zoe Ann Sparks, Jared Sparks. BA, U.Ala., 1992; MSW, U. Ala., 1994; postgrad., Tulane U., 1998—. LCSW 1998. Nephrology social worker U. Miss. Med. Ctr., Jackson, Miss., 1994—2000; transplant social worker Transplant Inst. New Orleans , 2000—. Mem.: New Orleans Kidney Patient Assn. (bd. dirs. 2001—), La. Coun. Nephrology Social Workers (bd.dirs. 2001—). Home: 5801 Cedar Creek #222C River Ridge LA 70123 Office: Transplant Inst of New Orleans 3535 Bienville St Ste 225 E. New Orleans LA 70119 Home Fax: 504-488-8121; Office Fax: 504-488-9672. Personal E-mail: jsparks2@tulane.edu. Business E-Mail: jared.sparks@tenethealth.com.

SPARKS, JOHN EDWARD, lawyer; b. Rochester, Ind., July 3, 1930; s. Russell Leo and Pauline Anna (Whittenberger) S.; m. Margaret Joan Snyder, Sept. 4, 1954; children: Thomas Edward, William Russell, Kathryn Chapman McCarthy. AB, Ind. U., 1952; LL.B., U. Calif., Berkeley, 1957; postgrad., London Sch. Econs., 1957-58. Bar: Calif. 1958. Assoc. Brobeck, Phleger & Harrison, San Francisco, 1958-66, ptnr., 1967-95, of counsel, 1996—. Adj. prof. law U. San Francisco, 1967-69; pres. Legal Aid Soc. San Francisco, 1978-79, dir., 1971-81. Editor U. Calif. Law Rev., 1956-57. Served to 1st lt. Q.M.C. U.S. Army, 1952-54, Korea. Recipient Wheeler Oak Meritorious award U. Calif., Berkeley, 1986. Fellow Am. Bar Found., Am. Coll. Trial Lawyers; mem. State Bar Calif., Bar Assn. San Francisco (bd. dirs. 1974-75), ABA, Am. Judicature Soc., Boalt Hall Alumni Assn. (pres. 1983-84), Pacific Union Club (San Francisco), Democrat. Office: Brobeck Phleger & Harrison Spear St Tower 1 Market Plz Fl 27 San Francisco CA 94105-1100 E-mail: jsparks@brobeck.com.

SPARKS, KENNETH R. association executive; b. Mar. 26, 1934; BS, Syracuse U., 1956, MS, 1961, PhD, 1964; JD, George Washington U., 1967. Dir. rsch. Voice of Am. USIA, Washington, 1964-67; dep. dir. pub. affairs U.S. Office Econ. Opportunity, 1967-68, dir., 1968-69; pres. U.S. Cultural and Trade Ctr. Commn., 1988-90; dep. dir. Fed. City Coun., 1970-72, exec. v.p., 1972—. Mem. Econ. Club of Wash. (sec. 1985—). Office: 1156 15th St NW Ste 600 Washington DC 20005-2431 E-mail: KRSPARKS@aol.com.

SPARKS, LINDSAY, information technology executive; Mainframe sys. programmer, 1980; from leader enterprise customer unit to corp. v.p. Microsoft, Redmond, Wash., 1992, corp. v.p. Office: One Microsoft Way Redmond WA 98052-6399*

SPARKS, ROBERT DEAN, medical administrator, physician; b. Newton, Iowa, May 6, 1932; s. Albert John and Josephine Emma (Kleinendorst) S.; children: Steven Robert, Ann Louise, John James. BA, U. Iowa, 1955, MD, 1957; D of Humanitarian Service, Creighton U., 1978. Diplomate Am. Bd. Internal Medicine. Intern Charity Hosp. of La., New Orleans, 1957-58, resident in internal medicine, 1958-59, asst. in medicine, 1958-59; fellow in gen. medicine and gastroenterology Tulane U. Sch. Medicine, 1959-62, instr. medicine, 1959-63, asst. prof., 1963-64, assoc. prof., 1964-68, prof., 1968-72, asst. dean, 1964-67, assoc. dean, acting dean, 1967-68, vice dean, 1968-69, dean, 1969-72, chief sect. gastroenterology, 1968-72; chancellor Med. Ctr. U. Nebr., 1972-76, prof. medicine, 1972-76; v.p. U. Nebr. System, 1972-76; health program dir. W.K. Kellogg Found., Battle Creek, Mich., 1976-81, v.p. programming, 1981-82, sr. v.p., 1982, pres., chief programming officer, 1982-86, pres., 1982-88, trustee, 1988, pres. emeritus, cons., 1988-92; pres., CEO, Calif. Med. Assn. Found., San Francisco, 1995-98, sr. assoc., 1998—. Cons. U. Tenn. Health Sci. Ctr., 1988-90, Boston U. Health Policy Inst., 1989-90; bd. dirs., mem. sci., compensation and trust rev. coms. Syntex Corp., Palo Alto, Calif., 1987-91, v.p. product safety and compliance, 1991-93; mem. overseers com. to visit Harvard U. Med. and Dental Schs., 1984-90; mem. vis. com. U. Miami Sch. Medicine, 1982-86; assoc. med. dir. for addiction treatment svcs., dir. for edn. and rsch., Battle Creek Adventist Hosp., 1990-91; v.p. Howe-Lewis Internat Inc., Menlo Park, N.Y., 1993-94, cons., 1994-95. Mem. editl. bd. Alcoholism Treatment Quar., 1985--; contbr. articles to profl. jours. Bd. dirs. Nat. Coun. on Alcoholism and Drug Dependence, N.Y.C., 1982-93, treas., 1986-88, chmn., 1989-90, past chmn., 1991-92; bd. dirs. Battle Creek Symphony Orch., 1981-88, Lakeview Sch. Dist., Battle Creek, 1979-83, 88-91; trustee Monsour Med. Found., Jeannette, Pa., 1976-90, interim pres. 1989, chmn. bd., pres., 1989-90; mem. President's Adv. Bd. on Pvt. Sector Initiatives, Washington, 1986-89; chmn. bd. dirs. Bard Coll. Health Policy and Practice Inst., 1988-96, Consumer Health Info. Rsch. Inst., 1990-95, Chelsea-Arbor Treatment Ctr., 1990-91; bd. dirs. Calhoun County Bd. Health, 1988-91, chmn., 1989-91; mem., bd. dirs. Mental Health and Addictions Found. Mich., Battle Creek, 1991-93. Recipient Harvard Dental award Harvard U. Sch. Dental Medicine, 1992, Disting. Alumni award for achievement U. Iowa Coll. Medicine, 1998, annual Robert D. Sparks Cmty. Health Leadership Achievement award CMA Found., 2000. Fellow ACP; mem. AMA, Nat. Acad. Scis. Inst. Medicine (com. study of treatment and rehab. svcs. for alcoholism and alcohol abuse, bd. mental health and behavioral medicine), Coun. Mich. Founds. (trustee 1986-88), Assn. Am. Med. Colls. (disting. svc. mem. 1975—). Phi Eta Sigma, Alpha Omega Alpha. Republican. Presbyterian. Avocations: tennis, bridge, reading, travel. Home and Office: PO Box 4620 El Dorado Hills CA 95762-0021 E-mail: sparksmd@pacbell.net.

SPARKS, ROBERT RONOLD, JR. lawyer; b. Bklyn., Dec. 4, 1946; s. Robert Ronold Sr. and Marjorie Anne (Boehm) S. BA, Va. Mil. Inst., 1969; JD, U. Va., 1972. Bar: U.S. Dist. Ct. (D.C. cir.) 1979, U.S. Dist. Ct. (ea. dist.) Va. 1979, U.S. Ct. Appeals (2d cir.) 1986, U.S. Ct. Appeals (D.C. cir.) 1975, Va. 1972, U.S. Ct. Appeals (4th cir.) 1982, U.S. Ct. Mil. Appeals 1976, U.S. Tax Ct. 1978, U.S. Supreme Ct. 1981, U.S. Dist. Ct. Md. 1993. From assoc. to ptnr. Sedam & Herge, McLean, Va., 1977-85; ptnr. Herge, Sparks & Christopher, 1985—. Mem. Bd. Regents James Monroe Law Office Mus. and Meml. Library, Fredericksburg, Va., 1983-86. Mem. Fairfax County Redevel. and Housing Authority, Fairfax, 1981-82; commr. Fairfax County Indsl. Devel. Authority, 1980-81, Fairfax County Planning Commn., 1983-89. Lt. USNR, 1972-77, Philippines. Mem. Va. Bar Assn., D.C. Bar Assn., Rotary (treas., bd. dirs. 1978-80). Roman Catholic. Home: 6448 Spring Ter Falls Church VA 22042-3141 Office: Herge Sparks Christopher 6862 Elm St Ste 360 Mc Lean VA 22101-3867

SPARKS, ROBERT WILLIAM, retired publishing executive; b. Seattle, Dec. 30, 1925; s. James Donald and Gladys (Simmons) S. Student, U. Wash., 1947-50; BA, U. Hawaii, 1954, MA, 1965. Editor, various publs., 1947-64; mng. editor U. Hawaii Press, 1964-66, dir., 1967-87. Cons. East-West Ctr., Jour. Hawaiian History, Japanese and Chinese book pubs., 1987-92; advisor New World Press, Beijing, 1986; mem. adv. bd. to pres. Kamehameha Schs. Author: Seattle, Sitka, San Francisco, 1955, Letters From an Island, 1962, New Endings, 1989, Riding Backwards, 2002; contbr. articles to internat. pub. jours. Served with AUS, 1944-46, PTO. Recipient McInerny editorship, 1953; Pacific House citation Pacific and Asian Affairs Council, 1974 Mem. Assn. Am. Univ. Presses, Assn. Am. Publishers, Internat. Assn. Scholarly Publishers, Soc. for Scholarly Pub., Hawaiian Hist. Soc., Hawaii Found. History and Humanities, Honolulu Acad. Arts, Bishop Mus. Assn. Home: 3634 Nihipali Pl Honolulu HI 96816-3307

SPARKS, SAM, federal judge; b. 1939; BA, U. Tex., 1961, LLB, 1963. Aide Rep. Homer Thornberry, 1963; law clk. to Hon. Homer Thornberry U.S. Dist. Ct. (we. dist.) Tex., 1963-65; assoc. to ptnr., shareholder Hardie, Grambling, Sims & Galatzan (and successor firms), El Paso, Tex., 1965-91; dist. judge U.S. Dist. Ct. (we. dist.) Tex., 1991—. Fellow Am. Coll. Trial Lawyers, Tex. Bar Found. (life); mem. Am. Bd. Trial Advocates (advocate), State Bar Tex. Office: US Dist Ct Judge 200 W 8th St Ste 100 Austin TX 78701-2333

SPARKS, STEPHEN STONE, lawyer; b. Kansas City, Mo., June 21, 1954; s. Billy Schley and Dorothy (Stone) S.; m. Martha Nelson, Oct. 19, 1979; children: Matthew Nelson, Adam Nelson. BA, New Coll. of U. of South Fla., 1976; JD with distinction, U. Mo., Kansas City, 1979. Bar: Mo. 1979, U.S. Dist. Ct. (we. dist.) Mo. 1979, U.S. Dist. Ct. Kans. 1998. Assoc. Linde, Thomson, Langworthy, Kohn & Van Dyke P.C., Kansas City, 1979-82, ptnr., 1982-91, Smith, Gill, Fisher & Butts, Kansas City, 1991-95, Bryan Cave LLP, Kansas City, 1995—. Mem. ABA, Kansas City Bar Assn., Lawyers Assn. K.C. Mo., Nat. Assn. Bond Lawyers, Milburn Country Club, Shadow Glen Golf Club. Democrat. Avocation: golf. Home: 10818 W 102nd St Overland Park KS 66214-2539 Office: Bryan Cave LLP 1200 Main St Fl 35 Kansas City MO 64105-2122 E-mail: sssparks@BryanCaveLLP.com.

SPARKS, THOMAS E., JR. lawyer; b. Little Rock, Jan. 11, 1942; children: Thomas Gunnar, Erik Richard, Andrew Pal. BS, Washington and Lee U., 1963; JD, U. Ark., 1968; LLM, Harvard U., 1970. Bar: Ark. 1968, Calif. 1970. Assoc. Pillsbury Madison & Sutro, San Francisco, 1970-76; ptnr. Pillsbury, Madison & Sutro, 1977-84, Baker & McKenzie, San Francisco, 1984-87, Pillsbury Madison & Sutro, San Francisco, 1987-2000, Pillsbury Winthrop, San Francisco, 2001—. Trustee Grace Cathedral, San Francisco. 1st lt. U.S. Army, 1965. Mem. ABA, Calif. Bar Assn., Olympic Club (San Francisco), Calif. Tennis Club (pres. 2000). Office: Pillsbury Winthrop 50 Fremont St San Francisco CA 94105-2230

SPARKS, WILLIAM SHERAL, retired seminary librarian; b. Alden Bridge, La., Oct. 30, 1924; s. Fred DeWitt and Truda (Bradford) S.; m. Joy Eleanor Young, Aug. 8, 1947; 1 child, David Frederick. AB, Phillips U., 1946; MDiv, Christian Theol. Sem., 1949; ThM, Iliff Sch. of Theology, 1955, ThD, 1957; MA, U. Denver, 1962. Pastor chs., 1950-60; asst. libr. Kans. Wesleyan U., Salina, 1962-66; dir. libr. and info. svcs. St. Paul Sch. of Theology, Kansas City, Mo., 1966-93, ret., 1993. Horowitz Found. fellow Hebrew Union Coll.-Jewish Inst. of Religion, 1949-52. Mem. Am. Theol. Libr. Assn.

SPARLING, MARY CHRISTINE, foundation executive; b. Collingwood, Ont., Can., July 8, 1928; d. Alexander and Catherine Henrietta (MacDonald) Malcolm; m. Wintfield Henry Sparling, June 17, 1950; children: Margaret, John. BA, Queen's U., Kingston, Ont., 1949; BEd (Gold medal 1970), St. Mary's U., Halifax, N.S., 1970; MA in Edn., Dalhousie U., 1978; DFA (hon), Nova Scotia Coll. Art & Design, 1994. Curator edn. N.S. Mus., Halifax, 1968-73; dir. art gallery Mt. St. Vincent U., 1973-94, also bd. dirs. Cons. in field; Atlantic regional coord. Can.'s Yr. of Asia Pacific, 1997; mem. organizing com. internat. symposium Design Week 2000, Halifax, N.S. Bd. govs. Mount St. Vincent U., Halifax, Nova Scotia, 1999. Recipient Ohio State award for film script The Artist in Nova Scotia, 1977, Queen's Silver Jubilee medal, 1977, Outstanding Cultural Exec. award N.S. Cultural Fedns., 1991; Warner-Lambert award for disting. arts adminstrn. in Can., 1993. Fellow Can. Mus. Assn. (pres. 1974-76, coun. 1972-78); mem. N.S. Coalition on Arts and Culture. Unitarian Universalist. Home: 6030 Jubilee Rd Halifax NS Canada B3H 2E4 E-mail: sparling@istar.ca.

SPARROW, EPHRAIM MAURICE, mechanical engineering scientist, educator; b. Hartford, Conn., May 27, 1928; s. Charles and Frieda (Gottlieb) S.; m. Ruth May Saltman, Nov. 2, 1952; 1 child, Rachel Bernarr. BS, MIT, 1948, MS, 1949; MA, Harvard Coll., 1950, PhD, 1956; Doutor Honoris Causa, U. Brazil, 1967. Heat transfer specialist Raytheon Mfg. Co., 1952-53; rsch. specialist Lewis Rsch. Ctr., NASA, Cleve., 1953-59; prof. mech. engring. U. Minn., 1959—, Inst. prof., 1994—, chmn. fluid dynamics program, 1968-80, Morse alumni disting. tchg. prof., 1980—. Program dir. NSF, 1986-87, dir. chem., biochem. and thermal engring. divsn., 1986-88; vis. prof., chief AID mission U. Brazil, 1966-67; adv. prof. Xi'an Jiaotong U., 1984—; cons. in field, 1960—; pres. 1st Brazilian Symposium on Heat Transfer and Fluid Mechanics, 1966; mem. solar energy panel Fed. Coun. on Sci. and Tech., 1972; U.S. sci. committeeman 5th Internat. Heat Transfer Conf., 1973-74. Author: (with R.D. Cess) Radiation Heat Transfer, 1966, 2nd edit., 1978; editor: Handbook of Numerical Heat Transfer, 1988, Advances in Numerical Heat Transfer, vol. 1, 1997, vol. 2, 2000; hon. mem. editorial bd. Internat. Jour. Heat Mass Transfer, 1964—, Internat. Comm. in Heat Mass Transfer, 1975—; sr. editor Jour. Heat Transfer, 1972-80; editor Series in Computational and Phys. Processes in Mechanics and Thermal Scis., 1980—; chmn. editorial adv. bd. Numerical Heat Transfer, 1978—; contbr. over 560 tech. articles to profl. jours. Recipient Ralph Coates Roe award Am. Soc. Engring. Edn., 1978, Outstanding Teaching award U. Minn., 1985, Fed. Engr. of Yr. award NSF, 1988, Sr. Rsch. award Am. Soc. Engring. Edn., 1989, Horace T. Morse award for outstanding contbns. to undergraduate teaching, 1993, Disting. Tchg. award Acad. Disting. Tchrs., U. Minn., 1997, 99, Donald Q. Kern award, Am. Inst. Chemical Engrs., 1999; named George Hawkins Disting. lectr. Purdue U., 1985. Fellow ASME (Meml. award for outstanding contbn. to sci. heat transfer 1962, Max Jakob award for eminent contbn. 1976, Centennial medal 1980, Disting. Svc. award heat transfer div. 1982, Charles Russ Richards Meml. award 1985, Worcester Reed Warner medal 1986, 50th Anniversary award heat transfer div. 1988, Disting. lectr. 1986-91, 93-94); mem. NAE, Biomed. Engring. Soc. (faculty advisor 1994—), Sigma Xi (Monie A. Ferst medal for contbn. to rsch. through edn. 1993), Pi Tau Sigma. Home: 2105 West Hoyt Ave Saint Paul MN 55108-1314 Office: U Minn Dept Mech Engring Minneapolis MN 55455-0111 E-mail: esparrow@umn.edu.

SPARROW, HERBERT GEORGE, III, lawyer, educator; b. Ft. Bragg, N.C., May 26, 1936; s. Herbert George and Virginia (Monroe) S.; m. Nancy Woodruff, Mar. 4, 1962; children: Amy Winslow, Edward Harrison, Herbert G. IV, Alison Kidder. AB cum laude, Princeton U., 1958; JD, U. Mich., 1961. Bar: Mich. 1961, Calif. 1964, D.C. 1979, U.S. Ct. Claims 1982, U.S. Tax Ct. 1983, U.S. Ct. Mil. Appeals 1962, U.S. Supreme Ct. 1976. Assoc. Dickinson Wright PLLC, Detroit, 1965-70, ptnr., 1970—. Adj. prof. Detroit Coll. Law, 1977—. Author numerous articles environ. law.; speaker in field. Bd. dirs. Family Life Edn. Coun., Grosse Pointe, Mich., 1982-88, Adult Well-Being Svcs., Inc., Detroit, 1995—. Capt. JAGC, U.S. Army, 1962-65. Mem. ABA, Mich. Bar Assn. (rep. assembly 1979-85, environ. law sect. coun. 1985-91), Calif. Bar Assn., D.C. Bar Assn., Detroit Bar Assn., Am. Arbitration Assn. (panel arbitrators 1975—), Mich. State Bar Found. (fellow 1989—), Environment Law Inst. (assoc.), Phi Delta Phi (pres. Kent Inn Assn., Ann Arbor 1985-97). Office: Dickinson Wright PLLC 500 Woodward Ave Ste 4000 Detroit MI 48226-3416

SPARROW, LAURA, secondary educator; b. Boston, June 15, 1947; d. John Henry Jr. and Laura Josephine (Thickens) Halford; m. William Talbot Sparrow, July 11, 1970. BA, U. Mich.; MAT, Johns Hopkins U., 1970. Cert. secondary tchr. Instr. social sci. C.C. of Balt., 1970; English tchr. North Farmington H.S., Farmington Hills, Mich., 1970-71; tchr. English and history Harrison H.S., 1971-95, tchr. English, chair dept., 1995—. Author: The White Wave, 1983, Hostages to Fortune, 1984, Firesigns, 1986, Seaswept, 1990. Incorporator Cascade Hemophilia Consortium, Ann Arbor, Mich., 1994. Named Oakland County Secondary Tchr. of Yr., Newsweek/WDIV-TV, 1998; Shakespeare study grantee NEH, 1992, Galileo leader Kellogg Found., 1999. Mem. ASCD, Nat. Coun. Tchrs. English, Humanities Task Force: Mich., Detroit Women Writers, Authors Guild. Avocations: travel, music, kayaking. Office: Harrison HS 29995 W 12 Mile Rd Farmington Hills MI 48334-3901

SPARTZ, ALICE ANNE LENORE, retired retail executive; b. N.Y.C., May 14, 1925; d. John Francis and Alice Philomena (Murray) Rattenbury; m. George Eugene Spartz, Oct. 29, 1949; children: Mary Elizabeth, James, Barbara, Anne, Thomas, William, Michael, John, Matthew, Clare, Robert, Richard. Student, Wright Coll., 1945-47, No. Ill. U., 1950; AA, Triton Coll., 1987. Svc. rep. Ill. Bell Tel., Chgo., 1945-46; stewardess United Airlines, Denver, 1947-49; ret. mgr. Family Life League Resale Shop, Oak Park, Ill., 1987-95; retired, 1995. Mem. Cicero (Ill.) Cmty. Coun., 1967—69, Park Dist. Oakk Park Com., 1973—74; active Ill. Right to Life Com., Chgo., 1971—, Com. Pro-Life Caths., Chgo., 1992—; mem. St. Martha's Roman Cath.. Ch.; former bd. dirs. Ill. Pro-Life Coalition, Family Life League; bd. trustees Trailwood Village; vol. canteen worker ARC, Chgo., 1942—45. Democrat. Roman Catholic. Avocations: travel, sewing, reading, swimming, pro-life activist. Office: 2026 Seven Oaks Dr Kingwood TX 77339

SPATAFORE, ANTHONY R. financial executive; b. Bklyn., Nov. 15, 1952; s. Anthony C. and Mercedes (Santiago) Spatafore. Student, Bklyn. Coll.; Cert. Fin. Planning, Adelphi U., 1982. Registered fin. planner; registered investment advisor, SEC. Agt. Paul Revere Ins. Co., N.Y.C., 1974-76; ins. cons. M.O.N.Y., 1976-79; fin. planner Home Life Ins. Co., 1979-82; pres., fin. planner ARS Fin. Svcs., Inc., Valley Stream, N.Y., 1982—. Contbr. articles to profl. jours. Mem. Internat. Assn. Registered Fin. Planners (bd. govs. 1987-89), Internat. Assn. Fin. Planning, Inst. Cert. Fin. Planners (local bd. dirs. 1987—, pres. L.I. Soc.), Nat. Assn. Securities Dealers. Republican. Roman Catholic. Avocation: tennis. Office: ARS Fin Svcs Inc 125 Franklin Ave Valley Stream NY 11580-2108

SPATARO, FRANCIS THOMAS, dentist, retired; b. Wateruliet, N.Y., Jan. 29, 1924; s. Carmelo Spataro and Mary (Concetta) S.; m. Catherine Theresa Spataro, Dec. 28, 1946; children: Sharyn, Jan, Francis Jr., Lauren, Melanie, Paul. BS in Biology, Siena Coll., 1948; MDM, Tufts U., 1950. Dentist, 1950—93. With U.S. Army, 1943-45. Mem. Troy Dental Soc. (exec. bd. 3d dist.), Holy Name Soc., Troy Dental Study Club (various chairs including pres.), Elks Club, K of C. Roman Catholic. Avocations: painting, carpentry, traveling, time with grandchildren. Home: 56 Joseph St Troy NY 12180

SPATARO, SANDRA ELIZABETH, finance educator, consultant; b. Sacramento, July 27, 1966; d. Sam Joseph and Susan Francoise Spataro. PhD, U. Calif., Berkeley, 2000. Tng. and documentation mgr. Oracle Corp., Redwood Shores, Calif., 1988—90, contract negotiator, 1990—91, bus. practices analyst Rewood Shores, 1991—94, tng. program mgr. Redwood Shores, 1994, sr. cons. Redwood Shore, 1994—95; asst. prof. Yale Sch. Mgmt., New Haven, 2000—. Cons. as individual contractor, Berkeley, 1994—2000. Author: (book chpt.) Research on Groups and Teams, 2001. Bd. dirs. New Haven Chorale, 2001—02. Mem.: APA, Acad. Mgmt. Democrat. Avocations: music, travel. Office: Yale Sch Mgmt Box 208200 135 Prospect St New Haven CT 06520

SPATCHER, DIANNE MARIE, finance executive; b. Reading, Pa., Feb. 1, 1959; d. Frederick Jacob and Claire Marie (Paskey) Seidel; m. Peter D. Spatcher. ASBA, Pa. State U., 1986; BA, Alvernia Coll., Reading, Pa., 1988. Office asst. Berks-Lehigh Valley Farm Credit Service, Fogelsville, Pa., 1977-80, sr. office asst., 1980, office supr., 1980-83, office mgr., 1983-86; chief fin. officer, 1986-88; exec. v.p. Keystone Farm Credit ACA, Lancaster, 1989-92, sr. v.p. fin. svcs., CFO, 1992-2000; treas. AAA Reading-Berks, Wyomissing, Pa., 2001—. Avocations: travel, cake decorating, classic cars. Home: 2413 Goddard Ave Sinking Spring PA 19608-9165 Office: 920 Van Reed Rd Wyomissing PA 19610 E-mail: pdspatch@aol.com.

SPATH, GREGG ANTHONY, lawyer; b. New Rochelle, N.Y., Nov. 13, 1952; s. Richard Dennis and Renee (Turtletaub) S.; m. Lois Lang, Mar. 18, 1979; 1 child, Emma Lang. Student, Coll. William and Mary, 1970-72; BA in English, U. Rochester, 1974; JD, New Eng. Sch. Law, 1977; LLM in Trade Regulation, NYU, 1979. Bar: N.Y. 1978, Pa. 1990, D.C. 2001. Spl. legal counsel Western Electric Co., N.Y.C., 1978-81; atty. St. Regis Paper Co., 1981-82; asst. gen. counsel, sec. patent com. United Mchts. and Mfrs., Inc., 1982-87; corp. counsel adidas USA, Inc., Warren, NJ, 1987-88; exec. v.p., corp. counsel Hy-Art Industries, Inc., Kingston, Pa., 1988-90; sec., treas., gen. counsel Regency Mfg. Co., Inc., Wilkes-Barre, 1990-93, Renee Mfg. Co., Inc., Exeter, 1993-95; corp. counsel real estate Nextel Comm., Inc., Reston, Va., 1996-99, corp. counsel intellectual property/licensing, 2000; of counsel Swidler Berlin Shereff Friedman LLP, Washington, 2000—. Contbr. New Eng. Law Rev., 1976, tech. editor, 1976-77. Mem. ABA (sects. of antitrust, patent, trademark and copyright law, comms. law). Avocations: fundraising, sports, music, theatre, cinema. Office: Swidler Berlin Shereff Friedman LLP 3000 K St NW Washington DC 20007 E-mail: gaspath@swidlaw.com.

SPATHIES, SHARON VERONICA, gifted education educator; b. Evergreen Park, Ill., Dec. 12, 1942; d. Anthony John and Charlotte Marie (Kras) Pavlik; m. William Spathies; 1 child, Mia Monique Bohlin. BEd, Chgo. Tchrs. Coll., 1964; MEd in Early Childhood Leadership and Advocacy, Nat. Louis U., 1995. Cert. tchr., Ill. Tchr. grade 2 Atwood Heights Elem. Sch., Alsip, Ill., 1965-66; tchr. intermediate grades Henderson Elem. Sch., Chgo., 1966-80; tchr. grade 3 Randolph Magnet Sch., 1980-82, tchr. gifted 1st grade, 1982-92, tchr. gifted 3d grade, 1992—2001. Reading chairperson 3d grade, 2000, reading rev. cons. Laidlaw Pub., River Forest, Ill., 1980-81; developer Parent Network System, 1992. Recipient educator awards Randolph PTA, 1982, 85, Thanks to Tchrs. award TV Sta. 2, Chgo. Tchrs. Coll., Ill. State Lottery, IBM and Carson, 1992, Reaching One Can Be Fun award, 1992; finalist Kohl Tchg. award, 1999; grantee Chgo. Found. Edn., 1988, 96, 99. Fellow Ill. Coun. Gifted, Chgo. Area Reading Assn. Evangelist. Avocations: piano, singing, reading, crocheting, Bible study. Home: 8320 Highpoint Cir Westmont IL 60561-5267 Office: Randolph Magnet Sch 7316 S Hoyne Ave Chicago IL 60636-3755

SPATOLA, JO-ANNE BUCCINNA, judge; b. N.Y.C., June 1, 1945; d. Nicholas Theodore and Catherine Buccinna; m. Joseph A. Spatola, Jan. 28, 1967; children: Michael J., Madeleine A. BA, U. Md., 1967; JD cum laude, Seton Hall U., 1977. Bar: N.J. 1977, U.S. Dist. Ct. N.J. 1977, U.S. Supreme Ct. 1985. Sch. tchr. G. Gardner Shugart Jr. H.S., Hillcrest Heights, Md., 1967-68; pvt. practice law Westfield, N.J., 1978-91; judge N.J. Superior Ct., Elizabeth, 1991—. Lawyer Union County Bd. Social Svc., Elizabeth, N.J., 1984-88. Coun. woman Scotch Plains (N.J.) Twp. Coun., 1985-91, dep. mayor, 1989, mayor, 1990. Mem. N.J. Coun. Family Ct. Judges. Roman Catholic. Office: 2 Broad St Elizabeth NJ 07201-2202

SPATT, ARTHUR DONALD, federal judge; b. 1925; Student, Ohio State U., 1943-44, 46-47; LLB, Bklyn. Law Sch., 1949. Assoc. Davidson & Davidson, N.Y.C., 1949, Lane, Winard, Robinson & Schorr, N.Y.C., 1950, Alfred S. Julien, N.Y.C., 1950-52, Florea & Florea, N.Y.C., 1953; pvt. practice, 1953-67, Spatt & Bauman, 1967-78; justice 10th judicial cir. N.Y. State Supreme Ct., 1979-82; adminstrv. judge Nassau County, 1982-86; assoc. justice appellate div. Second Judicial Dept., 1986-89; dist. judge U.S. Dist. Ct. (ea. dist.) N.Y., Bklyn., 1989-90, Uniondale, N.Y., 1990-2000, Central Islip, 2000—. Active Jewish War Vets. With USN, 1944—46. Mem. ABA, Assn. Supreme Ct. Justices State of N.Y., Bar Assn. Nassau County, Jewish Lawyers Assn. Nassau County, Bklyn. Law Rev. Assn., Long Beach Lawyers Assn., Theodore Roosevelt Am. Inn of Ct., Master of the Bench. Office: Long Island Courthouse 1024 Federal Plaza Central Islip NY 11722-4445

SPATT, ROBERT EDWARD, lawyer; b. Bklyn., Mar. 26, 1956; s. Milton E. and Blanche S. (Bakstansky) S.; m. Lisa B. Malkin, Aug. 11, 1979; 1 child, Mark Eric. AB, Brown U., 1977; JD magna cum laude, U. Mich., 1980. Bar: N.Y. 1981. Assoc. Simpson Thacher & Bartlett, N.Y.C., 1980-87, ptnr., 1987—. Mem. ABA, N.Y. State Bar Assn., City of N.Y. Bar Assn., Order of Coif, ACLU. Avocations: photography, boating, reading. Office: Simpson Thacher & Bartlett 425 Lexington Ave New York NY 10017-3954 E-mail: RSpatt@stblaw.com.

SPATZ, KENNETH CHRIS, statistics educator; b. Tyler, Tex., Mar. 25, 1940; s. Kenneth Christopher and Mary E. (Harton) S.; m. Thea Siria, May 31, 1961; children: Mark C., Kenneth S., Elizabeth A. BA, Hendrix Coll., 1962; PhD, Tulane U., 1966. Asst. prof. U. of the South, Sewanee, Tenn., 1966-69; assoc. prof. U. Ark., Monticello, 1971-73; prof. Hendrix Coll., Conway, Ark., 1973—. Author: Basic Statistics: Tales of Distributions, 1st edit., 1976, 7th edit., 2001. Fellow U. Calif., Berkeley, 1969-71. Office: Hendrix Coll Dept Psychology Conway AR 72032

SPAULDING, DAN, public relations executive; BA, MA, U. Mich. Commd. USN; aide, pub. affairs officer to comdr. Tng. Command U.S. Pacific Fleet, San Diego, 1969-72; news anchor/prodr./reporter Staf. WFRV-TV, Green Bay, Wis., Sta. WEYI-TV, Flint-Saginaw, Mich.; mem. faculty U. Wis., Green Bay; news dir. Sta. KOMU-TV, Columbia, Mo., Sta. WOTV-TV 8; with Seyferth & Assocs., Inc., Grand Rapids, Mich., 1989-94, exec. v.p., 1994—. Active West Mich. Environ. Action Com.; mem. bd., exec. com., chiar Ctmy. Wide Care Com., Heart of West Mich. United Way. Mem. Pub. Rels. Soc. Am. (accredited). Office: Seyferth & Assocs Inc 40 Monroe Center NW, Suite 202 Grand Rapids MI 49503-3003*

SPAULDING, FRANK HENRY, librarian; b. Danielson, Conn., July 12, 1932; s. Jacob Lindhurst and Frances (Upham) S.; m. Eugenia Jenewicz, May 25, 1963; children— Geoffrey Michael, Jennifer Anne AB, Brown U., 1957; MSL.S., Case Western Res. U., 1961. Supr. info. ctr. Colgate-Palmolive Co., Piscataway, N.J., 1961-65; group supr. library tech. processes Bell Labs., Holmdel, 1965-70, head library ops., 1970-84; mgr. library services AT&T Bell Labs., 1985-87, mgr. mktg. library network, 1984-86; library/info. cons., 1987—. Pres. Sp. Libraries. Assn. 1986-87; treas. Am. Soc. for Info. Sci., 1983-86; pres. Documentation Abstracts, N.Y.C., 1983-85; dir. Universal Serials and Book Exchange, Washington, 1984-85, Palinet, Phila., 1978-81. Compiler: Managing the Electronic Library, 1983; author: Today's Information Specialist-Tomorrow's Knowledge Counselor in 2006, International Information: International Librarianship; creator: Task Force on the Value of the Information Professional, 1987 Mem. Buten Mus. Wedgwood. Served to lt. USN, 1957-60. Mem. ALA (com. on accreditation 1989-93), Spl. Librs. Assn. (del. to Internat. Fedn. Libr. Assn. and Inst. 1987-89), Am. Soc. Info. Sci. and Tech. E-mail: frankspaulding@msn.com.

SPAULDING, JOHN PIERSON, public relations executive, marine consultant; b. N.Y.C., June 25, 1917; s. Forrest Brisbine and Genevieve Anderson (Pierson) S.; m. Eleanor Rita Bonner, Aug. 18, 1947; children: Anne Spaulding Balzhiser, John F., Mary T. Spaulding Calvert; m. 2d, Donna Alene Abrescia, May 15, 1966. Student Iowa State Coll., 1935-36, Grinnell Coll., 1936-38, U. Chgo., 1938-39. Reporter, Chgo. City News Bur., UPI, 1939-40; editor Cedar Falls (Iowa) Daily Record, 1940-41; picture editor Des Moines Register & Tribune, 1941-42, 47-50; pub. relations dir. Motor Club Iowa, Davenport, 1950-51; commd. 2d. lt. USAF, 1942, advanced through grades to maj., 1947, recalled, 1951, advanced through grades to lt. col.; ret., 1968; v.p. Vacations Hawaii, Honolulu, 1969-70; dir. pub. relations, mgr. pub. relations services Alexander & Baldwin, Inc., Honolulu, 1970-76; mgr. community relations Matson Navigation Co., Honolulu, 1976-81. Pres., Econ. Devel. Assn., Skagit County, Wash., 1983-85; pres., chmn. Fidalgo Island Ednl. Youth Found.; mem. Anacortes (Wash.) Sch. Bd., 1982-88; mem. Gov.'s Tourism Devel. Council, 1983-85; mem. adv. com. State Ferry System, 1982—, productivity coun., 1990—; chmn. Everett chpt. S.C.O.R.E., 1984-86, Bellingham chpt., 1991—; mem. citizens adv. com. Skagit County Transit, 1995—. Decorated Air medal. Mem. Pub. Relations Soc. Am. (pres. Hawaii chpt. 1974), Hawaii Communicators (pres. 1973), Nat. Def. Transp. Assn. (pres. Aloha chpt. 1980-81, Disting. Service award 1978-79), Air Force Assn., Can. Inst. Internat. Affairs, Anacortes C. of C., Sigma Delta Chi (life). Clubs: Propeller (pres. Port of Honolulu 1979-80), Honolulu Press, Fidelgo Yacht, Hawaii Yacht, Royal Hawaiian 400 Yacht (comdr. 1977-81), Rotary (sec. 1996-98). Home: 6002 Sands Way Anacortes WA 98221-4015

SPAULDING, KARLA RAE, lawyer; b. Breckenridge, Mich., Feb. 22, 1954; d. Donald Hugh and Shirley Ann (Federspiel) S. BA magna cum laude, Western Mich. U., 1975; JD, Northwestern U., 1980. Bar: Ohio 1980, Fla. 1987. Vis. prof. Grand Valley State Colls., Allendale, Mich., 1975-76; assoc. Baker & Hostetler, Cleve., 1980-83; asst. U.S. atty. U.S. Atty. Office, Tampa, Fla., 1983-88, Grand Rapids, Mich., 1988-89, chief maj. drug trafficking sect. Mid. Dist. Fla. Tampa, 1989-90, chief appellate div. Mid. Dist. Fla., 1990-92; asst. U.S. atty. Organized Crime and Drug Enforcement Task Force, 1992; chief fraud and econ. crime sect. So. Dist. Tex. U.S. Atty. Office, Houston, 1992-93; ptnr. Holland & Knight, Tampa, Fla., 1994; pvt. practice, 1994-97; U.S. magistrate judge U.S. Dist. Ct. (mid. dist.) Fla., Orlando, 1997—. Bd. editors, dep. editor-in-chief Fed. Bar Jour., 1992-95; contbr. articles to profl. publs. Recipient Dir.'s award IRS, 1988. Mem. ABA, FBA, Orange County Bar Assn. Office: George C Young US Courthouse 80 N Hughey Ave Orlando FL 32801-2231

SPAULDING, MAR, retired special education educator, therapist; b. Bellevue, Ky., Oct. 16, 1933; d. Mickey and Blanche Harris; m. Stan Lee Spaulding; children: Karla, Julie Underwood, Lisa Williams, Gregory. MA, Ea. Mich. U., 1978; BS, George Mason U., 1973. Cert. educator Emotionally/Neurologically Impaired, Pre-primary Impaired 1978. Head tchr. in nursery sch., Ann Arbor, Mich., 1973—75; intern Ypsilanti State Mental Instn., 1975—76; tchr. emotionally impaired and pre-primary impaired Monroe County Intermediate Dist., Monroe, 1978—93. Leader of groups of parents of handicapped children Monroe County Intermediate Sch. Dist., Monroe, MICH., 1978—93, mem. of grant com., MICH., 1980—96, tester on child find com., MICH., 1979—85. Author: (children's educational book) Kate Lynn's Fantastic Dream, 1999 (Spl. Edn. Tchr. of the Yr. in Monroe County, Mich., 1995), (companion book) Activities to use with Kate Lynn's Fantastic Dream. Includes cognitive, speech and language, fine motor, gross motor and behavioral, emotional skill areas for teachers and parents., 1999. Story lady Head Start, Baker Devel. Ctr., Punta Gorda, Fla., 1996—2002; tutor Continuing Edn. Ctr. and Even Start, Port Charlotte and Punta Gorda, 1996—2003; membership involvement chairperson Peace River Power Squadron, Punta Gorda, 1996—2003; pub. spkr. topics concerning early childhood edn. Early Childhood Edn. Assn. of SW Fla., 1999—2003. Recipient Writer's Award, US Power Squadrons, 2001. Mem.: US Sail and Power Squadrons, Thomas Paine Nat. Hist. Soc., Nat. Honor Soc., Phi Kappa Phi. Liberal. Avocation: travel, sailing (lived on 41 foot sailboat from 1993 to 1996),writing children's stories, swimming, biking, reading, playing the piano, attending concerts and plays, hiking.. Home: 1536 Islamorada Blvd Punta Gorda FL 33955 Personal E-mail: marstan@nut-n-but.net.

SPAULDING, WALLACE HOLMES, retired federal agency professional; b. Oakland, Calif., Sept. 3, 1928; s. Wallace Holmes and May Gibbons (Alves) S.; m. Dorothy Anne Wollon, Jan. 30, 1960; children: James Wallace, Anne Catherine Bridger. AB, U. Calif., Berkeley, 1950; MA, Johns Hopkins U., 1951; PhD, U. Pa., 1969. Rschr. CIA, McLean, Va., 1952-91; ret., 1991. Author: Is the Comintern Coming Back?, 1998; contbr. chpts. to books and articles to profl. jours. V.p. Fellowship of Concerned Churchmen, L.A.; pres. Found. for Christian Theology, Washington; Am. regional sec. Soc. of Mary, McLean. Col. USAR, 1950—81. Decorated Meritorious Svc. medal U.S. Army; Fulbright scholar, The Philippines, 1951-52. Mem. Phi Beta Kappa, Alpha Delta Phi, Pan Xenia. Avocations: hiking, cycling, domestic and foreign travel. Home: 1206 Buchanan St Mc Lean VA 22101-2943

SPAULDING, WILLIAM ROWE, investment consultant; b. Cambridge, Mass., Nov. 26, 1915; s. William Rowe and Jennie Jane (Gillam) S.; m. Gertrude Ellen Mowry, June 7, 1947; children: Edward Albert, William Mathews. BS, U. N.H., 1938; MBA, Harvard U., 1940. Trader Kidder Peabody & Co., N.Y.C., 1940-41; asst. exec. v.p. Mut. Savs. Cen. Fund, Inc., Boston, 1946-58; v.p. Vance Sanders & Co., 1959-63; trustee Century Shares Trust, 1963-71, mng. trustee, chmn., 1969-71; chmn. bd., chief exec. officer Wakefield Savs. Bank (Mass.), 1971-81, trustee, 1959-84, hon. trustee, 1994—; ind. non-affiliated dir., trustee Fidelity Group of Mut. Funds, Boston, 1972-87, active emeritus, 1988-89; ret., 1989. Dir. Mass. Congl. Fund, 1970-96; spkr. Investment Analyst Soc. of South Africa, Johannesburg Stock Exch. Auditorium, 1995; mem. Initiative for Edn. Sci. and Tech. South Africa Investment Mgmt. and Rsch. Assn., 1995. Trustee Melrose-Wakefield Hosp., 1973-84, Lakeside Cemetery Corp., Wakefield, 1973-2002; dir., fin. v.p. Citizens Scholarship Found., Wakefield, 1962—; mem. nat. adv. bd. Citizens' Scholarship Found. Am., 1989-92; mem. fin. com., mem. ho. of dels. Mass. Easter Seal Soc., 1972-97, v.i.p. telethon, 1990—; trustee Laudholm Farm Trust, Wells Nat. Estuarine Rsch. Res., 1982-94, hon. trustee, 1994—; exec. vol. Internat. Exec. Svc. Corps., Kingston, Jamaica, 1989, shirtsleeve amb., 1994—; citizen amb. People to People, 1994—; with Securities Industry Delegation to China, 1994; mem. Wakefield Hist. Commn., 1984-86; co-chmn. bd. advisors U. New Eng., Biddeford, Maine/Westbrook Coll., Portland, Maine, 1996-98. With AUS, 1942-45, MTO, ETO, lt. col. Decorated Bronze Star; Croix de Guerre (Belgium); named to Eagle Scout Boy Scouts Am., 1928; named Grand Marshall, Independence Day Parade, Wakefield, Mass., 1994. Mem. Pres.'s Coun. U. N.H., Boston Security Analyst Soc. Inc., Phi Kappa Phi. Congregationalist. Home and Office: PO Box 1999 Wells ME 04090-2337

SPEAKER, SUSAN JANE, lawyer; b. Dallas, Dec. 25, 1946; d. William R. and Jane E. (Aldrich) Turner; m. David C. Speaker, Dec. 21, 1968; children: David Allen, Melissa. BA, U. Ark., 1970, JD, 1985. Bar: Okla. 1985, U.S. Dist. Ct. (no., ea. and we. dists.) Okla. 1985. Assoc. Hall, Estill, Hardwick, Gable, Golden & Nelson, P.C., Tulsa, 1985-91; atty. Resolution Trust Corp., 1991-92; shareholder Speaker & Matthews, P.C., 1992-96; atty. Comml. Fin. Svcs., Inc., Tulsa, 1996-99; dir. properties and concessions Dollar Rent A Car Systems, Inc., 1999—. Editor U. Ark. Law Rev., 1983-85. Mem. ABA, ATLA, Okla. Bar Assn., Tulsa Bar Assn., Tulsa Title and Probate Lawyers Assn., Phi Beta Kappa, Delta Theta Phi.

SPEAKES, LARRY MELVIN, public relations executive, writer; b. Cleveland, Miss., Sept. 13, 1939; s. Harry Earl and Ethlyn Frances (Fincher) Speakes; m. Aleta Merkel, Oct. 5, 2001; children from previous marriage: Sondra LaNell, Barry Scott, Jeremy Stephen. Student, U. Miss., 1957-61; Litt. D. (hon.), Ind. Central U., 1982, BA in Journalism, 2001. News editor Oxford (Miss.) Eagle, 1961-62; news editor Bolivar Comml., Cleveland, 1962-63, mng. editor, 1965-66; dep. dir. Bolivar County Civil Def., 1963-65; gen. mgr. Progress Pubs., Leland, Miss., 1966-68; editor Leland Progress, Hollandale Herald, Bolivar County Democrat, Sunflower County News; press sec. U.S. Senator J.O. Eastland of Miss., 1968-74; staff asst. Exec. Office of Pres., Mar.-May 1974; press asst. to spl. counsel to Pres., May-Aug. 1974; asst. White House press sec., 1974-76, asst. press sec. to Pres., 1976-77; press sec. to Gerald R. Ford, 1977; v.p. Hill & Knowlton, Inc., internat. pub. relations and pub. affairs counsel, Washington, 1977-81; prin. dep. press sec. and asst. to Pres. of U.S., 1981-87; sr. v.p. Merrill Lynch & Co., Inc., N.Y.C., 1987-88; v.p. comm. No. Telecom Ltd., Washington and Toronto, Ont., Can., 1991-93; sr. v.p. corp. rels. U.S. Postal Svc., Washington, 1994-98, sr. advisor to postmaster gen., 1998—, mgr. of advt., 2001—. Corp. comm. cons., lectr. on press and politics, 1988-91. Author: Speaking Out: The Reagan Presidency From Inside the White House; contbr. Crisis Repsponse: Inside Stories on Managing Image Under Siege. Recipient Presdl. Citizens medal, 1987, Gen. Excellence award Miss. Press Assn., 1988, Disting. Journalism Alumni award U. Miss., 1981, Hall of Fame, 1985, Silver Em. Miss. Scholastic Press Assn., 1988, Spl. Achievement award Nat. Assn. Govt. Communicators, 1983, Silver Anvil award Pub. Rels. Soc. Am., 1988, NY Addy Gold TV comml. award; named to Top 100 PR Profls. of Century, PR Week mag., 1999, Pub. Rels. Hall of Fame, D.C. chpt. PRSA, 1999. Mem. Arthur Page Soc. (trustee), Pub. Rels. Seminar, Sigma Delta Chi, Kappa Sigma (Man of Yr. 1982), Lambda Sigma, Omicron Delta Kappa. Methodist.

SPEAKMAN, KEVIN LEROY, music educator, elementary school educator; b. Ponca City, Okla., Sept. 6, 1970; s. Larry Leroy and Nila Fern Speakman; m. Kristin Birkenfeld. BS in Edn., U. of Ark., 1993. Cert. Instrumental Music Edn. Okla., 1995. Band dir. Seneca R-7 Schs., Seneca, Mo., 1993—95, Shawnee Mid. Sch., Shawnee, Okla., 1995—97, Stillwater Mid. Sch., Stillwater, 1997—98, Sapulpa Mid. Sch., Sapulpa, 1998—. Band chmn. 2002 Okla. All-State Band; jr. H.S. band chmn. North Ctrl. Dir. Assn., 1998. Recipient Superior Ratings in Concert Band Performance at State Contest, Okla. Secondary Sch. Activities Assn., 1999, 2000. Mem.: Music Educators Nat. Conf., Okla. Music Educators Assn., Kappa Kappa Psi, Phi Mu Alpha, Phi Beta Mu. Ch. Of The Nazarene.

SPEALMAN, DONNA DENDE, elementary education educator, artist; b. Scranton, Pa., Nov. 13, 1952; d. Frank and Helen (Kotchick) D.; m. Alan D. Spealman, Aug. 6, 1977; children: Kristin, Brendan, Scott. BS, Pa. State U., 1974; cert. med. technician, Pa. Hosp., Phila., 1975. Rsch. asst. Temple U., Phila., 1975-77, ARC, Bethesda, Md., 1979-83; artist, mgr. Sugar & Frichtl Gallery, Kensington, 1985-88; ednl. asst. Holy Redeemer Sch., 1989-91, sci. mentor, judge, 1993—. tchr., ednl. cons., 1995—. Freelance artist, Kensington, 1990—. Avocations: classical piano, fossil hunting. Home: 3940 Baltimore St Kensington MD 20895-3906

SPEAR, ALLAN HENRY, former state senator, historian, educator; b. Michigan City, Ind., June 24, 1937; s. Irving S. and Esther (Lieber) S. BA, Oberlin Coll., 1958, LLD (hon.), 1997; MA, Yale U., 1960, PhD, 1965. Lectr. history U. Minn., Mpls., 1964-65, asst. prof., 1965-67, assoc. prof., 1967-2000; mem. Minn. State Senate, St. Paul, 1973-2000, chmn. jud. com., 1983-93; chmn. crime prevention com., 1993-2000; pres. Minn. State Senate, 1993—2000; vice chair Minn. Campaign Finance and Public Disclosure Bd., 2001—. Vis. prof. Carleton Coll., Northfield, Minn., 1970, Stanford U., Palo Alto, Calif., 1970. Author: Black Chicago, 1967. Mem. Internat. Network Gay and Lesbian Offcls., Com. on Suggested State Legislation of Coun. of State Govts. Mem. Dem. Farm Labor Party. Avocations: cooking, travel, reading, classical music. Home: 2429 Colfax Ave S Minneapolis MN 55405-2942 Office: Campaign Finance & Public Disclosure Board 190 Centennial Office Building 658 Cedar Street Saint Paul MN 55155-1603*

SPEAR, CHRIS, federal agency administrator; b. Auburn, Nebr. m. Michelle Spear; 2 children. B Polit. Sci., U. Wyo. Staff mem. Sen. Alan Simpson, Wyo., 1993; staff dir. Sen. Subcom. Employment, Safety and Tng.; legis. dir. Sen. Tim Hutchinson, Ark.; asst. sec. policy U.S. Dept. Labor, Washington, 2001—. Office: US Dept LAbor Policy 200 Constitution Ave NW Washington DC 20210*

SPEAR, HARVEY M. lawyer; b. Providence, May 24, 1922; s. Alfred and Esther (Marcus) S.; m. Ruth Abramson, June 27, 1965; children: Jessica Tjernberg, Elizabeth Anne. AB, Brown U., 1942; LL.B., Harvard, 1948; MA, George Washington U., 1949, LL.M., 1952, S.J.D, 1955. Bar: Mass. 1948, D.C. 1948, N.Y. 1954, U.S. Supreme Ct. 1954; CPA, Md. Asst. U.S. atty. D.C., 1948; legal asst. to chmn., asst. to vice chmn. SEC, 1948-50; spl. asst. to atty. gen. Dept. Justice, 1951-54; pvt. practice law N.Y.C. and Washington, 1956—; counsel Cadwalader Wickersham & Taft, N.Y.C., 1996—. Contbr. articles to legal jours. Founding trustee Harlem Prep. Sch., 1967; mem. Met. Opera Assn., 1961—. Served to maj. USMCR, 1942-45. Mem. ABA, Assn. of Bar of City of N.Y. Home: 765 Park Ave New York NY 10021-4254 Office: 100 Maiden Ln New York NY 10038-4818 Home: 78 Hither Ln East Hampton NY 11937

SPEAR, H(ENRY) DYKE N(EWCOME), JR. lawyer; b. New London, Conn., Feb. 26, 1935; s. Henry D. N. and Helene (Vining) S.; m. Karla A. Dalley, Sept. 9, 1995. BA, Trinity Coll., Hartford, Conn., 1958; JD, U. Conn., 1960. Bar: Conn. 1960. Pvt. practice matrimonial law, Hartford, 1961—. Mem. Conn. Bar Assn., Hartford County Bar Assn. Republican. Methodist. Office: 10 Trumbull St Hartford CT 06103-2404 E-mail: dykespear@attbi.com.

SPEAR, HILA J. nursing educator; b. Battle Creek, Mich., Aug. 19, 1951; d. William B. and Bette L. Hosack; m. Randl J. Spear, May 30, 1969; children: Lori, Amy, Ryan, Jason. AS, Kellogg Community Coll., 1975; BSN, Liberty U., 1986; MSN, U. Va., 1987. Cert. childbirth edn. specialist, cert. CPR instr. AHA. Student health nurse Lynchburg (Va.) Coll.; maternal child clin. instr. Va. Western Community Coll., Roanoke; assoc. instr. fundamentals Lynchburg Gen. Hosp. Sch. Nursing; isntr. community health nursing Liberty U., Lynchburg. Student advisor/fundraiser Am. Heart Assn., 1989.

SPEAR, RICHARD EDMUND, art history educator; b. Michigan City, Ind., Feb. 3, 1940; s. Irving S. and Esther Marion (Lieber) S.; m. Athena Tacha, June 11, 1965. BA, U. Chgo., 1961; M.F.A., Princeton U., 1963; PhD, 1965. Mem. faculty Oberlin (Ohio) Coll., 1964-2000, prof. art history, 1975-83, Mildred Jay prof. art history, 1983-2000; dir. Allen Meml. Art Mus., 1972-83; vis. disting. prof. U. Md., College Park, 1998—. Harn Eminent Scholar prof. U. Fla., 1997-98; disting. vis. prof. George Washington U., Washington, 1983-84; trustee Intermuseum Conservation Assn., 1972-83, pres., 1975-77 Author: Caravaggio and His Followers, 1971, 75, Renaissance and Baroque Paintings from the Sciarra and Fiano Collections, 1972, Domenichino, 1982, Domenichino, 1581-1641, 1996, The Divine Guido, 1997; editor-in-chief Art Bull., 1985-88; contbr. articles to profl. jours. Regional exec. bd. ACLU, 1974-76. Recipient Premio Daria Borghese Gold medal, 1972; Fulbright scholar Italy, 1966-67; Am. Coun. Learned Socs. fellow, 1971-72; NEH fellow, 1980-81, sr. fellow Ctr. Advanced Study in Visual Arts Nat. Gallery Art, 1983-84, Guggenheim fellow, 1987-88; Nat. Humanities Ctr. fellow, 1992-93, Rockefeller Found./Bellagio Ctr. fellow, 1996. Mem. Coll. Art Assn. Am. Democrat. Home: 3721 Huntington St NW Washington DC 20015-1817 Office: U Md Dept Art History & Archeol College Park MD 20742-0001

SPEAR, ROBERT CLINTON, environmental health educator, consultant; b. Los Banos, Calif., June 26, 1939; s. Clinton Wentworth Spear and Maytie Izetta (Patten) Gill; m. Patricia Warner, Dec. 15, 1962; children: Andrew Warner, Jennifer Ellen. BS, U. Calif., Berkeley, 1961, MS, 1962; PhD, Cambridge U., 1968. Registered profl. engr., Calif. Sys. engr. U.S. Naval Weapons Ctr., China Lake, Calif., 1962-65, 68-69; from asst. prof. to assoc. prof. environ. health U. Calif. Sch. Pub. Health, Berkeley, 1970-81, prof., 1981—, dir. No. Calif. Occupational Health Ctr., 1980-89, assoc. dean, 1988-91, dir. environ. engring. and health scis. lab., 1991-96; assoc. dean U. Calif. Coll. Engring., 1994-96; dir. Ctr. for Occupl. and Environ. Health U. Calif., 1992-2000. Vice-chair Berkeley divsn. Acad. Senate, 1998-99, chair, 1999-2000; hon. prof. Sichuan Inst. Parasitic Disease. Contbr. articles on engring. aspects of environ. health to profl. jours. Mem. Nat. Adv. Com. on Occupational Safety and Health, U.S. Dept. Labor, 1986-88. NSF grad. fellow Cambridge U., 1965-68, sr. internat. fellow Fogarty Ctr., NIH, Australian Nat. U., 1977-78, research grantee Nat. Inst. Occupational Safety and Health NIH, State of Calif., 1971— . Mem. ASME, AAAS, Am. Indsl. Hygiene Assn., Nat. Inst. Occupl. Safety and Health (bd. scientific counselors), Assn. Univ. Programs in Occupational Health and Safety (pres. 1984-85) Democrat. Avocation: sailing. Home: 1963 Yosemite Rd Berkeley CA 94707-1631 Office: U Calif Sch Pub Health Berkeley CA 94720-0001 E-mail: spear@uclink4.berkeley.edu.

SPEAR, SCOTT LAWRENCE, plastic surgeon; b. Chgo., Aug. 25, 1948; s. Louis and Esther S.; m. Cynthia Staley Spear; children: ALexandra, Geri, Louis. BA (hon.), U. Mich., Ann Arbor, 1968; MD, U. Chgo., 1972. Cert. Mass., 1986, Calif., 1992, Fla., 1990, Washington, 1981—, Md., 1982—, Va.,

1982—. Intern Beth Israel Hosp., Boston, 1972-73; jr. residency San Francisco Gen. Hosp., 1973-74, Beth Israel Hosp., Boston, 1974-75, sr. residency, 1976-78; plastic surgery residency U. Miami, 1978-80; asst. prof. plastic surgery U. Fla., Gainesville, 1980-81, Georgetown U. Sch. Medicine, Washington, 1981-86, assoc. prof. plastic surgery, 1988-90, prof. plastic surgery, 1990—. Dir. Nat. Capitol Tng. program, Washington, 1992—, Divsn. of Plastic and Reconstructive Surgery, Georgetown U. Sch. Medicine, Washington, 1992—; vis. prof. U., Tex., 1982, U. Fla., 1982, 84, 85, 86, 87, Nat. Naval Med. Ctr., 1983, 85. Contbr. articles to profl. jours. Mem. ACS, Med. Soc. of D.C., Plastic Surgery Ednl. Found., Am. Cleft Palata Assn., Nat. Capital Soc. of Plastic Surgeons, Am. Soc. of Maxillofacial Surgeons, Am. Soc. of Plastic and Reconstructive Surgeons, Northeastern Soc. of Plastic and Reconstructive Surgeons, Am. Assn. Plastic Surgeons, Am. Soc. for Aesthetic Plastic Surgery. Office: Georgetown U Med Ctr 3800 Reservoir Rd NW Washington DC 20007-2113 Fax: 202-687-2804. E-mail: spears@gunet.georgetown.edu.

SPEAR, THOMAS TURNER, history educator; b. Coral Gables, Fla., Dec. 23, 1940; BA, Williams Coll., 1962; MA, U. Wis., 1970, PhD, 1974; postgrad., Sch. Oriental and African Studies, 1976-77. Sr. lectr. La Trobe U., Melbourne, Australia, 1973-80; Charles R. Keller prof. Williams Coll., Williamstown, Mass., 1981-92; prof. U. Wis., Madison, 1993—, dir. African studies program, 1995-98, chair dept. history, 2001—. Reviewer NEH, Social Sci. Rsch. Coun./Am. Coun. Learned Socs., Am. Philos. Soc. Author: The Kaya Complex: A History of the Mijikenda Peoples of the Kenya Coast to 1900, 1978, Kenya's Past: An Introduction to Historical Method in Africa, 1981, (with Derek Nurse) The Swahili: Reconstructing the History and Language of and African Soc., 800-1500, 1985, Mountain Farmers: Moral Economics of Land and Agricultural Development in Arusha and Meru, 1997; editor: (with Richard Waller) Being Maasai: Ethnicity and Identity in East Africa, 1993, (with Isaria N. Kimambo) East African Expressions of Christianity, 1999; editor Jour. of African History, 1997-2001; contbr. articles to profl. jours. Grantee Williams Coll., 1984, 87-89, 91-92, NEH, 1984, Am. Coun. Learned Socs., 1982, La Trobe U., 1976-77; recipient A.C. Jordan prize U. Wis., 1972, Fgn. Area fellowship Social Sci. Rsch. Coun./Am. Coun. Learned Socs., 1970-72, Coll. Tchrs. fellowship NEH, 1987-88, Guggenheim fellowship, 1995-96, U. Wis., 1995—. Mem. Am. Hist. Soc. (contbr. Guide to Hist. Lit.), African Studies Assn., African Studies Assn. Australia (founder, exec. sec. 1978-80), Internat. African Inst. Office: U Wis Dept History 3211 Humanities 455 N Park St Madison WI 53706-1405

SPEARING, ANTHONY COLIN, English literature educator; b. London, Jan. 31, 1936; came to U.S., 1987; s. Frederick and Gertrude (Calnin) S. MA, Cambridge U., Eng., 1960. W.M. Tapp rsch. fellow Gonville-Caius Coll. Cambridge U., 1959-60, asst. lectr. in English, 1960-64, official fellow Queens' Coll., 1960-87, life fellow, 1987—, dir. studies in English, 1967-85, lectr. in English, 1964-85, reader in medieval English lit., 1985-87; vis. prof. English U. Va., Charlottesville, 1979-80, 84, prof. English, 1987-89, Kenan prof. English, 1989—. William Matthews lectr. Birkbeck Coll., London, 1983-84; invited lectr. numerous colls. and univs. in U.K., Europe, Can. and U.S.; Lansdowne vis. fellow U. Victoria, 1993. Author: Criticism and Medieval Poetry, 1964, rev. edit., 1972; (with Maurice Hussey and James Winny) An Introduction to Chaucer, 1965; The Gawain-Poet: A Critical Study, 1970, Chaucer: Troilus and Criseyde, 1976, Medieval Dream-Poetry, 1976, Medieval to Renaissance in English Poetry, 1985, Readings in Medieval Poetry, 1987, The Medieval Poet as Voyeur, 1993; editor: The Pardoner's Prologue and Tale (Chaucer), 1965, rev. edit., 1994, The Knight's Tale (Chaucer), 1966, rev. edit., 1995, The Franklin's Prologue and Tale (Chaucer), 1966, rev. edit., 1994; co-editor: (with Elizabeth Spearing) Shakespeare: The Tempest, 1971, Poetry of the Age of Chaucer, 1974, The Reeve's Prologue and Tale (Chaucer), 1979, Julian of Norwich: Revelations of Divine Love, 1998; translator: The Cloud of Unknowing and Other Works, 2001; contbr. numerous articles to profl. jours. Mem. Medieval Acad. Am., Internat. Assn. U. Profs. English, New Chaucer Soc. (trustee 1986-90). Office: Univ Va Dept English 219 Bryan Hall PO Box 400121 Charlottesville VA 22904-4121 E-mail: acs4j@virginia.edu.

SPEARING, KAREN MARIE, physical education educator, coach; b. Chgo., Apr. 17, 1949; d. John Richard and Naomi (Allen) Miller; m. Edward B. Spearing III, Apr. 28, 1973. BS in Phys. Edn., U. Wis., Whitewater, 1972; MS in Outdoor Edn., No. Ill. U., 1978. Cert. phys. edn. tchr., Ill.; cert. CPR instr., hunter safety instr., boating safety instr., master snowmobile instr., Ill. Tchr., coach Glenside Mid. Sch., Glendale Heights, Ill., 1973—, athletic dir., 1981-92, 95—, dept. chairperson, 1992-93. Hunter safety instr. State of Ill., 1988—, water safety instr., 1989—, snowmobile instr., 1990—, master snowmobile instr., 1995, CPR instr., 1996—. Amb. People to People Citizen Amb. Program, Russia and Belarus, 1993; awards chairperson U.S. Power Squadron, Chgo., 1987—93; mem. exec. com. DuPage Power Squadron., 1993—96, comdr., 2000—01, edn. officer, 1996—98, Adminst. Officer, 1998; mem. com. Ill. Hunting and Fishing Days, Silver Springs State Pk., 1993; mem. Outdoor Wilderness Leadership Class, 1997; pres. Allied Ill. Markswomen, 2001—02. Mem. AAHPERD, Ill. Assn. Health, Phys. Edn., Recreation and Dance, Ill. H.S. Assn. (volleyball referee). Avocations: clock collecting, hunting, fishing, boating. Office: Glenside Mid Sch 1560 Bloomingdale Rd Glendale Heights IL 60139-2734

SPEARMAN, DAVID HAGOOD, veterinarian; b. Greenville, S.C., Nov. 16, 1932; s. David Ralph and Elizabeth (Hagood) S.; m. Patsy Lee cordle, Dec. 18, 1954; children: Kathleen Elizabeth, David Hagood. Student, Clemson Coll., 1950-52, BS, 1975; DVM, U. Ga., 1956. With Cleveland Park Animal Hosp., Greenville, 1956-57; individual practice vet. medicine Easley, S.C., 1957—, Powdersville, 1957-96. Mem. S.C. State Bd. Vet. Examiners, 1981-87, chmn., 1987; advisor Pickins County Planning and Devel. Bd., 1972—; pres. Northside Parent-Tchr. Orgn., 1965-67; mem. adv. bd. vet. technicians program Tri-County Tech., 1975-76; mem. admissions com. Vet. Coll., U. Ga., 1975; mem. adv. com. pre-Vet Club, Clemson U.; chmn. Easley Zoning Bd., 1980-83; mem. S.C. Bd. Vet. Examiners, 1982-89, chmn., 1987. Mem. AVMA (alt. del. 1992-95, S.C. del. 1996-99), Blue Ridge Vet. Med. Assn. (founder, pres., sec.), S.C. Assn. Veterinarians (pres. 1974-75, publicity chmn. 1975—, chmn. animal health technician com., Veterinarianof Yr. 1985), Am. Animal Hosp. Assn. (assoc.), S.C. Wildlife, Pickens County Horse, Cattle and Fair Assn. (pres.), Jr. C. of C. (past officer, Key Man award 1959), Trout Unltd. (state dir.), Pickens County Foxhunters Assn., Clemson U. Tiger Lettermen Assn., Easley Boosters Club, Easley C. of C., World Wildlife Fund, Nat. Wildlife Fedn., Audubon Soc., Nature Conservancy, Internat. Platform Assn., Pickens County Hist. Soc., Lions (pres., internat. del. 1971, 73), Pendleton Farmers Soc., Eastatoee Valley Cmty. Club, Commerce Club, Cliffs at Glassy, Alpha Psi, Alpha Zeta. Presbyterian (deacon, elder, youth leader 1972-74, chmn. orgn. com. 1973-75, 83-85, pulpit com., chmn. nursery bldg. com., stewardship com.). Avocations: photography, fly fishing, bridge. Home: Burdine Springs PO Box 327 Easley SC 29641-0327 Office: 6714 Calhoun Memorial Hwy Easley SC 29640-3672

SPEARMAN, DAVID LEROY, elementary education educator, administrator; b. Chgo., June 4, 1959; s. Lee Roy and Florida Lee (Gordon) S.; m. Tina R. Smith, Aug. 20, 1994; 1 child, David Gordon. Student, Loyola U., Chgo., 1977-78, Moody Bible Inst., 1978-81; BA in Comm., Columbia Coll., Chgo., 1986; postgrad., DePaul U., 1987-89, Chgo. City Wide Colls., 1988—, Chgo. State U., 1992-93; MA in Ednl. Adminstrn., Governor's State U., 1994. Cert 03 tchr., lang. arts endorsement K-8, adminstrv. 020 endorsement, speech endorsement, Ill. Prodr., announcer, talk show host Sta. WYCA, Hammond, Ind., 1983-88; music dir., announcer Sta. WCFJ, Chicago Heights, Ill., 1988-89; tchr. Evangelical Christian Sch., Chgo., 1987-89; truant officer Chgo. Bd. of Edn., 1990-92; tchr. Truth Elem. Sch., Chgo., 1992-99; tchr. 7th grade Richard Byrd Acad., 1999—; video instr. dept. learning tech. Chgo. Pub. Schs., 1999—. 4th grade facilitator Truth Elem. Sch., Chgo., 1994-95, 3rd grade facilitator, 1995-97, chair dept. sci., 1993-96, chair social com., 1994-95, dir. summer sch., 1994, coord. social ctr., 1994; freelance camera operator Sta. WCFC-TV, Chgo., 1989—, Ctrl. City Prodns., Chgo., 1992—, Chgo. Cable Acess Prodns., 1992—; chief videographer DANA Videofilms Prodn. Co., 1995—. Author: (booklet) Teacher's Opinions of the Security and Safety Climate in Chicago Public Schools at Cabrini Green, 1993; contbr. articles to profl. jours., mags. and newspapers; producer documentaries Spirit Night, The Last Lifeboat. Youth counselor Cook County Juvenile Detention Ctr., 1979-80; scout leader Boy Scouts Am., Chgo., 1992—, asst. scoutmaster Chgo. Housing Authority scouting program, 1992-95; bd. dirs. ISO Aeronautics Chgo. Bd. Edn., 1994—. Recipient Tchr. Incentive award Oppenheimer Found., 1993-94, 95-96, Rochelle Lee Found. award, 1993-94, 96-97; named one of Outstanding Young Men of Am., 1989, 98; Chgo. Found. for Edn. grnatee, 1993-94, 94-95, 95-96, mini-grant libr. winner Chgo. Pub. Schs., 1998; tchr. honoree Chgo. State of City Address Dinner by Mayor Richard Daley, 1995; honored by visitation by U.S. Sec. of Edn. Richard Riley and Chgo. Pub. Schs. CEO Paul Vallas, 1995. Mem. Chgo. Tchrs. Union, Moody Bible Inst. Alumni, Columbia Coll. Alumni Govs. State U. Alumni, Internat. Platform Assn., United Negro Coll. Fund. Evangelical Pentecostal. Avocations: video editing and producing, freelance filmmaking. Office: Richard E Byrd Acad 363 W Hill St Chicago IL 60610-1872 E-mail: DanaVideofilms@aol.com.

SPEARMAN, MAXIE ANN, financial analyst, administrator; b. Piedmont, S.C., Sept. 14, 1942; d. J. Mac and Margaret Cecille S. BS, U. S.C., 1965; postgrad., Ga. State U., 1985; student, U. Ga. Acct. Shell Oil Co., Atlanta, 1965-66; internal auditor Sears, Roebuck & Co., 1966-67; acct. Econ. Opportunity Atlanta, 1967-68, City of Atlanta, 1968-78, fin. analyst, 1978-89, sr. fin. analyst planner, 1989—. Investment cons., Atlanta, Conyers, Ga., 1980—. Mem. Rep. Presdl. Task Force, 1985—, U.S. Senatorial Club, Rep. Nat. Com., 1988—, Ga. Rep. Party, 1990—, Atlanta Safety Com., 1985—, Mayor's Spl. Events Task Force, 1990; charter founder Ronald Reagan Rep. Ctr., 1988; del.-at-large Rep. Platform Planning Com., 1992, 94. Recipient safety award Atlanta City Govt., 1990, Presdl. Commn. Exec. Com. of Republican Party award, 1992; Order of Merit award Nat. Rep. Senatorial Com., 1996. Mem. AAUW, NAFE, Am. Mgmt. Assn., Ga. Assn. Med. Victims, Inc. (sec., treas. 1985—), Nat. Trust for Historic Preservation. Methodist. Avocations: writing, tennis, decorating, investing. Home: 1280 Vineyard Dr SE Conyers GA 30013-2466

SPEARMAN, PATSY CORDLE, real estate broker; b. Richmond, Va., Aug. 23, 1934; d. Lee Pierce and Kathleen Jeanette (Muhn) Cordle; m. David Hagood Spearman, Dec. 18, 1954; children: Kathleen Elizabeth, David Hagood. AA, Coll. William & Mary, 1952; student, U. Ga., 1953-54; grad., Realtors Inst., 1979. Copywriter Cabell Eanes Advt. Agy., Richmond, 1952; clk. athletic dept. U. Ga., Athens, 1954-55, sec. Coll. Agr., 1955-56; real estate saleswoman Merrill Lynch/C. Dan Joyner & Co., Inc. (now The Prudential), Greenville, S.C., 1978—. Past pres. Women of Ch.; Presbyn. Ch. Sunday sch. tchr. and youth leader. Recipient numerous awards for obtaining eye bank donors Lions Club and S.C. Eye Bank, Listing Agt. of Yr., 1985-87, 89, 90-93, Sales Agt. of Yr., 1987, 90, 91, 92. Mem. Nat. Assn. Realtors (cert. residential specialist), Real Estate Securities and Syndication Inst., S.C. Assn. Realtors, Greenville Bd. Realtors, Pickens County Bd. Realtors (chmn. cmty. svcs. com., edn. com., membership com. chmn.), Women's Coun. Realtors, Million Dollar Club (life, charter, Greenville and Pickens County), Am. Vet. M.A. Aux. (S.C. del. 1992-98, alt. del. 1999), S.C. Vet. Aux. (treas. 1988-92), Internat. Platform Soc., Inst. Noetic Scis., Smithsonian Assocs., Nat. Wildlife Fedn. (life), World Wildlife Fedn., Wilderness Soc., Sierra Club, Greenpeace, S.C. Wildlife Assn., Audubon Soc., Cousteau Soc., Smithsonian Inst., Better Homes (Easley) Club, Commerce Club Greenville (life), Greenville Little Theater, Eastatoee Valley Assn., Easley Foothills Theatre, Warehouse Theater, Nature Conservancy, Edisto Hist., Cliffs at Glassy Country Club. Home: 505 Asbury Cir Easley SC 29640-1343 Office: PO Box 327 Easley SC 29641-0327

SPEARMAN-LEACH, ANTHONY MAURICE PAUL, public policy and communications executive; b. Dec. 24, 1966; BS in Polit. Sci., History and Sociology, BS in Biology, Sociology, U. of the State of N.Y.; BA in Social and Behavioral Scis., Johns Hopkins U.; MBA Internat. Mgmt., U. London Royal Holloway Coll., 2000—. Fund raiser Stephen Dunn & Assocs. Inc., Southfield, Mich.; Southeastern Mich. polit. field dir. Mich. Rep. State Com., Detroit and Lansing; regional dir. Office of U.S. Senator Spencer Abraham, Southfield; sales asst. regional advt. sales office USA Networks, Troy; acct. exec. Viacom's CBS WWJ TV62. Arbitrator Met. Balt. Better Bus. Bur.; columnist The Mich. Chronicle. Vice chair bd. mgmt. Young Women's Chrisitan Assn. of Met. Detroit Interim Ho. Battered Women's Shelter Bd. of Mgrs., Detroit; bd. dirs. The Sphinx Orgn. Nat. String Competition; mem. 1995 Edn. Policy Summit; sec., bd. trustees, mem. scholarship and awards com. U. of the State of N.Y.; mem. United World Colls. U.S. Selections com. for Davis Scholars; bd. dirs. Chevron-Texaco Sphinx competition organization; mem. S.E. Mich. HIV/AIDS Coun.; mem., govtl. appointee Mich. Bd. of Phys. Therapy Mich. Dept. of Commerce, Lansing; coun. chair, mayoral appointee Downtown Detroit Citizen's Dist. Coun.; chmn. Hugh O'Brian Youth Leadership Seminar. Mem. Am. Mensa, Nat. Press Club, Ad Craft Club Detroit. Home: 9374 Penrod St Detroit MI 48228-1833 E-mail: spearman-leach@jhu.edu.

SPEARS, DIANA FAYE, computer scientist; b. N.Y.C., Aug. 17, 1952; d. Stanley R. and Vivian E. Sadin. BA, U. N.Mex., 1974; MA, U. Md., 1986, PhD, 1990. Programmer/analyst Goddard/NASA, Greenbelt, Md., 1978-80; computer scientist Nat. Bur. Stds., Gaithersburg, 1980-86, Naval Rsch. Lab., Washington, 1986-2001; prof. U. Wyo., Laramie, 2001—. Assoc. editor jour. in field. Mem. AAAI, Assn. Women in Sci., Women in Sci. and Engring., Am. Math. Soc., Sigma Xi. Avocations: art, skiing, hiking, biking. Office: Dept Computer Sci U Wyo Laramie WY 82071-3682 E-mail: dspears@cs.uwyo.edu.

SPEARS, DIANE SHIELDS, artist, retired art academy administrator; b. Seattle, May 21, 1942; d. Richard Keene McKinney and Dorothy Jean (Shields) Thacker; m. Howard Truman Spears, Sept. 3, 1977; 1 child, Truman Eugene. BA in Art, English, Edn., Trinity U., 1964; MA in Christian Counseling, San Antonio Theol. Sem., 1986, D of Christian Edn., 1988. Cert. tchr. secondary edn., elem. edn., ednl. supervision, Tex. Instr. ESL Dliel-Geb (Def. Lang. Inst.), San Antonio, 1973-74, Ceta/Ace Bexar County Sch. Bd., San Antonio, 1975-78; tchr. elem. edn., art, music New Covenant Faith Acad., 1983-89; instr. ESL Jewish Family Svc., 1991; tchr. elem. art Edgewood Ind. Sch. Dist., 1992-93, dist. art specialist, 1993-95, fine arts coord., 1995-98, dir. visual arts, 1998-99. Owner, operator Art for Kings, San Antonio, 1985—. Illustrator teacher-created materials-lit. activities for young children, 1989-90; author: (art curriculum) Art for Kings, 1987; editor: (art curriculum) Edgewood Ind. Sch. Dist. Elem. Art Curriculum, 1993; exhibited in group shows at Charles and Emma Frye Mus., Seattle, 1966, 68, Centro Cultural Aztlan Galerie Expression, 1998 (Best of Show 1998). Dir. intercessory prayer New Covenant Fellowship, San Antonio, 1980-90. Recipient awards for painting and graphics, San Antonio, 1996-98. Mem. Nat. Mus. for Women in Arts (charter), Tex. Art Edn. Assn. (1st pl. graphics divsn. 1995), San Antonio Art Edn. Assn. (1st pl. 1995). Republican. Avocations: water skiing, motorcycle riding, sewing, writing. Home: 264 Mountain Dr Lakehills TX 78063-6725 E-mail: dshieldsspears@earthlink.net.

SPEARS, DORIS ANN HACHMUTH, entrepreneur, writer, publisher, real estate and management consultant; b. Jersey City, July 6, 1951; d. Arthur Charles Hachmuth and Diana Sofia Moroz; m. Richard Alan Spears, May 13, 1969; children: Andrew, Mark, Daniel. B, Barry U., 1993, MS, 1997. Broker, owner Doris Spears Realty, Inc., Port Jervis, 1981-86, Spears & Spears, INc., Stuart, Fla., 1987-97; owner, pub. Arrow Pub., Inc., Palm City, 1988—2001; editor, pub. Today's Fla. Woman, Inc., 1994-96; owner, broker, sr. cons. Suncastle Realty, Inc., 1997—. Adj. instr. Indian River C.C., Ft. Pierce, Fla., 1994—; founder-owner Sunny Lifestyles TM, 1996. Author: Living Better for Less, 2000; (annual seminar) Building Wealth/Buying Property. Bd. dirs. Hibiscus Children's Ctr., Jensen Beach, Fla., 1993-96; sec. bd. dirs. Hibiscus Children's Found., Jensen Beach, 1996-99; mem. bus. adv. bd. Indian River C.C. Mem. Internat. Assn. Female Execs., Women's Coun. of Realtors, Real Estate Brokerage Mgrs. Coun., Martin County Bd. Realtors (bd. dirs. 1988-90), Realtor Assn. of Martin County, Nat. Spkrs. Assn., Sierra Club, Martin County C. of C., Nature Conservancy, Fla. Spkrs. Assn. Avocations: tennis, reading, travel. Office: 828 SW Palm City Rd Stuart FL 34994

SPEARS, GAY HOLMES, music educator; b. Blytheville, Ark., Oct. 2, 1958; d. Louis Lee and Dona Jene (Bohannon) H.; m. Jared Tozier Spears, July 20, 1985. BMus, U. Tenn., 1981; MMus, Ark. State U., 1984; DMus, U. Memphis, 1993. Prof. music Williams Coll., Walnut Ridge, Ark., 1983—. Organist First United Meth. Ch., Paragould, Ark., 1988—; clinician Ark. State U. Piano Camp, Jonesboro, 1987, Ark. Baptist Conv., Little Rock, 1988-89. Mem. ASCAP, Music Tchrs. Nat. Assn. (adjudicator 1990—), Southeastern Composers League, Federated Music Clubs, Sigma Alpha Iota, Pi Kappa Lambda. Home: 2304 Eagles Glen Ct Chesterfield MO 63017-7378

SPEARS, JAE, state legislator; b. Latonia, Ky. d. James and Sylvia (Fox) Marshall; m. Lawrence E. Spears; children: Katherine Spears Cooper, Marsha Spears-Duncan, Lawrence M., James W. Student, U. Ky. Reporter Cin. Post, Cin. Enquirer newspapers; rschr. Stas. WLW-WSAI, Cin.; tchr. Jiya Gakuen Sch., Japan; lectr. U.S. Mil. installations East Anglia, Eng.; del. State of W.Va., Charleston, 1974-80; mem. W.Va. Senate, 1980-1993. Mem. vis. com. W.Va. Extension and Continuing Edn., Morgantown, 1993-2000, W.Va. U. Sch. Medicine, 1992—; with state sen., 1980-93; apptd. to Jud. Hearing Bd., 1993-2000. Chmn. adv bd. Sta. WNPB, 1992-94; congl. liaison Am. Pub. TV Stas. and Sta. WNPB-TV, 1992-97; mem. coun. W.Va. Autism Task Force, Huntington, 1981-90; mem. W.Va. exec. bd. Literacy Vols. Am., 1986-90, 94—, pres., 1990-92; mem. Gov.'s State Literacy Coun., 1991-97; bd. dirs. Found. Ind. Colls. W.Va., 1986—; mem. regional adv. com. W.Va. Gov.'s Task Force for Children, Youth and Family, 1989; mem. USS W.Va. Commn., 1989; mem. exec. com. W.Va. Employer Support Group for Guard and Res., 1989, mem. steering com., 1990-92. Decorated Purple Heart (hon.); recipient Susan B. Anthony award NOW, 1982, edn. award Profl. Educators Assn. W.Va., 1986, ann. award W.Va. Assn. Ret. Sch. Employees, 1985, Meritorious Svc. award W.Va. State Vets. Commn., 1984, Vets. Employment and Tng. Svc. award U.S. Dept. Labor, 1984, award W.Va. Vets. Coun., 1984; named Admiral in N.C. Navy, Gov. of N.C., 1982, hon. Brigadier Gen. W.Va. N.G., 1984, One of 11 Women Pioneers of W.Va. Legislature, W.Va. U. Inst. for Pub. Affairs, 1997. Mem. DAR, VFW (aux.), Bus. and Profl. Women (Woman of Yr. award 1978), Nat. League Am. Pen Women (Pen Woman of Yr. 1984), Nat. Order Women Legislators, Am. Legion (aux.), Delta Kappa Gamma, Alpha Xi Delta. Democrat. Home and Office: PO Box 98 Shinnston WV 26431

SPEARS, JAMES GRADY, small business owner; b. Port Arthur, Tex., July 20, 1941; s. John Grady and Dorothy Nell (Haney) S. Grad. high sch., Port Arthur. Adminstr. Child Health & Devel. Studies, Oakland, Calif., 1962-69; sales mgr. Sunshine Biscuits Inc., Houston, 1969-75; owner, pres. S.W. Tookie Inc./Tookie's Restaurant, Seabrook, Tex., 1975—. Mem. Greater Houston Convention & Visitors Bur., Clear Lake Convention & Visitors Bur. With USN, 1959-62. Mem. Tex. Restaurant Assn., Houston Restaurant Assn., Seabrook Assn., Old Seabrook Assn. Republican. Roman Catholic. Avocations: collectibles, fine art, antiques, listening to records, self improvement. Home: 16310 Hickory Knoll Dr Houston TX 77059-5311 Office: SW Tookie Inc/Tookie's Restaurant 1202 Bayport Blvd Seabrook TX 77586-3406

SPEARS, JAMES WILLIAM, systems programmer, consultant; b. Mt. Clemens, Mich., Oct. 2, 1958; s. Arthur Jackson and Margaret Elizabeth (McLeod) S. Student, Oakland C.C., 1983-85, Northwestern U., 1976-78. Computer operator, tutor Oakland C. C., Farmington Hills, Mich., 1983-84; systems programmer, application programmer Nat. Wholesale Drug Co., Detroit, 1984-85; systems programmer Domino's Pizza, Inc., Ann Arbor, Mich., 1985-86; systems engr. Computer Assocs. Internat., Inc., Dearborn, 1987; cons. JWS and Assocs., Walled Lake, 1987-90; systems programmer Alexander Hamilton Life Ins., Inc., Farmington Hills, 1990-91; cons. level 2 support staff IBM, Poughkeepsie, N.Y., 1991-94; sr. tech. support rep. Legent Corp., Columbus, Ohio, 1994-95; lead tech. support specialist Cross Access Corp., Sunnyvale, Calif., 1995—. Mem. adj. faculty Oakland C.C., Farmington Hills, 1987-88. Mem. Nat. Systems Programmer Assn. Lutheran. Home: 655 S Fairoaks Ave Apt J114 Sunnyvale CA 94086-2056

SPEARS, KENNETH GEORGE, chemistry educator; b. Erie, Pa., Oct. 23, 1943; BS, Bowling Green State U., 1966; MS, PhD in Phys. Chemistry, U. Chgo., 1970. NIH predoctoral fellow U. Chgo., 1968-70; NRC-NOAA postdoctoral fellow NOAA, Boulder, Colo., 1970-72; prof. dept. chemistry Northwestern U., 1972—, mem. biomedical engring. dept., 1987—. Bd. editors The Rev. Scientific Instruments, 1980-83; conbtr. articles to profl.jours. Alfred P. Sloan Found. fellow, 1974-76. Fellow AAAS; mem. Am. Phys. Soc., Am. Chem. Soc. Office: Northwestern U Dept Chemistry 2145 Sheridan Rd Evanston IL 60208-3113 E-mail: k-spears@northwestern.edu.

SPEARS, LARRY JONELL, lawyer; b. Webb, Miss., Jan. 10, 1953; s. John Spears and Lillian Belle Embrey; m. Treycè L. Gaston, Jan. 14, 1989;children: Lyndzè Rae, Joshua Lawrence. BS, U. Ill., 1976, JD, 1979; MS, So. Ill. U., 1990. Bar: Ill. 1980. Asst. atty gen. Ill. Atty. Gen.'s Office, Murphysboro, 1980-84; asst. pub. defender Jackson County Pub. Defender's Office, 1985; lectr. Crime Study Ctr., Carbondale, Ill., 1985; sole practice, 1985-86; asst. state's atty. Peoria (Ill.) State's Atty. Office, 1986-90, Sangamon County State's Atty. Office, Springfield, Ill., 1990-94. Cons. Minority Contractors Assn., Carbondale, 1985; mem. Inmate Advocacy Group, Murphysboro, 1985-86; lectr. Sangamon State U., Springfield, 1990-96. Elijah P. Lovejoy scholar, 1972. Mem. Ill. State Bar Assn., McLean County Bar Assn., Adminstrn. of Justice Assn. (treas. 1984-85), Am. Soc. Criminology (discussant 1984-85), Midwest Criminal Justice Assn., Am. Judicature Soc., LWV, Sphinx Club (Carbondale), Phi Alpha Delta (treas. 1979), Alpha Phi Sigma. Republican. Baptist. Avocations: golf, fishing, songwriting, tennis, volleyball. Home: 1603 E Oakland Ave Bloomington IL 61701-5617 Office: Ill State U Student's Legal Svcs Normal IL 61761 E-mail: ljspear@mail.ilstu.edu.

SPEARS, MARCIA HOPP, nursing educator, health facility administrator; b. Rahway, N.J., July 29, 1927; d. Jacob and Ada (Dubow) Hopp; m. Harold Spears, Mar. 13, 1955 (dec. 1978); children: Ivy Hopp, Laura Suzanne, Douglas Mason (dec. 1984). Diploma in Nursing, Jersey City Med. Ctr., 1948; Cert. in Pub. Health, U. Pa., 1951, BS in Nursing Edn., 1953. RN, N.J., Md. Supr., asst. dir. nursing edn. Trenton (N.J.) Vis/ Nurses Assn., ., 1953-55; nursing supr. dept. of health City of Balt., 1955-56; assoc. prof. pub. health nursing Sch. Pub. Health Johns Hopkins U., Balt., 1955-56; nursing educator Middlesex Gen. Hosp., New Brunswick, N.J., 1964-66; health edn. nurse dept. spl. edn. City of Piscataway (N.J.), 1968-76; staff nurse, examiner Complete Health Care Svc., Inc., East Brunswick, N.J., 1985-88; staff nurse Portamedic, 1985-93; examiner World Wide Health Svcs., Clementon, N.J., 1985-86; mem. staff Rossmoor Community Med. Ctr., Jamesburg, 1988-98, ret., 1998. Vol. local chpt. ARC. Mem. ANA, APHA, Nat. League for Nursing (charter mem. local chpt.), Jersey Med. Sch. of Nursing Alumni. Home: 1367 Seminole Rd North Brunswick NJ 08902-1425

SPEARS, ROBERT FIELDS, lawyer; b. Tulsa, Aug. 1, 1943; s. James Ward and Berneice (Fields) S.; m. Jacquelyn Castle, May 10, 1961; children: Jeff, Sally. BBA, Tex. Tech. U., 1965; JD, U. Tex., 1968. Bar: Tex. 1968. Assoc. Rain, Harrell, Emery, Young & Doke, Dallas, 1968-73, ptnr., 1974-87, Locke Purnell Rain Harrell, Dallas, 1987-91; gen. counsel Fin. Industries Corp., Austin, Tex., 1991-96; gen. counsel, sec. Lone Star Technologies Inc., Dallas, 1996—. Pres. Sr. Citizens of Greater Dallas, 1988. Mem. ABA, Tex. Bar Assn., Dallas Bar Assn., Dallas Country Club, Phi Delta Phi. Republican. Baptist. Avocation: tennis. Office: Lone Star Technologies Inc PO Box 803546 Dallas TX 75380-3546

SPEARS, SALLY, lawyer; b. San Antonio, Aug. 29, 1938; d. Adrian Anthony and Elizabeth (Wylie) S.; m. Tor Hultgreen, July 15, 1961 (div. Jan. 1983); children: Dagny Elizabeth, Sara Kirsten, Kara Spears. BA, U. Tex., 1960, LLB, 1965. Bar: Tex. 1961, Ill. 1971. Practice law, Stamford, Conn., 1966-67, Chgo., 1970-71, Northbrook, Ill., 1972-73, Toronto, Ont., Can., 1973-81; assoc. firm Cummings & Lockwood, Stamford, 1966-67, Kirkland & Ellis, Chgo., 1970-71; sr. atty. Allstate Ins. Co., Northbrook, Ill., 1971-73; gen. counsel, sec. Reed Paper Ltd., Reed Ltd., Toronto, 1973-78, Denison Mines Ltd., Toronto, 1978-81; pvt. practice law San Antonio, 1981—. Apptd. by Sec. of Def. to serve on Def. Adv. Com., Women in the Svcs., 1997-99. Author: Call Sign Revlon: The Life and Death of Navy Fighter Pilot Kara Hultgreen, 1998. Mem. Tex. Bar Assn., San Antonio Bar Assn., Bankruptcy Bar Assn., Bexar County Women's Bar Assn., San Antonio Country Club, The Club at Sonterra. Home: 433 Evans Ave San Antonio TX 78209-3725 Office: Ste 106 8151 Broadway San Antonio TX 78209-1938 E-mail: sespears@swbell.net.

SPEARS, SAMUEL BRUCE, music educator; b. Atlanta, Aug. 2, 1972; MusB, Furman U., 1994; MusM, U. Cin., 1997. Instr. Emmanuel Coll., Franklin Springs, Ga., 1999—. Min. music 1st United Meth. Ch., Dacula, Ga. Mem.: Ga. Music Educators Assn., Nat. Assn. Tchrs. Singing, Am. Choral Dirs. Assn., Music Educators Nat. Conf., Phi Mu Alpha Sionfonia. Avocations: baseball, guitar.

SPEARS, VICTORIA ANGELIQUE, biochemist; b. Great Lakes, Ill., Apr. 15, 1974; d. Leslie Edwin and Laura Victoria Andrus; m. Victor Lee Spears, III, May 23, 1998. BS in Biochemistry and Cell Biology, U. Calif., San Diego, 1996; MS, U. Va., 1999. Life support scientist Hopkins Rsch. Inst. Stanford U., 2000—01; dir. life sci. Aegen Bioscis., 2001—. Mem. Officers Students Spouses Club (treas. 2000-01). Roman Catholic. Avocations: piano, racquetball, hiking, travel.

SPEAS, CHARLES STUART, human resources consultant, entrepreneur; b. Phila., Jan. 1, 1944; s. Austin LeRoy and Peggy Elaine (Drake) S.; m. Julie Ellen Royce, Apr. 10, 1965; children: Eric S. Speas, Robert Austin Speas. Student, Tri-State Coll., U. Notre Dame, Purdue U. Lic. agt. in life, accident and health ins., Ind. Sr. scheduling coord. Excel Industries, Elkhart, Ind., 1966-73; corp. dir. pers. EFP Corp., 1973-97; pvt. practice, 1997-98; founder Speas Enterprises, Inc., Hickory, NC, 1998—; human resources adv. Magellan Group, 2002—. Cons. various Elkhart, Hickory, Goshen area bus., 1980—. Contbr. articles profl. jours. Participant Soviet/Am. Conf. on Trade and Econ. Cooperation, Kremlin, 1991. With USAF, 1962-66. Mem. Ind. Pers. Assn., Goshen Indsl. Club (recipient cert. of appreciation 1990), Soc. for Human Resources Mgmt., Elkhart C. of C. (task force on healthcare availability/cost). Republican. Avocations: woodworking, fishing, gardening, golf. Office: 816 13th St NE Hickory NC 28601 Home: 104 E Holly St Maiden NC 28650-8323

SPECHLER, MARTIN CHARLES, economist; b. N.Y.C., Jan. 25, 1943; s. Sidney and Dorothy (Gelber) S.; m. Dina Rome, Aug. 30, 1964; children: Avraham Ravit, Michal Ya'arit. AB, Harvard Coll., 1964; MA, Harvard U., 1967, PhD, 1971. Teaching fellow in econs., social studies Harvard U., Cambridge, Mass., 1965-71; asst. prof., head tutor in econs., 1971-74; lectr. Hebrew U., Jerusalem, 1974-80; sr. lectr. Tel Aviv U., 1980-82; vis. assoc. U. Wash., Seattle, 1982-83, U. Iowa, Iowa City, 1983-84; assoc. prof. econs. Ind. U., Purdue U., Indpls., 1984-90; prof. econs. Ind. U., 1990—. Mem. faculty coun. Ind. U., 1993-97, 99—; cons. World Bank, Asian Devel. Bank, U.S. State Dept. Author: Perspectives in Economic Thought; mem. editorial bd. Comparative Econ. Studies; contbr. articles to profl. jours. Active Dem. Cen. Com., Monroe County, Ind., 1988—; pres. Beth Shalom, Bloomington, Ind. Jewish Community, 1999—; mem. exec. com. Assn. for Comparative Econ. Studies. With Israel Def. Forces, 1980-82. Mem. Am. Econ. Assn., Phi Beta Kappa, Hasty Pudding Club. Avocations: golf, tennis. Home: 4418 E Sheffield Dr Bloomington IN 47408-3135 Office: Cavanaugh 516 425 Univ Blvd Indianapolis IN 46202-5148 E-mail: spechler@indiana.edu.

SPECHT, ALICE WILSON, library director; b. Caracus, Venezuela, Apr. 3, 1948; (parents Am. citizens); d. Ned and Helen (Lockwood) Wilson; m. Joe W. Specht, Dec. 30, 1972; 1 child, Mary Helen. BA, U. Pacific, 1969; MLS, Emory U., 1970; MBA, Hardin-Simmons U., 1983. Libr. social scis. North Tex. State U., Denton, 1971-73; reference libr. Lubbock (Tex.) City and County Libr., 1974-75; system coord. Big Country Libr. System, Abilene, Tex., 1975-79; assoc. dir. Hardin-Simmons U., 1981-88, dir. univ. librs., 1988—. Apptd. Mayor's Task Force Libr. Svcs., 1995-96. Author bibliog. instrn. aids, 1981-90; editor; The College Man, For Pilots Eyes Only. Mem. mayor's task force Abilene Pub. Libr., 1995—96; mem. Libr. Sci. Art. Bd. for Tx. Recipient Boss of Yr., Am. Bus. Women's Assn., 1994. Mem.: ALA, Abilene Libr. Consortium (chair adminstrv. coun. 1990, 1993, 1998, 2002, coord. nat. conf. 1991, 1993, 2002), Tex. Libr. Assn. (chair com. 1978—84, sec.-treas. coll. and univ. librs. divsn. 1993—94, legis. com. 1994—), Texshare Ednl. Working Group (chair 1999, 2002), Rotary (chair com. 1989—90). Home: 918 Grand Ave Abilene TX 79605-3233 Office: Hardin-Simmons U PO Box 16195 2200 Hickory St Abilene TX 79601-2345

SPECHT, GORDON DEAN, retired petroleum executive; b. Garner, Iowa, June 3, 1927; s. Reuben William and Gladys (Leonard) S.; m. Cora Alice Emmert, May 24, 1952; children: Mary Ellen, Grant. BS in Chem. Engring., Iowa State U., 1950, MS in Chem. Engring., 1951; SM in Chem. Engring., MIT, 1954. Engr. Exxon Corp. Bayway Refinery, Linden, N.J., 1951-59, systemn services div. mgr., 1960-61, engring. services div. mgr., 1962-63, chem. coordination div. mgr., 1964; mgr. systems dept. Exxon Corp.-Exxon Chem. Co., N.Y.C., 1965-70; sr. advisor communications and computer scis. dept. Exxon Corp., Florham Park, N.J., 1971-76, assoc. cons., 1977-85; retired, 1986. Patentee in field. Asst. scoutmaster Boy Scouts Am., Westfield, N.J., 1986—; sr. qualified observer Sperry Obs., Cranford, N.J., 1986—; celestial navigation instr. U.S. Power Squadrons, 1990—. With U.S. Army, 1945-46, 1st lt. C.E., 1952-53, Korea. Decorated Bronze Star. Mem. Am. Inst. Chem. Engrs., Amateur Astronomers, Inc., No. N.J. Sail and Power Squadron, MIT Club of No. N.J., MIT Club of Princeton, Nat. Eagle Scout Assn., Tau Beta Pi, Phi Lambda Upsilon, Phi Kappa Phi, Tau Kappa Epsilon. Republican. Methodist. Avocations: astronomy, sailing, canoeing, swimming, bicycling. Home: 15 Normandy Dr Westfield NJ 07090-3431

SPECINER, MICHAEL, computer engineer; b. N.Y.C., Mar. 31, 1948; s. Edward and Esther S.; children: Dawn Perlner, Ray Perlner. SB in Math., SB in Physics, MIT, 1968. Programmer Composition Tech. Inc., Cambridge, Mass., 1973-74; sys. designer CAMEX, Boston, 1974-83, lead arch., 1986-93; group leader ZTEL, Wilmington, 1983-86; chief arch. Splash/ColorAge, Billerica, 1993-2000; sr. consulting engr. ThinkEngine Networks, Marlborough, 2001—02. Mem. coun. for arts MIT. Co-author: Network Security: Private Communication in a Public World, 2002; patentee in computer graphics. Mem. IEEE, Assn. for Computing Machinery, Am. Math. Soc. Avocations: composing, playing and listening to music, hiking. E-mail: ms@alum.mit.edu.

SPECK, DAVID DEAN, ophthalmologist; b. Auburn, N.Y., Mar. 19, 1953; s. Michael Stephen and Anne Margaret (Sopchak) S. AB in Chemistry, Cornell U., 1975, MD, 1979. Diplomate Am. Bd. Ophthalmology. Intern in medicine M. Bassett Hosp., Cooperstown, N.Y., 1979-80; resident ophthalmology St. Luke's-Roosevelt Hosp., N.Y.C., 1980-83; pvt. practice ophthalmology Auburn, 1983—. Mem. staff Auburn Meml. Hosp., 1985—. Vice chmn. Cmty. Preservation Com., Auburn, 1989-96; trustee, auditor St. Nicholas Ch., Auburn, 1989-93. Fellow Am. Acad. Ophthalmology; mem. AMA, Med. Soc. of the State of N.Y., Cayuga County Med. Soc., Golden Glow of Christmas Past, TESLA Coil Builders Assn. Avocations: antiques, electronics, stained glass, music, computers. Office: 35 Arterial W Auburn NY 13021-2730

SPECK, EUGENE LEWIS, internist; b. Boston, Dec. 17, 1936; s. Robert A. and Anne (Rosenberg) S.; m. Rachel Shoshana; children: Michael Robert, Keren Sara. AB, Brandeis U., Waltham, Mass., 1958; MS, U. Mass., 1961; PhD, George Washington U., 1966, MD, 1969. Diplomate Am. Bd. Internal Medicine with subspecialty in infectious diseases. Intern N.Y. Hosp.-Cornell, 1969-70; rsch. assoc. NIH, Bethesda, Md., 1970-72; resident Barnes Hosp.-Washington U., 1972-73; instr. medicine Washington U., St. Louis, 1972-73; fellow Strong Meml. Hosp.-U. Rochester, 1973-75; instr. medicine U. Rochester, N.Y., 1973-75, asst. prof. medicine, 1975-80, U. Nev., Las Vegas, 1980-85, assoc. prof., 1985-95, prof. medicine, 1995—; dir./co-dir. infectious disease unit U. Med. Ctr. of So. Nev., 1980—; ptnr. Infectious Diseases Consultants, 1983—. Cons. Clark County Health Dept., Las Vegas, 1980—, U. Med. Ctr. So. Nev., Las Vegas, 1980—. Sunrise Hosp., Las Vegas, 1980—, Valley Hosp., Las Vegas, 1980—. Contbr. articles to profl. jours., chpts. to books. Fellow ACP; mem. Am. Soc. Microbiology, Infectious Disease Soc. Am., Alpha Omega Alpha. Avocations: tennis, skiing, racquetball. Home: 2228 Chatsworth Ct Henderson NV 89074-5309 Office: Infectious Diseases Cons 3006 S Maryland Pkwy Ste 780 Las Vegas NV 89109-2292

SPECK, SAMUEL WALLACE, JR. state official; b. Canton, Ohio, Jan. 31, 1937; s. Samuel Wallace Sr. and Lois Ione (Schneider) S.; m. Sharon Jane Anderson, Jan. 20, 1962; children: Samuel Wallace III, Derek Charles. BA, Muskingum Coll., 1959; postgrad., U. Zimbabwe, Harare, 1961; MA, Harvard U., 1963, PhD, 1968. Prof. polit. sci. Muskingum Coll., New Concord, Ohio, 1964-83, asst. to pres., 1986-87, exec. v.p., 1987, acting pres., 1987-88, pres., 1988-99; assoc. dir. Fed. Emergency Mgmt. Agy., 1983-86; mem. Ohio Ho. of Reps., 1971-76; state senator from Ohio 20th Dist., 1977-83; dir. Dept. Natural Resources, mem. Gov's. cabinet State of Ohio, 1999—. Bd. dirs. Camco Fin. Corp., Cambridge, Ohio, Advantage Savs. Bank; pres. Eastern Ohio Devel. Alliance, 1990-92; Fund for Improvement of Postsecondary Edn., 1990-92, chmn. 1991. Contbr.: Southern Africa in Perspective, 1972; also numerous articles on African and Am. govt. and pub. policy. Bd. dirs. Ohio Tuition Trust Authority, 1991-93, Internat. Ctr. for Preservation Wild Animals, Lake Erie Commn., 1999—, Ohio Water Resources Coun., 1999—; mem. Great Lakes Commn., 1999—, chmn., 2002—; mem. Ohio Power Siting Bd., 1999—. Recipient Outstanding Legislator award VFW/DAV/Am. Legion, Conservation Achievement award State of Ohio. Mem. Assn. Ind. Colls. and Univs. of Ohio (chmn. 1992-94). Republican. Presbyterian. Home: 240 Greenbriar Ct Worthington OH 43085-3055 Office: Dir OH Dept of Natural Resources 1930 Belcher Dr # D-3 Columbus OH 43224-1392

SPECTER, ARLEN, senator; b. Wichita, Kans., Feb. 12, 1930; s. Harry and Lillie (Shanin) S.; m. Joan L. Levy, June 14, 1953; children: Shanin, Stephen. Student, U. Okla., 1947-48; BA Internat. Rels., U. Pa., 1951; LL.B., Yale U., 1956. Asst. counsel Warren Commn., Washington, 1964; magisterial investigator Commn. of Pa., 1965; asst. dist. atty. City of Phila., 1959-63, dist. atty., 1966-74; ptnr. Dechert Price & Rhoads, Phila., 1956-66, 74-80; U.S. senator from Pa., 1981—. Lectr. law Temple U., 1972-75, U. Pa., 1968-72; chmn. Appropriations Subcom. on Labor, Health and Human Svcs. and Edn. and Related Agys., Subcom. on Agr., Rural Deve. and Related Agys., Subcom. on Transp., Subcom. on Def., Subcom. on Fgn. Opers., Jud. Subcom. on Antitrusts, Bus. Rights, and Competition, Subcom. on Immigration, Subcom. on Terrorism, Tech. and Govt. Info., Govtl. Affairs Subcom. on Internat. Security, Proliferation and Fed. Svcs., Permanent Subcom. on Investigations, Subcom. on Oversight of Govt. Mgmt., Restructuring and D.C. Bd. editors Law Jour.; contbr. articls to profl. jours. Served to 1st U.S. Army, 1951-53. Recipient Youth Svcs. award B'nai B'rith, 1966; recipient Sons of Italy award, 1968, Community Humanitarian award Bapt. Ch., 1969, man of Yr. award, Temple Beth Ami, 1971, N.E. Cath. High Sch. Outstanding Achievement award, 1973. Mem. Phi Beta Kappa. Republican. Jewish. Office: US Senate 711 Senate Hart Bldg Washington DC 20510-0001*

SPECTER, RICHARD BRUCE, lawyer; b. Phila., Sept. 6, 1952; s. Jacob E. and Marilyn B. (Kron) S.; m. Jill Ossenfort, May 30, 1981; children: Lauren Elizabeth, Lindsey Anne, Allison Lee. BA cum laude, Washington U., St. Louis, 1974; JD, George Washington U., 1977. Bar: Mo. 1977, U.S. Dist. Ct. (ea. and we. dists.) Mo. 1977, U.S. Ct. Appeals (8th cir.) 1977, Ill. 1978, Pa. 1978, U.S. Dist. Ct. (ea. dist.) Ill. 1979, U.S. Ct. Appeals (7th cir.) 1979, Calif. 1984, U.S. Dist. Ct. (cen. dist.) Calif. 1985, U.S. Ct. Appeals (9th cir.) 1986, U.S. Dist. Ct. (so. dist.) Calif. 1987, U.S. Dist. Ct. (no. dist.) Calif. 1988, U.S. Supreme Ct. 1999. Assoc. Coburn, Croft, Shepherd, Herzog & Putzell, St. Louis, 1977-79; ptnr. Herzog, Kral, Burroughs & Specter, 1979-82; exec. v.p. Uniqey Internat., Santa Ana, Calif., 1982-84; pvt. practice law L.A. and Irvine, 1984-87; ptnr. Corbett & Steelman, Irvine, 1987—. Instr. Nat. Law Ctr. George Washington U. 1975. Mem. ABA, Ill. Bar Assn., Mo. Bar Assn., Pa. Bar Assn., Calif. Bar Assn. Jewish. Home: 37 Bull Run Irvine CA 92620-2510 Office: 18200 Von Karman Ave Ste 200 Irvine CA 92612-1086 E-mail: rspecter@corbsteel.com.

SPECTOR, ANITA FROHMANN, buyer; b. N.Y.C., Apr. 26, 1943; d. Ira and Minnie (Glazer) Friedman; m. Robert Frohmann, Dec. 24, 1961; 1 child, Edward Frohmann; m. Boris Spector, Apr. 21, 1985; stepchildren: Jeffrey Spector, Lori Spector Krein. BS, Adelphi U., 1984; MA, SUNY, 1992; PhD, Walden U., 1997. Buyer furniture-furnishings Colgate Palmolive Co., N.Y.C., 1983-87, buyer office supplies-forms, 1987-90, buyer fabric care packaging-household surface care packaging, 1990-95, materials sourcing project analyst, 1995-97, oral care buyer point of sale and packaging, 1997—. Mem. Colgate-Palmolive Sys. Applications Products in Data Processing (SAP) core team, 1997—, ergonomics team, 1997—, comml. print team, 2001-; mem. adv. bd. Adelphi U., Am. Biographical Inst. Profl. Women. Mem. adv. bd. Adelphi U. Named Disting. Alumni Adelphi U. U. Coll., 1998. Mem. AAUW, The Doctorate Assn. N.Y. Educators. Avocations: reading, travel, bicycling, music, decorating. Home: 4 Park Ave Apt 16C New York NY 10016-5311 Office: Colgate Palmolive Co 300 Park Ave Fl 4 New York NY 10022-7402

SPECTOR, ARTHUR ABRAHAM, physician, educator; b. Phila., May 14, 1936; s. Frank Lewis and Frances Berenbaum Spector; m. Jean Rosenberg, June 19, 1960; children: Ann Beck, Frank H., Hope Grimm. BA, U. Pa., 1956, MD, 1960. Intern Abington (Pa.) Hosp., 1960-61; rsch. fellow, rsch. med. officer Nat. Heart Inst., Bethesda, Md., 1963-68; from. asst. prof. to prof. U. Iowa, Iowa City, 1963-94, interim head dept. pharmacology, 1994-96, interim head dep. biochemistry, 1996-98, U. I. Found. Disting. prof., 1999—. Editor Jour. Lipid Rsch., 1994-99; assoc. editor Arteroe Thrombosis Vascular Biology, 1999—; contbr. articles to profl. jours. Lt. USN, 1961-63. Fellow: Am. Heart Assn. (mem. coun. artereo thrombosis vascular biology 1970—, chmn. coun. arteriosclerosis 1988—90, Spl. Recognition award 1998); mem.: Internat. Soc. Study Fatty Acids and Lipids (v.p. 1997—2000, pres. 2000—), Am. . Biochemistry Molecular Biology, Am. Soc. Clin. Investigation. Office: U Iowa Dept Biochemistry 4-403 BSB Iowa City IA 52242 E-mail: arthur-spector@uiowa.edu.

SPECTOR, ARTHUR JAY, federal judge; b. N.Y.C., Sept. 10, 1949; s. Nathan and Yetta S.; m. Kayla Dee Jaffe, Aug. 3, 1974; children: Joel, Andrew. BA, CCNY, 1971; JD cum laude, Boston U., 1974. Bar: N.Y. 1975, U.S. Ct. Appeals (2d cir.) 1975, U.S. Dist. Ct. (ea. dist.) N.Y. 1975, U.S. Dist. Ct. (so. dist.) N.Y. 1975, Mich. 1976, U.S. Dist. Ct. (ea. dist.) Mich. 1976, U.S. Ct. Appeals (6th cir.) 1981, U.S. Supreme Ct. 1979. Asst. dist. atty. N.Y. County, N.Y.C., 1974-76; assoc. Isackson and Neering, Bay City, Mich., 1976-79; ptnr. Pergande, Shaw and Spector, 1980; equity owner, assoc. Pergande, Shaw and Spector, later Pergande, Shaw, Spector and Wenzloff, 1980-84; judge U.S. Bankruptcy Ct., Bay City and Flint, 1984—, now chief bankruptcy judge. Contbg. editor: Norton Bankruptcy Law and Practice 2nd Edit. With U.S. Army, 1970-71. Mem. Nat. Conf. Bankruptcy Judges (6th cir. gov.), Am. Bankruptcy Inst. Office: US Bankruptcy Ct 111 First St PO Box 911 Bay City MI 48707-0911

SPECTOR, DANIEL EARL, historian, educator; b. Pensacola, Fla., Dec. 19, 1942; s. Joseph and Dorothy Margaret (Givens) S.; m. Esta Gelda Rappaport, Aug. 9, 1964; children: Warren Leigh, Susan Artemis (dec.). BA, George Washington U., 1963; postgrad., U. Fla., 1963-64; MA, U. Tex., 1972, PhD, 1975. Adj. instr. Jacksonville (Ala.) State U., 1975-77; chief skill qualification test br. U.S. Army Mil. Police Sch., Fort McClellan, Ala., 1975-80; supr. edn. specialist U.S. Army Chem. Sch., 1980-82; chief U.S. Army Chem. Sch. Standardization & Analysis Div., 1982-84; dep. dir. U.S. Army Chem. Sch. Directorate of Tng. & Doctrine, 1984-88; adj. prof. U. Ala., Birmingham, 1986—2001; chem. corps historian U.S. Army Chem. Sch., Fort McClellan, 1988-94. Accreditation coord. U.S. Army Chem. Sch., Ft. McClellan, 1984-90; accreditation team chief So. Assn. Colls. and Schs., Atlanta, 1985-90; U.S. Army rep. EURO-NATO nuc., biol. and chem. workgroups, 1984-90. Author: Chemical School Annual Historical Reviews, 1988-90. Mem. Jacksonville Kiwanis, 1981-92. Alumni scholar George Washington U., 1959-63; NDEA fellow U. Fla., 1963-64, NDFL fellow U. Tex. 1972-73. Mem. Middle Eastern Studies Assn., Middle East Inst., Am. Hist. Assn., Soc. Mil. History, Ala. Assn. Historians, MENSA, Temple Beth-El, Scottish Rite, Hiram Lodge, Ala. Master Gardener, Legion of Honor, Chapel of Four Chaplains, Phi Alpha Theta. Democrat. Jewish. Avocations: gardening, fishing, pistol shooting. Home: 1317 7th Ave NE Jacksonville AL 36265-1174 E-mail: spectord@aol.com.

SPECTOR, DAVID M. lawyer; b. Rock Island, Ill., Dec. 20, 1946; s. Louis and Ruth (Vinikour) S.; m. Laraine Fingold, Jan. 15, 1972; children: Rachel, Laurence. BA, Northwestern U., 1968; JD magna cum laude, U. Mich., 1971. Bar: Ill. 1971, U.S. Dist. Ct. (no. dist.) Ill. 1971, U.S. Ct. Appeals (7th cir.) 1977, U.S. Ct. Appeals (4th cir.) 1984, U.S. Dist. Ct. (cen. dist.) Ill. 1984. Clk. Ill. Supreme Ct., Chgo., 1971-72; ptnr., assoc. Isham, Lincoln & Beale, 1972-87; ptnr. Mayer, Brown & Platt, 1987-97, Hopkins & Sutter, Chgo., 1997-2001, Schiff, Hardin & Waite, Chgo., 2001—. Chmn. ABA Nat. Inst. on Ins. Co. Insolvency, Boston, 1986; co-chmn. ABA Nat. Inst. on Internat. Reins.: Collections and Insolvency, N.Y., 1988; chmn. ABA Nat. Inst. on Life Ins. Co. Insolvency, Chgo., 1993; spkr. in field. Editor: Law and Practice of Insurance Company Insolvency, 1986, Law and Practice of Life Insurer Insolvency, 1993; co-editor: Law and Practice of International Reinsurance Collections and Insolvency, 1988; contbr. articles to profl. jours. Mem. ABA (chair Nat. Inst. on Life Insurer Insolvency 1993), Chgo. Bar Assn., Lawyer's Club of Chgo. Office: Schiff Hardin & Waite 6600 Sears Tower Chicago IL 60606 Home: 1418 Lake Shore Dr Chicago IL 60611 E-mail: dspector@schiffhardin.com.

SPECTOR, ELEANOR RUTH, corporation executive; b. N.Y.C., Dec. 2, 1943; d. Sidney and Helen Lebost; m. Mel Alan Spector, Dec. 10, 1966; children: Nancy, Kenneth. BA, Barnard Coll., 1964; postgrad. sch. pub. adminstrn., George Washington U., 1965-67; postgrad sch. edn., Nazareth Coll., 1974. Indsl. investigator N.Y. State Dept. Labor, White Plains, 1964-65; mgmt. intern Navy Dept., Washington, 1965, contract negotiator, 1965-68, contract specialist, 1975-78, contracting officer/br. head, 1978-82, dir. div. cost estimating, 1982-84; dep. asst. sec. def. for procurement, 1984-91; dir. Def. Procurement, 1991-2000; v.p. contracts Lockheed Martin Corp., Bethesda, Md., 2000—. Advisor Nat. Contract Mgmt. Assn., 1984— Recipient Def. Meritoroius Civilian Svc. medal, 1986, 93, 96, Meritorious Svc. Presdl. award, 1989, 94, Disting. Civilian Svc. Presdl. award, 1990, 97, Def. Disting. Civilian Svc. medal, 1991, 94, 2000, Nat. Pub. Svc. award, 1998, Sec. Def. award for Excellence, 1997. Office: Lockheed Martin Corp MP 280 6801 Rockledge Dr Bethesda MD 20817-1877

SPECTOR, GERSHON JERRY, physician, educator, researcher; b. Rovno, Poland, Oct. 20, 1937; came to U.S., 1949; naturalized, 1956; m. Patsy Carol Tanenbaum, Aug. 28, 1965. BA, Johns Hopkins U., 1960; MD cum laude, U. Md., 1964. Intern Beth Israel Hosp., Boston, 1964-65; resident in surgery Sinai Hosp., Balt., 1965-66; resident in otolaryngology Mass. Eye and Ear Infirmary, Boston, 1966-69, Peter Bent Brigham Hosp., Boston, 1968-69; teaching fellow in otolaryngology Harvard U. Med. Sch., 1968-69; assoc. physician Ill. Crippled Children's Svc., Carbondale, 1971; mem. faculty Washington U. Med. Sch., St. Louis, 1971—, assoc. prof. otolaryngology, 1974-76, prof., 1976—; chief dept. otolaryngology St. Louis County Hosp., 1971-77. Mem. staff Washington U. Med. Ctr., Barnes Hosp.; dir. temporal bone bank, 1971-81; guest examiner Am. Bd. Otolaryngology, 1975-77; rsch. cons. neurosci. group, G.D. Searle Pharm. Corp. Mem. editl. bd. Laryngoscope, 1978, editor-in-chief, 1984-94; contbr. articles to med. jours. With U.S. Army, 1969-71. Hancock scholar, 1962. Fellow ACS; mem. AAAS, AMA, Am. Acad. Ophthalmology and Otolaryngology (Honor award 1979), St. Louis Med. Soc., St. Louis County Med. Soc., Am. Coun. Otolarygology, St. Louis Ear, Nose and Throat Club (pres. 1986), So. Med. Assn., Deafness Rsch. Found., Pan. Am. Assn. Otorhinolaryngology and Broncho Esophagology, Am. Soc. Head and Neck Surgery, Soc. Univ. Otolaryngologists, Am. Laryngological, Rhinological and Otological Soc. (Edmund Prince Fowler award 1974), Am. Soc. Cell Biology, Electron Microscopy Soc., N.Y. Acad. Scis., Am. Assn. Anatomists, Am. Acad. Facial Plastic and Reconstructive Surgery, Am. Neuro-Otology Soc., Gesellschaft fur Neurootologie und Aequilibrimoetrie A.V., Barany Soc., Am. Radium Soc., Assn. Acad. Surgery, Am. Fedn. Clin. Oncologic Socs., Am Otological Soc., Acoustical Soc. Am., Soc. for Neurosci., Internat. Skull Base Soc. (founding), Brazilian Skull Base Soc. (hon.), Centurion Club, Alpha Omega Alpha, Psi Chi. Home: 7365 Westmoreland Dr Saint Louis MO 63130-4241 Office: Washington U Med Sch Saint Louis MO 63110 E-mail: spectorg@msnotes.wustl.edu.

SPECTOR, JONATHAN MICHAEL, research psychologist, cognitive scientist; b. Pensacola, Fla. s. Joseph and Dorothy Margaret (Givens) S. (dec.); children: Randolph Conan, Julia May, Samuel Dylan, David Elijah, Miriam Pearl. BS with honors, USAF Acad., 1967; PhD, U. Tex., 1978. Commd. 2d lt. USAF, 1967, advanced through grades to 1st lt., 1968, intelligence officer Philippines, 1967-71, resigned, 1971; systems analyst systems devel. divsn. lab. IBM, Boulder, Colo., 1971-72; instr. philosophy U. Tex.-El Paso C.C., 1972-81; systems analyst Air Combat Maneuvering Instrumentation System Cubic Corp., Holloman AFB, N.Mex., 1981-83; sr. programmer Tower Telescope, Sunspot, 1983-84; prof. computer sci. Jacksonville (Ala.) State U., 1984-91; sr. scientist Instrnl. Design Br., Brooks AFB, Tex., 1991-97; Fulbright rsch. fellow dept. info. sci. U. Bergen, Norway, 1995-96, prof., dir. ednl. info. sci. Norway, 1997-2000; prof., chair instructional design, devel. and edn. Syracuse U., 2000—. Cons. Spector and Assocs., San Antonio, 1988-98; organizer, participant Advanced Rsch. Workshop, NATO, Spain, 1992, Advanced Study Inst., Norway, 1993. Editor: Automating Instructional Design, 1992, The Promise and Potential fo Distance Learning, 1992; editl. bd. Computers in Human Behavior, 1994—; book rev. editor Instrnl. Sci., 1994—; contbr. articles to profl. jours. Vol. Sherut La'am, Kiryat Shemona, Israel, 1971, Kitty Stone Elem. Sch., Jacksonville, 1984-87. Fulbright rsch. grantee U. Bergen, Norway, 1995-96. Mem. Am. Assn. Artificial Intelligence, Am. Edn. Rsch. Assn., Data Processing Mgmt. Assn. (chpt. pres. 1985-87), Assn. Devel. CBI Systems, Assn. Computing Machinery. Achievements include design of Advanced Instructional Design Advisor. Address: U Bergen Dept Info Sci N5020 Bergen Norway also: Syracuse U IDD&E 330 Huntington Syracuse NY 13244 E-mail: spector@syr.edu.

SPECTOR, JUDITH ANN, English educator; b. Klamath Falls, Oreg., Apr. 6, 1945; d. Samuel and Lillian (Hutchinson) S.; m. Sandor P. Vaci, May 14, 1966 (div. 1971); m. Thomas E. Ward, May 30, 1978 (div. 1985); m. John Michael Partridge, Sept. 15, 1989. BA in English magna cum laude, U. Mich., 1967; MA in English, Ind. U., 1975, PhD in English, 1977. Cert. tchr. ESL, Internat. House, London. Tchr. ESL The London Sch. English, 1967-70; assoc. instr. Ind. U., Bloomington, 1974-76; vis. asst. prof. Ind. U./Purdue U., 1977-78, asst. prof., 1978-83, assoc. prof., 1983-97, prof., 1997—. Editor, contbr.: Gender Studies: New Directions in Feminist Criticism, 1986; contbr. articles to profl. jours. Mem. MLA, Nat. Coun. Tchrs. English, Assn. for Humanistic Psychology, Phi Beta Kappa. Avocation: ballroom dance. Office: Ind U/Purdue U 4601 Central Ave Columbus IN 47203-1769 E-mail: jspector@iupui.edu.

SPECTOR, LARRY WAYNE, osteopath; b. Elkins Park, Pa., Sept. 1, 1968; s. Harvey M. and Rochelle M. (Fleishman) S. BA, U. Del., 1990; DO, Phila. Coll. Osteo. Medicine, 1994. Chief intern Grad. Hosp. Phila. Coll. Osteopathic Medicine, 1994-95; resident in internal medicine Med. Ctr. of Del., Newark, 1995-98. St. George's soc. grant, 1991. Mem. AMA (del. resident sect.), Am. Osteo. Assn., Pa. Osteo. Med. Assn. (del.), Delaware Med. Soc. (pres. resident sect.). Avocations: weight lifting, sports, movie watching, reading, sports fan. Home: 1851 Foothill Dr Huntingdon Valley PA 19006-7919

SPECTOR, LOUIS, retired federal judge, lawyer, arbitrator, consultant; b. Niagara Falls, N.Y., Apr. 4, 1918; s. Jacob and Gussie (Yochelson) S.; children: Gale Anne Spector Pasternack, Arthur George, James Aland. Student (N.Y. State scholar), Niagara U., 1936-37; LL.B. with honors, U. Buffalo (later State U. N.Y.), 1940. Bar: N.Y. bar 1940, D.C. bar 1972, U.S. Supreme Ct. bar 1971, U.S. Ct. Claims bar 1968. Asso. firm Saperston, McNaughton & Saperston, Buffalo, 1941-42; asst. chief legal div. U.S. Army C.E., Buffalo Dist., 1942-43; chief sect. claims appeals and litigation U.S. Army C.E. (Great Lakes Div.), Chgo., 1946, chief legal br. and real estate div. Buffalo Dist., 1946-53; exec. dir. Buffalo Port Authority, 1953-54; mem. Bd. Contract Appeals, Washington, 1954-59; chmn. Army panel Armed Services Bd. Contract Appeals, 1959-62, Unified Armed Services Bd. Contract Appeals, 1962-68; trial judge U.S. Ct. Claims, Washington, 1968-82, judge, 1982-85; cons., arbitrator, mediator Falls Church, Va., 1985—. Lectr., speaker, writer public contracts; Congressional appearances, 1953, 66, 69, 77 Contbr. articles to profl. publs. Served with C.E. U.S. Army, 1943-46. Recipient Freshman medal Niagara U., 1936, Sophomore medal, 1937 Fellow Am. Bar Found.; mem. ABA (chmn. sect. pub. contract law 1967-68); Fellow Nat. Contract Mgmt. Assn. (nat. bd. advisers 1967—); mem. ABA (ho. of dels. 1968-70), Fed. Bar Assn. (gen. editor jour. 1960-74, nat. chmn. com. govt. contracts and procurement law 1961-63, Distinguished Service award D.C. chpt. 1974), Lincoln Law Soc. (alumni pres. 1951) Clubs: Cosmos. Home: 6219 Beachway Dr Falls Church VA 22041-1425 *The concept of justice has been a central concern of my life. It is not a unique concern. Daniel Webster described it as "the great interest of man on earth . . . the ligament which holds civilized beings and nations together." And Reinhold Neibuhr reflected that: "Man's capacity for justice makes democracy possible; but man's inclination to injustice makes democracy necessary".*

SPECTOR, MELBOURNE LOUIS, retired foreign service officer; b. Pueblo, Colo., May 7, 1918; s. Joseph E. and Dora (Bernstein) S.; m. Louise Vincent, Nov. 23, 1948; 1 son, Stephen David. BA with honors, U. N.Mex., 1941. Intern U.S. Bur. Indian Affairs, 1941, Nat. Inst. Pub. Affairs, 1941; personnel asst. Office Emergency Mgmt., 1941-42; chief classification div. War Relocation Authority, 1942-43, Hdqrs. USAAF, 1943-45; employment officer UNRRA, 1945-46; pvt. employment, 1946-47; personnel officer Dept. State, 1947-49; detail Econ. Coop. Adminstrn., 1948; dep. dir. personnel Econ. Coop. Adminstrn., Marshall Plan, Paris, 1949-51; dep. dir., acting dir. personnel Econ. Coop. Adminstrn., Mut. Security Adminstrn., FOA, 1951-54; asst., dep. dir. Mission to Mexico, ICA, 1954-57, acting dir., 1957-59; chief C. Am., Mex. and Caribbean div. ICA, 1959-61; dir. Office Personnel Mgmt., AID, 1961-62; exec. dir. Bur. Inter-Am. Affairs, Dept. State, 1962-64; commd. consul gen., sec., 1964; counselor for adminstrv. affairs Am. embassy, New Delhi, India, 1964-66; seminarian Sr. Seminar Fgn. Policy, Dept. State, 1966-67; exec. dir. U.S.-Mex. Commn. for Border Devel. and Friendship, 1967-69, Am. Revolution Bicentennial Commn., 1969-71; mem. mgmt., policy and coordination staffs Dept. State, 1971-73; ret., 1973; cons., 1973—. Mem. Fgn. Svc. Grievance Bd., 1976-77; advisor Peace Corps Dir., 1979-80; exec. dir. Am. Consortium for Internat. Pub. Adminstrn., 1980-84, 93-94, dir. Marshall Plan Oral History Project, 1987-97. Mem. Cosmos Club, Am. Soc. Pub. Adminstrn., Pi Kappa Alpha, Phi Kappa Phi. Home: 6414 Bannockburn Dr Bethesda MD 20817-5430

SPECTOR, MICHAEL JOSEPH, agribusiness executive; b. N.Y.C., Feb. 13, 1947; s. Martin Wilson and Dorothy (Miller) S.; m. Margaret Dickson, Sept. 14, 1977. BS in Chemistry, Washington and Lee U., 1968. Rsch. chemist Am. Viscose, Phila., 1968-69; pres. MJS Entertainment Corp., Miami, Fla., 1970-84; also MJS Internat., Inc.; ptnr. Old Town Key West Devel. Ltd., Fla., 1977—. Pres. MJS Entertainment of Can., Inc., Toronto, Canada, Margo Farms, MJS Prodsn., Inc., N.Y.C.; chmn., CEO Margo Caribe, Inc., Dorado, PR, 1981—, bd. dir.; pres. Costa Del Norte Devel., Inc., Dorado, 1998—; bd. dir. Goodwill Industries So. Fla., v.p. fin., 1980; bd. dir. Plz. Bank of Miami; hon. Consul Belgium in P.R., U.S. V.I., 2000, Turks & Caicos Islands, West Indies; dir. Consular Corp. P.R., 2002. Internat. judge The Floralies Exhbn., Gent, Belgium, 2000. With AUS, 1969-70. Robert E. Lee rsch. grantee Washington and Lee U., 1967-68; named Agri-bus. Exec. of Yr., Govt. of P.R., 1999. Mem. Nat. Assn. Record Merchandisers (dir. Nova divsn., chmn. one-stop distbn. com. 1982-83), Country Music Assn., Dorado Beach Golf and Tennis Club, Bankers Club P.R., Ocean Reef Club (Key Largo, Fla.), Grove Isle Club (Coconut Grove, Fla.). Achievements include patent for synthetic stretching process. Home: PO Box 706 Dorado PR 00646-0706

SPECTOR, MICHAEL LEW, cardiothoracic surgeon; b. Cleve., Nov. 10, 1949; s. Samuel and Lillian (Hutchinson) S.; m. Kathryn Ann Melgun, June 3, 1978; children: Nicole, Samantha, Joshua. BS, U. Mich., 1972; MD, Case Western Reserve U., 1976. Diplomate Am. Bd. Surgery, Am. Bd. Thoracic Surgery. Intern Yale New Haven (Conn.) Hosp., 1976-77; resident in gen. surgery U. Hosp. of Cleve., 1977-81, resident in thoracic surgery, 1981-83; fellow pediatric cardiovascular surgery The Hosp. for Sick Children, Toronto, Ontario, Can., 1983-84; assoc. prof. Case Western Reserve U., Cleve., 1984—. Cardiac stds. subcom. Bur. for Children with Med. Handicaps, Columbus, 1985—. Mem. Acad. of Medicine of Cleve. (chmn. peer rev. med. surg. com. 1991—, bd. dirs. 1994—). Office: Childrens Hosp Med Ctr Akron One Perkins Sq Akron OH 44308 E-mail: mspector@chmca.org

SPECTOR, PHILLIP LOUIS, lawyer; b. L.A., July 15, 1950; s. Everett L. Spector and Rebecca (Horn) Newman; m. Carole Sue Lebbin, May 11, 1980; children: Adam, David. Student, U. Birmingham, Eng., 1970-71; BA with highest honors, U. Calif., Santa Barbara, 1972; M in Pub. Policy, JD magna cum laude, Harvard U., 1976. Bar: Calif. 1976, D.C. 1978, U.S. Ct. Appeals (D.C. cir.) 1983, U.S. Supreme Ct. 1983, U.S. Dist. Ct. D.C. 1985. Law clk. U.S. Ct. Appeals (2d cir.), Brattleboro, Vt., 1976-77; law clk. to U.S. Supreme Ct., Washington, 1977-78; assoc. asst. to Pres. U.S., 1978-80; assoc. Verner, Liipfert, Bernhard & McPherson, 1980-83; ptnr. Goldberg & Spector, 1983-92, Paul, Weiss, Rifkind, Wharton & Garrison, Washington, 1992-98; mng. ptnr., mem. mgmt. com., 1998—. Cons. U.S. exec. br. Close-Up Found., Alexandria, Va., 1980—. Co-author: Communications Law and Practice, 1995, Communications and Technology Alliances: Business and Legal Issues, 1996; mem. bd. editors Multimedia & Internet Strategist; contbr. articles to profl. jours. Mem. Coun. on Fgn. Rels., N.Y.C., 1980-85; moot ct. judge Nat. Assn. Attys. Gen., Washington, 1987—; adviser Dem. caucus U.S. Ho. Reps., Washington, 1981-83; speechwriter, podium prodr. Dem. Nat. Convs., N.Y.C., 1980, Phila., 1982, San Francisco, 1984, Atlanta, 1988, N.Y.C., 1992, Chgo., 1996, L.A., 2000. Recipient Disting. Achievement in Pub. Svc. Medal U. Calif., Santa Barbara, 1981, Close-Up Found. awards Via Satellite Mag., Vol. Recognition award Nat. Assn. Attys. Gen., 1993; named Leading Satellite Specialist in Washington, European Counsel, 2000. Mem. ABA (former chair internat. comm. law com.), Fed. Communications Bar Assn., Bethesda Country Club, Wintergreen Ptnrs., Phi Beta Kappa. Jewish. Office: Paul Weiss Rifkind Wharton & Garrison 1615 L St NW Ste 1300 Washington DC 20036-5694 E-mail: pspector@paulweiss.com.

SPECTOR, ROBERT DONALD, language professional, educator; b. N.Y.C., Sept. 21, 1922; s. Morris and Helen (Spiegel) S.; m. Eleanor Helen Luskin, Aug. 19, 1945; children: Stephen Brett, Eric Charles. BA, L.I. U., 1948, DHL, 1994; MA, NYU, 1949; PhD, Columbia U., 1962. Instr. L.I. U., Bklyn., 1948-59, asst. prof., 1959-62, asso. prof., 1962-65, prof. English, 1965-94, chmn. senate, 1966-67, 69-70, chmn. dept., 1970-75, dir. humanities and comm. arts, 1975-84, coord. div. of humanities and div. of comms. and performing arts, 1990—, dir. humanities, 1984-90, prof. emeritus, 1993—. Editor, cons. Johnson Reprint Corp., 1967-84 Author: English Literary Periodicals, 1966, Tobias George Smollett, 1968, updated edit., 1989, Pär Lagerkvist, 1973, Arthur Murphy, 1979, Tobias Smollett: A Reference Guide, 1980, The English Gothic, 1983, Backgrounds to Restoration and Eighteenth-Century English Literature, 1989, Political Controversy, 1992, Smollett's Women, 1994, Samuel Johnson and the Essay, 1997, Love Poems & Others, 1998, (poetry) Nature's Bounty in Brooklyn, 2000; co-author: (poetry) Mélange à Deux, 2000; editor: Essays on the Eighteenth Century Novel, 1965, Great British Short Novels, 1970, 9 other vols. English and Am. lit., revs. and articles, poetry, fiction. Trustee L.I. U., 1969-70; chmn. George Polk Award Com., 1977—. Served with USCGR, 1942-46. Recipient L.I. U. Trustee award for scholarly achievement, 1978, Tristram Walker Metcalfe Alumnus of Year, 1981; Swedish Govt. travel and research grantee, 1966; fellow Huntington Library, 1974; fellow Folger Library, 1975; fellow Newberry Library, 1976 Mem. MLA, Am.-Scandinavian Found. (publs. com. 1962-84), P.E.N., Acad. Am. Poets. Home: 1761 E 26th St Brooklyn NY 11229-2405

SPEDICK, MICHAEL JOHN, ophthalmologist; b. Trenton, N.J., Mar. 23, 1952; s. Michael Clifton and Marcella Verna (Ward) S.; m. Deborah Jane Camiscoli, July 10, 1977; children: Jennifer, Laura, Andrew, James. BS, Seton Hall U., 1974; MD, Rutgers U., 1978. Diplomate Nat. Bd. MEd. Examiners, Am. Bd. Internal Medicine, Am. Bd. Ophthalmology. Resident Rutgers Affiliated Hosps., 1978-81, Cleve. Clinic Found., 1982-85; fellow in pediat. ophthalmology Children's Hosp. Nat. Med. Ctr., Washington, 1985-86; ophthalmologist pvt. practice, Long Branch, N.J., 1986-88, Ocean Eye Inst., Toms River, 1987—. Clin. asst. prof. Rutgers U., Piscataway, N.J., 1993—, Hahnemann U., Phila., 1995—. Fellow: ACS, Am. Acad. Ophthalmology; mem.: AMA (Physicians award 1997, 2000), Ocean County Med. Soc. (trustee 1993—95, treas. 1995—97, sec. 1997—99, 2d v.p. 1999—2001, 1st v.p. 2001—, del. 1993—), Med. Soc. N.J. (trustee 1997—2000), Am. Assn. Pediat. Ophthalmology and Strabismus. Avocations: guitar, photography. Office: 601 Rte 37 W Toms River NJ 08755-8050

SPEE, JAMES CURTIS, management consultant, educator; b. Renton, WA, May 10, 1957; s. Ricarda Spee, Karl Jacob Spee; m. Paige Schindler. MBA, Claremont Grad. U., 1985, PhD, 1993; BS Engring. and Letters, Calvin Coll., Grand Rapids Mich., 1978; BSME, U. Wash., Seattle, 1980. Project coord. Christian Ref. World Relief Com., Bogra, Bangladesh, 1980—83; engr. Boeing Comml. Airplane Co., Seattle, 1984; grad. asst. Claremont Grad. U., Claremont, Calif., 1984—93; dir. devel. Union Sta. Found., Pasadena, 1986—86; exec. dir. Boys and Girls Club of Redlands, 1992—93; adj. faculty Pepperdine U., Culver City , 1994—95; assoc. prof. U. Redlands, 1995—. Presenter in field. Mem.: N.Am. Case Res. Assn. (western regional rep. 2002—), We. Case Writers Assn. (pres. 2001—02, pres. 2001—02). Avocation: travel, restoring antique airplanes, film. Office: Univ Redlands Sch Busi 1200 E Colton Ave Redlands CA 92374-3720 Office Fax: 909-335-5125.

SPEECE, HERBERT ELVIN, mathematician, educator; b. Meadowlands, Minn., Oct. 29, 1914; s. Ray M. and Grace Eva Speece; m. Ruth Ernestine Lowrance, July 28, 1945; children: Ray Elvin, Deborah Grace Speece Sykes. BA, York (Nebr.) Coll., 1938; MA, Tex. Christian U., 1943; M in Engring. Math., N.C.State U.; PhD, U. N.C., Chapel Hill. Sci. tchr. Sonora (Tex.) Pub. Sch., 1939—40; instr. in navigation USAF, Randolph Field, Tex., 1942—44; sci. tchr. Trinity H.S., Kerrville, 1945—47; instr. in physics Trinity U., San Antonio, 1947; prof. math. N.C. State U., Raleigh, 1947—90. Dir. earth sci. project N.C. Acad. Sci. Staff sgt/ USAF, 1942—45. Recipient Bond award, E. Carolina U., 1972, Svc. award, N.C. Coun. Math. Tchrs., 1979; grantee, NSF for engring. concepts curriculum project N.C. State U. Mem.: N.C. Coun. Tchrs. of Math. (Rankin award 1960), N.C. Acad. Sci. (pres. 1970—71), Masonic Lodge (lifetime instr. 1941—). Avocations: golf, reading, travel. Home: 112 Springmoor Dr Raleigh NC 27615-4300

SPEECE, KAREN A. See MARKS, KAREN ANNETTE SPEECE

SPEECE, RICHARD EUGENE, civil engineer, educator; b. Marion, Ohio, Aug. 23, 1933; s. Irvin Ward S. and Desta May (Speece); m. Jean Margaret Edscorn, Nov. 15, 1969; children: Eric Jordan, Lincoln Dana. BCE, Fenn. Coll., 1956; M of Engring., Yale U., 1958; PhD, MIT, 1961. Assoc. prof. civil engring. U. Ill., Urbana, 1961-65; prof. N.Mex. State U., 1965-70, U. Tex., Austin, 1970-74; Betz chair prof. environ. engring. Drexel U., Phila., 1974-88; Centennial prof. Vanderbilt U., Nashville, 1988—. Vis. scholar Cambridge (Eng.) U., 1994; cons. to govt., industry. Contbr. articles to profl. jours.; patentee in field. Recipient hon. mention for best paper Trans. Am. Fisheries Soc., 1973 Mem. Assn. Environ. Engring. Profs. (Disting. Faculty award 1970, disting. lectr. 1978, trustee 1981-83, Engring. Sci. award 1982), ASCE (J. James Cross medal 1983), Am. Soc. Microbiologists, Water Environ. Fedn. (Harrison Prescott Eddy medal 1966), U.S. ANC (Founder's award 1991), Internat. Assn. on Water Pollution Rsch. and Control. Office: Vanderbilt U Dept Civil Engring Nashville TN 37235

SPEED, LESLIE BOKEE, lawyer; b. Balt., Jan. 19, 1949; d. William George and Jean Alice (LaVine) Speed. BA, U. Colo., 1972; JD, U. Denver, 1977. Bar: Colo. 1978. Assoc. Holland and Hart, Denver, 1978-84, ptnr., 1984-93; dir., shareholder Parcel Mauro P.C., 1993-98; ptnr. Gallagher, Evelius & Jones, Balt., 1998—. Author: Corporate Powers, 1990; gen. editor U. Denver Law Rev., 1977. Bd. dirs. Denver Broncos Charities Fund, 1993-98, Colo. Lawyers Health Program, 1994-98, Bryn Mawr Sch. Alumnae Assn., 1999—; mem., sec. Colo. state adv. com. to U.S. Commn. on Civil Rights, Denver, 1974-77; sec. Denver Broncos Youth Found., 1984-98. Mem. ABA, Colo. Bar Assn. (co-chmn. gaming, entertainment and sports law com. 1994-95), Denver Bar Assn., Sports Lawyers Assn. (bd. dirs. 1988—), Order of St. Ives. Democrat. Episcopalian. Home: 2901 Boston St Apt 608 Baltimore MD 21224-4891 Office: Gallagher Evelius & Jones 218 N Charles St Ste 400 Baltimore MD 21201-4033

SPEED, LYNN ELIZABETH, nurse practitioner; b. Houston, Mar. 23, 1954; d. Thomas R. and Kathryn M. Schmidt; m. David L. Speed, Sept. 11, 1982; children: Barbara Kay, William David. BSN, U. Tex., Houston, 1977; M Nursing, U. Wash., 1983; cert. nurse practitioner, U. Colo., Denver, 1987. RN, N. Mex.; cert. family nurse practitioner. Nurse practitioner Santa Ana Family Health Ctr., Carlsbad, N.Mex., 1998—. Contbr. articles to nursing jours. Mem. ANA (cert. adult nurse practitioner). Home: 1618 Mission Ave Carlsbad NM 88220-9644 Office: Santa Ana Family Health Ctr 110 Halagueno #5 Carlsbad NM 88220

SPEER, JACK ATKESON, publisher; b. Wichita, Kans., July 3, 1941; s. Jack Shelley and Shannon C. Speer; m. Judith Ann Fuller, Aug. 5,1967; children: Martin Fuller, Elizabeth Speer Goodwin. BS in Bus. Adminstrn., Kansas. State U., 1966, ML, 1967; postgrad., U. Mo., 1967, U. So. Calif., 1969; IBM Pres.'s Class, Harvard U., 1980. Mem. advt., editorial, mech. staffs Wichita Eagle-Beacon, 1954-64; editorial asst. Emporia (Kans.) Gazette, 1964-65; supr. libr. data processing Kans. State U., Emporia, 1965-67, mgr. data processing ctr. Manhattan, 1967-69; mgr. systems and programming John Wiley Inc.-Becker & Hayes Inc., Bethesda, Md., 1969-72; dir. libr. info. systems Informatics Inc. Info. Systems Group, Rockville, 1972-77; v.p. ops. Arcata Real Estate Data Inc., Miami, Fla., 1977-79; mgr. electronic info. systems Arcata Publs. Group, Norwalk, Conn., 1979-83; v.p. mktg./sales, data imaging group The William Byrd Press, Richmond, Va., 1983-84; sr. v.p. ops. NewsBank Inc., New Canaan, Conn., 1984-85; pres., pub. Buckmaster Pub., Mineral, Va., 1986—. Mem. faculty Cath. U. Am. Libr. Sch., Kans. State U. Libr. Sch.; customer adv. coun. U.S. Postal Svc., 1996—. Author: Amateur Radio Call Directory, 1982—, Buckmaster's Ann. Stockholder Reports, 1986—, Front-Page-News (CD-ROM and Internet), 1989, HamCall (CD-ROM and Internet), 1988—; compiler Libraries and Automation: A Bibliography, 1967, The Living Bible Concordance, 1972. Trustee Jefferson-Madison Regional Libr., 1990-91; commr. Louisa County Planning Commn.; vice chmn. Louisa County Libr. Found. Mem. ALA, NRA, Am. Radio Relay League, Nat. Info. Standards Orgn. (CD-ROM com), D.C. Libr. Assn. (pres.), Rotary, Sigma Tau Gamma. Office: Buckmaster Pub 6196 Jefferson Hwy Mineral VA 23117-3425 E-mail: speerj@buck.com.

SPEER, JOHN ELMER, paralegal, reporter, counselor; b. Conrad, Mont., Mar. 19, 1956; s. Elmer Constant and Mildred Saphronia (LaBelle) S.; m. Sharron D. Knotts, May 23, 1982 (div. Mar. 1986); 1 child, Jeremy Keith; 1 foster child, Casey; m. Adah C. Corbett, March 10, 2000; stepchildren: Jody, Jay, Jill, Jessica. Paralegal assoc., Coll. of Great Falls, Mont., 1994; BS in paralegal studies, U. of Great Falls, Mont., 1999. Bar: Mont. 1996; cert. scuba diver. Farmer, Valier, Mont., 1956-73; janitor Shelby (Mont.) pub. schs., 1974-75; freelance news reporter Sta. KSEN, Shelby, 1980—, various TV stas., newspapers, Great Falls, 1980-90; office cleaner Parkdale Housing Authority, 1990-95; freelance paralegal, 1993—; law clk., paralegal Mont. State Dist. Judge Thomas McKittrick, 1993. Rschr. line-up identification appeal binder to U.S. Supreme Ct., 1993; trial assistance atty. Chas. Joslyn, spring 1996. Contbr. victim-witness assistance program operating manual, 1992. Counselor and adv. Victim-Witness Assistance Svcs., Great Falls, 1991-93. Mem. Mont. Big Sky Paralegal Assn., Am. Counseling Assn., Brain Injury Assn. of Mont. (chpt. v.p. 1997). Jehovah'S Witness. Avocations: hiking, fishing, cooking, travel, swimming. Address: PO Box 206 Great Falls MT 59403-0206

SPEER, JOHN KIRBY, judge; b. Glen Ridge, N.J., Mar. 25, 1929; s. John Kirby and Grace Stillwell (Holihan) S.; m. Deborah Doe, Nov. 28, 1959; children: John Kirby III, Philip MacKinnon. BA cum laude, Harvard U., 1951; MA, U. Va., 1953; LLB, Boston U., 1956. Bar: Mass. 1956, N.Y. 1988. Pvt. practice, Boston, 1956-57, 60-62; staff atty. Boston Legal Aid Soc., 1957-59; assoc. Donovan, Leisure, Newton & Irvine, N.Y.C., 1959; atty. Immigration & Naturalization Svc., 1962-80; acting asst. U.S. atty., 1969-70; immigration judge Dept. Justice, 1978-99. Alt. mem. Bd. Immigration Appeals, Washington, 1989; cons. to Rep. Frelinghuysen, 1999—. Contbr. articles to profl. jours. Mem. spl. events com. Am. Revolution Bicentennial Com., Morris County, N.J., 1973-74, bd. of ethics, 1998—; staff mem. Hands Across Am., Princeton, N.J., 1986. Mem. Nantucket Yacht Club, Morristown Club, Wharf Rat Club, Pacific Club, Sankaty Head Golf Club, Morristown Field Club. Republican. Avocations: golf, tennis. Home: 23 Bennington Rd Morristown NJ 07960-6128

SPEER, NANCY GIROUARD, health care administrator; b. Mankato, Minn., Sept. 14, 1941; d. Jared and Katherine (Schmitt) How; m. Robert L. Girouard, Aug. 29, 1964 (dec. Mar. 1983); children: Robert James Girouard, Mark Jared Girouard; m. David J. Speer, Dec. 21, 1985 (dec. Aug. 1999). BA, Wellesley Coll., 1963; MA in Tchg., Wesleyan U., 1965; cert. mgmt., Smith Coll., 1985. Tchr. secondary sch. Bunnell H.S., Stratford, Conn., 1964-65; tchr., class advisor Lincoln Sch., Providence, 1965-69; substitute tchr. Mankato, 1972-74; pub. info. dir. City of Mankato, 1974-78; univ. editor, dir. pub. affairs forum Mankato State U., 1978-79; comms. mgr. Humphrey Inst., U. Minn., Mpls., 1980-83, dir. external rels., 1983-87, dir. devel. and external rels., 1987-95; dir. devel. Breck Sch., 1996-2000; v.p. Abbott Northwestern Hosp., 2000—02, Planned Parenthood of Minn. and S.D., 2002—. Mem. steering com. Minn. Meeting, Mpls., 1990-96. Contbr. articles to mags. and periodicals; photographer for publs. and newspapers. Bd. dirs. Minn. Newspaper Found., St. Paul, 1985-91, chairperson, 1990-91, bd. dirs., vice-chairperson Cabrini House, Mpls., 1993-97; bd. dirs., sec. Minn. Ctr. for Book Arts, Mpls., 1990-97; bd. dirs. Minn. Landmark Ctr., St. Paul, 1994-2000; dir. Minn. Women's Campaign Fund, Mpls., 1994-2000, co-pres. bd., 1997; bd. dirs. Loft Lit. Ctr., 2000—; vice chair Metropolitan Airport Commn., 1999—, v. chmn. 2001—; mem. Leadership Mpls., Mpls. C. of C., 1982. Bush Leader fellow, 1985-87. Avocations: literature, nature, books.

SPEER, RICHARD JOHN, security consultant; b. Oxnard, Calif., Aug. 21, 1958; s. Richard McCord Speer and Betty Jean Wilson. Grad. H.S., Las Vegas, Nev. Enlisted U.S. Army, 1976, advanced through grades to sgt. first class, infantryman 82nd Airborne Divsn. N.C., 1976-81, infantry squad leader, 1981-87, infantry squad leader 4th Infantry Divsn. Ft. Carson, Colo., 1987-88, heavy weapons specialist Spl. Forces Ft. Bragg, 1988-94, project mgr. spl. projects, 1995-98, ret., 1998; ops. support mgr., nuclear security cons. Burns Internat. Security, Parsippany, N.J., 1998—. Life mem. Rep. Nat. Com., Washington, 1994—. Decorated Army Commendation medal 3rd award U.S. Army, 1984, Meritorious Svcs. medals U.S. Army, 1991, 96, 98. Mem. Heritage Found., N.Am. Hunting Club (life). Avocation: amateur philatelist.

SPEERS, ROLAND ROOT, II, lawyer; b. Jacksonville, Fla., Oct. 8, 1933; s. Roland Root and Alice (Calkins) S.; m. Florence Briscoe, Dec. 18, 1954; children: Kirsten, Guy, Gina Marie. BA cum laude, UCLA, 1955, JD, 1958. Bar: Calif. 1958, D.C. 1978. Dep. commr. corps. Calif. Dept. Corps., Los Angeles, 1958-59; sec., gen. counsel Suburban Cos., Pomona, Calif., 1959-64; sec. Amcord, Inc., Los Angeles, 1964-66, asst. to pres., 1968, v.p. corp. devel., 1969, v.p., gen. counsel Calif., 1970, sr. v.p., 1971, exec. v.p., 1972-75, pres., 1975-94; ptnr. Speers, Dana, Teal Balfour & MacDonald, Costa Mesa, Calif., 1977-97. Dir. Logicon, Inc., Torrance, Calif., Twelve Eleven Press, Newport Beach, Calif. Trustee Pitzer Coll., Pomona, 1975-80; bd. councillors Center Pub. Affairs U. So. Calif., 1976-81; bd. dirs. Newport Harbor Art Mus., 1977-82; sr. warden St. James Episcopal Ch., 1993. Mem. D.C. Bar Assn., State Bar Assn. Calif., UCLA Alumni Assn., UCLA Law Sch. Alumni Assn., Phi Alpha Delta. Clubs: Big Canyon Country (Newport Beach).

SPEICHER, CARL EUGENE, pathologist; b. Carbondale, Pa., Mar. 21, 1933; s. William Joseph and Elizabeth Marcella (Connolly) S.; m. Mary Louise Walsh, June 21, 1958; children: Carl E. Jr., Gregory, Erik. BS in Biology, King's Coll., 1954; MD, U. Pa., 1958; primary course in aeroship medicine, Sch. of Aerospace Medicine, Brooks AFB, Tex., 1969. Diplomate Am. Bd. Pathology. Intern U. Pa. Hosp., Phila., 1958-59, resident, 1959-63; chief lab. svcs. USAF Hosp., London, Eng., 1963-66, USAF Med. Ctr. Wright Patterson, Dayton, Ohio, 1966-70; dir. clin. labs. and chmn. dept. pathology Wilford Hall USAF Med. Ctr., San Antonio, 1971-77; prof. dept. pathology Ohio State U., Columbus, 1977—2000, vice chair dept. pathology, 1992—2000, prof. emeritus dept. pathology, 2000—; dir. clin. svcs. Ohio State U. Med. Ctr., 1977—2000; dir. clin. lab. Stoneridge Med. Ctr., Ohio State U., 2000—. Co-author: Choosing Effective Laboratory Tests, 1983; author: (book) The Right Test, 1990, 3d edit., 1998. Col. USAF, 1963-77. Decorated Legion of Merit, 1977, USAF; fellowship in med. chemistry SUNY, Syracuse, 1970-71. Mem. AMA (Physicians Recognition award), Ohio Soc. Pathologists, Ctrl. Ohio Soc. Pathologists, Royal Soc. of Medicine (Eng.), Coll. of Am. Pathologists, Am. Soc. Clin. Pathologists, Alpha Omega Alpha. Office: Ohio State U Med Ctr 410 W 10th Ave Columbus OH 43210-1228

SPEIDEL, DAVID HAROLD, geology educator; b. Pottsville, Pa., Aug. 10, 1938; s. Harold O. and Edith M. (Rosser) S.; m. Margaret Helen Liebrecht, Sept. 8, 1962. BS, Franklin and Marshall Coll., Lancaster, Pa., 1960; PhD, Pa. State U., 1964. Rsch. assoc. Pa. State U., 1964-66; asst. prof. to prof. dept. geology Queens Coll., CUNY, Flushing, 1966—, chmn. dept., 1980-88, dean faculty sci., 1970-79, chmn. faculty senate, 1992-96, provost, sr. v.p. acad. affairs, 1998-2000. Maj. projects sect. head, earth scis. NSF, 1988-89; vis. scholar Sr. Specialists div. Congl. Rsch. Svc., Washington, 1977-78 Author: (with A.F. Agnew) Natural Geochemistry of Our Environment; editor (with L. Ruedisili and A.F. Agnew) Perspectives on Water: Uses and Abuses; contbr. articles to profl. jours. Fellow Geol. Soc. Am.; mem. AAAS, Am. Ceramic Soc., Am. Geophys. Union, Am. Inst. Profl. Geologists, Nat. Hazards Soc., Soc. Environ. Geochemistry and Health, Sigma Xi. Office: Queens Coll Sch Earth & Environ Scis Flushing NY 11367 E-mail: david_speidel@qc.edu.

SPEIDEL, JOHN JOSEPH, physician, foundation officer; b. Iowa City, Sept. 17, 1937; s. Thomas Dennis and Edna (Warweg) S.; divorced; 1 child, Sabrina Brett; m. Melissa Jane Webster, Oct. 7, 2001. AB cum laude, Harvard U., 1959, MD, 1963, M.P.H., 1965. Diplomate: Nat. Bd. Med. Examiners, Am. Bd. Preventive Medicine. Intern St. Luke's Hosp., N.Y.C., 1963-64; resident N.Y.C. Dept. Health, 1965-67, dep. dir. maternal and infant care project, 1966-67; chief research div. Office of Population, AID, Dept. State, Washington, 1969-76; assoc. dir. Office of Population, 1977, dep. dir., acting dir. office, 1978-83; v.p. Population Action Internat. (formerly Population Crisis Com.), 1983-87, pres., 1987-95; program officer for population Hewlett Found., 1995—2001, program dir. for population, 2002—. Lectr. population and family planning Georgetown U., 1973-75 Contbr. articles to profl. jours.; Editor: (with others) Female Sterilization, 1971, Hysteroscopic Sterilization, 1974, Intrauterine Devices, 1974, Control of Male Fertility, 1975, Advances in Female Sterilization Technology, 1976, Risks, Benefits and Controversies in Fertility Control, 1978, Reversal of Sterilization, 1978, Pregnancy Termination, 1979, Vaginal Contraception, 1979. Served to maj. U.S. Army, 1967-69. Recipient Meritorious Unit citation Office of Population, 1969-71, Arthur S. Flemming award Washington Downtown Jaycees, 1972 Mem. Am. Pub. Health Assn. (Carl S. Shultz award 1982), Population Assn. Am. Office: William & Flora Hewlett Found 525 Middlefield Rd Ste 200 Menlo Park CA 94025-3448

SPEIER, JOHN LEO, JR. retired chemist; b. Chgo., Sept. 29, 1918; s. John L. and Mary Jane (Dickman) S.; m. A. Louise Kimmel, Oct. 21, 1944; children: Susan, Genevieve, Dorothy, Margaret, John L. III, Thomas J. B.Sc., St. Benedict's Coll., 1941; M.Sc., U. Fla., 1943; PhD, U. Pitts., 1947. Naval Stores research fellow U. Fla., 1941-43; research fellow Mellon Inst., Pitts., 1943, sr. fellow, 1947-56; mgr. organic research Dow Corning Corp., Midland, Mich., 1956-69, scientist in corp. research, 1969-75, sr. scientist in corp. research, 1975-93; retired, 1994. Contbr. numerous articles to profl. jours., 1950—; holder 100 patents prodn. organosilicon compounds and allied products. Named Indsl. Research and Devel. Scientist of Yr. Indsl. Research/Devel. mag., 1978 Mem. AAAS, Am. Chem. Soc. (Frederick Stanley Kipping award 1990), Sigma Xi.

SPEIER, PETER MICHAEL, mathematics educator; b. Bklyn., Nov. 4, 1946; s. Fred A. and Herta (Katz) S.; m. Patricia Carol Johnson, Nov. 27, 1976. BS, SUNY, Cortland, 1968; MEd, U. Ga., 1971; MS, Adelphi U., 1975. Dept. chair J. L. Mann High Sch., Greenville, S.C., 1971-72; tchr. Long Beach (N.Y.) Jr. High Sch., 1972-75; tchr., coord. Largo High Sch., Upper Marlboro, Md., 1975-89; tchr. Oxon Hill (Md.) High Sch., 1989-93; prof. Prince George's C.C., 1993—. Tchr. Cmty. Based Classroom, Lanham, Md., 1990; adj. prof. Prince George's C.C., Largo, Md., 1976-93. With U.S. Army, 1968-70, Vietnam. N.Y. State Regents scholar SUNY, 1964-68. Mem. NEA, VFW, DAV, Nat. Coun. Tchrs. Math., Am. Math. Assn., Two Yr. Colls., Md. Tchrs. Assn., Md. Coun. Tchrs. Math. Avocation: travel. Home: 6613 Pine Grove Dr Suitland MD 20746-3527 E-mail: speierpm@pg.cc.md.us.

SPEIGHTS, MICHAEL DAVID, newsletter editor; b. Owensboro, Ky., May 12, 1951; s. Marion Thomas and Joy Lee (Griffin) S. BA with honors, Northeastern U., 1973. Researcher, reporter Congl. Quar., Washington, 1974-77; staff asst. Senator Richard Schweiker, 1977; anchor, reporter Sta. WILM, Wilmington, Del., 1979-80; reporter, producer Sta. WUHY-FM, Phila., 1980-81, Sta. WABE-FM, Atlanta, 1982-83; editor Padres' Trail, St. Michaels, Ariz., 1984-88; campaign assoc. Ketchum, Inc., Pitts., 1988-89; editor Report on Literacy Programs Bus. Pubs., Inc., Silver Spring, Md., 1989—, editor Am. Marketplace and U.S. Census Report, 1989-96, editor Report on Edn. of the Disadvantaged, 1997-2000; editor HazMat Transport News, 2000—. Freelance reporter, producer Nat. Pub. Radio, 1980-83. Past assoc. editor Francisco. Vol. Navajo Nation Spl. Olympics, St. Michaels, 1986, Franciscan

Covenant Program, Ft. Defiance, Ariz., 1984-85. Mem. United Ch. Christ. Avocations: reading, travel. Home: 5805 Edson Ln Apt T2 Rockville MD 20852-2922 Office: Bus Pubs Inc 8737 Colesville Rd Ste 1100 Silver Spring MD 20910-3958

SPEILLER-MORRIS, JOYCE, English educator; b. Utica, N.Y., Nov. 11, 1945; d. Arnold Leonard Speiller and Sybil (Sall) McAdam; m. Joseph Raymond Morris, Mar. 17, 1984. BS, Syracuse U., 1968; MA, Columbia U., 1969. Cert. tchr., N.Y., Fla. Chmn. upper sch. social studies dept., tchr. grade 6 social studies and English Cathedral Heights Elem. Sch., N.Y.C., 1969-74; adj. prof. Broward Community Coll., Hollywood, Davie and Pompano, Fla., 1982-90, St. Thomas U., Miami, 1982-84, 90, 99, Miami-Dade Community Coll., 1983, Nova Southeastern U., Miami and Davie, 1983-84; semester lectr. U. Miami, Coral Gables, 1985-98, master tchr., 1990, 92, 94, faculty fellow, 1990-94, mem. curriculum devel., 1991-94. Contbr. presentation to Fla. Coll. English Assn., 1991-92, Wyo. Conf. English, 1991; guest spkr. in field of svc.-learning, 1992-94, 97; cons. svc.-learning curriculum design, 1994; acad. advisor U. Miami, 1994, 95, 96; U. Miami rep. to Ctrl. and South Fla. Higher Edn. Diversity Coalition, 1998; faculty acad. coach football, UCLA. Reviewer textbook McGraw Hill, 1993; contbr. instr.'s manual of textbook, 1994; contbr. poetry to revs., articles to profl. jours. Founder, dir. Meet the Author program, Coral Gables, 1989-98. Recipient V.P. award U. Miami, 1992, cert. recognition West Palm Beach, Fla., TV sta., 1992; grantee Fla. Office for Campus Vols., 1992, Dade Community Found., 1992. Mem. MLA, Nat. Soc. Experiential Edn., Fla. Coll. English Assn., Coll. English Assn., Nat. Coun. Tchrs. English, Fla. Chpt. of Tchrs. of English to Spkrs. of Other Langs. (spkr. conf. 1992), Conf. on Coll. Composition and Comm., Am. Correctional Assn., Phi Delta Kappa, Phi Lambda Theta. Avocations: reading, community svc. Home: PO Box 292104 Davie FL 33329-2104

SPEIR, BETTY SMITH, consultant, retired foundation administrator; b. Mar. 3, 1928; d. William Jasper and Carolyn (Pollock) Smith; m. David Ordway Speir, June 10, 1950; children: Carolyn G. Speir Brown, Christine St. Clair Speir Cameron. AB, Duke U., 1949; MA, East Carolina U., 1963. Tchr. English Farmville (NC) H.S., 1949—50, Bain H.S., Charlotte, 1950—51, Bethel H.S., 1961—70; cotton buyer Bethel Mfg. Co., NC, 1958—60; guidance counselor North Pitt H.S., Bethel, 1970—86; exec. dir. Pitt Edn. Found., 1986—91. Sec. NC Commn. on Edn. and Employment of Women, 1970—74; mem. NC State Bd. Edn., 1977—82, NC Gov.'s Crime Commn., 1982, NC Commn. on Length of Sentencing, 1981—82, Blue Ribbon Commn. to Study Needs of Tng. Schs., NC Commn. Edn. for Econ. Growth; chmn. B.N. Duke Scholarship Adv. Com.; trustee NC Ctr. for Advancement of Teaching, 1989—, East Carolina U., Explorers Mus, Pitt Edn. Found.; chmn. bd. trustees NC Meth. Retirement Homes, N.Mex.; vice chmn. NC Dem. Com., 1978—80, 1981—84, chmn., 1980; mem. Dem. Nat. Com., 1978—; del. Dem. Nat. Conv., 1980, 1984, 1988, 1989, mem. site selection com., 1992; bd. dirs. Pitt United Fund, 1991—. Named one of Winning Dem. Women of Decade, Nat. Fedn. Dem. Women, 1980. Mem.: NEA, NC Assn. Educators, Delta Kappa Gamma. Methodist. Home: PO Box 340 Bethel NC 27812-0340

SPEIR, SHANNON GAFFNEY, lawyer, healthcare company executive; b. Camp Springs, Md., June 11, 1968; d. Joseph Peter and Charlotte (Coleman) Gaffney. BA, Tulane U., 1989; JD, Cumberland Sch. Law, Birmingham, Ala., 1997. Fin. analyst Merrill Lynch, N.Y., Fla., 1989-90; product devel. mgr. Complete Health, Birmingham, Ala., 1991-93; v.p. corp. devel. Triton Health Sys., 1995-97; v.p. legal, regulatory Momentum Health Svcs., 1997-99; CEO, Advantage Health Plan, New Orleans, 1998—. Dir. Ala. HMO Guaranty Assn., Montgomery, 1996-97. Mem. ABA, Ala. Bar Assn. E-mail: sgspeir@charter.net.

SPEIR, WILLIAM ARTHUR, JR. critical care physician; b. Macon, Ga., July 18, 1939; s. William Arthur Speir and Esther Marie Garland; m. Mary Hazelton Lehmann, June 8, 1963; 1 child, Mary-Butler S. Mathieson. BS in Chemistry, U. Ga., 1961; MD, Med. Coll. Ga., 1965. Asst. prof. pulmonary medicine Med. Coll. Ga., Augusta, 1971-75, assoc. prof. pulmonary medicine, 1975-80, prof. medicine pulmonary/critical care medicine, 1980-2000, prof. emeritus medicine, 2000—, med. dir. med. ICU, 1977-79, 91-00, chief sect. pulmonary diseases, 1979-92; clin. prof. medicine Mercer U. Sch. Medicine, Macon, Ga., 2000—. Contbr. over 170 articles, abstracts to profl. jours., 4 chpts. to books. Bd. dirs. Augusta Opera Assn., 1973-80. Lt. comdr., surgeon USPHS, 1966-68. Recipient Pulmonary Acad. award Nat. Heart, Lung and Blood Inst., 1974-79, Order of St. Obscurus award RTH Laennec Assn., 1983; named Col., Hon. Order Ky. Cols., 1980—. Fellow Am. Coll. Chest Physicians (gov. for Ga. 1998-2002, bylaws com. 1993-99, steering com. sect. on respiratory pathophysiology 1984-86, com. undergrad. med. edn. 1976-79, pres. So. chpt. 1980-81, 93-94, Disting. Faculty award 1991), Am. Coll. Critical Care Medicine; mem. Am. Thoracic Soc. (edn. com. 1977-81, councilor-at-large 1980, Disting. Educator award 1972), So. Med. Assn. (chmn. sec. chest diseases 1980-81, 93-94, Paul A. Turner Meml. Lectr. award 1983, 86), Soc. Critical Care Medicine. Episcopalian. Avocations: painting, writing, cooking, music, gardening. E-mail: bandmspeir@mindspring.com.

SPEIRS, ALFRED C. plastic and reconstructive surgeon; b. Oct. 27, 1933; BA, Houghton Coll., 1955; MD, Jefferson Med. Coll., Pa., 1959. Diplomate Am. Bd. Plastic Surgery. Intern Dartmouth Med. Coll., Mary Hitchcok Meml. Hosp., N.H., 1959-60; resident in gen. surgery Mich. State U. Butterworth Hosp., Grand Rapids, Mich., 1960-63; resident in plastic surgery Henry Ford Hosp., Detroit, 1963-65, U. Mich., St. Joseph's Hosp., Ann Arbor, 1964; surgeon Speirs Clinic for Plastic Surgery, Colorado Springs, Colo., 1965—. Presented sci. rsch. to medical confs. and seminars. Fellow ACS; mem. AMA, Am. Soc. Plastic and Reconstructive Surgery, Am. Bd. Plastic and Reconstructive Surgeons, Am. Soc. for Aesthetic Plastic Surgery, Am. Soc. Laser Medicine and Surgery, Lipoplasty Soc. N. Am., Internat. Soc. Clin. Plastic Surgeons, Internat. Soc. Cosmetic Laser Surgeons, Internat. Soc. Ultrasonic Surgery, Rocky Mt. Assn. Plastic Surgeons, Am. Cleft Palate Assn., Colo. Med. Soc., El Paso County Med. Soc., Christian Med. and Dental Soc., Pikes Peak Range Riders, El Paso Club, Garden of the Gods Club, Broadmoor Golf Club. Avocations: horses, team penning, roping, golf, tennis, collecting med. antiques. Office: 1490 W Fillmore St Colorado Springs CO 80904-1166 E-mail: info@speirsclinic.com.

SPEIRS, CAROL LUCILLE, nurse, naval officer; b. Plainfield, N.J., Apr. 20, 1942; d. Alexander Walker and Catherine Lucille (McGovern) S. Diploma, St. Peters Med. Ctr., New Brunswick, N.J., 1963; student, Seton Hall U., 1972; BSN, Pacific Lutheran U., Tacoma, Wash., 1987-88; BA, San Diego State U., 1976; MA, Webster Coll., 1980. Staff nurse Muhlenberg Hosp., Plainfield, N.J., 1963-64, Burdette Tomlin Meml. Hosp., Cape May Court House, 1964, 65, Georgetown U. Hosp., Washington, 1964-65; pvt. duty nurse North Plainfield, N.J., 1965-66; staff nurse, charge nurse Raritan Valley Hosp., Greenbrook, 1966-72; commd. lt. (j.g.) U.S. Navy, 1973, advanced through grades to comdr., 1985; charge nurse Naval Regional Med. Center, San Diego, 1973-76, Iwakuni, Japan, 1977-78, Long Beach, Calif., 1978-83, Bremerton, Wash., 1983-86; patient care nurse coord., 1986; head ambulatory care nursing dept. Naval Hosp. Corpus Christi, 1989-90, head inpatient nursing dept., 1991-92; head male surg. nursing dept. Naval Hosp., Portsmouth, Va., 1992-94. Mem. Founders Ball Com, City of Cypress, Calif., 1981. Recipient Outstanding Cath. Young Adult award Diocese of Trenton, 1970. Mem. 2020 Com. of Stafford County Va., Nat. Assn. for Healthcare Quality, Am. Acad. Ambulatory Nursing, Fredericksburg Area Newcomers & Old Friends Club, Fredericksburg Regional Geneal. Soc., Scottish Soc. of the Fredericksburg Area, Sigma Theta Tau, Nat. Mus. Women in Arts. Republican. Roman Catholic. Home: 4317 Turnberry Dr Fredericksburg VA 22408-9547

SPEIRS, DEREK JAMES, diversified corporation financial executive; b. Montreal, Que., Can., Dec. 21, 1933; s. James B. and Marie C. (Hunt) S.; m. Carol Alice Cumming, Dec. 8, 1967 (div. Feb. 1989); children: Lara Marie, Gregory Ross, Scott Lawrence Gordon. B. Commerce with honors in Econs., McGill U., 1954, MBA, 1959. Chartered acct., Can., chartered corp. sec. Devel. dir. fine papers, corp. acctg. dir. Domtar, Inc., Montreal, 1970-72, dir. corp. devel., 1976-78, v.p. fin., corp. devel., 1978-89, sr. v.p. fin. and corp. devel., 1989-91; v.p., sec. fin. Consoltex, 1972-76, bus. cons., 1991—; pres. Speirs Fin. Inc., Speirs Cons. Inc., Speirs Capital Inc. Mem. Can. Inst. Chartered Accts., Fin. Execs. Inst., C.D. Howe Inst., Lac Marois Country Club, St. James Club, Montreal Amateur Athletic Assn. Avocations: travel, skiing. Home: 365 Stanstead Ave Ville Mont-Royal Montreal QC Canada H3R 1X5 Office: Ste 1100 2 Pl Alexis Nihon Montreal QC Canada H3Z 3C1 E-mail: speirsco@netcom.ca.

SPEISER, PHYLLIS WITZEL, endocrinologist, educator; b. Newark, Oct. 20, 1953; d. Irving R. and Frances Witzel; m. Mark A. Speiser, Apr. 8, 1979; children: David, Shoshana, Jonathan. BA, Brandeis U., 1975; MD, Columbia U., 1979. Intern, resident Bronx (N.Y.) Mcpl. Hosp., Albert Einstein Hosp., 1979-82; fellow in pediatric endocrinology N.Y. Hosp.-Cornell Med. Ctr., N.Y.C., 1982-84; asst. prof. Cornell U. Med. Coll., 1984-90, assoc. prof., 1990-99; prof. NYU Sch. Medicine, 1999—. Med. cons. Nat. Adrenal Disease Found., Long Island, 1993—; dir. pediatric endocrinology NS-LIJ Health System, 1999—. Contbr. articles to profl. jours. Mem. alumni admissions com. Brandeis U., Waltham, Mass. Mem. Soc. Pediatric Rsch., Endocrine Soc., Lawson Wilkins Pediatric Endocrinology Soc. Office: Schneider Childrens Hosp 269-01 76th Ave New Hyde Park NY 11040 E-mail: pspeiser@lij.edu.

SPEJEWSKI, EUGENE HENRY, physicist, educator; b. East Chicago, Ind., Sept. 15, 1938; s. Henry Louis and Carrie Jane (Fuss) S.; m. Norma Beverly Seekins, June 8, 1963; children: Maria Suzanne, Beverly Anne, Andrew John, Jeannette Michelle. BS, U. Notre Dame, 1960; PhD, Ind. U., 1966. Research assoc. Ind. U., Bloomington, 1965-67, Princeton U., 1967-69, instr., 1969-71; asst. prof. Oberlin Coll., Ohio, 1971-72; dir. UNISOR, Oak Ridge Assoc. Univs., 1972-85, mgr. SDS program, 1985-86, chmn. spl. projects div., 1986-89; v.p., dir. tng. and mgmt. systems div. Oak Ridge Inst. for Sci. and Edn., 1989-95, v.p., assoc. dir. for edn. and tng. group, 1995-98; cons. Oak Ridge Nat. Lab., 1999—. Vis. prof. physics U. Tenn., Knoxville, 1981-84, adj. prof.; mem., chmn. HHIRF Users Exec. Com., Oak Ridge Nat. Lab., 1982-84; referee U.S. Dept. Energy, various profl. jours. Co-editor: Future Directions in Studies of Nuclei Far from Stability, 1980; contbr. articles to profl. jours. Referee U.S. Soccer Fedn.; bd. dirs. Oak Ridge Community Playhouse, 1985-88, 95—. Mem. AAAS, Am. Phys. Soc., Am. Mgmt. Assn., Oak Ridge Sertoma Club (sec., treas., pres., chair bd. dirs.), Sigma Xi. E-mail: gene@mail.phy.ornl.gov.

SPELFOGEL, EVAN J. lawyer, educator; b. Boston, Jan. 28, 1936; s. Morris R. and Helen S. (Steinberg) S.; m. Beverly Kolenberg; children: Scott, Douglas, Karen. AB, Harvard U., 1956; JD, Columbia U., 1959. Bar: Mass. 1959, N.Y. 1964, U.S. Supreme Ct. 1969. Atty. Office of Solicitor, U.S. Dept. Labor, Washington, Boston, 1959-60, NLRB, Boston, N.Y.C., 1960-64; assoc. Simpson, Thacher & Bartlett, N.Y.C., 1964-69, Dewey, Ballantine, N.Y.C., 1969-77; ptnr. Fellner, Rovins & Gallay, 1977-80, Summit, Rovins & Feldesman, N.Y.C., 1981-91, Epstein Becker and Green, P.C., N.Y.C., 1991—. Adj. prof. law Baruch Coll., CCNY. Bd. editors Developing Labor Law: The Board, The Courts and the National Labor Relations Act, also co-editor-in-chief Supplements; bd. sr. editors Employee Benefits Law; contbr. articles to profl. jours. Fellow Coll. Labor and Employment Lawyers; mem. ABA (sect. on labor and employment law, exec. coun. 1978-86, co-editor sect. newsletter 1976-92, editl. bd. The Labor Lawyer 1986—, mem. ho. dels. 1987-90, sect. dispute resolution 1992—), FBA (coun. on labor law), N.Y. State Bar Assn. (chmn. labor and employment law sect. 1977-78, exec. coun. 1975—, ho. dels. 1978-79, com. on profl. discipline 1987-90), Assn. of Bar of City of N.Y. (labor com. 1968-71, 87-90, employee benefits com. 1992-96), Indsl. Resl. Rsch. Assn. (sec. N.Y. chpt. 1999-2000, pres. 2000-01), Am. Arbitration Assn. (nat. panel labor arbitrators), Harvard Varsity Club, Phi Alpha Delta. Home: 17 Parkside Dr Great Neck NY 11021-1042 Office: 250 Park Ave New York NY 10177-0001 E-mail: espelfogel@ebglaw.com.

SPELFOGEL, SCOTT DAVID, lawyer; b. Boston, Nov. 27, 1960; s. Evan. J. and Beverly (Kolenberg) S. BS, Boston U., 1982; JD, Syracuse U., 1985; LLM, Boston U., 1990. Bar: Mass. 1985, N.Y. 1986, U.S. Dist. Ct. (no. dist.) N.Y. 1986, U.S. Dist. Ct. Mass. 1987; lic. real estate broker, Mass., 1987. Assoc. Jeffrey M. McCrone, P.C., Syracuse, N.Y., 1985-87, Tatarian Law Offices, Boston, 1987-88; asst. gen. counsel The Berkshire Group, 1988-90, v.p., asst. gen. counsel, 1990-96, v.p., gen. counsel, 1996, sr. v.p., gen. counsel, 1997—. Mem. ABA, Am. Corp. Counsel Assn., Boston Bar Assn., N.Y. Bar Assn., Mass. Bar Assn. Home: 27 Sentry Hill Rd Sharon MA 02067-1521 Office: The Berkshire Group 1 Beacon St Ste 1500 Boston MA 02108-3116

SPELIOS, LISA GARONE, nurse, educator; b. L.I., N.Y., Sept. 27, 1961; d. Michael John and Gloria Josephine (Riggio) Garone; m. Louis G. Spelios, June 30, 1984; children: Gregory Louis, Zachary Michael, Jeremy Daniel. BS in Nursing, Fla. Internat. U., 1984. Operating rm. nurse Carroway Meth. Med. Ctr., Birmingham, Ala.; labor and delivery rm. nurse Brookwood Med. Ctr., med.-surg. nurse; tchr. Am. Med. Tng. Inst., Miami, Fla. Mem. Fla. Nurses Assn.

SPELKE, ELIZABETH SHILIN, psychology educator; b. N.Y.C., May 28, 1949; d. Alan Shilin and Ruth (Simon) Spelke; m. Elliott M. Blass, Oct. 23, 1988; children: Mae Bridget, Joseph Alan. BA, Radcliffe/Harvard U., 1971; PhD, Cornell U., 1978; Dr. Honoris Causa, Umeå (Sweden) U., 1993. From asst. prof. to assoc. prof. U. Pa., Phila., 1977-86; prof. Cornell U., Ithaca, N.Y., 1986-96, MIT, Cambridge, Mass., 1996—. Bd. editors for cognitive sci. MIT Press, Cambridge, Mass., 1984—. Recipient Fulbright Sr. Rsch. award Fulbright Commn., 1984-85; Guggenheim fellow John Simon Guggenheim Found., 1988-89, Cattell fellow, 1992-93. Fellow Am. Psychol. Soc., Soc. Exptl. Psychologists; mem. Cognitive Neurosci. Soc., Psychonomic Soc., Am. Acad. of Arts and Scis. Achievements include research on early development of perception by human infants; research on development of reasoning about objects, space, and number by children. Office: Detp Brain & Cognitive Sci MIT NE20-456 Cambridge MA 02139

SPELLACY, WILLIAM NELSON, obstetrician, educator, gynecologist, educator; b. St. Paul, May 10, 1934; s. Jack F. and Elmyra L. (Nelson) Spellacy; m. Lynn Larsen; children: Kathleen Ann, Kimberly Joan, William Nelson. BA, U. Minn., 1955, BS, 1956, MD, 1959. Diplomate subsplty. cert. in maternal and fetal medicine Am. Bd. Ob-Gyn. Intern Hennepin County Gen. Hosp., Mpls., 1959—60; resident U. Minn., 1960—63; practice medicine specializing in ob-gyn., 1963—67, Miami, Fla., 1967—73, Gainesville, 1973—79, Chgo., 1979—88; prof., head dept. U. Ill. Coll. Medicine, 1979—88; prof., chmn. dept. U. So. Fla. Coll. Medicine, Tampa, 1988—. Prof. dept. ob-gyn. U. Miami, 1967—73; prof., chmn. dept. U. Fla., 1973—79. Contbr. articles to med. jours. Mem.: ACOG, AMA, Inst. Medicine, Ill. Med. Soc., Soc. Perinatal Obstetricians, Ctrl. Assn. Obstetrics and Gynecology, South Atlantic Soc. Obstetrics and Gynecology, Perinatal Rsch. Soc., Am. Diabetes Assn., Assn. Profs. Gynecology and Obstetrics, Am. Fertility Soc., Endocrine Soc., Am. Assn. Obstetricians and Gynecologists, Soc. Gynecol. Investigation, Am. Gynecol. and Obstet. Soc., Am. Gynecol. Soc., Rotary. Episcopalian. Home: 845 Seddon Cove Way Tampa FL 33602-5774 Office: U South Fla Coll Medicine Dept OBGYN 4 Columbia Dr Ste 514 Tampa FL 33606-3589

SPELLBERG, DAVID MARK, urologist; b. Chgo., Aug. 28, 1960; BS, U. Ill., Champaign, 1982; MD, Rush Med., Chgo., 1986. Cert. Am. Bd. Urology, 1993, Am. Coll. Surgeons, 1993. Chief resident Rush Pres. St. Luke's Med. Ctr., Chgo., 1990-91; pvt. practice, sr. ptnr. Specialists in Urology, Naples, Fla., 1991—. Mem. adv. bd. Bay Area Renal Stone Ctr., St. Petersburg, Fla., 1996-97. Mem. bd. Am.Cancer Soc., Collier COunty, 1991-96. Named Best Doctor in Am., 1996-97, 97-99, 99-2000. Mem.: Collier County Med. Soc. (pres.-elect 2000—01, sec. 1998—99, treas. 1999—2000), Am. Urological Assn., Am. Assn. Clin. Urologists. Office: 800 Goodlette Rd N Naples FL 34102-5400

SPELLER, KERSTIN G. RINTA, psychologist; b. Washington, Nov. 18, 1949; d. Eugene and Saga (Lindberg) Rinta; Thomas Hughes Speller, Sept. 4, 1971; five children. AB, Ohio U., 1971, MS, 1972; PhD, SUNY, Buffalo, 1983. Cert. sch. psychologist. Sch. psychologist Iroquois Ctrl. Schs., Elma, N.Y., 1974-78; cons. psychologist Amherst, 1979-84; program dir. Child's Play Preschool Program, 1986-95; sch. psychologist Holland (N.Y.) Schs., 1995—. Project dir. ISO-9001 GEMCOR, Buffalo, 1993—, corp. dir. human rels., 1998—. Bd. dirs. Heritage Ctrs. (Assn. Retarded Children), Erie County, N.Y., 1983—, govt. affairs com. chair, 1995—. Mem. Nat. Assn. Sch. Psychologists, USTA (ea. mgmt. bd., regional v.p. western region 1996—, nat. awards com. 1999—), Country Club Buffalo, Buffalo Tennis and Squash Club, E. Aurora Pony Club, Village Glen Tennis & Fitness Club. Home: 1005 E Main St East Aurora NY 14052-2005

SPELLER, ROBERT ERNEST BLAKEFIELD, JR. choreographer; b. N.Y.C., Feb. 5, 1936; s. Robert E.B. and Flora Maxine Elliott (Watkins) S. Student, Duke U., 1954-56, NYU, 1958-59, New Sch. for Social Rsch., 1967-68. V.p. Robert Speller & Sons, Publishers, N.Y.C., 1963—; coordinator models New School Soc. Rsch., Parsons, 1972-2001; instr. Baruch Col., 1980-83. Choreographer many shows including Toulouse, 1981, The Ritz, 1983, Let's Misbehave, 1985-86; dir. I Died Yesterday, 1983; translator: The Mime (by Jean Dorcy), 1961. Mem. AFTRA, Actors' Equity Assn. (councillor, 1967-73), Screen Actors' Guild, Am. Guild Variety Artists, Soc. Stage Dirs. & Choreographers N.Y., N.Y. Genealogical and Biographical Soc. Episcopal. Office: Robert Speller and Sons 115 E 9th St New York NY 10003-5414

SPELLER, ROBERT ERNEST BLAKEFIELD, publishing executive; b. Chgo., Jan. 19, 1908; s. John Ernest and Florence (Larson) S.; m. Flora Maxine Elliott Watkins (dec. May 1997); children: Robert Ernest Blakefield, Jon Patterson. Student, Columbia U., 1929. Mng. editor Fgn. Press Svc., 1930-31; pres. Mohawk Press, 1931-32, Robert Speller Pub. Corp., 1934-52, Record Concerts Corp., 1940-53, Robert Speller & Sons, Pubs., inc., 1955—, Norellyn Press, Inc., 1960-83, Transglobal News Svc., Inc., 1960—. Corresp. Raleigh News & Observer, 1949-53; pub. Hough's Ency. Am. Woods, 1957—, mng. editor 1964-75; chmn. bd., pres., chief exec. officer Nat. Resources Publs., Inc., 1968-84; pres., dir. Transglobal Resources Devel. Corp., 1983—; owner, operator, prodr. Concert Theatre, N.Y.C., 1939-43, mgr. Otto Klemperer, Leon Barzin, Margaret Speaks, others; pub. East Europe Mag., 1970—; sec., dir. Encoder Research & Devel. Corp., 1971—, Pecos Internat., Inc., 1974-77; v.p., dir. Pecos Western Corp. of Del., 1973-83; dir. Gen. Research Corp., Fashion Form Mfg. Corp. Mem. founding bd. USO Trustee Philippa Schuyler Meml. Found. With Signal Corps, AUS, 1944-45. Mem. Gourmet Soc. (founder), Am. Legion, Local 38 Musicians Assn. AFL, Westchester Country Club, Lions Club, Columbia U. Club (N.Y.C.), Delta Chi. Episcopalian. Office: 115 E 9th St New York NY 10003-5414

SPELLERBERG, ELINOR M. riding instructor; b. Seymour, Ind., Feb. 27, 1927; d. Ellis Leroy and Edna (Linke) Hawk; m. Thomas Richard Spellerberg, May 10, 1947; children: Eric (dec.), Scott, Janet, Jeffrey, Lance. Student, Ohio State U., 1945-47. Horse breeder and trainer, Tiffin, Ohio, 1960-99; dressage instr., 1980-2001; judge dressage horses Am. Horse Show Assn., Lexington, Ky., 1982-2001; ret, 2002—. Head instr. Riding for Handicapped, Tiffin; mem. U.S. Equestrian Team, 1990-2001. Author, illustrator: The Test, 1995, (workbook) 4-H Dressage, 1990. Mem. exec. com. Elder Coll. Terra C.C., Fremont, Ohio, 1995-2001; mem. sch. bd. Mohawk H.S., Sycamore, Ohio, 1962-71; leader Seneca County 4-H, Tiffin, 1969-90; established Hope on Horseback, Tiffin, 1975-90, 1st 4-H Handicapped Riding Club and Program, Ohio, State 4-H Horse com.; sec. 4-H English divsn. Ohio State Fair. Named Woman of Yr., VFW, Tiffin, 1991, hon. chpt. farmer Future Farmers Am.; recipient Svc. award Kiwanis Club, Tiffin, 1990. Republican. Avocation: painting. Home: 1379 W Township Rd 58 Tiffin OH 44883

SPELLER-BROWN, BARBARA JEAN, pediatric nurse practitioner; b. Windsor, N.C., Feb. 8, 1958; d. Thomas Franklin and Esther Lee (Bond) Speller; m. Samuel Brown Jr., Nov. 16, 1985; children: Samuel, Shaun, Shea, Shanele, Samara. BSN, Howard U., 1981; MSN, U. Utah, 1993. Cert. PNP. Charge nurse Rosebud (S.D.) Indian Health Facility, 1981-82, Carl Albert Indian Health Facility, 1982-83; asst. head nurse Pitt County Meml. Hosp., Greenville, N.C., 1984-85; staff nurse St. Bernardine's Hosp., San Bernardino, Calif., 1986, San Bernardino Cmty. Hosp., 1986-87; staff nurse/charge nurse Gorgas Army Hosp., Republic of Panama, 1987-90; charge nurse Humana Hosp. Davis North, Layton, Utah, 1990-93; staff nurse Primary Children's Med. Ctr., Salt Lake City, 1990-93; clin. preceptor, PNP Cmty. Health Care Inc., Capital Heights, Md., 1994-95; faculty PNP Our Kids Ctr. Vanderbilt U. Med. Ctr., Nashville, 1995-2000; CPNP pediats. Walter Reed Army Med. Ctr., 2001—. Mem. Gospel choir The Word of God Bapt. Ch.; scholarship chairperson Watchcare. 1st lt. USPHS, 1981—83. Named Outstanding Young Woman Am. Delta Sigma Theta. Mem. ANA, Nat. Assn. PNPs, Am. Prof. Soc. on the Abuse of Children, Sigma Theta Tau, Phi Kappa Phi. Home: 11020 Lake Victoria Ln Bowie MD 20720 E-mail: momatwork05@aol.com.

SPELLING, AARON, film and television producer, writer, actor; b. Dallas, Apr. 22, 1923; s. David and Pearl (Wall) S.; m. Carole Gene Marer, Nov. 23, 1968; children: Victoria Davey, Randall Gene. Student, Sorbonne, U. Paris, France, 1945-46; BA, So. Meth. U., 1950. Actor Thomas-Spelling Prodns., L.A., 1953-69; screenwriter Zane Grey Series, 1972-76; prodr. Zane Grey Theater, 1977-86, The Dick Powell Show, L.A., 1986—; co-owner with Danny Thomas Thomas-Spelling Prodns., 1969-72; co-pres. Spelling-Goldberg Prodns., 1972-76; pres. Aaron Spelling Prodns., Inc., 1977-86, chmn., CEO, 1986—. Writer numerous TV plays and movies; producer or exec. prodr. over 58 TV series including The Mod Squad, The Rookies, Family, Nightingales, Dynasty, The Colbys, Love Boat, Hotel, Beverly Hills 90210, Charlie's Angels, Fantasy Island, Starsky and Hutch, T.J. Hooker, Matt Houston, Hart to Hart, Melrose Place, 7th Heaven, Savannah, Sunset Beach, Pacific Palisades, Charmed, Titans; also 130 TV movies for ABC, CBS, NBC, including After Jimmy, And the Band Played On; prodr. or exec. prodr. theatrical films including Mr. Mom, Knight Mother, Surrender, Loose Cannons, Cross My Heart, Soapdish, The Mod Squad, Charlie's Angels; author: Aaron Spelling-A Prime Time Life, 1996. Bd. dirs. Am. Film Inst. Served with USAAF, 1942-45. Decorated Bronze Star medal, Purple Heart with oak leaf cluster; recipient Eugene O'Neill awards, 1947, 48, NAACP Image awards 1970, 71, 73, 75, Winston Churchil medal of Wisdom, 1988, Lifetime Achievement award People's Choice Awards, 1996, Courage to Dream award Fulfillment Fund, 1996, GLADD award; named Man of Yr., Publicists Guild Am., 1971, Man of Yr. B'nai B'rith, Beverly Hills chpt., 1972, 85, NAACP Humanitarian of Yr., 1983, Man of Yr. Scopus award Am. Friends of Hebrew U., 1993; 1st prodr. honored by Mus. of Broadcasting, honored for contbns. to victims' rights by City of Las Vegas; inducted into TV Acad.'s Hall of Fame. Mem. Writers Guild Am. (award 1962), Prodrs. Guild Am., The Caucus of Prodrs., Writers and Dirs., Hollywood Radio and TV Soc., Hollywood TV Acad. Arts and Scis., Acad. Motion Picture Arts and Scis., Friars, Big Brothers of Am. Democrat. Jewish. Office: Spelling Entertainment Group 5700 Wilshire Blvd Fl 5 Los Angeles CA 90036-3659*

SPELLMAN, DOUGLAS TOBY, advertising executive; b. Bronx, N.Y., May 12, 1942; s. Sydney M. and Leah B. (Rosenberg) S.; m. Ronni I. Epstein, Jan. 16, 1966 (div. Mar. 1985); children: Laurel Nicole, Daren Scott; m. Michelle Ward, Dec. 31, 1986; 1 child, Dallas Ward Spellman. Media buyer Doyle, Dane, Bernbach, Inc., N.Y.C., 1964-66; various postions, 1966-72; media supr. Ogilvy & Mather, Inc., L.A., 1972-73; media dir. Vitt Media Internat., Inc., 1973-74; v.p., dir. West Coast ops. Ind. Media Svcs., Inc., 1974-75; owner Douglas T. Spellman, Inc., 1975-77, pres., chmn. bd., 1977-82; pres., COO Douglas T. Spellman Co. div. Ad Mktg., Inc., 1982-85; pres., CEO, chmn. bd. Spellbound Prodns. and Spellman Media divs. Spellbound Comms, 1984-86; gen. ptnr. Faso & Spellman, 1984-86; COO, pres. Yacht Mgmt. Internat., Ltd., 1984-86; v.p. media Snyder, Longino Advt. div. Snyder Advt., 1986-91; advt./media cons., 1986-90; gen. ptnr. Nucleus Nuance, L.A., 1987-88, Convention Photos Unltd., Hawaii, 1988-89; v.p. mktg. Pacific Med. Products, Inc., L.A., 1990-91; mgr. media and promotions Pleasant Holidays, LLC, 2002—. Media dir., Kennedy-Wilson Inc., L.A., 1991-94; dir. media and advt. svcs. Goddard & Claussen/First Tuesday, L.A., 1994-97; v.p. advt., mktg. Cosmetic Tech. Internat., Inc., L.A., 1997-98; mng. dir. Med. Mktg. and Advt., L.A., 1998-99; dir. media svcs., Publicis Dialog-FusionDM, San Francisco, 1999-2000; media dir., team leader Muse Cordero Chen & Ptnrs., L.A., 2001--; guest lectr. Sch. Bus. UCLA, 1964-69. Served with USAR N.G., 1964-69. Mem. Aircraft Owner and Pilots Assn., NRA, Calif. Pistol and Rifle Assn., Rolls royce Owners, Mercedes Benz Am., Aston Martin Owners, Phi Zeta Kappa, Phi Omega Epsilon.

SPELLMAN, MITCHELL WRIGHT, surgeon, academic administrator; b. Alexandria, La., Dec. 1, 1919; s. Frank Jackson and Altonette Beulah (Mitchell) S.; m. Billie Rita Rhodes, June 27, 1947 (dec.); children: Frank A., Michael A. (dec.), Mitchell A., Maria S. Weaver, Melva A., Mark A., Manly

A. (dec.), Rita S. Parks; m. Adrienne Foster Williams, Feb. 14, 2001 (dec. Dec. 2001). AB magna cum laude, Dillard U., 1940, LL.D. (hon.), 1983; MD, Howard U., 1944; PhD in Surgery (Commonwealth Fund fellow), U. Minn., Mpls., 1955; D.Sc. (hon.), Georgetown U., 1974, U. Fla., 1977. Intern Cleve. Met. Gen. Hosp., 1944-45, asst. resident in surgery, 1945-46, Howard U. and Freedmen's Hosp., Washington, 1946-47, chief resident in thoracic surgery, 1947-48, teaching asst. in physiology, 1948-49, chief resident in surgery, 1949-50, teaching asst. in surgery, 1950-51; asst. prof. surgery Howard U., 1954-56, assoc. prof., 1956-60, prof., 1960-68; dir. Howard surgery service at D.C. Gen. Hosp., 1961-68; fellow in surgery U. Minn., 1951-54; sr. resident in surgery U. Minn. Med. Sch. and Hosp., 1953-54; dean Charles R. Drew Postgrad. Med. Sch., Los Angeles, 1969-77, prof. surgery, 1969-78; asst. dean, prof. surgery Sch. Medicine, U. Calif. at Los Angeles, 1969-78; clin. prof. surgery Sch. Med., U. So. Calif., 1969-78; dean for med. svcs., prof. surgery Harvard Med. Sch., Boston, 1978-90, dean emeritus for med. svcs., 1990—, dean emeritus for internat. projects, 1990—, prof. surgery emeritus, 1990—; dir. internat. exch. programs Harvard Med. Internat., 1995—; exec. v.p. Harvard Med. Ctr., 1978-90. Fellow Ctr. for Advanced Study in Behavioral Scis.; vis. prof. Stanford, 1975-76; bd. dirs. Kaiser Found. Hosps., Kaiser Found. Health Plan, 1971-89; mem. D.C. Bd. Examiners in Medicine and Osteopathy, 1955-68; mem. Nat. Rev. Com. for Regional Med. Programs, 1968-70; mem. spl. med. adv. group, nat. surg. cons. VA, 1969-73; mem. Commn. for Study Accreditation of Selected Health Ednl. Programs, 1970-72; chmn. adv. com. br. med. devices Nat. Heart and Lung Inst., 1972; Am. health del. to visit People's Republic of China, 1973; hon. dir. State Mut. Cos., 1990—; mem. com. mandatory retirement in higher edn. NAS/NRC, 1989-91; mem. panel on internat. programs Nat. Libr. Medcine, 1996, 97. Mem. editorial bd.: Jour. Medicine and Philosophy, 1977-90; Contbr. articles on cardiovascular physiology and surgery, measurement of blood volume, and radiation biology to profl. jours. Past bd. dirs. Sun Valley Forum on Nat. Health; mem. ethics adv. bd. HEW, 1977-81; bd. dirs. Harvard Comty. Health Plan, 1979-84; former trustee Occidental Coll.; former bd. overseers com. to visit univ. health svc. Harvard, bd. overseers Harvard Comty. Health Plan, 1984-95; former regent Georgetown U., bd. dirs., 1986-92; former vis. com. U. Mass. Med. Ctr.; mem. bd. visitors UCLA Sch. Medicine; mem. corp. MIT; adv. bd. PEW Scholars Program in Biomed. Scis., 1984-86; bd. dirs. Med. Edn. for South African Blacks, 1985—. Markle scholar in med. scis., 1954-59; recipient Distinguished Alumnus award Dillard U., 1963; Distinguished Postgrad. Achievement award Howard U., 1974; Outstanding Achievement award U. Minn., 1979 Mem. AMA, AAAS, AAUP, ACS, Nat. Med. Assn. (William A. Sinkler Surgery award 1968), Soc. Univ. Surgeons, Am. Coll. Cardiology, Am. Surg. Assn., Inst. of Medicine of Nat. Acad. Scis. (chmn. program com. 1977-79, governing com. 1978-80), Nat. Acad. Practice in Medicine, Am. Assn. Sovereign Mil. Order of Malta (Knights and Dames of Malta), MIT Corp. (life mem. emeritus), Cosmos Club. Roman Catholic. Office: Harvard Medical Internat 1135 Tremont St Suite 900 Boston MA 02120

SPELLMAN, OLIVER B., JR. city official; m. Page Rander; 3 children. BA in Am. Studies, St. Michael's Coll.; JD in Criminal Justice, Howard U. Law asst. Office of Atty. Gen. of Ohio, 1978-79; instr. dept. criminal justice Ala. State U.; with N.Y.C. Criminal Justice Agy., N.Y.C. Dept. Pks. and Recreation, borough commr. Queens County, 1990-94; dir. Dept. Pks., Recreation and Properties City of Cleve., 1994-98, City of Houston, 1998—2002, chief of staff, 2002—. Chief Urban Pk. Svc., Adminstrv. Pks. and Recreation Mgr., Spl. Project Dir., N.Y.C. Dept. Pks. and Recreation. Office: Mayor's Office 901 Bagby Houston TX 77002

SPELLMAN, THOMAS JOSEPH, JR. lawyer; b. Glen Cove, N.Y., Nov. 11, 1938; s. Thomas J. and Martha H. (Erwin) S.; m. Margaret Mary Barth, June 23, 1962; children: Thomas Joseph, Kevin M., Maura N. BS, Fordham U., 1960, JD, 1965. Bar: N.Y. 1966, U.S. Dist. Ct. (so. and ea. dist.) N.Y. 1968, U.S. Ct. Appeals (2nd cir.) 1980, U.S. Supreme Ct. 1981. Staff atty. Allstate Ins. Co., N.Y.C., 1966-69; trial atty. Hartford Ins. Co., Hauppauge, N.Y., 1969-71; ptnr. Wheller & Spellman, Farmingville, 1971-76, Devitt, Spellman, Barrett, Callahan & Kenney, LLP, Smithtown, 1976—. Mem. grievance com. 10th Jud. Dist., Westbury, N.Y., 1984-92. Trustee Acad. St. Joseph, Brentwood, N.Y., 2000—; bd. govs. St. Catherine of Sienna Med. Ctr., Smithtown, NY, 2002--. Capt. USAR, 1960-68. Fellow: N.Y. Bar Found., Am. Bar Found.; mem.: N.Y. Bar State Bar Assn. (ho. of dels. 1989—, nominating com. 1992—93, v.p. 1996—98), Suffolk County Bar Assn. (bd. dirs., sec.-treas. v.p. 1982—, pres. 1992—93), Swordfish Club. Westhampton Beach, N.Y. (bd. dirs., sec. 2000—01). Home: 8 Highwoods Ct Saint James NY 11780-9610 Office: Devitt Spellman et al 50 Route 111 Ste 314 Smithtown NY 11787-3700

SPELLMIRE, GEORGE W. lawyer; b. Oak Park, Ill., June 10, 1948; Student, Brown U.; BA, Ohio State U., 1970; JD, De Paul U., 1974. Bar: Ill. 1974, U.S. Dist. Ct. (no. dist.) Ill. 1974, U.S. Tax Ct. 1984, U.S. Ct. Appeals (7th cir.) 1984, U.S. Supreme Ct. 1994. Ptnr. Hinshaw & Culbertson, Chgo., 1982-98, D'Ancona & Pflaum, Chgo., 1998—. Author: Attorney Malpractice: Prevention and Defense, 1988; co-author: Accounting, Auditing and Financial Malpractice, 1998, Accountants' Legal Liability Guide, 1990, Illinois Handbook on Legal Malpractice, 1982, Associates Primer for the Prevention of Malpractice, 1987. Mem. ABA, Am. Coll. Trial Lawyers, Soc. Trial Lawyers, Fed. Trial Bar, Internat. Assn. Def. Counsel (legal malpractice com., def. counsel practice mgmt. com.), Ill. State Bar Assn., Chgo. Bar Assn., Trial Lawyers Club Chgo. Office: D'Ancona & Pflaum 111 E Wacker Dr Ste 2800 Chicago IL 60601-4209

SPELMAN, DEIRDRE-HOLLY, clinical services administrator, social worker; b. Scranton, Pa. d. William F. and Florence R. Spelman. B in Psychology, Mansfield (Pa.) U., 1969; MSW, Marywood U., Scranton, Pa., 1972; paralegal cert., Pa. State U., 1987. Cert. social worker. Social worker Pa. Dept. Health, Wilkes Barre, 1969-77; sr. social worker Buckinghamshire County Coun., Milton Keynes, Eng., 1977-81; social worker dialysis, pediat., trauma Robert Packer Hosp., Sayre, Pa., 1981-88; dir. social svcs. Ideal Sr. Living Ctr., Endicott, N.Y., 1988-92; clin. svcs. dir. Childrens Home RTF Inc., Chenango Forks, 1995—. Mem. adv. bd. BEAR Program Mental Health Assn., Binghamton, N.Y., 1997—. Mem. cmty. devel. block grant adv. bd. City of Binghamton; vol. Dem. Com., Binghamton; mem. bd. Jewish Family Svcs., 1988. Mem. NASW (del. 1997—, bd. 1995—). Avocations: reading, travel, scrabble. Home: 38 Kneeland Ave Binghamton NY 13905-4108 Office: Childrens Home RTF Inc 638 Squirrel Hill Rd Chenango Forks NY 13746-2145

SPELMAN, NANCY LATTING, developmental psychologist; b. Oklahoma City, Sept. 13, 1945; d. Trimble Baggett and Patience Francelia (Sewell) Latting; m. Douglas Gordon Spelman, June 21, 1970; children: Brooke Patience, Erin Latting. BA in Polit. Sci., Boston U., 1967; MA in Psychology, Bucknell U., 1972; PhD in Psychology, U. Hong Kong, 1987. Tour guide UN, N.Y.C., summer 1966; tchr. emotionally disturbed and retarded pre-sch. children Mass. Dept. Mental Health, Boston, 1968-70; coord. vols. campaign for mayor Patience Latting, Oklahoma City, 1971; lectr. psychology Petaling Jaya Community Coll., Kuala Lumpur, Malaysia, 1987-88, George Mason U., Fairfax, Va., 1989; interactive skills observer, facilitator mgmt. programs Xerox Corp. Edn. and Tng., Leesburg, 1989-91; pers. officer Am. Inst. in Taiwan, Taipei, 1993-95; tchr. psychology U. Hong Kong, 1996-99; adj. fellow psychology Nat. U. Singapore, 2001—. Adj. fellow psychology Nat. U. Singapore, 2000. Bd. dirs. Internat. Sch. Kuala Lumpur, 1986-87, sec., 1987-88; bd. dirs. Golf Course Square Cluster, Reston, Va., 1991; com. mem. Hong Kong Soc. for Disabled, 1976-77. Democrat. Avocations: hiking, tennis. E-mail: spelman@pacific.net.sg.

SPELSON, NICHOLAS JAMES, engineering executive, retired; b. Oak Park, Ill., Sept. 10, 1923; s. James and Constance (Rellos) S. BS in Mech. Engring., Ill. Inst. Tech., Chgo., 1947. Mech. engr. pvt. industry, Chgo., 1947-60; mech. engr. USAF, 1960-65, Def. Logistics Agy., Dept. of Def., Chgo., 1965-82; br. chief ops. Def. Logistics Agy.-Def. Contract Adminstrn. Svcs. Region, 1982-90; br. chief quality assurance engring. Def. Logistics Agy.-Def. Contracts Dist., 1990-94. With U.S. Army, 1943-45. Mem. Am. Legion, Hellenic Profl. Soc. Ill. Greek Orthodox. Avocations: golf, travel.

SPELTS, RICHARD JOHN, lawyer; b. Yuma, Colo., July 29, 1939; s. Richard Clark and Barbara Eve (Pletcher) S.; children: Melinda, Meghan, Richard John Jr.; m. Gayle Merves, Nov. 14, 1992. BS cum laude, U. Colo., 1961, JD, 1964. Bar: Colo. 1964, U.S. Dist. Ct. Colo. 1964, U.S. Supreme Ct. 1968, U.S. Ct. Appeals (10th cir.) 1970, U.S. Dist. Ct. (ea. dist.) Mich. 1986. With Ford Motor Internat., Cologne, Germany, 1964-65; legis. counsel to U.S. Senator, 89th and 90th Congresses, 1967-68; minority counsel U.S. Senate Subcom., 90th and 91st Congresses, 1968-70; asst. U.S. atty., 1st asst. U.S. atty. Fed. Dist. of Colo., 1970-77; pvt. practice Denver, 1977-89; risk mgr. sheriff's dept. Jefferson County, Golden, Colo., 1990-91. Owner Video Prodn. for Lawyers, 1991—. Selected for Leadership Denver, 1977; recipient cert. for outstanding contbns. in drug law enforcement U.S. Drug Enforcement Adminstrn., 1977, spl. commendation for criminal prosecution U.S. Dept. Justice, 1973, spl. commendation for civil prosecution U.S. Dept. Justice, 1976. Mem. Fed. Bar Assn. (chmn. govt. torts seminar 1980), Colo. Bar Assn. (bd. govs. 1976-78), Denver Bar Assn., Colo. Trial Lawyers Assn., Denver Law Club, Order of Coif. Republican. Methodist. Home and Office: 9671 Brook Hill Ct Lone Tree CO 80124-5431 Fax: (303) 662-9957.

SPELTZ, MICHAEL JOHN, land use planner; b. Davenport, Iowa, Feb. 23, 1947; s. James Andrew and Elizabeth Jeanette (Bahnub) S.; m. Patricia Ann Honermann, Apr. 3, 1971; children: Michelle Ann, James Michael. BS in gen. engrng., U.S. Military Acad., 1969; MA in Russian, Univ. Wis., 1976; MA in Environ. Conservation, U. N.H., 2002. Artilery officer, fgn. area specialist U.S. Army, 1969-90; adv. U.S. Del. Strategic Arms Reduction Talks, Geneva, 1984-87; engr. program mgr. Raytheon Co., Bedford, Mass., 1990-2001; land protection specialist Soc. for Protection of NH Forests, Concord, 2002—. Co-author: University of Wisconsin-Platteville General Education Standards, 1989; contbr. articles to profl. jours. Del N.H. State Rep. Com., 1997—. Recipient Grad. fellowship Nat. Sci. Found., 1969. Mem. Soc. for the Protection N.H. Forests. Republican. Roman Catholic. Avocations: hiking, cross-country skiing, landscaping. Home: 55 White Plains Ave Londonderry NH 03053-4616 Office: Soc for Protection of NH Forests 54 Portsmouth St Concord NH 03301-5486

SPENCE, ANDREW, artist, painter; b. Bryn Mawr, Pa., Oct. 4, 1947; s. Thomas and Elizabeth Spence; m. Mary Stewart Stoll, June 24, 1977. BFA, Temple U., 1969; MFA, U. Calif., Santa Barbara, 1971. One-man shows include TransAvant Garde Gallery, Austin, Tex., 1989, Barbara Krakow Gallery, Boston, 1989, Barbara Toll Fine Arts, N.Y.C., 1982-83, 85, 87-88, 90, Compass Rose Gallery, Chgo., 1990, James Corcoran Gallery, L.A., 1990, Max. Protetch Gallery, N.Y.C., 1992-93, Barbara Scott Gallery, Miami, 1993, 96, Worcester (Mass.) Art Mus., 1991, Morris Healy Gallery, N.Y.C., 1996, Art Resources Transfer, N.Y.C., 2000, Edward Thorp Gallery, N.Y.C., 2001; exhibited in group shows including Corcoran Gallery of Art, Washington, 1987, Hirshhorn Mus. and Sculpture Garden, Smithsonian Instn., Washington, 1989, Whitney Mus. Am. Art, N.Y., 1989, 91-92, Met. Mus. Art, N.Y.C., 1993, Am. Acad. Arts and Letters, N.Y.C., 1994, Wall Street Rising, N.Y.C., 2002; represented in permanent collections including Balt. Mus. Art, Carnegie Mus. Art, Pitts., Cleve. Mus. Art, Cin. Art Mus., Hirshhorn Mus. and Sculpture Garden, Laguna Gloria Art Mus., Met. Mus. Art, N.Y.C., San Diego Mus. Contemporary Art, Walker Art Ctr., Whitney Mus. Am. Art, N.Y.C. Painting grantee Nat. Endowment for Arts, 1987; Guggenheim fellow, 1994.

SPENCE, A(NDREW) MICHAEL, dean, finance educator; b. Montclair, N.J., 1943; BA in Philosophy summa cum laude, Princeton U., 1966; BA, MA in Maths., Oxford U., 1968; PhD in Econs. with honors, Harvard U., 1972. Asst. prof. polit. econ. Kennedy Sch. Govt. Harvard U., Cambridge, Mass., 1971-75, prof. econs., 1977-83, prof. bus. adminstrn., 1979-83, George Gund prof. econs. and bus. adminstrn., 1983-86, vis. prof. econs. dept., 1976-77, chmn. bus. econs. PhD program, 1981-83, chmn. econs. dept., 1983-84, dean Faculty Arts and Scis., 1984-90; assoc. prof. dept. econs. Stanford (Calif.) U., 1973-75, Philip H. Knight prof., dean Grad. Sch. Bus., 1990-99, Philip H. Knight prof., dean emeritus, prof. econs., 1999—. Bd. dirs. BankAm. Corp., Gen. Mills, Inc., Nike, Inc., Siebel Syss., Sun Microsyss., VeriFone, Inc.; chmn. Nat. Rsch. Coun. Bd. on Sci., Tech. and Econ. Policy. Author: 3 books; mem. editl. bd. Am. Econs. Rev., Bell. Jour. Econs., Jour. Econ. Theory and Pub. Policy; contbr. over 50 articles to profl. jours. Mem. econs. adv. panel NSF, 1977-79; mem. econs. adv. com. Sloan Found., 1979—. Recipient Danforth fellow, 1966, Rhodes scholar, 1966, J.K. Galbraith prize for excellence in tchg., 1978, The Bank of Sweden Prize in Economic Sciences, 2001. Fellow AAAS, Econometric Soc.; mem. Am. Econ. Assn. (John Bates Clark medal 1981). Office: Stanford U Grad Sch Bus Bldg 350 Memorial Way Stanford CA 94305-5015

SPENCE, BARBARA E. publishing company executive; b. Bryn Mawr, Pa., July 8, 1921; d. Geoffrey Strange and Mary (Harrington) Earnshaw; m. Kenneth M. Spence Jr., June 29, 1944; children: Kenneth M. III, Christopher E., Hilary B. Grad. high sch. Movie, radio editor Parade Mag., N.Y.C., 1941-45; with Merchandising Group, 1946-47; exec. dir. Greenfield Hill Congl. Ch., Fairfield, Conn., 1958-74, dir. religious edn., 1968-74; assoc. Ten Eyck-Emerich Antiques, 1974-76; personnel dir. William Morrow & Co., Inc., N.Y.C., 1976-91; ret., 1991. Chmn. pub. relations, bd. dirs. ARC, 1951-56, Family Service Soc., Fairfield, 1956-57, 61-63; chmn. pub. relations Citizens for Eisenhower, 1952, Fairfield Teens Players, 1968-71; bd. dirs. Fairfield Teens, Inc., 1965-70, Planned Parenthood of Greater Bridgeport, 1969-75, chmn. pub. affairs, 1971-72, chmn. personnel, 1972-73, chpt. vice chmn., 1973-75; pres. steering com. Am. Playwrights Festival Theatre, Inc., Fairfield, 1969-70, v.p., bd. dirs., 1971—; bd. govs. Unquowa Sch., Fairfield, 1963-69; bd. dirs. Fairfield U. Playhouse, 1971-73, Downtown Cabaret Theatre, Bridgeport, 1975-76; bd. missions Southport Congl. Ch., 1998. Mem. AAP (compensation survey com.), Fairfield Women's Exch. (bd. dirs. 1993). Home: 101 Twin Brooks Ln Fairfield CT 06430-2834

SPENCE, CLARK CHRISTIAN, history educator; b. Great Falls, Mont., May 25, 1923; s. Christian Edward and Lela (Killion) S.; m. Mary Lee Nance, Sept. 12, 1953; children: Thomas Christian, Ann Leslie. BA, U. Colo., 1948, MA, 1951; PhD, U. Minn., 1955. Instr. Carleton Coll., Northfield, Minn., 1954-55; instr., then assoc. prof. Pa. State U., 1955-60; vis. lectr. U. Calif.-Berkeley, 1960-61; mem. faculty U. Ill., Champaign, 1961—, prof. history, 1964-90, prof. emeritus, 1990—, chmn. dept., 1967-70, assoc. mem. Ctr. for Advanced Study, 1975. Vis. lectr. Yale, summer 1964; vis. prof. U. Colo., summer 1967; disting. vis. prof. Ariz. State U., spring 1988. Author: British Investment and the American Mining Frontier, 1958, God Speed the Plow: The Coming of Steam Cultivation to Great Britain, 1960, Sinews of American Capitalism: An Economic History, 1964, The American West, 1966, Mining Engineers in the American West, 1970, Territorial Politics and Government in Montana, 1864-89, 1975, Montana: A Bicentennial History, 1978, The Rainmakers: American Pluviculture to World War II, 1980, The Salvation Army Farm Colonies, 1985, The Conrey Placer Mining Company, 1989, The Northern Gold Fleet: Twentieth Century Gold Dredging in Alaska, 1996, For Wood River or Bust: Idaho's Silver Boom of the 1880s, 1999. Served with USAAF, 1943-46. Fulbright fellow Eng., 1953-54; Ford Found. fellow, 1963-64; Guggenheim fellow, 1970-71; recipient ann. book award Agrl. History Soc., 1959 Mem. Western History Assn. (pres. 1969-70), Mining Hist. Assn. (pres. 1990-91), Phi Beta Kappa, Phi Alpha Theta. Home: 1107 Foley St Champaign IL 61820-6326

SPENCE, DIANNA JEANNENE, software engineer, educator; b. Mountain View, Calif., June 5, 1964; d. Ronald Kenneth and Susan (Durham) S. BA, Coll. William and Mary, 1985; MS, Ga. State U., 1996. Tchr. math. and computers Woodward Acad., College Park, Ga., 1985-90; software engr. Computer Comm. Specialists, Inc., Norcross, 1990-98; ind. cons., 1998—; instr. computer sci. Ga. Perimeter Coll., 1999, 2002—. Tutor, 1994—. Mem. Pi Kappa Phi, Pi Mu Epsilon. Jewish. Avocations: travel, writing, music, theater.

SPENCE, DONALD POND, psychologist, psychoanalyst; b. N.Y.C., Feb. 8, 1926; s. Ralph Beckett and Rita (Pond) S.; m. Mary Newbold Cross, June 2, 1951; children: Keith, Sarah, Laura, Katherine. AB, Harvard U., 1949; PhD, Columbia U., 1955. Lic. psychologist, N.Y., N.J. From rsch. asst. to prof. psychology NYU, 1954-74; prof. psychiatry Robert Wood Johnson Med. Sch., Piscataway, N.J., 1974-95; ret., 1995. Vis. prof. psychology Stanford (Calif.) U., 1971-72, Princeton (N.J.) U., 1975-95, Louvain-le-Neuve, Belgium, 1980, William Alanson White Inst., N.Y.C., 1992; mem. personality and cognition rsch. rev. com. NIMH, 1969-73. Author: Narrative Truth and Historical Truth, 1982, The Freudian Metaphor, 1987, The Rhetorical Voice of Psychoanalysis, 1994; mem. editl. bd. Psychoanalysis and Contemporary Thought, Psychol. Inquiry, Theory and Psychology; contbr. articles to profl. jours. With U.S. Army, 1944-46, ETO. Recipient rsch. scientist award NIMH, 1968-74; decorated 2 battle stars. Fellow APA (pres. theoretical and philos. divsn. 1992-93), Am. Psychoanalytic Assn., N.Y. Acad. Sci., Sigma Xi. Democrat. Home: 9 Haslet Ave Princeton NJ 08540-4913 E-mail: dpshaslet@aol.com.

SPENCE, EDELMIRA, social worker; b. Patillas, P.R., Sept. 27, 1942; BA, U. P.R., 1965. Elem. sch. tchr. Dept. of Edn., Patillas, PR, 1962—63, lunch supr. Arroyo, 1966, theater tchr. Guayama, 1966—67; employer interviewer Dept. of Labor, 1967—85; Hispanic out-reach worker Cath. Charities, Southbridge, Mass., 1986—91, area adminstr., 1991—. Mem. literacy vol. bd. Literacy Vol., Southbridge, 1988—; literacy amb. Literacy Vols., 1998. Recipient Angel Among Us award, Tri-Cmty. Aids Project, Southbridge, 2000.

SPENCE, FAYE YVONNE, elementary school educator; b. Raleigh, N.C., Nov. 11, 1952; d. Quinton and Martha (Wilkes) S. BA, N.C. Cen. U., 1974, MEd, 1982. Cert. middle childhood generalist Nat. Bd. Certification, 1998. Remedial reading tchr. Marboro County Schs., Bennettsville, S.C.; instr. Vance Granville Community Coll., Warrenton, N.C.; tchr. Durham (N.C.) City Schs., Warren County Schs., Warrenton, kindergarten tchr., tchr. grade 1, mentor tchr.; tchr. grade 3 Wake County Sch. Presenter math. workshop grades K-6. Named Outstanding Math. Educator for Region 3, 1991; Teaching Excellence and Math. Team fellow, 1991-95. Mem. NEA, ASCD, N.C. Assn. Educators (assn. rep. Warren County chpt., chairperson PACE), N.C. Tchrs. Math., N.C. Coun. Tchr. Educators (nat. bd. cert. mid. childhood generalist 1998). Home: 5921 Three Ponds Rd Holly Springs NC 27540-8878 Office: RR 4 Box 463 Warrenton NC 27589-9116

SPENCE, GERALD LEONARD, lawyer, writer; b. Laramie, Wyo., Jan. 8, 1929; s. Gerald M. and Esther Sophie (Pfleeger) S.; m. Anna Wilson, June 20, 1947; children: Kip, Kerry, Kent, Katy; m. LaNelle Hampton Peterson, Nov. 18, 1969. BSL, U. Wyo., 1949, LLB, 1952, LLD (hon.), 1990. Bar: Wyo. 1952, U.S. Ct. Claims 1952, U.S. Supreme Ct. 1982. Sole practice, Riverton, Wyo., 1952-54; county and pros. atty. Fremont County, 1954-62; ptnr. various law firms, Riverton and Casper, 1962-78; sr. ptnr. Spence, Moriarty & Schuster, Jackson, 1978—. Lectr. legal orgns. and law schs. Author: (with others) Gunning for Justice, 1982, Of Murder and Madness, 1983, Trial by Fire, 1986, With Justice for None, 1989, From Freedom to Slavery, 1993, How To Argue and Win Every Time, 1995, The Making of a Country Lawyer, 1996, O.J.: The Last Word, 1997, Give Me Liberty, 1998, A Boy's Summer, 2000, Gerry Spence's Wyoming: The Landscapes, 2000, Half Moon and Empty Stars, 2001, Seven Simple Steps to Personal Freedom, 2001. Mem. ABA, Wyo. Bar Assn., Wyo. Trial Lawyers Assn., Assn. Trial Lawyers Am., Nat. Assn. Criminal Def. Lawyers Office: Spence Moriarity & Schuster PO Box 548 Jackson WY 83001-0548

SPENCE, HOWARD TEE DEVON, judge, arbitrator, lawyer, consultant, insurance executive, government official; b. Corinth, Miss., Sept. 29, 1949; s. T. P. and Dorothy M.S.; m. Diane Earl Williams, Feb. 26, 1977 (div. June 1986); children: Derek, Tina, Steven. BA, Mich. State U., 1970, M in Criminal Justice Adminstrn., 1975, M in Labor-Indsl. Relations, 1981, MBA, 1983; JD, U. Mich., 1976, M in Pub. Adminstrn., 1977. Bar: Mich. 1976, U.S. Dist. Ct. (ea. dist.) Mich. 1976, U.S. Ct. Appeals (6th cir.) 1976, U.S. Supreme Ct. 1980, U.S. Dist. Ct. (we. dist.) Mich. 1986; cert. ins. examiner. Counselor State Prison of So. Mich., Jackson, 1971-76; personnel adminstr. Mich. Dept. Commerce, Lansing, 1976-77; asst. dir. Mich. Pub. Service Commn., 1977-78; dep. ins. commr. Mich. Ins. Bur., 1978-92; ptnr., cons. Spence & Assocs., 1983—; adminstrv. law judge State of Mich., 1992—. Arbitrator U.S. Dist. Ct. (we. dist.) Mich., Grand Rapids, 1986, Mich. Employment Rels. Commn., 1992-2002; adj. law prof. Thomas M. Cooley Law Sch., Lansing, 1977-80; adj. instr. Nat. Jud. Coll., Reno, 1993-98; presenter in field. Author short stories. Sec., v.p. Ingham County Housing Commn., Okemos, Mich., 1985-90; bd. dirs. Econ. Devel. Corp. City of Lansing, 1981-85. Mem.: NAACP (life), Ins. Regulatory Examiners Soc. (bd. dirs., nat. pres. 1990—91), Am. Judges Assn., Wolverine Bar Assn., Black Lawyers Assn., Nat.Conf. Adminstrv. Law Judges, Nat. Conf. Adminstrv. Law Judges, Mich. Assn. Adminstrv. Law Judges (pres. 1998), Assn. Black Judges Mich., Nat. Bar Assn., Mich. Bar Assn. (legal edn. com., mem. adminstrv. law sect. coun.), ABA (editor in chief NCALJ newsletter 1998—99), Blue Key, Kappa Delta Lambda (pres., chmn. bd. dirs., adminstr. Project Alpha, Edn. Found. Inc.), Alpha Phi Alpha. Mem. Ch. of Christ. Club: Renaissance, Economic (Detroit). Avocations: tennis, racquetball, camping, dancing. Home: 1637 Willow Creek Dr Lansing MI 48917-9643 E-mail: htspence@spence-associates.com.

SPENCE, JAMES ROBERT, JR. television sports executive, educator; b. Bronxville, N.Y., Dec. 20, 1936; s. James Robert and Mary Jeffery (Grant) S.; m. Betsy Jo Viener, June 16, 1992. BA, Dartmouth Coll., 1958. Prodn. asst. ABC Sports, Inc. (known as Sports Programs, Inc. through 1966), N.Y.C., 1960-63; asst. to exec. producer ABC's Wide World of Sports, 1963-66, coordinating producer, 1966-70; v.p. program planning ABC Sports, Inc., 1970-78, sr. v.p., 1978-86; pres. Sports Television Internat. Inc., N.Y.C., 1986—. Adj. assoc. prof. broadcasting NYU Sch. Continuing and Profl. Studies, N.Y.C., 1999—. Author: Up Close and Personal - The Inside Story of Network Television Sports, 1988. Served with U.S. Army, 1958-60. Mem.: Westchester Country (Rye, N.Y.). Office: Sports TV Internat Inc PO Box 6242 New York NY 10150-6242

SPENCE, JANET BLAKE CONLEY (MRS. ALEXANDER PYOTT SPENCE), civic worker; b. Upper Montclair, N.J., Aug. 17, 1915; d. Walter Abbott and Ethel Maud (Blake) Conley; m. Alexander Pyott Spence, June 10, 1939; children: Janet Spence Kerr, Robert Moray, Richard Taylor. Student, Vassar Coll., 1933-35; cert., Katharine Gibbs Sch., 1936. Active various community drives; chmn. Darien (Conn.) Assembly, 1955-56; sec., chmn. Wilton Jr. Assembly, 1961-63; subscription chmn. Candlelight Concerts Wilton, Conn., 1963-65; rec. sec. Pub. Health Nursing Assn. Wilton Bd., 1964-67; corr., rec. sec. Royle Sch. Bd., Darien, 1952-55; fund raiser Vassar Class of 1937; mem. Washington Valley Community Assn.; mem. N.J. Symphony Orch. League, treas. Morris County br. 1978-83, corr. sec. 1982-83, pres. 1985-89, acting pres. 1989—, state coun. mem. 1985-89, acting pres. Morris br. 1989-90; docent Macculloch Hall Historica Mus., Morristown, N.J., 1992—. Mem. Vassar Alumni Assn., Dobbs Alumni Assn., Jersey Hills Vassar Club Morristown (ann. fund raiser), Woman's Club, Wilton Garden Club (life), Washington Valley Cmty. Assn. (life corr. sec. 1977-82, pres. 1982-84, v.p. 1984-85, co-pres. 1985-86, chmn. membership com. 1987-89, archives com. 1988—, treas. 1990—), Washington Valley Home Econs. Club. Mem. United Ch. Of Christ. Home: Apt 5D 1212 Foulk Rd Wilmington DE 19803-2752 Address: 8 Evergreen Ave Kennebunk ME 04043

SPENCE, MARJORIE A. medical/surgical nurse; b. Pitts., Mar. 2, 1950; d. James Milton and Euphemia Martha (Brenner) McDowell; m. James L. Spence, Dec. 15, 1979. BSN, U. Evansville, 1972; MS in Nursing, U. Fla., 1989. Lic. advanced RN practitioner, Fla.; cert. adult nurse practitioner. Staff/charge nurse Gainesville (Fla.) VA Med. Ctr.; staff/charge nurse, relief supr. Transylvania Community Hosp., Brevard, N.C.; asst. head nurse Nairobi (Kenya) Hosp.; head nurse surg. fl. Lake City (Fla.) VA Med. Ctr.; head nurse rehab. unit Gainesville VA Med. Ctr., occupational health nurse, 1992—. Lt. USN, 1975-80. Mem. ANA (mem. coun. for advanced nursing practice, cert. med./surg. nurse), Sigma Theta Tau, Alpha Tau Delta.

SPENCE, MARY LEE, historian, educator; b. Kyle, Tex., Aug. 4, 1927; d. Jeremiah Milton and Mary Louise (Hutchison) Nance; m. Clark Christian Spence, Sept. 12, 1953; children: Thomas Christian, Ann Leslie. BA, U. Tex., 1947, MA, 1948; PhD, U. Minn., 1957. Instr., asst. prof. S.W. Tex. State U., San Marcos, 1948-53; lectr. Pa. State U., State College, 1955-58; mem. faculty U. Ill., Urbana-Champaign, 1973—, asst. prof., assoc. prof., 1973-81, 81-89, prof. history, 1989-90, prof. emerita, 1990—. Editor (with Donald Jackson) The Expeditions of John Charles Fremont, 3 vols., 1970-84, (with Clark Spence) Fanny Kelly's Narrative of Her Captivity Among the Sioux Indians, 1990, (with Pamela Herr) The Letters of Jessie Benton Fremont, 1993, The Arizona Diary of Lily Fremont, 1878-1881, 1997; contbr. articles to profl. jours. Mem. Children's Theater Bd., Urbana-Champaign, 1965-73. Grantee

Nat. Hist. Pub. and Records Commn., Washington, 1977-78, 87-90, Huntington Libr., 1992; recipient Excellent Advisor award Liberal Arts and Sci. Coll./U. Ill., 1986. Mem. Western History Assn. (pres. 1981-82), Orgn. Am. Historians, Phi Beta Kappa (exec. sect. Gamma chpt. 1985-89, pres. 1991-92), Phi Alpha Theta. Episcopalian. Home: 1107 Foley Avet Champaign IL 61820-6326 Office: U Ill Dept History 810 S Wright St Urbana IL 61801-3644 E-mail: c-spence@uiuc.edu.

SPENCE, PATRICK ANTHONY, international trade specialist; b. Pozzuoli, Italy, May 3, 1967; (parents Am. citizens); s. Robert Anthony and Felicitas Irene (Bienek) Spence. BA in Polit. Sci., U. Tenn., 1990; MBA in Internat. Bus., Ga. State U., 1996. Mgr. export trade Contrad Internat., Atlanta, 1996-97; ops. analyst Ctrl. Parking Corp., Nashville, 1997-2000; internat. trade specialist Internat. Trade Ctr., 2000—. Capt. USAR, 1990—. Mem.: World Trade Orgn. Avocation: historical preservation. Home: 1515 Holly St Nashville TN 37206

SPENCE, PAUL HERBERT, librarian; b. Geraldine, Ala., Dec. 25, 1923; s. John Clardy and Leila (Carrell) S.; m. Ruth Schmidt, May 9, 1954; children—John Carrell, Peter Schmidt, Robert McCollough AB, Emory U., 1948, MA, 1956; PhD, U. Ill., 1969. Asst. reference librarian Emory U., Atlanta, 1950-53; periodical reference librarian Air U., Maxwell AFB, 1953-56; dir. library Air Force Inst. of Tech., Wright-Patterson AFB, Ohio, 1957-58; asst. dir. social studies U. Notre Dame, South Bend, Ind., 1959-60, U. Nebr., Lincoln, 1960-63; history and polit. sci. librarian U. Ill., Urbana, 1963-66; assoc. dir. libraries U. Ga., Athens, 1966-70; dir. libraries U. Ala., Birmingham, 1970-84, collection devel. librarian, 1985-89, prof. emeritus, 1989—, libr. cons., 1990—. Bd. dirs. Southeastern Library Network, Atlanta, 1973-75. Served with U.S. Army, 1943-46, ETO Mem. ALA (council mem. 1976-78), Ala. Library Assn. (treas. 1975-76), Southeastern Library Assn. (pres. 1980-82) Democrat. Presbyterian. Home: 614 Warwick Rd Birmingham AL 35209-4426 Office: U Ala at Birmingham 172 Sterne Libr Birmingham AL 35294-0001 E-mail: pspence@beowulf.mhsl.uab.edu.

SPENCE, PHILIP WILLIAM, manufacturing executive, consultant; b. Chadwell Heath, Essex, Great Britian, June 9, 1947; came to U.S., 1960; S. Albert William and Alwen Dorothy S.; m. Sandra Lee Spence, Oct. 19, 1968; children: Philip D., Christian W., Meredith E. BS cum laude, U. Scranton, 1981; MA, Ind. U. Pa., 1986, Webster U., 1987. Commd. 2d U.S. Army, 1966; advanced through grades to col., 1987; chief opns. Nat. Guard Bus., Washington, 1989-90, dep. dir. support, 1990-93, dir. environ. programs, 1993-95, chief staff, 1995-96; v.p. McVey Co. Inc. Internat., Alexandria, Va., 1998—; dir. vets. svcs. Vols. of Am. Fla., Tampa, Fla. Advisor Drug Enforcement Adminstrn., Washington, 1993; cons. SAIC, McLean, Va., 1998—, Army Sci. Bd., WaAshington, 1999-2000. Master capt. USCG, 1966-87. Recipient Pres. Environ. Excellence award White House, 1995. Mem. Nat. Sojourners, Mason, William Daugherty Royal Arch, Officer Candidate Sch. Hall of Fame, Quantico Yacht Club (commodore 1993-94). Avocations: boating, running. Home: 4230 48th Ave S Saint Petersburg FL 33711 Office: Vols of Am 605 S Blvd Tampa FL 33606 E-mail: pspence1@tampabay.rr.com.

SPENCE, RICHARD DEE, former railroad executive; b. Tucumcari, N.Mex., Apr. 7, 1925; s. Andrew Dole and Myrtle Hannah (Roach) S.; m. Mary Ames Kellogg, July 24, 1976; children: Mary B., Ames T., Richard T.; children from previous marriage: Diana, Richard N. BS, UCLA, 1949; grad., Transp. Mgmt. Program, Stanford U., 1956, Sr. Execs. Program, MIT, 1962. With So. Pacific Transp. Co., San Francisco, 1946-75, asst. v.p. ops., 1967-69, v.p. ops., 1969-75; pres., chief oper. officer Consol. Rail Corp., Phila., 1975-78; pres. L&N R.R. Co., Louisville, 1978-80; exec. v.p. ops. Family Lines Rail System, 1980-84; cons. in field, 1984-90; dir., prin. Skippingdale Paper Products, England, 1986-97. With USN, 1943-46. Mem. Ponte Vedra Club, Sawgrass Club, Bohemian Club, Golf House Club of Elie (Scotland), Phi Kappa Sigma. Republican. Episcopalian. Home and Office: 339 Ponte Vedra Blvd Ponte Vedra Beach FL 32082-1813

SPENCE, ROBERT LEROY, publishing executive; b. Carlisle, Pa., Sept. 13, 1931; s. Leroy Oliver and Esther Helen (Lau) S.; m. Barbara Amelia Hunter, Sept. 1, 1954 (div. Sept. 1978); children— Robert Roy, Bonnie Leigh; m. 2d, Maryanne Elizabeth Yacono, Jan. 10, 1979 BA, Dickinson Coll., 1953; postgrad, Temple U., 1955-57, Rutgers U., 1956, 59-60, U. Pa., 1960. Cert. tchr., N.J. Chmn. dept. math. Haddon Heights High Sch., N.J., 1954-62; sr. editor Silver Burdett Co., Morristown, 1962-64; editor-in-chief Harcourt Brace Jovanovich, Inc., N.Y.C., 1964-81; v.p., pub. Harper & Row Publishers, Inc., 1981-85, Scribner Ednl. Pubs. div. Macmillan, Inc., N.Y.C., 1985; pres. R&M Spence, Inc., Sparta, N.J., 1985—. Author textbook series: Growth in Mathematics, 1978, Excel in Mathematics, 1989-90, Mathematics Plus: Multicultural Projects, 1993. Mem. Assn. Am. Pubs. (mem. exec. com. 1981-84), Nat. Council Tchrs. Math., Internat. Reading Assn., Am. Numismatic Assn. Avocations: rare coin collecting; coin newsletter author and publisher; artist; writer. Home and Office: 37 Heather Ln Sparta NJ 07871-3538 E-mail: rlsmys@tellurian.net.

SPENCE, SAMUEL STANFORD, tax accountant, day care provider; b. Kingston, Jamaica; came to U.S., 1965; s. Frederick Carlton and Maisie Evans (Hines) S.; children: Samuel Stanford, Tnoia Michelle, Kenneth Anthony, Aaron Matthew; m. Mary Frances Dunn. BS in Bus. Acctg., Fordham U., 1976; Ordained, Moravian Coll. and Sem., 1962. Tax acct., Phila.; pres. The Stanford Group, Day Car Providers, Phila. Elder Garden of prayer Ch. of God in Christ, Phila. Avocations: photography. Home: PO Box 17061 Philadelphia PA 19105-7061

SPENCE, SANDRA, retired professional administrator; b. McKeesport, Pa., Mar. 25, 1941; d. Cedric Leroy and Suzanne (Haudenshield) S. BA, Allegheny Coll., 1963; MA, Rutgers U., 1964. With Pa. State Govt., Harrisburg, 1964-68, Appalachian Regional Commn., Washington, 1968-75; legis. rep. Nat. Assn. Counties, 1975-77; fed. rep. Calif. Dept. Transp., 1977-78; dir. congl. affairs Amtrak, 1978-81, corp. sec., 1981-83; dir. computer svcs. Nat. R.R. Passenger Corp., 1983-84; co-owner Parkhurst-Spence Inc., 1985; owner The Spence Group, 1986-90; v.p. Bostrom Corp., Washington, 1990-92; exec. dir. Soc. Glass and Ceramic Decorators, 1992-2000. Chmn. legis. com. Womens Transp. Seminar, 1977-79, dir., 1982-83, v.p., 1983-84, chmn. edn. com., 1982-83; com. on edn. and tng. Transp. Rsch. Bd., 1982-85; mng. ptnr. Cambio Capital Club, 1996. Contbr. articles to profl. jours. Commnr. DC Commn. for Women, 1983—88, sec., 1983—88; pres. Found. for Work of Laity, 2001—; del. Ward III Dem. Com., 1982—90, 1st vice chmn., 1987—88; bd. dir. DC Habitat for Humanity, 1998—2002, chmn. devel. com., 1998—2000, sec., 2000—01. Fellow Eagleton Inst. Politics, 1963-64; recipient Achievement award Transp. Seminar, 1982, 83 Mem. Greater Washington Soc. Assn. Execs. (vice-chair law and legis. com. 1989-90, chmn. 1990-91, chmn. scholarship com. 1992-93, bd. dirs. 1993-96, Rising Star award 1989, Chmn.'s award for Govt. Rels. 1991), Am. Soc. Assn. Execs. (mgmt. cert. 1987), Phi Beta Kappa. Home: 3701 Appleton St NW Washington DC 20016-1807 E-mail: sandy_s@juno.com.

SPENCE, TERRY R. state legislator; b. Wilmington, Del., Nov. 30, 1941; m. Nancy Spence; children: Terry Jr., Mark, Greg, Laura. AS, Goldey Beacom Coll.; BBA, Wilmington Coll. Mem. Dist. 18 Del. Ho. of Reps., spkr. of house, 1987—, ethics and adminstrv. coms., legis. coun.; acct. exec. Brooks Courier Svc. Co., Wilmington, Del. Hon. mem. Wilmington Manor Vol. Fire Co. Recipient Disting. Legis. award MADD, 1987, Disting. Legis. Svc. award Del. Bar Assn., 1986. Mem. NRA, Del. Assn. Retarded Citizens, Del. Assn. Blind Athletes, Lions. Home: 26 Freeport Rd New Castle DE 19720-3019 Office: PO Box 1401 Dover DE 19903-1401 E-mail: tspence@legis.state.de.us.*

SPENCER, A. ARLENE, English educator; b. Seymour, Ind., Oct. 23, 1927; d. Herbert Austin and Elma Montgomery; m. Frank E. Spencer, Dec. 22, 1946 (dec. Apr. 1993); children: JoEllen Manship, James Spencer, Nancy Merbitz, Julie Blume. Student, Franklin Coll., 1945-47, U. Mich., 1947-48; BA, U. Indpls., 1970, MA, 1973. Secondary tchg. lic. Ind. Dept. Edn. English tchr. Beech Grove (Ind.) H.S., 1971-87; adminstrv. asst. Indpls. News, 1988-91; adj. faculty Ivy Tech. State Coll., Inpdls., 1993-2000; supr. tests McGraw-Hill, 1998—. Pvt. tutor Perry Twp. Schs., Indpls., 1996, adv. bd. mem., 1997. Author: We Can Print Anything, 1992; editor: Hugging the Heartland, 1991; columnist Indpls. Star/News, 1993-2000; author of poetry. Little Theater judge Encore, Indpls., 1993-97. Mem. Nat. League Am. Pen Women (historian 1988-89, nat. publicity 1989-2000, state pres. 2000-02, 1st prize poetry 1998), Ind. Ret. Tchrs., Beech Grove Ret. Educators (newsletter editor 2000—), Franklin Coll. Alumni Coun., Ind. Parent Tchrs. (life), Delta Zeta Alumni Orgn. Republican. Avocations: crossword puzzles, traveling, gardening, reading biographies. Home: 2036 Rosedale Dr Indianapolis IN 46227

SPENCER, ALBERT FRANKLIN, physical education and education educator; b. Pitts., Dec. 31, 1943; s. Albert Clair and Ann Mary (Kielbas) S. BS in Edn., Slippery Rock (Pa.) State, Coll., 1966; MS, Clarion (Pa.) State Coll., 1981; PhD in LS, Fla. State U., Tallahassee, 1985, PhD in Phys. Edn., 1992. Phys. edn. tchr., libr., coach St. John's Indian Sch., Komatke, Ariz., 1976-77, Duncan (Ariz.) H.S., 1977-79; tchr. math. and sci. Army and Navy Acad., Carlsbad, Calif., 1979-80; phys. edn. tchr., libr., coach Baboquivari H.S., Sells, Ariz., 1980-81; asst. men's intercoll. basketball coach Fla. State U., Tallahassee, 1981-83; asst. prof. phys. edn., dir. audiovisual svcs. St. Leo (Fla.) Coll., 1983-86; asst. prof. Atlanta U. and Emory U., Atlanta, 1986-87; assoc. prof. phys. edn./athletics, libr. dir., coach Ga. Mil. Coll., Milledgeville, 1987-90; asst. prof. edn. U. Nev., Las Vegas, 1991-94; asst. prof. phys. edn., dept. human performance/health scis. Rice U., Houston, 1994—. Cons. ednl. tech. Atlanta Pub. Schs., 1986-87; profl. basketball scout Bertka Agy. and L.A. Lakers, 1985-91; deptl. dir. KMart, New Kensington, Pa., 1972-74; dir. athletics YMCA, Kittanning, Pa., 1969. Contbg. author: Twentieth-Century Young Adult Writers, 1994; contbr. articles and revs. to profl. jours. Fundraiser KC, Las Vegas; vol. coach for youth league St. Anthony Elem. Sch., San Antonio, Fla.; scoutmaster Boy Scouss Am., New Kensington. Mem. AAHPERD, ALA, Am. Libr. and Info. Sci. Educators, Fla. Assn. for Health, Phys. Edn., Recreation and Dance, Tex. Assn. for Health, Phys. Edn., Recreation and Dance, U.S. Phys. Edn. Assn., Tex. Faculty Assn., Beta Phi Mu, Omicron Delta Kappa. Roman Catholic. Avocations: writing, golf, basketball, hiking. Office: Rice U Dept Human Perf/Hlth Svcs PO Box 1892 Houston TX 77251-1892

SPENCER, CAROL ANNE, computer systems analyst; b. Orange, N.J., Jan. 15, 1953; d. Robert Anthony and Mary Lee (Cumiskey) Prochazka; m. Kenneth Robert Spencer (div. Dec. 1994); children: Kyle Robert, Amy Eagan. BA, Bates Coll., 1974. Mktg. rep. IBM, various locations, 1974-85; v.p. mktg. P&S Software, Rockaway, N.J., 1985—; systems adminstr. info. tech. divsn. County of Morris, Morristown, 1993—. V.p. planning bd. Twp. of Denville, N.J., 1986-89, chmn. Rep. campaign com., 1987, councilwoman, 1990-95, mayor, 1996-99. Recipient Vol. Svc. award Morris Coun. on Alcoholism and Drug Abuse, 1989. Republican. Methodist. Home: 86 Woodstone Rd Rockaway NJ 07866-4132 E-mail: caspencer@att.net.

SPENCER, CHARLES DEWITT, physics educator; b. High Point, N.C., Aug. 20, 1943; s. Charles DeWitt and Eulalah (Mull) S. AB, Berea Coll., 1965; PhD, U. N.C., 1972. Grad. teaching and rsch. asst. U. N.C., 1965-72, instr., 1972-73; asst. prof. Ithaca (N.Y.) Coll., 1973-80, computing cons., asst. prof., 1980-82, asst. prof., 1982-87, assoc. prof., 1987-90, prof., 1990—, chair dept. physics, 1993-2000. Presenter in field. Author: Digital Design for Computer Data Acquisition, 1990, (software program) Physics Plot; contbr. articles to profl. jours. Grantee NSF, 1976, 77, 78, 81-84, 82-85, 88-92, 93-98. Mem. AAAS, Am. Phys. Soc., Am. Assn. Physics Tchrs., Phi Kappa Phi, Sigma Xi, Sigma Pi Sigma. Democrat. Avocations: travel, hiking. Home: 9 Penny Ln Ithaca NY 14850-6266 Office: Ithaca Coll Physics Dept Ctr for Natural Scis Ithaca NY 14850 E-mail: spencer@ithaca.edu.

SPENCER, CONSTANCE MARILYN, secondary education educator; b. New York, Jan. 2, 1942; m. Robert William Spencer, Dec. 30, 1966; children: Keane Thomas, Keith Lyle. BA, U. Calif., Santa Barbara, 1964; MA in English, U. West Fla., 1974. Cert. lang. devel. specialist, preliminary adminstr. Credentialed tchr. Valley Stream (N.Y.) N. H.S.; tchr. Workman Jr. H.S., Pensacola, Fla., Imperial Beach (Calif.) Elem. Sch.; substitute tchr. South Bay Union Sch., Imperial Beach; mgr. Geni, Inc., Pasadena, Calif., Avon Products, Inc., Pasadena; tchr. Walnut (Calif.) H.S., 1985—; pres. Am. Computer Instrn. Inc., Upland, Calif. Grant writer Walnut Valley Unified Sch. Dist., 1986-99, mentor tchr., 1988-2000; accreditation co-chair Walnut H.S., 1993-94. Mem., sec. Toastmistress, Ontario, Calif., 1977-86. Grantee Calif. Dept. Edn., 1987, Walnut Valley Unified Sch. Dist., 1988, Diamond Bar (Calif.) Walnut Valley Found., Rotary, 1994-2000. Republican. Roman Catholic. Avocation: writing. Home: 2238 Coolcrest Way Upland CA 91784-1290 Office: Walnut HS 400 Pierre Rd Walnut CA 91789-2535

SPENCER, DAVID ANTHONY, geologist, researcher; b. London, Nov. 7, 1963; s. Henry William George and Veronica Clair (Bonanno) S. BSc in Geology with honors, U. Exeter, Eng., 1986; Diploma, MSc in Structural Geology, U. London, 1988; Dr Natural Sci., Swiss Fed. Inst. Tech., Zurich, 1993. Chartered geologist, European geologist. Ins. claims broker Winchester Bowring Ltd., London, 1982-83; platinum exploration geologist Eastern Bushveld Complex, South Africa, 1986-87; rsch. fellow Swiss Fed. Inst. Tech., Zürich, 1988-89, rsch. and tchr. asst., 1989-92, vis. ETH rsch. fellow, 1992-93, vis. rsch. fellow, 1993-94, rsch. fellow in tectonics Zurich, 1994-97; vis. lectr. U. of the Punjab, Lahore, Pakistan, 1995; vis. scientist Tokyo Inst. Tech., Zurich, 1996; rsch. asst. prof., lectr. in structural geology U. Maine, Orono, 1997-98. Vis. scientist U. Beijing, 1986; vis. prof. U. of the Punjab, Lahore, 1997—; Himalayan regional coordinating com. Internat. Lithosphere Program, 1992-96, com. tectonic map of Himalaya, 1995; organizer confs. in field; founder, moderator, coord. HimNet, 1994-96; presenter, cons., lectr. in field. Contbr. numerous articles to profl. jours.; European regional editor Himalayan Notes, 1994-97; reviewer numerous internat. jours. in field. Sir John Cass Found. scholar, 1987-88, travel award, 1988; recipient travel award Swiss Geol. Soc., 1991, 93, Huber-Kudlich Found., 1992, Swiss Acad. Natural Scis., 1992, Pub. award Staub Fund, 1992; rsch. fellow Swiss Nat. Sci. Found., 1994-97; recipient Duke of Edinburgh Gold award, 1987. Fellow Geol. Soc., Royal Geog. Soc., Royal Soc. Arts, Am. Geog. Soc., Geol. Assn. of Can.; mem. AAAS, Inst. Petroleum, Royal Instn. of Gt. Britain, Royal Scottish Geog. Soc. (profl. assoc.), Order of Internat. Fellowship, Internat. Assn. Structural/Tectonic Geologists, Mineral. Soc., European Assn. Geoscientists and Engrs., Soc. for Sedimentary Geology, Geosci. Info. Soc., Computer Oriented Geol. Soc., European Union Geoscis., Am. Geophys. Union, Assn. Geoscientists for Internat. Devel., Geol. Soc Am., Geol. Soc. Switzerland, Geol. Soc. Pakistan, Geol. Soc. Punjab, Geol. Soc. Nepal, Swiss Mineral. and Petrological Soc., Soc. for Mining, Metallurgy and Exploration, Geochem. Soc., Am. Chem. Soc., Petroleum Exploration Soc. of Gt. Britain, Am. Assn. Petroleum Geologists, Nat. Geog. Soc., Assn. Am. Geographers, Can. Assn. Geographers, Brit. Assn. for Advancement of Sci., Sci. Exploration Soc., N.Y. Acad. Scis., Nat. Earth Sci. Tchrs. Assn., Nat. Assn. Geosci. Tchrs., Assn. for Sci. Edn., Himalayan Found., Himalayan Club, Himalayan Explorers Club, Nepal Studies Assn., Internat. Assn. for Ladakh Studies, Integrated Mountain Rsch. Soc., Internat. Mountain Soc., Brit. Mountaineering Coun., Sigma Xi. Avocations: mountaineering, guitar, long distance walking, sports.

SPENCER, DAWN JOYCE, librarian, educator; b. St. Louis, Nov. 7, 1938; d. Leslie Sylvan II and Iris Nunn (Burdick) S. AB, Syracuse U., 1964, MA, 1967, MA, 1995. Cert. secondary education educator, N.Y., Calif. Exec. sec. to permanent observer Rep. Korea to UN UN, N.Y.C., 1964-65; secondary level social studies tchr. Bd. Edn., Utica, N.Y., 1966-69; mgr. apt. complex Oakland, Calif., 1969-75; lectr. Fukushima (Japan) U., Fukushima Med. Coll., Sakura no Seibo Women's Coll., Kennedy Internat. Coll., 1975-94; dir. Bowerston (Ohio) Pub. Libr., 1996—. English fluency instr. to migrant workers N.Y. Dept. Edn., Clinton, summers 1967-68; sr. lectr. Fukushima Women's Coll., 1982-94. Pres. Syracuse-in-Asia, 1962-64; advisor U.S. Mil. Svc. Recruitment, Utica, N.Y., 1966-69; active ASPCA, HSUS, APL, Oakland, 1969-75, Fukushima Organic Farm Cooperative, 1982-94, Japan Animal Welfare Soc., Tokyo, 1993-94, African Wildlife Found., Am. Rivers, Best Friends Animal Sanctuary, Ctr. Marine Conservation, Defenders of Wildlife, numerous others. Mem. AARP, ASPCA, Bowerston Women's Club, Am. Legal Def. Fund, Greenpeace, Nat. Audubon Soc., African Wildlife Found., World Wildlife Fund, others. Democrat. Avocations: animal welfare, snow and water skiing, jazz, computers. Office: Bowerston Pub Libr 200 Main St Bowerston OH 44695 Fax: 740-269-8503. E-mail: djspence@tusco.net., spenceda@oplin.lib.oh.us.

SPENCER, DENNIS D. medical educator, director; b. Bedford, Iowa, Apr. 1, 1945; MD, Wash. U., St. Louis. Prof. of neurosurgery Yale, chair, chief of neurosurgery; dir. epilepsy program Yale; prof. in chief Yale-New Haven Hosp., 1987—; intern Barnes Hosp. , St. Louis, 1971—72; asst. neurosurgeon Yale-New Haven Hosp., 1977—80, assoc. neurosurgeon, 1977—80, residency, 1972—76. Achievements include first to in stero taxic cellular replacement therapy for patients with parkinson's desease. Office: Am Bd Neurological Surgery 6550 Fannin St Ste 2139 Houston TX 77030*

SPENCER, DOUGLAS LLOYD, chemist, manufacturing executive; b. Berkeley, Calif., July 19, 1952; s. Alma Glenn and Anna Lea (Lloyd) S.; m. Connie Jeanette Whitesel, Aug. 23, 1974; children: Jeanette Dawn, Jared Douglas, Jilissa Annette, Janine Marie, Janelle Renee, Jeffrey Brian. AA, Diablo Valley Coll., 1971; BS, Brigham Young U., 1974. Lab instr., chemistry dept. Brigham Young U., 1973-74; rsch. chemist Dow Chem. Western divsn., Pittsburg, Calif., 1975-80; pres. Sunset Distbg., Inc., Brentwood, 1980-82, Maier & Assocs., Inc., Brentwood, 1982-83, Doug Spencer & Assocs., Placerville, 1983-94; buyer, major wholesale merchandise distbr. Bacar, Inc., San Jose, 1995-97; life agt. Beneficial Life, Sacramento, 1997—2000; sales mgr. Fortel Traffic Inc., Hollister, 2001—. Mem. Brentwood Planning Commn., 1980-81; missionary, dist. zone leader Ea. States Mission, 1971-73; active Boy Scouts of Am. Rossmoor residents scholar, 1969-71, Brigham Young U. scholar, 1973-74. Republican. Mem. Lds Ch. Avocations: camping, fishing, gardening. Home: 2010 Clearview Dr Hollister CA 95023-6239 E-mail: sixjs@hollinet.com.

SPENCER, EDGAR WINSTON, geology educator; b. Monticello, Ark., May 27, 1931; s. Terrel Ford and Allie Belle (Shelton) S.; m. Elizabeth Penn Humphries, Nov. 26, 1958; children: Elizabeth Shawn, Kristen Shannon. Student, Vanderbilt U., 1949-50; BS, Washington and Lee U., 1953; PhD, Columbia U., 1957. Lectr. Hunter Coll., 1954-57; mem. faculty Washington and Lee U., 1957—, prof. geology, head dept., 1962-95, Ruth Parmly prof. Pres. Rockbridge Area Conservation Coun., 1978-79, 95-98; NSF sci. faculty fellow, New Zealand and Australia; dir. grant for humanities and pub. policy on land use planning Va. Found., 1975; dir. grant Petroleum Rsch. Fund, 1981-82; leader field trip Ctrl. Appalachian Mts. Internat. Geol. Congress, 1989. Author: Basic Concepts of Physical Geology, 1962, Basic Concepts of Historical Geology, 1962, Geology: A Survey of Earth Science, 1965, Introduction to the Structure of the Earth, 1969, 3d edit., 1988, The Dynamics of the Earth, 1972, Physical Geology, 1983, Geologic Maps, 1993, 2nd edit., 2000, Earth Science-Understanding Environmental Systems, 2002. Recipient Va. Outstanding Faculty award Va. Coun. of Higher Edn., 1990. Fellow Geol. Soc. Am., AAAS; mem. Am. Assn. Petroleum Geologists (dir. field seminar on fold and thrust belts 1987, 88-91), Am. Inst. Profl. Geologists, Am. Geophys. Union, Nat. Assn. Geology Tchrs., Yellowstone-Bighorn Rsch. Assn., Phi Beta Kappa (hon.), Omicron Delta Kappa (hon.), Sigma Xi. Home: PO Box 1055 Lexington VA 24450-1055

SPENCER, EDITHA MARY (EDITHA HAYES), artist; b. Oakland, Calif., Sept. 29, 1921; d. William Joseph and Edith Elizabeth (Carew) Hayes; m. Harold Edwin Spencer, Sept. 13, 1947; children: David Hayes, Robert Alan, Eric James, Mark Edward. BA, U. Calif., Berkeley, 1943. One-woman shows include U. Conn. Libr., Storrs, 1974, 83, Slater Meml. Mus., Norwich, Conn., 1994, 2000; exhibited paintings in invitational shows at Occidental Coll., L.A., 1963, Festival of Greater Hartford (Conn.), 1980, Slater Meml. Mus., 1990, Babbidge Libr., U. Conn., Storrs, 2002; exhibitor in juried art shows, 1946—; art editor/editor Oak Leaf (USN periodical), 1943-47; contbr. drawings to portfolio Architecture of Willimantic, 1976, block print bookplates to book Ex-Libris Artists VI, 1982, Am. Artists of the Bookplate: 1970-1990, 1990, linoleum block prints to book Julia Ayres Printmaking Techniques, 1993; block prints commd. by Joshua's Tract Conservation and Historic Trust, Storrs, Conn., 1982, U. Conn. Libr., Storrs, 1982, U. Conn. Found., 1983, Windham (Conn.) Regional Arts Coun., 1986, William Benton Mus. of Art, Storrs, Conn., 1996, Thomas J. Dodd Rsch. Ctr., U. Conn., 2001, Trinity Coll., Hartford, Conn., 2002. Active Ashford (Conn.) Conservation Commn., 1972-77; trustee Joshua's Tract Conservation and Hist. Trust, Storrs, Conn., 1974-79. Recipient numerous awards for paintings. Mem. Conn. Women Artists, Conn. Watercolor Soc., Conn. Acad. Fine Arts, Prytanean Alumnae, Inc., Phi Beta Kappa. Avocation: writing poetry. Home: 294 Mansfield Rd Ashford CT 06278-1414

SPENCER, ELEANOR ANN, foundation executive; b. Pace, Fla., Mar. 19, 1941; d. William Dexter and Eunice Love (Pitts) Gallops; m. William Clifton Spencer, Feb. 4, 1966 (div. 1980); children: Suzanne C. Spencer Collard, Kathleen L. Spencer Cole. Student, North Fla. Jr. Coll., 1959-60, Pensacola Jr. Coll., 1980. Dental asst. Dr. James Watson, Milton, Fla., 1963-66; community vol. Telcare, Inc., 1969-74; exec. dir. Santa Rosa County Council on Aging, 1975—. Bd. dirs. Santa Rosa Mental Health Assn., Milton, 1972, Santa Rosa Guidance Clinic, Milton, 1973-74; mem. council Ctr. on Aging, Pensacola, 1982—; bd. dirs. Fla. Council on Aging, Tallahassee, 1983—. Chair bd. mem. SSS, Local Bd. I, 1983—; mem. govt. affairs com. Santa Rosa C. of C., Milton, 1986—. Mem. Nat. Council on Aging, Nat. Inst. of Sr. Ctrs., Fla. Assn. Sr. Ctrs. (sec. 1984-86), Fla. Transit Assn., So. Gerontology Soc. Clubs: Tanglewood Country (Milton). Office: Santa Rosa County Council on Aging 609 Alabama St Milton FL 32570-4448

SPENCER, ELIZABETH, author; b. Carrollton, Miss., 1921; d. James Luther and Mary James (McCain) S.; m. John Arthur Blackwood Rusher, Sept. 29, 1956. BA, Belhaven Coll., 1942; MA, Vanderbilt U., 1943; LittD (hon.), Southwestern U. at Memphis, 1968; LLD (hon.), Concordia U. at Montreal, 1988; LittD (hon.), U. of the South, 1992; DLitt (hon.), U. N.C., Chapel Hill, 1998, Belhaven Coll., 1999. Instr. N.W. Miss. Jr. Coll., 1943-44, Ward-Belmont, Nashville, 1944-45; reporter The Nashville Tennessean, 1945-46; instr. U. Miss., Oxford, 1948-51, 52-53. Vis. prof. Concordia U., Montreal, Que., Can., 1976-81, adj. prof., 1981-86; vis. prof. U. N.C., Chapel Hill, 1986-92. Author: Fire in the Morning, 1948, This Crooked Way, 1952, The Voice at the Back Door, 1956, The Light in the Piazza, 1960, Knights and Dragons, 1965, No Place for an Angel, 1967, Ship Island and Other Stories, 1968, The Snare, 1972, The Stories of Elizabeth Spencer, 1981, Marilee, 1981, The Salt Line, 1984, Jack of Diamonds and Other Stories, 1988, (play) For Lease or Sale, 1989, On the Gulf, 1991, The Night Travellers, 1991, (memoir) Landscapes of the Heart, 1998, The Southern Woman, 2001; contbr. Recipient Women's Democratic Com. award, 1949, recognition award Nat. Inst. Arts and letters, 1952, Richard and Hinda Rosenthal Found. award Am. Acad. Arts and Letters, 1957, Fortner award for Lit., 1998; Guggenheim Found. fellow, 1953, 1st McGraw-Hill Fiction award, 1960, Henry Bellamann award for creative writing, 1968; Award of Merit medal for the short story Am. Acad. Arts and Letters, 1983, Salem award for lit., 1992, Dos Passos award for fiction, 1992, N.C. Gov.'s award for lit., 1994, Corrington award for lit., 1997, Richard Wright award for lit., 1997, award for non-fiction Miss. Libr. Assn. 1999, Brooks medal Fellowship of So. Writers, 2001; Kenyon Rev. fellow in fiction, 1957; Bryn Mawr Col. Donnelly fellow, 1962; Nat. Endowment for Arts grantee in lit., 1983, Sr. Arts Award grantee Nat. Endowment for Arts, 1988. Mem. Am. Acad. Arts and Letters, Fellowship of So. Writers (charter; vice chancellor 1993-97). Home: 402 Longleaf Dr Chapel Hill NC 27517-3042 E-mail: elizabeth0222@earthlink.net.

SPENCER, FRANK COLE, medical educator; b. Haskell, Tex., 1925; MD, Vanderbilt U., 1947. Intern Johns Hopkins U., Balt., 1947-48, fellow in surgery, 1947-48, asst. resident in surgery, 1953-54; resident in surgery Johns Hopkins Sch. Medicine, 1954-55; surgeon, outpatient dept. Johns Hopkins Hosp., 1955; resident in surgery Wadsworth VA Ctr. Hosp., 1949-50; fellow cardiovascular surgery USPHS, Los Angeles, 1951; asst. prof. surgery Johns Hopkins U., 1955-59, assoc. prof., 1959-61; prof. surgery U. Ky.; chmn. dept. surgery, George David Steward prof. surgery NYU, until 1998, now prof. surgery sch. medicine. Served to lt. M.C., USN, 1951-53. John and Mary R. Markle scholar in med. sci. Johns Hopkins U., 1956. Office: NYU Sch of Medicine Dept of Surgery 550 1st Ave New York NY 10016-6402

SPENCER, GAYLE, b. Charlotte, N.C., Aug. 14, 1947; BA in Health and Phys. Edn., U. S.C., 1969, MA in Health and Phys. Edn., 1973; postgrad., U. N.C., Charlotte, 1983, Coastal Carolina Coll. Tchr. Keenan Jr. High, Columbia, S.C., 1969, Saluda (S.C.) High, 1969-70, Hyatt Pk. Elem., Columbia, 1970-72; tchr. high sch. Providence Day Sch., Charlotte, 1973-84, tchr. elem.

and mid. sch., 1975-84; tchr. Waccamaw Elem., Conway, S.C., 1984-85, Conway Elem., 1984-85, Homewood Elem., Conway, 1986-93, Horry Elem., Aynor, S.C., 1986-91, St. James Mid. Sch., Surfside, 1994—97, Socastee Elem./Carolina Forest Elem., 97-98. Instr. Francis Marion Coll., Florence, S.C., 1973-74, Coastal Carolina Coll., Conway, 1974-75; dir. Tchrs. Understand Fun and Fitness (TUFF); mem. S.C. Tchr. Forum Leadership Coun., 1992-95; mem. Horry County Tchr. of Yr. Selection Com., 1992, 93, Horry County Tchr. Forum Steering Com., 1994—; coach various jr. high, high sch. and coll. athletic teams; presenter in field. Contbr. articles to profl. publs. Mem. Horry County Target 2000 Com., 1990, S.C. Health Frameworks Com., 1992-93; vol. ARC, Am. Heart Assn., Conway C. of C. Named Tchr. of Yr., Homewood Elem. Sch., 1991, 92, Horry County, 1992; scholar Sun News, 1990-91. Mem. NEA, S.C. Edn. Assn. (mem. delegate assembly 1993—), Horry County Edn. Assn. (sec. 1992-94, v.p. 1994-95, pres. 1995—), S.C Assn. Health, Phys. Edn., Recreation and Dance. Home: 182 Watersedge Dr Unit D3 Pawleys Island SC 29585-6449 E-mail: ggator2@aol.com., gspence@ses.sccoast.com.

SPENCER, GEORGE HENRY, lawyer; b. Vienna; s. Frank Henry and Lillian (Godin) S.; m. Joan Betty Spencer, Sept. 16, 1956 (dec.); children: Lucy, Margaret, Robert, Nancy; m. Mollie Cole Sabol, Oct. 31, 1987; stepchildren: Jeanne, Marta. BE, Yale U., 1948; JD, Cornell U., 1952. Bar: D.C., N.Y. Examiner U.S. Patent Office, 1952-54; sole practice N.Y.C., Washington, 1954-62; ptnr. Spencer & Frank, Washington, 1962-98, Venable, Washington, 1998—. Master of bench Prettyman-Leventhal Am. Inn of Ct.; lectr. World Trade Inst. Served to capt. JAGC, U.S. Army, 1956-62. Mem. ABA, Am. Patent Law Assn., Lawyer-Pilots Bar Assn., Am. Arbitration Assn. (panel of arbitrators), Cosmos Club (Washington). Avocations: aviation, music, German and French language studies, poetry. Home: 1102 Flor Ln Mc Lean VA 22102-1737 Office: Venable Attys at Law 1201 New York Ave NW Ste 1000 Washington DC 20005-3917 E-mail: specole@aol.com., ghspencer@venable.com.

SPENCER, HAROLD EDWIN, retired art educator, retired art historian, retired painter; b. Corning, N.Y., Oct. 1, 1920; s. Clayton Judson and Hazel Leona (McCaslin) Spencer; m. Editha Mary Hayes, Sept. 13, 1947; children: David Hayes, Robert Alan, Eric James, Mark Edward. BA, U. Calif., Berkeley, 1948, MA, 1949; PhD, Harvard U., 1968. Teaching asst., vis. instr. U. Calif., Berkeley, 1949, 50; chmn. art dept. Blackburn Coll., Carlinville, Ill., 1949-62; assoc. prof. art dept. Occidental Coll., L.A., 1962-68, chmn. dept., 1963—68; assoc. prof. art U. Conn., Storrs, 1968-69, prof., 1969-88, adminstrv. assoc. to dept. head, 1972-73, assoc. dept. head, 1977-79, coord. art history, 1984-87, prof. emeritus, 1988—. Guest curator William Benton Mus. Art, Storrs, 1979—80; mem. planning com. Weir Farm Trust, Wilton, Conn., 1988—89, bd. overseers, Conn., 1989—93, bd. dirs., v.p., Conn., 1995—; trustee Lyme Acad. Fine Arts, Old Lyme, Conn., 1993—98. Author: The Image Maker, 1975, Wilson Henry Irvine and the Poetry of Light, 1998; co-author: Connecticut and American Impressionism, 1980, Connecticut Masters, Connecticut Treasures, 1989, A Connecticut Place: Weir Farm, An American Painter's Rural Retreat, 2000; editor: Readings in Art History, 2 vols., 1969, Readings in Art History, 3d rev. edit., 1983, American Art: Readings from the Colonial Era to the Present, 1980; contbr. articles to profl. jours.; guest curator Florence Griswold Mus., Old Lyme, 1995—98, guest co-curator Weir Farm Nat. Hist. Site, 1997—2000; exhibitions include in regional and nat. juried and pvt. and pub. collections. With U.S. Mcht. Marine, 1942—46. Recipient various awards for art, 1941—; fellow Harvard U. Faculty Arts and Scis., 1960—61, Frank Knox Meml., 1964—65; grantee U. Conn. Rsch. Found., 1969, 1974—78; scholar U. Calif. James Phelan, 1948—49. Mem.: AAUP, Conn. Acad. Fine Arts, Conn. Acad. Arts and Scis., Coll. Art Assn., Phi Kappa Phi. Democrat. Avocations: reading, travel, poetry. Home: 294 Mansfield Rd Ashford CT 06278-1414

SPENCER, HARRY IRVING, JR. retired banker; b. Worcester, Mass., Feb. 3, 1925; s. Harry Irving and Bertha (Johnson) S.; m. Violet Virginia Bergquist, Sept. 16, 1950; children— Nancy Elaine, Harry Irving III, Carol Helen. BA, Clark U., 1950. With Worcester County Nat. Bank, 1950-82, asst. treas., 1954-58, cashier, 1958-62, v.p., 1966-69, sr. v.p., 1969-77, exec. v.p., cashier, 1977-82, clk., dir., 1980-82; exec. v.p., cashier, sec. Shawmut Worcester County Bank, N.A., 1982-88, also bd. dirs. Sec., treas., dir. Nobility Hill Realty Corp.; dir. Worcester Capital Corp., Wornat Leasing Corp. Bd. dirs. Worcester Taxpayers Assn. Methodist (trustee). Clubs: Kiwanis; Economic (Worcester, Mass.), Plaza (Worcester, Mass.). Home: 79 Birchwood Dr Holden MA 01520-1939 Office: 446 Main St Worcester MA 01608-2359

SPENCER, HEIDI HONNOLD, psychotherapist, writer, educator; b. Washington, June 30, 1943; d. John Otis and Annamarie (Kunz) Honnold; m. Charles David Spencer, Dec. 28, 1962; children: Hans Steven, Jason John, Tanya Anna. BA, U. Pa., 1965; MA, Columbia U., 1966; MSW, Cath. U., 1982; PhD in Adult and Family Psychology, Union Inst., Cin., 1990. Cert. clin. social worker, cert. nat. bd. addictions examiners; lic. social worker, D.C., Md., W.Va. Tchr. h.s. Peace Corps, Yap Island, 1966-68; faculty instr. Ctrl. Wash. State Coll., Ellensburg, 1972-75; parent group facilitator Individual Psychology Assocs., Chevy Chase, Md., 1975-79; group facilitator Georgetown U. Med. Sch., Washington, 1977-80; staff clinician D.C. Inst. Mental Health, 1980-86; pvt. practice in adult psychotherapy Bethesda, Md., 1985—; faculty Cath. U. Wa. Psychoanalytic Found., 1989-91; bd. dirs., cons., faculty, supr. Clin. Social Work Inst. Mem. bd. doctoral program for clin. social workers; counselor, tchr. The Spl. Sch. for Pregnant Teenagers, Seattle, 1969-71; crisis intervention counselor Montgomery County (Md.) Hotline, 1975-79; mental health intern No. Va. Mental Health Inst., Falls Ch., 1979-80; mem. part-time faculty Cath. U., Washington, 1991; cons., counselor Christ Child Soc., Rockville, Md., 1985-86; cons. Jewish Cmty. Ctr., Rockville, 1992, Brooklane Psychiat. Ctr., Hagerstown, Md., 1992, AmeriCorps, Washington, 1996, Affiliated Cmty. Counselors, Inc., Rockville, 1996—; insvc. instr. psychol. and learning ctr. Am. U., Washington, 1990—; chair, Conf. Washington Psychoanalytic Found., 1989-90; cons. The Bilingual Project/Project BUILD, Yakima, Wash., 1973-75; mem. curriculum com. Clin. Social Work Inst., 1991-94; spkr. and presenter in field. Author: (2 vols. book and record) Our Valley-Our Song, 1974, (book) Did I Do Something Wrong: A Supportive Guide for Parents and Loved Ones or People in Psychotherapy, 1995; columnist Family Therapy Acad., 1996-97. Trainer, cons. cmty.-based overflow shelters for homeless, Bethesda, 1989-94; vice chair bd. social concerns Cedar Ln. Unitarian Ch., 1986-87; active dr.-lawyer anti-drug program Fairfax Bar Assn., 1997. Mem. Greater Washington Soc. Clin. Social Work (v.p. for edn. 1992-94, at-large 1994-96, membership task force 1995-96). Baha'I. Avocations: violin, piano, accordion, gardening, writing.

SPENCER, HERBERT HARRY, structural engineering researcher, computer analyst; b. Vienna, Austria, Jan. 2, 1928; came to U.S., 1953; s. Ingenieur Oskar and Bronia (Steinberger) Schnabel; m. Margot Goldrei (div.); m. Sara Slomka, July 24, 1992; 1 child, Gil Oskar. BSc , U. London, 1948, PhD, 1976; MS, Poly. Inst. Bklyn., 1955. Jr. engr. asst. Tarmac Ltd., Coventry, England, 1944-45, George Wimpey & Co., Coventry, 1945-46, Kershaw & Kaufman, London, 1946-48; engr. William Halcrow & Ptnrs., 1948-49, Hydraulic Dept., Nazareth, Israel, 1949-50, Quibuts Eyn Hashofet, Galilee, Israel, 1950-51, Rendel Palmer & Tritton, London, 1951-53; rsch. asst. Poly. Inst. Bklyn., 1953-55; instr. Yale U., New Haven, 1955-56; rsch. asst., lectr. Columbia U., N.Y.C., 1956-59; asst. prof. San Diego (Calif.) State Coll., 1959-61; rsch. assoc. Caltech, Pasedena, Calif., 1961-62; asst. prof. U. So. Calif., L.A., 1961-65; sr. scientist Ford Instrument Co., Sperry Gyro, L.I.C., NY, 1965-66, Tech. Rsch. Group, Melville, N.Y., 1966-67; engr. cons. Spencer Rsch., N.Y.C. and London, 1967-77; sr. lectr. Hatfield (Eng.) Poly., 1970-77; vis. assoc. prof. U. Pitts., 1976-77; assoc. prof. La. State U., Baton Rouge, 1977-79; vis. rsch. cons. Columbia U., N.Y.C., 1979; asst. prof. Rutgers U., New Brunswick, N.J., 1979-82. Pres. Spencer Sci. Computing, New Brunswick, 1982—; vis. prof. Aero Lab., Technion, Haifa, Israel, 1988, Rutgers U., Piscataway, N.J., 1998—. Contbr. articles to rsch. publs. Mem. ASCE, ASME, Israeli Soc. Engrs. and Architects, Gesellschaft für Angewandte Mathematik und Mechanik, Structural Rsch. Coun., Mensa, Intertel. Home: 10-8M Landing Ln New Brunswick NJ 08901-1070 Office: Spencer Sci Comp PO Box 4191 Highland Park NJ 08904-4191 E-mail: hspencer@rci.rutgers.edu.

SPENCER, J. CLYDE, retired radiation oncologist, nuclear radiologist, educator; b. Ionia, Mich., 1929; MD, U. Mich., 1954. Diplomate Am. Bd. Radiology, Am. Bd. Nuc. Radiology. Intern Blodgett Meml. Hosp., Grand Rapids, Mich., 1954-55; resident in internal medicine U. Mich. Hosp., Ann Arbor, 1955, resident in radiology, 1957-60, chmn. dept. radiology, 1977-92, chief of med. staff, 1988-90; hon. staff Edward W. Sparrow Hosp., Lansing, Mich., 1992—. Assoc. clin. prof. Mich. State U. Capt. USMC, 1955-57.

SPENCER, JEAN, executive; b. Bklyn., Oct. 26, 1946; d. Frederic R. and Lucy Anne Spencer. BBA cum laude, Adelphi U., 1973, MBA, 1989; MS in Human Nutrition, U. Bridgeport, 1998. Notary public, 1986—. Exec. adminstrv. mgmt. Underwriters Labs., Inc., Melville, N.Y., 1966—; pres., CEO All Natural Health Corp., Seaford, 1990—. Vol., life mem. Nat. Ski Patrol, Colo. Recipient NASTAR, Bronze medal, Silver medal. Mem. Am. Coll. Nutrition, Am. Soc. Quality Control, Nat. Nutritional Foods Assn., Nat. Ctr. for Homeopathy. Avocations: snow skiing, bicycle riding, physical fitness, opera, theater. Office: All Natural Health Inc 3830 Sunrise Hwy Seaford NY 11783-2634

SPENCER, JOHN HEDLEY, biochemistry educator; b. Stapleford, Eng., Apr. 10, 1933; emigrated to Can., 1956; s. Thomas and Eva (Johnson) S.; m. Magdeliene Vera Kulin, Sept. 16, 1958; children— Robin Anne, David Thomas, Mark Stewart. BSc, U. St. Andrews, Scotland, 1955, BSc with honors, 1956; student, Montreal Cancer Rsch. Soc., 1956-59; PhD, McGill U., 1960. Damon Runyon Meml. Fund postdoctoral fellow Columbia U., N.Y.C., 1959-61; mem. faculty McGill U., Montreal, 1961-78, assoc. prof. biochemistry, 1966-71, prof., 1971-78; prof. biochemistry Queen's U., Kingston, Ont., 1978-98, head biochemistry, 1978-90, prof. emeritus, 1998—. Vis. scientist NICHHD/NIH, Bethesda, Md., 1987-88; vis. prof. U. Montreal, 1992-93. Author: The Physics and Chemistry of DNA and RNA, 1972; co-editor: Planet Earth: Problems and Prospects, 1995. Recipient Ayerst award Can. Biochem. Soc., 1972 Fellow Royal Soc. Can.; mem. AAAS, Can. Biochem. Soc. (treas. 1966-69, pres. 1979-80), Can. Fedn. Biol. Socs. (pres. 1981-82), Biochem. Soc., Am. Soc. Biochemistry and Molecular Biology, Royal Soc. Can., Sigma Xi. Home: 36 Kenwoods Cir Kingston ON Canada K7K 6Y1 E-mail: spencerj@post.queensu.ca.

SPENCER, JOHN HOWARD, radio astronomer; b. Washington, Apr. 23, 1945; s. John Wesley Hilldrup and Arabelle (Reed) S.; m. Jean Anne Rosen, Feb. 1, 1969; children: J. Michael, Julie R. BS Physics, U. N.C., 1967; PhD Physics, MIT, 1973. Physicist Naval Surface Warfare Ctr., Dahlgren, Va., 1963-73; radio astronomer Naval Rsch. Lab., Washington, 1973—. Patentee in field. Various to scoutmaster, chpt. adv. bd., Boy Scouts Am., Springfield, Va., 1983—; chmn. adminstrv. bd. local ch., Springfield, 1980-82. Mem. Am. Astron. Soc., Appalachian Trail Conf., Appalachian Mountain Club, Sigma Phi Sigma. Avocation: backpacking with Boy Scouts. Office: Naval Rsch Lab Washington DC 20375-0001 E-mail: spencer@rsd.nrl.navy.mil.

SPENCER, KEITH G. construction executive; b. Albany, N.Y., Feb. 15, 1943; s. Fred Mathias and Joan Spencer; m. Patricia Ann Miller, June 15, 1968 (annulled Aug. 18, 1981); 1 child Kevin Patrick. BS in Human Svcs., SUNY, Saratoga, 1993, MA in Labor Studies, 1996; fire adminstrn., Nat. Fire Acad., 1995; MSW, Brighton U. Lic. real estate N.Y., fire adjuster N.Y. Clk. U.S. Post Office, Albany, NY, 1965—67; multi-line adjuster Hartford Ins. Co., Delmar, 1967—73; gen. constrn. Spencer Constrn. Co., Latham, 1973—87, Albany, 1989—95; boys prefect The LaSalle Sch., 1987—89; tchr./semi-ret. St. Sophia Sch., 1998—2001. Inspector Kaplan Realtors, Delmar, NY, 1977—78. Author: Dunouer Cottage, 2001, Air Force Family 1942-1964, 2001, My Child's Keeper, 2002. Mgr., coach Little League, Pop Warner, Babe Ruth Latham Little League, 1978—82; asst. committeeman GOP, No. Colonie, NY, 1973—74; advanced cert. catechist Diocese of Albany, 1982—95. Sgt. USAR, 1964—70, sgt. USAR, 1987—90. Mem.: KC (vol. 1975—77), Elks Club. Roman Catholic. Avocations: reading, writing, golf, bowling, model ship building. Home: 115 Krumkill Rd Albany NY 12208

SPENCER, LARRY, member of parliament; Student, Met. Jr. Coll., Draughn's Bus. Coll.; diploma in Theology, So. Baptist Coll. Pastor Brown's Chapel Bapt. Ch., Paragould, Ark., 1970—74, Discovery Bapt. Ch., Regina, 1974—83, Covenant Bapt. Ch., Regina, 1983—87, Bapt. Union of We. Can., Swift Current, 1990—91, Discovery Bapt. Ch., 1991—; mem. House of Commons, Regina, Canada, critic human resources develop Can. family issues. Can. Alliance Caucus. Office: House of Commons Regina-Lumsden-Lake Ctr 6244 Rochdale Blvd Regina SK S4X 4K8 Canada Office Fax: 306-791-0701. E-mail: spencer.l@parl.gc.ca.*

SPENCER, LAVAL WING, retired physician; b. Lehi, Utah, Apr. 12, 1928; s. Lawrence Valdor and Mary Georgia (Wing) S.; m. Betty Jean Robertson, Nov. 10, 1950; children: Scott, Kelly, James, Debra Jean. AS, Weber Coll., 1956; BS, U. Utah, 1959, MD, 1963. Charter Diplomate Am. Bd. Family Practice. Amateur radio operator Extra Class, K7MD. Electronic technician Hill AFB, Ogden, Utah, 1950-53, med. officer, 1985-88; resident in gen. practice Dee Hosp., 1963-66; pvt. practice, 1966-85; hon. med. staff McKay-Dee Hosp., 1988—; ret., 1988. Mem. Utah emergency and comm. com. Utah Med. Assn., Salt Lake City, 1970-77; chmn. med. edn. and rsch. com. McKay-Dee Hosp., Ogden, 1972-73, pres. med. staff, 1973; clin. instr. U. Utah, Salt Lake City, 1978-88. Contbr. articles and essays to profl. publs. Sgt. USAAF, 1946-49, PTO. Recipient honoree award Women's Coun., 1995, Stewart Rehab. Ct., McKay-Dee Found. Fellow Am. Acad. Family Physicians (charter), Royal Soc. Health; mem. AMA, Utah Med. Assn., Weber County Med. Soc. (Doctor of Yr. 1999), Ogden Surg.-Med. Soc. (treas. 1970-75). Avocation: amateur radio operator. Home: 1365 Lark Cir Ogden UT 84403-2141

SPENCER, LONABELLE (KAPPIE SPENCER), political agency administrator, lobbyist; b. Owatonna, Minn., Aug. 3, 1925; d. Reuben Alvin and Florence Elizabeth (Wells) Kaplan; m. Mark Rodney Spencer, Sept. 14, 1947 (dec. May 1986); children: Gregory Mark, Gary Alan, Carol Ann (Spencer) Glumac, Dane Kaplan. BA, Grinnell Coll., 1947. State bd. legis. chair Am. Assn. Univ. Women, Iowa, 1978-82, nat. legis. com., 1980-83, nat. bd. legis. chair, 1982-83, nat. legis. and program coms., 1985-89, nat. bd. dir. for women's issues, 1985-89; founder, dir. Nat. Gender Balance Project, Sarasota, Fla., 1988—; bd. dirs., nat. steering com. Nat. Women's Political Caucus, Washington, 1992-97. Lobbyist, cmty. activist state legis. and congress, Fla. Iowa, Washington, 1974—; pub. policy cons. women's orgns., nationwide, 1978—; rep. Fla. women's pol. caucus ERA summit, Washington, 1992—. Author: (pub. policy manuals) Don't Leave It All to the Experts, 1981, Take An Unratified State to Launch, 1981, I Think We Need a Woman...It's a Man's World Unless Women Vote, 1983, Woman Power: It's a Capitol Idea, 1995, Gender Balance Project-USA: Politics and Decision Making, 1995, Whose Money Is It Anyway: Wills and Trusts for Women, 1999; exhibitor, presenter in field. U.S. rep. World Assn. Girl Guides Girl Scouts U.S., Acapulco, Mex., 1965, bd. dirs. Moingona Coun. Girl Scouts U.S., 1965-75; Rep. candidate Iowa senate, Des Moines, 1976; del., workshop presenter Internat. Fedn. Univ. Women, Netherlands, New Zealand, Finland, Sweden, 1983, 86, 89, workshop presenter U.S./China Joint Conf. on Women's Issues, Beijing, China, 1995, Nongovernmental Orgn. Forum, Huairou, China, 1995; trustee Grinnell (Iowa) Coll., 1993—; Iowa del. to Nat. Women's Conf., 1977; founder Fla. Women's Consortium, 1989; mem. People to People Internat.; tour leader Mission in Understanding to Cuba, 2001. Recipient Girl Scout awards Moingona Girl Scout Coun., Des Moines, 1969, 73, 78, Christine Wilson medal for Equality and Justice, Iowa Women's Hall of Fame, Des Moines, 1990; named gift honoree Am. Assn. Univ. Women, Des Moines and Sarasota, Fla. branches, Iowa and Vt. divsns., 1980, 82, 87, 92. Mem. AAUW (leader corps, various coms. 1975—), UN Fund for Women (UNIFEM), Nat. Assn. Commns. for Women, Vet. Feminists of Am. (Medal of Honor 2000), Women in Senate and House WISH-LIST (founder 1992—), Fla. Women's Consortium (founder, bd. dirs. 1989—). Republican. Avocations: travel. Home: 3735 Beneva Oaks Way Sarasota FL 34238-2524

SPENCER, M. RANDALL, lawyer; b. Champaign, Ill., June 2, 1961; s. Thomas Eugene and M. Josephine Spencer; m. Melissa Ann Spencer, July 30, 1988 (div. May 1998); m. Christine Anne Spencer, July 3, 1999. BA in Econs., Ball State U., 1983; JD, U. Notre Dame, 1991. Bar: Ind. 1991. Assoc. Miller, Carson, Boxberger & Murphy, LLP, Ft. Wayne, Ind., 1991—, ptnr. Active Ind. Leadership Forum, 1994, Leadership Ft. Wayne, 1998-99. Mem. Ind. State Bar Assn. Republican. Avocation: music. Home: 421 Arcadia Ct Fort Wayne IN 46807 Office: Miller Carson Boxberger & Murphy LLP 1400 One Summit Sq Fort Wayne IN 46802

SPENCER, MARGARET BEALE, researcher, educator; b. Philadelphia, Pa., Sept. 5, 1944; d. Junius Alton and Elizabeth Rebecca Beale; m. Charles Louis Beale, June 13, 1967; children: Tirzah, Natash, Charles Asramon. BS, Temple U., Sch. Pharmacy, Philadelphia, PA, 1967—67; MA, U. Kans., Dept. Psychology, Kansas, MO, 1970—70; PHD, U. Chgo., Com. Human Devel., Chicago, IL, 1976—76; MA (hon.) , U. Pa, Philadelphia, 1993—93. Registered pharmacist U. Kans. Med. Ctr., Kansas, Mo., 1967—69; asst. educator Emory U., Atlanta, 1977—83; clin. assoc. educator Morehouse Sch. Medicine, 1983—88; assoc. educator Emory U., 1983—91, educator, 1991—93; endowed educatorship U. Pa, Philadelphia, Pa., 1993—. Reserch project dir. U. Chgo., Chicago, Ill., 1974—77; dir. interdisciplinary studies human devel. U. Pennsylvani, Philadelphia, Pa., 1994—; dir. ctr. health achievement neighborhood growth & ethnic studies U. Pa, Philadelphia, Pa., 1994—, dir. w.e.b. du bois collective rsch. inst., Pa., 1998—. Editor: (book) Beginnings: Social and effective development of Black children. Fellow: Divsn. 45 APA, Divsn. 15 APA, Divsn. 7 APA; mem.: Soc. Rsch. Adolescence Coun. Mem., Found. Child Devel., Boysville Evaluation Ctr. (nat. adv. bd. 2000—02). Avocations: painting, reading. Office: University of Pennsylvania 3700 Walnut St Philadelphia PA 19104-6216

SPENCER, MARGARET GILLIAM, lawyer; b. Spokane, Wash., Aug. 30, 1951; d. Jackson Earl and Margaret Kathleen (Hindley) Gilliam; m. John Bernard Spencer, Feb. 21, 1993. BA in Sociology, U. Mont., 1974, MA in Sociology, 1978, JD, 1982. Bar: Mont. 1982, Colo. 1982. Assoc. Holland & Hart, Denver, 1982-84, Roath & Brega, P.C., Denver, 1984-88, shareholder, dir., 1988-89; spl. counsel Brega & Winters, P.C., 1989; corp. counsel CH2M Hill, Inc., 1989—. Democrat. Episcopalian. Avocations: skiing, scuba diving. Office: CH2M Hill Inc PO Box 22508 Denver CO 80222-0508

SPENCER, MARIAN ALEXANDER, volunteer; b. Gallipolis, Ohio, June 28, 1920; d. Harry McDonal and Rosanna (Carter) Alexander; m. Donald Andrew Spencer, Aug. 1940; children: Donald Andrew Jr., Edward Alexander. BA, U. Cin., 1942. Pres. Fellowship House, Cin., 1942-46, Cin. Chpt. Links, Inc., Cin., 1968-72, Woman's City Club, Cin., 1972-73, NAACP, Cin., 1980-82; trustee U. Cin., 1975-79; chairperson Ohio Adv. Com. on Civil Rights, Cin., 1980-86; vice-mayor City of Cin., 1983-85; mem. task force to monitor de-segregation of Cin. pub. schs., 1984-96. Recipient Recognition cert. Nat. Conf. of Christians and Jews, Cin., 1968, Black Excellence award Operation PUSH (People United to Save Humanity), Cin., 1972, Pres.'s award NAACP, Cin., 1980, Disting. Alumna award for outstanding leadership U. Cin., 1982, award NASW, Cin., 1986, A Life Dedicated to the Fulfillment of the Dream of Dr. Martin Luther King award Bapt. Mins. Conf., Cin., 1987, $10,000 Jacob E. Davis Vol. Leadership award Greater Cin. Found., 1993, Champion for Democracy award Ctr. for Voting and Democracy, Washington, 1994, Civil Rights Efforts award Urban League, Am. Jewish Com., Cin. Hist. Soc., 1995; named Woman of Yr., Cin. Enquirer, 1972; inductee Ohio Women's Hall of Fame, State of Ohio, 1984. Democrat. Methodist. Avocations: travel, swimming, drawing, reading, playing cards. Home: 940 Lexington Ave Cincinnati OH 45229-2726

SPENCER, MARK MORRIS, creative writing educator; b. Richmond, Va., Feb. 12, 1956; s. Howard Regan and Evelyn Roberta (Morris) S.; m. Diana Lynn Harvey, July 19, 1980 (div. Mar. 1992); children: Krista, David; m. Cindy Renee O'Brient, Oct. 17, 1994; 1 child, Brontë. BA, U. Cin., 1979; MFA, Bowling Green State U., 1981. Instr. English S.W. Mo. State U., Springfield, 1983-87; prof., chair English program Cameron U., Lawton, Okla., 1987—. Instr. Writer's Digest Sch., Cin., 1988—. Author: Spying on Lovers, 1989 (Bradshaw Book award 1988), Wedlock, 1990, Love and Reruns in Adams County, 1994, Only Missing, 1996 (Faulkner Soc. award 1996), The Weary Motel, 2000 (Omaha prize). Home: 1325 W Minnesota Ave Chickasha OK 73018-2951 Office: Cameron Univ English Dept 2800 W Gore Blvd Lawton OK 73505-6377 E-mail: marksp@cameron.edu.

SPENCER, MARY MILLER, civic worker; b. Comanche, Tex., May 25, 1924; d. Aaron Gaynor and Alma (Grissom) Miller; 1 child, Mara Lynn. BS, U. North Tex., 1943. Cafeteria dir. Mercedes (Tex.) Pub. Schs., 1943-46; home economist coord. All-Orange Dessert Contest Fla. Citrus Commn., Lakeland, 1959-62, 64; tchr. purchasing sch. lunch dept. Fla. Dept. Edn., 1960. Clothing judge Polk County (Fla.) Youth Fair, 1951-68, Polk County Federated Women's Clubs, 1964-66; pres. Dixieland Elem. Sch. PTA, 1955-57, Polk County Coun. PTA's, 1958-60; chmn. pub. edn. com. Polk County unit Am. Cancer Soc., 1959-60, bd. dirs., 1962-70; charter mem., bd. dirs. Lakeland YMCA, 1962-72; sec. Greater Lakeland Cmty. Nursing Coun., 1965-72; trustee, vice-chmn. Polk County Eye Clinic, Inc., 1962-64, pres., 1964-82; bd. dirs. Polk County Scholarship and Loan Fund, 1962-70; mem. exec. com. West Polk County (Fla.) Cmty. Welfare Coun., 1960-62, 65-68; mem. budget and audit com. Greater Lakeland United Fund, 1960-62, bd. dirs., 1967-70, residential chmn. fund drive, 1968; mem. adv. bd. Polk County Juvenile and Domestic Rels. Ct., 1960-69; sec. bd. dirs. Fla. West Coast Ednl. TV, 1960-81; mem. Polk County Home Econs. Adv. Com., 1965-71; mem. exec. com. Suncoast Health Coun., 1968-71; worker children's svcs. divsn. family svcs. Dept. Health and Rehab. Svcs., State of Fla., 1969-70, social worker, 1970-72, 74-82, social worker Overpayment Fraud Recoupment unit, 1977-81, with other pers. svcs., 1981-82, supr. Overpayment Fraud Recoupment unit, 1982-83, pub. assistance specialist IV, 1984-89; bd. dirs. Lake Region United Way, Winter Haven, 1976-81; mem. Polk County Cmty. Svcs. Coun., 1978-88; with other pers. svcs. Emergency Fin. Assistance Housing Program, 1990-96. Mem. AAUW (pres. Lakeland br. 1960-61), Nat. Welfare Fraud Assn., Fla. Congress Parents and Tchrs. (hon. life, pres. dist. 7 1961-63, chmn. pub. rels. 1962-66), Fla. Health and Welfare Coun., Fla. Health and Social Svc. Coun., Polk County Mental Health Assn., U. North Tex. Alumni Assn., Order Ea. Star. Democrat. Methodist. Home and Office: PO Box 2161 Lakeland FL 33806-2161

SPENCER, MELVIN JOE, hospital administrator, lawyer; b. Buffalo Center, Iowa, Jan. 2, 1923; s. Kenos W. and Jennie (Michaelsen) S.; m. Dena Joyce Butterfield, Mar. 1, 1952; children: Dennis Norman, Gregory Melvin, Shelly Lynn Spencer Goodnight. AB, U. Mich., 1948, JD, 1950. Bar: Iowa 1950, Mo. 1950, Okla. 1961. Practiced in, Kansas City, Mo., 1950-61, Oklahoma City, 1961—; assoc., then ptnr. Watson, Ess, Marshall & Enggas, 1950-61; ptnr. Miller & Spencer (and predecessor firm), 1961-75, of counsel, 1975-80; adminstr. Deaconess Hosp., 1975-92, cons., 1992-93. Dir. Union Bank & Trust Co., Oklahoma City, 1977-88, 89-96, adv. dir., 1996—; dir., sec. Hosp. Casualty Co., 1977-92; dir., treas. VHA of Okla., Inc., 1986-92. Assoc. editor Mich. Law Rev., 1949-50. Mcpl. judge City of Roeland Park, Kans., 1952, mem. city coun., 1954; area Rep. precinct chmn., 1968-69; del. Rep. State Conv., 1968, 96; bd. dirs. Deaconess Hosp., Oklahoma City, Christian Counseling Ctr., 1973-75; trustee Okla. Hosp. Assn., 1978-84, chmn. bd. trustees, 1983; trustee, vice chmn. bd. dirs. Ctrl. Coll., McPherson, Kans., 1972-86; trustee Okla. Ambulance Trust, 1984-87; mem. adv. bd. Okla. State U. Tech. Inst., 1980-92; bd. dirs. Emergency Med. Svcs. Ctrl. Okla., 1975-78, FMC Ministries, Inc.; mem. const. coun. Free Meth. Ch. World Fellowship, 1975-95; chmn. Free Meth. Found., 1988-99; gen. counsel Free Meth. Ch. N.Am., 1969-95, mem. bd. adminstrn., 1969-99, sec., 1985-95, mem. investment com., 1976-88, chmn. investment com., 1986-88. Capt. USAAF, 1943-46. Named Layman of Yr., Free Meth. Ch. N.Am., 1984; recipient W. Cleveland Rodgers Disting. Svc. award Okla. Hosp. Assn., 1985; fellow Cen. Coll. Acad. of Achievers, 1990. Mem. Okla. Bar Assn., Oklahoma County Bar Assn., Men's Dinner Club, Order of Coif, Phi Beta Kappa, Phi Kappa Phi. Home: 5910 N Shawnee Ave Oklahoma City OK 73112-1627

SPENCER, MILTON HARRY, economics and finance educator; b. N.Y.C., Mar. 25, 1926; m. Roslyn Pernick; children: Darcy, Robin, Cathy. BS, NYU, 1949, MA, 1950; PhD, Cornell U., 1954. Instr. econs., fin. Queens Coll., N.Y.C., 1949-52; rsch. asst. Cornell U., Ithaca, N.Y., 1952-54; economist Armour & Co., Chgo., 1954-55; assoc. prof. Wayne State U., Detroit, 1955-62, prof., 1962-91, prof. emeritus, 1991—. Vis. prof. U. Hawaii, Honolulu, 1965-66; lectr., U.S. and fgn. univs.; cons. U.S. Dept. State, several fgn. govt., various domestic and fgn. corps. Author: Basic Economics, 1951, Economic

Thought, 1954, Business and Economic Forecasting, 1958, Managerial Economics, 3 edits., 1959-68, Contemporary Economics, 8 edits., 1971-93; various monographs: contbr. numerous articles to profl. jours. Served as cpl. U.S. Army, 1943-45. Recipient Disting. Svc. awards from U.S. Dept. State, fgn. govts. E-mail: milspencer@aol.com.

SPENCER, PRISCILLA JAMES, physical education educator; b. Boston, Aug. 21, 1960; d. Richard P. and Gwendolyn (Williams) S. BA in Psychology, Bates Coll., Lewiston, Maine, 1983; MS in Phys. Edn. Recreation, So. Conn. State U., 1990; PhD in Phys. Edn., Temple U., 1999. Cert. educator in phys. edn. and health, Conn. Counselor Youth and Family Svcs., Westfield, Mass., 1983-85; phys. edn. tchr. Pleasant Valley Elem. Sch., South Winds, Conn., 1989-93; instr. kinesiology Pa. State U., 1998—. Cons. Pub. Schs., Conn., 1991—. Co-author: Popcorn's Travels Across America, 1992; author: Gymnastics for All, 1994. Named Outstanding Elem. Phys. Edn. Program Conn. Assn. Health, Phys. Edn. and Recreation, 1991; recipient Celebration of Excellence award State Conn. Dept. Edn., 1992; Fels Found. grantee, 1995; Pa. State Dept. Health cmty. grantee, 1999. Mem. AAHPERD. Home: 18 Saddle Ridge Dr West Hartford CT 06117-2330

SPENCER, RICHARD GLENN STEVENS, physician, nuclear magnetic resonance spectroscopist; b. Evergreen Park, Ill., July 23, 1955; s. Samuel and Getrude (Salant) S.; m. Christine Marie Stevens, Aug. 10, 1985; children: Sarah Naomi, Elizabeth Rose. BA in Astronomy summa cum laude, U. Calif., Berkeley, 1977, MA in Physics, 1983; PhD in Med. Physics, MIT, 1987; MD, Harvard U., 1988. Diplomate Am. Bd. Internal Medicine. Intern Faulkner Hosp., Jamaica Plain, Mass., 1988-89; post-doctoral fellow in chemistry MIT, Boston, 1989-91; attending physician Francis Scott Key Med. Ctr., Balt., 1992-94; asst. prof. medicine Johns Hopkins Med. Sch., 1993-99; assoc. prof. medicine, 1999—; chief in-vivo NMR unit NIH, Nat. Inst. Aging, Balt., 1991—, sr. investigator, 1993—; med. resident Johns Hopkins Med. Sch. Bayview Med. Ctr., 1994-96; attending physician Good Samaritan Hosp., Balt., 1997—. Rschr. in field. Contbr. articles to profl. jours. Fellow ACP. E-mail: spencer@helix.nih.gov.

SPENCER, RICHARD HENRY, lawyer; b. Kansas City, Mo., Nov. 29, 1926; s. Byron Spencer and Helen Elizabeth (McCune) Hockaday; m. Barbara G. Rau, Aug. 2, 1952 (div. 1955); 1 chlid, Christina G. Cuevas; m. Katherine Graham, Dec. 28, 1957; children: Elisabeth M., Katherine S. Rivard. BS in Engring., Princeton U., 1949; LLB, U. Mo., 1952. Bar: Mo. 1952, U.S. Dist. Ct (we. dist.) Mo. 1955. Assoc. Spencer, Fane, Britt & Browne, Kansas City, 1952-59, ptnr., 1959-94; ret. ptnr., 1995—. Co-author: Fiduciary Duties, Rights and Responsibilities of Directors, 1985. Sec., bd. dirs. Met. Performing Arts Fund, Kansas City, 1984—; trustee Barstow Sch., Kansas City, 2002--. Mem. ABA, Mo. Bar Assn., Lawyers Assn. Kansas City, Kansas City Club (pres. 1974), Kansas City Country Club (pres. 1986), Rotary. Republican. Episcopalian. Avocations: hunting, golf, traveling. Home: 77 Le Mans Ct Shawnee Mission KS 66208-5230 Office: Spencer Fane Britt & Browne 1400 Commerce Bank Bldg 1000 Walnut St Kansas City MO 64106-2140

SPENCER, RICHARD PAUL, biochemist, educator, physician; b. N.Y.C., June 7, 1929; s. David E. and Frances (Fried) S.; m. Gwendolyn Enid Williams, Apr. 7, 1956; children: Carolyn Roberts, Jennifer Holt, Priscilla James. AB, Dartmouth Coll., 1951; MD, U. So. Calif., 1954; MA (NSF fellow, Helen Hay Whitney fellow), Harvard U., 1958, PhD, 1961. Intern Beth Israel Hosp., Boston, 1954-55; practice medicine specializing in nuclear medicine; mem. faculty biophysics U. Buffalo, 1961-63; chief radioisotope service VA Hosp., Buffalo, 1961-63; asso. prof. nuclear medicine Yale Sch. Medicine, 1963-68, prof., 1968-74; prof., chmn. dept. nuclear medicine U. Conn. Health Center, 1974-97, prof., vice chmn. Dept. Diagnostic Imaging, 1997—2000, residency dir. nuclear medicine, 2000—. Author: The Intestinal Tract, 1960, (with others) Biophysical Principles, 1965, Radionuclide Studies of the Spleen, 1975, Clinical Focus on Nuclear Medicine, 1977, Handbook of Nuclear Medicine, 1977, Therapy in Nuclear Medicine, 1978, Radiopharmaceuticals: Structure-Activity Relationships, 1981, Interventional Nuclear Medicine, 1984, New Procedures In Nuclear Medicine, 1988; contbr. (with others) articles to profl. jours. Mem. Am. Physiol. Soc., AAAS, Soc. Nuclear Medicine, Biophys. Soc. Achievements include co-discovery of functional asplenia; developed first complete description of relationship of food intake to reproductive success and to longevity in a species. Office: U Conn Health Ctr Farmington CT 06030-2804 E-mail: rspencer@adp.uchc.edu.

SPENCER, RICHARD THOMAS, III, healthcare industry executive; b. Oak Park, Ill., Mar. 18, 1936; s. Richard Thomas Jr. and Lois Anne (Pollock) S.; m. Andrea B. Schlickeiser, June 29, 1962; 1 child, Richard Thomas IV. BA, U. Mich., 1959; postgrad., U. Pa., 1976, Stanford U., 1984, Clemson U., 1985. Mktg. group Mobil Oil Co., Detroit, 1962; internat. trade specialist U.S. Dept. Commerce, 1963-64; account exec. J. Walter Thompson Co., 1965-66; sales mgr. Sarns Inc., Ann Arbor, 1967-69; v.p. mktg. Cordis Dow Corp., Miami, Fla., 1970-81; pres. mktg. divsn. Cordis Corp., 1982-87; pres., CEO Uni-Med Internat. Corp., 1988—2000. Bd. dirs. Viacor Corp., Wilmington, Mass., Bioheart, Inc., Weston, Fla.; cons. in field. Contbr. articles to profl. jours. With U.S. Army, 1959-61. Republican. Avocations: skiing, scuba diving, running, stereo equipment, geopolits. Home and Office: 811 E Hill Rd North Troy VT 05859

SPENCER, RICHARD VAUGHN, investment bank executive; b. Waterbury, Conn., Jan. 18, 1954; s. Charles Eldridge and Catherine (Ahern) S.; m. Erin Wolf, Aug. 22, 1983; children: Averil Dickinson, Pierce Carlysle. BA in Econs., Rollins Coll., 1976. Asst. v.p. Bank of Boston, 1981-83, A.G. Becker, N.Y.C., 1983-84; v.p. Paine Webber, Atlanta, 1984-86, Goldman Sachs & Co., L.A., 1986-88; assoc. dir. Bear Stearns & Co., Inc., Boston, 1988—. Capt. USMC, 1976-81. Republican. Episcopalian. Office: 1 Federal St Fl 25 Boston MA 02110-2012

SPENCER, ROGER FELIX, psychiatrist, psychoanalyst, medical educator; b. Apr. 19, 1934; came to U.S., 1941; s. Eugene S. Spitzer and Santa Spencer; m. Barbara Ann Houser, Aug. 18, 1958; children: Geoffrey, Jennifer, Rebecca. BS, Yale Coll., 1956; MD, Harvard Med. Sch., 1959. Diplomate Am. Bd. Psychiatry. Intern N.C. Meml. Hosp., Chapel Hill, 1959-60, resident in psychiatry, 1960-63; instr. U. N.C. Sch. Medicine, 1963-66, asst. prof., 1966-69, assoc. prof., 1969-76, prof., 1976—. Dir. of liaison and cons., U. N.C., 1967-77, dir. out patient psychiatry, 1977-95. Contbr. more than 25 articles and short stories to profl. jours. and lit. mags. Recipient Career Tchr. award NIMH, 1965-67. Fellow Am. Psychiat. Assn. (life), Am. Psychoanalytic Assn.; mem. N.C. Psychoanalytic Soc. (past pres.), N.C. Neuropsychiat. Assn. (past pres.). Office: UNC Hosps Dept Psychiatry CB 7160 Chapel Hill NC 27599-7160 E-mail: roger_spencer@med.unc.edu.

SPENCER, ROZELLE JEFFERY, moving and storage company executive; b. Memphis, July 3, 1936; s. William Arthur and Octavia (McCormack) S.; m. Winifred L. Jones, July 5, 1968; children: Jeffery Christian, Derrick Christopher. Student, DePaul U., Chgo., 1956-59; BA, Northeastern Ill. U., Chgo., 1990, MA Candidate, 1990-91. Transp. rep. Santa Fe R.R., Chgo., 1956-64; employment supr. Trans World Airlines, 1964-70; pres., CEO Aaron Bros. Moving Systems Inc., 1969—; pres. Aaro Medicar Transport, 1976-85, Hyde Park Self Storage Inc., Chgo., 1990—. Mem. Chgo. Coun. Fgn. Rels., 1980's, Assn. African Historians, Chgo., 1980's and 90's, Task Force for Black Political Empowerment, Chgo., 1980's and 90's; assoc. Montford Point Marine Assn., Chgo., 1970's and 80's. Mem. Nat. Assn. Guardsmen, Plaza Club. Democrat. Baptist. Home: 10706 S Seeley Ave Chicago IL 60643-3315

SPENCER, SAMUEL REID, JR. education consultant, former university president; b. Rock Hill, S.C., 1919; m. Ava Clark; 1948; children: Samuel Reid, Ellen Spencer Henschen, Clayton, Frank. AB summa cum laude, Davidson Coll., 1940, LLD (hon.), 1964; MA, Harvard U., 1947, PhD, 1951; LHD (hon.), Oglethorpe U., 1977, Queens Coll., 1983, Bridgewater Coll., 1986, Marymount U., 1988, Hollins Coll., 1991, Mary Baldwin Coll., 1992; LittD (hon.), Washington and Lee U., 1991. With Vick Chem. Co., N.Y.C., 1940; research asst. to Grenville Clark, Dublin, 1947-48; asst. to pres. Davidson Coll., 1951-54, dean of students, asso. prof. history, 1954, dean of students, prof. history, 1955-57; pres. Mary Baldwin Coll., 1957-68, Davidson (N.C.) Coll., 1968-83, pres. emeritus, 1983—; pres. Va. Found. for Ind. Colls., Richmond, 1983-88; sr. cons. Acad. Search Consultation Svc., 1989—; interim pres. Hollins Coll., 1990-91. Dir. Piedmont Bank & Trust Co.; Fulbright lectr. U. Munich, 1965-66; mem. Bd. Fgn. Scholarships, 1980-83, chmn., 1982-83; bd. dirs. Assn. Am. Colls., 1976-83, chmn. assn., 1981-82; pres. So. Univ. Conf., 1979-80; mem. commn. govtl. relations Am. Council Edn., 1973-76 Author: Decision for War, 1917, 1953, Booker T. Washington and the Negro's Place in American Life, 1955, (with J. Garry Clifford) The First Peacetime Draft, 1986. Bd. dirs. Grenville Clark Fund, Dartmouth Coll., 1973—, Charlotte-Mecklenburg chpt. Urban League, 1979-83, 2000—; trustee Agnes Scott Coll., 1975-91, Mary Baldwin Coll., 1996—; trustee Union Theol. Sem., Richmond, Va., 1985-94, chmn., 1988-94. Maj. AUS, 1940-45. Austin fellow Harvard, 1947-48; Rosenwald fellow, 1948-49; Kent fellow Nat. Council on Religion in Higher Edn., 1949-51 Mem. Fulbright Assn. (bd. dirs. 1989-92), Phi Beta Kappa, Omicron Delta Kappa. Presbyterian (bd. Christian edn.). Address: PO Box 1117 Davidson NC 28036-1117 E-mail: samrs2@aol.com.

SPENCER, SUSAN NAMM, management consultant; b. Bklyn., June 28, 1939; d. William J. and Mildred (Henigson) Hammel; m. Arnold Namm, June 18, 1961 (div. 1978); children: Adam Edward Namm, Leslie Ellen Coplin; m. William I. Spencer, Feb. 14, 1994 (dec. Sept. 2001). BS, Emerson Coll., 1961. Pub. rels. dir. Burke Rehab. Ctr., White Plains, N.Y., 1975-76; v.p., exec. dir. So. Conn. & Westchester Health Plans, 1976-80; v.p. Citibank/Citicorp, N.Y.C., 1980-95; prin. mgmt. cons. No. Palm Beach, Fla., 1995—. Dir. Suprise Lake Camp, N.Y.C., 1995—. Mem. majority coun. Emilys List, Washington, 1994—; mem. nat. coun. The Conservationa Fund, 2001—; literacy and learning tutor Head Start, West Palm Beach, Fla., 1995—; bd. dirs. Surprise Lake Camp, N.Y.C., 1995—; trustee Emerson Coll., Boston, 1994—2002; founder, bd. dirs. Literacy and Learning Network of Westchester County, NY, 1999—; bd. dirs. Lighthouse Ctr. for Arts, Tequesta, Fla., 1995—. Mem.: Econ. Club N.Y. Avocations: golf, long distance biking, swimming, tennis, shooting. Home and Office: 11188 Turtle Beach Rd North Palm Beach FL 33408-3434 Home (Summer): 35 Chatsworth Ave Larchmont NY 10538

SPENCER, THOMAS MELVIN, III, soft drink company executive; b. Richmond, Va., Feb. 16, 1949; s. Thos Melvin Jr. and Frances (Lawson) S.; m. Leslie Graham Murray, Sept. 14, 1984. AB, U. N.C., 1972. With fountain sales dept. Coca-Cola U.S.A., Atlanta, 1973-80; with Russell Pierce and Assocs., Richmond, Va., 1980-81; mgr. fountain sales div. Allegheny Pepsi, 1982; corp. mktg. equipment mgr. Pepsi Bottling Ventures, LLC, Raleigh, N.C., 1983—. Mem. Nat. Soft Drink Assn. Democrat. Presbyterian. Home: 1115 Lakeside Dr NW Wilson NC 27896-2015 Office: Pepsi Bottling Ventures LLC 1800 Pepsi Way Garner NC 27529-7231

SPENCER, WALTER JESSE, accountant, consultant; b. Hamlet, N.C., Feb. 25, 1921; s. Walter Jordan and Willie Brigman Spencer; m. Evelyn Baldwin, Aug. 29, 1925; children: Walter Jesse Jr., John Baldwin. BS in Commerce, U. N.C., 1948. CPA, N.C. Staff acct. G.C. Lundin & Co., CPA, Laurinburg, N.C., 1948-51; ptnr. Lundin & Spencer, CPA, Rockingham, 1951-62, W. Jesse Spencer & Co., CPA, Rockingham, 1962-75, Dixon, Odom & Co., PLLC, High Point, N.C., 1975-86; pvt. practice Rockingham, 1986—. V.p. Kay's of Rockingham, 1986—; dir. adv. First Nat. Bank, Asheboro, N.C., 1990—. Bd. pres. Richmond C.C. Found., Hamlet, N.C., 1985—; pres. N.C. Bapt. Found., Cary, 1997-98, Found. for Richmon County, Rockingham, 1998—. With USNR, 1942-46, PTO. Named Citizen of Yr., Richmond C.C. Found., Hamlet, 1991. Mem. AICPA, N.C. Assn. CPA's (pres. 1981, bd. 1984), Rotary Club Rockingham (pres. 1988-89, Paul Harris 1989). Democrat. Baptist. Avocations: traveling, reading, golfing. Home and Office: 720 Scotland Ave Rockingham NC 28379-3149

SPENCER, WILLIAM CHRISTOPHER, English educator; b. Macon, Ga., June 30, 1957; s. Rock Thomas Sr. and Cindy Spencer; m. Carolyn Elkins, May 19, 1990; 1 stepchild, Farzad Sadjadi. BA, Mercer U., 1978; MA, U. Tenn., 1981, PhD, 1993. Tchg. assoc. U. Tenn., Knoxville, 1979-81; prof. English Delta State U., Cleveland, Miss., 1981—. Faculty advisor Lambda Iota Tau, Cleveland, 1995— (named Best Faculty Advisor in Nation, 2000). Contbr. articles to profl. jours. Bd. dirs. Univ. Press of Miss., Jackson, 1997—. Recipient Jessie Henly award Boy Scouts Am. Troop 420, 1998. Mem.: Miss. Philol. Assn. (sec. 1995—, editor 1998—), Cormac McCarthy Soc. (v.p. 1998—, editor 1997—98), Mensa (scholarship chair 1996). Home: 1715 College St Cleveland MS 38732 Office: Divsn Lang and Lit Delta State Univ Cleveland MS 38733 E-mail: bspencer@deltastate.edu.

SPENCER, WILLIAM COURTNEY, foundation executive, international business executive; b. Uniontown, Pa., Sept. 15, 1919; s. Clarence Ashley and Hazel (Stark) S.; m. Evelyn Van Cleve Bailey, Aug. 6, 1942; children: Courtney Lloyd, Henry Bailey, Edward Ashley. AB, Drew U., 1941; AM, Columbia U., 1946, EdD, 1952. Tchr. Scarsdale (N.Y.) Pub. Schs., 1946-49; dir. Univ. Sch. Columbia, 1949-52; prof. edn. and adminstrn. U. Del., 1952-55; prof., dir. grad. program tchr. edn. NYU, 1955-59, prof. higher edn. and internat. affairs, 1960-61; prof. adminstrn. U. Chile, Santiago, 1959-60; dir. Interam. affairs Inst. Internat. Edn. and asst. sec. gen. Coun. Higher Edn. in Am. Republics, 1961-65; assoc. dean Grad. Sch. Bus. Columbia U., 1965-67, spl. asst. to pres., 1967-69; pres. Western Coll., Oxford, Ohio, 1969-74, The Lindenwood Colls., 1974-79, Fund for Peace, 1979-80; v.p. Trans Internat. Mgmt. Corp., 1979-88; spl. adviser Fund for Higher Edn., 1979-82, pres., 1982-86; spl. asst. to pres. Internat. Exec. Svc. Corps, Stamford, Conn., 1988; dir. internat. devel. svcs. Nippon Manpower Ltd, Tokyo, 1988-91; pres. Trans Internat Exec. Svcs., 1988—. Cons. UNESCO Latin Am. major project in edn., Chile, 1959-60, project edn. and econ. planning, India, 1962; cons. Am. Coun. Edn., 1960-61; del. Pan-Am Assembly on Population, 1965; mem. standing com. on internat. edn. Coll. Entrance Exam. Bd., 1972-74; cons. Am. Med. Internat. Inc., 1980, McGraw Hill Internat. Book Co., 1981, AID, Indonesia, 1982, Thermo-Electron Corp., China, 1984, Internat. Exec. Svc. Corps, Jamaica, 1989, Costa Rica, 1991, 93, Hungary, 1991. Author: Education and World Responsibility, 1965, also articles; editor: Art and the University, 1964, University and National Development, 1965, Agriculture and the University, 1965. Bd. dirs. Internat. Sch. Svc., 1963-69, chmn., 1967-69; mem. Mo. master planning com. Coordinating Bd. Higher Edn., 1975-79; pres. Ind. Colls. and Univs. of Mo., 1977-79; bd. dirs. St. Louis Coun. on World Affairs, 1977-79; mem. scholarship bd. Timken Co. Ednl. Fund, 1971-76; bd. dirs. Internat. Inst. Energy Conservation, 1984-89, Conn. River Mus., 1988—. Lt. comdr. USNR, 1942-46. Decorated Purple Heart; commendation medals from Royal Navy, U.S. Navy. Mem. Coun. Fgn. Relations, N.Y. Yacht Club, Essex (Conn.) Yacht Club, North Cove Yacht Club. Home: Chester Woods 1004 317 W Main St Chester CT 06412-2339

SPENCER, WILLIAM EDWIN, telephone company executive, engineer; b. Mar. 22, 1926; s. Erwin Blanc and Edith Marie (Peterson) S.; m. Ferne Arlene Nieder, Nov. 14, 1952; children: Elizabeth Ann, Gary William, James Richard, Catherine Sue. Student, U. Kansas City, 1942; AS, Kansas City Jr. Coll., 1945; BSEE, U. Mo., 1948; postgrad., Iowa State U., 1969. Registered profl. engr., Kans. With Southwestern Bell Telephone Co., Kansas City, Mo., 1948-50, Topeka, 1952-61, sr. engr., 1966-69, equipment maintenance engr., 1967-76, engring. ops. mgr., 1976-79, dist. mgr., 1979—. Mem. tech. staff Bell Telephone Labs., N.Y.C., 1961-62, Holmdel, N.J., 1962-66; pres., owner W.E. Spencer Co.; mem. U.S. Senatorial Club, 1985—. Patentee in field. Mem. Rep. Presdl. Task Force, 1984—; supervising judge Shawnee County Election Commn.; trustee, bd. dirs. Brookwood Covenant Ch., also pres. Joy Sr. Group. With AUS, 1950-52. Recipient Best Kans. Idea award Southwestern Bell Telephone Co., 1972, cert. of appreciation Kans. Miss Teen Pageant, 1984, Rep. Presdl. League of Merit, 1992—. Mem. IEEE, NSPE, Kans. Engring. Soc., Topeka Engrs. Club (pres.), Telephone Pioneers Assn. (life mem., rep., Sunflower and Heartland chpt., Topeka life mem., coun. pres. and club pres.), Nat. Geog. Soc., Kans. Hist. Soc., Am. Assn. Ret. Persons, U. Mo.-Columbia Alumni Assn., Nat. Travel Club, Topeka Geog. Soc., Active Prime Timer. Republican. Home: 3201 SW Macvicar Ct Topeka KS 66611-1800 Office: 220 SE 6th Ave Topeka KS 66603-3507 E-mail: wespenc@attglobal.net.

SPENCER, WILLIAM FRANKLIN, SR. soil scientist, researcher; b. Carlinville, Ill., Mar. 4, 1923; s. Jesse H. and Mayme (Wohlert) S.; m. Marjorie Ann Hall, June 2, 1946; children: Barbara Annette, William Franklin Jr., Gary Alan. BS in Agr., U. Ill., 1947, MS in Chemistry, 1950, PhD in Agronomy, 1952. Asst. chemist U. Fla., Lake Alfred, 1951-54; soil scientist USDA Agrl. Rsch. Svc., Laramie, Wyo., 1954-55, Brawley, Calif., 1955-57; assoc. soil chemist U. Fla., Lake Alfred, 1957-62; rsch. leader USDA Agrl. Rsch. Svc., Riverside, Calif., 1962-95. Mem. Western Soil & Water Rsch. Com., Riverside, 1965-75; cons. Cen. U., Maracay, Venezuela, 1959. Contbr. articles to profl. jours. With U.S. Army, 1943-46, PTO. Fellow: AAAS, Soil Sci. Soc. Am., Am. Soc. Agronomy; mem.: Sigma Xi, Gamma Sigma Delta. Methodist. Achievements include research on behavior and fate of pesticides. Home: 2935 Arlington Ave Riverside CA 92506-4450 Office: U Calif Usda Agrl Rsch Svc Riverside CA 92521-0001

SPENCER, WINIFRED MAY, art educator; b. Tulsa, Oct. 7, 1938; d. Len and Madge (Scofield) S. BA in Comml. Art, U. Tulsa, 1961. Cert. comml. art, K-12 art, English/journalism tchr. Freelance comml. artist, Tulsa, 1962-63; art/sci. educator Pleasant Porter Elem., 1963-65; art educator, supervising tchr. Kendall Elem. Kendall Elem., 1965-70; art educator, team leader pilot program Bunche Elem., 1970-75; art educator Carnegie Elem., 1975-81; art educator, fine arts dept. chair Foster Jr. High, 1982-83, Foster Mid. Sch., 1983-97; freelance comml. artist, photographer Tulsa, 1997—2002. Judge Okla. Wildlife Arts Festival, Okla. Wildlife Assn., Tulsa, 1988; supervising tchr., tchr. tng. U. Tulsa, 1965-70, Northeastern State U., Tahlequah, Okla, 1965-70; pres. Tulsa Elem. Art Tchrs., Tulsa Pub. Schs., 1967-68, curriculum writing/curriculum cons., 1970-75, 91—; coord. summer arts/artists in the schs. program Tchr. Adv. Bd., Summer Arts Tulsa Arts and Humanities Coun., 1986-94. Exhibited in group shows at Tulsa City-County Ctrl. Libr., 1989, Philbrook Art Mus., 1993-94, Gillies Art Show, Gilcrease Mus., 1999. Mem. Rep. Nat. Com., 1994-96, 2000; art adv. PTA, Tulsa, 1970—; mem. Christian Sci. Ch., Tulsa, 1960-2002; mem. task force on cultural affairs Tulsa Goals for Tomorrow, 1995-98; del. Arts Edn. Summit Arts at the Core of Learning: Organizing for Action, Arts and Humanities Coun., Tulsa, 1998; mem. Gillies docent program Gilcrease Mus., Tulsa, 1999, 2000, 2001. Invited U.S.-China Joint Conf. on Edn., Citizen Amb. Program People to People Internat., 1992, U.S.-Spain Joint Conf. on Edn., 1995. Mem. AAUW, NEA, Okla. Edn. Assn., Okla. Mid. Level Edn. Assn. (del. 1994), Nat. Art Edn. Assn. (del. 1992, 94, 96), Okla. Art Edn. Assn., Internat. Platform Assn., Libr. of Congress Assn. Avocation: travel. Home and Office: 439 S Memorial Dr Tulsa OK 74112-2203

SPENDER, JOHN-CHRISTOPHER, dean, writer; b. Bishop's Stortford, Herts., Eng., July 26, 1936; arrived in U.S., 1982; s. Michael Alfred Spender and Erika Harmann; m. Barbara Ann Brimberg. BA, Oxford (Eng.) U., 1960, MA, 1965; PhD, Victoria U., 1980. Asst. prof. UCLA, 1981—85; prof. Glasgow (Scotland) U., 1988—90, Rutgers U., Newark, 1991—97; dean Sch. Mgmt. N.Y. Inst. Tech., N.Y.C., 1996—2000; dean Sch. Bus. Tech. Fashion Inst. Tech./SUNY, 2000—. Mem. U.S. Open U. Adv. Bd., 1999. Author: Industry Recipes, 1989; editor, author: Managerial and Organizational Cognition, 1998, editor, author: Scientific Management, 1996. Sub. Lt. RNVR, 1957. Fellow: Royal Soc. Arts; mem.: Landsdowne Berkeley Sq. Avocation: cruising sailor. Home: 411 E 57th St New York NY 10022-3066 Office: Fashion Inst Tech 7th Ave and 27th St New York NY 10001

SPENGLER, DAN MICHAEL, orthopedic surgery educator, researcher, surgeon; b. Defiance, Ohio, Feb. 25, 1941; s. Harold A. and Wilhelmina Spengler; m. Cynthia Niswonger; children: Christina, Craig. BS, Baldwin-Wallace Coll., 1962; MD, U. Mich., 1966. Diplomate Am. Bd. Orthopaedic Surgery (bd. dirs. 1988-97). Rotating intern King County Hosp., Seattle, 1966-67; resident in orthopedics U. Mich., Ann Arbor, 1970-73; asst. prof. U. Wash., Seattle, 1974-78, assoc. prof., 1978-83. Author: Low Back Pain, 1982. Bd. dirs. Musculoskeletal Transplant Found. Fellow: Am. Acad. Orthopaedic Surgeons; mem.: ACS, Internat. Soc. for Study of Lumbar Pain, Assn. Bone and Joint Surgeons, Am. Bd. Orthopaedic Surgeons (pres. 1993—94), Am. Orthopaedic Assn. (pres.-elect 2002—), U. Nashville Club. Avocations: flying, golf, running, skiing. Office: Vanderbilt U Dept Orthopedic Rehab 1161 21st Ave S #D4219MCN Nashville TN 37232-2550 E-mail: fly8@aol.com.

SPENGLER, PAUL ALBERT, foundation administrator; b. Buffalo, Feb. 18, 1947; s. Albert Henry and Hazel Mae Spengler; m. Cheryl Ann Spengler, June 22, 1985; stepchildren: Jennifer Ann MacFarlane, Mara Elizabeth Sroczyk. BS, SUNY, Buffalo, 1969, MA, 1973; PhD, U. Del., 1977. Dep. commr. Erie County Dept. Youth Svcs., Buffalo, 1984-87; dir. cmty. svcs. Salvation Army, 1988-93; dir. grants Niagara County C.C., Sanborn, N.Y., 1993-99; dir. found. giving Roswell Pk. Cancer Inst., Buffalo, 2000—. Cons. Edn. Devel. Ctr., Newton, Mass., 1978, Erie C.C., Buffalo, 1999-00, Genesee C.C., Batavia, N.Y., 1999, Adirondack C.C., Queensbury, N.Y., 1999; adj. instr. D'Youville Coll., Buffalo, 1988-90. Author: Yankee Swedish and Italian Aculturization and Economic Mobility in Jamestown New York from 1860 to 1920, 1980; contbr. articles to profl. jours. Sec. standing com. Episcopal Diocese Western N.Y., Buffalo, 1998—; vestryman Episcopal Ch. Good Shepherd, Buffalo, 1998—2001; mem. legis. commn. homelessness Erie County Legis., Buffalo, 1991-93. N.Y. State Regents scholar, 1965-69; Andelot fellow U. Del., 1973-74, 75-76, 76-77. Mem. Nat. Soc. Fundraising Execs. Democrat. Avocations: reading, gardening, classical music. Home: 26 Groveland St Buffalo NY 14214-1012 Office: Roswell Pk Alliance Elm And Carlton Sts Buffalo NY 14267-0001

SPENSER, IAN DANIEL, chemist educator; b. Vienna, Austria, June 17, 1924; m. Anita Fuchs, Sept. 5, 1951; children: Helen Ruth, Paul Andrew. B.Sc. with honors, U. Birmingham (Eng.), 1948; PhD in Biochemistry, U. London, 1952, D.Sc. in Organic and Biochemistry, 1969. Demonstrator in biochemistry King's Coll., U. London, 1948-52, asst. lectr. in biochemistry Med. Coll. St. Bartholomew's Hosp., 1952-54, lectr., 1954-57; postdoctoral fellow div. pure chemistry NRC Can., Ottawa, Ont., 1953-54; asst. prof. biochemistry McMaster U., Hamilton, Can., 1957-59, assoc.prof., 1959-64, prof., 1964-68, prof. chemistry, 1968-89, prof. emeritus, 1989—; Akademischer Gast Laboratorium für Organische Chemie/Eidgenössische Technische Hochschule, Zürich, Switzerland, 1971, 89; vis. prof. Inst. Organic Chemistry, Tech. U. Denmark, Lyngby, 1977, Inst. Organische Chemie/Univ. Karlsruhe, Fed. Republic Germany, 1981, Institut für Pharmazeutische Biologie, Universität Bonn, Federal Republic of Germany, 1989. Research in biosynthesis of alkaloids, biosynthesis of vitamin Bl and vitamin B6. Recipient Sr. Scientist award NATO, 1980; recipient Can.-Japan Exchange award, 1982-83, Univ. Club of Hamilton award, 1990. Fellow Royal Soc. Can., Chem. Inst. Can. (John Labatt Ltd. award 1982-83), Royal Soc. Chemistry (U.K.); mem. Biochem. Soc., Am. Soc. Biochemistry Molecular Biol., Am. Soc. Pharmacognosy, Phytochem. Soc. N. Am. Office: McMaster U Dept Chemistry Hamilton ON Canada L8S 4M1 E-mail: spenser@mcmaster.ca.

SPERAKIS, NICHOLAS GEORGE, artist; b. N.Y.C., June 8, 1943; s. George and Cathren (Cokatas) S.; m. Yolanda de Carmen Mesa, Feb. 1, 1983. Student, Pratt Inst., 1960, NAD, 1960-61, Art Students League N.Y., Pratt Graphic Art Center, 1961-63. Instr. Sumitt (N.J.) Art Center, 1971, New Sch. Social Research, N.Y.C., 1972—, Fashion Inst. Tech., N.Y.C., 1977—. Exhibited one-man shows at Paul Kessler Gallery, 1963, 64, Provincetown, Mass., Hinckley and Brohel Art Gallery, Washington, 1964, N.Y.C., 1965, Mari Galleries, Woodstock, N.Y., 1966, 67, 68, Larchmont, N.Y., 1967, Eric Schindler Galleries, 1965, Richmond (Va.) Art Gallery, N.Y. U. Student Loeb Center, 1969, L.I. U., 1971, Pratt Inst., 1971, Bienville Gallery, New Orleans, 1972, 74, Pace U., N.Y.C., 1972, Lerner-Heller Gallery, N.Y.C., 1975, 76, Daedal Gallery, Balt., 1976, Reading Mus. Art, (Pa.), 1977, Bklyn. Mus., 1977, Washington Irving Gallery, N.Y.C., 1982, Museo Universitario Del Chopo, Mexico City, 1984, Forum Gallery, N.Y.C., Mus. Contemporary Art, Bogota, The Atler Gallery, Munich, 1989, Galerieverein Blankenese, Hamburg, Fed. Republic Germany, 1988, Galeria Sextante, Bogota, 1989, La Francia, Centro de Arte, Medellin, Colombia, 1989, various woodcut exhbns., Alexander S. Onassis Ctr. N.Y.U., 1995, Claudia Carr Gallery, N.Y.C., 1997-98, The Old Print Shop, N.Y.C., 1998, Stephen Gang Gallery, N.Y.C., 2000, others; exhibited group shows, Mercy Hurst Coll., Erie, Pa., 1963, 64, Bklyn. Mus., 1964, 77, Jewish Mus., 1964, Chrysler Mus., 1964, 65, Assoc. Am. Artists Galleries, N.Y.C., 1965, Norfolk (Va.) Mus. Arts Scis., 1965, Long Beach (Calif.) Coll., 1969, Am. Acad. and Nat. Inst. Arts and Letters, 1969, 75, Mid West Mus-Am-Art, 1981, numerous others, print exhbns., France, Italy, Spain, other European Countries, Far East, 1970-71, Lerner-Heller Gallery, 1973, 76, Amherst Coll., 1974, Worcester (Mass.) Mus. Fine Art, 1977, Reading (Pa.) Mus. Art, 1977, Galeria El Museo Santate de Bogota, Colombia, 1992, Mus. Modern Art, Rio de Janeiro, Brazil, 1992, travel Ams., Europe, 1992, Rhino Horn, N.Y.C., 1994, WhiteHall, N.Y.C., 1993, 94, Barnard/Biderman Fine Art, N.Y.C., 1994, 10th Ann. Art Miami 2000, 2000, Siron Studios, N.Y.C., 2001; represented in permanent collections Bklyn.

Mus., Walter P. Chrysler Mus., Norfolk, Va., Norfolk Mus. Arts and Scis., N.Y.C. Public Library, Phila. Mus. Fine Arts, Worcester Mus. Fine Art, Flint (Mich.) Art Inst., Mus. Modern Art, N.Y.C., U. Conn., Storrs, Amherst Coll., Okla. Fine Arts Center Mus., Am. Acad. and Nat. Inst. Arts and Letters, Detroit Inst. Fine Art, Corcoran Gallery of Art, Midwest Mus. Am. Art, Exeter Acad., Conn., Mus. Modern Art, N.Y.C., print collections Nat. Mus. Am. Art Smithsonian Instn., DeHunter Mus. Art, Chattanooga, Libr. of Congress, Washington, High Mus. Art, Atlanta, Free Libr., Phila., Kunst Mus., Fine Arts Mus. Bern Switzerland, Australian Nat. Gallery, Canberra, Snite Mus. Art, U. Notre Dame, Ind., Bibliotheque Royale Albert/ER, Bruxelles, Belgium, Museo Rayo, Roldanillo, Colombia, Stedelijk Mus., Amsterdam, The Netherlands, Hirshhorn Mus., Washington, Mus. Modern Art Santa Fe de Bogota, Nordjyllands Kunstmus., Aalborg, Denmark, Banco Bozano Simonsen, Rio de Janeiro, Mus. Modern Art, Bogota, Rose Art Mus. Brandeis U., Conn.; organized (with others), Rhino Horn artist group, N.Y.C., 1970. Recipient First Prize Purchase award Mercy Hurst Coll., 1964; Lawrence and Hinda Rosenthal award Am. Acad. and Nat. Inst. Arts and Letters, 1969; Guggenheim graphics fellow, 1970; McDowell Colony summer resident, 1976 Mem. Soc. Am. Graphic Artists. Address: 245 W 29th St Fl 12A New York NY 10001-5208 *Art doesn't bring out the voters for candidates X or Z. Art brings forth an experience and enters the knowledge of the viewer, so it helps the individual consider new channels and modes of behavior. One of the reasons there is so much censorship of art is due to the power art has to transform people at the roots not into some action but in a more generalized manner in terms of understanding institutions and traditions for what they really are. I think art changes emotions more than it changes specific ideas.*

SPERANZA, PAUL SAMUEL, JR. lawyer; b. Rochester, N.Y., May 12, 1947; s. Paul Samuel and Rosemary Gloria (Patti) S.; m. Cheryl Ann Amering, June 27, 1969; children: Sarah, Martha. BS, Syracuse U., 1969; JD, U. San Francisco, 1971; LLM in Taxation, NYU, 1972. Bar: N.Y., Calif., Pa., U.S. Supreme Ct., U.S. Tax Ct., U.S. Ct. Appeals (2d cir.). Assoc. Martin, Dutcher, Cooke, Mousaw & Vigdor, Rochester, 1972-73; ptnr. Wegman, Mayberry, Burgess, Feldstein & Speranza, 1973-76; exec. officer, sr. v.p., gen. counsel, sec., 3-mem. bd. dirs. Wegmans Food Markets, Inc., 1976—. Chmn. fin., acctg., tax and human resources com., audit com., retirement plan com., risk mgmt. com. Wegmans Food Markets, Inc.; mem. govt. rels. tax and steering coms. N.Y. State Bus. Coun., Albany, 1984—, bd. dirs., mem. exec. policy com., 1997—; bd. dirs., counsel, sec. Wegmans Fed. Credit Union, Rochester, 1984-2001; bd. dirs., exec. com., nominating com., N.Y. rep., chmn. tax com., chmn. employee benefits com. C. of C. of U.S., 1998—. Contbr. articles to profl. publs.; frequent lectr. on various bus. and legal topics. Capt. fund raiser Syracuse U. Capital Fund, 1988; bd. dirs., chmn. various coms. Our Lady of Mercy H.S., Rochester, 1988—94, chmn. bd., 1990—93; bd. dirs., exec. com. audit fin. com., compensation com. Excellus, Inc., Blue Cross Blue Shield of Rochester, Syracuse, Utica and Watertown, NY, 1995—, vice chmn. fin. bd., 1998—2000, chmn. bd., 2000—02; mem. N.Y. State Gov.'s 25-mem. Taxpayer Adv. Coun., 1996—; chmn. tax com. Greater Rochester C. of C., mem. legis. com., 1996—, bd. dirs., 2000—; mem. local pub. libr. fin. com.; chmn. com. for Performing Arts Ctr., 2002, chmn. steering com.; mem. Monroe County Pub. Ofcl. Compensation Com. Mem. ABA (sects. on adminstrv. law, antitrust, closely held corps., tort and ins. practice, labor and employment law, real property, probate and trust law, taxation), Tax Execs. Inst., Food Mktg. Inst. (chmn. lawyers and economists com. 1991-93, mem. govt. rels., tax, lawyers and economists coms. 1983—), Am. Corp. Counsel Assn., N.Y. State Bar Assn. (sects. on labor, taxation, corp., negligence, antitrust, estates and trusts), Calif. Bar Assn., Pa. Bar Assn., Monroe County Bar Assn. (corp. counsel sect.), Syracuse U. Soc. of Fellows. Republican. Roman Catholic. Avocations: charitable and civic activities, helping economically disadvantaged youth, running, travel and foreign languages, food. Home: 45 Grosvenor Rd Rochester NY 14610-2513 Office: Wegmans Food Markets Inc PO Box 30844 Rochester NY 14603-0844 E-mail: paul.speranza@wegmans.com.

SPERBER, DANIEL, physicist; b. Vienna, Austria, May 8, 1930; came to U.S., 1955, naturalized, 1967; s. Emanuel and Nelly (Lieberman) S.; m. Ora Yuval, Nov. 29, 1963; 1 son, Ron Emanuel. M.Sc., Hebrew U., 1954; PhD, Princeton U., 1960. Tng. and rsch. asst. Israel Inst. Tech., Haifa, 1954-55, Princeton U., 1955-60; sr. scientist, rsch. adviser Ill. Inst. Tech. Rsch. Inst., Chgo., 1960-67; assoc. prof. physics Ill. Inst. Tech., 1964-67, Rensselaer Poly. Inst., Troy, N.Y., 1967-72, prof., 1972—. Nordita prof. Niels Bohr Inst., Copenhagen, 1973-74, NATO research fellow, vis., prof., 1974-77; vis. prof. G.S.I., Darmstadt, Fed. Republic Germany, 1983; sr. Fulbright research scholar, Saha Inst. Nuclear Physics, Calcutta, India, 1987-88. Contbr. over 100 sci. papers to profl. jours. Served to capt. Israeli Army, 1948-51. Fellow Am. Phys. Soc.; mem. Israel Phys. Soc., N.Y. Acad. Scis., Sigma Xi. Jewish. Home: 1 Taylor Ln Troy NY 12180-7162 Office: Rensselaer Poly Inst 110 8th St Dept Physics Troy NY 12180-3522 E-mail: sperbd@rpi.edu. *My goals are to further an understanding of nature by basic research in nuclear theory and to introduce a new generation to this research.*

SPERBER, MARTIN, pharmaceutical company executive, pharmacist; b. N.Y.C., Aug. 6, 1931; s. David and Gertrude (Besen) S.; m. Ellen Claire Marx, June 7, 1953; children— Steven Jay, Susan Barbara Parnes. BS, Columbia U., N.Y.C., 1952. Registered pharmacist. Pharmacist, dir. sales and mktg. Henry Schein, Inc., N.Y.C., 1953-65, v.p., 1965-80, pres., COO Melville, N.Y., 1980-89, vice chmn., 1989-93, also bd. dirs.; pres., COO Schein Pharm., Inc., Florham Park, N.J., 1985-89, chmn., chief exec. officer, 1989—, chmn., CEO, pres., also bd. dirs.; chmn., CEO Danbury Pharm. Inc. (owned by Schein Pharm., Inc.), Carmel, N.Y., 1989—, also bd. dirs.; chmn., CEO Schein Pharm. Inc., Phoenix, 1989—; also bd. dirs. Steris Labs., Inc. (owned by Schein Pharm., Inc.). Mem. coun. of overseers Arnold and Marie Schwartz Coll. Pharmacy, L.I. U.; bd. dirs. Am. Found. for Pharm. Edn. Mem. Am. Pharm. Assn. Office: Schein Pharm Inc 100 Campus Dr Florham Park NJ 07932-1006

SPERBER, MATTHEW ARNOLD, direct marketing company executive; b. N.Y.C., Dec. 17, 1938; s. Raymond and Sylvia (Pollock) S.; m. Jane L. Trautman; children: Sean S., Dawn E. BS in Architecture, CUNY, 1961. Mgr. advt. IBM, White Plains, N.Y., 1967-78; mgr. advt. and promotion Exxon Office Systems, Lionsville, Pa., 1979-81; dir. advt. and promotion Wang, Lowell, Mass., 1981-83; dir. mkgt. communication Datapoint, San Antonio, 1983-85; pres. Bus. to Bus. div. Harte Hanks Direct Mktg., 1985-88; pres. Internat. Direct Mktg., 1988—. Mgr. IBM Copier, 1970, QYX Electronic Typewriter, 1980; dir. Wang Personal Computer, 1982, Datapoint 32 Mini Computer, 1985. With U.S. Army, 1961-63. Mem. Am. Mktg. Assn. (exec.), Direct Mktg. Assn. (Best Indsl. Direct Mktg. award 1978). Republican. Avocations: tennis, basketball, aerobics, music, travel. Home: 331 Country Wood Dr San Antonio TX 78216-1610 Office: Internat Direct Mktg 8045 Antoine Dr Ste 109 Houston TX 77088-4301

SPERBER, STEVEN JAY, internist; b. N.Y.C., Oct. 1, 1956; BA magna cum laude, Franklin and Marshall Coll., 1978; MD, NYU, 1982. Diplomate Am. Bd. Internal Medicine, Am. Bd. Infectious Diseases. Intern, then resident in internal medicine SUNY, Stony Brook, 1982-85; clin. fellow in infectious diseases U. Va. affiliated hosps., Roanoke, 1985-86; rsch. fellow in infectious diseases U. Va. Sch. Medicine, Charlottesville, 1986-88; asst. prof. medicine Robert Wood Johnson Med. Sch., 1988-92; dir. med. resident rsch. program Hackensack (N.J.) U. Med. Ctr., 1992-97; clin. asst. prof. medicine N.J. Med. Sch.-U. Medicine and Dentistry N.J., 1992-99, clin. assoc. prof. medicine, 2000—. Contbr. articles to med. jours. Fellow ACP, Infectious Diseases Soc. Am.; mem. Am. Soc. Microbiology, Infectious Diseases Soc. N.J. (founding), Phi Beta Kappa. Avocation: photography. Office: Hackensack Univ Med Ctr 20 Prospect Ave Hackensack NJ 07601-1997

SPERBERG-MCQUEEN, C.M. information specialist; b. Borger, Tex., May 18, 1954; s. Lawrence R. and Elvira Tavizon S. and Miriam Culler S.; m. Marian R. McQueen, Sept. 15, 1979. AB in German Studies, AM in German Studies, Stanford U., PhD in Comparative Lit., 1985. Humanities computing specialist Princeton (N.J.) U., 1985-86; rsch. programmer U. Ill., Chgo., 1987-92, sr. rsch. programmer, 1992-99; mem. tech. staff World Wide Web Consortium, Cambridge, Mass., 1999—, arch. domain lead, 2001—. Co-chair Markup Techs., Chgo., Phila., 1998-99, Extreme Markup Langs. Cong., Montreal, Que., Can., 2000—; coord. Model Editions Partnership, 1995, 2002. Editor: Guidelines for Electronic Text Encoding and Interchange, 1994; editor-in-chief Text Encoding Initiative, 1988-99; contbr. articles to profl. jours. Vis. rsch. fellow U. Bergen, 1997-98, Deutscher Akad, Austauschdienst fellow, 1982-83. Mem. Assn. Computer and Humanities, Assn. literary and Linguistic Computing, Assn. Computational Linguistics. Home: 259 State Rd 399 Espanola NM 87532-3170 Office: World Wide Web Consortium MIT LCS 545 Tech Sq Cambridge MA 02139 Fax: 505-747-1424. E-mail: cmsmcq@acm.org.

SPERDUTO, ELISA BARBARA, social worker; b. White Plains, N.Y., Nov. 28, 1963; d. Robert Walter Dapice and Diane Florence (Kulesa) Kennedy; m. Robert Gerard Sperduto, July 22, 1989; children: Andrea Elizabeth, Michael Robert, Robert Gerard Jr. BA in Psychology, Marymount Coll., 1985; MSW, Fordham U., 1992. Cert. clin. social worker. Tech. writer, tech. support asst. Pergamon Press, Inc., Elmsford, N.Y., 1985-86; tech. writer, prodn. analyst The Bank of N.Y., Harrison, 1986-88, Pepsi Co., Inc., Purchase, N.Y., 1988-89; clin. social worker Westchester Assn. for Retarded Citizens, White Plains, 1990-91, Young Adult Inst., Tarrytown, 1991-92; pvt. practice White Plains, 1992—. Cons. YWCA, White Plains, NY, 1996—. Sec., bd. dirs. Haviland Manor Civic Assn., White Plains, 1994—, oncology unit Greenwich Hosp.; active Families for Greenwich (Conn.) Hosp. Com., 1996—; vol. oncology unit Greenwich Hosp. Marymount Coll. scholar, 1982-85. Mem. NASW (mem. clin. practice com. Westchester chpt. 1993—), Nat. Assn. for the Edn. Young Children, Westchester Country Club. Republican. Roman Catholic. Avocations: reading, writing, childrens issues, research. Home: 4 Laurel Rd White Plains NY 10605-4307 E-mail: eduto@aol.com.

SPERELAKIS, NICHOLAS, SR. physiology and biophysics educator, researcher; b. Joliet, Ill., Mar. 3, 1930; s. James and Aristea (Kayadakis) S.; m. Dolores Martinis, Jan. 28, 1960; children: Nicholas Jr., Mark (dec.), Christine, Sophia, Thomas, Anthony. BS in Chemistry, U. Ill., 1951, MS in Physiology, 1955, PhD in Physiology, 1957. Teaching asst. U. Ill., Urbana, 1954-57; instr. Case Western Res. U., Cleve., 1957-59, asst. prof., 1959-66, assoc. prof., 1966; prof. U. Va., Charlottesville, 1966-83; Joseph Eichberg prof. physiology Coll. Medicine U. Cin., 1983-96, chmn. dept., 1983-93, Eichberg prof. emeritus, 1996—. Cons. NPS Pharm., Inc., Salt Lake City, 1988-95, Carter Wallace, Inc. Cranbury, N.J., 1988-91; vis. prof. U. St. Andrews, Scotland, 1972-73, U. San Luis Potosi, Mex., 1986, U. Athens, Greece, 1994; Rosenblueth prof. Centro de Investigacion y Avanzades, Mex., 1972; mem. sci. adv. com. several internat. meetings, editl. bds. numerous sci. jours. Co-editor: Handbook of Physiology: Heart, 1979; editor: Physiology and Pathophysiology of the Heart, 1984, 2d edit., 1988, 3rd edit., 1994, 4th edit., 2000, Calcium Antagonists: Mechanisms of Action on Cardiac Muscle and Vascular Smooth Muscle, 1984, Cell Interactions and Gap Junctions, vols. I and II, 1989, Frontiers in Smooth Muscle Research, 1990, Ion Channels in Vascular Smooth Muscle and Endothelial Cells, 1991, Essentials of Physiology, 1993, 2d edit., 1996, Cell Physiology Source Book, 1995 (Outstanding Acad. Book, Choice Am. Libr. Assn. 1996, 98), 3d edit., 2001, Electrogenesis of Biopotentials, 1995; assoc. editor Circulation Rsch., 1970-75, 75-80, Molecular Cellular Cardiology; regional editor Current Drug Targets, 2000-2002; contbr. articles to profl. jours. Lectr. Project Hope, Peru, 1962. Sgt. USMC, 1951-53, Res., 1953-59. Recipient Disting. Alumnus award Rockdale (Ill.) Pub. Schs., 1958; U. Cin. Grad. fellow, 1989; NIH grantee, 1959-99. Mem. IEEE, Engring. in Medicine and Biology, Am. Physiol. Soc. (chair steering com. sect. 1981-82), Biophys. Soc. (coun. 1990-93), Am. Soc. Pharmacology and Exptl. Therapeutics, Internat. Soc. Heart Rsch. (coun. 1980-89, 92-98), Am. Hellenic Ednl. Progressive Assn. (pres. Charlottesville chpt. 1980-82), Ohio Physiol. Soc. (pres. 1990-91), Phi Kappa Phi. Independent. Greek Orthodox. Avocations: ancient coins, stamp collecting. Office: U Cin Coll Medicine 231 Bethesda Ave Cincinnati OH 45229-2827

SPERGEL, IRVING ABRAHAM, social worker, researcher; b. N.Y.C., Jan. 17, 1924; s. Julius and Freida Mann Spergel; m. Bertha Jampel Spergel, June 27, 1949 (dec. Nov. 1989); children: Barry Alexander, Mark Jonathan, Daniel Jeremy; m. Annot Mary McGiffin, Oct. 5, 1996. BSS, CCNY, 1946; MA, Columbia U., 1948, PhD in Social Work, 1960; MSW, U. Ill., 1952. Program asst. YM-YWHA, Wilmington, Del., 1948—49; gang worker, supr. N.Y.C., 1950, 1952; ct. rep. Youth Bd., 1954, 1958, 1960; dir. Neighbors United St. Club project Lenox Hill Neighborhood House, 1954—57; from asst. to assoc. prof. U. Chgo., 1960—66, prof., 1967—92, George Herbert Jones prof., 1993—. UN youth adv. Hong Kong Govt., 1970—71; external examiner social work Chung Chi Coll., 1978—97; cons. Hong Kong Coun. Social Svc., 1978—97; cons., rschr. in field. Author: Rocketville, Slumtown, Haulberg, 1964, Street Gang Work, 1966, Community Problem Solving, 1969, The Youth Gang Problem: A Community Approach, 1995. Mem. Ill. Gov.'s Commn. on Gangs, 1995—96, Nat. Youth Gang Adv. Com., Boys and Girls Clubs Am., 1989—91; mem. acad. adv. com. Ill. Criminal Justice Info. Authority, 1989—. With U.S. Army, 1943—46, ETO. Grantee, Ford Found., 1960, NIMH, 1960—61, U.S. Dept. Justice, 1988. Jewish. Office: U Chgo Sch Social Svc Adminstrn 969 E 60th St Chicago IL 60637

SPERIN, AMELIA HARRISON, medical/surgical nurse, pediatrics nurse, obstetrics/gynecological nurse; b. Eatonton, Ga., Apr. 5, 1961; d. Patrick Wesley and Mary Lee (Covert) Harrison; m. Phillip M. Sperin (div. Dec. 1987); children: Phillip Wesley, Lauren Heicha. LPN, Pickens Vocat. Tech. Sch., 1980; BSN, Med. Coll. Ga., 1984. RN, Ga. Med.-surg. nurse Cobb Gen. Hosp., Austell, Ga., 1983-85; nurse case mgr. N.W. Home Health, Jasper, 1991-93; nurse Northside Hosp.-Cherokee at R.T. Jones Campus, Canton, 1987—. Active mem. Jasper First Bapt. Ch. Office: Northside Hosp-Cherokee 201 Hospital Rd Canton GA 30114-2408

SPERL, JOHANN WOLFGANG KARL, pediatrician; b. Linz/Donau, Austria, May 15, 1956; s. Johann and Maria Sperl; m. Ingeborg Patauner-Sperl, May 22, 1988; 1 child Alexandra. Med. degree, U. Innsbruck, 1981, specialization in pediats., 1988; PhD, U. Nijmegen, 1992; Habilitation, U. Innsbruck, 1993. Assoc. prof. U. Innsbruck, 1992—96, prof. pediats., 1998; dir. Children's Hosp., Salzburg, 1996—. Contbr. articles to peer-reviewed jours. Recipient Eduard Wallnöfer prize, 1994, Nestle Alete prize, 1992. Mem.: Arbeitsgemeinschaft für pädiatrische Stoffwechselstörungen. Avocations: theater , skiing, climbing, sailing. Home: Vollerhofstr 533 A-5412 Puch Austria Office: Childrens Hosp Landeskliniken Salzburg Müllner Hauptstr A-5020 Salzburg Austria

SPERLIK, JR. ROBERT VAL, music educator, musician; b. Oak Park, Ill., Dec. 15, 1959; s. Robert Val and Dorothy J. Sperlik. BS in Music Edn., U. of Ill., Champaign-Urbana, 1982; MA in Music Performance, DePaul U., Chgo., 1986. Cert. Tchr. Ill., 1982. Dir. of percussion J. S. Morton HS, Berwyn-Cicero, Ill., 1983—96; dir. of percussion Morton Coll., Cicero, 1984—2000; band dir. Sch. Dist. 100, Berwyn, 1987—. Percussion cons. Shorewood H.S. Band, Shorewood, 1999—; founder-director Take-Ten Percussion Ensemble, Berwyn, Ill., 1996—; prin. percussionist Lake Shore Symphony, Chgo.; jazz band dir. Dist. 100 Heritage Mid. Sch., Berwyn, Ill., 1999—; prin. percussionist Classical Symphony Orch., Chgo., 1985—2001, Lincolnwood Chamber Orch., Lincolnwood, Ill., Salt Creek Ballet Co., Chgo., Chgo. Symphonic Wind Ensemble, Ill.; theatre percussionist Cir. Theatre, Forest Park, Ill. Musician: (percussion soloist) The World of Percussion, 1995, (marimba soloist) DePonte Concertino for Marimba, 2002. Recipient Ill. State Scholarship, State of Ill., 1984 through 1986, First Pl. Percussion Ensemble, Ill. H.S. Music Assn., 1983 through 1996, Divsn. 1 State Band Contest, Ill. Grade Sch. Music Assn., 1989, 1993, 1997, 1999, Dist. 100 Honor Band Day, City of Berwyn, 1997. Mem.: NEA, Chgo. Fedn. of Musicians, Percussive Arts Soc., Music Educators Nat. Conf., Ill. Edn. Assn. Episcopalian. Avocations: performing, bicycling, reading, sports, travel.

SPERLING, ALLAN GEORGE, lawyer; b. N.Y.C., Dec. 10, 1942; s. Saul and Gertrude (Lober) Sperling; m. Susan Kelz, 1965 (div. 2001); children: Matthew Laurence, Stuart Kelz, Jane Kendra; m. Ferne Goldberg, 2001. Bar: N.Y. 1969, U.S. Ct. Appeals (2d cir.) 1975. Law clk. to presiding justice U.S. Dist Ct., New Haven, 1967-68; assoc. Cleary, Gottlieb, Steen & Hamilton, N.Y.C., 1968-75, ptnr., 1976—. Editor Yale Law Jour. Bd. dirs. Vol. Lawyers for the Arts, 1998—, Merce Cunningham Dance Found., N.Y.C., 1985-98, 2000—, chmn. bd., 1992-98; chmn. bd. Rye (N.Y.) Arts Ctr. Inc., 1985-88, bd. dirs., 1990-94; bd. dirs. Friends of the Neuberger Mus. of Art, Purchase, N.Y., 1989—, chmn. bd., 1997-2000. Mem.: N.Y. State Bar Assn., Phi Beta Kappa, Order of the Coif. Home: 2 Fifth Ave New York NY 10011 Office: Cleary Gottlieb Steen & Hamilton 1 Liberty Plz Fl 43 New York NY 10006-1470

SPERLING, GEORGE, cognitive scientist, educator; s. Otto and Melitta Sperling BS in Math., U. Mich., 1955; MA in Psychology, Columbia U., 1956; PhD in Psychology, Harvard U., 1959. Rsch. asst. in biophysics Brookhaven Nat. Labs., Upton, N.Y., summer 1955; rsch. asst. in psychology Harvard U., Cambridge, Mass., 1957-59; mem. tech. rsch. staff Acoustical and Behavioral Rsch. Ctr., AT&T Bell Labs., Murray Hill, N.J., 1958-86; prof. psychology and neural sci. NYU, N.Y.C., 1970-92; disting. prof. cognitive scis., neurobiology and behavior U. Calif., Irvine, 1992—. Instr. psychology Washington Sq. Coll., NYU, 1962-63; vis. assoc. prof. psychology Duke U., spring 1964; adj. assoc. prof. psychology Columbia U., 1964-65; acting assoc. prof. psychology UCLA, 1967-68; hon. rsch. assoc. Univ. Coll., U. London, 1969-70; vis. prof. psychology U. Western Australia, Perth, 1972, U. Wash., Seattle, 1977; vis. scholar Stanford (Calif.) U., 1984; mem. sci. adv. bd. USAF, 1988-92. Recipient Meritorious Civilian Svc. medal USAF, 1993; Gomberg scholar U. Mich., 1953-54; Guggenheim fellow, 1969-70. Fellow AAAS, APA (Disting. Sci. Contbn. award 1988), Am. Acad. Arts and Sci., Optical Soc. Am.; mem. NAS, Assn. for Rsch. in Vision and Ophthalmology, Ann. Interdisciplinary Conf. (founder, organizer 1975—), Eastern Psychol. Assn. (bd. dirs. 1982-85), Soc. for Computers in Psychology (steering com. 1974-78), Psychonomic Soc., Soc. Exptl. Psychologists (Warren medal 1996), Soc. for Math. Psychology (chmn. 1983-84, exec. bd. 1979-85), Phi Beta Kappa, Sigma Xi. Office: U Calif SS Plz A Dept Cognitive Scis Irvine CA 92697-5100 E-mail: sperling@uci.edu.

SPERLING, GODFREY, JR. journalist; b. Long Beach, Calif., Sept. 25, 1915; s. Godfrey and Ida (Bailey) Sperling; m. Betty Louise Feldmann, June 22, 1942; children: Mary McAuliffe, John Godfrey. BS, U. Ill., 1937; JD, U. Okla., 1940. Bar: Ill. 1940. Pvt. practice, Urbana, Ill.; reporter Champaign-Urbana News-Gazette, 1940-41; mem. staff Christian Sci. Monitor, 1946—, Midwest bur. chief, 1957-62, N.Y. bur. chief, 1962-65, news mgr., asst. chief Washington bur., 1965-73, nat. polit. corr., 1970-83, chief Washington Bur., 1973-83, sr. Washington columnist, 1984—, cons. to pub., 2002—. Lectr. nat. affairs, 1955—; Woodrow Wilson vis. fellow, 1976—. Served to maj. USAAF, 1941—46, col. USAAF. Recipient Disting. Alumni award, U. Ill., 1987, Spl. citation, Nat. Press Found. for unique contbns. to Am. journalism, 1994. Mem.: Navy Officers Club, Gridiron Washington (pres. 1991), Overseas Wirters Club (Washington), Nat. Press Club (Washington), White House Press Corr. Assn., Congl. Press Corr. Assn., Mass. Bar Assn., Ill. Bar Assn., Okla. Bar Assn., Sperling Breakfast Group (host 1966—), Cosmos Club (Washington), Sigma Delta Chi. Christian Scientist. Home: 8101 Connecticut Ave Apt N500 Chevy Chase MD 20815-2827 Office: Christian Science Monitor 910 16th St NW Washington DC 20006-2903

SPERLING, IRENE R. publishing executive; Publisher Tradeshow Week, L.A. Office: Tradeshow Week 5700 Wilshire Blvd Ste 120 Los Angeles CA 90036-3644 E-mail: isperling@tsweek.com.

SPERLING, JOY HARMON, lawyer; b. Bklyn., Mar. 25, 1961; d. Aaron and Lenore Harmon; m. Norman Jay Sperling, July 1, 1984; 1 child, Daniel Steven. BA cum laude, Rutgers U., 1983, JD, 1986. Bar: N.J. 1986, U.S. Dist. Ct N.J. 1986, U.S. Ct. Appeals (3d cir.) 1995, U.S. Dist. Ct. (so. dist.) N.Y. 1998. Clk. to Hon W.P. Diana, Assignment and Chancery Judge Superior Ct. of N.J., Somerville, N.J., 1986-87; assoc. Pitney, Hardin, Kipp & Szuch, Morristown, 1987-95, ptnr., 1996—. Mem. ABA, N.J. State Bar Assn., Phi Beta Kappa. Home: 11 Argonne Farm Dr Bridgewater NJ 08807-1480 Office: Pitney Hardin Kipp & Szuch PO Box 1945 Morristown NJ 07962-1945 E-mail: jsperling@phks.com.

SPERLING, MARK A. physician, scientist; b. Lodz, Poland, Sept. 6, 1938; s. Josef and Celia S.; m. Vera R. Schreiber, June 7, 1966; children: Lisa N., Jonathan M. MBBS (MD), U. Melbourne, Victoria, Australia, 1962. Diplomate in pediatrics and pediatric endocrinology Am. Bd. Pediatrics. Intern Prince Henry Hosp., Melbourne, Australia, 1963-64; resident in pediatrics Royal-Childrens Hosp., 1964-67, registrar, 1967-68; fellow Childrens Hosp., Pitt., 1968-70; asst./assoc. prof. pediat. UCLA, 1970-78; prof. pediatrics Children's Hosp., Cin., 1978-89, U. Pitts., 1999—, chair dept. pediat., 1989—99; prof., chair emeritus dept. pediatrics Children's Hosp. of Pitts., 1999—. Mem. Nat. Diabetes Adv. Bd., 1992-96, Rsch. Adv. Bd., 1999—. Editor: Pediatric Endo, 1996; contbr. articles to profl. jours. Chair Sci. Am. Diab. Assn.; mem. Nat. Diab. Adv. Bd., 1992—96. Recipient Rsch. Career award NIH, 1975-80, Mary Jane Kugel award Juvenile Diabetes Found., 1977, Outstanding Faculty Tchr. award UCLA, 1973-74. Mem. Am. Pediat. Soc., Am. Soc. Clin. Investigation, Assn. Am. Physicians, Am. Diabetes Assn. (chair sci. program com.). Avocations: tennis, swimming. Home: 1405 Squirrel Hill Ave Pittsburgh PA 15217-1151 Office: Childrens Hosp 3705 5th Ave Pittsburgh PA 15213-2583 E-mail: masp@pitt.edu.

SPERLING, SCOTT EDWARD, software consultant, Bible expositor; b. Tucson, Jan. 11, 1961; s. Fritz Eric and Ruth Ann S.; m. Moon Hee, March 16, 1985; children: Scott Edward, Charlotte Moon. BSc in Applied Physics, Calif. Inst. Tech., Pasadena, 1983; BSc in Info. Computer Sci., U. Calif., Irvine, 1985. Software engr. Interstate Electronics, Anaheim, Calif., 1985-87, Hughes Aircraft, Fullerton, 1987-88, software cons. Azusa, 1991-92; software engr. Librascope Corp., Glendale, 1988-91; software cons. Litton Guidance & Control Sys., Woodland Hills, 1993—; prin., owner Scripture Studies Inc., SSper Inc., Foothill Ranch, 1994—, 1997—. Author, editor Scripture Studies, 1994—. Avocations: music, literature. Home and Office: Scripture Studies Inc 20 Pastora Foothill Ranch CA 92610 E-mail: ssper@aol.com.

SPERO, BARRY MELVIN, medical center executive; b. Richmond, Va., July 13, 1937; s. Stanley Leo and Jean (Marmorstein) Spero; m. Merle Burns, May 29, 1960; children: Amy, Robin, Melissa. BA, U. Richmond, 1959; MHA, Med. Coll. Va., 1961. Asst. adminstr. Bapt. Hosp., Nashville, 1963-66, adminstrv. dir., 1966-68; v.p., dir. hosp. adminstrn. Hosp. Affiliates, Inc., 1968-71; exec. dir. Bon Secours Hosp., Grosse Pointe, Mich., 1971-77; pres. The Mt. Sinai Med. Ctr., Cleve., 1977-85; pres., pres. NeWell Health Care System Newton-Wellesley Hosp., 1985-90; pres. Maimonides Med. Ctr., Bklyn., 1990-95; pres., CEO Masonicare, Wallingford, Conn., 1995—. Mem. pers. practice com. Combined Jewish Philantropies; chmn. United Way West Suburban Hosp. divsn.; regional bd. mem. Bay Bank Middlesex; mem. Perpetual Benevolent Fund Com., Blue Print 2000, Commonwealth Mass.; bd. dirs. Premier Health Alliance, chmn., 1981—84; bd. dirs. Premier Preferred Care, Healthfirst; trustee Villa Maria Nursing Ctr./Bon Secours Hosp., 1974—94, chmn., bd. dirs., 1988—94; bd. dirs. Conn. Assn. Not-for-Profit Providers for the Aging, League Vol. Hosps. and Homes, 1991—95, chmn.-elect, 1992—95; mem. State of Ohio Gov.'s Commn. on Health Care Cost, 1984—85; various coms. Coun. Tchg. Hosps., 1992—95; treas. Vol. Hosps. Am., Mass., 1986—90; chmn. hosp. adv. com. Blue Cross N.E. Ohio, 1983—85; trustee Med. Instrumentation Sys., 1978—84; mem. various coms. Am. Assn. Homes and Svcs. for the Aging, 1995—; adv. bd. Gateway Cmty. Coll. Fellow: Am. Coll. Healthcare Execs.; mem.: Greater New Haven C. of C. (bd. dirs.), Ohio Hosp. Assn. (bd. trustees 1981—85, exec. coun.), Mass. Hosp. Assn. (com. on health sys. 1986—90, bd. trustees 1987—90, com. on Medicare payment for outpatient svcs. 1989—90), Met. Boston Hosp. Coun. (chmn. 1988—90), New Eng. Healthcare Assembly (Blue Ribbon com. 1985—90), Greater Cleve. Hosp. Assn. (bd. trustees 1981—85, exec. coun.), Greater N.Y. Hosp. Assn. (bd. govs. 1992—94), Am. Assn. Homes Svcs. Aging (bd. dirs. 1997—,), Conn. Hosp. Assn. (bd. dirs. 1997—2000), Coun. Tchg. Hosps. (various coms. 1992—94), Am. Hosp. Assn. (com. on Medicare payment for outpatient svcs. 1989—90). Jewish. Avocation: Avocations: golf, tennis, scuba diving. Office: Masonicare PO Box 70 Wallingford CT 06492-7001

SPERO, C. MICHAEL, lawyer; b. N.Y.C., Oct. 13, 1936; s. Carl Mony and Mildred (Wolfe) S.; m. Joan Edelman, Nov. 9, 1969; children: Jason, Ben. BA, Amherst Coll., 1958; LLB, Yale U., 1961. Bar: N.Y. 1961, Fla. 1976. Assoc. Hughes, Hubbard & Reed, N.Y.C., 1961-64, Stroock & Stroock & Lavan, N.Y.C., 1964-70; ptnr. Wien, Malkin & Bettex, 1970-96, Salans, Hertzfeld, Heilbronn, Christy & Viener, N.Y.C., 1996—. Bd. dirs., past pres., Stanley Isaacs Neighborhood Ctr., advisor, Lincoln Ctr., Amherst Coll., United Jewish

Appeal-Fedn., N.Y.C. Mem. Frenchman's Creek Golf Club. Home: 1165 Park Ave New York NY 10128-1210 Office: Salans Hertzfeld Heilbronn Christy & Viener 620 5th Ave New York NY 10020-2402 E-mail: cmspero@salans.com.

SPERO, JOAN EDELMAN, foundation president; b. Davenport, Iowa, Oct. 2, 1944; d. Samuel and Sylvia (Halpern) Edelman; m. C. Michael Spero, Nov. 9, 1969; children: Jason, Benjamin. Student, L'Inst. d'Etudes Politiques, Paris, 1964-65; BA in Internat. Rels. with honors, U. Wis., 1966; MA, Columbia U., 1968, PhD, 1973; LLD (hon.), Amherst Coll., 1997. Asst. prof. Columbia U., N.Y.C., 1973-79; ambassador of U.S. to UN Econ. and Social Council, 1980-81; v.p. Am. Express Co., 1981-83, sr. v.p. internat. corp. affairs, 1983-89; treas., sr. v.p., 1989-91; exec. v.p. corp. affairs and communications Am. Express Co., 1991-93; under sec. for econ., bus. and agrl. affairs Dept. of State, Washington, 1993-97; pres. Doris Duke Charitable Found., N.Y.C., 1997—. Vis. scholar Fed. Res. Bank N.Y., 1976—77; dir. 1st Data Corp., Delta Air Lines Inc.; mem. adv. com. Japan Found. Ctr. for Global Partnership. Author: The Politics of International Economic Relations, 5th edit., 1997, The Failure of the Franklin National Bank, 1980; contbr. articles to profl. jours. Trustee Wis. Alumni Rsch. Found., 1997—, Brookings Instn., 1997, Columbia U., 1998; trustee emeritus Amherst Coll.; mem. Coun. Am. Ambs. Named to Acad. Women Achievers, YWCA, 1983; named Fin. Woman of Yr., Fin. Women's Assn., 1990; recipient George Washington U. Disting. Statesperson award, 1994; Woodrow Wilson fellow. Mem. Am. Acad. Diplomacy, Coun. on Fgn. Rels. (bd. dirs.), Am. Philos. Soc., Phi Beta Kappa. Democrat. Jewish. Avocations: writing; swimming. Office: Doris Duke Charitable Found 650 5th Ave 19th Fl New York NY 10019-6108

SPERO, JOSHUA B. political scientist, educator; b. Washington, Jan. 26, 1963; s. Robert H. and Janet N. Spero; m. Ellen Rewse, July 26, 1987; children: Samuel. PhD, Johns Hopkins U., 2000. Rsch. analyst Libr. of Congress, Washington, 1987—88; dep. asst. for europe and the ussr Office of the Sec. of Def., 1988—90; vis. nat. security fellow Nat. Def. U. Inst. for Nat. Strategic Studies, 1990—94; sr. civilian strategic planner Joint Chiefs of Staff, 1994—2000; vis. asst. prof. of polit. sci. Merrimack Coll., North Andover, Mass., 2000—. Cons. Ctr. for Def. Info., Washington, 2001—; adv. The NY Times, N.Y.C., NY, 2002; vis. asst. prof. govt. Dartmouth Coll., Hanover, NH, 2000—01. Contbr. articles, columns in newspapers. Nominee Nat. Pub. Svc. award, Joint Chiefs of Staff, 1997—98; fellow, Dartmouth Coll., 2000—01. Mem.: Women In Internat. Security, Internat. Inst. of Strategic Studies, Internat. Studies Assn., Coun. on Fgn. Rels. Avocations: reading, writing, running, travel. Office: Merrimack College Department of Political Science North Andover MA 01845 Business E-Mail: joshua.spero@merrimack.edu.

SPERO, KEITH ERWIN, lawyer, educator; b. Cleve., Aug. 21, 1933; s. Milton D. and Yetta (Silverstein) S.; m. Carol Kohn, July 4, 1957 (div. 1974); children: Alana, Scott, Susan; m. Karen Weaver, Dec. 28, 1975. BA, Western Res. U., 1954, LLB, 1956. Bar: Ohio 1956. Assoc. Sindell, Sindell & Bourne, Cleve., 1956-57, Sindell, Sindell, Bourne, Markus, Cleve., 1960-64; ptnr. Sindell, Sindell, Bourne, Markus, Stern & Spero, 1964-74, Spero & Rosenfield, Cleve., 1974-76, Spero, Rosenfeld & Bourne, LPA, Cleve., 1977-79, Spero & Rosenfield Co. LPA, 1979—. Tchr. bus. law U. Md. overseas div., Eng., 1958-59; lectr. Case-Western Res. U., 1965-69; instr.; nat. panel arbitrators Am. Arbitration Assn. Author: The Spero Divorce Folio, 1966, Hospital Libaiblity for Acts of Professional Negligence, 1979. Trustee Western Res. Hist. Soc., 1984—2000, exec. com., 1992—2000; v.p., chmn. libr. display and collections com. Western Res. Hist. Soc, 1992—95, chmn. history mus. com., 1995—99; commodore Dugway Creek Yacht Club, 1985—87; bd. dirs. Vail Valley Inst., 2000—. 1st lt. JAG USAF, 1957—60, capt. Res. USAF, 1960—70. Fellow Am. Acad. Matrimonial Lawyers; mem. ABA, Ohio Bar Assn., Cleve. Bar Assn., Cuyahoga County Bar Assn., Ohio Acad. Trial Lawyers (pres. 1970-71), Assn. Trial Lawyers Am. (state committeeman 1971-75, bd. govs. 1975-79, sec. family law litigation sect. 1975-76, vice-chmn. 1976-77, chmn. 1977-79), Am. Bd. Trial Advs., Order of Coif, Masons, Sonnenale Golf Club (edwards, Colo.), Phi Beta Kappa, Zeta Beta Tau, Tau Epsilon Rho. Jewish. (trustee, v.p. congregation 1972-78). Office: 440 Leader Bldg E 6th and Superior Cleveland OH 44114-1214 E-mail: keith@vail.net.

SPERO, MADDALENA ANN, nurse; b. S.I., N.Y., May 27, 1962; Cert. med. asst., Coll. S.I., 1984; diploma in nursing, St. Vincent's Sch. Nursing, S.I., 1986. RN N.Y., cert. in gen. nursing practice, ANCC, BLS, ACLS radiology image nurse, 2001, IV, 2001, ambulatory surgery/endoscopy staff nurse, 2001. Med. asst. S.I. Med. Group, 1983-84; rehab./phys. medicine staff nurse S.I. Univ. Hosp., 1986-92, employee health svc. staff nurse, 1992-98, pre-admission surg. testing, 1998-2001; vascular technician, office nurse S.I. Surg. Assocs., 1989-95; office nurse Pavillion for Cosmetic Surgery, S.I., 1996-97. V.p. student body St. Vincent's Sch. Nursing, S.I., 1984-86. Mem. N.Y. State Nurses Assn., Am. Assn. Office Nurses. Avocation: aerobics.

SPERO, MORTON BERTRAM, retired lawyer; b. N.Y.C., Dec. 6, 1920; s. Adolph and Julia (Strasburger) S.; m. Louise Thacker, May 1, 1943; children: Donald S., Carol S. Flynn. BA, U. Va., 1942, LLB, 1946. Bar: Va. 1946, U.S. Supreme Ct. 1961. Mem. legal staff NLRB, Washington, 1946-48; sole practice Petersburg, Va., 1948-70; sr. ptnr. Spero & Levinson, 1970-75, Spero & Diehl, Petersburg, 1975-85; sole practice, 1985-2001; retired, 2001. Chmn. The Community Bank, Petersburg, 1976-79, dir., 1976-91. Chmn. United Fund Drive, 1960, bd. dirs., 1999—; pres. Dist. IV Petersburg Coun. Social Welfare, Southside Sheltered Workshop, 1965, pres. Congregation B'rith Achim, 1973. Served to lt. USNR, 1943-45. Recipient Outstanding Mem. award Petersburg chpt. B'nai B'rith, 1966; Svc. to Law Enforcement award Petersburg Police Dept., 1965. Fellow Am. Acad. Matrimonial Lawyers; mem. Va. Bar Assn., Petersburg Bar Assn. (pres. 1981-82), Va. State Bar (coun. 1981-84, chmn. criminal law sect. 1972, chmn. family law sect. 1979, bd. dirs. litigation sect. 1983-86, Lifetime Achievement award for family law sect. 1995), Va. Trial Lawyers Assn. (v.p. 1972), Civitan Club (hon.), Rotary, Elks (exalted ruler 1968). Democrat. Jewish. Home: 9706 Bunker Ct Petersburg VA 23805-9125 Fax: 804-733-8809.

SPERO, RAND KEVIN, management consultant; b. Youngstown, Ohio, Apr. 10, 1955; s. Leslie Wayne and Elaine Carol (Grossfield) S.; m. Barbara Ann Hall, May 1, 1992; children: Emma, Daniel. BA in Psychology cum laude, Vassar Coll., 1977; MBA in Mktg., UCLA, 1980; EdM in Orgnl. Behavior, Harvard U., 1985. Staff Sen. Howard Metzenbaum, Washington, 1977; instr. Close Up Found., 1978; lectr. Northeastern Grad. Sch. Mgmt., Boston, 1987, 89, 90; corporate mktg. dir. Continental Cablevision, 1980-84; pres. Spero Assocs., Lexington, Mass., 1984—. Dir. WMXS, Brockton, Mass., 1987-88. Producer, host Career Crossroads (Cable TV) 1990-91; contbr. articles to profl. jours. Trustee Mass. Eye and Ear Infirmary, Boston, 1996—. Avocations: cycling, swimming, guitar. Office: Spero Assocs 11 Heritage Dr Lexington MA 02420-1104

SPEROU, ZESSE, retired social worker; b. Three Rivers, Mich., Aug. 21, 1929; s. Zesse Paul and Vasliki Areganan Sperou. BA in English-Journalism, Calif. State U., 1959, postgrad., 1959—63. Cert. tchr. Calif. Social worker Dept. Pub. Social Svc., L.A. County, 1965—86; ret., 1986. Author numerous poems. Foster care cons. Cmty. Assistance to Homeless Youngsters, 1972—81; parish coun. St. John Bapt. Greek Orthodox Ch., Anaheim, Calif., 1983—85. With USMC, 1950—51, Korea. Republican. Greek Orthodox. Home: 26679 Calle Emiliano Sun City CA 92585

SPERRAZZA, CAMILLE PEPE, journalist, educator; b. Brooklyn, Ny, Nov. 15, 1957; d. Joseph Pepe and Rose Albanese; children: Stephen, Nicky, Bernadette. MA, Bklyn Coll., Brooklyn, NY, 1999, BA, 1996; AA, Kingsborough, Brooklyn, NY, 1994. Contbg writer NY Tchr., New York, NY, 1995—; reporter Bklyn Baron, Brooklyn, 1997—98; journalism educator Bd. Edn., 1997—; editor New Image student paper, 1998—; reporter, critic Courier, Life Newspapers, 1998—; tchr. educator Bd. Edn., 2000—; adj. prof. Manhattan CC, New York, 2001—. Freelance writer Many Publications, New York, NY, 2002—; guest spkr. cuny Tchg. in NYC, New York, NY, 2001—01; newspaper competition judge Columbia Scholastic Press Assn., New York, NY, 2000—01; academic cons. Bd. Edn., New York, NY, 2002—02; curriculum writer United Fedn. Teachers, 1990—. Contbr. articles to profl. jours. Tchr. women's history Month Competition Essay Winners, 1997—2002; tchr., writing advisor Luth. Women's Health Ctr., Brooklyn, NY, 2000—01. Recipient Sam Caster Award, Excellence Journalism, Bklyn Coll., 1996, Louis B. Goodman Award Woman-Centered Work, 1995, Irwin Shaw Award Fiction, 1995. Mem.: United Fedn. Teachers, Phi Theta Kappa. Avocations: writing, traveling, traveling, journalism, women's studies. Personal E-mail: camstniber@aol.com.

SPERRIN, GRAHAM FREDERICK, marketing professional; b. London, Eng., Aug. 22, 1956; s. Frank Reginold and Joyce Ivy Sperrin; m. Kim Julie Hollox; children: Luke, Justin. Degree in Elec. & Electronic Engring., Thames Poly., London, 1979. Sr. design engr. Marconi Comm., Chelmsford, 1979—83; prin. design engr. Electro Optic Develop., Basildon, 1983—86; European product mktg. mgr. Anritsu Co., Luton, 1987—98, mktg. mgr. Richardson, Tex., 1998—. Contbr. articles. Mem.: IEEE, Inst. Elec. Engineers (chartered engr. 1980), Inst. Mgmt. (assoc.). Office: Anritsu Co 1155 E Collins Blvd Richardson TX 75081

SPERRY, EDMUND LYNN, real estate broker; b. Salt Lake City, Dec. 11, 1948; s. Edmund T. and Marjory (Matheson) S.; m. Anna Grace Bellis, Sept. 1, 1978; 1 child, Heather Anne Harris. Student, U. Utah, 1967, 70-71, U. N.C., 1971-73. Cert. real estate broker Utah. Sales assoc. Hooper Ballstaedt Realtors, Salt Lake City, 1971-79; bus. devel. cons. Realty World Intermountain Region, 1979-81; mgr. Commerce Residential Properties, 1981-82; owner broker E.L. Sperry Group Realtors, 1982-88; cons. Nat. Note, 1988-89; mng. ptnr. Bellis Sperry Group, 1989—. Dir. Hooper Ballstaedt, Salt Lake City, 1977-79, Commerce Properties, 1981-82, Utah Residential Real Estate, Salt Lake City, 1982-92. Author: Franchise Operations Manual, 1989; contbr. articles to profl. jours. Bd. dirs. Habitat for Humanity, Salt Lake City, 1981-84, Cmty. Housing Resource Bd., Salt Lake City, 1989-92, Utah Vet. Licensing Com., Salt Lake City, 1992-96, Physicians Licensing Bd., 1996—; mayors com. for critical needs housing Mayors Conf., Washington, 1993. Sgt. U.S. Army, 1967—. Mem. Salt Lake Bd. Realtors, Utah Assn. Realtors, Nat. Assn. Realtors. Avocations: sky diving, scuba diving, running, hiking, camping. Home: 2660 Highland Dr Salt Lake City UT 84106-2772

SPERRY, JAMES EDWARD, anthropologist, retired state official; b. Weeping Water, Nebr., May 17, 1936; s. John Edward and Augusta Anea (Frandsen) S.; m. Gail Louise Killen, Sept. 26, 1964; 1 child, Patrick Reuben. Student, Bethany Coll., Lindsborg, Kans., 1953-55; AB in Art and Anthropology, U. Nebr., Lincoln, 1962, MA in Anthropology, 1965; postgrad., Mus. Mgmt. Inst., 1984. Teaching asst. U. Neb., 1961-63, instr. anthropology, 1964-65; research archeologist State Hist. Soc. N.D., Bismarck, 1965-69, supt., 1969-98; sec. N.D. Heritage Found., 1973-76, N.D. Lewis and Clark Trail Council, 1970, chmn., 1971; hist. preservation officer State of N.D., Bismarck, 1969-98, coord. state records, 1975-93. Mem. Theodore Roosevelt Rough Rider award com., 1969-98. Editor: North Dakota History: Journal of the Northern Plains, 1969-1973; contbr. numerous articles profl. jours. Bd. dirs. Burleigh/Morton chpt. ARC, 1987-93, chmn., 1993, mem. N.D. State svc. coun., 1993-2000, chmn., 1995-98. Served with USAF, 1956-59. Recipient award Greater N.D. Assn. Tourism and Recreation Devel., 1996; Am. Assn. State and Local History fellow, 1967, Bush summer fellow, 1984. Mem. Sigma Xi, Delta Phi Delta, Sigma Gamma Epsilon. Home: 1811 Estate Ave Bismarck ND 58504-3043 E-mail: sperr04@attglobal.net.

SPERRY, MARTIN JAY, lawyer; b. Troy, N.Y., May 15, 1947; s. Raymond Leon and Selma (Jenkins) S.; children: Jana, Douglas, Jill. BSBA, U. Fla., 1969, JD, 1971. Bar: Fla. 1972, U.S. Dist. Ct. (mid. dist.) Fla. 1972, U.S. Dist. Ct. (so. dist.) Fla. 1974, U.S. Supreme Ct. 1976, N.Y. 1983. Sr. law clk. to chief judge U.S. Dist. Ct. (mid. dist.) Fla., Orlando, 1972-74; ptnr. Carey, Dwyer, Cole, Selwood & Bernard, Ft. Lauderdale, Fla., 1974-78, Krathen & Sperry, Ft. Lauderdale, 1978-84, Selwood & Sperry, Ft. Lauderdale, 1984-85, Sperry, Shapiro & Kashi, Ft. Lauderdale, 1985—. Mem. Fourth Dist. Ct. Appeals Judicial Nominating Commn., 1996-2000. Contbg. author: Casebook of Florida Constitutional Law, 1971. Served as capt. U.S. Army Reserves, 1969-77. Mem. Acad. Fla. Trial Lawyers (diplomate), Assn. Trial Lawyers Am. (sustaining), N.Y. State Bar Assn., Fla. Bar Assn. (bd. cert. civil trial lawyer), Fed. Bar Assn., Nat. Bd. Trial Advs. (cert. civil trial adv.), Am. Bd. Trial Advocates, Am. Inns of Ct. Lodges: B'nai B'rith. Democrat. Jewish. Avocations: sports, traveling. Office: 633 S Andrews Ave Ste 101 Fort Lauderdale FL 33301-2843 E-mail: ssklaw@aol.com.

SPERRY, SHARON E. foundation executive; b. St. Louis, July 29, 1938; d. Delbert Franklin and Opal (Barnes) Norton; m. Clyde David Sperry, Oct. 21, 1966 (div. 1983); children: Pamela, Michael, Cynthia, Janice, Curtis. BS in Econs., Washington U., St. Louis; cert. Adminstrn. and Health Services Mgmt., UCLA; cert. Health Planning, Adminstrn., U. So. Calif. Assoc. hosp. adminstr. for fin. Rancho Los Amigos Hosp., Downey, Calif., 1969-84; exec. dir. Harbor-UCLA Med. Found., Torrance, 1984—. Bd. dirs. Jemaru, Inc.; mem bus. com. Hosp. Council So. Calif., Los Angeles, 1984. Mem. planning commn. Calif. Assn. Rehab. Facilities, 1983-84. Awarded cert. recognition Los Angeles County Bd. Suprs., 1984. Mem. Healthcare Fin. Mgmt. Assn., Women in Health Adminstrn., Med. Group Mgmt. Assn., Health Services Mgmt. Assn., Nat. Mgmt. Assn., Healthcare Execs. of So. Calif. Mem. Society Of Friends. Home: 9240 S 50th St Phoenix AZ 85044-5644 Office: Harbor-UCLA Med Found Inc 1124 W Carson St Torrance CA 90502-2006

SPESER, PHYLLIS LEAH, social scientist, consultant; b. Buffalo, Mar. 17, 1951; s. David and Theodora (Cowen) S.; children: Arendt, Ariel. BA in Polit. Sci. and Journalism, Case Western Res. U., 1973; JD, SUNY, Buffalo, 1980, PhD in Polit. Sci., 1981. Spl. asst. for sci. and tech. Fedn. Am. Scientists, Washington, 1980-81; pres. Foresight Sci. and Tech., Port Townsend, Wash., 1981—. Wash. rep. Soc. Am. Archeology, 1982-89; exec. dir. Nat. Coalition for Sci. and Tech., Washington, 1985-89; session chair Nat. Biotech. Edn. Sharing Conf., Madison, Wis., 1991; cons. Office of Gov. State of N.Y., 1980; adj. prof. dept. anthropology Am. U., Washington, 1988; adv. panelist on univ. small bus. ctrs., NSF, Washington, 1985; steering com. Internat. Biotech. Edn. Leadership Conf., 1992—. Author: The Defense-Space Market, 1985, The Politics of Science, 1987, Technology Transfer Handbook, 1990, The Federal Laser and Optics Market, 1990, Small Business Guide to Federal Research and Development Funding, 1996, Forests In Jefferson County, 1993, others; author, editor numerous reports, articles. Founding chair Glen Echo (Md.) Park Found., 1987-88; bd. dirs. Jefferson County Edn. Found., Port Townsend, 1991-94, v.p. 1993-94; bd. dirs., exec. com. Jefferson County Econ. Devel. Coun., Port Townsend, 1991-93, v.p. 1992-93; bd. dirs. Wash. Tech. Ctr., 1994—; lead lobbyist Small Bus. Innovation Devel. Act of 1982; developer Port Townssend Sch. Dist.Magnet Ctr., 1992; founding pres. Olympic PeninsulaFound., 1993—; with Woodnet Mfg. Tech. Ctr. Grantee NSF, EPA, USDA, Small Bus. Adminstrn., Dept. Energy, Bullitt Found., U.S. West Found., Archibald Charitable Trust, others; Rose Hips Queen, Great Port Townsend Bay Kenetic Skulpture Race, 1998-99. Mem. AAAS, Am. Assn. Artificial Intelligence, Tech. Transfer Soc. (bd. dirs., chair task force on nat. tech. transfer policy 1988-91), Bar Assn. D.C. Democrat. Achievements include key role in many pieces of legislation, development of expert system for technology transfer services for small rural manufacturers, establishment of vocational-technical and science education programs in rural communities. Office: Foresight Sci & Tech Inc PO Box 6815 New Bedford MA 02742-6815

SPETH, CAMILLE, engineer; b. Midvale, Utah, Aug. 24, 1956; d. Gerald L. and Dora (Goff) S. Grad. high sch., Indpls. Systems coord. Allied Fidelity, Indpls., 1984-85; bus. analyst EDS/MIC, Detroit, 1985-91; local area network adminstr. EDS/GMAC, 1991-97; network engr. Elec. Data Systems, Corydon, Ind., 1997—. Author: (manuals) V4 Users Guide, 1985, Genealogy Training Manual, 1990, Network Users Guide, 1992, Site Administration Manual, 1997. Leader Ch. Young Women Camp, 1975-85, coach sports program, 1975-85. Mem. NAFE, Ind. High Sch. Athletic Assn. (high sch. sports referee 1976—), Netware Users Internat. Avocations: music, golf, woodworking. Home and Office: 1970 Lears Ln NE Corydon IN 47112-7657 E-mail: camispeth@earthlink.net.

SPETH, GERALD LENNUS, education and business consultant; b. Logan, Utah, July 14, 1934; s. Fredrick William and Elizabeth LaVern (Nuttall) S.; m. Dora Goff, Aug. 11, 1955; children: Camille, Michael Gerald, Mark Alan, Janell, Doreen. BS, Utah State U., 1956; MBA, Ind. U., 1969; EdD, Ball State U., 1988. Auditor Ernst & Ernst, Salt Lake City, 1956, 58-59; officer 1st and 2d lt. U.S. Army, 1956-58, officer capt. to col., 1959-82; controller Columbia Club, Indpls., 1982-83; sr. v.p. Allied Fidelity Corp., 1983-85; adj. faculty Ind. Cen. U., 1982-85; prof., dir. grad. bus. progs. U. Indpls., 1985-2001. Cons. in field. Counselor in stake presidency, bishop, area welfare dir., mission pres., high councilor LDS Ch., 1965—. Recipient Legion of Merit, 1971-80, Bronze Star medal, 1966. Mem. Am. Soc. Mil. Comptrollers, U.S. Govt. Accts. Assn., Beta Gamma Sigma, Sigma Iota Epsilon, Alpha Kappa Psi, Kappa Delta Psi, Delta Mu Delta. Home: 8337 Goldfinch Cir Indianapolis IN 46256-1629 Office: U Indpls 1400 E Hanna Ave Indianapolis IN 46227-3630

SPETH, JAMES GUSTAVE, dean, environmental studies educator, lawyer; b. Orangeburg, S.C., Mar. 4, 1942; s. James Gustave and Amelia St. Clair (Albergotti) S.; m. Caroline Cameron Council, July 3, 1965; children: Catherine Council, James Gustave, Charles Council. BA summa cum laude, Yale U., 1964, LLB, 1969; MLitt, Oxford U., 1966; LLD (hon.) , Clark U., 1995; MSE (hon.) , Coll. of the Atlantic, 2001. Bar: D.C. 1969. Law clk. to Justice Hugo L. Black U.S. Supreme Ct., 1969-70; sr. staff atty. Natural Resources Def. Council, Washington, 1970-77; mem. Council Environ. Quality, 1977-79, chmn., 1979-81; prof. law Georgetown U. Law Ctr., 1981-82; pres. World Resources Inst., 1982-93; adminstr. UN Devel. Program, N.Y.C., 1993-99; dean, prof. Yale Sch. Forestry and Environ. Studies Yale U., 1999—. Founded World Resources Inst.; organized Western Hemisphere Dialogue environ. and devel., 1990; chaired U.S. Task Force internat. devel. and environ. security. Contbr. articles to profl. jours.; speaker in field. Bd. dirs. World Resources Inst., Nat. Resources Def. Coun., Woods Hole Rsch. Ctr., Keystone Ctr., Leadership award 1994. Recipient Resources Def. award Nat. Wildlife Fedn., 1976, Barbara Swain award of honor Nat. Resources Coun. Am., 1992, Environ. Law Inst. Lifetime Achievement award, 1999; named to Global 500 Honor Role United Nations Environ. Program, 1988; Rhodes scholar, 1964-66. Mem. Coun. on Fgn. Rels. (N.Y.C.). Episcopalian. Home: 88 Mulberry Farms Rd Guilford CT 06437-3215 E-mail: gus.speth@yale.edu.

SPETH, MARK ALAN, telecommunications company executive; b. Junction City, Kans., Aug. 12, 1960; s. Gerald L. and Dora (Goff) S.; m. Tammara Ray Harris, Dec. 17, 1982; children: Steven T., Nathan M., Michelle H., Jonathan T. MBA with honors, U. Indpls., 1996. Missionary Ch. of Jesus Christ of Latter-Day Saints, Tahiti, 1979-81; asst. treas., corp. sec. Progressive United Corp., Carmel, Ind., 1982-85; sys. specialist Allied Fidelity Corp., Indpls., 1984-85; contr. J.C. Sipe, Inc., 1985-88, Gerwig Ventures, Indpls., 1988-94; mgr. data processing Telecomms. Computer Svcs., Carmel, 1994-95; v.p., contr. One Call Comms., 1995—. Stake clk. Ch. of Jesus Christ of Latter-Day Saints, Indpls., 1988-97; treas. Lawrence Soccer Club dba NYSL, Indpls., 1990—. Mem. Lds Ch. Office: One Call Comms 801 Congressional Blvd Ste 100 Carmel IN 46032-5650

SPETRINO, RUSSELL JOHN, retired utility company executive, lawyer; b. Cleve., Apr. 22, 1926; s. John Anthony and Madeline Spetrino; m. Marilyn Folk, July 17, 1954 (dec.); children: Michael J., Ellen A. Spetrino Raines; m. Mildred Pilkton, June 26, 1993. BS, Ohio State U., 1950; LL.B., Western Res. U., 1954. Bar: Ohio 1954. Asst. atty. gen., Ohio, 1954-57; atty.-examiner Public Utilities Commn. of Ohio, Columbus, 1957-59; atty. Ohio Edison Co., Akron, 1959-69, sr. atty., 1970-73, gen. counsel, 1973-78, v.p., gen. counsel, 1978-87, exec. v.p., gen. counsel, 1987-89, ret., 1989. Served with inf. U.S. Army, 1944-46. Mem. Portage Country Club. Republican. Home: 333 N Portage Path Unit 34 Akron OH 44303-1252 also: 6075 Pelican Bay Blvd # 104 Naples FL 34108 E-mail: rspetrino@aol.com. *The importance of— and the strength that can be derived from— simple intellectual honesty never ceases to amaze me. It is so much easier to deal successfully with others when every effort is made to understand their views, and your own views are based upon thoughtful, honest conviction.*

SPETSIERIS, PHOEBE G. physicist, scientific software engineer, researcher; b. Athens, Greece, Apr. 26, 1944; came to U.S., 1947; d. Elis P. and Helen Elis George; m. Spyridon Spetsieris, June 30, 1972; 1 child, Zoe. BS in Physics, U. Athens, 1968; MA in Physics, CCNY, 1970; MPhil in Physics, CUNY, 1979, PhD in Physics, 1980. Adj. lectr. in physics and math. CCNY, N.Y.C., 1968-77; rsch. asst. in physics CUNY, 1972-79; engr., sys. analyst Am. Electric Power Svc. Corp., 1979-83; sr. sci. programmer analyst Meml. Sloan-Kettering Cancer Ctr., 1984-89; sys. analyst, assoc. investigator Ctr. Neurosci. Functional Brain Imaging Lab. North Shore L.I. Jewish Rsch. Inst., Manhasset, N.Y., 1990—; rsch. assoc. prof. neurology NYU Sch. Medicine, 2001—. Presenter, cons. in field; adj. asst. prof. bioengring. Sch. Health Scis., Touro Coll., Dix Hills, NY, 1994—95; rsch. assoc. prof. of neurology NYU Sch. Medicine, 2001—. Contbr. articles to profl. publs. N.Y. State Regents scholar, 1962, CUNY scholar, 1971; CUNY rsch. fellow, 1976. Mem. IEEE Engring. in Medicine and Biology. Democrat. Greek Orthodox. Avocations: art, computer graphics, scientific visualization. Office: North Shore U Hosp Dept Neurology 350 Community Dr Manhasset NY 11030-3849 E-mail: pspetsie@nshs.edu.

SPEVACK, MARVIN, English educator; b. N.Y.C., Dec. 17, 1927; s. Nathan and Miriam (Propper) S.; m. Helga Husmann, May 28, 1962; 1 child, Edmund Daniel. BA, CCNY, 1948; MA, Harvard U., 1950, PhD, 1953. Instr. English CCNY, 1955-61; asst. prof. City Coll. N.Y., 1961-63; prof. English, U. Muenster, Germany, 1963-89, dir. English seminar Germany, 1964-89, dir. Inst. Erasmianum Germany, 1974-89; Fulbright lectr. U. Münster, Germany, 1961-62. Vis. prof. U. Munich, 1962-63, NYU, summer 1966, Harvard U., summer 1973, U. N.Mex., 1985-86, Bowling Green State U., fall 1989; fellow Folger Shakespeare Libr., 1970, 98; hon. rsch. fellow Univ. Coll., London, 1980-81, 94—; vis. fellow Wolfson Coll., Cambridge (Eng.) U., 1984; scholar-in-residence Ctr. for Renaissance and Baroque Studies, U. Md., spring 1989; vis. rsch. fellow Inst. for Advanced Studies in Humanities, U. Edinburgh, Scotland, 1991. Author: Harvard Concordance to Shakespeare, 1973, A Complete and Systematic Concordance to the Works of Shakespeare, 9 vols., 1968-80, Robert Burton, Philosophaster, 1984, Shakespeare: The second, Third, and Fourth Folios, 1985, New Cambridge Julius Caesar, 1988, Shakespeare-Text, Language and Criticism: Essays in Honor of Marvin Spevack, 1988, New Variorum Antony and Cleopatra, 1990, A Shakespeare Thesaurus, 1993, James Orchard Halliwell- Phillipps: A Classified Bibliography, 1997, A Victorian Chronicle: The Diary of Henrietta Halliwell-Phillipps, 1999, James Orchard Halliwell-Phillipps: The Life and Works of the Shakespearean Scholar and Bookman, 2001; also articles and editions. Served with AUS, 1953-55. Guggenheim fellow, 1973-74, Andrew W. Mellon Found. fellow Huntington Libr., 1992, Ctr. for Book fellow Brit. Libr., London, 1994-95. Mem. MLA, Internat. Assn. Univ. Profs. English, Internat. Shakespeare Assn., The Bibliog. Soc., Deutsche Shakespeare Gesellschaft W., Shakespeare Assn., Soc. Textual Scholarship, Harvard Club (N.Y.C.), Harvard of Rhein-Ruhr Club (Germany), Phi Beta Kappa. Home: 14 Potstiege 48161 Münster Germany Office: 12-20 Johannisstrasse 48143 Münster Germany

SPEWOCK, THEODOSIA GEORGE, principal, elementary school educator; b. Canton, Ohio, Sept. 11, 1951; d. George Eleftherios and Despina George (Ilvanakis) Sideropoulos; m. Michael Andrew Spewock, Aug. 23, 1974. BS, Kent State U., 1974; MEd in Reading, Pa. State U., 1978; postgrad., Ind. U. of Pa., 1989, 94, Pa. State U. Cert in early childhood edn., cert. elem. prin., Pa. Tchr. Winnisquam Regional Sch. Dist., Tilton, N.H., 1974-77; reading specialist Tyrone (Pa.) Area Sch. Dist., 1978-80, home-sch. liaison, 1980-98, title 1 coord., 1994—, elem. sch. prin., 1998—. Chair adv. bd. Family Ctr., Tyrone, 1994; steering com. Altoona Reading Inst., Altoona, Pa., 1991—; chair state reading conf. Keystone Reading Assn., 1994-96. Creator and host (weekly radio story hour): Mrs. Spewock & Friends, 1990-99; author: Just for Five's, 1995, Just for Four's, 1995, Just for Three's, 1995, Just for Two's, 1995, Just for One's, 1995, Just for Babies, 1995, Getting Ready to Read, 1996; contbr. articles to profl. jours. Mem. adv. bd. strategic planning Tyrone Area Sch. Dist., 1994; rep. Pa. in Washington D.C., 1992. Recipient Dist. Svc. award Tyrone Area Cmty. Orgn., 1992, Outstanding Employee award, 1989. Mem. Keystone State Reading Assn. (pres. 1995), Internat. Reading Assn., Blair County Reading Coun. (pres. 1986-88), Nat. Assn. Supervision and Curriculum Devel., Nat. Assn. Edn. Young Children, Nat. Assn. Elem. Sch. Prins., Pa. Assn. Fed. Program Coords., Phi Delta Kappa. Avocations: piano, reading, folk dancing, cross-country skiing, walking for fitness. Office: Tyrone Area Sch Dist 801 Clay Ave Tyrone PA 16686-1806 E-mail: tgspewock@tyrone.k12.pa.us.

SPEYER, DEBRA GAIL, lawyer; b. N.Y.C., Jan. 8, 1959; d. Frank R. and Lynn (Lederer) S.; m. Bruce H. Levin, Mar. 30, 1986. BBA, Hofstra U., Hempstead, N.Y., 1980, JD, 1984, MBA, 1988. Bar: N.Y. 1986, Pa. 1986,

Conn. 1986, Fla. 1988, D.C. 1988. Atty., v.p. Thomson McKinnon Securities, N.Y.C., 1984-87; pvt. practice North Miami, Fla., 1987-88; atty. Nat. Assn. Securities Dealers, Phila., 1988-90; pvt. practice, 1990—. Arbitrator NASD, N.Y. Stock Exch.; lectr. Phila. Bar Assn., 1996—, course planner; cons. Phila. Corp. for the Aging. Dir. Nat. Cong. Syn Youth, Merrick, N.Y., 1983-86; pres. A.F.S.I., 1988-90, bd. dirs., 1990—; bd. dirs. Heart to Heart, 1993—, Judicare Sr. Citizen Project, 1998—; pres. AMIT, 1994-98. Named One of Best Lawyers in Phila. Phila. Mag. Mem. ABA, N.Y. State Bar Assn., Conn. Bar Assn., Pa. Bar Assn., Phila. Bar Assn. (co-chair elder law com. 1997—), Am. Trial Lawyers Assn., D.C. Bar Assn., Fla. Bar Assn., Phi Alpha Delta (treas. 1982-83). Avocations: golf, art. Office: Ste 200 2 Penn Center Plz Philadelphia PA 19102 also: 2 Bala Plz Ste 300 Bala Cynwyd PA 19004 E-mail: debra@speyerlaw.com.

SPEZIALE, JOHN ALBERT, lawyer; b. Winsted, Conn., Nov. 21, 1922; s. Louis and Mary (Avampato) S.; m. Mary Kocsis, Aug. 12, 1944; children: John Albert, Marcia Jean. BA in Econs., Duke U., 1943, JD, 1947. Bar: Conn. 1948. Clk. Judiciary Com. of Conn. Gen. Assembly, 1949; judge Mcpl. Ct., Torrington, Conn., 1949-51; dir. CD, 1951-52; fed. atty. OPS, 1951-52; mem. Conn. State Jud. Council, 1955-59; sr. partner firm Speziale, Mettling, Lefebre & Burns, Torrington, 1958-61; city atty., 1957-59; treas. State of Conn., 1959-61; judge Conn. Ct. Common Pleas, 1961-65, Conn. Superior Ct., 1965-77; presiding judge Conn. Superior Ct. (Appellate div.), 1975-77, chief judge, 1975-77, mem. exec. com., 1975-84, chmn. exec. com., 1977-81; justice Conn. Supreme Ct., 1977-81, chief ct. adminstr., 1978-81, chief justice, 1981-84; sr. ptnr. Cummings & Lockwood, Hartford, 1984-92; of counsel, 1992—. Atty. trial referee Conn., 1986—; mem. exec. com. Nat. Conf. State Trial Judges, 1970-74; faculty advisor grad. session Nat. Coll. State Judiciary, U. Nev., 1973; mem. Conn. Jud. Rev. Coun., 1975-77; co-chmn. planning commn. criminal adminstrn. Conn. Justice Commn., 1975-78; mem. Conn. Commn. on Adult Probation, 1976-77, Adv. Coun. on Ct. Unification, 1976-78, Conn. Bd. Pardons, 1977-78; mem. exec. com. Nat. Bd. Trial Advocacy, 1983-88, dir. 1988—; mem. mediation com. Ctr. Pub. Resources, 1985—; chmn. State-Fed. Rels. Com. Conf. of Chief Justices, 1983-84; chmn. adv. bd. Use of Vol. Lawyers to Supplement Jud. Resources, Nat. Inst. Justice and Nat. Ctr. for State Ctrs., 1983-87; mem. lawyers com. Nat. Ctr. for State Cts., 1985-88; chmn. subcom. jud. decisions Nat. Assn. Ins. Commrs. Adv. Com. Environ. Liability Ins., 1985-87; mem. Panel of Trial and Appellate Judges, Asbestos Claims Facility, 1986—; arbitrator Ins. Arbitration Forums, Inc., 1986—, others. Trustee Conn. Jr. Republic, 1975-83; bd. dirs. Newington Children's Hosp. 1983-86, corporator 1983—; chmn. awards com. Freedoms Found. at Valley Forge, 1982, trustee Nat. Council, 1986—; fellow Pvt. Adjudication Found. Duke U. Sch. Law, 1986—. Lt. (j.g.) USNR, 1942-46, PTO. Recipient Conn. Trial Lawyers Jud. award, 1977; 1st Unico Nat. Disting. Key award, 1977; Citizen of Yr. award Elks, 1982; Alva P. Loiselle lifetime achievement award, 1984; Disting. Service award Nat. Ctr. for State Cts., 1985; Significant Practical Achievement award Ctr. for Pub. Resources Legal Program, 1985; Conn. Law Rev. award, 1985. Fellow Am. Bar Found. (life), Conn. Bar Found. (charter life fellow, chmn. James W. Cooper fellows 1994-97, John A. Speziale Symposia named in his honor); mem. ABA (vice chmn. 1984-86, com. on stds. jud. adminstrn. jud. adminstrn. divsn.), Inst. Jud. Adminstrn., Am. Judicature Soc. (dir. 1978-82), Conn. Bar Assn. (com. on alternative dispute resolution 1985-87, com. on liaison with state cts. 1986-92), Hartford Bar Assn., Litchfield County Bar Assn., Supreme Ct. Hist. Soc., Am. Arbitration Assn. (comml. panel arbitrators 1987-2001, panelist large complex case program 1993-2001), Am. Fedn. Musicians (life), Sons of Italy of Am., Conn. State Srs. Golf Assn., Inc., Litchfield County Univ. Club, Torrington Country Club, Unico Club (life), Bear Lakes Country Club (Fla.), K.C., Phi Beta Kappa. Roman Catholic. Home: 278 Windtree St Torrington CT 06790-7904 Office: Cummings & Lockwood 1 Cityplace Hartford CT 06103-3408 E-mail: judgespeziale@aol.com.

SPEZIALE, RICHARD SALVATORE, financial executive; b. N.Y.C., Jan. 27, 1957; s. Vito Anthony and Sally Ann (Buccheri) S.; m. Linda Candida Scro, May 31, 1986; children: Derek Joseph, Chiara Rose, Deanna Caterina. BSBA, L.I. U., 1983, MBA, 1988. Account exec. Dreyfus Corp., Garden City, N.Y., 1983-85; fin. advisor Home Life, Hauppauge, 1985-86; br. chief SEC, N.Y.C., 1986-91; 1st v.p., dept. mgr. Prudential Securities, 1991-94; dir. control divsn. Citigroup Corp. and Investment Bank, 1994—. Instr. NYU, N.Y.C., 1989-91, Securities Tng. Corp., N.Y.C., 1989-91. Cpl. U.S. Army, 1975-78. Mem. Securities Industry Assn. (mem. capital com. 1994—), Bond Market Assn. (mem. capital com. 1995—). Avocations: diving, bicycling, weight lifting. Home: 143 Tahlulah Ln West Islip NY 11795-5219 Office: Salomon Smith Barney Inc 388 Greenwich St New York NY 10013-2339

SPHIRE, RAYMOND DANIEL, anesthesiologist, educator; b. Detroit, Feb. 12, 1927; s. Samuel Raymond and Nora Mae (Allen) S.; m. Joan Lois Baker, Sept. 5, 1953; children— Suzanne M., Raymond Daniel, Catherine J. BS, U. Detroit, 1948; MD, Loyola U., Chgo., 1952. Diplomate Am. Bd. Anesthesiology. Intern Grace Hosp., Detroit, 1952-53; resident Harvard Anesthesia Lab.-Mass. Gen. Hosp., 1953-55; attending anesthesiologist Grace Hosp., Detroit, 1955-72, dir. dept. inhalation therapy, 1968-70; sr. attending anesthesiologist, dir. dept., dir. dept. respiratory therapy Detroit-Macomb Hosps. Assn., 1970—, trustee, 1978—, chief of staff, 1980—. Clin. asst. prof. Wayne State U. Sch. Medicine, 1967— ; clin. prof. respiratory therapy Macomb Community Coll., Mount Clemens, Mich., 1971— ; examiner Am. Registry Respiratory Therapists, 1972— ; insp. Joint Rev. Com. Respiratory Therapy Edn., 1972— Co-author: Operative Neurosurgery, 1970, First Aid Guide for the Small Business or Industry, 1978 With AUS, 1944-45; 1st lt. M.C., USAF, 1952 Fellow Am. Coll. Anesthesiologists, Am. Coll. Chest Physicians; mem. AMA, Am. Soc. Anesthesiologists, Wayne County Soc. Anesthesiologists (pres. 1967-69), Am. Assn. Respiratory Therapists, Soc. Critical Care Medicine, Detroit Athletic Club, Country Club of Detroit, Cumberland Club (Portland, Maine), Severance Lodge. Roman Catholic. Home: 19874 Westchester Dr Clinton Township MI 48038-6417 Office: 119 Kercheval Ave Grosse Pointe MI 48236-3696

SPICER, HAROLD OTIS, retired English language educator, communications educator; b. Gosport, Ind., Dec. 10, 1921; s. Otis R. and Hattie Grace (Wampler) S.; m. Hilda Jane Templeton, June 12, 1946 (dec. Nov. 1994); children: Sherry Lynne (dec. May 1987), Sylvia Jean, Stephen Michael, Zachary Ian. BA, DePauw U., 1947, MA, 1949; PhD, Ind. U., 1962. Instr. English DePauw U., Greencastle, Ind., 1947-49, asst. prof. English, 1957-63; from instr. to prof. English We. Ill. U., Macomb, 1949-57; adj. prof. English Ind. U., Indpls., 1960-63; assoc. prof. to prof. English Ind. State U., Terre Haute, 1963-85; ret., 1985. Sec. Main Street, Greencastle, 1983-95. Author: Covered Bridges of Putnam County, 1989, Organizational Handbook for Council on Aging, 1989 (Ameritech Tchr. Vol. award 1989), James Whitcomb Riley: Hoosier Poet, 1993; co-author: DePauw: Pictorial History, 1987. Pres. Ret. Tchrs. Putnam County, Greencastle, 1988-90, Putnam County Coun. on Aging, 1990-96 (Man of Yr. award 1994); bd. dirs. Heritage Preservation Soc., Greencastle, 1993—, Putnam County Found., 1995—, sec., 2000—; pres. West Ctrl. Ind. Area Agy. on Aging, 2000. Recipient Man of Yr. award Area 7 Agy. on Aging West Ctrl. Ind. Econ. Devel. Dist., Terre Haute, 1994; named Older Hoosier of Yr. Ind. Gov.'s Conf., Indpls., 1994, RSVP Vol. of Yr., 1995, Ameritech Vol. Tchr. of Yr., 1989, Martin H. Miller Vol. of Yr. award Ind. Family and Social Svcs. Adminstrn., 1999, Outstanding Leadership award in area/agy. on aging Ind. Assn. Area Agys. on Aging, 2000. Life mem. VFW; mem. Am. Legion, Am. Assn. Retired Persons (pres. Putnam County chpt. 1995-96, 99—), Greencastle C. of C. (Putnam County Citizen of Yr. 1996, bd. dirs. 1995-99), West Ctrl. Ind. Civil War Roundtable (v.p. 1998-2000), Kiwanis Club Greencastle. Avocations: music, writing, travel. Home: 706 Highwood Ave Greencastle IN 46135-1420 E-mail: halos@ccrtc.com.

SPICER, HOLT VANDERCOOK, retired speech and theater educator; b. Pasadena, Calif., Feb. 1, 1928; s. John Lovely and Dorothy Eleanor (Clause) S.; m. Marion Arel Gibson, Aug. 16, 1952; children: Mary Ellen, Susan Leah, Laura Alice, John Millard. BA, U. Redlands, 1952, MA, 1957; PhD, U. Okla., 1964. From instr. speech and theatre to prof. S.W. Mo. State Coll., 1952-93, emeritus prof., 1993—, head speech and theatre, 1967-71, dean Sch. Arts and Humanities, 1971-85. Chmn. Dist. 4 Nat. Debate Tournament Com., 1955, 58, 64, 68 Vestryman Episcopalian Ch., 1981—85, 1998—2001; bd. dirs. Springfield (Mo.) Cmty. Ctr., 1981—. Named Debate Coach of Decade U.S. Air Force Acad., 1965, Holt V. Spicer Debate Forum, 1988; recipient Alumni Achievement award in Speech and Debate U. Redlands, 1991, Alumni award of appreciation S.W. Mo. State U., 1996; team won CEDA Nat. Debate championship, 1992. Mem.: AAUP, Am. Forensic Assn., Speech Communication Assn. Episcopalian. Home: 2232 E Langston St Springfield MO 65804-2646 E-mail: holtspicer9@mchsi.com.

SPICER, JOHN AUSTIN, physicist; b. Rock Springs, W.Va., Sept. 25, 1930; s. Ernest Marvin and Ruth (Stevens) S.; m. Erika Gruendig, 1959; children: Cynthia, Michael, Marilynn. BS, U. Wyoming, 1956, MS, 1957; PhD, U. Freiburg, Germany, 1962. Mathematician Geotech. Corp., Laramie, Wyo., 1956-57; physicist Goodyear Aerospace Corp., Litchfield, Ariz., 1962-63; head engr. Aeroject Gen. Corp., Azusa, Calif., 1963-64; mathematical analyst North Am. Aviation Info. Systems Div., Downey, 1973-76; program mgr. Chrysler Space Systems Div., New Orleans, 1966-68; sr. research mathematician U. Dayton Research Inst., Ohio, 1968-70; ops. research analyst U. McCall Printing Corp. Systems Dept., Dayton, 1970-71; mathematician Systems Dyamics Br. AF Flight Dynamics La., 1971-72; physicist Radar and Microwave Tech. Br. Af Avionics lab., 1972-74, Analysis and Evaluation Br. AF Avionics Lab., 1974-89; physicist tech group, target recognition br. AF Avionics Lab., Dayton, Ohio, 1989-98. Contbr. articles on neural networks, wavelets and fractal methodology to profl. jours.; presenter in field. Achievements include inventing "exact stability," which is a numerical integration routine that yields a dead beat response, that is, always stable and controllable, reaches equilibrium in minimum time, and is always stable. Home: 4666 N State Route 235 Conover OH 45317-9601 Office: WL/AACR Bldg 620 Dayton OH 45433-7001

SPICER, KEVIN PAUL, history educator, priest; b. Washington, May 22, 1965; s. John Paul and Gloria Ann Spicer. BA, Stonehill Coll., 1987; MDiv, U. St. Michaels Coll., Toronto, Ont., Can., 1991; MA, Boston Coll., 1996, PhD, 2000. Joined Congregation of Holy Cross, 1988, ordained priest Roman Cath. Ch., 1992. Parochial vicar Holy Cross Ch., South Easton, Mass., 1992-94; asst. prof. Stonehill Col., Easton, 2000—. Mem. ch. rels. com. Ctr. for Advanced Holocaust Studies, U.S. Holocaust Meml. Mus., 2001—. Contbr. articles to books, profl. jours. Mem. Am. Cath. Hist. Assn., Am. Hist. Assn., German History Soc., German Studies Assn., New Eng. Hist. Assn. Democrat. Avocations: theater, reading, travel, film. Office: Stonehill Coll 320 Washington St Easton MA 02357 E-mail: kspicer@stonehill.edu.

SPICER, MICHAEL WILLIAM, university educator; b. Uffculme, Devon, Eng., July 18, 1949; s. William John Arthur and Annie Doreen Taverner Spicer; m. Claudia Ann Bevinger; 1 child Jeffrey Arthur. BS in Bus. Adminstrn., Ohio State U., 1971, MA in Pub. Adminstrn., 1972, PhD in Pub. Adminstrn., 1974. Lectr. in econs. U. Exeter, England, 1976; vis. asst. prof. pub. adminstrn. Ohio State U., Columbus, 1976—77; asst. prof. econs. and pub. adminstrn. U. Colo., Colorado Springs, 1977—81, assoc. prof. econs. and and pub. adminstrn., 1981—86, assoc. dean grad. sch. pub. affairs, 1983—86; assoc. dean coll. urban affairs Cleve. State U., 1986—92, prof. urban affairs and pub. adminstrn., 1992—. Bd. editors Adminstrv. Theory and Praxis, Omaha, 2000—02. Author: (book) The Founders, the Constitution, and Public Administration, 1995, Public Administration and the State: A Postmodern Approach, 2001; contbr. articles to profl. jours. Mem.: ASPA, Pub. Adminstrn. Theory Network, Am. Econ. Assn. Home: 23711 Cliff Dr Bay Village OH 44140 Office: Cleve State Univ 1717 Euclid Ave Cleveland OH 44115 Office Fax: 216-687-9342. Business E-Mail: mike@wolf.csuohio.edu.

SPICER, RONALD L. financial services educator; b. Louisville, Jan. 21, 1949; s. Robert Joseph and Ann (Stafford) S.; m. Joan E. Vining, Dec. 20, 1969 (div. June 1988); children: Jennifer Joan Spicer McMullen, Ronald Geoffrey; m. JoAnn F. Snyder, Feb. 18, 1989; 1 child, Veronica Michelle. BS in Psychology and Sociology, Carroll Coll., 1971; MA in Orgn. Mgmt., U. Phoenix, 1997; MBA in Bus., Regis U., 1999; postgrad., Capella U., 2000—. CPCU, CLU, CHFC, ARM. V.p. sales Alexander & Alexander, Atlanta, 1982-88; exec. v.p. Powell and Co., 1988-89; v.p. sales Corroon and Black, Balt., 1989-90; broker, owner Profl. Ins. Brokers, York, Pa., 1990-93; sr. account exec. Hilb, Rogal and Hamilton, Denver, 1993-95; ins. program coord. Pikes Peak C.C., Colorado Springs, 1995-97; pres., CEO Peak Profl. Svcs., Inc., 1997—, owner, 1997—. Adv. com. Ins. Inst. of Am., Malvern, Pa., 1995—; mem. next generation com., Life and Health Ins. Edn. Assn., N.Y.C., 1996-97. Author: (book) Colorado P&C PreLicense Course, 1998, Colorado Life and Health Pre-License Course, 1999; contbr. articles to profl. jours. Mem. Soc. CPCU (Pikes Peak chpt. pres. 1998-99), Soc. CLU/CHFC (v.p. 1998-99, pres. 2000—), Soc. Fin. Svc. Profls. (Pikes Peak chpt. pres. 2000-01), Optimist (pres. Uptown Club 1979-81), Masons. Republican. Episcopal. Avocations: skiing, camping, scuba diving. Office: Peak Profl Svcs Inc PO Box 2013 Colorado Springs CO 80901-2013 E-mail: vms1989@mindspring.com.

SPICER, WILLIAM EDWARD, III, physicist, educator, engineer; b. Baton Rouge, Sept. 7, 1929; s. William Edward II and Kate Crystal (Watkins) S.; m. Cynthia Stanley, June 12, 1951 (div. 1969); children: William Edward IV, Sally Ann; m. Diane Lubarsky, Apr. 24, 1969; 1 dau., Jacqueline Kate. BS, Coll. William and Mary, 1949, MIT, 1951; MA, U. Mo., 1953, PhD, 1955; D.Tech. (hon.), U. Linköping, Sweden, 1975. Scientist RCA Labs, 1955-61, Lawrence Radiation Lab., U. Calif.-Livermore, 1961-62; mem. faculty Stanford U., 1962—, prof. elec. engring. and materials sci. engring., 1965—, prof. by courtesy applied physics, 1976—, Stanford Ascherman prof. engring., 1978—, prof. Stanford Synchrotron Radiation Lab, 1992—; dir. Acad. Skills, Inc., Los Altos, Calif., 1971-73; dep. dir. Stanford Synchrotron Radiation Lab., 1973-75, cons. dir., 1975—, prof., 1992—, Stanford Linear Accelerator Ctr., 1993—. Cons. to govt. and industry, 1962—; mem. solid state scis. panel Nat. Acad. Sci.-NRC, 1965-73; cons., lectr. Chinese Univ. devel. project World Bank-Fudan U., 1983; mem. panel atomic and molecular physics div. Nat. Bur. Standards, 1966-73, chmn., 1971-73; mem. adv. group election devices Dept. Def., 1975-82; fellow Churchill Coll., Cambridge U., Eng., 1979; mem. panel Japanese tech. evaluation program U.S. Dept. Commerce and NSF, 1983-84; co-founder, acting dir. Stanford Radiation Lab., 1972; chmn. affiliated faculty Stanford Syncrotron Radiation Lab., 1988-92. Mem. editorial bd. Jour. Crystal Growth, 1981-85; author publs. theory and experiment solid state and surface physics and chemistry, photoemission, optical properties solids, electronic structure metals, semiconductors, insulators, high temperature superconductors; patentee in field. Bd. dirs. Princeton (N.J.) YMCA, 1960-62. Recipient Achievement award RCA, 1957, 60, mentor award Nat. Conf. Black Phys. Students, 1992; named Scientist of Yr., Indsl. Research and Devel. mag., 1981; Guggenheim fellow, 1978-79 Fellow IEEE, Am. Phys. Soc. (Oliver Buckley Solid State Physics prize 1980), Am. Vacuum Soc. (chmn. electronics material div. 1978-79, dir. 1979-80, trustee 1981-82, Medard W. Welch award 1984); mem. AAAS (Mentor award for Lifetime Achievement 2001), Amer Contract Bridge League (life master 1997, bronze life master 2000), Phi Beta Kappa. Home: 785 Mayfield Ave Palo Alto CA 94305-1043 Office: Stanford U Mccullough Bldg Stanford CA 94305 E-mail: dmspicer@aol.com.

SPICKLER, JOANN DOROTHY, secondary education educator; b. Valley City, N.D., Apr. 10, 1948; d. Roger W. and Dorothy H. (Berndtson) Lee; m. Harold R. Spickler, June 21, 1969; children: Heidi, Justin, David, Nathan. BS, Valley City (N.D.) State U., 1970. Tchr. English Glenfield (N.D.)-Sutton, 1970-74, Grace City (N.D.) Sch., 1978-91, Midkota Schs., Glenfield, 1991—. Speech coach, coach acad. team Midkota Schs., 1991—. Home: 8375 7th Pkwy NE Glenfield ND 58443-9321

SPICKNALL, JOAN, music educator; b. Arlington, Va., Feb. 13, 1942; d. Joseph Richard and Rhoda Louise (Beran) Singer; m. Marvin Herbert Spitz, Dec. 12, 1992; children from previous marriage: Lisa Sharon Spicknall Fruth, Richard Mark Spicknall. B of Mus, Peabody Conservatory, 1962, MusM, 1963; D of Musical Arts, U.Md., 1974. Grad. asst. U. Md., College Park, 1966-69; asst. prof. St. Mary of the Woods (Ind.) Coll., 1971-83; instr. piano pvt. practice, Columbia, Md., 1983-88; instr. Essex C.C., Balt., 1983-84, Loyola Coll., Balt., 1983-84, Howard C.C., Columbia, 1983-86; pres., dir. Suzuki Music Sch. Md., Inc., 1988—. Adj. prof. Rose-Hulman Inst. Tech., Terre Haute, Ind., 1973-83; piano tchr. Howard County Schs., 1986—; guest faculty, lectr. nat. and internat. music convs., 1991—. Contbr. articles to profl. jours. and newspapers. Mem. MTNA, SAA, Inc., ISA, AAUW, Mu Phi Epsilon, Delta Kappa Gamma. Home: 10659 Green Mt Cir Columbia MD 21044 Office: Suzuki Music Sch Md Inc PO Box 1284 Columbia MD 21044-0284 E-mail: director@suzukimusicschool.com.

SPICUZZA, JEANNE MARIE, actor, writer, artist, poet, producer; b. Milw., June 21, 1969; d. Robert Allen and Marianne Margaret (Jansen) S.; 1 child, Stephanie. BA, U. Wis., 1993. Retail sales various, Milw., 1988-95; graphic artist U. Wis., 1991-93; tchr., tutor self-employed, 1993-95; owner, CEO Seasons & a Muse, 1993—, tarot reader, 1990—; receptionist temporary, 1996; pres., founder hilde prdns., 1996—. Master herbalist, 1989—. Author numerous poems and plays, 1978—, children's stories, 1989—. Avocations: philosophy, art history, politics, cmty. studies. E-mail: jspicuzza@seasonsandamuse.com.

SPIEGEL, ALLEN, federal agency administrator; MD cum laude, Harvard Med. Sch., 1971. Intern and resident in internal medicine Mass. Gen. Hosp., Boston; mem. Nat. Inst. Diabetes and Digestive and Kidney Disease's Endocrinology Rsch. Tng. Program; sr. investigator Metabolic Diseases Branch, chief of molecular pathophysiology section, branch chief; scientific dir. Nat. Inst. Diabetes and Digestive and Kidney Disease, dir., 1999—. Recipient Komrower Meml. Lecture award, Soc. for the Study of Inborn Errors of Metabolism, 1996, Edwin B. Astwood Lecture award, Endocrine Soc., 1998. Office: 31 Center Dr Rm 9A04 Bethesda MD 20892*

SPIEGEL, ALLEN D. medical educator, consultant; b. N.Y.C., June 11, 1927; s. Max and Betty (Silver) S.; m. Lila Spiegel, Apr. 16, 1958; children: Merrill S., Marc B., Andrea M. AB, Bklyn. Coll., 1947; MPH, Columbia U., 1954; PhD, Brandeis U., 1969. Chief radio & TV unit N.Y.C. Health Dept., 1951-61; health edn. assoc. The Med. Found., Inc., Boston, 1961-69; prof. SUNY Downstate Med. Ctr. at Bklyn., 1969—. Cons. in field. Author, editor of numerous books including Strategic Health Planning, 1991, Home Health Care, 2d rev. edit., 1987, Risk Management in Health Care Institutions: A Strategic Approach, 1997, A. Lincoln, Esquire: A Shrewd Sophistacted Litigator, 2002; mem. editl.. adv. bd. Nation's Health; contbr. articles to profl. jours. NEH fellow, 1979, WHO study/travel fellow, 1974, Nat. Ctr. for Health Svcs. Rsch. fellow, 1966-69; recipient of citations from govtl. and pub. agys; seminar leader Profl. Continuing Edn. Programs (overseas), 1988. Mem. Am. Pub. Health Assn. (com. chmn.), Internat. Union for Health Edn., Columbia U. Sch. of Pub. Health Alumni Assn., Community Agy. Pub. Rels. Assn., Coun. on Med. Television, Soc. of Pub. Health Educators, Health Edn. Media Assn., Consumer Commn. on the Accreditation of Health Svcs. Home: 47 Jensen Rd Sayreville NJ 08872-1969 Office: SUNY Health Sci Ctr 450 Clarkson Ave Box 43 Brooklyn NY 11203-2056

SPIEGEL, EDNA Z. lawyer; b. N.Y.C., Oct. 27; m. Rubin E. Spiegel; children: Linda F. Spiegel Duboff, Joyce I., Bennett L. BS, NYU, 1948, MA, 1949; JD, Seton Hall U., 1986. Bar: N.J. 1988, U.S. Dist. Ct. N.J. 1988, U.S. Supreme Ct. 1993; lic. asst. prin., lic. prin. N.Y.C. Bd. Edn. Substitute tchr. music N.Y.C. Bd. Edn., 1950-52, tchr. music, 1952-81; pvt. legal practice River Edge, N.J., 1990—. Atty. River Edge Environ. Protection Commn., 1987—96; with cmty. outreach on advance directives Holy Name Hosp., Teaneck, NJ, 1994—97; trustee Bergen County Legal Svcs., Hackensack, 1999—; lawyer law day Divsn. Human Svcs. Bergen County, 1988—. Mem. Nat. Acad. Elder Law Attys. (charter mem. N.J. chpt.), N.J. Women Lawyers' Assn., N.J. State Bar Assn. (charter, elder law sect.), Bergen County Bar Assn. (charter, elder law com.), Women Lawyers in Bergen County, Hadassah/The Womens Zionist Orgn. of Am. (River Dell chpt., v.p. programs 1978-80, 96—, chmn. Am. affairs 1979—, Woman of the Yr. 1996, Nat. Leadership award 1997). Avocations: gardening, painting, cooking, swimming, collectibles. Office: 25 Wayne Ave River Edge NJ 07661-1809 E-mail: ezsesq@aol.com.

SPIEGEL, ELWYN, advertising agency executive, creative director; b. N.Y.C., Apr. 26, 1926; s. Morris and Rose Ann (Nemetzky) S.; m. Doris Kay, Apr. 25, 1954 (dec.); children: Elizabeth Ann Simendinger, Susan Gail Ambrose, Laura Faith Ciecierski. BSEE, N.C. State U., 1945; BS in Econs., Columbia U., 1950. Pres. Ad Infinitum, Inc., Hackensack, N.J., 1954-63; exec. v.p. Alden Advt. Agy., N.Y.C., 1964-81; pres. Spiegel/Labatt-Simon, Inc., 1981-88, Compris, Inc., N.Y.C., 1989-96, Elwyn Spiegel & Ptnrs., N.Y.C., 1996—. Cons. in field. Creative dir. TV commls. including Colorforms, 1976 (Clio award, 1976), creative dir. (mag.) Russell Fabrics, 1981; author: Get a New Life, The Jackknife Gypsies. Judge, Clio Awards, N.Y.C., 1975. Recipient Silver award, Neographics 1977, Addy (4), Am. Advt. Fedn., 1977-80, Desi (8), Graphics Design USA, 1981-82, Clio (3), Clio Adv. Bd., 1981. Mem. Nat. Trust for Hist. Preservation, Kiwanis (pres. 1954-55), Alpha Delta Sigma. Avocations: photography, music, sports cars, literature, writing. Office: Elwyn Spiegel & Ptnrs 325 E 41st St New York NY 10017-5955

SPIEGEL, EVELYN SCLUFER, biology educator, researcher; b. Phila., Mar. 20, 1924; d. George and Helen (Laurantos) Sclufer; m. Melvin Spiegel, Apr. 16, 1955; children: Judith Ellen, Rebecca Ann. BA, Temple U., 1947; MA, Bryn Mawr Coll., 1951; PhD, U. Pa., 1954. Asst. program dir. for regulatory biology NSF, Washington, 1954-55; instr. in biology Colby Coll., Waterville, Maine, 1955-59; rsch. assoc. Dartmouth Coll., Hanover, N.H., 1961-74, rsch. assoc. prof. biology, 1974-78, rsch. prof. biology, 1978-91; rsch. prof. biology emerita, 1991—. Vis. scholar Calif. Inst. Tech., Pasadena, 1964-65, U. Calif.-San Diego, La Jolla, 1970, Nat. Inst. for Med. Rsch., Mill Hill, Eng., 1971, NIH, Washington, 1975-76, U. Basel (Switzerland) Biocenter, 1979, 80, 81, 82, 85. Contbr. numerous articles to profl. jours., chpts. to books and book reviews. Mem. Soc. for Devel. Biology, Marine Biol. Lab. Corp. (trustee 1981-86, 88-92). Office: Dartmouth Coll Dept Biol Scis Hanover NH 03755

SPIEGEL, H. JAY, lawyer; b. Cleve., July 7, 1952; s. Martin and Thea (Lange) S. BS, Cornell U., 1974; JD, George Mason U., 1981. Bar: Va. 1981, U.S. Patent Office 1982, U.S. Ct. Appeals (fed. cir.) 1982, U.S. Dist. Ct. (ea. dist.) Va. 1982, U.S. Supreme Ct. 1984, D.C. 1986. Primary and asst. examiner U.S. Patent and Trademark Office, Arlington, Va., 1974-82; assoc. Sherman & Shalloway, Alexandria, 1982-88, of counsel, 1988; pvt. practice., 1988-96; pvt. practice, Mt. Vernon, Va., 1996—. Owner, pres. Premium Products, Inc., Alexandria, 1984—, Jumpstart. Patentee sporting goods and jewelry; inventor Toe-Tal Tee and Ground Zero Tee football tees, PENTA five panel football. Mem.: ATLA, Licensing Exec. Soc., Am. Intellectual Property Law Assn. Avocations: boating, travel. Office: H Jay Spiegel & Assocs PC PO Box 444 Mount Vernon VA 22121-0444 E-mail: jayspiegel@aol.com.

SPIEGEL, HERBERT, psychiatrist, educator; b. McKeesport, Pa., June 29, 1914; s. Samuel and Lena (Mendlowitz) S.; m. Natalie Shainess, Apr. 24, 1944 (div. Apr. 1965); children: David, Ann; m. Marcia Greenleaf, Jan. 29, 1989. BS, U. Md., 1936, MD, 1939. Diplomate: Am. Bd. Psychiatry. Intern St. Francis Hosp., Pitts., 1939-40; resident in psychiatry St. Elizabeth's Hosp., Washington, 1940-42; practice medicine specializing in psychiatry N.Y.C., 1946—; attending psychiatrist Columbia-Presbyn. Hosp., 1960—; faculty psychiatry Columbia U. Coll. Physicians and Surgeons, 1960—. Adj. prof. psychology John Jay Coll. Criminal Justice, CUNY, 1983— ; mem. faculty Sch. Mil. Neuropsychiatry, Mason Gen. Hosp., Brentwood, N.Y., 1944-46 Author: (with A. Kardiner) War Stress and Neurotic Illness, 1947, (with D. Spiegel) Trance and Treatment: Clinical Uses of Hypnosis, 1978; subject of book: (by Donald S. Connery) The Inner Source: Exploring Hypnosis with Herbert Spiegel, M.D.; Mem. editorial bd.: Preventive Medicine, 1972; Contbr. articles to profl. jours. Mem. profl. advisory com. Am. Health Found.; mem. pub. edn. com., smoking and health com. N.Y.C. div. Am. Cancer Soc.; mem. adv. com. Nat. Aid to Visually Handicapped. Served with M.C. AUS, 1942-46. Decorated Purple Heart. Fellow Am. Psychiat. Assn., Am. Coll. Psychiatrists, Am. Soc. Clin. Hypnosis, Am. Acad. Psychoanalysis, Internat. Soc. Clin. and Exptl. Hypnosis, William A. White Psychoanalytic Soc., N.Y. Acad. Medicine, N.Y. Acad. Scis.; mem. Am. Orthopsychiat. Assn., Am. Psychosomatic Soc., AASAS, AMA, N.Y. County Med. Soc. Office: 19 E 88th St New York NY 10128-0557

SPIEGEL, HERMAN D.J. architecture and structural engineer, educator; b. Boston, Dec. 31, 1924; s. Harry and Annie (Gittleman) S.; m. Sally Peery, June 2, 1957; children: Robert Stewart, William Steven. BS in Arch., RISD, 1953; M Structural Engring., Yale U., 1955. Registered profl. engr., Calif., Mass., R.I., D.C., Ky., Md., Va., Conn. Instr. archtl. engring. Yale U., New Haven, 1955-58, asst. prof. archtl. engring., 1958-64, assoc. prof. archtl. engring.,

1964-69, prof. archtl. engring., 1969-92, acting dean Sch. Arch., 1971, 82, dean Sch. Arch., 1971-76, sec. emeritus arch. engring., 1993—; founder, prin. Spiegel Zamecnik & Shah Cons. Structural Engrs., 1956—, Washington, 1971—. Mem. Bldg. Rsch. Inst., NSF. Lectr. on archtl. works of Antonio Gaudi and LeCorbusier. With U.S. Army, 1943-46, WW II, ETO and PTO. Recipient numerous awards. Fellow ASCE; mem. AIA (hon.), ASTM, Amigos de Gaudi (hon.), Assn. Collegiate Schs. Arch., Am. Concrete Inst., Am. Inst. Steel Constrn., Conn. Soc. Architects (hon.), Conn. bldg. Congress, Yale Engring. Soc., Army and Navy Club of Washington, Mory's Assn. Inc., Yale Club of N.Y.C., Yale Club of New Haven. also: Washington DC

SPIEGEL, JAYSON LESLIE, lawyer, organization executive; b. N.Y.C., Mar. 1, 1959; s. Jack and Frieda Rhoda (Michaelson) S.; m. Deborah Marie Scott, Nov. 1, 1986; children: Kyle Reid, Alicia Jean. AB, Georgetown U., 1980; JD, U. Va., 1983; postgrad., USMC Command and Staff Coll., 1991, Army Comd. & Gen. Staff Coll., 1996. Bar: Md. 1984, D.C. 1985, U.S. Ct. Appeals (D.C. cir.) 1986, U.S. Ct. Mil. Appeals 1987, U.S. Ct. Appeals (4th cir.) 1987, U.S. Supreme Ct. 1988, U.S. Ct. Claims 1990. Law clk. to assoc. judge Md. Ct. Appeals, Balt., 1983-84; assoc. Jordan, Coyne, Savits & Lopata, Washington, 1985-91, ptnr., 1991-94; dep. asst. sec. U.S. Army, 1994-99, acting asst. sec., 1997-98; exec. dir. Res. Officers Assn., 1999—. Lectr. law and transfusion medicine NIH, 1989, 91-94. Contbr. articles to profl. jours. Mem. recreation adv. bd. Montgomery County, Md., 1989-93. With USAR, 1981—, Desert Shield/Desert Storm, 1990-91. Mem. ABA (young lawyers mem. com. on law and nat. security, vice chair internat. criminal law com. 1991-94), D.C. Bar Assn. (founder, chmn. com. on law and nat. security 1987-94, Com. Chmn. of Yr. 1988, 91), Md. Bar Assn., Mil. Coalition (bd. dirs. 1999—), Am. Def. Preparedness Assn., Nat. Security Indsl. Assn., Res. Officers Assn. (life), U.S. C. of C. (com. of 100 assn. execs.), Army and Navy Club. Avocations: running, tennis. Office: Res Officers Assn One Constitution Ave NE Washington DC 20002

SPIEGEL, JERROLD BRUCE, lawyer; b. N.Y.C., Apr. 11, 1949; s. Seymour S. and Estelle (Minsky) S.; m. Helene Susan Cohen, Mar. 3, 1972; children: Dana Sean, Amy Barrett, Evan Tyler. BS, Queens Coll., 1970; JD cum laude, NYU, 1973. Bar: N.Y. 1974. Assoc. Austrian, Lance & Stewart, N.Y.C., 1973-75, Gordon Hurwitz Butowsky Baker Weitzen & Shalov, N.Y.C., 1975-79; ptnr. Shapiro Spiegel Garfunkel & Driggin, 1979-86, Frankfurt Garbus Kurnit Klein & Selz P.C., N.Y.C., 1986—. Editor Ann. Survey Am. Law, 1972-73, Mem. ABA (corp. law sect.), Order of the Coif, Omicron Delta Epsilon. Office: Frankfurt Garbus Kurnit Klein & Selz PC 488 Madison Ave Fl 9 New York NY 10022-5754

SPIEGEL, JOHN WILLIAM, banker; b. Indpls., Mar. 14, 1941; s. William Sordon and Elizabeth (Hall) S.; children: W. Robert, John F., Bradley H. BA, Wabash Coll., 1963; MBA, Emory U., 1965; postgrad., Nova Southeastern U., 1993-99. Rsch. assoc. IMEDE (Mgmt. Inst.), Lausanne, Switzerland, 1965-66; mgmt. trainee Trust Co. Bank, Atlanta, 1966-67, bond portfolio mgr., 1967-72; data processing mgr. Trust Co. Ga., 1972-78, treas., 1978-85; vice chmn., CFO SunTrust Banks Inc., 1985—. Mem. exec. com. CFO divsn. ABA, 1987-90, chair, 1989-90; former instr. Morehouse Coll. and Banking Schs. Mem. exec. com., bd. dirs. Alliance Theatre, Atlanta, 1985—92, pres., 1989—91; bd. dirs. High Mus. Art, 1985—, chmn., 1997—98; pres. Young Audiences Atlanta, Inc., 1981—84, bd. dirs., 1985, mem. adv. bd., 1986—, chmn., 1997—98; pres. bd. vis. Grady Meml. Hosp., 1983—90; v.p. exec. bd. Atlanta Area coun. Boy Scouts Am., 1983—92, treas., 1989—91, mem. adv. bd., 1992; mem. adv. coun. Ga. State U. Sch. Accountacy, 1981—85, chmn. curriculum subcom., 1983—84; mem. exec. com., trustee Morehouse Sch. Medicine, 1984—93, chmn. fin. com., 1987—90, chmn., 1990—92; mem. Leadership Atlanta, 1976—, trustee, 1990—94; trustee, mem. exec. com. Robert W. Woodruff Arts Ctr., Inc., 1976—, treas., 1976—83, chmn. fin. com., 1984—89, 1993—97, chmn., 1998—2001; chmn. fin. com., bd. dirs. Schenck Sch., 1986—88; exec. vice chmn. bd. trustees Holy Innocents Epsicopal Sch., 1976—79, bd. dirs., treas., 1987—90; bd. dirs. Atlanta Opera, 1986—98, United Way Met. Atlanta, 1994—98, Rock Tenn. Co., 1989—, Sallie Mae, 1993—97, Suburban Lodges Am., Inc., 1999—2002; mem. bd. visitors Emory U., 1991—95; trustee ESR Children's Health Care System, Inc., 1997—, bd. dirs., 1999—; trustee Wabash Coll., 1997—99; mem. dean's av. coun. Goizueta Bus. Sch., Emory U., 1994—99; bd. dirs., chmn. fin. com. Am. Cardiovasc. Rsch. Inst., 2002—, 2002—. Mem. Bank Adminstrn. Inst. (bd. dirs. 1987-92, rsch. oversight com. 1992-98, treas. 1999, chmn. 2000—). Episcopalian. Home: Unit 1701 3745 Randall Mill Rd NW Atlanta GA 30327-2747 Office: SunTrust Banks Inc 303 Peachtree St NE Atlanta GA 30308-3201

SPIEGEL, LAWRENCE HOWARD, advertising executive; b. N.Y.C., Oct. 9, 1942; s. Melvin Arthur and Rose (Black) S.; m. Christy Mansfield; children from previous marriage: Robert, David. BA, NYU, 1963. Print buyer William Esty Co., N.Y.C., 1964-65, broadcast buyer, 1965-66; media planner Batten, Barton, Durstine & Osborn, Inc., 1966-67, media supr., 1967-68, assoc. media dir., 1969-72, v.p., 1972-74; media group head Jack Tinker & Ptnrs., 1968-69; v.p. Tracy-Locke, Dallas, 1974-80, sr. v.p., 1980-84, exec. v.p., 1984-89; prin. The Richards Group, 1989—. Pres. Tex. Coun. Advt., 1991-97, Leading Agy. Network, 1997—; dir. Dream Fund, 1999—. Guest editor Mktg. and Media Decision mag., June 1982. Mem. Dallas Cable Bd., 1983-86; chmn. mktg. com. U. Tex., Dallas, 1984-89; pres. Cable Access Dallas, Inc., 1985-86; trustee Dallas Symphony Assn., 1978—; bd. dirs. Equest Inc., 1991-92, DREAM Fund, 1999—. Mem. Assn. Broadcasting Execs. Tex. (pres. 1975-76), Am. Women in Radio and TV, Inc. (bd. dirs. 1992-93). Republican. Avocations: skiing, sailing. Office: The Richards Group 8750 N Central Expy Ste 1200 Dallas TX 75231-6436

SPIEGEL, MELVIN, retired biology educator; b. N.Y.C., Dec. 10, 1925; s. Philip Edward and Sadie (Friedman) S.; m. Evelyn Sclufer, Apr. 16, 1955; children: Judith Ellen, Rebecca Ann. BS, U. Ill., 1948; PhD, U. Rochester, 1952; MA (hon.), Dartmouth Coll., 1967. Research fellow U. Rochester, 1952-53, Calif. Inst. Tech., 1953-55, 64-65; asst. prof. Colby Coll., 1955-59; mem. faculty Dartmouth Coll., Hanover, N.H., 1959—, prof. biology, 1966-93; prof. emeritus Dartmouth Coll; chmn. dept. biol. scis. Dartmouth Coll., 1972-74. Summer investigator Marine Biol. Lab., Woods Hole, Mass., 1954— ; sr. rsch. biologist U. Calif.-San Diego, 1970-71; vis. prof. biochemistry Nat. Inst. Med. Rsch., Mill Hill, London, 1971; vis. prof. Biocenter, U. Basel, 1979-82, 85; Wilson Meml. lectr. U. N.C., 1975; program dir. developmental biology NSF, 1975-76; mem. cell biology study sect. NIH, 1966-70 Editl. bd.: Biol. Bull., 1966-70, 71-75, Cell Differentiation, 1979-88 ; contbr. articles to profl. jours. Trustee Marine Biol. Lab. Corp.; mem. exec. com., trustee Marine Biol. Lab., 1976-80. Fellow AAAS; mem. Am. Soc. Cell Biology, Am. Soc. Devel. Biology, Internat. Soc. Devel. Biologists (sec.-treas. 1977-81, bd. dirs. 1981-85). Home: 15 Barrymore Rd Hanover NH 03755-2401 E-mail: melvin_spiegel@dartmouth.edu.

SPIEGEL, MERLE ANDREA, pharmaceutical company executive; b. N.Y.C., Oct. 28, 1947; d. Arnold Stuart and Betty Rosalind Dorfman; m. Mark Stefan Spiegel, June 16, 1968 (div. Dec. 1980); 1 child, Kathryn Emily. BA cum laude, Harvard Coll., 1968. Humanities editor Yale Univ. Press, New Haven, 1968-73; dir. publs. RCA Corp., N.Y.C., 1973-85; assoc. dir. corp. comm. Pfizer Inc., 1986-95; dir. comm. Perkin-Elmer Inc., Norwalk, Conn., 1996-99, N.Y. Acad. Scis., N.Y.C., 1999-2000; dir. corp. comm. Purdue Pharma L.P., Stamford, Conn., 2000—; dir. Stamford Mus., 2002—. Dir. Norwalk Emergency Shelter, 1997—; mem. task force Family and Childrens Agy., Norwalk, 1997-99. Mem. Internat. Assn. Bux. Communicators, N.Y. Acad. Scis. (com. on annals 1999—), Fairfield County Pub. Rels. Assn., Exec. Women's Golf Assn. (newsletter editor 1997-2000). Avocations: golf, bridge, mysteries. Home: 230 Saugatuck Ave # 13 Westport CT 06880 Office: Purdue Pharma LP One Stamford Forum Stamford CT 06901

SPIEGEL, PHYLLIS, public relations consultant, journalist; b. Bronx, N.Y. d. Bernard and Lillian (Horowitz) Finkelberg; m. Stanley Spiegel, Sept. 20, 1959 (div. 1981); children: Mark, Adam. BA, NYU. Feature writer various newspapers, pubs., 1960's-70's; dir. pub. rels. Mort Barish Assocs., Princeton, N.J., 1975-80; account exec. pub. rels. Keyes Martin, Springfield, 1980-84; pres. Phyllis Spiegel Assocs., Plainsboro, 1984—. Pub. rels. dir., founder Red Oak Coop. Nursery Sch., Middletown, N.J., 1960's, Matawan (N.J.) Student Enrichment Program, 1960s-70s; pub. rels. cons., event organizer New Philharm. of N.J., Morristown, 1991-93; mem. Child Placement Rev. Bd. of Family Ct., Mercer County, N.J., 1994-98. Recipient Commendation from Gov. N.J. for U. Med. and Dentistry of N.J. campaign, 1983, Commendation for N.J. Pharm. Assn. campaign Pub. Rels. News Assn., 1979. Mem. Soc. for Humanistic Judaism (bd. dirs. 1983-85). Avocations: film and theatre, classical music, reading, travel. walks. Office: Phyllis Spiegel Assocs PO Box 243 Plainsboro NJ 08536-0243

SPIEGEL, ROBERT ALAN, lawyer; b. N.Y.C., Apr. 1, 1952; s. Benjamin and Pauline Spiegel. BA, CUNY, 1974; JD, NYU, 1977; MPA, Syracuse U., 1984. Bar: Pa. 1978, D.C. 1985. Exec. rep. Found. Press., Mineola, N.Y., 1978-81; budget analyst Metro Studies Syracuse, 1982-83; policy analyst Nat. Conf. State Legislatures, Washington, 1983; from atty.-advisor mgmt., budget & fin. to intergovt. rels. HUD, 1984-87; from atty.-advisor procurement law to judgement claims GAO, 1987-96; atty.-advisor judgement claims FMS, Hyattsville, Md., 1996-2000, sr. advisor fin. acctg. & svcs. divsn., 2000—. Adj. asst. prof. urban studies CUNY, Flushing, 1981-82. Contbg. author: Middle-Class Blacks in a White Society, 1975, A State Legislator's Guide to Public Pensions, 2d edit., 1983, The President's National Urban Policy Report, 1986; editor: An Analytical Legislative History of the Medical Device Amendments of 1976, 1976. Mem. ABA, Pa. Bar Assn., Bar Assn. D.C. Jewish. Home: 1724 17th St NW Apt 41 Washington DC 20009-2428 Office: FMS 3700 East-West Hwy Hyattsville MD 20782-2015

SPIEGEL, S. ARTHUR, federal judge; b. Cin., Oct. 24, 1920; s. Arthur Major and Hazel (Wise) S.; m. Louise Wachman, Oct. 31, 1945; children: Thomas, Arthur Major II, Andrew, Roger Daniel. BA, U. Cin., 1942, postgrad., 1949; LLB, Harvard U., 1948. Assoc. Kasfir & Chalfie, Cin., 1948-52; assoc. Benedict, Bartlett & Shepard, 1952-53, Gould & Gould, Cin., 1953-54; ptnr. Gould & Spiegel, 1954-59; assoc. Cohen, Baron, Druffel & Hogan, 1960; ptnr. Cohen, Todd, Kite & Spiegel, 1961-80; judge U.S. Dist Ct. Ohio, 1980—; sr. status, 1995—. Served to capt. USMC, 1942-46 Mem. ABA, FBA, Ohio Bar Assn., Cin. Bar Assn., Cin. Lawyers Club. Democrat. Jewish. Office: US Dist Ct 838 US Courthouse 5th Walnut St Cincinnati OH 45202

SPIEGEL, SIEGMUND, architect; b. Gera, Germany, Nov. 13, 1919; came to U.S., 1938, naturalized, 1941. s. Jakob and Sara (Precker) S.; m. Ruth Josias, Apr. 13, 1945; children: Sandra Renee, Deborah Joan. Student, Colll. City N.Y., 1939-40, Columbia U., 1945-50; DHL (hon.), Hofstra U., 1993. Registered arch., N.Y., N.J., Mass., Md., Va., Pa., Conn., Ga., Vt., Tenn., N.H., Fla.; lic. profl. planner, N.J. Draftsman Mayer & Whittlesey, Archs., N.Y.C., 1941-47, office mgr., 1947-55; pvt. practice arch. East Meadow, N.Y., 1956—. Author: The Spiegel Plan; contbr. articles to Progressive Arch.; prin. works include Syosset (N.Y.) Hosp., 1962, Reliance Fed. Savs. and Loan Assn. Bank, Queens, N.Y., 1961, Louden Hall Psychiat. Hosp., 1963, Human Resources Sch., Albertson, N.Y., 1964, Nassau Ctr. for Emotionally Disturbed Children, 1968, Harbor Club Apt., Babylon, N.Y., 1968, Reliance Fed. Bank, Albertson, 1967, North Isle Club and Apt. Cmty., Coram, N.Y., 1972, County Fed. Savs. & Loan Assn., Commack, N.Y., 1972, Birchwood Glen Apt. Cmty., Holtsville, N.Y., 1972, Bayside Fed. Savs. & Loan Bank Plaza, Patchogue, N.Y., 1973, L.E. Woodward Sch. for Emotionally Disturbed Children, Freeport, N.Y., 1974, Birchwood Sagamore Hills, Blue Ridge and Bretton Woods Condominium Cmtys., Coram, N.Y., 1975, Maple Arms Condos, Westbury, N.Y., 1982, Dept. Pub. Works, Freeport, N.Y., Nuc. Molecular Resonance Bldg., 1983. Served with AUS, 1941-45, ETO. Decorated Purple Heart, Bronze Star, Croix de Guerre with palme (Belgium); recipient grand prize for instnl. bldgs. (for Syosset Hosp.), L.I. Assn., 1963, grand prize Human Resources Sch., 1966, grand prize Stony Brook Profl. Bldg., 1966, Beautification award, Town Hempstead, N.Y., 1969, Archi award for Harbour Club Apts., L.I. Assn., 1970, for Birchwood Blue Ridge Condominiums, 1974, Dr. Martin Luther King Jr. award Nassau County, 1986, Louise E. Yavner award N.Y. State Bd. Regents, 1992; fellow Acad. Mktg. Sci., L.I. U., 1971. Mem. AIA, N.Y. State Assn. Archs., East Meadow C. of C. (pres. 1966), Kiwanis Club. Home: Carlton Terr 6-D 10245 Collins Ave Bal Harbour FL 33154-1407

SPIEGELBERG, EMMA JO, business education educator, academic administrator; b. Mt. View, Wyo., Nov. 22, 1936; d. Joseph Clyde and Dorcas (Reese) Hatch; m. James Walter Spiegelberg, June 22, 1957; children: William L., Emory Walter, Joseph John. BA with honors, U. Wyo., 1958, MEd, 1985; EdD, Boston U., 1990. Tchr. bus. edn. Laramie (Wyo.) H.S., 1960-61, 65-93, adminstr., 1993-97; prin. McCormick Jr. H.S., Cheyenne, Wyo., 1997—2002. Author: Branigan's Accounting Simulation, 1986, London & Co. II, 1993; co-author: Glencoe Computerized Accounting, 1993, 2d edit., 1995, Microcomputer Accounting: Daceasy, 1994, Microcomputer Accounting: Peachtree, 1994, 3d edit., 2000, Microcomputer Accounting: Accpac, 1994, Computerized Accounting with Peachtree, 1995, 2000, 02. Mem. United Ch. of Christ; bd. dirs. Cathedral Home for Children, Laramie, 1967-70, 72—, pres., 1985-88, Laramie Plains Mus., 1970-79. Named Wyo. Bus. Tchr. of Yr., 1982, Wyo. Asst. Prin. of Yr., 1997. Mem.: NASSP, NEA, Wyo. Assn. Secondary Sch. Prins. (sec., treas. 1997—2001, exec. dir. 2001—), Albany County Edn. Assn. (sec. 1970—71), Wyo. Edn. Assn., Wyo. Bus. Edn. Assn. (pres. 1979—80), Internat. Soc. Bus. Edn., Mt. Plains Bus. Edn. Assn. (Wyo. rep. to bd. dirs. 1982—85, pres. 1987—88, Sec. Tchr. of Yr. 1991, Leadership award 1992), Nat. Bus. Edn. Assn. (bd. dirs. 1987—88, 1991—96, Sec. Tchr. of Yr. 1991), Wyo. Vocat. Assn. (exec. bd. 1978—80, pres. 1981—82, exec. sec. 1986—89, Outstanding Contbns. to Vocat. Edn. award 1983, Tchr. of Yr. 1985), Am. Vocat. Assn. (policy com. region V 1984—87, region V Tchr. of Yr. 1986), U. Wyo. Alumni Assn. (bd. dirs. 1985—90, pres. 1988—89), Laramie C. of C. (bd. dirs. 1985—88), Zonta Internat. (pres.-elect 2002—), Delta Pi Epsilon, Pi Lambda Theta, Chi Omega, Alpha Delta Kappa (state pres. 1978—82), Phi Delta Kappa, Kappa Delta Pi. Home: 3301 Grays Gable Rd Laramie WY 82072-5031

SPIEGELBERG, HARRY LESTER, retired paper products company executive; b. New London, Wis., Apr. 24, 1936; s. Harry Henry and Gladys Louise (Kalt) S.; m. Bonnie Faye Ludden, Jan. 23, 1960; children: Susan Faye Spiegelberg Schuldes, Sharon Louise Spiegelberg Kozlowski, Stephen Harry, Scott Charles. BSChemE, U. Wis., 1959; MS, Inst. Paper Chemistry, Appleton, Wis., 1963, PhD, 1966; MBA, U. Chgo., 1980. Teaching asst. U. Wis. Coll. Engring., Madison, 1957-59; engr. Kimberly-Clark Corp., Neenah, Wis., 1959-61, rsch. scientist, 1965-68, mgr. new concepts, 1968-73, dir. R & D, 1973-84, v.p. consumer tissue rsch., 1985-92, v.p. tech. and patent strategy, 1992-93, v.p. tech. transfer, 1993-96, ret., 1996. Mem., past chmn. vis. com. dept. chem. engring. U. Wis., 1985—, mem., past chmn. indsl. liaison coun. Coll. Engring., 1987-93; founder, vice chmn. Paper Industry Internat. Hall of Fame; past pres. Ctr. Project Inc.; paper industry bus. columnist, 1999—. Contbr. chpt. to book; patentee in nonwovens and tissue fields. Capt. C.E. USAR, 1959-67. Recipient Disting. Svc. citation U. Wis., 1986. Congregationalist. Avocations: bicycling, backpacking, kayaking, antique farm equipment. Home: 3624 S Barker Ln Appleton WI 54915-7038 E-mail: bspiegel@athenet.net.

SPIEGEL-HOPKINS, PHYLLIS, psychotherapist; b. Chgo., Oct. 28, 1947; d. Joseph Frank and Marie Ann (Hejhal) Spiegel; m. Daniel Mark Hopkins, Jan. 14, 1984. BS in Edn., Chgo. State U., 1968, MA in History, 1972; MA in Clin. Psychology, Ill. Sch. Profl. Psychology, Chgo., 1988; D in Clin. Hypnotherapy, Am. Inst. Hypnotherapy, Santa Ana, Calif., 1991. Diplomate Am. Psychotherapy Assn., Am. Coll. Forensic Examiners; cert./registered hypnotherapist, Internat. Med. and Dental Hypnotherapy Assn.; cert. clin. hypnotherapist; cert. master hypnotherapist and cert. hypnosis instr. Hypnodyne Found. Tchr. Holy Cross Grammar Sch., Chgo., 1968-69, Chgo. Bd. Edn., 1969-81, Mt. Asissi Acad., Lemont, Ill., 1981-82; police officer Chgo. Police Dept., 1982—; psychotherapist pvt. practice Chgo., 1988—. Mem. Assn. Past-Life Therapy and Rsch. (life), Internat. Assn. Counselors and Therapists (life).

SPIEGELMAN, JAMES MICHAEL, international affairs expert; b. Atlantic City, Aug. 13, 1958; s. William and Barbara (Cohen) S.; m. Elizabeth J. Kannan, Aug. 21, 1993; children: Jack Morrison, Elizabeth Margaret. Student, London Polytechnic, 1979; BA in Polit. Sci., U. Pa., 1980; MA in Internat. Affairs, Am. U., 1984. Account exec. United Expn. Svc. Co., Inc., Washington, 1980-82; rsch. fellow Congl. Rsch. Svc., U.S. Libr. Congress, 1984; writer, editor Hudson Rsch. Internat., Paris, 1985-90; dir. rsch. and programs Ctr. for Internat. Bus. and Trade, Georgetown U., Washington, 1986-91; dep. policy dir. U.S. Senator Bob Kerrey for Pres. Campaign, 1991-92; spl. asst. to George Soros, founder Soros Founds., N.Y.C., 1992-93; sr. internat. analyst Athena Global Investments, Greenwich, Conn., 1994; chief of staff UN Assn. of U.S.A., N.Y.C., 1995-96; cons. editor Bus. Week Exec. Programs, 1996-2000; editor The Global Challenge—Latin Am. in the World Economy, 1999—; dir. pub. affairs The Aspen Inst., Washington, 2001—. Co-editor: Impediments to U.S.-Arab Economic Relations: Progress in the Midst of Crisis, 1989; editor-in-chief CIB&T Analyst, quar. newsletter, 1986-90; contbr. numerous articles on U.S. politics and internat. affairs to newspapers and profl. pubs. Mem. World Affairs Coun., Washington. Mem. Am. Polit. Sci. Assn., UN Assn. of U.S., Nat. Geog. Soc., Penn Club of N.Y. Democrat. Office: The Aspen Inst One DuPont Cir NW Ste 7700 Washington DC 20036 E-mail: jspieg@ix.netcom.com., jim.spiegelman@aspeninst.org.

SPIELBERG, JOSHUA MORRIS, lawyer; b. Atlanta, July 31, 1955; s. Sol and Gisela (Meyer) S.; m. Anindita Banerji, May 31, 1977; children: Lela, Ben, Hannah. BA, Oberlin Coll., 1977; JD magna cum laude, U. Pa., 1981. Bar: Del. 1982, N.J. 1985, Pa. 1985, U.S. Ct. Appeals (3d cir.) 1984, U.S. Ct. Appeals (6th cir.) 1990, U.S. Supreme Ct. 1997. Law clk. to Judge Walter K. Stapleton U.S. Dist. Ct. Del., Wilmington, 1981-82; Reginald Heber Smith fellow Cmty. Legal Aid, 1982-84; atty., ptnr. Tomar, Simonof et al, Cherry Hill, N.J., 1984-2000; ptnr. Shivers, Spielberg, Gosnay & Greatrex, NJ, 2000—. Trustee Camden Regional Legal Svcs., 1993—,; mem. trust adv. com. DI Asbestos Disease Trust, Media, Pa., 1993-95; lectr. Rutgers Law Sch., Camden, 1993-99, adj. prof., 2000-01. Contbr. articles to law jours. Mgr. Little League baseball Haddon Twp. Athletic Assn., Westmont, N.J., 1994-2000; trustee Congregation M'Kor Shalom, Cherry HIll, 2002--. Recipient Fordham Human Rights award U. Pa. Law Sch., 1981, Outstanding Bd. Svc. award Legal Svcs. N.J., 2000. Mem. ATLA, N.J. Bar Assn. Democrat. Jewish. Avocations: baseball, bicycling, hiking. Home: 337 Westmont Ave Westmont NJ 08108-3536 Office: Shivers Spielberg & Gosnay 1415 Rte 70 E Ste 210 Cherry Hill NJ 08034 E-mail: jspielberg@ssglawfirm.com.

SPIELBERG, STEVEN, motion picture director, producer; b. Cin., Dec. 18, 1946; m. Amy Irving, Nov. 27, 1985 (div.); 2 children: Max Samuel, Sasha; m. Kate Capshaw; 5 children. BA, Calif. State Coll., Long Beach; Hon. Doctorate in Creative Arts, Brandeis U., 1986. Founder Amblin Entertainment (Universal Studios), Dreamworks SKG (with Jeffrey Katzenberg and David Geffen); directed segments of TV series Columbo; dir. TV movies Night Gallery, 1969, Duel, 1971, Savage, 1972, Something Evil, 1972; exec prodr. series: Steven Spielberg's Amazing Stories, Tiny Toon Adventures, Family Dog, Animaniacs, SeaQuest DSV, Steven Spielberg Presents Toonsylvania, 1998; Pinky, Elmyra & the Brain; films include (dir.): The Sugarland Express, 1974 (also story), Jaws, 1975, Close Encounters of the Third Kind, 1977 (also co-writer), 1941, 1979, Raiders of the Lost Ark, 1981, Indiana Jones and the Temple of Doom, 1984, Indiana Jones and the Last Crusade, 1989, Hook, 1991, Jurassic Park, 1993; (dir., prodr.): E.T. The Extra-Terrestrial, 1982, The Color Purple, 1985, Empire of the Sun, 1987, Always, 1989, Schindler's List, 1993 (Best Drama & Best Dir. Golden Globe awards, Best Picture & Best Dir. Acad. awards), Saving Private Ryan (Golden Globe award for Best Dir. 1999, Best Director Academy Award 1998, nominee Best Picture Academy award 1999), Artificial Intelligence, 2001 (also writer), Catch Me If You Can, 2002, Minority Report, 2002; (dir., exec. prodr.): Twilight Zone: The Movie, 1983; (prodr.): Poltergeist, 1982 (also co-writer), An American Tail: Fievel Goes West, 1991, Casper, 1995; (exec. prodr.): I Wanna Hold Your Hand, 1978, Used Cars, 1980, Continental Divide, 1981, Gremlins, 1984, The Goonies, 1985, Back to the Future, 1985, Young Sherlock Holmes, 1985, The Money Pit, 1986, An American Tail, 1986, Innerspace, 1987, *betteries not included, 1987, Who Framed Roger Rabbit?, 1988, The Land Before Time, 1988, Dad, 1989, Back to the Future Part II, 1989, Joe Verses the Volcano, 1990, Back to the Future Part III, 1990, Gremlins 2: The New Batch, 1990, Arachnophobia, 1990, Cape Fear, 1991, We're Back!: A Dinosaur's Story, 1993, The Flintstones, 1994, The Little Rascals, 1994, Balto, 1995, Men in Black, 1996, Twister, 1996, The Lost World, 1997, Amistad, 1997, Deep Impact, 1998, The Mask of Zorro, 1998, The Last Days, 1998, Jurassic Park III, 2001, Shrek, 2001, Price for Peace, 2001, Men in Black II, 2002; (actor): The Blues Brothers, 1980; exec. prodr. TV: Band of Brothers, 2001, (TV mini-series) (Emmy award for outstanding mini-series, 2002) The Unfinished Journey, 1999, Semper Fi, 2000, Shooting War, 2000, We Stand Alone Together, 2001. Recipient Man of Yr. award Hasty Pudding Theater, Harvard U., 1983, Outstanding Directorial Achievement award for feature films Dirs. Guild Am., 1985, Film award Brit. Acad. Film and TV Arts, 1986, Irving Thalberg Mem. award Acad. Motion Picture Arts and Scis., 1987, Golden Lion award for career achievement Venice Film Festival, 1993, Life Achievement award Am. Film Inst., 1995, Lifetime Achievement award, Dir. Guild Am., 2000. Fellow Brit. Acad. Film and TV Arts. Achievements include winning film contest with 40-minute war movie, Escape to Nowhere, at age 13; made film Firelight at age 16, and made 5 films while in coll.; became TV dir. at Universal Pictures at age 20. Office: CAA 9830 Wilshire Blvd Beverly Hills CA 90212-1804*

SPIELMAN, ANDREW IAN, biochemist; b. Tirgu Mures, Romania, June 23, 1950; arrived in Can., 1982; s. Joseph and Rachel S.; m. Kathy Szabó, Dec. 15, 1977; 1 child, Robert-Dan. DMD, U. Medicine and Pharmacy, Tirgu Mures, 1974; cert. specialist in oral surgery, Technion, Haifa, Israel, 1982; MSc, U. Toronto (Can.), 1985, PhD in Oral Biology and Biochemistry, 1988. Asst. mem. Monell Chem. Senses Ctr., Phila., 1988-89; clin. assoc. U. Pa. Sch. Dental Medicine, 1989-92; affiliate mem. Monell Chem. Senses Ctr., 1989—; prof. and chair dept. basic sci. and craniofacial biology NYU Coll. Dentistry, N.Y.C., 1996, assoc. dir. rsch., 1992-00, head biol. sci., medicine and surgery divsn., 1999—. Presenter in field. Author: (with others) Encyclopedia of Human Biology, 1991; editor: Experimental Cell Biology of Taste and Olfaction, 1995; contbr. articles to Brain Rsch., Chem. Senses, Jour. Dental Rsch., Archives Oral Biology, Experientia, Physiology and Behavior, Am. Jour. Physiology, Jour. Chem. Ecology, Jour. Neurophysiology, Critical Rev. in Oral Medicine and Biology, Jour. of Biol. Chemistry, Biochemistry, Nature (Neurosci.), also procs. V.p., bd. dirs. Trimethylaminuria Found., 2001—. Republican fellow Univ. of Medicine and Pharmacy, Tirgu-Mures, 1972, U. Toronto Open fellow, 1983, Med. Rsch. fellow Med. Rsch. Coun. can., 1983-88. Mem. AAAS, Internat. Assn. for Dental Rsch., N.Y. Acad. Sci., Assn. for Chemoreception Scis., Am. Assn. Oral Biologists (bd. dirs. 1996-99, pres.-elect 1999-2000, pres. 2000), Sigma Xi. Jewish. Achievements include research on the molecular basis of bitter taste mechanisms; on the interaction of saliva and taste; on identification of sweat-odor binding proteins in human axillary secretion. Office: NYU Coll of Dentistry 345 E 24th St New York NY 10010-4020

SPIELMAN, BARBARA HELEN NEW, editor, consultant; b. Canton, Ohio, June 28, 1929; d. Arthur Daniel and Helen Barbara (Rickenmann) New; m. David Vernon Spielman, Nov. 24, 1956; children: Daniel Bruce, Linda Barbara. BS in English and History Edn. cum laude, Miami U., Oxford, Ohio, 1951. Cert. tchr., Ohio, Tex. Tchr. Canton Pub. Schs., 1951-53; vets. aide U. Tex., Austin, 1954-57; copy editor, mng. editor U. Tex. Press, 1964-91; ret., 1991. Editorial cons. Chicago Manual of Style, 13th edit., 1975, Amon Carter Mus., Ft. Worth, 1970—, Ctr. for Mex. Am. Studies, Austin, 1980, Jack S. Blanton Mus. Art (formerly Archer M. Huntington Art Gallery), Austin, 1975—, 64 Beds Project for Homeless and Hungry, Austin, 1989—; mem. search com. for dir., U. Tex. Press, 1991. Troop leader Girl Scouts Am., Austin, 1970-73; officer PTA, Austin, 1964-73. Mem. Smithsonian Instn., Nat. Geog. Soc., Althenoi, Seton Med. Ctr. Aux., Phi Beta Kappa, Kappa Delta Pi, Sigma Sigma Sigma. Democrat. Presbyterian. Avocations: reading, gardening, piano, painting, drawing. Home: 3301 Perry Ln Austin TX 78731-5330

SPIELMAN, BARRY E, electrical engineer, educator, department chairman; b. Chicago, IL, Oct. 29, 1942; s. Herbert Spielman, Beatrice Freid Spielman; m. Louise W Wiant; children: Michael, Liza. PhD in electrical engineering, Syracuse University, Syracuse, New York, 1967—71; MS Electrical Engineering, Pennsylvania State University, University Park, Pennsylvania, 1964—67; BS Electrical Engineering, Illinois Institute of Technology, Chicago, Illinois, 1960—64; MS in electrical engineering, Pennsylvania State University, University Park, Pennsylvania, 1964—67; BS in electrical engineering, Illinois Institute of Technology, Chicago, Illinois, 1960—64. Research Assistant Ionosphere Research Laboratory, University Park, PA, 1964—67; Graduate Assistant Syracuse University , Syracuse, NY, 1967—71; Research Electronics Engineer Naval Research Laboratory, Washington , DC, 1971—78; Head, Solid State Circuits Section Naval Research Laboratory,

Washington, 1978—84; Head, Microwave Techology Branch Naval Research Laboratory, 1984—87; Professor and Chair Washington University Department of Electrical Engineering, St. Louis, 1987—2002. President Microwave Theory and Techniques Society Institute of Electrical and Electronics Engineers, New York, NY, 1988—89; President National Electrical Engineering Department Heads Association, Chicago, IL, 1998—99; Consultant McDonnell Douglas Corporation, St. Louis, 1988—89. Author: (Journal articles) IEEE Transactions on Microwave Theory and Techniques, 1972, (Journal article) , 1974, (Journal Article) IEE Electronics Letters, 1975; : IEEE Transactions on Microwave Theory and Techniques, 1977, (Conference presentation and article) 1998 Asia-Pacific Microwave Conference Proceedings, 1998, (Conference Presentation and Article) 1999 IEEE International Microwave Symposium, 1999. Trustee Board of Trustees Kehrs Mill Ridge Homeowners Association, Ballwin, MO, 1999—2001. Fellow: Institute of Electrical and Electronics Engineers. Avocation: running, walking, tennis. Home: 607 Kehrs Mill Ridge Drive Ballwin MO 63011 Office: Washington University One Brookings Drive Saint Louis MO 63130 Home Fax: 314-935-7500; Office Fax: 314-935-7500. Personal E-mail: bes@ee.wustl.edu. Business E-Mail: bes@ee.wustl.edu.

SPIELMAN, DAVID VERNON, retired insurance, finance and publications consultant; b. Humboldt, Iowa, Dec. 23, 1929; s. Elmo Bruce and Leona Belle (Blake) S.; m. Barbara Helen New, Nov. 24, 1956; children: Daniel Bruce, Linda Barbara. BA, U. Tex., 1966. Publs. engr. IBM Mil. Products Divsn., Kingston, N.Y., 1957-58; engring. writer Convair Astronautics div. Gen Dynamics Corp., San Diego, 1958-59; tech. publs. mgr. Ling-Temco Vaught, Inc., Garland, Tex., 1960-62; tech. writer Ken Cook Pubs. Co., Richardson, 1963-64; asst. coordinator Kuwait program U. Tex., Austin, 1964-66; ednl. writer Tex. Edn. Agy., 1967-74; cons. Dave Spielman Rsch. Assocs., 1974—. Cons. Nat. Ctr. Vocat. Edn., Columbus, Ohio, 1974-75, Tex. State Auditor, Austin, 1976-77, U.S. Dept. Labor, Washington, 1975-78; interview Fortune Mag.; exec. dir. Tex. Labor Ctr., Inc., 1978—. Counselor Distributive Edn. Clubs Am. Student Conf. Tex., Brenham, 1972; competition judge Tex. Carpenter's Apprentices, 1973-74; chpt. pres. Tex. Pub. Employees Assn., Austin, 1969-70; mem. Dem. Nat. Conv., 1988. Served to sgt. maj. U.S. Army, 1952-53, with USNR 1947-49, with Tex. N.G. 1949-50, cpl. USAF 1950-52. Recipient Outstanding Vocat. Edn. Contributor, Tex. House and Senate. Mem. Acctg. Computer Machinery Assn. (newsletter editor 1958-59), Soc. Tech Writers and Editors (chpt. pres. 1960-61), Soc. Tech. Writers and Pubs. (chpt. pres. 1961-62), Soc. Tech. Communications (membership chmn. 1983-84), Tex. State Tchrs. Assn., Delta Pi (local sec., treas.). Lodges: Masons. Democrat. Presbyterian. Avocations: chess, choral, novels, poetry, short story writing. Home and Office: 3301 Perry Ln Austin TX 78731-5330

SPIELVOGEL, LAWRENCE GEORGE, engineer; b. Newark, June 2, 1938; s. Joseph and Fanny (Ravitz) S. BSME, Drexel U., 1962. Asst. post engr. Walter Reed Med. Ctr., Washington, 1963-65; engr. Utility Survey Corp., Chgo., 1965-66; assoc. Werden & Assoc., Inc., Jenkintown, Pa., 1959-70; prin. Lawrence G. Spielvogel, Inc., King of Prussia, 1970—. Contbr. articles to profl. jours. Bd. dirs. Interfaith Coalition on Energy, Phila., 1980—. Mem. ASHRAE (Tech. Paper award 1974, Crosby Field award, 1981, Jour. Article of Yr. award 1980), Illuminating Engring. Soc. N.Am. (dir. 1976-79). Home and Office: Lawrence G Spielvogel Inc 203 Hughes Rd King Of Prussia PA 19406-3711

SPIELVOGEL, SIDNEY MEYER, investment banker; b. N.Y.C., July 14, 1925; s. Hyman and Rae (Mandel) S.; m. Beverly Anne Gold, Dec. 18, 1960; 1 son, Peter James. BSS., CCNY, 1944; A.M., Harvard U., 1946, MBA, 1949. Economist Treasury Dept., Washington, 1946-47; assoc. dept. mgr. Alexander's Dept. Stores, 1949-53; asst. to mdse. mgr., dept. mgr. Bloomingdale's Dept. Store, 1953-56; with Prudential-Bache Securities Inc., 1956-88, 1st v.p., 1971-75, sr. v.p., 1975-85, mng. dir., 1986-88. Dir. MoneyMart Assets Inc., 1976-96, pres., 1981-87; lectr. Hunter Coll., N.Y.C., 1963-68, The New Sch., 1993-96. Bd. dirs. Emanu-el Midtown YM-YWHA, N.Y.C., 1975-91; mem. Harvard Grad. Soc. Coun., 1983-88, 89-92, 94—, chmn., 1985-87. Mem. Phi Beta Kappa. Clubs: Harvard (N.Y.C.), Harvard Bus. Sch. (N.Y.C.), World Trade Center (N.Y.C.). Home: 245 E 19th St New York NY 10003-2639 Office: Corp Capital Cons Inc 230 Park Ave Rm 1000 New York NY 10169-0999

SPIER, KATHRYN ELIZABETH, economist, educator; b. Port Washington, NY, July 16, 1963; d. Peter Edward and Kathryn Madeleine Spier; m. James Dwight Dana, June 8, 1991; 1 child James Dwight Dana. BA summa cum laude, Yale U., 1985; PhD, MIT, 1989. Assoc. prof. Harvard U., Cambridge, Mass., 1989—94; vis. prof. U. Chgo., 1993—94; assoc. prof. Northwestern U., Evanston, 1994—. Bd. dirs., exec. com. Am. Law and Econs. Assn., New Haven, 1997—2000. Contbr. articles to profl. jours.; mem. editl. bd. Jour. Law Econs. and Orgn., 1996—; editor (assoc.): Rand Jour. Econs., 1996—. Fellow, Olin Found., 1988—89, 1992—94; grantee, NSF, 1985—88, 1991—93. Fellow: Nat. Bur. Econ. Rsch. Home: 2726 Payne St Evanston IL 60201 Office: Northwestern U Kellogg Sch 2001 Sheridan Rd Evanston IL 60208 Business E-Mail: k-spier@kellogg.northwestern.edu.

SPIER, PETER EDWARD, artist, author; b. Amsterdam, Netherlands, June 6, 1927; came to U.S., 1952, naturalized, 1958; s. Joseph Eduard and Albertine Sophie (Van Raalte) S.; m. Kathryn M. Pallister, July 12, 1958; children: Thomas P., Kathryn E. Student, Ryks Academie Voor Beeldende Kunsten, Amsterdam, 1945-47. Jr. editor Elsevier's Weekly, Amsterdam, 1950-51, Elsevier Pub. Co., Houston, 1952. Free-lance author, illustrator, N.Y.C., 1952— , speaker, lectr. schs. and libraries.; author, illustrator: 38 books, including: The Star-Spangled Banner, 1973, Fast-Slow, High-Low, 1972, Crash! Bang! Boom!, 1972, Tin Lizzie, 1975, Noah's Ark, 1977, Oh, Were They Ever Happy!, 1978, Bored— Nothing to Do, 1978, The Legend of New Amsterdam, 1979, People, 1980, Peter Spier's Village Books, 1981, Rain, 1982, Christmas!, 1983, The Book of Jonah, 1985, Dreams, 1986, We The People, 1987, Peter Spier's Circus, 1992, Father, May I Come?, 1993; illustrator over 150 books; contbr., illustrator many nat. mags. Historian Village of Shoreham, N.Y. Lt. Royal Netherlands Navy, 1947-58. Runner-up for Caldecott medal, 1960; recipient Christopher award, 1970, Boston Globe award, 1967, Caldecott medal, 1978, Christopher award, 1978, Nat. Religious Book award, 1978, Lewis Carroll Shelf award, 1978, Media award NCCJ, 1980, David McCord award, 1989, Empire State award N.Y. Lit. Assn., 2000. Mem. Shoreham Country Club (N.Y.). Address: PO Box 566 Shoreham NY 11786-0566 E-mail: spier11786@aol.com.

SPIERINGS, EGILIUS LEONARDUS HENDRICUS, pharmacologist, neurologist, headache specialist; b. Helmond, The Netherlands, Aug. 16, 1953; came to U.S., 1986; s. Egilius L.H. and Johanna A. (Schellekens) S.; m. Maria K.B. Zarska, Dec. 27, 1976; children: Sven E.J., Natalia M.K. BS cum laude, Erasmus U., Rotterdam, The Netherlands, 1974, MD, 1978, PhD in Experimental Pharmacology, 1980. Registered in medicine, cert. in neurology The Netherlands; lic. physician Mass. Intern in neurosurgery Univ. Hosp., Rotterdam, The Netherlands, 1980-81, resident in neurology The Netherlands, 1982-84; fellow in headache mgmt. Headache Rsch. Found., Boston, 1981-82; resident in psychiatry Hippolytus Hosp., Delft, The Netherlands, 1985; asst. prof. neurology Tufts U. Sch. Medicine, Boston, 1986-90; dir. Headache Rsch. Found., 1986-89, John R. Graham Headache Ctr., Boston, 1987-90; dir. headache sect. dept. neurology Brigham & Women's Hosp., 1990-94, dir. headache rsch. dept. neurology, 1994-96; dir. Boston Clin. Rsch. Ctr., Wellesley Hills, 1996—. Lectr. neurology Harvard Med. Sch., 1990-99, assoc. clin. prof. neurology, 1999—; spkr. in field. Author: The Pathophysiology of the Migraine Attack, 1980, Migraine, 1986, Migraine Questions & Answers, 1995, 2d edit., 2001, Management of Migraine, 1996, Headache, 1998; co-author: Hoofdpijn, 1984; sect. editor Office Practice of Neurology, 1996, 2002; editor: De Pathogenese van Migraine, 1982; contbr. numerous articles to profl. jours. and chpts. to books, over 40 radio and TV appearances. Edn. dir. Headache Coop. New Eng., 1991—. Fellow Am. Assn. Study of Headache (bd. dirs. 1991-93); mem. Netherlands Migraine Found. (bd. dirs. 1980-85), Netherlands Soc. Migraine Patients (bd. dirs. 1982-86), Internat. Headache Soc. (bd. dirs. 1985-86, assoc. editor Cephalagia, 1986-89). Home: 24 Algonquian Dr Natick MA 01760-6095 Office: 25 Walnut St Ste 102 Wellesley Hills MA 02481-2152 E-mail: Spierings@MediaOne.net.

SPIERS, ROBERT FRANKLIN, music educator; b. Richmond, Va., May 12, 1963; s. Jesse Lee and Edith Davis Spiers; m. Lisa Marie Edwards, July 18, 1987; children: Joel, Nathan. BM, James Madison U., Harrisonburg, VA, 1985. Band dir. Lancaster H.S., Lancaster, Va., 1985—. Mem.: Va. Band and Orch. Directors Assn., Va. Music Edn. Assn. R-Consevative. Baptist. Achievements include high school band has performed in 1998 Sugar Bowl and 2002 Orange Bowl halftime shows. Home: 390 Bald Eagle Rd White Stone VA 22578 Office: Lancaster High School 790 Mary Ball Rd Lancaster VA 22503 Office Fax: 804-462-5174. E-mail: rspiers@lcs.k12.va.us.

SPIERS, RONALD IAN, diplomat; b. Orange, N.J., July 9, 1925; s. Thomas Hoskins and Blanca (De Ponthier) S.; m. Patience Baker, June 11, 1949; children: Deborah Wood, Peter, Martha, Sarah. BA, Dartmouth Coll., 1948; M in Pub. Affairs, Princeton U., 1950. With AEC, 1950-54; officer-in-charge disarmament and arms control Dept. State, Washington, 1955-61, dir. NATO affairs, 1962-66; polit. counselor Am. Embassy, London, 1966-69; asst. sec. for Politico-Mil. Affairs U.S. Dept. State, 1969-73; amb. to Bahamas, Am. Embassy, Nassau, 1973-74, dep. chief of mission London, 1974-77; U.S. permanent rep. to CENTO Coun., 1977-79; amb. to Turkey, Am. Embassy, Ankara, 1977-80; asst. sec. for intelligence and rsch., mem. U.S. Intelligence Bd. U.S. Dept. State, Washington, 1980-81; amb. to Pakistan, Am. Embassy, Islamabad, 1981-83; under-sec. for mgmt. U.S. Dept. State, 1983-89; under-sec. gen. for polit. affairs UN, N.Y.C., 1989-92; internat. affairs cons. Dept. State, 1992—. Career ambassador U.S. Fgn. Svc., 1984. Served to lt. (j.g.) USN, 1943-46, PTO. Woodrow Wilson fellow Princeton U., 1948. Fellow Nat. Acad. of Pub. Adminstrn.; mem. Am. Fgn. Svc. Assn., Internat. Inst. Strategic Studies, Coun. on Fgn. Rels., Am. Acad. of Diplomacy, Washington Inst. Fgn. Affairs. Home: 1320 Middletown Rd South Londonderry VT 05155-9145 E-mail: embassy@sover.net.

SPIES, CHARLES ROBERT, lawyer; b. East Grand Rapids, Mich., Aug. 29, 1972; s. Frank S. Spies, Lynette K. Spies. BA, U. Mich., 1995; JD, Georgetown U., 1998. Atty. Carr Goodson Warner, Washington, 1998—99; execs. asst. to chmn. Darryl R. Wold Fed. Election Commn., 1999—2000; atty. Arent Fox Kintner Plotkin & Kahn, 2000—01; dep. counsel Rep. Nat. Com., 2001—. Office: Rep Nat Com 310 First St SE Washington DC 20003

SPIES, FRANK STADLER, lawyer; b. Adrian, Mich., Aug. 7, 1939; s. Charles F. and Lucille M. (Stadler) S.; m. Lynette K. Wells, July 25, 1964; children: Anne, Jane, Charles. BBA, U. Mich., 1961, LLB, 1964. Bar: Mich. 1964, U.S. Dist. Ct. (we. dist.) Mich. 1964, U.S. Ct. Appeals (6th cir.) 1971. Assoc. Schmidt, Smith, Howlett & Halliday, Grand Rapids, Mich., 1964-66; asst. city atty. City of Grand Rapids, 1966-69, U.S. Dept. Justice, Grand Rapids, 1969-77; U.S. atty. Western Dist. Mich., 1974-77; pvt. practice, 1977-81, 84-97; assoc. Kaufman, Payton & Kallas, 1981-84, Bensinger, Cotant, Menkes & Aardema, Grand Rapids, 1997—. Instr. bus. law Davenport Coll., Grand Rapids, 1967-68, Grand Valley State U., Grand Rapids, 1978-79. Recipient Dirs. Honor award U.S. Secret Svc., 1977. Mem. ABA, Grand Rapids Bar Assn., Nat. Assn. Former U.S. Attys., Grand Rapids East Rotary, Republican. Presbyterian. Home: 2122 Tenway Dr SE Grand Rapids MI 49506-4526 Office: 983 Spaulding Ave SE Grand Rapids MI 49546-3700 E-mail: fspies@bcma.net.

SPIES, JACOB JOHN, healthcare executive; b. Sheboygan, Wis., Jan. 27, 1931; s. Jacob Alfred and Julia Effie (Wescott) S.; m. Donna Dolores Jerale, June 17, 1954; children: Gary, Joni, Shari. BBA, U. Wis., 1955. V.p. health care systems Wausau (Wis.) Ins. Cos., 1972-77, v.p. mgmt. systems, 1977-79; dep. dir. Health Policy Inst. Boston U., 1979-85; pres., chief exec. officer Co-Med, Inc., Columbus, Ohio, 1984-85; sr. v.p. PARTNERS Nat. Health Plans, Irving, Tex., 1985-90; chmn. PARTNERS Health Plans of Colo., Denver, 1986-90; prin. The Furst Group, Dallas, 1990—. Pres., CEO Dallas/Ft. Worth Health Industry Coun., 1994—; bd. dirs. Integrated Healthcare Corp.; adv. bd. Healthcare Adminstrn.; chmn. Tex. Women's U. Co-author: A Corporations Experience with IPA-HMO, 1981, Health Care Cost Containment, 1983. Sgt. U.S. Army, 1952-54, Korea. Decorated Bronze Star, 1953. Mem. Group Health Assn. Am. (com. mem. 1988, 91), Am. Managed Care and Rev. Assn. (bd. dirs.), Nat. Assn. Employers on Health Care Actions (chmn.), North Tex. Med. Edn. Consortium (bd. trustees 1995—), LaCima Club, Denton Country Club. Episcopalian. Home and Office: The Furst Group 1941 Cordero Ct Lady Lake FL 32159-8566

SPIES, LEON FRED, lawyer; b. Blue Grass, Iowa, Oct. 8, 1950; s. Fred William and Alma Lois (Lineburg) S.; m. Janet Rae Peterson, July 15, 1979; children: Caitlin, Allison. BBA with distinction, U. Iowa, 1972, JD with distinction, 1975. Bar: Iowa 1975, U.S. Dist. Ct. (no. and so. dists.) Iowa 1975, U.S. Ct. Appeals 1975, U.S. Supreme Ct. 1987, U.S. Dist. Ct. (cen. dist.) Ill. 2000. Assoc. Heintz & Mellon, Iowa City, 1975-76; ptnr. Mellon & Spies, 1976—. Magistrate jud. dept. State of Iowa, 1978-83; instr. trial advocacy U. Iowa Coll. Law, 1996—. Bd. chmn. Johnson County Red Cross, Iowa City, 1982-84; bd. dirs. Big Bros./ Big Sisters, Johnson County, Iowa, 1985-89. Fellow Iowa Acad. Trial Lawyers; mem. ABA, ATLA, Iowa Bar Assn., Assn. Trial Lawyers Iowa, Am. Judicature Soc., Am. Inns of Ct. (master, pres. Dean Mason Ladd Inn 1995-96). Democrat. Methodist. Home: 2349 Kent Ct NE Iowa City IA 52240-9633 Office: Mellon & Spies 102 S Clinton St Iowa City IA 52240-4024

SPIES, PHYLLIS BOVA, information services company executive; b. Syracuse, N.Y., Nov. 10, 1949; d. Ralph Anthony and Elizabeth Margaret (Caputo) Bova; m. John William Spies, June 28, 1980; children: Fletcher, Logan. BA in Art History, SUNY, Cortland, 1971; MLS in Libr. and Info. Sci., Syracuse U., 1972. Libr. systems analyst Ohio Coll. Library Ctr., Columbus, 1973-78; mgr. libr. systems analysis OCLC Online Computer Libr. Ctr., Dublin, 1978-83, div. v.p., 1983-89, v.p. internat., 1989-92, v.p. mem. svcs., sales and internat., 1992—, OCLC Online Computer LIbr. Ctr., Dublin, 1994-98, v.p. worldwide sales, 1998—. Trustee Maps Micrographic Preservation Svc., Bethlehem, Pa., 1990—. Contbr. articles to profl. jours. Mem. Columbus Coun. World Affairs. Fellow The Gaylord Co., 1971. Mem. ALA, Internat. Fedn. Libr. Assns., Dublin Women in Bus. Avocations: gardening, cooking. Office: Online Computer Libr Ctr 6565 Frantz Rd Dublin OH 43017-5308

SPIESICKE, MARGRIT HERMA, retired counselor; b. Hannover, L. Saxonia, Germany, Dec. 29, 1925; came to U.S. 1960; d. Louis Adolf Otto Fritz and Else Herma (Meier) Becker; m. Horst Guenther Spiesicke, Nov. 9, 1949; 1 child, Marc Anthony. Cert. English/German Interpreter, Hannover (Germany) Lang. Coll., 1947; AA with hons., Broward C.C., Hollywood, Fla., 1983; BA in Humanities, Fla. Internat. U., 1989; postgrad., Nova U., 1992—. State interpreter British Mil. Govt., Hannover, 1947-49; sec., office mgr. Townsend Co., Montreal, Can., 1950-60; sec., adminstrv. asst. Wometco Enterprises, Miami, 1960-85; adminstrv. sec. Barry U., 1985-88; med. sec. Broward Correctional Instn., Pembroke Pines, Fla., 1988-90, instl. counselor, 1990-99; ret., 1999. Vol. group counselor Mancy Figueredo, M.D., Miami, 1988-89. Mem. Phi Kappa Phi. Republican. Lutheran. Avocations: music, reading, creative writing.

SPIESS, FRED NOEL, oceanographer, educator; b. Oakland, Calif., Dec. 25, 1919; s. Fred Henry and Elva Josephine (Monck) S.; m. Sarah Scott Whitton, July 25, 1942; children: Katherine Spiess Dallaire, Mary Elizabeth Spiess DeJong, John Morgen Frederick, Helen Spiess Shamble, Margaret Josephine Deligio-Spiess. AB, U. Calif., Berkeley, 1941, PhD, 1951; MS, Harvard U., 1946. With Marine Phys. Lab., U. Calif., San Diego, 1952—, dir., 1958-80, U. Calif. Inst. Marine Resources, 1980-88, Scripps Inst. Oceanography, La Jolla, 1964-65, prof. oceanography, 1961-90, prof. emeritus, rsch. prof., 1990—; chair U. Calif. Acad. Coun. and Assembly U. Calif. Bd. Regents, 1988-90. Mem. Naval Research Adv. Commn., 1978-81; mem. com. on geodesy Nat. Acad. Scis., 1980-84; mem. Def. Sci. Bd., 1976-79; chair Acad. Senate Task Force U. Calif., Merced, 1999-2001. Capt. USNR, 1941-79. Decorated Silver Star medal, Bronze Star medal; recipient John Price Wetherill medal Franklin Inst., 1965; Compass Disting. Scientist award Marine Technol. Soc., 1971; Robert Dexter Conrad award U.S. Sec. of Navy, 1974, Navy Disting. Pub. Svc. award, 1990; Newcomb Cleveland prize AAAS, 1981 Fellow Acoustical Soc. Am. (Pioneers of Underwater Acoustics medal 1985), Am. Geophys. Union (Maurice Ewing award 1983), Marine Tech. Soc. (Lockheed award 1985); mem. Nat. Acad. Engring., Phi Beta Kappa, Sigma Xi. Home: 9450 La Jolla Shores Dr La Jolla CA 92037-1137 Office: U Calif San Diego Scripps Inst Oceanogra La Jolla CA 92093-0205 E-mail: fspiess@ucsd.edu.

SPIETH, MARTHA MAXWELL, writer; b. Washington, Apr. 30, 1923; d. Thomas F. and Jessie (Anderson) Orr; m. George A. Maxwell; children: Christine, George A., Barbara; m. Walter Spieth. BA, U. Md., 1946, MA, 1948, PhD, 1960. Dir. reading & study skills program, assoc. prof. edn. U. Md., College Park, 1958-66; acad. advisor, dir., mem. grad. faculty U. Calif. Student Learning Ctr., Berkeley, 1968-79. Author: Skimming and Scanning Skills, 1968, Improving Student Learning Skills, 1978, rev. edit., 1997, Evaluating Academic Skills Programs: A Sourcebook, 1991, 2d edit., 1996; editor: When Tutor Meets Student, 1994, From Access to Success: A Book of Readings on College Development Education and Learning Assistance Programs, 1994. Recipient Nat. Assn. of Developmental Educators Pub. awards, 1979, 97; NSF grantee, 1979. Fellow Am. Coun. Devel. Edn. Assn., Am. Psychol. Assn. Counseling; mem. Am. Men Sci., Women of the South, Coll. Reading & Learning Assn. Avocations: biology, writing. Home: 322-4 Collington 10450 Lottsford Rd Mitchellville MD 20721-2734

SPILHAUS, ATHELSTAN FREDERICK, JR. oceanographer, association executive; b. Boston, May 21, 1938; s. Athelstan F. and Mary (Atkins) S.; m. Sharon Brown, June 11, 1960; children— Athelstan F. III, Ruth Emily, Mary Christina S.B. in Chem. Engring., MIT, 1959, S.M. in Geology and Geophysics, 1960, PhD in Oceanography, 1965. Cert. meeting profl. Phys. scientist U.S. Govt., Washington, 1965-67; asst. exec. dir. Am. Geophys. Union, 1967-70, exec. dir., 1970—. Bd. dirs. Renewable Natural Resources Found., Washington. Editor newspaper EOS. Chmn. Conv. Liaison Council, Washington, 1981-82. Fellow AAAS, Washington Acad. Sci., Am. Geophys. Union (hon.), Indian Geophys. Union, Geol. Soc. Am., Royal Astonomical Soc.; mem. Am. Soc. Limnology and Oceanography, Council Biology Editors, Am. Inst. Physics (mem. gov. bd. 1988—), Philos. Soc. Washington (pres. 1982-83), Geol. Soc. Can., Geol. Soc. Washington (2nd v.p. 1975), Soc. Exploration Geophysicists, Am. Soc. Assn. Execs., Assn. Am. Pubs. (div. exec. com. 1980-82, 94-97), Assn. Earth Sci. Editors (dir. 1972-78, pres. 1977), Council Engring. and Scientific Soc. Execs. (dir. 1976-82, pres. 1980-81), Internat. Union Geodesy Geophysics (mem. fin. com. 1987—, chair 1999—), Canadian Geophys. Union, European Geophys. Soc. Clubs: Cosmos (Washington, pres. 1992-93); Chesapeake Yacht (Md.). Home: 10900 Picasso Ln Rockville MD 20854-1710 Office: Am Geophys Union 2000 Florida Ave NW Washington DC 20009-1231

SPILKA, BERNARD, psychology educator; b. Bronx, N.Y., Aug. 12, 1926; BA, NYU, 1949; MS, Purdue U., 1950, PhD, 1952. Grad. teaching asst. Purdue U., Lafayette, Ind., 1950, sr. grad. rsch. asst. voice sci. lab., 1950-52; rsch. psychologist combat crew lab. Human Resources Rsch. Ctr., Randolph Field, Tex., 1952-53; staff psychologist tng. dept. human engring. U.S. Navy Spl. Devices Ctr., Sands Point, N.Y., 1953-55; asst. prof. psychology Washburn U., Topeka, 1955-57; instr. U. Kans. Extension, 1956-57; asst. prof. psychologyy U. Denver, 1957-61, assoc. prof. psychology, 1961-65, prof. psychology, 1965—97, prof. emeritus, 1997—. Cons. Fed. Youth Ctr., Englewood, Colo., Nat. Coun. Chs. of Christ, Community Rels. Commn. of Denver, Civil Rights Commn. of Colo., U.S. Office Edn., Indian Health Svc., Bur. Indian Affairs, Bur. Reclamation, Luth. Ch. Am., Reorganized Ch. LDS, Children's Hosp., Denver, Search Inst., Mpls. Author: Psychology in Literature: A Reader for Introductory Psychology, 1985, (with others) The Psychology of Religion: An Empirical Approach, 1985, 1996, Religion in Psychodynamic Perspective, 1996, Psychology of Religion: Theoretical Approaches, 1997; cons. editor Jour. for the Sci. Study of Religion, 1969-71, editorial reader, 1971—; assoc. editor Rev. of Religious Rsch., 1970—; mem. editorial bd. Omega, 1976—, Internat. Jour. of the Psychology of Religion, 1989—; book rev. editor Religious Studies Rev., 1983-85; contbr. articles to profl. jours. Recipient Commendation award USN, 1955, Cert. Appreciation award Am. Optometric Assn., 1961; NIMH grantee, 1965-68. Fellow APA (divsn. 36, chair fellows com. 1982-83, pres. 1985-86, chair awards com. 1987—, William James award 1982, Cert. Appreciation 1986, 90), Rocky Mountain Psychol. Assn. (chmn. conv. program 1965, pres. 1967-68, chmn. nominations com. 1968-69, chmn. membership and elections com. 1969-70, Disting. Svc. award 1978), Soc. for the Sci. Study of Religion (v.p. 1978-79, chair publs. com. 1977-79), Religious Rsch. Assn.; mem. AAUP (v.p. Washburn U. chpt. 1956-57, pres. U. Denver chpt. 1962-63, sec.-treas., 1966-67), Acad. Religion and Mental Health, Psi Chi, Sigma Xi, Phi Beta Kappa. Home: 1949 S Olive St Denver CO 80224-2255 Office: U Denver Dept Psychology Denver CO 80208-0001

SPILLANE, DENNIS KEVIN, lawyer; b. N.Y.C., Sept. 15, 1953; s. Denis Joseph and Mary Kate (Sullivan) S. BA magna cum laude, Manhattan Coll., 1974; JD, N.Y. Law Sch., 1978; MS in Taxation, Pace U., 1986, post-masters cert. in bus., 1992. Bar: N.Y. 1979, U.S. Dist. Ct. (ea. and so. dists.) N.Y. 1979, U.S. Tax Ct. 1986, D.C. 1988, U.S. Ct. Appeals (2d cir.) 1988, U.S. Supreme Ct. 1988, Conn. 1989. Asst. dist. atty. Borough of Bronx, N.Y.C., 1978-85; prin. atty. N.Y. State Tax Dept., 1985-87; supervising atty. Office of Profl. Discipline, N.Y. State Edn. Dept., 1987—. Prof. law and taxation Pace U., 1987—. Contbr. articles to profl. jours. Mem. Conn. Bar Assn, N.Y. State Bar Assn., D.C. Bar Assn. Conservative. Roman Catholic. Office: NY State Edn Dept 475 Park Ave S Frnt 3 New York NY 10016-6901 E-mail: dspillan@mail.nysed.gov.

SPILLANE, MARY CATHERINE, television producer; b. S.I., N.Y., Nov. 30, 1956; d. Joseph Bernard and Mary Catherine (Minoque) Spillane. BA, U. Hartford, 1978. Exec. sec. CBS Evening News, N.Y.C., 1978-80, asst. to prodr., 1980; weekend prodr./E.N.G. coord. Sta. KTVI-TV, St. Louis, 1981-82, spl. projects prodr., 1982-83, asst. news dir., 1983-86; assoc. prodr. CBS News, Detroit, 1986, N.Y.C., 1986-87, sr. prodr., 1987-89, Washington, 1989-93, prodr., 1993-99, CBS Weekend News, London, 1999—. Avocations: reading, travel, cooking, gardening. Office: CBS News 68 Knightsbridge London SW1X 7LL England

SPILLER, EBERHARD ADOLF, physicist, researcher; b. Halbendorf, Ger., Apr. 16, 1933; came to U.S., 1968; s. Walter Richard and Ruth Elfriede (Radzey) S.; m. Marga Dietz, Dec. 18, 1964; children— Michael, Bettina. Diploma, U. Frankfurt, Ger., 1960, PhD, 1964. Asst. U. Frankfurt, 1960-68, mem. faculty, 1966-68; physicist IBM Research Center, Yorktown Heights, N.Y., 1968-93; emeritus physicist IBM, 1993-97. Guest prof. Tech. U. Denmark, 1994-95, U. Ctrl. Fla., 1996; vis. scientist Nat. Inst. Stds. and Tech., 1997—, Lawrence Livermore Lab., Calif., 1997—. Author: Soft X-Ray Optics, 1994. Fellow AAAS, Am. Optical Soc.; mem. German Phys. Soc., Photo-Optic Instrumentation Soc. Achievements include research in solid state physics, laser and coherence optics, nonlinear optics, thin films, soft x-rays, x-ray microscopy, lithography; inventor multilayer x-ray optics, x-ray astronomy, x-ray lithography. Office: Lawrence Livermore Nat Lab MS-L395 Livermore CA 94551 E-mail: spiller@llnl.gov., espill@attglobal.net.

SPILLER, GENE ALAN, nutritionist, health facility administrator; b. Milan, Feb. 19, 1927; came to U.S., 1950, naturalized, 1962; s. Silvio and Beatrice (Galli) S. D of Chemistry, U. Milan, 1949; MS, U. Calif., Berkeley, 1968, PhD in Nutrition, 1972. Cert. nutrition specialist. Cons. nutrition rsch. and edn., L.A., 1952-65; rsch. chemist U. Calif., Berkeley, 1966-67, assoc. specialist physiology dept., 1968-72; prin. scientist, head nutritional physiology Syntex Rsch., Palo Alto, Calif., 1972-80; cons. clin. nutrition rsch. Los Altos, 1981—; head Health Rsch. and Studies Ctr., 1988—. Lectr. Mills Coll., Oakland, Calif., 1971-81, Foothill Coll., Los Altos, 1974—. Co-author: The Last Puff, 1990; editor: Fiber in Human Nutrition, 1976, Topics in Dietary Fiber, 1978, Medical aspects of Dietary Fiber, 1980, Nutritional Pharmacology, 1981, The Methylxanthine Beverages and Foods, 1984, CRC Handbook of Dietary Fiber in Human Nutrition, 1986, 3d edit., 2001, New Protective Roles for Selected Nutrients, 1989, The Mediterranean Diets in Health and Disease, 1991, The Superpyramid Eating Program, 1993, CRC Handbook of Lipids, 1995, Nutrition Secrets of the Ancients, 1996, Cancer Survivor's Nutrition & Health Guide, 1996—, Caffeine, 1997, Healthy Nuts, 2000, Calcium Power, 2000, Diagnosis Heart Disease, 2000, CRC Handbook of Dietary Fiber, 2001; rev. Jour. Am. Coll. Nutrition, 1976-95. Pres. SPHERA Found., 1990—. Mem. Am. Inst. Nutrition, Am. Soc. Clin. Nutrition, Brit. Nutrition Soc., Am. Assn. Cereal Chemists, Am. Diabetes Assn., Am. Coll. Nutrition, Alpine Hills Club..

Achievements include research on human nutrition; prin. investigator in human nutrition studies; dietary fibers, lipids, and carbohydrates effect on humna health; role of lesser known food components in nutrition; effect of whole foods vs. single nutrients; food antioxidants. Office: Health Rsch and Studies Ctr 340 2nd St Los Altos CA 94022-3624 E-mail: spiller@sphera.org.

SPILLERS, JAMES ANDREW, Bible and history educator, minister; b. Madison, Tenn., Mar. 29, 1968; s. Harold Loyd Spillers, Jr. and Marsha Lee (Hinkle) Mullen. AAS, Vol. State C.C., Gallatin, Tenn., 1988; BA, David Lipscomb U., 1992, MA in Religion, 1994; D Ministry, Theol. U. Am., 1998. Tchr. Bible, history Ezell-Harding Christian Sch., Antioch, Tenn., 1994—, chmn. dept. Bible, 1995—; adj. faculty/instr. David Lipscomb U., Nashville, 1995. Tchr. Bible Rivergate Ch. of Christ, Madison, Tenn., 1988-99, Mid-South Sch. Bibl. Studies, Madison, 1999—. Author: Study Guide to the Book of Numbers, 1993, Study Guide to the Book of Revelation, 1999. Mem. Sigma Tau Delta (life). Mem. Ch. of Christ. Avocations: writing, public speaking, art, philately. Home: 3211 Monthaven Park Pl Hendersonville TN 37075

SPILLERS, WILLIAM RUSSELL, civil engineering educator; b. Fresno, Calif., Aug. 4, 1934; s. William Horton and Marguerite Ester (Johnson) S.; m. Priscilla Watson, Sept. 10, 1960 (div. 1981); children: Sarah, William, Lars; m. Sandra Lynn Newsome, July 15, 1983 (div. 1995); m. Joy Bechard, Mar. 13, 2000. Student, Fresno State Coll., 1951-53; BS, U. Calif., Berkeley, 1955, MS, 1956; PhD, Columbia U., 1961. Registered profl. engr., N.Y., N.J. Structural engr. John Blume Assocs., San Francisco, 1956-57; teaching asst. Columbia U., N.Y.C., 1957-61, prof. civil engring. and engring. mechanics, 1961-76; prof. civil engring. Rensellaer Poly. Inst., Troy, N.Y., 1976-90; prof., chmn. civil and environ. engring. N.J. Inst. Tech., Newark, 1990—, disting. prof. civil and environ. engring., 1995—. Cons. Weidlinger Assoc., N.Y.C., 1957-76, Geiger Berger Assoc., N.Y.C., 1957-76, DeLeuw Oh Eocha, Manchester, Eng., 1974, Parsons Hawaii, L.A., 1983, Horst Berger Ptnrs., N.Y.C., 1980; organizer NSF workshop on design theory, Troy, N.Y., 1988. Author: Automated Structural Analysis, 1972, Iterative Structural Design, 1975, Intro Structures, 1985; (with R. Levy) Analysis of Geometrically Nonlinear Structures, 1995, Introduction to Structures, 2002; editor 4 books including Design Theory, 1988; contbr. over 140 articles to profl. jours. Named Educator of Yr. award, Cons. Engrs. Coun. N.J., 1998; NSF fellow, 1976, Guggenheim fellow, 1968. Mem. ASCE (numerous coms., chmn. exec. com. TCCP, 1987), Internat. Assn. Bridge & Structural Engrs. Democrat. Achievements include contribution to the development of fabric structures; initiated the science of design theory; participated in development of applications of digital computers to large structural systems. Home: 7 Oak Ave West Orange NJ 07052-2409 Office: NJ Inst Tech Dept Civil & Environ Engring Newark NJ 07102

SPILLETT, ROXANNE, social services administrator; 1 son, Keith. BA in Edn., SUNY; postgrad., St. Lawrence U., Hunter Coll., N.Y. Tchr., curriculum writer N.Y. State Schs., 1971-73; program specialist Girl Scouts U.S.A., 1973; dir. nat. health project Boys & Girls Clubs Am., Atlanta, 1978-79, dir. program svcs., 1979-91, asst. nat. dir. program svcs., 1991-1995, v.p. N.E. regional office, 1995, acting pres., 1995-96, pres., 1996—; vice chmn. Advisory Comm. on Safe Spaces, President's Summit for America's Future. Mem.: bd. of dir. National Assembly and American Humanities. Office: Boys & Girls Clubs Am 1230 W Peachtree St NW Atlanta GA 30309-3404*

SPILLIAS, KENNETH GEORGE, lawyer; b. Steubenville, Ohio, Nov. 8, 1949; s. George and Angeline (Bouyoucas) S.; m. Monica Mary Saumweber, May 10, 1975; children: Geoffrey David, Alicia Anne, Stephanie Marie. BA, Pa. State U., 1971; JD magna cum laude, U. Pitts., 1974. Bar: Pa. 1974, Fla. 1978, U.S. Supreme Ct. 1978, U.S. Ct. Appeals (2d, 3d, 4th, 5th, 6th cirs.) 1975, (11th cir.) 1981, U.S. Dist. Ct. (mid. dist.) Fla. 1979, U.S. Dist. Ct. (so. dist.) Fla. 1978; cert. cir. ct. mediator. Trial atty. U.S. Dept. Justice, Washington, 1974-76; asst. dist. atty. Dist. Atty. of Allegheny County, Pitts., 1976-78; asst. atty. gen. Fla. Dept. Legal Affairs, West Palm Beach, Fla., 1978-79; ptnr. Spillias & Mitchell, 1979-82, Considine & Spillias, West Palm Beach, 1982-83, Schneider, Maxwell, Spillias et al, West Palm Beach, 1984-86, Wolf, Block, Schorr et al, West Palm Beach, 1986-88, Shapiro & Bregman, West Palm Beach, 1988-91; of counsel Greenberg, Traurig et al, 1991; pvt. practice, 1991-97; ptnr. Lewis, Longman & Walker, P.A., 1997—. Instr. bus. law Coll. of the Palm Beaches, West Palm Beach, 1980-81; CLE lectr. Palm Beach County Bar Assn., 1983—. County commr. Bd. County Commrs., Palm Beach County, 1982-86; co-founder, mem. Children's Svcs. Coun., Palm Beach County, 1986-91; steering com. Fla. Atlantic U. Inst. of Govt., Boca Raton, 1983-94; bd. dirs. The Literacy Coalition of P.B.C., West Palm Beach, 1990-2000, health and human svcs. Fla. Dist. IX, 1995-98, Ctr. for Family Svc., West Palm Beach, 1992-96, Palm Beach County Coun. of Arts, 1987-1988, West Palm Beach Planning Bd., 1997—; mem. policy coun. Fla. Inst. Govt., Tallahassee, 1985-86; fund raising chmn. United Cerebral Palsey Telethon, West Palm Beach, 1984-85; judge Palm Beach Post Pathfinders Awards, 1992-98. Recipient Cmty. Svc. award Downtown Civitan Club, West Palm Beach, 1983, Man of the Day award United Cerebral Palsey, 1986, Spl. Honoree award Palm Beach County Child Advocacy Bd., 1986, Children's Trust award Exch. Club/Dick Webber Ctr. for Prevention Child Abuse, 1991, Up and Comers Award in Law, South Fla. Bus. Jour./Price Waterhouse, 1988, Achievement award Nat. Assn. Counties, 1986; named to Outstanding Young Men of Am., U.S. Jaycees, 1975, 84. Mem. ABA, Palm Beach County Bar Assn. (appellate practice com. 1990—), Am. Hellenic Ednl. Progressive Assn. Fla. Bar Assn. (pres. 2001-2002, appellate advocacy and city, county and local govt. sects.), Order of Coif, Kiwanis. Avocations: sports, writing, theater, reading, music. Home: 147 Gregory Rd West Palm Beach FL 33405-5029 Office: Ste 1000 1700 Palm Beach Lakes Blvd West Palm Beach FL 33401-2006

SPILLMAN, JANE SHADEL, curator, researcher, writer; b. Huntsville, Ala., Apr. 30, 1942; d. Marvin and Elizabeth (Russell) Shadel; m. Don Lewis Spillman, Feb. 18, 1973 (dec. Jan. 1999); children: K. Elizabeth, Samuel Shadel. AB, Vassar Coll., 1964; MA, SUNY, 1965. Rsch. asst. Corning (N.Y.) Mus. Glass, 1965-70, asst. curator, 1971-73, assoc. curator Am. glass, 1974-77, curator, 1978—, head of curatorial dept., 1994-99, dep. dir. collections, 1999—. Cons. The White House Curator's Office, Washington, 1987-90, other museums. Author: Complete Cut and Engraved Glass of Corning, 1979, rev. edit., 1997, Knopf Collectors Guide to Glass, Vol. 1, 1982, Vol. 2, 1983, White House Glassware, 1989, Masterpieces of American Glass, 1990, The American Cut Glass Industry: T.G. Hawkes and His Competitors, 1996, also 6 other books, numerous articles; editor The Glass Club Bull., 1999—. Mem. Am. Assn. Mus. (chairperson curators com. 1989-93), Nat. Early Am. Glass Club (bd. dirs. 1989-95), Glass Circle of London. Office: Corning Mus Glass 1 Museum Way Corning NY 14830-2253

SPILLMAN, NANCY ZOE, economics and law educator; b. Chgo.; d. Leo and Sarah S.; student Los Angeles City Coll., 1958-61; B.S. magna cum laude, U. So. Calif., 1963, M.B.A.,1965; postgrad. Claremont U., 1966-68, UCLA, 1969-73. Faculty, Los Angeles Trade Tech. Coll., 1968— , now prof. econs.; pres. Econ. Edn. Enterprises, cons. firm; mem. Calif. State Atty. Gen.'s Subcom. Consumer Edn.; former mem. consumer adv. council Fed. Res. Bd.; expert witness House subcom. on Consumer Affairs and Coinage and U.S. CPSC Comptroller of Currency Conf.; condr. radio program Consumer Mailbag, Sta. KJOI, Los Angeles. Bd. dirs. Consumer Credit Counselors, Los Angeles; mem. State of Calif. Retail Credit Adv. Com. (cons.); public mem. Calif. Beef Council. Recipient Freedoms Found. award, 1981. Mem. Am. Economic Assn., U.S. Metric Assn. (past nat. sec.), Standards Engring. Soc., Am. Council Consumer Interests (editor Consumer Edn. Forum), U. So. Calif. M.B.A. Alumni Assn. (former editor alumni bull.). Editor: Consumers: Personal Planning Reader; author: Bright Ideas for Consumer Educators; Personal Finance Study Guide; series of consumer articles Glendale Fed. and Silver Circle mags.; contbr. articles to profl. jours. Office: Los Angeles Trade Technical College 400 W Washington Blvd Los Angeles CA 90015-4108

SPILLMAN, ROBERT ARNOLD, architect; b. Bethlehem, Pa., May 21, 1931; s. Otto Henry and Ruth Meredith (Miller) S.; m. Cidney Jane Brandon, July 7, 1956; children: Catherine, Sarah, Peter. BArch, Cornell U., 1954. Registered arch., Pa., N.J. Archtl. designer Office Douglass Orr, New Haven, 1956-58; ptnr. Lovelace & Spillman, Archs., Bethlehem, 1959-70; sr. ptnr. Spillman Farmer Archs., 1971-82; pres. Spillman Farmer Shoemaker Pell Whildin, P.C., 1983—96, sr. prin., 1997—. Trustee Laros Found., Bethlehem, 1970—; pres. Bethlehem Libr. Bd., 1970-74, United Way Northampton and Warren Counties, 1979-81, Lehigh River Found., 1992-95; v.p. Lehigh Valley Indsl. Parks, 1985-96, pres., 1996-2001; chmn. Bethlehem Bd. Hist. Archtl. Rev., 1961-82; Olympic torchbearer, 1996. 1st lt. USAF, 1954-56. Fellow AIA (pres. Ea. Pa. chpt. 1969-70); mem. Pa. Soc. Archs. (disting. bldg. awards 1971, 76, 78, 94), Soc. Coll. and Univ. Planners, Bay Head Yacht Club (N.J.) (rear commodore 1985-87, vice commodore 1999-2001, commodore 2001—). Democrat. Episcopalian. Office: Spillman Farmer Shoemaker Pell 1 Bethlehem Plz Ste 1000 Bethlehem PA 18018-5716

SPILMAN, ROBERT HENKEL, furniture company executive; b. Knoxville, Tenn., Sept. 27, 1927; s. Robert Redd and Lila (Henkel) S.; m. Jane Bassett, Apr. 2, 1955; children: Robert Henkel Jr., Virginia Perrin, Vance Henkel. BS, N.C. State U., 1950. With Cannon Mills, 1950-57; with Bassett Table Co., Va., 1957-60; dir. Bassett Furniture Industries Inc., 1960—97, exec. v.p., 1966, pres., 1966-89, CEO, 1979—97, chmn., 1982—97, ret., 1997. Bd. dirs. Dominion Resources, Inc., Richmond, Va., Internat. Home Furnishing Ctr., High Point, N.C., Birmingham Steel Co.; adv. bd. Liberty Mut. Ins. Co. Trustee Va. Found. Ind. Colls., Darden Sch. Found., N.C. State U.; bd. dirs. Blue Ridge Airport Authority. Lt. U.S. Army, WWII and Korea. Recipient Best Chief Exec. Officer in Home Furnishing Industry award Wall Street Transcript, 1981, 82; named Humanitarian of Yr., City of Hope, 1982 Mem. Am. Furniture Mfrs. Assn. (James T. Ryan award 1984), Nat. Furniture Mfrs. Assn. (bd. dirs., past pres.), Furniture Factories Mktg. Assn. (past chmn., bd. dirs.), Va. Mfrs. Assn. (past dir. exec. com.), Bassett Country Club, Chatmoss Country Club, Commonwealth Club, Linville Golf Club, Grandfather Golf and Country Club (Linville, N.C.), The Country Club Va., Olde Farm (Bristol, Va.), Foundry Golf Club (Powhatan, Va.). Episcopalian. Avocation: fishing. Office: Spilman Industries PO Box 880 Bassett VA 24055 E-mail: bspilman@neocom.net.

SPINA, ANTHONY FERDINAND, lawyer; b. Chgo., Aug. 15, 1937; s. John Dominic and Nancy Maria (Ponzio) S.; m. Anita Phyllis De Orio, Jan. 28, 1961; children: Nancy M. Spina Okal, John D., Catherine M. Spina Samatas, Maria J. Spina Samatas, Felicia M. BS in Social Sci., Loyola U., Chgo., 1959; JD, DePaul U., 1962. Bar: Ill. 1962. Assoc. Epton, Scott, McCarthy & Bohling, Chgo., 1962-64; pvt. practice Elmwood Park, Ill., 1964-71; pres. Anthony & Spina, PC, 1971-84, Spina, McGuire & Okal, PC, Elmwood Park, 1985—. Codifier Rosemont Village Ordinances, 1971, Elmwood Park Bldg. Code, 1975, Leyden Twp. Codified Ordinances, 1987. Mem. Elmwood Pk. Bldg. Code Planning Commn. Bd. Appeals; bd. dirs. Sheridan Carrol Charitable Works Fund, 1994—; atty. Leyden Twp., Ill., 1969—89, Village of Rosemont, 1971; counsel for Pres. and dir. Cook County Twp. Ofcls. Ill., 1975—96; counsel for exec. dir. Ill. State Assn. Twp. Ofcls., 1975—96; counsel Elmwood Park Village Bd., 1967—89, Norwood Park St. Lighting Dist., 1988—, various Cook County Twps. including DuPage, 1980—82, Maine, 1981—97, Norwood Park, 1982—, Wayne, 1982—84, Berwyn Twp., 1997—99, Hanover Twp., 1997, Cook County Hwy. Commrs. Traffic Fine Litigation, 1974—96, 1999—2001, Hanover Twp. Mental Health Bd., 1991—, Glen Edens Assn., 1994—99, Berwyn Twp. Mental Health Bd., 1997—. Recipient Lacodaire medal, Deans Key Loyola U., Loyola U. Housing awards, 1965, 71, 76; Appreciation award Cook County Twp. Ofcls., av rating Martindale-Hubbel. Mem. ABA, Ill. Bar Assn., Chgo. Bar Assn., West Suburban Bar Assn. Cook County (past chmn. unauthorized practice law sect.), Am. Judicature Soc., Justinian Soc. Lawyers, Ill. State Twp. Attys. Assn. (past v.p., pres. 1982-86, dir. 1996-99, dir. emeritus 1999—), Nat. Inst. Town and Twp. Attys. (past v.p., pres. 1993-95, Ill. del.), Montclare/Leyden C. of C., Edgebrook C. of C. (past bd. dirs.), Nat. Assn. Italian Am. Lawyers, Joint Civic Com. Chgo. (exec. com.), World Bocce Assn. (dir.), St. Rocco Soc. Simbario, KC (scribe, trustee, past Grand Knight, bldg. corp. dir. 1967-99), Calabresi in Am. Orgn. (bd. dirs. 1991—), Fra Noi Ethnic Publ. (dir. 1995—), Blue Key, Delta Theta Phi, Tau Kappa Epsilon, Pi Gamma Mu. Roman Catholic. Office: 7610 W North Ave Elmwood Park IL 60707-4100 E-mail: spinalaw@aol.com.

SPINA, FRANCIS X. Supreme Court Judge; m. Sally O'Donnell; 2 children. BA, Amherst Coll.; JD, Boston Coll. Prosecutor, Berkshire County, Mass., 1979—83; pvt. law practice Pittsfield, 1983—93; judge Mass. Superior Ct., 1993-97, Appeals Ct., Pittsfield, 1997-99; assoc. justice Mass. Supreme Jud. Ct., Boston, 1999—. Office: Mass Supreme Ct New Ct House Pemberton Sq Boston MA 02108*

SPINA, HORACIO ANSELMO, psychiatrist, educator; b. Buenos Aires, Mar. 19, 1939; came to U.S., 1970; s. Antonio and Rosa Palma S.; m. Patricia Anne Duffy, Apr. 4, 1985; children: Alicia V., Cristina V., Mario A. Student, Nat. U. Cordoba, Argentina, 1968; MD in Psychiatry, U. Pitts., 1974. Diplomate Am. Bd. Psychiatry and Neurology. Resident psychiatry U. Pitts., 1971-74; rotating intern Shadyside Hosp., Pitts., 1970-71; med. dir. psychiat. svcs. and chem. dependence program St. Clair Mem. Hosp., 1980-2000; clin. asst. prof. psychiatry U. Pitts., 1986—90; med. dir. geriatric psychiatry St. Clair Meml. Hosp., 1996-2000, chmn. dept. psychiatry, 2001—. Mem. InterAm. Coll. Physicians and Surgeons, Cordoba Soc. Pharmacology and Therapeutics, N.Y. Acad. Scis., Am. Soc. Clin. Psychopharmacology, Acad. Psychosomatic Medicine, Nat. Alliance for Mentally Ill. Avocations: computers, music. Office: 1050 Bower Hill Rd Ste 303 Pittsburgh PA 15243-1869 E-mail: hspina@aol.com.

SPINA, MARY T. university official; b. Chgo., Nov. 24, 1961; d. Michael F. and Diane M. Nemeth; m. Philip V. Spina, Apr. 25, 1997. AA, Felician Coll., Chgo., 1980; BBA, Loyola U., Chgo., 1984. Cert. rsch. adminstr. Project contr., adminstr. dept. ob-gyn. Northwestern U. Med. Sch., Chgo., 1984-87, rsch. coord., 1987-91; dir. grants adminstrn. Rehab. Inst. Chgo., 1991-98; dir. sponsored rsch. and programs Ill. Inst. Tech., 1998—. Cons. Physicians Against Land Mines, Chgo., 1997-99. Contbr. articles to profl. jours. Recipient Founders award, Midwest sect. Soc. Rsch. Adminstrn., 1999, Hartford-Nicholsen award, Soc. Rsch. Adminstrn. Internat., 2001. Mem. Soc. Rsch. Adminstrs. Internat. (various offices 1992—), Rsch. Adminstrs. Cert. Coun. Avocation: scuba diving.

SPINDEL, ROBERT CHARLES, electrical engineering educator; b. N.Y.C., Sept. 5, 1944; s. Morris Tayson and Isabel (Glazer) S.; m. Barbara June Sullivan, June 12, 1966; children: Jennifer Susan, Miranda Ellen BSEE, Cooper Union, 1965; MS, Yale U., 1966, MPhil, 1968, PhD, 1971. Postdoctoral fellow Woods Hole Oceanographic Instn., Mass., 1971-72, asst. scientist, 1972-76, assoc. scientist, 1976-82, sr. scientist, 1982-87, chmn. dept. ocean engring., 1982-87; dir. applied physics lab. U. Wash., Seattle, 1987—. Mem. naval studies bd. NRC, 1987-99; mem. Naval Rsch. Adv. Com., 1998—. Contbr. articles to profl. jours.; patentee on underwater nav. Recipient A.B. Wood medal Brit. Inst. Acoustics, 1981, Gano Dunn medal The Cooper Union, 1989, Ocean Engr. Soc. Tech. Achievement award, 1990. Fellow IEEE (assoc. editor jour. 1982—), Acoustical Soc. Am., Marine Tech. Soc. (pres. elect 1991-93, pres. 1993-95), Oceanography Soc. (Munk award 2001). Independent. Jewish. Avocations: automobile restoration, hiking. Home: 14859 SE 51st St Bellevue WA 98006-3515 Office: U Wash Applied Physics Lab 1013 NE 40th St Seattle WA 98105-6606 E-mail: spindel@APL.Washington.edu.

SPINDEL, WILLIAM, retired chemist, consultant; b. N.Y.C., Sept. 9, 1922; s. Joseph and Esther (Goldstein) S.; m. Sara Lew, 1942 (div. 1966); children: Robert Andrew, Lawrence Marshall; m. Louise Phyllis Hoodenpyl, July 30, 1967. BA, Bklyn. Coll., 1944; MA, Columbia U., 1947, PhD, 1950. Jr. scientist Los Alamos Lab, Manhattan Dist., 1944-45; instr. Poly. Inst., Bklyn., 1949-50; assoc. prof. SUNY, 1950-54; rsch. assoc., vis. prof. Columbia U., 1954-57, vis. prof., sr. lectr., 1962-74; from assoc. prof. to prof. Rutgers U., 1957-64; prof., chmn. dept. chemistry Belfer Grad. Sch. Sci., Yeshiva U., 1964-74; exec. sec., office chemistry and chem. tech. NAS-NRC, 1974-81, also staff dir. bd. on chem. scis. and tech., prin. staff officer commn. phys. scis., math. and resources, 1982-90, sr. cons., 1990-97; ret., 1997. Vis. Am. scientist, Yugoslavia, 1971-72. Contbr. articles to profl. jours. Served with AUS, 1943-46. Recipient profl. staff award NRC, 1985, Lifetime Achievement award Bklyn. Coll., CUNY, 1999; Guggenheim fellow, 1961-62; Fulbright Research scholar, 1961-62 Fellow AAAS; mem. Am. Chem. Soc. Clubs: Cosmos. Achievements include research on separation of stable isotopes, isotope effects on chemical and biological processes; developed chemical exchange process for concentrating nitrogen-15. Home: 6503 Dearborn Dr Falls Church VA 22044-1116 E-mail: wspindel@cs.com. *Working at and for the sciences has yielded a most fulfilling professional life.*

SPINDLER, GEORGE DEARBORN, anthropologist, educator, writer, editor; b. Stevens Point, Wis., Feb. 28, 1920; s. Frank Nicholas and Winifred (Hatch) S.; m. Louise Schaubel, May 29, 1942 (dec. Feb. 1997); 1 dau., Sue Carol Spindler Coleman. BS, Central State Tchrs. Coll., Wis., 1940; MA, U. Wis., 1947; PhD, U. Calif. at Los Angeles, 1952. Tchr. sch. in, Wis., 1940-42; research asso. Stanford, 1950-51, mem. faculty, 1951—, prof. anthropology and edn., 1960-78, exec. head dept., 1963-67, 84; editor Am. Anthropologist, 1962-66. Cons. editor Holt, Rinehart & Winston, 1965-91, Harcourt, 1991-99, Wadsworth-Thomas, 2000—; vis. prof. U. Wis., 1979-85, U. Calif., Santa Barbara, 1986-91, Harvard U., 1999. Author: Menomini Acculturation, 1955, (with A. Beals and L. Spindler) Culture in Process, 1967, rev. edit., 1973, Transmission of American Culture, 1959, (with L. Spindler) Dreamers Without Power, 1971, rev. edit., 1984, Burgbach: Urbanization and Identity in a German Village, 1973, (with Louise Spindler) The American Cultural Dialogue and its Transmission, 1990; editor: Education and Anthropology, 1955, (with Louise Spindler) Case Studies in Cultural Anthropology, 1960—, Methods in Cultural Anthropology, 1965—, Case Studies in Education and Culture, 1966—, Basic Units in Anthropology, 1970; editor, contbr.: Education and Culture, 1963, Being An Anthropologist, 1970, Education and Cultural Process, 1974, rev. edit., 1987, 97, The Making of Psychological Anthropology, 1978, 2nd edit., 1994, Doing the Ethnography of Schooling, 1982, Interpretive Ethnography of Schooling at Home and Abroad, 1987, Pathways to Cultural Awareness: Cultural Therapy with Students and Teachers, 1994, Fifty Years of Anthropology and Education: A Spindler Anthology, 2000. Pres. Peninsula Sch. Bd., Menlo Park, Calif., 1954-56. Served with AUS, 1942-45. Recipient Lloyd W. Dinkelspeil award Stanford U., 1978, Disting. Svc. award Soc. Internat. Diplomacy and Third World Anthropologists, 1984, Disting. Career Contbn. award Com. on Role and Status of Minorities, Am. Edn. Rsch. Assn., Nat. Acad. Edn., 1994, Father of Ednl. Ethnography award Nat. Ednl. Ethnography Conf., 2000, George and Louise Spindler award for Excellence in Anthropology Stanford U., 2001; fellow Ctr. Advanced Study of Behavioral Scis., 1956-57; subject of Vol. 17 Psychoanalytic Study of Soc. essays, 1992. Fellow Am. Anthrop. Assn.; mem. Southwestern Anthrop. Assn. (pres. 1962-63), Coun. for Anthropology and Edn. (pres. 1982, George and Louise Spindler award for outstanding contbns. to ednl. anthropology 1987, disting. Scholar award 1998), Nat. Acad. Edn. Office: Ethnographics 1247 Alice St Davis CA 95616-2174 E-mail: geospinner@aol.com. *My major aims as a professional observer and interpreter of human behavior are to acquire knowledge by research and disseminate understanding to others by teaching, writing, and editing. As a person I try to keep love, work, play in balanced relationship to each other, and strive for tolerance at least, and hopefully appreciation for others who are different than myself.*

SPINDLER, JAMES ANDREW, not-for-profit executive; b. Morgantown, W.Va., Oct. 20, 1950; s. Garold Ralph and Elizabeth (Carroll) Spindler; m. Ann Bailie Trautman; children: James Andrew, Jr. AB, Harvard Coll., Cambridge, Mass., 1972; MPA, Princeton U., 1975, PhD, 1983. Bus. fellow The Brookings Instn., Washington, 1980—82; v.p. Continental Ill. Nat. Bank., Chgo., 1984—85, Fed. Res. Bank of N.Y., N.Y.C., 1985—89, sr. v.p., 1989—93; mng. dir. Fin. Svcs. Vol. Corps, 1993—95, exec. dir., 1995—. Prin. investigator The Russia Initiative Project of the Carnegie Corp. of N.Y., N.Y.C., 2000—01; mem. Basle Com. on Banking Supervision, Basle, Switzerland, 1991—93, G10 Com. on Payment and Settlement Systems, Basle, Switzerland, 1991—93. Author: The Politics of International Credit: Private Finance and Foreign Policy in Germany and Japan, 1984, (Op-Ed Pieces) International Herald Tribune, San Francisco Chronicle, and The Jakarta Post, 2001. Recipient Medal of Svc. for assistance in developing Russian fin. mkts., Ctrl. Bank of Russia and the Russian Finance Ministry, 1996. Mem.: Am. Coun. on Germany, Coun. on Fgn. Relations. Presbyterian. Avocations: classical music, travel, opera, running. Office: Financial Services Volunteer Corps 10 E 53d St 24th Flr New York NY 10022 Office Fax: 212-421-2162. Business E-Mail: jspindler@fsvc.org.

SPINDLER, JUDITH TARLETON, elementary school educator; b. Dayton, Tenn., Mar. 4, 1932; d. Frank Willson and Julia Elizabeth (Venable) S. BS in Edn., Longwood Coll., 1953; MA in Edn., Va. Commonwealth U., 1976. Tchr. Oceana, King's Grant Sch., Virginia Beach, Va., 1953-66, Ginter Park Elem. Sch., Richmond, 1966-67, Bon Air Elem. Sch., Chesterfield County, 1967-87; ret., 1987. Charter mem. Web of Hope sponsored by ARC (Humanitarian award). Recipient 80 ribbons for 1st, 2nd and 3rd pl. awards various knitting competitions, 5 Best in Show awards rosette competition, including blue ribbons State Fair Va., 1998, 6 ribbons Best in Show rosette Chesterfield County Fair, 1998, 2 Best in Show Chesterfield County Fair, 1 Best in Show State Fair of Va., 3 Blue Ribbons Chesterfield County Fair, 2000, 2 Red Ribbons, 1 White Ribbon Va. State Fair, 2000, 3 Blue Ribbons Chesterfield County Fair, 2 Red Ribbons, 1 White Ribbon Va. State Fair. Mem. NEA, Va. Edn. Assn., Knitting Guild Am. (qualified tchr.), Knit Wit Guild (founding mem.). Avocation: knitting. Home: 4103 Hyde Park Dr Chester VA 23831-4826

SPINDLER, PAUL, corporate executive, consultant; b. Chgo., May 2, 1931; s. Isaac Edward and Sophie (Stein) Spindler; m. Gail Klynn; children from previous marriage: Kevin, Makayla, Sydney, Jeffrey. BA in Journalism, Temple U., 1952. Reporter Akron Beacon Jour., Akron, Ohio, 1955-58, San Francisco Examiner, 1958-59; editor Santa Clara (Calif.) Daily Jour., 1959-63; dir. pub. affairs Litton Industries, Inc., Beverly Hills, Calif., 1963-68; dir. pub. relations Internat. Industries, 1968-70; pres. Paul Spindler & Co., L.A., 1970-75; exec. v.p. Manning Selvage & Lee, Inc., N.Y.C., 1975-85; pres. The Spindler Co., L.A., 1985-87; pres. Western div. GCI Group, 1987-91; pres. GCI Spindler, 1991-96; chmn. Bristol Retail Solutions, Inc., Newport Beach, Calif., 1996-98; pres. Paul Spindler Co., L.A., 1998—. Bd. dirs. Phoenix House Calif. Cpl. U.S. Army, 1952-54. With U.S. Army, 1952—54. Mem. Mountain Gate Country Club (L.A.). Democrat. Jewish. Office: Paul Spindler Co 5410 Wilshire Blvd Ste 906 Los Angeles CA 90036 E-mail: paul@spindlercompany.com.

SPINELLA, J(OSEPH) JOHN, insurance company executive; b. Queens, N.Y., Jan. 13, 1946; s. Peter Paul and Catherine (Vecchio) S.; m. MaryAnn D. Spinella, Feb. 1, 1969; children: Donna, Debra. BS in Math., SUNY, Cortland, 1972. Actuarial asst. Aetna Life & Casualty, Hartford, Conn., 1971-77; assoc. actuary INA Ins. Co., Phila., 1977-82; exec. v.p., chief operating officer Med. Mut. Liability Insurance Soc. of Md., Towson, 1982-85; pres., COO Med. Mut. Liability Ins. Soc. of Md., 1985, pres., CEO, 1986-87; pres. Spinella & Assocs., Inc., Balt., 1987-92, 95—; pres. med. profl. liability divsn. Great Am. Ins. Co., Hunt Valley, Md., 1992-95. Mem. Gov.'s commn. on health care providers profl. liability ins., 1983-85, Gov.'s joint exec. legis. task force on med. malpractice, 1985, Annapolis, Md.; bd. dirs. Interstate Automobile Ins. Co., 1990-92, 1995—, Commonwealth Mut. Ins. Co., 1995—. Mem. Md. Hosp. Assn. tort reform task force, Towson, 1985. Roman Catholic. Avocations: golf, tennis, squash. Home: 11 David Luther Ct Cockeysville Hunt Valley MD 21030-1741

SPINELLI, ANNE CATHERINE, elementary education educator; b. Chgo., Dec. 19, 1943; d. Stanley J. and Lucy A. (Schmidt) Malaski; m. Joseph P. Spinelli Jr., May 28, 1966. BS in Edn., Ohio U., 1965; postgrad., Ashland U., 1989—. Lic. tchr. kindergarten - 8th grade. Tchr. K-3 North Olmsted (Ohio) City Schs., 1965-70, master tchr., 1970-71, kindergarten tchr., 1971-74, Cloverleaf Schs., Lodi, Ohio, 1974—99; ret., 1999. Seminar presenter sci. dept. Ednl. Rsch. Coun. Am., Cleve., 1969-74, State of Ohio Supr. Assn., Columbus, 1986, Great Lakes Internat. Reading Assn., Chgo., 1993; panelist Ohio Coun. Elem. Sch. Sci. Conv., Akron, 1969; speaker Nat. Sci. Tchrs. Assn. Great Lakes Conf., Cleve., 1971, State of Ohio Proficiency Conf., Cleve., 1996, 97, 98, 2000. Co-author: North Olmsted Schools Motor Perception Book for Kindergarten, 1970, Kindergarten Home Activities Book, 1991—2002. Mem. Zoning Commn., Westfield Twp., Medina County, Ohio, 1978-90; area coord. Cancer Soc., Medina County, 1983, 85, 89, 98; mem. Zoning Bd. Appeals, Westfield Twp Medina County, Ohio, 1996-99. Jennings scholar Jennings Found., N.E. Ohio, 1987-88; named Outstanding Educator/Acad. Subjects Mid East Ohio/Spl. Edn. Regional Resouce Ctr., 1994, Medina County (Ohio) Tchr. of the Year, 1995; finalist Tchr. of Yr. for

Ohio, 1996. Mem. ASCD, NEA, Ohio Edn. Assn., No. Ohio Edn. Assn., N.E. Ohio Edn. Assn., Cloverleaf Edn. Assn. (bldg. reps. 1985-99), Internat. Reading Assn., Lizotte Reading Coun., Elem., Kindergarten, Nursery Sch. Educators. Avocations: travel, gardening. Office: Westfield Elem Sch 9055 S LeRoy Rd Westfield Center OH 44251

SPINELLI, JERRY, writer; b. Norristown, Pa., Feb. 1, 1941; s. Louis Anthony and Lorna Mae (Bigler) S.; m. Eileen Mesi; children: Kevin, Barbara, Lana, Jeffrey, Molly, Sean, Benjamin. BA, Gettysburg (Pa.) Coll., 1963; MA, Johns Hopkins U., 1964. Editor Chilton Co., Radnor, Pa., 1966-89. Author: Space Station Seventh Grade, 1982, Who Put That Hair in My Toothbrush?, 1984, Night of the Whale, 1985, Jason and Marceline, 1986, Dump Days, 1988, Maniac Magee, 1990 (Newbery medal 1991, Boston Globe/Horn Book award 1991), Bathwater Gang, 1990, There's a Girl in My Hammerlock, 1991, Dump Days, 1991, Fourth Grade Rats, 1991, Bathwater Gang Get Down to Business, 1992, Do the Funky Pickle, 1992, Report to the Principal's Office!, 1992, Who Ran My Underwear Up the Flagpole?, 1992, Picklemania, 1993, Crash, 1996, Blue Ribbon Blues, 1997, Wringer, 1997 (Newbery honor award 1997), The Libaray Card, 1997, Knots in My Yo-Yo String: The Autobiography of a Kid, 1998, Stargirl, 2000, Loser, 2002. Avocations: tennis, reading, country music, travel.

SPINELLI, R. L. (LOUIE), military association administrator; b. N.J., 1934; 6 children. Shop steward Oil, Chem. and Atomic Workers Union, v.p. N.J. indsl. coun., 1969—75. Decorated Purple Heart U.S. Army. Mem.: Mil. Order of the Purple Heart (nat. jr. vice commdr. 1999, sr.nat. vice commdr. 2000, nat. commdr. 2001). Office: Mil Order of the Purple Heart 5413R Backlick Rd Springfield VA 22151-2960 Office Fax: 703-642-2054. E-mail: info@purpleheart.org.

SPINKS, CARY WILLIAM, JR. literature educator; b. Whiteright, Tex., June 26, 1942; s. Cary William and Ella Gertrude Spinks; m. Clara Gay Hodges; children: Michael J., Cara R. BA, Wayland Bapt. U., 1964; MA, U. Nebr., 1965, PhD, 1970. Prof. lit. Trinity U., San Antonio, 1970—. Author: (books) Semiosis, Marginal Signs and Trickster, 1991, Peirce and Triadomania, 1991; editor: Trickster & Ambivalance, 2001; contbr. numerous articles to profl. jours. Mem. Semiotic Soc. Am. (editor of procs. 1995-2000). Office: 715 Stadium Dr San Antonio TX 78212-3104 Office Fax: (210) 999-7578.

SPINKS, JOHN LEE, retired engineering executive; b. Central City, Ky., June 19, 1924; s. William Lee and Lucy Susan (Greenwood) S.; m. Marion Louisa Mutz, Dec. 24, 1951; children— Susan Marie, Douglas John. BSM.E., U. Ky., 1951; postgrad., U. So. Calif., 1951-52, UCLA, 1957-58; grad., Res. Police Acad., 1977; PhD (hon.), World U., 1984. Registered profl. engr., Calif., La., Tex., Del., Wis., N.H., Okla., Ky., Miss.; diplomate Am. Acad. Environ. Engrs. Aerodynamicist Rockwell Internat., Los Angeles, 1951-52, Downey, Calif., 1954-55; engr. Bell Telephone Labs., Burlington, N.C., 1952-54, Mobil Oil Corp., Torrance, Calif., 1955-56; supervising engr. II S. Coast Air Quality Mgmt. Dist., El Monte, 1956-83; pres. Environ. Emissions Engring. Co., Palos Verdes Peninsula, 1983-95; ret., 1995. Dep. dir. civil engring. divsn., space divsn. USAFR, L.A. AFB, 1961-73; past cons. nat. and internat. govt. air quality agys. Co-author: Air Pollution Engineering Manual, 1967, 2d edit., 1973. Former res. police officer Hermosa Beach Police Dept.; mgr. Little League Baseball, 1966-70; instr. rock and ice mountaineering dir. AQMD Golf League, 1968-81; formre lectr. marathon running; usher St. Francis Episcopal Ch., Palos Verdes Estates, 1968-81. Lt. col. USAAF, 1943-46. Decorated Air Force Commendation medal; recipient U.S. Presdl. Sports award in running, 1977, Sierra Peaks emblem; named to Hon. Order Ky. Cols. Fellow Inst. for Advancement Engring.; mem. Am. Assn. Engring. Socs., Sierra Club, Triangle. Clubs: Srs. Track, Pacific Crest. Home: 26856 Eastvale Rd Palos Verdes Peninsula CA 90274-4007 *The achievement of one's personal goals in itself has little meaning. Complete fulfillment comes with guiding youngsters in their formative years, helping them reach higher levels of motivation and social behavior to insure saneness for tomorrow.*

SPINKS, PAUL, retired library director; b. London, Mar. 7, 1922; came to U.S., 1952; m. Clarice Ada Goode, Jan. 27, 1946 (dec. May 1996); 1 child, Philip Andrew BA, U. Okla., Norman, 1958, MLS, 1959. Catalog asst. Brit. Mus. Libr., London, 1939—52; from rsch. reports libr. to dir. librs. Naval Postgrad. Sch., Monterey, Calif., 1959—75, dir. libraries, 1975—93, prof. emeritus, 1993—. Author studies in field Recipient Civilian Svc. Meritorious award USN, 1993. Served with RAF, 1942-6. Mem. ALA, Spl. Libraries Assn., Am. Soc. Info. Sci. Clubs: Brit.-Am. (sec. Monterey 1982-85). Episcopalian. Home: 855 Capistrano Dr Salinas CA 93901-2420

SPINNATO, JOSEPH ANTHONY, II, obstetrician; b. Ketchikan, Alaska, May 10, 1949; s. Joseph Anthony and Ann S.; m. Diane Dusak, Apr. 26, 1969; children: Joseph Anthony III, Mark Andrew, Julie Anne. BS, U. Dayton, 1970; MD, U. Louisville, 1974. Diplomate Am. Bd. Obstetricians and Gynecologists. Resident on ob/gyn U. Louisville, 1974-77; asst. prof. ob/gyn Sch. Medicine Tex. Tech U., Lubbock, 1979-82; nutrition intern Montreal (Can.) Diet Dispensary, 1980; fellow in maternal-fetal medicine U. Tenn. Ctr. for Health Scis., Memphis, 1982-84, clin. instr. dept. ob/gyn, 1982-84; assoc. prof. divsn. maternal-fetal medicine dept. ob/gyn Coll. Medicine U. South Ala., 1984-88; dir., prof. divsn. maternal-fetal medicine dept. ob/gyn. Sch. Medicine/U. Louisville, 1988-99; prof., vice chair dept. ob/gyn. U. Cin., 2000—. Mem. ob/gyn staff Lubbock Gen. Hosp., 1979-82, City of Memphis Hosps., 1982-84, U. South Ala. Med. Ctr., Mobile, 1984-88, Norton Hosp., Louisville, 1988-99, U. Louisville Hosp., 1988-99; mem. birth defects adv. com., human resources dept. Commonwealth of Ky., 1992; dir. maternal transport Norton Hosp., 1988-93, dir. women's reproductive testing ctr., 1988-96; dir. improved pregnancy outcome project U. Louisville, 1988-93, 96-99; dir. Fetal Rev. Bd., 1990-92; dir. perinatology Christ Hosp. Cin.; presenter, lectr., rschr. in field. Spl. reviewer jours. in field; contbr. articles, abstracts to profl. publs. Dir. teenage parent program Emerson Sch., Louisville, 1988-92, 96—. Lt. comdr. Med. Corps USN, 1977-79. Nutrition intern March of Dimes, 1980; grantee Smith Kline French Labs., 1986, NIH, 1986, NKC Cmty. Trust Fund, 1988, 95-96, WHAS Crusade for Children, 1989-90, 92, 98, Ky. Human Resources Dept., 1990, 93-94; recipient Outstanding Tchr. award, 1991, 93, APGO Excellence in Tchg. award U. Louisville, 1994. Mem. Am. Coll. Obstetricians and Gynecologists, Assn. Profs. of Gynecology and Obstetrics (Excellence in Tchg. award 1994), Soc. Perinatal Obstetricians, Soc. for Maternal-Fetal Medicine, Nat. Perinatal Assn., Jefferson County Med. Soc., Louisville Obgyn Soc., Am. Inst. Ultrasound in Medicine. Avocations: tennis, golf, music, basketball. Office: U Cin PO Box 670526 Cincinnati OH 45267-0526 E-mail: spinnaja@ucmail.uc.edu.

SPINNER, GARY FREDERICK, physician assistant, healthcare administrator; b. Newark, Nov. 8, 1949; s. Harry Spinner and Adele (Spinner) Armm; m. Janet Crocker, July 14, 1974; children: Jacob Adam, Anna Ruth. BA, Rutgers U., 1972; cert. physician asst., Yale Sch. Medicine, 1983; MPH, U. Conn., 1993. Social worker Cath. Social Svcs., Syracuse, N.Y., 1974-78; paramedic, co-dir. Plenty Ambulance Svc., Bronx, 1978-81; physician asst. Alex Isgnt, MD, Newtown, Conn., 1983-84; physician asst., adminstr. managed care Hill Health Corp., New Haven, 1984—, dir. quality improvement, 1984—, COO. Corp. dir. Columbus House, New Haven, 1987—, 1st v.p.; chair Homeless Healthcare Network, New Haven, 1988-95; co-chair Conn. Dept. Social Svcs. Statewide Adv. Coun., Hartford, 1993-96; bd. dirs. Cmty. Health Network, Meridan, chair quality mgmt. and improvement com., 1995—; faculty Yale U. Sch. Medicine; presenter and lectr. in field. Chair New Haven (Conn.) Commn. on Homelessness. Recipient Humanitarian Svc. award Jack W. Cole Soc., 1986, Disting. Alumni award Yale Sch. of Medicine, 1998. Fellow Am. Acad. Physician Assts. (Outstanding Physician Asst. award 1990), Conn. Acad. Physician Assts.; mem. APHA. Avocations: computers, travel. Office: Hill Health Corp 400 Columbus Ave New Haven CT 06519-1233 E-mail: gary.spinner.med.83@aya.yale.edu., gspinner@hillhealthcenter.com.

SPINNER, LEE LOUIS, accountant; b. Hillsboro, Ill., Nov. 9, 1948; s. John Louis and Clara Mae (Brown) Spinner; m. Rosemary T. Dean, Mar. 2, 2002. BS in Acctg., U. Ill., 1971, MAS in Acctg., 1972; MS in Taxation, DePaul U., 1983. CPA, Ill. Sr. tax acct. Ernst & Young, Chgo., 1972-78; dir. tax returns and audits Sunbeam Corp., 1978-82; dir. tax compliance Sara Lee Corp., 1982-83; mgr. tax compliance AM Internat., Inc., 1983-85; mgr. taxes Household Mfg., Inc., Prospect Heights, Ill., 1985-89; mgr. internat. taxes Pittway Corp., Chgo., 1990-2000; dir. taxes Methode Electronics, Inc., Harwood Heights, Ill., 2000—. Instr. tax tng. program Ernst & Young, 1975-78; tax advisor Sta. WIND, Call Your Acct., Chgo., 1977-78. Sec. Grant Park Accts. Softball League, Chgo., 1976-77. Mem. AICPA, Ill. CPA Soc., U. Ill. Alumni Assn. (bd. assoc., audit com. 1997—), Top Social Athletic Club, Moose, KC. Democrat. Roman Catholic. Home: 435 W Wilshire Dr Palatine IL 60067-4788

SPINNER, ROBERT JAY, orthopedic surgeon; b. N.Y.C., Dec. 8, 1961; s. Morton and Paula (Lerner) S.; m. Alexandra Wolanskyj SB, MIT, 1984; M of Studies, Oxford (Eng.) U., 1985; MD, Mayo Clinic, 1989. Rsch. fellow, Luce scholar Prince of Wales Hosp., Hong Kong, 1989-90; intern in surgery Duke U., Durham, N.C., 1990-91, jr. resident in surgery, 1991-92, resident in orthopaedic surgery, 1992-96; resident in neurosurgery Mayo Clinic, Rochester, Minn., 1996-2000; fellow in peripheral nerve surgery David Kline M.D., New Orleans, 1998-99; asst. prof. neurologic surgery and orthopedics Mayo Clinic, Rochester, Minn., 2001—. Recipient Davison Tchg. award Duke U. Med. Sch., 1993, Goldner Rsch. award in Orthopaedic Surgery Duke U. Med. Ctr., 1996, Mayo Bros. Disting. Fellowship award, 2000, Karis award, 2001; Schilling scholar Mayo Found., 1985-87; Congress Neurol. Surg. Cushing Travel awardee, 2001; Mayo Found. scholar, 2001. Mem. Phi Beta Kappa, Sigma Xi, Alpha Chi Sigma. Avocations: travel, reading. E-mail: spinner.robert@mayo.com.

SPINOTTI, DANTE, cinematographer; b. Tolmezzo, Italy, Aug. 22, 1943; Cinematographer Mirsch Agy., L.A. Cinematographer: (films) Sotto, Sotto, 1984, The Berlin Affair, 1985, Manhunter, 1986, Choke Canyon, 1986, Crimes of the Heart, 1986, From the Hip, 1987, Illegally Yours, 1987, Beaches, 1988, Mamba, 1988, The Legend of the Holy Drinker, The Comfort of Strangers, 1989, Torrents of Spring, 1989, Hudson Hawk, 1990, True Colors, 1991, Frankie and Johnny, 1992, The Last of the Mohicans, 1992 (BAFTA winner), Blink, 1993, The Quick and the Dead, 1994, Nell, 1994, Heat, 1995, The Star Maker, 1995, (with Andrey Barkowyak) The Mirror Has Two Faces, 1995, L.A. Confidential, 1996, Goodbye Lover, 1997, The Other Sister, 1998, The Insider, 1999, Wonder Boys, 2000. Office: The Mirisch Agy Ste 700 101100 Santa Monica Blvd Los Angeles CA 90067

SPINRAD, RICHARD WILLIAM, oceanographer, researcher; b. N.Y.C., Apr. 6, 1954; s. Leonard William and Thelma (Zipkin) S.; m. Alanna Wynn Thompson, June 1, 1980; 1 child, Gary Brian. BA, Johns Hopkins U., 1975; MS, Oreg. State U., 1978, PhD, 1982. Rsch. asst. Oreg. State U., Corvallis, 1975-82; rsch. scientist Bigelow Lab. for Ocean Sci., West Boothbay Harbor, Maine, 1982-86, prin. investigator, 1986—94; pres. Sea Tech., Inc., Corvallis, 1986-87; program mgr. optical oceanography Office of Naval Research, Arlington, Va., 1987-89; div. dir. Office of Naval Rsch., 1989-94; dir. Consortium for Oceanographic Rsch. & Edn., 1994—99; tech. dir. Oceanographer of the Navy, 1999—. Adj. faculty George Mason U., 1994—, U.S. Naval Acad., 1997-99; trustee Bigelow Lab. for Ocean Scis., 1995—. Assoc. editor: Oceanography; contbr. sci. articles to profl. jours. Mem. AAAS, Am. Soc. Limnologists and Oceanographers, Am. Geophys. Union, The Oceanography Soc., Optical Soc. Am. (Johns Hopkins U. Schs. com.), Oceanography Soc. (coun. 1994—). Democrat. Jewish. Avocations: profl. banjo playing, outdoor activities, woodworking. Office: Oceanographer of Navy 3450 Massachusetts Ave NW Washington DC 20392

SPINRAD, ROBERT JOSEPH, computer scientist; b. N.Y.C., Mar. 20, 1932; s. Sidney and Isabel (Reiff) S.; m. Verna Winderman, June 27, 1954; children: Susan Irene, Paul Reiff. BS, Columbia U., 1953, MS (Bridgham fellow), 1954; PhD (Whitney fellow), MIT, 1963. Registered profl. engr., N.Y. Project engr. Bulova Research & Devel. Lab., N.Y.C., 1953-55; sr. scientist Brookhaven Nat. Lab., Upton, N.Y., 1955-68; v.p. Sci. Data Systems, Santa Monica, Calif., 1968-69; v.p. programming Xerox Corp., El Segundo, 1969-71, dir. info. scis., 1971-76, v.p. systems devel., 1976-78, v.p. research, 1978-83, dir. systems tech., 1983-87, dir. corp. tech., 1987-92, v.p. tech. analysis and devel., 1992-94, v.p. technology strategy, 1994-98; cons. in field, Palo Alto, Calif., 1998—. Contbr. articles to profl. jours. Mem. Nat. Acad. Engring., Calif. Coun. on Sci. and Tech., Sigma Xi, Tau Beta Pi. Achievements include patents in field. E-mail: robert@spinrad.com.

SPIOTTA, RAYMOND HERMAN, editor; b. Bklyn., Feb. 24, 1927; s. Michael Joseph and Olga Elizabeth (Schmidt) S.; m. Maria Theresa Attanasio, Apr. 17, 1949; children: Robert, Michael, Ronald, Mark, Sandra. B.M.E., Pratt Inst., 1953. Mfg. engr. Arma div. Am. Bosch Arma Corp., Garden City, N.Y., 1948-53; mng. editor Machinery mag., N.Y.C., 1953-65; editor Machine and Tool Blue Book, Wheaton, Ill., 1965-89; editorial dir. Machine and Tool Blue Book & Mfg. Systems, Carol Stream, 1989-90; cons. editor Cutting Tool Engring., Northbrook, 1992-95; acquisitions editor Hanser Gardner Publs., Cin., 1995-97, ret., 1997. Contbr. to Am. Peoples Ency. Yearbook; contbr. articles to profl. jours. Mem. DuPage County (Ill.) area council Boy Scouts Am., 1966-73. Served with AC USNR, 1944-48. Mem. Numerical Control Soc. of AIM-Tech., Soc. Am. Value Engrs., Soc. Mfg. Engrs., Am. Inst. Indsl. Engrs., Robotics Internat., Computer and Automated Sys. Assn. Roman Catholic. Home and Office: 1484 Aberdeen Ct Naperville IL 60564-9796 E-mail: r-mspiotta@mindspring.com.

SPIRA, JULIE MARGO, communications executive; b. Glen Rock, N.J., May 28, 1957; d. Hillard and Myra Regina (Schmertz) S. BS in TV and Radio, Ithaca Coll., 1979. Program dir., on-air personality WAAL-FM Radio, Binghamton, N.Y., 1977-79; N.E. sales mgr. Watermark Prodns., Hollywood, Calif., 1979-80; dir. nat. sales Golden Egg Prodns., 1980-81; dir. affiliate rels. RKO Radio Networks, N.Y. and L.A., 1981-87; v.p. broadcast sales and mktg. IDB Communications Group, Culver City, Calif., 1987—. Mem. Am. Women in Radio and TV, Internat. Radio and TV Soc., Soc. of Satellite Profls., Internat. TV and Radio Soc., Women in Communications. Avocations: painting, classical piano, theatre, skiing, golf. Home: 139 Voyage St Marina Del Rey CA 90292-7296

SPIRA, MELVIN, plastic surgeon; b. Chgo., July 3, 1925; s. Samuel and Jessie (Tivin) S.; m. Rita Silver, Nov. 27, 1952; children— Mary Ann, Joel Bennett, Pamela Beth Student, Wright Jr. Coll, Chgo., 1942-43, Franklin and Marshall Coll., Lancaster, Pa., 1943-44; DDS, Northwestern U., 1947, MSD, 1951; MD, Med. Coll. of Ga., 1956. Diplomate Am. Bd. Plastic Surgery (chmn. 1984-85). Intern Duke U. Hosp., Durham, N.C., 1956-57, jr. asst. resident, 1958-59, asst. resident, 1959-60; resident Jefferson Davis Hosp, Houston, 1960-61, asst. in surgery and plastic surgery; sr. attending physician Ben Taub Gen. Hosp, attending physician, Tex. Children's Hosp., Houston, St. Lukes Episcopal Hosp., Houston; prof. Baylor Coll. Medicine, past head divsn. plastic surgery. Past chmn. Am. Bd. Plastic Surgery. Served with USN, 1943-45, 48-50 Fellow ACS; mem. Houston Surg. Soc., Am. Soc. Maxillofacial Surgeons (pres. 1974-75), Am. Soc. Plastic and Reconstructive Surgeons, Harris County Med. Soc., Plastic Surgery Research Council, So. Med. Assn., Tex. Med. Assn., Am. Trauma Soc., G.V. Black Soc., Internat. Soc. for Burn Injuries, Am. Burn Assn., Am. Cleft Palate Assn., Am. Assn. Plastic Surgeons (pres. 1992-93), Acad. Plastic Surgery Forum, Internat. Soc. Reconstructive Microsurgery, Tex. Surg. Soc., Michael E. DeBakey Internat. Cardiovascular Soc., Baron Hardy Soc., Am. Soc. for Aesthetic Plastic Surgery, Alpha Omega Alpha, Sigma Xi Avocations: snow skiing, photography, painting, tennis, golf. Office: Baylor Coll Medicine Div Plastic Surgery 6560 Fannin St Ste 800 Houston TX 77030-2725

SPIRA, PATRICIA GOODSITT, association executive; b. Milw. d. Lawrence Manfred and Ruth Pauline (Miller) Goodsitt; m. Marvin Alfred Spira, July 12, 1952; children: David, James, Ann, Ellen. BA in History, U. Wis., Milw., 1967. Dir. group sales Swan Theatre and Supper Club, Milw., 1962-63; mgr. box office Performing Arts Ctr., 1969-80; dir. devel. St. Louis Conservatory and Schs., 1980-81; pres. The Internat. Ticketing Assn., N.Y.C., 1981—. Tchr. Creative Dramatics, Milw., 1962-66; adv. coun. Town Hall, N.Y.C., 1989—; bd. dirs. Theatre and Dance Co., N.Y.C., 1986-89. Bd. dirs. Milw. Chamber Music Soc., 1974-80, Soc. Preservation of Profl. Touring Entertainment History; chair bd. dirs. Great Am. Children's Theatre, 1977-80. Mem. Am. Soc. Assn. Execs. (cert.), N.Y. Soc. Assn. Execs. Avocations: reading, travel, theater. Office: The Internat Ticketing Assn 250 W 57th St Ste 722 New York NY 10107-0799 Fax: (212) 581-0885. E-mail: pspira@intix.org.

SPIRA, ROBERT ALAN, securities company executive; b. Chgo., Feb. 13, 1932; s. Leo and Tena Dolores (Sarnat) Spira; m. Nancy Ann Netzle (dec.); children: Leslie Gayle, James Michel; m. Barbara Lader (dec.). BA, Roosevelt U., Chgo., 1953. V.p. Walston & Co., Chgo., 1955-70; head new bus. Cowen & Co., N.Y.C., 1970-72; mem. instnl. sales staff Edwards & Hanly, 1975-77; pres. Haas Securities Corp., 1977-87; former pres., dir. Haas Devel. Corp.; mem. Wall St. Planning Group, 1976—. Past mem. Boston Stock Exch. (listing com.); chmn. bd. dirs. KIMG; chmn., CEO Berkeley Securities, 1988-90, Chapman, Spira & Carson, 1990—; bd. dirs. E-Data Corp.; pres., dir. Austin Davenport Assocs., Carlyle & Christie Capital Corp., Ulysses Capital Corp., Whitney, Sterling & Webster Corp., Am. Asian Enterprises, Inc., Peabody Sherman Capital Group, Inc., F.X. Knox & Co., Internat. Trading & Fin. Agy., Inc.; commentator ABC-TV fin. news, 1967-70; chmn. Russian Am. Cons. Group, Tran Eurasian Cons. Co., Inc., Advanced Techs. and Software N.Y. Trans Eurasian Materials and Testing Co., Inc.; advisor UN; lectr. Thunderbird Internat. Bus. Sch. Author: Diamonds are Forever, Almost, Ready or Not, Here Come the Banks; contbr. numerous articles on historic and econ. analysis to internat. publs. Bd. dirs. Boys Brotherhood Rep., Honest Ballot Assn., Rhumbline Advisers, Luscombe Aircraft Corp.; dir., chmn. KIMG Inc.; mem. Congl. Adv. Bd., Am. Security Coun., NTL Adv. Bd. With Green Berets U.S. Army, 1953-54. Mem. Nat. Option and Futures Soc., Nat. Assn. Securities Dealers (disting. bus. conduct com., arbitration panel and Wall St. planning group), Am. Commodities Exch. (listing com.), N.Y. Futures Exch., N.Y. Stock Exch., Am. Stock Exch. (allied mem., arbitration panel), Fin. Analysts and Money Mgrs. Assn., World Trade Ctrs. Assn., Am. Numismatic Assn., Am. Philatelic Soc., Nat. Options Soc. Pacific Cmty. Inst. (adv.), U.S. Senatorial Club, Big Apple Triathalon Club, Profl. Assn. Scuba Divers, NY Stock Exch. Club. Home and Office: Chapman Spira & Carson 30 Broad St 34th Fl New York NY 10004 E-mail: bobspira@chapmanspira.com.

SPIRA, ROBERT SIDNEY, gastroenterologist; b. N.Y.C., June 20, 1949; s. Bernhard and Molly (Linchitz) S.; m. Naomi Nutkis, Dec. 29, 1973; children: Daniele, Etan, Benjamin. BA, NYU, 1971, MD, 1975. Diplomate Nat. Bd. Med. Examiners, Am. Bd. Internal Medicine, Am. Bd. Gastroenterology. Resident in medicine NYU and N.Y. VA Med. Ctr., N.Y.C., 1975-79; fellow in gastroenterology N.Y. VA Med. Ctr., 1979-81; clin. asst. prof. medicine N.J. Sch. Medicine, Newark, 1983—; assoc. prof. medicine Sch. Post Grad. Medicine, Seton Hall U., 1988—; chief dept. gastroenterology St. Michael's Meml. Med. Ctr., 1992—. Bd. dirs. Caprius Corp. Presenter in field, 1981—. Fellow ACP, Am. Coll. Gastroenterology, Acad. Medicine N.J.; mem. N.J. Soc. Gastrointestinal Endoscopy (pres. 1990-91), N.J. Soc. Gastroenterology (exec. bd. 1987—, pres. 1994), Ileitis Colitis Found. Jewish. Avocations: tennis, skiing, opera. Office: 741 Northfield Ave Ste 101 West Orange NJ 07052-1104

SPIRES, ROBERT CECIL, foreign language educator; b. Missouri Valley, Iowa, Dec. 1, 1936; s. Roy C. and Ellen M. (Epperson) S.; m. Roberta A. Hyde, Feb. 2, 1963; children: Jeffrey R., Leslie Ann. BA, U. Iowa, 1959, MA, 1963, PhD, 1968. Asst. prof. Ohio U., Athens, 1967-69; asst. prof. dept. Spanish and Portuguese U. Kans., Lawrence, 1969-72, assoc. prof., 1972-78, prof., 1978—, chmn. dept., 1983-92. Author: La novela española, 1978, Beyond the Metafictional Mode, 1984, Transparent Simulacra, 1988, Post-Totalitarian Spanish Fiction, 1996; contbg. editor SigloXX/20th Century; editl. bd. Jour. of Interdisciplinary Literary Studies, 1993—, Ind. Jour. of Hispanic Lit., 1992—. Served with U.S. Army, 1959-61. NEH fellow, 1981-82, U.S.-Spain Joint Com. fellow, 1985-86, Hall Ctr. for Humanities fellow, 1992, Program Cultural Coop. fellow, 1993. Mem. Revista de Estudios Hispánicos (editorial bd. 1985—), Anales de Literatura Contemporánea (editorial bd. 1981—), Letras Peninsulares (editorial bd. 1987—), MLA (del. assembly 1989-91), MLA 20th Century Spain (exec. com. 1983-89), 20th Century Spanish Assn. Am. (v.p. 1989-92). Home: 2420 Orchard Ln Lawrence KS 66049-2710 Office: U Kans Dept Spanish & Portuguese Lawrence KS 66045-0001 E-mail: rspires@ukans.edu.

SPIRES, ROBERTA LYNN, small business owner; b. Gary, Ind., Sept. 4, 1952; d. Merle Russell and Kathryn Dias (Felts) Harris; m. Richard John Badovinich, Aug. 16, 1975 (div. 1989); m. Patrick Robert Spires, Mar. 14, 1992; 1 child, Zachary Robert. Grad. h.s., Griffith, Ind. Dep. clk. U.S. Bankruptcy Ct., Gary, 1970-80, chief dep. clk., 1980-97; owner, mgr. Spl. Touch, personal shopping svc., Griffith, 1997—; owner Specialized Secretarial Svcs., Highland, Ind., 1997-99, Special Touch Typing Svc., Griffith, 1999—. Mem. Fed. Ct. Clks. Assn., FBA (cert., lectr.). Democrat. Roman Catholic. Avocations: water skiing, boating, sewing, handcrafts, reading. Home and Office: 719 N Rueth Dr Griffith IN 46319-3817 E-mail: RSpires799@aol.com.

SPIRN, MICHELE SOBEL, communications professional, writer; b. Newark, Jan. 26, 1943; d. Jack and Sylvia (Cohen) Sobel; m. Steven Frederick Spirn, Jan. 27, 1968; 1 child, Joshua. BA, Syracuse U., 1965; MFA, The New Sch., 1999. Creative dir. Planned Communications Svcs., N.Y.C., 1966-72, EDL Prodns., N.Y.C., 1972-73; free-lance writer Bklyn., 1973-83; dir. pub. rels. Nat. Coun. Jewish Women, N.Y.C., 1983-90, dir. communications, 1990-95; freelance writer Bklyn., 1995—. Adj. lectr. CUNY, Bklyn., 1977—81; instr. The New Sch., N.Y.C., 1999—, NYU, 2002. Author: The Fast Shoes, 1985, The Boy Who Liked Green, 1985, The Know-Nothings, 1995; co-author: A Man Can Be..., 1981, A Know-Nothing Birthday, 1997, Birth Celebrations, 1998, New Year Celebrations, 1998; co-author: The Nutcracker, 1998, A Know-Nothing Halloween, 2000, The Know-Nothings Talk Turkey, 2000, The Bridges in London, 2000, All Washed Up, 2000, Racing To The Light, 2000, Wait Til The Midnight Hour, 2000, Jackie Joyner-Kersee, 2000, The Bridges in Paris, 2000, Race to the Sea, 2001, A Twist in Time, 2001; editor, columnist Children's Entertainment Rev. mag., N.Y.C., 1982; columnist The Phoenix newspaper, Bklyn., 1983. Pres. Tenth St. Block Assn., Bklyn., 1989-91; vol. Model Media Program, Bklyn., 1985—. Recipient Silver medal for pub. svc. film N.Y. Internat. Film and TV Festival, 1972. Mem. Mystery Writers Am., Soc. Children's Book Writers and Illustrators. Avocations: reading, gardening.

SPIRNAK, JOHN PATRICK, urologist, educator; b. Cleve., Mar. 17, 1951; s. John Joseph and Mary Barbara (Mancos) S.; m. Diane Lynne Miller, Sept. 15, 1979; children: Jennifer, Patrick, Christopher. BS in Zoology, Ohio U., 1973; MD, Emory U., 1977; degree in urology, Case Western Reserve U., 1983. Diplomate Am. Bd. Urology. Intern, gen. surg. resident U. Hosp., Cleve., 1977-79, resident in urology, 1980-83; nephrology rsch. resident Metro Health Med. Ctr., 1979-80, dir. urology, 1987—; sr. instr. divns. urology Case Western Reserve U., 1983-85, asst. prof. urology, 1985-91, assoc. prof. urology, 1991-2000, prof., 2000—. Adv. panel U.S. Pharmacopeia Urology, Washington, 1986—. Editor Urologic Decision Making, 1991, New Diagnostic Tests, 1996; manuscript reviewer Jour. Endourology, 1989—, Urology, 1993—, Jour. Urology, 1994—; contbr. articles to profl. jours. and chpts. to books. Named One of Top Doctors Cleve. Mag., 1996, 99. Fellow ACS; mem. AMA, Am. Assn. Surgery Trauma, Am. Urol. Assn., Cleve. Urol. Soc. (sec.-treas. 1986-88, pres. 1988-89). Avocations: sports, gardening. Home: 2178 Silveridge Trl Westlake OH 44145-1797 Office: Metro Health Med Ctr 2500 Metrohealth Dr Cleveland OH 44109-1900

SPIRO, HERBERT JOHN, political scientist, politician, educator, ambassador; b. Hamburg, Germany, Sept. 7, 1924; came to U.S., 1938, naturalized, 1944; s. Albert John and Marianne (Stiefel) S.; m. Elizabeth Anna Petersen, June 7, 1958 (div.); children: Peter John, Alexander Charles Stiefel; m. Marion Ballin, July 22, 1985. Student, San Antonio Jr. Coll., 1942-43; AB summa cum laude, Harvard U., 1949, MA, 1950, PhD, 1953; MA (hon.), U. Pa., 1971. Adminstrv. asst. U.S. War Dept., Vienna, Austria, 1945-46; mem. faculty Harvard U., Cambridge, Mass., 1950-61, asst. prof., 1957-61; assoc. prof. polit. sci. Amherst (Mass.) Coll., 1961-65; prof. polit. sci. U. Pa., Phila., 1965-73; mem. policy planning staff Dept. State, Washington, 1970-75; ambassador to Cameroon, 1975-77; amb. to Equatorial Guinea, 1975-76; fellow Woodrow Wilson Internat. Ctr. for Scholars, Smithsonian Instn., Washington, 1978; vis. prof. polit. sci. Def. Intelligence Sch., 1979-80; univ. prof. polit. sci. John F. Kennedy Inst. for N.Am. Studies, Free U. Berlin, 1980-89. Fulbright sr. research prof. U. Coll. Rhodesia and Nyasaland, 1959-60; cons. Brit. Commn. to Rev. Constn., Fedn. Rhodesia and Nyasaland, 1960, Japanese Commn. on Revision Constn., 1962; vis. assoc. prof. U. Chgo., 1961, Stanford (Calif.) U., 1963; chmn. Asian and African Studies program,

Amherst-Smith-Mt. Holyoke Colls., U. Mass., 1964-65; vis. prof. internat. affairs Woodrow Wilson Sch., Princeton (N.J.) U., 1966; mem. adv. council polit. sci. Haverford Coll., 1966-71; affiliated with Nuffield Coll., Oxford (Eng.) U., 1967-68; resident scholar Rockefeller Found. Study Ctr., Bellagio, Italy, 1968, 78; vis. prof. govt., guest scholar Ctr. for Internat. Affairs, Harvard U., 1983; vis. scholar U. Tex., Austin, 1984-89; life mem. Brit. studies faculty seminar U. Tex., Austin, 1983—; researcher Lyndon Baines Johnson Presdl. Library, 1985-86; fellow Aspen (Colo.) Inst. Humanistic Studies, 1986; adj. prof. govt. U. Tex., Austin, 1989-91; participant internat scholarly and diplomatic confs.; lectr. various univs.; founder Brackenridge H.S.-Wilhelm Gymnasium Exchange. Author: Politics of German Codetermination, 1958, (with others) Patterns of Government, 1958, 2d edit., 1962, Government by Constitution, 1959, Politics in Africa, 1962, 2d edit., 1975, Five African States, 1963, World Politics: The Global System, 1966, (with others) Authority, Nomos I, 1958, Responsibility, Nomos III, 1960, Privacy Nomos XIII, 1971, Why Federations Fail, 1968, Responsibility in Government, 1969, The Dialectic of Representation 1619-1969, 1969, Politics as the Master Science: From Plato to Mao, 1970 (with others), Theory and Politics, 1971 (with others), Between Sovereignty and Integration, 1974, A New Foreign Policy Consensus?, 1979, (with others) The Legacy of the Constitution, 1987, (with others) Anti-Americanism, 1988; editor, contbr.: (with others) Africa: The Primacy of Politics, 1966, Patterns of African Development, 1967, 'Privatization' of U.S. Foreign Relations, 1995; contbr. to: World Book Ency., Ency. Britannica, Intern. Ency. of the Social Scis.; host Spiro's Conversations, Austin Community TV, 1992-97, San Antonio TimeWarner Access TV channel 20, 1999—; contbr. articles to profl. jours. Del. Tex. State Rep. Conv., 1990-92; precinct chmn. Travis County; Rep. cand. for Tex. Ho. of Reps., 1991, U.S. House of Reps., 1992, 94, U.S. Senate, 1993. Decorated Bronze Star with oak leaf cluster, Purple Heart; grand officer Legion of Valor Cameroon, 1977; recipient Detur prize Harvard Coll., 1948, Bowdoin prize, 1952; John Harvard scholar, 1949-51, Holzer scholar, 1949-51; Guggenheim fellow, 1959-60, Social Sci. Research Council faculty fellow, 1962, 67-68, Rockefeller Found. fellow, 1958, Sheldon travelling fellow Harvard U., also Fulbright fellow, 1953-54; Moody grantee Lyndon Baines Johnson Found., 1985. Fellow Assn. for Diplomatic Studies; mem. African Studies Assn., Am. Polit. Sci. Assn. (coun. 1968-70, chmn. election com. 1969), Internat. Polit. Sci. Assn., Am. Soc. Polit. and Legal Philosophy, Coun. Fgn. Rels., Coun. Am. Ambs., Am. Fgn. Svc. Assn., Retired Fgn. Svc. Assn. of San Antonio, Mil. Order Purple Heart, San Antonio World Affairs Coun., Harvard Alumni Assn. (apptd. regional dir. Tex. 1994-97), San Antonio Coll. Alumni Assn. (dir. 1999—, Disting. Former Student award 2000), Wissenschaftliche Gesellschaft Berlin, Signet Soc., Harvard U. Faculty Club, Harvard Club (N.Y.C.), Harvard Club Berlin (pres. 1985-89), Harvard Club Austin (pres. 1990-92), Harvard Club San Antonio, Phi Beta Kappa (v.p. San Antonio assn.). Republican. Address: Apt 713 1 Towers Park Ln San Antonio TX 78209-6423 E-mail: herbspiro@earthlink.net.

SPIRO, HOWARD MARGET, physician, educator; b. Cambridge, Mass., Mar. 23, 1924; s. Thomas and Martha (Marget); m. Marian Freelove Wagner, Mar 11, 1951; children: Pamela Marget, Carolyn Standish, Philip Marget, Martha Standish. BA, Harvard, 1944, MD, 1947; MA, Yale, 1967. Intern Peter Bent Brigham Hosp., Boston, 1947-48, resident, 1948-51, Mass. Gen. Hosp., 1953-55; practice medicine, specializing in gastroenterology New Haven, 1955—. Chief gastrointestinal unit Yale Sch. Medicine, 1955-82, prof. medicine, 1967-99, dir. program for humanities in medicine, 1983-99. Author: Clinical Gastroenterology, 1970, 4th edit., 1993, Doctors, Patients and Placebos, 1986, The Power of Hope-A Doctor's Perspective, 1998; editor Jour. Clin. Gastroenterology, 1979-98, (with others) When Doctors Get Sick, 1987, Empathy and the Practice of Medicine, 1993, Facing Death—Where Culture, Religion and Medicine Meet, 1996, Doctors Afield, 1998. Served with USNR, 1943-45; Served with AUS, 1951-53. Mem. ACP (master) Clubs: Madison Beach. Home: 89 Middle Beach Rd Madison CT 06443-3006 Office: Conn Gastroenterology Cons 40 Temple St New Haven CT 06510-2715 E-mail: Howard.spiro@yale.edu.

SPIRO, MELFORD ELLIOT, anthropology educator; b. Cleve., Apr. 26, 1920; s. Wilbert I. and Sophie (Goodman) Spiro; m. Audrey Goldman, May 27, 1950; children: Michael, Jonathan. BA, U. Minn., 1941; PhD, Northwestern U., 1950. Mem. faculty Washington U., St. Louis, 1948—52, U. Conn., 1952—57, U. Wash., 1957—64; prof. anthropology U. Chgo., 1964—68; prof., chmn. dept. anthropology U. Calif., San Diego, 1968—99, prof. emeritus, 1999—. Author (with E.G. Burrows): An Atoll Culture, 1953; author: Kibbutz: Venture in Utopia, 1955, Children of Kibbutz, 1958, Burmese Supernaturalism, 1967, Buddhism and Society: A Great Tradition and Its Burmese Vicissitudes, 1971, Kinship and Marriage in Burma, 1977, Gender and Culture: Kibbutz Women Revisited, 1979, Culture and Human Nature, 1993, Oedipus in the Trobriands, 1982, Anthropological Other or Burmese Brother: Studies in Cultural Analysis, 1992, Gender Ideology and Psychological Reality, 1997; editor: Context and Meaning in Culture Anthropology, 1965. Bd. dirs. Social Sci. Rsch. Coun., 1960—62. Fellow: NAS, Am. Acad. Arts and Scis.; mem.: AAAS, Soc. for Psychol. Anthropology (pres. 1979—80), Am. Ethnol. Soc. (pres. 1967—68), Am. Anthrop. Assn. Home: 2500 Torrey Pines Rd La Jolla CA 92037-3400 Office: U Calif-San Diego 9500 Gilman Dr La Jolla CA 92093-0532 Business E-Mail: mspiro@ucsd.edu.

SPIRO, ROBERT HARRY, JR. foundation and business executive, educator; b. Asheville, N.C., Dec. 5, 1920; s. Robert Harry and Eoline Peterson (Shaw) S.; m. Terrie C. Gay, May 17, 1980; children by previous marriage: Robert Timothy, Elizabeth Susan, James Monroe. BS, Wheaton (Ill.) Coll., 1941; postgrad. Navy Supply Sch., Harvard U., 1943; postgrad., U. N.C., 1945-46; PhD, U. Edinburgh, Scotland, 1950; student, Union Theol. Sem., summers 1951-53; postdoctoral, Duke U., summer 1956; ScD (hon.), Fla. Inst. Tech. Assoc. prof. King Coll., Bristol, Tenn., 1946-50; prof. history Miss. Coll., 1950-57; pres. Blue Ridge Assembly, Black Mountain, N.C., 1957-60; dean Coll. Liberal Arts Mercer U., prof. history, 1960-64; pres. Jacksonville U., Fla., 1964-79; under sec. of Army, 1980-81; cons. to bus., 1981-84, 86-99; nat. exec. dir. Res. Officers Assn. U.S., 1984-86; chmn. RHS Imprinted Products Inc., 1988-99; past bd. mgrs. Voyager Variable Annuity of Fla., 1972-79. V.p. Am. Security Coun. Found., 1991—99, chmn., 2002—; pres. Nat. Security Caucus Found., 1997—2002; past pres. Fla. Assn. Colls. and Univs.; mem., past chmn. Ind. Colls. and Univs., 1964—79, chmn, 1967; sec.-treas. Assn. Urban Univs., 1968—76; past mem. Fla.-Columbia Ptnrs.; gen. chmn. Jacksonville Sesquicentennial Commn., 1970—72; mem. N.C. Tricentennial Commn., 1959—65; past mem. adv. coun. Robert A. Taft Inst. Govt., Inst. Internat. Edn.; pres. Nat. Security Caucus Found., 1998—. Editor (with D.F. Winkler and J.C. Reilly Jr.) Destroyer Dquadron Two From Leyte Gulf Through Okinawa, 2002; contbr. articles to profl. publs. and encys. Trustee Southwestern Bapt. Theol. Sem., 1968—78; chmn. bd. Bapt. Coll. and Sem., Washington, 1989—2001. Lt. USNR, 1941—45, ret. rear adm. USNR, 1978. Decorated Palmes Academique (France); recipient Disting. Civilian Svc. award, Dept. of Army, 1981, Disting. Alumnus award, Navy Supply Corps Sch., 2000. Mem. Navy League U.S. (former pres. Jacksonville coun.), Naval Res. Assn. (nat. adv. coun.), Res. Officers Assn. U.S. Naval Inst., Ret. Officers Assn., Am. Legion, Kiwanis (pres. Clinton, Miss. 1956-57; pres. Georgetown, D.C. Club 1991-92), Army-Navy Country Club (Arlington, Va.), Phi Delta Kappa, Alpha Kappa Psi, Phi Alpha Theta, Phi Kappa Phi. Home: 105 Follin Ln SE Vienna VA 22180-4957 E-mail: RHSpiro20@aol.com. *Esse Quam Videre "To Be Rather than to Seem" is an eloquent apothegm I learned in high school Latin classes. For me it has been a demanding goal for daily living, a worthy aspiration for each task in life and a challenging vision of what I wish and ought to be.*

SPIRO, THOMAS GEORGE, chemistry educator; b. Aruba, Netherlands Antilles, Nov. 7, 1935; s. Andor and Ilona S.; m. Helen Handin, Aug. 21, 1959; children: Peter, Michael. BS, UCLA, 1956; PhD, MIT, 1960. Fulbright rschr. U. Copenhagen, Denmark, 1960-61; NIH fellow Royal Inst. Tech., Stockholm, 1962-63; research chemist Calif. Research Corp., LaHabra, 1961-62; mem. faculty Princeton U., 1963—, prof. chemistry, 1974—, head dept., 1979-88, Eugene Higgins prof., 1981—. Author: (with William M. Stigliani) Environmental Issues in Chemical Perspective, 1980, Chemistry of the Environment, 1996; contbr. articles to profl. jours. Recipient Bomem-Michelson award Bomem Corp., 1986; NATO sr. fellow, 1972, Guggenheim fellow, 1990. Fellow AAAS; mem. Am. Chem. Soc., Phi Beta Kappa, Sigma Xi. Office: Princeton U Dept Chemistry Princeton NJ 08544-0001 E-mail: spiro@princeton.edu.

SPIRTOS, ANDREA C. columnist, muralist, office manager; b. Freeport, Ill., May 23, 1952; d. Carl E. H. and Eldora E. (Baker) DeFrane; m. Nicholas George Spirtos, Aug. 19, 1979. BA in Psych., BA in Edn. cum laude, U. Dubuque, 1973; MA in Guidance Counseling cum laude, U. Iowa, 1974; JD, Loyola U., L.A., 1983; EdD in Instl. Mgmt., Pepperdine U., 1994. Cert. rape crisis counselor, Calif. Tchr., counselor Kennedy H.S., Cedar Rapids, Iowa, 1973-74; counselor UCLA, 1974-77; youth cons. Am. Red Cross, 1977-79; dir. donor svcs. and shelter svcs. United Way, 1979-80; dir. youth svcs. Am. Heart Assn., 1980-82; pres. Comprehensive Office Sys. Technology, 1982; co-founder, corp. officer Pacific Multiple Sclerosis Rsch. Found., 1982-99; devel. dir. Junipero Serra H.S., 1987-88; v.p. Compensation Strategies, 1988; office mgr. Law Office of Nicholas G. Spirtos, 1982—; pres. Tekni-query Cons., 1990—; account rep. Met. Life, 1996; contbr. The Desert Woman Monthly, Palm Springs, Calif., 1997-99; columnist Charity Check The Desert Sun Gannet Pub., 1997-99; columnist Random Acts of Kindness Profile mag., 1999—; care giver, 2000—. Author: Not in My Wildest Dreams, 1995; co-editor, author: Cutting Edge Technologies: The Future of Community Colleges, 1993; columnist: Seventeen Mag., 1969-70, Freeport Jour. Standard, 1968-70, Freeport H.S. Gazette, 1967-70, Trumpeter, 1990-92; columnist, editor, layout Youth News, 1977-82. Decorated Legion of Merit; named Woman of Yr., ABI, 1997; recipient medallion of recognition, Joint Chiefs of Staff U.S., 1993, Presdl. Order of Merit, 1991; grantee Danforth Found., 1969—70. Mem. ACLU, Am. Pen Women, Internat. Platform Assn. (gov. 1994—, author poetry newsletter 1995-96, co-editor poetry anthology 1992, 93, 94, 95), Amnesty Internat., Kappa Delta Pi. Republican. Greek Orthodox. Avocations: painting, knitting, weight lifting, organic gardening, gourment cooking. Office: Law Office of Nicholas G Spirtos Ste D PMB 404 44489 Town Ctr Way Palm Desert CA 92260-2723 E-mail: rydnhd1@aol.com.

SPIRTOS, NICHOLAS GEORGE, lawyer, financial company executive; b. Youngstown, Ohio, Mar. 19, 1950; s. George Nicholas Spirtos and Tulla (Palaologos) Waldron; m. Andrea Carel DeFrane, Aug. 19, 1979. BA in Physics, Philosophy, UCLA, 1969, MA in Biochemistry, 1974, JD, 1978. Bar: Calif., 1978; cert. rape crisis counselor, Calif. Intelligence analyst, 1969-72; dir. product devel. Adolph's Food Products, Burbank, Calif., 1972-73; asst. to pres. Eckel Research and Devel., San Fernando, 1973-74; dep. State Public Defender Los Angeles, 1977-82; pvt. practice civil rights Pacific Palisades, Calif., 1982-94; pvt. practice Palm Desert, 1994—. Co-founder Tekni-Query Cons., 1990; appellate lawyer Calif. and U.S. Supreme Ct., 1982; exec. v.p. Gen. Counsel Compensation Strategies Group, Santa Ana, Calif., 1988-89; pro bono legal counsel Junipero Serra H.S., Gardena, Calif., 1987-88; cons. to U.S. Govt., 1982—; bd. dirs. Myelin Project, Washington, 1993-95. Patentee solubilization of Sodium CMC at room temperature, 1972. Founder, fund raiser Pacific Multiple Sclerosis Research Found., Beverly Hills, Calif., 1982—, coordinator with Reed Neurology Ctr. at UCLA; bd. dirs. John F. Kennedy Ctr. Performing Arts, Very Spl. Arts for Cachella Valley, 1996—. Westinghouse Sci. scholar, 1965; recipient Gregor Mendell award in genetics, 1962; named Jr. Engr. of Yr. Am. Assn. Aero. Engrs., 1963, Outstanding Speaker U. So. Calif., 1965. Mem.: Internat. Platform Assn., State Bar Calif., Am. Pen Women (assoc.), Am. Inns of Ct., Mensa. Greek Orthodox. Avocation: classic automobiles, hot rods, quantum mechanics. Office: Ste D PMB 404 44489 Town Center Way Palm Desert CA 92260-2789

SPISAK, JOHN FRANCIS, environmental company executive; b. Cleve., Mar. 27, 1950; s. Ernest Lawrence and Adele Marie (Chipko) S.; m. Barbara Ann Heisman, June 10, 1972; children: John Stefan, Theresa Rose. BS in Chemistry, BS in Biology with honors, Purdue U., 1972. Rsch. engr. Anaconda Minerals, Tucson, 1972-79; chief metallurgist Fed. Am. Uranium, Riverton, Wyo., 1979-80; v.p. ops. Anschutz Mining Corp., Denver, 1980-87; chmn. bd. dirs. Warrenton Refining (subs. of Anschutz Corp.), 1987-89; dir., owner BE&K/Terranext, Inc., 1989—. Mem. Western States-U.S. Senate Coalition for Superfund Reform; CEO, Am. Purificaion Corp., Newport Beach, Calif., Smart Truck Sys., Moreno Valley, Calif. Contbr. articles to profl. pubs.; patentee sequential flotation of sulfide ores. Named One of Fifty Colo. Top Bus. Leaders, Colo. Assn. Commerce and Industry. Mem. AIME, Soc. Mining, Metallurgy and Exploration, Nat. Assn. Environ. Mgrs. (co-founder, bd. dirs. Washington chpt., co-chmn. govt. liaison and advocacy com.), Denver Petroleum Club, Elks. Republican. Roman Catholic. Avocations: classical piano, cycling, model railroads. Home: 9384 Oakbrush Way Lone Tree CO 80124-3070 Office: Am Purification Inc 20101 SW Birch St Ste 140 Newport Beach CA 92660-1749 E-mail: jfsapi@aol.com.

SPISAK-SIEMIENTKOWSKI, SARA LOUISE, women's apparel, art, health and nutrition business; b. Parma, Ohio, Mar. 11, 1966; d. Frank Eugene and Mary Louise (Babjak) S.; m. Ronald John Siemientkowski, July 31, 1999. AA in Applied Bus., Mgmt., Mktg., Cuyahoga Community Coll. West, Parma, Ohio, 1985. Exec. fashion buyer, mdse. mgr. Rosenblum's Inc., Cleve., 1986-92; owner Elegance for Less, North Royalton, Ohio, 1994-97, SaRon Enterprises, Cleve., 1997—; ind. distbr. Body Sys. Tech., 1997—. Adviser Parma 60+ Mall Fashion Shows, 1986-90; fashion coord., model AAA Travel Agy, Cleve.; fashion coord., narrator, guest spkr. various vol. functions. Fashion coord. for Rosenblum's Fashion, Parma Jr. League, 1990, fashion coord., narration writer, Parma Area Fine Arts Coun. Fashion Show, 1991; hon. judge Miss Parma pageant, 1991, fashion coord., narration writer, guest speaker for North Royalton PTA Spring Luncheon and Fashion Show, 1996; sponsor Miss Greater Cleveland Scholarship prog., 1996, sponsor Cuyahoga C.C. Levy Campaign, 1996. Recipient Scholastic Art awards, Cleve. Inst. Art, 1983. Mem. NAFE, Nat. Assn. Investors Corp., Phi Theta Kappa. Byzantine Catholic. Avocations: travel, fashion shows, arts, crafts, health. Office: SaRon Enterprises PO Box 33085 Cleveland OH 44133-0085

SPITALERI, VERNON ROSARIO, newspaper publisher, manufacturing company executive; b. Pelham, N.Y., Aug. 2, 1922; s. Rosario S. and Martha (Landerer) S.; m. Marjorie A. Ferrar, Oct. 14, 1952; children: Marc, Eric, Kris, Lynn. BS, Carnegie Mellon U., 1942. Mgr. mech. dept. Am. Newspaper Pubs. Assn., N.Y.C., 1946-53; rsch. dir., gen. adminstr. Miami Herald and Knight Newspapers (Fla.), 1953-57; chmn. bd., pres. Sta-Hi Corp., Newport Beach, Calif., 1957-74; v.p. Republic Corp., 1974-76, Sun Chem. Corp., 1976-79. Chmn. bd. Sta-Hi Color Service, Sta-Hi Europe, Brussels, Concrete Floats-Huntington Engring. Corp., Huntington Beach, Calif., Kamalloy Alloys Corp.; editor, pub. Laguna Beach (Calif.) News-Post, 1967-81; pres. Laguna Pub. Co., Nat. Newspaper Found.; dir. Suburban Newspapers Am.; chmn. bd. Victory Profl. Products, Mango Surfware. Pres. Boys Club, Laguna Beach; mem. citizens adv. com. Laguna Beach; pres. Laguna Beach Libr. Bd., Laguna Playhouse, Laguna Coord. Coun.; bd. dirs. Sta-Hi Found.; dir. Opera Pacific, Festival of Arts. Lt. comdr. USNR, 1942-46. Decorated Purple Heart. Mem. Am. Mgmt. Assn., Nat. Newspaper Assn. (dir.), Calif. Newspaper Pubs. Assn. (dir.), Laguna Beach C. of C. (bd. dirs.), Dana Point Yacht Club, Alpha Tau Omega. Republican.

SPITALEWITZ, SAMUEL, nephrologist; b. Bklyn., Nov. 14, 1949; s. Hyman Louis and Harriet Spitalewitz; m. Maxine L. Spitalewitz; 2 children. BA magna cum laude, Bklyn. Coll., 1971; MD, NYU, 1975. Diplomate Am. Bd. Internal Medicine, Am. Bd. Nephrology. Intern in medicine The Brookdale Hosp. Med. Ctr., Bklyn., 1975-76, resident in medicine, 1976-78, fellow divsn. nephrology and hypertension, 1979-80, rsch. fellow divsn. nephrology and hypertension, 1980-81, physician-in-charge renal and hypertension clinics, 1981—, asst. attending physician divsn. nephrology and hypertension, 1981-85, assoc. attending physician, 1985-86, attending physician, 1987—. Asst. prof. medicine SUNY Health Sci. Ctr., Bklyn., 1984-99, assoc. prof. clin. medicine, 1999—. Contbr. articles to profl. jours. Grantee NIH, 1987-92, 88-93, ER Squibb Co., 1987-88. Fellow ACP; mem. AMA, AAAS, Am. Soc. Nephrology, Am. Heart Assn., Am. Fedn. Clin. Rsch., Am. Soc. Hypertension, Internat. Soc. Nephrology, Nat. Kidney Found., Coun. on Dialysis and Transplantation, Eastern Hypertension Soc., N.Y. Acad. Scis., Phi Beta Kappa. Office: Brookdale Plz Nephrology Assocs 1 Brookdale Plz Brooklyn NY 11212-3139

SPITZ, ARNOLDT JOHN, international trade professional, consultant; b. Koenigsberg, East Prussia, Germany, Nov. 20, 1929; s. Josef and Edith (Simon) S; m. Eleanor Marie; children: Allyson, Neil, Nicholas, Francesa. PhD, Ruprecht Karls U., Heidelberg, Fed. Republic Germany, 1952; MS, NYU, 1954; Hon. Doctorate in Internat. Econs., London Inst. Applied Rsch., 1992. Internat. economist Elektro Watt, Sindelfingen, Fed. Republic Germany, 1954-57, Arlen Industries, N.Y.C., 1957-66; sr. cons. and prof. Econ. Adv. Group Freiburg U., Fed. Republic Germany, 1966-70; exec. v.p. VAS Industries, Inc., NYC, 1970-74; exec. v.p., treas. Internat. Seaway Trading Corp., Boynton Beach, Fla., 1974-97; Unitech Steel Corp. (subs. Internat. Seaway), 1992-97; ret. Chardon, Ohio and Frankfurt, Germany, 1997—; pvt. cons. Internat. Trade, 1997—. Pres. emeritus bd. Geauga Campus Kent State U., 1974-97; sr. cons. Yonsei U., Seoul, Republic of Korea, 1982—; sr. cons. Beijing U., People's Republic of China, 1986—. Adv. Chardon (Ohio) Bd. Edn., 1987; dir. German-Am. Nat. Congress, Chgo., 1970-74. Recipient Spl. Recognition, George Washington U., 1979; named Hon. Prof., Inst. of Documentation and Study of Europe, Brussells, 1992; established Josef Spitz Meml. Scholarship Fund for Study of Humanities, Kent State U., 1985, Arnoldt J. Spitz Study of Humanities Fund, Ruprecht Karls U, 1988. Mem. Nat. Assn. Accts., Nat. Assn. Bus. Economists, Am. Econ. Assn., Soc. Govt. Econs., Rep. Nat. Com., Schurman Soc. at Heidelberg Univ., Ohio No. U. Coll. Bus. Roman Catholic. achcations: farming, horses, scouting. Home: 7580 Kimberly Ln Chesterland OH 44026-1328 E-mail: dr7580@aol.com.

SPITZ, BARBARA SALOMON, artist; b. Chgo., Jan. 8, 1926; d. Fred B. and Sadie (Lorch) Salomon; m. Lawrence S. Spitz, Mar. 19, 1949; children—Thomas R., Linda J., Joanne L. AB, Brown U., 1947; student, Art Inst. Chgo., 1942-43, R.I. Sch. Design, 1945. One-woman exhbns. include Benjamin Galleries, Chgo., 1971, 73, Kunsthaus Buhler, Stuttgart, Germany, 1973, Van Straaten Gallery, Chgo., 1976, 80, Elca London Studio, Montreal, Que., Can., 1977, Loyola U. Chgo., 1988, Schneider, Bluhm, Loeb gallery, Chgo., 1993, The Ctr. Gallery, 1994; group exhibitions include Am. Acad. Arts and Letters, Library of Congress traveling print exhbn., Tokyo Cen. Mus. Arts, Nat. Acad. Design, N.Y.C., Pratt Graphic Ctr., Honolulu Acad. Arts, Wadsworth Atheneum, Nat. Aperture, 1986—, Laguna Art Mus., others; represented in permanent collections, Phila. Mus. Art, DeCordova Mus., Okla. Art Ctr., Milw. Art Ctr., Los Angeles County Mus. Art, Art Inst. Chgo., Portland Mus. Art, med. arts program UCLA, Block Mus./Northwestern U., Smart Mus./U. Chgo. Vice-chmn. Chgo. area Brown U. Bicentennial Drive; treas. Hearing and Speech Rehab. Ctr., Michael Reese Hosp., 1960; fine arts patron bd. Newport Harbor Art Mus. Mem. Print Club Phila., Boston Printmakers, Arts Club of Chgo., Soc. Am. Graphic Artists. Address: 1106 Somerset Ln Newport Beach CA 92660-5629 E-mail: bsslss@aol.com.

SPITZ, HUGO MAX, retired lawyer; b. Richmond, Va., Aug. 17, 1927; s. Jacob Gustav and Clara (Herzfeld) S.; m. Barbara Steinberg, June 22, 1952; children: Jack Gray, Jill Ann Levy, Sally Spitz. AA, U. Fla., 1948, BLaws, 1951, JD, 1967. Bar: Fla. 1951, S.C. 1955, U.S. Dist. Ct. (so. dist.) Fla. 1951, U.S. Dist. Ct. (ea. dist.) S.C. 1956, U.S. Ct. Appeals (4th cir.) 1957. Asst. atty. gen. State of Fla., Tallahassee, 1951; assoc. Williams, Salomon & Katz, Miami, 1951-54, Steinberg & Levkoff, Charleston, S.C., 1954-57; sr. ptnr. The Steinberg Law Firm L.L.P., 1957-2001; ret., 2001. Lectr. S.C. Trial Lawyers Assn., Columbia, 1958—, S.C. U. Sch. Law, Columbia, 1975, S.C. Bar Assn., 1955—; assoc. mcpl. judge Charleston, 1972-74, chief mcpl. judge, 1974-76; commr. Charleston County Substance Abuse Commn., 1976-79; bd. govs. S.C. Patient's Compensation Fund, Columbia, 1978-97; adv. mem., atty. S.C. Legis. Coun. for Worker's Compensation; chmn. bd. dirs. Franklin C. Fetter Health Ctr., Charleston, 1977-78; mem. S.C. Appellate Def. Commn., 1985-86; founding sponsor Civil Justice Found., 1986—; bd. pres. Charleston Jewish Fedn., 1990-91, pres., 1991-92. Pres. Synagogue Emanu-El, 1969-71. With USN, 1945-46. Awarded Order of Silver Crescent, Gov. S.C., 2001. Fellow S.C. Bar Assn., U. S.C. Ednl. Found.; mem. ABA, Civil Justice Found., S.C. Law Inst., S.C. Trial Lawyers Assn. (founder and pres. 1985-86), S.C. Claimants' Attys. for Worker's Compensation (Hon. life bd. mem., founder, exec. com. 1986), S.C. Worker's Compensation Ednl. Assn. (bd. dirs. 1978-98), S.C. Law Inst., Am. Judicature Soc., Trial Lawyers Am. (mem. pres. council 1986-87, stalwart 2001), Nat. Rehab. Assn., Nat. Orgn. Social Security Claimants' Reps. S.C. Bar (chmn. trial and appellate sect. 1982-83, ho. of dels. 1984-85), So. Assn. Workmen's Compensation Adminstrs., Nat. Inst. for Trial Advocacy (com. chmn. 1985), Hebrew Benevolent Soc. (life, pres. 1974-75), Jewish Cmty. Ctr. (Charleston) (v.p. 1972-74), Hebrew Orphan Soc. (life, pres. 2000-01), B'nai B'rith, Elks (life). Democrat. Home: 337 Confederate Cir Charleston SC 29407-7430 E-mail: hspitz@comcast.net.

SPITZ, JACK GRAY, chemist; b. Charleston, S.C., Jan. 28, 1955; s. Hugo Max and Barbara Steinberg Spitz; m. Shelley Berlinsky Berlinsky; children: Cara Ann, Joshua Erin. BA in Microbiology, U. S. Fla., 1976; BS in Pharmacy, Med. U. S.C., 1979. Organic chemist Gen. Engring. Labs., Charleston, 1990—99; dir. Schneider Lab., Richmond, Va., 1999—2000; dir. ops. Great Smokies Diagnostic Lab., Asheville, NC, 2000—01. Jewish. Avocations: surfing, hiking. Home: 168 River Loop Dr Horse Shoe NC 28742 Office: Great Smokies Diagnostic Lab 63 Zillicoa St Asheville NC 28801-1132 Office Fax: 828-253-2237. Personal E-mail: jgspitz@yahoo.com. Business E-Mail: jacks@gsdl.com.

SPITZ, SEYMOUR JAMES, JR. retired fragrance company executive; b. Milw., Nov. 17, 1921; s. Seymour James and Marie (Spinette) S.; m. Elizabeth Taylor Parks, Feb. 7, 1948 (div. Aug. 1967); children: William Taylor, Elizabeth Seymour, Anne Bellin; m. Ellen C. Flynn, July 25, 1969; 1 dau., Ellen Christina. SB, MIT, 1943. With Newport Industries div. Heyden Newport Chem. Corp., Pensacola, Fla., 1946-65; asst. chief engr., 1955-57; asst. v.p., 1957-58; v.p. Newport Industries div. Heyden Newport Chem. Corp., 1959-60, exec. v.p., 1960-61, pres., 1961-65; v.p. parent co. Heyden Newport Chem. Corp., 1962-65, became group v.p., 1965; exec. v.p. Heyden Newport Chem. Corp. (now Tenneco Chems., Inc.), 1966; pres. Tenneco Chems., Inc., 1967-69; sr. v.p. parent co. Tenneco Inc.; pres. and dir. Internat. Flavors & Fragrances Inc., N.Y.C., 1970-85. Mem. MIT Corp. Devel. Com., 1977-86; trustee Spence Sch., 1982-88, Savannah (Ga.) Symphony, 1990-95, 98, Telfair Mus. Art, Savannah, 1993-96. With USN, 1943-46. Mem. Univ. Club (N.Y.C.), Larchmont Yacht Club (N.Y., trustee 1986-89), Landings Club, Oglethorpe Club (Savannah, bd. dirs. 1995-99). Home: 6 Brandenberry Rd Savannah GA 31411-2201

SPITZBERG, IRVING JOSEPH , JR. lawyer, corporate executive; b. Little Rock, Feb. 9, 1942; s. Irving Joseph and Marie Bettye (Seeman) S.; m. Roberta Frances Alprin, Aug. 21, 1966 (div. 1988); children— Edward Storm, David Adam; m. Virginia V. Thorndike, Dec. 24, 1988. BA, Columbia U., 1964; B.Phil., Oxford U., 1966; JD, Yale U., 1969. Bar: Calif. 1969, D.C. 1985, Va. 1995. Asst. prof. Pitzer Coll., Claremont, Calif., 1969-71; fellow Inst. Current World Affairs, N.Y.C., 1971-74; vis. lectr. Brown U., Providence, 1973; assoc prof. SUNY, Buffalo, 1974-80, dean of coll., 1974-78; gen. sec. AAUP, Washington, 1980-84; exec. dir. Coun. for Liberal Learning of Assn. Am. Colls., 1985-89; pres. The Knowledge Co., Fairfax, Va., 1985-2001; ptnr. Spitzberg & Drew, Washington, 1990-92; of counsel Spirer & Goldberg, 1993—; pvt. practice, 1993—. Coord. Alvan Ikoku Coll., Nigeria, 1979-80; cons. Bd. Adult Edn., Kenya, 1973-74, Philander Smith Coll., Little Rock, 1978-80; co-dir. nat. study on campus life for Carnegie Found. for Advancement Teaching, 1989-90. Author and editor: Exchange of Expertise, 1978, Universities and the New International Order, 1979, Universities and the International Exchange of Knowledge, 1980; author: Campus Programs on Leadership, 1986, Racial Politics in Little Rock, 1987; co-author: (with Berdahl and Moodie), Quality and Access in Higher Education, 1991, (with Virginia Thorndike) Creating Community on College Campuses, 1992. Founder Coalition for Ednl. Excellence, Western N.Y., 1978-80; founding mem. Alliance for Leadership Devel., Washington, 1985; counsel GASP, Pomona, Calif., 1969-71; Dem. Committeeman, Erie County, N.Y., 1978-80; founding pres. Internat. Found. for St. Catherine's Coll., Oxford, 1986-91; founder Coun. for Liberal Learning; mem. Ethical Culture Soc. Nat. winner Westinghouse Sci. Talent Search, 1960; Kellett scholar Trustees of Columbia U., 1964-66. Mem. Am. Immigration Lawyers Assn., Nat. Acad. Elder Law Attys., Assn. Study Higher Edn., Washington Ethical Soc., Columbia Club, Yale Club (Washington). Jewish. Avocations: kids, the Internet. E-mail: ijs@aol.com.

SPITZE, GLENYS SMITH, retired educator; b. Rozel, Kans., May 20, 1919; d. Harry H. and Mary Louisa (Mishler) Smith; m. LeRoy A. Spitze, Dec. 31, 1942 (dec. Nov. 1995); children: Randall LeRoy, Kevin Lance, Kimett Alvin, Terril Christian, Shawn Smith; 1 fosterchild, Theo Ritz-Spitze. Cert. tchg., U. Kans., 1939; AA, San Jose (Calif.) City Coll., 1963; BA in Psychology, San Jose State U., 1965, MA in Child Devel., 1968. Cert. tchr., counselor, Calif. Elem. sch. tchr. Topeka County Schs., Richland, Kans., 1939-40, Kinsley (Kans.) Pub. Schs., 1940-42; presch. substitute tchr. AAUW Kindergarten, Newark, 1945—46; presch. tchr. Meth. Ch. Facility, Campbell, Calif., 1956-58; guest lectr. Govt. Sch. Social Work, Colombo, Sri Lanka, 1965-66; instr. man-woman relationship San Jose State Free U., 1966-67; child devel. lab. psychol. examiner Child Labs San Jose State U., 1967-68; pvt. informal practice tchr., counselor, cons. Kailua, Hawaii. Vocal music dir. grades 1-3 Southside Sch., 1940-41; 6th dist. Calif. Congress Parent-Tchrs. Social Welfare dir., officer 6th dist. com. Calif. Coun. on Crime and Delinquency, San Jose, 1956-62; mem. kindergarten com. AAUW, Newark, Ohio, 1945-46; coord. Sangha Symposium, Asian Philosophy Club, San Jose State U., 1964-65; lectr. in field. Contbr. articles, poems to profl. publs. Hon. del. Gov. Brown's Conf. on Prevention of Juvenile Delinquency, Sacramento, 1963; co-organizer Post Polio Support Group, Kailua-Kona, HI, 2000. Mem. Psi Chi. Avocations: writing, reading, swimming, snorkeling, anthropology and archeology travel. Home: 78-6800 Alii Dr Apt 5-103 Kailua Kona HI 96740-4421 Home (Summer): Apt 5-103 78-6800 Alii Dr Kailua Kona HI 96740-4421 also: Gen Delivery Woodland Park CO 80863 E-mail: GMGlenys@webtv.net.

SPITZER, A. ROBERT, physician, electrical engineer; b. Bronx, N.Y., Aug. 13, 1955; s. Morris and Hedvig (Rosenthal) S.; m. Ann L. Silverman; children: Daniel, Rivka, Sarah, Rachel. BSEE, Columbia U., 1976; MD, Albert Einstein Coll. Medicine, 1980, 1980. Resident Westchester County Med. Ctr., Valhalla, N.Y., 1981-82, Tufts-New Eng. Med. Ctr., Boston, 1982-85; fellow Nat. Inst. Neurol. Disorders, Bethesda, Md., 1985-87; asst. prof. Wayne State U., Detroit, 1987-93, clin. assoc. prof., 1993—; pvt. practice Southfield, Mich., 1993—. Physician Braintree (Mass.) Hosp., 1982-84, South Shore Hosp., Weymouth, Mass., 1982-84, Harper Hosp., Detroit, 1987—, Detroit Receiving Hosp., 1987—, Huron Valley Hosp., Commerce, Mich., 1988—, Providence Hosp., Southfield, Mich., 1997—; physician Wm. Beaumont Hosp., Royal Oak, Mich., 1993—, mem. mgmt. info. com., 1995—; lectr. Pepperdine U., Malibu, Calif., 1990, Calif. State Polytech., Pomona, 1990, 91, U. Calif., Riverside, 1990, Met. Detroit chpt. Assn. Computing Machinery, 1990, U. Wis., LaCrosse, 1990, Winona (Minn.) State U., 1990, James Madison U., Va., 1990, U. Va., Charlottesville, 1990, U. Puget Sound, Takoma, Wash., 1991, Willamette U., Portland, Oreg., 1991, Northeastern U., Boston, 1991, Greater Boston chpt. Assn. Computing Machinery, 1991, Calif. State U., Fullerton, 1992, San Gabriel Assn. Computing Machinery, Jet Propulsion Lab., 1992, Citadel Coll., Charleston, S.C., 1992, U. S.C., Columbia, 1992, Southeastern Mich. on Artificial Intelligence, 1993, Tulane U., New Orleans, 1993, Loyola U., New Orleans, 1993, Nicolet Corp., Madison, Wis., 1991, Dantec Corp., Copenhagen, Denmark, 1991, Biomed. Engring. Soc., Charlottesville, Va., 1991, IEEE, Boston, 1991, Siemens Med. Electronics, Danvers, Mass., 1991, Wayne County Med. Soc., 1992, U. Calif. San Diego Neurology Grand Rounds, 1992, Technion U., Haifa, Israel, 1992, B'nai Zion Med. Ctr., Haifa, 1992, S.E. Mensa, 1994, among others. Contbr. articles to profl. jours. Inventor pad for preventing carpal tunnel syndrome. Grantee Whitaker Found., 1988-91, Upjohn Pharms., Kalamazoo, 1991-92, 92-93, Nervous Sys., Inc., 1993, NIMH. Mem. Am. Acad. Neurology, IEEE, Am. Assn. Electrodiagnostic Medicine (chmn. 1992-95), Mass. State Med. Soc., Assn. for Computing Machinery. Avocations: flying, photography, ham radio, sailing. Office: Basic Rsch & Investigative Neuroscis PC 20180 W 12 Mile Rd Ste 10 Southfield MI 48076-5412 Fax: 248 358 3299.

SPITZER, ADRIAN, pediatrician, medical educator; b. Bucharest, Rumania, Dec. 21, 1927; came to U.S., 1963, naturalized, 1968; s. Osias and Sophia S. S.; m. Carole Zelter, Oct. 31, 1951; 1 son, Vlad. BS, Matei Basarab Lyceum, Bucharest, 1946; MD, Med. Sch. Bucharest, 1952. Diplomate: Am. Bd. Pediatrics. Intern White Plains (N.Y.) Hosp., 1964; resident Hosp. Med. Coll. Pa., 1965-66; postdoctoral fellow pediatric nephrology Albert Einstein Coll. Medicine, 1966-67; postdoctoral fellow in renal physiology Cornell U. Med. Sch., 1967-68; practice medicine specializing in pediatric nephrology Bronx, N.Y., 1968—; asst. prof. pediatrics Albert Einstein Coll. Medicine, 1968-72, assoc. prof., 1972-76, prof., 1976—, dir. div. nephrology, 1973-99; mem. staff Bronx Mcpl. Hosp. Ctr., Hosp. Albert Einstein Coll. Medicine/Montefore Med. Ctr.; mem. Medicine B Study sect.-NIH, 1976-80. Prof. C. Donders rotating chmn. U. Utrecht, The Netherlands, 1990-91; Christiansen vis. fellow St. Catherine's Coll.; vis. fellow dept. biochemistry Oxford U., 1981-82; coord. Internat. Study Kidney Disease in Children; chmn. organizing com. 1st-7th Internat. Workshop on Devel. Renal Physiology, 1980-98, pres., 2001; mem. renal adv. com. N.Y.C. Dept. Health; sci. adv. bd. rsch. and grant com. Nat. Kidney Found., 1982; chmn. pediatric nephrology bd. Am. Bd. Pediat., 1982-83. Mem. editorial bd.: Pediatric Nephrology, Seminars in Nephrology; assoc. editor: Pediatric Renal Disease, 1979, 2d edit., 1992; editor: The Kidney Development, 1982. NIH spl fellow, 1967; John E. Fogarty Sr. Internat. fellow, 1981-82; grantee NIH, N.Y. State Health Research Council, Nat. Kidney Found.; recipient Bela Schick medal for extraordinary achievements in acad. and clin. pediatrics; The Scientific Advancement award of the Internat. Pediatr. Nephrol. Assoc. Mem.: Intersoc. Coun. for Kidney and Urinary Tract Rsch. (sec.-treas. 1984—89), Am. Pediat. Soc., Am. Acad. Pediat., Soc. Pediatric Rsch., Am. Physiol. Soc., Am. Fedn. Clin. Rsch., Am. Soc. Pediatric Nephrology (coun. 1977—80, pres. 1981—82), Am. Soc. Nephrology (com. on govtl. rels. 1999—2001), Internat. Pediatric Nephrology Assn. (hon. Sci. Advancement award), Salt and Water Club. Office: Albert Einstein Coll Medicine Montefiore Med Ctr 111 E 210th St Bronx NY 10467-2401 E-mail: spitzer@aecom.yu.edu.

SPITZER, CARY REDFORD, avionics consultant, electrical engineer; b. New Hope, Va., July 31, 1937; s. Clyde Burke and Marion Jeanette (Redford) S.; m. Carrie Laura Ruth Logan, June 18, 1960; 1 child, Stiegel Logan. BSEE, Va. Poly. Inst. & State U., 1959; MS in Engring. Mgmt., George Washington U., 1970. Rsch. engr., engring. mgr. Langley Rsch Ctr., NASA, Hampton, Va., 1962-94; founder, pres. AvioniCon, Inc., 1993—. Lectr. UCLA, 1989—, George Washington U., 1994. Author: Viking Orbiter Views of Mars, 1981, Digital Avionics Systems, 1987, 2d edit., 1993, Avionics Handbook, 2000; contbr. articles to sci. publs. 1st lt. USAF, 1959-62. Recipient Volare award Airline Avionics Inst., 1988; named Va. Peninsula Engr. of Yr., 1993; recipient Digital Avionics award Am. Inst. of Aeronautics and Astronautics, 1994 Fellow: IEEE (Centennial medal 1984, Millennium medal 2000), AIAA (assoc.); mem.: Aerospace and Electronic Systems Soc. of IEEE (pres. 1973—74, editor-in-chief Trans. 1996—99, chmn. IEEE-USA aerospace policy com. 1997—2000), Exch. Club (pres. Williamsburg 1985). Methodist. Avocations: kite flying, car mechanics. Home and Office: 3409 Foxridge Rd Williamsburg VA 23188-2499

SPITZER, ELIOT, state attorney general; m. Silda Spitzer; 3 children. Grad., Princeton U., 1981; JD, Harvard U., 1984. Clk. U.S. Judge Robert W. Sweet; assoc. Paul, Weiss, Rifkind, Wharton & Garrison, Skadden Arps Slate Meagher & Flom; ptnr. Constantine & Ptnrs., N.Y.C.; asst. dist. atty. State of N.Y., Manhattan, 1986—92, atty. gen. Albany, 1999—. Analyst, commentator on nat. news programs including NBC's Today Show, CNN's Burden of Proof, CNBC, Court TV. Editor: Harvard Law Rev.; contbr. articles in leading newspapers and legal jours. Founder Ctr. for Cmty. Interest; trustee Montifiore Med. Ctr. Office: Dept of Law The Capitol, 2nd Fl Albany NY 12224*

SPITZER, HUGH D. lawyer; b. Seattle, Feb. 14, 1949; s. George Frederick and Dorothy Lea (Davidson) S.; m. Ann Scales, Oct. 14, 1983; children: Johanna Spitzer, Claudia Spitzer, Jenny Spitzer. BA, Yale U., 1970; JD, U. Wash., 1974; LLM, U. Calif., 1982. Bar: Wash. 1974, U.S. Dist/ Ct. (ea. and we. dists.) Wash. 1975, U.S. Ct. Appeals (9th and D.C. cirs.) 1975, U.S. Supreme Ct. 1980. Program analyst N.Y.C. Health and Hosp. Corp., 1970-71; labor lawyer Hafer, Cassidy & Price, Seattle, 1974-76; legis. asst. Seattle City Coun., 1976-77; legal counsel to mayor City of Seattle, 1977-81; mcpl. bond lawyer Foster Pepper & Shefelman, PLLC, Seattle, 1982—. Affiliate prof. sch. law U. Wash. Contbr. articles to profl. jours. Vice chair Puget Sound Water Quality Authority Wash. State, 1989-96; chair Seattle Law Income Housing Levy Oversight com., 1988-96; chair Wash. State Affordable Housing Adv. Bd., 2000—; vice chair State Tax Structure Com., 2001--. Mem. Nat. Assn. Bond Lawyers, Pub. Legal Edn. Working Group, Am. Judicature Soc. (mem. exec. com. Coun. on Pub. Legal Edn.). Democrat. Avocations: piano, hiking, skiing. Office: Foster Pepper & Shefelman PLLC 1111 3rd Ave Bldg Ste 3400 Seattle WA 98101-3292 E-mail: spith@foster.com.

SPITZER, JACK J. banker; b. N.Y.C., Sept. 11, 1917; s. Ira I. and Jennie (Brody) S.; m. Charlotte May Braunstein, Dec. 21, 1941; children: Jil Spitzer-Fox, Robert Braunstein. BA, UCLA, 1938; LLD (hon.), Adelphi U., 1980, Ben-Gurion U.of the Negev. 1991. Pres., CEO Spitzer Co., L.A., 1951-59; pres., chief exec. officer Brentwood Savs. & Loan, 1959-66, Sterling Savs. & Loan, Riverside, Calif., 1966-72, Security Savs. & Loan, Seattle, 1972-78; chmn. bd. dirs. Cert. Reports, Kinderhook, N.Y., 1967—; chmn. bd. dirs., chief exec. officer Covenant Mortgage, Mercer Island, Wash., 1982—; chmn. Vitritek Environ., Inc., Columbia, Md., 1993—. Pres. United Way, Riverside, 1970; nat. chmn. David Ben-Gurion Centennial Com. of the U.S., Inc., 1985-87; mem. U.S. Del. to Inauguration of Pope John Paul II, apptd. by Pres. Carter, 1978; 1st v.p. Dem. County Ctrl. Com., L.A., 1953-62; Vice chmn., bd. govs. Ben-Gurion Univ. of Negev, 1984—, pres. Am. Assocs., 1985; founder, chmn. Seattle-Beer Sheva (Israel) Sister City Com., 1977, 2001; exec. committeeman Am. Jewish Joint Distbn. Com., 1985-96; v.p. Conf. on Jewish Material Claims, 1978—; vice chmn. bd. trustees Med. Edn. for South African Blacks, 1984-2001; chmn. bd. trustees B'nai B'rith Youth Orgn., 1996—; chmn. adv. coun. Cath. U. Am.-Internat. Ctr. for Global Aging.; apptd. to pub. del./amb. by Pres. Clinton 52d Session UN. Served to 2d lt. U.S. Army, 1943-46. Spitzer dept. of Social Work at Ben-Gurion Univ. named in his honor, 1986; recipient Outstanding Communal Svc. award Wurtzweiler Sch. Social Work, 1987, Gold medal for Humanitarian Svc., B'nai B'rith, 1994, Torch of Liberty award, Anti-Defamation League of B'nai B'rith, 1975. Mem. Meml. Found. for Jewish Culture (treas. 1978—, chmn. exec. com. 1990—, pres. 1994-96, hon. life pres. 1996—), Alexis de Tocqueville Soc., United Way, Rainier Club (Seattle), A.Z.A. of B'nai Brith (internat. pres. 1938-39, Harry Lapidus Communal Svc. award 1936, Sam Beber Outstanding Alumnus award 1970), B'nai Brith (west coast pres. 1968-69, internat. pres. 1978-82, hon. pres. 1982—, internat. chmn. susquicentennial celebration 1992-94), Rotary (World Cmty. Svc. award 1994). Avocation: ping pong. Home: PO Box 2008 Kirkland WA 98083-2008 Office: Covenant Mortgage Corp 9725 SE 36th St Ste 304 Mercer Island WA 98040-3896

SPITZER, JOHN BRUMBACK, lawyer; b. Toledo, Mar. 6, 1918; s. Lyman and Blanche (Brumback) S.; m. Lucy Ohlinger, May 10, 1941 (dec. Oct. 13, 1971); children: John B., Molly (Mrs. Edmund Frost), Lyman, Adelbert L.; m. Vondah D. Thornbury, July 3, 1972 (dec. Nov. 2001); stepchildren: Vondah, Barbara, James R. Thornbury. Grad., Phillips Andover Acad., 1935; BA, Yale U., 1939, LLB, 1947. Bar: Ohio 1947. Law clk. to U.S. Supreme Ct. Justice Stanley Reed, 1947-48; ptnr. Marshall, Melhorn, Cole, Hummer & Spitzer, Toledo, 1955-86, Hummer & Spitzer, Toledo, 1986-89; with Hummer Legal Svcs. Corp., Perrysburg, Ohio, 1990—. Pres. Spitzer Box Co., 1955-63; v.p. Spitzer Bldg. Co., 1960-91, pres. 1992—. Pres. Toledo Symphony Orch., 1956-58, v.p., sec., 1958-86. Maj. AUS, World War II. Mem.: Belmont Country Club. Congregationalist. Home: 29620 Gleneagles Rd Perrysburg OH 43551-3530 Office: Hummer Legal Svcs Corp 4841 Monroe St Ste 205 Toledo OH 43623-4352 E-mail: h/lsc@accessToledo.com.

SPITZER, LYNN CHRISTIAN, executive; b. Honolulu, Sept. 20, 1963; d. James Hulbert and Patricia Anne (Wassman) Christian; m. Allan Thomas Spitzer, Dec. 20, 1986; children: Michelle Anne Kapioláilehua, Andrew Kaleipaihala. BBA, U. Hawaii, 1985; postgrad., Hist. Preservation Cert. Course, Honolulu, 1988—. Adminstr., dir., life mem. Daughters Hawaii, Honolulu, 1985—. Branch mgr. Scholastic Book Fairs, HI. Contbr. articles to profl. jours. Rep. precinct officer 19th Precinct 9th Senatorial Dist., 1988—; donor Blood Bank Hawaii, Honolulu, 1984—, Bone Marrow Registry, Honolulu, Nat., 1990, Girl Scout leader, 1998—. Mem. Hist. Hawaii Found., Bishop Mus. Assn., Hawaii Mus. Assn., Nat. Trust for Hist. Preservation, Outrigger Canoe Club. Episcopalian. Avocations: water sports, cooking, writing, gardening, travel. Home and Office: 1422 Nanaloko Pl Kailua HI 96734-4069

SPITZER, MATTHEW LAWRENCE, retired retail store executive; b. Pitts., June 20, 1929; s. Martin and Ruth G. S.; children: Mark, Edward, Eric, Joseph. Student, U. Buffalo, 1948-50. Lic. airline transport pilot. Product line mgr. Gen. Dynamics, Rochester, N.Y., 1962-67; dir. contracts Friden divsn. Singer, San Leandro, Calif., 1968-69; asst. v.p. Talcott Computer Leasing, San Francisco, 1970-71; pres. Spitzer Music Mgmt. Co., Hayward, Calif., 1972-95, Spitzer Helicopter Leasing Co., Hayward. Chmn. bd. Leo's Audio and Music Techs., Oakland, Calif. Mem. Masons, Mensa.

SPITZER, MORTON EDWARD, insurance company executive; b. N.Y.C., Jan. 3, 1937; s. Henry Lawrence and Martha (Michel) S.; m. Nancy Dinetz, Oct. 10, 1965; children: Matthew, Douglas. BA, Bklyn. Coll., 1957; MS, N.C. State U., 1959; PhD, NYU, 1964. Dir./mgr. planning and analysis The Prudential Ins. Co. Am., Newark, 1964-74, v.p. S.W. ops. Houston, 1975-79, v.p. ordinary agys. Newark, 1979-87, pres. North Ctrl. ops. Mpls., 1988, sr. v.p. dist. agys. Newark, 1989, Woodland Hills, Calif., 1990-91; exec. v.p., COO Liberty Life Assurance Co. Boston, Dover, N.H., 1992—. Bd. dirs. Liberty Life Assurance Co., Boston, Liberty Assignment Co., Liberty Life Distbrs. LLC, Liberty Life Securities LLC, BARCO Lto, Barbados, Limra Internat.; bd. govs. ACLI Forum 500. Co-author: The Law and Personnel Testing, 1971. Bd. dirs. Nat. Soc. to Prevent Blindness, N.J., 1986-89, nat. bd. dirs., Chgo., 1989. Mem. APA, Am. Psychol. Soc., Ea. Psychol. Assn., Sigma Xi. Avocations: tennis, art. Home: 449 E Deering Rd Deering NH 03244 Office: Liberty Life Assurance Co of Boston 100 Main St Dover NH 03820-3835 E-mail: morton.spitzer@libertymutual.com.

SPITZER, PETER GEORGE, information systems executive, consultant; b. Oradea, Romania, July 16, 1956; married, 1985. BS in Bioelec. Engring., MIT, 1979, MS in Elec. Engring. and Computer Sci., 1980; MD cum laude, Harvard U., 1980; MBA, UCLA, 1986. Sr. systems analyst Nat. Cash Register Co., Los Angeles, 1976-77; dir. pathology diagnosis registry Peter Brigham Hosps., Boston, 1978-80; research analyst Mass. Gen. Hosp., 1978-80; resident obstetrics and gynecologist UCLA Ctr. for Health Scis., Los Angeles, 1980-81; asst. v.p. Am. Med. Internat., Info. Systems Group, Beverly Hills, Calif., 1981-87; chief info. officer Tex. Children's Hosp., Houston, 1988-90; asst. rsch. prof. pediatrics Baylor Coll. of Medicine, 1988-90; pres. Spitzer Assocs., 1990—. Cons. advanced info. tech., 1990—; sr. v.p. Deudrite Internat., 1999-2000; chief tech. officer Aspeon Inc., 2000. Smith-Kline Found. fellow, 1978-80. Fellow Healthcare Info. Mgmt. Systems Soc. (Clin. Syss. award 1995); mem. AMA, IEEE, Am. Hosp. Assn., Am. Coll. Physician Execs., Soc. for Info. Mgmt., Am. Soc. Quality Control, Am. Med. Info. Assn., European Community Com. for Standardization (CEN/TC251 - healthcare systems standardization com.), Eta Kappa Nu, Sigma Xi. Avocations: travel, reading, art, tennis, sailing. Office: 11718 Barrington Ct # 504 Los Angeles CA 90049-2930

SPITZER, ROBERT J. academic administrator; BBA, Gonzaga U.; MPhil, St. Louis U.; STB, Gregorian U., Rome; ThM, Weston Sch. Theology, Cambridge, Mass.; PhD in Philosophy, Cath. U. of Am. Tchr. Georgetown U., 1984-90, Seattle U., 1978-80, 90-98; pres. Gonzaga U., 1998—. Co-founder U. Faculty for Life; founder, adv. Life Principles. Office: Gonzaga U 502 E Boone Ave Spokane WA 99258-0001*

SPITZER, VLAD GERARD, lawyer; b. Bucharest, Romania, Mar. 3, 1956; came to U.S., 1963; s. Adrian and Carole Spitzer; m. Denise J. Borenstein, July 9, 1989; 1 child, Max Oliver. BA with honors, NYU, 1978; JD, Yeshiva U., 1981. Bar: N.Y. 1988, Conn. 1995, U.S. Dist. Ct. (so. and ea. dists.) N.Y. 1988, U.S. Dist. Ct. Conn. 1996, U.S. Ct. Appeals (2d cir.) 1994, U.S. Supreme Ct. 1995. Asst. dist. atty. Dist. Atty.'s Office of King's County, Bklyn., 1981-83; ptnr. Goldbergh & Spitzer LLC, N.Y.C., 1988-95, Stamford, Conn., 1995—. Adv. bd. Nat. Employee Rights Inst., Cin., 1997—; founding mem. Conn. Employee Rights Inst., Stamford, Conn., 1997; coop. atty. ACLU, N.Y. Civil Liberties Union; judge Wagner Nat. Lab. and Employment Law Moot Ct., N.Y. Law Sch., 1996-98. Belkin scholar, 1981. Mem. ATLA (labor and employment sect. 1996—), Assn. of the Bar of the City of N.Y., Nat. Employment Lawyers Assn., Conn. Bar Assn. (labor and employment sect. 1996—, employee benefits com. 1996—), Nat. Employee Rights Inst., Stamford-Norwalk Regional Bar Assn., Stamford Rotary Club. Office: Spitzer Sundheim & Brey LLC 350 Bedford St Ste 401 Stamford CT 06901-1741

SPITZER, WALTER OSWALD, epidemiologist, educator; b. Asuncion, Paraguay, Feb. 19, 1937; Canadian citizen; MD, U. Toronto, 1962; MHA, U. Mich., 1966; MPH, Yale U., 1970. Gen. dir. Internat. Christian Med. Soc., 1966-69; asst. prof. clin. epidemiology McMaster U., Hamilton, Ont., Can., 1969-73, assoc. prof. Can., 1973-75; prof. epidemiology McGill U., Montreal, 1975-95, prof. medicine, 1983-95, Strathcona prof. and chmn. dept. epidemiology and biostats., 1984-93, prof. emeritus, 1996—; pres. Methods in Epidemiology, Inc., 1997—; clin. prof. medicine Stanford U., 1996—. Cons. PanAm. Health Orgn., Washington, 1975, 77, Aga Khan Found., Geneva, 1983-84. Editor Jour. Clin. Epidemiology, 1981-95; contbr. articles to biomed. jours. Named Nat. Health Scientist of Can., 1981 Fellow Royal Coll. Physicians and Surgeons Can., Am. Coll. Epidemiology, Faculty of Pharm. Medicine of the Royal Colls. of Phys. of the U.K.; mem. Inst. Medicine of Nat. Acad. Scis. (U.S.). Avocations: music, sailing, photography.

SPITZER, WILLIAM JOHN, healthcare social work administrator, educator; b. Chgo., Jan. 31, 1949; s. William Carl and Violet (Kramer) S.; m. Eugena Ann Spitzer; 1 child, Colin William. BA, BS, U. Ill., 1971, MSW, 1973, PhD in Social Work, 1981. Lic. clin. social worker, Oreg., Tex; cert. sch. social worker, Ill. Dir. foster care svcs. Cath. Social Svcs., Grand Rapids, Mich., 1973-76, dir. residential group treatment, 1975-76; dir., founder Human Devel. Cons. Svcs., Urbana, Ill., 1977-89; dir. dept. social svcs. Sarah Bush Lincoln Health System, Mattoon, 1982-86; dir. dept. social work svc. Oreg. Health Scis. U., Portland, 1986-92; adj. asst. prof. social work Portland State U., 1986-92; dir. dept. socialwork svcs. Medical Coll. Va., 1992-2000; clin. assoc. prof. Va. Commonwealth Univ., 1992-99; pvt. practice. State clin. dir. Oreg. Critical Response Team, 1988-92; v.p. Interagy. Coun. Coles County, Ill., 1984-85; chmn. Area Child Abuse Mgmt. Team Coles County, Ill., 1986. Editl. bd. Health and Social Work, 1993-95, Social Work in Health Care, 1996—. Mem. NASW (ACSW 1976—, DCSW 1994, chair com. continuing edn. Oreg. chpt. 1988-92, LCSW advt. com. 1990-92, bd. dirs. Oreg. chpt. 1987-89, program com. Va. chpt. 1993-96, chair cont. edn. cert. program 1999-2001, exec. com. bd. dir. 1999-2001), Soc. Social Workers Admin. in Health Care (nat. bd. dirs. 1999—, nat. chmn. Hy Weiner leadership award com. 1988, v.p. ctrl. Ill. dist. 1984-86, pres. Oreg chpt. 1989-90, bd. dirs. 1987-89, chair., Oreg. chpt. continuing edn. com. 1988-92, nat. edn. for practice com. 1989-93, Oreg. social work dir. of the yr. award 1990, Oreg. social work program of the yr. 1990. 92, Oreg. pres. award 1990, 91), AHA/SSWAHC (pol. act. com. 1994-95, chair profl. devel. com. Va. chpt. 1993—, pres. elect Va. chpt. 1998, pres. Va. chpt. 1999-2000, Va. healthcare social work admin. of yr. 1996, Hy Weiner nat. healthcare social work leadership award 1998). Avocations: skiing, travel, motorcycling. Home and Office: 12208 Chadsworth Ct Glen Allen VA 23059-6931 E-mail: wjspitzer@aol.com.

SPITZLI, DONALD HAWKES, JR. lawyer; b. Newark, Mar. 19, 1934; s. Donald Hawkes and Beatrice (Banister) S.; children: Donald Hawkes III, Peter Gilbert, Seth Armstrong. AB, Dartmouth Coll., 1956; LL.B., U. Va., 1963. Bar: Va. 1963. Assoc. Willcox, Savage, Lawrence, Dickson & Spindle, Norfolk, Va., 1964-67, 68-70, ptnr., 1971-77; atty. Eastman Kodak Co., Rochester, N.Y., 1967-68; pres. Marine Hydraulics Internat., Inc., Chesapeake, Va., 1978-80; sole practice Virginia Beach, 1980—. Owner Chieftain Motor Inn, Hanover, N.H., 1980-87. Comdr. USNR, 1956-70. Episcopalian. Office: 281 Independence Blvd Ste 605 Virginia Beach VA 23462-2975 E-mail: airbuzzard24@aol.com.

SPITZNAGEL, JOHN KEITH, microbiologist, immunologist, physician; b. Peoria, Ill., Apr. 11, 1923; s. Elmer Florian and Anna S. (Kolb) S.; m. Anne Moulton Sirch, Feb. 2, 1947; children: John, Jean, Margaret, Elizabeth, Paul. BA, Columbia U., 1943, MD, 1946. Diplomate Nat. Bd. Med. Examiners, Am. Bd. Internal Medicine. Intern Johns Hopkins Hosp., Balt., 1946-47; resident in internal medicine Barnes Hosp., St. Louis, 1949-51; vis. investigator Rockefeller Inst., N.Y.C., 1952-53, Nat. Inst. Med. Research, London, 1967-68; mem. faculty U. N.C., Chapel Hill, 1957-79, prof. microbiology and infectious diseases, prof. medicine, 1957-79; cons. N.C. Meml. Hosp., Chapel Hill, 1974-79; ad hoc adviser NIH, 1971—; prof. microbiology and immunology, chmn. dept. Emory U., Atlanta, 1979-93, prof. emeritus microbiology and immunology, 1993—, assoc. dean rsch., 1997-98. Mem. study sect. bacteriology and mycology NIH, 1975-79, 85-89, chmn., 1977-79. Editor: Infection and Immunity, 1970-80, Jour. Immunology, 1973-80, Jour. Reticuloendothelial Soc, 1973-80. Served with M.C. AUS, 1947-57. Recipient Research Career Devel. award USPHS, 1957-67, Disting. Service award Sch. Medicine U. N.C., Chapel Hill, 1987; USPHS postdoctoral fellow, 1968; USPHS and AEC grantee; lectureship named in his honor, Spitznagel Lectureship on Host Antimicrobial Def., Emory U., 1998. Fellow ACP, Infectious Disease Soc.; mem. AAAS, AAUP, Am. Soc. Microbiology (div. group councilor 1977-79), Am. Assn. Immunologists, Reticuloendothelial Soc. (pres. 1982), Infectious Disease Soc., So. Soc. Clin. Rsch., Assn. Am. Med. Sch. Microbiology and Immunology Chmn. (pres. 1990-91), Sigma Xi. Achievements include research on cell biology of human neutrophil polymorphonuclear leukocytes, and oxygen ind. mechanisms of antimicrobial phagocytoses; first to demonstrate cationic antimicrobial proteins of polymorphonuclear leukocytes granules; co-discoverer of a cationic protein of polymorph granules with antimicrobial action and a powerful attractant for mononuclear phagocytes. Home: 95 Starcross Ln # 20804 Jasper GA 30143-7883 Office: 1510 Clifton Rd NE Atlanta GA 30322-4218 E-mail: spitzna@attglobal.net.

SPITZNAGEL, JOHN KEITH, periodontist, researcher; b. St. Louis, Feb. 22, 1951; s. John Keith and Anne Moulton (Sirch) S.; m. Susan Victoria Lipton, Jan. 2, 1981; children: Matthew, Katya. BS in Biology, U. N.C., 1977, DDS, 1982, cert. in Periodontology, 1992, PhD in Microbiology, 1994. Postdoctoral fellow Forsyth Dental Ctr., Boston, 1983-85; cons. in bioinformatics, 1984—; periodontic resident U. Tex. Health Sci. Ctr., San Antonio, 1985-91, dentist-scientist fellow, 1987-93; asst. prof. periodontology U. Tenn., Memphis, 1993-97, U. Md., Balt., 1997—. Contbr. articles to profl. jours. Scout leader Boy Scouts Am., Chapel Hill, N.C., 1978-81, Memphis, 1995-97, Balt., 1997—. With USCG, 1971-75. Recipient Dentist Scientist award Nat. Inst. Dental Rsch., 1987, R29 First Grant award, 1997—. Mem. ADA, AAAS, Am. Acad. Periodontology, Am. Soc. for Microbiology, Internat. Assn. Dental Rsch., Delta Sigma Delta, Omicron Kappa Upsilon. Episcopalian. Avocations: computers/electronics, amateur radio, fishing, sailing, soaring. Office: UMAB Dental Sch 666 W Baltimore St Baltimore MD 21201-1510

SPIVAK, ALVIN A. retired public relations executive; b. Phila., Nov. 30, 1927; s. Herman and Bella (Haimovitz) S.; m. Martha Barry, Nov. 26, 1965; 1 dau., Denise. BS, Temple U., 1949. With I.N.S., 1949-58, Senate reporter, also mem. gen. staff, 1951-58; with U.P.I., 1958-67, White House reporter, 1960-67; pub. affairs dir. Nat. Adv. Commn. on Civil Disorders, 1967-68, Democratic Nat. Com., 1968-70; corp. pub. affairs dir. Gen. Dynamics Corp., 1970-94, ret., 1994. Served with USAAF, 1946-47. Mem. Mil. Order of Carabao, Nat. Press Club, Beta Gamma Sigma. Home: 5726 W 1st Sq SW Vero Beach FL 32968-2256

SPIVAK, GAYATRI CHAKRAVORTY, humanities educator; b. Calcutta, India, Feb. 24, 1942; arrived in U.S., 1961; d. Pares Chandra and Sivani Chakravorty; m. Talbot Israel Spivak, Nov. 28, 1964 (div. 1977); m. Basudev Chatterji, May 3, 1987. BA in English, U. Calcutta, 1959; MA in English, Cornell U., 1962; PhD, 1967; LittD (hon.) , U. Toronto, Ont., Can., 2000. From instr. to full prof. U. Iowa, Iowa City, 1965—78; prof. U. Tex., Austin, 1978—84; Longstreet prof. Emory U., Atlanta, 1984—86; Andrew W. Mellon prof. U. Pitts., 1987—91; Avalon Found. prof. humanities Columbia U., N.Y.C., 1991—. Vis. prof. U. Paul Valéry, Montpellier, France, 1981; vis. fellow Jawaharlal Nehruy U., New Delhi, 1987; internat. adv. bd. Amsterdam (The Netherlands) Cultural Sch., Netherlands, 1990—; external advisor Soc. for Humanities Cornell U., Ithaca, NY, 1993—96; adv. bd. mem. Whitney Mus., N.Y.C., NY, 1997—, English Inst., 2001—. Editor, translator: Of Grammatology, 1976, Imaginary Maps, 1994; author: Outside in the Teaching Machine, 1993, A Critique of Postcolonial Reason, 1999. Active alternative devel. movements, Asian women's rights movements, rural literacy, various countries; founder, mem. So. Poverty Law Ctr., Montgomery, Ala., 1971—; sch. founder, tchr., trainer Paschimbangakheria, 1986—; activist Nomadic

Tribes Resistance Action, Calcutta, India, 1998—; publicist Asian Women's HR Coun., Kuala Lumpur, Malaysia, 1994. Recipient Tagore professorship, Sayajirao U., Baroda, India, 1995; fellow, Nat. Humanities Inst., U. Chgo., 1977—78, sr. fellow Humnaities Ctr., Australian Nat. U., Canberra, 1986, Guggenheim Found., 1995—96. Mem.: ACLU, AAUP, MLA, Soc. for African Philosophy, Nat. Women's Studies Assn., Am. Comparative Lit. Assn. Avocation: reading detective stories. Office: Columbia Univ 602 Philosophy Hall New York NY 10027

SPIVAK, JACQUE R. bank executive; b. San Francisco, Nov. 5, 1929; d. Robert Morris and Sadonia Clardine Breistein; m. Herbert Spivak, Aug. 26, 1960; children: Susan, Donald, Joel, Sheri. BS, U. So. Calif., 1949, MS, 1950, MBA, 1959. Mgr. Internat. Escrow, Inc., L.A., 1960-65, Greater L.A. Investment Co., 1965-75; mgr. escrow Transam. Title Ins. Co., 1975-78; mgr. escrow, asst. v.p. Wells Fargo Bank, Beverly Hills, 1979-80; adminstr. escrow, v.p. 1st Pacific Bank, 1980-85; escrow adminstr. Century City Savs. & Loan Assn., L.A., 1986-87; pres. Prodrs. Escrow Corp., Beverly Hills, 1987—. Recipient award, PTA, Girl Scouts U.S., Jewish Fedn. L.A. Mem.: Inst. Trustees Sales Officers, Calif. Escrow Assn., Nat. Assn. Bank Women, Hadassah (nat. bd. dirs., pres. L.A. chpt., mem. Nat. Young Yudea Scholarship bur., mem. audit com., award). Republican. Jewish. Office: Producers Escrow Corp PO Box 5771 Beverly Hills CA 90209-5771

SPIVAK, JOAN CAROL, healthcare communications specialist; b. Phila., May 12, 1950; d. Jack and Evelyn Lee (Copelman) S.; m. John D. Goldman, May 17, 1980; children: Jesse, Marcus. AB, Barnard Coll., 1972; M of Health Scis., Johns Hopkins U., 1980. Freelance writer, N.Y.C., 1980-84; project dir. Impact Med. Communication, 1984-87; exec. v.p., gen. mgr. health and sci. strategies Edelman Worldwide, 1987—2002; pres. Prime Medica, Inc., 2002—. Co-author: (pamphlet) Lead: New Perspectives on an Old Problem, 1978; contbr. The Book of Health, 1981, articles to profl. jours. Bd. dirs. May O'Donnell Dance Co., N.Y.C., 1983-85, Chamber Ballet U.S.A., N.Y.C., 1985-87, Nat. Child Labor Commn., 1991—, Cases, 1995—. Mem. N.Y. Acad. Sci. Democrat. Jewish. Avocations: pottery, sailing. E-mail: joan.spivak@prime-medica.com.

SPIVAK, KENIN MATHEW, executive; b. N.Y.C., May 14, 1957; s. Edwin Howard and Charlotte S. AB, Columbia U., 1977, MBA, JD, Columbia U., 1980. V.p. Merrill Lynch Capital Markets, 1985-88; COO, MGM/UA Comm. Co., 1988-90; pres. Island World Group, 1991-94; co-chmn., exec. com. Premiere Radio Network, L.A., 1995-97; chmn. Knowledge Exch., 1995-97; pres., CEO, Archon Comm., Inc., 1995-97; vice chmn. John Paul Mitchell Systems, Beverly Hills, Calif., 1994—; chmn., CEO, Spivak Sports, L.A., 1997-99; chmn. Aquarius Holdings, Inc., 1997-2000; chmn., CEO, Telemac Corp., 1998—. Editor: Knowledge Exchange Business Encyclopedia. Office: 6701 Center Dr W Ste 700 Los Angeles CA 90045-1565

SPIVAK, MAURICE SIDNEY, chief project management, consultant; b. Milford, Mass., Jan. 5, 1926; s. Phillip None and Esther Sarah Spivak; m. Annette Charlotte Mann; 1 child Michelle Kelley 1 child Myra Runge 1 child Jonah. BS, The Citadel, Charleston, S.C., 1950; MS, W. Va. U., Mogantown, 1955; PhD (hon.) , U.of Berkley, Southhill, Mich. Registered Profl. Engr., Wis., 1976. Biochemist Mass. Gen. Hosp., Boston, 1950—53, Worcester Found., Shrewsbury, 1955—56; chem. engr. U.S.Army, Springfield, 1956—67; project engr. U.S.Army Arsenal, Edgewood , Md., 1967—73; chief project mgmt. engring. U.S. Army Corps of Engrs., Norfolk, Va., 1973—86. Cons. U.S. Army Corps of Engrs., Norfolk, Va., 1986—99. Author: (Engineering Papers) Published in Govt. and Jour.Biolog. Chemistry, 1960 (Numerous awards, 1977). First V.P. B'rith Sholom, Norfolk, Va. Pvt. First Class U.S. Army, 1944—46, European Theater. Decorated Bronze Star Medal US Army, Combat Infantry badge; recipient Several Civilian Awards, Springfield Armory, 1956-1966, Numerous Awards, Edgewood Arsenal, 1967-1973, US Army Corps of Engineers, 1973-1986; fellow, Worcester Found., 1955, W. Va. U., 1955. Mem.: ASCE. Home: 821 Jennings St Virginia Beach VA 23464 Personal E-mail: MSpivak650@aol.com.

SPIVEY, BRUCE E. ophthalmologist, integrated healthcare delivery systems management executive; b. Cedar Rapids, Iowa, Aug. 29, 1934; s. William Lorancy and Grace Loretta (Barber) S.; children: Lisa, Eric; m. Patti Amanda Birge, Dec. 20, 1987. BA, Coe Coll., 1956; MD, U. Iowa, 1959, MS, 1964; MEd, U. Ill., 1969; DSc (hon.), Coe Coll., 1978. Diplomate Am. Bd. Ophthalmology (fellow, bd. dirs. 1975-83, chmn. oral exam 1976-81). Asst. prof. U. Iowa Coll. Medicine, Iowa City, 1966, assoc. prof., 1968-71; dean Sch. Med. Scis. U. Pacific, San Francisco, 1971-76; prof., chmn. dept. ophthalmology Pacific Med. Ctr. (now Calif. Pacific Med. Ctr.), 1971-87, pres., CEO, dir., 1976-91; exec. v.p., CEO Am. Acad. Ophthalmology, 1978-93; pres., CEO Calif. Healthcare System, Bay area, 1986-92; CEO Northwestern Healthcare Network, Chgo., 1992-97, Columbia Cornell Care, N.Y.C., 1997-2000, Columbia Cornell Network Physicians, N.Y.C., 1998-2000. Pres. Reliance Group Holdings Inc., Ophthalmic Pub. Co., Chgo., 1993—98; v.p. Am Bd. Med. Spltys., 1978—80, pres., 1980—82; pres. coun. Med. Splty. Soc., 2000—02, exec. v.p., 2002—; sec.-gen. Internat. Coun. Ophthalmology, 1994—; chmn. bd. dirs. Vol. Hosps. of Am.-No. Calif., 1985—87, nat. bd. dirs., 1991—96; mem. nat. adv. coun. NEI/NIH, 1987—92; mem. spl. med. adv. group Dept. Vets Affairs, 1987—93; trustee, bd. dirs., sec. bd. Ophthal. Mut. Ins. Co., 1988—, Phoenix Alliance, Inc., Mpls., 1993—99, MedEx, Mpls., 1999—, PrimeSight, San Francisco, 1996—99. Contbr. over 115 articles to profl. jours.; inventor instruments for eye surgery. Bd. dirs. Pacific Vision Found., San Francisco, 1978—, U.S.-China Ednl. Inst., 1979—; trustee Coe Coll., 1985—, Found. AAO, 1981—. Served to capt. U.S. Army, 1964-66. Decorated Bronze Star; recipient Emile Javal Gold medal Internat. Contact Lens Council, San Francisco, 1982, Gradle medal Pan-Am. Assn. Ophthalmol., others Fellow ACS, Am. Acad. Ophthalmology (Disting. Svc. award 1972, Sr. Honor award 1986, Guest of Honor 1996); mem. AMA, Am. Ophthal. Soc. (Howe medal 1993, bd. dirs. 1986-91, pres. 1994-95), Academia Ophthal. Internat. (Bernardo Streiff Gold medal), Soc. Med. Adminstrs. (pres. 1999-2001), Internat. Congress Ophthalmology (sec.-gen. 1978-82), Internat. Coun. Ophthalmology (sec.-gen. 1994—, trustee 1986—), Pacific-Union Club. (San Francisco), Chgo. Club, Chevy Chase Club (Northampton), Knickerbocker Club (N.Y.), Cosmos Club (Washington). Presbyterian. Office: One Beekman Pl New York NY 10022-8057 E-mail: bruce@spivey.org.

SPIVEY, STEPHEN DALE, lawyer; b. Clermont, Fla., Feb. 6, 1952; s. Herbert Basil Spivey and Marguerite Nordmann; previous marriage: Catherine Monohan; m. Rosemary Rosser, Sept. 7, 1990; children: Erin Alissa, Austin William. BA, BS, U. Ctrl. Fla., 1978; JD, Stetson Law Sch., St. Petersburg, Fla., 1980. Bar: U.S. Dist. Ct. (mid. dist.) Fla. Stockbroker, mgr. Merrill Lynch, Orlando, 1980—85; owner, ptnr. Chilton Fin., 1985—86; staff atty. 5th Jud. Cir. Ct., Ocala, Fla., 1987—92; cir. coord. U.S. Justice Dept., 1992—94; pvt. practice law, 1994—2000; mng. ptnr. Spivey & Rorex, PLC, 2000—01; pvt. practice Stephen D. Spivey, PA, Ocala, 2001—. Pres. bd. dirs. Recovery House, Inc., Ocala, 1990—; v.p. bd. dirs. Marion-Citrus Mental Health, 1995—99, pres. bd. dirs., 2000—02; coord., advisor Marion County Teen Ct., 1993—94, Marion County Drug Ct., 1996—97. Recipient Lewis F. Powell award, Am. Coll. Trial Lawyers, 1980, Chief Justice's Commendation for Exemplary Pub. Svc., Supreme Ct. Fla., 1998, Outstanding Svc. award, HRS Dist. III Planning Coun., 1994, Marion County Teen Ct., 1996. Mem. ABA, Fla. Bar Assn., Pub. Investors Arbitration Bar Assn., Elks. Republican. Avocations: hunting, fishing, scuba diving, underwater photography. Office: Spivey & Rorex PLC 3610 SE Ft King St Ocala FL 34470

SPIVEY, SUZAN BROOKS NISBET, association administrator, medical technologist; b. Princeton, Ky., Sept. 19, 1932; d. Dixon Franklin and Eva (Brooks) Nisbet; m. Herman Everette Spivey Jr., June 8, 1953; children: Eva Kathryn Spivey Bridges, Herman Everette III. Student, U. Louisville, 1950; BS, U. Ky., 1954; grad., Inst. Orgnl. Mgmt. U. Ga., 1990; postgrad., U. Ga., 1990—. Registered med. technologist. Med. technologist Madison (Wis.) Gen. Hosp., 1955-58, Fern Creek Clinic, Louisville, 1958-62; med. technologist, cons. Ga. Primary Health Care, Summerville, 1981—, Chattooga County Hosp., Summerville, 1983-86; grad. Inst. for Orgnl. Mgmt. U.S. Chamber U. Ga., 1990; pres. Chattooga County C. of C., Summerville, 1984—. Advisor Inst. for Orgnl. Mgmt. U.S. Chamber U. Ga., 1991; project coord. Impact 2000 FEMA, 2000—. Author: (newsletter) Essentials, 1985—; cons. adv. com.: (book) Becoming a Better Board Member, 1982; columnist You and Your Schs., 1973-80. Pres. memls., dir. Chattooga chpt. Ga. Dist. Field Svc. Am. Cancer Soc., mem., 1964—; mem. Ghattooga Bd. Edn., 1972-80, Ga. Assn. Leadership Communities, 1989—, Tri-State Coun., 1989-2000, Chattooga County 911 Com., 1996; bd. dir., advisor Chattooga County Parent/Child Ctr., 1972-92; bd. control N.W. Ga. Regional Edn. Svc. Agy., 1996-99; adminstrv. bd. Chattooga Early Learning Ctr., 1996-2000; bd. dirs. Lookout Mountain Pkwy. Assn., 1988—, Job Tng. Ptnrship. Act, Chattooga County, 1985-95, 7th Dist. Ga. Sch. Bds. Assn., Atlanta, 1974-80; pres. Bicentennial Com., Chattooga County, 1974-76; producer Hallelujah Players, Summerville, 1976-85; trustee Floyd Coll., 1988—; bd. dirs. Literacy Adv. Com. Walker Tech. Inst., 1991-99; mem. 7th dist. Ga. Congl. Adv. Com. on Health Care Reform, 1994; adminstrv. bd. Berry/Chattooga Early Head Start, 1996-98; sec., bd. dirs., Villa Internat., Atlanta, 1999, active Chattooga County 911 Com., 1996; bd. dirs. Blue Ridge AHEC, 1997—, Children's Adv. Ctr., 1998—, Chattooga County Family Connection, 1998—; trustee, bd. dirs. Villa Internat., Atlanta, 1996—; moderator Cherokee Presbytery, 1997; exec. bd. Chattooga Family Connection Collaborative, 1999—, bd. dirs., 2000—; adv. bd. rural enrichment and access program Mercer U. Sch. Medicine, 1999-2001, sec., 1999-2000. Recipient Excellence award Am. Cancer Soc., 1991; grantee Ga. Bd. Edn., 1990, 91, Ga. Gov.'s Commn., 1991, Martin Luther King, Jr. Cmty. Svc. award for Outstanding Svc. in Racial Rels., 1999. Mem. Am. Soc. Clin. Pathologists, Ga. Econ. Devel. Assn., Am. C. of C., Bus. and Profl. Women (Woman of Achievement award 1984), Ga. Assn. of Chamber Execs. (bd. dirs. 1999—), Am. C. of C. Execs. Assn. Democrat. Presbyterian. Avocations: reading, photography, needlework, writing, raising German Shepherds. Office: Chattooga County C of C 44 Highway 48 Summerville GA 30747-1531 E-mail: spivey@wavegate.com., chatcofc@wavegate.com.

SPIVEY, TED RAY, English educator; b. Fort Pierce, Fla., July 1, 1927; s. Theodore Roosevelt and Etty Pearl (Sumner) S.; m. Julia Brannon Douglass, June 30, 1962; children— Mary Leta, John Andrew. AB, Emory U., 1949; MA, U. Minn., 1951, PhD, 1954. Reporter Greenville Reporter, S.C., 1949-50; instr. Emory U., Atlanta, 1954-56; mem. faculty Ga. State U., 1956-89, assoc. prof. English, 1960-64, prof., 1964-89, Regents' prof., 1984-89, emeritus, 1989—. Author: (with Kenneth M. England) A Manual of Style, 1960, The Renewed Quest, 1969, The Coming of the New Man, 1971, The Journey Beyond Tragedy, 1980, Revival: Southern Writers in the Modern City, 1986, The Writer as Shaman: The Pilgrimages of Conrad Aiken and Walker Percy, 1986, To Die in Atlanta: Poems of the Civil War and After, 1987, Beyond Modernism: Toward a New Myth Criticism, 1988, A City Observed: Poems of the New Age, 1988, (with Arthur Waterman) Conrad Aiken: A Priest of Consciousness, 1989, Flannery O'Connor: The Woman, The Thinker, the Visionary, 1995, Airport: America Rediscovered, 1997, Time's Stop in Savannah: Conrad Aiken's Inner Journey, 1997, Bridges of Light: Four Poets of the Golden Isles, 2001. Served with USN, 1945-46. Urban Life Center grantee, 1977-80 Mem. So. Atlantic Modern Lang. Assn. Clubs: Brittany. Democrat. Episcopalian. Home: 104 Plemmons Dr Saint Simons GA 31522-9767 E-mail: TJSpivey@mindspring.com.

SPIVEY, WILLIAM FRANKLIN, JR. land planner, consultant; b. Sanford, Fla., Apr. 12, 1970; s. William Franklin Sr. and Nancy Ann (Pixley) S.; m. Sylvia Ann Moreland, July 30, 1994; children: Jack Tatum, Ethan James. AA in Geography (hon.), Seminole C.C., 1994; BA in Geography, U. N.C., 1997. Cons. City of Sanford, Fla., 1989-95, Byrd/Forbes Assocs., Inc., Greensboro, N.C., 1995-97; mktg. dir./land planner Bridge and Slaughter, LLP, Oxford, Miss., 1997-99; city planner City of Lake Mary, Fla., 1999—. Mem. Am. Inst. Cert. Planners, Am. Planning Assn., Fla. Planning and Zoning Assn. (bd. dirs. 2000—, v.p. 2002). Republican. Southern Baptist. Avocations: karate (2d degree black belt), basketball, power volleyball, soccer, archery. Home: 49 Sweetwater Creek Cir Oviedo FL 32765 Office: City of Lake Mary 100 N Country Club Rd Lake Mary FL 32746 Office Fax: 407-585-1464.

SPIZZIRI, JOHN ANTHONY, lawyer; b. Paterson, N.J., Sept. 2, 1934; s. Louis George and Carmella (Iacanone) S.; m. Alexandra Vitale, July 15, 1972; children: John A. Jr., Victoria Jean, Miriam. BS, Georgetown U., 1957, JD, 1960. Bar: N.J. 1961, U.S. Dist. Ct. N.J. 1961; cert. mediator. Pvt. practice, Wyckoff, N.J., 1961—; pros. Ramsey (N.J.) Borough, 1964-77, Oakland (N.J.) Borough, 1969-83, Borough Upper Saddle River, N.J.; counsel Franklin Lakes Planning Bd., 1970—; atty. Borough of Elmwood Park (N.J.), 1981—; police prosecutor Township of Wyckoff, 1964-66. Condemnation commr. Meadowlands Sports and Expn. Authority, presiding condemnation commr. Rte. 287; asst. counsel Bergen County (N.J.), 1970-71; judge Mcpl. Ct., Oakland, 1986; atty. Wyckoff Ambulance Corp., 1970—, Franklin Lakes Ambulance Corp., 1994—. Mem. Wyckoff Sewer Com., Wyckoff Planning Bd.; past co-chmn. Wyckoff Heart Fund; past vice chmn. N.W. Bergen County fund drive Boy Scouts Am.; mem. N.J. Gen. Assembly, 1971—77, minority whip and asst. minority leader; mayor Twp. of Wyckoff, 1969; past pres. Wyckoff Rep. League; Rep. mem. CVom. to Study Expenditures of Casino Gambling Revenue; state trustee, nat. del. Ducks Unltd., 2000—01; bd. dirs. 36 SSS; chmn. Hudson River Ducks Unltd., 1999—2001; N.J. state chmn. Ducks Unltd. Mem. ABA, N.J. Bar Assn., Bergen County Bar Assn., Nat. Wildlife Fedn., Allendale Field and Stream Assn., Wyckoff Vol. Ambulance Corps (hon.), Lawyers Club Bergen County (past pres.), State Feather Soc. (chmn. 2000-01), Lions (past bd. dirs., pres. Wyckoff chpt. 1989-90). Roman Catholic. Office: 356 Franklin Ave Wyckoff NJ 07481-1909

SPJUT, RICHARD WAYNE, botanist, consultant; b. San Francisco, Oct. 3, 1945; s. Richard Wangburg Spjut and Evelyn Panetta. BS in Wildlife Mgmt., Biology, Humboldt State U., 1969, MA in Biology, 1971. Pvt. practice botanist, Calif., 1970-72; support botanist USDA, Beltsville, Md., 1972-97; dir., plant explorer, collaborator World Bot. Assocs., Laurel, 1983—. Rsch. collaborator, assoc. Natural Mus. Natural History, Smithsonian Instn., 1973-76, 86-94. Contbr. articles and papers to profl. jours. Recipient Master Agreement award, NIH, 1988, NCI Contract, 2001—. Achievements include sample discovery of antitumor agents in mosses and liverworts; sample discovery of a species of smokebush leading to discovery of conocurvone, a potential new drug for AIDS treatment; described one new genus and more than 50 new species of lichens from Calif.; revised classification of fruit types. Home: PO Box 20261 Bakersfield CA 93390 Office: World Bot Assocs PO Box 880 Temecula CA 92593 E-mail: richspjut@aol.com.

SPLANE, RICHARD BEVERLEY, social work educator; b. Calgary, Alta., Can., Sept. 25, 1916; s. Alfred William and Clara Jane (Allyn) S.; m. Verna Marie Huffman, Feb. 22, 1971. BA, McMaster U., 1940, LLD (hon.), 1990; cert. social sci. and adminstrn., London Sch. Econs., 1947; MA, U. Toronto, 1948, MSW, 1951, PhD, 1961; LLD (hon.), Wilfrid Laurier U., 1988, U. B.C., Can., 1996. Exec. dir. Children's Aid Soc., Cornwall, Ont., Can., 1948-50; with Health and Welfare Can., Ottawa, 1952-72, exec. asst. to dep. minister nat. welfare, 1959-60, dir. unemployment assistance, 1960-62, dir. gen. welfare assistance and services, 1960-70, asst. dep. minister social allowances and services, 1970-72; vis. prof. U. Alta., Edmonton, 1972-73; prof. social policy Sch. Social Work, U. B.C., Vancouver, 1973—. Cons. Govt. Can., Govt. Alta., UNICEF. Author: The Development of Social Welfare in Ontario, 1965; (with Verna Huffman Splane) Chief Nursing Officers in National Ministries of Health, 1994, 75 Years of Community Service to Canada: Canadian Council on Social Development, 1920-1995. Served with RCAF, 1942-45. Recipient Centennial medal Govt. Can., 1967, Charles E. Hendry award U. Toronto, 1981, Commemorative medal for 125th anniversary of Confedn. of Can., 1992, Disting. Svc. award Internat. Coun. on Social Welfare, 1996. Mem. Can. Assn. Social Workers (Outstanding Nat. Svc. award 1985), Can. Inst. Pub. Adminstrn., Can. Hist. Assn., Can. Coun. on Social Devel. (Lifetime Achievement award 1995), Internat. Assn. Schs. Social Work, Internat. Confs. Social Devel., World Federalists of Can., UN Assns. Assn. of Can. (bd. dirs. Vancouver br.), Vancouver Club, Order of Can. Mem. United Ch. Can.

SPLETE, ALLEN PETERJOHN, association executive, educator; b. Carthage, N.Y., June 24, 1938; s. Howard Henry and Minnie Bertha (Peterjohn) S.; m. Marilyn Lois Detweiler, June 18, 1966; children— Heidi, Michael BA, St. Lawrence U., 1960; MA with distinction, Colgate U., 1962; PhD, Syracuse U., 1968; LHD, Campbellsville Coll., 1990; LLD, Davis and Elkins Coll., 1990; LHD, Mt. Union Coll., 1992, St. Thomas Aquinas Coll., 1992, U. Indpls., 1994, Juniata Coll., 1994, Hastings Coll., 1994; EdD, Marywood Coll., 1995; LHD, Holy Family Coll., 1996, Wesley Coll., 1996. Adminstrv. asst. to v.p. acad. affairs Syracuse U., N.Y., 1965-68, assoc. dean, exec. asst. to provost, 1968-70; v.p. for acad. planning St. Lawrence U., Canton, 1970-82; pres. Westminster Coll., New Wilmington, Pa., 1982-85; exec. v.p. Coun. Ind. Colls., Washington, 1985-86, pres., 1986-2000, pres. emeritus, 2000—. Dir. Nat. Prepaid Tuition Plan, 1988-91; cons. York Coll., Pa., 1974; mem. planning and research com. N.Y. State Com. on Ind. Colls. and Univs., 1975-82; mem. statewide higher edn. adv. com. N.Y. State Senate Com. on Higher Edn., 1979-82; mem. nat. adv. bd. Flaming Rainbow U., 1989-96; mem. adv. bd. Assn. Gov. Bds. Presdl. Search Consultation Svc., 1987-94, Academic Search Consultation Svc., 1989—, mem. Harvard Sem. for new pres. adv. bd., 1990—; bd. dirs. Tchr. Edn. Accreditation Coun., 1998—, chair, 2001—; mem. oversight and review com. leadership and orgnl. devel. program United Negro Coll. Fund, 1991-96, SCT adv. coun., 1996-2001; adv. bd. Eric Nat., 1996-2000, Boyer Ctr. for Advanced Studies, 1998—; UAW/Ford U. Help Steering Com., 1997-2001; bd. dirs. Project Pericles, 1999—. Co-author: Frederic Remington-Selected Letters, 1988, A Good Place To Work: Sourcebook for the Academic Workplace, 1991; editor: (with others) Confs. on Adirondack Park, 1972-82, Can.-Am. Relations, 1974-75, Presidential Essays — Success Stories, 2000; contbr. articles to profl. jours. Chmn. planning bd. Village of Canton, 1974-81; elder Neelsville Presbyn. Ch., 1986-89; trustee Adirondack Conservancy, Wilsboro, N.Y., 1980-82; trustee Millikin U., 2000—; mem. adv. bd. Sage Scholars, 2000—. Served to 1st lt. U.S. Army, 1960-62 Recipient Alumni citation, St. Lawrence U., 1987, Algernon Sydney Sullivan award, 1997, CIC Acad. Leadership award, 2000, Henry D. Paley award, NAICU, 2001; grantee, John Ben Snow Found., 1981. Mem. Pa. Assn. Colls and Univs. (govt. relations com. 1983-85), Middle States Assn. (team chmn. com. on higher edn. 1976-78, 81), Assn. Am. Colls. (project rev. cons. 1981-82), Soc. Educators and Scholars (bd. editors), Assn. Am. Colls. (pres. adv. com. 1977-78, reviewer Quill project 1978-79), St. Lawrence County Hist. Assn. (pres. 1977-82), Frederic Remington Mus. Assn., Beta Theta Pi (v.p. 1980-83) Republican. Home: 10821 Longmeadow Dr Damascus MD 20872-2240 Office: Coun Ind Colls 1 Dupont Cir NW Ste 320 Washington DC 20036-1137

SPLETTSTOESZER, WAYNE, music educator; b. New Britain, Conn., Nov. 25, 1970; s. James and Patricia Splettstoeszer; m. Wendi Splettstoeszer, June 24, 1995. BS in Edn. Music Edn., Cen. Conn. State U., 1994. Music tchr. St. Bernard H.S., Uncasville, Conn., 1994—96, Torrington (Conn.) H.S., 1996—. Office: Torrington H S Major Besse Dr Torrington CT 06790 E-mail: wsplettstoeszer@torrington.org.

SPLIETHOFF, WILLIAM LUDWIG, chemical company executive; b. Matamoras, Pa., Apr. 8, 1926; s. Oscar and Louisa (Rummel) S.; m. Dorothy Coffman, June 11, 1949; children: Christina Spliethoff Hansen, Karen Spliethoff Walker, William Mark; m. Marjorie Ann Johnson, Nov. 15, 1971. BS in Chemistry, Pa. State U., 1946, MS, 1948; PhD in Organic Chemistry, Mich. State U., 1953. Rsch. chemist E.I. duPont de Nemours & Co., Wilmington, Del., 1952-60; dir. market rsch. chem. divsn. Gen. Mills, Inc., Kankakee, Ill., 1960-62, mgr. comml. devel., 1962-67; asst. mng. dir. Polymer Corp., Sydney, Australia, 1967-69; v.p. Gen. Mills Chems., Inc., Mpls., 1969-77; exec. v.p. Henkel Corp., 1977-86; mgmt. cons. Chanhassen, Minn., 1986—, Naples, Fla., 1999—. Bd. dirs. Princess Soft Toys, Inc.; sr. v.p. Henkel of Am., N.Y.C., 1981-86; chmn. Habib-Gen., Ltd., Karachi, Pakistan, 1970-79, Nutralgum, S.P.A., Milan, 1972-85, Henkel Ireland Ltd., Cork, 1975-86; v.p. Chem-Plast, S.P.A., Milan, 1977-86, Poliamidas de Venezuela, S.A., Caracas, 1975-86, Gemisa, S.A. de C.V., Mexico City, 1979-86. Mem. bd. edn., Kankakee, 1964-67. Mem. Am. Chem. Soc., Chem. Market Rsch. Assn., Comml. Devel. Assn. (honor award 1982), Sigma Xi, Phi Lambda Upsilon. E-mail: wspliethof@aol.com.

SPLINTER, WILLIAM ELDON, agricultural engineering educator; b. North Platte, Nebr., Nov. 24, 1925; s. William John and Minnie (Calhoun) Splinter; m. Eleanor Love Peterson, Jan. 10, 1952 (dec. Jan. 1999); children: Kathryn Love, William John, Karen Ann, Robert Marvin; m. Elizabeth Butters Calhoun, Feb. 9, 2002. BS in Agrl. Engring., U. Nebr., 1950; MS in Agrl. Engring., Mich. State U., 1951, PhD in Agrl. Engring., 1955. Instr. agrl. engring. Mich. State U., East Lansing, 1953-54; assoc. prof. biology and agrl. engring. N.C. State U., Raleigh, 1954-60, prof. biology and agrl. engring., 1960-68; from prof., chmn. dept. agrl. engring. to interim dean U. Nebr., Lincoln, Nebr., 1968—2001; interim dean Coll. of Engring. and Tech., 2001—. Cons. engr. Mem. exec. bd. Am. Assn. Engring. Socs.; hon. prof. Shengyang (People's Republic of China) Agrl. U. Contbr. articles to tech. jours.; patentee in field. Vol. dir. L.F. Larsen Tractor Mus. Served with USNR, 1946-51. Recipient Massey Ferguson gold medal, 1978, John Deere gold medal, 1995, Kiwanis award for disting. svc., 1994; named to Nebr. Hall of Agrl. Achievement; named Disting. Alumni, U. Nebr.-Lincoln, 2000. Recipient George Howard-Loiuse Pound award, 2001. Fellow AAAS, Am. Soc. Agrl. Engrs. (pres., adminstrv. council, found. pres., Presdl. citation 1999); mem. Nat. Acad. Engring., Soc. Automotive Engrs., Am. Soc. Engring. Edn., Nat. Soc. Profl. Engrs., Sigma Xi, Sigma Tau, Sigma Pi Sigma, Pi Mu Epsilon, Gamma Sigma Delta, Phi Kappa Phi, Beta Sigma Psi. Home: 4801 Bridle Ln Lincoln NE 68516-3436 Office: U Nebr W181 Nebraska Hall 2000 N 35th St Lincoln NE 68588-0501 E-mail: wsplinter1@ual.edu.

SPODAK, MICHAEL KENNETH, forensic psychiatrist; b. Bklyn., Nov. 5, 1944; s. Harry and Betty (Rahn) S.; children: Lisa Beth, Brett David. BS, Union Coll., 1966; MD, SUNY-Syracuse, 1970. Diplomate: Nat. Bd. Med. Examiners, Am. Bd. Neurology and Psychiatry. Intern Mary Imogene Bassett Hosp., Cooperstown, N.Y., 1970-71; resident John Hopkins Hosp., Balt., 1974-77; practice medicine specializing in civil and criminal forensic psychiatry Towson, Md., 1977—; chief dept. psychiatry Balt. County Gen. Hosp., Randallstown, 1978-85; mem. staff Clifton T. Perkins Hosp. Ctr., Jessup, Md., 1977-92; clin. asst. prof. psychiatry U. Md. Hosp., Balt., 1983-97; psychiat. cons. Bur. Disability Ins., Social Security Adminstrn., Workmen's compensation Commn., 1981—; dir. community forensic services Mental Hygiene Adminstrn., Md., 1982-92; faculty Nat. Jud. Coll., 1988—. Mem. Md. Task Force on Somatic Therapies Contbr. numerous articles on forensic psychiatry to profl. jours., chpt. to book. Served with M.C. USN, 1972-74. Mem. Am. Acad. Psychiatry and Law, Am. Psychiat. Assn., Md. Psychiat. Soc. (chmn. peer rev. com. 2001), Md. Med. Soc. (chmn. occupational health com. 1983-90), Baltimore County Med. Soc. Office: 26 W Pennsylvania Ave Towson MD 21204-5001 E-mail: mkspodak@yahoo.com.

SPODEK, BERNARD, early childhood educator; b. Bklyn., Sept. 17, 1931; s. David and Esther (Lebenbaum) S.; m. Prudence Debb, June 21, 1957; children: Esther Yin-ling, Jonathan Chou. BA, Bklyn. Coll., 1952; MA, Columbia U., 1955, EdD, 1962. Cert. early childhood edn. tchr., N.Y. Tchr. Beth Hayeled Sch., N.Y.C., 1952-56, N.Y. City Pub. Schs., Bklyn., 1956-57, Early Childhood Ctr., Bklyn. Coll., 1957-60; asst. prof. elem. edn. U. Wis.-Milw., 1961-65; assoc. prof. early childhood edn. U. Ill., Champaign, 1965-68, prof. dept. curriculum and instrn., 1968-97, dir. dept. grad. programs, 1986-87, chair dept., 1987-89, dir. hons. program, Coll. Edn., 1984-86, mem. faculty Bur. Ednl. Rsch., 1981-85, prof. emeritus, 1997—; adv. prof. Hong Kong Inst. of Edn., 1999-2001. Dir. insts. Nat. Def. Edn. Act, 1965-67, dir. experienced tchr. fellowship program, 1967-69, co-dir. program for tchr. trainers in early childhood edn., 1969-74; vis. prof. Western Wash. State U., 1974, U. Wis., Madison, 1980; vis. scholar Sch. Early Childhood Studies, Brisbane (Australia) Coll. Advanced Edn., Delissa Inst. Early Childhood Studies, S. Australia Coll. Advanced Edn., 1985, Beijing Normal U., Nanjing Normal U., E. China Normal U., Shangai, People's Republic China, 1986; rsch. fellow Kobe U., Japan, 1996; adj. prof. Queensland (Australia) U. Tech., 2000. Author or co-author 31 books including: (with others) A Black Studies Curriculum for Early Childhood Eduication, 1972, 2d edit., 1976, Teaching in the Early Years, 1972, 3d edit., 1985, Early Childhood Education, 1973, Studies in Open Education, 1975 (Japanese trans.), Early Childhood Education: Issues and Perspectives, 1977, (with Nir-Janiv and Steg) International Perspectives on Early Childhood Education, 1982 (Hebrew trans.), with Saracho and Lee (Mainstreaming Young Children, 1984, (with Saracho and Davis) Foundations of Early Childhood Education, 1987, 2d edit. (Japanese trans.), 1991, (with Saracho) Right from the Start, 1994 (Chinese and Korean translations), Dealing with Individual Differences in the Early Childhood Classroom, 1994; editor: Handbook of Research in Early Childhood Education, 1982, Today's Kindergarten, 1986, (with Saracho and Peters) Professionalism and the Early Childhood Practitioner, 1988, (with Saracho) Early Childhood Teacher Education, 1990, Issues in Early Childhood Curriculum,

1991, Educationally Appropriate Kindergarten Practices, 1991, Issues in Childcare, 1992, Handbook of Research on the Education of Young Children (Portuguese translation), 1993, (Portuguese tranls.) (with Saracho), Language and Literacy in Early Childhood Education, 1993; (with Safford and Saracho) Early Childhood Special Education, 1994; (with Garcia, McLaughlin & Saracho) Meeting the Challenge of Cultural and Linguistic Diversity, 1995, (with Saracho) Issues in Early Childhood Educational Evaluation and Assessment, 1996, (with Saracho) Multiple Perspectives on Play in Early Childhood Education, 1998, (With Saracho and Pellegrino) Issues in Early Childhood Educational Research, 1998, (with Saracho) Contemporary Perspectives in Early Childhood Curriculum, 2002, (with Saracho) Contemporary Perspectives in Early Childhood Language and Literacy, 2002; series editor Yearbook in Early Childhood Education, early childhood edn. publs., 1971-79; guest editor Studies in Ednl. Evaluation, 1982, Early Education and Child Development, 1995; also contbr. chpts to books, articles to profl. jours. Mem. Am. Ednl. Rsch. Assn. (chair early childhood and child devel. spl. interest group 1983-84, publs. com. 1984-86), Nat. Assn. Edn. Young Children (sec. 1965-68, bd. govs. 1968-72, pres. 1976-78, editorial adv. bd. 1972-76, book rev. editor, 1972-74, cons. editor, 1985-87 Young Children jour., mem. tchr. edn. commn. 1981-88, chair commn. on appropriate edn. 4-5 yr. old children, 1984-85, cons. editor Early Childhood Rsch. Quar. 1987-90), Nat. Soc. for Study of Edn. (1972 yearbook com.). Office: U Ill Dept Curriculum & Instrn 1310 S 6th St Champaign IL 61820-6925 E-mail: b-spodek@uiuc.edu.

SPOEHEL, RONALD ROSS, communications company executive; b. L.A., Oct. 28, 1957; s. Edwin Henry and Geraldine Jean (Hoskins) S.; m. Deborah Elizabeth Bell, Jan. 29, 1994; children: Elizabeth Schuyler, James Henry. BS in Econ., U. Pa., 1979, MS in Engring., MBA, U. Pa., 1980. V.p. Bank Am., San Francisco, N.Y.C., L.A., 1980-85, Lehman Bros., N.Y.C., 1985-90; sr. v.p., chief fin. officer ICF Kaiser Internat., Washington, 1990-94; v.p. corp. devel. Harris Corp, Melbourne, Fla., 1994-2000; CEO Optinel Sys., Inc., Columbia, Md., 2000—02. Mem.: Cattail Creek Country Club, Metro Club (Washington).

SPOERI, LAURA LENHARDT, industrial engineer, consultant; b. Newport News, Va., May 12, 1959; d. Elgin H. and Joan C. Lenhardt; m. Randall K. Spoeri, Apr. 24, 1999. Bs in Indsl. engring. and Ops. Rsch., Va. Polytech. Inst. & State U., 1981; MBA, Wake Forest, 1989. Diplomate Am. Coll. Healthcare Execs. Mgmt. engr. SunHealth, Charlotte, N.C., 1981-84, cons., 1984-87, mgr., 1987-91; dir. quality resources Presbyterian Health Svcs., 1991-97; ind. contractor, 1997-99; mgr. Premier Co., 1999-2000; dir. performance mgmt. Somerset Med. Ctr., Somerville, N.J., 2000—. Adj. faculty Juran Inst., Wilton, Conn., 1996—. Grad., mem. Leadership Charlotte, 1995-96; chair United Way Campaign PHSC, Charlotte, 1996. Recipient Outstanding Alumna Va. Tech., 1996. Mem. Am. Soc. Quality (treas. 1994-96), Hosp. Info. Mgmt. Sys., Inst. Indsl. Engrs. (sr. mem., region III dir.).

SPOERI, RANDALL KEITH, healthcare company executive; b. Cleve., June 12, 1946; s. Theodore Warren and Marion (Barrick) S.; m. Kathleen Loma Bryden Hayes, Aug. 31, 1968 (div. Mar. 1981); 1 child, Jennifer Anne; m. Deborah Jean Hammett, June 20, 1981 (div. Nov. 1998); 1 child, Jason Randall; m. Laura Joan Lenhardt, Apr. 24, 1999. BS, Calif. Polytech. State U., 1968; MS, Tex. A&M U., 1970, PhD, 1976. Math. statistician U.S. Bur. of the Census, Suitland, Md., 1976-80; assoc. prof. U.S. Naval Acad., Annapolis, 1980-83; assoc. exec. dir. Am. Statis. Assn., Alexandria, Va., 1983-88; sr. corp. statistician Humana, Inc., Louisville, 1988-92; chief program coord. info. branch Health Care Fin. Adminstrn., Balt., 1993; asst. v.p. Nat. Com. for Quality Assurance, Washington, 1994-95; adminstrv. v.p. health care analysis NYLCare Health Plans, Inc., N.Y.C., 1995-98; v.p. med. and quality informatics HIP Health Plans, 1998—. Author: Quantitative Methods In Quality Management, 1991; contbr. articles to profl. jours. Mem. adv. com. Health Care Fin. Adminstrn., Balt., 1990-92, bur. dir. citation, 1993, adv. bd. Juran Inst., Wilton, Conn., 1995-98. 1st lt. U.S. Army, 1970-72. Recipient Svc. award Am. Statis. Assoc., Alexandria, 1994. Fellow AAAS, Am. Soc. for Quality (health care divsn. chair 1995-96); mem. Am. Statis Assn., Inst. Indsl. Engring., Inst. for Ops. Rsch. and the Mgmt. Scis., Am. Med. Informatics Assn., Acad. for Health Svcs. Rsch. and Health Policy. Avocations: sports, music. Home: 148 Top Of The World Way Green Brook NJ 08812-1839

SPOFFORD, ROBERT HOUSTON, advertising agency executive; b. N.Y.C., Apr. 3, 1941; s. Robert Knowlton and Linda Prieber (Houston) S.; m. Susan Proctor Allerton; children: Margaret, Robert Christopher. B.E.E., Cornell U., 1964. Account exec. Batten, Barton, Durstine & Osborn, Inc., N.Y.C., 1964-71, v.p., 1971-84, sr. v.p., 1984-88, exec. v.p., dir. strategic planning, 1988-96; exec. v.p. BBDO Univ., Barcelona, Spain, 1997—. Contbr. articles to advt. and data processing jours. Mem. Westchester County Democratic Com. N.Y. 1974-78; ch. organist First recipient Founder's medal Batten, Barton, Durstine & Osborn, Inc., 1985 Congregationalist. Home: 61 Dunfries Ter San Rafael CA 94901-2415 Office: BBDO LA 10960 Wilshire Blvd Los Angeles CA 90024-3702 E-mail: spoffo@bbdowest.com.

SPOFFORD, SALLY (SALLY HYSLOP), artist; b. N.Y.C., Aug. 20, 1929; d. George Hall and Esther (McNaull) Hyslop; m. Gavin Spofford, Mar. 11, 1950 (dec. Jan. 1976); children: Lizabeth Spofford Smith, Leslie Spofford Russell. Student, The China Inst., N.Y.C., 1949, The Art Students League, 1950; BA with high honors, Swarthmore Coll., 1952. Instr. Somerset Art Assn., Peapack, N.J., 1978-95, Hunterdon Mus. Art, Clinton, N.J., 1985—; adv. bd., lectr. Apollo Muses, Inc., Gladstone, N.J.; trustee Artshowcase, Inc. One-woman shows include Riverside Studio, Pottersville, N.J., 1985, Morris Mus., Morristown, N.J. 1989, Schering-Plough Gallery, Madison, N.J., 1989, Phoenix Gallery, N.Y.C., 1990, Robin Hutchins Gallery, Maplewood, N.J., 1992, Berlex Labs. Corp. Office, Wayne, N.J., 1992, Hunterdon Mus. Art, 1993, Newark Acad., Livingston, N.J., 1997; exhibited in group shows at Hickory (N.C.) Mus., 1983, Purdue U., 1983, Monmouth (N.J.), 1984, Nabisco Brands Gallery, E. Hanover, N.J., 1985, 89, Hunterdon Mus. Art, Clinton, N.J., 1988, 93, 99, Schering-Plough Gallery, Madison, 1988, Morris Mus., Morristown, 1989, Montclair (N.J.) State U., 1995, Williams Gallery, Princeton, N.J., 1997, Monmouth Mus., Lincroft, N.J., 1998, Newark Acad., Livingston, N.J., 2000; represented in permanent collections N.J. State Mus., Trenton, Newark Mus., Morris Mus., Morristown, N.J. Painting residency fellow Vt. Studio Ctr., 1992. Mem. Assoc. Artists N.J. (pres. 1985-87), N.J. Watercolor Soc., Federated Art Assns. of N.J. (panel mem. 1985, demonstrator 1991). Home: PO Box 443 Bernardsville NJ 07924-0443

SPOHN, HERBERT EMIL, psychologist; b. Berlin, Germany, June 10, 1923; s. Herbert F. and Bertha S.; m. Billie M. Powell, July 28, 1973; children: Jessica, Madeleine. BSS., CCNY, 1949; PhD, Columbia U., 1955. Research psychologist VA Hosp., Montrose, N.Y., 1955-60, chief research sect., 1960-64; sr. research psychologist Menninger Found., Topeka, 1965-80, dir. hosp. research, 1979-94, dir. research dept., 1981-94; ret., prof. emeritus for rsch., 1994—. Mem. mental health small grant com. NIMH, 1972-76, mem. treatment assessment rev. com., 1983-86, chmn. 1986-87. Author: (with Gardner Murphy) Encounter with Reality, 1968; assoc. editor: Schizophrenia Bull, 1970-87, 91—; contbr. articles to profl. jours. Served with AUS, World War II. USPHS grantee, 1964— Fellow Am. Psychopath. Assn.; mem. AAAS, N.Y. Acad. Sci., Soc. Psychopath. Research, Phi Beta Kappa, Sigma Xi. Office: Menninger Found PO Box 829 Topeka KS 66601-0829 E-mail: hspohn@prodigy.net.

SPOHN, JANICE, elementary education educator, consultant; b. Pitts., Jan. 12, 1952; d. James Arthur and Jean Edna (Smithyman) Rowan; m. Chester Michael Spohn II, Oct. 23, 1972; children: Chester M. III, Lisa Marie. BE, Clarion U., 1973; ME, Slippery Rock U., 1989; supervisory cert., Duquesne U., 1992. Cert. reading specialist, gifted edn., supervisor reading, Pa. Group supr. Butler County (Pa.) Children Ctr., 1974-87; temp. instr. Slippery Rock U., Slippery Rock, Pa., 1989; reading specialist North Allegheny Schs., Pitts., 1990—. Coord. Pa. Framework Network, North Allegheny Schs., 1991—; inservice com. Allegheny Intermediate Unit, 1993—; Pa. Framework steering com. Allegheny Intermediate Unit, 1993—. Co-author/editor: (book) Pennsylvania Framework-Portfolio Implementation Guide, 1993; author, instr. online course on Emergent and Early Reading. Mem. ASCD, Nat. Coun. Tchrs. of English, Internat. Reading Assn., Keystone State Reading Assn., Three Rivers Reading Coun., Butler County Reading Coun. Avocations: reading, crafts, camping. Home: 520 Herman Rd Butler PA 16002-9157 Office: Peebles Elem N Allegheny Schs 8625 Peebles Rd Pittsburgh PA 15237-5720 E-mail: cspohn@zoominternet.net., jspohn@northallegheny.org.

SPOHN, WAYNE ROBERT, mechanical engineer; b. Cleve., Dec. 13, 1949; s. Robert Lee and Ruth Mary (Hardman) S.; m. Ruth Elizabeth Wenzel, May 23, 1975; children: Ryan Wayne, Daniel Robert, Katrina Elizabeth. BA in Psychology, Cleve. State U., 1974. Sr. project engr. Childers Products, Eastlake, Ohio, 1974—2000, ITW Insulation Sys., 2001—. Republican. United Methodist. Avocations: softball, volleyball, computers. Office: ITW Insulations Sys 34799 Curtis Blvd Eastlake OH 44095-4014

SPOHN, WILLIAM GIDEON, JR. mathematician, musician; b. Lancaster, Pa., Mar. 8, 1923; s. William Gideon and Inza Mae (Huber) S.; m. Alice Liane Bailey, Sept. 13, 1946 (div.); children: Susan Jeannine Grochowina (dec.), William Gideon III (dec.), Peter Jonathan, Kathleen Anne Precht, Mary Louise; m. Evelyn Walsh Moreland, June 15, 1963 (div. Oct. 1978); m. Claire Louise Burgstahler, Dec. 19, 1987 (div. Sept. 1999). BA, St. Johns Coll., 1947; MA, U. Calif., Berkeley, 1950; PhD, U. Pa., 1962. Instr. math. Temple U., Phila., 1952-54, U. Del., Newark, 1954-56; mathematician Aberdeen Proving Ground, Md., 1954-55; instr. math. Bowling Green State U., 1956-59; mathematician, sr. staff Johns Hopkins U. Applied Physics Lab., Laurel, Md., 1959-84; singer, prodr. Spohn Music Co., Columbia, 1981-99. Contbr. articles to profl. jours. Served to lt. USNR, 1943-46, PTO. Johns Hopkins U. Applied Physics Lab. fellow, 1966-67. Mem. Math. Assn. Am. Home: 982A Tonia Ct Eldersburg MD 21784-4913

SPOKANE, ROBERT BRUCE, biophysical chemist; b. Cleve., Aug. 5, 1952; s. Herbert Norman and Marjorie Ellen (Firsten) S.; m. Linda Carol Wright, June 20, 1976; children: Lea, Hannah, Tara. BS in Chemistry, Ohio U., 1975; MS in Biophys. Chemistry, U. Colo., 1978, PhD in Biophys. Chemistry, 1981. Cert. full cave diver. Teaching asst. Dept. Chemistry, U. Colo., Boulder, 1975-77, rsch. asst., 1977-81; staff scientist Procter & Gamble Co., Cin., 1981-84; rsch. scientist Dept. Neurophysiology, Children's Hosp., 1984-90, YSI Co., Rsch. Ctr., Yellow Springs, Ohio, 1990—. Cons. Synthetic Blood Internat., Yellow Springs, 1992. Contbr. articles to profl. jours. Rescuer, treas. Boulder Emergency Squad, 1980; rescue diver Kitty Hawk Scuba, Dayton, Ohio, 1992. Recipient Merck Index award Ohio U., 1975. Mem. Am. Chem. Soc., N.Y. Acad. Sci., Am. Physiol. Soc., Nat. Speleological Soc. (cave diving sect.), Sigma Xi. Achievements include research in implantable glucose sensors; oxygen tonometer for peritoneal oxygen measurements; interferant removal system for biosensors for methanol, ethanol, glutamate, and glutamine, optical carbon dioxide sensor, water chemistry in submerged caves. Home: 1715 Garry Dr Bellbrook OH 45305-1362 Office: YSI Co 1725 Brannum Ln Yellow Springs OH 45387-1107 E-mail: rspokane@ysi.com.

SPOLAN, HARMON SAMUEL, lawyer; b. Phila., Dec. 12, 1935; s. Jay and Edythe (Greenberg) S.; m. Betty Jane Evnitz, Mar. 30, 1958; children: Michael, Suzanne. AB, Temple U., 1957, LLB, 1959; postgrad., Oxford U., 1966. Bar: Pa. 1960. Ptnr. Ravetz & Shuchman, Phila., 1960-68, Blair & Co., N.Y.C., 1968-72; v.p. Butcher & Singer, Phila., 1972-74; pres. Capital First Corp., 1974-75, State Nat. Bank, Rockville, Md., 1975-78, Jefferson Bank, Phila., 1978-99; pres., bd. dirs. JeffBanks, Inc., 1986-99; sr. mem. Cozen O'Connor, 1999—. Lectr. law U. Pa., Phila., 1964-68. Author: Federal Aids to Financing, 1970; contbr. articles to profl. jours. Former chmn. bd. Huntingdon Hosp., Willow Grove, Pa., 1982-89; bd. dirs. YMHA, Phila., 1978—; bd. dirs. Anti-Defamation League, 1982. Named Man of Yr., Nat. Assn. Women Bus. Owners, 1978, Disting. Alumnus, Central H.S., 1975. Mem. ABA, Phila. Bar Assn. Democrat. Jewish. Office: 1900 Market St Philadelphia PA 19103-3527 E-mail: hspolan@cozen.com.

SPOLAR-BLUMER, ANNE MARIE, insurance purchasing specialist; b. Tigerton, Wis., Sept. 2, 1956; d. Anthony R. and Bernadine G. (Donder) Spolar; m. William F. Blumer. A in Police Sci., Fox Valley Tech. Inst., Appleton, Wis., 1976; grad., Gemol. Inst. Am., 1990, 95. Cert. gemologist. Salesperson Spolar's Jewelry, Appleton, Wis., 1976-85; asst. mgr. customer svc. Paradise Printing, Madison, 1985-88; gemology instr. Gemological Inst. Am., Santa Monica, Calif., 1989-93; purchasing specialist State Farm Ins. Co., Bloomington, Ill., 1993—. Mem. NAFE, Am. Gem Soc., Nat. Assn. Watch and Clock Collectors, Women's Jewelry Assn., Gemology Inst. Am. Alumni Assn. Office: State Farm Ins Co # B4 1 State Farm Plz Bloomington IL 61710-0001

SPOLLEN, ANNE K. writer; b. S.I., N.Y., Feb. 19, 1958; d. Christopher Bartholomew Spollen and Anna Theresa Burns; m. Philip G. Pileggi; children: Christopher, Philip, Emma Mariah. MA in English Lit., SUNY, New Paltz, 1991. Cert. permanent cert. secondary English, permanent cert. in Spanish. Author: (short stories) The Green Hills Literary Lantern, 1998 (Pushcart Prize in Fiction nominee). Democrat. Roman Catholic. Personal E-mail: aspollen@juno.com.

SPONENBERG, CARL GEORGE, music educator; b. Berwick, Pa., Nov. 7, 1946; s. Olen and Mila Mae Sponenberg; m. Jean Dunn Sponenberg, Aug. 17, 1968; children: Krista, Rebecca, Carrie. BS, Wilkes Coll., Wilkes-Barre, PA, 1964—68; MM music edn., Eastman Sch. of Music, Rochester, NY, 1969—72. Music educator Big Sprig Sch. Dist., Newville, Pa., 1969—. Avocations: music, recreational sports. Home: 530 Springfield Road Shippensburg PA 17257

SPONG, DOUGLAS K. public relations executive; B in English, Iowa State U. With Colle & McVoy, sr. v.p., mng. dir., also bd. dirs.; mng. ptnr. Carmichael Lynch Spong, 1990—. Office: Carmichael Lynch Spong Pub Rels 800 Hennepin Ave Minneapolis MN 55403-1817*

SPONG, JOHN SHELBY, retired bishop; b. Charlotte, N.C., June 16, 1931; s. John Shelby and Doolie Boyce (Griffith) S.; m. Joan Lydia Ketner, Sept. 5, 1952 (dec. 1988); children: Ellen Elizabeth, Mary Katharine, Jaquelin Ketner; m. Christine Mary Bridger, Jan. 1, 1990. AB, U. N.C., 1952; M.Div., Va. Theol. Sem., 1955; D.D., St. Paul's Coll., 1976, Va. Theol. Sem., 1977; DHL (hon.), Muhlenburg Coll., 1998. Ordained to ministry Episcopal Ch., 1955, bishop, 1976; rector St. Joseph's Ch., Durham, N.C., 1955-57, Calvary Ch., Tarboro, 1957-65, St. John's Ch., Lynchburg, Va., 1965-69, St. Paul's Ch., Richmond, 1969-76; bishop Diocese of Newark, 1976-2000; ret., 2000. Mem. governing body Nat. Episc. Ch., 1973-76; lectr. Harvard U., 2000. Author: Honest Prayer, 1973, This Hebrew Lord, 1974, Dialogue--In Search of Jewish-Christian Understanding, 1975, Christpower, 1976, The Living Commandments, 1977, The Easter Moment, 1980, Into the Whirlwind: The Future of the Church, 1983, Beyond Moralism, 1986, Survival and Consciousness, 1987, Living in Sin? A Bishop Rethinks Human Sexuality, 1988, Rescuing the Bible from Fundamentalism--A Biship Rethinks the Meaning of Scripture, 1991, Born of a Woman, 1992, Resurrection: Myth or Reality?, 1994, Liberating the Gospels, Reading the Bible with Jewish Eyes, 1996, Why Christianity Must Change or Die, 1998, Here I Stand: My Struggle for a Christianity of Integrity, Love and Equality, 2000, A New Christianity for a New World, 2001; columnist: Beliefnet.com. Named Quartercentury Scholar Emmanuel Coll., Cambridge, Mass., 1992, William Belden Noble lectr. Harvard U., 2000. Mem.: Rotary. Home: 24 Puddingstone Rd Morris Plains NJ 07950-1114

SPONSLER, GEORGE CURTIS, III, research administrator, lawyer; b. Collingswood, N.J., Dec. 2, 1927; s. George Curtis and Mary Grace (Hollinberger) S.; m. Bridget Ruth Butcher, Sept. 3, 1955; children: Freda Grace, Naomi Margaret Bride, Curtis Alexander. BS in Engring. Physics, Princeton U., 1949, MA, 1951, PhD, 1952; JD, George Washington U., 1981. Bar: Md. 1981, D.C. 1982, U.S. Ct. Appeals (4th cir.) 1982, U.S. Ct. Appeals (fed. cir.) 1984. U.S. Supreme Ct. 1986. With Lincoln Lab., MIT, 1952-56; liaison officer Office Naval Research, London, 1956-58, head spl. projects br. Washington, 1958-59; sr. scientist Hoffman Sci. Center, Santa Barbara, Calif., 1959-60; chief sci., dir. tech. analysis and ops. research U.S. Navy Bur. Ships, 1960-63; dir. advanced planning, fed. systems div. IBM, 1963-66, dir. center exploratory studies, 1966-68; exec. sec. div. engring. Nat. Acad. Sci.-NRC, 1968-70; pres. Law Math. and Tech. Inc., 1970—2002. On leave, Congl. fellow U.S. Senate, Washington, 1987-88; mem. adv. com. to Office Emergency Planning, Nat. Acad. Sci., 1967-72, chmn. subcom. automation, 1966-68, mem. joint adv. com. on electromagnetic pulse, 1970-74; cons. Exec. Office of Pres., 1971-73 Contbr.: Tech. Innovation, Harper Ency. of Sci.; author articles in field. Fellow AAAS (electorate nominating com. 1980-83, chmn.-elect sect. X, 1983-84, chmn. 1984-85, mem. coun. 1985-86), Am. Physics Soc.; mem. IEEE (life, sr., chmn. subcom. on privacy of communications and info. policy com. 1982-85, aerospace R&D policy com. 1990-92), Phi Beta Kappa, Sigma Xi. Democrat. Episcopalian. E-mail: sponsler@worldnet.att.net.

SPOO, CHARISA MARYANN, diagnostic radiologist; b. Chgo., Apr. 26, 1960; d. Richard Henry and Theresa Margaret (Holoubek) Spoo; m. Lawrence Paul Giese, Oct. 13, 1984; children: Katrina, Melissa, Nicholaus, Brianna. BS, Loyola U. Chgo., 1982; DO, CCOM, Chgo., 1986. Resident Michael Reese & Mercy Hosp., Chgo., 1986—90; diagnostic radiologist Olympia Fields (Ill.) Osteo. Hosp., 1990-91, St. Anthony's Hosp., Effingham, Ill., 1991-96, Morris (Ill.) Hosp., 1996-99, Mt. Sinai Hosp., Chgo., 1999—, dir. vascular imaging, 1999—. Mem. Am. Coll. Radiology, Radiol. Soc. N.Am.

SPOON, ALAN GARY, venture capital company executive; b. Detroit, June 4, 1951; s. Harry and Mildred (Rudman) S.; m. Terri Alper, June 3, 1975; children: Ryan, Leigh, Randi. BS, MS, MIT, 1973; JD, Harvard U., 1976. Cons. The Boston Cons. Group, 1976-79, mgr., 1979-81, v.p., 1981, The Washington Post Co., 1982-84; v.p., contr. Washington Post, 1985-86, v.p. mktg., 1986-87; v.p. fin., CFO The Washington Post Co., 1987-89; pres. Newsweek mag., 1989-91; COO The Washington Post Co., 1991-2000, pres., 1993-2000; mng. gen. ptnr. Polaris Venture Ptnrs., Waltham, Mass., 2000—. Dir. Info. Industry Assn., Washington, 1982-83, 88-89; bd. dirs., trustee WETA-Pub. Broadcasting, 1986-92; bd. dirs. Danaher Corp. Washington, Ticketmaster, Inc., L.A., Human Genome Svcs, Rockville, Md., Internat. Data Group (IDG), Boston; regent Smithsonian Instn., Washington; mem. corp. MIT. Bd. dirs. Norwood Sch., 1989-93, chmn., 1993-95; bd. dirs. Smithsonian Nat. Mus. Natural History, Washington, 1994-99; dir. Info. Industry Assn., Washington, 1982-83, 88-89. Recipient award for scholarship and athletics Eastern Coll. Athletic Conf. and MIT, 1973 Office: Polaris Venture Partners 1000 Winter St Ste 3350 Waltham MA 02451-1476

SPOONER, BERNARD MYRICK, religious organization administrator; b. Pine Hill, Ala., Oct. 15, 1934; s. Earl William and Lomie (Vick) S.; m. Patricia Ann Fowler, June 8, 1957; children: Myra Joan Spooner Bush, Jane Ann Spooner Carlisle. BS, Miss. Coll., 1957; MA, Southwestern Bapt. Theol. Sem., 1962, PhD, 1975. Min. edn. First Bapt. Ch., Ruston, La., 1962-65, Immanual Bapt. Ch., Tulsa, 1965-66; min. edn. and adminstrn. Travis Ave. Bapt. Ch., Ft. Worth, 1966-77; prof. adminstrn. New Orleans Bapt. Theol. Sem., 1977-79; dir. Bible study discipleship ctr. Bapt. Gen. Conv. Tex., Dallas, 1979-2001, adminstr. curriculum devel. Baptistway Press, 2001—. Bd. dirs. The Sweet Shop, USA, Inc., Ft. Worth, 1983-93; ptnr. Center St. Properties, Ft. Worth, Tex., 1977-2000; chmn. Ch. Min. Rsch. Team, 1994-96. Co-author: You Can Reach People Now, 1971, The People Challenge, 1985; contbr. articles to various publs. Vice chair Christian edn. workgroup Bapt. World Alliance, 2000—; cons. ch. growth and adminstrn., 1975—. Capt. USMCR, 1957-60. Mem. Bapt. Assn. Christian Edn. (v.p. 1975-76, chmn. bd. dirs. 1990-92, pres. 1998-99, Metro Bapt. Religious Educators Assn. (chmn. 1974), Tarrant Bapt. Religious Educators Assn. (pres. 1970), Bapt. Religious Edn. Assn. of the S.W. (pres. 1976), State Sunday Sch. Dirs. Fellowship (pres. 1995-97). Avocations: investing, gardening, travel, reading. E-mail: Home: 330 Spyglass Dr Coppell TX 75019-5430 Office: Bapt Gen Conv Tex 333 N Washington Ave Dallas TX 75246-1782 E-mail: bspooner@aol.com.

SPOONER, BRIAN S. science educator; b. St. Louis, Dec. 27, 1937; s. William Kenneth and Dorothy Marie Spooner; m. Mary-Rita Sloan, Aug. 24, 1963; children: Brian, Beth Logsdon (Spooner), Megan, Matthew. AA, Hannibal LaGrange Coll., Hannibal, MO, 1956—59; BS degree, Quincy U., Quincy, Illinois, 1960—63; PhD degree, Temple U., Philadelphia, Pennsylvania, 1963—69; BS, Quincy U., Quincy, IL, 1960—63; PhD, Temple U., Philadelphia, PA, 1963—69. Postdoctoral fellow U. of Wash., Seattle, 1968—69, Stanford U., Stanford, Calif., 1969—71; asst. prof. of biology Kans. State U., Manhattan, Kans., 1971—75, assoc. prof. of biology, 1975—79; vis. prof. MRC Lab of Molecular Biology, Cambridge, Great Britain and Northern Ireland, 1977—78; prof. of biology Kans. State U., Manhattan, Kans., 1979—, u. disting. prof., 1999—, asst. prof., 1971—75, assoc. prof., 1975—79; vis. prof. MRC Lab Molecular Biology, Cambridge, England, 1977—78; prof. Kans. State U., Manhattan, Kans., 1979—, disting. prof., 1999—, dir. of biology. Dir., nasa ctr. Kans. State U., Manhattan, Kans., 1990—2000, dir., hhmi program, Kans., 1998—. Author: (scientific publications) Over 100 Publications. Recipient Disting. Grad. Faculty Mem., Kans. State U., 1991, Presdl. Outstanding Dept. Head, 1997, U. Disting. Professorship, 1999; fellow NIH Predoctoral Fellowship, NIH, 1966-1968, NIH Postdoctoral Fellowship, Nat. Institutes of Helath, 1969-1970; grantee Rsch. Grants, NIH, 1972-1986, Am. Heart Assn., 1980-1994, NASA, 1990-1999, Undergraduate Edn. Grants, Howard Hughes Med. Inst., 1998-2006. Mem.: Am. Soc. for Gravitational and Space Biology (bd. of directors 1992—95). Office: Kansas State University Division of Biology - Ackert Hall Manhattan KS 66506 Office Fax: 785-532-6653. E-mail: spoon1@ksu.edu.

SPOONER, DONNA, public administrator; b. Deland, Fla. d. Michael and Ruth Elizabeth Linkovich. BS, Fla. State U., 1971, MPA, 1993, PhD in Pub. Adminstrn. and Policy, 2001. Budget analyst Dept. Adminstrn./Exec. Office of Gov. State of Fla., Tallahassee, 1977-80, spl. projects adminstr./acting chief, Bur. of Employee Cert., 1980-81, sr. govtl. analyst Exec. Office of Gov., 1981-85, pub. and legis. affairs dir. Dept. Adminstrn., 1985-87, asst. dir. Gov.'s Drug and Crime Policy Office, 1987-90; statewide planning coord. alcohol, drug abuse, mental health Fla. Dept. Health and Rehab. Svcs., 1990-95; owner Spooner Energy Assocs., 1996—2000; dir., founder Ctr. for Policy and Mgmt. Strategies, 2001—. Mem. Am. Soc. Pub. Adminstrn., Am. Acad. Cert. Cons. and Experts, S.E. Evaluation Assn., Capital Women's Network, Pi Alpha Alpha. Avocations: reading, hiking. Home: PO Box 14595 Tallahassee FL 32317-4595 Home Fax: 850-385-6598. E-mail: cpmstrategies@worldnet.att.net.

SPOONER, FRANK CLYFFURDE, economic history educator; b. Cleveland, Australia, Mar. 5, 1924; s. Harry Gordon Morrison and Ethel Beatrice (Walden) S. BA, U. Cambridge, Eng., 1947, MA, 1949, PhD, 1953, LittD, 1985. Commonwealth Fund fellow U. Chgo., NYU, Columbia U., Harvard U., 1955-57, U. Paris, 1957-63; lectr. advanced studies U. Oxford, Eng., 1958-59; vis. lectr. econs. Harvard U., Cambridge, Mass., 1961-62; Irving Fisher rsch. prof. econs. Yale U., New Haven, 1962-63; mem. faculty U. Durham, Eng., 1963—, dir. Inst. European Studies Eng., 1969-76, prof. econ. history Eng., 1966-85, prof. emeritus Eng., 1985—. Author: The International Economy and Monetary Movements in France, 1493-1680, 1956, English lang. edit., 1972, The International Economy and Monetary Movements in France, 1493-1725, 1972, Risks at Sea, 1983. Sub-lt. Royal Navy, 1943-46, ETO. Recipient Prix Limantour Acad. Scis. Morales et Politiques, 1957; Leverhulme Fund fellow, 1976-78, 85-86. Fellow Royal Hist. Soc., Royal Numismatic Soc., Soc. Antiquaries London; mem. Econ. History Soc., Econ. History Assn., Verenigung Economisch-Historisch Archief, Royal Econ. Soc., Am. Econ. Assn., Cliometric Soc., Assn. Marc Bloch, Hakluyt Soc., Soc. Francaise Numismatique, Mark Twain Soc., Friends Nat. Librs., United Oxford and Cambridge U. Club. Home: 31 Chatsworth Ave Bromley Kent BR1 5DP England Office: U Durham Dept Econs 23-26 Old Elvet Durham DH1 3HY England

SPOONHOUR, JAMES MICHAEL, lawyer; b. San Antonio, Mar. 24, 1946; s. Robert W. and Marie C. (Schulze) S.; m. Terri Walker; children: Taylor, Erin, Whitney, Michael. BA, U. Nebr., 1968, MA, 1970; JD, Georgetown U., 1974. Bar: Fla. 1974, U.S. Dist. Ct. (mid. dist.) Fla. 1974. Assoc. Lowndes, Piersol, Drosdick & Doster, Orlando, Fla., 1974-76; asst. prof. law Loyola U., New Orleans, 1976-77; ptnr. Lowndes, Drosdick, Doster, Kantor & Reed, P.A., Orlando, 1977—. Lectr. on eminent domain and property taxes. Contbr. to profl. publs. Bd. dirs. Vis. Nurse Assn., Orlando, 1979-89, Croquet Found. Am., 2001—; chmn. sch. bd. The First Acad., Orlando, 1986-89. With USAF, 1970-72. Mem. ABA, Assn. Eminent Domain Profls., Fla. Bar, Orange County Bar Assn. Republican. Office: Lowndes Drosdick Doster Kantor & Reed PA 215 N Eola Dr Orlando FL 32801-2095 E-mail: james.spoonhour@lowndes-law.com.

SPOOR, JOHN EDWARD, physician; b. Laurens, N.Y., Nov. 14, 1935; s. Elmer Eugene and Helen Blanche (Stanton) S.; m. Donna Lou Crandall; children: Kevin Chandler, Brian Stephen. MD, U. Buffalo, 1966. Diplomate

Nat. Bd. Med. Examiners, Am. Bd. Emergency Medicine. Intern Lakeland (Fla.) Gen. Hosp., 1966-67; pvt. practice Laurens, N.Y., 1967-69; emergency physician Fox Hosp., Oneonta, 1969-85, dir. emergency dept., 1981-85; dir. health ctr. State U. Coll. Oneonta, 1977-81; dir. emergency dept. Park Ridge Hosp., Rochester, N.Y., 1978; dir. emergency svcs. M.I. Basstt Hosp., Cooperstown, 1985-92, chief emergency medicine, 1988-92; dir. emergency svcs. Cmty. Meml. Hosp., Hamilton, 1993-95, med. dir., 1993-95; pvt. practice, 1993-98; v.p. med. affairs Cortland (N.Y.) Meml. Hosp., 1995-97; pvt. practice cons. in med. mgmt., 1998—. Cons. emergency medicine Cortland Meml. Hosp.; cons. Schoharie County Cmty. Hosp., Cobleskill, N.Y., 1985-90; cons. to dir. ambulance svcs. Ministry of Health, Kuwait, 1989, 90; med. dir. Susquehanna Andirondack EMS Program, Binghamton, N.Y.; mem. adv. com. Otsego County Emergency Health Svcs., 1974-76, 79-92; mem. com. in emergency health svcs. Med. Soc. State N.Y., 1979-94; mem. Adirondack Appalachian Regional EMS Coun., 1984-90; mem. emd. adv. com. N.Y. State EMS Devel. Office, 1987-89; mem. adv. group Office Health Systems Mgmt., Syracuse, N.Y., 1994-96. Contbr. articles to profl. jours. Ostego County coroner, 1970-72; mem. bd. edn. Morris Ctrl. Sch., 1971-73; chpt. faculty Am. Heart Assn., Utica, N.Y., 1981-93, bd. dirs., 1986-88; chmn. N.Y. Stte Emergency Med. Svcs. Coun., Albany, 1982; mem. Otsego County Econ. Devel. Coun., Oneonta, 1988; cons., dir. ambulance svcs. Kuwait City, Kuwait, 1989, 90. With USN, 1953-57. Recipient svc. award Otsego County Emergency Squad Assn., Cooperstown, 1979, award for outstanding community svc. Fox Hosp., Oneonta, 198l, First Aider of Yr. award Cen. N.Y. Emergency Squad Assn., Norwich, 1974, recognition of svc. award Otsego County CD, Cooperstown, 1982. Mem. Am. Coll. Emergency Physicians (com. emergency resources 1987-91, chair sect. rural emergency medicine 1991-92, editor newsletter sect. rural emergency medicine 1992-93), Am. Coll. Physician Execs., Nat. Rural Health Assn. (mem. spl. task force on rural EMS 1988-90, bd. dirs. 1992), N.Y. State Med. Soc., Ostego County Med. Soc., Am. Acad. Med. Dirs. Avocations: wildlife improvement, reading, target shooting, skiing. Home and Office: 265 Ed Copes Rd Laurens NY 13796-2103

SPOOR, WILLIAM HOWARD, food company executive; b. Pueblo, Colo., Jan. 16, 1923; s. Charles Hinchman and Doris Field (Slaughter) S.; m. Janet Spain, Sept. 23, 1950; children: Melanie G., Cynthia F., William Lincoln. BA, Dartmouth Coll., 1949; postgrad., Denver U., 1949, Stanford U., 1965. Asst. sales mgr. N.Y. Export divsn. Pillsbury Co., 1949-53; mgr. N.Y. office Pillsbury Co., 1953-62, v.p. export divsn., 1962-68, v.p., gen. mgr. internat. ops., 1968-73, CEO, 1973-85, also bd. dirs., chmn. exec. com., 1987, pres., CEO, 1988, past chmn. bd. dirs. Bd. dirs. Coleman Co. Mem. regional export expansion coun. Dept. Commerce, 1966-74; bd. dirs. exec. Coun. Fgn. Diplomats, 1976-78; mem. bd. visitors Nelson A. Rockefeller Ctr., Dartmouth Coll., 1992-95; Minn. Orchestral Assn., United Negro Coll. Fund, 1973-75; chmn. Capitol City Renaissance Task Force, 1985; trustee Mpls. Found., 1985-92; mem. sr. campaign cabinet Carlson Com. U. Minn., 1985; mem. corps. rels. com. Nature Conservancy, 1985; mem. Nat. Cambodia Crisis Com., pres. pvt. sector Dept. Transp. task force, 1982, pres. pvt. sector survey on cost control, 1983; chmn. YWCA Tribute to Womwn in Internat. Industry. 2d lt. inf. U.S. Army, 1943-46. Recipient Golden Plate award, Am. Acad. Achievement, Disting. Bus. Leadership award, St. Cloud State U., Miss. Valley World Trade award, Outstanding Achievement award, Dartmouth Coll., Horatio Alger award, 1986, Medal of Merit, U.S. Savs. Bond Program; honored with William H. Spoor Dialogues on Leadership, Dartmouth Coll., honored Fair Player Minn. Women's Polit. Caucus, 1989. Mem. Grocery Mfrs. Am. (treas. 1973-84), Nat. Fgn. Trade Coun., Minn. Hist. Soc. (mem. exec. com. 1983, bd. dirs.), Minn. Bus. Partnership, River Club N.Y.C., Woodhill Country Club, Lafayette Club (Wayzata, Minn.), Mpls. Club (bd. govs. 1985, pres. 1986), Gulf Stream Bath and Tennis Club, Delray Beach Yacht Club, Gulf Stream Golf Club, Old Baldy Club (Saratoga, Wyo.), Alta Club (Salt Lake City), Phi Beta Kappa. Home: 622 Ferndale Rd W Wayzata MN 55391-9628 Office: 4900 IDS Ctr Minneapolis MN 55402

SPOR, MARY ABRAHAM, reading and English educator; b. Center Township, Pa., Feb. 11, 1944; d. Alex and Mary (Hart) Abraham; m. Robert William Spor, Sept. 23, 1967; children: Elizabeth Spor Taylor, Susan Lynn Spor. BS, Pa. State U., 1966; MEd, U. Pitts., 1969, PhD, 1986. Cert. English tchr., supr., reading specialist, reading supr., elem. prin. secondary prin., supt., asst. supt., Ohio. English tchr. Moon Area Sch. Dist., Coraopolis, Pa., 1966-70, 78-79, English/lang. arts supr., 1979-85; asst. prof. Cleve. State U., 1985-89; dir. of edn. Geauga County Bd. of Edn., Chardon, Ohio, 1990-92; assoc. prof. Lake Erie Coll., Painesville, 1992-95, U. Ala. in Huntsville, 1997—. Instrnl. cons. dept. of edn. State of Ala., Montgomery, 1995—. Mem. editl. bd., reviewer Coll. Ready Assn. Yearbrook, The Ready Tchr.; editor Content Reading Jour., 2002; contbr. articles to profl. jours. Pres. Westlake Bd. of Edn., 1988-91; mem. Edn. 2000 Com., State of Ohio, 1990-91; mem. reading panel State of Ala., 1975; mem. Ala. literacy workforce coun. State of Ala., 1996-97; bd. dirs. Morgan County Mental Health Assn., 1997, Cleve. Opera League, 1988-95; trustee Greater Cleve. Ecology Assn., 1989-95; chair ready comprehension Ala. Reading Initiative, Ala. Dept. Edn., 1985, mem. advanced study in reading com., 1998-99. Mem. Internat. Reading Assn. (by-laws com. 1995-97, chair content area reading spl. interest group 1995—), Coll. Reading Assn. (editl. adv. bd. 1993-98, Outstanding Masters and Dissertation Degree award selection com. 1996-2000), Nat. Coun. Tchrs. English, Phi Delta Kappa, Pi Lambda Theta, Sigma Tau Delta, also others. Office: Univ Ala in Huntsville 245 Morton Hl Huntsville AL 35899-0001 E-mail: nomobama@aol.com.

SPORE, KEITH KENT, newspaper executive; b. Milw., May 29, 1942; s. G. Keith and Evelyn A. (Morgan) S.; divorced; children: Bradley, Julie, Justine; m. Kathy Stokebrand. BS in Journalism, U. Wis., Milw., 1967. City editor Milw. Sentinel, 1977-81; asst. mng. editor/news Milw. Jour. Sentinel, 1981-89, mng. editor, 1989-91, editor, 1991-95, editl. page editor, 1995, pres., 1995—, pub., 1996—. Author: (novels) The Hell Masters, 1977, Death of a Scavenger, 1980. With U.S. Army, 1961-64. Recipient Freedom of Info. award Soc. Profl. Journalists, 1995; named Mass Comms. Alumnus of Yr., U. Wis.-Milw., 1994. Mem. Greater Milw. Com. Office: Milw Jour Sentinel PO Box 661 Milwaukee WI 53201-0661 E-mail: kspore@onwis.com.*

SPORLEDER, THOMAS LYNN, economist, researcher; b. Perrysburg, Ohio, Apr. 2, 1942; s. John Loren Sporleder, Ruth Cordelia Westrick; m. Marjorie Jean Stout; children: Thomas James, Candace Lynn. BS, Ohio State U., 1964, MS, 1965, PhD, 1968. Mgr. Agrl. Grading Sta. Campbell Soup Co., Napoleon, Ohio, 1961—64; prof. agrl. econs. Tex. A&M U., College Station, 1968—89; prof. agribusiness, income enhancement endowed chair Ohio State U., Columbus, 1989—. Vis. scholar USDA, Washington, 1974—75; rsch. economist Office Tech. Assessment, US Congress, Washington, 1976—77; bd. dirs. Internat. Food and Agribusiness Mgmt. Assn., Washington, Ctr. for Innovative Food Tech., Toledo, Heartland Agdeavor Assn., Columbus. Contbr. articles to profl. jours. Mem.: Am. Agrl. Econs. Assn. (pres. elect agribus. econs. and mgmt. sect.AEM sect. 2001—). Roman Catholic. Home: 4518 Elderberry Ct Upper Arlington OH 43220-3020 Office: Ohio State Univ 2120 Fyffe Rd Columbus OH 43210-1066 Office Fax: 614-292-4749. Personal E-mail: sporleder.1@osu.edu. Business E-Mail: sporleder.1@osu.edu.

SPORN, AARON ADOLPH, physician, educator; b. N.Y.C., Nov. 5, 1953; s. Herbert and Eleanor (Aron) S. BS, SUNY, Stony Brook, 1974; MD, Columbia U., 1978. Diplomate Am. Bd. Orthopaedic Surgery. Intern. gen. surgery Roosevelt Hosp., N.Y.C., 1978-79, resident gen. surgery, 1979-80; resident, chief resident in orthopaedic surgery NYU and Bellevue Hosp., 1980-83; fellow Midwest Inst. for Orthopaedics, Cin., 1983-84; v.p. medical affairs Inst. for Medicine in Sports, Trenton, N.J., 1984-85; clin. sr. instr. Hahnemann U. Med. Sch., Phila., 1986—; clin. instr. Rutgers U. Med. Sch., New Brunswick, N.J., 1986—; chief, dept. orthopaedic surgery Robert Wood Johnson U. Hosp. at Hamilton, 1994—, vice chmn., dept. surgery, 1993-95, chmn. dept. surgery, 1995—. Vis. clin. fellow Columbia U., N.Y.C., 1978-80, teaching asst. NYU, N.Y.C., 1982-83; com. mem. Arthroscopy Bd. N.Am. Exam Com., 1989-90; cons. N.J. State Police, Trenton, 1987-92; fundraising com. orthopaedics wing Hamilton Hosp., Trenton, 1989. Contbr. articles to profl. jours. Ind. Rsch. Project grantee NIMH, 1975, 88. Fellow Am. Acad. Orthopaedic Surgery, Arthroscopy Bd. N.Am.; mem. AMA, Greater Met. Sports Medicine Soc., Med. Soc. N.J. (alt. del. 1989, Physicians Recognition award 1991), Mercer County Med. Soc., Phi Beta Kappa. Avocations: opera, photography, history, music, numismatics. Office: Medical Arts Bldg 8 Quakerbridge Plz Trenton NJ 08619-1255

SPORN, STANLEY ROBERT, retired electronic company executive; b. N.Y.C., Dec. 10, 1928; s. Max and Mollie (Sporn; m. Audrey Brandfield, June 29, 1952; children: Lawrence (dec.), David, Howard. BEE, CCNY, 1950; MSEE, U. Tenn., 1951. Devel. engr. Arma div. AMBAC Industries, N.Y.C., 1951-55, sr. engr., 1958-60, supr., then sect. head, 1960-76, dir. engring., 1976-78; sr. devel. engr. Norden Labs., White Plains, N.Y., 1955-58; dir. engring. Gull Airborne Equipment, Smithtown, 1978-81, v.p. engring., 1981-86; v.p. advanced tech. Gull Electronic Systems Divsn. Parker Hannifin Corp., 1986-95; ret., 1995. Author: (with others) Mechanical Design and Systems Handbook, 1964; patentee accelerometers, servos, electronics. Mem. Tau Beta Pi, Eta Kappa Nu. Office: Gull Inc Electronic Systems Divsn PO Box 9400 Smithtown NY 11787-9400 E-mail: ssporn@worldnet.att.net.

SPOTO, ANGELO PETER, JR. internist, allergist; b. Tampa, Fla., Mar. 25, 1933; s. Angelo Peter and Zillah Marie (Renfroe) S.; m. Carolyn Jeanette Barbee, Aug. 30, 1958; children: Keith Peter, Elizabeth Anne, Jacqueline Marie. AA, U. Fla., 1953; BS in Medicine, Duke U., 1956, MD, 1957. Diplomate Am. Bd. Internal Medicine, Am. Bd. Allergy and Immunology. Intern Duke U. Med. Ctr., Durham, 1957-58, fellow in medicine (allergy), 1958-59; resident in internal medicine USAF Hosp., Lackland AFB, Tex., 1960-62; resident in allergy Walter Reed Army Med. Ctr., Washington, 1962-63; staff allergist Watson Clinic LLP, Lakeland, Fla., 1966—; ptnr., 1968—; med. staff Lakeland Reg. Med. Ctr., 1966—. Pres. Watson Clinic Found., 1984-93, 2001; clin. assoc. prof. medicine U. South Fla., Tampa, 1973-77; chmn. bd. dirs. Polk Internat., Inc., 1986-95; chmn. Am. Group Practice Corp., 1992-94. Contbr. articles to profl. jours. Ruling elder Presbyn. Ch., 1970—. Maj. USAF, 1959-66. Decorated Air Force Commendation medal. Fellow ACP, Am. Acad. Allergy; mem. AMA (alt. del. 1992), Polk County Med. Assn. (exec. com. 1971), Fla. Med. Assn., Fla. Allergy Soc. (pres. 1973-74, exec. com. 1972-78), Southeastern Allergy Assn., So. Med. Assn., Am. Med. Group Assn. (trustee 1985-94, pres. 1991-92), Assn. Cert. Allergists (bd. govs. 1971-75), Lakeland C. of C. (bd. dirs. 1987-89). Republican. Presbyterian. Avocation: golf. E-mai. Home: 2515 Hollingsworth Hill Ave Lakeland FL 33803-3236 Office: Watson Clinic LLP 1600 Lakeland Hills Blvd Lakeland FL 33805-3065 E-mail: kebeja@aol.com.

SPOTO, DONALD, writer, educator; b. New Rochelle, N.Y., June 28, 1941; s. Michael George and Anne Hortense (Werden) S. BA summa cum laude, Iona Coll., New Rochelle, 1963; MA, Fordham U., 1966, PhD, 1970. Instr. Fairfield U., Conn., 1966-68; prof. Coll. New Rochelle, 1968-74; mem. faculty CUNY, N.Y.C., 1974-75, New Sch. for Social Rsch., N.Y.C., 1975-86; adj. prof. U. So. Calif., L.A., 1987-89. Vis. lectr. Brit. Film Inst., Nat. Film Theatre, London, 1980-86; nat. lectr. Am. Film Inst., Washington, 1979-82. Author: The Art of Alfred Hitchcock, 1976, 2d edit., rev., 1992, Camerado, 1978, Stanley Kramer: Film Maker, 1978, The Dark Side of Genius: The Life of Alfred Hitchcock, 1983 (Edgar award Mystery Writers Guild 1984), The Kindness of Strangers: The Life of Tennessee Williams, 1985, Falling In Love Again, 1985, Lenya: A Life, 1989, Madcap: The Life of Preston Sturges, 1990, Laurence Olivier: A Biography, 1991, Blue Angel: The Life of Marlene Dietrich, 1992, Marilyn Monroe: The Biography, 1993, A Passion for Life: The Biography of Elizabeth Taylor, 1995, The Decline and Fall of the House of Windsor, 1995, Rebel: The Life and Legend of James Dean, 1996, Notorious: The Life of Ingrid Bergman, 1997, Diana, The Last Year, 1997, The Hidden Jesus: A New LIfe, 1999, Jacqueline Bouvier Kennedy Onassis: A Life, 2000; author numerous revs., essays; contbr. articles to mags. and newspapers. Mem. Authors Guild Am., Writers Guild Am. Roman Catholic. Office: care Elaine Markson Literary Agy 44 Greenwich Ave New York NY 10011-8347

SPRABARY, LARRY DREW, military analyst; b. Lewisville, Tex., Sept. 24, 1946; s. H. L. and Frankie Charlene (Lester) S.; married Patricia; 1 child, Christopher Lain. BS in Mgmt., Embry-Riddle Aero. U., 1979; MS in Human Resources, U. Ctrl. Tex., 1990. Commd. 2d lt. U.S. Army, 1967, advanced through grades to maj., 1977, inspector gen. HQ U.S. Army Europe and 7th Army Germany, 1979-82, test officer Tng. and Doctrine Command Ft. Hood, Tex., 1982-87, spl. asst. to CG Test and Experimentation Command, 1987-88, ret., 1988; staff analyst BDM Corp., Killeen, Tex., 1988-89; mil. plans analyst Test and Experimentation Command, Ft. Hood, 1989-91, 1991-97, sr. test mgr., 1997-2000; dir. ops. directorate Operational Test Command, 2000—. Decorated Air medal, Bronze Star, Army Commendation medal, Meritorious Svc. medal; named U.S. Army Civilian Tester of Yr., 1993; recipient Dr. Wilbur B. Payne Meml. award for excellence in analysis-group category, 1997. Baptist. Avocations: golfing, skiing, water sports. Office: Hdqs OTC CSTE-TEX-AC Fort Hood TX 76544-5068

SPRADLEY, GREGORY RAYMOND, music educator; b. St. Louis, Mar. 9, 1947; s. Francis Edward and Alcie Jane Spradley; m. Marjorie Gail Gowan, May 28, 1968; children: Troy, Tod, Jason. BA, S.W. Bapt. Coll., Bolivar, Mo., 1969. Cert. vocal & instrumental music tchr. Vocalffinstrumental music dir. Burch Tree (Mo.) - Mountain Veiw Schs., 1969—71; K-12 vocal/instrumental music dir. So. Reynolds R 2 Schs., Ellington, 1971—99; vocal music dir. Potosi (Mo.) H.S., 1999—. Music dir. 1st Bapt. Ch., Piedmont, Mo., 1994—2000. Mem.: S.E. Mo. Tchrs. Assn. (jr. high vocal v.p. 1995—99). Avocations: fishing, golf. Office: Potosi HS #1 Trojan Dr Potosi MO 63664 Personal E-mail: spradgr@il.net. Business E-Mail: spradgr@potosi.k12.mo.us.

SPRAFKIN, ROBERT PETER, psychologist, educator; b. N.Y.C., Dec. 18, 1940; s. Benjamin R. and Dora M. (Berman) S.; m. Barbara Marcus, July 19, 1964; children: Jeffrey P., Neal R., Noah M. AB, Dartmouth Coll., 1962; MA, Columbia U., 1964; PhD, Ohio State U., 1968. Lic. psychologist, N.Y. Asst. prof. psychology Syracuse (N.Y.) U., 1968-71, adj. assoc. prof., 1973-88, adj. prof., 1989—; chief day treatment ctr. VA Med. Ctr., Syracuse, 1971-95, dir. psychology tng. program, 1983-2001; cons. psychologist Enable United Cerebral Palsy Assn. of Syracuse, 2002—. Clin. assoc. prof. dept. psychiatry SUNY Health Sci. Ctr., Syracuse, 1973—95; cons. psychologist Assn. for Retarded Citizens, 1993—, ENABLE, United Cerebral Palsy Assn., 2002—; clin. prof. dept. psychiatry SUNY Upstate Med. U., 1995—; chief Behavioral Medicine Sect. Psychology Svc., 1994—2001, acting chief psychology svc., 1994—97, sr. psychologist, 1997—2001. Co-author: Skilltraining for Community Living, 1976, Skillstreaming the Adolescent, 1980, Social Skills for Mental Health, 1993. Mem. Onondaga County Legis. Coun. on Disabled, Syracuse, 1982-94; mem. cmty. svcs. bd. County Dept. Mental Health, 1987-97. Mem. APA, Assn. Advancement of Behavior Therapy, Soc. Behavioral Medicine, Cen. N.Y. Psychol. Assn. (pres.), Dartmouth Club (pres.). Office: 300 Burnet Ave Syracuse NY 13203

SPRAGGINS, JOHNNIE DAVID, social studies educator; b. Opelika, Ala., Oct. 13, 1954; s. John David and Alma Jean McCormick Spraggins; 1 child, Jada Ruth. BA, Auburn U., 1978, MA, 1988, U. Mich., 1993, PhD, 1995. Rsch. assoc. Auburn U., 1981-90; tchr. Madonna U., U. Mich.-Ann Arbor, 1990-96; prof. Randolph-Macon Coll., Ashland, Va., 1991-99; asst. prof. Our Lady of the Lake U., San Antonio, 2001—. Advisor Woman's Studies Coun., Randolph-Macon Coll., 1999—; vis. asst. prof. SUNY, Geneseo; vis. asst. prof. Asian divsn. U. Md., Sagamihara-shi, Japan; tchr. Kitasato U., Sagamihara-shi, Kanagawa-ken, 1996-98. Contbr. articles to profl. jours. Mem. Ctr. for Rsch. on Social Orgn. Democrat. Buddhist. Avocations: gardening, travel. Office: Randolph-Macon Coll Henry St Ashland VA 23005 Home: 243 Rolling Green Dr San Antonio TX 78228- E-mail: spraj@lake.ollusa.edu.

SPRAGUE, AMARIS JEANNE, real estate broker; b. Jackson, Mich., Feb. 18, 1935; d. Leslie Markham and Blanche Lorraine (Basnaw) Reed; m. John M. Vetterling, Oct. 1985; children by previous marriage, Anthony John, James Stuart. Student, Mich. State U., 1952-53; BS, Colo. State U., 1965. Cert. real estate broker. Real estate sales Seibel and Benedict Realty, Ft. Collins, Colo., 1968-69; salesman Realty Brokers Exch., 1969-72; broker, pres. Sprague and Assocs., Inc., Realtors, 1972-80; broker assoc. Van Schaack & Co., 1980-86; broker, ptnr. The Group, Inc., 1986—. Dir. Univ. Nat. Bank. Mem. bus. adv. council Colo. State U., 1976-84, chmn. 1979-80, mem. adv. council Coll. of Engring., 1981. Named Honor Alumni, Colo. State U., 1983. Mem. Nat. Assn. Realtors, Colo. Assn. Realtors, Ft. Collins Bd. Realtors, Ft. Collins C. of C. (bd. dirs. 1978-84, pres. 1982-83). Republican. Epsicopalian. Home: PO Box 475 Fort Collins CO 80522-0475 Office: 401 W Mulberry St Fort Collins CO 80521-2839

SPRAGUE, DALE JOSEPH, writer; b. Portland, Oreg., July 8, 1946; s. Gerald William Sprague and Ruth Marie (Majerus) Williams; children: Amber, Noah, Jonah, Rachel. BS in Biocybernetics, Western Wash. U., 1974. Tech. writer Boeing, Seattle, 1976—. Cyberspace mag. essayist. Contbr. prose/poetry to on-line Phoenix and profl. publs. With USN, 1965-69. Avocation: fly fishing. Home: 824 NW 52d St Apt 6 Seattle WA 98107-3601 E-mail: phoenix@nwlink.com.

SPRAGUE, EDWARD AUCHINCLOSS, retired association executive, economist; b. N.Y.C., Oct. 9, 1932; s. Irvin Auchincloss and Maude Browning (Fisher) S.; m. Patricia Ivy Cannon, Apr. 27, 1957; children: James Edward, Elizabeth Mary, Jennifer Ann. BA, Princeton U., 1954; MA, NYU, 1961. Rsch. analyst N.J. State C. of C., Newark, 1957-59; assoc. economist F.W. Dodge Corp., N.Y.C., 1959-62; economist Lehman Bros., 1962-67; v.p. Nat. Assn. Mfrs., N.Y.C. and Washington, 1967-77; dir. tax policy The Tax Found., Washington, 1977-82, sr. v.p., 1985-89; exec. dir. Tax Exec. Inst., 1982-85; v.p., exec. dir. The Tax Coun., 1979-82, 86-91, cons., 1991-92, Employers Coun. on Flexible Compensation, Washington, 1992-93; ret., 1993. Editor: Building Business, 1961-62; jour. The Tax Executive, 1983-85. With U.S. Army, 1955-57. Mem. Nat. Tax Assn. Republican. Home: 47921 Tranquility Ln Lexington Park MD 20653-3218

SPRAGUE, ELMER DELOS, JR. philosopher, art historian; b. Havelock, Nebr., Aug. 14, 1924; s. Elmer Delos Sprague and Gertrude Ola Dowd; m. Gretchen Louise Burnham, June 22, 1948; children: Emily, Jennifer, Timothy, Gilbert. BA, U. Nebr., 1948, Oxford (Eng.) U., 1950, DPhil, 1953. English instr. Kearney (Nebr.) State Tchrs. Coll., 1948; assoc. prof. philosophy Ark. Polytech. Coll., Russellville, 1953; instr. philosophy to assoc. prof. Bklyn. Coll., 1953-67, prof. philosophy, 1968-97, prof. emeritus, 1998—. Author: Persons and Their Minds, 1999, Metaphys. Thinking, 1978, What Is Philosophy?, 1961. Pres. Putnam Highlands Audubon Soc., Philipstown, NY, 1991—93; vol. archivist divsn. art and antiquities Dept. Parks and Recreation, N.Y.C., 1997—2001. Rhodes scholarship Oxford U., 1948; recipient Hanna Professorship Hamline U., 1987. Mem. Am. Philos. Assn., Mind Assn., Hume Soc., Phi Beta Kappa. Democrat. Avocations: sculpture watching, photography, hiking. Home: PO Box 350 Cold Spring NY 10516

SPRAGUE, FRANK HOMER, environmental engineer; b. Independence, Kans., Mar. 31, 1947; s. Mary LaVone Sprague and Oscar Franklin Baker; m. Janice Darlene Cochran; children: Margaret Stelling. BS, U. Md., 1984; MS in Environ. Engring., So. Meth. U., 1995; PhD, U. N.Mex., 1998. Registered environ. mgr. 1998. Emergency planning engr. Ill. Dept. Nuclear Safety, Springfield, 1985—90; nuclear & emergency planning engr. Babcock & Wilcox Naval Nuclear Fuel Divsn., Lynchburg, Va., 1990—91; program Engr. U.S. Dept. Energy, Albuquerque, 1991—. E-6 U.S. Army, 1964—78, Walter Reed Army Medical Center. Mem.: Health Physics Soc. Protestant. Avocation: creative writing.

SPRAGUE, JACK, race car driver; m. Rhonda Sprague. Race car driver Hendrick Motorsports, Harrisburg, NC. Named Champion Craftsman Truck Series, NASCAR, 1997, 1999, 2001, Champion Busch Series, 2002. Achievements include all-time leading money winner Busch Series, 2001. Avocation: motorcycling. Office: c/o Hendrick Motorsports PO Box 9 4400 Papa Joe Hendrick Blvd Harrisburg NC 28075

SPRAGUE, JAMES MATHER, medical scientist, educator; b. Kansas City, Mo., Aug. 31, 1916; s. James P. and Lelia (Mather) S.; m. Dolores Marie Eberhart, Nov. 25, 1959; 1 son, James B. BS, U. Kans., 1938, MA, 1940; PhD, Harvard U., 1942; AM (hon.), U. Pa., 1971. From asst. to asst. prof. anatomy Hopkins Med. Sch., 1942-50; asst. prof. to prof. anatomy U. Pa. Med. Sch., Phila., 1950-83, chmn. dept., 1967-76, Joseph Leidy prof. anatomy, 1973-83, emeritus Joseph Leidy prof., 1983—, dir. Inst. Neurol. Sci., 1973-80, chmn. univ. faculty senate, 1963. Vis. prof. Northwestern U., 1948, U. Oxford, 1949, Rockefeller U., 1955, Cambridge U., 1956, U. Pisa, 1966, 74-75, U. Leuven, 1984-95, Kyushu U., 1988; sci. cons. NIH, 1957-60. Co-editor: Progress in Psychobiology and Physiological Psychology, 1966-84; asso. editor: Acta Neurobiol. Exper., 1976; contbr. articles to profl. jours. Recipient Macy faculty award, 1974-75, Disting. Tchg. award Lindbach Found., 1965; Guggenheim fellow, 1948-49 Mem. NAS, Am. Assn. Anatomists (v.p. 1976-78), Japanese Assn. Anatomists (hon.), Soc. Neurosci. (founding coun.). Democrat. Home: 410 Lantern Ln Berwyn PA 19312-2011 Office: Dept Cell & Devel Biology Sch Medicine U Pa Philadelphia PA 19104-6058

SPRAGUE, JO ANN, state legislator; b. Nashville, Nov. 3, 1931; m. Warren G. Sprague; 6 children. BA, U. Mass., 1980. Mem. Mass. Ho. of Reps., Boston, 1992-98, mem. capital budget com., 1990-92; mem. Mass. Senate, 1998—. Mem. Walpole Prison Adv. Com., 1970-92, Rep. Town Meeting, 1979—. Bd. trustees Walpole Scholar Found., 1990-92; bd. advisors NE Sinai Hosp., 1999—. 2d lt. U.S. Army, 1950-53. Mem. Walpole Vis. Nurses Assn. (bd. dirs. 1989-92), Walpole LVW, Norfolk Am. Legion (Post No. 335). Republican. Home: 305 Elm St Walpole MA 02081-1903 Office: Room 206 State House Boston MA 02133 E-mail: jsprague@senate.state.ma.us., joann@joannsprague.com.

SPRAGUE, JOHN LOUIS, management consultant; b. Boston, 1930; s. Robert Chapman and Florence Antoinette (van Zelm) S.; m. Mary-Jane Whitney, June 19, 1952; children— John Louis, William Whitney, Catherine van Zelm, David Hyatt. AB, Princeton, 1952; PhD, Stanford, 1959. With Sprague Electric Co., North Adams, Mass., 1959-87, co-dir. engring. labs., sr. v.p. engring., 1964-65, v.p. research and devel., 1965-66, sr. v.p. semi-condr. div., 1967-76, pres., 1976-87, chief exec. officer, 1981-87; pres. John L. Sprague Assocs. Inc., 1988—. Bd. dirs. Sipex Corp., MRA Labs., Inc., Calif. Micro Devices, Aerospace Coating Sys., Inc. Chmn. Williamstown United Fund-ARC Campaign, 1961; trustee Pine Cobble Sch., 1978, Middlesex Sch., 1994-96. Lt. (j.g.) USNR, 1952-55. Mem. IEEE, Electrochem. Soc., Am. Chem. Soc., Sci. Research Soc. Am., Confrerie des Chevaliers du Tastevin, Confrerie de la Chaine des Rotisseurs, Mayflower Hist. Soc., Sigma Xi, Phi Lambda Upsilon. Clubs: Princeton (N.Y.C.). Home: 175 Bee Hill Rd Williamstown MA 01267-2703 E-mail: beehilljon@aol.com.

SPRAGUE, KELLIE, hematologist, oncologist; b. Westover AFB, Mass., Aug. 12, 1964; d. Kenneth Rodney and Karen Ann (Gaddis) S. BA, St. Anselm Coll., 1986; MD, U. Vt., 1991. Diplomate Am. Bd. Internal Medicine, Am. Bd. Med. Oncology, Am. Bd. Hematology. Intern New Eng. Med. Ctr., Boston, 1991-92, resident in internal medicine, 1992-94, fellow in hematol. oncology, 1994-97. Mem. AMA, Am. Soc. Clin. Oncology, Am. Soc. Hematology, Mass. Med. Soc. Roman Catholic. Office: New Eng Med Ctr 750 Washington St Boston MA 02111-1526

SPRAGUE, PETER JULIAN, software company executive, lecturer; b. Detroit, Apr. 29, 1939; s. Julian K. and Helene (Coughlin) S.; m. Tjasa Krofta, Dec. 19, 1959; children: Carl, Steven, Kevin, Michael. Student, Yale U., 1961, MIT, 1961, Columbia U., 1962-66. Chmn. Wave Sys., Inc.; bd. dirs. Enlighten Software Inc. Bd. dirs. vwink.com, Inc. Trustee Strang Clinic. Mem. Yale Club. Office: Wave Sys Corp 101 W 57th St New York NY 10019-2215

SPRAGUE, WILLIAM WALLACE, JR. retired food company executive; b. Savannah, Ga., Nov. 11, 1926; s. William Wallace and Mary (Crowther) S.; m. Elizabeth Louise Carr, Oct. 3, 1953; children: Courtney, Lauren Duane, William Wallace III, Elizabeth Louise BSME, Yale U., 1950. With Savannah Foods & Industries, Inc., 1952-94, ret., 1994, sec., 1961-62, v.p., 1962-72, pres., chief exec. officer, 1972-92, chmn. bd. dirs., CEO, 1993-94, also bd. dirs., 1999, chmn. emeritus, 1998—. Bd. dirs., pres. Adeline Sugar Factory Co., Ltd., Savannah, Coastal Mgmt. Corp., Savannah. Trustee Savannah Bus. Group; chmn. emeritus Youth Futures Authority, Savannah. With USN, 1945-46. Named Sugar Man of Yr. and recipient Dyer Meml. award B.W. Dyer & Co., 1985; named Industrialist of Yr. Internat. Mgmt. Coun., 1988. Mem. World Sugar Rsch. Orgn. (chmn. 1982-85), The Sugar Assn. (bd. dirs.),Carolina Plantation Soc., St. Andrews Soc., Oglethorpe Club, Century Club (Savannah). Office: Sprague Enterprises PO Box 1313 Savannah GA 31402-1313

SPRAKER, MARY KATHERINE, pediatric dermatologist; b. Madison, Wis., Feb. 15, 1948; d. Charles Lewis and Mary Ellen (Ames) S.; m. Gregory Neel Studdard; children: Henry Lawrence, Margaret Ellen, Mary Louise and Lydia Ann (triplets). BS, U. Wis., 1970, MD, 1974. Diplomate Am. Bd. Dermatology, Am. Bd. Pediat. Resident in pediat. Children's Hosp., Cin., 1974-77; resident in dermatology U. Oreg., Portland, 1978-81; assoc. prof. Emory U. Sch. Medicine, Atlanta, 1981—. Mem. Soc. Pediat. Dermatology (past pres.). Home: 1389 Cornell Rd NE Atlanta GA 30306-2401 Office: Emory Clinic 1365 Clifton Rd NE Atlanta GA 30322-1013

SPRANDEL, DENNIS STEUART, management consulting company executive; b. Little Falls, Minn, June 1, 1941; s. George Washington and Lucille Margaret (Steuart) S. AB, Albion Coll., 1963; MEd, U. Ariz., 1965; PhD, Mich. State U., 1973. Grad. tchg. asst. U. Ariz., Tucson, 1964-65; dir. athletics Owen Grad. Ctr., Mich. State U., East Lansing, 1965-68; prof., dir. student tchg. Mt. St. Mary's Coll., 1968-70; exec. dir. Mich. AAU, 1974-81, mem. numerous nat. coms., 1974-81; mem. U.S. Olympic Com., 1974-77; pres., chmn. bd. Am. Sports Mgmt., Ann Arbor, 1976—, Am. SportsVision, 1981—, Am. Sports Rsch., 1977—, Sprandel Group, 1984—; pres. Nat. Sports & Entertainment, Inc., 1984—; with Sprandel Assocs., 1984—, registered rep., 1988—, pres., 1996—, Sprandel Portfolio Mgmt., 2000—. Fin. advisor Prudential Preferred, 1988-95; bd. dirs. Nat. Golden Gloves, 1980—, bd. trustees, 1986, Port Huron TV Project, 1985—; pres. Detroit Golden Gloves Charities; pres. adminstrv. bd. Detroit Golden Gloves, 1985—; bd. dirs. Mich. Sports Hall of Fame, 1976—; cons. in field. Contbr. articles to profl. jours. Recipient Detroit Striders award, 1978, Emerald award, 1979, World TaeKwonDo award, 1979, Detroit Spl. Olympics award, 1978, Cmty. Svc. award Mich. State U., 1985. Mem. Am. Soc. Assn. Execs., Nat. Assn. Phys. Edn. in Higher Edn., AAHPER, Nat. Recreation and Pks. Assn., Nat. Assn. Life Underwriters, Internat. Boxing Fedn., N.Am. Boxing Fedn., U.S. Boxing Assn., World Boxing Assn., World Boxing Coun., Nat. Assn. for Girls and Women in Sport, Psi Chi. Home: 219 Hutchinson Big Rapids MI 49307-1715 Office: Sprandel & Assocs PO Box 6047 Ann Arbor MI 48106-6047 E-mail: dennwins@aol.com.

SPRANG, MILTON LEROY, obstetrician, gynecologist, educator; b. Chgo., Jan. 15, 1944; s. Eugene and Carmella (Bruno) S.; m. Sandra Lee Karabelas, July 16, 1966; children: David, Christina, Michael. Student, St. Mary's Coll., 1962-65; MD, Loyola U., 1969. Diplomate Am. Bd. Ob-gyn; Nat. Bd. Med. Examiners; CME accreditation. Intern St. Francis Hosp., Evanston, Ill., 1969-70, resident, 1972-75, sr. attending physician, 1985—; assoc. attending phsycian Evanston Hosp., 1975-79, attending physician, 1980-84, sr. attending physician, 1985—, v.p. med. staff, 1990-91, pres.-elect, 1991-92, pres., 1992-93; also bd. dirs., 1991-94; sec. exec. com. Evanston Hosp., 1993-94; chmn. ob-gyn Cook County Grad. Sch. Medicine, Chgo., 1983-91. Instr. Northwestern U. Med. Sch., Chgo., 1975-78, asst. prof., 1984-95, assoc. prof., 1995—; pres. Northwestern Healthcare Network Physician Leadership, 1994; lectr. acad. and civic groups OB-Gyn. Nat. Ctr. Advanced Med. Edn., 1991—; bd. dirs. Ill. Found. Med. Rev.; bd. trustees Ill. State Ins. Svcs., 1992—, chair, 1998-2000; bd. govs. Ill. State Med. Inter-Inst. Exch., 1987-92. Editor: Profl. Staff News, 1992-93; chmn. editorial bd. Jour. Chgo. Medicine, 1986-91; contbr. articles to profl. jours. Bd. dirs. Am. Cancer Sooc., chmn. profl. edn. com. North Shoore unit, 1982-85; bd. dirs. Chgo. Community Info. Network, 1994-95; mem. Nat. Rep. Congrl. Com., 1981—, Ill. Med. Polit. Action Com.; bd. advisors Nat. Youth Leadership Forum on Medicine, Chgo., 1998-. With USN, 1970-72. Fellow: ACOG (chmn. Ill. sect. 1975—76), ACS, Am. Soc. Colposcopy and Cervical Pathology; mem.: AMA (Physician Recognition award 1977, 1980, 1983), Chgo. Found. Med. Care (med. care evaluation and edn. com. 1980—83, nominating com. 1980—84, practice guidelines com. 1984), Edn1. and Scientific Found. (bd. dirs. 1994—98), Chgo. Med. Soc. (adv. com. advt. stds. 1978—84, physician's rev. com. 1980—85, exec. coun. north suburban br. 1981—82, trustee ins. bd. 1982—, v.p. 1984—85, chmn. 1985, 1985, nominating com. 1985—, exec. coun. north suburban br. 1986, treas. 1986—89, chmn. fin. com. 1986—89, trustee 1986—92, sec. 1989—90, pres.-elect 1990—91, chmn. bd. trustees 1990—91, pres. 1991—92, immediate past pres. 1992—93, chmn. ethical rels. com. 1994—, counselor), Ill. Med. Soc. (del. to AMA 1987—, govt. affairs com. 1988—, chmn. reference com. 1989, chmn. fin. com. 1992—94, sec.-treas. 1994—96, chmn. bd. trustees 1996—98, chmn. bylaws com. 1998—99, pres.-elect 1999—2000, 1999—2000, vice chair delegation 2001—02, immediate past pres. 2001—02, chair delegation 2003—, bd. trustees 2002—), Physician Benefit Trust (chmn. fin. com. 1993—2002). Roman Catholic. Avocations: reading, raising fish, swimming. Home: 4442 Concord Ln Skokie IL 60076-2606 Office: AGSO 1000 Central St Evanston IL 60201-1777

SPRATT, JOHN MCKEE, JR. congressman, lawyer; b. Charlotte, N.C., Nov. 1, 1942; s. John McKee and Jane Love (Bratton) S.; m. Jane Stacy, May 31, 1968; children: Susan Elizabeth, Sarah Stacy, Catherine Bratton. AB, Davidson Coll., 1964; MA, Corpus Christi Coll., Oxford U., 1966; LL.B., Yale U., 1969. Ops. analyst Office of Asst. Sec. of Def., 1969-71; ptnr. Spratt, McKeown & Spratt, York, S.C., 1971-82; pres. Spratt Ins. Agy., Ft. Mill, 1973-82, Bank of Ft. Mill, S.C., 1973-82; mem. U.S. Congress from 5th S.C. dist., Washington, 1983—; ranking Dem. budget com., sr. mem. armed svcs. com.; former dir. Bank of York. Chmn. bd. trustees Divine Saviour Hosp., York, 1980-82; bd. dirs. Piedmont Legal Services, Inc., 1978-82; bd. visitors Davidson Coll., 1978-80; chmn. bd. visitors Winthrop Coll., 1976. Served to capt. JAGC, U.S. Army, 1969-71. Mem. S.C. Bar Assn. (ho. of dels.), ABA. Democrat. Presbyterian. Office: US Ho of Reps 1536 Longworth Hob Washington DC 20515-4005*

SPRATT, JOHN STRICKLIN, surgeon, educator, researcher; b. San Angelo, Tex., Jan. 3, 1929; s. John Stricklin and Nannie Lee (Morgan) S.; m. Beverly Jane Winfiele, Dec. 27, 1951; children: John Arthur, Shelley Winfiele, Robert Stricklin. AS, U. Tex.-Arlington, 1947; BS with high honors, So. Methodist U., 1976; MD, U. Tex.-Dallas, 1952; MSPH, U. Mo., 1970; postgrad., Washington U., St. Louis, 1961. Asst. in physiology Southwestern Med. Sch. U. Tex., Dallas, 1952; intern Barnes Hosp. Washington U., St. Louis, 1952-53; asst. resident in surgery, 1955-57; resident Am. Cancer Soc. fellow in surgery, 1958-59; USPHS Cancer Research fellow in radiotherapy and surgery Mallinckrodt Inst. Radiology, St. Louis, 1957-58, chief resident, 1958-59; mem. surg. faculty Washington U., 1952-76; chief surgeon Ellis Fischel State Cancer Hosp., Columbia, Mo., 1961-76; practice medicine specializing in surgery Louisville, 1976—. Mem. staffs U. Louisville Hosp., Norton-Kosair Children's Hosp., VA Hosp., Bapt. Hosp. East, Jewish Hosp.; prof. surgery U. Mo.-Columbia, 1961-76; prof. surgery U. Louisville, 1976—, Am. Cancer Soc. prof. clin. oncology in surgery, 1978-83, prof. health systems, 1980—; adj. prof. surgery F. Edward Hebert Sch. Medicine Uniformed Svcs. U. Health Scis., Bethesda, Md., 1988. Contbr. numerous articles and books in cancer, surgery and med. edn. fields to sci. publs. Mem. editorial bd. Cancer mag., 1964-91, Am. Jour. Surgery, Jour. Surg. Oncology, Jour. Cancer Edn. Editor, editor-in-chief Louisville Medicine mag., 1979-82, Jour. Pelvic Surgery, 1995—, served to capt. USNR, 1952-93, (ret.). Grantee Nat. Cancer Inst., Am. Cancer Soc., recipient St. George medal, 1997. Fellow ACS, Am. Acad. Med. Adminstrs. (editl. bd. The Executive, diplomate), Royal Soc. Health; mem. AMA, Am. Coll. Physicians Execs., Am. Surg. Assn., Soc. Surg. Oncology, Res. Officers Assn., Naval Res. Assn., Assn. Mil. Surgeons U.S., Soc. Med. Cons. Armed Forces, Soc. Pelvic Surgeons, Ctrl. Surg. Assn., Soc. Surgery Alimentary Tract, Cell Proliferation Soc., Am. Assn. Cancer Edn., Soc. Univ. Surgeons, Am. Coll. Physician Execs., Alpha Omega Alpha. Clubs: Cosmos (Washington). Lodges: Rotary. Democrat. Baptist. Home: 2206 Bell Tavern Ct Louisville KY 40207-1215 Office: 529 S Jackson St Louisville KY 40202-3229 Fax: 502-583-4369.

SPRAY, PAUL ELLSWORTH, retired surgeon; b. Wilkinsburg, Pa., Apr. 9, 1921; s. Lester E. and Phoebe Gertrude (Hull) S.; m. Mary Louise Conover, Nov. 28, 1943; children: David C., Thomas L., Mary Lynn (Mrs. Thomas Branham). BS, U. Pitts., 1942; MD, George Washington U., 1944; MS, U. Minn., 1950. Diplomate Am. Bd. Orthopedic Surgery. Intern U.S. Marine Hosp., S.I., 1944-45; resident Mayo Found., Rochester, Minn., 1945-46, 48-50; practice medicine specializing in orthopedic surgery Oak Ridge, Tenn., 1950-98; retired, 1998; vol. physician Knoxville Interfaith Clinic, 1998—. Mem. active staff Oak Ridge Hosp., 1950-98, hon. staff, 98-2000, 2001—, mem. staff, 2000-01; courtesy staff Harriman Hosp., Tenn., ret., 1998; vol. vis. cons. CARE Medico, Jordan, 1959, Nigeria, 1962, 65, Algeria, 1963, Afghanistan, 1970, Bangladesh, 1975, 77, 79, Peru, 1980, U. Ghana, 1982; AMA vol. physician, Vietnam, 1967, 72; vis. assoc. prof. U. Nairobi, 1973; mem. tchg. team Internat. Coll. Surgeons to Peru, 1979, 84 ; vis. prof. orthop. surgery U. Khartoum, 1976; hon. prof. San Luis Gonzaga U., Ica, Peru, 1979; AmDoc vol. cons. U. Biafra Tchg. Hosp., 1969; vis. prof. Mayo Clinic, 1988; sec. orthops. overseas divsn. CARE Medico, 1971-76, sec. Medico adv. bd., 1974-76, vice chmn., 1976, chmn., 1977-79, v.p. CARE, Inc., 1977-79, pub. mem. CARE bd. dirs., 1980-90, mem. bd. overseers, 1991-99; chmn. Orthops. Overseas, Inc., 1982-86, treas., 1986-88, emeritus mem., 1994; mem. U.S. organizing com. 1st Internat. Acad. Symposium on Orthops., Tianjin, China, 1983; mem. CUPP Internat. Adv. Coun., 1986-99; invited guest spkr. Japan Orthop. Assn., 1994; mem. curriculum com. Oak Ridge Inst. Continual Learning, 1999—, chmn. med. programs subcom.; bd. mem. Meth. Med. Found., 2000—, chmn.-elect, 2002. Mem. editorial bd. Contemporary Orthopedics, 1984-96. V.p. Anderson County Health Coun., 1975, pres., 1976—77, hon. bd. dirs.; pres. health commn. Coun. So. Mountains, 1958—65, sec., bd. dirs., 1965—66; Tenn. pres. UN Assn., 1966—67; vice-chmn. bd. Camelot Care Ctr., Tenn., 1979—82, chmn., 1982—86; bd. dirs. Meth. Med. Ctr. of Oak Ridge Found., 2000—; hon. mem. World Orthopedic Concern, 1990; with del. to Vietnam People to People, citizen amb. to Vietnam, 1993; del. to Oak Ridge's Sister City Obninsk, Russia, 1993; trustee Vietnam Am. Scholarship Fund, 1992—95; Rotary vol. orthopaedic surgeon Kikuyu Hosp. Rehab. Ctr. of East Africa Presbyn. Ch., 1998. Named biographee, Mus. of Appalachia Hall of Fame; recipient Svc. to Mankind award, Serotoma, 1967, Humanitarian award, Lions Club, 1968, Freedom Citation, Sertoma, 1978, award, Amb. Goodwill Lions Club, 1979, Medico Disting. Svc. award, 1990, 1st Ann. Vocat. Svc. award, Oak Ridge Rotary, 1979, Tech. Comm. award, East Tenn. chpt. Soc. for Tech. Comm., 1983, Individual Achievement award, Meth. Med. Ctr. of Oak Ridge, 1991, Humanitarian award, Orthopaedics Overseas, 1992; fellow Melvin Jones fellow, Lions Club, 1993. Fellow ACS, Internat. Coll. Surgeons (Tenn. regent 1976-80, bd. councillors 1980-84, hon. chmn. bd. trustees 1981-83, trustee 1983-84, v.p. U.S. sect. 1982-83, mem. surg. teams com. 1983-90, Humanitarian award 1992); mem. AMA (Humanitarian Svc. award 1967, 72), Sociètè International Chirugie Orthopèdique et de Traumatologie, So. Orthopedic Assn., Western Pacific Orthopedic Assn., Am. Fracture Assn., Am. Acad. Orthopedic Surgeons (mem. com. on injuries 1980-86), Tenn. Med. Assn. (com. on emergency med. svcs. 1978-97), Peru Acad. Surgery (corr.), Peruvian Soc. Orthopedic Surgery and Traumatology (corr.), Clin. Orthopedic Soc., Mid-Am. Orthopaedic Soc., Rotary Club (Oak Ridge chpt., Paul Harris fellow). Home: 507 Delaware Ave Oak Ridge TN 37830-3902 Fax: 865-483-8657. E-mail: spray507@aol.com.

SPRAY, PAULINE ETHA MELLISH, retired elementary educator, writer; b. Byron Ctr., Mich., July 9, 1920; d. John Earl and Mary Rachel (Twining) Mellish; m. Russell Elbert Spray, Mar. 8, 1940; children: Sybil Marie (Spray) Musatics, Sue Anne (Spray) Smith. Student, Lapeer County Normal, 1938-39, Bethany Nazarene Coll., 1942, Ctrl. Mich. U., 1949-52, Grand Rapids Jr. Coll., 1967. Elem. sch. tchr. Lapeer County Bd. Edn., Mich., 1939-40, Shiawassee County Bd. Edn., 1949-52. Author: Daily Delights, 1968, Planned Programs for Women's Groups, 1968, RX for Nerves, 1975, How to Live with Less Tension, 1977, Coping with Tension, 1977, , 2d edit., RX for Happiness, 1978, The Autumn Years, 1979, Heritage of Hope, 1987, Confessions of a Preacher's Wife, 1985, Devotionals for Musicians, 1990, In the Valley of Decision, 1995, Devotionals for Musicians II, 2000; co-author: In the Footprints of Pioneers, 1983; contbr. other books and many articles and stories to religious newspapers of many denominations; also religious columns for secular newspapers including News Palladium, Benton Harbor, Mich., Sparta (Mich.) Reminder, Freeport (Mich.) News, Clarksville (Mich.) Record, The Lowell (Mich.) Ledger and The County Press, Lapeer, Mich., others. Mem. Mich. dist. coun. Nazarene World Missionary Soc. Mem. Pastors' Wives Fellowship (pres. 10 yrs.). Home: 1145 Adams St Lapeer MI 48446-1304

SPRAYBERRY, PHILLIP KENT, academic administrator; b. Summerville, Ga., July 24, 1954; s. Julius Edward and Thelma Ruth (Cooper) S. BA, Lipscomb U., 1976; MA, NYU, 1984. Dir. music and theater Boyd-Buchanan Sch., Chattanooga, 1976-84; chmn. dept. music and theater Faulkner U., Montgomery, Ala., 1984-90; lead tchr. arts and activities Booker T. Washington Magnet H.S., 1990-01; dir. pub. rels. Summerfun Theater, Montclair, N.J., 1995-99; media rels. coord. William Paterson U., Wayne, 2001—. Stage dir., actor, singer various theaters, 1976—. Presenter, spkr. numerous confs. Recipient Class Act award Sta. WSFA-TV, 1997, Friends award Janice Capilatato Ctr. for Deaf, 1997. Mem. Internat. Network of Performing and Visual Arts Schs. (Tchr. of Yr. 1998), Internat. Assn. Jazz Educators, E. Ctrl. Theatre Conf., Nat. Assn. Tchrs. of Singing, Am. Choral Dirs. Assn., Village Light Opera Group. Avocations: directing, acting, singing. Office: William Paterson U 300 Pompton Rd Wayne NJ 07470

SPRAYBERRY, ROSLYN RAYE, retired secondary school educator; b. Newnan, Ga., June 29, 1942; d. Henry Ray and Grace (Bernhard) S. BA, Valdosta State Coll., 1964; MA in Teaching, Ga. State U., 1976, EdS in Spanish, 1988; EdD, Nova U., 1993. Cert. tchr., Ga. Tchr. history Griffin (Ga.) High Sch., 1964-65; tchr. 6th grade Beaverbrook Elem Sch., Griffin, 1965-66; tchr. Spanish, chair fgn. lang. dept. Forest Park (Ga.) High Sch., 1969-77, Riverdale (Ga.) High Sch., 1977-99; ret., 1999. Correlator Harcourt, Brace, Jovanovich, 1989; adv. bd. So. Conf. Lang. Teaching, 1992-99; lectr. and speaker in field. Contbr. articles to The Ednl. Resource Info. Ctr. Clearinghouse on Langs. and Linguistics, Ctr. for Applied Linguistics, Washington; designed courses for the Gifted, Ga. Dept. of Edn. Cnvener Acad. Alliances-Atlanta II, Clayton County, Ga., 1982-99; advisor, workshop leader Ga. Fgn. Lang. Camp, Atlanta, 1983; dir. Clayton County Fgn. Lang. Festival, 1990-91. Recipient STAR Tchr. award Ga. C of C., 1982; Fulbright-Hays scholar, 1978; NEH grantee, 1977, 84. Mem. NEA, Am. Coun. Tchrs. Fgn. Langs., Am. Assn. Tchrs. Spanish and Portuguese, Ga. Assn. Educators, Fgn. Lang. Assn. Ga. (treas. 1977-85, assoc. editor jour. 1981-86, Tchr. of Yr. award 1976), Clayton County Edn. Assn., So. Conf. Lang. Teaching, KPS Leadership Specialists (co-founder 1993). Methodist. Avocations: guitar playing, traveling, reading, writing. Home: 104 Hickory Trail Stockbridge GA 30281-7361

SPRECHER, DAVID A. university administrator, mathematician; b. Saarbrucken, Fed. Republic Germany, Jan. 12, 1930; s. Wolfgang and Karolina (Jung) S.; children: Lorrie, Jeannie. Student, Hebrew U., 1952-54; AB, U. Bridgeport, 1958; PhD, U. Md., 1963. Instr. math. U. Md., 1961-63; asst. prof. Syracuse U., 1963-66; asso. prof. math. U. Calif.-Santa Barbara, 1966-71, prof., 1971-92, prof. emeritus, 1993—, chmn. dept., 1972-75, assoc. dean Coll. of Letters and Sci., 1975-78, dean Coll. of Letters and Sci., 1978-81, provost/dean, 1981-91. Author: Elements of Real Analysis, 1970, 2nd edit., 1987, Precalculus Mathematics, 1974, Finite Mathematics, 1976; (with P. Frank and A. Yaqub) A Brief Course in Calculus With Applications, 1971, 2nd edit., 1976; (with P. Frank) Calculus, 1975; contbr. articles to profl. jours. Served with Israeli Army, 1948-50. Mem. Am. Math. Soc., Math. Assn. Am.

SPRECHER, DREXEL ANDREAS, retired lawyer, writer; b. Independence, Wis., Mar. 25, 1913; s. Walter Edmund Sprecher and Florence LaVerne Maloy; m. Eleanor Rust Peirce, 1941 (div. 1946); m. Virginia Lee Sprecher, Sept. 24, 1949; children: Drexel A. Jr., Jenna Garman, Karen Maloy. Student, North Ctrl. Coll., Naperville, Ill., 1930-31; BA, U. Wis., 1934; JD, Harvard U., 1938. Bar: Wis. 1938, U.S. Supreme Ct. 1957. Trial atty. Nat. Labor Rels. Bd., Washington, 1938-42; from sgt. to capt. U.S. Army., 1942-46; asst. prosecutor Chief of Counsel for War Crimes, Nuremberg, Germany, 1945-49; asst. adminstr. Small Def. Plants Adminstrn., Washington, 1950-51; writer Chevy Chase, Md., 1972—. Pres. Potomac Constrn. Co., Chevy Chase, 1957-59; co-owner Ridgeland Farm Estates, Potomac, Md., 1957-65; pres., v.p. Leadership Resources, Inc., Washington, 1960-72. Author: Inside the Nuremberg Trial, 1998 (Ann. List Acad. Titles, Choice Mag. 1999); chief editor: Trials of War Criminals Before the Nuremberg Military Tribunals, 15 vols., 1948-51. Pres. Potomac Dem. Club, 1955-56; dep. chmn. Nat. Dem. Com., Washington, 1957-60. Unitarian Universalist. Avocations: gymnasium exercise, walking.

SPRECHER, BARON WILLIAM GUNTHER, pianist, composer, conductor, diplomat; b. Saarbrucken, Germany, Jan. 20, 1924; arrived in U.S., 1952; s. Wolf and Karoline (Jung) Sprecher; m. Blossom Tag, Aug. 6, 1952. Studied piano with Prof. Wittels, Tel Aviv; studied piano with Madame Vengerova, N.Y.C.; studied composition with Paul Ben-Haim, studied conducting with Georg Singer, , Tel Aviv; hon. degree, Inst. of Vocal Arts, 1957; Dr. honoris causa in Philosophy of Music, World Univ. Roundtable, 1988; MusD (hon.), London Inst. Applied Rsch., 1991, DFA (hon.), HHD, London Inst. Applied Rsch., 1993; MusD (hon.), Australian Inst. Coord. Rsch., 1991; diploma, Gran Premio Am., 1990, Paladino del Tricolore, 1990; D Musicology, Somerset U.; D Music (hon.), Atlantic Southeastern U.; Diploma, Acad. Argentina de Diplomacia; Assoc. (hon.), Inst. Affairs Internat., Paris, 1993; DD (hon.), The Christian Congregation; D rerum politicarum (hon.), LittD, U. Aeterna Lucina Vitama, 1991; DD (hon.), LittD, Eng., 1994; PhD (hon.), Germany, 1994. Korrepetitor Israel Folk Opera, Tel-Aviv, 1940-43; piano soloist Israel Philharm. Orch., 1946-48; pres., music dir. Bronx Philharm., N.Y.C., 1971-83; music dir. Sta. WEVD, 1969-85; asst. pianist accompanying Lotte Lenya, Richard Tucker, Jan Peerce, Itzhak Perlman, Jan Kiepura, Ilona Massey; prof. Inst. Hautes Etudes Economiques et Sociales. Rsch. prof. Alliance Universelle Paix Connaissance, Paris, 1991; prof. Haute Ecole de Recherche, Inst. des Hautes Etudes Economiques et Sociales; mem. coun. Inst. de Documentation et D'Etudes Europeennes; dep. mem., diplomat Internat. State Parliament; dep. mem. assembly Internat. Parliament for Safety and Peace. Composer: (Song Book) Yinglish, piano soloist 1st performance of Gershwin's Concerto in F in Israel; composer Piano Sonata, 1945, Jerusalem Concerto for Piano and Orch., 1967, (TV spl.) Great is Thy Faith, 1970; pianist-condr. 24 record albums; mem. The First Piano Quartet (Acad. award nomination, Peabody award). Consul Sovereign State Aeterna Lucina for State and City of N.Y.; comdr. fgn. rels. Island Du Caricom, 1995; diplomat World Jewish Congress; senator Coun. of States for Protection of Life and Human Rights, Palermo, Italy; del. at large Rep. Presdl. Task Force; active Nat. Rep. Senatorial Com., Nat. Com. to Preserve Social Security and Medicare, Ctr. for Am. Values, Sr. Coalition, Common Cause. Decorated noble knight Noble House of Amena, knight order Knight Templars of Jerusalem, knight comdr. Lofsensis Ursinius Order, baron Order of Bohemian Crown, comdr. Order of Golden Lance (Australia), Capt. Légion de L'Aigle Mer, Baron of Montsalvat, knight Holy Grail, count San Ciriaco, comdr. fgn. rels. Island du Caricom, 1995, Sen Maison Internationale Des Intellectuels, Sen European Parliament, Internat. Parliament for Safety and Peace, diplomat World Jewish Congress, Laird-Lord of Camster, Caithness, Scotland, 1995; recipient Diplomatic medal Internat. Parliament for Safety and Peace, 1995, Gold Cross of Honour, Albert Schweitzer Soc. Austria, Albert Einstein medal, Circulo Nobiliario Caballeros Universales, 1992, Swan Knight (Chevalier du Cygne), Order of the Swan, Knight of Yr. award Internat. Writers and Artists Assn., 1995, Medal of Merit, Rep. Presdl. Task Force, 1998, Noble Conquistador, Internat. Chivalric Order of the Knights of Justice, and other. Fellow United Writers' Assn. India; mem. ASCAP, Maison Internat. des Intellectuels, Internat. Parliament for Safety and Peace, World Parliament Confedn. of Chivalry (Grand Coun.), World Acad. Assn. of the Universe (life), Bronx Philharm. Symphony Soc., Inc. (founder, pres.), Internat. Platform Assn., Am. Fedn. Musicians, Robert Stolz Soc. Gt. Britain, World Univ. Roundtable (trustee, founder), Internat. Cultural Corr. Inst., Circulo Nobiliario de los Caballeros Universales (grandmaster U.S.), Royal Order Bohemian Crown (baron), Lègion de L'Aigle de Mer (capt.), USA United Srs. Assn. Inc. Avocations: walking, chivalry and heraldry, cats, collecting rare musical books and recordings, collecting rare medieval coins and antique Coptic Ethiopian Crosses.

SPREITZER, CYNTHIA ANN, computer programming professional; b. Chgo., July 16, 1953; d. John Herbert and Patricia Virginia (Tieman) S. BS in Math., Loyola U., Chgo., 1975. Cert. data processor, 1986. Sr. Arthur Andersen and Co., Chgo., 1975-80; lead analyst Larimer County, Ft. Collins, Colo., 1980—. Mem. Assn. Inst. Cert. Computer Profls., Computer Security Inst., Data Processing Mgmt. Assn. Roman Catholic. Avocations: reading, skiing, travelling, sailing, hiking. Home: 610 Grove Ct Loveland CO 80537-9372 Office: Larimer County PO Box 1190 Fort Collins CO 80522-1190

SPRENGER, CURTIS DONALD, choir conductor, educator; b. Loveland, Colo., Feb. 3, 1934; s. Fred John and Frieda Louise (Bangert) S.; m. Marlene Marian Banek, June 5, 1963; 1 child, Branden B. AB, U. No. Colo., 1959, MA, 1962, EdD in Music, 1969. Dir. choral activities Greeley (Colo.) H.S., 1961-65, Dickinson (N.D.) State Coll., 1966-68, Santa Rosa (Calif.) Jr. Coll., 1972—. Condr. Sonoma County Chorus, Santa Rosa, 1969-76, No. Calif. Chamber Chorale, Santa Rosa, 1971—, China Tour, 1985, Europe Tours, 1974, 76, 78, 82, 83, 85, 87, 88, 90, 92, 95, 97, 99, 01; lectr. Shanghai Conservatory of Music, 1985. With U.S. Army, 1953-56. Recipient Am. Choir Rep. award to French Celebration of Am. Bi-Centennial in Lyon, France, 1976; 5th prize Spittal Internat. Festival of Music, Austria, 1976, 1st prize Gdansk Festival of Music, Poland, 1978, Cmty. Coll. Performance award Western br. Conf. Am. Choral Dirs. Assn., Sacto., 1994, Santa Rosa C. of C. Excellence in Edn. award, 1997; named Outstanding Music Prof. Santa Rosa Jr. Coll., 1980-81. Mem.: Calif. Music Assn. Cmty. Colls. (choral rep. 1980—89, choral judge 1973—), Music Educations Assn., Am. Choral Dirs. Assn. (v.p. Calif. 1971—75, cmty. choir rep. Western br. 1986—2001), Theta Xi. Republican.

SPRENGER, ERNEST HENRY, pastor, translator; b. Elgin, N.D., Apr. 7, 1924; s. Christian and Martha (Schaible) Sprenger; m. Elizabeth May Strobel, June 20, 1947 (dec. Apr. 1973); children: Elizabeth Ann, Mark Randall, Scott Andrew, Cynthia Adele; m. Thelma Jean Koch McCormick, July 28, 1973; stepchildren: David Charles McCormick, Darlene Kay McCormick Hoefel. BA, Yankton Coll., 1946, B in Theology, 1947; B in Divinity, Hartford Sem., 1959; M in Sacred Theology, Pacific Sch. Religion, Berkeley, Calif., 1965. Pastor German Congl. Conf., S.D. and Colo., 1947-52; frat. worker in Germany World Coun. Chs., 1952-55; student pastor 2d Congl. Ch., Middle Haddam, Conn., 1955-59; prof. practical theology Sch. Theology Yankton (S.D.) Coll., 1959-62; pastor Phila. Congl. Ch., Ritzville, Wash., 1965-77, Zion Congl. Ch., Ritzville, 1977-86; ret. Author: Roots and Relatives, 1995. Bd. dirs. H.E. Gritman Sr. Ctr., Ritzville, 1970-86; mem. book com. Adams County Hist. Soc., 1968-90. Mem. Masons. Republican. Avocations: fishing, woodworking, traveling, translating German script.

SPRENKLE, CASE MIDDLETON, economics educator; b. Cleve., Aug. 18, 1934; s. Raymond E. and Helen K. (Middleton) S.; m. Elaine Elizabeth Jensen, June 22, 1957; children: David, Peter, Amy. BS, U. Colo., 1956; MA, Yale U., 1957, PhD, 1960. Instr. econs. Yale U., New Haven, 1959-60; mem. faculty U. Ill., Urbana, 1960-97, prof. econs., 1970-97, chmn. dept. econs., 1976-80, acting head dept. econs., 1995-96, asst. dean Coll. Commerce, 1962-65; dir. U. Ill.-U. Warsaw MBA program, 1991—; prof. emeritus U. Ill., 1997—. Faculty Econs. Inst., Boulder, Colo., 1965, 72, 81; vis. scholar London Sch. Econs., 1967, 74, 81, 88; vis. lectr. City of London U., 1981; cons. Ill. Revenue Commn., 1962; bd. dirs. Aggregate Equipment co. Contbr. articles to profl. jours. Bd. dirs. Champaign-Urbana Symphony, treas., 1972-74, pres., 1975-77; bd. dirs. Champaign County Arts and Humanities Coun., 1977-79; bd. dirs. Champaign-Urbana Mass Transit Dist., 1983-96, vice chmn., 1985, 93-94. Am. Bankers Assn. grantee, 1970-71 Mem. Am. Econs. Assn., Am. Fin. Assn., Omicron Delta Epsilon Presbyterian. Home: 3403 S Persimmon Cir Urbana IL 61802-7128 Office: U Ill Dept Econs 1201 S 6th St Champaign IL 61820 E-mail: csprenkel@uiuc.edu.

SPRICH, WILLIAM WALTERS DANIEL, neurosurgeon; b. St. Louis, June 7, 1952; s. Gene Frank and Roberta (Walters) S.; m. Gina Wiegand, May 20, 1977 (div. Oct. 1981); m. Kathy Susan Gerrish, June 25, 1988. BA magna cum laude, Washington U., St. Louis, 1973; MD, St. Louis U., 1977. Intern U. Cin., 1977-78, resident in neurosurgery, 1978-82; fellow in neuroendocrinology Yale U., New Haven, 1979; pvt. practice specializing in neurosurgery Belleville, Ill., 1982—. Fgn. house surgeon Nat. Hosp. for Nervous Diseases, London, 1982-83. Contbr. articles to profl. jours. Dep. sheriff St. Clair County Sheriff's Dept., 1987. Fellow Am. Assn. Neurol. Surgery; mem. AMA, St. Clair County Med. Soc. (pres. 1992—). Clubs: St. Louis. Presbyterian. Avocations: fgn. travel, wines, paintings, scuba, sports cars. Office: Neurol Svcs Belleville 6401 W Main St Belleville IL 62223-3801

SPRIESTERSBACH, DUANE CARYL, academic administrator, speech pathology/audiology services professional, educator; b. Pine Island, Minn., Sept. 5, 1916; s. Merle Lee and Esther Lucille (Stucky) Spriestersbach; m. Bette Rae Bartell, Aug. 31, 1946; children: Michael Lee, Ann. BEd, Winona State Tchrs. Coll., 1939; MA, U. Iowa, 1940, PhD, 1948. Asst. dir. pers. rels. Pacific Portland Cement Co., San Francisco, 1946-47; prof. speech pathology U. Iowa, Iowa City, 1948-89, prof. emeritus, 1989—, dean. Grad. Coll., v.p.

ednl. devel. and rsch., 1965-89, v. pres. and dean emeritus, 1989—, acting pres., 1981-82; v.p. ops. Breakthrough, Inc., Oakdale, 1993-94; cons., 1994—. Com. mem. Nat. Inst. Neurol. Disease and Blindess; chmn. dental tng. com. Nat. Inst. Dental Rsch., 1967—72, chmn. spl. grants rev., 1978—82; chmn. bd. dirs. Midwest Univs. Cons. Internat. Activities, Columbus, 1978—87. Author: (book) Psychosocial Aspects of Cleft Palate, 1973; author: (with others) Diagnostic Methods in Speech Pathology, 1978; co-editor: Cleft Palate and Communication, 1968, Diagnosis in Speech Language Pathology, rev. edit., 1999, The Way It Was: The University of Iowa 1964-1989, 1999. Pres. Iowa City Cmty. Theater, 1964, 1977, 1983. Served to lt. col. U.S. Army, 1941—46, ETO. Decorated Bronze Star; fellow Nat. Inst. Dental Rsch., 1971. Fellow: AAAS; mem.: Midwestern Assn. Grad. Schs. (chmn. 1979—80), Am. Cleft Palate Assn. (pres. 1961—62, disting. svc. award), Am. Speech and Hearing Assn. (pres. 1965, honor award), Assn. Grad. Schs. (pres. 1979—80), Cosmos Clug (Washington), Mortar Bd., Sigma Xi. Home: 2 Longview Knoll NE Iowa City IA 52240-9148 Office: Univ Iowa M212 Oakdale Hall Iowa City IA 52242-5000 E-mail: duane-spriestersbach@uiowa.edu.

SPRIETSMA, LEO C. priest; b. Phoenix, Jan. 29, 1928; s. William M. Sprietsma and Evalina Renaud. ThM, Franciscan Sch. Theology, Santa Barbara, Calif., 1954. Ordained priest to Roman Cath. Ch., 1953. Assoc. pastor St. Francis Parish, Sacramento, 1954—58, Spokane, Wash., 1958—60, St. Francis de Paula parish, Tularosa, N.Mex., 1950—64, St Anthony parish, Tigard, Oreg., 1964—66, St. Paschal Parish, Spokane, 1966—67; pastor St. Francis Parish, Parker, Ariz., 1967—69, Topawa Missions, Sells, 1968—71; chaplain Newman Ctr. U. Calif., Riverside, Calif., 1971—73; assoc. dir. Las Cruces Retreat, Mesilla Park, N.Mex., 1973—75; chaplain Calif. Rehab. Ctr., Norco, Calif., 1975—84; assoc.pastor San Antonio Mission, Jolon, pastor, 1988—90, Topawa Missions, Sells, Ariz., 1990—92; asssoc. pastor St. Charles Parish, Apache Junction, 1997—98; rector St. Anthony Chapel, Santa Barbara, 1998—. Author: (monograph) History of San Antonio Mission, 1996; contbr. articles to profl. jours. Conservative. Roman Catholic. Avocations: computers, video editing, reading, exercising, travel. Home: 2300 Garden St Santa Barbara CA 93105 Office: Franciscan Friars of California 2300 Garden St Santa Barbara CA 93105 Personal E-mail: sprietsma29@netscape.net.

SPRIGGS, DAVID RANDALL, healthcare administrator, educator; b. Chgo., May 12, 1950; s. Randall and Mary Spriggs; m. Nancy J. Gerlach, Jan. 22, 1973. BS, U. Wis., 1973, MD, 1977. Cert. Am. Bd. Internal Medicine; lic., N.Y. Fellow Dana Farber Cancer Inst., Boston, 1982-85; from instr. to assst. prof. Harvard U., 1985-89; asst. prof. U. Wis., Madison, 1989-93; mem., chief devel. chemotherapy, Winthrop Rockefeller chair med. oncology Meml. Sloan-Kettering Cancer Ctr., N.Y.C., 1993—. Sr. editor: (jour.) Clin. Cancer Rsch., 1996. Grantee Nat. Cancer Inst., 1994—. Mem. AAAS, Am. Assn. for Cancer Rsch., Am. Soc. Clin. Oncology. Avocations: golf, science fiction. Office: Meml Sloan Kettering Hosp 1275 York Ave New York NY 10021-6094

SPRIGGS, EVERETT LEE, lawyer; b. Safford, Ariz., July 30, 1930; s. Claude E. and Evelyn (Lee) S.; m. Betty Medley, Aug. 22, 1953; children: Claudia Lynn Reynolds, Lee M., Scott B. BS, Ariz. State U., 1955; JD, U. Ariz., 1958. Bar: Calif. 1960, U.S. Supreme Ct. 1983. City atty. criminal dept., Los Angeles, 1960-61; mem. firm Kinkle & Rodiger, Riverside, Calif., 1961-64; pres. Kinkle, Rodiger & Spriggs (P.C.), 1965—. Chmn. bd. dirs. Riverside Nat. Bank. With AUS, 1951-52. Mem. ABA, Calif. Bar Assn., Riverside County Bar Assn., L.A. County Bar Assn., Def. Rsch. Inst., So. Calif. Def. Counsel (editorial staff 1970-71), Assn. Trial Lawyers Am., Riverside Downtown Assn., Am. Bd. Trial Advocates, Supreme Ct. Hist. Soc., Def. Orientation Conf. Assn. Home: 1456 Muirfield Rd Riverside CA 92506-5576 also: 126 E Balboa Blvd Balboa CA 92661-1314 Office: Kinkle Rodiger & Spriggs 3333 14th St Riverside CA 92501-3809 also: 600 N Grand Ave Los Angeles CA 90012-2212 also: 837 N Ross St Santa Ana CA 92701-3419 also: 1620 5th Ave San Diego CA 92101-2747 also: 125 E De La Guerra St Santa Barbara CA 93101-2239

SPRIGGS, RICHARD MOORE, ceramic engineer, research center administrator; b. Washington, May 8, 1931; s. Lucian Alexander and Kathryn (Aber) S.; m. Patricia Anne Blaney, Aug. 1, 1953; children: Carolyn Elizabeth Spriggs Muchna, Richard Moore, Alan David BS in Ceramics, Pa. State U., 1952; MS in Ceramic Engring., U. Ill., 1956, PhD, 1958. Sr. research engr. Ferro Corp., Cleve., 1958-59; sr. staff scientist, group leader, ceramics rsch. AVCO Corp., Wilmington, Mass., 1959-64; assoc. prof. metall. engring. Lehigh U., Bethlehem, Pa., 1964-67, prof. metallurgy and materials sci. and engring., 1967-80, adminstrv. asst. to pres., 1970-71, asst. v.p. for adminstrn., 1971-72, v.p. for adminstrn., 1972-78, dir. phys. ceramics lab., 1964-70, assoc. dir. Materials Research Ctr., 1964-70; vis. sr. staff assoc. Nat. Materials Adv. Bd. NRC, Washington, 1979-80, sr. staff officer, staff scientist, 1980-87, staff dir. bd. on assessment of NBS programs, 1984-87; J.F. McMahon prof. ceramic engring., dir. NYS Ctr. Advanced Ceramic Tech. N.Y. State Coll. Ceramics, Alfred (N.Y.) U., 1987-97, dir. office of sponsored programs, 1988-97, prof. emeritus, 1997—. Affiliate staff scientist Pacific Northwest Lab., 1994—. Contbr. articles to profl. publs. Co-patentee in field Pres., bd. dirs. YMCA, Bethlehem, Pa., 1978-79. Served to lt. USNR, 1952-56 Fellow Armco Steel Corp., 1956-58, Am. Council on Edn., 1970-71; Centennial fellow Coll. Earth and Mineral Scis., Pa. State U., 1996, Alumni Achievement award, 1999, 30th Ann. SHS Medal of Honor, 1997. Fellow: Brit. Inst. Materials, Ceramic Soc. Japan (Centennial medal 1991), Am. Ceramic Soc. (trustee pension trust fund 1979—84, pres. 1984—85, coord. programs and meetings 1991—92, Ross Coffin Purdy award 1965, Hobard M. Kraner award Lehigh Valley sect. 1980, Orton lectr. 1988, McMahon lectr. 1988, Mueller lectr. 1996, Albert Victor Bleininger award Pitts. sect. 2000, disting. life); mem.: Serbian Acad. Scis. and Arts (fgn.), Ceramic Assn. N.Y. (sec.-treas. 1988—99), Fed. Materials Socs. (trustee 1978—84), Materials Rsch. Soc., Materials Rsch. Soc. Japan (hon.), Internat. Acad. Ceramics (trustee 1988—96), Brit. Ceramic Soc., Ceramic Ednl. Coun., Nat. Inst. Ceramic Engrs., Internat. Inst. for Sci. of Sintering, Rotary (dir. 1982—87, pres. 1985—86). Office: Alfred U Ctr Advanced Ceramic Tech NY State College of Ceramics Alfred NY 14802 E-mail: rmspriggs@exite.com.

SPRINCE, LEILA JOY, librarian; b. Toronto, Ont., Can., July 10, 1936; came to U.S., 1981; d. Harry and Anna Helen Caller; children: Alan Rosenthal, Joel Rosenthal; m. Arnold Joel Sprince, Feb. 16, 1982 BA, U. Toronto, 1957, B of Edn., 1962; MA, U. South Fla., 1987. Cert. tchr., Ont. Ballet dancer Volkoff Can. Ballet, Toronto, 1953-54; tchr. h.s. North York Bd. Edn., 1958-60; libr. Broward County Libr. Sys., Plantation, Fla., 1987-88, 91-93, Margate, 1988-91, head youth svcs. Coconut Creek, 1993-96, Ft. Lauderdale, 1996; ret., 2001. Advisor Omnigraphics Pub., Detroit, 1993—; cons. Gale/U*X*L* Pubs., N.Y.C., 1996—; state facilitator summer programs State Libr. Fla., 1993. Contbr. articles to profl. jours. Mem. nat. children and youth membership orgns. outreach com. ALA/ALSC, 2001—. Mem. ALA (Best Books for Young Adult Cmty. spkr. 1989, 90), Fla. Libr. Assn. (spkr.), B'nai B'rith Women (fin. sec. 1983, pres. 1984, 85), Phi Kappa Phi, Beta Phi Mu. Democrat. Jewish. Avocations: music/dance, computers, traveling, history. Fax: (954) 357-6122. E-mail: lsprince@aol.com.

SPRING, CARL C. , JR. medical writer; b. L.A., Nov. 17, 1936; s. Carl C. Spring, Sr. and Emilie Temple Spring; m. Alice W. Alice Waters, Oct. 7, 1967. BA , Calif. State U., 1960, MA, 1968. Writer, news editor, L.A.; med. writer Audio-Digest Found., Glendale, 1968—. Fellow Melvin Jones fellow, 2002. Mem.: Am. Med. Writers Assn. (v.p. 1973—74), Lions Club (editor of bull. 1994—, program chmn. 1994—), Bay Cities Shrine Club (pres. 2001—02). Liberal. Episcop. Avocations: beach walks, swimming, travel, meteorology. Home: 3490 Wade Street Los Angeles CA 90066 Office: Audio-Digest Foundation 1577 East Chevy Chase Drive Glendale CA 91206 Home Fax: 818-545-0831; Office Fax: 818-545-0831. Personal E-mail: ccspring55@earthlink.net. E-mail: cspring@audio-digest.org.

SPRING, GARY STEPHEN, civil engineer, educator, consultant; b. Pittsfield, Mass., June 24, 1953; s. Herbert Ronald and Gladys Adelia (Sykes) S.; m. Nancy Eileen Marshall, Oct. 28, 1989. AS in Civil Engring. Tech. cum laude, U. Lowell, 1980; BSCE cum laude, U. Mass., 1982, MSCE, 1984, PhD in Civil Engring., 1988. Registered profl. engr., Mass., N.C. Engr.'s aid Dept. Pub. Works Commonwealth of Mass., Lenox, 1972-81, jr. civil engr., 1981-85, sr. civil engr. Boston, 1985-86; assoc. prof. civil engring. N.C. Agrl. and Tech. State U., Greensboro, 1988—. Hwy. design, traffic engring., geographic info. systems and knowledge-based expert systems cons. various clients, Mass. and N.C., 1987—; lectr. profl. confs. and meetings. Author, co-author profl. reports; contbr. articles to profl. publs. Rsch. grantee U.S. Dept. Transp., 1989-91, 92-93, 94-95, N.C. Govt. Hwy. Safety Program, Greensboro, 1991-93, U.S. HUD, 1992—, N.C. Dept. Transp., 1995-96. Mem. ASCE (br. sec.-treas. 1989-90, v.p. 1990-91, pres. 1991-92, sect. pres.-elect 1995-96, sect. pres. 1996-97, sect. past pres. 1997-98, faculty advisor 1997-98, chair coms. on computing in transp. and hwy. and traffic safety 1999—), Am. Soc. Engring. Edn., Inst. Transp. Engrs. (coms. 1989—, faculty advisor 1994—), Transp. Rsch. Bd. (coms. 1989—, chair com. on artificial intelligence 2001—), Tau Beta Pi. Home: 11840 Forest Lakes Dr Rolla MO 65401-9734 Office: U Mo Dept Civil Engring Rolla MO 65409-0001

SPRING, KATHLEEN, writer; b. Mich. d. Edward and Mary Broilo; m. Samuel Taylor (div. 1984); 1 child, Justin; m. Paul Riethmeier (div. 1991) AD summa cum laude, Oakland C.C., 1990; BA cum laude, Wayne State U., 1993. Cert. holistic health profl. Adminstr. comm. dept. Wayne State U., Detroit, 1990-95; stringer The Daily Tribune, Royal Oak, Mich., 1992-98; writer, photographer Spring Times, Detroit, 1992-98; pub. rels. mktg., editor Fanclub Found. for Arts, Southfield, Mich., 1993-98; writer, tchr. Spring Times, Lyons, Colo., 1998—; travel cons. holistic svcs. Rocky Mt. Retreats, 1998—. Author: Small Towns, Detroits Crown, 1997, Birthing of Creative Writing and Capturing Random Memories, 2002, Finding Your Mission, A Powerful, Playful Process, 2002; (dir., author, exec. prodr.): (documentaries) Sandstone Quarry History: Our Stones Gather Moss, 2001. Vol. PBS-Detroit, 1982-95. Named Journalist of Yr., Wayne State U., 1992; scholar numerous acad. scholarships. Mem.: Denver Film Soc., Colo. Authors League, Film and Video Assn., Women in Comm., Soc. Profl. Journalists (1st v.p. 1993—98, Howard Dubin Outstanding Pro Chpt. Mem. 1996, Cir. of Excellence-Newsletter 1996). Avocations: travel, books, films, photography. Office: Spring Times PO Box 512 Lyons CO 80540-0512

SPRING, MICHAEL, editor, writer; b. N.Y.C., Oct. 14, 1941; s. Sol and Muriel (Roth) S.; m. Marjorie Hornblower Bauer, Mar. 1965 (div. 1980); children: Declan, Evan; m. Janis Abrahms, 1993. BA, Haverford Coll., Pa., 1964; MA, Columbia U., N.Y.C., 1970. Reporter Bergen Record, Hackensack, N.J., 1969-71; editor Scholastic Inc., N.Y.C., 1971-87; editorial dir. Fodor's Travel Publs., 1987-94, v.p., 1989-94; pub. Macmillan Travel, N.Y.C., 1994-99; pub. Frommer's Travel Guides John Wiley & Sons, 1999—2001; pub. Wiley Travel, 2001—. Broadcaster, writer WNCN-FM, N.Y.C., 1983-84. Author: Great Weekend Escape Book, 1982, 4th rev. edit. 1990, Student's Guide to Julius Caesar, 1984; editor: American Way of Working, 1980, 50 vol. Barron's Book Notes series, 1984, Scholastic Literature Anthologies, 4 vols., 1985, 87, Great European Itineraries, 1987, Touring Europe, 1990, 3d edit. 1994; contbg. editor Conde Nast's Traveler, 1987—; travel expert CNN Travel Show, 1991-94, WCBS Radio daily travel show, 1998—. Democrat. Jewish. Home: 20 Country Rd Westport CT 06880-2525 Office: John Wiley & Sons 909 3rd Ave New York NY 10022-4731 E-mail: mspring@wiley.com.

SPRINGATE, KAREN SPEARS, artist; b. Dallas, Jan. 24, 1955; d. William Charles and Georgia Maxine Spears; m. Larry G. Springate. AA, U. Louisville, 1974, BA, 1979; MFA, So. Ill. U., 1984. Instr. U. Louisville, 1983-86, Jefferson Cmty. Coll., Louisville, 1985-86; from asst. prof. to prof. dept. art Ea. Ky. U., Richmond, 1987—; instr. Ky. Inst. for Internat. Studies, Murray, 1988, 90, 94, U. Louisville Studies Abroad, 1985. Vis. artist U. Ga. Studies Abroad, Cortona, Italy, 1987, Am. Acad. In Rome, Italy, 1990; resident Va. Ctr. for the Creative Arts, Sweet Briar, Va., 1989. Vol. St. Joseph Hosp., 1995-96, Christ Ch. Cathedral, Lexington, 1995-96, First Presybn. Ch., 1996, Southland Christian Ch., 1998—. Fellowship Ky. Found. for Women, 1990, 98, Al Smith fellowship Ky. Arts Coun., 1991, 2000. Mem. Coll. Art Assn., Found. in Art Theory and Edn. Democrat. Avocations: skiing, gardening, travel, dogs. E-mial. Office: Dept of Art Ea Ky Univ 309 Campbell Bldg Richmond KY 40475 E-mail: karen.spears@eku.edu .

SPRINGER, CHRISTINE GIBBS, management consultant, business owner, educator; b. Portland, Oreg., Nov. 23, 1947; d. Robert Lambert and Barbara (Jones) Gresham; m. Bruce Gibbs (div. 1978); m. John Lambert Springer II, 1996; 1 child, Christe. BA in English, U. Ariz., 1968; MPA in Urban Planning, Ariz. State U., 1978; PhD in Pub. Policy Adminstrn., Ind. U., 1986. Dir. tech. assistance Gov.'s Office Ariz., Phoenix, 1976-78; dir. State Local Govt. Rels., Salt River Project, 1978-92; prin. Red Tape Ltd. LLC, 1992—. Adj. prof. Ariz. State U., Phoenix, 1986—. Author: Boundaryless Organizations, 1992, A Guide to Effective Use of Volunteers, 1992, Word of Mouth Marketing, 1994. Pres. Ctrl. Ariz. Homeles Shelter; pres. United Cerebral Palsy; examiner Ariz. Quality Alliance. Named one of Top 50 Women Bus. Owners in Ariz., award SBA, 1996; Alumnus of Yr. Ariz. State U., 1992. Mem. ASPA (past pres.) Westrends Coun. State Govts. (founding mem.), Ariz. Econ. Forum (founding mem.), Health Financial Authority, Nat. Acad. Pub. Adminstrn., Changler C. of C. (exec. com. 1998—), Soc. Human Resource Mgmt., Coll. Healthcare Execs. Republican. Presbyterian. Office: Red Tape Ltd Ste K593 4012 S Rainbow Blvd Las Vegas NV 89103 E-mail: cggs@aol.com.

SPRINGER, DOUGLAS HYDE, retired food company executive, lawyer; b. Englewood, N.J., Jan. 31, 1927; s. Arthur Hyde and Melicent Katherine (Messenger) S.; m. Virginia Helen Chouinard, Nov. 23, 1949; children: Susan Compton, Debora Lee. Student, Wesleyan U., 1944-45; AB, Yale U., 1947; LLB, Columbia U., 1950. Bar: N.Y. 1950. Atty. Port of N.Y. Authority, 1950-52; legal counsel Worthington Corp., Harrison, N.J., 1953-61, asst. sec., 1956-61; asst. counsel Campbell Soup Co., Camden, 1961-65, asst. sec., 1965, spl. assignments, 1966, dir. spl. studies, corp. planning, 1966-69, dir. corp. planning frozen foods, 1969-70, asst. treas., 1970-71, treas., 1971-73, v.p. fin. planning, 1973-75, v.p., controller, 1975-78, v.p., treas., 1978-88, v.p. investment mgmt., 1988-90. Trustee Meml. Health Alliance, 1981-99; trustee, treas. Virtua Health Hosp., 2000—, Meml. Hosp. Found., 1990—; mem. adv. bd. Pa. Liberty Mut. Ins. Co., 1971-88, Eastern regional adv. bd. Arkwright-Boston Mfrs. Mut. Ins. Co., 1985-90; exec. sec. Gov.'s Interstate Adv. Com., 1966; asst. to mem. Pres.'s Commn. on Postal Orgn., 1967-68; spl. asst. to chmn South Jersey Port Corp., 1969-71; mem. N.J. Econ. Devel. Council, 1972-76; mem. adv. coun. Tax Found., 1980-89. Trustee Nat. Food Processors Assn. Retirement Plan and Trust Indenture Fund, 1976-89, Perkins Ctr. for Arts, 1979-88, Ind. Coll. Fund, N.J., 1982-88; mem. exec. bd., v.p. fin. Camden County coun. Boy Scouts Am., 1978-90; mem. Y's Men's Club, Moorestown, N.J., 1990—, v.p., 1992-94, pres., 1994-95; mem. bd. Family "Y" of Burlington County, 1995-2000, sec. 2000—; mem. Yale Alumni Fund Bd., 1996-2002, exec. com. 1998-2002. With USNR, 1944-46. Mem. Nat. Assn. Corp. Treas. (bd. dirs. 1982-88), Phila. Treas. Club, Internat. Bus. Forum (bd. dirs. 1980-88), Phi Nu Theta, Phi Delta Phi, N.J. Soc. Pa. (pres. 1992-93, treas. 1994—). Clubs: Yale (Phila., N.Y.C.); Nassau (Princeton, N.J.), Laurel Creek (Mt. Laurel, N.J.). Home: 322 Laurel Creek Blvd Moorestown NJ 08057-3986

SPRINGER, FLOYD LADEAN, architect; b. Goodrich, N.D., Feb. 1, 1922; s. George Roy Springer and Louise Baumbach; m. Dorothy Mae Shepard (dec. Sept. 1995); children: Debra Louise, Tami June. Student, U. Denver, 1948-51; BS in Archtl. Engring., U. Colo., 1952; postgrad., U. Wash., 1953-54, U. Utah, Portland, Oreg., 1980. Apprentice to arch. Gilbert R. Horton AIA, 1946-48; job capt. Robert Hall and Ira Cummings, Archs., 1956-57; mem. archtl. staff Austin Co., 1964, Naramore, Bain, Brady and Johanson, 1965, Roland Terry and Assocs., 1967, John Graham & Co., 1967-68; mem. various archtl. firms Wash. and Alaska, 1952-69; prin. Floyd Springer/Arch., Seattle, 1969—. Arch. numerous pvt. comml. and residential projects, 1969—. Contbr. articles to profl. jours. Cpl. inf. U.S. Army, 1941-44, PTO. Decorated Silver Star. Mem. Masons. Presbyterian. Avocations: photography, ballroom dancing, leaded art glass, oil painting, writing. Home and Office: 18548 60th Ave NE Kenmore WA 98028-8725

SPRINGER, GEORGE STEPHEN, mechanical engineering educator; b. Budapest, Hungary, Dec. 12, 1933; came to U.S., 1959; s. Joseph and Susan (Grausz) S.; m. Susan Martha Flory, Sept. 15, 1963; children: Elizabeth Anne, Mary Katherine. B in Engring., U. Sydney, Australia, 1959; M in Engring., Yale U., 1960, MS in Engring., 1961, PhD, 1962; D (hon.), Tech. U. Budapest, 2000. Registered profl. engr., Mass. Asst. prof. mech. engring. MIT, Cambridge, Mass., 1962-67; prof. mech. engring. U. Mich., Ann Arbor, 1967-83; Paul Pigott prof. Stanford (Calif.) U., 1983—, chmn. dept. aeronautics and astronautics, 1990—2001. Author: Erosion by Liquid Impact, 1975; co-author, co-editor 12 books; contbr. over 200 articles to scholarly and profl. jours. Recipient Pub. Svc. Group Achievement award, NASA, 1988, Medal of Excellence in Composite Materials U. Del., 1999. Fellow AIAA (Engr. of Yr. 1995, Structures Structural Dynamics and Materials award 2000), ASME (Worcester Reed Warner medal 1994), Soc. Advancement Materials and Process Engring. (Delmonte award 1991); mem. Am. Phys. Soc., Soc. Automotive Engrs. (Ralph Teetor award 1978), Nat. Acad. Engring., Hungarian Nat. Acad. Sci. (fgn. mem.), Am. Soc. Composites (Outstanding Rschr. award 1997). Achievements include patent in field. Office: Stanford U Dept Aeronautics & Astronautics Stanford CA 94305

SPRINGER, LEONARD, musician, educator; b. Evanston, Ill., Mar. 11, 1953; s. George and Annemarie (Keiner) S.; m. Jennifer Susan Litz, Dec. 16, 1977 (div. Nov. 1993); 1 child, Benjamin Joseph; m. Deborah Kay Bushnell, June 25, 2001. BA, Ind. U., 1987; MEd, Vanderbilt U., 1991; PhD, Pa. State U., 1996. Co-owner Ribbon Rail Recording, Bloomington, Ind., 1976-81; musician Donna Fargo, Nashville, 1981, Brenda Lee, Nashville, 1981-85, Ronnie Reno, Hendersonville, 1985-90, Highwater, Junction City, Wis., 1998-2000; band leader Freddie Pate Jamboree, Crowley, La., 2001—; rsch. asst. Ctr. for Study of Higher Edn., University Park, Pa., 1992-96; rschr. Wis. Ctr. for Edn. Rsch., Madison, 1996-98; dir. Southern Wis. Bluegrass in the Schs., Verona, Wis., 2000—; band leader La.Purchase Bluegrass Band, Lafayette, 2001—; pres. South La. Bluegrass Assn., 2002—. Edn. and rsch. cons., Lafayette, La., 1998–; bd. dirs. Tommy Comeaus Fund for Traditional Music, Lafayette, 2001–. Contbr. articles to ednl. jours. Bd. dirs. coord. com. Shaarei Shamayim, Madison, 1998. Fellow Am. Edn. Rsch. Assn./Spencer Found., 1994, Nat. Inst. Sci. Edn., 1997. Democrat. Jewish. Avocations: horseback riding, sailing. Office: PO Box 51672 Lafayette LA 70505 E-mail: springer@acadian.net.

SPRINGER, LORENE HARGROVE, music educator; b. Clay County, Tex., Nov. 16, 1927; d. John Smith and Zetha Lucille (Barnett) Hargrove; m. Cecil Lee Springer, Sept. 7, 1950; 1 child, Michael John. MusB in Piano Performance, Hardin-Simmons U., 1954; MusM in Piano Performance, Howard Payne U., 1967. Cert. music and piano tchr., Tex. Freelance instr. piano, Ft. Worth, 1954-55, Brownfield, Tex., 1955-60; elem. tchr. Orange Cove (Calif.) Sch. Dist., 1960-61; tchr. music Abilene (Tex.) Ind. Sch. Dist., 1961-63; freelance tchr. piano, theory Abilene, 1963—. Judge for Nat. Guild Piano Tchrs., Austin, Tex., 1974—. Performed solo piano concert, 1989. Named Abilene Music Tchr. of Yr., 1989, to Hall of Fame Piano Guild U.S.A., 1971. Mem. Music Tchrs. Nat. Assn. (cert.), Abilene Music Tchrs. Assn. (pres. 1972-74, 90-91, Plaque 1974, 91), Beta Mu Kappa (sec. 1953-54). Baptist. Avocations: church music, reading, boating. Home: 3041 Ricsan Dr Abilene TX 79605-6629

SPRINGER, MICHAEL LOUIS, federal agency administrator; b. Sarasota, Fla., Jan. 28, 1938; s. Stewart and Vergie (Fayard) S.; m. Afife Camila Chamas, Aug. 31, 1963; children: Elizabeth Karime, Michele Renee, John David. BA, George Washington U., 1964; MPA, The Am. U., 1978. With fin. mgmt. office Nat. Libr. Medicine, Bethesda, Md., 1969-71; dep. dir. mgmt. and orgn. div. EPA, Washington, 1971-73, dir. mgmt. info. and data systems div., 1973-75; sr. mgmt. assoc. mgmt. improvement and evaluation U.S. Office Mgmt. and Budget, 1977-82; dep. dir. Office Adminstrn. NRC, 1982-86; staff dir. Office Consolidation, 1987-88; dir. Office Consolidation U.S. Nuc. Regulatory Commn., 1988-94, dir. divsn. facilities and property mgmt., 1994-96, dep. dir. Office of Adminstrn., 1997-99, dir. Office Adminstrn., 1999—. Bd. dirs. Transp. Action Partnership North Bethesda and Rockville, Md., 1988-98. Mem. Citizens Adv. Com. for North Bethesda Master Plan, Montgomery County, 1990-91. Roman Catholic. Office: Nuclear Regulatory Commn Mail Stop T-7 D57 Washington DC 20555-0001

SPRINGER, ROBERT DALE, retired air force officer, consultant, lecturer; b. Millheim, Pa., Jan. 17, 1933; s. Simon Peter and Ruth Olive (McCool) S.; m. Bonnie Joan Brubaker, Aug. 30, 1953; children: Robert Dale Jr., Debra K. Springer Miller, Curtis A., Michele L. Demmy, Tania. BA in Social Sci., George Washington U., 1964, MS in Internat. Affairs, 1969. Cert. command pilot. Commd. 2d lt. USAF; advanced through grades to lt. gen.; comdr. 435th Tactical Airlift Wing, Rhein-Main Air Base, Federal Republic Germany, 1978-80, 322d Airlift Divsn., Ramstein Air Base, Federal Republic Germany, 1980-81, Air Force Manpower and Pers. Ctr., Randolph AFB, Tex., 1982-84, 21 A.F., McGuire AFB, N.J., 1984-85; insp. gen. USAF, Washington, 1985-87; with DCS-pers. Mil. Airlift Command, Scott AFB, Ill., 1981-82, vice comdr.-in-chief, 1987-88; ret., 1988; pres. bsone, Inc., 1999—, NovaLogic Sys., 1999-2001. Media cons., lectr., 1989—; dir. Air Force Commissary Svc., San Antonio, 1982-84, Army-Air Force Exch. Svc., Dallas, 1982-84; chmn. bd. dirs. Air Force Welfare Bd., San Antonio, 1982-84; mem. adv. bd. First Bank; bd. dirs. NovaLogic, Inc. Exec. dir Air Force Meml. Found., 1992-96, pres. 1996-98, vice chmn., 1998—; trustee Aerospace Edn. Found., 1992-94, The Falcon Found., 1996—. Mem. Air Force Assn. (Presdl. Citation 1984), Airlift-Tanker Assn. (life mem., sr. v.p. 1989-94), Arnold Air Soc. (exec. dir. 1990-93, trustee 1993-2001), Ret. Officers Assn. (life), Daedalians (life), Masons (33 deg.). Lutheran. Avocations: tennis, golf, reading. E-mail: bsone@nc.rr.com.

SPRINGER, SALLY PEARL, university administrator; b. Bklyn., Mar. 19, 1947; d. Nathaniel Margulies and Fanny (Schoen) S.; m. Hakon Hope; children: Erik Jacob Hope, Mollie Liv Hope. BS, Bklyn. Coll., 1967; PhD, Stanford U., 1971. Postdoctoral fellow Stanford U. Med. Sch., Calif., 1971-73; asst. prof. SUNY, Stony Brook, 1973-78, assoc. provost, 1981-85, assoc. prof., 1978-87; exec. asst. to chancellor U. Calif., Davis, 1987-92, asst. chancellor, 1982-2001, assoc. chancellor, 2001—. Author: (with others) Left Brain, Right Brain, 1981 (Am. Psychol. Found. Disting. Contbr. award 1981), 5th rev. edit., 1998, How to Succeed in College, 1982; contbr. articles to profl. jours. Mem. Internat. Neuropsychol. Soc., Psychonomic Soc. Office: U Calif Office Chancellor Davis CA 95616 E-mail: sspringer@ucdavis.edu.

SPRINGER, STEVEN DAVID, director; b. Rochester , Minn., Dec. 3, 1964; s. Donna Springer. Degree in biology and animal sci., Virginia Tech., 1988. Cert. tchr. Calif., BCLAD. Vol. rural youth devel. U.S. Peace Corps, Guatemala, 1988—91; st. outreach Covenent House Calif., L.A., 1992—95; adult sch. tchr. ESL L.A. Unified Sch. Dist., 1997—99, tchr., 1992—2000; dir. cross-aged tutoring, mentoring intervention programs Action Learning Systems, L.A. Unified Sch. Dist., Monrovia , 2000—. Represented in permanent collections U. So. Calif., Sch. Denistry. Avocations: swimming, hiking, running, traveling. Office: LA Unified Sch Dist 450 N Grand Ave Los Angeles CA 90051

SPRINGER, WAYNE GILBERT, computer company executive; b. El Paso, Tex., Oct. 6, 1951; s. Wayne Gill and Constance A. (Courtney) S.; m. Dianne Louise Slaydon, Jan. 3, 1981; children: Courtney Lee, Carol Jeanne, Kent Slaydon. BS in Engring., U.S. Mil. Acad., 1973; MBA, So. Meth. U., Dallas, 1979, MSCE, 1980. Registered profl. engr. Commd. 2d lt. U.S. Army, C.E., 1973, advanced through grades to capt., 1977, resigned, 1978; grad. sch. instr. So. Meth. U., 1978-80; engr. Fluor Corp., Irvine, Calif. and Houston, 1980-82; coord. project devel. United Energy Resources, Houston, 1982-83; founder Computer Leasing Exch. Corp., 1983—. Founder Computer Helpline, Houston, 1984—, Network Systems Tech. Corp., 1993—; pres., founder Laser Express Corp., 1991; pres. Atiwa Computing, Inc., 1995—; ptnr. Springer Cons., Houston and Whittier, Calif., 1980-86. Author: Your Road Map to E-Commerce Success, 2000; contbr. articles to profl. jours.; inventor mech. devices. Mem. Houston Conv. and Visitors Coun., 1983—; mem. technology com. United Way. Mem. MIT Enterprise Forum, West Point Alumni Assn., Houston C. of C., Computer and Audio Visual Execs. Assn. (founder 1989), Nat. Speakers Assn., Rotary Club, Mensa, Plaza Oaks Club. Avocations: skiing, tennis. Office: Atiwa Computing Inc 1003 Wirt Rd Ste 100 Houston TX 77055-6862

SPRINGER, WAYNE RICHARD, healthcare system official, research biochemist; b. Milw., Nov. 16, 1946; s. Richard Andrew and Irma Edna (Richter) S.; m. Jane Bradley, Aug. 19, 1972; children: Matthew Bradley, Katherine Jane. BA, Northwestern U., 1968; PhD, U. Calif., Berkeley, 1977. Vol. Peace Corps, Somalia, Antigua, 1969-72; postdoctoral fellow U. Calif., San Diego, 1977-79, rsch. biochemist, 1979-92; assoc. project biochemist, 1992-99; rsch. biochemist VA Healthcare Sys., San Diego, 1979-99; chem. hygiene officer VA Med.

Ctr., 1992-94, biosafety officer, 1992—, chief environ. health and safety, 1994—. Judge Sci. Fair. Mem. Am. Biol. Safety Assn. Avocations: travel, gardening. Office: VA San Diego Healthcare Sys (138S) 3350 La Jolla Village Dr San Diego CA 92161-0002

SPRINGFIELD, DEMPSEY STEWART, physician, educator; b. Feb. 21, 1945; AB, Emory U., 1967; MD, U. Fla., 1971. Diplomate Am. Bd. Orthopaedic Surgery. Intern in surgery U. Ala., Birmingham, 1971-72; resident in orthopaedic surgery U. Fla., Gainesville, 1972-76, assoc. prof. Coll. Medicine, 1978-87, Harvard Med. Sch., Boston, 1987-96; prof., chair Mt. Sinai Sch. Medicine, N.Y.C., 1996—. Co-editor: Surgery for Bone and Soft-Tissue Tumor, 1998. Home: 5 E 98th St # 1188 New York NY 10029-6501 Office: Mt Sinai Sch Medicine Dept Orthopedics 5th and 100th St New York NY 10029

SPRINGFIELD, JAMES FRANCIS, retired lawyer, banker; b. Memphis, Nov. 5, 1929; s. C.L. and Mildred (White) S.; m. Shirley Burdick, June 1, 1951 (div.); children: Sidney, Susan, James Francis; m. Nancy Hardwick Ragan, Feb. 8, 1987 (dec. Jan. 1988); m. Donna Thomas Moore, Feb. 22, 1989. BA with distinction in econs., Southwestern at Memphis (now Rhodes Coll.), 1951; LLB, U. Memphis, 1960. Bar: Tenn. 1960. With Union Planters Nat. Bank, Memphis, 1951-94, exec. v.p., sr. trust officer, head trust dept., 1968-85, gen. counsel, sec. bd., 1985-94; sec. bd., exec. v.p., gen. counsel Union Planters Corp., 1985-94; ret., 1994. Mem. adv. bd. Memphis Alzheimer's Assn., 1999-2001; mem. president's coun. Rhodes Coll., Memphis, chmn., 1991-92, internat. chmn. ann. fund, 1995-96; chmn. bd. trustees So. Coll. Optometry, 1978-80; trustee Plough Found., Memphis Conf. United Meth. Ch. Found., 1978-85, U. Tenn. Med. Units Found., 1975-82, MidSouth Pub. Comm. Found., 1985-87, 98—; chmn. fin. com. Hutchinson Sch.; sec. bd. trustees Vision Edn. Found., 1977-78; bd. regents Tenn. Trust Sch., chmn., 1977; mem. president's adv. coun. Lambuth Coll., 1982-85; mem. exec. bd. Chickasaw coun. Boy Scouts Am., 1983-87; bd. visitors Memphis State U. Cecil C. Humphreys Sch. Law, treas. Balmoral Civic Club, 1967-68; pres., dir. Village of Bailey Station Homeowners Assn., Inc., 2000-2001. Lt. (j.g.) USNR, 1951-54. Mem. Tenn. Bar Assn. (chmn. interprofl. rels. com. 1976), Memphis and Shelby County Bar assn. (chmn. moral fitness com. 1972), Tenn. Bankers Assn. (chmn. legis.com. trust div. 1976-77, treas. 1972-73, pres. 1976-77, bd. dirs. 1976-77), Bank Adminstrn. Inst. (chmn. trust commn. 1981-82), Estate Planning Coun. Memphis (pres. 1973-74), Sigma Nu (div. comdr. 1967-68, treas., bd. dirs. House Corp. 1966-81), Omicron Delta Kappa (Rhodes Coll. chpt., pres. OKD Assocs. 2002—). Republican. Home: 1692 Village Ridge Rd Collierville TN 38017-9793 E-mail: jimmyspringfield@msn.com.

SPRINGGATE, CLARK FRANKLIN, physician, researcher; b. Champaign, Ill., Nov. 14, 1946; s. William F. and Marjorie E. (Fitch) S.; children from a previous marriage: Elizabeth, Benjamin; m. Diane Louise Rotnem, Oct. 19, 1991. AB in Biology, Boston U., 1967; PhD in Biochemistry, Boston Coll., 1972; MD, U. Miami, 1983. Diplomate Nat. Bd. Med. Examiners, Am. Bd. Pathology. Med. dir. Richardson Vicks Pharm., Shelton, Conn., 1989-91; v.p., med. dir. TSI Biomed. Rsch. Group, Medford, Mass., 1992-94. V.p. Scicor, Indpls., 1988-89; pres. Springgate Biotech, Guilford, Conn., 1991—, Biotech Regular Cons., Guilford, 1994—; designer/executor Phase I, Phase II, Phase III and Phase IV clin. trials in oncology, cardiology, rheumatology, endocrinology, infectious diseases, neurology. Contbr. articles to jours. Heart Transplant, Am. Soc. Hist. Immunogey. Bd. dirs. AIDS Protect New Haven, 1994-95; funding bd. Leap Youth Program, New Haven, 1991-92 Leukemia Soc. Am. fellow, 1972-74. Mem. AAAS, ACP Execs., Conn. State Med. Soc. Achievements include research in immune monitoring of heart transplant patients to prevent rejection and infection, diagnostic flow cytometry-oncology, gene therapy for cancer, heart disease, autoimmune disease and infectious disease. Home: 1320 Little Meadow Rd Guilford CT 06437-1659 E-mail: clarkmd@tx.netcom.com.

SPRING-MILLS, ELINOR JANE, anatomy and cell biology educator, researcher; b. Boston, June 24, 1938; d. Rennie Joseph and Katherine Barbara (Ehnes) Spring; divorced; 1 child, Rebecca Mills-Fallenius. AB, Vassar Coll., 1960; MA, Mt. Holyoke Coll., 1962; PhD, Harvard U., Boston, 1968. NIN rsch. fellow Nat. Inst. Arthritis, Metabolism, Digestive Diseases-Kidney, Bethesda, Md., 1967-70; rsch. biologist, asst. chief cell biology sect. VA Hosp., San Francisco, 1970-77; asst. prof., then assoc. prof. anatomy U. Calif. Med. Sch., 1970-77; assoc. prof. anatomy and urology SUNY Health Scis. Ctr., Syracuse, 1977-82, prof. anatomy, cell biology and urology, 1982—, acting chmn. anatomy and cell biology dept., 1982-83. Chmn. breast cancer working group Nat. Cancer Inst., NIH, Bethesda, 1984-87. Editor: Accessory Glands of the Male Reproductive Tract, 1979, Male Accessory Sex Glands, 1980, Prostatic Carcinoma: Biology and Dysfunction, 1981. Tutor Literacy Vols. Am., Syracuse, 1995. Recipient Outstanding Woman Faculty Mem. award SUNY Health Scis. Ctr., 1986, President's award, 1990, Chancellor's award, 1991, Armstrong award, 1992, 95. Avocations: antique collecting, gardening, music. Office: SUNY Health Scis Ctr Dept Anatomy-Cell Biology Irving Ave Syracuse NY 13210-1687

SPRINGSTEEL, FREDERICK NEIL, computer science educator; b. Bellingham, Wash., Aug. 8, 1940; s. Guy Stewart and Charlotte E. S.; 1 child, Ian Michael; m. Pamela Botts Reser, Aug. 3, 1985. AB in Math., U. Notre Dame, 1962; MA, U. Wash., 1964, PhD, 1967. Cert. Sys. Prof. Asst. prof. Bowdoin Coll., Brunswick, Maine, 1967-71; assoc. prof. U. Mont., Missoula, 1971-77; dir. undergrad. studies, 1977-81; assoc. prof. computer sci. U. Mo., Columbia, 1977-91, dir. grad. studies, 1992-95, prof. computer sci., 1991-2000, prof. emeritus, 2000—. Guest prof. computer sci. dept. Kaiserslautern (Germany) U., 1976-77; vis. assoc. prof. computer sci. Oreg. State U., Corvallis, 1985-86, U. Wash., Seattle, 1986. Contbr. articles, chpts., and revs. to profl. jours.; contbg. author: Encyclopedia of Information Sciences, 2000-2001. Treas., trustee Unitarian-Universalist Ch., Columbia, 1989-91, covenant chair, 1999-2001; v.p. St. Louis Unitarian-Universalist Area Coun., 1994-97; mem. tech. com. Columbia Pub. Schs., 1991-95, 2001—; ec. Boone County Indsl. Devel. Authority, 1993-9; sec. Energy and Environment Commn. of Columbia & Boone County, 2000-01. Rsch. grantee NSF, 1985-90, Fulbright grantee, Yugoslavia, 1986. AAUP (v.p. U. Mo. chpt. 1994-97), Assn. for Computing Machinery (rev. Computing Reviews 1981—, assoc. editor Sigmod Record, 1988-91, Spl. Interest Group on Computer Sci. Edn.). Avocations: classical ensemble singing, walking, biking. Office: Computer Sci & Engring Dept Univ Mo Columbia MO 65211-0001 E-mail: fsprings@coin.org.

SPRINKEL, BERYL WAYNE, economist, consultant; b. Richmond, Mo., Nov. 20, 1923; s. Clarence and Emma (Schooley) S.; m. Lory Kiefer, Aug. 29, 1993; children: Gary L., Kevin G. Student, N.W. Mo. State U., 1941-43, U. Oreg., 1943-44; BS, U. Mo., 1947; MBA, U. Chgo., 1948, PhD, 1952; LHD (hon.), DePaul U., 1975; LLD (hon.), St. Michael's Coll., 1981, U. Mo., 1985, U. Rochester, 1985, Govs. State U., 1988, U. Nebr., 1988; Doctor of Pub. Adminstrn., Marion Coll., 1988. Instr. econs. and fin. U. Mo., Columbia, 1948-49, U. Chgo., 1950-52; with Harris Trust & Savs. Bank, Chgo., 1952-81, v.p., economist, 1960-68, dir. rsch., 1963-69, sr. v.p., 1968-74, economist, 1968-81, exec. v.p., 1974-81; undersec. monetary affairs Dept. Treasury, Washington, 1981-85; chmn. Coun. Econ. Advisers, The White House, 1985-89, mem. Pres.'s Cabinet, 1987-89; pvt. cons. economist, 1989—. Cons. Fed. Res. Bd., 1955-59, Bur. of Census, 1962-70, Joint Econ. Com. U.S. Congress, 1958, 62, 67, 71, Ho. of Reps. Banking and Currency Com., 1963, Senate Banking Com., 1975; econ. adv. bd. to sec. commerce, 1967-69; bd. economists Time mag., 1968-80. Author: Money and Stock Prices, 1964, Money and Markets-A Monetarist View, 1971; co-author: Winning with Money, 1977 Pres. Homewood-Flossmoor (Ill.) Community High Sch., 1959-60. With AUS, 1943-45. Recipient Hamilton Bolton award Fin. Analysts Assn., 1968, Alexander Hamilton award U.S. Treasury, 1985, Disting. Alumnus award U. Chgo., 1986, Disting. Alumnus award U. Mo., 2000. Fellow Nat. Assn. Bus. Economists; mem. Am. Econ. Assn., Nat. Assn. Bus. Economists, Beta Gamma Sigma. Home: 20140 Saint Andrews Dr Olympia Fields IL 60461-1169 E-mail: sprinkelec@aol.com.

SPRINKLE, RALPH STEPHEN, podiatrist; b. Winston-Salem, N.C., Sept. 2, 1958; s. Robert Lee and Denise (Levesque) S.; m. Elizabeth Waters, Oct. 24, 1987; 1 child, Elizabeth Cathcart. BS, U. N.C., Greensboro, 1983; DPM, Dr. William Scholl Coll., Chgo., 1988. Diplomate Am. Bd. Podiatric Surgery. Pres. Georgetown (S.C.) Podiatry Group P.C., 1989—. Mem. adv. bd. Wachovia Bank, Georgetown, 1992—, Black River Dist., Georgetown, 1992-94. Fellow Am. Coll. Foot and Ankle Surgeons; mem. SAR, Sons Confederate Vets., S.C. Podiatric Med. Assn. (treas. 1990-99), Rotary (Paul Harris fellow 1995). Episcopalian. Avocations: outdoors, hunting, fishing, church, scouting. Office: 1101 Memorial Ln Georgetown SC 29440-3311

SPRINKLE, ROBERT LEE, JR. podiatrist; b. Winston-Salem, N.C., July 13, 1932; s. Robert Lee and Elton Elizabeth Sprinkle; children: Robert III, Karen, Ralph, Richard, Roy, Randy, Drouin; m. Nancy House Dixon. Student, Salem Coll., 1952; BS, Ohio Coll. Podiatry, 1956; DPM, Pa. Coll. Podiatry, 1970. Diplomate Am. Bd. Disability Analysts, Am. Coun. Cert. Podiatric Phys. and Surgeons, Sr. Acad. Ambulatory Podiatric Surgeons. Pvt. practice, Winston-Salem, 1957—. Chmn. N.C. Bd. Podiatry Examiners, 1968-74; clin. assoc. prof. Dr. William M. School Coll. Podiatric Medicine; researcher reconstructive surgery human foot and ankle; bd. dirs. Cmty. Gen. Hosp. Found., Thomasville, N.C.; bd. dirs. Am. Coun. Cert. Podiatric Phys. and Surgeons. Chmn. Mayor's Com. on Hiring the Handicapped, 1963-64; commr. Old Hickory Coun., Boy Scouts Am., 1970-71, v.p., 1973-74, Silver Beaver award, 1969, mem. adv. bd. Old North State Coun.; pres. St. Leo's Parochial Sch. PTA, 1969-70; dir. Halfway House, 1965-66; chmn. Bishop McGuiness PTA, 1976. Recipient St. George medal Charlotte Diocese, Roman Cath. Ch., 1971; Schering grantee, 1972-74. Mem. APHA, Am. Podiatric Med. Assn. (life mem.), N.C. Podiatry Assn. (past pres., Podiatrist of Yr. 1976), Piedmont Podiatry Assn., Acad. Ambulatory Podiatric Surgeons (life mem.), Internat. Analgesia Soc., Forsyth Country Club, Colonial Country Club, Twin City Club, KC (4th degree), SAR (life; pres. Bethabra chpt., mem. George Washington Found.), SCV, NRA (life), Rotary (Paul Harris fellow, dist. gov. 1976-77), St. Andrew's Soc., Sons of the Revolution (life; state chpt. sec.). Democrat. Roman Catholic. Home: 10 Mock St Thomasville NC 27360-4622 Office: ABC Family Foot and Ankle Clinic PO Box 366 17 W Main St Thomasville NC 27360-3934 also: ABC Family Foot & Ankle Clinic PO Box 5442 2057 Kerensky St Winston Salem NC 27103-3657 E-mail: foot1@earthlink.net.

SPRINKLE, WILLIAM MELVIN, audio-acoustical engineer, engineering administrator; b. Washington, Sept. 2, 1945; s. Melvin Cline and Gladys Virginia (Miller) S.; div.; children: Timothy William, Allison Anne. BS in Chemistry, Randolph-Macon Coll., 1967; M in Enging. Adminstrn., Va. Poly. Inst. & State U., 1990. Registered profl. engr., Va. Sr. cons. Sprinkle & Assocs., Kensington, Md., 1973-76; audio systems engr. Robertshaw Controls Co., Richmond, Va., 1976-80; sr. engr. TDFB-Engrs. & Architects, 1980-85; property mgmt. officer Signet Bank, 1985-87; asst. dir. engring. Va. Dept. Corrections, 1987—. Mem. summer adj. faculty Eastman Sch. Music, Rochester, N.Y., 1974-83. Editor newsletter Richmond Area Bicycling Assn.; contbr. Time Saver Standards for Architectural Design Data, 1982. Scoutmaster Boy Scouts Am., 1970-72, unit commr., 1990-92. Named Eagle Scout Boy Scouts Am. Mem. Acoustical Soc. Am., Pres. Soc. Randolph-Macon Coll., Pi Delta Epsilon (v.p.). Methodist. Office: Dept of Corrections 6900 Atmore Dr Richmond VA 23225-5646

SPRITZER, RALPH SIMON, lawyer, educator; b. N.Y.C., Apr. 27, 1917; s. Harry and Stella (Theuman) S.; m. Lorraine Nelson, Dec. 23, 1950; children: Ronald, Pamela. BS, Columbia U., 1937, LL.B., 1940. Bar: N.Y. bar 1941, U.S. Supreme Ct. bar 1950. Atty. Office Alien Property, Dept. Justice, 1946-51; anti-trust div. Dept. Justice, 1951-54, Office Solicitor Gen., 1954-61; gen. counsel FPC, 1961-62; 1st asst. to solicitor gen. U.S., 1962-68; prof. law U. Pa., Phila., 1968-86, Ariz. State U., Tempe, 1986—; gen. counsel AAUP, 1983-84. Adj. prof. law George Wasington U., 1967; cons. Adminstrv. Conf. U.S., Ford Found., Pa. Gov.'s Justice Commn. Served with AUS, 1941-46. Recipient Superior Service award Dept. Justice, 1960; Tom C. Clark award Fed. Bar. Assn., 1968 Mem. Am. Law Inst. Home: 1024 E Gemini Dr Tempe AZ 85283-3004 Office: Ariz State Univ Coll Law Tempe AZ 85287

SPRITZER, SAMUEL LEWIS, financial executive, computer consultant; b. Bklyn., Sept. 15, 1954; s. Murray Graham and Sylvia (Lerner) S.; m. Stephanie Gaudio, Oct. 7, 1979; children: Michael Stephen, Daniel Graham. BBA in Acctg., Pace U., 1976. Auditor N.Y. State Dept. Law, N.Y.C., 1976-81; sr. acct. Covenant House, 1981-82, mgr. gen. acctg., 1982-83, controller, 1983-88, dir. fin., treas., 1988-90; dir. acctg. and systems Edwin Gould Acad., Chestnut Ridge, N.Y., 1990-94; contr. Lang. Devel. Program, Tonawanda, 1994-97, Computer Task Group, Buffalo, 1997—. Mem. Nat. Assn. Accts. Avocations: computers, basketball, tennis, football. E-mail: spritzer@adelphia.net.

SPRIZZO, JOHN EMILIO, federal judge; b. Bklyn., Dec. 23, 1934; s. Vincent James and Esther Nancy S.; children— Ann Esther, Johna Emily, Matthew John. BA summa cum laude, St. John's U., Jamaica, N.Y., 1956; LLB summa cum laude, St. John's U., 1959. Bar: N.Y. 1960. Atty. U.S. Dept. Justice, 1959-63; asst. U.S. atty. so. dist. N.Y. Dept. Justice, N.Y.C., 1963-68, chief appellate atty., 1965-66, asst. chief criminal div., 1966-68; assoc. prof. Fordham U. Law Sch., 1968-72; ptnr. Curtis, Mallet-Prevost, 1972-81; dist. judge U.S. Dist. Ct. (so. dist.) N.Y., 1981—. Cons. Nat. Com. for Reform of Criminal Laws, N.Y.C., 1971-72; mem. Knapp Commn., 1971-72; assoc. atty. Com. of Ct. on Judiciary, N.Y.C., 1971-72 Co-contbr. articles to profl. law revs. Mem. ABA, D.C. Bar Assn., Assn. of Bar of City of N.Y. Office: US Dist Ct US Courthouse Foley Sq New York NY 10007-1501

SPROAT, CHRISTINE A. lawyer; b. Poughkeepsie, N.Y., Feb. 6, 1952; d. John and Jean (Hayes) Morabito; m. James P. Sproat, June 29, 1984; children: Ashley E., William C. AAS in Nursery Edn. cum laude, Dutchess C.C., Poughkeepsie, 1976; BS in Psychology, SUNY, New Paltz, 1978, postgrad., 1979-80; JD, Pace U., 1983. Bar: N.Y. 1984, U.S. Dist. Ct. (so. dist.) N.Y. 1996, U.S. Dist. Ct. (ea. dist.) N.Y. 1997. Atty. Michael Haggerty, Esq., Poughkeepsie, 1983-86; law clk. to Hon. Judith A. Hillery N.Y. Supreme Ct., 1986-96, prin. law clk., 2001—; atty. Gellert & Cutler, P.C., 1996—2001. Adj. lectr. law Marist Coll., Poughkeepsie, 1994-96. Editor, contbg. author Criminal Law Digest, 1987. Mem. Mid-Hudson Women's Network, Highland, NY, 1997—; pres. Beekman Women's Rep. Club, 1998—2000, 2002—; bd. dirs. YWCA, 1999—2002, treas., 2000—01; trustee Arlington Edn. Found., 2000—, Dutchess C.C., Poughkeepsie, 1997—. Mem.: Dutchess County Bar Assn. (asst. treas. 1998—99, treas. 1999—2000, sec. 2000—01, v.p. 2001—02, pres.-elect 2002—), Mid-Hudson Women's Bar (pres. 1986—87, 1999—2000), N.Y. State Bar Assn. Republican. Roman Catholic. Avocations: gardening, hiking. Office: Dutchess County Courthouse 10 Market St Poughkeepsie NY 12601 E-mail: csproat@courts.state.ny.us.

SPROAT, JOHN GERALD, historian, educator; b. L.A., Apr. 1, 1921; s. John Gerald and Grace (Elwell) Drummond S.; m. Ruth Christensen, Mar. 18, 1967; 1 child by previous marriage, Barbara BA, San Jose State Coll., 1950; MA, U. Calif.-Berkeley, 1952, PhD, 1959. Instr. Mich. State U., 1956-57; asst. prof. Williams Coll., 1957-63; prof. Lake Forest Coll., Ill., 1963-74; prof. history U. S.C., Columbia, 1974-92, chmn. dept., 1974-83; dist. prof. emeritus, 1992—; sr. fellow Inst. for So. Studies, 1992—. Fulbright prof. Hamburg U., Fed. Republic Germany, 1961-62; vis. fellow Cambridge U., Eng., 1970; vis. prof. U. Calif.-Berkeley, 1972; Fulbright prof. U. Munich, Fed. Republic Germany, 1982, Indonesia, 1993-94; Am. participant lectr. USIA, India, Pakistan, 1987; mem. S.C. Commn. Archives and History, 1974-83, chmn., 1979-83; mem. S.C. Bd. Rev. Hist. Places, 1974-86, chmn., 1978-83; del. Am. Council Learned Socs. Author: The Best Men: Liberal Reformers in the Gilded Age, 1968, 3d edit., 1972; (with others) The Shaping of America, 1972, Making Change: South Carolina Banking in the 20th Century, 1990; contbr. chpts. to books; exec. producer A Bond of Iron, S.C. ETV, 1979; gen. editor So. Classics Series. Past pres., trustee Columbia Mus. Art; pres. Historic Columbia Found., 1997-99. Served with USAAF, 1941-45. NEH grantee, 1976, 77, 79, 85; Shell Found. grantee, 1967, 70, 73; Lilly Endowment grantee, 1966-67 Mem. Am. Hist. Assn., Orgn. Am. Historians, So. Hist. Assn., Capital City Club. Home: 1686 Woodlake Dr Columbia SC 29206-4647 Office: U SC Inst For So Studies Columbia SC 29208-0001 E-mail: sproatj@gwm.sc.edu.

SPROAT, KEZIA VANMETER, communications executive, writer; b. Chillicothe, Ohio, Nov. 8, 1937; d. Joseph Vause and Helen Rose (James) Vanmeter; children: Cornelia Sisson Vanmeter, Eliza Bradford Delano. AB, Vassar Coll., 1959; MA, Ohio State U., 1963, PhD, 1975. Field dir. Miami Valley Campfire Girls, Dayton, Ohio, 1959-60; tchr. English Kingswood Sch. Cranbrook, Bloomfield Hills, Mich., 1960-61; grad. asst. Dept. English Ohio State U., Columbus, 1961-68, lectr. comparative lit., 1968-73, editor ctr. human resource rsch., 1979-85; dir. food for thought Univ. Ctr. Ministries, 1978-79; pres. Sproat Comm., Inc., 1985—. Editor, writer Ross Labs., Columbus, 1987-91; dir. Vanmeter Farm, Inc., Piketon, Ohio, 1993-2002; pres., founder Highbank Farm Peace Edn. Ctr., Chillicothe, 1994. Author, editor: National Longitudinal Surveys: Bibliography, 1985; editor: Malnutrition: A Hidden Cost, 1993 (2 Addy awards 1994); editor 7 books; editor Peace Grows Bull., 1996—. Founder, co-chair Community Film Assn., Columbus, 1979—; publicist Peace Grows, Inc., Columbus and Akron, Ohio, 1990—; coord. South Ctrl. Ohio Preservation Soc., 1992—; pres. Vassar Coll. Class of 1959, 1999-; mem. Martin Luther King, Jr. bd. sponsors Morehouse Coll., 2002-. Recipient Florence Howe award MLA, 1975, Mayor's award for vol. svcs Mayor of Columbus, 1980, Pres. award Abbott Labs., 1988; grantee Ohio Humanities Coun., 1977, 78. Mem. Lucy Webb Hayes Heritage Ctr., Women's Poetry Workshop. Avocations: collecting art, poetry. E-mail: keziav@aol.com.

SPROGER, CHARLES EDMUND, lawyer; b. Chgo., Feb. 18, 1933; s. William and Minnette (Weiss) Sproger. BA (David Himmelblau scholar), Northwestern U., 1954, JD, 1957. Bar: Ill. 1957. Practiced in, Chgo., 1958—; assoc. Ehrlich & Cohn, 1958-63, Ehrlich, Bundesen, Friedman & Ross, 1963-72; partner Ehrlich, Bundesen, Broecker & Sproger, 1972-77; pvt. practice, 1977—. Mem. adv. com. curriculum Ill. Inst. Continuing Legal Edn., Chgo., 1976— ; v.p. Mediation Coun. of Ill., 1986-87; arbitration panelist for Cir. Ct. Cook County, 1990—. Editor: Family Lawyer, 1962-63; contbr. articles to legal publs. Mediator Pastoral Psychotherapy Inst., 1982-86. Fellow Am. Acad. Matrimonial Lawyers (bd. examiners 1972-86, chmn. Law Day U.S.A. 1975); mem. ABA, Ill. Bar Assn. (chmn. coun. family law 1970-71), Chgo. Bar Assn. (matrimonial law com. 1958—), Am. Arbitration Assn. (divorce mediation com. 1983—), Decalogue Soc., U. Mich. Club Chgo. (pres. 1988-89), Phi Alpha Delta. Address: 2800 W Birchwood Ave Chicago IL 60645-1218

SPROLE, FRANK ARNOTT, retired pharmaceutical company executive, lawyer; b. Bklyn., Sept. 13, 1918; s. Frank Newland and Eleanor Arnott (Greenberg) S.; m. Sarah Louise Knapp, Sept. 23, 1944; children— Wendy Sprole Bangs, Frank J., Anne Sprole Mauk, Jonathan K., Sarah Sprole Obregon. BA, Yale U., 1942; LLB, Columbia U., 1949. Bar: N.Y. 1949. Assoc. firm Winthrop Stimson, Putnam & Roberts, N.Y.C., 1949-50; atty. Bristol-Myers Co., 1950-52, asst. sec., 1952-55, sec., 1955-67, v.p., 1965-73, sr. v.p., 1973-77, vice-chmn. bd., 1977-84; ret., 1984. Officer Proprietary Assn., Washington, 1978-84; dir., officer Knapp Fund, N.Y.C., 1960-93. Pres. bd. trustees Hotchkiss Sch., Lakeville, Conn., 1980-85; trustee Internat. Inst. Rural Reconstrn., N.Y.C., and Manila, 1983-87. Lt. comdr. USNR, 1942-45, PTO. Mem. Assn. of Bar of City of N.Y., Yale Club of N.Y.C., Wee Burn Country Club, Bohemian Club, John's Island Club, Riomar Country Club. Republican. Episcopalian. Avocation: golf. Home: 394 Mansfield Ave Darien CT 06820-2112

SPROSTY, JOSEPH PATRICK, producer, writer, weapons specialist; b. Cleve., Aug. 25, 1947; s. Joseph Patrick and Anna Margret (Louchka) S. Grad., Midpark H.S., Middleburgh, Ohio, 1965; student, San Diego City Coll., 1972-73. Class 2 firearms lic. Prop builder The Goulardi Show WJW-TV8, Cleve., 1962-65; sub-agent Internat. Artists Agy., San Diego and L.A., 1982-83; casting dir. Cinemode Films, 1982; operator, owner Actors Artists Agy., L.A., 1983-87; founder, prodr., dir. Magnum Prodns., 1985; founder Sprosty Prodns., 1990. Demonstrator weapons and handling of weapons, Propmaster TV Co., Van Nuys, Calif., 1992; expert witness Laser Weapon Scam, 1984; vis. lectr. firearms safety, handling, rules and regulations governing use of firearms in motion picture, TV prodn. U. So. Calif., 1996—; animal wrangler specializing in opossums. Scripwriter: (films) Vanishing Point II, The Apartment Manager, The Big House, Rambo III (optioned), Rambo IV (revised), Boneyard, Mister Ed - Talking Again, Mister Ed - Radio Talk, Brick, Life Plus One, Gun Slave, Fixation, Last Chance (renamed Terminal Virus), You're So Beautiful, Home Dead Home, Kung Fu Cop, The Fisherman, numerous others; prodr., dir. (video) Break Disc, 1985; location mgr., armorer, weapons splst.: (film) Heat from Another Sun (retitled Maladiction), 1988; armorer, 2nd asst. dir., assoc. prodr., weapons splst.: (film) Provoked, 1989; weapons splst., armorer: (film) Big City, 1990; co-prodr., animal wrangler, weapons splst.: (film) Opossum de Oro, 1996; weapons splst.: (tv shows) Jake and the Fat Man, Black's Magic, Hill Street Blues, Murder, She Wrote, On the Edge of Death, Emerald Point N.A.S., (7 episodes) America's Most Wanted, (3 episodes) FBI: The Untold Stories, numerous others, (films) Revolt, Rocky IV, Streets of Fire, Walk in the Sun, Cloak & Dagger, One Man's Poison, Killing Zoe, Desert Storm, The Movie, Live Shot, Outer Heat, Zipperhead, Four Minute Warning, The Robbery, Spirit, Texas Payback, High Adventure, The Waterfront, The Philadelphia Experiment II, Opossum de Oro, Harlem Nights, Tango & Cash, Die Hard, Provoked, Beverly Hills Cop II, Big City, numerous others. Spkr. Veterans Day Calif. State U., Dominguez Hills, 1993. Served with USN, 1965-67 (hon. discharge). Mem. AFTRA, SAG (charter mem. San Diego br.). Home: 337 W Maple St Glendale CA 91204-2014

SPROTT, DAVID ARTHUR, statistics and psychology educator; b. Toronto, Ont., Can., May 31, 1930; s. Arthur Frederick and Dorothy (Barry) S.; m. Muriel Doris Vogel; children: Anne, Jane. BA, U. Toronto, 1952, MA, 1953, PhD, 1955. Rsch. asst. Galton Lab., London, 1955-56; biogeneticist, clin. tchr. dept. psychiatry U. Toronto, 1956-58; assoc. prof. stats. U. Waterloo, Ont., 1958-61, prof., 1961-96, disting. prof. emeritus, 1996—, prof. psychology Ont., 1964-96, dean math., 1966-72, chmn. dept. stats., 1966-75; prof. Centro de Investigacion en Matematicas, Guanajuato, Mex., 1993—. Vis. prof. various univs. and colls. Author: Statistical Inference in Science, Springer Series in Statistics, 2000; contbr. numerous articles to profl. jours. Recipient Gold medal Statis. Soc. Can., 1988. Fellow Am. Statis. Assn., Inst. Math. Stats., Royal Soc. Can., Royal Photog. Soc.; mem. Internat. Statis. Inst., Statis. Soc. Can. (hon.). Avocations: photography, wine making. Office: U Waterloo Math Faculty Waterloo ON Canada N2L 3G1

SPROTT, RICHARD LAWRENCE, foundation administrator, researcher; b. Tampa, Fla., Aug. 9, 1940; s. Joseph Albert and Marie Marguerite (Goaper) S.; m. Margaret Ann Weidel, June 19, 1965; children— Lynn Marie, Deborah Ann Student, Franklin and Marshall Coll., 1958-60; BA, U. N.C., 1962, MA in Psychology, 1964, PhD in Psychology, 1965. Asst. prof. Oakland U., Rochester, Mich., 1967-69; assoc. staff scientist Jackson Lab., Bar Barbor, Maine, 1969-71, staff scientist, 1971-80; health scientist adminstr. Div. Research Resources, NIH, Bethesda, Md., 1980-81; br. chief Nat. Inst. on Aging, 1981-84, assoc. dir., 1984-98; exec. dir. Ellison Med. Found., 1998—. Editor: Hormonal Correlates of Behavior, 1975, Age, Learning Ability and Intelligence, 1980; mem. editorial bd. Exptl. Aging Research jour., 1978— ; contbr. articles to profl. jours. Mem. Bar Harbor Town Council, 1975-79, chmn., 1978-79; mem. bd. appeals Town of Bar Harbor, 1972-75, mem. warrant com., 1972-75 NIH fellow, 1965-67; NIH grantee, 1969-79; recipient Kent award Gerontologic Soc. Am., 1997. Fellow Am. Psychol. Assn.; mem. Behavior Genetics Assn. (membership chmn. 1979). Home: 11514 Regency Dr Potomac MD 20854-3733 Office: Ellison Med Found 4710 Bethesda Ave Ste 204 Bethesda MD 20814-5226 E-mail: rsprott@emf.ipmail.att.net.

SPROUL, JOAN HEENEY, elementary school educator; b. Johnstown, Pa., July 17, 1932; d. James L. and Grace M. (Dunn) Heeney; m. Robert Sproul, July 31, 1957; 1 child, Mary Claire. BS, Clarion U., 1954; MA, George Wash. U., 1963; postgrad., U. Va., 1966-88. Cert. tchr., Va. Kindergarten tchr. Jefferson Sch., Warren, Pa., 1954-55; primary grades tchr. Alexandria (Va.) Pub. Schs., 1955-64; elem. tchr. Fairfax County Schs., Springfield, Va., 1965-97; math. lead tchr. West Springfield (Va.) Sch., 1987-97, ret., 1997. Contbr. (with others) Virginia History, 1988. Advisor Springfield Young Organists Assn., 1971-83; mem. Fairfax County Dem. Com., 1988-94, West Springfield Civic Assn., 1965—, Women's Aux. Fairfax Co. Salvation Army. Grantee Impact II, 1985-86. Mem. AAUW, NEA, Nat. Fedn. Bus. and Profl. Women (pres., dir., dist. VIII 1984—, Woman of Yr. 1985, 88), Delta Kappa Gamma (2d v.p. Va. chpt. 1963—), Phi Delta Kappa, Sigma Sigma Sigma. Episcopalian. Avocations: reading, music, gardening, fashion design. Home: 8005 Greeley Blvd West Springfield VA 22152-3036

SPROUL, JOHN ALLAN, retired public utility executive; b. Oakland, Calif., Mar. 28, 1924; s. Robert Gordon and Ida Amelia (Wittschen) S.; m. Marjorie Ann Hauck, June 20, 1945; children: John Allan, Malcolm J., Richard O., Catherine E. AB, U. Calif., Berkeley, 1947, LL.B., 1949. Bar: Calif. 1950. Atty. Pacific Gas & Electric Co., San Francisco, 1949-52, 56-62, sr. atty., 1962-70, asst. gen. counsel, 1970-71, v.p. gas supply, 1971-76, sr. v.p., 1976-77, exec. v.p., 1977-89; gen. counsel Pacific Gas Transmission Co., 1970-73, v.p., 1973-79, chmn. bd., 1979-89, also bd. dirs. Atty. Johnson & Stanton, San Francisco, 1952-56; bd. dirs. Oreg. Steel Mills, Inc. Bd. dirs. emeritus Hastings Coll. Law. Served to 1st lt. USAAF, 1943-46. Mem. Calif. Bar Assn. (inactive), Pacific Coast Gas Assn., Pacific-Union Club, Orinda Country Club. Home: 8413 Buckingham Dr El Cerrito CA 94530-2531 Office: Pacific Gas & Electric Co Mail Code H17F PO Box 770000 San Francisco CA 94177-0001

SPROUL, MICHAEL FRANKLIN, economics educator; b. Burbank, Calif., Nov. 20, 1956; s. Hugo Franklin and Dorothy Leonora Sproul; m. Lorraine Annette Sproul, Aug. 21, 1982; children: Teresa, Carly. PhD, UCLA, 1990. Econs. lectr. Calif. State U., Northridge, 1980—, UCLA, 1993-99, U. Calif., Santa Barbara, 1999—. Author: Price Theory and Applications, 1986; contbr. articles to profl. jours. and newspapers. Mem. Am. Econ. Assn., Western Econ. Assn. Avocations: mechanics, camping, gardening. Office: Calif State U Dept Econs 18111 Nordhoff St Northridge CA 91330 E-mail: msproul@csun.edu.

SPROULL, ROBERT FLETCHER, research and development executive; b. Ithaca, N.Y., June 6, 1947; s. Robert L. and Mary L. Sproull; m. Lee Sonastine, June 26, 1971; 1 child, Katherine L. AB in Physics, Harvard U., 1968; MS in Computer Sci., Stanford U., 1970, PhD in Computer Sci., 1977. Mem. rsch. staff Xerox Palo Alto (Calif.) Rsch. Ctr., 1972-77; asst. prof. Carnegie Mellon U., Pitts., 1977-80, assoc. prof., 1980-83; v.p. Sutherland, Sproull & Assoc., 1980-90; v.p., fellow Sun Microsys., Burlington, Mass., 1990—. Mem. adv. com. NSF, Washington, 1990-97; mem. tech. adv. coun. R.F. Donnelley & Sons., Chgo., 1981-89. Co-author: Principles of Interactive Computer Graphics, 1979. Sr. asst. health svcs. officer USPHS, 1970-72; mem. sci. adv. bd. U.S. Air Force, 1997-99. Mem. Nat. Acad. Engring. Office: SUN Microsys 1 Network Dr Burlington MA 01803-2757 E-mail: bob.sproull@sun.com.

SPROULL, ROBERT LAMB, retired university president, physicist; b. Lacon, Ill., Aug. 16, 1918; s. John Steele and Chloe Velma (Lamb) S.; m. Mary Louise Knickerbocker, June 27, 1942; children: Robert F., Nancy M. Sproull Highbarger. AB, Cornell U., 1940, PhD, 1943; LLD (hon.), Nazareth Coll., 1983; DMusic (hon.), New Eng. Conservatory, 1997. Research physicist RCA labs., 1943-46; faculty Cornell U., 1946-63, 65-68, prof. physics, 1956-63, dir. lab. atomic and solid state physics, 1959-60, dir. materials sci. center, 1960-63, v.p. for acad. affairs, 1965-68; dir. Advanced Research Projects Agy., Dept. Def., Washington, 1963-65; v.p., provost U. Rochester, N.Y., 1968-70, pres., 1970-84, pres. emeritus, 1984—. Prin. physicist Oak Ridge Nat. Lab., 1952; physicist European Rsch. Assoc., Brussels, 1958-59; lectr. NATO, 1958-59; pres. Environ. Literacy Coun., 1997-99, chmn. 1999—; past bd. dirs., John Wiley & Sons, Charles River Labs., United Technols. Corp., Xerox Corp., Bausch & Lomb; mem. sci. adv. com. GM Corp., 1971-80, chmn., 1973-80; mem. Def. Sci. Bd., 1966-70, chmn., 1968-70; mem. Naval Rsch. Adv. Com., 1974-76, Sloan Commn. Higher Edn., 1977-79, N.Y. Regents Commn. Higher Edn., 1992-93. Author: Modern Physics, 1956, A Scientist's Tools for Business, 1997; Editor: Jour. Applied Physics, 1954-57. Trustee Deep Springs Coll., 1967-75, 83-87, Cornell U., 1972-77. Ctr. for Advanced Study in Behavioral Scis. fellow, 1973; Meritorious Civilian Svc. medal Sec. of Def., 1970. Fellow Am. Acad. Arts and Scis.; mem. Telluride Assn. (pres. 1945-47), Inst. of Def. Analysis (trustee 1984-92). Home: 16910 Bay St Jupiter FL 33477-1205 E-mail: lambspr@aol.com.

SPROUSE, EARLENE PENTECOST, special education educator; b. Hopewell, Va., Apr. 23, 1939; d. Earl Paige and Sophia Marlene (Chairky) Pentecost; m. David Andrew Koren, July 3, 1957 (div. Jan. 1963); children: David Andrew Jr., Elysia Marlene, Merri Paige; m. Wayne Alexender Sprouse, Sept. 2, 1964; 1 child, Michael Wayne. AS, Paul D. Camp C.C., Franklin, Va., 1973; BS in Comm. Disorders, Old Dominion U., 1975, MEd in Spl. Edn., 1977. Tchg. cert. with endorsement in speech lang. pathology, learning disabilities and emotional disturbance, Va. Speech lang. pathologist Southampton County Schs., Va., 1975-76; learning disabled tchr. itinerant Franklin (Va.) City Pub. Schs., 1976-78, emotionally disturbed/learning disabled tchr., 1978-85, speech lang. pathologist, 1986-91, ednl. diagnostician, 1992—, lead tchr. spl. edn., 2000—; resource specialist TideWater Acad., 1999—. Needs assessment com. Juvenile Domestic Rels. Ct., Franklin, 1993—; project leader curriculum guide Listening and Lang. Processing Skills, 1990-91. Mem. Career Edn. Adv. Com., Va. Dept. Edn., 1995—; mem. field-based cons. network Old Dominion U., Coll. of William and Mary, 1997—. Recipient Excellence in Edn. award C. of C., Hampton Roads, Va., 1988-89; grantee Va. Edn. Assn., Richmond, 1994—, Project UNITE Dept. Edn., Richmond, 1994—, Project Payroll, 1999-2000, DOE/VBEP Project Second Chance, 2000-01. Mem. Speech and Hearing Assn. Va., Franklin City Edn. Assn. (pub. rels. com., pres. 1980, 91), Internat. Dyslexia Assn., Coun. for Learning Disabilities. Methodist. Avocations: fishing, music. Home: 272 Colonia Dr Surry VA 23883-3130 Office: Franklin City Pub Schs 800 W 2nd Ave Franklin VA 23851-2162 E-mail: esprouse39@hotmail.com.

SPROUSE, JAMES MARSHALL, retired judge; b. Williamson, W.Va., Dec. 3, 1923; s. James and Garnet (Lawson) S.; m. June Dolores Burt, Sept. 25, 1952; children: Tracy Sprouse Ferguson, Jeffrey Marshall, Andrew Michael, Sherry Lee Sprouse Shinholser, Shelly Lynn Sprouse Schneider. AB, St. Bonaventure (N.Y.) U., 1947; LLB, Columbia U., 1949; postgrad. in internat. law, U. Bordeaux, France, 1950. Bar: W.Va. 1949. Asst. atty. gen. State of W.Va., 1949; with CIA, 1952-57; pvt. practice W.Va., 1957-72, 75-79; justice W.Va. Supreme Ct. Appeals, 1972-75; judge U.S. Ct. Appeals (4th cir.), Richmond, Va., 1979-92, sr. cir. judge, 1992-95; ret., 1995; pvt. practice, 1995—2001. With AUS, 1942-45. With AUS, 1942—45. Fulbright scholar. Mem. ABA, W.Va. State Bar, W.Va. Bar Assn., W.Va. Trial Lawyers Assn., Kanawha County Bar Assn., VFW, Am. Legion, Shriners, Aheppa. Democrat. Presbyterian. Office: 1404 Bedford Rd Charleston WV 25314-1915

SPROWL, CHARLES RIGGS, lawyer; b. Lansing, Mich., Aug. 22, 1910; s. Charles Orr and Hazel (Allen) S.; m. Virginia Lee Graham, Jan. 15, 1938; children: Charles R., Robert A., Susan G., Sandra D. AB, U. Mich., 1932, JD, 1934. Bar: Ill. 1935. Pvt. practice, 1934—; of counsel Taylor, Miller, Sprowl, Hoffnagle & Merletti, 1986—. Dir. Simmons Engring. Corp., Petersen Aluminum Corp. Mem. Bd. Edn., New Trier Twp. High Sch., 1959-65, pres. 1962-65; mem. Glencoe Zoning Bd. Appeals, 1956-76, chmn., 1966-76; mem Glencoe Plan Commn., 1962-65; bd. dirs. Glencoe Pub. Libr., 1953-65, pres. 1955-56; trustee Highland Park Hosp., 1959-69; bd. dirs. Cradle Soc., 1968-92. Fellow Am. Coll. Trial Lawyers; mem. Chgo. Bar Assn. (bd. mgrs. 1949-51), Ill. Bar Assn., ABA, Juvenile Protective Assn. (dir. 1943-53), Northwestern U. Settlement (pres. 1963-70, dir.), Soc. Trial Lawyers, Law Club (pres. 1969-70), Legal Club (pres. 1953-54), Univ. Chgo. Club, Skokie Country Club, Delta Theta Phi, Alpha Chi Rho. Presbyterian. Home: 380 Green Bay Rd Apt 2A Winnetka IL 60093-4051 Office: 33 N La Salle St Chicago IL 60602-2603

SPRUCH, GRACE MARMOR, physics educator; b. N.Y.C., Nov. 19, 1926; d. Isadore and Mollie (Pogel) Marmor; m. Larry Spruch, Jan. 8, 1950. BA, Bklyn. Coll., 1947; MS, U. Pa., 1949; PhD, NYU, 1955. Assoc. rsch. scientist NYU, N.Y.C., 1955-56, 58-63, 1965-67; instr. The Cooper Union, 1957-58; vis. assoc. prof. Rutgers U., Newark, 1964-65, assoc. prof., 1969-75, prof., 1975—. Sci. sec. Internat. Conf. Luminescence, N.Y.C., 1961; hon. rsch. assoc. in applied scis. Harvard U., Cambridge, Mass., 1977-78; hon. assoc. Nieman Found. for Journalism, Harvard U., Cambridge, 1977-78; mem. interview team China U.S. Physics Examination and Application Program, 1985, 86. Author: Such Agreeable Friends, 1983, Squirrels at my Window, 2000; co-author: The Ubiquitous Atom, 1974, 21 Astounding Science Quizzes, 1982; co-editor: Luminescence of Organic and Inorganic Materials, 1962; translator: (M. Françon) Holography, 1974; co-translator: (R. Jungk) The Big Machine, 1968; contbg. editor Internat. Sci. and Tech. Mag., 1955-60; referee Am. Jour. Physics, 1973—; contbr. articles to profl. jours. Fellow AAUW, Oxford (Eng.) U., 1963-64, Ctr. for Energy and Environ. Studies, Princeton U., 1981, Ctr. for Tech. Studies, N.J. Inst. for Tech., 1986-87; scholar N.Y. State Regents, Bklyn. Coll., N.Y.C., 1943-47; Humanities grantee Dept. Higher Edn., N.J., 1989-90. Mem. ACLU, Am. Phys. Soc., Phi Beta Kappa (chpt. pres. 1978-82), Sigma Xi, Sigma Pi Sigma, Pi Delta Epsilon (hon.). Avocations: listening to music, tennis, swimming, hiking, animals. Home: 14 E 8th St New York NY 10003-5917 Office: Rutgers Univ Physics Dept 101 Warren St Newark NJ 07102-1811 E-mail: spruch@andromeda.rutgers.edu.

SPRUDE, MARGARET, credit services company executive; b. 1946; BS in Bus., MS of Accountancy, Western Ill. U. CPA. Various fin.-exec.-level positions card divsn. including CFO Bank of Am., 1986-2000, mng. dir., CFO Household Internat. Credit Card Svcs. divsn., 2000—. Office: Household Internat Inc 1441 Schilling Pl Salinas CA 93901-4543 E-mail: masprude@household.com.

SPRUIELL, VANN, psychoanalyst, educator, editor, researcher; b. Leeds, Ala., Oct. 16, 1926; s. Vann Lindley and Zada (Morton) S.; m. Iris Taylor, Sept. 20, 1951 (div. Oct. 1966); children: Graham, Fain, Garth; m. Joyce Ellis, Feb. 11, 1967; stepchildren: Sidney Reavey, Catherine Ellis, Matson Ellis. BS, U. Ala., Tuscaloosa, 1948; MD, Harvard U., 1952. Resident Bellevue Hosp., N.Y.C., 1952-53, N.Y. Hosp., N.Y.C., 1953-55; fellow Tulane Sch. Medicine, New Orleans, 1955-57; pvt. practice, 1957—. Vis. rschr. Anna Freud Ctr., London, 1972-73; co-pub. JOURLIT and BOOKREV; pres. and founding mem. Psychoanalytic Archives CD-ROM Texts (PACT), New Orleans, 1993—; clin. prof. psychiatry La. State U. Sch. Medicine, Tulane U. Sch. Medicine; sec. Ctr. for Advanced Studies in Psychoanalysis, 1989—. Editl. bd. Psychoanalytic Quarterly, 1973—; N.Am. editor Internat. Jour. Psychoanalysis, London, 1988-93; editor Psychoanalysis South, 1996—; mem. various other editl. bds.; contbr. articles to profl. jours. and books. Sgt. U.S. Army, 1944-46. Mem. Psychoanalytic Assn. (sec. bd. on profl. stds. 1979-92), Wyvern Club. Avocations: interdisciplinary studies, sailing. Home: 215 Iona St Metairie LA 70005-4137

SPRUILL, HOWARD VERNON, former academic administrator, minister; b. South Norfolk, Va., Dec. 27, 1919; s. Veron B. and Mabel E. (Kirby) S.; m. Daisy Lee Singleton, Dec. 11, 1943; 1 child, Ruth Elaine. BS, Valley Forge Christian Coll., 1977; MDiv, Luther Rice Sem., 1978, DMin, 1980. Ordained to ministry Assemblies of God, 1953. Auditor U.S. Navy, Little Creek, Va., 1945-50; pastor Elk Garden, W.Va., 1950-52, Emporia, Va., 1952-57, Manassas, 1957-69; dist. sec., treas., 1968-74; pastor Silver Spring, Md., 1974-79; dist. supt. Potomac Dist. Coun., Assemblies of God Ch., 1979-91. Pres. Valley Forge Christian Coll., 1982; chmn. bd. regents, 1968-91; pres. Prince William County Ministerial Assn., 1966-68. Author: Deacon Servant to God and Man, 1980. Served with U.S. Army, 1937-45. Home: 122 Southern Oak Dr Hagerstown MD 21740

SPRUILL, KERRY LYNDON, judge; b. Alexandria, La., Sept. 1, 1954; s. Dwain H. and Alaine Sayes Spruill; m. Laura Roy, Oct. 18, 1975; 1 child, William C. BA, Northwestern State U., 1976; JD, La. State U., 1978. Bar: La. 1979. Judge 12th Jud. Dist. Ct. Divsn. A, Marksville, La. Mem.: La. State Bar Assn., Mansura C. of C., Marksville C. of C. Office: 12th Jud Dist Ct Divsn A PO Box 105 Marksville LA 71351-0105

SPRUNG, ARNOLD, lawyer; b. N.Y.C., Apr. 18, 1926; s. David L. and Anna (Stork) S.; m. Audrey Ann Caire; children: Louise, John, Thomas, Doran, D'Wayne. AB, Darmuth Coll., 1947; JD, Columbia U., 1950. Bar: N.Y. 1950, U.S. Dist. Ct. (so. dist.) N.Y. 1950, U.S. Patent Office 1952, U.S. Dist. Ct. (we. dist.) N.Y. 1954, U.S. Ct. Appeals (2d cir.) 1958, U.S. Ct. Customs and Patent Appeals 1958, U.S. Dist. Ct. (ea. dist.) N.Y. 1962, U.S. Dist. Ct. (no. dist.) Tex. 1971, U.S. Supreme Ct. 1971, and others. Sr. ptnr. Sprung, Kramer, Schaefer & Briscoe, Westchester, N.Y., 1950—. Lt. USN, 1943-46, PTO. Mem. ABA, N.Y. Intellectual Property Assn. Avocations: skiing, wind surfing, racquetball, biking, tennis. E-mail: asprung@aol.com.

SPRUNG, DAVID REICHERT, musician, conductor, educator; b. Jersey City, Oct. 24, 1931; s. Abraham Sprung and Natalie Ruth Reichert; m. Rita May Fallick, Feb. 21, 1957 (div. May 1967); m. Phyllis Gail Eddy, Aug. 17, 1967; children: Karen Ruth, Irene Joan Bruskin, Audrey Jane, Steven Mitchell. BA, Queens Coll., 1957; MFA, Princeton U., 1959. Lectr. music Coll. City of N.Y., N.Y.C., 1959-60, Queens Coll., Flushing, N.Y., 1959-60; asst. prof. in horn and theory Sch. Music, Wichita State U., 1963-66; asst. prof. music Sonoma State U., Rhonert Park, Calif., 1966-70; from assoc. prof. to prof. music Calif. State U., Hayward, 1970-92, prof. music emeritus, 1992—; music dir., condr. Flagler Symphonic Soc., Palm Coast, Fla., 2001. Hornist Met. Opera Orch., N.Y.C., 1960-61; prin. hornist Pitts. Symphony Orch., 1961-63; co-prin. hornist San Francisco Opera Orch., 1973—; prin. hornist Wichita Symphony Orch., 1964-66, San Francisco Ballet Orch., 1975-2001; music columnist Flagler Times, 2000—; composer: Trio for Violin, Cello and Piano, 1957 (Joseph Dillon Meml. prize 1957), Fantasy for Piano, 1958, String Quartet, 1959, Fanfare for Five, 1993; musician recs., opera and ballet videos; contbr. articles to profl. jours. With USN, 1951—55. Recipient Queens Coll. Orchestral Soc. award, 1957. Mem. Internat. Horn Soc., Am. Fedn. Musicians. Avocations: boating, reading, writing. Home: PO Box 354566 Palm Coast FL 32135 E-mail: dsprung@aol.com.

SPRUNG, DONALD WHITFIELD LOYAL, physics educator; b. Kitchener, Ont., Can., June 6, 1934; s. Lyall MacAulay and Doreene Bishop (Price) S.; m. Hannah Sueko Nagai, Dec. 12, 1958; children: Anne Elizabeth, Carol Hanako. BA, U. Toronto, Ont., 1957; PhD, U. Birmingham, Eng., 1961, DSc, 1977. Asst lectr. U. Birmingham, Eng., 1960-61; instr. Cornell U., Ithaca, N.Y., 1961-62; rsch. staff lab. nuclear sci. MIT, Boston, 1964-65; asst. prof. McMaster U., Hamilton, Ont., 1962-66, assoc. prof., 1966-71, physics prof., 1971—, dean faculty sci., 1975-84, 89, mem. bd. govs., 1986-90, chair dept. physics and astronomy, 1991-97. Vis. prof. U. Barcelona, Spain, 1991-92, 95. Contbr. articles to profl. jours. C.D. Howe fellow, 1969-70, Rotary Found. fellow, 1957-58. Fellow Royal Soc. Can.; mem. Can. Assn. Physicists (Herzberg medal 1972, medal for outstanding achievement 1997), Am. Phys. Soc.; mem. Inst. Physics. Avocations: bicycling, cabinet making. Office: McMaster Univ Dept Physics and Astronomy 1280 Main St W Hamilton ON Canada L8S 4M1 E-mail: dwsprung@mcmaster.ca.

SPRUNG, JURAJ, anesthesiologist, educator; b. Ploce, Croatia, Mar. 14, 1953; s. Maksimilijan and Margarita Sprung; m. Jasminka Sprung, Jan. 29, 1975; children: Katarina, Maksimilijan. MD, Med. Sch., Rijeka, Croatia, 1977; PhD, Med. Sch., Zabreb, Croatia, 1985. Anesthesiologist, Split, Croatia, 1979-86; rsch. fellow Mayo Clinic, Rochester, Minn., 1986-87; anesthesiologist Med. Coll. Wis., Milw., 1987-90; asst. prof. anesthesiology U. Md., Balt., 1990-94; assoc. prof. anesthesiology Cleve. Clinic, 1994-2001; prof. anesthesiology Mayo Clinic, 2001—. Mem. adv. bd. Biopure Corp., Boston, 1998—. Mem. editl. bd. ACTA Anaesthesiologica Croatica, 1996—; ad hoc reviewer Anesthesiology, Anesthesia Analgesia, Jour. Clin. Anesthesi; contbr. over 100 articles to profl. jours., chpts. to books. Mem. Am. Soc. Anesthesiologists, Am. Soc. Regional Anesthesia, Internat. Anesthesia Rsch. Soc. Home: 1902 Fair Oak Ln SW Rochester MN 55902-2534 Office: Mayo Clinic 200 First St SW Rochester MN 55905 Fax: 507-284-0120. E-mail: sprung.juraj@mayo.edu.

SPRY, DONALD FRANCIS, II, lawyer; b. Bethlehem, Pa., Nov. 17, 1947; s. Donald Francis and Carol Annette (Bolger) S.; m. Mary Frances, June 20, 1981; stepchildren: Michael Matlaga, Michelle Fehnel. BA, Moravian Coll., 1969; JD, U. Pitts., 1972. Bar: Pa. 1972, U.S. Dist. Ct. (ea. dist.) Pa. 1975. Assoc. Law Offices of Edmund P. Turtzo, Bangor, Pa., 1973-76; ptnr. Turtzo, Spry, Powlette & Sbrocchi, P.C., 1976-83, Turtzo, Spry, Powlette, Sbrocchi & Faul, P.C., Bangor and Stroudsburg, Pa., 1983-90, Turtzo, Spry, Sbrocchi, Faul & LaBarre, P.C., Bangor and Stroudsburg, 1990-2000; mem. King, Spry, Herman, Freund & Faul, LLC, Bethlehem, Pa., 2001—. Capt. USAR 1979-80. Mem. ABA (family law sect.), Pa. Bar Assn. (family law sect. edn. law com., zone del. Ho. of Dels.), Northampton County Bar Assn. (family law com.), North County Bar Assn. (pres.-elect 1989, pres. 1990), Pa. Sch. Bds. Assn., Nat Sch. Bds. Assn., ACLU, Edn. Law Assn., Pomfret Club. Republican. Methodist. Capt. USAR, 1979-80. Mem. ABA (family law sect.), Pa. Bar Assn. (family law sect. edn. law com., zone del. Ho. of Dels.), Northampton County Bar Assn. (family law com.), North County Bar Assn. (pres.-elect 1989, pres. 1990), Pa. Sch. Bds. Assn., Nat. Sch. Bds. Assn., ACLU, Edn. Law Assn., Pomfret Club. Republican. Methodist. also: 930 N 9th St Stroudsburg PA 18360-1208 Office: King Spry Herman Freund & Faul LLC 1 W Broad St Bethlehem PA 18018 E-mail: dfs@kingspry.com.

SPUHLER, JACILYN ERICKSON, librarian; b. Oct. 1, 1949; BA, U. Calif., Riverside, 1971; MLS, U. Hawaii, 1973. Dir. Garfield County Pub. Libr. Sys., New Castle, Colo., 1997—. Office: PO Box 320 New Castle CO 81647-0320 E-mail: jspuhler@marmot.org.

SPULBER, NICOLAS, economics educator emeritus; b. Bucharest, Romania, Jan. 1, 1915; m. Pauline, Aug. 5, 1950; 1 son, Daniel Francis. MA, New Sch. Social Rsch., 1950, PhD magna cum laude, 1952; D (hon.) , U. Bucharest, 2002. Rsch. assoc. Ctr. Internat. Studies, Mass. Inst. Tech., 1952-54; mem. faculty Ind. U., Bloomington, 1954—, prof. econs., from 1961, acting chmn. Inst. East European Studies, 1956-59, Disting. prof. econs., 1974-80, Disting. prof. emeritus, 1980—. Vis. prof. City Coll., City U. N.Y., 1963-64 Author: The Economics of Communist Eastern Europe, 1957, reissued 1976, The Soviet Economy: Structure, Principles, Problems, 2d edit., 1964, Soviet Strategy for Economic Growth, 1964, The State and Economic Development, 1966, Socialist Management and Planning, 1971, Organizational Alternatives in Soviet-Type Economies, 1979, Managing the American Economy from Roosevelt to Reagan, 1989, Restructuring the Soviet Economy: In Search of the Market, 1991, The American Economy: The Struggle for Supremacy in the 21st Century, 1995, reissued 1997, Redfining the State: Privatization and Welfare Reform in Industrial and Transitional Economies, 1997; co-author: Quantitative Economic Policy and Planning, 1976, Economics of Water Resources: From Regulation to Privatization, 1994, 2d edit., 1998, Russia Economic Transitions from Late Tsarism to the New Millennium, 2002; editor, co-editor 5 books; contbr. numerous articles to profl. jours. in U.S. and fgn. countries. Halle fellow, 1951-52; grantee Am. Philos. Soc., 1956; grantee Ford Found., 1962-63; rsch. fellow Ford Faculty Found., 1960-61; sr. fellow Internat. Devel. Rsch. Ctr., Ind. U., 1969-71 Mem. Am. Econ. Assn. Office: Ind U Dept Econs Wiley Hall Bloomington IN 47405

SPUNGIN, CHARLOTTE ISABELLE, retired secondary education educator, writer; b. Providence, June 12, 1929; d. Abraham Spungin and Golde Morrison. BA, U. R.I., 1951; MEd, U. Fla., 1966; EdS, Nova Southeastern U., Davie, Fla., 1981. Tchr., head dept. social sci. South Broward H.S., Hollywood, Fla., 1962-90. Cons. Fla. Atlantic U., Boca Raton, 1985-90, U. Miami, Fla., 1980-90, Broward County Sch. Dist., Ft. Lauderdale, Fla., 1990-96; tchr. trainer Fla. Performance Measurement Sys.; instr. psychology and sociology Broward C.C. Co-author: (books) (with N. Tallent) Psychology: Understanding Ourselves and Others, 1977, (with H. Besner) Gay and Lesbian Students: Understanding Their Needs, 1995, Training for Professionals Who Work with Gays and Lesbians in Educational and Workplace Settings, 1997, (curriculum guides) Creativity with Bill Moyers, 1984, World of Difference, 1987, Holocaust Curriculum Guide for the State of Florida, 1990, The Holocaust Remembered, 1986, (monograph) Southeast Asian Monograph on Comparative Educational School Systems: Singapore, Malaysia and the Indonesian Islands, 1971. Cons., bd. dirs. Holocaust Documentation Ctr., North Miami, Fla., 1985-90; bd. dirs. Fla. Coun. for Social Studies, Orlando and Tallahassee, 1979-85. Recipient Spirit of Excellence award Miami Herald, 1985, Skretting award Fla. Coun. for Social Studies, Wilma Simmons Golden Svc. award, 1985, Outstanding Svc. in Mental Health award Fla. divsn. Nat. Assn. Mental Health, Woman of Yr. in Edn. award Women in Comm., 1990; Fulbright fellow, 1970, 76; scholar NSF, 1965. Mem. APA, ASCD, Nat. Coun. on Social Studies, Fla. Coun. for Social Studies, Phi Delta Kappa, Phi Alpha Theta. Democrat. Jewish. Avocations: travel, writing, reading. Office: PO Box 8833 Fort Lauderdale FL 33310-8833 E-mail: spunbar@attbi.com.

SPUNT, SHEPARD ARMIN, real estate executive, management and financial consultant; b. Cambridge, Mass., Feb. 3, 1931; s. Harry and Naomi (Drooker) S.; m. Joan Murray Fooshee, Aug. 6, 1961 (dec. June 1969); children: Erica Frieda and Andrew Murray (twins). BS, U. Pa., 1952, MBA, 1956. Owner Colonial Realty Co., Brookline, Mass., 1953—, Cambridge, 1960—. Sr. assoc. Gen. Solids Assocs., 1956—; chmn. bd. Gen. Solids Sys. Corp., 1971-74; trustee Union Capital Trust, Boston; incorporator Liberty Bank & Trust Co., Boston; dir., clk. The Computer Co., Inc., Cambridge, 1986—, treas., 1997—; author, sponsor consumer protection, election law and pub. safety legislation Mass. Gen. Ct., 1969—, pub. safety U.S. Congress, 1998. Co-author: A Business Data Processing Service for Small Business Practitioners, 1956, A Business Data Processing Service for Medical Practitioners, 1956, rev. edit., 1959; patentee in field of automation, lasers, dieelectric bonding. Chmn. Com. for Fair Urban Renewal Laws, Mass., 1965—; treas. Ten Men of Mass., 1980; pres. New Eng. Coun. Young Reps., 1964-67, 69-71; vice chmn. Young Rep. Nat. Fedn., 1967-69, dir. region I, 1964-67, 69-71; mem. Brookline Rep. Town Com., 1960—, treas., 1996—; del. Atlantic Conf. Young Polit. Leaders, Brussels, 1973; bd. dirs. Brookline Taxpayers Assn., 1964—, v.p., 1971-72, pres., 1972—; dep. sheriff Norfolk County, 1998-99. Mem. Nat. Soc. Profl. Engrs., Rental Housing Assn., Greater Boston Real Estate Bd., Navy League, Boston Athenaeum, Copley Soc. Boston, Collector's Club N.Y., Masons, Shriners. Home: 177 Reservoir Rd Chestnut Hill MA 02467-1426 Office: 21 Elmer St Cambridge MA 02138-6107

SPURGEON, BARBARA, music educator; b. Norwalk, Conn., Jan. 24, 1964; d. Russell Dickinson and Betty Barbara Greaves; m. Sean Kevin Spurgeon, Aug. 29, 1987; children: Russell Dallas, Briana Blessing. BA in Spanish, MusB, Ga. So. U., 1986, MEd, 1988; EdD, U. Ga., 1998. Cert. tchr., Ga. Band dir. Jenkins County Bd. Edn., Millen, Ga., 1989-90, Loganville (Ga.) High Sch., 1990-92; asst. band dir. Cedar Shoals High Sch., Athens, Ga., 1993-97; band dir., music specialist Monroe (Ga.) Elem. Sch., 1997—. Prin. oboe Athens Symphony Orch., 1992—. Mem. Music Educators Nat. Conf., Internat. Double Reed Soc., Women Band Dirs. Internat. Home: 1947 Broadnax Mill Rd Loganville GA 30052-6118

SPURGEON, EDWARD DUTCHER, law educator, foundation administrator; b. Newton, N.J., June 2, 1939; s. Dorsett Larew and Mary (Dutcher) S.; m. Carol Jean Forbes, June 17, 1963; children: Michael Larew, Stephen Edward. AB, Princeton U., 1961; LLB, Stanford U., 1964; LLM in Taxation, NYU, 1968. Bar: Calif. 1965. Assoc. atty. Stammer McKnight et al, Fresno, Calif., 1964-67, Paul Hastings Janofsky and Walker, L.A., 1968-70, ptnr., 1971-80; prof. law U. Utah, Salt Lake City, 1980-90, Wm. H. Leary prof. law and policy, 1990-93, assoc. dean acad. affairs Coll. Law, 1982-83, dean Coll. Law, 1983-90; dean Sch. Law U. Ga., Athens, 1993-98, prof., 1993—; ptnr. Moyle & Draper, Salt Lake City, 2000—. Vis. prof. law Univ. Coll. London, fall 1990, Stanford U. Law Sch., spring 1991; ex-officio mem. Utah State Bar Commn., 1984-90. Co-author: Federal Taxation of Trusts, Grantors and Beneficiaries, 1st edit., 1978, 2d edit., 1989, 3d edit., 1997. Mem. Utah Gov.'s Task Force Officers and Dirs. Liability Ins., 1985-87, Utah Dist. Ct. Reorgn. Commn., 1986-87, Justice in 21st Century Commn., Utah, 1989-91; bd. visitors, exec. com. Stanford U. Law Sch., 1988-93; pres., dir. Albert and Elaine Borchard Found., 1983—; exec. dir. Ctr. on Law and Aging, 1998—; dir. Nat. Sr. Citizens Law Ctr., 1999—. Mem. ABA (Commn. on Legal Problems of the Elderly 1991-95, spl. advisor 1995—), Am. Bar Found. Office: U of Ga Law School Athens GA 30602

SPURGEON, ELIZABETH ANN, special education educator; b. Dalton, Ga., Sept. 30, 1946; d. John Wilbert and Alice Louise (Sanford) S. AA, Tarrant County Jr. Coll., Ft. Worth, Tex., 1969; BA, Tex. Wesleyan Coll., Ft. Worth, Tex., 1972; MEd, N. Tex. State U., Denton, 1986. Spl. edn. tchr. U.S. Peace Corps, Kenya, E. Africa, 1977-79, Ft. Worth State Sch., 1980-84, 86-87, Ft. Worth Ind. Sch. Dist. J.P. Moore Sch., 1987-91, Ft. Worth Ind. Sch. Dist. Jo Kelly Sch., 1991-92, Mansfield (Tex.) ISD Alice Ponder Elem. Sch., 1993—2001, Imogene Gideun Elem. Sch., 2001—. Democrat. Avocations: reading, collecting African art, poetry writing. Home: 5865 Rendon Estates Rd Mansfield TX 76063-3051 E-mail: libbyspurgeon@hotmail.com.

SPURGEON, NANNETTE SUANN (SUSIE SPURGEON), special education educator; b. Crawfordsville, Ind., Nov. 15, 1962; d. Dwight Cordell and Nancy Mae (Meagher) Spurgeon. BS, Stephen F. Austin State U., 1985; MS, Purdue U., 1990. Cert. elem. edn. tchr., deaf edn. tchr., learning disabilities educator. Tchr. 1st grade Aldine Ind. Sch. Dist., Houston, 1985-86; tchr. pre-Kindergarten Cypress-Fairbanks Ind. Sch. Dist., 1986-88, Disabilities Svcs., Inc., Crawfordsville, Ind., 1989; elem. hearing impaired tchr. Pleasant Hill Elem. Sch. North Montgomery Community Sch. Corp., 1990-91; tchr. learning disabilites, title 1, hearing impaired, reading recovery Hoover Elem. Sch. Crawfordsville Community Sch. Corp., 1991—. Tchr. aide Crawfordsville Community Sch. Dist., 1988-89; interpreter Christ the Good Shepard Cath. Ch., Houston, 1986-87; coach 7th grade volleyball Northridge Mid. Sch., 1990; volleyball coach Tuttle Mid. Sch., Crawfordsville, 1991—. Named to Alpha Chi, Kappa Delta Pi. Mem. Reading Recovery Coun. of N.Am., Coun. for Exceptional Children, Kappa Sigma Phi. Avocations: volleyball, softball, signed song interpretations. Home: 307 Jennison St Crawfordsville IN 47933-2748 E-mail: sspurgeon@cville.k12.in.us., sspurgeon@wico.net.

SPURLING, EVERETT GORDON, JR. architect, construction specifications consultant; b. Fallston, N.C., Sept. 5, 1923; s. Everett Gordon and Vera Mae (Lattimore) S.; m. Margaret Ball Duckworth, Sept. 9, 1944; children: David Steven, Diana Lynn, Norman Kent. AS, Mars Hill Coll., 1940-42; B in Archtl. Engrng. with high honors, N.C. State U., 1947, postgrad., 1948. Registered architect, N.C., Va., Md. Inspector aircraft Glenn Martin Co., Balt., 1942; draftsman, architect F. Carter Williams, Architect, Raleigh, N.C., 1947-52; staff architect C.E. Silling and Assocs., Charleston, W.Va., 1952-53, Greife and Daley, Architects, Charleston, 1953-55; ptnr. Hunter and Spurling, Architects, 1955-57; project architect, assoc. McLeod and Ferrara, Architects, Washington, 1957-64; owner, cons. E.G. Spurling Jr., Architect, Washington and Bethesda, Md., from 1964. Guest lectr. Montgomery Coll., Cath. U., U. Mo.-Rolla, George Washington U.; guest speaker, panelist numerous constrn. orgns. Contbr. articles to profl. jours. Served as sgt. C.E., U.S. Army, 1944-46, ETO. Recipient Design award GSA, 1990. Fellow AIA, Constrn. Specifications Inst. (hon. mem. 1995, cert. of appreciation 1971, 93, Ben John Small Meml. award 1979, edn. commendation 1979, Master Format spl. award 1983, Mid-Atlantic Region cert. of appreciation 1990, 92, Disting. svc. award 1998); mem. Am. Arbitration Assn. (panelist 1979-96), Specifications Cons. in Ind. Practice (pres. 1977-80), Tau Beta Pi, Phi Kappa Phi. Democrat. Baptist. Avocations: fishing, woodworking, art, fgn. travel. Died Apr. 1, 2001.

SPURLOCK, ISRAEL EMANUEL LEE, minister; b. LeFlore County, Miss., May 7, 1951; s. Will Spurlock Jr., Emma (Davis) Spurlock; m. Audrey Michell, May 7, 1973; children: Nikkia, Lakesha, Shaune, Latoyia;1 child Willie. M in Pastoral Counseling, Andersonville Bapt. Sem., 2001, D (hon.) of Counseling, 2002. Pres. Seven Enterprises, Champaign, Ill., 2000; CEO Seven Star Ministries, Rantoul, 2001—. Author: Victory Poetry Inspired Forty, 1996, The Power to Rise and Succeed, 1998, On the Wings of Faith, 2001. Sgt. USAF, 1971—75. Mem.: Toastmasters Internat. Avocations: horseback riding, bicycling, singing, basketball, football. Home: 613 Heath Dr Rantoul IL 61866

SPURRIER, JAMES JOSEPH, theater educator; b. Mexico, Mo., Oct. 1, 1946; s. Jack Joseph and Ruth Marilyn (Mundy) S.; m. Jean Madelon Alkire, June 5, 1976; children: Jenna, Jamie. BA, U. Mich., 1968; MA, UCLA, 1970; PhD, So. Ill. U., 1979. Tchr., dept. chmn. Alemany High Sch., Mission Hills, Calif., 1968-74; prof. speech, dir. theater Vincennes (Ind.) U., 1977—; chair dept. speech and theatre, 1999—. Composer various music selections, 1974-79. Choir dir. 1st Christian Ch., Vincennes, 1977-97, St. Paul's Luth. Ch., Vincennes, 1997—; bd. dirs. Arts Coun. Southwestern Ind., 1991-2001. Recipient Dir. Best Musical award Northridge (Calif.) Arts Coun., 1971; named Outstanding Young Man of Am., 1979, 82. Mem. Nat. Assn. Schs. of Theatre (ethics com. 1987-93, chmn. ethics com. 1990-93, nominations com. 1993-94, evaluator 1991—, chmn. nomination com. 2000-2001), Assn. for Theater in Higher Edn. (com. chmn. 1986-88), Ind. Theater Assn., Phi Kappa Phi, Kiwanis. Roman Catholic. Home: 2202 E Seminole Dr Vincennes IN 47591-1974 Office: Vincennes U Shircliff # 15 Vincennes IN 47591 E-mail: jspurrier@indian.vinu.edu.

SPURRIER, MARY EILEEN, investment advisor, financial planner; b. Mpls., Sept. 16, 1943; d. Charles Joseph and Ruth Eileen (Rowles) Dickman; m. Joseph Leo Spurrier, Jan. 16, 1965 (div. Aug. 1976); 1 child, Christopher Jude; m. Gary Albert Gutfrucht, July 8, 1988. BS, U. Minn., 1965. CFP; CDP; registered prin., registered investment advisor. Rsch. fellow, libr. Sch. Bus. Adminstrn. U. Minn., Mpls., 1965-68; exec. dir. Zero Population Growth, N.Y., 1972-76; fin. cons. Merrill Lynch, Rochester, 1977-84, Shearson/Smith Barney, 1984-89; investment cons. CitiCorp, Rochester, 1989-91; assoc. v.p. Essex Investment, 1991-95; pres. M. Spurrier Fin. Svcs., 1995—. Bd. dirs. Micro Bus. Alliance, Rochester; cons. Fund Devel. Rochester Women's Network, 1995-97, Women's Coun. C. of C., Rochester, 1992-97; spkr. in field. Advisor Blue Jean Mag.; contbr. articles to newspapers. Chmn. endowment campaign YWCA, Rochester, 1994-98, bd. dirs., mem. fin. com. 1997—; mentor Wilson Commencement Park, Rochester, 1993—; v.p., bd. dirs. N.Y. State Environ. Planning Lobby, 1973-75; bd. dirs. N.Y. State Family Planning Coalition, 1973-75; fin. dir. LWV, Rochester, 1989-90; capital campaign com. Susan B. Anthony House, 1997-99. Recipient Eminent Rochester Women award Upstate Mag., 1974. Mem. NAFE (spkr. 1990-95), Rochester Women's Network (bd. dirs. 1997—, v.p. 1999—), Women's Coun. C. of C. (chair W award 2000, nominee W award 1999), Nat. Assn. Women Bus. Owners (bd. dirs. Greater Rochester chpt. 1997-2000, chair Top Women's Bus. Owners Awards 1997-2000). Avocations: gardening, reading, walking. Office: 315 Westminster Rd Rochester NY 14607-3230

SPYERS-DURAN, PETER, librarian, educator; b. Budapest, Hungary, Jan. 26, 1932; came to U.S., 1956, naturalized, 1964; s. Alfred and Maria (Almasi-Balogh) S-D; m. Jane F. Cumber, Mar. 21, 1964; children: Kimberly, Hilary, Peter. Certificate, Free U. Budapest, 1955; MA in L.S, U. Chgo., 1960; Ed.D., Nova S Ea. U., 1975. Profl. asst. libr. adminstrn. div. ALA, Chgo., 1961-62; assoc. dir. librs., assoc. prof. U. Wis., 1962-67; dir. librs., prof. Western Mich. U., 1967-70; dir. librs., prof. libr. sci. Fla. Atlantic U., 1970-76; dir. libr. Calif. State U., Long Beach, 1976-83; prof. libr. and info. sci., dir. libr. Wayne State U., Detroit, 1983-86, dean, prof. libr. and info. sci. program, 1986-95, dean and prof. emeritus, 1995—; cons. Spyers-Duran Assocs., 1995—; acting univ. libr. Nova Southeastern U., Ft. Lauderdale, Fla., 1996-97. Vis. prof. State U. N.Y. at Geneseo, summers 1969-70; cons. publs., libr. and info. scis.-related enterprises; chmn. bd. internat. confs., 1970—. Author: Moving Library Materials, 1965, Public Libraries - A Comparative Survey of Basic Fringe Benefits, 1967; editor: Approval and Gathering Plans in Academic Libraries, 1969, Advances in Understanding Approval Plans in Academic Libraries, 1970, Economics of Approval Plans in Research Libraries, 1972, Management Problems in Serials Work, 1973, Prediction of Resource Needs, 1975, Requiem for the Card Catalog: Management Issues in Automated Cataloging, 1979, Shaping Library Collections for the 1980's, 1981, Austerity Management in Academic Libraries, 1984, Financing Information Systems, 1985, Issues in Academic Libraries, 1985; mem. editorial bd. Jour. of Library Adminstration, 1989-95. Mem. Kalamazoo County Library Bd., 1969-70; Bd. dirs. United Fund. Reciient G. Flint Purdy award for outstanding contbns. Wayne State U., 1999. Mem. ALA, Mich. Libr. Assn., Internat. Fed. Libr. Assns., Assn. Info. Sci., Fla. Libr. Assn., Calif. Libr. Assn., Fla. Assn. Community Colls., Boca Raton C. of C., U. Chgo. Grad. Libr. Sch. Alumni Club (pres. 1973-75), Solinet Mich. Libr. Consortium (founder charter bd. mem. 1973—, bd. dirs. 1973-76), Detroit Area Libr. Network (pres. bd. dirs. 1985-95), Mich. Ctr. for Book (pres. 1988-89), Am. Soc. Info. Sci., Assn. Libr. and Info. Sci. Edn. Republican. Methodist. Home: 7295 Maidencane Ct Largo FL 33777-4900 Office: Wayne State Univ Librs Detroit MI 48202 E-mail: PSpyers@aol.com.

SPYKER, HARRY A., III, music educator; b. Dayton, Ohio, Feb. 12, 1945; s. Donna M. Spyker; m. Renee' A. Arcella; 1 child Kelsey Justine. BS in Music Edn., Ctrl. State U., 1966; MusM, Ohio State U., 1972. Band dir. Fairborn (Ohio) Pub. Schs., 1966—68, Springfield (Ohio) North H.S., 1968—72, Deerfield Beach (Fla.) H.S./Middle Sch., 1973—86, Fla. Atlantic U., Boca Raton, 1986—87, Boca Raton (Fla.) Cmty. H.S., 1986—91, Santaluces H.S., Lantana, 1991—94, Congress Cmty. Middle Sch., Boynton Beach, 1994—. Clarinet player Springfield Symphony Orch., 1967—71; All-County Honor Band clinician/condr. 1991 and 1996 Broward County Pub. Schs., Ft.Lauderdale, Fla.; All-District Honor Band condr./clinician Palm Beach County Dist. 14 , West Palm Beach, Fla. Music curriculum writing team Palm Beach County Schools, West Palm Beach, 1987—89. Mem.: Fla. Music Educators Assn., Music Educators Nat. Conf., Am. Sch. Band Dirs. Assn. (nat. chmn. for marching bands 1983—85), Fla. Bandmasters Assn. (life; Fla. adjudicator for dist. band evaluations 1977—, dist. chmn., sec. 1978—82, Twenty Five Yr. award 1998). Roman Catholic. Avocations: jogging, golf, tennis, travel, reading. Home: 2820 SW 22nd Ave #203 Delray Beach FL 33445

SPYROPOULOS, GEORGE NICHOLAS, physician; b. Westwood, N.J., July 24, 1965; s. Nicholas George and Asimina Vasilios (Tassini) S.; m. Maria Evangelia Stavropoulos, May 3, 1968. BA in Biology, Franklin and Marshall, 1987; DO, Phila. Coll. Osteo. Medicine, 1992. Diplomate Am. Acad. Family Practice. Intern Crozer-Chester Med. Ctr., Springfield, Pa., 1992-93; resident family and community medicine Med. Ctr. Delaware, Wilmington, 1993-95; attending family physician West Chester, Pa., 1995—; team physician West Chester (Pa.) U., 1998—. Staff Christiana Hosp., Wilmington, 1995, So. Chester County Med. Ctr., Jennersville, Pa., 1996, Chester County Hosp., West Chester, 1996—; courtesy staff A.I. DuPont Children's Hosp., Wilmington, 1996; med. dir. Pepperridge Farm Downington, PA Plant. Vice pres. The Peloponnesian Soc. of Greater Delaware Valley, 1996-97. Recipient Ahepa Dist. scholarship, 1984-85. Mem. AMA. Am. Osteo. Assn., Am. Acad. Family Physicians, Am. Acad. Osteo. Family Physicians, Soc. Tchrs. of Family Medicine, Pa. Med. Soc., Delaware Med. Soc., Del. State Osteo. Med. Soc., Chester County Med. Soc., Hellenic U. Club of Phila., Hellenic Med. Soc. of Greater Delaware Valley. Avocations: travel, photography, sports, music. Home: 1104 Radley Dr West Chester PA 19382-8074 Office: 1646 West Chester Pike Ste 12 West Chester PA 19382- Office Fax: 610-738-9101.

SQUATRIGLIA, ROBERT WILLIAM, university dean, educator; b. Naugatuck, Conn., Nov. 23, 1937; s. P. William and Mary Elizabeth (Ogenskis) S.; m. Betty Lee Powell, Aug. 12, 1961; children: Robert Jr., Elizabeth, Katherine, Stephen. AB, Coll. of William & Mary, 1960, MA, 1965; PhD, U. S.C., 1970. Asst. dean of men Coll. of William & Mary, 1963-67; counselor, dir. VA U. S.C., Columbia, 1967-70, instr. sch. edn., 1969; dean student svcs. SUNY, Brockport, 1970-71, v.p. student affairs, 1971-72, assoc. dean students Albany, 1972-77; assoc. prof., v.p. student affairs, dean of students Coastal Carolina U., Conway, 1977—. Bd. dirs. United Way Horry County, 1997—. Capt. U.S. Army, 1961-63. Mmem. Rotary Internat. (dist. gov. 1987-88, task force chair 1995--; internat. tng. leader 1998, found. permanent fund nat. advisor 1999-2001, N.Am. affairs com. 1999-2000, gen. chmn. Zone 33 and 34 Inst. 2000, Disting. Svc. award 1993, Four Avenues of Svc. award 2000, Paul Harris fellow), Rotary Found. (benefactor), Bequest Soc. (aide to dir. 2001-02), Phi Delta Kappa (Meritorious Svc. award 2002). Roman Catholic. Home: 118 Wofford Rd Conway SC 29526-8815 Office: Coastal Carolina U PO Box 261954 Conway SC 29528-6054 E-mail: drbob@coastal.edu.

SQUATRITO, DOMINIC J. judge; BA, Wesleyan U., 1961; JD, Yale U., 1965. Judge U.S. Dist. Ct. Conn., 1994—. Office: US Dist Court 450 Main St Fl 2 Hartford CT 06103-3010

SQUAZZO, MILDRED KATHERINE (MILDRED KATHERINE OETTING), corporate executive; b. Bklyn., Dec. 22, 1927; d. William John and Marie M. Oetting. Student, L.I. U. Sec.-treas. Stanley Engrng., Inc. , 1960—68; v.p. Stanley Chems., Inc., 1960—68; founder, pres. ChemDynamics Corp., Scotch Plains, NJ, 1964—68; gen. adminstr., purchasing dir. Richardson Chem. Co., Metuchen, 1968—69; owner Berkeley Employment Agy. and Berkeley Temp. Help Svc., Berkeley Heights, 1969—91, Berkeley Employment Agy., Morristown, 1982—91, Bridgewater, 1987—91; pres. M.K.S. Bus. Group, Inc., Berkeley Heights, 1980—91; mgmt. cons.; pers. fin.; lectr. With Nurse Corps U.S. Army, 1946—47. Mem.: Nat. Bus. and Profl. Women's Club. Home and Office: 16 Heather Ln Warren NJ 07059-5258

SQUIBB, SAMUEL DEXTER, chemistry educator; b. Limestone, Tenn., June 20, 1931; s. Benjamin Bowman and Lou Pearl S.; m. JoAnn Kyker, Dec. 15, 1951; children: Sandra Lavanne, Kevin Dexter. BS, E. Tenn. State U., 1952; PhD, U. Fla., 1956. Assoc. prof., dir. chemistry Western Carolina U., Cullowhee, N.C., 1956-60; asst. prof., dir. chemistry Eckerd Coll., St. Petersburg, Fla., 1960-63, asso. prof., 1963-64; prof. chemistry U. N.C., Asheville, 1964-94, prof. emeritus, 1994—, chmn. dept., 1964-94. Vis. prof. U. N.C., Chapel Hill, 1976-81, 83-87, 92-95, Clemson U., S.C., 1982; cons. So. Assn. Colls. and Schs., State of W.Va. Author: Experimental Organic Chemistry, 1972, Understanding Chemistry One, 1979, rev. 1990, Two, 1981, rev. 1991, Three, 1981, rev. 1992, Four, 1981, rev. 1992, Five, 1981, rev. 1989, Six, 1984, Chemistry One, 1976, rev. 1987, Two, 1980, rev. 1990, Experimental Chemistry One, 1976, rev. 1988, Two, 1981, rev. 1991; contbr. articles to profl. jours. Mem. Grose United Meth. Ch. Disting. Tchr. award U. N.C.-Asheville, 1983; S.D. Squibb Disting. Chemistry Lectureship U. N.C., Asheville, established 1997; named to We. Carolina Fedn. Square and Round Dancing Hall of Fame, 2001; recipient Pres.'s Svc. award, Folk, Round and Square Dancing Fedn. N.C., 2001. Fellow Am. Inst. Chemists (life, nat. publs. bd. 1988-92); mem. Am. Chem. Soc. (Charles H. Stone award Carolina Piedmont sect. 1979, Disting. Chemist award Western Carolinas sect. 1993, chmn. Tampa Bay subsect. 1963, Western Carolina sect. 1981, editor Periodic News Western Carolina sect. 1980—, Disting. Chemist award 1993), N.C. Inst. Chemists (pres. 1977-79, sec. 1975-77, 85-91, Disting. Chemist award 1986), Skyland Twirlers Square Dance Club, Silver Spurs Advanced Square Dance Club, Double A's Advanced Square Dance Club, Skylarks Round Dance Club, Phi Beta Kap.

SQUIER, JACK LESLIE, sculptor, educator; b. Dixon, Ill., Feb. 27, 1927; s. Leslie Lee and Ruth (Barnes) S.; m. Jane Bugg, June 9, 1950. Student, Oberlin Coll., 1945-46; BS, Ind. U., 1950; M).F.A., Cornell U., 1952. Instr. Cornell U., 1952, asst. prof. art, 1958-61, asso. prof., 1961-65, prof., 1965—. Designer Howatt Pottery Co., N.Y.C., 1953; account exec. Jamian Advt. Co., N.Y.C., 1954-58; asst. prof. U. Calif., Berkeley, 1960; mem. Internat. Assn. Art, UNESCO, 1964-72, mem. exec. com., 1966-69, v.p., 1969-72 One-man shows include Alan Gallery, N.Y.C., 1956, 59, 62, 64, White Mus., Cornell U., 1959, 68, Instituto de Arte Contemporaneo, Lima, Peru, 1963, Landau-Alan Gallery, N.Y.C., 1966, 69, Herbert F. Johnson Mus., Cornell Univ. (retrospective of work , 1953-93); exhibited in group shows at Mus. Modern Art, N.Y.C., 1957, Whitney Mus., N.Y.C., 1952, 54, 56, 58, 62, 67, 78, Hirshhorn Mus., Washington, 1978, Mus. Fine Arts, Boston, 1958, Chgo. Art Inst., 1960, Brussel's Worlds Fair, 1956, competition, Auschwitz, Poland, 1957, Albright-Knox Mus., Buffalo, 1968, Claude Bernard Gallery, Paris, 1957, Hanover Gallery, London, 1958; represented in permanent collections Mus. Modern Art, N.Y.C., Whitney Mus. Art, Hirshhorn Mus., Instituto de Arte Contemporaneo, Everson Mus., Syracuse, N.Y., Stanford U. Mus., St. Lawrence U. Mus., SUNY at Potsdam, Ithaca Coll., Johnson Mus. at Cornell U., Houston Mus., Hamilton Coll. Mus., Hood Mus.-Dartmouth (N.H.) U., Castellani Mus., Niagara U., N.Y., Gogg Mus., Harvard U., Cambridge; bronze garden piece at Fogg Mus./Harvard U.; retrospective exhbn. Herbert F. Johnson Mus. Cornell U., 1993; work pub. in various, books, mags., newspapers, slide collections, catalogs. Served with AC USN, 1945-47. Office: Cornell U Dept Art 100 Tjaden Hall Ithaca NY 14853-7301

SQUIER, RITA ANN HOLMBERG, graphic designer; b. Norwalk, Conn., Jan. 4, 1967; d. Stig H. and Julia Mildred Tjader Holmberg; m. Michael Craig Squier, May 19, 1990. BS in Visual Arts, U. Bridgeport, 1988. Art dir., web designer Squier Design, Chatham, N.Y., 1995—; graphic designer, owner Studio 46, 1990-99. Mem. Mooresville Artist Guild, Columbia County Coun. on the Arts. Republican. Avocations: watercolor, pen and ink, gardening, acrylics, photography. Office: Squier Design 46 Payn Ave Chatham NY 12037-1427

SQUIERS, ELIZABETH C. healthcare administrator; b. Jan. 10, 1960; MD, Jefferson Med. Coll., 1983; BA, Pa. State U., 1979. Diplomate Am. Bd. Surgery. Transplant surgeon, asst. prof. surgery Geisinger Med. Ctr., Danville, Pa., 1990-94; dir. transplant program, assoc. prof. surgery SUNY Health Sci. Ctr., Syracuse, 1994-98; sr. dir. med. affairs Sangstat Med. Co., Fremont, Calif., 1998-99, sr. dir. clin. devel., drug safety officer, 1998—. Contbr. articles to profl. jours. Med. advisor Nat. Kidney Found. of Ctrl. NY, Syracuse, 1994-98. Fellow ACS, ASTS. Office: 6300 Dumbarton Cir Fremont CA 94555-3644

SQUILLACE, PAUL J, hydrologist, researcher; b. St Paul, Minn., July 7, 1955; s. Zanti D and Ruth Squillace; m. Sandra K Kessler; children: Timothy, Anna, Joseph, Maria, Emily, Rosemary. BA Geology, Winona State Coll., Minn., 1977. Sr. field asst. Armco, Marquette, Mich., 1979; field geologist Army Corps of Engineers, Nashville, 1983; cartographer Def. Mapping Agy. Aerospace Ctr., St Louis, Mo., 1983—84; hydrologist U.S Geol. Survey, Pitts., 1984—86, U.S. Geol. Survey, Iowa City, 1986—94, rsch. hydrologist Rapid City, SD, 1994—. Contbr. articles to profl. jours. Mem.: Am. Geophys. Union. Avocations: bicycling, swimming, weightlifting. Office: US Geol Survey 1608 Mt View Rd Rapid City SD 57702 Office Fax: 605-355-4523. E-mail: pjsquill@usgs.gov.

SQUIRE, ALEXANDER, management consultant; b. Dumfrieshire, Scotland, Sept. 29, 1917; s. Frederick John and Lillian (Ferguson) S.; m. Isabelle L. Kerr, June 23, 1945; children: Jonathan, David, Deborah, Stephen, Philip, Martha, Timothy, Rebecca, Elizabeth. BS, MIT, 1939. Research metallurgist Handy and Harman, Fairfield, Conn., 1939-41; devel. metallurgist Sullivan Machinery Co., Michigan City, Ind., 1941-42; head powder metallurgy br. Watertown Arsenal Lab., Mass., 1942-45; mgr. metall. devel. Westinghouse Electric Corp., Pitts., 1945-50; project mgr. Bettis Atomic Power Lab., 1950-62; gen. mgr. plant apparatus div. Westinghouse, 1962-69; dir. purchases and traffic Westinghouse Electric Corp., 1969-71; pres. Westinghouse Hanford Co., Richland, Wash., 1971-79; bus. cons., 1979-80; dep. mng. dir. Wash. Public Power Supply System, 1980-85, cons., 1985—. Mem. Nat. Acad. Engrng., Am. Nuclear Soc., Am. Soc. Metals, AIME, Am. Def. Preparedness Assn. Address: 2415 Winburn Ave Durham NC 27704-5145

SQUIRE, ANNE MARGUERITE, religious leader; b. Amherstburg, Ont., Can., Oct. 17, 1920; d. Alexander Samuel and Coral Marguerite Park; m. William Robert Squire, June 24, 1943; children: Frances, Laura, Margaret. BA, Carleton U., Ottawa, 1972, BA with honors, 1974, MA, 1975; LLD (hon.), Carleton U., 1988; DD (hon.), United Theol. Coll., 1979, Queen's U., 1985. Cert. tchr., Ont. Adj. prof. Carleton U., 1975-82; sec. div. ministry personnel and edn. United Ch. Can., Toronto, 1982-85, moderator, 1986-88. Author curriculum materials, 1959—; contbr. articles to profl. jours. Mem. bd. mgmt. St. Andrew's Coll., Saskatoon, Sask., 1982, Queens Theol. Coll., Kingston, Ont., 1999-2000; founding mem. Muslim-Christian Dialogue Group. Recipient Senate medal Carleton U., 1972. Mem. Can. Research Inst. for Advancement Women, Delta Kappa Gamma (pres. 1978-79). Office: 731 Weston Dr Ottawa ON Canada K1G 1W1 E-mail: asquire@netrover.com.

SQUIRE, LAURIE RUBIN, media consultant; b. N.Y.C., Jan. 30, 1953; d. Daniel and Ruth Thelma (Deutsch) Rubin; m. Herbert E. Squire Jr., Aug. 6, 1975; children: Amy Ruth, Julie Wynn. BA cum laude (scholar), Finch Coll., 1974; MA, NYU, 1976; postgrad., Columbia U., 1977—. Actress TV commls., 1960-65; arts editor Finch/Metro newspaper, N.Y.C., 1970-74; co-editor Finch Alumnae mag., 1971-72; intern producer Sta. WBAI-FM, N.Y.C., 1973; music prodn. coord. Ballet Theatre spl. Sta. WNET-TV, 1973; coll. bd. writer Mademoiselle mag., 1973; intern asst. pub. affairs dir. N.Y. Cultural Ctr., 1974; mdse. coord. Sta. WOR-AM, N.Y.C., 1974-76, contbg. writer Bob and Ray's Mary Backstage serial, contbr. nostalgia features Joe Franklin Show, producer Jean Shepherd Show and sydicated markets, 1975-77, producer Bernard Meltzer What's Your Problem, 1977-80; broadcast stage mgr. Texaco Met. Opera, 1976—. Dance critic Show Bus., theatre newspaper; bd. dirs. publicity and advt. L.I. Playhouse, 1982-84; press rep. Great Neck Pla. Contbg. writer Newsday, Can. Publs. Publicity cons. Nassau County Mus. Fine Art; v.p. pub. rels. United Community Fund. Recipient commendations for Leukemia Radiothons Peabody Broadcasting citation, 1983. Home and Office: 892 Middle Neck Rd Great Neck NY 11024-1400

SQUIRE, MOLLY ANN, organizational psychologist; b. Highland Park, Mich., Aug. 18; d. George Edward and Dorothy Laura (Molteni) Squirrell; m. Arthur Bruce Hanson, June 23, 1990; 1 child Mark Arthur Hanson. AA, NYU, 1978; BS cum laude, U. LaVerne, 1980; MA, Claremont (Calif.) Grad. Univ., 1982; PhD, Pacific-Western U., 1991. Cert. cons. to mgmt. Health svcs. adminstr. health care delivery orgns., 1978-82; nat. dir. Huntington's Disease Rsch. Project, Calif., 1981-82; CEO Claremont Mgmt. Cons. (now Squire Trainers), L.A., 1982—. Past statis. analyst to pres. L.A. City Coll.; past part-time instr. L.A. Trade Tech.; part=time instr. Glendale C.C., 1994—96. Editor: BEACON newsletter, 1989—96; contbr. Lt. 78th Fraser Highland Regiment San Juan Capistrano Bn. Decorated Knight Templar of Jerusalem, Internat. br. Netherlands; named a Krauthamer & Squire 'Thelma & Louise' Women's Scholarship, L.A. City Coll., 1993—; named Woman of Magic scholarship, 1997—; recipient Cert. Appreciation, City of Utah, Calif., 1984, We. Sqwuare Dance Assn., 1986, Am. Heart Assn., 1990, So. Calif. Skeptics, 1987, Pacific Bell, 1990, Achievement award, No. Am. Women's Inner Circle, 1991, Cert. Appreciation, L.A. City Coll., 1995, Clan MacKenzie Soc. So. Calif., 1996; fellow, Claremont Grad. Sch., 1980—82. Mem.: ASTD, APA, Soc. Indsl. and Orgnl. Psychologists, Nat. Bur. Profl. Cons. to Mgmt., Assn. Psychol. Type, Pacific Coast Assn. Magicians (golden cir.), Internat. Brotherhood Magicians (past pres. #254, sec., Best Mentalist trophy 1987, Cert. Appreciation, Blackstone Floating Ring), Arthurian Soc. Arthuret U.K. (life), Soc. Am. Magicians (life Zinger award, Cert. Appreciation, Merit award 1991, 1994, Best Character Act 1994, Peller Meml. trophy 1994), Mensa (proctor). Achievements include patents for bus. and health care products. Office: PO Box 41633 Los Angeles CA 90041-0633 E-mail: hansons@worldnet.att.net.

SQUIRE, PEVERILL, political science educator; b. Pasadena, Calif., Feb. 26, 1955; s. Hal E. and Margaret Lucille Squire; m. Janet Beth Lindstrom, Aug. 29, 1981; children: Russell, Emma. AB, U. Calif., Berkeley, 1977, MA, 1978, PhD, 1985. Prof. polit. sci. U. Iowa, Iowa City, 1985—; Marshall prof. polit. sci. Budapest (Hungary) U. Econ. Scis., 1999-2000. Vis. prof. Meiji U., Tokyo, 1990. Author: (book) The Politics of California Coastal Legislation, 1984, Dynamics of Democracy, 1997, Who Runs for the Legislature?, 2001; editor: The Iowa Caucuses and the Presidential Nominating Process, 1989, Legislatures: Comparative Perspectives on Representative Assemblies, 2002. Fulbright disting. lectr., 1999-2000. Home: 321 Windsor Dr Iowa City IA 52245 Office: U Iowa Dept Polit Sci Iowa City IA 52242 Office Fax: 319-335-3400. E-mail: peverill-squire@uiowa.edu.

SQUIRE, WALTER CHARLES, lawyer; b. N.Y.C., Aug. 5, 1945; s. Sidney and Helen (Friedman) S.; m. Sara Jane Abamson; children: Harrison, Russell, Zachary, Andrew. BA, Yale U., 1967; JD, Columbia U., 1971. Bar: N.Y. 1971, U.S. Dist. Ct. (so. and ea. dists.) N.Y. 1975, U.S. Ct. Appeals (2d cir.) 1974, U.S. Supreme Ct. 1977. Ptnr. Jones Hirsch Connors & Bull P.C., N.Y.C., 1986-98, Jacobson, Mermelstein & Squire, LLP, N.Y.C., 1998—; prin. Squire & Co., LLC, 1998—. Bd. govs. Arthritis Found. N.Y., Inc., 1993-99; bd. dirs. MedicAlert Found., N.Y., 1990-99. Mem. ABA, N.Y. State Bar Assn., Assn. of Bar of City of N.Y., Internat. Bar Assn., Licensing Execs. Soc., Chartered Inst. Arbitrators (London), Am. Arbitration Assn. (arbitrator 1975-2000, mediator 1993—), Am. Acad. Hosp. Attys., Risk Ins. Mgmt. Soc. (lectr. 1983-84), AIDA Reinsurance & Ins. Arbitration Soc. (cert.). Office: Jacobson Mermelstein et al 52 Vanderbilt Ave New York NY 10017-3808

SQUIRES, ARTHUR MORTON, chemical engineer, educator; b. Neodesha, Kans., Mar. 21, 1916; s. Charles Loren and Vera Amber (Moore) S. AB with distinction in Chemistry, U. Mo., 1938; Ph.D, Cornell U., 1947. Design engr. M.W. Kellogg Co., N.Y.C., 1942-46; asst. dir. process devel. Hydrocarbon Research, Inc., 1946-51, dir. process devel., 1951-59; cons. chem. process industries, 1959-67; prof. chem. engring. CUNY, 1967-74, disting. prof., 1974-76, chmn. dept. chem. engring., 1970-73; Vilbrandt prof. chem. engring. Va. Poly. Inst. and State U., Blacksburg, 1976-82, disting. prof., 1978-86, disting. prof. emeritus, 1986—. Author: The Tender Ship, 1986; editor: (with D.A. Berkowitz) Power Generation and Environmental Change, 1971; contbr. articles to profl. jours.; patentee in field Mem. N.Y. Pro Musica, 1953-60 Fellow Am. Acad. Arts and Scis., AAAS; mem. ASME, NAE, AIChE (inst. lectr.), Am. Chem. Soc. (Henry H. Storch award 1973), Internat. Soc. for Human Ethology, Human Behavior and Evolution Soc., Sigma Xi, Tau Beta Pi Avocation: performing medieval and Renaissance music. Home: 2710 Quincy Ct Blacksburg VA 24060-4124 Office: Va Poly Inst and State U Dept Chem Engring Blacksburg VA 24061 E-mail: verasqu@vt.edu.

SQUIRES, CONNIE JO, special education educator; b. Omaha, July 14, 1933; d. Paul Sydney Hilt, Lillian Elvera (Holstrom) Hilt; m. Daryl Jessup Squires, Sept. 2, 1955; children: Stephen George, Chadwick Jay, Scott Arthur. BEd, Whitworth Coll., 1955; MEd, Seattle Pacific U., 1978; postgrad., U. Wash., Ea. Wash. U. Cert. tchr. spl. edn. and reading Wash., sch. psychologist Wash., drug and alcohol counselor Wash. Tchr. elem. Mead Sch. Dist., Spokane, Wash., 1955—59; tchr. spl. edn. Cle Eleun Sch. Dist., 1959—60; tchr. elem. Goleta Sch., Santa Barbara, Calif., 1960—62, Anacortes Sch. Dist., Anacortes, Wash., 1962—63, Bellevue Sch. Dist., Bellevue, 1963—77; sch. psychologist/edni. specialist Spokane Sch. Dist., 1977—88; sch. psychologist

West Valley Sch. Dist., Spokane, 1990—98; ret., 1998. Counselor drug and alcohol, cons. Assocs. in Counseling, Spokane, 1984—99. Bd. dirs. Friends of Little Spokane River Valley. Mem.: Spokane Ret. Tchrs., Nat. Assn. Sch. Psychologists, Whitworth Women's Aux. Republican. Presbyterian. Avocations: writing, gardening, computers. Home: 1509 E Kaywood Way Spokane WA 99208

SQUIRES, JAMES RALPH, development company executive; b. Jan. 2, 1940; s. William Guilford and Ruby Alice (Whittington) S.; m. Ann Newton, Apr. 17, 1965; children: Samuel Guilford, James Drew. Student, pub. schs., Charlotte, N.C. With Squires Constrn. Co., 1959-62; pres. SBS Builders, Inc., Charlotte, 1968-70, Ralph Squires Homes, Charlotte, 1970-88, Squires & Assocs., Realtors, 1975-88. Bd. dirs., mem. exec. com. Park Meridian Bank, 1991, Dover Mortgage, First Landmark; chmn. Squires Enterprises, Inc. Mem. Charlotte Tree Commn., 1977; bd. dirs. Athletic Found. U. N.C., Charlotte, 1979-84, Providence Day Sch., 1981-84, Better Bus. Bur., 1983, MMAES Inn, 1983-87, Charlotte Symphony; pub. mem. N.C. State Bar, 1980-85; pres. Metrolina Home Owners, 1982, bd. dirs., 1983; bd. govs. Polit. Action Com. for Bldg. Industry; mem. bd. visitors Mercy Hosp., Charlotte, 1986; bd. dirs. Mercy Hosp. Found., chmn., 1993—; chmn. new bldg. fund United Cerebral Palsy; mem. exec. coun. Mecklenburg County coun. Boy Scouts Am., 1986-90; mem. exec. coun. Muscular Dystrophy Assn., Charlotte, 1987; mem. N.C. Wildlife Resources Commn., 1995-98 bd. dirs. Harris YMCA, N.C. March of Dimes, 1997. Recipient Profile award N.C. Blue Cross/Blue Shield, 1974, Albert Gallatin merit cert., 1974; named Charlotte Builder of Yr., 1977. Mem. Nat. Homebuilders Assn., N.C. Homebuilders Assn. (v.p. 1975), Charlotte Homebuilders Assn. (pres. 1974), Charlotte Bd. Realtors, Carolina Ambs., Quail Hollow Country Club, Old North State Country Club, Grandfather Golf and Country Club, Brays Island Plantation. Republican. Baptist. Home: 8811 Winged Bourne Rd Charlotte NC 28210-5941

SQUIRES, JEFFREY E. defender, lawyer; b. Bath, N.Y., Aug. 31, 1954; s. Raymond Campbell and Doris Wilcox Squires. BA, SUNY, Cortland, 1976; JD, Syracuse U., 1979. Bar: N.Y. 1980, U.S. Dist. Ct. (we. dist.) N.Y. 1980. Closing atty. Farm Credit of Western N.Y. ACA, Hornell, 1984—; town atty. Town of Bath, 1986—; pub. defender Steuben County, Bath, 1988—. Mem. Sons Am. Legion, Benevolent and Protective Order Elks. Republican. Episcopalian. Avocations: hunting, motorcycles. Home: 7920 Harrisburg Hollow Rd Bath NY 14810-8275 Office: 14 E Pulteney Sq Bath NY 14810

SQUIRES, JOHN HENRY, judge; b. Oct. 21, 1946; married; five children. AB cum laude, U. Ill., 1968, JD, 1971. Bar: Ill. 1971, U.S. Dist. Ct. (cen. dist.) Ill. 1972, U.S. Tax Ct. 1978. Assoc. Brown, Hay & Stephens, Springfield, Ill., 1971-76, ptnr., 1977-87; judge U.S. Bankruptcy Ct. No. Dist. Ill. ea. divsn., 1988—2001, reappointed, 2002—. Trustee in bankruptcy, 1984-87; adj. prof. law John Marshall Law Sch., Chgo., 1994, DePaul U., Chgo., 1995-96; lectr. Am. Bankruptcy Inst., Sangamon County Bar Assn., Winnebago County Bar Assn., Chgo. Bar Assn., Ill. Inst. CLE, Comml. Law League Am., DuPage County (Ill.) Bar Assn. Mem. Nat. Conf. Bankruptcy Judges, Am. Bankruptcy Inst., Fed. Bar Assn., Am. Bus. Club, Union League Club Chgo. Office: US Bankruptcy Ct No Dist Ill Ea Div 219 S Dearborn St #676 Chicago IL 60604-1702

SQUIRES, KATHERINE LANDEY, lawyer; b. N.Y.C., Mar. 28, 1959; BA, Clark U., 1980; JD, U. Dayton, 1982; LLM in Tax, Georgetown U., 1983; MDiv, Biola U., 1994, ThM, 1996. Bar: D.C. 1983, Calif. 1986, N.Y. 1999. Assoc. Kutak, Rock & Campbell, Washington, 1983-85; pres., CEO Plan Care, Inc., Irvine, Calif., 1985—88; ptnr. Finley, Kumble, Wagner et.al., Newport Beach, 1986-88, Sheppard, Mullin, Richter & Hampton, Newport Beach, 1988-89; prin. Law Office of Katherine L. Squires, Irvine, Calif., 1989-97; pres. LawPrep, Inc., LawPrep Press, Inc., 1989-97; atty., mgr. firm-wide tech. devel. tng. and forms Akin Gump Strauss Mauer & Feld, Dallas, 1997—; pres., COO, Legal EdNet.com., Atkin EdNet.com. and TrainEd.com, 1999-2000; chief learning officer, pres. CLE divsn. WebCE.com., LLC, 2000—; pres., chief learning officer Edway Online; CFO, COO, Fabricon, Inc., Dallas. Contbr. articles on taxation and comml. law to profl. jours. Rep. candidate for U.S. Senate, 1993-94; commr. Workers' Compensation Appeals Bd., 1994-96; mktg. mgr. Bowne Imaging Network, 1996. Mem. ABA (chmn. internat. law com. of gen. practice sect., 1986—), Orange County Bar Assn., Nat. Assn. Women Lawyers (chmn. bankruptcy com., 1983—), Nat. Assn. Women Execs., Newport Beach (Calif.) C. of C. Republican. Avocations: aviation, gourmet cooking, languages, architecture.

SQUIRES, NINA GRACE, artist; b. Point Fortin, Trinidad and Tobago, Mar. 25, 1929; came to U.S., 1986; d. Oswald De Freitas and Maude Rebecca (Bowen) Callender; m. George William Lamming, Mar. 29, 1950 (div. Apr. 1961); children: Gordon William, Natasha Anna Lamming-Lee; m. Cecil Noel Squires, Feb. 23, 1963; children: Ian Patrick, Richard St. Clair. Entrance to Brit. Libr. Assn., Ea. Caribbean Libr. Sch., Port of Spain, Trinidad, 1949; student in art, Hammersmith Sch., London, 1954, Ctrl. Sch. Arts and Crafts, 1954, Montgomery Coll., Takoma Park, Md., 1992-93. Libr. asst., cataloger Trinidad Pub. Libr., Port of Spain, 1949-51; clerical asst. High Commn. for India, London, 1952-54; libr. dir. U.S. Info. Svc. and State Dept., Port of Spain, 1955-65, specialist cultural affairs, ednl. cons., 1965-85; receptionist various depts. U. Miami, Fla., 1986-91; assistance info. mgr. EPA, Nat. Caucus and Ctr. on Black Aged, Inc., Washington, 1993—. Owner, dir. Nina's Art Gallery, Port of Spain, 1962-63. One-woman shows include Nat. Mus. and Art Gallery, Trinidad and Tobago, 1975, The Art Mart Gallery, Diego Martin, Trinidad, 1987, Takoma Park Pub. Libr., Md., 1993, Orgn. Am. States, Washington, 1998; exhibited in group shows Commonwealth Art Inst., London, 1962, Scotland, 1974, Inst. Cultura Hispanic, Madrid, 1963, Sao Paulo Bienal, Brazil, 1963, 73, 75, Carifesta, Guyana, 1972, Jamaica, 1976, Barbados, 1981, Museo de Bellas Artes de Caracas, Venezuela, 1977, Clark Humanities Mus., Calif., 1986, Paxtutent Art League, Md., 1994, Dundalk Gallery, Md., 1996, Smithsonian's Anacostia Mus., 1999; work documented in Internat. Rev. African Am. Art, Hampton U., 1989, 98; represented in permanent collections Trinidad and Tobago Govt., U. W.I., Trinidad Hilton Hotel, numerous others. Judge Trinidad Carnival Celebrations, Port of Spain, 1957-84; mem. Washington project for the Arts, 1997; vol. Bapt. Hosp., Miami, 1991, Montgomery Pub. Schs., 1992-93, S.W. Pub. Libr., Washington, 1993-95. Recipient 2d place prize UN Ednl. Sci. and Cultural Orgn., Port of Spain, 1972. Mem. Trinidad Art Soc., Smithsonian Instn. (nat. assoc.). Episcopalian. Avocations: reading, music, sports.

SQUIRES, NORMA JEAN, artist, writer; b. Toronto, Feb. 15, 1938; d. Ross and Ida (Rolland) S.; m. Gerald Hopman (div. 1996); 1 child, Jessica Hopman. BFA, The Cooper Union, N.Y.C., 1979; MA, Calif. State U., 1984. Instr. sculpture Lucinda Art Sch., Tenafly, N.J., 1967-68; artist, freelance writer L.A., 1969—; artists' rep. and cons., 1986-88; writer L.A. Artcore, 1990—. Juror Hudson River Mus., Yonkers, N.Y., 1967, Conejo Valley Art Mus., 1999; coord., organizer Thursday's Poets Cultural Affairs Dept. City of L.a., 1994-95. Illustrator: (children's books) I Am a Picture Book, 1977, The Witch Who Whistled, 1977, Mouse in the Magic Forest, 1977; one-woman shows include Palmcrest House, Long Beach, Calif., 1998, Orlando Gallery, Sherman Oaks, Calif., 1999, Nagasaki (Japan) Mus. Art, 2000, Internat. Art Festival, Seoul, Korea, 2000; represented in collections Sterling Forest Gardens, N.Y.C., Warner Bros. Records, Burbank, Calif., Perkins Bldg. of the City of Glendale, Calif., Siemans Pacesetter Sys., L.A., others; curator Quarks to Quasars, 1997, Angels, Ancestors and Spirit Guides, 1997; works rented to numerous movie and TV prodns. including Frasier, 1999. Mem. Women's Caucus for Art. Avocations: reading, flamenco dancing, singing, astronomy, aerobics. Home: 9347 Valjean Ave North Hills CA 91343-2834 E-mail: njsquires@earthlink.net.

SQUIRES, RICHARD FELT, research scientist; b. Sparta, Mich., Jan. 15, 1933; s. Monas Nathan and Dorothy Lois (Felt) S.; m. Else Saederup, 1 child, Iben. BS, Mich. State U., 1958; postgrad., Calif. Inst. Tech., 1958-61. Rsch. biochemist Pasadena Found. for Med. Rsch., 1961-62; chief biochemistry sect. rsch. dept. A/S Ferrosan, Soeborg, Denmark, 1963-78; neurochemistry group leader CNS Biology sect. Lederle Labs. div. Am. Cyanamid Co., Pearl River, N.Y., 1978-79; prin. rsch. scientist The Nathan S. Kline Inst. for Psychiat. Rsch., Orangeburg, 1979-2000, ret., 2000. Contbr. over 85 articles to profl. jours.; patentee in field. Nat. Inst. Neurol. and Communication Disorders and Stroke grantee, 1981-84. Mem. Soc. Neurosci., Collegium Internat. Neuro-Psychopharmacologicum, Internat. Soc. Neurochemistry, Am. Soc. Neurochemistry, Am. Soc. Biochemistry and Molecular Biology, Am. Soc. Pharmacology and Exptl. Therapeutics. Home: 861 Laugenour Ct Woodland CA 95776-4911 E-mail: else_dick@hotmail.com.

SQUIRES, SUSAN ELAINE, anthropologist, consultant; b. Malden, Mass., Feb. 10, 1956; d. William Raymond Squires and Dorothy Gertrude Pulaski; life ptnr. David T Ziegler. PhD, Boston U., Boston, Massachusetts, 1979—90. Dir./principle Tactics LLC, Pescadero, Calif., 1999—; dir. of interaction services GVO, Inc, Palo Alto, 1997—2001; mgr. Andersen Consulting, St. Charles, Ill., 1994—97; sr. rschr. The Network, Andover, Mass., 1991—94; asst. profession U. of NH, Dover, NH, 1990—92. Pres. Nat. Assn. for the Practice of Anthropology, Washington, 2000—. Editor: (non-fiction business book) Creating Breakthrough Ideas. Mem. Butano Mut. Water Assn., Pescadero, Calif., 2001—02. Mem.: High Plains Soc. for Applied Anthropology, Am. Evaluation Assn., Soc. for Applied Anthropology, Am. Anthropology Assn. Achievements include design of IDSA Excellence Award for Design Exploration with Ericsson Research/Cyberlab, Singapore. Office: Tactics LLC PO Box 881 Pescadero CA 94060 Office Fax: 650-879-9029. E-mail: tactics@inreach.com.

SQUIRES, WILLIAM ALLEN, distribution company executive; b. Springfield, Mass., May 30, 1949; s. Robert P. and Irma Ruth (Alpert) S.; m. Nancy Faye Weiner, Nov. 15, 1981; children: Maxine Rhea, Sarah Jill and Michelle Anne (twins). BA, U. Pa., 1971; postgrad., Temple U., 1971-74. V.p. Esquire Gas Products Co., Enfield, Conn., 1972-87, pres., 1987—. Mem. assoc. bd. Enfield (Conn.) Nat. Bank, 1989-91. Mem. 1000-voice choir for opening ceremonies of Spl. Olympics World Games, 1995; soloist Nat. Antjhem and God Bless America at numerous games.. CPR, first aid, sports safety tng. ARC, Farmington, Conn., 1978—; mem. local emergency planning com. Town of Enfield, 1988—; bd. dirs. Jewish Family Svc. Greater Springfield (Mass.), 1983-86, Goodwill Industries Springfield-Hartford Area, Inc., 1998—; bd. dirs. Congregation Kodimoh; mem. Kodimoh Brotherhood, v.p., 2001-02; mem. western Mass. athletic recruiting com. U. Pa., chmn., 1974—; life mem. Friends of Storrowton; mem. U. Pa. Western Mass. Secondary Sch. Com., chmn. 1974-84; torchbearer Olympic Torch Relay, 1996; mem. N.E. regional adv. bd., bd. assoc. alumni trustees U. Pa. Mem. Nat. Audubon Soc. (life), Nat. Wildlife Fedn. (life), U. Pa. Alumni Assn. (pres. Western Mass. club 1974—, Western New Eng. club 1975—, v.p. class of 1971, 1981—), Rotary (dist. sec. 1984-85, dist. gov.'s area rep. 1995-96, pres. Enfield 1982-83, Paul Harris fellow 1988, 2000), Delta Upsilon Alumni (treas. U. Mass. chpt. 1979-82). Jewish. Home: 33 Willow Cir Longmeadow MA 01106-2152 Office: Esquire Gas Products Co PO Box 281 156 Spring St Enfield CT 06082-3431

SQUIRES, WILLIAM RANDOLPH, III, lawyer; b. Providence, Sept. 6, 1947; s. William Randolph and Mary Louise (Gress) S.; m. Elisabeth Dale McAnulty, June 23, 1984; children: Shannon, William R. IV, Mayre Elisabeth, James Robert. BA in Econs., Stanford U., 1969; JD, U. Tex., 1972. Bar: Wash. 1973, U.S. Dist. Ct. (we. dist.) Wash. 1973, U.S. Dist. Ct. (ea. dist.) Wash. 1976, U.S. Ct. Appeals (9th cir.) 1976, U.S. Supreme Ct. 1976, U.S. Ct. Fed. Claims 1982. Assoc. Oles, Morrison, Rinker, Stanislaw & Ashbaugh, Seattle, 1973-78; ptnr., chmn. litig. group Davis Wright Tremaine, 1978-97; mem. Summit Law Group, 1997—. Fellow Am. Coll. Trial Lawyers; mem. ABA, Internat. Bar Assn., Wash. State Bar Assn., King County Bar Assn., Wash. Athletic Club, Rainier Club (Seattle). Episcopalian. Home: 5554 NE Penrith Rd Seattle WA 98105-2845 Office: Summit Law Group 1505 Westlake Ave N Ste 300 Seattle WA 98109-6211 E-mail: randys@summitlaw.com.

SRACIC, KAREN K. librarian; b. Sharon, Pa., Sept. 16, 1955; BFA, Pa. State U., 1977; postgrad., Ill. State U., 1978-80; MLS, Clarion U., 1991, postgrad., 1991—. Grad. teaching asst. art Ill. State U., Normal, 1978-80; libr. tech. asst. III, cataloging, Milner Libr., 1980-88; work-study libr. tech. svcs. dept. Pub. Libr. of Youngstown (Ohio) and Mahoning County, 1988-91; catalog and ref. libr., instr. McGill Libr. Westminster Coll., New Wilmington, Pa., 1991-93; union catalog liaison INFOHio Project, Youngstown, 1996—. Contbr., reviewer: Plays for Children and Young Adults: An Evaluative Index and Guide, 1991. Mem. ALA, Assn. for Libr. Collections and Tech. Svcs., Pa. State U. Alumni Assn., Beta Phi Mu.

SRACIC, PAUL ALBERT, political scientist, writer; b. Morristown, N.J., Mar. 23, 1962; s. Albert and Elizabeth Sracic; m. Susan Yvonne Mark, Aug. 10, 1991; children: Katya, Anna. PhD, Rutgers U., 1993. Assoc. prof. polit. sci. Youngstown (Ohio) State U., 1992—. Author: (novels) Encyclopedia of American Parties, Campaigns, and Elections, 1999; contbr. chapters to books. Mem.: Am. Polit. Sci. Assn. Republican. Roman Catholic. Home: 1346 Valley View Dr Youngstown OH 44512 Office: Youngstown State U 1 University Plz Youngstown OH 44555 Home Fax: 330-742-3439; Office Fax: 330-742-3439. Business E-Mail: pasracic@cc.ysu.edu.

SREDNI, CLARITA, artist, educator; b. Bogota, Colombia, Sept. 11, 1948; came to U.S., 1997; d. Marco and Ana W. Sredni; children: Nicole Kassin, Mauricio Kassin, Allan Kassin. Asst. art editor Arte en colombia, Sante Fe de Bogota, 1978-80; graphic design dir. Alvaro Sanchez Mayarino, 1980-81; fashion designer Yves Saint Laurent, 1982-83; curator Galleria La Leyenda, Pre-Colombian Art Gallery, 1980-85; fashion illustration instr. Taller 5, 1986-87; asst. dir. Corpoacero, 1988-92. Solo exhbns. include Galeria San Diego, Santa Fe de Bogota, 1973, Galeria Escala, Santa Fe de Bogota, 1975, Galeria Gobernacion, Cali, Colombia, 1976; exhibited in group shows at Boston U., 1965, David Manzur Sch. Arts, Santa Fe de Bogota, 1969, Galeria 70, Santa Fe de Bogota, 1970, 71, Union Panamericana, Washington, 1973, Salon Anual de Agosto, Santa Fe de Bogota, 1973, 74, U. Antioquia, Medellin, Colombia, 1975, Mus. Contemporary Arts, Santa Fe de Bogota, 1975, 76, 76, 77, 78, Nat. Mus., Santa Fe de Bogota, 1976, Mus. Modern Arts La Tertulia, Cali, 1980, Barry U., Miami, Fla., 1989, Van Cleef Fine Arts, Miami, 1991, South Miami Art Inst., Dania, Fla., others; contbr. articles to profl. jours. Recipient Gran Menclon award Mus. Contemporary Art, Santa Fe de Bogota, 1974. Home: 9801 Collins Ave Apt 15Y Bal Harbour FL 33154-1830

SREEBNY, LEO M. oral biology and pathology educator; b. N.Y.C., Jan. 8, 1922; s. Morris and Lillie (Bogdanoff) S.; m. Mathilda H. Sternfeld, Mar. 9, 1945; children— Oren, Daniel. BA, U. Ill., 1942, D.D.S., 1945, MS, 1950, PhD, 1954; D (hon.), Semmelweis Med. U., 2001. With dept. periodontics U. Ill., 1948-57, asso. prof., 1956-57; asso. prof., chmn. dept. oral biology U. Wash., Seattle, 1957-60, prof., 1960-75; dir. U. Wash. (Center for Research Oral Biology), 1967-75; dean Sch. Dental Medicine, SUNY-Stony Brook, 1975-79, prof. dept. oral biology and pathology, 1979—. Cons. VA Hosp., Seattle, 1960— ; mem. dental study sect. NIH, 1964-68, chmn., 1967-68; mem. com. on sci. policy Nat. Acad. Sci., 1973-74; mem. med. adv. coun. Internat. Conf. on Integrative Medicine, 1998-99. Author: (with Julia Meyer) Secretory Mechanisms in Salivary Glands, 1963, The Salivary System, 1987, (with I. Van der Waal) Diseases of the Salivary Glands, 1997; contbr. numerous articles to sci., biol. jours. Mem. med. adv. bd. Sjogren's Syndrome Found., 1997, bd. govs. 1998—. Served with AUS, 1942-45; with USNR, 1946-48. Recipient Internat. Assn. for Dental Research Sci. award, 1969; Silver medal for contbns. to dental sci. and art City of Paris, 1979; Salivary Research Group Award, 1987. Mem. Fedn. Dentaire Internat. (chmn. sci. assembly com. 1973— , rep. UN Conf. on Youth 1983-84), Internat. Assn. Dental Research (bd. govs. 1981), Fedn. Dentaire Internat. (list of honor 1988), Am. Assn. Dental Research, ADA. Home: 35 Gnarled Hollow Rd East Setauket NY 11733-2929 Office: SUNY Stony Brook Sch Dental Medicine Stony Brook NY 11794-0001 E-mail: lsreebny@usa.net.

SREERAMA, KARUN, civil engineer; b. Hyderabad, India, Oct. 30, 1963; s. Kannaiah Naidu and Kamala Naidu S.; m. Sai L., Sept. 21, 1990; 1 child, Abhijit. BS in Civil Engring., Osmania U., Hyderabad, 1983; MS in Earthquake Engring., U. Roorkee, India, 1985; CPGS in Soil Mechanics, Cambridge U., 1986; PhD in Civil Engring., U. Mo., Rolla, 1990. Reg. profl. engr. Lectr. U. Roorkee, 1985; rsch. scholar Cambridge (Eng.) U., 1985-86; lab. mgr. U. Mo., Rolla, 1986-90; staff engr. Environ. Svc., Inc., Houston, 1990-91; project engr. Law Engring. and Environ. Svc., Inc., 1991-93, project mgr., 1993-95, prin., 1995-96. Co-author: Paper Machine Found., 1994; contbr. articles to Jour. ASCE. Cambridge-Nehru scholar Cambridge Commonwealth, 1985; Overseas Rsch. scholar award Rsch. Soc., 1986; recipient Rsch. Achievement awrd Sigma Xi Soc., 1989. Fellow Cambridge Commonwealth Soc.; mem. ASCE, Tech. Assn. Pulp Paper Industries. Home: 4406 Orange Leaf Ct Houston TX 77059-3166

SRERE, BENSON M. communications company executive, consultant; b. Rock Island, Ill, Aug. 13, 1928; s. Jacob H. and Margaret (Weinstein) S.; m. Betty Ann Cerruti, June 20, 1957; children: David Benson, Anne Michele, Peter John. BA magna cum laude, U. So. Calif., 1949. Newsman U.P., Los Angeles, 1948-56; assoc. editor Good Housekeeping mag., N.Y.C., 1956-59, sr. editor, 1959-67, asst. mng. editor, dir. spl. publs. div., 1967-68, mng. editor, 1968-72, exec. editor, v.p., 1972-75, v.p., editorial dir., 1975-76; v.p., gen. mgr. King Features Syndicate, 1976-81; v.p. Hearst Metrotone News, 1976-81; exec. asst. to pres. Hearst Corp., 1981—, v.p., 1983-94. Dir. Hearst/ABC Video Svcs., Hearst/ABC Viacom Entertainment Svcs., A&E Cable Network, Lifetime Cable Network. Trustee Optometric Center of N.Y. Found., 1978-79. Served with U.S. Army, 1950-52. Mem. Soc. Profl. Journalists, Phi Beta Kappa, Phi Kappa Phi, Phi Eta Sigma. Home: 11 Lafayette Ct Greenwich CT 06830-5324

SRERE, LINDA JEAN, former advertising executive; b. N.Y.C., Aug. 14, 1955; d. Rudolph Joseph and Muriel Evelyn (Weigand) Forquignon. BA, SUNY, Oswego, 1975. Asst. account exec. to acct. exec. BBDO, Inc., N.Y.C., 1975-79; v.p., account supr. Ogilvy and Mather, Inc., 1979-82, McCaffrey and McCall, Inc., N.Y.C., 1982; with Rosenfeld, Sirowitz, Humphrey, & Strauss, Inc., 1983-94, exec. v.p., 1986-90, pres., 1990-94; chmn. Earle, Palmer, Brown/N.Y., 1992-94; exec. v.p., dir. bus. devel. Young & Rubicam N.Y., 1994-95, head global new bus., 1995-96, group mng. dir., 1996-97, pres., CEO, 1997—2001, vice chmn., 1998—2001. Mem. Am. Mgmt. Assn., Young Pres.'s Orgn., Advt. Women of N.Y.*

SRI-JAYANTHA, SRI MUTHUTHAMBY, mechanical engineer; b. Jaffna, Tamil-Eelam, Ceylon, Jan. 24, 1954; came to U.S., 1977; s. Eliathamby Muthuthamby and Suntharesway Sittambalam; m. Avis Stair Harrell, Sept. 1, 1985; children: Darren K.B., Loren S.H., Dylan V.C. BSc in Mech. Engring., U. Sri Lanka, Colombo, 1977; MS in Mech. Engring., Pa. State U., 1979; MA in Mech./Aero. Engring., Princeton U., 1980, PhD in Mech./Aero Engring., 1983. Rsch. asst. Princeton (N.J.) U., 1979-83; mgr., mem. rsch. staff IBM Rsch., Yorktown Heights, N.Y., 1983-89, rsch. mgr., 1989—. Patentee in field; contbr. articles to profl. jours. Soccer referee. Mem. IEEE, Ilankai Tamil Sangam (gen. sec.). Avocations: promoting global human rights issues, listening to music, carpentry. Home: 32 Sherwood Ave Ossining NY 10562-3541 E-mail: srij@us.ibm.com.

SRINATH, LATHA, physician; b. Bangalore, India, Jan. 1, 1958; came to U.S., 1985; d. Krishna and Shamanthaka (Ananthachar) Iyengar; m. Sampath Holevanahalli Srinath, Jan. 22, 1984; children: Shilpa, Preetha. BS, Bangalore U., 1978; MB, BChir, Bangalore Med. Coll., 1984; MD, Georgetown U., 1990. Diplomate Am. Bd. Internal Medicine. Fellow in infectious diseases U. Louisville, 1992-94; pvt. practice Boynton Beach, Fla., 1994—. Staff Bethesda Meml. Hosp., Boynton Beach, 1994—, JFK Med. Ctr., Boynton Beach, 1994—; cons. HIV Adv. Bd., Fla., 1997—. Contbr. articles to profl. jours. Nat. Merit scholar, India, 1975. Mem. Am. Assn. Physicians from India, Fla. Med. Assn., Palm Beach Med. Soc. Hindu. Avocations: travel, yoga, tennis, oil painting, athletics. Home: 473 N Country Club Dr Lake Worth FL 33462-1003 Office: ID Cons Inc 2623 S Seacrest Blvd Boynton Beach FL 33435-7501 E-mail: lsrinath@idconsults.net.

SRINIVASA, VENKATARAMANIAH, engineer; b. Mysore, India, Aug. 30, 1941; came to U.S., 1968; s. Venkataramaniah and Gowramma S.; m. Janakimala Muthiah, June 1972; children: Supreeth, Suman. BSc, Mysore U., 1962, MSc, 1964; MS, Rutgers U., 1972, PhD, 1975. Rsch. fellow CFTRI, Mysore, 1964-67; tech. officer Indian Inst. Packaging, Bombay, 1967; rsch. intern, rsch. tching. asst. Rutgers U., New Brunswick, N.J., 1972-75, fellow Bur. Engring. Rsch., 1972-75; sr. packaging engr. Abbott Labs., Abbott Park, Ill., 1975-78, sr. project engr., 1978-83, mgr., 1983—. Mem. Inst. Packaging Profls., Soc. Plastics Engrs., Am. Chem. Soc., Am. Soc. Engring. Mgmt., N.Y. Acad. Sci., Sigma Xi. Home: 2729 Sallmon Ave Waukegan IL 60087-3514 E-mail: vasa.srinivasa@abbott.com.

SRINIVASAN, MANDYAM M. management educator, researcher; b. Madurai, Tamil Nadu, India, Aug. 11, 1950; s. Mandayam and Mythili Parthasarathy; m. Kanchana Chari, May 31, 1979; children: Tanushree, Madhushree. M in Tech., Indian Inst. of Tech., 1973; diploma in Bus., Indian Inst. of Mgmt., 1977; PhD, Northwestern U., 1985. Jr. engr. Mahindra & Mahindra Ltd., Mumbai, India, 1973—75, sr. engr. India, 1977—79; systems mgr. Hindustan Motors, Ltd., Trivellore, India, 1979—80; asst. prof. The U. of Mich., Ann Arbor, Mich., 1985—92; from assoc. prof. to prof. The U. of Tenn., Knoxville, Tenn., 1992—2002, the ball corp. disting. prof. of bus., 2002—. Cons. De Royal Industries, Powell, Tenn., 1999—2000. Contbr. articles to profl. jours.; editor: Internat. Jour. Flexible Mfg. Sys., 1992—, IIE Transactions, 2001 (Cert. of Excellence award, 2002). Grantee Rsch. grant, NSF, 1995—98. Mem.: Inst. for Ops. Rsch. and Mgmt. Sci. (coun. mem. telecom. sect. 1993—96). Office: The University of Tennessee 611 SMC Volunteer Boulevard Knoxville TN 37996 Office Fax: 865-974-8636. E-mail: msrini@utk.edu.

SRINIVASAN, RANGASWAMY, chemical physicist; b. Madras, India, Feb. 28, 1929; came to U.S., 1953; s. K. Rangaswamy. BSc with honors, Madras U., India, 1949; PhD, U. So. Calif., 1956. Mgr., rsch. T.J. Watson Rsch. Ctr. IBM, Yorktown Heights, N.Y., 1961-90; chief exec. officer UV Tech Assocs., Ossining, 1990—. Vis. rsch. prof. chemistry Ohio State U., Columbus, 1966-67, Wellman Lab., Mass. Gen. Hosp., Boston, 1987-89, Columbia-Presbyn. Med. Ctr., N.Y.C., 1984-90. Editor: (books) Organic Photochemical Syntheses, Vol. 1., 1972, Vol. 2, 1976; contbr. over 200 articles to profl. jours. Guggenheim fellow, 1966; recipient award for creative invention Am. Chem. Soc., 1997, Essalen award for chemistry in the pub. interest, 1997. Fellow AAAS, Am. Physical Soc. (Biol. Physics prize 1998), N.Y. Acad. Scis., Am. Soc. Laser Medicine and Surgery; mem. NAE. Achievements include invention of Ablative Photodecomposition, a laser technique for removal of microscopic thickness of organic matter such as plastics (of use in microelectronics) or tissue (of use in eye surgery).*

SRINIVASAN, VENKATARAMAN, marketing and management educator; b. Pudukkottai, Tamil Nadu, India, June 5, 1944; came to U.S., 1968; s. Annaswamy and Jambagalakshmi Venkataraman; m. Sitalakshmi Subrahmanyam, June 30, 1972; children: Ramesh, Mahesh. B Tech., Indian Inst. Tech., Madras, India, 1966; MS, Carnegie-Mellon U., 1970, PhD, 1971. Asst. engr. Larsen & Toubro, Bombay, 1966-68; asst. prof. mgmt. and mktg. U. Rochester, N.Y., 1971-73, assoc. prof., 1973-74, Stanford (Calif.) U., 1974-76, prof., 1976-82, dir. PhD program in bus., 1982-85, Ernest C. Arbuckle prof. mktg. and mgmt. sci., 1982—; mktg. area coord., 1976-78, 88-93, 2000—. Cons. in field. Mem. editorial bd. Jour. Mktg. Rsch., 1988—, Mktg. Sci., 1980—, Mgmt. Sci., 1974-91; contbr. articles to profl. jours. Mem. Am. Mktg. Assn., Inst. Ops. Rsch./Mgmt. Scis. Hindu. Avocation: classical music.

SRINIVASARAGHAVAN, JAGANNATHAN, forensic psychiatrist; b. May 13, 1950; naturalized U.S. citizen; MD, Thanjavur Med. Coll./U. Madras, 1974. Diplomate in psychiatry and forensic psychiatry Am. Bd. Psychiatry and Neurology. Rotating intern Thanjavur Med. Coll. Affiliated Hosps., 1973-74; resident in internal medicine Madras Med. Coll. and Govt. Gen. Hosp., 1974-77; resident in psychiatry U. Health Scis./Chgo. Med. Sch. Affiliated Hosps., 1977-80; chief resident St. Mary of Nazareth Hosp., Chgo., 1979-80; staff psychiatrist VA Med. Ctr., North Chicago, 1981-86, ECT unit dir., 1990-94; acting chief psychiatry, 1993; various positions including chief psychiatry svc. VA Med. Ctr., Canandaigua, N.Y., 1994-98; med. dir. Clyde L. Choate Mental Health and Devel. Ctr., Anna, Ill., 1998—; clin. assoc. prof. psychiatry U. Rochester, N.Y., 1994-98; prof. clin. psychiatry So. Ill. U. Sch. Medicine, 1998—. Contbr. articles to Comprehensive Psychiatry, Violence and Victims, others. Recipient numerous awards and commendations. Fellow: Am. Psychiat. Assn. (pres. Asian Am. Caucus 1999—); mem.: India Assn. So. Ill. (v.p. 1999—2000), India Med. Assn., Am. Assn. Psychiatrists from India, Indo-Am. Psychiat. Assn. (life; treas. 1994—96, sec. 1996—98, pres.-elect 1998—2000, pres. 2000—02), Internat. Acad. Law and Mental Health, Am. Acad. Psychiatry and the Law (counselor, chair internat. rels. com.), Ill.

Psychiat. Soc. (downstate councilor 2001—). Office: Clyde L Choat MH and Devel Ctr 1000 N Main St Anna IL 62906-1652 also: So Ill U Sch Medicine PO Box 19230 Springfield IL 62794-9230

SRIVASTAVA, RADHEY SHYAM, scientist, researcher; b. Bahadurganj, India, June 7, 1931; s. Umeshwar Prasad and Ganesha Devi; m. Vijay Laxmi, Feb. 12, 1959; children: Suneeta, Sanjay, Sangita. BSc, Lucknow (India) U., 1951, MSc, 1953, PhD, 1963, cert. in French, 1957. Rsch. fellow, lectr. Lucknow U., 1954-56, 56-57; jr. sci. officer Def. Sci. Lab., New Delhi, 1958-61, sr. sci. officer, 1961-71, prin. sci. officer, 1971-80; dep. chief sci. officer Def. Sci. Ctr., 1980-91; pvt. rschr., 1991—. Postdoctoral rsch. fellow Royal Soc. London, Imperial Coll. Sci. and Tech., 1965; vis. scientist MRL, Melbourne, Australia, 1983, Inst. Aerospace Studies, Toronto, Can., 1980, Chiba U., 1991; vis. prof. Ernst Mach Inst., Freiburg, Germany, 1995, Tohoku U., Sendai, Japan, 2000, Chiba (Japan) U., 2000, Tokyo Denki U., 2001; mem. organizing com. winter sch. in physiol. fluid dynamics, 1975. Author: Turbulence (Pipe Flows), 1977, Interaction of Shock Waves, 1994; contbr. to profl. publs. Mem. gen. body Welfare Assn., New Delhi, 1985—. Grantee Def. Rsch. Can., 1980, USAF, 1980, Min. Def., New Delhi, 1983, Min. Edn. Japan, Chiba, 1991. Fellow Nat. Acad. Scis.; mem. Bharat Ganita Parishad (life), Indian Sci. Congress, Sci. Officer's Assn. Hindu. Achievements include development of Srivastava's Theory. Avocations: music, movies, sports. Home and Office: A-3/260 Janakpuri New Delhi 110058 India E-mail: ssmiriti@bol.net.in.

SRIVASTAVA, VISHNU CHANDRA, agronomy educator; b. Darvhanga, India, Jan. 20, 1943; s. Kailash and Chandrawati (Devi) Prasad; m. Kiran Verma, May 17, 1970; children: Rajinish, Manish. BS, Bihar U., Muzaffarpur, India, 1963; MS, Ranchi U., India, 1966; PhD, Moscow Agrl. Acad., 1973. Lectr. Ranchi Agrl. Coll., India, 1967-74; asst. prof., agronomist Birsa Agrl. U., Ranchi, 1974-78, assoc. prof., sr. scientist, 1978-86, additional dir. rsch., 1986-87, dean faculty agrl., 1994-95, 97—, prof., chief scientist, chmn., head agronomy, 1986-99. Cons. World Bank, Winrock Internat., 1993-94; cons. in field. Contbr. over 150 articles to profl. jours. Recipient Cert. of Appreciation for rsch. achievement USDA, 1991. Fellow Indian Soc. Agronomy (life), Indian Sci. Congress, Indian Soc. Soil Sci. Avocations: painting, photography, chess. Home: H/80 Argora Housing Colony Ranchi 834002 India Office: Birsa Agrl U Dept Agronomy Kanke Ranchi 834006 India

SROGE, MAXWELL HAROLD, marketing consultant, publishing executive; b. N.Y.C., Oct. 9, 1927; s. Albert N. and Goldie (Feldman) S.; children: Roberta, David, Marc, Sarah. Student, CCNY, 1946-48, NYU, 1948, New Sch. Social Research, 1948. Dir. sales Bell & Howell Co., Chgo., 1950-60, dir. prodn. planning, 1961-62, pres. Robert Maxwell div., 1962-63; pres. Maxwell Sroge Co., Inc., Chgo., 1965—, Telespond, Inc., Chgo., 1971—, Maxwell Sroge Pub., Inc., Chgo., 1976—. Chmn. JUF Comm. Industry, 1974-75, Transatlantic Catalogue Corp.; chmn. Direct Mktg. Svcs., Inc.; pub. Non-Store Mktg. Report, Inside Leading Mail Order Houses, Mail Order Industry Ann. Report, Best in Catalogs, How to Create Successful Catalogs, The Catalog Marketer, 101 Ideas for More Profitable Catalogs; bd. dirs. Tools Direct, DMSI; chmn. Telespond Inc. Mem. New Ill. Com., 1965; speakers bur. Percy for Gov., 1964, Citizens for Percy, 1972; co-chmn. Percy for Pres. Exploratory Com., 1974; mem. regional adv. bd. Nat. Jewish Hosp., 1974-75; mem. devel. com. WTTW-Channel 11, 1975-76, NCCJ; founder Save the Tarryall, Inc., 1982. Served with USNR, World War II. Mem. Direct Mail Mktg. Assn. (Gold Mail Box award 1978, Internat. Gold Carrier Pigeon award 1979), Nat. Retail Merchants Assn., Retail Advt. Conf., World Futures Soc. E-mail: msroge@catalog-news.com. *To succeed man must stretch himself, his mind, his heart, his grasp. Our capabilities far exceed our accomplishments. Within each of us there is the potential for greatness if we will dig deep enough to find it. Those of us who have been blessed to have discovered success owe a special responsibility to the world around us to make it a better place for all men to live.*

SROKA, JOHN WALTER, trade association executive; b. Perth Amboy, N.J., July 24, 1946; s. John and Mary (Teliszewski) S.; m. Paula J. Devitt, Aug. 17, 1968; children: Amanda, Alexandra. BA in Psychology, Fairleigh Dickinson U., 1968, postgrad., 1968-69; postgrad. in law, Am. U., 1972-73. Asst. exec. dir. Associated Gen. Contractors of Am., Washington, 1973-87; exec. v.p. Nat. Assn. Sheet Metal and Air Conditioning Contractors, Chantilly, Va., 1987—. Sgt. U.S. Army, 1969-71. Mem. Am. Soc. Assn. Execs. Roman Catholic. Office: SMACNA 4201 Lafayette Center Dr Chantilly VA 20151-1219 E-mail: jsroka@smacna.org.

STAAB, DIANE D. lawyer; BA, CUNY Hunter Coll., 1977; JD, Yeshiva U., 1980. Bar: N.Y. 1981. Assoc. atty. Hall, McNicol, Hamilton & Clark, 1980-84, Patterson, Belknap, Webb & Tyler, 1984-87; corp. counsel Internat. Paper Co., 1987—95; v.p., gen. counsel, corp. ethics/environ. compliance officer Ariz. Chem., Panama City, 1996—2001; gen. counsel Internat. Paper Europe, 2001—. Mem. ABA (mem. bus. law sect. fed. ref. of securities com. 1988-2001, vice-chmn. com. on corp. & bus. legis. subcom. on corp. governance 1992-98), Assn. of the Bar of the City of N.Y. (mem. spl. com. on election law 1987-89, mem. corp. law com. 1989-92, sec. com. on corp. law dept. 1992-93). Office: Internat Paper Europe Chausee de la Hulpe 166 1170 Brussels Belgium

STAAB, MICHAEL JOSEPH, lawyer; b. Hays, Kans., Oct. 12, 1955; s. Robert Joseph and Beatrice Agnes (Schenk) S.; m. Kathy Lee Brock, Jan. 11, 1986; children: Colton Brock, Matthew Michael. BA magna cum laude, Ft. Hays State U., 1978; JD, Drake U., 1981; LLM in Health Law, DePaul U., 1993. Bar: Idaho 1981, U.S. Dist. Ct. Idaho 1981, Utah 1986, U.S. Dist. Ct. Utah 1986, Ill. 1990, U.S. Dist. Ct. (no. dist.) Ill. 1990. Assoc. Quane, Smith, Howard and Hull, Boise, Idaho, 1981-83, Meuleman & Miller, Boise, 1983; pvt. practice, 1983-85; ptnr. Biele, Haslam & Hatch, Salt Lake City, 1985-89, Parsons, Behle & Latimer, Salt Lake City, 1989-90; assoc. Steinberg, Polacek & Goodman, Chgo., 1990-93, Ruff, Weldenaar and Reidy, Ltd., Chgo., 1994-96; ptnr. Gardner, Carton and Douglas, 1996—. Mem. Chgo. adv. bd. Drake U., 1996—2001; bd. counselors Drake U. Law Sch., 2001—; adv. bd. Health Law Inst., DePaul U. Coll. Law, 2002—; lectr. in field. Contbr. articles to legal publs. Bd. dirs. Winnetka Village Caucus, 1992—94, Big Bros./Big Sisters, Salt Lake City, 1985—89, Utah Head Injury Assn., Salt Lake City, 1988—90, Pediat. Brain Injury Assn., Salt Lake City, 1988—90; pack master Cub Scouts 15, 1999—. Mem. ABA, Ill. Bar Assn., Chgo. Bar Assn., Nat. Health Lawyers Assn., Nat. Order of Barristers, Order of Omega, K.C., Phi Kappa Phi, Phi Alpha Theta, Phi Eta Sigma. Roman Catholic. Avocations: bicycling, reading, basketball, baseball, antiques. Home: 173 De Windt Rd Winnetka IL 60093-3708 Office: 321 N Clark St Chicago IL 60610-4714 E-mail: mstaab@gcd.com.

STAAB, STEVEN ALAN, school counselor; b. Beaver Dam, Wis., Oct. 10, 1952; s. William Morton and Ruth Louise Staab; m. Margaret Ellen Brown, Dec. 20, 1986; children: Shane, Brenden. B of Social Welfare, U. Wis., Whitewater, 1975; M of Counseling, Ariz. State U., 1984. Lic. profl. counselor. Counselor, student affairs dir. Universal Tech. Inst., Phoenix, 1983-88; counselor Hilltop Inst., Running Springs, Calif., 1988—89; dir. guidance dept. Washakie Sch. Dist. #1, Worland, Wyo., 1989—. Adj. instr. N.W. Coll., Powell, Wyo., 1992-94; counselor Washakie Mental Health, Worland, 1990-96. Coord. Washakie Bridge Builders, Worland, 1999—; bd. dirs. Worland C. of C., 2000—; pres. bd. Big Horn Adolescent Programs, Basin, Wyo., 1992—; chmn. Washakie Youth Alternatives, Worland, 1992-98; mem. Wyo. Selective Svc. Bd., Cheyenne, 2000—. Mem. ACA, Assn. Career and Tech. Edn., Kiwanis (bd. dirs. 2000-2001). Avocations: reading, hiking, snow skiing. Office: Wakashie Sch Dist # 1 1900 Howell Ave Worland WY 82401

STAAB, THOMAS EUGENE, chemist; b. Peoria, Ill., Jan. 26, 1941; s. Leo Reuben and Mary Blanche (Griffin) S.; m. Donna Marie Murnighan, May 30, 1967; children: Lynn Anne, Thomas Patrick. BS in Chemistry, St. Louis U., 1963. R&D chemist for elastomers Victor Products divsn. Dana Corp., Chgo., 1963-65, application engr. for oil seals, 1965-68, application engring. supr. for oil seals, 1968-70, chief product engr. for oil seals, 1970-72, mgr. sales and engring. Ft. Wayne, Ind., 1973-75, prodn. supr., 1975-77, materials engr. for gaskets, 1977-79, mgr. oil seal engring. Lisle, Ill., 1979-82, chief devel. engr. materials, 1982-83, prodn. area mgr., 1983-84, mgr. materials devel., 1984-86, mgr. tech. svcs., 1986-90, environ. mgr., 1990-92, sen. tech. svc. engr., 1992-96, sr. materials engr., 1996-2001, Dana Corp., Victor Reinz divsn., Lisle, 2001—. New products mgr. Dana Corp., Lisle, 2001—. Alliance chief Y Indian Guides, 1975-76; mgr., coach Little League, 1978-81. Mem. Rubbers Mfrs. Assn. (past chmn. oil seal tech. com.), Soc. Automotive Engrs. (past mem. adv. bd. of sealing com.), Am. Chem. Soc. Roman Catholic. Achievements include, patentee hydrodynamic shaft seal, rotary shaft seals, antistick, non-liquid absorbing gasket, reinforced core heavy duty gasket. Home: 1 W Superior St Apt 4802 Chicago IL 60610-8865 Office: 1945 Ohio St Lisle IL 60532-2169

STAAB, THOMAS ROBERT, consumer product company financial executive; b. Beaver Falls, Pa., Apr. 23, 1942; s. Henry Louis and Margaret Constance (Clarke) S.; m. Angela Maria Simon, Aug. 6, 1965; children: Thomas II, Jennifer, Thea. BBA, U. Pitts., 1964, MBA, 1965. CPA, Pa. Sr. audit mgr. Price Waterhouse & Co., Pitts., 1970-77; practice fellow Fin. Acctg. Standards Bd., Stamford, Conn., 1978-80; dir. corp. acctg. and taxes Fieldcrest Cannon Inc., Eden, N.C., 1981-84, asst. contr., 1985, contr., 1986-91, v.p. fin., 1992-93, CFO, 1994-97; bd. dirs., sr. v.p., CFO Lorillard Inc., Greensboro, 1998—. Mem. adv. bd. Arkwright Mut. Ins. Co. Served to lt. USN, 1966-70. Mem. AICPA, Pa. Inst. CPAs. Republican. Roman Catholic. Home: 3726 NC # 65 Reidsville NC 27320 Office: Lorillard Inc PO Box 10529 714 Green Valley Rd Greensboro NC 27404-0529

STAATS, DEAN ROY, retired reinsurance executive; b. Somerville, N.J., Sept. 18, 1924; s. Roy Theodore and Mabel Ellen (Rhodes) S.; m. Marilyn Ann Hockenbury, 1947 (div. 1956; 1 child, Barry Clinton; m. Marilyn Lee Truitt, Dec. 16, 1961 B.Sc., Brown U., 1946, MA, 1948. Asst. actuary N.Am. Reassurance Co., N.Y.C., 1959-67, data processing officer, 1967-69, v.p., actuary, 1969-71, sr. v.p., 1971-84, exec. v.p., 1984-86; pres., dir. NARe Life Mgmt. Co., 1985-86; rep. Life Ins. Guaranty Corp, 1977-86; U.S. mgr. Can. Reassurance Co., 1984-86; cons. actuary, 1986-89. Served to lt. (j.g.), USN, 1943-46, PTO Fellow Soc. Actuaries; mem. Am. Acad. Actuaries N.Y. Jr. Actuaries Club (pres. 1960-61), Soc. Actuaries (reins. adminstrn. com. 1984-85) Clubs: Anchor and Saber (pres. 1959-60). Republican. Avocations: art collectibles; tennis; gardening; travel. Home and Office: 3 Post Run Newtown Square PA 19073-3014

STAATS, PETER S. pain medicine physician, surgeon; b. Phoenix, May 22, 1963; s. Arthur Wilbur and Carolyn (Kaiden) S.; m. Nancy Elizabeth Staats, Oct. 26, 1991; children: Alyssa, Dylan, Rachel. BSBA, JU. Calif., Santa Barbara, 1985; MD, U. Mich., 1989. Residency in anesthesia & critical care Johns Hopkins U., Balt., 1990-92, pain medicine fellow, 1992-94, chief, divsn. pain medicine, 1994—. Assoc. prof. anesthesia and oncology, Johns Hopkins U., 1994—. Contbr. more than 50 peer-reviewed articles to profl. jours.; inventor in field of pain management. Mem. Am. Pain Soc. (bd. dirs. 2000—), Nat. Pain Found. (bd. dirs. 1999—), Am. Neuromodulation Soc., So. Pain Soc. (pres. 2000—, Distinguished Svc. award 2001). Office: Johns Hopkins U 550 N Broadway Baltimore MD 21205 E-mail: pstaats@jhmi.edu.

STAATS, THOMAS ELWYN, neuropsychologist; s. Percy Anderson and Julia (Bourmorck) S.; m. Debra R.; children: Lauren Malu, Kara Kristyn, Stacy Rhnea, Ronald Derek. BA cum laude, Emory U., 1970; MA, U. Ala., 1972, PhD, 1974; postgrad., U. Tex., Tyler, 1992. Diplomate Am. Bd. Profl. Disability Cons.; lic. psychologist. Dir., chief psychologist Caddo Parish Diagnostic Ctr., Shreveport, La., 1974-81; exec. dir. Doctors Psychol. Ctr., 1979-91, Comprehensive Assessments, 1991—. Cons. to Charter Forest Hosp., Shreveport Impairment and Disability Evaluation Ctr.; neuropsychol. cons. dept. psychiatry La. State U. Med. Ctr.; clin. assoc. prof. psychology La. State U., Shreveport, 1977—, clin. assoc. prof. psychiatry Sch. Medicine, 1980-93; mem. faculty Am. Acad. Disability Evaluating Physicians, Health South Impairment Evaluation Lectr. Series, 1998—. Author: Manual for the Stress Vector Analysis Test Series, 1983, The Doctors Guide to Instant Stress Relief, 1987, Stress Management and Relaxation Training System Handbook; contbr. articles to profl. jours. and popular mags. Mem. Gov.'s Com. of 1000, La., 1979. Recipient AADEP award, 1991; Grad. Rsch. Coun. fellow, 1974. Fellow Am. Inst. Stress; mem. APA, Nat. Acad. Neuropsychology, Nat. Register of Health Svc. Providers. Episcopalian. Avocations: scuba diving, gun collecting, camping, boating, paintball competition. Home: 10816 Sunrise Pt Shreveport LA 71106-9357 Office: Comprehensive Assessments Inc 1801 Fairfield Ave Ste 201 Shreveport LA 71101-4460

STAB, MARTIN JOSEPH, SR. computer technician, writer; b. New Brunswick, NJ, Sept. 16, 1943; s. Oswald Stab; m. Elaine Rose Carbonarro; children: Paul, Charles, Brian, Martin, Jr. AA, Middlesex County Coll., Edison, N.J., 1975—78. Cert. A+ BancTec Corporation 2000. Comm. technician USAF, Vandenberg A.F.B., Calif., 1961—64; hardware instr. Unysis Corp., Princeton, NJ, 1979—81; tech. rep. Xerox Corp., 1966—84. Mem. Bd. of Adjustment, Lakehurst, NJ, 1982—83; Referee N.J. Youth Soccer Association, Belmar, 1982—86. E-4 Air Force, 1961—64, Vandenberg, Ca. Recipient Par Club, Xerox Corp., 1975. Roman Catholic. Avocation: woodworking.

STABA, EMIL JOHN, pharmacognosy and medicinal chemistry educator; b. N.Y.C., May 16, 1928; s. Frank and Marianna T. (Mack) P.; m. Joyce Elizabeth Ellert, June 19, 1954; children— Marianna, Joanna, Sarah Jane, John, Mark. BS cum laude, St. John's U., 1952; MS, Duquesne U., 1954; PhD, U. Conn., 1957. Asst. prof. U. Nebr., 1957-60, prof., chmn. dept., 1968; prof. dept. pharmacognosy U. Minn., 1968—; interim dir. R&D Tom's of Main, Kennebunk, 1996—. Pres. Plants Personified, Inc., 1995—; cons. econs. plants and plant tissue culture U.S. Army Q.M.C.; cons. on drug plants and plant tissue culture NASA; cons. N.C.I. at NIH on anti-cancer natural product prodn., 1991-92; cons. Govt. of Korea, food and pharm. industry cons. NSF-Egyptian Acad. Sci. Rsch. Tech., 1984—; internat. vis. prof. Dalhousie U., 1983; cons. on Indonesia biotech. devel. World Bank-Midwestern Univs. Consortium for Internat. Activities, 1985-90, Thailand, 1989; mem. natural products revision com. U.S. Pharmacopeia, 1980—, chair subcom. natural products, 1995-2000; mem. adv. coun. on life scis. NASA, 1984-87. Mem. editorial bd.: Jour. Plant Cell, Tissue and Organ Culture, 1980-86, plant cellular and developmental biology sect. of In Vitro, 1988— Served with USNR, 1945-46, PTO. Sr. fgn. fellow NSF, Poland, 1969; Fulbright fellow, Germany, 1970; Coun. Sci. and Indsl. Rsch.-NSF fellow, India, 1973, Pakistani Coun. Sci. and Indsl. Rsch.-NSF fellow, Pakistan, 1978; fellow U.K. Sci. Engring. Rsch. Coun., 1989. Fellow AAAS; mem. Am. Soc. Pharmacognosy (pres. 1971-72), Am. Assn. Colls. Pharmacy (chmn. tchrs. sect. 1972-73, dir. 1976-77), Tissue Culture Assn. (pres. plant sect. 1972-74), Am. Pharm. Assn. and Acad. (chmn. pharmacognosy and nat. products 1977), Soc. Econ. Botany, Am. Soc. Pharmacognosy (hon.), Am. Soc. Pharmacognosy, Plants Personified, Inc. (pres. 1995—). Home: 2840 Stinson Blvd Minneapolis MN 55418-3127 Office: U Minn Coll Pharmacy Unit F-9106 Minneapolis MN 55455 E-mail: staba001@tc.umn.edu.

STABEJ, RUDOLPH JOHN, computer consultant; b. Milw., Dec. 14, 1952; s. Rudolf and Katharina (Schaab) S. BS in Acctg., U. Ill., Chgo., 1975; MBA in Fin., De Paul U., 1981, MS in Computer Sci., 1986. Gen. acct. Field Mus. Nat. History, Chgo., 1975-77, Victor Bus. Products, Chgo., 1977-80, Northrop Def. Systems, Rolling Meadows, Ill., 1981-82; programmer Fed. Reserve Bank, Chgo., 1983-84; programmer/analyst Arthur Andersen & Co., 1984-85; cons./programmer Sycomm Systems Corp., 1985-86; pvt. practice computer cons., 1986—. Mem. Ind. Computer Cons. Assn., Assn. Info. Tech. Profls. Avocations: tennis, golf, stamp collecting. Home: 1004 Bayshore Dr Schaumburg IL 60194-1304

STABENAU, WALTER FRANK, systems engineer; b. Cleve., Apr. 24, 1942; s. Walter Kurt and Helen (Koris) S.; m. Mary Catherine Bishop, Nov. 20, 1971; children: Elizabeth Ann, Derek Walter. BS in Physics, Case Inst. Tech., 1964; PhD in Nuclear Sci., Cornell U., 1969. Computer programmer Air Force Logistics Commd., Wright Patterson AFB, Ohio, 1970-74; navigation analyst Logicon, Inc., Dayton, 1974-80; sonar engr. Gen. Electric, Syracuse, N.Y., 1980-84; prin. systems engr. RCA Corp., Moorestown, N.J., 1984-86, mgr. combat systems analysis, 1986-89, project mgr., 1989-92; cons. Sonalysts Inc., Willingboro, 1992-94; prin. analyst Applied Physics Lab., Laurel, Md., 1994-96; sr. tech. specialist Boeing Helicopters, Phila., 1996-99; lead mem. engring. staff Lockheed-Martin Naval Electronic Sys., Morrestown, N.J., 1999—. Contbr. articles to profl. jours. Mem. Am. Helicopter Soc. Avocation: stamp collecting. Home: 1543 Silo Rd Morrisville PA 19067-4259 E-mail: walter.f.stabenau@lmco.com., walter.stabenau@verizon.net.

STABENOW, DEBORAH ANN, senator, former congresswoman; b. Gladwin, Mich., Apr. 29, 1950; d. Robert Lee and Anna Merle (Hallmark) Greer; children: Todd Dennis, Michelle Deborah. BS magna cum laude, Mich. State U., 1972, MSW magna cum laude, 1975. With spl. svcs. Lansing (Mich.) Sch. Dist., 1972-73; county commr. Ingham County, Mason, Mich., 1975-78; state rep. State of Mich., Lansing, 1979—, state senator, 1990—94; mem. 103rd-106th Congress from Mich. 8th dist. U.S. Ho. Reps.; senator State of Mich., 2000—. Founder Ingham County Women's Commn.; co-founder Council Against Domestic Assault. Recipient Service to Children award Council for Prevention of Child Abuse and Neglect, 1983, Disting. Service to Mich. Families award Mich. Council Family Relations, 1983, Outstanding Leadership award Nat. Council Community Mental Health Ctrs., 1983, Snyder-Kok award Mental Health Assn. Mich., Awareness Leader of Yr. award Awareness Communications Team Developmentally Disabled, 1984, Communicator of Yr. award Woman in Communications, 1984, Lawmaker of Yr. award Nat. Child Support Enforcement Assn., 1985, Disting. Service award Lansing Jaycees, 1985, Disting. Service in Govt. award Retarded Citizens of Mich., 1986, Boxing Glove award Nat. Com. to Preserve Social Security and Medicare, 1999, Home Health Hero Nat. Assn. for Home Care, 1999, Friend of Farm Bur. Mich. Farm Bur., 1999, Leadership award Nat. Coun. of Space Grant Dirs., 1998, Outstanding Achievement Nat. Farmers Union, 1998, Legislator of Yr. award Nat. Multiple Sclerosis Soc., 1992, Assn. for Children's Mental Health, 1991, Mich. Assn. of Vol. Adminstrs., 1989, Citizens Alliace to Uphold Spl. Edn., 1989, Recognition award State 4-H Alumni, 1991, Cmty. award Mich. Mental Health, 1988; named One of Ten Outstanding Young Ams. Jaycees, 1986. Mem. NAACP, Lansing Regional C. of C., Delta Kappa Gamma. Office: US Senate 702 Hart Senate Office Bldg Washington DC 20510 E-mail: senator@stabenow.senate.gov.*

STABER, DOROTHEE BEATRICE, administrative assistant; b. Frankfurt am Main, Germany, Jan. 19, 1961; came to U.S., 1983; d. Rolf Joachim and Sibylle Dorothee (Grafin von Nostitz) Kundahl; m. Harley Joseph Staber; children: Marina Inez, Christopher Patrick. Student, Goethe U., Frankfurt, 1981-83; BBA, U. North Tex., 1987; postgrad., U. Dallas, 1990-93. Sales asst. Xerox Corp., Irving, Tex., 1987-88; asst. mgr. Pioneer Life Ins. Co., 1988-89; adminstrv. asst. Howard Hughes Med. Inst., Dallas, 1989—2001, lab. mgr., 2001—. Mem. Beta Gamma Sigma. Office: Howard Hughes Med Inst 5323 Harry Hines Blvd Dallas TX 75390-9050 E-mail: Dorothee.Staber@utsouthwestern.edu.

STABILE, BRUCE EDWARD, surgeon; b. Monterey Park, Calif., Apr. 14, 1944; s. Edward Emilio and Angela (Cramandozzi) S.; m. Caroline Graston, Sept. 18, 1967; children: Jessica, Drew. BA, UCLA, 1966; MD, U. Calif., San Francisco, 1970. Diplomate Am. Bd. Surgery. From asst. prof. to assoc. prof. UCLA Sch. Medicine, 1977-85; from assoc. prof. to prof. surgery U. Calif. San Diego Sch. Medicine, 1985-93; prof. surgery UCLA Sch. Medicine, 1993—, vice chmn. dept. surgery, 1993—. Chmn. dept. surgery Harbor-UCLA Med. Ctr., Torrance, 1993—, acting med. dir., 1997-98; interim assoc. dean UCLA Sch. Medicine, 1997-98, 93-; med. expert Med. Bd. Calif., 1980—. Fellow ACS (gov. 2002-), Am. Surg. Assn., Am. Bd. Surgery (dir.); mem. Soc. Univ. Surgeons, Assn. Acad. Surgery, Am. Gastroenterol. Assn., San Diego Soc. Gen. Surgeons (pres. 1992-93), L.A. Surg. Soc. (pres. 2000-01). Office: Harbor UCLA Med Ctr 1000 W Carson St Torrance CA 90502-2004

STABILE, CHRISTOPHER MICHAEL, secondary school educator; b. N.Y.C., Aug. 2, 1972; s. Louis Ralph and Elizabeth Ann Stabile. BS, Nova Southeastern U., 1994, MA, 1996, EdD, 2002. Cert. tchr. Fla. Grad. rschr. Nova Southeastern U., Ft. Lauderdale, 1994-96; social sci. tchr. Broward Sch. Bd., 1996-2001; instr. City Coll., 2000—. Mem. Dem. Orgn., Ft. Lauderdale, 1997. Mem. Am. Ednl. Rsch. Assn., Am. Philos. Assn., Cambridge Ctr. for Behavioral Studies, Phi Delta Kappa. Democrat. Avocations: collecting antiques and books, watching movies, collecting antique weapons, reading, water activities. Home: 5645 SW 87th Ave Cooper City FL 33328 E-mail: stabilem@nova.edu.

STABILE, DONALD ROBERT, economics educator, academic administrator; b. N.Y.C., Mar. 7, 1944; s. Jerome Joseph Stabile and Nancy Hope (Wishen) Lamb. BS, U. Fla., 1966; MA, U. Mass., 1972, PhD, 1979. Vice pres. Dixie Music Co., Ft. Pierce, Fla., 1966-68; statistician Standard & Poors Corp., N.Y.C., 1968-70; assoc. editor Nat. Assn. Accts., 1972-74; asst. prof. econs. Drury Coll., Springfield, Mo., 1978-80, St. Mary's Coll., St. Mary's City, 1980-85, assoc. prof., 1985-89, prof., 1989—, chair econs. dept., 1994—96, 1998—2002, assoc. provost, 1996—98, St. Mary's Coll. Md., St. Mary's City, 2002—; dir. St. Mary's Ctr. for Econ. Edn., 1982-94; NEH summer seminar leader St. Mary's Coll. Md., St. Mary's City, 1987, 93, liberal arts chair, 2000—. Columnist Enterprise newspaper, Lexington Park, Md., 1983-85; prin. rschr. CH Assocs., Inc., Silver Spring, Md., 1987-94; book reviewer Bus. Libr. Rev., 1990-2002; faculty fellow Students in Free Enterprise, 1991-92; mng. dir. Bayesian Edge Tech. Solutions, Inc., Ridge, Md., 2000—. Author: Prophets of Order, 1984, Activist Unionism, 1993, Work and Welfare, 1996, The Origins of American Public Finance, 1998, Community Associations, 2000; co-author: ABC's of Economics, 1985, The Public Debt of the U.S., 1991; assoc. editor for econs. Bus. Libr. Rev., 1993-2002; assoc. editor: Essays in Economic and Business History, 1998-99; mem. editorial bd. Jour. Econ. Issues, 1993-97; contbr. articles to profl. jours. and reference works. Vol. ride-a-bike Assn. for Retarded Citizens, Lexington Park, 1982-84; VITA organizer IRS, St. Mary's City, 1983; essay judge Hugh O'Brien Youth Found., Balt., 1984-2002. Recipient Faculty-Student Life award St. Mary's Coll., 1984, CDC Investment Mgmt. Corp. award, 1998. Fellow Lambda Alpha Internat. (Yeager Endowed Chair St. Mary's Coll. 2000—); mem. Am. Econ. Assn., Econ. and Bus. Hist. Soc., Bus. History Conf., Assn. for Evolutionary Econs., So. Econ. Assn., Indsl. Rels. Rsch. Assn., Social Sci. History Assn., Beta Gamma Sigma. Avocations: cycling, running, sailing. Home: PO Box 201 Park Hall MD 20667-0201 Office: St Marys Coll Md Saint Marys City MD 20686 E-mail: drstabile@smcm.edu.

STABLER, LEWIS VASTINE, JR. lawyer; b. Greenville, Ala., Nov. 5, 1936; s. Lewis Vastine and Dorothy Daisy Stabler; m. Monteray Scott, Sept. 5, 1958; children: Dorothy Monteray Scott, Andrew Vastine, Monteray Scott Smith, Margaret Langston. BA, Vanderbilt U., 1958; JD with distinction, U. Mich., 1961. Bar: Ala. 1961. Assoc. Cabaniss & Johnston, Birmingham, Ala., 1961-67; assoc. prof. law U. Ala., 1967-70; ptnr. Cabaniss, Johnston, Gardner, Dumas & O'Neal (and predecessor firms), Birmingham, 1970-91, Walston, Stabler, Wells, Anderson and Bains, Birmingham, 1991-97; pvt. practice, 1997—. Mem. com. of 100 Candler Sch. Theology, Emory U. Bd. editors: Mich. Law Rev, 1960-61. Fellow Am. Bar Found. (life); mem. Am. Law Inst., Ala. Law Inst. (mem. council, dir. 1968-70), ABA, Ala. Bar Assn., Birmingham Bar Assn., Am. Judicature Soc., Am. Assn. Railroad Trial Counsel, Order of Coif. Methodist (cert. lay speaker). Clubs: Country of Birmingham, Rotary. Home: 3538 Victoria Rd Birmingham AL 35223-1404 Office: PO Box 53-1161 Birmingham AL 35253-1161

STABLER, NANCY RAE, infosystems specialist; b. Elgin, Ill., June 15, 1946; d. Raymond Herman and Eleanora Marie (Gaedke) Redmer, m. Jay Stabler, Mar. 28, 1970; 1 child: Andrea Marie. AAS with honors, Elgin Community Coll., 1982, AA with Honors, 1985. Programmer, analyst Houghton-Mifflin, Geneva, 1966-77; project leader Kane County, 1978-83; sys. designer Burgess Norton, 1983-87; human resources telecomm. specialist Recon/Optical, Barrington, Ill., 1987-91; MIS project mgr., comml. sys. Advance Transformer, Rosemont, 1991—. Tutor Elgin (Ill.) Community Coll., 1983—. Home: 2305 Bluejay Trl Elgin IL 60123-4701 Office: Advance Transformer 10275 W Higgins Rd Fl 6 Rosemont IL 60018-5625

STABY, JACK BRADFORD, cost engineer, retired; b. Mineola, N.Y., Mar. 20, 1926; s. Ernest John and Arlene Katherine (Kramer) S.; m. Dorothy Louise Sheffield; children: John Bradford, Robert Stanford, Mary Katherine. BS in Indsl. Mgmt., L.I. U., 1964; AAS in Mktg. and Sales, Broome C.C., Binghamton, N.Y., 1994. With floor production dept. Grumman Aviation, Bethpage, N.Y., 1943-44; mfg. engr. Republic Aviation, Farmingdale, 1947-64, IBM, Endicott, 1964-70, cost engr., 1970-90; retired, 1990; owner, woodcarver The Yankee Crafter, Little Meadows, Pa., 1995—. Author: (with others) Tooling for Aircraft and Missile Manufacture, 1964. Pres. trustees United Methodist Ch., 1989—, mem. 1970—; councilman Borough Coun., Little Meadows, Pa., 1970-74; trustee Fire Dept., Little Meadows, 1974-78;

pres. Ch. Bd., Little Meadows, 1989—, mem. Amityville, N.Y., 1958-62; bd. dirs. Montrose Area Sch. Bd. Susquehanna, Pa., 1975-89; active Boy Scouts Am.; vol. SCORE, Binghampton, N.Y. and Susquehanna County, Pa. Mem. Phi Theta Kappa. Republican. Methodist. Avocations: gardening, stock market charting, oil and watercolor painting. Home: PO Box 475 Rte 858 Little Meadows PA 18830 Office: The Yankee Crafter Rt 858 Little Meadows PA 18830

STACEY, GLYN NIGEL, clinical scientist; b. Bishop's Stortford, Eng., Oct. 16, 1958; m. Geoffrey Collingwood and Valery Anne (Bedwell) S.; m. Alison Rose Gosney, July 1986; children: Emily Charlotte, Victoria Anne. BSc, U. Coventry, Eng., 1982; MPhil, U. Southampton, Eng., 1991; PhD, Open U., 1995. Med. sci. officer Pub. Health Lab. Svc., Coventry, 1980-81, Southampton, 1982-87; clin. scientist Ctr. for Applied Microbiology and Rsch., Porton Down, Eng., 1989-97; sr. scientist Nat. Inst. for Biol. Stds. and Control, South Mimms, Eng., 1998—. Co-organizer, initiator sci. interactions with U. Nottingham, 1991, Marasyk U., Brno, Czech Republic, 1992, 96, Oeiras, Portugal, 1996, U. Derby, 1997, Brescia, Italy, 1997. Editor: Safety in Cell and Tissue Culture, 1998. Rsch. grantee European Commn., 1996, Dept. Health, 1996. Fellow Inst. Biomed. Scis.; mem. Brit. Soc. Immunology, Soc. for Low Temperature Biology (treas. 1993-96), European Soc. for Animal Cell Tech. U.K., European Tissue Culture Soc., Biochem. Soc., Internat. Assn. Plant Tissue Culture, European Soc. for Animal Cell Tech.-UK (com. mem.), Soc. for In Vitro Biology (biosafety com. 1997), European Culture Collection Orgn. (sci. officer 1999—), Low Temp Biology (mtgs. sec. 1998-2000). Mem. Ch. of England. Achievements include standardization in cell culture and biosafety. Office: Nat Inst Biol Stds and Control (NIBSC) South Mimms EN6 3QG England

STACEY, JAMES HENRY, writer, columnist; b. Chgo., July 26, 1935; s. John James and Mary (Hollister) S.; m. Lelia West, Feb. 4, 1956 (div. Mar. 1978); children: Nicole, Michelle; m. Carol Ann Levenson, Apr. 26, 1980. BA, Grinnell Coll., 1957; MA, San Francisco State U., 1960. Asst. editor Bus. Week, Chgo., 1966-68; lectr. Northwestern U., Evanston, Ill., 1968-71; writer, devel. officer U. Chgo., 1972-76; nat. affairs editor Am. Med. News, Chgo., 1976-83, sci. news editor, 1983-86, dir. media rels., 1986-99; freelance writer Balt., 1999—. Author: Inside the New Temple, 1993, A Wounded Name, 2001; co-author: Severed Trust, 2001; contbr. articles to mags. Avocations: theater, travel, literature. Home: 230 Stony Run Ln #5D Baltimore MD 21210 E-mail: J.STACEY@WORLDNET.ATT.NET.

STACEY, JAMES ALLEN, retired judge; b. Norwalk, Ohio, Dec. 26, 1925; s. James Calvin and Glenna (Cleveland) S.; m. Marlyn Frederick, Aug. 21, 1948; children: James A., Libble M. Romigh, Lorrie Stacey Singler, David F., CamAllison Shenigo, Tricia Stacey Berger. Student, Bucknell U., 1943-44, Ohio Wesleyan U., 1944, 46, 47, U. N.C., 1944-45; JD, Cleveland-Marshall Law Sch., 1951. Bar: Ohio 1952, U.S. Dist. Ct. (no. dist.) Ohio 1955. Ptnr. McGory & Stacey, Sandusky, Ohio, 1954-56; assoc. Steinemann & Zieher, 1956-60; ptnr. Work, Stacey & Moyer, 1960-67; judge Sandusky Mcpl. Ct., 1967-95, ret., 1995. Mem. Ohio State Traffic Law Com., 1969-95, chmn., 1978-82. Mem. Erie-Ottawa Mental Health Bd., 1968-87; mem. Ex-Offenders for Help Bd., 1975-81; bd. dirs. Camp Fire Girls, 1956-60, L.E.A.D.S., 1984-86, Sandusky C. of C., 1984-86. Served with USNR, 1943-46. Mem. Ohio State Bar Assn., Ohio Mcpl. Judges Assn. (exec. bd. 1970-80), Am. Judicature Soc., Am. Judges Assn., Erie County Bar Assn., Amvets, Sandusky Exch. Club (bd. dirs. 1999—), Elks, Eagles Club, Italian-Am. Beneficial Club. Republican. Presbyterian. Home: 1407 Julianne Cir Sandusky OH 44870-7032

STACEY, RICHARD WAYNE, lawyer; b. Grand Junction, Colo., July 16, 1961; s. Donald Wayne and Roberta (Brawner) S.; m. Suzanne Nakao, Feb. 19, 1994; children: Kimberly, Nicole. BA in English Lit., Colo. Coll., 1983; JD, Boston Coll., Newton, Mass., 1987. Bar: Mass. 1987, U.S. Ct. Appeals (1st cir.) 1988, U.S. Dist. Ct. Mass. 1989, U.S. Ct. Appeals (9th cir.) 1991, Guam 1994, Hawaii 1995, U.S. Dist. Ct. Hawaii 1995. Jud. clk. N.H. Superior Ct., Concord, 1987-88; clk. McBride, Wheeler et al, Boston, 1988; asst. dist. atty. (ea. dist.) Mass., Salem, 1988-90; asst. atty. gen. Office Atty. Gen. Guam, Agana, 1990-95; spl. asst. U.S. atty., 1994-95; 1st asst. atty. gen. criminal divsn. Office Atty. Gen. Guam, Agana, 1993-94; dep. pros. aty. Dept. Pros. Atty., Honolulu, 1995—. Mem. Nat. Dist. Attys. Assn. Avocations: running, volleyball, surfing. Office: Dept Pros Atty 1060 Richards St Fl 10 Honolulu HI 96813-2920 E-mail: rstacey@co.honolulu.hi.us.

STACEY, TRUMAN, journalist, consultant; b. Port Arthur, Tex., Dec. 8, 1916; s. James Harrison and Billie (Davis) S.; m. Dorothy Mary Piboin, May 25, 1963 (dec.); m. Norma Elaine Trahan, Feb. 2, 1980 (dec.). B in Philosophy, U. Detroit, 1946, MA, 1954. Reporter Beaumont (Tex.) Enterprise, 1937-42, Oklahoma City Daily Oklahoman, 1943-44, Detroit Free Press, 1944-45; dir. pub. rels. U. Detroit, 1945-49; reporter Washington Times Herald, 1949-50; sports editor Lake Charles (La.) Am. Press, 1950-60, editor-in-chief, 1961-82; dir. communications Diocese Lake Charles, 1982-90, pres. Coun. of Cath. Men, 1990-92. Author: Louisiana's French Heritage, 1990, The Church Visible, 2000. Mem. Calcasieu Parish (La.) Family Svc. Agy., 1979-82; coord. SW La. Citizens for Ednl. Freedom, 1968-70;bd. dirs. La. Coun. Music and Performing Arts, 1967-79, Calcasieu Citizens for Decency, 1967-69, Lake Charles Symphony Orch., 1967-69. Sgt. U.S. Army, 1942-43. Recipient Merit award Sociedad Esañfiola de La., 1978, Silver Antelope award Boy Scouts Am., 1979, George Washington medal of Honor Freedom Found., 1980, Faith and Freedom award Religious Heritage Am., Inc., 1980, Harry J. O'Haire Meml. award Serra Internat., 1987, Pilgrim's Shell award Latin Patriarch Jerusalem, 1988, Nat. Silver Merit medal Knights Peter Claver, 1992, Stephen T. Victory Meml. award La. Bar assn., 1992, Past State Deputies award La. Knights Columbus, 1994, Spes Mundi-O'Connell award Internat. Cath. Com. on Scouting, 2000, Donald Millet Meml. award Southwest La. Hist. Assn., 2001; named to La. Sports Writers Hall of Fame, 1982, Columbian Hall of Fame, 1987; invested Chavalier, French Order of Merit, 1985. Mem.: NCCJ (Brotherhood award 1975), La. Press Assn. (bd. dirs. 1976—79), S.W. La. Hist. Assn. (pres. 2000—02), Inst. de la Maison Royale de France, Lake Charles C. of C. (Man of Yr. 1971), Am. Soc. Newspaper Editors, AP Mng. Editors Assn., La.-Miss. AP Assn. (pres. 1962—63, Merit citation 30 Yrs. Cmty. Svc. 1980), La. Sports Writers Assn. Avocations: reading, classical music, philately. Home: 1802 2nd Ave Lake Charles LA 70601-6432

STACEY, WESTON MONROE, JR. nuclear engineer, educator; b. Birmingham, Ala., July 23, 1937; s. Weston Monroe and Dorothy (Toole) S.; m. Penny Smith; children: Helen Lee, Weston Monroe III, Lucia Katherine. BS in Physics, Ga. Inst. Tech., 1959, MS in Nuclear Sci., 1963; PhD in Nuclear Engring., MIT, 1966. Nuclear engr. Knolls Atomic Power Lab., Schenectady, N.Y., 1962-64, 66-69; assoc. dir. applied physics divsn. and dir. fusion program Argonne Nat. Lab., Chgo., 1969-77; Callaway Regents prof. Ga. Inst. Tech., Atlanta, 1977—. Author 6 books; contbr. more than 200 articles to profl. jours. Recipient Cert. Appreciation Dept. Energy, Disting. Assoc. award Dept. Energy, 1990. Fellow: Am. Nuclear Soc. (bd. dirs. 1974—77, Outstanding Achievement award 1981, 1996, Seaborg medal), Am. Phys. Soc.; mem.: AAAS, Am. Soc. Engring. Edn. Office: Ga Inst Tech Nuclear Engring Dept 0425 Atlanta GA 30332-0001 E-mail: weston.stacey@nre.gatech.edu.

STACHOWIAK, DENNIS KENNETH, trading company executive; b. Buffalo, U.S., Dec. 28, 1943; arrived in Sweden, 1972; s. Edward Joseph and Sophie Anna (Syroczynski) S.; m. Ulla Charlotta Sunden; children: Erika, David. BA, SUNY, Buffalo, 1967. Tchr. Port Jefferson (N.Y.) Pub. Schs., 1967-70; mgr. Gylling & Co. AB, Stockholm, 1970-72; trading mgr. C. Itoh & Co., Ltd., 1972-95; sales exec. AB Ing. Fritz Egnell, 1995—. Contbr. articles to profl. publs. Bd. dirs. Trysil House Owners Assn., Norway, 1979-84; rep. Vendelso Home Owners Assn., Sweden, 1989. Mem. Vendelso Gard Boat Club (past pres.). Roman Catholic. Avocations: skiing, motorcycling. Home: Hovslagarv 6 S13673 Vendelso Gard Sweden Office: C Itoh & Co Ltd Ab Ing Fritz Egnell Sehlstedsg 4 10052 Stockholm Sweden E-mail: dennis_stachowiak@hotmail.com.

STACK, BEATRIZ DE GREIFF, lawyer; b. Medellin, Antioquia, Colombia, Feb. 3, 1939; came to U.S., 1967; d. Luis and Carolina (González) de Greiff; m. Norman L. Stack Jr., Dec. 18, 1972; children: Carolina M., Ingrid C. BS, Sch. Sacred Heart, Medellin, 1956; LLD, U. Pontificia Bolivariana, Medellin, 1961; cert. of attendance, Inst. Internat. Studies, Geneva, Switzerland, 1965; M in Comparative Law, George Washington U., 1974. Bar: Medellin 1963, Pa. 1983, Va. 1992. Trademarks examiner U.S. Patent and Trademark Office, Arlington, Va., 1977-78; legal rschr. Land and Natural Resources divsn. U.S. Dept. Justice, Washington, 1980-86; legal officer Food and Agr. Orgn., UN, Rome, 1986-89; legal counsel Pan Am. Health Orgn. Staff Assn., Washington, 1989-92; pvt. practice Mc Lean, Va., 1992—. City judge Caldas, Antioquia, 1989-92; city atty. City of Medellin, 1963; head polit. sci. inst. Antioquia State U., Medellin, 1965; instr. in lang. Peace Corps Vols., Mex., 1968; asst. exec. sec. Interam. Commn. Women, OAS, Washington, 1970; stats. asst. Pan Am. Health Orgn., Washington; cons. Inst. Internat. Law and Econ. Devel., Washington, 1974; ct. interpreter U.S. Magistrate Ct. Alexandria, Va.; legal cons. Mozambique, 1992. Sec. Cath. Daus. Am., Arlington, 1985-86; pres. Colombian Cultural Forum, 1991-94. Mem. Alumna Spanish Sacred Heart (v.p. 1990). Democrat. Roman Catholic. E-mail: degreiffst@aol.com.

STACK, DANIEL, lawyer, financial consultant; b. July 29, 1928; s. Charles and Gertrude (Heller) Stack; m. Jane Marcia Gordon, Apr. 18, 1953; children: Joan, Gordon. BA cum laude, Bklyn. Coll., 1949; LLB, Columbia U., 1952; LLM, Georgetown U., 1955. Bar: N.Y. 1956. Project adminstr. Am. Overseas Fin. Corp., 1957—58; asst. counsel. ABC-TV, N.Y.C., NY, 1959—60; gen. counsel IFC Securities Corp., 1961—63; exec. asst. to sr. v.p. N.Y. Stock Exch., 1963—64; sec. pension com. Consol. Foods Corp., Chgo., 1967—69; v.p. legal Seaway Multi Corp. Ltd., Toronto, Canada, 1969—72; v.p. mergers and acquisitions Acklands Ltd., 1972—74; sr. v.p., sec., counsel Greenwich Svs. Bank., N.Y.C., 1978—81; sole prctice, 1982—85; ptnr. Brennen and Stack, 1986—96; cons. venture capital, corp. fin., med. edn., health care, mining, and oil, 1982—. Pres. Bus. and Fin. Resources, Inc., 1982—84; adj. faculty NYU; officer and dir. various pub. cos.; bd. adv. Sch. of Bus., St. John's U.; chmn. sect. on mergers and acquisitions North Am. Soc. for Corp. Planning; lectr., guest spkr. on mergers and acquisitions Fac. of Mgmt. Studies, Univ. Toronto, 1974, SUNY, Buffalo, 1976; gen. counsel Greater N.Y. Safety Coun., 1980—. Info. officer U.S. Naval Acad., 1972—; mem. Congl. mil svc. acads, nominations com. and Civil Svc. intern selection com., 1978—. Lt. j.g. USNR, 1952—55, Capt. USNR, 1983, ret. Decorated Joint Svc. Commendation medal, Naval Order of US; scholar, N.Y. Regents, 1945—49. Mem.: N.Y. State Bar Assn., Ramapo Rep. Org. Republican. Home: 8 Linda Dr Suffern NY 10901-3004

STACK, EDWARD WILLIAM, business management and foundation executive; b. Rockville Centre, N.Y., Feb. 1, 1935; s. Edward Henry and Helen Margaret (Leitner) S.; m. Christina Carol Hunt, Aug. 19, 1967; children: Amy Alison, Kimberly Anne, Suzanne Gail. BBA, Pace U., 1956; LLD (hon.), Hartwick Coll., 1982; LHD (hon.), Pace U., 1991, L.I. U., 1994. With Clark Estates, Inc., N.Y.C., 1956-2000, pres., bd. dirs., 1990-2000. Trustee N.Y. State Hist. Assn., Cooperstown, 1975—2002, Mary Imogene Bassett Hosp., 1973—, Hartwick Coll., Oneonta, NY, Trooper Found. of State of N.Y.; sec. Nat. Baseball Hall of Fame and Mus., Inc., Cooperstown, 1961—77, pres., chmn., 1977—93, chmn., 1993—2000; mem. adv. bd. Salvation Army Nassau County and Greater N.Y. Ctr. for Family Life, Sunset Pk., Bklyn.; bd. dirs. Farmers' Mus., Inc., Cooperstown, 1991—, The Clark Found., N.Y.C., The Scriven Found., N.Y.C., United Meth. City Soc., St. Christopher-Ottilie, Sea Cliff, NY. Mem. Mohican Club (Cooperstown, N.Y.). Republican. Home: 25 Waverly St Glen Head NY 11545-1004 Office: 31st Fl One Rockefeller Plaza New York NY 10020 E-mail: ewstack@aol.com.

STACK, FRANK HUNTINGTON, painter, retired educator; b. Houston, Oct. 31, 1937; s. Maurice Z. and Norma Rose (Huntington) S.; m. Mildred Roberta Powell, June 12, 1959; children: Joan Elaine, Robert Huntington. BFA, U. Tex., 1959; postgrad., Sch. Art Inst. Chgo., 1960-61; MA, U. Wyo., 1963. Assoc. art editor Houston Chronicle, 1959-60; instr. U. Mo., Columbia, 1963-69, prof. art, 1969-95, Catherine P. Middlebush prof. humanities, 1995-2000, prof. emeritus, 2000—. Mem. regional adv. bd. Mo. Arts Coun., columbia, 1979-80; mem. exec. bd. U. Mo. Art and Archaeology Mus., Columbia, 1981-84; chmn. art dept. U. Mo., Columbia, 1981-83; mem. pers. com. U. Mo. Columbia Arts and Sci. Coll., Columbia, 1976-80; vis. artist W.Va. Arts Coun. and Exxon, Shepherd Coll., Shepherdstown, W.Va., 1983. Artist, author: (cartoons) The New Adventures of Jesus, 1963-95, (book of cartoons) Dorman's Doggie, 1990; illustrator artist: (graphic novel) Our Cancer Year, 1994 (Best Graphic Novel Harvey award 1995), Naked Glory: erotic art of Frank Stack. 1997; artist traveling exhibit Watercolors by Frank Stack, 1977-79; editor: (collection of comic strips) Alley Oop, 3 vols. 1946-47, 47-48, 48-49, 1990, 93, 95 (nominated Best Reprint 1991, 94, 96); mem. dv. bd. Jour. Cartoon and Comic Art, 1984—; contbg. writer The Comics Jour., 1989—. Mem. mus. rev. bd. U. Mo., 4 campus sys., Columbia, 1989. With U.S. Army, 1960-62. Recipient Rsch. Grants, U. Mo. Rsch. Coun., Columbia, 1969, 85, 93, 98, Gov.'s Arts awards Artist of Yr. Mo. Arts Coun., St. Louis, 1986. Mem. Kans. Watercolor Soc. (awards 1992, 96), Columbia Art League (adv. bd. 1978-82), Mo. Watercolor Soc. (award 2002). Avocations: historical research, art history, newspaper comics of 1930's and 40's. Home: 409 Thilly Ave Columbia MO 65203-3458 Office: U Mo Art Dept A-126 Fine Arts Columbia MO 65211-6911 E-mail: stackf@missouri.edu.

STACK, GEOFFREY LAWRENCE, real estate developer; b. Trinidad, British West Indies, Sept. 16, 1943; s. Gerald Francis and V. Louise (Bell) S.; m. Victoria Hammack, 1970 (div. 1986); 1 child, Kathryn; m. Nancy J. Haarer, Apr. 19, 1987; children: Alexandra, Natalie. BA, Georgetown U., 1965; MBA, U. Pa., 1972. Dir. acquisitions J.H. Snyder Co., L.A., 1972-75; from project mgr. to exec. v.p. Richards West, Newport Beach, Calif., 1975-77; pres. Regis Homes Corp., 1977-93; mng. dir. Sares-Regis Group, Irvine, Calif., 1993—. Bd. dirs. Arral & Ptnrs., Hong Kong, Calif. Housing Coun., Sacramento, Tejon Ranch Co., 1998. Bd. dirs. Nat. Multihousing Coun., 1987—. Capt. USMC, 1967—70. Decorated 2 Bronze Stars, 21 Air medals, Navy Commendation medal, Purple Heart. Mem. Young Pres. Orgn., Big Canyon Country Club, Pacific Club, Olympic Club. Democrat. Roman Catholic. Office: Sares Regis Group 18802 Bardeen Ave Irvine CA 92612-1521 E-mail: jstack@sares-regis.com.

STACK, GEORGE JOSEPH, philosopher, writer; b. N.Y.C. s. George Francis and Elizabeth (Sullivan) S.; m. Mary K. Di Maria, July 25, 1997; children: Diane, Christopher, stepchildren: Jena, Shelley. BA, Pace U., 1960; MA, Pa. State U., 1962, PhD, 1964. Instr. humanities Pa. State U., 1962-63; instr. philosophy L.I. U., 1963-64, asst. prof., 1964-67, SUNY, Brockport, 1967-68, asso. prof., 1968-70, prof., chmn., 1970-77, prof., 1977-95, prof. emeritus, 1995—, also advisor Center for Philosophic Exchange, 1970-82. Cons. to Choice. Author: Berkeley's Analysis of Perception, 1970, 2d edit., 1992, On Kierkegaard: Philosophical Fragments, 1976, Kierkegaard's Existential Ethics, 1977, 2d edit., 1992, Japanese transl., 1985, Sartre's Philosophy of Social Existence, 1978, reprinted 1992, Lange and Nietzsche, 1983; contbg. author: Nietzsche and Modern German Thought, 1991, Nietzsche and Emerson, 1992, Nietzsche: Man, Knowledge, Will to Power, 1994; editorial advisor: Folia Humanistica, 1970-97, Filosofia Oggi; contbr. numerous articles profl. jours. Office: PO Box 92 Grapevine TX 76099-0092

STACK, J. WILLIAM, JR. management consultant; b. Lansing, Mich., July 13, 1918; s. Joseph William and Helen (Dodge) S.; m. Wolcott Rorick, Sept. 25, 1948; children: Christopher D., Nathan S., Joseph W., David R., Peter S. BA, Yale U., 1940. With Gen. Motors Corp, 1945-57; dir. mktg. Gen. Motors Corp (AC Electronics div.), 1955-57; v.p. Kurth Malting Co., Milw., 1957-59; gen. sales mgr. Massey Ferguson, Inc., Toronto, Can., 1960-62; pres., founder Stancor Ltd., 1963-68; pres. William Stack Assocs. Inc., N.Y.C., 1968-98. Mem. Navy and Marine Corps Acquisition Rev. Com., 1974-75. Active Rep. Town Com. Lt. comdr. USNR, 1940-45. Mem. Yale Club of N.Y.C., New Canaan Country Club. Episcopalian. Home: 3185 Meadow Ridge Redding CT 06896-3227 E-mail: MSTAK@aol.com. *Success is measured by what you give back; not what you take. To help one person, to advance one worthy cause is the mark of total achievement.*

STACK, JANE MARCIA, lawyer; b. Bklyn., Aug. 11, 1928; m. Daniel Stack, Apr. 18, 1953; children: Joan, Gordon. Student, Ohio U., 1945-47; BA, NYU, 1949; JD, N.Y. Law Sch., 1983. Bar: N.Y., 1984; U.S. Dist. Ct. (ea. and so. dists.) N.Y. 1988. Assoc. Shannon, Flaherty, Purchase, N.Y., 1984-85, Schwall & Becker, New City, 1985-87; pvt. practice Suffern, 1987-90; sr. atty. N.Y. State Div. Human Rights, N.Y.C., 1990—. Vice-pres. Montebello (N.Y.) Civic Assn., 1988—. Republican. Home: 8 Linda Dr Suffern NY 10901-3004 Office: NY State Div Human Rights 1 Fordham Plz Bronx NY 10458-5871

STACK, MAURICE DANIEL, retired insurance company executive; b. N.Y.C., Dec. 15, 1917; s. Maurice E. and Margaret (Brooks) S.; m. Catherine T. O'Connor, Nov. 25, 1943; children: Mary Jane, Eileen, Peter, Clare. Student, U. Notre Dame, 1935-36; BBA, Manhattan Coll., 1939; MBA, Harvard, 1941. Investment analyst Carnegie Corp., N.Y.C., 1946-48; adminstrv. asst. Tchrs. Ins. & Annuity Assn., 1948-49; investment analyst First Nat. Bank N.Y., 1949-54; fin. sec. Atlantic Mut. Ins. Co., N.Y.C., 1954-56, v.p., 1957-60, fin. v.p., trustee, 1961-66, chmn. fin. com., 1966-83. Trustee emeritus Atlantic Mutual Ins. Co. Trustee emeritus, adviser St. Vincent's Hosp.; trustee emeritus YWCA. Maj., C.E., AUS, 1941-46. Mem. K.M. Club (N.Y.C.), Harvard Club (N.Y.C.). Home: 85 Lynbrook Ave Point Lookout NY 11569-0095

STACK, MAY ELIZABETH, library director; b. Jackson, Miss., Nov. 10, 1940; d. James William and Irene Thelma (Baldwin) Garrett; m. Richard Gardiner, Apr. 15, 1962; children: Elinor, Harley David. BS, Miss. State Coll. for Women, 1962; MBA, Western New Eng. Coll., 1981; MLS, So. Conn. State U., 1989. Clk. Western New Eng. Coll., Springfield, Mass., 1965-66, acquisitions staff, 1966-72, cataloger, 1972-84, asst. dir., 1984-89, acting dir., 1989-90, dir., 1990—. Chair Ctrl./Western Mass. Automated Resource Sharing Collection Devel. Com., Paxton, Mass., 1993-95, exec. bd., 1993-96. Mem. East Longmeadow (Mass.) Hist. Soc., 1989-92. Mem. ALA, Mass. Libr. Assn., Assn. Coll. and Rsch. Librs., Libr. and Mgmt. Assn., Libr. Info. and Technology Assn. Methodist. Avocations: horseback riding, show dogs. Office: Western New Eng Coll D'Amour Libr 1215 Wilbraham Rd Springfield MA 01119-2612 E-mail: mstack@wnec.edu.

STACK, PAUL FRANCIS, lawyer; b. Chgo., July 21, 1946; s. Frank Louis and Dorothy Louise Stack; m. Nea Waterman, July 8, 1972; children: Nea Elizabeth, Sera Waterman. BS, U. Ariz., 1968; JD, Georgetown U., 1971. Bar: Ill. 1971, U.S. Ct. Claims 1975, U.S. Tax Ct. 1974, U.S. Ct. Internat. Trade 1977, U.S. Supreme Ct. 1975. Law clk. U.S. Dist. Ct., Chgo., 1971-72; asst. U.S. atty. No. Dist. Ill., 1972-75; mng. dir. Stack & Filpi, 1976—. Bd. dirs. Riverside (Ill.) Pub. Libr., 1977-83, Suburban Libr. Sys., Burr Ridge, Ill., 1979-82; mem. Mayor's ad hoc adv. com. on Ctrl. Libr., Chgo., Ill., 1987-88; mem. bd. edn. Twp. H.S. Dist. 208, Riverside, Ill., 1989-97; pres. Village of Riverside, Ill., 1997-2001; mem. exec. com. Chgo. Area Transp. Study, 1999-2001. Mem. Chgo. Zool. Soc. (gov. 1980—, planned giving adv. com. 1996-99), Chgo. Bar Assn., Union League Club of Chgo. (bd. dirs. 1986-89). Home: 238 N Delaplaine Rd Riverside IL 60546-2035 Office: 140 S Dearborn St Ste 411 Chicago IL 60603-5201

STACK, STEPHEN S. manufacturing company executive; b. DuPont, Pa., Apr. 25, 1934; s. Steve and Sophie (Baranowski) Stasenko; m. Lois Sims Agnew, May 25, 1996. BSME, Case Western Res. U., 1956; postgrad., Syracuse Univ. reg. profl engr., Ill. Mech. engr. Kaiser Aluminum, Erie, PA, 1956-58; instr. Gannon Univ., 1958-60, Syracuse U., NY, 1960-61; engrg. supr. A.O. Smith Corp., Erie and Los Angeles, 1961-66; gen. mgr. Am. Elec. Fusion, Chgo., 1966-67; mgr.new products Maremont Corp., 1967-69; dir. market planning Gulf and Western Ind., Bellwood, IL, 1969-71; mgmt. and fin. cons. Stack & Assocs., Chgo., 1971-76; pres. Seamcraft, Inc., 1976—. Mem. Ill. Legis. Small Bus. Conf., 1980, Gov.'s Small Bus. Adv. Commn., 1984-94, Ill. State House Conf. on Small Bus., 1984, 86, 99; chmn. West Cell, 1988-2000, Bridge Pers. Svcs. Corp., 1989—; vice pres. Ind. Bus. Assn. Ill., 1993-94; mem. small bus. adv. counc. Fed. Res. Bank of Chgo., 1989-91, Nat. Fedn. Ind. Bus. mem. 1980—, del. White House Conf. on Small Bus., 1986, pres. Chgo. Marine Heritage Soc., 1999—, mem. Navy League of the U.S., 1991—, del. Congl. Small Bus. Summit, 1998, 2000, 02; with Ill. Small Bus. Leadership Coun., 2000—. Treas. Sem. Townhouse Assn., 1993-94; active Lincoln Park Conservation Assn., Sheffield Neighbors Assn.; mem. adv. coun., DePaul U. Coll. Commerce, 2000—. Recipient Am. Legion awd., 1948, Case Western Res. U. Honor key, 1956, Easgle Scout awd., 1949. Mem. Ill. Mfrs. Assn. (bd. dirs. 1986-98, vice chmn. 1995-98), Small Mfrs. Action Couns. (vice chmn. 1986-87, chmn. 1988-89), Mfrs. Polit. Action Com. (exec. com. 1987-98, vice chmn. 1993-95, chmn. 1995-98), Am. Mgmt. Assn., Pres. Assn., Blue Key, Beta Theta Pi, Theta Thau, Pi Delta Epsilon. Clubs: Chgo. Yacht, East Bank Club, Capitol Hill (Wash.), Fullerton Tennis (pres. 1971-79, treas. 1979-83, bd. dirs. 1983-86), Lake Shore Ski (v.p. 1982, 91), Lincoln Park Tennis Assn., Oak Park Tennis Club. Patentee in liquid control and metering fields. Office: 932 W Dakin St Chicago IL 60613-2922

STACK, STEVEN JOHN, JR. criminal justice educator; b. Providence, Dec. 20, 1947; s. Steven John and Alice Evelyn Stack; m. Dec. 20, 1968 (div. Aug. 1988); children: James Joseph, Timothy Allen, John Steven. BA in Math. and English, U. Conn., 1969, MA in Edn., 1970, MA in Sociology, 1973, PhD in Sociology, 1976. Asst. prof. Alma (Mich.) Coll., 1976-79, Ind. U., Indpls., 1979-81; assoc. prof. Pa. State U., State College, 1981-85; assoc. prof., then prof. Auburn (Ala.) U., 1985-90; prof. dept. criminal justice, dir., chmn. dept. Wayne State U., Detroit, 1990—. Mem. editl. bd. Suicide and Life Threatening Behavior 1984—, Jour. Crime and Justice, 1997—; assoc. editor Archives Suicide Rsch., 1995—; contbr. over 175 articles and revs. to profl. jours., including Sociol. Focus, Peninsular Papers: Jour. Mich. Sociol. Assn., Am. Sociol. Rev., Social Forces, Internat. Rev. Modern Sociology, Mich. Academician, Jour. Social Psychology, Western Sociol. Rev., Internat. Jour. Social Psychiatry, Jour. Marriage and Family, Aggressive Behavior, Jour. Comparative Family Studies, Social Psychiatry, Can. Jour. Polit. Sci., Jour. for Sci. Study Religion, Basic and Applied Social Psychology, Psychol. Reports, Jour. Family Issues, Sociol. Quar., Criminology, Deviant Behavior, Justice Quar., Quality and Quantity, Jour. Aging Studies, Family Perspective, Jour. Divorce and Remarriage, OMEGA: Jour. Death and Dying, Am. Jour. Criminal Justice, Internat. Rev. Modern Sociology, Am. Jour. Police, Death Studies, Suicide and Life Threatening Behavior, Transcultural Psychiatry, Jour. Crime and Justice, Contemporary Sociology, Social Pathology, also contbr. numerous chpts. to books and encys. Rsch. grantee Ind. Mental Health Dept., 1980, NIMH, 1985-88, Harry Frank Guggenheim Found., 1998-99. Mem. Am. Assn. Suicidology (sec. 1996-98, Edwin Shneidman rsch. award 1985), Am. Soc. Criminology, Nat. Coun. on Family Rels., Soc. for Sci. Study Religion, Acad. criminal Justice Scis. Roman Catholic. Office: Wayne State U Dept Criminal Justice 656 W Kirby St Detroit MI 48202-3622 Home: 6341 Parkview Dr Troy MI 48098-2241

STACKABLE, FREDERICK LAWRENCE, lawyer; b. Howell, Mich., Dec. 4, 1935; s. Lawrence Peter and Dorothea R. (Kiney) S. BA, Mich. State U., 1959; JD, Wayne State U., 1962. Bar: Mich. 1962, U.S. Dist. Ct. (ea. and we. dists.) Mich. 1964; U.S. Supreme Ct. 1968. Lawyer pvt. practice, Lansing, Mich., 1975—; commr., Ingham County Cir. Ct. V.p. Mich. Assn. Cir. Ct. Commrs., 1963, pres., 1967-70; 18th dist. rep. Ingham County Bd. Suprs.; mem. Com. on Mich. Law Revision Commn.; state rep. 58th House Dist., 1971, 72, 73, 74. County del. Rep. Party, Ingham County, Mich., 1969-70, state del., Mich., 1971-74; Lansing city atty., 1975. Recipient Disting. Alumni award Wayne State U. Sch. Law, Detroit, 1987. Mem. Mich. Bar Assn., Ingham County Bar Assn., Nat. Conf. Commrs. Uniform State Laws, Mich. Trail Riders Assn. (dir., past pres.), Mich. Internat. Snowmobile Assn., Sportsman's Alliance Mich., Cycle Conservation Club, Am. Judicature Soc. Avocations: horseback riding, snowmobiling, skiing, traveling. Office: 300 N Grand Ave Lansing MI 48933-1214

STACKELBERG, JOHN RODERICK, history educator; b. Munich, May 8, 1935; came to U.S., 1946; s. Curt Freiherr and Ellen (Biddle) von Stackelberg; m. Steffi Heuss, Oct. 10, 1965 (div. Apr. 1983); m. Sally Winkle, Mar. 30, 1991; children: Katherine Ellen, Nicholas Olaf, Emmet Winkle. AB, Harvard U., 1956; MA, U. Vt., 1972; PhD, U. Mass., 1974. Reading instr. Baldridge Reading Svcs., Greenwich, Conn., 1957-62; lang. tchr. Hartnackschule, Berlin, 1963-67; English and social studies tchr. Lake Region Union High Sch., Orleans, Vt., 1967-70; lectr. history San Diego State U., 1974-76; asst. prof. history U. Oreg., Eugene, 1976-77, U. S.D., Vermillion, 1977-78, Gonzaga U., Spokane, Wash., 1978-81, assoc. prof. history, 1981-88, prof. history, 1988—, Powers prof. of humanities, 1997—. Author: Idealism Debased, 1981, Hitler's Germany: Origins, Interpretations, Legacies, 1999, (with Sally A. Winkle) The Nazi Germany Sourcebook: An Anthology of Texts, 2002; contbr. articles to profl. jours. Pres. Spokane chpt. UN Assn.,

1986-90. With U.S. Army, 1958-60. Leadership Devel. fellow Ford Found., 1969-70. Avocations: chess, tennis. Home: 530 W 24th Ave Spokane WA 99203 Office: Gonzaga U Dept History Spokane WA 99258-0001 E-mail: stackelberg@gonzaga.edu.

STACKPOLE, H. C. government agency administrator; b. New Haven; Degree, Princeton U., N.J., George Washington U., Stanford U.; grad., Nat. War Coll., Naval Command and Staff Coll. Commd. U.S.M.C., advanced through grades to lt. gen., ret., comdr. III marine amphibious force/commanding gen. 3rd marine divsn. Japan, dir. plans and policy directorate (J-5) USCINCLANT Norfolk, Va., dir. plans, policies, and opers. Hqrs. Marine Corps. Washington, Marine Corps opers. dep. to Joint Chiefs of Staff; comdr. joint task force Sea Angel Bangladesh, 1991; comdr. Marine Forces Pacific U.S.M.C., Honolulu, 1992—94; pres. Loral Asia-Pacific, Tokyo, Asia-Pacific Ctr. Security Studies. Decorated Legion of Merit, Purple Heart with gold star, Vietnamese Cross of Gallantry; co-recipient Citation, Govt. of Bangladesh; recipient Japanese Order Rising Sun 3rd Order, Order of Nat. Security Merit, Rep. of Korea. Office: Asia Pacific Ctr Security Studies 2058 Maluhia Rd Honolulu HI 96815*

STACKPOLE, KERRY CLIFFORD, association executive; b. Putnam, Conn., Feb. 24, 1955; s. Howard Thompson Stackpole and Shyrlee Gladys Burr; m. Miriam Weisberg, July 29, 1984. MEd, Cambridge Coll., 1983. Gen. mgr. E.J. Ardon Co., Boston, 1978-82; ops. mgr. Fotobeam/Brookside, Waltham, Mass., 1982-83; assoc. dir. Printing Industries of New Eng., Natick, 1983—, v.p., 1989-91; exec. dir. Smaller Bus. Assn. New Eng., Waltham, Mass., 1991-93; pres., CEO, The Assn. for Work Process Improvement, Inc., 1993-97, EMA-The E-Bus. Forum, 1997-2000, Data Interchange Stds. Assn., Alexandria, Va., 2000-01; chmn. CEO, Neoterica Ptnrs., LLP, McLean, 2001—. Bd. dirs. Mass. Cert. Devel. Corp., EC Inst., Denver; mem. U.S. C. of C. Com. of 100, 2000—. Recipient HIRE Trust Fund award Graphic Arts Employers of Am., 1987, 2000. Fellow Am. Soc. Assn. Execs. (cert., mem. ann. meeting adv. com. 1996-97, mem. edn. com., 1996-99, chmn., exec. mgmt. sect. coun., 1997-98, bd. dirs., 1997-98, mem. key industries assn. com. 2000—); mem. Assocs. Advance Am. Com. (chmn. 1999-2000), New Eng. Soc. Assn. Execs. (committeeman 1983-84, membership devel. com. 1989-91, chmn. edn. com. 1991-93, bd. dirs. 1991—, treas.-sec. 1994-95, chmn.-elect 1995, chmn. bd. dirs. 1996—, immediate past chmn, 1997-98, Ralph Louis Towne award 1986). Avocations: reading, cross country skiing, ocean kayaking, jazz music buff. Office: Neoterica Ptnrs LLP PO Box 7763 Mc Lean VA 22106

STACKS, ROBERT DAVID, pediatrician; b. Apr. 17, 1941; BS, Mass. Coll. Pharmacy, 1962; MD, Med. Coll. Va., 1966. Intern Boston Floating Hosp., 1966-67, resident, 1967-69; chmn. dept. pediatrics St. Elizabeth's Hosp., Boston, 1980-93; pres. Roslindale Pediat. Assoc., P.C., 1988—; chief pediats. Faulkner Hosp., 1995—. Office: Roslindale Pediat Assoc PC 1153 Centre St Ste 31 Boston MA 02130-3446

STACY, CHARLES BRECKNOCK, lawyer; b. Charleston, W.Va., Sept. 2, 1924; s. George Palmer and Patti (Hubbard) S.; m. Judith Cook Willner, June 14, 1947 (dec. Jan. 1996); 1 child, Charles Brecknock. BS, Yale U., 1948, LLB, 1951. Bar: W.Va. 1951. Assoc. firm Spilman, Thomas & Battle, 1951-58; v.p. Lewis-Hubbard Corp., 1957; ptnr. Spilman, Thomas & Battle, Charleston, 1958-97, of counsel, 1997—. Mem. U.S. Circuit Ct. Judge Nominating Commn., 4th Circuit, 1977-79 Contbr. articles to law and tax publs. Pres. Kanawha-Charleston Vis. Nursing Assn., 1966-67; bd. dirs. Charleston Symphony Orch., 1960-70, pres., 1962-63; bd. trustees Woodberry Forest (Va.) Sch., 1970-76; pres. Woodberry Forest Alumni Assn., 1972-74; bd. dirs. Community Council of Kanawha Valley, Inc., 1971-79, pres., 1975-77; bd. dirs. United Way of Kanawha Valley, Inc., 1973-77, exec. com., 1975-77; trustee Greater Kanawha Valley Found., 1968-72, adv. bd., 1972—, chmn. bd., 1970-72; bd. dirs. W.Va. Tax Inst., 1958-67, pres., 1959-60; mem. adv. com. Charleston Area Med. Ctr. Found.; v.p., trustee Herscher Found.; pres., trustee Craik-Patton House Found. Fellow Am. Bar Found., Am. Coll. Trust and Estate Counsel, Am. Coll. Tax Counsel; mem. ABA (coun. 1977-83, vice chmn. adminstrn. sect. taxation 1980-83), Kanawha County Bar Assn., W.Va. State Bar (chmn. standing com. on state and fed. taxation 1959-70), W.Va. Bar Assn., Am. Law Inst., Am. Judicature Soc., Edgewood Country Club Charleston (gov. 1973-75, 83-86), Sea Pines Country Club (Hilton Head, S.C.), Yale Club N.Y.C., Rotary (bd. dirs. Charleston club 1979-80, 83-91, pres. 1989-90). Democrat. Presbyterian. Home: 1560 Thomas Cir Charleston WV 25314-1623 Office: Spilman Ctr 300 Kanawha Blvd E Charleston WV 25301-2532 E-mail: cstacy@spilmanlaw.com., cstacylhome@aol.com.

STACY, CHERYL R.K. consumer products company executive; b. Oakland, Calif., Dec. 15, 1956; d. Robert Walter Stacy and Romance Kim Yee; m. Jeffery Alan Weigle; children: C.R.G. Weigle, M.L. Weigle, K.D. Weigle. BA, U. Calif., Hayward, 1981. Channel mgr. Osborne Computer Corp., Hayward, 1980—83; dir. corp. and channel sales Breakthrough Software, San Francisco, 1983—87; v.p. sales CHRONOS Software, 1987—90; v.p. worldwides sales Tool Tech. Pub., Sausalito, 1990—92; dir. marcomm and inside sales UMAX Technologies, Fremont, 1992—94; v.p. sales and mktg. Plum Hall, Inc., Kamuela, 1995—97; v.p. sales Internet Image, Inc., Fremont, 1997—99; dir. corp. sales ValiCert, Inc., Mountain View, 1998—99; dir. Latin Am. bus. dev. Balt. Technologies, Dublin, 1999—2001. Owner iMagick Global Holdings Royal Palm Beach, 1989—; co-owner Kieke Assoc., Hayward, Hawaii, 1989—94, Kukui Onaona, Kilauea, Hawaii, 1994—97, Ecotropic Divers, Kawaihae, Hawaii, 1996—99, Accoutrements, West Palm Beach, Fla., 2000—02. Author: (biography) One Soul's Journey, 1997; instructor/choreographer (gorean dance) The Art of Seduction through Gorean Dance, 2001, website designer The Village, 1998 (HTML Guild, 1999); editor: (newsletter) LeatherFlash/LeatherZine, 2000; prodr.: (edn. workshops and seminars) LIVE, 2000; author: (book) PowerPlay, 2002. Mem. Ncsf, Washington, 1999—2002, Aclu, New York, NY, 1999—2002, Hrc, Washington, 1999—2002. Avocations: travel, scuba diving, writing, tarot reading. Office: iMagick Global Holdings 1128 Royal Palm Beach Blvd #281 Royal Palm Beach FL 33411 Office Fax: 561-795-9646. Business E-Mail: keiki@imagick.net.

STACY, DENNIS WILLIAM, architect; b. Council Bluffs, Iowa, Sept. 22, 1945; s. William L. and Mildred Glee (Carlsen) S.; m. Judy Annette Long, Dec. 28, 1968; 1 child: Stephanie. BArch, Iowa State U., 1969; postgrad., U. Nebr., 1972. Registered architect, Iowa, Tex., Colo., Mo. Designer Troy & Stalder Architects, Omaha, 1967, Architects Assocs., Des Moines, 1968-69, Logsdon & Voelter Architects, Temple, Tex., 1970; project architect Roger Schutte & Assocs., Omaha, 1972-73; architect, assoc. Robert H. Burgin & Assocs., Council Bluffs, 1973-75, Neil Astle & Assocs., Omaha, 1975-78; owner, prin. Dennis W. Stacy, AIA, Architect, Glenwood, Iowa, 1978-81; pres. Stacy Architects, Inc., Dallas, 1981—, Stacy Archtl. Studio, PLLC, 2002—. Archtl. works include: Davies Amphitheater, 1980, Addison Nat. Bank Bldg., 1985, Villa Roma, 1988, C.U. Performing Arts Ctr., 1989, Mercedes-Benz Distbn. Ctr., 1987, Dallas Chpt. AIA Offices, 1990, Janadria Festival Arena, 1994, Physicians Consultants Clinic, 1994, Horizon Pain Mgmt. Ctr., 1995, Rheumatology Assoc. Clinic, 1996, Addison Nat. Br. Bank, 1996, Cummins Southern Plains Distbn., Fabrication and Corp. Offices Ctr., 1998, Arthur Murray Dance Studio, 2001, Tatum Residence, 2001. Mem. City of Dallas Urban Design Adv. Com., 1992-96, chmn., 1995-96; dir. Greater Dallas Planning Coun., 1997-2002; chmn. Glenwood Zoning Bd. Adjustment, 1979-81; chmn. Mills County Plant Iowa Program, 1979-81; mem. S.W. Iowa Citizen's Adv. Com., Iowa State Dept. Transp., 1977-81; regional screening chmn. Am. Field Svc. Internat./Intercultural Programs, 1974-79, Iowa-Nebr. rep., 1978-80. With U.S. Army, 1969-71. Decorated Nat. Def. Svc. medal, Vietnam Svc. medal, Vietnam Campaign medal, Army Commendation medal; named Disting. Alumnus Iowa State U., 1999. Fellow AIA (chmn. nat. conv. 2000, recipient Iowa Design Honor award 1981, Dallas AIA commendation awards (2) 1990, 92, 95, 96, 97, 98, citation of honor award 1991, 92, 2001, Dallas Design awards (2) 1991, 96, 97, Tex. Design Honor award 1992, Dallas AIA Firm of Yr. award 1992, Dallas commr. design 1991, chmn. Dallas design awards 1992, pres. Dallas AIA 1996, Tex. Soc. Archs. (environ. resource com. 1994-95, chmn., Tex. arch. pub. com., 1992-98, chmn. 1997, 98), Nat. Coun. Archtl. Registration Bds., Iowa State U. Adv. Coun., 1997-2000, chmn. 1999-00, The 500 Inc. (outstanding mem. 1985), Glenwood Optimist (Disting. Svc. award 1982, pres. 1980-81), Masons. Home: 4148 Cobblers Ln Dallas TX 75287-6725 Office: 4148ACobblers Ln Dallas TX 75287-6725 E-mail: dstacyarch@aol.com.

STACY, DON MATTHEW, lawyer; b. Bluefield, W.Va., Dec. 7, 1954; s. Fred T. and Emma J. (Holey) S.; m. Nancy Jane Lusk, Mar. 20, 1982. BA in Econs., W.Va. U., 1975, JD, 1979. Bar: W.Va. 1979. Atty. United Mine Workers Am., Beckley, W.Va., 1979-81; ptnr. Stacy and Shunute Attys. at Law, Mt. Hope, 1981-82; pvt. practice Beckley, 1982—. Named one of Best Lawyers in Am., 1998-2002. Mem. ATLA, W.Va. State Bar Assn., Raleigh County Bar Assn., W.Va. Trial Lawyers Assn. Office: 600 Neville St Ste 200 Beckley WV 25801-5352

STADD, COURTNEY, federal agency administrator; With EarthWatch, Inc.; spl. asst. for space commercialization U.S. Dept. Commerce; dir. Office of Comml. Space Transp., U.S. Dept. Transp.; sr. dir. comml. space policy White House Nat. Space Coun.; founder, pres. PixSell Data Brokers Inc., Miss.; acting dep. assoc. adminstr. Office Advanced Concepts and Tech.' NASA, Washington, spl. asst. to adminstr., leader transition team, chief of staff, White House liaison. Bd. dirs. Alaska Aerospace Devel. Corp. Recipient pub. svc. award, Wash. Space Bus. Roundtable, Lloyd V. Berkner award, Am. Astron. Soc., 1994. Mem.: AIAA (sr.). Office: NASA Hdqrs Mail Code A 300 E St SW Washington DC 20546

STADDON, JOHN ERIC RAYNER, psychology, zoology, neurobiology educator; b. Grayshott, Hampshire, Eng. came to U.S., 1960; s. Leonard John and Dulce Norine (Rayner) S.; m. Lucinda Paris. BSc, Univ. Coll., London, 1960; PhD, Harvard U., 1964. Asst. prof. psychology U. Toronto, Ont., Can., 1964-67; from asst. prof. to prof. Duke U., Durham, N.C., 1967-72, prof., 1972-83, J.B. Duke prof. psychology, prof. neurobiology and zoology, 1983—. Author: Adaptive Behavior and Learning, 1983, The New Behaviorism, 2001, Adaptive Dynamics, 2001; editor Behavioural Processes, 1979-2001, Behavior and Philosophy, 1993; mem. editl. bd. Jour. Exptl. Analysis of Behavior, 1979-82. Recipient von Humboldt prize, 1985. Fellow AAAS, N.Y. Acad. Scis., Soc. Exptl. Psychologists; mem. Phi Beta Kappa (hon.), Sigma Xi. Avocations: history, philosophy of science, public policy. Office: Duke U Dept Psychol and Brain Scis PO Box 90086 Durham NC 27708-0086 E-mail: staddon@psych.duke.edu.

STADE, GEORGE GUSTAV, humanities educator, educator; b. N.Y.C., Nov. 25, 1933; s. Kurt Herman and Eva Bergit (Aronson) S.; m. Dorothy Louise Fletcher, Dec. 16, 1957; children: Bjorn, Eric, Nancy, Kirsten. BA, St. Lawrence U., 1955; MA, Columbia U., 1958, PhD, 1965. Tchr. Collegiate Sch., N.Y.C., 1957-58; instr. Bernard Baruch Sch. Bus., 1958-59, Bklyn. Poly. Inst., 1959-60, Rutgers U.-Newark, 1960-62, Columbia U., N.Y.C., 1962, asst. prof., 1965, assoc. prof., 1968, prof. English, 1971—. Cons. various law firms, N.Y.C., 1960— Author: Robert Graves, 1967, Confessions of a Lady-Killer, 1979; editor: European Writers, 13 vols., Selected Letters of E.E. Cummings, 1968, Six Modern British Writers, 1974, Six Contemporary British Writers, 1976, European Writers: Selected Authors, 3 Vols., 1992, British Writers Supplement II, 1992, British Writers Supplement III, 1995, British Writers Supplement IV, 1997; contbr. over 100 articles and reviews. Mem. PEN, N.Y. Book Critics Circle, Popular Culture Assn., MLA Home: 430 W 116th St New York NY 10027-7220 Office: Columbia U 604 Philosophy Hall New York NY 10027 E-mail: ggs3@columbia.edu.

STADELMAN, WILLIAM RALPH, chemical institution executive; b. Ont., Can., July 18, 1919; s. John Joseph and Lillian (Trachsell) S.; m. Jean MacLaren, Nov. 2, 1951; 1 child, Mary Laren. BASc, U. Toronto, 1941; MBA, U. Pa., 1949. Chief process engr. Can. Synthetic Rubber, Ltd., 1943-47; lectr. mktg. U. Pa., 1948-49; asst. to mgr. Pa. Salt Mfg. Co., 1950; sec.-treas. Ont. Research Found., Mississauga, 1950-64, pres., 1964-84, WRS Assocs., 1984—; dir., sr. exec. Inst. Chem. Sci. and Tech., 1985-89. Dir. Med. Tech. Investment Corp. Fellow World Acad. Art and Sci.; mem. Assn. Profl. Engrs. Ont., Innovation Mgmt. Assn. Can., Bd. Trade Met. Toronto, Club of Rome, Caledon Ski Club. Home and Office: WRS Assocs 31 Rykert Crescent Toronto ON Canada M4G 2T1

STADEM, CATHERINE JOSEPHINE, writer, editor, critic; b. Denver, June 3, 1938; d. Ray Vance Stocks and Josephine Margaret Way; m. Lester Kippenhan, Nov. 27, 1964 (div. June 1970); m. Per Ivar Norman Stadem, Aug. 14, 1971. BA, U. Alaska, 1984, MFA, 1997. Reporter, editor Anchorage Times, 1983-92, theater critic, 1983—; staff writer Alaska Mag., Anchorage, 1992-97; theater critic KSKA Pub. Radio, 1990—, Anchorage Daily News, 1992—. Adj. English instr. U. Alaska, Anchorage, 1997-2000; cmty. rels. writer, editor Cath. Social Svcs., Anchorage, 2000—. Co-author play: The Cost of Living, 1997. Recipient 1st pl. award in critics competition N.W. Drama Conf., 1983-84, numerous awards for writing. Fellow Nat. Critics Inst.; mem. Am. Theatre Critics Assn. (mem. ethic com., new play awards com., census com.) Democrat. Congregationalist. Avocations: cross country skiing, hiking. Home: 1826 E 26th Ave Anchorage AK 99508

STADLER, JAMES ROBERT, lawyer; b. Anderson, S.C., June 1, 1964; s. Robert Edgar and Dorothy Ann (Rhoads) S.; m. Laura Ann Rankin, Oct. 28, 1989. AB summa cum laude, Albion (Mich.) Coll., 1986; JD cum laude, U. Notre Dame, South Bend, Ind., 1989. Bar: Mich. 1989, U.S. Dist. Ct. (we. dist.) Mich. 1989, U.S. Dist. Ct. (ea. dist.) Wis., 1996, U.S. Dist. Ct. (ea. dist.) Mich. 1999, U.S. Dist. Ct. (no. dist.) N.Y. 1999, U.S. Ct. Appeals (7th cir.) 1995. Ptnr. Varnum, Riddering, Schmidt & Howlett LLP, Grand Rapids, Mich., 1989—. Contbr. articles to profl. jours. Sec. IRRA West Mich. Mem. ABA, Mich. Bar Assn., Grand Rapids Bar Assn., Phi Beta Kappa. Avocation: travel. Office: Varnum Riddering Schmidt & Howlett LLP PO Box 352 Grand Rapids MI 49501-0352

STADLER, KATHERINE LOY, advertising sales executive; b. N.Y.C., Mar. 26, 1930; d. William L. and Catherine Stadler. Student, St. John's U., 1948-49, Hunter Coll., 1957-59, NYU Mgmt. Inst., 1963-69. Br. mgr. Hull Travel Service, Inc., N.Y.C., 1959-63; with Loire Imports, Inc., 1963-69; dist. mgr. Sweet's divsn. McGraw-Hill Info. Sys. Co., 1969-74; nat. sales mgr. Floor Covering Weekly, 1974-76; account exec. Ziff-Davis Pub. Co., Hotel and Travel Index, L.A., 1976-81; founder Katherine Stadler & Assocs., 1981—83; regional mgr. Modern Salon, 1984-94; founder, CEO Bone Cancer Internat., Inc., 1999—. Mem. Nat. Cancer Inst./Consumer Advocates in Rsch. and Related Activities. Mem. Med. Mission Sisters, Roman Catholic. Ch., 1949-57; mem. Early Music Ensemble L.A., 1985-87. Named Sweet's Eastern Region Salesman of Yr., 1972, Salesman of Yr., Vance Pub., 1992. Mem. Nat. Assn. Profl. Saleswomen, L.A. Ad Club, Toastmasters. Home: 22 Robertson Way Newbury Park CA 91320-3939 E-mail: kayloy@earthlink.net.

STADLER, SELISE M. laboratory and x-ray technician; b. Portsmouth, Va., Dec. 27, 1960; d. William M. and Jorja Lee (Rigg) Gaidos; m. Stephen Michael McNeill, Feb. 29, 1988 (div. July 1993); 1 child, Stephen Michael Jr.; m. David Robert Stadler, June 15, 1996. Cert. chiropractic asst., Practice Mgmt. Assn., 1983; student, Tarrant County Coll., 2000—. Cert. radiologic technologist, instr. cert. World Modeling Assn., artificial external defibrilator, cardiopulmonary resuscitation and breath alcohol technician, bone scan technician. Chiropractic asst. Dr. Brad Hayes, D.C., Tulsa, Okla., 1982-84; adminstrv. asst. Dr. Wallace Gauntner, M.D., Pitts., 1984, sec., 1985-87; traffic mgr., office mgr. WVBS-AM/FM, Wilmington, N.C., 1985-87; med. asst. Dr. J. Bailey Bland, D.C., 1988-90; therapy/radiology supr. Dr. Roy L. Creasy Jr., D.C., 1990-91; sec. TRC Staffing Svcs., Ft. Worth, 1991; med. asst., radiologist Westside Clinic, Dallas, 1991-94; model, exec. instr. Aleksandra's Prodns., Ft. Worth, 1994-96; med. asst., radiologist Dr. Wayne R. English Jr., D.O., 1994-2000; x-ray lab. technician Med Care Now, Fort Worth, 2000—; x-ray/bone scan technician Kaner Med. Group, Bedford, 2002—. Author published poetry. Vol. Holy Family Cath. Ch., Ft. Worth, 1997-99. Mem. Tex. Soc. Radiologic Technologists (cert. in CPR and automated external defibrillation program). Episcopalian. Avocations: scuba diving, horseback riding, tennis, rollerblading. Office: Med Care Now 6340 N Beach St Fort Worth TX 76137

STADNICAR, JOSEPH WILLIAM, lawyer; b. Corpus Christi, Tex., Oct. 30, 1963; s. Edward and Carrie Louise (Garris) S.; m. Susan Marie Bitzel, Apr. 25, 1992. BBA, John Carroll U., 1986; MBA, Ohio State U., 1989, JD, 1990. Bar: Ohio 1990. Assoc. Gerald E. Schlafman Co., Fairborn, Ohio, 1991-95; pvt. practice Beavercreek, 1995-97. Asst. prosecuting atty. City of Fairborn, 1990-95; prosecuting atty. City of Beavercreek, 1990-2001; assoc. Hammond & Stier Law Office, Beavercreek, 1996-98, ptnr. Hammond, Stier and Stadnicar, 1998—. Trustee Family Violence Prevention Ctr. of Greene County, Xenia, Ohio, 1995—, Am. Heart Assn., Miami Valley, 1996—. Mem. ABA, Ohio Bar Assn., Greene County Bar Assn., Rotary, Beavercreek C. of C., Fairborn C. of C. Avocations: fishing, camping. Office: 3834 Dayton Xenia Rd Beavercreek OH 45432-2833 E-mail: stadnicar@aol.com.

STADTER, PHILIP AUSTIN, classicist, educator; b. Cleve., Nov. 29, 1936; s. John M. and Mary Louise (Jones) S.; m. Lucia Angela Ciapponi, July 6, 1963; children: Paul, Maria, Mark. BA, Princeton U., 1958; MA, Harvard U., 1959, PhD, 1963. Instr. U. N.C., Chapel Hill, 1962-64, asst. prof., 1964-67, assoc. prof., 1967-71, prof., 1971—, chmn. dept. classics, 1976-86, prof. comparative lit., 1991—, Falk prof. humanities, 1991—. Author: Plutarch's Historical Methods, 1965, The Public Library of Renaissance Florence, 1972, Arrian of Nicomedia, 1980, A Commentary on Plutarch's Pericles, 1989; editor: The Speeches of Thucydides, 1973, Plutarch and the Historical Tradition, 1992. Fulbright fellow Rome, 1960-61; Guggenheim fellow Florence, Italy, 1967-68; NEH fellow, 1974-75; fellow Am. Council Learned Socs., Oxford, Eng., 1982-83 Fellow Nat. Humanities Ctr.; mem. Am. Philol. Assn. (dir. 1977-80), Am. Assn. Ancient Historians, Soc. Promotion of Hellenic Studies, Classical Assn. Middle West and South Democrat. Roman Catholic. Office: U NC Dept Classics Chapel Hill NC 27599-3145

STADTLÄNDER, CHRISTIAN THOMAS KARL-HEINZ, microbiologist, researcher; b. Hanover, Germany, June 8, 1957; came to the U.S., 1989; s. Karl-Heinz Friedrich Johannes and Helga Marianne Ingrid (Steffen) S.; m. Jeanne Marie Parr, Feb. 12, 1994. BS in Biology, U. Hanover, Germany, 1982, MS in Biology, 1985; PhD in Microbiology, U. Hanover, 1987; MPH in Epidemiology, U. Ala., Birmingham, 1997. Postdoctoral fellow Progen Biotechnik, Heidelberg, Germany, 1987-88, The Vet. Sch., Hanover, 1988-89, U. Ala., Birmingham, 1989-91, rsch. assoc., 1992-93; scientist Hoechst, Frankfurt, Germany, 1991-92; asst. prof. Clemson (S.C.) U., 1993-94, rsch. assoc. prof., 1995-96; scientist, UAB Rsch. Found. U. Ala., Birmingham, 1996-97, scientist, sch. pub. health, 1996-2000. With German Navy, 1978-80. Rsch. fellow Deutsche Forschungsgemeinschaft, Germany, 1989, U. Ala., Birmingham, 1990. Mem. AAAS, Microscopy Soc. Am., Am. Soc. for Microbiology, Internat. Orgn. for Mycoplasmology, Vereinigung für Allgemeine und Angewandte Mikrobiologie, N.Y. Acad. Scis. Avocations: golfing, playing tennis, skiing.

STADTMAN, EARL REECE, biochemist, researcher; b. Carrizozo, N.Mex., Nov. 15, 1919; s. Walter William and Minnie Ethyl (Reece) Stadtman; m. Thressa Campbell, Oct. 19, 1943. BS, U. Calif., Berkeley, 1942, Ph.D, 1949. With Alcan Hwy. survey Pub. Rds. Adminstrn., 1942—43; rsch. asst. U. Calif., Berkeley, 1938—49, sr. lab. technican, 1949; AEC fellow Mass. Gen. Hosp., Boston, 1949—50; chemist lab. cellular physiology Nat. Heart Inst., 1950—58, chief enzyme sect., 1958—62, section chief lab. biochemistry, 1962—. Biochemist Max Planck Inst., Munich, Pasteur Inst., Paris, 1959—60; faculty dept. microbiology U. Md.; prof. biochemistry grad. program dept. biology Johns Hopkins U.; adv. com. Life Scis. Rsch. Office, Am. Fedn. Biol. Sci., 1974—77; chmn. dept. biochemistry Found. Advanced Edn. Scis., 1966—68; biochem. study sect. rsch. grants NIH, 1959—63; Julius Schultz Meml. vis. prof. U. Miami, 2002. Editor: Jour. Biol. Chemistry, 1960—65, Current Topics in Cellular Regulation, 1968—, Circulation Rsch., 1968—70; exec. editor: Archives Biochemistry and Biophysics, 1960—2001, exec. editor: Life Scis., 1973—75, exec. editor: Procs. NAS, 1975—81, exec. editor: Trends in Biochem. Rsch., 1975—78; mem. editl. bd. Biochemistry, 1969—76, 1981—. Recipient medallion, Soc. de Chemie Biologique, 1955, U. Pisa, 1966, Presdl. Rank award as Disting. Sr. Exec., 1981, Rsch. award, Am. Aging Assn., 1992, Lifetime Achievement and Mentoring award, NIH, 1998, Sci. and Humaity prize, Oxygen Club Calif., 2002, Trevor Slater award, Soc. for Free Rabical Rsch., 2002. Mem.: NAS (award in microbiology 1970), Washington Acad. Scis. (award biol. chemistry 1957, Nat. medal sci. 1979, meritorious exec. award 1980, Robert A. Welch award in chemistry 1991, Paul Glenn award in aging 1993), Am. Soc. Microbiology, Am. Acad. Arts and Scis., Am. Soc. Biol. Chemists (publs. com. 1966—70, coun. 1974—77, pres. 1983—, Merck award 1983), Am. Chem. Soc. (exec. com. biol. div 1959—64, chmn. div. 1963—64, Paul Lewis Lab. award in enzyme chemistry 1952, Hillebrand award 1969). Office: Nat Heart and Lung Inst 9000 Rockville Pike Bethesda MD 20892-0001

STADTMILLER, MARGUERITA W. advertising executive; b. Liverpool, Eng., June 14, 1942; came to U.S., 1963; d. William and Ada Lillian Melville; m. Gerald Carl Stadtmiller, Oct. 8, 1968. Grad., Ellergreen Coll., Liverpool, 1960; diploma, Liverpool Sch. Journalism, 1962. Cert. state gen. contractor, real estate salesperson, Fla. Editl. asst. Nat. Assn. Elec. Distbn., N.Y.C., 1963-65; asst. editor Nassau (Bahamas) Guardian, 1965-68; exec. sec. Ft. Lauderdale (Fla.) News, 1969-73, sales exec., 1973-78; suburban sales mgr. West, Lauderhill, Fla., 1978-80; retail advt. mgr. Sun Sentinel, Pompano Beach, 1980-83; retail sales mgr. Ft. Lauderdale News/Sun Sentinel, 1983-90; nat. travel sales mgr. Sun Sentinel Co., Ft. Lauderdale, 1990-96, diversity trainer, 1995-99; sr. sales mgr. Leisure Group, 1997-2000; travel cons., 2001—. Mem. leadership in giving United Way, Broward County, 1996-99. Mem. Newspaper Advt. Sales Assn. (sec., bd. dirs. 1993-99), Fla. Hotel Motel Assn., Bon Vivants, Am. Bus. Women's Assn. (pres. 1985, Woman of Yr. award 1986), Internat. Soc. Poets. Avocations: writing, golf, collectibles, travel.

STADTMUELLER, JOSEPH PETER, federal judge; b. Oshkosh, Wis., Jan. 28, 1942; s. Joseph Francis and Irene Mary (Kilp) S.; m. Mary Ellen Brady, Sept. 5, 1970; children: Jeremy, Sarah. BS in Bus. Adminstrn., Marquette U., 1964, JD, 1967. Bar: Wis. 1967, U.S. Supreme Ct. 1980. With Kluwin, Dunphy, Hankin and McNulty, 1968-69; asst. U.S. atty. Dept. Justice, Milw., 1969-74, 1st. asst. U.S. atty., 1974-75; with Stepke, Kossow, Trebon and Stadtmueller, Milw., 1975-76; asst. U.S. atty. Dept. Justice, 1977-78, dep. U.S. atty., 1978-81, U.S. atty., 1981-87; judge U.S. Dist. Ct. (ea. dist.) Wis., Milw., 1987—, chief judge, 1995—2002. Mem. 7th Cir. Jud. Coun., 1995—2002. Recipient Spl. Commendation award Atty. Gen. U.S., 1974, 80. Mem. ABA, State Bar Wis. (bd. govs. 1979-83, exec. com. 1982-83), Am. Law Inst., Fed. Judges Assn. (bd. dirs. 1995—, sec. 2001--). Clubs: University (Milw.). Republican. Roman Catholic. Office: 471 US Courthouse 517 E Wisconsin Ave Milwaukee WI 53202-4500

STAEGER, EARL, nurse; b. St. Louis, Apr. 17, 1947; s. Earl and Virginia (Tilton) S.; m. Carla Campbell; children: Brian, Kevin, Eric, Bruce. BA, S.W. Tex. State U., 1970. RN, Tex., N.Mex.; CCRN; cert. ACLS, advanced trauma life support. Formerly staff nurse CCU Columbia East Hosp., El Paso, Tex.; staff nurse ICU Las Cruces (N.Mex.) Meml. Hosp. Mem. AACN. Home: 9112 Lait Dr El Paso TX 79925-5948

STAEHELIN, LUCAS ANDREW, cell biology educator; b. Sydney, Australia, Feb. 10, 1939; came to U.S., 1969; s. Lucas Eduard and Isobel (Malloch) S.; m. Margrit Weibel, Sept. 17, 1965; children: Daniel Thomas, Philip Roland, Marcel Felix. Dipl. Natw., Swiss Fed. Inst. Tech., Zurich, 1963, PhD in Biology, 1966. Research scientist N.Z. Dept. Sci. and Indsl. Research, 1966-69; research fellow in cell biology Harvard U., Cambridge, Mass., 1969-70; asst. prof. cell biology U. Colo., Boulder, 1970-73, assoc. prof., 1973-79, prof., 1979—. Vis. prof. U. Freiburg, 1978, Swiss Fed. Inst. Tech., 1984, 92, U. Melbourne, Australia, 1998; mem. cellular biology and physiology study sect. NIH, Bethesda, Md., 1980-84; mem. DOE panel on rsch. directions for the energy bioscis., 1988, 92; mem. NSF adv. panel for cellular orgn., 1994-96; mem. plant biology panel NASA. Editor Jour. Cell Biology, 1977-81, European Jour. Cell Biology, 1981-90, Plant Physiology, 1986-92, Plant Jour., 1991-97, Biology of the Cell, 1996-99; editor: (with C.J. Antzen) Encyclopedia of Plant Physiology, Vol. 19, Photosynthesis III, 1986; contbr. numerous articles to sci. jours. Recipient Humboldt award Humboldt Found., 1978, Sci. Tchr. award U. Colo., 1984, Outstanding Faculty award U. Colo.-Boulder Parents Assn., 2001; grantee NIH, 1971—, USDA, 1994—, NASA, 1997—; hon. sr. fellow U. Melbourne, Australia, 1998. Mem. AAAS,

Am. Soc. Cell Biology, Am. Soc. Plant Physiology, German Acad. Natural Scis. Leopoldina. Home: 2855 Dover Dr Boulder CO 80305-5305 Office: Dept Molecular Cell U Colo 347 UCB Boulder CO 80309-0347 E-mail: staeheli@spot.colorado.edu.

STAEHLE, ROBERT L. foundation executive; b. Rochester, N.Y., Apr. 22, 1955; s. Henry Carl and Isabel Montgomery S. BS in Aero. and Astronautic Engring., Purdue U., 1977. Prin. investigator Skylab Expt. ED-31 (bacteria aboard Skylab), NASA/Marshall Space Flight Center, Huntsville, Ala., 1972-74, student trainee engring., 1974-77; sci. observation analyst Caltech/Jet Propulsion Lab., Pasadena, Calif., 1977-78; engr. advanced projects group, 1978-83; mem. tech. staff system integration sect. of Space Sta., 1983-87; mem. tech. staff and space sta., user ops. team leader, 1987-88; tech. mgr. Jet Propulsion Lab., Pasadena, Calif., 1988—, mgr. space sta. Freedom support office Pasadena ops., 1990-92, Pluto team leader, 1992-93, mgr. Pluto Express preproject, 1993-96, mgr. Ice and Fire preprojects, 1996-98, dep. mgr. outer planets/solar probe project, 1998-2000, dept. mgr. Europa Orbiter project, 2000—02. Prin. founder, pres. World Space Found., South Pasadena, Calif., 1979—; founding dir. So. Calif. Space Bus. Roundtable, 1987-95; bd. dirs. Altadena Foothills Conservancy, 2000—. Co-author: Project Solar Sail, New Am. Libr., 1990; contbr. articles to profl. jours. Mem. Cmty. Leaders Adv. Bd. for Irvine Scholars, Occidental Coll., L.A., 1996-97; bd. dirs. Caltech Y, 1987-93, Altadena Foothills Conservancy, 2000—. Nat. Space Club Goddard scholar, 1977; Charles A. Lindbergh Fund grantee, 1986. Fellow Brit. Interplanetary Soc.; mem. AIAA, Tau Beta Pi, Sigma Gamma Tau. Avocations: photography, hiking, mountain biking. Office: Jet Propulsion Lab Pasadena CA 91109 E-mail: robert.l.staehle@jpl.nasa.gov.

STAELIN, DAVID HUDSON, electrical engineering educator, consultant; b. Toledo, May 25, 1938; s. Carl Gustav and Margaret E. (Hudson) S.; m. Ellen Mahoney, June 16, 1962; children: Carl H., Katharine E., Paul H. SB, MIT, 1960, SM, 1961, ScD in Elec. Engring., 1965. Instr. elec. engring. MIT, Cambridge, 1965, asst. prof., 1965-69, assoc. prof., 1969-76, prof., 1976—, asst. dir. Lincoln Lab. Lexington, 1990—2001. Vis. asst. scientist Nat. Radio Astronomy Obs., Charlottesville, Va., 1968-69; cons. Jet Propulsion Lab., Pasadena, Calif., 1969, Wellesley, Mass., 1965—; dir. Environ. Rsch. and Tech., Inc., Concord, Mass., 1969-78; co-founder, chmn. PictureTel Corp., Peabody, Mass., 1984-87; mem. com. on radio frequency requirements for rsch., NAS, Washington, 1980-86, chmn. 1983-86; chmn. advanced microwave sounder working group NASA, Washington, 1981-82, mem. space applications adv. com.,NASA, 1983-86. Co-author: Made in America, 1989, Electromagnetic Waves, 1994; also articles; patentee grinding and polishing sheet glass, display of dynamic images, ribbon-beam cathode ray tube. Fellow IEEE, AAAS; mem. Am. Geophys. Union, Am. Meteorl. Soc., Internat. Union for Radio Sci. Office: MIT Rm 26-341 Cambridge MA 02139

STAELIN, EARL HUDSON, lawyer; b. Toledo, Apr. 24, 1940; s. Carl Gustav and Margaret E. (Hudson) S.; m. Carol Jane Keeney, Mar. 24, 1973 (div. 1995); 1 child, Vijay Hudson. BA, Yale U., 1962; LLB, U. Mich., 1966. Bar: Ohio 1966, U.S. Dist. Ct. (no. dist.) Ohio 1967, Tex. 1982, U.S. Dist. Ct. (we. dist.) Tex. 1988, U.S. Dist. Ct. (no. dist.) Tex. 1991, U.S. Ct. Appeals (5th cir.) 1994, Colo. 1998. Assoc. atty. Marshall, Melhorn, Toledo, 1966-69; pvt. practice, 1969; lectr. law U. Toledo Coll. Law, 1971-72; staff atty. Toledo Legal Aid Soc., 1969-71, dir., 1971-76, sr. staff atty., 1977-81; pvt. practice cons. nutrition Austin, Tex., 1981; staff atty. City of Austin Law Dept., 1982-86; pvt. practice Law Ofcs. of Earl H. Staelin, Austin and Aurora, Colo., 1986—. Presenter in field. Contbr. articles to profl. jours. Pres. Toledo Coun. on World Affairs, 1971-76; chmn. Mayors' com to rewrite Housing Code, Toledo, 1976; co-organizer Conferences on Nutrition and Crime, Austin, 1982, San Antonio, 1983. Mem. Colo. Bar Assn., State Bar Tex., Tex. Trial Lawyers Assn., Interfaith Alliance Colo. Democrat. Unitarian Universalist. Home: 12701 E Asbury Cir # 102 Aurora CO 80014-5317 Office: 12701 E Asbury Cir # 102 Aurora CO 80014-5317 E-mail: estaelin@attbi.com.

STAELIN, RICHARD, business administration educator; b. Larchmont, N.Y., Aug. 3, 1939; s. Richard Carl and Dorothy (Potts) S.; m. Julie Ann Fischer, Aug. 24, 1963; children: Adam, Kate. BSME, U. Mich., 1961, BS in Math., 1962, MBA, 1963, PhD, 1969. Market planner IBM, Harrison, N.Y., 1963-66; prof. Carnegie-Mellon U., Pitts., 1969-82; Edward and Rose Donnell prof. Duke U., Durham, N.C., 1982—, assoc. dean faculty affairs, 1982-91, assoc. dean exec. edn. NC, 2000—02, deputy dean, 2002—; mng. dir. GEMBA, 1995-97; exec. dir. Mktg. Sci. Inst., Cambridge, Mass., 1991-93; vis. prof. Australian Grad. Sch., Kensington, Australia, 1980-81. Author: Consumer Protection Legislation and the U.S. Food Industry, 1980; mem. editorial bd. Jour. Mktg. Rsch., 1974-82, Jour. Consumer Rsch., 1976-87; area editor Mktg. Sci., 1983-88; editor-in-chief Mktg. Sci., 1995-97. Mem. Pitts. Exec. Bd.; treas. Pitts. Arts and Crafts Ctr., 1976-79; bd. dirs. Dispute Settlement Ctr., Chapel Hill, N.C.; bd. vis. drama dept. Duke U., 1990-96. Recipient Best Mktg. Paper award Inst. Mgmt. Sci., 1985, hon. mention, 1986, NCNB Faculty award 1990, AMA/Irwin Disting. Mktg. Educators award, 1996, O'Dell award for Best Paper JMR, 1998; HEW grantee, 1972-74, NSF grantee, 1973-79. Mem. Am. Mktg. Assn. (Converse award 2000), Assn. Consumer Research, INFORMS. Office: Fuqua School of Business Science Dr Rm 339 Durham NC 27706-2597 E-mail: rick@staelin.com.

STAFFEL, EDWARD ROSS, JR. executive, consultant; b. San Antonio, June 7, 1963; s. Edward Ross and Moselle Mixson (Kouri). BA in Econ., U. Colo., 1987; MBA in Finance, Tex. Christian U., 1993. Mkt. rschr. Williams Distbn., Dallas, 1987—88; Cost analyst General Dynamics, Fort Worth, 1988-92; acct. Accts. on Call, 1993-95; project acct. Fairfield Devel., Grand Prairie, 1995-96; controller Advo Home Care, Fort Worth, 1996-98; pres. Staffel Enterprises, Inc., 1998—2001; treasury mgr. Chem. Lime Co. and Subs., Ft. Worth, 2001—. Mem. TCV MBA Alumni Assn. (v.p. 1996-97, exec. bd. 2000—), Colo. Alumni Assn., Nat. Soc. Accts., Am. Assn. Individual Investors. Avocations: golf, fishing, cooking, basketball, tennis. Home: 2448 Lofton Ter Fort Worth TX 76109-1123 Office: Staffel Enterprises Inc PO box 100762 Fort Worth TX 76185 E-mail: ross@staffel.com.

STAFFIER, PAMELA MOORMAN, psychologist; b. Passaic, N.J., Dec. 7, 1942; d. Wynant Clair and Jeannette Frances (Rentzsch) Moorman; m. John Staffier, Jr., Apr. 5, 1975; children: M. Anthony, C. Matthew. BA, Bucknell U., 1964; MA in Psychology, Assumption Coll., Worcester, Mass., 1970, CAGS, 1977; PhD, Union Inst., 1978. Psychologist Westboro (Mass.) State Hosp., 1965; prin. psychologist, also asst. to supt., 1973-76; psychologist Moriarty Mental Health Clinic; psychiat. cons. local gen. hosp. Rsch. psychologist Wrentham (Mass.) State Sch., 1966, Cushing Hosp., Framingham, Mass., 1967; prin. psychologist, also asst. to supt. Grafton (Mass.) State Hosp., 1967-72; dir. Staffier Clinic, 1978—. Mem. Am. Psychol. Assn. (assoc.), Am. Psychol. Practitioners Assn. (founding mem.), Mass. Psychol. Assn., Nat. Register Health Svc. Providers in Psychology. Achievements include research on state hosp. closings, biochem. basis of Schizophrenia. Home: PO Box 1103 Westborough MA 01581-6103 Office: 57 E Main St Westborough MA 01581-1464

STAFFORD, ABI, ballerina; b. Carlisle, Pa. Studied with, Ctrl. Pa. Youth Ballet, Carlisle; studied, Sch. Am. Ballet Summer Program, 1996—97, Sch. Am. Ballet, 1998. Apprentice N.Y.C. Ballet, 1999—2000, mem. corps de ballet, 2000—02, soloist, 2002—. Dancer prin. roles (ballets) George Balanchine's Ballo Della Regina, Divertimento No. 15, The Nutcracker, La Source, Symphony in C (3d Movement), Symphony in Three Movements, Tschaikovsky Pas de Deux, Valse-Fantaisie, featured roles Stars and Stripes, Swan Lake, Walpurgisnacht Ballet, Peter Martin's Sleeping Beauty, Miriam Mahdaviani's Appalachia Waltz, Fanfare, Martins' Viva Verdi, Swerve Poems, Mercurial Manoeuvres, Organon. Named Janice Levine dancer, 2000—01. Office: NYC Ballet NY State Theatre 20 Lincoln Ctr Plz New York NY 10023-6913*

STAFFORD, ARTHUR CHARLES, medical association administrator; b. Cleve., May 10, 1947; s. Charles Arthur and Florence Mildred (Hovey) S.; m. Patricia Anne Cz, Dec. 20, 1991. BS, Kent State U., 1977; MBA, Lake Erie Coll., 1984. Med. tech. VA, Cleve., 1977-81, supr. med. tech., 1981-97; lab. mgr. Univ. Hosps. Health System Meml. Hosp. of Geneva, 1998-99; instr. Lake Erie Coll., Painesville, 1980-82, Cuyahoga C.C., Cleve., 1988-91; mgr. customer svc. Giant Eagle Supermarket, Madison, 2001—02. Pres. Kent State U. Veterans Assn., 1974, mem. Kent State U Budget Review Com., 1975. Contbr. articles to profl. jour. Mem. Am. Legion, 1974, VFW, 1973. With USN, 1968-72. Mem.: Rock and Roll Hall of Fame, Founders Club. Republican. Avocations: genealogy, computers, antiques, chess, cooking. Home: 2193 Chimney Ridge Dr Madison OH 44057-2588 E-mail: czstafford@ncweb.com.

STAFFORD, CLAY, writer, film producer, director, actor, educator, public speaker; b. Chattanooga, Dec. 23, 1961; s. Joseph Edward and Katherine Louise (Parker) S.; m. Jacqueline Ellis, Aug. 12, 1995. Student, Freed-Hardeman Coll., Henderson, Tenn., 1979-80, U. Tenn., 1980-82; BA in Film and Video, Union Inst., 1989; MFA in Motion Pictures, U. Miami, 1992. Studio support staff Universal Studios, L.A., 1985-86; writer, prodr., dir. The Clay Stafford Co., L.A., Miami, Nashville, 1986—. Adj. prof. U. Miami, 1992-93, Union Inst., 1992-93, Miami Dade C.C., 1992, U. Tenn., 1995-97. Prodr., dir., writer WLRN-TV, Miami, 1987-90, Michael, 1989, Patterns of Power, 1990; dir., prodr.: Proud to be Me, 1989, New Horizons in Bonsai, 1990, We are Family, 1990, New Horizons in Bonsai II, 1992; dir., prodr., writer, actor: Mazatlan Mangle, 1986, Lost Amulet of Abalone Cove, 1987, For Lee's Sake, 1986, Bad Loch, 1986; prodr.: Sewing Without Pins IV, 1988; writer, prodr., actor: How to Win Auditions: An Actor's Guide to Success, 1994; writer: Marine Inboard Diesel Engine Maintenance, 1989, Marine Inboard Gasoline Engine Maintenance, 1989, Tell Me Why: Flight, 1989, Esquire Travel Series-Boston, 1991, Esquire Travel Series-California, 1991, Esquire Travel Series-Florida, 1991, Esquire Travel Series-New York, 1991; author: Know Business Like Show Business, 1986, The Tennessee Performer's Directory, 1995, The Georgia Performer's Directory, 1996, Mark Twains's Adventures of Huckleberry Finn-Discovery Spot edit., 2002; book editor: Thoughts for the day: Beyond the Blue, 1985, Sewing Without Pins IV, 1988, Lannom's Memory Methods, 1989, New Horizons in Bonsai, 1991, Kenneth Grahame's the Wind in the Willows-Discovery Spot edit., 2001; actor: The Wizard of Oz, 1972, Alice in Wonderland, 1973, Really Rosie, 1973, The Skin of Our Teeth, 1973, Willowsong, 1973, Winnie the Pooh, 1974, Endless Pavement, 1975, Free to Be, You and Me, 1976, You're a Good Man, Charlie Brown, 1977, The Lion in Winter, 1978, Our Town, 1978, Carnival, 1979, The King and I, 1980, Diary of Adam and Eve, 1981, Ten Little Indians, 1981, Lone Star, 1984, Angels Fall, 1984, Aesop's Fables, 1984, Androcles and the Lion, 1984, Tom Sawyer, 1985, Murder at La Quinta, 1986, Bank Job, 1986, Days of Our Lives, 1986, Gigolo, 1986, Chongqing Acrobats of China, 1986, The Fantasticks, 1986, Mining, 1987, Vampire, 1989, Reform, 1997, No Place That Far, 1998, Toyota Magic Summer, 2001. Valedictorian scholar U. Tenn., 1980, Paul Koblentz Meml. scholar, 1982, Chancellor's scholar, 1982, Vocal Performance scholar, 1982. Mem. AFTRA, SAG, Authors Guild, Authors League Am., Mystery Writers Am., Soc. Children's Book Writers and Illustrators, Tenn. Master Gardener Assn., Coun. for the Written Word (former chmn. bd.), Franklin Citizens' Police Acad. Alumni, FBI Citizens' Acad. Alumni, Toastmasters Internat., Mortarboard Soc., Pi Sigma Alpha. Avocations: reading, exercise, outdoors, music, movies. Office: The Clay Stafford Co/Am Blackguard PO Box 680686 Franklin TN 37068-0686

STAFFORD, DONALD GENE, chemistry educator; b. Valliant, Okla., Oct. 9, 1930; s. Otto Lewis and Rose Lavelle (Osterdock) S.; m. Jane Wright, July 5, 1951; children— Michael Royce, Robert Gene, Joel Dan. BS, U. Okla., 1957, PhD, 1969; MS, Okla. State U., 1961. Prof. sci. edn. East Cen. U., Ada, Okla., 1961-73, prof. chemistry, 1973—. Adj. prof. U. Okla., Norman, 1970—. Author: The Improvement of Science in Oklahoma (7-12), 1970, Guidelines and Successful Practices in Elementary Edn, 1970, Wings for a Dinosaur, 1972, Early Childhood Resource Book, 1972, Teaching Science in the Elementary School, 1973, 3d edit., 1979, Teaching Science in the Secondary School, 1973, Research, Teaching, and Learning with the Piaget Model, 1976, Investigations in Physical Science, 1976, The Learning Science Program K-6 (7 children's books and 7 tchr.'s guides), 1976, TOP, The Oklahoma Project, Chemistry, 1987, The Learning Cycle, 1988, The Lost City of Balee, A Novel for Young Teenagers, 2000, Don's Rhymes, A Book of Poetry, 2000. Served with AUS, 1948-53. Mem. Am. Chem. Soc., Nat. Sci. Tchrs. Assn., Okla. Sci. Tchrs. (pres. 1973-74, 78-79), Sigma Xi. Home: 2202 Fullview Dr Ada OK 74820-4436

STAFFORD, FRANK P. economist, educator; BA, Northwestern U., 1962; MBA, U. Chgo., 1964, PhD, 1968; married; two children. Asst. prof. econs. U. Mich., 1966-71, assoc. prof., 1971-73, 74-75, prof., 1978—, chmn., 1980-83; spl. asst. for econ. affairs Office Asst. Sec. Policy, Eval. and Rsch., Dept. Labor, Washington, 1975-76; vis. assoc. prof. Stanford U., 1973-74; vis. prof. U. Saarlands, Saarbruken, Rep. of Germany, 1986; vis. scholar Worklife Study Ctr. Stockholm, 1988; mem. small grants panel Dept. Labor, 1978-80; researcher Indsl. Inst. for Econ. and Social Rsch., Stockholm., 1979, 84. Editor: (with F. Thomas Juster) Americans' Use of Time, 1982; bd. editors Am. Econ. Rev., 1976-78; contbr. articles to profl. jours. Home: 3535 Daleview Dr Ann Arbor MI 48105-9686

STAFFORD, FRANK PETER, JR. economics educator, consultant; b. Chgo., Sept. 17, 1940; s. Frank Peter and Ida Gustava (Tormala) S.; m. Lilian Elisabeth Lundin, Aug. 8, 1964; children: Craig Peter, Jennifer Elisabeth, Christine Anna BA, Northwestern U., 1962; MBA, U. Chgo., 1964, PhD, 1968. Asst. prof. econs. U. Mich., 1966-71, assoc. prof., 1971-73, 74-75, prof., 1976—, chmn. dept. econs., 1980—, rsch. scientist Inst. Social Rsch., 1995—, chair budget study com., 1995—, assoc. dir. Inst. for Social Rsch., 2000—. Vis. assoc. prof. Grad. Sch. Bus.-Stanford U., 1973-74; spl. asst. for econ. affairs U.S. Dept. Labor, Washington, 1975-76; vis. prof. dept. econs. U. Saarlandes, Fed. Republic Germany, 1986; faculty rsch. assoc. Inst. Social Rsch., Ann Arbor, 1979—; vis. scholar Indsl. Inst. for Econs. and Social Rsch., Stockholm, 1979, 83, 90, Worklife Study Ctr., Stockholm, 1988, 90; Tinbergen Found. prof. U. Amsterdam, 1992, 94; panel mem. Social Sci. Rsch. Coun., N.Y.C., 1979—; rsch. assoc. Nat. Bur. Econ. Rsch., Cambridge, Mass., 1983—; prof. econs. Tinbsrgne Found. U. Amsterdam, 1992; vis. scholar U. Stockholm, 1994. Author, editor: Time Use Goods and Well Being, 1986, Studies in Labor Market Behavior: Sweden and the United States, 1981; mem. editorial bd.: Am. Econ. Rev., 1976-78; contbr. articles to profl. jours. Dir. Panel Study of Income Dynamics, 1995—. Grantee NSF, 1973, 80, 95—, NICHD, 1995—, Nat. Ins. on Aging, 1999—. Mem. Am. Econs. Assn. Home: 3535 Daleview Dr Ann Arbor MI 48105-9686 Office: U Mich Dept Econs Lorch Hall Rm 312 Ann Arbor MI 48105

STAFFORD, GEORGE TIMOTHY, surgeon; b. Oct. 16, 1938; BS, Wheaton Coll., 1960; MD, Med. Coll. Ala., 1964. Diplomate Am. Bd. Surgery. Pvt. practice, Birmingham, Ala., 1971-72; missionary physician Evang. Alliance Mission, Wheaton, Ill., 1972-98; surgeon San Luis Valley Med., Alamosa, Colo., 1998—. Office: 2115 Stuart Ave Alamosa CO 81101-2269

STAFFORD, JAMES FRANCIS, cardinal; Former archibishop of Denver; pres. Pontifical Coun. for Laity, Vatican, 1998—. Office: Pontifico Consiglio per i Laici Palazzo San Calisto 00120 Vatican City Italy E-mail: jfstafford@laity.va.

STAFFORD, JAMES POLK, JR. civil engineer; b. Oxford, Miss., Oct. 13, 1918; s. James Polk and Lottie Etoile (Smith) S.; m. Edna Earle Snyder, May 29, 1941; children: Jeanette Patricia, Pamela Anne. BS, Miss. State Coll., 1939; MS, Iowa State Coll., 1940. Registered profl. engr. Miss. Engr. Soil Conservation Svc., U.S. Dept. Agr., 1940, 46; officer U.S. Army Corps Engrs., 1941-45; civil engr. office engring. br., constrn. dvisn. U.S. Army Engr. Dist., Vicksburg, Miss., 1947-62; resident engr. DeGray Dam, Dike and Powerhouse, 1963-72; chief constrn. divsn. U.S. Army Engr. dist., Vicksburg, 1973-86, ret., 1986. Pres. Vicksburg Cmty. Chorus, 1975-76. With USAR, 1946-73. Recipient George Marshall Scholastic award Command and Gen. Staff Coll., Meritorious Svc. medal U.S. Army Res., 1973. Mem. Soc. Am. Mil. Engrs. (Goethals award 1974), ASCE, U.S. Soc. on Dams, Lions. Methodist.

STAFFORD, JEFFREY S. small business owner; b. Ridgewood, N.J., 1954; s. William Warren and June Elizabeth Stafford; m. Pamela Marguerite Stafford, Apr. 1, 1984; children: Gary, Mark. Student, Fairleigh Dickinson, 1973. Owner, pres. Stafford Tire Ctr., Inc., Red Bank, N.J., 1975—. Cmty. advisor Tinton Falls (N.J.) State Bank, 1999. Sponsor Men's Major Modified Ditch World Champs, 1993. Named Outstanding Citizen of the Yr. VFW, 1993. Republican. Avocations: softball, travel. Office: Stafford Tire Ctr Inc 400 Rte 35 Red Bank NJ 07701-5916

STAFFORD, JOHN ROGERS, pharmaceutical and household products company executive; b. Harrisburg, Pa., Oct. 24, 1937; s. Paul Henry and Gladys Lee (Sharp) S.; m. Inge Paul, Aug. 22, 1959; children: Carolyn, Jennifer, Christina, Charlotte. AB, Dickinson Coll., 1959; LLB with distinction, George Washington U., 1962, Degree (hon.), 1994. Bar: D.C. 1962. Assoc. Steptoe & Johnson, Washington, 1962-66; gen. atty. Hoffman-LaRoche, Nutley, N.J., 1966-67, group atty., 1967-70; gen. counsel Am. Home Products Corp., N.Y.C., 1970-74, v.p., 1972-77, sr. v.p., 1977-80, exec. v.p. Madison, N.J., 1980-81, pres., from 1981, chmn., CEO N.Y.C., 1986-2001, chmn., 2001—. Bd. dirs. The Chase Manhattan Corp., Honeywell Internat. Inc., Verizon Comm.; trustee Thiteen/WNET. Bd. dirs. Christopher Reeve Paralysis Found. Recipient John Bell Larner 1st Scholar award George Washington U. Law Sch., 1962, Outstanding Achievement Alumnus award, 1981 Mem.: NAM (bd. dirs.), ABA, DC Bar Assn., Baltusrol Club, Essex Fells (NJ) Country Club. Office: 5 Giralda Farms Madison NJ 07940-1021

STAFFORD, KENNETH VICTOR, SR. minister; b. Claremont, N.H., Dec. 30, 1926; s. Victor Ernest and Marion (Dodge) S.; m. Doreen Beverly Mossey, Apr. 12, 1947; children: Beverlee, Kenneth Jr., Marilee, Mark. Diploma in airframe/powerplant, Spartan Sch. Aeronautics, Tulsa, 1948, diploma in airport mgmt., 1949; B in Counseling, Valley Christian U., Fresno, Calif., 1981; M in Counseling, Valley Christian U., 1983; D Ministry in Christian Counseling, Christian Bible Coll. and Sem., Independence, Mo., 1997. Ordained to ministry Christian Ch., 1978; cert. counselor, 1990. Pres. Jacob's Well, Tulsa, 1974-78; dir. spiritual life Christian Broadcasting Network, Virginia Beach, Va., 1978, assoc. dir. counseling, 1978-83, dir. counseling, 1984, counselor tng. dir., 1985-87; founder, pres. Bearers of Light Ministries, Chesapeake, 1987—. Elder New Life Christian Fellowship, Chesapeake, 1990-2001. Author: Basic 8, 1982, revised edit., 1995, Handbook for Helping Others, 1986, revised edit., 1996, The Biblical Family, 1990, The Two Shall Become One, 1997, Parenting God's Way, 1997. Staff sgt. U.S. Army, 1945-46, PTO; staff sgt. USAF, 1950-51. Recipient First Line Mgmt. award Am. Mgmt. Assn., 1981, Supervising People award Batten, 1984. Office: Bearers of Light Ministries PO Box 2672 Chesapeake VA 23327-2672 E-mail: bolm@arilion.com. *I have found that the Bible, the written word of God, contains the keys to victorious living.*

STAFFORD, PATRICK PURCELL, poet, writer, management consultant; b. L.A., Mar. 13, 1954; s. Elsan H. Stafford and Ann (Ruelle) Lane; m. Liane Beale Stafford, Jan. 2, 1987; 1 child, David. Student, U.S. Armed Forces Inst., 1971, UCLA, 1980, 81. Head script writer Hollywood (Calif.) Radio Network, 1981-82; mgr. new bus. Harry Koff Agy., Encino, Calif., 1984-85; pres., mgr. Legal Experts, L.A., 1988-94, Creative Adminstrs., L.A., 1994—; office adminstr. Moneymaker & Kelley, 1989-90. Sales rep. Now Messenger Svc., L.A., 1993-98; staff mgr. Stafford Resume Svc., L.A., 1990—. Author: Homage to a Princess, 2000; feature writer Amateur Chef Mag.; contbr. poems, articles, short stories to profl. publs. Mem. Big Bros. of Greater L.A., 1991. With USMC, 1971-78, Vietnam. Recipient Concept/Essay award L.A. Rtd., 1990, Poetry Contest award Tradition Mag., 1991, Hon. Mention award Iliad Press, 1992, Wash. State Coll., 1990, Winner in Play-Reading Series, Altered Stage Theatre Co., 1991, 1st prize Jacobytebooks Poetry Contest, 2000. Mem. The Writer's Exch. (life), Marino's of Beverly Hills (charter). Libertarian. Avocations: classical music and films, martial arts, biking, boxing. Home and Office: 1775 Southgate Way Grants Pass OR 97527-7241 E-mail: thinksuccess@hotmail.com.

STAFFORD, REBECCA, academic administrator, sociologist; b. Topeka, July 9, 1936; d. Frank C. and Anne Elizabeth (Larrick) S.; m. Willard Van Hazel. AB magna cum laude, Radcliffe Coll., 1958, MA, 1961; PhD, Harvard U., 1964. Sociology lectr., dept. social rels. Sch. Edn., Harvard U., Cambridge, Mass., 1964-70, mem. vis. com. bd. overseers, 1973-79; assoc. prof. sociology U. Nev., Reno, 1970-74, prof., 1973-80, chmn. dept. sociology, 1974-77, dean Coll. Arts and Scis., 1977-80; pres. Bemidji (Minn.) State U., 1980-82; exec. v.p., prof. sociology Colo. State U., Ft. Collins, 1982-83; pres. Chatham Coll., Pitts., 1983-91, prof. sociology, 1992-93; pres. Monmouth U., West Long Branch, 1993—. Cons. higher edn., 1992—, U.S. Internat. U. on Acad. Planning, 1992-94, USDA, 1992-93, Integra Bank, 1992-93, Millsaps Coll, Jackson, Miss., 1991, U. Pitts. Med. Sch., 1992-93; co-dir. acad. leadership inst. Carnegie Mellon U., 1991-93, U. Tenn., Knoxville, 1992-93; vis. scholar dept. sociology Harvard U., 1991; mem. faculty coll. mgmt. program. Carnegie Mellon U., Pitts., 1984-93; cons. adult devel. grant Harvard U. Health Svcs., Cambridge, 1979, rsch. sociologist, 1964-69; dir. ednl. enrichment project Harvard Sch. Edn., 1966-67, 69-70. Mem. editl. bd. Sociometry, 1974-77, Sociol. Focus., 1974-77; contbr. articles to profl. jours.; presenter papers at profl. confs. Trustee Monmouth Med. Ctr., 1993—, Winchester-Thurston Sch., Pitts., 1986-91, Montefiore Hosp., Pitts., 1990-93; trustee Presbyn.-Univ. Hosp., Pitts., 1984-93, exec. planning com., 1986-89, fin. com., 1989-93; pres. Pitts. Coun. Higher Edn., 1990; mem. Found. Ind. Colls. Inc. Pa., 1984-91, sec., 1986; mem. Colo. Commn. Higher Edn. Task Force on Quality, 1981; mem. adv. bd. Animal Rescue League, Pitts., 1989-93; founder Bemidji Area Women's Network, Minn., 1980-82; mem. intergovtl. planning steering com. Bemidji, 1980-82; mem. cmty. rels. com. Girl Scouts Southwestern Pa., 1983-86; mem. brotherhood dinner coun. Nat. Conf. Christians and Jews, 1985; mem. hon. centennial com. Pa. Sch. Blind Children, Pitts., 1986; mem. citizens sponsoring com. Allegheny Conf. Cmty. Devel., Pitts., 1983-91; mem. five state regional bd. First Union Nat. Bank, 1996—; bd. dirs. Pitts. Symphony, 1984-93, First Fidelity Bank, N.A., N.J., 1993-95, Integra Bank, Pitts., 1987-97, Urban League, Pitts., 1984-87, Women's Ctr., Ft. Collins, Colo., 1982-83, Coun. Colls. Arts and Scis., 1978-81; chmn. Harvard U. Grad. Soc. Coun., 1987-93. Recipient McCurdy-Rinkle prize for rsch. Eastern Psychiat. Assn., 1970; named Woman of Yr. in Edn., City of Pitts., 1986, Vectors/Pitts., 1987, Woman of Yr. in Edn., YWCA Tribute to Women, 1989, Women of Distinction award Muscular Dystrophy Assn., 1999, Women of Leadership award Monmouth County Girl Scouts Am., 1995, Woman of Achievement in Edn. award Monmouth County Adv. Commn. on Status of Women, 1994, Salute to Policymakers award Exec. Women in N.J., 1994; grantee Am. Coun. Edn. Inst. Acad. Deans, 1979, Inst. Ednl. Mgmt., Harvard U., 1984. Mem. Assn. Ind. Colls. and Univs. of N.J. (v.p. 1999—, sec. 1998-99, treas. 1994-98, pres. northeastern conf. 1995-99, bd. dirs. 1993—), Am. Coun. on Edn., Assn. Am. Colls., Soc. for Coll. and Univ. Planning (mem. instl. decision making and resource planning acad. 1994—), Ind. Coll. Fund (treas. 1995-96, bd. dirs. 1993—), Nat. Coun. Family Rels., Harvard U. Alumni Assn. (bd. dirs. 1985-87), Phi Beta Kappa, Phi Kappa Phi. Office: Monmouth University West Long Branch NJ 07764

STAFFORD, ROBERT THEODORE, lawyer, former senator; b. Rutland, Vt., Aug. 8, 1913; s. Bert L. and Mable R. (Stratton) S.; m. Helen C. Kelley, Oct. 15, 1938; children— Madelyn, Susan, Barbara, Dianne. BS, Middlebury Coll., 1935, LL.D., 1960; postgrad., U. Mich., 1936; LL.B., Boston U., 1938, LL.D., 1959, Norwich U., 1960, St. Michaels Coll., 1967, U. Vt., 1970. Bar: Vt. bar 1938. City prosecutor, Rutland, 1939-42; state's atty. Rutland County, 1947-51; dep. atty. gen. Vt., 1953-54; atty. gen., 1954-56; lt. gov., 1957-58; gov., 1959-60; mem. 87th to 92d Congresses, Vt.-at-large; apptd. U.S. Senate, 1971, mem., 1972-89, chmn. com. on environment and public works, 1981-87, chmn. edn. subcom., 1981-87, ranking mem., 1987-89; ptnr. Stafford, Abiatell & Stafford, 1938-46; sr. ptnr. Stafford & LaBrake, 1946-51. Chmn. UN-U.S.A. Assn. Panel UNESCO, 1989—. Lt. comdr. USNR, 1942-46, 51-52; capt. Res. Named Disting. Scholar U. Vt., 1989, Disting. Prof. Pub. Affairs Castleton State Coll., 1989. Mem. V.F.W., Am. Legion. Clubs: Elk. Home and Office: 108 Gables Pl Rutland VT 05701-9448 Office: Castleton Coll Coolidge Libr Bldg Castleton VT 05735

STAFFORD, WILLIAM BUTLER, retired psychology educator; b. Pitts., Feb. 6, 1931; s. Lee Elmer and Helen Huston (Butler) S.; m. Barbara Anne Svoboda, Aug. 11, 1956; children: Mark William, Debra Anne. Student, Adrian (Mich.) Coll., 1949-50; AB, Ohio U., 1954, MA, 1955; EdD, Ind. U., 1965. Cert. tchr., dir. guidance svcs., Ind., nat. bd. cert. counselor. Residence counselor Ohio U., 1954-55; counselor dean of students' staff DePauw U., Ind., 1955-57; instr. Ind. U., Bloomington, 1957-65, asst. prof. edn., 1965-67; counselor Univ. Sch., Ind., 1957-65, dir. pupil pers. svcs., 1965-67; asst. prof. edn. Lehigh U., Bethlehem, Pa., 1967-72, assoc. prof. counseling psychology, 1972-94, prof. emeritus, 1994—. Mem. clin. staff Impact Project, 1996-98; cons. North Ctrl. Assn. Secondary Schs. and Colls., Ind. Dept. Public Instrn., Pa. Dept. Edn. Patients rights and rev. com. Allentown State Hosp. Author:

Schools Without Counselors: Guidance Practices for the Teacher in the Elementary School, 1975. Mem. adv. bd. Lehigh Valley Child Care, Inc. Jesse Smith Noyes fellow, 1980. Mem. ACA, APA (counseling psychology divsn.), Am. Sch. Counselor Assn., Assn. Counselor Educators and Suprs., Am. Ednl. Rsch. Assn., Pa. Counseling Assn., Pa. Sch. Counselors Assn. (Pa. Counselor Educator of Yr. 1994), Internat. Alliance Invitational Edn. (adv. coun., mem. editl. bd., editor Jour. Invitational Theory and Practice), Pa. Alliance Invitational Edn. (editor newsletter), Chi Sigma Iota (chpt. advisor). Episcopalian. Home: 1586 Pinewind Dr Alburtis PA 18011-2704 E-mail: wbs0@lehigh.edu.

STAGE, BRIAN, hotel executive; BSBA, Coll. William and Mary, 1974; grad. mgmt. exec. program, U. Minn., 1995. Mgr. Sheraton Boston Hotel and Towers, 1981; ops. mgr. Inn Am., area dir. ops. and corp. dir. sales and mktg.; v.p. sales and mktg. Inn Am. Corp.; regional v.p. ops. Radisson Hotels Worldwide, 1990-95, exec. v.p. sales and mktg., 1995-97, pres., COO, 1997-99; exec. v.p. sales, reservations and distbn. Carlson Hotels Worldwide, 2000—. Overseer Radisson Mktg. Assn. Office: Carlson Hotels and Worldwide Carlson Pky PO Box 59159 Minneapolis MN 55459-8204 E-mail: bstage@radisson.com.

STAGE, GINGER ROOKS, psychologist; b. Allentown, Pa., Sept. 23, 1946; d. John Myers Rooks and Catherine Estelle (Graser) Rooks Bistritz; m. Robert Roy Stage, Aug. 23, 1969; 1 child, Stephen. BA in Psychology magna cum laude, Moravian Coll., 1968; MA in Psychology, Temple U., 1969. Lic. psychologist, Pa.; cert. clin. hypnotherapist Nat. Bd. Clin. Hypnotherapists. Instr. Beaver campus Pa. State U., Monaca, 1969-74; staff psychologist St. Francis Cmty. Mental Health Ctr., Pitts., 1974-83; pvt. practice family therapy Coraopolis, Pa., 1977—. Mem. Greenstein Family Therapy Consultation Group, Pitts., 1981-00; mem., spkr. Human Sexuality Alliance, Pitts., 1989-91; spkr. in field. Mem. APA, Greater Pitts. Psychol. Assn., Western Pa. Family Ctr. Episcopalian. Avocations: needlework, guitar, exercise, walking. Home: 112 Wessex Hills Dr Coraopolis PA 15108-1021 Office: 409 Mill St Coraopolis PA 15108-1607

STAGE, KEY HUTCHINSON, urologist; b. Washington, June 12, 1947; s. Anson H. and Lucie T. Stage; m. Jo-Ellen Arpin; children: Jennifer, Amanda. BA, Linfield Coll., 1969; MD, U. Oreg., 1973. Diplomate Am. Bd. Urology. Intern U.S. Naval Regional Med. Ctr., Oakland, Calif., 1973-74; resident in urology U. Tex. Southwestern Med. Sch., Dallas, 1977-81; pvt. practice, 1981—; assoc. prof. U. Tex. Southwestern Med. Sch.; chief urology Parkland Mem. HOsp., Dallas. Lt. comdr. USNR, 1973-77. Fellow ACS; mem. Am. Urol. Assn. Episcopalian. Office: U Tex Southwestern Med Sch Dept Urology 5323 Harry Hines Blvd Dallas TX 75390-9110 E-mail: key.stage@email.swmed.edu.

STAGE, MARY-BETH, clinical social worker, educator; b. Dallas, Mar. 21, 1945; d. Francis Marion Jr. and Janelle Fowler (Walton) S.; m. Donald Howard Lynx, June 27, 1969 (div. June 1979). BA in Psychology, Centenary Coll., 1969; MSW, U. Ill., 1982; cert. in Family, Washington U., St. Louis, 1984. Case mgr. Dept. Children and Family Svcs., Charleston, Ill., 1978-84; social worker Bossier Parish Pub. Schs., Bossier City, La., 1984-88; family advocacy therapist Mental Health Clinic of 2d Strategic Hosp., Barksdale AFB, 1988-89; primary group therapist Greentree Ctr. Psychiat. Medicine Humana Hosp.-Brentwood, Shreveport, 1989-90; group and family therapist Schumpert Med. Ctr., 1990—; pvt. practice, 1984—. Mem. NASW (vendorship com.), La. Group, Hoover Watercolor (publicity com.), Kappa Kappa Iota. Methodist Episcopal. Avocations: potter, water colorist. Office: 1002 Highland Ave Shreveport LA 71101-4143

STAGE, RICHARD LEE, consultant, retired utilities executive; b. Byesville, Ohio, Nov. 5, 1936; s. Clifford Earl Stage and Evelyn Virginia (Nunley) Rolston; m. Joan Eleanor Bednarz, Feb. 1, 1958; 1 child, Julie Marie. B in Mgmt., Malone Coll., 1987. Fleet office supr. Ohio Power Co., Canton, 1954-77; supr. automotive acctg. and leasing Am. Electric Power, 1977-83, dir. fleet mgmt. Columbus, 1983-95; fleet mgmt. cons., Canton, 1995—. Mem. Soc. Automotive Engrs. (chmn. utilities com. 1988-89, exec. com.), Edison Electric Inst. (fleet mgmt. com. 1983-95), Masons. Republican. Avocations: golf, woodworking. Home and office: 1329 Davis St SW Canton OH 44706-4503 E-mail: rlstage@sssnet.com.

STAGE, THOMAS BENTON, psychiatrist; b. Marietta, Ohio, July 23, 1926; s. John Douglas and Grace (Shawhan) S.; m. Doris Jeane Weinstock, Dec. 22, 1951; children: Samuel Ray, Amy Elizabeth, James Robert; m. Alicia Anderson Marsh, June 7, 1993. BA cum laude, Marietta Coll., 1949; MD, Ohio State U., 1952. Diplomate: Am. Bd. Psychiatry and Neurology. Intern Detroit Receiving Hosp., 1952-53; psychiat. resident, fellow Menninger Sch. Psychiatry, Topeka, 1953-56; sect. chief, chief psychiatry VA Hosp., 1956-62, adminstr. Sheridan, Wyo., 1962-66, dir. Salem, Va., 1967-72; dep. asst. chief med. dir. for ambulatory care VA Central Office, Washington, 1972-74; dir. No. Va. Mental Health Inst., Falls Church, 1974-78; asst. commr. for mental health State of Va., Richmond, 1978-79; dir. clin. services Fairfax-Falls Church Community Services Bd., Vienna, 1979-82, psychiat. cons. for med. affairs, 1982-99, med. dir. Fairfax, 1999—. Instr. Menninger Sch. Psychiatry, 1958-62, U. Wyo. Sch. Nursing, 1963-66; assoc. prof. U. Va. Med. Sch., 1972-74; cons. surveyor Joint Commn. on Accreditation of Hosps., 1976—; cons. Crow-No. Cheyenne USPHS Hosp., 1963-66, Ala. Dept. Mental Health (Wyatt Com.), 1986-91; psychiatric cons. on accreditation Commonwealth of Va. Dept. Mental Health, Mental Retardation and Substance Abuse, 1982—; mem. Comprehensive Mental Health Ctr. Com., 1968-73, Gov.'s Adv. Commn. on Mental Health, 1971-74; chmn. Drug Abuse Rehab. Com., 1970-73; cons. adminstrv. psychiatry NIMH, 1975-78; chmn. steering com. Asso. Faculties Program Community Psychiatry, Washington, 1975-77; mem. State Health Coordinating Coun., 1976-89. Contbr. articles to profl. jours. Served wtih USNR, 1944-46, PTO. Fellow Am. Psychiat. Assn. (life); mem. Am. Assn. Psychiat. Adminstrs., Washington Psychiat. Soc., Psychiat. Soc. Va., Am. Assn. Community Psychiatrists. Home: 11410 Hollow Timber Way Reston VA 20194-1906 Office: Fairfax-Falls Ch Cmty Svcs Ste 800 12011 Government Center Pkwy Fairfax VA 22035-1100

STAGEBERG, ROGER V. lawyer; B of Math. with distinction, U. Minn., 1963, JD cum laude, 1966. Assoc. Mackall, Crounse & Moore, Mpls., 1966-70, ptnr., 1970-86; shareholder and officer Lommen, Nelson, Cole & Stageberg, P.A., 1986—. Co-chmn. joint legal svcs. funding com. Minn. Supreme Ct., 1995-96. Mem. U. Minn. Law Rev. Bd. dirs. Mpls. Legal Aid Soc., 1970—, treas., 1973, pres., 1977, dir. of fund, 1980—, chmn. of fund, 1998-2000; chmn. bd. trustees Colonial Ch. of Edina, 1975, chmn. congregation, 1976, pres. found., 1978; officer, trustee Mpls. Found, 1983-88. Mem. Minn. State Bar Assn. (numerous offices and coms., pres. 1994), Hennepin County Bar Assn. (chmn. securities law sect. 1979, chmn. attys. referral svc. com. 1980, sec. 1980, treas. 1981, pres. 1983), Order of Coif. Office: Lommen Nelson Cole & Stageberg PA 1800 IDS Center 80 S 8th St Minneapolis MN 55402-2100 E-mail: roger@lommen.com.

STAGER, DONALD K. retired construction company executive; Chmn., pres., CEO Dillingham Constrn. Holdings Inc., Pleasanton, Calif., 1982-99; with Guy F. Atkinson Co., 1952—82; ret., 1999. Recipient, Roebling award Am. Soc. of Civil Engineers, 1995, Golden Beaver award for Mgmt Beavers, Inc., 1998. Office: 957 Wapato Way Manson WA 98831-9595

STAGG, CLYDE LAWRENCE, lawyer; b. St. Petersburg, Fla., May 22, 1935; s. Milton Gurr and Clyda Montese (Lawrence) S.; m. Betsy Barron, Aug. 22, 1959; children: Sharon, Brian, Lauren, Stephen. BSJ, U. Fla., 1956, LLB, 1959. Bar: Fla. 1959, U.S. Dist. Ct. (mid. dist.) Fla. 1959, U.S. Ct. Appeals (5th cir.) 1969, U.S. Supreme Ct. 1971, U.S. Ct. Appeals (11th cir.) 1987. Assoc. Shackleford, Farrior, Tampa, Fla., 1959-60; asst. solicitor Hillsborough County Solicitor's Office, 1960-61; chief asst. state atty. State Atty.'s Office, 1963-64, asst. state atty., 1961-63; ptnr. Whitaker, Mann & Stagg, Knight, Jones & Whitaker, Tampa, 1965-67, Holland & Knight, Tampa, 1968-74, 80-86, Stichter, Stagg, Hoyt, et al, Tampa, 1974-79, Stagg, Hardy, Ferguson, Murnaghan & Mathews P.A., Tampa, 1986-93, Akerman, Senterfitt & Eidson P.A., Tampa, 1993—. Bd. dirs. Fla. Lawyers Mut. Ins. Co. Mem., sec. Hillsborough Area Regional Transit Authority, Tampa, 1979—85; mem., sec., vice chmn., chmn. Tampa Sports Authority, 1985—89; spl. counsel U.S. Senator Bob Graham, 1988; spl. counsel nat. conf. of commrs. Uniform State Laws, 1997—; bd. dirs. United Way Greater Tampa, Inc., Tampa, 1988—91, Fla. Blood Svcs., Inc., Tampa, 1989—, treas., 2001—. Mem. ABA, Am. Bar Found., Fla. Bar (bd. govs. 1974-75), Hillsborough County Bar Assn. (pres. 1970-71, Outstanding Lawyer award 1998), Fla. Bar Found., Am. Bd. Trial Advocates, Greater Tampa C. of C. (bd. dirs. 1988-91), Am. Inn Ct. (master emeritus of bench). Home: 3303 W San Nicholas St Tampa FL 33629-7034 Office: Akerman Senterfitt & Eidson PA PO Box 3273 Tampa FL 33601-3273

STAGG, LOUIS CHARLES, English language and literature educator; b. Jan. 3, 1933; s. Louis Anatol and Gladys (Andrews) S.; m. Mary Casner, June 5, 1959; children: Robert Charles, Helen Marie. BA in English, La. Coll., 1955; MA in English, U. Ark., 1957, PhD in English, 1963. Tchg. asst. English U. Ark., 1955-59; asst. prof. William Jewell Coll., 1959-60; instr. Stephen F. Austin State U., 1960-62; asst. prof. Memphis State U. (now U. Memphis), 1962-69, assoc. prof., 1969-77, prof. English lang. and lit., 1977-98, prof. emeritus, 1998—, dir. grad. studies in English, 1985-88, dir. English Drama Players, 1968-92, dir. undergrad. advising for English, 1970-80, 88-91, chair policies and procedures com. for English, 1983-95, tenure and promotion com. for English, 1978-80, 82-86, 89-97, now cons. for 2001 program. Chmn. acad. policies com. Memphis State U. Senate, 1981-82, 88-90, 93-94, 95-96, mem. exec. com. senate, 1987-91, 93-96, parliamentarian of senate, 1987-88, 90-91, 94-96, humanities rep. budget adv. com. dean Coll. Arts and Scis., 1992-93, mem. adv. bd. Acad. Exch. Quar., 1997—, mem. steering com., chair of schedules, originator Alliance Creative Theatre, Edn. and Rsch. series, 1986, 89, 90, 92, 94, 96, 98; cons. NEH, 1975, 76, 78, Ohio State U. Press, summer 1985, 86, U. Jordan, Amman, 1985; chair policies and procedures subdivsn. Eng. dept. so. assn. colls., schs. self study, mem. steering com. 1992-93; cons. Memphis State U. Learning Media-Ctrs. catalogue Shakespeare holdings, 1992-93, rev., 1993-94, 94-95. Author: (with J. Lasley Dameron) Poe's Critical Vocabulary, 1966; author series: Index to the Figurative Language of John Webster's Tragedies, 1967, of Ben Jonson's Tragedies, 1967, of Thomas Heywood's Tragedies, 1967, of George Champman's Tragedies, 1970, of Thomas Middleton's Tragedies, 1970, of Cyril Tourneur's Tragedies, 2d edit., all 7 under title Index to the Figurative Langauge of the Tragedies of Shakespeare's Chief 17th Century Contemporaries, 1977, 3d edit., 1982, Index to the Figurative Language of the Tragedies of Shakespeare's Chief 18th Century Contemporaries, 1984; contbr. to Great Writers of the English Language Dramatists, 1979, 87; circulation editor Interpretations, 1976-80; contbr. articles on English and Am. drama to profl. jours., publs. on Shakespeare, other lit. publs. Mem. Memphis Oratorio Soc. Chorus, 1969-92, diction coach, 1987; mem. Memphis Symphony Chorus, 1993—, mem. symphony chorus newsletter com., 1999-2000; mem. Memphis in May Sunset Symphony Choir, 1996, Martin Luther King Tribute Concert Choir, 1995, 96, 99—, City of Memphis Faure Requiem Concert, 2001, Memphis Symphony Chorus and Orch. prodn. Rolling Requiem for 9/11/02; lay reader Episcopal Ch.; program chair Friends of Univ. Librs., 2000—. Recipient summer stipend NEH, 1967; Memphis State U. grantee, 1965, travel grantee to U.S. Libr. Congress, summer 1971. Mem. MLA (life mem.), So. Humanities Coun. (sec.-treas. 1974-76, exec. com. 1976-83, 94-96, chmn. coun. 1993-94, chmn. sect. humanities in pluralistic soc. 1984, ad hoc com. on crisis in tchg. humanities 1977, chmn. local arrangements for convs. 1975, 94, chmn. sect. on Thomas Hardy 1996), Tenn. Philol. Assn. (pres. 1976-77, exec. com. 1977, local arrangements chmn. 1965, 69, 75, 87, chmn. Shakespeare sect. 1996), Marlowe Soc. Am. (book reviewer 1984, 86, 87, 88, 93), Am. Soc. for Theatre Rsch., Samuel Beckett Soc., Conf. on Christianity and Lit., South Cen. Conf. on Christianity and Lit. Soc. for Study of Works of Harold Pinter (asst. constn. revision 1988, asst. with planning 1992, treas. 1994-98, mem. exec. com. 1994-98, lifetime mem. 1997—), Ark. Philol. Assn., Shakespeare Assn. Am. (local arrangements host com. 1985), Stratford-upon-Avon Shakespeare Festival, Eng., Eugene O'Neill Soc., Alliance for Creative Theatre, Edn. and Rsch. (chmn. schedules com., originator of proposal 1986, 89, 90, 92, 94, 96, 98, cons. residency S.E. Mo. State U. 1997), Internat. Shakespeare Assn., Am. Soc. Theatre Rsch., Internat. Soc. Theatre Rsch., Medieval and Renaissance Drama Soc., Renaissance Soc. Am., South Cen. Renaissance Conf. (chmn. nominations 1976, exec. com. 1978-80, program com. 1981-83, chmn. sect. Shakespeare 1981, 85, 95, 99, 2002, 16th Century lit. 1982, chmn. local arrangements 1983, symposium on humanism 1984, chmn. Shakespeare on film and the tchg. of Brit. drama 1986, chmn. music in Shakespeare's plays, 1987, chmn. sect. Thematic Approaches to Tudor/Stuart Drama 1988, chmn. sect. Medieval Influences on Renaissance drama 1993, chmn. Shakespeare's Villains: Stage and Page 1995, Adaptions of Renaissance Drama 1993, chmn. local arrangements for convention 1990, chmn. spl. session 1989, 95, Shakespeare II sect. 1996, chair Renaissance Drama Section 1999, 2001; SCRC (hon. life mem 1998—), chmn. Performing Rennaissance Drama 2001, South Cen. MLA (assoc. editor for English, South Cen. Bull. 1982-84, nominations com. 1985-86, 95-96, book reviewer South Cen. Rev. 1983, 85, 86, sec. English I.B. Renaissance, 1986, chair, 1987, sec. spl. sect. Renaissance Drama, 1988, chair Shakespeare's Tragi-comedies and tragi-comic romances, 1989, co-chair local arrangements, 1999, chair panel on renaissance drama criticism 1995, sec. renaissance drama sect. 1997, sect. chmn. 1998, mem. com. Conv., Memphis, 1999, hon. life mem. 2000—), South Atlantic MLA, South Ctrl. Coll. English Assn. (sec.-treas. 1980-81, v.p. 1981-82, pres. 1982-83, exec. com. 1983-90, co-host 1982, com. constitution revision 1989), Coll. English Assn., Internat. Patristic Medieval and Renaissance Conf. (sect. chmn. Medieval drama 1977, chair Shakespeare session 1994, chair Renaissance drama section 1995, chmn. 17th century Brit. lit. sect. 1996, chmn. Milton sect. 1996), Am. Theatre Assn. (chmn. sect. combining Brit. lit. and theatre in teaching of drama 1983, chmn. Shakespeare sect. 1994), Marlowe Soc. Am., Eugene O'Neill Soc., The Stratford Can. Shakespeare Festival, AAUP (sec. treas. Memphis State U. chap. 1982-86, v.p. 1986-88, pres. 1988-90), Phi Beta Kappa (pres. memphis alumni assn. 1985-88, mem. spl. panel The Soc. and the New Scholarship at 37th triennial conv. 1994), Friends of U. Memphis Libraries (program chair 2000-02, v.p. 2002—), Alpha Chi. Democrat. Home: 5219 Mason Rd Memphis TN 38117-2104

STAGG, TOM, federal judge; b. Shreveport, La., Jan. 19, 1923; s. Thomas Eaton and Beulah (Meyer) S.; m. Margaret Mary O'Brien, Aug. 21, 1946; children: Julie, Margaret Mary. BA, La. State U., 1943, JD, 1949. Bar: La. 1949. With firm Hargrove, Guyton, Van Hook & Hargrove, Shreveport, 1949-53; pvt. practice law, 1953-58; sr. ptnr. firm Stagg, Cady & Beard, 1958-74; judge U.S. Dist. Ct. (we. dist.) La., 1974-84, 91-92, chief judge, 1984-90, sr. judge, 1992—. Pres. Abe Meyer Corp., 1960-74, Stagg Investments, Inc., 1964-74; mng. partner Pierremont Mall Shopping Center, 1963-74; v.p. King Hardware Co., 1955-74; Mem. Shreveport Airport Authority, 1967-73, chmn., 1970-73; chmn. Gov.'s Tidelands Adv. Council, 1969-70; del. La. Constl. Conv., 1973-74; chmn. rules com., com. on exec. dept.; mem. Gov.'s Adv. Com on Offshore Revenues, 1972-74 Active Republican party, 1950-74, del. convs., 1956, 60, 64, 68, 72; mem. Nat. Com. for La., 1964-72, mem. exec. com., 1964-68; Pres. Shreveport Jr. C. of C., 1955-56; v.p. La. Jr. C. of C., 1956-57. Served to capt., inf. AUS, 1943-46, ETO. Decorated Bronze Star, Purple Heart with oak leaf cluster, Combat Inf. badge. Mem. Am., La., Shreveport bar assns. Office: US Dist Ct 300 Fannin St Ste 4100 Shreveport LA 71101-3123

STAGGERS, KERMIT LEMOYNE, II, history and political science educator, state legislator, municipal official; b. Washington, Nov. 2, 1947; s. Kermit LeMoyne and Christine Ruby (Scherich) S.; m. June Ann Wenda, Aug. 22, 1970; children: Ayn Kristen, Kyle Lee. BS, U. Idaho, 1969, MA, 1975; PhD, Claremont Grad. U., 1986. Instr. history Troy (Ala.) State U., 1975-76, U. Idaho, Moscow, 1977, Northwestern Coll., Orange City, Iowa, 1979-80, Coll. Lake County, Grayslake, Ill., 1981-82; lectr. history Chapman Coll., Orange, Calif., 1979, U. Md.-Europe, Heidelberg, Germany, 1988-89; vis. instr. history Trinity Internat. U., Deerfield, Ill., 1980; ad. instr. history Coll. St. Francis, Joliet, 1982; prof. history and polit. sci. U. Sioux Falls (S.D.), 1982—; mem. S.D. Senate, Pierre, 1995—2002, Sioux Falls City Coun., 2002—. Lectr. Diplomatic Acad. Ukrainian Fgn. Ministry and Nat. U. Kiev-Mohyla Acad., 2001; expert analyst on polit. and social issues for local radio and TV. Contbr. to profl. publs. Chair Senate Transp. Com., 1997-99. Capt. USAF, 1970-76. Recipient Guardian Small Bus. award Nat. Fedn. Ind. Bus., 1996; Malone Faculty fellow, 1993. Mem. Orgn. Am. Historians, Great Plains Polit. Sci and Pub. Affairs Assn. (pres. 2000-01), Conf. on Faith and History, Federalist Soc., Fulbright Assn., Hist. Soc., Kiwanis, Phi Alpha Theta, Phi Kappa Phi. Republican. Avocations: book collecting, travel. Home: 1135 S Walts Ave Sioux Falls SD 57105-0543 Office: U Sioux Falls Dept History/Polit Sci 1101 W 22nd St Sioux Falls SD 57105-1699 E-mail: kermit.staggers@usiouxfalls.edu.

STAGGS, BARBARA J. vice mayor; b. Trotwood, Ohio, Aug. 25, 1944; d. Campbell Cester and Zelma Ann (Barlow) Phillips; m. Edward Lowell Staggs, June 10, 1961; children: Terrence Lee, Deann Lorraine Staggs Roesdiger, Eric Justin. Lic. real estate salesperson, Ohio. In retail sales, Dayton; secretarial aide, tchrs. aide Trotwood (Ohio) Sch. Sys.; real estate agt. Hussman Realty, Dayton, 1988-90, Dever-Schenk Realty, Trotwood, 1990-93; mem. city coun. City of Trotwood, 1994—; exec. dir. Trotwood C. of C., 1990—2001. Advisor Civil Svc. Commn., Trotwood; bd. dirs. Miami Valley Career Tech. Ctr., Job Adv. Bd., Clayton, Choices in Cmty. Living, Dayton. Pres. Cmty. Investment, Trotwood; bd. dirs. Northwest Devel. Assn., Trotwood, Resolution Commn., Nat. League of Cities, human devel. policy com., info. tech. and comm. policy com., coun. re. zoning appeals bd., program planning com. Mem.: Women in Govt., Trotwood Rotary. Avocations: doll collecting, building doll houses, sewing and crafts. Home: 19 W Sunrise Ave Trotwood OH 45426-3525 Office: City of Trotwood 35 Olive Rd Ste 2 Trotwood OH 45426-2698

STAGLIANO, JAMES JOSEPH, physical science educator, scientist; b. Kenosha, Wis., Nov. 15, 1965; s. James Joseph and Hazel May (Mastin) S.; m. Susan Elizabeth Cain, May 20, 1994 (div. July 14, 2000); children: James, Mary. BS in Math., U. Wis., Kenosha, 1987; MS in Physics, PhD in Physics, Auburn U., 1994. Asst. prof. physics Jacksonville (Ala.) State U., 1994-97; rschr. dept. physics Auburn (Ala.) U., 1995, lectr. in physics, summer 1996; software engr. Enterprise (Ala.) Electronics Corp., 1997-2000; adj. prof. sci. Enterprise State Jr. Coll., 1998-2000; sr. systems analyst Enterprise Electronics Corp., 2000—02, sr. scientist, 2002—. Contbr. articles to profl. jours. Mem., bd. dirs. Ala. Family Rights Assn., Huntsville, 1998-2001; mem. Citizens for Legal Accountability and Reform in Ala., Dothan, 1999-2001; pres., bd. dirs. Coffee County CASA, Inc., Enterprise, 2000—. Mem. Am. Inst. Physics, Am. Math. Soc., N.Y. Acad. Scis. Office: Enterprise Electronics Corp 128 S Industrial Blvd Enterprise AL 36330 E-mail: james_stagliano@hotmail.com.

STAGLIANO, VITO ALEXANDER, federal agency administrator, utilities executive; b. Catanzaro, Calabria, Italy, May 13, 1942; came to U.S., 1956; s. Filippo and Maria Stagliano; m. Julie Ann Werth, Sept. 30, 1967; children: Jason Vito, Carlos Otobed. Program analyst U.S. Office Econ. Opportunity, Washington, 1968-69; exec. dir. Palau Cmty. Devel. Agy., 1969-71; program officer U.S. Peace Corps, Ghana, 1971-73, dir. Mauritania, 1973-74, dir. West Africa, 1974-77; counselor Interstate Commn. on Drought Control, Ouagadougou, Bourkina Faso, 1977-79; staff asst. Sec. of Energy, Washington, 1979-81; dir. River Basins Devel. Office, Dakar, Senegal, 1981-85; dir. Office of Energy Demand Policy, U.S. Dept. Energy, Washington, 1986-89, assoc. dep. undersec. of energy, 1990-91, dep. asst. sec. energy for policy planning, 1991-93; vis. scholar Resources for Future, 1993-95; dir. Energy Security Analysis, Inc., Washington, 1996-98; v.p. Commonwealth Edison Co., Chgo., 1998-2000, Calpine Corp., 2001—. Mem. adv. bd. Sch. Advanced Internat. Studies, Johns Hopkins U., GAO, U.S. Office Tech. Assessment; guest lectr. Harvard U., Tufts U., Nat. Def. U., Va. Mmil. Inst., École Nationale Superièure, France. Author: A Policy of Discontent: The Making of a National Energy Strategy, 2001; co-author: A Shock to the System: Restructuring America's Electricity Industry, 1996, Energy and National Security in the 21st Century, 1995; contbr. articles to profl. jours. Peace corps vol., Mauritania, 1966-67; founder Micronesia Legal Svcs. Program, 1971; mem. foster care review bd. State of Md. Ampart fellow USIA, 1981; recipient Silver Medal for Meritorious Svc., U.S. Dept. Energy, Bronze medal for exceptional svc., awarded rank of meritorious sr. exec. by Pres. George Bush. Mem. NAACP (legal def. fund), Amnesty Internat. Avocations: Roman and medieval history, 20th century poetry. Home: 30 E Division St Chicago IL 60610-5292 E-mail: vitostagliano@earthlink.net.

STAGLIN, GAREN KENT, computer service company executive, venture capitalist; b. Lincoln, Nebr., Dec. 22, 1944; s. Ramon and Darlene (Guilliams) S.; m. Sharalyn King, June 8, 1968; children: Brandon Kent, Shannon King. BS in Engring. with honors, UCLA, 1966; MBA, Stanford U., 1968. Assoc. Carr Mgmt. Co., N.Y.C., 1971-75; v.p. Crocker Nat. Bank, San Francisco, 1975-76; dir. fin. Itel Corp., 1976-77, pres. ins. services divsn., 1977-79; corp. v.p., gen. mgr. ADP Automotive Svcs. Group, San Ramon, Calif., 1978-91; chmn., CEO Safelite Glass Corp., Columbus, Ohio, 1991-97, chmn., 1998-2000; owner Staglin Family Vineyard, Rutherford, Calif., 1985—; pres., CEO, eOne Global L.L.C., Napa, 2000—. Bd. dirs. Certive Corp., Specialized Bicycle Corp., Dashboard Enterprises, Quick Response Svcs., Inc., 1st Data Corp. Bd. dirs. Peralta Hosp. Cancer Inst., 1977-78, Berkeley Reportory Theatre, 1979-85; trustee Justin Sienna H.S., Napa, Calif., 1995-2000; chmn. major gifts program East Bay region Stanford (Calif.) U., 1989-92; mem. adv. bd. Stanford Bus. Sch., 1995-2000; chmn. 75th anniversary campaign Stanford Grad. Sch. Bus., 1998-2000; chmn. capital campaign, pres. bd. trustees Am. Ctr. Wine, Food and Arts, Napa, Calif., 1998—. Lt. USN, 1968-71. Recipient Gold Spike award, Stanford U., 2000. Mem. Stanford Assocs. (bd. govs. 1985-92), World Pres. Orgn., Internat. Inst. Soc. (bd. govs. 1985-92). Democrat. Lutheran. Home: PO Box 680 1570 Bella Oaks Ln Rutherford CA 94573 E-mail: gstaglin@coveglobal.com.

STAHL, ALICE SLATER, psychiatrist; b. Vienna, Austria, Jan. 28, 1913; came to U.S., 1938; d. Sam and Helen (Bluman) Slater; widowed; chidlren: Kenneth Lee, June Audrey. Baccalaureate, Gymnasium, Vienna, 1932; Med. Dr., U. Vienna Med. Sch., 1938. Intern Williamsport (Pa.) Gen. Hosp., 1939-40; resident in psychiatry Gallinger Mcpl. Hosp., Washington, 1940-41, Independence State Hosp., 1941-42, Bellevue Hosp., N.Y.C., 1942-43, attending psychiatrist, 1945-48; staff psychiatrist Jewish Bd. of Guardians, 1943-45; attending psychiatrist Jamaica Hosp., Queens, N.Y., 1948-52; dir. adolescent pavilion Hillside Hosp., Glen Oaks, 1954-96, staff psychiatrist, 1982—; supervising psychiatrist Bergen Regional Hosp., Paramus, N.J., 1987—. Asst. prof. clin. psychiatry Yeshiva U. Med. Sch., 1978-96. Fellow AMA (life), Am. Psychiat. Assn. (life); mem. Am. Psychoanalytic Assn. (life), Am. Soc. for Adolescent Psychiatry (life) Avocations: swimming, hiking, gardening, grandmotherhood. Home and Office: 305 Joan Pl Wyckoff NJ 07481-2818

STAHL, CHARLES JAY, III, forensic, anatomic and clinical pathologist; b. Phila., Aug. 5, 1930; s. Charles John and Myrtle Mae (Esher) S.; m. Ellen Carolyn Baran, Nov. 20, 1954; children: Charles, Marcia, Kim. BS, Ursinus Coll., Collegeville, Pa., 1952; MD, Jefferson Med. Coll., 1956. Diplomate Am. Bd. Pathology. Rotating intern Naval Hosp., Phila., 1956-57, resident in anatomic and clin. pathology, 1957-61; resident in forensic pathology Armed Force Inst. Pathology, Washington, 1962-63; commd. ensign USN, 1953, advanced through grades to capt., 1971; chief lab. svc. U.S. Naval Hosp., Guam, 1963-65; dep. med. examiner Territory of Guam; chmn. dept. forensic scis. Armed Forces Inst. Pathology, Washington, 1965-75; chmn. dept. lab. medicine Nat. Naval Med. Ctr., Bethesda, Md., 1975-80; ret., 1980; chief lab. svc. VA Med. Ctr., Johnson City, Tenn., 1980-83; asst. chief med. examiner State of Tenn., 1983—86; prof. pathology East Tenn. State U., Johnson City, 1980-86; chief staff VA Med. Ctr., Dayton, Ohio, 1986-91; dep. med. insp. U.S. Dept. Vet. Affairs, Washington, 1991-92; armed forces chief med. examiner Armed Forces Inst. Pathology, 1992-96; adminstrv. hearing officer Office of Justice Programs Dept. of Justice, 2000—. Cons. in forensic pathology Navy Bur. Medicine and Surgery, Washington, 1970-75, cons. in lab. medicine, 1975-80; mem. sci. adv. bd. Armed Forces Inst. Pathology, 1976-80; prof. pathology George Washington U. Sch. Medicine, Washington, 1975-80, Georgetown U. Sch. Medicine, Washington, 1976-80, Uniformed Svcs. U. Sch. Medicine, Bethesda, 1976-79; prof., asst. dean vet. affairs Wright State U. Sch. Medicine, Dayton, 1986-91. Assoc. editor Jour. Forensic Scis., 1971-72, 79-92, editor, 1972-74; contbr. over 60 articles to med. jours., chpts. to books. Alumni trustee Thomas Jefferson U., Phila., 2002—; mem. mid-county citizens adv. bd. Montgomery County Md., 2000—02. Decorated Legion of Merit. Recipient Ann. Alumni award Ursinus Coll., 2000. Fellow Am. Acad. Forensic Scis. (disting.), Coll. Am. Pathologists, Am. Soc. Clin. Pathologists, Am. Coll. Legal Medicine (hon.); mem. Nat. Assn. Med. Examiners (pres. 1993-94, Milton Helpern Laureate 1998), Assn. Mil. Surgeons U.S., Soc. Med. Cons. to Armed Forces.

STAHL, DAVID, orchestra and opera conductor; b. N.Y.C., Nov. 4, 1949; s. Frank L. and Edith (Cosmann) S.; m. Karen Doss Shehan, Feb. 25, 1989; children: Sonya Leonore, Byron David, Anna June. B.Mus., Queens Coll., 1972, MA, 1974; studied with, Leonard Bernstein and Seiji Ozawa, Tanglewood, 1975, Gunther Schuller, Joseph Rosenstock, Walter Susskind, Max Rudolf; LLD, Coll. of Charleston. Carnegie Hall debut with Youth Symphony Orch. of N.Y., 1973; music dir., Doctors' Orchestral Soc., N.Y.C., 1973-76, asst. condr., N.Y. Philharm., 1976, assoc. condr., Cin. Symphony Orch., 1976-79, music dir. St. Louis Philharm., 1976-81, Charleston (S.C.) Symphony Orch., 1984—; guest condr., prin. guest condr., Bavarian Staatstheater am Gartnerplatz, Munich, 1996-99, Lyric Opera of Chgo., NDR Orch., Hamburg, Germany, Staatskappelle Dresden, Dusseldorf, Bamberg, Frankfurt, Hanover, Symonig orchs., Munich Philharm., Orchestre de Lyon, France, Pitts., Atlanta, Buffalo, St. Louis, Nat., Am., N.J., Dallas, Edmonton, Louisville, Toronto Syphony, Balt., Winnipeg, Indpls. Symphony orchs., Cin. Opera, Teatro Comunale di Genoa, Spoleto Festival USA, Israel Festival, Concertgebouw, Amsterdam, Stadtheater Mannheim, Staatstheatre Darmstadt, Staatsphilharmonic Rheinlandpfalz, Festival of Two Worlds, Spoleto, Italy, N.Y.C. Opera, Wash. Opera, Lake George Opera Festival, Omaha Opera, Dayton Opera, Mich. Opera Theatre, Montreal Opera, Tulsa Opera, Hawaii Opera Theatre, Teatro Massimo di Palermo, Orchestre Colonne, Long Beach Opera, Leonard Bernstein Festival, Holland, RAI Orchestra Rome, Seoul (Dem. Republic Korea) Philharm., Orchestra del Sodre, Montevideo, Uruguay; music dir.: Broadway and internat. tour. West Side Story, Porgy and Bess, Israel Fest. Recipient Gov.'s award for Excellence in the Arts, S.C. Order of Palmetto Exxon/Arts Endowment Condr. award, 1976-79, S.C. Verner award 1996. Mem. Am. Symphony Orch. League.*

STAHL, DAVID EDWARD, trade association administrator, retired; b. Chgo., Apr. 10, 1934; s. Archie Edward and Dorothy Stahl; m. Carolyn Downs Stahl, June 23, 1956; children: Stephen, Michael, Kurt, Thomas. BS, Miami U., 1956. Exec. v.p. Republic Realty Mortgage Corp., Chgo., 1963-66; dep. mayor City of Chgo., 1966-70, city comptroller, 1971-73; exec. v.p. Urban Land Inst., Washington, 1973-76, Nat. Assn. Home Builders, Washington, 1977-84; pres. Nat. Forest Products Assn., 1984-87; exec. v.p. Urban Land Inst., 1987-92; exec. dir. Young Pres.'s Orgn., Irving, Tex., 1992-95; ret., 1996. Del. 6th Ill. Constl. Conv., Springfield, 1970 City adminstr., Annapolis, Md., 2001—02. Served to lt. USAF, 1956—59. Mem. Wayfarers Club, Annapolis Yacht Club, Eastport Yacht Club, Naples Sailing and Yacht Club. Roman Catholic. Home: 100 Severn Ave Apt 607 Annapolis MD 21403-2688

STAHL, DONALD CHARLES, orthopedic surgeon; b. Newark, Dec. 2, 1931; s. John J. and Madeleine E. Stahl; m. Linda Heyman, Aug. 30, 1958 (div. Oct. 1974); children: Carolyn, Douglas, Susan; m. Amy Babcock, June 2, 1978; children: Christopher, Gretchen. AB, Princeton U., 1953; MD, Yale U., 1957. Diplomate Am. Bd. Orthopedic Surgeons. Intern Yale-New Haven Med. Ctr., 1957-58; resident Hosp. Spl. Surgery, N.Y.C., 1962-66; attending orthopedic surgeon Morristown (N.J.) Meml. Hosp., 1966-98, chief orthopedic surgery, 1975-80, chief of staff, 1986-87. Trustee Morristown Meml. Hosp., 1980-87. Bd. dirs. United Way, Morris County, N.J., 1984, Stickley Mus. at Craftsman Farms, Parsippany, N.J., 1997--. Lt. USNR, 1958-62, 2d Marine Air Wing, 1959-62. Fellow Am. Coll. Surgeons, Am. Acad. Orthopedic Surgeons; mem. AMA, Med. Soc. N.J., Morris County Med. Soc. (pres. 1983-84). Democrat. Episcopalian. Home: 53 Seney Dr Bernardsville NJ 07924

STAHL, DONNA LAURA, surgeon; b. Davenport, Iowa, 1945; d. Donald Howard and Elta Loretta (Waage) S. BA, Augustana Coll., 1967; MD, U. Iowa, 1971. Diplomate Am. Bd. Surgery. Intern U. Cin./Cin. Hosp., 1971-72, resident in surgery, 1972-78; ptnr. group practice Cin., 1989—. Staff Good Samaritan Hosp., Cin., 2000; courtesy staff Christ Hosp., 1986—, Jewish Hosp., 1989—. Fellow ACS. Office: 3d flr 4850 Red Bank Expy Cincinnati OH 45227

STAHL, FRANK LUDWIG, civil engineer; b. Fuerth, Germany; came to U.S., 1946, naturalized, 1949; s. Leo E. and Anna (Regensburger) S.; m. Edith Cosmann, Aug. 31, 1947; children: David, Robert. BSCE, Tech. Inst. Zurich, Switzerland, 1945. With Ammann & Whitney, Cons. Engrs., N.Y.C., 1946-93, project engr., 1955-67, assoc., 1968-76, sr. assoc., 1977-81, chief engr. Transp. div., 1982-93; pvt. cons., 1994—. Expert in field. Prin. works include: Verrazano-Narrows Bridge, Throgs Neck Bridge, Walt Whitman Bridge, Improvements to Golden Gate Bridge, rehab. of Williamsburg Bridge, N.Y.C. Royal Gorge Bridge, Colo., Interstate-10 Deck Tunnel, Phoenix, Ariz.; contbr. articles to profl. jours. on bridge design and construction. Recipient Gold award The James F. Lincoln Arc Welding Found., 1986, John A. Roebling medal Internat. Bridge Conf., 1992. Fellow ASCE (Thomas Fitch Rowland prize 1967, Innovation in Civil Engring. award of mert 1983, Metro. Civil Engr. of Yr. award 1987, Roebling award 1990), ASTM (vice chmn. com. A-1 on steel, stainless steel and related alloys 1978-83, chmn. steel reinforce-subcom. 1971-82, award of merit 1982); mem. Am. Inst. Steel Constrn. (Prize Bridge award 1986), Engring. Found. (rsch. coun. on structural connections), Internat. Assn. Bridge and Structural Engring., Internat. Bridge Tunnel and Turnpike Assn. Home: 20911 28th Rd Flushing NY 11360-2412 E-mail: bridgfrank@aol.com.

STAHL, GARY EDWARD, neonatologist; b. N.Y.C., Mar. 19, 1951; s. Louis and Susan (Stein) S.; m. Deborah Susan Levy, July 1, 1973; children: Adam Louis, Eric Alexander. BS, BSEE, MIT, 1973; MD, U. Rochester, 1977. Diplomate Am. Bd. Pediat. subbd. neonatal-perinatal medicine. Pediat. resident Children's Hosp., Phila., 1977-80; neonatal fellow U. Pa., 1980-83; asst. prof. pediat. U. Pa. Sch. Medicine, 1983-90; assoc. prof. pediat. Hahnemann U. Sch. Medicine, 1991-93, U. Med. Dentistry N.J., Cambden, 1993—. Head, divsn. neonatology, vice chief dept. pediats. Children's Regional Hosp., Camden, 1993—. Contbr. articles to profl. jours. Fellow Am. Acad. Pediat.; mem. Nat. Perinatal Soc., Pa. Perinatal Soc., Phila. Perinatal Soc., Physicians for Social Responsibility, Sigma Xi. Office: Children's Regional Hosp at Cooper 1 Cooper Plz Camden NJ 08103-1461

STAHL, JACK LELAND, real estate company executive; b. Lincoln, Ill., June 28, 1934; s. Edwin R. and Edna M. (Burns) S.; m. Carol Anne Townsend, June 23, 1956; children: Cheryl, Nancy, Kellea BS in Edn., U. N.Mex., 1957. Tchr. Albuquerque Public Schs., 1956-59; pres. House Finders, Inc., Albuquerque, 1959-65; v.p. N.Mex. Savs. & Loan Assn., 1965-67; chmn. bd. Hooten-Stahl, Inc., 1967-77; mem. N.Mex. Ho. of Reps., 1969-70; pres. The Jack Stahl Co., Albuquerque, 1977—; mem. N.Mex. Senate, 1981-86; lt. gov. State of N.Mex., 1987-90. Mem. N. Mex. Ho. of Reps., 1969-70, exec. bd. Gr. S.W. Coun. Boy Scouts Am, 1982-89; bd. dirs. BBB N. Mex., 1968-82, pres. 1975-76; trustee Univ Heights. Hosp.,1980-85; vice chmn. N. Mex. Bd. Fin., 1987-90, N. Mex. Cmty. Devel. Coun., 1987-90; bd. dirs. Ctr. for Entrepreneurship and Econ. Devel., 1994-96; mem. Gov.'s Bus. Adv. Coun., 1995-97. Named Realtor of Yr., Albuquerque Bd. Realtors, 1972. Mem. Nat. Assn. Realtors, Nat. Homebuilders Assn., N.Mex. Amigos, 20-30 Club (pres. 1963-64), Rotary. Republican. Methodist. Office: 1911 Wyoming Blvd NE Albuquerque NM 87112-2865 E-mail: Jstahl@webtv.net.

STAHL, LADDIE L. electrical engineer, manufacturing company executive; b. Terre Haute, Ind., Dec. 23, 1921; s. Edgar Allen and Martha (Llewellyn) S.; m. Thelma Mae Beasley, Dec. 11, 1942; children: Stephanie, Laddie L., Craig. BSCE, Purdue U., 1942; MS in Engring., Johns Hopkins U., 1950. With GE, 1954-90, mgr. planning and resources, electronics sci. and engring., corp. research and devel. N.Y., 1974-76, mgr. electronics systems programs ops., elec. sci. and engring., 1976-84, mgr. spl. programs and project devel. operation, 1984-90; dir. tech. transfer program Data Storage Systems Ctr. Carnegie Mellon U., Pitts., 1990—. Chmn. adv. group U.S. Army Electronics Command, 1971-74; mem. U.S. Army Sci. Bd., 1978-87; cons. in field. Contbr. articles to profl. publs. Mem. alumni bd. dirs. Purdue U., 1979-82. Served with U.S. Army, 1942-54, ETO; maj. gen. Res. (ret.), 1954-77. Decorated D.S.M., Legion of Merit. Mem. AIAA (sr.), IEEE (life), Am. Def. Preparedness Assn., Army and Navy Club (Washington), Tau Beta Pi, Chi Epsilon. Home: 29 Fairway Ln Rexford NY 12148-1213 Office: Carnegie Mellon U Data Storage Sys Ctr ECE Dept 5000 Forbes Ave Pittsburgh PA 15213-3815 E-mail: laddie@ece.cmu.edu.

STAHL, LESLEY R. journalist; b. Lynn, Mass., Dec. 16, 1941; d. Louis and Dorothy J. (Tishler) S.; m. Aaron Latham; 1 dau. BA cum laude, Wheaton Coll., Norton, Mass., 1963. Asst. to speechwriter Mayor Lindsay's Office, N.Y.C., 1966-67; rschr. N.Y. Election unit CBS News, 1967-68; rschr. London-Huntley Brinkley Report, NBC News, 1969; producer, reporter WHDH-TV, Boston, 1970-72; news corr. CBS News, Washington, from 1972, White House corr., 1979-91; moderator Face the Nation, 1983-91; co-editor, corr. CBS News, 60 Minutes, 1991—. Trustee Wheaton Coll. Recipient Tex. Headliners award, 1973, Dennis Kauff award for lifetime achievement in journalism, Fifth Estate award Broadcasting Mag. Hall of Fame, 1992, Fred Friendly First Amendment award, 1996; named Best White House Corr., Washington Journalism Rev., 1991. Office: CBS News 60 Minutes 524 W 57th St New York NY 10019-2924*

STAHL, MADONNA, retired judge; b. Robinson, Ill., Sept. 26, 1928; d. Lawrence Joy and Inez Lucille (Kennedy) S.; children: Khushro Ghandhi, Rustom Ghandhi, Behram Ghandhi. BS, U. Ill., 1950; JD, Albany Law Sch., 1973. Bar: N.Y. 1974, U.S. Dist. Ct. (no. dist.) N.Y. 1974, U.S. Ct. Appeals (2nd cir.) 1975, U.S. Supreme Ct. 1978. Atty. trainee N.Y. State Dept. Commerce, Albany, 1973-74; atty. Legal Aid Soc., 1974-76; ptnr. Powers, Stahl & Somers (and predecessor firms), 1976-89; part-time judge Albany City Ct., 1984-89, full-time judge, 1990-97; ret., 1997. Mem. com. on character and fitness N.Y. State Supreme Ct. A.D. 3d Dept., Albany, 1980-86; jud. hearing officer State of N.Y., 1997-2000. Lobbyist Com. for Progressive Legislation, Schenectady, 1968-70. Mem. N.Y. State Bar Assn., Women's Bar Assn. State N.Y. (Capital dist. pres. 1983-84). Democrat. Unitarian Universalist. E-mail: judge_stahl@yahoo.com.

STAHL, MARILYN BROWN, interior designer; b. Boston, Dec. 11, 1929; d. Benjamin M. and Nettie D. (Glazer) Brown; m. Alvan L. Stahl, July 1, 1951; children: Robert, Barry, Kim. BS in Art Edn., Mass. Coll. Art, 1951. Instr. painting, Newton, Mass.; freelance fabric designer, 1960-63; owner gallery Newton, 1963-66, M.B. Stahl Interiors, Chestnut Hill, Mass., 1966—. Founder, pres. Maab Inc., mfrs. French furniture, 1979; pres. Decorators' Clearing House, Newton Upper Falls, Mass. Mem. Nat. Home Fashions League, Am. Soc. Interior Designers Industry Found., Nat. Home Fashions League Industry Found. Home: 390 Commonwealth Ave Apt 201 Boston MA 02215-2824 Office: M B Stahl Interiors 1381 Washington St West Newton MA 02465 E-mail: MBSinteriors@aol.com.

STAHL, MARY GAIL, elementary educator; b. Chgo., July 3, 1943; d. Thomas Finbar and Dorothy Helen (Eley) Hagan; m. John Louis Fish, Aug. 19, 1967 (dec. Sept. 1969); m. Harry Anthony Stahl, Feb. 5, 1972. BS, Edgewood Coll., 1966. Cert. elem. tchr., Wis. Tchr. 2d grade Palatine (Ill.) Pub. Schs., 1966-68; tchr. 1st and 2d grades Wauwatosa (Wis.) Pub. Schs., 1968-75, St. Eugene Sch., Fox Point, Wis., 1977—. Reading cons. Palatine Pub. Schs., 1967; report card cons. Wauwatosa Pub. Schs., 1970-72; presenter Milw. Archdiocese Math Seminar, 1990; student tchr. supr. Cardinal Stritch U., Milw., 1979—. Author: (booklet) Turning on the Accelerated Learner, 1990, (workbook) Weather & Seasons, Building a Nation, 2000. Crusade chair Am. Cancer Soc., Waukesha, Wis., 1972-75. Named Elem. Tchr. of Yr., Milw. Archdiocese, 1991. Mem. Nat. Cath. Edn. Assn., Wis. State Reading Assn. Avocations: reading, gardening, cooking. Home: 1057 Woodview Dr Grafton WI 53024-9759 Office: St Eugene Sch 7600 N Port Washington Rd Fox Point WI 53217-3127

STAHL, NORMAN H. federal judge; b. Manchester, N.H., 1931; BA, Tufts U., 1952; LLB, Harvard U., 1955. Law clk. to Hon. John V. Spalding Mass. Supreme Ct., 1955—56; assoc. Devine, Millimet, Stahl & Branch, Manchester, NH, 1956—59, ptnr., 1959—90; dist. judge U.S. Dist. Ct. (N.H. dist.), 1990—92; cir. judge U.S. Ct. Appeals (1st cir.), Concord, NH, 1992—. Del to Rep. Nat. Conv., 1988. Mem.: N.H. Bar Assn. Office: US Courthouse Ste 8730 1 Courthouse Way Boston MA 02210

STAHL, NORMAN A. educator; b. San Francisco, Apr. 21, 1949; AA, City Coll. San Francisco, 1969; BA, San Francisco State U., 1971, MA, 1976; PhD, U. Pitts., 1983. Rsch. assoc. U. Pitts., 1980-82; asst. prof. divsn. devel. studies Ga. State U., Atlanta, 1982-87; assoc. prof. dept. curriculum & instrn. No. Ill. U., DeKalb, 1987-93, prof., chair dept. curriculum & instrn., 1994-99, chair dept. literacy edn., 1999—. Contbr. articles to profl. jours. Pres. DeKalb Edn. Found., 1999-2001. Recipient Disting. Rsch. award Coll. Reading & Learning Assn., 1990, N.Y. Coll. Learning Skills Assn., 1996. Mem. Coll. Reading Assn. (pres. 1991-92, treas. 1985-88), Internat. Reading Assn. (pres. history reading spl. interest group 1992-94), Am. Reading Forum (chair bd. dirs. 1996-97), Nat. Reading Conf. (historian 1998—), Coll. Reading Assn. (pres. 1991-92). Office: No Ill U Dept Literacy Edn Dekalb IL 60115 E-mail: stahl@niu.edu.

STAHL, PHILIP ANTHONY, physics educator; b. Milw., July 6, 1946; s. Curtis Philip and Magdalen Mary (Polacheck) S.; m. Janice Anne Johnson, Aug. 9, 1975. BA in Astronomy, U. South Fla., 1971; MPhil in Physics, U. W.I., St. Michael, Barbados, 1984. Sci. tchr. U.S. Peace Corps, Barbados, W.I., 1971-75; head sci. dept. West St. Joseph Secondary, 1975-77, Garrison Secondary, St. Michael, Barbados, 1977-82; asst. tutor Barbados Community Coll., 1982-83; lectr. physics Harrison Coll., 1985-91; tech. writer Nucletron Corp., Columbia, Md., 1993-96. Dir. Solar Rsch. Sect., Harry Bayley Observatory, St. Michael, 1984-91; tech. writer, cons. in field. Author: Metacosmos: Cosmic Connections and Self-Actualizing Universe, 1997, The Atheist's Handbook to Modern Materialism, 2000; contbr. articles to profl. jours. Mem. Barbados Environ. Assn., St. Michael, 1987—, Barbados Cancer Soc., St. Michael, 1986—, Barbados and Latin Am. Mus. Soc., 1988—, Mensa, 1993—. Recipient Studentship award Solar Physics Div. Am. Astron. Soc., 1984, Postgrad. Rsch. grant, 1980-84. Mem.: Dynamical Astron. divsn. of Am. Astron. Soc., Solar Physics divsn. of Am. Astron. Soc., Am. Astron. Soc., Barbados Astron. Soc. (pres. 1977—80), Am. Geophys. Union, Am. Math. Soc. Achievements include development of first astronomy syllabus used at secondary level by Caribbean Examination Coun.; discovery of basic relationship between sudden ionospheric disturbances and specific types of H-alpha flare assoc. with sunspot. Home and Office: 2720 Nogal Ct Colorado Springs CO 80917 E-mail: jpstahl@msn.com.

STAHL, RAY EMERSON, freelance writer, historian, researcher; b. Latrobe, Pa., Mar. 24, 1917; s. Curtis E. and Josephine (King) S.; m. Faith Worrell, Aug. 25, 1941; children: Ellen Josephine Carpenter, Ray Emerson Jr. AB, Bethany Coll., 1938; MDiv, Butler U., 1943; EdM, U. Pitts., 1946; postgrad., St. Vincent Coll., 1939, Pitts. Sch. Accountancy, 1939-40, U. Ky., 1955; MA, Ohio State U., 1969; LittD, Milligan Coll., 1995. Ordained to ministry Disciples of Christ Ch., 1941. Min. Brentwood Christian Ch., Pitts., 1943-46, 1st Christian Ch., Erwin, Tenn., 1946-50; exec. sec. in charge bus. adminstrn. and pub. rels. Miligan Coll.ate U., Johnson City, 1950-68; dir. pub. rels., pub. info. East Tenn. State U., 1968-78. Author: How to Finance the Local Church, 1953, Six Decades of Progress, 1976, History of Tennessee-Virginia Energy Corporation, 1981, Money, Wealth, the Bible and You, 1983, Greater Johnson City, A Pictorial History, Tennessee, A Pictorial History, 1983, rev. 2nd edit., 1986, A Beacon to Health Care, 1989; contbr. articles to profl. jours. Bd. dirs. United Way, ARC, Am. Cancer Soc., Reece Mus., Tipton-Haynes Hist. Assn., Johnson City Symphony; elder Christian Ch. Mem. Pub. Rels. Soc. Am. (accredited 1974—), Coun. for Advancement of Small Colls. (chmn. pub. rels. 1957-61), East Tenn. Edn. Assn. (chmn. pub. rels. 1968-76), Johnson City C. of C. (bd. dirs., ofcl. city historian 1986-99), Washington County Tenn. Hist. Assn. (pres.), Johnson City Execs. Club (pres. 1961-62), Kiwanis (sec.-treas. 1983-84, bd. dirs., Kiwanian of Yr. 1995), Theta Phi, Kappa Tau Alpha. Republican. Home and Office: 699 Stadium Dr Boone NC 28607-5423

STAHL, ROBERT ALAN, manufacturing executive, consultant; b. Bklyn., Dec. 27, 1942; s. William Leonard and Marion Teresa (Saunders) S.; m. Patricia Ann Loughery, Oct. 26, 1968; children: Robert Jr., Matthew. BS in Econs., Villanova U., 1966. Mgr. prodn. control Continental Can Co., Patterson, N.J., 1971-73; materials mgr. Schatz-Fed. Co., Poughkeepsie, N.Y., 1973-75, E.G.& G. Sealol, Inc., Warwick, R.I., 1975-81; prin. cons. Comserv Corp., Mnpls., 1981-82; pres. Oliver Wight Assoc., Attleboro, Mass., 1982-88; R.D. Garwood Assoc., 1988-92; Ptnrs. for Excellence Assn., Attleboro, 1992-2000; Supply-Chain Partnership, 2000—. Co-author: (books) Sales Forecasting, Master Scheduling; contbr. articles to profl. jours.; speaker in field. Mgr. Attleboro Little League, 1977-89, Seekonk (Mass.) Youth Hockey, 1975-79, Attleboro Babe Ruth League, 1981-85. Served to lt. USN, 1966-71, Vietnam. Mem. R.I. Agile Alliance, Am. Prodn. and Inventory Control Soc. (cert.). Lodges: KC. Roman Catholic. Home and Office: 6 Marlise Dr Attleboro MA 02703-6535

STAHL, S. SIGMUND, dean, dental educator; b. Berlin, June 16, 1925; came to U.S., 1939; s. Abraham L. and Rosa (Kleinmann) S.; m. Phyllis Schloff, 1947 (div. 1968); 1 child, Jacquelyn; m. Benita Novick. DDS, U. Minn., 1947; MS, U. Ill., 1949. Diplomate Am. Bd. Periodontology. From lectr. to prof. Coll. of Dentistry NYU, N.Y.C., 1950-68; chair dept. periodontics, prof. Sch. of Dentistry U. So. Calif., L.A., 1969-71, chair dept. peridontics, prof. Coll. of Dentistry, 1971-89, assoc. dean acad. affairs, prof. Coll. of Dentistry, 1978—. Cons. USN, N.Y.C., 1971—; mem. dental study sect. NIH, Washington, 1968-72. Contbr. numerous articles to profl. jours. Capt. U.S. Army, 1953-55. Fellow Am. Acad. Peridontology (pres. Chgo. chpt. 1979-80); mem. ADA, Am. Bd. Periodontology (chmn. Chgo. chpt. 1976-77), Internat. Assn. Denta Rsch. (pres. peridontology sect. 1973-74). Jewish. Avocation: philosophy. Home: 111 Bleecker St New York NY 10012-1811 Office: NYU Coll of Dentistry 421 1st Ave New York NY 10010-4001

STAHL, STEPHEN LEE, theater director, writer, producer; b. Phila., Mar. 15, 1949; s. Myer and Fridel (Goldstein) S.; m. Cornell DeFanis, Dec. 29, 1969 (div. May 1976); 1 child, Meredith. Student, Lee Strasburg Actors Studio, 1981. Artistic dir. Studio 3 Prodns., Phila., 1979-82; artistic dir., tchr. drama Actors Ctr., 1982-85; dir. Troyvay Internat., Paris, London, 1985-87, Theatre of Living Arts, Phila., 1987—, Theatre on the Sq., San Francisco; tchr. drama Freez Frame Inc., Phila., 1987—. Dir., writer, prodr. Music Found. Awards, 1989-93; instr. Duality Playhouse, N.Y.C., 1995-96. Writer, dir. plays Porno Stars at Home, Full Bloom, 1998, Queen of Hearts, 1999—, Lady Day, 1986-87 (Bay City award 1987, Creative Drama award 1987), Philly's Beat, 1985 (citation City of Phila. 1985); dir. plays Hosanna, 1981, Coupla White Chicks, 1983, He Plays Piano, 1984, Danny and the Deep Blue Sea, 1984, Sister Mary ... etc., 1985-87, Tallulah, 1987, Psycho Beach Party, 1994, Sophie, Totie and Belle, 1994, We Love Lucy, 1994, P.S. Bette Davis, 1994, 30,000 Pigs Roamed the City, 1995-96, Judy at the Wall Inn, 1995-96, Leany, 1995-96, The Passion, 1995-96, Skirts, 1995-96, Airborn From Deerborn, Chicago Gangstertown, Full Bloom; co-producer play Heart Strings, 1990, Jerker, 1993, Women Behind Bars, 1993, Chicago's Gangsters, 1996-97. Bd. dirs. Max Goldstein Outreach, Phila., 1979-82, Young Persons Apprenticeship Program, Phila., 1979-82. Democrat. Avocations: art, design, tennis. Home: 11 N Main St # A New Hope PA 18938-1314

STAHLMAN, MILDRED THORNTON, pediatrics and pathology educator, researcher; b. Nashville, July 31, 1922; d. James Geddes and Mildred (Thornton) Stahlman. AB, Vanderbilt U., 1943, MD, 1946; MD (hon.) , U. Goteborg, Sweden, 1973, U. Nancy, France, 1982. Diplomate Am. Bd. Pediat., Am. Bd. Neonatology. Intern Boston Children's Hosp., 1947—48; resident Vanderbilt Univ. Hosp., 1948—49; fellow Royal Caroline Inst. Medicine, Sweden, 1949—50; cardiac resident La Rabida Sanitarium, Chgo., 1951; instr. pediat. Vanderbilt U., Nashville, 1951—58, instr. physiology, 1954—60, asst. prof. pediat., 1959—64, asst. prof. physiology, 1960—62, assoc. prof. pediat., 1964—70, prof., 1970—, prof. pathology, 1982—, Harvie Branscomb Disting. prof., 1984, dir. divsn. neonatology, 1961—89, now prof. pediat. and pathology. Editor: Respiratory Distress Syndromes, 1989; contbr. over 175 articles to profl. publs., chpts. to books. Recipient Apgar award, Am. Acad. Pediat., 1987; grantee NIH, 1954—. Mem.: AAAS, Inst. Medicine NAS, Royal Swedish Acad. Scis., So. Soc. Pediatric Rsch. (pres. 1961—62), Am. Physiology Soc., Soc. Pediatric Rsch., Am. Pediatric Soc. (pres. 1984, John Howland award 1996). Episcopalian. Home: 538 Beech Creek Rd S Brentwood TN 37027-3421 Office: Vanderbilt U Med Ctr A-0109 Med Ctr N 21st Ave S Nashville TN 37232-2370 E-mail: mildred.stahlman@mcmailvanderbilt.edu.

STAHMANN, ROBERT F. education educator; b. Peoria, Ill., Nov. 26, 1939; s. Fred Soeffner and Mary Emma (Thompson) S.; m. Kathleen Cook, Dec. 21, 1965; children: Benjamin C., John C., Paul C., Mark C., Anne. BA, Macalester Coll., 1963; MS, U. Utah, 1965, PhD, 1967. Research fellow U. Utah, 1966-67; sr. counselor U. Iowa, Iowa City, 1967-71, coordinator counseling service, 1971-72, dir. counseling service, 1972-75, asst. prof. edn., 1967-71, asso. prof., 1971-75; prof. family scis. Brigham Young U., Provo, Utah, 1975—, chmn. dept. family scis., 1983-89, dir. Marriage and Family Counseling Clinic, 1976-83, coordinator program in marriage and family therapy, 1977-83; program dir. marriage and family therapy, 2001—. Vis. prof. sex and marital therapy clinic Coll. Medicine, U. Utah, 1980-81. Mem. Utah State Marriage and Family Therapy Licensing Bd., 1982-92; mem. Commn. Accreditation for Marriage and Family Therapy Edn., 1989-94, chair, 1990-94. Co-author: Premarital Counseling, 1980, 2d edit., 1987, Dynamic Assessment in Couples Therapy, 1993, Premarital and Remarital Counseling, 1997; co-editor: Ethical and Professional Issues for Marital and Family Therapists, 1980; co-editor, contbr.; Counseling in Marital and Sexual Problems: A Clinician's Handbook, 1977, 3d edit., 1984; assoc. editor: Jour. Coll. Student Pers., 1971-77; editor: Jour. Assoc. Mormon Counselors and Psychotherapists, 1977-78; contbr. chpts. to books., articles to profl. jours. Scoutmaster Boy Scouts Am., 1969-72, 83-87, cubmaster, 1976-79; mem. Orem City Beautification Commn., 1976-77; mem. adv. bd. Ret. Sr. Vol. Program for Utah County, 1987-89. Fellow Am. Assn. Marriage and Family Therapy (bd. dirs. 1977-79); mem. ACA, Internat. Family Therapy Assn., Am. Assn. Sex Educators, Counselors and Therapists (cert.), Utah Assn. Marriage and Family Counselors (pres. 1978-80), Nat. Coun. on Family Rels., Utah Coun. on Family Rels. (pres. 1987-88), Sigma Xi, Phi Kappa Phi. Mem. Lds Ch. Office: Brigham Young Univ 240 TLRB Provo UT 84602 E-mail: robert_stahmann@byu.edu.

STAHR, CURTIS BRENT, photographer, art association administrator, educator; b. West Union, Iowa; s. Freman H. and Lucile M. (Schreiner) S. AA, Ellsworth Coll., 1966; BFA, Peru (Nebr.) State U., 1968. Cert. tchr., Iowa, Colo., Ariz. Art dir. Iowa Falls (Iowa) High Sch., 1968-70, Wiley (Colo.) Schs., 1971-72, Judson Sch., Scottsdale, Ariz., 1973-79; freelance graphic artist, photographer and mktg. dir., 1979-88; prof. photography, photography dir. Des Moines Area C.C., 1988—; art dir. Homestead Assn., Des Moines, 1993-98. Bd. dirs. Homestead Corp., Alpha Inst., Unoged Corp., v.p., 1999; v.p. Young Masters Photographic Art Collection, 1998—; pres. Interpretive Photography, 1999; art dir. Starland Design Band Group, 1979-86, graphic effects dept. Bischoff's, 1987-88; photographic dir. ednl. exchange trip to China. Exhibited in 16 one-man art shows, in 34 invited/juried art shows; represented in numerous pvt. collections; photographer numerous field trips including migration of Am. eagle from Alaska to Fla., all 99 Iowa County Courthouses, Yellowstone Nat. Park, Grand Teton Nat. Park, Waterton-Glacier Internat. Peace Park (U.S. and Can.), Isle Royale Nat. Park, Grand Canyon Nat. Park, Denali Nat. Park, Arctic Nat. Park & Preserve, Canyon de Chelly Nat. Monument, Rainbow Bridge Nat. Monument, Devils Tower Nat. Monument, Effigy Mounts Nat. Monument, Yosemite Nat. Park, Sequoia Nat. Park, Kings Canyon Nat. Park, Japser Nat. Park (Can.), Glacier Nat. Park (Can.), Banff (Can.) Nat. Park, Terra Nova Nat. Park (Newfoundland), Boundary Waters Canoe Area Wilderness, Quetico Provincial Park, Can., North Magnetic Pole, Can., Canyonlands (Utah), Auyuittuq Nat. Park Res., Can., Ellesmere Island Nat. Park Res, Can. Yoho Nat. Park, Can., Kootenay Nat. Park, Can., Angel Falls, Venezuela, Machu Picchu, Peru; numerous cross coutnry trips to U.S., Can., Mex., Cen. Am., S.Am., Yukon Territory and Arctic Cir. Speaker Ariz.-Calif. Lecture Series, 1982-84; chairperson art evaluation com. State of Iowa, 1970; bd. dirs. Ariz. Arts Festival, 1974-79, Muscular Dystrophy Assn. Fund Drive, Ariz., 1982-85. Recipient 8 purchase awards. Democrat. Office: Des Moines Area CC 2006 S Ankeny Blvd Ankeny IA 50021-8995

STAHR, ELLEN MARIE, secondary school educator; b. Chgo., Dec. 20, 1946; d. Thomas Leo and Joan Marie Stahr.; 1 child, Audrey. AB in English, MacMurray Coll., 1968; MA in Lit., Sangamon State U., 1979. Cert. 6-12 grade tchr., Ill. English, French and humanities tchr. Waverly (Ill.) H.S., 1968—; composition and humanities instr. Lincolnland C.C., Springfield, Ill., 1981—. Mem. MLA, NEA, AAUW, Nat. Coun. Tchrs. English, Am. Fedn. Tchrs. Fgn. Lang., Ill. Fedn. Fgn. Lang. Tchrs., Ill. Edn. Assn., Waverly Edn. Assn. (pres., negotiator). Democrat. Avocations: foreign travel, reading, film. Home: 420 W Tremont St Waverly IL 62692-9527 Office: Waverly HS 201 N Miller St Waverly IL 62692-1041

STAHR, REBECCA, interior designer; b. New Orleans, Aug. 30, 1951; d. John Harold and Helen Theresa (Falanga) Mutter; m. Garrett Miles Stahr, Sept. 10, 1988. BS in Merchandising, La. State U., 1973; BFA, Ga. State U., 1985. Buyer Rich's Dept. Store, Atlanta, 1973-81; account exec. Comml. Interior Design, 1981-86; prin. interior designer builder divsn. KBG Interiors, 1986-87; interior designer Rebecca, Inc., Marietta, Ga., 1987—; co-owner Design Strategies, Inc. Speaker design seminar Atlanta Symphony Showhouse, 1990. Design editor Peachtree mag., 1989-92; contbr. articles to various publs. and newspapers. Mem. exec. com. Ga. Coun. for Internat. Visitors, Atlanta, 1992-93; mem. internat. com. Festival of Trees, Atlanta, 1991-93; home delivery vol. Meals on Wheels, Roswell, Ga., 1993-95; co-chairperson Quality of Life event Am. Cancer Soc., Atlanta, 1991. Recipient awards for Best Kitchen, Best Furnishings, Best Interior Design, and Best of Show Street of Dreams, Atlanta, 1987. Mem. AIA (allied mem.), Am. Soc. Interior Designers (legis. task force 1990), Women Healthcare Execs., Nat. Coun. on Aging, Am. Soc. on Aging, Am. Assn. Homes for Aging, Nat. Inst. Srs. Housing, Ga. Coun. on Aging, Sr. Living Assn. Ga. Office: 5675 Commons Ln Alpharetta GA 30005-4689

STAIGER, NANCY LEE, science center executive, accountant; b. Cin., June 8, 1953; d. Russell Louis and Vera (Girten) S.; m. John H. Davis, June 7, 1980 (div. 1990); children: John Henry III, Justin Russell. BBA, U. Cin., 1971-76, MBA, 1976-77. CPA. Auditor Arthur Young & Co., Cin., 1977; acctg. mgr. Richardson Vicks Inc., Wilton, Con., 1978-82; controller New England Info. Systems, St. Johnsbury, Vt., 1983-85, G.TECH Corp., Orlando, Fla., 1986-88; dir. fin. and adminstrn. Orlando Sci. Ctr., 1989—. Seminar instr. in field. Vol. United Arts of Cen. Fla., Orlando, 1990-91, Orlando Sci. Ctr. Guild, PTA Arbor Ridge Elem. Sch. Mem. AICPA, Assn. Sci. & Tech. Ctrs., Fla. Inst. CPAs, U.S. Taedwondo Ctr., Delta Delta Delta. Republican. Avocations: taekwondo, running, snow skiing. Office: Orlando Sci Ctr 810 E Rollins St Orlando FL 32803-1221

STAINBACK, JOHN PHILIP, privatization development executive; b. Henderson, N.C., Aug. 27, 1948; s. John Marvin and Helen Grace (Knight) S.; m. Cynthia Rodgers Working, June 11, 1972 (div. Aug. 1979); m. Ramona Lyn Hightower, Apr. 19, 1985 (div. May 1986); m. Barbara Furr, Oct. 27, 1989. BA, U. Md., 1972, BArch, 1973; M.City Planning, MArch, U. Pa., 1977. Architect, urban designer Pennsylvania Ave. Devel. Corp., Washington, 1973-74; project mgr. Wallace, McHarg, Roberts & Todd, Phila., 1974-75; assoc. The Arroyo Group, Pasadena, Calif., 1977-78; project dir. Daniel, Mann, Johnson & Mendenhall, L.A., 1978-81, assoc. v.p., mng. dir. Houston, 1981-86; dir. devel. Barker Interests Ltd., 1986-88, Decoma Venture Houston Tex. (Privatization Consortium); chmn., pres., chief exec. officer Privatization Devel. of Am. Inc., (subs. 3D Internat.), Houston, 1988-89; pres., CEO Privatization Internat., Inc., N.Y.C., 1989-92; CEO Privatization for Am., Inc., PFA Acquisition and Devel. Co., Houston, 1992—95; prin. and nations dir. public/pvt. devel. Ernst & Young LLC, L.A., 1995—99; sr. v.p. LCOR, Inc., Pa., 1999—2001; mng. ptnr. Stainback Public/Pvt. Real Estate LLC, Malvern, 2001—. Founding mem. Urban Futures Group, L.A., 1980—; design critic, lectr. U. Md., College Park, U. Kans., Manhattan, Rice U., 1974-83; chmn. real estate/pub. facility task force Nat. Coun. for Pub./Private Partnerships, 1993—; chmn. Conf. on New Pub./Private Partnerships for Real Estate and Pub. Facilities, 1994. Author: Public/Private Finance and Development, 2000; contbr. articles to profl. jours. Bd. advisors Mus. Dist. Devel. Assn. of Houston, 1986-89; chmn. internat. policy bd. The Privatization Coun., 1989—; vice chmn. 4th Nat. Privatization Conf., Washington; sponsor mem., bd. dirs. The Privatization Coun., 1989—, v.p. bd. dirs. 1991—; bd. advisors Mackinac Ctr. Pub. Policy, 1993—; mem. Urban Land Inst., 1993—; chmn. real estate, pub. facility task force, Nat. Coun. for Pub.-Pvt. Partnerships, 1993—; chmn. Conf. on New Pub.-Pvt. Partnerships for Real Estate and Pub. Facilities, 1994. Recipient New Mem. of Yr. award Soc. Mktg. Profl. Svcs., 1986; U. Pa. scholar, Phila., 1976, 86-89. Mem. Rice Design Alliance (bd. dirs. 1986-89), Houston C. of C. (chmn. subcom.). Republican. Home: 3 Somerset Ln Malvern PA 19355

STAINE, ROSS (ROSS DONAN ALLISON JR.), lawyer; b. El Paso, Tex., July 13, 1924; s. Ross Donan Allison and Dennie Joe (Stowe) S.; m. Mary Louise Sibert, Aug. 15, 1947; children: Martha Louise, Julie Ann, Ross. BA, Tex. A&M U., 1947; LL.B., U. Tex., 1950. Bar: Tex. Assoc. Baker & Botts, Houston, 1947, ptnr., 1962—. Served with AUS, 1943-46; served to 1st lt. U.S. Army, 1950-52, PTO. Mem. State Bar Tex., Houston Bar Assn., Tex. Law Rev. Assn., Chancellors, Forest Club (Houston), Order of Coif, Phi Delta Phi. Baptist. Home: 5555 Del Monte Dr Apt 807 Houston TX 77056-4117 Office: Baker & Botts 3000 One Shell Plaza Houston TX 77002 E-mail: rdall@swbell.net.

STAINES, CHARLES L. entomologist, researcher; b. Balt., Oct. 19, 1949; s. C. Leroy and Betty E. Staines; m. Susan L. Shanks, June 12, 1971. BS, U. Md., 1972. Lab. technician Alfalfa Weevil Parasite Program, dept. entomology U. Md., College Park, 1971, lab. technician Insect Pathology Lab., dept. entomology, 1971—72; summer worker mosquito control program Md. Dept. Agr., 1971; plant pest inspector USDA, Beltsville, 1972—73; entomologist plant protection sect. Md. Dept. Agr., Annapolis, 1973—97; freelance entomologist Edgewater, 1997—. Contbr. over 100 articles to profl. jours. Recipient Disting. Svc. award, Horticultural Inspection Soc., 1994, Carl Carlson award, Nat. Plant Bd., 1996. Mem.: Md. Entomol. Soc. (pres., Disting. Svc. award 1993), Entomol. Soc. Washington, Cleopterists Soc. Home: 3302 Decker Pl Edgewater MD 21037

STAINES, DAVID MCKENZIE, English educator; b. Toronto, Aug. 8, 1946; s. Ralph McKenzie and Mary Rita (Hayes) S. BA, U. Toronto, 1967; AM, Harvard U., 1968, PhD, 1973. Asst. prof. English Harvard U., Cambridge, Mass., 1973-78, vis. assoc. prof., summers 1980, 82; assoc. prof. English U. Ottawa, Ont., 1978-85, prof., 1985—, vice-dean faculty of Arts, 1994-95, dean faculty of arts, 1995—. Author: Tennyson's Camelot, 1982, Beyond the Provinces: Literary Canada at Century's End, 1995; contbr. articles and revs. Arthurian lit., medieval drama and romance to profl. jours.; editor: The Canadian Imagination, 1977, The Forty-ninth and Other Parallels, 1986, Margaret Laurence: Critical Reflections, 2001; editor Jour. Can. Poetry, 1984—; gen. editor New Can. Libr., 1988—; translator The Complete Romances of Chrétien de Troyes, 1990; co-editor Elements of Literature, 1990, The Short Story in English, 1991. Recipient Lorne Pierce medal, 1998; Ind. study fellow NEH, London, 1977-78, fellow Huntington Libr., San Marino, Calif., 1979. Mem. Medieval Acad. Am. (chmn. com. on ctrs. and regional assn. 1981-87), MLA, Internat. Arthurian Soc., Assn. Can. Univ. Tchrs. English. Roman Catholic. Avocations: theater, bridge. Home: 222 Clemow Ave Ottawa ON Canada K1S 2B6 Office: Univ Ottawa Office of Dean Faculty Arts Ottawa ON Canada K1N 6N5 E-mail: dstaines@uottawa.ca.

STAINES, MAVIS AVRIL, artistic director, ballet principal; b. Cowansville, Que., Can., Apr. 9, 1954; d. David Russell and Betty (Knott) S.; m. Jyrki Virsunen, Feb. 4, 1988. Student, Nat. Ballet Sch., 1968-73, 81-83. Dancer Nat. Ballet of Can., 1973-78, 1st soloist, 1975-78; dancer Dutch Nat. Ballet, 1978-81; artistic dir. Nat. Ballet Sch., Toronto, Ont., Can., 1989—. Mem. artistic staff Nat. Ballet Sch., 1982, assoc. artistic dir., 1984; juror Prix de Lausanne, Switzerland, 1993, 94, 95, guest spkr., 1997; presenter Prix de Lausanne Internat. Symposium, 1997; mem. task force on classicl ballet tng. DANCE/USA, Phila., 1994; pres. Prix de Lausanne, 1998, 99, artistic pres. designate, 2001, artistic pres., 2002; bd. dirs. Kala Nidhi Fine Arts of Can. Recipient Toronto Arts award for performing arts, 1998. Office: The Nat Ballet Sch 105 Maitland St Toronto ON Canada M4Y 1E4

STAINES, MICHAEL LAURENCE, oil and gas production executive; b. Guildford, Eng., May 30, 1949; came to U.S., 1958; s. John Richard and Myrra (Smith) S.; children: Leslie Myrra, Claire Alexandra, Julia Wallis, Cameron Sutton. BS, Cornell U., 1971; MBA, Drexel U., 1976. Asst. comptr. grants U. Pa., phila., 1976-78; sr. analyst Sun Co., Radnor, Pa., 1978-80, Penn Cen. Energy Group, Radnor, 1980-83; v.p., sec. Bryn Mawr Energy Co., Bala Cynwyd, Pa., 1983-88; sr. v.p. Resource Am., Inc., Phila. and Akron, Ohio, 1988—, dir., sec., 1988-2000; COO Atlas Pipeline Ptnrs., 2000—. Chmn. stewardship com. St. Mary's Episc. Ch., Radnor, vestry, 1999—, chmn. fin. com., 1999, search com., 1999—. Winner Silver medal in coxless pair rowing, 1976 Olympic Games, Montreal; named Oarsman of Yr. Schuylkill Navy, Phila., 1976; U.S. Nat. Rowing Champion, 1971, 72, 73. Mem. Ohio Oil and Gas Assn., Oil and Gas Assn. N.Y., Bachelors Barge Club (Phila.), Vesper Boat Club (capt. 1973). Avocations: classic automobiles and motorcycles, sailing. Office: Resource Am Inc 1521 Locust St Philadelphia PA 19102 E-mail: mstaines@resourceamerica.com.

STAINROOK, HARRY RICHARD, retired banker; b. Phila., Jan. 11, 1937; s. Millward M. and Janet (Cruickshank-Smith) S.; m. Judith Ann Swann, May 21, 1966; children: Jennifer, Eric. BA, Rutgers U., 1970. Mgr. bank ops. First Pa. Bank, Phila., 1956-61, asst. v.p. br. dept., 1964-73, v.p., mgr. London office, 1973-75, v.p. internat. dept., 1975-78, sr. v.p. comml. group, 1978-81, exec. v.p., trust and investments, 1981-85; exec. v.p. trust and investments Mfrs. and Traders Trust Co., Buffalo, 1985-97; ret., 1997. Former chmn., bd. dirs. Greater Buffalo Opera Co.; former pres. Buffalo Philharm. Orch.; pres. Acad. Vocal Arts, Phila. With U.S. Army, 1961-64. Mem. World Future Soc., English Speaking Union, Saturn Club. Lutheran. Home: 150 Columbus Ave Apt 4A New York NY 10023-5964 E-mail: hs01@email.msn.com.

STAIR, THOMAS OSBORNE, physician, educator; b. Richmond, Va., Jan. 10, 1950; s. Frederick Rogers Jr. and Martha (Osborne) S.; m. Lucy Caldwell, Dec. 28, 1973; children: Rebecca Caldwell, Peter Caldwell. AB, U. N.C., 1971; MD, Harvard U., 1975. Diplomate Am. Bd. Emergency Medicine (examiner 1982-88). Residency dir. emergency dept. Georgetown U. Sch. Medicine, Washington, 1979-85, asst. dir. emergency dept., 1979-89, asst. dean for continuing med. edn., 1985-89, chair dept. emergency medicine, 1989-95; prof. U. Md., Balt., 1995-98; assoc. prof. Harvard Med. Sch., 1998—; attending emergency physician Brigham and Women's Hosp., Boston, 1998—. Co-author: Common Simple Emergencies, 1985, Emergency Medicine, 1997, Minor Emergencies, 1999. Recipient Excellence in Teaching award Emergency Medicine Residents Assn., 1986. Fellow Am. Coll. Emergency Physicians; mem. Soc. Acad. Emergency Medicine, Am. Med. Informatics Assn. Home: 46 Woodcliff Rd Newton MA 02461-1825 Office: 75 Francis St Boston MA 02115-6110 E-mail: tstair@partners.org.

STAIR, WILSON ALFRED, JR. urban planner, landscape architect; b. St. Louis, Feb. 9, 1946; s. Wilson Alfred Stair and Teresa Kathleen Donahoe; m. Jan Hanson, Nov. 1, 1968. BS in Environ. Design, U. Okla., 1973, BArch, MArch, U. Okla., 1974. Registered landscape arch., Ariz., N.Mex., Fla., S.C. Urban designer divsn. urban redevelopment City of St. Petersburg, Fla., 1976-81; design dir., project mgr. D.V. Preiser Designs, Inc., Tampa, 1982-83; project mgr. H.L. Yoh Co., Inc., 1983-86; urban design mgr. dept. planning and mgmt. City of Tampa, 1986—. Mem. Livable Roadways Com., Tampa, 1992—; design rev. com. Fla. Dept. Transp., Tampa, 1992—; bd. dirs. Mayor's Beautification Program, Tampa. Project designer Janus Landing, 1981, Tampa Downtown Riverwalk, 1989, CBD Streetscape. Staff sgt. USAF, 1966-70. Recipient Recognition award for ednl. contbn. to dept. landscape arch. U. Fla., 1992. Mem. Am. Soc. Landscape Archs., Tau Sigma Delta. Democrat. Methodist. Avocations: martial arts, motorcycling, hiking, watercolor painting. Home: Unit 206 782 Village Lake Ter N Saint Petersburg FL 33716-3146 Office: City of Tampa Dept Planning and Mgmt 306 E Jackson St Tampa FL 33602-5223 E-mail: wilson.stair@tampagov.net.

STAIRS, DENIS WINFIELD, political science educator; b. Halifax, N.S., Can., Sept. 6, 1939; s. Henry Gerald and Freda (Winfield) S.; m. Valerie Downing Street, Aug. 10, 1963 (div. Dec. 1986); children: Robert Woodliffe, Christopher Winfield; m. Jennifer Smith, July 18, 1987. BA, Dalhousie U., 1961, Oxford U., 1964, MA, 1968; PhD, U. Toronto, 1969. Asst. prof. dept. polit. sci. Dalhousie U., 1966-70, assoc. prof., 1970-75, dir. Centre Fgn. Policy Studies, 1971-75, prof. polit. sci., 1975—, McCulloch prof., 1995—, chmn. dept., 1980-85, v.p. acad. and rsch., 1988-93. Bd. dirs. Atlantic Coun. Can., 1979—, Inst. Rsch. Pub. Policy; mem. coun. Social Sci. and Humanities Rsch. Coun. Can., 1981-87; mem. rsch. coun. Can. Inst. Advanced Rsch., 1986-97; bd. dirs. Orgn. for Study of Nat. History of Can., 1995-98. Author: The Diplomacy of Constraint: Canada, the Korean War, and the United States, 1974; editl. bd. Internat. Jour., 1997—. Rhodes scholar, 1961; J.W. Dafoe postgrad. fellow internat. studies, 1965-66; Can. Council leave fellow, 1972-73; Social Scis. and Humanities Research Council Can. leave fellow, 1979-80 Fellow Royal Soc. Can.; mem. Can. Polit. Sci. Assn. (pres.), Can. Inst. Internat. Affairs, Internat. Studies Assn. Clubs: Royal N.S. Yacht Squadron. Office: Dalhousie U Dept Polit Sci Halifax NS Canada B3H 4H6

STAKER, ROBERT DALE, cost analyst, computer scientist, biologist, educator; b. Newport, R.I., July 3, 1945; s. Ray Nicholas and Garnet Louise (Hyland) S.; m. Carolyn Rita Kleinhenz, Feb. 16, 1985; children: Patrick, Katrina, Theresa. BS, U. Dayton, Ohio, 1967, MBA with honors, 1981, MA, 1984; MS, U. Ariz., 1971, PhD, 1973; AS in Math., Sinclair Coll., 1999. Cert. in fin. mgmt. IBM operator Rsch. Ctr./U. Dayton, 1963-67; grad. tchr. asst. dept. biology U. Ariz., Tucson, 1967-73; rsch. biologist dept. biology U. P.E.I., Charlottetown, Can., 1973-75; marine scientist N.Y. Ocean Sci. Lab., Montauk, 1975-79; asst. to dean U. Dayton, 1979-81; program analyst Wright-Patterson AFB, Fairborn, Ohio, 1994-95, cost analys, computer scientist, 1981—. Adj. prof. biol. scis. Wright State U., Fairborn, 1996—99, Sinclair Coll., Dayton, 2001—. Contbr. articles to profl. jours. Cub scout pack leader Boy Scouts Am., Beavercreek, Ohio, 1995-98, boy scout leader, 1995-98, quartermaster, 1998-99, treas. 1999—. NSF grantee Woods Hole Oceanographic Inst., 1970. Mem. Sigma Xi. Roman Catholic. Avocations: hiking, travel, biking, swimming. Home: 3542 Woodgreen Dr Beavercreek OH 45434-5942 Office: MSG/ILI Wright Patterson AFB 4375 Chidlaw Rd C027 Dayton OH 45433-5006 E-mail: robert.staker@wpafb.af.mil.

STAKER, ROBERT JACKSON, federal judge; b. Kermit, W.Va., Feb. 14, 1925; s. Frederick George and Nada (Frazier) S.; m. Sue Blankenship Poore, July 16, 1955; 1 child, Donald Seth; 1 stepson, John Timothy Poore. Student, Marshall U., Huntington, W.Va., W.Va. U., Morgantown, U. Ky., Lexington; LL.B, W.Va. U., 1952. Bar: W.Va. 1952. Practiced in, Williamson, 1952-68; judge Mingo County Circuit Ct., 1969-79; U.S. dist. judge So. Dist. W.Va., Huntington, 1979-95, sr. U.S. dist. judge, 1995—. Served with USN, 1943-46. Democrat. Presbyterian. E-mail: robert_staker@wvsd.uscourts.gov.

STAKIAS, G. MICHAEL, lawyer, merchant banker; b. Norfolk, Va., Feb. 2, 1950; s. George and Gloria Stakias. BA, William & Mary, 1972; JD, Thomas M. Cooley Law Sch, 1976; LLM, NYU, 1977. Bar: Mich., 1976, D.C. 1980, Pa. 1980, N.Y. 1994. Atty. U.S. SEC, Washington, 1977-80; ptnr. Blank, Rome, Comisky & McCauley, Phila., 1980-98, chmn. bus. and corp. dept., 1996-98; ptnr. Liberty Ptnrs., LP, N.Y.C., 1998—. Co-chmn. atty. adv. com. Pa. Securities Commn. Bd. dirs. Thomas M. Cooley Law Sch., Lansing, Mich., 1988—. Mem. ABA (bus. law sect.), Patrons Found. Office: Liberty Partners LP Floor 34 1370 Ave of the Americas New York NY 10019-4602

STALBAUM, BERNARDINE ANN, English language educator; b. Passaic, N.J., May 14, 1942; d. Michael and Anna (Filakowski) Vasel AB, Montclair State U., 1964; MA, Montclair (N.J.) State U., 1969, post grad., 1981. Cert. secondary Eng. tchr. acctg. and gen. bus.; reading specialist, supr., prin. English tchr. Clifton (N.J.) Bd Edn., 1964-82, 90—, reading specialist, 1982-96, dept. resource person, 1982—; G.E.D. instr., student tchr. supr. Clifton (N.J.) Evening Sch. Div., 1984-98; computer instr. lang. arts mid. and H.S., Clifton Bd. Edn., 2000—. Rschr. in field; mem. clin. faculty Montclair State U., 1998—. Mem. NEA, Parent Tchr. Student Assn., Nat. Coun. Tchrs. English, N.J. Edn. Assn., Passaic County Edn. Assn., Clifton Tchrs.' Assn. (sch. del. 1964-92), N.J. Coun. Tchrs. English, N.J. Network Ednl. Renewal, Clifton HS Faculty Orgn. (welfare chmn.), Montclair State U. Alumni Assn. (v.p. membership and programming 1984-95). Home: 279 Pershing Rd Clifton NJ 07013-3718 Office: Clifton High Sch 333 Colfax Ave Clifton NJ 07013-1701

STALBERG, ZACHARY, newspaper editor; b. Phila., Apr. 6, 1947; m. Deborah Lock, Sept. 2, 1990. Student polit. sci., Temple U., 1968. Reporter Bucks County Courier Times, Levittown, Pa., 1970-71; reporter Phila. Daily News, 1971-75, city editor, 1975-77, mng. editor, 1977-79, exec. editor, 1979-84, editor, exec. v.p., 1984—. Served with U.S. Army, 1968-70 Mem. Am. Soc. Newspaper Editors Office: Philadelphia Daily News 400 N Broad St Philadelphia PA 19130-4015*

STALCUP, JOE ALAN, lawyer, clergyman; b. Hooker, Okla., Feb. 13, 1931; s. Herbert I. and Ruby (Gantt) S.; m. Nancy Jo Vaughn, Sept. 3, 1950; children: Melinda, Sondra Jo, Cheri Ann. BBA cum laude, So. Methodist U., 1951, JD magna cum laude, 1959, M.Th. magna cum laude, 1978. Bar: Tex. 1959. Tchr. Dallas Ind. Sch. Dist., 1951-57; assoc. mem. firm Locke, Purnell, Boren, Laney & Neely, Dallas, 1959-66; assoc. atty., partner firm Geary, Brice & Lewis, 1966-67; founder, sr. partner firm Stalcup, Johnson, Meyers & Miller (and predecessor firm), 1968-75; dean Sch. Theology for the Laity, 1978-80, 92-96. Pres. Dallas County Young Democrats, 1952-54; Bd. dirs., mem. exec. com. N. Tex. Christian Communications Commn., 1972-78; bd. dirs., v.p. Greater Dallas Council Chs., 1972-75; bd. dirs., chmn. Christian Ch. Found., 1976-84, 86-91, Christian Bd. Publ., 1991-98. Mem. ABA, Tex. Bar Assn., Dallas Bar Assn., Am. Judicature Soc., Phi Alpha Delta. Mem. Disciples of Christ (minister). Home: 7594 Benedict Dr Dallas TX 75214-1903 Office: 6510 Abrams Rd Dallas TX 75231-7217

STALERMAN, RUTH, civic volunteer, poet; b. N.Y.C., Mar. 18, 1919; d. Samuel and Minnie (Weckstein) Kosson; m. Joseph Stalerman, June 5, 1949 (dec. Aug. 1986); children: Helene, Enid. Student, Modern Machines Bus. Sch. Various bookkeeping positions, to 1951. Poetry pub. Am. Anthology Contemporary Poetry, Nat. Libr. Poetry, A Far Off Place, Songs on the Wind, Tears of Fire, numerous other pubs. and jours. Co-editor, then editor newsletter PTA; dist. dir. Girl Scouts U.S., 1958-62; pres. White Plains chpt. B'nai B'rith, cons. on membership, programming; mem. White Plains Hosp. Aux., mem. instnl. rev. bd.; USO hostess, Temple Emanuel, N.Y.C., WWII. Recipient Editor's choice awards for outstanding achievement in poetry, 1994, 95, 96, Best Poems of the 90s, Best Poems of 1997. Mem. Jewish War Vets. (chaplain, contbr. to newsletter), Internat. Soc. Poets Home: 50 Lawrence Dr White Plains NY 10603-1503

STALEY, BRADLEY WAYNE, music educator, set designer; b. Richmond, Va., May 30, 1977; s. David Wayne and Jane (Potter) Staley; m. Kerri Michelle Kelly, Mar. 13, 2002. BS in Edn., State Coll., Institute, W.Va., 2000. Lic. Tchr. Va., N.C., W. Va., 2001. Band dir. 6-12 Logan County Schs., Logan, W.Va., 2000—01; band dir. 9-12 Northside H.S., Jacksonville, NC, 2001—. Theatre asst. / cultural activities W.Va. State Coll., Institute, W.Va., 1996—2000, resident asst., 1998—2000. Musician: (performance in euphonium and trumpet) Various Works, 1998 (Selected Soloist W.Va. Music Educators Conf., 1999). Guest spkr. to W. Va. Legislature mems. Leadership Program, W.Va. State Coll., Institute, W.Va., 2000. Named Most Outstanding Musician, W.Va. State Coll., 1998; recipient Music Dept. Scholarship, 1995-1999. Mem.: NC Bandmasters Assn., NC Music Educators Assn., Music Educators Nat. Conf. (pres., student chpt. 442 1997—99, Nat. Growth Award 1997), Kappa Delta Pi, Omicron Delta Kappa. Methodist. Avocations: bowling, camping, fishing, golf. Home: 2100 Country Club Rd Apt 1705 Jacksonville NC 28546 Office: Northside HS 365 Commons Dr S Jacksonville NC 28546 Home Fax: 910-353-7520. Personal E-mail: bstaley@ocs.onslow.k12.nc.us.

STALEY, DAWN, basketball player; b. Phila., May 4, 1970; Grad., U. Va., 1992. Basketball player US Nat. Women's Basketball Team, Olympics 1996, 1999, 2000; basketball player, guard Charlotte Sting, 1997—. Scholar U. Va.; named 1994 USA Basketball Female Athlete of Yr, named to Eastern Conf. All-Star Team, 2001. Avocations: played professional basketball Italy, Brazil, Spain and France. Office: 100 Hive Dr Charlotte NC 28208-7707*

STALEY, HENRY MUELLER, manufacturing company executive; b. Decatur, Ill., June 3, 1932; s. Augustus Eugene, Jr. and Lenore (Mueller) S.; m. Violet Lucas, Feb. 4, 1955; children— Mark Eugene, Grant Spencer. Grad., Governor Dummer Acad., 1950; BS in Psychology, Northwestern U., 1954, MBA in Finance, 1956. Salesman Field Enterprises, Chgo., 1953; salesman A.E. Staley Mfg. Co., 1951, mgmt. trainee, 1956-57, ins. mgr., 1957-59, asst. treas., 1959-65, treas., asst. sec., 1965-73, v.p., treas., asst. sec., 1973-77, v.p. bus. and econ. analysis, 1977-87, also dir., 1969-85; pvt. investor Decatur, 1987—. Dir. Staley Continental, Inc., 1985-88. Crusade chmn. Macon County unit Am. Cancer Soc., 1964-65, mem. bd. dirs., 1965-71, vice chmn. bd., 1965-66, chmn. bd., 1966-69; bd. dirs. United Way Decatur and Macon County, 1972-74; mem. adv. council Millikin U., 1968-91, chmn. adv. coun., 1970-71; mem. Decatur Meml. Hosp. Devel. Council, 1969-71, mem. finan. com., bd. dirs., 1970-79, mem. long-range planning com., 1976-77, mem. devel. and community relations com., 1977-78. Mem. Decatur C. of C. (dir. 1967-72), Sigma Nu. Clubs: Decatur, Decatur Country. Home and Office: 276 N Park Pl Decatur IL 62522-1952 also: 74 Ironwood Ln Lahaina HI 96761-9062

STALEY, JOHN FREDRIC, lawyer; b. Sidney, Ohio, Sept. 26, 1943; s. Harry Virgil and Fredericka May (McMillin) S.; m. Sue Ann Bolin, June 11, 1966; children: Ian McMillin, Erik Bolin. AB in History, Fresno State Coll., 1965; postgrad., Calif. State U., Hayward, 1967-68; JD, U. Calif., San Francisco, 1972. Bar: Calif. 1972. Ptnr. Staley, Jobson & Wetherell, Pleasanton, Calif., 1972—. Lectr. U. Calif. Hastings Coll. Law, San Francisco, 1973-74; founding mem. Bank of Livermore (now U.S. Bank); del. U.S.-China Joint Conf. on Law, Beijing, 1987. Mem. Livermore City Coun., 1975-82, vice mayor, 1978-82; bd. dirs. Alameda County Tng. and Employment Bd., Alameda-Contra Costa Emergency Med. Svcs. Agy., Valley Vol. Ctr. With M.I., U.S. Army, 1966-67. Fellow Am. Acad. Matrimonial Lawyers; mem. ABA, Calif. State Bar, Alameda Bar Assn., Amador Valley Bar Assn., Calif. Assn. Cert. Fmaily Law Specialists (pres. 1988-89, Hall of Fame award 1994), Hastings Coll. Law Alumni Assn. (bd. dirs.). Office: Staley Jobson & Wetherell Ste 310 5775 Stoneridge Mall Rd Pleasanton CA 94588-2838

STALEY, KENNETH BERNARD, civil engineer; b. Dec. 31, 1948; s. Kinzy and Bernice Florence (Williams) S.; m. Sheila Ruth Keeys, Apr. 26, 1975; children: Tabbatha, Christina, Harrison. ThM, Villanova U., 1971, MA, 1976, DD, 1978. Registerd profl. engr.; ordained to ministry Bapt. Ch., 1978. Cost estimator Joseph A. McCollum Inc., Marlton, N.J., 1967-69; expeditor R. V. Rulon Inc., Riverton, 1971; field engr. United Engrs., Phila., 1971-72; civil engr., v.p., dir. Kinzy Staley & Sons, Inc., 1972—. Vol. Aid Sickle Cell Anemia, 1974, Mendenhall Ministries, Miss.; asst. pastor Christian Stronghold Bapt. Ch., Phila., 1978—; bd. dirs. Christian R&D, Phila., Germantown Cmty. Devel., Phila.; bd. advisors Manna Bible Inst., Phila.; trustee Ctr. Urban Theol. Studies, Conservative Bapt. Sem., Phila. Prison Sys. Mem. Nat. Soc. Profl. Engrs., Assn. Cost Engrs., Am. Arbitration Assn., Am. Ceramic Soc., Am. Concrete Inst., Phila. Engrs. Club, Alpha Phi Alpha. Democrat. Home: 1130 Lakeside Ave Philadelphia PA 19126-2308 Office: Covenant Cons Group PO Box 698 Bala Cynwyd PA 19004-0698

STALEY, THOMAS FABIAN, language professional, academic administrator; b. Pitts., Aug. 13, 1935; s. Fabian Richard and Mary (McNulty) S.; m. Carolyn O'Brien, Sept. 3, 1960; children: Thomas Fabian, Caroline Ann, Mary Elizabeth, Timothy X. AB, BS, Regis Coll., 1957; MA, U. Tulsa, 1958; PhD, U. Pitts., 1962; D.H.L., Regis Coll., 1979. Asst. prof. English Rollins Coll., 1961-62; mem. faculty U. Tulsa, 1962-88, prof. English, 1969-88, dean Grad. Sch., 1969-77; dir. Grad. Inst. Modern Letters, Trustees prof. modern lit. U. Tulsa (Grad. Sch.), 1977—; dean Coll. Arts and Scis. U. Tulsa, 1981-83, provost, v.p. acad. affairs, 1983-88, McFarlin prof. modern lit., 1988—; prof. English, dir. Ransom Humanities Rsch. Ctr. U. Tex., Austin, 1988—, Chancellor's Centennial prof. of the Book, 1989-92, Harry Huntt Ransom chair liberal arts, 1992—. Fulbright prof., Italy, 1966-67; Fulbright lectr., 1971; Danforth assoc., 1962-67; chmn. Internat. James Joyce Symposium; dir. Grad. Inst. Modern Letters, 1970-81. Author: James Joyce Today, 1966, James Joyce's Portrait of the Artist, 1968, Italo Svevo: Essays on His Work, 1969, (with H.J. Mooney) The Shapeless God: Essays on the Modern Novel, 1968, (with B. Benstock) Approaches to Ulysses: Ten Essays, 1970, Approaches to Joyce's Portrait: Ten Essays, 1977, Jean Rhys: A Critical Study, 1979; editor: Il Punto Su Joyce, 1973, Dorothy Richardson, 1975, Ulysses: Fifty Years, 1974, Twentieth-Century Women Novelists, 1982, British Novelists, 1890-1929, Traditionalists, Dictionary of Lit. Biography, Vols. 34, 36, 70, 77, An Annotated Critical Bibliography of James Joyce, 1989, Joyce Studies: An Annual edit., 1990—, Studies in Modern Literature Series, 1990—. Reflections on James Joyce: Stuart Gilbert's Paris Journal, 1993, Writing the Lives of Writers, 1998, James Joyce Quar., 1963-89; adv. editor Twentieth-Century Lit., 1966—, Jean Rhys Rev., 1986—; bd. dirs. Eighteenth-Century Short Title Catalogue/North America, 1990; editl. bd. Tulsa Studies in Women's Literature, Jour. Modern Lit., 1989—; contbr. articles to profl. jours. Bd. dirs. Tulsa Arts Coun., 1969-76, NCCJ, 1979—; pres. James Joyce Found., 1968-72; chmn. bd. Undercroft Montessori Sch., 1968-70, Marquette Sch., 1969-70; bd.

dirs. Cascia Hall Prep. Sch.; chmn. disting. authors com. Tulsa Libr. Trust, 1984; mem. bd. commrs. Tulsa City-County Libr., chmn., 1980-82; mem. adv. coun. Tex. Inst. for Humanities; trustee Regis U., 1992—; bd. dirs. Libr. of Am., 1994—, Harlick Trust, 1994—; mem. symposium com. Lyndon Baines Johnson Presdl. Libr., 1993—. Recipient Am. Council Learned Socs. award, 1969, 80 Mem. MLA, Internat. Assn. Univ. Profs. English, Anglo-Irish Studies Assn., Am. Com. for Irish Studies, Assn. Internat. de Bibliophilie, James Joyce Soc., Hopkins Soc., Tex. Philos. Soc. (bd. dirs. 1991—), U.S. Tennis Assn., Tulsa Tennis Club, Westwood Country Club, The Athenaeum Club (London), Grolier Club (N.Y.), Edgecomb Tennis Club (Kennebunk, Maine), Tarry House, Phi Beta Kappa. Home: 2528 Tanglewood Trl Austin TX 78703-1540 also: 4 Surf Ln Kennebunk ME 04043

STALFORT, JOHN ARTHUR, lawyer; b. Balt., June 9, 1951; s. John Irving and Libby Jean (Adams) S.; m. Rebecca Higgins, Aug. 21, 1976 (div. 1984); m. Anne Cheesman, July 19, 1985. BA, U. Va., 1973, MBA, JD, 1977. Bar: Md. 1977. Assoc. Miles & Stockbridge, Balt., 1977-84, ptnr., 1984—. Author: Commercial Financing Forms-Maryland, 1986. Sec. Roland Pk. Rds. and Maintenance Corp., Balt., 1978-83. Mem. ABA, Md. State Bar Assn. (chmn. sect. bus. law 1995-96), Nat. Assn. of Bond Lawyers, Balt. Country Club, Md. Club, Talbot Country Club, Phi Beta Kappa. Republican. Presbyterian. Avocations: skiing, golf, lacrosse, running. Office: Miles & Stockbridge 10 Light St Ste 1100 Baltimore MD 21202-1487 E-mail: jstalfort@milesstockbridge.com.

STALICK, WAYNE M. chemistry educator, law firm consultant; b. Oregon City, Oreg., Aug. 24, 1942; s. Anton and Caroline Stalick; m. Judith K. Stalick, June 24, 1967 (div. June 2000); 1 child, Jonathan. BA, U. Oreg., 1964; PhD, Northwestern U., 1969. Vis. asst. prof. San Jose (Calif.) State U., 1969-70; postdoctoral fellow, instr. Ohio State U., Columbus, 1970-72; asst. prof. chemistry George Mason U., Fairfax, Va., 1972-76, assoc. prof., 1976-87, prof., 1987—. Vis. scientist Naval Rsch. Labs., Washington, 1955-88; patent law cons. Foley & Lardner, Washington, 1997-98; session chmn. organic chemistry divsn. Pacific Chemistry Conf., Honolulu, 2000. Co-author: Base-Catalyzed Reactions of Hydrocarbons and Related Compounds, 1977, Organic Chemistry Laboratory Manual, 2d edit., 1990; contbr. articles to sci. jours. Pres. Beech Ridge Civic Assn., Fairfax, 1978-87; mem. Fairfax County Parks Adv. Com., 1982—. Grantee NSF, 1995-2000, grantee Thomas F. and Kate Miller Jeffress Meml. Trust, 2000—. Mem. Am. Chem. Soc., Internat. Soc. Heterocyclic Chemistry, Va. Acad. Sci., Chem. Soc. Washington, Capital Area Triumph Owners Club, Vintage Triumph Register Car Club. Office: George Mason U MS 3E2 Chemistry Dept Fairfax VA 22030 E-mail: wstalick@gmu.edu.

STALKER, JACQUELINE D'AOUST, academic administrator, educator; b. Penetang, Ont., Can., Oct. 16, 1933; d. Phillip and Rose (Eaton) D'Aoust; m. Robert Stalker; children: Patricia, Lynn, Roberta. Teaching cert., U. Ottawa, 1952; tchr. music, Royal Toronto Conservatory Music, 1952; teaching cert., Lakeshore Tchrs. Coll., 1958; BEd with honors, U. Manitoba, 1977, MEd, 1979; EdD, Nova U., 1985. Cert. tchr. Ont., Man., Can. Adminstr., tchr., prin. various schs., Ont. and Que., 1952-65; area commr. Girl Guides of Can., throughout Europe, 1965-69; administr., tchr. Algonquin Community Coll., Ottawa, Ont., 1970-74; tchr., program devel. Frontenac County Bd. Edn., Kingston, 1974-75; lectr., faculty advisor dept. curriculum, edn. U. Man., Can., 1977-79; lectr. U. Winnipeg, Man., Can., 1977-79; cons. colls. div. Man. Dept. Edn., 1980-81, sr. cons. programming br., 1981-84, sr. cons. post secondary, adult and continuing edn. div., 1985-88, dir. post secondary career devel. br. and adult and continuing edn. br., 1989; asst. prof. higher edn., coord. grad. program in higher edn. U. Man., 1989-92, assoc. prof., coord. grad. program in higher edn., 1992-95. Cons. lectures, seminars, workshops throughout Can. Contbr. articles to profl. jours.; mng. editor Can. Jour. of Higher Edn., 1989-93. Mem. U. Man. Senate, 1976-81, 86-89, bd. govs., 1979-82; Can. rep. Internat. Youth Conf., Garmisch, Fed. Republic of Germany, 1968; vol. Can. Cancer Soc.; mem. Assn. RN Accreditation Coun., 1980-85; chair Child Care Accreditation Com., Man., 1983-90; chair Task Force Post-Secondary Accessibility, Man., 1983; vol. United Way Planning and Allocations; provincial dir., mem. nat. bd. Can. Congress for Learning Opportunities for Women. Recipient award for enhancing the Outreach activities of the univ. U. Man., 1994. Mem. Can. Soc. Study Higher Edn., Man. Tchrs. Soc., U. Man. Alumni Assn., Women's Legal Edn. and Action Fund. Home: 82 McNulty Crescent Winnipeg MB Canada R2M 5H4

STALL, ALAN DAVID, packaging company executive; b. Moose Jaw, Sask., Can., June 14, 1951; came to U.S., 1982; s. Joel and Evelyn (Schwartz) S.; m. Carol I. Johnston; children: Jeffrey, Jennifer, Michael, Timothy. BSME, U. Sask., 1973; MBA, Lewis U., 1986. Registered profl. engr., Ont. Devel. engr. DuPont Can., North Bay, Ont., 1973-76; project engr. Union Carbide Corp. Can., Lindsay, 1976-79, engring. mgr., 1979-82; mgr. shirring rsch. Union Carbide Corp., Chgo., 1982-85; dir. engring. tech. Viskase Corp., 1985-90, v.p. engring., 1990-95; gen. mgr. Kuko Corp., Gross-Gerau, Germany, 1995-98; pres. Films Casings Tech. Inc., Woodridge, Ill., 1996—; gen. mgr. Alfacel Inc., 1998—. Patentee breathable plastic, shirring apparatus, sausage stuffing machine, cellulose casings, cellulose regeneration. Rotary bus. exchange fellow, London, l982. Mem. Engring. Inst. Can., Can. Soc. Mech. Engrs., Soc. Plastics Engrs., Assn. Profl. Engrs., Ont., Am. Mensa, Can. Club Chgo. Home: 23W540 James Way Naperville IL 60540-9552 Office: Alfacel Inc PO Box 5415 Woodridge IL 60517-0415

STALL, RICHARD J., JR. lawyer; b. Covington, Ky., July 5, 1941; BS with distinction, Purdue U., Lafayette, Ind., 1963; JD, Stanford U., Calif., 1966. Bar: Calif., U.S. Supreme Ct., U.S. Dist. Ct. (ctrl. dist.), U.S. Ct. Appeals (9th cir.). Assoc. Lawler, Felix & Hall (now Arter & Hadden), L.A., 1966-70; ptnr. pvt. practice, 1971-93, Stall, Astor & Goldstein, L.A., 1994—. Contbg. author: Ins. Jour. Mem.: ABA, Culver-Marina Bar Assn. (past pres., dir.), Santa Monica Bar Assn., Nat. Assn. Railroad Trial Counsel, L.A. County Bar Assn., Calif. State Bar Assn. (real estate sect.), Beverly Hills Bar Assn. (real estate sect.), Assn. Bus. Trial Lawyers, Am. Arbitration Assn., Lion's Club (past pres.), Tau Beta Pi, Sigma Chi (Delta Delta Chpt. past pres.). Office: Law Office Richard J Stall Jr Ste 200 10507 W Pico Blvd Los Angeles CA 90064-2319 Fax: 310-470-3673. E-mail: rstall@picolaw.com.

STALLAERTS, ROBERT, librarian, researcher; b. Antwerp, Belgium, Apr. 26, 1947; s. Raymond and Gabriela (Van Den Oever) S. Lic. in moral scis., U. Belgium, 1972, lic. in devel. econs., 1975; postgrad., Inst. Ekonomskih Nauka, 1978-81; D in Devel. Econs., State U. Ghent, Belgium, 1981. Rschr. State U. Ghent, 1999—. Contbr. articles to profl. jours.; translator Yugoslav lit. Home: Ellebogten 66 B-9070 Heusden Belgium

STALLINGS, CHARLES HENRY, retired physicist; b. Durham, N.C., Dec. 28, 1941; s. Henry Harroll and Dorothy (Powers) S.; m. Elizabeth Bright, Sept. 4, 1965; children: Deborah, Sharon. BS, N.C. State U., 1963, MS, 1964; PhD, U. Wis., 1970. Sr. physicist Physics Internat. Co. (now Maxwell Physics Internat.), San Leandro, Calif., 1970-73, dep. dept. mgr., 1974-76, dept. mgr., 1976-79, dir. satellite x-ray test facility office, 1979-81, dir. bus. devel., 1981-83, v.p., dir. rsch. devel., v.p., gen. mgr., 1983—2001; ret., 2001. Contbr. articles to tech. jours. Mem. Gen. Plan Rev. Com., Pleasanton, Calif., 1983. Mem. Am. Phys. Soc., IEEE (mem. pulsed power sci. and tech. com. 1996—, chmn. 12th internat. pulsed power conf. 1999). Home: 1717 Courtney Ave Pleasanton CA 94588-2692

STALLINGS, FRANK , JR. industrial engineer; b. Concord, N.C., Aug. 21, 1954; s. Frank and Theresa Ann (Iorlano) S. BS in Indsl. Engring., N.C. State U., 1976; MS in Adminstrn., George Washington U., 1979. Jr. indsl. engr. Naval Air Rework Facility, Norfolk, Va., 1974-75; indsl. engr. Babcock & Wilcox, Lynchburg, 1977-79; sr. prin. engr. NCR Corp., Columbia, S.C., 1979-82; mgr. indsl. engring. Mars Electronics, Ltd., Reading, Eng., 1982-84; liaison between European/U.S. mfg. divsns., sr. indsl. engr. M&M/MARS, Inc., Waco, Tex., 1982-84, mgr. quality assurance, 1984-87, mgr. indsl. engring., 1988-96, inbound logistics mgr., 1996-97; mng. prin. Oracle Corp., 1998—2001, practice mgr., 2001; dir. applications ATC Logistics, 2001—. Coach Heart of Tex. Soccer League, Waco, 1985-87; Sunday sch. tchr. Columbus Ave. Bapt. Ch., Waco, 1988-97, mem. Missions com., 1991-96, Bapt. Youth leader, 1990-97, mem. ch. singles coun., 1989-91; Sunday sch. tchr. First Bapt. Hartsville (S.C.) Ch., 1998-2000; exec. mem. singles coun. Waco Bapt. Assn.; counselor Royal Ambs., 1990-96; children's leader Bible Study Fellowship, 1995-97. Mem. Inst. Indsl. Engrs. (sr.), Am. Soc. Quality Control, Am. Prodn. and Inventory Control Socl., Am. Radio Relay League, Project Mgmt. Inst. (cert.), Radio Amateurs Civil Emergency Svcs., Amateur Radio Emergency Svcs., Ten-10 Internat. Amateur Radio Network, Waco Amateur TV Soc. (bd. dirs. 1995-96), Appalachian Trail Soc. (life). Republican. Avocations: camping, boating, running, cycling, amateur radio operator. Home: PO Box 77958 Fort Worth TX 76177-0958 E-mail: frank@stallings.com.

STALLINGS, JIM ALLEN, painter; b. Waco, Tex., Dec. 27, 1960; s. Jim Moye and Dorothy Lee Stallings. BA in graphic advt., Ctrl. State U., 1982—86. Cert. internat. advt. diploma 1986. Artist Sargent's Fine Art Gallery, Lahaina, Hawaii, 1992—97, owners, 1998—2001. Painting live symphony music. Home: 3111 Ber Air Dr. #5D Las Vegas NV 89109

STALLINGS, NORMAN (CHARLES NORMAN STALLINGS), lawyer; b. Tampa, Fla., Apr. 3, 1914; s. Otto Pyromus and Minnie Henderson (Mitchell) S.; m. Mary Phillips Powell, Feb. 6, 1943 (dec. 1999); children: Charles Norman, Jean Katherine (dec.), Mary Anne. AB, U. Fla., 1935; JD, Harvard U., 1938, LL.M., 1940. Bar: Mo. 1939, Fla. 1940, D.C. 1941, Ga. 1946. Asso. firm Ryland, Stinson, Mag & Thomson, Kansas City, Mo., 1938-39, Sutherland, Tuttle & Brennan, Washington, 1940-41, Atlanta, 1946-49; mem. firm Shackleford, Farrior, Stallings & Evans, Tampa, Fla., 1949-84, of counsel, 1984—. Vice chmn. Hillsborough County (Fla.) Aviation Authority, 1955-61. Served to lt. col. U.S. Army, 1941-46, ETO. Decorated Bronze Star; Croix de Guerre avec Palma, Belgium. Fellow Am. Coll. Trial Lawyers; mem. ABA, Hillsborough County Bar Assn. (past pres.), Fla. Bar (past gov.), Univ. Club (past pres.), Tampa Yacht and Country Club (past gov.), Ye Mystic Krewe of Gasparilla (past capt. and king), Phi Delta Phi, Kappa Alpha. Republican. Episcopalian. Home: 1901 S Ardsley St Tampa FL 33629-5930 Office: PO Box 3324 Tampa FL 33601-3324

STALLINGS, RONALD DENIS, lawyer; b. Evansville, Ind., Feb. 22, 1943; s. Denis and Gertrude (Tong) S.; m. Vicki Lee Chandler, Aug. 21, 1965; children: Courtnay, Claire, Ryan. B in Indsl. Engring., Ga. Inst. Tech., 1965; LLB, U. Va., 1968. Bar: Ga. 1968. Assoc. Powell, Goldstein, Frazer & Murphy LLP, Atlanta, 1968-75, ptnr., 1976-2000, co-counsel, 2001—; sr. v.p., gen. counsel, corp. sec. Reliance Trust Co., 2001—. Co-author: Georgia Corporate Forms, 1988. Mem. ABA, Ga. Bar Assn., Atlanta Bar Assn., Nat. Assn. Bond Lawyers, Am. Soc. Corp. Secs., Phoenix Soc. Atlanta (trustee 1987-93). Roman Catholic. Home: 4601 Polo Ln NW Atlanta GA 30339-5345 Office: Reliance Trust Co Ste 900 3384 Peachtree Rd NE Atlanta GA 30326-1106 E-mail: rstallings@relico.com.

STALLINGS, VALERIE A. physician, state official; b. N.Y.C., Nov. 27, 1943; BS in Zoology, Duke U., 1964; MD, U. N.C., 1968, MPH, 1988. Intern, resident Pediats. Med. Coll. Va., 1968-71; physician Va. Dept. Health Bur. Crippled Children, Norfolk, 1971-75, Portsmouth (Va.) Health Dept., Portsmouth, Va., 1971-77; dir. Tidewater Child Devel. Clin., Norfolk, 1977-82; dep. dir. Norfolk Dept. Pub. Health, 1982-89, dir., 1989—. Office: Norfolk Dept Pub Health 830 Southampton Ave Norfolk VA 23510-1001

STALLINGS, VIOLA PATRICIA ELIZABETH, systems engineer, educational systems specialist; b. Norfolk, Va., Nov. 6, 1946; d. Harold Albert and Marie Blanche (Welch) S.; m. (div. Oct. 1984); 1 child, Patricia N.P. Stallings. BS in Psychology, Va. State U., 1968; MBA with distinction, U. Pa., 1975; postgrad., Temple U., 1972-74, Calif. State U., San Francisco, 1973; EdD with specialization in tech., Nova Southeastern U., Ft. Lauderdale, Fla., 1996. Cert. exec. project mgr., project mgmt. profl. Project Mgmt. Inst. Tchr., supr. Peace Corps, Liberia, West Africa, 1968-71; tchr. Day Care Ctr., disruptive h.s. students Tioga Comm. Youth Ctr., 1972-73; tchr. Phila. Sch. Dist., 1972-76; bus. cons. Phila., 1976; sr. sys. engr./sr. industry svcs. specialist, project mgr. IBM/K-12 Edn. and IBM Global Industry, Mt. Laurel, N.J.; cert. exec. project mgr. IBM Global Svcs. Task force leader IBM Corp., 1990—91. Bd. dirs. Unity Ch. of Christ, 1993—95, 2000—02, sec., 2000—01. Recipient Outstanding Svc. award IBM Black Workers Alliance, Washington, 1984. Mem. AAUW, World Affairs Coun., Project Mgmt. Inst., St. Joseph's Carpenter Soc. (bd. dirs. 1999—), Women of Arts, Beta Gamma Sigma. Baptist. Avocations: reading, writing, drawing, gardening, cooking, dancing, sewing. Office: IBM Global Svcs Atrium I 5th Fl 1000 Atrium Way Mount Laurel NJ 08054-3902

STALLMAN, DONALD LEE, corporate executive; b. Rochester, N.Y., Feb. 20, 1930; s. William F. and Clara Elizabeth (Boulle) S.; m. Dolores Anita Putney, Nov. 8, 1958; stepchildren: Nancy, Terri, Jeff. Student, Hobart Coll., Geneva, N.Y., 1948-49, U. Rochester, 1953-54. V.p. Kolstad Assocs., Inc., Rochester, N.Y., 1954—; pres. Water Treatment Assocs., Latham, 1975—, KB Fabrications, Latham, 1977—. Dir. Kolstad Assocs., Inc.; chmn. bd. Water Treatment Assocs.; vice chmn. bd. K.B. Fabrications; adv. bd., pres. Bruner Corp., Milw., 1982-83. Designer Chock-o-Lette Spl. Aircraft Wheel Chock, 1978, Water Treatment Skid for Oil Field Applications, 1980; inventor in field. Cons. Capital Dist. Planning Commn., Albany, 1980-81. With U.S. Army, 1951-53. Decorated Bronze Star medal, Purple Hearts (2). Mem. Am. Soc. Plumbing Engrs., Water Quality Assn., Quiet Birdman Soc., Latham Area C. of C. (mem. transport com. 1985—), Sigma Chi. Republican. Roman Catholic. Avocations: flying, boating, golf. Home: 16 Hillcrest Rd Latham NY 12110-4133 also: 111 Royal Park Dr Fort Lauderdale FL 33309-5893 Office: Water Treatment Assocs PO Box 367 Latham NY 12110-0367

STALLMAN, RICHARD MATTHEW, software developer; b. N.Y.C., 1953; BA in Physics, Harvard U., 1974; PhD (hon.), Royal Inst. Tech., Stockholm, 1996, U. Glasgow, 2001. Software developer MIT, Cambridge, 1971-83. Chief GNUisance, GNU Project, 1984—; founder, pres. Free Software Found., Boston, 1985—. Author: (software) EMACS, 1975, GNU EMACS, 1984, GNU C Compiler, 1988. Bd. dirs. League Programming Freedom, 1989-95, pres., 1989-92. Recipient Grace Hopper award Assn. Computing, 1990, MacArthur prize fellowship MacArthur Found., 1990, Pioneer award Electronic Frontier Found., 1998, Yuri Rubinski Insight Found. award, 1999, Takeda prize for social/econ. betterment, 2001. Avocations: Balkan folk dance, Balinese and Javanese gamelan music, reading, eating. Office: Free Software Found 59 Temple Pl Ste 330 Boston MA 02111-1307

STALLMAN, ROBERT, JR. concert flutist, recording artist, editor, arranger; b. Boston, June 12, 1946; s. Robert Wooster and Virginia (Blume) S.; m. Hannah Day Woods, Sept. 26, 1981. MusB, New Eng. Conservatory Music, 1968, MusM, 1971; studied with, James Pappoutsakis, Boston, Alain Marion, Gaston Crunelle, Paris, J.P. Rampal. Debut Merkin Concert Hall, N.Y.C., 1980. Tchr. New Eng. Conservatory Music, 1978—82, CUNY Queens Coll., 1980—, Nat. Conservatory of Mex., 1982, Nat. U. Mex., 0199—2001, Domaine Forget, Que., Canada, 1982—85, Académie Internationale d'Eté, Nice, France, 1985, Boston Conservatory, 1986—90, Hochschule für Musik, Mannheim, Germany, 2000; founder, artistic dir. Cambridge Chamber Players & Marblehead Music Festival, 1976—96. Musician: (solo appearances) Libr. of Congress, Carnegie Hall, Alice Tully Hall, Avery Fisher Hall, Symphony Hall, Phila. Acad. Music, Wigmore Hall, Salle Pleyel, Suntory Hall, (soloist with maj. orchs. including) Am. Symphony, Mostly Mozart Festival, Royal Philharm. Orch., No. Sinfonia, Suk Chamber Orch.; guest musician (orch.) Lincoln Ctr. Chamber Music Soc. , Mendelssohn, Orion, Alexander, Martinu, St. Lawrence, string quartets, festivals in Can., Spain, Yugoslavia, Czech Republic, Holand, Finland, France, Mex., U.S.; editor: (flute music) Internat. Music Co., 1984—, G. Schirmer, 1996—; author: (publs.) Flute Workout, 1995—, The Flutist's Détaché Book, 1997—, Cadenzas to the Mozart Flute Concertos, 2001—; musician: (premiere performances include works by) E. Carter, —, R. Danielpour, —, S. Dodgson, —, J. Harbison, —, —, K. Husa, —, R. Helps, —, —, W. McKinley, —, (recorded for) ASV, —, VAI Audio, —, Biddulph Recs., —, CBS Masterworks, —, MHS, —, Centaur, —, CRI, —, New World, —, Northeastern, —, Owl, —, Crown (Japan), —, (solo recs. include) American Flute, —, The Lyric Flute, —, Gypsy Flute, —, The Nightingale in Love, —, Incantations, —, Bach Sonatas, —, Blavet Sonatas, —, Handel Sonatas, —, Schubert Sonatas, —, Telemann Concertos, —, Vivaldi Concertos, —, Dodgson Concerto, —, McKinley Concerto, —. Fulbright grantee, 1968-69, Arcadia Found. grantee, 1994; Koussevitsky fellow, 1970; recipient Chadwick medal, 1968, C.D. Jackson prize, Tanglewood, 1970, 1st prize USA Nat. Assn. Collegiate Artists Competition, 1971; NEA Solo Recitalist grantee, 1983. Avocations: travel, swimming, reading, French culture. Address: 1530 Locust St Philadelphia PA 19102-4415 also: 175 W 73d St 14E New York NY 10023 E-mail: flute@robertstallman.com.

STALLMEYER, JAMES EDWARD, engineer, educator; b. Covington, Ky., Aug. 11, 1926; s. Joseph Julius and Anna Catherine (Scheper) S.; m. Mary Katherine Davenport, Apr. 11, 1953; children: Cynthia Marie, James Duncan, Michael John, Catherine Ann, John Charles, Gregory Edward. BS, U. Ill., 1947, MS, 1949, PhD, 1953. Jr. engr. So. Ry. System, 1947; research asst. U. Ill., Urbana, 1947-49, research asso., 1951-52, asst. prof. civil engring, 1952-57, assoc. prof., 1957-60, prof., 1960-91, prof. emeritus, 1991—. Cons. on structural problems various indsl. and govt. agys. Author: (with E.H. Gaylord Jr.), Design of Steel Structures; editor: (with E.H. Gaylord Jr.) Structural Engineering Handbook; contbr. to Shock and Vibration Handbook. Served with USN, 1944-46. Standard Oil fellow, 1949-51; recipient Adams meml. award, 1964, Everitt award for teaching excellence, 1981 Mem. ASCE, Am. Concrete Inst., Am. Ry. Engring. Assn., ASTM, Am. Welding Soc., Am. Soc. Metals, Soc. Exptl. Stress Analysis, Scabbard and Blade, Sigma Xi, Chi Epsilon, Sigma Tau, Tau Beta Pi, Phi Kappa Phi. Clubs: KC. Republican. Roman Catholic. Office: Newmark Civil Engring 205 N Mathews Ave Urbana IL 61801-2350

STALLONE, SYLVESTER ENZIO, actor, writer, director; b. N.Y.C., July 6, 1946; s. Frank and Jacquline (Labofish) S.; m. Sasha Czack, Dec. 28, 1974 (div.); children: Sage, Seth; m. Brigitte Nielsen, Dec. 15, 1985 (div. 1987). Student, Am. Coll. of Switzerland, 1965-67, U. Miami, 1967-69. Formerly, usher, fish salesman, horse trainer, delicatessen worker, truck driver, bouncer, zoo attendant, short order cook, pizza demonstrator, phys. edn. tchr., motel supt., bookstore detective Appeared in motion pictures Lords of Flatbush, 1973, Capone, 1974, Rocky, 1976, (Oscar for Best Picture 1976, Golden Globe award for best picture 1976, Donatello award for best actor in Europe 1976, Christopher Religious award 1976, Bell Ringer award Scholastic Mag. 1976, Nat. Theatre Owners award 1976) F.I.S.T, 1978, Paradise Alley, 1978, Rocky II, 1979, Nighthawks, 1981, Victory, 1981, Rocky III, 1982, First Blood, 1982, Rhinestone, 1984, Rambo: First Blood Part II, 1985, Rocky IV, 1985, Cobra, 1986, Over the Top, 1987, Rambo III, 1988, Lock Up, 1989, Tango and Cash, 1989, Rocky V, 1990, Cliffhanger, 1993, Demolition Man, 1993, The Specialist, 1994, Judge Dredd, 1995, Assassins, 1995, Firestorm, 1996, Daylight, 1996, Copland, 1997, An Alan Smithee Film: Burn Hollywood Burn, 1998; producer, dir. film Staying Alive, 1983; author: Paradise Alley, 1977, The Rocky Scrapbook, 1977, Rocky II, 1979. Recipient Star of the Year award 1977, named Show West actor of the year 1979, Artistic Achievement award Nat. Italian Am. Found., 1991, Order of Arts and Letters, French Ministry, 1992, Caesar award for Career Achievement, 1992. Mem. Screen Actors Guild, Writers Guild, Stuntmans Assn. (hon.), Dirs. Guild. Achievements include being nominated for two Oscars (acting and writing) in same year (1976); occurred for only 3d time in history. *Once in one's life, for one mortal moment, one must make a grab for immortality; if not, one has not lived.*

STALLONE, THOMAS MICHAEL KEARNEY, clinical psychologist; b. N.Y.C., Dec. 5, 1952; s. Vito Joseph and Mary Ellen (Kearney) S.; m. Bonnie Elizabeth Wenk, May 30, 1982; 1 child, Thomas Lucius. B of Profl. Studies, N.Y. Inst. Tech., 1987; MA, Spalding U., 1991; PsyD, Pacific U., 1994. Lic. psychologist, Wash.; cert. psychol. assoc. in clin. psychology, Ky.; cert. rational emotive therapist; diplomate and fellow Am. Bd. Forensic Examiners. Internat. banker Sumitomo Bank, Ltd., N.Y.C., 1980-82, Bank of N.Y., N.Y.C., 1982-87; pvt. practice hypnosis cons. LaGrange, Ky., and N.Y.C., 1982-90; rehab. specialist Goodwill Industries Ky., Louisville, 1989; psychol. assoc. div. mental health Ky. Corrections Cabinet, La Grange, 1989-91; teaching asst. Pacific U., Forest Grove, Oreg., 1991-93; psychotherapist Portland, 1991-95; clin. psychologist Vancouver, Wash., 1995—; dir. Attention Deficit Disorders Clinic Vancouver, 1997—. Author: The Boke of Taliesyne, 1979, The Effects of Psychodrama on Inmates Within a Structured Residential Behavior Modification Program, 1993, Panic Symptoms in Asthma, 1994, Rational Emotive Behavior Therapy and Subpersonalities, 1997. Cons. Hist. Arms, Ltd., N.Y.C., 1983-87, N.Y. Medieval Festival, 1984-86; dir., cons. Whitestone (N.Y.) Creative Arts Workshop, 1977, Ky. Shakespeare Festival, Louisville, 1987-88; treas., advisor 4H Exec. Coun., La Grange, 1988-91; advisor Columbia River chpt. Children & Adults with Attention Deficit Disorder, 1998—; mem. Clark County Human Resources Rev. Com. Decorated Grant of Arms Chief Herald of Ireland, Irish Family Sept Chieftain of Kearney of Ely/Oriel His Highness Eile O'Carroll Prince of Eile Chief of the Name and of Clan Cian; named to Honorable Order of Ky. Col. Mem. APA, Wash. State Psychol. Assn. (media rels. and pub. edn. com.), Am. Soc. Group Psychotherapy and Psychodrama, Internat. Soc. for Profl. Hypnosis, Wash. State Psychol. Assn., Ancient Order Hibernians, Mensa. Avocations: hypnosis, meditation, Martial Arts, Medieval history, teaching. E-mail: drtms@pacifier.com.

STALLWORTH, CHARLES DEROTHA, JR. psychologist; b. Riderwood, Ala., July 4, 1940; s. Charles D. and Annie (Horn) S. BS, Tenn. State U., Nashville, 1963; MS, Tenn. State U., 1966; postgrad., Calif. Sch. Profl. Psychology, 1977-79, U. South Ala., 1967, Tuskegee Inst., 1968, U. Ky., 1980; PhD in Psychology, Internat. Coll., 1983; cert. in mental disability law, N.Y. Law Sch., 2001. Diplomate Am. Bd. Psychotherapy, Am. Coll. Mental Health Practitioners, Am. Coll. Profl. Health Practitioners, Am. Coll. Cert. Forensic Counselors. Psychiat. asst. Hubbard Hsop., Nashville, 1964-66; counselor, tchr. North Ctrl. H.S., Chatom, Ala., 1966-68; tchr. Washington County H.S., 1969-70; supr. adult edn. Washington County Bd. Edn., Chatom, 1968-70; dir. counseling ctr. Albany State Coll., Ga., 1970-92; pvt. practice, 1993—. Staff assistance Auburn U., 1969; cons. Peace Corps, 1979-82; cons. Peace Corps., 1979-82. Bd. dirs. Dougherty County CODAC, Inc., Albany, 1973-77. Recipient Eagle Scout award, 1955; Grantee HEW, 1970-77, U.S. Office Edn., 1972. Mem. Am. Psychol. Assn. (assoc.), Am. Psychotherapy Assn. (diplomate, Acad. Cert. Neurotherapists, Alpha Phi Alpha. Democrat. Baptist. Achievements include research on impact of affective domain on learning outcomes and on application of cognitive therapies as a means of controlling negative effects. Home: 805 E 4th Ave Albany GA 31705-1203 E-mail: cd7400@earthlink.

STALLWORTH-BARRON, DORIS A. CARTER, librarian, educator; b. Ala., June 12, 1931; d. Henry Lee Carter and Hattie Belle Stallworth; m. George Stallworth, 1950 (dec.); children: Annette LaVerne, Vanzette Yvonne; m. Walter L. Barron, 1989. BS, Ala. State U., 1955; MLS, CUNY, 1968; postgrad., Columbia U., St. John's U., NYU. Cert. supr. and tchr. sch. libr. media, N.Y. Libr. media specialist N.Y.C. Bd. Edn.; head libr. Calhoun County High Sch., Hobson City, Ala. Cons. Libr. Unit, N.Y.C. Bd. Edn.; cons. evaluator So. Assn. Secondary Schs., Ala.; supr., adminstr., liason rep. Community Sch. Dist. #24 N.Y.C. Sch. System; previewer libr. media Preview Mag., 1971-73; mem. ednl. svcs. adv. coun. Sta. WNET, 1987-89; mem. coun. N.Y.C. Schs. Libr. System, 1987-90, mem. N.Y.C. bd. examiners for tchr. librs., 1972-89; turn-key tchr. trainer N.Y. State Dept. Edn., 1988; spl. guest speaker and lectr. Queens Coll., City U., Community Sch. Dist. #24, PTA, N.Y. City Sch. System, Libr. unit, 1980-90; curriculum writer libr. unit N.Y.C. Bd. Edn., 1985-86. Contbr. articles to ednl. pubs. Mem. State of Ala. Dem. Exec. Com., 1994—; active A+ for Kids. Mem. NAFE, ALA, Am. Assn. Sch. Librs. (spl. guest speaker and lectr. for conv. 1987), Am. Sch. Libr.'s Assn., Nat. Assn. Black Pub. Adminstrs., N.Y. State Libr. Assn., N.Y.C. Sch. Librs. Assn., Nat. Forum for Black Pub. Adminstrs., N.Y. Coalition 100 Black Women, Lambda Kappa Mu Sorority, Inc., Alpha Kappa Alpha Sorority Inc.

STALOFF, ARNOLD FRED, financial executive; b. Dover, N.J., Dec. 12, 1944; s. William and Ida (Greenberg) S.; m. Sharon Marcia Teplitsky, June 10, 1967; children: Kimberly, Lindsay. BBA, U. Miami, 1967. Statistician U.S. Census Bur., Washington, 1967-68; fin. analyst SEC, 1968-71; sr. v.p. Phila. Stock Exch., 1971-78; v.p. Securities Industry Automation Corp., N.Y.C., 1978-80; pres. Fin. Automation Corp., Phila., 1980-83, Phila. Bd. Trade, 1983-89; pres., CEO Commodity Exch., Inc. (COMEX), N.Y.C., 1989-90; CEO Bloom Staloff Corp., Phila., 1990—. Bd. dirs. Lehman Bros. Fin. Products, Inc.; bd. govs. Phila. Stock Exch., 1991-97. Bd. dirs. Variety Club for Handicapped Children, Phila., 1987-92; mem. adv. bd. Phila. Internat. Airport, 1988—; mem. U. Miami Pres.'s Cir. Mem. Nat. Futures Assn. (bd. dirs. 1987-90). Avocations: fly fishing, golf, skiing. Office: Bloom Staloff Corp 2000 Market St Fl 18 Philadelphia PA 19103-3294

STALON, CHARLES GARY, retired economics educator, institute administrator; b. Cape Girardeau, Mo., Oct. 26, 1929; s. Charles Douglas and Lucy Idell (Row) S.; m. Marie Allene Hitt, Mar. 15, 1952; children: Connie Lucille

Stalon Estopinal, Donna Jean Stalon Williams. Student, Ohio State U., 1955-56; BA, Butler U., 1959; MS, Purdue U., 1963, PhD, 1966. Econs. instr. Purdue U., Lafayette, Ind., 1962—63; econs. prof. So. Ill. U., Carbondale, 1963—77; rsch. economist Fed. Power Commn., Washington, 1969—70; commr. Ill. Commerce Commn., Springfield, 1977—84, Fed. Energy Regulatory Commn., Washington, 1984—89; dir. Putnam, Hayes & Bartlett, Inc., 1989—91; dir. Inst. Pub. Utilities, prof. econs. Mich. State U., East Lansing, 1991—93; ret. Pres. Mid-Am. Regulatory Commn., Chgo., 1983-84; mem. adv. coun. Gas Rsch. Inst., 1982-84, 91-99; bd. dirs. Ga. Transmission Corp. Author: (book chpt.) Papers in Quantitative Economics, 1968, The Future of Electrial Energy, 1986; contbr. articles to profl. jours. With USN, 1948-49, 52-54. Mem. Am. Econ. Assn., Transp. and Pub. Utility Group, Nat. Soc. Rate of Return Analysts (bd. dirs. 1982-90), Nat. Assn. Regulatory Utilities Commns., Nat. Regulatory Rsch. Inst. (bd. dirs. 1983-84, 91-94), Inst. for Study of Regulation (bd. dirs. 1984-87). E-mail: stalon@ldd.net.

STALTER, ERIC RAYMOND, social services executive; b. Colonia, N.J., Jan. 21, 1965; s. Raymond Harold Stalter and Joan Jacqueline (Robedee) S.; m. Karen Louise Bates, Nov. 11, 1989. BA, Glassboro State Coll., 1987, MA, 1989. Counselor Together Inc., Glassboro, N.J., 1984-85, Youth Adv. Program, Harrisburg, Pa., 1985-87, Bancroft Sch., Haddonfield, N.J., 1987, Group Homes of Camden County, Camden, 1987-88; dir. Youth adv. Program, 1988-89, Easter Seal Soc., Milltown, 1989—. Head coach varsity wresting Deptford High Sch., 1986-94. Mem. N.J. Children's Coord. Coun., Hammonton, N.J., 1991—, Gloucester County Juvenile Conf. Com., Woodbury, N.J., 1993—. Mem. ACA, Assn. Marriage and Family Counselors. Avocations: sports, sailing, boating. Home: 130 Cumberland Ave Sewell NJ 08080-1209 Office: Blackwood Med Ctr 141 S Black Horse Pike Ste 204 Blackwood NJ 08012-2959 Address: 130 Cumberland Ave Sewell NJ 08080-1209

STALTER, RICHARD ALAN, museum administrator; b. Dayton, Ohio, Apr. 27, 1934; s. Chester Clayton and Alverta Miller Stalter. BSBA, Ohio State U., 1956. Artist, Gaylordsville, Conn., 1964-94; mus. pres. Mus. of Contemporary Impressionism, New Milford, 1994—. Exhibited at Fulton Gallery, N.Y.C., 1966-96, Gregory James Gallery, New Milford, Conn., 1996—. With U.S. Army, 1956-62. Office: Mus of Contemporary Impressionism PO Box 67 New Milford CT 06776-0067

STALTER, RICHARD B. biology educator, researcher; b. Montvale, N.J., Jan. 16, 1942; s. Lester C. and Betty R. Stalter; divorced; 1 child, Laurie. BS, Rutgers U., 1963; MS, U. R.I., 1966; PhD, U. S.C., 1968. Asst. prof. High Point (N.C.) Coll., 1968-69, Pfeiffer Coll., Misenheimer, N.C., 1969-70; fish kill expert S.C. Pollution Control Authority, Columbia, 1970-71; prof. biology St. John's U., Jamaica, N.Y., 1971—. Cons. So. Engring. Co., Atlanta, 1972-75, Cabot Corp., Boston, 1974-75; trustee N.Y. Ocean Sci. Lab., Montauk, N.Y., 1974-82. Author: Barrier Island Botany, 1992, Barrier Island Botany The Southeastern United States, 1993, Man in the Environment, 1996; contbr. articles to profl. jours. Mem. Torrey Bot. Club, Assn. S.E. Biologists, So. Appalachian Bot. Club, N.E. Weed Sci. Soc., Skull and Cir. Honor Soc., S.C. Acad. Sci., Sigma Xi, Phi Sigma. Republican. Episcopalian. Home: 36 Glade Ln Levittown NY 11756-3918

STALTER, TODD ANDREW, music educator; b. Peoria, Ill., Aug. 19, 1966; s. Larry Wagner and Karen Lucille Stalter; m. Angie Sue Tibbs, May 27, 1989; children: Evan. MusB Edn. (cum laude), Ill. State U., 1988—2008, MusM Performance, 1990. Cert. K-12 tchr. Ill. Dir. of bands Eureka (Ill.) H.S., 1991—. Prin. trumpet Grace Presbyn. Ch. Brass Ensemble, Peoria, Ill., 1996—. Author: (guest column) School Music Dealer Magazine, 2002, composer (arranger) religious brass ensemble music. Recipient Marching Band State Champions (Class 1A), 2000—01, Mar. Madness Ofcl. Tournament Band, Ill. H.S. Assn., 1998, 2000, 2002. Mem.: NEA, Music Educators Nat. Conf., Ill. Edn. Assn., Ill. Music Educators Assn. Republican. Avocations: birdwatching, golf. Office: EurekaHS 200 W Cruger Ave Eureka IL 61530 Office Fax: 309-467-2648. E-mail: ehs_bands@hotmail.com.

STALZER, MARK ANTHONY, computer scientist, technical director; b. Canoga Park, Calif., June 11, 1962; s. Dennis L. and Barbara J. (Pierce) S.; m. Julie F. Hopkins, July 2, 1983; children: Ashley M. Brittany A. BS in Physics and Computer Sci., Calif. State U., Northridge, 1984; MS in Computer Sci., U. So. Calif., 1988, PhD in Computer Sci., 1993. Prin. engr., mgr. software engring. Trace Instruments, Canoga Park, 1981-91; assoc. Merrill Lynch, N.Y.C., 1995-96; staff computer scientist Hughes Rsch. Labs., Malibu, Calif., 1991-95; sr. staff computer scientist Hughes Rsch. Labs. (name now HRL Labs.), 1996-98; sr. rsch. scientist and mgr. computational physics dept. HRL Labs., 1998-99, mgr. info. scis. lab., 1999-2000, dir. Info. Scis. Lab., 2000—. Mng. ptnr. Oak Park Speculation, 1996-98. Contbr. articles to sci. jours.; inventor in field. Mem. IEEE (sr. mem.), Assn. for Computing Machinery, Sigma Xi. Avocation: running. Office: HRL Labs 3011 Malibu Canyon Rd Malibu CA 90265-4797

STAM, DAVID HARRY, librarian; b. Paterson, N.J., July 11, 1935; s. Jacob and Deana B. (Bowman) S.; m. Deirdre Corcoran, May 15, 1963; children—Julian, Wendell, Kathryn. AB, Wheaton Coll., 1955; postgrad., New Coll., U. Edinburgh, 1955-56; MLS, Rutgers U., 1962; postgrad., CUNY, 1963-64; PhD, Northwestern U., 1978. Asst. editor library publs., reference librarian, manuscript cataloguer New York Pub. Library, 1959-64; librarian Marlboro (Vt.) Coll., 1964-67; head tech. services dept. Newberry Library, Chgo., 1967-71, assoc. librarian, 1969-73; librarian Milton S. Eisenhower Library, Johns Hopkins U., Balt., 1973-78; Andrew W. Mellon dir. rsch. libraries N.Y. Pub. Library, N.Y.C., 1978-86; Univ. librarian Syracuse U., 1986-98, sr. scholar, History Dept., 1998—. Trustee Gladys K. Delmas Found. Author: Wordsworthian Criticism, 1974, International Dictionary of Library Histories, 2001; co-author (with Rissa Yachnin): Turgenev in English: A Checklist of Works by and about Him, 1960; contbr. articles to profl. jours. Served with USNR, 1956-58. Brit. Acad. Overseas fellow, 1975, Brit. Libr. fellow, 1995-96. Mem.: Am. Antiquarian Soc., Am. Hist. Assn., Groller Club (N.Y.C.), Princeton Club N.Y. Office: Syracuse U History Dept Eggers Hall Syracuse NY 13244 E-mail: dhstam@syr.edu.

STAM, LAWRENCE E. nephrologist; b. Bklyn., Mar. 12, 1953; BA, Columbia Coll., 1974; MD, SUNY, 1978. Diplomate Am. Bd. Nephrology, Am. Bd. Internal Medicine. Intern St. Elizabeth's Hosp., Boston, 1978-79, resident internal medicine, 1979-81; nephrology fellow Bklyn. Jewish Hosp., 1982-84; attending physician N.Y. Meth. Hosp., Bklyn., 1984—. Clin. asst. prof. SUNY Downstate, Bklyn., 1986—, Sch. Medicine Cornell U. Office: NY Meth Hosp 506 6th St Brooklyn NY 11215-3645

STAMAS, STEPHEN, not-for-profit administrator; b. Salem, Mass., Apr. 26, 1931; s. Theodore and Georgia (Fotopulos) S.; m. Elaine Heidi Zervas, Apr. 24, 1955; children: Heidi, Theodore. AB, Harvard, 1953, PhD, 1957; B.Phil. (Rhodes scholar), Oxford U., 1955. Budget examiner Bur. Budget, Washington, 1957-59; loan officer Devel. Loan Fund, 1959-60; mgr. internat. divsn. treasurer's dept. Standard Oil Co. (N.J.), N.Y.C., 1960-63, dep. European fin. rep. London, Eng., 1963-64; govt. rels. mgr. Esso Europe, 1964-67; petroleum planning mgr. Esso Internat., 1967-68; dep. asst. sec. for fin. policy Dept. Commerce, Washington, 1968-69; chief economist Standard Oil Co. (N.J.), N.Y.C., 1969-70, dep. mgr. pub. affairs dept., 1971; v.p., pub. affairs Exxon Corp., N.Y.C., 1973-86; pres. Wallace Funds, 1986-87, N.Y. Philharm., 1984-89, chmn., 1989-96. Trustee, pres. Am. Ditchley Found.; trustee emeritus Rockefeller U.; chmn. Am. Assembly, Columbia U., Marlboro Sch. Music; mem. bd. overseers Harvard Coll., 1979-85; bd. dirs. N.Y. Philharm.-Symphony Soc.; bd. dirs. emeritus Lincoln Ctr. for the Performing Arts; bd. dirs. The Greenwall Found., Seacor SMIT, Inc.; co-chmn. Am. Trust for Brit. Libr. Mem. Coun. Fgn. Rels., Acad. Polit. Sci., Am. Coun. on Germany, Scarsdale Golf Club (NY), Phi Beta Kappa. Clubs: Harvard (N.Y.C.), Century Assn. (N.Y.C.), Manursing Island (Rye, N.Y.). Home: 325 Evandale Rd Scarsdale NY 10583-1505 E-mail: astolatz@aol.com.

STAMATAKIS, CAROL MARIE, lawyer, former state legislator; b. Canton, Ohio, Apr. 27, 1960; d. Emmanuel Nicholas and Catherine Lucille (Zam) S.; m. Michael Shklar, Mar. 23, 1985. BA in Criminology and Criminal Justice, Ohio State U., 1982; JD, Case Western Res., 1985. Bar: N.H. 1985, U.S. Dist. Ct. N.H. 1985. Atty. Elliott, Jasper & Stamatakis, Newport, N.H., 1990-93; state rep. N.H. State Legislature, 1988-94; staff atty. N.H. Dept. Health and Human Svcs., Keene, 1994-99; legal coord. Divsn. of Elderly and Adult Svcs., Concord, N.H., 1999—. Instr. Am. Inst. Banking, Claremont, 1987-88, 91-92, 95. Asst. editor: (jours.) Health Matrix: The Jour. of Health Services Mangement, 1983-85. Treas., mem. Town of Lempster N.H. Conservation Commn., 1987—; bd. dirs. Orion House, Inc., Newport, N.H., 1987-91; town chair N.H. Dem. Party, 1987—; mem. Town of Lempster Recycling Com., 1988—, Community Task Force on Drug and alcohol Abuse, 1988. Mem. N.H. Bar Assn., Sierra Club, Upper Valley Group (former vice chair and solid waste chair). Avocations: drawing, painting. Home: PO Box 807 Newport NH 03773-0807

STAMATY, CLARA GEE KASTNER, artist; b. Piqua, Ohio, May 15, 1919; d. Sam and Dina (Glad) Kastner; m. Stanley Stamaty, Apr. 27, 1944 (dec. Sept. 1979); 1 child, Mark Alan; m. Milton Ziment, Aug. 12, 1984. Grad. high sch., Piqua, Ohio; grad., Cin. Art Acad., 1943; postgrad., Art Students League, N.Y.C., 1959, Pratt Graphic Workshop, 1968-69, Prints Divsn. Libr., 1969-70. Artist Air Svc. Command/Paterson Field, Dayton, Ohio, 1943-45; supr. art Colony Surf Club, West End, N.J., 1960-66; tchr. Stamaty Studios, Elberon, 1962-81. Mem. graphic design adv. com. Brookdale C.C., Lincroft, N.J., 1974-80; guild del. to ann. sems. Federated Art Assns. N.J., Westfield, 1974-80. One-man shows include Monmouth County Libr., Monmouth YM-YWHA, West Long Branch Libr., Long Branch Libr., Temple Beth Miriam, Guild Creative Art, Shrewsbury, N.J., 1999, Unitarian Meeting House, Lincroft, N.J., 2001, exhibited in group shows at Monmouth Festival of Arts, 1970—, Jewish Cmty. Ctr. Greater Monmouth County, Guild of Creative Art, 1999—, MCAC at Monmouth Mus., Lincroft, N.J., 2001—, Am. Watercolor Soc., N.Y.C. Nat. Acad. Galleries, Cin. Art Mus., Dayton Art Inst., Butler Art Inst., exhibited in group shows at Monmouth Coll., N.J. Watercolor Soc., Morris Mus., Brookdale Coll., Garden State Watercolor Soc., Princeton, Monmouth Mus., Garden State Art Ctr. Celebrity House, Represented in permanent collections Ford Co., Detroit, United Meth. Ch., Red Bank, N.J., Ranney Sch., Rumson, N.J., Monmouth Reform Temple, Tinton Falls, N.J., others; illustrator What's Cookin'?, 1957—; author, editor: What's Cookin'?, 1957; author: Ginny, 1967—; illustrator Ginny, 1967—; contbr. cartoons and illustrations. Recipient 8 1st prize awards Three Arts Club, 1939-42, Spl. award Dayton Art Inst., 1945, Gold medal Long Branch Cmty. Ctr., 1962, Purchase award Meth. Ch., Red Bank, 1965. Mem.: Monmouth County Arts Coun. (guild del. 1996—98, 2000—02, adv. bd.), Monmouth Arts Found., Art Alliance N.J., Guild of Creative Art (exhibiting artist 1960—, sec. 1967—68, gallery dir. 1968—70, publicity dir. 1972—75, v.p. 1974—75, bd. dirs. 1997—2000, 2001—02), Nat. Cartoonist Soc. (life), Ea. Star. Avocations: writing poetry, yoga, walking, reading, dancing. Home and Office: Stamaty Studios 1019 Woodgate Ave Long Branch NJ 07740-4631

STAMATY, MARK ALAN, cartoonist, author, artist; b. Bklyn., Aug. 1, 1947; s. Stanley and Clara Gee Stamaty. B.F.A., The Cooper Union, 1969. Mem. faculty Parson's Sch. Design, N.Y.C., 1977-81. Author-illustrator: (children's books) Who Needs Donuts?, 1973 (Bklyn. Art Books For Children award 1974), Small in the Saddle, 1975, Minnie Maloney & Macaroni, 1976, Where's My Hippopotamus?, 1977, Too Many Time Machines, 1999, (comic strip collections) Macdoodle St., 1981, Washingtoon, 1983; cartoonist: Macdoodle St. Village Voice newspaper, 1978-79, Carrrttoooonnn, Village Voice newspaper, 1980-81, (Washington Post and syndication) Washingtoon, 1981-94, Boox, N.Y. Times Book Review, 2001—; polit. cartoonist TIME mag., 1994-96, Doodlennium, 1996-98; contbr.: Slate Mag., 1996—; illustrator various publs., including: (children's book) Yellow Yellow, 1971, (Bklyn. Art Books for Children award); cartoon coverage of Milan fashion show for GQ Mag., 2000—. Recipient Purchase award N.J. State Mus., about 1969, Gold medal Soc. Illustrators, 1974 Mem. PEN Am. Ctr. Avocations: impersonating Elvis Presley; watching the world; softball; swimming.

STAMBAUGH, ARMSTRONG A., JR. restaurant and hotel executive; b. Cleve., Nov. 1, 1920; s. Armstrong Alexander and Beatrice (Snyder) S.; m. Janet Turley Marting, July 26, 1943 (div. 1958); children— Susan Reed (Mrs. Roy H. Beaton, Jr.), Sally Russell (Mrs. Michael H. Huber), Elizabeth Renshaw (Mrs. Michael C. Warr); m. Aagot Hinrichsen Cain, June 10, 1972. BA, Dartmouth Coll., 1942; Indsl. Adminstr., Harvard U., 1943, MBA, 1946. Research asst., then instr. bus. adminstrn. Harvard Grad. Sch. Bus. Adminstrn., 1946-48; with Gulf Oil Corp., 1948-66, coord. sales devel. mktg. hdqrs., 1962-63, v.p. Eastern marketing region Phila., 1963-66; exec. v.p. adminstrn. Howard Johnson Co., Inc., 1966-70, exec. v.p. ops. and adminstrn., 1970-79, exec. v.p., asst. to pres., 1979-81, dir., 1969-81; operator, developer food and lodging facilities, 1981-98. Pres. trustees Fox Chapel Country Day Sch., Pitts., 1955-57; div. vice chmn. Boston United Fund, 1961; bd. dirs. Houston Internat. Trade and Travel Fair, 1962-63, World Affairs Coun. Phila., 1964-65; dir. Phila. C. of C., 1964, 65, 66; bd. overseers Hanover Inn, Dartmouth Coll., 1979-85, chmn., 1984-85; trustee Old Sturbridge Village, Mass., 1979-01. Served to lt. (j.g.) USNR, 1943-46. Mem. Pine Valley Golf Club (N.J.), Weston (Mass.) Golf Club, Kittansett Golf Club (Mass.), Boston Skating Club, Vineyard Haven Yacht Club (Mass.), Harvard Faculty Club (Cambridge), Paradise Valley Country Club (Ariz.), Delta Tau Delta. Home and Office: 5 Blossom Ln Weston MA 02493-1103 E-mail: aastam@flash.net.

STAMBAUGH, HARRIETT MCCARDELL (HARRIETT WYNN MCCARDELL), social worker; b. Philipsburg, Pa., May 10, 1922; d. Horace Andrew and Vivian Annabel (Wynn) McCardell; m. James Arthur Stambaugh Sr., May 1, 1954; children: James Arthur Jr., David Monroe, Richard Thomas. BA, Juniata Coll., 1942; MS in Social Svc., Boston U., 1947. Instr. in pediatrics Southwestern Med. Sch. U. Tex. Health Sci. Ctr., Dallas, 1966-67, asst. prof. pediatrics, 1968-80; dir. dept. clinical social work Children's Med. Ctr. of Dallas, 1967-80; dir. clin. social work dept. U. N.Mex. Hosp., Albuquerque, 1981-84; contract therapist Family Counseling Svcs., Inc., 1984-85; supr. Chaparral Maternity and Adoption Svcs., 1985-87; interim exec. dir. Family & Children Svcs., Inc., 1987-88; part-time clin. social worker Chaparral Maternity Adoptions div. Chaparral Maternity and Adoption Svcs., 1988-92; exec. dir. Family and Children's Svc's., Inc., 1992. Cons. Terrell (Tex.) State Hosp., 1966-67, Tex. Child Welfare Dept., Dallas, 1966-67, Dallas Assn. for Retarded Citizens, 1966-67, Community Mental Health Program, Corsicana, Tex., 1968, Britain Nursing Home, Irving, Tex., 1968-70, Turtle Creek Nursing Home, Dallas, 1969, North Tex. Hemophilia Found., Dallas, 1969, Four Seasons Nursing Home, Dallas, 1970-71, YWCA Park North Br., Dallas, 1972, Children's Hosp. of Phila., 1972, Dialysis Ctr., Inc., Albuquerque, 1982-84, Carrie Tingley Hosp., Albuquerque, 1982-84; adj. prof. Dept. of Sociology adn Social Work Tex. Women's U., Denton, 1977-80. Contbr. articles to profl. jours. Mem. Child Care Coun. of Dallas County, 1971-74; mem. Human Devel. Fund Rev. Com. City of Dallas, 1975-77, mem. Children and Youth Adv. Com., 1975-80; mem. Profl. Adv. Com. Parents Without Ptnrs., 1967-74, Creative Learning Ctr., 1968-74, Mental Health Assn. Greater Dallas 1966-72, 1976-79, bd. dirs. 1972-80, Dallas County Community Action Com., 1967-68, Routh St. Ctr., 1972-80; profl. adv. com. Epilepsy Assn., 1971-80, Vis. Nurse Assn., 1977-80; mem. med. adv. com. March of Dimes, and others. Mem. NASW (chmn. subcom. to est. responsibilities for summer employment 1964-65, chmn. profl. stds. divsn. 1967-68, chmn. battered child com. 1968-73, v.p. Dallas chpt. 1974-75), Nat. Registry Clin. Social Workers, Acad. Cert. Social Workers. Methodist. Avocations: genealogy, travel, walking. Home: 5023 Calle De Luna NE Albuquerque NM 87111-2918

STAMBAUGH, JOHN EDGAR, oncologist, hematologist, pharmacologist, educator; b. Everett, Pa., Apr. 30, 1940; s. John Edgar and Rhoda Irene (Becker) S.; m. Shirley Louise Fultz, June 24, 1961; 4 children. BS in Chemistry cum laude, Dickinson Coll., 1962; MD, Jefferson Med. Coll., 1966, PhD, 1968. Intern Thomas Jefferson U. Hosp., Phila., 1968-69, resident, 1968-69; oncology fellow Jefferson Med. Coll., 1970-72, instr. pharmacology, 1969-70, asst. prof., 1970-74, assoc. prof., 1974-82, prof., 1982—. Pvt. practice med. oncology, hematology and cancer pain, Woodbury, N.J.; staff physician Cooper Med. Ctr., Camden, N.J., 1972—, Underwood Meml. Hosp., Woodbury, 1972—, West Jersey Hosp., 1973—, J.F. Kennedy Hosp., 1978—, Our Lady of Lourdes Hosp., 1990—. Contbr. articles to profl. jours. Fellow: Am. Soc. Pain Mgmt., Am. Acad. Pain Mgmt., Am. Coll. Clin. Pharmacology; mem.: Am. Assn. Clin. Rsch., Am. Pain Soc., Internat. Assn. for Study of Pain, Am. Assn. for Cancer Rsch., Am. Soc. Clin. Oncology, Am. Soc. for Pharmacology and Exptl. Therapeutics, Camden County Med. Soc., Gloucester County Med. Soc., N.J. Med. Soc. (trustee), Am. Soc. Clin. Pharmacology, AMA, ABA, Sigma Xi. Office: 17 W Red Bank Ave Ste 101 Woodbury NJ 08096-1630 also: 100 Carnie Blvd Ste 3 Kirkwood Voorhees NJ 08043-4512

STAMBAUGH, ROBERT F. finance educator; b. Camden, N.J., Oct. 18, 1952; s. Jacob Forney and Mildred E. Stambaugh; m. Catherine A. Williams, Aug. 17, 1974. AB, Dickinson Coll., Carlisle, Pa., 1974; MBA, U. Chgo., 1976, PhD, 1981. Fin. analyst Ford Motor Co., Dearborn, Mich., 1976-77; from asst. prof. to prof. of fin. U. Chgo., 1983-88; lectr. and asst. prof. fin. U. Pa., Phila., 1979-83, Ronald O. Perelman prof. fin., 1989—. Cons. Daiwa Securities SB, Tokyo, 2000—, Deutsche Asset Mgmt., N.Y.C., 2001—. Contbr. articles to profl. jours. Recipient Fama-DFA prize, 1999, 2000, Smith-Breeden prize, 1996; Marvin Bower fellow, Harvard U., 1997-98, Batterymarch Fin. Mgmt. fellow, 1985-86. Mem. Nat. Bur. Econ. Rsch. (rsch. assoc. 1990-2001), Am. Fin. Assn. (bd. dirs. 1988-90), Soc. of Fin. Studies (editor, assoc. editor Rev. of Fin. Studies 1984-92). Office: Univ of Pennsylvania The Wharton Sch Philadelphia PA 19104-6367 E-mail: stambaugh@wharton.upenn.edu.

STAMBERGER, EDWIN HENRY, farmer, civic leader; b. Mendota, Ill., Feb. 16, 1916; s. Edwin Nicolaus and Emilie Anna Marie (Yost) S.; m. Mabel Edith Gordon, Oct. 6, 1937; 1 child, Larry Allan. Farmer seed corn, livestock, machinery devel., Mendota, 1939—; bd. dirs. Mendota Coop. & Supply Co., 1949-67, pres., 1958-67. Mem. coun. Mendota Luth. Ch., 1958-64, chmn., 1964, treas. N.W. conf., 1966-68, trustee Bible camp; mem. Mendota Watershed and Flood Ctrl. Com., 1966-73, 77-79, started flood control City of Mendota, Ill., rev. and comment com. subregion and region Ill. Ctr. Comprehensive Health Planning Agy., 1974-76; asst. in devel. Mendota Hosp., Mendota Lake; chmn. bldg. com. Mendota Luth. Home, 1972-73; bd. dirs. LaSalle County Mental Health Bd., 1969-74, U. Ill. County Extension, 1963-67, chmn., 1966-67; bd. dirs. Soil and Water Dist., 1968-73, vice chmn., 1971-73. Recipient Future Farmers Am. award, Honor award R.R. Mus., 1998; Disting. Svc. medal Railroad Mus. Mem. Am. Soc. Agrl. Engrs., Ill. Coun. Watersheds, Smithsonian Inst., Mental Health Assn., People-to-People Internat., Internat. Platform Assn., Mendota C. of C. (Honor award 1974), Mendota Sportsman's Club, Loyal Order of Moose, Odd Fellows, Lions (bd. dirs. Mendota chpt. 1965-67, Honor award 1981, Legacy of Lions 1998). Home and Office: Sabine Farm 4429 E 250th Rd Mendota IL 61342-9426

STAMBLER, IRWIN, publishing executive; b. Bklyn., Nov. 20, 1924; s. Sidney and Bessie (Levine) S.; m. Constance Gay Lebowitz, Nov. 5, 1950; children: Amy Ruth Champeau, Alice Joan Seidman, Lyndon Sidney, Barrett Charles. Cert. in Mech. Engring., Tex. A&M, 1944; B in Aero. Engring., NYU, 1947, M in Aero. Engring., 1949. Design engr., project mgr. Chase Aircraft, N.Y.C., 1950-53; structures engr. Republic Aviation, Farmingdale, N.Y., 1953-54; engring. editor Space Aero., N.Y.C., L.A., 1954-66; western editor, corr. Rsch. & Devel., L.A., 1967—. Author: Encyclopedia of Pop, Rock and Soul Music, 1974, 89, Encyclopedia of Folk, Country and Western, 1969, 82, 97 (Reference Book of Yr., Libr. Jour. 1982); 45 other books; co-author: (with Lyndon Stambler) Folk and Blues Encyclopedia, 2001; field editor Gas Turbine World, 1970—; pub., editl. dir. Tech. Forecasts, 1969—, Alternative Energy, 1979—. Chmn. com. Boy Scouts Troop 17, Beverly Hills, 1968-70; coach Little League, Beverly Hills, 1976-80. With U.S. Army, 1944-46. Avocations: jogging, softball. Office: PWG Publ 205 S Beverly Dr Ste 208 Beverly Hills CA 90212-3867

ŠTAMBUK, NIKOLA, research scientist; b. Varaždin, Croatia, Mar. 25, 1959; s. Ranko and Vjera (Mrakovčić) Š.; m. Ana Lazić, Nov. 12, 1988; 1 child, Albert. MD, Zagreb (Croatia) U., 1984, MS, 1988; PhD, Inst. Med. Rsch. Occup. Health, Zagreb, 1991. Intern Sisters of Mercy Clin. Hosp., Zagreb, 1984-85; resident Railway Health Ctr., 1986-88; postdoctoral fellow Mc Gill U., Montreal, Can., 1991-92; rschr. Rugjer Bošković Inst., Zagreb, 1994—. Sci. com. Internat. Conf. on Math. and Computer Modelling and Sci. Computing, Berkeley, Calif., 1993, Boston, 1995, Washington, 1997. Contbr. articles to profl. jours. Mem. Internat. Assn. for Math. and Computer Modelling, Internat. Ocular Inflammation Soc., Internat. Soc. for Thymology and Immunotherapy. Achievements include the discovery of necklace model, I Ching and horseshoe map representation of the genetic code (SCA procedure), rsch. in models of artificial barriers constrn., protein transfer and molecular recognition, computer-aided drug design, compartmental volume-pressure relationships. Home: Šubićeva 16 HR-10000 Zagreb Croatia Office: Rugjer Bošković Inst Bijenička 54 HR-10000 Zagreb Croatia E-mail: stambuk@rudjer.irb.hr.

STAMELMAN, RICHARD HOWARD, French and humanities educator; b. Newark, Mar. 7, 1942; s. Louis Robert and Golda (Senzer) S.; children: Emily, Gibson, Jeremy White. BA, Hamilton Coll.; PhD, Duke U. Asst. prof. French and humanities Wesleyan U., Middletown, Conn., 1967-74, assoc. prof., 1974-79, prof., 1979-93, William R. Kenan Jr. prof. humanities, 1983-92, dean humanities, 1986-89, dir. Ctr. for the Humanities, 1976-82, dir. humanities devel., 1982-85; dir. Weston Ctr. for Fgn. Langs., Lits. and Cultures Williams Coll., Williamstown, Mass., 1992-97, prof. Romance langs., lit. studies, 1992—; chmn. dept. French and Italian U. Colo., Boulder, 1991-92. Organizer (study group) Ecrire le Livre: Autour d'Edmond Jabès, Cerisy-la-Salle, France, 1987; co-dir. Edouard Morot-Sir Summer Inst. for French Cultural Studies, Hanover, N.H., 1994. Author: The Drama of Self in Guillaume Apollinaire's Alcools, 1976, Claude Garache: Prints, 1965-85, 1985, Lost Beyond Telling: Representations of Death and Absence in Modern French Poetry, 1990; editor: Contemporary French Poetry, Studies in 20th Century Literature, 1989, Ecrire le Livre: Autour d'Edmond Jabès, 1989, Italian transl., 1991, French Poetry since the War, L'Esprit Créateur, 1992; editor, prin. translator: The Lure and the Truth of Painting, Selected Essays by Yves Bonnefoy, 1995; translator: The Grapes of Zeuxis and Other Fables by Yves Bonnefoy, 1987, Once More the Grapes of Zeuxis by Yves Bonnefoy, 1989, The Last Grapes of Zeuxis by Yves Bonnefoy, 1993, Transmorphoses by Yves Bonnefoy, 1998; mem. editorial bd. French Forum; contbr. articles to profl. jours. Recipient Chevalier dans l'ordre des Palmes Académiques award French Govt., 1993; NEH fellow, 1973, John Simon Guggenheim Meml. Found. fellow, 1999; Am. Council Learned Socs. grantee, 1983 Mem. MLA (regional del. 1987-90, mem. program com. 1996-99), Societe Francaise des Parfumeurs. Home: PO Box 1624 Norwich VT 05055 Office: Williams Coll Weston Ctr Fgn Langs Lits Culture 995 Main St Williamstown MA 01267-2615 E-mail: Richard.H.Stamelman@dartmouth.edu., rstamelm@williams.edu.

STAMELOS, ELECTRA GEORGIA, artist; b. Jersey City, May 28, 1927; d. Byron D. and Eulalia (Gerachis) Mousmoules; m. William Stamelos, Apr. 26, 1953. BFA, Wayne State U., 1970; MFA, Eastern Mich. U., 1976. Instr. Nat. Art Sch., Washington, 1945-48, YWCA, Redford, Mich., 1969-73, Ann Arbor (Mich.) Art Assn., 1977—, Birmingham-Bloomfield (Mich.) Art Ctr., 1980—; lectr. fine and applied arts U. Mich., Dearborn, 1980—, dir. art collections and exhbns., 1984-92. Shows include Burpee Mus., Rockford, Ill., Springfield (Ill.) Art Mus. Watercolor USA, 1977, 80, 99, Butler Mus. of Am. Art, Youngstown, Ohio, 1998; one-woman shows include Cantor-Lemberg Gallery, Birmingham, Mich., Habitat Gallery, Southfield, Mich., Slusser Gallery, Ann Arbor, Shapolsky Gallery, N.Y.C., Mickelson Gallery, Washington, Indigo Gallery, Boca Raton, Fla., 1995-98; represented in permanent collections Jesse Bessard Mus., Alpena, Mich., Battle Creek (Mich.) Art Ctr., Flint Inst. of Art, Mich., Beaumont Hosp., Renal Ctr. Commn., Birmingham, Mich., 1998; author: (bibliography) Georgia O'Keefe, 1976, Splash I Flowers in Watercolor, 1991, Splash II Understanding Watercolor, 1991; contbr. articles to profl. jours. Chartered commr. Livonia (Mich.) Arts Commn., 1972; commr. Livonia Hist. Dist. Study Commn., 1973; pres. Friends of the Barn, Livonia, 1972; treas. Women's Caucus for Art, Detroit, 1980. Mem. Nat. Watercolor Soc. (Purchase Signature Honor 1976, 83), Midwest Watercolor Soc., Mich. Watercolor Soc. (pres. 1975-79), Rocky Mountain Nat. Water Media Soc., Watercolor USA Honor Soc. (treas. 1993-95, pres. 1995-98), The Art Exchange (co-founder 1971), Jaycees (v.p. Livonia chpt. 1962). Greek Orthodox. Avocations: photography, travel, swimming, stain glass designer. Home: 38131 N Vista Dr Livonia MI 48152-1067

STAMELOS, ELLEN ANNE, librarian; b. Pasadena, Calif., Sept. 21, 1941; d. Richard Franklin and Sarah Ellen (Nixon) Bird; m. Heron Klearchos Stamelos, Jan. 29, 1967 (div. Apr. 1980). B in Music, U. Mich., 1963; diploma, Sch. of Fine Arts, Fontainebleau, France, 1963; M in Music, U. Mich., 1965; MLS, Rutgers U., 1976. Assoc. prof. music No. State Coll., Aberdeen, S.D., 1966-67; libr. West N.Y. Pub. Libr., 1977-78, Bergenfield (N.J.) Pub. Libr., 1978-79; audiovisual cataloger Wm. Paterson Coll., Wayne, N.J., 1979-81;

automated cataloging mgr. Dallas Pub. Libr., 1982-85, catalog divsn. mgr., 1985—2002, materials processing mgr., 2002—. Mem. Grand Prairie (Tex.) Arts Commn., 1983-85; v.p. for presentations Grand Prairie Arts Coun., 1983-84. Mem. ALA, Music Libr. Assn., Tex. Libr. Assn., Beta Phi Mu, Kappa Lambda, Mu Phi Epsilon. Office: Dallas Pub Libr 1515 Young St Dallas TX 75201-5499 E-mail: estamelos@dallaslibrary.org.

STAMES, WILLIAM ALEXANDER, realtor, cost management executive; b. Douglas, Ariz., Mar. 26, 1917; s. Alex Basil and Teresa (Ruis) S.; m. Marguerite Winifred Nelson, June 11, 1943; 1 child, Wynn Lorain. AA, Long Beach Coll., 1941; postgrad., U. Calif., Berkeley, 1962-64; cert. mgmt. practice, Naval Offices CIC Sch., Glenview, Ill., 1955; grad., Real Estate Inst., Calif. Lic. real estate assoc.; grad. Realtors Inst. Owner Stames Beverage Co., Brawley, Calif., 1945-50; liaison engr. Lockheed Missiles & Space Co., Sunnyvale, 1958-60, sr. liaison engr., 1960, adminstr., 1960-62, staff adminstr., 1962-63, sr. liaison engr., sr. design engr., 1965-70; owenr, mgr. Cost Reduction Equipment Sales & Tech., 1967-76; realtor Cornish & Carey, Palo Alto, Calif., 1988-99; real estate assoc. Coldwell Banker, Coronado, 1999—. Dir. ret. activities office Naval Amphibious Base, Coronado, Calif. Author: Polaris Electrical Subsystems Design History, 1964, Poseidon Subsystem Invention, 1971. Comdr. USNR, 1941-69, ret., World War II, Korea, Vietnam. Decorated DFC, Air medal with 4 gold stars. Mem. Am. Mgmt. Assn., Mountain View Real Estate Bd. (pres.), Calif. Assn. Realtors (bd. dirs.), Tailhook Assn., Commonwealth San Francisco. Ret. Officers Club (-past pres. Peninsula chpt.), Lions. Home: 1060 Coronado Ave Coronado CA 92118-2439

STAMEY, THOMAS ALEXANDER, urologist, educator; b. Rutherfordton, N.C., Apr. 26, 1928; s. Owen and Virginia (Link) S.; m. Kathryn Simmons Dec. 1, 1973; children: Fred M., Charline, Thomas A. III, Allison, Theron. BA, Vanderbilt U., 1948; MD, Johns Hopkins U., 1952. Diplomate Am. Bd. Urology. Intern, then resident Johns Hopkins Hosp., 1952-56; asst. prof. urology Johns Hopkins U. Sch. Medicine, Balt., 1958-60, assoc. prof., 1960-61; assoc. prof., chmn. divsn. urology Stanford (Calif.) U., 1961-64, assoc. prof., 1964-90, prof., 1991—, chmn. dept., 1964-95. Author: Renovascular Hypertension, 1967, Pathogenesis and Treatment of Urinary Tract Infections, 1980, Urinalysis and Urinary Sediment: A Practical Guide for the Health Science Professional, 1985; editor: Campbell's Urology, edits. 4-6, 1978-92, Monographs in Urology, 1980-99. Capt. M.C., USAF, 1956-58. Recipient Sheen award ACS, 1990, Ferdinand C. Valentine award N.Y. Acad. Medicine, 1991. Mem. Am. Urol. Assn. (Ramon Guiteras award 1995, John K. Lattimer award 2000, Eugene Fuller Triennial Prostate award 2001), Am. Surg. Assn. (sr.), Inst. Medicine of NAS. Avocations: fishing, astronomy. Office: Stanford U Med Ctr Dept Urology S 287 300 Pasteur Dr Stanford CA 94305-5118 E-mail: tstamey@stanford.edu.

STAMM, ALAN, lawyer; b. Galesburg, Ill., Nov. 22, 1931; s. Gustave Frederick and Miriam (Simon) S.; m. Shelley Lynn Ramage, Mar. 19, 1978; 1 child, Lucinda Anne. Student, Universidad Nacional de Mex., summer 1950; AB, Yale U., 1952; JD, Harvard U., 1957. Bar: Calif. 1957, U.S. Supreme Ct. 1963. Assoc. Thelen, Marrin, Johnson & Bridges, San Francisco, 1957-60; staff atty. Litton Industries Inc., Beverly Hills, Calif., 1960-66, asst. sec., 1963-66; sec., gen. counsel Internat. Rectifier Corp., L.A., 1966-69, v.p., 1968-69; v.p., gen. counsel Republic Corp., 1969-71, also bd. dirs., 1970-71; v.p., gen. counsel Sat. Rev. Industries, N.Y.C., 1971-72, Mattel Inc., Hawthorne, Calif., 1972-74, staff cons., 1974-75; of counsel Long & Levit, L.A., 1975-82, O'Donnell & Gordon, L.A., 1983-87, Hedges, Powe & Caldwell, L.A., 1988-90; pvt. practice, 1990—. Judge pro tem Mcpl. Ct. L.A. Jud. Dist., 1977—; arbitrator L.A. Superior Ct. 1979—, judge pro tem L.A. Superior Ct. 1989—, arbitrator Nat. Assn. Securities Dealers, 1981—. Founding trustee Ctr. for Law in the Pub. Interest; trustee Marlborough Sch., L.A.; bd. govs. Century City Hosp., L.A.; counsel bus. and profl. com. L.A. Philharmonic; bd. dirs. Yale Alumni Fund. Lt. (j.g.) USNR, 1952-54; lt. comdr. Res.; ret. Mem. ABA, Calif. Bar Assn., L.A. Bar Assn., Am. Jewish Com., Harvard Law Sch. Assn., L.A. County Art Mus., Am. Arbitration Assn. (nat. panel arbitrators), NAACP, Sierra Club, Nat. Assn. Yale Alumni (former bd. govs.), Yale Club of So. Calif. (former dir.), Harvard Club of So. Calif., Phi Beta Kappa. Home: 422 Denslow Ave Los Angeles CA 90049-3507 Office: Ste 810 1801 Avenue of the Stars Los Angeles CA 90067-5801

STAMM, GEOFFREY EATON, retired arts administrator; b. Washington, July 30, 1943; s. George Edward Stamm and Dorothy Bourne (Baden) Elliott; m. Florence Theresa Ryan, Nov. 19, 1983. AB, Hamilton Coll., 1965; diploma in arts adminstrn., Harvard U., 1974. Mus. tech. Indian Arts and Crafts Bd., Washington, 1965-67, rsch. asst., 1967-69, coord. spl. projects, 1969-74, asst. to gen. mgr., 1974-78, asst. gen. mgr., 1978-93, gen. mgr., 1993-94, dir., 1994-97; ret., 1997. Chmn. Foggy Bottom and West End Adv. Neighborhood Commn., Washington, 1983-86; pres. St. Mary's Ct. Housing Devel. Corp., Washington, 1988-93. Mem. Am. Assn. Mus., Am. Craft Coun., Native Am. Art Studies Assn.

STAMM, ROBERT JENNE, building contractor, construction company executive; b. Albuquerque, Nov. 17, 1921; s. Roy Allen and Elizabeth C. (Baldridge) S.; m. Florence I. Bradbury, May 14, 1943; children— R. Brad, Susan Stamm Evans. BSCE, U. N.Mex., 1942; postgrad. in Naval Architecture, U.S. Naval Acad., 1943. Registered profl. engr. and surveyor, N.Mex. With Bradbury Stamm Constrn. Co., Albuquerque, 1946—, chmn., 1983—, former CEO, pres.; comdr./ret. USNR, 1943-69. Mem. U. N.Mex. Found., 1982-94, N.Mex. Commn. on Higher Edn., 1986-95; mem. centennial exec. com. U. N.Mex., chmn. devel. fund, 1984-85, 89-94; trustee Albuquerque Cmty. Found., 1983-2001; trustee Albuquerque Mus., 1993-02, chmn. 1995-97, trustee Nat. Conservancy/N.Mex., 1998—; trustee N.Mex. Mus. Natural History Found., 1995-2001; bd. dirs., pres. Albuquerque Bus.-Edn. Compact, 1987-88, Albuquerque Mus. Found., 1986-91, 96-97, Indsl. Found. Albuquerque; past bd. dirs. United Way, Girl Scouts U.S.A., Boy Scouts Am., Presbyn. Hosp. Ctr. Found., Presbyn. Heart Inst., Greater Albuquerque Cmty. Ednl. Alliance, N.Mex. First, Albuquerque Econ. Forum, Albuquerque YMCA, Anderson-Abruzzo Internat. Balloon Mus. Recipient Regents Recognition medal U. N.Mex., 1986, Zimmerman award U. N.Mex., 1988, U. N.Mex. Centennial Alumnus award Nat. Assn. State Univ. and Land Grant Colls., 1987, Disting. Pub. Svc. award State N.Mex., 1990, Award of Excellence, Presbyn. Health Fedn., 1991, Disting. Citizen award Boy Scouts-Great S.W. Coun., 1994, Disting. Alumni award Coll. Engring. U. N.Mex., 1999, United Way Lifetime Achievement award, 1999, N.Mex. Ethics in Bus. Individual award, 2000; named Most Admired Co., N.Mex. Pvt. 100, 1991, 92, 94, 95, 96, 97, 98; named to Albuquerque Sr. Citizen Hall of Fame, 1994; named for N.Mex. Outstanding Philanthropic Leadership, 1994. Mem. NSPE (Albuquerque Engr. of Yr. 1987, N.Mex. Lifetime Svc. award 1995), Assoc. Gen. Contractors N.Mex. (pres. bldg. br. 1962), Econ. Forum Albuquerque (bd. dirs. 1998-2002), Exec. Assn. Greater Albuquerque, Albuquerque country Club (bd. dirs. 1972-76, 87-89), Albuquerque Tennis Club (bd. dirs. 1978-80). Avocations: tennis, golf. Home: 1524 Las Lomas Rd NE Albuquerque NM 87106-4532 Office: Bradbury Stamm Constrn Inc PO Box 10850 Albuquerque NM 87184-0850 E-mail: rstamm@bradburystamm.com.

STAMM, RUDOLF ARMIN, journalist; b. Winterthur, Switzerland, May 28, 1937; arrived in U.S., 1999; s. Alfred Stamm and Elsbeth Meier; m. Gerlinde Anna Schwarz, Aug. 29, 1969; children: Christian Armin, Stefan Armin. PhD, U. Zurich, 1964. Dep. editor, corr. Basler Nachrichten, Paris, 1965-71; editor Woche, Olten, 1972-73; corr. Eastern Europe Neue Zurcherzeitung, Vienna, 1974-88, corr. Rome, 1988-99, Washington, 1999—. Chmn. Swiss Sch. Bd., Rome, 1995—97. Author: (book) Alltag und Tradition in Osteuropa, 1985; co-author: Keine Angst vor Europa, 1991. Mem.: Fgn. Press Assn. (chmn. 1978—80). Avocations: Roman and Greek history, Italian Renaissance. Home and Office: 3808 Woodley Rd Washington DC 20016

STAMOS, JOHN JAMES, judge; b. Chgo., Jan. 30, 1924; s. James S. and Katherine (Manolopoulos) S.; m. Helen Voutiritsas, Sept. 3, 1955 (dec. 1981); children— James, Theo, Colleen, Jana; m. Mary Sotter, March 21, 1986. LL.B., DePaul U., 1948. Bar: Ill. 1949. Since practiced in, Chgo.; asst. corp. counsel City Chgo., 1951-54; asst. states atty. Cook County, 1954-61; chief criminal div. States Attys. Office, 1961-64, 1st asst. states atty., 1964-66, states atty., 1966-68; judge Appellate Ct. of State of Ill., 1968-88; Judge Ill. Supreme Ct., Springfield, 1988-90; ret., 1990; of counsel Stamos and Trucco, Chgo., 1991—. Served with AUS, 1943-45.

STAMOS, MICHAEL JERRY, colon and rectal surgeon, educator; b. Miami Beach, Fla., Sept. 22, 1959; s. Peter and Carol Sue (Adams) S.; m. Bridget Thompson, Mar. 3, 1990. BA, Case Western Res. U., 1981, MD, 1985. Diplomate Am. Bd. Colon and Rectal Surgery. Intern and resident U. Miami/Jackson Meml. Hosp., 1985-90; fellow in colon and rectal surgery Ochsner Clinic, New Orleans, 1990-91; asst. prof. surgery UCLA, 1991-97, assoc. prof. surgery, 1997—2002; chief sect. colon and rectal surgery Harbor UCLA Med. Ctr., Torrance, 1992—2002; prof. surgery U. Calif., Irvine, 2002—; chief divsn. colon and rectal surgery U. Calif. Irvine Med. Ctr., 2002—. Contbr. articles to med. jours., chpt. to books. Fellow ACS (adv. coun. colon and rectal surgery 1995-2002), Am. Soc. Colon and Rectal Surgeons; mem. Soc. Am. Gastrointestinal Endoscopic Surgeons, Internat. Soc. Univ. Colon and Rectal Surgeons, Southwestern Surg. Congress. Avocations: bicycling, raquetball, hiking, skiing. Office: U Calif Irvine Med Ctr Bldg 55 Rte B1 101 The City Dr Orange CA 92868

STAMPER, EWA SZUMOTALSKA, psychologist; b. Warsaw, Poland, Sept. 8, 1954; came to U.S., 1984; d. Tadeusz and Regina (Sobczak) S.; m. Ryszard Zwierowicz, Dec. 30, 1980 (div. Jan. 13, 1986); m. Allen Malcolm Stamper, Oct. 23, 1992. MA in Clin. Psychology, U. Warsaw, Poland, 1978; PhD in Psychology, New Sch. U., N.Y.C., 1992. Staff therapist Marital Therapy Counseling Ctr., Warsaw, 1978-79, Ctr. for Psychotherapy and Personality Growth, Warsaw, 1978-80; sr. staff therapist Lab. for Psychoedn. Polish Psychol. Assn., Poland, 1981-85; postgrad. affiliate Washington Square Inst. for Psychotherapy, N.Y.C., 1990-92; police psychologist Honolulu Police Dept., 1993-98; pvt. practice, Honolulu, 1994—. With Tng. Ctr. for Family Therapy, Warsaw, 1976—78, Stuyvesant Poly., N.Y.C., 1988—89, North Ctrl. Bronx (N.Y.) Hosp., 1988—89, Yale Psychiat. Inst., 1989—90, Castle Med. Ctr., Kailua, Hawaii, 1993—94; co-chmn. Crystal Methamphetamine Forum, Honolulu, 1996—99. Mem. APA, Am. Acad. Experts in Traumatic Stress, Internat. Critical Incident Stress Found., Hawaii Psychol. Assn. (clin. divsn. rep. 1998-99). Avocations: horseback riding, raising German Shorthaired Pointers and Siamese cats, gardening, fiction writing, running. Office: 1188 Bishop St Ste 1607 Honolulu HI 96813-3313

STAMPER, JAMES M. retired English language educator; b. Roxana, Ky., Sept. 26, 1917; s. Marion and Amanda (Combs) S.; m. Diane C. Mahoney, Aug. 12, 1967. BS in Edn., Union Coll., 1941; MA in English, U. Ky., 1946. Subs. tchr. Ermine Elem. Sch., Dry Fork Elem. Sch., 1936-37; elem. tchr. various schs., 1937-41; h.s. Eng. tchr. Whitesburg H.S., Ky., 1941-46; instr. English U. Ky., Lexington, 1946-49, U. Md., College Park, 1949-52; instr. bus. English DePaul U., Chgo., 1952-62; English tchr., cons. in high sch. English Bd. Edn., 1962-72; ret. Chgo. Area Schs., 1972; subst. tchr. Chgo. Area schs., 1972-82. Vis. instr. in English Jacksonville (Fla.) U. Co-author: A Handbook on Oral Reading Diagnosis, Resource Materials for Essential English in the Secondary Schools, A Syllabus in Basic English; contbr. articles to profl. jours. Scholar Knights of Columbus, Union Coll., U. Ky. Mem. AARP. Home: 4501 Concord Ln Northbrook IL 60062-7163

STAMPER, JOE ALLEN, lawyer; b. Okemah, Okla., Jan. 30, 1914; s. Horace Allen and Ann (Stephens) S.; m. Johnnie Lee Bell, June 4, 1936; 1 child, Jane Allen (Mrs. Ernest F. Godlove). BA, U. Okla., 1933, LL.B., 1935, JD, 1970. Bar: Okla. bar 1935. Practice in, Antlers, 1935-36, 46—; mem. firm Stamper, Hadley & Reasor, 1974—; atty. Pushmataha County, 1936-39; spl. justice Okla. Supreme Ct., 1948. Mem. Okla. Indsl. Commn., 1939-40; pres. Antlers Sch. Bd., 1956-67, Pushmataha Found., 1957— ; mem. Okla. Bicentennial Com., 1971— ; vice chmn. bd. U. Okla. Law Center, 1975-78; mgr. Okla. Democratic party, 1946, dist. chmn., 1946-50; alt. del. Dem. Nat. Conv., 1952. Served to col. AUS, 1935-46, E O. Decorated Bronze Star. Fellow Am. Bar Found., Am. Coll. Trial Lawyers, Am. Bd. Trial Advocates (advocate); mem. ABA (del. 1974-91, state del. 1975-86, mem. com. on law book pub. practices 1974-76, bd. govs. 1986-89, standing com. on fed. jud. improvement 1989-92), SAR, Okla. Bar Assn. (bd. govs. 1969-73, Pres.'s award 1977, 80, 93, 2001), Okla. Bar Found. (pres. 1977), Mil. Order World Wars, Pi Kappa Alpha. Baptist (deacon). Clubs: Petroleum (Oklahoma City). Lodges: Masons, Shriners, Lions. Home: 1006 NE 2nd St Antlers OK 74523-2822 Office: PO Box 100 112 N High St Antlers OK 74523-2250

STAMPER, MALCOLM THEODORE, publishing company executive; b. Detroit, Apr. 4, 1925; s. Fred Theodore and Lucille (Cayce) S.; m. Marion Philbin Guinan, Feb. 25, 1946; children: Geoffrey, Kevin, Jamie, David, Mary, Anne. Student, U. Richmond, Va., 1943-44; BEE, Ga. Inst. Tech., 1946; postgrad., U. Mich., 1946-49; DHumanities, Seattle U., 1994. With Gen. Motors Corp., 1949-62; with Boeing Co., Seattle, 1962-90, mgr. electronics ops., v.p., gen. mgr. turbine div., 1964-66; v.p., gen. mgr. Boeing Co. (747 Airplane program), 1966-69, v.p., gen. mgr. comml. airplane group, 1969-71, corp. sr. v.p. ops., 1971-72; pres. Boeing Co., 1972-85, vice chmn., 1985-90; CEO, Storytellers Ink Pub., Seattle, 1990—, also chmn. bd. dirs. Bd. dirs. Pro-Air Inc.; trustee The Conf. Bd., 1988—. Candidate for U.S. Ho. of Reps., Detroit, 1952; trustee, chmn. Seattle Art Mus.; nat. bd. dirs. Smithsonian Assocs. With USNR, 1943-46. Named Industrialist of Year, 1967; recipient Educator's Golden Key award, 1970, Elmer A. Sperry award, 1982, AIEE award, Ga. Inst. Tech. award, Sec. Dept. Health and Human Services award, Silver Beaver award Boy Scouts Am., 1989, Literary Lions award, 1995; named to Engring. Hall of Fame. Mem. Nat. Alliance Businessmen, Phi Gamma Delta.

STAMPER, ROBERT LEWIS, ophthalmologist, educator; b. N.Y.C., July 27, 1939; m. Naomi T. Belson, June 23, 1963; children: Juliet, Marjorie, Alison. BA, Cornell U., 1957-61; MD, SUNY-Downstate, 1965. Diplomate Am. Bd. Ophthalmology (assoc. examiner 1976-92, bd. dirs. 1992-99). Intern Mt. Sinai Hosp., N.Y.C., 1965-66; resident in ophthalmology Washington U.-Barnes Hosp., St. Louis, 1968-71; Nat. Eye Inst.-NIH fellow dept. ophthalmology Washington U., 1971-72, from instr. ophthalmology to asst. prof. dept. ophthalmology, 1971-72; asst. prof. dept. ophthalmology Pacific Presbyn. Med. Ctr., San Francisco, 1972-76, assoc. prof. ophthalmology, 1976-87; chmn. dept. ophthalmology Calif. Pacific Med. Ctr. (formerly Pacific Presbyn. Med. Ctr.), 1987-96; vice-chmn. dept./prof. clin. ophthalmology, dir. glaucoma U. Calif., San Franciso, 1999—. Asst. ophthalmologist Barnes Hosp., St. Louis, 1971-72, Harkness Hosp., San Francisco, 1973-74; dir. ophthalmic photography and fluorescin angiography, dept. ophthalmology Washington U., St. Louis, 1969-72; dir. resident tng. Pacific Presbyn. Med. Ctr., 1972-89, dir. glaucoma svc., vice-chmn. dept. ophthalmology, 1974-87; chief ophthalmology svc. Highland Hosp., Oakland, Calif., 1974-76; clin. instr. dept. ophthalmology U. Calif., San Francisco, 1974-77, prof. clin. ophthalmology, 1998—; clin. asst. prof. ophthalmology U. Calif., Berkeley, 1974-78, asst. clin. prof. ophthalmology, 1978-85; sr. rsch. assoc. Smith-Kettlewell Inst. Visual Scis., San Francisco, 1972-89; project co-dir. ophthalmic curriculum for med. students Nat. Libr. Medicine, 1973-75; commr. Joint Commn. on Allied Health Pers. in Ophthalmology, 1975-87, bd. dirs., 1978-88, sec., 1980, v.p., 1982-83, pres., 1984-85; provisional asst. chief dept. ophthalmology Mt. Zion Hosp., San Francisco, 1976-87, assoc. chief dept. ophthalmology, 1982-86; ophthalmic cons. Ft. Ord, Calif., 1976—, Oakland Naval Hosp., 1978-83; instr. Stanford (Calif.) U., 1977—; glaucoma cons. U. Calif., Davis, 1978-84; vis. lectr. dept. ophthalmology Hadassah Hebrew U. Med. Ctr., Jerusalem, 1978, Oxford (Eng.) U. Eye Hosp., 1986; ind. med. examiner State of Calif., 1979—; mem. appeals hearing panel Accreditation Coun. for Grad. Med. Edn., 1986-93, mem. residency rev. com. for ophthalmology, 1993-98; mem. provisional courtesy staff Peralta Hosp., Oakland, 1988-92; mem. ophthalmic devices adv. panel USFDA, 1989-92; presenter, lectr. in field. Editor Ophthalmology Clinics of North Am., 1988—; mem. editl. adv. com. Ophthalmology, 1982-89, mem. editl. bd., 1983-94; sr. author: Becker and Shaffer's Diagnosis and Management of the Glaucomas, 7th edit., 1999; contbr. articles to profl. jours. Chmn. bd. Agy. for Jewish Edn., Oakland, 1986-89; bd. dirs. Jewish Fedn. Greater East Bay, Oakland, 1992-94; bd. dirs. Found. for Glaucoma Rsch.; mem. glaucoma adv. com. Nat. Soc. to Prevent Blindness, 1981—; mem. Am. Diabetes Assn. Surgeon USPHS, 1966-68. Recipient Nat. Soc. for Performance and Instrn. award for self-instrnl. material in ophthalmology, 1975, Honor award Am. Acad. Ophthalmology, 1982, Sr. Honor award, 1992, Statesmanship award Joint Commn. on Allied Health Pers. in Ophthalmology, 1989, Troutman Master Tchr. in Ophthalmology award, 2000; N.Y. State Regents scholar, 1961, N.Y. State scholar in medicine, 1965; Blalock student fellow UCLA Sch. Medicine, 1961, Fight for Sight student fellow dept. ophthalmology N.Y. Hosp. and Cornell Med. Ctr., 1962, 63, 64. Fellow Am. Acad. Ophthalmology and Otolaryngology (rep. to joint commn. on allied health pers., faculty home study course sect. X, chmn. sect. VIII 1983-85, bd. councilors, editl. adv. com. Opthalmology jour. 1982-89, editl. bd. Ophthalmology jour. 1983-94, and many others), ACS; mem. AMA (Physician's Recognition award 1989), Am. Ophthalmologic Soc., Assn. for Rsch. in Vision and Ophthalmology, Calif. Med. Assn. (asst. sec. sect. ophthalmology, chmn., sci. bd. rep. adv. panel on ophthalmology 1985-91), Nat. Soc. Prevent Blindness (mem. glaucoma adv. com. 1981—, bd. dirs. 1986—), No. Calif. Soc. Prevent Blindness, Calif. Assn. Ophthalmology, Pan Am. Ophthal. (bd. dirs. 1992-2000), Soc., N.Y. Acad. Scis., Las Vegas Ophthal. Soc. (hon.), Am. Glaucoma Soc. (v.p. 1997-99, pres. 1999-2000), Glaucoma Rsch. Found. (bd. dirs.). Office: Dept Opht UCSF Med Ctr 8 Kirkham St San Francisco CA 94143-0001 E-mail: stamper@itsa.ucsf.edu.

STAMPFL, CATHERINE MARGARET, physicist, research scientist; b. Warracknabeal, Victoria, Australia, July 25, 1963; d. Athol Harry and Joyce Arden (Oulton) Tickner; m. Anton Patrick Joseph Stampfl, Nov. 29, 1959. BSc with honors, La Trobe U., Melbourne, Australia, 1985, PhD in Physics, 1991. Trainee actuary Nat. Mut., Melbourne, 1986; postdoctoral fellow Fritz-Haber-Inst der Max-Planck-Gesellschaft, Berlin, Germany, 1991-94, staff scientist Germany, 1995-96, 98. Vis. rsch. scientist Xerox Parc, Palo Alto, Calif., 1997, sr. rsch. assoc. Northwe. U., Evanston, Ill., 1999—. Contbr. articles to profl. jours. Recipient David Meyers award, 1985, Commonwealth Postgrad. award, 1987-90, 3d Yr. prize in Physics, 3d Yr. prize in Applied Math., 1984. Mem. Australian Inst. Physics, Am. Vacuum Soc., Materials Rsch. Soc. Home: 1512 Lakeview Dr Apt 335 Darien IL 60561-4936 Office: NW Univ Dept Physics 2145 Sheridan Rd Evanston IL 60208-0834

STAMPKE, STUART REH, physicist, researcher; b. Burbank, Calif., Apr. 20, 1950; BS in Physics summa cum laude, Calif. State U., Northridge, 1973; PhD in Physics, Calif. Inst. Tech., Pasadena, 1982. Rsch. fellow in physics Calif. Inst. Tech., Pasadena, 1982; rsch. assoc. Mich. State U., East Lansing, 1982-86; scientist I Superconducting Super Collider Lab., Waxahachie, Tex., 1989-94; sr. scientist Aura Sys., Inc., El Segundo, Calif., 1996—. From vis. asst. prof. to vis. assoc. prof. U. Notre Dame, Ind., 1986-88; mem. part-time faculty Calif. State U., Northridge, 1994-96. Contbr. articles to profl. jours. on particle physics, detectors, and accelerator physics. Mem. IEEE, Am. Phys. Soc., Internat. Solar Energy Soc., Am. Solar Energy Soc. Home: 17803 Superior St Apt 215 Northridge CA 91325-4795 Office: Aura Sys Inc 2335 Alaska Ave El Segundo CA 90245-4822 E-mail: s.stampke@ieee.org.

STAMPS, GEORGE MORELAND, communications consultant, facsimile pioneer; b. Kuling, Jiangxi, China, June 15, 1924; came to U.S., 1926 (parents Am. citizens); s. Drew Fletcher and Elizabeth Camilla (Belk) S.; m. Helen Leone Paty, Nov. 29, 1946; children: Margaret Evalyn, Robert Fletcher, Thomas Paty, John Belk. BS magna cum laude, Wake Forest U., 1947; MA in Physics, Columbia U., 1949; postgrad., Poly. Inst. Bklyn., 1950-52. Instr. physics and math. SUNY Maritime Coll., Bronx, 1949-51; asst. chief engr., dir. tech. sales Hogan Labs. Inc., N.Y.C., 1951-59; chief engr., asst. to pres. mktg. Telautograph Corp., Los Angeles, 1960-62; program mgr. Magnafax Program Magnavox Co., Torrance, Calif., 1963-65, mgr indsl. mktg. Urbana, Ill., 1965-71, mgr. bus. devel., 1971-73; corp. mgr. bus. devel. Xerox Corp., Stamford, Conn., 1973-76; pres. GMS Consulting, Westport, 1976-86, Oxford, Ga., 1986—. Expert witness on facsimile-visual scis. N.Y. Supreme Ct., 1982; chmn. numerous sci. and profl. confs. Contbr. over 35 articles on facsimile and telecommunication scis. to profl. jours. and govt. coms. Patentee in field. Del. Conn. Dem. Conv., Hartford, 1980; bd. dirs. Champaign-Urbana (Ill.) Symphony Orch., 1968-72, Newton County Red Cross, 1988-94; sec. Newton County Hist. Soc., 1991-93, v.p., 1993-95, pres., 1995-96; v.p. Friends of Newton County Porter Meml. Libr., 1988-91, pres., 1991-93; pres. Newton County Facilities Bd., 1997—; chmn. Newton County Facilities Bd., 1997—; co-chair Newton County Impact Fee Adv. Com., 1999—. Decorated Air medal with two oak leaf clusters; named Friend of Newton County Libr., 1994; named Wake Forest U. Alumnus of Yr., 1997, recipient Disting. Svc. citation for sci. and tech., 1997. Mem. IEEE, Computer Soc. of IEEE, Comm. Soc. of IEEE (officer Ft. Wayne chpt. 1972-73), Geosci. and Remote Sensing Soc. of IEEE, Electronics Industries Assn. (chmn. comm. terminals and interfaces sect. 1963-73, founder TR-29 facsimile systems and equipment engring. com. 1961), Armed Forces Comm. and Electronics Assn., Am. Phys. Soc., Kiwanis (pres. Covington club 1993-94, lt. gov. 21st divsn. 1996-97), Phi Beta Kappa, Omicron Delta Kappa. Presbyterian. Home: 1280 Lake Stone Lea Dr PO Box 1299 Oxford GA 30054-1299 E-mail: patystamps@prodigy.net.

STAMPS, LORI MUSSELWHITE, school counselor; b. Buford, Ga., Feb. 13, 1975; d. Autley Musselwhite; d. Dennis Lamar (stepfather) and Marilyn Ann Bruce; m. Shane Gregory Stamps, Feb. 24, 1972. MEd, Clemson U., 2000. Nat. cert. counselor. Rsch. asst. Ga. State U., Atlanta, 1996-97; nutrition cons. Health Weigh, Anderson, S.C., 1999—. Faculty scholar Ga. State U., 1997. Mem. ACA, Psi Chi, Phi Kappa Phi. Republican. Presbyterian. Avocations: aerobics, running, cycling. Home: 1162 Buford Hwy Buford GA 30518 Office: Dacula Mid Sch Dacula GA 30519 E-mail: lrstamps@aol.com.

STAMPS, THOMAS PATY, lawyer, consultant; b. Mineola, N.Y., May 10, 1952; s. George Moreland and Helen Leone (Paty) S.; children: Katherine Camilla, George Belk, Elizabeth Margaret, Carley Lynn, Walker Paty; m. Diana Lynn Whittaker, Dec. 11, 1993. BA, U. Ill., 1973; postgrad., Emory U., 1975-76; JD, Wake Forest U., 1979. Bar: Ga. 1979, N.C. 1979. Pers. dir. Norman Jaspan, N.Y.C., 1973-74; assoc. Macey & Zusmann, Atlanta, 1979-81; prin. Zusmann, Small, Stamps & White PC, 1981-85; mem. Strategic Capital Am., L.L.C., 1998—. Ptnr. Destin Enterprises, Atlanta, 1983-85. Author: Study of a Student, 1973, History of Coca-Cola, 1976; asst. editor Ga. Jour. So. Legal History, 1991-94. Atty. Vol. Lawyers for Arts, Atlanta, 1981—94, Atlanta Vol. Lawyers Found.; active High Mus. Art, 1986—, Atlanta Hist. Soc., Atlanta Bot. Gardens, Atlanta Symphony Orch., Ga. Trust Hist. Preservation, Ind.; sec. Friends of Woodrow Wilson, 1988—, chmn. dinner, 1990—; trustee Ga. Legal History Found., 1989—; pres. N. Springs H.S. Touchdown Club, 2000—01; founding dir. Sandy Springs Youth Basketball Program, 1999—2000; mem. Dem. Party Ga., Atlanta, 1983—; mem. Bench and Bar Com. State Bar Ga., 1996—; chmn. Summer Law Inst., Atlanta, 1981—85; panel mem. U.S. Bankruptcy Trustees No. Dist. Ga., 1982—92. Named to Honorable Order of Ky. Colonels; recipient Svc. award Inst. Continuing Legal Edn., Athens, Ga., 1981, 86. Fellow Ga. Bar Found.; mem. Atlanta Bar Assn. (com. chmn. 1981-85, bd. dirs. litigation sect. 2001—, mem. jud. selection com. 2001—, chmn. history com. 2001—), N.C. Bar Assn., Lawyers Club, North Springs H.S. Touchdown Club (pres. 2000-01), Phi Alpha Delta (justice, Atlanta 1982-83, emeritus 1983). Office: 7715 Jett Ferry Rd Atlanta GA 30350-5419

STAMSTA, JEAN F. artist; b. Sheboygan, Wis., Nov. 2, 1936; d. Herbert R. and Lucile Caroline (Malwitz) Nagel; m. Duane R. Stamsta, Aug. 18, 1956; children: Marc, David. BS, BA, U. Wis., 1958. Guest curator Milw. Art Mus., 1986; resident artist Leighton Artist Colony, Banff, Alta., Can., 1987. One-woman shows Am. Craft Mus., N.Y.C., 1971, Winona (Minn.) State U., 1986, Lawrence U., Appleton, Wis., 1990, Walkers Point Ctr. Arts, Milw., 1990, U. Wis. Ctr., Waukesha, 1995, U. Wis. Ctr., Sheboygan, 1998, Wis. Luth. Coll., Milw., 1999; exhibited in group shows, incuding Cleve. Mus. Art, 1977, Milw. Art Mus., 1986, 88, Nat. Air and Stace Mus., Smithsonian Instn., Washington, 1986, Madison (Wis.) Art Ctr., 1987, 90, Paper Press Gallery, Chgo., 1988, North Arts Ctr., Atlanta, 1990, Dairy Barn Cultural Arts Ctr., Athens, Ohio, 1991, Paper Arts Festival, Appleton, 1992, Fine Arts Mus., Budapest, Hungary, 1992, Tilburg Textile Mus., The Netherlands, 1993, U. Wis. Union Gallery, 1994, Holland Area Arts Coun. Gallery, U. Mich., Ann Arbor, 1996; Self-Portraits, Charles Allis Art Mus., Milw., 1996, Bergstrom-Mahler Mus., Neenah, Wis., 1998, West Bend Mus. Art, Wis., 2000. NEA craftsman fellow, 1974. Avocations: swimming, travel. Home: 9313 Center Oak Rd Hartland WI 53029 E-mail: jstamsta@aol.com.

STANALAND, BRETT ERIC, allergist, clinical immunologist, internist; b. Orlando, Fla., Nov. 22, 1959; s. Billy Dow and Betty Jean (Holliday) S.; m. Linda Monique Susca, June 27, 1987; children: Brett Eric II, Kyle Patrick, Tiffany Erica. AA, Valencia C.C., Orlando, 1980; BS, U. Ctrl. Fla., 1983, MS, 1985; MD, U. South Fla., 1989. Diplomate Am. Bd. Internal Medicine. Resident in internal medicine Wake Forest U., Winston-Salem, N.C., 1989-92; fellow in clin. lab. immunology U. South Fla., Tampa, 1992-94, asst. clin.

prof. medicine divsn. allergy and immunology, 1995—; pvt. practice, Naples, Fla., 1995—. Chmn. dept. medicine Naples Cmty. Hosp., 2000-2002; mem. spkr. burs. Pfizer, Schering, Key, Glaxo, Astra, HMR. Fellow Am. Assn. Immunologists, Am. Acad. Allergy, Asthma and Immunology; mem. ACP, Am. Coll. Allergy and Immunology, Fla. Med. Assn. Office: 1000 Goodlette Rd N Ste 200 Naples FL 34102-5449

STANARD, CHRISTOPHER LEON, statistician; b. Washington, 1967; s. Leon and Willie Louise Stanard B of Indsl. Engring., Ga. Tech., 1990, MS in Indsl. Engring., 1992. Process tech. engr. Michelin Tire Co., Lexington, S.C., 1992-94; statistician GE Corp. Rsch. and Devel., Schenectady, N.Y., 1996—. Founding sec. Awareness of Career and Ednl. Opportunities Inc., Atlanta, 1992. Contbr. poetry to Drumvoice mag., 1992, 93, 96, Catch the Fire, 1998, Spirit & Flame, 1997, Dark Eros, 1997; book reviewer Technometrics. Plant sect. coord. Michelin Walk Am. March of Dimes, 1993, 94. NSF grad. minority fellow, 1990-92, 94-95. Mem. Am. Soc. Quality (organizing com., Web master 1999), Nat. Soc. Black Engrs. (tech. profls. conf. pub. rels. chair 2000, mem. region I and II Profl. Devel. Conf. com. 1998, asst. nat. publs. chair 1989-90, Alumni Extension Region I Mem.-at-Large of the Yr. 1998), Inst. Indsl. Engrs., Internat. Inst. of Forecasters, Am. Statis. Assn. (minority affairs com. 2001—), Tau Beta Pi. Office: GE Corp Rsch and Devel 1 Rsch Ctr Niskayuna NY 12309 E-mail: stannard@crd.ge.com.

STANBERRY, D(OSI) ELAINE, English literature educator, writer; b. Elk Park, N.C. m. Earl Stanberry; 1 child, Anita St. Lawrence. Student in Bus. Edn., Steed Coll. Tech., 1956; BS in Bus. and English, East Tenn. State U., 1961, MA in Shakespearean Lit., 1962; PhD, Tex. A&M U., 1975; postgrad., North Tex. State U., U. South Fla., NYU, Duke U., U. N.C. Prof. Manatee Jr. Coll., Bradenton, Fla., 1964-67; Disting. prof. English Dickinson State U., N.D., 1967-81; retired, 1981. Author: Poetic Heartstrings, Mountain Echoes, Love's Perplexing Obsession Experienced by Heinrich Heine and Percy Bysshe Shelley, Poetry from the Ancients to Moderns: A Critical Anthology, Finley Forest, Chapel Hill's Tree-lined Tuck, (plays) The Big Toe, The Funeral Factory; contbr. articles, poetry to jours., mags. Recipient Editor's Choice award Nat. Libr. Poetry, 1988, 95, Distinguished Professor of English Award, Dickinson State U., 1981; included in Best Poems of 1995. Mem. Acad. Am. Poets, N.C. Writers Network, N.C. Poetry Soc. (Carl Sandburg Poetry award 1988), Poetic Page, Writers Jour., Poets and Writers, Friday-Noon Poets, Delta Kappa Gamma. Home: Finley Forest 193 Summerwalk Cir Chapel Hill NC 27517-8642

STANBERY, ROBERT CHARLES, veterinarian; b. Conneaut, Ohio, Apr. 5, 1947; s. Robert James and Ruth Virginia Stanbery; student Miami U., Oxford, Ohio, 1965-67; D.V.M., Ohio State U., 1971; m. Constance Ann Coutts, July 24, 1971; children: Scott Andrew, Mark Donald. Veterinarian, Lexington (Mass.) Animal Hosp., 1971-74, Avon Lake Animal Clinic Inc. (Ohio) 1974-76; pres., treas. Bay Village Animal Clinic Inc., Ohio, 1976—. Mem. AVMA, Ohio Vet. Med. Assn., Animal Hosp. Assn. Cleve. Acad. Vet. Medicine, Lorain County Vet. Assn. Internat. Platform Assn., Bay Village C. of C. (bd. dirs.), U.S. Jaycees (Outstanding Young Man of Am. 1976). Fundamentalist Christian. Home: Avon Lake, Ohio. Died Mar. 27, 2001.

STANBURY, JOHN BRUTON, physician, educator; b. Clinton, N.C., May 15, 1915; s. Walter A. and Zula (Bruton) S.; m. Jean F. Cook, Jan. 6, 1945; children: John Bruton, Martha Jean, Sarah Katherine, David McNeill, Pamela Cook. AB, Duke U., 1935; MD, Harvard U., 1939; MD (hon.), U. Leiden (Netherlands), 1975, U. Pisa, Italy, 1994. House officer Mass. Gen. Hosp., 1940-41, asst. resident, 1946, chief med. resident, 1948, mem. med. staff, 1949—; research fellow pharmacology Harvard Med. Sch., 1947; vis. prof. medicine U. Leiden, 1955; prof. exptl. medicine MIT, Cambridge, 1966-80, emeritus, 1980—. Cons. Pan Am. Health Orgn., WHO, UNICEF, U.S. AEC. Author: Endemic Goiter: The adaptation of man to iodine deficiency, 1954, Metabolic Basis of Inherited Disease, 5th edit., 1984, The Thyroid and Its Diseases, 5th edit., 1984, Endemic Goiter, 1969, Human Development and the Thyroid, 1972, Endemic Goiter and Endemic Cretinism, 1980, Prevention and Control of Iodine Deficiency Disorders, 1987, A Constant Ferment, 1991, The Damaged Brain of Iodine Deficiency, 1994, The Inborn Errors of the Thyroid System, 1994, Iodine in Pregnancy, 1998. Served from lt. (j.g.) to comdr. USNR, 1941-45. Recipient Delmar S. Fahrney medal Franklin Inst., 1993, Prince Mahidol award, Thailand, 1994. Mem. Am. Assn. Physicians, Soc. Clin. Investigation, Am. Thyroid Assn. (pres. 1969), Am. Acad. Arts and Scis., Endocrine Soc., Endocrine Socs. Finland, Colombia, Peru, Ecuador and Argentina, Internat. Coun. for Control of Iodine Deficiency Disorders (chair emeritus). Democrat. Episcopalian. Home: 43 Circuit Rd Chestnut Hill MA 02467-1802 E-mail: john_stanbury@hms.harvard.edu.

STANCATI, RICHARD EMANUEL, cleaning company and restaurant executive; b. N.Y.C., June 18, 1936; s. Louis L. and Susan S. (Cecare) S.; m. Lollie M. Stancati, Nov. 11, 1939; children: Lisa, Ricky, Robert. BS, Adelphi Coll., 1961, BS, Y. Mgr. U.S. Merchant Marine Acad., Kings Point, N.Y., 1991; pres. The Kitchen Restaurant, N.Y.C., 1980-91, Ea. Queens Cleaning, N.Y.C., 1980-91. Producer, host Cablevision Bus. to Bus. and Beyond, 1989—. Chmn. bd. Great Neck Village Bus. Assn., N.Y.C., 1990—; bd. dirs. Great Neck Cmty. Fund, N.Y.C., 1988-92. Named Friend of Edn. Great Neck Tchrs. Assn., 1992. Mem. Great Neck C. of C. (dir. 1989—, Small Bus. of yr. 1989). Avocations: photography, electronics. Home: 14 Burbury Ln Great Neck NY 11023-1308

STANCELL, ARNOLD FRANCIS, chemical engineering educator, retired oil executive; b. N.Y.C., Nov. 16, 1936; s. Francis and Maria (Lucas) S.; m. Constance Newton, Apr. 21, 1973; 1 child, Christine. BChemE, CCNY, 1958; ScD, MIT, 1962. Registered profl. engr., N.Y. 1972rsch. scientist, mgr. Mobil Oil Corp., Edison, NJ, 1962, chem. planning assoc., mgr. N.Y.C., 1972—75, v.p. chem. divsn. Macedon, NY, 1976—79, mgr. corp. planning N.Y.C., 1980—81, regional exec. mktg. and refining London, 1982—84, planning v.p. mktg. and refining N.Y.C., 1985—86, v.p. U.S. exploration and prodn. Fairfax, Va., 1987—88, v.p. internat. exploration and producing, 1989—93; prof. chem. engring. Ga. Inst. Tech., Atlanta, 1994—2001, endowed chair prof. chem. engring., 2001—. Vis. prof. MIT, Cambridge, 1998, adv. bd., 1976—; adv. bd. CCNY, 1990—, Carnegie Mellon U., 1999—. Contbg. author: Polymer Science and Materials, 1971; contbr. articles to Jour. Applied Polymer Sci., AIChE Symposia Series, Jour. Macromolecular Sci. Inducted NAE. Recipient Profl. Achievement award, NOBCChE, 1975, Career Achievement award CCNY, 1993, Black Engineer of Yr. award U.S. Black Engr., 1992, Outstanding Tchr. award Ga. Tech., 1997, Chem. Engring. Practice award AIChE, 1997. Mem. AIChE, Sigma Xi, Tau Beta Pi, Phi Lambda Upsilon. Achievements include management and growth of large dollar billions scale domestic and international chemical, oil and natural gas businesses; patents for petrochemical and polymer processes and plasma processes at surfaces. Office: Ga Inst Tech 778 Atlantic Dr NW Atlanta GA 30332-0100 E-mail: arnold.stancell@che.gatech.edu.

STANCER, KENNETH WILLIAM, elementary school educator; b. Beaver Dam, Wis., Jan. 10, 1963; s. William Arnold and Janice Elaine Stancer; m. Lisa Lane Stancer, Feb. 25, 1989; children: Nicholas Lane, Tyler Lane. MusB Edn., U. Wis., Whitewater, 1986. Cert. svc. playing Am. Guild Organists, 1998. Elem. music tchr. Cambridge (Wis.) Elem. Sch., 1991—; music dir. Faith Luth. Ch., Columbus, 1986—. Artistic dir. Columbus (Wis.) Area Cmty. Choir, 1995—. Musician: New Organ Dedications. Recipient Walmart Tchr. of the Yr. award, Walmart Found., 1997. Mem.: Soc. Am. Music, Wis. Alliance for Composers, Music Educators Nat. Conf., Am. Guild of Organists. Democrat. Lutheran. Avocations: swimming, gardening, painting. Home: 219 South Spring St Columbus WI 53925 Office: Cambridge Elem Sch 802 West Water St Cambridge WI 53523

STANCIL, IRENE MACK, family counselor; b. St. Helena Island, Sept. 29, 1938; d. Rufus and Irene (Wilson) Mack; m. Nesby Stancil, Dec. 29, 1968; 1 child, Steve Lamar. BA, Benedict Coll., 1960, CUNY, 1983; MA, New World Bible Coll., 1984; SSD, United Christian Coll., 1985; cert., Mercy Coll., 1993. Supr. City of New York; tchr. local bd. edn., S.C.; supr, case worker, counselor City of New York. Mem. Am. Ctr. for Law & Justice.

STANCILL, JAMES MCNEILL, finance educator, consultant; b. Orange, N.J., July 30, 1932; s. James Sr. and Anne Jeanne (Sauter) S.; m. Catherine Jackson, Sept. 25, 1954; children: Martha A., Mary C., Christine E. AB, George Washington U., 1954, MBA, 1957; PhD in Fin. and Econs., U. Pa., 1965. Buyer Melpar Inc., Falls Church, Va., 1954-59; instr., adminstrv. officer U. Pa., Phila., 1959-64; prof. fin. U. So. Calif., L.A., 1964—. Prin. Stancill & Assocs., Pasadena, Calif., 1964—; chmn. S.W. Products Co., 1991-97. Author: Management of Working Capital, 1970, Entrepreneurial Finance: Management of New and Emerging Businesses; contbr. numerous articles to Harvard Bus. Rev., 1977—. Avocations: genealogy, sailing. Office: U So Calif Marshall Sch Bus Los Angeles CA 90089-0001

STANCZYK, BENJAMIN CONRAD, judge; b. Detroit, Apr. 4, 1915; s. Bruno and Josephine (Tarczynski) S.; m. Stephanie W. Wojsowski, June 4, 1946; children: Benjamin Conrad Jr., Kathy Jo Thibault. AB, Wayne State U., 1936; JD, U. Mich., 1939. Bar: Mich. 1939, U.S. Dist. Ct. (ea. and we. dists.) Mich. 1939, U.S. Ct. Appeals (6th and 10th cir.) 1943. Pvt. practice, Detroit, 1939-49; asst. pros. atty., 1949-57; judge Common Pleas Ct., 1957-75; vis. judge State of Mich., 1975-97. Chmn. Income Tax Study Commn., Detroit, 1960-62; adv. bd. Madonna Coll., 1961-65; chmn. Tri-County Dental Health Coun., Detroit, 1962-68, pres., 1962-65; judge advocate Am. Legion Mich., 1962-63, DAV Dept. of Mich. 1966-70; Nat. Legis. Officer, Polish Legon of Am. Vets., 1961-63; exec. bd. Sr. Judges Mich., 1992—. Pub. Poles in Michigan. Pres. Polish Nat. Alliance 167, Detroit, 1949-57, Ctrl. Citizens Commn., Polish Coordinating Coun., Detroit, 1951-58, Cass Tech H.S. Assn., 1964-65; spokesmen Detroit's Polish Cmty. in Pol. and Cult. Matters, 1950-75, mem. Adv. Com. on Sch. Needs, Detroit, 1956-58; trustee Hist. Soc. Mich., 1988-96; adv. dem. Platform Comm. of Fgn. Affairs, 1952, 56; mem. exec. bd. Detroit's 250th Birthday Com., 1951; mem. Mich. Soccer and Football Commn., 1956-58; pres., mem. adv. bd. Vols. Am., 1977-80; organizer family music concerts Detroit Symphony Orch., 1954; active NAACP. With U.S. Army, 1942-46. Mem. ABA, NRA, NAACP, Grosse Point Camera Club (pres. 1993-94, 96-97), Am. Trial Lawyers Assn., Detroit Press Club (charter), Lions (pres. Detroit chpt. 1966-67, 96-97, Melvin Jones award 1998), Pi Sigma Alpha, Delta Sigma Rho. Democrat. Roman Catholic. Avocations: travel, photography, horology, firearms, numismatics. Office: 22811 Mack Ave Ste 211 Saint Clair Shores MI 48080-2054

STANCZYK, PIOTR, ballet dancer; b. Poznan, Poland; arrived in Can., 1997; Student, State Ballet Sch., Poznan, Nat. Ballet Sch., Can., 1997. Mem. corps de ballet Nat. Ballet Can., Toronto, Canada, 1998—2001, second soloist, 2001—. Dancer (ballets) Don Quixote, The Nutcracker, Swan Lake, Giselle, The Four Seasons, The Comforts of Solitude. Office: Walter Carsen Ctr for Nat Ballet Can 470 Queens Quay W Toronto ON Canada M5V 3K4 Office Fax: 416-345-8323.*

STANDBERRY, HERMAN LEE, school system administrator, educational consultant; b. Oran, Mo., Feb. 22, 1945; s. Willie Standberry and Bettie Mae (Thompson) Standberry-Taylor; m. Barbara Irene Palmer, July 1, 1942; children: Donna, Debra, Nina, Miriam, Miranda, Gretchen, Charles, Mary, Dwayne, Helena, Regina, Lakesha. BS, So. Ill. U., 1968; MA, Newport U., 1981, LHD (hon.), 1990; EdD, Walden U., 1992; D Ministry, Am. Christian Coll. and Sem., 1992; MEd, Ind. Wesleyan U., 1997. Cert. supt., gen. adminstr., curriculum, tchr., sch. counselor; approved profl. devel. provider Ill. State Bd. Edn. and Ill. State Tchr. Cert. Bd. Tchr. Community H.S. Dist. 428, Blue Island, Ill., 1968-70; exec. dir., dep. dir. program planner, HeadStart dir. Kane County Coun. for Econ. Opportunity, Batavia, 1970—75; case mgr., youth supr., educator State of Ill., Dept. Pub. Aid., Dept. Corrections, Chgo., Joliet and St. Charles, 1975—85; adminstrv. asst. to prin. Bloom High Sch. Dist. 206, Chicago Heights, 1992-93; asst. prin. Rogers High Sch., Michigan City, Ind., 1994-95; prin. Mich. City (Ind.) Area Alternative H.S., 1995—. Chmn. bd. dirs. Greater Chgo. Coun. of Religious Orgns., 1985-89; mem. George Bush's Rep. Presdl. Task Force, Washington, 1989; nominated mem. U.S. Rep. Senatorial Inner Cir., Washington, 1989; interim supt. LaPorte Cmty. Schs., 2002; supt., prin. United Ednl. Cultural Acad., 2002—. Author (curriculum) Business Law I & II, 1968, Career Counseling and Survival, 1978. Bd. dirs. United Way, Elgin, Ill, 1972, City of Elgin-Fremont Youth Orgn., 1971-72; host agy. rep. Dept. Human Svcs., Chgo., 1985-90; sustaining mem. Ill. Rep. Party, Springfield, 1989; host agy. Percy Julian High Sch., Chgo., 1989-90, 2002, Ill. Dept. Pub. Aid, Chgo., 1987. Recipient NBC 5/Chgo. and AT&T Je4fferson award; grantee Ill. Dept. Pub. Aid, 1984-87, hon. award Christian World Affairs Conf., 1985-86. Mem. Internat. Assn. Police and Community Rel. Officers, United Evangelistic Consulting Assn. (chmn. bd. dirs., pres. 1985—). Home: 803 E 193rd St Glenwood IL 60425-2011 Office: United Evangelistic Assn 1236 W 103rd St Chicago IL 60643-2361

STANDBRIDGE, PETER THOMAS, retired insurance company executive; b. Norristown, Pa., Mar. 30, 1934; s. Henry Kay and Helen Margaret (Ballard) S.; m. Jean Ann Sire, Sept. 29, 1956; children: Kevin Scot, Keith Alan, Kathryn Ann, Steven Todd. AB, Lafayette Coll., Easton, Pa., 1955. Regional mgr. Kemper Group, Richmond, Va., 1961-63, div. sales mgr. Syracuse, Summit, N.Y., N.J., 1963-73, spl. planning officer Long Grove, Ill., 1973, v.p. mktg., 1973-86, sr. v.p., 1986-87, exec. v.p., 1988-96; dir. Kemper County Mut. Ins., Garland, Tex., 1978-85, Am. Protection Ins. Co., Long Grove, 1976-96, Acord Corp., Oradell, N.J., 1978-82. Mem. Henrico County (Va.) Rep. Com., 1960-64; trustee Village of Manlius, N.Y., 1966-68; bd. govs. Good Shepherd Hosp., Barrington, Ill., 1983-92; chmn. Marquis Soc. Lafayette Coll., 1984-86; bd. dirs. Buehler YMCA, Palatine, Ill., 1989-92; trustee Lafayette Coll., 1991-93; dir. Savannah Runaway Home, 1997—. Mem.: The Landings Club (Ga.). Republican. Episcopalian. Home: 5 Moonrise Cir Savannah GA 31411-2944

STANDER, RICHARD RAMSAY, SR. retired civil engineer and construction engineer; b. Mansfield, Ohio, Jan. 3, 1919; s. Carl H. and Eula (Ramsay) S.; m. Bette Penhorwood, Mar. 8, 1941; children: Richard Jr., William, Susan, Sally. BCE, Ohio State U., 1940. Registered profl. engr., Ohio. Gen. mgr. to chmn. Mansfield Asphalt Paving co., 1946-93; ret., 1993. Chmn. The Rd. Info. Program, Washington, 1985—87; pres. Mohican Constrn. Co.; bd. dirs. First Buckeye Bank, Mansfield, Ohio, mem. exec. com., Ohio, 1972—85; mem. emeritus Asphalt Pavement Constrn. Com. of Transp. Rsch. Bd., Nat. Acad. Sci., Washington. Pres. Richland County Regional Planning Commn., 1953; mem. Ohio Transp. Rsch. Bd., Marysville, 1973-88, The State Parking Commn., Columbus, Ohio, 1987-94; cand. Ohio Senate Dist. 19, Columbus, 1986. Capt. U.S. Army, 1941-46. Recipient Centennial Alumnus award, Ohio State U., 1970, Disting. Alumnus award, Coll. Engring. Ohio State U., 1970, Rebuilding Am. award, CIT Corp., 1986, 40 Yrs. Svcs. to Transp. Industry, Am. Assn. State Hwy. and Transp. Ofcls., 2001. Fellow ASCE (life); mem. NSPE (life), Assn. Asphalt Paving Techs. (life, bd. dirs. 1969), Soc. Am. Mil. Engrs. (life), Transp. Rsch. Bd. (assoc.), Am. Rd. and Transp. Bldrs. Assn. (life; chmn. 1978, Nello Teer award 1988, Significant Achievement award 1996), Nat. Asphalt Pavement Assn. (life; pres. 1963-65, Hall of Fame award 1990), Internat. Soc. for Asphalt Pavements (charter), Ohio Contrs. Assn. (life, pres. 1963, Hall of Fame award 1971) Elks, Pres.'s Club (Ohio State U.), Mansfield Kiwanis Club (pres. 1953). Democrat. Presbyterian. Avocations: fishing, hunting, history. Home: 746 Clifton Blvd Mansfield OH 44907-2283

STANDFAST, SUSAN J(ANE), retired state official, educator, researcher; b. Callicoon, N.Y., July 2, 1935; m. Theodore P. Wright Jr., 1967; children: Henry S., Margaret S., Catherine B. AB in Biology and Chemistry, Wells Coll., 1957; MD, Columbia U., 1961; MPH in Epidemiology, U. Calif., Berkeley, 1965. Diplomate Am. Bd. Preventive Medicine. Intern King County Hosp., Swedish Hosp, Seattle, 1961-62; pediatric resident U. Wash., 1963; sr. resident in epidemiology N.Y. State Health Dept., 1965-67; instr. dept. cmty. health Albany (N.Y.) Med. Coll., 1965-67, asst. prof. dept. preventive and cmty. medicine, 1968-72, cons. in epidemiology, 1968-72, adj. asst. prof. preventive and cmty. medicine, 1975-80, adj. assoc. prof., 1980-91, cons. preventive medicine dept. family practice, 1983-91; rsch. physician bur. cancer control divsn. epidemiology N.Y. State Dept. Health, Albany, 1975-83, dir. cancer surveillance unit cancer control sect. bur. chronic disease prevention, 1983-85, asst. to dir. divsn. epidemiology, 1985-86, dir. injury control program divsn. epidemiology, 1986-90; physician pub. health, 1983-95; ret., 1995; dir. disability prevention program, 1988-91; cons. epidemiologist div. family health N.Y. State Dept. Health, Albany, 1991-95. Vis. lectr. G.S. Med. Coll., Bombay, 1969-70, London Sch. Hygiene, 1974-75, Coll. Cmty. Medicine, Lahore, Pakistan, 1991; cons. in epidemiology Bombay Cancer Registry Tata Meml. Hosp., Bombay, 1969-70; cons. infectious diseas sect. VA Med. Ctr., Albany, 1979; mem. ad hoc task force on data resource devel. for dir. epidemiology and biometry rsch. program Nat. Inst. Child Health and Human Devel., Bethesda, Md., 1979-80; assoc. prof. epidemiology Sch. Pub. Health, SUNY, 1987-97, adj. prof. epidemiology, 1997-99, co-dir. master's pub. health program, 1991-97; instr. AARP 55 Alive, 1996-99; human svcs. coord. Colonic Sr. Svc. Ctrs., 1999-2000; lectr. in field. Contbr. articles to profl. jours. Mem. med. adv. bd. Hudson-Mohawk chpt. Nat. Found. SIDS, 1976-84; mem. med. adv. bd coun. on human sexuality Planned Parenthood, Albany, 1971-88; mem. Physicians for Social Responsibility, 1984—, also numerous pub. health task forces and coms.; bd. dirs. Eddy Cmty. Care, Troy, N.Y., Albany-Tula Alliance, 2000--; vol. Colonie Sr. Svcs. Ctr., Newtonville, N.Y., 1996-2002; vol. Glen Eddy Retirement Cmty., 2002--. Recipient Disting. Alumnae award Wells Coll., 1994. Fellow Am. Coll. Preventive Medicine, Am. Coll. Epidemiology; mem. APHA. Home: 17 Wellington Way Niskayuna NY 12309

STANDIFER, RICK M. lawyer; b. Paris, Apr. 1, 1959; s. John B. and Betty J. (Watson) S.; m. Tina Y. Roberts, Dec. 14, 1985; children: Bailee Hollen, Sabre Savannah. AA, Paris Jr. Coll., 1979; BA, U. Tex., 1981; JD, U. Houston, 1984. Bar: Tex. 1984, Okla. 1990. Mng. ptnr. Clifford & Standifer, Paris, 1986—. Coll. scholar U. Tex., 1980 Mem. Lamar County Bar Assn. (pres. 1991-92), Am. Trial Lawyers Assn., Tex. Trial Lawyers Assn. Avocations: hunting, collecting Indian artifacts. Home: 2305 Wildwood Ln Paris TX 75462 Office: Clifford & Standifer 2765 NE Loop 286 Paris TX 75460-3427 E-mail: standifer@neto.com.

STANDING, KIMBERLY ANNA, educational researcher; b. Hagerstown, Md., Mar. 24, 1965; d. Thomas Townsend and Ruth Annadeane (Powell) Stone; m. Christopher G. Standing, May 20, 1989; children: Iain Christopher, Leah Elizabeth. BA in Math., St. Mary's Coll., 1988; MA in Higher Edn. Adminstrn., George Washington U., 1996, postgrad. Sr. analyst Westat, Inc., Rockville, Md., 1988—. Mem. Am. Ednl. Rsch. Assn., Assn. Study Higher Edn. Home: 11545 Brundidge Ter Germantown MD 20876-5500 Office: Westat Inc RW2564 1650 Research Blvd Rockville MD 20850-3195 E-mail: KimStanding@westat.com.

STANDING BEAR, ZUGGUELGERES GALAFACH, criminologist, forensic scientist, educator; b. Boston, Jan. 10, 1941; m. Nancy Lee Karlovic, July 13, 1978 (div. Aug. 1985); m. Virginia Anne Red Hawk, Mar. 22, 1988. BS, U. Nebr., 1971; MS in Forensic Sci., George Washington U., 1974; postgrad. cert. in forensic medicine, Armed Forces Inst. Pathology, 1974; MSEd, U. So. Calif., 1976; MPA, Jacksonville State U., 1981; PhD in Criminology, Fla. State U., 1986. Diplomate Am. Bd. Forensic Examiners, Am. Bd. Forensic Medicine, chmn. 2002-03; cert. coroner, Ga., 1988-92; cert. criminal justice instr., Calif., Ga. Criminal investigator U.S. Army, 1965; dist. comdr. 7th region U.S. Army Criminal Investigation Command, Seoul, 1974-77; course mgr. U.S. Army Mil. Police Sch., Ft. McClellan, Ala., 1978-81; ret. U.S. Army, 1981; instr. Fla. State U., Tallahassee, 1981-85; asst. prof. No. Ariz. U., Flagstaff, 1985-86; program coord., prof. Valdosta (Ga.) State U., 1986-95; assoc. prof. Colo. State U., Ft. Collins, 1995—2001, U. Colo., 2001—; adminstr. The Flash and Thelma Meml. Hedgehog Rescue of N.Am., Inc., 1998—. V.p. Bearhawk Cons. Group, Ft. Collins, 1996—; chair Am. Bd. Forensic Examiners. Editor Jour. Contemporary Criminal Justice, 1992. Mem., task group coord. Com. for Sexual Assault Evidence Stds., ASTM, 1993— Com. Colo State U.; mem. leadership coun. Cmty. Policing Project, Valdosta, Ga., 1993-95; treas. and v.p. edn. and rsch. No. Colo. WOLF rescue, edn., and rsch. project, LaPorte, Colo., 1995—; mem. Nat. Am. lang. preservation com. Colo. State Univ. Decorated Bronze Star medal, Meritorious Svc. medal (with oak leaf cluster). Fellow Am. Acad. Forensic Scis. (gen. sec. 1987-88, gen. chmn. 1988-90, gen. program co-chair 1995-96, Gen. Sec. Meritorious Svc. award 1996), Am. Coll. Forensic Examiners, Internat. Assn. Forensic Nurses (disting. fellow, mem. exec. bd. dirs., cons. and permissions exec., chmn. ethics com.); mem. ASTM (co-coord. sexual assault evidence stds. task group), Am. Sociol. Assn., Acad. Polit. Sci., Am. Soc. Criminology, Acad. Criminal Justice Scis. (program com. 1996-97), So. Criminal Justice Assn., Am. Assn. of U. Profs., Harley Owners Group, Internat. Hedgehog Assn, (treas.). Haudenosaunee (Native Am.). Avocations: hedgehog and wolf behavior, traditional Native American religious counseling, motorcycling. Office: Forensic Health Sci Programs Beth-El Coll Nursing and Health Scis U Colo Colorado Springs CO 80918 Home: 514 Hopi Circle Divide CO 80814

STANDISH, JOHN SPENCER, textile manufacturing company executive; b. Albany, N.Y., Apr. 17, 1925; s. John Carver and Florence (Spencer) S.; m. Elaine Joan Ritchie, Oct. 20, 1962 (div. 1984); children: John Carver, Christine Louise; m. Patricia Hunter, Nov. 9, 1985. BS, MIT, 1945. Asst. to prodn. mgr. Forstmann Woolen Co., Passaic, N.J., 1945-52; various positions Albany Internat. Corp., 1952-72, v.p., 1972-74, exec. v.p., 1974-76, vice chmn., 1976-84, chmn., 1984-98, also bd. dirs., 1958-98, chmn. emeritus, 1998—. Bd. dirs. Albany chpt. ARC, 1966-92, chpt. chmn., 1971-74, bd. govs., Washington, 1980-86; bd. dirs. United Way Northeastern N.Y., Albany, 1980-97, pres., 1984-85 ; trustee Albany Med. Coll. and Ctr., 1984-93, Sienna Coll., Loudonville, N.Y., 1987—; chmn. U. Albany Fund, 1982-87, 89-92; pres. U. Albany Found., 1992-98. Sgt. U.S. Army, 1945-46. Mem. Am. Mgmt. Assn., World Econ. Forum, Ft. Orange Club, Wolferts Roost Country Club, Schuyler Meadows Country Club, John's Island Club (Fla.). Republican. Episcopalian. Avocations: bridge, tennis, golf. Home: 1 Schuyler Meadow Club Rd Loudonville NY 12211-1423 Office: Albany Internat Corp PO Box 1907 Albany NY 12201-1907

STANDISH, SAMUEL MILES, oral pathologist, college dean; b. Campbellsburg, Ind., July 6, 1923; s. Irvin Arthur and Etta May (Smedley) S.; m. Gertrude Elizabeth Eberle, Aug. 6, 1949; children— Nancy Jo, Linda Sue. D.D.S., Ind. U., 1945, MS, 1956. Diplomate: Am. Bd. Oral Pathology (dir. 1973-80), Am. Bd. Forensic Odontology. Practice dentistry, specializing in oral pathology, Indpls., 1948-58; mem. faculty Sch. Dentistry Ind. U., 1958-88, emeritus prof. oral pathology, 1967-88, chmn. div. clin. oral pathology, 1967-77, asst. dean sch., 1969-74, asso. dean, 1974-88. Cons. Nat. Cancer Inst., 1969-73, Nat. Bd. Dental Examiners, 1966-74, ADA, 1971-77. Author: (with others) Oral Diagnosis/Oral Medicine, 1978, Maxillofacial Prosthetics: Multidisciplinary Practice, 1972, Outline of Forensic Dentistry, 1982. Served with USNR, 1945-47. Fellow Am. Acad. Oral Pathology (pres. 1972-73); mem. ADA, Internat. Assn. Dental Research, Am. Acad. Forensic Sci., Sigma Xi, Omicron Kappa Upsilon, Xi Psi Phi. Home: 4548 Manning Rd Indianapolis IN 46228-2768 Office: Ind U Sch Dentistry Indianapolis IN 46202

STANDISH, WILLIAM LLOYD, judge; b. Pitts., Feb. 16, 1930; s. William Lloyd and Eleanor (McCargo) S.; m. Marguerite Oliver, June 12, 1963; children: Baird M., N. Graham, James H., Constance S. BA, Yale U., 1953; LLB, U. Va., 1956. Bar: Pa. 1957, U.S. Supreme Ct. 1967. Assoc. Reed, Smith, Shaw & McClay, Pitts., 1957-63; ptnr., 1963-80; judge Ct. Common Pleas Allegheny County (Pa.), 1980-87, U.S. Dist. Ct. (we. dist.) Pa., 1987—. Solicitor Edgeworth Borough Sch. Dist., 1963-66. Bd. dirs. Sewickley (Pa.) Cmty. Ctr., 1981-83, Staunton Farms Found., mem., 1984—, trustee, 1984-92; corporator Sewickley Cemetery, 1971-87; trustee Mary and Alexander Laughlin Children's Ctr., 1972-90, Leukemia Soc. Am., 1978-80, We. Pa. chpt., 1972-80, We. Pa. Sch. Deaf, 1983—, YMCA of Sewickley, 1996—; bd. dirs. Pitts. Theol. Sem., 2001—. Recipient Pres. award Leukemia Soc. Am., 1980. Mem. ABA, Pa. Bar Assn., Allegheny County Bar Assn., Am. Judicature Soc., Acad. Trial Lawyers Allegheny County (treas. 1977-78, bd. dirs. 1979-80), Am. Inn of Ct. (Pitts. chpt. 1993—). E-mail: Judge William. Office: US Dist Ct 605 US Post Office Ct House 700 Grant St Pittsburgh PA 15219-1906 E-mail: Standish@pawd.uscourts.gov.

STANDLEY, JOHN ROBERT, city official; b. Dallas, May 16, 1928; s. Robert Richard and Lillian Mae (Glenn) S.; m. May Pearl Jones, Sept. 16, 1946 (dec. Oct. 1998); 1 child, Vicki Renee; m. Susan Ann Miller Page, Jan. 16, 2000. BBA in Indsl. Mgmt., So. Meth. U., 1958. Regional traffic mgr. Catalog Order Plant, Sears Roebuck Co., Dallas, 1944-70, mgr. traffic svcs. S.W. ter., 1970-80; transp. specialist Tex. Shippers Assn., 1983-88; exec. dir. Buffalo (Tex.) Housing Authority, 1989—. Gen. chmn. S.W. Shippers Adv. Bd., Dallas, 1963-65. Treas. Citizens Traffic Safety Commn., Dallas, 1965-70; arbitrator Am. Arbitration Assn., 1970-80. With U.S. Army AC, 1946-47; staff sgt. USAF, 1951-52. Mem.: Knights of the York Cross of Honor, Tex. York Rite Coll. 14, Karem Shrine, Order Ea. Star (past worthy patron), KT (Dallas

Commandery past comdr., Teague Commandery past comdr.), Scottish Rite, Buffalo Masons (past master), Tannehill Masons. Mem. Ch. of Christ. Office: Buffalo Housing Authority PO Drawer L Buffalo TX 75831

STANDLEY-BURT, NANCY VILMA, psychologist, educator, retired; b. Chgo., Aug. 6, 1934; d. Joseph and Anna (Tichna) Pav; m. Fred L. Standley, Sept. 8, 1956 (div. Mar. 1982); m. Jesse W. Burt, Dec. 18, 1982. BS, Northwestern U., 1957; MA, MacMurray Coll., Jacksonville, Ill., 1960; PhD, Fla. State U., 1969. Cert. sch. psychologist and counselor; nat. cert. counselor; lic. psychologist, Fla. Tchr. English Niles Twp. High Sch., Skokie, Ill., 1957-59; counselor, psychologist Maine Twp. High sch., Park Ridge, 1960-63; instr. English Fla. State U., Tallahassee, 1963-65, asst. prof., 1965-70; assoc. prof. Fla. A&M U., 1970-75, prof., 1975—2001, dir. career devel. ctr., 1973-75, dir. tchr. edn. ctr., 1982-92; ret., 2001. Adj. prof. Tallahassee Ctr. for Bibl. Studies, 2002. Author: (with Fred Standley) James Baldwin : A Reference Guide, 1979, Critical Essays: James Baldwin, 1984; contbr. articles to profl. jours. and monographs. Danforth Found. Assoc. award, 1969, 74; Salley Eckert Stevenson scholar, 1955-57. Mem. ACA, So. Assn. Counselor Edn., Fla. Counseling Assn., Fla. Assn. Counselor Edn., Big Bend Counseling (past pres.), Leon Mental Health Assn., Assn. for Counselor Edn. and Supervision, Psi Chi. Democrat. Methodist. Home: 2466 Thornton Rd Tallahassee FL 32308-6020

STANDRIDGE, JEAN, real estate executive, real estate broker; b. Danville, Ala., July 14, 1931; d. Elbert Eugene and Pearl May Rogers Brown; m. Arch Standridge, Jr., June 21, 1952; 1 child, Terry Brian. Grad., Burroughs Bus. Sch., Birmingham, 1951, Am. Real Estate Inst., 1975; student, Jefferson State Coll., Birmingham, 1980. Cert. real estate broker. Bookkeeper Mac Wates Coal Co., Birmingham, Ala., 1952-57; music tchr. County Schs., Blount County, 1957-75; real estate broker, owner Standridge Realty, Hayden, 1977—. Organist Meth. Ch., Hayden, 1957-77; sponsor Young Boys Soft Ball, Hayden, 1985-86; city coun. mem. Town of Hayden, 1988-92. Mem. Nat. Assn. Realtors, Ala. Assn. Realtors, Birmingham Assn. Realtors. Avocations: photography, indoor gardening, reading, music. Home: 177 Main St Hayden AL 35079-6452 Office: Standridge Realty Inc 177 Main St Hayden AL 35079-6452 also: 177 Main St Hayden AL 35079-6452

STANDRING, JAMES DOUGLAS, real estate developer; b. Fresno, Calif., Dec. 2, 1951; s. James Robert Pusey and Jacquelin (Moore); children: Craig Douglas, Ryan Scott, Melinda Jean, Kevin Paul. BS, Calif. State U., Fresno, 1975. Pres. Westland Industries, Inc., Portland, Oreg., 1976—; ptnr. Aloha Land and Cattle, Inc., 1982—. Bd. dirs. Tualitin Valley Econ. Devel. Corp., Portland, 1988-95; co-founder, bd. dirs. People for Washington County Charities, Beaverton, Oreg., 1985-88; mem. Westside Econ. Alliance, 1000 Friends of Oreg.; mem. steering com. Oreg. Med. Laser Ctr., 1995—. Named Portland Metro. Builder of Yr., 1992, Oreg. Builder of Yr., 1992; named to Oreg. Housing Hall of Fame, 2000. Mem. Homebuilders Assn. Metro Portland (v.p. 1988-90, pres. 1990-91), Oreg. Bldg. Industry Assn. (v.p. 1993-96, pres. 1996-97), Nat. Assn. Homebuilders, BUILD-PAC (Oreg. trustee 1992—, exec. com. 1994-2000). Republican. Episcopalian. Home: 5 Nansen Smt Lake Oswego OR 97035-1029 Office: Westland 12670 SW 68th Ave Ste 400 Portland OR 97223-8370

STANEART, LARRY WILLIAM, technology company marketing executive; b. Pawnee, Okla., Oct. 19, 1943; s. Arthur William and Della Lorin Staneart; m. Tracy Elaine Armand, Feb. 29, 1970 (div. Apr. 1983); children: Stacy, Marci. BS, Okla. State U., 1965. Br. mgr. Xerox Corp, Tampa, Fla., 1980-83, region sales mgr. New Orleans, 1983-86, region mgr. ea. U.S. Atlanta, 1986-93, v.p. bus. svc. Rochester, N.Y., 1993-95, v.p., gen. mgr. Miami, Fla., 1995-99, v.p. indsl. transition, 1999, v.p. mktg., 1999—. Bd. dirs. Sterling Quality Coun., Fla., 1995—; mem. coun. of 100 Fla. Internat. U., Miami, 1995—. Capt. U.S. Army, 1965-68, Korea. Mem. Miami C. of C. (trustee 1995—). Avocations: golf, tennis. Home: 3020 Paddock Rd Weston FL 33331-3605

STANEK, ALAN EDWARD, music educator, performer, administrator, retired; b. Longmont, Colo., July 3, 1939; s. Edward Thomas and Mary Rose (Hicks) Stanek; m. Janette Elizabeth Swanson, Aug. 23, 1963; children: Michael Alan, Karen Leigh. B in Music Edn., U. Colo., 1961; MusM, Eastman Sch. Music, 1965; DMusArts, U. Mich., 1974. Dir. instrumental music Ainsworth Pub. Sch., Nebr., 1961-64, Cozad Pub. Sch., 1965-67; asst. prof. music Hastings Coll., 1967-76; prof., chmn. music dept. Idaho State U., Pocatello, 1976-2001, ret., 2001. Contbr., editor, reviewer profl. jours. including Clarinet, Idaho Music Notes, Nebr. Music Educator. Mem. Music Educators Nat. Conf., Idaho Music Educators Assn. (chmn. higher edn. 1978-86, 97-98, pres. 1988-90, chair state solo contest 1990-92), Internat. Clarinet Assn. (sec. 1978-84, v.p. 1986-88, pres. 1996-98), Coll. Music Soc., Nat. Assn. Coll. Wind and Percussion Instrs. (chmn. Idaho 1978-88), Nat. Assn. Schs. Music (sec. N.W. region 1979-82, vis. evaluator 1990—, chair N.W. region 1991-94), Rotary (pres. Gate City chpt. 1994-95). Office: Idaho State U Dept Music PO Box 8099 Pocatello ID 83209-0001 E-mail: stanalan@isu.edu.

STANEK, BRUNO L. software developer, author, commentator; b. Rorschach, Switzerland, Nov. 9, 1943; s. Leopold A. and Gertrud (Siebert) S.; m. Erika E. Schraner, Nov. 28, 1979; children: Ganymed, Oliver. Diploma in math., Swiss Fed. Inst. Tech., Zurich, 1968, DSc in Math., 1971. Asst. Inst. Applied Math., Swiss Fed. Inst. Tech., 1968-70; freelance book and TV author, Switzerland, 1971-75; prof. math., physics and computer sci. Engring. Coll., Brugg, Switzerland, 1976-79; founder, CEO, Ärztesoftware, Arth, Switzerland, 1980-2001, Astrosoftware, Arth, 1994—. Space commentator Swiss Nat. TV and other stas., 1968—; over 1000 pub. lectures on space and astronomy, Switzerland, Germany, 1968—; med. emergency software planner for Swiss cities, 1991-96. Author: Der Weg ins All, 1969, Kursbuch für das Sonnensystem, 1971, Bildatlas des Sonnensystems, 1974, Space Shuttle, 1975, Neuland Mars, 1976, Hallwag-Taschenbuch 111, 1977, Space Art-Weltraumkunst, 1980, Raumfahrtlexikon, 1983 (CD- and DVD-ROM yearly edit. 1998—), Planetenlexikon, 1979 (last edit. 1992, also yearly edit. 1998—), Sparer leben gefährlich, 1987, Tragbare Opfer, 1988, (software) Air Traffic Control Simulator, 1996, (med. software) Ganymed; contbr. numerous articles on space and astronomy to Swiss and fgn. publs. Mem. supervising bd. high sch. graduation KKS Schwyz, 1996—. Mem. Swiss Frieds U.S.A., Lions (pres. Zurich 1977-78). Avocations: studying United States culture, travel. Home and Office: Wybergliweg 62 CH-6415 Arth Switzerland E-mail: Bruno@Stanek.ch.

STANEK, GENA STIVER, critical care clinical nurse specialist; b. Washington, Feb. 9, 1958; d. William Earl and Norma A. (Cull) Stiver; m. Andrew Henry Stanek, July 1, 1984; children: Amiel Benjamin, Alyssa Anna. BSN, U. Md., 1980, MS, 1985. RN, Md. Clin. nurse specialist Johns Hopkins Hosp., Balt.; clin. nurse critical care Shock Trauma Ctr. U. Md. Med. System; rsch. cons.. U. Md.; clin. nurse specialist shock trauma U. Md. Med. Sys. Mem. AANN, AACN, ASPEN, U. Md. Sch. of Nursing Alumni Assn., Phi Kappa Phi, Sigma Theta Tau. Home: 5217 Lynngate Ct Columbia MD 21044-1437

STANFEL, LARRY EUGENE, business educator; b. Waukegan, Ill., Feb. 6, 1940; s. Paul P. and Lola C. Stanfel; m. Jane Ellen Yetter, Sept. 1, 1962; children: Kenneth, Larry, Christine, Rebecca. BS in Math., Ill. Inst. Tech., 1962; MS in Indsl. Engring. & Mgmt. Sci., Northwestern U., 1965, PhD, 1966. Asst. prof. indsl. engring. U. Fla., Gainesville, 1966-69; assoc. prof. mech. engring. Colo. State U., Fort Collins, 1969-72; prof. indsl. engring. U. Tex., Arlington, 1972-80; prof. mgmt. Clarkson Coll., Potsdam, N.Y., 1980-84; prof. quantitative bus. analysis La. State U., Baton Rouge, 1984-88; prof. mgmt. sci. U. Ala., Tuscaloosa, 1988—. Cons. Def. Info. Systems Agy., Reston, Va., 1988-90, 92, 94, Bur. Land Mgmt., Denver, 1991, Esca Corp., Bellevue, Wash., 1981-85, U.S. Army, White Sands Missile Range, 1969, 72-73, 77. Author: Optimization Techniques, 1975, Analysis of Systems in Operations Research, 1975; contbr. articles to profl. jours. Fellow Royal Norwegian Coun. for Sci. and Engring., 1975-77, 94-95. Mem. Inst. for Mgmt. Sci., Ops. Rsch. Soc. Am., Internat. Info. Mgmt. Assn., Sigma Xi, Beta Gamma Sigma. Roman Catholic. Avocations: mineralogy, writing, skiing, short wave radio. Office: U Ala Mgs Dept Tuscaloosa AL 35487-0001 Address: Myrdalskogen 288 5095 Ulset Norway

STANFILL, DENNIS CAROTHERS, business executive; b. Centerville, Tenn., Apr. 1, 1927; s. Sam Broome and Hattie (Carothers) S.; m. Therese Olivieri, June 29, 1951; children: Francesca, Sara, Dennis Carothers. BS, U.S. Naval Acad., 1949; MA (Rhodes scholar), Oxford U., 1953; LHD (hon.), U. S.C. Corporate finance specialist Lehman Bros., N.Y.C., 1959-65; v.p. finance Times Mirror Co., Los Angeles, 1965-69; exec. v.p. 20th Century-Fox Film Corp., 1969-71, pres., 1971, chmn. bd., chief exec. officer, 1971-81; pres. Stanfill, Bowen & Co., 1981-90; chmn. bd. dirs., chief exec. officer AME, Inc., 1990-91; co-chmn., co-CEO Metro-Goldwyn-Mayer, Inc., 1992-93; sr. advisor Credit Lyonnais, 1993-95; pres. Dennis Stanfill Co., 1995—. Trustee Calif. Inst. Tech.; bd. dirs. Weingart Found. Served to lt. USN, 1949-59; politico-mil. policy div. Office Chief Naval Ops., 1956-59.

STANFILL, LATAYNE COLVETT, non-fiction writer; b. Atwood, Tenn., Apr. 23, 1914; d. Benjamin Franklin and Geneva Wilson (Carter) Colvett; m. Homer Lawrence Stanfill, June 4, 1932 (dec. Mar. 1990); children: Lawrence Colvett, Suzanne Latayne. Grad., Alamo (Tenn.) H.S., 1929. Pres., hist. rschr., cons. Heirloom Press, Glendale, Calif., 1990—. Author: Colvett Family Chronicles: The History of the Colvett Family of Tennessee 1630-1990, 1991, Wings of Morning, a coll. of poetry and prose, 1995; contbr. articles to hist. and geneal. mags. Dist. collection chmn. L.A. area ARC, 1950-52; active various ch. and mission activities, Los Angeles County, 1972-83. Mem. DAR (chaplain 1989-99, Calif. State Librs. award 1992), Daus. of War of 1812, Hugueonot Soc. of Founders of Manakin in the Colony of Virginia 1699, Calif. Cameo Club. Avocations: reading, painting, sewing, poetry readings, gardening. Office: Heirloom Press PO Box 250916 Glendale CA 91225-0916

STANFILL, PATRICIA MAE, accountant; b. Bowman, N.D., Feb. 9, 1975; d. Bob L. and Dixie L. Justice; m. Jay T. Stanfill, July 13, 1996. BS magna cum laude, Nat. Coll., 1997. CPA. Acct. Robert Martin, atty. at law, Rapid City, S.D., 1996-97, Forest Products Distributors, Rapid City, 1997, Ortt and Co. CPAs, Billings, Mont., 1997—. Office: 1437 Wyoming Ave Billings MT 59102-5333

STANFORD, HENRY KING, college president; b. Atlanta, Apr. 22, 1916; s. Henry King and Annie Belle (Callaway) S.; m. Laurie Ruth King, Sept. 19, 1936; children: Henry, Lowry, Rhoda, Peyton. AB, Emory U., 1936, MA, 1940, LLD, 1961; postgrad., U. Heidelberg, Germany, 1936-37; MS in Govt. Mgmt. (Alfred P. Sloan Found. fellow 1941-43), U. Denver, 1943, LLD, 1962; PhD (Tax Found. fellow 1943-44), NYU, 1949; DCL Jacksonville (Fla.) U, 1963; LLD, Loyola U., New Orleans, 1968, U. Akron, Kyung Hee U., Seoul, Korea, 1968, Rollins Coll., 1977, Barry Coll., 1979; DHL, U. Tampa, 1969; DLitt, U. R.I., 1970; D in Higher Edn., U. Miami, 1981; DHL, Birmingham-So. Coll., 1987. Instr., Emory U., 1937-40; asst. prof. Ga. Inst. Tech., 1940-41; instr. NYU, 1943-46; prof. pub. administrn., also dir. sch. pub. administrn. U. Denver, 1946-48; pres. Ga. Southwestern Coll., Americus, 1948-50; dir. U. Center in Ga., 1950-52; asst. chancellor U. System of Ga., 1952-53; pres. Ga. State Coll. for Women, Milledgeville, 1953-56; chief of party NYU-Internat. Cooperation Adminstrn. Contract, Ankara, Turkey, 1956-57; pres. Birmingham-So. Coll., 1957-62, U. Miami, Fla., 1962-81, pres. emeritus, 1981—; interim pres. U. Ga., 1986-87, pres. emeritus, 1987—. Bd. dirs. DWG, Southeastern Pub. Service; research asst. Tax Found., N.Y.C., 1943-44; staff N.A.M. com. exec., 1944-46; chmn. Fed. Res. Bank Atlanta, 1969, 72 Trustee Knight Found., 1982-97; vice chmn. Invest-in-Am., 1984-86, chmn. 1986-87; chmn. Dade County Community Rels. Bd., 1969-71; bd. visitors Air U., Maxwell AFB, Ala., 1963-66; trustee Caribbean Resources Devel. Found., 1978-85, pres., 1978-83, chmn., 1983-84; chmn. Jimmy Carter Hist. Site Adv. Commn., 1990-2001. Decorated Star of Africa medal Liberia; officer Order of Merit Fed. Republic of Germany; recipient Eleanor Roosevelt-Israel Humanitarian award, 1965, Outstanding Civilian Svc. award U.S. Army, 1966, Silver Medallion Fla. Region NCCJ, 1968, Ga. Region, 1987, Disting. Svc. award Ga. Coll., 1979, hon. alumnus, 1996, C.H.I.E.F. award Ind. Colls. and Univs. Fla., 1983, Sibley award Ga. Mil. Coll., 1991, Emory medal, 1991, Adrian Dominican Ednl. Leadership award Barry U., 1991, Atlanta Boys' High Alumnus award, 1992, James Blair Humanitarian award Americus, Ga., 1993, Westmeyer award pub. svc. NYU, 1993. Mem. So. Assn. Colls. and Schs. (chmn. commn. colls. 1960-62, pres. 1972-73), Nat. Assn. Ind. Colls. and Univs. (dir. 1976-80), Assn. Caribbean Univs. and Rsch. Insts. (v.p. 1965-79), Golden Key Honor Soc. (bd. dirs. 1982-91), Internat. Assn. Univ. Pres. (exec. com. 1977-81), Delta Phi Alpha, Phi Beta Kappa, Omicron Delta Kappa, Phi Sigma Iota, Alpha Kappa Psi, Phi Mu Alpha, Phi Kappa Phi, Rotary (pres. 1984-85). Methodist. Office: PO Box 1065 Americus GA 31709-1065 *The greatest literary influence on my life has been Goethe's Faust, Part I. Reading it in the original German as a college student, I was struck immediately with the demands Faust made of himself in concluding the contract with Mephistopheles: he would lose his soul if he ever chose a "bed of ease," succumbed to flattery, opted for pleasure alone, or said to any one moment, "Linger awhile; you are so nice!" In other words, whenever he ceased striving, he was lost.*

STANFORD, JACK ARTHUR, biological station administrator; b. Delta, Colo., Feb. 18, 1947; s. LeRoy and Wilma (Tucker) S.; children: Jake, Chriss. BS in Fisheries Sci., Colo. State U., 1969, MS in Limnology, 1971; PhD in Limnology, U. Utah, 1975. Fisheries biologist Alaska-Fish and Game, Dillingham, 1968-69; rsch. biologist and limnologist instr. U. Mont., Missoula, 1973-74, dir. Flathead Lake Biol. Sta. Polson, 1980—, research prof. zoology Missoula, 1983-86, Jessie M. Bierman prof. Mont., 1986—; prof. N. Tex. State U., Denton, 1974-81. Panelist div. biotic system NSF, Washington, 1985—; chmn. Coun. of Aquatic Scis., 1998-2002. Editor: Ecology of Regulated Streams, 1979, Groundwater Ecology, 1994; editor Regulated Rivers: Rsch. and Mgmt., 1985-99, Ecol. Applications, 1996-2002; contbr. over 120 articles to profl. jours. Advisor Nature Conservancy, Boulder, Colo., 1982—. Named Bierman Prof. Ecology U. Mont., 1986—; grantee EPA, U.S. Army, U.S. Bur. Reclamation, NSF, U.S. Nat. Park Svc.; disting. scholar U. Mont., 1997. Fellow AAAS: mem. Mont. Acad. Aci., Am. Soc. Limnology and Oceanography, Ecol. Soc. Am. (pub. affairs com., 1984—), N.Am. Benthological Soc. (exec. com. 1979, 1988-89, pres. 1997). Avocations: fly fishing, skiing. Office: U Mont Flathead Lake Biol Sta 311 Bio Station Ln Polson MT 59860-9659 E-mail: stanford@selway.umt.edu.

STANFORD, JANE HERRING, management consultant and educator, author; b. Lockhart, Tex., Dec. 17, 1939; d. John William and Frances Argyra (Cheatham) H. Jr.; m. Rube Valton Stanford, Sept. 17, 1966; children: (Steven) Scott, Lisa Ann. BS, Texas A&M U., Kingsville, 1965; MS in Counseling, Texas A&M U., Corpus Christi, 1982; MBA, Texas A&M U., Kingsville, 1988; PhD in Orgn. Theory and Strategic Mgmt., U. North Tex., 1992. Cert. secondary sch. tchr., coun., Tex. Tchr. h.s. pub. sch., Tobstown, Tex., 1965—78; owner, mgr. retail bus., Portland, 1978-81; instr. cmty. coll., Corpus Christi, 1981—88; tchg. fellow U. North Tex., Denton, 1988-90; assoc. prof. bus. policy and internat. mgmt., pres. faculty senate Texas A&M U., Kingsville, 1990—99, full mem. grad. faculty, 1992-99, grad. rsch. advisor, MBA program, Coll. Bus., 1992-98, head, asst. v.p. acad. affairs, 1998-99, ret., 1999; mgmt. cons. Strategic Mgmt. Solutions, Inc., 1999—, pres., primary cons., 2000—; adj. prof., mgmt. Texas A&M U., 2002—. Chair univ. assessment, budgeting and planning com. Tex. A&M U., 1997—98; internat. lectr. strategic mgmt. within internat. context, Columbia, Argentina; workshop leader and participant in acad. issues; paper presenter internat. conf. Soc. for the Advancement Mgmt., 1998—2002. Author: Building Competitiveness: U.S. Expatriate Management Strategies in Mexico, 1995; contbr. articles to profl. jours. and conf. procs. Finalist Disting. Svc. award, Tex. A&M U., 1997, 1998, 1999; named Leadership Corpus Christi Class of XXX, 2001—02; fellow Sys. Chancellor's fellow in leadership in higher edn. program, Tex. A&M U., 1997. Mem.: Soc. ADvancement Mgmt., Acad. Mgmt., Inst. Mgmt. Cons., Strategic Mgmt. Soc., Delta Signa Pi, Kappa Delta Pi (life). Presbyterian. Avocations: book collecting, photography, art, travel. Home: 13526 Carlos Fifth Ct Corpus Christi TX 78418-6913 Office: Strategic Mgmt Solutions Inc 13526 Carlos Fifth Ct Corpus Christi TX 78418-6913 E-mail: planyourbiz@aol.com.

STANFORD, JOSEPH STEPHEN, diplomat, lawyer, educator; b. Montreal, Que., Can., May 7, 1934; s. Walter Albert and Geraldine (O'Loghlin) S.; m. Agnes Mabelle Walker, Nov. 16, 1957; children: Kevin, Karen, Michael. BA, U. Montreal, 1953; LLB, U. Alta., Edmonton, Can., 1956. Bar: Alta. 1957; called to Queen's Counsel 1984. Mem. Greenan, Cooney & Stanford, Calgary, Alta., 1957-60; joined Fgn. Svc., Dept. External Affairs, Govt. of Can., 1960; amb. to Israel Tel Aviv, 1979-82; also Can. high commr. to Cyprus; asst. dep. min. for Africa and Mid. East Dept. External Affairs, Ottawa, Ont., 1983-85, asst. dep. min. for Europe, 1985-87, assoc. undersec. of state for external affairs, 1987-88; dep. solicitor gen. Govt. of Can., 1988-93; ret., 1994; sr fellow, conflict mgr. Canadian Center Mgmt. Devel., Ottawa, 1993-96; assoc., bd. dirs. Conflict Mgmt. Group, Cambridge, Mass., 1994-97, chmn. bd. dirs., 1997-99. Cons. Conflict Mgmt. Group, Cambridge, Mass., 1994—97. Contbr. articles on internat. law, fgn. investment and conflict resolution to profl. jours. Roman Catholic. Avocations: wilderness canoeing, tennis, skiing. Home: 58 Amberwood Cres Ottawa ON Canada K2E 7C3 E-mail: stanfrdj@magi.com.

STANFORD, KATHLEEN THERESA, secondary school educator; b. Belize City, Belize, Sept. 28, 1933; d. Frederick Gill and Ila Mae (Cherrington) Hyde; m. Herman Emanuel Stanford., Oct. 3, 1970 (dec. Feb., 1989). Student (summer), S. We. La. U., Lafayette, 1958; BA, Seton Hill Coll., 1962; student (summer), Xavier U., New Orleans, 1956, 68; postgrad., Southern U. and A&M Coll., 1962, 67, Adelphi U., 1988, C.W. Post, N.Y., 1988. Cert. sci. tchr., La. (life). Tchr. Mem. Sisters of Holy Family Order, various cities, U.S. & Belize, 1953-69; sci. tchr., moderator Sisters of Holy Family, Grand Coteau, La., 1967-68, Lafayette, 1968-70; laicized, 1970; sci. tchr., sponsor of sci. fair N.Y.C. Bd. of Edn., Bklyn., 1981—. Sci. coord. La. Sci. Acad., Lafayette, 1968-70; mem. U.F.T. /IHS sci. com., N.Y.C., 1984-85. Contbr. poetry to Poetry Mags., 1974—. Hon. mem. Pres. Clinton's 2d Term Com., Washington, 1997; sci. sponsor Ford Future Scientists of Am., 1968, Dist. Sci. Fair, Bklyn., 1984; sec. Belize Parkfest of N.Y., Inc., 1990-92 Recipient Commendation for pupils 20th Internat. Sci. Fair, 1969, poetry awards Am. Poetry Assn., 1989, 90, cert. for leadership, Dem. Nat. Com., Washington, 1997. Mem. Belize Cosmopolitan Benevolent Assn. (v.p.). Democrat. Avocations: writing poetry, photography, bird watching, swimming, walking, singing.

STANG, ARNOLD, actor, director, writer; b. N.Y.C., Sept. 28, 1928; s. Harold Louis and Anna (Chest) S.; m. JoAnne Taggart, Sept. 21, 1949; children: David Donald, Deborah Jane Stang-Healy. Ind. actor, dir., writer, N.Y.C., 1936—. Actor: (Broadway prodns.) Front Page, A Funny Thing Happened On the Way to the Forum, Wallflower, All in Favor, (TV shows) Bonanza, Ed Sullivan Show, McHale's Navy, Bewitched, Milton Berle Show, Jack Benny Show, Jackie Gleason Show, Top Cat, Emergency, Robert Klein Show, Playhouse 90, Frank Sinatra Spls., Bob Hope Spls., What's My Line, Bill Cosby Show, Tales From The Dark Side, numerous others, (stock theatrical prodns.) Don't Drink the Water, Death Knocks, Charley's Aunt, Finian's Rainbow, Three Men on a Horse, The Gazebo, Wish You Were Here, Pajama Game, Let 'Em Eat Cake, Anything Goes, Luv, Tobacco Road, Play It Again, Sam, Annie Get Your Gun, (starring film roles) Double for Della, Arnold the Benedict, Honorable Myrtle, The Expectant Father, Dondi, The Wonderful World of the Brothers Grimm, The Aristocats, Hello Down There, Alakazam the Great, The Man With the Golden Arm, The Cottonwood, Hercules in New York, Skidoo, My Sister Eileen, Seven Days Leave, Let's Go Steady, It's A Mad, Mad, Mad World, Dennis the Menace, numerous featured roles; rec. artist numerous albums including Winnie & Baby Pooh, Winnie the Pooh, Peter and the Wolf, Arnold Stang Meets Gus Edwards, Beezy the Sneezy Bee, The Hippy Hippo, Chester the Chimp, Further Adventures of Harry the Horse. Mem. Screen Actors Guild, Acad. Motion Picture Arts and Scis., Actors Equity Assn., AFTRA. Clubs: Players (N.Y.C.). Avocations: gardening, poetry, carpentry, social work. Office: 350 E 54th St Apt 1-h New York NY 10022-5049

STANG, ROLF KRISTIAN, vocalist, teacher, writer, advertising executive; b. Rockford, Ill., Sept. 19, 1939; s. Trygve Ingvald and Kirsten (Anfinsen-Kristiansen) S. BA, Augustana Coll., 1961; MA, Columbia U., 1963; performance/repertoire cert., opera div., Musikhochschule, Hamburg, Germany, 1964. Vocal soloist Christoph-Weber-Barock Ensemble, Hamburg, 1965-67; German and music faculty Coll. of White Plains, N.Y., 1968-73; sec. Internat. Percy Grainger Soc., White Plains, 1974-79, pres., 1979—. Music critic Norway Times, N.Y.C., 1970—; advt. exec. The Frank Vos Co AS/VP, 1973-83; lectr. recital Songs of Frederick Delius, Cambridge U., 1984—; multimedia lectr. on career of Wagnerian singer Kirsten Flagstad, 1995—; lectr. on life and music of English composer Frederick Delius and singer of Delius' songs, 1966—. Translator Songs of Grieg, 1988-93; composer "Backward Tracings" (for solo voice, chorus and orchestra)/commd. Tallahassee Sesquicentennial Assn., 1974, "Train Window Thoughts" (song cycle for soprano/15 stringed instruments), "Hymns in Praise of Night/Nietzschean Nocturnes" (for chorus/6 instruments), Lied/Romanse Art Song and opera rep. (Am., English, German, Norwegian, Swedish, 1968—); concert vocalist appearances 44 states, numerous countries in recital, 1963—; author and actor touring with one-man play on Norwegian composer Edvard Grieg, U.S., Norway, Eng., 1993—; Millennium characterization of Viking-age voyager Icelander Leif Eriksson, 2000—; touring as Danish author Hans Christian Andersen telling his stories throughout U.S., 1994—; touring as Askeladden throughout U.S. telling Norwegian fairytales and singing traditional Norse songs, 1995—. Vol. Cath. Ctr. for Deaf, N.Y.C., 1975-79, Children to the Beach prog., N.Y.C., 1978-83, Reaching Out to the Homeless, N.Y.C., 1988—. Created knight (Norway); decorated St. Olav medal King Harald V of Norway, 1997; inductee Scandinavian-Am. Hall of Fame, 1998; recipient Leif Eriksson citation, 2000. Mem. SAG, Am. Choral Dirs. Assn. (life), Nordmanns Forbundet/Norsemen's Fedn. (hon., life), Delius Assn. of Fla. (life), Delius Soc. of Great Britain, Sons of Norway Internat., Delius Soc. of Phila. (life), Am.-Scandinavian Soc. of N.Y., Soc. for Advancement of Scandinavian Studies (life), Edvard Grieg Soc. Great Britain (hon., life). Lutheran. Avocations: furniture making, carpentry, gardening, promoting Nordic culture and music. Home: The Monks Cell 29 W 65th St New York NY 10023-6630 E-mail: rolf_k_stang@hotmail.com.

STANGE, JAMES HENRY, architect; b. Davenport, Iowa, May 25, 1930; s. Henry Claus and Norma (Ballhorn) S.; m. Mary Suanne Peterson, Dec. 12, 1954; children: Wade Weston, Drew Dayton, Grant Owen. BArch, Iowa State U., 1954. Registered architect, Iowa, Nebr., Kans., Mo., Okla. Designer Davis & Wilson, Lincoln, Nebr., 1954-62, v.p., 1962-68; v.p., sec. Davis, Fenton, Stange, Darling, 1977-92, pres., 1976—93, chmn., 1978—94. Mem. State Bd. Examiners for Engrs. and Architects, 1989-92, chmn. region V NCARB, 1991. Prin. works include Dorsey Labs., 1960, East H.S., Lincoln, 1966, Lincoln Gen. Hosp., 1967, Lincoln Airport Terminal, Sq. D Mfg. Plant, Lincoln, Bryan Meml. Hosp. (masterplans and additions), 1970, 80, 90, Bryan Ambulatory Care Ctr. Med. Office Bldg., Same Day Surgery Conf. Ctr., Parking Garage, 1993-95, Nebr. Wesleyan Theatre, Lincoln, Hasting (Nebr.) YMCA, various structures U. Nebr., Lincoln, ctr. and br. offices Am. Charter Fed. Savs. & Loan, S.E. H.S. (addition), 1984, U. Nebr. Animal Sci. Bldg., 1987, Beadle Ctr., UNL, 1991, Carriage Park Parking Garage, 1995. V.p. Nebr. Jazz Orch., 1995, 2000—, pres., 1997, Nebr. Art Assn., 1996—99; deacon 1st Presbyn. Ch., 1960, chmn. bd. trustees, 1968—90, elder, 1972—87, 1997—99, chmn. property com., 1998—2000; bd. dirs. Capitol Assn. Retarded Citizens, 1968—72, 1994—, pres., 1970; chmn. United Way Campaign, 1986, chmn. bd., 1988; chmn. endowment com. Bryan Hosp. Found., 1988—90; bd. dirs. Delta Dental, 1987—92, Downtown Lincoln Assn., 1985—94, mem. steering com., 1989; mem. mayor's com. Study Downtown Redevel., 1989, pub. bldg. commn., masterplan rev. com., 1994; pres. Lincoln Ctr. Assn., 1979. Recipient Honor award Conf. on Religious Architecture-First Plymouth Ch. Addition, 1969, also numerous state and nat. awards from archtl. orgns. Mem. AIA (Nebr. bd. dirs. 1964-65, treas. 1965, sec. 1966, v.p. 1967, pres. Nebr. 1968, mem. com. on architecture for health 1980-94, Regional Design award 1976, 88, 96), Am. Assn. Health Planners, Interfaith Forum on Religion, Art, Architecture, Lincoln C. of C. (bd. dirs. 1982), Exec. Club (pres. 1972), Crucible Club, 12 Club, Hillcrest Country Club (pres. 1977), Lincoln U. Club (sec. 1992, bd. dirs. 1991-97, pres. 1995, 96). Avocations: travel, photography, golf. Home: 3545 Calvert St Lincoln NE 68506-5744 Office: Davis Design 211 N 14th St Lincoln NE 68508-1616 E-mail: JimSustange@aol.com.

STANGE, KURT C. medical educator; MD, Albany Med. Coll., 1983; PhD, U. N.C., 1989. Diplomate Am. Bd. Family Practice, Am. Bd. Preventive Medicine. Prof. family medicine, epidemiology, biostatistics, oncology and sociology Case Western Reserve U., Cleve.; physician, tchr., rschr. dept. family medicine U. Hosps. Cleve.; assoc. dir. prevention, control and population rsch. Ireland Cancer Ctr. at U. Hosps. Cleve. and Case Western Reserve U.; dir., Family Medicine Res. Div. Case Western Reserve U., Cleve.

Mem. Inst. Medicine, Rsch. Assn. Practicing Physicians. Office: Case Western Reserve U Sch Medicine Dept Family Medicine 10900 Euclid Ave Cleveland OH 44106-1712 also: Dept Family Medicine U Circle Rsch Ctr 11001 Cedar Ave Ste 306 Cleveland OH 44106-3043 Fax: 216-368-4348. E-mail: kcs@po.cwru.edu.*

STANGE, TERRENCE V. education educator; b. Aberdeen, S.D., Sept. 6, 1951; m. Cheryll Lynn Stange, Aug. 30, 1975. BS, No. State U., 1975, MS, 1981; PhD, U. Okla., 1993. Instr. Redfield (S.D.) State Hosp., 1975-78; remedial tchr. Simmons Jr. H.S., Aberdeen, 1978-82; adj. prof., rsch. asst. U. Okla., Norman, 1986-93; asst. prof. Ohio State U., Lima, 1993-96, Ark. State U., Jonesboro, 1996-2000; assoc. prof. Midwestern State U., Wichita Falls, Tex., 2000—. Reading cons. Ohio Lit. Coun., Lima, 1994-95; program cons. edn. program County Econ. Devel., Lima, 1994-96; mem. adv. coun. ednl. success program Valley View Schs., Jonesboro, 1997-2000. Contbr. articles to profl. jours. Dir., vol. tutored children Faith-based Social Outreach Reading Program, Jonesboro, 1996-2000; book buddy reading to K-4 students Nettleton Pub. Schs., Jonesboro, 1999; appt. editor newsletter Profs. of Reading Tchrs. Educators, Whitewater, Wis., 2000—. Mem. AAUP, ASCD, Internat. Reading Assn., Tchg. as a Rsch. Profession, Org. of Tchr. Educators in Reading, Mid-South Rsch. Assn., Nat. Coun. Tchrs. of English, Phi Delta Kappa, Kappa Delta Pi. Democrat. Lutheran. Avocations: rollerblading, cross-country skiing, drawing, biking, reading. Office: 3410 Taft Blvd Wichita Falls TX 76308-2095 Home: PO Box 1147 Wichita Falls TX 76307-1147 E-mail: terrence.stange@nexus.mwsu.edu.

STANGEL, PHILIP DAVID, secondary school educator; s. Benjamin Wencil and Beverly Ann Stangel; m. Mary Lee Egger, Apr. 12, 1959; children: David, Matthew. MusB Edn., St. Norbert Coll., De Pere, Wis., 1979. Cert. instrumental music edn. Wis., 1979. Grades 7 - 9 band instr. Green Bay (Wis.) Pub. Schools, 1979—80; grades 5 - 12 band instr. Freedom (Wis.) Area Pub. Schools, 1980—99; grades 9 - 12 band instr. / woodwind emphasis Pulaski (Wis.) Cmty. Schools, 1999—. Recipient Teachers are Tops award, NBC Channel 26, 1998—99. Mem.: NEA, Green Bay City Band, Nat. Band Assn., N.Am. Saxophone Alliance, Am. Fedn. Musicians, Music Educators Nat. Conf., Wis. Band Masters Assn. (pres. 1997—98), Harley Owners Group, Nat. Railroad Mus. Democrat. Roman Catholic. Avocations: tour guide, bicycling, reading, performing. Office: Pulaski High Sch 1040 South Saint Augustine Street Pulaski WI 54162 Office Fax: 920-822-6707. E-mail: pdstangel@pulaski.k12.wi.us.

STANGER, ILA, writer, editor; b. N.Y.C. d. Jack Simon and Shirley Ruth (Nadelson) S. BA, Bklyn. Coll., 1961. Feature and travel editor Harpers Bazaar, N.Y.C., 1969-75; exec. editor Travel and Leisure mag., 1975-85; editor in chief Food and Wine Mag., 1985-89, Travel and Leisure mag., N.Y.C., 1990-93; mng. editor More mag. Writer on arts, features and travel. Mem. Am. Soc. Mag. Editors Office: More Magazine 125 Park Ave New York NY 10017-5529 E-mail: istanger@mdp.com.

STANGER, ROBERT HENRY, psychiatrist, educator; b. N.Y.C., N.Y., May 19, 1937; s. Sidney and Mary (Strassner) S.; m. Andrea Rogin, Aug. 28, 1960; children: Lee Ann, David Neal. AB, Guilford Coll., 1959; MD, Emory U., 1964. Intern in internal medicine Wake Forest U., 1964-65; resident in gen. psychiatry U. Pitts., Western Psychiat. Inst. and Clinic, 1967-70; pvt. practice gen. psychiatry Monroeville, Pa., 1970-2001; med. dir. Allegheny Valley Mental Health-Mental Retardation Ctr., New Kensington, 1970-76; dir. psychiat. svcs. Allegheny Valley Hosp., Natrona Heights, 1983-96, chmn. dept. psychiatry and behavioral medicine, 1983-96; pvt. practice, 1984-97. Clin. instr. psychiatry U. Pitts. Sch. Medicine, 1970-79, clin. asst. prof., 1980—; cons. Westinghouse Elec. Corp., East Pitts., 1977-87; mem. ethics com. human rsch. Allegheny Valley Hosp., 1976-97; chmn. dept. psychiatry Citizens Gen. Hosp., 1978-88. Capt. M.C., U.S. Army, 1965-67, Vietnam. Mem. AMA, Am. Psychiat. Assn. (del. 1986-88), Pa. Psychiat. Soc. (councilor 1976-79, treas. 1979-80, sec. 1980-81, v.p. 1981-82, pres.-elect 1982-83, pres. 1983-84), Pitts. Psychiat. Soc. (councilor 1974-76, sec. 1977-78, pres.-elect 1978-79, pres. 1979-80), Allegheny County Med. Soc. Home and Office: 3910 Old William Penn Hwy Pittsburgh PA 15235-4837

STANGO, JULIETTE MARY, composer, music publisher, educator; b. Phila., Aug. 15, 1962; d. Dominick A. and Rita F. Stango. Diploma in arts, Sessione Senese Musica l'Arte, Siena, Italy, 1990. Composer, pub. Juliette Stango Pub., Phila., 1990—. Staff condr., composer Sessione Senese per La Musica e L'Arte, 1987, 90; MMC rec. artist Slovak Radio and TV Orch.; commd. work for Musica 2000 The Symphony Orch. Composer: (aria) Hopeless, 1990, (solo piano work) Nice Weather for a War, 1992; commd. composer (orchestral composition) Sol Per Dirti Adio, 1994; commd. composer and lyricist (aria) Heathcliff's Lament, 1998; commd. by Alberto Barbetti Pub., Siena, 1987, 93, Millennial Arts Prodn., N.Y.C., 1998; live TV performance Siena Palio, RAI, 1986; with Music Art Co., N.Y.C., 1987-88; music therapist Golden Slipper Uptown Home, Phila., 1988-90, HCR-Manor Care, Huntingdon Valley, Pa., 1997-99. Mem. World Affairs Coun. Phila. Democrat. Roman Catholic. Avocations: swimming, travel, languages and cultural studies. Office: 9747 Susan Rd Philadelphia PA 19115-2918

STANHOPE, RICHARD GRAHAM, pediatric endocrinologist, consultant, pilot; b. London, June 12, 1950; s. Richard Frank and Marion Logan (Broad) S.; children: Oliver Every, Sophie Caroline. BSc in Biochemistry with honors, London U., 1971, MD, 1989; MB BS, St. Bartholmew's Hosp., London, 1974. Lic. comml. pilot, airline transport pilot. Flying instr., 1973—; pre-registration house physician St. Bartholmew's Hosp., 1974; registrar various hosps., 1976-82; registrar in pediats. Ctrl. Middlesex Hosp./Middlesex Hosp., 1982-84; rsch. fellow Middlesex Hosp., 1984-86; lectr. pediat. endocrinology Gt. Ormond St./Inst. Child Health, London, 1986-89, cons., 1989—. Airline pilot capt. Dan Air Lines, London, 1980-85, Air Europe Ltd., London, 1987-91. European editor Jour. Pediat. Endocrinology and Metabolism, 2000—; contbr. more than 200 articles to profl. jours. Freedom City London, Guildhall, 1985—. Fellow Royal Coll. Physicians, Royal Soc. Medicine (sec. endocrine sect.), Royal Coll. Pediats. and Child Health; mem. Royal Coll. Obs., Royal Aero. Soc., Soc. Endocrinology (joint program sec. 1994-98), Am. Dndocrine Soc., European Soc. Paediat. Endocrinology, South African Pediat. Assn. Office: Gt Ormond St Hosp Children Dept Endocrinology London WC1N 3JH England E-mail: r.stanhope@ich.ucl.ac.uk.

STANISCI, THOMAS WILLIAM, lawyer; b. Bkln., Nov. 16, 1928; s. Vito and Angela Marie (Martino) S.; m. Catherine Ellen Cullen, June 4, 1955; children: Thomas, Marianne, Ellen, William, Peter. BA, St. John's Coll. Men, 1949, JD, 1953, postgrad., 1954. Bar: N.Y. 1953, U.S. Dist. Ct. (so. and ea. dists.) N.Y. 1956, U.S. Supreme Ct., 1981; diplomate Am. Bd. Profl. Liability Attys. (trustee). Assoc. Diblasi Marasco & Simone, White Plains, N.Y., 1954-60; mem. Simone Brant & Stanisci, 1960-66, Shayne Dachs Stanisci & Harwood, Mineola, N.Y., 1966-83; sr. mem. Shayne Dachs Stanisci Corker & Sauer, 1983—. Lectr. Practising Law Inst., 1975-79; instr., lectr. Am. Mgmt. Assn., 1976-77, N.Y. State Bar Assn., 1993, 94; guest lectr. Adelphi U., Hofstra U., 1975-79; guest speaker, panelist network and local TV programs. Contbr. articles in field. With U.S. Army, 1950-52. Mem. Am. Arbitration Assn., Am. Bd. Trial Advs., Nassau Suffolk Trial Lawyers Assn. (bd. dirs. 1978-90, treas. 1991, sec. 1992, vice chmn. 1993-94, chmn. 1995-96), Nassau County Bar Assn. (bd. dirs. 1993-96, lectr. acad. law), Columbian Lawyers.

STANISLAO, JOSEPH, consulting engineer, educator; b. Manchester, Conn., Nov. 21, 1928; s. Eduardo and Rose (Zaccaro) S.; m. Bettie Chloe Carter, Sept. 6, 1960. BS, Tex. Tech. U., 1957; MS, Pa. State U., 1959; Eng.ScD, Columbia U., 1970. Registered profl. engr., Mass., Mont. Asst. engr. Naval Ordnance Research, University Park, Pa., 1958-59; asst. prof. N.C. State U., Raleigh, 1959-61; dir. research Darlington Fabrics Corp., Pawtucket, R.I., 1961-62; from asst. prof. to prof. U. R.I., Kingston, 1962-71; prof., chmn. dept. Cleve. State U., 1971-75; prof., dean N.D. State U., Fargo, 1975-94, acting v.p. agrl. affairs, 1983-85, asst. to pres., 1983—, dir. Engring. Computer Ctr., 1984—, prof. emeritus indsl. engring. and mgmt., 1994—; pres. XOX Corp., 1984-90; chmn. bd., chief exec. officer ATSCO, 1989-94, chief engr., 1993—; prof. emeritus N.D. State U., 1994. Adj. prof. Mont. State U., 1994—, dir. indsl. and mgmt. engring. program, 1996—, mfg. rsch., sponsored by Nat. Sci. Found. 1997—; v.p., co-owner, bd. dirs. D.T.&J., Inc., Fargo, N.D., 1999—; v.p. engring. Roll-A-Ramp and Rolla-A-Latter, 2000—; cons. to healthcare sys., 1999—. Contbr. chpts. to books, articles to profl. jours.; patentee pump apparatus, pump fluid housing; patents pending roll-a-ramp and roll-a-latter. Served to sgt. USMC, 1948-51. Recipient Sigma Xi award, 1968; Order of the Iron Ring award N.D. State U., 1972, Econ. Devel. award, 1991; USAF recognition award, 1979, ROTC appreciation award, 1982 Mem. Am. Inst. Indsl. Engrs. (sr.; v.p. 1964-65), ASME, Am. Soc. Engring. Edn. (campus coord. 1979-81), Acad. Indsl. Engrs. Tex. Tech U., Lions, Elks, Am. Legion, Phi Kappa Phi, Tau Beta Pi (advisor 1978-79). Roman Catholic. Home: 8 Park Plaza Dr Bozeman MT 59715-9343

STANKEE, GLEN ALLEN, lawyer; b. Clinton, Iowa, Sept. 27, 1953; s. Glen Earl and Marilyn Jean (Clark) S.; m. Carol Ann Prowe, Feb. 19, 1984. BSBA, Drake U., 1975; MBA, Mich. State U., 1977; JD, U. Detroit, 1979; LLM in Taxation, U. Miami, 1983. Bar: Mich. 1980, U.S. Dist. Ct. (ea. dist.) Mich. 1980, U.S. Ct. Appeals (6th cir.) 1980, U.S. Tax Ct. 1980, Fla. 1981, U.S. Ct. Appeals (11th cir.) 1981, U.S. Dist. Ct. (so. dist.) Fla. 1982, U.S. Dist. Ct. (mid. dist.) 1984, U.S. Supreme Ct. 1987; CPA, Fla. Assoc. Raymond & Dillon P.C., Detroit, 1980-81, West Palm Beach, Fla., 1981-85, prin., 1985-86, Ft. Lauderdale, 1987-93; ptnr. Ruden, McClosky, Smith, Schuster & Russell, P.A., 1993—. Contbr. articles to profl. jours. Mem. ABA, Fed. Bar Assn., Fla. Bar Assn., Mich. Bar Assn., Am. Inst. CPA's, Fla. Inst. CPA's, Palm Beach County Bar Assn., South Fla. Republican. Avocation: golf. Office: Ruden McClosky Smith Schuster & Russell PA PO Box 1900 Fort Lauderdale FL 33302-1900 E-mail: glen.stankee@ruden.com.

STANKEWICH, PAUL JOSEPH, lawyer; b. Meriden, Conn., Apr. 15, 1968; s. Joseph Paul and Linda Marie (D'Agostino) S. BA in Polit. Sci., U. Conn., 1989, BA in Econs., 1990, JD, 1993. Atty. Pfizer, Inc., Groton, Conn., 1993, pvt. practice, Storrs, 1993-95, Bergman, Horowitz & Reynolds, New Haven, 1995-2000; corp. counsel USCO Logistics, Hamden, 2000—02, assoc. gen. counsel, 2002—. Assoc. editor Conn. Jour. Internat. Law, 1992-93. Recipient Hartford County Fed. Bar Assn., 1993. Mem. ABA, Am. Corp. Coun. Assn., Conn. Bar Assn., New Havan Bar Assn. Avocations: collecting sports memorabilia, writing, hiking, travel. Office: USCO Logistics 2319 Whitney Ave Hamden CT 06518 Fax: 203-597-6890. E-mail: pstankewich@usco.com.

STANKIEWICZ, ANDRZEJ JERZY, physician, biochemistry educator; b. Lidzbark, Poland, Sept. 28, 1948; came to U.S., 1981; s. Wincenty and Zofia (Plawgo) S. MD, Med. Sch., Gdansk, Poland, 1972, PhD, 1976. Asst. prof. Med. Sch., Gdansk, 1972-77, adj. prof., lectr., 1978-81; rsch. fellow Harvard U. Med. Sch., Boston, 1981-84; resident Brown U. Sch. Medicine, Providence, 1984-87, fellow in oncology, 1987-90; pvt. practice, 1990—. Contbr. articles to profl. jours. Fellow Internat. Union Biochemistry; mem. ACP, Societas Scientiarum Gedanensis. Roman Catholic. Achievements include evolution of adenine metabolizing systems, rare abnomalities of blood coagulation interactions between hemostasis and complement system. Office: St Josephs Hosp 200 High Service Ave North Providence RI 02904-5113

STANKIEWICZ, RAYMOND, design engineer; b. Bklyn., Sept. 3, 1932; s. Benjimen and Stella (Baer) S.; m. Ann F. Carpenter, May 1, 1955; children: Michael Raymond, Stacy Ann, Raymond Thomas. Cert. tool design, SUNY, 1959; BS in Indsl. Engring., Allied Inst. Tech., 1967; MS in Engring. Tech., Am. Western U., 1982; D Design Engring., World U., 1991. Founder, owner Am. Engring. Model Co., Bohemia, L.I., N.Y., 1959-83; project engr., program mgr. Russell Plastice Tech. Inc., Lindenhurst, L.I., 1983-86, tool design mgr., machine shop mgr., 1986; sr. devel. and methods mgr. Symbol Tech., Inc., Bohemia, L.I., 1986-91; dir. ops. U.S. Air Tool Co., Inc., Ronkonkoma, 1991—. Bd. dirs. Skills Unltd., Oakdale, N.Y., 1980-84, Gurrney's Inn, Montauk, N.Y., 1985, Suffolk County Spl. Olympics, 1985-86. Cpl. U.S. Army, 1951-54. Recipient Design Innovation award GE,. 1987, Cert. of Recognition, Rep. Nat. Com., 1991-92. Mem. Inst. Indsl. Engrs., Soc. Plastic Engrs., Soc. Mech. Engrs., Soc. Mfg. Engrs., Soc. Mil. Engrs., Res. Officers Assn. Roman Catholic. Avocations: pistol shooting, boating. Office: US Air Tool Co Inc 60 Fleetwood Ct Ronkonkoma NY 11779-6907

STANKUS, ANTHONY VYTAUTAS, science librarian, educator, analyst; b. Worcester, Mass., Mar. 9, 1951; s. Frank and Anna Elfrieda (Rauch) S.; m. Mary Frances Doyle, Nov. 4, 1978 (div. 2000); children: Andrew (dec.), Peter (dec.). BA summa cum laude, Coll. Holy Cross, 1973; MLS, U. R.I., 1975. Accredited libr. ALA. Sci. libr. Coll. Holy Cross, Worcester, Mass., 1974—; adj. prof. U. R.I., Kingston, 1982—. Author: Science Librarianship at America's Liberal Arts Colleges, 1992, Making Sense of Journals in the Physical Sciences, 1992, Making Sense of Journals in the Life Sciences, 1992, Scientific and Clinical Literature for the Decade of the Brain, 1993, Special Format Serials and Issues in the Sciences, 1995, Electronic Expectations: Science Journals on the Web, 1999, the Journals of the Century, 2001 and 3 others; contbg. editor, columnist Reference and User Svcs. Quar., Technicalities, Sci. and Tech. Librs., Serials Libr. and others; contbr. over 70 articles to profl. jours. Named Disting. Alumnus of Yr., U. R.I. Grad Sch. Libr. and Info. Studies, 1992; ranked 2d Most Productive Author Nationally Among Acad. Librs. in 1980's, Coll. and Rsch. Librs., 1991, 2000. Republican. Roman Catholic. Avocation: vegetable gardening. Home: 26 Calumet Ave Worcester MA 01606-2104 Office: Holy Cross Coll Sci Libr 1 College St Worcester MA 01610-2322 E-mail: TStankus@HolyCross.edu.

STANLEY, BRIAN JORDAN, corporate lawyer; b. Duncan, Okla., Sept. 10, 1954; s. Elmer E. and Betty Sue Stanley; m. Ruth Anne Lynn Stanley, Apr. 6, 1979 (div. Mar. 1989); children: Lindsey Jordan, Brent Alan; m. Francine Michelle La Valle, Oct. 18, 1996. BA in Polit. Sci., U. Okla., 1979; JD with honors, Oklahoma City U., 1985. Bar: (Okla.) 1985, (U.S. Dist. Ct. (we. dist.) Okla.). Sports writer The Norman (Okla.) Transcript, 1979-80; oil and gas landman Milt McCullough, Oklahoma City, 1980-81; trust officer Liberty Nat. Bank & Trust, 1981-83; atty. Michael P. Rogalin, 1985-86, William H. Mattoon, Norman, 1986-87, Fed. Deposit Ins. Corp., Oklahoma City, 1987, Reed, Shadid & Pipes, Oklahoma City, 1987-88, Mosburg, Sears, Kunzman & Bollinger, Oklahoma City, 1988; v.p., corp. gen. counsel The Hefner Co., Inc., 1989—. Bd. dirs. The Hefner Co., Inc.; trustee Dr. Brent Hisey Irrevocable Trust, Oklahoma City, 1998—. Contbr. articles to profl. jours. Mem.: ABA, Mensa. Republican. Episcopalian. Avocations: Italian language, theology, politics. Office: The Hefner Co Inc PO Box 2177 Oklahoma City OK 73101-2177 E-mail: vito1954@hotmail.com.

STANLEY, COVIA LEVANCE, physician, clergyman; b. Longwood, N.C., Aug. 3, 1946; s. Covia and Lou Mina (Moore) S.; m. Lillian C. Stanley, June 27, 1969; children: Covia L. II and Quenton C. BS, N.C. Ctrl. U., Durham, 1968, MS, 1974; MD, U. Buffalo, 1978; MDiv, Va. Union U., Richmond, 1995. Pvt. practice ob-gyn., Whiteville, N.C., 1982-87; ob-gyn clinician Richmond City Health Dept., 1987-93, dir., dep., acting, 1993-97; pastor Mt. Rona Bapt. Ch., Newport News, Va., 1993-96; dist. health dir. Waccamaw Pub. Health Dist., Conway, S.C., 1998—; pastor Mt. Calvary Bapt. Ch., 1999—. Mem. steering com. Turning Point, R.W. Johnson Found., Columbia, S.C., 1999; mem. Obstet. Task Force S.C. Dept. Health and Environ., Columbia, 1998, Commrs. Task Force Eliminating Health Disparities, 1999—. Lt. col. USAF Res., 1988—. Mem. AMA, APHA, Nat. Assn. City and County Ofcls., EveReady Lodge, Shriners, Alpha Phi Alpha (life, pres. Conway chpt., cert. of merit 1997). Baptist. Avocations: travel, preaching, tennis, playing guitar. Home: PO Box 3053 Conway SC 29528-3053 Office: Waccamaw Pub Health Dist 2830 Oak St Conway SC 29526-4560 also: Mt Calvary Bapt Ch 5916 Highway 905 Conway SC 29526-7170 E-mail: mercylcs@scgorst.net.

STANLEY, CRAIG (MALCHAN CRAIG STANLEY), school system administrator, psychologist; b. Boston, Nov. 19, 1948; s. Harry Eugene and Ruth (Shultz) S.; 1 child, Jessica. BA in Psychology, Antioch Coll., Yellow Springs, Oh., 1971; MEd, Boston State Coll., 1975; EdD, Boston Coll., 1992. Counselor Fernald Sch., Waltham, Mass., 1970-71, psychologist, 1975; tchr. Boston Pub. Schs., 1972-74; sch. psychologist EdCo, Inc., Brookline, Mass., 1975-76, Greater Lawrence Ednl. Collaborative, Lawrence, 1976-77, exec. dir., 1977—. Sec. adv. commn. Mass. Dept. Edn., 1981-84; treas. Mass. Orgn. Ednl. Collaboratives, 1988-93, pres., 1993-95. Chmn. Greater Lawrence Interagy. Task Force, 1980—83; clk. Middleton Planning Bd., 1991—96; trustee Middleton Congl. Ch., 2001—. Mem.: USCG Aux., ASCD, Assn. Ednl. Svc. Agys. (exec. coun. 1997—2000), Mass. Assn. Sch. Supts., Am. Assn. Sch. Adminstrs., Phi Delta Kappa. Home: 19 Gates Rd Middleton MA 01949-1924 Office: 480 Broadway Methuen MA 01844 E-mail: craig77@attbi.com., cstanley@glec.org.

STANLEY, DOUGLAS PARNELL, county planner, administrator; b. Hampton, Va., July 7, 1969; s. Henry Herbert and Ann Marie (Vause) S.; m. Jenny Lee Springer, Dec. 30, 1995. BA in Geography, Mary Washington Coll., 1992; M in Urban and Regional Planning, Va. Commonwealth U., 1994; certificate in pub. adminstrn., Shenandoah U., 1998. Cert. zoning adminstr. Zoning adminstr. Warren County, Front Royal, Va., 1994-96, planning dir., 1996—, county adminstr., county planner, 2000—. Mem. Am. Inst. Cert. Planners (Outstanding Student award 1994), Am. Planning Assn. (awards com. Va. chpt. 1996-2000, chmn. 1998-2000), Va. Assn. Zoning Officials, High Knob Owners Assn. (bd. dirs. 1999—, sec. 1999-2001), Front Royal Rotary Club. Home: 960 High Knob Rd Front Royal VA 22630-5749 Office: Warren County 220 N Commerce Ave Ste 100 Front Royal VA 22630-3201

STANLEY, DUFFY B. architect; b. Midland, Tex., Feb. 14, 1923; s. Benjamin M. and Mary L. (White) S.; m. Irene M. Muller, July 31, 1948; children: Sheila, Lars, Brock, Sonya, Sharon. BArch, Tex. A&M U., 1948; hon. diploma, U. Autonoma de Cd. Juarez, Mex., 1977. Registered architect, Tex., N.Mex.; cert. Nat. Coun. Archtl. Registration Bds. Draftsman, designer J.J. Black, Architect, Midland, 1948-51; job capt. Carroll & Daeuble Architects, El Paso, Tex., 1951-57; pvt. practice, 1957—. Lectr. in field. Author: Open Space in the El Paso Region, 1970. Vice chmn. Citizens Environ. Coun. of El Paso, 1972—73; chmn. GARC com. West Tex. Coun. Govts., El Paso, 1977; chmn. El Paso County Hist. Commn., 1978, Zoning Bd. of Adjustment, El Paso, 1970; mem. Open Space Com., 1970—71; bd. dirs. Mission Heritage Assn. of El Paso, 1977—84. Capt. U.S. Army, 1943—46, ETO. Decorated Combat Inf. badge, Bronze Star, Silver Star with three oak leaf clusters; recipient Caudill awrd, Tex. Assn. Sch. Bds. and AIA Tex., 1996. Mem. AIA (chpt. pres. 1964, Design award 1995, Service to Profession award 1991), FAIA. Avocations: tennis, reading, travel, family activities. Office: 303 Texas Ave Ste 402 El Paso TX 79901-1452 Business E-Mail: ivolta@dzn.com.

STANLEY, EDWARD ALEXANDER, geologist, forensic scientist, technical and academic administrator; b. N.Y.C., Apr. 7, 1929; s. Frank and Elizabeth (Wolf) S.; m. Elizabeth Ann Allison, June 7, 1958; children: Karen (dec.), Scott. BS, Rutgers U., 1954; MS, Pa. State U., 1956, PhD, 1960. Geologist Amoco Petroleum Co., Tulsa, Okla., 1960-62; prof. U. Del., 1962-64, U. Ga., 1964-77; assoc. dean rsch., chmn. geology dept. Indiana (Pa.) U., 1977-81; supr. Phillips Petroleum Co., Bartlesvill, Okla., 1981-86; dir., comdg. officer N.Y.C. Police Dept. Crime Lab., 1986-94. Cons. geology, forensic sci., microscopy 1994-97; assoc. Internat. Environtl. Svcs., 1997—; cons. geology, Athens, Ga., 1963-77, Indiana, Pa., 1977-81. Contbr. articles to profl. jours. Served to sgt. USAF, 1947-50. NSF grantee, 1965-68, 74, Office Water Resources Rsch. grantee, 1965-68; NAS exch. prof. Soviet Union, 1968-69, 73; invited guest Moscow Police Dept. Forensic Labs., 1990; invited speaker FBI Internat. Symposium on Forensic Trace Evidence, 1991, 98; recipient Commemorative medal of the lab. Dept. Botany, Jozsef Attilla U., Szeged, Hungary, 2000, Millenium medal, 2000. Fellow AAAS, Geol. Soc. Am.; mem. Am. Assn. Petroleum Geologists, Am. Acad. of Forensix Sci., Am. Soc. Crime Lab Dirs., Am. Assn. Stratigraphic Palyologists, Sigma Xi. Presbyterian. Avocations: photography, music, firearms. Home: 2004 Haverford Rd Ardmore PA 19003-3010 E-mail: eastanley@netreach.net.

STANLEY, ELLEN MAY, historian, consultant; b. Dighton, Kans., Feb. 3, 1921; d. Delmar Orange and Lena May (Bobb) Durr; m. Max Neal Stanley, Nov. 5, 1939; children: Ann Y. Stanley Epps, Janet M. Stanley Horsky, Gail L. Stanley Peck, Kenneth D., Neal M., Mary E. Stanley McEniry. BA in English and Journalism, Ft. Hays (Kans.) State U., 1972, MA in History, 1984. Pvt. practice local/state historian, cons., writer local history, Dighton, 1973—; cons. genealogy, 1980—. Vice chmn. State Preservation Bd. Rev., Kans., 1980-87; area rep. Kans. State Mus. Assn., 1978-84. Author: Early Lane County History: 12,000 B.C.--A.D. 1884, 1993, Cowboy Josh: Adventures of a Real Cowboy, 1996, Early Lane County Development, 1993 (recipient award Am. Assn. for State and Local History, 1994), Golden Age, Great Depression and Dust Bowl, 2001; contbr. Precinct woman com. Alamota Township, Kans., 1962-86; mem. Dem. State Affirmative Action Com., 1975. Recipient hon. mention for photography Ann. Christian Arts Festival, 1974, Artist of Month award Dane G. Hansen Mus., 1975. Mem. Kans. State Hist. Soc. (pres. 1990-91), Lane County Hist. Soc. (sec. 1970-78). Methodist. Avocations: fossil hunting, walking, photography, antiques. Home: 100 N 4th Dighton KS 67839 Office: 110 E Pearl St Dighton KS 67839

STANLEY, GEORGE EDWARD, writer; m. Gwen Stanley; 2 children: James, Charles. BA, MA, Tex. Tech. U.; PhD, U. Port Elizabeth, South Africa. Tchr. writing, fgn. langs.; chmn. for pers., dept. English, fgn. langs., journalism Cameron U., Lawton, Okla., 1970—. Author: Writing Short Stories for Young People, 1987, Rats in the Attic, 1995, Happy Deathday to You, 1995, The Day the Ants Got Really Mad, Bugs for Breakfast, There's a Shark in the Swimming Pool, Mrs. O'Dell's Third Grade Class is Shrinking, Who Invited Aliens to My Slumber Party, The New Kid in School is a Vampire Bat, A Werewolf Followed Me Home, Vampire Kittens of Count Dracula; (under pseudonym M. Masters) The Case of the Phony Frankenstein, 1984, The Case of the Clever Marathon Cheat, 1985; (under pseudonym Laura Lee Hope) The Bobbsey Twins and the Case of the Runaway Money, 1987; (under pseudonym M.T. Coffin) Billy Baker's Dog Won't Stay Buried, 1995, Where Have All the Parents Gone?, 1995, Check it Out and Die, 1995, Don't Go the the Principal's Office, 1996, The Dead Kid Did It, 1996, Pet Store, 1996, The Haunted Museum, 1996, We Wish You a Scary Christmas, 1996, The Curse of the Cheerleaders, 1997, Circus F.R.E.A.K.S., 1997, The Secret Ingredient, 1999, Frogs' Legs for Dinner, 2000, The Battle of the Bakers, 2000, Ghost Horse, 2000, Snake Camp, 2000, The Clue of the Left-Handed Envelope, 2000, The Puzzle of the Pretty Pink Handkerchief, 2000, Nancy Drew-The Mystery in Tornad Alley, 2000, Geronimo, 2001, Adam Sharp-The Spy Who Barked, 2002 others; contbr. numerous articles and short stories to young reader mags. Mem. MLA, Am. Assn. Tchrs. of Arabic, Am. Assn. Tchrs. of Turkish Langs., Am. Assn. Netherlandic Studies, Mystery Writers of Am., Soc. Children's Book Writers and Illustrators. Home: PO Box 6538 Lawton OK 73506-0538 E-mail: georges@cameron.edu.

STANLEY, GEORGE JOEL, social services administrator, advocate; b. Wethersfield, Vt., Sept. 1, 1947; s. George and Lucretia (Lincoln) Stanley. BA, U. Mass., 1990, MEd, 1997. Lic. real estate agt. Mass. Min., missionary Watchtower Soc., Bklyn., 1960-81; founder, dir. Carefree Living Ctrs., Springfield, Mass., 1970—, Networks, Springfield, 1980—, Cult Busters, Springfield, 1981—, Free at Last, Springfield, 1981—, Caring Cmty., Vt., N.H. and Mass., 1980—, Essential Svcs., New Eng. area, 1972—, Live Free or Die, Keene, N.H., 1997—. Owner, operator thrift shops and drop-in ctrs., 1972—; bd. dirs., founder Valley Singles, Northampton, 1985—, Paradise Coalition, Northampton, Mass., 1990—97. Author: The Patriarch and Prodigal Son, 1981; contbr. articles to profl. publs. Past guardian ad litem, conservator for homeless, indigent, disabled; candidate for Mass. Senate People's Party, Springfield, 1995; vol. Michael Dukakis for Pres., 1975—83. Mem.: APA, Artists Alliance Against Violence, Nat. Artists for Mental Health. Unitarian/Episcopalian. Avocations: naturism, spirituality, community building, anything experimental.

STANLEY, HAROLD WATKINS, political science educator; b. Enterprise, Ala., June 14, 1950; s. James Franklin and Muriel Louise (Brooks) Stanley; m. Marie Regine Denise Gelineau, Jan. 3, 1976 (div. 1999); children: Margaret Louise, Duncan Gelineau. BA magna cum laude, Yale U., 1972, PhD, 1981; MPhil in Politics, Oxford U., 1975. Instr. polit. sci. U. Rochester, NY, 1979—82, asst. prof., 1982—88, assoc. prof., 1988-98, prof., chair dept. polit. sci., 1996-99. Vis. rsch. prof. U. Ala., Tuscaloosa, 1987—88, So. Meth. U., Dallas, 2000—01. Author: Senate vs Governor, Alabama, 1975, Voter Mobilization and the Politics of Race, 1987; editor: Vital Statistics on American Politics, 1988, 8th edit. retitled VSAP, 2001—02; contbr. articles. Rhodes scholar, 1972-75. Mem. Am. Polit. Sci. Assn., So. Polit. Sci. Assn. (v.p., program chair 1997-98, pres.-elect 1999-2000, pres. 2000-2001), Midwest Polit. Sci. Assn., Phi Beta Kappa. Democrat. Mem. Soc. Of Friends. Office: U Rochester Dept Polit Sci RC Box 270146 Rochester NY 14627-0146 E-mail: harold.w.stanley@rochester.edu.

STANLEY, H(ARRY) EUGENE, physicist, educator; b. Norman, Okla., Mar. 28, 1941; s. Harry Eugene and Ruth S.; m. Idahlia Dessauer, June 2, 1967; children: Jannah, Michael, Rachel. BA in Physics (Nat. Merit scholar),

Wesleyan U., 1962; postgrad. (Fulbright scholar), U. Cologne, W. Ger., 1962-63; PhD in Physics, Harvard U., 1967; PhD (hon.), Bar-Ilan U., Ramat-Gan, Israel, 1994, Roland Eötvös U., Budapest, Hungary, 1997, U. Liege, 2001, U. Dortmund, 2001. NSF predoctoral rsch. fellow Harvard U., 1963-67; mem. staff Lincoln Lab MIT, 1967-68, asst. prof. physics, 1969-71, assoc. prof., 1971-73; Miller rsch. fellow U. Calif., Berkeley, 1968-69; Hermann von Helmholtz assoc. prof. health scis. and tech. Harvard U.-MIT Program in Health Scis. and Tech., 1973-76; vis. prof. Osaka (Japan) U., 1975; univ. prof., prof. physics, prof. physiology Sch. Medicine, dir. Ctr. Polymer Studies Boston U., 1976—. Joliot-Curie vis. prof. Ecole Superieure de Physique et Chimie, Paris, 1979; vis. prof. Peking U., 1981, Seoul Nat. U., 1982, 30th Ann. Saha Meml. Lecture, 1992; Sigma Xi nat. lectr., 2002; dir. NATO Advanced Study Inst., Cargese, Corisca, 1985, 88, 90, IUPAP Internat. Conf. on Thermodynamics and Statis. Mechanics, 1986, Enrico Fermi Sch., Varenna, Italy, 1996, Gordon Rsch. Conf. on Water and Aqueous Solutions, 1998, NATO advanced rsch. workshop, 1999, 2001; cons. Sandia Nat. Lab., 1983-94, Dowell Schlumberger Co., 1982-92, Elscint Co., 1983-85; nat. co-chmn. Com. of Concerned Scientists, 1974-76. Author: Introduction to Phase Transitions and Critical Phenomena, 1971, From Newton to Mandelbrot: A Primer in Theoretical Physics, 1990, Fractal Forms, 1991, Fractal Concepts in Surface Growth, 1995, Cours de physique, 1999, Introduction to Econophysics: Correlations & Complexity in Finance, 2000; editor: Biomedical Physics and Biomaterials Science, 1972, Cooperative Phenomena Near Phase Transitions, 1973, On Growth and Form: Fractal and Non-Fractal Patterns in Physics, 1985, Statistical Physics, 1986, Random Fluctuation and Pattern Growth, 1988, Correlations and Connectivity: Geometric Aspects of Physics, Chemistry and Biology, 1990, Fractals in Science, 1994, Disordered Materials and Interfaces, 1996, Physics of Complex Systems, 1997, Statistical Mechanics in the Physical Biological and Social Sciences, 1997, Application of Statistical Mechanics to Practical Problems, 1999, Structure and Function of Biological Systems under Extreme Conditions, 2002, Statistical Physics, 2000, Statistical Mechanics: From Rigorous Results to Applications, 2000, Scaling in Disordered Systems, 2002, New Kinds of Phase Transitions, 2002; editor Physica A., 1988—. Recipient Choice award Am. Assn. Book Pubs., 1972, Macdonald award, 1986, Venture Rsch. award British Petroleum, 1989, Mass. Prof. of Yr. award Coun. Advancement and Support of Edn., 1992, Floyd K. Richtmyer prize, 1997, Turnbull prize, 1998, NSF Disting. Tchg. prize, 2001, Memory Ride prize, 2001; John Simon Guggenheim Meml. fellow, 1979-80. Fellow AAAS, Am. Phys. Soc. (chmn. New Eng. sect. 1982-83; Centennial lectr. 1997); mem. Non-Linear Sci. Panel of Nat. Acad. Sci., Hungarian Phys. Soc. (hon.). Home: 50 Metacomet Rd Waban MA 02468-1465 Office: Boston U Ctr for Polymer Studies Boston MA 02215 E-mail: HES@bu.edu. *The greatest joy of my professional life is to share in the excitement of learning something new—however minor—about the workings of Nature. The greatest joy of my personal life is to be able to imagine that I've done my very best to meet the needs of my family and my co-workers. The greatest obstacle to happiness is the persistent feeling that it is impossible to find that tortuous path whereby both joys may occasionally be experienced.*

STANLEY, HELEN CAMILLE, composer, musician; b. Tampa, Fla. d. Edward and Lucy Gage (Crehore) S.; widowed; 1 child, Helen Marjorie. MusB, Cin. Conservatory Music, 1951; MusM, Fla. State U., 1954; BS, Muskingum Coll., 1961. Instr. music and fine arts Jacksonville (Fla.) U., 1962-67; instr. music in communications Jones Coll., Jacksonville, 1965-66; composer, condr. St. Paul's by-the-Sea, Jacksonville Beach, Fla., 1976; composer-in-residence, pianist Fla. Contemporary Ensemble, Jacksonville, 1986; ind. composer, lectr., pianist, 1963—. Cons. Beaches Fine Arts Series, Neptune Beach, Fla., 1973—. Composer Rhapsody for Electronic Tape and Orchestra, 1972 (Composition Commn. award), Allegro, Passacaglia, Sonata for trombone and piano, various instrumental and vocal works, Evocation I for piano; orchestral works on CD include: Fanfare for Orchestra (Warsaw Nat. Philharmonic Orch. and Owensboro Symphony), 1994, Passacaglia (St. Petersburg Philharmonic), Concerto Romantico, Prague, 1997, Fanfare for Orchestra (All American Celebration by Owensboro Symphony), 1999. Mem. Nat. Soc. Arts and Letters, Soc. Mayflower Descs., 1987—. Recipient Pogner Music Composition award, Cin., 1950, C. Hugo Ensemble Composition award, Cin., 1951, Anthem Descant award St. Paul's by-the-Sea, 1980, Art Ventures Fund award, 1992, Jacksonville Comty. Found. award, 1994; named Outstanding Achievements Classical Music, Jacksonville, 1997. Mem. ASCAP, Am. Music Ctr., Am. Keyboard Artists, Performing Arts Directory, Pi Kappa Lambda. Avocations: art, walking, dancing. Home: 1768 Emory Cir S Jacksonville FL 32207-7707 Studio: Aladdin Farm 12047 Aladdin Rd Jacksonville FL 32223-3201

STANLEY, HUGH MONROE, JR. lawyer; b. Ft. Lewis, Wash., Oct. 25, 1944; s. Hugh Monroe Sr. and Rita (McHugh) S.; m. Patricia Page, Aug. 17, 1968; children: Allison Michelle, Matthew Monroe, Trevor Marshall. BA magna cum laude, U. Dayton, 1966; JD, Georgetown U., 1969. Bar: Ohio 1969, U.S. Ct. Appeals (6th cir.) 1983, U.S. Supreme Ct. 1979. Assoc. Arter & Hadden, Cleve., 1969-76, ptnr., 1976—, chmn. litigation dept., 1983-96. Staff editor Georgetown Law Jour., bd. editors. Fellow Am. Bar Found., Bar Assn. Greater Cleve., Am. Coll. Trial Lawyers, Internat. Acad. Trial Lawyers, Internat. Soc. Barristers, Nat. Assn. R.R. Trial Counsel; mem. ABA, Fed. Bar Assn., Def. Rsch. Inst., Cleve. Assn. Civil Trial Attys., Ohio Assn. Civil Trial Attys. Republican. Roman Catholic. Avocation: reading. Office: Arter & Hadden 1100 Huntington Bldg 925 Euclid Ave Ste 1100 Cleveland OH 44115-1475

STANLEY, JEAN-DANIEL, geological oceanographer; b. Metz, France, Apr. 14, 1934; came to U.S., 1941, naturalized, 1946; s. Paul Emile and Madeleine (Simon) Streisguth; m. Adrienne N. Ellis, Mar. 5, 1988; children: Marc Michel, Eric Paul, Brian Northrop, Natalie Anne, Susan N. B.Sc., Cornell U., 1956; M.Sc., Brown U., 1958; D.Sc., U. Grenoble, France, 1961. Rsch. geologist French Petroleum Inst., Paris, 1958-61; asst. to dir. U.S. Waterways Expt. Sta., Vicksburg, Miss., 1961-63; asst. prof. geology Ottawa U., Ont., Can., 1963-64; rsch. assoc. prof. Dalhousie U., Halifax, N.S., Can., 1964-66; sr. scientist, oceanographer, dir. Geoarchaeology-Global Change Program div. sedimentology Smithsonian Instn., Washington, 1966—; adj. prof. U. Québec, 1992—2001. Cons. to govts. Mediterranean countries; sci. expert Internat. Ct. Justice, 1981—. Editor: New Concepts of Continental Margin Sedimentation, 1969, Mediterranean Sea: A Natural Sedimentation Laboratory, 1972, Marine Sediment Transport and Environmental Management, 1976, Sedimentation in Submarine Canyons, Fans and Trenches, 1978, The Shelfbreak: A Critical Interface on Continental Margins, 1983, Geological Evolution of the Mediterranean Basin, 1985, Nile Delta, A Geological Excursion, 1997; contbr. chpts to books, articles to profl. jours. Bd. dirs. Geoarchaeology and Deltas Programs. Served to capt. C.E., U.S. Army, 1961-63. Recipient médaille Alpes Maritimes, France, 1976, F.P. Shepard medal Soc. for Sedimentary Geology, 1990, Gold Trident medal Italian Acad., 1998; named Hon. Prof., East China U., 1995; grantee in field. Fellow Geol. Soc. Am., AAAS, Geol. Soc. Belgium; mem. Internat. Assn. Sedimentologists, Am. Assn. Petroleum Geologists, Soc. Econ. Paleontologists and Mineralogists, Geol. Soc. Washington, Cosmos Club (Washington), Sigma Xi. Clubs: Cosmos (Washington). Republican. Office: Smithsonian Instn Mus Natural History Washington DC 20560-0001

STANLEY, JULIAN CECIL, JR. psychology educator; b. Macon, Ga., July 9, 1918; s. Julian Cecil and Ethel (Cheney) S.; m. Rose Roberta Sanders, Aug. 18, 1946 (dec. Nov. 1978); 1 child, Susan Roberta Willhoft; m. Barbara Sprague Kerr, Jan. 1, 1980 (dec. 2001). BS, Ga. So. U., 1937; Ed.M., Harvard U., 1946, Ed.D., 1950; D of Ednl. Excellence (hon.), U. North Tex., 1990; LHD (hon.), State U. of West Ga., 1997. Tchr. Fulton and West Fulton high schs., Atlanta, 1937—42; instr. psychology Newton (Mass.) Jr. Coll., 1946—48; instr. edn. Harvard U., 1948—49; assoc. prof. ednl. psychology George Peabody Coll. Tchrs., 1949—53; assoc. prof. edn., 1953—57; prof. edn., 1957—62; prof. ednl. psychology, 1962—67; chmn. dept., 1962—63; dir. lab. exptl. design U. Wis., Madison, 1961—67; prof. edn. and psychology Johns Hopkins U., 1967—71, prof. psychology, 1971—99, dir. study mathematically precocious youth, 1971—, prof. emeritus, 1999. Mem. rsch. adv. coun. Coop. Rsch. Br., U.S. Office Edn., 1962—64; mem. com. examiners for aptitude tests Coll. Entrance Exam. Bd., 1961—65, chmn., 1965—68; mem. rsch. com. Ednl. Testing Svc., 1962—67; fellow Social Sci. Rsch. Coun. Inst. Math. for Social Scientists U. Mich., summer, 1955; postdoctoral fellow stats. U. Chgo., 1955—56; Fulbright rsch. scholar U. Louvain, Belgium, 1958—59; Fulbright lectr. New Zealand and Australia, 1974; cons. U. Western Australia, 1980; fellow Ctr. for Advanced Study in Behavioral Sci., 1965—67, vis. scholar, 1983; hon. prof. Shanghai (People's Republic of China) Tchrs. U.; disting. tchr. Commn. on Presdl. Scholars, 1987, 92; vis. prof. U. Ga., 1947, U. Hawaii, 1960, Harvard U., 1963, U. North Tex., 1990, U. NSW, 1992; mem. adv. bd. Tex. Acad. Math. and Sci., 1988—89; trustee Ctr. for Excellence in Edn., 1989—93, Advanced Acad. Ga., 1999—, Ga. Acad. Math., Engrng. and Sci., 1996—; cons. Ctr. for Talented Youth, 1998—. Author: Measurement in Today's Schools, 4th edit., 1964, (with D.T. Campbell) Experimental and Quasi-Experimental Designs for Research, 1963, 66, (with Gene V Glass) Statistical Methods in Education and Psychology, 1970, (with K.D. and B. Hopkins) Educational and Psychological Measurement and Evaluation, 3d edit., 1990, (with K.D. Hopkins, G.H. Bracht) Perspectives in Educational and Psychological Measurement, 1972; editor: Improving Experimental Design and Statistical Analysis, 1967, Preschool Programs for the Disadvantaged, 1972, Compensatory Education for Children, Ages 2-8, 1973, (with D.P. Keating, L.H. Fox) Mathematical Talent: Discovery, Description, and Development, 1974, (with W.C. George, C.H. Solano) The Gifted and the Creative: A Fifty-Year Perspective, 1977, Educational Programs and Intellectual Prodigies, 1978, (with W.C. George, S.J. Cohn) Educating the Gifted: Acceleration and Enrichment, 1979, (with C.P. Benbow) Academic Precocity: Aspects of Its Development, 1983; adv. editor jours. Served with USAAC, 1942-45. Julian C. Stanley chair in ednl. psychology created U. Wis., Madison, 1995; recipient awards Mensa Ednl. Rsch. Found., 1989, 97, four awards for excellence in rsch., Lifetime Achievement award, 2000. Fellow APA (pres. div. ednl. psychology 1965-66, div. evaluation and measurement 1972-73, Thorndike award for disting. psychol. contbns. to edn. 1978, divsn. evaluation and measurement Lifetime Contbn. award 1997, divsn. gen. psychology George Miller award 1999), AAAS, Am. Statis. Assn., Am. Psychol. Soc. (J. McKeen Cattell award 1994); mem. Nat. Council Measurement Edn. (pres. 1963-64), Am. Ednl. Research Assn. (pres. 1966-67, award for disting. contbns. to research in edn. 1980), Nat. Assn. for Gifted Children (2d v.p. 1977-79, Disting. Scholar award 1982), Psychometric Soc. (past dir.), AAUP (past chpt. pres.), Tenn. Psychol. Assn. (past pres.), Nat. Acad. Edn., Phi Beta Kappa (past chpt. pres.), Phi Beta Kappa Assocs., Sigma Xi, Phi Delta Kappa Office: CTY 2701 N Charles St Baltimore MD 21218-4351 Fax: 410-516-0108. E-mail: jstanley@jhu.edu. *I am deeply indebted for my graduate education to the G.I. Bill following World War II.*

STANLEY, KAREN FRANCINE MARY LESNIEWSKI, human resources professional; b. Amsterdam, N.Y., Oct. 10, 1948; d. Francis Raymond and Genievive Mary (Klementowski) Lesniewski; m. Mark Anthony Stanley, Nov. 11, 1972. BA, Alliance Coll., 1970; MA, The Coll. St. Rose, 1976, CAS, 1987. English tchr. Middle Country Sch., Centereach, N.Y., 1970-71; English and social studies tchr. Mt. Carmel, Gloversville, 1971-72; English tchr. Bishop Scully H.S., Amsterdam, 1972-80, Shenendehowa Ctrl., Clifton Park, N.Y., 1980-82; English tchr., head dept. Broadalbin (N.Y.) Ctrl. Sch., 1982-86; adminstrv. intern Saratoga Springs (N.Y.) City Sch. Dist., 1986-87, dir. for human resource svcs., 1987—. Bd. dirs. N.Y. State Staff Devel. Coun., 1990-92. Mem. Am. Soc. for Human Resource Mgrs., N.Y. State Assn. Women Adminstrs., Nat. Assn. Schs., Colls. and Univs., Nat. Assn. Ednl. Negotiators, Soroptimist Internat. (sec. Saratoga County chpt. 1991-92, del. Dist. I 1992-93, 96-97, asst. treas. 1994-95, treas. 1995-96, del. 1996-98), Ednl. Adminstrn. Assn./Coll. St. Rose (bd. dirs., sec. 1986-89, pres. 1989-92). Republican. Roman Catholic. Avocations: gardening, reading, sailing, golf. Office: Saratoga Springs City Schs 5 Wells St Saratoga Springs NY 12866-1205

STANLEY, KURT EDWARD, plant ecologist; b. Schuylkill Township, Pa., Dec. 2, 1954; s. Roland Glenn and Bethel Grabo Stanley; m. Julie Ann Juenemann, June 21, 1980. BS, Mich. State U., 1977, PhD in Plant Ecology, 2000. Cert. wetland profl. in tng. Jr. secondary sch. tchr., vol. Peace Corp, Fiji, 1978-79; biochemistry technician dept. surgery U. Pa., Phila., 1979-80; comml. multi-line ins. underwriter Mich. Millers Mutual Ins. Co., Lansing, 1980-82; property/casualty ins. sales staff Juenemann Ins. Agy., Harper Woods, Mich., 1982-83; mgmt. trainee Advance Auto Parts, Roanoke, Va., 1983-85, store mgr., 1985-86; owner/operator Plymouth (Mich.) Carquest Auto Parts, 1986-92; wetland scientist Tilton & Assocs., Ann Arbor, Mich., 2001—. Mem. environment com. Friends of the Rouge, Detroit, 1994. Grad. fellow Rob and Bessie Welder Wildlife Found., Tex., 1994-98, rsch. fellow Botany and Plant Pathology Mich. State U., East Lansing, 1994-2000; Sigma Xi grantee-in-aide of rsch., 1994. Mem. Ecol. Soc. Am. (cert. assoc. ecologist), Soc. Wetland Scientists, Soc. for Ecol. Restoration, Mich. Bot. Club. Avocations: bird watching, travel. Office: Tilton & Assocs Inc 501 Avis Dr Ste 5C Ann Arbor MI 48108 Fax: (734) 769-3164. E-mail: kstanley@tiltoninc.com.

STANLEY, LILA GAIL, political scientist, antique appraiser; b. Marietta, Ga., Mar. 23, 1941; d. James Miller and Louise (Land) S. AB cum laude, Randolph-Macon Woman's Coll., 1963; MA in Polit. Sci., Emory U., 1964; cert. appraisal studies decorative arts, George Washington U., 1997. Polit. sci. instr. U. West Ga., Carrollton, 1964-66; Am. history tcrh. Foxcroft Sch., Middleburg, Va., 1966-67; staff asst. Rep. John J. Flynt U.S. Ho. Reps., Washington, 1967-74; legis. asst. Sen. Robert C. Byrd U.S. Senate, 1974-80; asst. to arch. Arch. of the Capitol, 1980-97; appraiser Gail Stanley Appraisers, 1997—. Participation Winter Inst., Winterthur (Del.) Mus., 2000. Vol. worker various nat. polit. campaigns Dem. Orgn., Washington, 1968-80; bd. dirs., 1st v.p., treas. Watergate East Inc., Washington, 1986-96; vol. rsch. asst. Nat. Mus. Am. History, Smithsonian Instn., Washington, 1999—; docent, curatorial vol. Tudor Pl., Washington, 1999—. Mem. DAR, Am. Soc. Appraisers, Washington Decorative Arts Forum, Zeta Tau Alpha. Democrat. Methodist. Home and Office: 2510 Virginia Ave NW Washington DC 20037-1904

STANLEY, MARGARET KING, performing arts administrator; b. San Antonio, Dec. 11, 1929; d. Creston Alexander and Margaret (Haymore) King; children: Torrey Margaret, Jean Cullen. Student, Mary Baldwin Coll., 1948-50; BA, U. Tex., Austin, 1952; MA, U. Incarnate Word, 1959. Tchg. cert. Elem. tchr. San Antonio Ind. Sch. Dist., 1953-54, 55-56, Arlington County Schs., Va., 1954-55, Ft. Sam Houston Schs., San Antonio, 1955-57; art and art history tchr. St. Pius X Sch., 1959-60; English tchr. Trinity U., 1963-65; designer-mfr., owner CrisStan Clothes, Inc., San Antonio, 1967-73; founder, exec. dir. San Antonio Performing Arts Assn., 1976-92; founder Arts Coun. of San Antonio, 1962; founding chmn. Joffrey Workshop, San Antonio, 1979; originator, founding chairwoman Student Music Fair, 1963; host On Stage with Margaret Stanley Sta. KTRU-FM, 1983-98. Tchg. fellow Trintiy U., San Antonio, 1964-66; mem. Met. Opera Nat. Coun., 1969-80; pres. San Antonio Symphony League, 1971-74; v.p. Arts Coun. San Antonio, 1975; bd. govs. Artists Alliance San Antonio, 1982; founding organizer Musica San Antonio, 1997-98; v.p., founder San Antonio Opera Guild, 1974-76, founder Early Music Festival, San Antonio, 1990-92; adv. bd. Hertzberg Circus Collection, San Antonio Dance Umbrella, Houston Early Music, Morgan-Scott Ballet; artistic advisor, dir. presentation San Antonio Symphony, 1992-94; v.p. Instnl. Devel. Carver Cultural Ctr. Originator of the idea for a new ballet created for the City of San Antonio, "Jamboree," commd. from the Joffrey Ballet, world premiere in San Antonio, 1984. Recipient Outstanding Tchr. award Arlington County Sch. Dist., 1954, Emily Smith award for outstanding alumni Mary Baldwin Coll., 1973, Today's Woman award San Antonio Light Newspaper, 1980, Woman of Yr. in Arts award San Antonio Express News, 1983, Erasmus medal The Dutch Consulate, 1992, Mary Baldwin Sesquicentennial medallion, 1992; named to Women's Hall of Fame, San Antonio, 1984, Disting. Alumnae, St. Mary's Hall, 1995, Opera Guild award 2000. Mem.: S.W. Performing Arts Presenters (chmn. 1988—92), Battle Flowers Assn., Jr. League San Antonio (Vol. Extraodinaire 2001), Women in Comm. (Headliner award 1982), Assn. Performing Arts Presenters, Internat. Soc. for Performing Arts (hon.; regional rep. 1982—85, bd. dirs. 1991—97). Avocations: traveling, reading, cooking, music, dance.

STANLEY, MARGARET DURETA SEXTON, retired speech therapist; b. Wells County, Ind., Aug. 7, 1931; d. James Helmuth and Bertha Anna (Kizer) Roberts; m. Gale Sexton, Nov. 21, 1950; children: Cregg Alan, Donna Sue, Sheila Rene; m. Charles Stanley, Mar. 24, 1979. BS, Ball State U., 1952, MA, 1963. Speech and hearing clinician Hamilton (Ohio) City Schs., 1955-59, Kettering (Ohio) Pub. Schs., 1959-60; speech, lang. and hearing clinician Muncie (Inc.) Community Schs., 1960-93; asst. prof. speech pathology Ball State U., 1993-97. Dir. Psi Iota Xi Summer Clinic, Decatur, Ind., 1964, Ball State U., 1965-77, asst. prof., 1993-97; supr. clinician Tri-County Hearing Impaired Assn., 1978-81. Compiler, editor curriculum for speech, lang. and hearing clinicians of Muncie Community Schs. Mem. NEA, Am. Speech and Hearing Assn., Ind. Edn. Assn., Ind. Coun. Suprs. Speech and Hearing (pres. 1982-84), Speech and Hearing Area Educators Ind. (founder, 1st pres. 1984-86, Disting. Svc. award 1991, Honors of Assoc. 1992), Delta Kapa Gamma (1st v.p. 1992-94, pres. 1994-96). Republican. Methodist. Home: 5245 Pelayo Rd SW Deming NM 88030-1781

STANLEY, MARLYSE REED, horse breeder; b. Fairmont, Minn., Sept. 19, 1934; d. Glenn Orson and Lura Mabel (Ross) Reed; m. James Arthur Stapleton, 1956 (div. 1976); 1 child, Elisabeth Katharene; m. John David Stanley, Oct. 22, 1982. BA, U. Minn., 1957. Registered breeder Arabian horses in Spain, 1976-94. Chmn. bd. dirs. Sitting Rock Spanish Arabians, Inc., Greensboro, N.C., 1978-81, pres. Hollister, Calif., 1981-91, Stanley Ranch, Yerington, Nev., 1991—. Bd. dirs. Glenn Reed Tire Co., Fairmont, Minn. Author Arabian hunter/jumper rules Am. Horse Shows Assn.; contbr. articles to horse jours. Named Palomino Queen of Minn., 1951, Miss Fairmont, 1954, Miss Minn., 1955. Mem.: AAUW, World Arabian Horse Assn., Assn. Española de Criadores de Caballos Arabes (Spain), Am. Paint Horse Assn. (nat. bd. dirs. 1967—70), Minn. Arabian Assn. (bd. dirs. 1972—75), Internat. Arabian Assn. (Minn. and Wis. 1973—76, nat. chmn. hunter-jumper com. 1976—81, chair IAHA sport horse rules com. 1998—2001, bd. dirs. region 10), Arabian Horse Registry Am., U.S. Nat. Arabian Sport Horse Finals--Show Commn., Alpha Xi Delta. Republican. Episcopalian. Avocations: fox hunting, fishing, breeding and importing Arabian horses.

STANLEY, MARY ELIZABETH, judge; AB, Mt. Holyoke Coll., 1970; JD, Univ. of Va., 1973. Bar: W.Va., U.S. Dist. Ct. (so. dist.) W.Va., U.S. Ct. Appeals (4th cir.). Atty. Columbia Gas Transmission Corp., 1973-76; law clk. to Judge Dennis R. Knapp, 1976-77; asst. U.S. atty. Charleston, W. Va., 1977-92; magistrate judge U.S. Dist. Ct. (so. dist.) W. Va., Bluefield, 1992-01, Charleston, 2001—. Office: Robert C Byrd US Courthouse Rm 5408 300 Virginia St E Charleston WV 25301

STANLEY, MYRTLE BROOKS, minister, educational and religious consultant; b. Balt., May 13, 1929; d. Benjamin Franklin and Ora Estell (Robinson) Brooks; m. Theodore Freeland Stanley, June 4, 1949; children: Theodora Stanley Snyder, Benjamin Brooks, Jonathan Stephen. BS, Morgan State Coll., 1951, MS, 1972; MA in Theology, St. Mary Sem. and U., Balt., 1987; postgrad., Fordham U., 1989-91; PhD, Am. U., 2001. Tchr., curriculum coord. Balt. City Pub. Schs., 1958-83; dir. propagation of faith Archdiocese of Balt., Roman Cath. Ch., Balt., 1984-95; coord. rite of Christian initiation for adults St. Matthew Roman Cath. Ch., 1996—; instr. Ch. Leadership Inst., Archdiocese of Balt., 1999—. Author, prodr. play It's Your Own Funeral, 1980, Miracle on 22d Street, 1980. Bd. dirs. Balt. Clergy and Laity Concerned, 1984-94, Towson (Md.) Cath. H.S., 1993-95, Good Samaritan Hosp., Balt., 1994-96; coord. Internat. Sisters in Struggle, 1991—. Mem. AAUW, Religious Sisters of Mercy of the Ams. (assoc.), Phi Delta Kappa.

STANLEY, NANCY JANE, medical records administrator, municipal official; b. Rome, Oct. 13, 1935; d. Jack Stanley and Lennie Lee (Fountain) Stanley-Smith; m. Harold Dean Lewis, Feb. 7, 1953 (div. June 1971); children: Doris Anne Goforth, Millissa Gale Lewis, Terry Allan Lewis, Scott Dale Lewis; m. Tony Welles Wallace, July 1, 1971 (dec. Mar. 1987). BS, U. Tex. Sch. Allied Health, Galveston, 1989. Cert. records adminstr. Supr. med. records MS Anderson Cancer Ctr., Houston, 1989-92; dir. med. records Mercy Hosp., Waldron, Ark., 1989, Harris County Sheriffs Dept., Houston, 1992—. Advisor 3 coll. record programs, Houston, 1994-99; tchr. Lee Cmty. Coll., Baytown, Tex., 1995-99, reviewer for cert., 1995-99. Asst. editor Tex. Health Info. Mgmt. Assn. Jour., 1991-92; spkr. profl. panels; editor newspaper Coll. of the Mainland, 1985. Campaign worker Ross Perot for Pres., 1992. Mem. Nat. Commn. Correctional Health Care (advisor divsn. profl. stds. for jails and prisons 1995), Phi Theta Kappa. Lutheran. Avocations: creative and profl. writing, painting. Office: Harris County Sheriffs Dept 1301 Franklin St Houston TX 77002-1978

STANLEY, PETER WILLIAM, academic administrator; b. Bronxville, N.Y., Feb. 17, 1940; s. Arnold and Mildred Jeanette (Pattison) Stanley; m. Mary-Jane Cullen Cosgrove, Sept. 2, 1978; 1 child Laura. BA magna cum laude(hon.) , Harvard U., 1962, MA, 1964, PhD, 1970; LHD (hon.) , Occidental Coll., 1994. Asst. prof. history U. Ill., Chgo., 1970—72, Harvard U., 1972—78, lectr. history, 1978—79; dean of coll. Carleton Coll., Northfield, Minn., 1979—84; program officer in charge edn. and culture program Ford Found., 1984—87, dir. edn. and culture program, 1987—91; pres. Pomona Coll., Claremont, Calif., 1991—. Lectr. Fgn. Service Inst., Arlington, Va., 1977—89. Author: A Nation in the Making: The Philippines and the United States, 1974; co-author: Sentimental Imperialists: The American Experience in East Asia, 1981; editor: Reappraising an Empire: New Perspectives on Philippine-American History, 1984; contbr. articles to profl. jours. Trustee The Coll. Bd., 1991—99, vice-chmn., 1993—94, chmn., 1994—96, Barnard Coll., 2000—; humanities and scis. coun. Stanford U., 1986—; nat. adv. coun. Nat. Fgn. Lang. Ctr., 1992—; exec. com. Consortium Financing Higher Edn., 1992—95; pres.' coun. divsn. III NCAA, 2000—; bd. dirs. Nat. Assn. Latino Elected Ofcls. Edn. Fund, Commn. on Internat. Edn., Am. Coun. Edn., 1992—95, The James Irvine Found., 1997—, The Hitachi Found., 1993—, Assn. Am. Colls. and Univs., 1995—, vice-chmn., 1998—99, chmn., 1999—; bd. fellows Claremont Grad. U. and Claremont U. Ctr., 1991—. Fellow Frank Knox Meml. fellow, Harvard U., 1962—63, Charles Warren Ctr. for Studies in Am. History fellow, 1975—76. Mem.: Coun. on Fgn. Rels., Assn. Asian Studies, Am. Hist. Assn., Phi Beta Kappa. Home: 345 N College Ave Claremont CA 91711-4408 Office: Pomona Coll Pres Office Claremont CA 91711-6301

STANLEY, RICHARD HOLT, consulting engineer; b. Muscatine, Iowa, Oct. 20, 1932; s. Claude Maxwell and Elizabeth Mabel (Holthues) S.; m. Mary Jo Kennedy, Dec. 20, 1953; children: Lynne Elizabeth, Sarah Catherine, Joseph Holt. BSEE, BSME, Iowa State U., 1955; MS in Sanitary Engrng., U. Iowa, 1963. Lic. profl. engr., Iowa. With Stanley Cons. Inc., Muscatine, Iowa, 1955—, pres., 1971-87, chmn., 1984—, also bd. dirs. Bd. dirs. Dover Resources, Inc.; bd. dirs. HON Industries, Inc., vice-chmn., 1979—; chmn Nat. Constrn. Industry Coun., 1978, Com. Fed. Procurement Archtl.-Engrng. Svcs., 1979; pres. Ea. Iowa C.C., Bettendorf, 1966-68; mem. indsl. adv. coun. Iowa State U. Coll. Engrng., Ames, 1969-97, chmn., 1979-81. Contbr. articles to profl. jours. Bd. dirs. N.E.-Midwest Inst., 1989-95, treas., 1991-93, chmn., 1993-95; bd. dirs. Stanley Found., 1956—, pres., 1984—, chmn., 1995—; bd. dirs. Muscatine Health Support Found., pres., 1984—; bd. dirs. Muscatine United Way, 1969-75, Iowa State U. Meml. Union, 1968-83, U. Dubuque, Iowa, 1977-93, Inst. Social and Econ. Devel., 1992-2001, Unity Health Sys., 1999—, chmn. 1999—; bd. govs. Iowa State U. Achievement Found., 1982-96. Recipient Young Alumnus award Iowa State U. Alumni Assn., 1966, Disting. Svc. award Muscatine Jaycees, 1967, Profl. Achievement citation Coll. Engrng., Iowa State U., 1977, Anson Marston medal Iowa State U., 1991, Harry S. Truman disting. svc. award Am. Assn. C.C., 1998; Disting. Alumni Achievement award U. Iowa Alumni Assn., 1999, award for Citizen Diplomacy, Nat. Coun. for Internat. Visitors, 2000, Hoover medal, 2001; named Sr. Engr. of Yr., Joint Engrng. Com. Quint Cities, 1973; named to Disting. Engrng. Alumni Acad., U. Iowa, 1998; inducted into Muscatine H.S. Hall of Honor, 2000. Fellow ASCE, Am. Cons. Engrs. Coun. (pres. 1976-77, Cmty. Svc. award 1997, Disting. Award of Merit 1998), Iowa Acad. Sci.; mem. IEEE (sr.), ASME, Am. Soc. Engrng. Edn., Nat. Soc. Profl. Engrs., Cons. Engrs. Coun. Iowa (pres. 1967), Iowa Engrng. Soc. (pres. 1973-74, John Dunlap-Sherman Woodward award 1967, Disting. Svc. award 1980, Voice of Engr. award 1987, Herbert Hoover Centennial award 1989), Muscatine C. of C. (pres. 1972-73), C. of C. of U.S. (constrn. action coun. 1976-91), Rotary, Tau Beta Pi, Phi Kappa Phi, Pi Tau Sigma, Eta Kappa Nu. Presbyterian (elder). Home: 516 Hogan Ct Muscatine IA 52761-2740 Office: Stanley Cons Inc Stanley Bldg Muscatine IA 52761 E-mail: rhstanley@machlink.com., rstanley@stanleygroup.com.

STANLEY, RICHARD P. mathematics educator; b. N.Y.C., June 23, 1944; s. Alan and Shirley (Silver) S.; m. Doris S. Skulsky, July 4, 1971; children: Kenneth, Sharon. BS, Calif. Inst. Technology, 1966; PhD, Harvard U., 1971.

Math. instr. MIT, Cambridge, Mass., 1970-71; Miller research fellow Miller Inst., Berkeley, Calif., 1971-73; asst. prof. applied math. MIT, Cambridge, 1973-75, assoc. prof. applied math., 1975-79, prof. applied math., 1979-2000, Norman Levinson prof. applied math., 2000—. Cons. in field. Author: Combinatorics and Commutative Algebra, 1983, 2d edit., 1996, Enumerative Combinatorics, Vol. 1, 1986, Vol. 2, 1999. Recipient SIAM Polya Prize Soc. Indsl. and Applied Math., Guggenheim Fellowship, Guggenheim Found., 1983-84, Steele prize for math. exposition, 2001. Fellow Am. Acad. Arts and Scis.; mem. Nat. Acad. Scis., Am. Math. Soc., Math. Assn. Am. Office: MIT Dept Math 2-375 77 Massachusetts Ave Cambridge MA 02139-4307 E-mail: rstan@math.mit.edu.

STANLEY, ROBERT ANTHONY, artist, educator; b. Defuniac Springs, Fla., Mar. 10, 1942; m. Jane Tumosa, May 11, 1973; children: Daiva, Thomas, Daniel. BA cum laude, U. Dayton, 1964; MS, Pratt Inst., N.Y.C., 1969. Dir. art program Upward Bound project Earlham Coll., Richmond, Ind., 1967-68; lectr. art dept. U. Dayton, Ohio, 1967-68; asst. prof. art and humanities Harrisburg (Pa.) C.C., 1969-71; prof. art Oakton Coll., Des Plaines, Ill., 1971—2002, prof. emeritus, 2002—. Mem. com. League for Humanities Study Grant, Des Plaines, 1988-89; assoc. dir. Inst. for Environ. Response, N.Y.C., 1968-70; presenter League for Innovation Conf., 1994, Mid-Am. Art Conf., 1997. Author: Exploring the Film, 1968 (Maxi award 1969), (interactive multimedia) VisLang, 1994; contbr. articles to profl. jours.; shows include William Penn Mus., Harrisburg, Pa., New Horizons in Art Chgo., 1974, Internat. All on Paper, Buffalo, 1979, Zaner Gallery, Rochester, N.Y., 1983, Joy Horwich Gallery, Chgo., 1988, 95, U. Oreg., Portland, 1991, Atrium Gallery, N.Y.C., 1991, Shelter Gallery, Chgo., 1992, Matrix Gallery, Chgo., Museé d'Art Contemporain, Chamalieres, France, 1994, 97, Blank Arts Ctr., Michigan City, Ind., 1997, No. Ind. Ctr. Visual and Performing Arts, Munster, Ind., 1998, Contemporary Art Ctr., Peoria, Ill., 1999, Gov.'s Mansion, Indpls., 1998, Vichy, FR, 2000, Blank Art Ctr., M.C., Ind., 2001, Koehnline Gallery, Des Plaines, 2002. Vol. Ctr. of Concern, Park Ridge, Ill., 1993—; bd. dirs. Kloempken Prairie Restoration, Des Plaines, 1987-89, Brickton Art Ctr., 1998—. Grantee OCC Ednl. Found., 1989; recipient 2d Place Paragon award for video Nat. Coun. Cmty. Rels., 1985, 1st place Gold award for graphics Art Ctr. Show, Dayton Art Inst., 1969, award of merit Internat. Works on Paper, 1979, Prix de la Ville de Vichy Chamalieres Triennial, 1997, Merit award Chesteron Ind. Regl. 2000. Mem. NEA, Ill. Higher Art Edn. Assn. (founding mem., bd. dirs. 1975-76, 83-84). E-mail: rstanley@oakton.edu.

STANLEY, RONNIE L., JR. theology educator, college dean, clergyman; b. Washington, Aug. 26, 1961; s. Ronnie L. and Marilyn Patricia Stanley; m. Vera Frances Allen, Nov. 23, 1986; children: Ashley, Lauren, Taya, Amanda. BS, Columbia (S.C.) Internat. U., 1994; ThM, Dallas Theol. Sem., 1999. Ordained to ministry Independant Evang., 1998. Supervision specialist Alston Wilkes Soc., Columbia, 1991-93; instr. comm. Columbia Internat. U., 1992-93; urban missionary, mentor The S.T.E.P. Found., Dallas, 1994-97; dir. Ctr. for Christian Growth, Oak Cliff Bible Fellowship, 1996-98, missions dir., 1998-99; prof. theology, acad. dean Carver Bible Coll., Atlanta, 1999—; pastor Christian edn. New Calvary Missionary Bapt. Ch., 1999—. Bd. dirs. Renaissance Enterprises, Dallas; mem. Ctr. for Christian Leadership Thinktank, Dallas, 1996-97. Bd. dirs. Mt. Sinai Outreach Ctr., Washington, 1986. Mem. Evang. Tchrs. Assn. (cert.). Republican. Avocations: reading, writing, skating. Home: 437 Nelson St SW Atlanta GA 30313-1333 Office: Carver Bible Coll 437 Nelson St SW Atlanta GA 30313-1333 E-mail: revstanley@hotmail.com.

STANLEY, SCOTT, JR. editor; b. Kansas City, Kans., July 11, 1938; s. Winfield Scott and Irene Mae (Flint) S.; m. Janice Johns, Aug. 30, 1959 (dec. July 1992); children: Leslie, Scott, Margaret; m. Cynthia Ward, Dec. 30, 1995; 1 child, Elizabeth. BA, Earlham Coll., 1960. Mng. editor Am. Opinion mag., Boston, 1961-85; editor Rev. of The News mag., 1965-85; editor-in-chief Conservative Digest, Washington, 1985-88, Am. Press Internat., Washington, 1987—; pres. USA Tech., 1991-92; mng. editor Nutrition and Healing, 1994-2000; dep. editor Insight on the News, Washington, 1995—. Mem. nat. bd. dirs. Young Ams. for Freedom, 1960-62; public speaker and univ. lectr., 1962— Keynote speaker Am. Party Nat. Conv., 1976; pres. Ams. Legal Def. Fund, 1977— ; bd. govs. Council for Nat. Policy, 1981—; bd. dirs. Free Congress Polit. Action Com., 1985-88; pres. Scott Stanley Real Estate Trust, 1988—. Recipient award of merit Young Ams. for Freedom, Freedom award Nat. Congress for Freedom. Mem.: Nat. Press, Meganset Yacht. Episcopalian.

STANLEY, STEVEN MITCHELL, paleobiologist, educator; b. Detroit, Nov. 2, 1941; s. William Thomas and Mildred Elizabeth (Baker) S.; m. Nell Williams Gilmore, Oct. 11, 1969. AB with highest honors, Princeton U., 1963; PhD, Yale U., 1968. Asst. prof. U. Rochester, 1967-69; asst. prof. paleobiology Johns Hopkins U., 1969-71, assoc. prof., 1971-74, prof., 1974, chmn. dept. Earth and planetary Scis., 1987-88, chmn. MS program in environ. scis. and policy. Assoc. in rsch. Smithsonian Instn., 1972—; mem. bd. earth scis. NRC, 1985—, vice chmn., 1988, mem. bd. earth scis. resources, 1988-88, com. on solid earth scis., exec. and steering com., 1988, com. on geoscis., environ, and resources, 1990-96. Author: Relation of Shell Form to Life Habits in the Bivalvia, 1970, (with D.M. Raup) Principles of Paleontology, 1971, Macroevolution: Pattern and Process, 1979, The New Evolutionary Timetable: Fossils, Genes, and the Origin of species, 1981, Earth and Life Through Time, 1986, Extinction, 1987, Exploring Earth and Life Through Time, 1992, Children of the Ice Age: How a Global Catastrophe Allowed Humans to Evolve, 1996, Earth System History, 1999; mem. editl. bd. Am. Jour. Sci., 1975—, Paleobiology, 1975-82, 88—, Evolutionary Theory, 1973—. Recipient Outstanding Paper award Jour. Paleontology, 1968, Allan C. Davis medal Md. Acad. Scis., 1973, Outstanding Tech. Paper award Washington Geol. Soc., 1986, Bownocker medal Ohio State U., 1997; Guggenheim fellow, 1981 Fellow NAS, Am. Acad. Arts and Scis., Geol. Soc. Am. (chmn. Penrose com. 1978, councilor 2002—); mem. Paleontol. Soc. (councilor 1976-77, sr. councilor 1991-93, pres. 1993-94, Charles Schuchert award 1977), Soc. for Study Evolution (councilor 1982-84), Am. Geophys. Union (pub. affairs com.), Paleontol. Rsch. Inst., Am. Geol. Inst. (mem. exec. com. 1996-99, pres. 2001—). Office: Johns Hopkins U Dept Earth Planetary Sciences Baltimore MD 21218 E-mail: stanley@jhu.edu.

STANLEY-CHAVIS, SANDRA ORNECIA, special education educator, consultant; b. Jersey City, July 6, 1950; d. McKinley and Thelma Louise (Newberry) S. BA, Ottawa (Kans.) U., 1972; MS in Edn., U. Kans., 1975, PhD (fellow), 1980; postgrad. St. George's U. Sch. Medicine, Grenada, W.I. Dir., head tchr. Salem Bapt. Nursery Sch., Jersey City, 1972-73; spl. ednl. instr. Joan Davis Sch. Spl. Edn., Kansas City, Mo., 1975-76; instructional media/materials trainee, then rsch. asst. U. Kans. Med. Ctr., 1976-79; rsch. asst. U. Kans., Lawrence, 1979; dir., coord. tng. and observation Juniper Gardens Children's project Bur. Child Rsch., U. Kans., Kansas City, 1979-82, rsch. assoc., 1980; psychol assoc., ednl. cons. family crisis unit Internat. Youth Orgn., 1988-93; ednl. cons. Renaissance Ctr., 1994; exec. dir. 2000 Friends, 1994; asst. prof. and coord. spl. edn., Albany (Ga.) State U., 1995-2000; pres. Ednl. Expansion, Inc.; lectr., speaker, cons. edn. and med. sci. Author papers and manuals in field. Past mem. adv. bd. Rainbows for All God's Children. Christian Community Health fellow; scholar Coll. Women, Inc., 1977; Easter Seal grantee, 1975; recipient various awards, plaques, certs. of recognition. Mem. Christian Med. and Dental Soc., The Coun. of Exceptional Children, Assn. for Supervision and Curriculum devel., Nat Coun. for Learing Disability. E-mail: educationalexpansion@yahoo.com. Home: 2301 Beattie Rd Albany GA 31707-2105

STANLEY-HERMANNS, MELINDA LOUISE, mental health nurse; b. Tyler, Tex., July 13, 1971; d. Jerry Luther and Joyce Louise (Kinard) S. ADN, Tyler Jr. Coll., 1992; BSN magna cum laude, U. Tex., Tyler, 1995, MSN, 1998. RN Tex., cert. bd. cert. psychiat./mental health nursing, ANCC, 2000. Grad. nurse East Tex. Med. Ctr. Hosp., Tyler, 1992; staff nurse Tyler Rehab. Hosp., 1993-94, East Tex. Med. Ctr. Behavioral Health, Tyler, 1996-2000; nursing lab. coord. U. Tex., 1998-2000. Presenter, lectr. on cmty. cancer awareness, prevention of breast cancer, Tyler, 1994—; adj. prof. U. Tex., Tyler, 1999; sr. lectr., course coord. mental health nursing U. Tex., Tyler, 2000—. Bd. dirs. Tyler Civic Chorale. Mem. ANA, Am. Psychiat. Nurses Assn., Tex. Nurses Assn., U. Tex. Alumni Assn., Tyler Jr. Coll. Alumni Assn., Alpha Chi, Sigma Theta Tau. Avocations: cooking, travel, singing.

STANLEY-STEVENS, LESLIE, sociologist; b. Dallas, May 15, 1961; d. William Henry and Mary Lurline (Smith) Stanley; m. Christopher Lee Stanley-Stevens, Dec. 28, 1985; children: Parker Alan, Forrest Alexander. BS in Secondary Edn. and English, Tex. Tech. U., 1983; MA in Religion, Asbury Theol. Sem., Wilmore, Ky., 1985; PhD in Sociology, U. North Tex., 1994. Assoc. dir. Louisville Coun. on Ministries Louisville Conf. of United Meth. Ch., 1986—88; min. Christian edn. Arapaho United Meth. Ch., Richardson, Tex., 1988—89; rsch. project mgr. U. North Tex., Denton, 1989—94; asst. prof. sociology Tarleton State U., Stephenville, Tex., 1995—2002, assoc. prof. sociology, 2002—. Movie reviewer Stephenville Empire-Tribune, Tex., 1999—, Hood County News, Granbury, Tex., 1999—; John Wesley fellow Found. for Theol. Edn., 1990—. Contbr. Active hwy. trash pick-up Tex. Adopt-a-Hwy. Program, Stephenville, 1998—; vol. Chamberlin Elem., 1999—. Fellow Outstanding Tchg. fellow, U. North Tex., 1994; grantee 6 rsch. grants. Mem.: Am. Sociol. Assn. Democrat. United Methodist. Avocations: photography, travel, racquetball, reading. Office: Tarleton State U Dept Sociology TSU Box T-0665 Stephenville TX 76402

STANN, JOHN ANTHONY, investment banker; b. San Francisco, Nov. 10, 1947; s. John Peter and Mary Jane (Erny) S.; m. Judith Darlene Knapp, Apr. 27, 1973; children: John Andrew, Theodore Joseph, Rebecca Marie. BA in Econs. and Math., U. Mo., 1969. Cost acct. Monsanto Co., St. Louis, 1971-73, acctg. supr., 1973-76, salesman Brighton, Mo., 1976-79, market mgr. St. Louis, 1979-81; mfr's. rep. Farbenfabriken, Bayer, Davos & Others, 1981-82; A.G. Edwards & Sons, Inc., 1982-2000; pres. Stann Fin., 2000—. Investment banking advisor to numerous pvt. cos.; Dev. Comm. of Neriny Hall H.S., 1994-97. Fundraiser Archdiocese of St. Louis, 1981-84, 87-92, YMCA, St. Louis, 1987; chmn. fin. com. St. Clare Parish, St. Louis, 1982-84; mem. Assumption Parish Coun., 1988-90, chmn., 1989-90; youth baseball mgr. Affton Athletic Assn., St. Louis, 1985-86; poll worker Danforth for Senate, St. Louis, 1982. Lt. USNR, 1969-71. Named Man of Yr. St. John's Men's Club, 1978. Mem. Fox Run Golf Club. Republican. Roman Catholic. Avocations: handball, golf. Home: 9148 Fox Bridge Dr Saint Louis MO 63127-1362 Office: Stann Financial LLC PO Box 270001 Saint Louis MO 63127 E-mail: john@stannfinancial.com.

STANNETT, VIVIAN THOMAS, chemical engineering educator; b. Langley, Eng., Sept. 1, 1917; came to U.S., 1947, naturalized, 1957; s. Ernest and Dorothy Grace (Rustell) S.; m. Flora Susanne Sulzbacher, May 30, 1946; 1 dau., Rosemary Anthia. BS, London Poly., 1939; PhD, Poly. Inst. Bklyn., 1950. Chemist, govt. and industry, Eng., 1939-47; research assoc. Mellon Inst., Pitts., 1950-51; research chemist Koppers Co., 1951-52; prof. polymer chemistry State U. Coll. Forestry, Syracuse, N.Y., 1952-61; asso. dir. Camille Dreyfus Labs., Research Triangle Inst., Durham, N.C., 1961-67; Camille Dreyfus prof. chem. engring. N.C. State U., Raleigh, 1967—, vice provost, dean Grad. Sch., 1975-82. Author: Cellulose Acetate Plastics, 1950, Handbook of Chemical Technology, 1953; contbr. articles to profl. jours. Recipient Borden award Am. Chem. Soc., 1974, Anselm Payen award, 1974, O. Max Gardner award U. N.C., 1984, Polymer Chemistry award Am. Chem. Soc., 1987. Olney medal Am. Assn. Textile Chemists and Colorists, 1995. Fellow Royal Soc. Chemistry, TAPPI (Silver medal synthetic divsn. 1967), N.Y. Acad. Scis., Soc. Plastics Engrs. (Internat. award and gold medal 1978, N.C. Sci. medal 1981); mem. NAE. Home: 2801 Glenwood Gardens Ln # 106 Raleigh NC 27608- E-mail: Deanvivian@aol.com.

STANNY, GARY, infosystems specialist, computer scientist; b. Detroit, Aug. 2, 1953; s. Richard Telesfor and Gertrude Mildred (Senbach) Stanny. AS, Washtenaw C.C., 1973; B in Computer Sci., Ea. Mich. U., 1975. Programmer Ann Arbor (Mich.) Terminals, 1976-78; sr. programmer, analyst Mfg. Data Systems Inc., Ann Arbor, 1978-83; sr. software specialist Digital Equipment Corp., Farmington Hills, Mich., 1983-85; sr. systems cons. Tierra del Fuego Ltd, Whitmore Lake, 1985-87, v.p. R & D, 1987—, also bd. dirs. Bd. dirs. RTS Enterprises, South Lyon, Mich.; dir. R & D, Lynn-Arthur Assocs., 1993-97. Author: Ingres RMS Benchmarks, 1986, The S&P Premium Matrix, 1991; inventor in field; developer software WTDF-lib, 1998. Counselor Drug Help, Ann Arbor, 1971-77, Rep. candidate senate, Ann Arbor, 1976; mem. Students Dem. Soc. State of Mich. Competitive Sci. grantee, 1971. Mem. Am. Assn. Artificial Intelligence Rsch. (computing machinery), Digital Equipment Computer Users Soc., Decus Artificial Intelligence Spl. Interest Group, Soc. Machine Intelligence, Mensa. Avocations: geopolitics, backpacking, travel, computers, artificial intelligence research. Office: Tierra del Fuego Ltd 7725 Shady Beach St Whitmore Lake MI 48189-9514

STANO, MARY GERARDINE, writer, tax accountant; b. Milw., Sept. 28, 1953; d. Stephen A. and Vera D. (Gulas) S. Newsletter editor Lake Havasu City (Ariz.) Police Dept., 1984-85; entertainment columnist Today News, Lake Havasu City, 1985-87; hist. columnist Las Vegas Rev.-Jour., 1988-89; editor Guide to the Western Sunbelt, Lake Havasu City, 1989-92, Destination Havasu, Lake Havasu City, 1995—; article writer True West, Stillwater, Okla., 1988—, Wild West, Leesburg, Va., 1994—. Mem. Nat. Writers ASsn. Republican. Roman Catholic. Avocations: reading books, hiking, bowling, biking.

STANSBERRY, JAMES WESLEY, air force officer; b. Grafton, W.Va., Dec. 29, 1927; s. William Adrian and Phyllis Gay (Robinson) S.; m. Audrey Mildred Heinz, May 7, 1950; children: Nora G., Amy G. Stansberry Goodhand, Lisa Porten. BS, U.S. Mil. Acad., 1949; MBA, Air Force Inst. Tech., 1956. Advanced through grades from pvt. to lt. gen. USAF; chief prodn. (Kawasaki Gifu Contract Facility), Gifu, Japan, 1956-57; dep. asst. to Sec. of Def. for atomic energy Washington, 1970-71; dep. dir. procurement policy U.S. Air Force, 1972-73; dep. chief staff contracting and mfg. (Hdqrs. Air Force Systems Command), Andrews AFB, Md., 1977-81; comdr. Electronic Systems Div. Hanscom AFB, Mass., 1981-84; pres. Stansberry Assocs. Inc., 1984—. Decorated DSM with oak leaf cluster, Legion of Merit with oak leaf cluster; named Disting. grad. Lancaster (N.Y.) H.S. Methodist. Home: 43 Monadnock Dr Westford MA 01886-3021 E-mail: us49@aol.com. *The real secrets are enthusiasm, competence and good luck; and it helps immensely to marry a good woman. Work and persistence define us, accomodating various levels of talent and intelligence. Work and persistence prevail, buttressed by discipline and determination, and perhaps supported by a sense of humor.*

STANSBERY, DAVID HONOR, biology diversity educator, malacologist; b. Upper Sandusky, Ohio, May 5, 1926; s. Honor Gerald and Daisy Elizabeth (Kirby) S.; m. Mary Lois Pease, June 16, 1948; children: Michael David, Mark Andrew, Kathleen Mary, Linda Carol. BS, Ohio State U., 1950, MS, 1953, PhD, 1960. Instr. Ohio State U., Columbus, 1956-62, asst. prof., 1962-66, assoc. prof., 1966-71; state curator of natural history Ohio State Mus., 1962-72; vis. scientist Smithsonian Instn., Washington, 1973-74; sr. rsch. assoc. The Ohio State Mus., Columbus, 1972—; dir. mus. of zoology Ohio State U., 1970-92, prof. zoology, 1971-91, curator of mollusks Mus. of Biol. Diversity, 1962-2000, prof. emeritus, 1991—, curator emeritus, 2001—. Adv. bd. Ohio Biol. Survey, 1961-72; exec. com. Ohio Acad. of Sci., 1961-69; chair collection stds. Coun. of Systematic Malacologists, 1977-81; bd. govs. The Nature Conservancy, 1979-86; rsch. adv., guest lectr. Huazhong Agrl. U., Wuhan, Hubei, China, 1992; mem. faculty Upper Cumberland Biol. Sta. Tenn. Tech. U., 1987-91; presenter in field. Assoc. editor: Ohio Jour. Sci., 1960-61, editor, 1961-64; contbr. articles to profl. jours. Bd. trustees Columbus Audubon Soc., 1969-73; bd. dirs. Am. Rivers Cons. Coun., 1973-88. Recipient Oak Leaf award Nature Conservancy, 1977, Ohio Conservation Achievement award Ohio Dept. Natural Resouces, 1974, Lifetime Achievement award Freshwater Mollusk Conservation Soc., 1999, Herbert Osborn award Ohio Biol. Survey, 1999; grantees U.S. Dept. Interior, U.S. Dept. Commerce, U.S. Army Corps of Engrs., Battelle, Am. Electric Power, and others. Fellow AAAS, Ohio Acad. of Sci., Acad. of Zoology; mem. Am. Malacol. Union (pres. 1970-71), Sigma Xi (pres. 1974-75). Achievements include building the world's largest freshwater bivalve mollusk collection at the Ohio State University Museum of Biological Diversity. Avocations: geology, history of science, evolution of ethics, linguistics. Home: 32 Amazon Pl Columbus OH 43214-3502 Office: Mus of Biol Diversity Ohio State Univ 1315 Kinnear Rd Columbus OH 43212-1157 Fax: 614-292-7774. E-mail: stansbery.1@osu.edu.

STANSBURY, HARRY CASE, state commissioner; BS in Gen. Studies, La. State U., 1968; JD, Loyola U., New Orleans, 1971; student, Oxford (Eng.) U., 1985, Harvard U., 1988; MBA, U. New Orleans, 1998; MA, Columbia U., 2000. Bar: La., N.Y., D.C., U.S. Supreme Ct., U.S. Ct. Appeals (1st-11th cirs., D.C. cir., fed. cir.), U.S. Ct. Mil. Appeals, U.S. Ct. Fed. Claims, U.S. Ct. Internat. Trade, U.S. Tax Ct., U.S. Dist. Ct. (ea., mid. and we. dists.) La., U.S. Dist. Ct. (ea., no., so. and we. dists.) N.Y., U.S. Dist. Ct. D.C. Staff atty. La. Securities Commn., New Orleans, 1971-75, dep. commr. securities, 1975—. Mem. liaison com. fed. securities code project Am. Law Inst.-ABA, 1974-80; speaker, expert witness in field. Contbr. articles to profl. jours. Mem. ABA (sect. bus. law, sect. internat. law and practice, sect. legal edn. and admissions to bar, mem. subcom. derivative instruments fed. regulation securities com. 1993—), N.Am. Securities Adminstrs. Assn. (mem. registration exemption com. 1991—), La. State Bar Assn. (sect. corp. and bus. law, mem. internat. law com. 1991-92), N.Y. State Bar Assn. (banking, corp. and bus. law sect.), D.C. Bar Assn. (corp., fin. and securities law divsn.), Assn. of Bar of City of N.Y., Assn. of Bar of D.C., New Orleans Bar Assn. (vice chair corps. and bus. law com. 1992-94, chair 1994—), Fed. Bar Assn. (fin. instns. and economy sect.), Internat. Bar Assn. (sect. bus. law, mem. issues and trading in securities com. 1991—), La. State U. Alumni Assn., Loyola Law Alumni Assn., Harvard Law Sch. Assn., Am. Friends Rewley House, Supreme Ct. Hist. Soc. Address: 10001 Lake Forest Blvd Ste 803 New Orleans LA 70127

STANSBURY, JAMES PATRICK, anthropologist, researcher; b. L.A., May 26, 1953; s. John Gilbert Stansbury and Dorothy Alice Stansbury-Gleeson; m. Brenda S. Stidham, Oct. 4, 1997; 1 child, Melanie Ann. BA, U. N.Mex., 1975, MA, 1986; PhD, U. Ky., 1996. Asst. prof. U. Fla., Gainesville, 1997—. Vol. Internat. Voluntary Svcs., San Julian, Santa Cruz, Bolivia, 1991-92. Grantee NSF, 2000. Mem. Am. Anthropol. Assn., Soc. Applied Anthropology. Home: 5530 SW 98th Ter Gainesville FL 32608 Office: Dept Anthropology U Fla Gainesville FL 32611-7305 Fax: (352) 392-6929. E-mail: jstansbu@ufl.edu.

STANSELL, LELAND EDWIN, JR. lawyer, mediator, educator; b. Central, S.C., July 13, 1934; s. Leland Edwin and Hettie Katherine (Hollis) S.; children: James Leland, Susan. BS, Fla. So. Coll., 1957; LLB, U. Miami, Fla., 1961, JD, 1968. Bar: Fla. 1961; cert. civil mediator Fla. Supreme Ct., U.S. Dist. Ct. Fla. Assoc. Wicker & Smith, Miami, 1961-62, ptnr., 1962-75; pvt. practice, 1975-99, Leland E. Stansell, Jr., P.A., 1995—. Chmn. Appellate Jud. Nominating Com., Dade County (Fla.), 1983-87; mem. adv. com. Am. Arbitration Assn., 1975-90. Served with U.S. Army, 1957. Mem. ABA (ho. of dels. 1982-86), Fla. Bar (bd. govs. 1966-70, 70-80), Dade County Bar Assn. (dir. 1969-72, exec. com. 1974-75, pres. 1975-76), U Miami Law Alumni Assn. (dir., officer, pres. 1968-69), Fla. Criminal Def. Attys. Assn. (treas. 1964-66), Am. Judicature Soc., Am. Bd. Trial Advs., Internat. Assn. Def. Counsel, Fla. Acad. Profl. Mediators, Fedn. Ins. Counsel, Miami Beach Rod and Reel Club (pres.), Coral Reef Yacht Club, Bankers Club, Ocean Reef Yacht Club, Delta Theta Phi (pres. Miami alumni chpt. 1966, regional dir. 1968. Office: 19 W Flagler St Miami FL 33130-4400

STANSELL, RONALD BRUCE, investment banker; b. Hammond, Ind., Apr. 9, 1945; s. Herman Bruce and Helen Rose Stansell; m. Kathie Van Atta, Oct. 2, 1976; children: Kelsey, Kymberlie. BA, Wittenberg U., 1967; MA, Miami U., Oxford, Ohio, 1969. Investment officer First Nat. Bank, Chgo., 1969-73; mgr. investments Chrysler Corp., Detroit, 1973; asst. v.p. A.G. Becker, Chgol, 1973-76; v.p. Blyth Eastman Dillon, Chgo., 1976-79, Dean Witter Reynolds Inc., Chgo., 1979-82, First Boston Corp., 1982-88; sr. v.p. Prudential-Bache Securities, Chgo., 1988-90; ptnr. William Blair & Co., 1991-99; pres. Oakmont of Carolina, 1999—2001; 1st v.p. Legg, Mason, Wood, Walker, 2001—. Mem. Mettawa (Ill.) Zoning Bd., 1978-80; treas. Village of Mettawa, 1977-78, trustee, 1980-91. With USMCR, 1968-74. Mem. Bond Club Chgo., Investment Analyst Soc., Fixed Income Group, Bob O'Link Golf Club, Grandfather Golf Club, Forest Creek Golf Club, Belfair Golf Club, Berkeley Hall Club, Old Chatham Club, Diamond Creek Golf Club, Univ. Club.

STANSFIELD, CHARLES W. educational administrator; m. Charlene Rivera, Sept. 6, 1989. BA in Spanish, Fla. State U., 1968, MA in Fgn. Lang. Edn., 1969, MS in Teaching English as Second Lang., 1970, PhD in Fgn. and Second Lang. Edn., 1973. Tchr. English, Centro Colombo-Americano, Bogota, Colombia, 1966; 2jr. high sch. tchr. Spanish Fla. State U. Demonstration Sch., 1968-69; instr. Spanish, U. Colo., Boulder, 1970-73, asst. prof., 1973-80, assoc. prof., 1980-81; assoc. program dir. lang. programs Ednl. Testing Svc., Princeton, N.J., 1981-86; dir. fgn. lang. edn. and testing div. Ctr. for Applied Linguistics, Washington, 1986-94, dir. ERIC Clearinghouse Lang. and Linguistics, 1986-94; pres. Second Lang. Testing, Inc., Bethesda, Md., 1994—. Dir. Peace Corps Tng. Ctr., Managua, Nicaragua, 1978; mem. exec. com. Joint Nat. Com. on Langs., 1988-93; conf. coord. Interagy. Lang. Roundtable Invitational Symposium on Lang. Aptitude Testing, Rosslyn, Va., 1988; mem. adv. bd. Nat. Fgn. Lang. Resources Ctr., U. Hawaii, 1991-93; numerous presentations at profl. meetings, 1970—. Author: Cuaderno de ejercicios, 1976, rev. edit., 1981; co-author: Manual de laboratorio, 2d rev. edit., 1981, The Test of Spoken English as a Measure of Communicative Ability in the Health Professions,: Validation and Standard Setting, 1983, (with, others) Multiple-Choice Cloze Items and the Test of English as a Foreign Language, 1988; co-editor: Second Language Proficincy Assessment: Current Issues, 1988, Language Aptitude Reconsidered, 1990; also numerous articles. Named Outstanding Alumnus Fla. State U., 1994; Colo. Congress Fgn. Lang. Tchrs. scholar, 1981. Mem. Am. Assn. Tchrs. Spanish and Portuguese (life), Am. Coun. on Teaching Fgn. Langs. (Paul Pinsleur award 1984), Am. Ednl. Rsch. Assn., Internat. Assn. Applied Linguistics, Nat. Assn. for Bilingual Edn., Nat. Coun. on Measurement in Edn., Internat. Lang. Testing Assn. (pres. 1992-93), Tchrs. English to Speakers Other Langs., Washington Area Tchrs. English to Speakers Other Langs., Colo. Tchrs. English to Speakers Other Langs. (Gladys Doty award 1987). Home and Office: 10704 Mist Haven Ter Rockville MD 20852-3437 E-mail: cstansfield@2LTI.com.

STANSIL, SHERYL, medical/surgical nurse; b. Birmingham, Ala., May 17, 1963; d. Willie Caesar and Irene (Fisher) Stansil; 1 child Tyler Christina. BSN, Dillard U., 1987; MSN in Trauma Nursing, U. Ala. in Birmingham, 1992. Asst. prof. nursing BSN program Coppin State Coll., Balt., 1997-99; staff nurse Progressive Care Ctr., Colorado Springs, Colo., 1995-96; clin. instr. nursing Beth-El Coll. Nursing, 1995; staff nurse VA Med. Ctr., Balt., 1996—, Nursefinders of Balt., 1996—; staff nurse surgery Johns Hopkins Hosp., Balt., 1997-99; nurse care mgr. VA Med. Ctr., 1999—. Past instr. clin. nursing Beth-El Coll. Nursing; past asst. prof. and clin. instr. BSN program Coppin State Coll. Mem.: AACN, ANA, State Nurses Assn., Am. Assn. Managed Care Nurses, Sigma Theta Tau Internat.

STANTON, BENJAMIN R. investment company executive; b. N.Y.C., Oct. 25, 1930; s. Lionel and Nettie (Voloshen) S.; m. Melinda Koch, 1959 (div. 1969); children: Wendy, Carol; m. H. Elizabeth Tonning, Apr. 30, 1970; children: Natasha, Nicholas. BA, Emerson Coll., 1950; postgrad., Harvard U., 1960. V.p. Parvin Dohrman, L.A., 1960-70; v.p. operating div. Beatrice Foods, Chgo., 1970-78; dir. Damson Oil, N.Y.C., 1978-79; exec. v.p. Globe Glass, Chgo., 1979-88; pres. Sun Distrbrs. Glass, Rosemont, Ill., 1988-93; exec. v.p. Nat. Autoglass Coop., Winston-Salem, N.C., 1992-93, Lake Forest, Ill., 1993-95; ptnr. AVM Fin., Chgo., 1995—; investment banker Stanton & Co. Investment Banking Svcs., Lake Forest, 1997—. Lt. USN, 1950-55, Korea. Mem. Mason Darcy Lodge. Republican. Avocations: geopolitics, golf, travel. Home: 3069 Sumter Valley Cir Henderson NV 89052-6893 Office: Stanton & Co 3069 Sumter Valley Cir Henderson NV 89052 Business E-Mail: bstan001@worldnet.att.net.

STANTON, DAVID LONGJOHN, lawyer; b. Colorado Springs, Oct. 23, 1968; s. Stephen Slaughter and Barbara Ann Stanton. AA, Arapahoe C.C., 1992; BA, St. John's Coll., 1996; JD, U. Calif., Berkeley, 1999. Bar: Calif. 1999. Atty. Troy & Gould Profl. Corp., L.A., 1999—. E-mail: dlstanton@lawyer.com.

STANTON, DAVID MANSFIELD, writer, communications executive; b. Summit, N.J., Feb. 7, 1962; s. George Basil Jr. and Jane Gray Mansfield Stanton; m. Barbara Ann Somogyi, Dec. 15, 1955; children: Sara Louise, Christopher David. BA in Print Journalism, U. So. Calif., 1984. Copy editor PC Mag., N.Y.C., 1989-90; sr. copy writer Book-of-the-Month Club, 1990-97; dir. mktg. comm. Statis. Rsch., Inc., Cranford, NJ, 1997—; freelance copywriter advt. and direct mail, 1990—. Contbg. editor The Croton Rev., 1983-88;

contbr. articles to various jours., publs. Fellow Bread Loaf Writers' Conf. Avocations: drumming, writing poetry, photography, collecting, concert-going. Home: 2219 Westfield Ave Scotch Plains NJ 07076 E-mail: d.m.stanton@worldnet.att.net.

STANTON, DONALD SHELDON, academic administrator; b. Balt., June 8, 1932; s. Kenneth Gladstone and Dorothy Erma (Hetrick) S.; m. Barbara Mae Hoot, June 25, 1955; children: Dale Richard, Debra Carol, Diane Karen. AB, Western Md. Coll., 1953; Litt.D., Oglethorpe U., 1999; LLD, Western Md. Coll., 1981; MDiv magna cum laude, Wesley Theol. Sem., 1956; MA, Am. U., 1960; Ed.D., U. Va., 1965; L.H.D., Columbia Coll., 1979; Litt.D., Albion Coll., 1983. Ordained to ministry United Methodist Ch., 1956; pastor Balt. and Va. confs. United Meth. Ch., 1953-59; dir. Richmond (Va.) Area Wesley Found., 1959-63; chaplain, dean of students Greensboro Coll., 1963-65; chaplain Wofford Coll., 1965-69; dir. office coll. services United Meth. Div. Higher Edn., Nashville, 1969-75; v.p. for devel. Wesleyan Coll., 1975-78; pres. Adrian Coll., 1978-88, Oglethorpe U., Atlanta, 1988-99, pres. emeritus, 1999—. Adminstr., prof. European internat. ednl. programs, summers 1960, 69-71, 73; chmn. pres.'s assn. Mich. Intercollegiate Athletic Assn., 1986-87. Contbr. articles, revs. to profl. publs. in U.S., Japan, Argentina, chpts. to books; editor: Faculty Forum, 1972-74; bass-baritone soloist. Bd. dirs. Toledo (Ohio) Symphony, 1980-83, Lewanee County Jr. Achievement, 1980-83, Found. Ind. Higher Edn., 1996-99, Nat. Conf. for Cmty. and Justice, Atlanta Region, Atlanta Area Coun. Boy Scouts Am.; chair bd. trustees U. Ctr. Ga., 1994-96; chair So. Collegiate Athletic Conf., 1994-95. Adminstrn. bldg. at Adrian Coll. named in honor of Stanton and his wife, 1988. Mem. Am. Assn. Univ. Adminstrs. (bd. dirs. 1990-93), Ga. Assn. Colls. (pres. 1992), Soc. Wesley (Disting. Alumni Recognition award 1988), Ga. Found. for Ind. Colls. (vice chair 1992), Nat. Assn. Ind. Colls. and Univs. (past mem. pub. rels. com.), Assn. Pvt. Colls. and Univs. Ga. (treas. 1996-97), Rotary, Omicron Delta Kappa, Order of Omega, Tau Kappa Epsilon, Psi Chi, Phi Eta Sigma. Home: 312 Tillman Rd Lake Junaluska NC 28745-9779 E-mail: stantons@primeline.com.

STANTON, EDWARD SPIRES, surgeon; b. Edenton, N.C., Mar. 22, 1953; m. Linda Stanton; children: Craig, Jeffrey, Scott. BA in Chemistry magna cum laude, Duke U., 1975, MD, 1979. Diplomate Am. Bd. Surgery. Intern, then resident in gen. surgery Hosp. U. Pa., Phila., 1979-81; resident in gen. surgery Lankenau Hosp., 1981-84; hon. registrar dept. clin. surgery and clin. breast cancer U. Edinburgh, Scotland, 1983; extern in gen. surgery Washington County Hosp., Plymouth, N.C., 1976, 77, 78; attending staff divsn. surgery Ctrl. Carolina Hosp., Sanford, 1984—, chief of surgery, 1989, 98, chief of staff, 1993; gen. surgeon, ptnr. Sanford Surg. Clinic, PA, 1984—. Clin. asst. prof. surgery U. N.C., Chapel Hill, 1991—; presenter in field. Contbr. articles to profl. publs. Bd. dirs. Ctrl. Carolina Hosp., 1995-97. Am. Scandinavian Found. scholar U. Göteborg, 1975; recipient Outstanding Citizen award Pa. State Police, 1983. Fellow ACS; mem. Soc. for Surgery of Alimentary Tract, Am. Soc. Gen. Surgeons, N.C. Med. Soc. Office: Sanford Surg Clinic PA 1816 Doctors Dr PO Box 1169 Sanford NC 27331-1169 E-mail: esstanton@sanfordsurgical.com.

STANTON, FRANK LAWRENCE, JR. graphic designer, illustrator, educator; b. St. Louis, Feb. 5, 1929; s. Frank Lawrence and Rose Margaret (Haas) S.; m. Elizabeth Ann Buehrle, Oct. 16, 1965; children: Laura Ann, Carol Beth. BFA, Washington U., St. Louis, 1955; MFA, Syracuse (N.Y.) U., 1979. Illustrator New Ctr. Studio, Detroit, 1955, The Illustrators, St. Louis, 1955-60; designer, illustrator Frank Stanton Art Studio, 1960-66, The Stantons' Studio, St. Louis, 1966—; prof. art St. Louis Cmty. Coll., 1966-92, prof. emeritus, 1992—. Mem. graphic comms. adv. bd. Washington U., St. Louis, 1974-75. Illustrator: (with others) Curbstone Dragons, 1972; (cookbook) Creative Homemakers-Times/Mirror, 1973, Reading for Concepts, 1970; stained glass designer Little Sisters of the Poor, St. Louis, 1958, designer, muralist, 1971; designer, muralist Bellefontaine Habilitation Ctr., St. Louis, 1981; stained glass designer: Carmelite Convent, Springfield, Mo., 1964, 1st Presbyn. Ch., Tucumcari, N.Mex., 1964, Grace Meth. Ch., Springfield, 1980, St. Monica Ch., Creve Coeur, Mo., 1982, Our Lady of Providence, St. Louis, 1988, Calvary Cemetary Mausoleum, DeSoto, Mo., 1992, St. George Ch., St. Louis, 1995, St. Catherine Laboure Ch., St. Louis, 2000, Ch. of Incarnate Word, St. Louis, 2001, Timothy Luth., St. Louis, 2001; designer, sculptor St. Monica, St. Louis, 1982, St. Philip Neri-Cath. Ctr., U. Tulsa, 1993. With USN, 1951-53. Recipient nat. tchg. excellence award U. Tex. Study, Austin, 1989. Mem. St. Louis Art Dirs. Club (1st v.p. 1971-72, awards of excellence 1960, 61, 72). Home: 12540 Pepperwood Dr Saint Louis MO 63146-3814

STANTON, GEORGE BASIL, JR. engineering executive, chemical engineer; b. Bklyn., Nov. 3, 1926; s. George B. and Despina Stanton B in Chem. Engring., Poly. Inst., Bklyn., 1945, M in Chem. Engring., 1948; MBA, NYU, 1971, MA in Safety and Health, 1975. Registered profl. engr., N.J., cert indsl. hygienist, safety profl. Chief occupl. health Dept. Labor State of N.J., 1971-74; cons. engr. N.J., 1974-79; pres. Am. Hazard Control Cons., Inc., Caldwell, 1979—. Adj. prof. N.J. Inst. Tech., 1974-92, Ctr. for Safety NYU, 1977-84; organizer, pres. Essex Fells Found. for Ednl. Excellence, Inc., 1994-95; ASME rep. Joint Coun. for Health, Safety and Environ. Edn. of Profls., 1995—. Fellow Royal Soc. Health; mem. ASME (Centennial medal 1980), Am. Soc. Safety Engrs. (award 1980). Office: Am Hazard Control Cons Inc PO Box 231 Caldwell NJ 07006-0231

STANTON, GEORGE PATRICK, JR. lawyer; b. Fairmont, W.Va., Nov. 21, 1933; s. George Patrick and Wilma Roberta (Everson) S.; m. Shirley Jean Champ, Sept. 3, 1956; children: George Patrick, Edward Scott. BS in Bus. Adminstrn., Fairmont Coll., 1956; MBA in Fin., U. Dayton, 1969; JD, U. Balt., 1977. Bar: Md. 1978, U.S. Dist. Ct. Md. 1978, W.Va. 1979, U.S. Dist. Ct. (so. dist.) W.Va. 1979, U.S. Dist. Ct. (no. dist.) W.Va. 1980, U.S. Ct. Appeals (4th cir.) 1985. Auditor 1st Nat. Bank Fairmont, 1955-61; asst. cashier S.C. Nat. Bank, Columbia, 1961-64; sr. sys. analyst Chase Manhattan Bank, N.Y.C., 1964-65; asst. v.p. Winters Nat. Bank, Dayton, Ohio, 1965-69, Md. Nat. Bank, Balt., 1969-74; v.p. Equitable Trust Co., 1974-79; gen. ptnr. Stanton & Stanton Attys. at Law, Fairmont, 1979—. Staff sect. leader, mem. faculty Sch. for Bank Adminstrn. U. Wis.-Madison, 1978-89. Treas. Mountaineer Area coun. Boy Scouts Am., Fairmont, 1982-90; pres. Three Rivers Coal Festival, Inc., Fairmont, 1984-85, pres., 1985-86, bd. dirs., 1982-86; pres. Appalachian Coal Festival, 1985-86, bd. dirs., 1985—; mem. adv. bd. Inst. for Living, Fairmont, 1983-85; pres. Firemans' CSC, Fairmont, W.Va., 1992-96. Mem. ABA, ATLA, Comml. Law League Am., W.Va. Bar Assn. (Kaufman award 1997), Marion County Bar Assn., Md. Bar Assn., W.Va. Trial Lawyers Assn., Marion County C. of C. (bd. dirs. 1983—), Fairmont State Coll. Alumni Assn. (bd. dirs. 1982—, pres. 1992-94, Alumnus of Yr. 2002), Fairmont Field Club, Rotary, Masons. Home: 2 W Hills Dr Fairmont WV 26554-5015 Office: Stanton & Stanton PO Box 968 WesBanco Bldg Ste 707 Fairmont WV 26555-0968

STANTON, JEANNE FRANCES, retired lawyer; b. Vicksburg, Miss., Jan. 22, 1920; d. John Francis and Hazel (Mitchell) S. Student, George Washington U., 1938-39; BA, U. Cin., 1940; JD, Salmon P. Chase Coll. Law, 1954. Bar: Ohio 1954. Chief clk. Selective Svc. Bd., Cin., 1940-43; instr. USAAF Tech. Schs., Biloxi, Miss., 1943-44; with Procter & Gamble, Cin., 1945-84, legal asst., 1952-54, head advt. svcs. sect. legal divsn., trade practice dept., 1954-73, mgr. advt. svcs., legal divsn., 1973-84, ret., 1984. Team capt. Cmty. Chest Cin., 1983; mem. ann. meeting com. Archaeol. Inst. Am., 1983; trustee, asst. corr. sec., statutory agt. Friends of Bronze Age Archaeology in the Aegean area, 1987—. Mem. ABA (chmn. subcom. D of com. 307 copyright sect. 1987-88, 89, 90), Ohio Bar Assn. (chmn. uniform state laws com. 1968-70), Cin. Bar Assn. (sec. law day com. 1965-66, chmn. com. on preservation hist. documents 1968-71), Vicksburg and Warren County Hist. Soc., Cin. Hist. Soc., Intercontinental Biog. Assn., Lawyers Club Cin. (exec. com., pres. 1983). Home: 3580 Shaw Ave Apt 323 Cincinnati OH 45208-1454 *Personal philosophy: Most people are good and honest. If a person does the most honorable thing, that is its own reward.*

STANTON, JOHN JEFFREY, editor, print and broadcast journalist, government programs director, analyst, professional society administrator; b. Wichita Falls, Tex., July 19, 1956; s. John Joseph Jr. and Joan (Marley) S.; m. Scylla Maria Silva, Jan. 6, 1981; 1 child, Damien Kristian. BS in Pub. Adminstrn. and Bus. Adminstrn., Nichols Coll., 1978; M in Pub. Adminstrn., U. Detroit, 1980. Rsch. asst. Am. Enterprise Inst., Washington, 1977; rep. aide R.I. Ho. of Reps., Providence, 1977-78; mng. editor Am. Politics, Washington, 1982, assoc. editor, 1983, corp. advisor, 1984, sr. editor, 1985-87; editor, govt. programs mgr. ENTEK, Alexandria, Va., 1988-90; govt. programs dir., cons. Tuckerman Group, Springfield, 1991; analyst, writer Nat. Security Issues, Arlington, 1991—; program dir. TeleStrategies, McLean, 1991-93; Washington corr., mem. editl. bd. Tech. Transfer Jour., 1994-98; editor Tech. Transfer Newsletter; asst. to pres., info. transfer specialist Am. Def. Preparedness Assn., Arlington, 1994-97; contbg. writer Nat. Def. Mag., 1996—; adminstrn. dir. Nat. Def. Indsl. Assn., Arlington, 1997—; Washington corr. Australian Def. Mag., 1998-99; editor Voice of the Indsl. Base NDFA, 1998—. Creator, co-host (radio programs) Power Breakfast, Sta. WNTR, Washington, 1987, Am. Politics Radio, 1987; frequent guest broadcast journalist Stas. WNTR, WAMU-NPR, Washington, WBAL, Balt. and Washington areas. Polit.-mil. analyst CBS News, CNN, ABC, 2001—; contbg. writer: Am. Behavioral Scientist, 2001—; Pravda, newsinsider, onlinejournal, Counter Punch Mag. Polit. campaign cons. to Glenn Tenney, 1992—; commr. Arlington Little League Baseball, 1993, coach 1997—; mentor Arlington County Ct. Sys., 1997; varsity football coach Wakefield H.S., Arlington, Va., 1998—. Recipient Doers Honoree The Washington Times, 1988. Avocations: coaching youth sports programs. E-mail: jstanton@ndia.org.

STANTON, JOHN W. communications executive; b. Seattle; BA in Polit. Sci., Whitman Coll.; MBA, Harvard U. Chmn., CEO Western Wireless, Bellevue, Wash.; chmn. Telocator, 1986—95; chmn., CEO VoiceStream Wireless, 1999; cons. cellular and long-distance bus.; v.p. McCaw Comms., 1983; exec. v.p., COO McCaw Cellular, 1985—88, vice-chmn., 1988—91; dir. McCaw and LIN Broadcasting, 1991—94; co-founder Stanton Comms., 1988; founder, chmn., CEO Pacific N.W. Cellular, 1992. Bd. dirs. Advanced Digital Info. Corp., Columbia Sportswear, Pacific Sci. Ctr.; trustee Whitman Coll. Mem.: Cellular Telecomms. Industry Assn. (chmn. emeritus). Office: Western Wireless Ste 400 3650 131st Ave SE Bellevue WA 98006

STANTON, LOUIS LEE, federal judge; b. N.Y.C., Oct. 1, 1927; s. Louis Lee and Helen Parsons (La Fétra) S.; m. Berit Eleonora Rask; children: L. Lee, Susan Helen Benedict, Gordon R., Fredrik S. BA, Yale U., 1950; JD, U. Va., 1955. Assoc. Davis Polk Wardwell Sunderland & Kiendl, N.Y.C., 1955-66, Carter, Ledyard & Milburn, N.Y.C., 1966-67, ptnr., 1967-85; sr. judge U.S. Dist. Ct. (so. dist.) N.Y., 1985—. Served to 1st lt. USMCR, 1950-52. Fellow Am. Coll. Trial Lawyers, N.Y. Bar Found.; mem. Va. Bar Assn.

STANTON, PAMELA FREEMAN, interior designer, writer; b. Jacksonville, Tex., July 18, 1941; d. William Thomas and Ruth Ethel (Branton) Freeman; m. Karl F. Edmonds, Jr., Jan. 28, 1961 (div. 1966); m. Charles Calvin Stanton, Sept. 1, 1973; 1 child, Julie Anne. AA in Bus., Kilgore Coll., 1961. Design cons., Denver, Boston and Salem, Oreg., 1963-69; exec. sec. Alexander: Alexander of Tex. Inc., Dallas, 1967-69; interior designer Milmac Furniture, 1969-73, Homestead House, Denver, 1973-76; case aide counselor Eliot Cmty. Mental Health Ctr., Concord, Mass., 1980-82; pres., owner Stancom Designs, Virginia Beach, Va., 1990-2000; interior designer Willis Furniture Co., 2000—. Author: I Am That I Am, 1994 (Best Book of Yr., N.Am. Bookdealers Exch. 1995). Recipient Cert. of Appreciation for vol. work Emerson Hosp., Concord, 1981. Republican. Avocations: collecting art, travel, gardening, theatre-plays, entertaining. Home and Office: 4401 Leatherwood Dr Virginia Beach VA 23462-5704

STANTON, PATRICK MICHAEL, lawyer; b. Phila., Sept. 8, 1947; s. Edward Joseph and Helen Marie (Coghlan) S.; m. Kathleen Ann Fama, Aug. 22, 1970; children: Cheryl Marie, Susan Elizabeth. BS in History, St. Joseph's U., 1969; JD, U. Va., 1972; MBA, Fairleigh Dickinson, 1984. Bar: Ohio 1972, U.S. Dist. Ct. (so. dist.) Ohio 1972, N.J. 1982, U.S. Dist. Ct. N.J. 1982, N.Y. 1984. Assoc. Taft, Stettinius & Hollister, Cin., 1972-80; labor counsel Union Camp Corp., Wayne, N.J., 1980-83; dir. labor rels., equal employment oppurtunity programs W.R. Grace & Co., N.Y.C., 1983-86; of counsel Shanley & Fisher, P.C., Morristown, N.J., 1986-89, ptnr., chmn. labor and employment group, 1989-95; dir. Stanton, Hughes, Diana, Cerra, Mariani & Margello, P.C., 1995—. Adj. prof. bus. law Fairleigh Dickinson Univ.; pres. Sidney Reitman employment law Am. Inn. Ct., 1997-2001. Pres., bd. dirs. N.Y. State Adv. Coun. on Employment Law, Inc., N.Y.C., 1985-86. DuPont scholar U. Va., 1970. Mem. ABA, N.J. State Bar Assn. (exec. com. labor employment law sect. 1989—, rec. sec. 1995-97, treas. 1997-99, 2d vice chair 1999-2001, 1st vice chair 2001—), Phi Alpha Theta, Delta Mu Delta. Roman Catholic. Home: 292 Forest Ave Glen Ridge NJ 07028-1808 Office: Stanton Hughes Diana Cerra Mariani & Margello PC 10 Madison Ave Ste 402 Morristown NJ 07960-7303 Fax: 973-656-1611. E-mail: pstanton@stantonhughes.com.

STANTON, ROBERT JAMES, JR. geologist, educator; b. L.A., June 17, 1931; s. Robert James and Audrey (Franke) S.; m. Patricia Ann Burns, Sept. 13, 1953; children— John, Carol. BS, Calif. Inst. Tech., 1953, PhD, 1960; MA, Harvard U., 1956. Research geologist Shell Devel. Co., Houston, 1959-67; mem. faculty Tex. A&M U., 1967—, prof. geology, 1972-86, Ray C. Fish prof. geology, 1986-98, head dept., 1979-83, prof. geology emeritus, 1998—. Vis. prof. U. Nuremburg-Erlangen, Germany, 1984; rsch. assoc. invertebrate paleontology Natural History Mus. L.A. County. Co-author: Paleoecology: Principles and Applications, 1981, 2d edit., 1990. Served with AUS, 1953-55. Fellow Geol. Soc. Am.; mem. Internat. Paleontol. Union, Paleontol. Soc., Paleontol. Research Inst., Soc. Econ. Paleontologists and Mineralogists (Outstanding Paper award 1970), Sigma Xi, Tau Beta Pi. Home: 2297 Valleyfield Ave Thousand Oaks CA 91360 Office: Nat Hist Mus LA County Dept Invertebrate Paleontol 900 Exposition Blvd Los Angeles CA 90007 E-mail: robertstanton@adelphia.net.

STANTON, ROBERT JOHN, JR. English language educator; b. Manhattan, N.Y., July 7, 1942; s. Robert John Stanton and Mary McGinty; m. Felicia Lena Giancola, Nov. 15, 1959; children: Robert III, Sharon. BA, Hofstra U., 1970; MA, U. Mass., Amherst, 1972, postgrad., 1974-79. Instr. English Flagler Coll., St. Augustine, Fla., 1972-74; tchg. asst. U. Mass., Amherst, 1974-77, lectr. in Rhetoric, 1979-81; English tchr. Bishop Kenny H.S., Jacksonville, Fla., 1982-83, Duval County Pub. Schs., Jacksonville, 1984-87; asst. prof. English Jacksonville U., 1987-91, assoc. prof. English, 1992—, chmn. divsn. humanities, 1993-97. Author: Seventeen British Novelists, 1978, Gore Vidal, 1978, Truman Capote, 1980, Views From A Window: Conversations with Gore Vidal, 1980; (poems) Collected Word Paintings, 2000; co-author: Beneath Mad River Mansion, 1992, Noah's Orbella, 1994, The Devil's Rood, 1996. Mem. MLA, Nat. Assn. Tchrs. English, Fla. Assn. Depts. English (pres. 1996), Swift River (Mass.) Hist. Soc. Democrat. Avocations: astronomy, reading, writing, observing the universe. Home: 614 15th Ave S Jacksonville Beach FL 32250 Office: Jacksonville Univ Jacksonville FL 32211 E-mail: bstanto@ju.edu.

STANTON, ROGER D. lawyer; b. Oct. 4, 1938; s. George W. and Helen V. (Peterson) S.; m. Judith L. Duncan, Jan. 27, 1962; children: Jeffrey B., Brady D., Todd A. AB, U. Kans., 1960, JD, 1963. Bar: Kans. 1963, U.S. Dist. Ct. Kans. 1963, U.S. Ct. Appeals (10th cir.) 1972, U.S. Supreme Ct. 1973. Assoc. Stanley, Schroeder, Weeks, Thomas & Lysaught, Kansas City, 1968-72, Weeks, Thomas & Lysaught, Kansas City, 1969-80, also bd. dirs., chmn. exec. com., 1981-82, Stinson, Mag & Fizzell, Kansas City, 1983-96, chmn. products practice group, also bd. dirs., 1993-95; ptnr. Berkowitz, Feldmiller, Stanton, Brandt, Williams & Shaw, Prairie Village, Kans., 1997—. Chmn. bd. editors Jour. Kans. Bar Assn., 1975-83; contbr. articles to profl. jours. Active Boy Scouts Am., 1973-79; pres. YMCA Youth Football Club, 1980-82; co-chmn. Civil Justice Reform Act com. Dist. of Kans., 1991-95; bd. dirs. Kans. Appleseed Found., 2000—. Fellow Am. Coll. Trial Lawyers (state chmn. 1984-86); mem. Internat. Assn. Def. Counsel, Exec. com., 1994-99 East Kansas/West Miss. Chpt., Am. Bd. Trial Adv., Def. Rsch. Inst. (state co-chmn. 1979-90, Exceptionl Performance award 1979), Kans. Bar Assn. (Pres.'s award 1982), Johnson County Bar Found. (pres., trustee), Chmn. Bench/Bar Com. of Johnson Co. Bar Assn., Kans. Assn. Def. Counsel (pres. 1977-78), Kans. Inn. Ct., U. Kans. Sch. Law Alumni Assn. (bd. dirs. 1972-75, 2001-), U. Kans. Kansas City Alumni (bd. dirs. 2001--). Office: Berkowitz Feldmiller Stanton Brandt Williams & Stueve 4121 W 83rd St Ste 227 Prairie Village KS 66208

STANTON, SHANNON KATHLEEN, elementary school educator, writer; b. Reno, May 11, 1977; d. Connie Ray (Butler) and Tommie Lee Stanton. BA, Mid. Tenn. State U., 2000. Cert. tchr. Author: (short stories) Winter's Resurrection, 1998, (novels) Shades of Grey, 2001. Named Hostess of the Yr., O'Charley's Restaurant, 1999; recipient Right Stuff award, U.S. Space and Rocket Ctr., 2001. Avocations: reading, writing, travel, movies. Personal E-mail: Shanabrightstar@hotmail.com.

STANTON, SYLVIA DOUCET, artist, art gallery owner; b. New Orleans, Sept. 21, 1935; d. Clifton Leo Sr. and Maria Del Vel (Alfonso Swiber) Doucet; m. Robert Elmer Stanton, Jan. 3, 1953; children: Robert, Sylvia, Barbara, Richard, Laura, Cheri. Grad. high sch., New Orleans, 1952. Real estate agt. Century 21, Slidell, La., 1982-88; ptnr. Doucet's Jewelry, 1969-82; owner Plantation Antiques, 1974-88, Magnolia Plantation, Slidell, 1988-97, Doucet-Stanton Ltd., Slidell, 1988-97, Gallery at Milbrook, Picayune, Miss., 2001—. Appraiser jewelry, antiques, real estate, 1969—; artist, painter, 1950—. Exhibited in group shows at Montserrat Gallery, N.Y.C., Abita Gallery, Abita Springs, La., The Gallery at Millbrook, Picayune, Miss., Serenity Gallery, Bay St. Louis, Miss. Founder Le cotillion, Slidell, 1975; founding chmn. Pres. Coun. of Le Cotillion, 1987. Recieved title of nobility Countess De Miron Del Vel, Greece, 1988. Mem.: Allied Artists of Am., New Orleans Art Assn., Inner Wheel (dist chmn. 6840 1990—91, founding pres. Slidell 1989), World Trade Ctr., Albuquerque Art League, Bayou Liberty Garden Club (sec. 1988—), Picayune Garden Club, Ozone Camellia Club. Republican. Roman Catholic. Avocations: art, collecting antiques, landscape gardening, home decor. Home: 2105 Waynewood Dr Picayune MS 39466-2139

STANTON, THOMAS MITCHELL, lawyer, educator; b. Vicksburg, Miss., Sept. 30, 1922; s. John Francis and Hazel Florence (Mitchell) S.; m. Jean Aldrich Herron, Oct. 31, 1953; children: Lucinda S. Duddy, Amy S. Conklin, Thomas Herron. BS, Harvard U., 1943, JD, 1948. Bar: Ohio 1949, Wis. 1962. Pvt. practice law, Cin., 1949-56; corp. atty. Kroger Co., 1957-61; with Kimberly-Clark Corp., Neenah, Wis., 1962-86, v.p., gen. counsel, 1971-84, v.p., internat. counsel, 1985-86, ret., 1986; pvt. practice law Neenah, 1987—. Trustee Friends of Bronze Age Archeology in the Aegean Area. Capt. AUS, 1943-46. Mem. ABA, Wis. Bar Assn., Am. Corp. Counsel Assn. (internat. legal affairs com.), North Shore Golf Club, Univ. Club. Home: 390 Park St Menasha WI 54952-3428 Office: 101 W Canal St Ste 25 Neenah WI 54956-3093

STANTON, VICTORIA MEAD, lawyer; b. Albany, N.Y., Feb. 19, 1960; d. Douglas Rhodell and Marjorie Lemka S.; m. R. Matthew Sweeney, Jan. 21, 1989. BA, U. Rochester, N.Y., 1982; JD, Albany (N.Y.) Law Sch., 1987; LLM in Taxation, N.Y.U. Sch. Law, 1990. Bar: N.Y. 1988. Assoc. Rogers & Wells, N.Y.C., 1987-89, McNamee, Lochner, Titus & Williams, Albany, N.Y., 1989-91; exec. v.p., gen. counsel, sec. Farm Family Ins. Co., 1991—. Chair N.Y. Ins. Assn., Albany, 2000-01. Mem. Jr. League of Albany, 1990—. Office: Farm Family Ins Co PO Box 656 Albany NY 12201-0656

STANTON, VIVIAN BRENNAN (MRS. ERNEST STANTON), retired educator; b. Waterbury, Conn.; d. Francis P. and Josephine (Ryan) Brennan; B.A., Albertus Magnus Coll.; M.S., So. Conn. State Coll., 1962, 6th yr. degree, 1965; postgrad. Columbia U.; m. Ernest Stanton, May 31, 1947; children— Pamela L., Bonita F., Kim Ernest. Tchr. English, history, govt. Milford (Conn.) High Sch., 1940-48; tchr. English, history, fgn. Born Night Sch., New Haven, 1948-54, Simon Lake Sch., Milford, 1960-62; guidance counselor, psychol. examiner Jonathan Law High Sch., Milford, 1962-73, Nat. Honor Soc. adv., 1966-73, mem. Curriculum Councils, Graduation Requirement Council, Gifted Child Com., others, 1940-48, 60-73; guidance dir. Foran High Sch., Milford, 1973-79, career center coordinator, 1976-79, ret., 1979. Active various community drives; mem. exec. bd. Ridge Rd PTA, 1956-59; mem. Parent-Tchr. council Hopkins Grammer Sch., New Haven; mem. Human Relations Council, North Haven, 1967-69; vol., patient rep. surg. waiting rm. Fawcett Meml. Hosp., P.C., Sun City Ctr. Emergency Squad, Good Samaritans. Mem. Nat. Assn. Secondary Schs. and Colls. (evaluation com.; chmn. testing com.), AAUW, LWV, Conn. Personnel and Guidance Assn., Conn. Sch. Counselors Assn., Conn. Assn. Sch. Psychol. Personnel, Conn., Milford (pres. 1945-47) edn. assns. Clubs: Univ., Charlotte Harbor Yacht, Sun City Ctr. Golf and Racquet. Home: 237 Courtyard Blvd Apt 202 Sun City Center FL 33573-5779

STANTON, WILLIAM JOHN, JR. marketing educator, author; b. Chgo., Dec. 15, 1919; s. William John and Winifred (McGann) S.; m. Imma Mair, Sept. 14, 1978; children by previous marriage: Kathleen Louise, William John III. BS, Ill. Inst. Tech., 1940; MBA, Northwestern U., 1941, PhD, 1948. Mgmt. trainee Sears Roebuck & Co., 1940-41; instr. U. Ala., 1941-44; auditor Olan Mills Portrait Studios, Chattanooga, 1944-46; asst. prof., assoc. prof. U. Wash., 1948-55; prof. U. Colo., Boulder, 1955-90, prof. emeritus, 1990—; head mktg. dept. U. Colo., 1955-71, acting dean, 1963-64; assoc. dean U. Colo. (Sch. Bus.), 1964-67. Author: Economic Aspects of Recreation in Alaska, 1953; (with Rosann Spiro) Management of a Sales Force, 10th edit., 1999 (also Spanish, Portuguese and Chinese transls.), (with others) Challenge of Business, 1975, (with M. Etzel and B. Walker) Marketing, 12th edit., 2001 (also Spanish, Portuguese, Indonesian and Chinese transls.), (with M.S. Sommers and J.G. Barnes) Can. edit. Fundamentals of Marketing, 8th edit., 1998, (with K. Miller and R. Layton) Australian edit., 3d edit., 1994, (with R. Varaldo) Italian edit., 2d edit., 1990, (with others) South African edit., 1992; monographs on Alaska Tourist Industry, 1953-54; contbr. articles to profl. jours. Mem. Am. Mktg. Assn., Western Mktg. Assn., Beta Gamma Sigma. Roman Catholic. Home: 1445 Sierra Dr Boulder CO 80302-7846

STANTON-HICKS, MICHAEL D'ARCY, anesthesiologist, educator; b. Adelaide, Australia, June 3, 1931; came to U.S., 1972; s. Cedric Stanton-Hicks and Florence (Haggett) Perrin; m. Kristina Litsmark, Aug. 4, 1969 (div. Aug. 1984); children: Erik Michael, Leif Neal; m. Ursula Koch, Aug. 27, 1985. MB, BChir, Adelaide U., 1962; Dr. med., U. Dusseldorf, 1984. Bd. equivalent Am. Bd. Anesthesiology; diplomate Am. Bd. Pain Medicine. Intern Queen Elizabeth Hosp., Adelaide, 1961-62, tutor, staff anesthesiologist, 1970-72; resident Royal Postgrad. Med. Sch., London and Lasarettet Köping, 1966-68; asst. dir. anesthesiology intensive care Södersjükhuset, Stockholm, 1968-69; instr. anesthesiology U. Wash. Med. Sch., Seattle, 1969-70, asst. prof., 1972-75; prof., chmn. dept. U. Mass. Med. Sch., Worcester, 1975-83; prof. U. Colo. Health Scis. Ctr., Denver, 1983-86, vice chmn. dept., 1983-85, acting chmn., 1985-86; prof., dir. pain clinic and rsch. Johannes Gutenberg U., Mainz, Germany, 1986-88, prof. Germany, 1986—; dir. pain mgmt. ctr. Cleve. Clinic Found., 1988-98, vice chmn. pain mgmt. and rsch. divsn. anesthesia, 1998—. Med. examiner Indsl. Commn. Ohio; mem. Ohio Pain Adv. Com., Dept. Health; mem. liaison com. med. bd. Ohio Pain Com.; advisor Am. Acad. Disability Evaluating Physicians, 2000—; bd. dirs. World Inst. of Pain, 1995—. Author, editor: Regional Anesthesia: Advances and Selected Topics, 1978, Chronic Low Back Pain, 1982; author (with Raj and Nolte): Illustrated Manual of Regional Anesthesia, 1988 (Most Beautiful Book of Yr. award Frankfurt, Fed. Republic Germany Pubs. Book Conv., 1989); author: Pain and Sympathetic Nervous System, 1989; author: (with Janig and Boas) Reflex Sympathetic Dystrophy, 1989; author: (with Janig) Reflex Sympathetic Dystrophy: A Reappraisal, 1996; exec. editor: Pain Practice Jour., 2001—, sect. editor: Complete Regional Pain Syndrome. Squadron leader res. Royal Australian Air Force, 1962-65. Named Scientist of Yr., Am. Herschel Soc., 1991-92; Australian Univs. Commn. mature age scholar, 1953-60. Fellow Royal Coll. Surgeons (faculty anesthetists), Royal Coll. Anesthetists, Am. Acad. Pain Medicine; mem. Internat. Assn. Study Pain (chmn. spl. interest group on sympathetically maintained pain 1990—), Am. Soc. Regional Anesthesia (bd. dirs. 1979-91, pres. 1989-90, Disting. Svc. award, 1998), Assn. Anesthetists Gt. Britain and Ireland, Ohio State Med. Assn., Cleve. Acad. Medicine, Am. Acad. Med. Infrared Imaging (bd. dirs. 1991-95, pres. 1994-95, William Hobbins Rsch. award 1993), Am. Acad. Disability Evaluating Physicians (adv. com. mem. complex regional pain syndrome 2000—), Am. Pain Soc., Am. Acad. Pain Medicine, Am. Neuromodulation Soc. (pres. 1994-98, bd. dirs. 1998—), Army-Navy-Air Force Club. Republican. Anglican. Avocations: skiing, photography, travel, flying. Home: 198 Woodsong Way Chagrin Falls OH 44023-6703 Office: Cleve Clinic Found 9500 Euclid Ave Cleveland OH 44195-0001

STANVICK, DAVID J. information scientist; b. Haverhill, Mass., Apr. 15, 1967; s. Joseph W. and Andrea R. (Marquis) S. BS, North Adams (Mass.) State Coll, 1986; cert. advanced study in network engring., Boston U., 1994. Office mgr. CBT Archs., Boston, 1986-88; sys. adminstr. Mahoney, Hawkes & Goldings, 1988-93; v.p. of tech. Iprax, Lexington, Mass., 1993-96; pres. H2C, Haverhill, 1996-97; sr. analyst Dartmouth Hitchcock Med. Ctr., Lebanon, N.H., 1997-98; v.p. mktg. Vality Tech. Inc., Boston, 1998-2001, Knowledge Impact, Wayland, Mass., 2001—. Democrat. Jewish. Avocations: travel, cooking, reading. Office: Knowledge Impact 321 Commonwealth Rd Wayland MA 01778 E-mail: dstanvick@kimpact.com.

STAPLES, DONALD EDWARD, radio, film and television educator; b. N.Y.C., Apr. 15, 1934; s. Edward Daniel and Ethlyne Babcock Staples; m. Diane Staunton, June 2, 1956 (div. July 1980); children: Douglas Arthur, Daniel Charles; m. Kristen Petersen, Nov. 26, 1982; stepchildren: Julia Lynn Smith, Susan Smith Milner. BS in Speech, Northwestern U., 1955; MA in Cinema, U. So. Calif., 1959; PhD, Northwestern U., 1967. Instr. So. Ill. U., Carbondale, 1959-63; lectr. Northwestern U., Evanston, Ill., 1963-65; asst. prof. Ohio State U., Columbus, 1965-68, assoc. prof., 1968-69; prof. NYU, N.Y.C., 1969-79, Vassar Coll., Poughkeepsie, N.Y., 1972-74, U. North Tex., Denton, 1979—. Author, editor: American Cinema, 3d edit., 1991; co-author: Film Encounter, 1973; contbr. articles, film revs. to profl. jours. Mem. Greater Denton Arts Coun., 1980—, Denton Cmty. Theatre, 1980—; bd. dirs. Nat. Mus. Comms., Irving, Tex., 1983-93; juror film festivals, 1969—; mem. adv. bd. Arts and Humanities Citation Index, Phila., 1979—. Lt. (j.g.) USN, 1955-57. Univ. scholar U. So. Calif., 1957-59, Northwestern U., 1963-65; Danforth Found. assoc., 1968-85. Mem. SAG, Soc. for Cinema Studies (pres. 1974-75), Univ. Film and Video Assn. (pres. 1975-77, life mem.), Internat. Congress of Schs. of Film and TV (v.p. 1982-86), Univ. Film and Video Found. (trustee emeritus), Dallas Corinthian Yacht Club (bd. dirs. 1995-98). Methodist. Avocations: sailing, golf. Home: 2901 Montecito Dr Denton TX 76205-8513 Office: U North Tex Dept Radio/TV/Film Denton TX 76203

STAPLES, LYLE NEWTON, lawyer; b. Radford, Va., Feb. 16, 1945; s. Lester Lyle and Velma Jean (King) S.; m. Christie Mercedes Carr, Feb. 1, 1971; children: Scott Andrew, John Randolph, Brian Matthew, Melissa Ann. BA, U. Md., 1967, JD, 1972; LLM in Taxation, Georgetown U., 1977. Bar: Md. 1973, U.S. Supreme Ct. 1978, U.S. Tax Ct. 1981, U.S. Dist. Ct. Md. 1981, U.S. Ct. Appeals (4th cir.) 1981. Tax law specialist IRS, Washington, 1972-77; assoc. Hessey & Hessey, Balt., 1978-82, Rosenstock, Burgee & Welty, Frederick, Md., 1982-84; sole practice Hampstead, 1984-91; mem. firm Johnson, Parker & Hess, Westminster, 1991-96; pvt. practice, 1996—. Vis. asst. prof. Towson (Md.) State U., 1981—82. Treas., bd. dirs. Literacy Coun. of Carroll County, Inc., 1993-98. Served with U.S. Army, 1968-69, Vietnam. Mem. ABA, Md. Bar Assn., Fin. Planning Assn., Carroll County C. of C. Democrat. Methodist. Home: 813 Clearview Ave Hampstead MD 21074-2325 Office: Ste 210 79 E Main St Westminster MD 21157-5026

STAPLES, LYNNE LIVINGSTON MILLS, retired psychologist, educator, consultant; b. Detroit, Sept. 18, 1934; d. Robert Livingston Mills Staples and Lyda Charlotte (Diehr) Staples; m. Lee Edward Burmeister, July 16, 1955 (div. 1982); children: Benjamin Lee, Lynne Ann. BS, Ctrl. Mich. U., 1957; MA, U. Mich., 1965; student, Marygrove Coll., Cen. Mich. U., 1971-74. Ltd. lic. psychologist, sch. psychologist; cert. social worker, elem. permanent cons. and tchr. for mentally handicapped. First grade tchr. Shepherd (Mich) Schs., 1957-59; tchr. Kingston (Mich.) Schs., 1959-65; tchr. educationally handicapped Rialto (Calif.) Unified Sch. Dist., 1965-66; tchr., cons. Tuscola Int. Sch. Dist., Caro, Mich., 1966-71; sch. psychologist Huron Int. Sch. Dist., Bad Axe, 1971-74, Tuscola Int. Sch. Dist., Caro, 1974-89; instr. Delta Coll., University Center, Mich., 1976-88; tchr. spl. day classes Victorville (Calif.) High Sch., 1989; sch. psychologist Bedford (Ind.) Schs., 1990-91; clin. psychologist ACT team and outpatient therapy Sanilac County Mental Health Svcs., Sandusky, Mich., 1991-99; ret., 1999. Cons. sch. psychologist Marlette (Mich.) Schs., 1982-86, Bartholomew Pub. Schs., Columbus, Ind., 1989, Johnson County Schs., Franklin, Ind., 1990; clin. psychologist Thumb Family Counseling, Caro, 1985-88; personnel com. Team One Credit Union, 1993; instr. St. Clair C.C., 1993. Conf. presenter in field. Del. NEA-Mich. Edn. Assn. Rep. Assemblies, 1970—89; pres., auction chmn. Altrusa Club, Marlette, 1982—88; style show chmn. Marlette Band Boosters, 1983; mem. exec. bd. Lawrence County Tchrs. Assn., Bedford, 1991; mem. Meth. Choir, 2000; dist. dir. social action United Meth. Women, 2000—02; mem. pit orch. prodn. Bye Bye Birdie, Sandusky, 2001; bd. dirs. Team One Credit Union, 1994—2002, Vassar City Band, 1998—2002, Flint Concert Band, 2000—02, Bay City Concert Band, 2000—02, Sanilac Three-Minute Band, 2001, Unionville-Sebewaing Cmty. Band, 2001, Vassar Orch., 2001, Honsinger Wind Ensemble, 2001; mem. Marlette First United Meth. Praise Band, 1999—2000, Sanilac Symphonic Band, 1993—2000, Sanilac Three Minute Band, 1995—2001, Sandusky Pit Orch., 2001. Fed. govt. grantee Wayne State U., 1968. Mem.: Ind. Assn. Sch. Psychologists (pub. rels. bd. 1990—91), Ind. State Tchrs. Assn. (rep. assembly del. 1991), Am. Federated State and Mcpl. Employees (chairperson #219 1993, chairperson #15 chpt. 1993—96), Mich. Edn. Assn. (Thumb area sec. 1995—2002), Emmaus Reunion Group, Lions (bd. dirs. 1996—99, 2d v.p. 1999). Democrat. Methodist. Avocations: antiques, swimming, gardening, pets, traveling. Home: 6726 Clothier Rd Clifford MI 48727-9501

STAPLES, MARK ANDREW, biochemist; b. Norton, Kans., July 28, 1954; s. Austin Joyce and Virginia Lila (Gates) S.; m. Argie Inez Koons, Mar. 5, 1977. BA in Chemistry and Biochemistry with honors, U. Kans., 1975, BA in English, PhD in Biochemistry, U. Kans., 1979; MBA, Northeastern U., 1985. Postdoctoral fellow Med. Sch. Harvard U., Boston, 1979-80; chemist New England Nuc., 1980-82, prodn. supr., 1982-84; mgr. analytical biochemistry Seragen, Lexington, 1985-86; project mgr. Hopkinton, 1986-87; rsch. scientist Immunogen, Cambridge, 1987-88; process scientist Biogen, 1988-89, sr. process scientist, 1989-92, group leader, 1992-97; dir. pharm. scis. Praecis Pharms., Inc., 1997—2002, sr. dir. pharm. scis., 2002—. Session chmn. BIO 2000. Contbr. articles to profl. jours. Mem. Am. Assn. Pharm. Sci. (mem. chmn. biotech. sect. 2002), Am. Chem. Soc., Parenteral Drug Assn. (treas. N.E. chpt. 1993—). Avocations: literature, museums, travel. Home: 10 Rogers St Apt 906 Cambridge MA 02142-1251 Office: Praecis Pharms Inc 830 Winter St Waltham MA 02451 E-mail: mstaples@attbi.com., mark.staples@praecis.com.

STAPLES, RICHARD FARNSWORTH, lawyer; b. Providence, Nov. 24, 1919; s. Harold E. and Margaret (Smith) S.; m. Mary Kingsbury, June 20, 1942; children: Richard Farnsworth, Jr., Benjamin T., Edward K. AB, Harvard U., 1941, LLB, 1949. Bar: R.I. 1949. Ptnr. Tillinghast, Collins & Graham, Providence, 1949-81, Hinckley, Allen & Snyder, Providence, 1981-87, of counsel, 1987—. Mem. commn. on jud. tenure and discipline, 1987-93; mem. ethics adv. panel R.I. Supreme Ct., 1995-97. Chmn. sch. com. Town of Barrington (R.I.), 1956-62, mem., 1957-62; mem. State Bd. Edn., Providence, 1964-69, chmn., 1968-69; pres. R.I. Hist. Soc., 1981-83. Served to 1st lt. U.S. Army, 1943-46. Decorated Bronze Star Mem. ABA, R.I. Bar Assn., Soc. Colonial Wars, Providence Art Club, Harvard Club. Home: 180 Slater Ave Providence RI 02906-5723 also: 79 Loon Lake Rd Freedom NH 03836-0298

STAPLETON, HARVEY JAMES, physics educator; b. Kalamazoo, Dec. 22, 1934; s. Herbert James and Viola Delia (Early) S.; m. Joan Eilleen Sylvander, June 22, 1957; children: Patricia Lynne, Susan Joan, Jeffrey Denis. BS, U. Mich., 1957; PhD, U. Calif., Berkeley, 1961. Faculty physics U. Ill., Urbana, 1961—, prof., 1969-95, prof. emeritus, 1995—, assoc. dean Grad. Coll., 1980-95, assoc. vice chancellor for rsch., 1987-95; interim dean Grad. Coll., 1992; interim vice chancellor for rsch. U. Ill., 1992. Alfred P. Sloan fellow, 1962-64 Contbr. articles to profl. jours. Fellow Am. Phys. Soc.; mem. Phi Beta Kappa, Sigma Xi, Phi Sigma Kappa, Phi Kappa Phi, Phi Eta Sigma. Roman Catholic. Home: 3806 Gulf Of Mexico Dr Unit 310 Longboat Key FL 34228-2733 E-mail: hjstapleton@earthlink.net.

STAPLETON, JAMES HALL, statistician, educator; b. Royal Oak, Mich., Feb. 8, 1931; s. James Leo and Dorothy May (Hall) S.; m. Alicia M. Brown, Apr. 3, 1963; children: James, Lara, Sara. BA, Eastern Mich. U., 1952; MS, Purdue U., 1954, PhD, 1957. Statistician Gen. Electric Co., 1957-58; asst. prof. stats. and probability Mich. State U., East Lansing, 1958-63, assoc. prof., 1963-72, prof., 1972—, chmn. dept., 1968-75, grad. dir., 1985—. Cons. Gen. Telephone Co. of Ind.; vis. prof. U. Philippines, 1978-79 Mem. USS-Mich. Swim Com., AAU, 1976-84, chmn., 1976-78; mem. Mich. AAU Exec. Bd., 1976-81. NSF fellow, 1966-67 Mem. Inst. Math. Stats., Am. Statis. Assn. Office: Mich State U Dept Statistics East Lansing MI 48823

STAPLETON, JAMES FRANCIS, lawyer; b. Bridgeport, Conn., June 30, 1932; s. James M. and Lucy V. (Moran) S.; m. Margaret M. Daly, July 13, 1957; children: James F., Mark T., Paul and Kathleen. BSS, Fairfield U., 1954; LLB, Boston Coll., 1957; LLM, Georgetown U., 1958. Bar: Conn. 1957, U.S. Dist. Ct. (ea. and so. dists.) N.Y. 1979, U.S. Ct. Appeals (2d cir.) 1966, U.S. Dist. Ct. Conn. 1961, Mass. 1957, U.S. Supreme Ct. 1965, U.S. Ct. Appeals (D.C. cir.) 1958. Atty., Appellate Sect., Antitrust Divsn. U.S. Dept. Justice, 1957-58; assoc., ptnr. Marsh, Day & Calhoun, Bridgeport, 1958-73; city atty. City of Bridgeport, 1971-73; legis. counsel Conn. Bankers Assn., 1971-73; judge Conn. Superior Ct., 1973-78; chmn. Criminal Justice Commn. State of Conn., 1991-95; ptnr. Day, Berry & Howard, Stamford, Conn., 1978—. Mem. Bridgeport Bd. Edn., 1960-69. Fellow Am. Bar Found., Am. Coll. Trial Lawyers (chmn. state com. 1994-96, regent 1996-2000); mem. ABA, Am. Bd. Trial Advocates, Conn. Bar Assn. (bd. govs., ho. of dels., v.p., pres.), Fed. Bar Coun. Found. for 2d Circuit (v.p.), Bridgeport Bar Assn., Stamford-Darien Bar Assn. Home: 225 Winton Rd Fairfield CT 06430-3858 Office: Day Berry & Howard One Canterbury Green Stamford CT 06901 E-mail: jfstapleton@dbh.com.

STAPLETON, JEAN, journalism educator; b. Albuquerque, June 24, 1942; d. James L. and Mary (Behrman) S.; m. John Clegg, Apr. 15, 1965 (dec. Sept. 1972); m. Richard Paul Bright, Jan. 13, 1973 (div. 1985); children: Lynn, Paul Bright; m. William Walter Farran, Nov. 9, 1996. BA, U. N.Mex., 1964; MS in Journalism, Northwestern U., 1968. Reporter Glenview (Ill.) Announcements, 1967-68, Angeles Mesa News Advertiser, L.A., 1968-69, City News Svc., Radio News West, L.A., 1969-71; press sec. polit. campaign, 1972; instr. journalism East L.A. Coll., 1973-75, prof., dept. chair, 1975—. Author: Equal Marriage, 1975, Equal Dating, 1979. Mem. NOW (pres. L.A. chpt. 1973-74), Assn. Women in Comm., Soc. Profl. Journalists, Ninety Nines, L.A. Poets Writers Collective. Democrat. Methodist. Home: 3232 Philo St Los Angeles CA 90064-4719 Office: East LA Coll 1301 Avenida Cesar Chavez Monterey Park CA 91754-6001

STAPLETON, KATHARINE HALL (KATIE STAPLETON), food broadcaster, writer; m. Benjamin Franklin Stapleton; children: Benjamin Franklin III, Craig Roberts, Katharine Hall. BA, Vassar Coll., 1941. Prodr., writer, host Cooking with Katies live on-hour weekly Sta. KOA, 1979-89. Guest broadcaster Geneva Radio, 1974, London Broadcasting Corp., 1981, 82; tour leader culinaries to Britain, France and Switzerland, 1978-85. Eng., 1978. Author: Denver Delicious, 1980, 3d edit., 1983, High Notes, 1985—. Chmn. women's divsn. United Fund, 1955-56; founder, chmn. Denver Debutante Ball, 1956, 57; hon. chmn. Nat. Travelers Aid Assn., 1952-56, 93-96; commr. Denver Centennial Authority, 1958-60; trustee Washington Cathedral, regional v.p., 1967-73; trustee Colo. Women's Coll., 1975-80; sole trustee Harmes C. Fishback Found.; hon. chmn. Le Bal à Versailles, 1999, 2002. Decorated Chevalier de L'Etoile Noire, France; recipient People-to-People citations, 1960, 66, Beautiful Activist award, Colo.-Wyo. Restaurant Assn. award, 1981, Humanitarian of Yr. award Arthritis Found., 1995, Arts award Colo. Symphony, 1998; named Chevalier du Tastevin, 1989, Outstanding Vol. Fundraiser, Nat. Philanthropy Day, 1995. Mem. Denver Country Club. Republican. Episcopalian. Home: 8 Village Rd Cherry Hills Village CO 80110-4908

STAPLETON, RONALD JAMES, trust company administrator; b. Gary, Ind., Jan. 4, 1941; s. Roger John Stapleton and June Sarah (Transeau) Patterson; m. Sue Ellen Tillett, Dec. 28, 1963; children: Laura, Ronald, Amy. BBA, U. Notre Dame, 1963; MBA, Calif. State U., Sacramento, 1969. Chartered fin. analyst, Tex. Credit rep. Shell Oil Co., San Francisco, 1970-73, dist. credit mgr. San Diego, 1973-74, fin. analyst Houston, 1974-76; supr. investment acctg. Shell Pension Trust, 1976-78, investment analyst, 1978-79, money mkt. portfolio mgr., 1979-80, fixed income analyst, 1980-82, fixed income portfolio mgr., 1982-86, mgr. fixed income portfolios, 1986-93, mgr. fixed income, 1993—. Mem. City of Houston Investment Com. Treas. Norchester Maintenance Fund, Inc., Houston, 1986, pres., 1987. Capt. USAF, 1963-69. Mem. Assn. Investment Mgmt. and Rsch., Houston Soc. Fin. Analysts (pres., dir.), Fixed Income Analysts Soc. (com. on investment of employee benefit assets), Raveneaux Country Club. Republican. Roman Catholic. Avocations: tennis, golf, gardening. Home: 8711 Ashridge Park Dr Spring TX 77379-6810 Office: Shell Pension Trust 910 Louisiana St Houston TX 77002-4916

STAPLETON, WALTER KING, federal judge; b. Cuthbert, Ga., June 2, 1934; s. Theodore Newton and Elizabeth Grantland (King) Stapleton; m. Georgianna Duross Stapleton; children: Russell K., Theodore N., Teryl J. BA, Princeton, 1956; LLB, Harvard, 1959; LLM, U. Va., 1984. Bar: Del. Assoc. Morris, Nichols, Arsht & Tunnell, Wilmington, Del., 1959—65; dep. atty. gen. State of Del., 1963; ptnr. Morris, Nichols, Arsht & Tunnell, 1966—70; judge U.S. Dist. Ct. , Wilmington, Del., 1970—85, chief judge, 1983—85; judge U.S. Ct. Appeals (3d cir.), 1985—. Dep. atty. gen., Del., 1964; mem. Jud. Conf. U.S., 1984—85. Bd. dirs. Am. Bapt. Chs., 1978. Baptist. Office: US Ct Appeals 844 N King St Wilmington DE 19801-3519

STAPLIN, DAVID EARL, civil engineer; b. Rochester, N.Y., Aug. 20, 1947; s. William Ray and Mable Dean (Marx) S.; m. Jane Marie Mills, Aug. 4, 1973; children: Jennifer Marie, Alison Jane. BSCE, U. Mich., 1969; MBA, Jacksonville U., 1985. Registered profl. engr., Pa. Chief engr. planning U.S. Railway Assn., Washington, 1974-76; mgr. rehab. planning Conrail, Phila., 1976-80, div. engr., 1980-81; dir. planning and valuation Seaboard System Railroad, Jacksonville, Fla., 1981-86; dir. quality control CSX Transp., 1987-88, asst. chief engr., 1989-90, asst. to v.p. engring., 1990-92; avp and chief engr. Amtrak, Phila., 1992-95; exec. dir. Am. Ry. Engring. Assn., Washington, 1995-98; dir. rail ops. LTK Engring. Svcs., Blue Bell, Pa., 1998—. Contbg. author: The Track Cyclopedia, 1985; contbr. articles to profl. jours./publs. Mem. ASCE, assn. Am. R.R.s (mem. vehicle/track steering com. 1991-92, chmn. rail working group/track maintenance rsch. com. 1978-92, mem. track adv. com. 1988—, heavy axle load econ. rev. com. 1988-91, engr. mgmt. com. 1992—), Roadmasters and Maintenance of Way Assn. (pres. 1985), Am. Ry. Engring. Assn., Am. Ry. Bridge and Bldg. Assn., Permanent Way Assn. Methodist. Achievements include development of economic models for railway maintenance. Home: 6 Tunbridge Ln Malvern PA 19355-1042 Office: LTK Engring Svc 512 Township Line Rd Blue Bell PA 19422-2700

STAPP, DAN ERNEST, retired lawyer, utility executive; b. New Orleans, July 1, 1934; s. James Frank, Jr. and Marguerite Edna (Joubert) S.; m. Barbara Allan Wilmot, June 10, 1961; children: Marguerite Wilmot (dec.), Mary Darby, Paul Wilmot (dec.), James Andrew. BBA, Loyola U., New Orleans, 1955, LL.B., 1957. Bar: La. 1957. With New Orleans Pub. Service Inc., 1958-68, asst. to v.p., 1965-68; with Entergy Svcs. (formerly MSU System Svcs. Inc.), New Orleans, 1968-92; v.p., sec., asst. treas. Entergy Svcs., 1968-80; sr. v.p., 1980-92. Sec. System Fuels, Inc., New Orleans, 1972-92, Entergy Corp. (formerly Middle South Utilities, Inc.), New Orleans, 1974-92, Systems Energy Resources, Inc., Jackson, Miss., 1974-91, Electec, Inc., 1984-91, Entergy Ops., Inc., 1990-91, Enterg Power, Inc., 1990-92. Trustee Mercy Hosp., New Orleans, 1973-80, pres., 1975, chmn. bd. devel., 1971-72; mem. pres.'s coun. Loyola U., 1975-85, chmn., 1980-82; adv. coun. Coll. Bus. Adminstrn., 1969-70; mem. adv. bd. Asso. Cath. Charities, 1979-82; gen. chmn. United Way Greater New Orleans, 1978, trustee, 1978-84; mem. exec. bd. New Orleans Area coun. Boy Scouts Am., 1980-85, pres., 1984-85. 2d lt. AUS, 1957. Mem. ABA, La. Bar Assn., New Orleans Country Club, Pickwick Club, Blue Key (past chpt. pres.), Alpha Sigma Nu, Delta Theta Phi. Republican. Roman Catholic. Home: 401 Bellaire Dr New Orleans LA 70124-1014

STAPRANS, ARMAND, electronics executive; b. Riga, Latvia, Feb. 28, 1931; s. Theodore and Elvira (Ulmanis) S.; m. Vija Spalvins, Sept. 25, 1955; children: Silvija, Armin, Erik. Student, Willamette U., 1949-52; BSEE, U. Calif., Berkeley, 1954, MSEE, 1955, PhDEE, 1959. Rsch. asst. dept. elec. engring. U. Calif., 1955-57; engr. microwave tube div. Varian Assocs., Palo Alto, Calif., 1957-60, engring. mgr., 1960-68, ops. mgr., 1978-78, 86-89, chief engr., 1978-86, gen. mgr. coupled cavity tube divsn., 1989-92, v.p., 1990-95; gen. mgr. microwave power tube products, 1992-95; pres. microwave power tube products divsn. Comms. and Power Inds., Palo Alto, Calif., 1995-98; mgmt. cons., 1999—. Contbr. articles to profl. jours., chpt. to book; patentee microwave tubes field. Fellow IEEE (electron device adminstrv. com. 1983-88). Home: 445 Knoll Dr Los Altos CA 94024-4732 Office: Comm & Power Inds M S B 100 Microwave Power Tube Prod Divsn PO Box 50750 Palo Alto CA 94303-0665 E-mail: AStaprans@aol.com.

STARCHER, GEORGE WILLIAM, management consultant; b. Columbus, Ohio, June 25, 1933; arrived in France, 1964; s. George William and Cynthia Margaret Starcher; m. Diane Lindsay Chamberlin, June 24, 1956; children: Loren King, Bruce Gregory. BA, Yale U., 1954; MBA, Harvard U., 1956. Cert. mgmt. cons. Dir. McKinsey & Co., N.Y., Paris, Milan,Geneva, 1959-80; profl. assoc. The MAC Group, Paris, 1980-93; sec. gen. European Baha'i Bus. Forum, Chambery France, 1990—. Dir. European Continuing Edn. Ctr., Fontainebleau, France, 1970—. Author: Entrepreneurship, 1993, Ethics and Entrepreneurship: An Oxymoron?, 1995, Corporate Social Responsibility and Business Success, 1997. Lt. U.S. Army, 1956-59. Mem. Nat. Spiritual Assembly of Baha'is of France (chmn. 1986-89). Avocations: mountaineering, skiing. Home and Office: European Baha'i Bus Forum 35 Ave Jean Jaures 73000 Chambéry France

STARCHER, LARRY VICTOR, state supreme court justice; b. Rocksdale, W.Va., Sept. 25, 1942; AB cum laude, W.Va. U., 1964, JD, 1967. Bar: W.Va. 1967. Former judge and chief judge W.Va. Ct. (17th jud. cir.), 1977-96; now justice W.Va. Supreme Ct. Appeals, 1997—. Pvt. practice, Morgantown, 1976—; dir. North Ctrl. W.Va. Legal Aid Soc., 1969-76; former instr. law, pub. adminstrn., and history W.Va. U.; contract adminstr. W.Va. U., 1966-67, asst. to v.p., 1967-69. Editor W.Va. Law Rev.; contbr. articles to profl. jours. Mem. City Coun. Morgantown, 1971-72; former mem. Young Dems. Fellow Harvard U., summer 1978. Mem. Am. Correctional Assn., W.Va. Jud. Assn., W.Va. State Bar, Monongalia County Bar Assn., Beta Theta Pi, Phi Delta Phi, Phi Alpha Theta, Pi Sigma Alpha. Avocations: carpentry, gardening, skiing. Office: Supreme Ct Appeals State Capital Rm E 307 Charleston WV 25305*

STARCHER-DELL'AQUILA, JUDY LYNN, special education educator; b. Cuyahoga Falls, Ohio, Sept. 20, 1956; d. James Calvin and Jane Yvonne (Hart) Starcher; m. Richard Paul Dell'Aquila, July 16, 1983; 1 child, Jessica Lynn Dell'Aquila. BS in Hearing & Speech Scis., Ohio U., 1978; MEd in Deaf Edn., U. Cin., 1980; PhD in Spl. Edn., Kent State U., 1996. Cert. supr. and tchr., Ohio. Tchr. deaf Parma (Ohio) City Schs., 1978-79, Mayfield (Ohio) City Schs., 1980-81; tchr. deaf, low incidence work study coord. Trumbull County Ednl. Svc. Ctr., Warren, Ohio, 1981-84; work study coord. Cuyahoga Ednl. Svc. Ctr., Valley View, 1984-88; instr., student tchg. supr. Kent (Ohio) State U., 1993-95; project dir. Children's Hosp. Med. Ctr./Family Child Learning Ctr., Tallmadge, Ohio, 1995-2000; coord. spl. edn. Cleveland Heights/University Heights (Ohio) City Sch. System, 2000—. Am. Sign Lang. instr. Cuyahoga C.C., Cleve., 1993-2000; dir. adv. bd. Hearing Impaired Toddler Infant & Families Program, Tallmadge, 1995-2000; mem. County Collaborative Group, Medina, Summit counties, Ohio, 1995-2000; state trainer SKI—HI, Logan, Utah, 1997—. Mem. Coun. Exceptional Children. Grantee Job Tng. & Partnership Act, Cleve., 1982, 86-88; Univ. fellow Kent State U., 1991. Democrat. Avocations: antique collector, exercise, reading. Home: 151 E Pleasant Valley Rd Seven Hills OH 44131-5601 Office: Cleveland Hgts/Univ Hgts Bd Edn 2155 Miramar Blvd University Heights OH 44118

STARCHMAN, DALE EDWARD, medical educator; b. Wallace, Idaho, Apr. 16, 1941; s. Hubert V. and Lottie M. (Alford) S.; m. Erlinda Socrates, Dec. 13, 1969; children: Ann, Cindy, Julie, Mark. Student, Rockhurst Coll., 1959-61; BS in Physics, Pitts. (Kans.) State U., 1963; MS in Radiation Biophysics, U. Kans., 1965, PhD in Radiation Biophysics, 1968. Cert. Radiol. Physicist, Health Physicist, Med. Physicist. Chief health physicist IIT Rsch. Inst., Chgo., 1968-71; radiol. physicist Mercy Hosp. Inst. of Radiation Therapy, 1968-71; prof., head radiation biophysics Northeast Ohio U. Coll. of Medicine, Rootstown, Ohio, 1971—; pres. Med. Physics Svcs., Inc., Canton, 1971—. Author: (with Wayne R. Hedrick and David L. Hykes) Ultrasound Physics and Instrumentation, 3rd edit., 1995; contbr. numerous articles in profl. jours., chpts. in books, monographs. Fellow Am. Coll. Radiology; mem. Am. Assn. Physicists in Medicine (bd. mem. at large 1984-86, pres. Penn-Ohio chpt. 1975-76, rec. sec. midwest chpt. 1970, mem. edn. coun. 1980-83, chmn. Am. assn. med. dosimetrists task group 1976-78, mem. diagnostic radiology task group on quality control 1975—, mem. numerous other coms. 1975-83), Health Physics Soc. (chmn. summer sch. sub. com. 1977-78), Radiol. Soc. N.Am. (assoc. scis. com. 1976-86, task force chmn. 1983-86, mem. 1975-86), Sigma Xi, Kappa Mu Epsilon. Achievements include research areas including selection, quality assurance and acceptance testing of diagnostic x-ray units, design of radiology facilities; effects of tissue inhomogeneities on electron therapy, radiation atrophy in bone, large field therapy swing technique, polymer dosimetry, photon spectra through thick shields, fetal effects, ultrasound, mammography. Home and Office: 5942 Easy Pace Cir NW Canton OH 44718-2216

STARCK, CHRISTIAN WALTER, jurist; b. Breslau, Germany, Jan. 9, 1937; s. Walter and Ruth (Hubrich) S.; m. Brigitte Edelmann, Aug. 31, 1965; children: Annette, Johannes, Marie-Christine. Student, U. Kiel, 1957, U. Freiburg, 1958-59; Dr. iur., U. Würzburg, 1963, Habil., 1969. Clk. Fed. Constl. Ct., 1964-67; govt. ofcl., 1968-69; lectr. U. Würzburg, 1969-71; prof. pub. law U. Göttingen, Germany, 1971—, rector, 1976-77; judge Constl. Ct. Lower Saxony, Fed. Republic Germany, 1991—. Vis. prof. U. Paris-Sorbonne, 1987; mem. TV bd. Zweites Deutsches Fernsehen, 1978-92; pres. TV bd. ARTE, 1991-2000. Author: Der Gesetzesbegriff des Grundesetzes, 1970, Spanish edit., 1979, Das Bundesverfassungsgericht im politischen Prozess, 1976, Japanese edit., 1978, Der demokratische Verfassungsstaat, 1995, La Constitution, cadre et mesure du droit, 1994, Das Bonner Grundgesetz Kommentar, 4th edit., 1999, 2000, 2001; editor: Studien und Materialien zur Verfassungsgerichtsbarkeit, 90 vols., 1973—; co-editor: Juristenzeitung, 1978—; contbr. over 200 articles to law jours. and festschriften, —. Fellow Inst. for Advanced Study, Berlin; mem. Internat. Assn. Constl. Law (exec. com. 1981—), Acad. Scis. Gôttingen, Assn. German Profs. Pub. Law (exec. com. 1988-89, pres. 1998-99), German Assn. Comparative Law (exec. com. 1985—). Home: Schlegelweg 10 D-37075 Göttingen Germany Office: Georg August Univ Platz U Gôttingen Sieben 6 D-37075 Gôttingen Germany E-mail: c.starck@gwdg.de.

STARE, PETER KNUT JOHAN, human resource consultant; b. Stockholm, Oct. 30, 1936; s. Erik and Karin Margareta (Rydberg) S.; m. Gudvor Eyderfelt, Aug. 19, 1960 (div. 1980); children: Karin, Gunilla, Gunnar; m. Elise Christina Fellborn, Sept. 15, 1992. Law degree, U. Stockholm, 1962. Negotiator Govt. Negotiating Bd., Stockholm, 1962-66, 85-93; dep. dir. gen. Nat. Rd. Bd., 1966-71; head negotiating dept. Employers Orgn. of State Owned Cos., 1971-77; v.p. personal dept. Sara Co. Ltd., 1977-85; cons. advisor Police Ctr. Bd., 1993-95. Bd. dirs. Govt. Pension Found. Author: Handbook of Labour Law, 1976, 11th edit. 1998, Summeries of the Judgement From the Labour Court, 1977—, Management Guide, 1998, To Employ for a Given Period, Labour Law for County Councils, 2002. Capt. Royal Air Force, 1958-93. Home: Tegnergatan 48 11329 Stockholm Sweden

STARER, BRIAN DOUGLAS, lawyer; b. Utica, N.Y., 1945; BS, U.S. Merchant Marine Acad., 1967; JD, Union U., 1972. Bar: N.Y. 1972, U.S. Dist. Ct. (no., so. and ea. dists.) N.Y., U.S. Ct. Appeals (2nd, 3rd and 5th cirs.) 1973, U.S. Ct. Appeals (9th cir.) 1976, U.S. Supreme Ct. 1977, U.S. Ct. Internat. Trade 1977, U.S. Ct. Customs and Patent Appeals 1980. Mem. Haight Gardner Holland & Knight, N.Y.C., new exec. ptnr. Mng. editor Albany Law Rev., 1971-72; contbr. articles to profl. jours. Named to, Maritime Hall of Fame, 2002. Mem. ABA, Maritime Law Assn. U.S., Internat. Bar Assn., N.Y. State Bar Assn. Office: Haight Gardner et al 195 Broadway Fl 24 New York NY 10007-3189 E-mail: bstare@hklaw.com.

STARER, DAVID, funds management executive; b. Bournemouth, England, Mar. 25, 1955; came to U.S., 1996; s. Benedict and Herculine Davyna (Kriel) S.; m. Marion Kay Harper; children: Briony Jennifer, Mark. BS, Capetown U., South Africa, 1980; M in Engring., Pretoria U., South Africa, 1983; MS, Yale U., 1985, PhD, 1990. Registered patent agt. Rsch. engr. Siemens, Pretoria, 1980-83; rsch. mgr. Fuchs Electronics, Johannesburg, South Africa, 1983-87;

rsch. fellow Yale U., 1987-90; sci. advisor Fish & Neave, N.Y.C., 1990-91, F.B. Rice & Co., Sydney, Australia, 1991-93; funds mgmt. exec. Lend Lease Investment Mgmt., Australia, 1993-96; sr. quantitative analyst Jacobs Levy Equity Mgmt., Roseland, N.J., 1996—. Contbr. articles to profl. jours.; reviewer sci. papers. Mem. IEEE, Q-Group of Australia, Yale Club of Sydney, Sigma Xi. Office: Jacobs Levy Equity Mgmt 3 A D P Blvd Roseland NJ 07068-1724

STARER, ROBERT, composer, educator; b. Vienna, Austria, Jan. 8, 1924; came to U.S., 1947, naturalized, 1957; s. Nison and Erna (Gottlieb) S.; m. Johanna Herz, Mar. 27, 1942; 1 child, Daniel. Student, State Acad., Vienna, 1938-39, Jerusalem Conservatory, 1939-42; postgrad. diploma, Juilliard Sch. Music, 1949; PhD (hon.), SUNY, 1996. Mem. faculty Juilliard Sch. Music, 1949-74; assoc. prof. Bklyn. Coll., 1963-66, prof., 1966-91, Disting. prof., 1986-91, ret., 1991. Composer: Symphony 1, 1950, Symphony 2, 1951, Piano Concerto 1, 1947, Piano Concerto 2, 1952, Concerto a Tre, 1954, Viola Concerto, 1958, Ariel, 1959, Joseph and His Brothers, 1966; opera The Intruder, 1956, Concerto for Violin Cello and Orch, 1967, Six Variations with Twelve Notes, 1967, On The Nature of Things (chorus), 1968, Symphony 3, 1969; ballets The Dybbuk, 1960, Samson Agonistes, 1961, Phaedra, 1963, Mutabili, 1965, Third St. Overture, 1970, (opera), Pantagleize, 1971, Concerto Piano 3, 1972, Images of Man, 1973, Stone Ridge Set, Mandala, Profiles in Brass, 1974, The Last Lover (opera), 1975, Journals of a Songmaker; text by Gail Godwin, 1975, The People, Yes; text by Carl Sandburg, 1976, Piano Quartet, 1977; song cycle Transformations, 1978; operas Apollonia, 1978, Anna Margarita's Will, 1979; chorus Voices of Brooklyn, 1980, Evanescence, 1981; Violin Concerto, 1982, Hudson Valley Suite, 1983, Concerto a Quattro, 1984, Piano Trio, 1985, Remembering Felix, 1986, Kaaterskill Quartet, 1987, Cello Concerto, 1987, Duo for violin and piano, 1988, Angel Voices for brass and organ, 1989, Night Thoughts for chorus and synthesizer, 1990, Yizkor and Anima Eterna for flute and harpsichord, 1991, Clarinet Quintet, 1992, Episodes for Viola, Cello and Piano, 1993, Concerto for Two Pianos, 1994, String Quartet No. 2, 1995, String Quartet No. 3, 1996; piano quintet, 1997; The Other Voice, 1998, Maverick Variations, 2000; also chamber music, choral, piano music, songs.; author: Rhythmic Training, 1969, Continuo: A Life in Music, 1987, The Music Teacher, 1997; Symphonic works premiered by N.Y. Philharmonic condrs., other leading condrs. in, U.S., abroad, ballets commd. by Martha Graham, 1961-63, CBS TV for Anna Sokolow, 1964, Lincoln Center for John Butler, 1967. With Royal Air Force, 1943-46. Recipient award Am. Acad. and Inst. Arts and Letters, 1979, Austrial Presdl. medal for arts and scis., 1996; Guggenheim fellow, 1957, 63; Fulbright postdoctoral research grantee, 1964; Nat. Endowment for Arts grantee, 1974, 77. Mem. ASCAP, Am. Music Ctr. (dir. 1962-64), Am. Acad. Arts and Letters. Home: Woodstock, NY. Died Apr. 22, 2001.

STARESNICK, JULIE CHIH, school psychologist; b. San Francisco, Sept. 1, 1950; d. Yu-Ju and Dorothy (Wei) Chih; m. Michael Staresnick, Aug. 20, 1973 (div. April 2000); children: Michelle, Jennifer, Brian. BA, Ind. U., 1972, MS, 1973. Cert. sch. psychologist; lic. clin. social worker; cert. sch. psychologist. Sch. psychologist Gary (Ind.) Schs., 1973-76; dir. svcs. Marshall-Starke Devel. Ctr., Plymouth, Ind., 1978-79; sch. psychologist Hammond (Ind.) Schs., 1981-89, Carmel (Ind.)-Clay Schs., 1989—. Clin. specialist Southlake Mental Health Ctr., Merrillville, Ind., 1980s; adj. faculty Ind. U. Northwest, Gary, 1975; adj. faculty mem. Purdue U. Calumet campus, 11976. Past pres. Parent-Faculty Orgn. Belzer Mid. Sch., Indpls., 1989-90. Recipient Belzer Outstanding Parent award, 1996—97. Mem. Nat. Assn. Sch. Psychologists (mem. exec. coun. 1999—, Ind. state del. 1994-2001), Ind. Assn. Sch. Psychologists (pres. 1989-90, 2002-). Avocations: movies, working out/fitness, racquetball, tennis, travel.

STARFIELD, BARBARA HELEN, pediatrician, educator; b. Bklyn., Dec. 18, 1932; d. Martin and Eva (Illions) Starfield; m. Neil A. Holtzman, June 12, 1955; children: Robert, Jon, Steven. AB, Swarthmore Coll., 1954; MD, SUNY, 1959; MPH, Johns Hopkins U., 1963. Teaching asst. in anatomy Downstate Med. Ctr., N.Y.C., 1955—57; intern in pediat. Johns Hopkins U., 1959—60, resident, 1960—62, dir. pediatric med. care clinic, 1963—66, dir. cmty. staff comprehensive child care project, 1966—67, dir. pediatric clin. scholars program, 1971—76, prof. health policy, joint appointment in pediatrics, 1975—, disting. univ. prof., 1994—. Mem. Nat. Com. Vital Stats., 1994—2002; cons. DHHS; mem. nat. adv. coun. Agy. for Health Care Policy and Rsch., 1990—94; adv. subcom. on Health Systems and Svcs. RSch. Pan Am. Health Orgn., 1988—92, 1995—; cons. Health Care Fin. Adminstrn., 1980—. Editl. bd. Med. Care, 1977—79, Pediat., 1977—82, Internat. Jour. Health Svcs., 1978—, Med. Care Rev., 1980—84, Health Svc. Rsch., 1996—, assoc. editor Ann. Rev. Pub. Health, 1996—2001; contbr. articles to profl. jours. Recipient Dave Luckman Meml. award, 1958, HEW Career Devel. award, 1970—75, APHA Martha May Eliot award, 1995, Disting. Investigator award, Assn. Health Svcs. Rsch., 1995, 1st Primary Care Achievement award, Pew Charitable Trust Fund, 1994, 1st Ann. Rsch. award, Ambulatory Pediatric Assn., 1990. Fellow: Am. Acad. Pediat.; mem.: APHA (Martha May Eliot award 1995), Internat. Soc. for Equity in Health (pres. 2000—02), Ambulatory Pediatric Assn. (pres. 1980), Internat. Epidemiologic Assn., Soc. Pediatric Rsch., NAS Inst. Medicine (governing coun. 1981—83), Alpha Omega Alpha, Sigma Xi. Office: Johns Hopkins Sch Hygiene 624 N Broadway Baltimore MD 21205-1900

STARING, GRAYDON SHAW, lawyer; b. Deansboro, N.Y., Apr. 9, 1923; s. William Luther and Eleanor Mary (Shaw) S.; m. Joyce Lydia Allum-Poon, Sept. 1, 1949; children: Diana Hilary Agnes, Christopher Paul Norman. AB, Hamilton Coll., 1947; JD, U. Calif., Berkeley, 1951. Bar: Calif. 1952, U.S. Supreme Ct. 1958. Atty. Office Gen. Counsel, Navy Dept., San Francisco, 1952-53; atty. admiralty and shipping sect. U.S. Dept. Justice, 1953-60; assoc. Lillick & Charles (now Nixon Peabody), 1960-64, ptnr., 1965-95, of counsel, 1995—. Titulary mem. Internat. Maritime Com.; bd. dirs. Marine Exchange at San Francisco, 1984-88, pres. 1986-88; instr. pub. speaking Hamilton Coll., 1947-48; adj. prof. Hastings Coll. Law, 1996-97, Boalt Hall, U. Calif., 1999. Author: Law of Reinsurance, 1993; assoc. editor Am. Maritime Cases, 1966-92, editor, 1992—; contbr. articles to legal jours. Mem. San Francisco Lawyers Com. for Urban Affairs, 1972-90; bd. dirs. Legal Aid Soc., San Francisco, 1974-90, v.p., 1975-80, pres., 1980-82. With USN, 1943-46, comdr. USNR. Fellow Am. Bar Found., Am. Coll. Trial Lawyers; mem. ABA (chmn. maritime ins. com. 1975-76, mem. standing com. admiralty law 1976-82, 86-90, chmn. 1990, ho. dels. 1986-90), FBA (pres. San Francisco chpt. 1968), Bar Assn. San Francisco (sec. 1972, treas. 1973), Calif. Acad. Appellate Lawyers, Maritime Law Assn. U.S. (exec. com. 1977-88, v.p. 1980-84, pres. 1984-86), Brit. Ins. Law Assn., Brit.-Am. C. of C. (bd. dirs. 1987-2001), World Trade Club San Francisco, Tulane Admiralty Inst. (permanent adv. bd.), Assocs. Maritime Mus. Libr. (dir. 1990-2001, pres. 1992-94). Office: 2 Embarcadero Ctr Ste 2700 San Francisco CA 94111-3900 E-mail: gstaring@nixonpeabody.com., Starlaw@aol.com. *"How small, of all that human hearts endure,/That part which laws or kings can cause or cure!".*

STARK, ALBERT MAXWELL, lawyer; b. Trenton, N.J., May 3, 1939; m. Ellen Stark, Nov. 20, 1966; children: Jared, Rachel. BA, Darmouth Coll., Hanover, N.H., 1960; LLD, U. Pa., Phila., 1963. Bar: N.J. 1964. Asst. to gov. of N.J., 1964; asst. atty. City of Trenton, 1965-66; asst. prosecutor Mercer County, N.J., 1967-68. Host radio programs Lawline, WHWH, 1985-95, In the Pub. Interest, WIMG, 1996. Recipient Humanitarian award Thomas A. Edison State Coll., 2000, award Trial Attys. of N.J., 2000. Mem. ABA, N.J. Bar Assn., Mercer County Bar Assn., Mercer County C. of C. (Citizen of Yr. 1994), Rotary Internat. (Fred Harris fellow 1996). Avocations: writing, tennis, skiing. Office: Stark & Stark 993 Lenox Dr Ste 301 Lawrenceville NJ 08648-2316

STARK, ANTONY ALBERT, astronomer; b. Seattle, Oct. 29, 1953; s. Leon Theodore Stark and Marie (Heise) Ross; m. Ellen Alice Garber, Sept. 5, 1976. BS, Calif. Inst. Tech., 1975; MA, Princeton U., 1977, PhD, 1979. Mem. tech. staff AT&T Bell Labs., Holmdel, N.J., 1979-91; astronomer Smithsonian Astrophys. Obs., Cambridge, Mass., 1991—. Vis. lectr. Princeton U., 1981-92, Harvard U., 1991—. Mem. Am. Astronomical Soc., Internat. Astronomical Union. Republican. Office: Smithsonian Astrophys Obs 160 Concord Ave Cambridge MA 02138-2306

STARK, BRANDY B. news correspondent, educator, artist; b. St. Louis, May 30, 1975; BA (2), U. S. Fla., 1998, MA in Religious Studies, 2000; student in avant garde program, Tampa Mus. Art, 2002—. Artist Stark Images, St. Petersburg, 1996—; times corr. St. Petersburg (Fla.) Times, 2000—; contbg. writer Bayside News, 2000—; guest instr. Creative Clay, Safety Harbor, 2000—. Dj. instr. St. Petersburg Coll., 2002—; guest presenter Dali Mus., St. Petersburg, 2001. Artist (hand wrapped wire metal sculpture) Mystical Merman , 2000 (Best in 3-D Dragoncon Art Show, 2000), (collaborative project) Flag of Hands, 2001; author: (short stories) The Decision, 1998 (Best Short Story submission Omnibus Mag., 1998), The Books, 2001. Mem.: The Exhibiting Soc. Artists, Women Artists Rising, Tampa Bay Pug Club (rescue coord. 2001—02), Phi Alpha Theta (sec. 1997—98). Avocations: parapsychology, exercise, ancient cultures, world mythology. Home and Office: 745 26th Ave N Saint Petersburg FL 33704 E-mail: stark_brandy@hotmail.com.

STARK, BRUCE GUNSTEN, artist; b. Queens, N.Y., Feb. 17, 1933; s. Richard M. and Karen (Gunsten) S.; m. Joan Patricia Lauer, Nov. 19, 1960; children: Robert, Ronald. Student, Sch. Visual Arts, N.Y.C., 1955-58. Artist, cartoonist N.Y. Daily News, N.Y.C., 1961—. One-man shows Art Inst., Pitts., 1968, U. Kutztown, Pa., 1970, N.Y. Bank for Savs., N.Y.C., 1971; group shows Nat. Art Mus. Sport, N.Y.C., 1971; represented in permanent collections Everett Dirksen Library, L.D. Johnson Library, Baseball Hall Fame, Cooperstown, N.Y., Basketball Hall Fame, Mass. Served with USN, 1952-54. Recipient Nat. Cartoonist Soc.'s Rueben Catagory awards for sports, 1966, 75, spl. features, 1968; Page One award for best sports cartoon, 1970, 73 N.Y.C., 71; 3d, 4th, 6th prizes Internat. Salon de Caricatures Montreal, 1966, 68, 69; Most Outstanding Achievement award Sch. Visual Arts, 1982 Achievements include having original cartoons requested by Pres. Nixon, Johnson; 1st color cartoon appearing on front page of N.Y. Daily News. Home: 3139 Stonewater Dr Lakeland FL 33803-2572 *My goals, ideas, principles and standards of conduct are all helpfully outlined for me by God in His holy word— the Bible. I really need no other source. Whatever success has come to me, I think, is because of this, and what God has done for me, through His Son, Jesus Christ.*

STARK, DENNIS EDWIN, university official; b. Springfield, Ill., Dec. 24, 1937; s. Edwin C. and Ida (Fentem) S. BS, Ill. Wesleyan U., 1959; Sanxay fellow practical ethics, Princeton U., 1959-60; MBA, Harvard U., 1962. Adminstrv. asst. to chmn. bd. Industrial Valley Bank, Phila., 1962-64; fin. analyst E.I. DuPont de Nemours, Wilmington, Del., 1964-65; asst. treas. Old Stone Bank, Providence, 1965-68, treas., 1968-71; sr. v.p., treas., sec. Old Stone Bank and Old Stone Corp., 1971-76; exec. v.p., chief fin. officer Old Stone Corp., Old Stone Bank, 1976-86, Dime Bank, N.Y.C., 1986-88; ptnr. Bank Mgmt. Ptnrs., 1988-90; sr. v.p., CFO, corp. sec. Cen Fed Bank, Pasadena, Calif., 1990-92; exec. v.p., CFO, corp. sec. Ea. Bank, Lynn, Mass., 1992-96; ptnr. Fin. Mgmt. Ptnrs., Pawtucket, R.I., 1996-99; v.p. bus. and fin. U. R.I., Kingston, 1999—. Mem. bd. overseers, chmn. human resources com. Peabody Essex Mus., Salem, Mass.; bd. dirs., chmn. fin. com. Preservation Soc. Pawtucket; mem. bd. visitors Ill. Wesleyan U., Bloomington; trustee, chmn. fin. com. Preserve R.I.; chmn. fin. com., mem. Diocesan Coun. Episcopal Diocese; vestry, treas. St. Martins Episcopal Ch.; dep. to gen. conv. Episcopal Ch. USA; bd. dirs. exec. com. and fin. com. R.I. Philharm. Mem. Fin. Execs. Inst., Harvard Bus. Sch. Assn. of R.I., Acacia (co-founder Ill. Wesleyan U. chpt.), Providence Art Club, Hope Club, Univ. Club (R.I.), Harvard Club (N.Y.C.), Agawam Hunt, Dunes Club. Republican. Episcopalian. Avocations: philately, numismatics. Home (Summer): 41 Courtway St Narragansett RI 02882-3610 Office: U RI Carlotti Adminstrn Bldg 75 Lower College Rd Kingston RI 02881-1966 E-mail: destark@uri.edu.

STARK, EVELYN BRILL, poet, musician; b. N.Y.C., Sept. 12, 1913; d. Henry Brill and Rae Hessberg; m. Morton W. Stark, Apr. 27, 1933; 1 child, Henry. BA, Barnard Coll., 1933; artist student of Edouard Dethier, Juilliard Sch. Music, 1933-40. Bd. dirs., violinist Nat. Found. Mus. Therapy, N.Y.C., 1940-50; violinist ARC Hosp. Music Unit, 1950-70, Hosp. Music Unit, Protestant Coun. Chs., N.Y.C., 1950-70; bd. dirs., violinist Music Therapy Ctr., 1960-80; founder, sponsor Nora Hellen Music Friends, 1970-80; ret., 1980. Mem. editl. bd., contbr. Music Jour., 1969-70; contbr. articles and poetry to Sci. of Thought Rev., Eng., 1982—, Beyond (jour.), Eng., 1982-94; recorded tapes with original programs distbd. internationally to librs., hosps., and homes for the aged; author: (book of poetry) Never Apart, 1992, (autobiography) Life is a Poem, 1999; dramatic presentations of Life is a Poem, Hartford, Conn., 2000, Essex, Conn., 2000, Brooklyn, Conn., East Haddam, Conn., Middleton, Conn.; performer (record) All About the Violin, 1969. Donated 3 violins (Amati, Carcassi, Gragnani) to the Met. Mus. Art, N.Y.C., 1974, 80, 97. Recipient 1st prize poetry contest award Altrusa Internat. of Middletown, Conn., 1997, 98, Editors' Choice awards for poetry Nat. Libr. of Poetry, 1996, 97, 98; named Poet Laureate of Conn. Gilbert and Sullivan Soc., 1998; inductee Internat. Poetry Hall of Fame, 1998. Mem. Internat. Soc. Poets. Address: 317 W Main St Chester CT 06412-1057

STARK, FORTNEY HILLMAN (PETE STARK), congressman; b. Milw., Nov. 11, 1931; s. Fortney Hillman Sr. and Dorothy M. (Mueller) S.; children: Jeffrey Peter, Beatrice Ann, Thekla Brumder, Sarah Gallun, Fortney Hillman Stark III; m. Deborah Roderick; children: Hannah Marie, Andrew Peter. BS, MIT; MBA, U. Calif. Teaching asst. MIT, Cambridge, 1953-54; prin. Skaife & Co., Berkeley, Calif., 1957-61; founder Beacon Savs. & Loan Assn., Antioch, 1961; pres., founder Security Nat. Bank, Walnut Creek, 1963-72; mem. U.S. Congress from 13th (formerly 9th) Calif. dist., 1973—; mem. ways and means com., formerly chmn., now ranking minority mem. health subcom.; mem.joint econ. com. Bd. dirs. ACLU, 1971, Common Cause, 1971, Starr King Sch.; del. Dem. State Cen. Com.; trustee Calif. Dem. Coun. Capt. USAF, 1955-57. Mem. Delta Kappa Epsilon. Office: Ho of Reps 239 Cannon Ho Office Bldg Washington DC 20515-0001

STARK, FRANCIS C(IO), JR. horticulturist, educator; b. Drumright, Okla., Mar. 19, 1919; s. Francis C. and Maude Salena (Crowder) S.; m. Dorothy Lucille Moore, Sept. 14, 1941; children: Carolyn P. Stark Reich, Francis C. III. BS, Okla. A&M Coll., 1940; MS, U. Md., 1941, PhD, 1948. Asst. prof. horticulture U. Md., College Park, 1945-49, asso. prof., 1949-51, prof., 1951-80, prof. emeritus, 1980—, head dept. horticulture, 1964-74, chmn. food sci. program, 1966-73, provost agr. and life scis., 1974-80, acting vice chancellor acad. affairs, 1981-82, spl. asst. to v.p., 1982—; archivist/historian Am. Soc. Hort. Sci., 1997—. Contbr. articles to profl. jours. Mem. Md. Gov.'s Commn. on Migratory Labor, 1959-79, chmn., 1963-76; bd. dirs. Capital Area Christian Ch., 1961-66, 89-94, pres., 1963-66; bd. dirs. Christian Ch. Facilities for aging, 1965-96, pres., 1975-80; trustee Lynchburg (Va.) Coll., 1970-79. With USAAF, 1942-45. Recipient Hon. State Farmer award, Md. Future Farmers Assn., 1966, Disting. Alumnus award, Okla. State U., 1999. Fellow Am. Soc. Hort. Sci., AAAS. Clubs: Rotary. Office: U Md Acad Affairs College Park MD 20742-5031

STARK, GEORGE ROBERT, health science association administrator; b. N.Y.C., July 4, 1933; s. Jack and Florence (Israel) S.; m. Mary Susan Beck, Aug. 19, 1956; children: Robert Braden, Janna Elizabeth. BA in Chemistry, Columbia Coll., N.Y.C., 1955; PhD in Chemistry, Columbia Coll., 1959. Rsch. assoc., asst. prof. Rockefeller U., N.Y.C., 1959-63; asst. prof. dept. biochemistry Stanford (Calif.) U., 1963-66, assoc. prof., 1966-71, prof., 1971-83; sr. scientist Imperial Cancer Rsch. Fund, London, 1983-85, asst. dir. rsch., 1985-89, assoc. dir. rsch., 1989-92; chair Lerner Rsch. Inst. Cleve. Clinic Found., 1992—. Reilly lectr. Notre Dame U., 1972; mem. physiol. chemistry study sect. NIH, 1974-77, study sect. Am. Cancer Soc., 1981-83; mem. European Molecular Biology Orgn. Coun., 1990; mem. sci. com. Cancer Rsch. Campaign, 1990-92 Mem. editl. bd. Jour. Biol. Chemistry, 1970-75, Cell, 1983-88, European Molecular Biology Orgn. Jour., 1990-93; contbr. over 180 articles to profl. jours. including European Molecular Biology Orgn. Jour., Jour. Biol. Chemistry, Molecular Cellular Biology, Nature, Oncogene, Proceedings of the Nat. Acad. Scis., among others. Trustee Cleve. Playhouse, 1993—. Guggenheim fellow, 1970-71, Josiah Macy, Jr. fellow, 1977-78; Yamagiwa-Yoshida Study grantee Internat. Union Against Cancer, 1981; named H.A. Sober Meml. lectr. Am. Soc. Biol. Chemists. Fellow Royal Soc.; mem. NAS, Am. Soc. Biochemistry Molecular Biology (rep. U.S. nat. com. biochemistry 1995—), European Molecular Biology Orgn. Achievements include discoveries in enzyme chemisry, interferon signaling and mammalian genetics; contributions to methodology in protein chemistry and molecular biology. Home: 2900 W Park Blvd Shaker Heights OH 44120-1812 Office: Cleve Clinic Found 9500 Euclid Ave Cleveland OH 44195-0001

STARK, JOAN SCISM, education educator; b. Hudson, N.Y., Jan. 6, 1937; d. Ormonde F. and Myrtle Margaret (Kirkey) S.; m. William L. Stark, June 28, 1958 (dec.); children: Eugene William, Susan Elizabeth, Linda Anne, Ellen Scism; m. Malcolm A. Lowther, Jan. 31, 1981. BS, Syracuse U., 1957; MA (Hoadly fellow), Columbia U., 1960; Ed.D., SUNY, Albany, 1971. Tchr. Ossining (N.Y.) High Sch., 1957-59; free-lance editor Holt, Rinehart & Winston, Harcourt, Brace & World, 1960-70; lectr. Ulster County Community Coll., Stone Ridge, N.Y., 1968-70; asst. dean Goucher Coll., Balt., 1970-73, asso. dean, 1973-74; assoc. prof., chmn. dept. higher postsecondary edn. Syracuse (N.Y.) U., 1974-78; dean Sch. Edn. U. Mich., Ann Arbor, 1978-83, prof., 1983-2001, prof. and dean emeritus, 2001—; dir. Nat. Ctr. for Improving Postsecondary Teaching and Learning, 1986—91. Editor: Rev. of Higher Edn., 1991-96; contbr. articles to various publs. Leader Girl Scouts U.S.A., Cub Scouts Am.; coach girls Little League; dist. officer PTA, intermittently, 1968-80; mem. adv. com. Gerald R. Ford Library, U. Mich., 1980-83; trustee Kalamazoo Coll., 1979-85; mem. exec. com. Inst. Social Research, U. Mich., 1979-81; bd. dirs. Mich. Assn. Colls. Tchr. Edn., 1979-81. Mem. Am. Assn. for Higher Edn., Am. Ednl. Rsch. Assn. (Div. J. Rsch. award 1998), Assn. Study Higher Edn. (dir. 1977-79, v.p. 1983, pres. 1984, Rsch. Achievement award 1992, svc. award 1998, Disting. Career award 1999), Assn. Innovation Higher Edn. (nat. chmn. 1974-75), Assn. Instl. Rsch. (disting. mem., Sidney Suslow award 1999), Assn. Colls. and Schs. Edn. State Univs. and Land Grant Colls. (dir. 1981-83), Acctg. Edn. Change Commn., Phi Beta Kappa, Phi Kappa Phi, Sigma Pi Sigma, Eta Pi Upsilon, Lambda Sigma Sigma, Phi Delta Kappa, Pi Lambda Theta.

STARK, NANCY LYNN, critical care nurse; b. Clinton, Ind., July 31, 1956; d. William and Martha Louise (Reed) Gray; m. Matthew Topping Stark, Aug. 4, 1979; children: Matthew Gray, Kyle Reed. BSN, Ind. State U., 1978; MSN, Ind. U., Indpls., 1985. RN, Ind., Ga. Staff nurse Union Hosp., Terre Haute, Ind., 1978-81, St. Vincent Hosp. and Health Care Ctr., Indpls., 1981-85; head nurse Med. Coll. Ga., Augusta, 1985-86, 91-93, nurse educator, 1986-91, clin. instr., adj. faculty Sch. Nursing, 1990—2001, acting dir. nursing, critical care divsn., 1992-93, DON critical care divsn., 1993-97, DON patient care svcs., 1998—2001, clin. instr. Sch. Nursing. Cons. on dimensions of critical care nursing, 1989-94. Contbg. author: Nursing Theorists and Their Work, 4th edit., 1998, Clinical Medical-Surgical Nursing: A Decision-Making Reference, 2002. Mem.: ANA, AACN (pres. CSRA chpt. 1990—91), Cardiovascular Nursing Coun., Am. Heart Assn., Soc. Critical Care Medicine, Am. Trauma Soc., Sigma Theta Tau. Republican. Presbyterian. Home: 595 Country Place Ln Evans GA 30809-3911 Office: Med Coll Ga 15th St EB-208 Augusta GA 30901-1014 E-mail: nstark@mail.mcg.edu., n.graystark@home.com.

STARK, NATHAN J. medical administrator, health policy consultant, lawyer; b. Mpls., Nov. 9, 1920; s. Harold and Anna (Berlow) Stark; m. Lucile D. Seidler, Nov. 28, 1943; children: Paul S., David H., Robert, Margaret J. AA, Woodrow Wilson Jr. Coll., Chgo., 1940; BS, U.S. Mcht. Marine Acad., 1943; JD, Ill. Inst. Tech., 1948; LLD (hon.) (hon.) , Park Coll., 1969, U. Mo., 1980; DHL, Scholl Coll., Hahnemann U., 1987. Bar: Ill. 1947, Mo. 1952. Plant mgr. Englander Co., Inc., Chgo., 1948—51; partner law firm Downey, Abrams, Stark & Sullivan, Kansas City, Mo., 1952—53; v.p. Rival Mfg. Co., 1954—59; sr. v.p. ops. Hallmark Cards, Inc., 1959—74, dir., 1960—74; pres., chmn. Crown Center Redevel. Corp., 1971—74; sr. vice chancellor health scis. Schs. Health Professions, U. Pitts., 1974—84, sr. vice chancellor emeritus, 1984—, also pres. Univ. Health Center, 1974—79, also prof. Grad. Sch. Public Health; undersec. HEW, Washington, 1979—81; of counsel Fort & Schlefor; lawyer, treas., pres., CEO Nat. Acad. of Social Ins., 1992—95, also pres. Univ. Health Center, 1981—. Dir. ERC Corp., 1970—79, Hallmark Continental Ltd., Ireland, 1971—73; mem. exec. bd. Nat. Bd. Med.; mem. sci. adv. bd. NE Regional Ctr., 2000—. Contbr. articles. Legal counsel Lyric Opera Theater, Kansas City, Mo., 1958—72; mem. com. undergrad. med. edn. AMA, 1966—73; chmn. cmty. hosp.-med. staff group practice program Robert Wood Johnson Found., 1974—79; vice chmn. health ins. benefits adv. com. HEW, 1965—70; sec. Task Force on Medicaid, 1960—70, chmn. adv. commn. incentive reimbursement experimentation, 1968—70; chmn. capital investment conf. HEW-HRA, 1976; mem. liaison com. Am. Assn. Med. Colls.-AMA, 1970—74; chmn. task force life-long learning opportunities Kellogg Found., 1975—77; mem.-a-large Nat. Bd. Med. Examiners; mem. bd. Blue Cross Western Pa., 1975—79, Am. Nurses Found., 1975—77, Health Sys. Agy. SW Pa., 1976—; v.p. Kansas City Philharm. Assn., 1954; sec. Eddie Jacobson Meml. Found., 1960—; mem. tech. bd. Milbank Meml. Fund, 1976—78; pres., chmn. Kansas City Gen. Hosp. and Med. Ctr., 1962—74; trustee Allegheny Found., 1975—, Pitts. Ballet Theater, 1977—79, Pitts. Chamber Opera Theater, 1978—; mem. VA Scholars Bd. Governance, 1979—; hon. fellow, trustee Hastings Ctr., 1981; v.p. Pitts. Opera; adv. bd. trustees St. Joseph Coll., trustee, 1994. Recipient Chancellor's medal, U. Mo. at Kansas City, 1969, Pro-Meritus award, Rockhurst Coll., 1967, Layman award, AMA, 1974. Fellow: Am. Acad. Pediatrics (hon.); mem.: Nat. Acad. Social Ins. (bd. trustees, pres. 1992—94, treas. 1994—), Am. Coll. Hosp. Adminstrs., Inst. Medicine of NAS (coun. 1973—76), Am. Hosp. Assn. (hon. Trustee award 1968). Home: Apt 132B 4000 Cathedral Ave NW Washington DC 20016-5249

STARK, NORMAN, secondary school educator; b. Bronx, N.Y., Sept. 15, 1940; s. Martin and Margaret (Neuman) S.; m. Betty Joanne Kelton, Sept. 4, 1994 (dec. May 1998); 1 child, Michelle Allison; m. Lois Marie Ricketson, Dec. 25, 2001. Student, Newark State Coll., Union, 1963-69. Creative writing tchr., acting tchr., singles forum tchr., film tchr. Plantation (Fla.) High Sch., 1988; Hoover Mid. Sch. and Palm Bay H.S., Melbourne, Fla., 1995. Editor West Palm Beach News, 1979; screenplay writer, actor. With U.S. Army, 1963-69. Avocations: reading, puzzles, movies. Home: 2732 Locksley Rd Melbourne FL 32935-2433 E-mail: norman915@aol.com.

STARK, PATRICIA ANN, psychologist; b. Ames, Iowa, Apr. 21, 1937; d. Keith C. and Mary L. (Johnston) Moore. BS, So. Ill. U., Edwardsville, 1970, MS, 1972; PhD, St. Louis U., 1976. Counselor to alcoholics Bapt. Rescue Mission, East St. Louis, Ill., 1969; rschr. alcoholics Gateway Rehab. Ctr., 1972; psychologist intern Henry-Stark Counties Spl. Edn. Dist. and Galesburg State Rsch. Hosp., Ill., 1972-73; instr. Lewis and Clark C.C., Godfrey, 1973-76, asst. prof., 1976-84, assoc. prof., 1984, coord. child care svcs., 1974-84; mem. staff dept. psychiatry Meml. Hosp., St. Elizabeth's Hosp., 1979-2001; supr. various workshops in field, 1974-84. Supr. various workshops in field, 1974-84; dir. child and family svc. Collinsville Counseling Ctr., 1977-82; clin. dir., owner Empas-Complete Family Psychol. and Hypnosis Svcs., Collinsville, 1982—; cons. cmty. agys., 1974—; mem. adv. bd. Madison County Coun. on Alcoholism and Drug Dependency, 1977-80. Mem. APA, Ill. Psychol. Assn., Midwestern Psychol. Assn., Nat. Assn. Sch. Psychologists, Am. Soc. Clin. Hypnosis, Internat. Soc. Hypnosis. Office: 2802 Maryville Rd Maryville IL 62062

STARK, RAY, motion picture producer; Student, Rutgers U. Publicity agt.; lit. agt.; talent agt. Famous Artist Agy., to 1957; co-founder Seven Arts Prodn. Co., 1957; ind. film producer, 1966—. Producer : (films) The World of Suzie Wong, 1960, The Night of the Iguana, 1964, Reflections in a Golden Eye, 1967, Funny Girl, 1968, The Owl and the Pussycat, 1970, Fat City, 1972, The Way We Were, 1973, Funny Lady, 1975, The Sunshine Boys, 1975, Murder By Death, 1976, Smokey and the Bandit, 1977, The Goodbye Girl, 1977, The Cheap Detective, 1978, California Suite, 1978, Chapter Two, 1979, The Electric Horseman, 1979, Seems Like Old Times, 1980, Annie, 1982, Blue Thunder, 1983, Nothing in Common, 1986, Peggy Sue Got Married, 1986, The Secret of My Success, 1987, Biloxi Blues, 1988. Steel Magnolias, 1989, Revenge, 1990, Lost in Yonkers, 1993, Barbarians at the Gate, 1993 (Emmy award Outstanding Made to Television Movie 1993), Mr. Jones, 1993, Dr. Jekyll and Ms. Hyde, 1995, Mariette in Ecstacy, 1996, To Gillian on Her 37th Birthday, 1996, Harriet the Spy, 1996, Random Hearts, 1999. Recipient Thalberg award Acad. Motion Picture Arts and Scis., 1980 Office: 1990 S Bundy Dr Ste 200 Los Angeles CA 90025

STARK, RICHARD BOIES, surgeon, artist; b. Conrad, Iowa, Mar. 31, 1915; s. Eugene and Hazel (Carson) S.; m. Judy Thornton, Oct. 31, 1967 AB, Stanford U., 1936; postgrad., U. Heidelberg, 1936-37; MD, Cornell U., 1941. Diplomate Am. Bd. Plastic Surgery (pres. 1967-68). Intern Peter Bent Brigham Hosp., Boston, 1941-42; asst. resident surgery Childrens Hosp., 1942; plastic surgeon Northington Gen. Hosp., Ala., 1945-46, Percy Jones Gen. Hosp., Mich., 1946; postwar fellow anatomy and embryology Stanford U., 1946-47; from asst. resident to resident in head and neck surgery VA Hosp., Bronx, N.Y., 1947-50; asst. resident, resident surgery, plastic, head and neck and gen. surgery N.Y. Hosp., 1947-50; instr. surgery Cornell U., 1950-52, asst. prof., 1952-55, assoc. prof., 1955; asst. attending surgeon N.Y. Hosp., 1950-55; asst. prof. surgery Columbia U., 1955-58, assoc. prof., 1958-73, prof. clin. surgery, 1973—; assoc. attending surgeon St. Luke's Hosp., N.Y.C., 1955-58, founding attending surgeon dept. plastic surgery, 1958—; founder dept. plastic surgery, 1955. Cons. Walter Reed Med. Ctr., 1970-77 Author: Plastic Surgery, 1962, Cleft Palate, 1968, Plastic Surgery at the New York Hospital 100 Years Ago, 1952, Aesthetic Plastic Surgery, 1980, Total Facial Reconstruction, 1985, Plastic Surgery of the Head and Neck, 1986; contbr. 51 chpts. to books, 219 articles to profl. jours.; assoc. editor: Plastic Reconstructive Surgery, 1977-82; founding editor: Annals Plastic Surgery, 1978-81; 21 one-person art shows, 1946—; rep. in permanent art exhibit, N.Y. Hosp. Chmn. Medico Adv. Bd., 1976-77; mem., v.p. CARE Bd.; v.p. Wellborn Found., N.Y.C. Served with AUS, 1943-46 Decorated Bronze Star (U.S.); Medal of Honor (2) (Vietnam); cavallero Order of San Carlos (Colombia), Dieffenbach medal (Berlin), Gold medal Nat. Inst. Social Scis. Fellow ACS; mem. Am. Assn. Plastic Surgeons, Am. Soc. Plastic and Reconstructive Surgery (pres. 1966, Spl. Achievement award), Found. Am. Soc. Plastic and Reconstructive Surgery (pres. 1961-65), Am. Surg. Assn., Soc. Univ. Surgeons, French Soc. Plastic Surgeons, Brasilian Soc. Plastic Surgeons, Colombian Soc. Plastic Surgeons, Argentina Soc. Plastic Surgeons, Brit. Assn. Plastic Surgery, Peruvian Acad. Surgeons, N.Y. Surg. Soc., N.Y. Acad. Medicine (pres. Friends Rare Book Room), Plastic and Reconstructive Surgery (sec., pres. 1966), N.Y. State Med. Soc. (pres., sec., med. history), N.Y. Regional Soc. Plastic and Reconstructive Surgery (pres. 1064-65), Halsted Soc. (pres. 1973-74), James IV Assn. Surgeons, Am. Soc. Aesthetic Plastic Surgery (pres. 1974-75), Nat. Arts Club (exhibiting mem.), Century Club (profl. artist), Artist Fellowship. Home: 35 E 75th St New York NY 10021-2761

STARK, ROBERT MARTIN, mathematician, civil engineer, educator; b. N.Y.C., Feb. 6, 1930; s. Alexander and Julia (Gross) S.; m. Carol LaSage, Jan. 13, 1955 (dec. Mar. 1988); children: Bradley R., Timothy D., Steven M., Candice B. AB, Johns Hopkins U., 1951; MA, U. Mich., 1952; PhD, U. Del., 1965. Rsch. scientist Bausch and Lomb, Rochester, N.Y., 1955; instr. Rochester Inst. Tech., 1956-57; asst. dean engring., asst. prof. math. Cleve. State U., 1957-62; instr. U. Del., 1962-64, asst. prof. civil and environ. engring., math. scis., 1964-68, assoc. prof., 1968-76, prof., 1976—; pres., cons. applied sci. R.M. Stark & Co., Inc. Vis. assoc. prof. MIT, 1972-73; chmn. grad. program in ops. rsch.; cons. in field. Author: (with R.L. Nicholls) Mathematical Foundations for Design: Civil Engineering Systems, 1972; (with R.H. Mayer, Jr.) Quantitative Construction Management: Uses of Linear Optimization, 1983; (with R. Engelbrecht-Wiggans and M. Shubik) Auctioning, Bidding and Contracting, 1983; (with C. Sloyer, et al) Contemporary Applied Mathematics Series, 1987, Mathagrams, 1996. Bd. dirs. Geriatrics Svcs. Del., Inc., 1989—, Wilmington Sr. Ctr., 1994—, Meals on Wheels Found.; bd. dirs. Del. Acad. Sci., 1990—, pres., 1994-96; bd. dirs., v.p. White Clay Watershed Assn., 1992-97; commr. Del. Heritage Commn., 1990—; sec. Pencader Heritage Area, 1999—. Recipient Outstanding Alumnus award U. Del. Dept. Civil and Environ. Engring., 1999; grantee Office Naval Rsch., 1974-81, NSF, 1969-70, U.S. Army Rsch. Office, 1966-68. Mem. AAAS, ASCE, Nat. Coun. Tchrs. Math., Inst. Mgmt. Sci., Ops. Rsch. Soc. Am., Phila. Ops. Rsch. Soc. (pres. 1970). Avocations: research, publs. ops. rsch., applied probability. Home: One Fox Ln Newark DE 19711 Office: U Del Dept Math Sci Newark DE 19716 E-mail: rstark@udel.edu.

STARK, ROBIN CARYL, psychotherapist, consultant; b. Yonkers, N.Y., Apr. 16, 1953; d. Louis and Bernice (Cooper) S. BA in Psychology cum laude with honors, Hunter Coll., 1979; MSW, NYU, 1982. Diplomate Am. Bd. Clin. Social Work; lic. social worker, N.Y.; cert. psychoanalytic psychotherapy, psychotherapy of eating disorders. Pvt. practice psychotherapy, N.Y.C., 1983—. Mem. adj. field faculty Grad. Sch. Social Svc. Fordham U., N.Y.C., 1986—87, Grad. Sch. Social Work, Hunter Coll., N.Y.C., 1987—88; coord. patient care svces. Achievement and Guidance Ctrs. Am., Inc., N.Y.C., 1988—89; staff psychotherapist Ctr. for Study of Anorexia and Bulimia, 1990—94, facilitator wellness support chronic & life-challenging illness, 1993—; bd. dirs. N.Y. Met. Cmty. of Mindfulness, 1999—2000. Recipient service award Young Adult Inst., 1987; N.Y.C. Youth Bur. grantee, 1983-85. Mem. NASW, Acad. Cert. Social Workers. Office: 410 E 57th St Ste 1A New York NY 10022-3059

STARK, S. DANIEL, JR. gaming industry executive; b. Port Hueneme, Calif., Mar. 26, 1953; s. S. Daniel and Eloise Marie (Fisher) S.; m. Pauline Laube Finley, June 7, 1997; 1 child, Kaitlyn Elizabeth. BS, Calif. Poly. U., Pomona, 1981; cert. in exec. mgmt., Claremont Grad. U., 1989, MA in Mgmt., 1992. Driver-guide San Diego Wild Animal Pk./Zool. Soc. San Diego, Escondido, Calif., 1974-76; attractions host Disneyland divsn. The Walt Disney Co., Anaheim, 1976-80, mgmt. intern, 1981, supr. ops., 1981-82, area supr. ops., dept. mgr., 1982-87; mgmt. cons. S.D. Stark, Jr., Las Vegas, 1985—; dir. mktg. Ramada Express Hotel & Casino, Laughlin, Nev., 1988-89; exec. dir. San Bernardino (Calif.) Conv. and Visitors Bur., 1989-98; pres., CEO Panama City Beach Conv. & Visitors Bur., 1998-99; exec. dir. Bay County (Fla.) Tourist Devel. Coun., 1998-99; dir. mktg. Boyd Gaming Corp., Las Vegas, 1999—. Part-time instr. mgmt. and mktg. So. Calif. campus U. Phoenix, 1997-98, Nev. campus, 1999—, area chair for mktg., 2001--; cons. Hemmeter Devel. Corp., Honolulu, 1985, Calif. Authority Racing Fairs, Sacramento, 1987-88, USIA for Latvian Ministry Transp., tourism divsn., 1992, U.S. Bur. Land Mgmt., tourism mgmt. project U. Alaska Sch. Mgmt.; adj. prof. Sch. Bus. and Pub. Admisntrn., Calif. State U., San Bernardino, 1992-93. Bd. dirs. Leadership So. Calif., 1993-98, grad. pub. affairs tng., 1993; congl. appointee del. White House Conf. on Travel and Tourism, 1995; mem. regional econ. strategies consortium So. Calif. Assn. Govts., 1996-98; mem. Visit Fla. Mktg. Com., 1998-99; bd. dirs. Fla. Assn. Conv. and Visitors Burs., 1998-99, Speedway Childrens Charities Las Vegas Chpt., 1999—, treas., 2000-01, chmn., 2001—. Recipient resolution Calif. Assembly, 1989, 98, San Bernardino County Bd. Suprs., 1989, City of San Bernardino Mayor and Coun., 1989, 98, Calif. Senate, 1989, 98; selected as one of 1991 Up and Coming Young Bus. Leaders in San Bernardino County; named one of Inland Empire Bus. All Stars, 1991; recipient World Champion Trail Horse award Am. Jr. Quarter Horse Assn., 1972, Calif. Tourism award for Best Spl. Event-Rt. 66 Rendezvous, 1997. Mem. Am. Horse Shows Assn. (life), Am. Quarter Horse Assn (life), Assn. Travel Mktg. Execs., Internat. Assn. Conv. and Visitors Burs. (cert. comm., conv. mktg., tourism mktg.), Pub. Rels. Soc. Am. (bd. dirs. Calif. Inland Empire chpt. 1990-95, Polaris award 1997), Calif. Festivals and Events Assn. (pres. 1997-98, 2002—, bd. dirs. 1994-98, 2002--), Inland Empire Tourism Coun. (bd. dirs. 1996-98, exec. com. 1996-98, treas. 1997-98), Calif. Travel Industry Assn., Tourism Assn. So. Calif. (bd. dirs. 1990-95, vice chair 1992-95), Western Assn. Convs. and Vis. Bur. (chmn. Calif. coun. 1992-94), FarmHouse Fraternity (internat. bd. dirs. 1986-94, v.p. 1990-92, Snyder Alumni award 1984). Avocations: boating, fishing, films, equestrian competition. Office: 2950 Industrial Rd Las Vegas NV 89109-1150

STARK, SUSAN, medical technician; b. Phila., Apr. 27, 1962; d. Frank Joseph and Mariana Caroline (Peranteau) Hetherington; m. Todd Ian Stark, Feb. 4, 1984; children: Ian Michael, Nicholas Andrew, Jessica Sara. BS in Med. Tech., Hahnemann U., 1985. Chief med. technologist Parkview Hosp., Phila., 1989—98, Lower Bucks Hosp., Bristol, 1998—. Chief technologist Hematology and Oncology Assocs., Phila., 1990—93; bd. advisors Med. Lab. Oberserver, Phila., 1996—99; aquatic dir. Camp Cherokee, Bensalem, Pa., 1998—2000, Sumerton Springs Swim Club, Feasterville, Pa., 2001. Eucharistic min., lector, cantor Maternity B.V.M. Ch., Phila., 1993—. Mem.: AAAS, Am. Soc. Clin. Pathologists (cert. med. technologist). Avocations: scuba diving, classical singing. Home: 1738 Megargee St Philadelphia PA 19152

STARKE, HAROLD E., JR. lawyer; b. Richmond, Va., Aug. 1, 1944; BA, Randolph-Macon Coll., 1967; JD, U. Richmond, 1971; LLM in Taxation, NYU, 1973. Bar: Va. 1971, D.C. 1981. Mem. Troutman Sanders LLP, Richmond. Editor U. Richmond Law Rev., 1970-71. Bd. trustees Randolph-Macon Coll., 1983-85, 95-97, 99—. Fellow Am. Coll. Tax Counsel; mem. ABA (taxation sect.), Va. State Bar (chmn. taxation sect. 1985-86), D.C. Bar, Richmond Estate Planning Coun., Randolph-Macon Estate Planning Coun. (chmn. 1985—), McNeill Honor Soc., Phi Delta Phi. Office: Troutman Sanders LLP Bank of Am Center PO Box 1122 Richmond VA 23218-1122

STARKEY, ELIZABETH LARUFFA, accountant; b. Franklin, Ky., May 23, 1947; d. Albert A. and Alma L. (Duer) LaRuffa; m. Jerry L. Starkey, June 14, 1969; children: James, Jonathan. AA, Miami-Dade Jr. Coll., 1967; BS in Math., Fla. State U., 1969; MS in Acctg., U. Houston, 1984. Cert. public acct., math. tchr. Tchr. Dade County, Miami, Fla., 1969-75; mgr. Ernst & Young, Houston, 1984-90; prin. Starkey & Co, 1990—. Bd. dirs. St. Thomas H.S. Found., 1994-2000, Miami-Dade C.C. Found., 1997-99 ; bd. dirs. Am. Cancer Soc., Houston, 1985-87, 90-2000, mem. legacy and planned giving com.; bd. dirs., treas. Univ. Houston Alumni Orgn., 2000—; mem. Planned Giving and Coun. Houston, Houston Estate and Fin. Forum. Mem. AICPAs, Tex. Soc. CPAs (Houston chpt.), Nat. Soc. Tax Profls., Beta Gamma Sigma, Beta Alpha Psi, Omicron Delta Kappa. Roman Catholic. Home: 4410 Merwin St Houston TX 77027-6714 Office: Starkey & Co PO Box 22166 Houston TX 77227-2166 E-mail: estarkey@starkeycpa.com.

STARKEY, RUSSELL BRUCE, JR. utilities executive; b. Lumberport, W. Va., July 20, 1942; s. Russell Bruce and Dorotha Mable (Field) S.; m. Joan McClellan, May 27, 1966; children: Christine, Pamela, Joanne. BS, Miami U., Oxford, Ohio, 1964; grad. student, U. New Haven, 1972-73, N.C. State U., 1974-75. U.S. Navy Schs., 1964-66, 68. From sr. engr., nuclear generation sect. to prin. engr. Carolina Power & Light Co., Raleigh, NC, 1973—75; quality assurance supr. to supt. tech. and administrn. Brunswick Steam Electric Plant, Southport, 1975—77; plant mgr. H. B. Robinson Steam Electric Plant, Hartsvile, S.C., 1977-83, mgr. environ. services Raleigh, 1984-85, mgr. nuclear safety and environ services dept., 1985-88; exec. dir. nuc. prodn. Pub. Svc. ind., Jeffersonville, 1983-84; mgr. Brunswick Nuclear Project Dept., 1988-89, v.p., 1989-92, v.p. Nuclear Svcs. Dept., 1992-93, cons., 1993-94; exec. v.p. energy mgmt. divsn. Hesco, Inc., 1994; from dir. indsl. electrotech. lab. to v.p. gen. tech. mgr. Advanced Energy Corp., 1994—97; cons. U.S. Enrichment Corp., 1997—98, tng. mgr., 1998—2001, plant gen. mgr., 2001—. With USN, 1964-73. Mem.: Am. Nuclear Soc. Home: 1227 Beresford Way Paducah KY 42001-6552 Office: Bldg C-100 PO Box 1410 Paducah KY 42002-1410

STARKMAN, BETTY PROVIZER, genealogist, writer, educator; b. Detroit, July 18, 1929; d. Jack and Rose (Bodenstein) Provizer; m. Morris Starkman, Dec. 25, 1952; children: Susan Lynn Starkman Rott, Robert David Starkman. AB, Wayne State U., 1951; postgrad., U. Wis., 1949; MA, Wayne U., 1954. Cert. social worker, Mich. Social worker Wayne County Social Aid, Detroit, 1951-54, B'nai B'rith Youth Orgn., Detroit, 1951-54; genealogist, historian Birmingham, Mich., 1979—. Tchr. Midrasha Coll., Southfield, Mich., 1986-88, Coll. Jewish Studies, Birmingham, 1986-88; lectr. Jewish Cmty. Ctr., West Bloomfield, Mich., 1986-89. Editor jour. Generations, 1986; contbr. articles to Jwish News, Generations, Search, others. Bd. dirs. Anti Defamation League,Detroit, 1980—, Jewish Cmty. Coun., Southfield, 1980—, Tribute Fund, Detroit, 1979-85; v.p. Maimonides, Detroit, 1966-67; bd. dirs. Am. Mogen David for Israel, Mich. br.; del. 1st conf. Jews of Old China, Harvard U., 1992; mem. archives com. Jewish Welfare Fedn. Mich., 1993—. Recipient Humanitarian award State of Israel Bonds, 1980; Helping Hand award Israel Red Cross, 1980, Humanitarian award, 1991; honored by Mich. region Am. Red Mogen Dovid for Israel, 1997, Jewish Geneal. Soc. Mich., 1997. Mem. Jewish Genealogy Soc. Mich. (founder, pres. 1982-84, bd. dirs. 1995—), Jewish Genealogy Soc. Ill., Jewish Genealogy Soc. Inc., Jewish Hist. Soc. (Mich. bd. dirs. 1986-88), Jewish Genealogy Soc. L.A., Jewish Genealogy Soc. Phila., Jewish Genealogy Soc. Washington, Jewish Genealogy Soc. Toronto, Polish Genealogy Soc. Mich. Avocations: travel, reading, collecting art, music, archaeology. Home and Office: 1260 Stuyvessant Rd Bloomfield Hills MI 48301-2141

STARKMAN, GARY LEE, lawyer; b. Chgo., Sept. 2, 1946; s. Oscar and Sara (Ordman) S. AB, U. Ill., 1968; JD cum laude, Northwestern U., 1971. Bar: Ill. 1971, U.S. Dist. Ct. (no. dist.) Ill. 1972, U.S. Ct. Appeals (7th cir.) 1972, U.S. Supreme Ct. 1974, Trial Bar U.S. Dist. Ct. (no. dist.) Ill. 1982, U.S. Ct. Appeals (3d cir.) 1984, U.S. Ct. Appeals (D.C. cir.) 1984. Asst. U.S. Atty. No. Dist. Ill., 1971-75; gen. counsel, dir. rsch. Citizens for Thompson Campaign Com., 1975-77; counsel to Gov. of Ill., 1977-81; ptnr. Ross & Hardies, Chgo., 1990—; admissions com. U.S. Dist. Ct. (no. dist.) Ill., 1982-90. Co-author: (textbook) Cases and Comments on Criminal Procedure, 1974, 5th edit., 1998; contbr. articles to profl. jours.; reviewer in field. Chmn. state agys. divsn. Jewish United Fund Met. Chgo., 1978-81; chmn. Ill. Racing Bd., 1991-96; bd. dirs. Internat. Assn. Racing Commn., 1992-94; cmty. adv. bd. Jr. League Chgo., 1979-83. Recipient John Marshall award for appellate litigation Atty. Gen. U.S., 1974, Nat. Svc. award Tau Epsilon Phi, 1968; named one of Ten Outstanding Young Citizens, Chgo. Jr. C. of C., 1978. Mem. ABA (litigation sect.), Chgo. Bar Assn. (constl. law com.), Decalogue Soc., Northwestern U. Law Alumni Assn. Office: Ross & Hardies 150 N Michigan Ave Ste 2500 Chicago IL 60601-7567 E-mail: gary.starkman@rosshardies.com.

STARKS, CHARLES WILEY, minister; b. Bastian, Va., June 27, 1954; s. Clarence Eugene and Mattiline Mae (Compton) S.; m. Angela D. Marshall; 1 child, Olivia Grace Starks. BA, Emory and Henry Coll., 1976; MDiv, Emory Univ., 1979, D of Ministry, 1988. Lic. to ministry, 1972; ordained to ministry United Meth. Ch. as deacon, 1977, as elder, 1981. Pers. recruiter and trainer A Christian Ministry in the Nat. Parks, N.Y.C., 1979—80; min. Meadowview United Meth. Ch., Meadowview, Va., 1980—84, Pleasant View United Meth. Ch., Abingdon, 1984—93, First United Meth. Ch., Newport, Tenn., 1993—97, Asbury United Meth. Ch., Greeneville, 1997—2002; dist. supt. Wytheville Dist. of United Meth. Ch., Va., 2002—. Adj. prof. of philosophy/religion Va. Highlands Cmty. Coll., Abingdon, 1986-93; coord. Abingdon Dist. Youth, 1980-84; New Life Missioner, 1983—; apptd. counseling elder Holston Conf., supervising pastor, 1985—; mem. Abingdon Dist. Com. on Superintendency, 1985-93, Holston Conf. Bd. of Ordained Ministry exec. com., 1985-92, chmn. psychol. testing and assessment com., 1987-92, com. on the Episcopacy, 1990-97, task force on conf. strategy and structure for ministry and mission, 1990-92; mem. alumni exec. com. Candler Sch. Theology. Vol. Big Bro., Washington County Big Bro./Big Sister Orgn., 1985-88; chmn. Washington County Office on Youth Svcs. Citizens Bd., 1988-90; mem. Washington County Commonwealth Alliance for Drug Rehab. and Edn., 1989-90, Washington County Multi-Discipline Bd., 1989-90, Washington County Fed. Emergency Mgmt. Authority Bd., 1987-93; mem. bio-med. ethics com. Johnston Meml. Hosp., 1991-93; bd. dirs. Holston Home for Children, 1993-97; bd. trustees Hiwassee Coll., 1997—. Named to Outstanding Young Men in Am., 1985; Chaplain of the Day U.S. Senate, Washington, 1989. Mem. United Meth. Assn. of Ch. Bus. Adminstrs., Kiwanis (religious affairs com. 1988), Mason, others. Home: 290 Scenic View Cir Wytheville VA 24382 Office: Wytheville Dist United Methodist Ch PO Box 925 Wytheville VA 24382 *Increasingly it seems, for individuals, families and nations, life becomes more complex and knotty to the point that people resign themselves to hopelessness. But, in giving ourselves to maturing relationships with God and others, based on trust, hopelessness can be uprooted. Confidence can flourish. Peace of mind and simplicity in living can be restored.*

STARKS, FLORENCE ELIZABETH, retired special education educator; b. Summit, N.J., Dec. 6, 1932; d. Edward and Winnie (Morris) S. BA, Morgan State U., 1956; MS in Edn., CUNY, 1962; postgrad., Fairleigh Dickinson U., 1962-63, Seton Hall U., 1963, Newark State Coll. Cert. blind and visually handicapped and social studies tchr., N.J. Tchr. adult edn. Newark Bd. of Edn.; ret., 1995; tchr. N.Y. Inst. for Edn. of the Blind, Bronx. Developer first class for multiple handicapped blind children in pub. sch. system, Newark, 1960; ptnr. World Vision Internat. Mem. ASCD, AFL-CIO, AAUW, Coun. Exceptional Children, Am. Assn. U. Women, Nat. Assn. Negro Bus. and Profl. Women's Club Inc., N.J. Edn. Assn., Newark Tchrs. Assn., Newark Tchrs. Union-Am. Fedn. Tchrs., World Vision Internat. (ptnr.). Home: 4 Park Ave Summit NJ 07901-3942

STARKS, FRED WILLIAM, chemical company executive; b. Millford, Ill., Aug. 16, 1921; s. Otis Earl and Evelyn Viola S.; m. Minnie Jane Reynolds, Sept. 4, 1946; children: David F., Steven J., Daniel J. B.S., U. Ill., 1943, M.S., 1947; Ph.D., U. Nebr., 1950. Supr., U.S. Rubber Co., Torrance, Calif., 1943-44; supr. DuPont, Niagara Falls, N.Y., 1950-57; pres. Starks Assocs., Inc., Buffalo, N.Y., 1957-89, chmn., 1989—; spl. lectr. U. Buffalo, 1959-63. Lt. (j.g.) USNR, 1944-46. Avery fellow, 1948-49; USPHS fellow, 1949-50. Mem. Am. Chem. Soc., N.Y. Acad. Sci., Am. Inst. Chemists, Sigma Xi. Clubs: Buffalo, Cosmos, Chemists. Patentee in field. Home: 742 Highland Ave Buffalo NY 14223-1645 Office: Starks Assocs Inc 1280 Niagara St Buffalo NY 14213-1592

STARKSCHALL, GEORGE, medical physicist; b. Weiden, Germany, Sept. 11, 1946; came to U.S., 1947; s. Nathan and Rosa (Ginsberg) S.; m. Carol Sue Eisenberg, Apr. 20, 1974; children: Jessica Michelle, Andrea Debra. SB, MIT, 1967; PhD, Harvard U., 1972. Diplomate Am. Bd. Radiology, Am. Bd. Med. Physics. Rsch. assoc. U. Chgo., 1972-74; radiol. physicist Hines VA Hosp., 1974-75, St. Francis Hosp., Evanston, Ill., 1975-77; asst. prof. Chgo. Med. Sch., 1977-80, U. Kans. Med. Sch., 1980-85; physicist U. Tex.-M.D. Anderson Cancer Ctr., Houston, 1985—. Editor: Quality Assurance in Radiotherapy Physics, 1991, Clinical Implementation of 3-D Radiation Therapy, 1999; contbr. articles to sci. jours. Achievements include research on radiation oncology treatment planning and radiation oncology imaging. Office: MD Anderson Cancer Ctr Dept Radiation Physics 1515 Holcombe Blvd Houston TX 77030-4009

STARKWEATHER, FREDERICK THOMAS, retired data processing executive; b. Sioux City, Iowa, Feb. 24, 1933; s. Fred Ervin and Gertrude Faye (Madden) S.; m. Margot Glassen, Nov. 19, 1959; children: Thomas Frederick, Jerry Russell, Michael Glassen. BA in Math. and Physics, U. Nebr., Omaha, 1955. Mathematician Flight Determination Lab., White Sands Missile Range, N.Mex., 1955-56; supervisory mathematician Analysis & Computation, 1956-81; chief data scis. div. Nat. Range Ops., 1981-98; ret. Nat. council rep. Am. Def. Preparedness Assn., Washington, 1980—; pres. White Sands Pioneer Group, White Sands Missile Range, 1983-86; bd. dirs. Assn. U.S. Army, Washington. Author hist. and genealog. books; contbr. book reviews and articles to newspapers and mags. Chmn. El Paso (Tex.) City Planning Commn., 1980-84; bd. dirs. El Paso County Hist. Soc., 1983-87; mem. El Paso County Hist. Commn., 1983—. With USAR, 1955-63. Recipient Profl. Secs. Internat. Exec. of Yr. award, 1987, Conquistador award City of El Paso, 1980; named Disting. Alumnus U. Nebr., Omaha, 1985; named to Hon. Order of St. Barbara U.S. Field Arty. Assn., 1988; cited for svcs. to mankind El Paso chpt. Sertoma, 1985. Mem. Fed. Mgrs. Assn. (bd. dirs.), Freedom Found. at Valley Forge (pres. El Paso chpt., George Washington Hon. medal 1982), El Paso C. of C. (assoc. dir. 1984—, bd. dirs.), Toastmasters (dist. gov. 1970-71), Masons, Tau Kappa Epsilon (Hall of Fame 1986). Avocations: numismatics, genealogy, books, weaponry.

STARKWEATHER, TERESA MADERY, artist, educator; b. L.A., June 12, 1950; d. Earl and Maureen Madery; m. Lee A. Starkweather, May 29, 1977; children: Ashley, Chelsea. Student, Art Ctr. Coll. Design, L.A., 1970-72; BFA, Atlanta Coll. Art, 1973; credential, Calif. State U., Northridge, 1994-96. artist Chaleur, Torrance, Calif., 1991, Prestige Graphics, L.A., 1993-95; artist, designer Zarah Co., Topanga, Calif., 1991-95. Artistic dir. Echoes Cards, Topanga, Calif., 1991-94. Contbg. artist Am. Artist Mag., spring 1991, The Best of Watercolor, 1995, Splash 4 The Splendor of Light, 1996, Splash 5, 1997, Painting the Many Moods of Light, 1999, Keys to Painting Textures and Surfaces, 2000, Keys to Painting Fruit and Flowers, 2000; exhibited Lankershim Arts Ctr., Calif., 1990, L.A. City Hall, 1990, Orlando Gallery, Sherman Oaks, Calif., 1991, Watercolor West Nat. Exhbn., Calif., 1991, 95, 97, Century Gallery, L.A., 1992, L.A. Mcpl. Art Gallery, 1993, Artspace Gallery, L.A., 1993, Springfield Art Mus., Mo., 1994, Foothills Art Ctr., Colo., 1994, Orlando Gallery, Sherman Oaks, 1996, Nan Miller Gallery, Rochester, N.Y., 1998. Recipient Bronze medal Art Calif. Mag. Discovery Awards, 1992, 93, 1st pl. award Valley Watercolor Assn., Artspace Gallery, L.A., 1993, 98, Patron Purchase award Watercolor U.S.A., Springfield, Mo., 1994, 2d pl. award Nat. Watercolor Soc. Show, 1997, Best of Show award Valley Watercolor Soc. Show, 1998; finalist The Artist's Mag. Awards, 1996, 97; named Signature Mem., Watercolor West, 1997. Avocations: horseback riding, tennis.

STARLING, LARRY EUGENE, auditor; b. Nashville, Aug. 15, 1954; s. Thomas Edward and Montoria (Dickson) S.; m. Deborah Denise Askins, Sept. 8, 1984; children: Ryan Thomas, Sean Michael. BS, Tenn. State U., 1979. Tax auditor III State Tenn., Nashville, 1979-83; tax analyst No. Telecom Inc., 1983-90; state tax specialist Burlington Industries, Inc., Greensboro, N.C., 1990—. Office: Burlington Industries Inc 3330 W Friendly Ave Greensboro NC 27410-4800

STARLING, VIRGINIA R. music educator, consultant; b. Loraine, TX, Apr. 26, 1929; d. Lawrence Livingston and Ruth Cleo (Martin) Trott; widowed; children: Catherine, Caroline, Randall. B of Music Edn., Mary Hardin Baylor U., 1950; MusM, 1976; MS in Psychology, Coll. of Southwest, 1989. Choir dir. Methodist Ch., Belton, TX, 1949-50; music instr. Monahans (Tex.) Pub. Schs., 1950-52, Lovington (N.Mex.) Pub. Schs., 1952-54, N.M. Jr. Coll., Hobbs, 1976-79; pvt. sch. music tchr. N.M., 1987-93; ch. organist, pvt. tchr. Lovington, Hobbs, 1952-99; ch. organist, cons. Cloudcroft, 1999—. Soloist: (CD) Enduring Devotion; composer piano solos for children, Just For You, 2000; concert performances in Hobbs, N. Mex., Carnegie Hall. Bd. dirs. Southwest Symphony. Mem. Music Tchrs. Nat. Assn., Profl. Music Tchrs. of N.Mex. (bd. dirs.), Lee County Music Forum, Sigma Alpha Iota. Baptist. Avocations: gardening, travel, history, music. Home: PO Box 1003 Cloudcroft NM 88317-1003 E-mail: skyhigh@zianet.com.

STARN, BARBARAJEAN, healthcare administrator; b. Elyria, Ohio, June 1, 1948; d. Andrew and Eugenia Tomoko; m. Richard W. Starn, Feb. 13, 1971; children: Heather, DeAnna, Jennifer. Student, M.B. Johnson Sch. Nursing, 1969, Baldwin Wallace Coll., 1970. RN, Ohio, Mo., Pa. Staff nurse Elyria Meml. Hosp.; supr. Medi Ctr. of Am., Springfield, Mo.; asst. dir. nursing Manor Care Nursing Ctr., Olmsted, Ohio; nurse coord. Parkside Health Mgmt. Corp., Middleburg Heights, client svc. rep.; asst. dir. nursing The Oakridge Home, Westlake, Ohio; DON, Oakridge Home, Edinboro (Pa.) Manor, 1996-99, regional dir. quality assurance Healthcare Facilities (HCF), Inc., 1999—. Zaharas scholar. Home: 10783 Konneyaut Trail Ext Conneaut Lake PA 16316-3333

STARNER, BARBARA KAZMARK, marketing, advertising and export sales executive; b. Detroit, Sept. 2, 1940; d. Eugene Anthony and Lucille Ann Kazmark; m. G. Frederick Starner, June 30, 1962; 1 child, Natasha Lucienne. BA with honors, U. Mich., 1962; BS, Ohio State U., 1965. Tchr. art Columbus (Ohio) Pub. Schs., 1965-68, Mt. Olive Pub. Schs., Budd Lake, N.J., 1968-71; stained glass designer Barbara Designs, LaCrosse, Wis., 1975-87; from trade show mgr. to v.p. advt., mktg., export sales Kart-A-Bag divsn. Remin, Joliet, Ill., 1978—. Advt. and mktg. cons. Starner Mktg., L.A., 1987-95; ptnr. PreciousGem, L.A., 1999—. Mem., pres. East Bank Artists, LaCrosse, 1979-86; co-founder, dir. crafts Great River Traditional Music & Crafts Festival, LaCrosse, 1975-87; chmn. Spiritual Frontiers Fellowship, Mpls., 1979-85, 85-87; co-chmn. Spiritual Sci. Fellowship, 1985-87; fund raiser, mem./cook 1st crew Sloop Clearwater Restoration, Maine-N.Y., 1969 (Hudson River pollution clean-up). Democrat. Mem. Universalist Ch. Avocations: landscape and portrait painting. Office: Kart-A-Bag 510 Manhattan Rd Joliet IL 60433-3099

STARNER, DON EDWARD, radiologist, educator; b. Zanesville, Ohio, June 28, 1959; s. Larry and Sara Ann Starner; m. Carla Marcote, Aug. 31, 1991; children: Ryan. BS, The Ohio State U., 1982. Cert. Radiographer Am. Registry of Radiologic Technologists, 1982, Quality Mgmt. Radiographer Am. Registry of Radiologic Technologists, 2002, lic. Radiologic Technologist Fla. Dept. Health, 1988. X-ray technologist The Ohio State U. Hospitals, Columbus, Ohio, 1982—88; from clin. instr. to program dir. West Boca Med. Ctr. Sch. of Radiography, Boca Raton, Fla., 1988—91, program dir., 1991—96; dir. of clin. radiography edn. Indian River CC, Ft. Pierce, 1996—. Contbr. chapters to books; actor: (films) Brubaker, 1980. Mem.: AAUP, Fla. Assn. of C.C., Am. Soc. of Radiologic Technologists, Am. Registry of Radiologic Technologists. Home: 6717 NW Dorothy St Port Saint Lucie FL 34983 Office: Indian River Community College 3209 Virginia Ave Fort Pierce FL 34981

STARNES, EARL MAXWELL, urban and regional planner, architect; b. Winter Haven, Fla., Sept. 14, 1926; s. Thomas Lowe and Kathryn Maxwell (Gates) S.; m. Dorothy Jean Prather, Aug. 21, 1949; children: Tom, Will, Janet, Patricia. Student, Fla. So. Coll., 1946-48; BArch cum laude, U. Fla., 1951; MS in Urban and Regional Planning, Fla. State U., 1973, PhD, 1977. Registered architect, Fla. Assoc. Courtney Stewart (Architect), Ft. Lauderdale, Fla., 1951-52, William Bigoney, Architect, Ft. Lauderdale, 1952-53, William T. Vaughn, Architect, Ft. Lauderdale, 1953, Alfred B. Parker, Architect, Miami, Fla., 1953-55, Rufus Nims, Architect, Miami, 1955-57; ptnr. Starnes & Rentscher, Architects, 1957-63, Starnes, Rentscher & Assocs., Architects, Miami, 1963-71; dir. div. mass transp. Fla. Dept. Transp., Tallahassee, 1971-72; dir. div. state planning Fla. Dept. Adminstrn., 1972-75; engaged in research and cons. service Tallahassee, 1975; prof., chmn. urban and regional planning Coll. Architecture U. Fla., Gainesville, 1976-88, prof. urban and regional plan coord., doctoral studies, 1989-93, prof. emeritus, 1993—. Instr. architecture U. Miami, 1953; adj. asst. prof. dept. urban and regional planning Coll. Social Scis., Fla. State U., 1971-74; mem. adv. panel B8-15, Nat. Coop. Hwy. Research Program, Transp. Research Bd., NRC-Nat. Acad. Scis., 1974—; mem. adv. bd. Pub. Tech., Inc., 1974—; mem. North Central Fla. Regional Planning Com., 1980-85, Fla. Substate Dist. Com., 1985-87; co-chmn. Joint Liaison Com. on Div. Responsibility for Urban Services, Dade County, Fla., 1965-71; chmn. joint policy com. U. Miami-Dade County Jackson Med. Center, 1966-71; chmn. Cape Fla. State Park Adv. Council, 1966-69, Dade County Landscape Ordinance Study Com., 1967-70, South Fla. Everglades Area Planning Council, 1969-71; vis. lectr. Calif. Poly. State U., San Luis Obispo, 1988-89; cons. Urban Planning Fla. and Caribbean. Prin. works include 1st Unitarian Ch., Miami; contbr. article on archtl. planning relationship Ency. Architecture Planning, 1987, chpt. to Growth Management, 1992, chpt. and preface (with Ivonne Audivac) to Rural Sustainability in America, 1996; contbr. chpts. to books, articles on land use and urban devel. policies, wetland protection, state planning, greenways and rural sustainability to profl. jours. Active South Dade Mental Health Soc., 1967-68, Cape Fla. Acquisition Com., 1966, Dade County Downtown Govtl. Center Com., 1967-71, Miami Downtown Devel. Authority, 1970, Gov.'s Task Force on Resource Mgmt., 1971-72, Nat. Task Force on Natural Resources and Land Use Info. and Tech., 1973-74, Fla. Gov.'s Commn. on Property Rights, 1993-94; county commr. Dist. 7, Dade County, 1964-71; vice mayor, 1964, 68; mem. adv. com. Legis. Council Subcom. on Constrn. Industry Study, 1966-68; bd. dirs., chmn. retirement and compensation com. State Assn. County Commrs., 1968-71; mem. Alachua County Budget Study Com., 1978, Fla. Land Use Adv. Com. for Phosphate Lands, 1978-80, Suwanee River Water Mgmt. Bd., 1982-87, 91-98, chmn. 1987-88; chmn. Fla. Inst. Phosphate Research, 1984-87; bd. dirs. 1000 Friends of Fla, 1986—; active Fla. Greenway's Commn., 1991-93, Fla. Greenway Coordinating Coun., 1998-99; gov.'s adv. commn. on coastal mgmt., 1997. With USCG, 1944-46. Fellow: AIA (urban design com. 1976—80), Am. Inst. Cert. Planners; mem.: Assn. Collegiate Schs. of Planning (bd. dirs. 1986—88), Nat. Inst. Bldg. Scis. (steering com. for rsch. 1979—80), Gargoyle Soc., Phi Kappa Phi. Democrat. Unitarian Universalist. Office: PO Box 234 Cedar Key FL 32625-0234

STARNES, EDWARD CLINTON, public relations executive; b. Marquette, Mich., Jan. 19, 1950; s. Edward Erwin and Florence Irene (Lemieux) S.; m. Claire Marie Brisebois, Apr. 12, 1973; children: Sean, Bryan. Student, Western Ill. U., 1968-69. Journalist, editor U.S. Army, Ft. Monroe, Va., 1969-72; spl. projects officer U.S. Continental Army Command, 1972-73; pub. affairs intern U.S. Tng. and Doctrine Command, 1973-75; dep. pub. affairs officer Air Defense Artillery Ctr. U.S. Army, Ft. Bliss, Tex., 1975-87; also pub. affairs officer to Gen. of the Army Omar N. Bradley, 1975-81; chief corp. affairs U.S. Army Ordnance Ctr. and Sch., Aberdeen Proving Ground, Md., 1987—; pub. affairs officer U.S. Army Sexual Harassment Hotline, 1996. Sec. pub. affairs coun. Fed. Exec. Bd., Balt., 1988-93; pub. affairs cons. U.S. Interagy. Task Force for Indo-China Refugees, Ft. Indiantown Gap, Pa., 1975. Contbr. articles to profl. publs. Exec. bd. El Paso County (Tex.) Hist. Soc., 1985-86; bd. dirs. Reach for a Star, El Paso, 1983-86; asst. varsity soccer coach Perryville High Sch., 1990-96, head coach, 1997-98; active EMT-B, Water Witch Vol. Fire Co. Named Visitante Distinguido Presidente Municipal, Cuidad Juarez, Mexico, 1985, 87, Harford County Schs. Bus. Vol. of the Yr., 1990; recipient Cert. Appreciation Juvenile Ct. City of El Paso, 1985. Mem. Assn. U.S. Army, Noncommd. Officer Assn., Air Def. Arty. Assn. (life), Royal Neighbors Am., Nat. Assn. EMTs, Nat. Soccer Hall of Fame. Episcopalian. Avocations: writing, art. Home: PO Box 9 Conowingo MD 21918-0009 Office: US Army Ordnance Corps Corp Affairs Office Aberdeen Proving Ground MD 21005-5201 E-mail: starnese@rcn.com, edward.starnes@ocs.apg.army.mil.

STARNES, JAMES WRIGHT, lawyer; b. East St. Louis, Ill., Apr. 3, 1933; s. James Adron and Nell (Short) S.; m. Helen Woods Mitchell, Mar. 29, 1958 (div. 1978); children: James Wright, Mitchell A., William B. II; m. Kathleen Israel, Jan. 26, 1985. Student, St. Louis U., 1951-53; LLB, Washington U., St. Louis, 1957. Bar: Mo. 1957, Ill. 1957, Fla. 1992. Assoc. Stinson, Mag & Fizzell, Kansas City, Mo., 1957-60, ptnr., 1960-90, Mid-Continent Properties Co., 1959-90, Fairview Investment Co., Kansas City, 1971-76, Monticello Land Co., 1973-99; of counsel Yates, Mauck, Bohrer, Elliff, Croessmann & Wieland, P.C., Springfield, Mo., from 1995. Sec. Packaging Products Corp., Mission, Kans., 1972-89; chmn., treas. Galerie of Naples (Fla.), Inc., 1990-92. Adv. bd. Washington U. Law Quar., 1957-90. Bd. dirs. Mo. Assn. Mental Health, 1968-69, Kansas City Assn. Mental Health, 1966-78, pres., 1969-70; bd. dirs. Heed, 1965-73, 78-82, pres., 1966-67, fin. chmn., 1967-68; bd. dirs. Kansas City Halfway House Found., exec. com., 1966-69, pres., 1966; bd. dirs. Joan Davis Sch. for Spl. Edn., 1972-88, v.p., 1972-73, 79-80, pres., 1980-82; bd. dirs. Sherwood Ctr. for Exceptional Child, 1977-79, v.p., 1978-79. With AUS, 1957. Mem. ABA, Mo. Bar, Fla. Bar, Springfield Bar Assn., Kansas City Bar Assn., Washington U. Law Alumni Assn. (bd. govs. 1990-92). Presbyterian (deacon). Home: Springfield, Mo. Deceased.

STARNES, JANE SMITH, women's health nurse; b. Albermarle, N.C., June 18, 1947; d. James Cornelius and Lois (Spoon) Smith; m. John Henderson Starnes Jr., Aug. 1, 1976; stepchildren: John Richard, Roy Henderson. Diploma, Presbyn. Hosp. Sch. Nursing, Charlotte, N.C., 1968. Staff nurse gynecology Presbyn. Hosp., Charlotte, 1968-69; clin. instr. Montgomery Tech. Inst., Troy, N.C., 1969-70; asst. DON, Biscoe (N.C.) Nursing Home, 1970; clin. nurse labor and delivery Presbyn. Hosp., Charlotte, 1970—, recruiter blood drive, 1980, quality assurance and quality improvement nurse, 1990-99, mem. quality demonstration team, 1995, also advisor for interns. Leader, cons. Girl Scouts Am., Charlotte, 1989-92. Recipient nursing Excellence award Presbyn. Healthcare, 1999. Mem.: Am. Assn. Women's Health Obs. and Neonatal Nurses, Presbyn. Hosp. Sch. Nursing Alumni (Home Base chpt. treas. 1994—95, v.p. 1995—96, pres. 1997—99, interim v.p. 2000, advisor Home Base chpt., co-chmn. PHSON 2001—02). Avocations: gardening, knitting, crocheting, crafts, antiques.

STARNES, SUSAN SMITH, elementary education educator; b. Grinnell, Iowa, Oct. 8, 1942; d. Edwin Fay Smith Jr. and Miriam Jane (Spaulding) Smith Simms; m. Wayman J. Starnes, Apr. 25, 1964; children: Michele Ann Starnes Hoffman, Mary Shannon Starnes Zornes. BS in Edn. summa cum laude, Mo. Bapt. Coll., 1991. Cert. early childhood tchr., elem. tchr. 1-8. Adminstr. Presbyn. Ch. in Am. Hist. Ctr., St. Louis, 1985-90; tchr. 3rd grade Ctrl. Christian Sch., 1991-98; subst. tchr. Ctrl. Christian Sch., Kirk Day Sch., Twin Oaks Christian Sch., 1998—. Mem. chapel com. Ctrl. Christian Sch., St. Louis, 1991-98. Children's dir. Canaan Bapt. Ch., St. Louis, 1991—96, Bible study fellowship children's leader, 1986—89, mission trip vol., 1992, 1993, 1999, 2000, 2001, 2002; camp counselor Youth for Christ, Kansas City, 1992, 1993, Awana leader, 1996—. Mem. Kappa Delta Pi. Avocations: biking, swimming, scuba diving.

STARNES, WILLIAM HERBERT, JR. chemist, educator; b. Knoxville, Tenn., Dec. 2, 1934; s. William Herbert and Edna Margaret (Osborne) Starnes; m. Maria Sofia Molina, Mar. 4, 1986. BS with honors, Va. Poly. Inst., 1955; PhD, Ga. Inst. Tech., 1960. Rsch. chemist Esso Rsch. & Engring. Co., Baytown, Tex., 1960-62, sr. rsch. chemist, 1962-64, polymer additives sect. head, 1964-65, rsch. specialist, 1965-67, rsch. assoc., 1967-71; instr. and rsch. assoc. dept. chemistry U. Tex., Austin, 1971-73; mem. tech. staff AT&T Bell Labs., Murray Hill, NJ, 1973-85; prof. chemistry Poly. U., Bklyn., 1985-89, head dept. chemistry and life scis., 1985-88, assoc. dir. polymer durability ctr., 1987-89; Floyd Dewey Gottwald Sr. prof. chemistry Coll. William and Mary, Williamsburg, Va., 1989—, prof. applied sci., 1990—. Invited lectr. several fgn. countries and U.S.; ofcl. guest USSR Acad. Scis., 1990, Russian Acad. Scis., 1992; disting. vis. prof. Beijing Inst. Tech., 1996; vis. scientist Tex. Acad. Scis., 1964—67; mem. bd. doctoral thesis examiners Indian Inst. Tech., New Delhi, 1988, McGill U., Montreal, 1989, MacQuarie U., Sydney, Australia, 1991, McMaster U., Hamilton, Canada, 1994; panelist, reviewer NSF Acad. Rsch. Facilities Modernization Program, 1990; channel program mentor U. Cairo, 1994—95; mem. opinion leader panel Wall St. Jour., 1995—; charter mem. dept. chemistry adv. coun. Va. Poly. Inst. and State U., 1998—; sci. advisor European Multinational Environ. Rsch. Project on PVC in Soil and Landfills, 1995—99; cons. numerous indsl. cos., govtl. and pvt. agys.; course dir. continuing edn. Editor-in-chief: Jour. Vinyl and Additive Tech., 1998—, mem. adv. bd., bd. reviewers: Jour. Vinyl Tech., 1981—83, mem. adv. bd., bd. reviewers: Jour. Chem. and Biochem. Kinetics, 1992—, mem. editl. bd.: Polymer Degradation and Stability, 1997—; contbr. articles to profl. jours.; mem. editl. bd.: Internat. Jour. Coatings Sci. , 2001—; contbr. chapters to books. Named honoree Plastics History and Artifacts Program, Plastics Pioneers Assn., 2001; recipient Profl. Progress award, Soc. Profl. Chemists and Engrs., 1968, Disting. Tech. Staff award, AT&T Bell Labs., 1982, Polymer Sci. Pioneer award, Polymer News, 1988, Honor Scroll award, N.J. Inst. Chemists, 1989; fellow NSF, 1958—60; grantee, NSF, 1989—, Nat. Bur. Stds. Ctr. Fire Rsch., Internat. Copper Rsch. Assn., Va. Ctr. Innovative Tech., GenCorp Found., several indsl. cos. Fellow: AAAS (Project 2061 1985—86, chmn. chemistry subpanel 1985—86, mem. panel on phys. scis. and engring. 1985—86), Soc. Plastics Engrs. (nat. publs. com. 1998—2001, thesis advisor nat. award Vinyl Plastics divsn. 1996, 1998), N.Y. Acad. Scis., Am. inst. Chemists (life); mem.: Va. Acad. Sci., Soc. Plastics Engrs., Am. Chem. Soc. (bd. dirs. southeastern Tex. sect. 1970, spkrs. bur. divsn. polymer chemistry 1976—, mem.-at-large exec. com. Va. sect. 1995), Phi Lambda Upsilon (pres. Va. Poly. Inst. chpt. 1954—55), Sigma Xi (M. A. Ferst award Ga. Inst. Tech. chpt. 1960), Phi Kappa Phi (life). Achievements include patents in field; research in on degradation, stabilization, flammability, microstructures and polymerization mechanisms of synthetic polymers, especially poly(vinyl chloride); free radical chemistry; carbon-13 nuclear magnetic resonance and organic synthesis; subspecialities include organic chemistry, polymer chemistry. Office: Coll William and Mary Dept Chemistry PO Box 8795 Williamsburg VA 23187-8795 E-mail: whstar@wm.edu.

STARNES-VINCENT, CAROLYN ANN, music educator; b. Chattanooga, July 8, 1956; BS, George Peabody Coll. for Tchrs., Nashville, 1977; MS, Peabody Coll. of Vanderbilt U., 1980. Cert. music edn., PreK-12 Ga., Tenn. Piano instr. Cadek Conservatory of Music, U. Tenn., Chattanooga, 1983—85, Swinnett Sch. of Music, Stone Mountain, Ga., 1985—88, Clayton State Coll., Morrow, 1988—89; elem. gen. music specialist Swint Elem./Clayton County, Jonesboro, 1988—94, Sumner County Schs., Hendersonville, Tenn., 1994—95, Austin Rd. Elem./Henry County, Stockbridge, Ga., 1995—. Adj. music instr. Gordon Coll., Barnesville, Ga., 2000—; interviewer Ga. Dept. Edn./Gov.'s Honor Program, Atlanta, 1986—90; rep. State of Tenn. PBS Broadcast, 1996; participant World's Largest Concert Music Educators Nat. Conf., 1995. Co-author: (workbook) The Big Theory Book for Little Fingers, 1989. Mem.: Music Educators Nat. Conf. Office: Austin Rd Elem 50 Austin Rd Stockbridge GA 30281

STAROSOLSZKY, ÖDÖN, civil engineer; b. Veszprèm, Hungary, Dec. 26, 1931; s. Sándor and Irma (Benkö) S.; m. Erzsébet Zilahi-Kiss, Apr. 1, 1961. Dipl.Ing., T.U., Budapest, 1954, DEng, 1968; DSc, Hungarian Acad. Sci., 1995. Engring. diplomate. Rsch. engr. Rsch. Inst. Water Rsch., Budapest, 1954-60, head sect., dept., 1960-71; head dept. Nat. Water Authority, 1971-76; dir. Inst. of Hydraulics, 1976-89; dep. gen. dir. Water Res. Rsch. Ctr., 1989-91, gen. dir., 1991-98; expert on hydrological measurements, network devel. UN-UNDP, India, Sri Lanka, Nigeria, Egypt, 1980-86. Chmn. com. on water scis. Hungarian Acad. Scis., Budapest, 1990-97; pres. Commn. for Hydrology, WMO, Geneva, 1984-92. Author: Civil Engineering Hydraulics, 1971; co-author/editor: Hydraulic Engineering, 1973, Applied Surface Hydrology, 1987; co-editor: Hydrology of Disasterw, 1989. Recipient Széchenyi prize, 2000. Mem. Hungarian Hydrol. Soc. (chmn. com. internat. affairs 1990-96, pres., 1996—, Vásárhelyi prize 1986, 92), Internat. Assn. Hydraulic Rsch. (v.p. 1988-91), Hungarian Soc. Environment. Roman Catholic. Achievements include rsch. results in the field of hydrology, hydraulics, hydraulic engineering and water management. Office: Water Resources Rsch Ctr Kvassay Jenöut 1 Box 27 H-1453 Budapest Hungary E-mail: starosolszky@vituki.hu.

STARR, CHARLES CHRISTOPHER, foundation executive, priest; b. Atlanta, Jan. 15, 1952; s. David Homer and Margaret Mary (Bussey) S.; m. C. Kathy Wright, Dec. 15, 1984; 1 child, Anna Katherine. BA in Philosophy, St. Mary's Coll., 1975; MDiv, St. Vincent de Paul, 1980. Ordained to ministry Roman Cath. Ch., 1980; received into ministry Episcopal Ch., 1993. Assoc. pastor Sacred Heart Ch., Atlanta, 1980-82, Immaculate Heart of Mary, Atlanta, 1983, Cathedral Christ the King, Atlanta, 1983-84; vice chancellor Archdiocese of Atlanta, 1982-84; v.p. Lehfeldt and Assocs., 1985-89; dir. devel. Winship Cancer Ctr., 1989-91; exec. dir. Henry W. Grady Found., 1992-95; assoc. rector Ch. of Atonement, Atlanta, 1993—; exec. dir. Nat. Kidney Found. of Ga., 1995—. Pres. Transition House, Atlanta, 1988-92. Mem. Nat. Soc. Fund Raising Execs. (cert., bd. dirs. Ga. chpt. 1992—). Home: 1726 Coventry Pl Decatur GA 30030-1005 Office: Nat Kidney Found of Ga 2951 Flowers Rd S Ste 211 Atlanta GA 30341-5533

STARR, CHAUNCEY, research institute executive; b. Newark, Apr. 14, 1912; s. Rubin and Rose (Dropkin) Starr; m. Doris Evelyn Debel, Mar. 20, 1938; children: Ross M., Ariel E. EE, Rensselaer Poly. Inst., 1932, PhD, 1935, DEng (hon.) , 1964, Swiss ETH, 1980; DSci (hon.) , Tulane U., 1986. Rsch. fellow physics Harvard U., 1935—37; rsch. assoc. Mass. Inst. Tech., 1938—41; rsch. physicist D.W. Taylor Model Basin, Bur. Ships, 1941—42; staff radiation lab. U. Calif., 1942—43, Tenn. Eastman Corp., Oak Ridge, 1943—46, Tenn. Eastman Corp. (Clinton Labs.), 1946; chief spl. rsch. N. Am. Aviation, Inc., Downey, Calif., 1946—49, dir. atomic energy rsch. dept., 1949—55, v.p., 1955—66; gen. mgr. N. Am. Aviation, Inc. (Atomics Internat. divsn.), 1955—60; pres. divsn. N. Am. Aviation, Inc. (Atomics Internat. div.), 1960—66; dean engring. U. Calif. at LA, 1966—73; cons. prof. Stanford U., 1974—; pres. Electric Power Rsch. Inst., 1973—78, vice chmn., 1978—87, pres. emeritus, 1987—. Dir. Atomic Indsl. Forum. Contbr. sci. articles to profl. jours. Decorated Legion of Honor France; recipient Henry D. Smyth award, Atomic Indsl. Forum, 1983, Nat. medal of Tech., 1990. Fellow: AAAS (dir.), Am. Phys. Soc. (Pake prize), Am. Nuc. Soc. (past pres.); mem.: AIAA (sr.), Royal Swedish Acad. for Engring. Scis., Nat. Acad. Engring., Am. Power Conf., Sigma Xi, Eta Kappa Nu. Home: 95 Stern Ln Atherton CA 94027-5422 E-mail: cstarr@epri.com.

STARR, DAVID, newspaper editor, publisher; b. N.Y.C., Aug. 1, 1922; s. Aaron and Helen (Simon) S.; m. Marjorie Giffen, Aug. 3, 1943; children: Pamela, Peter. BA, Queens Coll., 1942. Reporter, rewriteman L.I. Daily Press, 1942-50; exec. editor Nassau Daily Rev. Star, 1950-53; asst. editor Newark Star-Ledger, 1954-56; asso. editor L.I. Press, 1953-54, 56-62, mng. editor, 1962-69, editor, 1969-77; sr. editor Newhouse Newspapers, 1971—; pub. Springfield Union-News, Sunday Republican, 1977-99, pres., 1999—. Pres. Springfield Ctrl., Inc., 1978-88, chmn., 1989-95. Trustee Nassau C.C., SUNY, 1959-66; bd. dirs. Springfield Libr. and Mus. Assn., chmn., 1988-90; mem. Mass. Cultural Coun., 1980—; bd. dirs. Am. Arts Alliance, 1988-92, chmn., 1989-92. Mem. Am. Soc. Newspaper Editors, Am. Newspaper Pubs. Assn. E-mail: dstarr@union-news.com.

STARR, HAROLD PAGE, lawyer; b. Phila., June 17, 1932; s. Isaac and Edith Nelson (Page) S.; m. Emily W. Churchman, Sept. 3, 1960; children: Elizabeth Twells, Edith Nelson, Harold Page Jr., Alice Churchman, Isaac Barclay. BS, Yale U., 1954; LLB, Harvard U., 1961. Bar: Pa. 1962. Assoc. Pepper, Hamilton & Scheetz, Phila., 1961-69, ptnr., 1970-81; pvt. practice, 1982—. Lt. (j.g.) USNR, 1955-58. Office: 8411 Stenton Ave Wyndmoor PA 19038-8445 E-mail: hpstarr@bellatlantic.net.

STARR, HARVEY, political scientist, educator; b. N.Y.C., Nov. 11, 1946; s. Nathan and Betty (Brand) S.; m. Madonna Kissel, June 1, 1969 (div. Dec. 1979); m. Dianne C. Luce, July 2, 1994. BA, SUNY, Buffalo, 1967; M of Philosophy, Yale U., 1970, PhD, 1971. Acting instr. Dept. Polit. Sci., Yale U., New Haven, 1970-71; visiting fellow in politics Dept. Politics, U. Aberdeen, Scotland, 1971-72, 78-79; asst. prof. Dept. Polit. Sci., Ind. U., Bloomington, 1972-77, assoc. prof., 1977-83, prof., 1983-89; prof. in internat. affairs Dept. Govt. & Internat. Studies, U. S.C., Columbia, 1989—, chair dept., 1998—. Editl. bd. Am. Polit. Sci. Rev., 1985-89, 91-95, Internat. Studies Quar., 1985-90, Jour. of Politics, 1988-97, Comparative Polit. Studies, 1979-92, Internat. Interactions, 1985-91, editor, 1991-2000; assoc. editor Teaching Polit. Sci., 1978-81, Jour. Politics, 2000—. Author: Henry Kissinger: Perceptions of International Politics, 1984, Anarchy, Order, and Integration, 1997; co-author: Inquiry, Logic and International Politics, 1989, World Politics: Menu for Choice, 1981, 85, 89, 92, 96, The Diffusion of War: A Study of Opportunity and Willingness, 1991, Agency, Structure and International Politics, 1997; contbr. articles to profl. jours. Grantee NSF, 1982-84, 98—. Mem. Peace Sci. Soc. (pres. 2000-2001), Peace Sci. Soc. Midwest (pres. 1978-80), Ind. Consortium for Security Studies (dep. dir. 1980-89), Data Devel. in Internat. Rsch. (exec. coun. 1986-87, 89-92), Conflict Processes Sect., Am. Polit. Sci. Assn. (exec. coun. 1989-91, pres. 1992-95, v.p. 1995-96), So. Polit. Sci. Assn. (exec. coun. 1991-94). Office: U SC Dept Govt Internat Studies Columbia SC 29208-0001 E-mail: starr-harvey@sc.edu.

STARR, ILA MAE, educator; b. La Grande, Oreg., Dec. 27, 1917; d. Samuel Fulmer Andrew and Ida Luella Perry; m. James Marion Starr, Mar. 2, 1940; children: Jacqueline Ann Starr Brandon, James Steven Starr. BA, U. Wash., 1939; BS, Eastern Oreg. Coll., LaGrande, Oreg., 1960, Tchr. Cert. Oreg., 1940. Cert. Wash. 1962, Calif. 1974. Mus. tchr. La Grande (Oreg.) Pub. Schs., 1939-40; girl scout exec. Girl Scouts of Am., Grand Coulee, Wash., 1940-41; Elem. Sch. Tchr. Centralia (Wash.) Pub. Schs., 1954; elem. sch. tchr. Wenatchee (Wash.) Pub. Schs., 1956-64, Lancaster (Calif.) Pub. Schs., 1964-68, Marysville (Calif.) Pub. Schs., 1968-79. Pvt. mus. tchr., Seattle, Grand Coulee and Wenatchee, Wash., 1940—. Bd. dirs. Community Concert Assn., Yuba City, Calif., 1986-88; inspiration chmn. Republican Women, Yuba City, 1986-88. Recipient Hon. Pub. Sch. Award, Masonic Lodge 437, Lancaster, 1966; Nominee for Tchr. of Yr., Marysville Pub. Schs., 1978. Mem. Am. Assn. U. Women (program v.p. 1976; Grant Honoree 1977), PTA (hon. life mem. 1965), The Seminar Club (program chmn.), Innerwheel Club (pres. 1985-86). Mem. Lds Ch. Avocations: mus. vocal soloist, choir dir.

STARR, ISIDORE, law educator; b. Bklyn., Nov. 24, 1911; BA, CCNY, 1932; LLB, St. John's U., Jamaica, N.Y., 1936; MA, Columbia U., 1939; JSD, Bklyn. Law Sch., 1942; PhD, New Sch. Social Rsch., 1957. Bar: N.Y. 1937. Tchr. various high schs., N.Y.C., 1934-61; from assoc. prof. to prof. edn. Queen's Coll., 1961-75, prof. emeritus, 1975—. Dir. Inst. on Law-Related Edn., Lincoln-Filene Ctr., Tufts U., 1963; dir. Law Studies Inst., N.Y.C., 1974; adv. on Our Living Bill of Rights Film Series (6 films) Ency. Brit. Ednl. Corp.; mem. Ariz. Ctr. for Law-Related Edn.; mem. coun. on pub. legal edn. State of Wash., 2001—; cons. in field. Author: The Lost Generation of Prince Edward COunty, 1968, The Gideon Case, 1968, The Feiner Case, 1968, The Mapp Case, 1968, The Supreme Court and Contemporary Issues, 1968, Human Rights in the United States, 1969, The American Judicial System, 1972, The Idea of Liberty, 1978, Justice: Due Process of Law, 1981; co-editor Living American Documents, 1971. Bd. dirs. Phi Alpha Delta Juvenile Justice Program, 1981—. 1st lt. U.S. Army, 1943-46. John Hay fellow, 1952-53; recipient Outstanding Citizen award Philip Morris Co., 1992. Mem. ABA (hon. chair adv. commn. on Youth Edn. for Citizenship, Isidore Starr award for Spl. Achievment in Law Studies, Leon Jaworski award 1989), Am. Judicature Soc., Am. Soc. Legal History, Am. Legal Studies Assn., Nat. Coun. Social Studies (past pres.), Washington Coun. Pub. Legal Edn., Phi Beta Kappa, Phi Alpha Delta (cert. of appreciation 1981). Address: 12501 Greenwood Ave N Apt C110 Seattle WA 98133-8000

STARR, JAMES EDWARD, logistics management executive; b. Iowa City, June 12, 1944; s. Donald Edward and Lucille (Waggoner) S. BBA, U. Iowa, 1967; M in Sys. Mgmt., Colo. Tech. U., 1996. Supr. bus. ops. various orgns., Chgo., 1973-82; logistics prog. analyst 442 Fighter Wing, Richards-Gebaur AFB, Mo., 1983-87; dir. plans, logistics prog. analyst 302 Airlift Wing, Peterson AFB, Colo., 1987-98; logistics mgmt. specialist HQ USAF Pentagon Strategic Logistics Plans Divsn., Washington, 1998—. Capt. USAF, 1967-73, lt. col. res., 1975-98. Named Resource Officer of Yr. USAF Res., Robins AFB, Ga., 1985, Unit of Yr., 1989. Mem. Air Force Assn., Res. Officers Assn. U.S. (pres. Colo. State 1990-91, nat. officer 1981-82, various state offices 1978—, chmn. nat. AF com. 1992-93, Air Force nat. exec. committeeman 1993-95, nat. v.p. Air Force 1999-2000), U. Iowa Alumni Assn., Colorado Springs Club (chmn. 1988-96), Alpha Kappa Psi, others. Lutheran. Avocations: golf, internat. affairs, reading. Home: 307 Yoakum Pkwy Apt 803 Alexandria VA 22304-4020 E-mail: james.starr@pentagon.af.mil.

STARR, JOYCE IVES, special education educator; b. Guilford, N.Y., Jan. 25, 1932; d. Paris Otto and Alta Lena (Wade) Ives; m. Leonard E. Cornell, July 7, 1956 (dec. Mar. 1973); children: Stephen, Lorrinda, Teresa, David; m. Donald Fay Starr, May 8, 1976 (dec. Apr. 1982); stepchildren: Donald Fay II, Matthew, Mark, Thor (dec. May 1986). Student, Rochester (N.Y.) Inst. of Tech., 1949-51; BS. in Edn., SUNY, New Paltz, 1955; student, Syracuse U., summers 1967-68. Art tchr. Oxford (N.Y.) Acad. and Cen. Sch., 1954-57; spl. edn. tchr. junior high sch. Liberty (N.Y.) Cen. Sch., 1966-67, spl. edn. tchr. primary grades, 1967-71; spl. edn. tchr. Del. Acad. and Cen. Sch., Delhi, N.Y., 1971-87; resource rm. tchr. Sidney Ctrl. Sch., 1993. Pres. Tchrs. Assn., Bd. Coop. Sch. Ednl. Services, Liberty, N.Y., 1970-71; organizing com. of N.Y. Heartland Bioregion, 1996—; mem. Made in Chenago Gallery, Inc., 1997-99. Vol., coach Spl. Olympics, Liberty, Delhi, N.Y., 1974-87; chairperson Chenango County Environ. Mgmt. Coun., 1991-93; mem. Upper Catskill Community Coun. Arts; deacon Guilford Ctr. Presbyn. Ch., 1991-93, treas. ladies aid, 1995-99, elder, 1999; mem. planning bd. Town of Guilford, 1999. Mem. N.Y. State Tchrs. of Handicapped, Assn. Children with Learning Disabilities, Del. Acad. Faculty Assn. (region polit. action com. 1982-83), Three Rivers Project, Chenango County Bird Club (sec. 1995-96, editor newsletter 1997—), Tri-Town Hikers, Delhi Art Group. Avocations: gardening, hiking, freelance art, nature study. E-mail: jivesstarr@mkl.com.

STARR, KEVIN, librarian, educator; BA, U. San Francisco, 1962; MA, Harvard U., 1965, PhD, 1969; MLS, U. Calif., Berkeley, 1974; postgrad., Ch. Div. Sch. Pacific, Berkeley, 1983-84. From asst. to assoc. prof. Am. lit. Harvard U., Cambridge, Mass., 1969-74; city libr. San Francisco, 1973-76; prin. Kevin Starr Assocs., 1983-85; prof. comm. arts U. San Francisco, 1981-89; prof. Sch. Planning and Devel. U. So. Calif., 1989—; state libr. Calif., 1994—. Allston Burr sr. tutor Eliot House Harvard U., Cambridge, 1970-73; cons. Beyl and Boyd, Inc., San Francisco, 1979-83; sr. cons. Hill and Knowlton USA, San Francisco, 1983-84; vis. assoc. prof. English U. Calif., Berkely, 1974, vis. lectr. polit. sci., 1976, lectr. librarianship, 1978; adj. prof. humanities San Francisco State U., 1975-76; Regent's lectr. polit. sci. U. Calif., Riverside, 1977; adj. prof. English Santa Clara (Calif.) U., 1977-78; vis. prof. history U. Calif., Davis, 1985-86; vis. scholar, media fellow Hoover Inst., 1986-88; vis. fellow Ctr. Humanistic Studies, Claremont McKenna Coll., 1987; faculty master Embassy Residential Coll., 1990-94. Sr. editor New West Mag., 1977; vatican corr. Hearst Newspapers, Rome, 1978; columnist Examiner, San Francisco, 1977-83; contbng. editor L.A. Times, 1994—; contbr. articles to profl. jours., chpts. to books. Exec. aide to mayor San Francisco, 1973; bd. trustees Am. Issues Forum, 1975-76, Calif. Hist. Soc., 1992—; co-chmn. sister city com., San Francisco and Sydney, Australia, 1981-86; advisor Jr. League San Francisco, 1982-84; canidate San Francisco Bd. Suprs., 1984; councilor Am. Antiquarian Soc., 1996—; mem. Calif. Coun. Humanities, 1996—; regent Cathedral St. Mary Assumption, San Francisco, 1996—. Lt. German Army, 1962-64. Office: Calif State Lib PO Box 942837 Sacramento CA 94237-0001*

STARR, LEON, retired chemical research company executive; b. Bronx, N.Y., May 2, 1937; s. Michael and Bella (Foux) S.; m. Joan Gail Linett, June 19, 1960; children— Michael Jason, Jennifer Nicole BS, Poly. Inst., Bklyn., 1958; PhD, U. Mo., 1962. Teaching asst. U. Mo., Columbia, 1958-62; chem. rschr. Mobil Chem. Co., Edison, N.J., 1962-67; various mgmt. positions then dir. tech. Celanese Corp., N.Y.C., 1967-83, corp. v.p. tech., 1983-86; pres. Celanese Rsch. Co., 1983-90; pres., corp. v.p. tech. Hoechst Celanese Corp., Chatham, N.J., 1986-90, ret., 1990; pres. Lee Starr Assocs., 1991—. Adv. bd. U. Pa. 1988-90; adv. coun. Hampton U., 1988-97; nat. adv. coun. Synthesis Coalition on Engring. Edn. 1991-96; ptnr. Internat. Think-Tank Group, 1995-97; bd. dirs Internat. Fibers Corp., 2000—. Contbr. chpt. to book; patentee in field. Mem. conservation com. Town of Westport, 1996—; chmn. Land Acquisition Com., Westport, 1998—. Fellow Phillips Corp., U. Mo., 1961-62, Poly. Inst. N.Y., 1985. Mem. AAAS, Assn. Rsch. Dirs. (bd. dirs 1995-97), Am. Chem. Soc. (corp. assoc. 1983-90, bd. govs.), Natural Sci. Assn., N.Y. Acad. Scis., Soc. Chem. Industry, Chem. Mfrs. Assn. (chmn. chem. regulations and adv. com. 1977-82), Am. Inst. Chemists, Sales and Mktd. Execs. Internat. (v.p. 1972-73), STAR Residential (bd. dirs. 1994-98), Sigma Xi. Avocations: tennis, golf, sailing, collecting antique scientific instruments. E-mail: LStarr1@prodigy.net.

STARR, MIRABAI PAULA, philosophy and religious studies educator, writer; b. Bklyn., May 2, 1961; d. Ian and Susanna (Lehrer) S.; children: Daniela, Jennifer (dec.). BA with distinction, U. N.Mex., 1983, MA with distinction, 1985. Tchr. humanities Mid-Peninsula H.S., Palo Alto, Calif., 1986-88; mgr. Rancho Encantado, Quintana Roo, Mex., 1988-89; founder, dir. studies chamisa Mesa H.S., Taos, N.Mex., 1989-92; dir. programs Rancho Encantado, Quintana Roo, 1992—; instr. philosophy and religious studies U. N.Mex. Taos Edn. Ctr., Taos, 1992—. Group facilitator lama Found., Taos, 1990—. Neem Karoli Baba Ashram Taos, 1997—; lectr. bilingual literacy program. Author: Dark Night of the Soul , 2002. Mem. Authors Guild, Soc. of Muse of the Southwest. Mem. Green Party. Avocations: Eastern religions, meditative practices, East Indian music, Spanish mysticism.

STARR, MIRIAM CAROLYN, telecommunications company executive; b. Pitts., Apr. 13, 1951; d. Donald Curtis and Virginia Ruth (Weise) S. BS in Math., Bucknell U., 1973; MBA in Fin., Drexel U., 1984. Mgmt. trainee Bell Pa., Allentown, 1973-75, from equipment engr. to short range planner Phila., 1975-77, chief switchman Langhorne, 1977-78, from long range planner to cost analyst Phila., 1978-81, price/demand analyst, 1981-83; from inventory analyst to budget analyst AT&T, Parsippany, N.J., 1983-87, expense analyst, 1987-88, asst. controller gen. bus. systems, 1988-90, regional fin. mgr. Irvine, Calif., 1990-92, dist. mgr. comms. products group fin. staff Basking Ridge, N.J., 1992-93, dist. mgr. multimedia products and svcs. group fin. staff, 1993; div. mgr. Fin. Mgmt. Architecture, Morristown, 1993-95; project leader distributed gen. ledger AT&T, 1995-96, divsn. mgr. performance measurements, 1996-97, fin. planning and analysis dir., 1997-98; release mgmt. dir. Lucent Techs., Warren, N.J., 1998-1999; dir. fin IT applications Enterprise Resource Planning, Lucent Tech., 2000—. Treas. Stone Run II Neighborhood Assn., 1987-90, trustee, 1989-90. Named to Achievers Club, 1991. Mem. NAFE, Fin. Execs. Networking Group, Exec. Womens Golf Assn., Delta Zeta. Avocations: reading, golfing. Home: 32 Windmill Dr Morristown NJ 07960-5967 Office: Lucent Techs 283 King George Rd Warren NJ 07059-5134 E-mail: mstarr@avaya.com.

STARR, MONICA, program director; b. Chgo., Oct. 8, 1958; d. Myrtis (Saville) Harrold; 1 child, Kristopher. BS, U. Ill., 1980. News dir., announcer, prodn. dir., program dir. Sta. KXOK, St. Louis, 1989-93; music rsch. dir. promotions, sales coord., announcer Sta. KMJM, 1989-91; announcer, programming asst. Sta. WPEG, Charlotte, N.C., 1993-94; program dir. Sta. WEJM, Chgo., 1994-96, Sta. WMXD, Detroit, 1996—. Conf. chairperson Midwest Radio and Records Assn., 1995; cons. Multiverse Networks, L.A., 1996. Spkr. Minority Spkrs. Bur., 1997. Recipient GRIOT award Midwest Radio and Records Assn., 1996, Music Pioneer award Columbia's Music Assn., 1996; named Outstanding Young Woman of Yr., 1982, 85, 97. Mem. Nat. Black Programmers Coalition (treas., v.p., pres., nat. chpt. Spirit award 1994, FM Personality of Yr. nat. chpt. 1994, Carolina's chpt. 1994). Avocations: computers, bike riding, writing, photography. Office: Sta WMXD-FM 645 Griswold St Detroit MI 48226-4105

STARR, NANCY BARBER, pediatric nurse practitioner; b. Carlsbad, N.Mex., Dec. 7, 1954; d. John Thomas and Janet Lee (Fleehart) B. BSN cum laude, Tex. Christian U., 1976; MS, U. Colo., 1980. Cert. pediatric nurse practitioner; RN, Colo., Tex. Staff nurse/team leader The Children's Hosp., Denver, 1976-79, clin. nurse specialist, 1980-83; pediatric nurse practitioner Nancy Byrd, M.D., P.C., Houston, 1984-89, Aurora (Colo.) Pediatric Assocs., 1989—. Interim dir. edn. Nat. Assn. Pediat. Nurse Assocs. & Practitioners, Cherry Hill, N.J., 1995-96. Author: Pediatric Primary Care Textbook, 1996, 2d edit., 2000, Pocket Reference for Pediatric Primary Care, 2000; dept. editor Jour. Pediat. Health Care, 1994—, mem. editl. bd., 1995-2001; contbr. articles to profl. jours. Deacon, mem. outreach steering com. Greenwood Cmty. Ch., Denver, 1991-94; tchr. Bethel Ind. Ch., Houston, 1985-89; mem., leader Bible Study Fellowship, Houston and Denver, 1985-91, 94-95. Fellow Nat. Assn. Pediatric Nurse Assocs. and Practitioners (exec. bd., program chair 1989-93, Rocky Mt. chpt. AAP liaison 1992-95, Houston area chpt. pres. 1988-89); mem. Colo. Nurses Assn., Sigma Theta Tau. Office: Aurora Pediatric Assocs 5657 S Himalaya # 100 Aurora CO 80015-3572

STARR, PHILLIP HENRY, psychiatrist, educator; b. Poland, Nov. 16, 1920; arrived in Can., 1922; s. Harry and Jennie (Amsterdam) S.; children: Eric, Craig, Susan. MD, U. Toronto, Ont., Can., 1944. Diplomate Am. Bd. Psychiatry and Neurology, Am. Bd. Child Psychiatry. Intern Hamilton Gen Hosp., Can., 1944-45; residence St. Louis Children's Hosp., 1946-49; fellow St Louis Children's Hosp, 1949-51; dir. Cmty. Child Guidance Clinic, Washington U., St. Louis, 1952-54; chief children's outpatient clinic Nebr. Psychiat. Inst., Omaha, 1955-60; pvt. practice, 1955-84, Scottsdale, Ariz., 1984-99. Staff psychiatrist Student Health Ctr., Ariz. State U., Tempe, 1992-99. Capt. Can. Army, 1942-44. Fellow Am. Psychiat. Assn., AMA. Home and Office: 7246 E El Caminito Dr Scottsdale AZ 85258-2721 Mailing: PO Box 5973 Scottsdale AZ 85261

STARR, ROSS MARC, economist, educator; b. Oak Ridge, Nov. 14, 1945; s. Chauncey and Doris E. S.; m. Susan S. Strauss, July 2, 1967; children: Daniel, Diana. BS, Stanford U., 1966, PhD, 1972. Cons. Rand Corp., summers 1966, 67, Western Mgmt. Sci. Inst., Grad. Sch. Mgmt., UCLA, summers 1967, 71; Cowles Found. staff rsch. economist Yale U., New Haven, 1970, faculty, 1970-74, assoc. prof. econs., 1974, U. Calif., Davis, 1975-76, prof. econs., 1976-80, San Diego, 1980—, chmn. dept., 1987-90. Vis. lectr. London Sch. Econs., 1973-74, Peoples U. China, Beijing, 1987; vis. scholar U. Calif., Berkeley, 1978-80, vis. prof., 1997. Author: General Equilibrium Theory: An Introduction, 1997; co-editor: Essays in Honor of Kenneth J. Arrow, 1986: v.1, Social Choice and Public Decision Making, v.2, Equilibrium Analysis, v.3, Uncertainty, Information and Communication; editor: Gen. Equilibrium Models of Monetary Economies, 1989; contbr. articles to profl. jours. NDEA fellow, 1966-69, Yale jr. faculty fellow, 1973-74, Guggenheim fellow, 1978-79; NSF grant, 1979-81, 83-85. Office: U Calif San Diego Dept Econs 0508 9500 Gilman Dr La Jolla CA 92093-0508 E-mail: rstarr@ucsd.edu.

STARR, STEVEN DAWSON, photographer; b. Albuquerque, Sept. 6, 1944; s. Richard Vernon and Carol (Harley) S.; m. Marilynne Sue Anderson, Aug. 6, 1965; 1 child, Stephen Richard. Student, Antioch Coll., 1962-63, Bethel Coll., 1963-64; BA, San Jose State Coll., 1967. Photographer San Jose Mercury-News, Calif., 1966-67; photographer, picture editor A.P., 1968-73; audiovisual producer Starr Productions, Inc., Coral Gables, Fla., 1974-85; photographer Picture Group Agy., 1986-88, Saba Press, N.Y.C., 1988—. Recipient Pulitzer prize for spot news photography, 1970, Nat. Headliners award, 1970, George Polk Meml. award, 1970, Pictures of Year hon. mention, 1970 Office: Corbis/Saba Press 902 Broadway 4th Fl New York NY 10010 E-mail: steve@stevestarr.com.

STARR, TERRELL, state senator; b. Clayton County, Ga., June 5, 1926; m. Celeste McKinney; children: Terry, JoAnn Kennedy. Grad., Atlanta Law Sch. Real estate broker, ins. agent; mem. Ga. Senate, Atlanta, 1968—, pres. pro tempore, 2002—; chmn. fin. and pub. utilities com.; vice chmn. appropriations com.; mem. banking and fin. instns., reapportionment coms.; also health and human svcs., edn. coms. Past mem. Clayton County Commn., Clayton County Libr. Bd., Clayton County Bd. Health, Atlanta Regional Met. Planning Commn.; past trustee Forest Park Sch. Dist. Youth Ctr.; deacon, former chmn. bd. of deacons First Baptist Ch., Forest Park. With USN, 1944-46. Recipient Ga. Legis. of Yr. award Ga. Sch. Counselors Assn., Nat. Legis. of Yr. award Am. Sch. Counselors Assn., Legis. of Yr. award Ga. Parks and Recreation Assn., Disting. Svc./Citizen of Yr. award C. of C.; honores received Ga. Mcpl. Assn., Ga. Assn. Children with Learning Disabilities, Ga. Moose Assn., Ga. Assn. Home Health Agys., Elem. Sch. Prins. Assn., Ga. Assn. Edn. Leaders, Gridiron Hon. Society, Am. Acad. Pediats., Nat. Assn. Home Health Care; park named in his honor City of Forest Park; Terrell Starr Human Svcs. Ctrl named in his honor Jonesboro. Mem. Peace Officers Assn. Ga. (hon., life), Jaycees (past pres., Disting. Svc. award), Rotary, Masons, Royal Arch, Tara Club, Kiwanis (past pres.), Yaareb Temple. Democrat. Office: Rm 321 State Capitol Atlanta GA 30334 also: 541 Forest Pkwy Ste 3 Forest Park GA 30297-2147*

STARRATT, PATRICIA ELIZABETH, writer, actress, composer, pianist; b. Boston, Nov. 7, 1943; d. Alfred Byron and Anna (Mazur) S. AB, Smith Coll., 1965; grad. prep. dept., Peabody Conservatory Music, 1961; postgrad., Saybrook Grad. Sch./Rsch. Ctr., San Francisco, 1999. Tchg. asst. Harvard U. Grad. Sch. Bus. Adminstrn., 1965-67; mng. dir. INS Assocs., Washington, 1967-68; adminstrv. asst. George Washington U. Hosp., 1970-71; legal asst. Morgan, Lewis & Bockius, Washington, 1971-72; profl. staff energy analyst Nat. Fuels & Energy Policy Study U.S. Senate Interior Com., 1972-74; cons., exec. asst. energy resource devel. Fed. Energy Adminstrn., Washington, 1974-75; sr. cons. energy policy Atlantic Richfield Co., 1975-76; energy cons. Alaska, 1977-78; govt. affairs assoc. Sohio Alaska Petroleum Co., Anchorage, 1978-85; legal asst. Hughes, Thorsness, Gantz, Powell and Brudin, 1989-90; writer, media specialist corp. affairs Alyeska Pipeline Svc. Co., 1990-95; legal asst. Hughes Thorsness Powell Huddleston & Bauman LLC, 1996-97; sr. paralegal Brit. Petroleum, 1997-98; writer, editor Inst. Circumpolar Health Studies U. Alaska, Anchorage, 1998—; exec. dir. Anchorage Cmty. Theatre, 1999—2002. Mem. econ. devel. commn. Municipality of Anchorage, 1981. Actress, asst. dir. Brattle St. Players, Boston, 1966-67, Washington Theater Club, 1967-68, Gene Frankel, Broadway, 1968-69; actress Aspen Resident Theater, Colo., 1985-86, Ranyevskya (The Cherry Orchard), Anchorage, 1994, Bonfila (SLAVS!), Frau Schmidt (The Sound of Music), Anchorage, 1995, Maria (Moonlight), Anchorage, 1997, Olga (Three Sisters), Eccentric Theatre Co., Anchorage, 1998, Mrs. Barker (The American Dream), 7th Ann. Edward Albee Theatre Conf., Valdez, Alaska, 1999, Ethel (Moon Over Buffalo), Eccentric Theatre Co., Anchorage, 1999; writer, assoc. prodr.: Then One Night I Hit Her, 1983, Stephanie (Yardsale) 9th Ann. Edward Albee Theatre Conf., Valdez, Alaska, 2001, Prudence (Landfall) Loblolly Theatre Co., Pensacola, Fla., 2002; screenwriter, prodr., actress, composer, pianist: A Call to Live, 1995, Marmee (Little Women), 1997; appeared off-Broadway in to Be Young, Gifted and Black; performed as Mary in Tennessee, Blanche in A Streetcar Named Desire, Stephanie Dickinson in Cactus Flower, Angela in Papa's Wine, Elizabeth Procter in The Crucible, Candida in Candida, Zeuss in J.B., Martha in Who's Afraid of Virginia Woolf, Amy in Dinny and the Witches, as Columbina in Servant of Two Masters, as Singer in Death of Morris Biederman, as Joan in Joan of Lorraine, as Mado in Amadee, as Mrs. Rowlands in Before Breakfast, as the girl in Hello Out There, as Angela in Bedtime Story, as Hannah in Night of the Iguana, as Lavinia in Androcles and the Lion, as Catherine in Great Catherine, as Julie in Lilliom, as First Nurse in Death of Bessie Smith, as Laura in Tea and Sympathy, as Amelia Earhart in Chamber Music; appeared at Detroit Summer Theatre in Oklahoma, Guys and Dolls, Carousel, Brigadoon, Kiss Me Kate, Finnian's Rainbow; asst. to dir. Broadway plays A Cry of Players, A Way of Life, Off-Broadway play To Be Young, Gifted and Black; screenwriter Challenge in Alaska, 1986, Martin Poll Films; asst. dir. Dustin Hoffman, 1974; contbr. articles on natural gas and Alaskan econ. and environ. to profl. jours. Bd. dirs. Anchorage Comty. Theatre, Alaska Assn. Legal Assts., 1996-98; industry rep. Alaska Eskimo Whaling Commn.; mem. Alaska New Music Forum. Mem. Actors' Equity. Episcopalian. Avocations: skiing, horseback riding, biking, hiking. Home: 6920 Sea Turtle Cir Navarre FL 32566 E-mail: starward1@yahoo.com.

STARRETT, FREDERICK KENT, lawyer; b. Lincoln, Nebr., May 23, 1947; s. Clyde Frederick and Helen Virginia (Meyers) Starrett; m. Linda Lee Jensen, Jan. 19, 1969; children: Courtney, Kathryn, Scott. BA, U. Nebr., 1969; JD, Creighton U., 1976. Bar: Nebr 1976, Kans 1977, US Dist Ct Nebr 1976, US Dist Ct Kans 1977, US Ct Appeals (8th and 10th cirs) 1983, Mo 1987, US Dist Ct (we dit) Mo 1987, US Supreme Ct 1993. Pvt. practice law, Great Bend, Kans., 1976-77, Topeka, 1977-86; ptnr. Miller, Bash & Starrett, P.C., Kansas City, Mo., 1986-90, Lathrop Norquist & Miller, 1990-91, Lathrop and Norquist, Overland Park, Kans., 1991-95, Lathrop & Gage L.C., Overland Park, 1996—. Judicial nominating comnr 10th Judicial Dist, 2000—. Lt (jg) USNR, 1969—72. Mem.: ABA, Mo Orgn Def Lawyers, Def Research Inst (state rep Kans 1998—2001), Am Bd Trials Advs (pres Kans chpt 1997), Kans Bar Asn (pres litigation sect 1985—86), Civitan Club (pres 1985—86, Distinguished Pres Award 1985—86). Democrat. Presbyterian. Avocations: aviation, scuba diving. Office: Lathrop & Gage LC Bldg 82 10851 Mastin Blvd Ste 1000 Shawnee Mission KS 66210-2007 E-mail: fstarrett@lathropgage.com.

STARRETT, GREGORY, anthropologist, educator; b. Denver, 1961; PhD, Stanford U., 1991. Assoc. prof. anthropology U. N.C., Charlotte, 1992—. Author: Putting Islam to Work: Education, Politics, and Religious Transformation in Egypt, 1998. Office: Dept Anthropology U NC Charlotte 9201 University City Blvd Charlotte NC 28223

STARRETT, KEITH, lawyer; b. McComb, Miss., July 15, 1951; s. Melvin and Mary (Roberts) S.; m. Barbara O'Neal, Dec. 18, 1971; children: Josh, Whit, Leah Claire. BS, Miss. State U., 1972; JD, U. Miss., 1974. Bar: Miss. 1974, U.S. Dist. Ct. (no. and so. dists.) Miss. 1974. Ptnr. Statham, Watkins & Starrett, Magnolia, Miss., 1975-79; pvt. practice, 1980-89, McComb, 1989-92; cir. judge 14th Cir. Dist., 1992—. Baptist. Avocations: backpacking, jogging, canoeing. Office: 299 Apache Dr Mc Comb MS 39648-6307 E-mail: starrett@telapex.com.

STARRETT, WILLIAM, dancer, artistic director; b. Indio, Calif., Oct. 18, 1959; s. George Lester and Arleen (LaDroute) S. Soloist Royal Winnipeg (Can.) Ballet, 1974-76, Eglevsky Ballet, N.Y.C., 1977; mem. Am. Ballet Theater, 1977; prin. Joffrey Ballet, N.Y.C., 1978-81; guest artist Ballet West, Salt Lake City, 1981, Atlanta Ballet, 1982, No. Ballet Theatre, Manchester, England, 1983; artistic dir. Columbia (S.C.) City Ballet, 1986—. Named Sr. Medalist Jackson (Miss.) U.S. Ballet Competition, 1979; recipient Key to City, Singapore, 1985. Mem. Leadership Columbia. Office: Columbia City Ballet PO Box 11898 Columbia SC 29211-1898*

STARRFIELD, SUMNER GROSBY, astrophysics educator, researcher; b. L.A., Dec. 29, 1940; s. Harold Ernest and Eve (Grosby) S.; m. Susan Lee Hutt, Aug. 7, 1966; children: Barry, Brian, Sara. BA, U. Calif., Berkeley, 1962; MA, UCLA, 1965, PhD, 1969. From lectr. to asst. prof. Yale U., New Haven, 1967-71; rsch. scientist IBM, Yorktown Heights, N.Y., 1971-72; asst. prof. Ariz. State U., Tempe, 1972-75, assoc. prof., 1975-80, prof., 1980—2001, Regents' prof., 2002—. Vis. assoc. prof. Steward Observatory, Tucson, 1978-79; vis. staff mem. Los Alamos (N.Mex.) Nat. Lab., 1974-94. Author numerous scientific papers. Grantee Ariz. State U., 1973, NSF, 1974—, NASA, 1981—; Los Alamos summer fellow, 1974, 86; Joint Inst. Lab. Astrophysics fellow, 1985-86. Fellow Royal Astron. Soc., Am. Phys. Soc. (astrophysics divsn.); mem. Internat. Astron. Union, Am. Astron. Soc. (high energy astrophysics div., mem. publs. bd. 1978-81, chmn. publs. bd. 2002--). Achievements include discovery of thermonuclear runaway theory of nova outburst; co-discovery of hottest known class of pulsating variable stars and the cause of their pulsations, ultraviolet studies of nova cygni, 1992; HST and CHANDRA X-ray studies of novae in outburst. Office: Ariz State U Dept Physics/Astronomy PO Box 871504 Tempe AZ 85287-1504 E-mail: starrfield@asu.edu.

STARRS, ELIZABETH ANNE, lawyer; b. Detroit, Jan. 1, 1954; d. John Richard and Mabel Angeline (Gilchrist) S. BA, U. Mich., 1975; JD, Suffolk U., 1980. Bar: Mass. 1980, Colo. 1983, U.S. Dist. Ct. Mass. 1981, U.S. Ct. Appeals (1st. cir.) 1981, Colo. 1983, U.S. Dist. Ct. Colo. 1983, U.S. Ct. Appeals (10th cir.) 1983. Assoc. Denner & Benjoya P.C., Boston, 1980-83, Kennedy & Christopher P.C., Denver, 1983-86, ptnr., 1986—, pres., mng. ptnr., 1994-2000. Mem. jud. nominating commn. 2d Jud. Dist., Colo., 2000-06. Troop leader Girl Scouts U.S., Denver, 1984-85; pres. Colo. Women's Bar Assn. Found., 1992-94. Fellow Am. Coll. Trial Advs., Colo. Bar Found.; mem. ATLA, FBA, Colo. Bar Assn. (litigation coun. 1989-96, chair 1993-94, profl. liability chair 1991-93), Denver Bar Assn. (pres.-elect 2001—), Colo. Women's Bar Assn. (bd. dirs. 1984-85, v.p. 1989-90), U.S. Dist. Ct. Colo. (com. conduct 1997—), Am. Bd. Trial Advs., Def. Rsch. Inst., Faculty of Fed. Advs. Roman Catholic. Office: Kennedy & Christopher PC 1050 17th St Ste 2500 Denver CO 80265

STARRS, JAMES EDWARD, law and forensics educator, consultant; b. Bklyn., July 30, 1930; s. George Thomas and Mildred Agatha (Dobbins) S.; m. Barbara Alice Smyth, Sept. 6, 1954; children: Mary Alice, Monica, James, Charles, Liam, Barbara, Siobhan, Gregory. BA, LLB, St. John's U., Bklyn., 1958; LLM, NYU, 1959. Bar: N.Y. 1958, D.C. 1966, U.S. Ct. Mil. Appeals 1959, U.S. Dist. Ct. (so. and ea. dists.) N.Y. 1960. Assoc. Lawless & Lynch, N.Y.C., 1958; tchg. fellow Rutgers U., Newark, 1959-60; asst. prof. law DePaul U., Chgo., 1960-64; assoc. prof. law George Washington U., Washington, 1964-67, prof. law, 1967—, prof. forensic scis., 1975—. Cons. Nat. Commn. Reform Fed. Criminal Laws, Washington, 1968, Cellmark Diagnostics, Germantown, Md., 1987—, Time-Life Books, 1993; participant re-evaluation sci. evidence and trial of Bruno Richard Hauptmann for Lindbergh murder, 1983; participant reporting sci. re-analysis of firearms evidence in Sacco and Vanzetti trial, 1986; project dir. Alfred G. Packer Victims Exhumation Project, 1989, A Blaze of Bullets: A Sci. Investigation into the Deaths of Senator Huey Long and Dr. Carl Austin Weiss, 1991, Meriwether Lewis Exhumation Project, 1992—, Frank R. Olson Exhumation Project, 1994, Jesse W. James Exhumation Project, 1995, Samuel Washington-Harewood Excavations, 1999, The Boston Strangler Re-Investigation, 2000, The Exhumation of Carl E. Williams, Sr., 2001; Snider lectr. U. Toronto, 1999, Boston Strangler Re-Investigation, 2000. Author: (with Moenssens and Inbau) Scientific Evidence in Criminal Cases, 1986; (with Moenssens, Inbau and Henderson) Scientific Evidence in Civil and Criminal Cases, 1995; editor: The Noiseless Tenor, 1982; co-editor: (review) Scientific Sleuthing, 1976—; mem. editl. bd. Jour. Forensic Sci., 1980-98, Encyclopedia of Forensic Sciences; contbr. articles to profl. jours. Sgt. U.S. Army, 1950-53, Korea. Recipient Vidocq Soc. award, 1993; Ford Found. fellow, 1963; vis. scholar in residence USMC, 1984. Fellow Am. Acad. Forensic Sci. (chmn. jurisprudence sect. 1984, 94, 95, bd. dirs. 1986-89, 98-2001, Jurisprudence Sect. award 1988, Disting. fellow 1996); mem. ABA (emeritus), Mid-Atlantic Assn. Forensic Sci., Assn. Trial Lawyers Am., Internat. Soc. Forensic Sci. (chmn. jurisprudence sect. 1988), Internat. Assn. for Identification (co-chmn. historic cases sect. 1998—). Roman Catholic. Home: 8602 Clydesdale Rd Springfield VA 22151-1301 Office: George Washington U Nat Law Ctr 720 20th St NW Washington DC 20006-4306 E-mail: jstarrs@main.nlc.gwu.edu.

STARRY, DONN ALBERT, former aerospace company executive, former army officer; b. N.Y.C., May 31, 1925; s. Don Albert and Edith (Sortor) S.; m. Leatrice Hope Gibbs, June 15, 1948; children: Michael, Paul, Melissa, Melanie. BS, U.S. Mil. Acad., 1948; MS in Internat. Affairs, George Washington U., 1966. Commd. 2d lt. U.S. Army, 1948, advanced through grades to gen., 1977; svc. in Europe, Korea and Vietnam; comdr. 11th armored cavalry rgt. Vietnam, Cambodia, 1969-70; assigned Dept. Army Staff, 1970-72; comdr. Armor Center and Ft. Knox, Ky., 1973-76, V Corps, Europe, 1976-77; comdr. Tng. and Doctrine Command Ft. Monroe, Va., 1977-81; comdr. in chief U.S. Readiness Command, 1981-83, ret., 1983; v.p. mission analysis and tech. affairs Ford Aerospace and Communications Corp., Detroit, 1983-84, v.p., gen. mgr. space missions group, 1984-86; exec. v.p. Ford Aerospace Corp., Arlington, Va., 1987-90; spl. asst. to pres. BDM Internat., McLean, 1988-90. Chmn. bd. Maxwell Techs. Inc., San Diego, 1995-97, Universal Voltronics, Brookfield, Conn., 1998—; author, lectr., counselor to govt. and industry. Mem. Def. Sci. Bd., 1985—93, Order of Aaron and Hur, Friends of Fifth of May; mem. bd. Eisenhower Found., 1995—; chmn. bd. U.S. Cavalry Meml. Found., 1995—; mem. bd. Army Hist. Found., 2000—. Decorated Def. D.S.M., Army D.S.M. with oak leaf cluster, Silver Star, Bronze Star with V, Soldier's medal, Purple Heart, Legion of Merit with 2 oak leaf clusters, French Ordre Nationale du Merite, German Knight Commdr.'s Cross of Order of Merit with Badge and Star, Disting. Flying Cross, Air Medal with 9 oak leaf clusters; named to U.S. Army Ft. Leavenworth Command and Gen. Staff Coll. Hall of Fame, 1993; recipient Gold medal The Order of St. George. Mem. U.S. Armor Assn., Assn. U.S. Army. Episcopalian. Office: 11401 Lilting Ln Fairfax Station VA 22039-1717 E-mail: dastarry@earthlink.net.

STARTUP, WILLIAM HARRY, chemist; b. Port Jervis, N.Y., Oct. 24, 1945; s. William George and Robina Victoria S.; m. Frances Williams, Nov. 6, 1976; 1 child, Elizabeth. BS in Chemistry, SUNY, Cortland, 1974. Sr. flavor analyst PFW-Hercules, Middletown, N.Y., 1975-91; analytical supr. Tastemaker, Cin., 1991-96; mgr. analytical svcs. Degussa Flavors and Fruit Sys., 1996—. Bd. dirs. Humane Soc. Middletown N.Y., 1985-91. Sgt. USAF, 1966-70. Mem. Am. Chem. Soc., Assn. of Ofcl. Analytical Chemists. Home: 892 Sabino Ct Cincinnati OH 45231-4905 Office: Degussa Flavors and Fruit Sys 10311 Chester Rd Cincinnati OH 45215-1224

STARTZ, RICHARD, economist; b. White Plains, N.Y., July 19, 1952; s. Arthur and Adele (Kersh) S.; m. Shelly Joyce Lundberg, Jan. 8, 1983; children: Meredith Lundberg, Glynis Lundberg. BA, Yale U., 1974; PhD, MIT, 1978. Asst. prof. fin. U. Pa., Phila., 1978-84; assoc. prof. U. Wash., Seattle, 1984-91, prof. econs., 1991—, Castor prof. econs., 1999—, chmn. dept. econs., 1995-2000. Author: 8087/80287/80387 For the IBM PC, 1983, 85, 87, Working with 1-2-3, 1985; co-author: Macroeconomics, 1997, 2d edit., 2000. Avocations: computer programming, playing with my children. Office: Univ of Washington Dept Econs PO Box 353330 Seattle WA 98195-3330 E-mail: startz@u.washington.edu.

STARY, FRANK EDWARD, chemistry educator; b. St. Paul, Jan. 3, 1941; s. Frank C. and Elaine E. S.; m. Sonja G. Dalsbo, Aug. 30, 1964 BChem, U. Minn., 1963; PhD in Inorganic Chemistry, U. Cin., 1969. Undergrad. researcher U. Minn., Mpls., 1960-63; instr., postdoct. fellow U. Calif., Irvine, 1968—72; rsch. assoc. U. Mo., St. Louis, 1972-74; asst. prof. chemistry Maryville Coll., 1974-78; assoc. prof. chemistry, 1978-82; prof. chemistry Maryville U., St. Louis, 1982—. Contbr. articles to profl. jours. Mem. ACS, Gateway V.W. Club, Phi Lambda Upsilon, Sigma Xi. Avocations: shito ryu, tai chi, French, keyboards. Office: Maryville U 13550 Conway Rd Saint Louis MO 63141-7299 E-mail: stary@maryville.edu.

STARYK, STEVEN SAM, violinist, concertmaster, educator; b. Toronto, Ont., Can., Apr. 28, 1932; s. Peter and Mary Staryk; m. Ida Elisabeth Busch, May 17, 1963; 1 child, Natalie. Student, Royal Conservatory of Music, Toronto, 1942-48, Harbord Collegiate Inst., 1945-48; LittD (hon.), York U., Toronto, 1980. Soloist, concertmaster CBC-Radio Can., Toronto, 1951-55, Royal Philharmonic Orch., London, 1956-59; 1st concertmaster, tchr. Concertgebouw Orch. and Amsterdam Conservatory, 1960-63; concertmaster Chgo. Symphony Orch., 1963-67; prof. of violin Oberlin (Ohio) Coll. Conservatory, 1968-72, Acad. of Music, Vancouver, B.C., Can., 1972-75, Royal Conservatory of Music, Toronto, 1975-87; concertmaster Toronto Symphony, 1982-87; prof. of violin, chair string div. U. Wash. Sch. Music, Seattle, 1987-97, prof. emeritus, 1997—. Faculty music U. Toronto, 1980-87; vis. prof. U. Victoria, 1972, U. Ottawa, 1975, Northwestern U., 1965-66; founding mem. Quartet Can., 1975-80. Soloist, recitalist, N.Am., Europe and the Far East; recording artist on EMI-HMV, CBC, Everest, Orion, other labels; biography (by Thane Lewis) Fiddling with Life, 2000. Recipient 2 Arts awards Can. Coun., Ottawa, 1968, 75, Queen's Silver Jubilee medal Govt. of Can., Toronto, Shevchenko medal, Winnipeg, Man., Can.; biography "Fiddling with Life" by T. Lewis and S. Staryk, 2002. Home: 12068 E Bella Vista Cir Scottsdale AZ 85259-6034 Office: U Wash Sch Music Mail Stop DN-10 PO Box 353450 Seattle WA 98195-3450

STARZINGER, VINCENT EVANS, political science educator; b. Des Moines, Jan. 12, 1929; s. Vincent and Genevieve (Evans) S.; m. Mildred Hippee Hill, June 16, 1953; children: Page Hill, Evans. AB summa cum laude, Harvard U., 1950, LLB, 1954, PhD, 1959; AM (hon.), Dartmouth Coll., 1968.

Bar: Iowa 1954. Practice with firm Bannister, Carpenter, Ahlers & Cooney, Des Moines, 1954; teaching fellow, then instr. govt. Harvard, 1957-60; mem. faculty dept. govt. Dartmouth, 1960-94, chmn. dept. govt., 1972-77, 83-85, Joel Parker prof. law and polit. sci., 1976-94, prof. emeritus, 1994—. Author: Middlingness: Juste Milieu Political Theory in England and France, 1815-48, 1965, repub. as The Politics of the Center, 1991; also articles. Served with AUS, 1955-56. Sheldon traveling fellow, 1950-51; Social Sci. Research Council fellow, 1958-59; Dartmouth faculty fellow, 1963-64; Am. Philos. Soc. award and Earhart Found. fellow, 1970-71 Mem. ABA, Am. Polit. Sci. Assn., Iowa Bar Assn., Am. Alpine Club, Cambridge (Mass.) Boat Club, Phi Beta Kappa.. Home: Elm St Norwich VT 05055 Office: PO Box 981 Hanover NH 03755-0981

STARZL, THOMAS EARL, physician, educator; b. Le Mars, Iowa, Mar. 11, 1926; s. Roman F. and Anna Laura (Fitzgerald) S.; m. Barbara Brothers, Nov. 27, 1954 (div.); children: Timothy, Rebecca, Thomas; m. Joy D. Conger, Aug. 1, 1981. BA, Westminster Coll., 1947, DSc (hon.), 1965; MA, Northwestern U., 1950, MD, PhD, 1952; DSc (hon.), N.Y. Med. Coll., 1970, Westmar Coll., 1974, Med. Coll. Wis., 1981, Northwestern U., 1982, Bucknell U., 1985, Muhlenberg Coll., 1985, Mt. Sinai Sch. Medicine, 1988; MD (hon.), U. Louvain, Belgium, 1985, U. Genova, 1988, U. Rennes, 1988; LLD (hon.), U. Wyo., 1971; LHD (hon.), LaRoche Coll., 1988. Intern Johns Hopkins U. Hosp., Balt., 1952-53, fellow, surg., 1953-54, resident, 1955-56; mem. faculty Northwestern U. Med. Sch., Evanston, Ill., 1958-61, U. Colo. Med. Sch., Denver, 1962-80, prof. surgery, 1964-80, chmn. dept. surgery, 1972-80; prof. surgery, dir. of Transplantation Inst. U. Pitts. Sch. Med., 1981—. Mem. staff Presbyn. Hosp., Univ. Hosp., Children's Hosp. of Pitts., Pitts. VA Hosp. Author: Experience in Renal Transplantation, 1964, Experience in Hepatic Transplantation, 1969; contbr. articles to profl. jours. Recipient award Westminster Coll., 1965, Achievement award Lund U., 1965, Eppinger award Soc. Internat. de Chirurgie, 1965, Eppinger prize, Freiburg, 1970, William S. Middleton award for outstanding research in VA system, 1968, Merit award Northwestern U., 1969, Disting. Achievement award Modern Medicine, 1969, Creative Council award U. Colo., 1971, Colo. Man of Yr. award, 1967, Brookdale award AMA, 1974, David Hume Meml. award Nat. Kidney Found., 1978, Pitts. Man of Yr. award, 1981; Markle scholar, 1958. Fellow ACS (Sheen award 1982), Am. Acad. Arts and Scis.; mem. Soc. Univ. Surgeons, Soc. Vascular Surgery, Am. Surg. Assn., Transplantation Soc., Deutsche Gesellschaft für Chirurgie, numerous others. Address: Thomas E Starzl Transplant Inst 4th Fl Falk Med Bldg 3601 5th Ave Pittsburgh PA 15213-3403 Office: U Pitts Sch Med 3601 5th Ave 4th Fl Falk Clinic Pittsburgh PA 15213*

STASACK, EDWARD ARMEN, artist; b. Chgo., Oct. 1, 1929; s. Clifford Clement and Elizabeth Frances (Mallek) S.; m. Mary Louise Walters, June 20, 1953 (div. 1972); children: Caren Marie, Jennifer Elizabeth, John Armen, Michael Clifford; m. Diane Miura Hirsch, June 26, 1993; 1 stepchild, David K. Hirsch. BFA with high honors, U. Ill., Urbana, 1955, MFA, 1956. Instr. in art U. Hawaii, 1956-61, prof. art, chmn. dept. art, 1969-72, program chmn. in printmaking, 1975-83, prof. emeritus, 1988; affiliate Downtown Gallery, N.Y.C., 1960-70. Author: (with J. Halley Cox) Hawaiian Petroglyphs, 1970, (with Georgia Lee) Petroglyphs of Kaho'olawe, 1993, Ka'upulehu Petroglyphs, 1994, Spirit of Place, Petroglyphs of Hawaii, 1999, (with Diane Stasack) Rock Art of Hawaii Volcanoes National Park, Nine Reports, 1995-2001; one-man shows include Honolulu Acad. Arts, 1961, 66, 69, 76, 87, U.S. embassies Istanbul and Izmir, Turkey, 1976, Am. Cultural Ctr., Bucharest, Romania, 1976, Cleve. Inst. Art, 1976, Hilo (Hawaii) Coll. Gallery, 1976, Amfac Plaza Gallery, 1978, Ryan Gallery, 1981, Art Loft, Honolulu, 1983, Commons Gallery, U. Hawaii, 1996, Hawaii Volcano Nat. Park Art Ctr., 1996; group shows include Carnegie Inst., Pitts., 1964, Krakow (Poland) Biennial, 1966, 68, Smithsonian Instn., Washington, 1967, Mexico City Mus. Modern Art, 1968, Leicester Gallery, London, 1965, Art Mus. Manila, The Philippines, 1982, 2d Internat. Biennial Print Exhibit Republic of China, 1986, Yuma Art Ctr., 1990; represented in permanent collections Mus. Modern Art, N.Y.C., Met. Mus. Art, N.Y.C., Chgo. Art Inst., Bklyn. Mus., Honolulu Acad. Arts, Hawaii State Found. Culture and the Arts, Libr. of Congress, Phila. Mus. Art, Boston Pub. Libr. Served with U.S. Army, 1952-54. Recipient numerous prizes, including; Boston Printmakers Mems. prize, 1967; Juror's awards Honolulu Printmakers, 1957, 58, 59, 62, 63, 66, 67, 68, 74, 77, 87; Soc. Am. Graphic Artists prizes, 1956, 57, 61, 62, 63, 68, 73, 78, 79, 80, 91; Tiffany Found. fellow, 1958, 62; Rockefeller Found. grantee, 1959, Hawaii Cmty. Found. grantee. 1997-2001; MacDowell Colony fellow, 1971, 75; Hawaii State and U.S. Bicentennial Commns. fellow, 1975 Mem. Soc. Am. Graphic Artists, Australian Rock Art Rsch. Assn., Rock Art Assn. Hawaii (emeritus pres.), Am. Rock Art Rsch. Assn., Soc. Hawaiian Archaeology, Sharlot Hall Mus., Smoki Mus. Office: 1623 Morning Stone Dr Prescott AZ 86305-5282

STASH, SUSAN MICHELE, critical care nurse; b. Inglewood, Calif., Mar. 28, 1965; d. Michael Paul and JoAnn Patricia (Margan) S. BSN, Westminster Coll., Salt Lake City, 1987. RN, Calif.; cert. med.-surg. nurse ANCC. Staff nurse gen. surg. unit St. Joseph Hosp., Orange, Calif., 1987-91; staff nurse gen. med. surg. unit Castle Med. Ctr., Kailua, Hawaii, 1992-94; staff nurse renal/pulmonary/telemetry unit Mary Washington Hosp., Fredericksburg, Va., 1994-95; intermediate med. care unit staff nurse Onslow Meml. Hosp., Jacksonville, N.C., 1995-97; staff nurse progressive care unit Swedish Med. Ctr., Englewood, Colo., 1998—; staff nurse subacute ICU Hoag Meml. Hosp. Presbyn., Newport Beach, Calif., 1999—. Mem. ANA, AACN, Am. Assn. Cert. Nurses, Sigma Theta Tau.

STASHOWER, DANIEL MEYER, writer; b. Cleve., Sept. 21, 1960; s. David L. and Sally (Weiss) S.; m. Alison Corbett, May 18, 1996. BA, Northwestern U., 1982; MFA, Columbia U., 1984. Magician, 1978—; author, 1986—. Author: The Ectoplasmic Man, 1985, Elephants in the Distance, 1989, Teller of Tales: The Life of Arthur Conan Doyle, 1999, The Dime Museum Murders, 1999, The Floating Lady Murder, 2000, The Houdini Specter, 2001, The Boy Genius and the Mogul, 2002. Recipient Raymond Chandler Fulbright fellowship U.S.-U.K. Fulbright Commn., 1992-93, Edgar Allen Poe award Mystery Writers Am., 2000. E-mail: daniel@stashower.com.

STASTNY, JOHN ANTON, real estate executive; b. Chgo., June 30, 1921; s. John Joseph and Bozena (Brezina) S.; m. Elizabeth Regina Ossowski, Jan. 2, 1943; children: Mary Elizabeth, John Bernard. Grad. high sch., Chgo. Owner, pres. Stastny Builders, Berwyn, Ill., 1945—; founder, pres. John A. Stastny & Co., Inc., 1954—, Care Ctr. Profls. Inc., Berwyn, 1961-95, Fairfax Health Care Ctr., Berwyn, Ill., 1975-95; chmn. bd. Fairview Health Care Ctr., LaGrange Park, 1983-95. Pres., adv. bd. Fed. Nat. Mortgage Assn., Washington, 1971-73; chmn. bd. Fed. Home Loan Bank, Chgo., 1972-78. Contbr. articles to profl. jours.; co-founder (tech. jour.): Compendium of Multi-Family Housing, 1965. Bd. dirs. Avery Coonley Sch., Downers Grove, Ill., 1956-60, MacNeal Meml. Hosp., Berwyn, 1978-95; founding gov. West Towns Cmty. Nursing Svc., Berwyn, 1968, Washington Sq. retirement housing, Hinsdale, Ill., 1986; elected del. Cmty. Caucus, Hinsdale, 1955. With U.S. Army, 1942-43. Named Presdl. Appointee Constrn. Industry Collective Bargaining Com., Washington, 1969-71, advisor to U.S. Del. to Econ. Commn. for Europe, U.S. State Dept., Geneva, Switzerland, 1971; named to Housing Hall of Fame, Washington, 1980. Mem. Chgo. Home Builders Assn. (life mem., bd. dirs., pres. 1964-65, Award of Merit 1961), Nat. Assn. Home Builders (life bd. dirs., pres. 1971, numerous disting. service awards 1965-78), Nat. Housing Ctr. (gov., chmn. 1974), Lambda Alpha Internat. (Key award 1964). Clubs: Edgewood Valley Country (LaGrange, Ill.). Republican. Avocations: fishing, golf. Home: 3231 Golfside Dr Naples FL 34110-7006 E-mail: STAZDAD@aol.com.

STASZESKY, FRANCIS MYRON, independent energy consultant; b. Wilmington, Del., Apr. 16, 1918; s. Frank J. and Ruth (Jones) S.; m. Barbara F. Kearney, May 30, 1943; children— Francis Myron, John B., Barbara J., Faith A., Paul D. BSME, MIT, 1943; MSME, Mass. Inst. Tech., 1943. Mech. engr. Union Oil Co. Calif., L.A., 1943-45; with E.I. duPont de Nemours Co., Wilmington, Del., 1946-48; joined Boston Edison Co., 1948, supervising engr. design and constrn., 1948-57, supt. engrng. and constrn. dept., 1957-64, v.p., asst. to pres., 1964-67, exec. v.p., 1967-79, pres., chief operating officer, 1979-83; cons., 1983—; dir. Boston Edison Co., 1968-83. Fellow ASME (life); mem. IEEE (sr., life), Nat. Acad. Engrng., Engrng. Soc. New Eng. (pres. 1961-62). Address: 166 Bank St Harwich Port MA 02646-1321

STATEN, BEVERLY JANET, political action administrator; b. Columbus, Ohio, Aug. 28, 1954; d. Charles Christopher DeWeese and Margaret Fuller Gilmer; m. Joe Richard Staten, Apr. 23, 1977; children: Anastasia, Christopher, Joseph. Student, Franklin U., 1980. Asst. exposition mgr. Ohio Exposition Ctr., Columbus, 1987-93; rules sec., spkr. Ohio Ho. of Rep., 1993, exec. asst. minority leader, 1994-95; asst. 23d dist. senator Ohio Senate, 1996-97; PAC adminstr. Limited, Inc., 1997-2001; aide 54th House Dist., Ohio Ho. of Reps. , 2001—. Home: 6407 Plankton Dr Columbus OH 43213 Office: Ohio Ho of Reps 77 S High St Columbus OH 43215

STATEN, DONNA KAY, elementary school educator; b. Temple, Tex., Apr. 17, 1958; d. Paul James and Doris Mary (Kleypas) Hoelscher; 1 child, Ryan. BS in Edn., U. Mary Hardin-Baylor, Belton, Tex., 1980. Cert. tchr. in art, elem. edn., health, phys. edn., recreation, gifted and talented edn., Tex. Art tchr. Meridith Magnet Sch., Temple, 1980-84, 1991-2001; bank officer mktg. Tex. Am. Bank, Houston, 1985-88; pvt. practice art tchr., designer, 1989; tchr. ESL Aldine Ind. Sch. Dist., 1990; art tchr. Kennedy-Powell Acad., Temple, 2000—. Exec. dir. Visual Arts Friends of the Cultural Activities Ctr., Temple, 1993-95, Temple Sister Cities Corp., Temple, 1994-97; chmn. fine arts team Meridith Campus, 1993-96; state rev. panelist Tex. Edn. Agy., 1997; curator Artsonia-.com student art gallery, 2002. Curator Internat. Children's Art Exhbn., 1996, art exhibit From Russia with Love, 1992-95. Mem. Contemporaries, Temple, 1994—2001; treas. Oaks Homeowners Assn., 1994—95, sec. bd. dirs., 1997—99; mem. Temple Mayor's Panel; bd. sec. Keep Temple Beautiful, 1997—99; Tchr.'s Honor Scroll Internat. Project, 2001—02; singer St. Luke's Ch. Choir, Temple, 1991—; mem. St. Luke's Women's Soc., 1993—. Recipient honorable mention in Christmas Decorating Contest Women's Day mag., 1989, cert. of recognition Crayola/Binney & Smith, 1993-94, 95-96, 97-2001; Focus on Edn. grantee, Wal-Mart, 2001. Mem. ASCD, AAUW, Fine Arts Network, Internat. Soc. for Edn. Through Art, Nat. Art Edn. Assn., Tex. Classrm. Tchrs. Assn., Am. Craft Coun., Soc. Craft Designers, Tex. Computer Edn. Assn., Tex. Fine Arts Assn., Tex. Art Edn. Assn., Nat. Mus. of Women in the Arts, Cultural Activities Ctr., Temple Assn. for the Gifted, Electronic Media Interest Group, Tex. Alliance Edn. and the Arts., Friends of the Temple Libr., Tex. Assn. Gifted and Talented. Roman Catholic. Avocations: gardening, painting and drawing, singing. Office: Kennedy-Powell Acad 3707 W Nugent Ave Temple TX 76504 Address: 2420 Holly Ln Temple TX 76502-2669 E-mail: donna.staten@temple.isd.org.

STATHIS, NICHOLAS JOHN, lawyer; b. Calchi, Greece, Feb. 27, 1924; Republican. s. John and Sylvia (Koutsonouris) S. Student, Columbia U., 1942-43, 44-48, AB, 1946, JD, 1948. Bar: N.Y. 1949. Assoc. James Maxwell Fassett, NYC, 1948—50; asst. counsel to spl. com. to investigate organized crime in interstate commerce U.S. Senate, Washington, 1951; trial atty. Fidelity & Casualty Co., NYC, 1952; law sec. to Harold R. Medina Judge U.S. Ct. Appeals (2d cir.), 1952—54; spl. dep. atty. gen. N.Y. State Election Frauds Bur., Dept. Law, N.Y.C., 1956; assoc. Watson, Leavenworth, Kelton & Taggart, NYC, 1954—60, ptnr., 1961—81, Hopgood, Calimafde, Kalil, Blaustein & Judlowe, NYC, 1981—84, Botein, Hays & Sklar, NYC, 1984—89; of counsel White & Case, 1989—93; corp. coun., dir. intellectual property Aphton Corp., 1993—. Lectr. Practising Law Inst., N.Y.C., 1968-69. Contbr. articles to profl. jours. on trademarks. Pres., exec. dir., chmn., bd. dirs. Found. Classic Theatre and Acad., 1973—; bd. dirs. Concert Artists Guild, 1974-91, Pirandello Soc., 1976—, Bklyn. Philharm. Orch., 1986-91, Orpheon, Inc., 1986-98, Friends of Young Musicians, 1998—. With AUS, 1943-44. Mem. ABA, Assn. of Bar of City of N.Y., N.Y. State Bar Assn., Fed. Bar Coun., Am. Intellectual Property Law Assn., N.Y. Intellectual Property Law Assn. Greek Orthodox. Home: 1885 John F Kennedy Blvd Jersey City NJ 07305-2113 Office: 515 Madison Ave Ste 2511 New York NY 10022-5403

STATHOPOULOS, PETER, internist; b. Hackensack, N.J., Mar. 24, 1952; s. Anastasios and Vasiliki S.; m. Diane Menichella. MD, U. Thessaloniki, 1981. Diplomate Am. Bd. Internal Medicine. Intern St. Vincent's Med. Ctr., S.I., 1981-82, resident in internal medicine, 1982-84, attending physician, 1985—. Office: 856 Castleton Ave Staten Island NY 10310-1809

STATHOPOULOS, THEODORE GEORGE, civil engineering educator; b. Athens, Greece, Sept. 30, 1947; arrived in Can., 1973; s. George Theodore and Helen (Tsakotos) S.; m. Theodora Kourtelessi, Aug. 15, 1979; children: George, Helen. Diploma in civil engring., Nat. Tech. U., Athens, 1970; M Engring. Sci., U. Western Ont., 1976, PhD, 1979. Registered engr., Greece, Can. Rsch. assoc. Ctr. for Bldg. Studies, Concordia U., Montreal, Que., Can., 1979, asst. prof. bldg. engring. Can., 1979-82, assoc. prof. Can., 1982-87, prof. Can., 1987—, assoc. dir. Ctr. Can., 1983—. Author books; contbr. over 100 articles on bldg. aerodynamics to profl. jours. Ensign Greek Navy, 1970-73. Grantee Natural Scis. and Engring. Rsch. Coun. Can., 1980—. Fellow ASCE; mem. Can. Wind Engring. Assn., Wind Engring. Rsch. Coun., Tech. Chamber Greece. Christian Orthodox. Avocation: stamp collecting. Office: Concordia Ctr Bldg Studies 1455 de Maisonneuve Blvd W Montreal QC Canada H3G 1M8

STATKUS, JEROME FRANCIS, lawyer; b. Hammond, Ind., June 13, 1942; s. Albert William and Helen Ann (Vaicunas) S.; children: Wesley Albert, Nicholas Jerome. BA, So. Ill. U., 1964; JD, U. Louisville, 1968; MA, U. Wyo., 1974. Bar: Wyo. 1971, U.S. Dist. Ct. Wyo. 1971, Wis. 1989, D.C. 1977, U.S. Ct. Claims 1973, U.S. Supreme Ct. 1974, U.S. Ct. Appeals (10th cir.) 1973, U.S. Ct. Appeals (7th cir.) 1992. Law clk. U.S. Dist. Ct., So. Dist. Ill., Peoria, 1968-69; asst. atty. gen. State of Wyo., Cheyenne, 1971-75; legis. asst. to U.S. Senator Clifford Hansen Washington, 1975-76; asst. U.S. atty. U.S. Dept. Justice, Dist. of Wyo., 1976-77; sole practice Cheyenne, 1978-79; assoc. Horisky, Bagley & Hickey, 1979-81; ptnr. Rooney, Bagley, Hickey Evans & Stratkus, 1981-88; exec. dir. Wyo. State Bar, 1988-89; trustee Village of Germantown, Wis., 1991-93; office share Ladewig and Rechlicz, 1990-93; pvt. practice Douglas, Wyo., 1993-96; asst. pub. defender State of Wyo., 1993-96. Pres. Ret. Sr. Vol. Program, Cheyenne, 1982-83; treas. Pathfinder (drug rehab.), Cheyenne, 1982-85; bar commr. 1st Jud. Dist., 1985-87; mem. Future Milw., 1991; chair Waukesha County Devel. Disability Adv. Coun., 1996—; mem. Washington County Econ. Devel. Com. Served with USNR, 1969-70. Mem. Wyo. Bar Assn., D.C. Bar Assn., Wis. State Bar Assn., Wyo. Trial Lawyers Assn. (bd. dirs. 1984-85), KC, VFW. Republican. Roman Catholic. Office: W156N 11340 Pilgrim Rd Germantown WI 53022 Home: Apt 912 9301 N 76th St Milwaukee WI 53223-1071

STATLER, CHARLES WILLIAM, television advertising executive, sportscaster, consultant; b. Abilene, Tex., Oct. 3, 1956; s. Tivis Edward Jr. and Naomi (Favors) S.; m. Sherri Todd, July 23, 1983. Student, Cisco (Tex.) Jr. Coll., 1975-77, Tarleton State U., 1977, U. Md., Fed. Republic Germany, 1978-80; B Applied Studies, Abilene Christian U., 1996. Mgr. J.T. Morrow Texaco, Breckenridge, Tex., 1973-74; asst. mgr. Winn Dixie Supermarkets, Breckenridge and Granbury, Tex., 1974-78; sales mgr., news dir. Sta. KSTB, Breckenridge, 1981-83; sportscaster Abilene Christian Univ. Sports Network, 1986-89; sportswriter Abilene Reporter News, 1987—; advt. exec. Sta. KTAB-TV, Abilene, 1983—. Sportswriter McMurry U., 1990-96, Abilene Christian U., 1996-97, Diamond Shamrock Radio Network, 1990-96. Producer, writer news stories, commls., documentaries; prodr. Spl. Reports from Dallas Cowboy Tng. Camp, 1992—; tv and radio play-by-play announcer various tourneys and championships. Mem. fund raising bd. Ben Richey Boys Ranch, Abilene; bus. drive chmn. Taylor County Cancer Soc., Abilene, 1986; bd. dirs. Stephens County Red Cross, Breckenridge, 1981-83, Mend-A-Child, 1988-90, Abilene Conv. and Vis. Bur., 1995-97, Abilene Crimestoppers Inc., 1996—; bd. dirs., mem. mktg. com. Hillcrest Ch. of Christ, Abilene, 1983-90, Univ. Ch. of Christ, 1994—; mem. Abilene Citizens Police Acad., 1997. Served with U.S. Army, 1978-81. Mem. Abilene Advt. Fedn. (bd. dirs. 1983—), Abilene C. of C. (mil. affairs com. 1988—, vice chmn. Redcoats 1983—, chmn. 1988-89), TV Bur. of Advt., Abilene Fine Arts Mus., Abilene Preservation League, Assn. Chamber Ambs. (life, nat. v.p. 1990, nat. pres. 1991-93), Abilene North Rotary (bd. dirs. 1996—, sgt. at arms 1996-97, comm. svc. dir. 1997—), Kiwanis (publicity chmn. Breckenridge club 1981-83), Abilene Citizens Police Acad. Alumni Assn. Republican. Mem. Ch. of Christ. Avocations: gardening, fishing, softball, golf. Office: 804 Highland Ave Abilene TX 79605-3208

STATLER, IRVING CARL, aerospace engineer; b. Buffalo, Nov. 23, 1923; s. Samuel William and Sarah (Strauss) S.; m. Renee Roll, Aug. 23, 1953; children: William Scott, Thomas Stuart BS in Aero. Engring., BS in Engring. Math., U. Mich., 1945; PhD, Calif. Inst. Tech., 1956. Research engr. flight research dept. Cornell Aero. Lab., Inc., Buffalo, 1946-53, prin. engr. flight research dept., 1956-57, asst. head aero-mechanics dept., 1957-63, head applied mechanics dept., 1963-70, sr. staff scientist aeroscis. div., 1970-71; research scientist U.S. Army Air Mobility Research and Devel. Lab., Moffett Field, Calif., 1971-73, dir. Aeromechanics Lab., 1973-85, dir. AGARD, 1985-88; sr. staff scientist NASA Ames Rsch. Ctr., 1988-92, chief Human Factors Rsch. Divsn., 1992—. Research scientist research analysis group Jet Propulsion Lab., Pasadena, Calif., 1953-55; chmn. flight mechanics panel adv. group aerospace research and devel. NATO, 1974-76; lectr. U. Buffalo, Millard-Fillmore Coll., Buffalo, 1957-58 Served with USAAF, 1945-46 Fellow AIAA (Internat. Cooperation in Space Sci. medal 1992), AAAS, German Aerospace Soc., Royal Aero Soc.; mem. Am. Helicopter Soc., Sigma Xi. Home: 1362 Cuernavaca Circulo Mountain View CA 94040-3571 Office: NASA Ames Rsch Ctr MS 262-7 Moffett Field CA 94035 E-mail: istatler@mail.arc.nasa.gov.

STATLER, JOHN DANIEL, radiologist; b. Wilmington, Del., Oct. 10, 1967; BA, Johns Hopkins U., 1990; MD, Jefferson Med. Coll., 1994. Diplomate Am. Bd. Radiology. Commd. 2d lt. U.S. Army, 1994, advanced through grades to maj., 2000; intern in gen. surgery Walter Reed Army Med. Ctr., Washington, 1995, radiology resident, 1995—, attending radiologist, 2000—. Asst. prof. Uniformed Svcs. Univ. of the Health Scis., Bethesda, Md., 1999—. Mem. Am. Roentgen Ray Soc. Presbyterian.

STATON, CANDI MARIA, singer; b. Hanceville, Ala., Mar. 13; m. John Sussewell, Dec. 1, 1979 (div. 1999); children: Marcel, Marcus, Terry, Cassandra, Clarence Jr. H.s. diploma, Jewell Acad., Nashville, 1958. Recording artist Unity Records, Nashville, 1968, Minaret Records, Nashville, 1968, Capitol Records, N.Y.C., 1969-72, United Artists Records, N.Y.C., 1972-74, Warner Bros. Records, N.Y.C., 1974-80, Sugar Hill Records, N.J., 1981-82, Beracah Records, Atlanta, 1983—, Intersound Records, Roswell, 1995-99, React Records, 1999—2000. Author: This Is My Story, 1994, For Parents Only: What to Do When Your Child Turns to Crime, 2000, Young Hearts Fun Free, 2000; singer: (CD) Nite Lites, 1983, It's Time, 1995, The Best of Candi Staton, 1995, Cover Me, 1997, Outside In, 2000, Here's a Blessing for You Love, Candi, 2000, Sypscious Minds: Best of Candi Staton , 2001, Christmas in My Heart, 2001. Bd. dirs. Say Yes Found., Bahamas, 1994—. Nominee Grammy award NARAS, 1971, 73, 83, 87. Office: Capital Entertainment PO Box 66661 Washington DC 20035-6661

STATON, CECIL POPE, JR. religious and academic publisher, educator; b. Greenville, S.C., Jan. 26, 1958; s. Cecil Pope and Shirley Ann (Hughes) .; m. Catherine Lynn Davidson, Aug. 23, 1986. BA, Furman U., 1980; MDiv, Southeastern Bapt. Theol. Sem., 1982, ThM, 1985; DPhil, U. Oxford, 1988. Assoc. minister Washington Ave. Bapt. Ch., Greenville, S.C., 1977-79; pastor Maple Heights Bapt. Ch., 1979-80, Trinity Bapt. Ch., Arcadia, N.C., 1983-85; prof. Christianity Brewton-Parker Coll., Mount Vernon, Ga., 1989-91; pub., pres. Smyth & Helwys, Macon, 1990—, also bd. dirs., 1990. Assoc. provost for acad. publs., pub. Mercer U. Press, Macon, 1991—; assoc. prof. Coll. Liberal Arts, Mercer U., 1991—. Editor: Interpreting Isaiah for Preaching and Teaching, 1991, Interpreting Hosea for Preaching and Teaching, 1993, Interpreting Amos for Preaching and Teaching, 1995, Why I Am a Baptist: Preserving the Baptist Heritage for the 21st Century, 1999; contbr. articles to profl. jours. Recipient Am. scholarship Regent's Park Coll., 1986-87, G. Henton Davies Prize in Hebrew, 1985, R.T. Daniel award in Old Testament, 1983, Baggott award Furman U., 1980, Richard Furman Bapt. Heritage award Furman U., 2000. Mem. Soc. Biblical Lit., Am. Acad. Religion, Nat. Assn. Bapt. Profs. Religion, Rotary (local chpt.). Home: 103 Plantation Oaks Dr Macon GA 31220-8757 Office: 6316 Peake Rd Macon GA 31210-3960

STATON, DAVID MICHAEL, JR. public relations executive; b. Parkersburg, W.Va., Mar. 8, 1970; s. David Michael and Lynn Spencer Staton. B in Polit. Sci., W.Va. U., 1992, MPA, 1994; Campaign Mgmt. Cert., Leadership Inst., Washington, 1995. V.p. Capitol Link, Inc., Leesburg, Va., 1994—2002. Vol. Mick Staton for Congress, Charleston, 1978—82; Sterling coord. Jerry Kilgore for Atty. Gen., 2001; Sugarland Run coord. Mark Earley for Gov., Sterling, 2001. Mem.: Loudoun Taxpayers Coalition (bd. dirs. 2002), Loudoun County Young Reps. (chmn. 2002—03), Loudoun County Rep. Com. (precinct capt. 2001), Kappa Sigma. Avocations: reading, golf, politics. Home: 13 Simeon Ln Sterling VA 20164 Office: Capitol Link, Inc Ste E 831 South King St Leesburg VA 20175 Home Fax: 703-444-8906; Office Fax: (703) 443-2315. Personal E-mail: mjr@caplink.com. Business E-Mail: mjr@caplink.com.

STATON, DONNA ELLEN, interior designer; b. Newman, Ga., Feb. 26, 1955; d. Ezra Eugene Whittle and Jackie Ruth (Dukes) Jones; m. William Russell Staton, Sept. 22, 1973 (div. Feb. 1977). AA, Art Inst. Atlanta, 1984. Legal sec. Schwall and Huett, Atlanta, 1975-76; word processor Sears, Roebuck and Co., 1976-79; legal sec. Garland Nuuckolls and Kadish, 1979-80; legal word processor Dennis Corry Webb and Carlock, 1980-84; contract sales rep. Seabrook Wallcoverings, Inc., 1984-86; interior designer BAker Interiors, Chamblee, Ga., 1986-87; prin. interior designer Design II and Assocs., Inc., Atlanta, 1987—. Interpreter for the Deaf Marietta First United Meth. Ch., Cobb County, 1986-87; vol. safeway house Safe Night Rest, Marietta, 1987, 88. Mem. Nat. Assn. for Female Execs., Internat. Soc. Internat. Designers, Cobb C. of C. Methodist. Avocations: cross stitch, crochet, water skiing, aerobics, racquetball. Office: Design II and Assocs Inc 200 Sandy Springs Pl Suite 301 Atlanta GA 30328

STATTEL, ROBERT JOHN, music educator; b. Washington, June 9, 1959; s. Raymond John and Henrietta Maria Stattel; m. Mary Therese Harrington, Aug. 5, 1995. MusB, U. Md., 1986; MusM, U. Mich., 1987. Cert. tchr. music grades k-12. Trombone and euphonium player N.Y. Area, N.Y.C., 1995—; instrumental music tchr. New Rochelle Pub. Schs., 1999—2001; band dir. Suffern H.S., 2001—02. Pvt. music tchr., Yonkers, NY, 1995—. With U.S. Army, 1977—80. Recipient 2d pl. award in instrumental competition, Mu Phi Epsilon, 1985, Joseph Delli Carri Meml. Fund award, Lehman Coll. Music Dept., 1999. Mem.: Am. Fedn. Musicians, Internat. Trombone Assn., Internat. Tuba Euphonium Assn. Democrat. Avocations: birdwatching, hiking, camping, photography. Home: 610 Palisade Ave Yonkers NY 10703 Personal E-mail: rodstaple@aol.com.

STATZ, SHELLY ROSE, social worker; b. Sauk City, Wis., May 26, 1976; d. Frank Werner and Susan Ann Statz. B Social Work, U. Wis., 1998; MSW, U. Md., Balt., 1999. Lic. social worker. Adolescent case mgr. Taylor Manor Hosp., Ellicott City, Md., 1999; adolescent and family therapist Robert A. Pascal Youth and Family, Severna Park, 2000-01; social worker Harbor Hosp., Balt., 2001—, Mercy Hosp., Balt., 2001. Therapist Md. Psychol. Laurel, Md. Acting dir. adolscent mental health & addictions Act II, Laurel, Md., 2000—01. Mem. NASW, Nat. Assn. Christian Social Workers, Epiphany Assn. Roman Catholic. Avocations: vocalist, musician. E-mail: Shellysw99@yahoo.com.

STAUB, AUGUST WILLIAM, drama educator, theatrical producer, director; b. New Orleans, Oct. 9, 1931; s. August Harry and Laurel (Elfer) S.; m. Patricia Gebhardt, Nov. 22, 1952; 1 child, Laurel Melicent. BA, La. State U., 1952, MA, 1956, PhD, 1960. Instr., tech. dir. La. State U., 1955; instr. Ea. Mich. U., 1956-58; assoc. dir. Dunes Summer Theatre, Michigan City, Ind., summers 1957-60; asst. prof., assoc. dir. univ. theatre U. Fla., 1960-64; assoc. prof. U. New Orleans, 1964-66, prof., chmn. dept. drama and communications, 1966-76; prof., head drama dept. U. Ga., 1976-95. Exec. producer Jekyll Island Mus. Comedy Festival, 1984-88, Highlands (N.C.) Playhouse, 1989-2000, Ga. Repertory Theatre, 1991-95; staff dir. Theatre in the Square, Marietta, Ga.; exec. sec. Theatres of La.; v.p. New Orleans Internat. Jazz Festival, 1967-69; pres. S.W. Theatre Conf., 1973-74. Author: Lysistrata, 1968, The Small Chicken, 1969, A Small Bare Space, 1970, Introduction to Theatrical Arts, 1971, Creating Theatre, 1973, Varieties of Theatrical Arts, 1980, 83, 94; gen. editor: Artists and Ideas in the Theatre (Peter Lang), 1989—; assoc. editor Speech Tchr., 1966-68, So. Speech Comm. Jour., 1974-77, Quar. Jour. Speech, 1977-79. Bd. dirs. Friends Ga. Mus., Athens, Ga. Symphony, Coun. Arts for Children, New Orleans, New Orleans Ctr. Creative Arts, Athens Arts. Commn., Ga. Alliance Arts Edn. Lt. AUS, 1952-54. Recipient Creativity in Rsch. medallion U. Ga., 1987, Disting. Svc. award S.W. Theater Conf., 1985; La. State U. Found. Disting. Faculty fellow, 1970-71. Fellow Coll. of Fellows of Am. Theatre (bd. dirs. 1999-2001), Coll.

of Fellows of the S.W. Theatre Assn.; mem. Am. Theatre Assn. (pres. 1985-86, bd. dirs.), Univ. and Coll. Theatre Assn. (pres. 1974-75), Nat. Assn. Schs. Theatre (pres. 1981-83), Univ. Resident Theatre Assn. (bd. dirs. 1976-79), Inst. European Theatre, Nat. Theatre Conf., Am. Soc. Theatre Rsch., Internat. Fedn. Theatre Rsch. Home: 190 Ravenwood Ct Athens GA 30605-3340 E-mail: gusstaub@earthlink.net. *How good it is to be able to spend a lifetime doing what one loves to do.*

STAUB, MARTHA LOU, retired elementary education educator; b. Cumberland, Md., May 29, 1939; d. Walter W. and Velma Grace (Darr) McCoy; m. Paul L. Staub, Apr. 11, 1964; children: Desiree, Paul, Sharon, Lucy, Charles. BS, Frostburg State U., 1961; postgrad., We. Md. State U., 1983; MS, Towson State Coll., 1983; student, Loyola Coll., 1988. Cert. tchr. 1st-mid. sch., Md. Elem. tchr. Cumberland Valley, Bedord, Pa., Garrett County, Oakland, Md., Carroll County, Westminster, Balt. County Bd. Edn., Towson, Md. With peer coaching, 1990-93, master learning, 1989-91. Recipient Excellence in Edn. award Baltimore County, 1990-91; honored by Randallstown Elem. PTA, 1989; donation made in her honor Christa McAuliffe scholarship fund, 1990. Mem. ASCD, NEA (Excellence in Teaching honor 1992), Md. State Tchrs. Assn., Tchr.'s Assn. of Balt. County Orgn., PTA, Md. Coun. Tchrs. Math., Women Educators of Balt. County Orgn., Delta Kappa Gamma. Home: 710 Melendez Way Lady Lake FL 32159-9265

STAUB, SHALOM DAVID, cultural organization administrator; b. Bklyn., Jan. 28, 1956; s. Daniel Marvin and Miriam (Rosen) S.; m. Janet Eleanor Frankel, Sept. 2, 1979; 2 children. BA, Wesleyan U., 1977, MA, 1978; PhD, U. Pa., 1985. Dir. folklife program Pa. Heritage Affairs Commn., Harrisburg, 1982-87, exec. dir., 1987-95; pres., CEO Inst. Cultural Partnerships, 1995—. Vis. prof. dept. religion and anthropology Dickinson Coll., Carlisle, Pa., 1987, 2001—. Author: Yemenis in New York City, 1989, Craft and Community, 1989; editor Jewish Folklore & Ethnology Rev., 1979-91. Active Jewish Burial Soc., Harrisburg, 1984—; chmn., instr. High Sch. of Jewish Studies, Harrisburg, 1995—. Fgn. Lang./Area Studies fellow U.S. Dept. of Edn., 1980-82; recipient Ione Vargus Multicultural award Multicultural Rsch. and Tng. Inst., Temple U., 1993. Fellow: Soc. Applied Anthropology, Am. Anthrop. Assn.; mem.: Am. Folklore Soc. (exec. sec.-treas. 1991—2000, editor newsletter 1991—2000). Avocations: tae kwon do, skiing, biking. Office: Inst Cultural Partnerships 3211 N Front St Ste 104 Harrisburg PA 17110-1342 E-mail: staub@culturalpartnerships.org.

STAUB, W. ARTHUR, health care products executive; b. Detroit, Dec. 25, 1923; s. Edward Elmer and Emma Josephine (Fleury) S.; m. Alla Elizabeth Edwards, June 26, 1948; children: James Randall, Sally Ann, David Scott. BS, Dartmouth Coll., 1944; MD, Temple U., 1947. Intern Muhlenberg Hosp., Plainfield, N.J., 1947-48; resident in pediatrics Abington (Pa.) Meml. Hosp., 1950-51; practice medicine specializing in pediatrics Westfield (N.J.) Med. Group, 1948-63; assoc. med. dir. Ciba Pharm. Co., Summit, N.J., 1963-66; med. dir., v.p. life sci. div. Becton-Dickinson and Co., Rutherford, 1966-70; v.p. med. affairs C. R. Bard Co., Murray Hill, 1970-88, also bd. dirs. Bd. dirs. Crestmont Fed. Savs. and Loan Assn., Edison, N.J., Colonial Trust Nat. Bank, North Palm Beach, Fla.; cons. Children's Specialized Hosp., Westfield, 1948-88, Overlook Hosp., Summit, 1948-88. Contbr. articles to profl. jours. Deacon Presbyn. Ch., Westfield, 1959—. Ensign USNR, 1944—50, to capt. USAF, 1944—50. Fellow Am. Coll. Physician Execs.; mem. AAAS, Assn. Advancement Med. Instrumentation, Health Industry Mfrs. Assn. (chmn. med. and sci. steering com.). Clubs: Echo Lake Country (Westfield) (bd. trustees 1984-88); Lost Tree (North Palm Beach, Fla., bd. govs. 1989-94, sec. 1989-94); Skytop (Pa.). Republican. Presbyterian. Avocations: golf, physical fitness, reading, sailing, travel. Home: 3330 Devonshire Way Palm Beach Gardens FL 33418 E-mail: DoctorWAS@aol.com.

STAUBER, CYNTHIA B. medical/surgical nurse; b. Pitts., Oct. 26, 1962; d. Joseph and Antoinette (D'Onofrio) Berg; m. Mark W. Stauber, May 26, 1984; children: Eric Joseph, Ryan Matthew, Brad Michael. BS in Biology, BS in Sociology cum laude, LaRoche Coll., 1984; RN, Louise Suydam McClintic Sch., Nursing, St. Margaret Meml. Hosp., Pitts., 1986. Med./surg. clin. level 3 staff nurse U.P.M.C. Passavant Hosp., Pitts.; level 1 and 2 clin. nursing instr. C.C. of Allegheny County. Recipient Elizabeth Montgomery Nursing Scholarship, 1985, Arthur Murtland Scully award for High Scholastic Achievement, 1986. Mem. St. Margaret Meml. Alumni Assn., LaRoche Coll. Alumni Assn.

STAUBER, MARILYN JEAN, retired secondary and elementary school; b. Duluth, Minn., Feb. 5, 1938; d. Harold Milton and Dorothy Florence (Thompson) Froehlich; children: Kenneth D. and James H. Atkinson; m. Lawrence B. Stauber Sr., Jan. 11, 1991. BS in Edn., U. Minn., Duluth, 1969, MEd in Math., 1977. Cert. elem. and secondary reading tchr., remedial reading specialist, devel. reading tchr., reading cons. Sec. div. vocat. rehab. State Minn., Duluth, 1956-59; sec. Travelers Ins. Co., 1962-66; lead tchr. Title 1 reading and math. Proctor, Minn., 1969-98. Mem. choirs and Choral Soc. John Duss Music, chairperson Outreach, Forbes Meth. Ch., proctor. Mem. NEA, VFW, Internat. Reading Assn., Nat. Reading Assn., Minn. Arrowhead Reading Coun., Elem. Coun. (pres. 1983-84, 86-87), Proctor Fedn. Tchrs. (recert. com. 1980—, treas. 1981-86), Proctor Edn. Assn. (chairperson recert. com.), Am. Legion, Phi Delta Kappa. Home: 6713 Grand Lake Rd Saginaw MN 55779-9782

STAUBITZ, ARTHUR FREDERICK, lawyer, healthcare products company executive; b. Omaha, Mar. 14, 1939; s. Herbert Frederick Staubitz and Barbara Eileen (Dallas) Alderson; m. Linda Medora Miller, Aug. 18, 1962; children: Michael, Melissa, Peter. AB cum laude, Wesleyan U., Middletown, Conn., 1961; JD cum laude, U. Pa., 1964. Bar: Ill. 1964, U.S. Dist. Ct. (no. dist.) Ill. 1964, U.S. Ct. Appeals (7th cir.) 1964, Pa. 1972. Assoc. Sidley & Austin, Chgo., 1964-71; sr. internat. atty., asst. gen. counsel, dir. Japanese ops. Sperry Univac, Blue Bell, Pa., 1971-78; from asst. to assoc. to dep. gen. counsel Baxter Internat. Inc., Deerfield, Ill., 1978-85, v.p., dep. gen. counsel, 1985-90; v.p. Baxter Diagnostics, 1990-91; sr. v.p., sec., gen. counsel Amgen, Inc., Thousand Oaks, Calif., 1991-92; v.p., gen. mgr. Ventures Group Baxter World Trade Corp., Deerfield, Ill., 1992-93; v.p., sec., gen. counsel Baxter Internat. Inc., 1993, sr. v.p., gen. counsel, 1993-97, sr. v.p. portfolio strategy, 1997-98. Bd. dirs. Aastrom Bioscis., Inc. Mem. Planning Commn., Springfield Twp., Montgomery County, Pa., 1973-74, mem. Zoning Hearing Bd., 1974-78; bd. dirs. Twp. H.S. Dist. 113, Deerfield and Highland Park, Ill., 1983-91, pres., 1989-91; trustee Food and Drug Law Inst., 1991-92, 93-96, Carthage Coll., Kenosha, Wis., 1996—, exec. com., 1999—; bd. dirs. Music of the Baroque, 1994-2001, vice-chmn. Mem. ABA. Episcopalian. Home: 6251 E Placita Aspecto Tucson AZ 85750 E-mail: staubitz@msn.com.

STAUBUS, GEORGE JOSEPH, accounting educator; b. Brunswick, Mo., Apr. 26, 1926; s. George Washington and Florence Lidwina (Pittman) S.; m. Sarah Mayer, Apr. 11, 1949; children: Lindsay, Martin, Paul, Janette. BS, U. Mo., 1947; MBA, U. Chgo., 1949, PhD, 1954. C.P.A., Ill. Instr. U. Buffalo, 1947-49, U. Chgo., 1950-52; asst. prof. then prof. acctg. U. Calif.-Berkeley, from 1952, now Michael N. Chetkovich prof. emeritus. Vis. prof. NYU, 1965, London Bus. Sch., 1966-67, U. Kans., 1969-70; Erskine lectr. U. Canterbury, New Zealand, 1972, 91. Author: A Theory of Accounting to Investors, 1961, Activity Costing and Input-Output Accounting, 1971, Making Accounting Decisions, 1977, An Accounting Concept of Revenue, 1980, Activity Costing for Decisions, 1988, Economic Influences on the Development of Accounting in Firms, 1996, The Decision-Usefulness Theory of Accounting: A Limited History, 2000. Served with USN, 1944-46. Recipient Disting. prof. Calif. Soc. C.P.A.s, 1981 Fellow Acctg. Researchers Internat. Assn. (treas. 1981-83); mem. Am. Acctg. Assn. (disting. internat. lectr. 1982), Am. Inst. C.P.A.s, Fin. Execs. Inst. Office: UC Berkeley Haas Sch Bus Berkeley CA 94720-0001

ST AUBYN, FREDERIC CHASE, French language educator; b. Russell, Kans., Sept. 30, 1921; s. Ernest Leicester and Beulah Elvira (Chase) St. A. B, S.W. Mo. State U., Springfield, 1942; M, Yale U., 1947, D, 1952. Instr. SUNY, Harpur Coll., Endicott, 1950-54; asst. prof. U. Del., Newark, 1954-61; assoc. prof., prof. Elmira (N.Y.) Coll., 1961-72; prof. French U. Pitts., 1972-86, prof. emeritus, 1986—. Author: Stéphane Mallarmé, 1969, 89, Arthur Rimbaud, 1975, 88, Charles Péguy, 1977; (catalogue) William J. Jones Collections, 1986; co-editor: Sartre: Les Mouches, 1963, 3 Pièces Surréalistes, 1969; lit. critic 51 articles, 1949—, 160 revs, 1953—. Sgt. USAF, 1942-45. Recipient Chevalier, French Govt. Ordre des Palmes Académiques, 1986. Mem. MLA (life), Am. Assn. Tchrs. French (life). Democrat. Presbyterian. Avocations: literary critic, Arthur Rimbaud/Michel Butor publications collecting. Home: 200 Leeder Hill Dr Apt 338 Hamden CT 06517-2728

STAUDER, MICHAEL H. lawyer; b. St. Louis, Nov. 20, 1944; s. Harry W. and Mary Jane S.; m. Theresa L. Stauder; children: Michael Stauder Jr., C. Brooke Stauder, Kelly Morrison, Kristen Morrison, Marissa Lynn Stauder. BA in Bus. Adminstrn., Christian Bros. U., 1966; JD, U. Miss., 1969. Bar: Miss. 69, Fla. 72. Spl. agt. FBI, Washington, 1969-72; pvt. practice North Palm Beach, Fla., 1972—. Mem. ATLA, Fla. Trial Lawyers Assn., Soc. Former FBI Agts. (pres. Palm Beach chpt. 1975-76). Office: 1201 US Highway One Ste 315 North Palm Beach FL 33408 E-mail: staudmike@adelphia.net.

STAUDERMAN, ALBERT PHILIP, JR. media consultant; b. Englewood, N.J., Dec. 14, 1936; s. Albert Philip Stauderman and Martha Louise (Dodd) Williamson; m. Helen MacKenzie Layton, Dec. 27, 1958; children: Elizabeth, Sarah, Edward (Ted). BSc, Syracuse U., 1958. Audio-visual prodn. supr. Luth. Ch. in Am., Phila., 1960-64; TV comml. prodn. supr. Procter & Gamble, Cin., 1964-71, assoc. mgr., 1971-82; dir. advt. prodn. Richardson-Vicks, Wilton, Conn., 1982-85; chmn., CEO Bird Bonette Stauderman Inc., Westport, 1985—; co-chmn., dir. Bird Bonette Stauderman Europe Ltd., London, 1996-2000, chmn., dir., 2000—, founder Sao Paulo, Brazil, 2001—; ptnr. Stauderman/Petray, LLC, Westport, Conn., 2001—. Pres. Dikaia Found., Inc., 1995—2001. Author: TV Commercial Production Cost Trends, 1985, 2d. edit., 1986; writer, dir. various pub. svc. TV Commls., 1970-82; actor Golden Age TV programs, 1949-56. Commr. Wilton (Conn.) Water and Inland Wetlands Commns., 1988—; founding pres. Syracuse U. Newhouse Sch. Alumni Assn., 1985—87; mgmt. com. vice chmn. office for comms. Luth. Ch. in Am., NY, 1978—86; chmn. comms. unit Ohio Synod of Luth. Ch. in Am., Columbus, 1978—82; pres. congregation and coun. St. Michael's Luth. Ch., New Canaan, Conn., 1999—2001. Recipient Alumni Svc. award Syracuse U., 1981. Mem. Sprite Island Yacht Club (chmn. race com. 1993-98), Williams Club (N.Y.C.). Republican. Avocations: sailing race management official.

STAUDERMAN, BRUCE FORD, writer, advertising executive; b. Jersey City, Mar. 17, 1919; b. Herbert Henry and Helen Ann (Jacobus) S.; m. Claude Outhier, Mar. 23; 1946. Student, Syracuse U., 1936-38, TV Workshop, N.Y.C., 1949-50, Sch. TV Technique, 1950. V.p. TV, radio, films Meldrum & Fewsmith, Inc. (advt. agy.), Cleve., 1954-62, exec. v.p., chmn. plans bd., exec. creative dir., 1973-79; v.p., creative dir. Ogilvy & Mather (advt. agy.), N.Y.C., 1962-69, Kenyon & Eckhardt, Inc. (advt. agy.), N.Y.C., 1979-83, Barnhart & Co. (advt. agy.), Denver, 1983-84; pres. Stauderman Advt., 1984—; v.p., creative dir. Mktg. Resources Group (advt. agy.), 1985-88. Dir. TV, Intermarco-Elvinger (advt. co.), Paris, 1969-73; TV cons. gov., Ohio, 1958; mem. coun., judge C.L.I.O. Festival, 1960— ; chmn. Paris jury, 1969-73; jury mem. Internat. Advt. Film Festival, Cannes, Venice, 1976— Radio, TV program writer: House of Mystery, The Big Story, Columbia Workshop, 1946-51; writer, producer, dir., WXEL-TV, Cleve., 1951-54. Mem. men's com. Cleve. Playhouse, 1958-62; chmn. TV com. Cleve. United Fund, 1958-59. Served from pvt. to 2d lt. AUS, 1941-46; to 1st lt. N.G. Essex Troop AUS, 1948-50. Mem. Am. Assn. Advt. Agys. (TV and radio adminstrs. com. 1958-62), Am. Fedn. TV and Radio Artists, Naval Club (London). Home: 8647 Falcon Green Dr West Palm Beach FL 33412-1576 E-mail: bfswriter@aol.com.

STAUDINGER, HERIBERT WOLFGANG, pulmonologist; b. Werl, Germany, Dec. 25, 1951; s. Hugo and Hilde (Kröger) S.; m. Ursel Lange; children: Philipp, Lucas. MD, Albert Ludwigs U., Freiberg, Germany, 1978. Asst. physician Hamburg (Germany) Gen. Hosp., 1979-83, Wandsbek Gen. Hosp., Hamburg, 1983-87; head of dept. Byk-Gulden Pharm., Konstanz; therapeutic area head respiratory medicine Boehringer Ingelheim (Germany) GmbH, 1990-96; group dir. asthma and allergy Rhone-Poulenc-Rorer, Paris, 1996-98, v.p. clin. rsch. allergy, asthma and clin. immunology Kennilworth, N.J., 1998—. Contbr. articles to profl. jours. Scholar German Acad. Exch. Svc., Eng. Mem. Hosp. Drs. Assn. (pres. 1980-82), Am. Thoracic Soc., European Respiratory Soc. Mem. Social Dem. Party. Avocation: mountain biking. Home: 53 Vanderveer Dr Basking Ridge NJ 07920 Office: 2015 Galloping Hill Rd Kenilworth NJ 07033 E-mail: heribert.staudinger@spcorp.com.

STAUFF, WILLIAM JAMES, college official; b. Providence, Mar. 2, 1949; s. William A. and Charlotte A. (Thorpe) S.; m. Bertha Nichols, Jan. 22, 1972; children: William J., Heidi A., Anneliese C. BSBA, Northea. U., Boston, 1977; MBA, Suffolk U., 1983; ABS, Moody Bible Inst. Chgo., 1992-97; ThD, Bethany Theol. Sem., Dothan, Ala., 1997. Process writer, indsl. engr. Rockwell Internat., Hopedale, Mass., 1972-77; bus. mgr., acct. Luth. Svc. Assn. New Eng., Framingham, 1977-80; mgr. acctg. and fin. Office Info. Tech. Harvard U., Cambridge, 1980-89; dir. bus. ops. facilities mgmt. U. Va., Charlottesville, Va., 1989-97; mgr. commitment sys. Billy Graham Evangelistic Assn., Mpls., 1997-2000; v.p. Erskine Coll., Due West, S.C., 2000—. Pub. acctg. auditor Charles Murphy/Paul Haggerty, CPAs, Framingham, 1977-80. Mem. Assn. Higher Edn. Facilities Officers. Avocations: gardening, music, teaching. E-mail: stauff@erskine.edu.

STAUFFER, ELIZABETH CLARE, elementary school educator, music choral director, consultant; b. Waterbury, Conn., May 15, 1948; d. Harold Henry and Minerva May (Mattoon) S. B.A., Fairleigh Dickinson U., 1970; M.S., So. Conn. State U., 1973, 6th year diploma, 1978; postgrad., Christ Ch. Coll., Oxford (Eng.) U., 1994, 95—. Cert. tchr. elem. edn., music edn., intermediate adminstrn. and supervision, Conn., Sexual Assault Crisis Counselor, Conn. Tchr. music pub. schs., Clyde, N.Y., 1970-71; tchr. Children's Corner, Inc., Stamford, Conn., 1973-79; tchr. pub. schs., Naugatuck Conn., 1972— ; cons., adviser Children's Corner, Inc., Stamford, 1979-84; dir. Sweet Adelines, Inc., Waterbury, 1981— . Contbr. articles to profl. jours.; arranger songs for barbershop harmony, 1983. Mem. Republican Town Com., Seneca Falls, N.Y., 1971; edn. chmn. Town Bicentennial Com., Naugatuck, 1975-76; v.p. PTO, Naugatuck 1975-77. Mem. Naugatuck Tchrs. League (bldg. rep. 1972, 75, 78, 85, 99-03), Negotiations Com., 1985,87, 90, 92, 95, 98, 2001, 02, Conn. Edn. Assn. (rep. assembly), NEA, Adminstrn. and Supervision Assn., AAUW. Republican. Episcopalian. Avocations: tennis; sailing. Home: 50 Hickory Ln Naugatuck CT 06770-1725 Office: Naugatuck Bd Edn Naugatuck CT 06770

STAUFFER, ERIC P. lawyer; b. Tucson, Feb. 1, 1948; s. Robert D. and Jeanne E. (Catlin) S.; m. Jane F. Snyder, Aug. 2, 1969; children: Curtis Austen, Marcus Elias, Laura Afton. BA, New Coll. of Fla., 1969; JD, Yale U., 1972. Bar: Ariz. 1972, Maine 1974, D.C. 1979. Spl. asst. to gov., fed. state coord. State of Maine, 1973-75; Maine alt. to New England Regional Commn., 1973-75; gen. counsel Maine State Housing Auth., 1976-77; adminstrv. asst. to chmn. Dem. Nat. Com., 1977-78; mem. Preti, Flaherty, Beliveau Pachios & Haley, LLC, Portland, Maine, 1978—. Bd. dirs. Jr. Achievement Maine, Inc., 1995-98; pres. Goodwill Industries No. New Eng., 1981-82, bd. dirs., 1979-93, 99—. Mem. Am. Health Lawyers Assn., Maine State Bar Assn., Ariz. State Bar, D.C. Bar, Maine Real Estate Devel. Assn. (bd. dirs. 1991—, Pub. Svc. award 1992, Founder's award 2002). Office: Preti Flaherty Beliveau Pachios & Haley LLC PO Box 9546 One City Ctr Portland ME 04112-9546 E-mail: estauffe@preti.com.

STAUFFER, JOANNE ROGAN, steel company official; b. Coatesville, Pa., Oct. 15, 1956; d. Joseph Chester and Anne Mary (Kauffman) Rogan; m. Robert Lee Marvin Stauffer, Oct. 15, 1988. AS in Bus. Adminstrn., Harrisburg Area C.C., 1979, student, 1986-88; BS in Leadership, Duquesne U ., 2000. Store acct. Giant Foods, Harrisburg, Pa., 1977—79; payroll clk. Bethlehem Steel (name changed to Pa. Steel Techs.), Steelton, 1980—83, material and cost acct., 1983—86, cost analyst, 1986—96, bus. mgr. for gen. mech. dept., 1996—2002, coord. steelmaking dept., 2002—. Treas. Pot of Gold Investors, 1997—. Mem. Internat. Platform Assn., Am. Bus. Women's Assn. (corr. sec. Rainbow Valley charter chpt. 1991-92, v.p. 1992-93, pres. 1993-94), Steelton Plant Engrs. Club (sec. 1982-85, v.p. 1985-86, pres. 1986-87). Republican. Avocations: outdoor activities, swimming, horses, reading, crafts. Home: 401 Sheetz Rd Halifax PA 17032-9695

STAUFFER, JOHN EUGENE, engineering company executive; b. Bronxville, N.Y., Sept. 16, 1932; s. Hans and Virginia L. (Deimel) S.; m. Valerie Brown, June 5, 1956; children: Jill, Karen, John Christian, Peter Eugene. BS, Princeton U., 1954; ChemE, MIT, 1957; PhD, Worcester Poly. Inst., 1960. With Stauffer Chem. Co., Westport, Conn., 1960-83; pres. Stauffer Tech., Greenwich, 1093—. Author: Quality Assurance of Food, 1988; numerous patents in field. Mem. Greenwich Planning and Zoning Commn., 1972-76. Office: Stauffer Tech 6 Pecksland Rd Greenwich CT 06831-3738

STAUFFER, JOHN WILLIAM, cultural historian; b. Lincoln, Nebr. s. William Albert and Jean Stanley Stauffer. MALS in Humanities, Wesleyan U., 1991; MA in Am. Studies, Purdue U., 1993; PhD in Am. Studies, Yale U., 1999. Asst. prof. Harvard U., Cambridge, Mass., 1999-2001, assoc. prof., 2001—. Spkr. in field. Author: The Black Hearts of Men, 2002; contbr. articles to profl. jours. Rec. clk. New Haven Friends, 1997. Newhouse fellow in writing Yale U., 1996-97, Rsch. fellow, 1994-95, History and Am. Studies Rsch. fellow, 1996, Marcia Brady Tucker fellow, 1994-95, New Britain Mus. of Am. Art fellow New Britain Mus., 1994, Charlotte Newcombe fellow Woodrow Wilson Nat. Fellowship Found., 1997-98; grantee NEH, 1999; recipient Ralph Henry Gabriel prize, 1999, Jan Thaddeus Tchg. award Harvard U., 2002, Frederick Douglass Book prize, 2002. Mem. Soc. for Values in Higher Edn., Orgn. of Am. Historians (presenter ann. mtg. 1998), SHEAR, Am. Studies Assn. (Ralph Henry Gabriel prize 1999), Daguerreian Soc., Phi Kappa Phi. Avocation: dance (jazz, ballet), photography. Home: 13 Ware St Apt 14 Cambridge MA 02138-4010 Office: Harvard U Dept English Barker Ctr 12 Quincy St Cambridge MA 02138-3804 E-mail: stauffer@fas.harvard.edu.

STAUFFER, RONALD EUGENE, lawyer; b. Hempstead, N.Y., Jan. 22, 1949; s. Hiram Eugene and Florence Marie (Hintz) S.; m. Vicki Lynn Hartman, June 12, 1973; children: Eric Alan, Craig Aaron, Darren Adam. SB, MIT, 1970; JD magna cum laude, Harvard U., 1973. Bar: D.C. 1973, U.S. Ct. Mil. Appeals 1976, U.S. Tax Ct. 1979. Ptnr. Hogan & Hartson, Washington, 1977-87, Sonnenschein Nath & Rosenthal, Washington, 1988—. Contbr. articles to profl. publs. Capt. U.S. Army, 1970-77. Mem. ABA (chair TIPS Employee Benefits Com. 1977—), D.C. Bar Assn., Tau Beta Pi, Sigma Gamma Tau. Avocations: running, water skiing. Home: 10207 Woodvale Pond Dr Fairfax Station VA 22039-1658 Office: Sonnenschein Nath & Rosenthal 1301 K St NW Ste 600 Washington DC 20005-3317

STAUFFER, SCOTT WILLIAM, lawyer, accountant; b. Oshkosh, Wis., Aug. 17, 1954; s. Robert Edward and Shirley Lydia (Wrasse) S.; m. Debralee Bowland, Nov. 14, 1987. BBA in Acctg., U. Wis., 1975; JD, U. Denver, 1979. Bar: Colo. 1979; CPA, Colo. Tax acct. Arthur Andersen & Co., Denver, 1979-82; tax mgr. Gary-Williams Oil, Englewood, Colo., 1982-85; pvt. practice Aurora, 1986—. Pres. Colo. Chorale, Denver, 1984-85, 92-93. Mem. ABA, AICPA, Colo. Bar Assn. (mem. multidisciplinary practice taskforce 2000—, ethics com. 1997-99), Denver Bar Assn. (chmn. law office mgmt. com. 1993-95, intraprofl. com. 1997—), Colo. Soc. CPAs (chmn. fed. tax com. 1994-96, mem. 1999-2000, bd. dirs. 2000—), Am. Assn. Atty.-CPAs., Denver Tax Assn. Lutheran. Avocations: golf, travel, reading, computer. Home: 8147 W Frost Pl Littleton CO 80128-4325 Office: 2851 S Parker Rd Ste 720 Aurora CO 80014-2728 E-mail: swstauff@ix.netcom.com.

STAUFFER, STANLEY HOWARD, retired newspaper and broadcasting executive; b. Peabody, Kans., Sept. 11, 1920; s. Oscar S. and Ethel L. (Stone) S.; m. Suzanne R. Wallace, Feb. 16, 1945 (div. 1961); children: Peter, Clay, Charles; m. Elizabeth D. Priest, July 14, 1962 (div. 1991); children: Elizabeth, Grant; m. Madeline A. Sargent, Nov. 27, 1992. AB, U. Kans., 1942; DHL (hon.), Washburn U., 2001. Assoc. editor Topeka State Jour., 1946-47; editor, pub. Santa Maria (Calif.) Times, 1948-52; rewrite and copy editor Denver Post, 1953-54; staff mem. AP (Denver bur.), 1954-55; exec. v.p. Stauffer Publs., Inc., 1955-69; gen. mgr. Topeka Capital-Jour., 1957-69; pres. Stauffer Comm., Inc., 1969-86, chmn., 1986-92. Bd. dirs., chmn. Morris Comm. Fnd. Past pres. Topeka YMCA; past chmn. adv. bd. St. Francis Hosp.; past chmn. Met. Topeka Airport Authority; trustee William Allen White Found., Menninger Found., Midwest Rsch. Inst., Washburn U. Endowment Assn. With USAAF, 1942-45. Named Chpt. Boss of Yr. Am. Bus. Women's Assn., 1976, Outstanding Kans. Pub. Kappa Tau Alpha, 1980, Legion of Honor De Molay, Topeka Phi of Yr., 1971 Mem. Kans. Press Assn. (past pres.), Inland Daily Press Assn. (past dir.), Air Force Assn. (past pres. Topeka), Kans. U. Alumni Assn. (past dir.), Kans. C. of C. and Industry (past chmn.), Def. Orientation Conf. Assn., Topeka Country Club, Top of the Tower Club, Garden of the Gods Club, La Quinta (Calif.) Country Club, Masons (32d deg.), Arab Shrine, Phi Delta Theta (past chpt. pres.), Sigma Delta chi (past chpt. pres.). Episcopalian (past sr. warden).

STAUFFER, THOMAS GEORGE, retired hotel executive; b. Akron, Ohio, Mar. 4, 1932; s. Caldwell E. and Rose C. (Ortscheidt) S.; m. Lois Campsey, June 18, 1960. BS, Case Western Res. U., 1954. Cert. hotel adminstr. Pres. Renaissance Hotels Internat. (Ams.), 1954-98; ret., 1998. Trustee Cleve. Bot. Garden. Recipient Legion of Honor, Order of DeMolay. Mem. Am. Hotel and Motel Assn., Urban Land Inst., Nat. Restaurant Assn. (dir.), Rolling Rock Club, Lakewood Country Club, Masons, Shriners, Sigma Chi (Significant Sigma Chi). Home: 19 Warwick Ln Cleveland OH 44116-2305 Office: Renaissance Hotels Internat Marriott Dr Washington DC 20058-0001 E-mail: tomgstau@aol.com.

STAUFFER, THOMAS MICHAEL, former university president; b. Harrisburg, Pa., Dec. 5, 1941; s. John Nisley and Louise Lee Stauffer; m. Marion Walker, Aug. 26, 1966 (div. Dec. 1989); children: Amity Juliet, Courtney Amanda, Winston Thomas; m. Deborah Whisnand, May 16, 1993; 1 stepchild, Elizabeth Stinson. Student, Juniata Coll., 1959-61; BA cum laude, Wittenberg U., Ohio, 1963; Cert. in E. European Politics, Freie U. Berlin, 1964; MA, PhD, U. Denver, 1973. Asst. dean coll., asst. prof. polit. sci. Keene State Coll., 1968-72; dir. fellows in acad. adminstrn., office leadership devel. Am. Coun. Edn., 1972-78; v.p., dir. div. external relations Am. Council on Edn., Washington, 1978-82; CEO Young Pres. Orgn. Internat., 1994-99. Exec. sec. Fedn. of Assn. of the Acad. Health Care Professions, 1975-80; chmn. task force on the future of Am. Coun. on Edn., 1978; exec. dir. Bus.-Higher Edn. Forum, 1978-81, Nat. Commn. on Higher Edn. Issues, 1980-81; pres., prof. pub. policy U. Houston, Clear Lake, 1982-91; pres., prof. pub. policy and internat. rels. Golden Gate U., 1992—; spl. asst. to adminstr. NASA, 1992; cons. NSF, Dept. State, Coun. for Internat. Exch. Scholars, Japan External Trade Orgn.; mem. Bay Area Internat. Forum; chair nat. bd. Challenger Ctr. for Space Sci. Edn., 1987-89, Ctr. for Advanced Space Studies, 1990-94; mem. dels. on higher edn. and econ. devel. to People's Republic of China, S.E. Asia, Japan, Rwanda, Sri Lanka, United Arab Emirates, 1978-98. Exec. editor Ednl. Record and Higher Edn. and Nat. Affairs, 1978-82; contbr. articles to profl. jours., newspapers, monographs, chpts. to books. Chmn. com. advanced tech. Tex. Econ. Devel., 1984, Houston Com. on Econ. Diversification Planning, 1984, Houston World Trade Ctr. Task Force, 1985, East Tex. 2000 Com. on Econ. Devel., S.E. Tex. Higher Edn. Coun., 1989, Clear Lake Area Econ. Devel. Found.; v.p. Inter-Am., U. Coun. for Econ. and Social Devel., Houston World Trade Assn.; vice chmn. Tex. Sci. and Tech. Coun., 1986; pres. St. John Hosp.; bd. dirs. Houston Hosp. Coun. Found., Tex. Coun. on Econ. Edn., Tex. Senate Space Industry Tech. Commn., Tex. Innovation Info. Network Sys., San Francisco C. of C.; vice-chair San Francisco World Trade Assn.; chair San Francisco Consortium on Higher Edn.; mem. steering com. Houston Econ. Devel. Coun., blue ribbon com. City Coll., Bay Area Coun., Silicon Valley Mfrs. Group; chair San Francisco Mayor's Blue Ribbon Com. on Econ. Devel. Recipient Disting. Alumni award Grad. Sch. Internat. Studies U. Denver, 1989, Tex. Senate Resolution of Commendation, 1991, Challenger Ctr. Nat. award, 1990, ACE Fellow Anniversary award, 1990, Leadership H.S. Do the Right Thing award, 1998; Am. Coun. on Edn. fellow in acad. adminstrn., 1971, Ford Found. and Social Sci. Found. fellow, 1963-68, sr. fellow Am. Leadership Forum. Mem. AAAS, Internat. Studies Assn. (co-chmn. ann. meeting 1978), Am. Hosp. Assn., Policy Studies Orgn., Internat. Assn. Univ. Pres., San Francisco Com. on Fgn. Rels., Oakland C. of C., Sacramento C. of C., San Francisco C. of C. (150th anniversary com.), Commonwealth Club, San Francisco World Trade Club, City Club (bd. govs.), Univ. Club San Francisco. Home: 1806 Green St San Francisco CA 94123-4922 Office: Golden Gate U Office of Pres 536 Mission St San Francisco CA 94105-2967

STAUFFER, VALERIE VILAS, civic volunteer; b. N.Y.C., Aug. 29, 1935; d. Frank Jay and Kathleen Vilas Brown; m. John Eugene Stauffer, June 5, 1956; children: Jill Stauffer Cobbs, Karen Stauffer Murphy, John Christian, Peter Eugene. BA, Wellesley Coll., 1956. V.p. Stauffer Tech., Greenwich,

Conn., 1985—. Editor: (nonfiction) Quality Assurance of Food, 1988, (newsletter) Round Hill Association Newsletter, 1991-92; contbr. Greenwich Rev. mag., 1971-73. Mem., vice chmn. dist. 7 Rep. Town Meeting, Greenwich, Conn., 1984—, chmn. social svcs. com., 1997; chmn. Friends of Greenwich Libr., 1997—99; trustee, exec. com. Greenwich Libr., 1999—. Mem. Greenwich Garden Club (pres. 1999—). Home: 6 Pecksland Rd Greenwich CT 06831-3738 Office: Stauffer Tech 6 Pecksland Rd Greenwich CT 06831-3738 Fax: (203) 618-0479. E-mail: stauftek@aol.com.

STAVELY, KEITH WILLIAMS FITZGERALD, librarian; b. New Brunswick, N.J., May 13, 1942; s. Homer Eaton and Elizabeth (Williams) S.; m. Kathleen Fitzgerald, Aug. 19, 1978; 1 child, Jonathan Keith. BA, Yale U., 1964, PhD, 1969; MLS, Simmons Coll., 1980. Asst. prof. English Boston U., 1969-74, Ohio State U., 1990-91; lectr. in English Boston Coll., 1975-80; adult svcs. libr. Watertown (Mass.) Free Pub. Libr., 1979-89, br. libr., 1984-89, head adult svcs., 1989-90; reference libr. Somerville (Mass.) Pub. Libr., 1991-92; asst. adminstr. Fall River (Mass.) Pub. Libr., 1992-99, adminstr., 1999—. Author: Puritan Legacies: Paradise Lost and the New England Tradition, 1630-1890, 1987, paperback edit., 1990, The Politics of Milton's Prose Style, 1975; co-author: Family Man: What Men Feel About Their Wives, Their Children, Their Parents, and Themselves, 1978; contbr. articles and revs. to profl. publs. Fellow Fulbright Found., India, 1964-65, Am. Coun. Learned Socs., 1988-89, John Simon Guggenheim Meml. Found., 1989. Mem. MLA (Prize for Ind. Scholars 1987), ALA, Mass. Libr. Assn., Phi Beta Kappa.

STAVERT, ALEXANDER BRUCE, bishop; b. Montreal, Apr. 1, 1940; s. R. Ewart and Kathleen H. (Rosamond) S.; m. Diana Greig, June 26, 1982; children: Kathleen, Rosamond, Timothy. Student, Lower Can. Coll., Montreal, 1957; BA, Bishop's U., 1961; STB, U. Toronto, Ont., Can., 1964, ThM, 1976, DD (hon.), 1986. Ordained to ministry Anglican Ch. as deacon, 1964, as priest, 1965. With Mission of Schefferville, Que., 1964-69; fellow, tutor in div. Trinity Coll., U. Toronto, 1969-70, chaplain, 1970-76; with St. Clement's Mission East, St. Paul's River, Que., 1976-81; chaplain Champlain Regional Coll., Bishop's U., 1981-84; dean, rector St. Alban's Cathedral, Prince Albert, Sask., Can., 1984-91; consecrated bishop Anglican Diocese of Que., Quebec, 1991—. Address: Diocese of Que 31 rue des Jardins Quebec QC Canada G1R 4L6 E-mail: diocese_of_quebec@sympatico.ca.

STAVES, SUSAN, English educator; b. N.Y.C., Oct. 5, 1942; d. Henry Tracy and Margaret (McClemon) Staves. AB, U. Chgo., 1963; MA, U. Va., 1964, PhD, 1967. Woodrow Wilson intern Bennett Coll., Greensboro, N.C., 1965-66; from asst. prof. to prof. Brandeis U., Waltham, Mass., 1967-93, Paul Proswimmer prof. of Humanities, 1993—2001, dept. chair, 1986-89, 95-98, prof. emerita, 2001—. Clark prof. UCLA, 1989—90. Co-author (with John Brewer): Early Modern Conceptions of Property, 1994; co-author: (with Cynthia Ricciardi) Elizabeth Griffith's Delicate Distress, 1997; author: Players' Scepters: Fictions of Authority in the Restoration, 1979, Married Women's Separate Property in England, 1660-1833, 1990, Eighteenth Century: Theory and Interpretation, Studies on Voltaire and the 18th Century, (essays) Fetter'd or Free?: Collected Essays on 18th Century Women Novelists, 1986, History, Gender, and 18th Century Literature, 1994, Woman and Political Writing, 1998; contbr. articles to profl. jours. Mem. ACLU, 1967—; assoc. mem. Belmont Dem. Town Com., Belmont, Mass. Fellow Woodrow Wilson fellow, 1963—64, Woodrow Wilson Dissertation fellow, 1966—67, Harvard Liberal Arts fellow, 1980—81, John Simon Guggenheim fellow, 1981—82. Mem.: AAUP, MLA (exec. com. divsn. on late 18th century English lit. 1984—86), English Inst., Am. Soc. for 18th Century Studies (exec. bd. 1987—90). Episcopalian. Avocations: hiking, squash. Office: Brandeis U Dept English MS 023 Waltham MA 02454

STAVIG, MARK LUTHER, English language educator; b. Northfield, Minn., Jan. 20, 1935; s. Lawrence Melvin and Cora (Hjertaas) S.; m. Donna Mae Ring, July 3, 1957; children— Anne Ragnhild, Thomas Edward, Rolf Lawrence BA, Augustana Coll., 1956, Oxford U., 1958, MA, 1962; PhD, Princeton U., 1961. Instr. to asst. prof. English U. Wis., Madison, 1961-68; from assoc. prof. to prof. English Colo. Coll., Colorado Springs, 1968—2001; ret., 2001—. Author: John Ford and the Traditional Moral Order, 1968, The Forms of Things Unknown: Renaissance Metaphor in Romeo and Juliet and A Midsummer Night's Dream, 1995; editor: Ford, 'Tis Pity She's a Whore, 1966. Fellow Danforth Found., 1956-61, Woodrow Wilson Found., 1956-57; Fulbright scholar Oxford U., 1956-58 Mem. MLA, Shakespeare Assn. Am. Democrat. Home: 1409 Wood Ave Colorado Springs CO 80907-7348 Office: Colo Coll Dept English Colorado Springs CO 80903

STAVIS, ROGER LEE, lawyer; b. N.Y.C., Nov. 5, 1958; s. Nathan Joshua and Francine (Green) S.; m. Randy Beth Bielsky, Nov. 22, 1987; 1 child, Allyson P. BA magna cum laude, CUNY, Queens, 1979; JD with honors, George Washington U., 1982. Bar: N.Y. 1983, U.S. Dist. Ct. (so. and ea. dists.) N.Y. 1983, U.S. Ct. Appeals (2d cir.) 1986, U.S. Supreme Ct. 1986, U.S. Ct. Mil. Appeals 1988, U.S. Ct. Appeals (4th cir.) 1991, U.S. Ct. Appeals (3d cir.) 1993. Asst. dist. atty., supervising appellate atty. Bronx County, N.Y., 1982-86; assoc. Litman, Asche, Lupkin and Gioiella, N.Y.C., 1986-88; ptnr. Kartagener and Stavis, 1988-93; pvt. practice, 1993-99; ptnr. Stavis & Kornfeld, LLP, 1999—. Author: (with others) Criminal Trial Advocacy, 1992, Criminal Defense Techniques, 1991. Regents scholar State of N.Y., 1975; recipient Profl. Achievement award George Washington U. Law Alumni Assn., 1995. Mem. ABA, N.Y. State Bar Assn., Assn. Bar City N.Y., N.Y. County Lawyers Assn. Democrat. Jewish. Avocations: golf, reading, antiques. Home: 19 Fernwood Rd Larchmont NY 10538-1704 Office: Stavis & Kornfeld LLP 820 2nd Ave New York NY 10017-4504

STAVITSKY, ABRAM BENJAMIN, immunologist, educator; b. Newark, May 14, 1919; s. Nathan and Ida (Novak) S.; m. Ruth Bernice Okney, Dec. 6, 1942; children: Ellen Barbara, Gail Beth. AB, U. Mich., 1939, MS, 1940; PhD, U. Minn., 1943; VMD, U. Pa., 1946. Research fellow Calif. Inst. Tech., 1946-47; faculty Case Western Res. U., 1947—, prof. microbiology, 1962—, prof. molecular biology and microbiology, 1983-89, emeritus, 1989; mem. expert com. immunochemistry WHO, 1963-83; mem. microbiology fellowship com. NIH, 1963-66; mem. microbiology test com. Nat. Bd. Med. Examiners, 1970-73; chmn. microbiology test com. Nat. Bd. Podiatry Examiners, 1978-82. Mem. editl. bd. Jour. Immunological Methods, 1979-88, Immunopharmacology, 1983-96. Vice pres. Ludlow Community Assn., 1964-66. Fellow AAAS; mem. Am. Assn. Immunologists, Am. Soc. Microbiology, Sigma Xi. Home: 14604 Onaway Rd Cleveland OH 44120-2845 Office: 2119 Abington Rd Cleveland OH 44106-2333

STAVITSKY, LESLEY ALISSON, nonprofit executive, fundraising executive; b. Plainfield, N.J. d. Albert B. Stavitsky and Jayne Marut. BA, Marymount Manhattan Coll., 2000; postgrad., CUNY, 2001; student, Ind. U., 1987. Dir. devel. Legal Aid Soc., N.Y.C., 1987-90; capital campaign dir. NAACP Legal Def. and Ednl. Fund, Inc., 1990-93; dir. devel. Cmty. Svc. Soc., 1993-94, MFY Legal Svcs., Inc., N.Y.C., 1995-99, Partnership with Children, Inc., N.Y.C., 2000—. Cons. Leonore Blitz Assocs., N.Y.C., 1994. Vol. Clinton Presdl. Election Campaign, N.Y.C., 1992, N.Y. CARES, N.Y.C., 1994, Epiphany Roman Cath. Ch.; pediat. vol. NYU Med. Ctr., N.Y.C., 1992-95. Mem.: Assn. Fundraising Profls., Marymount Manhattan Coll. Alumni Assn., Cath. Alumni Club of Archdiocese of NY. Avocations: fine arts, theater, films, photography, creative writing.

STAVOLA, JOHN JOSEPH, retired obstetrician-gynecologist; b. Hartford, Conn., Feb. 4, 1929; MD, N.Y. Med. Coll., 1956. Diplomate Am. Bd. Ob-Gyn., 1964. Intern St. Francis Hosp., Hartford; resident in ob-gyn. Hartford Hosp., 1957-60, asst. dir. ob-gyn., 1965-90; clin. asst. prof. ob-gyn. U. Conn.; pvt. practice, 1962-96; retired, 1996. With USN, 1960-62. Recipient Disting. Svc. award Hartford Hosp., 1997. Fellow Am. Coll. of Ob-Gyn. Home: 3 Danforth Ln West Hartford CT 06110-2435

STAVREV, KRASSIMIR K. chemist, researcher; b. Shumen, Bulgaria, Nov. 11, 1958; s. K. Stavrev and Penka P. Iovcheva; m. Galina N. Nikolova, Sept. 20, 1978 (div. Jan. 1982); 1 child, Nikolay; m. Galina I. Georgieva, Feb. 3, 1985 (div. July 2001); children: Lidia, Iordan; m. Antonia M. Smillova, May 7, 2002. PhD, Sofia U., Bulgaria, 1988. Asst. prof. Sofia U., 1988-92; postdoctoral fellow Scuola Normale Superiore, Pisa, Italy, 1992-94, U. Fla., Gainesville, 1994-97; dir. sci. support Hypercube, Inc., 1997-98; asst. dir. Coll. Medicine, 1998—; rschr. Quantum Theory Project, Gainesville, 1999—. Home: 10000 SW 52d Ave Gainesville FL 32608 Office: Univ of Florida PO Box 100177 Gainesville FL 32610-0177 Home Fax: (603) 794-2408; Office Fax: 352-265-8047. E-mail: krasimir@hpe.ufl.edu.

STAVRO, STEVE A. professional hockey team executive; b. Gavro, Greece, Sept. 27, 1927; m. Sally Stavro; 4 children. Chmn. bd., chief exec. officer Toronto Maple Leafs, Ont., Can.; gov. NHL. Office: Toronto Maple Leafs 60 Carlton St Toronto ON Canada M5B 1L1*

STAVROPOULOS, ROSE MARY GRANT, community activist, volunteer; b. Decatur, Ill. d. Walter Edwin and Ora Lenore (Kepler) Grant; m. Stan Stavropoulos; children: Becky Ann Stavropoulos Betian, Stephanie Diane. BS, Ea. Ill. U., 1954. Cert. elem. edn. Tchr. 2nd grade Garfield Sch., Decatur, 1954-55; bd. dirs. Wilmot Sch. Bd. PTA, Deerfield, 1971-73, Moraine Girl Scout Coun., Deerfield, 1968-75, also bd. dirs. Ill., 1984-89; chmn. Human Rels. Commn., 1975-84; mem. sr. citizen adv. com. Deerfield Park Dist., 1984-89; pres. Lake County (Ill.) LWV, 1979-81; chmn. Deerfield Village Caucus, 1980-82; pres. Caring For Others, Inc., Deerfield, 1986-88, Deerfield Area LWV, 1972-89; bd. mem., pres. Deerfield Area United Way, 1988-89, pres., 1976-93. Mem. Deerfield Village Caucus Adv. Coun., 1980-81, 92-97. Recipient Deerfield Human Rels. Humanitarian award, 1984, Lerner Life's Citizen of Month, 1987. Mem. Deerfield Area Hist. Soc., Highland Park Hosp. Aux, Legacy at Bryant Ranch Home Assn. (bd. dirs. 2001—, treas. 2001—02, sec. 2002-), Delta Zeta. Home: 23959 Sanctuary Pkwy Yorba Linda CA 92887

STAVROPOULOS, WILLIAM S. chemical executive; b. Bridgehampton, N.Y., May 12, 1939; m. Linda Stavropoulos; children: S. William, Angela D. BS in Pharm. Chemistry, Fordham U.; PhD in Medicinal Chemistry, U. Washington; LLD (hon.) , Northwood U., 1998. Rsch. chemist in pharm. rsch. Dow Chem. Co., Midland, Mich., 1967, rsch. chemist for diagnostics product rsch., 1970, rsch. mgr. diagnostics product rsch., 1973, bus. mgr. diagnostics product rsch., 1976, bus. mgr. polyolefins, 1977, dir. mktg. plastics dept., 1979; comml. v.p. Dow Chem. Co. Latin Am., Coral Gables, Fla., 1980; pres. Dow Latin Am., 1984; comml. v.p., basics and hydrocarbons Dow Chem. Co. U.S.A., Midland, 1985-87, group v.p., 1987-90; pres. Dow U.S.A., 1990—; v.p. The Dow Chem. Co., 1990, sr. v.p., 1991, pres., COO, 1993—95, CEO, 1995—2000, chmn., 2001—. Bd. dirs. Dow Corning Corp., The Dow Chem. Co., Marion Merrel Dow Inc.; CEO Essex Chem Corp, 1988-92. Recipient Ellis Island Medal of Honor, 1998, Palladium Medal award, Societe de Chimie Industrielle, 2001. Office: Dow Chem Co 2030 Dow Ctr Midland MI 48674-0001*

STAVROS, PETER JAMES, lawyer; b. N.Y.C., Sept. 16, 1966; s. James P. and Suzanne T. Stavros. BA in English, Duke U., 1988; grad. in creative writing, Harvard U., 1989; JD, U. Ky., 1995. Bar: Ky. 1995, U.S. Dist. Ct. (ea. and we. dists.) Ky. 1995, U.S. Ct. Appeals (6th cir.) 1995, U.S. Ct. Appeals (fed. cir.) 1996, U.S. Supreme Ct. 2000. Reporter AP, Louisville, 1990, Charleston, W.Va., 1990, Indpls., 1991; law clk. Supreme Ct. Ky., Frankfort, 1995-96; assoc. Frost Brown Todd LLC, Louisville, 1996—. Articles editor Ky. Law Jour., 1995. Mem. ABA, Ky. Bar Assn., Louisville Bar Assn. Avocation: triathlons. Office: Frost Brown Todd LLC 400 W Market St Fl 32 Louisville KY 40202-3346 E-mail: pstavros@fbtlaw.com.

STAVROULAKIS, ANTHEA MERRIE, biology educator; b. Bklyn., Nov. 9, 1959; d. Zachary Stavroulakis and Evangeline Stella Spirakis. AA, CUNY, 1978; BA, NYU, 1981, MS, 1984, PhD, 1992. Grad. rsch. asst. in biology NYU, N.Y.C., 1981-92, adj. instr., 1984-89; adj. instr. sci. Borough of Manhattan C.C.-CUNY, 1986-92; asst. prof. CUNY, 1992; adj. instr. natural sci. York Coll.-CUNY, 1989-90; assoc. prof. biol. sci. Kingsborough C.C.-CUNY, 1992—. Adj. instr. biology Suffolk County C.C., 1991-92; jr. rsch. asst. in biology Brookhaven Nat. Lab., 1991-92. Author: Laboratory Manual-General Biology II, 1996, Laboratory Manual: General Biology I, 1999; contbr. articles to profl. jours. Grantee N.Y. State Edn. Dept., 1995-96, C.C. Sci. and Tech. Equipment Fund, N.Y., 1995, Eelgrass Remediation in Jamaica Bay, 1996, 98-2000, Eppley Found., 1999-2000, 2000—. Mem. AAAS, Am. Soc. for Microbiology, Nat. Assn. Biology Tchrs., N.Y. Acad. Scis., Profl. and Staff Congress CUNY. Democrat. Greek Orthodox. Avocations: gourmet cooking, aviculture, gardening, travel. E-mail: E-mail: astravroulakis@kbcc.cuny.edu.

STAWICKI, JOSEPH JOHN, JR. marketing executive; b. New Haven, Nov. 27, 1944; s. Joseph J. Sr. and Tonya (Bolash) S.; m. Barbara Jean Schneider, Jan. 19, 1968, children: Laura, Kevin, Dennis. BS, St. Joseph Coll., 1966; MBA, No. Ill. U., 1968. Investment adminstr. Phoenix Equity Planning Corp., Hartford, Conn., 1971-74; asst. prof. Cen. Conn. State U., New Britain, 1975-81; trade officer New Eng. Trade Assistance Ctr., Boston, 1981-83; dir. ops. Multimate Internat. Corp., East Hartford, Conn., 1983-84; pres. Mercor Resources Corp., Winsted, 1985—, also bd. dirs.; pres. Stawicki Realty, 1988—. Mem. Elks, Sigma Iota Epsilon. Roman Catholic. Home: PO Box 416 Winsted CT 06098-0416 Office: Mercor Resources Corp 135 W Wakefield Blvd Winsted CT 06098-2929

STAWNYCHY, ZORIANA MARIA, financial executive; b. N.Y.C., May 31, 1953; d. Walter and Eugenia (Hanusczcak) Salak; m. Yuri Andrij Stawnychy, Oct. 26, 1985. BA, Fordham U., 1975. Cert. fin. planner, registered investment advisor. Fin. planner Cigna, N.Y.C., 1978-83, 85-90; mgr. Bruce Raines Assocs., 1983-84; sr. fin. counselor Ind. Fin. Services, White Plains, N.Y., 1984-85; owner Stawnychy Fin. Svcs., Inc., Kinnelon, N.J., 1991—. Mem. Fin. Planning Assn. Avocation: tennis.

STAYIN, RANDOLPH JOHN, lawyer; b. Cin., Oct. 30, 1942; s. Jack and Viola (Tomin) S.; children: Gregory S., Todd R., Elizabeth J. BA, Dartmouth Coll., 1964; JD, U. Cin., 1967. Bar: Ohio 1967, U.S. Dist. Ct. (so. dist.) Ohio 1968, U.S. Dist. Ct. D.C. 1977, U.S. Ct. Appeals (6th cir.) 1968, U.S. Ct. Appeals (fed. cir.) 1986, U.S. Supreme Ct. 1974, U.S. Ct. Appeals (D.C. cir.) 1976, U.S. Ct. Internat. Trade, 1985. Assoc. Frost & Jacobs, Cin., 1967-72; exec. asst., dir. of legislation U.S. Sen. Robert Taft, Jr., Washington, 1973-74, chief of staff, 1975-76; assoc. Taft, Stettinius & Hollister, 1977, ptnr., 1978-88, Barnes & Thornburg, Washington, 1988—. Mem. adv. coun. U.S. and FGN. Comml. Svc., U.S. Dept. Commerce. Chmn., mem. numerous coms., chmn., worker campaigns for local politicians Rep. Party state and local orgns.; mem. Citizens to Save WCET-TV, 1967-72, Fine Arts Fund, 1970-72, Cancer Soc., 1970-72; chmn. agy. rels. com. Hamilton County Mental Health and Mental Retardation Bd., 1969-71, vice chmn., 1971, chmn., 1971-72; v.p. Recreation Commn., City of Cin., 1970-72; mem. funds mgmt. com. Westwood 1st Presbyn. Ch., 1968, v.p., 1969, pres., 1970, trustee, 1970, elder, 1971-72; bd. dirs. Evans Mill Pond Owners Assn., v.p., 1986, pres., 1987; chmn. Washington Nat. Cathedral Fund Com., mem. devel. com. Mem.: ABA (sect. on internat. law and practice, vice chmn.com.on nat. legislation 1977—79, internat. sect., anti-trust sect.), D. C. Bar Assn. (com. on internat. law), Internat. Bar Assn., Am. Soc. Assn. Execs. (legal sect., internat. sect.). Avocations: theater, tennis, skiing, travel, reading. Office: Barnes & Thornburg 1401 I St NW Ste 800 Washington DC 20005-2225

STAYTON, THOMAS GEORGE, lawyer; b. Rochester, Minn., May 1, 1948; m. Barbara Joan Feck, Aug. 8, 1970; children: Ryan, Megan. BS, Miami U., Oxford, Ohio, 1970; JD, U. Mich., 1973. Bar: Ind. 1973, U.S. Dist. Ct. (so. dist.) Ind. 1973, U.S. Ct. Appeals (7th cir.) 1977. Ptnr. Baker & Daniels, Indpls., 1973—. Recipient Sagamore of the Wabash Gov. of Ind., 1988. Mem. ABA, Ind. State Bar Assn., Indpls. Bar Assn. Clubs: Indpls. Athletic. Office: Baker & Daniels 300 N Meridian St Ste 2700 Indianapolis IN 46204-1782 E-mail: tstayton@bakerd.com.

ST CLAIR, JAMES SHELDON, agricultural economics educator; b. Pomona, Calif., Aug. 18, 1919; s. Maurice Sheldon and Ruth Joy (Hogan) St. C.; m. Betty Jane Dobson, June 12, 1942; children— Virginia Jill, John Maurice, David Dobson. B.S., U. Calif.-Berkeley, 1941; M.S., U. Ill., 1947, Ph.D., 1956. Instr., Calif. State Poly. U., San Luis Obispo, 1946-50; asst. agrl. economist U. Ariz., Tucson, 1951-55; agrl. economist USDA, Tucson, 1955-57; assoc. prof. agrl. econs. U. Wyo., Laramie, 1957-59, prof., 1959-84, agrl. economist, 1959-84, prof. emeritus, 1984— , acting head div. agrl. econs., 1973, 82-83. Served with USAAF, 1942-45. USDA grantee, 1979-83. Mem. Western Agrl. Econs. Assn. (v.p. 1961-62, pres. 1969-70, Research Achievement award 1959), Am. Agrl. Econs. Assn., Alpha Zeta, Gamma Sigma Delta, Sigma Xi. Democrat. Congregationalist. Home: 711 E Lyons St Laramie WY 82072-2134

STEAD, EUGENE ANSON, JR. physician; b. Atlanta, Oct. 6, 1908; s. Eugene Anson and Emily (White) Stead; m. Evelyn Selby, June 15, 1940; children: Nancy White, Lucy Ellen, William Wallace. BS, Emory U., 1928, MD, 1932. Intern Peter Bent Brigham Hosp., Boston, 1932—33, surg. intern, 1934—35, assoc. medicine, 1939—42, acting physician-in-chief, 1942; rsch. fellow medicine Harvard, 1933—34; asst. resident medicine Cin. Gen. Hosp., 1935—36, resident, 1936—37; instr. medicine U. Cin., 1935—37; resident phys. Thorndike Meml. Lab.; asst. medicine Harvard and Boston City Hosp., 1937—39; from instr. medicine to assoc. Harvard, 1938—42; prof. medicine Emory U.; physician-in-chief Grady Hosp., Atlanta, 1942—46; dean Emory U., 1945—46; physician in chief Duke Hosp., 1947—67; prof. medicine Duke U. Sch. Medicine, 1947—78; disting. physician VA, 1978—85. Editor: Circulation, 1973—78, N.C. Med. Jour., 1983—92; contbr. articles to profl. jours. Mem.: Am. Soc. Clin. Investigation, Assn. Am. Physicians, Am. Fedn. Clin. Rsch., N.C. Med. Soc., Phi Beta Kappa, Sigma Xi, Alpha Omega Alpha. Methodist. Home: 5113 Townsville Rd Bullock NC 27507-9438 Office: Duke U Dept Medicine Durham NC 27710-0001

STEAD, JAMES JOSEPH, JR. securities company executive; b. Chgo., Sept. 13, 1930; s. James Joseph and Irene (Jennings) S.; m. Edith Pearson, Feb. 13, 1954; children: James, Diane, Robert, Caroline. BS, DePaul U., 1957, MBA, 1959. Asst. sec. C. F. Childs & Co., Chgo., 1957-62; exec. v.p., sec. Koenig, Keating & Stead, Inc., Chgo., 1962-66; 2d v.p., mgr. midwest mcpl. bond dept. Hayden, Stone Inc., Chgo., 1966-69; sr. v.p., nat. sales mgr. Ill. Co. Inc., 1969-70; mgr. instl. sales dept. Reynolds and Co., Chgo., 1970-72; partner Edwards & Hanly, 1972-74; v.p., instnl. sales mgr. Paine, Webber, Jackson & Curtis, 1974-76; v.p., regional instl. sales mgr. Reynolds Securities, Inc., 1976-78; sr. v.p., regional mgr. Oppenheimer & Co., Inc., 1978-88; sr. v.p., regional mgr. fixed income Tucker Anthony, 1988—; instr. Mcpl. Bond Sch., Chgo., 1967— . With AUS, 1951-53. Mem. Security Traders Assn. Chgo., Nat. Security Traders Assn., Am. Mgmt. Assn., Mcpl. Fin. Forum Washington. Clubs: Execs., Union League, Mcpl. Bond, Bond (Chgo.); Olympia Fields Country (Ill.); Wall Street (N.Y.C.). Home: 1005 Hickory Ridge Ct Frankfort IL 60423-2114 Office: 1 S Wacker Dr Chicago IL 60606-4614

STEAD, WILLIAM WHITE, physician, educator, public health administrator; b. Decatur, Ga., Jan. 4, 1919; s. Eugene Anson and Emily (White) S.; m. Ethel Barnett, June 14, 1947 (div.); 1 child, Richard Barnett; m. Joan Jordan DeVore, Apr. 22, 1975. AB, Emory U., 1940, MD, 1943. Intern Grady Meml. Hosp., Atlanta, 1944; resident in medicine Emory U., 1944-45, U. Cin., 1946-48, U. Minn., 1948-49, faculty med. schs., 1949-57, U. Fla., 1957-60; prof. medicine Med. Coll. Wis., Milw. County Gen. Hosp., Milw., 1960-72; med. dir. Muirdale Sanatorium, 1963-72; prof. medicine U. Ark. Med. Sch., 1972—; chief pulmonary diseases service VA Hosp., Little Rock, 1972-73, cons., 1973—; dir. Tb control Ark. Health Dept., Little Rock, 1973—; ret., 1998. Cons. VA Hosp., Wood, Wis., 1960-72 Author 3 books on Tb, also numerous articles. Served to lt. (j.g.) M.C. USNR, 1945-46; capt. M.C. AUS, 1953-54. Recipient Tom T. Ross award Ark. Public Health Assn., 1981; Robert S. Abernathy award for excellence in medicine Am. Coll. Physicians, 1984, James D. Bruce award Am. Coll. Physicians, 1988, Emily Bisseel Award, Am. Lung Assn., 2001; research grantee in pulmonary emphysema, 1957-65 Master ACP; mem. AAAS, Am. Fedn. for Clin. Rsch. (nat. sec. 1955-58, v.p. 1958-59, pres. 1959-60), Ctrl. Soc. Clin. Rsch., Am. Soc. Clin. Investigation, Am. Thoracic Soc. (Trudeau medal 1988), Am. Coll. Chest Physicians. Achievements include research on unitary concept of Tb and epidemiology of Tb in prisons and among elderly in nursing homes; chemotherapy of Tb; variation in susceptibility to Tb infection; history of Tb as a global epidemic; suggestion for genetic engineering of material to enhance resistance to initial infection with Tb; prevention of Tb transmission in crowded places by proper use of ultraviolet irradiation.

STEADHAM, RICHARD LYNN, magazine art director; b. Sacramento, Sept. 3, 1951; s. Lyndell Harvey and Dorothy Mae (Dennis) S.; m. Karen Jean Stoner, May 2, 1971; children: Taylor Ryan, Erin Danielle, Nathan Lynn. Book designer/staff illustrator Rev. and Herald Pub. Assn., Hagerstown, Md., 1982-87; art dir. Governing Mag./Congrl. Quarterly, Washington, 1987—. Freelance illustrator, Hagerstown, Md., 1982-88, Woodbridge, Va., 1988—. Editor and designer Art Dirs. Club Newsletter, Halfbleed, 1995. Recipient Merit award Soc. Illustrators, N.Y., 1985, Comm. Arts Illustration Ann., 1994. Mem. Art Dirs. Club of Met. Washington (v.p. publs. 1994-96, Merit award 1993, editor, designer newsletter Halfbleed 1995), Soc. Pub. Designers (Merit award 1994), Va. State Soc. (George Washington chpt.), Nat. Soc. of SAR (editor, designer newsletter The Surveyor, George Washington chpt. 1988-2000, Timen Stiddem Soc. (founding officer, editor, designer of the award-winning newsletter NGS 1998, 99, 2000). Avocations: travel, gardening, family history. Office: Gov Mag-Congrl Quarterly 1100 Connecticut Ave NW Washington DC 20036-4101 E-mail: rsteadham@governing.com.

STEAD LEE, POLLY JAE **See LEE, PALI JAE**

STEADMAN, DAVID ROSSLYN AYTON, business executive, corporate director; b. Wembley, Eng., June 7, 1937; came to U.S., 1980; s. Eric and Iris Sina (Smith) S.; m. Beryl Ellen Giles, Jan. 5, 1963 (div.); children: Michael, Christopher, Timothy. B.Sc. in Engring. with honors, City U., London, 1960. Mng. dir. Cossor Electronics, Harlow, Eng., 1974-78; chmn. EMI med. Electronics, London, 1978-80; pres. Raytheon Data Systems, Norwood Mass., 1980-84, Raytheon Ventures, Lexington, 1985-87; chmn., CEO GCA Corp., Andover, Mass., 1987-88; pres. Atlantic Mgmt. Assocs., Inc., Bedford, N.H., 1988—; chmn. Brookwood Cos., Inc., 1989—, Visibility, Inc., 1996-2000, CEO, 1999-2000; chmn. Visaer, Inc., 2000—. Bd. dirs. Tech/Ops-Sevcon, Inc., Aavid Thermal Techs., Inc., Telequip Corp., Express Point Tech. Svcs., Inc. Fellow Instn. Elec. Engrs. (U.K.); mem. Inst. Mgmt. (U.K.; companion), Inst. Mech. Engrs. (U.K.). Avocations: music, sailing. Office: Atlantic Mgmt Assocs Inc PO Box 10670 Bedford NH 03110-0670 E-mail: drsteadman@aol.com.

STEADMAN, DAVID WILTON, retired museum official; b. Honolulu, Oct. 24, 1936; s. Alva Edgar and Martha (Cooke) S.; m. Kathleen Carroll Reilly, Aug. 1, 1964; children: Alexander Carroll, Kate Montague. BA, Harvard U., 1960, MAT., 1961; MA, U. Calif.-Berkeley, 1966; PhD, Princeton U., 1974. Lectr. Frick Collection, N.Y.C., 1970-71; asst. dir., acting dir., assoc. dir. Princeton U. Art Mus., 1971-73; dir. galleries Claremont Colls., (Calif.), 1974-80; art cons. Archtl. Digest, L.A., 1974-77; rsch. curator Norton Simon Mus., Pasadena, Calif., 1977-80; dir. Chrysler Mus., Norfolk, Va., 1980-89, Toledo Mus. Art, Ohio, 1989-99; ret., 2000. Author: Graphic Art of Francisco Goya, 1975, Works on Paper 1900-1960, 1977, Abraham van Diepenbeeck, 1982. Chester Dale fellow Nat. Gallery Art, Washington, 1969-70 Mem. Coll. Art Assn., Am. Assn. Mus. Dirs. Episcopalian.

STEADMAN, E. THOMAS, gynecologist; b. Passaic, N.J., Nov. 14, 1926; s. E. TenBroeck and Rosalie (Schieb) S.; m. Marcia Winder, June 15, 1948; children: E. TenBroeck, Tracy, Dirk, Webb, Coe. BA, Amherst Coll., 1950, MA, 1953; MD, Cornell U., 1957. Diplomate Am. Bd. Ob-Gyn. Intern St. Luke's Hosp., 1957-58; resident N.Y. Hosp., 1958-63, attending ob/gyn., 1985—. Clin. prof. Cornell U. Med. Coll., N.Y.C., 1985—. Fellow ACS, Am. Coll. Ob-Gyn.; mem. Am. Fertility Soc., N.Y. Gynecol. Soc., N.Y. Med. and Surg. Soc. (pres. 1984-85), N.Y. Obstet. Soc. (pres. 1978-79). Office: 449 E 68th St New York NY 10021-6310

STEADMAN, GREG, race car driver; b. Tampa, Fla. Mem. racing car crew Petty Enterprises, Randleman, NC, 1995—2000, crew chief, 2000—. Office: Petty Enterprises 311 Bronson Mill Rd Randleman NC 27317-8008

STEADMAN, JOHN MARCELLUS, III, English educator; b. Spartanburg, S.C., Nov. 25, 1918; s. John Marcellus and Medora Rice (Rembert) S. AB, Emory U., 1940, MA, 1941, DHL (hon.), 1976; MA (T.W. Hunt scholar), Princeton U., 1948, PhD, 1949; DHL (hon.), St. Bonaventure U., 1998. Instr. English Ga. Inst. Tech., 1941-42; asst. prof. U. N.C., 1949-51; ind. study and rsch. in English lit., 1953-61; from rsch. assoc.to sr. rsch. assoc. Henry E.

Huntington Libr., San Marino, Calif., 1962—2002; mem. faculty U. Calif., Riverside, 1966—, prof. English, 1967—, faculty rsch. lectr., 1977, prof. emeritus, 1989—. Vis. disting. prof. City U. N.Y., fall, 1974 Author numerous books including Milton and the Renaissance Hero, 1967, Milton's Epic Charters, 1968, The Myth of Asia, 1970, Disembodied Laughter: Troilus and the Apotheosis Tradition, 1972, The Lamb and The Elephant: Ideal Imitation and the Context of Renaissance Allegory, 1974, Epic and Tragic Structure in Paradise Lost, 1976, Nature into Myth: Medieval and Renaissance Moral Symbols, 1979, Milton's Biblical and Classical Imagery, 1984, The Hill and the Labyrinth: Discourse and Certitude in Milton and His Near-Contemporaries, 1984, The Wall of Paradise: Essays on Milton's Poetics, 1985, Milton and the Paradoxes of Renaissance Heroism, 1987, Redefining a Period Style: "Renaissance," "Mannerist," and "Baroque" in Literature, 1990, Ryoanji Temple and Other Poems, 1993, Moral Fiction in Milton and Spenser, 1995, Reconnaissances: Poems, 1995, Winter Harvest, A Retrospective, 1996, In Earnest or Game: A Seriocomic Medley. Verses Early or Late, 1998, Siege of Contraries: Rumors of Wars Real or Metaphorical, Stories and Sketches, 1998; co-editor latest being A Milton Ency., vols. I-IX, 1978-83; editor: latest being Huntington Libr. Quar., 1962-81; mem. numerous edit. and advisory bds.; contbr. articles to profl. jours. Served to capt. USAAF, 1942-46; capt. AUS, 1951-52. Grantee Huntington Libr., 1961-62; Procter fellow Princeton U., 1949, Guggenheim fellow, 1979. Mem. Milton Soc. Am. (pres. 1973, honored scholar 1976), So. Calif. Renaissance Conf., Phi Beta Kappa, Chi Phi, Fine Arts Club. Democrat. Home: 250 S Oak Knoll Ave Apt 109 Pasadena CA 91101-2995

STEADMAN, JOHN MONTAGUE, appellate court judge; b. Honolulu, Aug. 8, 1930; s. Alva Edgar and Martha (Cooke) S.; m. Alison Storer Lunt, Apr. 8, 1961; children— Catharine N., Juliette M., Eric C. Grad., Phillips Acad., Andover, Mass., 1948; BA summa cum laude, Yale U., 1952; LLB magna cum laude, Harvard U., 1955. Bar: D.C. 1955, Calif. 1956, U.S. Supreme Ct. 1964, Hawaii 1977. Assoc. Pillsbury, Madison & Sutro, San Francisco, 1956-63; atty. Dept. Justice, 1963-64; dep. under sec. army for internat. affairs, 1964-65; spl. asst. to sec. and dep. sec. def. Dept. Def., 1965-68; gen. counsel Dept. Air Force, 1968-70; vis. prof. law U. Pa. Law Sch., 1970-72; prof. law Georgetown U. Law Ctr., Washington, 1972-85, assoc. dean, 1979-84; assoc. judge D.C. Ct. Appeals, 1985—. Instr. Lincoln Law Sch., San Francisco, 1961-62, San Francisco Law Sch., 1962-63; vis. prof. U. Mich. Sch. Law, 1976, U. Hawaii Sch. Law, 1977; of counsel firm Pillsbury, Madison & Sutro, Washington, 1979-85 Editor: Harvard Law Rev, 1953-55. Sinclair-Kennedy Traveling fellow, 1955-56 Mem. Am. Law Inst., Cosmos Club, Phi Beta Kappa, Delta Sigma Rho, Zeta Psi. Episcopalian. Home: 2960 Newark St NW Washington DC 20008-3338 Office: DC Ct Appeals 500 Indiana Ave NW Washington DC 20001-2131 E-mail: jsteadman@dcca.state.dc.us.

STEADMAN, LYDIA DUFF, symphony violinist, retired elementary school educator; b. Hollywood, Calif., Dec. 31, 1934; d. Lewis Marshall and Margaret Seville (Williams) Duff; m. John Gilford Steadman, Apr. 14, 1961 (dec.). Student, Pepperdine U., 1952-55; BA in Music Edn., U. So. Calif., 1957. Cert. spl. secondary music, edn. tchr., Calif. Instrumental music tchr. Lancaster (Calif.) Sch. Dist., 1957-62, Simi Sch. Dist., Simi Valley, Calif., 1962-70, elem. tchr., 1970—2001. Tchr. Polynesian culture, dances, games, 1970—; hist. play wright for elem. grades, organizer elem. sch. dance festivals; dir. All Dist. Orch., Lancaster, Simi Valley Schs., 1957-70; compile Japanese Culture Study Unit for elem. grades Ventura County. 1st violinist San Fernando Valley Symphony, Sherman Oaks, Calif., 1962-75, Valley Symphony, Van Nuys, 2001--. Simi Valley's Santa Susana Symphony, Conejo Valley Symphony, Thousand Oaks, 1975-81, tour concert mistress, 1980; 2d violinist Ventura County Symphony, Santa Susana Symphony, 1981-95, L.A. Drs. Symphony, 2001-; prin. 2d violinist Calif. Luth. U. Orch. Pres. San Fernando Cmty. Concerts, Van Nuys, Calif., 1982-94; free lancing with pit orch. Cabrillo Music Theatre, Conejo Players Theater, Moorpark College Theatre, Newbury Park H.S. Theater Orch., 2001--; organizer ann. sch. Jump Rope-a-Thon for Am. Heart Assn., Nat. Geog. Geography Bee; bd. dirs. East Ventura County Cmty. Concert Assn. Mem. AAUW, NAFE, L.A. World Affairs Coun., Bus. and Profl. Women of Conejo Valley (pres. Golden Triangle chpg. 1988-90, 95-96, issues and mgmt. chair 1990, ways and means chair Coast chpt. 1990, editor Golden Triangle newsletter 1988-90, treas. 1992-93, sec. 1993-94, v.p. 1994—), Pacific Asia Mus., Armand Hammer Mus., Sigma Xi. Republican. Lutheran. Avocations: hula dancing, walking, collecting world coins, world traveling, violin. Home: 32016 Allenby Ct Westlake Village CA 91361-4001

STEADMAN, ROBERT KEMPTON, oral and maxillofacial surgeon; b. Mpls., July 8, 1943; s. Henry Kempton and Helen Vivian (Berg) S.; m. Susan E. Hoffman; children: Andrea Helene, Darcy Joanne, Richard Kempton, Michael Dean. BS, U. Wash., Seattle, 1969, DDS, 1974. Diplomate Am. Bd. Oral and Maxillofacial Surgery. Residency USAF, Elgin AFB, Fla., 1974-75; resident oral and maxillofacial surgery U. Okla., 1977-80, La. State U., Shreveport, 1980-81; pvt. practice Spokane, Wash., 1981—. Cons. Group Health Coop., 1989—; mem. adv. bd. Osteoporosis Awareness Resource, 1988— Select recruiting ptnr. U. Wash. Sch. Dentistry, 1990. Fellow Am. Acad. Cosmetic Surgery, Internat. Assn. Oral and Maxillofacial Surgery, Am. Coll. Oral and Maxillofacial Surgery, Am. Soc. Oral and Maxillofacial Surgery, Acad. Gen. Dentistry; mem. Internat. Soc. Plastic, Aesthetic and Reconstructive Surgery, Am. Acad. Cosmetic Surgery, Delta Sigma Delta (pres. 1987-88). Office: 801 W 5th Ave Ste 212 Spokane WA 99204-2800

STEADMAN, STEPHEN GEOFFREY, physicist; b. Rochester, N.Y., June 28, 1942; s. Luville T. and Elizabeth (Genung) S.; m. Brigitte M. Kreuzer, Aug. 1, 1975; children: Claudia, Mark, William. BS, U. Rochester, 1964; MS, Rutgers U., 1966, PhD, 1969. Vis. scientist Univ. Erlangen-Nurnberg, Erlangen, Germany, 1969-71; asst. Univ. Freiburg, Germany, 1971-72; sr. rsch. assoc. MIT, Cambridge, Mass., 1972-74, asst. prof., 1975-79, assoc. prof., 1979-82, sr. rsch. scientist, 1982-98; guest scientist Max Planck Inst., Heidelberg, Germany, 1974-75; sr. nuc. physics advisor U.S. Dept. Energy, Germantown, Md., 1998—. Program dir. nuc. physics NSF, Arlington, Va., 1994—97; E866 co-spokesman Brookhaven Nat. Lab., Upton, NY, 1992—98. Contbr. articles to profl. jours. Watertown provincial guard, 1998—; mem. Arsenal Reuse Com., Watertown, Mass., 1992—97. Mem. AAAS, Am. Phys. Soc., Watertown Provincial Guard. Episcopalian. Avocations: piano, tropical fish. Office: US Dept Energy SC-23 19901 Germantown Rd Germantown MD 20874-1207

STEAHLY, LANCE PRESTON, ophthalmologist, educator; b. Oak Ridge, Tenn., June 5, 1944; s. Frank Lester and Vivian (Emrick) S.; m. Harriet Taylor, July 11, 1964; children: Lance Jr., Christian W., Taylor Reed, Charles Stuart. BS magna cum laude, U. Charleston, 1963; BA, Johns Hopkins U., 1964; MD, W.Va. U., 1968. Diplomate Am. Bd. Ophthalmology. Intern Johns Hopkins Hosp., Balt., 1968-69, fellow in retinal surgery, 1978-79; commd. U.S. Army, 1969; advanced through grades to col.; resigned, 1982; resident Walter Reed Army Hosp., Washington, 1969-70, Greater Balt. Med. Ctr., 1972-73, Tripler Army Med. Ctr., Honolulu, 1973-75; chief surgery and ophthalmology U.S. Army Hosp., Heidelberg, Fed. Republic Germany, 1975-78; chief retinal svc. Fitzsimons Army Med. Ctr., Denver, 1979-82; assoc. clin. prof. U. Tex., Galveston, 1982-86; prof., chmn. dept. ophthalmology So. Ill. U. Sch. Medicine, Springfield, 1986—. Contbr. articles to profl. jours. Col. USAR, 1982—. Fellow ACS, Am. Acad. Ophthalmology. Republican. Episcopalian. Home: 1303 S Wiggins Ave Springfield IL 62704-3365 Office: So Ill U Sch Medicine 801 N Rutledge PO Box 19230 Springfield IL 62794-9230

STEAMER, ROBERT JULIUS, political science educator; b. Rochester, N.Y., Oct. 14, 1920; s. William August and Lotte (Becker) S.; m. Jean Worden, Apr. 12, 1947; children: Gregg Robert, James Worden. BA in Social Sci., Bucknell U., 1947; MA in Polit. Sci., U. Va., 1952; PhD, Cornell U., 1954; postgrad. law, Oxford (Eng.) U., 1968-69. Asst. prof. Oglethorpe U., 1952-55, U. Mass., 1955-56; assoc. prof. La. State U., 1956-62; prof. polit. sci., chmn. dept. Lake Forest (Ill.) Coll., 1962-72; prof. U. Mass., Boston, 1972-88, dean Coll. II, 1974-76, vice chancellor for acad. affairs, provost, 1976-79. Vis. summer prof. Tulane U., 1958, Cornell U., 1960, UCLA, 1965; staff cons. La. sect. U.S. Commn. Civil Rights, 1961 Author: The Constitution: Cases and Comments, 1959, The Supreme Court in Crisis, 1971, The Supreme Court: Constitutional Revision and the New Strict Constructionism, 1973, Chief Justice: Leadership and the Supreme Court, 1986; sr. co-author: American Constitutional Law: Cases and Commentary, 1991; contbr. articles to profl. jours. Served with USAAF, 1942-46. Recipient Gt. Tchr. award Lake Forest Coll., 1965; Lilly Found. Research award, 1967; Major Research award Project 87, 1981; hon. research fellow U. Exeter, Eng., 1981 Mem. Am. Polit. Sci. Assn., Midwest Polit. Sci. Assn. (v.p. 1970-71), New Eng. Polit. Sci. Assn. (pres. 1979-80) Home: 439 Kilbourn Rd Rochester NY 14618-3635

STEARLEY, ROBERT JAY, retired packaging company executive; b. Brazil, Ind., Sept. 6, 1929; s. Melvin George and Hila Mona (Bolin) S.; m. Helen Louise Dellacca, Nov. 25, 1950; children: Rhonda Jo, Robert Thomas. BS in Mech. Engring., Rose Hulman Inst. Tech., 1957; postgrad., Harvard U., 1979. Gen. mgr. Poly Tech Corp., Mpls., 1961-63; gen. mgr. plastics Gt. Plains Bag Corp., Stamford, Conn., 1963-66, v.p., 1966-71, v.p. ops., 1971-75, pres., 1975-84, dir., 1966-84; v.p. Jefferson Smurfit Corp., Alton, Ill., 1984—. Mem. Paper Shipping Sack Mfg. Assn. (dir. 1980-82), Am. Legion Clubs: Norwood Hills Country (St. Louis). Lodges: Elks. Republican. Methodist. Home: 2 Country Estates Pl Saint Louis MO 63131-3411

STEARMAN, WILLIAM LLOYD, military association executive, author; b. Wichita, Kans., June 22, 1922; s. Lloyd Carlton and Virtle Ethyl (Trusty) S.; m. Joan Crotty, May 5, 1984. BA in History and Math., U. Calif., Berkeley, 1944; MA in Internat. Rels., U. Geneva, Switzerland, 1948, PhD in Polit. Sci., 1961. Fgn. correspondent Mutual Broadcasting Sys., Austria and Ea. Europe, 1948-50; officer U.S. Fgn. Svc., Washington, Austria, Germany, Vietnam, 1950-78; mem. nat. sec. coun. staff The White House, 1971-76, 81-93; dep. asst., asst. dir. U.S. Arms Control and Disarmament Agy., 1976-77; adj. prof. internat. affairs Georgetown U., 1977-93; exec. dir. U.S. Naval Fire Support Assn., 1996—. Author: The Soviet Union and the Occupation of Austria, 1962; contbr. articles to profl. jours. Lt. U.S. Naval Res. WWII PTO. Mem. Cath. Acad. Scis. (academecien), Diplomatic and Consular Officers Retired, Izaak Walton League, Knight of the Holy Sepulcre. Republican. Roman Catholic. Avocations: outdoor activities, art, music, history. Home: 10416 Rockville Pike Apt 301 Bethesda MD 20852-3322

STEARNS, CLIFFORD BUNDY, congressman, business executive; b. Washington, Apr. 16, 1941; s. Clifford Robert and Emily Elizabeth (Newlin) S.; m. Joan Bette Moore, 1973; children: Douglas Moore, Clifford Bundy Jr., Scott Newlin. BSEE, George Washington U., 1963. Mgr. Control Data Systems, Inc., L.A., 1967-69; sr. contract adminstr. CBS, Inc., Stamford, Conn., 1969; account exec. Kutola Advt. Agy., Greenwich, 1970-71, Images 70/Wilson Haight Welch, Inc., Greenwich, 1971-72; motel owner Hatfield, Mass., 1972-77; pres., motel mgr. Stearns House, Inc., Silver Springs, Fla., 1972—88; mem. U.S. Congress from 6th Fla. dist., 1989—, mem. banking, fin. and urban affairs com., vets. affairs com., mem. energy subcom. and commerce com., subcoms. energy and power, commerce, consumer protection and competetiveness; mem. commerce and vets. coms., subcoms. telecom. and fin., healthcare, energy and power. Broker Silver Springs (Fla.) Real Estate, 1981-88. Trustee, vice chmn. Monroe Regional Hosp., Ocala, Fla., 1984-89; bd. dirs. Boys Club of Ocala, 1980-84; pres. Toastmaster Club L.A., 1962. Capt. USAF, 1963-67. Mem. Am. Hotel/Motel Assn., Fla. Hotel/Motel Assn., Am. Assn. Realtors, Fla. Assn. Realtors, Marion County Motel Assn. (pres. 1979), Marion C. of C. (bd. dirs. 1987—), Kiwanis (pres. Ocala club 1984). Republican. Presbyterian. Avocations: basketball, swimming, computers. Office: US Ho of Reps 2227 Rayburn Hob Washington DC 20515-0001 also: 115 SE 25th Ave Ocala FL 34471-9179*

STEARNS, ELLIOTT EDMUND, JR. retired surgeon; b. Cleve., Jan. 11, 1923; s. Elliott Edmund and Sarah (Hoyt) S.; m. Martha Hudson Small, June 26, 1945; children: Michael Elliott, Philip Hoyt, Daniel Arthur. Student, Williams Coll., 1941-43; BS, U. Calif., Berkeley, 1945; MD, U. Calif., San Francisco, 1948. Diplomate Am. Bd. Urology. Intern U.S. Pub. Health Hosp., San Francisco, 1949-50; resident Sonoma Co. Hosp., Santa Rosa, Calif., 1950-51; fellow urology Cleve. Clinic, 1952-54; chief resident urology Cin. (Ohio) Gen. Hosp., U. Cin., 1954-56; med. staff St. Mary's Hosp., Tucson, 1956-87, St. Joseph's Hosp., Tucson, 1956-87, Tucson (Ariz.) Med. Ctr., 1956-87, Pima County Hosp., Tucson, 1956-87; ret., 1987. Exec. com. mem. Pima County Med. Soc., Tucson, 1970s; chief of surgery St. Joseph's Hosp., Tucson, 1980s. Author: Catapult, 1994. Capt. USAF, 1954-56. Fellow ACS. Home: 2926 N Cascada Cir Tucson AZ 85715-3421 E-mail: mestearns@aol.com.

STEARNS, FRANK WARREN, lawyer; b. Washington, July 20, 1949; s. Robert Maynard and Ermyntrude (Vaiden) S.; m. Judith Anne Ketcheson, Sept. 7, 1974; children: Frank W. Jr., Brian S., Joe G. BA, Washington & Lee, 1971; JD with honors, George Washington U., 1974. Bar: Washington DC 1975, Va. 1980, U.S. Supreme Ct. 1980, U.S. Dist. Ct. DC 1975, U.S. Ct. Appeals (DC cir.) 1975, U.S. Ct. Appeals (4th cir.) 1985. Law clk. Superior Ct. D.C., Washington, 1974-75; asst. corp. counsel Office of the Corp. Counsel, 1975-79; asst. county atty. County Atty's Office, Fairfax County, Va., 1979-80; mng. ptnr. Wilkes Artis P.C., Fairfax, 1984-2001; ptnr. Venable, Baetjer & Howard, LLP, McLean, 2001—. Bd. dirs. No. Va. Bldg. Industry Assn., 1987-94; trustee Greater Washington Bd. Trade, 1987—; chmn. tech. adv. com. NVBIA, Loudoun, Va., 1986-90. Coun. Excellence in Govt., Washington, 1989—98; Commr. Arlington County Econ. Devel. Commn., Arlington, Va., 1987—91. Mem. Barristers, Counsellors. Avocations: tennis, golf. Office: Ste 300 Towers Crescent Dr Vienna VA 22182 E-mail: fwstearns@venable.com.

STEARNS, FREDERIC WILLIAM, dermatologist; b. Battle Creek, Mich., Feb. 12, 1943; s. William Frank and Leora Stearns; m. Linda Comfort, Sept. 23, 1978; children: Gillian Lind, Victoria Cornell. AB, Harvard U., 1964; MD, Baylor U., 1968; postgrad., U. Minn., 1964, SUNY, Buffalo, 1976. Diplomate Am. Acad. Dermatology. Intern, 1968-69; resident in internal medicine Rochester (N.Y.) Gen. Hosp., 1972-73; resident in dermatology SUNY, Buffalo, 1973-76; pvt. practice Williamsville, N.Y., 1976-78, Springer Clinic, Tulsa, 1978-87, 1987—. Col. USAF, ret. Fellow Am. Acad. Dermatology; mem. AMA, Okla. Dermatological Soc. (pres., sec., treas. Tulsa chpt.), Tulsa Dermatological Soc. (pres.), Okla. Med. Assn., Cen. States Dermatological Soc. (sec., treas.). Avocation: flying. Office: Southcrest Med Plaza 8803 S 101st E Ave Ste 335 Tulsa OK 74133

STEARNS, MILTON SPRAGUE, JR. financial executive; b. N.Y.C., June 3, 1923; s. Milton Sprague and Katherine (Stieglitz) S.; m. Virginia McCormick; children— Virginia Parker Stearns King, John Brackett (dec.), Barbara Ellison Stearns Terry, Kathryn Trowbridge Stearns Sergio, Elizabeth Sprague (dec.). Grad., Phillips Exeter Acad., 1942; BS cum laude, Harvard U., 1946, MBA, 1948. With The Fidelity Bank, Phila., 1948-72, group v.p. nat. lending div.; pres. Charter Fin. Co., Radnor, Pa., 1972—. Main Line Adult Day Ctr., 1997-99; chmn., chief exec. officer Judson Infrared, Inc., 1976-87. Ret. trustee Franklin Inst., Bryn Mawr Presbyn. Ch., pres. 1993-95. Served with USNR, WWII; lt. (j.g.) Res. ret. Mem. Robert Morris Assoc. (pres. Phila. chpt. 1961-62), Spee Club Cambridge, Mass., Merion Golf Club, Merion Cricket Club, Phila. Skating and Humane Soc., Union League Club of Phila., Delray Beach (Fla.) Club, Delray Beach Yacht Club, Country Club of Fla., Gulfstream Bath and Tennis Club, Pine Tree Golf Club, The Little Club. Home: 43 Righters Mill Rd Gladwyne PA 19035-1548 Office: 290 King Of Prussia Rd Ste 300 Radnor PA 19087-5107 E-mail: msscharter@aol.com.

STEARNS, NEELE EDWARD, JR. investment executive; b. Chgo., Apr. 2, 1936; s. Neele Edward Sr. and Grace (Kessler) S.; m. Bonnie Ann Evans; children: Katherine Stearns Sprenger, Kendra Stearns Drozd. BA magna cum laude, Carleton Coll., 1958; MBA with distinction, Harvard U., 1960. Audit staff Arthur Andersen Co., 1962-66, audit mgr., 1966-67; asst. gen. mgr. internat. divsn. Imperial-Eastman Corp., 1967-68; asst. treas. Allied Products Corp., 1968-69, treas., 1969-72; v.p. Henry Crown (Ill.) and Co., 1972-75, v.p., controller, 1975-79; exec. v.p., COO, Henry Crown and Co., 1979-86; pres., CEO, CC Industries, Inc., Chgo., 1986-95; chmn. exec. com. Barnes Internat., Inc., Northbrook, 1996-99; chmn. Wallace Computer Svcs., Inc., 2000, Fin. Investments Corp., Chgo., 2001—. Dir. Maytag Corp., 1989—, Wallace Computer Svcs., Inc., 1990—, Footstar, Inc., 2000—. Trustee Evanston Northwestern Healthcare. Mem. Commercial Club Chgo., Econ. Club Chgo., Country Club Fla., Chgo. Club, OldElm Club, Skokie Country Club, Phi Beta Kappa. Office: Financial Investments Corp 405 N Wabash River Plz 2E Chicago IL 60611

STEARNS, PETER NATHANIEL, history educator; b. London, Mar. 3, 1936; (parents Am. citizens); s. Raymond P. and Elizabeth (Scott) S.; m. Nancy Driessel (div. 1976); children: Duncan, Deborah; m. Carol Zisowitz, Mar. 26, 1978 (div. 1999); children: Clio Elizabeth, Cordelia Raymond; m. Margaret Brindle. AB, Harvard U., 1957, MA, 1959, PhD, 1963. From instr. to assoc. prof. U. Chgo., 1962-65; prof., chmn. history dept. Rutgers U., New Brunswick, N.J., 1965-74; Heinz prof. history Carnegie Mellon U., Pitts., 1974—, chmn. dept. history, 1986-92, dean Coll. Humanities and Social Scis., 1992-2000; provost George Mason U., 2000—. Co-dir. Pitts. Ctr. for Social History, 1986-92; chmn. acad. adv. coun. N.Y.C. Coll. Bd., 1982-85; chmn. Pacesetter World History commn., Coll. Bd., 1992-95, Coll. Bd. Advanced Placement World History, 1997—; mem. adv. bd. Liberal Education, 2001—. Author: The Working Classes and the Rise of Socialism , 1971, European Society in Upheaval: Social History since 1800, 1967; : European Society in Upheaval: Social History since 1800, 1975, (3d ed.) , 1991, Priest and Revolutionary: Lamennais and the Dilemma of French Catholicism, 1967, (Polish tranl.) , 1967, Modern Europe, 1789—1914, 1969, Revolutionary Syndicalism and French Labor: a cause without rebels , 1971, (with Harvey Mitchell) Workers and Protest: The European Labor Movement, The Working Classes and the Rise of Socialism, 1890—1914, The European Experience since 1815, 1972, 1848: The Revolutionary Tide in Europe, 1974, (publ. in England) The Revolutions of 1848, Lives of Labor: Work in Maturing Industrial Society , 1975, (German tranl.) , 1975, Old Age in European Society , 1977, Face of Europe, 1977, Paths to Authority: Toward the Formation of Middle Class Consciousness, 1978, Be A Man! Males in Modern Society, 1979, (rev. ed.) , 1990, (with Linda Rosenzweig) Themes in Modern Social History , 1985, (with Carol Stearns) Anger: The Struggle for Emotional Control in America's History , 1986, World History: Patterns of Change and Continuity, 1987, (rev.ed.) , 1994, (3d ed.) , 1998, (4th ed.) , 2001, (with others) Makers of Modern Europe, 1987, (rev. ed.) , 1994, (with others) Readings in World History, Vol.1: The Great Tradition and Vol. 2: The Modern Centuries , 1987, Expanding the Past: A Reader in Social History , 1988, Life and Society in the West, The Modern Centuries, 1987, Expanding the Past: A Reader in Social History , 1988, Life and Society in the West, The Modern Centuries, 1988, (with C. Stearns) Emotion and Social Change, Toward a New Psychohistory, 1988, (with Andrew Barnes) Social History and Issues in Consciousness and Cognition, 1989, Jealousy: Evolution of an Emotion in American History , 1989, Interpreting the Industrial Revolution , 1991, (with Michael Adas and Stuart Schwartz) World Civilizations, 1991, (rev. ed.) , 1995, (3d edit.) , 2000, Meaning Over Memory: Issues in Humanities Education, 1993, The Industrial Revolution in World History, 1993, (rev. ed.) , 1998, (Swedish tranl.) , American Cool: Developing a 20th Century Emotional Style, 1994, Turbulent Passage: A Global History of the 20th Century, 1994, (with Ron Harre) Discursive Psychology in Practice, 1995, Millenium III, Century XXI, 1996, (rev. ed.) , 1998, (with Hinshaw) Encyclopedia of the Industrial Revolution, 1996, (rev. ed.) , 1998, Fat History: Bodies and Beauty in the West, 1997, Fat History: Bodies and Beauty in the West, rev. edit., 2002, Schools and Students in Industrial Society: Japan and the West, 1997, History in Documents, 1998, (with Lewis) Emotional History of the U.S., 1998, World History in Documents: and Comparative Analysis in World History , 1998, Battleground of Desire: The Struggle for Self-Control in Modern America , 1999, Experiencing World History, 2000, Teaching, Learning and Knowing History , 2000, Gender in World History, 2000, Consumerism in World History, 2001, (with Brinkle) Facing Up to Management, 2001, Cultures in Motion, 2001; editor: Century for Debate, 1969, The Impact of the Industrial Revolution, 1972, (with Walkowitz) Workers in the Industrial Revolution, 1974, The Other Side of Western Civilization, 1979, (rev. ed.) , 1984, (4th ed.) , 1991, The Rise of Modern Women, 1977, (with Michael Weber) The Spencers of Amberson Avenue: A Turn-of-the-Century Memoir, 1983, (with Van Tassel) Old Age in a Bureaucratic Society, 1986, Encyclopedia World History, 2000, Encyclopedia of European Social History, 1999; contbg. editor: History of Emotions series NYU Press; contbr. over 150 articles to prof. and popular jours. Guggenheim Found. fellow, 1973-74; NEH grantee, 1981-84, 86, 90, Rockefeller Found. grantee, 1982-83. Fellow Internat. Soc. for Rsch. on Emotion; mem. Am. Hist. Soc., World History Assn., Am. Hist. Assn. (v.p., head teaching div. 1995-98), Nat. Bd. Profl. Tchg. Standards. Democrat. Avocations: racquet sports, travel. Home: 6310 Barsky Ct Fairfax Station VA 22039 Office: George Mason Univ Fairfax VA 22030

STEARNS, RICHARD GAYLORE, judge; b. L.A., June 27, 1944; s. Gaylore Rhodes and Jeannetta Viola (Hofheinz) S.; m. Patricia Ann McElligott, Dec. 21, 1975. BA, Stanford U., 1968; MLitt, Oxford U., Eng., 1971; JD, Harvard U., 1976. Bar: Mass. Dep. campaign mgr. McGovern for Pres., Washington, 1970-72; spl. asst. U.S. Senate, 1972-73; asst. dist. atty. Norfolk County, Dedham, 1976-79, 80-82; del. dir. Kennedy for Pres., Washington, 1979-80; asst. U.S. atty. U.S. Dept. Justice, Boston, 1982-90; assoc. justice Superior Ct. Mass., 1990-94; U.S. dist. judge U.S. Dist. Ct. Mass., 1994—. Author: Massachusetts Criminal Law: A Prosecutor's Guide, 21st edit., 2001. Mem. jud. conf. com. on federal-state jurisdiction, mem. mass torts working group; trustee Vincent Meml. Hosp., Boston. Rhodes scholar, 1968. Mem. ABA, Mass. Bar Assn., Phi Beta Kappa. Office: US Courthouse 1 Courthouse Way Ste 7130 Boston MA 02210-3009

STEARNS, ROBERT LELAND, curator; b. L.A., Aug. 28, 1947; s. Edward Van Buren and Harriett Ann (Hauck) S.; m. Sheri Roseanne Lucas, Oct. 2, 1982 (div. 1994); children: Marissa Hauck, Caroline Lucas. Student, U. Calif., San Diego, 1965-68, BFA, 1970; student, Calif. Poly. State U., San Luis Obispo, 1968. Asst. dir. Paula Cooper Gallery, N.Y.C., 1970-72; prodn. asst. Avalanche Mag., 1972; dir. Kitchen Ctr. for Video/Music, 1972-77, Contemporary Arts Ctr., Cin., 1977-82; dir. performing arts Walker Art Ctr., Mpls., 1982-88; dir. Wexner Ctr. for Arts, Columbus, Ohio, 1988-92; mem. Wexner Ctr. Found., 1990-92; dir. Stearns & Assocs./Contemporary Exhbn. Svcs., Ohio, 1992—2000; sr. prgm. dir. Arts Midwest, Minneapolis, 1998—. Adj. prof. dept. art, assoc. dean Coll. Art, Ohio State U., Columbus, 1988-92; lectr. Sch. of the Art Inst. Chgo., 2002; cons. McKnight Found., St. Paul, 1978, Jerome Found., 1978-79; chmn. Artists TV Workshop, N.Y.C., 1976-77; bd. dirs., chmn. Minn. Dance Alliance, Mpls., 1983-88; bd. dirs. Haleakala, Inc., N.Y.C.; mem. various panels Nat. Endowment for Arts, Washington, 1977-91; mem. pub. arts policy Greater Columbus Arts Coun., 1988-90; adv. coun. Bklyn. Acad. Music, 1982-84, Houston Grand Opera, 1991-93. Author, editor: Robert Wilson: Theater of Images, 1980, Photography and Beyond in Japan, 1995; author: Mexico Now: Point of Departure, 1997, Robert Wilson: Scenografie e Installazioni, 1997, Illusions of Eden: Visions of the American Heartland, 2000, Aspirations: Toward a Future in the Middle East, 2001, Staking Middle Ground: Recent Pictures from Central Europe and the American Midwest, 2002, Staking Middle Ground: Central Europe and Middle America, 2002; editor: Dimensions of Black, 1970; exec. editor: Breakthroughs, 1991; author and editor numerous catalogues. Decorated chevalier Order of Arts and Letters (France); Jerome Found. travel grantee, 1986, Japan Found. travel grantee, 1991. E-mail: arts2020@aol.com.

STEARNS, ROBERT MARRON, librarian; b. Bristol, Pa., Feb. 23, 1955; s. Robert Louis and Irene Marron Stearns. MS in Libr. Sci., Clarion U. Pa., 1996. Music therapist Fairmount Inst., Phila., 1988—95; libr. Temple U. Tyler School of Art, Elkins Park, 1997—98; centralized svcs. libr. Norristown (Pa.) State Hosp., 1998—99; corrections libr. State Correctional Instn. at Chester, 1999—. Contbr. articles to profl. jours.; , author short stories. Scholar Elizabeth Rupert scholar, Clarion U. Libr. Sci. Dept., 1996. Mem.: Beta Phi Mu. Avocations: writing, composing music. Office: SCI-Chester 500 East 4th St Chester PA 19013 Personal E-mail: rstearns@axs2000.net.

STEARNS, STEPHEN JEROLD, history educator, writer; b. Boston, Dec. 24, 1935; s. Maurice and Minna Stiller Stearns; m. Anna Brennen (div. Apr. 1973); 1 child, Lisa Deborah Stearns Deal; m. Lee Jeffries Whedon (dec. May 1992); stepchildren: Samuel Whedon, Matthew Whedon, Joss Whedon. BA, Harvard Coll., 1957; MA, Columbia U., 1959; PhD, U. Calif., Berkeley, 1967. Tchg. asst. U. Calif., Berkeley, 1964-65; asst. prof. history dept. Vassar Coll., Poughkeepsie, N.Y., 1965-67, Richmond Coll., S.I., 1967-72; assoc. prof. Coll. of S.I., 1972—. Adj. assoc. prof. Columbia Tchrs. Coll., N.Y.C., 1986. Editor, author introduction: (books) Great Illusion (N. Angell), 1970, In Savage Times (L. Woolf), 1970, International Government (L. Woolf), 1971, Paris (L. Hart), 1972. Fulbright grantee U.S. Edn. Commn. U.K., 1962-63,

63-64. Mem. Am. Hist. Assn., Conf. on Brit. Studies. Democrat. Jewish. Home: 895 W End Ave New York NY 10025-3500 Office: Coll of S I CUNY 2800 Victory Blvd Staten Island NY 10314-6609

STEARNS, STEWART WARREN, charitable association executive; b. Denver, Apr. 8, 1947; s. Vinton H. and Marjorie L. (Tedro) S.; m. Marjorie L. Fuller, Jan. 25, 1969; children: Theresa Lyn, Gregory Robert. BS, Ea. N.Mex. U., 1970; MA, No. Ill. U., 1973; postgrad., SUNY, Albany, 1974—. Mng. editor Studies in Linguistics, DeKalb, Ill., 1972-73; instr. No. Ill. U., 1972-73; cons. AID, Guatemala, 1973-74; instr. Skidmore Coll., Saratoga Springs, N.Y., 1975; OAS fellow Guatemala, 1976-77; asst. dir. Chaves County Cmty. Action Program, Roswell, N.Mex., 1977-78; exec. dir. United Way Chaves County, 1978-83, Levi Strauss Found., Dallas, 1983-85, Cmty. Trust Met. Tarrant County, Ft. Worth, 1985-88; pres., CEO, Cmty. Found., Sarasota County, 1989—. NDEA fellow, Dallas, 1970-71. E-mail: stearns@sarasota foundation-.org. Business E-Mail: sstearns@sarasota-foundation.org.

STEARNS, SUSAN TRACEY, lighting design company executive, lawyer; b. Seattle, Oct. 28, 1957; d. Arthur Thomas and Roberta Jane (Arrowood) S.; m. Ross Alan De Alessi, Aug. 11, 1990; 1 child, Chase Arthur. AA, Stephens Coll., 1977, BA, 1979; JD, U. Wash., Seattle, 1990. Bar: Calif. 1990, U.S. Ct. Appeals (9th cir.) 1990, U.S. Dist. Ct. (no. dist.) Calif 1990, U.S. Dist. Ct. (we. dist.) Wash. 1991, Wash. 1991. TV news prodr. KOMO, Seattle, 1980-86; atty. Brobeck, Phleger & Harrison, San Francisco, 1990-92; pres. Ross De Alessi Lighting Design, Seattle, 1993—. Author periodicals in field. Alumnae Assn. Coun. Stephens Coll., Columbia, Mo., 1995—. Named Nat. Order of Barristers U. Washington, Seattle, 1990. Mem. ABA (mem. state labor and employment law subcom.), Wash. State Bar Assn. (mem. bench-bar-press com.), State Bar Calif., King County Bar Assn., Bar Assn.San Francisco, Wash. Athletic Club. Avocations: travel, dance. Office: Ross De Alessi Lighting Design 3313 W McGraw Seattle WA 98199

STEBBINS, ELIZABETH JOSEPH HINTON, management and statistics educator, researcher; b. L.A., Sept. 14, 1923; d. James Thomas and M. Evangeline (Russell) Hinton; m. James Frederick Stebbins, July 7, 1945 (dec.); children: James Wyatt (dec.), John Russell. BA Archeology, Anthropology, Fine Arts, U. So. Calif., 1945, postgrad. in Edn.; MA in Psychology and Fine Arts, Chapman U., 1963; PhD in Human Behavior-Leadership, U.S. Internation U., 1989. Elem. tchr. L.A. Unified Sch. Dist. and Orange County Sch. Dists.; sch. administr. Covina Valley (Calif.) Sch. Dist.; cons. curriculum and evaluation L.A. County Schs., 1965-71; project mgr. for innovative sch. model State of Calif., 1971-72; v.p. The Bradford Group-Exec. Search, Newport Beach, Calif., 1978-84; commodity broker, 1975-78; prof. mgmt. and supervision Coastline C.C., 1979—; prof. mgmt., stats. and counseling U. Phoenix, Orange County, Calif., 1990—. Owner, pres. profl. career advisement Hinton Cons. Recipient Nat. Inst. for Staff and Orgnl. Devel., 1992. Mem. Calif. Assn. for Measurement & Evaluation in Counseling (past-pres.), Nat. Counsel Measurement in Edn., Am. Ednl. Rsch. Assocs., Calif. Assn. Counseling and Devel., Chi Phi. Avocation: oil and water color painting. Address: 23592 Windsong Apt 41A Aliso Viejo CA 92656-1392

STEBBINS, GREGORY KELLOGG, foundation executive; b. Lafayette, Ind., Jan. 10, 1951; s. Albert Kellogg and Nancy Ruth (Osborn) S. BS in Data Processing, Calif. Poly., Pomona, 1974; MBA, U. So. Calif., 1976; EdD, Pepperdine U., 1985. Account exec. ADP, Long Beach, Calif., 1977-78; salesman Grubb & Ellis, L.A., 1978-81, v.p. Beverly Hills, Calif., 1981-83; regional mgr. Hanes Co., 1983-85; treas. U. Santa Monica, L.A., 1983—; pres. Stebbins Consulting Group, Santa Monica, 1989—; chair Santa Monica Inst., 1994—. Mem. ASTD, Sigma Xi. Avocations: flying, scuba diving, photography. Office: Santa Monica Inst 944 Princeton Dr Marina Del Rey CA 90292

STEBBINS, LEROY JOSEPH (LEE STEBBINS), not-for-profit organization executive; b. Hartford, Conn., Sept. 25, 1945; s. Leroy Joseph and Eleanor Ann (Joseph) S.; m. Marjorie Ann Gould, Oct. 5, 1973 (div.); children: Daniel Chapman, David Liam. BA, U. Conn., 1967. Asst. dir. community health and safety programs ARC, Farmington, Conn., 1971-75, exec. dir. Greenwich, 1975-80, asst. mgr. Farmington, 1980-83; mng. dir. Region III, Ea. Ops. Hdqrs., ARC, Alexandria, Va., 1983-92; exec. dir. Am. Speech-Lang.-Hearing Found., 1992-95; dir. chpt. svcs. Am. Soc. Tng. and Devel., 1995-96; v.p., COO D.C. C. of C., 1996-98; COO Nat. Capital Area Chpt., ARC, 1998—. Disaster fund raising specialist Ea. Field Office, ARC, 1978-83; faculty health and safety symposium Conn. Health Dept., Hartford, 1976. Mem. gov.'s adv. com. Conn. Health Dept., 1973—76; campaign account exec. United Way of Capital Area, Hartford, 1982; mem. adminstrv. com. Leadership Fairfax, 2001; select soccer coach Fairfax (Va.) Police Youth Club, 1986—90; asst. soccer coach Fairfax H.S.; vol. World Cup organizing com. World Cup USA '94; pres. nat. capital chpt. U. Conn. Alumni Assn., Washington, 1999—2002. Mem. U. Conn. Alumni Assn. (pres.). Republican. Roman Catholic. Avocations: golf, youth soccer, college basketball. Home: 9280 Bailey Ln Fairfax VA 22031-1930 Office: 2131 K St NW Washington DC 20037-1898

STEBBINS, ROBERT ALAN, sociology educator; b. Rhinelander, Wis., June 22, 1938; s. William Nelson and Dorothy May (Guy) S.; m. Karin Yvonne Olson, Jan. 11, 1964; children: Paul, Lisa, Christi. BA, Macalester Coll., 1961; MA, U. Minn., 1962, PhD, 1964. Assoc. prof. Presbyterian Coll., Clinton, S.C., 1964-65; assoc. prof.to prof. Meml. U. Nfld., St. John's, Can., 1965-73; prof. U. Tex.-Arlington, 1973-76; prof. sociology U. Calgary, Alta., Can., 1976-99, faculty prof. social scis. Can., 2000—, dept. head Can., 1976-82; head dept. sociology and anthropology Meml. U. Nfld., 1968-71. Author: Commitment to Deviance, 1971, The Disorderly Classroom: Its Physical and Temporal Conditions, 1974, Teachers and Meaning, 1975, Amateurs, 1979, The Magician, 1984, Sociology: The Study of Society, 2d edit., 1990, Canadian Football: The View from the Helmet, 1987, Deviance: Tolerable Differences, 1988, The Laugh-Makers: Stand-Up Comedy as Art, Business, and Life-Style, 1990, Amateurs, Professionals and Serious Leisure, 1992; co-editor: Fieldwork Experience, 1980, The Sociology of Deviance, 1982, Experiencing Fieldwork, 1991, Career, Culture, and Social Psychology in a Variety Art, 1993, Predicaments: Moral Difficulty in Everyday Life, 1993, The Franco-Calgarians: French Language, Leisure and Linguistic Lifestyle in an Anglophone City, 1994, The Connoisseur's New Orleans, 1995, The Barbershop Singer: Inside the Social World of a Musical Hobby, 1996, Tolerable Differences: Living with Deviance, 2d edit., 1996; After Work: The Search for an Optimal Leisure Lifestyle, 1998, The Urban Francophone Volunteer: Searching for Personal Meaning and Community Growth in a Linguistic Minority, 1998, The French Enigma: Survival and Development of Canada's Francophone Societies, 2000, Exploratory Research in the Social Sciences, 2001, New Directions in the Theory and Research of Serions Leisure, 2001. Pres. St. John's Orch., 1967-68; mem. Dallas Civic Symphony, 1973-76, Orch. Soc. of Calgary, 1978-97. Can. Coun. Sabbatical Leave fellow, 1972-72, Calgary Inst. for Humanities fellow, 1987-88, Killam resident fellow, 1990; NEH summer stipend, 1976; Acad. Leisure Scis. fellow, 1996—, Royal Soc. Can. fellow, 1999—. Mem. Leisure Studies Assn., Can. Sociology and Anthropology Assn. (pres. 1988-89), Internat. Sociol. Assn., Assn. for Can. Studies, World Leisure and Recreation Assn. (bd. dirs. 1997—), Social Sci. Fedn. Can. (pres. 1991-92), Can. Assn. for Leisure Studies (v.p. 1993-96). Home: 144 Edgemont Estates Dr NW Calgary AB Canada T3A 2M3 Office: U Calgary Dept Sociology 2500 University Dr NW Calgary AB Canada T2N 1N4

STEBBINS, VRINA GRIMES, retired elementary school educator, counselor; b. Columbus, Ohio, Aug. 24, 1939; d. Marion Edward and Vrina Elizabeth (Davis) Grimes; m. Gary Frank Stebbins, Dec. 23, 1959; 1 child, Gregory Gary. Student, Ohio U., 1957-59; BS in Edn., Miami U., Oxford, Ohio, 1965; MS in Edn., St. Francis Coll., 1971; Counseling Endorsement, Ind.-Purdue U., Ft. Wayne, 1988. Cert. elem. classroom educator K-6, sch. counselor, social worker, Ind. 1st grade tchr. Greenville (Ohio) Pub. Schs., 1963-68; elem. educator East Allen County Schs., New Haven, 1969-84, elem. sch. counselor, 1984-98; ret., 1998. Presenter at Ind. profl. orgns., 1985-92, 1st Presbyn. Ch., Ft. Wayne, 1984—, Project 2000, Ft. Wayne, 1992—; participant Bus.-Edn. Exchange, Ft. Wayne C. of C., 1993. Mem. ACA, Ind. Counseling Assn. (com. mem. 1992-93, Ind. Elem. Counselor of Yr. 1991), East Allen Educators' Assn. (chair com. 1989-98, East Allen County Schs. Elem. Educator of Yr. 1989, 95), Arts United, Phi Delta Kappa, Delta Kappa Gamma (1st v.p. Ind. state 1993-95, Ind. state pres. 1995-97). Democrat. Presbyterian. Avocations: travel, collecting antiques and angels. Home: 5712 Sandra Lee Ave Fort Wayne IN 46819-1118 Fax: 260-747-0789. E-mail: vstebbinsg@aol.com.

STEBLAY, RAYMOND WILLIAM, immunopathologist, researcher; b. Chgo., Mar. 28, 1922; s. Joseph Bernard Jr. and Margaret (Kobadich) S. AB magna cum laude, Princeton U., 1947; MD, U. Chgo., 1952. Asst. prof. dept. ob-gyn. U. Chgo., 1959-67, asst. prof. depts. pathology and medicine, 1967-69; rsch. assoc prof. dept. pathology Albany (N.Y.) Med. Sch., 1969-72; rsch. physician N.Y. State Kidney Disease Inst., Albany, 1969-83. Contbr. articles to profl. jours. Recipient Disting. Svc. award U. Chgo., 1986. Mem. Am. Soc. Nephrology, Am. Assn. Pathologists, Am. Assn. Immunologists. Presbyterian. Achievements include the first experimental models of autoimmune glomerulonephritis and autoimmune tubular-interstitial nephritis identifying the corresponding human diseases. Home: 107 Heritage Rd Apt 11 Guilderland NY 12084-9662

STEBLER, JUDITH ANNE, medical/surgical nurse, critical care nurse; b. Pitts., Jan. 1, 1959; d. Edward A. Stebler and Ruth E. (Kemmler) Bartholomew. AS in Med. Lab., George Washington. U., 1990; BSN magna cum laude, Columbia Union Coll., Takoma Park, Md., 1991; MS in Health Care Adminstrn., Ctrl. Mich. U., 1998. Cert. med. lab. technician, med. lab. technologis; BLS instr. trainer, PALS instr., ACLS instr., CCRN. Enlisted USN, 1977; emergency room corpsman, trauma nurse core curriculum instr. Nat. Naval Med. Ctr., Bethesda, Md., 1978-79, med. lab. technician, 1980-85, instr. Advanced Med. Lab. Sch., Naval Sch. Health Scis., 1985-89; staff nurse surgery unit Naval Hosp., 1992-96, staff nurse ICU, 1994-96, staff nurse PACU Jacksonville, Fla., 1996-97, staff nurse ICU divsn. officer, 1999—2000; ret., 2000. Decorated Navy Achievement medal, Navy Commendation medal. Mem. Regents of the Nightingale Soc., Alpha Chi. Roman Catholic. Avocations: photography, softball, bowling. Home: 110 Ridgefield Ct Orange Park FL 32065-5773

STEC, JOHN ZYGMUNT, real estate executive; b. Stalowawola, Poland, Jan. 21, 1925; Came to U.S.A. 1947. s. Valenty and Maria (Madej) S. m. Wanda G. Baca, Oct. 13, 1956; children: David, Maria, Monica. Student, Poland, 1941-44, Kent St. U., Oh., 1965-66, student, 1966-67. Cert. Master of Corporate Real Estate. With The Singer Co., Cleve., 1952-54, dis. mgr., 1954-60, sales supr., 1960-67, dir. real estate Detroit and Chgo., 1967-73; v.p. Fabri Center of Am., Beachwood, Ohio, 1973—; sr. v.p. real estate Fabri-Centers of Am., Inc., 1987—. With U.S. Army 1950-52 With U.S. Army, 1950-52. Mem. Nat. Assoc. of Corporate Real Estate (speaker, organizer 1974-77, audit Com. 1977-79, bd. dirs. 1970-82, Outstanding Achievement award 1982). Chagrin Valley Club. Repulican. Roman Catholic. Avocations: swimming, hiking, reading. Home: 725 Sagewood Dr Chagrin Falls OH 44023-6733 Office: JoAnn Stores Inc 5555 Darrow Rd Hudson OH 44236-4011 E-mail: johnstec@jo-annstores.com. *Personal philosophy: Think success and you'll be successful. Perseverence of any goal leads to achievement. Learning is knowledge. Knowledge is the most powerful key that leads to greatness and opens any door.*

STECICH, RITA LOUISE, secondary education educator; b. Chgo., Oct. 1, 1949; d. Thomas Filbert Fahey and Ada Helen Tambellini; m. John Patrick Stecich, July 1, 1972; children: Eric John, Thomas John. BA in English, U. Ill., 1971; MS in Reading, Chgo. State U., 1976. Cert. secondary edn. tchr., Ill. Tchr. English and reading Tilden H.S., Chgo., 1971-77, Evergreen Park (Ill.) Comm H.S., 1990—. Union pres. Evergreen Park Tchrs. Assn., 1998—. Bd. dirs. Local Redevel. Bd. Mt. Greenwood, Chgo., 1997-99. Named Tchr. of Yr., PTA, 1998. Mem. Nat. Tchrs. English, Ill. Reading Assn.

STECK, WARREN FRANKLIN, retired chemical company executive, biochemist; b. Regina, Sask., Can., May 10, 1939; m. 1963; 2 children. B in Eng., McGill U., 1960; PhD in Organic Chemistry, U. Sask., 1964. Rsch. assoc. Rsch. Inst. Okla. U., 1963-64; asst. rsch. officer Nat. Rsch. Coun. Can., 1964-70, assoc. rsch. officer, 1970-76, sr. rsch. officer, 1976-80, asst. dir., 1980-81, assoc. dir., 1982-83, dir. Plant Biotech. Inst., 1983-90, dir. gen. Plant Biotech Inst., 1991-94; asst. pres. Fytokem Inc., Saskatoon, Sask., 1995-97, v.p. tech., 1997—99; pres. Steck & Assoc. Inc., 1999—. Mem. Phytochem. Soc. N.Am., Soc. Cosmetic Chemists. Achievements include rsch. in insect sex attractants and pheromones, chem. ecology.

STECKEL, ANITA, artist; b. Bklyn. d. Hyman and Dora (Slavin) Arkin. Student, Cooper Union, 1947-51, Alfred U., 1952-53, Art Students League, N.Y.C., 1959-61. Tchr. Art Students League; lectr. Sarah Lawrence Coll., New Sch. for Social Rsch., CCNY, NYU, Hobart and William Smith Coll., Rutgers U., Coll. New Rochelle, U. R.I., Queens Coll., Baruch Coll., also others. One-woman shows, 1961-2001, including Hacker Gallery, 1961, 63, Rutgers U., Seawolf Gallery, Razor Gallery, N.Y.C., 1985-87, Kenkeleba Gallery, 1991, Art in Gen., N.Y.C., 1984, Alex Rosenberg Gallery, Rockland Community Coll., 1971, Seawolf-EEast Hampton, 1983, 85, 86, 87, Rutgers U., N.J., 1985, Kingsboro Coll., N.Y., 1988, Kenkeleba Gallery, N.Y., 1991, 94, 95, PDG Gallery, N.Y., 1993, 94, 96, Mitchel Algus Gallery, N.Y.C., 2000, 01; exhibited in group shows, 1969-89, including Whitney Mus., 1969, Chung-Esing Mus., Aldrich Mus., 1975, Portland (Maine) Mus., 1974, Bowers Mus., Calif., 1975, Kipp Mus., Pa., 1975, Bronx Mus., 1976, Krannert Mus., Ill., 1977, Elehjem Mus., Madison, Wis., 1977, Rochester Meml. Mus., N.Y., 1977, Mex. Palace Fine Arts, 1982, Mich. Mus. Art, Bienale Colombia, S.Am., 1977, Amazona Gallery, Holland, Moda-Kassel Germany, 1981, Lanam Mus., 1983, Radford Mus., 1995, Roanoke (Va.) Mus., 2000, Attleboro (Mass.) Mus., 2001, 02, ARmory Show, N.Y.C., 2001, 02, also numerous colls. and univs.; represented in permanent collections Lanan Mus., Radford Mus.; work reviewed in Art in Am., Arts, Art News, N.Y. mags., N.Y. Times, (books) The Male Nude, Feminist Art Criticism-An Anthology, The Art of N.Y., Women Artists Self Portraits, others. Nat. Endowment for Arts grantee, 1983; only work selected to represent 20 Yrs. of Women's Art, 20th Anniversary of Ms. Mag., 1993, pub. in book "New Feminist Criticism", 1997.

STECKEL, BARBARA JEAN, retired city financial officer; b. L.A., Mar. 9, 1939; d. John Herschel and Bernice Evelyn (Selstad) Webb Banta; m. Jimmie Raeburn Lugenbeel, Feb. 16, 1957 (div. 1962); Leanna Virgina, Debra Lynn; m. Dale Robert Steckel, Mar. 16, 1962; 1 child, Richard Alan. AA in Bus., Anchorage Community Coll., 1975; BBA, U. Alaska, Anchorage, 1980. City clk., treas. City of Kotzebue, Alaska, 1973-74, city mgr., treas., 1974-76; grants adminstr. Municipality of Anchorage, 1976-79, contr., 1979-82, mcpl. mgr., 1982-84, chief fiscal officer, 1984-87; fin. dir., treas. City of Riverside, Calif., 1988-98; ret., 1998. Bd. dirs. Riverside Cmty. Health Svcs. Corp.; chmn. Cmty. Health Corp. Mem. adv. coun. sch. bus. and pub. adminstrn. U. Alaska, Anchorage, 1982-85; bd. dirs. Anchorage Parking Authority, 1984-87, ICMA Retirement Corp., 1985-93, Police and Fire Retirement Sys. Mcpl. of Anchorage, 1982-87, chmn., 1986; devel. com. mem. Am. Heart Assn., Anchorage, 1987. Mem. Govt. Fin. Officers U.S. and Can. (bd. dirs. 1984-87), Mcpl. Fin. Officers Alaska (pres. 1981-82), Nat. Assn. Accts. (bd. dirs. 1986-87), Am. Soc. Women Accts., Calif. Soc. Mcpl. Fin. Officers (chmn. cash mgmt. com. 1989-91, bd. dirs. 1992-95, pres. elect 1995-96, pres. 1996-97), Mcpl. Treas. Assn. (R.E. Phillips award, Svc. award, debt com. chmn. 1992-95), Calif. Mcpl. Treas. Assn., Internat. City Mgrs. Assn., U. Alaska Alumni Assn., Rotary, Elks. Avocations: reading, sewing. Address: PO Box 1027 Sterling AK 99672-1027

STECKEL, RICHARD HALL, economist; b. Milledgeville, Ga., June 28, 1944; s. Richard Hoch and Lillian Blanche (Hall) S.; m. Barbara Jean Bullard, Sept. 26, 1972; children: Sarah Elizabeth, Anna Kathryn. AB, Oberlin (Ohio) Coll., 1966; MA in Econs., MA in Math., U. Okla., 1970; MA in Econs., U. Chgo., 1973, PhD in Econs., 1977. Instr. Ohio State U., Columbus, 1974-77, asst. prof., 1977-81, assoc. prof., 1981-89, prof., 1989—. Rsch. assoc. Nat. Bur. Econ. Rsch., Cambridge, 1982—. Author: The Economics of U.S. Slave and Southern White Fertility, 1985; co-editor: Health and Welfare During Industrialization, 1997, A Population History of North America, 2000. Grantee NSF. Mem. Am. Econ. Assn., Econ. History Assn. (chair program com. 1999, v.p. 1999-2000), Am. Hist. Assn., Population Assn. Am., Social Scis. History Assn. (chair program com. 1985-86, chair nomination com. 1991-92), Cliometrics Soc., Am. Assn. Phys. Anthropologists. Avocations: music, golf, skiing, traveling. Office: Ohio State U 1945 N High St Columbus OH 43210-1120 E-mail: steckel.1@osu.edu.

STECKEL, RICHARD J. radiologist, academic administrator; b. Scranton, Pa., Apr. 17, 1936; s. Morris Leo and Lucille (Yellin) Steckel; m. Julie Raskin, June 16, 1960; children: Jan Marie, David Matthew. BS magna cum laude, Harvard U., 1957, MD cum laude, 1961. Diplomate Am. Bd. Radiology. Intern UCLA Hosp., 1961-62; resident in radiology Mass. Gen. Hosp., Boston, 1962-65; clin./rsch. assoc. Nat. Cancer Inst., 1965-67; faculty UCLA Med. Sch., 1967—, prof. radiol. scis. and radiation oncology, 1974-94; chmn. dept. radiol. scis. UCLA Med. Ctr., 1994-2000, prof. emeritus, 2000—; pres. Assn. Am. Cancer Insts., 1981. Dir. Jonsson Comprehensive Cancer Ctr., 1974—94. Contbr. Fellow: Am. Coll. Radiology; mem.: Assn. Univ. Radiologists, Am. Roentgen Ray Soc., Radiol. Soc. N.Am. Office: 1126 Bel Air Dr Santa Barbara CA 93105-

STECKERL, SHALLY A. executive recruiter; b. Santa Fe, Nov. 3, 1971; s. Doris J. Steckerl and Paul Schraps; life ptnr. Stefanie A. Butts. BS, Rochester Inst. Tech., 1993. Sr. recruiter Kenda Sys., Atlanta, 1996—97; mgr. Western region Support Techs., Scottsdale, Ariz., 1997—98; sr. Internet recruiter Motorola, Inc., Tempe, 1998—99; sr. Internet recruitment and rsch. analyst Cisco Sys., Phoenix, 1999—2001, sr. CI analyst, 2001. Cons. JobMachine, Inc., Scottsdale, 1997—; v.p. Breckenridge Group, 2002—. Author: (courses and resource Website) JobMachine, 2000. Jewish. Avocations: travel, music, Web surfing, strategy gaming. Home: 2913 Ridge Brook Tr Duluth GA 30096 Office: PO Box 921762 Norcross GA 30010 Home Fax: 661-457-3726; Office Fax: 661-457-3726. Personal E-mail: shally@jobmachine.net. Business E-Mail: shally@jobmachine.net.

STECKLER, JESSICA ANN, continuing nursing education educator; b. York, Pa., June 26, 1941; d. Edward A. and Mary Elizabeth (Hoffman) Debes; divorced; 1 child, Scott Edward. Diploma Sch. Nursing, Bryn Mawr (Pa.) Hosp., 1963; BS in Edn., Millersville State Coll., 1971; MEd, Gannon U., 1979; doctoral candidate in edn., Pa. State U., 1992. Cert. in staff devel., continuing edn., ANA; cert. in med. ethics consultation, U. W.Va. Instr. practical nursing York (Pa.) County Vocat.-Tech., 1966-73; instr. Sch. Nursing Hamot Med. Ctr., Erie, Pa., 1973-75; instr. nursing Behrend Coll. Pa. State U., 1989-92; assoc. dir. Erie (Pa.) VA Med. Ctr., 1981—, chairperson med. ethics team, 1988—; acting CHEP dir., ednl. specialist Employee Edn. Sys. VA, 1997—. Contbg. author: Transcultural Health Care: A Culturally Competent Approach, 1997, 2d edit., 2002; contbr. articles to profl. jours. Recipient Recognition award for promoting excellence in evaluation in edn., Nat. Nursing Staff Devel. Orgn., 1994, Customer Svc. Star award Erie VA Med. Ctr., 2000, Spl. Contbn. award Vets. Health Adminstrn., 2002. Mem. Pa. Nurses Assn. Home: 6124 Washington Ave Erie PA 16509-2726 Office: 135 E 38th St Erie PA 16504-1559

STECKLER, LARRY, publisher, editor, writer; b. Bklyn., Nov. 3, 1933; s. Morris and Ida (Beekman) S.; m. Catherine Coccozza, June 6, 1959 (div. June 1999); m. Lorraine Mary Rubsamen, Oct. 16, 1999 (div. June 1999); children: Gail Denise, Glenn Eric, Kerri Lynn, Adria Lauren; m. Lorraine Rubsamen, Oct. 16, 1999. Student, CCNY, 1951. Assoc. editor Radio-Electronics mag., N.Y.C., 1957-62, editor, 1967-85; pub., editor in chief Radio Electronics mag., 1985-92; electronics editor Popular Mechanics mag., N.Y.C., 1962-65; assoc. editor Electronic Products mag., Garden City, N.Y., 1965-67; editorial dir. Merchandising 2-Way Radio mag., N.Y.C., 1975-77; v.p., dir. Gernsback Publs., 1975-84, pres., dir., 1984—; pub., editorial dir. Spl. Projects mag., 1980-84, Radio-Electronics Ann., 1982-84; pub., editor in chief Hands-On Electronics, 1984-88, Computer Digest, 1985-90, Experimenters Handbook, 1986-96, Modern Short Stories, 1987-90, Video/Stereo Digest, 1989-91, Popular Electronics Mag., 1988-99, GIZMO, 1988-99, Hobbyists Handbook, 1989-96, Sci. Probe! mag., 1989-93, StoryMasters, 1989—, Electronics Shopper, 1990-99, Electronics Market Ctr., 1991-99, Electronics Now Mag., 1992-99, Radio Craft, 1993-96, Poptronix Handbook, 1996—; pres. Claggk, Inc., 1986—, Silicon Chip, 1993-94, Sci. Probe Inc., 1989-93, Poptronix Inc., 1997—; pub., editor-in-chief Poptronix online, 1997—. Mem. electronics adv. bd. Bd. Coop. Ednl. Svcs., Nassau County, NY, 1975—77; pres. Electronics Industry Hall of Fame, 1985—2001; bd. dirs. Pub. Hall of Fame, 1987—89. Author books, handbooks; pub., editor-in-chief Poptronics, 2000—, Poptronics Shopper, 2000—, PC Tech, 2000—; co-editor The Shofar, 1998—; pub.; contbr. articles to profl. jours. Bd. dirs. Nassau County coun. Camp Fire Girls, 1971-72; 1st v.p. bd. dirs. Temple Beth Am, Las Vegas, 1998—, pres. 2001-02. Served with U.S. Army, 1953-56. Recipient Coop. award Nat. Alliance TV and Electronic Services Assns., 1974, 75; inducted into Electronics Industry Hall of Fame, 1985; ISCET Gov's. award, 1998, FESA Pres. award, 1998. Mem.: L.A. Press, Soc. Profl. Journalists, Internat. Performing Magicians (exec.dir.), Internat. Underwater Explorers Soc., Am. Mgmt. Assn., Nat. Electronics Sales and Svc. Dealers Assn. (rec. sec. N.Y. State 1976—78, treas. 1991—94, Man of Yr. award 1975, 1985, M.L. Finneyberg Excellence award 1994), Internat. Soc. Cert. electronic Technicians (chmn. 1974—76, 1979—81, dir.-at-large 1991—93, rep. to NESDA bd. 1991—93, chmn. 1993—95, Region 9 dir. 1995—97, chmn. 1999—2001, Chmn.'s award 1985), IEEE, Am. Soc. Bus. Press Editors (sr.), Radio Club Am. Home: 9072 Lawton Pine Dr Las Vegas NV 89129-7044 *Do not be afraid to try the unaccepted. Do not be afraid to do the undesirable. Do what you enjoy. . .do it well. . .and after it is done. . .never regret having done it. . .only regret what you have not yet done.*

STECKLER, PHYLLIS BETTY, publishing company executive; b. N.Y.C. d. Irwin H. and Bertha (Fellner) Schwartzbard; m. Stuart J. Steckler; children: Randall, Sharon Steckler-Slotky. BA, Hunter Coll.; MA, NYU. Editorial dir. R.R. Bowker Co., N.Y.C., Crowell Collier Macmillan Info. Pub. Co., N.Y.C., Holt Rinehart & Winston Info. Systems, N.Y.C.; pres., CEO Oryx Press, Scottsdale, Ariz., 1973-76, Phoenix, 1976-01, Zephyr Info., Inc., Phoenix, 2001—. Adj. prof. mktg. scholarly publs. Grad. History dept., Ariz. State U., Tempe; mem. dean's coun. Coll. of Extended Edn., Ariz. State U., Phoenix. Past chmn. Info. Industry Assn.; past chair Ariz. Ctr. for the Book; past pres. Contemporary Forum of Phoenix Art Mus.; founding mem. Nat. Edn. Network, U.S. Dept. Edn.; past pres. Friends of the Librs., U.S.A.; mem. Ariz. Women's Forum. Recipient Women Who Make a Difference award The Internat. Women's Forum, 1995, Excellence in Pub. award Ariz. Book Pub. Assn., 1997, The Pub. History Program Ariz. State U. Founding Friend award, 2000; elected to Hunter Coll. Hall of Fame. Mem.: Univ. Club of Phoenix, Ariz. Libr. Assn., ALA. Home and Office: 6446 N 28th St Phoenix AZ 85016-8946 E-mail: pbs.zephyr@cox.net.

STEDGE-FOWLER, JOYCE, retired clergywoman; b. Spring Valley, N.Y., Mar. 2, 1926; d. Sidney and Lila Mae (Joyce) Kearsing; m. Leland Stedge, Sept. 4, 1948 (div. Apr. 1978); children: Leland Jr., Deborah Stedge-Stroud, David, Donald, Claudia, Douglas; m. Joseph Charles Fowler, June 23, 1985. BA in Liberal Arts, U. Iowa, 1947; MDiv, Union Theol. Sem., N.Y.C., 1973. Ordained to ministry Ref. Ch. in Am., 1973; cert. elem. tchr., N.Y. Elem. tchr. Ramapo I Sch. Dist., Suffern, N.Y., 1966-68, Ramapo II Sch. Dist., Spring Valley, 1968-69; pastor Rochester Ref. Ch., Accord, N.Y., 1973-76; NIMH clin. pastoral intern in mental health St. Elizabeths Hosp., Washington, D.C., 1976-77, clin. pastoral resident in supervision and consultation, 1977-79; pastor-at-large New Castle Presbytery, Wilmington, Del., 1979-82; interim pastor Coop. Parish St. George's, Port Penn, Del. City, Pencader Presbyn. chs., 1980; interim pastor 1st and Olivet Presbyn. Ch., Wilmington, 1980, Hanover Presbyn. Ch., Wilmington, 1981, Ocean City (Md.) Presbyn. Ch., 1982; pastor Christ Presbyn. Ch., Martinsville, N.J., 1982-85; min. to elderly United Presbyn. Ch., Plainfield, 1985-91; ret., 1991. Chaplain Robert Wood Johnson Health Care Ctr., Plainfield, 1985-91; cons., clin. pastoral educator and therapist, 1975-95; mem. task force on abortion Nat. Coun. Chs., 1970-73, mem. Commn. on Women in Ministry, 1973-80, mem. women's ecumenical coordinating group, 1973-79; mem. justice for women com. Elizabeth Presbytery, 1982—, mem. social issues com., 1986-91, moderator, 1991-92, mem. gen. coun., 1990-91, mem. pers. com., 1991-95; del. to Gen. Assembly, Presbyn. Ch. (U.S.A.), 1985, 91. Former leader Rockland County coun. Girl Scouts U.S.A.; former treas., fin. chmn., bd. dirs. LWV; com. mem. Water, Sewer and Fgn. Policy Rockland County Study, 1955-73; former program chmn. Women's Assn., former adult edn. chmn. Spring Valley Ref. Ch.; former mem. coun. and edn. chmn. Ctrl. Rockland Ecumenical Witness, Spring Valley; bd. dirs. Somerset Chaplaincy to Elderly, 1985-91, Somerset Chaplaincy to Ex-Offenders, 1982-86, NAMI-Familya, 1999—. Democrat.

Achievements include becoming the 1st woman ordained in the Reformed Church in America by Rockland-Westchester Classis. Avocations: reading, swimming, walking, children and grandchildren. Home: 10 Summit Park Rd Spring Valley NY 10977-1510

STEDINGER, JERY RUSSELL, civil and environmental engineer, researcher; b. Oakland, Calif., June 22, 1951; s. Russell Phillip and Vivian Lavina (Nelson) S.; m. Robin Lee Gray, June 30, 1973; children: Matthew, Carolyn. BA, U. Calif., Berkeley, 1972; AM, Harvard U., 1974, PhD, 1977. Math. programmer Lawrence Livermore Lab., Livermore, Calif., 1973; rsch. asst., teaching fellow Engr. and Applied Physics, Harvard U., Cambridge, Mass., 1974-77; asst. prof. Civil and Environ. Engr., Cornell U., Ithaca, N.Y. 1977-83; hydrologist U.S. Geol. Survey, Resten, Va., 1983-84; assoc. prof. Civil and Environ. Engr., Cornell U., Ithaca, N.Y., 1989-93, prof., 1989—. Cons. Pacific Electric and Gas Co., San Francisco, 1989-98, U.S. Army Corps Engrs., 1999. Author: Water Resources Systems Planning and Analysis, 1981; contbr. articles to profl. jours. Scoutmaster Troop 2, Boy Scouts Am., Ithaca, N.Y., 1988-2002. Recipient Editor's Citation for Excellence in Reviewing award Am. Geophys. Union, 1983, 90, 93; named Presdl. Young Investigator, NSF, 1984-90, CEE Prof. of Yr., Chi Epsilon, 1979-80, 99-2000. Fellow Internat. Water Acad.; mem. ASCE (Huber Civil Engring. Rsch. prize 1989, Julian Hinds award 1997), Am. Geophys. Union, Inst. Mgmt. Scis., Soc. for Risk Analysis. Office: Cornell U Sch Civil Environ Engring 213 Hollister Hall Ithaca NY 14853-3501

STEDMAN, MYRTLE LILLIAN, artist; b. Charleston, Ill., Feb. 5, 1908; d. Edward Bullard and Myrtie (Harrell) Kelly; m. Wilfred Henry Stedman, Nov. 15, 1928 (dec. 1950); children: Thomas Wilfred, Wilfred Donald. Student, Mus. Fine Arts, Houston, 1927-34, Art Student's League, N.Y.C., 1979-80. Fine artist, illustrator Stedman Studio, Houston, 1927—34. Designer, builder Tesuque Home Builder, 1952-87. Prin. works include preservation of historic homes Adobe Morada, Taos, N.Mex., 1954, redesign of Tesuque Elem. Playground and Parking Lot, 1974; author, illustrator: The Way Things Are Or Could Be: A New Consciousness, 1996, Ongoing Life, 1993, Artists in Adobe, 1993, A House Not Made With Hands, 1993, Rural Architecture of Southern Colorado and Northern New Mexico, Featuring Barns, Fences, and Corrals, 1990, Of One Mind, 1974, Adobe Architecture, 1936-73, 86, Adobe Remodeling and Fireplaces, 1973, 86, Of Things to Come, 1998, The Ups and Downs of Living Alone in Later Life, 2000. Mem. bd. Las Tres Villas, Tesuque, 1973-83, Santa Fe (N.Mex.) Water Basin, 1970-80, Pojoaque (N.Mex.) Water Bd., 1960's; mem. County Recreational Adv. Com., Santa Fe, 1960's. Recipient Visual and Lit. Arts award N.Mex. Arts Commn., Mayor's award City of Santa Fe, 1994, Old Santa Fe Assn. award, 1993, Watercolor awards Houston Fine Arts Mus., 1933, N.Mex. Gov.'s award for Excellence in the Arts Art/Arch., 1997; named Living Treasure Santa Fe Networks, 1985. Mem. PEN/USA/West, Mus. N.Mex. Found. (life), Inst. Noetic Scis. (charter), Women in the Arts Nat. Mus. (charter), Santa Fe Hist. Found., Old Santa Fe Assn. Avocations: keeping scrapbooks, photography, walking, reading. Home: 225-A County Rd 73 Santa Fe NM 87506-0005

STEDMAN, R VANGORDEN, artist, art historian radio and television personality; b. N.Y., 1965; s. Richard J. and Joyce (Allen) S. Student, SUNY, New Paltz, 1990, SUNY, Purchase, 1994; BA in Art History, SUNY, Binghamton, 1996. Curatorial intern Roberson Ctr. for Arts and Scis., Binghamton, 1982-83; photography, publicity and graphic design mgr. The Switch, Endicott, N.Y., 1984; emcee The Jolt, East Aurora, 1984; TV guest host WSKG Pub. TV, Binghamton, 1984-85; radio fine arts commentator Talk Am. Radio Network Stas. WENE, WGUL, WNFB, WVOX, Upstate N.Y., also Fla., 1986-99; studio and archive dir., mgr. estates of artists Henryk Glickenstein, Emmanuel Romano, others, St. Petersburg, Fla., 1989—. Panelist Personal FX, Fox TV Network, N.Y., 1994; curator Otto Bierhals Family Collection and Archive, Greenwich, Conn., 1991—; acting curator The Gallery at Gran Finale, St. Petersburg, 1998-99. Exhibited works in shows including Tracy St. Collective, 1985, Purchase Coll., 1995, others; author fine arts and related topics article series Antiquer's Guide, Sidney, N.Y., 1986-87; art appraisal commn. Cornell U., Ithaca, N.Y., 1996; lectr., rschr. Mem. Zodiac Group/Salvador Dali Mus., 1998-99. Office: 204 37th Ave N # 351 Saint Petersburg FL 33704-1416

STEDMAN, RICHARD RALPH, retired lawyer; b. Columbus, Ohio, July 18, 1936; s. Ralph Dale and Kathleen (Smith) S.; m. Elizabeth Ann Witschey, Dec. 18, 1965; children: Gretchen Kathleen, Richard Ralph II, Patrick Christopher Raymond. BBA, Ohio State U., 1958, JD, 1964. Bar: Ohio 1964; CPA, Ohio. Staff acct. Price Waterhouse & Co., Columbus, 1958-60; salesman Royal McBee Co., 1960; assoc. Vorys, Sater, Seymour & Pease, 1964-69, ptnr., 1970-99. Contbr. articles to profl. jours. Trustee Found. Cath. Diocese of Columbus, 1985—; trustee Ohio Dominican Coll., 1990-96, St. Charles Prep. Sch., 1990—, Edward Orton, Jr. Ceramic Found., 1994—. Merson fellow Ohio State U., 1963-64. Mem. Athletic Club Columbus, Columbus Club, Brookside Golf and Country Club, Zanesfield Rod and Gun Club, Equestrian Order of Knights Holy Sepulchre of Jerusalem, Order of St. Gregory the Great. Republican. Avocations: golfing, tennis, fishing, photography.

STEDMAN, WILLIAM PRESTON, music educator; b. Austin, Tex., Feb. 10, 1923; s. Nathan Alexander and Mary Lucille (Sneed) S.; m. Helen Margaret Slessor, Aug. 3, 1946 (div. May 1968); children: Preston Slessor, Alexander Winship; m. Leslie Clark McNeill, June 5, 1971. BA, Tex. Christian U., 1944, MMus, 1948; PhD, U. Rochester, N.Y., 1953. Asst. bus. mgr. Ft. Worth Civic Opera Assn., 1946-47; asst. prof. music Sul Ross State Coll., Alpine, Tex., 1947-51; asst. prin. viola El Paso (Tex.) Symphony Orch., 1948-51; teaching asst. Eastman Sch. Music, Rochester, 1952-53; instr. music Ind. U., Bloomington, 1953-55; music chair, prof. music Tex. A&I U., Kingsville, 1955-66; dean Conservatory of Music U. Pacific, Stockton, Calif., 1966-76; prof. music Calif. State U., Fullerton, 1976—; exec. dir. Pacific Symphony Orch., 1978-79. Dir. Western Opera, San Francisco Opera, 1975-78; v.p. exec. bd. Pacific Symphony Orch., Costa Mesa, Calif., 1978-93; examiner Western Assn. Schs./Colls., Oakland, Calif., 1966-92; cons. Calif. Arts Coun., Sacramento, 1968-76; fiscal cons. Calif. Assn. Profl. Music Tchrs. Author: Intro to Stylistic Theory, 3 vols., 1988, The Symphony, Research and Information Guide, 1990, Mexico's Musical Evolution, 1992, The Symphony, 2nd edit., 1993. Lay reader Episcopal Ch., Alpine, Tex., Stockton, Calif., Kingsville, Tex., 1950-76; pres. Kingsville Cmty. Concerts Assn., 1964-66; bd. mem. Fine Arts Commn.,Fullerton, Calif., 1980-84. Lt. (j.g.) USN, 1943-46, PTO. Faculty rsch. grantee Ind. U., Bloomington, 1954, Tex. A&I U., Kingsville, 1963. Mem. Assn. Calif. Symphony Orchestra (bd. mem., v.p. 1988-90), Music Tchrs. Nat. Assn. (chmn. theory composition S.W. divsn. 1958-66). Avocations: hiking, camping, back-packing, politics. Home: 731 E Avocado Crest Rd La Habra Heights CA 90631-8132

STEEB, ROSEMARIE CHRISTINA, accountant, consultant; b. Buffalo, Feb. 23, 1966; d. Anthony George and Carmela Maria (Federico) S. BSBA, Rockhurst Coll., 1987. CPA. Sr. tax staff mem. Arthur Young, Kansas City, Mo., 1985-89, Ernst & Young, Buffalo, 1989-92, tax mgr., 1992-94, area dir. compliance Pitts., 1994-97, tax compliance mgr. Charleston, W.Va., 1997-98, sr. engagement coord., 1998—. Dir. Excalibur Leisure Skills Ctr., Buffalo, 1992—; tchr. U. Buffalo Grad. Tax Inst., 1993—, Becker CPA review, Buffalo, 1997—. Mem. AICPA, Am. Inst. Individual Investors, N.Y. State Soc. CPA. Roman Catholic. Office: Ernst & Young LLP 1400 Key Twr 50 Fountain Plz Buffalo NY 14202 E-mail: rosemarie.steeb@ey.com.

STEED, CONNIE MANTLE, nurse; b. Ft. Riley, Kans., Oct. 6, 1956; d. Ronald James Jr. and Ivey Coene (Jenkins) Mantle; m. Thomas Joseph Steed, Jr., Aug. 27, 1979; children: Christopher Michael, Robert James. ADN, Columbus Coll., 1976; postgrad. RN, S.C.; cert. in infection control. Nurse aide Bradley Ctr. Psychiatric Hosp., Columbus, Ga., 1975-76; staff nurse West Ga. Med. CTr., LaGrange, 1976-78, nurse epidemiologist, 1978-87, nurse edn. coord., 1987-88; employee health coord. Spartanburg Regional Med. Ctr., S.C., 1988-89; nurse epidemiologist Greenville Meml. Hosp., 1989—. Nat. infection control adv. bd. mem. SmithKline and Beecham, Inc., 1991-92; nat. adv. com. mem. Standard Textiles, Inc., Cin., 1993-94; cons. Kimberly Clark Healthcare Divsn., Roswell, Ga., 1992, B. Braun, Inc., Bethlehem, Pa., 1992-93; mem. regulatory affairs com. S.C. Hosp. Assn., 1995, 96; chmn. S.C. TB Task Force, 1993-98. Co-author: Home Health Infection Control Manual, 1988; contbr. articles to profl. jours. Recipient scholarship for abstract devel. Palmetto Hosp. Trust, Inc., 1995. Mem. Am. Heart Assn. (dist. 4 chmn. 1984-87, Ray Johnson award for edn. achievement Ga. affiliate 1987), Assn. for Profls. in Infection Control and Epidemiology, Inc. (Horizon award Palmetto chpt. 1995, nat. govt. affairs com. mem. 1994, 95), Nat. Assn. for Profls. in Infection Control and Epidemiology, Ga. Infection Control Network (mem. of yr. award 1988), Inc. (chmn. bd. 1982-91, award 1988). Republican. Avocations: reading, softball. Office: Greenville Meml Hosp 701 Grove Rd Greenville SC 29605-4295

STEED, KELLY RENÉE, writer, poet; b. Detroit, Apr. 6, 1965; d. Kenneth Calvin and Edna Jean (Hughes) R.; m. Richard Dale Steed, Nov. 22, 1991. BS in History, No. Mich. U., 1989. Cert. secondary tchr., Mich. Hist. site interpreter Heritage Hill State Park, Green Bay, Wis., 1990, Henry Ford Museum and Greenfield Village, Dearborn, Mich., 1991-92; proofreader of subpeonas Record Copy Svc., Detroit, 1990-91; substitute tchr. Grosse Pointe (Mich.) Pub. Schs., 1991-92; novelist, poet Harrison Twp., Mich., 1995—. Author: Stasis, 2001; contbr. poetry, short stories and essays to various publs. (Editor's Choice award 1995, 96, 97, 2000), including America at the Millennium. Recipient 2d Pl. award First Page Novel Contest, 1997; named to Internat. Poetry Hall of Fame, 1996, hon. mention Rotten Romance Contest, 2001, finalist May/June Creative Jour. Contest. Mem. Internat. Soc. Poets (disting.), VFW Aux. (life, 5-yr. pin 1997), Mil. Order Cooties. Republican. Avocations: historical reenacting, period clothing reconstruction, collecting science fiction movie and television memorablia, aiding writers via internet. E-mail: kellysteed@authorsden.com.

STEED, MICHELLE ELNORA, special education educator, counselor; b. Raleigh, N.C., Sept. 23, 1967; d. Johnnie Wilbert and Ednell (Thornton) S. BA, N.C. State U., 1989, MEd, 1990. Cert. spl. edn. Tchr. Franklin County Schs., Youngsville, N.C., 1999—. N.C. State U. fellow, 1989-90, All Am. scholar N.C. State U. Democrat. Baptist. Avocations: pianist, organist. Home: 5512 Thornton Rd Raleigh NC 27616-5728

STEED, THERESA JEAN, manufacturing company executive; b. Grapeland, Tex., Mar. 10, 1932; d. Robert Tresband and Alma Inez (Denson) Bobbitt; m. Jarvis Lacy Steed, July 8, 1950; children: Judy Karen, Pamela Kay, Kim Lacy. Grad., Elliott Bus. Sch., Houston, 1949; BMus. Edn., So. Coll. Fine Arts, Houston, 1956; postgrad., U. Tex., 1961, Sul Ross U., Alpine, Tex., 1962; M. of Rhymes (hon.), Duke U., 1961. Exec. sec. various cos., Houston, 1950-57; elem. sch. tchr. Rosenburg (Tex.) Ind. Sch. Dist., 1957-58; kindergarten/music edn. tchr. Sonora (Tex.) Ind. Sch. Dist., 1959-65; elem. sch. tchr. Houston Ind. Sch. Dist., 1965-67, Conroe (Tex.) Ind. Sch. Dist., 1968-70; co-founder, co-owner Steed Tile & Mfg. Co., Conroe, 1965—. Author: Audio-Visual Curriculums for Music Education: Kindergarten Through Eighth Grade, 1962. Mem. Dem. Nat. Com., Washington, 1993—, Dem. Senatorial Campaign Com., Washington, 1997. Mem.: Order Eastern Star (assoc. matron 1963), Nat. Trust for Hist. Preservation, Women in Constrn. (charter, reporter 1970—75), Pilot Club, Delta Kappa Gamma (publicity chmn. 1962—65). Methodist. Avocations: cooking, gardening, grandparenting, politicking. Home: 17595 W FM1097 Montgomery TX 77356-8471

STEEDMAN, DORIA LYNNE SILBERBERG, organization executive; b. L.A. d. Mendel B. and Dorothy H. (Howell) Silberberg; m. Richard Cantey Steedman, Feb. 19, 1966; 1 child, Alexandra Loren. BA summa cum laude, UCLA. Producer EUE/Screen Gems, N.Y.C., 1963-66, Jack Tinker & Ptnrs., N.Y.C., 1966-68, Telpac Mgmt., N.Y.C., 1968-72; v.p. broadcast prodn. Geer DuBois Advt., 1973-78, account mgr., dir. ops., 1979-92; exec. v.p., pro bono dir. creative devel. Partnership for a Drug-Free America, 1992—. Bd. dirs. Friends of the Earth. Recipient Andy award Art Dirs. Club, 1968, 71; named one of 100 Best and Brightest Women in Advt., Advt. Age mag.; named Advt. Woman of Yr., 1996. Mem. Advt. Women N.Y. (pres. 1993-95), Advt. Women N.Y. Found. (pres. 1995-97), Phi Beta Kappa. Office: Partnership for a Drug-Free Am 405 Lexington Ave New York NY 10174-0002 E-mail: doria_steedman@drugfree.org.

STEEG, MOISE S., JR. lawyer; b. New Orleans, July 25, 1916; s. Moise S. and Carrie (Gutmann) S.; m. Marion B., Sept. 14, 1943 (dec.); children: Barbara Steeg Midlo, Marion, Robert M.; m. Melba Law, Nov. 29, 1969. LLB, Tulane U., 1937. Bar: La. 1937, U.S. Dist. Ct. (ea. dist.) La. 1939, U.S. Ct. Appeals (5th cir.) 1946, U.S. Supreme Ct. 1950, U.S. Ct. Appeals (11th cir.) 1981. Practice, New Orleans, 1937—; assoc. Rittenberg & Rittenberg, 1937-38; sole practice, 1938-46; founder Gertler & Steeg, 1946-48, Steeg & Morrison, 1948-50, Marcus & Steeg, 1950-54, Steeg & Shushan, 1954-71; sr. ptnr. Steeg & O'Connor, 1972—. Bd. dirs. Loyola U., chmn., 1979—, mem. search com. for dean Coll. Law; chmn., founder New Orleans Hist. Dist. and Landmarks Com.; bd. dirs. chmn. bd. New Orleans Mus. Art, 1980; bd. overseers Hebrew Union Coll.; bd. dirs. Delgado Jr. Coll., New Orleans Symphony; founder, dir. New Orleans Ednl. and Rsch. Corp.; bd. dirs. Louise Davis Sch. for Retarded Children, Touro Infirmary, 1963-69; mem. Ochsner Found. Hosp. Bd., 1985—; bd. visitors Trinity Episcopal Sch., 1989—; organizer, sec. New Orleans Bus. Coun., 1986; pres. Temple Sinai, 1966-67; chmn. Anti-Defamation League, Jewish Community Ctr., chmn. Acquarium Drive, Acquarium of Ams.; local counsel Nat. Dem. Party, 1966. Served to capt. USAF, 1942-46. Recipient Brotherhood Award, NCCJ, 1980, Disting. Alumnus award Tulane Law Sch., 1991, Isidore Newman Sch., Svc. award Newcomb Coll. Soc., Cmty. Svc. award New Orleans Bar Assn. Mem. Paul Tulane Honor Soc. Home: One River Place 3 Poydras St New Orleans LA 70130-1665 Office: 201 Saint Charles Ave Ste 3201 New Orleans LA 70170-1032

STEEL, DANIELLE FERNANDE, author; b. N.Y.C., Aug. 14, 1947; d. John and Norma (Stone) Schuelein-Steel Student, Parsons Sch. Design, 1963, NYU, 1963-67. Vice pres. pub. relations and new bus. Supergirls Ltd., N.Y.C., 1968-71; copywriter Grey Advt., San Francisco, 1973-74. Author novels Going Home, 1973, Passion's Promise, 1977, Now and Forever, 1978, The Promise, 1978, Season of Passion, 1979, Summers End, 1979, To Love Again, 1980, The Ring, 1981, Loving, 1980, Love, 1981, Remembrance, 1981, Palomino, 1981, Once in a Lifetime, 1982, Crossings, 1982, A Perfect Stranger, 1982, Thurston House, 1983, Changes, 1983, Full Circle, 1984, (non-fiction) Having A Baby, 1984, Family Album, 1985, Secrets, 1985, Wanderlust, 1986, Fine Things, 1987, Kaleidoscope, 1987, Zoya, 1988, Star, 1988, Daddy, 1989, Message from Nam, 1990, Heartbeat, 1991, No Greater Love, 1991, Jewels, 1992, Mixed Blessings, 1992, Vanished, 1993, Accident, 1994, The Gift, 1994, Wings, 1994, Lightning, 1995, Five Days in Paris, 1995, Malice, 1996, The Ghost, 1997, The Ranch, 1998, The Long Road Home, 1998, The Klone & I, 1998, Silent Honor, 1997, His Bright Light, 1998, Mirror Image, 1998, Bittersweet, 1999, Granny Dan, 1999, Irresistible Forces, 1999, The Wedding, 2000, The House on Hope Street, 2000, Journey, 2000, Lone Eagle, 2001, Leap of Faith, 2001, The Kiss, 2001, The Cottage, 2002, (children's) Martha's Best Friend, Martha's New School, Martha's New Daddy, Max's New Daddy, Max and The Babysitter, Max's Daddy Goes To The Hospital; contbr. poetry to mags., including Cosmopolitan, McCall's, Ladies Home Jour., Good Housekeeping Home: PO Box 1637 New York NY 10156-1637 Office: care Dell Publishing 1540 Broadway New York NY 10036-4039

STEEL, DUNCAN GREGORY, physics educator; b. Cleve., Jan. 11, 1951; s. Robert John and Mildred (Graham) S.; children: Adam, Benjamin. BA, U. N.C., 1972; MS, U. Mich., 1973, 75, PhD, 1976. Physicist Exxon Rsch. and Engring., Linden, N.J., 1977-78, Hughes Rsch. Labs., Malibu, Calif., 1975-85; prof. U. Mich., Ann Arbor, 1985—; sr. rsch. scientist Inst. Gerontology Sch. Medicine, U. Mich., 1986—, sr. rsch. scientist biophys. rsch. divsn., 1992—, Peter S. Fuss prof. engring., 1999—, area chair optical scis., dir. optical sis. lab., 1989—. Topical editor Jour. Optical Soc., Washington, 1986-92. Contbr. articles to profl. jours. Guggenheim fellow, 1999. Fellow IEEE, Optical Soc. Am., Am. Phys. Soc. Achievements include development of first phase conjugate laser; first high resolution nonlinear laser spectroscopy of semiconductor heterostructures; research in of collision induced resonances in atoms; low noise (below the standard quantum limit) room temperature semiconductor lasers; of first demonstration of coherence optical control and wave function engineering in quantum dots; of first demonstration of wave function engineering; first deimonstration quantum entanglement in a single quantum dot; demonstration of in vitro tryptophan phosphorescence for studies of protein structure in solution; discovery of of structural annealing in proteins during protein folding. Office: U Mich Physics Dept 500 E University Ave Ann Arbor MI 48109-1120

STEEL, KUNIKO JUNE, retired artist; b. San Francisco, June 3, 1929; d. Jirohei and Moriyo (Shiraishi) Nakamura; m. John Schulein-Steel, Jan. 26, 1963 (dec. May 1978). Student, U. Calif., 1948-49; diploma, Am. Acad. Art, Chgo., 1951; student, Academic Julian, Paris, 1952-53, Art Inst. Chgo., 1954-55, Art Students League, N.Y.C., 1959-62, 79-85. Exhibited in group shows at Rafilson Gallery, Chgo., 1954, Arts of N.E., Silvermine, Conn., 1966, 79, 90, 92, Modern Maturity Traveling Exhibit, 1990-92, Schoharie Exhibit, Cobleskill, N.Y., 1993-94, Mus. of Modern Art, Miami, Coral Gables, Fla., 1993, 37th Chautaqua Nat. Exhibit of Am. Art, 1994, Montclair State U., 1994, 95. Vol., crafts tchr. Hosp. for Spl. Surgery, N.Y.C., 1967-84; vol. Japanese Gallery Met. Mus., 1994; past vol. costume conservation Met. Mus., N.Y.C., 1979-94. Recipient scholarship Palo Alto Quota Club, 1948, Art Students League, 1960. Avocations: designing arts and crafts, painting.

STEEL, PHILIP S. architect, artist; b. Phila., Nov. 1, 1934; s. Robert Wenzing and Beryl (Vanhorn) S.; m. Joan Crawford, June 1, 1979; children: Philip, Amy, Eric, Robert. BArch, Pa. State U., 1957; MArch, U. Calif., Berkeley, 1963. Registered architect, Fla., Maine, Pa., N.J.; Nat. Coun. Archs. Registration Bd. cert. Prin. Philip Steel & Assoc., AIA, West Chester, Pa., 1964-75, Palm Beach, Fla., 1975-88, Ft. Pierce, 1988—. Past mem. Fla. State Bd. Bldg. Codes and Stds. Works exhibited in group shows McBridge Gallery, Annapolis, Md., Patricia Cloutier Art Gallery, Tequesta, Fla., Arnold Art Store, Newport, R.I., Admiralty Gallery, Vero Beach, Fla., Geary Gallery, Darien, Conn. Chmn. Landmark Commn. for Palm Beach, Fla.; chmn. Under Oaks Show and Fla. Competitive, Ctr. for the Arts, Vero Beach; bd. mem. Cultural Affairs Coun. St. Lucie County; mem. St. Lucie County Seaport Adv. Commn., St. Lucie County U. Task Force. Lt. comdr. USNR, 1957-59. Recipient Disting. Bldg. award Pa. Soc. Architects, 1969, 1st honor award, 1971, Internat. Torchburner award Am. Hotel and Motel Assn., 1985, 2nd place watercolor Backus Gallery, Ft. Pierce, Fla., 1994, 1st place watercolor Backus Gallery, Ft. Pierce, 1995, 96, Sanford Studio award N.E. Water Color Soc.'s Ann. Nat. Exbhn., Kent Art Assn., 1996, 2d place award St. Lucie County Profl. Arts League Regional Exhbn., 1997, Silver Brush award Fla. Watercolor Soc., Melvin Gallery, Lakeland, Fla., 1997. Mem. AIA (pres. Palm Beach chpt., state dir. Indian River chpt.), Pa. Soc. AIA (past state dir., past pres.), Rotary Club Palm Beach. Avocations: sailing, music, tennis. Office: 2030 Harbortown Dr Fort Pierce FL 34946-1438

STEEL, RONALD LEWIS, writer, historian, educator; b. Morris, Ill., Mar. 25, 1931; BA magna cum laude, Northwestern U., 1953; MA, Harvard U., 1955. Vice consul U.S. Fgn. Service, 1957-58; editor Scholastic mag., N.Y.C., 1959-62; sr. assoc. Carnegie Endowment for Internat. Peace, 1982-83; fellow Woodrow Wilson Internat. Ctr. Scholars, 1984-85; prof. internat. relations U. So. Calif., Los Angeles, 1986—; fellow Wissenschaftskolleg zu Berlin, Federal Republic of Germany, 1988. Vis. fellow Yale U., 1971-73; vis. prof. U. Tex., 1977, 79, 80, 85, Wellesley Coll., 1978, Rutgers U., 1980, UCLA, 1981, Dartmouth Coll., 1983, Princeton U., 1984; Shapiro prof. internat. rels. George Washington U., 1995-97. Author books including: The End of Alliance: America and the Future of Europe, 1964, (with G. Kimble) Tropical Africa Today, 1966, Pax Americana, 1967, Imperialists and Other Heroes, 1971, Walter Lippmann and the American Century, 1980, Temptations of a Superpower, 1995, In Love With Night: The American Romance with Robert Kennedy, 2000; editor various publs. for H.W. Wilson Co., 1961-67; contbr. to N.Y. Rev. Books; contbg. editor New Republic. Served with U.S. Army, 1954-56. Recipient Sidney Hillman award, 1968, Washington Monthly book award, 1980, Los Angeles Tims book award for non-fiction, 1980, Nat. Book Critics Circle award, 1981, Bancroft prize Columbia U., 1981, Am. Book award for biography, 1982; Guggenheim fellow, 1973-74 Mem. Council on Fgn. Relations Office: U So Calif Sch Internat Rels Los Angeles CA 90089-0001

STEEL, SHAWN, political party official; m. Michelle Park; 2 children. M in History, JD, U. So. Calif. Atty. Shawn Steel & Assocs., Rolling Hills, Calif.; former treas. bd. dirs., former vice chmn. Calif. Rep. Party, chair, 2001—. Mem.: LA Lincoln Club. Office: 1903 W Magnolia Blvd Burbank CA 91506 also: Shawn Steel & Assocs 27520 Hawthorne Blvd Ste 270 Palos Verdes Peninsula CA 90274 Office Fax: 818-841-6668.*

STEELE, ANA MERCEDES, former government official; b. Jan. 18, 1939; d. Sydney and Mercedes (Hernandez) S.; m. John Hunter Clark, June 2, 1979. AB magna cum laude, Marywood Coll., 1958. Actress, 1959-64; sec. Nat. Endowment for Arts, Washington, 1965-67, dir. budget and rsch., 1968-75, dir. planning, 1976-78, dir. program coordination, sr. exec. svc., 1979-81, assoc. dep. chmn. programs, dir. program coordination, 1982-93, acting chmn., acting sr. dep. chmn., 1993, sr. dep. chmn., sr. exec. svc., 1993-96, dep. chmn. mgmt. and budget, sr. exec. svc., 1996-98; ret., 1998. Guest lectr. George Washington U., 1987; trustee Marywood Coll., 1989-96, Marywood U., 1997-98. Author, editor report: History of the National Council on the Arts and National Endowment for the Arts During the Johnson Administration, 1968; editor: Museums USA (Fed. Design Coun. award of Excellence 1975), 1974, National Endowment Arts, 1965-85: A Brief Chronology of Federal Involvement in the Arts, 1985. Former reader Rec. for the Blind, N.Y.C.; former tutor Future for Jimmy, Washington. Named Disting. Grad. in Field of Arts, Marywood Coll., 1976; recipient Sustained Superior Performance award Nat. Endowment for Arts, 1980, Disting. Svc. award, 1983, 84, 85, 89, 92, 96, presdl. medal Marywood U., 2000; named to Disting. Alumnae Hall of Fame, Ursuline Acad., 2001. Mem. Actors' Equity Assn., Screen Actors Guild, Delta Epsilon Sigma, Kappa Gamma Pi. Home: 2475 Virginia Ave NW Apt 604 Washington DC 20037-2639

STEELE, ANTONIO L. retired principal, educator; b. Charlotte Amalie, St. Thomas, V.I., Oct. 4, 1947; s. Oliver O. and Viola A. (Smith) Steele; m. Floria R.; children: Monifa N., Renael E., Renan O., Rissah M. BA, Coll of V.I., 1970; MA, NYU, Washington Sq., 1977; postgrad., U. Ill., Taff Inst. Elem. tchr. George Washington Sch., St. Thomas, 1970; tchr. Eulalie Rivera Sch., St. Croix, V.I., 1971-73, Alfredo Andrews Sch., St. Croix, 1973, tchr. environ. edn., 1974, asst. prin., 1975-80, Juanita Gardina Elem. Sch., St. Croix, 1980, Evelyn M. Williams Elem. Sch., St. Croix, 1981, prin., 1982-97, Claude O. Markoe Elem. Sch., 1998—2000. Leader and presenter workshops, task force leader; mem. V.I. Commn. on Edn. Active ch. and cmty. roles. Mem. LEAD (adv. bd.), Am. Fedn. Sch. Adminstrs., St. Croix Edn. Adminstrn. Assn. (pres. 1987-2000, adminstr. adult basic edn. 1989—), C.L.C. of V.I. (treas. 1996).

STEELE, C. WILLIAM, scouting organization administrator; b. Dayton, Ohio, Oct. 17, 1948; s. Charles William Sr. and Helen Marie Steele; m. Janet Lynn Fitzsimmons, Sept. 9, 1978; children: Brian, Audrey. BS, Ind. U., 1973. Profl. scouter Boy Scouts Am., San Antonio, 1980-96, scout exec. Bartlesville, Okla., 1996-2001, assoc. nat. dir. Irving, Tex., 2001—. Author: Yochib: The River Cave, 1985; contbr. chpt. to books. Mem. Explorers Club. Democrat. Episcopalian. Avocation: exploring caves. Office: 1325 W Walnut Hill Ln Irving TX 75038-3008

STEELE, CARL LAVERN, academic administrator; b. Patoka, Ill., Aug. 22, 1934; s. Boyd Alfa and Effie Jane (Corson) S.; m. Lula Irene Saliba, June 11, 1961; children: Jeffrey Van, Gregory Michael, Douglas Alan. BEd, So. Ill. U., 1956, MEd, 1960; MLS, No. Ill. U., 1971. Tchr. Shawneetown (Ill.) Community High. Sch., 1956-57; GED instr. U.S. Army, Ft. Hood, Tex. and Ulm, Fed. Republic of Germany, 1957-59; tchr. Forrest-Strawn-Wing Unit Dist., Forrest, Ill., 1959-61, Richwoods Community High Sch., Peoria, 1961-66; asst. dir. instructional materials Sauk Valley Coll., Dixon, 1966-68; dir. Ednl. Resources Ctr., Rock Valley Coll., Rockford, 1968-93; ret., 1993. Part-time traffic safety instr. Rock Valley Coll., 1992—. Asst. World Record sec. Nat. Fresh Water Fishing Hall of Fame, Hayward, Wisc., 1977-79. Served with U.S. Army, 1957-59. Mem. ALA, Assn. Ednl. Communications and Technology, Ill. Assn. Ednl. Communications and Technology (conv. chmn. 1976), No. Ill. Media Assn. (conv. chmn.), Learning Resource Commn. ICCCA (chmn. 1981). Democrat. Presbyterian. Avocations: fishing, travel, reading, woodworking, gardening. Home: 5758 Weymouth Dr Rockford IL 61114-5569 E-mail: lsteele@steele.com.

STEELE, CHARLES GLEN, retired accountant; b. Faulkton, S.D., July 24, 1925; s. Clifford D. and Emily O. (Hanson) S.; m. Shirley June Ferguson, Nov. 9, 1947; children: Richard Alan (dec.), Deborah Ann Steele Most. BBA, Golden Gate U., San Francisco, 1951, MBA, 1962. With Deloitte Haskins & Sells, 1951-86, partner, 1963-86, partner charge Chgo. office, 1973-76, partner charge personnel and adminstrn., 1976-78, chmn., chief exec. officer, 1978-86. Instr. evening program Golden Gate U., 1952-58. Served with USNR, 1943-48. Recipient Elijah Watts Sells Gold medal for highest grade in U.S. for C.P.A. exam., 1951 Mem. Am. Inst. C.P.A.s. Home and Office: 5 Stonecrest Circle Rancho Mirage CA 92270

STEELE, CHARLES RICHARD, biomedical and mechanical engineering educator; b. Royal, Iowa, Aug. 15, 1933; married, 1969; 4 children. BS, Tex. A&M U., 1956; PhD in Applied Mechanics, Stanford U., 1960; PhD (hon.), Zaporozhye State U., Ukraine, 1997. Engring. specialist aircraft structure Chance-Vought Aircraft, Dallas, 1959-60; rsch. scientist shell theory Lockheed Rsch. Lab., Palo Alto, 1960-66; assoc. prof. Stanford (Calif.) U., 1966-71, prof. applied mechanics, 1971—. Lectr. U. Calif., Berkeley, 1964-65; vis. prof. Swiss Fed. Inst. Technology, Zurich, 1971-72, U. Luleå, Sweden, 1982, Chung Kung U., Taiwan, 1985, U. Cape Town, South Africa, spring 1993, U. Trento, Italy, fall 1999; tech. dir. Shelltech Assoc. Editor-in-chief: Internat. Jour. Solids Structures, 1985—. Recipient NIH Claude Pepper award, 1988, Humboldt award, 1994; named Eminent Academician Ukrainian Acad., 1998. Fellow ASME (chmn. exec. com. applied mechanics divsn. 1983-84, Warner T. Koiter medal 1999), Am. Acad. Mechanics (pres. 1989-90); mem. AIAA, NAE, Acoustical Soc. Am. Achievements include research in asymptotic analysis in mechanics; thin shell theory; mechanics of the inner ear; noninvasive determination of bone stiffness; and morphology of plants. Office: Stanford U Divsn Mechanics & Computat Durand Bldg 355A Stanford CA 94305-4040

STEELE, CHERYL A. oncology nurse; b. Pitts., July 17, 1952; d. Thomas Smith and Lois Eleanor (Sherrick) S. BSN, Indiana U. Pa., 1978; MSN, U. Pitts., 1987; MPM, Carnegie Mellon U., 1997. RN, Pa.; advanced oncology cert. nurse. Critical care nurse Western Pa. Hosp., Pitts., 1974-78; head nurse, oncology clin. specialist Forbes Health Sys., Monroeville, Pa., 1978-89; clin. dir. outpatient svcs., breast care ctr., cmty. sites U. Pitts. Cancer Inst., 1989—. Adj. faculty U. Pitts. Sch. Nursing Grad. Program, 1991—. Contbr. chpts. to books, articles to profl. jours. Am. Cancer Soc. scholar, 1985, award, 1988. Mem. Nat. Oncology Nursing Soc., Assn. Cmty. Cancer Ctrs., Nat. Assn. Vascular Access Networks, Sigma Theta Tau. Presbyterian. Home: 217 Heather Dr Monroeville PA 15146-1747 Office: U Pitts Cancer Inst Montefiore Hosp 3459 5th Ave Pittsburgh PA 15213-3236 E-mail: steeleca@msx.upmc.edu.

STEELE, CLARENCE HART, retired otolaryngologist; b. Sabetha, Kans., Feb. 21, 1914; MD, U. Kans., 1940. Cert. in otolaryngology. Intern Kansas City Gen. Hosp., 1940-41; resident in otolaryngology Tulane Ear Nose and Throat Hosp., New Orleans, 1941-43; Am. Bd. Otolaryng, 1944; hon. Bethany Med. Ctr., Kansas City, Kans., 1990-92, Providence Health Ctr., Kansas City, 1992-95; ret., 1995. Fellow ACS; mem. Am. Acad. Otolaryngology-Head and Neck Surgery, Am. Acad. Otolaryngic Allergy, Am. Coll. Allergy and Immunology, Am. Laryngol., Rhinol. and Otol. Soc. (1997 Centennial Yr. Honor for Svc. v.p., 1974, 97).

STEELE, EARL LARSEN, electrical engineering educator; b. Denver, Sept. 24, 1923; s. Earl Harold and Jennie (Larsen) S.; m. Martha C. Hennessey, June 27, 1953; children: Karl Thomas, Earl Robert, Karen Lynn, Kevin Douglas, Lisa Louise, Colleen Carol. BS with honors, U. Utah, 1945; PhD, Cornell U., 1952. Research physicist Gen. Electric Co., 1952-56; chief device devel. Motorola, Inc., 1956-58; mgr. devel. lab. Hughes Aircraft Co., 1958-64; research scientist N.Am. Rockwell Corp., 1964-69; prof. elec. engring. U. Ky., Lexington, 1969-90, prof. emeritus, 1991—, chmn. dept., 1971-80, 1988-89. Affiliate prof. Ariz. State U., 1956-58, U. Calif.-Irvine, 1966-69; adviser So. Calif. Coll., Costa Mesa, 1963-64; charter mem. Orange County Academic Decathlon (Calif.); bd. dirs. Southeastern Center for Elec. Engring. Edn., 1975—, treas., 1980-81, v.p., 1981-82, resident dir., 1981-82, 89-90, pres., 1982-83, mem. coun. of pres.', 1983—. Author: Optical Lasers in Electronics; contbr. articles to profl. jours. Fellow IEEE; mem. Am. Soc. Engring. Edn. (U. Ky. Coll. Engring. rep. to ASEE, 1988-90), Am. Phys. Soc., Internat. Soc. Hybrid Microelectronics, Sigma Xi, Tau Beta Pi, Eta Kappa Nu (dir. 1974-76, v.p. 1983-84, pres. 1984-85). Mem. Lds Ch. Home: 313 Blueberry Rd Lexington KY 40503-2004

STEELE, ERNEST CLYDE, retired insurance company executive; b. Corbin, Ky., May 11, 1925; s. J. Fred and Leona (McFarland) S.; m. Cora Jones, June 17, 1944 (dec. Nov. 1988); children: Gerald R., David. P.; m. Helen LeCoultre, July 7, 1990. BS with honors, U. Ky., 1948, MS, 1950. Asst. actuary Peninsular Life Ins. Co., Jacksonville, Fla., 1950-54; actuary Pioneer Life & Casualty Co., Gadsden, Ala., 1955; v.p., actuary Guaranty Savs. Life Ins. Co., Montgomery, 1956-57; exec. v.p., actuary Am. Investment Life Ins. Co., Nashville, 1958-59; pres., actuary Appalachian Nat. Life Ins. Co., Knoxville, Tenn., 1959-67; sr. v.p., chief investment officer, ops. analyst Coastal States Life Ins. Co., Atlanta, 1968-71, exec. v.p., dir., 1971-74, pres., dir., 1974-79, Occidental Life Ins. Co. of N.C., 1979-85, chmn., 1986-88; pres., dir. Peninsular Life Ins. Co., 1981-83, chmn., 1986-88; exec. v.p. investments MCM Corp., 1985-88; ret., 1988. Past pres. Ga. Assn. Life Inst. Cos., 1976-77. Mem. devel. coun. U. Ky. Served to 2d lt. U.S. Army, 1943-45. Fellow Life Mgmt. Inst.; mem. Life Office Mgmt. Assn. (past chmn. bd.), Am. Council Life Ins. (past dir.), U. Ky. Alumni Assn. (past bd. dirs.), Am. Acad. Actuaries, Pi Mu Epsilon. Republican. Baptist. Home: 103 Newell Village Cir Seymour TN 37865-5931 E-mail: ecsteele@webtv.net. *My success in life is measured by the success of those with whom I have been associated.*

STEELE, FRANK RICHARD, retired consumer products company executive; b. N.Y.C., Apr. 1, 1922; s. Sidney Richard and Hilda Maude Steele; m. Barbara Mae Haley; children: Joan, Gary; children: Joan, Gary, Michael. Grad., Stuyvesant HS, N.Y.C., 1940. Dir. manpower planning domestic oper. Johnson & Johnson, New Brunswick, NJ, 1972—76, dir. adminstrv. svcs. corp. hdqs., 1976—84. Adj. gen. corps U. S. Army, various Army Posts, world-wide, 1940—65; mgmt. analyst Port Authority, N.Y. & N.J., 1965—67; dir. adminstrn. hdqs. Nat. Urban League, N.Y.C., 1967—72. Author: Story of a Buffalo Soldier, 2002. Pres. Bloomsdale Gardens-Fleetwing Estates Civic Assn., Bristol, 1965. Maj. U.S. Army.

STEELE, GEORGE PEABODY, retired marine transportation executive; b. San Francisco, July 27, 1924; s. James Mortimer and Erma (Garrett) S.; m. Elizabeth Yates Fahrion, July 11, 1944 (div. May 1988); children: Jane Yates Steele Marcum, James Fahrion; m. Betty McDonnell, May 20, 1988. BS, U.S. Naval Acad., 1944. Commd. ensign USN, 1944; advanced through grades to vice adm., 1973; service aboard submarines in Pacific World War II, 1945; comdr. U.S.S. Hardhead, 1955-56, comdr. nuclear powered U.S.S. Seadragon (made 1st NW passage under ice to North Pole), 1959-61, comdr. Polaris missile sub U.S.S. Daniel Boone, 1963-66; head politico-mil. policy div. Europe/NATO br. Office Chief Naval Ops., 1966-68, comdr. Naval Forces Korea, chief Naval adv. group, Korean Navy, comdr. Naval Component UN Command, 1968-70, comdr. Anti-Submarine Warfare Group 4, 1970-72; dep. asst. chief of staff Supreme Allied Comdr. SHAPE, Europe, SHAPE, Belgium, 1972-73; comdr. U.S. 7th Fleet, 1973-75, ret., 1975; exec. v.p. Interocean Mgmt. Corp., Phila., 1976-78, pres., 1978-81, chmn., chief exec. officer, 1981-89, dir., 1989-94. Chmn. bd. trustees Fgn. Policy Rsch. Inst., 1980-89, trustee, 1989-93. Author: Seadragon, Northwest Under the Ice, 1962, (with H. Gimpel) Nuclear Submarine Skippers and What They Do, 1962, Vengeance in the Depths, 1963; contbr. articles to profl. publs. and newspapers. Decorated D.S.M., Legion of Merit with 4 gold stars, Navy Cross (Peru), Order of Rising Sun (Japan), Cloud and Banner (China), Order Nat. Security of Merit (Republic Korea); recipient John B. Diman Disting. Grad. award St. George's Sch., 1994, Lowell Thomas award for submarine Arctic exploration Explorers Club, 1997, Elisha Kent Kane Gold medal for Arctic svc., 2001. Mem. Am. Polar Soc. (hon. membership medallion 2000), U.S. Naval Inst., Univ. Club, N.Y. Yacht Club, Army-Navy Club. Episcopalian. Home: 6 Upland Rd Apt 2B Baltimore MD 21210-2258

STEELE, GLENN DANIEL, JR. surgical oncologist; b. Balt., June 23, 1944; m. Diana; 1 child, Joshua; m. Lisa; children: Kirsten, Lara. AB magna cum laude, Harvard Coll., 1966; MD, NYU, 1970; PhD, Lund U., Sweden, 1975. Intern, then resident Med. Ctr. U. Colo., Denver, 1970-76; fellow NIH in immunology Univ. Lund, Sweden, 1973-75; asst. surgeon Sidney Farber Cancer Inst., Boston, 1976-78; cons. surgeon Boston Hosp. for Women, 1977-80; clin. assoc. surgical oncology Sidney Farber Cancer Inst., 1978-79; jr. assoc. in surgery Peter Bent Brigham Hosp., Boston, 1976-82; instr. surgery Med. Sch. Harvard, 1976-78; asst. prof. surgery Med. Sch. Harvard Coll., 1978-81; asst. physician surgical oncology Sidney Farber Cancer Inst., 1979-82; assoc. prof. surgery Med. Sch. Harvard Coll., 1981-84; surgeon Brigham & Women's Hosp., 1982-84; assoc. physician surgical oncology Dana-Farber Cancer Inst., 1982-84, physician surg. oncology, 1984-95; chmn. dept. surgery, deaconess Harvard Surg. Svc. New England Deaconess Hosp., Boston, 1985-95; William V. McDermott prof. surgery Med. Sch. Harvard Coll., 1985-95; prof. Univ. Chgo., 1995—2001, dean biological scis. divsn. and Pritzker Sch. Medicine, 1995—2001, v.p. medical affairs Pritzker Sch. Medicine, 1995—2001; chair. Am. Bd. Surgery, Phila., 1999-; pres, CEO Geisinger Health System, Danville, 2001—. Assoc. editor Jour. of Clin. Oncology, 1986—, Jour. of Hepatobiliary-Pancreatic Surgery, 1993—; mem. editorial bd. Annals of Surgery, Annals of Surg. Oncology, British Jour. of Surgery, Surgery, Surgical Oncology; contbr. numerous articles to profl. jours. Recipient NIH fellow 1973-75, Am. Cancer Soc. fellow 1972-73, 76-79, various other rsch. grants. Fellow Am. Coll. Surgeons (chmn. patient care and rsch. com. commn. on cancer 1989-91, mem. bd. govs. 1991-95, chmn. commn. on cancer 1991-93, mem. exec. com. commn. on cancer 1992-93); mem. Am. Assn. Immunologists, Am. Bd. Surgery (dir. 1993-98, vice-chmn. 1998—), Ill. Surgical Soc., Am. Bd. Med. Specialties, Am. Soc. Clin. Oncology, Am. Surg. Assn., Assn. Program Dirs. in Surgery, Assn. for Surgical Edn., Internat. Fedn. Surg. Colls., Internat. Surg. Group, Soc. Surg. Oncology (treas. 1994-97, v.p. 1997, pres.-elect 1998), New England Cancer Soc., and numerous other mems. Office: Geisinger Health System 100 North Academy Ave Danville PA 17822*

STEELE, HOWARD LOUCKS, economic development consultant, author; b. Pitts., Jan. 27, 1929; s. Howard Bennington and Ruby Alberta (Loucks) S.; m. Sally E. Funk, June 6, 1952 (div. 1977); children: John F., David A., Patricia A.; m. Jane R. Cornelius, July 30, 1977 (div. 1996); 1 child, Jennifer L.; m. Elaine Haddock, Aug. 23, 1997. BS, Washington and Lee U., 1950; MS, Pa. State U., 1952; PhD, U. Ky., 1962. Sales mgr. Greenville (Pa.) Dairy Co., 1952-56; owner H.L. Steele Bulk Milk Hauling, Greenville, 1955-60; asst. prof. Clemson (S.C.) U., 1956-57, assoc. prof., 1957-64, Ohio State U., Columbus, 1964-71; with Fgn. Agrl. Svc./Internat. Coop. and Devel. U.S., Dept. Agr., Washington, 1971-97; ret.; econ. devel. cons., 1997—. Project mgr. AID, Guatemala, 1976-77, Bolivia, 1977-80, Honduras, 1980-82, Sri Lanka, 1982-84, Bur. L.Am. and Caribbean USAID, Washington, 1984-88, office of the dir. tech. assistance divsn., 1988-90, with office of dep. adminstr., 1990-97; USDA liaison officer Inter-Am. Inst. Coop. in Agr., 1993-97; instr. U. Md., College Park, 1974-76; vis. prof. U. Sao Paulo, Piracicaba, Brazil, 1964-66; ptnr. Kingwood Acres Farm, Rockwood, Pa., 1966-98. Author: Commercial-izacao Agricola, 1971, A 200 Year History of Some Descendents of the Pioneer James Steel of Castleblaney, Ireland and Mt. Pleasant, Pennsylvania, 1994, Your Tax Dollars at Work (I'd Rather Have Gone Business Class!), 1998, Food Soldier, 2002; contbr. articles to profl. jours. Recipient Nat. Forensic Union award; named One of Outstanding Young Men U.S., U.S. Jaycees, 1965; cert. of merit Dept. Agr., 1975, 92. Mem. Am. Agrl. Econs. Assn., Internat. Assn. Agrl. Economists, SAR, Masons, Shriners, Gamma Sigma Delta, Sigma Nu. Home: 5204 Holden St Fairfax VA 22032-3418 E-mail: ehsteele@juno.com.

STEELE, IAN MCKAY, research scientist, consultant; b. Syracuse, N.Y., June 19, 1944; s. Alister Watt Donald Steele and Anna Frances Padget; m. Barbara Jean Argumedo. BS, Rensselaer Poly. Inst., 1966; PhD, U. Ill., 1971. Sr. rsch. assoc. U. Chgo., 1971—. Materials cons., Michiana Shores, 1986—. Coun. mem. Town Coun., Michiana Shores, 2000—02. Fellow: Meteoritical Soc., Mineral. Soc. Am.; mem.: Mineral. Soc. Gt. Britian. Avocation: antique restoration. Home: 221 Pokagon Trail Michigan City IN 46360 Office: U Chgo 5734 S Ellis Ave Chicago IL 60637 Home Fax: 773-702-9505; Office Fax: 773-702-9505. Personal E-mail: iansteele@attbi.com. Business E-Mail: steele@geosci.uchicago.edu.

STEELE, JAMES EUGENE, school system administrator, educator; b. South Norfolk, Va. s. James Edward and Blanche Eugenia (Munden) S. BS in Music Edn., William & Mary Coll., 1961; MEd in Ednl. Adminstrn. and Supervision, Temple U., 1972; EdD in Ednl. Adminstrn., Nova U., 1976. Cert. tchr., Va. Piccoloist Va. Symphony Orch., 1951-73; dir. choral music Hampton (Va.) City Schs., 1960-65, supr. music, 1965—. Guest flute soloist Music Tchrs. Assn., Great Britain, 1962. Dir. fine arts divsn. Hampton Assn. Arts Humanities, 1967—. Mem. NEA, Va. Edn. Assn., Hampton Edn. Assn., Va. Assn. Sch. Execs., Hampton Instrnl. Suprs. Assn., Tidewater Regional Suprs., Va. Assn. Sch. Curriculum Devel., Va. Music Suprs. Assn., Va. Music Educators Assn., Music Educators Nat. Conf., Va. Choral Dirs. Assn., Va. Band and Orch. Dirs. Assn., Va. String Tchrs. Assn. Home: 132 Fayton Ave Norfolk VA 23505-4428 Office: 1819 Nickerson Blvd Hampton VA 23663-1026

STEELE, JAMES HARLAN, former public health veterinarian, educator; b. Chgo., Apr. 3, 1913; s. James Hahn and Lydia (Nordquist) S.; m. Aina Oberg, 1941 (dec. 1969); children: James Harlan, David, Michael; m. Maria-Brigitte Meyer, 1969. DVM, Mich. State Coll., 1941; MPH, Harvard U., 1942. With Ohio Dept. Health, 1942-43; with USPHS, 1943-71; advancing through grades to asst. surgeon gen. for vet. affairs and chief vet. officer; chief vet. pub. health activities Communicable Disease Center, Atlanta, 1947-71; prof. environ. health U. Tex. Sch. Pub. Health, Houston, 1971-83, prof. emeritus, 1983—. Cons. WHO, 1950—, Pan-Am. Health Orgn., 1945—, FAO, UN, 1960, German Health Svc., 1986-93; vis. prof. Tex. A&M U., 1976—, all univ. prof., 1981-82. Author: (with J. Arthur Myer) Bovine Tuberculosis Control in Man and Animals, 1969, rev. (with Charles Thoen), 1995; editor-in-chief CRC Zoonoses Handbooks, 1979-84, cons. editor, 1994, 8 vols. transl. into Russian and Farsi, Bacterial & Viral Zoonoses, 2 vols. rev. by Beran; mem. editl. cons. bd. APHA Control Communicable Disease, 1960-2000; contbr. articles to profl. jours. and sects. to books on food hygiene and irradiation. Recipient Mich. State U. Alumni award, 1958, USPHS Order of Merit, 1963, Karl F. Meyer Gold Head Cane award, 1966, Disting. Svc. award USPHS, 1971, Mich. State U. Coll. Vet. Medicine award, 1972, hon. mem. Epidemic Intelligence Svc., 1975, James Law award Cornell U., 1983, Centennial award U. Pa., 1984, Am. Vet. Med. Assn. Internat. Vet. award, 1984, Pub. Svc. award, 1993; James H. Steele Vet. Pub. Health award World Vet. Epidemiology Soc., 1975, Disting. Svc. award Am. Vet. History Soc., 1995, James H. Steele award Ctr. for Disease Control, 1998, Disting. Alumni award Mich. State U., 2001; James H. Steele ann. lectr. established in his honor U. Tex. Health Sci. Ctr., 1993, James H. Steele Pub. Health Professorship, 1996. Fellow Am. Pub. Health Assn. (emeritus, 1984; Bronfman award 1971, Centennial award 1972), Am. Coll. Epidemiology (founding fellow); mem. Conf. Pub. Health Vets. (founder), Am. Soc. Tropical Medicine (emeritus), Am. Coll. Vet. Preventive Medicine (founder, hon. diploma 1983, Pres.'s award 1994), Nat. Acad. Health Practitioners, World Vet. Epidemiology Soc. (founder, pres. 1971), Am. Vet. Epidemiology Soc. (pres. 1966-88), World Vet. Assn. (hon.), Philippines Vet. Med. Assn. (hon.), Peru Vet. Med. Assn. (hon.), Hellenic Vet. Soc. (Athens Greece, hon. diploma, 1977), U.S. Animal Health Assn. (life), U.S.-Mex. Pub. Health Assn. (hon., life), Mil. Surgeons Assn. (hon. life), Infectious Disease Soc. Am. (emeritus), Internat. Epidemiology Soc. (emeritus), XXI World Vet. Congress (Moscow, hon. diploma 1979), German Health Svc. (hon. diploma, 1988, Order of Merit 1993), Harvard U. Alumni Assn. (Alumni award 1998), Mich. State U. Alumni Assn., Alpha Psi. Episcopalian. Home: 10722 Riverview Way Houston TX 77042-1391 Office: School of Public Hlth University of Texas Houston TX 77225 *I have believed firmly throughout my career that I should share my knowledge and expertise with my fellow man, be he American or citizen of the world. Those of us who are more fortunate to be endowed with intellectual advantages have an even greater responsibility to share.*

STEELE, JEFFREY ALLEN, English language educator; b. Berkeley, CAlif., Feb. 15, 1947; s. Charles William Steele and Eleanor Jean Townsend; m. Jocelyn Carol Riley, Sept. 4, 1971; children: Doran, Brendan. BA magna cum laude, Carleton Coll., 1969; MAT, Harvard U., 1971, MA, 1977, PhD, 1981. Asst. prof. English U. Wis., Madison, 1981-87, assoc. prof. English, 1987-92, prof. English, 1992—. Author: (books) Unfolding the Mind: The Unconscious in American Romanticism and Literary Theory, 1987, The Representation of Self in the American Renaissance, 1987, Transfiguring America: Myth, Ideology, and Mourning in Margaret Fuller's Writing, 2001; editor: (anthology) The Essential Margaret Fuller, 1992 (Outstanding Acad. Book Choice 1993). Asst. scoutmaster troop 13 Boy Scouts of Am., Madison, 1990-93, 96—. Named one of Top 100 Educators at U. Wis.-Madison, Wis. Student Assn., 1991; Initial fellow U. Wis. Tchg. Acad., 1993, Vilas Assocs. fellow U. Wis.-Madison, 1990-92, fellow U. Wis. Inst. for Rsch. in Humanities, 1984, Arthur Lehman fellow Harvard U., 1978, traveling fellow Thomas J. Watson Found., 1969; summer stipend NEH, 1989. Mem.: Margaret Fuller Soc. (1st v.p. 1999—), Phi Beta Kappa. Office: U Wis Dept English Madison WI 53706 E-mail: jsteele@facstaff.wisc.edu.

STEELE, JERE RANDALL, elementary school educator; b. Cairo, Apr. 30, 1945; s. Louise Holst Steele; children: Jere, Thomas. BS, Coll. Charleston, 1976, MEd, 1979; EdS, U. Fla., 1988. Cert. Elem. Edn. 1976. Instr. Charleston County Schs., Charleston, SC, 1976—78; adminstr. Charleston County Schools, 1979—80; asst. prof. P.K.Yonge Devel. Rsch. Sch., Gainesville, Fla., 1982—. Consulting faculty Challenger Ctr., Washington, 1990—99; dir. Space Camp for Disadvantaged Youth, Gainesville, FLA., 1989—94; adj. instr. U. of Fla., Gainesville, FLA., 1986, Valdosta State Coll., Ga., 1982. Author: (novel) Second Island Out, 2002. Mem. City Beautification Bd., Gainesville, FLA., 1986. Sgt. USMC, 1966—72, Vietnam. Fellow Christa McCauliffe fellowship, US Dept. of Edn., 1990; grantee Bingham Environ. Fellowship, U. of Fla., 1995. Mem.: Fla. Alliance Social Studies Educators, Nat. Assn. of Lab. Schools, VFW. Republican. Lutheran. Avocation: sailing, bicycling, woodworking, gardening, travel. Home: 7817 SW 95th Ln Gainesville FL 32608 Office: P.K.Yonge Devel Rsch Sch 1080 SW 11th St Gainesville FL 32601 Business E-Mail: jsteele@pky.ufl.edu.

STEELE, JOHN HYSLOP, marine scientist, oceanographic institute administrator; b. Edinburgh, U.K., Nov. 15, 1926; s. Adam and Annie H.; m. Margaret Evelyn Travis, Mar. 2, 1956; 1 son, Hugh. B.Sc., Univ. Coll., London U., 1946, D.Sc., 1964. Marine scientist Marine Lab., Aberdeen, Scotland, 1951-66, sr. prin. sci. officer, 1966-73, dep. dir., 1973-77; dir. Woods Hole Oceanographic Instn., Mass., 1977-89, pres., 1986-91. Mem. NAS/NRC Ocean Sci. Bd., 1978-88, chmn., 1986-88; mem. rsch. and exploration com. Nat. Geog. Soc.; mem. Arctic Rsch. Commn., 1988-92; trustee U. Corp. Atmospheric Rsch., 1987-91, Bermuda Biol. Sta., R.W. Johnson Found.; del. Internat. Coun. Exploration Sea; hon. prof. U. Aberdeen. Author: The Structure of Marine Ecosystems, 1974; Contbr. articles to profl. jours. Served with Brit. Royal Air Force, 1947-49. Recipient Alexander Agassiz medal Nat. Acad. Sci., 1973 Fellow Royal Soc. London, AAAS, Royal Soc. Edinburgh, Am. Acad. Arts and Scis. Home: PO Box 25 Woods Hole MA 02543-0025 Office: Woods Hole Oceanographic Inst Woods Hole MA 02543

STEELE, JOHN THOMAS, surgeon, military officer; b. Marietta, Ga., July 2, 1961; MD, Med. U. S.C., 1987. Diplomate Am. Bd. Surgery. Commd. ensign USN, 1983, advanced through grades to commdr., 1998; intern Med. Coll. Ohio, Toledo, 1987-88, resident in gen. surgery, 1988-92; dir. surg. svcs. Naval Hosp., Patuxent River, Md., 1992-94; trauma/critical care fellow U. Calif., San Diego, 1994-96; staff surg. critical care Naval Med. Ctr., 1996—2000, asst. chmn. dept. gen. surgery, 1999, vice chmn. navy com. on trauma, 1999; staff surgeon trauma and critical care Palomar Med. Ctr., Escondido, 2000—. State faculty advanced trauma life support, 1996. Fellow: ACS; mem.: AAST. Office: 488 E Valley Pkwy Ste 311 Escondido CA 92025

STEELE, KAREN KIARSIS, retired state legislator; b. Haverhill, Mass., Sept. 26, 1942; d. Victor and Barbara (McFee) Kiarsis; m. Edward E. Steele, Apr. 16, 1966; children: Shawn Robert, Gretchen Garvey. BA, U. Vt., 1964. Tchr. Waterbury Sch. System, 1964-65, Burlington (Vt.) Sch. System, 1965-67; legislator State of Vt., Montpelier, 1982-2000; ret., 2000. Trustee Ctrl. Vt. Hosp., Berlin, Woodridge Nursing Home, Berlin. Mem. Am. Legis. Exch. Coun. (mem. exec. com. health and human svcs. task force). Republican. Avocations: golf, swimming, reading. Home: 1553 Perry Hill Rd Waterbury VT 05676-9633 E-mail: kksteele@aol.com.

STEELE, KAREN DORN, journalist; b. Portland, Oreg., Oct. 27, 1943; d. Ronald Gottche and Margaret Elizabeth (Cates) Moxness; m. Charles Stuart Dorn, Oct. 30, 1965 (div. Oct. 1982); children: Trilby Constance Elizabeth Dorn, Blythe Estella Dorn; m. Richard Donald Steele, July 4, 1983. BA, Stanford U., 1965; MA, U. Calif., Berkeley, 1967. Prodr. Sta. KSPS-TV, Spokane, Wash., 1970-72, dir. news and pub. affairs, 1972-82; reporter Spokesman-Rev., 1982-87, environ./spl. projects reporter, 1987—. Contbr. articles to sci. publs. (Olive Br. award NYU Ctr. War, Peace & The Media 1989). Bd. dirs. Women Helping Women, Spokane, 1994; trustee St. George's Sch., Spokane, 1988-92. Mid-career fellow Stanford Knight Fellowship Program, 1986-87, Arms Control fellow Ctr. for Internat. Security and Arms Control, Stanford U., 1986-87; Japan Travel grantee Japan Press Found., Tokyo, 1987, rsch. grantee John D. and Catherine T. MacArthur Found., 1992; recipient Gerald Loeb award Anderson Sch. Mgmt. UCLA, 1995, George Polk award L.I. U., 1995, William Stokes award U. Mo., 1988, Nat. Headliner award, Excellence in Legal Journalism award, Wash. State Bar Assn., 2000; inductee State Hall of Journalistic Achievement, Wash. State U., Pullman, 1995. Unitarian Universalist. Office: Spokesman Rev PO Box 2160 999 W Riverside Ave Spokane WA 99201-1098 E-mail: karend@spokesman.com.

STEELE, KENNETH FRANKLIN, JR. science educator, director; b. Statesville, N.C., Jan. 16, 1944; s. Kenneth Franklin and Ruth Virginia (Wilhelm) S.; m. Sheila Kay Stumpf, Sept. 3, 1966 (dec.); children: Krista Robin, Celisa Anne. BS in Chemistry, U. N.C., 1966, PhD in Geology, 1971. Registered profl. geologist, Ark., registered hydrogeologist. From instr. to assoc. prof. geology U. Ark., Fayetteville, 1970-83, dir. Ark. Water Resources Ctr., 1988—2002, prof., 1983—. Mem. State Bd. Registration for Profl. Geologists, 1992-96, 2000–, chmn., 1996, vice chmn., 2001-02; cons. in field. Contbr. numerous articles to profl. jours., chpts. to books; editor: Animal Waste and the Land-Water Interface. Summer faculty fellow Oak Ridge Associated Univs., 1981, 83, 85. Mem. Assn. Ground-Water Scientists and Engrs., Geol. Soc. Am. (regional bd. dirs. 1980-82, 84-86), Am. Water Resources Assn. (bd. dirs. 1991-94), Ark. Ground Water Assn. (bd. dirs. 1988-90, 93-95, v.p. 1991, pres. 1992), Nat. Assn. Water Inst. Dirs. (counselor 1990-93), Nat. Inst. Water Resources (bd. dirs. 1998-2001). Achievements include research on the importance of rainstorms on spring water chemistry, nitrate and pesticide contamination of ground water. Home: 1115 Valley View Dr Fayetteville AR 72701-1603 Office: U Ark Dept Geoscis 113 Ozark Hall U Ark Fayetteville AR 72701-4040 E-mail: ksteele@mail.uark.edu.

STEELE, KEVIN EDWARD, lawyer; b. Gary, Ind., Nov. 24, 1967; s. Charles Walter and Petra Agnes (Manning) S.; m. Laura Therese Gordon, Nov. 11, 1995. BA, U. Notre Dame, Ind., 1990; JD, Ind. U., 1993. Bar: Ind. 1993, U.S. Dist. Ct. (no. and so. dist.) Ind. 1993, U.S. Ct. Appeals (7th cir.) 1993. Ptnr. Burke, Costanza & Cuppy LLP, Merrillville, Ind., 1993—. Mem. ABA, Ind. Bar Assn., Lake County Bar Assn. Office: Burke Costanza & Cuppy LLP 9191 Broadway Merrillville IN 46410-5661

STEELE, MYRON THOMAS, lawyer; b. Taunton, Mass., July 28, 1945; s. Myron Thetus and Coleen Amelia (Polk) S.; m. Beverly June Heaps, Feb. 4, 1967; children— Clayton Carter, Jenness Farnham. B.A., U.Va., 1967, J.D., 1970. Bar: Va. 1970, Del. 1970, U.S. Dist. Ct. Del. 1970, U.S. Ct. Appeals (3d cir.) 1974. Assoc. Prickett, Ward, Burt & Sanders, Dover, Del., 1970, 73, ptnr., 1974; dep. atty. gen. State of Del., 1971-72; v.p., dir. Prickett, Jones, Elliott, Kristol & Schnee, Dover, Del., 1974-88; assoc. judge Superior Ct., 1988-90, resident judge, 1990-94, vice chancellor Ct of Chancery (Del.), 1994—; chmn. Ctrl. De. Health Care Corp., 1990-93. Mem. exec. com. Del. Democratic State Com., 1974-88; bd. dirs. Childrens Bur. Del., Del. News Council; chmn. Consumer Affairs Bd., 1974. Served to 1st lt. U.S. Army, 1970, Del. N.G., 1974—, col. ret. Mem. ABA, Del. Bar Assn. (past v.p.), Va. State Bar, Kent

County Bar Assn. (past pres.), Commn. on Ct. 2000 (Del.), Wilmington Club, Rehobeth Beach Country Club, Kiwanis (past pres.), Del-Vets, Masons. Episcopalian. Office: 417 S State St Dover DE 19901-6723*

STEELE, REBECCA HARRISON, lawyer, educator; b. Durham, N.C., Sept. 18, 1956; d. Thomas H. Harrison and Betty H. Inteman; m. Thomas T. Steele, Dec. 13, 1986; children: Sarah Elizabeth, Miranda Katherine. BA, U. S. Fla., 1978; postgrad., Carnegie-Mellon U., 1979-81; JD magna cum laude, Stetson U., 1995. Bar: Fla., U. S. Ct. Appeals (11th cir.), U. S. Dist. Ct. (so., mid. and no. dists.) Fla., U.S. Supreme Ct. Free-lance stage dir., theater mgr. various theater, 1975—94; adj. prof. U. S. Fla., Tampa, 1987—88, U. Tampa, 1990—91; assoc. Shackleford, Farrior, Tampa, 1995—97, Holland & Knight, Tampa, 1997—99; law clk. to Hon. Charles R. Wilson 11th Cir. Ct. Appeals, 1999—2000; with Trenam, Kemker, Scharf, Barkin, Frye, O'Neill & Mullis, 2000—. Adj. prof. Stetson U. Coll. Law, St. Petersburg, Fla., 1998—2000. Articles editor Stetson Law Rev. Mem. ABA (labor and employment law, employee benefits com. 1997—), Tampa Bay Pension Coun., West Coast Employee Benefits Coun., Athena Soc., Fla. Bar Assn. (labor and employment law, past chair employee benefits com.), Hillsborough Assn. of Women Lawyers (v.p., bd. dirs.). Office: Ste 2700 101 E Kennedy Blvd Tampa FL 33602 E-mail: rsteele@trenam.com.

STEELE, RICHARD DONALD, researcher, linguist, physicist; b. Modesto, Calif., Jan. 12, 1943; s. Warren Nelson, Jr. and Fern Marjorie (Thompson) S.; m. Karen Moxness Dorn, July 4, 1983; children: Trilby Dorn, Blythe Dorn. BS in Physics, Stanford U., 1964; MA, Harvard U., 1966, PhD in Slavic Langs., Linguistics, 1973. Asst. prof. Cornell U., Ithaca, N.Y., 1973-74; lectr. Harvard U., Cambridge, Mass., 1974-75, MIT, Cambridge, 1975-76; asst. prof. Grinnell (Iowa) Coll., 1976-80; rsch. health scientist Rehab. Rsch. Devel. Ctr., VA Med. Ctr., Palo Alto, Calif., 1982-90; mgr. comm. products Tolfa Corp., 1990-96; chief scientist LingraphiCARE Am., Oakland, 1996—. Rev. rehab. proposals NIH, Washington, 1991-94. Mem. editl. bd. Assistive Tech., 1988-91; contbr. articles to Neuropsycologia, Aphasiology, Brain Lang., Archives Phys. Med. Rehab., Stroke, others. Organizing com., official Clean Air Car Race, MIT, Calif. Inst. Tech., 1970; co-organizer aphasia spkrs. series Stanford U., 1988-89. Recipient Info. Resources Mgmt. award U.S. Govt. Interagy. com., 1987, Excellence in Tech. Transfer award Tech. Utilization Found., 1993; grantee World Rehab. Fund, 1987. Mem. IEEE, Sierra Club, Phi Beta Kappa. Democrat. Achievements include research in computer aided visual communication for aphasics, dissemination of rehabilitation technologies; 3 patents for a method of communicating using graphical elements, a method of communication using sized icons. Home: 1325 E 20th Ave Spokane WA 99203-3437 Office: LingraphiCARE Am 425 Jackson St Oakland CA 94607-4329

STEELE, RICHARD J. management consultant; b. Elkhart, Ind., Sept. 27, 1925; s. Cornelius H. and Harriett (Poel) S.; m. Shirley P. Ballard, Sept. 28, 2001; children: Barbara, Cheryl, Patricia, Thomas, Richard Jr., Marjorie, Gregory, Susan, Kathleen. SB, MIT, 1946; MBA, Ind. U., 1949. Cert. mgmt. cons. V.p. Fry Cons.'s, Inc., Chgo., 1950-70; pres. Richard Steele and Ptnrs., Inc., N.Y.C., 1970-72, Richard Steele Cons.'s, Inc., Columbia, Md., 1978-96; group v.p. Macro Systems, Inc., Silver Spring, 1972-78; sr. v.p. Birch & Davis Assocs., Inc., 1979-94. Counselor Nat. Health Coun., N.Y.C., 1971-94. Author: (with others) Determinants of HMO Success, 1988. Trustee Village of Riverwoods, Ill., 1967. Lt. USNR, 1943-75, WWII, Korea. Recipient Award of Merit Am. Heart Assn., 1974. Mem. Inst. Mgmt. Cons. Unitarian Universalist. Home and Office: Unit 201 20918 Island Sound Cir Estero FL 33928-8951 E-mail: rjsteele@alum.mit.edu.

STEELE, ROBERT DENNIS, radio producer, announcer, actor; b. Cin., Feb. 27, 1956; s. John Robert and Martha Adelaide (Friedmann) S.; m. Denise Elizabeth Rinear, Sept. 1, 1979; children: John Rinear, Benjamn Rinear, Allison Rinear, Emily Rinear. BFA in Radio, TV, Film, U. Cin., 1978. Announcer WSAI-AM, Cin., 1977; prodn. asst. WEBN-FM, 1977-78; prodn. dir. KGGO-FM, Des Moines, 1978-79, WWCK-FM, Flint, Mich., 1979-80; prodn. dir., then prodn. dir. and morning co-host WYSP-FM, Phila., 1980-81, 83-85; freelance producer, announcer Steele Creative Svcs., 1981-83, 87—; TV and radio writer, dir. programming Denny Somach Prodns., Havertown, Pa., 1984-87. Cons. Olympia Networks, St. Louis, 1988 Producer, writer radio spls. including Billy Crystal's Countdown to Christmas, 1985, Nat. Rock Test, 1986, 20th Ann. Salute to the Doors, 1987, Am. Comedy Network Awards, 1990, Led Zeptember, 1993, The World Premiere Broadcast of The Beatles Anthology II, 1996; radio series include: Psychedelic Psnack, 1985-87, John Madden's Sports Calendar, 1988-99; co-producer series Continuous History of Rock and Roll, 1981-83; producer, writer numerous comml s. Recipient Addy award Des Moines Advt. Profls., 1979, Flint Advt. Fedn., 1979, 80, Phila. Advt. Club, 1982, 84, 87, 2002, Silver Microphone Finalist award, 1986. Roman Catholic. Avocations: tennis, music, reading, cinema, theater. Home and Office: 215 Comrie Dr Villanova PA 19085-1402 E-mail: rdsteele@mindspring.com.

STEELE, ROBERT EDWIN, orthopedic surgeon; b. Kansas City, Mo., Jan. 8, 1937; s. Robert Edwin and Margaret Jane (Levens) S.; m. Emily Wells Stephens, May 9, 1964; children: Edward Stephen, Thomas McKewon, Linda Katherine. AB, U. Mo., 1959; MD cum laude, Harvard U., 1963. Diplomate Am. Bd. Orthopedic Surgery; cert. Am. Acad. Orthopedic Surgeons, Assn. Arthritic Hip and Knee Surgery. Intern Mass. Gen. Hosp., Boston, 1963-64; resident in orthopedics Harvard U., 1966-71; instr. in orthopedic surgery Harvard Med. Sch., Boston, 1971; mem. med. staff Good Samaritan Hosp., Corvallis, Oreg., 1971—. Bd. dirs. Good Samaritan Hosp., 1984-88, pres. med. staff, 1985, chmn. peer rev. com., 1994. Author: Studies on Osteonecrusis, 1979. Lt. USNR, 1964-66, Vietnam. Recipient Kappa Delta award for Outstanding Orthopedic Rsch., Am. Acad. Orthopedic Surgeons, 1978. Mem. Corvallis Orthopedic Surgeons (pres. 1990). Achievements include performance of total knee replacement. Avocations: camping, cycling, hiking, skiing, white water boating. Address: 560 NW Tyler Ave Corvallis OR 97330

STEELE, RODNEY REDFEARN, judge; b. Selma, Ala., May 22, 1930; s. C. Parker and Miriam Lera (Redfearn) S.; m. Frances Marion Blair, Aug. 1, 1964; children: Marion Scott, Claudia Redfearn, Parker Blair. AB, U. Ala., 1950, MA, 1951; LLB, U. Mich., 1954. Bar: Ala. 1954, U.S. Dist. Ct. (mid. dist.) Ala. 1959, U.S. Ct. Appeals (5th cir., now 11th cir.) 1981. Law clk. Ala. Ct. Appeals, 1956-57; assoc. Knabe & Nachman, Montgomery, Ala., 1957-61; asst. U.S. atty. Dept. Justice, 1961-66; staff atty. So. Bell T&T Co., Atlanta, 1966-67; judge U.S. Bankruptcy Ct., Mid. dist. Ala., Montgomery, 1967—, chief judge, 1985-99; ret., 1999—. Served with U.S. Army, 1954-56, Korea. Mem. ABA, Ala. State Bar, Montgomery County Bar Assn. Democrat. Episcopalian. Home: 1227 Magnolia Curv Montgomery AL 36106-2136

STEELE, SAMUEL MCDOWELL, urologist; b. Osawatomie, Kans., Mar. 16, 1939; s. Samuel McDowell and Maxine Rose (Meek) S.; m. Olivia Ann Smith, June 4, 1960; 1 child, Rodney Andrew. BS, Pitts. State U., 1961, MS, 1962; MD, U. Kans., 1968. Commd. officer USN, 1964; advanced through grades to capt., 1980; sr. med. officer Armed Forces Exam and Entrance Sta., Kansas City, Mo., 1970-71; urology resident Naval Reginal Med. Ctr., Phila., 1971-75; chmn. dept. urology Naval Hosp., Camp LeJeune, N.C., 1975-78, chmn. dept. urology, dir. urology resident tng. Portsmouth, Va., 1978-81; dir. combat casualty care course-task force Ft. Sam, Houston, 1981-84; physician advisor quality assurance, staff urologist Navy Hosp., Bethesda, Md., 1985-86; asst. chief staff plans and ops. Pacific Region Naval Med. Command, Barbers Point, Hawaii, 1986-89; comdr. joint med. readiness tng. ctr. Ft. Sam, 1989-93; ret. USN, 1993; staff mem. Cannon Meml. Hosp., Linville, NC, 1993—. Staff urologist Tripler Army Med. Ctr., Honolulu, 1987-89, Brooke Army Med. Ctr., Ft. Sam, 1990-93. Contbr. articles to profl. publs. Recipient Col. John F. Patton award Soc. Govt. Svcs. Urologists, 1983. Mem. AMA (award of appreciation 1984), Am. Coll. Physician Execs., Uniformed Svcs. Univ. Surgical Assocs., Am. Assn. Clin. Urologists. Avocations: scuba, snow skiing, running, reading, attending ethnic festivals. also: Cannon Meml Hosp Banner Elk NC 28604 also: Spruce Pine Cmty Hosp Spruce Pine NC 28777 Office: 177 New Vale Rd Newland NC 28657

STEELE, THOMAS JOSEPH, English language educator, writer; b. St. Louis, Nov. 6, 1933; s. Harry L. and Genevieve E. (Harder) S. BA, St. Louis U., 1957, licentiate in Philosophy, 1958, MA, 1959, licentiate in Theology, 1965; PhD, U. N.Mex., 1968. Tchr. Chaplain Kapaun High Sch., Wichita, Kans., 1959-61, Regis Coll., Denver, 1968—. Vis. prof. U. N.Mex., Albuquerque, 1982—. Author: Santos and Saints, 1994, (with others) Penitente Self-Government, 1985, Fraser Haps and Mishaps, 1990, Guidebook to Zen & The Art of Motorcycle Maintenance, 1990. Regis Centenary scholar, 1977. Mem. Soc. of Jesus. Roman Catholic. Avocations: golf, art, fishing, ranching. Office: Regis Jesuit Community 3333 Regis Blvd Denver CO 80221-1154

STEELE, THOMAS LEE, lawyer; b. Kearney, Nebr., Oct. 16, 1959; s. Clyde M. and L. Lorene S.; m. Sarah E. Owens, May 8, 1992; 1 child, Andrew. BA, U. Mo., 1984; JD, Creighton U., 1987. Bar: Nebr. 1987, Mo. 1988, Kans. 1989, U.S. Supreme Ct. 1993. Gen. counsel Gen. Fin. Svcs., Inc., Wichita, 1995—, Dunes Hotels and Casinos, Inc., 2000—. Bd. dirs. The Inland Corp., Norwich, Kans. Precinct chmn. Wichita Rep. Com., 1996—; exec. bd. Quivira coun. Boy Scouts Am., 1993—. Mem. ABA, Am. Assn. Sales Profls. (bd. dirs. 2000—), Mo. Bar Assn., Kans. Bar Assn., Nebr. Bar Assn., Pi Omicron Sigma. Presbyterian. Home: 156 Belmont Pl Wichita KS 67208 Office: Gen Fin Svcs Inc 8441 E 32d St N Wichita KS 67226

STEELE, THOMAS MCKNIGHT, law educator; b. Bartlesville, Okla., June 4, 1948; s. James Robert and Erma Blanche (McKnight) S.; m. Barbara Van Curen, Mar. 23, 1973 (div. 1985); children: James Robert, Ryan Thomas, David Christopher Joyce, Justin Daniel Joyce; m. Martha Bolling Swann, Apr. 1985 (div. 1990); m. LeAnn P. Joyce, Jan. 1995. BA in History, Okla. State U., 1969; MLS, U. Oreg., 1974; JD, U. Tex., 1977. Adminstrv. asst. Tarlton Law Libr. U. Tex., Austin, 1975-77; acting law librarian Underwood Law Libr. So. Meth. U., Dallas, 1977-78, asst. law librarian, 1978-79; assoc. prof. law, dir. Franklin Pierce Law Ctr., Concord, N.H., 1979-82; asst. prof., dir. U. Miss. Law Libr., University, 1982-85; assoc. prof., dir. Wake Forest U. Sch. Law Libr., Winston-Salem, N.C., 1985-91; dir. Profl. Ctr. Libr. Wake Forest U., NC, 1991—99, prof. law, 1991—. Cons. in field; exec. dir. SCRIBES--Am. Soc. Writers on Legal Subjects, 1988-97. Editor (newsletter) Scrivener, 1986-88; mng. editor Scribes Jour. Legal Writing, 1989-91; editor Pub. Librs. and Pub. Laws, 1986-88; compiler bibliography IDEA, 1981-83, Jour. Air Law and Commerce, 1977-81; co-author: A Law Library Move: Planning Preparation and Execution, 1994. With U.S. Army. Mem. Am. Assn. Law Librs. Democrat. Baptist. Office: Wake Forest U Sch Law PO Box 7206 Winston Salem NC 27109-7206

STEELE, VICTORIA LEE, librarian; b. L.A., Feb. 24, 1952; d. John Wilms and Marjorie (Lee) Erpelding; m. Timothy Reid, Jan. 14, 1979. BA, UCLA, 1974, MLS, 1981; MA, U. So. Calif., 1993, PhD, 2000. Libr. Belt Libr. of Vinciana UCLA, 1981-82, head history and spl. collections Biomed. Libr., 1983-86, dir. devel. librs., 1986-88; head spl. collections Young Rsch. Libr., 2000—; head spl. collections U. So. Calif., L.A., 1988-2000. Fundraising cons.; mem. adv. bd. KUSC Radio, 1997-2000. Author: Becoming a Fundraiser, 1992, 2d edit., 2000; prodr. film: Every time I See a Patient..., 1994; contbr. articles to profl. publs. Mem. adv. bd. Fulbright Program for So. Calif., 1995—, Mus. Found. Fashion Inst. Design and Merchandising, 2000—, Archives of Am. Art, 2000—; mem. adv. coun. Annenberg Sch. for Comm. U. So. Calif., 1994-2000; founder L.A. Preservation Network; vol. Save Outdoor Sculpture, 1995—; bd. dirs. Heritage Preservation. U. Calif. rsch. grantee, 1979, U. So. Calif. rsch. grantee, 1995; Fulbright fellow (U.K.), 1995, fellow L.A. Inst. for Humanities, 2000—. Mem. ALA (3M/JMRT award 1982, G.K. Hall award 1995), Calif. Hist. Soc. (bd. dirs. 2000—). Office: UCLA Young Rsch Libr Dept Spl Collections Box 951575 Los Angeles CA 90095-1575

STEELMAN, FRANK (FRANK SITLEY), lawyer; b. Watsonville, Calif., June 6, 1936; s. Frank S. Sr. and Blossom J. (Daugherty) S.; m. Diane Elaine Duke, June 27, 1960; children: Susan Butler, Robin Thurmond, Joan Bentley, David, Carol Pina. BA, Baylor U., 1958, LLB, 1962. Spl. agt. IRS, Houston, 1962-64, atty. for estate tax, 1964-68; trust officer First City Nat. Bank, 1968-71; sr. v.p., trust officer First Bank & Trust, Bryan, Tex., 1971-73; assoc. Goode, Skrivanek & Steelman, College Station, 1973-74; pvt. practice Bryan, 1974—. Vis. lectr. Tex. A&M U., College Station, 1974-75; mcpl. judge City of Bryan, 1986-88. Bd. dirs. Bryan Devel. Found., 1994-97; mem. Bryan Zoning Bd. Adjustments, 1992-94; pres. Brazos Valley Estate Planning Coun., 1973-74, Am. Heart Assn., 1975-76; deacon, mem. ch. choir, Sunday sch. tchr. So. Bapt. Ch.; v.p. bd. dirs. Bryan Bus. Coun., 1998-99. Mem. Rotary (bd. dirs. Bryan club 1973-74). Avocations: walking, golf. Office: 1810 Greenfield Plz Bryan TX 77802-3492 E-mail: fssteelman@aol.com.

STEELMAN, ROBERT JOE, pediatric dentist, researcher, pediatric intensivist; b. Richland, Wash., Apr. 11, 1949; s. Earl and Betty Catherine (Young) S.; m. Marie Carol Hobson, Dec. 20, 1980. BA, U. Wash., 1972; AM, Washington U., St. Louis, 1974, DMD, 1982; MS, Baylor U., 1989; MD, W. Va. U., 1993. Diplomate Am. Bd. Pediats. Ecology rschr. Washington U., St. Louis, 1974-76, med. rschr., 1976-78; resident in oral and maxillofacial surgery Emory U., Atlanta, 1982-83; pediatric dentist U. Tex. Health Sci. Ctr., Dallas, 1983-87; asst. prof. pediatric dentistry W.Va. U., Morgantown, 1989—91, ntern pediats. and anesthesia, 1994, clin. assoc. prof. oral maxillofacial surgery, 1995—2000, resident in pediatrics, 1996, fellow critical care medicine, 1997, asst. prof. pediatrics, 1999—; med. dir. pediat. critical care St. John's Hosp., Springfield, Mo., 2000—01; asst. prof. pediats. Oreg. Health Sci. U., Portland, 2001—, W.Va. U., 1999—2000, clin. asst. prof. oral and maxillofacial surgery, 2002—. Contbr. articles to profl. jours. Dental officer, USPHS, 1983-87. Pediatric dental fellow Children's Med. Ctr., 1987-89, Tex. Scottish Rite Hosp., Dallas, 1987-89. Fellow Am. Assn. Hosp. Dentists, Am. Acad. Pediatrics, Am. Acad. Pediatric Dentistry, Royal Coll. Surgeons (faculty dental surgeons); mem. AMA, Am. Acad. Pediatrics, Soc. Critical Care Medicine, Acad. Dentistry for Persons with Disabilities, Sigma Xi, Omicron Kappa Upsilon, Alpha Epsilon Delta. Office: Oreg Health Scis U Pediat Critical Care 707 SW Gaines Rd MCCDRC-P Portland OR 97201 E-mail: steelmar@ohsu.edu.

STEELMAN, SARA GERLING, state legislator; b. Wichita, Kans., Apr. 24, 1946; d. Paul Henry and Amy (Gessner) Gerling; m. John Henry Steelman; 1 child, Amy. BS in Zoology, U. Chgo., 1967; PhD in Behavior Genetics, Stanford U., 1976. Instr. dept. psychology No. Ill. U., DeKalb, 1974-75; instr. Fullerton (Calif.) Jr. Coll., 1976-80; postdoctoral fellow dept. psychobiology U. Calif., Irvine, 1976-80; asst. prof. dept. biology Skidmore Coll., Saratoga Springs, N.Y., 1980-83; staff writer Saratogian, 1983-86; contbg. writer Indiana Gazette, 1987-93; elected mem. Pa. Ho. of Reps., Harrisburg, 1990—. Contbr. articles to sci. publs. Co-chair com. on women in politics Pitts. Inst. Politics, 1993—. Rsch. fellow Nat. Inst. Aging, 1979-80. Mem.: LWV, AAUW (Notable Woman 1991), Ind. Symphony Soc. (bd. dirs. 1992—). Democrat. Avocations: gardening, music, horseback riding. Office: 325 South Office Bldg House Box 202020 Harrisburg PA 17120-2020 E-mail: ssteelma@pahouse.net.

STEEN, CARLTON DUANE, private investor, former food company executive; b. Walnut Grove, Minn., June 12, 1932; s. Conrad Wendell and Hilda (Eng) S.; m. Dorothy Corinne Sorknes, Aug. 16, 1953; children: James, Craig, Jennifer. BA in Econs. cum laude, St. Olaf Coll., 1954; MA in Indsl. Relations, U. Minn., 1957. Job analyst Exxon Corp., Roselle, N.J., 1958-59; personnel adminstr. Kraft Inc., Chgo., 1959-65, compensation mgr., 1965-69, plant mgr. Decatur, Ga., 1969-70, Champaign, Ill., 1971-74, v.p. prodn. Chgo., 1974-76; pres. Indsl. Foods div., Memphis, 1976-82, Indsl. Foods Group, 1982-87. Served to capt. USAF, 1955-57. Republican. Lutheran.

STEEN, JOHN, health policy company executive, consultant; b. Bklyn., Dec. 14, 1941; m. Carol Nolde, June 3, 1978 (div. Nov. 2001); 1 child, Thoa Flaherty. BA, NYU, 1962, MA, 1964, PhD, 1965. Cert. of Need. Asst. dir. Health Systems Agy. of N.Y.C., 1976-86; mgr. C.O.N./planning Munns & Dobbins, CPAs, Scarsdale, N.Y., 1986-92; exec. dir. Essex & Union Adv. Bd. for Health Planning, Inc., South Orange, N.J., 1992-95; rsch. asst. prof. Seton Hall U., 1992-95; dir. regulatory compliance State Health Planning Agy., Atlanta, 1996-97; prin. John Steen & Assocs., Ewing, NJ, 1997—. Vis. prof., lectr 7 colls. and univs. Contbr. articles to profl. jours. Mem. health task force Cmty. Coun. of Greater N.Y., 1971-74, chmn. state health issues com., 1974-76; chmn. project rev. com. Comprehensive Health Planning Agy. of N.Y.C., 1974-76; officer, chmn. health and hosps. com. Cmty. Bd. #2, Staten Island, N.Y., 1973-76; chmn. landmarks com. Borough Coun., Mountain Lakes, N.J., 1984-92, borough historian, 1993-97; bd. dirs. Morris County Trust for Historic Preservation, Morristown, 1998-2000. Mem. APHA, Am. Health Planning Assn. (bd. dirs., chair pub. policy), Am. Coll. Med. Quality, Mensa. Office: John Steen & Assocs 114 Scenic Dr Ewing NJ 08628-2201 E-mail: jwsteen@att.net.

STEEN, JOHN THOMAS , JR. lawyer; b. San Antonio, Dec. 27, 1949; s. John Thomas and Nell (Donnell) S.; m. Ida Louise Clement, May 12, 1979; children: John T. III, Ida Louise Larkin, James Higbie Clemernt. AB cum laude, Princeton U., 1971; JD, U. Tex., 1974. Bar: Tex. 1974, U.S. Dist. Ct. (we. dist.) Tex. 1976, U.S. Ct. Appeals (5th cir.) 1989. Assoc. Matthews & Branscomb, San Antonio, 1977-82; ptnr. Soules, Cliffe & Reed, 1982-83; sr. v.p., gen. counsel, dir. Commerce Savs. Assn., 1983-88; pvt. practice, 1988—. Trustee San Antonio Acad., 1976-81, 87-93, chmn. bd., 1989-91; adv. coun. San Antonio Acad., 1991—; v.p. Bexar County Easter Seal Soc., San Antonio, 1976-77; trustee, vice-chmn. San Antonio C.C. Dist., 1977-82; bd. dirs. Tex. Easter Seal Soc., Dallas, 1977-80, San Antonio Rsch. and Planning Coun., 1978-81, Cmty. Guidance Ctr., 1983-84, Accord Med. Found., 1987-92; vice-chmn. Leadership San Antonio, 1978-79; dir. Fiesta San Antonio Commn., 1982-83, 93-96, 98-2001; commr. Bexar County, San Antonio, 1982, Tex. Commn. on Economy and Efficiency in State Govt., 1985-89; adv. bd. Coliseum, 1985-91, chmn. bd. 1990-91; pres. San Antonio Performing Arts Assn., 1984-85; bd. trustees World Affairs Coun. San Antonio, 1982—, chmn. bd., 1984-86; trustee United Way, San Antonio, 1985-92, Tex. Cavaliers Charitable Found., 1994-97, Austin Coll., 1996-2001; mem. adv. bd. U. Tex., San Antonio, 1987—; active Pan-Tex. Assembly, 1985—; commr. Tex. Alcoholic Beverage Commn., 1998—, chmn., 2002-; exec. com. Rep. Eagles, 2000—. 1st lt. USAR. Named Chevalier Confrérie de Chevaliers du Tastevin, Sous-Commanderie de So. Tex., 1994—. Fellow San Antonio Bar Found., Tex. Bar Found. (life); mem. Tex. Bar Assn., San Antonio Acad. Alumni Assn. (pres. 1976-77), Ivy Club (Princeton, N.J.), San Antonio German Club (pres. 1982-83), Order of Alamo, Tex. Cavaliers (bd. dirs. 1989-92, 94-97, comdr. 1994-95, King Antonio LXXIV 1996-97, Kings coun. 1997—), San Antonio Country Club (bd. govs. 1990-93, v.p. 1992-93), Argyle Club, Conopus Club (bd. dirs. 1989-90), Princeton Club San Antonio and South Tex. (pres. 1980-81), Maclean Soc. Princeton U., Chevalier, Confrérie des Chevaliers du Tastevin, Sous-Commanderie of Southern Tex., Phi Delta Phi. Republican. Home: 601 Garraty Rd San Antonio TX 78209-6148 Office: 300 Convent St Ste 2440 San Antonio TX 78205-3710

STEEN, LINDA PETERSON, interior designer; b. Portland, Oreg., Sept. 24, 1938; d. Rudolph Ernest and Blanche Pauline Peterson; m. Norman Frank Steen, June 24, 1961; 1 child, Michelle Dickes. BS in Sociology, U. Oreg., 1960; cert. interior design, Parsons Sch. Design, 1984. Interior designer Lind-Elle Designs, Greenwich, Conn., 1984-89, 90—; corp. interior rsch. libr. Corp. Planning Group, Stanford, 1989-90; interior planner Contract Assocs., Los Alamos, N.Mex., 1999—. Interior design program cons., coord., instr. Santa Fe C.C., 1998-99; cmty. instr., 1996-98. Chairperson mus. project Jr. League L.A., Inc., 1977-79; pres. Mother's Club, Marymount Jr. Sch., L.A., 1978-80; bd. dirs. Jr. League L.A., 1977-79. Mem. Am. Soc. Interior Designers (bd. dirs. 1996—, pres.-elect 1999-00, chair No. group 1997-98, 99-00, pres. 2000-01, nomanating chair 2001—). Republican. Avocations: tennis, skiing. E-mail: linda@lind-elle.com.

STEEN, LOWELL HARRISON, retired physician; b. Kenosha, Wis., Nov. 27, 1923; s. Joseph Arthur and Camilla Marie (Henriksen) S.; m. Cheryl Ann Rectanus, Nov. 20, 1969; children: Linda C., Laura A., Lowell Harrison Jr., Heather J., Kirsten M. BS, Ind. U., 1945, MD, 1948. Intern Mercy Hosp.-Loyola U. Clinics, Chgo., 1948-49; resident in internal medicine VA Hosp., Hines, 1950-53; pvt. practice Highland, Ind., 1953—; ret., 1999. Pres., CEO Whiting Clinic, 1960-85; mem. hon. staff St. Catherine Hosp., East Chicago, Ind.; hon. staff Cmty. Hosp., Munster, Ind.; bd. commrs. Joint Commn. Accreditation of Hosps. With M.C., AUS, 1949-50, 55-56 Recipient Disting. Alumni Svc. award Ind. U., 1983 Fellow ACP; mem. AMA (trustee 1975, chmn. bd. trustees 1979-81), Ind. Med. Assn. (pres. 1970, chmn. bd. 1968-70), World Med. Assn. (dir. 1978-82, chmn. 1981-82, del. world assembly), Ind. Soc. Internal Medicine (pres. 1963), Am. Soc. Internal Medicine (Disting. Internist award 1981), Lake County Med. Soc., Ind. U. Sch. Medicine Alumni Assn. (pres. 1989-90, Disting. Alumnus award 1981). Presbyterian. Home: 8800 Parkway Dr Highland IN 46322-1520 E-mail: lhsteenmd@earthlink.net.

STEEN, LYNN ARTHUR, mathematician, educator; b. Chgo., Jan. 1, 1941; s. Sigvart J. and Margery (Mayer) S.; m. Mary Elizabeth Frost, July 7, 1940; children: Margaret, Catherine. BA, Luther Coll., 1961; PhD, MIT, 1965; DSc (hon.), Luther Coll., 1986, Wittenberg U., 1991, Concordia Coll., Minn., 1996. Prof. math. St. Olaf Coll., Northfield, Minn., 1965—. Vis. scholar Inst. Mittag-Leffler, Djursholm, Sweden, 1970-71; writing fellow Conf. Bd. Math. Sci., Washington, 1974-75; exec. dir. Math. Sci. Edn. Bd., Washington, 1992-95. Author: Counterexamples in Topology, 1970, Everybody Counts, 1989; editor: Mathematics Today, 1978, On the Shoulders of Giants, 1990, Math. Mag., 1976-80, Why Numbers Count, 1997, Mathematics and Democracy, 2001; contbg. editor: Sci. News, 1976-82. NSF Sci. faculty fellow, 1970-71, Danforth Found. grad. fellow, 1961-65. Fellow AAAS (sec. math. sect. 1982-88); mem. Am. Math. Soc., Math. Assn. Am. (pres. 1985-86, Disting. Svc. award 1992), Coun. Sci. Soc. Pres. (chmn. 1989), Sigma Xi (Bd. Dirs. Spl. award 1989). Home: 716 Saint Olaf Ave Northfield MN 55057-1523 Office: St Olaf Coll Dept of Math Northfield MN 55057 E-mail: steen@stolaf.edu.

STEEN, NANCY, artist; b. Denver, Feb. 7, 1949; d. John and Petrita (Pino) Ciddio; m. Charles A. Steen, Nov. 13, 1968 (div. June 1976); children: Monica Lee Steen, Charles A. Steen III; m. Ben Q. Adams, Dec. 31, 1985. BA cum laude, Gonzaga U., 1973; postgrad., N.Mex. State U., 1973-74, U. N.Mex., 1974-76. Pub., owner New Leaf Press, Walnut Creek, Calif., 1974-79, The Leaf Press, Santa Monica, 1974-79, New Leaf Press, Albuquerque, 1974-79; rsch. adminstr. Taos Editions, 1981-89; asst. dir. Western Graphics, 1983—, R.C. Gorman pub., 1983-91. Author: R.C. Gorman: The Graphic Works, 1988, Who is R.C. Gorman?: An Insiders Portrait, 1996; exhibited in one-woman and group shows including Art Outdoors, Albuquerque, 1980, Mus. of Art, Albuquerque, 1980, 81, Susanne Brown, Scottsdale, Ariz., 1981, Mus. of Art, Santa Fe, 1982, Am. Design, Dallas, 1983, Phoenix Art Mus., 1983, Nabisco World Headquarters, East Hanover, N.J., 1984, Gallery One, Dallas, 1986, Gallery One, Denver, 1986, 87, Gallery Mach, Seattle, 1988, Mus. of the Permain Basin, Odessa, Tex., 1989, Silver City (N.Mex.) Mus., 1990, Santa Fe Style, Madison, Wis., 1990, Denver Art Mus., 1993, Dartmouth Street Gallery, 1994, Fiesta Del Carazon Creative Response to AIDS, Albuquerque, 1994, Live at the KIMO, Albuquerque, 1994; exhibited in numerous permant collections include L.A. County Mus. of Art, Oakland Mus. of Art, San Jose Mus. of Art, Phoenix Art Mus., U. Nev., Koofenay Sch. of Art, U. Calgary, U. Wash., N.Mex. State U., Maderia Sch., Tamarind Inst., Crocker Gallery, Western Graphics Collection, Mus. of Fine Art, Monterey Peninsula Mus. of Art, many others. Chairperson NAMES Project-Quilt Dis., Albuquerque, 1994; bd. dirs. NMAPLA-N.Mex. Assn. of People Living with AIDS, Albuquerque, 1993-94; fundraiser Make A Wish, Denver, 1994, Am. Heart Assn., Honolulu, Albuquerque, 1994-97. Grantee N.Mex. State U., 1973. Mem. Pi Beta Phi. Democrat. Roman Catholic. Avocations: gardening, reading, music. Home: PO Box 375 Corona NM 88318-0375 Office: Western Graphics Workshop PO Box 373 Corona NM 88318-0373

STEEN, NANCY G. volunteer, retired rare books librarian; b. Mar. 4, 1939; BA, Bowling Green State U., 1961, MA in History, 1963; AMLS, U. Mich., 1966. Rare books libr. Bowling Green (Ohio) State U., 1982-90; discography editor newsletter José Carreras Soc. Am., Elkins Park, Pa., 1996—. Vol. José Carreras Internat. Leukemia Found., Barcelona and Seattle, 1995—; mem. Met. Opera Guild, N.Y.C., 2002--, patron Met. Opera, 1998-2002; mem. Playwright's Circle, Stratford Festival of Can. Mem. Friends of Librs. at Bowling Green State U., Order Eastern Star.

STEEN, PAUL JOSEPH, retired broadcasting executive; b. Williston, N.D., July 4, 1932; s. Ernest B. and Inez (Ingebrigtson) S.; m. Judith Smith; children— Michael M., Melanie. BA, Pacific Luth. U., 1954; MS, Syracuse U., 1957. Producer, dir. Sta. KNTV, San Jose, Calif., 1957-58, Sta. KVIE, Sacramento, 1958-60; asst. prof. telecommunications Pacific Luth. U., Tacoma, 1960-67; dir. ops. Sta. KPBS San Diego State U., 1967-74; gen. mgr., 1974-93; prof. telecommunications and film, 1974-93; dir. univ. telecommunications. Co-chmn. Office of New Tech. Initiatives. Dir. (tel. program) Troubled Waters (winner Nat. Ednl. TV award of excellence 1970). With AUS. Named Danforth Assoc. Mem. Pacific Mountain Network (bd. dirs., chmn., bd. of govs. award 1993), NATAS, Assn. Calif. Pub. TV Stas. (pres.), Pi Kappa Delta. Home: 6068 Caminito De La Taza San Diego CA 92120-5323 E-mail: psteen@mail.sdsu.edu.

STEENBERGEN, GARY LEWIS, computer aided design educator; b. Detroit, Jan. 23, 1959; s. Edwin P. and Pauline (Bright) S.; m. Barbara Earlene Snyder, June 2, 1979; children: Christopher Lewis, Stephanie Brooke. AAS in Pre-engring., Sue Bennett Coll., London, Ky., 1987; BS in Indsl. Edn. Tech., Ea. Ky. U., 1996. Archtl. draftsman Laminated Timbers, London, 1977; archtl. designer Ea. Ky. Homes, Corbin, 1979-80; detail draftsman East Ky. Steel, Barbourville, 1979-80; quality control technician Elicon divsn. Nat. Standard, Corbin, Ky., 1980-82, plant engring. technician, 1984-90; CAD instr. Ky. Tech., Pineville, 1990-95; assoc. prof. Cumberland Valley Tech. Coll. Chmn. Craft Adv. Com. for Vo-Tech Edn., Corbin, 1980-90; adj. prof. Southeast C.C., Middlesboro, Ky. Scoutmaster Boy Scouts Am., Corbin, 1982—; chess coach U.S. Chess Found., Corbin, 1988—. Recipient Scouters award Boy Scouts Am., 1985, Scoutmaster award, 1985, Scoutmaster Merit award, 1994. Mem. Am. Fedn. Tchrs., Sue Bennett Alumni, Ea. Ky. U. Alumni, Golden Key Honor Soc., Mortar Bd., Kappa Delta Pi. Republican. Pentecostal Ch. Home: 390 Hart Mine Rd Corbin KY 40701-5009

STEEN CRAWFORD, ANDREA, village manager; b. Chgo., July 20, 1963; d. John G. III and Susan M. Crawford; m. Stephen L. Steen; children: Collin, Julia, Gabrielle. BA, Kalamazoo Coll., 1985; MPA, U. Wis., 1987. Budget and planning analyst I State of Wis., Madison, summer 1986; adminstrv. intern City of Madison, 1986-87; adminstrv. asst. Village of Wilmette, Ill., 1987-89, asst. fin. dir., 1989-90; village adminstr. Village of Maple Bluff, Wis., 1990-97; village mgr. Village of Elm Grove, 1997—. Bd. dirs. Wis. Ctr. for State and Local Govt., Madison, 1995-96; pres. LaFollette Inst. Alumni Bd., Madison, 1992-94; trustee State of Wis. Investment Bd., 2000—. Mem. Internat. City Mgmt. Assn., Wis. City Mgmt. Assn. (pres. 1996-97), Ill. City Mgmt. Assn., Rotary. Office: Village of Elm Grove 13600 Juneau Blvd Elm Grove WI 53122-1679

STEENHAGEN, ROBERT LEWIS, landscape architect, consultant; b. Grand Rapids, Mich., July 11, 1922; s. Abraham and Rena (Vanden Broek) S.; m. Doris Brisentine, Aug. 2, 1952; children: Deborah, Cynthia, James. A.S., Grand Rapids Jr. Coll., 1942; BS, Mich. State U., 1949. Chief landscape design Eastern design office Nat. Park Service, Phila., 1963-66; capt. planning team Nat. Park Service, Washington, 1966-70, asst. mgr. N.E. area Design Office Denver, 1971-77, assoc. mgr., 1978-80; cons. landscape architecture Lakewood, Colo., 1980—. Served to sgt. U.S. Army, 1942-45, PTO. Recipient Meritorious Service award Nat. Park Service, 1971; recipient Performance award for Nat. Bicentennial Program, 1976 Fellow Am. Soc. Landscape Architects Home: 2473 S Carr Ct Denver CO 80227-3104

STEEN-HINDERLIE, DIANE EVELYN, social worker, musician; b. Duluth, Minn., June 13, 1947; d. Julian Sem and Evelyn Synnove (Helgaas) Steen; m. John Peter Hinderlie, June 27, 1971 (div. Sept. 1987); children: Peder Donald, Erik Steen; m. John Richard Olson, July 21, 1989. BA in Asian Studies/Social Psychology cum laude, St. Olaf Coll., 1969; MusB equivalency, U. Minn. and other instns., 1970-91; postgrad., Hamline U., 1989-91. Lic. social worker, Minn.; cert. music tchr. Music Tchrs. Nat. Assn. Social worker child care licensing Hennepin County Welfare Dept., Mpls., 1970-73; mem. clergy team exch. program Luth. World Fedn., Göppingen, Germany, 1973-77; mem. clergy team, music dir. Jubilation Singers Bethel Luth. Ch., Rochester, Minn., 1978-83; mem. clergy team, music dir. youth choir First Luth. Ch., St. Louis Park, 1983-86; adminstr. Family Child Care facility, 1986-90; mem. faculty, tchr. Stenson Suzuki Studios and Home Studio, 1988-92; small group leader, tchr. vol. Mt. Olive Ch., Children's Hosp., Mpls., 1993, 96-98; mem. workshop and children's ministry Augsburg Coll. Youth and Family Inst. and Trinity Congregation, 1998—; founding dir. Fair Pay Inst., Mpls., 1995—; trainer United for a Fair Economy, 1997—. Founder orgn. and curriculum Early Childhood Orgn. for Edn. with Singing, 1993—, co-leader German-Am. youth group exch., 1979-82; co-founder Family DayCare Cert. Program and Babygarten (B-12 edn.) classes, 1970-73; bd. dirs. Midwest Coun., Nat. Peace Inst. Found., Grinnell, Iowa, 1991; presenter in field.; mem. root causes of violence action team Initiative for Violence-Free Families, 4th Jud. Dist. Minn., 1997—. Author: (tng. manual) Mother Tongue Singing/Voice Method, 1988, (study packet) School Start Time/Teen Sleep Deprivation, 1996-97; rec. artist, mem. ensemble record/cassettes Nowell Sing We, 1986; performer Nordic Am. Psalmodikon Forbundet, 1997—. Vol. People of Faith Peacemakers, Feminists in Faith/ReImagining, Jewish Cmty. Rels. Coun., Muslim-Christian Rels. Coun., Joint Religious Legis. Coalition, Bread for the World; founder People for Reforming Early Start Time for Teens Orgn., Mpls., 1993—; mem. steering com. Progressive Cmty. and FairVote, Minn., 1994-99; local host youth com. NAACP Conv., Mpls., 1995; vol. Common Cause, St. Paul and Washington; charter mem. U.S. Holocaust Mus., 1993. Recipient appreciation plaque Christian Boy/Girl Scouts Germany; Svc. pin Am. Luth. Ch. Women; listed in Minn. Profiles, Minn. Hist. Soc. A Tribute to Outstanding Minn. Women by Marilyn Chelstrom, 2001; named Asset Builder of Month, St. Louis Park Children First Initiative, 1997; named to Honor Roll, Mendota Mdewakanton Dakota Cmty., 1999. Mem.: MADD, Minn. Music Tchrs. Assn. (first early childhood music chair 2001—), Assn. Pre- and Perinatal Psychology and Health, Wash. Nat. Cathedral, Early Childhood Music and Movement Assn., Soc. for Psychol. Studies of Social Issues, Interfaith Alliance Minn., Nat. Luth. Choir Acad., Suzuki Assn. Americas (study area co-organizer, editl. adviser), Internat. Suzuki Assn., Nat. Assn. Tchrs. Singing and VoiceCare Network, UN Assn., Sojourner Project, Inc., World Wildlife Fund, Ctr. for Victims of Torture, Minn. Parenting Assn., Amnesty Internat., Nat. Peace Found., Germanic-Am. Inst., Am.'s Jr. Miss. Coun., Sons of Norway (lodge trustee 1991—), Phi Beta Kappa, Am. Mensa. Green. Lutheran. Avocations: reading, political activism, concerts, travel, memory albums. Office: Fair Pay Inst PO Box 16031 Minneapolis MN 55416-0031

STEENSGAARD, ANTHONY HARVEY, federal agency administrator; b. Rapid City, S.D., Mar. 21, 1963; s. Harvey Hans and Dorothy Lorraine (Hansen) S. Student, Anchorage C.C., 1983-84; BSCE, U. Alaska, 1985; AAS in Indsl. Security, C.C. Air Force, 1989; BS in Criminal Justice, Wayland U., 1989; MS in Computer Systems Engring., U. Calif., San Diego, 1996. Lic. pilot, radio operator; cert. hostage negotiator FBI, Fed. Air Marshall Sch., FAA, Instr. Am. Soc. Protection Profls., fed. emergency mgmt. agy. level III incident comdr. Bookseller B. Dalton Bookseller, Rapid City, 1978—81, Anchorage, 1981-83; warehouseman Sears, Roebuck & Co., 1983-85; air res. technician Alaska Air N.G., 1985—88; agt., draftsman, engring. cons., asst. intelligence officer U.S. Border Patrol, El Centro, Calif., 1988—. Computer cons., 1994-2000; computer criminal investigator, 1999—. Author: Unit Security Manager's Guide Book, 1988. Vol. Spl. Olympics, Rapid City, 1981; observer Civil Air Patrol, Anchorage, 1981, sr. pilot Rapid City, 1996, pub. affairs officer, 1996—98, aerospace edn. officer, 1998—2000, wing dir. aerospace edn., 2000—; Vol. U.S. Senator George McGovern's Campaign, 1980, Congressman Tom Daschle's Campaign, Rapid City, 1980. With USNR, 1980—81, With USMC, 1981—85, With USAF, 1985—98. Recipient Hon. Sci. award Bausch and Lomb, 1984, commendation State of Alaska, 1987, 2d commendation, 1988, Brigadier Gen. Charles E. Yeager Aerospace Achievement award, 2000, Blanchard trophy, 1990. Mem. U.S. Cavalry Assn. (heritage mem.), HTML Writer's Guild, Am. Legion, Air Force Assn., VFW, Fraternal Order Eagles, S.D. Sheriff's Assn., Fraternal Order of Police, Virtual Geog. League, WWII Meml. Soc. (charter mem.), Nat. D-Day Mus. Found. Avocations: reading, flight simulations, aviation, history, wargaming. Office: US Border Patrol 1111 N Imperial Ave El Centro CA 92243-1795 E-mail: ahsteensgaard@yahoo.com.

STEENSLAND, RONALD PAUL, librarian; b. Dothan, Ala., Dec. 16, 1946; s. Maurice John and Claire Folkes S.; m. Nancy Hollister, Dec. 20, 1970; 1 child, Ronald Paul. BA, Fla. State U., 1969, MS, 1970; postgrad., Miami (Ohio) U., 1972, U. Md., 1980, U.S. Army War Coll., 1995. Dir. Davidson County Pub. Libr., Lexington, N.C., 1970-73, Hidalgo County Libr. System, McAllen, Tex., 1973-76, Los Alamos County Libr., 1976-77, Lexington (Ky.) Pub. Libr., 1977—. Chmn. John Cotton Dana Library Public Relations Awards, 1977 Treas. Hildago County chpt. ARC, 1975. Served to col. USAR, 1969-70. Recipient Service award United Way. Mem. ALA, Res. Officers Assn. (sec.-treas. chpt. 100), Assn. U.S. Army (sec. Bluegrass chpt.), U.S. Chess Fedn., Southeastern Library Assn., Ky. Library Assn., Lexington C. of C., Alpha Tau Omega. Clubs: Lafayette, Pres.'s, Lexington Chess, Rotary. Baptist. Office: Lexington Pub Libr 140 E Main St Lexington KY 40507-1318 E-mail: ron@lexpublib.org.

STEEPLES, DOUGLAS WAYNE, retired university dean, consultant, researcher; b. Great Bend, Kans., Mar. 30, 1935; s. Marion Wayne and Dorothy Augusta (King) S.; children from previous marriage: Donald Bruce, John Douglas, Sheila Margaret; m. Christine Marie Webster, Dec. 8, 1990. BA summa cum laude, U. Redlands, 1957; MA, U. N.C., 1958, PhD, 1961; cert., Inst. Ednl. Mgmt., Harvard U., 1981. Asst. prof. history Calif. State U.-Northridge, 1961-64; prof. history Earlham Coll., Richmond, Ind., 1963-80; acad. v.p. Wartburg Coll., Waverly, Iowa, 1979-80; exec. v.p. Westminster Coll., Salt Lake City, 1980-83; provost Ohio Wesleyan U., Delaware, Ohio, 1983-85, acting pres., winter 1984; dean Coll. Liberal and Fine Arts, U. So. Colo., Pueblo, 1985-89; v.p. for acad. affairs Aurora (Ill.) U., 1989-94; dean, prof. history Coll. Liberal Arts, Mercer U., Macon, Ga., 1994-2000; ret., 2000. Cons. higher edn. mgmt.; cons., reader advanced placement program Ednl. Testing Service, Princeton, N.J., 1976-93; cons., evaluator North Central Assn. Schs. and Colls., Chgo., 1985—; bd. dirs. Western Ind. Colls. Fund, Salt Lake City, 1980-83; bd. dirs. Am. Con. of Acad. Deans, 1995, sec.-treas., 1998-99; bd. trustees Econ. and Bus. Hist. Soc., 1995—, pres., 1998-99. Editor, contbg. author: Institutional Revival: Case Histories, 1986, Successful Strategic Planning Case Studies, 1989, Managing Change in Higher Education, 1990, Treasure from the Painted Hills: Calico California, 1882-1907, 1999, (with David O. Whitten) Democracy in Desperation: The Depression in the 1890s, 1998; editor John Randolph Spears, Illustrated Sketches of Death Valley, 2000, Advocate for American Enterprise: William Buck Dana and the Commercial and Financial Chronicle, 1865-1910, 2001; assoc. editor Bus. Libr. Rev., 1996-2001; contbr. some 45 articles and 80 book revs. to various publs. Mem. adv. bd. Pueblo Symphony Orch., 1987—89; mem. allocations coms. United Way, Richmond, 1976—79, Pueblo, 1988—89, Aurora, 1990—94; vol. in svc. Ho-Chunk (Wisconsin Winnebago) Nation, 2001, spl. cons. to pres., 2001; mem. Mayor's Commn. on Restoration of Ft. Hawkins, Macon, Ga., 1997—; pres. Luth. Inter-parish Coun., Richmond, 1975—78; bd. dirs. Soc. for Use and Preservation of Resources, 1976—79. Scholar U. Redlands, Calif., 1953-57; Danforth fellow, 1957-61; Woodrow Wilson fellow, 1957-58; Found. for Econ. Edn. fellow in bus., 1963; Am. Philos. Soc. grantee, 1966 Mem. Am. Hist. Assn., Orgn. Am. Historians, So. Hist. Assn., Sierra Club, Palaver Club, Phi Beta Kappa (senator united chpts. 1973-79), Omicron Delta Kappa. Lodges: Rotary (bd. dirs. 1983-84). Republican. Avocations: mountaineering, running, bagpiping. Office: 656 River North Blvd Macon GA 31211-6340 E-mail: marliesesteeples@aol.com.

STEERE, ALLEN CARUTHERS, JR. physician, educator; b. Apr. 11, 1943; m. Margaret Mercer, 1969; children: Allen Caruthers III, Margaret Hamilton, Samuel Mercer, John Summers. BA, Columbia U., 1965, MD, 1969; DSc. (hon.), Indiana U., 1992, SUNY, 1997. Diplomate Am. Bd. Internal Medicine; lic. rheumatologist, N.Y., Ga., Ct., Mass. Intern St. Luke's Hosp., N.Y.C., 1969-70, asst., sr. resident, 1970-72, chief resident, instr. medicine, 1972-73; chief resident, instr. medicine Coll. Physicians and Surgeons Columbia U., 1972-73; clin. fellow in rheumatology Yale U., New Haven, 1975-77, asst. prof. medicine, epidemiology and pub. health, 1977-81, assoc. prof. medicine, 1981-87; prof. medicine, chief rheumatology and immunology New Eng. Med. Ctr. Tufts U., Boston, 1987—, Natalie V. & Milton O. Zucker prof. rheumatology/immunology, 1998—. With USPHS, 1973-75. Recipient Citation for Elucidation of Lyme disease, Infectious Diseases Soc. Am., 1984, Ciba-Geigy Rheumatology prize, Internat. League Against Rheumatism, 1985, award for discovery of Lyme disease, Nat. Inst. Arthritis and Musculoskeletal Skin Diseases, 1988, Richard and Hinda Rosenthal award, ACP, 1990, Joseph Mather Smith prize, Coll. Physicians and Surgeons, Columbia U., 1990, Zucker Faculty prize, Tufts U., 1990, award for studies Lyme disease, Nat. Health Coun., 1990, Lee C. Howley Sr. prize, Arthritis Found., 1993, Gold medal, Albert Sabin Vaccine Inst., 1998, Astute Clinician award, NIH, 1999, award, Am. Lyme Disease Found., 2000, Columbia Coll. of Phys. and Surgeon's Alumni award for Disting. Acad. Accomplishment, 2001. Mem. Am. Soc. Clin. Investigation, Am. Fedn. Clin. Rsch., Am. Coll. Rheumatology (Howard and Martha Holley rsch. prize in rheumatology 1995). Office: Tufts U Sch Medicine New Eng Med Ctr # 406 750 Washington St Boston MA 02111-1526

STEERE, ANNE BULLIVANT, retired student advisor; b. Phila., July 27, 1921; d. Stuart Lodge and Elizabeth MacCuen (Smith) B.; m. Richard M. H. Harper Jr., Nov. 14, 1942 (div. Oct. 1967); children: Virginia Harper Kliever, Richard M. H. Harper III, Patricia Harper Flint, Stuart Lodge Harper, Lucy Steere, Grace Steere; m. Bruce Middleton Steere, July 5, 1968. BS in Sociology, So. Meth. U., 1978, M in Liberal Arts, 1985. Asst. to dir. Harvard Law Sch. Fund, Cambridge, Mass., 1958-68; advisor to older students So. Meth. U., Dallas, 1976-85. Contbr. articles to profl. jours. Trustee Pine Manor Coll., Chestnut Hill, Mass., 1983—; bd. dirs. Planned Parenthood, Dallas, 1975-85. Mem. New Eng. Hist. and Geneal. Soc., Alpha Kappa Delta, Chilton Club (Boston), Jr. League Club. Episcoplian. Avocations: reading, needlepoint, sailing. Home: 369 S Lake Dr # 5D Palm Beach FL 33480-6509 also: 59 Snow Inn Rd Harwich Port MA 02646-2413

STEERE, CAROL Z. volunteer; b. N.Y.C., Oct. 10, 1930; d. Albert and Mary Zimmerman; widowed; children: Kenneth, Kathryn, James, Nancy, Edward. BS in Nursing cum laude, Syracuse U., 1953; M in Health Svcs. Adminstrn., George Washington U., 1983. V.p., sec. Hoste Sys., Inc., Fairfax, Va., 1970-78, pres., 1978-86; asst. to adminstr. Rockville (Md.) Nursing Home, 1986; devel. mgr. Fairfax County C. of C., Vienna, 1987; fin. clerk Fairfax County Office Tax Adminstrn., Fairfax, 1987-97; ret., 1997. Mem., pres. Sutton Area Civic Assn., Vienna, Va., 1960-92; mem. Fairfax County Complete Census CHE, Northeast Vienna Civic Assn., Va. Mem. AAUW (v.p. Falls Church Area br. 1963-65), LWV (bd. dirs., adminstrv. asst.), Parents Without Ptnrs. Sail and Power Club (bd. dirs., chmn). Avocations: sailing, cruising, reading, investing, travel. Home: 416 Creek Crossing Rd NE Vienna VA 22180-3566

STEERE, WILLIAM CAMPBELL, JR. pharmaceutical company executive; b. Ann Arbor, Mich., June 17, 1936; s. William Campbell and Dorothy (Osborne) S.; m. Lynda Gay Powers, Jan. 29, 1957; children: William, Mark, Christopher. BS, Stanford U., 1959. Sales rep. Pfizer & Co., Modesto, Calif., 1970-72; v.p., dir. ops. Pfizer Labs, N.Y.C., 1982-84; sr. v.p., dir. ops. Pfizer Pharms., 1982-84, exec. v.p., 1984-86, pres., 1986-91; pres., CEO Pfizer Inc., 1991-92, CEO, 1991—2000, chmn., 1992—2001, chmn. emeritus, 2001—. Bd. dirs. Texaco Inc., NYU Med. Ctr., Minerals Techs. Inc., Met Life, Dow Jones, WNET-TV. Trustee N.Y. Bot. Garden; bd. overseers Meml. Sloan-Kettering Cancer Ctr. Mem. Pharm. Rsch. and Mfrs. Am. (bd. dirs.), Bus. Coun. (bd. dirs.), Bus. Roundtable, Univ. Club, N.Y. Yacht Club. Avocations: sailing, skiing. Office: Pfizer Inc 235 E 42nd St New York NY 10017-5755*

STEFAN, VLADISLAV, academic administrator, researcher, educator; b. Yugoslavia, Feb. 5, 1948; Came to U.S., 1981; s. Bozhidar and Rosanda Stefan.; 1 child, Andrej. BSEE, U. Belgrade, Yugoslavia, 1972, MSc, 1975; DSc, Russian Acad. Scis., Moscow, 1978. Rsch. scientist Inst. Nuc. Scis., Belgrade, 1973-79, Russian Acad. Scis., 1977-81; assoc. prof. U. Belgrade, 1979-81; vis. prof. MIT, Cambridge, 1981-82; cons. Jaycor, Inc., San Diego, 1983—; pres. The Stefan U., La Jolla, 1998—. Editor (and author): Physics and Society, 1992; editor: Nonlinear and Relativistic Effects in Plasmas, 1992, Research Trends in Physics, 1989—. Mem. AAAS, Am. Phys. Soc., Am. Soc. Genomic Medicine (pres.). Avocations: painting, music, rock climbing. Office: The Stefan U PO Box 2946 7596 Eads Ave La Jolla CA 92038-2946 E-mail: vs@stefan-university.edu.

STEFANCICH, DONNA LEE, information security specialist; b. West Islip, N.Y., Jan. 13, 1961; d. Stanley Frank and Irene Eleanor (Soullard) S. AAS in Archtl. Tech., SUNY, Farmingdale, 1981; BS in Computer Sci. summa cum laude, NY Inst. of Tech., 1985, postgrad., 1993—98. Programmer, analyst Fairchild Republic Co., Farmingdale, N.Y., 1985-87; sr. computer security analyst Grumman Data Systems, Bethpage, 1987-94; mgr. data security and controls Nationar, Woodbury, 1994-95; mgr. network security Cablevision Systems Corp., 1995—96; data security analyst Arrow Electronics, Melville, NY, 1996—. Mem. Nat. Computer Security Assn., Computer Security Inst., Nu Ypsilon Tau. Avocations: golf, in-line skating, jogging, gardening. Home: 17 Taca Blvd Deer Park NY 11729-3442 Office: Arrow Electronics 50 Marcus Dr Melville NY 11747

STEFANIAK, NORBERT JOHN, business administration educator; b. Milw., Jan. 12, 1921; s. Peter Stephen and Mary Ann (Schlaikowski) S.; m. Elizabeth Jean Horning, Aug. 27, 1949; children— John, Mary, Jane, Beth, Joel, Peter, James, Thomas, Anne, Jean. BBA, U. Wis., 1948, MBA, 1950, PhD, 1960. C.P.A. Instr. U. Wis., Milw., 1950-53; treas., controller Wauwatosa (Wis.) Realty Co., 1953-56; prof. bus. adminstrn. U. Wis., Milw., 1957-75, prof. emeritus. Author: Real Estate Marketing, monograph and articles in field. Past commr. West Allis (Wis.) Planning Commn.; bd. dirs. Internat. Exch. Found.-Poland and Milw. County, Wis.; condemnation commr. Milw. County; bd. review City of West Allis, Wis. With USAAF, WWII. Named Polish-Am. Man of Yr., Polish Nat. Alliance (Milw. Soc.), 1990. Mem. Am. Real Estate and Urban Econs. Assn. (past pres.), Wis. Realtors Assn. (past dir.), Wis. Real Estate Exam. Bd. (past vice chmn.), Am. Soc. Real Estate Counselors (emeritus), Polish Nat. Alliance. Home: 865 S 76th St Milwaukee WI 53214-3026 E-mail: walker@milwpc.com.

STEFANICS, CHARLOTTE LOUISE, retired mental health nurse; b. Leechburg, Pa., Dec. 30, 1927; d. George J. and Mary Magadelene (Boronyak) S. Diploma Sch. Nursing, St. Elizabeth Hosp., 1948; BSN, Seton Hall U., 1968; MS, Ohio State U., 1971; EdD, U. Sarasota, 1982. Diplomate Logotherapy. Various nursing positions, 1952-69; staff nurse Med. Ctr. NYU, N.Y.C., 1969-70; pvt. practice, 1971-73; instr. Sch. Nursing Duke U., Durham, N.C., 1974-77; clin. nurse specialist VA Med. Ctr., Bay Pines, Fla., 1977-93; ret., 1993. Instr., pvt. practice Community Hosp. Springfield, Ohio; cons. in field; part-time chaplain Miami Valley Hosp., Dayton, Ohio; lectr. U. South Fla. Coll. Nursing, 1978-92. Co-author (with G. Niklas): Ministry to the Sick, 1982; co-author: (with R. Peck) Learning to Say Good-bye, 1987; co-author: (with R. Henrion) The Power of the Human Spirit, 2002. Vol. community classes and workshops; vol. Habitat for Humanity Internat. Hungary, nursing exchange with Chinese Nurses Assn. Mem. Inst. Logo Therapy, Assn. Death Educators and Counselors (cert.), Assn. Christian Therapists, Nurses Orgn. Vet. Affairs. Home: 1342 Rosehaven Cir Dayton OH 45429-5744

STEFANIK, JEAN MARIANNE, educator, naturalist; b. Springfield, Mass., June 10, 1949; d. Edward Carl and Suzanne Florence (Chelkonas) S. BS in Elem. Edn.; MEd, Am. Internat. Coll.; postgrad., Norwich U., U. Vt., Merrimack Valley Coll., Franklin Pierce Coll., U. Mass., U. Hawaii. Reading specialist Easthampton (Mass.) Schs., 1973-74; dir. curriculum Barre Town (Vt.) Sch. Dist., 1974-80; dir. extended edn. program Anherst (N.H.) Sch. Dist., 1980—. Part-time educator Computer Ctr., Tandy Corp., Manchester, N.H., 1981-82; part-time instr. Notre Dame Coll., Manchester, 1981-83, Merrimack Valley Coll., 1981-86, U. N.H. Coll. for Lifelong Learning, 1982-87, 92—, sabbitical including work for Smithsonian Inst. Marine Sys. Lab. and New England Aquarium's Right Whale Rsch. Team, 1987-88; mem. Alaska Oil Spill and Ecology Info. Ctr., Juneau, 1989; mem. Earthwatch/Rsch. Teams Giant Clams of Tonga, 1988, Fijian Coral Reefs, 1993, field svc. rep., 1993-95. Mem. ASCD (internat., bd. dirs. 1979-80, 82-2000, mem. elem. global edn. pilot project 1992-94, issues com. 1995-96, mem. conf. local arrangements com. 1991), Vt. ASCD (pres. 1970-80, treas. 1977-79), N.H. ASCD (pres. 1982-84, 86-87, bd. dirs. 1981—, exec. dir. 1999-2000), New Eng. Aquarium Self-Contained Underwater Breathing Apparatus Club (pres. 1990-93), United Divers N.H. (pres. 1996-97), N.H. Orchid Soc. (trustee 1996-98), Seamark (chmn. 1993), Mensa, Phi Delta Kappa, Alpha Chi. Home: 285 Beaver St Manchester NH 03104-5569 E-mail: jstefanik@sprise.com.

STEFANILE, LAWRENCE VINCENT, management coumsulting company executive; b. Jersey City, Jan. 24, 1939; s. Angelo Anthony and Agnes Antoinette (Altomonte) S.; m. Margaret Ann Marzell, Apr. 2, 1967. AB, Seton Hall U., 1961; MA, Niagara U., 1962; doctoral equivalency, St. John's U., 1968; EdD, U. Am., 1991. Cert. sch. adminstr., N.J.; cert. Am. Coll. Hosp. Adminstrs. Coord. internat. tchr. devel. program at Ohio U. U.S. Dept State, 1963-64; vice prin. Marist High Sch., Bayonne, N.J., 1964-68; dir. coll. rels. St. peter's Coll., Jersey City, 1968-72; COO St. Francis Hosp., 1972-81; pres. Vanguard Mgmt. Svc., Short Hills, N.J., 1981—; with U.S. Dept. Vets. Affairs, N.Y.C., 1993—, Phila., 1993—. Cons. Village of Ridgefield Park, N.J., 1968—, U.S. Dept. Vets. Affairs, Newark, 1992—, Borough of Little Ferry, N.J., 1992—. Author: The Art of The Search: A Guide to Successful Job Placement, 1991, A Systems Approach to Job Search and Placement, 1992. Trustee St. Francis Hosp., Jersey City, 1978; bd. dirs. Hudson chpt. ARC, Jersey City, 1978; commr. Manpower Commn.-Hudson, Jersey City, 1979; mem. Hosp. Reimbursement coun. N.J. Dept. Health, Princeton, 1980. Seton Hall U. scholar, 1957; fellow Niagara U., 1961, Fulbright Found., 1962, Ohio U., 1962; named to Internat. Tchr. Devel. Program, Fulbright Exch., 1962. Mem. Seton Hall U. Alumni, Niagara U. Alumni Assn., U. Am. Alumni Assn. Office: Vanguard Mgmt Svc Mountainside Crossing 1108 Springfield Ave Mountainside NJ 07092-2906

STEFANINI, MARIO, physician, pathologist; b. Chieri, Piedmont, Italy, June 11, 1916; s. Eleuterio and Therese (Trivereau) S.; m. Elizabeth J. Just, Feb. 12, 1949; children: Marie T., Virginia E. MD, U. Rome, 1939; MS in Biochemistry, Marquette U., 1947. Diplomate Am. Bd. Pathology, Am. Bd. Hematology, med. chemistry, blood banking. Instr. in biochemistry Marquette U. Med. Sch., Milw., 1947-49; asst. prof. to prof. Tufts U. Med. Sch., Boston, 1949-61; dir. of rsch. St. Elizabeth Hosp., 1955-61; assoc. pathologist St. Joseph Hosp., Chgo., 1962-65; pathologist, dir. of labs. St. Elizabeth Hosp., Danville, Ill., 1965-79; pathologist Clinch Valley Med. Ctr., Richlands, Va., 1979—. Cons. VA Hosp., Boston, 1955-58, West Roxbury, Mass., 1958-61; cons. several hosps. in New Eng. area. Author: Hemorrhagic Disorders, 1955, rev. edit. 1962 (award 1960); editors (book series, 9 vols.) Progress in Clinical Pathology, 1966-85; contbr. articles to profl. jours. Named sr. rsch. fellow, USPHS, NIH, 1947—49, Damon Runyon clin. cancer rsch. fellow, Damon Runyon-Walter Winchell Fund, N.Y., 1950—52, established investigator, Am. Heart Assn., N.Y., 1953—58; recipient cert. merit, AMA, Chgo., 1952, first prize, Am. Assn. Blood Banks, Chgo., 1952—58. Fellow Am. Coll. Nuclear Physicians, Am. Coll. Nuclear Medicine (Disting.), Am. Soc. Investigative Pathology, Soc. for Exptl. Biology and Medicine, Am. Soc. Clin. Investigation, Internat. Soc. Hematology, Col. of Am. Pathologists, Am. Soc. Clin. Pathologists. Achievements include the devel. of techniques for transfusing platelets; discovery of syndrome of disseminated intravascular coagulation (DIC); early work in clin. use of thrombolytic agts. Home: 710 Sandy Ln Richlands VA 24641-2640 Office: Clinch Valley Med Ctr 2949 W Frnt Richlands VA 24641-2010

STEFANO, JOSEPH WILLIAM, film and television producer, writer; b. Phila., May 5, 1922; s. Dominic and Josephine (Vottima) S.; m. Marilyn Epstein, Dec. 5, 1953; 1 son, Andrew Dominic. Ed. pub. schs. Pres. Villa di Stefano Prodns., 1962—. Toured as song and dance man in Student Prince, 1945, Merry Widow, 1946; composer music and lyrics popular songs, night club revues, indsl. shows, others, 1946-57; author screenplays The Black Orchid, 1958, The Naked Edge, 1960, Psycho, 1960, Anna di Brooklyn, 1962, Eye of the Cat, 1969, Futz, 1970, The Kindred, 1986, Blackout, 1989, Psycho IV: The Beginning, 1990, Two Bits, 1995, Psycho, 1998; TV drama Made in Japan, 1959, movies for TV, 1970-78; prodr., author TV series The Outer Limits, 1963-64, Swamp Thing, 1990; exec. con. The Outer Limits, 1995—. Recipient Robert E. Sherwood award for Made in Japan, Fund for Republic, 1959, Edgar Allen Poe award for Psycho, Mystery Writers Am., 1960, Columbia award Federated Italo-Ams. Calif., 1964, Pres.'s award Acad. Sci.-Fiction Fantasy and Horror Films, 1987, Movieguide commendation for Two Bits, One of Ten Best Films of 1995; inducted into Cultural Hall of Fame, South Phila. H.S. Mem. ASCAP, Writers Guild Am., Dirs. Guild Am., Producers Guild Am., Acad. Motion Pictures Arts and Scis., Mystery Writers Am. Home: 10216 Cielo Dr Beverly Hills CA 90210-2035 *For me it has always been important to succeed first in my own eyes. This personal sense of success seems warmer and surer and more likely to maintain the spirit during those moments when worldly success dances to tunes other than my own. Goals are golden. Guidelines are lines on a street map; they show how many different ways there are to go from where to when.*

STEFANON, ANTHONY, lawyer; b. Bellefonte, Pa., Sept. 6, 1949; s. Severino and Dorothy (Albright) S.; m. Elizabeth Jo Windsor, Nov. 22, 1969; children: Dyon, Justin. BS in Aerospace Engring., Pa. State U., 1971; JD, Dickinson U., 1977. Bar: Pa. 1977, U.S. Dist. Ct. (mid. dist.) Pa. 1977, U.S. Ct. Appeals (3rd cir.) 1991. Assoc. Myers & Potteiger, Harrisburg, Pa., 1977-79; ptnr. Myers, Potteiger & Stefanon, 1979-82; assoc. Thomas & Thomas, 1982-85; ptnr. Stefanon & Lappas, 1985-88; pvt. practice, 1988—. Mem. Assn. of Trial Lawyers of Am., Pa. Trial Lawyers Assn., Pa. Bar Assn., Dauphin County Bar Assn. Avocations: squash, auto racing, restorations. Office: 407 N Front St Harrisburg PA 17101-1221

STEFANSCHI, SERGIU, dancer; b. Komralid, Romania, Mar. 2, 1941; emigrated to Can., 1971, naturalized, 1977; s. Alexander and Lidia S. Diploma, Acad. Dance, Leningrad, 1960. Tchr. Nat. Ballet Sch. and Nat. Ballet of Can., Toronto, 1978—. Prin. dancer, Bucharest (Romania) Opera, 1960-68, Jeunesse Musicale de France, 1969-70, Theatre Francaise de la Dance, Paris, 1970, Nat. Ballet of Can., Toronto, Ont., 1971-78, appeared with, Belgrade (Yugoslavia) Opera, 1966, 68, Coob Marieta (Ga.) Ballet, 1976 (Recipient Silver medal I, Internat. Ballet Concourse, Varna, Bulgaria 1964), Internat. Guest Theater. Mem. Actors Equity Can. Mem. Romania Orthodox Ch. Home: 319 Ave Keewatin Toronto ON Canada M4P 2A4 Office: 111 Maitland St Toronto ON Canada M4Y 1E4

STEFANSEN, PEGGY ANN, special education educator; b. Newton, Kans., Sept. 16, 1953; d. Manny E. and Marjorie M. (Covalt) Osburn; m. Todd Stefansen, June 9, 1976; 1 child, Tyler L. BA, Oral Roberts U., 1975; MA, Tulsa U., 1981. Cert. tchr. educable mentally handicapped, trainable mentally retarded, learning disabilities, elem. edn., Okla. Tchr. learning disabilities Prague (Okla.) Pub. Schs., Chandler (Okla.) Pub. Schs., Skiatook (Okla.) Pub. Schs.; tchr. Prague Pub. Schs. Mem. NEA, Learning Disabilities Assn., Okla. Edn. Assn., Okla. Reading Coun. Home: Rte 1 Box 22A Paden OK 74860 Office: Prague Elementary NBU # 3504 Prague OK 74864-2031

STEFENELLI, GEORGE EDWARD, physician; b. Bklyn., Sept. 27, 1948; s. George Edward and Ann Marie (Mandel) S.; m. Rosemary Elizabeth Stefenelli, June 16, 1973; children: Stephanie, Rory, George, Samantha. BSN, SUNY, Stony Brook, 1975; DO, Phila. Sch. Osteo. Medicine, 1986. Diplomate Am. Bd. Ob-Gyn., lic. physician N.J., Pa., Md., S.C., Ga. Intern Interfaith Med. Ctr., Bklyn., 1986-87; resident U. Medicine and Dentistry of N.J., Stratford, 1987-91; asst. prof. clin. ob-gyn. U. Medicine and Dentistry N.J., 1992-93; ptnr. Potomac Ob-Gyn., Waynesboro, Pa., 1993-2000; chief svc. ob-gyn. dept. Waynesboro Hosp., 1994-96, 98-00, v.p. med. staff, 1999-2000; pvt. practice Women's Health Care of Clarion, Pa., 2000—01, Meriwether Ob/Gyn Assocs., 2001—; chief of surgery, chief ob-gyn. Ga. Bapt. Meriwether Hosp., 2002—. Sgt. USMC, 1966-70, capt. U.S. Army, 1976-82. Mem. Am. Osteo. Assn., Am. Coll. Osteo. Ob-Gyn., Am. Coll. Ob-Gyn., Am. Soc. Colposcopy and Cervical Pathology, Am. Assn. Gynecologic Laparoscopists, Am. Soc. for Reproductive Medicine, Tri-County Med. Soc. Ga. (v.p. 2002—). Home: 737 John Lovelace Rd Lagrange GA 30241 Office: Profl Bldg 5995 Spring St Warm Springs GA 31830

STEFFA, JOHN AMON, music educator, composer; s. Robert Karl and Dorothy Grace Steffa; m. Nancy Margaret Scarborough; 1 child Matthew 1 child Scott Chappell. BA Edn., U. Northern Iowa, 1969, M Music, 1978; D Musical Arts, U. Tex., 1985. Orch. tchr. Cedar Falls (Iowa) Pub. Sch. Sys., 1969—72, Charleston County Sch. Dist., Charleston, SC, 1972—77, Marshalltown (Iowa) Cmty. Sch. Dist., 1978—82, Temple (Tex.) Ind. Sch. Dist., 1985—87; music prof. Bowling Green (Ohio) State U., 1987—88, Murray State U., Murray, Ky., 1988—. Music dir. Charleston County Youth Symphony, Charleston, SC, 1973—77. Composer: (Transcription) Pines of Rome (for clarinet and electronics), 2001, (Music Composition) Bahiana (for percussion ensemble), 1990, Scherzo (for piano trio), 1991, A Jangada (for percussion ensemble), 1991, A Jangada (for wind ensemble), 1991, Tangents (a variation suite for piano), 1992 (Ky. Music Teachers Assn. Commn. award, 1992), Character Pieces for orchestra and electronics, 1993 (Ky. Arts Coun. grant support, 1993), Dialogue (for violin and viola), 1995, Piano Piece (for solo piano), 1995, Jazzy (for alto saxophone and electronics), 1995, Dialogue (for flute and string bass with electronics), 1995, Slide Talk (for eight trombones), 1997, Canyon Music (for clarinet and piano), 2000, Canyon Music (for clarinet and electronics), 2001, (Incidental Music for Public Radio) Voices, 2000, (songs) Dance Music No. 1, 1990, Trilogy (for chorus, organ, percussion and dancers), 1996, Songs in Tribute (for flugel horn, English horn and electronics), 2001. Recipient citation, Distance Edn. Report Magna Publs., 2000; grantee Profl. Assistance grant, Ky. Arts Coun., 1992. Mem.: Ky. Music Tchrs. Assn. (composer of yr. award 1992), Music Educators Nat. Conf., Coll. Music Soc. Office: Murray State U 524 Fine Arts Bldg Murray KY 42071 Business E-Mail: john.steffa@murraystate.edu.

STEFFAN, WALLACE ALLAN, entomologist, educator, museum director; b. St. Paul, Aug. 10, 1934; m. Sylvia Behler, July 16, 1966; 1 child, Sharon. BS, U. Calif., Berkeley, 1961, PhD, 1965. Entomologist dept. entomology Bishop Mus., Honolulu, 1964-85, head diptera sect., 1966-85, asst. chmn., 1979-85; dir. Idaho Mus. Natural History, Idaho State U., Pocatello, 1985-89, U. Alaska Mus., 1989-92; prof. biology, dir. U. Alaska, Fairbanks, 1989—92; exec. dir. Gt. Valley Mus. Natural History, 1992-94, Sun Cities Mus. Art, 1995-97, Burpee Mus. Natural History, Rockford, Ill., 1997-00, West Valley Art Mus., 2000—. Mem. grad. affiliate faculty dept. entomology, U. Hawaii, 1969-85; reviewer NSF, 1976-94; mem. affiliate faculty biology, Idaho State U., 1986-89. Acting editor Jour. Med. Entomology, 1966; assoc. editor Pacific Insects, 1980-85. Bd. dirs. Idaho State U. Fed. Credit Union, 1986-89; mem. adv. coun. Modesto Conv. and Visitors Bur., 1992-95; mem. Ft. Hall Replica Commn., 1986-89; judge Hawaii State Sci. and Engring. Fair, 1966-85, chief judge sr. display divsn., 1982, 83, 84; advisor to bd. Fairbanks Conv. and Visitors Bur., 1989-91; mem. vestry St. Christopher's Episcopal Ch., 1974-76, St. Matthew's Episcopal Ch., Fairbanks, 1990-91; pres. Alaska Visitors Assn., Fairbanks, 1991; advisor Fairbanks Conv. and Visitors Bur. Bd., 1989-91; bd. dirs. Kamehameha Fed. Credit Union, 1975-77, chmn., mem. supervisory com., 1980-84. With USAF, 1954-57. Grantee NIH, 1962, 63, 67-74, 76-81, 83-85, U.S. Army Med. Rsch. and Devel. Command, 1964-67, 73-74, NSF, 1968-76, 83-89, City and County of Honolulu, 1977, U.S. Dept. Interior, 1980, 81. Mem. Entomol. Soc. Am. (standing com. on systematics resources 1983-87), Pacific Coast Entomol. Soc., Soc. Systematic Zoology, Hawaiian Entomol. Soc. (pres. 1974, chmn. coms. 1966-85, editor procs. 1966), Hawaiian Acad. (councillor 1976-78), Sigma Xi (pres. San Joaquin chpt. 1994-95), Northwest Passage Immigrants and Ingenuity (pres. exec. com. 1998-00, v.p.), Ill. Assn. Museums (bd. dirs. 1998-00), Assn. Midwest Mus. (chair local arrangements com.), N.W. Valley C. of C. (bd. dirs. 2001—). Office: West Valley Art Mus 17420 N Ave of Arts Surprise AZ 85374

STEFFEL, SUSAN ELIZABETH, English language and literature educator; b. Muskegon, Mich., Feb. 9, 1951; d. Sherman Burgess and Geraldine (Westerman) Bos; m. Andrew John Steffel, July 12, 1975. BA, Hope Coll., 1973; MA in English, Mich. State U., 1978, PhD in English, 1993. Tchr. secondary English Maple Valley Schs., Vermontville, Mich., 1973-91; prof. English Ctrl. Mich. U., Mt. Pleasant, 1991—, Towle prof., 1998—. Supr. secondary student tchrs. dept. English Ctrl. Mich. U., 1991—, vice-chair profl. educators, 1994-95, chair profl. educators coun., 1995—, chair com. on coms., 1997-98. Co-author: High School English: A Process for Curriculum Development, 1985, 20th Century Children's Authors, 1994, Fantasy Literature for Children and Young Adults, 1998. Recipient Excellence in Edn. award Lansing Regional C. of C., 1985, 86, 88, 89, 90, Excellence in Teaching award Ctrl. Mich. U., 1996, outstanding tchr. award Sigma Delta Tau, 1997, outstanding educator award Kappa Delta Pi, 2000; named Towle Prof., 1998. Mem. ASCD, AAUW, Am. Assn. Colls. for Tchr. Edn., Am. Ednl. Rsch. Assn., Nat. Coun. Tchrs. English (guest reviewer 1993—), Mich. Coun. Tchrs. English (mem. steering com. 1985—, v.p. 2001-02, asst. editor jour. 1993-98, editor jour. 1999—), Assembly Lit. for Adolescents, Conf. English Edn., Golden Key Honor Soc. (hon.), Phi Kappa Phi, Phi Delta Kappa (sec. 1995-96). Avocations: reading, gardening, pets, needlework. Office: Ctrl Mich U 204 Anspach Hl Mount Pleasant MI 48859-0001

STEFFEN, ALAN LESLIE, entomologist; b. Ansonia, Ohio, Feb. 27, 1927; s. Henry William and Maude Moiselle (DuBois) S.; m. Genevieve Carlyle, Dec. 27, 1950 (dec. Jan. 6, 1989); m. Doris Mae Rable, Jan. 20, 1990. AB, Miami U., 1948; MSc in Entomology, Ohio State U., 1949; diploma, Malaria Tng. Ctr., 1959; postgrad., WHO, Sri Lanka and The Philippines, 1967, 68. Registered profl. entomologist. Malaria specialist Agy. for Internat. Devel., Jakarta, Indonesia, 1959-65, chief malaria advisor Kathmandu, Nepal, 1966-72, Addis Ababa, Ethiopia, 1972-76, Kathmandu, 1976-78, Islamabad, Pakistan, 1978-80; malaria specialist Ctr. Disease Control, Songkhla, Thailand, 1965-66; tropical disease cons. Ill., 1981—. Cons. U.S. AID, Port Au Prince, Haiti, 1981, WHO, Geneva, 1981—, Tifa, Ltd., Millington, N.J., 1982, John Snow, Inc., Boston, 1984, Vector Biology and Control Project, Arlington, Va., 1986. Mem. Nature Conservancy, Washington, 1986-88. With U.S. Army, 1945-46, ETO. Recipient Meritorious Honor award U.S. Dept. State, 1972. Fellow Royal Soc. Tropical Medicine; mem. Entomol. Soc. Am., Am. Registry Profl. Entomologists, Nat. Assn. Ret. Fed. Employees (life), Am. Fgn. Svc. Assn., Ohio State Alumni Assn. (life), VFW. Avocations: stamp collecting, study of Asian art. Home and Office: 3666 E Cromwell Ln Springfield MO 65802-2487

STEFFEN, KENNETH CHARLES, priest, lawyer; b. Effingham, Ill., Feb. 25, 1958; s. Delbert Steffen and Alma Jansen. BA, Cardinal Glennon Coll., St. Louis, 1979; MA, MDIV, MDVI, Kenrick Sem., St. Louis, 1984; DMIN, Grad. Theol. Inst., Donaldson, 1993; JCL, Cath. U., Washington, 1996; DMIN, Grad. Theol. Inst., Donaldson, 1993; JCL, Cath. U., Washington, 1996. Assoc. pastor Little Flower, Springfield, Ill., 1984—89, St. Agnes, Springfield, 1987—94; jud. vicar Tribunal, 1987—; cons. Family Life Office, 1987—; instr. Lay Ministry Program, 1987—; co-pastor St. James, Riverton, 1994—, St. Katharine Drexel, Springfield, 2001—. Mem.: Midwest Canon Law Soc., Canon Law Soc. of Am. Roman Catholic. Office: Catholic Pastoral Center 1615 W Washington Springfield IL 62702 Office Fax: 217-698-0802.

STEFFEN, KONRAD, geology educator; b. Zurich, Zurich, Switzerland, Jan. 2, 1952; s. Ernst S. and Maria Steffen-Kurzynski; m. Regula Dorothee Werner, Feb. 10, 1952; children: Anico, Simon. PhD, Swiss Fed. Inst. Tech., Zurich, Switzerland, 1976. Prof. geology U. Colo., Boulder, 1990—, assoc. dir. CIRES, 1997—. Editor: (albums) article in Annals of Glaciology, 1993. Master: NASA (chair adv. panel for DAAC 1991—2000), World Meteorol. Orgn. (chair ACSYS/CliC OPP panel 1998—2003); mem.: Am. Meteorol. Soc. (assoc. editor Jour. Appl. Meteorolgy 1996—2001), Glaciol. Soc. (mem. executive bd. 1992—96). Reformed Ch. Avocations: photography, travel, mountaineering. Personal E-mail: konrad.steffen@colorado.edu. Business E-Mail: konrad.steffen@colorado.edu.

STEFFEN, LLOYD HOWARD, minister, religion educator; b. Racine, Wis., Nov. 27, 1951; s. Howard C. and Ruth L. (Rode) S.; m. Emmajane S. Finney, Feb. 14, 1981; children: Nathan, Samuel, William. BA, New Coll., 1973; MA, Andover Newton Theol. Sch., 1978; MDiv, Yale U., 1978; PhD, Brown U., 1984. Ordained to ministry United Ch. of Christ, 1983. Chaplain Northland Coll., Ashland, Wis., 1983-90, assoc. prof., 1982-90, Lehigh U., Bethlehem, Pa., 1990-97, chaplain, 1990—, prof., 1997—, chair dept. religion studies, 2000—. Mem. theol. com. Wis. Conf. United Ch. of Christ, Madison, 1985—87; mem. div. ch. and ministry NW assn. Wis. Conf., Eau Claire, 1987—90; mem. ecumenical commn. Penn N.E. Conf., 1994—96; mem. Common Ground, Bethlehem, Pa., 1994—97, chair, Pa., 1995—97; mem. ch. & ministry com. Pa. Northeast Conf., 1997—; mem. ethics com. St. Luke's Hosp., Bethlehem, Pa., 1998—; mem., vice-chair, bd. dirs. Religious Coalition for Reproductive Choice; non-govtl. orgn. rep. UN; 10th Curtis Lectr. Sacred Heart Univ., 1999; Frederick C. Wood Lectr. Cornell U., 2002. Author: Self-Deception and the Common Life, 1986, Life/Choice: The Theory of Just Abortion, 1994, Abortion: A Reader, 1996, Executing Justice: The Moral Meaning of the Death Penalty, 1998; contbr. articles to profl. jours. Town supr. Town of La Pointe, Wis., 1984-87. Recipient 1st Pilgrim Press Church and Soc. Book award, NEH Inst. award, Harvard U., 1988, East-West Ctr., 1995; fellow Univ. fellow, Brown U., 1982; grantee faculty devel. grantee, Northland Coll., 1986, 1990, Lehigh U., 1994, 1998. Mem. Soc. Christian Ethics, Am. Acad. Religion, Assocs. for Religion and Intellectual Life, Assn. for Coordination of Univ. Religious Affairs. Home: 1349 Woodland Cir Bethlehem PA 18017-1636 Office: Lehigh U Johnson Hall # 36 Bethlehem PA 18015 E-mail: lhs1@lehigh.edu.

STEFFEN, MAXINE LYNN, small business owner; b. Geneva, Aug. 14, 1955; d. Edwin and Leta Lucille Domeier. BS, U. Nebr., 1976. Owner Landry & Assocs., Oklahoma City, 1983-86; regional sales mgr. Staley Foodservice, Chgo., 1986-87; sales Marvene Fischer Sales, Northbrook, Ill., 1987-88; owner Am. Food Brokers, Inc., Chgo., 1988—, Flagworks, Lincoln, Nebr., 1997—, Stars & Stripes Antiques, Lincoln, 1999—. Mem. Women Bus. Owners Network, Univ. Pl. Bus. Orgn., Soroptomist (pres. 1997—). Republican. Avocations: piano, tennis, golf, theatre, reading. Office: 332 S 33d St Lincoln NE 68510

STEFFENS, ANNIE LAURIE, sign language educator, interpreter; b. N.Y.C. d. Robert William and Irene Marie (Hoecker) S. Cert., U. Ariz., Tucson, NYU, Gallaudet U., Washington D.C. Cert. sign lang. interpreter, sign lang. educator. Sign language interpreter high sch., Brattleboro, Vt., Longmeadow, Mass.; tchr. sign language pvt. sch., Putney, Vt., Main Street Arts, Saxtons River, Cmty. Coll., Greenfield, Mass., Cheshire Hosp., Keene, N.H., YMCA, Keene, Brattleboro Sr. Ctr., Brattleboro Recreation Ctr.; pvt. practice. Developer new program using Am. sign lang., 1995—; mem. sign lang. choir Gallaudet U., NYU; poetry educator Main Street Arts; mem. new Am. Sign Lang. program Grace Cottage Hosp., Townsend, Vt., 1996; developer, designer Am. Sign Lang. Mentorship, 1997—, Am. Sign Lang. Linguistics program, 1998—. Author: (poem) Down Peaceful Paths. Advocate Women's Shelter, Brattleboro; counselor Vt. respite care project Mental Health of Southeastern Vt., Brattleboro. Named Am. Sign Language Tchr. of Excellence, 1998. Mem. Nat. Assn. Deaf, Sign Instrs. Guidance Network. Avocations: signing to music, dancing, singing, poetry, painting abstract designs. Home: 14 Spruce St Brattleboro VT 05301-2716

STEFFENS, BRIAN LEE, communications executive; b. Mt. Clemens, Mich., July 1, 1949; s. Alvin Oliver Charles and Leola (Vance) S.; m. Linda Wood, July 1, 1972 (div. Dec. 1979); m. Martha Moutoux, Aug. 9, 1980; children: Jonathan Jaquess, Jeffrey Nash, Lauren Endicott. BS in Journalism, Bowling Green (Ohio) State U., 1971. Reporter Flint (Mich.) Jour., 1972-73; copy editor, asst. news editor, photographer, picture editor Detroit News, 1973-77; picture editor Miami Herald, 1977-79; graphics editor St. Paul Pioneer Press, 1979-81; asst. mng. editor Orange County Register, Santa Ana, Calif., 1981-84; news editor San Diego Union, 1984-87; graphics editor, news editor L.A. Times Orange County edit., Costa Mesa, Calif., 1987-91; editor Quill Mag., Greencastle, Ind., 1991-95; exec. v.p., COO Giles Comm., Mt. Kisco, N.Y., 1995-98; sr. v.p. news, editor Editor & Pub. Co., N.Y.C., 1998—99. Cons. Field Newspaper Syndicate, Irvine, Calif., 1981-83, AAA Tex./N.Mex./Hawaii mem. mags., 1996-97; spkr., faculty Am. Press Inst., Reston, Va., 1983-87; invited participant Poynter Inst. for Media Studies, St. Petersburg, Fla., 1983-92; spkr., faculty Soc. Newspaper Design, Reston, 1983-94. Editor Quill, 1991-95; contbr. articles to mags. Named to Journalism Hall of Fame, Bowling Green State U., 1993. Mem. Soc. Profl. Journalists, Soc. Newspaper Design (com. chair, publs. dir. 1983-87, invited judge internat. competition 1995, 3 bronze awards, 5 awards of excellence 1982-91). Avocations: music, golf, tennis. Office: C/O Editor and Publisher 11 W 19th St Fl 10 New York NY 10011-4209

STEFFENS, DAVID CARL, geriatric psychiatrist; b. San Diego, June 25, 1962; s. Carl Arthur Steffens and Diane Elisabeth Coulter; m. Lori Anne Bastian, July 14, 1990; children: Eleanor Bastian Steffens, Catherine Grace Steffens. BA, Rice U., 1984; MD, U. Tex., Houston, 1988. Diplomate Am. Bd. Psychiatry, added qualifications in geriatric psychiatry. Intern, resident psychiatry Duke U. Med. Ctr., Durham, NC, 1988-92, assoc. psychiatrist, 1992-97, asst. prof. psychiatry, 1997—2001, assoc. prof., 2002—. Mem. spkr.'s bur. Pfizer Inc., 2001—, Novartis Inc., 2001—, Janssen Inc., 2001—. Contbr. articles to profl. jours. Mem.: Am. Assn. Geriatric Psychiatry (CME com. 2001—), Am. Psychiat. Assn. Office: Duke U Med Ctr Box 3903 Durham NC 27710-0001

STEFFENS, JOHN HOWARD, cytotechnologist; b. Glendale, Calif., Aug. 5, 1941; s. Amzel Emmet Steffens and Wanda Elgain (Haylock) Clark; m. Yvonne Marie Croxen, Sept. 9, 1966; children: Roberta Mae, Deena Marie, Adam Kemp. BS, Warner Pacific Coll., Portland, Oreg., 1970; cert. cytotech., U. Kans., 1973. Cert. cyto-technologist. Messenger, orderly Palo Alto (Calif.) Stanford Hosp., 1957-62; warehouse worker Loma Linda Foods, Riverside, Calif., 1962-64; apiary worker Albert Knoefler Honey Co., 1962-65; cyto-technician United Med. Labs., Portland, 1966-70; mgr. Independence (Mo.) Fire & Safety Equipment Co., 1970-72; res. and substitute tchr. Independence Sch. System, 1970-72, 90-95; cyto-technologist, med. technologist U. Health Scis., Kansas City, Mo., 1973-85; cyto-technologist Kansas City VA Hosp., 1973—, Martin Luther King Jr. Hosp., Kansas City, Mo., 1975, Rsch. Med. Ctr., Kansas City, 1984-90, Johnson Med. and Reference Labs., Independence, 1990-96, Midwest Anatomic Pathology Lab., Kansas City, 1999—. Cons. Univ. Diagnostic Sys. Inc., Independence, 1992-98; quality control supr. United Med. Labs, Portland, 1968-70; lab. safety officer U. Health Scis., Kansas City, 1980-84. Mem. Burroughs Aubudon Soc., Independence, Cmty. Assn. for the Arts. Recipient Performance award Kansas City VA Hosp., 1987, Svc. award, 1988, Outstanding Rating Cert., 1988, 94, 95. Mem. Heart of Am. Assn. Cytotechnologists, Am. Beekeeping Fedn., Mo. Beekeepers Assn., Midwestern Beekeepers Assn. (bd. dirs. 1987-89, pres. 1990, honey plants com., Beekeeper of Yr. award 1990), Nat. Audubon Soc., Pathfinder Club (bd. dirs. 1973-76, dep. dir. 1974-76). Republican. Seventh Day Adventist. Home: 913 Main Rd Independence MO 64056-2417 Office: Kansas City VA Hosp 4801 E Linwood Blvd Kansas City MO 64128-2226

STEFFENSEN, DWIGHT A. former medical products and data processing services executive; b. Fresno, Calif., 1943; BA, Stanford U., 1965. Corp. contr. Synergex Corp. (merged with Bergen Brunswig Corp. 1985), Orange, Calif., 1969-72, chief fin. officer, v.p., 1972-80, chief oper. officer, chief fin. officer, exec. v.p., treas., 1980-83, pres., chief exec. officer, 1983-85, exec. v.p., 1985—; pres. Drug Service Inc., 1975-80; pres., coo, dir. Bergen Brunswig Corp.; chmn. & CEO Merisel, Inc., El Segundo, Calif., 1996—2000.*

STEFFER, ROBERT WESLEY, clergyman; b. Spokane, Wash., June 24, 1934; s. Harold Wesley and Kathryne (Trumble) S.; m. Diane DeMoisey, Aug. 19, 1960; children: Erika Kirsten, Beauregard Gregory Robert. BA, Whitworth Coll., 1956; BD, Lexington Theol. Sem., 1959; MA, Ind. U., 1966, PhD, 1967. Ordained to ministry Christian Ch. (Disciples of Christ), 1959. Civilian dir. religious edn. U.S. Army Armor Ctr., Ft. Knox, Ky., 1960-64; assoc. min. Christian Ch. (Disciples of Christ), Oklahoma City, 1967-71; prof. Phillips U., Enid, Okla., 1971-76; fraternal worker div. overseas ministries Christian Ch. (Disciples of Christ), Barrow-in-Furness, Cumbria, Eng., 1976-79; Lilly vis. prof. religious edn. Christian Theol. Sem., Indpls., 1979-81; dir. edn. for mission Christian Ch. (Disciples of Christ), 1981-87; exec. regional min. Christian Ch. (Disciples of Christ) in Can., Guelph, Ont., 1987-97; interim sr. minister Eureka (Ill.) Christian Ch., 1997-98; curator Cane Ridge Hist. Preservation Project, 1998—. Sec. Coll. Chs. of Christ in Can., Guelph, 1987-97. Editor Cane Ridge Bull., 1999—; contbr. articles to religious publs. and ency. Col., chaplain USAR ret., 1964—. Lilly Found. fellow in adult edn. Ind. U., 1964-66. Mem. Disciples of Christ Hist. Soc. (life, trustee 1990-94), Religious Edn. Assn. (bd. dirs. 1994-97), Conf. Regional Mins. and Moderators (2nd v.p.), Ch. Fin. Coun. (bd. dirs. 1995-96, exec. com. 1995), Phi Delta Kappa, Theta Phi. Democrat. Avocations: gardening, reading, travel, music. Office: PO Box 26 Paris KY 40362-0026 Mailing: PO Box 5226 Paris KY 40362-5226 Home: 1655 Cane Ridge Rd Bourbon County KY E-mail: canerdgmtg@aol.com.

STEFFEY, EUGENE PAUL, veterinary medicine educator; b. Reading, Pa., Oct. 27, 1942; s. Paul E. and Mary M. (Balthaser) S.; children: Michele A., Bret E., Michael R., Brian T. Student, Muhlenberg Coll., 1960-63; D in Vet. Medicine, U. Pa., 1967; PhD, U. Calif., Davis, 1973. Diplomate Am. Coll. Vet. Anesthesiologists (pres. 1980). NIH spl. research fellow U. Calif., San Francisco, 1973, asst. prof. Davis, 1974-77, assoc. prof., 1977-80, prof. vet. medicine, 1980—, also chmn. dept. vet. surgery, 1980-93. Mem. scientific reviewers Am. Jour. Vet. Research, Schaumburg, Ill., 1984-87. Contbr. more than 150 articles to profl. jours. Mem. AVMA, Am. Coll. Vet. Anesthesiologists, Am. Physiol. Soc., Am. Soc. Pharmocology Exptl. Therapeutics, Am. Soc. Anesthesiologists, Assn. Vet. Anaesthetists, Calif. Soc. Anesthesiologists, European Coll. Vet. Anesthesia, Internat. Anesthesia Rsch. Soc., Pa. Vet. Med. Assn., Royal Coll. Vet. Surgeons (hon. assoc.), Sigma Xi, Phi Zeta. Office: U Calif Dept Surg Radiol Scis School of Vet Medicine Davis CA 95616

STEFFY, JOHN RICHARD, nautical archaeologist, educator; b. Lancaster, Pa., May 1, 1924; s. Milton Grill and Zoe Minerva (Fry) S.; m. Esther Lucille Koch, Oct. 20, 1951; children: David Alan, Loren Craig. Student, Pa. Area Coll., Lancaster, 1946-47, Milw. Sch. Engring., 1947-49. Ptnr. M.G. Steffy & Sons, Denver, 1950-72; ship reconstructor Kyrenia Ship Project, Cyprus, 1972-73, Inst. Nautical Archaeology, College Station, Tex., 1973—; from lectr. to prof. anthropology Tex. A&M U., 1976-88, Sara W and George O. Yamani prof. nautical archaeology, 1989-90, prof. emeritus, 1990—. Lectr. on ship constrn. Author: Wooden Shipbuilding and the Interpretation of Shipwrecks, 1994; co-editor: The Athlit Ram, 1991; contbr. chpts. to books and articles to profl. jours. Sec. Denver Borough Authority, Pa., 1962-72. Served with USN, 1942-45. MacArthur Found. fellow, 1985. Republican. Methodist. Office: Tex A&M U Inst Nautical Archaeology College Station TX 77845

STEFUNEK, PAUL CHRISTOPHER, executive search company executive; b. Bronx, N.Y., Sept. 17, 1965; s. John and Millie Ann Stefunek; m. Kathleen Ann Kutrubs, May 23, 1992; children: Jacob, Natalie. BBA in Mktg., Pace U., 1987. Sales rep. Pitney Bowes, White Plains, N.Y., 1988-91; dist. mgr. Automatic Data Publ., Cleve., 1991-92; product mgr., sales rep. Pitney Bowes, 1992-93; cons. Christian & Timbers, 1993-96; v.p., co-founder Stratford Group, 1996—2001; co-founder, pres. Paul Lawrence Assocs., 2002—; CEO, HighBridge Assocs. , 2002—. Mem. Assn. Online Profls. Avocations: baseball, ice hockey, reading. Office: HighBridge Assocs 1330 Corporate Dr Ste 400 Hudson OH 44236

STEG, LEO, research and development executive; b. Vienna, Austria, Mar. 30, 1922; came to U.S., 1941, naturalized, 1946; s. Jacob and Clara (Gellert) S.; m. Doreen Ethel Ray, June 12, 1947; children: Paula Jamie, Ellen Leslie, Audrey Leigh. BS, CCNY, 1947; MS, U. Mo., 1948; PhD, Cornell U., 1951. Registered profl. engr., Pa. Chief engr. Fed. Design Co., N.Y.C., 1946-47; instr. mech. engring. U. Mo., Columbia, 1947-48; instr. applied mechanics and materials Cornell U., Ithaca, N.Y., 1948-51, asst. prof., 1951-55; sys. engr., missile and space divsn. GE, Phila., 1955-56, mgr. space sci. lab., 1956-79, chief scientist, 1980-81; sr. v.p. University City Sci. Ctr., 1981-82; pres. Steg, Ray & Assocs., Villanova, Pa., 1980—; sci. and pub. policy fellow Brookings Inst., Washington, 1982-84; pres. Tech. Applications Internat., Inc., McLean, Va., 1990-97. Adj. prof. Drexel U.; cons. to space scis. bd. NAS, other govt. agencies. Contbr. articles to profl. jours.; editor 2 books. Assoc. trustee U. Pa. Named Engr. of Yr. Phila., 1965 Fellow AIAA (editor-in-chief jour. 1963-67), AAAS; mem. Phila. Acad. Scis. (founding), Franklin Inst. Phila. (past mem. bd. mgrs.), Long Beach Island Found. Arts and Scis. (past chmn. bd.), Sigma Xi, Phi Kappa Phi. Clubs: Cosmos, Cornell of N.Y. Home and Office: c/o Polk 225 Windsor Gate Cove Atlanta GA 30342

STEGALL, MARK D. surgeon, medical educator; b. Lubbock, Tex., June 24, 1957; BA, Harvard Coll., 1979; postgrad., Trinity Coll., Oxford (Eng.), 1979; MD, Columbia U., 1984. Diplomate Am. Bd. Surgery. Resident in surgery Presbyn. Hosp., N.Y.C., 1984-91; post-doctoral rsch. scientist Columbia U., 1987-89; fellow in transplantation U. Wis., Madison, 1991-93; asst. prof. surgery, dir. pancreas and islet transplantation U. Colo., Denver, 1993-98; dir. kidney and pancreas transplantation surgery Mayo Clinic, Rochester, Minn., 1998—, chmn. divsn. transplantation surgery, 2002—; assoc. prof. surgery Mayo Med. Sch., 1998—. Post-Doctoral Rsch. fellow N.Y. State Diabetes Fund, 1987-88; recipient NIH-NIAID Individual Nat. Rsch. Svc. award, 1988-89, Upjohn prize N.Y. State Transplantation Soc., 1988. Mem. Am. Soc. Transplant Surgeons (Upjohn award 1989, Ortho Faculty Devel. award 1995), Soc. Univ. Surgeons, Assn. Acad. Surgery. Office: Mayo Clinic Campus Box C-318 200 1st St SW Rochester MN 55905-0002

STEGALL, WILLIAM R. retired brokerage house executive; b. Thomasville, Ga., Feb. 26, 1942; s. Willie W. and Alberta Stegall; m. Constance A. Rogato, July 12, 1997; children: William, Kimberly Johnson, Andrea, Kelley, John McNeill, Kimberly McNeill. Student, Univ. Md., 1966—74. Officer CIA, Washington, 1962—92; chmn., pres. WorldWide Logistics, Inc., North Fort Myers, Fla., 1992—2002; ret., 2002. Author: (novels) Shadow Over The Caribbean, 2000, From The Mouth Of The Mamba, 2002. Avocation: sailing.

STEGER, CHARLES WILLIAM, university administrator; b. Richmond, Va., June 16, 1947; s. Charles William and Virginia Belle (Garrett) S.; m. Janet Grey Baird, Sept. 13, 1969; children: Christopher B., David C. BArch, Va. Poly. Inst. & State U., 1970, MArch, 1971, PhD, 1978. Registered architect, Va. Project planner, architect Wiley & Wilson Inc., Lynchburg, Va., 1971-72, mgr. urban planning dept., 1973-74; dir. Environ. Design Consortium Inc., Blacksburg, 1974-85; inst. grad. urban design program Coll. Architecture and Urban Studies , Va. Poly. Inst. and State U., 1974-76, chmn. grad. urban design program, 1976-81; dean Coll. Architecture and Urban Studies, Va. Poly. Inst. and State U., 1981-93; acting v.p. for pub. svc. Va. Poly. Inst. and State U., 1990-93, v.p. for devel. and univ. rels., 1993-99; pres. Va. Tech. U., 2000—. Bd. dirs. Va. Found. Architecture, Richmond, Innovative Tech. Authority; mem. Gov.'s Secure Va. Tech. Initiative, 2001-02; mem. Gov.'s Va. Preparedness and Security Panel, 2001-02; bd. mem. Va. Advanced Shipbuilding and Carrier Integration Ctr., 2001--. Contbr. articles to jours. in field. Bd. dirs. Hollins Coll., Roanoke, Va., 1987-96, Boswil (Switzerland) Found., 1986—, Ctr. in the Square, Roanoke, 1993-99; v.p. Va. Tech. Found., Inc., 1993-99; adv. coun. Va. Ctr. on Rural Devel., 1992—; commr. Govs. Commn. on Population Growth and Devel., Richmond, 1989-94. Fellow AIA (bd. dirs. ACSA Health Facilities Rsch. Program, Washington 1989—, ACSA Coun. on Arch. Rsch., 1987—); mem. Am. Planning Assn., Am. Inst. Cert. Planners, Commonwealth Club (Richmond, Va.), Shenandoah Club (Roanoke, Va.). Avocations: cattle farming, golf, canoeing. Office: Va Tech Pres 210 Burruss Hall Blacksburg VA 24061

STEGER, EDWARD HERMAN, chemist; b. New Orleans, Dec. 11, 1936; s. Herman Christoph and Katherine (Walther) S.; m. Amy Patricia Duvall, July 29, 1960; children: David B., Sandra E. BS, Tulane U., 1958. Analytical chemist Atlantic Rsch. Corp., Gainesville, Va., 1960-64, head control lab., 1964—. Presenter at profl. confs. Contbr. articles to Fine Particle Soc. Jour. Lt. USNR, 1958-60. Mem. Am. Chem. Soc., N.Y. Acad. Scis., Phi Beta Kappa, Phi Eta Sigma, Alpha Chi Sigma. Baptist. Home: 4311 Alta Vista Dr Fairfax VA 22030-5302 Office: Atlantic Rsch Corp 5945 Wellington Rd Gainesville VA 20155-1633

STEGER, EVAN EVANS, III, retired lawyer; b. Indpls., Oct. 24, 1937; s. Charles Franklin and Alice (Hill) S.; m. Suzy Gillespie, July 18, 1964; children: Cynthia Anne, Emily McKee. AB, Wabash Coll., 1959; JD, Ind. U., 1962. Bar: Ind. 1962, U.S. Dist. Ct. (so. dist.) Ind. 1962, U.S. Ct. Appeals (7th cir.) 1972, U.S. Tax Ct. 1982, U.S. Supreme Ct. 1982. Assoc. Ice, Miller, Donadio and Ryan and predecessor firm Ross, McCord, Ice and Miller, Indpls., 1962-69, ptnr., 1970-96, mng. ptnr., 1996-99, ret., 1999. Fellow Am. Coll. Trial Lawyers. Democrat. Presbyterian. Office: Ice Miller Box 82001 1 American Sq Indianapolis IN 46282-0020 E-mail: esteger565@aol.com.

STEGER, JOSEPH A. university president; Formerly sr. v.p. and provost U. Cin., pres., 1984—. Office: U Cin PO Box 210063 Cincinnati OH 45221-0063

STEGER, RALPH JAMES, chemist; b. Meridian, Okla., Jan. 24, 1940; s. Daniel Bose and Opal Creola (Brothers) S. BS in Chemistry and Math., Langston U., 1962. Cartographer Aeronautical Chart and Info. Ctr. ACIC USAF, St. Louis, 1962-63; lab. technician Sigma Chem. Co., 1963; phys. scientist U.S. Army Chem. Corps, Edgewood Arsenal, Md., 1963-65; rsch. chemist Chem. Rsch., Devel. and Engring. Ctr. SMCCR Rsch. Lab., Analytical Div., Aberdeen Proving Ground, 1965-86; chemist Chem. Rsch., Devel. and Engring. Ctr. SMCCR-Detection, Detection Technology, 1986-97. Adv. com. Garrison Gents, Balt., 1980—; ACOR monitoring govt. contracts, Balt., 1987—. Contbr. articles to profl. publs. Mem. Okla. Hist. Soc. Mem. AAAS, N.Y. Acad. Sci., Okla. Hist. Soc. Office: CBDCOM-RTE Aberdeen Proving Ground MD 21010-5423 E-mail: rjsteger@erols.com.

STEGER, WILLIAM MERRITT, federal judge; b. Dallas, Aug. 22, 1920; s. Merritt and Lottie (Reese) S.; m. Ann Hollandsworth, Feb. 14, 1948; 1 son, Merritt Reed (dec.). Student, Baylor U., 1938-41; LL.B., So. Meth. U., 1950. Bar: Tex. 1951. Pvt. practice, Longview, 1951-53; apptd. U.S. dist. atty. Eastern Dist. Tex., 1953-59; mem. firm Wilson, Miller, Spivey & Steger, Tyler, Tex., 1959-70; U.S. dist. judge Ea. Dist. Tex. U.S. Dist. Ct. (ea. dist.) Tex., 1970—, sr. judge, 1988—. Republican candidate for gov. of Tex., 1960; for U.S. Ho. of Reps., 1962; mem. Tex. State Republican Exec. Com., 1966-69; chmn. Tex. State Republican Party, 1969-70. Pilot with ranks 2d lt. to capt. USAAF, 1942-47. Mem. ABA, State Bar Tex., Masons (32 degree, Shriner). Home: 801 Meadowcreek Dr Tyler TX 75703-3524 Office: US Courthouse PO Box 1109 Tyler TX 75710-1109

STEGMAYER, JOSEPH HENRY, housing industry executive; b. Teaneck, N.J., Jan. 4, 1951; s. Arthur Harry and Alicia (Ward) S.; m. Delene Russell. BS in Fin., U. Louisville, 1973. Spl. projects Worthington Industries Inc., Columbus, Ohio, 1973-75, dir. investor rels., 1975-77, dir. corp. rels., 1977-80, v.p. corp. devel., 1980-82, v.p., CFO, treas., 1982-93, also bd. dirs.; pres., vice chmn. Clayton Homes, Inc., Knoxville, Tenn., 1993-98, also bd. dirs.; pres. retail & CFO Champion Enterprises, Inc., Auburn Hills, Mich., 1998-2000; chmn., CEO Centex Mfg. Housing Group, Dallas, 2000—. Editor: We've Only Scratched the Surface, 1981. Chmn. YMCA, Columbus, 1981-83; pres. Columbus Zoo, 1987-90, chmn., 1990-93; bd. dirs. Muskingum Coll., 1984-93, Knoxville Zoo, Found. of Diocese of Columbus, United Way Knoxville; fin. chmn. Ronald McDonald House, Columbus; mem. chancellor's assocs. bd. U. Tenn. Named Citizen of Yr., Columbus Jaycees, 1984; recipient Outstanding Achievement in Fin. award Phi Beta Kappa, 1984. Mem. Fin. Execs. Inst. Roman Catholic. Avocations: scuba diving, travel, investing. Office: Centex Corp 2728 N Harwood Dallas TX 75201

STEHLE, EDWARD RAYMOND, secondary education educator, school system administrator; b. Pitts., May 30, 1942; s. Edward August and Mary Josephine (Veverka) S.; m. Alberta McConnell; 1 child, Christian Dollison. BA, U. Pitts., 1964; MA, Columbia U., 1966, doctoral student, 1966-68. Instr. European history C.W. Post Coll., Long Island U., Greenville, N.Y., 1967-68, Middlebury (Vt.) Coll., 1968-69; history master The Lawrenceville (N.J.) Sch., Lawrenceville, N.J., 1969—, dir. day students, 1978-83, asst. dir. coll. counseling, 1983-88, chmn. history dept., 1988-94; asst. dir. The N.J. Scholars Program, 1981, dir., 1982-91, chmn. bd., 1988-96, also bd. dirs. Cons. U. Del. Sea Grant Coll., Newark, 1981-82; cons. on history of migrations Statue of Liberty-Ellis Island Found., N.Y.C., 1985-88; mem. selection com. Morris County (N.J.) Summer Opportunities for Tchrs. Program, Morristown, 1985-86; trustee Craftsbury Chamber Players, Greensboro, Vt., 1985-89; N.E.H. Coun. for Basic Edn. fellowship ind. study in the humanities, 1997. Co-author: A Guide to Programming in Basic Plus, 1975; contbr. Harper's Encyclopedia of the Modern World, 1972. Vice pres. Assoc. Mems., Ch. of Christ, Greensboro, 1974-76, pres., 1976-78. Vis. scholar Cambridge (Eng.) U., 1996. Mem. Am. Hist. Assn., Nassau Club (Princeton, N.J.), Mountainview Country Club (Greensboro, Vt.), N. Am. Conf. British Studies. Democrat. Episcopalian. Avocation: painting. Home: 2810 Main St Lawrenceville NJ 08648-1017 Office: The Lawrenceville Sch Main St Lawrenceville NJ 08620-2310 E-mail: estehle@lawrenceville.org.

STEHLI, FRANCIS GREENOUGH, geologist, educator; b. Upper Montclair, N.J., Oct. 16, 1924; s. Edgar and Emily (Greenough) S.; m. Irene Comfort, June 19, 1948; children: Anne, Robert, John, Edgar. BS, St. Lawrence U., 1949, MS, 1950; PhD, Columbia U., 1953. Asst. prof. invertebrate paleontology Calif. Inst. Tech., 1953-56; tech. group supr. research dept. Am. Petroleum Corp., 1956-60; prof. geology, chmn. dept. Case Western Res. U., 1960-73, Samuel St. John prof. earth scis., 1973-80, acting dean sci., 1975, acting dean sci. and engring., 1976, dean sci. and engring., 1977-80; dean grad. studies and research U. Fla., Gainesville, 1980-82; dean Coll. Geoscis. U. Okla., Norman, 1982-86; chmn. sci. adv. com. DOSECC, Inc., 1986—; rsch. assoc. Archeol. Rsch. Team, 1993—. Geol. cons., 1960— Author articles in field. Served with USNR, 1943-46. Fellow Geol. Soc. Am., AAAS; mem. Geochem. Soc., Paleontol. Soc. (pres.), Am. Soc. Engring. Edn., No. Ohio Geol. Soc. Home: PO Box 163 Smithville Flats NY 13841-0163 Office: 5561 SW 91st Ter Gainesville FL 32608-4369 also: Archeol Rsch Team 1519 NW 25th Ter Gainesville FL 32605-5120

STEHLIN, JOHN SEBASTIAN, JR. surgeon; b. Brownsville, Tenn., June 16, 1923; s. John Sebastian and Princess (King) S.; m. Mary Elizabeth Cleary, Sept. 19, 1950 (div. 1962); 1 child, Mary Cleary. Student, Vanderbilt U., 1941-42, Notre Dame U., 1943-44; MD, Med. Coll. Wis., 1947. Diplomate: Am. Bd. Surgery. Intern Milw. Hosp., 1947-48; resident pathology Bapt. Hosp., Memphis, 1948-49; resident surgery Milw. Hosp., 1949-52; fellow surgery Lahey Clinic, Boston, 1952-53; sr. fellow surgery U. Tex., M.D. Anderson Hosp. and Tumor Inst., Houston, 1955-56; fellow surgery Lahey Clinic, Boston, 1956; mem. surg. staff U. Tex., M.D. Anderson Hosp. and Tumor Inst., Houston, 1957-67, asst. surgeon, 1957-60, asso. surgeon, 1961-67; asst. prof. surgery U. Tex. Postgrad. Sch. Medicine, Houston, 1957-60, asso. prof., 1961-63; asso. prof. surgery U. Tex. Postgrad. Sch. Medicine (Grad. Sch. Biomed. Scis.), 1963-67; clin. asso. prof. surgery Baylor Coll. Medicine, Houston, 1967—; mem. surg. staff St. Joseph Hosp., 1967—. Hon. prof. faculty medicine U. Republic Uruguay, 1965; founder, sci. dir. Stehlin Found. Cancer Research, Houston, 1969— Contbr. over 100 articles to sci. jours. Served to capt. USAF, 1953-55. Recipient humanitarian award B'nai B'rith, 1982; named to City of Houston Hall of Fame, 1985 Fellow ACS; mem. Am. Assn. Cancer Research, AAAS, AMA, Cancer Assn. Argentina (hon.), Cancer Soc. Chile (hon.), Internat. Platform Assn., Soc. Surg. Oncology, Inc., Pan Am. Med. Assn., Soc. Dermatology Uruguay (hon.), Surg. Soc. Chile (hon.), Royal Soc. Medicine, Western Surg. Assn., Southwestern Surg. Congress, So. Med. Assn., Tex. Med. Assn., Tex. Surg. Soc., N.Y. Acad. Scis., Salem Surg. Soc. (hon.), Phoenix Surg. Soc. (hon.), Harris County Med. Soc., Houston Surg. Soc., Am. Judicature Soc. Office: 1315 Calhoun St Ste 1800 Houston TX 77002-8234

STEHMAN, BETTY KOHLS, financial and management consultant; b. Glencoe, Minn., Dec. 23, 1952; d. Clarence Otto and Pearl Amelia (Tuman) K.; m. Carl Knottwell Stehman, Feb. 12, 1984; 1 child, Sandra. BA, Winona State U., Minn., 1975. CPA, Md.; cert. internal auditor. Staff auditor Wells Fargo Bank Minn., N.A., Mpls., 1975-78; acctg. mgr. Regan Mgmt., Bloomington, 1978-79; sr. internal auditor Bemis Co., Inc., Mpls., 1980; internal audit mgr. Hartzell Corp., St. Paul, 1980-82; corp. contr. Ragon Electronics, 1982-85; contr. Gustafson Construction Inc., St. Louis Park, 1985-88; pres., CEO Entrepreneurial Fin. Svcs., Inc., Eden Prairie, Minn., 1985-88, Greenbelt, Md., 1988—; independent sales cons. Discovery Toys, Livermore, Calif., 1988-92. Cons. in field. Chairperson Immanuel Luth. Ch., Eden Prairie, 1981-84; asst. treas. Berg for Congress Campaign, St. Paul, 1980; vol. acct. Children's Miracle Network Telethon, Mpls., 1984, 85; pres. Citizens Assn., 1991-96; treas. St. Stephen Luth. Ch., 1991-94. Mem. Inst. Internal Auditors, Nat. Assn. Tax Practitioners, Nat. Soc. Pub. Accts., Md. Soc. Accts., Kensington Bus. and Profl. Women's Group, Montgomery County Women Bus. Owners. Lutheran. Avocations: downhill skiing, reading, crafts. Office: 8957-J Edmonston Rd Greenbelt MD 20770 E-mail: betty@efsnet.com.

STEHN, LORRAINE STRELNICK, physician; b. Richmond, Ind., Aug. 27, 1950; d. Daniel H. and Eleanor Gayle (Robertson) Strelnick; m. Thomas Veasey Stehn, June 16, 1973; children: Alexander Veasey, Andrew Thomas. BA, Carleton Coll., 1972; DO, Coll. Osteo. Medicine & Surg., 1976. Diplomate Am. Bd. Family Practice. Intern Pontiac (Mich.) Osteo. Hosp., 1976-77; vol. med. officer U.S. Peace Corps, Swaziland, 1977-79; resident family practice St. Mary's Hosp., Port Arthur, Tex., 1980-82; family practice osteo. medicine Aransas Pass, 1982—; med. adv. Christian Svc. Ctr., 1983—. Chief staff Coastal Bend Hosp., Aransas Pass, 1985, 90, 95; chief staff elect North Bay Hosp., 2002. Pres. bd. dirs. Corpus Christi (Tex.) Chorale, 1995-96; pres. Aransas Pass H.S. Band Booster, 1998-2000. Recipient Svc. award Aransas Pass Jr. High, 1984. Fellow Am. Acad. Family Practice (pres. bd. dirs. profl. counseling svcs.); mem. Tex. Med. Assn., SPAR County Med. Soc. (pres. 2001—). Democrat. Home: 1613 S Saunders St Aransas Pass TX 78336-3107 E-mail: TStehn@interconnect.net.

STEIER, MICHAEL EDWARD, cardiac surgeon; b. N.Y.C., Mar. 22, 1942; s. Philip (deceased) and Gertrude S.; m. Sheila Elaine Finkelstein, June 9, 1963; children: Douglas, James, Lauren. BA, Long Island U., 1964; MD, Univ. Health Scis., Chgo., 1968. Diplomate Am. Bd. Surgery, Am. Bd. Thoracic Surgery. Resident in gen. surgery St. Vincent's Hosp., N.Y.C., 1969-73; resident in thoracic surgery Mayo Clinic, Rochester, Minn., 1973-75; cardiac surgeon S.W. Fla. Regional Med. Ctr., Ft. Myers, Fla., 1975—, Lee Meml. Hosp., Ft. Myers, 1975—, Cape Coral (Fla.) Hosp., 1977—, Naples (Fla.) Cmty. Hosp., 1996—; pres. Cardiac Surg. Assocs. West Fla., Ft. Myers; ret. Chief surgery, S.W. Fla. Regional Med. Ctr., Ft. Myers, 1980-82, pres. med. staff, 1982; cons. Naples Cmty. Hosp., 1996—. Capt., USAR, 1969-78. Fellow ACS, Am. Coll. Chest Physicians, Am. Coll. Cardiology; mem. Soc. for Thoracic Surgeons, N.Y. Acad. Scis., Cardiac Surg. Assn. S.W. Fla. (pres. 1993-99), Explorers Club. Office: Cardiac Surgical Assocs SW Fla 2675 Winkler Ave Fort Myers FL 33901-9342

STEIG, DONALD BARRY, management consultant; b. Bklyn., Dec. 27, 1933; s. Israel and Jean (Lerner) S.; m. Janet Barbara Feldman, Sept. 13, 1959; children: Jenifer Anne, Adam Brett, Jordan Scott. BS, MIT, 1955; MS, Columbia U., 1956. Cert. mgmt. cons. Systems analyst Curtiss-Wright Corp., Carlstadt, N.J., 1956-59; systems engr. IBM Corp., N.Y.C., 1959-61; dir. data processing Data Processing Systems, Inc., Rochester, N.Y., 1961-64; corp. systems cons. Celanese Corp., Newark, 1964-65; group mgr. systems devel. Hoffmann-LaRoche, Inc., Nutley, N.J., 1965-78; dir. mgmt. info. systems Pub. Clearing House, Port Washington, N.Y., 1978-82; v.p. info. svcs. Margrace Corp., Middlesex, N.J., 1982-85; pres. Practical Computer Solutions, Short Hills, 1985—. Mem. adj. faculty Seton Hall U., South Orange, N.J., 1964-65, Rutgers U., New Brunswick, N.J., 1965-78, Adelphi U., Garden City, N.Y., 1980-82; nat. lectr. Assn. for Computing Machinery, 1969-70. Contbr. articles to profl. publs. Bd. dirs. Neighborhood Assn., Millburn, N.J., 1987-90; regional chmn. MIT Ednl. Council, No. N.J., 1982-93. With USN, 1958-59. Mem. Inst. Mgmt. Cons. (pres. N.J. chpt. 1990-91, 96-97), Ind. Computer Cons. Assn. (bd. dirs. 1986-88), Soc. Info. Mgmt., Am. Arbitration Assn., MIT Club (No. N.J. chpt. pres. 1969-70). Jewish. Avocations: hiking, skiing, swimming, tennis. Home and Office: Practical Computer Solutions 43 Mohawk Rd Short Hills NJ 07078-3003

STEIGBIGEL, ROY THEODORE, infectious disease physician and scientist, educator; b. Bklyn., Nov. 23, 1941; s. Samuel and Lillian I. (Parker) S.; m. Julia Ann Enterline, June 10, 1967 (div. 1983), children: Keith D., Glenn N.; m. Sidonie Ann Morrison, Oct. 15, 1985; 1 child, Andrew M. BA, Carleton Coll., 1962; MD, U. Rochester, 1966. Diplomate Am. Bd. Internal Medicine, Am. Bd. Infectious Disease. Resident U. Rochester, N.Y., 1966-68, Stanford U., Palo Alto, Calif., 1970-71, fellow, 1971-73; from asst. to assoc. prof. U. Rochester, N.Y., 1973-83; prof. SUNY, Stony Brook, 1983—. Mem. adv. bd. infectious disease U.S. Pharmacopea, Rockville, Md., 1980—; mem. adv. panels NIH, Bethesda, Md., 1985-87. Contbr. over 10 chpts. to books and over 95 articles to profl. jours. Served in USPHS, 1968-70. Fellow NIH, 1971-73, grantee, 1985—. Fellow ACP, Infectious Disease Soc. Am. Office: SUNY Stony Brook School of Medicine Hsc T 15 080 Stony Brook NY 11794-8153 E-mail: rsteigb@mail.som.sunysb.edu.

STEIGER, PAUL ERNEST, newspaper editor, journalist; b. N.Y.C., Aug. 15, 1942; s. Ernest and Mary Agnes (Walsh) S.; children: Erika Maren, Laura Arlene, Isabelle Amanda, William Ernest. BA, Yale U., 1964. Staff reporter Wall Street Jour., San Francisco, 1966-68, asst. mng. editor N.Y.C., 1983-85, dep. mng. editor, 1985-92, mng. editor, 1991—, also v.p., 1992—; bus. writer Los Angeles Times, 1968-71, econ. corr. Washington bur., 1971-78, bus. editor L.A., 1978-83. Mem. Pulitzer Prize Bd., 1999. Co-author: The 70's Crash, 1970. Recipient G.M. Loeb award UCLA, 1971, 74, 78, John Hancock award, 1971 Office: Wall Street Journal Dow Jones & Co Inc 200 Liberty St New York NY 10281-1003*

STEIGER, SHELDON GERALD, lawyer; b. Cleve., May 27, 1945; s. Max and Fannie (Axelrod) S.; m. Sally Blumental, Sept. 6, 1971; children: Jeremy M., Suzanna L., Melissa R. BA, Ohio State U., 1967; JD, Cleve. State U., 1971. Bar: Ohio 1972, U.S. Dist. Ct. (no. dist.) Ohio 1975. Asst. dir. law City of Cleve., 1973-74; assoc. Berger & Kirschenbaum, Cleve., 1974; pvt. practive, 1975—. Mem. Ohio Bar Assn., Cleve. Bar Assn. Home: 4426 Silsby Rd University Heights OH 44118-3939 Office: 75 Public Sq Ste 650 Cleveland OH 44113-1901 E-mail: steiger@winstarmail.com.

STEIGERWALD, DOUGLAS GARDINER, economics educator; b. Torrance, Calif., June 19, 1959; s. Jack and Eileen Steigerwald; m. Julia Lowell, May 22, 1995; 1 child Gregory. PhD, U. Calif., Berkeley, 1988. Rsch. asst., bd. govs. Fed. Res., Washington, 1981-83; prof. econs. U. Calif., Santa Barbara, 1988—. Assoc. editor Econometric Revs., 1999—. Regents jr. faculty fellowship U. Calif., 1991. Office: Econs Dept U Calif Santa Barbara CA 93105

STEIGERWALD, LOUIS JOHN, III, corporate executive; b. Syracuse, N.Y., Dec. 24, 1953; s. Louis John Jr. and Virginia (Irving) S.; m. Mary Rescorl, May 31, 1980; children: Amy Elizabeth, Louis John IV. BS, St. Lawrence U., 1976. Salesperson Cathedral Candle Co., Syracuse, 1976-80, v.p., 1980-2001, pres., 2001—. Bd. dirs. Cathedral Candle Co., Syracuse. Account exec. United Way Ctrl. N.Y., Syracuse, 1982-83, sect. chmn., 1984-85; active Boy Scouts Am., 1992—. Mem. Nat. Ch. Goods Assn. (bd. dirs. 1990-2000, pres. 1997, 98), Nat. Candle Assn. (bd. dirs. 1989-99), Ea. Ch. Goods Guild. Avocations: golf, tennis, woodworking, skiing, music. Office: Cathedral Candle Co 510 Kirkpatrick St Syracuse NY 13208-2100

STEIGMAN, ANDREW L. academic dean; b. N.Y.C., Aug. 30, 1933; s. Nathan and Sarah (Levine) S.; m. Meryl Fialka, June 20, 1959; children: Daria H., Jonathan S. AB summa cum laude, Princeton U., 1954; postgrad., London Sch. Econs., 1954-55, Am. U., Washington, 1958-60. Fgn. svc. officer Dept. State, various locations, 1958-69; first sec. Dept. State, U.S. Embassy, Paris, 1969-72, polit. counselor Lagos, Nigeria, 1972-75, U.S. ambassador to Gabon Libreville, Gabon, 1975-77; dir. nat. intelligence tasking office Intelligence Community Staff, Washington, 1978-80; dep. asst. sec. for personnel Dept. State, 1981-84; asst. dean/prof. internat. relations Georgetown U., 1985—, assoc. dean, 1996. Vis. fellow Woodrow Wilson Fellowship Found., Princeton, 1987-93; mem. edn. com. Atlantic Council, Washington, 1989-98. Author: The Foreign Service of the United States, 1985. With U.S. Army, 1955-57. Wilbur Carr award, U.S. Dept. State, 1985. Mem.: Am. Fgn. Svc. Assn., Am. Hist. Assn. Office: Georgetown U Sfs Icc # 301 Washington DC 20057-0001

STEIGMAN, CARMEN KAY, pathologist; b. Dallas, May 14, 1956; d. Walter Benjamin and Margaret Louise (Patton) S. BS, N.E. La. U., 1977; MD, La. State U., 1983; MPH, St. Louis U., 1994. Diplomate in anat., clin. and pediatric pathology Am. Bd. Pathology; diplomate Am. Bd. Quality Assurance and Utilization Rev. Physicians. Pathology resident Fairfax Hosp., Falls Church, Va., 1983-87; pediatric pathology fellow Children's Hosp. of Phila., 1987-89; pathologist Sparrow Hosp., Lansing, Mich., 1989-90; asst. prof. pathology St. Louis U. Sch. Medicine, 1990-96; pathologist Cardinal Glennon Childrens Hosp., 1990-96; dir. Pub. Health Lab. City of St. Louis Dept. Health and Hosps., 1996-99; pathologist Garden City (Mich.) Hosp., 1999—. Fellow Coll. Am. Pathologists; mem. Soc. for Pediatric Pathology, Am. Coll. Physician Execs., Am. Pathology Found.

STEIGMEIER, ROGER JAMES, adult educator, poet; b. N.Y.C., Mar. 31, 1942; s. Roger Leon and Ruth Edna Steigmeier; m. Diana Steigmeier, May 23, 1970. BA, Empire State Coll., N.Y.C., 1992; MA, NYU, 1994. Civil servant City of N.Y., 1960-95; adj. mentor Empire State Coll., N.Y.C., 1994-96; adj. instr. Aims C.C., Loveland, Colo., 2001—. Author: Light Traveling Dark Traveling Light, 1984, Ideology and Transcendence, 1995, The Amfortas Legacy, 1998. With U.S. Army, 1964-67. Mem. Poets and Writers Inc. Green Party.

STEIL, GEORGE KENNETH, SR. lawyer; b. Darlington, Wis., Dec. 16, 1924; s. George John and Laura (Donahoe) S.; m. Mavis Elaine Andrews, May 24, 1947; children: George Kenneth, John R., MIchelle Steil Bryski, Marcelaine Steil-Zimmermann. Student, Platteville State Tchrs. Coll., 1942-43; JD, U. Wis., Madison, 1950. Bar: Wis. 1950, U.S. Tax Ct. 1971, U.S. Dist. Ct. (western dist.) Wis. 1950. Assoc. J. G. McWilliams, Janesville, 1950-53; ptnr. McWilliams and Steil, 1954-60, Brennan, Steil, Basting & MacDougall, Janesville, 1960-72; pres. Brennan, Steil, Basting & MacDougall (S.C., and predecessor), 1972—. Lectr. law U. Wis., 1974; bd. dirs. Acuity Ins. Co., Sheboygan, Wis., Blain Supply Inc., Blain's Farm & Fleet Stores, 1993-00; trustee, bd. dirs. Roman Cath. Diocese of Madison; mem. Wis. Supreme Ct. Bd. Atty. Profl. Responsibility, 1982-87, chmn., 1984-87; chmn. Gov.'s Adv. Coun. Jud. Selection, State of Wis., 1987-92; chmn. Wis. Lottery Bd., 1987-90; bd. dirs. Acuity Bank, SSB, Tomah, Wis., chmn. 2000—. Bd. dirs. St. Coletta Sch. for Exceptional Children, Jefferson, Wis., 1972-76, 78-84, 86-89, chmn., 1982-83; bd. regents U. Wis., 1990-97, pres., 1992-94; bd. dirs. U. Wis. Hosp. Authority, 1996—, chmn., 2002-; bd. dirs., chair U. Wis. Med. Found., 1996-99. Recipient Disting. Svc. award U. Wis. Law Alumni, 1991, Cath. Leadership awrd Diocese of Madison, 1998; named Knight of St. Gregory, Pope John Paul II, 1997. Fellow Am. Bar Found. (life), Am. Coll. Trust and Estate Counsel; mem. ABA, Jamesville Area C. of C. (pres. 1970-71), State Bar Wis. (pres. 1977-78), Wis. Bar Found. (bd. dirs. 1976—, Charles L. Goldberg Disting. Svc. award 1990). Roman Catholic. Home: 2818 Cambridge Ct Janesville WI 53545-2797 Office: 1 E Milwaukee St Janesville WI 53545 Fax: 608-756-9000. E-mail: gkss@bsbmlaw.com.

STEIL, JANICE M. social psychology educator; b. Fall River, Mass., Mar. 1, 1941; d. Alfred Edward Ingham and Rita Hindle; m. M. Peter Steil Jr., June 28, 1970; children: Justin Peter, Alexis Ingham. BA, U. Mass., 1962; EdM, Boston U., 1965; PhD, Columbia U., 1979. Lectr. Boston U., 1966, Brandeis Coll., Waltham, Mass., 1967, 69; project dir. Nat. Commn. on Resources for Youth, N.Y.C., 1971-73; rsch. scientist State of N.Y., 1978-79; prof. social psychology Adelphi U., Garden City, N.Y., 1979—, dir. rsch. tng., 1997—, chair univ.-wide self-study for re-accreditation, 1997-99. Presenter in field.; scholar in-residence Catalyst, N.Y.C., 1997-98; mem. steering com. Feminist Conf. Series, 1993-94. Assoc. editor Psychology of Women Quar., 1993-98; author: Marital Equality: Its relationship to the well-being of husbands and wives, 1997; contbr. numerous articles to profl. jours., chpts. to books; ad hoc reviewer numerous jours. in field. Fellow APA; mem. Am. Psychol. Soc., Internat. Soc. for Study of Personal Relationships, Internat. Network on Personal Relationships, Ea. Psychol. Assn. (program com. 1988-91). Office: Adelphi U Derner Inst Garden City NY 11530

STEIL, VALERIE GLADYS, interior designer; b. Beloit, Wis., Aug. 18, 1957; d. Melbourne and Dolores Leona (Radtke) S. BS, U. Wis., Stevens Point, 1979. Free lance designer Giltspur Exhibits, Chgo., 1979; prof. interior design Valparaiso (Ind.) U., 1989-90, 94; interior designer Marc T. Nielsen Interiors, Valparaiso, 1980—2000; owner, pres. Marc T. Nelsen Interiors, 2000—. Mem. Am. Soc. Interior Designers. Lutheran. Avocations: textile arts, illustration, aerobics, biking, skiing, gardening. Home: 1601 Burlington Beach Rd Valparaiso IN 46383-1566 Office: Marc T Nielsen Interiors 734 N Old Suman Rd Valparaiso IN 46383-9716

STEILING, DANIEL PAUL, retired railroad conductor, writer, geographer; b. San Jose, Calif., June 28, 1944; s. Paul Henry and Lois Kathryn (Barton) S. Right of way agt. Caltrans - Calif. State Dept. Transp., San Francisco, 1969-70; owner Dan's Bicycle Shop, Santa Cruz, 1970-83; soil inspector Soil Svcs. Inc. divsn. Applied Soil Mechanics, Inc., San Jose, 1983-84; sr. mfg. specialist disk products divsn. IBM, 1984-92; R.R. condr. Amtrak, 1993-97; ret., 1997; substitute tchr. history, geography, sci. Murrieta Valley Unified Sch. Dist., 1999—2001; instr. geography Riverside C.C., 2001—. Author: Operation and Maintenance of TRACOR Thickness Measuring Guage (Liquid Nitrogen Cooled), 1987. With USAF, 1966-68. Mem. Assn. Am. Geographers, Antique Auto Club Am., Fallbrook Vintage Car Club, Ford Falcon Club Am., Early Ford v/8 Club Am. Avocations: bicycle touring, photography, antique auto restoration. Home: 42033 Via Renate Temecula CA 92591

STEIN, ALBERT, sales professional; b. Long Branch, N.J., Jan. 30, 1925; s. Jacob and Minnie Stein; m. Ann Lee Stein; children: Jay, Mark. BS, NYU, 1957. Store mgr. Robert Hall, N.Y.C., 1951-53; salesman Krain & Canton, 1953-57, Newark Star Ledger, Newark, 1957-75; sales exec. New House Newspapers, N.Y.C., 1975-97; owner advt. splty. bus., 1997—. Mem. Joseph Warren Gothic Lodge. Republican. Avocations: photography, golf, swimming, walking, biking. Home and Office: Jay Mart Co 66 Clubhouse Ln Marlboro NJ 07746 E-mail: albert.stein@gte.net.

STEIN, ALLAN MARK, lawyer; b. Montreal, Quebec, Can., Oct. 18, 1951; came to U.S., 1977; s. Boris and Beatrice (Fishman) S. B in Commerce, Sir George Williams, 1972; BA, Loyola, Montreal, 1973; B in Civil Law, McGill U., 1976, LLB, 1977; JD, Nova U., 1979. Bar: Fla. 1979, U.S. Dist. Ct. (so. dist.) Fla. 1979, U.S. Ct. Appeals (5th cir.) 1980, U.S. Ct. Appeals (11th cir.) 1983, U.S. Dist. Ct. Ariz. 1993. Assoc. Law Offices of Paul Landy Beiley, Miami, Fla., 1980, Heitner & Rosenfeld, Miami, 1980-85, Rosenfeld & Stein,

Miami, 1985-90, Rosenfeld, Stein & Sugarman, Miami, 1990-94, Rosenfeld & Stein P.A., Miami, 1994—. Mem. North Dade Bar Assn. (bd. dirs. 1985-90). Republican. Jewish. Avocation: photography, HISTORY. Office: 18260 NE 19th Ave Ste 202 Miami FL 33162-1632

STEIN, ALLISON, media specialist; b. Prince George's County, Md., Feb. 4, 1963; d. Archie James Jr. and Ann Patton (McCoy) Stein; m. Walter M. Best Jr., Nov. 25, 1989 (div. Mar. 1999). BA in Journalism, U. S.C., 1985. Stringer, obit clk. The State Newspapers, Columbia, S.C., 1983-85; editor Sandlapper Pub. Co., Orangeburg, 1985-87; media rels. asst. S.C. C. of C., Columbia, 1987-88; pub. rels. intern S.C. Econ. Devel. Bd., 1988; lead writer Policy Mgmt. Systems Corp., 1988-94; sr. editor Trozzolo Resources, Kansas CIty, 1994-95; dir. media rels. Cerner Corp., 1995-98; e-commerce industry analyst NetSales, Inc., Overland Park, Kans., 1998-2000; mktg. mgr. Thazar Solutions, Kansas City, 2001—02. Author: 365 Scary Stories, 1998; editor Manifest Destiny Jour., 1995-97, E-Scape: The Digital Jour. Speculative Fiction, 1998—. Bd. dirs., treas. Sci. Fiction & Fantasy Hall of Fame, 1996-98. Recipient writing & editing awards Media Women S.C., 1988-2002. Mem. Nat. Fedn. Press Women (parliamentarian 1995-97, bd. dirs. 1992-2002, webmaster 1997—, writing & editing awards 1988—), Mo. Press. Women (pres. 1997—, v.p. 1994-97, Communicator of Achievement 1997, writing & editing awards 1994—)), Kansas City Sci. Fiction & Fantasy Soc. Avocations: reading science fiction, writing, editing, photography. Home: 210 E 73d Terr Kansas City MO 64114 Office: Thazar Solutions 9201 State Line Rd Kansas City MO 64114 E-mail: astein@noblefusion.com.

STEIN, ARLENE J. sociology educator, writer; b. N.Y.C., Mar. 18, 1959; d. Lawrence Stein and Pearl Sugarman; m. Nancy J. Solomon; 1 child, Lewis Solomon-Stein. BA in History, Amherst U., 1980; MA in Sociology, U. Calif., Berkeley, 1988, PhD in Sociology, 1993. Lectr. sociology U. Essex, Colchester, U.K., 1993-94; asst. prof. sociology U. Oreg., Eugene, 1994—. Chair sexualities sect. Am. Sociol. Assn., Washington, 1998-99; mem. nat. rsch. adv. bd. Gay and Lesbian Alliance Against Defamation, N.Y.C., 1999—. Author: Sex and Sensibility, 1997; editor: Sisters, Sexperts, Queers, 1993. Postdoctoral fellow Social Sci. Rsch. Coun., Sexuality Rsch. Fellowship Program, N.Y.C., 1997-99. Mem. Phi Beta Kappa. Office: Dept Sociology Univ Oreg Eugene OR 97403 E-mail: astein@orgon.uoregon.edu.

STEIN, ARTHUR OSCAR, pediatrician; b. Bklyn., Apr. 3, 1932; s. Irving I. and Sadie (Brander) S.; m. Judith Lenore Hurwitz, Aug. 27, 1955; children: Susan, Jeffrey, Benjamin. AB, Harvard U., 1953; MD, Tufts U., 1957; postgrad., U. Chgo., 1963-66; BFA, San Jose State U., 1998. Intern U. Chgo. Hosps., 1957-58, resident, 1958-59, N.Y. Hosp.-Cornell U. Med. Ctr., 1959-61; pediatrician, 1963-70, Healthguard Med. Group, San Jose, Calif., 1970-72, Permanente Med. Group, San Jose, 1972-95; ret., 1995. Instr. pediat. Cornell U. Med. Sch., 1960-61, U. Chgo. Sch. Medicine, 1963-66, asst. prof., 1966-70; tchg. asst. photography San Jose (Calif.) State U., 1995—. Author: (CD) The Sketch Class. V.p. Jewish congregation 1969-70, pres. 1972-73. Capt., M.C., AUS, 1961-63. USPHS Postdoctoral fellow, 1963-66. Fellow Am. Acad. Pediat., Santa Clara County Med. Assn., Calif. Med. Assn.; mem. Light and Shadow Camera Club (pres. San Jose 1978-80), Ctrl. Coast Counties Camera Club (v.p. 1980-81, pres. 1981-82), Santa Clara Camera Club (pres. 1991). Achievements include co-discovery (with Glyn Dawson) of genetic disease lactosylceramidosis. Home: 956 Redmond Ave San Jose CA 95120-1831 E-mail: artform2@pacbell.net.

STEIN, BARRY EDWARD, medical educator; BA, CUNY, Queens, 1966, MA, 1969; PhD, CUNY, 1971. Prof. dept. physiology Med. Coll. Va.-Va. Commonwealth U., Richmond, 1982-94, affil. prof., 1994—; prof., chair dept. neurobiology and anatomy Wake Forest U Sch. Medicine, Winston-Salem, N.C., 1994—. Bd. trustees The Gwendolyn Hardy Williams and Oliver Williams Found., Inc., 1992—; lectr. in field. Co-author: The Merging of the Senses, 1993; contbr. chpts. to books including The Cognitive Neurosciences, 1995, 99, Electrophysiology of Vision, 1991, The Development of Intersensory Perception: Comparative Perspectives, 1994, others; contbr. numerous articles to profl. pubs. including Jour. Neurophysiology, Jour. Neurosci., Sci., Jour. Comparative Neurology, others; mem. editl. bd. Somatosensory and Motor Rsch., Jour. Cognitive Neuroscience, The Behavioral and Brain Sciences. Home: 1825 Georgia Ave Winston Salem NC 27104-3101 Office: Wake Forest School of Medicine Med Ctr Blvd Winston Salem NC 27157-0001 E-mail: bestein@wfubmc.edu.

STEIN, BENJAMIN J. television personality, writer, lawyer, economist; b. Washington, Nov. 25, 1944; s. Herbert and Mildred (Fishman) S.; m. Alexandra Denman, June 22, 1968. BA, Columbia U., 1966; LLB, Yale U., 1970. Bar: Conn. Trial lawyer FTC, Washington, 1970-72; speech writer The White House, 1973-74; columnist The Wall St. Jour., N.Y.C., 1974-76; writer, commentator, columnist The Los Angeles Herald-Examiner, 1978-87; currently TV personality Win Ben Stein's Money Comedy Ctrl., 1996—, host Turn Ben Stein On, 1999—2001. Fin. cons. LAACO, Inc., Los Angeles; contbg. editor The Am. Spectator, 1980—; law and econs. tchr. Pepperdine, Malibu, 1992—. Author: On The Brink. 1977, The View from Sunset Boulevard, 1978, DREEMZ, 1978, Moneypower, 1980, 'Ludes, 1981, Financial Passages, 1986, A License to Steal, 1992, Tommy and Me, 1999; author numerous articles on leveraged buy-outs and other fin. frauds for Barrons, 1984—. Recipient Emmy award for Best Game Show Host, 1999. Mem. Writers Guild Am., Screen Actors' Guild, Am. Fedn. TV and Radio Actors, Yak Club N.Y.C., Friars, L.A. Athletic Club, Calif. Yacht Club. Republican. Jewish. Office: 8787 Shoreham Dr West Hollywood CA 90069-2231 E-mail: benstein@aol.com.

STEIN, BERNARD, stockbroker; b. N.Y.C., Nov. 24, 1913; s. Abraham and Fannie (Zoob) S.; m. Marion Charlotte Holtsberg, Feb. 24, 1946; children: Robert Frederick, Ellen Frances (Mrs. Howard Lazarus). Student, Sch. Commerce, NYU, 1930-32. Ptnr. firm Ralph E. Samuel & Co., N.Y.C., 1947-70, Neuberger & Berman, Inc., 1970—99; sr. v.p., treas., dir. Energy Fund, N.Y.C., 1962-80, pres., 1980-91, dir. emeritus; former vice chmn. Neuberger & Berman Mgmt. Co. Served with USAAF, 1942-45. Mem.: Quaker Ridge Golf (Scarsdale); Beach Point (Mamaroneck, N.Y.). Home: 8 Split Tree Rd Scarsdale NY 10583-7900 Office: Neuberger & Berman 605 3rd Ave Fl 21 New York NY 10158-3698

STEIN, BERNARD ALVIN, business consultant; b. Winnipeg, Can., June 4, 1923; s. Herman Louis and Rebecca (Harris) S.; m. Dorothy Lock, Jan. 1, 1942; 1 dau., Marilynn Stein Lakein. Vice-pres. food drug div. Giant Food, Inc., Washington, 1951-69; v.p., gen. mgr. Read Drug Stores, Balt., 1969-70; pres. Scotty Stores div. Sav-A-Stop, Jacksonville, Fla., 1970-71; pres., gen. mgr. Liberal Markets, Dayton, Ohio, 1971-72; pres. Pueblo Supermarkets, San Juan, P.R., 1972-74, Hills Supermarkets, Brentwood, N.Y., 1974-75, Allied Supermarkets, Detroit, 1976-78, Chatham Supermarkets, Detroit, 1978-81; CEO Network Assocs., Chgo., 1981-92; bus. cons. Balt., 1992—. Mem. Presdl. Com. for Emergency Food Controls, 1969. Served with USAAF, 1943-45. Decorated Air medal. Home: 43 Stone Pine Ct Baltimore MD 21208-1038

STEIN, BERNARD L. journalist; b. Cleve. m. Marguerite Adams; 1 child, Anna. BA in Lit., Columbia U., 1963; postgrad., U. Calif., Berkeley, 1964-66; DHL (hon.), Manhattan Coll., 1999. Editor Riverdale Press, 1978—, co-pub., 1980—. Mem. team of scholars editing Mark Twain's writing for pub. U. Calif. Press, James H. Ottaway Disting. vis. prof., SUNY, New Paltz, 2002. Winner 1998 Pulitzer Prize for editl. writing, finalist 1987 & 88; Recipient First Amendment award Soc. Profl. Journalists, 1989; named Writer of the Yr., N.Y. Press Assn., 1986. Office: c/o Riverdale Press 6155 Broadway Bronx NY 10471-3136

STEIN, CAROLE RUTH, social services administrator, researcher; b. N.Y.C., Nov. 9, 1932; d. William Nathan and Faye Zelda (Simon) Popper; m. Jerry Stein, July 11, 1953; children: Marc, Pamela, Todd. BS in Bus. Edn., Packard Coll., N.Y.C., 1952. Planner community devel. Ind. Family and Social Svcs. Adminstrn., Indpls., 1977—, policy analyst fed. rels. Office Commr., 1991—; v.p. family bus. Indpls. and N.Y.C., 1980-92; legis. advocate Nat. Coun. of Jewish Women, Washington and N.Y.C., 1980-90, Ind. Alliance Better Child Care, Washington and N.Y.C., 1986-91. Researcher nat. ednl. goals Gov.'s Office Ind., Indpls., 1992. Founder Ind. Women's Polit. Network, Indpls., 1989—, Dialogue Today, Inc. Black/Jewish Rels., Indpls., 1985—, Sojourner Shelter for Battered Women, Indpls., 1984—, Ind. Children and Youth Legis. Task Force; mem. hon. bd. Jewish Community Rels. Coun., 1980—; pres., chair Coalition for Human Svcs., 1981-83, founder; vice chair Gov. Juvenile Justice Delinquent Prevention, 1983—. Recipient Spl. Recognition award Gov. Juvenile Justice Delinquent Prevention, 1991, David Cook award Jewish Community Rels. Coun., 1984, Sagamore of Wabash award State of Ind., 1982, Hannah G. Solomon award Nat. Coun. Jewish Women, 1984, Hoosier Edn. award Ind. Assn. Edn. Young Children, 1989. Democrat. Jewish. Avocations: reading, aerobics/fitness, traveling, voluntarism. Home: 7420 Colony Cir Indianapolis IN 46260-3412 Office: Ind Family & Social Svcs 402 W Washington St Indianapolis IN 46204-2739

STEIN, DANIEL ALAN, public interest lawyer; b. Washington, Mar. 9, 1955; s. Edward Seymour and Ann Rose Stein; m. Sharon McCloe, Oct. 18, 1986; children: Claire, Corrieanne. BA, Ind. U., 1977; JD, Cath. U. Am., 1984. Bar: D.C. 1984, U.S. Dist. Ct. D.C. 1985, U.S. Ct. Appeals (D.C. cir.) 1987, U.S. Tax Ct. 1987. Profl. staff mem. select com. on narcotics abuse and control U.S. Ho. of Reps., Washington, 1977-81; pvt. practice, 1984-89; exec. dir. Immigration Reform Law Inst., 1986-88, Fedn. for Am. Immigration Reform, Washington, 1982-86, 89—. Mem. adv. bd. Social Contract periodical, Petosky, Mich., 1990—. Mem. Capitol Hill Club, Nat. Press Club. Republican. Avocations: trombone, American history, western civilization, jazz, antique books. Office: Fedn for Am Immigration Reform 1666 Connecticut Ave NW Ste 400 Washington DC 20009-1039

STEIN, DANIEL SCOTT, physician, researcher; b. N.Y.C., Mar. 6, 1958; BS, Pace U., 1978; MD, SUNY, N.Y.C., 1982. Diplomate Am. Bd. Internal Medicine and Infectious Diseases. Asst. prof. U. Tenn., Memphis, 1988-90; med. officer DAIDS NIAID, NIH, Bethesda, Md., 1991-94; assoc. prof., dir. Clin. Pharmacology Studies Unit Albany (N.Y.) Med. Coll., 1994-98; dir. antivirals/anti-infective clin. pharmacology Glaxo-Wellcom, Research Triangle Park, N.C., 1998-2001; therapeutic head, antivirals Glaxo SmithKline, 2001—02; clin. assoc. prof. medicine U. N.C. Hosp. and Clinics, 1998—; head exploratory med. scis., antivirals Glaxo SmithKline, Research Triangle Park, 2002—. Mem. editl. bd. Antimicrobial Agts. and Chemotherapy, 1996-98, 2002—; contbr. over 90 articles to profl. jours. Achievements include research in clinical trials that have lead to licensing or refining the clinical use of several antivirals and anti-HIV agents. Office: Glaxo-Wellcome 5 Moore Dr Research Triangle Park NC 27709 E-mail: dss94020@gsk.com.

STEIN, DAVID FRED, investment executive; b. N.Y.C., May 17, 1940; s. William Howard and Phoebe Louise (Hockstader) S.; m. Susan Vail Berresford, June 17, 1963 (div. 1970); 1 child, Jeremy Vail; m. Ellen Gail Cohen, Sept. 16, 1973; children: Katharine Ellen, Nicholas David. BA, Harvard U., 1962; MBA, Harvard Grad. Sch. Bus. Adminstrn., 1965. Assoc. Bache & Co., N.Y.C., 1965-68; assoc., then gen. ptnr. Kuhn Loeb & Co., 1969-77; mng. dir. Lehman Brothers Kuhn Loeb, 1977-83, Shearson Lehman Am. Express, N.Y.C., 1983-86; sr. exec. v.p., dir. Am. Express Bank, 1986-87; mng. dir. Shearson Lehman Hutton, 1987-89; mng. dir., mem. exec. com. The Stamford Co., 1989-90; mng. dir J & W Seligman & Co., 1990-96, vice chmn., 1997—; co-chmn. Seligman Henderson Co., 1991-98. Bd. dirs. Griffin Land & Nurseries Inc. Trustee P.R. Traveling Theatre, N.Y.C., 1970-72, Altro Health and Rehab. Ctr., Bronx, N.Y., 1975-82, Blythedale Children's Hosp., Valhalla, N.Y., 1977-2001, hon. trustee, 2001-, Montefiore Med. Ctr., Bronx, 1990—; trustee, chmn. fin. com. Riverdale Country Sch., Bronx, 1988-2000, chmn. bd. trustees, 1997-2000; trustee Children's Aid Soc.; mem. Coun. on Fgn. Rels. With U.S. Army, 1962-63. Mem. Nat. Assn. Security Dealers (internat. com. 1970-85), Century Country Club (Purchase, N.Y.), River Club (N.Y.C.), Harvard Club (N.Y.C.), Edgartown (Mass.) Yacht Club, Mill Reef Club (Antigua, Brit. V.I.), Chappaquiddick Beach Club (Edgartown). Democrat. Avocations: reading, sailing, fishing, skiing. Home: 875 Park Ave New York NY 10021-0341 Office: J & W Seligman 100 Park Ave Fl 8 New York NY 10017-5516 E-mail: dstein@jwseligman.com.

STEIN, DAVID KIDD, infectious diseases physician, educator; b. Queens, N.Y., Nov. 3, 1958; s. Samuel and Roberta E. (Ellis) S.; m. M. Valerie Marrero, Jan. 10, 1987; children: Matthew P., Catherine E., Courtney R. BA, U. Pa., 1980; MD, N.Y. Med. Coll., 1984. Med. resident Thomas Jefferson U. Hosp., Phila., 1984-87; infectious diseases fellow Boston U. Med. Ctr., 1987-91; asst. prof. medicine and infectious diseases Albert Einstein Coll. Medicine, Bronx, 1991—; attending physician Jacobi Med. Ctr., N.Y., 1991—. Dir. AIDS Inpatient Cons. Svc., Jacobi Med. Ctr., Bronx, 1992-93, prin. site coord. AIDS clin. trial unit, 1993-97; prin. investigator mycoses study group Albert Einstein Coll. of Medicine, 1992—; mem. Mycoses Systemic Pathogen Study Group/AIDS Clin. Trials Group, 1992-94; prin. site investigator cmty. programs for clin. rsch. on AIDS, Jacobi Med. Ctr., 1998—, dir HIV Clinic, 2002--; dir. adult HIV rsch. activities North Bronx Healthcare Network, 2001—. Contbr. articles to profl. jours. Mem. AIDS curriculum adv. bd. Mahopac (N.Y.) Schs., 1995-96. Mem. ACP, AAAS, Am. Soc. Microbiology, Infectious Diseases Soc. Am. (Gilbert Dalldorf fellow in med. mycology 1989), Alpha Omega Alpha, Alpha Epsilon Delta. Office: Jacobi Ambulatory Care Pavilion Ste 607 Pelham Pkwy S Bronx NY 10461

STEIN, DAVID TIMOTHY, minister; b. Chillicothe, Mo., Apr. 25, 1936; s. Frederick Carl and Irene Edith (Kroggel) S.; m. Judith Ann Ritchhart, June 6, 1959; children: Laurie Beth, David Scott, Timothy Christian, Michelle Ann. BA in Humanities, Concordia Coll., St. Louis, 1958; diploma in theology, Concordia Sem., St. Louis, 1961; MA in Speech, St. Louis U., 1962, PhD in Higher Edn. Adminstrn., 1979. Ordained to ministry Luth. Ch.-Mo. Synod, 1962. Prof. Concordia U., River Forest, Ill., 1962-79, dean of students, asst. to pres., dir. pub. rels., dir. placement, 1962-79; dir. parish rels. and lay tng. Luth. Gen. Hosp., Park Ridge, 1979-85; exec. adminstr. Park Ridge Ctr. Luth. Gen. Health Care System, 1985-89; sr. pastor Evang. Luth. Ch. of the Apostles, Melrose Park, Ill., 1989-91, Evang. Ch. of the Holy Spirit, Elk Grove Village, 1991—. Trustee Luth. Film Assocs., N.Y.C., 1968-80; mem. com. on campus life Luth. Ch.-Mo. Synod, Chgo., 1979-82; assoc. Hastings Inst., 1985—; pres. Ethics Mgmt. Cons. Svc., River Forest, 1988—, DayStar.net., Inc., 1999—. Author: A Circle of Love, 1967; editor Chronical of Pastoral Care, 1980-88; producer film College With a Cause, 1964 (award San Francisco Film Festival). Co-chair coll. and sch. div. Community Chest, Oak Park/River Forest, Ill., 1964-65, coach, sponsor Little League Assn., River Forest, 1970-78; active Citizens Adv. Com., River Forest, 1975-78; bd. mgrs. Gen. PTA, River Forest, 1977-78; bd. dirs. Luth. Community Svcs. for the Aged, Arlington Heights, Ill., 1985—, United Way, Luth. Child and Family Svcs. Ill., 1996—; mem. com. on human rsch. Concordia U., River Forest, 1996—; bd. trustees United Way of Elk Grove Village, Ill., 1996—. Recipient citation N.Y. Graphic Arts Soc., 1967, Chgo. Graphic Arts Soc., 1968; Aid Assn. for Luths. fellow, 1973. Mem. Park Ridge Assocs., Oak Park/River Forest Clergy Assn., Religious Pub. Rels. Coun. Inc. (pres. Chgo. chpt., nat. gov. 1986-90, DeRose Hinkhouse award 1968-87). Home: 550 Clinton Pl River Forest IL 60305-1910 Office: Evang Luth Ch of the Holy Spirit 150 Lions Dr Elk Grove Village IL 60007-4200 E-mail: dtsteinlb@aol.com. *The most significant dilemma the religious communities and traditions face in a world of diminishing services is the allocation of resources, moral, spiritual, social, educational, economic, and their applications to the growth of artificial intelligence.*

STEIN, ELEANOR BANKOFF, judge; b. N.Y.C., Jan. 24, 1923; d. Jacob and Sarah (Rashkin) Bankoff; m. Frank S. Stein, May 27, 1947; children: Robert B., Joan Jenkins, William M. Student, Barnard Coll., 1940-42; BS in Econs., Columbia U., 1944; LLB, NYU, 1949; grad. Ind. Jud. Coll., 1986. Bar: N.Y. 1950, Ind. 1976, U.S. Supreme Ct. 1980. Atty. Hillis & Button, Kokomo, Ind., 1975-76, Paul Hillis, Kokomo, 1976-78, Bayliff, Harrigan, Kokomo, 1978-80; judge Howard County Ct., Kokomo, 1981-89; ret., 1989; co-juvenile referee Howard County Juvenile Ct., 1976-78. Mem. Republican Women's Assn. Kokomo, 1980—; bd. dirs. Howard County Legal Aid Soc., 1976-80; dir. Howard County Ct. Alcohol and Drug Svcs. Program, 1982-89; bd. advisors St. Joseph Hosp., Kokomo, 1979—; bd. dirs. Kokomo Human Rels. Commn., 1967-70, Howard County Children's Ctr., 1993—. Mem. law rev. bd. NYU Law Rev., 1947-48. Mem. Am. Judicature Soc., Ind. Jud. Assn., Nat. Assn. Women Judges, ABA (apptd. Ind. del. jud. adminstrn. div. 1987), Ind. Bar Assn., Howard County Bar Assn. Jewish. Clubs: Kokomo Country, Altrusa. Home: 2804 May Ave Redondo Beach CA 90278-1533

STEIN, ELEANOR BENSON (ELLIE STEIN), playwright, writer; b. New Haven, Feb. 18, 1922; d. Harry Lorin and Bertha Adeline (Schwolow) Benson; m. Louis Stein; children: Eleanor Smith, Patrice Forgues, Mary Kelly, Paul Stein. Student, Rockland C.C., Suffern, N.Y., 1966-67, S.D. State U., 1969-70, Mesa Coll., 1975, S.D. City Coll., 1976. Office mgr. Thatcher & Hurst Attys., San Diego, 1968-73. Author: (plays) Squeeze, 1989, Emily Dickinson, 1996; prodr. (plays) Epitaph, Edgar Allan Poe: The Man, The Legend, Paul Revere: An American Rebel, 60 and Holding, Always, Harriet Tubman: A Woman Called Moses, Sacagawea: Indian Guide to Lewis and Clark Expedition, Hans Christian Andersen: An Ugly Duckling, Frederick Douglass: An American Slave. Bd. dirs., v.p. NewWorks Theatre. Recipient Roll of Honored Women Unitarian Universalist Women's Fedn., 1978, Aurelia Reinhardt Roll of Honored Women, 1983, Unitarian Universalist award for cmty. svc. First Unitarian-Universalist Ch., 1990, Woman of Yr. So. Regional Conf. Women, 1991. Mem. Nat. League Am. Pen Women, Older Women's League, Actors' Alliance San Diego, Dramatists Guild, U.U. Women's Fedn., Scripteasers, Poets in Profile, Looking Glass Mobile Theatre. Home and Office: 4870 1/2 Old Cliffs Rd San Diego CA 92120-1144

STEIN, ELLEN F. music therapist, songwriter; b. Bklyn. d. Henry Allen and Elizabeth Firestone; m. Richard M. Stein, June 12, 1954; children: Julie Brockway, Eric, Adam. Student, Bennington (Vt.) Coll.; BA, Bklyn. Coll., 1; MEd, William Paterson Coll., Wayne, N.J. Cert. tchr. N.Y., N.J., tchr. handicapped N.J., music therapist Cert. Bd. Music Therapists. Tchr. kindegarten N.Y.C. Bd. Edn., 1954-57; music therapist Presch. Instruction for Exceptional, Northvale, N.J., S.E. Sr. Ctr. for Independent Living, Englewood, Early Childhood Learning Ctrs. N.J., Morristown and Ridgefield, Assn. Retarded Citizens Children's Ctr., Blauvelt, N.Y.; music therapist, insvc. tng. cons. Divsn. Youth and Family Svcs. Day Care Ctrs., Jersey City. Cons. insvc. tng. workshops for tchrs., music therapists. Composer: (songs) From Everything-A Song, 1990, 1992, 1994, 1997, Pronunciation (Rap), 2000. Active Closter Bd. Edn.; chair PIE adv. coun. Northern Valley (N.J.) Pre-Sch. Instrn. for Exceptional program. Mem. Am. Music Therapy Assn., Mid-Atlantic Region Music Therapy Assn., N. N.J. Orff-Schulwerk Assn. (recording sec.), Am. Orff-Schulwerk Assn. (at large), N.J. Assn. Music Therapy, Children's Entertainment Assn. (edn. com.), Nat. Assn. Edn. Young Children, Phi Beta Kappa, Kappa Delta Pi, Pi Lamba Theta. Home: 26 Collins Ave Closter NJ 07624 Office: Dr Goose Music PO Box 31 26 Collins Ave Closter NJ 07624 Fax: 201-768-4771. E-mail: Steinre@aol.com.

STEIN, ELLEN GAIL, executive manager; b. N.Y.C., May 19, 1951; d. Manuel W. and Bella (Skutel) Stein. BA, SUNY, Stony Brook, 1972; M of Urban Planning, Hunter Coll., 1976; cert. program execs. state/local govt., Harvard U., 1985. Sr. rsch. assoc. Nassau Suffolk (N.Y.) Regional Med. Program, 1976-77; sr. planner N.Y.C. Dept. Correction, 1977-79; group leader criminal justice Mayor's Office, Dept. Ops., N.Y.C., 1979-81, dep. asst. dir. citywide spl. projects, 1981, dir. citywide audit implementation, 1981-84; adminstr. Bur. Supplied N.Y.C. Bd. Edn., 1984-90; mgmt. cons. Project Provide Hope, Russia, Citizen's Budget Commn., 1990-94; pres., CEO FEDVentures Inc., 1994-99; assoc. commnr., dir. Office of CIO N.Y.C. Dept. Tech. and Telecomm., 1999—. Mem. Nat. Assn. Purchasing Mgmt., Am. Women Econ. Devel., Ctrl. Women's Focus, Gov.'s Procurement Coun. (N.Y.), Human Svcs. Coun. (contracting com.). Home: 67 Park Ter E New York NY 10034-1445 Office: 75 Park Pl Fl 7 New York NY 10007-2146 E-mail: estein@doitt.nyc.gov., egstein@hotmail.com.

STEIN, ELLIOT, JR. business executive; b. St. Louis, Jan. 31, 1949; s. Elliot and Mary Ann (Bleiweiss) S.; m. Pamela Sztybel, Oct. 4, 1997. BA, Claremont McKenna Coll., 1971. Assoc. Lehman Bros., N.Y.C., 1972-79; chmn. Caribbean Internat. News Corp., San Juan, P.R., 1985—; ptnr. Commonwealth Capital Ptnrs., N.Y.C., 1988—. Bd. dirs. ACX Pacific, Inc., Playpower, Inc., VTG Holdings, Inc., Cloud Corp., LLC; mem. adv. bd. Investigative Group Internat., 1998—. Trustee Claremont Grad. U., 1980—, New Sch. U., 1990—; bd. councillors Annenberg Sch. Comm., U. So. Calif., 1998—. Democrat. Office: Commonwealth Capital Ptnrs 444 Madison Ave Ste 703 New York NY 10022-6903

STEIN, FRANKLIN JOSEPH, computer systems analyst, organist; b. Eau Claire, Wis., Mar. 26, 1945; s. Herbert Charles Stein and Gwenn Marie Lassek. BS in Secondary Edn., U. Wis., Eau Claire, 1968; BS in Computer Sci., Coleman Coll., 1989, MIS in Info. Systems, 1995. Cert. tchr. Wis. Biology, sci., Spanish tchr. Stanley (Wis.)-Boyd H.S., 1968-71; dept. mgr. Day Music Co., Eau Claire, 1972-75; store mgr. Tropic Waters Pet Store, 1975-76, Thearle Music Co., San Diego, 1977—82; 6th grade tchr. St. Paul's Luth. Sch., Pacific Beach, 1977-78; profl. theatre organist Organ Power Pizza Restaurants, San Diego, 1977-85; store mgr. Organ Stop Inc., 1982—89; computer programmer analyst Health Examinetics, Rancho Bernardo, 1989-91; clin. computer systems specialist SHARP HealthCare, San Diego, 1991—97; systems programmer/clin. analyst U. Calif., 1997—2002; sr. computer systems analyst SHARP HealthCare, 2002—. Profl. concert organist, San Diego, 1965—; Cath. music dir./organist USMC. Author: Technician's Manual of Thermography, 1987; editor: Manual of Thermography, 1988. Cath. music dir./organist U.S. Marine Corps Air Station, Miramar, Calif.; sponsor Childreach, 2000—. Recipient Silver medal Piano Performance Wis. Music Educators, 1962, 63, Cert. of Merit for Excellence in Sci. Wis. Jr. Acad. of Sci., 1963. Mem. Am. Guild of Organists, Am. Theatre Organ Soc. Roman Catholic. Avocations: reading, concerts, traveling. Home: 10227 Kamwood Pl San Diego CA 92126-5139 Office: SHARP HealthCare/Info Sys 8695 Spectrum Center Ct San Diego CA 92123 Fax: 619-543-3675. Business E-Mail: frank.stein@sharp.com. E-mail: fjstein@msn.com.

STEIN, GARY S. state supreme court justice, retired, lawyer; b. Newark, June 13, 1933; s. Morris J. and Mollie (Goldfarb) S.; married, July 1, 1956; children— Jill, Carrie, Michael, Terri, Jo; m. Et Tilchin, July 1, 1956 AB, Duke U., 1954, LL.B. with distinction, 1956; D.H.L. (hon.), N.J. Inst. Tech., 1985. Bar: D.C. 1956, Ohio 1957, N.Y. 1958, N.J. 1963. Research asst. U.S. Senate AntiTrust and Monopoly Subcom., Washington, 1955; assoc. Kramer, Marx, Greenlee & Backus, N.Y.C., 1956-65; sole practice Paramus, N.J., 1966-72; ptnr. Stein & Kurland, Esquires, 1972-82; dir. Gov.'s Office of Policy and Planning, Trenton, 1982-85; assoc. justice Supreme Ct. N.J., Hackensack, 1985—2002, ret., 2002; counsel Pashman Stein, 2002—. Mcpl. atty., Paramus, 1967-71; counsel N.J. Election Law Revision Commn., 1970; atty. Bd. Adjustment, Teaneck, N.J., 1973-82 Mem. editorial bd. Duke Law Jour., 1954-56, assoc. editor, 1955-56. Mem. Dist. Ethics Com. for Bergen County, N.J., 1977-80, chmn. 1981. Served with U.S. Army, 1957-58, 61-62 Mem. ABA, N.J. State Bar Assn. (com. on state legislation 1973-79, chmn. 1973-76, jud. selection com. 1976-81, Constl. amendment com. 1977-79, court modernization com. 1976-79), Bergen County Bar Assn., Order of Coif. Jewish. Avocation: tennis. Office: Pashman Stein 45 Essex St Hackensack NJ 07601-5415

STEIN, GEORGE HENRY, historian, educator, administrator; b. Vienna, Austria, May 18, 1934; came to U.S., 1939, naturalized, 1948; m. Dorothy Ann Lahm, Nov. 22, 1963; 1 child, Kenneth. BA with honors (State Regents scholar), Bklyn. Coll., 1959; MA in History (Regents fellow), Columbia U., 1960, PhD in History (Pres.'s fellow), 1964. Lectr. history City Coll., CUNY, 1962-63; instr. dept. history Columbia U., N.Y.C., 1963-65, asst. prof., 1965-66; assoc. prof. dept. history SUNY-Binghamton, 1966-70, prof., 1970-73, disting. teaching prof., 1973-98, emeritus, 1998—, vice chmn. grad. affairs, 1974-76, v.p. acad. affairs, 1976-87, provost, 1985-87, acting pres., 1986-87. Manuscript evaluator and cons. to numerous publishers, 1964—Author: The Waffen SS: Hitler's Elite Guard at War, 1939-45, 1966, paperback edit., 1984 (transl. into German, 1967, French, 1967, Spanish, 1973, Portuguese, 1970, Japanese, 2002); contbr. articles on modern European history to scholarly publs.; editor: Hitler, 1968; contbr. book revs. to hist. jours. Served with USAF, 1953-57. NEH fellow, 1970-71 Mem. Am. Hist. Assn. (mem. conf. group on cen. European history, conf. group for use of psychology in history), Acad. Polit. Sci., Assn. of Contemporary Historians, Am. Assn. Higher Edn., Nat. Assn. State Univs. and Land Grant Colls. (mem. council acad. affairs 1976-87), Am. Counc. Edn. (exec. com. nat. coun. chief acad. officers 1983-85), Com. Internat. d'Histoire de la Deuxieme Guerre Mondiale, WWII Studies Assn. Home: 2300 Hemlock Ln Vestal NY 13850-2633 Office: SUNY Dept History Binghamton NY 13902-6000

STEIN, GERALD HERBERT, medical educator; b. Phila., Oct. 11, 1936; s. Harry N. and Rose (Miller) S.; Lona Livingston, May 30, 1962 (div.); children: Alexander, Lauren; m. Sara Morton, Jan. 4, 1990; children: Katherine, Frances. BA, U. Pa., 1958, MD, 1962. Asst. prof. U. Fla. Coll. Medicine, Gainesville, 1972-95; staff physician VA Med. Ctr., 1972-92; dir. med. edn., prof.-in-residence Kameda Med. Ctr., Kamogawa, Japan, 1992-99; assoc. clin. prof. dept. medicine U. Hawaii, Honolulu, 1996—; courtesy asst. prof. medicine U. Fla., Gainesville, 1995—. Commd. cons. USN, Yokosuka, Japan, 1993-99; teaching cons. Shonan Kamakura Hosp., Japan, 1994—; dir. Mammatech Corp., Gainesville, 1979-84; pres. Corp. Pub. Medicine, Gainesville, 1981-95; physician advisor Gainesville VA Med. Ctr., 2000—. Patentee in field. Mem. sch. adv. com. Alachua County Sch. Bd., Gainesville, 1982-90, Capt. U.S. Army Res., 1964-66. Fellow ACP, Am. Coll. Rheumatology; mem. Am. Soc. Hypertension, Phi Beta Kappa, Alpha Omega Alpha. Democrat. Jewish. Avocations: classical music, jogging, windsurfing, computers. Office: 4700 SW Archer Rd #90 Gainesville FL 32608

STEIN, HOWARD, economics educator; b. Toronto, Ont., Can., Aug. 4, 1952; came to U.S., 1977; s. David Solomon and Beulah (Tanner) S.; m. Alisa Erika Koch, June 19, 1988; children: Joshua Walter, Daniel Nathan. BA, U. Toronto, 1975; MA, U. Ottawa, Can., 1977; PhD, U. Calif., Riverside, 1983. Lectr. Dept. Econs. U. Dar es Salaam, Tanzania, 1980-82; assoc. prof. dept. econs. Roosevelt U., Chgo., 1983—. Vis. scholar Ctr. Rsch. on Econ. Devel., U. Mich., Ann Arbor, 1990-91, Sch. Internat. Svc., Am. Univ., Washington, 1995, Sch. of Oriental and African Studies, U. London, 1998; vis. prof. Inst. Econ. Rsch., Hitotsubashi U., Tokyo, 1995-96. Co-editor: Tanzania and the IMF: The Dynamics of Liberalization, 1992, Deregulation and the Banking Crisis in Nigeria: A Comparative Study, 2002; editor: Asian Industrialization and Africa: Studies in Policy Alternatives to Structural Adjustments, 1995. Doctoral fellow Soc. Social Sci. and Humanities Rsch. Coun. Can., 1979; Nat. Endowment for Humanities grantee, 1985; recipient U.S. Info. Agy. Spkr. and Specialist award, 1999. Mem. Am. Econ. Assn., African Studies Assn. Avocations: ice hockey, gardening. Home: 1527 William St River Forest IL 60305-1138 Office: Roosevelt U 430 S Michigan Ave Chicago IL 60605-1394

STEIN, HOWARD S. banker; b. N.Y.C., Dec. 27, 1939; s. J. Zachary and Adele (Epstein) S. BA, U. Mich., 1961; MBA, Harvard U., 1963. Mem. treas.'s staff Gen. Motors Corp., N.Y.C., 1963-69; dep. dir., dir. fiscal ops. Human Resources Adminstrn., City of N.Y., 1969-71, dep. adminstr., 1972-74, 1st dep. adminstr., 1974-78; asst. commr. Manpower and Career Devel. Agy., N.Y.C., 1971-72; dep. commr. rent and housing maintenance Housing and Devel. Adminstrn., City of N.Y., 1972; v.p. Citicorp Credit Services Inc., N.Y.C., 1979-86; sr. v.p. Citicorp Retail Services Inc., 1986-87; exec. dir. Landmark Mut. Funds Group of Citibank, N.A., 1987-88; v.p. br. banking sect. devel. div. Citibank NA, 1989-91, sr. credit officer worldwide securities svcs. div. Fin. Instns. Group, 1991-94; group risk mgr. Global Transaction Svcs., 1995—2001, head operational risk mgmt., emerging markets and transaction svcs., 2002—. Lectr. human resources policy Nova U., Ft. Lauderdale, Fla., 1973-74; field instr. adminstrn. specialization NYU Sch. Social Work, 1976-77; mem. risk mgmt. com. Participants Trust Co., 1995-99. Past Bd. dirs., chmn. program com. Vol. Urban Cons. Group, Inc.; chmn. bd. dirs. Nova Inst; past treas., past pres., bd. dirs. Child Study Assn. Am./Wel-Met, Inc., 1963-85; past treas., bd. dirs. Career Center for Social Services Greater N.Y., Inc.; past treas., past pres. bd. dirs. Cavalier King Charles Spaniel Club U.S.A., Inc.; past bd. dirs., past sec. Child Welfare Info. Services; treas., bd. dirs., chmn. fin. com. WNYC Radio; bd. dirs. Senate Residence Owners Inc., New Goddard-Riverside Housing Devel. Fund Co., N.Y.C. Health and Hosps., Corp., 1976, Homes for the Homeless; mem. corp. Children's Mus., Boston; bd. dirs., treas., mem. fin. com. Goddard Riverside Neighborhood Houses; mem. Dept. Disciplinary com. Supreme Ct. State N.Y. Appellate Divsn. 1st Jud. Dept.; mem. corp. adv. com. U. Mich., Coll. Lit., Sci and the Arts; bd. dirs. The Childrens' Cause. Mem.: Harvard (N.Y.C., past mem. admissions com.). Home: 1158 5th Ave New York NY 10029-6917 Office: 111 Wall St New York NY 10005 E-mail: howard.s.stein@citi.com.

STEIN, JACOB, computer programmer, analyst; b. N.Y.C., Aug. 20, 1960; s. John H. Kliever and Ann DuBois; m. Sara Wallach, Aug. 18, 1981 (div. 1991); m. Miriam Tichomirov, Oct. 4, 1994; children: Samson and Abigail (twins). Student, Kazon Ish Rabbinical Inst., 1981-86; cert. programmer, Cope Inst., 1988. Programmer Eastern Systems, Bklyn., 1988-90, Presidential Life, Nyack, N.Y., 1990-94, Group Health Inc., N.Y.C., 1995—. Mem. Mensa. Republican. Jewish. Avocations: Talmudic research, theological writing, hiking, genealogy. Office: Group Health Inc 9th Ave New York NY 10001 Home: 164 Saddle River Monsey NY 10952 E-mail: jstein@ghi.com.

STEIN, JAY MARTIN, planning and design educator, consultant; b. N.Y.C., Dec. 21, 1946; s. Samuel and Helen S.; children: Danielle Eva, Melissa Ilana, Jessie Phillips. BA, Harpur Coll., 1968; MA, York U., Toronto, Ont., Can., 1971; PhD, U. Mich., 1976. Cert. planner. Lectr. U. Mich., Ann Arbor, 1974-76; asst. prof. planning Ga. Inst. Tech., Atlanta, 1976-81, assoc. prof., 1981-86; prof., chmn. dept. SUNY, Buffalo, 1986-89, acting dean, 1988; prof., chmn. dept. urban and regional planning U. Fla., Gainesville, 1989—, interim dean Coll. Design, Constrn. and Planning, 1999-2001, dean Coll. Design, Constrn. and Planning, 2001—. Vis. prof. Stanford (Calif.) U., 1984-85; prin. Jay M. Stein Assocs.; cons. Legal Svcs. Corp. Ga., Atlanta, 1980-84, Atlanta Regional Commn., 1982, Legal Svcs. Corp. Ala., Montgomery, 1983-84, New Orleans Legal Svcs., 1988-89. Editor: Public Infrastructure, 1988, Growth Management: The Planning Challenge of the 1990s, 1992, Classic Readings in Urban Planning, 1995, Classic Readings in Real Estate and Development, 1996, (with Kent Spreckelmeyer) Classic Readings in Architecture, 1999; mem. editl. bd. Jour. Arch. and Planning Rsch., Jour. Infrastructure Sys., Jour. Pub. Works Mgmt. and Policy; contbr. chpts. to books, articles to profl. jours. Mem. Am. Inst. Cert. Planners, Am. Planning Asasn. (mem. jour. editl. bd. 1984-88, 95—), Assn. Collegiate Schs. Planning (exec. com. 1980-82), Urban Land Inst. (affiliate), Assn. Collegiate Schs. of Architecture (affiliate), Fla. Planning and Zoning Adminstrn., Am. Soc. Landscape Architects (affiliate). Avocations: tennis, photography. Office: U Fla Coll Design Constrn PO Box 115701 Gainesville FL 32611-5701 E-mail: jmstein@ufl.edu.

STEIN, JEROME LEON, economist, educator; b. Bklyn., Nov. 14, 1928; s. Meyer and Ida (Shapiro) S.; m. Hadassah Levow, Aug. 27, 1950; children: Seth, Gil, Ilana. BA summa cum laude, Bklyn. Coll., 1949; MA, Yale U., 1950, PhD, 1955; Docteur honoris causa, U. de la Méditerranée, 1997. Instr. Brown U., Providence, 1953-56, asst. prof., 1956-60, assoc. prof., 1960-62, prof., 1962-70, Eastman prof. polit. economy, 1970-94, prof. emeritus, 1994—. Vis. prof. Hebrew U., Jerusalem, 1965-66, 72-73, 78; Ford Found. rsch. prof. econs. U. Calif., Berkeley, 1979-80, Sorbonne, U. Paris, 1982, Tohoku U., Sendai, Japan, 1983, Haute Etudes Comml., France, 1987, Monash U., Melbourne U., Australia, 1989, U. Aix-en-Provence, Marseille, France, 1992, 95, 96, 97, 98, U. Munich, 1994, La Sapienza, Rome, 1994; vis. prof. applied math. Brown U., 1996—. Author: Essays in International Finance, 1962, (with G.M. Borts) Economic Growth in a Free Market, 1964, Money and Capacity Growth, 1971, Monetarism, 1976, Monetarist, Keynesian and New Classical Economics, 1982, Economics of Futures Markets, 1986, International Finance Markets, 1991, Fundamental Determinants of Exchange Rates, 1995; bd. editors Am. Econ. Rev., 1974-80; assoc. editor Jour. Fin., 1964-70. Ford Found. faculty fellow, 1961-62; Social Sci. Research Council grantee, 1965-66; Guggenheim fellow, 1972-73 Mem. Am. Econ. Assn. Home: 77 Elton St Providence RI 02906-4505 Office: Brown U 182 George St Providence RI 02912-9056 Fax: 401-863-1355. E-mail: Jerome_Stein@BROWN.EDU.

STEIN, JOHN C. lawyer; b. Flint, Mich., May 8, 1939; s. Joseph Aloyosius and Gertrude (Carlin) S.; m. Dorothea Ruel, Nov. 20, 1965; children: John Jr., Christian, Peter, Thea. BA, U. San Francisco, 1963; JD, U. Calif. Hastings, San Francisco, 1966; cert., Mil. Justice Sch., Newport, R.I., 1968. Bar: Calif. 1966, U.S. Dist. Ct. (no., ctrl. and so. dists.) Calif. 1969. Dep. city atty. City of San Francisco, Office of City Atty., 1969-71; with The Boccardo Law Firm, San Francisco, 1971-81, mng. ptnr. San Jose, Calif., 1981-99. Judge pro tem San Francisco County Superior Ct., 1978—, Santa Clara County Superior Ct., 1981—; lectr. U. Santa Clara Law Sch., 1985—, Hastings Coll. of Law, U. C. San Francisco. Bd. dirs. Katherine Delmar Burke Sch. Girls, San Francisco, 1988-92, Planning Orgn. for The Richmond, San Francisco, 1985-88. Capt. USMC, 1966-69. Fellow Am. Coll. Trial Lawyers; mem. ATLA, Consumer Attys. of Calif., Am. Bd. Trial Advocates. Democrat. Roman Catholic. Avocations: golf, skiing, SCUBA diving. Office: Boccardo Law Firm 111 W Saint John St Ste 1100 San Jose CA 95113-1107

STEIN, JOSEPH, playwright; b. N.Y.C. s. Charles and Emma S.; m. Elisa Loti, Feb. 7, 1975; children by previous marriage: Daniel, Harry, Joshua; children of present marriage: John, Jenny Lyn. BSS, CCNY, 1934; MSW, Columbia U., 1937. Psychiat. social worker, N.Y.C., 1938-45. Writer: radio shows, including Raleigh's Room, 1948-49, Henry Morgan Show, 1949-52; TV shows, including Your Show of Shows, 1952-54; Sid Caesar Show, 1954-55; playwright Plain and Fancy, 1955; Mr. Wonderful, 1957, Juno, 1959, Take Me Along, 1959, Enter Laughing, 1963, Fiddler on the Roof, 1964 (Am. Theatre Wing Tony award for best musical, 1965, N.Y. Drama Critics Circle award Best Musical 1965), Zorba, 1968 (Tony nomination), Irene, 1975, King of Hearts, 1978, Carmelina, 1979, The Baker's Wife, 1983, (Olivier award nomination London 1989), Rags, 1986 (Tony nomination); screenplays Enter Laughing, 1970; Fiddler on the Roof, 1972 (Screen Writers Guild award). Mem. Authors League, Screen Writers Guild (award recipient), Dramatists Guild Coun. Home: 1130 Park Ave New York NY 10128-1255

STEIN, KAREN LOUISE, elementary music education educator, composer; b. Wichita, Kans., Jan. 25, 1955; d. Ralph Wesley Sr. and Flavia Elizabeth Goodman; m. Richard Allen Stein, Jan. 7, 1954; children: Jeremy, Andrea. BA in Music Edn., Olivet Nazarene U., Kankakee, Ill., 1977; MMus in Composition/Theory, U. No. Iowa, 1989. Licensed tchr., Ark., Ky. Tchr. kindergarten Sonshine Sch., Canton, Ohio, 1978-79; pvt. instr. music, 1977-2000; music specialist Maryville Elem. Sch., Louisville, 1989-2000, Stephens Elem. Sch.-Little Rock Sch. Dist., 2000—01; instrumental instr. Oaklawn Visual and Performing Arts Magnet Sch., Hot Springs, Ark., 2001—. Panel mem. Ky. std. setting study for Praxis series, 1995. Dir. (drama prodn.) The Best Christmas Pageant Ever, 1997; composer jazz compositions; performed at All-County Music Festival, Bullitt County, Ky., 1999. Dir. Payne (Ohio) Cmty. Children's Choir, 1984-85, Children's Choir, Farmdale Ch. of Nazarene, Louisville, 1990-98, 1st Ch. of Nazarene, Little Rock, 2000—; mem. Louisville Chorus, 1999-2000. Recipient Disting. Svc. award Internat. Ch. of Nazarene, 1998; named Tchr. of Yr. Maryville Elem. Sch. PTA, 1992; Raymond Hubbell Musical scholar, ASCAP, 1987. Mem. NEA, Music Educators Nat. Conf., Ark. Edn. Assn., Ark. Music Educators Assn., Litte Rock Classroom Tchrs. Assn., Ky. Congress Parents and Tchrs. (hon. life). Republican. Avocation: golf. Home: 1407 Westhampton Dr Little Rock AR 72211 Office: Oaklawn Magnet Sch 301 Oaklawn Blvd Hot Springs National Park AR 71903 E-mail: steinr@prodigy.net.

STEIN, LAWRENCE A. lawyer; b. Balt., Mar. 18, 1965; s. Hersh and Ellen (Hart) S.; m. Diane Wells, June 23, 1991; children: Joshua A., Julie E. AB, U. Chgo., 1988; JD, No. Ill. U., 1993. Bar: Ill. 1993, U.S. Dist. Ct. (no. dist.) Ill. 1993, U.S. Ct. Appeals (7th cir.) 1993, Md. 1994, U.S. Dist. Ct. Md. 1994, U.S. Supreme Ct. 1997. Shareholder Huck, Bouma, Martin, Jones & Bradshaw, Wheaton, Ill., 1993—. Advisor Prairie State Legal Svcs., Carol Stream, Ill., 1993—. Commr. Glen Ellyn (Ill.) Architecture Review Commn., 1994-97. Recipient Am. jurisprudence award for excellence in appellate advocacy Lawyers Coop., 1991. Mem.: ABA, Am. Inns Ct., Ill. State Bar Assn., DuPage County Bar Assn., Phi Delta Phi. Republican. Jewish. Home: 69 Ott Ave Glen Ellyn IL 60137-5632 Office: Huck Bouma Martin Jones & Bradshaw 1755 S Naperville Rd Ste 200 Wheaton IL 60187-8144 E-mail: lstein@huckbouma.com.

STEIN, LYNN ANDREA, computer scientist, educator, engineering educator; b. June 27, 1965; children: Sara, Miriam, Joshua. AB in Computer Sci. cum laude, Harvard U., 1986; MSc in Computer Sci., Brown U., 1987, PhD in Computer Sci., 1990. Asst. prof. dept. elec. engring. and computer sci. MIT, 1990—92, class of 1957 asst. prof. dept. elec. engring. and computer sci., 1992—94, class of 1957 assoc. prof. dept. elec. engring. and computer sci., 1994—95, assoc. prof. dept. elec. engring. and computer sci., 1995—2001; prof. computer sci. and engring., mem. founding faculty Franklin W. Olin Coll. Engring., 2000—. Sci. scholar Mary Ingraham Bunting Inst., 1997—98, Radcliffe Coll., 1998—99; adj. prof. dept. computer sci. Brandeis U., 2000—; cons. in field; lectr. in field. Contbr. chapters to books, articles to profl. jours. Grantee, NSF, 1993—99, Mitsubishi Electric Rsch. Labs., 1993—99, DARPA/Rome Labs., 1994—99, DARPA/ONR Multidisciplinary U. Rsch. Initiative, 1995—2000, Microsoft U. Curriculum Program, 1998, Nippon Tel. and Telegraph, 1999—2000, Merrill Lynch, 1999—2000, NSF, 1999—2002, DARPA Agt. Markup Lang. Program, 2000—02, Rome Labs., 2001, others. Office: FW Olin Coll Engring 1000 Olin Way Needham MA 02492-1245

STEIN, MARK RODGER, allergist; b. Phila., Apr. 24, 1943; s. Eli and Norma Stein; m. Phyllis Feinstein, Dec. 27, 1964; children: Amy Lynn, Philip Warren. BA, LaSalle Coll., Phila., 1964; MD, Jefferson Med. Coll., Phila., 1968. Diplomate Nat. Bd. Med. Examiners, Am. Bd. Internal Medicine, Am. Bd. Allergy and Immunology. Intern Abington (Pa.) Meml. Hosp., 1968-69; resident internal medicine Letterman Army Med. Ctr., San Francisco, 1972-75; fellow allergy and clin. immunology Fitzsimons Army Med. Ctr., Denver, 1975-77; pvt. practice West Palm Beach, Fla., 1979—. Asst. prof. depts. medicine and pediatrics Uniformed Svcs. U. Health Scis. Sch. Medicine, Bethesda, Md., 1978—79; clin. asst. prof. dept. internal medicine U. South Fla. Coll. Medicine, Tampa, 1979—83, Tampa, 1997—2000; clin. care cons. Clin. Ctr., NIH, Bethesda, 1978—79; mem. active staff Good Samaritan Hosp., West Palm Beach, Fla., chief svc. dept. allergy, 1990—98, 2001—; mem. active staff, chief dept. allergy St. Mary's Hosp., West Palm Beach, 1985—98; mem. active staff Palm Beach Gardens Med Ctr., Jupiter Med. Ctr.; chief allergy svc. Intracostal Health Sys., 2000—01. Editor Gastroesophageal Reflux Disease and Airway Disease, 1999; contbr. articles to profl. jours. Trustee Am. Lung Assn., West Palm Beach, 1984-93, 95—. Fellow ACP, Am. Acad. Allergy, Asthma and Immunology, Am. Coll. Allergy, Asthma and Immunology (chmn. geriat. com. 1988-90), Am. Assn. Cert. Allergists; mem. Am. Thoracic Soc., Mil. Allergists, Fla. Med. Assn., Palm Beach County Med. Assn., Asthma and Allergy Found. Am., Fla. Allergy and Immunology Soc. (pres. 1987-88), Southeastern Allergy Assn. Jewish. Avocations: tennis, golf. Office: 840 Us Highway 1 North Palm Beach FL 33408-3830 E-mail: latallergy@aol.com.

STEIN, MARSHALL DAVID, lawyer; b. Greensboro, N.C., Dec. 17, 1941; s. Joseph and Celia (Feuer) S.; m. Helene Sue Weiner, Mar. 20, 1965; children: Lisa D., Daniel R. BA, Brandeis U., 1964; LLB, Boston U., 1967. Bar: Mass. 1968, U.S. Dist. Ct. Mass. 1970, U.S. Ct. Appeals (1st cir.) 1971, U.S. Dist. Ct. Vt. 1978, U.S. Supreme Ct 1981. Asst. U.S. Atty. Office of U.S. Atty., U.S. Dist. Ct. Mass., 1974-76; chief staff atty. U.S. Ct. Appeals (1st cir.), Boston, 1976-78; ptnr. Cherwin & Glickman, 1982-96, Cherwin, Glickman & Theise, LLP, Boston, 1996-2000; of counsel Cherwin, Theise, Adelson & Loria, LLP, 2001—. Assoc. editor Mass. Law Rev., Boston, 1980-90; contbr. articles to profl. jours. Panelist issues in housing discrimination U.S. Commn. Civil Rights, Washington, 1985. Mem. Mass. Bar Assn., Boston Bar Assn. (chmn. jud. pay raise subcom. 1993-96). Jewish. Office: Cherwin Theise Adelson & Loria LLP 1 International Pl Ste 1120 Boston MA 02110-2622 E-mail: mstein@ctallaw.com.

STEIN, MARVIN, psychiatrist, historian; b. St. Louis, Dec. 8, 1923; s. Samuel G. and Dora (Kline) S.; m. Ann Hackman, May 5, 1950; children: Leslie, David, Lisa. BS, MD, Washington U., St. Louis, 1949; grad., Phila. Psychoanalytic Inst., 1959. Intern St. Louis City Hosp., 1949-50; asst. resident in psychiatry Barnes Hosp., St. Louis, 1950-51; fellow in psychiatry Hosp. U. Pa., 1953-55; asst. prof., then assoc. prof. psychiatry U. Pa. Med. Sch., 1956-63; prof. psychiatry Cornell U. Med. Sch., N.Y.C., 1963-66; prof., chmn. dept. psychiatry SUNY Downstate Med. Ctr., Bklyn., 1966-71; chmn. dept. psychiatry Mt. Sinai Sch. Medicine, N.Y.C., 1971-87, Esther and Joseph Klingenstein prof. psychiatry, 1971-94, Esther and Joseph Klingenstein prof. emeritus, 1994—. Mem. fellowships rev. panel NIMH, 1961-64, chmn. mental health extramural rsch. adv. com., 1968-71, chmn. rev. com. Mental Health Aspects of AIDS, 1988-90; mem. rsch. adv. com. VA, 1965-68, mem. rsch. svc. merit rev. bd. in behavioral sci., 1972-75; chmn. Mental Health Rsch. Career Award Com., 1963-67; chmn. bd. dirs. Founds. Fund for Rsch. in Psychiatry, 1967-70; mem. behavioral medicine study sect. NIH, 1981-83, geriatric rev. com., 1986-88. Contbr. articles on brain and behavior and immune function to med. jours. USPHS postdoctoral fellow, 1951-53; mental health career investigator, 1956-61; sr. fellow grantee, 1961-63 Mem. Am. Psychiat. Assn. (chmn. rsch. coun. 1981-84), N.Y. Acad. Medicine (Salmon com. 1984—), Alpha Omega Alpha. Home: 5700 Arlington Ave Bronx NY 10471-1503 Office: Mt Sinai Sch Medicine 1 Gustave L Levy Pl New York NY 10029-6500 E-mail: marvin.stein@mssm.edu.

STEIN, MELVIN A. accountant; b. N.Y.C., Sept. 7, 1932; s. William H. and Lillian (Goldberg) S.; m. Barbara Blumencranz, Dec. 17, 1955 (dec.); children: Susan, Karen; m. Marie Sacco, Nov. 1, 1992. BS, NYU, 1953. Pvt. practice acctg., Jericho, N.Y., 1961-75; pres. Stein & Stein, P.C., Hicksville, 1975-81, Stein, Stein & Feit, P.C., Hicksville, 1982—. Bd. dirs. Stern Sch. Bus., NYU, 1990-92, treas., 1991-92, v.p., 1995—; mem. alumni bd. dirs. NYU. Mem. AICPA, N.Y. State Soc. CPAs, N.J. Soc. CPAs, C.W. Post Tax Inst., NYU Club, Princeton Club. Jewish. Home: 7 Ingleside Ln White Plains NY 10605-5009 Office: 1 Frederick Pl Hicksville NY 11801-4205 also: Buccaneer Mall Saint Thomas VI 00801 E-mail: CPA35@aol.com.

STEIN, M(EYER) L(EWIS), journalist, magazine editor, writer; b. Escanaba, Mich., July 30, 1920; s. Alexander and Fannie Stein; m. Romana Susan Paal, Apr. 15, 1981 (dec. Feb. 1994); children: Andrea, Jeannine; stepchildren: Adam Paal, Edith Paal. BJ, U. Mo., 1942; MA, Stanford U., 1961. Reporter, telegraph editor Daily Tribune, Royal Oak, Mich., 1946-51; reporter San Francisco Examiner, 1951-60; prof., chair dept. journalism and mass comm. NYU, 1961-74; prof., chair dept. journalism Calif. State U., Long Beach, 1974-87; west coast editor Editor & Publ. mag., Palo Alto, Calif., 1981-99. Author 17 books including: Freedom of the Press, 1970, Reporting Today, 1971, How to Write Plain English, 1976, Shaping the News, 1974, When Presidents Meet the Press, 1969, Under Fire: Story of American War Correspondents, 1995, (with Susan Paterno) Introduction to Journalism, 1998, (with Susan Paterno) Talk Straight, Listen Carefully: The Art of Interviewing, 2001; contbr. over 500 articles to newspapers and mags. Sgt. U.S. Army, 1942-45, Africa, Italy. Gannett fellow, 1980. Mem. Assn. Edn. in Journalism and Mass Comm. (chmn. freedom and responsibility com. 1964), Am. Soc. Journalists and Authors. Avocation: travel. Home and Office: 10 Bella Rosa Irvine CA 92602 Fax: (949) 362-1544. E-mail: mlsteinav@aol.com.

STEIN, MICHAEL ALAN, cardiologist, medical educator; b. Chgo., May 31, 1958; s. Harold Marc and Carlyne Mae (Skirow) S.; m. Ann Palmer Coe, June 9, 1984; children: Sarah Elizabeth, David Benjamin, Kathryn Marie. BA magna cum laude, Lawrence U., 1980; MD, U. Ill., 1984. Diplomate in internal medicine, cardiovas. diseases and interventional cardiology Am. Bd. Internal Medicine. Intern, resident in medicine U. Ill., Chgo., 1984-87; fellow in cardiology, then interventional cardiology U. Iowa, Iowa City, 1987-91; asst. prof. Emory U., Atlanta, 1991-95; dir. cardiology dept. Lower Fla. Keys Health Sys., 1997-98; clin. asst. prof. U. Wis., Madison, 1998—2001. Med. dir. CCU Atlanta VA Med. Ctr., Decatur, Ga., 1991—95; med. dir. cardiac catheterization lab. Dunwoody Med. Ctr., Atlanta, 1994—95; staff cardiologist Cardiology Cons., Pensacola, Fla., 1995—96, So. Med. Group, Key West, Fla., 1996—98, U. Wis., 1998—2001; staff cardiologists St. Mary's Hosp., Madison, Wis., 2001—; dean Med. Ctr., 2001—; v.p. Fond du Lac (Wis.) City Coun., 2000—01. Mem. Fond du Lac City Coun., 2000—01, v.p., 2000—01. Recipient clin. investigator award NIH, 1990-95. Fellow Am. Coll. Cardiology, Am. Heart Assn. (coun. clin. cardiology, Clin. Scientist award 1990-95); mem. AAAS, Soc. for Cardiac Angiography & Interventions. Avocations: sailing, sailboat racing, hiking, scuba diving, fishing. Office: St Mary's Hosp Cardiology Dept 707 S Mills St Madison WI 53715 Home: 7104 Park Shores Ct Middleton WI 53562 E-mail: mastein@chorus.net.

STEIN, MILTON MICHAEL, lawyer; b. N.Y.C., Sept. 18, 1936; s. Isidore and Sadie (Lefkowitz) S.; m. Jacqueline Martin, June 17, 1962; children: April, Alicia. AB, Columbia U., 1958, LLB, 1961. Bar: N.Y. 1962, Pa. 1971, U.S. Supreme Ct. 1971. Asst. dist. atty. N.Y. County, 1962-67; sr. counsel Nat. Commn. for Reform of Fed. Criminal Law, Washington, 1967-70; asst. dist. atty., chief of appeals City of Phila., 1970-73; asst. dir. Nat. Wire Tapping Commn., Washington, 1973-75; dir. D.C. Law Revision, 1975-77; spl. asst. HUD, 1977-79; asst. gen. counsel U.S. Commodity Futures Trading Commn., 1979-83; v.p. N.Y. Futures Exch., N.Y.C., 1983-89, N.Y. Stock Exch., N.Y.C., 1989—. Mem. ABA, N.Y. State Bar Assn., Assn. of Bar of City of N.Y. Democrat. Jewish. Home: Hudson House PO Box 286 Ardsley On Hudson NY 10503-0286 E-mail: m.stein@nyse.com.

STEIN, MITCHELL BRIAN, physician; b. Queens, N.Y., Nov. 11, 1954; s. Philip and Doris (Kramer) S.; m. Barbara Ellen Pollard, Mar. 24, 1980; children: Julie, Laura. BA, Columbia Coll., 1975; MD, Albert Einstein Coll. Medicine, 1979. Diplomate Am. Bd. Internal Medicine, Am. Bd. Ophthalmology. Pvt. practice, Mt. Kisco, NY, 1987—; asst. clinical prof. Albert Einstein Coll. Medicine, Bronx, N.Y., 1994—; vol. attending physician Northern Westchester Hosp. Ctr., Mt. Kisco, 1996—. Office: 69 S Moger Ave Mount Kisco NY 10549-2217

STEIN, OTTO LUDWIG, botany educator; b. Augsburg, Germany, Jan. 14, 1925; came to U.S., 1939, naturalized, 1944; s. Julius and Margaret (Haas) S.; m. Diana Borut, June 15, 1958; children: Deborah Lee, Judith Ann, Suzanne Beth, Jonathan Henri Richard. BS with distinction, U. Minn., 1949, MS, 1952, PhD, 1954. Instr. botany U. Mo. at Columbia, 1955; USPHS research fellow Brookhaven Nat. Lab., 1955-57, research collaborator, 1958-68; asst. prof. botany U. Mont., Missoula, 1957-63, asso. prof., 1963-64; asso. prof. botany U. Mass., Amherst, 1964-70, prof. botany, 1970-90, prof. emeritus, 1990—, head dept., 1969-74; dir. U. Mass./U. Freiburg (Germany) Exchange Program, 1979. Vis. asst. prof. botany U. Calif., Berkeley, 1961-62 Served with AUS, 1944-46. NATO sr. research fellow Imperial Coll., London, Eng., 1971-72 Fellow Linnean Soc. (London), AAAS; mem. Bot. Soc. Am. (chmn. developmental sect. 1963-65), Soc. Developmental Biology, Soc. Exptl. Biology, Sigma Xi., Gamma Sigma Delta, Alpha Zeta, Gamma Alpha. Home: 140 Red Gate Ln Amherst MA 01002-1845 Office: U Mass Dept Biology Amherst MA 01003

STEIN, PAUL ARTHUR, financial services executive; b. St. Louis, Aug. 20, 1937; s. Harry Arthur and Julia (Vandivort) S.; m. Ann Garwood, Oct. 8, 1960 (dec. 1993); m. Marjorie Orr MacIver, 1996; children: Valerie Suzanne, Paul Garwood. AB, Dartmouth U., 1959. From trainee to dir. spl. market offices Merrill Lynch, N.Y.C. and Princeton, 1959—. Chmn. bd. dirs. VPI, Inc. Mem. Beacon Hill Club (Summit, N.J.), N.J. Ctr. for Visual Arts (officer and trustee), Securities Industry Inst. (former trustee). Episcopalian.

STEIN, PAULA JEAN ANNE BARTON, hotel real estate executive, broker; b. Chgo., July 29, 1929; m. Marshall L. Stein; children: Guy G., George L.; guardian of Bradley Stein, Gregory Stein. BA, Lake Forest (Ill.) U., 1951; postgrad., Roosevelt U., Chgo., 1955-77, UCLA, 1978-79. Adminstrv. asst. publicity Kefauver for Pres., Chgo., 1951; adminstrv. asst. Wells Orgns., 1952; rschr., writer Employers Assn. Am., 1951-52; writer Woodworking Jobbers Assn., 1953; cons. L.A., 1978-80; pres. Steinvest, Inc., Chgo., 1980—; freelance writer, 1996—. Cons., hotels Nat. Diversified Svcs., Inc., Chgo., 1990—, Beach Hotel, Inc., Monterey, Calif., IBA Women's Adv. Bd., 1999; advicate for learning disorder causes. Script for first TV bus. prog. on WGN-TV, 1951-52. Mem. Ragdale Found., Lake Forest, Ill. IBA fellow, 1990. Mem. World Future Soc. (profl.), Sisters in Crime, Mystery Writers Am., Chgo. Bot. Soc., So. Poverty Law Ctr., others. Avocations: oil painting, grandparenting, social services causes, citizen-diplomacy, mystery writing. Home and Office: Steinvest Inc 2291 Hybernia Dr Highland Park IL 60035-5509 E-mail: steinvest@msn.com.

STEIN, PAULA NANCY, psychologist, educator; b. N.Y.C., Aug. 23, 1963; d. Michael and Evelyn (Graber) S.; m. Andreas Howard Smoller, Sept. 2, 1991; children: Rebecca Leigh Smoller, Rachel Jordan Smoller. BA, Skidmore Coll., 1985; MA with distinction, Hofstra U., 1986, PhD, 1989. Lic. clin. psychologist, N.Y.; cert. in sch. psychology, N.Y. Intern NYU Med. Ctr.-Rusk Inst., N.Y.C., 1988-89; instr. Mt. Sinai Med. Ctr., 1989-93, asst. prof. rehab. medicine, 1993-95. Chief psychologist Fishkill (N.Y.) Consultation Group, 1991—. Contbr. chpt. to book, articles to profl. jours. Kraewic scholar Skidmore Coll., 1985. Mem. APA, Assn. for Advancement of Behavior Therapy, Phi Beta Kappa. Jewish. Avocations: skiing, swimming. Office: Fishkill Consultation Group 1092 Main St PO Box 446 Fishkill NY 12524-0446

STEIN, RICHARD ALAN, cardiologist, educator; b. N.Y.C., Apr. 7, 1942; BA, Columbia Coll., N.Y.C., 1963; MD, NYU, 1967. Diplomate in internal medicine, cardiovascular diseases, geriatrics and sports medicine Am. Bd. Internal Medicine; lic. physician, N.Y., Conn.; lic. handler radioactive materials, N.Y.C. Intern, then resident in medicine Downstate Med. Ctr.-Kings County Hosp., Bklyn., 1967-69, cardiology fellow, 1972-74; chief resident in medicine Kings County Hosp., 1971-72, attending physician; prof. medicine, chief cardiology divsn. dept. medicine SUNY-Health Sci. Ctr., Bklyn., 1985-95; chief preventive and rehab. cardiology Lenox Hill Hosp., N.Y.C., 1995-99; attending physician SUNY Hosp., Bklyn.; chief of cardiology The Bklyn. Hosp. Ctr., 1999—. Mem. vis. faculty Yale-New Haven Hosp., 1982; dir. cardiology fellowship program Bklyn. VA Hosp., Brookdale Hosp., S.I. U. Hosp., 1985—95; dir. cardiac rehab. program 92d St. YM-YWHA, N.Y.C.; prof. clin. medicine Weill-Cornell Med. Ctr., 1999—. Mem. editorial bd. Preventive Cardiology, Nephron, Jour. Cmty. Health; contbr. chpt. to: Coronary Rehabilitation for the Practicing Physician, 1979, Sports Medicine for the Primary Care Physician, 1984, Anesthesia as Co-Existing Heart Disease, 1993, (with others) Diabetic Renal-Retinal Syndrome, 1980; sect. editor: Heart Disease: A Jour. of Cardiovasc. Disease; contbr. or co-contbr. articles to med. jours., 1977-93. Maj. USAF, 1969-71. Recipient Acad. Career award, Preventive Cardiology Acad. award NIH, 1985-90. Fellow ACS, Am. Coll. Cardiology, Am. Coll. Chest Physicians, Am. Coll. Sports Medicine, N.Y. Cardiol. Soc. (bd. dirs.), N.Y. Acad. Medicine; mem. Am. Heart Assn. (fellow coun. on clin. cardiology), Assn. Profs. Cardiology, Am. Fedn. for Clin. Rsch., Am. Heart Assn. (Heritage affiliate, chair task force on profl. edn., grantee in aid 1979-81), Sigma Xi. Office: 201 E 81st St New York NY 10028-3215 E-mail: rastein@msn.com.

STEIN, RICHARD PAUL, lawyer; b. New Albany, Ind., Sept. 2, 1925; s. William P. and Lillian M. (Russell) S.; m. Mary Charlotte Key, June 22, 1959; children: Richard Paul, William, Patricia. Student, Miligan (Tenn.) Coll., 1943-44, Duke, 1944-45; JD, U. Louisville, 1950. Bar: Ind., 1950. With labor relations Goodyear Engring. Co., Charlestown, Ind., 1952-54; ptnr. Naville & Stein, New Albany, 1954-61; pros. atty. 52d Jud. Circuit Ind., 1956-61; U.S. atty. So. Dist. Ind., 1961-67; chmn. Pub. Service Commn. of Ind., 1967-70; legis. counsel Eli Lilly Co., Indpls., 1970-74; v.p. pub. affairs Pub. Service Co. Ind., 1974-90; atty., pub. affairs cons., 1990-98; of counsel Stewart, Irwin, 1999—. Dir. Indpls. Indians; Co-counsel New Albany-Floyd County Bldg. Authority, 1960-62; mem. State Bd. Tax Commrs. Adv. Bd., Jud. Study Commn. Sec. New Albany Dist. Dem. Com., 1956-61; chmn. New Albany United Way, 1957. Served to lt. USNR, 1943-46, 50-51; lt. Res. Named Floyd County Young Man of Yr. Floyd County Jr. C. of C., 1955, Outstanding Young Man of Yr. New ALbany Jaycees, 1958. Mem. Ind. Bar Assn., Marion County Bar Assn., Ind. Prosecutors Assn. (pres. 1960-61), Ind. Electric Assn. (dir.), Am. Legion, Plum Creek Country Club, Skyline Club, K.C. Roman Catholic. Avocations: tennis, golf, reading. Home: 12414 Medalist Pkwy Carmel IN 46033-8933

STEIN, RICHARD STEPHEN, chemistry educator; b. N.Y.C., Aug. 21, 1925; s. Isidor and Florence (Lewengood) S.; m. Judith Elma Balise, May 27, 1951; children: Linda Ann, Anne Marie, Carol Joan, Lisa Jean. BS, Poly. Inst. Bklyn., 1945; MA, Princeton U., 1948, PhD, 1949; DS (hon.), U. Ulm, Fed. Republic Germany, 1989; DSc (hon.), U. Mass., 1992, Poly. U., 1999. Postdoctoral fellow Cambridge U., 1948-49; rsch. assoc. Princeton U., 1949-50; asst. prof. U. Mass., Amherst, 1950-57, assoc. prof., 1957-59, prof., 1959-61, Commonwealth prof., 1961-80, Goessmann prof. chemistry, 1980-92, Goessmann prof. emeritus, 1992—, founder, dir. Polymer Research Inst., 1961—. Co-editor: Electromagnetic Scattering, 1967, Structure and Properties of Polymer Films, 1973; contbr. numerous articles to profl. jours. Recipient Internat. award Soc. Plastics Engrs., 1969, Bingham award Rheology Soc., 1972, Award for Disting. Svc. for Advancement of Polymer Sci., Soc. Polymer Sci. Japan, 1988, Gordon Res. Conf. Huggins award, 1987, von Hippel award Materials Rsch. Soc., 1999, Disting. Alumnus award Poly. U., 2000. Mem. NAS, NAE, AAAS, AAUP, Am. Acad. Arts and Scis., Am. Chem. Soc. (Bordon award 1972, Polymer Chemistry award 1983), Am. Phys. Soc. (award in high polymer physics 1976), Rheology Soc., Sigma Xi. Achievements include being the founder of sci. rheo-optics of polymers. Home: 5 Berkshire Ter Amherst MA 01002-1301

STEIN, ROBERT A. writer, educator; b. Duluth, Minn., Aug. 5, 1933; s. Abe A. and Grace (Wichterman) S.; m. Betty Lou Pavlik, Nov. 5, 1955; children: Robert Jr., David K., Steven J. BS in Commerce, U. Iowa, 1956, MA in Counselor Edn., 1968, MA in Writing, 1986. Cert. tchr. Iowa; cert. profl. counselor. Commd. 2d lt. USAF, 1956, advanced through grades to col., ret., 1977; asst. prof. aerospace studies U. Iowa, Iowa City, 1964-66, assoc. prof., 1966-68, prof., 1975-77; dir., safety and security U. Iowa Hosps./Clinics, Iowa City, 1977-85, ret., 1985; mem. faculty divsn. writing Kirkwood C.C., Iowa City & Cedar Rapids, Iowa, 1984-89; writer, tchr. Iowa City, 1985—. Writer, tchr. Iowa City/Johnson County Sr. Citizens Ctr., Iowa City, 1994—. Author: (novels) Apollyon: A Novel, 1985, The Chase, 1988, The Black Samaritan, 1997, 2d edit., 2000, The Vengeance Equation, 2000, hardcover edit., 2001, (fiction) Death Defied, 1988 (Internat. Literary award 1988); co-author (screenplay) WGAW-Registered, 2001. Decorated Bronze Star, 1969. Mem. Authors Guild, Authors League Am., Air Force Assn. (life), Military Affairs Assn. (charter), Daedalians, Nat. Iowa Lettermen's Club (past pres.), Nat. Iowa Varsity Club (exec. bd., pres.-elect, 2002-03, lifetime achievement award 1999, pres.-elect 2002-03), Rotary (Paul Harris fellow), Phi Delta Kappa. Avocations: flying, international travel, reading, sports announcer U. Iowa, swimming. Home and Office: 2020 Ridgeway Dr Iowa City IA 52245-3238

STEIN, ROBERT ALAN, electronics company executive; b. Chgo., Oct. 18, 1930; s. Manfred and Mildred (Rosenfield) S.; m. Frances Roslyn Berger, Dec. 25, 1960; 1 dau., Marcia Beth. BA, U. Chgo., 1950, MBA, 1953. C.P.A., Ill. Sr. auditor Scovell, Wellington & Co., Chgo., 1955-63; supr. corp. acctg. Mack Trucks, Inc., Montvale, N.J., 1963-65; v.p. fin., treas. Lionel Corp., N.Y.C., 1965-82; pres. ITI Electronics, Inc., Fairfield, N.J., 1982—. Served with U.S. Army, 1953-55. Mem. Am. Inst. CPAs. Home: 32 Stonewall Dr Livingston NJ 07039-1822 Office: 12 Kulick Rd Fairfield NJ 07004-3308 E-mail: itielect@aol.com.

STEIN, ROBERT FOSTER, astrophysicist, educator; b. N.Y.C., Mar. 4, 1935; s. Arthur H. and Louise (Halpern) S.; m. Laura Cooper, Dec. 21, 1958; children: Karen, Tamara. BS, U. Chgo., 1957; PhD, Columbia U., 1966. Lectr. CCNY, N.Y.C., 1959-61; rsch. fellow Mt. Wilson and Palomar Obs., Pasadena, Calif., 1966-67, Harvard Coll. Obs., Cambridge, Mass., 1967-69; asst. prof. astrophysics Brandeis U., Waltham, 1969-76; assoc. prof. astronomy Mich. State U., East Lansing, 1976-80, prof. physics and astronomy, 1981—. Cons. Smithsonian Astrophys. Obs., Cambridge, 1969-79, NASA, Washington, 1980-82, Jet Propulsion Lab., Pasadena, 1983-88; vis. fellow Joint Inst. Lab. Astrophys., Boulder, 1973-74. Author: Stellar Evolution, 1966; contbr. numerous articles to sci. publs. Mem. Am. Astron. Soc., Internat. Astron. Union, Norwegian Acad. Sci. and Letters, Lansing Area Folklore Soc. (dance coord. 1977-87, membership coord. 1989-92, co-treas. 1992—). Avocations: square and contra dancing. Office: Dept Physics/Astronomy Mich State U East Lansing MI 48824

STEIN, ROGER RICHARD, microcomputer specialist, educator; b. N.Y.C., Apr. 2, 1942; s. Ronald H. and Gertrude (Savine) S. BA, C.W. Post Coll., 1963; MS in Edn., Hofstra U., 1967. Cert. sch. libr. N.Y., N.J., Fla. Sch. libr. Hicksville (N.Y.) Pub. Schs., 1963-64, Massapequa (N.Y.) Pub. Schs., 1964-70, N.Y.C. Pub. Schs., 1970-76, 80-85; mgr. software configuration libr. ITT Avionics, Nutley, N.J., 1985-87; computer systems specialist Tech. Devel. Ctr., Clearwater, Fla., 1988—. Adj. instr. St. Petersburg Jr. Coll., 1990—; cert. adminstr. Novell Netware. Editor Added Entries newsletter, 1965-68; contbr. articles to newsletters. Avocations: music, theater, reading. Home: 127 Irwin St E Safety Harbor FL 34695-2763 Office: Pinellas County Govt MIS Info Ctr 400 S Fort Harrison Ave Clearwater FL 33756-5113

STEIN, RUTH ELIZABETH KLEIN, physician; b. N.Y.C., Nov. 2, 1941; d. Theodore and Mimi (Foges) Klein; m. H. David Stein, June 9, 1963; children: Lynn Andrea Stein Melnick, Sharon Lisa, Deborah Michelle. AB, Barnard Coll., 1962; MD, Albert Einstein Coll. Medicine, 1966. Diplomate Am. Bd. Pediat. Intern, then resident Bronx Mcpl. Hosp. Ctr., 1966-68; sr. resident, fellow; instr. dept. pediats. George Washington U., Washington, 1968-70; with Albert Einstein Coll. of Medicine, Bronx, 1970-77, assoc. prof. pediats., 1977-83, prof., 1983—; vice-chmn. dept. pediats. Albert Einstein Coll., 1992—, dir. office of acad. affairs, dept. pediats., 1997—; pediatrician-in-chief, dir. pediats. Jacobi Med. Ctr. (formerly Bronx Mcpl. Hosp. Ctr.), 1992-97. Vis. prof. pub. health dept. epidemiology Yale U. Sch. of Medicine, New Haven, 1986-87; scholar-in-residence United Hosp. Fund, N.Y., 1995-97; dir., prin. investigator Preventive Intervention Rsch. Ctr. for Child Health, N.Y., 1983-94, Nat. Child Health Assessment Planning Project, N.Y., Behavioral Pediatric Tng. Program, N.Y.; dir. gen. pediatrics Pediat. Divsn., N.Y., 1992-97; apptd. to Montefiore Med. Ctr., North Ctrl. Bronx Hosp., Jacobi Med. Ctr.; bd. dirs. Ctr. for Child Health Rsch. of Am. Acad. Pediatrics, mem. exec. com., 1999—. Editor: Caring for Children with Chronic Illness: Issues and Strategies, 1989, Health Care for Children: What's Right, What's Wrong, What's Next, 1997; mem. editorial bd. Jour. Behavioral and Devel. Pediatrics, Jour. Ambulatory Pediatrics; contbr. articles to profl. jours. Fellow Am. Acad. Pediats.; mem. APHA, Am. Pediatric Soc., Soc. for Pediat. Rsch., Ambulatory Pediat. Assn. (bd. dirs. 1982-89, pres. 1987-88, rsch. award 1995, Ray Helper award 1999), N.Y. Acad. Medicine (chmn. N.Y. forum on child health 2001--), Soc. for Devel. and Behavioral Pediats., Alpha Omega Alpha. Jewish. Home: 91 Larchmont Ave Larchmont NY 10538-3748 Office: Albert Einstein Coll Med Montefiore Med Ctr Centennial 1 111 E 210 St Bronx NY 10467-2804 E-mail: rstein@montefiore.org., rstein@aecom.yu.edu.

STEIN, SEENA DEBORAH, real estate executive; b. Bronx, N.Y., Apr. 20, 1941; d. Al Israeloff and Esther (Barcan) Wallace; m. Fred Heiman, June 22, 1968 (div. 1973); m. Sanford Stein, Nov. 2, 1974; children: Neil, Hope, Rachel, Sara, Rachel. BS, Purdue U., 1963; MLS, Rutgers U., 1970, MBA, 1978. Dir. info. Engelhard, Edison, N.J., 1967-72, Coll. Medicine and Dentistry N.J., Piscataway, 1972-76; rsch. assoc. Wall Street, N.Y.C., 1978; sr. v.p. Archie Schwartz, East Orange, N.J., 1979-82; pres., owner Seena Stein, Inc., Somerset, 1982-83; v.p., dir. sales Helmsley-Spear, Inc., Secaucus, 1983-85; with Jacobson Goldfarb & Tanzman, Woodbridge, 1985; sr. v.p., dir. sales and leasing Jacobson, Goldfarb & Tanzman, 1985-93; pres. Newmark Real Estate of N.J., Inc., Rutherford, 1993—2001. Mem. Nat. Assn. Corp. Real Estate Execs. (bd. dirs.), Indsl. and Office Real Estate Brokers Assn. (bd. dirs.), Indsl. and Comml. Real Estate for Women (mem. exec. com. 1984—), Nat. Assn. Indsl. and Office Parks, Assn. Exec. and Profl. Women (N.J. chpt.), Soc. Indsl. and Office Realtors. Jewish. Home: 108 Rumson Rd Rumson NJ 07760-1241 Office: Newmark Real Estate of NJ 301 Route 17 Rutherford NJ 07070-2575

STEIN, SEYMOUR, electronics scientist; b. Bklyn., Apr. 4, 1928; s. Louis Harry and Clara (Roth) S.; m. Corinne Leader, Sept. 14, 1954; children: Paul M., Emily L. BEE, CCNY, 1949; MS in Applied Physics, Harvard U., 1950, PhD in Applied Physics, 1955. Sr. engring. specialist Applied Rsch. Lab., GTE Sylvania, Waltham, Mass., 1954-56, sr. scientist, 1959-64, assoc. dir., 1964-66; dir. Communications Systems Lab., GTE Sylvania, 1966-69; staff mem. Hermes Electronics, Cambridge, Mass., 1956-59; pres. Stein Assocs. div. Adams-Russell Co. Waltham, 1969-79; with SCPE, Newton Centre, Mass., 1979—. Co-author: Communications Systems and Techniques, 1966, 2nd edit., 1995, Modern Communication Principles, 1967. Fellow IEEE. Jewish. Office: SCPE 56 Great Meadow Rd Newton MA 02459-2748

STEIN, SOL, publisher, writer, editor in chief; b. Chgo., Oct. 13, 1926; s. Louis and Zelda (Zam) S.; m. Patricia Day, Mar. 31, 1962 (div. Oct. 1997); children: Kevin David, Jeffrey Lewelyn, Leland Dana, Robert Bruce, Andrew Charles, David Day, Elizabeth Day; m. Edith Tennenbaum Shapiro, Nov. 25, 2000. BSS, CCNY, 1948; MA, Columbia U., 1949, postgrad., 1949-51. Lectr. social studies CCNY, 1948-51; sr. editor, ideological adv. staff Voice of Am., U.S. State Dept., 1951-53; gen. editor, originator Beacon Press Paperbacks, Boston, 1954—; cons. to pres. Harcourt, Brace, Jovanovich, N.Y.C., 1958-59; exec. v.p. The Mid-Century Book Soc., 1959-62; pres., editor in chief Stein & Day Pubs., Briarcliff Manor, N.Y., 1962-89; pres. The Colophon Corp., Scarborough, 1983-95, The WritePro Corp., 1989—, The Stein Software Corp., 1993—. Lectr., playwright Columbia U., 1958-60, Dialogue for Writers, Pub., U. Calif., Irvine, 1990-93; treas. The Forensic Found., N.Y.C., 1959-62; founding mem. Playwrights Group, The Actors Studio, 1957. Author: (plays) The Illegitimist, 1953 (1st prize Dramatists Alliance), A Shadow of My Enemy, 1957, (novels) The Husband, 1969, The Magician, 1971. Living Room, 1974, The Childkeeper, 1975, Other People, 1979, The Resort, 1980, The Touch of Treason, 1985, A Deniable Man, 1989, The Best Revenge, 1991 (computer software) WritePro, The Stein Creative Writing Program, 1989—, FirstAid for Writers, 1991, FictionMaster, 1993, WritePro for Business, 1996; (non-fiction) A Feast for Lawyers, 1989, Stein on Writing, 1995, How to Grow a Novel, 1999; also articles, revs. poetry. Exec. dir. Am. Com. for Cultural Freedom, 1953-56; mem. exec. com. Am. Friends of Captive Nations. Served to 1st lt. AUS, 1945-47. Fellow Yaddo Found., 1952, MacDowell Colony, 1952-56. Recipient Disting. Instr. award U. Calif. at Irvine, 1992. Mem. New Dramatists Com. (coun. mem.), Internat. Brotherhood Magicians (hon. life), Writers Guild Am. East, Authors Guild, Phi Beta Kappa. Avocations: tennis, inventing computer software programs. Office: 277 E South Broadway Tarrytown NY 10591-5322 E-mail: solstein@aol.com.

STEIN, STEPHEN WILLIAM, lawyer; b. N.Y.C., Apr. 12, 1937; s. Melvin S. and Cornelia (Jacobowitz) S.; m. Judith N., Jan. 22, 1966. AB, Princeton U., 1959; LLB, Columbia U., 1962; LLM, NYU, 1963. Bar: N.Y. 1962, Fla. 1962. Assoc. White & Case, N.Y.C., 1963-67; atty. advisor U.S. Agy. Internat. Devel., Washington, 1967-69, regional legal advisor Mission to India New Delhi, 1969-71, asst. gen. counsel Washington, 1971-73; assoc. ptnr. Delson & Gordon, N.Y.C., 1973-87; ptnr. Kelley Drye & Warren, 1987—. Mem. U.S. exec. com. Indonesian Trade, Tourism & Investment Promotion Program, 1990-92; mem. U.S.-Indonesia Trade & Investment Adv. Com., 1989-92; vis. instr. internat. Devel. Law Inst., 1993; lectr. Internat. Law Inst., Washington, 1984, 85; spkr. in field. Mem. ABA (mem. sect. internat. law, co-chair African law com. 1999-2002), Internat. Bar Assn. (mem. sect. energy resources law, sect. bus. law, mem. various coms.), Assn. Bar of City of N.Y. (mem. com. project fin. 1997—, mem. com. Asian affairs 1992—, former mem. others), Am. Indonesian C. of C. (bd. dirs. 1986—, pres. 1989-96). Home: 320 Central Park W New York NY 10025-7659 Office: Kelley Drye & Warren 101 Park Ave Fl 30 New York NY 10178-0062 E-mail: sstein@kelleydrye.com.

STEIN, THEODORE ANTHONY, biochemist, educator; b. St. Louis, Aug. 30, 1938; s. Leonard A. and Mathilda M. S.; m. Virginia M. Loos, 1994. BS, St. Louis U., 1960; MS, So. Ill. U., 1970; PhD, CUNY, 1987. Rsch. instr. surgery Washington U. Sch. Medicine, St. Louis, 1972-75; rsch. supr. surgery L.I. Jewish-Hillside Med. Ctr., New Hyde Park, N.Y., 1975-76, rsch. coord. surgery, 1977-93; asst. prof. surgery SUNY, Stony Brook, 1978-89, Albert Einstein Sch. Medicine, Bronx, N.Y., 1989—. Dir. rsch. and dir. vascular lab. L.I. Vascular Ctr., Roslyn, N.Y., 1994—; biostats. cons. NIH grantee, 1962; Am. Liver Found. grantee, 1984. Contbr. articles to profl. jours., chpts. to books. Mem. AAAS, N.Y. Acad. Scis., Am. Fedn. Clin. Rsch., Am. Pub. Health Assn., Am. Gastroenterol. Assn., Sigma Xi. Republican. Roman Catholic. Achievements include development of chromatographic methods to determine prostaglandin and leukotriene content in tissues using fluorescent agents to increase sensitivity, elastase activity in the aorta with disease, and active anabolites of 5-fluoracil in tumors; improvement of regulation of liver growth after surgery by diet; demonstration of diagnostic value of liver function tests, surgery on obese patients interferes with sugar metabolism and intestinal function; research in etiology of pancreatitis and pharmacological modification of pancreatic function; effect of stress on the stomach and colon; investigation of the mediators of inflammatory bowel disease, the long-term reduction of stroke after carotid endarterectomy, the benefit of composite grafts for distal limb salvage, the value of completion angiography for distal bypass, risk factors which may be related to rapid growth of abdominal aortic aneurysms, the value of axillo-axillary bypass grafts. Home: 10 Glamford Rd Port Washington NY 11050-2437 Office: LI Vascular Ctr 1050 Northern Blvd Roslyn NY 11576-1503 E-mail: tajcs@optonline.net.

STEIN, THOMAS HENRY, social science educator; b. Elmhurst, Ill., May 17, 1949; s. Peter Leonard and Marion Edith (Zirbel) S.; m. Alberta Piazza, July 10, 1971; 1 child, Heather. BA in Polit. Sci., Loyola U., Chgo., 1971; postgrad., Loyola U., 1972-76; MS in Edn., Pacific Western U., 1988, PhD in Edn., 1989. Cert. tchr., Ill. Budget analyst U.S. Dept. Def., Gt. Lakes Naval Sta., Ill., 1971-72; tchr. social sci., coach bowling, softball Mother Guerin High Sch., River Grove, 1972—; tchr. Highland Park (Ill.) High Sch., 1981-84. Instr. Franklin Park (Ill.) Park Dist., 1977—; tchr. Triton Coll., River Grove, 1990-91; evaluator Chgo. Met. History Fair, 1980-89; faculty adviser Scholastic, Inc., N.Y.C., 1990—; dir. Students Against Animal Cruelty, River Grove, 1991—; mod. Nat. Honor Soc., 1993—. With Ill. N.G., 1971-77. Recipient Outstanding Achievement award Am. Express/Assn. Am. Geographers, 1989. Fellow Acad. Polit. Sci.; mem. ASCD, Nat. Coun. Social Studies, Nat. Hist. Soc., Ctr. Study of the Presidency, Nat. Cath. Edn. Assn., Orgn. History Tchrs., Am. Polit. Sci. Assn. Democrat. Roman Catholic. Avocations: bowling, politics, baseball, animal activism, fitness training. Home: 3601 Emerson St Franklin Park IL 60131-1713 Office: Mother Guerin High Sch 8001 W Belmont Ave River Grove IL 60171-1096

STEIN, TOMIKO, infectious disease specialist; b. New Delhi, July 27, 1966; s. George Jay and Mitsue (Tokuzawa) S. BA, Smith Coll., 1988; MD, MPH, Tulane U., 1992. Intern Baylor Coll. Medicine, Houston, 1992-93, resident in internal medicine, 1993-95; fellow in infectious diseases L.A. Co-Harbor UCLA Med. Ctr., Torrance, 1995-97, fellow in HIV, 1997-98; physician AIDS Healthcare Found., L.A., 1999—. Mem. ACP, Infectious Disease Assn. Calif. (assoc.), Infectious Disease Soc. Am. (assoc.). Office: AIDS Healthcare Found 1300 N Vermont Ave Ste 407 Los Angeles CA 90027-6005 Business E-Mail: tomikos@aidshealth.org.

STEINACHER, RONALD, music educator; b. Carrollton, Ill., Feb. 25, 1955; s. Eugene Carl and Catherine Alfreda Steinacher. BA, Ea. Ill. U., Charleston, IL, 1977; MS, Ill. State U., Normal, IL, 1986, Cert. Advanced Study, Edn. Adminstrn., 1990. Tchr.: grades 5-8 gen. music, 6-12 choir Reed Custer Sch. Dist. #255U, Braidwood, Ill., 1977—79, tchr.: grades 5-8 gen. music, 5-8 choir, 6th grade english, 1979—84, tchr.: grade 4, classroom, 1984—94; tchr.: grade k-5 gen. music, elem. band Reed Custer Sch. Dist. #225U, 1994—99; tchr.: grade 1-5 gen. music, elem. band Reed Custer Sch. Dist. #255U, 1999—. Curriculum revision, negotiating team, staff devel., superentendent cabinet mem., team leader, mentor tchr. Reed Custer Dist. #255U, Braidwood, Ill., 1977—. Exec. sec. Reed Custer Ednl. Assn., Braidwood, Ill., 1989—91. Mem.: Universalist Unitarian Ch.: fund raising. Universalist Unitarian. Avocations: gardening, choral singing, choral singing, restauranting. Home: 23236 Pilcher Road Plainfield IL 60544 Office: Reed Custer School District #255U 255 Comet Drive Plainfield IL 60544 Personal E-mail: ronsteinacher@hotmail.com.

STEINBACH, HAROLD I. lawyer; b. Bronx, N.Y., Aug. 31, 1956; s. Aaron and Phyllis (Feldfeber) S.; m. Beryl Joy Schwartz, Mar. 14, 1982; children: Sarah Brandl, Rachel Beth, Avi Michael. BA, SUNY, Binghamton, 1978; JD, NYU, 1981. Bar: N.Y. 1982, N.J. 1983, U.S. Dist. Ct. (so. dist.) N.Y. 1982. Assoc. Flemming, Zulack & Williamson, N.Y.C., 1981-83; assoc., then ptnr. Kleinberg, Kaplan, Wolff & Cohen, P.C., 1983-2000; ptnr. Parker Duryee Rosoff & Haft, PC, 2000—01; ptnrr. Harold I. Steinbach, P.C., Hackensack, NJ, 2002—. Trustee Jewish Braille Inst. Am., Inc., 1992—. Mem. N.Y. State Bar Assn. (bus. law and property law sects.), Phi Beta Kappa. Jewish. Home: 665 Ogden Ave Teaneck NJ 07666-2203 Office: Univ Plz Ste 412 Hackensack NJ 07601 Office Fax: 201-584-0353. E-mail: harold@steinbachesq.com.

STEINBACH, MEREDITH LYNN, novelist; b. Ames, Iowa, Mar. 18, 1949; d. Christopher Gene and Joy Janice (Johnson) Steinbach; m. Charles Ossian Hartman, May 5, 1979 (div. Dec. 1991); 1 child Zachary Steinbach Hartman. BGS, U. Iowa, 1973, MFA, 1976. Teaching fellow U. Iowa, Iowa City, 1975-76; writer in residence Antioch Coll., Yellow Springs, Ohio, 1976-77; lectr. in fiction Northwestern U., Evanston, Ill., 1977-79; vis. asst. prof. U. Washington, 1979-82; Bunting fellow Harvard-Radcliffe, Cambridge, Mass., 1982-83; asst., assoc. prof. Brown U., Providence, 1983-97, prof. English, 1997—. Author: Zara, 1982, Here Lies the Water, 1990, Reliable Light, 1990, The Birth of the World As We Know It, Or, Teiresias, 1996, In the Realm of Which There Is No Sign, 1995. Recipient Pushcart prize Best of the Small Presses, 1976, R.I. award for Excellence in Lit., R.I. Coun. on Arts, 1986-87, O'Henry award for the short story, 1990, creative writing fellow in fiction Nat. Endowment for Arts, 1978; Thomas J. Watson travel grantee Thomas J. Watson Inst. for Internat. Study, France and Greece, 1993-94. Mem. PEN, Amnesty Internat., Assoc. Writing Programs. Office: Brown U Dept of English Box 1852 Providence RI 02912 E-mail: Meredith_Steinbach@Brown.edu.

STEINBARGER, KIMBERLY ANN, physical therapist, educator; b. Charleston, SC, Mar. 13, 1967; d. Bruce Richard and Mary Ann McKenna; m. Everett Jeremy Steinbarger, Sept. 18, 1993. BS, Daemen Coll., 1989; earning M of Health Sci., U. Indpls., 1996—. lic. physical therapist, Michigan, Indiana. Physical therapist Queens Hosp., Honolulu, 1989-92; instr. Kapiolana Cmty. Coll., Kailua, HI, 1991; physical therapist Nova Care, Napa, CA, 1992-94, Sturgis, MI, 1994-95; clin. coord. Concept Rehab., Kalamazoo, 1995-97; instr. Michiana Coll., South Bend, IN, 1997-98, program dir., 1998—2000. Guest lectr. Western Mich. U., Kalamazoo, 1999-01; item writer Fedn. of State Bds. Physical Therapy, Alexandria, Va., 1999. Mem. Am. Physical Therapy Assn., Arthritis Found. Office: Michiana College 1030 E Jefferson Blvd South Bend IN 46617-3123 E-mail: Kimberste@hotmail.com.

STEINBAUER, ROBERT A. retired music educator; b. Niles, Mich., May 20, 1926; s. Perley J. and Myrta Eva Steinbauer; m. June Louise Young, Sept. 6, 1947; children: Jeffrey R., Martha June. MusB, U. Mich., 1950, MusM, 1951; MusD, Ind. U., 1959. Cert. music tchr. Head music dept. SC Sch. for Blind, Spartanburg, 1951—53; head keyboard dept. Drury U., Springfield, Mo., 1953—59, Wichita (Kans.) State U., 1959—69, U. Nev., Las Vegas, 1969—70; head music dept. Kans. State U., Manhattan, Kans., 1970—88; ret., 1988. Instr. music history, art history Edison C.C., Ft. Myers, Fla., 1989—98; instr. music history and piano U. Mary Hardin Baylor, Belton, Tex., 1999—. Founder, editor: Music Svc. Guild newsletter; contbr. articles to profl. publs. Chmn. edn. bd. Nat. Piano Found., Chgo., 1977—85; pres. Manhattan Rotary Club, 1983—85; mem. ambassadors Manhattan C. of C., 1980—88; chmn. United Way, 1977; v.p. mil. affairs Manhattan C. of C., 1978, chmn. cultural affairs, 1975; founder Manhattan Cultural Arts Assn., Kans. State U. Music Svc. Guild. Sgt. U.S. Army, 1944—46. Mem.: Coll. Music Soc., Am. Coll. Musicians (bd. dirs.), Music Tchrs. Nat. Assn. (bd. dirs.), Nat. Assn. Schs. of Music, Sinfonia. Democrat. Presbyterian. Avocations: landscaping, golf, travel. Home: 513 Neches Dr Belton TX 76513

STEINBERG, ALAN WOLFE, investment company executive; b. Bklyn., Oct. 26, 1927; s. Benjamin F. and Gertrude (Wolfe) S.; m. Suzanne Nichols, Oct. 12, 1958; children: Carol Albanese, Laura Frohman, Benjamin T. AB with honors and spl. distinction in math, Columbia U., 1947, MS, 1950. Indsl. engr. USDA, Washington, 1948-50; ops. rschr. Port of N.Y. Authority, 1950-55; prof. engring. NYU, 1956-63; pres. Am. Computing Ctrs., N.Y.C., 1962-66; v.p., dir. TBS Computer Ctrs., 1967-76; mng. ptnr. Alan W. Steinberg Partnership, N.Y.C. and Coral Gables, Fla., 1974—. Contbr. articles to profl. jours. Nat. advisor automation United Jewish Appeal, N.Y.C., 1965-75; trustee Fla. Nature Conservancy, Winter Park, 1990—, treas., 1990—; bd. dirs., treas. Fla. Audubon Soc., Casselberry, 1984-95, Defenders of Wildlife, Washington, 1985-95, chmn. bd. dirs. 1995-98; 1st v.p. Tropical Audubon Soc., South Miami, 1983-93. Recipient Chmn.'s award Fla. Audubon Soc., 1989, 93; funded named scholarship Columbia Coll. Fellow Fairchild Tropical Garden; mem. Columbia Coll. Alumni Assn. (bd. dirs. 1992-93, sustaining), Phi Beta Kappa. Home: 5522 Riviera Dr Coral Gables FL 33146-2747 Office: 1501 Venera Ave Ste 205 Coral Gables FL 33146-3052 E-mail: SteinbergX@aol.com.

STEINBERG, AMY WISHNER, dermatologist; b. N.Y.C., Nov. 19, 1959; d. Arnold Blaine and Sylvia Fay (Bernoff) Wishner; m. Alan Lloyd Steinberg, June 15, 1986; children: Joshua Darren, Arielle Dana, Natalie Tara. BS, Northwestern U., Evanston, Ill., 1981; MD, Northwestern U., Chgo., 1983. Clin. instr. Univ. Hosp., Stony Brook, N.Y., 1987—; pvt. practice, 1987—. Fellow Am. Acad. Dermatology; mem. Suffolk Dermatology Soc., Internat. Soc. Dermatology, N.Y. State Dermatology Soc. Office: 2500 Route 347 Bldg 5 Stony Brook NY 11790-2527

STEINBERG, ARTHUR IRWIN, periodontist, educator; b. Pitts., Sept. 16, 1935; s. Ben and Sylvia (Jacobs) S.; m. Barbara Fay Ehrenkranz, May 23, 1959; chldren: Sharon Jill, Mindy Ruth, Michael Eli. BS in Microbiology, U. Pitts., 1957, DMD cum laude, 1963, postgrad. in radiobiology, 1957-59; diploma in periodontology-immunology, Harvard U., 1966. Asst. prof. periodontology SUNY, Buffalo, 1966-67; assoc. prof. periodontology Temple U., Phila., 1967-68, assoc. prof. grad. periodontology, 1968-70; attending periodontist Phoenixville (Pa.) Hosp., 1971—; clin. assoc. prof. U. Pa. Sch. Dental Medicine, 2001—. Mem. infections control com., by-laws com., religious affairs com., 1977—, credentials com., 1982—; mem. staff Suburban Gen. Hosp. Norristown, Pa., 1971-80, Phoenixville Hosp., 1968-95; asst. prof. periodontics U. Pa., 1973-82, clin. assoc. prof., 1982—; lectr. continuing edn., off-campus program U. Pitts., 1973-93; Fulbright-Hays lectr. Nat. U. Ireland, Cork, 1970-71; vis. prof. Cork Dental Sch. and Hosp., 1971—; lectr. Periodontology Soc. Madrid, 1980, 5th Region Soc. Periodontology Viña Del Mar, Chile, 1985; dentist in pediatrics Charlestown (Mass.) Boys Club, 1965-66; spkr. Periodontists Conv., Chgo., 1966, N.J. Coll. Medicine and Dentistry, Conn. Dental Assn., 1967, U. Ind. Schs. Dentistry and Medicine, Phila. Ann. Dental Sci. Session, 1969, N.J. Dental Assn., 1970, Wilmington chpt. Sigma Epsilon Delta, 1974, Lehigh Valley Dental Soc.m 1974, Inst. Medicine, Bucharest, Romania, 1976, Irish Dental Assn., 1992, other confs., and convs.; participant Project Head Start, Childrens Hosp., Boston, 1966; mem. fund-raising subcom. Harvard U. Sch. Dental Medicine, 1980—; mem. faculty U. Pitts., 1988-93; commencement spkr. U. Pa. Sch. Dental Medicine, 1988, Harcum Coll. Dental Hygiene Program, 1994-95; presenter Phila. County Dental Soc., Ann. Meeting Liberty Dental Conf., 1988, 90, Acad. Gen. Dentistry Ann. Meeting, 1988; judge divsn. medicine and healthcare Del. Valley Sci. Fair, 1997. Contbg. author: The Fulbright Experience, 1987, Dentistry and the Allergic Patient, 1973; contbr. numerous articles to profl. jours. Named to Phoenixville Hosp. Hall of Honor, 1996; USPHS fellow. Fellow Acad. Dentistry Internat., Internat. Acad. Dental Studies, Am. Coll. Dentists, Coll. Physicians Phila., Pierre Fuchard Acad.; mem. AMA, AAUP, Harvard Dental, Fulbright alumni assns., Harvard Odontological Soc., Fulbright Assn., Nat. Fulbright Alumni Assn. (a founder 1976, v.p.fin. affairs 1976-79), Am. Acad. Periodontology (ins. com. 1969, hosp. care com. 1973-74, continuing edn. spkr. 1976 conv., 1983 conv., nominating com. chmn. Pa. region to exec. coun. 1975, nat. clin. affairs com. 1984), Am. Coll. Clin. Pharmacology, Northea. Soc. Periodontists, Acad. Stomatology Phila., Phila. Acad. Scis., Sigma Xi, Omicron Kappa Upsilon, Psi Omega (dep. councillor Zeta chpt. 1977-79), Masons (32 degree Shriner), Legion Honor Chapel Four Chaplains, Rotary (dir. 1973-76, chmn. found. com., chmn. internat. svc. 1974-76), B'nai B'rith, Hadassah (assoc. mem.), Harvard of Phila., 25 Yr. Club U. Pa., Area Study (pres. 1976-77), Am. Soc. of Ret. Dentists. Home and Office: 1681 Pheasant Ln Norristown PA 19403-3331 E-mail: arthurst@pobox.upenn.edu.

STEINBERG, DANIEL, preventive medicine physician, educator; b. Windsor, Ont., Can., July 21, 1922; came to U.S., 1922; s. Maxwell Robert and Bess (Krupp) S.; m. Sara Murdock, Nov. 30, 1946 (dec. July 1986); children: Jonathan Henry, Ann Ballard, David Ethan; m. Mary Ellen Strathaus, Aug. 11, 1991; 1 stepchild: Katrin Seifert. BS with highest distinction, Wayne State U., 1941, MD with highest distinction, 1944; PhD with distinction (fellow Am. Cancer Soc. 1950-51), Harvard U., 1951; MD (hon.), U. Gothenburg, 1991. Intern Boston City Hosp., 1944-45; physician Detroit Receiving Hosp., 1945-46; instr. physiology Boston U. Sch. Medicine, 1947-48; joined USPHS, 1951, med. dir., 1959; research staff lab. cellular physiology and metabolism Nat. Heart Inst., 1951-53, chief sect. metabolism, 1956-61, chief of lab. metabolism, 1962-68; lectr. grad. program NIH, 1955, mem. sci. adv. com. ednl. activities, 1955-61, com. chmn., 1955-60; mem. metabolism study sect. USPHS, 1959-61; chmn. heart and lung research rev. com. B Nat. Heart, Lung and Blood Inst., 1977-79; vis. scientist Carlsberg Labs., Copenhagen, 1952-53, Nat. Inst. Med. Research, London, 1960-61, Rockefeller U., 1981; pres. Lipid Research Inc., 1961-64, adv. bd., 1964-73; prof. medicine Sch. Medicine, U. Calif., San Diego, 1968—. Former editor Jour. Lipid Research; mem. editorial bd. Jour Clin. Investigation, 1969-74, Jour. Biol. Chemistry, 1980-84, Arteriosclerosis, 1980— ; exec. editor Analytical Biochemistry, 1978-80; contbr. articles to profl. jours. Bd. dirs. Found. Advanced Edn. in Scis., 1959-68, pres., 1956-62, 65-67. Served to capt. M.C. AUS, World War II. Mem. Nat. Acad. Scis., AAAS, Am. Acad. Arts and Scis., Am. Heart Assn. (mem. exec. com. coun. on arteriosclerosis 1960-63, 65-73, chmn. coun. arteriosclerosis 1967-69), Fedn. Am. Scientists (exec. com. 1957-58), Am. Soc. Biol. Chemists, Am. Soc. Clin. Investigation, Assn. Am. Physicians, Am. Fedn. Clin. Rsch., Inst. Medicine, European Atherosclerosis Discussion Group, Alpha Omega Alpha. Home: 7742 Whitefield Pl La Jolla CA 92037-3810 Office: U Calif San Diego Dept Medicine 9500 Gilman Dr La Jolla CA 92093-0682 E-mail: dsteinberg@ucsd.edu., dsteinb1@san.rr.com.

STEINBERG, DAVID ISAAC, economic development consultant, educator; b. Cambridge, Mass., Nov. 26, 1928; s. Naaman and Miriam (Goldberg) S.; m. Isabel Maxwell, 1951 (div. 1962); 1 child, Christopher; m. Ann Myongsook Lee, May 15, 1964; children: Alexander L., Eric D. BA, Dartmouth Coll., 1950; MA, Harvard U., 1955; DLitt (hon.), Sungkunkwan U., Seoul, Republic of Korea. Analyst Nat. Security Coun., Washington, 1951-53; program officer Asia Found., N.Y.C., 1956-58, asst. rep. Burma, 1958-62, Hong Kong, 1962-63, rep. Republic of Korea, 1963-68, Washington, 1968-69; cons., sr. fgn. svc. officer AID, Washington and Bangkok (Thailand), 1969-86; ret., 1986; pres. Mansfield Ctr. for Pacific Affairs, Helena, Mont., 1986-87, Sr. Resources Internat., 1989-94; disting. prof. Korea Studies Georgetown U., Washington, 1990-94; rep. The Asia Found., Seoul, Republic of Korea, 1994-97; dir. Asian studies Sch. Fgn. Svc. Georgetown U., Washington, 1997—; Disting. prof., 1997—. Pvt. cons., Washington, 1987—, World Bank, 1987—, Woodrow Wilson Ctr. for Scholars of the Smithsonian Instn., Dept. of State and the Agy. for Internat. Devel., the Can. Internat. Devel. Agy., Devel. Assocs., Inc., and others; founding mem. Burma Studies Found., De Kalb, Ill., 1987. Author: Burma's Road Toward Development, 1981, Burma, 1982, The Republic of Korea Economic Transformation and Social Change, 1988, The Future of Burma, 1990, Burma: The State of Myanmar, 2001. 1st lt. U.S. Army, 1953-55. Fellow Lingnan U., Canton, China, 1948, Dartmouth Coll., 1950; named Disting. Prof. of Korea Studies, Georgetown U. Mem. Assn. Asian Studies, Oriental Ceramic Soc., Asia Devel. Roundtable (chmn. 1984-86, 87—), Siam Soc., Royal Asiatic Soc. (life Korea br.), Burma Rsch. Soc. (life), Asia Soc. (cons. 1988—), Cosmos Club, Royal Bangkok (Thailand) Sports Club. Home: 6207 Goodview St Bethesda MD 20817-6101 Office: Georgetown U Sch Fgn Svc 6207 Goodview St Bethesda MD 20817 E-mail: tafko2@mcimail.com., stienbdi@georgetown.edu.

STEINBERG, DAVID JOEL, academic administrator, historian, educator; b. N.Y.C., Apr. 5, 1937; s. Milton and Edith (Alpert) S.; m. Sally Levitt (div. Dec., 1986); children: Noah, Jonah; m. Joan Diamond, Aug. 28, 1987. BA magna cum laude, Harvard U., 1959, MA, 1963, PhD, 1964; LittD, Kyung Hee U., Seoul, Korea, 1989; LLD (hon), Keimyung U., Daegu, Korea. Prof. history U. Mich., 1964-73; exec. asst. to pres. Brandeis U., Waltham, Mass., 1973-77, v.p., univ. sec., 1977-83; pres. L.I. U., Brookville, N.Y., 1985—. Testified before Com. on Fgn. Affairs, U.S. Ho. of Reps., Fgn. Affairs Com. of U.S. Senate; cons. The Ford Found., UN Fund for Population Activities. Author: Philippine Collaboration in World War II, 1967 (Univ. Press award 1969), The Philippines: A Singular and a Plural Place, 1982, rev. edit., 2000; author (with others) In Search of Southeast Asia: A Modern History, 1970, rev. edit., 1987, Asia in Western and World History: A Guide for Teaching, 1993. Chmn. Commn. Ind. Colls. and Univs.; past pres. Cambridge (Mass.) Ctr. for Adult Edn., chmn. L.I. Group. English Speaking Union Exch. scholar, Malvern Coll., NDEA scholar, Fulbright Found. exch. scholar. Mem. Coun. Fgn. Rels., Assn. Asian Studies (chmn. fin. com.), Harvard Club (N.Y.C.), Century Club (N.Y.C.). Democrat. Jewish. Office: LI Univ Off Pres 700 Northern Blvd Greenvale NY 11548-1320

STEINBERG, DONALD KENNETH, diplomat; b. L.A., Mar. 25, 1953; s. Warren Linnington and Beatrice (Blass) S. BA in Econs., Reed Coll., 1974; MA in Polit. Economy, U. Toronto, Ontario, Can., 1975; MS in Journalism, Columbia U., 1984. Fgn. svc. office gen. U.S. Embassy, Bangui, Ctrl. African Republic, 1976-78; econ.-comml. officer U.S. Consulate, Rio de Janeiro, 1978-80; econ. officer U.S. Embassy, Kuala Lumpur, Malaysia, 1981-83, dep. chief of mission Port Louis, Mauritius, 1984-86; congressional fellow Congressman Richard Gephardt U.S. Ho. Reps., Washington, 1986-87; dir. divsn. textile affairs Econ. and Bus. Bur. Dept. of State, 1987-88; chief textile negotiator (acting) Office U.S. Trade Rep. Exec. Office Pres., 1988-89; dir. Ho. Reps. Task Force on Trade and Competitiveness, 1989; sr. advisor for fgn. affairs and defense Office Majority Leader U.S. Ho. Reps., 1989-90; officer in charge and counselor econ. and comml. affairs U.S. Embassy, Praetoria, S. Africa, 1990-93; dep. white house press sec. for nat. security affairs spl. Pres. asst., sr. dir. Pub. Affairs Nat. Security Coun., Washington, 1993-94; spl. asst to Pres., sr. dir. for African affairs Nat. Security Coun., 1994-95; sr. fgn. svc. officer rank of minister-counselor U.S. Dept. State, 1992—; U.S. ambassador Angola, 1995-98; spl. rep. of Pres. and sec. of state Global Humanitarian Demining, 1998—2001; spl. Haiti coord. Dept. of State, 1999-2001, dep. asst. Sec. State for population, refugees, and migration, 2000-01, prin. deputy dir. for policy planning, 2001—. Lectr. on U.S. Trade Policy, Germany, Italy, Austria, U.S. Info. Agy., 1988. Contbr. articles to mags. including The Nation, Asian Jour., African Econ. Digest. Recipient Joseph A. Pulitzer Travelling fellowship Columbia U. Grad. Sch. Journalism, 1984, Commendation Office Equal Employment Opportunity, 1993, Presdl. Meritorious Svc. award, 1994, Robert C. Frasure Meml. Peace award, 1996, Disting. Honor award, 2002. Office: Dept of State Rm 7311 Washington DC 20520-0001 E-mail: d.steinberg@state.gov.

STEINBERG, GREGG MARTIN, financial and management consultant, investment banker; b. Columbus, Ind., Mar. 26, 1962; s. Jerry H. and Sharla C. (Waitzman) S.; m. Stacy A. Schneider, Nov. 6, 1988; 2 children. BSBA, U. Ariz., 1982; M in Mgmt., Am. Grad. Sch. Internat. Mgmt., Glendale, Ariz., 1984. V.p. fin. Bera Hotels Ltd., Phoenix, 1984-85; gen. mgr. Les Jardains Hotel, 1985-87; asst. dir., sr. negotiator GVA Mergers & Acquisitions, 1987-88; pres. Gregg M. Steinberg Ltd., Phoenix and Chgo., 1987—; prin. Berger, Goldstein Capital Group, Inc., Chgo., 1989-91; pres. Internat. Profit Assocs., 1992—, Integrated Bus. Analysis, Toronto, 1994—. Bd. dirs., chmn. N.W. com. Jewish Coun. for Youth Svcs., Chgo., 1989-92; bd. dirs. J.C.C., 1997—. Avocations: golf, squash. Office: Integrated Business Analysis 40 King St W Ste 4900 Toronto ON Canada M5H 4A2

STEINBERG, HOWARD ELI, lawyer, holding company executive, public official; b. N.Y.C., Nov. 19, 1944; s. Herman and Anne Rudel (Sinnreich) S.; m. Judith Ann Schucart, Jan. 28, 1968; children: Henry Robert, Kathryn Jill. AB, U. Pa., 1965; JD, Georgetown U., 1969. Bar: N.Y. 1970, U.S. Dist. Ct. (so. and ea. dists.) N.Y. 1973, U.S. Ct. Appeals (2d cir.) 1976. Assoc. Dewey, Ballantine, Bushby, Palmer & Wood, N.Y.C., 1969-76, ptnr., 1977-83; exec. v.p., gen. counsel Reliance Group Holdings, Inc., 1983-2000, exec. v.p., chief corp. ops., 2000—01; exec. v.p., gen. counsel Prudential Securities Inc., 2001—. Chmn. N.Y. State Thruway Authority, 1996-99; dep. chmn. L.I. Power Authority, 1999—. Editor Georgetown Law Jour., 1968-69. Bd. dir. Puerto Rican Legal Def. and Edn. Fund. Inc., 1993-95, Sheltering Arms Childrens Svc., 1997—; bd. regents Georgetown U., 1999—; bd. overseers U. Pa. Sch. Arts and Scis., 1989—. Capt. JAGC, USAR, 1972-74. Mem. ABA, N.Y. State Bar Assn., Assn. of Bar of City of N.Y. (com. on securities regulation 1984-87, com. on corp. law 1987-90, com. on fed. legis. 1990-93, chair ad hoc com. on Senate Confirmation Process 1991-92), Securities Industry Assn. (mem. fed. regulation com. 2001-, mem. elective com. compliance and legal divsn. 2001-), Univ. Club. Office: Prudential Securities Inc One Seaport Plaza New York NY 10292

STEINBERG, JANET ECKSTEIN, journalist; d. Charles and Adele (Ehrenfeld) Eckstein; m. Irvin S. Silverstein, Oct. 22, 1988; children: Susan Carole Steinberg Somerstein, Jody Lynn Steinberg Lazarow. BS, U. Cin., 1964. Travel cons., 1994—; pub. Paine Webber Vantage Living website, 2000—; guest lectr. Tri State Travel Sch., 1999—2001. Freelance writer: ; guest appearance Braun & Co., Sta. WLW-TV, Sta. WMK-TV; contbr. articles to newspapers, mags., and books; travel editor Am. Israelite, 1996—, Jewish News, 1996—, N.J. Jewish News, 1997—; travel editor: Miami Herald Jewish Star Times, 2002—; travel editor S. Fla. Single Living, 1988—92, Cin. Post, 1978—86, Ky. Post, 1978—86, Cin. Enquirer, 1986—94, MetroWest Jewish News, N.J., 1996—, Jewish News-New Orleans, 1996—, L.A. Jewish Jour., 1997—, NJ Jewish News, 1997—, Miami Herald's Jewish Star Times, 2002—; contbg. editor: Travel Agt., 1986—88, Birnbaum Travel Guides, 1988—98, The Writer, 1988, 1992, 1998, Entree, 1986—97; travel columnist Northeast Mag., 1986—88, South Fla. Single Living, 1984—92, Eastside Weekend Mag., 1994—96. Recipient Lowell Thomas Travel Journalism award, 1984, 1985, 1990, Henry E. Bradshaw travel journalism award, 1st pl., best of show, 1988, Buckeye Travel award, Ohio Divsn. Travl & Tourism, 1992, Cipriani Best Overall WRiter award, 1981, 13 awards, Soc. Am. Travel Writers, 1981—96, 14 awards, Midwest Travel Writers, 1981—99. Home: 900 Adams Xing Ste 9200 Cincinnati OH 45202-1677 E-mail: jxs4travel@aol.com.

STEINBERG, JEFFREY MARC, lawyer, accountant; b. Newark, July 30, 1956; s. Marvin E. and Barbara (Nebret) S.; m. Melanie B. Grabowski, May 22, 1983; 1 child, Jonathan. BSBA, Boston U., 1978; MBA, Fairleigh Dickinson U., 1980; JD, N.Y. Law Sch., 1984. Bar: N.J. 1985, N.Y. 1988. Assoc. Jaffe & Schlesinger, Springfield, N.J., 1987-92; sole practitioner real estate and bankruptcy law, 1992—. Home: 9 Alder Ln Basking Ridge NJ 07920-3708 Office: 32 Commerce St Springfield NJ 07081-3004

STEINBERG, JONATHAN ROBERT, judge; b. Phila., Jan. 3, 1939; s. Sigmund Hopkins and Hortense B. (Gottlieb) S.; m. Rochelle Helene Schwarts, May 30, 1963; children: Andrew Joshua, Amy Judith. BA, Cornell U., 1960; LLB cum laude, U. Pa., 1963. Bar: D.C. 1963, U.S. Ct. Appeals (D.C. cir.) 1964. Law clk. to judge U.S. Ct. Appeals (D.C. cir.), 1963-64; atty. advisor, then dep. gen. counsel Peace Corps, Washington, 1964-69; com. on labor and pub. welfare, counsel subcom. vets. affair U.S. Senate, 1969-71, counsel subcom. on R.R. retirement, 1971-73, counsel spl. subcom. on human resources, 1972-77, chief counsel com. on vets affairs., 1977-81, minority chief counsel and staff dir. com. on vets. affairs, 1981-87, chief counsel and staff dir. com. on vets. affairs, 1987-90; judge U.S. Ct. of Appeals for Vets. Claims, 1990—. Contbr. to legal jours. Bd. dirs. Bethany West Recreation Assn., Bethany Beach, Dels., 1973-84, 86-90. Mem. ABA, D.C. Bar Assn., Order of Coif. Democrat. Jewish. Office: US Ct of Appeals for Vets Claims 625 Indiana Ave NW Ste 900 Washington DC 20004-2917

STEINBERG, JOY NATHANIA, communications executive, graphic media specialist; b. Flemington, N.J., Aug. 2, 1959; d. Rafael Mark and Tamiko (Okamoto) S.; m. Thomas William Malnight, May 5, 1990 (div. July 1992); m. Robert Winslow Graham, Mar. 26, 1994; 1 child, Logan Sei Graham. BA, Bard Coll., 1981. Word processor RMS Word Processing, N.Y.C., 1981-84, office mgr., 1986-88; edtl. asst. to editor chief Vanity Fair Mag., 1984-85; freelance artist, illustrator Cambridge and Boston, Mass., 1988—; pres., co-founder Audio Visual Group, Arlington, 1992-96, Mediactive, Inc., Arlington, 1996—. Asst. visual projects dept. Vanity Fair Mag., N.Y.C., 1985. Interface designer: (CD ROM) Multiple Media Tour, 1992; graphic illustrator: (CD ROM) SAT CD ROM, 1995; graphic support: (CD ROM) Kerouac Romnibus CD ROM, 1995 (Invision award 1996), Dime-DC Health, 1995-96 (Invision award 1995-96); interface designer, illustrator: (CD ROM) Changing Your Mind-Drugs in the Brain, 1996. Avocations: windsurfing, cross country skiing, biking. Home: 15 Medford St Arlington MA 02474-3132 Office: Mediactive Inc 7 Mystic St Arlington MA 02474-1109

STEINBERG, LAURA, lawyer; b. Phila., Feb. 3, 1948; d. Leonard and Pearl (Zeid) S.; children: Seth, Adam, Bree. BA magna cum laude with honors, Bryn Mawr Coll., 1968; JD cum laude, Harvard U., 1972. Bar: Mass. 1972, U.S. Dist. Ct. Mass. 1972, U.S. Dist. Ct. R.I. 1974, U.S. Ct. Appeals (1st cir.) 1973, U.S. Ct. Appeals (10th and D.C. cirs.) 1986, U.S. Ct. Appeals (4th cir.) 1988, U.S. Claims Ct. 1979, U.S. Supreme Ct. 1988. Assoc. Sullivan & Worcester, Boston, 1972-79, ptnr., 1979—, mem. mgmt. com., 1988-2000, head litigation dept., 1988-99. Dir. Greater Boston Legal Svcs., 1987-90. Bd. dirs. Law Firm Resources Project, Boston, 1980-86, Lawyers Com. for Civil Rights Under Law, 1998—; pres. Peirce Extended Day Program, Inc., West Newton, Mass., 1983-86. Spl. career fellow U. Calif., Berkeley, 1968-69; Fulbright scholar, 1968. Mem. Boston Bar Assn. (vice-chmn. litigation sect. 1992-94, chmn. 1994-95). Avocations: reading, tennis. Office: Sullivan & Worcester LLP Ste 2300 One Post Office Sq Boston MA 02109-2129 E-mail: lsteinberg@sandw.com.

STEINBERG, LAWRENCE EDWARD, lawyer; b. Dallas, Nov. 25, 1935; s. Oscar J. and Pearl L. (Soloman) S.; children: Adam Joseph, Ilana Sara, Oliver David. BBA, U. Tex., 1958; JD, So. Methodist U., 1960. Bar: Tex. 1960. Since practiced in, Dallas; partner firm Steinberg Soloman & Meer, 1971-88, Johnson & Steinberg, Dallas, 1988-93; of counsel Jenkins & Gilchrist, 1994-98; chmn., CEO Eagle Equity, Inc., 1991—. Mem. Urban Rehab. Stds. Bd., Dallas, 1975-76; mem. adv. com. affirmative action program Dallas Ind. Sch. Dist., 1974-76; regional bd. chmn. Anti-Defamation League of B'nai Brith, 1974-77, nat. exec. com., 1977—, nat. law com., 1974-87; trustee Edna Gladney Home, 1975-92; v.p., trustee Shelton Sch., 1987-90; trustee Temple Emanu-El, 1992-94, Dallas Jewish Cmty. Found., 1990-2001; pres. U. Tex. Hillel Found., 2001—; bd. dirs. Jewish Fedn. Greater Dallas, 1984-87, 91-94, Dallas Coun. on World Affairs, 1998—, Stephen Wise, Acad., 1998—, Dallas Holocaust Ctr., 1998—, JINSA, 1999—; regional bd. chmn. Am. Israel Pub. Affairs Com., 1997-2001. 2d lt. U.S. Army, 1959-60. Mem. Lincoln City Club, Columbian Club, Masons, Shriners, Zeta Beta Tau., Phi Delta Phi, Beta Gamma Sigma, Pi Tau Pi (nat. pres. 1964-66). Home: 10131 Hollow Way Rd Dallas TX 75229-6634 Office: 5430 LBJ Fwy Ste 1575 Dallas TX 75240

STEINBERG, LEO, art historian, educator; b. Moscow, July 9, 1920; came to U.S., 1945; s. Isaac N. and Anna (Esselson) S. PhD, NYU Inst Fine Arts, 1960; PhD (hon.), Phila. Coll. Art, 1981, Parsons Sch. Design, 1986, Mass. Coll. Art, 1987, Bowdoin Coll., 1995. Assoc. prof. art history Hunter Coll., CUNY, N.Y.C., 1961-66, prof., 1966-75; prof. Grad. Ctr. CUNY, 1969-75; Benjamin Franklin prof. art. history U. Pa., Phila., 1975-91, prof. emeritus, 1991—. Charles Eliot Norton lectr. Harvard U., 1995-96; Mellon lectr. Nat. Gallery Art, 1981-82. Author: Other Criteria, 1972, Michelangelo's Last Paintings, 1975, Borromini's San Carlo alle Quattro Fontane, 1977, The Sexuality of Christ in Renaissance Art and in Modern Oblivion, 1983, 2d enlarged edit., 1996, Encounters with Rauschenberg, 2000, Leonardo's Incessant Last Supper, 2001. Recipient award in lit. Am. Acad. and Inst. Arts and Letters, 1983; fellow Am. Acad. Arts and Scis., 1978, Univ. Coll., London U., 1979, MacArthur Found., 1986; recipient Frank Jewett Mather award, 1956, 84 Mem. Coll. Art Assn. Am. Home: 165 W 66th St New York NY 10023-6508

STEINBERG, LINDA SUE, interior designer; b. Dallas, Aug. 24, 1945; d. Nathan Charles and Fannie (Rosenbloom) Goidl; m. Lawrence Edward Steinberg, Aug. 31, 1967 (div. 1994); children: Adam Joseph, Ilana Sara. BA, So. Meth. U., 1967; Degree in Interior Design, cert. interior design, El Centro Coll., 1987. Cert. interior designer Tex., nat. cert. interior designer. Assoc. Silvergold Interiors, Dallas, 1979-82; owner LS Design Group Inc., 1986—. Spkr. in field. Mem. Am. Soc. Interior Designers (honor cert. in profl. devel. 1992), Dallas Assoc. (chmn. 1995-96, bd. dirs. Tex. chpt. 1993-95, pres. Tex. chpt. 1999-2000), Interior Designers Guild (pres. 1994-96), Adventure Investment Club (pres. 1993-95). Jewish. Avocations: walking, skiing, weight training, traveling. Fax: (972) 774-9657. E-mail: lindas@dhc.net.

STEINBERG, LOIS SAXELBY, marketing executive; b. New Rochelle, N.Y., Sept. 13, 1926; d. John J. and Ruth (Taussig) Saxelby; m. Jack Steinberg, Nov. 27, 1947 (div. 1980); children: Eric, Mark. BA, Hunter Coll., N.Y.C., 1952; MA, Columbia U., N.Y.C., 1964; PhD, Fordham U., Bronx, 1978; MPS, Sarah Lawrence Coll., Bronxville, N.Y., 2000. Account exec. The Rowland Co., N.Y.C., 1956-64; rsch. asst. Columbia U., 1965-67; rsch. assoc. CUNY, 1967-72; staff asst. Community Svc. Soc., N.Y.C., 1972-74; rsch. assoc. Inst. for Responsive Edn., Boston, 1976-77, Designs for Change, Chgo., 1977-78; sr. study dir. Nat. Opinion Rsch. Ctr., U. Chgo., 1979-81; rsch. spr. BBDO, N.Y.C., 1981-82, Marsteller, Inc., Chgo., 1982-83; v.p. Sorkin-Enenstein Rsch. Svc., Inc., 1984-98; rsch. assoc health advocacy program Sarah Lawrence Coll., Bronxville, 2000—01; vol. coord. Medicare Rights Ctr., N.Y.C., 2001—. Contbr. articles to profl. jours. Fordham U. fellow, 1974; Columbia U. fellow, 1964. Mem. APHA, Am. Sociol. Assn. Address: 3 Washington Sq Apt 3C Larchmont NY 10538-2026 E-mail: lstein5325@aol.com.

STEINBERG, LOUIS MARSHALL, dentist, researcher; b. Bklyn., Aug. 1, 1954; s. Jack and Nancy Steinberg; m. Carolyn Preska Steinberg, June 9, 1954; children: Asher, Merrill. BA, Columbia U., 1976, MS, 1984; DDS, NYU, 1980. Postdoctoral fellow Inst. Human Nutrition Columbia U., N.Y.C., 1983-86, clin. rsch. assoc. Ctr. Clin. Rsch., 1986-92; pvt. practice West New York, N.J., 1989—; clin. asst. prof. N.J. Dental Sch., Newark, 1994—. Cons. McNeil Specialty Products, New Brunswick, N.J. Contbr. articles to profl. jours. N.Y. State Regents scholar NYU, 1977-80. Mem. AAAS, Internat. Assn. Dental Rsch., Acad. Gen. Dentistry, Sigma Chi (hon.). Jewish. Avocations: gardening, aquaria. Office: 6050 Boulevard E West New York NJ 07093-3901 E-mail: drlmsteinberg.lms@verizon.net.

STEINBERG, MALCOLM SAUL, biologist, educator; b. New Brunswick, N.J., June 1, 1930; s. Morris and Esther (Lerner) S.; children: Jeffery, Julie, Eleanor, Catherine; m. Marjorie Campbell, 1983. BA, Amherst Coll., 1952; MA, U. Minn., 1954, PhD, 1956. Postdoctoral fellow dept. embryology Carnegie Instn., Washington, 1956-58; asst. prof. Johns Hopkins, Balt., 1958-64, assoc. prof., 1964-66; prof. biology Princeton U., 1966-90, Henry Fairfield Osborn prof. biology, 1975—, prof. molecular biology, 1990—. Instr.-in-charge embryology course Marine Biol. Lab., 1967-71, trustee, 1969-77; chmn. Gordon Rsch. Conf. on Cell Contact and Adhesion, 1985; apptd. to NAS/NRC Bd. on Biology, 1986-92. Mem. editl. bd. Bioscience, 1976-82, Integrative Biology, 1997-99; contbr. articles to profl. jours. Fellow AAAS; mem. AAUP, Soc. Comparative Integrative Biology (program officer divsn. devel. biology 1966-69, chmn. elect, then chmn. 1982-85), Am. Soc. Cell Biology, Internat. Soc. Devel. Biologists, Internat. Soc. Differentation (bd. dirs. 1995-2000), Soc. Devel. Biology (trustee, sec. 1970-73), Sigma Xi. Home: 86 Longview Dr Princeton NJ 08540-5642 E-mail: msteinberg@princeton.edu.

STEINBERG, MARSHALL, retired toxicologist; b. Pitts., Sept. 18, 1932; s. Harry Lionel and Eva (Goldstein) S.; m. Patricia Louise Zobac, Nov. 3, 1962; children: Leslie Renee, Michael Allan, Maureen Sara. BS, Georgetown U., 1954; MS, U. Pitts., 1956; PhD, U. Tex., 1966. Commd. U.S. Army, 1956, advanced through grades to col., 1957-74, ret., 1976; prin. investigator Tracor Jitco, Rockville, Md., 1977, v.p., chief ops., 1977-78; v.p., dir. life scis. Hazleton Labs. Am., Vienna, 1978-83; v.p., sci. dir. Hazleton Labs. Corp., 1983-87, v.p. Asian ops., 1987-90; v.p. health and environment Hercules, Inc., Wilmington, Del., 1990-98, ret., 1998. Chmn. safety panel Fed. working Group on Pest Mgmt., Washington, 1973—74; cons. Office of Pesticide Programs, EPA, Washington, 1975—77; mem. expert in pharmacology and toxicology French Govt., 1985—90; chmn. safety com. Internat. Pharm. Excipients Coun., 1990—, chmn., 1999—2000, Internat. Pharma. and Excipients Auditing, Inc., 2000—; bd. dirs. Brandywine Valley Assn. Author articles, govt. reports. book chpts. Bd. dirs. Del. chpt. Am. Lung Assn.; trustee Health Environ. Scis. Inst.; mem. sci. adv. bd. Digene, 1986-89. Decorated Legion of Merit. Fellow Acad. Toxicol. Scis. (councillor 1982-85, v.p. 1990-91), Royal Soc. Medicine; mem. Soc. Toxicology (sec. 1983-85), Am. Coll. Toxicology (pres. 1986), Am. Indsl. Hygiene Assn., Toxicology Lab. Accredidation Bd. (sec. 1985-91), Internat. Soc. Regulatory Toxicology and Pharmacology, Brandywine Valley Assn. (bd. dirs.). Jewish. Avocation: hunting. E-mail: msteinbe@bellatlantic.net.

STEINBERG, MARTIN H. hematologist, educator; b. N.Y.C., July 2, 1936; s. Meyer and Anne (Palatnik) S.; m. Susan Elizabeth McDaniel, Nov. 24, 1973; 1 child, Elizabeth Anne. AB, Cornell U., 1958; MD, Tufts U., 1962. Diplomate Bd. Internal Medicine, Am. Bd. Hematology. Intern Cornell Med. Svc., Bellevue Hosp., N.Y.C., 1962-63; USAF Med. Corps, 1963-66; resident in medicine New Eng. Med. Ctr., Boston, 1966-68, fellow in hematology, 1968-70; asst. prof., U. Miss., 1970-74; hematologist VA Med. Ctr., Jackson, Miss., 1970-74, chief of rsch., 1974-2000; prof. medicine U. Miss., 1977—. Vis. prof. Tufts U., Boston, 1987; prof. medicine and pediat. Boston U., 2000—; sickle cell adv. com. NIH-Nat. Heart, Lung, Blood Inst., Bethesda, Md., 1988-2000. Editorial bd. Am. Jour. Hematology, 1978—, Am. Jour. Med. Sci., 1986—; assoc. editor Hemoglobin; contbr. chpts. to books, articles to sci. jours. Capt. USAF, 1963-66. Grantee VA, 1970—, NIH, 1975—; recipient Founders' medal. Fellow AAAS; mem. Assn. Am. Physicians, Am. Soc. Clin. Investigation, So. Soc. Clin. Investigations. Achievements include original research in sickle cell disease and thalassemia. Office: Boston U Sch Medicine 88 E Newton St Boston MA 02118 E-mail: msteinberg@medicine.bu.edu.

STEINBERG, MARVIN EDWARD, orthopaedic surgeon, educator; b. New Brunswick, N.J., Aug. 31, 1933; s. David and Fannie (Karshmer) S.; m. Delores Gusky White, Nov. 22, 1956; children: David, James, Susan, Julie. BA, Princeton U., 1954; MD, U. Pa., 1958; MA (status pro tem), U. Oxford,

Eng., 1964. Cert. Am. Bd. Orthopaedic Surgery, re-cert.; lic. Pa., N.J. Asst. prof. orthopaedic surgery U. Pa., Phila., 1968-73, assoc. prof., 1973-80, vice chmn., 1977-2000, prof. orthopaedic surgery, 1980—, prof. orthopaedic surgery in medicine, 1988—, interim chmn., 1994-95. Dir. Joint Reconstrn. Ctr., Hosp. U. of Pa., Phila., 1987-97; examiner Am. Bd. Orthpaedic Surgeons, Chgo., 1977-97. Editor, author: The Hip and Its Disorders, 1991, Revision Total Hip Arthroplasty, 1998; guest editor, author: Seminars in Arthroplasty, 1998; guest editor: Orthopaedic Clinics of N.America, 1982, (jour.) Seminars in Arthroplasty, 1991; editl. cons. Clin. Orthopaedics and Related Rsch., 1987; assoc. editor Jour. Bone & Joint Surgery, 1992-2000; contbr. numerous articles to jours. and textbooks. Named one of The Best Drs. in Phila., Phila. Mag., 1984, 87, 94; Fulbright scholar, Oxford, 1963-64; fellow Arthritis Found., Oxford, 1963-64. Fellow ACS, Am. Acad. Orthopaedic Surgeons; mem. AMA, Assn. for Acad. Surgery, Ea. Orthopaedic Assn. (pres. 1975-76), Orthopaedic Rsch. Soc., Internat. Soc. for Orthopaedic Surgery and Traumatology (sec.-treas. 1997-2000, chmn. elect 2000-2002, chmn. 2002-), Am. Orthopaedic Assn., Hip Soc., Girdlestone Soc., Assn. Rsch. Circulation, Lupus Found. Jewish. Avocations: travel, sailing, boating, photography. Home: 221 Winding Way Merion Station PA 19066-1217 Office: Hosp of U of Pa 3400 Spruce St Philadelphia PA 19104-4206 E-mail: marvin.steinberg@uphs.upenn.edu.

STEINBERG, MEYER, chemical engineer; b. Phila., July 10, 1924; s. Jacob Louis and Freda Leah S.; m. Ruth Margot Elias, Dec. 24, 1950; children: David Martin, Jay Louis. BSChemE, Cooper Union, 1944; MSChemE, Bklyn. Poly. Inst., 1949. Registered profl. engr. N.Y. Jr. chem. engr. Manhattan dist., Kellex Corp., Oak Ridge, Los Alamos, 1944-46; asst. chem. engr. Deutsch & Loonam, 1947-50; chem. engr. Guggenheim Brothers, Mineola, N.Y., 1950-57; head process sci. div. Brookhaven Nat. Lab., Upton, 1957—. Expert in fossil and nuclear energy. Contbr. articles to profl. jours. Served with AUS, 1944-46. Recipient IR-100 award, 1970; Wasson award Am. Concrete Inst., 1972, Engr. of Year award, 1985, Ind. award Quest, 1985, Greenman award Internat. Energy Agy. IEA Greenhouse Program, 1996. Fellow Am. Nuclear Soc., Am. Inst. Chem. Engrs. (dir. L.I. sect.); mem. Am. Chem. Soc., AAAS, Am. Concrete Inst., Inst. Assos. Hydrogen Energy, Sigma Xi. Democrat. Jewish. Achievements include research on nuclear and fossil energy. Home: 15 Alderfield Ln Melville NY 11747-1724 Office: Brookhaven Nat Lab Upton NY 11973

STEINBERG, MICHAEL, music critic, educator; b. Breslau, Germany, Oct. 4, 1928; came to U.S., 1943, naturalized, 1950; s. Siegfried and Margarethe (Cohn) S.; m. Jane Bonacker, July 26, 1953 (div. 1983); children: Peter Sebastian, Adam Gregory; m. Jorja Fleezanis, July, 1983. AB, Princeton U., 1949, M.F.A., 1951; Mus. D. (hon.), New Eng. Conservatory Music, 1966. Free-lance writer, 1952—; head history dept. Manhattan Sch. Music, N.Y.C., 1957-64; music critic Boston Globe, 1964-76; dir. publs. Boston Symphony Orch., 1976-79; artistic adviser San Francisco Symphony, 1979-89, program annotator, lectr., 1989-99; artistic adviser Minn. Orch., 1989-92; artistic dir. Minn. Sommerfest, 1990-92; program annotator, lectr. N.Y. Philharmonic, 1995-2000. Vis. mem. faculty Hunter Coll., 1954, U. Sask. (Can.), 1959, Smith Coll., 1964, Brandeis U., 1964-65; faculty New Eng. Conservatory Music, 1968-71, Wellesley Coll., 1971-72, Brandeis U., 1971-72, Mass. Inst. Tech., 1973; disting. vis. prof. McMaster U., Hamilton, Ont., 1982; cons. NEH, Nat. Endowment for Arts, Mass. Council of Arts and Humanities, Calif. Arts Council, Rockefeller Found.; free-lance writer, lectr. Author: The Symphony: A Listener's Guide, 1995, The Concerto: A Listener's Guide, 1998. Served with U.S. Army, 1955-57. Recipient Sang prize for criticism in arts, 1969; citation for Excellence in Criticism Am. Guild Organists, 1972 Mem. Am. Internat. musicological socs. Home: 6828 Valley View Rd Edina MN 55439-1646 E-mail: fleeberg@earthlink.net.

STEINBERG, MILTON, civilian military employee; b. Cornwall, N.Y., Apr. 3, 1941; s. Samuel Lewis Steinberg, Anna Ethel Steinberg; m. Francine Steinberg (div.); children: Daniel B., Rachel T. Rubenstein; m. Rimma Steinberg, Sept. 14, 1986; stepchildren: Marina Harary, Galina Ziegler. BA in Psychology, UCLA, 1963; MS in Adminstrv. Scis., City U., London, 1968. Cert. tng., responsibility involvement and preparation of claims U.S. Dept. Vet. Affairs, N.Y. State Divsn. Vet. Affairs and Am. Legion. Sales rep. Gen. Tng. Svc., N.Y.C., 1969—70; caseworker N.Y.C., Bronx, 1970—71; state vet. counselor N.Y. State, Spring Valley, 1971—. Vol. Congressman Benjamin A. Gilman campaign, Rockland County, NY, 1991—; sec. B'nai Jeshurun Synagogue, Monsey, 1987—. Specialist 4th class U.S. Army, 1963—65. Recipient Cert. of Honor, Town of Ramapo, N.Y., 1995, Cert. of Humanitarianism, 1993, 1995, Cert. of Appreciation, Rockland County Am. Legion, 1997, 2000. Mem.: DAV (life), Nat. Mus. Am. Jewish Mil. History, Vietnam Vets. Am., Am. Legion (county svc. officer, post svc. officer), Jewish War Vets. (state svc. officer, post svc. officer, nat. svc. officer, Cert. Appreciation 1999, 2001, Cert. Merit 1995). Republican. Jewish. Avocations: travel, gardening, reading, photography, music. Office: NY State Divsn Vet Affairs 9-B Perlman Dr Spring Valley NY 10977 E-mail: amerivet@hotmail.com.

STEINBERG, MORTON M. lawyer; b. Chgo., Feb. 13, 1945; m. Miriam C. Bernstein, Aug. 25, 1974; children: Adam Michael, Shira Judith. AB with honors, U. Ill., 1967; JD, Northwestern U., 1971. Bar: Ill. 1971, DC 1994, Colo. 1995, U.S. Dist. Ct. (no. dist.) Ill. 1971, U.S. Dist. Ct. Colo. 1998, U.S. Ct. Appeals (7th cir.) 1971, U.S. Supreme Ct. 1974. Assoc. Caffarelli & Wiczer, Chgo., 1971-73, Arnstein, Gluck, Lehr, Barron & Milligan, Chgo., 1974-76, ptnr., 1977-86, Piper, Rudnick and predecessor, 1986—. Speaker in field. Sr. editor Jour. Criminal Law and Criminology, Northwestern U., 1969-71. Chmn. Chgo. region Leaders Tng. Fellowship, 1962-63; bd. dirs. Camp Ramah in Wis., Inc., Chgo., 1974—, sr. v.p., 1992-94, pres. 1994—, bd. dirs., pres. Ramah Day Camp, Inc., Chgo., 2001-; bd. dirs., v.p. Camp Ramah in Wis. Endowment Corp., 1993—; bd. dirs. North Suburban Synagogue Beth-El, Highland Park, Ill, 1978—, corp. sec., 1983-87, pres. 1989-91, chmn. bd. trustees, 1991-93, trustee, 1991—; mem. Nat. Ramah Commn., 1987—, v.p., 1994—; bd. dirs. Found. Conservative Judaism in Israel, 1985-90; Midwest region bd. dirs. United Synagogue of Conservative Judaism, 1989-91, 94—; mem. editor's cir. Jewish Forward Newspaper, 1997-2000; trustee Am. Jewish Hist. Soc., 1998—; charter mem. U.S. Holocaust Meml. Mus., 1992; pro bono counsel Frank Lloyd Wright Preservation Trust, Oak Park, Ill., 1996—. Served with USAR, 1969-75. Recipient Youth Leadership award Nat. Fedn. Jewish Men's Clubs, N.Y.C., 1963; cert. of merit U.S. Dist. Ct. Fed. Defender Program, Chgo., 1969. Mem. ABA, Internat. Wine Law Assn., D.C. Br, Std. Club, Ill. State Bar Assn., Chgo. Bar Assn. Jewish. Home: 1320 Lincoln Ave S Highland Park IL 60035-3459 Office: Piper Rudnick Ste 1800 203 N La Salle St Chicago IL 60601-1225 E-mail: morton.steinberg@piperrudnick.com.

STEINBERG, NORMAN MICHAEL, lawyer; b. Montreal, Feb. 10, 1950; s. Jack and Faigie (Pekeles) S.; m. Renee Kessler, May 8, 1974; children: Marc, Tara. BS, McGill U., 1971, B of Civil Law, 1975. Bar: Que. 1976. Ptnr., mem. mgmt. com. Ogilvy Renault, Montreal, 1976—. Bd. dirs., sec. Shreve Crump & Low Co. Ltd., Boston, 1992—; bd. dirs. Schwarzschild Jewelers, Inc., Richmond, Va., Global-GIX Can. Inc., Montreal, Gildan Active Wear, Inc., Lennox Industries, Ltd., Can. Bd. dirs. Centaur Theatre, Montreal, 1992—, Montreal Symphony Orch., 1990—, treas., mem. exec. com. Mem. Can. Club Montreal (past pres.), Univ. Club Montreal, Mt. Royal Club Montreal. Jewish. Avocation: photography. Office: Ogilvy Renault Ste 1100 1981 McGill College Ave Montreal QC Canada H3A 3C1

STEINBERG, PAUL, allergist, immunologist; b. N.Y.C., Nov. 5, 1937; s. Harry and Mary Steinberg; m. Vivian Claire Gallo, June 26, 1960; children: David Charles, Douglas Allen. BS, CCNY, 1959; MD, Johns Hopkins U., 1963. Diplomate Am. Bd. Allergy and Immunology. Intern, resident dept. medicine Strong Meml. Hosp., Rochester, N.Y., 1963-65; epidemic intelligence svcs. officer Nat. Communicable Disease Ctr., Atlanta, 1965-67; staff assoc. NIH, Bethesda, Md., 1967-70; spl. fellow div. clin. immunology Johns Hopkins U., Balt., 1970-72; asst. prof. dept. medicine U. Mich., Ann Arbor, 1972-76; dir. allergy sect. Park Nicollet Med. Ctr., Mpls., 1980-85; clin. prof. dept. medicine U. Minn., 1983-98; dir. allergy and immunology divsn. Hennepin County Med. Ctr., 1985-97, Bassett Healthcare, Cooperstown, N.Y., 1997—; clin. prof. medicine Columbia U., N.Y.C. Clin. prof. medicine dept. medicine Columbia U., N.Y., 1998—. Contbr. numerous articles to profl. jours. and chpt. to book. Exec. bd. dirs. Minn. chpt. Asthma and Allergy Found. of Am., Mpls., 1984-88. Served to surgeon USPHS, 1965-67. Fellow Am. Acad. Allergy and Immunology, Am. Coll. Allergy and Immunology; mem. Minn. Allergy Soc. (pres. 1983-84, 87-89), Minn. Med. Assn. (Inter-specialty Coun. rep. 1987—), Sigma Xi, Phi Beta Kappa. Avocations: fishing, book collecting. Office: Bassett Healthcare One Atwell Rd Cooperstown NY 13326-1394

STEINBERG, PAUL JAY, psychiatrist; b. Norwalk, Conn., Mar. 5, 1948; s. Benjamin and Ethel (Friedman) S.; m. Helen Katz; children: Miritte, Arielle. BA, U. Pa., 1970; MD, SUNY, Bklyn., 1974. Diplomate Am. Bd. Psychiatry and Neurology. Intern U. Rochester, Rochester, N.Y., 1974-75; resident George Washington U., Washington, 1975-78; staff psychiatrist Psychiat. Inst. D.C., 1978-81; psychiatrist U. Md., College Park, 1981-89; assoc. dir. counseling and psychiat. svc. Georgetown U., Washington, 1989—. Coord. drug and alcohol treatment U. Md., College Park, 1981-89. Contbr. articles to profl. jours. Mem. Am. Psychiat. Assn., Am. Soc. Adolescent Psychiatry, Am. Coll. Health Assn., D.C. Med. Soc. Jewish. Avocation: tennis. Office: Georgetown U Counseling and Psychiat Svc 37th And O Sts NW Washington DC 20057-1005

STEINBERG, ROBERT PHILIP, lawyer; b. Danville, Ill., Apr. 4, 1931; s. Frederick Philip and Beulah Iona (Olmsted) S.; m. Doris Elizabeth Blank, May 10, 1958; children: Susan Elizabeth, Mary Louise. BA, DePauw U., 1953; LLB, N.Y. U., 1956. Bar: N.Y. 1956, Pa. 1959. Assoc. Shearman & Sterling, N.Y.C., 1956, Drinker Biddle & Reath, Phila., 1958-65, ptnr., 1965-97, chmn., 1992-94, of counsel, 1997-98; ptnr. Commons & Commons LLP, 1998—. V.p. Germantown Hist. Soc., Phila., 1991-95, The Phila. Theatre Co., 1992-96; pres. E. Falls Cmty. Coun., 1997-2000. Mem. Phila. Bar Assn. (treas. 1970-72). Home: 3906 W Netherfield Rd Philadelphia PA 19129-1014 Office: Commons & Commons 2967 W School House Ln Philadelphia PA 19144-5222 E-mail: philip.steinberg@att.net.

STEINBERG, ROY BENNETT, television producer, director, educator; b. N.Y.C., Mar. 24, 1951; s. Seymour and Flora Joyce (Matthews) S.; m. Marlena Lustik, Sept. 8, 1984, 1 child, Alexa Catherine. BA, Tufts U., 1973; MFA, Yale U., 1978. Guest artist various univs., 1978-87; dir. Circle Repertory Co. Lab., N.Y.C., 1985-90; artistic dir. John Michael Kohler Arts Ctr., Sheboygan, Wis., 1988; prodr. Guiding Light, CBS-TV, N.Y.C., 1990-98; dir. One Life To Live, 1999; prodr., dir. Days of Our Lives, NBC; prof. Muhlenberg Coll., 1999—. Freelance drama coach, N.Y.C., 1978—; script cons. Circle Repertory Co. Lab., N.Y.C., 1985-90; casting dir. Theatre Matrix, N.Y.C., 1981-83; adv. bd. Sch. Film & TV, N.Y.C., 1995—. Actor: (play) Wings, 1979 (Tony nomination 1979), (TV spl.) The Wall, 1980, (soap opera) Another World, 1985, (film) The Man Who Envied Women, 1986; dir. (play) Private Lives, 1987, Absent Friends, 1987, Broadway Bound, 1988, The Miser, 1989, The Learned Ladies, 1989, The Marriage Fool, 1989, Othello, 1989, Children, 1996, Blithe Spirit, 1997, Intuition, 1997. Five Towns Music & Art Found. scholar, 1969, 4 Emmy nominations, 1990-93. Mem. AFTRA (nat. del. 1988), Actors Equity Assn. (dep.), Soc. Stage Dirs. and Choreographers, Dirs. Guild Am., Screen Actors Guild. Avocations: travel, cooking, movies, sports, reading. Home: 3951 Sunswept Dr Studio City CA 91604

STEINBERG, RUSSELL MAX, behavioral pediatrician, educator; b. Salinas, Calif., Aug. 18, 1941; s. Martin and Eve S. AB in Zoology, UCLA, 1963, MA in Zoology and Endocrinology, 1964, PhD in Zoology and Endocrinology with distinction, 1969; MD, Med. Coll. Ohio, Toledo, 1972. Diplomate Nat. Bd. Med. Examiners. Intern in pediatrics Affiliated Hosps. U. Calif., Irvine, 1972-73, resident in pediatrics Affiliated Hosps., 1973-74; chief resident in pediatrics then mem. staff Childrens Hosp. of Orange County and U. Calif.; fellow in behavioral pediatrics and learning disabilities UCLA, 1975-76; behavioral pediatrician Childrens Med. Group, Anaheim, Calif., 1976-79; physician in child devel. program Fairview Devel. Ctr., Costa Mesa, 1979-81, physician behavior adjustment program, 1981—, past chief med. staff, 1990-94; asst. clin. prof. pediatrics U. Calif., Irvine, 1990-94. Adj. asst. prof. zoology UCLA, 1969, instr. pediatrics, 1976; adj. asst. prof. pharmacy, U. Toledo, 1970-71; vis. lectr. Tchr. Edn. U. Calif., Irvine, 1980-93; lectr. and presenter in field. Contbr. articles to profl. jours. Rsch. fellow Ford Found., 1966, U.S. Pub. Health Svc., 1965-69. Mem. Am. Acad. Pediatrics (assoc.), Soc. for Behavioral Pediatrics, Orange County Pediatric Soc., Sigma Xi. Office: Fairview Devel Ctr Behavior Adjustment Program 2501 Harbor Blvd Costa Mesa CA 92626-6143

STEINBERG, SAUL PHILLIP, holding company executive; b. N.Y.C., Aug. 13, 1939; s. Julius and Anne (Cohen) S.; m. Barbara Herzog, May 28, 1961 (div. 1977); children: Laura, Jonothan, Nicholas; m. Laura Sconocchia, Dec. 21, 1978 (div. Dec. 1983); 1 child, Julian; m. Gayfryd McNabb, Jan. 22, 1984; children: Rayne, Holden. BS, Wharton Sch., U. Pa., 1959. Founder, chmn., chief exec. officer, dir., COO Reliance Group Holdings Inc., N.Y.C. Bd. dirs. Symbol Techs. Inc. Chmn. bd. overseers Wharton Sch. U. Pa.; mem. bd. overseers Cornell U. Med. Coll., N.Y.C.; trustee Jewish Med. Ctr., N.Y.C., U. Pa., N.Y. Pub. Libr. Jewish. Home: 680 Madison Ave New York NY 10021-7246 Office: Reliance Group Holdings Inc 5 Hanover Sq New York NY 10004

STEINBERG, STEPHEN ARTHUR, information technology executive, consultant; b. Hartford, Conn. m. Lois Shapiro. B in Elec. Engring., Rensselaer Poly. Inst., 1966; MBA, U. Chgo., 1968. Sr. systems cons. Mobil Oil Corp., N.Y.C., 1968-71; v.p. systems and tech. Citibank, N.A., 1972-88; sr. v.p., dir. info. systems Capital Markets Assurance Corp., 1989-97; exec. v.p., chief info. officer Enhance Fin. Svcs. Group Inc., 1998-2000; pres. Chatsworth Solutions Inc., 2001—. Mem. IEEE Computer Soc. Avocation: jazz drummer. E-mail: ssteinberg@chatsworthinc.com.

STEINBERG, STEPHEN PHILLIP, university administrator, philosopher, writer; b. Chgo., Mar. 9, 1949; s. David Louis and Dena Sudow Steinberg. AB in Philosophy with distinction, U. Mich., 1971; MS in Journalism, Columbia U., 1972; MA in Philosophy, New Sch. for Social Rsch., 1982; PhD in Philosophy, U. Pa., 1989. News writer WGN-TV and Radio, Chgo., summer 1970; writer USIA, Washington, summer 1971; staff writer Med. Tribune, Inc., N.Y.C., 1972-73; account exec. Joseph Dermer and Assoc., Inc., 1974-75; account assoc. Bruce Porter Co., Inc., 1975-76; devel. officer, adj. instr. humanities Pratt Inst., 1977-78; asst. dean Sch. Arts and Scis., U. Pa., Phila., 1978-87, lectr. dept. philosophy, 1981—. Acad. and career advisor Coll. Gen. Studies, U. Pa., 1978-87, asst. dir. grad. programs, adminstr. Coll. Gen. Studies, 1982-87, dir. MA and Profl. Studies program, 1985-87, coord. Faculty Coun. on Undergrad. Edn., 1986-87, coord. provost's coun. on undergrad. edn., 1987-92, coord. provost's coun. on undergrad. admissions, 1987-92, coord. coun. of undergrad. deans, 1987-92, acting exec. asst. to provost, spring 1990, coord. coun. of grad. deans, 1987-90, coord. planning com. on undergrad. edn., 1987-89, coord. planning com. on doctoral edn., 1987-89, faculty advisor Coll. Arts and Scis., 1990—, asst. to pres., 1990—; exec. dir. Penn Nat. Commn. on Society, Culture and Cmty., 1996—; interim dir. 21st Century Project for Undergrad. Experience, 1997-98, affiliated faculty Solomon Asch Ctr. for Study of Ethno-polit. Conflict, 1999—; exec. dir. Penn Pub. Talk Project, 1999—. Contbr. articles to profl. jours. Mem. bd. dirs., exec. com. Jewish Cmty. Rels. Coun., Phila., 1984—; mem. bd. dirs., trustee Hillel of Greater Phila., 1988—. Mem. Am. Philos. Assn., Soc. for Phenomenology and Existential Philosophy, Assn. for Study of Ethnicity and Nationalism. Avocations: horseback riding, wilderness camping. Home: 515 S 22nd St Philadelphia PA 19146-1247 Office: Univ Pa 502 Hollenback Ctr 3000 South St Philadelphia PA 19104-6325 E-mail: sps@pobox.upenn.edu.

STEINBERG, SYLVAN JULIAN, lawyer; b. New Iberia, La., July 25, 1933; s. Emanuel and Myrtle (Weil) S.; m. Judith Ann Benson, Sept. 7, 1959; children: Jeanne Wyn, Susan Beth, Jonathan Michael. BBA with honors, Tulane U., 1955, JD with honors, 1957. Bar: La. 1957, U.S. Dist. Ct. (ea. dist.) La. 1958, U.S. Supreme Ct. 1963, U.S. Ct. Appeals (5th cir.) 1976, U.S. Ct. Appeals (11th cir.) 1981, U.S. Dist. Ct. (mid. dist.) La. 1984, U.S. Dist. Ct. (we. dist.) 1989. Assoc. Weinstein and Bronfin, New Orleans, 1958-62; ptnr. Bronfin & Heller, 1962-99; of counsel Heller, Draper, Hayden, Patrick & Horn LLC, 2000—. Gen. adv. bd. cont. legal edn. Tulane Law Sch. Mem. editorial staff Tulane U. Law Rev., 1955-57, book rev. editor, 1957, mem. bd. adv. editors. Mem., former pres. bd. advisors B'nai B'rith Hillel Found. of Tulane U., Loyola U. and U. New Orleans; past pres. Tikvat Shalom Synagogue, New Orleans; cmty. rels. com., past trustee New Orleans Jewish Welfare Fedn., budget com.; former mem. New Orleans regional adv. bd. Anti-Defamation League; former mem. tech. adv. com. regional econ. devel. Regional Planning Commn.; past bd. dirs. Jewish Family and Children's Svc.; profl. adv. com. Jewish Endowment Found.; past chmn. bd. commrs. Cmty. Improvement Agy. for City of New Orleans; bd. dirs. New Orleans Redevel. Authority, 1994-95; former v.p. B'nai B'rith State of La. Maj. JAGC, U.S. Army, and USAR, 1957-66. Mem. ABA, New Orleans Bar Assn. (chmn. gen. practice com. 1986 mem. continuing legal edn. com., chmn. legis. com., chmn. sr. lawyers com.), Fed. Bar Assn. (Fed. Ct. Bench bar liaison com.), La. Bar Assn. (mem. task force selection, election judges 1988), La. Assn. Def. Counsel, New Orleans C. of C. (mem. com. on housing), Masons, B'nai B'rith (v.p.). Home: 2710 Chestnut St New Orleans LA 70130-5731 Office: Heller Draper Hayden Patrick & Horn LLC 650 Poydras St Ste 2500 New Orleans LA 70130-6103 E-mail: ssteinberg@hellerdraper.com.

STEINBERG, TERESA SHERWOOD, paralegal, legal administrator; b. Valdosta, Ga., May 30, 1950; d. J.C. and Irma Lou (Williams) Sherwood; m. James Miller Steinberg, Apr. 18, 1970; children: James Jr., William Sherwood. Cert. legal asst., Valdosta State U., 1989. Legal sec., paralegal Dover, Sherwood, & Shelton, Valdosta, 1986-90; indigent def. adminstr. Lowndes County Bd. Commrs., 1990—. Mem. juvenile justice com. Ga. Indigent Def., Atlanta, 1996-97. Mem., past officer, chmn. Valdosta Jr. Svc. League, 1979—; chmn. Lowndes Youth Leadership League, 2002—; bd. dirs. Class of 1998 Leadership Lowndes, v.p., alumni treas.; bd. dirs. Wesley Found. Valdosta State U., ARC. Mem. Nat. Paralegal Assn., South Ga. Assn. Legal Assts. (edn. chmn. 1989—), Valdosta-Lowndes County C. of C. Methodist. Avocations: gardening, cooking, sewing, designing. Office: Lowndes County Indigent Def Office Lowndes County Govtl. Bldg. 2d Flr Annex 300 N Patterson St Valdosta GA 31601-5507

STEINBERG, WARREN LINNINGTON, school principal; b. N.Y.C., Jan. 20, 1924; s. John M. and Gertrude (Vogel) S.; m. Beatrice Ruth Blass, June 29, 1947; children: Leigh William, James Robert, Donald Kenneth. Student, U. So. Calif., 1943-44; BA, UCLA, 1949, MEd, 1951, EdD, 1962. Tchr., counselor, coach Jordan H.S., Watts, L.A., 1951-57; tchr., athletic coord. Hamilton H.S., L.A., 1957-62; boys' vice prin. Univ. H.S., 1962-67, Crenshaw H.S., L.A., 1967-68; cons. Ctr. for Planned Change, L.A. City Sch., 1968-69; instr. edn. UCLA, 1965-71; boys' vice prin. LeConte Jr. J.S., L.A., 1969-71, sch. prin., 1971-77; adminstrv. cons. on integration L.A. Unified Sch. Dist., 1977-81, adminstr. student-to-student interaction program, 1981-82; cprin. Gage Jr. H.S., Huntington Park, Calif., 1982-83; prin. Fairfax H.S., L.A., 1983-90. Pres. Athletic Coords. Assn., L.A. Unified Sch. Dist., 1959-60; v.p. P-3 Enterprises, Inc., Port Washington, N.Y., 1967-77, Century City (Calif.) Enterprises, 1966-88. Contbr. articles on race rels., youth behavior to profl. jours. and newspapers. V.p. B'nai B'rith Anti-Defamation League, 1968-70; mem. adv. com. L.A. City Commn. on Human Rels., 1966-71, 72-76, commr., 1976—, pres., 1978-87, also chmn. edn. com.; mem. human rels. commn. L.A. Unified Sch. Dist., 1999—, mem. citizens adv. com. for student integration, 1976-79; mem. del. assembly Cmty. Rels. Conf. So. Calif., 1975-91; chmn. So. Calif. Drug Abuse Edn. Month com., 1970; bd. dirs. DAWN, The Seedling, 1993-95, Project ECHO—Entrepreneurial Concepts, Hands-On, 1996—; mem., chmn. case conf. human rels. West L.A. Coordinating Coun. With USMCR, 1943-46. Recipient Beverly Hills B'nai B'rith Presdl. award, 1965, Pres.'s award Cmty. Rels. Conf. So. Calif., 1990, Lifetime Achievement award L.A. City Human Rels. Commn., 1996, award L.A. Unified Sch. Dist. Bd. Edn., 1997, commendation L.A. City Coun., 1968, 88. Mem. Beverly-Fairfax C. of C. (bd. dirs. 1986-88), Lions (bd. dirs. 1960-62), Kiwanis. Home: 2737 Dunleer Pl Los Angeles CA 90064-4303

STEINBERGER, JACK, physicist, educator; b. Bad Kissingen, Germany, May 25, 1921; came to U.S., 1935; s. Ludwig Lazarus and Berta (May) S.; m. Joan Beauregard, 1943, (div. 1962); children: Joseph, Richard Ned; m. Cynthia Eva Alff; children: Julia Karen, John Paul. BS in Chemistry, U. Chgo., 1942, PhD in Physics, 1948; hon. degree, Ill. Inst. Tech., 1989, U. Glasgow, 1990, Dortmund U., 1990, Columbia U., 1990, U. Autonoma de Barcelona, Spain, 1992, U. Blaise Pascal, Clermont-Ferrand, France, 1995, U. Würzburg, 1997. Mem. Inst. for Advanced Study, Princeton, N.J., 1948-49; asst. U. Calif., Berkeley, 1949-50; prof. Columbia U., N.Y.C., 1950-68, Higgins prof., 1968-72; staff mem. European Orgn. for Nuclear Research, Geneva, 1968-86, dir., 1969-72; prof. physics Scuola Normale, Pisa, Italy, 1986—. Pfc. U.S. Army, 1943-46. Co-recipient Nobel prize in physics, 1988; recipient Nat. Medal of Sci., 1988, Mateuzzi medal Societa Italiane delle Scienze, 1991; fellow Guggenheim Found., Sloan Found. Mem. NAS, Am. Acad. Arts and Scis., Heidelberg Acad. Scis., Academia Europea, Academia Nationale dei Lincei. Home: 25 Chemin des Merles CH 1213 Onex Switzerland Office: European Ctr for Nuclear Rsch CH 1211 Geneva 23 Switzerland

STEINBERGER, JEFFREY WAYNE, lawyer, consultant; b. Bronx, N.Y., Nov. 27, 1947; s. Martin and Shirley (Blumen) S.; m. Marlene Zimmelman, Apr. 28, 1976 (div. June 1983); 1 child, Darren William. BS, Queens Coll., 1968; JD, U. Western Los Angeles, 1976. Sole practice, 1979—. Owner Jeridean Industries, Los Angeles, 1968-75; mgr., artist Clout Agy., Beverly Hills, Calif., 1972-76; real estate broker Nat. Real Estate, Beverly Hills, 1974—; dist. atty. City of Los Angeles, 1976-77; cons. City of Hope, San Fernadino, Calif., 1979; judge pro tem Los Angeles Mcpl. Ct., 1984-2002. Producer, developer, host TV show Jeffs Law, 1979—; cast mem. (TV show) Power of Attorney. Developer, founder Coalition for Child Care, Beverly Hills, 1985. Served with USAR, 1969-70. Mem. Los Angeles Bar Assn., Beverly Hills Bar Assn., Assn. Trial Lawyers Am., Calif. Trial Lawyers Assn., Beverly Hills Trial Lawyers Assn., Los Angeles Bd. of Realtors, Beverly Hills Bd. of Realtors, Mensa. Avocations: karate-do, scuba exploration, hatha yoga, triathalons. Office: 8383 Wilshire Blvd Ste 1032 Beverly Hills CA 90211-2409

STEINBOCK, JOHN THOMAS, bishop; b. L.A., July 16, 1937; Student, L.A. Diocesan sems. Ordained priest Roman Cath. Ch., 1963. Aux. bishop Diocese of Orange, Calif., 1984-87; bishop Diocese of Santa Rosa, 1987-91; titular bishop of Midila, 1984; bishop Diocese of Fresno, Calif., 1991—. Office: Diocese of Fresno 1550 N Fresno St Fresno CA 93703-3788 Fax: 559-488-7464.

STEINBRENNER, GEORGE MICHAEL, III, professional baseball team executive, shipbuilding company executive; b. Rocky River, Ohio, July 4, 1930; s. Henry G. and Rita (Haley) S.; m. Elizabeth Joan Zieg, May 12, 1956; children: Henry G. III, Jennifer Lynn, Jessica Joan, Harold Zeig. BA, Williams Coll., 1952; postgrad., Ohio State U., 1954-55. Asst. football coach Northwestern U., 1955, Purdue U., 1956-67; treas. Kinsman Transit Co., Cleve., 1957-63; pres. Kinsman Marine Transit Co., 1963-67, dir., 1965—; pres., chmn. bd. Am. Ship Bldg. Co., 1967-78, chmn. bd., 1978—; prin. owner N.Y. Yankees, Bronx, 1973-90, 93—, limited ptnr., 1990-93; owner Bay Harbor Inn, Tampa, Fla., 1988—. Bd. dirs. Gt. Lakes Internat. Corp., Gt. Lakes Assocs., Cin. Sheet Metal & Roofing Co., Nashville Bridge Co., Nederlander-Steinbrenner Prodns. Mem. Cleve. Little Hoover Com., group chmn., 1966; chmn. Cleve. Urban Coalition; vice chmn. Greater Cleve. Growth Corp., Greater Cleve. Jr. Olympic Found.; founder Silver Shield Found., N.Y.C.; chmn. Olympic Overview Commn.; v.p. U.S. Olympic Com., 1989—. Served to 1st lt. USAF, 1952-54. Named Outstanding Young Man of Yr. Ohio Jr. C. of C., 1960, Cleve. Jr. C. of C., 1960; Chief Town Crier, Cleve., 1968; Man of Yr., Cleve. Press Club, 1968. Mem. Greater Cleve. Growth Assn. (bd. dirs.). Office: NY Yankees Yankee Stadium E 161st St & River Ave Bronx NY 10451*

STEINBRING, JOHN HENRY (JACK STEINBRING), archaeologist; b. Oshkosh, Wis., July 1, 1929; s. Arthur Edward and Lillian (Koller) S.; m. Sandra . Sund, June 14, 1958; children: Christian, Albert, Amelia, Frederick, Eric. MA, U. Wis., 1959; PhD, U. Minn., 1975. Prof. anthropology U. Winnipeg, 1980-91, U. Wis., Oshkosh, 1995—. Adj. prof. Anthropology U. Wis. (Oshkosh), 1995—. Author: Archaeology on the Winnipeg River, 1980; editor: Time and Space, 1994, Rock Art of the Americas, 1995, Rock Painting Sites of Manitoba, 1998; mem. editl. com. IFRAO-BREPOLS Rock Art Series. Mem. Preservation Commn., Ripon, 1996—. Grantee Social Sci. & Humanities Rsch. Coun. Can., 1984-86, Ont. Ministry Culture, 1983, Saskatchewan Heritage Found., 1989-94, U. Winnipeg, 1980, 86; sr. scholar U. Winnipeg, 1990-95; adj. scholar Ripon (Wis.) Coll., 1988—. Mem. Am. Rock Art Rsch. Assn., Mid-Am. Geographic Found. (bd. dirs., internat. rep.),

Australian Rock Art Rsch. Assn., Wis. Archaeol. Survey, Wis. Archaeol. Soc., Wis. Rock Art Assn., Internt. Fedn. Rock Art Orgns. (sec.-gen. 1998-99, pres. 1999), Princeton Hist. Soc. (v.p.). Avocations: book collecting, historic restoration, hiking, photography, ornithology. Home: 610 Liberty St Ripon WI 54971-1220 Office: Ripon Coll 300 Seward St Ripon WI 54971 Fax: (920) 748-7243. E-mail: steinbringj@ripon.edu.

STEINBRUCKNER, BRUNO FRIEDRICH, foreign language educator; b. Linz/Donau, Austria, Aug. 22, 1941; came to U.S., 1965, naturalized, 1973; s. Bruno and Michaela Maria (Wimberger) S.; m. Claudia Jane Frey, Mar. 9, 1973. PhD, U. Innsbruck, 1965. Asst. U. Innsbruck, spring 1965; mem. faculty Am. U., 1965—, prof. German studies, 1973—, chmn. dept. lang. and fgn. studies, 1975-79; dir. The Am. U. Ctr., Vienna, 1985-96, Inst. on Contemporary German-speaking Europe, 1999—2001. Author: Dialektographie des oberen Mühlviertels, 1976, Ludwig Thoma, 1978; also articles.; contbg. author: Encyclopedic Dictionary of Religion, 1979; Contbg. author: Die deutsche Literatur, Germany in World Politics, 1979; contbg. author: Federal Republic of Germany, 2d edit., 1982, Germany, 1996. Mem. Am. Goethe Soc. (pres. 1971-73), Am. Assn. Tchrs. German (chpt. corr. sec. 1965-66), Nat. Humanities Faculty. Home: PO Box 747 Mc Lean VA 22101-0747 Office: PO Box 314 A-1191 Vienna Austria E-mail: bfst@american.edu.

STEINBUCHEL, CARLA FAYE, organizational development professional; b. Wichita, Kans., Aug. 6, 1949; d. Conrad Vernon Sr. and Dolores Mae (Jacobs) Jansson; m. Mark Joseph Steinbuchel, June 5, 1969; children: Carla Lara, Cara Nicole, Haley Elisabeth. BS in Nursing, Wichita State U., 1978, M of Nursing, 1985; Cert. Pediatric Nurse Practitioner, U. Ala., Birmingham, 1997. Nurse supr. Osteopathic Hosp., Wichita, 1978-85; nurse Wesley Med. Ctr., 1982-85, Huntsville (Ala.) Hosp., 1985-86; neonatal outreach coordinator North Ala. Perinatal Outreach Ctr., Huntsville, 1986-90; clin. instr.Coll. Nursing U. Ala., 1990-92; pediatric and neonatal clin. nurse specialist Med. Ctr. Hosp. Huntsville, 1991-95; pediatric clin. nurse specialist Huntsville Hosp. System, 1995-98, pediatric nurse mgr., 1997-98, clin. edn. specialist, 1998-2000; mgr. organizational devel. and tng., 2000—. Manuscript reviewer Neonatal Network, Petaluma, Calif., 1987-88. Mem. AACN (past sec. pres.), Nat. Assn. Pediatric Nurses and Practitioners. Democrat. Methodist. Avocations: travel, reading, writing. Home: 2511 Galahad Dr SE Huntsville AL 35803-1809 Office: Huntsville Hosp System 101 Sivley Rd SW Huntsville AL 35801-4421

STEINDL, FRANK GEORGE, economist, educator; b. Chgo., Aug. 26, 1935; s. Frank and Anna (Bumeder) S.; m. Joyce Ann Becker, Aug. 26, 1961; children: David F., Andrew M., Peter E., Matthew T. BA, DePaul U., Chgo., 1957; AM, U. Ill., 1958; PhD, U. Iowa, 1963. Asst. prof. Okla. State U., Stillwater, 1962-65, assoc. prof., 1965-70, prof., 1970-89, regents prof. of econs., 1989—, Ardmore prof. bus. adminstrn., 1994—. Economist Fed. Res. Bank Cleve., 1966-67; economist, counselor budget com. U.S. Senate, Washington, 1976; vis. prof. U. Munich, 1986—; Konrad Zuse guest prof. U. Bamberg, Germany, 1991; vis. scholar London Sch. Econs. Brown U., 1993-94, U. Iowa, 2000-01. Author: Monetary Interpretations of the Great Depression, 1995; contbr. articles to profl. jours. Mem. sch. bd. St. Francis Sch., Stillwater, 1973-77; scoutmaster Boy Scouts Am., 1984-86. Named Disting. Lectr., Mid-Am. State Univs. Assn., 1981-82. Mem. Am. Econ. Assn., So. Econ. Assn (trustee 1989-91), Midwest Econs. Assn. (v.p. 1974), Southwestern Econ. Assn. (pres. 1974). Avocations: gardening, walking, opera. Home: 2206 Tanglewood Cir Stillwater OK 74074-1713 Office: Okla State Univ Dept Econs Stillwater OK 74078-1104

STEINDLER, HOWARD ALLEN, lawyer; b. Cleve., June 12, 1942; s. Sidney and Lois Jean (Rosenberg) S.; children: Rebecca, Allison, Daniel. BS, Miami U., Oxford, Ohio, 1964; JD, Ohio State U., 1967. Bar: Ohio 1967. Mem. firm Benesch, Friedlander, Coplan & Aronoff, Cleve., 1967—. Pres. bd. trustees Cleve. Scholarship Program, 1987-97, trustee, 1997—; trustee Downtown Cleve. Partnership, Inc., The Ratner Sch. Office: Benesch Friedlander Coplan & Aronoff 2300 BP Tower 200 Public Sq Cleveland OH 44114-2371 E-mail: hsteindler@bfca.com.

STEINDLER, MARTIN JOSEPH, chemist; b. Vienna, Austria, Jan. 3, 1928; came to U.S., 1938; s. J.P. and M.G. S.; m. Joan Long, Aug. 16, 1952; children: M.H., T.P. PhB, U. Chgo., 1947, BS, 1948, MS, 1949, PhD, 1952. Chemist Argonne (Ill.) Nat. Lab., 1953-74, sr. chemist, 1974—, assoc. dir. div. chem. engring., 1978-84, dir. chem. tech. div., 1984-93, sr. tech. advisor, 1993—. Mem. adv. com. on nuclear waste NRC, Washington, 1988-96, chmn. 1995; adminstrv. judge ASLBP, 1973-90. Contbr. articles to profl. publs.; patentee in field. Pres. Matteson-Park Forest (Ill.) Sch. Bd., 1959-78. Recipient Disting. Performance medal U. Chgo., 1992, Meritorious Svc. award for Scientific Excellence, U.S. NRC, 1996. Mem. AAAS, Am. Nuclear Soc., Am. Inst. Chem. Engrs. (Robert E. Wilson award 1990), Sigma Xi. Office: Argonne Nat Lab 9700 Cass Ave Argonne IL 60439-4803

STEINDLER, WALTER G. retired lawyer; b. N.Y.C., Dec. 2, 1927; s. Mortimer B. and Ray (Feingold) S.; m. Carol A. Halpin, June 28, 1969; children: Michael, Morty, Melissa, Amy, Ellen. BA, Queens Coll., 1950; JD, NYU, 1953. Bar: N.Y. 1953, U.S. Supreme Ct. 1965, U.S. Dist. Ct. (ea. dist.) N.Y. 1972, U.S. Dist. Ct. (so. dist.) 1974, U.S. Ct. Appeals (2d cir.) 1974. Ptnr. Borden Skidell Fleck & Steindler, Jamaica, N.Y., 1955-62; pvt. practice law Babylon, 1962-67; town atty. Town of Babylon, 1967-69; asst. county atty. Suffolk County, N.Y., 1970-71; ptnr. Sarisohn, Carner, Steindler, Lebow, Braun & Castrovinci, Commack, 1976-93; ret., 1993. Capt., judge adv. 2d area command N.Y. Guard, N.Y.C., 1965-70; guardian ad litem 20th Jud. Cir. Lee County, Fla., 1995-98. With U.S. Army, 1946-47. Mem. Free Sons Israel (pres. 1953), Masons. Office: 350 Veterans Memorial Hwy Commack NY 11725-4330

STEINEGER, MARGARET LEISY, non-profit organization officer; b. Newton, Kans., Feb. 8, 1926; d. Ernest Erwin and Elva Agnes (Krehbiel) L.; m. John Francis Steineger, Dec. 2, 1949; children: John Steineger III, Cindy Blair, Melissa, Chris. B., So. Meth. U., 1947; M. in Social Work, U. Kans., 1949. County vice-chair United Way, Kansas City, Kans., 1960-61; bd., sec., treas. Wyandotte County Bar Aux., 1960-63; bd. Jr. League of Kansas City, 1962-66, County Coun. PTA, Wyandotte County, 1963-66, KCK Friends of the Arts, Kansas City, 1974-77; pres. Grinter Place Mus. Friends, Kans., 1977-78; bd. Kaw Valley Arts Coun., Kansas City, 1982-86; commr. Landmarks Commn., 1985-87; bd. Arts with the Handicapped, Wyandotte County, 1986—. Bd. dirs. Kans. Arts Adv. Bd., Grinter Place Friends, Kans., Tri-County Tourism Coun., Kans. V.p. Kans. Legis. Wives, Topeka, 1975-76; bd. dirs. KCK Friends of the Libr., Kansas City, 1984—, Shepherd's Ctr., 1996—; founder Wyandotte County Libr., 1963-64, Creative Experiences, Kansas City, 1967; commr. Kans. Arts Commn., 1965-85; mem. Kaw Valley Arts and Humanities Bd., 1988-92; mem. adv. bd. Parents as Tchrs., 1992-99; mem. Kansas City Ballet Guild.; bd. dirs. Shepherd's Ctr., 1996—. Recipient Humanities award Kans. Com. for the Humanities, 1989; named Citizen of Yr. Kansas City, Kans., 1978. Mem. Kappa Kappa Gamma (C.C. Endowment Bd. 1989—). Democrat. Methodist. Avocations: skiing, sailing, inventing. Home: 6400 Valleyview Ave Kansas City KS 66111-2013 Office: Security Bank Building Ste 600 Kansas City KS 66101

STEINEM, GLORIA, writer, editor, lecturer; b. Toledo, Mar. 25, 1934; d. Leo and Ruth (Nuneviller) S.; m. David Bale, Sept. 3, 2000. BA, Smith Coll., 1956; postgrad. (Chester Bowles Asian fellow), India, 1957-58; D. Human Justice, Simmons Coll., 1973, PhD (hon.). Co-dir., dir. edl. found. Ind. Rsch. Svc., Cambridge, Mass. and N.Y.C., 1959-60; contbg. editor Glamour Mag., N.Y.C., 1962-69; co-founder, contbg. editor New York Mag., 1968-72; feminist lectr., 1969—; co-founder, editor Ms. Mag., 1971-87, columnist, 180-87, cons. editor, 1987—. Active various civil rights and peace campaigns including United Farmworkers, Vietnam War Tax Protest, Com. for the Legal Def. of Angela Davis (treas., 1971-72); active polit. campaigns of Adlai Stevenson, Robert Kennedy, Eugene McCarthy, Shirley Chisholm, George McGovern; Co-founder, bd. dirs. Women's Action Alliance, 1970—; co-founder, convenor, mem. nat. adv. com. Nat. Women's Polit. Caucus, 1971—; co-founder, pres. bd. dirs. Ms. Found. for Women, 1972-1990; founding mem. Coalition of Labor Union Women, 1974; mem. Internat. Women's Year Commn., 1977, pres. Choice USA, co-founder, chmn. Liberty Media for Women, 1998- ; editorial cons., Conde Nast Publications, 1962-69, Curtis Publishing, 1964-65, Random House Publishing, 1988—, McCall Publishing. Author: The Thousand Indias, 1957, The Beach Book, 1963, Wonder Woman, 1972, Outrageous Acts and Everyday Rebellions, 1983, Marilyn: Norma Jeane, 1986, Revolution from Within: A Book of Self-Esteem, 1992, Moving Beyond Words, 1994; contgb. corr. NBC Today Show, 1987-88; contbr. to various anthologies. Pres. Voters for Choice, 1979—. Recipient Penney-Missouri Journalism award, 1970, Ohio Gov.'s award for Journalism, 1972, Bill of Rights award ACLU of So. Calif., 1975; named Woman of the Yr. McCall's mag., 1972; Woodrow Wilson Internat. Ctr. for Scholars fellow, 1977; inducted into Nat. Women's Hall of Fame, 1993. Mem. NOW, AFTRA, Nat. Press Club, Soc. Mag. Writers, Authors' Guild, Phi Beta Kappa. Office: Ms Magazine 20 Exchange Pl Fl 22 New York NY 10005-3201 also: Choice USA 1010 Wisconsin Ave NW Ste 410 Washington DC 20007*

STEINER, ALAN P. military officer, government agency administrator; Commd. USN, 1976—; advanced through grades to master missile technician; chief of boat USS Rhode Island; courier security team leader submarine re-supply ships Victoria, Marshfield and Vega; with Submarine Tng. Facility, Charleston, SC, Strategic Weapons Facility, Atlantic; master chief missile technician Naval Space Command, Dahlgren, Va., 1999—. Decorated Navy Commendation medal, Marine Corps Commendation medal with 2 gold stars, Navy and Marine Corps Achievement medal with 3 gold stars, Humanitarian Svc. medal. Office: Naval Space Command Attn: Public Affairs 5280 Fourth St Dahlgren VA 22448-5300*

STEINER, CHARLES HARRIS, sports broadcaster, journalist; b. N.Y.C., July 17, 1949; s. Howard Stanley and Gertrude (Harris) S. Student, Bradley U., Peoria, Ill., 1967-71. Newscaster WIRL, Peoria, 1969-70, KSTT, Davenport, Iowa, 1970-74; news dir. WAVZ Radio, New Haven, 1972-73, All-News WPOP Radio, Hartford, Conn., 1973-77, All-News WERE Radio, Cleve., 1977-78; sports broadcaster WOR Radio, N.Y.C., 1978-86; sports dir. RKO Radio Network, 1980-86; play-by-play announcer N.Y. Jets WABC Radio, 1986-88; anchorman ESPN, Bristol, Conn., 1988—. Play-by-play announcer NCAA football, maj. league baseball, NBA basketball. Recipient Emmy award Nat. Acad. TV Arts and Scis., 1993, Cable Ace award Nat. Acad. Cable Programming, 1994, Clarion award Women in Comm., 1993; named to Bradley U. Hall of Fame, 1995. Office: ESPN ESPN Pla Bristol CT 06010 E-mail: steinerc@espn.com.

STEINER, DAVID MILLER, lawyer; b. Phoenix, Apr. 9, 1958; s. Paul Miller and Nan (Adamson) S. BA, Columbia U., 1980; MALD, Tufts U., 1985; JD, Cornell U., 1988; M of Internat. and Pub. Affairs, Columbia U., 1989; LLM in Taxation, NYU, 1993. Bar: N.Y. 1988. English tchr. Peace Corps, Tahoua, Niger, 1980-82; law clk. to Judge Jane Restani U.S. Ct. Internat. Trade, N.Y.C., 1989-91; law clk. to Judge Reynaldo Garza U.S. Ct. Appeals (5th cir.), Brownsville, Tex., 1991-92; assoc. Wasserman, Schneider and Babb, 1993-95; with N.Y.C. Law Dept. Office of the Corp. Counsel, 1995—2002, U.S. Dept. Justice, Washington, 2002—. Mem. ABA, Assn. Bar City N.Y. (state and local tax com.), N.Y. County Lawyers Assn. (com. on taxation), Fgn. Policy Assn., Apollo Cir.-Met. Mus. Art, Univ. Club, Columbia Club. Avocations: ballroom dancing, backgammon, running. Home: 2298 17th St NW # 3 Washington DC 20009- Office: US Dept Justice Tax Divsn PO Box 55 Ben Franklin Sta Washington DC 20044- E-mail: sirius_001@yahoo.com.

STEINER, DONALD FREDERICK, biochemist, physician, educator; b. Lima, Ohio, July 15, 1930; s. Willis A. and Katherine (Hoegner) S. BS in Chemistry and Zoology, U. Cin., 1952; MS in Biochemistry, MD, U. Chgo., 1956; D Med. Sci. (hon.), U. Umea, 1973, U. Ill., 1984, Technische Hochschule, Aachen, 1993, U. Uppsala, 1993, Mt. Sinai Sch. Medicine, N.Y.C., 1998. Intern King County Hosp., Seattle, 1956-57; USPHS postdoctoral research fellow, asst. medicine U. Wash. Med. Sch., 1957-60; mem. faculty med. sch. U. Chgo., 1960—, chmn. dept. biochemistry, 1973-79, A.N. Pritzker prof. biochemistry, molecular biology and medicine, 1985—, sr. investigator Howard Hughes Med. Inst., 1986—. Jacobaeus lectr., Oslo, 1970; Luft lectr., Stockholm, 1984. Co-editor: The Endocrine Pancreas, 1972, discoverer proinsulin. Recipient Gairdner award Toronto, 1971, Hans Christian Hagedorn medal Steensen Meml. Hosp., Copenhagen, 1970, Lilly award, 1969, Ernst Oppenheimer award, 1970, Diaz-Cristobal award Internat. Diabetes Fedn., 1973, Banting medal Am. Diabetes Assn., 1976, Banting medal Brit. Diabetes Assn., 1981, Passano award, 1979, Wolf prize in medicine, 1985, Frederick Conrad Koch award Endocrine Soc., 1990. Mem. Nat. Acad. Scis., Am. Soc. Biochemists and Molecular Biologists, AAAS, Am. Diabetes Assn. (50th Anniversary medallion 1972), European Assn. Study Diabetes, Am. Acad. Arts and Scis., Sigma Xi, Alpha Omega Alpha. Home: 2626 N Lakeview Ave Apt 2508 Chicago IL 60614-1821 E-mail: dfsteine@midway.uchicago.edu.

STEINER, GEORGE (FRANCIS STEINER), author, educator; b. Paris, Apr. 23, 1929; s. Frederick George and Elsie (Franzos) S.; m. Zara Shakow, 1955; children: David Milton, Deborah Tarn. BA, U. Chgo., 1949; MA, Harvard U., 1950; PhD, Oxford U., 1955; DLitt (hon.), Trinity Coll., Dublin, 1996; LittD (hon.), Louvain U., 1980, Mount Holyoke Coll., 1983, Durham U., 1995; D honoris causa, U. Bristol, 1989; DLitt (hon.), U. Glasgow, 1990, U. Liége, 1990, U. Ulster, 1993, U. Durham, 1995, Kenyon Coll., 1996, U. Rome, 1998, U. Sorbonne, 1998, U. Salamanca, 2002. Mem. staff Economist, London, 1952-56; mem. staff Inst. Advanced Study Princeton (N.Y.) U., N.J., 1956-58, Gauss lectr., 1959-60; Massey lectr., 1974; First Lord Weidenfeld prof. Comp. Lit. Oxford U., 1994—; Charles Eliot Norton prof. poetry Harvard U., 2001—. Cons. and lectr. in field; Maurice lectr. U. London, 1984, Leslie Stephen lectr. Cambridge U., 1985, W.P. Ker lectr. U. Glasgow, 1986; lectr. Page-Barbour Lectures U. Va., 1987, Gifford lectr., 1990; vis. prof. Coll. France, 1992; First Lord Weidenfield vis. prof. comparative lit., Oxford U., 1994—. Author: Tolstoy or Dostoevsky, 1958, The Death of Tragedy, 1960, Anno Domini, 1964, Language and Silence, 1967, Extraterritorial, 1971, In Bluebeard's Castle, 1971, The Sporting Scene: White Knights in Reykjavik, 1973, After Babel, 1975 (adapted for TV as The Tongues of Men, 1977), Heidegger, 1978, On Difficulty and Other Essays, 1978, The Portage to San Cristobal of A.H., 1981, Antigones, 1984, George Steiner: A Reader, 1984, Real Presences, 1989, Proofs and Three Parables, 1992, Homer in English, 1996, No Passion Spent, 1996, The Deeps of the Sea, 1996, Errata, An Examined Life, 1997, Grammars of Creation, 2001; editor: The Penguin Book of Modern Verse Translation, 1966, Homer: A Collection of Critical Essays (with Robert Flagles), 1962. Decorated chevalier de la Legion d'Honneur (France); Churchill Coll. fellow, 1961—; Hon. Royal Academician (London), Commandeur dans l'Ordre des Arts et des Lettres (Paris); hon. fellow Balliol Coll., Oxford, Eng., 1995, St. Anne's Coll., Oxford; Fulbright prof., 1958-69; recipient O. Henry Short Story award, 1958, Guggenheim fellowship, 1971-72, Zabel award Nat. Inst. Arts and Letters, U.S., 1970, King Albert medal Royal Belgian Acad., 1982, P.E.N. Internat. Fiction prize, 1993; Faulkner Fiction grantee P.E.N., 1983; Le Prix du Souvenir, 1974, Truman Capite Lifetime award for Lit., 1999, Prince of Asturias prize in humanities, 2001. Fellow British Acad.; mem. Am. Acad. Arts and Scis. (hon.), English Assn. (pres. 1975), German Acad. Lit. (corr.) Office: Churchill Coll Cambridge England

STEINER, GEORGE, management science, operations research educator; b. Budapest, Hungary, Sept. 11, 1947; arrived in Can., 1974; s. Aladar and Magda (Klein) S.; m. Judit Csizmazia, Sept. 21, 1974; children: Adam, David. Diploma in math. cum laude, Eötvös Lorand U., Budapest, 1971; PhD in Math., U. Waterloo, Ont., Can., 1982. Ops. rsch. analyst Infelor Systems Engring. Inst., Budapest, 1970-73; systems analyst Steel Co. Can., Hamilton, Ont., 1974-80; asst. prof. mgmt. sci. McMaster U., 1981-85, assoc. prof., 1985-92, prof., 1992—, chmn. mgmt. sci. and info. systems dept., 1989-93. Vis. prof. U. Bonn, Germany, 1987; vis. sci. U. Montpellier, France, 1993. Contbr. articles on math., ops. rsch. and combinatorial optimization to profl. jours. Grantee Natural Scis. Engring. Rsch. Coun. Can., 1981-82, 1983—; fellow Social Scis. and Humanities Rsch. Coun. Can., 1986-87, German Acad. Exch. Svc., 1987. Fellow Inst. of Combinatorics and Its Applications. Avocations: racquetball, theatre, books, music, chess. Office: McMaster U 1280 Main St W Hamilton ON Canada L8S 4M4

STEINER, GLORIA LITWIN, psychologist; b. Newark, Oct. 21, 1922; d. David Milton and Minna (Krasner) Litwin; m. Charles Steiner, Aug. 29, 1942; children: Charles Jr., Susan Steiner Sher, Jeanne. BA, U. Pa., 1944; MS, CCNY, 1956; EdD, Columbia U., 1965. Psychologist St. Michael's Hosp. and Mt. Carmel, Newark, 1956-62; chief psychologist Children's Hosp., 1965-78; prof. psychology, dir. psychol. svc. Child Study Ctr., Kean Coll., Union, N.J., 1971-78; vis. assoc. prof. grad. sch. applied and profl. psychology Rutgers U., Piscataway, 1976-94; clin. assoc. prof., former dir. psychology tng. U. Medicine and Dentistry N.J.-N.J. Med. Sch., Newark, 1978—. Psychology cons. Nat. Pediatric HIV Resource Ctr., 1991-94; bd. trustees Sister Rose Edoument dept. Jewish Christian Studies Seton Hall U.; bd. govs. Am. Jewish Com. Co-author: Traumatic Abuse/Children, 1980; co-editor: Children, Families and HIV/AIDS: Psychosocial and Psychotherapeutic Issues, 1995; contbr. articles to profl. jours.; mem. editl. bd. Jour. Psychotherapy, 1981-96. Mem. N.J. State Task Force on AIDS, 1986-89, N.J. State Bd. Psychol. Exam., 1978-84, Regional Health Planning Coun., N.J., 1984-85, child adv. com. Mental Health Assn., N.J., 1974-80; trustee, founder N.J. Acad. Psychology, 1978-83, bd. trustees, 1994-97. Grantee tng. health care workers Regional AIDS Edn. and Tng. Ctr. U. Medicine and Dentistry N.J., Newark, 1990, Nat. Pediat. HIV Resource Ctr., Newark, 1991-94. Fellow Am. Orthopsychiat. Assn.; mem. N.Y. Acad. Scis., N.J. Assn. for the Advancement Family Therapy (vice-chmn. 1979-81), Am. Psychol. Assn. Avocation: grandchildren. Home and Office: 4D 321 N Wyoming Ave Apt 4D South Orange NJ 07079-1671 E-mail: glorcharsteiner@csi.com.

STEINER, HENRY JACOB, law and human rights educator; b. Mt. Vernon, N.Y., June 14, 1930; s. Meier and Bluma (Henigson) S.; m. Pamela Pomerance, Aug. 1, 1982; stepchildren: Duff, Jacoba. BA magna cum laude, Harvard U., 1951, MA, LLB magna cum laude, Harvard U., 1955. Bar: N.Y. 1956, Mass. 1963. Law clk. to Hon. John M. Harlan U.S. Supreme Ct., 1957-58; assoc. Sullivan and Cromwell, N.Y.C., 1958-62; asst. prof. sch. law Harvard U., Cambridge, Mass., 1962-65, prof., 1965—, Jeremiah Smith Jr. prof. law, 1986—. Founder, dir. Law Sch. Human Rights Program, 1984—; chmn. univ. com. on human rights studies Harvard Law Sch., 1992—; bd. dirs. U. Middle East project, 1996—99, chair bd. dirs., 2000—; vis. prof. Yale U., 1972—73, Stanford U., 1965; cons. AID, 1962—64, Ford Found., 1966—69. Co-author: (textbook) Transnational Legal Problems, 4th edit., 1994, Tort and Accident Law, 2d edit., 1989, International Human Rights in Context: Law, Politics, Morals, 2d edit., 2000; author: Moral Argument and Social Vision in the Courts, 1987, Diverse Partners: Non-Governmental Organizations in the Human Rights Movement, 1991; former devels. editor Harvard Law Rev.; contbr. articles to profl. jours. Office: Harvard U Law Sch Cambridge MA 02138 E-mail: hsteiner@law.harvard.edu.

STEINER, HENRY-YORK, English langauge educator; b. Chgo., Mar. 12, 1932; s. Richard Morrow and Deborah (Lantz) S.; m. Margaret Gray, June 3, 1957 (div.); children: Anne Elizabeth, Edward Yagi, Riley Jane; m. Leonor Coleman Flores, Jan. 13, 1990. BA, Grinnell Coll., 1956; MA, Yale U., 1957; PhD, U. Oreg., 1963. Instr. Grinnell (Iowa) Coll., 1957-59, assoc. prof., assoc. dean faculty, 1964-68; instr. U. Oreg., Eugene, 1959-62; assoc. prof. Yankton (S.D.) Coll., 1959-62; dean undergrad. studies Ea. Wash. U., Cheney, 1968-77, prof. English, 1977—. Chmn. Wash. State Folklife Coun., Olympia, 1988-92. Editor: (autobiobraphy) St. Peter & I, 1967, (anthology) 12 Poets, 1967; contbr. articles to profl. jours., including Internat. Edn. Chmn. Spokane (Wash.) Cmty. Action, 1971-76; bd. dirs. Expo '74, Spokane World's Fair, 1972-75; dir. 49 Degrees N. Ski Patrol, Chewelah, Wash., 1982-86, 97—; sect. chief Inland Empire region Nat. Ski Patrol, Spokane, 1994-97. Named Patroller of Yr., Inland Empire region Nat. Ski Patrol, 1998, Patrol Dir. of Yr., Pacific N.W. divsn., 1998; Fellow Yale U. and Ford Found., 1957. Mem. AAUP (sec. Wash. State coun. 1993-98). Avocations: skiing, sailing, gardening. Home: 2627 W Gardner Ave Spokane WA 99201 Office: Ea Wash U Dept English Cheney WA 99004

STEINER, HERBERT MAX, physics educator; b. Goeppingen, Germany, Dec. 8, 1927; came to U.S., 1939, naturalized, 1944; s. Albert and Martha (Epstein) S. BS, U. Calif., Berkeley, 1951, PhD, 1956. Physicist Lawrence Berkeley Lab., Berkeley, Calif., 1956—; mem. faculty U. Calif., 1958—, prof. physics, 1966-2000, prof. emeritus, 2000—, William H. McAdams prof. physics, chmn. dept., 1992-95; vis. scientist European Center Nuclear Research, 1960-61, 64, 68-69, 82-83, Max Planck Inst. Physics and Astrophysics, Munich, 1976-77; vis. prof. Japanese Soc. Promotion Sci., 1978. Vis. prof. physics U. Paris, 1989-90; vis. scientist Deutsches Electron Synchrotron Lab., 1995-96. Author articles in field. Served with AUS, 1946-47. Recipient Sr. Am. Scientist award Alexander von Humboldt Found., 1976-77; Guggenheim fellow, 1960-61 Fellow Am. Phys. Soc. Office: U Calif Berkeley Dept Physics 7300 Berkeley CA 94720-0001

STEINER, JEFFERY ALLEN, project engineer, executive; b. Longview, Wash., June 22, 1954; s. Glyn Elmer and Betty Jean (Shuster) S.; m. Cynthia Gene Schoppey, June 5, 1976; children: Peter, David, Scott. BSME, U.S. Naval Acad., 1976; MSCE, Oreg. State U., 1982. Registered profl. engr., Calif., Minn. Commd. ensign USNR, 1976; gunnery officer U.S.S. Bradley, San Diego, 1976-79; maintenance officer Naval Base, Guantanamo Bay, Cuba, 1979-81; co. comdr. Amphibious Constrn., San Diego, 1982-85; engr. City of Chula Vista (Calif.), 1985-86; project mgr. Mayo Clinic, Rochester, Minn., 1986—. Tech. advisor Minn. Pollution Control Agy., St. Paul, 1988-93. Bd. trustees Ronald McDonald House, Rochester, Minn., 1990—, pres. 1995-96; bd. govs. Grace Evang. Free Ch., Stewartville, Minn., 1990-94. Decorated Navy Achievement, Navy Battle Excellence; named Cmty. Hero Participant Olympic Torch Relay, 1996. Mem. Minn. Soc. Profl. Engrs. (sec.-treas. 1992, v.p. 1993, pres. 1994, bd. dirs. 1995-96), Toastmasters (Competent Toastmaster). Achievements include development of concepts, drawings and environmental review for the waste management facility for the Mayo Clinic, Rochester; started business to manufacture products from all grades of recycled plastics in 1995. Office: Mayo Clinic 200 1st St SW Rochester MN 55905-0002

STEINER, JEFFREY JOSEF, industrial manufacturing company executive; b. Vienna, Austria, Apr. 3, 1937; came to U.S., 1958; s. Beno and Paula (Bornstein) S.; m. Claude Angel, Apr. 11, 1957 (div. 1972); children: Eric, Natalia, Thierry; m. Linda Schaller, Mar. 6, 1976 (div. June 1983); children: Benjamin, Alexandra. Student textile design, U. London, 1956; student textile mfg., Bradford Inst. Tech., London, 1957; HHD (hon.), Yeshiva U., 1996. Mgmt. trainee Metals and Controls div. Tex. Instruments, Attleborough, Mass., 1958-59, mgr. internat., 1959-60, pres. Argentina, Brazil, Mex., Switzerland, France, 1960-66, Burlington Tapis, Paris, 1967-72; chmn., pres. Cedec S.A. Engring. Co., 1973-84; chmn., CEO Fairchild Corp., N.Y.C., 1985—, Banner Aerospace, 1993—. Bd. dirs. Copley Fund, Fall River, Mass., Comms. Intelligence Corp., Corp. Express, Inc. Trustee Montefiore Med. Ctr., N.Y.C.; bd. dirs. Israel Mus., Yeshiva U. Bus. Sch. Decorated Knight of Arts (France), knight Indsl. Merit of France, chevalier de L'Ordre des Arts et des Lettres, 1990, chevalier de L'order National du Merite (France), commandatore de la Republica (Italy); recipient mayor's medal City of Paris, 1990. Mem. City Athletic Club, Racing Club, Polo Club. Jewish. Avocations: tennis, sailing. Office: Fairchild Corp 45025 Aviation Dr Ste 400 Dulles VA 20166-7516

STEINER, JOHN WILLIAM, retired biophysicist; b. Chgo., Feb. 3, 1934; s. John Deacon Steiner and Bernice Marguerite Taylor; m. Phyllis Irene Rendell, July 12, 1958; children: John Alfred, Jay William. BA in Chemistry, Boston U., 1964. Analytical chemist MIT Nuc. Reactor, Cambridge, Mass., 1965—66; rsch. biophysicist biophysics dept. Boston U. Med. Ctr., Boston, 1967—99; ret., 1999. Contbr. Vestryman, mem. various coms. Ch. of Our Redeemer, Lexington, Mass., 1985—. Col. USAR, 1952—86. Mem.: Employer Support of Guard/Res., Res. Officers Assn. (Mass. state pres. 1967—). Republican. Episcopalian. Avocations: philately, numismatics, genealogy. Home: 22 Estabrook Rd Lexington MA 02421-7540

STEINER, KAREN RUTH, physician's assistant; b. Milw., Nov. 25, 1953; d. Carl Gustav Martin and Lois Pauline Edna (Koch) S.; m. Christian Joseph Nichols, Sept. 15, 1990. AA in Sci., Glendale Community Coll., 1974; cert. of surg. tech., Maricopa County Tech. Coll., 1976; AA physician asst. pgrm., Essex Community Coll., Balt., 1980. Registered physician asst., Ariz.; lic. phys. asst., Mich.; cert. Nat. Commn. Cert. Physician's Assts. and Nat. Bd. Examiners. Operating room technician Maricopa County Gen. Hosp., Phoenix, 1976-77, Greater Balt. Med. Ctr., 1977-78; resident dept. surgery Franklin Square Hosp., Balt., 1980-811; physician's asst. urgent care unit Ariz. Health Plan, Phoenix, 1981-82; physician's asst. family practice unit CIGNA Health-plan, Tempe, Ariz., 1982-83; physician's asst. cardiac-thoracic surgery dept.

Henry Ford Hosp., Detroit, 1983-87, Thoracic Surgeon's Assocs., Grand Rapids, Mich., 1987-88; physician's asst. surg. White Mountain Hosp., 1988-89; physicians asst. Grace Hosp., Detroit, 1989-91, St. John Hosp., 1991—, Women's Health Ctr., Clarkston, Mich., 1993, Livonia (Mich.) Family Physicians, 1994-96, Emergency Med. Physician's Group, Ann Arbor, Mich., 1996—. Choral Mem. Ariz. State U., Tempe, 1977, 82, Balt. Choral Arts Soc., 1978, White Mtn. Chorale, 1988. Fellow Am. Acad. Physician's Assts., Assn. Physician Assts. in Cardiovascular Surgery, Mich. Acad. Physician Assts. Democrat. Lutheran. Avocations: music, playing guitar, cats, antiques, gardening.

STEINER, MARK DAVID, engineering executive; b. Erie, Pa., Feb. 27, 1961; s. William George and Joyce Elaine (Alexis) S.; m. Melissa Ann Suain, Dec. 30, 1983; children: Jonathan, Michelle. BSEE, Penn State U., 1983. Electronics engr. spl. payloads divsn. NASA-Goddard, Greenbelt, Md., 1983-86, 88-89, elec. systems mgr. satellite servicing project, 1986-88, sect. head. payload devel. sect., 1989-91, sect. head. payload design sect., 1991-94, mgr. Spartan 204 Mission (STS-63), 1992-95, mgr. Spartan 207 Inflatable Antenna Expt. (STS-77), 1995-97, mgr. Spartan 251, 1997-2001, sr. sys. engr., 2001—. Recipient NASA Group Achievement Honor award, 1996, Spl. Achievement award NASA-Goddard Space Flight Ctr., 1985, Group Achievement award, 1985, 93, Outstanding Achievement award, 1984, 90, 91, 93, 95, 96, 98, 2000, NASA Acquisition Improvement award, 2001, Spl. Art awards, 2002. Mem. IEEE, Am. Astronautical Soc., Tau Beta Pi, Eta Kappa Nu. Lutheran. Office: NASA-GSFC Code 531 Greenbelt MD 20771-0001 E-mail: mark.steiner@gsfc.nasa.gov.

STEINER, MICHAEL LOUIS, pediatrician; b. Youngstown, Ohio, Jan. 27, 1937; s. Morris Louis and Blanche Evelyn Steiner; m. Diane W. Martin, Dec. 24, 1961; children: Jocelyn, Mindy, Susan. AB, U. Pa., 1958; MD, St. Louis U., 1962. Diplomate Am. Bd. Pediatrics. Intern U. Fla. Teaching Hosp., Gainesville, 1962-63, resident in pediatrics, 1963-65, instr. pediatrics, 1965; practice medicine specializing in pediatrics and pediatric cardiology Palm Beach Gardens, Fla., 1967—. Cons. cardiology div. children's med. services State of Fla., 1968—. Contbr. articles to profl. jours. Served to capt. U.S. Army, 1965-67. Recipient Physician Recognition award AMA, 1970—. Fellow Am. Acad. Pediat.; mem. Am. Heart Assn. (rsch. com. 1970—), Fla. Pediat. Soc. Republican. Jewish.

STEINER, PAUL ANDREW, retired insurance executive; b. Woodburn, Ind., Feb. 17, 1929; s. Eli Gerig and Emma Mae (Yaggy) Steiner; m. Ruth Edna Henry, Sept. 1, 1950; children: Mark, Nancy, Jonathan, David. AB, Taylor U., 1950. CPCU. Owner feed and grain, lumber and constrn. firms, Bluffton, Ohio, 1951-64; home office rep. Brotherhood Mut. Ins. Co., Ft. Wayne, Ind., 1964-65, dir. claims, 1966-71, v.p., treas., 1968-71, pres., 1971-94, chmn. bd., 1974-2000. Trustee emeritus Taylor U.; past chmn. Summit Christian Coll.; past pres. Ft. Wayne Rescue Mission; sec. bd. dirs. William Taylor Found. Mem.: Soc. CPCU (past nat. ethics com., past pres. No. Ind. chpt.), Mut. Ins. Cos. Assn. Ind. (past pres.), Conf. Casualty Ins. Cos. (past pres.), DEVCO Mut. Assn. (past chmn.), Nat. Assn. Mut. Ins. Cos. (past chmn. bd., Merit award 1973), Christian Bus. Men's Com. Ft. Wayne, Nat. Assn. Evangs. (past treas., Layman of Yr. 1977), Am. Bible Soc., Ft. Wayne Rotary Club (past pres.). Republican. Mem. Evang. Mennonite. Home: 1825 Florida Dr Fort Wayne IN 46805-5036

STEINER, PETER OTTO, economics educator, dean; b. N.Y.C., July 9, 1922; s. Otto Davidson and Ruth (Wurzburger) S.; m. Ruth E. Riggs, Dec. 20, 1947 (div. 1967); children: Mary Catherine, Alison Ruth, David Denison; m. Patricia F. Owen, June 2, 1968. AB, Oberlin Coll., 1943; MA, Harvard, 1949, PhD, 1950. Instr. U. Calif., Berkeley, 1949-50, asst. prof. econs., 1950-57; assoc. prof. U. Wis., Madison, 1957-59, prof., 1959-68; prof. econs. and law U. Mich., Ann Arbor, 1968-91, prof. emeritus, 1991—, chmn. dept. econs., 1971-74, dean Coll. Lit., Sci. and Arts, 1981-89. Vis. prof. U. Nairobi, Kenya, 1974—75; cons. U.S. Bur. Budget, 1961—62, Treasury Dept., 1962—63, various pvt. firms, 1952—. Author: An Introduction to the Analysis of Time Series, 1956, (with r. Dorfman) The Economic Status of the Aged, 1957, (with R.G. Lipsey) Economics, 10th edit., 1993, On the Process of Planning, 1968, Public Expenditure Budgeting, 1969, Mergers: Motives, Effects, Policies, 1975, Thursday Night Poker: Understand, Enjoy and Win, 1996; contbr. articles to profl. publs. Served to lt. USNR, 1944-46. Social Sci. Research Council Faculty Research fellow, 1956; Guggenheim fellow, 1960; Ford Faculty Research fellow, 1965 Mem. Am. Econ. Assn., Econometric Soc., AAUP (chmn. com. Z 1970-73, pres. 1976-78) Home: 502 Heritage Dr Ann Arbor MI 48105-2556 Office: U Mich Law Sch 625 S State St Ann Arbor MI 48109-1215 E-mail: psteiner@umich.edu.

STEINER, RAYMOND JOHN, art critic, editor; b. Bklyn., May 1, 1933; s. Rudolph Caspar and Anne Catherine (Spring) S.; m. Barbara Caldara (div. 1979); children: Barbara Ann Jonason; m. Cornelia Seckel, Oct. 12, 1980. BA, SUNY, New Paltz, 1966, MA, 1971. Cert. tchr., N.Y. Tchr. Kingston (N.Y.) Consolidated Schs., 1966-82; instr. Ulster County C.C., Stone Ridge, N.Y., 1975-78; editor, critic Art Times/CSS Pub. Inc., Saugerties, 1984—. Judge, curator art shows, N.Y., 1984—; lectr. in field. Author: The Vessel of Splendor, 1978, Heinrich J. Jarczyk: Toward A Vision of Wholeness, 1992, Quarry Rubble, 1993, Heinrich J. Jarczyk: Etchings 1968-98, 1998, The Art Students League of New York: A History, 1999. With U.S. Army, 1953-55, 57-60. Recipient Support of State of N.Y. Exec. Chamber of Arts citation Gov. Office, 1994. Mem. Nat. Arts Club, Nat. Press Club, Am. Soc. Aesthetics, Artists Fellowship Inc. (v.p.), Assn. Internat. Art Critics. Avocations: gardening, painting. Office: Art Times PO Box 730 Mount Marion NY 12456-0730 E-mail: rjs@arttimesjournal.com.

STEINER, RICHARD C. semitic linguist, educator; b. N.Y.C., Nov. 7, 1945; s. Frederick Steiner and Pearl Weiss; m. Sara K. Rosenschein, June 1, 1969; children: Chana, Shana, Rachel. BA, Yeshiva U., 1966; student, Hebrew U., Jerusalem, 1963-64; B in Hebrew Lit., Yeshiva U., 1966; postgrad., Uppsala (Sweden) U., 1966-67; PhD, U. Pa., 1974. Asst. prof. Dropsie U., Phila., 1972-73, Touro Coll., N.Y.C., 1973-75; asst. to assoc. prof. semitic langs. and lit. Yeshiva U., Bernard Revel Grad. Sch., 1975-84, prof. semitic langs. and lit., 1984—. Vis. assoc. prof. U. Chgo., 1981; Gerard Weinstock vis. prof. Jewish studies, Harvard U., 1999. Author: The Case for Fricative-Laterals in Proto-Semitic, 1977, Affricated Sade in the Semitic Languages, 1982; co-author: A Quantitative Study of Sound Change in Progress, 1972; contbr. articles to profl. jours. (Bibl. Archeology Soc. award 1984); editl. bd. Hebrew Ann. Rev., 1981-87, Jour. Afroasiatic Langs., 1986-92. Fellow Inst. Advanced Studies, Jerusalem, 1983-84, 94-95, Am. Scandinavian Found., 1966-67, Humphrey Inst. Social Ecology, Beersheba, Israel, 1989; rsch. grantee NEH, 1978-81, 84-88. Fellow Am. Acad. Jewish Rsch., Am. Friends of Acad. Hebrew Lang. (pres. 1998—). Office: Yeshiva U Revel Grad Sch 500 W 185th St New York NY 10033-3299 E-mail: rsteiner@ymail.yu.edu.

STEINER, RICHARD RUSSELL, textile & apparel company executive; b. Chgo., Feb. 26, 1923; s. Frank Gardner and Ruth (Cowie) S.; m. Colleen M. Kearns, Dec. 6, 1949; children— Robert C., Kevin K., Sheila M. BA, Dartmouth Coll., 1948. With Steiner Corp., Salt Lake City, 1948—, divisonal dir., v.p., 1951-59, pres., 1959-2000, chmn., 2000—. Dir. Am. Uniform Co. Served with USAAF, 1942-46. Decorated D.F.C. Mem. Phi Beta Kappa. Clubs: Alta, Salt Lake Country. Office: 505 E South Temple Salt Lake City UT 84102-1004

STEINER, ROBERT FRANK, biochemist; b. Manila, Philippines, Sept. 29, 1926; came to U.S., 1933; s. Frank and Clara Nell (Weems) S.; m. Ethel Mae Fisher, Nov. 3, 1956; children: Victoria, Laura. AB, Princeton U., 1947; PhD, Harvard U., 1950. Chemist Naval Med. Research Inst., Bethesda, Md., 1950-70, chief lab. phys. biochemistry, 1965-70; prof. chemistry U. Md., Balt., 1970—, chmn. dept. chemistry, 1974—; prof. emeritus, 1996—; dir. grad. program in biochemistry U. Md., Balt., 1985. Biophysics study sect. NIH, 1976. Author: Life Chemistry, 1968, Excited States of Proteins and Nucleic Acids, 1971, The Chemistry of Living Systems, 1981, Excited States of Biopolymers, 1983, A Pilot's Tale and Other Stories, 1998, The Decoy and Other Stories, 1999, The Student Pilot and Other Stories, 2000, The Beauty Contest and Other Stories, 2002; editor Jour. Biophys. Chemistry, 1972—, Jour. Fluorescence, 1991; contbr. over 160 articles to profl. jours. Served with AUS, 1945-47. Recipient Superior Civilian Achievement award Dept. Def., 1966; NSF rsch. grantee, 1971-77, NIH, 1973-93. Fellow Washington Acad. Sci., Japan Soc. for Promotion Sci.; mem. Am. Soc. Biol. Chemists. Clubs: Princeton (Washington). Achievements include development of fluorescence techniques for studying proteins. Home: 2609 Turf Valley Rd Ellicott City MD 21042-2021 Office: 5401 Wilkens Ave Baltimore MD 21250-1000 E-mail: xuzw63A@aol.com.

STEINER, ROBERT LISLE, retired language consultant; b. Tehran, Iran, May 21, 1921; s. Robert Lisle and Lois (Foresman) S.; m. Margaret S. Sherrard, June 4, 1944; children— Patricia Jean, Robert Lisle III, William Sherrard, John Scott. Grad., Mercersberg (Pa.) Acad., 1938; BA, Wooster (O.) Coll.; M.I.A., Columbia, 1948. Cons. Commn. Chs. on Internat. Affairs, 1948-49; cultural attache Am. embassy, Iran, 1950-52; educationist U.S. Office Edn., 1952-54; program dir. Am. Friends of Middle East, 1954-59; v.p. Vershire Co., Vt., 1959-62; dir. Peace Corps, Kabul, Afghanistan, 1962-66; regional dir. North Africa, Near East and South Asia, 1966-69; dir. Washington office Devel. & Resources Corp., 1969-70; dir. Ctr. for Cross-Cultural Tng. and Research, adviser to univ. pres. on internat. affairs U. Hawaii, Honolulu, 1971-72; dir., gen. mgr. Hawaii Pub. Broadcasting Authority, 1972-73; exec. dir. N.J. Edn. Consortium, Princeton, 1973-78; pres. InterLink Lang. Ctrs., 1979-91, chmn., 1992—. Tchr. U. Kansas City, Mo., 1957, Bradford (Vt.) Acad., 1961; poultry cons. Middle East Tech. U., Ankara, Turkey, 1963. Councilman, v.p. Shanks Village Assn., Orangeburg, N.Y., 1948; chmn. Kabul Sch. Bd., 1965. Served as pilot USNR, 1943-46. Mem. Princeton Mid. East Soc. (sec. 1986-88, treas. 1993-95). Democrat. Presbyterian. Home: 1898 Villa Ct Lancaster PA 17603-2386 Office: Interlink Lang Ctrs 1898 Villa Ct Lancaster PA 17603-2386

STEINER, ROBERTA PEARL, not-for-profit foundation administrator; b. N.Y.C., July 11, 1948; d. Charles and Ethel (Fier) S. BA, U. Calif., Berkeley, 1969, MLS, 1973. Specialist community resources, Sch. Resource Vols. Berkeley Pub. Schs., 1975-77; chief librarian Am. Insts. for Research, Palo Alto, Calif., 1973-77; assoc. in bibliography and instr. library sch. U. Calif., Berkeley, 1975-77; dir. Cen. Pacific Region B'nai B'rith Women, Daly City, Calif., 1977-84. Dir. Found. Ctr. San Francisco office. Bd. dirs. Jewish Vocat. Svcs., 1984-88, San Francisco Jewish Community Ctr., 1984-90, mem. exec. com.; trustee Brandeis Hillel Day Sch., San Francisco, San Rafael, Calif., 1996-2002. Jewish.

STEINER, ROGER JACOB, linguistics educator, writer, researcher; b. South Byron, Wis., Mar. 27, 1924; s. Jakob Robert and Alice Mildred (Cowles) S.; m. Ida Kathryn Posey, Aug. 7, 1954 (dec. May 1992); children: David Posey, Andrew Posey, Anthony Wright. BA cum laude, Franklin & Marshall Coll., 1945; MDiv, Union Theol. Sem., 1947; MA, U. Pa., 1958, PhD, 1963. Ordained to ministry, Meth. Ch., 1947. Clergyman United Meth. Ch., N.Y., Wis., Pa., 1945-61; lectr. U. Bordeaux, France, 1961-63; instr. dept. langs. & lit. U. Del., Newark, 1963-64, asst. prof., 1964-71, assoc. prof., 1971-80, prof., 1980-85, dept. linguistics U. Del., Newark, 1985-96, prof. emeritus, 1998—. Cons. Charles Scribner's Sons, N.Y.C., 1972-75, Larousse, N.Y.C., 1981-84, Houghton-Mifflin, Boston, 1981-84, Macmillan, 1994-99. Author: Two Centuries of Spanish and English Bilingual Lexicography (1590-1800), 1970, New College French and English Dictionary, 1972, 1988; editor: Simon & Schuster's International Spanish Dictionary, 2d edit., 1997, Cuyás Spanish and English Dictionary, 3d edit., 1999, New College Spanish and English Dictionary, 3d edit., 2002; contbr. articles to profl. jours., chpts. to books. Recipient fellowship Am. Philos. Soc., Phila., 1971, Lilly Found., Phila., 1979-81. Mem. MLA (founder lexicography group 1974-75, chmn. 1976, 77, 80, 85), Dictionary Soc. N.Am., Phi Beta Kappa (pres. chpt. 1975-76). Republican. Avocations: languages, photography. Office: U Del Dept Linguistics Newark DE 19716-2551 E-mail: rsteiner@udel.edu.

STEINER, SHARI YVONNE, publisher, editor, journalist; b. Colorado Springs, Colo., Mar. 3, 1941; d. Evan Keith and Blanche Marie (Ketzner) Montgomery; m. Clyde Lionel Steiner, June 24, 1962; children: Vienna Kay, Marco Romano. BA, Adams State Coll., 1962; cert. in sociology, London Sch. Econs., 1978; postgrad., U. Calif., Berkeley, 1988—. Lic. real estate broker, Calif. Freelance journalist various publs., 1964—; owner, mgr. SREI Group, San Francisco, 1985-87; tng. design developer 1st Nationwide Bank, 1987-90; pub., editor Ind. Info. Publs., 1990—; pres. The SREI Group. Feature writer Internat. Herald Tribune, Rome, 1964-79; acct. exec. Allen, Ingersol & Weber, Rome, 1970-72; gen. ptnr. Greenhaven Park, Sacramento, 1990—, Port Chicago Indsl., Concord, Calif., 1991-98, Star/Steiner, 1997—. Author: The Female Factor: A Report on Women in Europe, 1972, 2d edit., 1996, Steiners' Complete How to Move Handbook, 1997, 2d edit., 1999, Steiners' Complete How to Talk Mortgage Talk, 1998, 2d edit., 1999, Relocation Guru, 2000; editor The Bottom Line newsletter, 1985-92; assoc. editor The Semaphore, 1990-92; columnist Country's Best Log Homes, 1999--. Coord. urban reforestation Friends of Urban Forest, San Francisco, 1989; co-founder New Sch. for Internat. Elem. Students, Rome, 1970. Recipient internat. journalism award Guida Monaci, 1970, award of merit Lotus Club, N.Y.C., 1975; corr. in archives Am. Heritage Ctr., U. Wyo. Mem. Nat. Assn. Realtors (multiple listing svc. selection com. 1986, 91, investment real estate group 1991), Comml. Real Estate Women (editor, bd. dirs. 1985—), Am. Soc. Journalists and Authors (exec. bd. dirs. 1998—), PEN Internat., Employee Relocation Coun. Avocation: gardening.

STEINER, STANLEY F. literature educator; b. Richardton, N.D., July 18, 1952; s. John F. and Anna Maria (Greff) Steiner; m. Katherine Radloff, July 20, 1973 (div. May 1978); 1 child Benjamin Matthew ; m. Joy Lynn Steiner, Mar. 31, 1983; children: Lea Christine, Avi John. AA, Bismarck State Coll., 1972; BA, U. Mary, Bismarck, 1974; MS, Northern State U., Aberdeen, S.D., 1976; PhD, U. Wyo., 1992. Tchr., asst. prin. Bismarck Pub. Schs., ND, 1974—78, Teton County Sch. Dist., Jackson Hole, Wyo., 1978—89; prof. Boise State U., 1992—. Author: (novels) Promoting A Global Community, 2001; editor Frierian Pedagogy: Problems, Praxis, and Possibilities, 2000. Adv. bd. dirs. Idaho Human Rights Commn. Mem.: NCTE, Am. Libr. Assn., Internat. Reading Assn. (Notable Books for Global Soc. award 2002). Avocations: childrens literature specialist, woodworker, hiking, cooking. Home: 1105 Pueblo St Boise ID 83702-4152 Office: Boise State U 1910 University Dr Boise ID 83725 Business E-Mail: ssteine@boisestate.edu.

STEINER, STUART, college president; b. Balt., July 24, 1937; s. Louis and Lillian (Block) S.; m. Rosalie Weiner, Sept. 12, 1962; children— Lisa, Susan, David, Robyn. AA, Balt. Jr. Coll., 1957; BS, U. Md., 1959; grad. cert., Fla. State U., 1962; MSW, U. Pa., 1963; JD, U. Balt., 1967; MA, Tchrs. Coll., Columbia U., 1972; EdD, Columbia U., 1987. Caseworker, then supr. and dir. juvenile ct. services Balt. Dept. Social Services, 1960-64; dir. referral center Health and Welfare Council Met. Balt., 1964; dir. admissions and placement Harford Jr. Coll., Bel Air, Md., 1965-67; dean of students Genesee Community Coll., Batavia, N.Y., 1967-68, dean of coll., 1968-75, pres., 1975—. Pres. SUNY West, acting dep. to chancellor for community colls., 1985, pres. of assn. Pres. of Pub. Community Colls., 1987-89; acting pres. Fashion Inst. Tech., N.Y.C., 1997-98; CEO Ednl. Found. Fashion Industries, 1997-98; bd. dirs. Workforce Investment Bd.; commr. Commn. of Higher Edn., Mid. States Assn., 1999—. Contbr. articles to profl. jours. Bd. dirs. St. Jerome Hosp., Genesee County Community Chest, campaign chmn.; bd. dirs. Health Sci. Agy., Western N.Y.; trustee Villa Maria Coll.; trustee, v.p. N.Y. Chiropractic Coll.; bd. dirs. St. Jerome Hosp., Genesee Mercy Healthcare, United Meml. Med Ctr.; pres. Genesee County United Way, Community Coll. of Balt. Hall of Fame. Sigma Delta scholar U. Md., 1958-59, Heuisler scholar U. Balt. Law Sch., 1960-61, Kellogg fellow, 1971-72; recipient CEO award Assn. of C.C. Trustees (N.E. region) 1997. Mem. Pvt. Indsl. Coun. (bd. dirs. 1983-2000, workforce investment bd. 2000-02). Home: 33 Woodcrest Dr Batavia NY 14020-2721 Office: Genesee Community Coll 1 College Rd Batavia NY 14020-9703 E-mail: ssteiner@genesee.edu.

STEINER-HOUCK, SANDRA LYNN, interior designer; b. Columbia, Pa., May 29, 1962; d. Howard Jr. and Mary Louise Steiner; children: Brandon Paul, Brittany Leigh. AA in Interior Design, Bauder Fashion Coll., 1981. Cert. kitchen designer. Designer Bob Harry's Kitchen Ctr., Inc., York, Pa., 1982-87, Leggett, Inc., Camp Hill, 1987-90, Mother Hubbard's Kitchen Ctr., Mechanicsburg, 1990-93; owner ind. design svc., 1994—. Designer: Bath Industry Technical Manuals Vol.3, 1993; contbr. designs to profl. jours. Recipient 1st pl. award and Best of Show Resdl. Bath Design, 1986, Showroom Design, 1989, 3d pl. award Resdl. Kitchen, 1992, Resdl. Bath Design, 1992, Heritage Custom Kitchens Mfr.'s Design award, 1986, 94, 3 Nat. Design. awards Resdl. Kitchen, 1994, Kasmar Kitchen Design award 1994, 95, 96, 2d pl. Nat. Design award Kitchen Design, 1997, 1st pl. Nat. Design award Bath Design, 1997, 2000. Mem. Am. Soc. Interior Design, Soc. Cert. Kitchen Designers. Home: 515 Mockingbird Dr Columbia PA 17512-8438 Office: 3 Kacey Ct Ste 201 Mechanicsburg PA 17055-9213 Fax: 717-591-0563.

STEINETZ, BERNARD GEORGE, JR. endocrinologist; b. Germantown, Pa., May 30, 1927; s. Bernard George Sr. and Hazel Scott (Jefferds) S.; m. Jane Rutledge Nash, June 17, 1949; children: Scott Jefferds, Ann Rutledge Steinetz Barton. AB, Princeton U., 1950; PhD, Rutgers U., 1954. Sr. scientist Warner-Chilcott Co., Morris Plains, N.J., 1954-58; sr. rsch. assoc. Warner-Lambert Rsch. Inst., 1958-67; head reprod. endocrinology CIBA Pharm. Co., Summit, N.J., 1967-71; mgr. cartilage rsch. and endocrinology CIBA-Geigy Corp., Ardsley, N.Y., 1971-84; rsch. assoc. prof. Lab. Exptl. Medicine and Surgery in Primates NYU Med. Ctr., Tuxedo, 1984—, rsch. prof., 1991—; rsch. prof. environ. medicine Nelson Inst. Environ. Medicine NYU Sch. Medicine, 1997—. Mem. conf. orgn. com. N.Y. Acad. Scis., N.Y.C., 1968-70. Contbr. more than 150 articles to profl. jours. Mem. Drug Utilization Rev. Coun. of the State of N.J., Trenton, 1977-86. Fellow CIBA Rsch. CIBA Pharm. Co., 1968, fellow N.Y. Acad. Sci., 1971; grantee March of Dimes, 1987-89, 95-97, Morris Animal Found., 1987-93, NIH (NICHHD) 1994—, Cancer Rsch. Found. of Am., 1999—. Mem. Endocrine Soc., Am. Physiol. Soc., Soc. for Study Reproduction, N.Y. Acad. Scis., Orthopaedic Rsch. Soc., Brookside Racket & Swim Club, Franklin Lakes Racket Club. Achievements include patents for method of determining pregnancy in dogs. Home: 336 Longbow Dr Franklin Lakes NJ 07417-2122 Office: NYU Sch Med Nelson Inst Eviron Medicine 57 Old Forge Rd Tuxedo Park NY 10987-5007 E-mail: steinetz@env.med.nyu.edu.

STEINFELD, BARBARA NICHOLAS, language educator; b. Bossier City, La. d. Elias N. Nicholas and Daisy Loretta Killinger-White; m. James Henry Steinfeld, May 25, 1973; children: Mark Christian, David Lawrence. BA, Montclair State U., 1965; MS, Ind. U., 1966, EdS, 1967; PhD, Mich. State U., 1971. Cert. tchr. Fla. Asst. prof. Ball State U., Muncie, Ind., 1970—73; assoc. prof. English Brevard C.C., Melbourne, Fla., 1989—95; English tchr. Orange County Pub. Schs., Orlando, 1995—99, Sch. Bd. Brevard County, Melbourne, 1993—94, 1999—; instr., prof. Columbia Coll., Patrick AFB, 2000. Author: Language Arts Labcon, 1997. Recipient Disney Teacherrific award, Disney, Orlando, 1997, award, The Darden Found., Orlando, 1997, Sch. to Work award, Sch. to Work Partnership, Orlando, 1998, 1999. Avocations: golf, non-fiction reading, home and garden research.

STEINFELD, JEFFREY IRWIN, chemistry educator, consultant, writer; b. Bklyn., July 2, 1940; s. Paul and Ann (Ravin) S. B.Sc., MIT, 1962; PhD, Harvard U., 1965. Postdoctoral fellow U. Sheffield, Yorkshire, Eng., 1965-66; asst. prof. chemistry MIT, Cambridge, 1966-70, assoc. prof., 1970-79, prof., 1980—. Author: Molecules & Radiation, 1974; co-author: Chemical Kinetics and Dynamics, 1989, 2d edit., 1999; editor: Laser and Coherence Spectroscopy, 1977, Laser-Induced Chemical Processes, 1981; co-editor: Spectrochimica Acta, 1983-98; contbr. articles to profl. jours. Treas. Ward 2 Democratic Com., Cambridge, 1972-73 NSF fellow Harvard U., Cambridge, 1962-65; NSF fellow Sheffield U., 1965-66; Alfred P. Sloan Found. research fellow MIT, 1969-71; Guggenheim fellow, 1972-73 Fellow Am. Phys. Soc.; mem. AAAS, Union Concerned Scientists, Fedn. Am. Scientists, Sigma Xi, Phi Lambda Upsilon. Jewish. Office: MIT Room 2-221 Cambridge MA 02139

STEINFELD, MANFRED, furniture manufacturing executive; b. Josbach, Germany, Apr. 29, 1924; s. Abraham and Puala (Katten) S.; m. Fern Goldman, Nov. 13, 1949; children: Michael, Paul, Jill. Student, U. Ill., 1942; BS in Commerce, Roosevelt U., 1948, LLH (hon.), 1997. Rsch. analyst State of Ill., 1948-50; v.p. Shelby Williams Industries, Inc., Chgo., 1954-63, pres., 1964-72, chmn. bd., 1973-96, chmn. exec. com., 1996—. Bd. dirs. Amalgamated Trust & Savs. Bank. Mem. adv. bd. Shc. Human Ecology, U. Tenn., 1981-87, devel. coun., 1982-87; mem. adv. bd. dept. interior design Fla. Internat. U., 1981-85; life trustee Roosevelt U., Chgo.; past pres. Roosevelt U. Bus. Sch. Alumni Coun.; hon. governing mem. Art Inst. Chgo., mem. com. 20th century decorative art; bd. dirs. Jewish Fedn. Chgo., 1986-90; gen. chmn. Jewish United Fund, 1987, 97; nat. vice chmn. United Jewish Appeal, 1988-94; chmn. bd. dirs. Jewish Fedn. Chgo., 1988—. Served to 1st lt. AUS, 1942-45, 50-52. Decorated Bronze Star, Purple Heart; named Small Bus. Man of Yr., Ctrl. REgion, 1967; established Manfred Steinfeld Hospitality Mgmt. Program at Roosevelt U., Chgo., 1988; established Manfred Steinfeld Hospitality mgmt. Program at Roosevelt U., Chgo., 1988; established Fernand Manfred Steinfeld Chair Judaic Studies U. Tenn., Knoxville, 1995; recipient Horatio Alger awrad of disting. Ams., 1981, Outstanding Bus. Leader award Northwood Inst., 1983, Vol. of Yr., U. Tenn., 1996, Lifetime Achievement award Hospitality Design Mag., 1999. Mem. Horation Alger Assn. (bd. dirs. 1986-92), Standard Club, Bryn Mawr Country Club, Bocaire Country Club (Boca Raton, Fla.), Beta Gamma Sigma. Home: 1300 N Lake Shore Dr Apt 34D Chicago IL 60610-5165 Office: Mdse Mart Rm 11-111 Chicago IL 60654 also: Shelby Williams Industries Inc 150 Shelby Williams Dr Morristown TN 37813-1138

STEINFELD, RAY, JR. food products executive; b. Portland, Oreg., Nov. 21, 1946; s. Ray and June Catherine (Cox) S.; children: Erik, Blair. Student, Wheaton Coll., 1964-66, Drew U., 1967; BS in Polit. Sci., Lewis and Clark Coll., 1968. Sales rep. Continental Can Co., L.A., 1969-72; co-chmn. bd., CEO, Steinfeld's Products Co., Portland, Oreg., from 1972. Chmn. Oreg. Mus. Sci. in Industry, 1992-94. Treas., bd. dirs. Portland Recycling Team, 1973—; pres. exec. bd. Stop Oreg. Litter and Vandalism, 1973-92, pres., 1976; chmn., exec. com. Oreg. Landmark of Quality, 1985-87, Oreg. Ballet Theatre, 1994—, bd. dirs., 1995—, v.p. devel., 1997—, pres., 1998—; pres. exec. com. William Temple House, 1985-91; vestry mem. Trinity Episcopal Ch., 1987-90; chmn. Oregn. Strategic Plan Agrl. Dept., 1988, World Trade Week, Portland, 1989; mem. Gov. Robert's Task Force, Salem, Oreg., 1991-92; bd. dirs. Oreg. Enterprise Forum, 1992-96, chmn., 1995; bd. dirs. Portland Advocates for Student Arts, 1999—. Mem. Pickle Packers Internat. (mem. mdse. com.), Portland C. of C. (bd. dirs. 1995-99). Democrat. Episcopalian. Avocations: tennis, golf, bridge. Home: Portland, Oreg. Deceased.

STEINFELD, THOMAS ALBERT, publisher; b. N.Y.C., June 17, 1917; s. Albert and Marjorie (Lesser) S.; m. Joan Rollinson, July 29, 1945 (dec. Nov. 1973); children: Geoffrey T., Jill R.; m. Viviane Barkey, June 20, 1977. Student, G. Phillips Exeter Acad., 1934, Harvard U., 1934-35. Salesman John Orr Products, N.Y.C., 1935-36; asst. advt. mgr. Bloomingdale's, 1936-37; with Playbill mag., 1937—, pub., 1962-65, pres., 1962-68, v.p., nat. sales dir., nat. sales dir. emeritus, cons., 2000—. Served to capt. AUS, 1942-46, CBI. Mem.: The Wings Club (N.Y.C.), Aspetuck Valley Country Club (Weston, Conn.). Home: 83 W Meadow Rd Wilton CT 06897-4722 Office: 525 7th Ave New York NY 10018

STEINFINK, HUGO, chemical engineering educator; b. Vienna, Austria, May 22, 1924; s. Mendel and Malwina (Fiderer) S.; m. Cele Intrator, Mar. 21, 1948; children: Dan E., Susan D. BS, CCNY, 1947; MS, Columbia U., 1948; PhD, Bklyn. Poly. Inst., 1954. Rsch. chemist Shell Devel. Co., Houston, 1948-51, 53-60; T. Brockett Hudson prof. chem. engring. U. Tex., Austin, 1960-2000, prof. emeritus, 2000. Contbr. articles to profl. jours. With AUS, 1944-46. Fellow Am. Mineral Soc.; mem. AIChE, Am. Chem. Soc., Am. Crystallographic Assn. (pres.-elect 1994, pres. 1995, past pres. 1996), Materials Rsch. Soc., Phi Beta Kappa, Sigma Xi, Phi Lambda Epsilon. Home: 3811 Walnut Clay Dr Austin TX 78731-4011

STEINGLASS, PETER JOSEPH, psychiatrist, educator; b. N.Y.C., Mar. 1, 1939; s. Sam and Bella Sarah (Bernstein) S.; m. Abbe Stahl, July 1, 1962; children: Matthew Aaron, Joanna Eowyn. AB, Union Coll., 1960; MD, Harvard U., 1965. Diplomate, Am. Bd. Psychiatry and Neurology. Head clin. rsch. program Nat. Inst. Alcohol Abuse and Alcoholism, Washington, 1971-74; asst. prof. psychiatry George Washington U., 1974-77, assoc. prof. psychiatry, 1977-81, prof. psychiatry and behavioral sci., 1981-90; exec. dir. Ackerman Inst. for the Family, N.Y.C., 1990—. Vis. prof. psychiatry Hebrew U., Jerusalem, 1981-82; clin. prof. psychiatry Cornell U. Med. Coll., 1993—. Author: The Alcoholic Family, 1987; contbr. articles to sci. publs. Lt. comdr. USPHS, 1969-71. Fellow Am. Psychiat. Assn., Am. Assn. Marriage and Family Therapy (cumulative contbn. award 1992), Assn. Clin. Psychosocial Rsch.; mem. Am. Family Therapy Acad. (charter, bd. dirs. 1987-89, v.p.

1989-91, Disting. Contbn. award 1987), Aesculapian Soc., Phi Beta Kappa. Democrat. Jewish. Avocations: photography, classical music. Office: Ackerman Inst for the Family 149 E 78th St New York NY 10021-0405 E-mail: psteinglass@ackerman.org.

STEINGRABER, FREDERICK GEORGE, management consultant; b. Mpls., July 7, 1938; s. Frederick F. and Evelyn (Luger) S.; m. Veronika Agnes Wagner, Aug. 9, 1974; children: Karla, Frederick. BS, Ind. U., 1960; MBA, U. Chgo., 1964. Cert. mgmt. cons. Internat. banker Harris Trust, Chgo., 1960-61; with comml. loan and credit No. Trust Co., 1964—68; assoc. A.T. Kearney, 1969—72, prin., 1972—, officer/ptnr., 1972—, pres., COO, 1981—82, CEO, 1983—2000, chmn. bd., 1983—2000, also bd. dirs. Bd. dirs. Continental AG, Maytag Corp., John Hancock Fin. Trend Funds; bd. mem. Inst. for Ill. , 1986. Chief crusader United Way Crusade of Mercy, Chgo., 1983—90; divsn.chmn., bd. dirs.l Ill. Coalition, 1989; fin. rsch. aand adv. com. City of Chgo., 1989—; mem., past chmn. dean's adv. coun. U. Ind. , Bloomington, 1985—; bd. dirs. Ind. U. Cound.; mem. coun. Grad. Sch. Bus. U. Chgo.; mem. Northwestern U. Assocs., Evanston, Ill.; exec. com. Mid. Am. Com., 1985—; mem. Chgo. Com. , 1994—; bd. dirs. Northwestern Healtcare Network, 1989—96, Children's Meml. Hosp., Chgo., 1985—. Recipient Disting. Alumnus award U. Chgo., 1996, Disting. Corp. Exec. award U. Chgo., 1996, Disting. Corp. and Comm. Leadership award Am. Jewish Com., 1998, Disting. Alumnus award Ind. U., 2000. Mem. NAM (bd. dirs.), Inst. Mgmt. Cons., Chgo. Coun. Fgn. Rels. (bd. dirs., chair devel. com.), Ill. State C. of C. (bd. dirs. 1982-88, exec. com. 1984-88, chmn. Ill. Alliance for Econ. Initiatives), Exec. Club Chgo., Acad. Alumni Fellows Ind. U. (award), Chgo. Club, Econ. Club (bd. dirs.), Comml. Club, Met. Club, Glenview Club, Beta Gamma Sigma, others. Home: 615 Warwick Rd Kenilworth IL 60043-1149 Office: AT Kearney Inc 222 W Adams St Ste 2500 Chicago IL 60606-5307

STEINGRABER, LARRY LEE, quality engineer; b. Manawa, Wis., June 5, 1954; s. Clarence M. and Viann M. (Vaughn) S.; m. Kathleen L. Rein, Aug. 12, 1978; 1 child, Daniel J. BS in Archtl. and Bldg. Constrn. Engring, Milw. Sch. Engring., 1980. Registered profl. engr., Wis.; cert. playground safety inspector. Engr. Inryco-Milcor, Milw., 1980-85, Inryco-Bldg. Panels, Milw., 1985-87, BCI Burke Co., Inc., Fond du Lac, Wis., 1988—, BCI Burke Co. Inc., 1988-97, BCI Burke Co., LLC, 1997—. Mem. ASTM, NSPE, ASM Internat., Soc. Plastics Engring., Nat. Recreation and Parks Assn., Soc. Mfg. Engrs., Wis. Soc. Profl. Engrs., Corvair Soc. Am., soc. of Plastics Engrs. Lutheran. Achievements include patent for enclosed rubber spring. Home: 287 Hartford Rd Slinger WI 53086-9545 Office: BCI Burke Co LLC 660 Van Dyne Rd Fond Du Lac WI 54937-1447

STEINGRABER, SANDRA KATHRYN, biologist, ecologist, writer; b. Champaign, Ill., Aug. 27, 1959; d. Wilbur Francis and Kathryn Marie (Maurer) Steingraber; m. Brian Wayne Burt, May 21, 1982 (div. Sept. 1994); m. Jeffrey Peter de Castro, Oct. 18, 1996; children: Faith Kathryn, Elijah Jeffrey. BA, Ill. Wesleyan U., 1981; MS, Ill. State U., 1982; PhD, U. Mich., 1989; LHD (hon.) , Ill. Wesleyan U., 2001. Prof. biology Columbia Coll., Chgo., 1990-93; vis. scholar Northeastern U., Boston, 1994—. Vis. asst. prof. Ctr. for the Environment, Cornell U., 1999—. Author: The Spoils of Famine, 1988, Post-Diagnosis, 1995, Living Downstream: An Ecologist Looks at Cancer and the Environment, 1997, Having Faith: An Ecologist's Journey to Motherhood, 2001. Pub. spkr. Women's Cmty. Cancer Project, Cambridge, Mass., 1993—. Named Woman of Yr., Ms. Mag., 1997; recipient Jenifer Altman Found. Pub. Svc. award, 1998, Med. Comms. award, Am. Med. Writers Assn., 1998, Rachel Carson Leadership award, Chatham Coll., Pitts., 2001; fellow Bunting Inst. fellow, Cambridge, 1993, U. Ill. fellow in Women's Pub. Health Policy, 1996. Mem.: APHA, Radcliffe Fellows Soc., Nat. Writers' Union, Associated Writing Programs, Phi Beta Kappa. Avocations: hiking and backpacking, running, literature. Home: 201 Thomas Rd Ithaca NY 14850-9687 Office: Ctr for Environ Cornell U 110 Rice Hall Ithaca NY 14853-5601

STEINGRUB, JAY STANLEY, critical care physician, educator; b. N.Y.C., Feb. 29, 1952; m. Milagrow C. Rosal, Oct. 17, 1993. BA, SUNY, Buffalo, 1973; MD, SUNY, Syracuse, 1977. Diplomate Am. Bd. Internal Medicine (question provider, relevancy reviewer, critical care medicine test and policy com. 1992—), Am. Bd. Critical Care Medicine. Intern in medicine Rochester (N.Y.) Gen. Hosp.-U. Rochester, 1977-78, resident in medicine, 1978-80; clin. fellow in critical care medicine Univ. Health Ctr. Pitts., 1980-81, rsch. fellow in critical care medicine, 1981-82; assoc. prof. medicine Tufts U. Sch. Medicine, Boston, 1982—, asst. prof. surgery, 1995—; assoc. dir. adult critical care ctr. Baystate Med. Ctr., Springfield, Mass., 1982—, dir. med. ICU, 1985—. ICU physician Park Ridge Hosp., Rochester, 1978-80; emergency room physician Allegheny Gen. Hosp., Pitts., 1980-81; lectr. in field, 1982—. Contbr. articles to med. jours. Grantee NIH, Miles, Cortech, Ohmeda PPD, Liposomal Co., Glaxo, Pfizer, RAR, ICOS, Lilly, Wyeth. Fellow ACP, Am. Coll. Chest Physicians (abstract reviewer 1993—); mem. Critical Care Soc., Shock Soc., Soc. Critical Care Medicine (cert. course instr. for fundamental critical care support, abstract reviewer 1992—, rep. internal medicine sect. to rsch. award selection com. 1995—), N.Y. Acad. Scis., Arista, Phi Beta Kappa. Office: Baystate Med Ctr 759 Chestnut St Springfield MA 01199-1001

STEINHARDT, NANCY SHATZMAN, art historian, educator; b. St. Louis, July 14, 1954; d. Ben and Miriam (Levin) Shatzman; m. Paul Joseph Steinhardt; children: Charles, Joseph, William, Cynthia. AB, Washington U., 1974; AM, Harvard U., 1975, PhD, 1981. Lectr. Bryn Mawr (Pa.) Coll., 1981-83; lectr. art history U. Pa., Phila., 1982-86, asst. prof., 1986-91, assoc. prof. Asian and Middle Eastern studies, 1991-97, prof. Asian and Middle Eastern studies, 1997—, curator Chinese art, 1997—. Author: Chinese Traditional Architecture, 1984, Chinese Imperial City Planning, 1990, Liao Architecture, 1997; contbr. articles to profl. jours. Getty Sr. fellow, 1990; grantee Fulbright-Hays, 1976-77, NEH, 1983, 92, 94, Am. Coun. Learned Socs., 1984, 89, Graham Found., 1989, 2001, Am. Philos. Soc., 1992, 98, Asian Cultural Coun., 1993, Social Sci. Rsch. Coun., 1995, Guggenheim Found., 2001, Chiang Ching-Kuo Found., 2001. Mem. Coll. Art Assn., Assn. Asian Studies, Soc. Archtl. Historians. Home: 154 Christopher Dr Princeton NJ 08540-2322 Office: U Pa Dept Asian-Mid Ea Studies Philadelphia PA 19104-6305 E-mail: nssteinh@sas.upenn.edu.

STEINHAUER, JODY, retail executive; Pres., chief visionary officer The Bargains Group Ltd., Toronto. Office: The Bargains Group Ltd 153 Brideland Ave Unit # 1 Toronto ON Canada M6A 2Y6

STEINHAUER, KARSTEN, neuroscientist, researcher; b. Itzehoe, Schleswig-Holstein, Germany, Sept. 1, 1960; s. Werner Steinhauer, Lieselotte Marie Steinhauer; m. Clare L. Foa. Dr.rer.nat., Free U. Berlin. Rsch. fellow Max Planck Inst. Cognitive Neuroscience, Leipzig, Germany, 1995—2000; postdoctoral fellow Georgetown U., Washington, 2000—, rsch. asst. Author: (book) Hirnphysiologische Korrelate prosodischer Satzverarbeitung bei gesprochener und geschriebener Sprache, 2001; contbr. articles to profl. jours. Mem.: AAAS, Cognitive Neuroscience Soc. Office: Georgetown Univ 3900 Reservoir Rd NW Washington DC 20007 Office Fax: 202-687-6914. Business E-Mail: steinhau@giccs.georgetown.edu.

STEINHAUER, SHERRI, professional golfer; b. Madison, Wis., Dec. 27, 1962; Student, U. Tex. Golfer LPGA, 1986—; winner du Maurier Classic, 1992, Sprint Championship, 1994, Weetabix Women's British Open Championship, 1998, 99; mem. U.S. Solheim Cup Team, 1994, 98, 2000, Japan Airlines Big Apple Classic, 1999. Achievements include 3 LPGA career hole-in-ones. Office: c/o LPGA 100 International Golf Dr Daytona Beach FL 32124-1082

STEINHAUS, JOHN EDWARD, physician, medical educator; b. Omaha, Feb. 23, 1917; s. Emil F. and Pearl (Haynie) S.; m. Mila Jean Pinkerton, Feb. 21, 1943; children: Kathryn, Carolyn, Barbara, William, Elizabeth. BA, U. Neb., 1940, MA, 1941; MD, U. Wis., 1945, PhD, 1950. Diplomate: Am. Bd. Anesthesiologists. Pvt. practice specializing in anesthesiology, Madison, Wis., 1951-58, Atlanta, 1958—; faculty U. Wis., 1951-58; mem. faculty Emory U., Atlanta, 1958—, prof. anesthesiology, 1959-87, prof. emeritus, 1987—, chmn. dept., 1959-85; chief anesthesiology service Grady Meml. Hosp., 1959-77, Emory U. Hosp., 1958-85. Author: Medical Care Divided; contbr. articles to profl. jours. Pres. Anesthesia Found. Mem. Am. Soc. Anesthesiologists (past pres., Disting. Service award 1982), So. Soc. Anesthesiologists (past pres.), AMA, AAAS, Assn. U. Anesthetists (past pres.), Anesthesiology History Assn. (pres), Soc. Pharm. Exptl. Therapeutics, Phi Beta Kappa, Sigma Xi, Alpha Omega Alpha. Home and Office: 836 Castle Falls Dr NE Atlanta GA 30329-4114 E-mail: jsteinh@emory.edu.

STEINHAUSER, JANICE MAUREEN, arts administrator, educator, artist; b. Oklahoma City, Apr. 3, 1935; d. Max Charles and Charlotte (Gold) Glass; m. Stuart Z. Hirschman, Dec. 30, 1954 (div. 1965); children: Shayle, David, Susan; m. Sheldon Steinhauser, May 2, 1965; children: Karen, Lisa Steinhauser Hackel. BFA, U. Colo., Denver, 1972; student, U. Mich., 1953-55. Community affairs adminstr. United Bank Denver, 1973-76; dir. visual arts program Western States Arts Found., Denver, 1976-79; exec. dir. Artreach, Inc., 1980-82; v.p. mktg. Mammoth Gardens, 1982-83; dir. pub. rels. Denver Ctr. for Performing Arts, 1983-86; founder, pres. Resource Co., Denver, 1986-88; dir. liberal studies div. Univ. Coll. U. Denver, 1992-97; sculptor, 1997—. Bd. dirs. Met. Denver Arts Alliance, 1982-85, Denver Internat. Film Festival, 1983-86, Colo. Nat. Abortion Rights Action League, 1991-95. Mem. Women's Forum Colo., Colo. New Music Assn. (bd. dirs. 1987-91), Asian Performing Arts Colo. (bd. dirs. Mizel Mus. of Judaica, 1995-2000), Phi Beta Kappa, Kappa Delta Phi. Democrat. Jewish. Avocations: travel, reading, films. E-mail: jansart3@aol.com.

STEINHAUSER, JOHN WILLIAM, retired lawyer; b. Akron, Ohio, June 25, 1924; s. John Hugo and Francis Lillian (Pearson) S.; m. Patricia E. Mooney, Dec.1, 1956; children: John, Christian, Mark, Sharon. BSBA, Ohio State U., 1949; JD, U. Mich., 1950. Bar: Mich. 1950, Colo. 1972. Atty., dir. L.Am., dir. export sales, gen mgr. Africa-Far E. Chrysler Corp., dir. Chrysler Internat., dir. Africa-Far East, 1950-71; atty. Denver, 1971—; founder, dir., pres. Pearson Energy Corp., 1977—. Founder, chmn. Sharon Energy, Ltd., Denver, 1980, also dir., 1971-97. Active Colo. Rep. Com.; sponsor Denver Symphony; pres. John and Patricia Steinhauser Found. With USNR, 1943—46. Mem. ABA, Colo. Bar Assn., Mich. Bar Assn., Soc. Internat. Law, Rocky Mountain Mineral Law Found., Cherry Hills Country Club, Royal Poinciana Golf Club, Rotary. Home: 46 Charlou Cir Englewood CO 80111-1103 E-mail: jwsteinhauser@prodigy.com.

STEINHAUSER, SHELDON ELI, sociology and gerontology educator, diversity and development consultant; b. N.Y.C., Aug. 11, 1930; s. Charles W. and Helen (Rosenstein) S.; m. Frances Goldfarb, June 28, 1953 (div. 1963); children: Karen, Lisa Steinhauser Hackel; m. Janice M. Glass, May 2, 1965; children: Shayle, David, Susan Hirschman. BS, L.I. U., 1963; DPS (hon.), Regis U., 1994. Community cons. Anti-Defamation League, Columbus, Ohio, 1951-57, regional dir. Denver, 1957-85, dir. nat. field svcs., 1977-85, dir. nat. community svcs. divsn., 1979-81, western area dir., 1975-85; exec. v.p. Allied Jewish Fedn. of Denver, 1985-91; pres. Sheldon Steinhauser & Assocs., Denver, 1991—; instr. sociology Met. State Coll., 1969-71, assoc. prof., 1994—. Arbitrator Am. Arbitration Assn., Denver, 1988—; pres. Anti-Defamation League profl. Staff Assn., Agy. Execs. Orgn., Denver, 1963; past cons. EEOC. Mem. editl. bd. Sustainable Cmtys. Rev. Missions to Egypt and Israel, 1982, 83; staff dir. Mission to Israel, 1986, 87, 90; former mem. Denver Anti-Crime Coun.; chmn. Mountain States Inst. of Judaism, Denver, 1958-59; past pres. Adult Edn. Coun. Met. Dever; past mem. cmty. adv. bd. Jr. League Denver; cons. U.S. Dept. Justice Cmty. Rels. Svc., 1994; past mem. Colo. Martin Luther King Holiday Planning Com., Latin Am. Rsch. and Svc. Agy., founding bd. mem.; mem. adv. com. Regis U. Inst. Common Good; Equal Opportunity Adv. Coun., Met State Coll., Denver; past mem. cmty. working group Nat. Civilian Cmty. Corps.; congl. del. White House Conf. on Aging, 1995. Recipient M.L. King Jr. Humanitarian award Colo. M.L. King Commn., Denver, 1986, 1st Ann. Human Rels. award Colo. Civil Rights Commn., Denver, 1965, Humanitarian award NAACP, Denver, 1980, ADL Civil Rights Achievement award, 1989; named to Gallery of Fame, Denver Post, 1979, 80. Mem. Diversity Assocs. Internat., Western Social Sci. Assn., Am. Sociol. Assn. (sect. on aging), Colo. Jewish Reconstructionist Fedn., Am. Soc. on Aging, Sociol. Practice Assn., Assn. for Gerontology in Higher Edn. (nat. pub. policy com.), Gerontol. Soc. Am., Colo. Gerontol. Soc., Am. Arbitration Assn. (Rocky Mountain adv. com.), B'nai B'rith. Avocations: travel, photography, tennis, running, cantorial music. E-mail: sheldon53@aol.com.

STEINHERZ, LAUREL JUDITH, pediatric cardiologist; b. N.Y.C., Jan. 5, 1947; d. Bernard and Adeline Weinberger; m. Peter Gustav Steinherz, July 4, 1967; children: Jennifer, Jonathan, Daniel, David. Student, Hebrew U., Jersualem, l966; BA with distinction, U. Rochester, l967; MD, Albert Einstein Coll. Medicine, 1970. Diplomate Am. Bd. Pediatrics, sub-bd. pediatric cardiology. Intern in pediatrics N.Y. Hosp.-Cornell Med. Ctr., N.Y.C., 1970-71; pediatric cardiology fellow N.Y. Presbyn. Hosp.-N.Y. Weill Cornell Med. Ctr. (formerly N.Y. Hosp. Cornell U. Med. Ctr.), 1973-75, asst. attending pediatrician, 1978-85, assoc. attending pediatrician, 1985—; resident in pediatrics St. Louis Children's Hosp., 1971-72; attending pediatrician State U. Hosp. and King County Med. Ctr., Bklyn., 1975-77; asst. prof. pediatrics SUNY Downstate, 1975-77, Cornell U. Med. Coll., N.Y.C., 1977-85, assoc. prof. pediatrics, 1985—; from asst. to assoc. attending pediatrician Meml. Sloan Kettering Cancer Ctr., 1977—, dir. pediatric cardiology, 1977—, asst. clin. mem., 1984-92, assoc. mem., 1997—. Contbg. author Adolescent Medicine II, 1976, Principles and Practice of Oncology, 1992, 1996, 2001, Supportive Care of Children With Cancer, 1993, 1997, Cardiac Toxicity After Treatment for Childhood Cancer, 1993, Progress in Pediat. Cardiology, 1998; contbr. articles to profl. jours. Hutzler Found. grantee, 1987. Fellow: Am. Coll. Cardiology, Am. Acad. Pediatrics; mem.: Children's Oncology Group, Am. Heart Assn. Avocations: photography, swimming, Star Trek. Office: Meml Sloan Kettering Cancer Ctr 1275 York Ave New York NY 10021-6094

STEINHOFF, ANTHONY JAMES, European history educator; b. Moscow, Aug. 13, 1967; s. Raphael John and Jeanne Margaret (Joubert) S. BA, Brandeis U., 1989; MA, U. Chgo., 1990, PhD, 1996. Asst. prof. history U. Tenn., Chattanooga, 1999—. Vis. asst. prof. history, Miami U., Oxford, Ohio, 1997-98, Coll. Charleston, S.C., 1998-99. Inst. European History fellow, Mainz, Germany, 1994, dissertation fellow, Friedrich Ebert Stiftung, 1992-93, short-term rsch. fellow, German Acad. Exch. Svc., 1992. Mem. Am. Hist. Assn., German Studies Assn., Soc. French Hist. Studies, Phi Beta Kappa. Avocation: music. Office: U Tenn (2052) 615 McCallie Ave Chattanooga TN 37403 Fax: (423) 785-2138.

STEINHOFF, RAYMOND O(AKLEY), consulting geologist; b. Hart, Mich., Apr. 22, 1925; m. Anne M. Steinhoff, 1952; 1 child, Kirk O. BS, MS, So. Meth. U., 1948; PhD in Geology, Tex. A&M, 1965. Instr. geology Tex. A&M U., Coll. Sta., Tex., 1948-51; geologist Atlantic Rich., Wichita, Kans., 1951-53, Humble Oil and Refining Co., New Orleans, 1953-57; asst. prof. geology Tulane U., 1957-65, assoc. prof., 1965-70, chmn. dept., 1969-70; prof. and dept. head geology Stephen F. Austin State U., Nacogdoches, Tex., 1970-78; divsn. geologist Buttes, New Orleans, 1978-79; cons. geologist Graham, 1979-83. Cons. Trinexco, New Orleans, 1964-69. Sgt. U.S. Army, 1944-46; 1st lt. USAF, 1952-53, Korea. Mem. Am. Assn. Petroleum Geologists (emeritus), New Orleans Geol. Soc. (emeritus), Phi Kappa Phi. Home: 6 North H St Pensacola FL 32501-4420

STEINHORN, IRWIN HARRY, lawyer, educator, corporate executive; b. Dallas, Aug. 13, 1940; s. Raymond and Libby L. (Miller) Steinhorn; m. Deborah Kelley Steinhorn, Apr. 7, 2002; 1 child Leslie Robin. BBA, U. Tex., 1961, LLB, 1964. Bar: Tex. 1964, U.S. Dist. Ct. (no. dist.) Tex. 1965, Okla. 1970, U.S. Dist. Ct. (we. dist.) Okla. 1972. Assoc. Oster & Kaufman, Dallas, 1964-67; ptnr. Parness, McQuire & Lewis, 1967-70; sr. v.p., gen. counsel LSB Industries, Inc., Oklahoma City, 1970-87; v.p., gen. counsel USPCI, Inc., 1987-88; ptnr. Hastie & Steinhorn, 1988-95; mem., officer, dir. Conner & Winters, 1995—. Adj. prof. law Oklahoma City U. Sch. Law, 1979—; lectr. in field. Mem. adv. com. Okla. Securities Commn., 1986—; mem. exec. adv. bd. Oklahoma City U. Sch. Law, 2000—; bd. dirs. Okla. Venture Forum, 2000—. Served to capt. USAR, 1964-70. Mem. ABA, Tex. Bar Assn., Okla. Bar Assn. (bus. assn. sect., sec.ptreas. 1986-87, chmn. 1988-89), Com. to Revise Okla. Bus. Corp. Act, Rotary, Phi Alpha Delta. Republican. Jewish. Home: 224 NW 18th St Oklahoma City OK 73103 Office: Conner & Winters One Leadership Sq 211 N Robinson Ave Ste 1700 Oklahoma City OK 73102-7136 E-mail: isteinhorn@cwlaw.com.

STEINKE, GREG A, music educator, administrator, composer, oboist; b. Fremont, Mich., Sept. 2, 1942; s. Donald Ferdinand John and Ella Louise (Clute) S.; m. Karen Florence Larsen, June 5, 1971; children: Carl Asa, Kyle Alban. MusB, Oberlin Conservatory, 1964; MMus, Mich. State U., 1967, PhD, 1976; MFA, U. Iowa, 1971. Instr. music U. Idaho, Moscow, 1967-68, dir. Sch. Music, prof. music, 1983-86; chmn. dept. music, prof. San Diego State U., 1986-88; instr. music U. Md., College Park, 1968-72; asst. prof. music Calif. State U., Northridge, 1973-75; mem. faculty Evergreen State Coll., Olympia, Wash., 1975-79; chmn. music dept., prof. Linfield Coll., Mcminnville, Oreg., 1979-83; asst. dir. U. Ariz. Sch. Music, Tucson, 1988-91; prof., dir. Sch. Music Ball State U., Muncie, Ind., 1991-96; prof., dean Coll. fine Arts Millikin U., Decatur, Ill., 1996-97; mem. faculty No. Ariz. U., Flagstaff, 1997-98; chmn. art and music dept., assoc. dean undergrad. studies Marylhurst (Oreg.) U., 1999-2001, Joseph Naumes endowed chair music, 1999-2001, ret., 2001. Guest composer Contemporary Music Festival Western Ill. U., 1982, 90-91, Charles Ives Ctr. for Am. Music, New Milford, Conn., summer 1982, 91, 1st Ann. Festival of New Music, bowling Green State U., 1980, New Music Fest XV Memphis State U., 1987, 5th Symposium for New WWQ5 Mus., U. Ga., 1988,l Biennial Festival New Music Fla. State U., 1989, 91, 93, 96, S.W. Tex. U., 1990, Birmingham So. U., 1990; finalist Seoul Internat. Competition for Composers, 2001; composer-participant numrous music festivals, Atlantic Ctr., for Arts Assn., 1995. Contbr. articles to profl. jours.; author music theory books; numerous compositions for voice, piano, instrumental chamber orch., wind ensemble, miscellaneous, incidental music for plays; also arrangements of music; oboe performer, 1961—. Com. mem. Lake Oswego (Oreg.) Arts Commn., 1999-2001, Moscow City Arts Commn., 1984-86. Recipient numerous awards including: commn. Western Arts Music Festival, laramie,, Wyo., 1986, awards Standards Awards panel of ASCAP, 1979—, Phi Mu Alpha Composition winner Sam Houston State U., 1975; fellow Tucson/Pima Arts Coun. Composition, 1991; grantee Ariz. Arts Commn. Spl. Project Grant, 1990. Mem. McMinnville Arts Assn. (bd. dirs. 1980-81), Am. Music Ctr., Soc. Composers Inc. (past chmn. region IX, editor monograph series, pres., chair nat. coun. 1988-97), ASCAP, Am. Composers Forum, Alban Berg Soc., Ernest Bloch Soc., Coll. Music Soc., Internat. Double Reed Soc., Nat. Assn. Composers, Soc. Oreg. Composers (past pres.). E-mail: oboegreg@yahoo.com.

STEINLAUF, MICHAEL CHARLES, historian; b. Paris, Feb. 19, 1947; came to U.S., 1950; s. William Robert and Doris (Wald) S.; m. Meri Adelman, July 2, 1989; children: Zev-Noah Sar, Benjamin Dov-Lior. BA, Columbia U., 1967, MA, 1969; PhD, Brandeis U., 1988. Asst. prof. Univ. Mich., Ann Arbor, 1988, Brandeis Univ., Waltham, Mass., 1989-90; project dir. U.S. Holocaust Mus., Washington, 1990; asst. prof. Gratz Coll., Melrose Park, Pa., 1991-93; scholar in residence Franklin and Marshall Coll., Lancaster, 1993-94, asst. prof., 1994-96; sr. rsch. fellow YIVO Inst. Jewish Rsch., N.Y.C., 1996-98; assoc. prof. Gratz Coll., Melrose Park, Pa., 1998—. Author: Bondage to the Dead: Poland and the Memory of the Holocaust, 1997; editor Polin; mem. editl. bd. Jewish Scholarship in Eastern Europe; contbr. to profl. jours. Fellow Fulbright, 1983-84, Am. Coun. Learned Soc., 1988-89. Mem. Am. Hist. Assn., Assn. Jewish Studies, Polish Inst. Arts and Sci. Office: Gratz Coll 7605 Old York Rd Melrose Park PA 19027-3010 Home: 330 W Duval St Philadelphia PA 19144-3102

STEINMAN, BETTY JO, civic worker; b. Enid, Okla., Jan. 8, 1935; d. Joseph Edward and Gladys Opal (Johnson) Grimm; m. Henry A. Steinman Jr., June 7, 1953; children: Sharon, Kathy, Nancy, Sherrie and Carrie (twins), Beth and Henry A. III (twins). Tchr.'s cert., Seeger Sch. Cake Decorating, Toledo, 1969; student, Ogden Sch. Cake Decorating, Columbus, Ohio, 1971, San Diego Sch. Decorating, 1975, May's Sch. Decorating, Dallas, 1977. Hostess Foods of World, cable TV show, 1974-76. Demonstrator Mich. State Fair, 1976-79, Betty Ho's Monroe Sch. Cake Decorating, 1969-87, Betty Jo's Cake and Candy Shop, Dundee, Mich., 1977-80; traveling tchr. Editor, author: Cakes and Techniques, 1977. Pres. St. Michael's We Care Inc., 1986-90, former CareTelethon coordinating dir., pres., 1987-88. Named Vol. of Yr., St. Michael's We Care, 1986, Ky. Col., Gov. of State of Ky., 1983; recipient Golden Heart award City and County of Monroe, 1987, Minuteman award State of Mich., 1989, Kelly Svc. Green Derby award, 1990, U.S. Fidelity & Guaranty Co. Award of Excellence, 1990. Mem. Internat. Cake Exploration Soc. (founder, Hall of Fame award 1985), Mothers Club, Twins Club. Home: 176 Troy Ln Hohenwald TN 38462-4013

STEINMAN, CHARLES ROBERT, rheumatologist; b. N.Y.C., Aug. 3, 1938; s. Alan and Estelle Steinman; m. Patricia Steinman; children: Tibbon, Lily. AB, Princeton U., 1959; MD, Columbia U., 1963. Diplomate Am. Bd. Internal Medicine, Am. Bd. Rheumatology. Intern Presbyn. Hosp., N.Y.C., 1963-64, resident, 1964-65, 68-69, fellow in rheumatology, 1967-68, 69-70; physician, faculty mem. Mt. Sinai Sch. of Medicine, 1970-84, SUNY, Bklyn., 1984-90, Stony Brook, 1990—. Staff assoc. NIH, Bethesda, Md., 1965-67; med. adv. bd. Arthritis Found., Atlanta, 1995-97, Lupus Found., 1985—, L.I. chpt. Arthritis Found., 1990—, bd. dirs. Contbr. articles to profl. jours.; patentee in field. Comdr. USPHS, 1965-67. Rsch. grantee NIH, Arthritis Found. E-mail: steinman@epo.som.sunysb.edu.

STEINMAN, H. ROBERT, dean; PhD Physiology, Wayne State U.; DDS, U. Detroit; MSD., cert. in endodontics, Ind. U. Chmn. dept. endodontics U. Detroit-Mercy, 1980—, dean, 2000—, chmn. dept. physiology, dept. basic scis. Office: 8200 W Outer Dr Box 98 Detroit MI 48219*

STEINMAN, JOAN ELLEN, law educator; b. Bklyn., June 19, 1947; d. Jack and Edith Ruth (Shapiro) S.; m. Douglass Watts Cassel, Jr., June 1, 1974 (div. July 1986); children: Jennifer Lynn, Amanda Hilary. Student, U. Birmingham, Eng., 1968; AB with high distinction, U. Rochester, 1969; JD cum laude, Harvard U., 1973. Bar: Ill. 1973. Assoc. Schiff, Hardin & Waite, Chgo., 1973-77; asst. prof. law Chgo.-Kent Coll. Law Ill. Inst. Tech., 1977-82, assoc. prof., 1982-86, prof., 1986-98, Disting. prof., 1998—, interim dean, 1990-91. Cons. in atty. promotions Met. Dist. Greater Chgo., 1981, 85. Contbr. articles to law jours. Coop. atty. ACLU Ill., Chgo., 1974, Leadership Coun. for Met. Open Cmtys., Chgo., 1975, Better Bus. Bur. Met. Chgo., 1987; apptd. bd. arbitrators Nat. Assn. Security Dealers, 1989—2000; apptd. to Ill. Gov.'s Grievence Panel, 1987; bd. dirs. Pro Bono Advocates, 1995—99. Recipient Julia Beveridge award Ill. Inst. Tech., 1996, Ralph L. Brill award Chgo. Kent Coll. Law, 1997; Norman and Edna Frehling scholar Chgo.-Kent Coll. Law, 1989-93. Mem. ABA, Am. Law Inst. (advisor Fed. Jud. Code Revision project 1996-2001, cons. group complex litigation project 1990-93, restatement of the law, third, torts, products liability 1993, transnat. rules of civil procedure 2000-02), Am. Assn. Law Schs. (exec. com. civil procedure sect. 1998-99), Soc. Am. Law Tchrs., Chgo. Coun. Lawyers (fed. cts. com.), AAUW (legal advocacy network 1987-2000), Chgo.-Lincoln Am. Inn. of Ct. (master 1991), Order of Coif, Phi Beta Kappa. Democrat. Jewish. Office: Chgo Kent Coll Law 565 W Adams St Chicago IL 60661-3613

STEINMAN, JOHN FRANCIS, psychiatrist; b. N.Y.C., May 5, 1916; s. David Barnard and Irene Stella (Hoffman) S.; m. Helen G. Meyer (div. 1963); children: James, Judith, Jill; m. Roxane Bear (div. 1972); m. Ellen M. Sears, Nov. 16, 1985. AB with hons., Columbia U., 1936, MD, 1940. Diplomate Am. Bd. Psychiatry and Neurology. Intern Strong Meml. Hosp., Rochester, N.Y. and Cin. Gen. Hosp., 1940-43; resident psychiatry Nebr. Psychiat. Inst., 1948, 58, R.I. Med. Ctr., 1961; psychiatrist, dir. Lincoln (Nebr.) and Lancaster County Child Guidance Ctr., 1948-61; instr. pediatrics, psychiatry and neurology U. Nebr., Lincoln, 1951-52; postdoctoral fellow in psychiatry Yale U., New Haven, 1962-64; psychiatrist U. Conn., Storrs, 1964-69, Community Mental Health Services, San Francisco, 1971-79; pvt. practice psychiatry, 1979—. Delgate, chmn. Nebr. health com. White House Conf. Children and Youth, Washington, 1960. Served to capt. M.C., AUS, 1943-46, PTO. Mem. Am. Psychiat. Assn. (life), Am. Orthopsychiat. Assn., N.Y. Acad. Scis., Phi Beta Kappa. Home and Office: 164 Otsego Ave San Francisco CA 94112-2536 E-mail: steinman334@gateway.net.

STEINMAN, LISA MALINOWSKI, English literature educator, writer; b. Willimantic, Conn., Apr. 8, 1950; d. Zenon Stanislaus and Shirley Belle Malinowski; m. James A. Steinman, Apr. 1968 (div. 1980); m. James L. Shugrue, July 23, 1984. BA, Cornell U., 1971, MFA, 1973, PhD, 1976. Asst. prof. English Reed Coll., Portland, Oreg., 1976-82, assoc. prof., 1982-90, prof., 1990—, Kenan prof. English lit. and humanities, 1993—. Cons. NEH, Washington, 1984-85. Author: Lost Poems, 1976, Made in America, 1987, All That Comes to Light, 1989, A Book of Other Days, 1992, Ordinary Songs, 1996, Masters of Repetition, 1998; editor: Hubbub Mag., 1983—; mem. editl.

bd. Williams Rev., 1991—, Stevens Jour., 1994—; contbr. articles to profl. jours. Fellow Danforth Found., 1971-75, NEH, 1983, 96, Oreg. Arts Commn., 1983, Nat. Endowment for Arts, 1984; Rockefeller Found. scholar, 1987-88; recipient Pablo Neruda award, 1987, Oreg. Inst. Lit. Arts award, 1993. Mem. MLA, Poets and Writers, PEN (N.W. chpt., co-founder, officer 1989-93). Home: 5344 SE 38th Ave Portland OR 97202-4208 Office: Reed Coll Dept English 3203 SE Woodstock Blvd Portland OR 97202-8138 E-mail: lisa.steinman@reed.edu.

STEINMAN, THEODORE IRVING, nephrologist, educator; b. Phila., May 16, 1938; s. Jacob and Lena (Rosenberg) S.; m. Carol Zeldon, June 9, 1964; children: Kenneth, Michael Jay. BS, Pa. State U., 1960; MD, Georgetown U., 1964. Diplomate Am. Bd. Internal Medicine, Am. Bd. Nephrology. Intern in medicine Cedars-Sinai Med. Ctr., L.A., 1964-65, jr. asst. resident in medicine, 1965-66; sr. asst. resident in medicine Beth Israel Hosp., Boston, 1968-69, asst. physician, 1971-76, assoc. physician, 1976-87, physician, 1988—; teaching fellow in medicine Harvard Med. Sch., 1968-69, instr. in medicine, 1971-74, asst. clin. prof. medicine, 1974-80, assoc. clin. prof. medicine, 1980-93, prof. medicine, 1993—; rsch. fellow in nephrology, teaching fellow in medicine and nephrology Tufts New England Med. Ctr., 1969-71; attending physician and cons. in nephrology West Roxbury VA Hosp., 1971-76; assoc. in medicine Brigham and Women's Hosp., 1981-82, physician, 1982—. Cons. in nephrology Dept. Health, Edn. and Welfare, Bur. Health Ins., Washington, 1973-75, New Eng. Sinai Hosp., Stoughton, Mass., 1974-90; sr. officer in medicine Nat. Naval Med. Ctr., Bethesda, Md., 1967-68; rsch. assoc. Nat. Naval Rsch. Unit, Bethesda, 1967-68; vis. prof. nephrology Tulane U., New Orleans, 1975, Wayne State U., Detroit, 1988, U. Medicine and Dentistry of N.J., Robert Wood Johnson Sch. of Medicine, New Brunswick, N.J., 1990, La. State U., New Orleans, 1991; vis. prof. medicine Marshfield (Wis.) Clinic, 1985, Lehigh Valley Med. Ctr., Allentown, Pa., 1990; manuscript reviewer in field. Mem editl. bd. Perspectives in Hypertension and Renal Disease, 1988-91, Nephrology News and Issues; contbr. articles to profl. jours., chpts. to books. With USN, 1966-67, Vietnam. NIH grantee, 1984-88, 85-87, 88-93; Brigham-Beth Israel Med. Group Rsch. and Edn. Fund grantee, 1982-84; R.W. Johnson Pharm. Rsch. Inst. grantee, 1989-93; Kovlar grantee Med. Edn. South African Blacks, 1992-93; Marion Merrill Dow Co. grantee, 1993; recipient Disting. Svc. award Nat. Kidney Found., 1988, Gift of Life award Nat. Kidney Found. of Mass., 1989. Fellow ACP (guidelines for transplant physicians programs com. 1990-92); mem. Am. Heart Assn. (coun. on the kidney), Am. Fedn. Clin. Rsch., Am. Israeli Nephrology Assn., Am. Soc. Artificial Internal Organs, Am. Soc. Nephrology (manpower com. 1990, ann. program com. 1991, 92, 93), Am. Soc. Transplant Physicians (program com. 1983-85, chmn. patient care and edn. com. 1985-88), Am. Coll. Physician Execs. (awards com. 1993-94), Internat. Soc. Nephrology, Internat. Soc. Renal Nutrition and Metabolism, Internat. Soc. Artificial Organs (program com. 2nd Internat. Soc. Artificial Organs, 1979, chmn. symposium continuing ambulatory peritoneal dialysis 1979), Nat. Kidney Found. of Mass. (bd. dirs. 1978—, v.p. 1980-82, pres. 1982-85), Nat. Kidney Found. (bd. dirs. 1993—), Intersoc. Coun. Rsch. of the Kidney and Urinary Tract (exec. coun. 1993-95), Renal Physicians Assn. (bd. dir. 1985-97, nat. v.p. 1989-91, pres. 1992-93), Renal Physicians No. New England (v.p. 1985-86, pres. 1986-88), Polycistic Kidney Rsch. Found. (bd. dirs. 1995-96, vice chair 1997, chair 1998-2000), Coun. Am. Kidney Socs. (exec. com. 1998-2000), Am. Soc. Transplantation (chair clin. practices com. 1999-2000). E-mail: tsteinma@caregroup.harvard.edu.

STEINMANN, ALWIN F. physician, educator; b. N.Y.C., Jan. 23, 1958; s. Vernon Richard and Violet Theresa; m. Kathleen Steinmann, Feb. 23, 1985; children: Kevin, Kathryn, Antonette. BS, Manhattan Coll., 1980; MD, NYU, 1984. Diplomate Am. Bd. Internal Medicine. Intern Albany Med. Ctr., Albany, N.Y., 1984-85, resident, 1985-87, physician emergency dept., 1987-88; faculty internal medicine Albany Med. Coll., instr. medicine, 1988-92, asst. prof. medicine, 1992-98, assoc. prof. medicine, 1998—; program dir. internal medicine residency program Albany Med. Ctr., 1997—, vice chmn. acad. affairs dept. medicine, 2000—. Fellow Am. Coll Physicians; mem. ACP, Assn. Program Dirs. in Internal Medicine. Office: Albany Med Coll 43 New Scotland Ave # Mc-17 Albany NY 12208-3412 E-mail: SteinmA@mail.amc.edu.

STEINMANN, JOHN COLBURN, architect; b. Monroe, Wis., Oct. 24, 1941; s. John Wilbur and Irene Marie (Steil) S.; m. Susan Koslosky, Aug. 12, 1978 (div. July 1989). BArch, U. Ill., 1964; postgrad., Ill. Inst. Tech., 1970-71. Registered architect, Wash., Oreg., Calif., N.Mex., Ariz., Utah, Alaska, Wis., Ill. Project designer C.F. Murphy Assocs., Chgo., 1968-71, Steinmann Architects, Monticello, Wis., 1971-73; design chief, chief project architect State of Alaska, Juneau, 1973-78; project designer Mithun Assos., architects, Bellevue, Wash., 1978-80; owner, prin. John C. Steinmann Assos., Architect, Kirkland, 1980-94; supr. head facilities sect. divsn. fin. Dept. Edn. State of Alaska, Juneau, 1994-96; docs. mgr. Loschky Marquardt and Nesholm, Architects, Seattle, 1996-98; project mgr. Dept. Gen. Adminstrn. Divsn. Engring. and Archtl. Svsc., State of Wash., Olympia, 1998-99; project mgr. URS Architects, Seattle, 2000—. Bd. dirs. Storytell Internat.; lectr. Ill. Inst. Tech., 1971-72. Prin. works include Grant Park Music Bowl, Chgo., 1971, Menomonee Falls (Wis.) Med. Clinic, 1972, Hidden Valley Office Bldg., Bellevue, 1978, Kezner Office Bldg., Bellevue, 1979, The Pines at Sunriver, Oreg., 1980, also Phase II, 1984, Phase III, 1986, The Pines at Sunriver Lodge Bldg., 1986, 2d and Lenora highrise, Seattle, 1981, Bob Hope Cardiovascular Rsch. Inst. lab animal facility, Seattle, 1982, Wash. Ct., Bellevue, 1982, Anchorage Bus. Park, 1982, Garden Townhouses, Anchorage, 1983, Vacation Internationale, Ltd. Corp. Hdqrs., Bellevue, 1983, Vallarta Torres III, Puerto Vallarta, Mex., 1987, Torres Mazatlan (Mex.) II, 1988, Canterwood Townhouses, Gig Harbor Wash., 1988, Inn at Ceres (Calif.), 1989, Woodard Creek Inn, Olympia, Wash., 1989, Northgate Corp. Ctr., Seattle, 1990, Icicle Creek Hotel and Restaurant, Leavenworth, Wash., 1990, Bellingham (Wash.), Market Pl., 1990, Boeing Hot Gas Test Facility, Renton, Wash., 1991, Boeing Longacres Customer Svc. Tng. Ctr. Support Facilities, Renton, 1992, Boeing Comml. Airplane Group Hdqrs., Renton, 1996, U. Wash./Cascade C.C., Bothell, 1999, Wash. State U., Pullman, Wash., Sea-Tac Airport Comm. Control Ctr., Seattle, 2000, McCarty, Internet Cafe and Residence Hall Renovation, U. Wash., Seattle, 2001, K'ima Med. Ctr. Dental Clinic, Hoopa, Calif., 2001, Sea-Tac Airport Flight Info. Mgmt. Sys., 2002; also pvt. residences. Served to 1st lt. C.E., USAR, 1964-66, Vietnam. Decorated Bronze Star. Mem. AIA, Am. Mgmt. Assn., Nat. Coun. Archtl. Registration Bds., U. Wash. Yacht Club, Columbia Athletic Club, Alpha Rho Chi. Republican. Roman Catholic. Address: 4316 106th Pl NE Kirkland WA 98033-7919

STEINMETZ, MICHAEL, biochemist; b. Luebeck, Germany, July 4, 1947; s. Ludwig Max and Anne-Marie (Wiemann) S.; m. Cornelia Wessel, Mar. 10, 1972; children: Lars, Stephanie, Silja, Thomas. Diploma in Chemistry, U. Hamburg, 1973; Dr. Rer. Nat., U. Munich, 1977. Scientific asst. Inst. Physiol. Chemistry, Munich, 1971-80; rsch. fellow Calif. Inst. Tech., Pasadena, 1980-83; mem. Basel Inst. for Immunology, 1983-86; assoc. dir., head biology dept. F. Hoffmann-La Roche, Ltd., Basel, 1986-91; v.p. dept. biotechnology rsch. F. Hoffmann-La Roche, Inc., Nutley, N.J., 1991-92, v.p. preclin. rsch., 1992-94; v.p. pre-clin. R&D Hoffmann-La Roche, Inc., 1994-97; gen. ptnr. MPM Capital, Cambridge, Mass., 1997—. Contbr. numerous articles to profl. jours. Lievre fellow Am. Cancer Soc.; recipient Young Investigator award Am. Assn. for Clin. Histocompatibility Testing, 1983; Venia Docendi, U. Basel, 1985. Mem. Acad. Europaea, European Molecular Biology Orgn., European Network of Immunology Institutes, The Human Genome Orgn. Avocations: reading, skiing, swimming, windsurfing. Office: MPM Capital 111 Huntington Ave Boston MA 02199 E-mail: msteinmetz@mpmcapital.com.

STEINMETZ, RICHARD BIRD, JR. lawyer; b. Orange, N.J., Mar. 27, 1929; s. Richard Bird and Charlotte (Quinby) S.; m. Merriam Holly Miller, June 9, 1956; children: Richard Blair, Jonathan Bird, Edward Quinby. BA, Yale U., 1950; JD, Harvard U., 1955. Bar: N.Y. 1955. Assoc. Chadbourne and Parke, N.Y.C., 1955-59; with Anaconda Co., 1959-79, v.p., gen. counsel, 1971-79; v.p. Colt Industries Inc., 1979-82; v.p., gen. counsel Pittston Co., Greenwich, Conn., 1982-84; exec. v.p. Case, Pomeroy and Co., N.Y.C., 1984-94. Bd. dirs. Case, Pomeroy and Co. Served to capt. USMC, 1950-52. Mem. ABA, Assn. of Gen. Counsel. Republican. Episcopalian. Home: 275C Park St New Canaan CT 06840-5739

STEINMETZ, SEYMOUR, pediatrician; b. Czechoslovakia, Oct. 6, 1934; s. Nathan and Gisela S. BA, Yeshiva U., N.Y.C., 1956; MD, Albert Einstein Coll. Medicine, Bronx, N.Y., 1960. Diplomate Am. Bd. Pediatrics. Intern UCLA Hosp., L.A., 1960-61, resident in pediat., 1961-62; chief resident in pediat. Montefiore Hosp., Bronx, N.Y., 1964-65; fellow in child psychiatry Jacobi Hosp., 1965-66; pvt. practice, Gt. Neck, 1966-74; pvt. practice Fremont (Calif.) Pediatric Med. Group, 1974—, pres., 1984—. With M.C. USAF, 1962—64. Fellow Am. Acad. Pediatrics. Office: Fremont Pediatric Med Group 3755 Beacon Ave Fremont CA 94538-1411

STEINMEYER, ROBERT JAY, lawyer; b. Clatonia, Nebr., Aug. 10, 1921; s. William F. and Willie (Davis) S.; m. Susie Levicki, Dec. 23, 1948; children— William Bruce, James Jay, Sharon Sue. B.S., U. Nebr., 1943; postgrad. Albany law Sch., 1947-48; LL.B., George Washington U., 1949. Bar: D.C. 1950, Calif. 1958. Devel. engr. Gen. Electric Co., Schenectady, 1943-46, patent atty., 1947-53, patent counsel, 1953-57; patent counsel Beckman Instruments, Inc., Fullerton, Calif., 1957-63, gen. counsel, 1963-71, v.p.-legal, 1971-85, dir., 1984-85; sole practice, 1985-86; of counsel, Karon, Morrison & Savikas, Ltd., 1986— . Mem. ABA, Am. Patent Law Assn., Assn. Corp. Patent Counsel (pres. 1975-76), Order of Coif, Sigma Tau, Pi Mu Epsilon. Home: 609 Lemon Hill Ter Fullerton CA 92832-1024 Office: 2500 N Harbor Blvd Fullerton CA 92835-2600

STEINMILLER, JOHN F. professional basketball team executive; b. Mt. Prospect, Ill. m. Corinne Steinmiller; children: John Henry, Mary Kate. V.p. bus. ops. Milw. Bucks, 1977—. Bd. dirs. M.W. Athletes Against Childhood Cancer Fund, Milw. Big Bros.-Big Sisters, Metro Milw. YMCA, Milw. Convention Visitors Bur.; mem. Greater Milw. Com. Recipient Contardi Commitment award MACC Fund, 1991, Vol. of Yr. award YMCA, 1996. Office: Milw Bucks 1001 N 4th St Milwaukee WI 53203-1314 E-mail: jsteinmiller@milwaukeebucks.com.

STEINMULLER, KAREN ANNE, accountant; b. Washington, Nov. 15, 1954; d. Herbert M. and Edith Frieda (Bley) S. B.B.A., Coll. William and Mary, 1977. C.P.A., Va. Staff acct. Aaron Roesen & Co., Newport News, Va., 1977-80; sr. staff acct. Hart Adams & Scollin, P.C., Hampton, Va., 1980-83; sr. to mgr. Hart Adams & Toney, P.C., Hampton, 1983-85; shareholder John T. Hart & Assocs., P.C., Hampton, 1985— . Mem. Am. Inst. C.P.A.s, Va. Soc. C.P.A.s, Am. Woman's Soc. C.P.A.s, Nat. Assn. Female Execs. Luthern. Avocations: music; reading; sewing; aerobics. Office: John T Hart & Assocs PC 2101 Executive Dr Tower PO Box 30 Hampton VA 23669-0030

STEINPARZ, FRANZ XAVER, information scientist, consultant, educator; b. Steyr, Austria, June 16, 1947; s. Franz and Juliane (Omer) S.; m. Waltraud Elizabeth Wirth, Sept. 13, 1985. Diploma in Math. Engring., Johannes Kepler U., Linz, Austria, 1980, Dr. in Tech. Scis., 1983. Lectr. in computer sci. Johannes Kepler U., Linz, 1980-86; sr. lectr. computer sci. U. Zürich, Switzerland, 1986-87, Johannes Kepler U., 1987-94; prof. computer sci. Hohere Technische Bundeslehranstalt (polytechnic), Leonding, 1994—. Author: Computer & Kommunikation, 1988, Message Handling Systems, 1988; contbr. articles to profl. jours. Mem. IEEE, Assn. Computing Machinery, Arbeitsgemeinschaft fur Datenverarbeitung (province chmn. 1985-92). Home: Starhembergstr 27 A-4020 Linz Austria

STEINWALL, SUSAN DEBORAH, lawyer; b. St. Paul, May 13, 1952; AB, Grinnell Coll., 1974; MA, U. Wis., Madison, 1981; JD, U. Minn., 1991. Bar: Minn. 1991, U.S. Dist. Ct. Minn. 1992; cert. real property law specialist Minn. State Bar Assn. 1998. Newspaper reporter various newspapers Oconomowoc, Wis., Janesville, Wis., Duluth, Minn., 1974-80; archivist U. Minn., U. Wis.-River Falls, State Hist. Soc. Wis., 1981-88; rsch. asst. Minn. Ho. of Reps., St. Paul, 1990-91; shareholder Fredrikson & Byron, P.A., Mpls., 1991—. Instr. St. Mary's Coll. Grad. Ctr., Mpls., 1989, Met. State U., St. Paul, 1993. Co-author: MDLA Release Deskbook; contbr. articles to law jours. Office: Fredrikson & Byron 1100 Internat Ctr 900 2d Ave S Minneapolis MN 55402-3397 E-mail: ssteinwall@fredlaw.com.

STEINZOR, SETH A. state attorney general; b. San Jose, Calif., June 19, 1952; BA, Middlebury Coll., Vt., 1974; JD, U. Maine, 1979. Bar: Vt. 1985, Mass. 1979. State investigator, civil rights Office of Atty. Gen., State of Vt., Montpelier, 1985—90, asst. atty. gen., 1990—. Avocation: building furniture, hand crafting bamboo fly fishing rods.

STEITZ, ELLA EMMA ANTPUSAT, artist, educator; b. Bklyn. d. August and Anna (Pimat) Antpusat; children: Lanning Dennis, Judith Lynn Weis. Art cert., Maironius Art Acad., Kaunas, Lithuania; student, Pratt Inst., Bklyn., Nassau C.C., 1988. Pub. rels. speaker Nat. Bank N.Am., West Hempstead, N.Y., 1962-75; instr. art Village of Lynbrook, 1981-85, City of Glen Cove, 1987-90, Rockville Centre (N.Y.) Recreation Dept., 1976—. Spkr., demonstrator Nat. Coun. State Garden Clubs, 1965—, master flower show judge, 1970—. Author: Pressing Flowers for Fun and Profit, 1970; exhibited in group shows in Southampton (N.Y.) Gallery, 1976, Lever House Gallery, N.Y.C., 1984, 96, Hutchins Gallery, Greenvale, N.Y., 1986; pvt. collections, U.S. Chair Civic Beautification Com., Garden City, N.Y., 1985—; master gardener Cornell Coop. Ext., Plainview, N.Y., 1989—; sec. Salvation Army, Garden City, 1965-82. Recipient Grumbacher award Ind. Art Soc., 1980, Creativity award Federated Garden Clubs, 1985, numerous awards from flower and art shows. Mem. Tri-County Art League (A. Roos Meml. award 1986), Art League Nassau County (Excellence award 1980), Floral Park Art League (Best in Show award 1985, 87), Village Art Club (Winsor and Newton award, Newton award 1986), Village Garden Club (pres. 1973-75, Tri Color award 1965). Avocations: organic gardening, photography, travel. Home: 127 Oxford Blvd Garden City NY 11530-2715

STEITZ, PHILIP WAKEFORD, research corporation owner; b. Evanston, Ill., Apr. 7, 1925; s. Philip Walter and Suzanne (Wakeford) S.; m. Marjorie Stevens Eberly, Nov. 17, 1951; children: Nancy, Philip, Mark, Paul, David. BS, Georgetown U., 1949; MA, Columbia U., 1951. Interviewer recruiter J.A. Ward Rsch., N.Y.C., 1951-53; mdse. coord. Puck the Comic Weekly, 1953-54; mng. editor Pubs. Syndicate, Chgo., 1955-64; assoc. dir. VISTA, Washington, 1965-69; asst. dir. Peace Corps, 1969-71; cons. Philip W. Steitz Assocs., 1971-74; owner, dir. Survey Rsch. Corp., 1974—. Vice pres. Helping Children Grow, Washington, 1980-2001. Sgt. maj. U.S. Cavalry, 1943-45. Mem. Nat. Press Club. Democrat. Avocation: biking. Home: 582 Brummel Ct NW Washington DC 20012-1859 Office: Survey Rsch Corp 12th Fl 818 Connecticut Ave NW Fl 12 Washington DC 20006-2702 E-mail: srcsteitz@aol.com.

STEJSKAL, JOSEPH FRANK, JR. carbohydrate chemist; b. Oak Park, Ill., Jan. 16, 1932; s. Joseph Frank and Bertha Helen (Urban) S.; m. Dorothy May Milas, Nov. 28, 1953; children: Patricia Anne, Joseph Frank III. BS, Wheaton Coll., 1953. Chemist Corn Products Refining Co., Argo, Ill., 1953-89; phys. sci. asst. U.S. Army Food Container Inst., Chgo., 1955-57; chemist Am. Maize Products Co., Hammond, Ind., 1987-96; ret. Cerestar USA, Inc., 1996. Patentee in field. Mem. Brookfield (Ill.) Hist. Commn., 1993-02; elder, treas. Presbyn. Ch. USA, gen. assembly del., 1951-96, nat. del. 1970); instnl. rep. Boy Scouts Am., 1961-90, cmty. svc. award 1978, silver beaver award 1987. Mem. Hollywood Citizens Assn. (historian). Republican. Presbyterian. Avocations: golf, chess, local history, church and community activities. Home: 3611 Rosemear Ave Brookfield IL 60513-1738

STEKLER, HERMAN O. finance educator; b. Vienna, Austria, Nov. 4, 1932; arrived in U.S., 1939; s. Walter and Gisela Stekler; m. Joan Pinchak, June 1957 (div. 1965); m. Lois E. Stekler, Feb. 19, 1967; children: Beth Ann, Joanne Donna. AB, Clark U., 1955; PhD, MIT, 1959. Asst. prof. bus. adminstrn. U. Calif., Berkeley, 1959-66; prof. econs. SUNY, Stony Brook, 1968-79, Indsl. Coll. Armed Forces Nat. Def. U., Washington, 1982-94; rsch. prof. George Washington U., 1994—. Economist Bd. Govs. Fed. Res. Sys., Washington, 1966—68, Inst. Def. Analyses, Alexandria, Va., 1979—82. Author: (book) Structure and Performance of the Aerospace Industry, 1965, Economic Forecasting, 1970; contbr. articles to profl. jours.; assoc. editor: Internat. Jour. Forecasting, 1984, book rev. editor: , 1994—2001. Fellow: Internat. Inst. Forecasters (bd. dirs. 2001—); mem.: Am. Econ. Assn. Avocations: stamp collecting, tennis. Office: George Washington U Dept Econ Washington DC 20052-0001

STELCK, CHARLES RICHARD, geology educator; b. Edmonton, Alta., Can., May 20, 1917; s. Robert Ferdinand and Florella Maud (Stanbury) S.; m. Frances Gertrude McDowell, Apr. 24, 1945; children— David, Brian, Leland, John (dec.) B.Sc., U. Alta., 1937, M.Sc., 1941; PhD, Stanford U., 1951. Registered profl. geologist Alta. Field geologist B.C. Dept. Mines, Victoria, Can., 1939-41; field geologist Canol Project, Norman Wells, N.W.T., Can., 1941-43, Imperial Oil Co., Calgary, Alta., 1943-49; from lectr. to prof. emeritus geology U. Alta., Edmonton, 1946—. Contbr. numerous articles principally on biostratigraphy of Cretaceous to sci. publs. Decorated officer Order of Can.; recipient Disting. Educator award Am. Assn. Petroleum Geologists, 2001. Fellow Royal Soc. Can.; mem. Assn. Profl. Engrs., Geologists and Geophysicists Alta. (Centennial award 1979), Geol. Assn. Can. (Logan medal 1982), Geol. Soc. Am., Can. Soc. Petroleum Geologists (Douglas medal 1994, Stanley Slipper gold medal 2002), Order of Can. (officer 1997). Conservative. Office: U Alta Dept Earth & Atmospheric Scis Edmonton AB Canada T6G 2E3

STELLA, JOHN ANTHONY, investment company executive; b. Jessup, Pa., Feb. 3, 1938; s. John Anthony and Alda (Parri) S.; m. Aurelia M. Arre, Feb. 20, 1965; children— John C., Matthew A., Krista R. BS, U. Detroit, 1960; MBA, NYU, 1965. Bus. evaluation cons. Allied Chem. Co., N.Y.C., 1965-70; treas. Spinnerin Yarn Co., Hackensack, N.J., 1970-72, Penn-Dixie Cement Corp., N.Y.C., 1972-74; v.p. finance Halecrest Co., 1974-76; treas. Rsch.-Cottrell, 1976-84, v.p., contr./treas., 1984-88; pres. John A. Stella & Assocs., Plainfield, N.J., 1988-91; sr. v.p. Investment Support Systems, Inc., Bloomfield, 1991-95. Pres. State Tax Auditing and Rsch., Inc. , Bethlehem, 1993—. Served with AUS, 1960. Office: State Tax Auditing & Rsch Inc 1775 Arden Ln Bethlehem PA 18015-5829

STELLAR, ARTHUR WAYNE, educational administrator; b. Columbus, Ohio, Apr. 12, 1947; s. Fredrick and Bonnie Jean (Clark) S. BS, Ohio U., 1969, MA, 1970, PhD, 1973. Tchr. Athens (Ohio) City Schs., 1969-71; curriculum coord., tchr. Belpre (Ohio) City Schs., 1971-72; prin. elem. schs., head tchr. learning disabilities South-Western City Schs., Grove City, Ohio, 1972-76; dir. elem. edn. Beverly (Mass.) Pub. Schs., 1976-78; coord. spl. projects and systemwide planning Montgomery County Pub. Schs., Rockville, Md., 1978-80; asst. supt. Shaker Heights (Ohio), 1980-83; supt. schs. Mercer County Pub. Schs., Princeton, W.Va., 1983-85, Oklahoma City Pub. Schs., 1985-92, Cobb County, Ga., 1992-93; dep. supt. Boston Pub. Schs., 1993-95, acting supt., 1995-96; supt. Kingston (N.Y.) Sch. Dist., 1996—2001; pres., CEO High/Scope Ednl. Rsch. Found., Ypsilanti, Mich., 2001—. Adj. prof. Lesley Coll., Cambridge, Mass., 1976-78; adj. faculty Harvard U., 1992-93. Author: Educational Planning for Educational Success, Effective Schools Research: Practice and Promise; editor: Effective Instructional Management; cons. editor, book rev. editor Jour. Ednl. Pub. Rels.; mem. editl. bd. Jour. Curriculum & Supervision, Reading Today's Youth; contbr. articles to profl. jours. Bd. govs. Kirkpatrick Ctr.; mem. Oklahoma City Com. Econ. Devel.; founding bd. dirs. Oklahoma Alliance Against Drugs, Oklahoma Zool. Soc. Inc.; selected for Leadership Oklahoma City, 1986; bd. dirs. Leadership Oklahoma City, ARC; bd. dirs. Okla. Centennial Sports Inc., Rip Van Winkle Coun. BSA; mem. Oklahoma Acad. for State Goals, State Supt.'s Adv. Coun.; mem. clin. experiences adv. com. U. Okla. Coll. Edn.; trustee Arts Coun. Oklahoma City, Omniplex Sci. and Arts Mus., Oklahoma City Area Vocat.-Tech. Dist. 22 Found.; mem. Urban Ctr. Ednl. Adv. Bd., U.S. Dept. Edn. Urban Supt. Network, Coun. Great City Schs. Bd., Urban Edn. Clearing House Adv. com., U. Okla. Adminstrn. cert. program com., Cmty. Literacy Coun. Bd.; chmn. bd. dirs. Langston U.; chairperson United Way Greater Okla., Sch. Mgmt. Study Group, Okla. Reading Coun. (Okla. literacy coun. reading award 1-89), Oklahoma City PTA; bd. dirs. Oklahoma County chpt. ARC, Jr. Achievement Greater Oklahoma City Bd., Oklahoma State Fair Bd., Horace Mann League Bd., 1993-2000, v.p. 2000-01, pres.-elect, 2001-2002, pres. 2002-; v.p. Last Frontier Coun. Bd.; v.p. N.Y. State PTA, 1996-2000, Kingston Chpt. Rip Van Winkle Coun., Boy Scouts Am., 1996-2001, membership chmn., 1996-97; exec. bd. Nat. Dropout Prevention Ctr. Network, 1998—; mem. curriculum com. N.Y. State Coun. Sch. Supts., 1996-2001; bd. dirs. Friends Historic Kingston, 1996-2001, Friends Senate House, Kingston, 1996-2001. Recipient Silver Beaver award, Boy Scouts Am., 1990, Amb. award, Horace Mann League, 1995, 1996, 1997, 1998, 1999, 2000, 2001, 2002; fellow, Charles Kettering Found. IDEA, 1976, 1978, 1980, NEH, Danforth Found., 1987—88. Mem. ASCD (exec. coun., pres.-elect 1993-94, pres. 1994-95, rev. coun. 1997-2002), Mass. ASCD, Ohio ASCD, Okla. ASCD (Publ. award 1989), N.Y. ASCD, Internat. Soc. Ednl. Planning, Nat. Soc. Study Edn., Nat. Planning Assn., Nat. Assn. Gifted Children (life), Nat. Coun. Tchrs. English (life), Music Educators Nat. Conf. (life), Nat. Orgn. Legal Problems Edn., Nat. Policy Bd. Ednl. Adminstrn., Am. Assn. Sch. Adminstrs. (life, Leadership for Learning award 1991), Coll. Bd. Advanced Placement Spl. Recognition award 1991, Nat. Assn. Elem. Sch. Prins. (life), Am. Edn. Fin. Assn., Nat. Assn. Edn. Young Children (life), Nat. Sch. Pub. Rels. Assn. (Honor award 1991), Am. Mus. Natural Hist. (assoc.), World Coun. Curriculum and Instrn. (life, bd. dirs. N.Am. chpt. 1996-2000, pres. 2000-02), Coun. Basic Edn., Ohio Assn. Elem. Sch. Adminstrs., Buckeye Assn. Sch. Adminstrs., Ohio U. Coll. Edn. (disting. alumnus award 1991), Okla. Assn. Sch. Adminstrs., Mass. Assn. Sch. Adminstrs., Okla. Coalaition Pub. Edn., Okla. Commn. Ednl. Leadership, Urban Area Supts. (Okla. br.), Ohio U. Alumni Assn. (nat. dir. 1975-78, pres. Ctrl. Ohio chpt. 1975-76, pres. Mass. chpt. 1976-78, life mem. trustee's acad.), World Future Soc. (life) Greater Oklahoma City C. of C. (bd. dirs.), Oklahoma Heritage Assn., H eritage Hills Assn. (bd. dirs.), Victorian Soc. (New England chpt.), Nat. Eagle Scout Assn., Aerospace Found. (hon. bd. dirs.), PLATO, Learning, Inc. (bd. dirs.), Am. Bus. Card Club, Coca Cola Collectors Club, Internat. Club, Mgmt. Consortium (bd. advisors), Rotary (Boston), Tau Kappa Epsilon Alumni Assn. (regional officer Mass. 1976-78, named Alumni Nat. Hall of Fame 1986, Nat. Alumnus of Yr. 1993, Excellence in Edn. award 1993), Kappa Delta Pi (life, advisor Cen. Okla. chpt., nat. publs. com.), Phi Delta Kappa (life). Methodist.

STELLE, ROBERT E. physician, retired educator; b. Kalamazoo, Feb. 7, 1930; s. Earl Clarkson and Norma Lillian Stelle; m. Barbara Lutz, Apr. 29, 1955; children: Amy, Mark, Nancy. BA, Kalamazoo Coll., 1955; MD, U. Mich., 1959. Diplomate Am. Bd. Family Practice (charter). Intern Toledo Hosp., 1959-60; mng. ptnr. Falls Clinic P.C., Crystal Falls, Mich., 1960-79; assoc. prof. Mich. State U., Lansing, 1974-79, U. Wis., Madison, 1979-81; prof., vice chmn. dept. U. Mo., Kansas City, 1981-82, U. Colo., Denver, 1982-85; med. dir. Hertzler Clinic, Wichita, Kans., 1985-86; cons. Locum Tenens Contractors Inc., Colorado City, Colo., 1986—99. Home and Office: PO Box 19051 7710 Charles Colorado City CO 81019

STELLMACH, ALBERT JOHN, music educator; b. Milw., Sept. 30, 1959; s. Albert Joseph Stellmach and Delia Estrada; m. Bianca Andrea Combagnoni, Nov. 20, 2001. MusB Edn., U. Miami, Coral Gables Fla., 1984—84, MA in Music Edn., 1988. Cert. Tchr. Music Fla., 1984. String tchr. WR Thomas Jr. H.S., Miami, Fla., 1984; music tchr. Campbell Dr. Elem., Homestead, 1984—90; itinerant string music tchr. Tampa Schools, 1990—94; string orch. cons. Southwood Mid. Sch., Miami, 1994—95; magnet string music tchr. Perrine (Fla.) Elem., 1997—. Dir. South Atlantic Youth Orch., Homestead, Fla., 1987—90. Author: (book) Historical Celebrity Sites of South Florida, 2002. Polit. union steward United Teachers of Dade, Miami, Fla., 1999—2002. Recipient Boys State of Fla., Am. Legion, 1978, 1st Pl. Jr. Divsn., Orlando Performing Arts Festival, 1992. Mem.: Fla. Orch. Assn., Music Educators Nat. Conf. (bass auditioner 1984—2002). Democrat. Roman Catholic. Avocations: football, art, movies, travel. Home: 3241 SW 105 Ave Miami FL 33165 Office: Perrine Elem Sch for Arts 8851 SW 168th St Miami FL 33157 Personal E-mail: stellma@attglobal.net.

STELLMAN, JEANNE MAGER, public health educator; b. Bensheim, W. Ger., May 27, 1947; arrived in U.S., 1948, permanent resident, 1951; d. Abraham and Rosalie (Shapiro) Mager; m. Steven D. Stellman, Sept. 10, 1967; children: Andrew Benjamin, Emma Deborah. BS in Chemistry, CCNY, 1968; PhD in Phys. Chemistry, CUNY, 1972. Asst. to pres. for health and safety Oil, Chem. and Atomic Workers Internat. Union, Denver, 1972—75; chief divsn. occupl. health and toxicology Am. Health Found., N.Y.C., 1977—80; exec. dir. Women's Occupational Health Resource Ctr., 1978—91; clin. assoc. prof. rsch. medicine Sch. Medicine, U. Pa., Phila., 1975—80; prof. clin. pub. health Sch. Pub. Health, Columbia U., N.Y.C., 1980—. Trainee NASA, 1968—69; adj. prof. Labor Edn. Ctr. Rutgers U., 1971—76; vis. assoc.

prof. U. Medicine and Dentistry N.J., Piscataway, 1987—; cons. Am. Occupl. Health Nurses Assn., 1983—85, Port Authority N.Y. and N.J., 1983—84, IVA Office Safety and Health, 1980—82, N.Y. State Dept. Health, 1982—84, Coalition Labor Union Women, 1975—80, Nat. Union Hosp. and Health Care Workers, 1975—85; cons. to spl. master Agt. Orange Vet. Payment Program, 1987—96; mem. merit peer rev. com.-cancer control Nat. Cancer Inst., 1979—81; mem. expert panel for guidelines on pregnant working women Am. Coll. Ob-Gyn., 1978; mem. environ health task force Am. Lung Assn., 1976—80; mem. task force on preventing disease, workgroup on occupl. health U.S. Surgeon Gen.'s Office, 1979; mem. adv. com. for 14 chem. carcinogens U.S. Sec. Labor, 1972; mem. tech. rev. coms. for criteria documents on cadmium, mercury, sulfur dioxide and benzene Nat. Inst. Occupl. Safety and Health; spkr. on occupl. health hazards U.S. and Can. Author (with S.M. Daum): (book) Work Is Dangerous to Your Health (translated into Italian, Portuguese, French, Spanish), 1973; author: Women's Work, Women's Health: Myth and Realities (translated into Italian, French, Japanese); author: (with Mary Sue Henifin) Office Work Can Be Dangerous to Your Health, 1984; editor-in-chief: Ency. Ency. Occupl. Health and Safety, 4th edit., 1991—98; contbr. ; contbg. editor: (jour.) Environment, 1975—76; mem. editl. bd.: jour. Women and Health, 1983—85; editor, 1985—. Named one of 80 Women to Watch in the 80's, Ms. Mag., 1980; recipient Preventive Oncology Acad. award, Nat. Cancer Inst., 1980—85, Commendation award, Vietnam Vets. Am., 1990, citation for meritorious svc., Am. Legion, 1991; fellow, N.Y. State Regents, 1970—72, Guggenheim Found., 1989—90; grantee, NSF, 1969—70. Mem.: AAAS, APHA (governing coun. 1981—83), Sigma Xi, Am. Indsl. Hygiene Assn., N.Y. Acad. Scis., Soc. Occupl. and Environ. Health, Am. Phys. Soc., Am. Chem. Soc. (com. chem. safety 1973—79, chmn. task force on benzene 1978—79, task force safe lab practices 1978—79). Democrat. Jewish. Office: Found for Worker Vet & Environ Health Inc 117 Saint Johns Pl Brooklyn NY 11217-3401 also: Columbia U Mailman Sch Pub Health 600 W 168th St 6th Fl New York NY 10032

STELLMAN, STEVEN DALE, epidemiologist; b. Toronto, May 7, 1945; s. Samuel David and Lillian (Mandlsohn) S.; m. Jeanne Esther Mager, Sept. 10, 1967; children: Andrew, Emma. BS in Chemistry, Ohio State U., 1966; PhD in Phys. Chemistry, NYU, 1971; MPH in Health Policy and Mgmt., Columbia U., 1992. Rsch. assoc. biochem. sci. Princeton (N.J.) U., 1971-73; lectr. in chemistry U. Colo., Denver, 1973-74; chief div. computing and biostats. Am. Health Found., N.Y.C., 1975-80, chief divsn. epidemiology, 1991—; asst. v.p. epidemiology Am. Cancer Soc., 1980-88; asst. commr. biostat. and epidemiol. rsch. N.Y.C. Dept. Health, 1988-91; adj. assoc. prof. dept. cmty. medicine Mt. Sinai Sch. Medicine, N.Y.C., 1981-99. Sci. cons. agt. orange vet. payment program U.S. Dist. Ct., Bklyn., 1985—; mem. adv. bd. pub. health grad. program Robert Wood Johnson Sch. Medicine, Piscataway, N.J., 1986—; cons. in epidemiology and biostats. Meml. Sloan-Kettering Cancer Ctr., N.Y.C., 1993—; prof. epidemiology Mailman Sch. Pub. Health, Columbia U., 2001—. Author Women and Cancer, 1986; editor Vital Stats. Summaries, N.Y.C., 1988-91; assoc. editor Women and Health, 1991—; contbr. articles to profl. pubs.; co-author spl. issue Environ. Rsch., 1988. Condr. DeRossi singers Kane St. Synagogue. Fogarty Sr. Internat. fellow NIH, 1992-93. Mem. APHA, Am. Coll. Epidemiology, Soc. for Epidemiologic Rsch., Am. Chem. Soc. Democrat. Jewish. Achievements include study of health effects of agent orange, cancer prevention study of 1.2 million Ams. Home: 117 Saint Johns Pl Brooklyn NY 11217-3401 Office: Am Health Found 1 Dana Rd Valhalla NY 10595 E-mail: sds91@columbia.edu.

STELLWAGEN, ROBERT HARWOOD, biochemistry educator; b. Joliet, Ill., Jan. 6, 1941; s. Harwood John and Alma Dorothy (Handorf) S.; m. Joanne Kovacs, June 15, 1963; children: Robert Harwood, Alise Anne. AB, Harvard U., 1963; PhD, U. Calif.-Berkeley, 1968. Staff fellow NIH, Bethesda, Md., 1968-69; postdoctoral scholar U. Calif.-San Francisco, 1969-70; asst. prof. biochemistry U. So. Calif., L.A., 1970-74, assoc. prof., 1974-80, prof., 1980—, chmn. dept., 1981-86, vice chmn. dept., 1993—. Vis. scientist Nat. Inst. for Med. Research, Mill Hill, Eng., 1979. Contbr. articles to profl. jours. Recipient Henderson prize Harvard U., 1963; NSF fellow, 1963-67; NIH grantee, 1971-84 Mem. AAAS, Am. Soc. Biochemistry and Molecular Biology, Sierra Club, Phi Beta Kappa. Democrat. Office: U So Calif Keck Sch Medicine 2011 Zonal Ave Los Angeles CA 90089-0110 E-mail: stellwag@hsc.usc.edu.

STELMACH, WALTER JACK, physician, medical education administrator; b. Kansas City, Kans., Mar. 7, 1926; s. Jacob and Stella (Wanchuk) S.; m. Patricia Ann Scherrer, June 19, 1948; children: Christopher Stephen, Cheryl Anne, Jeffrey David BA, U. Mo., Kansas City, 1949; MD, Kans. U., Kansas City, 1953. Diplomate Am. Bd. Family Practice (bd. dirs. 1980-85, mem. exec. com. 1980-82, pres. 1983). Intern St. Mary's Hosp. and Children's Mercy Hosp., Kansas City, Mo., 1953-54; practice family medicine, 1954-74; clin. prof. medicine Sch. Medicine U. Mo., 1974—, asst. dean, chmn. coun. on evaluation, 1974-75, chmn. dept. cmty. and family medicine Truman Med. Ctr., 1977-78; pres. med. staff Bapt. Meml. Hosp., 1967-68, chmn. sect. gen. practice, 1969-71, dir. family practice residency program, 1974-93, chmn. Residency Assistance Program project bd., 1975-80; v.p. med. affairs Bapt. Med. Ctr., 1993-96. Preceptor Sch. Medicine, U. Mo., Columbia; chmn. sect. family practice Rsch. Hosp., 1969-71; participant Ditchley Park Conf. on Devel. of Health Svcs. and Med. Care, Brit., Can., U.S., 1972; mem. Grad. Med. Edn. Nat. Adv. Com., 1976-80, chmn., 1976-78; bd. dirs. Coun. of Med. Splty. Socs., 1979-81, pres., 1980-81; chmn. Coun. for Med. Affairs, 1981 Contbr. articles to med. jours., presentations to profl. confs. Pres. Family Health Found. Am., 1980-85; trustee U. Mo., Kansas City, 1981. With USN, 1943-46 Recipient John G. Walsh award, 1981, Max Cheplove award, 1981, Alumni award U. Mo., Kansas City, 1981; W. Jack Stelmach Resident Edn. Fund established in his honor Bapt. Med. Ctr., 1996. Charter fellow Am. Acad. Family Physicians (del. 1969-74, mem. commn. on edn. 1971-76, chmn. 1974-75, 75-76, bd. dirs. 1974-77, chmn. bd. 1976-77, pres. 1978-79); mem. AMA, Mo. State Med. Assn. (del. 1964-73), Mo. Acad. Family Physicians (bd. dirs. 1966-69, pres. 1973-74), Kansas City Acad. Family Physicians (pres. 1965-66), Jackson County Med. Soc. (sec. 1960-61), S.W. Clin. Soc. (sec. 1967-68, bd. dirs. 1967-69, assoc. dir. clinics 1972-73), dir. clinics 1975), Kansas City Acad. Medicine, Kans. U. Med. Alumni (1st v.p. 1972-73), Alpha Omega Alpha. Mem. Unity Ch. Home: 5252 Sunset Dr Kansas City MO 64112-2356

STELPSTRA, WILLIAM JOHN, minister; b. Paterson, N.J., Nov. 1, 1934; s. Duke and Nellie (Stapert) S.; m. Anna Rizkovsky, Sept. 6, 1958; 1 child, Linda Mae. BA, Alma White Coll., 1957; B. of Religion, Zarephath Bible Sem., 1958. Ordained to ministry Pillar of Fire Ch., 1954. Pastor Pillar of Fire Ch., Little Falls, N.J., 1956-60; evangelist Wesleyan Meth. Ch., 1960-64; founder, dir. Bethel Children's Home, Paterson, N.J., 1964-71, Bethel Ranch Rehab. for Men, West Milford, 1971—; founder, pres. World for Christ Crusade, Inc., N.J., Fla., 1960—, dir. fgn. missions, 1980—; adminstr. Fellowship House, Bloomfield, N.J., 1979—, Bright Side Manor, Teaneck, 1978—. Mem. Ocean Grove C. of C. Republican. Wesleyan Ch. Avocations: painting with oils, swimming, boating, travel, gardening. Home: 1005 Union Valley Rd West Milford NJ 07480-1220

STELSON, KIM ADAIR, mechanical engineering educator; b. Pitts., Feb. 24, 1952; s. Thomas Eugene and Constance Anne (Semon) S.; m. Caren Ann Barzelay, July 16, 1978; children: Aaron, Elisabeth. BS, Stanford U., 1974; SM, MIT, 1977, ScD, 1982. Asst. prof. U. Minn., Mpls., 1982-87, assoc. prof. mech. engring., 1987-94, prof., 1994—. Cons. 3M, St. Paul, 1986-90; vis. sr. lectr. Hong Kong U. Sci. and Tech., 1992-93; vis. assoc. prof. U. Auckland, 1996; vis. prof. U. Bath., 2001-2002; chmn. Japan-USA Symposium on Flexible Automation (Robotics) Conf., 1996; dir. design and mfg. divsn. Dept. Mech. Engring., U. Minn., 1994—, dir. grad. studies, MS in Mfg. Syss., 1997—. Co-editor: Sensors and Controls for Automated Manufacturing and Robotics, 1984; co-author: Safari, 1988; assoc. tech. editor ASME Jour. Mfg. Sci. and Engring., 1997—, Jour. Mgr. Process, 1999-; mem. editl. bd. IMechE Jour. of Engring. Mfg., 2000-; internat. editor Trans. on Control, Automation and Systems Engring., 2000-; contbr. articles to profl. jours.; co-inventor pressbrake having springback compensating adaptive control, 1983, closed loop control system, 1991. NSF fellow, Washington, 1974-77, NSF Presdl. Young Investigator award, 1985, Dow award Am. Soc. Engring. Edn., 1987. Mem. AAAS, ASME (assoc. tech. editor 1995—, Minn. Young Engr. of Yr. 1985), N.Am. Mfg. Rsch. Inst., Soc. Mfg. Engrs., Sigma Xi, Phi Beta Kappa, Tau Beta Pi. Unitarian Universalist. Achievements include research in metal forming, precision engring., composite materials and starch-based plastics. Avocations: travel, music, outdoor activities, gardening. Home: 5605 Hillside Ct Minneapolis MN 55439-1219 Office: U Minn Dept Mech Engring 111 Church St SE Minneapolis MN 55455-0150

STELTER, PAUL JAMES, editor, freelance writer; b. Park Ridge, Ill., Nov. 1, 1967; s. James E. and Susan C. Stelter. BA in Govt., U. Notre Dame, 1989; MA in Internat. Affairs, George Washington U., 1991. Intern for Congressman Les Aspin. Ho. of Reps., Washington, 1991-92; electronic file editor, proofer Bur. Nat. Affairs, 1993-94, editor, writer, 1995—, copy editor, proofer Union Labor Report newsletter, 1998—, article writer Union Labor Report, 1998-99. Freelance music writer, columnist Washington Times, 2001—. Vol. Tom Ward congl. campaign, South Bend, Ind., 1986 Mem. Newspaper Guild, Washington Psychotronic Film Soc., D.C. Film Soc., Kennedy Ctr. for Performing Arts. Democrat. Avocations: reading, film, music, restaurants, writing. Home: 1600 N Oak St Apt 1523 Arlington VA 22209

STELTZLEN, JANELLE HICKS, lawyer; b. Atlanta, Sept. 18, 1937; d. William Duard and Mary Evelyn (Embrey) Hicks; divorced; children: Gerald William III, Christa Diane. BS, Okla. State U., 1958; MS, Kans. State U., 1961; JD, U. Tulsa, 1981. Bar: Okla. 1981, U.S. Dist. Ct. (no., ea. and we. dists.) Okla. 1981, U.S. Tax Ct. 1982, U.S. Ct. Claims 1982, U.S. Ct. Appeals (10th cir.) 1983, U.S. Ct. Appeals (Fed. cir.) 1984, U.S. Supreme Ct. 1986; lic. real estate broker. Pvt. practice, Tulsa, 1981-97. Lectr. Coll. of DuPage, Glen Ellyn, Ill., 1976, Tulsa Jr. Coll., 1981-88; dietitian, Tulsa; res. dep. for Tulsa County Sheriff's Office; 2d dep., legal Tulsa County Clk., 1997-2000. Christian counselor 1st United Meth. Ch., Tulsa, 1986—, coord. legal counseling ministry, 1985—, lay pastor, 1987—; mem. Tulsa County Bd. Equalization and Excise Tax Bd., 1989-90; mem. Leadership Tulsa XX, 1993—; recipient of Leadership Tulsa Paragon award, 1996; bd. dirs. Sister Cities Tulsa/San Luis Potosi, 1988—, South Peoria Neighborhood Connection Found., 1991—, pres., 1995-96; active Tulsa County Tax Oversight Com., 1994—, Tulsa Home Rule Charter Com., 1994—. Recipient Okla. Sr. Olympics medal. Mem. Okla. Bar Assn., Tulsa County Bar Assn., Vol. Lawyers Assn. (bd. dirs.), Am. Dietetic Assn., Tulsa Dist. Dietetic Assn., Kiwanis Internat., Mensa, DAR, Delta Zeta. Republican. Avocations: swimming, scuba diving, jogging, bicycling, reading, painting, needlework, photography. Home: 6636 S Jamestown Pl Tulsa OK 74136-2615

STELZER, GUSTAV R. retired automotive executive; b. St. Louis, June 1, 1915; s. Martin J. Stelzer and Alma Mangelsdorf; m. Lorraine Louise Sueme, Feb. 3, 1940; children: Gail Messett, John J. Stelzer. Grad. in acctg. and comml. law, Mo. Bus. Sch., St. Louis, 1929. Acct. Craig Furniture Co., St. Louis, 1930-32; sales rep. Newsom & Stelzer, 1933-34; various positions GM Corp., various cities, 1935-66, sr. exec. regional mgr. Chevrolet Motor Divsn. Kansas City, Mo., 1966-76; ret., 1976. Author: Free Trade and the Constitution, 1987, 89, 94, The Nightmare of Camelot, An Expose of Free Trade, 1994, The State Against Religion, The Case for Equal Protection, 2001; contbr. over 130 articles to profl. pubs.; appeared numerous radio and TV talk shows. Mem. World Affairs Coun., San Diego, 1981-85, Inst. of the Ams., San Diego, 1982-86; mem. adv. coun., U. San Diego Sch. Edn., 1983-85. Avocations: golf, travel, writing. Home: 1836 163d Pl SE Mill Creek WA 98012 E-mail: gusstelzer@aol.com.

STELZER, IRWIN MARK, economist; b. N.Y.C., N.Y., May 22, 1932; s. Abraham and Fanny (Dolgins) S.; m. Marian Faris Stuntz, 1981. BA cum laude, NYU, 1951, MA, 1952; PhD, Cornell U., 1954. Fin. analyst Econometric Inst., 1952; tchg. fellow Cornell U., 1953-54; instr. U. Conn., 1954-55; rschr. Twentieth Century Fund, 1953-55; economist W.J. Levy, Inc., 1955-56; sr. cons., v.p. Boni, Watkins, Jason & Co., Inc., 1956-61; rschr. Brookings Instn., 1956-57; pres. Nat. Econ. Rsch. Assocs., Inc., 1961-85, I.M. Stelzer Assocs. Inc., 1986—; dir. Energy and Environmental Ctr., Harvard U., 1987-90. Dir. regulatory policy studies Am. Enterprise Inst., 1990-98; bd. dirs. Regulatory Policy Inst., Oxford U., 2000—; dir. regulatory studies Hudson Inst., 1998—; adv. coun. Electric Power Rsch. Inst.; adv. com. revision of rules of practice and procedure FERC; chmn. com. on adequate power supply FPC; bd. dirs. The Energy Adv. Group of the Keystone Ctr; mng. dir. Rothschild, Inc.; assoc. mem. Nuffield Coll., Oxford U.; mem. publs. com. The Pub. Interest; lectr. in field. Author: Selected Antitrust Cases: Landmark Decisions, 1955, The Antitrust Laws: A Primer, 1993; econ. columnist The Sunday Times, London, 1986—; contbg. editor The Weekly Standard; columnist Courier Mail, Australia; contbr. articles to econs. field; mem. publ. com. The Pub. Interest. Mem. Mayor's Energy Policy Adv. Group for N.Y.C.; adv. panel Pres.'s Nat. Commn. for Rev. of Antitrust Laws and Procedures; mem. Gov.'s Adv. Panel on Telecom., bd. governing trustees Am. Ballet Theatre; bd. dirs. U.S. Nat. Com., World Energy Conf., Regulatory Policy Inst., Oxford U.; mem. Fed. Energy Regulatory Com. Task Force on Pipeline Competition. Mem. Am. Econ. Assn., Reform Club, Cosmos Club, Phi Beta Kappa. Home: PO Box 1008 Aspen CO 81612-1008 Office: 1101 17th St NW Ste 202 Washington DC 20036-4722 E-mail: stelzer@aol.com.

STELZER, PATRICIA JACOBS, retired secondary school educator; b. Springfield, Ohio, Sept. 7, 1936; d. George Kenneth and Beatrice Snook Jacobs; m. James Glea Stelzer, May 12, 1956; children: Michael G., Samantha S. Moehn, James Todd. BS in Edn., Wright State U., 1973, MA in History, 1997. Reporter, features writer, columnist Springfield News-Sun, 1962—65; social studies tchr. Schaefer Jr. H.S., 1975—77, 1978—81, South H.S., Springfield, 1977—78, 1981—2000; ret., 2000; chmn. social studies dept. South H.S., Springfield, 1991—2000. Adj. prof. history Clark State C.C., Springfield, 2001—; cons. Ohio test scholastic achievement State of Ohio Dept. Edn., Columbus, 1985—87; participant cert. assessment pilot program social studies program Nat. Bd. Profl. Tchg. Stds., 1998. Pres. Springfield Civic Theater, 1984—85; performer, mem. pub. rels. com. Music-Stage Theater, 1964—68, 1975; dir., choreographer Northwestern H.S. and South H.S., 1977—91. Lutheran. Avocations: golf, travel, theater , writing. Home: 6541 Troy Rd Springfield OH 45502 Office: Clark State CC 570 E Leffel Ln Springfield OH 45501

STELZMANN, RAINULF ALEXANDER, retired humanities educator, writer; b. New Orleans, Sept. 30, 1924; s. Alexander and Ella Louise Stelzmann; m. Janet Joyce Hanley, June 6, 1957; children: Andrew, Mary, Juliet, Susan, Paul. PhD, Albert-Ludwig U., Freiburg, Germany, 1953; pedagog. diploma in higher edn., Essen (Germany)Pedagog. Sem., 1956. Tchg. asst. Aloisius Kolleg, Bonn, Germany, 1954—55; prof. Xavier U. of La., New Orleans, 1957—63, U. South Fla., Tampa, 1963—2001. Author: Die Romane Wilkie Collins: Struktur und Stil: Eine Studie zum Element des Melodramatischen in der englischen Literatur, 1953, Religiöse und philosophische Aspekte des zeitgenössischen amerikanische Romans, 1999, Thinking of Germany at Night: A Personal View of the Years 1927 to 1956, 2001; author, editor: Aegidius Albertinus: Christi Königreich und Seelengejaidt, 1983. Avocations: bicycling, swimming, windsurfing. Home: 18705 Lakeshore Dr Lutz FL 33549

STELZNER, PAUL BURKE, textile company executive; b. Iowa City, Jan. 1, 1935; s. Glenn W. and Ruth (Schroder) S.; m. Martha Jane Schneeberger, Aug. 23, 1958; children: Martha Elizabeth Beuke and Barrie Jane Lubbering. BS, Muskingum Coll., 1960; postgrad., Akron U., 1961-65. Tech. dir. Buckeye Fabric Finishing Co., Coshocton, Ohio, 1963-74; sec., sales mgr. Excello Fabric Finishers Inc., 1966-74; gen. mgr. Mineral Fiber Mfg. Corp., 1974-76, dir., 1998—; v.p., gen. mgr. Kellwood Co. Recreation Group, 1976-85; v.p. Am. Recreation Products, Inc., New Haven, 1985-88; v.p., gen. mgr. John Boyle & Co., Statesville, NC, 1989-93, pres., 1993—, dir., 1999—. Pres. Coshocton County Young Rep. Club, 1960-62; mem. Coshocton County Rep. Exec. Com., 1960-62; pres. Coshocton Park Bd., 1972-76; mem. Coshocton City Planning Commn., 1972-76; chmn. indsl. div. United Fund, 1973; dist. commr. St. Louis Council Boy Scouts Am., 1977-79, pres. Gateway Amica, 1986-87. Served with USN, 1953-57. Mem. ASTM, Indsl. Fabrics Assn. Internat. (assoc. dir. 1973-74, 82-88, 94-99, dir. 1998-2002), Am. Assn. Textile Colorists and Chemists, Soc. Plastics Engrs. (sr.). Presbyterian. Home: 210 Brierwood Rd Statesville NC 28677-5408 Office: John Boyle & Co Inc 1803 Salisbury Rd Statesville NC 28677-6219

STELZRIED, CHARLES THOMAS, engineer; b. L.A., Sept. 14, 1928; s. Charles Edward Stelzried and Dorothy Claire (Morgan) Mercer; m. Virginia Stelzried, 1962 (div. Jan. 1974); children: Camile Traci, Charles Thomas; m. Kay Stelzried, Apr. 4, 1977. BS, UCLA, 1957, MS, 1959; PhD, U. So. Calif., 1969. With NASA/Jet Propulsion Lab., Pasadena, Calif., 1953—, team mem. deep space radio sci. Mariner 10, 1967-81, tracking and data sys. mgr. for various deep space missions, 1981-86, DSN advanced sys. dep. program mgr., 1986—. Contbr numerous articles to profl. publs. With USN, 1946-53. Fellow IEEE (life); mem. AAAS, Sigma Xi, Tau Beta Pi. Office: Jet Propulsion Lab MS303-402 4800 Oak Grove Dr Pasadena CA 91109-8001

STEM, CARL HERBERT, business educator; b. Eagleville, Tenn., Jan. 30, 1935; s. Marion Ogilvie and Sara Elizabeth (Jones) S.; m. Linda Marlene Wheeler, Dec. 28, 1963; children: Anna Elizabeth, Susan Kathleen, John Carl, David Leslie. *Great-great-great-great-grandfather Jacob Stem-of Pennsylvania Dutch ancestry-migrated from the Philadelphia region after the Revolutionary War to Granville County, N.C., where there is still a farming village named Stem. In the 1830s several sons migrated to Middle Tennessee. Great-great-grandfather John Richard Stem was a lieutenant in the 55th (McKoins) Tennessee Infantry (CSA). Great-grandfather Marion Luther Stem was the first to "leave the farm", owning general merchandise stores. Grandfather Charles R. Stem practiced country dentistry for more than 50 years. Father Marion Ogilvie Stem died at the age of 28 in 1941.* BA, Vanderbilt U., 1957; AM (Woodrow Wilson fellow, Harvard scholar), Harvard U., 1960, PhD, 1969. Internat. fin. economist, bd. govs. Fed. Res. System, Washington, 1963—70; from assoc. prof. to prof. econs. Tex. Tech. U., Lubbock, 1970—75; from assoc. prof. to prof. internat. fin. Tex. Tech U., 1970—2001; from chmn. fin., adminstr. grad. programs, exec. assoc. dean to dean Tex. Tech U. Coll. Bus. Adminstrn., 1971—97, dean emeritus, 1997—. Sr. econ. adviser Office Fgn. Direct Investments, U.S. Dept. Commerce, Washington, 1973-74; cons. U.S. Dept. Treasury, 1974-75; mem. faculty Grad. Sch. Credit and Fin. Mgmt., Lake Success, N.Y., 1974-87; adj. scholar Am. Enterprise Inst. Pub. Policy Rsch., Washington, 1974-88; treas. Mission Jour., Inc., 1969-88. Editor (with Makin and Logue) Eurocurrencies and The International Monetary System; contbr. articles to profl. jours. Trustee St. Mary Plains Hosp., Lubbock, Tex., 1987-92, chmn., 1992; v.p. Tex. Coun. of Collegiate Edn. for Bus., 1977-78, pres., 1978-79; mem. acad. adv. bd. United Arab Emirates U., Al Ain, 1996—; mem. Coun. on Podiat. Med. Edn., Washington, 1998—; bd. visitors Abilene Christian U., 1998—; elder Broadway Ch. of Christ, Lubbock, 2001-. Capt. Security Agy. AUS, 1961-62. Fulbright scholar U. Reading, Eng., 1957-58. Fellow Phi Beta Kappa; mem. Southwestern Bus. Adminstrn. Assn. (pres. 1982-83), Nat. Assn. Bus. Economists, So. Bus. Adminstrn. Assn. (v.p. 1985-86, pres. 1986-87), Lubbock Econ. Coun. (pres. 1973), Am. Assembly Collegiate Schs. Bus. (stds. com. 1981-84, bd. dirs. 1993-96), Lubbock Club (pres. 1986-87), Omicron Delta Kappa, Phi Kappa Phi, Beta Gamma Sigma, Tau Kappa Alpha, Phi Beta Kappa. Home: 6218 Louisville Dr Lubbock TX 79413-5429 E-mail: cstem@ba.ttu.edu. *Most important to me are the ever timely values of our Judeo-Christian heritage- faith in God and a deep appreciation for the inherent value of man. These values have underpinned my aspirations and sustained me through disappointments. They have generated the perseverance and continual hope so vital to me as I have worked for self-growth and to make a contribution to the institutions and people with which I have been associated in various periods of my life.*

STEMERMAN, DAVID H. radiologist; b. Elmira, N.Y., Aug. 2, 1966; BA, Emory U., 1988; MD, Boston U., 1992. Diplomate Nat. Bd. Med. Examiners; bd. cert. Am. Bd. Radiology. Intern Mass. Gen. Hosp., Boston, 1992-93; resident Temple U., Phila., 1993-97; fellow NYU, N.Y.C., 1997-98; assoc. radiologist Abington (Pa.) Meml. Hosp., 1998-99, St. Joseph's Med. Ctr., 1999—2000, St. Barnabas Hosp., 2000—01; pres. GDS Imaging PC, Larchmont, NY, 2001—. Fax: (914) 722-9409.

STEMMER, EDWARD ALAN, surgeon, educator; b. Cin., Jan. 20, 1930; s. Edward Purcell and Helen Marie (Smith) S.; m. Lois Jean Moss, May 1, 1954; children: Susan Helen, Linda Diane, Paul Frederick, Nancy Joan, Carol Jean. BA, U. Chgo., 1949, MD, 1953. Diplomate Am. Bd. Surgery, Am. Bd. Thoracic Surgery. Resident in surgery U. Chgo., 1953-60; chief resident in surgery Stanford U., Palo Alto, Calif., 1960-62, instr. surgery, 1962-64; asst. prof. surgery U. Utah, Salt Lake City, 1964-65; from asst. prof. surgery to prof. surgery U. Calif., Irvine, 1966—. Acting chmn. surgery U. Calif., Irvine, 1978-80; chief surg. svc. VA Hosp., Long Beach, Calif., 1965—. Editor: Vascular Disease in the Elderly, 1997; contbr. articles to profl. jours., chpts. to books. Capt. USAF, 1955-57, maj. USAFR, 1957-72. Grantee NIH, Am. Heart Assn., 1962-72; recipient disting. svc. award Am. Heart Assn., 1971. Mem. Am. Assn. Thoracic Surgery, Assn. VA Surgeons (pres. 1979-80, disting. svc. award 1995), Am. Surg. Assn., Am. Coll. Surgeons (pres. So. Calif. chpt. 1974-75), L.A. Surg. Soc. (pres. 1986-87), Sigma Xi. Avocations: carpentry, gardening, electronics. Home: 136 College Park Dr Seal Beach CA 90740-2527 Office: VA Med Ctr 5901 E 7th St Long Beach CA 90822-5201 E-mail: edward.stemmer@med.va.gov.

STEMMER, JAY JOHN, safety engineer, consultant; b. Wilkes-Barre, Pa., Apr. 29, 1939; BSCE, N.J. Inst. Tech., 1962; MBA, Calif. State U., Long Beach, 1969. Registered profl. engr., Calif.; cert. safety profl. Engr. Factory Mut., N.J., 1973-77; cons. McKay & Assoc., Calif., 1977-81, Index Research, 1981-83, Fireman's Fund, 1983-85, AIG Cons., 1985-87; sr. cons. Argonaut, 1987—. Assoc. prof. Sierra Coll., Los Angeles, 1979-80. Author: Medical Manual of Industrial Toxicology, 1965, Latin America, A Study of Air Transport Development and Potential in the Decade Ahead, 1970. Served to lt. USAF, 1962-65. Mem. NSPE, SAG, AFTRA, AEA, Calif. Soc. Profl. Engrs., Am. Soc. Safety Engrs. Avocations: graphology, duplicate bridge, photography, white water rafting, pub. speaking. Home: 1935 Alpha Rd Apt 225 Glendale CA 91208-2135

STEMMERMANN, GRANT NICHOLAS, pathologist, educator; b. N.Y.C., Oct. 28, 1918; s. Charles and Agnes Stuart (Grant) S.; m. Jean Elizabeth Gammon, Sept. 7, 1944 (dec. June 25, 1976); children: Ruth (dec.), Maile Anne; m. Nell Jane Nelson, Dec. 23, 1977; children: Mele, Rachel. Student, Trinity Coll., 1935-37, Cornell U., 1937-39; MD, McGill Coll., Montreal, Can., 1943. Intern Montreal Gen. Hosp., 1943-44; resident Halloran VA Hosp., Staten Island, N.Y., 1946-50; lab dir. Hilo (Hawaii) Meml. Hosp., 1951-58, Kuakini Med. Ctr., Honolulu, 1952-83; pathologist Japan Hawaii Cancer Study, 1983-93; prof. U. Cin., 1993—. Cons. Japan Hawaii Cancer Study, 1998—. Contbr. artilces to profl. jours. Capt. Med. Corps., 1944-46. Office: U Cin Dept Pathology 231 Albert Sabin Way Cincinnati OH 45267-0529 E-mail: stemmegn@email.uc.edu.

STEMMLER, EDWARD JOSEPH, physician, retired association executive, retired academic dean; b. Phila., Feb. 15, 1929; s. Edward C. and Josephine (Heitzmann) Stemmler; m. Joan C. Koster, Dec. 27, 1958; children: Elizabeth, Margaret, Edward C., Catherine, Joan. BA, La Salle Coll., Phila., 1950, ScD (hon.) , 1983; MD, U. Pa., 1960; ScD (hon.) , Ursinus Coll., 1977, Phila. Coll. Pharmacy and Sci., 1989; LHD (hon.) , Rush U., 1986, Med. Coll. Pa., 1994; ScD (hon.) , SUNY, Syracuse, 1994; ScD, Georgetown U., 1998. Diplomate Am. Bd. Internal Medicine. Intern U. Pa. Hosp., 1960—61, resident in internal medicine, 1961—63, fellow in cardiology, 1963—64, chief med. resident, 1964—65, chief med. outpatient dept., 1966—67; chief of medicine U. Pa. Med. Svc., VA Hosp., Phila., 1967—73; deans com. VA Hosp., 1974—88; instr. medicine grad. divsn. medicine U. Pa., 1964—66, NIH postdoctoral rsch. trainee, dept. physiology, grad. divsn. medicine, 1965—67, assoc. in medicine grad. divsn. medicine, 1966—67; assoc. in physiology Grad. Div. Medicine, 1967—72, from asst. prof. medicine to prof., 1967—91, Robert G. Dunlop prof., 1981—91, prof. emeritus, 1991—; assoc. dean Univ. Hosp. Sch. Medicine, 1973, assoc. dean student affairs, 1973—75, from acting dean to dean, 1974—88, dean emeritus, 1989—; exec. v.p. U. Pa. Med. Ctr., 1986—89, Assn. Am. Med. Colls., 1990—94, sr. adv. to pres., 1994—95. Nominating and ad hoc governance coms. Nat. Bd. Med. Examiners , 1985, exec. com., 1986—99, vice-chmn., 1987—89, treas., 1989—91, chmn., 1991—95; ednl. policy com. Nat. Fund for Med. Edn., 1975—77; deans com. VA Hosp., 1974—89; chmn. Pa. Deans Com., 1976—87, Mid-Ea. Regional Med. Libr. Svcs., 1978—81; adv. com. dept. medicine U. Ala., Birmingham, 1985—89; vis. com. Tufts U. Sch. Medicine, 1990—94, Med. U. S.C., 1990—99, U. Calif., Davis, 1993—. Contbr. articles to profl. jours. Trustee

Dorothy Rider Pool Healthcare Trust, 1991—2000, Ursinus Coll., 1991—, Wintergreen Nature Found., 1996—2001, Saw Cmty. Found., 2000—. Recipient Frederick A. Packard award, 1960, Albert Einstein Med. Ctr. staff award, 1960, Roche award, 1960, Disting. Svc. award, Nat. Bd. Med. Examiners, 1999. Master: ACP (treas., chmn. investment com. 1975—80, Laureate award Ea. Pa. region 1986, Disting. Svc. award); mem.: AMA, Am. Clin. and Climatological Soc. (pres. 1997—98), Coll. of Physicians of Phila. (bd. censors, coun. 1979—85, coun. 1990—92), Assn. Am. Med. Colls. (ad hoc external exam. rev. com. 1980—82, exec. coun., coun. of deans adminstrv. bd. 1980—85, chmn. 1983—85, nat. chmn.-elect 1985—86, chmn. assembly 1986—87), Inst. Medicine, Alpha Omega Alpha. Republican. Mem. Christian Ch. Home: RR 1 Box 676 Roseland VA 22967-9209

STEMPEL, GUIDO HERMANN, III, journalism educator; b. Bloomington, Ind., Aug. 13, 1928; s. Guido Hermann Jr. and Alice Margaret (Menninger) S.; m. Anne Elliott, Aug. 30, 1952; children: Ralph Warren, Carl William, Jane Louise. Student, Carnegie Tech., 1945-46; AB in Journalism, Ind. U., 1949, AM in Journalism, 1951; PhD in Mass Communication, U. Wis., 1954. Sports editor Frankfort (Ind.) Times, 1949-50; instr., asst. prof. Sch. Journalism, Pa. State U., University Park, 1955-57; from assoc. prof. to prof. Dept. Journalism, Cen. Mich. U., Mt. Pleasant, 1957-65; assoc. prof. Sch. Journalism, Ohio U., Athens, 1965-68, prof., 1968-82, Disting. prof., 1982-97, dir., 1972-79, Disting. prof. emeritus, 1997—. Rsch. cons. Ohio Newspaper Assn., Columbus, 1985—; chmn. rsch. com. Coll. Media Advisors, 1963-69, 79-84; mem. adv. bd. dept. comm. arts U. West Fla., 1987—; survey cons. Scripps Howard News Svc., 1992—. Co-author: The Media in the 1984 and 1988 Presidential Campaigns, 1991; assoc. editor, Newspaper Rsch. Jour., 1992-2001; co-editor Web Jour. of Mass Comm. Rsch., 1997—; editor, co-author: The Practice of Political Communication, 1994; co-editor, co-author: Research Methods in Mass Communications, 1981, 2d edit., 1989, The Media in the 1984 and 1988 Presidential Campaigns, 1991; co-editor: Historical Dictionary of Political Communication in the United States, 1999, Mass Communication Research and Theory, 2002; editor: Journalism Quar., 1972-89; contbr. articles to profl. jours. Mem. bd. visitors Def. Info. Sch., Ft. Meade, 1985-96. Recipient Chancellor's award U. Wis., 1977. Mem. Assn. for Edn. in Journalism and Mass Communication (chmn. rsch. com. 1968-71; Eleanor Blum award 1989, Trayes tchr. of yr. award 1997, Disting. Svc. award 1999), Soc. Profl. Journalists, Rotary (pres. Athens unit 1984-85). Democrat. Methodist. Home: 7 Lamar Dr Athens OH 45701-3730 Office: Ohio Univ Sch of Journalism Athens OH 45701 E-mail: stempel@ohio.edu.

STEMPEL, JOHN DALLAS, international studies educator; b. Easton, Pa., July 26, 1938; s. John Emmert and Mary Roberts (Farmer) S.; m. Nancy A. Dean, Feb. 11, 1961 (div. Jan. 1990); m. Susan Hodgetts, May 18, 1991; children: Amy, Alix, Jill. AB cum laude, Princeton U., 1960; MA with distinction, U. Calif., Berkeley, 1963, PhD, 1965. Jr. officer U.S. Embassy U.S. Fgn. Svc., Conakry, Guinea, 1966, acting dep. chief mission U.S. Embassy Bujumbura, Burundi, 1966-68, watch officer State Dept. Ops. Ctr. Washington, 1968-70, staff asst. to dep. sec. state, 1968-70, Ghana desk officer, 1970-72, polit.-econ. officer U.S. Embassy Zambia, 1972-74, from sr. internat. polit. reporter to dep. chief sect. to acting polit. counselor U.S. Embassy Tehran, Iran, 1975-79; diplomat-in-residence, mem. faculty U.S. Naval Acad., Annapolis, Md., 1979-81; dir. ops. ctr. Dept. State U.S. Fgn. Svc., Washington, 1981-83, dir. Office Near East and South Asian Affairs Bur. Internat. Security Affairs Dept. Def., 1983-84, spl. asst. Persian Gulf affairs, 1984-85, consul gen. Madras, India, 1985-88; prof. internat. studies, assoc. dir. Patterson Sch. Diplomacy and Internat. Commerce U. Ky., Lexington, 1988-93, prof. internat. studies, dir. Patterson Sch. Diplomacy, 1993—. Adj. prof. George Washington U., Washington, 1968-72, 80-85, Am. U., Washington, 1975; prof. Regional Coop. and Devel. Coll., Tehran, 1975-78; rsch. assoc. Mershon Ctr. Ohio State U., 1972. Author: Inside the Iranian Revolution, 1981, Faith, Diplomacy and the International System, 2000; (monograph) Theory and Practice in Foreign Affairs: Why Two Worlds Seldom Meet, 1972; contbr. articles to profl. jours. With USN, 1960-62, lt. USNR, 1962-70. Mem. Internat. Studies Assn., N.Y. Coun. on Fgn. Rels. (mem. U.S. Dept. Commerce Export Coun. Ky.). Avocations: tennis, reading, railroads, philosophy. Office: U Ky Patterson Sch Diplomacy Patterson Tower Rm 455 Lexington KY 40506-0027

STEMPL, ROBERT C. energy company executive; b. 1932; Pres. GM Corp., 1987-90, chmn., CEO, 1990-92; mem. bd. mgrs. GM Ovonic; chmn. Ovonic Battery; sr. bus. and tech. advisor to chmn. Energy Conversion Devices, Inc., Troy, Mich., chmn. bd. dirs., exec. dir., 1999—. Bd. dirs. United Solar and Ovonyx, Alliance Bd. of Ovonic Media, Southwall Technologies, Inc.; mem. mgmt. com. Texaco Ovonic Fuel Cell Co., Bekaert ECD Solar Systems; others. Office: Energy Conversion Devices Inc 2956 Waterview Dr Rochester MI 48309

STEMPLER, JACK LEON, government and aerospace company executive; b. Newark, Oct. 30, 1920; s. Morris and Ida (Friedman) S.; m. J. Adelaide Williams, Oct. 28, 1950; children: Mark N., Sandra J., Carrie B. BA, Montclair (N.J.) State U., 1943; LL.B., Cornell U., 1948. Bar: N.Y., D.C. 1949. Atty. com. uniform code mil. justice Dept. Def., 1948-49, atty. adviser legis. div., 1949-50; asst. counsel Munitions Bd., 1950-53; counsel Armed Forces Housing Agy., 1952-54, Advanced Research Projects Agy., 1958-65; asst. gen. counsel logistics Dept. Def., 1953-65, asst. to sec. def. for legislative affairs, 1965-70; gen. counsel Dept. Air Force, 1970-77; asst. to sec. of def. for legis. affairs, 1977-81; v.p. legis. affairs LTV Aerospace, Washington, 1982-92; ret., 1992. Cons. in field. Served to 1st lt. USMCR, 1942-46, PTO. Recipient Outstanding Civilian Performance award Dept. Def., 1959, Distinguished Civilian Service award, 1965, Distinguished Civilian Service award with palm, 1969, with 2d bronze palm, 1970; Exceptional Civilian Service award USAF, 1973, 75, 77; awarded Presdl. rank of Disting. Exec., 1980; recipient Disting. Public Service award Dept. Def., 1981 Mem. Fed. Bar Assn., D.C. Bar Assn., Cornell Law Sch. Assn. Home: 4701 Newcomb Pl Alexandria VA 22304-1506

STEMPLESKI, SUSAN, English language professional, writer; d. John Adam Stempleski and Helen Marie (Fitzgerald) Sutter. BA in English Lit., Boston U., 1964; MA in Bilingual, Bicultural Studies, Boston State Coll., 1973; MEd, Columbia U. Tchr.'s Coll., 1989, postgrad. Tchr. French, math. Matignon High Sch., Cambridge, Mass., 1964-65; rsch. asst. Boston U., 1965-66; coord. ABE, ESL Boston Pub. Schs., 1966-72; coord. ESL program Harvard U., Cambridge, 1972-74, tng. rep., 1974-76; lectr. ESL Emerson Coll., Boston, 1976-77; coord. bilingual programs Newbury Jr. Coll., 1976-77; tchr. EFL, tchr. trainer The Cleve. Inst., Paris, 1977-80; mng. dir. Caf(é)-Th(é)atre de la Rosais, Jugon-les-Lacs, France, 1980-81; instr. ESL CUNY, 1981-89; lectr. in TESOL Columbia U. Tchr.'s Coll., N.Y.C., 1988—. Cons. EFL/ESL materials devel., program design tchr. tng. and devel.; Fulbright lectr., Chile, 1987; mem. adv. bd. BBC English by TV, Encyclopedia Britannica; cons. ESL English Advantage Video, 1990; dir. ESL Hello America, 1991; advisor Encounter English, 1990, Am. Lang. Hello, 1991. Author: Getting Together, 1986, Explorations, 1988, Video in Action, 1990, Focus on the Environment, 1992, Video in Second Language Teaching, 1992, Earth Watch, 1993, Cultural Awareness, 1993, That's English, 1994, American English OK!, 1998, English Today, 1998, Film, 2001; contbr. articles to profl. jours. Recipient Duke of Edinburgh commendation, 1990; grantee U.S. Info. Agy. Acad. Specialist, 1985, 87, 89, 91, 94, Disting. Am. Specialist award, 1994; Fulbright scholar Bolivia, 1987. Mem. TESOL (exec. bd. 1993-96, founding chair video interest sect. 1989-90, local com. conv. N.Y.C. 1985, dir. video theater ann. conv. San Antonio 1989, San Francisco 1990, pres. Mass. affiliate 1976-77, v.p. 1975-76, mem.-at-large exec. bd. 1973-75, chair ann. conf. 1975, 76, video liaison officer 1987—), Internat. Assn. Tchrs. English as Fgn. Lang. (video spl. interest group com. 1987—), Assn. Binational Ctrs. in L.Am. (proposal com. 1989), Kappa Delta Pi. Avocations: theater, film, opera. Home: 504 W 111th St Apt 54 New York NY 10025-1939 Office: Columbia U Tchrs Coll Box 66 TESOL Program 525 W 120th St New York NY 10027-6625

STEMPSEY, WILLIAM EDWARD, medical philosopher; b. Albany, N.Y., Jan. 26, 1952; s. William Edward and Helen Theresa (Kuras) S. BS in Biology/Psychology magna cum laude, Boston Coll., 1974; MD, SUNY, Buffalo, 1978; AM in Philosophy, Loyola U., Chgo., 1988; MDiv, Jesuit Sch. Theology, Berkeley, Calif., 1991; STM in Moral Theology, Jesuit Sch. Theology, 1992; PhD in Philosophy, Georgetown U., 1996. Diplomate Nat. Bd. Med. Examiners; joined S.J., Roman Cath. Ch., 1982, ordained priest, 1992. Intern in anatomic pathology Boston City Hosp., 1978-79; resident in clin. pathology U. Hosp., Boston, 1980-82; resident in pediatric pathology Children's Hosp., 1984-85; teaching fellow Boston U. Sch. Medicine, 1981-82; clin. fellow in pathology Harvard Med. Sch., Boston, 1984-85; clin. scholar Ctr. for Clin. Bioethics, Georgetown U. Med. Ctr., 1995-96; asst. prof. philosophy Coll. of the Holy Cross, Worcester, Mass., 1996—. High sch. tchr. Claver Coll., Punda Gorda, Belize, 1983; hosp. minister Youville Hosp., Cambridge, 1983; mem. ethics com. St. Mary's Hosp. and Med. Ctr., San Francisco, 1989-92; mem. admissions com. Jesuit Sch. Theology, Berkeley, 1989-90; rsch. asst. for dir. Kennedy Inst. Ethics, Georgetown U., 1992-94; guest retreat dir. Mercy Ctr., Burlingame, Calif., 1990, 91; pastoral care minister Loyola Med. Ctr., Maywood, Ill., 1986-87, St. Francis Hosp., Evanston, Ill., 1987-88. Author: Disease and Diagnosis: Value-Dependent Realism, 1999; contbr. articles to profl. publs. Vol. Shelter, Inc., Cambridge, Mass., 1982; mem. bioethics commn. Diocese of Worcester, Mass., 1997—; mem. ethics com. Fallon Clinic, Worcester, 1998—; mem. regional ethics com. Vis. Nurses Assn. Care Network, Worcester, 1998—. Mem. Am. Philos. Assn., Soc. for Health and Human Values, Kennedy Inst. Ethics, Hastings Ctr. (assoc.), Alpha Epsilon Delta. Avocations: music, piano, accordion, fishing. Office: Coll of the Holy Cross Dept Philosophy 1 College St Worcester MA 01610-2395

STENBERG, ADAM W. financial advisor, investment company executive; b. Mpls., May 11, 1970; s. Michael Glenn and Donna Rae S.; m. Sharalyn V. Deming, June 20, 1992; children: Georgia, Everett. BS in Econs., U. Minn., 1992, BA in Polit. Sci., 1993. Registered investment adv., Minn. Sys. adminstr. U.S. Rep. Jim Ramstad, Washington, 1994; sr. legis. asst. U.S. Rep. Gil. Gutknecht, 1995-96; fin. adv. Prudential Securities, Mpls., 1997-98, Paradigm Investments, Mpls., 1998—. Cons. Am. Express Fin. Advs., Mpls., 1999—. Mem. First Bapt. Ch., 1988—, dir. men's ministry, 1998—, trustee, chmn., 1999—; candidate Minn. State Rep., Mpls., 1998, 00. Recipient Spl. Svc. award U.S. Treasury, 1991. Mem.: U. Minn. Alumni Assn. Republican. Avocations: web development, politics, basketball, softball, backpacking. Office: Paradigm Investments 4920 Ewing Ave S Minneapolis MN 55410-1750

STENBERG, CARL W., III, public administration educator, dean; b. Pitts., July 8, 1943; s. Carl W. and Mildred (Baggs) S.; m. Kirstin D. Thompson; children: Erik Anders, Kerry Cathryn, Kaameran Baird. BA, Allegheny Coll., 1965; MPA, SUNY, Albany, 1966, PhD, 1970. Research asst. N.Y. State Div. Budget, Albany, 1967; analyst, then sr. analyst U.S. Adv. Commn. on Intergovtl. Relations, Washington, 1968-77, asst. dir. for policy implementation, 1977-83, acting exec. dir., 1982; exec. dir. Council of State Govts., Lexington, Ky., 1983-89; prof., dir. Weldon Cooper Ctr. for Pub. Svc. U. Va., Charlottesville, 1989-95, Disting. prof. pub. svc., 1991-95; prof., dean Yale Gordon Coll. Liberal Arts U. Balt., 1995—. Mem. Am. Part Program USIA, 1987; adj. prof. George Washington U., 1971, 81, Am. U., 1972-80, 82, U. Md., 1976, U. So. Calif., 1984-87; v.p. Bureaucrat Inc., Washington, 1973-77, mng. editor, 1973-77. Feature editor Pub. Mgmt. Forum Pub. Adminstrn. Rev., 1977-83, editor U. of Va. newsletter, 1994-95; co-editor-in-chief The Regionalist, 1997-2002. Pres. Reston Home Owners' Assn., Va., 1973-74; mem. U.S. del. Ad Hoc Group on Urban Problems, OECD, 1980-82. Vivien Stewart vis. fellow Cambridge U., Eng., 1980; recipient Disting. Alumni award Polit. Sci. Dept. Rockefeller Coll., 1985. Fellow: Nat. Acad. of Public Adminstrn. (vice-chair, bd. dirs. 2002—); mem.: Va. Alliance for Pub. Svc. (pres. 1991—92), Am. Soc. Pub. Adminstrn. (pres. 1990—91, Marshall E. Dimock award, Louis Brownlow award, Donald Stone award). Home: 2 Johnson Mill Rd Baltimore MD 21204-3549 Office: U Balt 1420 N Charles St Baltimore MD 21201-5720 E-mail: cstenberg@ubalt.edu.

STENBERG, DONALD B. state attorney general; b. David City, Nebr., Sept. 30, 1948; s. Eugene A. and Alice (Kasal) Stenberg; m. Susan K. Hoegemeyer, June 9, 1971; children: Julie A., Donald B. Jr., Joseph L., Abby E. BA, U. Nebr., 1970; MBA, JD cum laude, Harvard U., 1974. Bar: Nebr. 1974, U.S. Dist. Ct. Nebr. 1974, U.S. Ct. Appeals (fed. cir.) 1984, U.S. Ct. Claims 1989, U.S. Ct. Appeals (8th cir.) 1989, U.S. Supreme Ct. 1991. Assoc. Barlow, Watson & Johnson, Lincoln, Nebr., 1974—75; ptnr. Stenberg and Stenberg, 1976—78; legal counsel Gov. of Nebr., 1979—82; sr. prin. Erickson & Sederstrom, 1983—85; pvt. practice, 1985—90; atty. gen. State of Nebr., 1991—. Mem.: Phi Beta Kappa. Republican. Office: Office of Atty Gen 2115 State Capitol Lincoln NE 68509-8000

STENBIT, JOHN PAUL, federal agency administrator; b. Oakland, Calif., June 1, 1940; s. Paul Charles and Antoinette (Inguglia) S.; m. Albertine Heederik, Aug. 19, 1966; children: Elisabeth Francesca, Antine Elaine. BS, Calif. Inst. Tech., 1961, MS, 1962; postgrad., Stanford U., 1981. Rsch. fellow Technische Hogesch., Eindhoven, The Netherlands, 1962-63, 65-67; engr. Aerospace Corp., El Segundo, Calif., 1962-68; prin. dep. dir. Office Sec. Def., Washington, 1973-77; engr. TRW, Redondo Beach, Calif., 1968-73, 77—, engr., v.p., gen. mgr. systems integration group Fairfax, Va., 1977—, exec. v.p.; asst. secy. command, control, commun. and intel. U.S. Dept. Defense, Washington, 2001—. Mem. adv. bd. Dir. Naval Intelligence, Washington, 1982-91; mem. sci. adv. group Def. Communications Agy., Arlington, Va., 1989—; cons. Def. Sci. Bd., Washington. Chmn. Internat. Children's Festival, Fairfax, 1991-92. Recipient medal for outstanding pub. svc. Sec. Def., 1977; Fulbright fellow, The Netherlands, 1962-63, Aerospace Corp., The Netherlands, 1965-67. Mem. NAE, AIAA, Security Affairs Support Assn. (bd. dirs. 1990—), Electronic Industries Assn. (bd. dirs. 1991—), Armed Forces Communications and Electronics Assn., Va. Bus. Coun., Korean-Am. Bus. Coun., Met. Club (Washington). Republican. Office: US Dept Defense Command, Control, Commun and Intel 6000 Defense Pentagon Washington DC 20301-6000 Office Fax: 703-614-8060.*

STENCER, MARK JOSEPH, academic administrator, consultant; b. Pitts., Mar. 19, 1955; s. Frank C. and Ramona (Calabrese) S. BFA, Carnegie-Mellon U., 1976; BA in Liberal Arts, U. Mich., 1979; MA in Mgmt., NYU, 1982. Asst. dir. NYU Office Acad. Devel., N.Y.C., 1980-82; program dir. John B. Cummings Co., Inc., Fundraising and Pub. Rels. Cons., 1982-84; assoc. dir. The Statue of Liberty, Ellis Island Found., 1984-86; dir. devel. Fordham U., 1986-91; exec. v.p. Cambridge U., England, 1991-94; exec. campaign dir. Cmty. Counselling Svc. Co., Inc., N.Y.C., N.J., 1995-2000. Exec. sr. dir., U. Chgo., N.Y. Regional Divsn., 2000—. Named Outstanding Young Man Am., 1985, 86. Mem. Nat. Assn. Fundraising Execs., Coun. Advancement and Support of Edn. Republican. Roman Catholic. Avocation: pianist. Home: 201 Saint Pauls Ave Apt 11K Jersey City NJ 07306-3763

STENCHEVER, MORTON ALBERT, obstetrician, gynecologist; b. Paterson, N.J., Jan. 25, 1931; s. Harold and Lena (Suresky) Stenchever; m. Diane Bilsky, June 19, 1955 (dec. 1999); children: Michael A., Marc R., Douglas A.; m. Luba Kane, Sept. 8, 2001. AB, NYU, 1951; MD, U. Buffalo, 1956. Diplomate Am. Bd. Ob-gyn., 1988. Intern Mt. Sinai Hosp., 1956-57; resident obstetrics and gynecology Columbia-Presbyn. Med. Center, N.Y.C., 1957-60; asst. prof., Oglebey research fellow Case-Western Res. U., Cleve., 1962-66, asso. prof. dept. reproductive biology, 1967-70, dir. Tissue Culture Lab., 1965-70, coordinator Phase II Med. Sch. program, 1969-70; prof., chmn. dept. obstetrics-gynecology U. Utah Med. Sch., Salt Lake City, 1970-77; prof. ob-gyn. U. Wash. Sch. Medicine, Seattle, 1977-98; prof. emeritus, 1998—; chmn. dept. U. Wash. Sch. Medicine, Seattle, 1977-96. Chmn. test com. for ob-gyn. Nat. Bd. Med. Examiners, 1979-82; cons. in urogynecology Fedn. Internat. for Gynecology & Obstetrics, 1998—. Author: Labor: Workbook in Obstetrics, 1968, Labor: Workbook in Obstetrics, 2d edit., 1993, Human Sexual Behavior: A Workbook in Reproductive Biology, 1970, Human Cytogenics: A Workbook in Reproductive Biology, 1973, Introductory Gynecology: A Workbook in Reproductive Biology, 1974; co-author: Comprehensive Gynecology, 1987, Comprehensive Gynecology, 4th edit., 2001, Caring for the Older Woman, 1991, Caring for the Older Woman, 2d edit., 1996, Health Care for the Older Woman, 1996, Office Gynecology, 1992, Office Gynecology, 2d edit., 1996, Good Health, Good Sex After 40: A Woman's Guide, 1997; sr. editor: Atlas of Gynecology, 5 vols., 1997—99, assoc. editor: Ob-Gyn., 1986—2001, assoc. editor: Ob-Gyn. Survey; editor: Clinical Updates in Women's Health Care, 2001—, ACOG Review, 2001—; mem. editl. bd.: Western Jour. Medicine; contbr. articles. Served to capt. USAF, 1960-62. Fellow Am. Coll. Obstetricians and Gynecologists (com. on residency edn. 1974-80, learning resource commn. 1980-86, vice chmn. 1982-83, chmn. prolog self-assessment program 1982-86, vice chair com. health care for the underserved women 1995-97), Am. Assn. Obstetricians and Gynecologists, Am. Gynecol. Soc., Am. Soc. Ob-Gyn., Pacific Coast Ob-Gyn. Soc.; mem. AAAS, AMA, Am. Bd. Ob-Gyn. (bd. dir. 1988-, v.p. 1990-92, treas. 1992-96, chmn. 1996-98, mem. resident rev. com. 1993-97, chmn. divsn. female pelvic medicine/reconstructive surgery), Assn. Profs. Gynecology and Obstetrics (chmn. steering com. teaching methods in ob-gyn. 1970-79, v.p. 1975-76, pres. 1983-84, v.p. Found. 1986-87, pres. Found. 1987-91), Pacific N.W. Ob-Gyn. Soc., Wash. State Med. Assn., Seattle Gynec. Soc. (v.p. 1981, pres.-elect 1982, pres. 1982-83), Pacific Coast Ob-Gyn. Soc., Am. Soc. Human Genetics, Ctrl. Assn. Ob-Gyn., Soc. Gynecologic Investigation, Wash. State Obstet. Soc., Tissue Culture Assn., N.Y. Acad. Sci., Utah Ob-Gyn. Soc., Utah Med. Assn., Teratology Soc., Am. Fertility Soc. Home: 8301 SE 83rd St Mercer Island WA 98040-5644 Office: Ob-Gyn 130 Knickerson St Ste 211 Seattle WA 98109

STENDAHL, KRISTER, retired bishop; b. Stockholm, Sweden, Apr. 21, 1921; came to U.S., 1954, naturalized, 1967; s. Olof and Sigrid (Ljungquist) S.; m. Brita Johnsson, Sept. 7, 1946; children: John, Anna, Daniel. Teol. kand., U. Uppsala, Sweden, 1944, teol. lic., 1949, teol.dr., 1954; Litt. D. (hon.), Upsala Coll., 1963; D.D., St. Olaf Coll., 1971, Harvard U., 1985, St. Andrews U., 1987, Calif. Luth. U., 1995; LL.D., Susquehanna U., 1973; L.H.D. (hon.), Hebrew Union Coll./Jewish Inst. Religion, 1980, Brandeis U., 1981, Loyola U., New Orleans, 1992; Teol. dr., U. Helsinki, 2000. Ordained priest Ch. of Sweden, 1944. Chaplain to students Uppsala U., 1948-50, instr. O.T., N.T. exegesis, 1951-54, docent, 1954; asst. prof. N.T., 1954-56; asso. prof. Harvard U. Div. Sch., 1956-58, John H. Morison prof. N.T. studies, 1958-63, Frothingham prof. Bibl. studies, 1963-68, dean, John Lord O'Brian prof. div., 1968-79, Andrew W. Mellon prof. div., 1981-84, prof. emeritus, 1985—; pastor Luth. Ch. Am., 1968-84; Robert and Myra Kraft and Jacob Hiatt Disting. prof. Christian studies Brandeis U., 1991-93; moderator consultation on ch. and Jewish people World Council Chs., 1975-85; co-dir. Osher Ctr. for Tolerance and Pluralism Shalom Hartman Inst., 1994-98. Author: The School of St. Matthew, 1954, 2d edit., 1968, The Bible and the Role of Women, 1966, Holy Week, 1974, Paul Among Jews and Gentiles, 1976, Final Account, 1995, 2d edit., Energy for Life, 1999. Recipient Disting. Service award Assn. Theol. Schs., 1988. Fellow Am. Acad. Arts and Scis.; mem. Nathan Soederblom Soc. Business E-Mail: krister_stendahl@harvard.edu.

STENDER, BRUCE WILLIAM, business executive; b. Monroe, Wis., Feb. 15, 1942; m. Kaye Lee; 4 children. AB, Marquette U., 1964, MEd, 1967; PhD, Fla. State U., 1969; LLD (hon.), Coll. of St. Scholastica, 1981. Asst. to dean of faculty Boston Coll., 1969-71; dean of coll. Maryville Coll., 1971-74; pres. Coll. of St. Scholastica, Duluth, Minn., 1975-81; pres., CEO, prin. Labovitz Enterprises, 1981—; CEO Labovitz Corp. Bd. dirs. ALLETE. Trustee C.K. Blandin Found.; active numerous bus., health care and comty. bds. and coms. Named one of Ten Outstanding Minnesotans, 1978. Mem. Internat. Assn. Holiday Inn Owners. Office: 227 W 1st St Ste 880 Duluth MN 55802-1913 Fax: (218) 727-7362. E-mail: Bruce_Stender@LionInvestment.com.

STENDER, ROBIN, protective services official; b. Chestertown, Md., Apr. 27, 1976; d. Donald and Jean Carter; m. Eric Stender. Grad. H.S., Venice, Fla. Police dispatcher City of Venice Police Dept., 1998—. Author: (Poetry,Rhyming Stories, etc...) Prayer For A Child, 2001, poetry and stories. Avocations: writing, research. Personal E-mail: heresruby@aol.com.

STENEHJEM, WAYNE KEVIN, state attorney general, lawyer; b. Mohall, N.D., Feb. 5, 1953; s. Martin Edward and Marguerite Mae (McMaster) Stenehjem; m. Tama Lou Smith, June 16, 1978 (div. Apr. 1984); 1 child Andrew Stenejhem ; m. Beth D. Bakke, June 30, 1995. AA, Bismarck (N.D.) Jr. Coll., 1972; BA, U. N.D., 1974, JD, 1977. Bar: N.D. 1977. Ptnr. Kuchera & Stenehjem, Grand Forks, ND, 1977—2000; spl. asst. atty. gen. State of N.D., 1983—87, atty. gen., 2000—; mem. N.D. Ho. Reps. , 1976—80, N.D. State Senate, 1980—2000, pres. pro tempore, 1998—99. Chmn. Senate Com. on Social Svcs., 1985—86, Senate Com. on Judiciary, 1995—2000, Interim Legis. Judiciary Com., 1995—2000, Legis. Coun., 1995—2000; mem. Nat. Conf. Commrs. on Uniform State Laws, 1995—, Gov.'s Com. on Juvenile Justice. Bd. dirs. N.D. Spl. Olympics, 1985—89; chmn. Dist. 42 Reps., Grand Forks, 1986—88; bd. dirs. Christus Rex Luth. Ch., pres., 1985—86. Named Champion of People's Right to Know, Sigma Delta Chi, 1979, N.D. Friend of Psychology, N.D. Psychol. Assn., 1990; named one of Outstanding Young Man of N.D, Jaycees, 1985; recipient Excellence in County Govt. award, N.D. Assn. Counties, 1991. Mem.: Grand Forks County Bar Assn., N.D. State Bar Assn. (Legis. Svc. award 1995). Home: 1216 Crestview Ln Bismarck ND 58501 Office: Office of the Atty Gen State Capitol Bldg 600 E Boulevard Ave Bismarck ND 58505

STENERSON, JOHN GORDEN, lumber and building materials executive; b. Ft. Rucker, Ala., Mar. 24, 1952; s. Robet Gorden and Georgiann S.; m. Shirley Mae, Nov. 14, 1981; children: Michael David, Sarah Ann, Robert John. Studetn, Moorhead State U., 1970-71; AA, Moorhead Area Vocat. Inst., 1973. Hardware mgr. Stenerson Lumber, Moorhead, Minn., 1973-74, outside sales, 1974-75, asst. mgr. Detroit Lakes, Minn., 1975-84, hardware merchandising coord. office Moorhead, 1984-85, yard mgr., 1986-94, asst. gen. mgr. corp. office, 1994-95, gen. mgr. corp. office, 1996—. Mem. city coun. City of Moorhead, 1992—; park adv. bd. chair Moorhead Park Bd., 1997—; v.p. Moorhead Healthy Cmty. Initiative, 1995-96. Mem. Jaycees (dir., v.p. 1975-83, Wiliam Brownfield award 1977), Lions. Republican. Lutheran. Avocations: snowmobiling, ice hockey, water skiing. Home: 1702 1st Ave N Moorhead MN 56560-2304

STENGEL, ROBERT FRANK, engineering and applied science educator; b. Orange, N.J., Sept. 1, 1938; s. Frank John and Ruth Emma (Geidel) S.; m. Margaret Robertson Ewing, Apr. 8, 1961; children: Brooke Alexandra, Christopher Ewing. SB, MIT, 1960; MS in Engring., Princeton U., 1965, MA, 1966, PhD, 1968. Aerospace technologist NASA, Wallops Island, Va., 1960-63; tech. staff group leader C.S. Draper Lab., Cambridge, Mass., 1968-73, Analytic Scis. Corp., Reading, 1973-77; assoc. prof. Princeton (N.J.) U., 1977-82, prof. engring. and applied sci., 1982—, assoc. dean engring., 1994-97. Cons. GM, Warren, Mich., 1985-94; mem. com. strategic tech. U.S. Army NRC, 1989-92; vice chmn. Congl. Aero. Adv. Com., Washington, 1986-89; mem. com. on trans-atmospheric vehicles USAF Sci. Adv. Bd., 1984-85; mem. com. on low altitude wind shear and its hazard to aviation Nat. Rsch. Coun., 1983, Navy Theater Missile Defense com. NRC, 2000-01. Author: Stochastic Optimal Control: Theory and Application, 1986, reprinted as Optimal Control and Estimation, 1994; N.Am. editor Cambridge Aerospace Series, Cambridge Univ. Press, 1993-98; contbr. over 200 tech. papers to profl. publs.; patentee wind probing device. Lt. USAF, 1960-63. Recipient Apollo Achievement award NASA, 1969, Cert. of Commendation, MIT, 1969, Excellence in Aviation award FAA, 1997, John R. Ragazzini Edn. award, AACC, 2002. Fellow IEEE, AIAA (Mechanics and Control of Flight award 2000). Avocations: photography, music, bicycling. Home: 329 Prospect Ave Princeton NJ 08540-5330 Office: Princeton U D202 Engineering Quadrangle Princeton NJ 08544-0001 Fax: (609) 258-6109. E-mail: stengel@princeton.edu.

STENGEL, RONALD FRANCIS, management consultant; b. Lock Haven, Pa., Oct. 18, 1947; s. Elmer S. and Elizabeth (Heivley) S.; m. Margaret Linda Dezack, Aug. 23, 1969. BSME, U. Pa., 1969, MBA, 1976. Mfg. engr. Control Data Corp., Valley Forge, Pa., 1969-70; mgr. mfg. svcs. Knoll Internat., East Greenville, 1970-75; ptnr. mgmt. cons. Touche Ross & Co., Phila., 1976-85; pres. RF Stengel & Co. Inc., Valley Forge, 1985—.

STENGEL, TONY, television producer; b. Columbus, OH; Prodr.(tv comedy): Generation Next, 1996; actor(film, tv, stage): Too Many To List; prodr.(promotional video): Visit Tahiti, 2000; contbr. . Vol. Amnesty Internat., Washington, 1994—, The Drug Policy Found., Washington, 1995—2001; vol. instr. Am. Film Inst., Hollywood, Calif., 1995—; vol. Actors and Others for Animals, 1995—. Mem.: AFTRA, Screen Actors Guild, Native Am. Indian Com. Non-Partisan. Avocation: Avocations: world adventure travel - over 30 countries and islands, camping/hiking, concerts, martial arts, produce and direct independent TV/film projects. Office: Soxon Productions 3153 Future st Los Angeles CA 90065-1919

STENHOLM, CHARLES W. congressman; b. Stamford, Tex., Oct. 26, 1938; m. Cynthia Ann Watson; children: Chris, Cary, Courtney Ann. Card., Tarleton State Jr. Coll., 1959; BS in Agrl. Edn., Tex. Tech U., 1961, MS in Agrl. Edn., 1962; LL.D. (hon.), McMurry Coll., 1983, Abilene Christian U., 1991. Farmer, Tex.; past pres. Rolling Plains Cotton Growers and Tex. Electric Coops.; mem. U.S. Congress from 17th Tex. dist., Washington, 1979—; ranking Dem. mem. agr. com. Co-chmn. Congl. Leaders United for a Balanced Budget. Active Bethel Luth. Ch., Ericksdahl, Tex.; charter trustee Cotton Producer Inst.; former mem. state Dem. exec. com. Recipient Gerald W. Thomas Outstanding Agriculturalist award Tex. Tech U., 1979, Am. Farmer Degree Future Farmers Am., 1979, Disting. Alumnus award Tarleton State U., 1979, Pres. Coun. award Tex. Future Farmers Am., 1981, Disting. Alumnus award Tex. Tech U., 1987, MORE Common Sense Sound Dollar awards, 1988, 90, Guardian of Small Bus. awards, 1980-92, Watchdogs of the Treasury awards, 1980-92, Legis. award Nat. Rural Health Assn., 1991, Disting. Svc. award Tex. Soc. Biomed. Rsch., 1993, Disting. Svc. award Tex. Med. Assn., 1993, Dr. Nathan Davis award AMA, 1993, Leadership in Advocacy for Children's Health award Nat. Assn. Children's Hosps., 1996, Meritorious Health Svc. award Nat. Assn. Cmty. Health Ctrs., 1997, Golden Plow award Am. Farm Bur. Fedn., 1988, 92, 96, golden Triangle award Nat. Fermers Union, 1994, Thomas Jefferson award Food Distbn. Industry, 1994, 95, Progressive Fermer Man of Yr. award, 1993, Econ. Patriot award, 1997; named Legislator of Yr. Chem. Prodrs. and Distbrs. Assn., 1992, Man of Yr. Progressive Farmer, 1993, Cooperative Hall of Fame, 1998. Mem. Tex. State Soc. (Washington, past pres.), Tex. Breakfast Club (Washington, past pres.), Rolling Plains Cotton Growers (past pres.), Stamford C. of C. (past pres.). Democrat. Lutheran. Office: 1211 Longworth Ho Office Bldg Washington DC 20515-4317*

STENHOUSE, EVERETT RAY, clergy administrator; b. Minco, Okla., May 15, 1931; s. George E. and Jessie Loraine (Dean) S.; m. Alice Irene English, Aug. 22, 1948; children: Brenda Jones, Judy Lundberg, Stephen, Andrew. Student, U. Calif. Berkeley, U. Athens, 1969-71. Ordained to ministry Assemblies of God, 1955. Pastor Wayside Chapel, Bakersfield, Calif., 1955-59, Bethel Temple, Bakersfield, 1960-63; dist. dir. youth So. Calif. Dist. Assemblies of God, Costa Mesa, Calif., 1963-67; assoc. pastor 1st Assembly of God, San Diego, 1968-69; missionary Assemblies of God Fgn. Missions, Athens, Greece, 1969-73; pastor Bethany Ch., Alhambra, Calif., 1974-79; supt. So. Calif. Dist., Assemblies of God, Costa Mesa, 1979-85; asst. gen. supt. Gen. Coun. Assemblies of God, Springfield, Mo., 1986-94. Bd. adminstrn. Nat. Assn. Evangs., Wheaton, Ill., 1986-94, Pentecostal Fellowship of No. Am., Ont., Can., 1986-94; chmn., bd. dirs. Assemblies of God Theol. Sem., Springfield, 1991-94, Ministers Benefit Assn., Springfield, 1986-94. Contbr. articles to various mags. Home: 77696 Westbrook Ct Palm Desert CA 92211-0416

STENHOUSE, RICHARD, artist; b. Charlotte, N.C., Dec. 10, 1944; s. James Allen and Louise Hunter Stenhouse; m. Joan Marie Alexander, June 25, 1965 (div. 1973); m. Pamela Jean Claude, Apr. 20, 1984. BA, U. N.C., Charlotte, 1970; MFA, U. N.C., Greensboro, 1975. Profl. visual artist, Charlotte, 1975—. Represented in permanent collections 18 museums, univs. and instns., and over 500 corp. and pvt. collections. Grantee So. Arts Fedn., Atlanta, 1986, N.C. Arts Coun., Raleigh, 1996. Mem.: MONA (v.p., mem. bd. 1999—2002). Avocations: travel, reading, inventing, designing, tinkering. Home and Studio: 2426 Arnold Dr Charlotte NC 28205

STENITZER, GEORGE IGNATIUS, corporate communications executive; b. Granite City, Ill., June 30, 1956; s. George Ignatius and Beatrice Marie (Cuenca) S.; m. Donna Dwyer, Jan. 16, 1982; children: Jody Bea, Jonathan Jacob. BA in English, Quincy Coll., 1977. Editor Alton (Ill.) Citizen, 1978-80; writer Sverdrup Corp., St. Louis, 1980-84; advt. mgr. Consol. Aluminum, 1984-85; mgr. advt. Southwestern Bell Telecom, 1985-90; corp. mgr. news rels. Southwestern Bell Corp., 1990-94; dir. corp. positioning Ameritech Corp., Chgo., 1994-99; v.p. corp. comm. R.R. Donnelley & Sons., 1999-2000, Tellabs, Chgo., 2000—. Mem. Bus. Profl. Advt. Assn. (treas. 1985-87, v.p. profl. devel. 1987-88, pres. 1988-89, publisher The St. Louis Bus. Profl. Advt. Assn. Communicator 1989-90), Nat. Investor Rels. Inst. (dir. Chgo. chpt. 2000-2001), Pub. Rels. Soc. Am. (dir. Chgo. chpt. 2000—, exec. v.p. 2002—), Bus. Mktg. Assn. (dir. Chgo. chpt. 2001-). Roman Catholic. E-mail: george.stenitzer@tellabs.com., geo4747@yahoo.com.

STENMARK, JEAN KERR, mathematics educator; b. Davis, Calif., Aug. 25, 1922; d. Norman and Rachel Kerr; m. Roy M., Aug. 24, 1952, (div. July 1975); children: Ruthann, John, Jane. BA, U. Calif., Berkeley, 1942; MS, Calif. State U., Hayward, 1978. Cert. elem. tchr., Calif. With civil svc. U.S. Navy-Aviation Supply, Oakland, Calif., 1942-45; acct. various acctg. firms, San Francisco, 1945-56; tchr. Oakland Unified Sch. Dist., 1969-80; maths. specialist EQUALS and Family Math. Programs U. Calif., Berkeley, 1980-95. Cons. Calif. Assessment Program, Sacramento, 1975-92, New Standards Assessment Project, Oakland, Calif., 1991—. Editor: 101 Short Problems, 1995, Mathematics Assessment: Myths, Models, Good Questions and Practical Suggestions, 1991; author: Assessment Alternatives in Mathematics, 1989; co-author: Family Math, 1986, Math for Girls and Other Problem Solvers, 1981, Family Math for Young Children: Comparing, 1997; co-editor: Mathematics Assessment: a practical handbook for grades 3-5, 2001; co-writer, core advisor: Mathematics Assessment: A Video Library, K-12 Guide, 1998. Mem. Nat. Coun. Tchrs. Maths., Calif. Maths. Coun., PTA (hon. life mem.). Democrat. Protestant. Avocations: piano lessons, walking, reading. Home and Office: 242 Ashbury Ave El Cerrito CA 94530-4104 E-mail: jkstenmark@aol.com.

STENNER, ROBERT DAVID, environmental and health research engineer, toxicologist; b. Fennimore, Wis., Mar. 12, 1946; s. Arno F. and Edna M. (Mill) S.; m. Vicki S. Muller, June 12, 1965; children: James Brian, Heidi Diane. BS in Power Mechanics with honors, U. Wis., Menomonie, 1970; MS in Nuc. Engring., Idaho State U., 1981; PhD in Toxicology, Wash. State U., 1996. Environ. engr. Gaston County Air Pollution Control, Gastonia, N.C., 1973-77; environ. engring. specialist environ. divsn. State of Idaho, Pocatello, 1977-81; chem. and radiation protection engr. Pacific Gas and Electric Co., San Francisco, Eureka, Calif., 1981-84; rsch. engr. sci. III, IV and V Battelle N.W. Labs., Richland, Wash., 1984—. Mem. audit team Assurance Program for Remedial Action, Dept. of Energy, Washington, 1984-86; risk assessment rep. Environ. Mgmt. Ops. Cons. Selection Team, Richland, Wash., 1988-89; mem. chem. protection initiative team Battelle N.W. Labs., 1989-90, point of contact-Life Sci. Ctr., 1993—; mem. tech. team Ctr. for Risk Excellence, Dept. of Energy, 1998—; pres., chmn. bd. SEA, Inc., 1999—; tech. lead Exposure to Dose-Environ. Health Initiative; mem. tech. bd., 1999. Contbr. articles to profl. jours. Sec. Lions Club, Bessemer City, N.C., 1974-77; youth program counselor United Meth. Chs., numerous cities, 1973-95; vol. ARC, Kennewick, Wash., 1989; chmn. bd. dirs. Pacific N.W. Cross Connection Youth Mission; bd. mem. Ingalls Creek Enrichment Ctr. Recipient Merit award Menomonie Area C. of C., 1970. Mem. ASTM (chair E47.14 subcom.), Soc. Toxicology, Pacific N.W. Assn. Toxicologists, Soc. Risk Analysis. Democrat. Avocations: outdoor recreation, European sports car restoration, travel, music. Home: 1238 Glenwood Ct Richland WA 99352-9404 Office: Battelle NW Labs PO Box 999 Richland WA 99352-0999 E-mail: robert.stenner@pnl.gov.

STENNETT, STEVE MARSHALL, software systems engineering executive; b. Ridgway, Ill., Nov. 6, 1951; s. Alvin and Pearl (Fryman) S.; m. Linda Kay Harman, Sept. 14, 1976 (div. 1983); children: Stefanie Marie, Kristin Lynn. AA in Computer Sci., Catonsville Community Coll., 1979; BS in Computer Sci., U. Md., 1981. Asst. engr. Westinghouse Elec. Corp., Balt., 1975-80, sr. engr., 1985-86; sci. programmer Unisys Corp., Lanham, Md., 1980-81, sr. sci. programmer, 1981-83, prin. systems analyst, 1983-85, 86-87, mgr. systems engring., 1987-88; mgr. Digital Equipment Corp., 1988—. Pres. Micro Software Services, Inc., College Park, Md., 1985—. Patentee security transeiver unit, test exec. algorithm. Served with USAF, 1971—. Mem. IEEE, Digital Equipment Computer Users Soc. Avocations: racquetball, golf. Home: 11417 Jordan Ln Great Falls VA 22066-1313 Office: Digital Equipment Corp 6406 Ivy Ln Greenbelt MD 20770-1443

STENNETT, WILLIAM CLINTON (CLINT STENNETT), television station executive, state legislator; b. Winona, Minn., Oct. 1, 1956; s. William Jessie and Carole Lee (Halsey) Stennett. BA in Journalism, Idaho State U., 1979. Gen. mgr. Wood River Jour., Hailey, Idaho, 1979-85, pres., pub., 1985-87; pres. Sta. KSVT-TV, Ketchum, Sta. KSKI-FM, Sun Valley; mem. Idaho Ho. of Reps., Boise, 1990-94; mem., minority leader Idaho Senate, Dist. 21, 1996—. Recipient Gen. Excellence award Idaho Newspaper Assn., 1985, 86-87; named Legislator of the Yr. Idaho Soil Conservation Dists., 1994, Idaho Wildlife Found., 1996, Idaho Assn. Recyclers, 2002. Mem. Idaho Broadcasters (bd. dirs.), Ketchum Sun Valley C. of C. (bd. dirs. 1990-95), Rotary. Democrat.

STENSETHER, JOHN ELDON, minister; b. Mpls., Feb. 28, 1944; s. John H. and Gertie Marie (Stensaas) S.; m. Barbara L. Erickson, Sept. 3, 1966; children: Julie Lyn, Kevin John. BA, U. Minn., 1966; postgrad., Fuller Theol. Sem., Pasadena, 1966-69; PhD, Calif. Grad. Sch. Theology, Glendale, 1970. Ordained to ministry Evang. Free Ch. Am., 1972. Sr. pastor Del Rey Hills Evang. Free Ch., Playa del Rey, Calif., 1968-72, Calvary Evang. Free Ch., Essex Fells, N.J., 1972-76, Trinity Evang. Free Ch., South Bend, Ind., 1976-80, Evang. Free Ch., Turlock, Calif., 1980—. Vis. prof. Northeastern Bible Coll., Essex Fells, N.J., 1973-75; staley disting. Christian scholar; speaker various Colls., sems. and confs. Fellow Evang. Free Ch. of Am. Ministerial, Turlock Evang. Assn. of Ministers. Office: Evang Free Ch 1360 N Johnson Rd Turlock CA 95380-3507 E-mail: jstensether@efcturlock.org. *The older I grow, the more I experience life, the greater is my confidence in, and reliance upon, the Sovereignty of God.*

STENSON, WILLIAM FREDERICK, gastroenterologist; b. Rome, Dec. 2, 1945; s. Frederick Vincent and Mary Catherine (Tucker) S.; m. Janet Marie Breaugh, Dec. 28, 1968; children: Catherine, Karen, Thomas. BS, Providence Coll., 1967; MD, Washington U., 1971. Diplomate Am. Bd. Internal Medicine and Gastroenterology. Intern Barnes Hosp., St. Louis, 1971-72, resident in medicine, 1972-73, 75-76; chief gastroenterology Jewish Hosp. of St. Louis, 1981—; assoc. prof. medicine Washington U., St. Louis, 1985-91, prof. medicine, 1991—. Co-author: Manual of Nutritional Therapeutics, 1st edit., 1983, 2d edit., 1988, 3rd edit., 1995; editor: (book) Inflammatory Bowel Disease, 1991, Gastrointestinal Pharmacology, 1992. Maj. USAF, 1973-75. Office: Washington U Sch Medicine PO Box 8124 Saint Louis MO 63156-8124

STENSTROM, MICHAEL KNUDSON, civil engineering educator; b. Anderson, S.C., Nov. 28, 1948; s. Edward Farnum and Virginia Frances (Garrett) S.; m. Linda Ann Moxley, Aug. 15, 1974 (div. Nov. 1976); m. Margaret Merle Allen, Jan. 13, 1977 (div. Apr. 1994). BSEE, Clemson U., 1971, MS in Environ. Engring., 1972, PhD in Environ. Engring., 1976. Registered profl. engr., Calif. Project mgr. Amoco Oil Co., Naperville, Ill., 1975-77; asst. prof. civil engring. UCLA, 1977-81, assoc. prof., 1981-84, prof., 1984—, dir. Engring. Computer Ctr., 1985-89, asst. dean, 1989—92, chair dept. Civil Engring. 1991—98, assoc. dean, 2001—. Cons. on pollution control to numerous cos. and state and city govts. Contbr. articles to profl. jours. Chmn. sci. adv. bd. Heal-the-Bay, L.A., 1987-88. With USAF, 1969-70. Recipient numerous grants. Mem. ASCE (Walter L. Huber award 1989), Am. Acad. Environ. Engrs., Assn. Environ. Engring. Profs., Water Environ. Fedn. (Harrison Prescott Eddy medal 1992), Internat. Assn. on Water Quality, Am. Chem. Soc., Blue Key, Sigma Xi, Tau Beta Pi. Democrat. Avocations: photography, stamp collecting. Home: 1829 S Crescent Heights Blvd Los Angeles CA 90035-4616 Office: UCLA 5714 Boelter Hall Los Angeles CA 90095-1593

STENSVAD, ALLAN MAURICE, minister; b. Melstone, Mont., Mar. 27, 1934; s. Arthur Leonard and Mabel Violet (Rykken) S.; m. Margaret Lillian Fountain, Aug. 21, 1954; children: Sondra Louise, Joy Lynn, Jill Linda, Janiece Lorraine, Sharla Lee. BA in History, Cascade Coll., 1956; ThM, Dallas Theol. Sem., 1960. Ordained to ministry Conservative Bapt. Assn. Am., 1962. Interim pastor Trinity Bapt. Ch., Walla Walla, Wash., 1960-61; missionary to Brazil Unevangelized Fields Mission, Bala Cynwyd, Pa., 1962-71; min. of evangelism Bible Bapt. Ch., Auburn, Wash., 1972-75; pastor 1st Bapt. Ch., Dayton, 1975-80, Berean Bapt. Ch., Eugene, Oreg., 1980-93, First Bapt. Ch., Philomath, 1994—. Dir. No. Evang. Christian Sem., Sao Luis, Brazil, 1966-71; trustee Conservative Bapt. Assn. Wash., 1976-80, Conservative Bapt. Assn. Oreg., N.W. Conservative Bapt. Assn., 1985-91; mem. consolidation com. Conservative Bapt. Assn. Oreg./Wash., 1985, ann. meeting program chmn., 1986-91; vis. lectr. Seminário Cristão Evangélico do Norte, São Luís, Brazil, 1998, tng. seminar for Russias pastors, Tyumen, Siberia, 2001. Mem. Philomath Ministerial Assn. (chmn. 1995—). Republican. Home: PO Box 1078 2355 Applegate St Philomath OR 97370-9365 Office: First Bapt Ch PO Box 1420 335 S 26th St Philomath OR 97370-9239 E-mail: amstens@casco.net.

STENT, ANGELA E. political scientist, educator, director; b. London, Feb. 24, 1947; arrived in U.S., 1970; d. Ronald Walter and Gabriele Stent; m. Daniel H. Yergin, Aug. 10, 1975; children: Alexander Yergin, Rebecca Yergin. BA in Econs. and History with honors, Cambridge (Eng.) U., 1969; MSc with distinction, London Sch. Econs., 1970; AM in Soviet Studies, Harvard U., 1972, PhD in Govt., 1977. Assoc. prof. dept. govt. Georgetown U., Washington, 1983—, prof. dept. govt. and Sch. Fgn. Svc., 1998—, dir. Ctr. for Eurasian, Russian and East European Studies, 2001—. Sr. policy advisor Office Policy Planning U.S. Dept. State, Washington, 1999—2001; adv. bd. mem. U.S.-Russia Bus. Coun., Women in Internat. Security, Am. Inst. for Contemporary German Studies. Author: From Embargo to Ostpolitik, 1981, Russia and Germany Reborn, 1999; contbr. articles to profl. jours. Mem.: Coun. Fg. Rels. N.Y., Cosmos Club. Office: Ctr for Eurasian Russian and East European Studies Georgetown Univ Washington DC 20057

STENT, GUNTHER SIEGMUND, molecular biologist, educator; b. Berlin, Germany, Mar. 28, 1924; came to U.S., 1940, naturalized, 1945; s. George and Elizabeth (Karfunkelstein) S.; m. Inga Loftsdottir, Oct. 27, 1951; 1 son, Stefan Loftur. BS, U. Ill., 1945, PhD, 1948; DSc (hon.), York U., 1984. Research asst. U. Ill., 1945-48; research fellow Calif. Inst. Tech., 1948-50, U. Copenhagen, Denmark, 1950-51, Pasteur Inst., Paris, France, 1951-52; asst. research biochemist U. Calif., Berkeley, 1952-56, faculty, 1956—, prof. molecular biology, 1959-94; prof. emeritus, 1994—; prof. arts and scis. U. Calif., 1967-68, chmn. molecular biology, 1980-86, chmn. molecular and cell biology, 1987-92, dir. virus lab., 1980-86. Document analyst U.S. Field Info. Agy. Tech., 1946-47; mem. genetics panel NIH, 1959-64, NSF, 1965-68; fellow Inst. Advanced Studies, Berlin, 1985-90. Author: Papers On Bacterial Viruses, 2d edit., 1966, Molecular Biology of Bacterial Viruses, 1963, Phage and the Origin of Molecular Biology, 1966, The Coming of the Golden Age, 1969, Function and Formation of Neural Systems, 1977, Morality as a Biological Phenomenon, 1978, Paradoxes of Progress, 1978, Molecular Genetics, 2d edit., 1978, Nazis, Women and Molecular Biology, 1998; mem. editl. bd. Jour. Molecular Biology, 1965-68, Genetics, 1963-68, Zeitschrift für Vererbungslehre, 1962-68, Ann. Revs. Genetics, 1965-69, Ann. Revs. Microbiology, 1966-70, Jour. Neurosci., 1988-96; contbr. numerous sci. papers to profl. lit. Merck fellow NRC, 1948-54; sr. fellow NSF, 1960-61; Guggenheim fellow, 1969-70; Fogarty Research Scholar NIH, 1990-92. Mem. NAS, Am. Acad. Arts and Scis., Soc. Neurosci., Am. Philos. Soc., Acad. Scis. and Lit. of Mainz (Germany), European Acad. Scis. and Arts, Cosmos Club. Home: 145 Purdue Ave Kensington CA 94708-1032 E-mail: stent@uclink4.berkeley.edu.

STENTZ, STEVEN THOMAS, writer, researcher, project consultant; b. Sidney, Nebr., May 4, 1951; s. Howard William and Orletha Maxine (Gardner) S.; m. Patricia Marie Thompson, Oct. 9, 1971 (div. 1979); 1 child, Carrie Lee; m. Barbara Ann Willie, Dec. 29, 1990. BA magna cum laude, We. Wash. U., 1979; MS, U. Wash., 1982, doctoral postgrad., 1982-85. Computer, rsch. cons. U. Wash., Seattle, 1982-85, instr., 1986, We. Wash. U., Bellingham, 1986-88; rschr., project cons. Wash. Supreme Ct., Olympia, 1986-2001; owner, cons. Sonntag & Stentz, 2000—. Mem. Human Subjecs Rev. Com. U. Wash., Seattle, 1982-85. Contbr. articles to profl. jours.; author software reference manuals. Spkr. Jud. Conf., 1987-91, Dist. and Mcpl. Judges Spring Conf., 1988-90, 96-98, Wash. State Assn. County Clks., 1988-92, 94-98, 2001. With U.S. Army, 1971-72. Avocations: land and seaplane pilot, pianist, racquetball, boating. E-mail: ststentz@attbi.com.

STENWICK, MICHAEL WILLIAM, retired internist, geriatric medicine consultant; b. Red Wing, Minn., Nov. 12, 1941; s. Vincent Ferdinand and Geraldine Frances (Veith) S.; m. Judith Ann Nelson, June 10, 1961; children: Scott Michael, Gregg William. BS cum laude, Hamline U., 1963; MD, U. Minn., 1969. Diplomate Am. Bd. Internal Medicine. Fellow dept. pharmacology U. Minn., Mpls., 1966-68; intern in internal medicine Northwestern Hosp., 1969-70, resident in internal medicine, 1970-73; sr. internist internal medicine sect. Bloomington Lake Clinic, 1973—2000; ret., 2000. Bd. dirs. Bloomington Lake Clinic, Mpls., pres. 1977, v.p. 1989-97, fin. com., 1987—, chmn. properties, 1984—, chmn. trustees profit sharing; med. adviser Kimberly Quality Care, St. Paul, 1990-94; internal medicine cons. Fairview Multiple Sclerosis Ctr. and Rehab. Unit, Mpls., 1986-91; informal adviser internal medicine sect. Minn. Relative Value Index, Mpls., 1971; mem. task force Riverside Med. Ctr., Mpls., 1988-91, chmn. critical care com., 1986-91, reviewer quality assurance subcom., 1989-90. Contbr. articles to profl. jours. Mem., co-organizer, 1st pres. Cyrus Barnum Soc., U. Minn. Med. Sch., Mpls.; bd. dirs. Signal Inn Beach and Racquetball Club, Sanibel Island, Fla., 1983-84, 89-98, Signal Inn Condominium Assn., Sanibel Island, 1983-84, 89-98; co-emcee Nursing Talent Show, Northwestern Hosp., Mpls., 1969; 1st med. dir. Beltrami Health Ctr., Mpls., 1970-72. Recipient scholarship Charles and Alora Allis Found., 1960-63, Walter Kenyon award, 1963, grant U. Minn., 1963. Fellow Am. Coll. Physicians; mem. AMA, Am. Soc. Internal Medicine, Minn. Med. Assn., Hennepin County Med. Assn., Mpls. Soc. Internal Medicine. Republican. Lutheran. Achievements include research in drug specificity that could be defined even in an alkylating agent. Office: Bloomington Lake Clinic 3017 Bloomington Ave Minneapolis MN 55407-1771

STENZEL, KURT HODGSON, physician, nephrologist, educator; b. Stamford, Conn., Nov. 3, 1932; s. Alfred B. and Aurelie C. (Hodgson) S.; m. Carolyn Briggs, Dec. 21, 1957; children— Matthew, Jennifer, Mary. BA magna cum laude, N.Y. U., 1954; MD, Cornell U., 1958. Intern Bellevue Hosp., N.Y.C., 1958-59; resident, 1959-60, 62-63; asst. in medicine Cornell U. Med. Coll., N.Y.C., 1959-60, asst. prof. medicine, 1965-68, asso. prof. biochemistry and surgery, 1969-75, prof. biochemistry, medicine and surgery, 1976—, chief div. nephrology (medicine), 1979-92, dir. Rogosin Kidney Ctr., 1970—; attending physician, surgeon N.Y. Hosp., N.Y.C., 1976—. Diplomate Am. Bd. Internal Medicine and Nephrology. Contbr. articles to profl. publs. Served to lt., M.C. USNR, 1960-62. Recipient Nat. Kidney Found. Hoenig award for excellence in renal medicine Fellow ACP; mem. Am. Soc. Biol. Chemists, Am. Soc. Nephrology, Transplantation Soc., Am. Fedn. Clin. Research, Am. Assn. Immunologists, Am. Soc. for Artificial Internal Organs, Phi Beta Kappa. Achievements include research on cell biology, cellular immunology, transplantation and dialysis. Office: The Rogosin Inst 505 E 70th St New York NY 10021-9809 E-mail: stenzek@rockvax.rockefeller.edu.

STENZEL, LARRY GENE, writer; b. Arlington, Minn., July 20, 1949; s. Albin Ludwig and Mildred Sophia (Bartels) S. BA, U. Minn., 1971. Owner Samuel Powell Publ. Co., Sacramento, 1979—; cons. Mogavero Notestine Assocs., 1984—; assoc. Barry Cassidy Rare Books, 1985—. Author: Tales to Tell, 1979, Afraid of the Dark, 1981, Lillie Seline's Confession, 1982, A Vacation From Worry, 1984, Alms at Beautiful Gate, 1991, How Weeping Spends the Night, 2001. Bd. dir. Resources for Independent Living, Sacramento, Calif., 1986—, Sacramento Housing Alliance, 1999-2001; mem. ch. coun. St. John's Luth. Ch., Sacramento, 1992-97. Independent. Lutheran. Home: 2202 I St Sacramento CA 95816-4008 E-mail: lgstenzel@juno.com.

STENZEL, WILLIAM A. consulting services executive; b. Cambridge, Mass., Jan. 21, 1923; s. Herman Rheinhold and Helen (Proskurniak) S.; m. Pallie Jean Bottorff, July 25, 1952; children: Jeffrey Rheinhold, Anne Virginia, Peter Deane, Christopher James. BA cum laude, Harvard U., 1944, MBA, 1948. Advt. mgr. Waltham Watch Co., Mass., 1948-54; v.p. Tracer Lab. Inc., Waltham, 1954-62; sr. v.p. Premier Indsl. Corp., Cleve., 1962-85, Mex. Info. and Cons. Svcs., Inc., 1985—; v.p. Edn. Techs. and Cons., Inc. Bd. dirs. Greater Cleve. chpt. ARC, 1983-86, bd. dirs., mem. exec. com. Orange City chpt., Calif.; fundraiser Cleve. Orch., 1977-81; trustee Mid Town Corridor, 1985-87, Dunham Tavern Mus., 1985-87; bd. dirs., mem. fin. devel. com. Orange City chpt. ARC; bd. dirs. Blood, tissue svcs. So. Calif. region ARC, 1992-95; pres. San Clemente Friends of the Libr., 1995-98; treas. Friends of the Libr. Found., Orange County, 1997-98. Fellow Rowfant Club, 1985—. Mem.: Harvard Bus. Sch., Rowfant (Cleve.). Home and Office: 124 Avenida Cota San Clemente CA 92672-3327 E-mail: stenzelwa@cs.com.

STENZL, ARNULF KARL MARBOD, urologist; b. Klagenfurt, Austria, Aug. 2, 1955; s. Walter and Olga (Brauner) Stenzl; m. Birgit Ursula Koeck, Jan. 17, 1961; children: Anna Katharina, Benedikt, Clara. MD, U. Graz, Austria, 1980. Diplomate Austrian Bd Urology, Austrian Bd Surgery. Staff fellow urol. oncology, vis. prof. urology UCLA, 1988-89; staff urologist U. Graz, 1989-90, U. Berne, Switzerland, 1990-92, U. Innsbruck, Austria, 1992—, head urol. oncology Austria, 1993—, prof. urology Austria, 1996, vice chmn. Austria, 1999—. Chmn Interdisciplinary Working Group, Innsbruck, 1993—; co-chmn Project Nat Bank Fund, Vienna, 1995—97. Author: (video) Jour Urology, 1994; editor (sect ed): (jour) European Urology; mem exec bd: jour Brit Jour Urology Int. Recipient Cert Commendation, City of Los Angeles, 1989, GE Voges Prize, Bavarian Urological Soc, 1996. Fellow: European Asn Urology (Diploma 1991); mem.: Austrian Surgeons Asn (Billroth Prize 1997), German Urological Soc, Swiss Urological Soc, Soc Urological Oncology (corr.), Am Urological Asn (corr.), Am Cancer Research Asn (corr.), Austrian Urological Soc, European Urological Asn (Mgmt Comt Prize 1996). Avocations: flying, mountain climbing, languages. Home: 16 Hechenbergweg A-6170 Zirl Austria Office: U Innsbruck-Kliniken Dept Urology A-6020 Innsbruck Austria E-mail: arnulf.stenzl@uibk.ac.at.

STEP, EUGENE LEE, retired pharmaceutical company executive; b. Sioux City, Iowa, Feb. 19, 1929; s. Harry and Ann (Keiser) S.; m. Hannah Scheuermann, Dec. 27, 1953; children: Steven Harry, Michael David, Jonathan Allen. BA in Econs., U. Nebr., 1951; MS in Acctg. and Fin., U. Ill., 1952. With Eli Lilly Internat. Corp., London and Paris, 1964-69, dir. Elanco Internat. Indpls., 1969-70, v.p. marketing, 1970-72, v.p. Europe, 1972; v.p. mktg. Eli Lilly and Co., 1972-73, pres. pharm. div., 1973-86, exec. v.p., 1986—. Bd. dirs. Scios Cell-Genesys, Guidant Corp. 1st lt. U.S. Army, 1953-56. Mem. Pharm. Mfrs. Assn. (bd. dirs. 1980-92, chmn. 1989-90), Internat. Pharm. Mfrs. Assn. (pres. 1991-92). Home: PO Box 8997 Rancho Santa Fe CA 92067-8997

STEPAK, ASA MARTIN, writer; b. Bklyn., Nov. 23, 1950; s. Louis and Anna (Leyter) S. BA cum laude, NYU, 1973. Author: Southern Rhapsody, 1995, Southern Heritage Potpourri, 1995, Southern Heritage Revisited: A Compendium of Behind the Scene E-mail's, 2000, Cognitive Linguistics: Oral Metaphor Construction, 2000.

STEPAN, FRANK QUINN, chemical company executive; b. Chgo., Oct. 24, 1937; s. Alfred Charles and Mary Louise (Quinn) S.; m. Jean Finn, Aug. 23, 1958; children: Jeanne, Frank Quinn, Todd, Jennifer, Lisa, Colleen, Alfred, Richard. AB, U. Notre Dame, 1959; MBA, U. Chgo., 1963. Salesman Indsl. Chems. div. Stepan Chem. Co., Northfield, Ill., 1961-63, mgr. internat. dept., 1964-66, v.p. corporate planning, 1967-69, v.p., gen. mgr., 1970-73, pres., 1973-84; pres., chmn., CEO Stepan Co., 1984-99, chmn., CEO, 1999—, also bd. dirs. Mem. liberal arts council Notre Dame U., South Bend, Ind., 1972—; bd. dirs. Big Shoulders, Chgo. 1st lt. AUS, 1959-61. Mem. Chem. Mfrs. Assn. (bd. dirs.), Soap and Detergent Assn. (bd. dirs., exec. com., chmn.), Ill. Bus. Roundtable (policy com., sec.), Econ. Club Chgo., Exmoor Country Club, Bob O'Link Golf Club, Everglades Club, Sailfish Club Fla. Home: 200 Linden St Winnetka IL 60093-3862 Office: Stepan Co Edens & Winnetka Rds Northfield IL 60093

STEPANEK, DAVID LESLIE, financial services company executive; b. Atchison, Kans., Oct. 1, 1929; s. Henry William and Helen Louise (Howarth) S.; m. Carmen Mercedes Comez, Aug. 22, 1960; children: Karen L. Barrow, James W. BS in Petroleum Engring., U. Calif., Berkeley, 1952; MBA in Fin., UCLA, 1962. CFP, registered investment advisor. Petroleum engr. Creole Petroleum Corp., Venezuela, 1952-64, mgr. budget dept. Venezuela, 1964-66, mgr. planning sect. Venezuela, 1966-69; sr. advisor in prodn. dept. Exxon Corp., N.Y.C., 1969-77, sr. advisor in coal dept. Coral Gables, Fla., 1977-82, mgr. planning dept. Abu Dhabi, United Arab Emirates, 1983-87; pres. DLS Tax Preparation, Inc. and DLS Fin. Planning, Inc., Thomasville, Ga., 1989—; franchise owner H & R Block franchises, Thomasville, Quitman, Cairo, 1991—. Republican. Avocations: tennis, golf. Home: 1522 Millpond Rd Thomasville GA 31792-7407 Office: H & R Block 123 E Jackson St Thomasville GA 31792-5136 E-mail: dlstepanek@netscape.net.

STEPANEK, JOSEPH EDWARD, industrial development consultant; b. Ellinwood, Kans., Oct. 29, 1917; s. Joseph August and Leona Mae (Wilson) S.; m. Antoinette Farnham, June 10, 1942; children: Joseph F., James B., Antoinette L., Debra L. BSChemE, U. Colo., 1939; DEng in Chem. Engring., Yale U., 1942. Registered profl. engr., Colo. Engr. Stearns-Roger Mfg., Denver, 1939-45; from asst. to assoc. prof. U. Colo., Boulder, 1945-47; from cons. to dir. UN, various countries, 1947-73; cons. internat. indsl devel., U.S.-China bus. relations Boulder, 1973—. Bd. dirs. 12 corps., 1973—. Author 3 books on indsl. devel.; contbr. 50 articles to profl. jours. Exec. dir. Boulder Tomorrow, 1965-67. Recipient Yale Engring. award Yale Engring. Assn., 1957, Norlin award U. Colo. 1978, Annual award India League of Am., 1982. Mem. AAAS. Democrat. Unitarian Universalist. Avocation: ranching. Home: 1622 High St Boulder CO 80304-4224

STEPANOV, SERGEI VALENTINOVICH, consultant, researcher; b. Orenburg, Russia, Apr. 5, 1957; s. Valentin Ananyevitch and Albina Nikolayevna (Lobkovskaya) S.; 1 child, Victoria. Degree in linguistics, Inst. Fgn. Langs., Minsk, Belarus, 1980; degree in law, State U. Belarus, Minsk, 1990; postgrad., Inst. USA and Can. Studies, Moscow, 1990; expert lectr. info. and comm., Coun. of Europe, 1994. Cert. interpreter. Pres. ATM, Minsk, 1985-95. Programmer projects, programs Anti-chernobyl Project, 1993; freelance rschr. RAND, Santa Monica, Calif., 1996, 97, 98. Author project Democracy In Action, 1994. Mem. support group Svc. Civil Internat., 1993-94. Served with anti-missile unit USSR armed forces, 1975-77. European Union grantee, 1994. Mem. Assn. Internat. Youth Work (pres. 1987-95, bd. dirs. 1995-96), Mobility Internat. (award). Russian Orthodox. Avocations: research, ocean swimming. Home: 6857 Franklin Ave # 29 Hollywood CA 90028 E-mail: stepanov@earthlink.net.

STEPANOVICH, PAUL, management educator; b. Butler, PA, June 15, 1956; m. Pamela Hopkins. AB, Grove City Coll., 1978; MBA, Clarion U. Pa., 1979; PhD, Med. U. S.C., 1995. Analyst, mgr. Ford New Holland, Pa., 1980—91; asst. prof. Wilkes U., Wilkes-Barre, 1995—99, Old Dominion U., Norfolk, Va., 1999—. Contbr. articles to profl. jours. Mem.: Am. Coll. Health Care Execs., Sys. Dynamics Soc., Inst. for Behavioral and Applied Mgmt. (bd. mem. 1992—96). Office: Old Dominion Univ 129 Spong Hall Norfolk VA 23529

STEPANSKI, ANTHONY FRANCIS, JR. computer software company executive; b. Jersey City, June 29, 1941; s. Anthony Francis and Gertrude Stepanski; m. Jane Ellen Schuler, Sept. 5, 1965; children— Matthew A.W., Melinda Kate BA in Physics, Clark U., 1963. Sales rep. IBM Corp., N.Y.C., 1964-68; from sales rep. to sr. v.p. AGS Computers, Inc., N.Y.C. and Mountainside, N.J., 1968-82, exec. v.p. Mountainside, 1982-93; pres., CEO AGS Info. Services, Inc., 1986-93, Origin Tech., N.A. (subs. Origin, BV, Amsterdam), 1994-97; also bd. dirs. AGS Computers, Inc., a NYNEX Co., Mountainside, mng. dir.; pvt. investor Melmatt Ptnrs., LLP, 1998-2000; CEO, bd. mem. IZODIA, plc, London, 2001—. Pres., CEO, Origin Technology, N.A. (subs. Origin/Amsterdam, The Netherlands), 1994-97. Trustee Clark U., Worcester, Mass., 1987, Children's Specialized Hosp. Found., Mountainside, 1989-96; bd. dirs. Westchester Artificial Kidney Ctr., Valhalla, N.Y., 1982-97, Westfield Symphony Orch., N.J., 1983-96. Served with USAR, 1965-66.

STEPHAN, ALEXANDER FRIEDRICH, German language and literature educator; b. Lüdenscheid, Fed. Republic Germany, Aug. 16, 1946; came to U.S., 1968; s. Eberhard and Ingeborg (Hörnig) S.; m. Halina Konopacka, Dec. 15, 1969; 1 child, Michael. MA, U. Mich., 1969; PhD, Princeton U., 1973. Instr. German Princeton U., N.J., 1972-73; from asst. prof. to prof. German UCLA, 1973-85; prof. German U. Fla., Gainesville, 1985-2000, chmn., 1985-93; prof. German, Ohio Eminent Scholar, mem. Mershon Ctr., Ohio State U., 2000—. Author: (literature critiques) Christa Wolf, 1976, Die deutsche Exilliteratur, 1979, Christa Wolf (Forschundbericht), 1981, Max Frisch, 1983, Anna Seghers im Exil, 1993, Im Visier dem FBI, paperback edit 1998, English translation Cafion Communazis, 2000, 1995, Vanna Seghers: Das siebte Kreuzi Welt und Wirkung eines Romans, 1997; editor: Peter Weiss: Die Asthetik des Widerstands, 1983, 3d edit., Exil. Literatur und die Künste, 1990, (literature critiques) Exil-Studien, 1993—, Christa Wolf: The Author's Dimension , 1993—, 2d edit., 1995—, Themes and Structures, Uwe Johnson: Speculations about Jakob and Other Writings, 2000; co-editor: Studies in GDR Culture and Society, 1981—90, Schreiben in Exil, 1985, The New Sufferings of Young Werther and Other Stories from the GDR, 1997; editor: (biography) Peter Weiss Jahrbuch, 1994; co-prodr.: (documentaries) In Visier des FBI, 1995; co-editor: Rot Brauu Brecht Dialogs, 2000, (Book of Essays) Nationalsozialimus und Stalinismus bei Brecht und Zeitgenossen, 2000; co-prodr.: (documentaries) Das FBI und Marlene Dietrich, 2000, Das FBI und Brecht's Telephone, 2001, Exilauten und der CIA, 2002, Thomas Mann und der CIA, 2002. Humboldt Found. fellow, 1988, 94, 98-99, 2002-03, Guggenheim Found. fellow, 1989, VG Wort fellow, 1992, UCLA faculty fellow, 1984; grantee Feuchtwanger Meml. Libr., 1998, Internat. Rsch. and Exchs. Bd., 1993, German Acad. Exch. Svcs., 1993, 97, NEH, 1974, 84, 97, Am. Coun. Learned Socs., 1976-77, 84, Sch. Theory and Criticism, 1978, Am. Philos. Soc., 1979, 81, 92, Weichmann Stiftung, 1998. Mem.: German PEN, Internat. Anna Seghers Soc., Soc. for Exile Studies, Internat. Lion Feuchtwanger Soc. Office: Ohio State U Dept Germanic Lang/Lit 314 Dieter Cunz Hall Columbus OH 43210-1229

STEPHAN, EGON, SR. cinematographer, film equipment company executive; b. Leipzig, Germany, Nov. 25, 1933; came to U.S., 1952; 1 child, Egon Jr. Engr. Reeves Sound, Inc., N.Y.C., 1952-55, Camera Equipment Co., N.Y.C., 1955-57; instr. U.S. Army Signal Corps., 1957-59; camera rental mgr. F&B Ceco, Miami, Fla., 1959-66; freelance cinematographer, 1966—; owner, pres. Cine Video Tech., Inc., Miami, 1968—. Recipient Cine Golden Eagle award Coun. on Internat. Nontheatrical Events, 1973, Gold Camera award U.S. Indsl. Film Festival, 1974, Emmy award Nat. Acad. TV Arts and Scis., 1981, Fisher Meml. award South Fla. Film and Tape Prodrs. Assn., 1981. Mem. Soc. Motion Picture and TV Engrs., Fla. Motion Picture and TV Assn. (chmn. 1978), Internat. Assn. Theatrical Stage Employees. Office: Cine Video Tech Inc 7330 NE 4th Ct Miami FL 33138-5005 E-mail: cinecamera@earthlink.net.

STEPHAN, JOHN JASON, historian, educator; b. Chgo., Mar. 8, 1941; s. John Walter and Ruth (Walgreen) S.; m. Barbara Ann Brooks, June 22, 1963. BA, Harvard U., 1963, MA, 1964; PhD, U. London, 1969. Rsch. assoc. Social Sci. Ctr., Waseda U., Tokyo, 1969-70; mem. faculty U. Hawaii, Honolulu, 1970—, prof. history, 1977-2001, emeritus prof. history, 2001—, chmn. East Asian studies program, 1973-74, dir. program on Soviet Union in Pacific-Asia region, 1986-88. Rsch. prof. Japan Found.; fellow U. Hokkaido, 1976-77; vis. prof. Inst. of Far East, Moscow, 1982, Inst. Econ. Rsch., Khabarovsk, USSR, 1982-83, Stanford U., 1986, Kennan Inst. for Advanced Studies, 1987; adj. rsch. assoc. East-West Ctr., 1988-92; Sanwa disting. lectr. Tufts U. Fletcher Sch. Law and Diplomacy, 1989. Author: Sakhalin: A History, 1971, The Kuril Islands: Russo-Japanese Frontier in the Pacific, 1974, The Russian Fascists, 1978, Hawaii Under the Rising Sun, 1984, Soviet-American Horizons on the Pacific, 1986, The Russian Far East, 1994. Sr. assoc. mem. St. Antony's Coll., Oxford (Eng.) U., 1977; Bd. dirs. Library Internat. Relations, Chgo., 1976-87; Hawaii rep. U.S.-Japan Friendship Commn., 1980-83. Recipient Kenneth W. Baldridge prize Hawaii chpt. Phi Alpha Theta, 1996; Fulbright fellow, 1967-68; Asia Found. grantee, 1974. Mem. AAUP, Am. Hist. Assn., Am. Assn. Advancement Slavic Studies, Assn. Asian Studies, Authors Guild, Internat. House of Japan, Can. Hist. Assn. Home: 4334 Round Top Dr Honolulu HI 96822-5021 Office: U Hawaii Dept History 2530 Dole St Honolulu HI 96822-2303 E-mail: stephan@hawaii.edu.

STEPHAN, MARK TYLER, radiologist; b. Lafayette, La., Dec. 14, 1955; s. John Edward and Beulah (Dupré) S.; m. Wanda Robertson, July 2, 1987; 1 child, Sophie Justinn. BS, U. Southwestern La., 1978; MD, La. State U., New Orleans, 1982. Diplomate Am. Bd. of Radiology with certification in diagnostic radiology, interventional radiology and neuroradiology. Fellow in radiology Ochsner Clinic, New Orleans, 1982-86, M.D. Anderson Hosp., Houston, 1986-87; angiographer Northwest Radiologists, Indpls., 1987-88; diagnostic radiologist Acadiana Radiology, Lafayette, 1988—. Contbr. articles to profl. jours. Recipient AMA Physician's Recognition award, 1985, 92, 95, 98, 01. Mem. Am. Coll. Radiology, Am. Roentgen Ray Soc., Am. Soc. Neuroradiology, Radiol. Soc. of La., Lourdes Physician Hosp. Orgn. (bd. dirs. 1995-98). Avocations: cooking, hi fi. Office: ARG Inc c/o Our Lady of Lourdes 611 Saint Landry St Lafayette LA 70506-4627

STEPHAN, PAULA ELIZABETH, economics educator, university official; b. Menomonie, Wis., Mar. 31, 1945; d. A. Stephen and Margaret (Shaffer) S.; m. William D. Amis, July 27, 1974; 1 child, David. BA, Grinnell Coll., 1967; MA, U. Mich., 1970, PhD, 1971. Asst. prof. econs. Ga. State U., Atlanta, 1971-76, assoc. prof. econs., 1976-81, prof. econs., 1981—, assoc. dean Andrew Young Sch., 1996—2001. Vis. scholar Sci. Ctr., Berlin, 1992, 93, 94; mem. com. on equal opportunities in Sci. NSF, 1999-2002; mem. adv. bd. SBE, 2001—; mem. various coms. NRC. Author: Striking the Mother Lode in Science, 1992; contbr. over 30 articles to profl. jours. Mem. bd. dirs. Paideia Sch. Endowment, Atlanta, 1983—, chair, 1991-98. Grantee, Alfred P. Sloan Found., 1993—95, 1999, Andrew Mellon Found., 1995, 2000, NSF, 1983—85, 1990—91, 2000—02. Avocations: reading, traveling. Home: 2101 Black Fox Dr NE Atlanta GA 30345-4124 Office: Ga State Univ Andrew Young Sch 33 Gilmer St SE Atlanta GA 30303-3083 E-mail: pstephan@gsu.edu.

STEPHANI, NANCY JEAN, social worker, journalist; b. Garden City, Mich., Feb. 19, 1955; d. Ernest Helmut Schulz and Margaret Mary Fowler Thompson; m. Edward Jeffrey Stephani, Aug. 29, 1975; children: Edward J., Margaret J., James E. AA, Northwood Inst., Midland, Mich., 1975; student in theology, Boston Coll., 1991; BS summa cum laude, Lourdes Coll., Sylvania, Ohio, 1992; MSW, Ohio State U., 1995. Lic. ind. social worker; cert. cognitive behavioral therapist, master addictions counselor. Profl. facilitator Parents United, Findlay, Ohio, 1989-94; contbg. writer Cath. Chronicle, Toledo, 1988-95; mem. ministry formation faculty Cath. Diocese of Toledo, 1992-96; crisis intervention specialist John C. Hutson Ctr., 1994-98; contbg. writer Sunset Gazette, Findlay, Ohio, 1996-98; mgr. Century Health Svcs., 1998, dir. emergency mental health svcs., 1998—, co-chair strategic planning action team, 1999-00. Social work clinician Family Svc. Hancock County, coord. clin. svcs. Family Svc., 1997—98, Blanchard Valley Home Health Social Svc.; trustee, bd. dirs. Hope House for Homeless, Findlay, 1990—99, v.p., 1996—97, pres., 1997—99; mem. Hancock County Cluster on Elderly; adult edn . coord. St. Michael Parish, Findlay, 1986—93, mem. strategic plan core com., 1989—91, v.p., pres. parish coun., 1985—89; program planning com. Family Life Conf., Cath. Diocese, 1994—95, mem. accreditation com. ministry formation dept.; profl. facilitator Hope Plus Program through Hancock County Common Pleas Ct., 1996—; coord. critical incident stress mgmt. team Hancock County, 1997—; profl. facilitator Hancock County Survivors of Suicide group, 1997—2000; field instr. dept. social work U. Findlay, 1996—, mem. social work adv. coun., 1998—; field instr. Capital U., Bowling Green State U., Heidelberg U., 1997—98; mem. adj. faculty Owens Tech. Coll., Findlay; trustee City Mission, 2000—; co-program coord., field edn. coord. MSW program Ohio State U., Lima, 2001—. Founder Food Coop., MPBA, Findlay, 1981; founding mem. Chopin Hall, Findlay, 1983; mem. Hancock County AIDS Task Force, 1994-98; strategic planning com. mem., co-chair goal setting com. Findlay Pub. Schs., 1994, steering com., Call to Action Northwest Ohio, 1997—; trustee City Mission, 1999—. Nat. Inst. Food Svcs. grantee, 1974; Diocese of Toledo grantee, 1991; Ohio State U. Coll. Social Work grantee, 1994. Mem. NOW, NASW (mem. ethics com. Ohio 1997—, v.p. bd. trustees 2000—, nat. com. on nominations and leadership 2001—, region VII rep nat. leadership identification com.), Social Worker of Yr. Region 1, 2000), AAUW (legis. chair Findlay chpt.), Am. Assn. on Child Abuse, Transpsychol. Assn., Friends of Creation Spirituality, Cognitive/Behavioral Profl. Soc., Call to Action, Pax Christi, Women in Ch. Leadership. Avocations: jogging, hiking, cooking, travel. Home: 2615 Goldenrod Ln Findlay OH 45840-1025 E-mail: NancyStephani@hotmail.com.

STEPHANICK, CAROL ANN, dentist, consultant; b. South Amboy, N.J., Feb. 5, 1952; d. Edward Eugene and Gladys (Pionkowski) S. BS, Rutgers U., 1974; MS, Med. Coll. Pa., 1980; DMD, Temple U., 1984. Lic. dentist, Pa., N.J., Vt. Med. technologist Jersey Shore Med. Ctr., Neptune, N.J., 1975-76, South Amboy Meml. Hosp., 1976-78, Smith-Kline Clin. Labs., King of Prussia, Pa., 1981; instr. dept. biology St. Peter's Coll., Jersey City, 1976-78; instr., edn. coord. Coll. Allied Health, Hahnemann U., Phila., 1978-80; instr. dept. oral radiology Sch. Dentistry, Temple U., 1984-87; assoc. dentist Personal Choice Dental Assocs., South Amboy, 1985-86, Marcucci and Marcucci, P.C., Phila., 1986-90, Gwynedd Dental Assocs., Springhouse, Pa., 1990-92. Spl. events coord. Liberty Dental Conf., Phila., 1990—. Neighbor patrol Sprague St. Neighbors Town Watch, Phila., 1986-93. Named to Legion of Honor, Chapel of Four Chaplains, 1987. Mem. ADA, Pa. Dental Assn., Philadelphia County Dental Soc. (publicity coord. 1990—, pub. info. coord. 1991, semi-finalist judge sr. smile contest 1990—, com. on concerns of women dentists, select com. 1988—), Delaware Valley Assn. Women Dentists, Am. Assn. for Functional Orthodontics, Am. Soc. Clin. Pathologists (med. technologist), Delta Sigma Delta. Roman Catholic. Avocations: reading, weight training, walking, sailing, dog training. Home: PO Box 386 Haddonfield NJ 08033-0310 Office: 777 White Horse Pike S Hammonton NJ 08037-2029

STEPHEN, DENNIS JOHN, financial planner; b. Allentown, Pa., Apr. 25, 1948; s. Martin Paul and Bernice Evelyn (Baumer) S.; m. Constance Rose Wilcox, Jan. 20, 1996; children: Christopher Matthew, Erin Marie. BS in Edn., Millersville U., 1970; postgrad., Marywood Coll., 1971-72, Pa. State U., 1971-73, Coll. Fin. Planning, Denver, 1981-83. CFP; registered investment advisor. Tchr., coach Boyertown (Pa.) Area Sch., 1970-77; ins. cons. W.H. Seward Agy., Reading, 1973-84; registered rep. First Buffalo Corp., 1973-89, Keogler Morgan & Co. Inc., 1989-97, Royal Alliance, 1997-2000; insr. cons. J.K. Lengel and Assocs., Reading, 1985-90; owner, fin. cons. Dennis J. Stephen CFP, Boyertown, 1977—; pres., registered investment advisor Dennis J. Stephen Assocs. Ltd, 1988—; owner, ins. cons. Wyomissing (Pa.) Fin. Group, 1989-2000; registered rep. Nat. Planning Corp., 2000—. Guest WBC-TV, 1985. Fin. chmn. St. Columbkill Roman Cath. Ch., Boyertown, 1985-98; adv. bd. Helping Hands, Inc., Bechtelsville, Pa., 1979—; bd. v.p. Boyertown Area Sch. Bd., 1983-85, bd. dirs., singer Hosanna Music Ministry, Boyertown, 1983-84; singer, mem. Alpha Music Ministry, Boyertown, 1985-95; cubmaster, dist. com. Cub Scouts and Explorers, Boy Scouts Am., Boyertown, 1970-2002—; cantor St. Columbkill Roman Cath. ch., 1978—; bd. dirs. Brookeside Montessory, 1999—. Recipient Disting. Sales award Sales and Mktg. Execs., 1981, Life Quality award Investment Guaranty Life, 1979. Mem. Am. Bus. Clubs, Inst. Cert. Fin. Planners, Northeastern Pa. Soc. Inst. Cert. Fin. Planners (pres. 1992), Boyertown Lions Club (com. chmn. 1977-2002), Full Gospal Businessmen's Fellowship, Boyertown Area Bus. Assn. (pres. 1982, bd. dirs. 1977-81, 82-88). Democrat. Avocations: hunting, toy train collecting. Home: 1480 Orchard Ln Boyertown PA 19512-8934 also: Dennis Stephen Assoc Ltd 1260 E Philadelphia Ave Gilbertsville PA 19525-0516 E-mail: djsdsal@aol.com.

STEPHEN, ELIZABETH HERVEY, sociologist, educator; b. Fort Collins, Colo., Jan. 19, 1953; d. Donald Franklin Hervey and Bettie Culbertson Wilcox; m. Todd I. Malkoff, Nov. 24, 1990; children: Anne Malkoff. PhD, U. of Tex., Austin, 1985. Asst. prof. Georgetown U., Washington, 1987—93, assoc. prof., 1993—. Contbr. articles to profl. jours. Mem.: Population Assn. of Am. (sec.-treas. 1996—99). Democrat-Npl. Unitarian Universalist. Avocations: bicycling, quilting. Home: 10015 Leafy Ave Silver Spring MD 20910 Office: Georgetown Univ Sch of Fgn Svc ICC 301 Washington DC 20057 Office Fax: 202-687-1431. Business E-Mail: stepheel@georgetown.edu.

STEPHEN, JOHN ERLE, lawyer, consultant; b. Eagle Lake, Tex., Sept. 24, 1918; s. John Earnest and Vida Thrall (Klein) S.; m. Gloria Yzaguirre, May 16, 1942; children: Vida Leslie Stephen Renzi, John Lauro Kurt. JD, U. Tex., 1941; postdoctoral, Northwestern U., 1942, U.S. Naval Acad. Postgrad. Sch., Annapolis, 1944; cert. in internat. law, U.S. Naval War Coll., Newport, R.I., 1945; cert. in advanced internat. law, U.S. Naval War Coll., 1967. Bar: Tex. 1946, U.S. Ct. Appeals (D.C. cir.) 1949, U.S. Tax Ct. 1953, U.S. Supreme Ct. 1955, U.S. Dist. Ct. D.C. 1956, U.S. Ct. Appeals (2nd cir.) 1959, U.S. Ct. Appeals (7th cir.) 1964, U.S. Dist. Ct. (so. dist.) N.Y. 1964, U.S. Dist. Ct. (so. dist.) Fla. 1969, D.C. 1972, U.S. Dist. Ct. (no. dist.) Ill. 1974, U.S. Dist. Ct. (we. dist.) Wash. 1975, Mich. 1981, U.S. Dist. Ct. (we. dist.) Mich. 1981, U.S. Dist. Ct. (so. dist.) Tex. 1981. Gen. mgr., corp. counsel Sta. KOPY, Houston, 1946; gen. atty., exec. asst. to pres. Tex. Star Broadcasting Co. and affiliated cos., 1947-50; ptnr. Hofheinz & Stephen, 1950—56; sr. v.p., gen. counsel TV Broadcasting Co., Tex. Radio Corp., Gulf Coast Network, 1953—56; spl. counsel, exec. asst. Mayor, City of Houston, 1953-57; spl. counsel Houston C. of C., 1953—57; sr. v.p., gen. counsel Air Transp. Assn. Am., Washington, 1958-70; v.p., gen. counsel Amway Corp. and affiliated cos., Ada, Mich., 1971-82; counsellor, cons. Austin, Tex., 1983—. Chief protocol City of Houston, 1953-56; advisor Consulates Gen. of Mex., San Antonio, Houston, New Orleans, Washington, 1956-66; atty. Gen. Creighton W. Abrams, Comdr. U.S. Mil. Assistance Command, Vietnam, Saigon/Washington, 1970-71; mem. adv. bd. Jour. of Air Law and Commerce, 1966-72; vis. lectr. Harvard Bus. Sch., Pacific Agribus. Conf., The Southwestern Legal Found., Inter-Am. Law Conf., Inst. Aerospace Law; apptd. by Pres. of U.S. legal advisor, del. U.S. Diplomatic Dels. to Internat. Treaty Confs., Paris, London, Rome, Tokyo, Madrid, Bermuda, Guadalajara, Dakar, 1961-71, Internat. Air-Rte. Dels. to U.K., France, Spain, Portugal, Belgium, The Netherlands, Japan, Rep. of Korea, Mex., Australia, Argentina, Soviet Union, and Brazil, 1960-70; legal advisor, del. U.S. dels. to UN Specialized Orgns., Montreal, Geneva, 1964-71; U.S. rep. Internat. Conf. on Aircraft Disturbance, London, 1966; hon. faculty mem., vis. lectr. sch. of law, sch. of bus., U. Miami, 1968—; accredited corr. UN, Rep. and Dem. Nat. Convs.; exec. officer USNR Pub. Affairs Co. 8-7, 1950-57. Author, editor, media prodr. Comm. and transp. group chief Harris County/Houston CD, 1952-56; chmn. legal com. Nat. Aircraft Noise Abatement Coun., Washington; mem. adv. bd. Houston Mus. Fine Arts, 1953-57; bd. dirs. Contemporary Arts Assn., 1952-57; mem. exec. com. Tex. Transp. Inst., 1964-72; apptd. conferee Global Strategy Conf.; commdr. Naval War Coll., 1958. Comdr. USNR, 1941-46, PTO; mem. staff comdr. Supreme Allied Command, NATO. Recipient Jesse L. Lasky award RKO Pictures-CBS, Hollywood, Calif., 1939, H.J. Lutcher Stark prize U. Tex., 1939, 40, Walter Mack award PepsiCo, U. Tex., 1941, Best U.S. Pub. Svc. Broadcasts award CCNY, 1946, First-FM (West) award Frequency Modulation Assn., Houston, 1947, Tex. State Network award mobile coverage Nat. Presdl. Convs., Phila., 1948, Chgo., 1952, Trusonic Wireless Microphone award Acad. Motion Picture Arts & Scis., Beverly Hills, 1951, Frank White award, Mutual Broadcasting Sys., N.Y., 1953, H.M.S. SHEFFIELD citation Brit. Royal Navy U.S. Cruise, 1954, C.R. Smith Aviation Devel. award, Am. Airlines, N.Y., 1955, KLM Royal Dutch Airlines award, Washington, 1956, Capt. Eddie Rickenbacker Air Transport Advancement award Eastern Air Lines, N.Y., 1956, Padre Alvarez award Boys Town Chorale World Tour, Canavati Industries, Monterrey, 1957, Allied Rod & Gun Club Triple Crown trophy, Gander, Nfld., 1958, Iron Duke award No. Va. Lit. Soc., Arlington, 1962, President's Outstanding commendation, U.S. Naval War Coll., Newport, 1967, IBM Corp. Exec. Computer Concepts prize, San Jose, Calif., 1976, M.Y. ENTERPRISE award Peter Island, Brit. V.I., 1978, Glacier Bay award M.V. MALIBU, Sitka, Alaska, 1980. Mem. ABA (past chmn., coun. sect. pub. utility, comms. and transp. law, standing com. on aero. law), The Am. Law Inst. (advisor Restatement (2d) of Torts), World Peace Through Law Ctr. Geneva (past chmn. internat. aviation law com., advisor world air piracy treaty), The Fed. Bar Assn. (exec. com. transp. coun., comm. coun.), The D.C. Bar, State Bar Tex. (50 Yr. Meritorious Practice award 1996), State Bar Mich., Fed. Comms. Bar Assn., Assn. ICC Practitioners, Am. Judicature Soc., Washington Fgn. Law Soc. (vis. lectr. 1967-68), USS ST. PAUL Assn. (hon.), Japanese Air Law Soc. (hon. 1966—), Venezuelan Air and Space Law Soc. (hon.), SOVEDAE (hon. Caracas), USS PRESIDENT ADAMS Assn., Naval Submarine League, Naval War Coll. Found., Internat. Club (Washington), Explorers Club (Washington), Houston Polo Club, Lake Shore Club (Chgo.), Nat. Aviation Club (Washington), Saddle and Cycle Club (Chgo.), Breakfast Club (Houston), Execs. Club (Houston), Order Ky. Cols. (amb. Ark.), Ark. Travelers, Tex. Navy Adm., Flying Col., Quintana Roo Safari, Phi Eta Sigma, Delta Sigma Rho (pres. Tex. chpt. 1940). Home: 6904 Ligustrum Cv Austin TX 78750-8352 E-mail: magnusmedia@aol.com.

STEPHENS, B. CONSUELA, minister, consultant; b. Bkyn., May 12, 1947; d. Bernadine (Whitley) King and Mortimer (Montiphus) King (DeReyes). PhD in Religion, Clayton Theological Inst., 1983. Pastor Chenaniah Missionary Ch., Hollis, NY, 1986—. Cons. Chenaniah Missionary Ch., Hollis, United States, 1986—. Author: (book) Behold, I Shew You A Mystery, 1998. Pres. Henderson Ave. Civic Assn., Hollis, NY, 1991—2002. Mem.: Fedn. Civic Assn. (pres. 2001—), United For Progress Dem. Club. Avocation: gardening. Home: 18625 Henderson Ave Hollis NY 11423-3132 Office: Chenaniah Missionary Ch 18625 Henderson Ave Hollis NY E-mail: alien512@msn.com.

STEPHENS, BART NELSON, former foreign service officer; b. Norfolk, Va., May 29, 1922; s. Bart Dannelly and Lura Lee (Cannon) S.; m. Barrett Krausz, Jan. 7, 1950; children: Tracey Rainier, Schuyler Barrett, Holly Cannon, Sinah Kendall Lee. AB, Duke, 1943; grad., USNR Midshipman Sch., Norte Dame, 1944; A.M., Harvard, 1947; lang. tng., Fgn. Service Inst., 1962, 66, 76. Divisional asst. Greece-Turkey-Iran sect., pub. affairs overseas program staff Dept. State, 1948-49; asst. pub. affairs officer Thessaloniki, Greece, 1950; asst. info. officer Athens, 1950-51; pub. affairs officer Patras, Greece, 1951-54 and, Thessaloniki, 1954; dir. Amerika Haus, Nuernberg, Germany, 1955-59; mem. cultural council City of Nuernberg, 1958-59; mgmt. analyst USIA, Washington, 1959-61; cultural attache Am. Embassy, Warsaw, Poland, 1963-65; dir. Am. Cultural Center, Saigon, Vietnam, 1967-68; 1st sec., regional projects officer Am. Embassy, Vienna, Austria, 1968-70; consul, pub. affairs officer Am. consulate gen. Stuttgart, Germany, 1970-73; area coordinator (Europe) USIA, Washington, 1973, seminar-conf. Programming officer, 1973-74; dep. dir. Office Internat. Arts Affairs, Dept. State, 1974-76; counselor cultural affairs officer Am. Embassy, Bangkok, 1977-82; counselor Sr. Fgn. Service. Contbr. articles to profl. jours. Vice chmn., bd. dirs. Thailand-U.S. Ednl. Found., 1977-82; bd. dirs. John F. Kennedy Found., Thailand, 1977-82, John E. Peurifoy Found., 1979-82, Lynchburg Symphony Orch., 1992-93; exec. sec. Eisenhower Exch. Fellowship Selection Com., Thailand, 1977-82; mem. winter forums com. Sweet Briar Coll., 1990-96. Lt. (j.g.) USNR, 1944-46, PTO. Decorated Bronze Star with combat V, Purple Heart.; recipient Meritorious Svc. award USIA, 1956, medal for civilian service in Vietnam, 1968, Civilian award U.S. European Command, 1973. Mem. Am. Fgn. Svc. Assn., Soc. Lees of Va., Siam Soc., Westwood Country Club (Vienna, Va.), Boonsboro Country Club, Phi Beta Kappa, Omicron Delta Kappa, Phi Eta Sigma, Pi Kappa Phi. Home: 201 Saint James Pl Lynchburg VA 24503-4226
Personal responsibility should be an essential principle for all of us, in the family, job and community. My 34 years in the U.S. Foreign Service gave me a wonderfully stimulating and rewarding career and a profound belief: the diplomatic service is America's first line of defense.

STEPHENS, BETSY BAIN, retired elementary school educator; b. Bessemer, Ala., Apr. 1, 1927; d. Herman Merritt and Lorene Burnice (Waldrop) Bain; m. Merton Von Stephens, June 23, 1947; children: Marc Von, Timothy Merton, Martha Katherine. Diploma, Wheeler Bus. Coll., Birmingham, Ala., 1945; B, U. Montevallo, 1949; MA, U. Ala., Birmingham, 1972. Tchr. Lee County Bd. Edn., Auburn, Ala., 1950-52, Jefferson County Bd. Edn., Birmingham, 1964-89. Mem. Nat. Coun. Tchrs. of English, Bessemer Music Club, Jefferson County Ret. Tchrs. Assn., Ala. Ret. Tchrs. Assn., Soc. of Ala. Retirees, Alpha Delta Kappa. Home: 7373 Warrior River Rd Bessemer AL 35023-7019

STEPHENS, BILLIE LOWELL, information assurance manager; b. Eunice, N.Mex., Apr. 4, 1950; children: Michael, David. BS in Mgmt., Calif. Coast U., 1994, MBA, 1997. Microsoft cert. engr. Chief network engr. Def. Info. Security Agy., Washington, 1999—2000; instr. nat. learning ctr. IRS, Austin, Tex., 2000—01; info. assurance mgr. SAIC, Columbia, Md., 2001—. Author: Coastal Del Rey and Mesa De Lagrimas, 2001, The Dome, 2002. Bd. dirs. Writers League Tex., Austin, 2001—01. With U.S. Army, 1969—81. Mem.: Writers League of Tex. (bd. dirs., v.p. 2002—), Tex. Assn. for Hist. Preservation (pres. 2001—02). Baptist. Avocations: golf, writing, travel, history. Home: RR 4 Box 606A Lampasas TX 76550 Personal E-mail: sierrav8@hotmail.com.

STEPHENS, BOBBY GENE, college administrator, consultant; b. Glendale, S.C., Mar. 8, 1935; s. Dewey and Bertha Cordelia (Mott) S.; m. Sandra Elizabeth White, June 27, 1957; children: Elaine, Ward, Todd, Adam. BS, Wofford Coll., 1957; MS, Clemson U., 1961, PhD, 1964; LHD (hon.), MacMurray Coll., 1987. Textile chemist Reeves Bros., Fairforest, S.C., 1957-58; grad. asst. Clemson (S.C.) U., 1960-63; instr. chemistry Wofford Coll., Spartanburg, S.C., 1963-64, asst. prof., 1964-67, assoc. prof., 1967-72, prof., v.p. acad. affairs, 1972-80; pres. MacMurray Coll., Jacksonville, Ill.,

1980-86; v.p. research and enrollment Wofford Coll., Spartanburg, S.C., 1986-91, v.p. sci. and tech., 1991—, prof. chemistry emeritus, 2000—. Project dir. Howard Hughes Med. Inst., 1992—; cons. colls. and industry Contbr. articles to sci. jours.; inventor extractions with propylene carbonate, 1975; producer: TV series The Psychology of Interpersonal Behavior, 1974. Co-chmn. Daniel Morgan Restoration Com., 1986-88; vice chmn. Spartanburg County Pollution Control Authority, 1970-74; bd. dirs. S.C. Lung Assn., Spartanburg, 1970-75, Comms. Svcs., Inc., 1977-80; sect. maj. United Way, 1975-77. 1st lt. U.S. Army, 1958-60. Recipient Jefferson award S.C. Acad. Sci., 1969; recipient 1st prize graphics div. 2d Edit. Art Contest, 1971, 2d and 3d prizes Lawson's Fork Creek Photography Contest, 1978, Alumni Disting. Svc. award Wofford Coll., 2001; USPHS grantee; NSF grantee Mem. Am. Chem. Soc., Nat. Assn. Gifted Children, Assn. Ednl. Communications and Tech., Phi Beta Kappa. Methodist. Home: 460 S Fairview Ave Spartanburg SC 29302 Office: Wofford College 429 N Church St Spartanburg SC 29303-3663 E-mail: stephensbg@wofford.edu.

STEPHENS, BRENDA WILSON, librarian; b. Durham, N.C., Oct. 22, 1952; d. Leroy Thomas and Lucy Mae (Umstead) Wilson; m. Gregory Frederick Stephens, Mar. 6, 1977; children: Seth, Sara. Student, Vincennes U., 1970-71; BA, Winston-Salem State U., 1974; MLS, N.C. Cen. U., 1981. Cert. pub. libr., N.C. From bookmobile coord. to county libr. Orange County Pub. Libr., Hillsborough, N.C., 1976-92, regional libr. dir., 1992—. Sec. United Way of Greater Orange County, 1991—93; elected mem. Orange County Sch. Bd., 1998—, chair, 2001—02; sec. Lipscomb Bapt. Ch., 1998—2002. With U.S. Army, 1974—76. Mem.: ALA, N.C. Pub. Libr. Dirs. Assn. (officer, pres. 2001), N.C. Libr. Assn. (chair adult sect. 1987—93, co-chair 1985—87, lit. com. 1983—85), A.L. Stanback Mid. Sch. PTO (pres. 1991—92), Kiwanis Club (pres. 1992—93). Democrat. Baptist. Avocation: quilting. Home: 5807 Craig Rd Durham NC 27712-1008 Office: Orange County Pub Libr 300 W Tryon St Hillsborough NC 27278-2438

STEPHENS, CARSON WADE, minister; b. San Angelo, Tex., Mar. 12, 1950; s. Allison Carson and Betty Jo Justice (Ellis) S.; m. Jeanette Martha Zett, June 19, 1971; children: Jennifer Hope, Bethany June. MusB, U. Tex., 1974; DMin, Drew U., 1991; postdoctoral, Tex. A&M U., 1996; postdoctoral fellow, U. Tex., Austin, 1996. Tchr. Manor (Tex.) Ind. Schs., 1970-73; minister Three Rivers (Tex.) Ch. of Christ, 1976-77, East Main Ch. of Christ, Holdenville, Okla., 1977-83, Sharpstown Ch. of Christ, Houston, 1983-86, Clear Lake Ch. of Christ, Houston, 1986-99; intern dept. of univ. advancement and pub. rels. Rice U., 1996; intern dept. univ. advancement and pub. rels. U. Tex.-Houston Health Sci. Ctr., 1996. Guest lectr. Fred-Hardeman U., Henderson, Tenn., 1992, Pepperdine U., 1996; dir. devel. Lifeline chaplaincy Tex. Med. Ctr., 1999—. Author: Evangelization, 1991, In the Beginning, Vol. 1, 1992, Vol. 2, 1993. Bd. dirs. Edgar A. Smith YMCA, Houston, 1987-94; mem. Mayor's Com. for Drug Prevention, Houston; active Pasadena Mcpl. Band, Pasadena Mcpl. Orch.; past pres. Summer Repertoire Theatre. Mem. Am. Acad. Ministry, Rotary (youth chair Space Ctr. chpt. 1988-89, bd. dirs. 1990, Presdl. award 1989, 90, chmn. drug awareness program, 1989, 992-93, 93-94, Paul Harris fellow 1993). Avocations: music composition and performance, drama, writing, reading. Office: Clear Lake Ch of Christ 938 El Dorado Blvd Houston TX 77062-4020 Home: 112 Mountain Laurel Way Bastrop TX 78602-7468

STEPHENS, CECILE HIGDON, artist, art educator; b. Linden, Ala., July 12, 1925; d. Cecil Rudolph and Mildred (Thomas) Hinson; m. William Travis Higdon, Jr., June 28, 1947 (div. Dec. 1971); children: William Travis III, Kent Thomas, Dean Gregory; m. John Pearson Stephens, June 29, 1973. BFA, Auburn U., 1968; MA, U. South Ala., 1971; 2d MA, U. Miss., 1976; postgrad., Nova U., 1973-80. Head art program, art instr. Miss. Gulf Coast C.C., Gautier, 1968-80; art instr. William Carey Coll., Gulfport, Miss., 1982-83. Art instr. U. So. Miss., Hattiesburg, 1968-73; juror and judge various art shows, 1975-85. Exhibited in solo shows at Birmingham So. U., 1960, Auburn U., 1968, La Font Gallery, Pascagoula, Miss., 1991, U. Miss., Oxford, 1994, Singing River Depot Gallery, Pascagoula, 1995, Eastern Shore Art Ctr., Fairhope Ala., 1995, Space 504 Gallery, N.Y.C., 1996, others; group shows include U. Ala., Tuscaloosa, Birmingham So. U., Biloxi (Miss.) Art Mus., Montgomery (Ala.) Mus. Art, Mobile (Ala.) Coll., Palais des Congres, Paris, Auburn U., U. So. Miss., Hattiesburg, James Russell Gallery, Gautier, Miss., Nat. Mus. of Women in the Arts, Washington. Mem. Rep. Women, Pascagoula, 1984-97; past state chmn., pres. gen.'s project DAR, Pascagoula, 1988-92, past regent, Pascagoula, 1988-92; v.p., bd. mem. cmty. concerts, Gautier, Pascagoula and Moss Point, Miss., 1986-90; ship christening com. mem. Ingalls Ship Bldg., Pascagoula, 1997; mem. adv. bd. Melange Dance Co., Pascagoula, 1995-97. Recipient Exemplary Achievement Alumna award Auburn U. Centennial of the Admission of Women, 1992, Unsung Hero's award Moss Point Miss. C. of C., 1996. Mem. Am. Soc. Portrait Painters, Washington Soc. Portrait Artists (charter), Nat. Mus. Women in the Arts (charter), Jackson County Arts Coun. (bd. mem.), Mobile Mus. Art, Ea. Shore Miss. Mus. Art, Walter Anderson Mus. Art (mem. adv. bd.). Episcopalian. Avocations: gardening, antique collecting, traveling. Home: 3855 River Rd Moss Point MS 39563-3711

STEPHENS, DEBORAH LYNN, health company executive; b. Newton, Iowa, May 30, 1952; d. Clarence Harry and Nancy Elizabeth (Gass) Wright; m. David K. Brender, Dec. 18, 1971 (div.); m. Michael E. Stephens, May 21, 1988 (div.). BS, U. Iowa, 1974; postgrad., U. Wis., Milw., 1978-80, U. Calif., Berkeley, 1987. Asst. to dean of fin. U. Iowa Coll. Medicine, Iowa City, 1975-77; contract audit acct. Miller Brewing Co., Milw., 1977-79; asst. contr. Unicare Health Facilities, 1979-81; v.p. fin. Sacred Heart Rehab. Hosp., 1981-84; COO, exec. v.p. Sacred Heart Rehab. Hosp., Med. Rehab. Inst., 1984-88; CEO, prin. founding mem. Behavioral Health Sys., Birmingham, Ala., 1989—, also bd. dirs. Cons. on rehab., fin., multi-corp. planning and zero-base budgeting 1988; founding mem. Am. Rehab. Network, Inc., Washington, 1986-87; mem. oral exam. bd. City of Milw., 1984-86, Jefferson County, Ala., 1995; mem. prospective payment adv. com. HHS, Washington, 1986; nat. presenter on zero-base budgeting, corp. reorgns., managed care, and planning. Contbr. articles to profl. jours. Mem. healthcare cost containment com. Bus. Coun. Ala., Rotary Club of Birmingham. Named one of Top 5 Thriving Bus. Women in Birmingham, Bus. to Bus., 1995, one of Top 78 nat. Entrepreneurs, Entrepreneur mag., 1996; featured in Healthwatch, Open Minds, Entrepreneur mag., Birmingham Post Herald, Birmingham News. Mem. Hosp. Fin. Mgmt. Assn. (governing bd. 1981-88), Nat. Forensic League (life), Nat. Assn. Accts., Nat. Assn. Rehab. Facilities (prospective payment adv. bd. 1986-88, com. on med. oriented facilities 1983-88), Ga. Managed Care Assn. (bd. dirs. 1995), Birmingham C. of C. (Small Bus. Person of Yr. award 1995), Venture Club, Kappa Kappa Gamma. Avocations: dancing, skiing, jogging, travel, reading. Office: Behavioral Health Systems 2 Metroplex Dr Ste 500 Birmingham AL 35209-6812 E-mail: deborahlstephens@aol.com., dstephens@bhs-inc.com.

STEPHENS, DONALD R(ICHARDS), investor; b. San Francisco, June 28, 1938; s. Donald Lewis and Anona Marie (O'Leary) S.; m. Christina Brinkman, Sept. 11, 1971 (div. 1996); m. Patricia Hamilton, Oct. 21, 2000; children: Lane B., Justin H., Nicholas W., Adam H. BS, U. So. Calif., 1961; JD, Hastings Coll., 1969. Pres. Campodonico & Stephens, San Francisco, 1963-65; pres., owner Union Investment Co., 1966-69; assoc. Law Offices of Louis O. Kelso, 1969-72; pres. D.R. Stephens & Co., San Francisco, 1972—. Chmn., CEO Bank of San Francisco Co., 1978-91, also bd. dirs.; chmn. N.Am. Trust REIT, also bd. dirs.; bd. dirs. Charles Schwab Family of Funds Inc. Bd. dirs. Bay Area Coun.; trustee St. Francis Meml. Hosp., San Francisco, 1976-82; mem. policy adv. bd. U. Calif., 1985—. Mem. Urban Land Inst., World Bus. Coun., Bohemian Club, Reserve Palm Desert. Republican. Presbyterian. Avocations: tennis, golf. E-mail: drs1220@aol.com.

STEPHENS, EDWARD CARL, communications educator, writer; b. L.A., July 27, 1924; s. Carl Edward and Helen Mildred (Kerner) S.; children: Edward, Sarah, Matthew. AB, Occidental Coll., 1947; MS, Northwestern U., 1955. Advt. exec. Dancer-Fitzgerald-Sample Inc., N.Y.C., 1955-64; prof. Medill Sch. Journalism, Northwestern U., Evanston, Ill., 1964-76; prof., chmn. dept. advt. S.I. Newhouse Sch. Pub. Communications, Syracuse U., N.Y., 1976-80, dean, 1980-89; prof. comms. S.I. Newhouse Sch. Pub. Comms. Syracuse U., 1990-92, prof. emeritus, 1992—. Cons. Foote, Cone & Belding Communications Author: (novels) A Twist of Lemon, 1958, One More Summer, 1960, Blow Negative!, 1962, Roman Joy, 1965, A Turn in the Dark Wood, 1968, The Submariner, 1974, (nonfiction) Submarines, 1960. Mem. George Polk Awards Com. With USN, 1943-46, 1950-53. Capt. USNR (ret.). Decorated Purple Heart Mem. Am. Acad. Advt. (pres. 1976-77), Assn. Edn. Journalism and Mass Communication, The Army and Navy Club, Authors League, Century Club of Syracuse, Alpha Tau Omega. Episcopalian.

STEPHENS, ELISA, academic administrator; Pres. Acad. of Art Coll., San Francisco, 1992—. Office: 79 New Montgomery St 6th Fl San Francisco CA 94105-3410

STEPHENS, GARY RALPH, American literature and journalism educator; b. Wichita, Kans., Mar. 4, 1943; s. Hubert Hal and Iris Lenore (Edgar) S.; m. Swati Niru Desai, May 13, 1978; children: Anaar, Joshua. AB, Wichita State U., 1965; MA, Brandeis U., 1969, PhD, 1972. Asst. prof. English, Queens Coll., CUNY, Flushing, 1971-75, N.Y. Inst. Tech., Old Westbury, 1976-81, assoc. prof., 1982-88, chmn. dept., 1979—93, prof. N.Y.C., 1989—; assoc. in journalism Grad. Sch. Journalism, Columbia U., 1986-97; chmn. dept. N.Y. Inst. Tech., Old Westbury, 1999—. Cons. in field. Contbr. articles to profl. publs. J.W. Fulbright fellow India, 1993; fellow Woodrow Wilson Found., 1965, Rockefeller Found., 1966, NEH, 1981. Office: NY Inst Tech 1855 Broadway New York NY 10023-7692

STEPHENS, GEORGE EDWARD, JR. lawyer; b. Lawrence, Kans., Mar. 26, 1936; s. George Edward and Mary Helen (Houghton) Stephens; m. Gretel Geiser, Dec. 31, 1965; children: Thaddeus Geiser, Edward Houghton. Student, U. Colo., Boulder, 1954-57, U. Colo., Denver, 1957-59; LLB, Stanford U., 1962. Bar: Calif. 1963, U.S. Dist. Ct. (cen. dist.) Calif. 1963, U.S. Ct. Appeals (9th cir.) 1971. Law clk. to judge U.S. Dist. Ct., L.A., 1962-64; assoc. ptnr. Pollock & Palmer, 1964-69; ptnr. Gates, Morris, Merrill & Stephens, 1969-72, Paul, Hastings, Janofsky & Walker, L.A., 1972—. Mem. Coordinating Coun. on Lawyer Competence, Conf. Chief Justices, 1983-86; chmn. probate sect. L.A. County Bar Assn., 1979-80. Nat. chmn. Stanford (Calif.) U. Law Fund Quad Program, 1980-87; mem. bd. visitors Stanford Law Sch., 1982-85; founder mus. Contemporary Art, L.A., 1982; bd. dirs. Pacific Oaks Coll., 1990-94. Recipient Stanford Assocs. award, 1982. Fellow: Fellows of Contemporary Art (bd. dirs. 1991—92), Internat. Acad. Probate and Trust Law, Am. Coll. Trust and Estates Counsel, Am. Bar Found.; mem.: Stanford Law Soc. (pres. 1972—73, chmn. 1998—99), ABA (chmn. standing com. specialization 1979—82, standing com. lawyer referral svcs. 1969—76, consortium delivery legal svcs. and the pub. 1979—82), The Athenaeum, Valley Hunt (Pasadena, Calif.), Annandale Golf (Pasadena, Calif.), Chancery (L.A.). Episcopalian. Office: Paul Hastings Janofsky & Walker 515 S Flower St 25th Fl Los Angeles CA 90071-2300

STEPHENS, JACK EDWARD, civil engineer, educator; b. Eaton, Ohio, Aug. 17, 1923; s. Harry M. and Mary Elizabeth (Galloway) S.; m. Virginia May Ives, June 19, 1948; children: Jay Edward, Jerry Edward, Jill Louise, Jana Lynn. BS in Engring., U. Conn., 1947; MS in Engring., Purdue U., 1955, PhD, 1959. Registered profl. engr., Conn. Jr. hwy. engr. Conn. Dept. Hwys., New Haven, 1949-50; instr. U. Conn., Storrs, 1947-48, asst. prof., then assoc. prof. civil engring., 1950-62, prof. civil engring., 1962-88, head civil engring. dept., 1965-72, prof. emeritus, 1989—, dir. Conn. Advanced Pavement Lab., 1995—. Soils cons. A.J. Macchi Engrs., Hartford, Conn., 1958-65; pavement cons. Conn. Dept. Hwys., Hartford, 1962-63, Consumers Union Auto Test Facility, Colchester, Conn., 1991—; prin. Jack E. Stephens Soil and Materials Test Lab., Storrs, 1958—. Contbr. jour. articles to Procs. Assn. Asphalt Paving Tech., Trans. Rsch. Bd., others. Cpl. U.S. Army, 1943-46, ETO. Fellow Automobile Safety Found., Washington, 1958-59; recipient citation for teaching excellence Western Electric Fund, Washington, 1974. Mem. ASCE (life, B. Wright award Conn. sect. 1989), NSPE, AAUP, Assn. Asphalt Paving Tech. (life), Conn. Acad. Sci. and Engring. (chmn. transp. com. 1984-94), Am. Rd. and Transp. Bldrs. Assn., Transp. Rsch. Bd., Am. Assn. Engring. Edn., Am. Soc. for Photogrammetry and Remote Sensing, Sigma Xi. Office: U Conn Transp Inst Box U-202 Storrs Mansfield CT 06269-5202 E-mail: jack.stephens@uconn.edu.

STEPHENS, JAMES LINTON, mechanical engineer; b. Stamford, Conn., Nov. 1, 1956; s. James Regis and Beatrice Helen (Johnson) S.; m. Laura Lynn Holmes, Sept. 6, 1980; children: Mark Linton, Jaimee Lee, Matthew James. BS in Mech. Engring., BS in Biomed. Engring., Northwestern U., 1980; profl. devel. degree in engring., U. Wis., 2001. Registered profl. engr., Wis. Mfg. engr. Parker Hannifin Corp., Des Plaines, Ill., 1980-81, St. Mary's, Ohio, 1981-84; mfg. engr. Ohmeda divsn. BOC Group, Madison, Wis., 1984-91, sr. mfg. engr. Ohmeda divsn., 1991-95; sr. engr. CNH Global N.V., Racine, 1995—. Mem. steering com. for engring. profl. devel. program U. Wis., Madison, 1994. Ill. State scholar, 1975. Mem. Soc. Mfg. Engrs. (treas. Madison chpt. 1984-85, 2d vice chmn. 1985-86, 1st vice chmn. 1986-87, chmn. 1987-88, certification chmn. 1988—, fundraiser 1987—, seminar and workshop leader 1987—, Chmn. plaque 1988, elected to machining tech. assn. bd. advisors 1996—). Avocations: swimming, tennis, reading science fiction. Office: CNH Global NV 7000 Durand Ave Racine WI 53406

STEPHENS, JAY B. Federal Agency Administrator, Lawyer; b. Akron, Iowa, Nov. 5, 1946; s. Lyle R. and Marie (Borchers) S. BA magna cum laude, Harvard U., 1968, JD cum laude, 1973. Bar: D.C. 1973, U.S. Supreme Ct., 1979. Assoc. Wilmer, Cutler & Pickering, Washington, 1973-74; asst. spl. prosecutor Watergate Spl. Prosecution Force, 1974-75; assoc. gen. counsel Overseas Pvt. Investment Corp., 1976-77; asst. U.S. atty. Dept. Justice, 1977-81, spl. counsel to asst. atty. gen., 1981-83, dep. assoc. atty. gen., 1983-85, assoc. dep. atty. gen., 1985-86; dep. counsel to Pres. Reagan, 1986-88; U.S. atty. for D.C. Office U.S. Atty., 1988-93; ptnr. Pillsbury Madison & Sutro, Washington, 1993-97; v.p. and dep. gen. counsel Honeywell, Morristown, NJ, 1997—2001; assoc. atty. gen. U.S. Dept. Justice, Washington, 2001—. Contbr. articles to profl. publs. Knox fellow Oxford, Eng., 1968-69 Mem. D.C. Bar Assn., Asst. U.S. Atty. Assn., Nat. Assn. Former U.S. Attys., Federalist Soc., Supreme Ct. Hist. Soc., Phi Beta Kappa. Republican. Presbyterian. Office: US Dept Justice Assoc Atty Gen 950 Pennsylvania Ave NW Washington DC 20530-0001

STEPHENS, JERRY WAYNE, librarian, library director; b. Birmingham, Ala., Sept. 10, 1949; s. William Larkin and Odell (Kerr) S.; m. Lisa Brown, June 2, 1972; children— Jeramy Wayne, Elizabeth Ashley, John Larkin BS in Acctg., U. Ala.-Birmingham, 1974, MBA, 1976; M.L.S., U. Ala., 1977, PhD in Adminstrn. Higher Edn., 1982. Svc. mgr. Hammond Organ Studios, Birmingham, 1973-74; acct. Mervyn Sterne Libr., U. Ala., 1974-75, asst. to dir., 1975-76, asst. dir., 1976-85, libr., dir., 1985—; interim fiscal officer Univ. Coll. U. Ala., 1982, interim asst. v.p. for acad. affairs, 1989-91. Vice chmn. Network Acad. Librs., 1985-86, 95-96, chmn., 1986-88, 96, 2000-01; cons. Birmingham Pub. Libr., 1977—; cons. Southeastern Libr. Assn., Atlanta, 1979-80; bd. dirs. Southeastern Libr. Network, treas., 1992-93, chmn., 1993-94; mem. user's coun. Online Computer Libr. Ctr., 1997—, pres.-elect, 2000-01, pres., 2001-2002. Contbr. articles to profl. publs. Sponsored exec. United Way, Birmingham, 1978, sr. exec., 1982; foster parent Dept. Pensions and Securities, Birmingham, 1982-83; elder Homewood Cumberland Presbyn. Ch., Birmingham, 1982-84, 88-90. With USN, 1972-73 Named one of Outstanding Young Men Am., U.S. Jaycees, 1978, 79 Mem. ALA, SE Libr. Assn., Ala. Libr. Assn. (treas. 1977-78), Am Mgmt. Assn. Avocations: camping; softball. Home: 2621 Kemp Ct Birmingham AL 35226-1982 Office: U Ala-Birmingham Mervyn H Sterne Libr University Sta Birmingham AL 35294-0001 E-mail: jerry@beowulf.mhsl.uab.edu.

STEPHENS, JOANNE B. engineer; b. Owensboro, Ky., July 9, 1951; d. Herman J. Barr and Ernestine Hamilton; m. George W. Stephens, May 30, 1970; children: Christy Jacondino, Jason, Julie Stewart, Jeremy, Leah. AAS in Elec. Engring. Tech., Owensboro C.C., 1995; BS in Electro-Mech. Engring. Tech., Western Ky. U., 1998. Bus. mgr. Tri-State Welding and Constrn., Owensboro, 1988—95; customer support engr. Owensboro Mcpl. Utilities, 1998—. Divsn. chair United Way of Daviess County, Owensboro, Ky., 1999—. Mem.: Power Engrs. Assn. of Ky. (treas., sec., v.p., pres. 2000—). Home: 820 Worthington Rd Owensboro KY 42301 Office: Owensboro Mcpl Utilities 2070 Tamarack Rd Owensboro KY 42301 Personal E-mail: mcgyver105@aol.com. E-mail: stephensjb@omu.org.

STEPHENS, JOHN FRANK, association executive, researcher; b. Malone, N.Y., Nov. 9, 1949; s. J. Frank and Marjorie (Drew) S.; m. Smaroula Georgina Paras, Sept. 1, 1989; 1 child, Georgina Elizabeth. BA, Harpur Coll., 1971; MA, SUNY-Binghamton, 1973, PhD, 1977. Research assoc. Fernand Braudel Ctr., SUNY-Binghamton, 1977; asst. to provost U. Md., College Park, 1978; vis. instr. St. Mary's Coll. Md., St. Mary's City, 1978-79; dir. Alexandria Regional Preservation Office, Va., 1980-83; exec. dir. Am. Studies Assn., Washington, 1983—; cons. (in field); reviewer U.S. Dept. Interior, NEH, HEW, USIA, PBS, Washington, 1983—. Author: (with Immanuel Wallerstein) Libraries and Our Civilizations, 1978, (with others) Archaeology in Urban America: A Search for Pattern Process, 1982; bd. dirs. Songmasters, The Am. Rd. Exec. bd. dirs. Nat. Humanities Alliance, 1992-99. Fulbright-Hays fellow, 1974-75; Spanish Govt. fellow, 1974-75 Mem. Am. Studies Assn., Fulbright Assn. Home: 4631 Bettswood Dr Olney MD 20832-2042 Office: Am Studies Assn 1120 19th St NW Ste 301 Washington DC 20036-3614

STEPHENS, JOHN JOSEPH, JR. materials engineer; b. Canton, Ohio, Sept. 11, 1955; s. John J. and Ann L. S.; m. Linda J. Brown, July 19, 1986. BA in Physics, Cornell U., 1977; MS in Metallurgical Engring., Stevens Tech. Inst., Hoboken, N.J., 1980; PhD in Materials Sci. and Engring., Stanford U., 1985. Rsch. technician Exxon Rsch. & Engring. Co., Linden, N.J., 1977-80; grad. rsch. fellow Stanford U., Palo Alto, Calif., 1980-84; prin mem. tech. staff Sandia Nat. Labs., Albuquerque, 1985-87, 88—; mem. tech. staff Lockheed Missiles & Space, Palo Alto, 1987-88. Inventor in field. Recipient Best Tech. Paper award Internat. Metallographic Soc., 1987, AWS Peasley award for best paper in brazing, 1999, 2000. Mem.: TMS (chmn. refractory metals com. 1989—92), ASM (mem. chpt. devel. task force 1992—94), ASTM (co-chair subcom. F1.03 1993—, 1st vice chair electronics com. F-1 1999—, Charles Marsden award 1995).

STEPHENS, JOHN RICHARD, writer; b. San Diego, 1958; s. Richard Clark and LaVerne Adelle Stephens. BA Rsch. Psychology, San Jose State U., 1982; DDiv (hon.) , United World Assembly. Author: (book) Weird History 101, 1997. Mem.: Horror Writers Assn., Authors Guild. Office: Fern Canyon Press PO Box 1708 Cambria CA 93428-1708

STEPHENS, KITTY FRANCES, academic administrator; b. Thomasville, N.C. d. Willie Edward and Dorothy Lee Harper; children: Rodney, Jamel. BS, Livingstone Coll., 1970; MPA, U. Balt., 1981. Unit adminstr. Hosp. U. Md., Balt., 1971-79, asst. to dir. ops. Hosp., 1979-82, bus. mgr. Sch. Medicine, 1991-93; asst. to chief solid waste Howard County Govt., Ellicott City, 1984-90; customer svc. rep. Am. W. Airlines, Balt., 1990-93; budget analyst MD. State Dept. Human Resources, 1993-95; adminstrv. officer Md. Income Maintenance Adminstrn., 1995; ops. mgr. Cmty. Inst. Behavioral Svcs., 1995-96; office asst. N.C. A&T State U., Greensboro, 1997; grants and contracts mgr. Bennett Coll., 1997-99; asst. v.p. devel. Johnson C. Smith U., Charlotte, N.C., 1999—. Kresge fellow Kresge Found. and So. Edn. Found., 2000. Mem. Coun. Advancement and Support Edn., Nat. Assn. Title III Adminstrs., Nat. Sponsored Programs Adminstrs. Alliance, Delta Sigma Theta. Democrat. Methodist. Avocations: travel, reading. Office: Johnson C Smith U 100 Beatties Ford Rd Charlotte NC 28216-5398 Fax: 704-378-3521. E-mail: kstephens@jcsu.edu.

STEPHENS, LARRY DEAN, engineer, consultant; b. Sterling, Colo., Sept. 1, 1937; s. John Robert and Shirley Berniece (Rudel) S.; m. Carol Ann Wertz, Sept. 1, 1957 (div. May 1975); children: Deborah Lynn, Janell Diane, Dana Larry, Hilary Elizabeth Melton; m. Neslihan Ozlen, Aug. 18, 2000. BS in Engring., Colo. State U., 1960; MBA, U. Colo., 1967. Registered profl. engr., Colo. Engr. Bur. Reclamation, Denver, 1960-90, cons., 1991—. Exec. v.p. U.S. Com. on Irrigation and Drainage, Denver, 1971—; exec. dir. U.S. Soc. on Dams, Denver, 1986—. V.p. Internat. Commn. on Irrigation and Drainage, 1989-92. With USNG, 1961-62. Mem. Am. Soc. Agrl. Engrs., Assn. State Dam Safety Ofcls., Colorado River Water Users Assn., Coun. on Engring. and Sci. Soc. Execs., Univ. Club Denver. Republican. Methodist. Home: 1625 Larimer St Apt 1505 Denver CO 80202-1532 Office: USCID 1616 17th St Ste 483 Denver CO 80202-1277 E-mail: stephens@uscid.org.

STEPHENS, LAURENCE DAVID, JR. linguist, investor, oil industry executive; b. Dallas, July 26, 1947; s. Laurence D. Sr. and Amy Belle (Schickram) S.; m. Susan Leigh Foutz, Apr. 16, 1988; 1 child, Laurence David III. MA, Stanford U., 1972, PhD, 1976. Vis. fellow Yale U., New Haven, summer 1979; rsch. fellow U. S.C., Columbia, 1980; asst. prof. U. N.C., Chapel Hill, 1982-88, assoc. prof., 1989—; pres. Colgate Mgmt. Co., Inc., Dallas, 1997—; gen. ptnr. Moorman, Schickram & Stephens, Ltd., 1997—. Co-author: Two Studies in Latin Phonology, 1977, Language and Metre, 1984, The Prosody of Greek Speech, 1994, Discontinuous Syntax, 1999: editor ann. vol. L'Année Philologique, 1987-92; contbr. numerous articles to profl. jours. Mem. Univ. Pk. Cmty. League, Park Cities Hist. Soc., Nat. Trust for Hist. Preservation, Washington, 1989—, Dallas Opera Guild, 1992—, The Dallas Symphony Assn. Ann. Fund, Metro. Opera Guild, N.Y.C., 1992—, Wythe County VA Hist. Soc., 1998—. Grantee L'Année Philologique, NEH, 1987-89, 89-91, 91-93. Mem. Am. Philol. Assn., Greek and Latin Linguistic Assn. (chmn. 1987-92), N.Y. Acad. Scis., Indogermanische Gesellschaft, Internat. Soc. Bibliographie Classique, Sigma Xi. Achievements include discovery of language universal regularities concerning labiovelar phonemes, laws of palatalization, the law of catathesis in Greek (pitch lowering), and grammatical, semantic, pragmatic (information structure) regularities of discontinuous constituency and nonconfigurational syntactic structures in Greek; co-developer of Justeson-Stephens probability distribution for cognates between unrelated languages, Justeson-Stephens probability distribution of the numbers of vowels, consonants, and total phonological inventory size in the languages of the world; research on the law of the quantitative form of diachronic polysemy growth, semantic universals of aspect and modality, universals of writing systems and their evolution. Home: 3319 Greenbrier Dr Dallas TX 75225-4818 Office: Univ NC Chapel Hill Dept Classics Cb 3145 212 Murphey Hl Chapel Hill NC 27599-0001 Address: Moorman Schickram & Stephens Ltd 4020 Colgate Ave Dallas TX 75225-5425 E-mail: lsteph8694@aol.com.

STEPHENS, LAWRENCE JAMES, chemistry educator, program director; b. Chgo., Aug. 11, 1940; s. James Jenkyn and Mary Catherine (Caughlin) S.; m. Theresa Ann Duster, Aug. 8, 1964; children: Anne Marie, Mark, Susan. BS, Loyola U., 1963; PhD, U. Nebr., 1969. Postdoctoral rsch. assoc. Stanford (Calif.) U., 1968-69; asst. prof. chemistry Findlay (Ohio) Coll., 1969-73; from asst. prof. chemistry to prof. Elmira Coll., Elmira, NY, 1973—96, Georgia Harkness prof. natural sci., 1996—. Author textbooks; contbr. articles to ednl. jours. Pres. Chemung County Gen. Edn. Bd., Elmira, 1976-79. Mem. Am. Chem. Soc. (sect. chair 1986, 2000), Ancient Order Hibernians (divsn. pres. 1988, 89, 97-99, dir. 2001—). Republican. Roman Catholic. Home: 613 Mooreland Pl Elmira NY 14904-1622 Office: Elmira Coll. Elmira NY 14901 E-mail: lstephens@elmira.edu.

STEPHENS, MARLA JEAN, lawyer; b. Milw., Mar. 1, 1952; m. Robert J. Dvorak. BA, U. Wis., 1978; JD, Marquette U., 1981. Bar: Wis. 1981, U.S. Dist. Ct. Wis. 1981. Asst. pub. defender, Milw., 1981-94; 1st asst. pub. defender Office Wis. Pub. Defender, 1994-96, dir. appellate divsn. Milw. and Madison, 1996—. Mem. Wis. Jud. Coun., Madison, 1996—, chair, 2000—. Mem. Nat. Assn. Criminal Def. Lawyers, Assn. Criminal Def. Lawyers, Wis. Assn. Criminal Def. Lawyers, Assn. for Women Lawyers, Milw. Bar Assn., State Bar Wis. (appellate practice bd. 1999—). Office: Office Wis Pub Defender Appellate Divsn 735 N Water St Ste 912 Milwaukee WI 53202 E-mail: stephensm@mail.opd.state.wi.us.

STEPHENS, MARTIN R. state official; b. Ogden, Utah, Mar. 26, 1954; m. Carole Stephens. BSin Bus. Adminstrn., Webder State U. Mayor Farr West City, Utah, 1986-88; house speaker State of Utah, 1999—. Coun. mem. Farr West City, 1984-85, vice chair Weber Area Coun. of Govts., 1986-87, chair, 1988, elected Utah rep. White House Conf. Small Bus., Washington, 1986, majority leader, 1993-94, chair legis. mgmt. com., judiciary standing com., govt. ops. standing com., retirement com., exec. appropriations com. (chair 1993-94), commerce and revenue appropriations com., 1999—. Recipient Roy B. Gibson Freedom of Information award Soc. Profl. Journalists, 1991. Office: Utah Legis 318 State Capitol Salt Lake City UT 84114 also: 3159 N Higley Rd Farr West UT 84404-9380*

STEPHENS, MICHAEL THORYNE, librarian; b. Cedartown, Ga., June 14, 1955; s. Thomas Herschel and Bertie (Moncrief) S.; m. Cindy Yvonne Coley July 1, 1977 (div. Apr. 1986); children: Jada, Joey. AA, Floyd Coll., 1993; BA,

Jacksonville State U., 1996. Mgr. Rite Aid Corp., Rome, 1993—94, Revco Drug Co., Rome, 1996; librarian, reference serials specialist Rome-Floyd County Libr., 1999—. Mem. Ga. Libr. Assn., Pi Sigma Alpha, Omicron Delta Kappa. Democrat. Baptist. Avocation: fishing, hiking, climbing, darts. Home: 233 Houseal St Cedartown GA 30125-2831 Office: Sara Hightower Regional Library 205 Riverside Pky Rome GA 30161 Fax: (706)236-4605. E-mail: stephen_m76@hotmail.com.

STEPHENS, NORVAL BLAIR, JR. marketing consultant; b. Chgo., Nov. 20, 1928; s. Norval Blair and Ethel Margaret (Lewis) S.; m. Diane Forst, Sept. 29, 1951; children: Jill E., John G., Sandra J. (dec.), Katherine B., James N. BA, DePauw U., 1951; MBA, U. Chgo., 1959. Asst. to v.p. ops. Walgreen Drug Co., Chgo., 1953-56; with Needham, Harper Worldwide (formerly Needham, Harper & Steers), 1956-86, v.p., 1964-70, sr. v.p., 1970-72, exec. v.p. internat., 1972-74, exec. v.p., mng. dir., 1974-75; exec. v.p. Chgo. office Needham, Harper & Steers, 1975-82, exec. v.p. internat., 1982-86; also dir.; pres. Deltacom, N.Y.C., 1971-76; pres. Norval Stephens Co., 1987—90; exec. dir. Internat. Comms. Agy. Network, 1988-98. Bd. advisors Barrington Area Arts Coun., 1985-86, bd. dirs., 1987-89; bd. dirs. N.W. Cmty. Hosp. Found., Arlington Heights, 1976-89, vice chmn., 1987-89; bd. dirs. Harper Coll. Ednl. Found., Palatine, Ill., 1977-86, pres., 1980-86; bd. dirs. Barrington Area Devel. Coun., 1978—, pres., 1994-96; bd. visitors, dir. alumni bd. DePauw U., 1979-83, pres., 1981-83, trustee, 1983—, vice chmn., 1995-99; bd. dirs., pres. Barrington Area Cmty. Found., 1998—. With USMCR, 1951-53. Named Young Man of Yr., Arlington Heights Jaycees, 1964, Barrington Area Citizen of Yr., 1999; recipient Rector award DePauw U., 1976, Old Gold Goblet award for outstanding svc. DePauw U., 1994, Outstanding Greek Vol. award N.Am. Interfraternity Conf., 2001; named to Sr. Hall of Fame, Barrington, Ill., 2002. Mem. Internat. Advt. Assn. (v.p. Midwest chpt. 1986-87), Am. Mgmt. Assn., Am. Mktg. Assn., DePauw Alumni Assn. (pres. 1977-79), Phi Beta Kappa, Delta Tau Delta (bd. dirs. edn. found. 1987—, vice chmn. 1994-95, chmn. 1995—, 2d v.p. Arch chpt. 1988-90, 1st v.p. 1990-92, pres. 1992-94). Republican. Methodist. Home and Office: 107 Fox Hunt Trl Barrington IL 60010-3418 E-mail: norval@norvalstephens.com. *I view my life not as a passage but a daily renewing challenge: to be better; to be a better father, husband, brother, son; to return each day an honest day's work; to bear witness to my beliefs and my faith; to serve my fellowman. I seek a whole life and a life of rewarding parts, each a lesson and an experience.*

STEPHENS, PATRICIA ANN, marketing professional; b. Gulfport, Miss., Feb. 1, 1945; d. James Marshall and Edna Mathilda (Hogan) S. BA, St. Louis U., 1967; MA, Memphis State U., 1971. Lic. secondary educator speech, theatre, English, religion. Exec. v.p. Prodns. Unltd., Memphis, 1971-73; chairperson speech dept. Southaven (Miss.) High Sch., 1973-77; instr. speech N.W. Jr. Coll., Southaven, 1974-76; pub. rels. dir., instr. St. Agnes Acad., Memphis, 1977-78; religion and English instr. Memphis Cath. High Sch., 1978-82; resource tchr. communications Mobile (Ala.) City Schs., 1982-84; mktg. devel. specialist/mktg. mgr. Prime Health Ala., Mobile, 1984-85; mktg. mgr. Blue Cross Blue Shield Fla./Health Options, Lakeland and Orlando, Fla., 1986-92; ind. agt., 1992-94; nat. mktg. and svc. coord. Delta Care, PMI, Tampa, 1994—, mgr. client svcs. ea. region, 2002—. Bd. mem. Red Balloon Players, Memphis, 1971-73, Downtown Dream Machine, Memphis, 1980-82, Cir. Playhouse/Playhouse on the Square, Memphis, 1980-82, WIFS Ctrl. Fla., 2002--. Newspaper Fund fellow Wall St. Jour. Newspaper Fund, U. Oreg., 1968, writing fellow Greater Memphis Writing Project, Memphis State U., 1980, part-time masters fellow Memphis State U., 1981-82; recipient Pres.'s Club BCBSF/Health Options Sales Mgr. award Health Options of Polk County, 1987. Democrat. Roman Catholic. Home: 4128 Sunny Land Dr Lakeland FL 33813-3946 Office: Delta Dental Ins Co Ste 350 258 Southhall Ln Maitland FL 32751-7427

STEPHENS, PAUL ALFRED, dentist; b. Muskogee, Okla., Feb. 28, 1921; s. Lonny and Maudie Janie (Wynn) S.; m. Lola Helena Byrd, May 7, 1950; children: Marsha Stephens Wilson, Paul Alfred Jr., Derek M. BS cum laude, Howard U., 1942, DDS, 1945. Instr. dentistry Howard U., Washington, 1945-46; gen practice dentistry Gary, Ind., 1947—; chmn. bd. Assocs. Med. Ctr., Inc. Sec. Gary Ind. Sch. Bldg. Corp., 1967-85; pres. Bd. Health, 1973-81; Ind. State Bd. Dental Examiners, 1975-83. Mem. adv. bd. Ind. U.-Purdue U. Calumet Campus, 1973; bd. dirs. Urban League Northwest Ind.; pres. Gary Ednl. Devel. Found., 1990—. With AUS, 1942-44. Fellow Internat. Coll. Dentists, Acad. Dentistry Internat., Acad. Gen. Gen. Dentistry (pres. chpt. 1973, nat. chmn. dental care com. 1977, Midwestern v.p., nat. bd. dirs. 1984-89, v.p. 1990-91, pres. 1992-93), Am. Coll. Dentists; mem. ADA, Nat. Dental Assn., N.W. Ind. Dental Assn. (bd. dirs., pres. 1976-77, Disting. Svc. award 1993), Am. Soc. Anesthesia in Dentistry, Am. Acad. Radiology, Gary C. of C., Alpha Phi Alpha (pres. Gary Ednl. Found. 1988, pres. Gary Ednl. Devel. Found. 1990—), Acad. Gen. Dentistry (pres. 1992-93). Baptist. Home: 1901 Taft St Gary IN 46404-2759 Office: 2200 Grant St Gary IN 46404-3439

STEPHENS, RALPH RENNE, massage therapy educator; b. Vinton, Iowa, Apr. 19, 1948; s. E.O. and Carrie D. S.; m. Sara Ann Beckley. BS in Indsl. Edn., Iowa State U., 1971; Natural Therapeutics Splst., N.Mex. Sch. Natural Therapeutics, 1986. Lic. massage therapist Iowa, N.Mex., massage therapy instr. N.Mex., cert. therapeutic massage and bodywork Nat. Cert. Bd. Therapeutic Massage and Bodywork, St. John method neuromuscular therapy. Pvt. practice Helping Hands Body Therapy Ctr., Iowa City, 1986-92; staff instr. Carlson Coll. Massage Therapy, Cedar Rapids, Iowa, 1987-92; instr. St. John Neuromuscular Therapy Seminars, 1991-99; pvt. practice Ralph Stephens Seminars, Cedar Rapids, 1992—. Dir. sports massage Iowa City Annual Hospice Road Race Com., 1986-88; cons., sys. engr., equipment supplier to workshop and seminar presenters Helping Hands Audio/Video, 1989-94; chairperson Iowa Bd. Examiners Massage Therapy, Des Moines, 1995-2000; sec. Iowa Bd. Examiners Massage Therapy, Des Moines, 1992-95; presenter in field. Author: Massage Therapy Principles and Practice, 1999; contbr. articles to profl. jours.; prodr. videos Seated Therapeutic Massage, Vol. 1, Back and Neck, 1995, Vol. 2, Shoulder, 1996, Vol. 3, Forearm, Wrist and Hand, 1996, Feel Great Hands on Health Series (4 tapes) Feel Great Every Day, Posture Yourself and Move Right, Massage Made Easy, Stretching that Works, 1998, Event Sports Massage, 1998, Side-Lying Therapeutic Massage, 1999, Therapeutic Sports Massage for the Lower Extremity, 1999, Anatomy of the Lower Extreminty, 1999, Medical Massage for the Cervical Region, 2001, Medical Massage for the Lumbar Region, 2002; monthly editl. columnist Massage Today, 2000-. Trustee Am. Massage Therapy Assn. Found., 1990-93, 95-96; chairperson Walford (Iowa) Disaster Preparedness Com., 1999. Mem. Am. Massage Therapy Assn. (cert. sports massage therapist, registered massage therapist cert., organizer, chair Iowa sports massage team 1986-88, 1st v.p., convention coord. Iowa chpt. 1988-89, edn. chair Iowa chpt. 1988-89, pres. Iowa chpt. 1989, ctrl. dist. rep. nat. bd. dirs. 1990-93, media spokesperson nat. media rels. team 1991-96, nat. nominating com. 1994, mem.-at-large nat. bd. dirs. 1995-96, nat. nominating commn. 1998-99, Disting. Nat. Officer award 1993, 96, Meritorious award Iowa chpt. 1997, Nat. Meritorious award 1997), Himalayan Inst. Yoga Sci. and Philosophy. Republican. Avocations: golf, yoga, meditation. Home: PO Box 8267 Cedar Rapids IA 52408-8267 Office: Ralph Stephens Seminars LLC PO Box 8267 Cedar Rapids IA 52408-8267 Business E-Mail: ralph@ralphstephens.com.

STEPHENS, ROBERT DAVID, environmental engineering executive; b. La Follette, Tenn., Nov. 8, 1949; s. Robert Oscar and Billie Jean (Maples) S.; m. Donna Jean Reece, July 11, 1970 (div. Apr. 1984). BA in Biology, Berea (Ky.) Coll., 1971; postgrad., U. Cin., 1973-74. Cert. environ. assessor Fla., environ. trainer, registered environ. propery assessor, environ. mgr. Environ. specialist Ky. Dept. Health, Ludlow, 1971-74; project mgr. Pedco Environ. Specialists, Cin., 1974-77; environ. control mgr. Mobil Chem. Corp., Richmond, Va., 1978-84; v.p. Environ. Analysis Corp., 1984-85; mgr. Environ. Rsch. and Tech. Group GSX Corp., Greensboro, N.C., 1985-86; mgr. regulatory affairs and cmty. rels. Internat. Tech. Corp., Knoxville, Tenn., 1986-88, mgr. environ. studies Tampa, Fla., 1988-90; gen. mgr. First Environment, Inc., 1990-91; co-owner Bruder Stephens, Inc., 1991—. Faculty Fla. C. of C. Environ. Seminars, 1988—; adj. faculty U. Fla. Treeo Ctr.; adj. faculty U. South Fla. Coll. Pub. Health; expert witness in environ. mgmt., sampling and analysis, environ. risk mgmt. Contbr. articles to profl. jours. Co-founder Berea Community Theater, 1970; bd. dirs. So. Waste Info. Exch., Inc.; mem. adv. bd. Ctr. for Environ./Occup. Risk Analysis and Mtmg., U. South Fla. Coll. Pub. Health. Mem. Fla. Bar Assn. (assoc., environ and land use sect.), Fla. Environ. Assessors Assn. (pres. 1996-97, bd. dirs. 1993—), Water Polution Control Fedn., Va. Orchid Soc. (pres. 1980-85, del. World Orchid Congress, Miami 1984), Ridge Orchid Soc., Tampa Club (bd. dirs. 1999—), Ye Loyal Krewe of Samuel Bellamy (co-founder, bd. dirs. 2000—), Outback Bowl (bd. dirs. 2001—). Republican. Avocations: orchid horticulture, guitar. Home: PO Box 145 Mango FL 33550-0145 Office: 14409 N Nebraska Ave Ste A Tampa FL 33613-2226 E-mail: rd-stephens@usa.net.

STEPHENS, ROBERT ERNEST, retired educator; b. Whitley City, Ky., Feb. 9, 1921; s. Arthur and Jewell Reed Stephens; m. Helen Carmack (div. 1972); children: Monty N'Neal, Randy Craig, Robert James; m. Beatrice Lawson, Nov. 8, 1973; 1 child, Robert Ernest Jr. BA, U. Louisville, 1972, MEd, 1974; LLB, Blackstone Sch. Law, 1959. Cert. secondary sch. supr., Ky. Commd. USMC, 1941, advanced through grades to 1st lt.; accountable officer Marine Corp Air Sta., Cherry Point, N.C., 1952; navy supply officer Marine Aircraft Group, Po Hang Dong, Korea, 1953-56; helicopter liaison officer Aviation Supply Office, Phila., 1960-62; ret., 1962; supply chief 47th Rifle Co. Marine Corps Tng. Ctr., Louisville, 1970-72; fin. officer McCreary County Schs., Whitley City, 1972, prin., 1975-79; math. and sci. tchr. Valley High Sch., Louisville, 1973-75; indsl. engr., pers. officer Devoe & Reynolds Co. Chmn. provisioning Sikorsky Helicopters, Bridgeport, Conn., 1961. Author: Historical and Cemetery Inventories, 1996-98 (Genealogy Soc. award 1997), (play) Princess Cornblossom Maiden of the River, 1998, (history) A Lost Hearitage for a Changing People, 1999. Sec. Big South Fork Devel., Ky. and Tenn., 1976; chmn., sec., treas. McCreary County Sportsman Club, Whitley City, 1978; chmn. McCreary County Farm Bur., Whitley City, 1980s; mem. Com. to Prepare Ky. Health Plan, Frankfort, 1982; chmn. bd. suprs. McCreary County Soil Conservation Dist., Whitley City, 1983-95; chmn. Rural Abandoned Mine Reclamation Com., Ky., 1994-97; candidate for county judge McCreary County Rep. Primary. Recipient Cert. of Appreciation, East Ky. Health Sys. Agy., Inc., 1982, Outstanding Svc. award McCreary Farm Bur., 1984, Disting. Svc. award McCreary County Conservation Dist., 1994. Mem. VFW, Ky. Ret. Tchrs. Assn., Ky. Farm Bur., Orie S. Ware Lodge (sec. 1990-94). Republican. Baptist. Avocations: hiking, gardening, farming, reading, photography. Home: 1200 Lick Creek Rd Whitley City KY 42653-4109

STEPHENS, RONALD DANIEL, physician; b. Corpus Christi, Tex., Apr. 19, 1958; s. Ronald Theron and Dora Coleen (Isaacs) S.; m. Martha Lyn Strong, Jan. 3, 1981; children: Wesley Daniel, Katelyn Elizabeth. BS, Tex. A&M U., 1980; MD, Tex. Tech. Sch. Medicine, 1986. Diplomate Am. Bd. Family Physicians, Am. Acad. Hospice and Palliative Medicine. Resident Meml. Med. Ctr., Corpus Christi, 1986-88, chief resident, 1988-89; physician Parkview Med. Surg. Clinic Hosp., Mexia, Tex., 1989-2000; med. dir. Parkview Med. Surg. Clinic, 1993-94, 1996-2000; pvt. practice, 2001—. Med. dir. Hospice of Mercy, Mexia, 1990-2000; chief of staff Parkview Regional Hosp., Mexia, 1991-93, 98-99, pres. bd. dirs., 1993-95, vice chmn. bd. govs., 1996—; founding pres. Parkview Regional Hosp. Found., Mexia, 1995-96. Fellow Am. Bd. Family Practice; mem. Am. Acad. Family Practice, Acad. Hosp. Palliative Medicine, Tex. Acad. Family Practice, Tex. Med. Assn. (com. access to health care 1992—). Avocations: golfing. Office: Office Dr R Stephens 514 Bonham Ste J Mexia TX 76667

STEPHENS, SHERYL LYNNE, family practice physician; b. Huntington, W.Va., Dec. 11, 1949; d. William Clayton Stephens and Virginia Eleanor (Hatten) Stephens Terry; 1 child, William Earl Hicks III (dec.); m. Lannie Dale Rowe, Jan. 17, 1981; 1 child, Seton Christopher. BA, U. Ky., 1972; MA, Marshall U., 1982, MD, 1988. Tchr. Wayne County Bd. Edn., Ceredo, W.Va., 1973-83; real estate developer Huntington, 1981-88; resident in family practice Grant Med. Ctr., Columbus, Ohio, 1988-91; gen. practice indigent care physician Columbus (Ohio) Health Dept., 1991—; med. dir. Billie Brown Jones Family Health Ctr., Columbus, 1993-98; sch. physician Columbus Bd. Edn., 1994—; med. dir. St. Stephens Health Care Ctr., Columbus, 1995-98, Billie Brown Jones Family Health Care Ctr., Columbus, 1993-98, lead physician, 1998—. Chair Coll. Health Dept. Com. on Pharmacy and Therapeutics, 1994-2000; rschr., 1976-81. Counselor, instr. Contact of Huntington, 1975-88; polit. activist pro choice movement and ratification of equal rights amemdment, 1976-81. Recipient Leadership award Marshall U., 1985. Mem. Am. Assn. Family Practitioners (pres. 1984-85, Leadership award 1985), Am. Med. Women's Assn. (sec. 1985-86), NOW (pres. 1976-78, 79-81, v.p. Huntington 1978-79, sec. 1981-82), Nat. Abortion Rights Action League. Democrat. Avocations: horseback riding, reading, boating, skiing (snow and water), travel. Home: 9323 Mccord Rd Orient OH 43146-9518 Office: Billie Brown Jones Family Health Ctr 1060 Mount Vernon Ave Columbus OH 43203-1518

STEPHENS, SHIRLEY LYNNE, writer, editor; b. Glendale, Ariz., Mar. 11, 1934; d. Burrell G. and Kathryn Sullivan Stephens; m. William H. Stephens; children: Laura, Paula Baker, Greg, Carol. BA, Grand Canyon U., Phoenix, AZ, 1958; MDiv, So. Bapt. Theol. Sem., Ft. Worth, TX, 1967. Contract writer Lifeway Christian Resources, Nashville, 1968—94; writer self-employed, 1968—2002; v.p. Authors Book Nook, Brentwood. Co-author (book) Under the SS Shadow; author: (book) A New Testament View of Women, Breaking Crime's Viscious, My Daughter Susan Smith. Avocations: sports, movies, esl teaching. Office: Authors Book Nook PO Box 513 Brentwood TN 37024-0513 Office Fax: 615-377-1033. E-mail: w-s.stephens@nashville.com.

STEPHENS, SIDNEY DEE, chemical manufacturing company executive; b. St. Joseph, Mo., Apr. 26, 1945; s. Lindsay Caldwell and Edith May (Thompson) S.; m. Ellen Marie Boeh, June 15, 1968 (div. 1973); m. Elizabeth Ann Harris, Sept. 22, 1973; 1 child, Laura Nicole. BS, Mo. Western State U., 1971; MA, U. Houston, 1980; advanced cert. employment law, Inst. Applied Mgmt. and Law, 1998. Cert. Stephen Covey programs facilitator, 1997. Assoc. urban planner Met. Planning Commn., St. Joseph, 1967-71; prodn. acctg. assoc. Quaker Oats Co., 1971-72, office mgr., pers. rep. Rosemont, Ill., 1972-73, employee and cmty. rels. mgr. New Brunswick, N.J., 1973-75, Pasadena, Tex., 1975-80; mgmt. cons., Houston, 1981—; regional mgr. human resources Syngenta Crop Protection Inc., 2001—. Contbr. articles to profl. jours. With USNR, 1963-65. Mem. ASTD, Nat. Soc. for Human Resources Mgmt., Houston Human Resources Mgmt. Assn. (cmty. and govtl. affairs com. 1984-85, 85-86). Republican. Methodist. Home: 16446 Longvale Dr Houston TX 77059-5420 Office: Syngenta Crop Protection Inc 5757 Underwood Rd Pasadena TX 77507-1031 E-mail: sid.stephens@syngenta.com.

STEPHENS, STEVE ARNOLD, real estate broker; b. Irby, Cheshire, Eng., May 25, 1945; came to U.S., 1983; s. Harold Dennis George and Hilda Leonora (Howell) S.; m. Lynn Williams, Apr. 14, 1983. Student, Manchester U., Eng., 1967-69. Lic. pvt. detective, Ill.; cert. comml. investment mem. From cadet to detective Cheshire (Eng.) Police, 1961-69; acting detective sgt. Merseyside (Eng.) Police, 1969-75; acting sgt. Hampshire (Eng.) Police, 1975-77; retail store owner Horsham, West Sussex, Eng., 1977-79; pvt. detective Carratu Internat., London, 1979-83, D.A.C. Stephens, Aurora, Ill., 1983-86; broker Coldwell Banker Comml.-Primus Realty, Oswego, 1986-98; broker, owner Stephens Comml. Real Estate, Aurora, 1998—. Bd. dirs. Aurora Crimestoppers, pres., 1995-96. Recipient Rep. Legion of Merit award, Rep. Order of Merit award. Mem. Nat. Assn. Realtors (CCIM), CCIM Inst. (cert., bd. dirs. Ill. CCIM chpt. 1992-97, sec.-treas. 1994, v.p. 1995, pres. 1996, v.p. region 7 1999-2001, nat. governing coun. 1999—), No. Ill. Comml. Assn. Realtors (dir. 1995-97), Internat. Assn. Chiefs of Police, Ill. Assn. Realtors, Greater Aurora C. of C., Aurora Country Club. Avocations: travel, literature, golf. Home: 7 Saddlewood Ct Aurora IL 60506-9175 Office: 518 N Lake St Aurora IL 60506-3105 E-mail: sstephens@ccim.net. *Work hard. Tell the truth and shame the Devil!.*

STEPHENS, THOMAS M(ARON), education educator; b. Youngstown, Ohio, June 15, 1931; s. Thomas and Mary (Hanna) S.; m. Evelyn Kleshock, July 1, 1955. BS, Youngstown Coll., 1955; MEd, Kent State U., 1957; EdD, U. Pitts., 1966. Lic. psychologist, Ohio. Tchr. Warren (Ohio) public schs., 1955-57, Niles (Ohio) public schs., 1957-58; psychologist Montgomery County, Ohio, 1958-60; dir. gifted edn. Ohio Dept. Edn., Columbus, 1960-66; assoc. prof. edn. U. Pitts., 1966-70; prof. edn. Ohio State U., 1970—, chmn. dept. exceptional children ., 1972-82, chmn. dept. human services edn., 1982-87, assoc. dean Coll. Edn., 1987-92, prof., 1987-92, prof. emeritus, 1992—; clin. prof. edn. U. Dayton, Ohio, 1993—; exec. dir. Sch. Study Coun. Ohio, Columbus, 1993—. Mem. Higher Edn. Consortium for Spl. Edn., chmn., 1976-77; pub., pres. Cedars Press, Inc. Author: Directive Teaching of Children with Learning and Behavioral Handicaps, 2d edit, 1976, Implementing Behavioral Approaches in Elementary and Secondary Schools, 1975, Teaching Skills to Children with Learning and Behavioral Disorders, 1977, Teaching Children Basic Skills: A Curriculum Handbook, 1978, 2d edit., 1983, Social Skills In The Classroom, 1978, 2d edit., 1991, Teaching Mainstreamed Students, 1982, 2d edit., 1988, Social Behavior Assessment Scale, 1991; dir.: Jour. Sch. Psychology, 1965-75, 80—; exec. editor: The Directive Tchr.; assoc. editor: Spl. Edn. and Tchr. Edn., Techniques, Behavioral Disorders, Spl. Edn. and Remedial Edn.; contbr. articles to profl. jours. Named to Ohio State U. Coll. of Edn. Hall of Fame, 1999; U.S. Office of Edn. fellow, 1964-65. Mem. APA, NASP (charter), State Dirs. for Gifted (pres. 1962-63), Coun. for Exceptional Children (gov., Tchr. Educator of Yr. tchr. edn. divsn. 1985), Coun. Children with Behavioral Disorders (pres. 1972-73). Home: 551 E Cooke Rd Columbus OH 43214-2813 Office: Sch Study Coun of Ohio 4807 Evanswood Dr # 300 Columbus OH 43229-6294

STEPHENS, WANDA BREWER, social services administrator, investor; b. Bolckow, Mo., Nov. 6, 1932; d. Perry Clark and Mary Carolyn (Fisher) Brewer; m. Lloyd Wesley Stephens, June 19, 1954; children: Ruth Ann, Susie Jo, John Allen, Donna Lynn. BS in home econs., U. Ark., 1954, MS, 1958. Cert. secondary edn. Home economics tchr. West Fork (Ark.) High Sch., 1954-58; pres. Devel. Child Care Assn., Fayetteville, Ark., 1971-74; pres., founding bd. Infant Devel. Ctr., 1972-75, treas., 1975-81; edn. chmn., fin. com., admin. bd. Cen. United Meth. Ch., 1976-79; pres. League of Women Voters, 1979-83, Nat. Orgn. Women, Fayetteville, 1983-89; state legis. v.p. NOW, 1985-90, 93-98; state pres. Nat. Orgn. Women Ark., 1991-93, 98—. Bd. sec., headstart, Econ. Opportunity Agy., Fayetteville, 1969-70; treas. Mama's Mink Investment Club, 1970-72. Co-author: Bylaws for Economic Opportunity Agy., 1969; co-editor: Washington County, Ark., 1982. Fundraiser United Fund, 1972-75; polit. organizer NOW, 1986; treas. Washington County Dem. Women, 1990-92; organizer/staff/fund Women's Libr., 1982-91, 99-2000; cons./organizer Ctrl. Child Care Ctr., 1977-78. Recipient Internat. 4-H Youth Exch., 1953-54, Infant Devel. Ctr. Founders Plaque Univ. Ark., 1987; Fayetteville Women's History honoree, 2001; named Lay Person of Yr., Ctrl. United Meth. Ch., 1977. Mem. Mental Health Assn. (Cmty. Svc. award 1972), AAUW (pres. Fayetteville 1975-77, state treas. 1996-2000, Edn. Found. fellow 1984), ACLU (Susan B. Anthony award 1985, Disting. Svc. award 1999), Ark. Women's Polit. Caucus (Uppity Woman award 1987, 92). Democrat. Methodist. Avocations: genealogy, reading, investing. Home: 1177 E Ridgeway Dr Fayetteville AR 72701-2612 E-mail: wandasteph@aol.com.

STEPHENS, WILLIAM THEODORE, lawyer, business executive; b. Balt., Mar. 31, 1922; s. William A. and Mildred (Griffin) S.; m. Arlene Alice Lesti, June 2, 1958; children: William Theodore Jr., Renée Adena. Grad., Balt. City Coll., 1941; student, U. Md., 1946-47; AB, JD, George Washington U., 1950, postgrad., 1951. Bar: D.C. 1951, Md. 1950, Va. 1959. Assoc. J.L. Green, Washington, 1950-51; with J.M. Cooper, 1952-54; sr. ptnr. Stephens Law Firm, 1955—. Gen. counsel Exotech, Inc., Gaithersburg, Md.; prin. owner BARBCO, Inc., Va., Fairfax Raquet Club; gen. counsel various nat. corps. and assns. Author: Rental Contracts - Contracts for the Rental of Personal Property, 2000. 1st lt. AUS, 1941-45. Mem. ABA, D.C. Bar Assn. (sect. taxation 1959—, sect. corps, banking and bus. law 1960—), Bar Assn. D.C. (sec. taxation 1959-68), XVI Corps Assn. (pres. 1967), Commonwealth Club, Univ. Club, Capitol Hill Club, Army-Navy Country Club, Regency Sport and Health Club, Jockey Club, LaCosta Country Club, Racquet Club Internat., Kappa Alpha (preceptor, ct. of honor, James Ward Wood Province 1988-91), Delta Theta Phi. Home: 1800 Old Meadow Rd Mc Lean VA 22102-1819 also: 881 Ocean Dr Key Biscayne FL 33149-2609 Office: PO Box 1096 Mc Lean VA 22101-1096 Address: PO Box 1169 Rancho Santa Fe CA 92067-1169 E-mail: wstephens@stephenslawfirm.org.

STEPHENSON, ALAN CLEMENTS, lawyer; b. Wilmington, N.C., Nov. 7, 1944; s. Abram Clements and Ruth (Smith) S.; m. Sherri Jean Miller, Dec. 19, 1970; children: Edward Taylor, Anne Baldwin. AB in Hist., U. N.C., 1967; JD, U. Va., 1970. Bar: N.Y. 1971. Assoc. Cravath, Swaine & Moore, N.Y.C., 1970-78, ptnr., 1978-88; mng. dir. Wasserstein, Perella and Co. Inc., 1988-92; ptnr. Cravath, Swaine & Moore, 1992—. Mem. external adv. bd. undergrad. honors program U. N.C., 1998—. Bd. trustes Poly Prep Country Day Sch., N.Y.C., 2000—. Morehead scholar John M. Moorehead Found., 1963. Mem. N.Y. State Bar Assn., Assn. of Bar of City of N.Y., The Brook Club, The Links Club, Tuxedo Club, Union Club, Phi Beta Kappa. Home: 1107 5th Ave New York NY 10128-0145 Office: Cravath Swaine & Moore 825 8th Ave Fl 38 New York NY 10019-7475

STEPHENSON, ANN, artist; b. Fayetteville, W.Va., June 30, 1933; d. George W. and Eva J. (Weatherford) Booth; m. Roger Allen Stephenson, July 19, 1958 (div. May 1993); 1 child, David. AA, Ctrl. Acad. Art, Cin., 1955. Fashion artist Mabley & Carew, Cin., 1957—60, May D and F, Denver, 1960—61, Shillito's Dept. Store, Cin., 1961, Gidding/Jenny, Cin., 1964; head fashion artist McAlpin's Dept. Store, 1964-77; art dir., dir. phtography Rogers Dept. Store, Grand Rapids, Mich., 1977-95; art dir., owner Ann Stephenson Designs, Charleston, W.Va., 1996—. Author, artist: Introduction to Fashion Art, 1981; fine art watercolor exhibits, Mich. and Ga., 1992, 94; exhibit of 38 yrs. of original fashion illustrations, 2002. Recipient six Addy awards, 1975, 78. Mem. Nat. Mus. Women Arts, Rivertown Artist Guild (historian 1992). Avocations: watercolor, reading, hiking, drying flowers. Address: 209 1/2 Gilmore St Blackshear GA 31516-2531

STEPHENSON, ARTHUR EMMET, JR. corporate and investment company executive; b. Bastrop, La., Aug. 29, 1945; s. Arthur Emmet (dec.) and Edith Louise Stephenson; m. Toni Lyn Edwards, June 17, 1967; 1 child, Tessa. BS in Fin. magna cum laude, La. State U., 1967; MBA (Ralph Thomas Sayles fellow), Harvard U., 1969. Chartered fin. analyst. Adminstrv. aide to U.S. Sen. Russell Long of La., Washington, 1966; security analyst Fidelity Funds, Boston, 1968; chmn. bd., pres. Stephenson & Co., Denver, Stephenson Mcht. Banking Inc., Circle Corp.; sr. ptnr. Stephenson Ventures, Stephenson Properties; founder, chmn. Gen. Comm., Inc., Denver; founder, chmn. bd. dirs. StarTek, Inc. Bd. dirs. Danaher Corp.; co-founder Pub. Network, Inc.; founder Charter Bank and Trust, chmn., 1980-91; mem. adv. bd. First Berkshire Fund, Capital Resources Ptnrs., L.P.; former pub. Law Enforcement Product News, Colo. Book, Pub. Safety Product News, 1990-98, Colo. Book, Denver mag., Denver Bus. mag. Past mem. assocs. coun. Templeton Coll. at Oxford U., Eng.; nat. trustee Nat. Symphony Orch. at John F. Kennedy Ctr. for Performing Arts, 1995-98; past mem. nat. steering com. Norman Rockwell Mus., Stockbridge, Mass.; past mem. Colo. small bus. coun.; del. White House Conf., 1980; bd. dirs. Ptnrs. in Excellence La. State U. Recipient Hall of Fame award Inc. mag., 1994, Albert Einstein Tech. medal, 1999; named to Hall of Distinction, La. State U. Coll. Bus. Adminstrn., 1998. Mem. Harvard U. Bus. Sch. Assn. (internat. pres. 1987-88), Chief Execs. Orgn., World Pres.'s Orgn., Colo. Investment Advisors Assn. (treas., bd. dirs. 1975-76), Denver Soc. Security Analysts (bd. dirs. 1975-77), Colo. Press Assn., Colo. Harvard Bus. Sch. Club (pres. 1980-81, chmn. 1981-82), Thunderbird Country Club (Rancho Mirage, Calif.), Annabel's (London), Jonathan Club (L.A.), Pinnacle Club, Harvard Bus. Sch. Clubs (So. Calif. and Orange County), Omicron Delta Kappa, Phi Kappa Phi, Beta Gamma Sigma, Kappa Sigma, Delta Sigma Pi. Office: 100 Garfield St Denver CO 80206-5597

STEPHENSON, DAVID ALAN, manufacturing engineer; b. Moline, Ill., Feb. 1, 1959; s. Lawrence Aaron and Marion Moody Stephenson; m. Maria Clelia Milletti, Jan. 15, 1983; children: Francesca Laura, Luke Andrew. BSME, MIT, 1981, MS in Mech. Engring., 1983; PhD in Mech. Engring., U. Wis., 1985. Engring. group mgr. GM Corp., Detroit, 1986—. Author: (book) Metal Cutting Theory and Practice, 1997; contbr. . Recipient Campbell Applied Sci. award, GM Corp., 2001. Mem.: ASME (exec. com. mfg. engring. divsn. 2001—, assoc. tech. editor ASME Transactions 1994—2000, Blackall Machine Tool award 1994), Soc. Mfg. Engrs. (assoc. tech. editor 1998—, Outstanding Young Mfg. Engr. award 1994). Home: 19389 Canterbury Detroit MI 48221

STEPHENSON, DONALD GRIER, JR. government studies educator; b. DeKalb County, Ga., Jan. 12, 1942; s. Donald Grier and Katherine Mason (Williams) S.; m. Ellen Claire Walker, Aug. 15, 1967; children: Todd Grier, Claire Walker. AB, Davidson Coll., N.C., 1964; MA, Princeton U., 1966, PhD,

1967. Research assoc. Nat. War Coll., Washington, 1968-70; asst. prof. govt. Franklin and Marshall Coll., Lancaster, Pa., 1970-73, assoc. prof. govt., 1973-81, prof. govt., 1981—, Charles A. Dana prof., 1989—, dept. chair, 1976-79, 99—. Mem. adv. coun. to dean of the chapel Princeton U., 1974-85; Commonwealth lectr. Pa. Humanities Coun., Phila., 1987-88, 90, 92-95, 98-99. Co-author: American Constitutional Development, 1977, co-author: American Government, 1992, co-author: , 1994, co-author: American Constitutional Law, 2002; author: The Supreme Court and the American Republic, 1981, An Essential Safeguard, 1991, Campaigns and the Court, 1999; contbr. Elder, mem. session First Presbyn. Ch., Lancaster, 1973-76, 96-99; judge Pa. constl. competition Dickinson Coll., 1988-94. Capt. U.S. Army, 1968-70. Woodrow Wilson fellow, 1964-65, 66-67; Nat. Endowment for Humanities grantee, 1972, 85-89. Mem. Am. Polit. Sci. Assn. (Corwin award com. 1978, nominating com. Law and Courts sect. 1995), Pa. Polit. Sci. Assn. (editl. bd. Polity 1972-78), Supreme Ct. Hist. Soc. (editl. award 1990). Presbyterian. Home: 62 Oak Ln Lancaster PA 17603-4762 Office: Franklin and Marshall Coll PO Box 3003 Lancaster PA 17604-3003 E-mail: g_stephenson@email.fandm.edu.

STEPHENSON, DOROTHY MAXINE, volunteer; b. Hanna, Ind., July 16, 1925; d. William John and Inez Louisa (Werner) Hunsley; m. Orville Lee Stephenson, Mar. 10, 1945 (dec. Oct. 1985). Grad. high sch., Hanna. Postal clk. U.S. Post Office, Hanna, 1943-44; bookkeeper LaPorte Co Farm Bur. Coop Assn., 1944-45; news correspondent Ind., 1950—; organist Wanatah (Ind.) United Meth. Ch., 1959-60, Bethel Presbyn. Ch., Union Mills, Ind., 1960—. Publicist LaPorte chpt. OES, 1992—, Starke County Geneal. Soc., 1999—, LaPorte County Geneal. Soc., 1984—. Compiler: Werner-Wentz Connections, 1982, Inez Scribblins/Dot's Jottings, 'N Nibblins, 1986, abstractions Hanna H.S. Alumni records, 1990, record books II, III and IV for Bethel Presbyn. Ch., 1992; compiler, pub. Poetry, Music of the Soul, 1995. Publicity person Am. Heart Assn. (Ind. affiliate), LaPorte, 1982-85, LaPorte County Geneal. Soc., 1984—, Starke County Geneal. Soc., 1999—. Recipient Golden Poet award World of Poetry, 1988, hon. mention, 1987-88, Editor's Choice award Nat. Libr. of Poetry, Best Poems of 90's and the 1990 Nat. Anthology award, Echoes of Yesterday, 1994; Voices of America by Sparrowgrass Poetry anthologies, 1989, 90, 91, 92, Amherst Soc. anthologies, 1990, 92, Iliad Press anthologies, 1992, 93, Quill Books, 1993, Outstanding Poets of Am. anthology, 1994, Distinguished Poets of America anthology, 1993. Mem. Merry Prairie (treas. 1964—), Order Ea. Star (worthy matron 1953, 85-90, publicity person LaPorte chpt. 1992—). Democrat. Presbyterian. Avocations: sewing, reading, writing, photography, knitting. Home and Office: 12805 S Hunsley Rd Hanna IN 46340-9736

STEPHENSON, FRANK ALEX, engineer, consultant; b. Helena, Mont., May 4, 1940; s. Alex Banning and Phyllis Jean (Smith) S.; m. Lorann Marcella Berg, July 9, 1962 (div. Aug. 1970); children: Patty Jo, Scott Alex; m. Brenda Mae Vitales, June 21, 1986; 1 child, Jennifer Jean. BS in Civil Constrn. Engring., Mont. State U., 1967; MS in Sanitary Engring., Delft U., 1973; PhD in Environ. Engring., Exeter U., 1975. Registered profl. engr., Ariz., Mont., S.D., Colo., N.Mex., Wyo., Kans. Constrn. engr. Al Johnson Co., Mpls., 1967-70; sr. engr. Stearns Roger Inc., Denver, 1975-79; ptnr. Thomas Group Inc., San Jose, Calif., 1979-85; sr. engr. CH2M Hill Inc., 1985-87; dir. engring. western divsn. Dames & Moore, Phoenix, 1987-93; dir. techs. Terranext, 1993-97; systems engr. Sumitomo-Sitix, Phx., 1997-98; prin. engr. Harding Lawson Assoc., 1998—. Recipient Ernest Cook Rsch. fellowship Royal Acad. Sci., London, 1973. Mem. AIChE, Hazardous Waste Soc., diplomate Am. Coll. Forensic Engrs. Presbyterian. Achievements include development of technology for on-line total organic carbon analysis using ultraviolet light and resistivity changes; design and installation of first reverse osmosis unit used in a nuclear (electric power) reactor. Avocations: model railroading, fishing, swimming, bicycling. Home: 1702 E Aurelius Ave Phoenix AZ 85020-5508 Office: EOS Engring Inc 5016 S Ash Ave Ste 101 Tempe AZ 85282-6845

STEPHENSON, GARY VAN, electro-optics systems engineer; b. Huron, S.D., Mar. 25, 1958; s. Phillip Carlyle Stephenson and Barbara Jean (O'Leary) Young; m. Sandra Lynn Deault, June 4, 1977 (div. Feb. 1989); m. Nancy Watkins Gossett, July 19, 1991. BS in Physics, BA in Philosophy, Mont. State U., 1983. Mem. tech. staff Hughes Aircraft Co., El Segundo, Calif., 1983-86; sr. engr. ITT-Aerospace Optical Div., Ft. Wayne, Ind., 1986-88; electro-optics engr. Weyerhaeuser Co., Federal Way, Wash., 1988-89; systems engr. Hughes Aircraft Co., Seattle, 1989—97, The Boeing Co., Seattle, 1997—. Pres. Seculine Consulting, Bellevue, Wash., 1989—. With U.S. Army, 1976-79. Mem. AIAA, Sigma Pi Sigma. Democrat. Episcopalian. Avocations: skiing, cycling, hiking. Home: 16501 SE 57th Pl Bellevue WA 98006-5537 Office: The Boeing Co Kent Space Ctr PO Box 3999 Seattle WA 98124-2499

STEPHENSON, HELENE RUTH, painter, consultant; b. Phila., Aug. 6, 1926; d. Eugene Frank and Ida Gertrude (Loeffert) Schweitzer; m. Robert Louis Stephenson, June 12, 1948; children: John, Wayne, Cynthia. Diploma, Phila. Coll. Art, 1948. One-woman shows include Woodmere Art Mus., Phila., 1976, Gallery 500, Elkins Park, Pa., 1983, 91, Toro Gallery, Huntingdon Valley, Pa., 1998; exhibited in group shows Woodmere Art Mus., 1966, 81, Allentown (Pa.) Mus., 1977, Tel-Aviv Mus., 1978, Pa. State Mus., Harrisburg, 1992, others; represented in permanent collections Wills Eye Hosp., Anheuser-Busch, Bryn Mawr Coll., American Design, Ltd., others. Pres., dir. Old York Rd. Art Guild, Alverthorpe, Abington, Pa.; bd. dirs. Woodmere Art Mus.; recording sec. Artists' Equity, Phila. Mem. James Michener Art Mus., Woodmere Art Mus. Avocations: gardening, needlepoint. Home: 1501 County Line Rd Huntingdon Valley PA 19006-1406

STEPHENSON, HERMAN HOWARD, retired banker; b. Wichita, Kans., July 15, 1929; s. Herman Horace and Edith May (Wayland) S.; m. Virginia Anne Ross, Dec. 24, 1950; children: Ross Wayland, Neal Bevan, Jann Edith. BA, U. Mich., 1950; JD with distinction, U. Mo., Kansas City, 1958, LLD (hon.), 1993. Bar: Kans. 1958. With City Nat. Bank, Kansas City, Mo., 1952-54, City Bond & Mortgage Co., Kansas City, 1954-59, Bank of Hawaii, Honolulu, 1959-94, CEO, 1989-94, ret. chmn., 1994-2000. Bd. dirs. Friends of Cancer Rsch. Ctr. Hawaii. Bd. dirs. Maunalani Found.; chmn., bd. dirs. Pacific Fleet Submarine Meml. Assn. With U.S. Army, 1950-52. Mem.: Pacific Forum/CSIS (bd. govs.), Navy League U.S., Waialae Country Club, Oahu Country Club, Eagle Bend Country Club, Rotary, Pi Eta Sigma, Kappa Sigma.

STEPHENSON, IRENE HAMLEN, biorhythm analyst, consultant, editor, educator; b. Chgo., Oct. 7, 1923; d. Charles Martin and Carolyn Hilda (Hilgers) Hamlin; m. Edgar B. Stephenson, Sr., Aug. 16, 1941 (div. 1946); 1 child, Edgar B. Author biorhythm compatibilities column Nat. Singles Register, Norwalk, Calif., 1979-81; instr. biorhythm Learning Tree Open U., Canoga Park, 1982-83, instr. biorhythm personality analysis, 1980—, instr. biorhythm compatibility, 1982—; owner, pres. matchmaking svc. Pen Pals Using Biorhythm, Chatsworth, 1979—. Editor newsletter The Truth, 1979-85, Mini Examiner, Chatsworth, 1985—; rschr. biorhythm personality and compatibility, 1974—, biorhythm columnist Psyhic Astrology Horoscope, 1989-94, True Astrology Forecast, 1989-94, Psychic Astrology Predictions, 1990-94, Con Artist Types, 1995, Pedophile (child molester) Types, 1995-2000, Personality Types, 1996, Trouble-Addict (Suicide) Types, 1997, Domineering/Nag Types, 1998, Con Artists, Sweetheart Swindlers, Super Con Artist Types, 1998, Bully types, 2000, Deadly Compatibility Combination, 2000, Fatal Attraction Types, 2000, Sadism, Sadistic, Sadistic Predators, 2000, Salesperson, Practical Joker Types, 2000, Doormat Types, 2000, Famous/Queen Bee/Rescuer Types, 2000, Prostitution, 2000. Author: Learn Biorhythm Personality Analysis, 1980, Do-It-Yourself Biorhythm Compatibilities, 1982; contbr. numerous articles to mags. Office: PO Box 3893 Chatsworth CA 91313-3893

STEPHENSON, JANE ELLEN, educational association administrator; b. Banner Elk, N.C., Apr. 2, 1938; d. Braxton Leo and Mary Helen (Barlow) Baucom; m. John Bell Stephenson (dec. 1994); children: Jennifer Stephenson McLamb, Rebecca, David. AA, Lees McRae Coll., 1957; BS in Secretarial Adminstrn./Edn., U. N.C., Greensboro, 1959; MA in Bus. Edn., Appalachian State U., 1962; MS in Higher Edn. Adminstrn., U. Ky., 1976; Doctorate (hon.), Berea Coll., 1995. Acad. intern continuing edn. U. Ky., Lexington, 1977, coord. student svcs., 1978-80, dir. acad. support svcs., 1980-83, dir. human rels. ctr., 1983-84; exec. dir. Berea (Ky.) C. of C., 1988-89; found., dir. New Opportunity Sch. for Women, Berea, 1987—. Asst. prof. bus. and econs. Berea Coll., fall 1987. Author: (book) Courageous Paths: Stories of Nine Appalachian Women, 1995. Bd. dirs. Berea Hosp., 1985—, Mountain Assn. for Comty. Econ. Devel., 1995-96, Ky. Nat. Identification Program for Advancement of Women in Higher Edn. Adminstrn., 1984-86; mem. adv. bd. Ency. of Appalachia, 1996—; vol. coord. Berea Forum, 1985-95; mem. adv. bd. Ea. Ky. Women's Leadership, 1996—; mem. Leadership Madison County, Richmond, Ky., 1988; mem., bd. dirs. Ky. Women's Leadership Network, Lexington, 1993; chairperson state adv. bd. Elderhostel, 1987-94; mem. Foster Care Rev. Bd., 1990-91; commr. Ky. Commn. on Women, 1993-97, Ky. Appalachian Commn., 1995—; Appalachian dir. Steele-Reese Found., 1997—. Recipient Woman Advocate for Women award Women Mean Bus. Conf., 1996, Anderson medal Commonwealth of Ky., 1991, Women of Achievement State and Local award Bus. and Profl. Women Ky., 1988; named Citizen of Yr., Berea Lions Club, 1989. Mem. AAUW (Women as Agts. of Change award 1990), LWV. Presbyterian. Avocations: reading, piano. Home: 3121 Grantham Way Lexington KY 40509-2373 Office: New Opportunity Sch for Women 204 Chestnut St Berea KY 40403-1538

STEPHENSON, LARRY KIRK, stategic planner, management, geography educator; b. Seattle, Sept. 22, 1944; s. Norman Eugene and Virginia Dare (Frost) S.; m. Margery Alsever, Aug. 15, 1992; children: Matthew Alan, Leah Anela. BS, Ariz. State U., 1966, MA, 1971; PhD, U. Cin., 1973. Manpower rsch. analyst Employment Security Commn. of Ariz., 1969-70; asst. prof. geography U. Hawaii, Hilo, 1973-76, assoc. prof., 1976-78, chmn. dept. geography, 1975-77; planner Ariz. Dept. Health Svcs., Phoenix, 1978-84; strategic planner City of Glendale, Ariz., 1984-92; pub. health analyst Gila River Indian Comty., 1992-98, econ. devel. planner, 1998—. Vis. lectr. dept. geography Ariz. State U., 1978, adj. assoc. prof., 1979—; vis. assoc. prof. dept. geography, area devel. and urban planning U. Ariz., 1978; mem. faculty U. Phoenix, 1979—; adj. prof. Golden Gate U., 1981—; ptnr. Urban Rsch. Assocs., Phoenix, 1981—; adj. prof. Coll. St. Francis, 1982—; mem. faculty Troy State U., 1990—. Author: Statistics for Health Managers, 1981; co-author: Student Study Guide and Instructor's Manual to accompany Geography: A Modern Synthesis, 4 edits., 1975-83; editor: Kohala keia: Collected Expressions of a Community, 1977; contbr. articles to profl. jours., chpts. to textbooks. Mem. Hawaii Island Health Planning Coun., 1974-78, Glendale Comty. Colls. Pres.'s Coun. , 1986-92. With U.S. Army, 1966-68. NDEA fellow 1971-72. Mem. Am. Inst. Cert. Planners, Am Planning Assn., Assn. Am. Geographers, Ariz. Planning Assn. (pres. 1987—), S.W. Profl. Geog. Assn., Lambda Alpha. Unitarian Universalist. Home: 9825 S 30th Dr Laveen AZ 85339 Office: PO Box 97 Sacaton AZ 85247-0097 E-mail: Lstephe739@aol.com.

STEPHENSON, LAURA L. music educator, therapist; b. Woodville, Tex., July 28, 1973; d. Ernest L. and Rosalie (Saunders) M. BMus in Music Therapy cum laude, Sam Houston State U., 1996. Registered music therapist. Piano tchr., 1989—. Music therapist Brazos Valley Health and Wellness, College Station, Tex., 1997; elem. music tchr. Neal Elem., Bryan, Tex., 1997-99, Milam Elem. Sch., Bryan, 1999—. Mem. Am. Music Therapy Assn., Tex. Music Tchrs. Assn., Music Tchrs. Nat. Assn., Am. Coll. Musicians, Southwestern Regional Assn. for Music Therapy, Golden Key, Pi Kappa Lambda. Home: 2412 Pleasant Rose Cir Bryan TX 77808-2222 Office: Milam Elem 1200 Ridgedale St Bryan TX 77803-3521

STEPHENSON, MARIA I. O'BYRNE, lawyer; b. Cali, Valle, Colombia, Nov. 12, 1951; came to U.S., 1965; d. Alvaro and Maria Teresa (Malvehy) O'Byrne; m. John Edward Stephenson, May 31, 1975; children: Teresa Maria, Phillip David. BA, Tulane U., 1973; JD, U. Houston, 1975. Bar: Tex. 1975, La. 1976. Assoc. Grisbaum & Kleppner, Metairie, La., 1976-78; ptnr. Bryan, Nelson, Allen, Schroeder & Stephenson, New Orleans, 1978-86; of counsel Maria I. O'Byrne Stephenson, 1986-95, Stephenson Matthews & Chavarri LLC, New Orleans, 1996—. Active Pan Am. Commn., Baton Rouge, 1993-94; bd. dirs. Shared Housing, New Orleans, 1994—. Recipient Diploma Al Merito, Consulate of Mex., 1994, Tributo de Reconcimiento, Consulate of Colombia, 1999; named Hon. Consul of Peru, New Orleans, 2000—. Mem. La. Bar (bd. dirs. internat. law sect. 1993-94), La.-Mex. Trade Assn. (officer 1991-94), Hispanic Lawyers Assn. (officer 1981-97, pres. 1997). Roman Catholic. Avocations: trade, travel, golf, tennis. Office: Stephenson Matthews Et Al 2305 World Trade Ctr New Orleans LA 70130

STEPHENSON, MASON WILLIAMS, lawyer; b. Atlanta, May 29, 1946; s. Donald Grier and Katherine Mason (Williams) S.; m. Linda Frances Partee, June 13, 1970; children: Andrew Mason, Walter Martin. AB cum laude, Davidson Coll., 1968; JD, U. Chgo., 1971. Bar: Ga. 1971, U.S. Dist. Ct. (no. dist.) Ga. 1985. Assoc. Alston, Miller & Gaines, Atlanta, 1971-76, ptnr., 1976-77, Trotter, Bondurant, Griffin, Miller & Hishon, Atlanta, 1977-82, Bondurant, Miller, Hishon & Stephenson, Atlanta, 1982-85, King & Spalding, Atlanta, 1985—, mng. ptnr. Atlanta office, 2001—. Mem. fin. com. Atlanta Olympic Organizing Com., 1988-90. Mem. ABA (sect. bus. law, real property, probate and trust sect.), Am. Coll. Real Estate Lawyers, State Bar Ga. (exec. com., real property law sect. 1989-97, chair intangible rec. tax com. 1994-97), Atlanta Bar Assn. (chair real estate sect. 1981-82), Causeway Club, Capital City Club, Phi Beta Kappa, Phi Delta Phi. Avocations: sailing, skiing, jogging. Office: King & Spalding 191 Peachtree St NE Ste 4900 Atlanta GA 30303-1740

STEPHENSON, NANCY LOUISE, medical products company professional; b. Bemidji, Minn., Nov. 7, 1945; d. Raymond Julian and Dorothy Marion Stephenson. BSN, Pacific Luth. U., 1972. RN, Wash., Minn. ICU/CCU nurse various hosps., Tacoma and Mpls., 1967-72; instr. med. nursing Luth. Deaconess Hosp., Mpls., 1972-73; clin. rsch. assoc. Medtronic, 1973-76, clin. evaluation mgr., 1976-82, sr. clin. evaluation mgr., 1982-86, mgr. physicians rels., 1986-98, dir. physician rels., 1998—. Vol. Big Bros./Big Sisters Am., St. Paul, 1978-82; bd. dirs. Sight and Hearing Assn., Mpls., 1998—, Heartbeat Internat., Tampa, 2000—. Mem. N.Am. Soc. Pacing and Electrophysiology, Am. Heart Assn. Coun. Cardiovasc. Nursing, Am. Coll. Cardiology (corp. liaison bd. mem. 1996-2002, 50th Anniv. com. 1998-99), Order of Eastern Star. Democrat. Methodist. Avocations: internat. and domestic travel, reading, writing poetry. Home: 4895 Kent Dr Saint Paul MN 55126-2073 Office: Medtronic USA Inc 7000 Central Ave NE Minneapolis MN 55432-3576

STEPHENSON, PATRICIA ANN, public health researcher, educator; b. Washington, July 21, 1954; arrived in Sweden, 1990; d. Stanley Edwin and Mary Virginia (Brenneman) S.; m. Marsden Grigg Wagner, Dec. 14, 1990. BS, Calif. State U., Hayward, 1979; ScD, Johns Hopkins U., 1986. RN, Calif. Asst. prof. Sch. Pub. Health U. Wash., Seattle, 1986-90, adj. asst. prof. Sch. Nursing, 1987-90; sr. rschr. Ctr. for Pub. Health Rsch., Karlstad, Sweden, 1990-94; cons. health policy analyst, ops. rschr. Copenhagen, 1990-97; sr. advisor maternal, child health and nutrition USAID, Washington, 1998—. Vis. assoc. prof. Sch. Pub. Health U. Mich., Ann Arbor, 1995-96; cons. WHO, 1989, UNICEF, 1990—, World Bank, 1995-96. Mng. editor, co-founder European Jour. Pub. Health, 1991-94; author, editor: Tough Choices - InVitro Fertilization and the New Reproductive Technologies, 1993; contbr. articles to profl. publs. Women's health policy fellow John D. and Catherine T. MacArthur Found., 1995; recipient Commendation for work in fertility U.K. Parliament/House of Commons, 1989. Mem. APHA, Global Health Council, Delta Omega. Avocations: equestrian sports, dressage, show jumping, ballet, opera. Home: 123 Sherman Ave Takoma Park MD 20912 E-mail: pstephenson@usaid.gov.

STEPHENSON, RICHARD ISMERT, lawyer; b. Augusta, Kans., Oct. 13, 1937; s. Paul Noble and Dorothy May (Ismert) S.; m. Mary Lynn Bryden, July 2, 1967 (div. 1973); 1 child, Richard William; m. Linda Cox, Apr. 5, 1976. BA, U. Kans., 1958; JD, U. Mich., 1965. Bar: Kans. 1965, U.S. Dist. Ct. Kans. 1965, U.S. Ct. Appeals (10th cir.) 1965. Assoc. Fleeson, Gooing, Coulson & Kitch, Wichita, Kans., 1965-72, ptnr., 1973-95; gen. counsel RAGE Inc. and Affiliated Cos., 1995—. Lt. (j.g.) USNR, 1959-62. Recipient Hilden Gibson award U. Kans., 1958. Mem. ABA (forum on franchising), Def. Rsch. Inst., Internat. Assn. Def. Counsel, Kans. Bar Assn., Wichita Bar Assn., Wichita Country Club, Pi Sigma Alpha, Beta Theta Pi. Avocations: golf, fishing. Home: 9203 Killarney Wichita KS 67206-4027 Office: RAGE Inc 1313 N Webb Rd Ste 200 Wichita KS 67206-4077

STEPHENSON, RICHARD WALTER, librarian, historian, geographer; b. Washington, Nov. 22, 1930; s. Charles Herbert and Marie Viola (Umhau) S.; m. Sally Joan Larrison, Jul. 20, 1951; children: Cheryl Ann Graziano, Deborah Marie Riegert. BA, George Washington Univ., 1966; MA, Catholic Univ. Am., 1976. Libr. asst. Geography & Map Divsn. Libr. of Congress, Washington, 1951-54, reference librarian, 1954-66, head aquisitions sect., 1966-70, head reference & bibliography sect., 1970-87, specialist in Am. Cartographic History, 1987-92; cons., lectr. history of cartography , Stephens City, Va., 2002—. Instr. Sch. of Libr. Sci. Catholic Univ. Am., 1975-94; instr. geography dept. George Mason Univ., 1980-98. Author: A Plan Whol(l)y New, 1993, The Cartography of Northern Virginia, 1983, Civil War Maps, 1989; co-editor: Map Collections in the U.S. and Canada, 1985, A Geographical Bibliography for American Libraries, 1985, Virginia in Maps, 2000. Bd. dirs. Handley Regional Libr., Winchester, Va., 1995—, chair bd. dirs. 1999—; bd. dirs. Winchester-Frederick County Hist. Soc., 1996-99; acad. advisor Philip Lee Phillips Soc. Libr. Congress, 1995—. Recipient Superior Svc. award Libr. Congress, 1992, Spl. Achievement award, 1990, Honors award Spl. Libr. Assn., 1977, Outstanding Svc. to Surveying and Mapping Prof. Am. Congress on Surveying & Mapping, 1988. Mem. Washington Map Soc. (pres. 1982-83), Soc. for the History of Discoveries (coun.2000—), Historical Soc. of Washington D.C., Winchester-Frederick Co. Historical Soc. (v.p. for publ. 1997-99). Episcopalian. Avocation: golf. Home and Office: 106 Coopworth Ct Stephens City VA 22655 E-mail: rstephen_l@msn.com.

STEPHENSON, ROSCOE BOLAR, JR. state supreme court justice; b. Covington, Va., Feb. 22, 1922; AB, Washington and Lee U., 1943, JD, 1947, LL.D. (hon.), 1983. Bar: Va. 1947. Ptnr. Stephenson & Stephenson, Covington, 1947-52; commonwealth's atty. Alleghany County, Va., 1952-64; ptnr. Stephenson, Kostel, Watson, Carson and Snyder, Covington, 1964-73; judge 25th Jud. Cir. Ct. Commonwealth Va., 1973-81; justice Va. Supreme Ct., Richmond, 1981-97, sr. justice, 1997—. Recipient Covington Citizen of Yr. award, 1973, Outstanding Alumni award Covington H.S., 1973, Disting. Alumnus award Washington and Lee U., 1997. Fellow Am. Coll. Trial Lawyers; mem. Va. State Bar (council 1969-73), Va. Bar Assn., Va. Trial Lawyers Assn., Order of Coif, Omicron Delta Kappa. Home: North Ridge Hot Springs VA 24445 Office: Va Supreme Ct 214 W Main St PO Box 198 Covington VA 24426-0198 also: Va Supreme Court Supreme Court Bldg 100 N 9th St Richmond VA 23219-2335

STEPHENSON, SAMUEL EDWARD, JR. retired physician; b. Bristol, Tenn., May 16, 1926; s. Samuel Edward and Hazel Beatrice (Walters) S.; m. Janet Sue Spotts, May 16, 1970; children: Samuel Edward III, William Douglas, Dorothea Louise, Judith Maria. BS, U. S.C., 1946; MD, Vanderbilt U., 1950. Intern Butterworth Hosp., Grand Rapids, Mich., 1950-51; instr. to asso. prof. surgery Vanderbilt U., 1955-67; prof. surgery U. Fla., 1967-95, emeritus prof. clin. surgery, 1995—. Chmn. dept. surgery Univ. Hosp., Jacksonville, 1967-78 Asst. editor So. Med. Jour., 1968-88; contbr. articles to profl. jours. Co-chmn. Fla. Burn and Trauma Registry, 1974-77. Served with USNR, 1944-45. Fellow ACS; mem. Am. Coll. Chest Physicians, Masons. Home: 10553 Scott Mill Rd Jacksonville FL 32257-6227

STEPHENSON, SAMUEL FLOYD, JR. music educator; b. Cleve., Dec. 19, 1955; s. Samuel Floyd Stephenson Sr. and Lula Pearl Stephenson; m. Deborah Ann Dixon, Apr. 10, 1982; children: Allan, Aaron, Adam. BA in Music Edn., Livingstone Coll. Music tchr. Ea. Clev. City Schs., Ea. Cleve., Ohio, 1979—82; tchr. Cleve. Urban Luth. Sch., Cleve., 1985—88; substitute music tchr. Cleve. City Schs., 1988—90; tchr. Warrensville Heights City Schs., Warrensville Heights, 1990—. Music tchr. Shaw H.S., Ea. Cleve., 1983, cons., 83; music instr. Rainey Inst., Cleve., 1981—83, Sannaa Music Sch., Cleve., 1984—87. Avocations: sports, travel, music, attending concerts, family activities. Home: 1052 Elbon Rd Cleveland Heights OH 44121 Office: Warrensville Heights City Schools 4270 Northfield Rd Warrensville Heights OH 44128

STEPHENSON, STEVEN LEE, biologist, educator; b. Washington, Mar. 28, 1943; s. Elbert Arnold and Madine Scott Stephenson; m. Barbara Jane Creel; children: Rebecca. BS, Lynchburg Coll., 1968; MS, Va. Poly. Inst. and State U., 1970, PhD, 1977. Prof. of biology Fairmont State Coll., W.Va., 1976—2002. Editor: (book) Upland Forests of West Virginia, 1993. Grantee travel grant, Fulbright Commn., 1987. Mem.: Sthn. Appalachian Botanical Soc., Mycological. Soc. Am., W.Va. Acad. Sci. (pres. 1988—90). Home: 1115 Morningstar Lane Fairmont WV 26554-2470 Office: Fairmont State College 1201 Locust Avenue Fairmont WV 26554-2470 Personal E-mail: sstephenson@mail.fscwv.edu. Business E-Mail: sstephenson@mail.fscwv.edu.

STEPHENSON, TONI EDWARDS, publisher, investment management executive, communications executive; b. Bastrop, La., July 23, 1945; d. Sidney Crawford and Grace Erleene Little; m. Arthur Emmet Stephenson Jr., June 17, 1967; 1 child Tessa Lyn. Grad. owner/pres. mgmt. program, Harvard Bus. Sch. Pres., dir. Gen. Comm., Inc., Denver; sr. v.p., founder Stephenson & Co., 1971—; gen. ptnr. Viking Fund; ptnr. Stephenson Properties, Stephenson Ventures, Stephenson Mgmt. Co.; v.p. Startek, Inc. Bd. dirs. Startek Europe Ltd., Startek Pacific, Ltd.; v.p., dir. corp. commn. Startek, Inc. Past. pres. Children's Hosp. Assn. Vols.; past troop leader Girl Scouts Am.; v.p. Anchor Ctr. for Blind Children; past dir. The Children's Hosp., St. Joseph's Hosp., Cherry Creek H.S. Parent Tchr. Conf. Orgn. Mem. Harvard Bus. Sch. Club Colo., DAR, Delta Gamma, Jonathan Club, Annabel's (London), Thunderbird Country Club, Glenmoor Country Club, Denver Petroleum Club.

STEPHERSON, BRIAN EDWARD, psychological social worker, artist, writer; b. N.Y.C. s. Lemuel Arthur and Margaret Sue (Badgett) S. BA, Columbia U., 1965; postgrad., Hunter Coll., 1981-83. In psychol. social work, N.Y.C. Writer prose, essays and non-fiction. Recipient Pres.'s achievement award Pres. Ronald Reagan, 1984. Mem. Columbia Coll. Club. Republican. Episcopal. Avocation: writing. Home: 50 E 18th St E9 Brooklyn NY 11226

STEPIEN, CAROL ANN, molecular geneticist, fisheries educator; b. Cleve., Apr. 21, 1958; d. Theodore John and Anna M. (Bowerman) Stepien. BS, Bowling Green U., 1979; MS, U. So. Calif., 1980, PhD, 1985. Lectr. U. San Diego, 1984-86; rsch. assoc. Hubbs Marine Research Inst., San Diego, 1985-86, NSF and Scripps Instn. Oceanography, La Jolla, 1986-88; Sloan postdoctoral fellowship in molecular evolution, 1989-91; rsch. assoc. NRC/Marine Fisheries/NOAA, 1991-92; asst. prof. molecular evolutionary biology Case Western Res. U., Cleve., 1992-2000; prof., dir. Gt. Lakes Environ. Genetics Lab. Cleve. State U., 2000—. Editor: (with Thomas D. Kocher) Molecular Systematics of Fishes, 1997; contbr. articles to profl. jours. NSF fellow, 1986-88; Lerner Marine grantee Am. Mus. Natural History, 1982-84. Mem. Am. Soc. Ichthyologists and Herpetologists (Best Paper 1983), Soc. Systematic Biologists, Am. Fisheries Soc., Soc. for Study of Evolution, Soc. Systematic Biology. Avocations: scuba diving, underwater photography. Office: Cleve State U MC-219 Ctr Environ Sci-Tech-Policy Cleveland OH 44114-4434 Fax: 216-687-5393. E-mail: c.stepien@csuohio.edu.

STEPKE, RUSSELL, investment banker, lawyer; b. Milw., May 7, 1942; s. Richard F. and Esther M. Stepke; m. Sandra A. Reese, Sept. 15, 2001; children: Chad, Carrie, Bret, Rachel. BA, Marquette U., 1965, JD, 1968. Bar: Wis. 68. Ptnr. Hersh, Stupar, Stepke & Gollin, 1968—71; mng. ptnr. Stepke, Kossow, Trebon & Stadtmueller, 1970—79; CEO Resource Fin. Corp., Chgo., 1980—. Pres. Fox Point (Wis.) Sch. Bd., 1982—88; trustee Village of Fox Point, 1976—80. Mem.: ABA, Wis. Bar Assn., Chgo. Club. Avocations: golf, platform tennis, skiing, scuba. Office: Resource Fin Corp 190 S LaSalle St 60603 Office Fax: 312-673-7125.

STEPKOSKI, ROBERT JOHN, automobile dealership executive; b. Floral Park, N.Y., Mar. 15, 1933; s. John Vincent and Mary Victoria (Rudnicki) S.; m. Caryl Diane Henderson, June 20, 1953; 1 child, Caryl Dale Stepkoski Yarley. 1000 hour cert., L.I. Drafting Sch., Freeport, N.Y., 1952; cert. in forms design, NYU, 1957; AAS, C.W. Post Coll., 1961; continuing edn. certs., Clemson U., 1981-82. Distbn. mapper and planner L.I. Lighting Co., Roslyn and Hicksville, 1952-57, records analyst Hicksville, 1957-58, statis. analyst Mineola, 1958-65, mgr. budget divsn., 1965-70, econ. analyst, 1970-71; sec.-treas., bus. mgr. Hunter Chevrolet Co., Hendersonville, N.C., 1971-85; compt., asst. sec., asst. treas. Hughes Chem. Corp., Fletcher, 1985-86; contr. Raleigh (N.C.) Toyota, 1986-87; dir. ops. Boyd Pontiac-Cadillac-Buick, Inc.,

Hendersonville, 1988-95; fin. cons., 1995—. With U.S. Army, 1953-55. Mem. Hendersonville Country Club, Kiwanis (bd. dirs. Hendersonville 1976-79, fund raising treas. 1976-86, Outstanding Committeeman award 1976, Disting. Svc. award 1981, Outstanding Svc. award 1995, 97, 25 Yr. Legion of Honor award 1999). Avocations: golf, model trains. Home: 15 White Squirrel Ln Hendersonville NC 28739-8360

STEPONAITIS, VINCAS PETRAS, archaeologist, anthropologist, educator; b. Boston, Aug. 10, 1953; s. Vincas and Elena (Povydis) S.; m. Laurie Cameron, Dec. 31, 1976; children: Elena Anne, Lillian Kazimiera. AB in Anthropology magna cum laude, Harvard U., 1974; MA in Anthropology, U. Mich., 1975, PhD in Anthropology, 1980. From lectr. to assoc. prof. dept. anthropology SUNY, Binghamton, 1979-87; assoc. prof. U. N.C., Chapel Hill, 1988-94, prof., 1995—, dir. Rsch. Labs. Archaeology, 1988—. Bd. dirs. Archael. Conservancy, Cr. for Maya Rsch.; guest worker Nat. Bur. Standards, 1979; adj. lectr. dept. anthropology SUNY, Binghamton, 1979; lectr. and presenter in field. Author: Ceramics, Chronology, and Community Patterns, An Archaeological Study at Moundville, 1983, Archaeology of the Moundville Chiefdom, 1998, (CD-Rom) Excavating Occaneechi Town, 1998; editor Southeastern Archaeology, 1984-87; regional editor Investigations in Am. Archaeology, 1987-91; mem. editl. bd. Prehistory Press, 1990-97, Southern Cultures, 1992—, Am. Archaeology, 1996-2000; contbr. articles to profl. jours. Smithsonian Instn. fellow, 1978-79; grantee NSF, 1978-80, 83, 89-92, 94, 2000, Wenner-Gren Found., 1981, 86-88, Nat. Geographic Soc., 1987-88, Z. Smith Reynolds Found., 1992-94. Fellow Am. Anthrop. Assn.; mem. Soc. Am. Archaeology (Presdl. Recognition award 1993-94, exec. com. 1983-84, treas. 1992-94, pres. 1997-99), bd. dirs., Archaeological Conservancy, 2000-, bd. dirs., Center for Maya Research, 2002- Southeastern Archaeol. Conf. (editor 1984-87, pres. 1990-92), N.C. Archaeol. Soc. (exec. sec. 1988-91, sec. 1991-96), N.C. Archaeol. Coun. (exec. com. 1988-92), Archaeol. Soc., S.C., Ala. Archaeol. Soc., Miss. Archaeol. Soc., La. Archaeol. Soc., Tenn. Anthrop. Assn. Office: U NC Rsch Labs Archaeology Alumni Bldg Cb 3120 Chapel Hill NC 27599-0001

STEPPUTTIS, SUSAN LYN, management consultant, educator; b. Martins Ferry, Ohio, July 28, 1953; d. Edward Joseph and Louise Irene (Kolb) Kowalczyk; m. Richard Dale Stepputtis, Aug. 20, 1977. BA in History, Muskingum Coll., 1975; diploma in gen. banking, Ohio Sch. Banking, 1982; grad. banking diploma, Grad. Sch. Banking, 1986; Am. Inst. Banking mgmt. diploma, Wheeling Jesuit U., 1983; MBA, Franciscan U., 1989. Asst. v.p. Belmont County Nat. Bank, St. Clairsville, Ohio, 1975-84; v.p. Buckeye Savs. and Loan Co., Bellaire, 1984-86; lectr., instr. Grad. Sch. Banking, Madison, 1989—. Adj. prof. W.Va. No., Wheeling, 1982-83, Belmont Tech. Coll., St. Clairsville, 1983—; pres., CEO Staff Mgmt. Cons., Inc., St. Clairsville, Ohio, 1986—; adv. St. Clairsville City Sch. Bus. Adv. Coun., 1990—. Contbr. articles to mags. Chairwoman, dir. New Covenant Acad., St. Clairsville, Ohio, 1990—96; exec. com. Belmont County Rep. Party, 1996—, ctrl. committeewoman, 1996—; chairwoman county chpt. Christian Coalition, 1996—2000; founder Concerned Christian Citizens, 1998—2000. Recipient Woman of Yr. Award Belmont County Young Reps., 1998, Pronouncer's award Belmont County Spelling Bee, 1998. Mem.: Am. Inst. Banking (2nd v.p. 1980—85, dir.), Rotary (charter dir. St. Clairsville Sunrise 1996—, chairwoman vocat. svc. St. Clairsville Sunrise 1996—98, 1st v.p. St. Clairsville Sunrise 1999, pres.-elect St. Clairsville Sunrise 2000, pres. St. Clairsville Sunrise 2001, asst. dist. govt. #6690 2002—). Republican. American Baptist. Avocations: piano, golf, swimming, reading. Office: Staff Mgmt Cons 212 Maple Ave Saint Clairsville OH 43950-9289

STEPTOE, JAVAKA, writer, illustrator; b. N.Y.C., Apr. 19, 1971; s. John Steptoe and Stephanie Douglas. BFA, Cooper Union for Advancement of Sci. and Art, 1995. Cons. Harlem Textile Works, N.Y.C. Illustrator, poet: In Daddy's Arms I Am Tall, 1997 (Coretta Scott King Illustrator award, ALA Notable Children's Book, Reading Magic award Parenting mag., Tex. Bluebonnet award Master List, Soc. Illustrators Original Art Show), illustrator: Do You Know What I'll Do?, 2000, illustrator: A Pocketful of Poems, 2001;exhibitions include Hostos C.C., N.Y.C., 1997, Children's Mus. Manhattan, 1998, Creative Arts Workshop, New Haven, 1998, Soc. Illustrators, N.Y.C., 1998, commd., exhibitions include Meml. Art Gallery, Rochester, NY, 2000, Art Inst. Chgo., 2000—01, Bklyn. Pub. Libr., 2001; contbr. Recipient award, NY Found. on Arts, 2001. Mem.: Writers Union. Avocations: pool, wind surfing, music. Mailing: PO Box 330-170 Brooklyn NY 11233-0170

STERBENZ, JAMES PHILIP GUENTHER, computer network scientist; s. Bertram L. Jr. and Lois Sterbenz; m. Kristine L.G. Sterbenz; 1 child, Katarina. BSEE, BSCS, ABEcon, Wash. U., 1981, MS, 1986, DSc, 1991. Adv. engr., scientist IBM Rsch., Milford, Conn., Hawthorne, N.Y.; prin. MTS GTE Labs., Waltham, Mass.; sr. network scientist BBN Technologies, Cambridge, mgr. mobile wireless and active networking. Chair steering com. Protocols for High-Speed Networks, 2000—. Author: High Speed Networking, 2001; editor: Protocols for High Speed Networks, 1999; mem. editl. bd. IEEE Network, Computer Networks, 1999—, Jour. Comm. and Networks, 2000—. Mem.: IEEE (sr.; chmn. ComSoc TCGN 1994—99, steering com. 1999—), Protocols for High-Speed Networks (keynote address 1994, program chair 1999, steering com. chair 2000—), Internat. Fedn. Info. Processing Soc., Interplanetary Chpt. Internet Soc., Assn. Computing Machinery (vice chair SIGCOMM 99 conf.). Avocation: railway signaling. Home: PO Box 187 Hopkinton MA 01748-0187 Office: BBN Technologies 10 Moulton St Cambridge MA 02138-1191 E-mail: jpgs@acm.org.

STERCHI, THOMAS NEAL, lawyer; b. Olney, Ill., Aug. 6, 1945; s. Alfred Rhodell and Gladys Marie (Chaplin) S.; m. Mary-Michael Kelly, Dec. 31, 1990; children: Laura, Neal, Sarah, Megan. BS, Ea. Ill. U., 1967; JD, U. Mo., 1972. Bar: Mo., U.S. Dist. Ct. (we. and ea. dists.) Kans., U.S. Ct. Appeals (8th and 10th cirs.), U.S. Supreme Ct. 2000. Assoc. Watson, Ess, Marshall & Enggas, Kansas City, Mo., 1972-79, ptnr., 1979-82; founding ptnr. Baker Sterchi Cowden & Rice, L.L.C., 1982—. Past chmn. pharm. med. device litigation section Fedn. Def. Corp. Counsel , 1997—99; mem. products liability section, mem. devel. com., new mems. com. and admissions com. Fedn. Def. Corp. Counsel; past nat. coordinating trial counsel E.R. Squibb & Sons, Inc.; nat. coordinating trial counsel Bracco Diagnostics Inc. ; product liability adv. coun. Def. Rsch. Inst. Author: Case notes and Comments Mo. Law Review, 1972, Mo. Product Liability Case Survey, 1991; contbr. author: TIPS Jour. 1999 Annual Survey. Pub. relations com. Jackson Cmty. Med. Soc., Kansas City, Mo., 1979-80; commr. Great Am. Basketball League, Johnson City, Kans., 1992-97; pres. Western Mo. Def. Lawyers Orgn., 1985-87. With U.S. Army, 1969-71. Mem.: ATLA, ABA (litigation and tort and ins. practice sects.), Kansas City Claims Assn., Kansas City Met. Bar Assn., Mo. Orgn. Def. Lawyers (bd. dirs. 1989—95), Fedn. Def. and Corp. Counsel, Internat. Assn. Ins. Law. Avocations: golf, tennis. Office: 2400 Pershing Rd Ste 500 Kansas City MO 64108-2504 Fax: 816-472-0288. E-mail: sterchi@bscr-law.com.

STERLING, ARTHUR JAMES, legal assistant; b. Pineville, La., July 27, 1944; s. Leon Henry and Dorothy Mae Sterling; children: Hope, Monique, Heather. AA in Bus. Adminstrn., Compton C.C., 1986; student, U. Southern Calif., 1988-89; AA in Bus. Paralegal, Cerritos C.C., Norwalk, 1994; PhD, U. of Life, 2000. With U.S. Naval Weapons Sta., Seal Beach, Calif., 1979-83, Norwalk Superior Ct., 1991; law clk.; guidance counselor, 2000—02. Dave Holt Meml scholar, K.T. Skula meml. scholar, Johnson Controls, Inc. Fund scholar, Amy Welch Meml. scholar. Mem. Soc. for Advancement of Mgmt., Phi Beta Lambda. Democrat. Avocations: computers, cooking, reading. Home: 4216 Carlin Ave #C Lynwood CA 90262-5208

STERLING, DAVID MARK, graphic designer; b. Okla., Apr. 28, 1951; s. Paul J. and Roberta Myrtice (Rousseau) S. BA, Oklahoma City U., 1973; MFA, Cranbrook Acad. Art, Bloomfield Hills, Mich., 1978. Exhibit designer Omniplex, Oklahoma City, 1973-76; art dir. ID Mag., N.Y.C., 1979-81; prin. Doublespace, 1982-94; founder, prin. World Studio and World Studio Found., 1992—. Graphic design faculty Sch. of Visual Arts, N.Y.C., 1992—. Pub. mags. Fetish, 1979-81, Sphere, 1994—; works included in books: Graphic Style: From Victorian to Post-Modern, 1988, New American Design, 1988, Low Budget/High Quality Design, 1990, Cranbrook Design: The New Discourse, 1990, Contemporary Graphic Design, 1991, Mixing Messages: Graphic Design in Contemporary Culture, 1996; represented in permanent collections at Cranbrook Acad. Art, Libr. of Congress, Michael C. Rockefeller Arts Ctr., Cooper Hewitt Nat. Design Mus., Smithsonian Instn. Recipient Am. Inst. Graphic Arts awards for Cover Show, N.Y., 1984, for Comm. Graphics, N.Y., 1986, 90; recipient Type Dirs. Club award, 1990, 92, Best of Category award Design Rev., N.Y., 1986, Am. Assn. of Mus., 1986, 88, Am. Ctr. for Design, 1990, Indsl. Design Rev. award, 1985, 86, 88, 93, N.Y. Festival awards, Bronze Apple award Indsl. Designers Soc. Am., 1996; featured Internat. Design Mag., ID40, 1996, 2001. Democrat. Office: World Studio 9th Fl 225 Varick St Fl 9 New York NY 10014-4304

STERLING, DONALD EUGENE, civil engineer; b. Rootville, Pa., May 30, 1939; s. Blanche Marie (Phelps) Vanik; m. Janet Leigh Wotring, Apr. 23, 1983. A in Engring., Pa. State U., 1966; BSCE, W.Va. Inst. Tech., 1981; MS in Engring., W.Va. Coll. Grad. Studies, Charleston, 1987. Cert. engr. technician. Hwy. drafting technician W.Va. Dept. Transp., Charleston, 1965-67, hwy. engr. technician, 1967-82, design rev. engr., 1982-89, sr. rev. engr., 1989-94; civil engr. Woolpert Cons., W.Va., 1994-96; asst. project mgr. Michael Baker Jr. Inc. Cons. Engrs., 1998-99. Tutor Charleston Dist. Outreach Ministries, 1981-83, counselor Camp For Under Privileged Children, 1982; treas., v.p. Kanawha City Midget Football Team, 1978. Sgt. USAF, 1959-63, with Pa. Nat. Guard, 1956-59. Recipient certs. Appreciation Kanawha City Midget Football Team, 1978, Charleston Dist. Outreach Ministries, 1981-83. Mem. ASCE (W.Va. sect. pres. 1990-91, v.p. 1989-90; pres. Charleston Br. 1988-89, sec., treas. 1987-88; corr. mem. nat. com. on employment conditions 1989-91). Democrat. Methodist. Home: 821 Scenic Dr Charleston WV 25311-1522 Office: Michael Baker Cons Engrs 5088 Washington St W Charleston WV 25313-1536 E-mail: don.jan.sterling@worldnet.att.net.

STERLING, ELEANOR J. science association director; PhD in Anthropology and Forestry and Environ. Studies, Yale U., 1993. Adj. prof. in conservation biology Columbia U.; dir. Ctr. for Biodiversity and Conservation, Am. Mus. Natural History, N.Y.C. Office: Ctr for Biodiversity and Conservation Am Mus Natural History Central Park W at 79th St New York NY 10024*

STERLING, ERIC EDWARD, lawyer, legal policy advocate; b. N.Y.C., Oct. 25, 1949; s. Bowen and Helen (Champnella) S.; m. June S. Beittel, Oct. 1996; 1 child, Maya Rebecca. BA, Haverford Coll., 1973; JD, Villanova (Pa.) U., 1976. Bar: Pa. 1976, U.S. Supreme Ct. 1980. Asst. pub. defender Del. County, Media, Pa., 1976-79; asst. counsel sub. on criminal justice U.S. Ho. Reps., Washington, 1979-81, counsel subcom. on crime, 1981-89; pres. The Criminal Justice Policy Found., 1989—. Cons. Dem., Rep. and Libertarian Party orgns. and candidates, 1982—; cons. The Brookings Instn., 1990, Office of Pers. Mgmt., 1990, GAO, 1992, Nat. News Media, 1989—; lectr. Am. U. Sch. Pub. Affairs, Washington, 1984-86, U. Colo. Conf. on World Affairs, 1990-99, others. Founder, dir. Nat. Drug Strategy Network, 1989-2000; mem. D.C. Mayor's Adv. Com. on Drug Abuse, 1990, Baltimore Mayor's Task force on Drug Policy, 1993; mem. steering com. D.C. Safe Streets Project, 1990-91; bd. dirs. Families Against Mandatory Minimums Found., 1991—, Forfeiture Endangers Am. Rights, 1993-95, William Penn House, 1992-98, Marijuana Policy Project, 1995—, Vol. Com. of Lawyers, 1995—. Recipient Cert. of Appreciation, U.S. Bur. Alcohol, Tobacco and Firearms, 1982, U.S. Postal Inspection Svc., 1988, Justice Gerald LeDain award for achievement in law Drug Policy Found., 1999. Mem. ABA (individual rights and responsibility sect.), APHA, Am. Soc. Criminology, Nat. Assn. Criminal Def. Lawyers. Mem. Soc. Of Friends. Avocations: swimming, bicycling, hiking. Office: The Criminal Justice Policy Found 8730 Georgia Ave Ste 400 Silver Spring MD 20910-3649 E-mail: esterling@cjpf.org.

STERLING, KEIR BROOKS, historian, educator; b. N.Y.C., Jan. 30, 1934; s. Henry Somers and Louise Noel (de Wetter) S.; m. Anne Cox Diller, Apr. 3, 1961; children: Duncan Diller, Warner Strong, Theodore Craig. BS, Columbia U., 1961, MA, 1963, profl. diploma, 1965, PhD, 1973. Asst. to dean Sch. Gen. Studies Columbia U., N.Y.C., 1959-65; rsch. grantee Eng., 1965-66; instr. history Pace U., N.Y.C. and Pleasantville, N.Y., 1966-71, from asst. prof. to assoc. prof., 1971-77, adj. prof., 1977-83; ordnance br. historian U.S. Army Ordnance Ctr. and Sch., Aberdeen Proving Ground, Md., 1983-94, Ft. Lee, Va., 1994-98; historian U.S. Army Combined Arms Support Command, 1998—. Lectr. gen. counseling Bklyn. Coll., CUNY, 1967-68; asst. acad. dean, adj. asst. prof. history, coord. Am. studies program, dir. summer session Marymount Coll., Tarrytown, N.Y., 1968-71; asst. dean Rockland C.C., SUNY, Suffern, 1971-73; vis. prof. Mercy Coll., Westchester C.C., King's Coll., Nyack Coll., U. Wis., 1971, 75, 78-80, 83, Harford (Md.) C.C., 1987-94; adj. instr. Army Logistics Mgmt. Coll., Ft. Lee, 1995—; co-project dir. Am. Ornithologists Union Centennial Hist., Project, 1976-89; cons. Arno Press, Inc., 1973-78, Coun. State Colls. of N.J., 1984-85, NSF, 1983—, Am. Trust for Brit. Libr., 1986-89; active Columbia U. Seminar on History and Philosophy of Sci., 1976-83; archivist, historian mem. steering com. sect. mammalogy Internat. Union Biol. Scis., 1985—. Author: Last of the Naturalists: The Career of C. Hart Merriam, 1974, 77; editor: Notes on the Animals of North America (B.S. Barton), 1974; assoc. editor: Am. Nat. Biog., 1989-98; editor, contbr.: Natural Sciences in America, 1974, 68 vols., 1974, Biologists and Their World, 1978, 77 vols.; gen. editor, contbr.: The International History of Mammalogy, 1987—; sr. editor, contbr. (with R. Harmond, G. Cevasco, and L. Hammond) Biographical Dictionary of American and Canadian Naturalists and Environmentalists, 1997; editor, contbr. to numerous works in history, Am. natural scis., and Am. mil. history. With U.S. Army, 1954—56. Grantee Theodore Roosevelt Meml. Fund, Am. Mus. Natural History, 1967, Nat. Geog. Soc., 1977, NSF/Am. Soc. Mammalogists, 1978, NSF, 1981-82, IREX, 1982. Mem.: Assn. Bibliography of History (mem. coun. 1994—), Am. Soc. Environ. History (sec., mem. governing bd., editor newsletter), Am. Ornithologists Union (co-chmn. centennial hist. com., mem. archives com., grantee 1976, 1977), Am. Soc. Mammalogists (mem. archives com., mem. 75th ann. com.), Phi Delta Kappa, Sigma Tau Delta, Phi Alpha Theta. Democrat. Episcopalian. Home: 7104 Wheeler Rd Richmond VA 23229-6939 Office: 3901 A Ave Ste 100 Fort Lee VA 23801-1807 E-mail: kbs1934@cs.com, sterlink@lee.army.mil.

STERLING, MICHAEL ERWIN, lawyer; b. Chgo., Feb. 3, 1944; s. Dave and Roselle (Yarowsky) Silverman; m. Alicia Ruth Hayes, June 10, 1966; children: Aaron, Isaac, Jacob. BSC, DePaul U., 1965, JD, 1967; LLM, NYU, 1970. Bar: Ill., 1967, N.Y., 1969, Wash., 1970, U.S. Tax Ct., 1969, U.S. Ct. Appeals (9th cir.), 1970, U.S. Supreme Ct., 1971. Tax atty. J.K. Lasser, N.Y.C., 1968-70; staff atty. Preston, Gates & Ellis, Seattle, 1970-72; tax counsel PACCAR, Inc., Bellevue, Wash., 1972-79; pvt. practice Bellevue and Issaquah, 1979—. Mem. AICPA, Wash. Bar Assn. (chmn. sect. taxation 1981-82, vice chmn. 1979-80), Tax Execs. Inst. (v.p. 1979-80). Republican. Office: 4411 186th Ave SE Issaquah WA 98027-9759

STERLING, PHILLIP DUNCAN, English educator; b. Pontiac, Mich., Nov. 10, 1950; s. James Foster and Barbara Jane Sterling; m. Debra Jean Stack, Dec. 7, 1974 (div. Aug. 1998); children: Matthew, Rachel, Sarah, Andrew. BA, Centre Coll., Danville, Ky., 1972; MA, Ctrl. Mich. U., 1974; PhD, Bowling Green State U., 1979. From asst. prof. to assoc. prof. Keuka Coll., Keuka Park, N.Y., 1979-87; prof. English, Ferris State U., Big Rapids, 1987—. Sr. Fulbright lectr. Cooun. for Internat. Exch. Scholars, Belgium, 1992-93, Poland, 1997-98. Author: (poetry) Mutual Shores, 2000. Recipient Disting. Faculty award Mich. Assn. Governing Bds., 1992. Mem. Poetry Soc. Am., Acad. Am. Poets, Poets and Writers, Fulbright Assn. (life). Avocation: cycling. Home: 20600 Edgewood Dr Big Rapids MI 49307 Office: Ferris State U 820 Campus Dr Big Rapids MI 49307 Fax: 231-591-2910. E-mail: sterling@ferris.edu.

STERLING, RAYMOND LESLIE, civil engineering educator, researcher, consultant; b. London, Apr. 19, 1949; came to U.S., 1966; s. Richard Howard and Joan Valeria (Skinner) S.; m. Linda Lee Lundquist, Aug. 8, 1970 (div. Sept. 1982); children: Paul, Juliet, Erika; m. Janet Marie Kjera, Aug. 20, 1983; 1 child, Zoey. B in Civil and Structural Engring. with 1st class honors, U. Sheffield, Eng., 1970; MS in Geol. Engring., U. Minn., 1975, PhDCE, 1977. Registered civil engr., Minn.; chartered structural engr., Eng. Engr. trainee Met. Water Bd., London, 1968; civil engr. Egil Wefald and Assocs., Cons. Engrs., Mpls., 1969-71; structural engr. Husband and Co., Cons. Engrs., Eng., 1971-73; rsch. asst. U. Minn., Mpls., 1973-77, dir. Underground Space Ctr., 1977-95, asst. prof. dept. civil and mineral engring., 1977-83, assoc. prof., 1983-95; project. coord., structural engr. Setter, Leach and Lindstrom, Inc., 1976-77; prin. cons. Itasca Cons. Group, Inc., 1981-94; prof. civil engring. La. Tech. U., Ruston, 1995—, dir. Trenchless Tech. Ctr., 1995—. Vice-chmn. U.S. Nat. com. on tunneling tech. NRC, NAS, 1990-91, chmn. 1992-94, mem. com. on infrastructure, 1991-93, mem. bd. infrastructure and the constructed environment, 1994-96; acting co-dir. Minn. Cold Climate Bldg. Rsch. Ctr. U. Minn., 1987-89, co-dir. Bldg. Energy Rsch. Ctr., 1986, mem. speaker's bur., active numerous other u. coms.; mem. energy adv. com. Legis. Com. on Minn. Resources, 1989-95; mem. com. on moisture control in bldgs. U.S. Bldg. Thermal Envelope Coordinating Coun., 1985-86; mem. program planning com. on bldg. founds. U.S. Dept. Energy, 1985-95; mem. adv. bd. for energy efficient residence demonstration project Nat. Assn. Home Builders, 1980; mem. Gov's. Exxon Oil Overcharge Adv. Task Force, 1986, Mpls. Energy Future Com., 1980-81, Scientist's Inst. for Pub. Info., N.Y.; cons. U.S. Army Corps. Engrs., UN, N.Y., Opus Corp., Mpls., Dames & Moore Internat., London, City of Mpls., Larson Engring., White Bear, Minn., Pilsbury Co., Mpls., Colgate Divsn. Sch., Rochester, N.Y., many others; adv. prof. Chongqing Jianzhu U., Sichuan, People's Republic China, 1985—; vis. rschr. Nat. Inst. Pollution and Resources MITI, Japan, 1991; vis. prof. U. Mo., Rolla, 1979; Shimizu prof. civil and mineral engring., U. Minn., 1988-95; adv. prof. Tongji U., Shanghai, 1996—; mem. eminent speaker program Instn. Engrs., Australia, 1993; hon. prof. Changsha Rwy. U., China, 1998—; lectr., presenter numerous profl. meetings. Author: Earth Sheltered Housing Design: Guidelines, Examples and References, 1978, transl. into Chinese, French, Spanish and Russian, 2d. edit., 1985, (with others) Earth Sheltered Community Design: The Design of Energy-Efficient Residential Communities, 1980 (award for Best Book in Architecture and Urban Planning Profl. and Scholarly div. Assn. Am. Pubs. 1981), transl. into Spanish, 1981, Underground Building Design, 1983, translated into Japanese and Russian, others, Building Foundation Handbook, 1988, Underground Space Design, 1993, others; editor: (with others) Key Questions in Rock Mechanics: Proc. 29th U.S. Symposium on Rock Mechanics, 1988; contbr. articles to profl. jours. including Jour. Agrl. Engring., Internat. Jour. Rock Mechanics and Mining Scis., Exptl. Mechanics, many others. Recipient Young Engr. of Yr. award Minn. Fedn. Engring. Soc., 1982, Applied Rsch. award in rock mechanics NRC; elected fgn. mem. Acad. Engring. of Russian Fedn., 1993; grantee Shimizu Constrn. Co., 1987-93, Nat. Assn. Homebuilders, 1989, U.S. Dept. Energy, 1989-90, NSF, 1991, Minn. Dept. Transp., 1991, ASHRAE, 1991-92, many others. Fellow ASCE (pres. Minn. sect. 1990-91, bd. dirs. 1985-92, Young Civil Engr. of Yr. award 1982), Instn. Civil Engrs., Inst. Structural Engrs., Royal Soc. Arts, Mfrs. & Commerce; mem. NSPE, Am. Underground Constrn. Assn., Internat. Tunneling Assn. (coordinating editor jour. 1986—, co-sr. editor 1996—, animateur working group on direct/indirect advantages of underground structures 1997—), N.Am. Soc. Trenchless Tech. (bd. dirs. 1996—, treas. 1997, internat. rep. 1998—, vice chmn. 1999). Achievements include research in underground construction, underground space utilization, trenchless technology, rock mechanics, and energy use in buildings. Office: Trenchless Technology Ctr Louisiana Tech U PO Box 10348 Ruston LA 71272

STERLING, RICHARD LEROY, English and foreign language educator; b. Atlantic City, Feb. 18, 1941; s. Richard Leroy and Anne (Bass) S. BA, Am. U., 1968; MA, Cath. U., 1971; PhD, Howard U., 1990. Head Start tchr. D.C. pub. schs., summer 1968; tchr. French and English, adult and continuing edn. D.C. Pub. Schs., Washington, 1969-71, 76-83; instr. French Howard U., 1973-76, grad. teaching asst., 1983-85, instr., lectr. in French, 1985-89; tchr. English Community-Based Orgns., D.C. Pub. Schs., 1989-91; asst. prof. French and English Bowie (Md.) State U., 1991-97, assoc. prof. French, 1997—. Tchr. summer enrichment program for gifted children Sch. Edn., Howard U., summers 1985, 86; tchr. ESL, D.C. Pub. Schs., summer, 1989, 94; asst. coord. Humanities Immersion Program, Project Access for H.S. Students, Bowie State U., summer 1997-98; vice-chmn. World Centennial Conf.; French, Am. and Planetary Dimensions of Saint-John Perse, U. D.C., 1987; mem. adv. coun. Northeast Conf. Teaching Fgn. Langs; NAACP-ACT-SO competition humanities judge 1997-2000; adj. assoc. prof. English, Southeastern U. Washington, summer 1998—; judge D.C. Pub. Schs. World Langs. Festival, 2001; presenter, book reviewer in field. Author: The Prose Works of Saint-John Perse: Towards an Understanding of His Poetry, 1994; contbr. articles to profl. jours. Active Assn. Democratique des Francais a L.Etranger, 1988—, Senegal friendship com. Office Cmty. and Ethnic Affairs, Prince George's County Govt., Md., 1993-94, Inst. for Haitian Cultural and Sci. Affairs, 1992-94, local arrangements com. Conf. Coll. Composition and Communication, Washington, 1995, Friends of the Corcoran, 1999; membership com. and outreach com. St. John's Ch., Washington, 1993, ch. growth com., 1995. With U.S . Army, 1964-66. Mem. MLA, Coll. Lang. Assn., Middle Atlantic Writers Assn. (chmn. essay contest com. 1995-2000, bd. dirs. 2000—), Samuel Beckett Soc., Societe des Professeurs Francais et Francophones d'Amerique, Zora Neale Hurston Soc., Am. Assn. Tchrs. French (sec.-treas. Washington chpt. 1986-90), Nat. Cathedral Assn., Md. Fgn. Lang. Assn. (bd. dirs. 1997-2001), Coun. Internat. d'Etudes Francophones, Friends D.C. Superior Ct. (bd. dirs. 1996—), Univ. Club (Washington), Pi Delta Phi, Sigma Tau Delta. Democrat. Episcopalian. Avocations: classical music, history, travel. Office: Bowie State U Dept English & Modern Langs Bowie MD 20715 E-mail: rsterling@bowiestate.edu.

STERLING, ROBERT LEE, JR. investment company executive; b. Cleve., June 12, 1933; s. Robert Lee and Kathryn (Durell) S.; children from previous marriage: Robert Livingston, William Lee, Cameron Platt; m. Joyce Lanier Milner, June 4, 1994. Student, U. Edinburgh, Scotland, 1955; BA, Brown U., 1956; MBA, Columbia U., 1962. Corp. rsch. analyst Morgan Guaranty Trust, N.Y.C., 1962-63; asst. comptr. Western Hemisphere CPC Internat., 1963—76; v.p. White, Weld & Co., Inc., 1976—78, Merrill Lynch Asset Mgmt., 1978-80, Wood, Struthers & Winthrop Mgmt. Corp., N.Y.C., 1980-83; sr. v.p. Shearson Lehman Bros. Asset Mgmt., 1983-88; v.p., sr. portfolio mgr. Chase Manhattan Bank, 1988-93; sr. v.p., sr. portfolio mgr. Melhado, Flynn & Assocs., Inc., N.Y.C., 1993—; mng. ptnr. Winthrop Asset Mgmt., 1995—. Mem. adv. bd. Mus. Modern Art, Oxford U., Eng.; trustee Soc. of the Four Arts, Palm Beach, Norton Mus. of Art, Palm Beach, Preservation Soc., Palm Beach, Comty. Chest, United Way, Palm Beach, Game Coservancy, U.S. Mem. New Eng. Soc. (past pres., J.P. Morgan medal), St. Nicholas Soc., Pilgrims, N.Y. State Soc. of Cin. (past pres.), Univ. Club (N.Y.C.), Everglades Club (Palm Beach, Fla.), Piedmount Driving Club (Atlanta), Charokee Country Club (Atlanta), Bath and Tennis Club (Palm Beach, Fla.), Anabell's (London), Alpha Delta Phi, Alpha Kappa Psi. Home: 200 Regent Park Palm Beach FL 33480 Office: Melhado Flynn & Assocs Inc 530 5th Ave New York NY 10036-5101

STERLING, SCOTT, political party official; Chmn. Dem. Party. Office: 900 Susitna Dr Wasilla AK 99654 also: PO Box 104199 Anchorage AK 99510 Business E-Mail: sasjmm@alask.net.*

STERLING, WILLIAM CARLISLE, physician assistant; b. Toledo, Oct. 18, 1942; s. Robert Kelso and Maryellen Ruth S.; m. Christina A. Clark, June 1, 1995; children: Sean Carlisle, Lyle Brent, Nelson Anthony. Student, U. Toledo, 1960-61, 65-69. Physician asst. Grand Rapids (Ohio) Med. Clinic, 1969-76, GM, Toledo, 1983-93, Brownville (Tex.) Cmty. Health, 1993-98, Excalibur Health Assocs., Brownsville, 1998—. Med. dir. Brownsville Cmty. Health, 1995-97; founder, dir. Emergency Squad Unit, Inc., Grand Rapids, 1973-83. With USN, 1961-65. Decorated Commendation medal. Mem. Am. Acad. Physicians Assts., Am. Assn. Physician Assts. Occupational Medicine (v.p.), Ohio Assn. Physician Assts., Tex. Assn. Physician Assts. Home: 805 Rose Ct Pemberville OH 43450-9437

STERMAN, GAIL K. MENDELSON, public relations specialist; b. Cleve., Mar. 18, 1940; d. Joseph S. and Ida (Horr) Kreinberg; m. Robert Louis Mendelson, June 26, 1960 (div. May 1991); 1 child, Rebecca Mendelson Schwam; m. Irving Sterman, July 2, 1995. BS in Edn., Miami U., Oxford, Ohio, 1962. Pvt. practice pub. rels. specialist, Waterloo, Iowa, 1966-68; mtg. planning cons. Wheeling, W.Va., 1970-82; cable TV prodr., host WACO TV, 1978-79; reporter WWVA radio, W.Va., 1980-82; dir. pub. and coll. rels. Wheeling Jesuit Coll., 1982-92; fundraising cons. Ketchum, Inc., Pitts., 1992-93; dir. devel. Park Sch. of Buffalo, 1993-95; pvt. practice pub. rels., mktg., fundraising cons. Boynton Beach, Fla., 1995-2000, Jacksonville, 2000—; mem. consumer adv. bd. US Airways, Washington, 2000—. Bd. dirs. Healthy Mothers/Healthy Babies of Palm Beach, 1996-2000, pres. bd., 1999-2000, mem. devel. com., 1995-2000, chmn. fund raising, mem. exec. com., 1997-2000; bd. dirs. Florence Fuller Child Devel. Ctr., Boca Raton, Fla.,

1997-99; chmn. cmty. rels. com. Florence Fuller Child Devel. Ctr., Boca Raton, Fla., 1997-98; mem. adv. bd. Innonet, Inc., Washington, 1992-97; mem. CASE/Europe task force Coun. Advancement Support Edn., Washington, 1989-91; bd. dirs. W.Va. Pub. Radio, Charleston, 1990-92, Big Bros./Big Sisters, Wheeling, 1988-92; mem. Women for Downtown, Buffalo, 1993-95; mem. mktg. com. Jacksonville Cmty. Coun., Inc., 2001—; founding mem. Women's Giving Alliance, Jacksonville, 2002—; bd. mem. Jewish Family Cmty. Svcs., Jacksonville, 2002—. Fulbright fellow, 1990. Mem. Fulbright Assn. (mem. devel. com. 1994-97). Avocations: working out, reading, golf, travel, concerts. Home: 13153 Summit Creek Rd Jacksonville FL 32224-8423 E-mail: turkeyII@aol.com.

STERMER, DUGALD ROBERT, designer, illustrator, writer, consultant; b. Los Angeles, Dec. 17, 1936; s. Robert Newton and Mary (Blue) S.; m. Jeanie Kortum; children: Dugald, Megan, Chris, Colin, Crystal. BA, UCLA, 1960. Art dir., v.p. Ramparts mag., 1965-70; freelance designer, illustrator, writer, cons. San Francisco, 1970—; founder Pub. Interest Communications, 1974; chmn. illustration dept. Calif. Coll. Arts and Crafts, 1994—. Bd. dirs. Am. Inst. Graphic Arts, Illustration Partnership Am.; mem. San Francisco Art Commn., 1997—. Cons. editor: Communication Arts mag., 1974-90; designer: Oceans mag., 1976-82; editor: The Environment, 1972, Vanishing Creatures, 1980; author: The Art of Revolution, 1970, Vanishing Creatures, 1980, Vanishing Flora, 1994, Birds and Bees, 1994; designer 1984 Olympic medals; illustration exhbn. Calif. Acad. Scis., 1986; one-man show Jernigan Wicker Gallery, San Francisco, 1996. Mem. Grand Jury City and County San Francisco, 1989; bd. dirs. Delancey St. Found., 1990—. Recipient various medals, awards for design and illustration nat. and internat. competitions. Office: 600 The Embarcadero # 204 San Francisco CA 94107-2121

STERMER, JEREMIAH COLLETT, artist; b. Balt., Nov. 3, 1946; s. Edward Collett and Phyllis Margurete (Stegman) S.; m. Nonni Mary Costantini, Feb. 14, 1992. Student, Md. Inst. Coll. Art, Balt., 1966-68. Art dir., illustrator Columbia (Md.) Tag & Label, 1978-81; artist, illustrator AAI Corp., Cockeysville, Md., 1981-84; fine easel painter Balt., 1984-88; art dir. Printing Corp. Am., 1988-90; graphic artist, illustrator JS Graphics, 1990-95. One man shows include Wright Gallery, N.Y.C., 1996, 97; exhibited in group shows at U. Balt., 1982, Sch. 33 Gallery, Balt., 1983, Macon (Ga.) Fine Arts Gallery, 1997, Marin Price Galleries, Chevy Chase, Md., 1997-98; represented in permanent collection Hickory (N.C.) Mus. Art. Recipient various awards for painting. Avocations: music, photography, cinematography. Home: 626 Piccadilly Rd Towson MD 21204-3821

STERN, ADRIENNE EHRLICH, interior designer; b. Chgo., May 19, 1932; d. Louis and Rose Judith (Sherman) Ehrlich; m. Charles Stern, Jan. 10, 1954; children: Corey Alan, Todd Merrill. Student, U. Ill., 1949-50. Interior designer Ehrlich Bros., Lincolnwood, Ill., 1974—; calligrapher, 1965—; aquanastics instr. Village of Lincolnwood, 1981—. Mem. at large nat. bd. dirs. City of Hope Med. Ctr., 1981—, pres. Bobby Flechman chpt., 1969-71. Democrat. Jewish. Avocation: sculpting. Home: 3815 W Greenleaf Ave Lincolnwood IL 60712-2523

STERN, ANNIE WARD, development executive; b. Jacksonville, Fla., Oct. 18, 1944; d. Peter Otey and Annie (Boyd) Ward; m. Edward J. Stern, Dec. 23, 1968; children: Robert W., Ward Preston. BA, Sweet Briar Coll., 1966; MS in Edn., U. Va., 1969. Tchr. pub. schs., Indpls., 1967-77; dir. community svcs. Ind. Repertory Theatre, 1977; adminstrv. asst., then program dir. Young Audiences of Ind., 1978-83; dir. pub. rels., alumnae dir. Oak Knoll Sch. of Holy Child, Summit, N.J., 1983-84, dir. devel., 1984-92, Summit Country Day Sch., 1992—. Vol. pub. rels. and fundraising Indpls. Mus. Art, 1970-80, Ind. Repertory Theatre, 1970-80, St. John's Luth. Ch., Summit, 1985—. Mem. Nat. Soc. Fund Raising Execs. (bd. dirs. N.J. chpt., nat. recognition award 1989, bd. dirs. Greater Cin. chpt.), N.J. Assn. Ind. Schs. (pres., v.p., devel. dirs. 1984-92), Coun. for Advancement and Support Edn., Greater Cin. Planned Giving Coun., Ind. Sch. Mgmt. Assn., Maplewood Club, Spring Valley Hounds Hunt Club, Sweet Briar Coll. Club (v.p.). Avocations: horseback riding, tennis, theater. Office: The Summit Country Day Sch 2161 Grandin Rd Cincinnati OH 45208-3300 E-mail: stern_a@summitcds.org.

STERN, ARTHUR ALEXANDER, retired pediatrician; b. N.Y.C., May 5, 1922; s. Max and Beatrice (Fleischer) S.; m. Muriel H. Schneider, Dec. 24, 1946; children: Ellen Hope, Teri Beth. BS, U. Chgo., 1945; BS in Medicine, U. Ill., Chgo., 1948. Intern Coney Island Hosp., Bklyn., 1948-49, asst. resident, 1949-50, Mamonides Hosp., Bklyn., 1950-51; asst. contagious diseases Kingston Hosp., 1951-52; attending pediatrics Good Samaritan Hosp., Suffern, N.Y.; sr. attending pediatrics Nyack (N.Y.) Hosp., 1965-80, chief pediatrics, 1972-78; ret., 1980. Cons. in field, organized pediatric ICU Nyack Hosp. Avocations: golf, photography, stamps. Home: 7956 Rockford Rd Boynton Beach FL 33437-2526

STERN, ARTHUR PAUL, electronics company executive; b. Budapest, Hungary, July 20, 1925; arrived in U.S., 1951; s. Leon and Bertha (Frankfurter) Stern; m. Edith M. Samuel; children: Daniel, Claude, Jacqueline. Diploma in Elec. Engring., Swiss Fed. Inst. Tech., Zurich, 1948; MSEE, Syracuse U., 1955. Mgr. electronic devices and applications lab. GE, Syracuse, N.Y., 1957-61; dir. engring. Martin Marietta Corp., Balt., 1961-64; dir. ops. Bunker Ramo Corp., Canoga Park, Calif., 1964-66; v.p., gen. mgr. advanced products divsn. Magnavox, Torrance, 1966-79; pres. Magnavox Advanced Products and Systems Co., 1980-90; vice chmn., bd. dirs. Magnavox Govt. and Indsl.Electronics Co., Ft. Wayne, Ind., 1987-90; pres. Ea. Beverly Hills Corp., 1991—. Pres. Calif.-Israel C. of C., 1994—98, chmn. bd. dirs., 1998—2000; mem. governing coun. Am.-Jewish Congress, 1997—98; bd. dirs. Jewish Coun. Pub. Affairs, 1996—, Progressive Jewish Alliance, 1999—; non-resident staff mem. MIT, 1956—59; instr. GE Bus. Mgmt., 1955—57. Author: (book) Transistor Broadcast Receivers, 1954; co-author: Transistor Circuit Engineering, 1957, Handbook of Automation, Computation and Control, 1961; contbr. articles to profl. jours. Mem. adv. bd. dept. elec. engring. U. Calif., Santa Barbara, 1980—92; mem. Sch. Engring. Adv. and Devel. Coun. Calif. State U., Long Beach, 1985—90; chmn. bd. dirs. Calif. Humanitarian Found. for Holocaust Survivors, 2000—; regional co-chair Ams. for Peace Now, 2002—; chmn. engring. divsn. United Jewish Appeal, Syracuse, 1955—57; bd. dirs. Bur. Jewish Edn., L.A., 1995—, chmn. investment com., 2000—; vice-chmn. Jewish Cmty. Rels. Com. of Jewish Fedn. of L.A., 1998—. Recipient Justice-Tzedeu award, Labor Zionist Alliance, 2001. Fellow: IEEE (pres. 1975, bd. dirs., officer 1970—77, guest editor spl. issue IEEE Trans. on Circuit Theory 1956, invited guest editor spl. issue Procs. IEEE on Integrated Electronics 1964, Centennial medal 1984, Millennium medal 2000, Haraden Pratt award 2001), AAAS. Achievements include patents in field.

STERN, BRUCE L. finance educator; b. Portland, Oreg., Nov. 28, 1945; s. Reuben L. and Goldie K. Stern; m. Sheila A. Resnikoff, June 15, 1969; children: Brian G., Robert S. BS, Portland State U., 1967, MBA, 1969; PhD, Ariz. State U., 1974. Instr. Pacific U., Forest Grove, Oreg.; asst. prof. mktg. Ill. State U., Normal, 1973—75; prof. bus. adminstrn. Portland (Oreg.) State U., 1975—. Editor Mktg. Edn. Rev., Portland, Oreg., Jour. of Mktg. Edn., Portland, Oreg.; mktg. and rsch. cons., Beaverton, Oreg., 1975—. Contbr. articles to profl. jours. Chair, Crescendo Oreg. Symphony, Portland, Oreg., 1999—2002. Recipient Mktg. Educator of Yr. award, Mktg. Edn. Assn., 1992. Mem.: Am. Acad. of Advt. (chair fin. com. 1993—94), Soc. of Mktg. Advances (conf. track chair 1998—99), Am. Mktg. Assn. (pres. Oreg. chpt. 1981—82), Phi Kappa Phi (pres., Portland State U. chpt. 1999—2000). Jewish. Avocations: travel, fishing, impressionist art. Home: 8655 SW Pacer Ct Beaverton OR 97008 Office: Portland State University PO Box 751 Portland OR 97207 Personal E-mail: brucel@hevanet.com. E-mail: bruces@sba.pdx.edu.

STERN, CARL LEONARD, former news correspondent, federal official; b. N.Y.C., Aug. 7, 1937; s. Hugo and Frances (Taft) S.; m. Joy Elizabeth Nathan, Nov. 27, 1960; children: Lawrence, Theodore. AB, Columbia U., 1958, MS, 1959; JD, Cleve. State U., 1966, JD (hon.), 1975, New Eng. Coll. Law, 1977. Bar: Ohio 1966, D.C. 1968, U.S. Supreme Ct. 1969. Law corr. NBC News, Washington, 1967-93; dir. Office of Pub. Affairs U.S. Dept. Justice, 1993-96; Shapiro Prof. of Media and Pub. Affairs George Washington U., 1996—. Lectr. Nat. Jud. Coll.; adj. prof. George Washington U., Stanford U. Editorial bd.: The Dist. Lawyer. Mem. Dept. Transp. Task Force on Assistance to Families in Aviation Disasters, 1997; mem. nat. adv. coun. Cleveland-Marshall Law Sch. Recipient Peabody award, 1974, Emmy award, 1974, Gavel award, 1969, 74, Headliner Club award, 1991, Edmond J. Randloph award U.S. Dept. Justice. Mem. ABA (vice chmn. criminal justice sect. com. on criminal justice and the media, gov., forum com. on communications law, working group intelligence requirements and criminal code reform, mem. standing com. on strategic comms.), AFTRA (nat. exec. bd. 1984-86, first v.p. Washington, Balt. chpt. 1985-87). Home: 2956 Davenport St NW Washington DC 20008 Office: George Washington U #400 805 21st St NW Washington DC 20052 Personal E-mail: sterncarl@aol.com. E-mail: cstern@gwu.edu.

STERN, CARL WILLIAM, JR. management consultant; b. San Francisco, Mar. 31, 1946; s. Carl William and Marjorie Aline (Gunst) S.; m. Karen Jaffe, Sept. 7, 1966 (div. Mar. 1972); 1 child, David; m. Holly Drick Hayes, Mar. 21, 1985; children: Kenneth, Matthew. BA, Harvard U., 1968; MBA, Stanford U., 1974. Cons. Boston Cons. Group, Inc., Menlo Park, Calif., 1974-77, mgr., 1977-78, London, 1978-80, v.p. Chgo., 1980-87, sr. v.p., 1987-97, pres., CEO, 1998—. Lt. USNR, 1968-71. Office: Boston Consulting Group Inc 200 S Wacker Dr Ste 2700 Chicago IL 60606-5846

STERN, CLAUDIO DANIEL, medical educator, embryological researcher; b. Montevideo, Uruguay, Feb. 9, 1954; came to U.S., 1994; s. Erico and Trude Stern. BSc with honors, U. Sussex, 1975, DPhil, 1978; MA, U. Oxford, 1985, DSc, 1994. Asst. prof. anatomy dept. Cambridge (England) U., 1984-85; assoc. prof. dept. human anatomy U. Oxford (England), 1985-93; prof., chmn. dept. genetics and devel. Coll. Physicians and Surgeons Columbia U., N.Y.C., 1994—. Contbr. articles to profl. jours.; mng. editor Mechanisms of Devel.; mem. editorial adv. bd. Devel.; mem. editorial bd. Internat. Jour. Devel. Biology, Cell. Rsch. fellow U. Coll. London, 1978-84, fellow Christ Ch. Coll., 1985-93. Office: Columbia U Dept Genetics & Devel 701 W 168th St Dept & New York NY 10032-2704

STERN, DANIEL, author, executive, educator; b. N.Y.C., Jan. 18, 1928; s. Morris and Dora (Hochman) S.; m. Gloria Shapiro, Nov. 9, 1963; 1 son, Eric Branfman. Sr. v.p., mng. dir., mem. bd. mgmt. McCann-Erickson Advt., Inc., N.Y.C., 1964-69; v.p. advt. and publicity worldwide, also dir. Warner Bros., 1969-72; v.p., dir. mktg. Longchamps, Inc., N.Y.C., 1972-73; v.p., creative dir. Lubar-Southard, Inc., 1973; fellow Ctr. for Humanities, Wesleyan U., 1969, vis. prof. letters and English, 1976-79; v.p. promotion East Coast CBS Entertainment, N.Y.C., 1979-86; pres. entertainment divsn. McCaffrey & McCall, Advt., 1986; prof. English and creative writing U. Houston, 1992—, Cullen disting. prof. English, 1993—. Dir. Humanities, 92nd St. YMHA, 1988. Author: Girl with Glass Heart, 1953, The Guests of Fame, 1955, Miss America, 1959, Who Shall Live, Who Shall Die, 1963 (Internat. Remembrance award for fiction Bergen Belsen Assn. 1973), After the War, 1967, The Suicide Academy, 1968, The Rose Rabbi, 1971, Final Cut, 1975, An Urban Affair, 1980, Twice Told Tales, 1989 (Richard and Hinda Rosenthal Fiction award AAAL 1990), Twice Upon a Time, 1992, One Day's Perfect Weather, 1999, In the Country of the Young, 2001. With U.S. Army, 1946-47. Recipient Brazos prize for best short story Tex. Inst. Letters, 1996. Mem. PEN, Nat. Book Critics Circle, Author's League.

STERN, DAVID M. dean, educator; BS, Yale U., 1973; MD, Harvard U., 1978. Prof. physiology, grad. studies Med. Coll. Ga., sr. v.p. clin. activities, dean medicine, dean, 2002—. Office: 1120 15th St Augusta GA 30912*

STERN, DONALD KENNETH, lawyer; BA, Hobart Coll., 1966; JD, Georgetown U., 1969; LLM, U. Pa., 1973. Intern Dist. Atty.'s Office, Mineola, N.Y., 1967, Citizen's Adv. Ctr., Washington, 1968; staff atty. Defender Assn. Phila., Cmty. Legal Svcs., Phila., 1969-71; adj. prof. law, supervising atty. Boston Coll. Law Sch., Boston Coll. Legal Assistance Bur., 1971-73, asst. prof. law, dir. clin. programs, supervising atty., 1973-75; asst. atty. gen., dir. atty. gen. clin. program, Mass. Atty. Gen.'s Office, Boston Coll. Law Sch., 1975-77, asst. prof. law, dir. atty. gen. clin. program, spl. asst. atty. gen., 1977-78, asst. atty. gen., dir. atty. gen. clin. program, 1978-79; chief govt. bur. Mass. Atty. Gen.'s Office, 1979-82; assoc. Hale and Dorr, Boston, 1982-85, jr. ptnr., 1985-87, sr. ptnr., 1987, 91-93, of counsel, 1990-91; chief legal counsel to Gov. Mass., 1987-90; U.S. atty. Dist. Mass., 1993—2001; ptnr. Bingham McCutchen, LLP, 2001—; lectr. Harvard Law Sch., 2002—. Office: Bingham McCutchen LLP Federal St Boston MA 02210-1726 E-mail: donald.stern@bingham.com.

STERN, EDITH LOIS, counselor, hypno-therapist; b. Paterson, N.J., Apr. 20, 1928; d. Meyer Zenack and Helen Rebecca (Jarvis) Zenack-Kollin; m. Eugene Stern, June 23, 1949 (div. Dec. 1978); children: Michael, Jonathan, Andrew. BA in Edn., Bklyn. Coll., 1949; MS in Counseling, C.W. Post U., 1971. Cert. counselor, N.Y. Tchr. Pub. Sch. 70, Bklyn., 1949-53; counselor Jericho (N.Y.) H.S., 1972, Farmingdale (N.Y.) H.S., 1973, 75, Uniondale (N.Y.) H.S., 1974; dir. New Directions, Massapequa, N.Y., 1971-91. Mem. adv. bd. Mid-Queens Cmty. Coun., Jamaica, N.Y., 1957-64, Peacesmith's, Inc., Massapequa, 1972-75, Nassau Women's Polit. Caucus, Mineola, 1973-80; dir. Kaplan Meml. Libr., Mineola, N.Y., 1968-80; counselor Nassau County CETA, Hempstead, N.Y., 1977-81; tax agt. N.Y. State Dept. Taxation, Hempstead, 1982-92. Editor (editl.) Temple Judea Newsletter, 1967. Pres. PTA Pub. Sch. 165, Flushing, N.Y., 1962-64; committeewoman Nassau County Dem., Massapequa, 1965-85; campaign mgr. Krupsak for Lt. Gov., Nassau County, 1974. Mem. NOW, Am. Pers. and Guidance Assn., Am. Assn. Ret. Persons, N.Y. State Ret. Pub. Employees Assn., Hawaiian Gardens Women's Club (v.p. 1995-97, pres. 1997-99), Ilana Hadassah (corr. sec. 1995-97, pres. 1997—). Jewish. Avocations: reading, attending the theatre, writing. Home: Apt D210 5041 W Oakland Park Blvd Fort Lauderdale FL 33313-1517

STERN, EDWARD ABRAHAM, physics educator; b. Detroit, Sept. 19, 1930; s. Jacob Munich and Rose (Kravitz) S.; m. Sylvia Rita Sidell, Oct. 30, 1955; children: Hilary, Shari, Miri. BS, Calif. Tech., 1951, PhD, 1955. Post-doctoral fellow Calif. Tech., Pasadena, 1955-57; asst. prof. U. Md., College Park, 1957-61, assoc. prof., 1961-64, prof., 1964-65, U. Wash., Seattle, 1965—2000, emeritus, 2000—. Contbr. over 200 articles to profl. jours.; editor; three books. Recipient B. Warren award Am. Crystallography Assn., 1979, Outstanding Achievement award Internat. XAFS Soc., 2000; named Guggenheim fellow, Cambridge, Eng., 1963-64, NSF Sr. Post-doctoral fellow, Haifa, Israel, 1970-71, Fulbright fellow, Jerusalem, Israel, 1985-86. Fellow AAAS, Am. Physical Soc. Achievements include patent for x-ray focusing device; development of x-ray absorption fine structure technique; research on surface plasmons, nonlinear reflection from surfaces, electronic properties of alloys, structural phase transition. Office: U Wash Dept Physics PO Box 351560 Seattle WA 98195-1560 E-mail: stern@phys.washington.edu.

STERN, EDWARD MAYER, lawyer, educator; b. Albany, N.Y., Feb. 18, 1946; s. William Barnet and Louise (Mayer) S.; m. Ann Swanson, Jan. 22, 1972; children: Jared William, Jordan Carl. BS in Civil Engring., Tufts U., 1968; JD, Boston U., 1972; diploma for a dental technician, 1969. Bar: Mass. 1972, U.S. Dist. Ct. Mass. 1973, U.S. Supreme Ct. 1980, N.Y. 1983. Civil engr. Std. Engring. Corp., Albany, N.Y., 1966-67; environ. engr. Fed. Water Pollution Control Adminstrn., Needham Heights, Mass., 1968-69; civil engr. Anderson-Nichols Engring. Co., Boston, 1970; legal aid law student Multi-Service Ctr., South Boston, Mass., 1971-72; staff atty. Boston Legal Assistance Project-Juvenile Ct. Adv. program, 1972-74; legal counsel Treatment Alternative to Street Crime-Juveniles Youth Activities Commn., Boston, 1974-75; staff atty., project dir. Action Plan for Legal Svcs., 1976; lawyer in residence U. Mass., 1976-77; pvt. practice Newton, Mass., 1976—; v.p., gen. counsel real estate developer Triangle Devel. Corp., Newton Centre, 1987-90; pres. Mass. Funding Group, Inc., 1988-97. Asst. dean for pre-law advising Boston U., 1977—; vis. lectr. dept. sociology U. Mass., 1977—; lectr. continuing edn. Tufts-New Eng. Med. Ctr., Boston, 1973—75; bd. dirs. Pre-Law Advisors Nat. Coun., 1986—88; bd. visitors Walnut Hill Sch., 1995—97; adv. bd. paralegal studies program Boston U., 1994—, coach mock trial team, 1993—; pres. N.E. Assn. Pre-Law Advs., Inc., 1987—88, bd. dirs., 1982—84. Co-author (with Emily Soltanoff): The NAPLA Pre-Law Advisors Guide, 1982—94; author, 1987, Charting a Law School Course, 1982; mo. columnist The Mass. Psychologist, 2000—, performer Action Plan for Legal Services (Criminal), 1977—; co-author (with Gerald Wilson): The Book of Law School Lists, 1998—2001; contbr. Mem. Gov.'s Com. Prevention of Drug Abuse; bd. dirs., pres. Citizens for Juvenile Justice, 1997—; mem. med. policy rev. com. Nat. Neurofibromatosis Found., Inc., 1987—, Pub. Svc. award, 1990; mem. pub. affairs com. and civil rights com. Anti Defamation League, Boston. With USAR, 1968—69, with res. USAR, 1968—74. Named Outstanding Participant, Nat. Coll. Juvenile Justice, 1975; recipient Merit award Boston Mayor's Office Youth Activities Commn., 1973, Pub. Svc. award Nat. Neurofibromatosis Found., Inc., 1990. Mem. ABA, Mass. Bar Assn. (adminstrn. justice com., family law com.), N.E. Assn. Pre-Law Advisors, Inc. (pres. 1987-88), Nat. Neurofibromatosis Found. (med. policy com. 1987—). Jewish. Home: 178 Nehoiden Rd Waban MA 02468-1344 Office: 60 Austin St Ste 210 Newton MA 02460-1857 E-mail: stern@bu.edu.

STERN, ELIZABETH ESPIN, lawyer; b. Prince Georges County, Md., June 21, 1961; d. Cesar A. and M. Cecilia (Salvador) E.; m. Michael L. Stern, May 16, 1992; 1 child, Alexander. BA magna cum laude, U. Va., 1983, JD, 1986. Bar: Va. 1986, U.S. Dist. Ct. (ea. dist.) Va., D.C. 1988. Ptnr. comml. immigration Shaw, Pittman, Potts & Trowbridge, Washington, 1986—. Moderator Counsel Connects Immigration Discussion Group. Mem. editorial bd. Bus Law Inc., 1987—; editor-in-chief Free-Market Cuba Bus. Jour; contbg. writer Tech. Law Notes, 1987—, The Changing Workplace, 1991—. Past chair young lawyers sect. Vol. Bar Assn. D.C. Recipient Martin Preis award Vol. Bar Assn. D.C., 1992. Mem. NAFE, Am. Immigration Lawyers Assn., Va. Bar Assn., D.C. Bar Assn. (internat. sec. 1986—, del. to ABA, chair young lawyers sect. 1992-93, Young Lawyer of Yr. 1994), Immigration Tech. Assn. Am. Republican. Avocation: journalism. Home: 8529 Century Oak Ct Fairfax Station VA 22039-3343 Office: Shaw Pittman Potts & Trowbridge 2300 N St NW Fl 5 Washington DC 20037-1172

STERN, FRITZ RICHARD, historian, educator; b. Breslau, Germany, Feb. 2, 1926; came to U.S., 1938, naturalized, 1947; s. Rudolf A. and Catherine (Brieger) S.; m. Margaret J. Bassett, Oct. 11, 1947 (div. 1992); children: Frederick P., Katherine Stern Brennan; m. Elisabeth Niebuhr Sifton, Jan. 1, 1996. BA, Columbia U., 1946, MA, 1948, PhD, 1953; DLitt (hon.), Oxford U., 1985; LLD (hon.), New Sch. for Social Rsch., 1997, Columbia U., 1998. Lectr., instr. Columbia U., 1946-51, faculty, 1953—, prof. history, 1963—, Seth Low prof. history, 1967-92, univ. prof., 1992-96, provost, 1980-83; acting asst. prof. Cornell U., 1951-53; univ. prof. emeritus Columbia U., 1997—; tchr. Free U. Berlin, 1954, Yale U., 1963; permanent vis. prof. U. Konstanz, West Germany, 1966—; sr. adviser U.S. Embassy, Bonn, 1993-94. Élie Halévy prof. U. Paris, spring 1979; Phi Beta Kappa vis. scholar, 1979-80; Tanner lectr. Yale, 1993. Author: The Politics of Cultural Despair, 1961, The Failure of Illiberalism-Essays in the Political Culture of Modern Germany, 1972, rev. edit., 1992, Gold and Iron: Bismarck, Bleichroeder and the Bldg. of the German Empire, 1977 (recipient Lionel Trilling award Columbia U.), Dreams and Delusions: The Drama of German History, 1987, rev. edit. 1999, Einstein's German World, 1999; editor: The Varieties of History, 1956, 71, (with L. Krieger) The Responsibility of Power, 1967; mem. editorial bd. Foreign Affairs, 1978-92; contbr. articles to profl. jours.; reviewer Fgn. Affairs, 1963-95. Trustee German Marshall Fund, 1981-99, Aspen Inst. of Berlin, 1983—; senator Deutsche Nationalstiftung, 1994—; mem. Trilateral Commn., 1983-90. Decorated Officer's Cross Order of Merit Fed. Republic of Germany; fellow Center Advanced Behavioral Scis., 1957-58; fellow Social Sci. Research Council, 1960-61; fellow Am. Council Learned Socs., 1966-67; fellow Netherlands Inst. Advanced Study, 1972-73; mem. Nuffield Coll., Oxford, 1966-67, Inst. Advanced Study Princeton, 1969-70; Guggenheim fellow, 1969-70; Ford Found. grantee, 1976-77; vis. scholar Russell Sage Found., 1989, spring 1993; recipient Leopold-Lucas-prize Evang. Faculty U. Tübingen, 1984, Peace prize German Book Trade Frankfurt Book Fair, 1999. Mem. Am. Hist. Assn., AAAS, Am. Philos. Soc., Coun. Fgn. Rels., Deutsche Akademie für Sprache und Dichtung (corr.), Berlin Brandenburgische Akademie der Wissenschaften (corr.), Orden Pour le Mérite, Germany, Phi Beta Kappa (senator-at-large 1973-78). Clubs: Century (N.Y.C.). Home: 15 Claremont Ave New York NY 10027-6802 E-mail: fs20@columbia.edu.

STERN, GAIL FRIEDA, historical association director; b. Atlantic City, May 18, 1950; d. Herbert and Faith (Beldegreen) Stern; m. Irwin Allen Popowsky (div.); m. Shawn Paul Aubitz (div.); 1 child Jonathan. Student, Brown U., 1972; postgrad., U. Pa., 1973. Asst. in decorative arts Phila. Mus. Art, 1972-75; asst. curator Wheaton Mus. Glass, Millville, N.J., 1973-74; assoc. dir. Pa. Humanities Coun., Phila., 1976-79; mus. curator The Balch Inst. for Ethnic Studies, 1979-83, mus. dir., 1984-93; dir. Hist. Soc. Princeton, N.J., 1993—. Chair Pa. Task Force on Folk Arts and Culture, 1981-82; vice chmn. crafts panel Pa. Coun. on the Arts, Harrisburg, 1988-89; chair cultural conservation com., Pa. Heritage Affairs Commn., Harrisburg, 1990-92; participant Internat. Partnership in Mus., Singapore, 1991. Recipient pub. programming award, NJ Coun. Humanities, 1996, award for outstanding contbns. to NJ history, NJ Hist. Commn., 1999. Mem. Mus. Coun. Phila. (v.p. 1982-83), Am. Assn. Mus./Internat. Coun. Mus. (bd. dirs. 1991-97), N.J. Mus. Assn. (bd. dirs., sec. 1993-98, John Cotton Dana award 2000), Am. Assn. for State and Local History Awards (N.J. chair 1994-95), Mid-Atlantic Assn. Mus. (bd. dirs. 1997-98). Home: 41 Lafayette Street Hopewell NJ 08525 Office: Hist Soc Princeton 158 Nassau St Princeton NJ 08542-7006 E-mail: gailfstern@aol.com.

STERN, GEOFFREY, lawyer, disciplinary counsel; b. Columbus, Ohio, Nov. 29, 1942; s. Leonard J. and Anastasia (Percin) S.; m. Barbara Shnider; children: Emily Staheli, Elizabeth; stepchildren: Courtney, Jennifer, Brian Feuer. Student, Williams Coll., 1960-63; BA cum laude, Ohio State U., 1965, JD summa cum laude, 1968. Bar: Ohio 1968. Assoc. Alexander, Ebinger, Holschuh & Fisher, Columbus, Ohio, 1968-72; ptnr. Folkerth, Calhoun, Webster & O'Brien, 1972-80, Arter & Hadden, Columbus, 1980-93; disciplinary counsel Supreme Ct. of Ohio, 1993-97; counsel Kegler, Brown, Hill & Ritter, Columbus, 1997-2000, dir., 2000—. Nat. coordinating counsel for asbestos litigation Combustion Engring. Inc. and Basic, Inc., 1985-93; lectr. on legal ethics and profl. responsibility; mem. Spl. Commn. to Review Ohio Ethics Rules, 1995-98, Spl. Commn. on Legal Edn., 1995-98; mem. symposium on ethics and Chinese legal sys., Shanghai, 1998; keynote spkr. Faith and Law Symposium, 1999; spl. investigator Bd. Commrs. Character and Fitness Ohio Supreme Ct., 1998. Sr. editor Ohio State Law Jour., 1967-68. Pres. Bexley (Ohio) City Coun., 1977-80, mem., 1973-80, mem. Bexley Civil Svc. Commn., 1983-85; v.p., trustee Creative Living, Columbus, 1981-89, Ohio Citizens Com. for Arts, Columbus, 1982-88; mem. Nat. Def. Com. on Asbestos in Bldgs. Litigation, 1986-92; pub. mem. Ohio Optical Dispensers Bd., Columbus, 1978-82. Recipient Am. Jurisprudence Evidence award Ohio State U. Coll. Law, 1967. Fellow Am. Bar Found., Columbus Bar Found., Ohio State Bar Found.; mem. Ohio State Bar Assn. (com. on legal ethics and profl. conduct, sec. 1981-90, vice chmn. 1990-92, chmn. 1992-93), Columbus Bar Assn. (profl. ethics com. 1975-86, 90-93, Liberty Bell award for Cmty. and Profl. Svc. 1998), Order of Coif, Phi Beta Kappa, Pi Sigma Alpha. Home: 278 Crossing Crk N Columbus OH 43230-6108 Office: Kegler Brown Hill & Ritter 65 E State St Ste 1800 Columbus OH 43215-4213 E-mail: gstern@kbhr.com.

STERN, GERALD MANN, lawyer; b. Chgo., Apr. 5, 1937; s. Lloyd and Fannye (Wener) S.; m. Linda Stone, Dec. 20, 1969; children: Eric, Jesse, Maia. BS in Econs., U. Pa., 1958; LL.B. cum laude, Harvard, 1961. Bar: D.C. 1961, Calif. 1991, U.S. Supreme Ct. 1971. Trial atty. civil rights div. U.S. Dept. Justice, 1961-64; assoc. firm Arnold & Porter, Washington, 1964-68, ptnr., 1969-76; founding ptnr. Rogovin, Stern & Huge, Washington, 1976-81; exec. v.p., sr. gen. counsel Occidental Petroleum Corp., 1981—92; spl. counsel fin. instn. fraud and health care fraud U.S. Dept. Justice, 1993-95; ind. legal cons. pvt. practice, 1995—; cons. Antitrust divsn. U.S. Dept. Justice, 1998—2001. Author: The Buffalo Creek Disaster, 1976; co-author: Southern Justice, 1965, Outside the Law, 1997. Trustee Facing History and Ourselves, 1996—. Mem. ABA. Home and Office: 3322 Newark St NW Washington DC 20008-3330 Fax: 202-364-2595. E-mail: GMS37@aol.com.

STERN, GERD JAKOB, poet, import/export company executive; b. Saarbrücken, Germany, Oct. 12, 1928; arrived in U.S., 1936; s. Otto and Lilly Stern; m. Sara Shaw Stern (div. 1999); children from previous marriage: Zalman, Radha, Eric, Abram. Pub. Poems in Folio, Sausalito, Calif., 1956—59; pres. Intermedia Found., Garnerville, NY, 1967—; assoc. in edn. Harvard U., Cambridge, Mass., 1972—74; pres. Intermedia Sys. Corp., 1974—82, Galilee Imports, Cresskill, NJ, 1990—96; owner Gerd Stern Etcetera, 1996—. Author: (book of poems) First Poems and Others, 1948,

Afterimage, 1965, Oral History Gerd Stern, 2001. Grantee, Cosper Found., Ariz., 1999, 2000, 2001, NEA, NEH. Mem.: Acad. Am. Poets, Poetry Soc. Am. Home and Office: 111 Madison Ave Cresskill NJ 07626

STERN, HAROLD PETER, business executive; b. Frankfurt, Germany, Oct. 16, 1923; s. Hugo H. and Lily C. (Strauss) S.; m. Annette B. Kaplan, Nov. 28, 1958; children: Steven B., Eric K., Robert (dec.). Student, NYU, Columbia U., 1940-43. V.p., pres. Rector Internat. Corp., Mt. Vernon, N.Y., 1948—, Rector Internat. Equipment Corp., Mt. Vernon, 1984—, Rector Mineral Trading Corp., Mt. Vernon, 1948—. Exec. sec. Cork Inst. Am., N.Y.C. Elected to Rep. State Com., Albany, N.Y.; vice chmn. Rep. Town Com., Harrison, N.Y.; mem. Nat. Coun./Small Bus. Adminstrn., Washington; commr./chmn. Westchester County Police Bd. Lt. Col. N.Y. Guard. Recipient John Egar Hoover Gold medal Am. Police Hall of Fame, Excellent Police Duty medal Nat. Assn. Chiefs of Police, Police Disting. Svc. medal Westchester County Dept. Pub. Safety, Westchester County Disting. Svc. medal Westchester County Exec. Fellow Nat. Law Enforcement Acad. (hon.). Avocations: boating, skiing, hunting, fishing. Office: Rector Internat Corp 9030 Lakes Blvd West Palm Beach FL 33412-1560

STERN, HARRIAN MICHA BURTTSCHELL, educational diagnostician; b. Houston, June 30, 1951; d. Henry August and Barbara Ruth (Banks) Burttschell; m. Stephen Stern, May 28, 1972; children: Barrett Avonn, Ashley Beth. BS in Spl. Edn./Psychology, Tex. Woman's U., 1973, MEd in Spl. Edn./Ednl. Diagnostician, 1975, PhD in Child Devel./Spl. Edn. Diagnostic, 1989. Cert. tchr., adminstr. elem. mentally retarded, ednl. diagnostician lang./learning disabilitis, spl. edn. supr., mid-mgmt. adminstr., emotionally disturbed, Tex.; registered profl. ednl. diagnostician. Spl. edn. resource tchr. Dallas Ind. Sch. Dist., 1972-75, ednl. diagnostician, 1975-79, 80-82, 92-98, spl. edn. early childhood tchr., 1980, specialist IV, diagnostician supervisor, 1998—; diagnostic resource tchr., 1987-89; ednl. diagnostician Irving (Tex.) Ind. Sch. Dist., 1982-83; pvt. practice in testing, cons., speaking, tutoring Psychoednl. Diagnostic Svcs., Dallas, 1982—. Tchr. U. Tex., Dallas, 1982, Richland Jr. Coll., 1990. Pres. Starlight B'nai B'rith Women, 1982-83, pres. Dallas coun., 1990-91; pres. Shearith Israel Sisterhood, 1987-89; v.p. S.W. br. Women's League for Conservative Judaism, 1987-92, nat. bd. dirs., 1988—, pres. S.W. br., 1992-94, nat. trainer, 1994—, mem. editl. bd. Outlook mag., 1994-96, 98—, nat. v.p. 1998-2000, nat. cons., 1999—, features editor, 2002-. Mem. Tex. Ednl. Diagnosticians Assn. (state pres. 1984-85), Tex. Profl. Edn. Diagnosticians Bd. of Registry (bd. dirs. 1983-89, chmn. 1987-89), Assn. Children with Learning Disabilities, Orton Dyslexia Soc., Coun. Exceptional Children, Phi Delta Kappa, Pi Lambda Theta. Avocations: reading, travel, gourmet cooking. E-mail: hbsphd13@aol.com.

STERN, HERBERT JAY, lawyer; b. N.Y.C., Nov. 8, 1936; s. Samuel and Sophie (Berkowitz) S.; children: Jason Andrew and Jordan Ezekiel (twins), Samuel Abraham, Sarah Kathrine. BA, Hobart Coll., 1958; JD (Ford Found. scholar), U. Chgo., 1961; LL.D. (hon.), Seton Hall Law Sch., 1973, Hobart Coll., 1974; L.H.D. (hon.), Newark State Coll., 1973; D.C.L. (hon.), Bloomfield Coll., 1973; Litt.D. (hon.), Montclair State Coll., 1973. Bar: N.Y. 1961, N.J. 1971. Asst. dist. atty., New York County, 1962-65; trial atty. organized crime and racketeering sect. Dept. of Justice, 1965-69; chief asst. U.S. atty. Dist. of N.J., Newark, 1969-70, U.S. atty., 1971-74, U.S. dist. judge, 1974-87; ptnr. Stern, Greenberg & Kilcullen, Roseland, N.J., 1990—. Adv. com. U. Chgo. Law Sch. Author: Judgment in Berlin, 1984 (Valley Forge award Freedoms Found. 1984, Torch of Learning award Am. Friends of Hebrew U. 1987), Trying Cases to Win, Vol. I, 1991, Vol. II, 1992, Vol. III, 1993, Vol. IV, 1995; co-author: Trying Cases to Win, Anatomy of A Trial, 1999, Trying Cases to Win: Evidence Weapons for Winning, 2000; subject of book Tiger in the Court, 1973. Trustee Hobart and William Smith Colls. Named One of America's 10 Outstanding Young Men U.S. Jr. C. of C., 1971; Swartzer scholar U. Chgo. Law Sch., 1985; recipient Dean's Club award U. Akron Sch. Law, 1986, medal of excellence Hobart Coll., 1990, Citizen's award N.J. Acad. Medicine, 1997. Fellow ABA, Am. Law Inst. (Clarence Darrow award), Internat. Platform Assn.; mem. ABA, N.J. Bar Assn., Fed. Bar Assn. (past pres. Newark chpt., recipient William J. Brennan, Jr. award 1987), Essex County Bar Assn., Am. Judicature Soc., Phi Alpha Delta. Achievements include being subject of book Tiger in the Court, 1973. Office: 75 Livingston Ave Roseland NJ 07068-3701

STERN, ISAAC, violinist, performing arts executive; b. Kreminiecz, Russia, July 21, 1920; came to U.S., 1921; s. Solomon and Clara S.; m. Nora Kaye, Nov. 10, 1948; m. Vera Lindenblit, Aug. 17, 1951; children: Shira, Michael, David; m. Linda Reynolds, Nov. 3, 1996. Student, San Francisco Conservatory, 1930-37; numerous hon. degrees including, Dalhousie U., 1971, U. Hartford, 1971, Bucknell U., 1974, Hebrew U., Jerusalem, 1975, Yale U., 1975, Columbia U., 1977, Johns Hopkins U., 1979, U. Md., 1983, Tel Aviv U., 1983, NYU, 1989, U. Ill., 1992, Harvard U., 1992. Pres. Carnegie Hall, N.Y.C. Recital debut San Francisco, 1934; orchestral debut San Francisco Symphony Orch., 1936; N.Y. debut, 1937; Carnegie Hall recital debut, 1943; N.Y. Philharm. debut (Arthur Rodzinski condr.), 1944; participated Prades Festival with Pablo Casals, 1950-52; soloist for first orchestral and recital performances at Kennedy Ctr., Washington; first Am. to perform in USSR after World War II, 1956; mem. Istomin-Rose-Stern trio, 1962-83 (Beethoven cycle w/Istomin & Rose 1970-71); performed in China at invitation of Chinese govt., 1979; performed world premieres of violin works by Bernstein, Dutilleux, Hindemith, Maxwell Davies, Penderecki, Rochberg, Schuman and Bolcom; has played with major orchestras, given countless recitals and performed at important festivals in the U.S., Europe, Israel, Far East, Australia and S. Am. Over 100 records, cassettes and CD's for CBS/Sony, named Artist Laureate 1984 CBS Masterworks; made soundtrack for motion pictures Humoresque (Warner Bros.) and Fiddler on the Roof (United Artists); starred in soundtrack Tonight We Sing (20th Century Fox) and Journey to Jerusalem with Leonard Bernstein; documentary film From Mao to Mozart-Isaac Stern in China (Academy award 1981, Cannes Film Festival Special Mention), Carnegie Hall: The Grand Reopening, 1987 (Emmy award), Isaac Stern-A Life, 1991; author: My First 79 Years, 1999. Chmn. emeritus Am.-Israel Cultural Found.; founder Jerusalem Music Ctr.; originating mem. Nat. Endowment for the Arts; pres. Carnegie Hall, N.Y.C., 1960—. Decorated comdr. Order de la Couronne, comdr. Legion d'Honneur; comdr.'s cross (Order of Dannebrog (Denmark); recipient numerous Grammy awards, Grammy Lifetime Achievement award, 1987, Hall of Fame Induction medal Am. Classical Music, Nat. medal of Honor, 1991, Presdl. medal of Freedom, 1992, numerous local city awards, Japan's Order of the Rising Sun, 1998, Polar prize, 2000, ECHO Schallplatenpreis, 2000; named Musician of Yr., ABC/Musical Am., 1986; Fellow of Jerusalem, 1986. Died Sept. 22, 2001.

STERN, JAMES ANDREW, investment banker; b. N.Y.C., Oct. 1, 1950; s. Arthur and Lenore (Oppenheimer) S.; m. Jane Yusem, April 13, 1975; children: Peter, David. BS, Tufts U., 1972; MBA, Harvard U., 1974. Assoc. Lehman Bros. Inc., N.Y.C., 1974-79, v.p., 1979-82, mng. dir., 1982-94; chmn. The Cypress Group, 1994—. Dir. Lear Corp., Southfield, Mich., Cinemark U.S.A., Inc., Amtrol, Inc., West Warwick, R.I., Wesco Inc. Trustee Tufts U., Medford, Mass., 1982—, Jewish Mus., N.Y.C.; bd. dirs. Cystic Fibrosis Found. Mem. Quaker Ridge Golf Club, Beach Point Club. Clubs: Quaker Ridge Golf (Scarsdale, N.Y.), Beach Point (Mamaroneck, N.Y.). Avocations: golf, reading. Office: The Cypress Group Inc 65 E 55th St New York NY 10022-3219 Business E-Mail: jstern@cypressgp.com.

STERN, JAMES COPER, sales executive; b. N.Y.C., Dec. 12, 1925; s. George Charles and Ruth (Coper) S.; m. Judith Vinson, Oct. 31, 1963 (div. Mar. 1974); children: Hillary Anne, Renee Jean; m. Ruth Nussbacker Szold, Aug. 22, 1982. BA, NYU, 1949. Trainee, exec. asst. Gardner Advt. Co., N.Y.C., 1949-50; advt. mgr. NOPCO Chem. Co., Harrison, N.J., 1950-53; account exec. Ziv TV Programs, N.Y.C., 1954-56; sales rep. United Artists Associated, 1957-61; v.p., sales mgr. Allied Artists TV, 1961-70; exec. v.p., gen. sales mgr. ITC Entertainment, Inc., Studio City, Calif., 1970-89; pres. JCS Syndication Svcs., L.A., 1990—. Cpl. U.S. Army, 1944-46, ETO. Mem. Internat. Radio and TV Soc., Nat. Assn. TV Program Execs., Ind. TV Program Execs. Republican. Jewish. Avocations: watercolor painting, skiing, golf, art. Home: 1414 N Harper Ave #3 West Hollywood CA 90046- Office: JCS Syndication Svcs 1414 N Harper Ave #3 West Hollywood CA 90046-

STERN, JOAN NAOMI, lawyer; b. Phila., Mar. 7, 1944; d. Clarence J. and Diana D. (Goldberg) S. BA, U. Pa., 1965; JD, Temple U., 1977. Bar: Pa. 1977. Assoc. Blank, Rome, Comisky & McCauley, Phila., 1977-83, ptnr., 1983—, co-chair pub. fin. group, 1983-92, chair pub. fin. group, 1993, chair pub. fin. dept., 1994—. Cons. counsel Phila. Charter Commn., 1993-94. Contbr. articles to profl. jours. Mem. Sch. Dist. Task Force on Regulatory Reform, Phila., 1987, Tax Policy and Budget Com., Phila., 1989, Phila. Mayor's Fiscal Adv. Com., 1990; chair Sch. Dist. of Phila. Task Force on Alternate Financing Strategies, 1995; bd. mgrs. Moore Coll. Art and Design, Phila., 1993—, vice chair bd. trustees, bd. mgrs., 1995—; bd. dirs. Police Athletic League, Phila., 1994—, Jewish Fedn. of Greater Phila., 2000—, Am. Jewish Congress, 1995—, Urban Three Connection, 2000- Fellow Am. Bar Found. (life); mem. ABA, Nat. Assn. Bond Lawyers, Phila. Bar Assn., Phila. Bar Assn. (chmn. mcpl. govt. com. 1983-97), Pa. Assn. Bond Lawyers. Office: Blank Rome Comisky & McCauley LLP One Logan Square Philadelphia PA 19103-6998 E-mail: stern@blankrome.com.

STERN, JOANNE THRASHER, elementary school educator; b. Norfolk, Va., Oct. 18, 1932; d. Thomas Williams and Mary Ellen Thrasher; m. Milford Josiah Stern, Apr. 29, 1956; children: Milford J. III, Thomas Thrasher, William Byrd. BS, James Madison U., 1952; MEd, U. Va., 1963. Cert. elem. tchr. Tchr. 5th grade City of Chesapeake, 1952-54; tchr. Va. Beach Pub. Schs., 1957-60, Norfolk (Va.) City Pub. Schs., 1966-68; life insurance agent Spain, 1977-78; tchr. Def. Dependent Schs., Fed. Republic Germany, 1985; tchr. English Madison Middle Sch., 1987-89; tchr. ESOL 1st grade, 1988-91; 1st grade tchr., reading tchr. Toussaint Louverture Elem. Sch., 1989-2000; tchr. grade 2 Campbell Dr. Elem. Sch., Leisure City, Fla., 2000—; real estate agt. Prudential Keyside Properties, Tavernier. Real estate agent Gregory Realty Corp., 1964-83; tchr. English Nan Ping Tchrs. Coll., summer 1993; tchr. piano Hess Conservatory Music, 1997-2000. Organist 1st Bapt. Ch. of North Miami Beach (Fla.); tchr. Holiday Bible Club, Pembrokeshire, Wales, 1996. Mem. AAUW, Women Leaders Round Table (life), Chesapeake Bay Bus. and Profl. Women, First Baptist Ch. Key Largo, Kappa Delta Pi. Home: 225 Saint Croix Pl Key Largo FL 33037-4316

STERN, JOHN JULES, lawyer; b. Paterson, N.J., Apr. 15, 1955; s. Howard and Muriel (Lubowitt) S.; m. Joyce Levine; children: Julianne Lauren, David Charles; stepchildren: Robert Malcomnson, Aaron Malcomnson, Jarred Malcomnson. Student, Northwestern U., 1972-73; BA, Brandeis U., 1976; M in Pub. Adminstrn., JD, U. So. Calif., 1979. Bar: Calif. 1979, U.S. Dist. Ct. (cen. dist.) Calif. 1979, U.S. Ct. Appeals (9th cir.) 1979, N.J. 1980, U.S. Dist. Ct. N.J. 1980, U.S. Ct. Appeals (3d cir.) 1982, U.S. Supreme Ct. 1997, U.S. Ct. Claims; cert. civil trial atty. Supreme Ct. N.J., 2000. Law sec. to chancery judge N.J. Superior Ct., Paterson, 1979-80; assoc. Stern, Steiger, Croland, Tanenbaum & Schielke, Paramus, N.J., 1980-83, ptnr., 1983-95; atty. Planning Bd., Montvale, 1989-93, Borough of Montvale, 1993-99; ptnr. Forman Stern P.C., Paramus, 1995-97; sr. ptnr. Stern Berenbroick, P.A., N.J., 1997-2001, Williams, Caliri, Miller, Otley & Stern, P.C., Wayne, 2001—. Lectr. land use and planning Nat. Bus. Inst., 1999—. Contbr. articles to profl. jours. Mem. ABA (jud. adminstrn. div., antitrust div. 1979—), N.J. Bar Assn., Calif. Bar Assn., Trial Attys. N.J. (trustee 1987-89), N.Y. Acad. Scis., Passaic County Bar Assn. (chmn. equity jurisprudence com. 1984—, chmn. com. civil and constl. rights 1984—), Bergen County Bar Assn., Morris County Bar Assn., Am. Judicature Soc. Democrat. Jewish. Avocations: sailing, soccer, golf.

STERN, JOSEPH SMITH, JR. former footwear manufacturing company executive; b. Cin., Mar. 31, 1918; s. Joseph S. and Miriam (Haas) S.; m. Mary Stern, June 14, 1942; children: Peter Joseph, William Frederick, Peggy Ann Graeter. AB, Harvard U., 1940, MBA, 1943; HHD (hon.), Xavier U., 1988; DSc(hon.), U. Cin., 1989. With R. H. Macy & Co., N.Y.C., 1940-41; with U.S. Shoe Corp., Cin., 1941-68, v.p., 1951-65, pres., 1965-66, chmn. bd., chief exec. officer, 1966, chmn. exec. com., 1966-68, dir., 1956-70. Prof. bus. policy emeritus U. Cin. Pres. bd. trustees Cin. and Hamilton County Pub. Libr.; chmn. Cin. Bicentennial Com., Greater Cin. Tall Stacks Commn.; trustee Cin. Music Hall Assn., Cin. Hist. Soc., Children's Hosp. Med. Center, Cin. Symphony Orch., Cin Country Day Sch., 1956-72, Family Svc., Cin., 1964-82; trustee, pres. Cin. Mus. Festival Assn.; pres. bd. trustees Children's Convalescent Hosp., Cin., 1972-75; bd. overseers vis. com. univ. libr. Harvard U. Served to lt. USNR, 1943-46. Recipient Disting. Community Svc. award NCCJ, 1986, Great Living Cincinnatian award Cin. C. of C., 1989, Disting. Svc. award U. Cin. Coll. Bus., 1992. Mem. Am. Footwear Industries Assn. (life; dir.) Jewish (past pres. temple). Clubs: Literary (Cin.), Harvard (Cin.) (pres. 1965), Queen City (Cin.), Queen City Optimists, Harvard (N.Y.C.). Home: 3 Grandin Pl Cincinnati OH 45208-3402

STERN, JUDITH SCHNEIDER, nutritionist, researcher, educator; b. Bklyn. d. Sidney and Lillian (Rosen) Schneider; m. Richard C. Stern; 1 child, Daniel Arthur. BS, Cornell U., 1964; MS, Harvard U. Sch. Pub. Health, 1966, ScD, 1970. Rsch. asst., dept. food sci. and nutrition MIT, Cambridge, 1964-65; rsch. assoc. dept. human behavior and metabolism The Rockefeller U., N.Y.C., 1969-72, asst. prof. dept. human behavior and metabolism, 1972-74; contbg editor Vogue Mag., Conde Nast Publs., 1974; asst. prof. nutrition U. Calif., Davis, 1975-77, assoc. prof. dept. nutrition, 1977-82, dir. food intake lab. group, 1980—, prof. dept. nutrition, 1982—, prof. divsn. endocrinology, clin. nutrition & vasc. biology, 1988—. Mem. editl. bd. Internat. Jour. Obesity, 1976-85, Appetite, 1990, Obesity Rsch., 1993—, Nutrition Today, 1999—. Mem. nutrition adv. bd. Avocado Growers Calif., 1975—98; bd. sci. advisors Am. Coun. Sci. and Health, 1980; mem. U.S. Dept. Agr. Dietary Guidelines Adv. Com., 1983—85; bd. advisors Inst. Behavioral Edn.; mem. obesity task force NIDDK, 1996—2002, AAAS; mem. expert com. U.S. Pharmacopeia Bioavailability and Nutrient Absorption, 2000—; mem. adv. bd. USDA Nat. Agrl. Rsch. Ext., Edn. and Econs., 2000—. NIH tng. grant, 1979—. Mem. Am. Soc. Clin. Nutirition (pres. 1995-96), Am. Dietetic Assn., N.Am. Assn. for Study of Obesity (pres. 1992-93), Inst. Medicine NAS, Inst. Food Technologists, Am. Obesity Assn. (v.p. 1995—), Am. Soc. Nutrition Sci. (chair pub. info. com. 1992-94), Sigma Xi, Delta Omega. Office: U Calif Dept Nutrition 1 Shields Ave Davis CA 95616-5271 E-mail: jsstern@ucdavis.edu., sternshome@aol.com.

STERN, KATE MACOMBER, writer, educator; b. Iowa City, Aug. 19, 1952; d. Richard Gustave and Ruth Gay (Clark) S.; m. Jeffrey Jay Baron, Dec. 27, 1980; children: Liza Cady, Alexander Macomber. BA in English, Washington U., St. Louis, 1973; MA in English, U. Iowa, 1976; PhD in English, Loyola U., Chgo., 1983. With sch. dept. Holt, Rinehart and Winston, N.Y.C., 1973-74; press sec. Congressman Clarence Long, Washington, 1979; legis. corr. Senate Fin. Com., 1980; lectr. Georgetown U., 1983-85. Author: Christina Stead's Heroine, 1989; contbr. book rev. to literary jours. Mem. MLA, Am. Assn. Australian Lit. Studies. Avocations: Japanese language, Arabic language. Home: 5513 Mckinley St Bethesda MD 20817-3729

STERN, LEO G. lawyer; b. Mpls., Apr. 10, 1945; s. Philip J. and June I. (Monasch) S.; m. Christine E. Lamb, June 29, 1968; children: Alison M., Zachary A. BA, U. Calif., Davis, 1967; JD cum laude, U. Minn., 1970. Bar: Minn. 1970, U.S. Dist. Ct. Minn. 1971, Calif. 1971, U.S. Ct. Appeals (6th, 7th and 8th cirs.) 1985, U.S. Supreme Ct. 1993, Wis. 1999; cert. mediator and arbitrator, Minn. Ptnr. Cox, King & Stern, Mpls., 1970-77, Wright, West & Diessner, Mpls., 1977-84, Fredrikson & Byron, P.A., Mpls., 1984—. Mem. Minn. Bar Assn. (governing coun. environ. and natural resources law sect. 1989-95, governing coun. litigation sect. 1995-99), Am. Arbitration Assn. (arbitrator, mediator). Avocations: sailing, jogging. Home: 206 Central Ave S Wayzata MN 55391-1818 Office: Fredrikson & Byron PA 1100 International Ctr 900 2nd Ave S Minneapolis MN 55402-3314 E-mail: lstern@fredlaw.com

STERN, LEONARD, physician; b. Buffalo, Apr. 7, 1950; s. Henry and Sarah S.; m. Joan Stern, Sept. 8, 1974; children: Rebecca, Jeffrey. BA, CUNY, Bklyn., 1972; MD, N.Y. Med. Coll., 1975. Diplomate Am. Bd. Internal Medicine, Am. Bd. Nephrology. Intern and resident Albert Einstein Coll. of Medicine, Bronx, N.Y., 1975-78; fellowship in nephrology Montefiore Hosp. and Med. Ctr., 1978-79, Yale New Haven (Conn.) Hosp., 1979-81; dir. Dialysis Ctr. Columbia U., N.Y.C., 1995—, dir. peritoneal dialysis, 1985—; asst. prof. clin. medicine Columbia U. Coll. Physicians and Surgeons. Contbr. articles to profl. jours. Fellow ACP; mem. Am. Soc. Nephrology, Internat. Soc. Nephrology, Internat. Soc. for Peritoneal Dialysis. Avocations: outdoor activities, hiking, skiing, sailing. Office: NY Presbyn Hosp Columbia Presbyn Campus 622 W 168th St New York NY 10032-3720

STERN, LEONARD BERNARD, television and motion picture production company executive; b. N.Y.C., Dec. 23, 1923; s. Max and Esther (Marton) S.; m. Gloria Jane Stroock, Aug. 12, 1956; children: Michael Stroock, Kate Jennifer. Student, NYU, 1944. Dir. TV, L.A., 1946-53; writer, dir., producer Jackie Gleason Show/Honeymooners, Sergeant Bilko, Steve Allen Show N.Y.C., 1953-60; founder Price-Stern-Sloan, L.A., 1959-64, v.p., 1964-69, dir., 1969-80; pres. Heyday Prodns., L.A., 1962-69, 75-97; v.p. Talent Assocs./Norton Simon, L.A. and N.Y.C., 1965-75; pres. Tallfellow Prodns., L.A., 1997—. Author: (with Roger Price) Mad Libs, 1958, What Not to Name the Baby, 1960, Dear Attila the Hun, 1985; (with Roger Price and Larry Sloan) The Baby Boomer Book of Names, 1985, (with Diane L. Robison) A Martian Wouldn't Say That, 1994; writer, dir.: (motion pictures) Just You and Me, Kid, 1979, Target, 1985, Missing Pieces, 1990; creator, writer, dir. 21 TV series, including Get Smart, McMillan and Wife and He and She, 1953-89; mem. editor Dialogue newsletter. Mem. adv. coun. Sch. of Arts, NYU; bd. dirs. Nat. Coun. for Families and TV, Inst. for Mental Health Initiatives. Recipient Peabody award U. Ga., Writers Guild award 1956, 66, Nat. Assn. TV Arts and Scis. award 1956, 66-67, Emmy award 1956, 1966. Mem. Writers Guild Am., Dirs. Guild Am., Caucus for Producers, Writers and Dirs. (co-chmn., Mem. of Yr award 1987, Disting. Svc. award 1987), Producers Guild Am. (pres.), Bd. Motion Picure and TV Fund Found. Office: Tallfellow Prodns 1180 S Beverly Dr Ste 320 Los Angeles CA 90035-1154

STERN, LOUIS WILLIAM, marketing educator, consultant; b. Boston, Sept. 19, 1935; s. Berthold Summerfield Stern and Gladys (Koch) Cohen (deceased); m. Rhona L. Grant; children: Beth Ida, Deborah Lynn. AB, Harvard U., 1957; MBA in Mktg, U. Pa., 1959; PhD in Mktg, Northwestern U., 1962. Mem. staff bus. research and consumer mktg. sects. Arthur D. Little, Inc., Cambridge, Mass., 1961-63; from asst. prof. bus. orgn. to prof. Ohio State U., Columbus, Ohio, 1963—70, prof. mktg., 1970—73; from A. Montgomery Ward prof. mktg. to prof. emeritus Northwestern U., 1975—2001, John D. Gray disting. prof. mktg., 2001—; on leave as exec. dir. Mktg. Sci. Inst., Cambridge, Mass., 1983-85; Thomas Henry Carroll Ford Found. vis. prof. Harvard U. Grad. Sch. Bus. Adminstrn., 1984-85. Mem. staff Nat. Commn. on Food Mktg., Washington, 1965-66; vis. assoc. prof. bus. adminstrn. U. Calif., Berkeley, 1969-70; guest lectr. York U., U. Minn., U. Ky., UCLA, Ohio State U., U. N.C., Duke U., U. Wis., U. Pitts., U. Chgo., MIT, U. Mich., U. Pa., Cornell U., U. Mo., Norwegian Sch. Econs. and Bus. Adminstrn.; faculty assoc. Hernstein Inst., Vienna, Austria, 1976-77, Mgmt. Centre Europe, 1988-96; faculty assoc. Gemini Cons. Inc., Montvale, N.J., 1977-96, mem. midwest adv. bd., 1989-94; Xerox research prof. Northwestern U., 1981-82; cons. to FTC, 1973, 80; vis. scholar U. Calif., Berkeley, 1997-2001; mem. faculty adv. bd. CSC Index, 1997-98. Author: Distribution Channels: Behavioral Dimensions, 1969, (with Frederick D. Sturdivant and others) Managerial Analysis in Marketing, 1970, Perspectives in Marketing Management, 1971, (with John R. Grabner, Jr.) Competition in the Marketplace, 1970, (with Anne T. Coughlan, Erin Anderson and Adel I. El-Ansary) Marketing Channels, 6th edit., 2001, (with Thomas L. Eovaldi) Legal Aspects of Marketing Strategy: Antitrust and Consumer Protection Issues, 1984; (with Adel I. El-Ansary and James R. Brown) Management in Marketing Channels, 1989; mem. editl. bd. Jour. Mktg. Rsch., 1976-82, Jour. Mktg., 1979-83, Mktg. Letters, 1988-94; contbr. articles on mktg. to profl. jours. Mem. exec. com. Northwest Area Coun. on Human Rels., Columbus, 1971—72. Rsch. grantee: Ohio State U., 1964-73, Mktg. Sci. Inst., 1976-77, 88-90, 92-94; recipient Harold H. Maynard award best article Jour. Mktg., 1980; named Mktg. Educator of Yr. Sales and Mktg. Execs. Internat., 1989, also Chgo. chpt. 1990, Outstanding Profl. of Yr. award, 1992, and named One of Top 6 Profs. in Kellogg Sch., Northwestern U., Grad. Mgmt. Assocs., 1984-94, (named 6 times Outstanding Prof. Exec. Masters Program), One of Top 12 Tchrs. in U.S., Bus. Week. Mem. AAUP, Am. Mktg. Assn. (mem. program com. educators conf. 1971, chmn. com. 1978, Paul D. Converse award 1986, Richard D. Irwin Disting. Mktg. Educator of Yr. 1994), Hellenic Inst. Mktg. (hon.), Beta Gamma Sigma. Home: 522 Church St Apt 2D Evanston IL 60201-4575 Office: Northwestern U JL Kellogg Sch Mgmt Dept Mktg Evanston IL 60208-2001 E-mail: lwstern@kellogg.northwestern.edu.

STERN, MADELEINE BETTINA, rare books dealer, author; b. N.Y.C., July 1, 1912; d. Moses Roland and Lillie (Mack) S. BA, Barnard Coll., 1932; MA, Columbia U., 1934. Tchr. English N.Y.C. High Schs., 1934-43; ptnr. Leona Rostenberg Rare Books, N.Y.C., 1945—, Leona Rostenberg and Madeleine B. Stern Rare Books, N.Y.C., 1980—. Lectr. history of book, feminism, pub. history, lt. Author: The Life of Margaret Fuller, 1942, Louisa May Alcott, 1950, new edit., 1996, Purple Passage: The Life of Mrs. Frank Leslie, 1953, Imprints on History: Book Publishers and American Frontiers, 1956, We the Women: Career Firsts of Nineteenth Century America, 1962, new edit., 1994, So Much in a Lifetime: The Story of Dr. Isabel Barrows, 1965, Queen of Publishers' Row: Mrs. Frank Leslie, 1966, The Pantarch: A Biography of Stephen Pearl Andrews, 1968, Heads and Headlines: The Phrenological Fowlers, 1971, Books and Book People in 19th-Century America, 1978, Antiquarian Bookselling in the United States: A History from the Origins to the 1940s, 1985, Nicholas Gouin Dufief of Philadelphia Franco-American Bookseller, 1776-1834, 1988, The Life of Margaret Fuller: A Revised Second Edition, 1991, Louisa May Alcott: From Blood & Thunder to Hearth & Home, 1998; (with Leona Rostenberg) Old and Rare: Forty Years in the Book Business, 1974, rev. edit. 1988, Between Boards: New Thoughts on Old Books, 1978, Bookman's Quintet: Five Catalogues about Books, 1980, Quest Book-Guest Book: A Biblio-Folly, 1993, Connections: Our Selves-Our Books, 1994, Old Books in the Old World: Reminiscences of Book Buying Abroad, 1996, Old Books, Rare Friends: Two Literary Sleuths and Their Shared Passion, 1997, New Worlds in Old Books, 1999, Books Have Their Fates, 2001, Bookends: Two Women, One Enduring Friendship, 2001, From Revolution to Revolution: Perspectives on Publishing and Bookselling, 2002; editor: Women on the Move, 4 vols., 1972, Victoria Woodhull Reader, 1974, Louisa's Wonder Book-An Unknown Alcott Juvenile, 1975, Behind a Mask: The Unknown Thrillers of Louisa May Alcott, 1975, new edit., 1995, Plots and Counterplots: More Unknown Thrillers of Louisa May Alcott, 1976, Publishers for Mass Entertainment in 19th-Century America, 1980, A Phrenological Dictionary of 19th-Century Americans, 1982, Critical Essays on Louisa May Alcott, 1984, A Modern Mephistopheles and Taming a Tartar by Louisa May Alcott, 1987, Louisa May Alcott Unmasked: Collected Thrillers, 1995, Modern Magic by Louisa May Alcott, 1995, The Feminist Alcott: Stories of a Woman's Power, 1996, Louisa May Alcott: Signature of Reform, 2002; co-editor: Selected Letters of Louisa May Alcott, 1987, A Double Life: Newly Discovered Thrillers of Louisa May Alcott, 1988, The Journals of Louisa May Alcott, 1989, Louisa May Alcott: Selected Fiction, 1990, (co-editor) Freaks of Genius: Unknown Thrillers of Louisa May Alcott, 1991, From Jo March's Attic: Stories of Intrigue and Suspense, 1993 (Victorian Soc. award), The Lost Stories of Louisa May Alcott, 1995. Guggenheim fellow, 1943-45; recipient Medalie award Barnard Coll., 1982, Victorian Soc. award, Disting. Alumna award Barnard Coll., 1997. Mem. Antiquarian Booksellers Assn. Am. (gov. 1966-68, 78-80), Internat. League Antiquarian Booksellers, MLA, Am. Printing History Assn. (co-recipient award 1983), Authors League, Manuscript Soc. (former trustee), Phi Beta Kappa Jewish. Home: 40 E 88th St New York NY 10128-1176

STERN, MARGARET BASSETT, retired special education educator, author; b. Bklyn., June 6, 1920; d. Preston Rogers and Jeanne (Mordorf) Bassett; m. Fritz R. Stern Oct. 11, 1947 (div. Dec. 1992); children: Frederick Preston, Katherine Stern Brennan. BA, Wellesley Coll., 1942; MEd, Bank Street Coll. Edn., N.Y.C., 1943, 74. Propr. Castle Sch., N.Y.C., 1944-51; dir. Mothers' Coop. Nursery Sch., Ithaca, N.Y., 1952-54; tchr. sci. and math. The Brearley Sch., N.Y.C, 1956-57. Cons., lectr. Head Start, Tuskegee, Ala., 1964; cons. in math. The Gateway Sch., N.Y.C., 1967-90; spl. lectr. Columbia U. Tchrs. Coll., N.Y.C., 1990-94; condr. workshops in Eng., 1960-88. Author: (with Catherine Stern and Toni Gould) Structural Reading Program, Workbooks and Teachers Guides A through E, 1963, 3d edit., 1978, Structural Arithmetic Workbooks and Teachers Guides Grades 1-3, 1965, 2d edit., 1966, (with Stern) Children Discover Arithmetic, 1971, (with Gould) Spotlight on Phonics, Four Workbooks and Teachers Guides, 1980, Sound/Symbol Activities and Decoding Activities, 1980, 2d edit., 1994; Experimenting with Numbers, 1988, Structural Arithmetic, 1-3, 1992. Recipient award, Orton Dyslexia Soc. N.Y., 1989, Bank St. Coll. Edn., 1998. Mem. Nat. Coun. Tchrs. Math., Orton Dyslexia Soc. Home: 116 Pinehurst Ave Apt J44 New York NY 10033-1755

STERN, MARILYN, photographer, writer, picture editor; b. Detroit, Nov. 8, 1953; d. Julian and Phyllis Stern. BA, Brown U., 1976. Photographer's asst., N.Y.C., 1976-82; freelance photographer, 1976—; freelance writer, 1985—; picture editor Across the Board mag., 1990-96; tchr. Internat. Ctr. of Photography, 2001. Photographer, organizer: (book) Masked Culture: The Greenwich Village Halloween Parade, 1994; author, photographer: Kval! Die Walfanger der Lofoten, 1990; solo exhbn. Profil Gallery, Bratislava, 2001; several group exhbns., 1976--; represented in permanent collection Detroit Inst. Arts, also numerous pvt. collections. Travel Study grantee Royal Norwegian Consulate to Norway in the U.S., 1987, Am.-Scandinavian Found., 1986.

STERN, MARVIN, psychiatrist, educator; b. N.Y.C., Jan. 6, 1916; s. Jacob and Mary (Kappel) S.; m. Libby Rifkin, Jan. 18, 1942; children: Carol S., Robert M., Theodore A. BS, CCNY, 1935; MD, NYU, 1939. Diplomate Am. Bd. Psychiatry and Neurology. Intern in medicine and surgery Bellevue Hosp., N.Y.C., 1939-40, resident in medicine and psychiatry, 1940-42, fellow in psychiatry, 1946-47; practice medicine specializing in psychiatry, 1947—; asst. prof. psychiatry NYU Med. Ctr., 1948-55, assoc. prof., 1955-62, prof., 1962-79, Menas S. Gregory prof. psychiatry, 1979-86, prof., 1986-95; prof. emeritus, 1995—, NYU Med. Ctr., N.Y.C., 1995—, exec. chmn. dept. psychiatry, 1976-86. Mem. staff NYU Hosp., Bellevue Hosp.; cons. psychiatrist VA Hosp.; cons. psychiatrist emeritus Brookdale Hosp. Served to maj. AUS, 1942-46. Fellow Am. Psychiat. Assn. (sec. dist. br. 1956-63, pres. dist. br. 1964, area chmn. 1962-63); mem. Am. Psychosomatic Assn., N.Y.C. Acad. Medicine, Harvey Soc., NYU Med. Alumni Assn. (pres. 1979-80), Phi Beta Kappa, Sigma Xi, Alpha Omega Alpha Home: 300 E 33rd St Apt 12C New York NY 10016-9415 Office: NYU Sch Medicine 550 1st Ave New York NY 10016-6402

STERN, MICHAEL LAWRENCE, psychologist; b. N.Y.C., July 3, 1948; s. Abraham Isaac and Etta (Silverberg) S.; m. Karen Beth Rivard, July 26, 1981; children: Joshua Ethan, Rachel Lynn. BA, Calif. State U., Long Beach, 1970; PhD, U. Wash., 1977. Diplomate Am. Bd. Med. Psychotherapists; cert. employee assistance profl., sex therapist. Intern St. Elizabeth's Hosp. NIMH, Washington, 1973-74; instr. dept. psychology U. Wash., Seattle, 1975-77; rsch. assoc. dept. psychiatry U. Tenn. Med. Sch., Memphis, 1977-78; clin. dir. drug abuse program Fed. Correction Inst., Danbury, Conn., 1978-85, chief psychologist, 1985-86; dir. outpatient recovery ctr. Briarcliff Manor, N.Y., 1986-88; pvt. practice clin. psychology, 1981-86; cons. Addiction Recovery Corp, Westchester, 1987-88; adj. faculty Fairfield U., 1981-86; dir. OMNI Health Assn. U. Tenn. postdoctoral fellow, 1977-78. Mem. Am. Psychol. Assn. (cert. addictions), Assn. Advancement Behavior Therapy, Am. Assn. Sex Educators, Counselor, and Therapists, Conn. Psychol. Assn. Family Firm Inst. Cons. editor TSA News, 1977-78. Home: Saw Mill Ridge Rd Newtown CT 06470 Office: Green Knoll Profl Ctr 60 Old New Milford Rd Brookfield CT 06804-2430

STERN, MORT(IMER) P(HILLIP), journalism and communications educator, academic administrator, consultant; b. New Haven, Feb. 20, 1926; s. Bernard and Louise Eleanor (Spiro) S.; m. Patricia Ruth Freeman, Jan. 10, 1946; children: Susan C., Margaret L. AB, U. Ark., 1947; MS, Columbia U., 1949; postgrad., Harvard U., 1954-55; PhD, U. Denver, 1969. Reporter S.W.-Am., Ft. Smith, Ark., 1946-47; night bur. mgr. UPI, Little Rock, 1947-48; reporter, polit. writer, state editor Ark. Gazette, 1949-51; reporter, rewrite man Denver Post, 1951-53, night city editor, 1953-54, asst. editor Rocky Mountain Empire sect., 1955-56, mng. editor, 1956-58, assoc. editor, 1958, editorial page editor, 1958-65, asst. to pub., 1965-70, editorial page editor, 1971-73; dean Sch. Pub. communication U. Ala., 1973-74; dean Sch. Journalism U. Colo., Boulder, 1974-77; lectr. journalism U. Denver, 1953-54, adj. prof., 1970, exec. dir. pub. affairs, 1977-78, exec. asst. to chancellor, 1978-84; prof., chmn. dept. journalism and mass communication U. No. Colo., Greeley, 1985-90; pres. P. Paty & Co., Georgetown, Colo., 1989—. Atwood prof. journalism U. Alaska, Anchorage, 1981-82. With USAAF, 1944-45. Elected to Georgetown, Colo. Bd. of Selectmen, Apr. 7, 1997-99. Nieman fellow Harvard U., 1954-55; named Disting. Alumnus dept. journalism U. Ark., 1999; inducted to Fulbright Coll. Alumni Acad. U. Ark., 1999. Mem.: Assn. for Edn. in Journalism, Georgetown Libr. Assn. (v.p. 1999—, bd. dirs., pres. 2001—), Phi Beta Kappa, Sigma Delta Chi, Omicron Delta Kappa. Baptist. Home: PO Box 549 Georgetown CO 80444-0549 E-mail: stemegrit@aol.com.

STERN, NANCY FORTGANG, mathematics and computer science, educator; b. N.Y.C., July 15, 1944; d. Murray and Selma (Karp) Fortgang; m. Robert A Stern, Sept. 3, 1964; children: Lori Anne, Melanie. AB, Barnard Coll., 1965; MS, NYU, 1968; MA, SUNY, 1974, PhD, 1978. Programmer analyst ATT, N.Y.C., 1965-67; asst. prof. Nassau Community Coll., Garden City, N.Y., 1965-68; adj. prof. Dowling Coll. SUNY, 1968-77; disting. prof. Hofstra U., Hempstead, N.Y., 1977—. Rsch. cons. Am. Inst. Physics, N.Y.C., 1976-77; adv. editor John Wiley & Sons, 1977—. Author 12 textbooks on computing; asst. editor in chief Annals of the History of Computing, 1977-87; contbr. articles to profl. jours. Mem. Charles Babbage Inst., Nat. Computing Com. E-mail: nancy.stern@hofstra.edu.

STERN, PAUL CLINTON, social scientist; b. N.Y.C., Dec. 23, 1944; s. Sydney Clinton and Anne Lillian (Schechtman) S.; m. Susan Parkison, July 13, 1968; 1 child, Sarah R. (dec.). BA, Amherst Coll., 1964; MA, Clark U., 1969, PhD, 1975. From instr. to asst. prof. psychology Elmira (N.Y.) Coll., 1971-78; postdoctoral fellow, rsch. assoc. Yale U., New Haven, 1978-80; study dir., prin. staff officer U.S. Nat. Rsch. Coun., Washington, 1980—; rsch. prof. sociology George Mason U., Fairfax, Va., 1993—; pres. Social and Environ. Rsch. Inst., Leverett, Mass., 1996—. Peer ptnr. Danish Environ. Rsch. Program, Denmark, 1997. Author: (book) Evaluating Social Science Research, 1979, (with others) Home Energy Conservation: Issues and Programs for the 1980s, 1981, Environmental Problems and Human Behavior, 1996, Evaluating Social Science Research, 2d edit., 1996; editor: (with others) Energy Use: The Human Dimension, 1984, Improving Energy Demand Analysis, 1984, Energy Efficiency in Buildings: Behavioral Issues, 1985, Perspectives on Deterrence, 1989, Behavior, Society, and Nuclear War, vol. 1, 1989, vol. 2, 1991, vol. 3, 1993, Global Environmental Change: Understanding the Human Dimensions, 1992, Perspectives on Nationalism and War, 1995, Understanding Risk: Informing Decisions in a Democratic Society, 1996, Environmentally Significant Consumption: Research Directions, 1997, People and Pixels: Linking Remote Sensing and Social Science, 1998, Making Climate Forecasts Matter, 1999, The Aging Mind: Opportunities in Cognitive Research, 2000, International Conflict Resolution After the Cold War, 2000, The Drama of the Commons, 2002, New Tools for Environmental Protection: Education, Information, and Voluntary Measures, 2002; co-editor: Jour. Socio-Econs., 1991-98; assoc. editor: (jours.) Evaluation Rev., 1986-89, Environment and Behavior, 1997—; contbr. articles to profl. jours., chpts. to books. Fellow AAAS, APA; mem. Soc. for Psychol. Study of Social Issues, Soc. for Personality and Social Psychology, Soc. for Human Ecology. Office: Nat Rsch Coun 2101 Constitution Ave NW Washington DC 20418-0007 E-mail: pstern@nas.edu.

STERN, PETER R. lawyer; b. East Orange, N.J., Nov. 2, 1947; s. Ralph and Jacqueline Rene (Piot) S. BA, Columbia U., 1969, JD, 1972. Bar: N.Y. 1973, U.S. Dist. Ct. (so. and ea. dists.) 1973, U.S. Ct. Appeals (2d cir.) 1975, U.S. Ct. Appeals (3d cir.) 1995, U.S. Ct. Appeals (D.C. cir.) 2001, U.S. Supreme Ct. 1979. Law clk. to judge U.S. Dist. Ct., N.Y.C., 1972-74; assoc. Winthrop, Stimson, Putnam & Roberts, 1974-80; founding ptnr. Berger, Steingut, Weiner, Fox & Stern, 1980-85; ptnr. Berger & Steingut, 1986-90, Berger Steingut Tarnoff & Stern, N.Y.C., 1990-93, Berger, Steingut & Stern, N.Y.C., 1993-94, Berger, Stern & Webb, LLP, N.Y.C., 1994—. Bd. dirs. Kitchen Ctr., N.Y.C., 1978-90; bd. advisors Franklin Furnace, 1984-97; law adv. coun. Internat. Found. for Art Rsch., 1988—. Bd. dirs. Vol. Lawyers for Arts, 1995—, chmn. 1999—. Mem. ABA, N.Y.C. Bar Assn., Fed. Bar Coun., N.Y. State Bar. Office: 900 3rd Ave New York NY 10022-4728 E-mail: pstern@bswny.com.

STERN, PHYLLIS NOERAGER, nursing educator; b. San Mateo, Calif., Sept. 2, 1925; d. Philip Julius and Grace Ann (Zoellen) Noerager; m. David Arthur Hungerford, May 20, 1949 (div. Sept. 1956); 1 child, Paula Ann; m. Milton Stern, July 5, 1960 (dec. Jan. 2001). AA, Coll. San Mateo, 1968; BS magna cum laude, San Francisco State U., 1970; MS, U. Calif., San Francisco, 1971, D of Nursing Sci., 1976. Asst. prof. Calif. State U., Hayward, 1971-76, U. Calif., San Francisco, 1976-80; prof. Northwestern State U. La., Shreveport, 1980-82; prof., dir. Dalhousie U., Halifax, N.S., Can., 1983-87, prof. Can., 1987-91; prof., dept. chair Ind. U., Indpls., 1991-96, prof., 1996—. Editor, author: Women Health and Culture, 1986; editor: Childbirth and Childcare, 1988, Lesbian Health Care, 1991; editor-in-chief: Health Care for Women Internat., 1983-2001; co-editor: (with R.S. Schricber) Grounded Theory for Nurses (Am. Jour. Nursng Book of Yr. award 2001), 2001. Health educator Battered Women's Shelter, Indpls., Salvation Army, Indpls., 1994-96. Named Disting. Alumna U. Calif., San Francisco, 1995; rsch. grantee Ind. U., 1995; Glenn W. Irwin Jr. Rsch. scholar, 1999. Fellow Am. Acad. Nursing (mem. expert panel 1989-96), Am. Acad. Practice Coun. (Disting. Practitioner 1992), Coun. Gen. Internat. on Women's Health Issues (co-founder 1984—), Am. Acad. Anthropology, Sigma Theta Tau. Avocations: film, reading, walking, mentoring. Office: Ind U 1111 Middle Dr Indianapolis IN 46202-5243 E-mail: pnstern@aol.com., pstern@iupui.edu.

STERN, RALPH DAVID, lawyer; b. Longview, Tex., June 20, 1943; children: Eric, Justin. AB, Bucknell U., 1963; JD, U. Chgo., 1966. Bar: D.C. 1967, Ill. 1967, Calif. 1970, U.S. Supreme Ct. 1970. Law clk. Ill. Appellate Ct., Chgo., 1966-67; assoc. Ressman & Tishler, 1968-70; exec. asst. Orange County Bd. Suprs., Santa Ana, Calif., 1970-71; gen. counsel San Diego City Schs., 1971-83; ptnr. Whitmore, Kay & Stevens, Palo Alto, Calif., 1983-88, Stern & Keebler, San Mateo, 1988-90; gen. counsel Schs. Legal Counsel, Hayward, 1990—2001; chief sch. counsel Sch. and Coll. Legal Svcs. of Calif., 2002—. Chmn. Nat. Coun. Sch. Attys., 1982-83; pres. Leagal Aid Soc. San Diego, 1976-79, Nat. Orgn. on Legal Problems of Edn., 1981-82. Editor: Law and the School Principal, 1978; contbr. articles to profl. jours. Mem. exec. bd., county membership chair Boy Scouts Am., San Diego, 1979-81; vice chmn. Laurels for Leaders, San Diego, 1980-83; mem. ednl. adminstrn. adv. com. U. San Diego, 1981-86.; mem. adv. com. West's Ednl. Law Reporter, 1981-85. Named Outstanding Young Citizen, San Diego Jaycees, 1977. Office: Sch and Coll Legal Svcs 313 W Winton Ave Rm 372 Hayward CA 94544-1136

STERN, RICHARD DAVID, investment company executive; b. New Rochelle, N.Y., Nov. 5, 1936; s. Leo and Grace Marjorie (Phillips) S.; m. Phyllis Marlene Edelstein, Nov. 20, 1966; children: Marjorie Anne, Andrew Howard. AB, Princeton U., 1958; MBA, Harvard U., 1962. CFA. 1st v.p. Newburger, Loeb & Co., N.Y.C., 1962-74, also bd. dirs., 1969-74; sr. investment officer Ctrl. Trust Co., Cin., 1974-76, owner bus. valuation cons. co., 1976-78; v.p. Gt. Western Bank & Trust Co. (now Wells Fargo Bank), Phoenix, 1978-84; pres. Stern, Ludke & Co. (now Stellar Capital Mgmt. LLC.), 1984—, mng. mem., 2000—. Co-author: Air Cushion Vehicles, 1962. Trustee endowment trust Phoenix Chamber Music Soc., 1982-91; v.p., 1986-90, bd. dirs., 1982-91, 93-94; pres. Cen. Ariz. chpt. Arthritis Found., 1982-84, chmn. planned giving com., 1986-91, mem. nat. planned giving com., 1987-89; chmn. endowments and trusts com. Temple Beth Israel, Phoenix, 1980-83; dir., investment com. Endowment Found., Temple Solel, Paradise Valley, 1990—; pres. Am. Jewish Com., Phoenix, 1983-84, bd. dirs., 1980-84, adv. bd., 1985—; bd. dirs. Asian Arts Coun., Phoenix Art Mus., 1987-93, v.p., 1989-90, pres., 1990-92; trustee Ariz. Theatre Co., 1990-97, mem. regional nominating com., 1995-97, chmn., 1995-96, asst. treas., 1996-97; panelist Phoenix Arts Commn., 2002. Mem. Phoenix Soc. Fin. Analysts (chmn. profl. conduct com. 1980-83, membership com. 1990-91, bd. dirs.), Anti-Defamation League (dir. Ctrl. Ariz. chpt. 1986—, exec. bd. 1989—, chair nominating com. 1990-94, 2001—, chair bd. devel. 1993-94, treas. 1994—, assoc. nat. commr. 1998—), Princeton Alumni Assn. No. Ariz. (alumni schs. com. 1992—), Univ. Club Phoenix (bd. dirs. 1990-92, fin. com. 1990-91), Harvard Bus. Sch. Club Ariz. (bd. dirs. 1991—, pres. 1993-95, treas. 1995—). Republican. Home: 7547 N Lakeside Ln Paradise Valley AZ 85253-2857 Office: 2200 E Camelback Rd Ste 130 Phoenix AZ 85016-3455 E-mail: rstern@stellarmgt.com.

STERN, RICHARD GUSTAVE, writer, educator; b. N.Y.C., Feb. 25, 1928; s. Henry George and Marion (Veit) S.; m. Gay Clark, Mar. 14, 1950 (div. Feb. 1972); children: Christopher Holmes, Kate Macomber, Andrew Henry, Nicholas Clark; m. Alane Rollings, Aug. 9, 1985. BA, U. N.C., 1947; MA, Harvard U., 1950; PhD, State U. Iowa, 1954. Mem. faculty U. Chgo., 1955—, prof. English, 1965—, Helen Regenstein prof. English, 1990—2002, prof. emeritus, 2002. Author: Golk, 1960, Europe and Up and Down with Baggish and Schreiber, 1961, In Any Case, 1962, Teeth, Dying and Other Matters, 1964, Stitch, 1965, 1968: A Short Novel, An Urban Idyll, Five Stories and Two Trade Notes, 1970, The Books in Fred Hampton's Apartment, 1973, Other Men's Daughters, 1973, Natural Shocks, 1978, Packages, 1980, The Invention of the Real, 1982, A Father's Words, 1986, The Position of the Body, 1986, Noble Rot: Stories, 1949-88, 1989 (book of yr. award Chgo. Sun-Times 1990), Shares and Other Fictions, 1992, One Person and Another, 1993, A Sistermony, 1995 (Heartland award, nonfiction book of year), Pacific Tremors, 2001, What Is What Was, 2002; editor: Honey and Wax, 1966. Recipient Longwood Found. award, 1960, Friends of Lit. award, 1963, fiction award Nat. Inst. Arts and Letters, 1968; Nat. Coun. Arts and Humanities fellow, 1967-68, Carl Sandburg award for fiction, 1979, Arts Coun. awards, 1979, 81, Am. Acad. and Inst. of Arts and Letters medal of Merit for Novel, 1985; Rockefeller fellow, 1965, Guggenheim fellow, 1973-74. Fellow Ctr. Advanced Studies in the Behavioral Scis.; mem. Am. Acad. Arts and Scis. Office: U Chgo Dept English Chicago IL 60637 E-mail: rstern@midway.uchicago.edu.

STERN, RICHARD HENRY, advertising executive; b. N.Y., Sept. 9, 1936; s. Henry Leo and Harriet Caroline (Koll) S.; m. Alicia Bishko, May 7, 1960; children: Jeffrey, Steffan, Elizabeth. BS, Fordham U., 1958. Mgr. advt. devel. Consol. Edison Co., N.Y., 1959-66; account exec. Reach McClinton & Co., 1966-73; account supr. Bozell & Jacobs, Inc., 1973-78, group v.p. Union, N.J., 1980-84; account supr. Marsteller, Inc., N.Y., 1978-80; advt. sales promotion mgr. Automatic Switch Co., N.J., 1985-99; ret., 1999; owner Dee Ess Comm., Towaco, N.J., 1984-87. Mem. adv. bd. Nat. Mfg. Week. Dep. mayor Montville Twp., 1988-89, mayor, 1990, councilman, 1976-87; mem. Montville Twp. Planning Bd., 1981-90; mem. Montville Twp. Zoning Bd., 2001—; pres. bd. trustees Montville Twp. Pub. Libr.; legis. Aide, N.J. State Assembly, 1996-99, N.J. State Senate, 1973-77. Republican. Roman Catholic. Avocations: decoy carving, woodworking, gardening, travel. Home: 5 Tumbling Brook Dr Towaco NJ 07082-1021 : 254 Pompano Dr Loveladies NJ 08008 E-mail: rdeeess@aol.com.

STERN, ROBERT, psychiatrist; b. Aug. 12, 1928; BS, Swiss Fed. Inst. Tech., Zurich, 1951; MS, Yale U., 1953, PhD, 1956; MD, Case Western Res. U., 1966. Diplomate Am. Bd. Psychiatry and Neurology; lic. physician, Conn. Asst. prof. chemistry Wesleyan U., Middletown, Conn., 1957-58, Conn. Coll., New London, 1959-60; supr. bio-organic chem. rsch. Arthur D. Little, Inc., Cambridge, Mass., 1960-62; vis. fellow medicine Mass. Gen. Hosp., 1964; rsch. assoc. biol. chemistry Harvard Med. sch., Boston, 1964, tchg. fellow psychiatry, 1967-68; intern medicine King County Hosp./U. Wash., Seattle, 1966-67; resident in psychiatry McLean Hosp., Belmont, Mass., 1967-68; jr./sr. asst. resident internal medicine Yale-New Haven Hosp., 1968-70, clin. fellow medicine, 1970-71; postdoctoral fellow psychiatry Yale U. Sch. Medicine, 1971-73, asst. clin. prof. psychiatry, 1974-86, assoc. clin. prof. psychiatry, 1986—; pvt. practice New Haven, 1973—. Cons. Child Guidance clinic of Southeastern Conn., New London, 1973-82; cons. CHAMPUS peer reviewer Qualidigu, Inc., Middletown, 1994-98; lectr. in field. Contbr. articles to profl. jours. Fellow Am. Psychiat. Assn., 1989-99, life fellow, 1999—; mem. New Haven Individual Practice Assn. (co-chmn. psychiatry panel 1985-98, quality assurance com. 1989-98, bd. dirs. 1986-89), Conn. Psychiatry Soc. (councilor-at-large 2001—, councilor 2000-2001, pres. New Haven/Middlesex chpt. 1999-2000, treas. 1996-99, managed care com. 1996-98, com. on 3d party payors 1985-96, ins. com. 1980-85, pvt. practice com. 1979-80), New Haven Individual Practice Assn. (co-chmn. psychiatry panel 1985-98, quality assurance com. 1989-98, bd. dirs. 1986-89), Conn. State Med. Soc., New Haven County Med. Assn (New Haven pvt. practice com. 1995—). Office: 340 Whitney Ave New Haven CT 06511-2317

STERN, ROBERT C. physician, educator; b. N.Y.C., Dec. 13, 1938; s. Samuel and Lily S. BA, Drew U., 1959; MD, Albert Einstein Coll. Medicine, 1963. Diplomate Nat. Bd. Med. Examiners, Am. Bd. Pediat., Am. Bd. Pediatric Pulmonology. Intern pediat. U. Hosps. Cleve., Babies and Childrens Hosp. Divsn., 1963-64, jr. asst. resident pediat., 1964-65; sr. asst. resident pediat. Bronx Mcpl. Hosp. Ctr., N.Y.C., 1965-66; fellow cystic fibrosis/pediat. pulmonary diseases Case Western Res. U. Sch. Medicine, Cleve., 1968-70; sr. instr. pediat. Case Western Res. U., 1970-71, asst. prof., 1971-77, assoc. prof., 1977-83, prof., 1983—. Cons. Cystic Fibrosis Founds. various countries, 1990—, various pharm. and med. tech. cos., 1990—. Author: Treatment of Hospitalized Cystic Fibrosis Patients, 1998, Treatment of Cystic Fibrosis, 2000; contbr. numerous chpts. to Nelson's Textbook of Pediatrics, 1979—, also over 100 articles to med. jours. Pres., CEO, Children's Lung Found., Cleve., 1983—. Capt. USAF, 1966-68. Recipient David Stuckert award Cystic Fibrosis Rsch. Inst., San Francisco, 1997. Mem. Am. Thoracic Soc., Soc. Pediat. Rsch. Achievements include introduction of heparin lock for intermittent administration of intravenous drugs; research in cystic fibrosis. Avocations: reading, running, chess, writing humor, mathematics. Home: 2300 Overlook Rd Apt 406 Cleveland Heights OH 44106-2391 Office: Univ Hosp Cleve 11100 Euclid Ave Cleveland OH 44106-1736 E-mail: rcs1@prodigy.net.

STERN, ROBERT D. publishing executive; b. N.Y.C., Sept. 30, 1929; s. Morris and Jean (Gordon) S.; m. Natalie Greenberg, Sept. 5, 1952 (div. 1978); children: Mitchell, Bradley; m. Roslyne Paige, June 5, 1978. BA, Syracuse U., 1950; JD, NYU, 1953, LLM, 1958. Bar: N.Y. 1955, U.S. Dist. Ct. (D.C. cir.) 1953, U.S. Supreme Ct. 1967. Ptnr. Fink, Weinberger, Levin & Gottschalk, N.Y.C., 1957-59, 1957—72; chmn. Rudor Consol. Industries, 1972—99, Dance Mag., Inc., N.Y.C., 1985—2001, AGC/Sedgwick Inc., Princeton, N.J., 1990—. Bd. dirs. Ctr. for Graphic Comms. Mgmt. and Tech., NYU, N.Y.C., 1979—; chmn. bd. dirs. AGC Sedgwick, Princeton, N.J., Rudor Consol. Ind. Inc.; pub. Stern's Performing Arts Directory, 1989-98. Bd. dirs. YMCA, N.Y.C., 1987-90 Mem. ABA, N.Y. State Bar Assn., Sheldrake Yacht Club (Mamaroneck, N.Y.), Birchwood Country Club (Westport, Conn.). Avocations: tennis, skiing, sailing. Home: 2 Imperial Lndg Westport CT 06880-4934

STERN, ROBERT MASON, lawyer; b. Balt., May 9, 1944; s. Albert L. and Margaret E. (Jones) S.; m. Joan E. Venezia, Sept. 4, 1971; 1 child, Ryan. Student, Am. U., 1965; BA, Pomona Coll., 1966; JD, Stanford U., 1969. Bar: Calif. 1970, U.S. Dist. Ct. (no. dist.) Calif. 1970. Teaching fellow Stanford (Calif.) Law Sch., 1969-70; counsel assembly elections com. Calif. State Legis., Sacramento, 1971-72; elections counsel Calif. Sec. of State's Office, 1973-74; gen. counsel Fair Polit. Practices Commn., 1975-83; co-dir., gen. counsel Calif. Commn. on Campaign Financing, L.A., 1983-99; pres. Ctr. Govtl. Studies, 1999—. Host cable TV program Polit. Potpourri, L.A., 1989-93; election night polit. commentator Sta. KSMC Channel 30, Santa Monica, Calif., 1988, 90, 92; host cable TV program Rodney King Beating Trial, L.A., 1992; cons. L.A. City Ethics Commn., 1990-97; adminstr. Coun. on Govtl. Ethics Laws, 1994-99; expert witness in campaign fin. cases. Co-author: The New Gold Rush, 1985, Money and Politics in Local Elections, 1989, Democracy by Initiative: Shaping California's Fourth Branch of Government, 1992, The Price of Justice, 1995, Campaign Money on the Information Highway, 1998; contbr. articles to profl. jours. Co-author Polit. Reform Act-Proposition 9 state-wide initiative, Calif., 1974; French horn player Palisades Symphony. Recipient Annual Ethics award Coun. on Govtl. Ethics, Orlando, Fla., 1988, Good Govt. award Calif. Common Cause, 1982. Mem. Americans for Nonsmokers Rights (bd. dirs. 1986-97). Avocation: playing French horn. Home: 18057 Coastline Dr Apt 6 Malibu CA 90265-5713 Office: Ctr for Governmental Studies 10951 W Pico Blvd # 120 Los Angeles CA 90064-2126 E-mail: stern@cgs.org.

STERN, ROBERT MORRIS, gastrointestinal psychophysiology researcher, psychology educator; b. N.Y.C., June 18, 1937; s. Irving Dan and Nellie (Wachstetter) S.; m. Wilma Olch, June 19, 1960; children: Jessica Leigh, Alison Rachel. AB, Franklin and Marshall Coll., 1958; MS, Tufts U., 1960; PhD, Ind. U., 1963. Research assoc. dept. psychology Ind. U., 1963-65; asst. prof. psychology Pa. State U., 1965-68, assoc. prof., 1968-73, prof., 1973—, disting. prof., 1992—, head dept., 1978-87. Author: (with W.J. Ray) Biofeedback, 1977, (with W.J. Ray and C.M. Davis) Psychophysiological Recording, 1980, (with K.L. Koch) Electrogastrography, 1985, (with W.J. Ray and K.S. Quigley) Psychophysiological Recording, 2d edit., 2001; contbr. articles to profl. jours. Recipient Nat. Media award Am. Psychol. Found., 1978 Mem. Am. Psychol. Soc., Aerospace Med. Assn., Soc. Psychophysiol. Rsch., Am. Gastroent. Assn., Internat. EGG Soc., Functional Brain-Gut Rsch. Assn., Internat. Brain-Gut Soc. Home: 1360 Greenwood Cir State College PA 16803-3232 Office: Pa State U 512 Moore Bldg University Park PA 16802-3105 E-mail: RS3@psu.edu.

STERN, ROBERT STUART, dermatologist; b. New Haven, Sept. 23, 1944; s. Jack and Ann (Bercutt) S.; m. Gail Ann Howrigan, July 28, 1985; children: Elizabeth Preston, Julia Paige. AB, Harvard U., 1966; MD, Yale U., 1970. Intern Mt. Sinai Hosp., N.Y.C., 1970-71; rsch. assoc. NIH, Bethesda, Md., 1971-73; resident Mass. Gen. Hosp., Boston, 1973-76; from instr. to prof. dermatology Harvard U. Med. Sch., 1976-97, prof., 1997—, Carl J. Herzog prof., 2000—; chair dept. dermatology Beth Israel Deaconess Med. Ctr., 2000—. Cons. Health Sci. Industries Coun., Washington, 1971-73; mem. exec. com. U.S. Pharm. Conv., Rockville, Md., 1988-2000. Contbr. articles to profl. jours. With USPHS, 1971-73. Fellow Mass. Gen. Hosp., 1975-76, Milton Fund fellow, 1985. Mem. Phi Beta Kappa. Home: 39 Clinton Rd Brookline MA 02445-5812 Office: Beth Israel Deaconess Med Ctr 330 Brookline Ave Boston MA 02215-5400 E-mail: rstern@caregroup.harvard.edu.

STERN, ROSLYNE PAIGE, magazine publisher; b. Chgo., May 26, 1926; d. Benjamin Gross and Clara (Sniderman) Roer; m. William E. Weber, May 3, 1944 (div. Mar. 1956); m. Richard S. Paige, June 28, 1958 (div. Apr. 1978); children: Sandra Weber Porr, Barbara Paige Kaplan, Elizabeth Paige (dec.); m. Robert D. Stern, June 5, 1978. Cert., U. Chgo., 1945. Profl. model, singer, 1947-53; account exec. Interstate United, Chgo., 1955-58; sales mgr. Getting To Know You Internat., Great Neck, N.Y., 1963-71, exec. v.p., 1971-78; pub. After Dark Mag., N.Y.C., 1978-82; assoc. pub. Dance Mag., 1978-85, pres., pub., 1985—2001, pres. emeritus, 2001—. Bd. dirs. Rudor Consol. Industries, Inc., N.Y.C., AGC/Sedgwick, Inc., Princeton, N.J. Founding pres. Dance Mag. Found., N.Y.C., 1984-86; life mem. nat. women's com. Brandeis U., Waltham, Mass., 1958—; bd. dirs. Westport Arts Ctr.; The Internation Com. for Dance Libr. of Israel. Recipient Disting. Svc. award Dance Notation Bur., 1996, Am. Coll. Dance Festival award, 1998, Pres.'s award Dance Masters of Am., Inc., 1998, Documents of Dance award Dance Library of Israel, 1999. Mem. Pub. Relations Soc. Am., LWV, Am. Theatre Wing, Nat. Arts Club. Democrat. Jewish. Avocations: dance, theater, opera, visual arts, travel. Home: 2 Imperial Lndg Westport CT 06880-4934

STERN, RUTH SZOLD, business executive, artist; b. Bronx, N.Y., Oct. 14, 1929; d. Albert and Margaret (Karl) Nussbacher; m. Martin Szold, Apr. 10, 1949 (div. Sept. 1978); children: Lauren, Terry; m. James C. Stern, Aug. 22, 1982. Student, Hunter Coll., N.Y.C., 1947; cert. in writing, UCLA, 1988; BFA, Calif. Inst. Arts, 1994, MFA, 1996. Exec. legal sec. to sr. ptnr. Paul, Weiss, Rifkind, Wharton & Garrison, N.Y.C., 1958-62; asst. to pres. M.E. Green & Co. brokerage, 1962-65; demonstrator, cons. various cosmetic cos., 1965-85; founder, pres. Ruth Szold Promotional Models, 1968-84, Cosmetic Art, Inc., 1979-85, founder, pres., designer, promoter cosmetic line, 1979-85; columnist Fire Island News, Ocean Beach, N.Y., 1985-89; asst. to pres., CEO Gladden Entertainment, L.A., 1989-90; exec. adminstr. C&O Cogent Light and Techs., 1990-91. Demonstrator-lectr. for TV, also videotapes; condr. cosmetic workshops for N.Y. Salute to Fashion Industries, 1981; chmn. earthquake com. Fountainview Assn., 1989-98, bd. dirs., 1997-98; cons. in field; tchr. art to homeless Found. House, West Hollywood, Calif., 2000. One-woman shows include Fire Island Transmission, 1997; group exhbns. include SPLICE Side St. Projects, Santa Monica, Calif., 1997-98, 5th Ann. Miracle on 18th St. Side St. Projects, Santa Monica, 1997, (video) Mel and Alice's Wedding 1950, 2000, Santa Barbara Contemporary Arts Forum, 2002, (edible books) Occidental Coll., 2002. Mem. coun. Girl Scouts U.S.A., 1964-69; bd. dirs. Bleecker Tower Tenants Corp., N.Y.C., 1979-80, chmn. architecture and design com., 1979-80, chmn. maintenance, 1980-85, pres., 1981-82; mem. Hunger Project, Fin. Family; lectr., panelist Am. Women's Econ. Devel. Corp.,

1981. Recipient gold medal Deborah Fund Raising Dinner, 1955. Mem. Foragers of Am., Nat. Retail Mchts. Assn., Fragrance Found., Cosmetic Exec. Women, Brandeis U. Club, Hadassah Club. Home: 8455 Fountain Ave Apt 515 Los Angeles CA 90069-2543

STERN, SAMUEL ALAN, lawyer; b. Phila., Jan. 21, 1929; AB, U. Pa., 1949; LLB, Harvard U., 1952. Bar: Mass. 1952, D.C. 1958. Ptnr. Wilmer, Cutler & Pickering, Washington, 1962-88, Dickstein, Shapiro & Morin, Washington, 1988-92; pvt. practice law and bus. Washington and St. Petersburg, Russia, 1992-94; counsel Rogers & Wells, Washington, N.Y.C., 1994-97; pvt. practice law and bus. Washington, 1997-98; gen. counsel Global Energy Investors, Inc., 1997-2000; ptnr. Hills & Stern, 1999—; pres. Hills Enterprises, 1999—; counselor Hills & Co., 1999—. Vis. prof. law Harvard U., Cambridge, Mass., 1976; dir. Internat. Law Inst. Georgetown U., 1971—, adj. prof. law, 1979—92; asst. counsel Warren Commn., 1964; cons. UN, 1984—96; bd. dirs. Hills Enterprises, Ltd., Global Energy Investors Inc., Stern & Co., Warp Broadband Corp., iSign, Macrobuild.com, Lexsite.com, India; lectr. profl. confs. on project fin., privatization, cross-border investment and dispute resolution. Contbr. articles to legal jours. Bd. dirs. Internat. Ctr., Washington. Mem. ABA, Am. Law Inst., Internat. Bar Assn., D.C. Bar Assn. Home: 2336 California St NW Washington DC 20008-1637 Office: 1200 19th St NW Washington DC 20036-2412 E-mail: sastern@hillsandstern.com.

STERN, SANDOR, film writer, director; b. Timmins, Ont., Can., July 13, 1936; s. Stephen Mendel and Ann (Gurevitch) S.; m. Marlene Greenstein, May 19, 1957 (div. 1976); children: Shawn, Mark, Adam, Jamie; m. Kandy Lea Cave, Jan. 26, 1980; children: Lauren, Seth. BA, U. Toronto, 1957, MD, 1961. Intern New Mount Sinai Hosp., Toronto, 1961-62; physician Can., 1962-68; writer L.A., 1968—; dir., 1974—. Writer (films) The Amityville Horror, 1978, Fastbreak, 1979 (NAACP Image award); writer, dir. (film) Pin, 1988, (TV films) Web of Deceit, 1990, Deception: A Mother's Secret, 1991, Dangerous Pursuit, 1989, John and Yoko, 1985, Muggable Mary: Street Cop, 1981, (TV miniseries) Woman on the Run: The Lawrencia Bembeneck Story, 1992-93; dir. (TV films) Glitz, 1988, Passions, 1984, Heart of a Child, 1993, The Stranger Beside Me, 1995, Gridlock, 1995, Badge of Betrayal, 1996, In My Sister's Shadow, 1997; co-writer, dir. (TV films) Jericho Fever, 1992, Duplicates, 1992, A Child's Cry for Help, 1994, (episodes for TV shows) Touched by an Angel, 1997, 98, 99, Promised Land, 1997, 98, 99. Mem. Writers Guild Am., Dirs. Guild Am., Producers Guild Am. Office: Jamson Prodns Inc 9116 1/2 W Pico Blvd Los Angeles CA 90035-1321 E-mail: esgees@aol.com.

STERN, SCOTT, finance educator; b. Hempstead, NY, Jan. 1, 1969; s. Eitan and Sandra Stern; m. Catherine Fazio, June 10, 1995. PhD, Stanford U., 1990—95. Non-resident sr. fellow Brookings Inst., Washington; assoc. prof. Kellogg Grad. Sch. of Mgmt., Evanston, Ill., 2001—. Faculty rsch. fellow Nat. Bur. of Econ. Rsch., Cambridge, Mass., 1996—. Contbr. articles. Office: Kellogg Grad Sch of Mgmt Leverone 609 Chicago IL 60628 Business E-Mail: s-stern2@northwestern.edu.

STERN, S(EESA) BEATRICE, executive secretary, registered nurse; b. Atlantic City, Feb. 13, 1919; d. Max and Gussie (Thierman) Rosen; m. Francis H. Stern, June 29, 1958 (dec. Feb. 1973); m. Bernard N. Abelson, Dec. 5, 1973 (div. Feb. 1992). AA, AS in Nursing, Miami-Dade C.C., Fla., 1982. RN, Fla., N.J., Nev. Sec. N.J. State Highway Dept., Trenton, 1938-41; columnist N.J. Herald, 1939-41; sec. U.S. Army, various locations, 1941-46; legal sec. Gus Feuer, Atty. at Law, Miami, 1946-47; exec. sec. to pres. Pharms., Inc., N.Y.C., 1947-58; med. sec. Phila., 1958-72; nurse Mt. Sinai Med. Ctr., Miami Beach, Fla., 1982-83, Atlantic City Med. Ctr., 1983-84. Vol. Hollywood Med. Ctr., 1992-96, Aventura Med. Ctr., 1992—; mem. bd. govs. Brith Sholom, 1970-2000. Mem. Brith Sholom Women (nat. pres. 1970-72), Phi Theta Kappa. Avocations: swimming, handcrafts, reading, crossword puzzles.

STERN, SHIRLEY, lawyer, author; b. Bklyn., Aug. 16, 1929; d. Bernard and Bessie (Tasgal) Gartenstein; m. Leonard W. Stern, Dec. 24, 1949; children: Erwin Samuel, Elana Debra, Gil Avram. BA, CUNY, 1950, MA, 1956; JD, St. John's U., 1982. Bar: N.Y. 1983. Freelance writer, New Hyde Park, N.Y., 1972—; sole practice, New Hyde Park, 1983—. Author: Exploring Jewish History, 1979; Exploring Jewish Wisdom, 1980; Exploring Jewish Holidays, 1981; Exploring the Prayerbook, 1982; Exploring the Torah, 1984. Mem. Nassau County Bar Assn. Democrat. Jewish. Office: 26 Birchwood Dr New Hyde Park NY 11040-3744

STERN, STANLEY, psychiatrist; b. N.Y.C., Apr. 5, 1933; s. Frank and Gussie S.; children: Marcus F., David S. BA cum laude, N.Y. U., 1953; MD, SUNY, 1957. Intern Ohio State U. Hosp., Columbus, 1957-58; resident in psychiatry Inst. Living, Hartford, Conn., 1958-60, Austen Riggs Ctr., Stockbridge, Mass., 1960-61; psychoanalytic tng. We. New Eng. Inst. for Psychoanalysis, New Haven, 1965-73; asst. clin. prof. psychiatry Yale U., 1975-81; assoc. clin. prof. psychiatry U. Calif., San Diego, 1982-84; pvt. practice New Haven, 1965-82, La Jolla, Calif., 1982-84, Phoenix, 1984—. Mem. faculty San Diego Psychoanalytic Inst., 1980-84; pres. Ariz. Psychoanalytic Study Group, Phoenix, 1986-88, Phoenix Psychoanalytic Study Group, 1986-88; tng. and supervising analyst So. Calif. Psychoanalytic Inst., 1989; chmn. edn. com. Ariz. Psychoanalytic New Tng. Facility, 1990-91; lectr., presenter, participant seminars and confs. in field. Contbr. article to profl. jours. Trustee, Gesell Inst., New Haven, 1986-88, Ctr. for the Exceptional Patient, New Haven; bd. dirs. ACLU. Capt. USAF, 1961-63. Mem. Am. Coll. Psychoanalysts, Am. Psychoanalytic Assn. (cert.), Am. Psychiatric Assn., Am. Acad. Psychoanalysts, Irene Josselyn Group Advancement of Psychoanalysis, So. Calif. Psychoanalytic Inst. and Soc. (faculty), San Diego Psychoanalytic Inst., Council for the Advancement of Psychoanalysis (treas. 1972-73, pres.-elect 1973-74, pres. 1974-75, councillor 1975-80), Phi Beta Kappa, Beta Lambda Sigma, Psi Chi. Home and Office: 3104 E Camelback Rd # 601 Phoenix AZ 85016 Address: 4438 E Arlington Rd Phoenix AZ 85018-1262 *Personal philosophy: "Be a little kinder to each other" Aldous Huxley.*

STERN, STEVEN ALAN, sports development owner; b. Chgo., Dec. 5, 1943; s. Sidney J. and Leona (Bernstein) S.; m. Helena Kerner, July 12, 1975; children: Jeremy, Jessica. BA, Brandeis U., 1965; postgrad., Columbia U., 1965-66. CPCU, Ill. Trust officer First Nat. Bank Chgo., 1966-69; ptnr. Equicon, Inc., Chgo., 1970-74; coord. Singer for Mayor, 1974-75; mgr. underwriting policy CNA Ins., 1976-79; project dir. Gov.'s Blue Ribbon Panel, Denver, 1979-81; dir. capital budget State of Colo., 1981-82; exec. dir. Ctr. Bus. and Econ. Forecasting U. Denver, 1982=85; v.p. pub. fin. Kirchner Moore Divsn. George K. Baum & Co., Denver, 1986-93; sr. v.p. pub. fin. Donaldson, Lufkin & Jenrette Securities Co., 1993-95, William R. Hough & Co., 1995-99; mng. dir. Scheer Game Sports Devel., 1999—2002, CEO, 2002—. Sr. fin. cons. Greenville (S.C.) Auditorium Dist., 1994-98, Stamfair Sports, 1996-99, City of Manchester, N.H., 1997—, Harbor Devel. Co., 1999-2000, Met. Denver Major League Baseball Stadium Dist., 1989-92; mem. adv. task force to capital devel. com. Colo. Gen. Assembly, 1985-87, chmn. adv. task force subcom. on privatization, 1986-87; em. adv. coun. Colo. Advanced Tech. Inst., 1986-90; guest lectr., 1982, 93; adv. task forces on capital budgeting, transp. Denver C. of C., 1980-91; spkr. Bond Buyer Ann. Stadium and Arena Fin. Conf., 1997, co-chmn., 1998; spkr. ann. meetings Nat. Assn. State Mental Health Program Dirs., 1987-89, Nat. Assn. State Mental Retardation Program Dirs., 1987, Nat. Assn. State Alcohol and Drug Abuse Dirs., 1988, Corp. Trust Conf. Am. Bankers Assn., 1998, Sports Fin. Forum, 1999, bd. dirs. Mental Health Resources Ctr., Renaissance Ctr., 1993-94; prin., program mgr. Arsna and ballpark projects City of Jacksonville, Fla., 2001—. Author: Colorado Capital Investment Budget, 1982, (with others) Colorado: Investing in the Future, 1981; editor: Techniques of Economic Research, 1981. Spkr. Adopt-A-Sch., Denver Pub. Schs., 1983, 86, Brandeis U. Alumni Admissions Coun., 1990-93, numerous other orgns.; participant Leadership Denver, 1983-84; sec.-treas. Colo. Student Obligation Bond Authority, 1984-86, also bd. dirs.; bd. dirs. Circus Arts Found., 1985-86; chmn. devel. com. Stanley Brit. Primary Sch., Denver, 1984; mem. Denver Baseball Commn., 1987-89; bd. dirs., chmn. corp. gifts Epilepsy Found., Chgo., 1977-79. Mem. Brandeis U. Alumni Assn. Jewish. Office: 25 2nd St S Jacksonville Beach FL 32250-6827

STERN, STEVEN NEAL, economics educator; b. N.Y.C., July 22, 1958; s. Henry Leon and Doris (Bliss) S.; m. Sandra Mae Lichtenstein, May 20, 1984; children: Doriana Rivka, Aaron Amit. BA, BS, U. Pa., Phila., 1979; PhD, Yale U., 1985. Lectr. Yale U., New Haven, 1984-85; asst. prof. U. Va., Charlottesville, 1985-90, assoc. prof., 1990-96, prof., 1996—. Cons., Charlottesville, 1985—. Contbr. articles to profl. jours. Chmn. Social Devel. Commn., Charlottesville, 1992-93, chmn. Godsey-Stilfried Freedom Fund, Charlottesville, 1988-94, Charlottesville-Albemarle Children and Youth Task Force on Teenage Pregnancy Prevention; pres. Jefferson Area United Transp., 1994-95. NIH grantee, 1986-91, NIMH grantee, 1992—. Democrat. Jewish. Avocations: music, tennis, canoeing. Office: U Va Dept Econs Charlottesville VA 22901

STERN, T. NOEL, political scientist, educator; b. Pitts., July 7, 1913; s. Leon Thomas (LeFevre) and Elizabeth Gertrude (Limburg) S.; m. Katherine Frances Kirk, Dec. 28, 1940; children: S. Yolanda, Roland Craig, Ellen Cornog, Joan Thrush. BA with honors, Swarthmore Coll., 1934; postgrad., U. Lyons, France, 1934-35; MA in Polit. Sci. U. Pa., 1940, PhD in Polit. Sci, 1942. Tchr. Lycée des Garçons, Roanne, France, 1934-35; prof., acting chmn. dept. govt. Boston U., 1945-53; Fulbright prof. U. Rennes, U. Strasbourg, 1952; dir. Fondation des Etats-Unis, U. Paris, France, 1953-56; acting chief UN Pub. Adminstrn. Mission to Ethiopia, 1956-57; dir. research and stats. Pa. Dept. Revenue, 1957-60; pres. West Chester State Coll., Pa., 1960-61; research prof. govt. African Studies program Boston U., 1962-63; also chief pub. adminstrn. team Boston U./US Aid, Guinea, West Africa; prof., past chmn. dept. polit. sci. U. Mass., Dartmouth, 1964-69, prof., 1969-85, prof. emeritus, 1985—, also past chmn. acad. coun. Frequent guest on radio, Boston, 1948-53, New Bedford, Fall River and Providence, 1964—. Author: Community Forests in Pennsylvania for Allegheny Forest Experiment Station, 1941, Secret Family, 1988, Your Guide to Dartmouth Town Government, 1991; past mem. editl. bd. Internat. Rev. History and Polit. Sci., Revue de la Cité, Paris; contbr. to Boston U. Law Rev., Sch. and Society, New Republic, Progressive mag., Christian Sci. Monitor, Friends Jour., Quaker Life, Quaker History, Boston Globe, Providence Jour.-Bull, New Bedford Standard-Times, U. Pa. Gazette, also others; collective writings deposited in Archives of Friends Hist. Libr., Swarthmore Coll. and Libr. U. Mass., Dartmouth; frequent contbr. to internet discussion group Quaker-Spectrum In the Past. Past mem. permanent bd. New Eng. Yearly Mtg. of Friends; past mem. exec. com. Friends Gen. Conf., Phila.; past mem. adminstrv. bd. William Penn House, Washington; past clk. North Dartmouth Friends Mtg., past presiding clk. Sandwich Quar. Mtg. of Friends; trustee, chmn. Dartmouth Town Librs., 1992-98; bd. dirs. Cmty. Ctr. for Non-Violence, New Bedford, Mass., 1994-98; mem. governing com. New England Friends Home, Hingham, Mass., 1996-98. Mem. AAUP (past pres. U. Mass.-Dartmouth chpt.), Am. Polit. Sci. Assn., LWV (acting pres. New Bedford-Fall River area 1990-91). Home: The Village House 1155 Indian Springs Rd Indiana PA 15701

STERN, WALTER EUGENE, neurosurgeon, educator; b. Portland, Oreg., Jan. 1, 1920; s. Walter Eugene and Ida May (McCoy) S.; m. Elizabeth Naffziger, May 24, 1946; children: Geoffrey Alexander, Howard Christian, Eugenia Louise, Walter Eugene III. AB cum laude, U. Calif., MD, 1943. Diplomate: Am. Bd. Neurol. Surg. (vice chmn. 1975-80). Surg. intern, asst. resident surgery and neurol. surgery U. Calif. Hosp., 1943-46, asst. resident neurol. surgery and neuropathology, 1948; clin. clk. Nat. Hosp. Paralyzed and Epileptic, London, Eng., 1948-49; Nat. Research fellow med. sci. Johns Hopkins, 1949-50; asst. resident, resident U. Calif. Service, 1951; NIH spl. fellow univ. lab. physiology Oxford U., 1961-62; clin. instr. U. Calif., 1951; asst. prof. neurosurgery UCLA, 1952-56, assoc. prof., 1956-59, prof., 1959-87, now emeritus, chief div. neurosurgery, 1952-85, chmn. dept. surgery, 1981-87. Cons. neurosurgery, Wadsworth VA Hosp. Former mem., chmn. editorial bd. Jour. Neurosurgery; contbr. articles to sci. jours., chpts. in books. Lt. to capt. M.C. AUS, 1946-48. Fellow ACS (sec.); mem. AMA, Am. Surg. Assn., Pacific Coast Surg. Assn., L.A. Surg. Soc. (pres. 1978), Am. Assn. Neurol. Surgeons (pres. 1979-80, Cushing medalist, 1992), James IV Assn. Surgeons, Western Neurosurg. Soc. (past pres.), Soc. Neurol. Surgeons (past pres., Disting. Svc. award 1999), Neurosurg. Soc. Am., Am. Neurol. Assn., Soc. Univ. Surgeons, Soc. Brit. Neurol. Surgeons (hon.), Phi Beta Kappa, Sigma Xi, Alpha Omega Alpha. Republican. Episcopalian. Home: 435 Georgina Ave Santa Monica CA 90402-1909 Office: U Calif Sch Med PO Box 95-7039 Los Angeles CA 90095-7039

STERN, WALTER PHILLIPS, investment executive; b. N.Y.C., Sept. 26, 1928; s. Leo and Marjorie (Phillips) S.; m. Elizabeth May, Feb. 12, 1958; children: Sarah May, William May, David May. AB, Williams Coll., 1950; MBA, Harvard U., 1952. With Lazard Freres & Co., N.Y.C., 1953-54; assoc. Burnham & Co., Inc. (predecessor firm to Drexel Burnham Lambert Group, Inc.), 1954-60, ptnr., 1960-71, sr. exec. v.p., 1972-73; vice-chmn., mng. dir. Ea. ops. Capital Rsch. Co., 1973-95; chmn. bd. New Perspective Fund, Inc., 1973—; chmn. Capital Internat. Inc., 1973—. Chmn. Europacific Growth Fund, Inc., 1984—99; chmn. bd. dirs. Emerging Markets Growth Fund Capital Group Internat., Inc., chmn., 1984—2002; dir. Temple-Inland, Inc., 1969; past mem. pub. bd. Mcpl. Securities Rulemaking Bd., 1984—87; trustee Fin. Analysts Rsch. Found.; chmn. bd. trustees Hudson Inst.; instr. investment mgmt. and fin. NYU, 1956—62; dir. Birla Advantage Fund Birla Capital Internat. AMC Ltd., Bombay, 1994—98; mem. adv. bd. South African Growth Fund, 1996—2002, CyberCity Capital LLC, 1999—2002. Contbr. articles to profl. jours. Dir. Jewish Cmty. Rels. Coun. N.Y.; mem. Coun. Fgn. Rels.; chmn. fin. adv. com. Haddassah; trustee Am. Jewish Com., Tel Aviv U., Jaffee Inst. Strategic Studies, Tel Aviv; mem. publ. com. Commentary, 1995—; editl. adv. bd., Moment, 1998—; dir. Am.-Israel Friendship League, 1996—; gov. Anti-Defamation League; bd. dirs. Am. Friends of Tel Aviv U.; v.p., mem. exec. com. Washington Inst. Near East Policy; chmn. steering com. Freedom Trade with Israel; adv. bd. Am. Committees on Fgn. Rels., 1998—; bd. visitors Monterrey Inst., 2001—. Mem. N.Y. Soc. Security Analysts (bd. dirs.), Fin. Analysts Fedn. (pres. 1971-72, bd. dirs.), Inst. Chartered Fin. Analysts (pres. 1976-77, bd. dirs.), Assn. Investment and Mgmt. Rsch. (bd. dirs., exec. com. 1990-92), Harvard Club, Econ. Club, Sunningdale Country Club, Calif. Club, Phi Beta Kappa. Jewish. Home: 450 Fort Hill Rd Scarsdale NY 10583-2413 Office: Capital Group Inc 630 5th Ave Ste 36 New York NY 10111-0100 also: Capital Group Inc 333 S Hope St Los Angeles CA 90071-1406 E-mail: wps@capgroup.com.

STERN, WILLIAM LOUIS, botanist, educator; b. Paterson, N.J., Sept. 10, 1926; s. Abram and Rose (Chrisman) S.; m. Floraet Selma Tanis, Sept. 4, 1949 (dec.); children: Susan Myra, Paul Elihu. BS, Rutgers U., 1950; MS, U. Ill., 1951, PhD, 1954. Instr., then asst. prof. Yale Sch. Forestry, 1953-60; curator div. plant anatomy Smithsonian Inst., 1960-64, chmn. dept botany, 1964-67; prof. botany U. Md., College Park, 1967-79, U. Fla., Gainesville, 1979—, chmn. dept., 1979-85. Emeritus prof. U. Fla., Gainesville, 2002; forestry officer FAO, 1963-64; mem. sci. adv. bd. Nat. Tropical Bot. Garden, 1969-83; mem. sci. adv. com. Winterthur Mus., 1973-86 ; vis. com. Arnold Arboretum of Harvard U., 1971-77; vice chmn. Arnold Arboretum of Harvard, 1973-76; asesor cientifico U. de los Andes, Merida, Venezuela, 1975; program dir. systematic biology NSF, 1978, 79; rsch. assoc. The Kampong, 1996—. Editor: Tropical Woods, 1953-60, Plant Sci. Bull., 1962-64, Biotropica, 1968-73; asso. editor: BioSci, 1963-65, Econ. Botany, 1966-75, Phytomorphology, 1996—; mem. editorial com.: Am. Jour. Botany, 1967-69. Bd. dirs. Fairchild Tropical Garden, 1980-86; trustee Kampong Fund, 1995— . Served with USNR, 1944-46, PTO. Fellow Linnean Soc. of London; mem. Bot. Soc. Am. (pres. 1984-86), Am. Inst. Biol. Scis. (bd. dirs. 1987-89), Internat. Assn. Wood Anatomists (hon., council), Am. Soc. Plant Taxonomists (pres. 1981), Soc. Econ. Botany (treas. 1988-91), Bot. Soc. Am. (Cert. Merit 1987), Torrey Bot. Club (editor Memoirs 1971-75), Washington Bot. Soc. (pres. 1972), Internat. Soc. Tropical Foresters, Soc. Advancement Research (Philippines), Assn. for Tropical Biology, Internat. Wood Collectors Soc. (life), Phi Beta Kappa, Sigma Xi, Delta Phi Alpha, Phi Kappa Phi, Phi Sigma. Office: U Fla Dept Botany Gainesville FL 32611-8526 E-mail: wstern@botany.ufl.edu.

STERNBERG, DAVID EDWARD, psychiatrist; b. Norfolk, Va., Jan. 18, 1946; s. Theodore and Bella (Rosenblatt) S.; m. Frances Toby Glazer, Aug. 23, 1970; children: Jonathan Theodore, Daniel Alexander. BA in Biopsychology, U. Chgo., 1967; MD with hons., Tufts U., 1971. Diplomate Nat. Bd. Med. Examiners, Psychiatry and Addiction Psychiatry, Am. Bd. Psychiatry and Neurology. Intern SUNY Upstate Med. Ctr., Syracuse, 1971—72; resident in psychiatry Yale U., New Haven, 1972—75; clin. asst. prof. psychiatry Georgetown U., Washington, 1975-79; mem. faculty Washington Sch. Psychiatry, 1977-79; staff psychiatrist, dir. alcohol rehab. Nat. Naval Med. Ctr., Bethesda, Md., 1975-77; rsch. coord., staff psychiatrist Biol. Psychiatry br. NIMH, 1977-79; asst. prof., chief clin. rsch. unit Yale U., New Haven, 1979-83; med. dir. Falkirk Hosp., Central Valley, N.Y., 1983-88, Kansas Inst., Olathe, 1988-90; dir. Psychiatry Assocs., Chartered, Overland Pk., Kans., 1990—; med. dir. Dual Diagnosis Program Two Rivers Psychiat. Hosp., Kansas City, 1991—98. Lectr. Karl. Menninger Sch. Psychiatry, Topeka, 1988-91, dept. psychiatry Yale U., New Haven, 1983-92; assoc. clin. prof., U. Kans., Kansas City, 1988—. Author: Evaluation and Treatment of Drug Abuse, 1990; author: (with others) Dual Diagnosis: Addiction and Psychiatric Disorders, 1988; contbr. more than 87 articles to profl. jours., 12 chpts. to books; reviewer: Am. Jour. Psychiatry, reviewer: Archives of Gen. Psychiatry, reviewer: Biol. Psychiatry. Lt. comdr. USN, 1975-77, comdr. USPHS, 1977-79. Mem. Am. Psychiat. Assn., Soc. for Biol. Psychiatry, Soc. Neurosci., Acad. Clin. Psychiatrists, Am. Acad. Psychiatrist in Alcoholism and Addictions. Avocations: running, swimming, tennis, classical music. Office: 110 E Poplar St Olathe KS 66061 Fax: 913-498-0523. E-mail: sternbergmd@hotmail.com.

STERNBERG, ESTHER MAY, neuroendocrinologist, immunologist, rheumatologist; b. Montreal, May 9, 1951; came to U.S., 1980, naturalized, 1991; d. Joseph and Ghitta (Wexler) Sternberg; 1 child, Penny Rebecca Herscovitch. BSc with great distinction, McGill U., 1972, MD, 1974. Diplomate Nat. Bd. Med. Examiners; lic. physician, Can., Mo. Intern Royal Victoria Hosp./McGill U., Montreal, 1974-75, resident II in medicine, 1977-78, clin. fellow rheumatology, 1978-79, clin. and rsch. fellow rheumatology, 1979-80; gen. practice medicine Mount Royal, Que., 1975-77; rsch. assoc. divsn. allergy/clin. immunology Washington U., St. Louis, 1981-83, rsch. assoc. Howard Hughes Med. Inst., 1983-84, assoc. Howard Hughes Med. Inst., 1984-86, instr. divs. rheumatology, 1984-86; attending physician Barnes Hosp., 1984-86; tenured sr. scientist NIMH/NIH, Bethesda, 1991—, med. officer, chief unit on neuroendocrine immunology, 1991-95, assoc. br. chief clin. neuroendocrinology br., 1994-2000, med. officer, chief sect. neuroendocrine immunology, 1995—, dir. integrative neural-immune program, 1999—. Vis. scientist Nat. Inst. Arthritis Musculoskeletal and Skin Disease, NIH and head Inter-Inst. Unit on Neuroendocrine Immunology and Behavior, NIMH and Nat. Inst. Arthritis, Musculoskeletal and Skin Diseases, Bethesda, 1989-90; rsch. full prof. Am. U., Washington, 1995—; temporary advisor WHO, 1991; ad hoc mem. NIH/NIMH/Libr. Congress Human Genome Project liaison com., 1990-91; invited expert CDC, Atlanta, 1989-93; spl. cons. Inst. Health (Hygienic) Scis., Min. of Health, Japan, 1992-94; med. adv. bd. Scleroderma Fedn., 1993-95; cons. John D. and Catherine T. MacArthur Found. Network on Mind-Body Interactions, 1994—; participant WHO/Pan Am. Health Orgn. Collaborating Ctr. for Health of the Elderly Work Group meeting, 1995; mem. com. on military nutrition rsch. Inst. of Medicine of NAS, 1998—; advisor Nat. Libr. of Medicine Planning Com., Breath of Life: An Exhbn. on Asthma, 1997-98, NIMH/NIH Ctr. for Sci. Rev., 1998; reviewer FDA's Office of Women's Health, 1998; co-dir. Exhibition on Emotions and Disease Nat. Libr. Medicine, 1996-97, others; dir. NIMH Program on Integrative Neural-Immune, 1999—; co-chair/chair/organizer numerous confs. Author: The Balance Within. The Science Connecting Health and Emotions; editl. bd. Brain, Behavior and Immunity, Jour. Neuroimmunology, Neuroimmunomodulation, Molecular Psychiatry, Immunologic Rsch.; invited guest series editor Jour. Clin. Investigation, 1997; reviewer Jour. Clin. Investigation, New Eng. Jour. Medicine, Jour. Immunology, Endocrinology, Jour. Clin. Endocrinology and Metabolism, Arthritis and Rheumatism, Am. Jour. Physiology, Jour. Neuroimmunology, Brain, Behavior and Immunity; editor: Stress: Mechanisms and Clinical Implications, 1995, Neuroimmune Interactions: Molecular, Integrative Systems and Clinical Implications, 1998; assoc. editor Brain, Behavior and Immunity, Neuroimmunomodulation; contbr. chpts. to books and articles to profl. jours.; patentee in field. Recipient Arthritis Found. Met. Washington William R. Felts award for excellence in rheumatology rsch. pubs., 1991, FDA's Commr.'s Spl. Citation, 1991, USPHS Superior Svc. award, 1994; McGill U. scholar, 1967-68, 68-71; Am. Acad. Allergy/Schering Travel grantee, 1982, United Scleroderma Found. grantee, 1985-86, 86-87, Scleroderma Found. Greater Washington, 1987, 88; NIH New Investigator awardee, 1985-88, others. Fellow Am. Coll. Rheumatology; mem. AAAS, Soc. Neurosci., Am. Soc. Clin. Investigation, Am. Assn. Immunologists, N.Y. Acad. Scis., Can. Med. Assn., Internat. Soc. Neuroimmunology (mem. internat. adv. com. 1995), PsychoNeuroImmunology Rsch. Soc. (councillor 1997—), Soc. for Neuroimmunomodulation (sec. 1997-99, pres. 1999—). Office: NIMH/NIH Bldg 10 10 Center Dr MSC-1284 Bethesda MD 20892-1284 Fax: 301-496-6095. E-mail: ems@codon.nih.gov.

STERNBERG, HARRIET ELAINE, psychiatric social worker; b. Greensboro, Vt., July 18, 1924; d. Celon and Isabel (Silver) S. BA, U. Mass., 1948; MA in Edn., Clark U., 1953; MSW, U. Conn., 1961. Asst. psychiat. social worker Foxboro (Mass.) State Hosp., 1955-58; caseworker Children's Svcs. Conn., Torrington, 1958-59, field placement social worker Hartford, 1959-61; psychiat. social worker Mental Health Svcs., Springfield, Vt., 1961-67; assoc. psychiat. social worker Waterbury (Conn.) Hosp., 1967-68; clin. social worker Franklin County Mental Health Ctr., Greenfield, Mass., 1968-90; social worker Valley Clin. Assocs., 1969-97. Mem. Phi Kappa Phi. Avocations: travel, music. Home: 128 Briar Way Greenfield MA 01301-3807

STERNBERG, PAUL, retired ophthalmologist; b. Chgo., Dec. 18, 1917; s. David M. and Sarah (Kopeka) S.; m. Dorie Betty Feitler, Dec. 24, 1949; children— Daniel P., Patricia F., Paul, Susan P., David. BS, Northwestern U., 1938, MD, 1940. Intern Michael Reese Hosp., Chgo., 1940-41, resident ophthalmology, Ill. Eye & Ear Infirmary U. Ill.; spl. fellow ophthalmology Cornell U. Med. Center, N.Y. Hosp., Wilmer Inst. Johns Hopkins, 1941-44; practice medicine, specializing in ophthalmology Chgo., from 1945. Attending ophthalmologist Cook County Hosp., Michael Reese Hosp., Highland Park (Ill.) Hosp., Louis Weiss Meml. Hosp.; prof. ophthalmology Chgo. Med. Sch., U. Ill. Med. Sch. Contbr. sci. articles to med. and ophthal. jours. Trustee Art Inst. Chgo. Fellow A.C.S.; mem. Assn. for Research in Ophthalmology, Am. Assn. Ophthalmology, Am. Acad. Ophthalmology, Chgo. Ophthal. Soc., Pan-Am. Congress Ophthalmology, Merit Country Club, Standard Club, Lake Shore Country Club. Home: 359 Surfside Pl Glencoe IL 60022-1723 Office: 225 W Washington St Ste 2150 Chicago IL 60606-3483

STERNBERG, SEYMOUR, insurance company executive; b. Bklyn., June 24, 1943; s. Max and Mollie Sternberg; m. Roslyn Jacobowitz, June 14, 1965 (div.); children: Jodi, Donna; m. Laurette Zolty, Sept. 14, 1980; 1 child, Matthew. BSEE, CCNY, 1965; MSEE in Computer Sci., Northeastern U., 1968. Mgr. Raytheon Co., Bedford, Mass., 1965-73; mgr. Data Architects, Waltham, 1973-75; dir. info. services Mass. Mut. Life Ins. Co., Springfield, 1975-76, 2d v.p., 1976-77, v.p. info. services, 1977-81, sr. v.p. group life and health div., 1981-84, exec. v.p. group life and health div., 1984-87, sr. exec. v.p., 1987-88; sr. v.p. group ops. N.Y. Life Ins. Co., 1989, exec. v.p., 1991, vice chmn., pres., 1995-97, also bd. dirs., chmn., pres., CEO, COO, 1997—, chmn., pres., CEO; also bd. dirs. Mass. Mut. Life Ins. Co., Springfield. Bd. dirs. Bank of New Eng. West. US Rep. APEC Bus. Advisory Council; bd. of gov. United Way Tri-State; bd. of trustees Hackley School, Terrytown, NY, Big Bros./ Big Sisters of NYC. Mem.: US-China Business Council, CUNY Business Leadership Council, NYC Partnership and Chamber of Comerce (bd. mem.), BRT, ACLI (bd. dir.). Avocations: stamp collecting; tennis. Office: NY Life Ins Co 51 Madison Ave Rm 1304 New York NY 10010

STERNBERG, STEPHEN STANLEY, pathologist, educator; b. N.Y.C., July 30, 1920; s. Morris and Clara (Nussberg) S.; m. Norma Wollner; children: Alessandra, Susan. BA, Colby Coll., 1941; MD, NYU, 1944. Diplomate Am. Bd. Pathology and Anatomic Pathology. Intern Mt. Sinai Hosp., Cleve.; resident in pathology Charity Hosp., New Orleans, 1947-49; fellow Meml. Hosp., N.Y.C., 1949-50, attending pathologist, 1972—; prof. pathology Cornell U. Med. Ctr., 1979—. Mem. Sloan-Kettering Inst. for Cancer Rsch., N.Y.C., 1984—, prof. pharmacology and therapeutics, 1981—. Contbr. articles to profl. jours.; editor: Diagnostic Surgical Pathology, 1989. Capt. (flight surgeon) USAF, 1945-47. Fellow N.Y. Acad. Scis.; mem. Am. Assn. for Cancer Rsch., Soc. for Toxicology, Am. Coun. on Sci. and Health (chmn. bd. dirs. 1986-89). Republican. Jewish. Office: Meml Hosp 1275 York Ave New York NY 10021-6094

STERNBERGER, LUDWIG AMADEUS, neurologist, educator; b. Munich, Germany, May 26, 1921; s. Hugo and Emy (Welinger) S.; m. Nancy Jeanne Hoy, Dec. 13, 1961. BA, Am. U. Beirut, 1941, MD, 1945. Fellow Sloan

Kettering Meml. Cancer Ctr., N.Y.C., 1948-50; sr. med. biochemist N.Y. State Dept. Health, Albany, 1950-54; asst. prof. medicine Northwestern U., Chgo., 1954-55; chief basic scis. div. Med. Research Labs., Edgewood Arsenal, Md., 1957-78; prof. brain research U. Rochester Med. Ctr. (N.Y.), 1978-86; prof. neurology, pathology and anatomy U. Md., Balt., 1986-92; sci. co-dir., treas. Sternberger Monoclonals, Inc., 1992—. Author: Immunocytochemistry, 1974, 3d edit, 1986; mem. editoral bd. Cell and Tissue Research, Histochemistry, Jour. Histochemistry and Cytochemistry, Jour. Neurosci. Methods, Jour. Neuroimmunology, Histochem. Jour., Electron Microscopy in Biology. Served to maj. M.C., U.S. Army, 1955-57. Recipient Paul A. Siple prize, 1972; recipient Humboldt prize for sr. U.S. scientists, 1980, Classic Author citation Inst. Sci. Info., 1983; Senator Jacob K. Javits neurosci. investigator award, 1984; 25th most frequently cited author in sci. lit. of 1984; author of one of 17 Newcomer Superstar papers among 100 most cited of all time. Mem. Histochem. Soc. (pres. 1977-78), Am. Soc. Neurochemistry (program com. 1983-84), Am. Assn. Immunologists, Endocrine Soc., Am. Acad. Allergy, Am. Assn. Neuropathologists Lutheran. Home: 10 Burwood Ct Lutherville Timonium MD 21093-3502 E-mail: sternbmonoc@att.net.

STERNE, JOSEPH ROBERT LIVINGSTON, newspaper editor, educator; b. Phila., Apr. 25, 1928; s. Robert Livingston and Edith Eisner (Heymann) S.; m. Barbara Adele Greene, Feb. 10, 1951; children: Robert Greene, Paul Livingston, Edward Joseph, Adam Heymann, Lee Winslow Greene. BA cum laude, Lehigh U., 1948; MS, Columbia U., 1950. Reporter Salt Lake Telegram, Salt Lake City, 1948-49, Wall Street Jour., N.Y.C., 1950-51, Dallas Morning News, 1951-53; reporter Balt. Sun, 1953-72, editorial page editor, 1972-97; sr. fellow Inst. for Policy Studies Johns Hopkins U., 1997—. Mem. Am. Soc. Newpaper Editors, Hamilton St. Club, Phi Beta Kappa. Home: PO Box 599 Sparks MD 21152-0599 Office: Johns Hopkins U Inst Policy Studies 3400 N Charles St Baltimore MD 21218-2680 E-mail: sterne@jhunix.hcf.jhu.edu.

STERNER, FRANK MAURICE, industrial executive; b. Lafayette, Ind., Nov. 26, 1935; s. Raymond E. and Maudelene M. (Scipio) S.; m. Elsa Y. Rasmusson, June 29, 1958; children: Mark, Lisa. BS, Purdue U., 1958, MS, 1959, PhD, 1962. Sr. staff specialist Gen. Motors Inst., Flint, Mich., 1962-63; dir. personnel and orgnl. research Delco Electronics, Milw., 1963-66, dir. personnel devel. and research, 1966-68; partner Nourse & Sterner, Inc., Milw., 1968-69; pres., 1969-73; assoc. dean, prof. Krannert Grad. Sch. of Mgmt., Purdue U., West Lafayette, Ind., 1973-79; v.p. human resources mgmt. Johnson Controls, Inc., Milw., 1979-89; pres., chief exec. officer E.R. Wagner Mfg. Co., 1989—; pres., owner Ridgeway Devel. Inc., Milw., 1993—. Bd. dirs. Wausau Homes, Inc., E.R. Wagner Mfg. Co., Ridgeway Devel. Inc. Mem. rsch .com. Am. Lung Assn., Wis.; mem. Greater Milwaukee Com., 1997—; mem. Wis. Tobacco Control Bd., 2000—; bd. dirs. Children's Hosp. of Wis. Found. Mem.: Reamer. Home: 1440 E Standish Pl Milwaukee WI 53217-1958 Office: ER Wagner Mfg Co 4611 N 32nd St Milwaukee WI 53209-6000 E-mail: frank.sterner@erwagner.com.

STERNER, MICHAEL EDMUND, international affairs consultant; b. N.Y.C., Dec. 26, 1928; s. Harold Walther and Leonie (Knoedler) S.; m. Courtenay Read, Mar. 30, 1957; children: Lucian, Marcellin. AB, Harvard Coll., 1951. Govt. rels. rep. Arabian-Am. Oil Co., Dhahran, Saudi Arabia, 1951-54; joined Fgn. Svc., 1956; vice consul Aden, 1957-58; polit. officer Cairo, 1960-64; desk officer Near Eastern Affairs Dept. State, 1964-70, dir. Egyptian affairs, 1970-74; amb. to United Arab Emirates Abu Dhabi, 1974-76; dep. asst. sec. state for Near East and South Asian affairs, 1977-81; mng. dir. The IRC Group, Inc., 1982—. Mem. bd. govs. Mid. East Inst. With AUS, 1954-56. Mem. Coun. Fgn. Rels. Home: 2712 36th St NW Washington DC 20007-1421 Office: 1320 19th St NW Ste 410 Washington DC 20036-1644 E-mail: sternerm@starpower.net.

STERNFELD, MARC HOWARD, investment banker; b. N.Y.C., July 12, 1947; s. Joseph and Jeane (Richstein) S.; m. Arleen Estelle Weinreb, Aug. 25, 1968; children: Joshua, Jonathan. BA, Queens Coll., 1968; MS, NYU, 1970; MBA, Columbia U., 1971; student, Jewish Theol. Sem., 2001—. Spacecraft programmer Grumman Aero., 1968-70; fin. analyst CBS, N.Y.C., 1971-72; rsch. asst. Nat. Bur Econ. Rsch., 1970-71; sr. analyst N.Y.C. Police Dept., 1972-75; prtnr. Arthur Andersen & Co., N.Y.C., 1975-88; prin. Morgan Stanley, 1987-94; mng. dir. Salomon Bros., 1994-96; pres. Trans-Form L.L.C., 1995—; mng. dir. Deutsche Bank Global Ops. and Tech., 1996—; CEO Settlement-.com, 2000-01. Adj. prof. Columbia U. Internat. bd. dirs., exec. com. United Synagogue Conservative Judaism; past pres. Marlboro Jewish Ctr.; v.p. World Counsel of Synagogues; dean's coun. Tisch Sch. Arts. Mem. Jazz Vt. Avocation: piano. Home: 13 Evan Dr Morganville NJ 07751-1062

STERNHAGEN, FRANCES, actress; b. Washington, Jan. 13, 1930; Student, Vassar Coll., Perry-Mansfield Sch. of Theatre; studied with Sanford Meisner, N.Y. Tchr. Milton Acad., Cath. U. Ams., Mass.; actress Arena Stage, Washington, 1953-54. Debut Thieves Carnival, N.Y., 1955; plays include The Carefree Tree, The Admirable Bashville (Clarence Derwent award, Obie award), Ulysses in Night Town, Red Eye of Love, Misalliance, The Return of Herbert Bracewell, Laughing Stock, The Displaced Person, The Pinter Plays (Obie award); Broadway shows include The Skin of Our Teeth, Viva Madison Avenue, Great Day in the Morning, The Right Honorable Gentleman, The Cocktail Party, Cock-a-Doodle Dandy, Playboy of the Western World, The Sign in Sidney Brustein's Window, The Good Doctor (Tony award 1973), Equus (Drama Desk award), Angel, On Golden Pond (Drama League award), The Father, Grownups, Summer, You Can't Take It With You, Home Front, Driving Miss Daisy, Remembrance, A Perfect Ganesh, The Heiress (Tony award 1995), Long Day's Journey into Night, 1998, The Exact Center of the Universe, 1999; actress films including Up The Down Staircase, Starting Over, 1979, Outland, 1981, Independence Day, 1983, Romantic Comedy, 1983, Bright Lights, Big City, 1988, See You in the Morning, 1989, Communion, 1989, Misery, 1990, Doc Hollywood, 1991, Raising Cain, 1992, Curtain Call, Land Fall, 1997, The Rising Place, 1998; (TV series) Love of Life, The Doctors, Secret Storm, Cheers, Golden Years, Under One Roof, The Road Home, E.R., Sex and the City, The Laramie Project; (TV movies) Who Will Save Our Children?, 1978, Prototype, 1982, Resting Place, 1986, Follow Your Heart, 1990, She Woke Up, 1992, Labor of Love: The Arlette Schweitzer Story, 1993, Reunion, 1994, Tales from the Crypt, Outer Limits, Law and Order, 1990, 96, The Con, 1997, To Live Again, 1997, New York: A Documentary Film, 1999.

STERNIK, ALEXANDER VADIMOVICH, diplomat, historian, linguist; b. Moscow, Russia, Jan. 20, 1966; came to U.S., 1998; s. Vadim Isaakovich and Iolana Vassilievna S.; m. Anna Igorevna, Dec. 5, 1992; children: Milana, Maxim. Degree in World's History, Moscow State, 1989. Interpreter Embassy of USSR to Ethiopia, Addis Abeba, 1989-91, attaché, 1991-94; third sec. Ministry of Foreign Affairs, Moscow, 1994-95, second sec., 1995-97, first sec., 1997-98, Permanent Mission of the Russian Fedn. to UN, N.Y.C., 1998—. Avocations: horseback riding, swimming, bodybuilding. Office: Permanent Mission of the Russian Fedn to UN 136 E 67th St New York NY 10021-6137

STERNITZKE-HOLUB, ANN, elementary school educator; b. Oklahoma City, May 5, 1952; d. James Francis and Doris Josephine (Lahr) Sternitzke; m. James Robert Holub, Apr. 4, 1987. AA, Golden West Coll., Huntington Beach, Calif., 1972; BS, Calif. State U., Fullerton, 1975, postgrad., 1976. Cert. secondary multiple subject, phys. edn. and English tchr. grades kindergarten-12, Calif.; life cert. educator Calif. Cmty. Colls. Phys. edn. and fencing instr. Fullerton Coll., 1976-82; fencing instr. Golden West Coll., Huntington Beach, 1977-83, Calif. State U., Fullerton, 1983-86; elem. phys. edn. specialist Placentia-Yorba Linda (Calif.) Unified Sch. Dist., 1989-93, elem. tchr. Bryant Ranch Sch., 1993—. Puppeteer Adventure City Amusement Park, Anaheim, Calif., E. Free Ch., Fullerton, Everlasting Arms, Fullerton. Mem. support staff 1984 Olympics, Long Beach, 1984; entertainer Stagelight Family Prodns., Brea, Calif., 1993—. Recipient Calif. Dept. Agr. award, 1999; grantee, Placentia-Yorba Linda Found., 1997—98, Disney Performing Arts, 1996—2001, others, Org. County Music/Arts Adminstrs., 2001. Mem. AAHPERD, U.S. Fencing Assn., U.S. Fencing Coaches Assn., Calif. State U. Alumni Assn., Vets. Fencing Assn. Republican. Avocations: dance, musical theatre, puppetry, fencing, costuming. Office: Bryant Ranch Sch 24695 Paseo De Toronto Yorba Linda CA 92887-5116 E-mail: annholub@yahoo.com.

STERNLICHT, BENO, research and development company executive; b. Nowy Sacz, Poland; came to U.S., 1949, naturalized, 1950; s. Hugo Charles and Helena (Anisfield) S.; m. Lisa Spilberg; children: Mark David, Eric Alan, Joshua Hugh, Aaron Jonathan. BSEE, Union Coll., Schenectady, N.Y., 1950; MS, Columbia U., 1951, PhD, 1954, DSc (hon.), 1970. Staff engr. thermal power systems, gen. engring. lab. Gen. Electric Co., 1951-54, specialist applied mechanics, 1954-58, cons. engr., 1958-61; co-founder, 1961; since chmn. bd., tech. dir. Mech. Tech., Inc., Latham, N.Y.; pres. Benjosh Mgmt. Corp., N.Y., 1983, Ameast, N.Y.C., 1981—, Arben Internat. LLC MTI, N.Y.C., 1994—. Dir. Small Diesels Ltd., India, New Eastern India Ltd., Plug Power LLC; chmn. com. energy tech. and space propulsion NASA, 1969-72, mem. rsch. adv. coun., 1970-72; Pres. Vols. Internat. Tech. Assistance, 1965-71, chmn. bd., 1971-73, Comfortex Corp, 1995—; Mem. Nat. Energy Task Force, 1981; advisor to Pres. Carter on Innovation and Energy, to Pres. Reagan and Pres. Bush on Energy; cons. to PRC, Israel. Author; patentee in field. Fellow ASME (Machine Design award 1966); mem. AIAA, Nat. Acad. Engring., Am. Soc. Lubrication Engrs., NavyLeague, Sigma Xi, Tau Beta Pi. Address: 123 Partridge Run Schenectady NY 12309-1321 E-mail: LISBEN26@aol.com.

STERNLICHT, SANFORD, English and theater arts educator, writer; b. N.Y.C., Sept. 20, 1931; s. Irving Stanley and Sylvia (Hilsenroth) S.; m. Dorothy Hilkert, June 4, 1950 (dec. 1977); children: David, Daniel. BS, SUNY, Oswego, 1953; MA, Colgate U., 1955; PhD, Syracuse U., 1962. Instr. SUNY, Oswego, 1959-60, asst. prof., 1960-62, prof. and dir. grad. studies in English, 1962-72, chmn. dept. theater, 1972-84; adj. prof. English Syracuse (N.Y.) U., 1984—. Leverhulme vis. prof. English U. of York, Eng., 1965-66. Author: Gull's Way, 1961, The Blue Star Commodore, 1961, Love in Pompeii, 1967, John Webster's Imagery and the Webster Canon, 1972, John Masefield, 1977, McKinley's Bulldog, 1977 (Mil. Book Club award, Saturday Evening Post Book Club award), C.S. Forester, 1981, Padraic Colum, 1985; (with E.M. Jameson) The Black Devil of the Bayous, 1971; (with E.M. Jameson) U.S. F. Constellation: Yankee Racehorse, 1981, John Galsworthy, 1986, R.F. Delderfield, 1988, Stevie Smith, 1990, Stephen Spender, 1992, Siegfried Sassoon, 1993, All Things Herriot: James Herriot and His Peaceable Kingdom, 1995, Jean Rhys, 1997, A Reader's Guide to Modern Irish Drama, 1998, C.S. Forester and the Hornblower Saga, 1999, Chaim Potok: A Critical Companion, 2000, A Reader's Guide to Modern American Drama, 2002; editor: The Selected Short Stories of Padraic Colum, 1985, The Selected Plays of Padraic Colum, 1986, The Selected Poems of Padraic Colum, 1988, In Search of Stevie Smith, 1991, New Plays from the Abbey Theatre, 1993-1995, 1996, New Plays from the Abbey Theatre, 1996-1998, 2001, A Reader's Guide to Modern American Drama, 2002. Lt. (j.g.) USN, 1955-59, comdr. USNR, ret. Recipient New Poets award Writer mag., 1960, Chancellor's award SUNY, 1974; fellow Poetry Soc. Am., 1964; rsch. grantee SUNY, 1963-70; named Tchr. of Yr. Syracuse U., 1986. Mem. MLA, NAACP, PEN, Shakespeare Assn. Am., Am. Conf. Irish Studies. Democrat. Jewish. Home: 128 Dorset Rd Syracuse NY 13210-3048 Office: Syracuse U Dept English Syracuse NY 13244-0001 E-mail: svsternl@syr.edu.

STERNLIEB, LAWRENCE JAY, marketing professional, writer; b. Akron, Ohio, Aug. 19, 1951; s. Max and Mollie (Atleson) S. BA in English, BA in Sociology, Kent State U., 1974, MA in Sociology, 1977. Lic. social worker, Ohio. Social program specialist State of Ohio, Cleve., 1976-79; sr. mktg. exec. Xerox Corp., 1979-82; nat. acct. mgr. NCR Corp., Independence, Ohio, 1983-85; sr. acct. mgr. McDonnell Douglas Corp., 1985-87; sr. mktg. rep. Prime Computer Inc., 1987-90; acct. exec. GE Cons. Svcs., 1990-94; sr. sales and mktg. exec. Decarlo, Paternite and Assoc., 1994-96; major acct. mgr. General DataComm, Inc., Cleve., 1996—. Instr. Cuyahoga C.C., Cleve., 1980-81, 92. Author: Barry Storm, 1995. Mem. Cleve. Playhouse. Avocations: acting, modeling, writing, sports, physical fitness. Home: 950 Tollis Pkwy Apt 610 Broadview Heights OH 44147

STERNMAN, JOEL W. lawyer; b. N.Y.C., Oct. 20, 1943; s. Abraham and Sarah (Simon) S.; children: Mark S., Cheryl A.; m. Barbara E. Shiers, March 31, 1985; children: Matthew S., Julia S. AB, Dartmouth Coll., 1965; LLB, Yale U., 1968. Bar: N.Y. 1970, U.S. Dist. Ct. (so. and ea. dists.) N.Y. 1971, U.S. Ct. Appeals (2d cir.) 1972, U.S. Supreme Ct. 1984, U.S. Ct. Appeals (6th cir.) 1985, U.S. Ct. Appeals (9th cir.) 1994, U.S. Tax Ct. 1996, U.S. Dist. Ct. (ea. dist.) Mich. 1997. Law clk. to judge U.S. Dist. Ct., New Haven, 1968-69; assoc. Rosenman Colin Freund Lewis & Cohen, N.Y.C., 1969-77; ptnr. Rosenman & Colin LLP, 1977—, Katten Muchin Zavis Rosenman, 2002—. Editor Yale Law Jour., New Haven, 1966-68. Mem. Phi Beta Kappa. Office: Katten Muchin Zavis Rosenman 575 Madison Ave New York NY 10022-2585 E-mail: j.sternman@kmzr.com.

STERNS, HARVEY LEONARD, psychologist, gerontologist; b. Waterville, Maine; s. Fredrick James and Sarah (Hoos) S.; m. Ronni Susan Small, Nov. 14, 1964; children: Anthony Alexander, Randy Rose, George Herbert. Bachelor, Bard Coll., 1965; Master, SUNY, Buffalo, 1968; PhD, W.Va. U., 1971. Lic. psychologist. Prof. psychology U. Akron, Ohio, 1971—, dir. Inst. Life-Span Devel. and Gerontology, 1975—; rsch. prof. gerontology Northeastern Ohio Univs. Coll. Medicine, Rootstown, 1978—. Prin. Creative Action Inc., Akron, 1988—. Editor: Gerontology in Higher Education: Perspectives and Issues, 1978, Gerontology in Higher Education: Building Institutional and Community Strength, 1979; contbr. chpts. to books and articles to profl. jours. Bd. trustees Ohio Presbyn. Retirement Communities, Columbus, 1989-2000; pres. Jewish Family Svcs., Akron, 1991-93, Mature Svcs., Inc., Akron, 1998—; chair City of Akron Sr. Citizens Adv. Commn., Akron, 1995—. Recipient award Andrus Found., 1976, 77, 78, award Dept. HEW, 1977-79, award Nat. Inst. Disability and Rehab. Rsch., 1992-2001, award Ohio Dept. Aging, 1993. Fellow APA (mem.-at-large 1983-87, editor Adult Devel. and Aging News 1997-2002, pres. 2002—), Assn. Gerontology in Higher Edn. (pres. 1983-84, Clark Tibbitts award 1994), Gerontol. Soc. Am. (mem.-at-large Behavioral and Social Sci. 1988-90), Ohio Acad. Sci. (v.p. psychology sect. 1973-74), Sigma Phi Omega (life, nat. pres. 1985-86). Democrat. Jewish. Avocations: sailing, old house restoration, old car restoration. Home: 680 N Portage Path Akron OH 44303 Office: Univ Akron Inst Li-Span Dev&Geron Arts & Scis Bldg Ste 310 Akron OH 44325-4307 Home Fax: 330-867-6899; Office Fax: 330-972-5174. E-mail: hsterns@uakron.edu.

STERNS, JOEL HENRY, lawyer; b. N.Y.C., Apr. 13, 1934; s. Barney and Yvetta S.; m. Joanne Glickman, Nov. 19, 1961; children: Racel, Leslie, David. BS in Journalism, 1956; MPA, Princeton U., 1958; JD, NYU, 1967. Bar: N.J., D.C. Exec. asst. to commr., acting commr. N.J. Dept. Conservation and Econ. Devel., 1958-61; exec. asst. to adminstr. Bur. Security and Consular Affairs, U.S. Dept. State, 1961-62; regional programs coord. Alliance for Progress, 1962-64; exec. asst. to pres. Export-Import Bank U.S., 1964; dep. commr. N.J. Dept. Cmty. Affairs, 1967-68; counsel to gov. N.J., 1968-70; pres. firm Sterns, Herbert & Weinroth (P.A.), Trenton, N.J., 1970-88; mem. exec. com., compensation com. and mktg. com. Sterns, Herbert & Weinroth (merged with Hannoch-Weisman 1988), Roseland, 1988-91; pres. Hannoch-Weisman, 1991-93, Sterns & Weinroth, Trenton, 1994—. Mem. lawyers adv. com. U.S. Dist. Ct. N.J., 1995—. Mem. ABA, Am. Law Inst., Am. Judicature Soc., N.J. Bar Assn. (trustee), Mercer County Bar Assn., Assn. Princeton U. Grad. Alumni (trustee 1975-77), NYU Alumni Assn. N.J. (Disting. Alumni award 1987). Home: 28 Heritage Hills Dr Washington Crossing PA 18977 Office: Sterns & Weinroth PO Box 1298 50 W State St Ste 1400 Trenton NJ 08607

STERNSTEIN, ALLAN J. lawyer; b. Chgo., June 7, 1948; s. Milton and Celia (Kaganove) S.; m. Miriam A. Dolgin, July 12, 1970 (div. July 1981); children— Jeffery A., Amy R.; m. Beverly A. Cook, Feb. 8, 1986; children: Cheryl L., Julia S. B.S., U. Ill., 1970; M.S., U. Mich., 1972; J.D., Loyola U., 1977. Bar: Ill. 1977, U.S. Dist. Ct. (no. dist.) Ill. 1977, U.S. Dist. Ct. (no. dist.) Ohio 1977, U.S. Dist. Ct. (ea. dist) Mich. 1986, U.S. Dist. Ct. (we. dist.) Mich. 1990, U.S. Ct. Customs and Patent Appeals 1978, U.S. Ct. Appeals (7th cir.) 1979, U.S. Ct. Appeals (Fed. cir.) 1982. Patent agent Sunbeam Corp., Oak Brook, Ill., 1972-76; ptnr. Neuman, Williams, Anderson & Olson, Chgo., 1976-84; div. patent counsel Abbott Labs., North Chgo., Ill., 1984-87; ptnr. Brinks Hofer Gilson & Lione, Chgo., 1987—, mng. ptnr., 1996-99; adj. prof. of law John Marshall Law Sch., 1989-90, DePaul Univ., 1990-92, Univ. Ill., 1992—; lectr. Nat. Sci. and Tech. Devel. Agy. Chunlangkon U., Bangkok, Thailand, 1994; arbitrator Cir. Ct. Cook County, Ill., 1996—. Co-author: Designing an Effective Intellectual Property Compliance Program; contbr. article to profl. jour. Legal advisor Legal Aid Soc., Chgo., 1974-76, Pub. Defender's Office, Chgo., 1974. Teaching fellow U. Mich., 1971-72; research grantee U. Mich., U.S. Air Force, 1971-72. Mem. ABA, Chgo. Bar Assn., Patent Law Assn. of Chgo. (com. chmn. 1982), Am. Intellectual Property Law Assn., Licensing Execs. Soc., Tau Beta Pi, Sigma Tau, Sigma Gamma Tau, Phi Eta Sigma. Jewish. Office: Brinks Hofer Gilson & Lione Ste 3600 455 N Cityfront Plaza Dr Chicago IL 60611-5599

STERRETT, JAMES KELLEY, II, lawyer; b. St. Louis, Nov. 26, 1946; s. James Kelley and Anastasia Mary (Holzer) S.; 1 child, Brittany. AB, San Diego State U., 1968; JD, U. Calif., Berkeley, 1971; LLM, U. Pa., 1973. Bar: Calif. 1972, U.S. Dist. Ct. (so. dist.) Calif. 1972. From assoc. to ptnr. Gray, Cary, Ames & Frye, San Diego, 1972-83; ptnr. Lillick, McHose & Charles, 1983-90, Pillsbury, Madison & Sutro, San Diego, 1991-96, Dostart Clapp Sterrett & Coveney, LLP, 1996-99; sole practice, 1999—. Contbr. articles to profl. jours. Bd. dirs. Holiday Bowl, San Diego, 1980—, Mus. Photog. Arts, San Diego, 1985-88, San Diego Internat. Sports Coun., 1980—, pres., 1990, chmn., 1992. Capt. USAFR, 1972. Fellow U. Pa. Ctr. Study Fin. Instns., 1971-72. Mem. ABA, Calif. Bar Assn., San Diego County Bar Assn. Clubs: Fairbanks Ranch Country (Rancho Santa Fe) (bd. dirs. 1985-87). Republican. Episcopalian. Avocations: golf, college football, hiking. Office: Ste 291 3525 Del Mar Heights Rd San Diego CA 92130

STERRETT, JAMES MELVILLE, accountant, business consultant; b. Chicago, Dec. 25, 1949; s. James McAnlis and Antoinette (Galligan) S.; m. Joyce Mieko Motoda, Sept. 1, 1989; 1 child, Victoria Hanako. BS in Acctg., Chaminade U., Honolulu, 1988; MBA, Chaminade U., 1991. CPA, Hawaii. Cons. Profitability Cons., Honolulu, 1985-87; pres. Sterrett Cons. Group, 1987-88; auditor Deloitte & Touche, 1988-90; acct., cons. pvt. practice, 1990—. Mem. Nat. Soc. Pub. Accts., Nat. Assn. Tax Practitioners, Hawaii Soc. CPA's, Delta Epsilon, Sigma. Office: 1314 S King St Ste 855 Honolulu HI 96814-1979

STERRETT, SAMUEL BLACK, lawyer, former judge; b. Washington, Dec. 17, 1922; s. Henry Hatch Dent and Helen (Black) S.; m. Jeane McBride, Aug. 27, 1949; children: Samuel Black, Robin Dent, Douglas McBride. Student, St. Albans Sch., 1933-41; grad., U.S. Mcht. Marine Acad., 1945; BA, Amherst Coll., 1947; LLB, U. Va., 1950; LLM in Taxation, NYU, 1959. Bar: D.C. 1951, Va. 1950. Atty. Alvord & Alvord, Washington, 1950-56; trial atty. Office Regional Counsel, Internal Revenue Service, N.Y.C., 1956-60; ptnr. Sullivan, Shea & Kenney, Washington, 1960-68; municipal cons. to office vice pres. U.S., 1965-68; judge U.S. Tax Ct., 1968-88, chief judge, 1985-88; ptnr. Myerson, Kuhn & Sterrett, Washington, 1988-89; of counsel Vinson & Elkins, 1990—2002; pvt. practice Law Offices of Samuel B. Sterrett, 2002—. Bd. mgrs. Chevy Chase Village, 1970-74, chmn., 1972-74; 1st v.p. bd. trustees, mem. exec. com. Washington Hosp. Center, 1969-79, chmn. bd. trustees, 1979-84, mem. bd. trustees, 1999—; chmn. bd. trustees Washington Healthcare Corp., 1982-87; chmn. bd. trustees Medlantic Healthcare Group, 1987-89; mem. audit com. Medstar Health, 1990—; mem. Washington Cathedral, 1973-81, 99—, mem. fin. com., 1998—, chmn., 1999—; mem. governing bd. St. Albans Sch., 1977-81; trustee Louise Home, 1979-89. Served with AUS, 1943; Served with U.S. Mcht. Marine, 1943-46. Fellow Am. Bar Found.; mem. ABA, D.C. Bar Assn., Am. Coll. Tax Counsel, Soc. of the Cincinnati, Coun. for Future, Am. Inns. of Ct., Chevy Chase Club (bd. govs. 1979-84, pres. 1984), Met. Club, Lawyers Club, Alibi Club, Alfalfa Club, Ch. of N.Y. Club, Beta Theta Pi. Episcopalian. Office: Law Offices of Samuel B Sterrett 1455 Pennsylvania Ave NW Fl 7 Washington DC 20004-1013

STERTZ, STEPHEN ALLEN, historian, educator; b. N.Y.C., Aug. 2, 1944; s. Philip Bernard and Anne (Herman) S. BS, Columbia U., 1968; PhD, U. Mich., 1974. Rschr. Bronx (N.Y.) County Hist. Soc., 1978-82, 83—. Adj. asst. prof. history Rutgers U., Newark, 1980—82, 1986, Dowling Coll., Oakdale, NY, 1991—, Mercy Coll., Bronx, 1996—; vis. asst. prof. classics U. Ill., Urbana, 1982—83; adj. lectr. classics and history St. Peter's Coll., Jersey City, 2000—, Fordham U., N.Y.C., 2000, Montclair State Coll., Upper Montclair, NJ, 2002—. Author: Jonathan Swift's Gulliver's Travels, 1996; editor: Concordantia in Orationem Quae Aristidis Fertur Eis Basilea, 1996; contbr articles to profl. jours. Candidate N.Y. State Legislature, 1970. Travel to Collections grantee NEH, Washington, 1984; rsch. grantee Wilbur Found., Mecosta, Mich., 1992, Soc. Farsaratul, L.I. City, N.Y., 1992, Richter Found., N.Y.C., 1996. Mem. Am. Hist. Assn., Am. Philol. Assn., Archaeol. Instn. Am. (nat. coun. 1977-78). Avocations: reading, book collecting. Office: St Peters Coll Dept Modern and Classical 2641 Kennedy Blvd Jersey City NJ 07306

STERZER, FRED, research physicist; b. Vienna, Austria, Nov. 18, 1929; came to U.S., 1947, naturalized, 1952; s. Karl and Rosa (Trumer) S.; m. Betty Distel, Sept. 5, 1964 (dec.). BS in Physics, CCNY, 1951; MS in Physics, NYU, 1952, PhD in Physics, 1955. With RCA, 1954-87, RCA Labs., David Sarnoff Research Ctr., Princeton, N.J., 1956-87, dir. microwave tech. center, 1972-87; dir. microwave research lab. David Sarnoff Research Ctr., 1987-88; pres. MMTC, Inc., Princeton, 1988—. Herbert J. Kayser research prof., City Coll., CUNY, 1986-87. Contbr. numerous articles to profl. publs. Fellow IEEE; mem. Am. Phys. Soc., Nat. Acad. Engring., Sigma Xi, Phi Beta Kappa. Achievements include condr. research on optical components, microwave solid-state devices and circuits, med. microwave tech. Home: 4432 Province Line Rd Princeton NJ 08540-4368 Office: MMTC Inc 12 Roszel Rd Princeton NJ 08540-6234 E-mail: sterzer@mmtc.com.

STETINA, PAMELA ELEANOR, nursing educator; b. Cambridge, Mass., Nov. 11, 1964; d. Charles and Eleanor Mary (Jennison) Toth; m. Francis Lee Stetina Jr., Aug. 15, 1987. BSN, Salisbury (Md.) State U., 1987; cert. in gerontology, U. Denver, 1990; M in Nursing, U. Phoenix, Englewood, Colo., 1996. RN; cert. oncology nurse. Grad. nurse, RN Dorchester Gen. Hosp., Cambridge, Md., 1987-89; staff nurse Salisbury Med. Ctr., 1988-89; staff/charge nurse Porter Care Hosp., Denver, 1989-91; floating nurse Summit Health Profls., 1991-96; clin. nurse NMC Home Care, Englewood, 1992-95; mem. faculty, asst. dir. nursing Concorde Career Inst., Denver, 1994-96; coord. nursing Pueblo C.C.-S.W., Durango, Colo., 1996-2000; asst. prof. Tex. A&M U., Corpus Christi, 2000—. Mem. curriculum com., faculty whole com., libr. com. Tex. A&M U., Corpus Christi, 2000—. Contbr. Jour. Nursing Jocularity. Instr. CPR Am. Heart Assn., Colo., 1994—. Named Educator of Yr., Colo. Pvt. Sch. Assn., Denver, 1995. Mem. Nat. League for Nursing, Oncology Nursing Soc., So. Nursing Rsch. Soc., Sigma Theta Tau. Avocations: reading, hiking. Office: Tex A&M U Sch Nursing 6300 Ocean Dr Corpus Christi TX 78412 E-mail: pstetina@juno.com.

STETLER, RUSSELL DEARNLEY, JR. private investigator; b. Phila., Jan. 15, 1945; s. Russell Dearnley and Martha Eleanor (Schultz) S. BA with honors in Philosophy, Haverford (Pa.) Coll., 1966; postgrad., New Sch. Social Research, 1966-67. Research asst. to Bertrand Russell, 1967; lectr. Hendon Coll., London, 1968-69; pres. Archetype, Inc., Berkeley, Calif., 1971-78; pub. Westworks, 1977-80; pvt. investigator, 1980-90; chief investigator Calif. Appellate Project, 1990-95; dir. of investigation and mitigation N.Y. State Capital Defender Office, N.Y.C., 1995—. Cons., dir. Ramparts Press, Palo Alto, 1971-80; editorial cons. Internews, Berkeley, 1973-78; faculty Caribbean Sch., Ponce, P.R., 1978-80 Author: The Battle of Bogside, 1970; co-editor: The Assassinations: Dallas and Beyond, 1976. Research grantee Atlantic Peace Found., 1969-70 Mem. Calif. Assn. Lic. Investigators, Nat. Assn. Legal Investigators, Calif. Soccer Referees Assn.-North (treas. Marin County chpt. 1982-90), Amigos de las Americas (pres. Marin chpt. 1985-88). Clubs: Mill Valley Soccer (dir. 1981), Albany-Berkeley Soccer (pres. 1977-78). Office: Capital Defender Office 217 Broadway Fl 9 New York NY 10007-2909 E-mail: rstetler@nycdo.org.

STETLER, STEPHEN H. state legislator; b. York, Pa., July 5, 1949; m. Polly Stetler. Student, St. James Sch., 1967; BA, Drew U., 1971, MDiv., 1974; MS, John Hopkins U., 1983. Tchr. Nat. Cathedral Sch. for Girls, Washington, 1975-77; with Commonwealth of Pa. Dept. Revenue, 1977-89, dep. sec. for taxation, 1987-89; with D.E. Stetler's & Sons, Inc., York, Pa., 1989—; rep. 95th state dist. Pa. Ho. of Reps., 1991—. Address: 266 E Market St York PA 17403-2013

STETSON, EUGENE WILLIAM, III, film producer; b. Norwalk, Conn., Mar. 31, 1951; s. Eugene William Jr. and Grace Stuart (Richardson) S.; m. Jane White Watson, June 14, 1993. AB, Harvard U., 1982, postgrad. in Sch. Arts and Scis., 1986. Assoc. exec. dir. Conn. River Watershed Coun.,

Easthampton, Mass., 1978-81; v.p. Fairhill Oil & Gas Corp. (Fairhill Oil Ltd.-Can.), N.Y.C., Calgary, Alta., Can., 1981-84, pres., 1984-92; film and TV writer and producer, 1991—. Bd. dirs. Piedmont Fin. Co., Greensboro, N.C., 1978-80, Chisolm Mgmt. Corp., N.Y.C., 1983—; supr. Ottauquechee Conservation Dist., Woodstock, Vt., 1978-82; pres. Boatwright Found., N.Y.C., 1981—; exec. com. Westminster Sch., Simsbury, Conn., 1984-86; gov. Smith Richardson Found., N.Y., 1984—; trustee Proctor Acad., Andover, N.H., 1985—; co-founder River Watch Network, Montpelier, Vt., 1987—; pres. bd. dirs. Vt. Film Commn., 1996—. Mem. Vt. Gov.'s Coun. of Environ. Advisors, 1992—, Vt. Gov.'s Coun. on Bus. and the Environment, 1994—; pres. Vt. Film Commn., 1996—. Mem. Harvard-Radcliffe Club Vt. (v.p. 1994—), Harvard Club N.Y.C., Hasty Pudding Club. Home: 139 Elm St Norwich VT 05055-9445

STETSON, PETER BRAILEY, astronomer; b. Middleboro, Mass., Aug. 30, 1952; s. George Robert and Estelle Marie (Ives) Stetson; m. Frances Eileen Bogucki, Aug. 5, 1979; children: Whitney Ann, Brailey Marie, Garrett Wilson, Leete Anthony. BA, MA, Wesleyan U., 1974; MS, Yale U., 1975, PhD, 1979. Postdoctoral astronomy dept. Yale U., New Haven, 1979-80; Carnegie fellow Mt. Wilson and Las Campanas Obs., Pasadena, Calif., 1980-83; rsch. assoc. Dominion Astrophys. Obs., Victoria, B.C., Can., 1983-84, asst. rsch. officer Can., 1984-86, assoc. rsch. officer Can., 1986-89, sr. rsch. officer Can., 1989—; adj. prof. U. Victoria, 1988—. Contbr. articles to Astrophysical Jour., Jour. of Royal Astron. Soc. Can., Annual Reviews of Astronomy and Astrophysics, Astron. Jour., Publ. Astron. Soc. of Pacific. Recipient R.M. Petrie prize lectr. Can. Astron. Soc., 1991, Gold medal Sci. Coun. B.C., 1994, Maria and Eric Muhlmann award Astron. Soc. Pacific, 2000. Office: Dominion Astrophys Obs 5071 W Saanich Rd Victoria BC Canada V9E 2E7 E-mail: peter.stetson@nrc.ca.

STETSON, ROBERT FRANCIS, retired metallurgist; b. N.Y.C., Oct. 20, 1928; s. Ralph Jerome and Margaret Mary Stetson; m. Rita Marie Jubach, Dec. 30, 1950 (dec. May 31, 1994); 1 child Barbara A. ; m. Mary Jane McKinney, June 10, 1999. CE in Metallurgy, Pa. State U., 1955. ICET A NSPE. Lab. technologist & inspection Babcock & Wilcox Co., Beaver Falls, Pa., 1949—58; tech. specialist materials sci. Gen. Atomics, San Diego, 1958—86, cons., 1986—98; ret., 1998. With AC U.S. Army, 1945—47, ETO. Recipient Nat. Engring. Assocs. Achievement award, Am. Soc. Metals, 1979, James F. Lincoln Arc Welding Found. award, 1979. Fellow: Am. Soc. Metals Internat. (exec. bd. San Diego chpt. 1964—96, chmn. San Diego chpt. 1972—73). Achievements include patents for plasma orifice tip. Avocation: genealogy. Home and Office: 6754 El Banquero Pl San Diego CA 92119-1130 Personal E-mail: bobstetson@cox.net.

STETTLER, CARLA RICE, marketing executive; b. Louisville, Nov. 21, 1947; d. Rudolph Carl and Mildred N. (Sharp) Rice; m. John Austin Stettler, Sept. 19, 1967; children: Susan Romaine, Melissa Ann, Jennifer Jon. BA in Communications, Spalding U., Louisville, 1988. Freelance reporter Fern Creek Neighbor Newspaper, Louisville, 1978-79, Courier-Jour., Louisville, 1978-79; sec.-treas. Fern Creek United Meth. Ch., 1979-84; circulation mgr. Fern Creek Neighbor Newspaper, 1984-85; exec. sec. Spalding U., 1985-89; mktg. coord. Genequip, Inc., Louisville, 1989-94; pres. Bluegrass Foliage, Inc., 1995—. Troop leader Girl Scouts Am., Louisville, 1974-80; adminstrv. bd. Fern Creek United Meth. Ch., 1979-84, 1991—, trustee, 1992-96. Mem. NAFE, Women in Comm., Louisville Bus. and Profl. Women. Avocations: music, writing, reading, travel.

STETTLER, STEPHEN F. performing company executive; b. Phila., May 1, 1952; s. Wallace Frederick and Catherine Sue (Brill) S. AB summa cum laude, Kenyon Coll., 1974; MFA in Directing, Cath. U. Am., 1982; MLitt in Theatre, Lincoln Coll., Oxford, Eng., 1983. Dir. dramatics Westminster Sch., Simsbury, Conn., 1975-80; acting coach Hartke Conservatory Cath. U., Washington, 1982; chair drama dept. St. Albans and Nat. Cathedral Schs., 1980-84; dir., instr. acting Nat. Theatre Inst. O'Neill Theater Ctr., Waterford, Conn., 1984-93; artistic dir. TNT/New Theatre Bklyn., 1985-90; producing dir. Weston (Vt.) Playhouse, 1988—. Lit. asst. Arena Stage Co., Washington, 1983-84; site evaluator theatres Nat. Endowment for Arts, Washington, 1990—; panelist project grants com. Vt. Coun. Arts, Montpelier, 1993-01; mem. capital grants com. N.Y.C. Dept. Cultural Affairs, 1989; cons. various ind. schs., 1986—; guest instr. directing Teatret Vart, Norway; ednl. theatre cons., guest artist Mercersburg (Pa.) Acad., Pa. Wyoming Seminary, Pa. Dir.: Who's Afraid of Virginia Woolf?, Dancing at Lughnasa, Animal Fair, Rough Crossing, Nora, Donkeys' Years, Floyd Collins (Moss Hart award for best prodn. in New Eng.), Sweeney Todd, Six Degrees of Separation, A Midsummer Night's Dream (Best Play award Folger Shakespeare Libr. competition). Mem. Phi Beta Kappa. Office: Weston Playhouse 703 Main St Weston VT 05161 E-mail: steve@westplay.com.

STETTNER, EDWARD A. political science educator; b. N.Y.C., Feb. 18, 1940; s. Frederick Albert and Celia Carolyn (Everard) S.; m. Laura Gagliardi, July 17, 1966; children: Victoria, Jeffrey, Thomas. BA, Brown U., 1962; MA, Princeton U., 1964, PhD, 1968. Lectr. polit. sci. Rutgers U., New Brunswick, N.J., 1965-66; instr. polit. sci. Wellesley (Mass.) Coll., 1966—68, asst. prof. polit. sci., 1968—74, assoc. prof., 1974—80, prof. polit. sci., 1980-95, Ralph Emerson and Alice Freeman Palmer prof. polit. sci., 1995—, assoc. dean of the coll., 1977-86, dean of the faculty, 1986-88. Author: Shaping Modern Liberalism: Herbert Croly and Progressive Thought, 1993; editor: Perspectives on Europe, 1970. Trustee Mount Ida Coll., Newton, Mass., 2000—. Mem. AAUP (mem. nat. coun. 1970-73, pres. Mass. State Conf. 1975-77), Am. Polit. Sci. Assn., New Eng. Polit. Sci. Assn., Phi Beta Kappa. Democrat. Episcopalian. Home: 869 Charles River St Needham MA 02492-1007 Office: Wellesley College 106 Central St Wellesley MA 02481 E-mail: estettner@wellesley.edu.

STETTNER, JERALD W. retail drugs stores executive; b. Miami, Fla., Mar. 31, 1952; s. Richard A. and LeJean D. (Haberman) S.; m. Linda G. Day, Dec. 22, 1978; children: Kelly R., Jarrod M., Zachary A. BS in Behavioral Mgmt., Ga. Inst. Tech., 1974. Various mgmt. positions Eckerd Drug Co., Clearwater, Fla., 1974-87; regional v.p. Eckerd Corp., 1987-98, sr. v.p., 1998—. Mem. Ga. Tech. Alumni Assn., Phi Delta Theta. Avocations: tennis, golf, skiing. E-mail: JWStettner@aol.com.

STEUER, GARY PAUL, art association administrator; b. Newport, R.I., Nov. 28, 1955; s. Irwin And Wilma S.; m. Renee Perez, Dec. 30, 1983; children: Rachel, Emma. BA, NYU, 1977, M in Arts Adminstrn., 1981. Aide Congressman Ted Weiss, N.Y.C., 1976-79; dir. programs Alliance Resident Theatres, 1981-84; mng. dir. Vineyard Theatre, 1984-88; mgr. Capital Funding Initiative N.Y. State Coun. on Arts, 1988-91; exec. dir. Nat. Actors Theater, 1991-92; pres., CEO Arts & Bus. Coun., Inc., 1993—. Bd. dirs. Early Stages, Inc., N.Y.C., Alliance for Nonprofit Mgmt., Washington; mem. steering com. N.Y.C. Arts Coalition, Arts Action for NY State, 1999—. Contbr. articles to profl. jours.; spkr. in field. Office: Arts & Bus Coun Inc 520 8th Ave Fl 3 Ste 319 New York NY 10018 E-mail: gsteuer@artsandbusiness.org.

STEUER, RICHARD MARC, lawyer; b. Bklyn., June 19, 1948; s. Harold and Gertrude (Vengar) S.; m. Audrey P. Forchheimer, Sept. 9, 1973; children: Hilary, Jeremy. BA, Hofstra U., 1970; JD, Columbia U., 1973. Bar: N.Y. 1974, U.S. Dist. Ct. (ea. and so. dists.) N.Y. 1974, U.S. Ct. Appeals (2d cir.) 1974, U.S. Supreme Ct. 1979, U.S. Dist. Ct. (no. dist.) N.Y. 1984, U.S. Dist. Ct. (we. dist.) N.Y. 1997, U.S. Ct. Appeals (3d cir.) 1987, U.S. Ct. Appeals (5th cir.) 1995. Ptnr. Kaye Scholer LLP, N.Y.C., 1973—, chair antitrust practice group, 1996—. Adj. assoc. prof. law NYU, 1985; lectr. in field; neutral evaluator U.S. Dist. Ct. Ea. Dist., N.Y. 1994-96. Author: A Guide to Marketing Law: Law and Business Inc., 1986; contbr. articles to profl. jours. Fellow: Am. Bar Found. (others); mem.: ABA (lectr. 1969, 1978, chmn. monograph com. refusals to deal and exclusive distributorships 1983, editl. bd. antitrust devel. vol. 1984—86, lectr. 1985, vice-chmn. program com. 1988—91, lectr. 1989, chmn. spring meeting program com. 1991—92, Sherman Act sect. 1 com. 1991—93, coun. sect. antitrust law 1993—96, chmn. publs. com. 1996—98, lectr. 1997, 1998, editl. chmn. Antitrust mag. 1998—2001, lectr. 1999, 2000, coun. sect. antitrust law 2001—), Assn. Bar City N.Y. (chmn. antitrust and trade regulation 1995—98, antitrust and trade regulation, internat. trade, lectures and CLE coms). Office: Kaye Scholer LLP 425 Park Ave New York NY 10022-3506 E-mail: rsteuer@kayescholer.com.

STEURER, JEFFREY M, music educator; b. Geneva, Oct. 20, 1974; s. Michael Ray and Karen Ann Steurer; m. Karen Elizabeth Nelson, July 29, 2000. BA, Judson Coll., Elgin, IL, 1997; MM, No. Ill. U., DeKalb, IL, 2000. Choral music tchr. Rockford Christian Schools, Rockford, Ill., 1997—2000; dir. of music First Bapt. Ch., Belvidere, 1997—2000; music tchr. Hiawatha CUSD #426, Kirkland, 2000—02; dir. of worship Covenant Bapt. Ch., Marengo, 2000—; music methods instr. Judson Coll., Elgin, 2000—; music tchr. Rockford Pub. Sch #205, Rockford, 2002—. Piano and voice tchr. self-employed, Belvidere, Ill., 1996—2001. Composer: (songs) Thinking You (Billboard Top 500, 1999). Mem.: Ill. Music Educators Assoc, Am. Choral Directors Assoc. Baptist. Avocations: composing, travelling, history (civil war studies), history (civil war studies), history (civil war studies). Office: Ellis Arts Academy-Rockford Sch #205 Central Ave Rockford IL 61104 E-mail: jsteurer@judson-il.edu.

STEUTERMAN, ERIKA C. government agency administrator; Student Air Force Res. Officer Tng. Corps program, Purdue U., West Lafayette, Ind. Commd. USAF, 1977, advanced through grades to brig. gen., individual mobilization asst. to commdr. of Air Intelligence Agy. Tex. Office: Lackland AFB 102 Hall Blvd Ste 201 San Antonio TX 78243-7009*

STEVENS, ALICE MARIE, educational consultant; b. Colorado Springs, Colo., Jan. 18, 1954; d. Charles C. and Gladys Marie (Craft) S. BS, S.W. Bapt. U., 1976; MEd, U. Mo., 1983; PhD, Purdue U., 2001. Cert. tchr. reading, learning disabilities, Mo. Sci. tchr. Lincoln County R-IV Schs., Winfield, Mo., 1976-78; sci. instr. Ricks Inst., Monrovia, Liberia, West Africa, 1978-79; learning specialist Total Learning Clinic, Columbia, Mo., 1982-89; homebound instr. Rusk Rehab. Ctr., 1988-91; instr. Columbia Coll., 1989, 91; learning disabilities specialist Columbia (Mo.) Pub. Schs., 1989-91; tchr., rsch. asst. Purdue U., West Lafayette, Ind., 1991-98; ednl. cons., 1991-97; asst. dir. Cerebral Palsy Assn. Greater Lafayette, 1993-94; instr. Frostburg (Md.) State U., 1998-2000; dir. prevention programs Brain Injury Assn., Alexandria, Va., 2000—. Asst. dir. Cerebral Palsy Assn. Greater Lafayette, 1993-94. Mem. ASCD, AAE, Nat. Sci. Tchrs. Assn. (conf. presenter 1993), Coun. for Exceptional Children (conf. presenter), Soc. for Prevention Rsch., Kappa Delta Pi, Phi Delta Kappa. Office: Brain Injury Assn 105 N Alfred Alexandria VA 22314 E-mail: amstevens@biausa.org.

STEVENS, ALLAN WOODARD, electrical engineer; b. White Plains, N.Y., Aug. 10, 1958; s. Allan B. and Margaret (Woodard) S.; m. Bonnie Groudan, Sept. 25, 1983; 1 child, Julie L. BSEE, Clarkson U., 1980. Registered profl. engr., N.J., Wis. Asst. engr. Princeton (N.J.) U. Plasma Physics Lab., 1980-81, assoc. engr., 1981-84, staff engr., 1984-92, project engr., 1992-97; supervising elec. engr. Washington Group Internat., Princeton, 1997—2001. Presdl. scholar Clarkson U., 1976, N.Y. State Regents scholar, 1976. Mem. IEEE. Home: 16 Willis Ct East Brunswick NJ 08816-2885 Office: Washington Group Internat 510 Carnegie Ctr Princeton NJ 08540-6241 E-mail: allan.stevens@wgint.com., allan.stevens@ieee.org.

STEVENS, ALLYSSA ELIZABETH, retail executive; b. Townshend, Vt., Nov. 27, 1961; d. William Francis and Elizabeth Jane (Stevens) K.; m. Cedric Vaughn Stevens, Jan. 31, 1988; 1 child, William Vaughn Reuben Stevens. Student, Simmons Coll., 1979-80; cert. in purchasing, Bryant Coll., 1987. Sec., asst. to supt. Tehran (Iran) Am. Sch., summer 1979; asst. to pres., office mgr. Town & Country Furniture, S. Burlington, 1981-86; mgr. Center Store, Burlington, 1986-87; gen. mgr., contr. residential and contract divsns. Novello Inc., Montpelier, Vt., 1988—; various towns; ind. distbr. skin care and nutrition bus. Network Mktg., Skin Care and Nutrition, Hinesburg, 1991—. Cons. Ctr. Store/Health Fun Inc., Burlington, 1987—; with Tehran Am. Sch., Iran, summer 1979. Forum mem. Govt. Commn. on Econ. Devel., Montpelier, 1989; pub. speaker Iran Hostage Crisis. Mem. Vt. Retail Assn. Roman Catholic. Avocations: quilting, needlepoint, fishing, camping. Office: Novello Inc Barre-Montpelier Rd PO Box 309 Montpelier VT 05601-0309 E-mail: aestevens@novellofurniture.com.

STEVENS, ART, public relations executive; b. N.Y.C., July 17, 1935; m. Eva Sandberg, Mar. 19, 1972. BA, CCNY, 1957. Pub. relations dir. Prentice Hall, Inc., Englewood Cliffs, N.J.; account exec. William L. Safire Public Relations Inc., N.Y.C., 1966-69, v.p., 1967-68, pres., 1968-69, Lobsenz-Stevens Inc., N.Y.C., 1970—; instr. Fairleigh Dickinson U.; chmn. & CEO Publicis Dialog, N.Y.C., 1999—. Weekly humor commentator WINK-TV, Ft. Myers, Fla. Author: The Persuasion Explosion, 1985, Sanibel Shell Shocked, 1992; weekly columnist Sanibel-Captiva (Fla.) Islander; contbr. articles to profl. jours. Bd. dirs. United Way of Putnam County, N.Y.; trustee Gotthelf Lupus Rsch. Inst. Inducted City Coll. N.Y. Comms. Alumni Hall Fame, 2001. Mem.: Public Relations Soc. Am. (nat. bd., pub. rels. com., chair-elect tri-state dist., exec. com., chmn. eligibility com., counselors acad. sect.), Publicity Club N.Y. (Disting. Svc. award 1969), Gipsy Trail (pres., chmn. Carmel, N.Y.). Home: 201 E 21st St New York NY 10010-6401 Office: Publicis Dialog 460 Park Ave S New York NY 10016-7315 E-mail: astevens@publicis-usa.com. *Life is not an accident. The events in one's life are not accidents either. When I look back at what I have done and the lives that have been interwined with mine, it's as though it's all been scripted by a higher power.*

STEVENS, BERTON LOUIS, JR. data processing manager; b. Chgo., Apr. 4, 1951; s. Berton Louis Sr. and Mary Cover (Kochavaris) S.; m. Janet Alene Madenberg, May 20, 1990. Student, Ill. Inst. Tech., Chgo., 1969-73. Systems and applications programmer Judge & Dolph, Ltd., Elk Grove Village, Ill., 1978-91, mgr. data processing, 1991-99; bus. sys. coord. Meml. Med. Ctr., Inc., 2000-2001, lead sys. analyst, 2001—02; svc. ctr. mgr. Siemens Health Sys., 2002—. Instr. Adler Planetarium and Astron. Mus., Chgo., 1980-86; dir. Desert Moon Observatory #448. Editor and author newsletter Bert's Bull., 1987-90; editor newsletter No. Lights, 1990-98. Recipient Regional award North Ctrl. Region Astron. League, 1989. Mem. Nat. Assn. Sys. Programmers, Internat. Occultation Timing Assn. (sec. 1975-78), Chgo. Computer Soc., Chgo. Astron. Soc. (pres. 1977, 80, 84), Racine Astron. Soc. (pres. 1979), Astron. League (exec. sec. 1993-95, webmaster 1995-02), Desert Moon Observatory (dir.), Astron. Soc. Las Cruces (pres, 2001). E-mail: bstevens@zianet.com., Berton.stevens@smed.com.

STEVENS, BETSY A. hotel and hospitality management educator; b. Detroit, July 4, 1948; d. Roger Lee Emish and Sara Louise Drake; m. Kenneth W. Stevens, June 22, 1974 (div. Nov. 1986). BA, U. Cin., 1970, MA, 1971; PhD, Wayne State U., 1992. Asst. dir. career svcs. U. Mich., Ann Arbor, 1983-86; dir. human resources Archdiocese of Detroit, 1986-87; lectr. U. Mich., Ann Arbor, 1987-94; asst. prof. Cornell U., Ithaca, N.Y., 1994—. Cons. in field. Author: How to Travel as an Air Courier, 1997; contbr. numerous articles to profl. jours. Fulbright sr. scholar U.S. Govt. Info. Agy., Tomsk, Russia, 1998. Mem. Assn. Bus. Comm., Rotary Club. Avocations: traveling to foreign countries. Office: Elon Univl Elon NC 27244 Home: 602 Brookfield Dr Gibsonville NC 27249-3348

STEVENS, CHARLOTTE WHITNEY, artist, retired art educator; b. N.Y.C., Dec. 13, 1923; d. Philip Charles Lamm and Edna May (Carson) Decker; m. William Kuebler Whitney, Aug. 26, 1946 (dec. Oct. 1985); children: Charlene Edwards, Alice Webb; m. Arthur Raymond Stevens, Feb. 21, 1997. BFA, George Washington U., 1945; MFA, Cranbrook Acad. Art, 1446. Art tchr. Roeper Sch., Bloomfield Hills, Mich., 1950-59, Olivet (Mich.) Cmty. Sch., 1959-60, 72-89; artist Olivet, 1989—. Part-time art tchr. Bloomfield Hills H.S., 1946-48; part-time art instr. Olivet Coll., 1965-75. Author: Children's Art, 1965. Chairperson Olivet Planning Com., 1973-83; vol. restoration project downtown storefronts, Olivet, 1965-75. Mem. Eaton Art League. Congregationalist. Avocation: swimming. Home: PO Box 305 205 S Main St Olivet MI 49076-9610 E-mail: cwhitney@voyager.net.

STEVENS, COLLEEN NEWPORT, artist; b. San Diego, May 4, 1951; d. Lyle Burton and Carroll Louise Newport; m. Ronnie Marion Stevens, Sept. 12, 1986; children: Laura, Mike. BFA, Eastern Wash. Univ., 1979. V.p. Ariz. Watercolor Soc., Phoenix, 1984-85; workshop chmn. Tenn. Watercolor Soc., 1987-88; pres. Memphis Germantown Art League, Memphis, 1990-91; owner/ptnr. Madison Ave. Art Gallery, 1991-96. Painting workshop instr., Indian Nations, 1993, Edisto Art League, 1995, and various others. Included in books: Best of Watercolor, 1995, Splash 3, 1994, Creative Watercolor, 1996, Portrait Inspirations, 1997, Watercolor Magic, 1996, 2nd edit., 1999, 200 Great Ideas for Artists, 1998, Easy Solutions, 1998, Watercolor Expressions, 1999; exhibited at over 100 mus. and galleries; illustrator: (cover) Christian Sci. Herald, Christian Sci. Sentinel. Counselor Cancer Support Ctr., vol. Flying Colors. Recipient Memphis in May Artist award City of Memphis, 1997, Arts and Humanities Gold medal for Visual Arts, Germantown Arts Alliance, 2000. Avocations: painting, hiking, computers, fishing, cooking. Home: 8386 Meadow Run Cv Germantown TN 38138-6244 E-mail: newportpainting@aol.com.

STEVENS, CONNIE, actress, singer; b. Bklyn., Aug. 8, 1938; d. Peter and Eleanore (McGinley) Ingolia; m. Maurice Elias; m. Edwin Jack Fisher (div.); children: Joely, Tricia Leigh. Pres. Forever Spring Cosmetics; founder Windfeather Foundation. Show bus. debut as vocalist with, The Three Debs, Hollywood, at age 16; appeared in: Finians Rainbow for Hollywood Repertory Co.; numerous motion pictures, including Way, Way Out, Scorchy, Eighteen and Animals, Young and Dangerous, Drag Strip Riot, Rock-a-bye Baby, Parish, Susan Slade, Palm Springs Weekend, The Grissom Gang, Never Too Late, Grease II, 1983, Back to the Beach, 1987, Bring Me the Head of Dobie Gillis, 1988, Love Is All There Is, 1996; starred in TV series Wendy and Me and TV series Hawaiian Eye, 1959-62, Head Over Heals, 1997, Titus, 2002-, TV films for ABC-TV Movie-of-the-Week; Call Her Mom, 1972, Playmates, Mister Jericho, Cole Porter in Paris, The Sex Symbol, 1974, Starting From Scratch, 1988, James Dean: Live Fast, Die Young, 1997; guest star on TV with, Bob Hope, Red Skelton, Englebert Humperdinck, Tom Jones, Perry Como and Laugh-In; TV appearance comedy spl. Harry's Battles; headliner at Flamingo Hotel, Las Vegas, also, Hilton Internat., Sands Hotel, Desert Inn, Aladdin, MGM, Sahara, 1969-76; stage appearances include The Wizard of Oz at Carousel Theatre in So. Calif., Any Wednesday at Melodyland, Anaheim, Calif.; made Broadway debut in Star Spangled Girl, 1967; accompanied Bob Hope around world on his Christmas tour, 1969, Persian Gulf Christmas tour, 1987; dir., prodr., writer, editor, cinematographer: A Healing, 1997 (Santa Clarita Internat. Film Festival Award, 1998). Bd. dirs. Ctr. for Plastic and Reconstructive Surgery, South Vietnam. Recipient Lady of Humanities Award, Shriners Hospital, 1991, Humanitarian of the Year, Sons of Italy, 2001, Distinguished Civilian Service Medal, 2002.*

STEVENS, DALE MARLIN, civil engineer; b. Boyd, Minn., June 11, 1940; s. Leslie Dale Stevens and Hazel Margaret Anderson Neumann; m. Renee Joy Pflueger, Apr. 21, 1967 (div. 1977); children: Joan Marie, Jeffrey Michael; m. Marianne Jean Solting, Feb. 10, 1979. BSCE, S.D. State U., 1962; MSCE, S.D. Sch. Mines & Tech., 1973. Registered profl. engr., S.D., Ala. Commd. U.S. Army, 1962-83, advanced through grades to lt. col., 1979; staff engr. U.S. Army C.E., Huntsville, Ala., 1983-86; sr. engr. The BDM Corp., 1986-89; mgr. bus. devel. Wyle Labs., Inc., 1989; sr. systems engr. Teledyne Brown Engring., 1990—2002. Mem. civil and environ. adv. coun. U. Ala., Huntsville, 1990-96, chmn. civil and environ. program adv. coun., 2000—. Coun. mem. St. Mark's Luth. Ch., Huntsville, 1986-87, chmn., 1987. Named Civil Engr. of the Yr. Huntsville Assn. Tech. Soc., 1988-89, 94-95. Fellow ASCE (br. pres. 1988, dir. Ala. sect. 1995-97, sec-treas. Ala. sect. 1996-98, 1st v.p. Ala. sect.); mem. Am. Concrete Inst., Soc. Am. Mil. Engrs. (post v.p. 1991), Prestressed Concrete Inst., Ret. Officers Assn., Elks, Chi Epsilon. Republican. Lutheran. Home: 2101 Greenslope Trl NE Huntsville AL 35811-2609 Office: Earth Tech Inc 4955 Corporate Dr Huntsville AL 35805

STEVENS, DANIEL FRANCIS, author; b. Bklyn., Feb. 8, 1922; s. Thomas Francis and Mae Agnes (McClorey) S.; m. Florinda Camile Del Ferraro, Aug. 16, 1952; children: Nina Christina Girolamo-Stevens, Paula Stevens. BA cum laude, U. Notre Dame, 1943; MA, Columbia U., 1949, profl. diploma, 1954, EdD, 1958. Cert. social studies tchr., elem. tchr., elem. and secondary prin., supts. Counselor, testing tech. N.Y. State Dept. Labor/Employment Svc., Hempstead, 1949-52; elem. and high sch. tchr. Oyster Bay (N.Y.)-East Norwich Ctrl. Sch. Dist., 1952-58, elem. prin., 1958-70, asst. supt. instrn., 1970-81, supt. schs., 1981-83; ret., 1983; pvt. practice counselor Syosset, N.Y., 1983-94; ret., 1994. Adj. prof. edn. C.W. Post Ctr., L.I. U., Greenvale, N.Y., 1968-78, project mem. ednl. adminstrn. adv. com., 1973-80; dir. rsch. projects on middle sch. studentsproblem solving skills. Author: (young adult books) Rhea and the Fireflies, 1991, Adventures Mad Anthont-The Art, 1991, Magic of the Brass Ring, 1991, Riding a Sunbeam, 1993, Letter to Lincoln, 1997. Congl. rep. White House Golden Anniversary Conf. on Children and Youth, Washington, 1960; rep. N.Y. State Conf. on Children and Youth, Albany, 1970; vol. mem. adv. bd. St. Anthony's Guidance Clinic/Divsn. Cath. Charities, 1972-75; vol. advisor to registrants Nat. Selective Svc. System, Great Neck, N.Y., 1952-78; motivational spkr. to encourage children to read, Internat. Reading Assn., N.Y. State Libr. Assn. Ret. lt. USNR, 1942-59. Mem. AAUP, Am. Assn. Sch. Adminstrs. (ret.), Assn. for Measurement and Evaluation, Nat. Vocat. Guidance Assn., Am. Pers. and Guidance Assn., Phi Delta Kappa, Lions Club. Home and Office: 67 Calvin Ave Syosset NY 11791-2136 E-mail: maeagnes@aol.com.

STEVENS, DENNIS LEROY, physician, researcher; b. Fort Benton, Mont., Nov. 26, 1941; s. John Gunnard and Alma Hope (Myers) S.; children: Karsten Erik, Marisa Lee. BA in Microbiology, U. Mont., 1964; PhD in Microbiology, Mont. State U., 1967; MD, U. Utah, 1971. Cert. medicine and infectious diseases Am. Bd. Internal Medicine. Intern, then resident U. Utah; staff physician Ft. Lee (Va.) Army Med. Ctr., 1974-75; infectious disease fellowship Brooke Army Med. Ctr., San Antonio, 1975-77, asst. chief infectious diseases, 1977-79; chief infectious diseases Vets. Affairs Med. Ctr., Boise, Idaho, 1979—; assoc. prof. medicine Univ. Wash., Seattle, 1986—, prof. of medicine. Mem. task force in streptococcal infections CDC, Atlanta, 1991—; fellowship Univ. Belgrade, Yugoslavia, 1971. Author: Streptococcal Infections, 2000. Tribal chief YMCA Indian Guides, Boise, 1980-83; basketball coach YMCA Basketball Program, Boise, 1985-88; pres. Idaho Lung Assn., 1988-90. Recipient Meritorious Svc. award U.S. Army, 1979, Disting. Alumni award U. Mont., 1991, Citation Infectious Disease Soc. of Am., 2000, Altemeir award, Surgical Infection Soc., 2001. Fellow Am. Coll. Physicians, Infectious Disease Soc. Am.; mem. Assn. of Am. Physicians, Am. Assn. of Physicians, Am. Soc. Microbiology, Am. Fedn. for Clin. Rsch., Western Soc. of Clin. Investigating, Western Assn. of Physicians, Sigma Xi. Avocations: photography, tennis, skiing, backpacking, gardening. Home: 4461 E Victory Rd Meridian ID 83642 Office: Veterans Affairs Med Ctr 500 W Fort St Boise ID 83702-4535

STEVENS, DENNIS MAX, audit director; b. Jersey City, Sept. 3, 1944; m. Susan Gail Brown, Mar. 15, 1969; children: Julie Ayn, Daniel Ross. BBA, Rutgers U., 1966; MA in Acctg., U. Mo., 1968. CPA, Mo. Staff Peat, Marwick, Mitchell and Co., St. Louis, 1968-80, ptnr., 1980-84; sr. v.p. and internal auditor Southwestern States Bankcard Assn., Dallas, 1985-86, sr. v.p. and chief fin. officer, 1986-89; corp. planner NCH Corp., Irving, 1989-95, dir. corp. audit, 1995—2002; auditor Alamo Group, Seguin, 2002—. Contr. articles to profl. jours. 1st lt. U.S. Army, 1969-70. Mem. AICPA (mem. electronic data processing auditing stds. com. 1979-84), Inst. Internal Auditors, Beta Gamma Sigma, Beta Alpha Psi. Home: 2325 Fountain Head Dr Plano TX 75023-6413 E-mail: den.stevens@attglobal.net.

STEVENS, DIANA LYNN, elementary education educator; b. Waterloo, Iowa, Dec. 12, 1950; d. Marcus Henry and Clarissa Ann (Funk) Carr; m. Paul John Stevens; 1 child, Drew Spencer. BS, Mid Am. Nazarene Coll., 1973; M in Liberal Arts, Baker U., 1989. Elem. tchr. Olathe (Kans.) Sch. Dist. #233, 1975—. Artwork appeared in traveling exhibit ARC/Nat. Art Edn. Assn., 1968, Delta Kappa Gamma Bull., 2001. Mem. Cedarhouse Aux., Olathe, 1986—; pres. Artists' League, Olathe, 1990—. Olathe Sch. Dist. Action grantee, 1996-97. Mem. NEA, Kans. Edn. Assn., Olathe Edn. Assn. (social com.), Nat. Art Edn. Assn., Delta Kappa Gamma (profl. affairs com. mem.), Coll. Ch. of the Nazarene. Avocations: portrait art, reading biographies, power walking, exhibiting artwork. Home: 217 S Montclaire Dr Olathe KS 66061-3828

STEVENS, DONALD KING, retired aeronautical engineer, consultant; b. Danville, Ill., Oct. 27, 1920; s. Douglas Franklin and Ida Harriet (King) S.; m. Adele Carman de Werff, July 11, 1942; children: Charles August, Anne Louise, Alice Jeanne Stevens Kay. BS with high honors in Ceramic Engring., U. Ill., 1942; MS in Aeros. and Guided Missiles, U. So. Calif., 1949; grad., U.S. Army Command and Staff Coll., 1957, U.S. Army War Coll., 1962. Served with Ill. State Geol. Survey, 1938-40; air defense officer Eng., North Africa, Italy, 1942-44; regimental staff officer 473d Infantry Regiment, Italy, 1944-45; ceramic engr. Harbison-Walker Refractories Co., Pitts., 1945-46;

commd. 2d lt. U.S. Army, 1942, advanced through grades to col., 1963, with Arty. Sch. Tex., 1949-52, supr. unit tng. and Nike missile firings N.Mex., 1953-56; mem. Weapons Systems Evaluation Group, Office of Sec. of Def., Washington, 1957-61; comdr. Niagara-Buffalo Def., 31st Arty. Brigade U.S. Army, Lockport, N.Y., 1963-65; study dir. U.S.A. ballistic missile def. studies DEPEX and X-66 for Sec. Def., 1965-66, chief Air Def. and Nuclear br. War Plans divsn., 1965-67; chief Strategic Forces divsn. Office Dep. Chief of Staff Mil. Ops. U.S. Army, Washington, 1967—69; chief spl. weapons plans, J5, U.S. European Command Germany, 1969-72; ret. U.S. Army, 1972. Guest lectr. U.S. Mil. Acad., 1958-59; cons. U.S. Army Concepts Analysis Agy., Bethesda, Md., 1973-95; cons. on strategy Lulejian & Assocs., Inc., 1974-75; cons. nuclear policy and plans to Office Asst. Sec. of Def., 1975-80, 84-93; cons. Sci. Applications, Inc., 1976-78. Contbr. articles to profl. jours. Asst. camp dir. Piankeshaw Area coun. Boy Scouts Am., 1937' mem. chancel choir, elder First Christian Ch., Falls Church, Va., 1957-61, 65-69, 72-2002; elder, trustee Presbyn. Ch., Niagara Falls, N.Y., 1963-65. Decorated D.S.M., Legion of Merit, Bronze Star. Mem. Am. Ceramic Soc., Assn. U.S. Army, U. Ill. Alumni Assn., U. So. Calif. Alumni Assn., Rotary, Keramos, Niagara Falls Country Club, Ill. Club (Washington), Terrapin Club, Sigma Xi, Sigma Tau, Tau Beta Pi, Phi Kappa Phi, Alpha Phi Omega. Achievements include pioneer in tactics and deployment plans for Army surface-to-air missiles. Address: 5916 5th St N Arlington VA 22203-1010 E-mail: dkstevens@erols.com.

STEVENS, EARL PATRICK, minister; b. Vicksburg, Miss., Nov. 21, 1925; s. Elton Alva and Mary Elizabeth (Keathley) S.; m. Vonda Jean Tuttle, Aug. 7, 1949; children: Teresa Darlene, Deborah Lalene, Earl P. II, David Paul. BA, Abilene Christian U., 1949; BRE, Coll. of the Bible, 1966; MA, MRE, Nat. Christian U., 1968, ThM, PhD, ThD, Nat. Christian U., 1969; DD (hon.), Ohio Christian Coll., 1968. Ordained to ministry Ch. of Christ, 1943; cert. neuropsychiat. technician. Minister Ch. of Christ, Olden, Tex., 1946-49, Barrackville, W.Va., 1949-62, Parkersburg, 1962-66, St. Mary's, 1966-77, Shinnston, 1977-90, Fairmont, 1990-96, Mt. Nebo, 1990-96, Pleasant Valley, 1996—. Instr. Ohio Valley Coll., Parkersburg, 1964-66; prof. Nat. Christian U., Ft. Worth, 1968-78. Author: The Glory of Christ, 1963, Doctrinal Study of I Timothy, 1987, 100 Years Preaching, 1995, Doctrines of Scripture Preservation, 1997, 17 other books. Served with USN, 1944-46. Named to Eagle Scout, Boy Scouts Am., 1942; recipient Golden Record award Word Records, 1968, Colin Anderson award Colin Anderson Ctr., 1968. Mem. So. Assn. Marriage Counselors, Am. Numismatic Assn. Democrat. Avocations: writing, stamps, hunting and fishing, golf, bowling. Home and Office: 204 Russell St Fairmont WV 26554-1860 *Every life has value; the strong must protect the weak; men belong together; friendship is a two-way street; everyone must mould his heart, shape his life and enrich his mind. These are living guidelines for my life and all others, too. Neglect any or all and we are the poorer for it.*

STEVENS, EDWARD IRA, information systems educator; b. York, Pa., Oct. 13, 1937; s. Francis DeHaven and Myra Jane (Foust) S.; m. Marjorie Eleanor Bisson, Aug. 29, 1959 (div. Oct. 1978); children: Mark Edward, Whitney Lynne, Kimberly Lauren; m. Kathleen Susan Berg, May 30, 1983. AB, Davidson (N.C.) Coll., 1959; MDiv, Harvard U., 1962; PhD, Vanderbilt U., 1965. Asst. prof. psychology, then assoc. prof. Eckerd Coll. (formerly Fla. Presbyn. Coll.), St. Petersburg, 1965-69, dir. research and ednl. services, 1969-73, dir. planning, exec. asst. to pres., 1977-84, from assoc. prof. info. sys. to prof., 1984-2000, prof. emeritus, 2000—, dir. instl. rsch. and planning, 1993-97, dir. libr. svcs., 1995-2000, dir. info. svcs. & tech., 1996—; dean acad. affairs Northland Coll., Ashland, Wis., 1973-75, v.p., 1974-75; pres. Lyndon State Coll., Lyndonville, Vt., 1975-77; v.p. rsch. St. Clair Software Systems, Inc., Clearwater, Fla., 1985-87. Cons. and lectr. in field. Contbr. articles to profl. jours. Am. Council Edn. fellow, Washington, 1969-70; Fund for Improvement Post-Secondary Edn. grantee, Washington, 1976-78. Mem. EDUCAUSE, ALA, Phi Beta Kappa. Presbyterian. Avocations: art, antiques, photography. Home: 504 W Sullivan St Olean NY 14760 Office: Eckerd Coll 4200 54th Ave S Saint Petersburg FL 33711-4744 E-mail: ed_stevens@post.harvard.edu.

STEVENS, ELISABETH GOSS (MRS. ROBERT SCHLEUSSNER JR.), writer, journalist, graphic artist; b. Rome, Aug. 11, 1929; d. George May and Elisabeth (Stryker) Stevens; m. Robert Schleussner, Jr., Mar. 12, 1966 (dec. 1977); 1 child, Laura Stevens BA, Wellesley Coll., 1951; MA with high honors, Columbia U., 1956. Editorial assoc. Art News Mag., 1964-65; art critic and reporter Washington Post, Washington, 1965-66; free-lance art critic and reporter Balt., 1966—; contbg. art critic Wall Street Jour., N.Y.C., 1969-72; art critic Trenton Times, N.J., 1974-77; art and architecture critic The Balt. Sun, 1978-86. Author: Elisabeth Stevens' Guide to Baltimore's Inner Harbor, 1981, Fire and Water: Six Short Stories, 1982, Children of Dust: Portraits and Preludes, 1985, Horse and Cart: Stories from the Country, 1990, The Night Lover: Art & Poetry, 1995, In Foreign Parts, 1997, Household Words, 1999, 2000, Eranos, 2000, Cherry Pie & Other Stories, 2001; one-woman show includes Coll. Notre Dame of Md., 1997, Galerie Francoise, Lutherville, Md., 2000; exhibited in group shows at The Corcoran Gallery of Art, Washington, Towson State U., Balt., Atelier A/E, N.Y.C., Stephen Gang Gallery, N.Y.C., Govt. House, Annapolis, U. Minn., Morris, Cooperstown Art Assn., N.Y.; contbr. articles, poetry and short stories to jours., nat. newspapers and popular mags. Recipient A.D. Emmart award for journalism, 1980, Critical Writing citation Balt.-Washington Newspaper Guild, 1980, fiction awards Md. Poetry Rev., 1992, 93, 94, 2d prize Lite Circle, 1994, 1st prize in fiction Lite Circle, 1995, 96, Balt. Writers Alliance Play Writing Contest award, 1994; art critics' fellow NEA, 1973-74, fellow MacDowell Colony, 1981, Va. Ctr. for Creative Arts, 1982-85, 88-90, 92, 93, 95, 97, 2000, Ragdale Found., 1984, 89, Yaddo, 1991, Villa Montalvo, 1995; Work-in-Progress grantee for poetry Md. Art Coun., 1986, Creative Devel. grantee for short fiction collection Balt. Mayor's Com. on Art and Culture, 1986. Mem. Coll. Art Assn., Authors Guild, Fla. Printmakers Assn., Poetry Soc. Am., Am. Soc. Graphic Artists, Nat. Book Critics Circle, Women Contemporary Artists Sarasota. Home: Bards Castle 5353 Creekside Trail Sarasota FL 34243-

STEVENS, ELIZABETH, psychotherapist, consultant; b. Evanston, Ill., Jan. 11, 1950; d. Kenneth M. and C. Jane (Reynolds) S.; m. David W. Handy, Oct. 3, 1986. BA in Psychology, U. Fla., 1973; MA in Clin. Psychology, Kent State U., 1976. Lic. profl. counselor; lic. marriage and family therapist. Exec. dir. Genesis Women's Shelter, Dallas, 1986-87; dir. outpatient svcs. Green Oaks Hosp., 1987-88; mgmt. cons. Houston, 1977—; pvt. practice, 1990—; founder Integrated Clin. Resources, Inc., The Stevens Co., healthcare cons., Humble, Tex., 1995—. Cons., amb. St. Joseph Hosp., 1977—; co-founder N.E. Hospice, Med. Affiliates, Support N.E. Cancer Workers, Emergency Support Systems for Police, fire Dept. and Ambulance Svc.; founder Stevens Counseling Ctrs., The Psychoimmunology Ctr., Stevens, Lancaster and Assocs.; co-founder Associated Mental Health Group, Inc.; cons. to devel. utilization rev. Kelsey-Seybold Clinics, 1992—; cons. creating feasibility studies for venture capitalists; cons. devel. triage, regional dir. Behavioral Health Svcs. Sisters of Charity for Southeast Tex., 1997-99; co-founder Integrated Clin. Resources, Inc.; owner Budget Mini Warehouses, Lake Houston Equestrian Ctr. and Stevens Handy Ranch; cons. Charter Corp, 1998; exec. dir. Integrated Psychiat. Medicine. Contbr. articles to profl. jours., mags., and newspapers. Vol. Mental Health Assn., Houston and Harris County, chair nominating com., membership com., sec. exec. com.; bd. advisors N.E. Hospice, mem. strategic planning teams; founder Lake Houston Dressage Ctr., 1999; sponsor Lake Houston Pride 2000; host Autumn Classic Horseshow Houston Dressage Soc., 2001; bd. dirs. Mental Health Assn., Houston and Harris County, 1988—. Named Exceptional Vol. of Yr. Mental Health Assn., Speakers Bur. award. Mem. Walden Country Club.

STEVENS, ELLIOTT WALKER, JR. allergist, pulmonologist; b. Wilmington, N.C., Sept. 11, 1940; s. E. Walker Sr. and Margaret Ardelle (Hester) S.; m. Blanche Bonner, July 10, 1965; children: Elliott W. III, Margaret Baker. AB in French, U. N.C., 1962, MD, 1966. Diplomate Am. Bd. Internal Medicine, Am. Bd. Allergy and Immunology, Am. Bd. Pulmonery Diseases. Intern U. N.C. Hosp., Chapel Hill, N.C., 1966-67; resident Duke U., Durham, 1969-70, fellow Allergy and pulmonary diseases, 1970-72; allergist and pulmonologist Greensboro Chest Disease and Allergy Associates, Greensboro, 1972—. Capt. USAF, 1967-69. Fellow Am. Coll. Allergy and Immunology, Am. Coll. Chest Physicians. Republican. Episcopalian. Avocations: skiing, sailing. Home: 4 Round Hill Ct Greensboro NC 27408-3709 Office: Greensboro Chest Diseases and Allergy Assocs and Allergy Assocs 1018 N Elm St Greensboro NC 27401-1488 E-mail: wstev7970@aol.com.

STEVENS, GAIL LAVINE, community health nurse, educator; b. Glens Falls, N.Y., June 10, 1938; d. Paul E. and Doris E. (Shippey) Lavine; m. Gary R. Stevens, Apr. 1, 1961; children: Ginelle Tonia, Gavin Wesley, Gordon Rickard. BSN, Syracuse (N.Y.) U., 1961; MA, U. South Ala., 1975, MS in Nursing, 1989; EdD, U. So. Miss., 1979. Instr. nursing Providence Sch. Nursing, Mobile, Ala., 1961-63, Mobile Infirmary Sch. Nursing, 1963-75; asst. and assoc. prof. nursing Mobile Coll., 1975-89; prof. nursing U. Mobile, 1989—, chair Baccalaureate Dept. Nursing, 2002—. Contbr. articles to profl. jours. Mem. ANA, Syracuse U. Nurses Alumni Assn., Sigma Theta Tau. Home: 2710 Palao Ct Mobile AL 36693-2722 E-mail: gailstevens@free.umobile.edu.

STEVENS, GEORGE ALEXANDER, real estate broker; b. Loma, Mont., Nov. 10, 1923; s. Otto Oliver and Josephine (Dale) S.; m. Martha Evie Fultz, Sept. 16, 1944 (div. 1978); children: Gary, Kathleen, Arlene, Tina; m. Arleen Dorothea Largent, Nov. 14, 1978. A in Bus Admisntrn., SUNY, 1992. Prin. George Stevens Farm, Loma, Mont., 1946-93, George Stevens, Real Estate Broker, Loma, 1957-93; pres. George A. Stevens Corp., 1976-93, Gold and Silver Realty, Inc., Great Falls, Mont., 1993—, Cowboys n Plowboys, Inc., Great Falls, 2000—. Trustee Sch. Dist. # 32, Loma, 1947-50; election judge Precinct # 7, Loma, 1953-88. With USN, 1944-46, PTO. Mem.: VFW (life), Eagles Lodge (life), Elks (life), Am. Legion (life). Democrat. Lutheran. Home: 810 8th Ave N Great Falls MT 59401-1036 E-mail: gastevens@montana.com., thecowboy@montana.com.

STEVENS, GEORGE RICHARD, business consultant, public policy commentator; b. Chgo., Sept. 6, 1932; s. George and Irene (Kaczmarek) S.; m. Jeanne E. Sowden, Aug. 2, 1957; children: Stacey, Samantha, Pamela. BS with honors, Northwestern U., 1954. CPA, Ill. With Arthur Andersen & Co., 1954-78, mng. ptnr. Belgium, 1957-71, ptnr. Chgo., 1971-78; pres. Daubert Industries, Oak Brook, Ill., 1978-80, G.R. Stevens Group, 1981—; founder, pres. Stevens Ctr. for Pub. Policy Studies, 1981—. Mem. Chgo. Com., 1979—; commr. Ill. Ednl. Facilities Authority, 1989—. Commr. Ill. State Scholarship Commn., 1981-87; vice chmn. Ill. Ind. Higher Edn. Loan Authority, 1982-88. Home and Office: 22615 N Las Lomas Ln Sun City West AZ 85375-2022

STEVENS, GLADSTONE TAYLOR, JR. industrial engineer; b. Brockton, Mass., Dec. 16, 1930; s. Gladstone Taylor and Blanche Ruth S.; m. Jane A. Crouch, July 20, 1953; children— Robert, Bartlett. BSM.E., U. Okla., 1956; MSM.E., Case Inst. Tech., 1962; PhD in Indsl. Engring, Okla. State U., 1966. Registered profl. engr., Tex., Okla. Project engr. E.I. duPont, Orange, Tex., 1956-59; research engr. Thompson-Ramo-Wooldridge, Cleve., 1960-62; asst. prof. mech. and indsl. engring. Lamar U., Beaumont, Tex., 1962-64; asst. prof. to asso. prof. indsl. engring. Okla. State U., Stillwater, 1966-75; prof., chmn. dept. indsl. engring. U. Tex., Arlington, 1975-98. Author: (with J.E. Shamblin) Operations Research: A Fundamental Approach, 1974, Economic and Financial Analysis of Capital Investments, 1993; Engineering Economy, 1983. Served with AUS, 1948-52. Recipient E.L. Grant award, 1974, AMOCO Teaching award, 1979, Wellington award, 1992. Fellow Am. Inst. Indsl. Engrs.; mem. Sigma Xi, Alpha Pi Mu (nat. pres.), Tau Beta Pi, Sigma Tau, Omicron Delta Kappa. Home: 2501 Spanish Trl Apt 212 Arlington TX 76016-1410 Office: U Tex Indsl Engring Arlington TX 76019-0001

STEVENS, HELEN JEAN, retired elementary school educator, musician; b. Nevada, Iowa, July 11, 1934; d. Paul Ellison and Helen Margaret (Ives) S. MusB, U. So. Calif., L.A., 1956. Cert. secondary music tchr., Calif. Tchr. San Francisco Sch. Dist., 1956-58; prin. oboist Marin Symphony Orch., San Rafael, Calif., 1956-94, Santa Rosa (Calif.) Symphony, 1956-86; tchr. Santa Venetia Mid. Sch., San Rafael, 1958-83; asst. prof. music Sonoma State Coll., Rohnert Park, Calif., 1963-76; tchr. Davidson Mid. Sch., San Rafael, 1984-89; tchr. oboe students. Organist, choir dir. Korean Meth. Ch., L.A., 1953-56; oboist Evenings on the Roof Series, L.A., 1953-56, Debut TV Show, L.A., 1954-56, Carmel (Calif.) Bach Festival, 1954-82; prin. oboist Light Opera Curren Theatre, San Francisco, 1966-67, Marin Opera Co., San Rafael, 1980-84. Leader Sonoma County 4-H Guide Dog Project, Guide Dogs for the Blind, Inc., 1974-87; organist, choir dir. United Meth. Ch., St. James, Mo., 2002. Recipient Svc. award PTA, 1974, Golden Bell award Marin County Office of Edn., 1984; named Outstanding Tchr., Marin Edn. Found., 1986, Continuing Svc. award Calif. Congress Parents, Tchrs. and Students, Inc, 1989. Mem. German Shepherd Dog Club Am. Avocations: computers, animals. Home: 14713 State Rt BB Saint James MO 65559 E-mail: stevfam@fidnet.com.

STEVENS, HENRY AUGUST, insurance agent, educator; b. Frankfurt, Main, Germany, July 21, 1921; came to U.S., 1940; m. Rosemary O'Neil, Mar. 23, 1963; children: Michael, Patrick; children from previous marriage, H. Jack Fay, Sondra Fay. Student, U. Wis., 1943-44; grad., Dale Carnegie Sch., Richland, Wash., 1974. Theatre mgr. Sterling Theatres, Seattle, 1946-54, Alliance Amusement Co., Chgo., 1955-68; ins. agt. N.Y. Life Ins. Co., Richland, 1968—. Regional v.p. Washington Assn. Life Underwriters, Richland, 1980; mem. adv. com. Wash. State Ins., Olympia, 1983-89. Chmn. bd. Richland YMCA, 1968; commr. Benton County Dyking Dist., Richland, 1970; chmn. Benton-Franklin Counties Bi-Centennial Commn., Tri-Cities, Wash., 1976; dist. chmn. Rep. Party, Benton County, 1980-96, 98—; bd. dirs. Salvation Army, 1999—, Tri-City Salvation Army. Staff sgt. U.S. Army 1943-46. Recipient Nat. Quality award, Nat. Sales Achievement award. Mem. Tri-Cities Life Underwriters Assn. (pres. 1975, bd. dirs.), Tri-Cities Estate Planning Coun. (pres. 1984), Wash. State Assn. Life Underwriters (dist. chmn. 1997), Kiwanis (pres. Chgo. club 1963, Richland club 1986-87, lt. gov. Pacific N.W. dist. 1983, chmn. dist. conv. 1971, 81, 91, sec. Pacific N.W. Found. 1994-01, sec. Kiwanis Found. 2001—), Tri-City Stamp Club (pres. 1999—). Avocations: stamp collecting, preparing family tree. Home: 712 Riverside Dr Richland WA 99353-5216 Office: NY Life Ins Co 8203 W Quinault Ave Kennewick WA 99336-7117

STEVENS, HERBERT FRANCIS, lawyer, law educator; b. Phila., Nov. 19, 1948; s. Herbert F. and Lois Marie (Kenna) S.; m. Jane Pickard, 1994; children: Sarah, Ben. SB, MIT, 1970; JD, Catholic U. Am., 1974; ML in Tax, Georgetown U, 1983. Bar: D.C., 1975; U.S. Supreme Ct., 1980. Law clk Md. Ct. of Spl. Appeals, 1974-75; with Morgan, Lewis & Bockius, Washington, 1975-78, Lane & Edson, P.C., Washington, 1979-89, Kelley Drye & Warren, Washington, 1989-93, Nixon Peabody LLP, Washington, 1993—; adj. prof. Georgetown U. Law Ctr., 1983-98. Spkr. nat. confs., seminars, TV Editor: Real Estate Aspects of the 1984 Tax Law, 1984; author: Real Estate Taxation: A Practitioner's Guide, 1986, Developer's Guide to Low Income Housing Tax Credit, 4th edit., 2000. Bd. dirs. Ctr. for Mental Health, Inc., 1987-2000 (exec. com.); bd. dirs. Nat. Fund for U.S. Botanic Garden, 1992—, exec. com. Mem. ABA, D.C. Bar Assn. Democrat. Presbyterian. Home: 8301 Hackamore Dr Potomac MD 20854-3877 Office: Nixon Peabody LLP 401 9th St NW Washington DC 20004-2128 E-mail: hstevens@nixonpeabody.com.

STEVENS, JAMES CRAIG, neurologist, educator; b. Greenville, S.C., May 14, 1957; s. Melvin Gene and Ida ZeNora Stevens; m. Laurel Stevens, Aug. 15, 1981; children: Benjamin Lee, Kathryn Sara. BS, Ind. U., 1979; MD, Ind. U., Indpls., 1983; neurology, Indiana U. schl. of med. Diplomate Am. Bd. Psychiatry and Neurology, Am. Bd. Sleep Medicine. Neurologist, sleep disorders medicine specialist Ft. Wayne (Ind.) Neurology, 1987—; assoc. prof. Ind. U. Med. Ctr., Ft. Wayne, 1990—; intern. Internal med. Methodist Hosp. Indianapolis. Med. dir. Sleep Disorders Ctr., Ft. Wayne, 1990—; bd. dirs. Luth. Hosp. Ind. Contbr. articles to profl. jours. Dir. Ft. Wayne Citadel Soccer Club, 1996—; rep. Ind. Youth Soccer Assn., Indpls., 1996-99. Fellow Am. Acad. Neurology, Am. Sleep Disorders Assn.; mem. AMA, Nat. Bd. Med. Examiners, Ind. Neurol. Soc. (v.p. 1999—), Phi Beta Kappa, Alpha Omega Alpha. Avocations: wine collecting, art collecting, tennis, skiing, hiking. Office: Ft Wayne Neurology 7910 W Jefferson Blvd Fort Wayne IN 46804-4159

STEVENS, JAMES HERVEY, JR. retired financial advisor; b. Balt., June 22, 1944; s. James H. and Hilda (Pearce) S.; m. Patricia Carol Donohue, Aug. 27, 1967 (div. Mar. 1983); children: James III, Carol; m. Lisa Gay Landrum, Apr. 29, 1984. BA, Duke U., 1966; MS in Fin. Scis., Am. Coll., Bryn Mawr, Pa., 1981. CLU; ChFC; CFP; registered health underwriter. Supr. New Eng. Life, Overland Park, Kans., 1969-75, agt., 1969—; v.p., treas. Creative Planning, Inc., 1980-95; pres. Hokanson, Lehman & Stevens, Inc., 1982-95; founder, chmn. Wings Over Mid-Am., Inc., 1995-97, chmn. emeritus, 1997—; chmn. Air Care Alliance, 1997—; chmn. emeritus Wings Over Mid-Am., Inc., 1997—; founder, chmn. Angel Flight Control, Inc., Kansas City, Mo. Contbg. editor monthly tax topics Kansas City Bus. Jour.; contbg. editor Pvt. Pilot Mag.; contbr. articles to profl. jours. Bd. dirs. Mo. div. Am. Cancer Soc., Kans. and Mo., 1982-84, Apple Valley Homes Assn., Overland Park, 1990—, pres. 1992, Cen. United Meth. Ch., Kansas City, Mo., 1990-92., North Cross United Meth., 1991—. Recipient Outstanding Young Man award, 1977; named one of Top 200 Fin. Advisors, Money Mag., 1987, Boss of Yr., Kansas City LICOMA, 1983. Mem. Kansas City Life Underwriters (pres. 1980-82, Herbert A. Hedges award 1987), Kansas City CLU & ChFC Soc. (pres. 1981-83), Mo. Life Underwriters (pres. 1984-86), Am. Soc. CLU & ChFC (vice chmn., bd. dirs.). Republican. Avocations: model railroading, collecting post-war "Lionel", airline transport pilot, instrument flight instr. Home: 5200 W 98th Ter Shawnee Mission KS 66207-3221 Office: Angel Fly Ctrl Inc 10 Redwoods Rd Kansas City MO 64113

STEVENS, JAMES WALTER, manufacturing representative; b. Albany, N.Y., Apr. 8, 1932; s. George Walker and Alma Catherine (Sill) S.; m. Winifred Palmer, June 18, 1955; children: George, Deborah, Marc. AA, SUNY, Canton, 1956. Vice pres., sales mgr. Lewis Equipment Co., Albany, 1957-86; br. mgr. Plattsburg Supply, 1986-90; contract food equipment specialist Sysco Corp., 1990-96; mfrs. rep. R.A. Meyer Assocs., Oneida, N.Y., 1996—. Guest lectr. Rochester (N.Y.) Inst. Tech., 1985—. Author: Food Equipment Facts, 1981, Manual of Equipment and Design, 1989, Food Equipment Digest, 1995; columnist Restaurant Mgmt. mag., 1987-88; inventor food equipment. Sgt. USAF, 1950-54, Korea. Mem. Food Equipment Distbrs. Assn., K.C. (sec.-treas. 1975-77), Am. Legion. Republican. Roman Catholic. Home: 253 Hudson Ave Rensselaer NY 12144-3743 Office: RA Meyer Assocs 149 Cedar St Oneida NY 13421-1736

STEVENS, JANE, curator; b. Chgo., Oct. 1, 1947; d. John. J. and Mattie S. BA in Anthropology, U. Ill., 1972; MA in Media Study, SUNY, Buffalo, 1981; cert. arts mgmt., U. Mass., 1994. Asst. curator Chgo. Hist. Soc., 1978-85; instr. photography Morton Coll., Cicero, Ill., 1987—; curator, asst. adminstr. Ill. Art Gallery, Chgo., 1985—. Coord. fine arts seminar Chgo. Met. Ctr., 1999-00; affiliate mem. Ceres Gallery, N.Y.C., 1993—; dir. ARC Ednl. Found., Chgo., 1992-93, mem. adv. bd., 1999—, grantwriter, 1996-99. Guest artist House of Good Shepherd, Chgo., 1997—; panelist Ill. Assn. Mus., 1996; city arts visual arts panelist City of Chgo., Cultural Affairs, 1994-97; moderator, panelist Art Culture Nature Assn., U. Wash., 1999; editor, writer (exhbn. catalogue) Artists Residents Chgo. Gallery, 20th Anniversary, 1995; curator, writer (exhbn. brochure) Ill. State Mus., 1996; guest writer (newsletter) YLEM/Internat. Soc. Electronic Arts Conf., 1996; editor, curator (exhbn. catalogue) Electronic Immersions, 1997. Recipient Purchase award Fla. State U., 1985, Spl. Projects award Ill. Arts Coun., 1998; Project Completion grantee Ill. Arts Coun., 1983. Mem. Am. Assn. Mus. (mem. curator com. 1996—), Assn. Humanistic Psychology, Coll. Art Assn., Chgo. Artists Coalition. Avocations: travel, reading, photography, film, modern dance. Home: 1631 N Nagle Ave Chicago IL 60707-4016 Office: Ill Art Gallery Ill State Mus 100 W Randolph St Ste 2-100 Chicago IL 60601-3219 E-mail: jstevens@museum.state.il.us.

STEVENS, JEROME HEBERT, media specialist; b. Paris, Apr. 24, 1959; came to U.S., 1991; s. Francois Hébert-Stevens and Claude Arthaud; m. Valerie Travert, Dec. 28, 1996; 1 child, Arthur. MD, U. Paris VII, 1987; diploma in health economics, U. Paris V, 1989; MBA, U. Pa., 1994. Attending physician Hosp. de Paris, 1987-90; med. dir. Lyonnaise Santé, Paris, 1989-92; cons. CSC Healthcare, N.Y.C., 1994-99; founder Direct Medica, Paris, 2000—. Co-author: Reengineering the Operating Room, 1996; participant med. TV series Entretiens de Bichat, 1990. Bd. dirs. GERO 92 Geriat. Assn., Paris, 1989-92. With French Army, 1985-86. Mem. Am. Coll. Physician Execs. Avocations: sailing, golf, modern art. Home: 666 5th Ave No 239 New York NY 10103-0001 E-mail: jstevens@directmedica.com.

STEVENS, JESSE, financial executive; b. Detroit, Sept. 28, 1951; s. Jesse James and Carmen O. (Slaughter) S.; m. Gweneth Merilyn Lloyd, Sept. 13, 1986; children: Christopher Lloyd, Olivia Stevens Carumey. BS in Christian Ministry, Ea. Mennonite U., 1980; MSW, Columbia U., 1984; MBA, Pace U., 1986; DBA, U. Sarasota, 2002. Cert. lic. SEC, Nat. Assn. Security Dealers, lic. to ministry Bapt. Ch. Account exec. Dean Witter Reynolds, N.Y.C., 1986-88; fin. cons. Smith Barney Inc., Newburgh, N.Y., 1988-2001, 2d v.p. investment NY, 1999—. Instr. Orange County C.C., Middletown, N.Y., 1989—. Mem. at-large, bd. dirs. Boy Scouts Am., Middletown, N.Y., 1993—. With U.S. Army, 1973-75, Germany. Recipient Outstanding Vol. Svc. award Prison Fellowship, washington, 1993. Mem. Orange County C. of C. Democrat. E-mail: jessestevens@rssmb.com.

STEVENS, JILL WINIFRED, project expediter; d. William Horace Routledge and Winifred Mabel (Richards) S. Asst. to radio prodr. BBC, London, 1963; governess pvt. home, Hillsboro, Calif., 1965; adminstrv. asst. Cambridge U., Eng., 1966; expediter, buyer, technician Bechtel Petroleum Inc., San Francisco, 1967-87, control sys. technologist Houston, Bechtel Power Corp., Houston; material planner for electrical and control systems Union Carbide/Bechtel Assn., 1988-97; control sys. expediter multi-project acquisition group Bechtel Corp., 1997-99; project expediter Bechtel Nat., Inc., 1999-2000; field project expeditor Aberdeen Proving Ground, Md., 2000—. Recipient awards in English lang. and English lit. with honors, Royal Soc. Arts and Scis., City London Day Coll. Mem. Instrument Soc. Am., Soc. Women Engrs. (assoc.). Home: 832 Revolution St Havre De Grace MD 21078 Office: Bechtel Nat Inc Aberdeen Proving Ground MD 21010 E-mail: jwsteven@bechtel.com.

STEVENS, JOHN PAUL, United States supreme court justice; b. Chgo., Apr. 20, 1920; s. Ernest James and Elizabeth (Street) Stevens; m. Elizabeth Jane Sheeren, June 7, 1942; children: John Joseph, Kathryn Stevens Jedlicka, Elizabeth Jane Stevens Sesemann, Susan Roberta Stevens Mullen; m. Maryan Mulholland, Dec. 1979. AB, U. Chgo., 1941; JD magna cum laude, Northwestern U., 1947. Bar: Ill. 1949. Practiced in, Chgo.; law clk. to Hon. Wiley Rutledge U.S. Supreme Ct , 1947—48; assoc. Poppenhusen, Johnston, Thompson & Raymond, 1949—52; assoc. counsel sub-com. on study monopoly power, com. on judiciary U.S. Ho. of Reps., 1951; ptnr. Rothschild, Stevens, Barry & Myers, 1952—70; judge U.S. Cir. Ct., 1970—75; assoc. justice U.S. Supreme Ct., 1975—. Lectr. anti-trust law Northwestern U. Sch. Law, 1952—54, U. Chgo. Law Sch., 1955—58; mem. Atty. Gen.'s Nat. Com. to Study Anti-Trust Laws, 1953—55. With USNR, 1942—45. Decorated Bronze Star. Mem.: Am. Law Inst., Fed. Bar Assn., Ill. Bar Assn., Am. Bar Assn., Chgo. Bar Assn. (2d v.p. 1970), Order of Coif, Phi Delta Phi, Psi Upsilon, Phi Beta Kappa. Office: US Supreme Ct Supreme Court Bldg One 1st St NE Washington DC 20543*

STEVENS, JOHN RICHARD, architectural historian; b. Toronto, Ont., Can., Mar. 19, 1929; came to U.S., 1954; s. Walter John and Florence Rosalie (Warr) S.; m. Marion Frances Moore, May 7, 1964. Student, Columbia U., 1966-67. Comml. artist, tech. illustrator, Toronto, Ont., Can. and New Haven, Conn.; asst. to curator Mystic Seaport, 1957; curator Maritime Mus. Can., Halifax, 1960-63; with dept. no. affairs Hist. Sites Divsn., 1963-66; surveyor early bldgs. Halifax, Quebec, Fredericton, Woodstock, St. John River Valley, Ea. Twps. of Quebec; lighthouses of Great Lakes, Nova Scotia, New Brunswick; with Archtl. Heritage, Inc., 1967-70; prin. John R. Stevens Assocs., Greenlawn, N.Y., 1970—. Cons. hist. restoration Old Bethpage Village Restoration, 1967-94, Soc. for the Preservation L.I. Antiquities, Roslyn Preservation Corp., Smithtown Hist. Soc., Colonial Farmhouse Restoration Soc., numerous others; restorations include Van Nostrand-Starkins House, Revolutionary War "Arsenal", two c.1900 Am.-built streetcars for City of Detroit, 1976, 80, 1878 N.Y. elevated railroad car, 1983, first electric freight locomotive, 1988, c. 1880 horsecar for Rochester Mus., 1987; lectr. Dutch-Am. bldgs., street railway history. Author: Old Time Ships, 1949, H.M. Schooner Tecumseth, 1961, Ships of the North Shore, 1963, (guidebook) Ride Down Memory Lane, 1965, 2d rev. edit., 1984, Early History of Street Railways - The New Haven Area, 1982, The Derby Horse Railway and the

World's First Electric Freight Locomotive, 1987; co-author/editor: Pioneers of Electric Railroading, 1991; contbr. articles on hist. bldg. tech., book revs. to profl. publs. Bd. trustees Roslyn Landmark Soc., 1980—. With U.S. Army, 1955-57. Mem. Branford Electric Rlwy. Assn. (bd. trustees 1957, 74, 80-81, 83-85, supt. equipment 1974-75, supt. bldgs. and grounds 1980-82, chmn. bd. trustees 1983, pres. 1984, 85, contbr. articles to jour.). Home and Office: 1 Sinclair Dr Greenlawn NY 11740-2607

STEVENS, JOSEPH CHARLES, psychology educator; b. Grand Rapids, Mich., Feb. 28, 1929; s. Joseph, Jr. and Anne Katheryn Stevens. AB, Calvin Coll., Grand Rapids, 1950; MA, Mich. State U., 1953; PhD, Harvard U., 1957. Instr., then asst. prof. psychology Harvard U., 1957-66; fellow John B. Pierce Found. Lab., also sr. research scientist Yale U., 1966—. Cons. in field. Author: Laboratory Experiments in Psychology, 1965; co-editor: Sensation and Measurement, 1974; mem. editorial bds. profl. jours.; contbr. numerous articles to profl. jours. Grantee NSF; Grantee NIH; Grantee Air Force Office Sci. Research. Fellow AAAS, Am. Psychol. Soc., N.Y. Acad. Scis.; mem. Acoustical Soc. Am., Optical Soc. Am., Soc. Neurosci., Eastern Psychol. Assn., Gerontol. Soc. Am. Office: 290 Congress Ave New Haven CT 06519-1403

STEVENS, JULIE ANN, lawyer; b. Normal, Ill., June 3, 1961; d. James E. and Janice J. (Richey) S. BSN with honors, Baylor U., 1984; JD magna cum laude, St. Louis U., 2000. RN, Tex., Mo. Nurse intern operating rm. Parkland Meml. Hosp., Dallas, 1984-85, staff nurse, 1985-89; charter employee, staff nurse Zale Lipshy U. Hosp. at Southwestern Med. Ctr., 1989-92, clin. coord. neurosurgery, 1992-96; staff nurse Med. City Dallas Hosp., 1996-97; clk. Hullverson & Hullverson, L.C., 1998-2000; assoc. Morgan & Weisbrod, LLP, 2000-01; jud. law clk. Mo. Ct. Appeals, 2001—. Recipient Order of Woolsack award. Mem. Mo. Bar Assn., Tex. Bar Assn., Ill. Bar Assn., DAR, Internat. Order of Job's Daus. (past Honored Queen). Methodist. Home: 3000 Autumn Lakes Ct Maryland Heights MO 63043 E-mail: julieastevens@hotmail.com.

STEVENS, KENNETH NOBLE, b. Toronto, Ont., Can., Mar. 23, 1924; arrived in U.S., 1948, naturalized, 1962; s. Cyril George and Catherine (Noble) Stevens; m. Phyllis Fletcher, Jan. 19, 1957 (div. 1979); children: Rebecca, Andrea, Michael Hugh, John Noble; m. Sharon Manuel, Jan. 14, 1994; 1 child Kendra Wenyu Manuel. BASc., U. Toronto, 1945, MASc., 1948; Sc.D., MIT, 1952. Instr. U. Toronto, 1946—48; faculty MIT, Cambridge, 1948—, prof. elec. engring., 1963—, Clarence J. LeBel prof., 1977—. Vis. fellow Royal INst. Tech., Stockholm, 1962—63; cons. to industry, 1952—; vis. prof. phonetics U. Coll., London, 1969—70; mem. Nat. Adv. Coun. on Neurol. and Communicative Disorders and Stroke, NIH, 1982—86. Author (with A.G. Bose): Introductory Network Theory; author: Acoustic Phonetics, 1998; contbr. articles to profl. jours. Trustee Buckingham Browne and Nichols Sch., 1974—80. Recipient Quintana award, Voice Found., 1992, medal, European Speech Comm. Assn., 1995, Nat. Medal of Sci., 1999; fellow, Guggenheim, 1962. Fellow: IEEE, Am. Acad. Arts and Scis., Acoustical Soc. Am. (exec. com. 1963—66, v.p. 1971—72, pres.-elect 1975—76, pres. 1976—77, Gold medal 1995); mem.: NAE, NAS. Home: 51 Montrose St Somerville MA 02143-1212 Office: MIT 77 Massachusetts Ave Cambridge MA 02139-4307

STEVENS, KENNETH ALLEN, retired defense department worker; b. Exeter, N.H., June 21, 1933; s. Albert Howard and Helen Susan (Sewall) S. BA, U. N.H., 1961. With Dept. Def., 1961-88. Bd. dirs. Columbia (Md.) Dem. Club, 1988-90; mem. Howard County (Md.) Dem. Ctrl. Com., 1990-94; vol. Office Human Rights, Howard County, 1989-2001. Staff sgt. USAF, 1953-57. Mem. ACLU (coord. Howard County chpt. 1988-98). Democrat. Avocations: computer games, crossword puzzles. E-mail: kasteve@smart.net.

STEVENS, LAUREN ROGERS, writer, environmentalist; b. Phila., May 3, 1938; s. Lewis Miller and Elizabeth (Morgan) S.; m. Beverly Decker, June 20, 1964 (div. Dec. 1987); children: Rebecca Fasciano, Jeffrey L., Jennifer B. BA, Princeton U., 1960; MA, U. Iowa, 1962. Tchr. English lang. & environ. studies Williams Coll., Williamstown, Mass., 1963-81, dean of freshmen, 1970-81; founder, pub., editor Advocate Newsweekly, 1981-83. Writer, freelance, Williamstown, 1983—. Author: The Double Axe, 1961 (Athenaeum of Phila. literary award 1961), Hikes and Walks in the Berkshire Hills, 1990, Skiing: Downhill and Cross Country, 1991; co-author (with Deborah Burns) Most Excellent Majesty, 1988; (with Richard W. Babcock) Old Barns in the New World: Reconstructing History, 1996, The Berkshire Book, 6th edit., 2000; contbr. articles to mags. and newspapers. Founder Hoosic River Watershed Assn., Williamstown, 1986, co-pres., 1994-96, exec. dir., 1997—; leader Mahican-Mohawk Trail, N.Y., Vt., Mass., 1992—; co-founder Greylock A Better Chance, Williamstown, 1968; deacon First Congregational Ch., Williamstown, 1985—, moderator 2000—. Mem. Mass. Audubon, Appalachian Mountain Club, Williamstown Rotary (pres. 1990-91), Phi Beta Kappa. Democratic. Congregationalist. Avocations: hiking, canoeing, cross country skiing. Home: 24 Mountain View St Williamstown MA 01267-2246 E-mail: lstevens@berkshire.net.

STEVENS, LEONARD BERRY, educational consultant; b. Fall River, Mass., Sept. 19, 1938; s. Henry Bennett and Manetta (Berry) S.; m. Elizabeth Holihen, Aug. 17, 1963; children: Lisa M., Christopher M., Andrew B., Rosa B. A. BS, Boston U., 1960; EdD, U. Mass., 1978. Cert. supt., Mass. Edn. writer Providence Jour.-Bull., 1963-67; sr. editor Cowles Comms., Inc., N.Y.C., 1967-68; exec. editor Change in Higher Edn. Mag., 1968-70; spl. asst. to Chancellor N.Y.C. Bd. Edn., 1970-73; rsch. asst. U. Mass., Amherst, 1973-76; dir. Greater Cleve. Project, 1976-78; dir. Office Sch. Monitoring and Cmty. Rels. U.S. Dist. Ct. (no. dist.) Ohio, Cleve., 1978-88; dir. Compact for Ednl. Opportunity, Milw., 1988-90; race-related sch. planning cons. Sarasota, Fla., 1990—. Cons. as racial/cultural diversity and sch. desegregation planning expert and analyst to state edn. depts., pub. sch. dists., parties in litigation; expert witness in over 25 sch. desegregation cases; lectr. in field at univs. and seminars. Co-author: Make Your Schools Work, 1975; contbr. articles to profl. jours. and mass media publs. Trustee Inst. Child Advocacy, Cleve.; bd. dirs. Com. on Cath. Cmty. Action, Cleve., 1981-88. Lt. (j.g.) USN, 1960-63. Office: PO Box 2479 Sarasota FL 34230

STEVENS, LEOTA MAE, retired elementary education educator; b. Waverly, Kans., Mar. 27, 1921; d. Clinton Ralph and Velma Mae (Kukuk) Chapman; m. James Oliver Stevens, Nov. 7, 1944 (dec.); children: James Harold, Mary Ann Hooker Tibbits. BA, McPherson Coll., 1954; MS, Emporia U., 1964, postgrad., 1969-77, Wichita U., 1977. Educator Pleasant Mound Sch., Waverly, 1940-41; prin. educator Halls Summit Sch., 1941-42; educator Waverly Grade Sch., 1942-43, Ellinwood (Kans.) Jr. H.S., 1943-45, Hutchinson (Kans.) Grade Sch., 1945-48, Lincoln Sch., Darlow, Kans., 1948-49; educator prin. Mitchell-Yaggy Consol. Sch., Hutchinson, 1949-57; educator elem. Hutchinson Sch. Dist. 308, 1957-85, ret., 1985. V.p. Reno County Tchrs. Assn. Hutchinson, 1956-57, pres. Assn. Childhood Edn. Internat., 1978-79. Author of numerous poems; compiler The Alexander-Kukuk Descendants: 1754 to 1998. Mem. Worker ARC Blood Mobile, 1986—, Hutchinson Cmty. Concerts , 1970—; historian Women's Civic Ctr., 1988—92, art com. chmn, 1992—96; den mother Cub Scouts, 1963—66; leader Girl Scouts Ellinwood, 1944—45; bell ringer ARC Blood Mobile, 1986—2000; ch. sch. tchr. Trinity United Meth. Ch., 1959—71, attendance chair, 1994. Mem. AAUW (news reporter 1984-87, legis. chmn. program com. 1991-94, 2d v.p., 1994—), Ret. Nation State and Local Edn. Assn., Reno County Tchrs. Assn. (v.p. 1956-57), Assn. Childhood Edn. Internat. (pres. 1978-79), Reno County Extension Homemaker Coun. (rep. 1987—), Rainbow Extension Club (pres. 1986-92), Hutchinson Area Ret. Tchrs. Assn. (historian 1996-99), Am. Legion Aux., Friends of Preservation, Delta Kappa Gamma (sec., v.p. 1972-80, grant chmn. 1980-88, publicity com. 1990-93, legis. chmn. 1994—). Republican. Avocations: art, music, traveling, gardening, camping, genealogy. Home: 805 W 23rd Ave Hutchinson KS 67502-3765

STEVENS, LINDA LOUISE HALBUR, addiction counselor; b. Huron, S.D., Oct. 28, 1960; d. Alvin LeRoy and Esther Louise (Schroeder) Halbur; m. Lowell Eugene Stevens, July 26, 1980 (div. 1995); children: Lowell John, Tracie Lynn. BSW, U. N.D., 1991; MEd, N.D. State U., 1993. Lic. addiction counselor, bd. cert. counselor reciprocal Minn. Tracker Luth. Soc. Svcs., Hillsboro, N.D., 1990-94; addiction counselor Heartland Med. Ctr., Fargo, 1993-94, S.E. Human Svc. Ctr., Fargo, 1994—; dual diagnosis Off Main Program, 1995; addiction counselor, SMI day treatment provider Koochiching Counseling Ctr., International Falls, Minn., 1997; OTR driver Gainey Transp. Svcs., 1998; inpatient substance abuse case mgr. New Ulm Med. Ctr., 1998—. Local/state officer N.D. Women of Today, Hillsboro, 1982-87. Recipient Presdl. Excellence award N.D. women of Today, 1986-87. Mem. New Ulm Police Res. Officers. Avocations: golf, sewing, pets, cross country skiing. Home: 1217 N Spring St New Ulm MN 56073-1131 Office: 1324 5th North St New Ulm MN 56073-1514 E-mail: linda.stevens@allina.com.

STEVENS, LYDIA HASTINGS, community volunteer; b. Highland Park, Ill., Aug. 2, 1918; d. Rolland T.R. and Ruth Shotwell (Beebe) Hastings; m. George Cooke Stevens, Nov. 2, 1940; children: Lydia Stevens Gustin, Priscilla Stevens Goldfarb, Frederick S., Elizabeth Stevens MacLeod, George H., Ruth Stevens Stellard. BA, Vassar Coll., 1939. State rep. 151st Dist. of Conn., Greenwich, 1988-92. Cons. Nat. Exec. Svc. Corps, N.Y.C., 1985. Pres. Greenwich YWCA, 1971-74, Greenwich Housing Coalition, 1982-86; v.p. planning Greenwich United Way, 1973-76; sr. warden Greenwich Christ Episcopal Ch., 1981-86; chmn. rev. commn. Episcopal Diocese of Conn., 1985-87; bd. dirs. Greenwich Libr., 1985-93; chmn. Greenwich Commn. Aging, 1986-88; pres., bd. dirs. Greenwich Broadcasting Corp., 1977-79; bd. dirs. Fairfield County Cmty. Found., 1992, United Way of Greenwich, Save the Sound, 1996—, League Conservation Voters Conn., 1999. Recipient Golden Rule award J.C. Penney, 1987, President's award Greenwich YWCA, 1992, Braua award, 1994, Conn. Assn. for Human Svc. Dirs. award, 1992; named Layperson of Yr., Coun. Chs. and Synagogues, 1995. Republican. Episcopalian. Avocations: sailing, organic gardening.

STEVENS, MARILYN RUTH, editor; b. Wooster, Ohio, May 30, 1943; d. Glenn Willard and Gretchen Elizabeth (Ihrig) Amstutz; m. Bryan J. Stevens, Oct. 11, 1969; children: Jennifer Marie, Gretchen Anna. BA, Coll. Wooster, 1965; MAT, Harvard U., 1966; JD, Suffolk U., 1975. Bar: Mass. 1975. Tchr. Lexington (Mass.) Pub. Schs., 1966-69; with Houghton Mifflin Co., Boston, 1969—, editl. dir. sch. depts., 1978-81, editl. dir. math. scies. sch. divsn., 1981-84, mng. editor sch. pub., 1984—. Mem. Mass. Bar Assn. Office: Houghton Mifflin 222 Berkeley St Fl 7 Boston MA 02116-3764

STEVENS, MARK ALAN, lawyer, environmental engineer; b. Phila., July 30, 1949; BA, Brandeis U., 1971; MSc in Engring., Wash. State U., Pullman, 1976; JD, Temple U., 1987. Bar: Pa., N.J. Prof. assoc. U. Man., Winnipeg, Can., 1976-78; tech. cons. BCM Engrs., Plymouth Meeting, Pa., 1978-86; ptnr. Langsam Stevens , Phila., 1995—. Mem. ABA (litigation sect.), Pa. Bar Assn., N.J. State Bar Assn., Phila. Bar Assn. Office: 1616 Walnut St Ste 1700 Philadelphia PA 19103-5308 E-mail: mstevens@langsamstevens.com.

STEVENS, MARTIN BRIAN, publisher; b. N.Y.C., Dec. 29, 1957; s. David Robert and Shirley Stevens. Grad. high sch. Advt. artist Unitron Pubs., N.Y.C., 1977, Westchester Publs., Elmsford, N.Y., 1978; pub. Retailers Forum, Centerport, 1981—, Swap Meet mag., Centerport, 1990—; founder, CEO, Forum Pub. Co., 1981—. Pub. 8 bus. directories, rep. 6 bus. book pubs.; founder Rodeo Dr. Limousine Svc., 1990-93, Mercedes-Benz Limousine Svc., 1990-93. Named Top Mail Order Dealer, Nat. Mail Dealers Counsel, 1978. Mem. Mail Order Bus. Bd. (pres. 1978-80), Better Bus. Bur., Nat. Assn. Self-Employed, Nat. Assn. Desktop Pub., L.I. Assn., Can. Direct Mail Assn. Avocations: weight training, reading. Office: Forum Pub Co 383 E Main St Centerport NY 11721-1538

STEVENS, MAY, artist; b. Boston, June 9, 1924; d. Ralph Stanley and Alice Margaret (Dick) S.; m. Rudolf Baranik, June 5, 1948; 1 child, Steven. BFA, Mass. Coll. Art, 1946; postgrad., Academie Julian, Paris, 1948-49, Art Students League, 1948. Mem. faculty Sch. Visual Arts, N.Y.C., 1964-96, Skowhegan Sch. Painting and Sculpture, 1992, Vt. Studio Ctr., 1997, Santa Fe Art Inst., 2000. Lectr. Royal Coll. Art, London, 1981, U. Wis.-Racine, 1973, Coll. Art Assn., Washington, 1975; sole juror Am. Drawing Biennial, Coll. William and Mary, Williamsburg, Va., 2000; lectr. Coll. Santa Fe, 1998. One-woman shows: Terry Dintenfass Gallery, N.Y.C., 1971, Cornell U., 1973, Douglass Coll., Rutgers U., 1974, Lerner-Heller Gallery, N.Y.C., 1975, 76, 78, 81, Clark U., 1982, Boston U. Art Gallery, 1984, Frederick S. Wight Gallery, UCLA, 1985, U. Md., College Park, 1985, Real Art Ways, Hartford, Conn., 1988, New Mus. Contemporary Art, 1988, Orchard Gallery, Derry, No. Ireland, 1988, Kenyon Coll., Gambier, Ohio, 1988, Greenville County (S.C.) Art Mus., 1991, Herter Gallery, U. Mass., Amherst, 1991, U. Colo., Boulder, 1993, U. N.Mex., Albuquerque, 1996, Mary Ryan Gallery, N.Y.C., 1996, 97, 99, 2001, Mus. Fine Arts, Boston, 1999, LeWallen Contemporary, Santa Fe, 1998; exhibited in group shows: Inst. Contemporary Arts, London, 1980, Gemeente Mus., The Hague, 1979, Whitney Mus., 1970, Gedok, Kunsthaus, Hamburg, Germany, 1972, Everson Mus., Syracuse, N.Y., 1976, Clocktower, N.Y.C., 1986, Guerrilla Girls Exbn. at Palladium, N.Y.C., 1985, One Penn Pla., 1985, Pentonville Gallery, London, 1986, Heckscher Mus., N.Y., 1987, Univ. Art Mus., Berkeley, Calif., 1987, Mus. Modern Art, 1988, Exit Art, N.Y.C., 1988, Sao Paulo (Brazil) Mus. Modern Art, 1989, Blum Helman Gallery, N.Y.C., 1989, Univ. Art Mus., Long Beach, Calif., 1990, Angels Gate, San Pedro, Calif., 1990, Newark Mus., 1990, Städtliche Kunsthalle, Düsseldorf, Germany, 1990, DeCordova Mus., Lincoln, Mass., 1991, Exit Art, N.Y.C., 1994, Mary Delahoyd Gallery, N.Y.C., 1995, Mary Ryan Gallery, N.Y.C., 1995, Gwenda Jay Gallery, Chgo., 1995, Lizardi Harp Gallery, L.A., 1995, ACA Galleries, N.Y.C., 1996, Nassau County Mus., Roslyn, N.Y., 1997; represented in permanent collections: Metropolitan Mus. of Art, N.Y.C., Mus. Modern Art, N.Y.C., Moca, L.A., San Francisco Mus. Art, New Mus. Contemporary Art, Whitney Mus., Bklyn. Mus., Herbert F. Johnson Mus., Cornell U., Mus. Fine Arts Boston, De Cordova Mus., Lincoln, Mass.; contbr. articles to various mags. Recipient Childe Hassam Purchase awards Nat. Inst. Arts and Letters, 1968, 69, 75, N.Y. State Coun. on Arts award, 1974, Disting. Alumna award Mass. Coll. Art, 1997, Disting. Artist award Coll. Art Assn., 2001, Andy Warhol Found. grant for project space Headlands Ctr. for Arts, Sausalito, Calif., 2001; MacDowell Colony fellow, 1971, 72, 74, 75, 81, 82, 84, Bunting Inst. fellow Radcliffe Coll., 1988-89; grantee NEA, 1983, Guggenheim, 1986; honoree Women's Caucus for Art, 1990. Mem. Coll. Art Assn.

STEVENS, MURIEL KAY, elementary educator; b. Pulaski, Ohio, Mar. 9, 1937; d. Loren Wyatt and Eleanor F. (Fisher) Chamberlain; m. Leland LeRoy Stevens, Jan. 26, 1957; children: Sheila Dawn, Shane Scott, Shara Lea. BS in Edn., Defiance Coll., 1968; postgrad., Miami U., Oxford U., Bowling Green State U., St. Francis Coll., Ft. Wayne, Ind. Lic. elem. tchr. Elem. tchr. Pulaski-Jefferson Elem. Sch., Bryan, Ohio, 1959-64, North Cen. Schs., Pioneer, 1965-70, Bryan City Schs., 1970-92; ret., 1992. Instr. Project TEACH, Bowling Green (Ohio) State U., 1977-79; workshop presenter Effective Classroom Techniques, 1975—; tour cons. Adventure Travel, Evelyn's Excursions. Designer copyrights "Me" Doll, Family Tree, Puppet, 1987. V.p. Williams County Rep. Women, Bryan, 1983-86; membership chmn., pres. Williams County Concert Assn., 1988-95; sec. Ohio Edn. Assn. Ret. Divsn., 1993—; co-founder support group for parents of attention deficit disorder children S.O.C.K., 1993—; presenter ADD/ADHD, 1993; presenter William County Hist. Soc., Montpelier, Ohio, 1986—; pres. Williams County Ret. Tchrs. Assn. Mem. NEA (pub. rels. com. 1984-88), Assn. Classroom Tchrs. (pres. S.E. region 1981-82, Emory O. Jackson Top Leadership award 1985, Humanitarian Meml. award 1988), Ohio Edn. Assn. (IPD commn. 1983-90, div. classroom tchrs. 1980-90), Northwest Ohio Edn. Assn. (disting. svc. to edn. award 1989), Williams County Ret. Tchrs. Assn. (pres.), Bryan Edn. Assn. (Friend of Edn. award 1986), Bryan Bus. and Profl. Women (legis. chmn. 1986-88), Order Eastern Star, Alpha Delta Kappa (past pres. 1968—). Mem. Brethren Ch. Avocations: geneologies, travel, crafts, writing, photography. Home and Office: 5488 County Road 13 Bryan OH 43506-8983 E-mail: murielks@earthlink.net.

STEVENS, PAUL EDWARD, lawyer; b. Youngstown, Ohio, July 22, 1916; s. Raymond U. and Mary Ann (Pritchard) S.; m. Janet L. Weisert, Mar. 9, 1946; 1 son, Mark O. LL.B., Ohio State U., 1941. Bar: Ohio 1941. Practiced in, Youngstown, 1941—; ptnr. Green, Schiavoni, Murphy & Stevens, 1962-71, Burdman, Stevens & Gilliland, 1971-75, Stevens & Toot, 1976-77, Paul E. Stevens Co., 1977—. Prof. law Youngstown Coll. Sch. Law, 1946-60; gen. counsel Animal Charity League of Ohio, 1965—; sec.-treas. CASTLO Community Improvement Corp., 1986—. Trustee Poland Twp., Ohio, 1960-69; Republican candidate for U.S. Congress, 1959; dist. adminstrv. asst. Congressman Charles J. Carney, 19th Ohio dist., 1970-80; pres. Welsh Nat. Gymanfa Ganu Assn., 1988-90. With AUS, 1942-46. Mem. ABA, Ohio Bar Assn. (chmn. membership com. 1955), Mahoning County Bar Assn. (pres. 1953-54), Mahoning County Planning Assn. (chmn. 1990-98). Unitarian Universalist. Home: 7191 N Lima Rd Youngstown OH 44514-3749 Office: 780 Boardman Canfield Rd Youngstown OH 44512-4344 *To be allowed to practice law is an honor. Therefore, an attorney must be fair and honest, but most of all, he must have respect for and love his fellow man.*

STEVENS, PAUL IRVING, manufacturing company executive; b. Lawrence, Kans., Mar. 22, 1915; s. Ira F. and Ida M. S.; m. Artie Faye Womack, Nov. 10, 1935; children: Richard Irving, Constance Irene. Student bus. adminstrn., Pasadena (Calif.) Coll., 1933-35. Indsl. engr. Consol. Aircraft Co., San Diego, 1940-49; founder, prin. stockholder, pres. United Machine Co., Ft. Worth, 1950-61; exec. v.p. Clary Corp., San Gabriel, Calif., 1962-65; pres., owner Stevens Corp., Ft. Worth, 1965-69; pres., chief exec. officer Waltham Industries, N.Y.C., 1969-71, Stevens Industries, La Jolla, Calif., 1972—, Campbell Industries, San Diego., 1976-79; chmn., pres. Stevens Air Systems, El Cajon, Calif., 1974-81; pres. Womack Motors, Inc., El Centro, 1982-90. Chmn. bd. dirs., CEO Stevens Graphics Corp., Ft. Worth, 1986-95; bd. dirs. Rancho Santa Fe Nat. Bank, Calif., 1982-85, chmn. 1985-95; chmn., CEO Stevens Internat., Inc., 1995—; bd. dirs. Rancho Santa Fe. Mem. Nat. Mgmt. Assn. (exec. com.), Presidents Assn., Civic Round Table, La Jolla Country Club, Colonial Country Club, Canyon Country Club, University Club, Ft. Worth Club, Shady Oaks Country Club. Republican. Methodist. Home: 2585 Calle Del Oro La Jolla CA 92037-2005 Office: PO Box 950 La Jolla CA 92038-0950

STEVENS, PAUL SCHOTT, lawyer; b. New Orleans, Nov. 19, 1952; s. Miles Gordon and Rosemary Louise (Schott) S.; m. Joyce Lynn Pilz, Aug. 18, 1979; Paul Schott Jr., Alexander Holmes, Andrew Colby, Carl Bernard. BA magna cum laude, Yale U., 1974; JD, U. Va., 1978. Bar: D.C. 1979, U.S. Dist. Ct. D.C. 1979, U.S. Ct. Appeals (D.C. cir.) 1979, U.S. Ct. Appeals (fed. cir.) 1983, U.S. Supreme Ct. 1982. Assoc., prin. Dickstein, Shapiro & Morin, Washington, 1978-85, ptnr., 1989-93; dep. dir., gen. counsel Pres.'s Blue Ribbon Commn. on Def. Mgmt., 1985-86; legal adviser NSC, 1987, exec. sec., 1987-89; spl. asst. to Pres. for nat. security affairs The White House, 1987-89; exec. asst. to Sec. of Defense, 1989; sr. v.p., gen. counsel Investment Co. Inst., 1993-97; sr. v.p., gen. counsel Mut. Funds and Internat. Enterprise, Charles Schwab & Co., Inc., San Francisco, 1997-99; ptnr. Dechert, Washington, 1999—. Lectr. law Washington Coll. Law, Am. U., Washington, 1980-83; trustee M.G. Stevens Corp., New Orleans, 1978—; mem. quality of markets com. NASDAQ Stock Market, Inc., 1997, mem. investment cos. com. NASD Regulation, Inc., 1999; mem. adv. bd. Ctr. Banking & Fin. Law, Boston U., 1996—. Author: U.S. Armed Forces and Homeland Defense: The Legal Framework, 2001. Chmn. bd. dirs. Student Conservation Assn., Charlestown, N.H., 1986-87, bd. dirs., 1985-91, 94-96, sec., gen. counsel, 1991-93. Recipient medal for disting. pub. svc. Dept. Def., 1989; Bates fellow Yale U., 1973, Scholar of House, 1973-74; Rotary Internat. Found. grad. fellow, 1978, U.S.-Japan Leadership fellow Japan Soc., 1989-90, assoc. fellow Saybrook Coll., Yale U., 1993—. Mem.: ABA (chmn. standing com. law and nat. security 1995—98), Federalist Soc. (vice chmn. internat. and nat. security law practice group), Internat. Bar Assn., DC Bar Assn., Fed. Bar Assn., Coun. Fgn. Rels., Cosmos Club, Elizabethan Club, Yale Club, Met. Club. Republican. Roman Catholic. Office: Dechert 1775 Eye St NW Washington DC 20006-2402 E-mail: paul.stevens@dechert.com.

STEVENS, PHYLISS ELIZABETH, fine art dealer, consultant, publisher, lecturer; b. Balt., Dec. 30, 1953; d. Lawrence and Frances Elizabeth Stevens. BS, Va. Commonwealth U., 1977. Gallery dir. KenWest Gallery, L.A., 1979-84; fine art cons. La Mirage Gallery, 1984-86; gallery dir. West 43rd St. Gallery, 1986-89; pres. Vibrant Fine Art, 1990—. Pres., founder, organizer Art in Pub. Places, L.A., 1984-86; creative dir. The Black Child/Art, L.A., 1986-88; art cons. NBC-TV Segment Series, Hill St. Blues, Hollywood, Calif., 1982. Editor Art Forum, 1984, American Black Artists Newsletter, 1988. Recipient Top Cons. Design Workshop award West Coast Art Stars, 1978, Community Involvement In the Arts award Founder's Women Club, 1980. Mem. NAFE, Am. Artist Club (pres. 1986-88). Democrat. Avocations: reading, creative writing, theatre, travel. Office: Vibrant Fine Art 3931 W Jefferson Blvd Los Angeles CA 90016-4211 E-mail: vibrant2@earthlink.net.

STEVENS, RHEA CHRISTINA, lawyer; b. Chgo., Dec. 25, 1964; d. Samuel Nowell and Rhea Mae (Lipham) S.; m. Peter Linzer, June 20, 1992; 1 child, Grayson Nowell. BS in Psychology, U. Houston, 1989; MEd, Cambridge Coll., 1987; JD, U. Houston, 1992. Bar: Tex. 1992. Instr., client liaison Hippocrates Health Inst., Boston, 1985-86; reorganization cons. Psychotechnics, Inc., Cary, Glenview, Ill., 1987-88; pvt. practice law Houston, 1992—. Founder, owner Aristic Enterprises I and II, 1995, breeder Great Danes, Anatolian Shepherds, Papillons and Dobermans for svc. orgns. and show-August Kennels, 1988—; canine behaviorist; founder DemiSance Ctr., 1999. Rep. mid-Am. chpt. ARC to Nat. Conv., 1980; bd. dirs., treas. Clark Rd. Found., Houston, 1990-92, Houston ACLU, 1990-92; counsellor Boston Area Rape Crisis Ctr., 1986-87. Recipient cert. commendation ARC, 1979-80. Mem. State Bar Tex. (disability issues com. 1996—, Pro Bono Coll. 1995—). Avocations: training and exhibiting dogs, locksmithing, computer consulting. Office: 6655 Arabia Ln Ste 100 Sealy TX 77474

STEVENS, RICHARD GORDON, political scientist, educator; b. Chgo., Dec. 29, 1925; s. Philip Jacob and Almyra (DeVillery) Solomon; m. Norma Jean Duncan, Oct. 14, 1949; children: Dennis Gordon, Laura Louise, Patricia Jean. AM in Polit. Sci., U. Chgo., 1956, PhD in Polit. Sci., 1963. Asst. prof. Coll. William and Mary, Williamsburg, Va., 1959-62; tutor honors divsn. U. Santa Clara, Calif., 1963-66; asst. prof. U. Wash., Seattle, 1966-69; assoc. prof. U. Waterloo, Ont., Can., 1969-73; prof., chmn. Rockford (Ill.) Coll., 1973-75; prof. Georgetown U., Washington, 1981-85; prof., assoc. dean Def. Intelligence Coll., 1984-92; prof. Nat. Def. U., 1992-94; lectr. Inst. World Politics, 1994-2000. Cons. Pub. Adminstrn. Svc., McLean, Va., 1975—, Office Sec. Def., Washington, 1977; Fulbright prof. law U. Hong Kong, 1986-87. Author: The American Constitution and Its Provenance, 1997, Frankfurter and Due Process, 1987, Sober as a Judge, 1999; co-author: American Political Thought, 1973, 83; contbr. articles to profl. jours. Comdr. USNR, 1943-85. Carnegie fellow in law and govt. Harvard Law Sch., Cambridge, Mass., 1962-63; Salvatori fellow Free Congress Found., Washington, 1994-95. Mem. Am. Polit. Sci. Assn., Nat. Assn. Scholars, Naval Res. Assn., Assn. Former Crewmembers USS Intrepid, Harvard Law Sch. Assn. E-mial. Home: 8350 Greensboro Dr # 307 McLean VA 22102 E-mail: stevensrg@aol.com.

STEVENS, RICHARD YATES, retired county official; b. Raleigh, N.C., Dec. 12, 1948; s. Floyd L. and Luna (Yates) S.; m. Jere Ann Gilmore, Sept. 13, 1980; children: Charles Andrew, Katherine Elizabeth. BA in Polit. Sci., U. N.C., 1970, JD, 1974, MPA, 1978. Bar: N.C. 1974. Asst. dean mean U. N.C., Chapel Hill, 1970-71, asst. residence dir., 1971-75, asst. Office Student Affairs, 1973-75; pvt. practice, 1974-76; adminstrv. asst. City of Durham (N.C.), 1975-76, budget officer, 1976-78, dir. adminstrn., 1978-79, dir. fin. and program devel., 1979-80; asst. county mgr. Wake County (N.C.), 1980-84, county mgr., 1984-2000. Adj. prof. polit. sci. N.C. State U., 1980, 92, 94; coord. N.C. State Govt. intern program, Inst. Govt., summer, 1971; sr. budget advisor N.C. Gov.'s Transition Team, 2000—01. Mem. bd. visitors U. N.C., Chapel Hill, 1991—95, trustee, 1995—, chmn., 1997—99; chmn. bd. dirs. U. N.C. Endowment Fund, 1997—99; chmn. U. N.C. Found., 1997—99. Mem. Internat. City/County Mgmt. Assn., ASPA (Nat. Pub. Svc. award 2000), Nat. Assn. County Adminstrs. (bd. dirs. 1989-92), N.C. Bar Assn., N.C. City-County Mgmt. Assn. (bd. dirs. 1991-92, 2d v.p. 1997-98, 1st v.p. 1998-99, pres. 1999-2000), N.C. Mus. Natural Scis. Soc. (bd. dirs. 1987-88, treas. 1988-89, pres.-elect 1989-90, pres. 1990-91), U. N.C. Pub. Adminstrn. Alumni Assn. (pres. 1977-79, dir. 1982-84, Disting. Pub. Svc. award 1998), U. N.C. Gen. Alumni Assn. (dir. 1978-80, 83-84, 85-88, treas. 1988-98, chmn.-elect 1999-2000, chmn. 2000-01, Disting. Svc. medal 1994), Carolina Club (vice chmn. 1993-94, chmn. 1994-98, 2002—), Cary Acad. (bd. dirs.), Yates Mill Assn. (bd. dirs.). Home: 132 Lochwood Dr W Cary NC 27511-8301

STEVENS, RISË, performing arts company administrator; b. N.Y.C. m. Walter Surovy; 1 child, Nicolas. Student, Juilliard Sch.; Hon. Degree Smith Coll., Coll. of Senecas, Russell Sage Coll., Rider Coll., U. Pa., Baylor U., Rice U., Mercy Coll., Mannes Coll Music, Hobart Coll., Cleve. Inst. Music, Va. Commonwealth U. Co-gen. mgr. Met. Opera Nat. Co., N.Y.C., 1980-88; pres.

The Mannes Coll. Music, 1975-78; mng. dir. Met. Opera Bd. Performer Prague Opera, Vienna State Opera, Royal Opera, NY Met. Opera, 1938-61; starred in films, concerts, TV, and radio. Mem. Nat. Endowment for Arts (co-chair music panel 1981-83), N.Y. State Coun. on Arts (chmn. music panel), Met. Opera Guild (bd. dirs.), Wagnerian Soc. Buenos Aires, Sigma Alpha Iota. Office: Met Opera Assn Lincoln Ctr New York NY 10023

STEVENS, ROBERT BOCKING, lawyer, educator; b. U.K., June 8, 1933; naturalized, 1971; s. John Skevington and Enid Dorthy (Bocking) S.; m. Katherine Booth, Dec. 23, 1985; 1 child, Robin; children by previous marriage: Carey, Richard. BA, Oxford U., 1955, BCL, 1956, MA, 1959, DCL, 1984; LLM, Yale U., 1958; LLD (hon.), N.Y. Law Sch., 1984, Villanova U., 1985, U. Pa., 1987; D.Litt. (hon.), Haverford Coll., 1991. Grays Inn bencher, 1999. Barrister-at-law, London, 1956; tutor in law Keble Coll. Oxford U., 1958-59; asst. prof. law Yale U., 1959-61, assoc. prof., 1961-65, prof., 1965-76; provost, prof. law and history Tulane U., 1976-78; pres. Haverford Coll., 1978-87; chancellor, prof. history U. Calif., Santa Cruz, 1987-91; counsel Covington and Burling, Washington and London, 1991—2002; master Pembroke Coll., Oxford, 1993-2001; mem. Essex Court Chambers, 1966—; sr. rsch. fellow Univ. Coll., London, 2001—. Vis. prof. U. Tex., 1961, U. East Africa, 1962, London Sch. Econs., 1963, Stanford U., 1966, Brookings Instn., 1967-68, U. Coll. London, 1991-94; cons. UN, HEW, U.S. Dept. State. Author: The Restrictive Practices Court, 1965, Lawyers and the Courts, 1967, In Search of Justice, 1968, Income Security, 1970, Welfare Medicine in America, 1974, Law and Politics, 1978, The Law School, 1983, The Independence of the Judiciary, 1993, The English Judges, 2002. Chair Marshall Memorial Commn., 1994—2001; mem. Nat. Humanitarian Coun., 1982—86. Named hon. fellow, Pemebroke Coll., Oxford U., 2001; fellow Russell Sage Found., 1967—68, NEH, 1973—74, Nuffield Found., 1975, hon. fellow, Pemebroke Coll., Oxford U., 2001; grantee, Rockefeller Found., 1962—64, Ford Found., 1962—64, 1973—74, NEH, 1973—74, Nuffield Found., 1975. E-mail: steven@cov.com.

STEVENS, ROBERT DAVID, librarian, educator; b. Nashua, N.H., Aug. 11, 1921; s. David Philip and Ruth (Ackley) S.; m. Helen Medora Conrad, Jan. 16, 1943; children: Ruth Wilson Robertson, Hope Conrad. AB magna cum laude, Syracuse U., 1942; BS in L.S. with honors, Columbia, 1947; MA, Am. U., 1955, PhD, 1965. With Library of Congress, Washington, 1947-64, coordinator pub. law 480 programs, 1962-64; dir. Library East West Center, Honolulu, 1964-65; dean Grad. Sch. Library Studies U. Hawaii, 1966-75; chief cataloging div. Copyright Office, 1975-80, coordinator copyright collections, 1980; lectr. grad. Sch. Library Studies, U. Hawaii, 1981-91; chief exec. officer Molesworth Inst. West, Inc., 1984-91, chmn., 1991-96. Fulbright lectr. U. Indonesia, 1971; U.S. del. Intergovtl. Conf. Planning Nat. Libraries Infrastructures, 1974 Author: Role of the Library of Congress in International Exchange of Government Publications, 1955, Toshokan Kyoryoku, 1970, Documents of International Organizations, 1974, Japanese and U.S. Research Libraries at the Turning Point, 1977, Short History of the School of Library and Information Studies, 1991; contbr. articles to profl. publs. Served to lt. USNR, 1943-46. Mem. Hawaii Library Assn. (pres. 1966-67), ALA (mem. council 1967-70, mem. U.S.-Japan adv. com. 1972-79, chmn. 1974-76, Rlms policy and research com. 1977-81), Assocs. U. Hawaii Library (vice chmn. 1981-84), Japan Library Assn., Hui Dui, Phi Beta Kappa, Pi Sigma Alpha. Clubs: 15 (Honolulu). Home: 3-3400 Kuhio Hwy Apt C208 Lihue HI 96766-1084

STEVENS, ROBERT EDWARD, engineering company executive; b. Kansas City, Mo., Oct. 30, 1957; s. Kenneth E. and Nina (France) S. BS in Chem. Engring., U. Mo.-Rolla, 1980, MS in Engring. Mgmt., 1985. Process design engr. The Pritchard Corp., Kansas City, Mo., 1981-83; process engr. Procter & Gamble, Cape Girardeau, 1986-87, tech. mgr., 1987-90; project engring. mgr. Bechtel, 1990, mgr. engring., 1990-93, project mgr., 1993-99, site mgr., 1998-99, engring. mgr. Mex., 1999-2000, project mgr., 2000-01, engring. mgr. Egypt, 2001—. Contbr. to Physical Properties of Gases and Liquids, 1987. Chmn. bd. dirs. Wesley Found., St. Louis, 1993-98; mem. corp. devel. coun. U. Mo.-Rolla, chair benchmarking com., 1996-2000, chair distance learning com., 2001—, mem. chem. engring. indsl. adv. bd., 2001—. Recipient Stan Adams Reliability award P & G Paper Div., 1990, Pres.'s award for team excellence Shell Oil Co., 1994, Performance Plus award Bechtel, 1994; Nat. Merit scholar, 1976. Mem. AIChE, Nat. Fire Protection Assn., Project Mgmt. Inst., Am. Soc. Engring. Mgmt., U. Mo. Rolla-Wesley Found. Alumni Assn. (pres. 1988-97, Outstanding Contbr. 1983, 88), Alpha Chi Sigma (Chpt. Appreciation 1991), Tau Beta Pi. Methodist. Home and Office: 11220 W Florissant # 369 Florissant MO 63033-6741

STEVENS, ROBERT JAY, magazine editor; b. Detroit, July 25, 1945; s. Jay Benjamin and Louise Ann (Beyreuther) S.; m. Dahlia Jean Conger, Aug. 15, 1970; children— Sandra Lee, Julie Ann. Student, Huron (S.D.) Coll., 1963-66, Wayne State U., 1968-71. Sr. staff writer Automotive News, Detroit, 1968-71; editor Excavating Contractor mag., Cummins Pub. Co., Oak Park, Mich., 1971-78, Chevrolet's Pro Jour., Sandy Corp., Southfield, 1978—79, Cars and Parts mag., Cars and Parts Corvette mag. Amos Press, Sidney, Ohio, 1979—; truck editor Automotive Design & Devel. mag., 1971-78. Lectr., speaker in field. Author articles, poems. Served with AUS, 1966-68, Vietnam. Decorated Air medal, Bronze star, Commendation medal; recipient Alphomega Publs. award, 1965—, Robert F. Boger Meml. award for outstanding constrn. journalism, 1975, U.L.C.C. nat. editl. award, Am. Pub. Works Assn., 1978, Moto award for outstanding automotive journalism, Internat. Automotive Media Conf., 1997, 1998, 1999, 2000, 2001, Best of Divsn. award, 2001, Folio mag. Editl. Excellence award, 2001. Mem. Detroit Auto Writers (past dir.), Internat. Motor Press Assn., Antique Automobile Club Am. Republican. Presbyterian. Home: 653 Ridgeway Dr Sidney OH 45365-3432 Office: PO Box 482 911 Vandemark Rd Sidney OH 45365 E-mail: bstevens@carsandparts.com.

STEVENS, ROBERT WILLIAM, church administrator; b. Coquille, Oreg., Mar. 23, 1936; s. Stanton Frank and Eva R. (Mossholder) S.; m. Marilyn Ludlow, Sept. 10, 1957; children: Paul, Ruth. BA in Econs., Willamette U., 1958; postgrad., U. Wash., 1958-59. Treas. Pacific N.W. Ann. Conf., United Meth. Ch., Seattle, 1966—. Del. Western Jurisdictional Conf., United Meth. Ch., 1968, 72, 76, 80, 84, 88, 92, 96, Gen. Conf., 1976, 80, 84, 88, 92, 96, mem. com. audit and rev. Gen. Coun. Fin. and Adminstrn., 1972-76, mem. Gen. Coun. Fin. and Adminstrn., 1976-84, mem. Gen. Bd. Pensions, 1984-92, v.p., 1988-92; chairperson Denominational Health Care Task Force, United Meth. Ch., 1989-91. Trustee Seabeck Christian Conf. Camp, Wash., 1973-84, 92-98, pres., 1982-84. Home: 13011 20th Ave NE Seattle WA 98125-4121 Office: United Meth Ch NW Ann Conf 2112 3rd Ave Ste 300 Seattle WA 98121-2394

STEVENS, ROGER ROSS, lawyer; b. N.Y.C., Nov. 7, 1951; s. Stanley and Miriam S.; m. Nina Iaria, July 17, 1977; 1 child, Alexis. Student, NYU, 1969-71; BBA cum laude, Pace U., 1974, JD, 1979. Bar: N.Y. 1980, U.S. Dist. Ct. (ea. and so. dists.) N.Y. 1980. Supt. John T. Brady & Co., New Rochelle, N.Y., 1970-72, office mgr., 1973-79, corp. counsel, 1980-84; pvt. practice New Rochelle, 1985-86; asst. gen. counsel George A. Fuller Co., N.Y.C., 1986-94; gen. counsel PMS Cons. Mgmt. Corp., New Rochelle, N.Y., 1994—. Elected mem. Representative Town Meeting, Greenwich, 1980-98. Mem. N.Y. State Bar Assn., Am. Arbitration Assn. (arbitrator). Avocations: trap shooting, off road trucking, tennis. Office: PMS Cons Mgmt Corp 92 North Ave New Rochelle NY 10801-7413 E-mail: pmscm@aol.com.

STEVENS, ROGER TEMPLETON, writer; b. Syracuse, N.Y., Jan. 11, 1927; s. Raymond Alfred and Mable Eunice Stevens; m. Mildred Lorraine Hasbrouck, June 12, 1948 (dec. Aug. 1978); children: Margaret Ann, David Keith; m. Barbara Ann Wilkinson, July 14, 1979. AB in English, Union Coll., Schenectady, N.Y., 1949; MA in Math., Boston U., 1959; MS in Systems Engring., Va. Inst. Tech., 1975; PhD in Elec. Engring., Calif. We. U., 1978. Tech. writer Raytheon Mfg. Co., Waltham, Mass., 1950—51; engr. Lab. for Electronics, Boston, 1951—55; sr. engr. Spencer Kennedy Labs., 1955—56, Avco Mfg. Co., Boston, 1956—57, Electronics Systems, Inc., Boston, 1957—60; supr., video and display Sanders Assocs., Nashua, NH, 1960—65; sr. rsch. engr. The Dikewood Corp., Albuquerque, 1967—70; sect. head EG & G Inc., 1974—81; mem. tech. staff The Mitre Corp., Bedford, Mass., 1965—67, 1970—74, 1983—92. Author: Operational Test and Evaluation, 1979, Graphics Programming in C, 1988, Fractal Programming with C, 1989, Fractal Programming with Turbo Pascal, 1990, Advanced Fractal Programming in C, 1990, Fractal Programming and Ray Tracing with C++, 1991; author: (with Christopher Watkins) Advanced Graphics Programming in C and C++, 1991, Advanced Graphics Programming with Turbo Pascal, 1991; author: The C Graphics Handbook, 1992, Learning C with Fractals, 1993, Quick Reference Guide to Computer Graphics Terms, 1993, Object Oriented Graphics Programming in C++, 1994, Using PCX Graphics Files, 1995, Understanding Self-Similar Fractals, 1995, The C++ Graphics Handbook, 1996, Graphics Programming with Java, 1997, Computer Graphics Dictionary, 2002. With USN, 1945—46, Pacific. Mem.: AF and AM, Shriners. Avocations: computers, photography. Home: 17 Castle Rock Rd Rio Rancho NM 87124

STEVENS, RON A. lawyer, public interest organization executive; b. Indpls., Sept. 4, 1945; s. Granville Thomas and Charlotte May (Wheeler) S.; m. Judy Rohde, June 15, 1968; children: Samuel Thomas, Alison Elizabeth. BA, Okla. State U.; JD with honors, Ill. Inst. Tech., 1976. Bar: Ill. 1976. Staff atty. Legal Assistance Found. Chgo., 1976-79; staff atty., dir. housing agenda Bus. and Profl. People for Pub. Interest, Chgo., 1979-81; chief housing divsn. Office of Cook County State's Atty., 1981-82; campaign coord. north lakefront Washington for Mayor, 1982-83; program officer The Joyce Found., 1983-86; pres. Citizens for a Better Environment, 1986-89, United Way Santa Fe County, 1989—. Adv. bd. state support ctr. on environ. hazards Nat. Ctr. for Policy Alternatives, Washington, 1987-89; chair Local Bd. EFSP, 1989—, Santa Fe Affordable Housing Roundtable, 1992-97; chair Exec. Leadership Coun. for Cmty. Schs, 1998—; bd. dirs. No. N.Mex. Grantmakers Assn., v.p., 1999, pres., 2000. Mem. bldg. code enforcement com. Mayor's Transition Team Housing Task Force, Chgo., 1983, steering com. Chgo. Ethics Project, 1986-88; founder, chmn. Progressive Chgo. Area Network, 1981-84; bd. dirs. Uptown Recycling Sta., Chgo., 1987-89; mem. South Ctrl. Regional Coun., United Way of Am., 1993-98. Mem. Chgo. Coun. Lawyers (chmn. housing com. 1978-81, bd. govs. 1981-83, bd. dirs. Fund for Justice, 1986-88), Chgo. Area Runners Assn. (founder, v.p. 1977-81). Home: 739 Gregory Ln Santa Fe NM 87505-1657 Office: United Way Santa Fe County 440 Cerrillos Rd Santa Fe NM 87501-0261

STEVENS, ROSEMARY A. medicine and public health historian; b. Bourne, Eng. came to U.S., 1961, naturalized, 1968; d. William Edward and Mary Agnes (Tricks) Wallace; m. Robert B. Stevens, Jan. 28, 1961 (div. 1983); children: Carey, Richard; m. Jack D. Barchas, Aug. 9, 1994. BA, Oxford (Eng.) U., 1957; Diploma in Social Adminstrn., Manchester (Eng.) U., 1959; MPH, Yale U., 1963, PhD, 1968; LHD (hon.), Hahnemann U., 1988; DSc with honors, Northeastern Ohio U. Coll. Medicine, 1995. Various hosp. adminstrv. positions, Eng., 1959-61; rsch. assoc. Med. Sch. Yale U., 1962-68, asst. prof. Med. Sch., 1968-71, assoc. prof. Med. Sch., 1971-74, prof. pub. health Med. Sch., 1974-76; master Jonathan Edwards Coll., 1974-75; prof. dept. health systems mgmt. and polit. sci. Tulane U., New Orleans, 1976-78, chmn. dept. health systems mgmt., 1977-78; prof. history and sociology of sci. U. Pa., Phila., 1979—, chmn. dept., 1980-83, 86-91, UPS Found. prof., 1990-91, dean Sch. Arts and Scis., Thomas S. Gates prof., 1991-96, Stanley I. Sheerr prof., 1997—2001, prof. emeritus, 2002—. Prof. emeritus U. Pa., Phila., 2002-; vis. lectr. Johns Hopkins U., 1967-68; guest scholar Brookings Instn., Washington, 1967-68; acad. visitor London Sch. Econs., 1962-64, 1973-74. Author: Medical Practice in Modern England: The Impact of Specialization and State Medicine, 1966, new edit., 2002, American Medicine and the Public Interest, 1971, rev. edit., 1998, In Sickness and in Wealth: American Hospitals in the Twentieth Century, 1989, rev. edit., 1999, (with others) Foreign Trained Physicians and American Medicine, 1972, Welfare Medicine in America, 1974, new edit., 2002, Alien-Doctors: Foreign Medical Graduates in American Hospitals, 1978. Bd. dirs. Milbank Meml. Fund. Rockefeller Humanities fellow, 1982-83, Guggenheim fellow, 1984-85; Bellagio Study and Conf. scholar, 1984; recipient Frohlich medal Royal Soc. Medicine, London, 1986, Baxter Found. prize distinction in health svcs. rsch., 1990, James A. Hamilton Book award Am. Coll. Healthcare Execs. best book, 1990, Welch medal distinction in history of medicine Am. Assn. History Medicine, 1990, Arthur Viseltear award history pub. health Am. Pub. Health Assn., 1990, Nicholas E. Davies award Piedmont Hosp., Atlanta, 1997, Investigator award in health policy rsch. Robert Wood Johnson Found., 1998-, Carlson award for extraordinary contbns. to history of medicine Cornell U., Weill Med. Coll., 2000., Lifetime Achievement award Am. Assn. History Medicine, 2002. Fellow Am. Acad. Arts and Scis.; mem. AAAS (chmn. sect. history and philosophy of sci.), Inst. Medicine of Nat. Acad. Sci., Am. Sociol. Assn., Am. Assn. for History of Medicine, Coll. Physicians of Phila. (pub. mem. exec. com.), Am. Bd. Med. Specialities, Cosmopolitan Club. Home: 1900 Rittenhouse Sq # 18 A Philadelphia PA 19103-5767 Office: U Pa 324 Logan Hall 249 South 36th St Philadelphia PA 19104-6304 E-mail: rstevens@sas.upenn.edu.

STEVENS, ROY W. sales and marketing executive; b. Ottumwa, Iowa, Oct. 28, 1924; s. Manley O. and Ruth (Worrell) S.; m. Donna R. Borman, June 7, 1952 (dec. Jan. 1973); children: Katharine Anne Stevens Dillon, Thomas W., John M.; m. Beth A. Murphy, Apr. 20, 1974; children: Carrie Theresa, Elizabeth Mary. BSC., U. Iowa, 1948. With Coca-Cola Co., 1948-54, Gen. Foods Corp., 1954-67; exec. v.p. Riviana Foods, Houston, 1967-73; v.p. mktg. Hiram Walker Inc., Detroit, 1973-75, pres., 1975-80, Maidstone Wine & Spirits Inc., L.A., 1980-91, Kahlua Group (Allied Domecq), 1987-91; exec. v.p. The Century Coun., Los Angeles, 1991-98. Bd. dirs., past chmn. Detroit Met. YMCA; bd. dirs. L.A. Met. YMCA. Lt. (j.g.) USN, 1943-46. Mem. Sigma Alpha Epsilon, Jonathan Club, Annandale Golf Club (Pasadena, Calif.). Episcopalian. Home: 1444 S Marengo Ave Pasadena CA 91106-4228

STEVENS, ROY W. microbiologist, researcher; BS, SUNY, Albany, 1956, MS, 1958; PhD, Albany Med. Coll., 1965. Diplomate Am. Bd. Med. Microbiology. Rsch. scientist Wadsworth Ctr., N.Y. State Dept. Health, Albany, 1967-70, assoc. rsch. scientist, 1970-73, prin. rsch. scientist, 1973-79; dir. labs. diagnostic immunology Wadsworth Ctr., N.Y.State Dept. Health, 1979-85; dir. retrovirology and immunology labs. Wadsworth Ctr., N.Y. State Dept. Health, 1985-91; adj. prof. microbiology and immunology Albany Med. Coll., 1982-92; assoc. prof. sch. pub. health SUNY, Albany, 1988-98; pres. Biomed. Resource Group, 1991—. Trustee Bender Sci., Albany, 1986—. Fellow Am. Acad. Microbiology (emeritus), Assn. Med. Lab. Immunologists (pres. 1989), Am. Soc. Microbiology (chmn. clin. and diagnostic immunology divsn. 1997-98). Home: 507 Acre Dr Schenectady NY 12303-5226 Office: Biomedical Resource Group PO Box 12393 Albany NY 12212-2393

STEVENS, SALLY ANN, interior and costume dsigner; b. Enid, Okla., Sept. 15, 1944; d. Ralph Leopold and Martha Loretta (Meyer) Richter; m. Donald Thompson Stevens, Jr., June 2, 1966; children: Zhawn, Angela, Amanda, Andrea. BEd, Phillips U., 1966, MEd, 1968; diploma interior design, LaSalle U., Chgo., 1972-91. Cert. educator, Okla. Freelance designer SASI's (Sally Ann Stevens Interiors), Enid, 1970—. Fashion designer under name Bare-None; instr. edn. St. Paul's Parochial Sch., Enid. Sustaining mem. Jr. Welfare League. Mem. NAFE, S.W. Home Furnishings Assn., P.E.O., Pi Beta Phi. Republican. Avocations: arts, humanities. Office: SASI's Ill E Maine Enid OK 73703

STEVENS, SANDY See STEVENSON, AMANDA

STEVENS, SCOTT, professional hockey player; b. Kitchener, Ont., Canada, Apr. 1, 1964; Capt. St. Louis Blues, 1990-91, NJ Devils, 1991—. Played in NHL All-Star Game, 1985, 89, 91-94, 96; mem. Stanley Cup Championship Team, 1995; named to NHL All-Rookie Team, 1982-83, Sporting News All-Star Second Team, 1987-88, NHL All-Star First Team, 1987-88, 93-94, NHL All-Star Second Team, 1991-92, Sporting News All-Star First Team, 1993-94. Office: c/o NJ Devils Continental Airlines Arena PO Box 504 East Rutherford NJ 07073-0504*

STEVENS, SHANE, novelist; s. John and Caroline (Royale) S. MA, Columbia U. Mem. numerous writers confs. including Bread Loaf, Santa Barbara Writers Conf. Author: Go Down Dead, Way Uptown in Another World, Dead City, Rat Pack, By Reason of Insanity, The Anvil Chorus; (as J.W. Rider) Jersey Tomatoes (Best Novel award), Hot Tickets; contbr. articles to pubs. including N.Y. Times, Life, Washington Post; screenwriter: By Reason of Insanity, The Me Nobody Knows. Mem. Authors Guild, Writers Guild Am.

STEVENS, SHEILA MAUREEN, teachers union administrator; b. Glendale, Calif., Nov. 1, 1942; d. Richard Chase and Sheila Mary (Beatty) Flynn; m. Jan Whitney Stevens, Sept. 12, 1964; children: Ian Whitney, Bevin Michelle. AA in Liberal Arts, Monterey Peninsula Coll., Calif., 1963; BA in Anthropology, Calif. State U., Long Beach, 1969; postgrad. studies in Edn., U. Guam, 1976-77. Tchr. U.S. Trust Territory of the Pacific, Koror, Palau Island, 1968-72, Kolonia, Ponape Island, 1972-76, Dept. Edn., Agana, Guam, 1976-79; newspaper editor Pacific Daily News (Gannett), 1979-83; comm. dir. Guam Fedn. of Tchrs., 1983-84, exec. dir., 1984-85, Alaska Fedn. Tchrs., Anchorage, 1985-87; labor rels. specialist N.Y. State United Tchrs., Watertown, 1987-93, regional staff dir. Potsdam, 1993—. Mem. Gov.'s Blue Ribbon Panel on Edn., Agana, Guam, 1983-85; leadership devel. coord. Am. Fedn. Tchrs., Washington, 1983—; trainer positive negotiations program Situation Mgmt. Sys., Hanover, Mass., 1988—. Author, editor: Pacific Daily News, 1981-83 (Guam Press Club awards 1981, 82, 83); contbr. articles to mag. and jours. Mem. task force on labor policy, com. on self determination, Govt. of Guam, Agana, 1984-85, Adult Basic Edn. Planning Com., 1985; mem. labor studies adv. bd., Anchorage, Alaska, 1989, regional compact coalition N.Y. State Edn. Dept., Albany, 1994. Named Friend of Edn., Carthage (N.Y.) Tchrs. Assn., 1990. Mem. NOW, ACLU, ASCD, AAUW, Am. Fedn. Tchrs. Comm. Assn. (Best Editorial award 1984), Indsl. Rels. Rsch. Assn. Democrat. Methodist. Avocations: travel, reading, free-lance writing, cross-country skiing. Office: NY State United Tchrs 12 Elm St Potsdam NY 13676-1812

STEVENS, STANLEY CARLSON, economics educator, investment advisor, farmer; b. Sumner, Iowa, June 12, 1943; s. William Delano and Marjorie Elanor (Carlson) S.; m. Janet Pauline Gettings, Feb. 15, 1969; children: Carlson Delano, Andrew Gettings, Sarajane Denton. BS, Iowa State U., 1964; MA, U. Ill., 1970, PhD, 1972. Farmer, Sumner, Iowa, 1964-67; teaching asst. U. Ill., Champaign, 1967-71; instr. St. Olaf Coll., Northfield, Minn., 1971-72; investment advisor Compdex, Inc., Champaign, Ill., 1971-77; farmer Sumner, Iowa, 1977-84; assoc. prof. econs. U. Minn., St. Paul, 1985—. Pres. Worthington Corp., Dundas, Minn., 1985—. Contbr. articles to profl. jours. With USAFNG, 1963-69. Mem. Am. Agrlt. Econ. Assn. Avocation: postal chess. Home: 3265 130th St E Dundas MN 55019-4004 Office: U Minn 130 Classroom Office Bldg Saint Paul MN 55108

STEVENS, STANLEY DAVID, local history researcher, retired librarian, archivist, archivist; b. San Francisco, Nov. 10, 1933; s. David Franklyn and Ellen Myrtle (Wixson) S.; m. Carli Ann Lewis, Sept. 3, 1960; adopted children: Alexander Lewis, Nikolas Harriman, Brooke Cayton Stevens Rich. BA, San Jose State U., 1959. Conf. officer polit. and security com. 14th Gen. Assembly, UN, N.Y.C., 1959; map libr. U. Calif., Santa Cruz, 1965-93, ret., 1993, coord. Hihn-Younger Archive, Univ. Libr., 1994—. Mem. Cartographic Users Adv. Coun., 1976-86, chmn., 1982-86; presenter in field, 1971—; adj. prof. libr. sci. San Jose (Calif.) State U., 1989, 91. Author: Indes to Guinn's Biographical Record of Santa Cruz, San Benito, Monterey and San Luis Obispo Counties, Catalog of aerial photos by Fairchild Aerial Surveys, Inc. now in the collections of the Department of Geography, University of California at Los Angeles, 1982, Correspondence of Charles B. Younger Sr. and Charles B. Younger Jr., Santa Cruz, California Attorneys and Counsellors at Law, (vols. 1-15 of approx. 70 completed to date), 1996—, indexed edit. Santa Cruz County, California, 1997, (index to biographies) 1903 Biographical Record of Santa Cruz, San Benito, Monterey and San Luis Obispo Counties, 2002; editor, Santa Cruz County History Journal, 1994-96, 98; also 10 others related to Hihn-Younger Archive; prodn. editor: Index to Boulder Creek Mountain Echo, 1896-1916, 1999; contbr. over 100 articles and book revs. to profl. jours. Mem. adv. com. archaeol. program Cabrillo Coll., Aptos, Calif., 1985—; bd. dirs. Santa Cruz County Hist. Soc., 1985-94, chmn. publs. com., 1985-96, mem. programs adv. coun., 1994-95; mem. Santa Cruz Orgn. for Progress and Euthenics, 1987—; bd. dirs. Friends of U. Calif.-Santa Cruz Libr., 1994-97; founding mem. Rschr. Anonymous, Santa Cruz, 1994—; mem. U. Calif.-Santa Cruz Emeriti Group, sec.-treas. 1996—; mem. collections adv. com. Santa Cruz City Mus. Natural History, 1995—. With U.S. Army, 1954-56. Recipient honors award geography and map div. for outstanding achievement in map librarianship Spl. Librs. Assn., 1981, cert. of commendation Santa Cruz Hist. Soc., 1986, appreciation cert. for svcs. Assn. Info. and Image Mgmt., 1989, Proclamation of Honor, Santa Cruz County Bd. Suprs., 1998, Historian of Yr. award Mus. Art & History of Santa Cruz, 2001, Historian of Yr. award History Forum of Santa Cruz Mus. of Art and History, 2001; grantee Librs. Assn. U. Calif., 1981-82, rsch. grantee Office of Pres., U. Calif., 1985-86. Mem. ALA (publs. com. Map and Geography Round Table 1985-86, editl. bd. Meridian 1989-2000, honors award Map and Geography Round Table 1992), ACLU (chmn. bd. dirs. Santa Cruz County chpt. 1962-68, bd. dirs. no. Calif. br. 1973-76), Western Assn. Map Librs. (hon. life, founding pres. 1967-68, treas. 1968-89, editor Info. Bull. 1969-84, Exec. Com. award 1984, Stanley D. Stevens Hon. Map presented at 30th anniversary meeting 1997), Calif. Hist. Soc., Calif. Map Soc., Pajaro Valley Hist. Assn., Santa Cruz County Geneal. Soc., Capitola Hist. Soc., El Paso de Robles Hist. Soc. (life). Democrat. Avocations: researching local history, listening to jazz and classical music. Home: 231 13th Ave Santa Cruz CA 95062-4831 Office: U Calif Dean E McHenry Libr Santa Cruz CA 95064 E-mail: sstevens@library.ucsc.edu.

STEVENS, STEPHEN EDWARD, psychiatrist; b. Phila. s. Edward and Antonia S.; m. Isabelle Helen Gallacher, Dec. 27, 1952. BA cum laude, LaSalle Coll., 1950; MD, Temple U., Phila., 1954; LLB, Blackstone Sch. Law, 1973. Diplomate Am. Bd. Psychiatry and Neurology. Intern Frankford Hosp., Phila., 1954-55; resident in psychiatry Phila. State Hosp., 1955-58; practice medicine specializing in psychiatry Woodland Hills, Calif., 1958-63, Santa Barbara, 1970-77; asst. supt. Camarillo (Calif.) State Hosp., 1963-70; cons. ct. psychiatrist Santa Barbara County, 1974-77; clin. dir. Kailua Mental Health Ctr., Oahu, Hawaii, 1977—. Author: Treating Mental Illness, 1961, Survival and the Fifth Dimension, 1997, Psychiatry, Survival and God, 1998. Served with M.C., USAAF. Decorated Purple Heart. Fellow Am. Geriatrics Soc. (founding); mem. Am. Acad. Psychiatry and Law, AMA, Am. Psychiat. Assn., Am. Legion, DAV (Oahu chpt. 1), Caledonia Soc, Am. Hypnosis Soc., Am. Soc. Adolescent Psychiatry, Hawaiian Canoe Club, Honolulu Club, Elks (BPOE 616), Aloha String Band (founder, pres.). Home: PO Box 26413 Honolulu HI 96825-6413

STEVENS, SUZANNE DUCKWORTH, artist, educator; b. Richmond, Ind., Feb. 1, 1946; d. Delbert Raymond and Virginia (Grosvenor) Duckworth; married, 1970 (divorced 1979); 1 child, Neil D. Stevens. BA in Painting and Drawing with honors, Fla. State U., 1968; MA in Painting and Drawing, Goddard Coll., Plainfield, Vt., 1978. Substitute counselor Crisis Intervention Home, Virginia Beach, Va., 1978-85; art instr. Contemporary Art Ctr. Va., 1979—; pvt. art instr. and artist Fine Art Studio, Virginia Beach, 1978—. Artist in residence Virginia Beach Sch. Sys., 1991, 93; curator student shows Contemporary Art Ctr. Va., 1990—; instr. Va. Marine Sci. Mus., Virginia Beach, 1993. One-woman shows include Decker Studios, Virginia Beach, 1986, Contemporary Art Ctr. Va., 1990—, Commons Gallery, Norfolk, Va., 1990, Waterworks Visual Arts Ctr., Salisbury, N.C., 1991, Artists at Work Gallery, Virginia Beach, 1992, Ramada Plaza Resort, 1992—2000, exhibited in group shows at Peninsula Fine Arts Ctr., Newport News, Va., 1982, 1983, 1984, Contemporary Art Ctr. Va., 1986, 1988, 1994, 1995, 1996, Maritime Mus., Virginia Beach, 1988, Seashore State Park, 1992, Represented in permanent collections Chrysler Mus., Norfolk, Exhibited in group shows at Va. Waterfront Internat. Arts Festival Poster. Recipient Outstanding Tchr. award, Gov.'s Sch. for Visual and Performing Arts, U. Richmond, Va., 1990, 1992, 1998, 1999. Mem. Women in the Arts Mus., Classics Plus Dance Orgn., Tadems Dance Orgn. Democrat. Avocations: dancing, piano, tennis, reading, gardening. Home: 1401 Rylands Rd Virginia Beach VA 23455-3929

STEVENS, THEODORE FULTON, senator; b. Indpls., Nov. 18, 1923; s. George A. and Gertrude (Chancellor) S.; m. Ann Mary Cherrington, Mar. 29, 1952 (dec. 1978); children— Susan B., Elizabeth H., Walter C., Theodore Fulton, Ben A.; m. Catherine Chandler, 1980; 1 dau.; Lily Irene. BA, U. Calif. at Los Angeles, 1947; LL.B., Harvard U., 1950. Bar: Calif., Alaska, D.C., U.S. Supreme Ct. bars. Pvt. practice, Washington, 1950-52, Fairbanks, Alaska, 1953; U.S. atty. Dist. Alaska, 1953-56; legis. counsel, asst. to sec., solicitor Dept. Interior, 1956-60; pvt. practice law Anchorage, 1961-68; mem. Alaska Ho. of Reps., 1965-68, majority leader, speaker pro tem, 1967-68; senator for Alaska U.S. Senate, 1968—, asst. Rep. leader, 1977-85; chair, Senate Appropriations com., 1997—2001; ranking mem. Senate Appropriations Com.

U.S. Senate. Served as 1st lt. USAAF, World War II. Mem. ABA, Alaska Bar Assn., Calif. Bar Assn., D.C. Bar Assn., Am. Legion, VFW. Lodges: Rotary, Pioneers of Alaska, Igloo #4. Home: PO Box 100879 Anchorage AK 99510-0879 Office: US Senate 522 Hart Senate Bldg Washington DC 20510-0001*

STEVENS, THOMAS CHARLES, lawyer; b. Auburn, N.Y., Oct. 17, 1949; s. Alice (Kerlin) S.; m. Christine Eleanor Brown, June 2, 1973; children: Erin, Leigh, Timothy. BA, SUNY, Albany, 1971; JD, Duke U., 1974. Bar: Ohio 1974. Mng. ptnr. Thompson, Hine & Flory, Cleve., 1991-96; vice-chmn., chief adminstrv. officer, sec. KeyCorp., 1996—. Trustee Greater Cleve. Growth Assn., 1993-96, Greater Cleve. Roundtable, 1993—, Playhouse Sq. Found., 1998—; active Leadership Cleve., 1992-93, Young Audiences, 1999—, 1999 United Way Campaign. Mem. ABA, Cleve. Bar Assn., Am. Soc. Corp. Secs., Nisi Prius. Office: KeyCorp 127 Public Sq Cleveland OH 44114-1306 E-mail: thomas_stevens@keybank.com.

STEVENS, TOM GRANVILLE, psychologist, educator; b. Jan. 9, 1942; MTh, Claremont Sch. Theology, 1968; PhD in Psychology, U. Hawaii, 1973. Mem. faculty Honolulu C.C., 1971-72, Whittier Coll., Calif., 1972-73; counselor, mem. faculty Calif. State U., Long Beach, 1973—. Author: A Guide to Better Self-Management and Career Planning, 1976, You Can Choose to be Happy, 1998. Office: Counseling Ctr Calif State U 1250 N Bellflower Blvd Long Beach CA 90840-0006

STEVENS, WARREN, actor; b. Clark's Summit, Pa., Nov. 2, 1919; s. Albert Clifford and Helen Dodd (Blakeslee) S.; m. Barbara Helen Fletcher, Sept. 9, 1969; children— Adam Fletcher, Matthew Dodd; 1 son by previous marriage, Laurence Blakeslee. Student, U.S. Naval Acad., 1939-40. Appeared on: New York stage in Gallileo, 1947, Sundown Beach, 1948, Smile of the World, 1949, Detective Story, 1949; appeared in numerous motion pictures, since 1950, including, Barefoot Contessa, Forbidden Planet; appeared on: numerous television shows, including Richard Boone Rep. With USN, 1937-40; with USAAF, 1942-46. Mem. Actors Studio.

STEVENS, WILBUR HUNT, accountant; b. Spencer, Ind., June 20, 1918; s. John Vosburgh and Isabelle Jane (Strawser) S.; m. Maxine Dodge Stevens, Sept. 28, 1941; children: Linda Maxine Piffero, Deborah Anne Augello. BS, MBA, U. Calif., Berkeley, 1949. CPA, Calif.; cert. fraud examiner, fin. svcs. auditor; diplomate Am. Bd. Forensic Acctg. Staff acct. McLaren, Goode, West & Co., San Francisco, 1949-52; mng. ptnr. Wilbur H. Stevens & Co., Salinas, Calif., 1952-70; regional ptnr. Fox & Co., CPAs, 1970-73, nat. dir. banking practice Denver, 1973-80; pres., chmn. Wilbur H. Stevens, CPA, PC, Salinas, 1980-94; chmn. Stevens, Sloan & Shah, CPAs, 1994—. Adj. prof. acctg. U. Denver, 1975-78; faculty mem. Assemblies for Bank Dirs., So. Meth. U., Dallas, 1976-81, Nat. Banking Sch., U. Va., Charlottesville, 1979-87; chmn., dir. Valley Nat. Bank, 1963-71, Pacific Ag Credit, Inc., 1997—; dir. World Travel, Inc.; v.p., dir. Dirs. Coun. Ind. Banks, Global Uplift, Inc. Editor Issues in CPA Practice, 1975; contbr. articles to profl. jours. Capt. AUS, 1942-53. Decorated Bronze Star; Frank G. Drum fellow U. Calif., Berkeley, 1949. Mem. AICPA (v.p. 1971), Am. Acctg. Assn., Am. Assembly Collegiate Schs. Bus. (accreditation coun. 1975-78, 81-84), Nat. Assn. State Bds. Accountancy (pres. 1976-77, strategic initiatives com. 1997-99), Inst. Internal Auditors (fin. svcs. group), Am. Acad. Cert. Consultants and Experts, Calif. Soc. CPAs (pres. 1968-69, Disting. Svc. award 1988), Acctg. Rsch. Assn. (pres. 1973-75), Acad. Acctg. Historians, Assn. Cert. Fraud Examiners, Am. Coll. Forensic Examiners, Ctrl. Calif. Past Masters Assn. (pres. 1998), Burma Star Assn., CBI Vets. Assn., 14 AF Assn., Hump Pilots Assn., Salinas C. of C. (pres. 1960), Commonwealth Club Calif., Masons (master 1992, 97, Hiram award 1998, grand lodge com. taxation), Knight Templar (comdr. 2000), Royal Arch (high priest 1998, grand chpt. inspector 1999-2000), Cryptic Masons (illus. master 2000), Knight Masons Am., Royal Order Scotland, 32 degree Scottish Rite, Nat. Sojourners (pres. Monterey Bay chpt. 1996), Heroes of '76 (comdr. John C. Fremont chpt. 1996-97), Fed. for Collingwood Libr. and Mus., Red Cross of Constantine, Salinas High Twelve Club (pres. 1995), Philalethes Soc., QCCC, London, Rotary (dist. gov. 1983, chmn. internat. fellowship accounts 1994-96, Paul Harris fellow 1973), Phi Beta Kappa, Beta Gamma Sigma (v.p. 1949), Beta Alpha Psi. Republican. Methodist. Home: 38 Santa Ana Dr Salinas CA 93901-4136 Office: 975 W Alisal St Ste D Salinas CA 93901-1148

STEVENS, WILLIAM C., JR. pharmaceutical executive; b. Portsmouth, Va., June 30, 1967; s. William C. and Shelby B. Stevens. PhD, U. Va., 1996. Postdoctoral trainee Mpls. Med. Rsch. Found., 1997-99; sr. scientist ArQule-Pfizer, Medford, Mass., 1999—. Mem. Am. Chem. Soc. Avocation: surfing. Office: ArQule Pfizer 200 Boston Ave Boston MA 02155 Fax: 617-551-3431. E-mail: combinatorial@telocity.com.

STEVENS, WILLIAM DOLLARD, consulting mechanical engineer; b. Bayonne, N.J., Aug. 4, 1918; s. William B. and Beatrice (Dollard) S.; m. Mary E. King, Oct. 12, 1940; children: Sandra A. (Mrs. Jeffrey N. Melin), Barbara E. (Mrs. Dennis Gallagher), William K. BSME, Rensselaer Poly. Inst., 1940; postgrad., Case Inst. Tech., 1958; DSc (hon.), N.J. Inst. Tech., 1986. Various engrng. and mgmt. positions Babcock & Wilcox Co., N.Y.C., 1940-62; v.p. equipment div. Foster Wheeler Corp., Livingston, N.J., 1962-73, sr. v.p., 1972-74, exec. v.p., 1974-78, chmn. bd., 1978-81, dir., 1974-86, dir. emeritus, 1986-90; bd. of dir. Am. Soc. for Macro Engrng., 1992—. Instr. Pratt Inst., 1946-47; bd. overseers N.J. Inst. Tech., 1978-94. Contbr. articles to profl. jours.; patentee in field Chmn. fund drive ARC, Hackensack, N.J., 1956; planning commr., Hackensack, 1955-58; trustee Bergen County Mental Health Consultation Ctr., 1955-58; bd. dirs. Metals Properties Coun.; mem. coun. Rensselaer Polytech. Inst., 1983—. Lt. USNR, 1943-45. Fellow ASME; mem. Nat. Acad. Engrng., Sigma Xi, Tau Beta Pi, Phi Kappa Tau, Pi Tau Sigma. Methodist. Home and Office: 4 Stonybrook Dr North Caldwell NJ 07006-4025

STEVENS, WILLIAM FREDERICK, III, software engineer; b. Paducah, Ky., Aug. 13, 1954; s. William Frederick Jr. and Imogene (Outland) S. Student, Case Western Res. U., 1973-77. Software engr. Allen Bradley Co., Cleve., 1977-80; sr. analyst Mark Bus. Systems, 1980-82, Datacomp Corp., Cleve., 1982-84; sr. cons. GE, 1984-87; sr. engr. Micro Dimensions Inc., 1987-94, Codonics, Inc., Middleburg Heights, Ohio, 1994—. Bd. dirs., pres. N.E. Ohio Apple Corps. Mem. Assn. for Computing Machinery, Maths. Assn. of Am. Avocations: science fiction, computers, theater. Home: 50 S Rocky River Dr Apt 505 Berea OH 44017-2541

STEVENS, WILLIAM J. lawyer; b. Chgo., Jan. 26, 1940; s. Richard James and Jane (Collidge) S.; m. Peggy Hess, Sept. 17, 1960; children: Mark, David. BA, U. Chgo., 1962; JD, Chgo. Kent, 1966. Bar: Ill. 1966, Ind. 1983, U.S. Dist. Ct. (no. dist.) Ill. 1966, Mich. 1996. Assoc. Tenney & Bentley, Chgo., 1966-70; ptnr. Foss Schuman & Drake, 1970-86; pvt. practice, 1986-98; assoc. Kopka Landau & Pinkus, Crown Point, Ind., 1998-2001, Hettinger & Hettinger, Kalamazoo, Portage, Mich., 2001—. Contbg. author: Illinois Trial Guide, 1991. Office: Hettinger & Hettinger 7215 S Westnedge Ave Portage MI 49002 Fax: (616) 344-3601. E-mail: butterflypeggy@qtm.net.

STEVENS, WILLIAM KENNETH, lawyer; b. Chgo., Apr. 19, 1917; s. Ernest James and Elizabeth (Street) S.; m. Anne Hughes, Jan. 4, 1943; children: Anne Elizabeth Stevens Fishman, William Hughes Stevens, Mary Carol Stevens Williams, Martha Street Stevens Gingrich. AB cum laude, U. Calif., Berkeley, 1938; MA, U. Chgo., 1940; JD, Harvard U., 1948. Bar: Ill. 1948, Fla. 1977. With First Nat. Bank Chgo., 1948-74, asst. v.p., 1958-61, v.p., 1961-74; ptnr. McDermott, Will & Emery, Chgo., 1974-85, Myers Krause & Stevens, Naples, Fla., 1986—2001; of counsel Fowler White Myers Krause, 2001—. Author: Illinois Estate Administration, 1968. Chmn. Ill. Inst. Continuing Legal Edn., 1971-72; pres. Hinsdale (Ill.) Pub. Libr., 1977-79. Lt. USNR, 1941-45. Recipient Disting. Svc. award Chgo. Estate Planning Coun., 1981. Fellow Am. Coll. Trust and Estate Counsel; mem. ABA, Am. Law Inst., Chgo. Bar Assn., Ill. Bar Assn., Fla. Bar Assn. (bd. cert. estate planning and probate lawyer), Internat. Acad. Estate and Trust Law. Clubs: Mid-Day, Hinsdale Golf; Chikaming Country (Lakeside, Mich.), The Club at Pelican Bay (Naples). Home: 314 S Lincoln St Hinsdale IL 60521-4008 Office: Ste 600 5811 Pelican Bay Blvd Naples FL 34108-2711 E-mail: wstevens@fwmk.com.

STEVENS, WILLIAM TALBERT, financial services executive; b. Houston, Mar. 11, 1952; s. Talbert Maxton and Peggy Elizabeth (Cagle) S.; m. Christine Leslie Treml, May 24, 1975; 1 child, Anne Kathleen. BBA, Pacific Western U., 1988. Mgr. Capital Fin. Svcs., Akron, Ohio, 1975-80, Beneficial Mgmt., Columbus, 1980-85; v.p. Mid Am. fed. Savs. and Loan, 1985-87, Lender's Svc., Inc., Pitts., 1987-89; pres. Equity Mgmt. Svcs., Inc., 1989-90; divsn. gen. mgr. CBC Cos., 1990-97, sr. v.p., 1997—, Gen. Am. Corp., Pitts., 2001—. Mem. faculty, bd. govs. Nat. Inst. Consumer Credit Mgmt. Marquette U., Milw., 1988-94. Recipient Pres.'s Disting. Achievement Beneficial Mgmt., 1982, 83. Avocation: golf. Office: Gen Am Corp 700 Grant St Pittsburgh PA 15219 also: CBC Cos 520 E Main St Carnegie PA 15106-2051

STEVENS, WILLIS A. music educator; b. Saratoga, Ny, Apr. 4, 1926; s. Willis Alvin and Elizabeth Rieger Stevens; m. Elizabeth Rieger Stevens, June 1, 1957; children: Elizabeth Ann, Peter Dunsmors. BA, Columbia U., New York, NY, 1948, MA, 1953; MS, Juilliard, New York, NY, 1955; Ph.D, Eastman Sch. of Music, Rochester, NY, 1961. Instr. Salem Coll., Winston Salem, NC, 1955—58; assoc. prof. North Tex. State U., Denton, Tex., 1960—62; asst. prof. Whitman Coll., Walla Walla, Wash., 1962—65; assoc. prof. So. Ill. U., Edwardsville, Ill., 1965—67; music chmn. prof. St. Marys Coll., Notre Dame, Ind., 1967—61; dir. Piano Sch., Wayne, Pa., 1971—. Mem.: Phila. Music Teachers Assn. (v.p.). Achievements include Three Town Hall recitals in New York City. Home: 230 Lansdowne Ave Wayne PA 19087

STEVENSON, A. BROCKIE, retired artist; b. Montgomery County, Pa., Sept. 24, 1919; s. Alfred Brockie and Caroline Lansdale (Sill) Stevenson; m. Jane Merriman Mackenzie, Dec. 23, 1978. Student, Pa. Acad. Fine Arts, 1940-41, 46-50, Barnes Found., 1946-48, Skowhegan Sch., Maine, 1950. Instr. Sch. Fine Arts, Washington U., St. Louis, 1960-62; head dept. painting and drawing Corcoran Sch. Art, 1965-81, from assoc. prof. to prof. design, painting, drawing & watercolor, 1965-98; ret., 1998. One-man shows include War Paintings, London and Salisbury, Eng., 1944, Instituto Cultural Peruano-Norteamericano, Lima, Peru, 1953, Art Ctr., Miraflores, Peru, 1958, 1960, Assn. Cultural Peruano-Britanica, Lima, 1959, Mickelson Gallery, Washington, 1970, Pyramid Galleries Ltd., 1973, No. Va. C.C., 1974, Fendrick Gallery, Washington, 1978, 1984, 1988, exhibited in group shows at Nat. Gallery Art, London, 1944, Pa. Acad. Fine Arts, Phila., 1948—51, Sociedad Bellas Artes del Peru, Lima, 1953—56, SUNY, Potsdam and Albany, 1971, Columbia (S.C.) Mus. Art, 1971, EXPO '74, Spokane, Wash., 1974, Corcoran Gallery, Washington, 1980, retrospective, Represented in permanent collections Corcoaran Gallery Art, Washington, Dept. Def., Nat. Mus. Am. Art, Phillips Collection, Fed. Res. Bank, Richmond, Va., Woodward Found., Washington, Ogunquit (Maine) Mus. Art, Brown U. Libr. Milit. Coll., Providence. With U.S. Army, 1941—45, ETO. Home: 6106 Yale Ave Glen Echo MD 20812-1122

STEVENSON, ADLAI EWING, III, lawyer, former senator; b. Chgo., Oct. 10, 1930; s. Adlai Ewing and Ellen (Borden) S.; m. Nancy L. Anderson, June 25, 1955; children: Adlai Ewing IV, Lucy W., Katherine R., Warwick L. Grad., Milton Acad., 1948; AB, Harvard U., 1952, LL.B., 1957. Bar: Ill. 1957, D.C. 1977. Law clk. Ill. Supreme Ct., 1957-58; assoc. Mayer, Brown & Platt, Chgo., 1958-66, ptnr., 1966-67, 81-83, of counsel, 1983-91; treas. State of Ill., 1967-70; U.S. senator from Ill., 1970-81; chmn. SC&M Internat. Ltd., Chgo., 1991-95, pres., 1995-98, chmn. of bd., 1998—. Mem. Ill. Ho. of Reps., 1965-67; Dem. candidate for gov. of Ill., 1982, 86. Capt. USMCR, 1952-54. Office: 20 N Clark St Ste 750 Chicago IL 60602

STEVENSON, AMANDA (SANDY STEVENS), librettist, composer, document examiner; b. Bklyn., Oct. 24, 1943; d. Haakon and Grace Svendsen. Grad., Bay Ridge H.S., Bklyn., 1961. Cert. Nat. Bur. Document Examiners. Composer, librettist, Nellie Bly, Victorine, (screenplay) The Last Assignment Mem. Actors Equity Assn., GMI, Songwriters Guild. Democrat. Unitarian Universalist. Avocations: chess, art history, pen pals. Home and Office: 3543 84th St Apt 327 Jackson Heights NY 11372

STEVENSON, BEN, artistic director; b. Portsmouth, Eng., Apr. 4, 1936; came to U.S., 1968; s. Benjamin John and Florence May (Gundry) S.; m. Joan Toastivine, Jan. 6, 1968. Grad., Arts Ednl. Sch., London, 1955. Dir. Houston Ballet Acad. Mem. dance panel Tex. Commn. Arts, 1977; guest tchr. Am. Ballet Theatre, Joffrey Ballet, Royal Ballet, London, Beijing Dance Acad. Dancer Theatre Arts Ballet, London, 1952-54, Sadler's Wells Theatre Ballet, 1955-56, Royal Ballet, 1956-60, London Festival Ballet, 1960-62; appearances in Wedding in Paris, 1954-55, Music Man, London, 1962-63, Half a Sixpence, also, Boys in Syracuse, London, 1964; prin. dancer, ballet master, London Festival Ballet, 1964-68; artistic dir. Harkness Ballet Youth Dancers, 1968-71, Chgo. Ballet, 1974-75, Houston Ballet, 1976—; co-dir. Nat. Ballet, Washington, 1971-74; prin. ballets choreographed include Three Faces of Eve, 1965, Cast Out, 1966, Sleeping Beauty (full length), 1967, 71, 76, 78, Fervor, 1968, Three Preludes, 1968, Forbidden, 1969, Cinderella (full length), 1969, 71, 73, 74, 76, Bartok Concerto, 1970, Nutcracker (full length), 1972, 76, Symphonetta, 1972, Courant, 1973, Swan Lake (full length), 1977, L, 1978, Britten Pas de Deux, 1979, Four Last Songs, 1979, Space City, 1980, Peer Gynt (full length), 1981, Zheng Ban Qiao, 1982, The Prince of Pagodas, 1986 Recipient 1st prize London Choreographic competitions, 1965, 66, 67, 1st prize modern ballet choreography Internat. Ballet Competition, Varna, Bulgaria, 1972, Gold medal for choreography Internat. Ballet Competition, 1982, Dance mag. award, 2000; named Order of Brit. Empire, 1999. Asso. mem. Royal Acad. Dancing (Adeline Genee Gold medal 1955) Office: Houston Ballet 1921 W Bell St Houston TX 77019-4813*

STEVENSON, CANDACE J. museum director; Exec. dir. N.S. Mus., Halifax, N.S., Can. Office: NS Mus PO Box 456 Halifax NS Canada B3J 2R5

STEVENSON, DAVID JOHN, planetary scientist, educator; b. Wellington, New Zealand, Sept. 2, 1948; came to U.S., 1971; s. Ian McIvor and Gwenyth (Carroll) S. BSc, Victoria U., New Zealand, 1971; PhD, Cornell U., 1976. Rsch. fellow Australian Nat. U., Canberra, Australia, 1976-78; asst. prof. UCLA, L.A., 1978-80; assoc. prof. Calif. Inst. Tech., Pasadena, 1980-84, prof., 1984—, George van Osdol prof., 1995—. Chmn. divsn. geol. & planetary scis. Calif. Inst. Tech., 1989-94. Contbr. about 100 articles to profl. jours. Named Fulbright scholar, USA, 1971-76. Fellow Am. Geophysical Union (Harry H. Hess medal 1998), Royal Soc. London, 1993; mem. AAAS, Am. Astron. Soc. (Urey prize 1984). Office: Calif Inst Tech 1200 E California Blvd Pasadena CA 91125-0001 E-mail: djs@gps.caltech.edu.

STEVENSON, DENISE L. business executive, banking consultant, realtor; b. Washington, Sept. 18, 1946; d. Pierre and Alice (Mardrus) D'Auga; m. Walter Henry Stevenson, Oct. 17, 1970 (div. 1990). AA, Montgomery Coll., 1967; BA in Econs./Bus. Mgmt., N.C. State U., 1983; cert. legal asst., Meredith Coll., 1989; cert. in Mgmt., Fin. Women Internat., 1990. Lic. ins. agt. Savs. counselor Perpetual Bldg. Assn. (now Crestar Bank), Washington, 1968—70; regional asst. v.p. 1st Fed. Savs. (now Centura Bank, Rocky Mount), 1971—83; pres., owner Diversified Learning Svcs., Raleigh, 1983—; pres., treas. Daily Life Svcs., Inc., 1994—99; realtor Prudential Carolinas Realty, 2002—. Realtor Prudential Carolinas Realty, 2002—; instr. Inst. Fin. Edn., Raleigh, 1983—89, Am. Inst. Banking, 1986. Mem. Am. Bus. Women's Assn. (Woman of Yr. 1982), Fin. Women Internat. (cert. leader 1987, Mem. of Yr. award 1992, N.C. Woman of Yr. 1992), Laurel Hills Women's Club (pres. 1974-75, Raleigh), Omicron Delta Epsilon. Avocation: fishing. Office: Diversified Learning Svcs PO Box 33231 Raleigh NC 27636-3231 E-mail: divlrnserv@aol.com.

STEVENSON, EARL, JR. civil engineer; b. Royston, Ga., May 8, 1921; s. Earl and Compton Helen (Randall) S.; B.S. in Civil Engring., Ga. Inst. Tech., 1953; m. Sue Roberts, Apr. 25, 1956; children— Catherine Helen, David Earl. Engr., GSA, Atlanta, 1959-60; engr., pres. Miller, Stevenson & Steinichen, Inc., Atlanta, 1960— ; sr. v.p. Stevenson & Palmer, Inc., Camilla, 1984— ; dir. Identification & Security Products, Inc., Atlanta. Served with USAAF, 1944-45. Registered profl. engr., Ga., Ala., S.C., Miss. Mem. Ga. Soc. Profl. Engrs., Water Pollution Control Fedn. Methodist. Home: 3208 Whiteoak Cir SE Smyrna GA 30082-3363 Office: 2430 Herodian Way SE Smyrna GA 30080-2980

STEVENSON, EDWARD WARD, retired physician, surgeon, otolaryngologist; b. Chester, S.C., Jan. 9, 1926; s. Thomas M. and Annie Lou (Ward) S.; m. Dorothy Giles, Sept. 2, 1947; children: Sally Anne Stevenson Yeilding, Laura Stevenson Healy, Nancy Stevenson Schonbeger (dec.), Molly Stevenson Walker. B in Medicine, Duke U., 1945; MD, U. Md., Balt., 1949. Intern Bapt. Meml. Hosp., Memphis, 1949-50; resident Med. Coll. Va. Hosp., Richmond, 1953-55; fellow Ochsner Found. Hosp., New Orleans, 1955-56; staff otolaryngologist Ochsner Clinic, 1956-57; pvt. practice Birmingham, 1957-60, 65-94; instr., clin. asst. prof. surgery U. Ala., 1957-94; pvt. practice Decatur, Ala., 1960-65; ret., 1994. Faculty Tulane U. Sch. Medicine, 1956-57; staff Bapt. Med. Ctr.-Montclair, Birmingham. Contbr. articles to profl. jours. Bd. dirs. So. Mus. Flight, Birmingham, 1989—, Ala. Aviation Hall of Fame; pres. Birmingham Aero Club, 1996. Mem. AMA, ACS, Am. Laryngol., Rhinol. and Otol. Soc. (sec.- treas. so. sect. 1990-93, v.p. so. sect. 1993-94), Am. Soc. Head and Neck Surgery, Am. Acad. Otolaryn., Jefferson County Med. Soc., Ala. Oolaryn. Soc. (founder, pres. 1971), Med. Assn. State Ala., Morgan County Med. Soc. (pres. 1964-65), Tri-State Otolaryn. Assembly (co-founder), Birmngham Otolaryn. Soc. (pres. 1984), Birmingham Aero Club (pres. 1996), Birmingham Downtown Rotary Club. Methodist. Avocations: aerobatic flying, world travel. Home: 4249 Antietam Dr Birmingham AL 35213-3221 E-mail: flypitts1@aol.com.

STEVENSON, FRANCES KELLOGG, museum program director; b. Boston; d. Charles Summers and Alice deGueldry (Stevens) S.; m. James Richard Wein, 1971 (div. 1989). BA, Wells Coll., Aurora, N.Y., 1967; MA, Oxford U., 1972; MBA, U. Pa., 1992. Publs. officer Nat. Portrait Gallery Smithsonian Instn., Washington, 1974—2001, strategic planning officer, 2001—. Mem. St. John's Episcopal Ch., Lafayette Sq. James E. Webb fellow Smithsonian Instn., 1988-89. Mem. Sulgrave Club. Episcopalian. Home: 2724 Ordway St NW Apt 4 Washington DC 20008-5047 Office: Smithsonian Instn Nat Portrait Gallery 750 Ninth St NW Ste 8300 Washington DC 20560-0973

STEVENSON, GARTH, social sciences educator; b. Montreal, Que., Can., Apr. 7, 1943; s. Andrew Archibald Stevenson and Ruth Graham (Scott) Swinton; m. Carol Barbara Krell, Aug. 10, 1968 (div. 1983); children: Colin, Fiona, Moira; m. Yvonne Brown, Aug. 5, 1983; 1 child Jacqueline. BA, McGill U., Montreal, 1963, MA, 1965; PhD, Princeton U., 1971. Asst. prof. Carleton U., Ottawa, Canada, 1968—76, assoc. prof. Canada, 1976—78, U. Alberta, Edmonton, Canada, 1978—82, prof. Canada, 1982—87, Brock U., St. Catharines, Canada, 1987—. Vis. prof. Duke U., Durham, NC, 1992—93. Author: (novels) The Politics of Canada's Airlines, 1987, Ex Uno Plures, 1993, Community Besieged, 1999. Candidate in Canadian Gen. Election New Democratic Party, Edmonton North, 1984. Mem.: Canadian Polit. Sci. Assn. (bd. dirs. 1998—2000), Am. Polit. Sci. Assn. Anglican Ch. Of Canada. Home: 35 October Dr St Catharines ON Canada Office: Brock U POB 1600 Glenridge Ave St Catharines ON Canada L2S 3A1 Address: Brock U Polit Sci Dept PO Box 1600 Lewiston NY 14092-5000 Office Fax: 905-988-9388. Business E-Mail: stevenson@spartan.ac.brocku.ca.

STEVENSON, GELVIN LEE, investment consultant, writer; b. Chelsea, Okla., Nov. 6, 1944; s. George Joseph and Mary Ellen (Milam) S.; m. Clara Elsie Rodriguez, June 7, 1969; children: Clara Gelvina, José Angel. BA in Econs., Carleton Coll., 1966; MA in Econs., Washington U., 1968, PhD in Econs., 1973. Dir. referral program Manpower Office N.Y.C. (N.Y.) Addiction Svcs. Agy., 1973; with Charter Revision Commn. for N.Y.C., N.Y., 1973-74; cmty. organizer, co-founder, chmn. Grass Roots Orgn., South Bronx, 1974-77; assoc. econs. editor/staff, editor corp. fin. Bus. Week Mag., N.Y.C., 1977-85; pvt. practice cons., 1985-90, 91-92; dir. investment responsibility N.Y.C. (N.Y.) Comptr., 1990-91; pvt. practice fin. cons., 1991—. Adj. instr. U. Coll., Washington U., St. Louis, 1968, C.W. Post Ctr., L.I. U., 1974, Lehman Coll., CUNY, Bronx, 1974; adj. prof. Manhattan Coll., Bronx, 1998, Iona Coll., New Rochelle, 2000; vis. scholar Columbia U. Divsn. Urban Planning, 1975; bd. dirs. First Nations Devel. Inst., Environ. Rsch. Found., Cmty. Resource Exch., Am. Indian Cmty. House; dir. bus. devel. for web site, 2001—; lectr. in field. Contbr. articles to profl. jours. Democrat. Cherokee. Avocations: running, string figures. Office: Ste 3B 2160 Bolton St Apt 3B Bronx NY 10462-1325

STEVENSON, HOWARD HIGGINBOTHAM, business educator; b. Salt Lake City, June 27, 1941; s. Ralph Shields and Dorothy Dee (Higginbotham) S.; m. Fredericka O'Connell; children: William, Charles, Andrew. BS, Stanford U., 1963; MBA, Harvard U., 1965, DBA, 1969. Asst. prof. bus. Harvard U., Cambridge, Mass., 1968-72, assoc. prof., 1972-78, Sarofim Rock prof., 1982—, sr. assoc. dean for fin. adminstrn., 1991-94, sr. assoc. dean external rels., faculty chair. Owner, pres., mgr. Program in Exec. Edn., 1998—2000; chmn. publs. rev. bd. Harvard Bus. Sch. Press, 1999—2000; faculty chmn. Latin. Am. Adv. Bd., 1999—2001; v.p. Simmons Assocs., Boston, 1970—72; v.p. fin. adminstrn. Preco Corp., West Springfield, Mass., 1978—81; bd. dirs. Landmark Comms., Norfolk, Va., Camp Dresser and McKee Inc., Cambridge, The Baupost Group, Inc., Boston, Commonwealth Capital Ptnrs., Boston, Bessemer Securities Corp., N.Y.C. Co-author: Policy Formation and Administration, 1984, New Business Ventures and the Entrepreneur, 1985, 89, 94, 5th edit., 1999, Entrepreneurial Ventures, 1992, 2d edit., 1999, Do Lunch or Be Lunch: The Power of Predictability in Creating Your Future, 1997, (with David Amis) Winning Angels: The Seven Fundamentals of Early Stage Investing, 2001. Trustee Rural Land Found., Lincoln, Mass., 1973-78, Boston Ballet, Suffield Land Conservancy, Conn., 1978-82; dir. Sudbury Valley Trustees, 1991—, pres. bd. trustees, 96-2000. IBM Nat. Merit scholar, 1959; Ford Found. fellow, 1965. Mem. Fin. Execs. Inst., Acad. Mgmt., Harvard Club (N.Y.C.). Office: Harvard Bus Sch South Hall 314 Boston MA 02163

STEVENSON, IAN, psychiatrist, educator; b. Montreal, Que., Can., Oct. 31, 1918; s. John Alexander and Ruth Cecilia (Preston); m. Octavia Reynolds, Sept. 13, 1947 (dec. Nov. 1983); m. 2d, Margaret H. Pertzoff, Nov. 29, 1985. Student, U. St. Andrews, Scotland; BS, McGill U., 1942, MD, CM, 1943. Cert. Am. Bd. Psychiatry, 1953. Asst. prof. psychiatry La. State U., New Orleans, 1949-52, assoc. prof. psychiatry, 1953-57; prof. psychiatry, chmn. U. Va. Sch. Medicine, Charlottesville, 1957-67, Carlson prof. psychiatry, head div. of personality studies, 1967—2001, rsch. prof. psychiatry, 2001—; assoc. mem. Darwin Coll., U. Cambridge, 1981-96. Author: The Diagnostic Interview, 1960, Twenty Cases Suggestive of Reincarnation, 1966, Reincarnation and Biology, 1997, 10 other books; contbr. 250 articles to profl. jours. Fellow Am. Psychiat. Assn. (life); mem. AAAS, Soc. for Psychical Rsch. London (coun. mem. and pres. 1988-89), Am. Soc. for Psychical Rsch., Soc. for Sci. Exploration (founding com.), Colonnade Club (U. Va.), Oxford and Cambridge Club (London). Office: U of Va Health Sys PO Box 800152 Charlottesville VA 22908-0152 E-mail: ips6r@virginia.edu.

STEVENSON, JAMES LARAWAY, communications engineer, consulting; b. Detroit, Oct. 25, 1938; s. Joseph Morley and Kittie Harriet (Laraway) S.; m. Jeanie Lorraine Minkstein, Aug. 7, 1965; children: Amy Jean, Brian Morley. AAS, U.S. Armed Forces Inst., 1958; BSEE, MIT, 1960, MSEE, 1962. Cert. master radio and telecommunications engr. FCC. With USN Mercury Space Project, 1957-63, Office of Naval Rsch., 1962—63; engr. Sta. WBCM-FM, Bay City, Mich., 1964-65; chief engr. Sta. WCRM, Clare, 1965-66, Sta. WSMA, Marine City, 1966; engr. Sta. WWJ-AM-FM-TV, Detroit, 1966-79; owner, mgr. Twin Oaks Comms. Engring. (name now Twin Oaks Comms. Engring. P.C.), North Branch, 1972—. Charter pilot, flight & ground instr. G. B. DuPont Co., Almont Marlette Aviation Inc., 1977-82; cons. electronics engr. various cos., 1968—; expert legal witness, 1968—; mem. corp. edn. dean's adv. coun. Colls. Bus. Adminstr., Sci., Engring. & Tech., Saginaw Valley State U., 1997—; mem. curriculum adv. com. ITT Tech. Inst., Canton, Mich., 2002—. Contbr. articles to profl. jours. Sr. div. judge Detroit Met. Sci. and Engring. Fair, 1975—, Mich. State Sci. & Engring. Fair, 2000—; spl. awards judge Intel Internat. Sci. & Engring. Fair, Detroit, 2000; search & rescue pilot, mission comdr., capt. Mich. wing CAP, 1961-81; cubmaster Pack 457 Boy Scouts Am., North Branch, 1983-85; mem. adv. bd. jacknabbit.com., Issaquah, Wash., 1999-2001; hon. state chmn. bus. adv. coun. Rep. Congl. Com., 2002-. Recipient appreciation award CAP, 1980, North Branch Area Schs., 1985, Century award Boy Scouts Am., 1984 Mem. AIAA, IEEE (sr., chmn. N.E. Mich. sect. 1987-88, 95—, bd. dirs. 1984—), NSPE, Am. Soc. for Engring. Edn. (profl. mem.), Nat. Assn. Radio Telecomm. Engrs. (sr.), Am. Inst. Physics (assoc.), Mich. Soc. Profl. Engrs. (flint chpt.), Saginaw Valley Engring. Coun. (chmn. 1990-91, 2000-01, sec.-treas. 1992-95, Outstanding

Leadership award 1991, 2001), Engring. Soc. Detroit (profl.), Profl. Activities Coun. Engrs. (chmn. U.S. activities bd. 1985—), Nat. Pilots Assn. (sr. pilot citation, safe pilot award 1978), Aircraft Owners and Pilots Assn., North Branch C. of C. (charter), Tri-County Econs. Club, Am. Legion, Lions (pres. North Br. club 1990-91), Radio Club Am. Avocations: computers, amateur radio, flying. Office: Twin Oaks Comms Engring PC 2465 Johnson Mill Rd PO Box 340 North Branch MI 48461-0340

STEVENSON, JAMES D(ONALD), JR. psychologist, counselor; b. Ft. Wayne, Ind., July 6, 1943; s. James Donald Sr. and Charlotte Eileen (Starnes) S.; m. Sharon Sue Kearns, Nov. 26, 1965 (div. 1978); 1 child, E. Willow; m. Diane Kulesza, Apr. 13, 1980 (div. 1987); 1 child, James Wesley; m. Christine Berthold, Aug. 8, 1992. BA, Whittier (Calif.) Coll., 1965; MA, Calif. State U., Northridge, 1974; PhD, Calif. Coast U., 1986. Lic. counselor, Calif. Auditor State Compensation Ins. Fund, Arcadia, Calif., 1965-66, supervising auditor, 1969-74; dir. social svcs. Buena Vista Acad., Ventura, 1974-76, benefits counselor, 1976-77; counselor Calif. Dept. of Rehab., Thousand Oaks, 1977-82, vocat. psychologist Pleasant Hill, 1982—. Prin. James Stevenson Pub., 1994—, Career Interest Testing Svc., Ventura and Contra Costa Counties, 1980-83; instr. Ventura Coll., 1975; cons. Ctr. for Career Evaluation, Oakland, Calif., 1986-87, St. Vincent DePaul Soc., Pittsburg, Calif., 1986-97, Allied Fellowship Svcs., Oakland, 1990. Contbr. articles to profl. jours. Bd. dirs. Solano County (Calif.) Hist. Records Commn., pres., 1997-99, v.p., 1999-2001, pres., 2001-03. With U.S. Army, 1965-67, ETO. Mem. AACD, Nat. Rehab. Assn. (exec. bd. San Francisco chpt. 1986-93, pres. San Francisco East Bay divsn. 1991-92), Ventura County Mental Health Assn. (bd. dirs. 1978-81), Los Padres Rehab. Assn. (pres. Ventura chpt. 1978-79), Sons Am. Revolution, Napa County Hist. Soc., Solano County Geneal. Soc. Avocations: genealogy, hiking. Office: James Stevenson Publ 1500 Oliver Rd Ste K-109 Fairfield CA 94533- E-mail: jimstevenson@jspub.com.

STEVENSON, JAMES RALPH, school psychologist, writer; b. Kemmerer, Wyo., June 29, 1949; s. Harold Ralph and Dora (Borino) S.; m. Alice M. Paolucci, June 17, 1972; children: Tiffany Jo, Brian Jeffrey. BA, U. No. Colo., 1971, MA, 1974, EdS, 1975. Diplomate Am. Psychotherapy Assn.; lic. elem. sch. counselor, sch. psychologist, Colo.; nationally cert. sch. psychologist. Sch. psychologist Jefferson County Pub. Schs., Golden, Colo., 1975-87, 89-91, Weld County Sch. Dist. 6, Greeley, 1987-89, Weld Bd. Coop. Edn. Svcs., LaSalle, 1991-95, spl. edn. coord., 1995; sch. psychologist Fort Lupton (Colo.) Schs., 1995-98; coord. of spec. edn. and gifted progs. Fort Lupton Sch. Dist., 1998-2000; dir. spl. edn. programs Fort Lupton/Keenesburg Schs. Consortium, 2000—. Ltd. pvt. practice sch. psychologist Pathways, Greeley, 1994—. Asst. coach Young Am. Baseball, Greeley, 1989, 90, head coach, 1992, 93; asst. basketball coach Recreation League for 6th-7th Grades, 1992, 93. U. No. Colo. scholar, 1974. Mem. NASP (alt. del. Colo. chpt. 1975-77, dir. Apple II users group Washington chpt. 1989-95), APA, Coun. Adminstrs. Spl. Edn., Coun. for Exceptional Children, Colo. Assn. Sch. Execs., Assn. Play Therapy, Inc., Colo. Soc. Sch. Psychologists (chmn. task force on presch. assessment 1991-96), Jefferson County Psychologists Assn. (sec. 1986-87), Colo. Assn. for Play Therapy. Democrat. Roman Catholic. Avocations: travel, reading, sports events, plays, music. Home: 1937 24th Ave Greeley CO 80634-6027 Office: Fort Lupton Schs 301 Reynolds St Fort Lupton CO 80621-1329 Personal E-mail: pshrynk@aol.coom. Business E-Mail: jstevenson@ftlupton.k12.co.us.

STEVENSON, JAMES RICHARD, radiologist, lawyer; b. Ft. Dodge, Iowa, May 30, 1937; s. Lester Lawrence and Esther Irene (Johnson) S.; m. Sara Jean Hayman, Sept. 4, 1958; children: Bradford Allen, Tiffany Ann, Jill Renee, Trevor Ashley. BS, U. N.Mex., 1959, JD, 1987; MD, U. Colo., 1963. Diplomate Am. Bd. Radiology, Am. Bd. Nuc. Medicine, Am. Bd. Legal Medicine, 1989: Bar: N.Mex. 1987, U.S. Dist. Ct. N.Mex. 1988. Intern U.S. Gen. Hosp., Tripler, Honolulu, 1963-64, resident radiology Brook, San Antonio, 1964-67; radiologist, ptnr. Van Atta Labs., Albuquerque, 1970-88, Radiology Assocs. of Albuquerque, 1988—, pres., 1994-96. Radiologist, ptnr. Civerolo, Hansen & Wolf, Albuquerque, 1988-89; adj. asst. prof. radiology U. N.Mex., 1970-71; pres. med. staff AT & SF Meml. Hosp., 1979-80, chief of staff, 1980-81, trustee, 1981-83. Author: District Attorney manual, 1987. Participant breast screening Am. Cancer Soc., Albuquerque, 1987-88; dir. profl. divsn. United Way, Albuquerque, 1975. Maj. U.S. Army, 1963-70, Vietnam; col. M.C. USAR, 1988—. Decorated Bronze Star; Allergy fellow, 1960; Med.-Legal Tort scholar, 1987. Fellow Am. Coll. Radiology (councilor 1980-86, mem. med. legal com. 1990-96), Am. Coll. Legal Medicine, Am. Coll. Nuc. Medicine, Am. Coll. Nuc. Physicians, Radiology Assn. Albuquerque; mem. AMA (Physicians' Recognition award 1969—), Am. Soc. Law & Medicine, Am. Arbitration Assn., Albuquerque Bar Assn., Soc. Nuc. Medicine (v.p. Rocky Mountain chpt. 1975-76), Am. Inst. Ultrasound in Medicine, N.Am. Radiol. Soc. (chmn. med. legal com. 1992-95), N.Mex. Radiol. Soc. (pres. 1978-79), N.Mex. Med. Soc. (chmn. grievance com.), Albuquerque-Bernalillo County Med. Soc. (scholar 1959), Nat. Assn. Health Lawyers, ABA (antitrust sect. 1986—), N.Mex. State Bar, Albuquerque Bar Assn., Sigma Chi, Albuquerque Country Club, Elks, Masons, Shriners. Republican. Methodist. Home: 3333 Santa Clara Ave SE Albuquerque NM 87106-1530 Office: Medical Arts Imaging Ctr A6 Med Arts Sq 801 Encino Pl NE Albuquerque NM 87102-2612

STEVENSON, JEAN MYERS, education educator; b. Racine, Wis., July 24, 1947; d. Alfred Richard and Nora Elizabeth (Edmands) Myers; m. Robert James Stevenson, May 17, 1969; children: Peter, Katharine, Philip. BS in Edn., U. Wis., Oshkosh, 1969; MS in Child Study and Edn., U. N.D., 1986, PhD in Tchr. Edn., 1989. Tchr., libr. Duluth (Minn.) Pub. Schs., 1969-70, Racine Pub. Schs., 1970-73; instr. U. N.D., Grand Forks, 1986-88; asst. prof. Dominican U., River Forest, Ill., 1989-93; assoc. prof. edn. Tenn. Wesleyan Coll., Athens, 1993—2002, chmn. edn. dept., 1996—2002; asst. prof. edn. U. Minn., Duluth, 2002—. Contbr. articles to books. Mem. Nat. Coun. Tchrs. English, Children's Lit. Assn., Internat. Reading Assn., Cherokee Reading Coun., N.D. Study Group on Evaluation, Phi Delta Kappa, Pi Lambda Theta. Avocations: reading, cooking, quilting, needlepoint. Office: U Minn Duluth Dept Edn 120 Montague Hall 10 University Plz Duluth MN 55812

STEVENSON, JOANNE SABOL, older adults care provider, educator, researcher; b. Steubenville, Ohio, June 8, 1939; d. Joseph A. and Susan (Ploskunak) Sabol; m. Robert J. Stevenson, Aug. 6, 1966; children: James J., Michael J. BS, Ohio State U., 1963, MS, 1964, PhD, 1970. Prof. Ohio State U., Columbus, 1970-95, dir. Ctr. for Nursing Rsch. Coll. Nursing, 1972-84, emeritus prof. dept. adult health and illness, 1995—, assoc. dean acad. affairs and rsch., 1998—2002; prof. emeritus Rutgers U., Newark, 2002—. Author books; editor Ann. Rev. of Nursing Rsch.; contbr. articles to profl. jours. Pres. bd. trustees Friendship Village Columbus. NIH predoctoral fellow; Fulbright scholar to Brazil, 1995-96; recipient Am. Jour. Nursing Book of Yr. award, 1977, 94, 95, 96, others. Fellow AAAS, Am. Acad. Nursing (chmn. knowledge devel. and utilization think tank); mem. AAUP, ANA (cabinet on rsch., coun. nurse researchers), Ohio Nurses Assn., Midwest Nursing Rsch. Soc. (pres. 1991-93), Am. Coll. Sports Medicine, Sigma Theta Tau (chmn. rsch. com.), Alpha Tau Delta, Phi Beta Delta. Home: 4954 Wintersong Ln Westerville OH 43081-4440 Office: 180 University Ave Newark NJ 07102-1803 E-mail: stevenson@nursetech.rutgers.edu.

STEVENSON, JOHN FRANCIS, beverage company administrator; b. Miami, Fla., Feb. 16, 1959; s. Thomas Charles and Mary Kathryn (Murphy) S.; m. Sharon Louise Keever, Jan. 25, 1986; 1 child, Katherine Reed. BA, DePauw U., 1981; MBA, Pepperdine U., 1989. Account exec. NBI, Inc., Chgo., 1981-83, group sales instr. Boulder, Colo., 1983-84, mgr. European sales ops. London, 1985-86, br. mgr. L.A., 1986-88; v.p., gen. mgr. MGI of Calif., Inc., 1988-91; mgr. sales ops. and planning Pepsi-Cola Co., 1991-92, gen. mgr. Denver metro market, 1992—. Bd. dirs. Pres.'s Leadership Coun., Colo. State U., Ft. Collins, 1993—. Recipient Thorton F. Bradshaw fellowship Claremont Grad. Sch., 1990. Mem. Colo. Soft Drink Assn. (pres.), Lakewood Country Club. Republican. Roman Catholic. Office: Pepsi Cola Co 3801 Brighton Blvd Denver CO 80216-3693

STEVENSON, JOSIAH, IV, cultural arts administrator; b. Jamaica, N.Y., Oct. 4, 1935; s. Josiah and Ruth Lillian (Leech) S.; m. Jane Margaret Kupfer, Sept. 1, 1957; children: Josiah V., Todd Sander. AB, Dartmouth Coll., 1957; MBA, Amos Tuck Sch. Bus., 1958. Instr. U. Md.-Far East, 1959-61; account supr. Benton & Bowles, Inc., N.Y.C., 1961-66; group product mgr., gen. mgr. Japan Chesebrough-Pond's Inc., Greenwich, Conn., 1967-77; dir. devel. Dartmouth Coll., 1977-84, Boston Symphony Orch., 1984-95; v.p. Curtis Inst. Music, Phila., 1995—; mng. ptnr. Dover Stevenson & Assocs., 1987—. With USAF, 1958-61. Mem. U.S. C. of C., Assn. Fund Raising Profls. (Mass. chpt. bd. dirs., v.p. 1993-95, Greater Phila. chpt. bd. dirs., v.p. fin. 1996—), Dartmouth Club, Tokyo Lawn Tennis Club, Yale-Dartmouth Club (N.Y.C.), Badminton and Tennis Club (Boston). Independent. Presbyterian. Home: Spring Pond Rd PO Box 1810 Norwich VT 05055-1810 Office: Curtis Inst Music 1726 Locust St Philadelphia PA 19103-6187 E-mail: JosiahS4@aol.com.

STEVENSON, KATHERINE HOLLER, federal agency administrator; b. Jan. 20, 1948; d. Jacob W. and Sheila Holler; m. Donald Stevenson, aug. 14, 1982; 2 children. BA, Skidmore Coll., 1969; MA, U. Del., 1971. Researcher Nat. portrait Gallery, Smithsonian Inst., Washington, 1971; with Nat. Park Svc., 1972-80, Denver, 1980-87, Phila., 1987-95, assoc. dir. Washington, 1995—. Co-author: Houses by Mail, 1983. Recipient Meritorious Svc. award Dept. Interior, 1994. Office: Nat Park Svc Cultural Resource 1849 C St NW Washington DC 20240-0001 E-mail: Kate_Stevenson@nps.gov.

STEVENSON, KENNETH LEE, chemist, educator; b. Ft. Wayne, Ind., Aug. 1, 1939; s. Willard Henry and Luella Marie (Meyer) S.; m. Virginia Grace Lowe, Dec. 26, 1959 (dec. Mar. 1991); children: Melinda Anne, Jill Marie; m. Carmen Ramona Kmety, May 9, 1992. BS, Purdue U., 1961, MS, 1965; PhD, U. Mich., 1968. Tchr. Ladoga High Sch., Ind., 1961-63; tchr. Central High Sch., Pontiac, Mich., 1963-65; prof. chemistry Ind.-Purdue U., Ft. Wayne, 1968—, chmn. dept. chemistry, 1979-86, 87—, acting dean Sch. Sci. and Humanities, 1986-87. Sabbatical visitor Solar Energy Research Inst., Golden, Colo., 1980; vis. faculty N.Mex. State U., Las Cruces, 1975-76 Author: Charge Transfer Photochemistry of Coordination Compounds, 1993, also numerous rsch. papers. Mem. Am. Chem. Soc. (chmn. Northeastern Ind. sect. 1978-79, Chemist of Yr. 1979, 93), Inter-Am. Photochem. Soc., Phi Kappa Phi, Sigma Xi. Office: Ind U-Purdue U Dept Chemistry Fort Wayne IN 46805 E-mail: stevenso@ipfw.edu.

STEVENSON, LAURA CAROLINE, writer, educator; b. Ann Arbor, Mich., Sept. 8, 1946; d. Charles Leslie and Louise Ellen (Destler) S.; m. Michael William O'Connell, Sept. 27, 1969 (div. July 1981); children: Katharine O'Connell, Margaret O'Connell; m. Franklin D. Reeve, Dec. 22, 1997. AB with highest honors, U. Mich., 1968; MPhil, Yale U., 1971, PhD, 1974. Lectr. history U. Calif., Santa Barbara, 1970-71; prof. humanities Bradford Coll., Haverhill, Mass., 1980-83, Marlboro (Vt.) Coll., 1986—. Author: Praise and Paradox, 1984, Happily After All, 1990, The Island and the Ring, 1991, All the King's Horses, 2001. Mem. Vt. Natural Resources Coun., Windham County Farm Bureau. Recipient Grant-in-Aid, Am. Coun. Learned Socs., Andrew W. Mellon Faculty fellowship Harvard U., 1982-83, NEH rsch. fellow, 1996-97. Mem.: AAUW, Authors Guild, Royal Oak Found., Assn. Late-Deafened Adults, Beatrix Potter Soc., Phi Beta Kappa. Quaker-Soc. of Friends. Mem. Soc. Of Friends. Avocations: horseback riding, farming. Home: PO Box 14 Wilmington VT 05363-0014 Office: Marlboro Coll Dept Humanities Marlboro VT 05344 E-mail: lsteve@marlboro.edu.

STEVENSON, MICHAEL E. metallurgical engineer; b. New Orleans, July 16, 1976; s. Michael and Marilyn Stevenson; m. Julie S Simon. BS in Metall. Engring., U. Ala., 1998, MS in Metall. Engring., 1999, PhD in Metall. Engring., 2001. Metall. engr. USM Corp., New Orleans, 1998—2000; rsch. assoc. U. Ala., Tuscaloosa, 1998—2001; chief forensic metallurgist QORE Inc. - Materials Engring. Divsn., Suwanee, Ga., 2001—. Office: QORE Inc. Materials Engring Divsn 1039 Industrial Ct Suwanee GA 30024

STEVENSON, NANCY NELSON, museum executive; b. Annapolis, Md., Oct. 23, 1950; d. Perry Waldemar and Grace Anne Nelson; m. Roger Stevenson Jr., Nov. 18, 1972; children: Jennifer Loren, Matthew Austin. BA, Sarah Lawrence Coll., 1972. Tchr. Montgomery County (Md.) Pub. Schs., 1972—76; bd. dirs. Jr. League of Washington, 1988—89, 1990—92; trustee Nat. Mus. Women in the Arts, 1996—, sec. bd. of trustees, 1997—98, treas. bd. of trustees, 1998—2002, v.p. bd. trustees, 2002—. Co-author French immersion curriculum, 1974. Pres. Country Pl. Citizens Assn., Potomac, Md., 1983-84. Office: Nat Mus Women in the Arts 1250 New York Ave NW Washington DC 20005-3970

STEVENSON, PAUL MICHAEL, physics educator, researcher; b. Denham, Eng., Oct. 10, 1954; came to U.S., 1983; s. Jeremy and Jean Helen (Jennings) S. BA, Cambridge (Eng.) U., 1976; PhD, Imperial Coll., London, 1979. Rsch. assoc. U. Wis., Madison, 1979-81, 1983-84; fellow European Orgn. for Nuclear Rsch., Geneva, 1981-83; sr. rsch. assoc. Rice U., Houston, 1984-86, asst. prof. physics, 1986-89, assoc. prof., 1989-93; prof. physics, 1993—. Contbr. articles to profl. jours. Avocation: music. E-mail: stevenson@physics.rice.edu.

STEVENSON, ROBERT BENJAMIN, III, prosthodontist, writer; b. Topeka, Feb. 13, 1950; s. Robert Benjamin and Martha (McClelland) S.; m. Barbara Jean Sulick, June 6, 1975; children: Jody Ann, Robert Woodrow. BS, U. Miami, Coral Gables, Fla., 1972; DDS, Ohio State U., 1975, MS, MA, cert. in prosthodontics splty. tng., Ohio State U., 1980. Practice dentistry specializing in prosthodontics, Columbus, Ohio, 1981—; clin. asst. prof. Ohio State U., 1981-87, 98—. Chmn. oral cancer com. Columbus Dental Soc., 1981-85, Am. Cancer Soc., Columbus, 1985-97; trustee Ohio Divsn, 1997-2000; vol. dentist Provodencialis Ctr., Turks and Chicos Islands, Brit. West Indies, 1982-87. Editor Columbus Dental Soc. Bull., 1981-87, 89-92; assoc. editor Ohio State U. Dental Alumni Quar., 1982—, Am. Med. Writer's Assn. Ohio Newsletter, 1983-86, Ohio State Journalism Alumni Assn. Newsletter, 1986-88, alumni spotlight editor, 1995—; assoc. editor Jour. Prosthetic Dentistry, 1987-92; mem. editl. coun. Jour. Prosthetic Dentistry; inventor intraoral measuring device. Vol. Am. Cancer Soc., Columbus, 1982—, Gahanna and Reynoldsburg, Ohio, 1983, 84; fundraiser Columbus council Boy Scouts of Am., 1984; Served to capt. USAF, 1975-78. Mem. ADA, Am. Coll. Prosthodontists, Ohio Dental Assn. (alt. del. 1982-89, del. 1990-92, 97—, editor new products newsletter 1988-97), Carl Boucher Prosthodontic Conf. (editor 1987-92, sec. 1992-98, treas. 1998—), Procrastinator's Club Am, Columbus Downtown Quarterback Club. Avocations: playing electric organ, golf, music, reading. Home: 1300 Southport Cir Columbus OH 43235-7642 Office: Riverview Profl Village 3600 Olentangy River Rd Columbus OH 43214 E-mail: stevenson.113@osu.edu.

STEVENSON, ROBERT B. software company executive, application developer; b. Tampa, Fla., Apr. 30, 1973; s. Robert Barclay and Eleanor Sue Stevenson. BS in Design, N.C. State U., 1995, postgrad., 1996. Cert. MSOUS Expert - Project '98 1999. Freelance design and programming various, Raleigh, NC, 1992—96; rschr., programmer Virtual Environments Lab, 1993—96; designer/prodr. Interactive Magic, Research Triangle Park, 1995—99; sr. prodr. Virtus Entertainment, Cary, 1999; v.p. product devel. iROCK Interactive, 2000—. Bd. dirs. North Carolina Online, Raleigh, 1998—2000. Contbr. articles; programmer (software) Architectural Courseware, 1994, Harpoon, 1997, Warbirds 2.0, 1998, Operation Flash Point, 1999, Savage Skies, 2002. Recipient Louis Sullivan Design Competition award, Constrn. Specification Inst./NC Brick, 1995, 3D Studio r3 Student Work - Siggraph award, Autodesk, 1995. Mem.: Internat. High IQ Soc., Project Mgmt. Inst., DirectX Adv. Coun., Assn. for Computing Machinergy, Internat. Game Developers Assn.

STEVENSON, ROBERT MURRELL, music educator, educator; b. Melrose, N.Mex., July 3, 1916; s. Robert Emory and Ada (Ross) S. AB, U. Tex., El Paso, 1936; grad., Juilliard Grad. Sch. Music, 1938; MusM, Yale, 1939; PhD, U. Rochester, 1942; STB cum laude, Harvard U., 1943; BLitt, Oxford (Eng.) U.; Th.M., Princeton Theol. Sem.; DMus honoris causa, Cath. U. Am., 1991; LHD honoris causa, Ill. Wesleyan U., 1992; LittD honoris causa, Universidade Nova de Lisboa, 1993. Instr. music U. Tex., 1941-43, 46; faculty Westminster Choir Coll., Princeton, N.J., 1946-49; faculty research lectr. UCLA, 1981, mem. faculty to prof. music, 1949—. Vis. asst. prof. Columbia, 1955-56; vis. prof. Ind. U., Bloomington, 1959-60, U. Chile, 1965-66, Northwestern U., Chgo., 1976, U. Granada, 1992; adj. prof. Cath. U. Am., 1991—; cons. UNESCO, 1977; Louis Charles Elson lectr. Libr. of Congress, Washington, 1969; inaugural prf. musicology Nat. U. Mex., 1996; spkr. Dumbarton Oaks Pre-Columbian Music Workshop, 1998, Internat. Colonial Music Congress, Lima, Peru, 2000; lectr. Tureck Bach Rsch. Found., Oxford U., 2000; hon. prof. Conservatorio Nacional, Peru, 2000. *He was the national winner of the Joseph M. Bearns Composition prize awarded by Columbia University in 1942. He headlined an entire program of his compositions at Town Hall, New York, in March 1947. Leopold Stokowski conducted the Philadelphia Orchestra in premiere performances of two of his compositions in 1961. In Spain on May 8, 1997, he received in person the third gold medal awarded by the Real Conservatorio Superior. On July 17, 1997, he was Keynote Speaker at the 1997 Inter-American Conference on Black Music Research in Chicago. On March 13, 1999, he received the first Lifetime Achievement Award bestowed by the National Society for American Music. In November 2001 he was inducted as an honorary member of the America Musicological Societ at its national meeting.* Author: Music in Mexico, 1952, Patterns of Protestant Church Music, 1953, La musica en la catedral de Sevilla, 1954, 85, Music Before the Classic Era, 1955, Shakespeare's Religious Frontier, 1958, The Music of Peru, 1959, Juan Bermudo, 1960, Spanish Music in the Age of Columbus, 1960, Spanish Cathedral Music in the Golden Age, 1961, La musica colonial en Colombia, 1964, Protestant Church Music in America, 1966, Music in Aztec and Inca Territory, 1968, Renaissance and Baroque Musical Sources in the Americas, 1970, Music in El Paso, 1970, Philosophies of American Music History, 1970, Written Sources for Indian Music Until 1882, 1972, Christmas Music From Baroque Mexico, 1974, Foundations of New World Opera, 1973, Seventeenth Century Villancicos, 1974, Latin American Colonial Music Anthology, 1975, Vilancicos Portugueses, 1976, Josquin in the Music of Spain and Portugal, 1977, American Musical Scholarship, Parker to Thayer, 1978, Liszt at Madrid and Lisbon, 1980, Wagner's Latin American Outreach, 1983, Spanish Musical Impact Beyond the Pyrenees, 1250-1500, 1985, La Música en las catedrales españolas del Siglo de Oro, 1993; contbg. editor: Handbook Latin Am. Studies, 1976—; editor Inter-Am. Music Rev., 1978—; contbr. to New Grove Dictionary of Music and Musicians, 17 other internat. encys. Served to capt. U.S. Army, 1943-46, 49. Decorated Army Commendation ribbon; fellow Ford Found., 1953-54, Gulbenkian Found., 1966, 81, Guggenheim Found., 1962, NEH, 1974, Comité Conjunto Hispano-Norteamericano (Madrid), 1989; recipient Fulbright rsch. awards, 1958-59, 64, 70-71, 88-89, Carnegie Found. tchg. award, 1955-56, Gabriela Mistral award OAS, 1985, Heitor Villa Lobos Jury award OAS, 1988, OAS medal, 1986, Cert. Merit Mexican Consulate San Bernardino, Calif., 1987, Silver medal Spanish Ministry Culture, 1989, Gold medal Real Conservatorio Superior, 1994, 97, 1st Lifetime Achievement award Sonneck Soc., 1999. Mem. Am. Musicol. Soc. (hon. life, Pacific SW chpt.), Real Academia de Bellas Artes, Hispanic Soc. Am., Am. Liszt Soc. (cons. editor), Heterofonia (cons. editor), Brazilian Musicol. Soc. (hon.), Portuguese Musicol. Soc. (hon.), Argentinian Musicol. Soc. (hon.), Am. Musicol. Soc. (hon.), Orden Andrés Bello, Primera Clase, Venezuela, 1992. Avocation: playing piano. Office: UCLA Dept Music 405 Hilgard Ave Los Angeles CA 90095-9000 Fax: 310-206-9203.

STEVENSON, SARAH SCHOALES, rancher, business owner; b. N.Y.C., Sept. 1, 1944; d. Dudley Nevison and Virginia Jocelyn (Vanderlip) Schoales; m. David Earl Hollatz, Jan. 27, 1968 (div. June 1985); children: Melissa Virginia, Peter David; m. Richard Stevenson, Sept. 1, 1995. BS, U. Wis., 1966; postgrad., U. So. Calif., L.A., 1966. Copywriter Max W. Becker Advt., Long Beach, Calif., 1966-67; advt. dir. officers news USN, Coronado, 1968-70; with syndicate dept. Morgan Stanley & Co., N.Y.C., 1970-72; lay-out asst. North Castle News, Armonk, N.Y., 1972-75; performer, writer Candy Band, Pound Ridge, 1975-82; owner, mgr. Circle Bar Guest Ranch, Utica, Mont., 1983—. Bd. dirs. Park Inn, Lewistown, Mont.; co-founder, producer, dir. The Garage Theater, 1998. Artist, composer: Play Me a Song, 1978, Going Home, 1980; composer: (mus. play) Elsie Piddock, 1979, Secret Garden, 1981, Windows, 1989. Soloist Hobson (Mont.) Meth. Ch., 1983—; founder What the Hay, Utica, 1990—. Mem. Mont. Emergency Med. Assn. (bd. dirs. 1990—), Dude Rancher's Assn. (bd. dirs. 1989—, pres. 1996, 97). Episcopalian. Avocations: horse breeding, literature, finance. Home and Office: Circle Bar Guest Ranch Utica MT 59452

STEVENSON, THOMAS HERBERT, management consultant, writer, adult education educator; b. Covington, Ohio, Oct. 16, 1951; s. Robert Louis and Dolly Eileen (Minnich) S.; m. Jackie Lowe, June 1, 1997. BA in Econs./Comm., Wright State U., 1977; MA in Psychology, Cleve. State U., 2001. Cert. regulatory compliance mgr. Am. Bankers Assn., 1990; cert. Gestalt Practitioner, Gestalt Inst. Cleve., 1999. Teaching asst., rsch. asst. Wright State U., Dayton, Ohio, 1975-77; teaching asst. Bowling Green (Ohio) State U., 1978; loan officer Western Ohio Nat. Bank & Trust Co., 1979-80, asst. v.p. adminstrs., 1981-82, v.p. mgmt. svcs. div., 1983-85; bank mgmt. cons. Young & Assocs., Inc., Kent, Ohio, 1985-86, exec. v.p., 1987-2000; mem. faculty Gestalt Inst. Cleve., 2001—, Cleve. State U., 2002—. Legis. impact analyst Community Bankers Ohio, 1985-94, Community Bankers Ga., 1988-94; mem. exec. com. Owl Electronic Banking Network 1981-85; mem. faculty Gestalt Inst. Cleve., 2001—. Author: Compliance for Community Banks, 1987, Compliance Deskbook, 1988, Internal Audit for Community Banks, 1989, Truth in Lending for the Community Bank, 1989, Bank Protection for the Community Bank, 1989, Community Reinvestment Act for the Community Bank, 1989, Executive Management Guide to an Effective Board of Directors, 1990, The Board of Directors, 1990, The Home Mortgage Disclosure Guide, 1990, A Guide to Flood Insurance, 1990, Insider Lending, 1990, A Guide to the Equal Credit Opportunity Act, 1990, Investment Management, 1990, Contingency Planning, 1990, Insider Conduct, 1990, Currency Transaction Reporting Deskbook, 1990, Property Appraisal Deskbook, 1991, Bank Protection Deskbook, 1991, Regulatory Management Deskbook, 1991, Record Retention Deskbook, 1991, Environmental Deskbook for Financial Institutions, 1992, Deposit Compliance Deskbook, 1992, Fair Housing Deskbook, 1992, Insider Lending Deskbook, 1992, CRA Deskbook, 1992, Investment Mgmt. Deskbook, 1992, Internal Audit Deskbook, 1993; contbr. articles to profl. jours. Mem. adv. bd. Upper Valley Joint Vocat. Sch. for Fin. Instns., 1981-85, Am. Indian Edn. Ctr., Cleve. Cpl. USMC, 1972-73. Recipient George Washington medal of Honor Freedom's Found., 1974. Mem. Nat. Mus. Am. Indian (charter), Am. Inst. Banking (adv. bd. 1982-85), Native Am. Heritage Assn., Inst. Noetic Scis., Eagles Club, Gestalt Inst. Cleve. Republican. Mem. Ch. of Brethren. Home and Office: 3750 Chagrin River Rd Chagrin Falls OH 44022-1130 E-mail: Therbstevenson@aol.com.

STEVENSON, THOMAS RAY, plastic surgeon; b. Kansas City, Mo., Jan. 22, 1946; s. John Adolph and Helen Ray (Clarke) S.; m. Judith Ann Hunter, Aug. 17, 1968; children: Anne Hunter, Andrew Thomas. BA, U. Kans., 1968, MD. Diplomate Am. Bd. Plastic and Reconstructive Surgery, Am. Bd. Surgery. Resident in gen. surgery U. Va., Charlottesville, 1972-78; resident in plastic surgery Emory U., Atlanta, 1980-82; asst. prof. surgery U. Mich., 1982-88, assoc. prof. surgery, 1988-89. Chief plastic surgery Ann Arbor VA Hosp., 1982—, U. Calif., Davis, 1989—. Served to maj. USAR, 1978-80. Fellow ACS; mem. Am. Soc. Plastic and Reconstructive Surgery. Office: UC Davis Divsn Plas Surg 4301 X St Ste 2430 Sacramento CA 95817-2214

STEVENSON, WARREN HOWARD, mechanical engineering educator; b. Rock Island, Ill., Nov. 18, 1938; s. Joseph Howard and Camilla Irene (Darnall) S.; m. Judith Ann Fleener, June 7, 1959; children: Kathleen, Kevin, Kent. BSME, Purdue U., 1960, MSME, 1963, PhD, 1965. Engr. Martin Co., Denver, 1960-61; rsch. asst., instr. Purdue U., West Lafayette, Ind., 1961-65, asst. prof., 1965-68, assoc. prof., 1968-74, prof., 1974—, asst. dean engring., 1992-97, assoc. dean engring., 1997—. Guest prof. U. Karlsruhe, Germany, 1973-74; vis. prof. Ibaraki U., Hitachi, Japan, 1993; mem. tech. conf. coms. various profl. groups. Editor: Laser Velocimetry and Particle Sizing, 1979; mem. editorial bd. Jour. Laser Applications, 1988-98; contbr. articles to profl. jours.; patentee in field. U.S. sr. scientist Alexander von Humboldt Found., Fed. Republic Germany, 1973. Fellow Laser Inst. Am. (bd. dirs. 1984—, pres. 1989); mem. ASME, Optical Soc. Am. Avocations: sailing, photography. Office: Purdue U Sch Mech Engring Engring Adminstrn West Lafayette IN 47907

STEVENSON, WILLIAM ALEXANDER, retired justice of Supreme Court of Canada; b. Edmonton, Alta., Can., May 7, 1934; s. Alexander Lindsay and Eileen Harriet (Burns) S.; m. Patricia Ann Stevenson; children: Catherine, Kevin, Vivian, James. BA, U. Alta., Edmonton, 1956, LLB, 1957; LLD (hon.), U. Alta., 1992. Called to Alta. bar, 1958. Ptnr. Hurlburt Reynolds Stevenson &

Agrios, Edmonton, 1957-68; prof. U. Alta., 1968-70; ptnr. Reynolds Stevenson & Agrios, Edmonton, 1970-75; judge Dist. Ct. Alta., 1975-79; justice Ct. of Queens Bench Alta., 1979-80, Ct. of Appeal Alta., Edmonton, 1980-90, Supreme Ct. Can., Ottawa, Ont., 1990-92. Officer Order of Can., 1997. Co-author: Civil Procedure Guide, 1995. Mem. Can. Bar Assn., Can. Inst. for Adminstrn. Justice (pres. 1983-85, hon. dir.), Nat. Jud. Inst. (hon. dir.). Home: 7 Laurier Pl Edmonton AB Canada T5R 5P4

STEVENSON, WILLIAM EDWARD, chemical engineer; b. Farmington, Mo., Apr. 21, 1938; s. Herbert Coleman and Mary Jeannetta (Harrington) S.; m. Ramona Ann Shrum, Aug. 29, 1959; children: Marjorie Ellene, Gretchen Faithe. BS in ChemE, Washington U., St. Louis, 1971. Lab tchnician Internat. Oil Burner, St. Louis, 1959-61; maintenance supt. Lever Brothers Co., 1961-74; mgr. hose dept. Haywood Co., Brownsville, Tenn., 1974-95, safety mgr., 1995—. Pres. Haywood County Band Boosters, 1981-83, Haywood County Edn. Task Force, 1985-86; chmn. Haywood County Indsl. Com., 1989-91, mem., 1994—; chmn. Haywood County Job Svc. Employers Com., 1991—, Haywood County Ptnrs. in Edn. Com., 1987-94, Haywood County Rep. Com., 1995—; pres. bd. elders Luth. Ch., 1987-90; chmn. bd. edn. Concordia Luth. Ch. and Sch., 1990-93; v.p. Haywood County Arts Coun., 1994, 95, pres., 1995-96; mem. distbn. com. United Way, 1996-97; bd. dirs. Jackson Tenn. Symphony, 1999. Mem. ASSE, Haywood County C. of C., Brownsville Rotary (pres. elect 1996, pres. 1998). Avocations: fishing, golf, gardening. Home: 127 Hillcrest St Brownsville TN 38012-2702 Office: Haywood Co 751 Dupree Rd Brownsville TN 38012-6255

STEVENSON, WILLIAM EDWARD, III, language educator; b. Balt., Aug. 4, 1948; s. William Edward and Gladys Margaret (Kaufman) S. BA, Johns Hopkins U., 1970, MA, 1972, MEd, 1974; PhD, U. Pa., 1975. Cert. tchr., Md. Grad. instr. Johns Hopkins U., Balt., 1970-72; cons. Stevenson & Kelly, 1975-78; tchr. lang. City of Balt. pub. schs., 1978—. Cons. S.A.T. Prep, Balt., 1986-87, Morgan State U., Balt., 1989-90; adj. prof. Essex C.C., 1999, 2000-01. Author: Pathological Grotesque in Greek and Roman Art, 1975. Head adult sch. Grace Meth. Ch., 1994—. Fellow Daniel Coit Gilman fellow, Johns Hopkins U., 1970—72, David and Lucille Packard fellow, Am. Sch., Athens, Greece, 1972, NEH, 1987, Rockefeller fellow, 1987. Democrat. Methodist. Avocations: photography, painting, drawing, sculpture, coin collecting. Office: Roland Park Sch (233) 5207 Roland Ave Baltimore MD 21210-1334 Fax: 410-396-7662. E-mail: mhardiman@bepsk12md.us.

STEVENSON, WILLIAM ROBERT, retired military historian, genealogist; b. Vero Beach, Fla., Aug. 27, 1920; s. Albert "Bert" Noble and Laura Belle (Atkin) S.; m. Beatrice Ruth Levy, Dec. 13, 1947; children: Fredrick Philip (dec.), Robert John, William Rudolph, Earl Marion, Edith May Doland. AB, Ind. U., 1948. Ednl. advisor USAF, Germany, 1950-51, mil. historian Germany, 1951-56, Mobile (Ala.) Air Material Area, 1956-58; tech. writer Missile Command, Huntsville, Ala., 1958-60; mil. historian White Sands (N.Mex.) Missile Range, 1960-63, Electronics Command, Eatontown, N.J., 1963-77. Merit badge councilor Boy Scouts Am., Vero Beach, Fla., 1984—, troop committeeman troop 551, 1987—. With USN, 1939-45. Mem. SAR (registrar, genealogist Fla. chpt. 1985—), War of 1812 (registrar, registrar, genealogist Treasure Coast chpt., genealogist Fla. chpt. 1997—), Descs. Washington's Army at Valley Forge (registrar Fla. brigade). Republican. Methodist. Avocation: genealogy.

STEVENS-SOLLMAN, JEANNE LEE, artist; d. Ernest Gustave and Virginia Hawes; m. Philippus Steven Sollman, Oct. 16, 1971. BS, R.I. Coll., 1968, BFA, 1970; MFA in Ceramics, Pa. State U., 1972, postgrad., 1986-87. Artist in residence, instr. ceramics Juniata Coll., Huntingdon, Pa., 1975-76; artist in residence State Coll. (Pa.) Area H.S., 1995; instr. ceramics Haystack Mountain Sch. Crafts, Deer Isle, Maine, 1977, Pa. State U., University Park, 1978. Coord., dir. Trout Run Medallic Symposium, St. Marys, Pa., 1997, 99, 2001; juror Am. delegation Fedn. Internat. de la Medaille, The Hague, The Netherlands, 1998; juror, coord. Am. Medallic Sculpture Assn., Polish Artist Union Exhibit, Colorado Springs, 2001, Polish medals from Collection of Medallic Mus. Art, Wraclaw, Poland, Hands Across the Sea exhibit, 2002, F.I.D.E.M., Paris Mint; cons. in field. One-person shows include Handcrafters Gallery, Portland, Maine, 1984, Soc. Arts and Crafts, Boston, 1984, Susan McLeod Gallery, Sarasota, Fla., 1984, Palisander Gallery, Taos, N.Mex., 1986, 15 Steps, Ithaca, N.Y., 1987, Am. Numismatic Soc., N.Y.C., 1999, Shippensburg (Pa.) U., 2001; recent group exhbns. include The Pen and Brush Club, N.Y., 1997, 98 (Medallic Art Co. award), 99 (Margaret Sussman Meml. award), 2000, 01, 02 (Charlotte Dunwiddie Meml. award 2002), Art Show at the Dog Show, Wichita, Kans., 2002, Rack and Hamper Gallery, N.Y., 1997, 99, 2000, Gallery Heian, Kyoto, Japan, 1997, Art Alliance Gallery, Lemont, Pa., 1997, U. Park Campus Mall Pa. State U., University Park, 1998, Sculptures at Sea Mus., The Hague, 1998, Benson Park, Loveland, Colo., 1998, 99, 2000, Bedford (Pa.) Art Arts Coun., 1999, So. Alleghenies Mus. Art, Loretto, Pa., 1999, University Park Campus Pa. State U., 1999, 2000, Mus. of the Dog, St. Louis, 1999, Altoona (Pa.) Campus Pa. State U., 1999, Queensboro (N.Y.) C.C., 2000, Goethe Nat. Mus., Weimar, Germany, 2000, HUB Pa. State U., 2001, Shippensburg (Pa.) U., 2001, Maguro Mus. Art, Tokyo, 2001, Nat. Sculpture Soc., 2001, numerous others. Co-partitioner Patton Concerned Citizens, Centre County, Pa., 1990. Recipient Dutch Art Metal award Dutch Art Metal Soc., The Hague, 1998, Distinction in Sculpture award So. Alleghenies Mus. Art, Loretto, Pa., 1997, 1st prize sculpture Rural Am. 2000, Harrisburg, Pa., 2000, J. Sanford award for signal achievement in the art of the medal. Fellow Am. Numismatic Soc. (J. Sanford Saltus award 1999); mem. Am. Sculpture Assn., Nat. Sculpture Soc., Pen and Brush (Margaret Sussman Meml. award 1999), Fedn. Internat. de la Medaille (co. del., vice del. for USA 1999—), Am. Medallic Sculpture Assn. (2d v.p. 1987—, pres. 2001—), Art in Common. Avocations: gardening, dogtrials & showing, shepherding. Studio: Stevens Sollman Studios 318 N Fillmore Rd Bellefonte PA 16823-9047 E-mail: stevsollmn@aol.com.

STEVENTON, ROBERT WESLEY, marketing executive; b. Allentown, Pa., Nov. 2, 1948; s. Robert Wesley and Catherine May (Feineur) S; m. Deborah Damon Barrett, Aug. 29, 1977; children: Calvin Nathaniel, Alexander MacAuley. BA, Pa. State U., 1970; MA, U. Minn., 1975; Cert. Resident, Cambridge U., Eng., 1992. Mktg. specialist U.S. Bur. of Census, Washington, 1975-77; mktg. mgr. Am. Chem. Soc., 1978-83; account exec. Kreitlow & Assocs., Silver Spring, Md., 1983-84; sr. account exec. Mktg. Gen., Inc., Washington, 1984-85, v.p. Alexandria, Va., 1985-89, sr. v.p., 1989-94; pres. AB&C Mktg., McLean, 1994-2000; mng. ptnr. iMark Comms. Ltd., Fairfax, 2000—. Dir. Intelmark Corp., 1995—, Immedia Corp., 1999—, InfoQuest Comms. Corp., 1999—, InfoQuest Comm. Corp., 2000—; advisor Euro Broadcasting Corp., 1996-99; lectr. Direct Mktg. Assn., Washington, 1988-92, Coun. Engring. and Sci. Soc. Execs., N.Y.C., 1988-98; gen. chmn. Direct Mktg. Days Conv. Com., Washington, 1988. Mem. com. econ. devel. bur. Greater Washington Bd. Trade, 1989-92, bus. mktg. com., 1993-96; mem. Greater Washington Initiative, 1999—; vol. Christ House, Alexandria, Va., 1987—. With U.S. Army, 1970-73. Recipient Capital award Nat. Leadership Coun., 1992. Mem. Am. Soc. Assn. Execs. (membership com. 1989—), Am.-European Cmty. Assn., Brit. Am. Bus. Assn., Direct Mktg. Assn. Washington (bd. dirs. 1983-85), Soc. for Assn. Mktg. Internat. (pres. 1991-94), Assn. Svcs. Group (chmn. bd. 1996-2000), Order St. Etheldreda (officer 1993), Manorial Soc. Gt. Britain (life), Army and Navy Club Washington, Salisbury Club (U.K.), Kappa Tau Alpha. Republican. Episcopalian. Avocations: downhill skiing, bicycling, golf. Office: iMark Comm Ltd Ste 380 13135 Lee-Jackson Hwy Fairfax VA 22033-1907

STEVER, DONALD WINFRED, lawyer; b. Altoona, Pa., Jan. 25, 1944; s. Donald Winfred and June Lily (Bargfrede) S.; m. Betsy Jean Seaman, May 28, 1968 (div. Oct. 1975); 1 child, Heather Elene; m. Margo Leaman Taft, July 30, 1976; children: David Whittaker, James Taft. BA, Lehigh U., 1965; JD, U. Pa., 1968. Bar: Conn. 1968, N.H. 1969, D.C. 1983, N.Y. 1983, U.S. Dist. Ct. N.H. 1969, U.S. Dist. Ct. Conn. 1986, U.S. Dist. Ct. (so. dist.) N.Y. 1985, U.S. Dist. Ct. (no. and we. dists.) N.Y. 1990, U.S. Ct. Appeals (1st cir.) 1974, U.S. Ct. Appeals (10th cir.) 1980, U.S. Ct. Appeals (5th, 11th and Fed. cirs.) 1982, U.S. Ct. Appeals (2d cir.) 1990, U.S. Supreme Ct. 1972. Atty. Aetna Life & Casualty co., Hartford, Conn., 1968-69, Office of N.H. Atty. Gen., Concord, 1969-72, asst. atty. gen., chief environ. protection, 1972-77; atty. pollution control sect. U.S. Dept. Justice, Washington, 1978-79, chief pollution control sect., 1979-80, chief environ. def. sect., 1980-82; prof. Pace U. Sch. Law, White Plains, N.Y., 1982-87, adj. prof. environ. law, 1987-92; ptnr. Sidley and Austin, N.Y.C., 1987-93, Dewey Ballantine, N.Y.C., 1993—. Bd. dirs. Environ. Law Inst., Washington, chmn., 1996-97, Hudson Valley Writers Ctr. Inc., Tarrytown, N.Y. Author: Seabrook and The Nuclear Regulatory Commission, 1980; Law of Chemical Reation and Hazardous Waste, 1986; editor: Environmental Law & Practice, 1992; co-editor Environmental Law & Practice, 1992. Bd. dirs. Biddeford Pool (Maine) Improvement Assn., 1989-93; mem. adv. com. North Tarrytown (N.Y.) Conservation, 1989—. Mem. Biddeford Pool Yacht Club (treas. 1989-92, sec. 1992—), Sleepy Hollow Country Club, Abenakee Club, Mill Reef Club. Avocations: golf, tennis, sailboat racing, early music. Home: 157 Millard Ave North Tarrytown NY 10591-1412 Office: Dewey Ballantine 1301 Avenue Of The Americas New York NY 10019-6022

STEVER, HORTON GUYFORD, aerospace scientist and engineer, educator, consultant; b. Corning, N.Y., Oct. 24, 1916; s. Ralph Raymond and Alma (Matt) Stever; m. Louise Risley Floyd, June 29, 1946; children: Horton Guyford, Sarah, Margarette, Roy. AB, Colgate U., 1938, Sc.D. (hon.) , 1958; PhD, Calif. Inst. Tech., 1941; LL.D., Lafayette Coll., U. Pitts., 1966, Lehigh U., 1967, Allegheny Coll., 1968, Ill. Inst. Tech., 1975; D.Sc., Northwestern U., 1966; DSc, Waynesburg Coll., 1967, U. Mo., 1975; D.Sc., Clark U., 1976; DSc, Bates Coll., 1977; DH, Seton Hill Coll., 1968; D.Engring., Washington and Jefferson Coll., 1969, Widener Coll., Poly. Inst. N.Y., 1972, Villanova U., 1973, U. Notre Dame, 1974; DPS, George Washington U., 1981. Staff radiation lab. MIT, Cambridge, Mass., 1941—42, asst. prof., 1946—51, assoc. prof. aero. engring., 1951—56, prof. aero. and astro., 1956—65, head depts. mech. engring., naval architecture, marine engring., 1961—65, assoc. dean engring., 1956—59, exec. officer guided missiles program, 1946—48; chief scientist USAF, 1955—56; pres. Carnegie-Mellon U., Pitts., 1965—72; dir. NSF, Washington, 1972—76; sci. adviser, chmn. Fed. Council Sci. and Tech., 1973—76; dir. Office Sci. and Tech. Policy, sci. and tech. adviser to Pres., 1976—77, sci. cons., corp. trustee, 1977—. Secretariat guided missiles com. Joint Chiefs of Staff, 1945; sci. liaison officer London Mission, OSRD, 1942—45; guided missiles tech. evaluation group Rsch. and Devel. Bd., 1946—48; sci. adv. bd. to chief of staff USAF, 1947—69, chmn., 1962—69; steering com. tech. adv panel on aeros. Dept. Def., 1956—62; chmn. spl. com. space tech. NASA, chmn. rsch. adv. com. missile and spacecraft aerodynamics, 1959—65; mem. Nat. Sci. Bd., 1970—72, ex-officio, chmn. exec. com., 1972—75; mem. Def. Sci. Bd., 1962—68; adv. panel U.S. Ho. Reps. Com. Sci. and Astronautics, 1959—72; mem. Pres.'s Commn. on Patent System, 1965—67; chmn. U.S.-USSR Joint Commn. Sci. and Tech. Cooperation, 1973—77, Fed. Council Arts and Humanities, 1972—76; Pres. com. Nat. Sci. medal, 1973—77. Author: Flight, 1965; contbr. articles to profl. jours. Past trustee Colgate U., Shady Side Acad., Sarah Mellon Scaife Found., Buckingham Sch.; trustee Univ. Rsch Assn., 1977—, pres., 1982—85; trustee Woods Hole Oceanographic Inst., 1980—. Sci. Svc., 1982—, Univ. Corp. for Atmospheric Rsch., 1980—83; bd. dirs. Saudi Arabia Nat. Ctr. for Sci. and Tech., 1978—81; bd. govs. U.S. Israel Binat. Sci. Found., 1972—76, chmn., 1972—73; mem. Carnegie Commn. on Sci., Tech. and Govt., 1988—93. Recipient Pres.'s Cert. of Merit, 1948, Exceptional Civilian Svc. award, USAF, 1956, Scott Gold medal, Am. Ordinance Assn., 1960, Disting. Pub. Svc. medal, award, Dept. Def., 1969, NASA, 1988, Nat. Medal of Sci., 1991. Fellow: AAAS, AIAA (hon.; pres. 1960—62), Am. Phys. Soc., Royal Soc. Arts, Am. Philos. Soc., Am. Acad. Arts and Scis., Royal Aero. Soc.; mem.: NAE (chmn. aero. and space engring. bd. 1967—69, fgn. sec. 1984—88), NAS (chmn. assembly engring. 1979—83, chmn. policy divsn. 1995—97), Royal Acad. of Engring. of Great Britain (fgn. mem.), Acad. Engring. of Japan (fgn. mem.), Bohemian, Cosmos Club, Phi Beta Kappa, Tau Beta Pi, Sigma Gamma Tau, Sigma Xi. Episcopalian. Office: 588 Russell Ave Gaithersburg MD 20877-2868

STEVES, GALE C. retired editor-in-chief, publishing executive, marketing professional, writer; b. Mineola, N.Y., Dec. 20, 1942; d. William Harry and Ruth (May) S.; m. David B. Stocker, Mar. 31, 1972 (div. Apr. 1978); m. Philip L. Perrone, Aug. 14, 1983. BS, Cornell U., 1964; MA, NYU, 1966. Editorial asst. Ladies Home Jour., N.Y.C., 1966-69; seafood consumer specialist U.S. Dept. Commerce, 1969-73; editor food Homelife mag., 1973-74; editor food and equipment Co-Ed mag., 1974-76, Am. Home mag., N.Y.C., 1976-78; editor kitchen design and equipment Woman's Day mag., 1979-83; editor-in-chief Woman's Day Spls., 1983-91; v.p., editor-in-chief Home Mag. Group, 1991—2001. Bd. dirs. Les Dames d'Escoffier, N.Y.C., Coun. Sr. Ctrs. and Svcs. of N.Y.C., 1982-98, The Catskill Ctr. for Cons. and Econ. Devel.; mem. editl. bd. Sr. Summary, N.Y.C., 1982-88; co-chmn. Alder Lake Restoration Soc. Author: Game Cookery, 1974, The International Cook, 1980, Creative Microwave Cooking, 1981, (with Lee M. Elman) Country Weekend Cooking, Home Magazine's Best Little Houses, 1998. Chmn. alumni adv. bd. Coll. Human Ecology, Cornell U., 1993-97, mem. univ. coun., 1996-2000, mem. Pres.'s Coun. for Cornell Women, 1992—; mem. adv. bd. Cornell Plantations. Mem. Internat. Furnishings and Design Assn., Am. Soc. Mag. Editors, Garden Writers Assn. Am., Acad. of Women Achievers at YWCA of N.Y.C. Office: Open House Prodns 185 West End Ave Ste 26C New York NY 10023-5551

STEVOS, JOYCE LOUISE, education director; b. Providence, May 22, 1943; d. Josephus Caldwell and Patricia Anita (Strong) Caldwell Smith; m. Manuel Joseph Stevos, Oct. 22, 1966 (div. Jan. 1981); 1 child, Manuel Joaquim. BEd, R.I. Coll., 1965. Cert. tchr. and prin., R.I. Tchr. Providence Sch. Dept., 1975-76, social studies dept. head, 1971-76, supr. social studies, 1976-90, dir. program and staff devel., 1990-92, dir. strategic planning and profl. devel., 1992—. Cons. in field. Author: The Constitution, 1977, 87. Pres. Urban League R.I., Providence, 1983-87. Recipient Never Again award Jewish Fedn. R.I., 1983, Community Svc. award John Hope settlement House, 1987, Edn. award Providence NAACP, 1991, Nat. Educator award Milken Family Found., 1992. Mem. NCCJ (trustee, program com.), DAR, Nat. Coun. for Social Studies (membership com., sec. 1979-80, Carter G. Woodson Book Award com. 1994—), Social Studies Suprs. Assn. (sec. 1979-80), R.I. Black Heritage Soc. (pres. 1989-95), Delta Sigma Theta (treas. 1989-91, scholarship). Avocations: cooking, family history, reading. Home: 57 Althea St Providence RI 02907-2801 Office: Providence Sch Dept 797 Westminster St Providence RI 02903-4045

STEWARD, ALETA JOANNA, artist; b. Bethpage, N.Y., Dec. 18, 1957; d. John L. and Loretta Rossi; m. Steve M. Steward, June 10, 1978; children: Luke, Bill, Nathan. Student, Art Students League, 1977. Artist, Alturas, Calif., 1979-87, Cape Cod, Mass., 1987—. One woman show including Trees Place, 1995—, Cape Cod Mus. of Natural History, 1988, 90; exhibited in group exhibitions Schaff Gallery, Cin., 1996, Gallery 503, Klamath Falls, Oreg., 1986-87, Marine Arts Gallery, Salem, Mass., 1996-97. Mem. Rep. Nat. Com., 1997—. Recipient multiple nat., regional and local art awards, 1985—. Mem. Nat. Assn. Photoshop Profls., Copley Soc. of Boston. Republican. Avocations: astronomy, photography, interior design, computers. Home: 57 Colonial Way Harwich MA 02645-1456 E-mail: ajsteward@earthlink.net.

STEWARD, HAROLD DAVID (HAL STEWARD), author, journalist, retired army officer; b. East St. Louis, Ill., Dec. 2, 1918; s. Owen Bob and Margaret Alice S. LLB, La Salle Ext. U., Chgo., 1948; BS, Boston U., 1961; PhD, Columbia Pacific U., San Rafael, Calif., 1979. Cert. flight instr. and instrument-rated pilot, FAA. Enlisted U.S. Army, 1937, advanced through grades to lt. col., former intelligence and pub. info. officer, unit comdr., gen. staff; staff officer NATO; comdg. oficer Hdqs. and Hdqs. Bn., Ft. Leonard Wood, Mo.; asst. chief staff G-2; ret., 1961; reporter L.A. Examiner, 1961-62, San Diego Union, 1962-65; corr. Copley News Svc., 1965-66, N.Am. Newspaper Alliance, 1967-75; exec. editor Daily Chronicle, Centralia, Wash., 1975-79; roving corr. Newsletter on Newsletters, Rhinebeck, N.Y., 1980-99. Spkr. in field. Author: The Successful Writer's Guide, 1970, Money Making Secrets of the Millionaires, 1972, Winning in Newsletters, 1989, also 3 others; contbr. over 500 articles to nat. mags. including Mil. Rev., Arty. Jur., Coast Arty. Jour., Mil. Engr., Mil. Transp. Jour., Armed Forces Digest. Asst. dir. Calif. Dept. Human Resources, Sacramento, 1970-71; asst. to lt. gov. State of Calif., Sacramento, 1971. Recipient Copley journalism award, 1963; named to U.S. Army Pub. Affairs Hall of Fame, 2000, U.S. Army Officer Candidate Sch. Hall of Fame, 2000. Mem. Authors Guild, Nat. Press Club, San Diego Press Club, Rancho Bernardo Press Club (pres. 2000). Republican. Avocations: travel, reading, walking. Home: 5240 Fiore Ter Apr J-306 San Diego CA 92122

STEWARD, JERRY WAYNE, air transportation executive, consultant; b. Tulia, Tex., Mar. 22, 1945; s. Joe M. and Mary Evelyn (Boggs) S.; m. Peggy L. Thomas, Nov. 18, 1978; children: Eric, Chalynda, Julie. AMT, Spartan Aeronautics, Tulsa, 1965. Designated Airworthiness Rep., U.S. FAA. Dir. quality control Braniff, Dallas, Orlando, Tex., Fla., 1966-90; dir. tech. svcs. Polaris Aircraft Leasing, San Francisco, 1990-94; cons. Roanoke, Tex., 1994—. With U.S. Army, 1966-69. Avocations: hunting, fishing, travel. Home and Office: 1820 Summer Ln Roanoke TX 76262-4921 E-mail: planerep@aol.com.

STEWARD, LINDA SUSAN, accountant; b. Columbus, Ohio, Oct. 26, 1956; d. James B. and Josephine (Johnson) S. BA in Econs. Lake Forest Coll., 1978; BS in Acctg. and Fin., Franklin U., 1979. econ. devel. profl. Acct. Nationwide Ins. Co., Columbus, 1976-79; acct. Kinnear Mfg. Co., Columbus, 1979-80; investment analyst devel. State of Ohio, Columbus, 1980—; v.p. SRA & Assocs., 1986; pres. Number Crunchers Acctg. & Tax Service, 1986; tax cons. Taxes Unlimited, 1988; mng. ptnr. Lynch, Brown and Assocs., 1989. Bd. dirs. Nat. Devel. Council, 1987; treas. Columbus Habitat for Humanity, 1992, Ohio Bus. Women's Resource Network, 1993; regional housing mgr. United Ch. Homes, 1991-92; dir. Ctrl. Ohio Small Bus. Devel. Ctr., 1993; dir. women's bus. initiative Greater Columbus C. of C., 1992; pres. Prosperous Solutions, Inc., 1992. Mem. Am. Mgmt. Assn., Am. Soc. Exec. and Profl. Women, Nat. Assn. Accts., Nat. Soc. Tax Profls., Assn. Bus. and Profl. Women in Constrn., Ohio Soc. C.P.A.s, Am. Mktg. Assn., Am. Women's Soc. C.P.A.s, Tech. Alliance Central Ohio, Columbus C. of C., Columbus Leadership Forum, Lake Forest Alumni Assn., Franklin U. Alumni Assn. Researcher in field. Office: 1582 E Livingston Ave Ste A Columbus OH 43205-2929

STEWARD, MARSH, JR. obstetrician, gynecologist; b. Plano, Ill. s. Charles Marsh and Louise (Warnock) S.; m. Huguette Gabriell Dulondel, Nov. 14, 1964 (div. Jan. 1991); children: Lewis Olivier, John Jacques. BS, Northwestern U., 1945, MD, 1948; JD, Western State U., 1987. Diplomate Am. Bd. Ob-Gyn. Intern Cook County Hosp., Chgo., 1948-49, resident, 1953-55; mem. staff St. Jude Hosp., Fullerton, Calif., Placentia (Calif.)-Linda Hosp.; pvt. practice Fullerton. Clin. prof. ob-gyn. U. Calif.-Irvine. Fellow Am. Coll. Legal Medicine, ACOG, Calif. Assn. Ob-Gyn. (pres. 1980); mem. AMA, Calif. Med. Assn., Orange County Ob-Gyn. Soc. (pres. 1967). Office: PO Box 5977 Fullerton CA 92838-0977 E-mail: msmdjd@aol.com.

STEWARD, WELDON CECIL, architecture educator, architect, consultant; b. Pampa, Tex., Apr. 7, 1934; s. Weldon C. and Lois (Maness) S.; m. Mary Jane Nedbalek, June 9, 1956; children: Karen A., W. Craig. Cert. in architecture and planning, Ecole des Beaux Arts, Fontainebleu, France, 1956; B.Arch., Tex. A&M U, 1957; MS in Architecture, Columbia U., 1961; LHD (hon.), Drury Coll., 1991. Registered architect, Tex., Nebr. Designer Perkins & Will, Architects, White Plains, N.Y., 1961-62; asst. prof. architecture Tex. A&M U., College Station, 1962-67, assoc. chmn. Sch. Architecture, 1966-69, assoc. dean, prof. Coll. Environ. Design, 1969-73; dean, prof. Coll. Architecture U. Nebr., Lincoln, 1973-2000, emeritus dean, prof. arch. and planning, 2000—; founding pres. Joslyn Castle Inst. Sustainable Cmtys., Omaha, 1996—; W. Cecil Steward dist. chair sustainable arch. U. Nebr., Lincoln, 2000—02. Adj. prof. Sch. Arch. U. Hawaii, 1999—; ednl. cons. People's Republic of China, 1979--; project dir. Imo State U. Planning, Nigeria, 1981-88; vis. prof. Tong ji U., Shanghai, 1984; hon. prof. N.W. Inst. Architects Engrs., Xian, 1989; specialist Design USA, USSR, 1990; co-chmn. nat. coordination com. AIA Nat. Coun. Archtl. Registration Bd. Intership, Washington, 1980-81; bd. visitors Drury Coll., 1980-97, Coll. Arch. U. Miami, Fla., 1993-96, Judson Coll., 1998-2000; mem. nat. design rev. bd. GSA, Washington, 1994—; mem. founding bd. dirs. East/West Pacific Arch., U. Hawaii, 1995—; vice chmn. Design Futures Coun., Reston, Va., 1995—; sr. fellow Design Futures Coun., 1999. Designer, Quinnipiac Elem. Sch., New Haven, Conn., 1961 (Am Assn. Sch. Adminstrs. Exhibit 1969), J.J. Buser Residence, Bryan, Tex., 1969, Steward Urban Residence, Lincoln, Nebr., 1994. Mem. Lincoln Architects, Engrs. Selection Bd., 1979-88; mem. Nat. Com. for U.S.-China Rels., N.Y.C., 1981—, Nebr. Capitol Environ. Commn., 1989-97; bd. dirs. Downtown Lincoln Assn., 1996—, KZUM Pub. Radio, 1997-2001; mem. Lincoln Planning Commn., 1996—; bd. dirs. Lincoln Children's Mus., 1996-2001; profl. adviser nat. design competition Wick Alumni Ctr., Lincoln, 1981; steering com. Internat. Coun. Tall Bldgs., 1992-96. Named Disting. Alumnus, Tex. A&M U., 1998; Grad. fellow Columbia U., 1960 Mem. AIA (pres. Brazos chpt. 1969, chmn. profl. devel. com. 1979, bd. dirs. 1979-90, dir. Cen. States 1987-90, nat. pres. 1991-92, Coll. of Fellows 1983, Tri-Nat. com. 1991--, Nebr. Gold medal 1997, nat. AIA/ACSA Topaz award for excellence in architecture 1999); mem. Am. Planning Assn. (chair Dubai Internat. award for sustaining cmty. 2000), Nebr. Soc. Architects (bd. dirs. 1977-2000), Archtl. Found. Nebr. (bd. dirs. 1981-94, treas. 1981-94), Assn. Collegiate Schs. Architecture (bd. dirs. 1975-79), Nat. Archtl. Accrediting Bd. (bd. dirs. 1986-89, pres. 1988-89), Kazakhstan Union Architecture, Assn. Siamese Architects, Royal Inst. Canadian Architects, Fedn. Mexican Architects, Japan Inst. Architects (hon.), Tau Sigma Delta (medal 1999), Phi Kappa Phi, Phi Beta Delta. Home: 125 N 11th St Lincoln NE 68508-3605 Office: U Nebr Coll Architecture Lincoln NE 68588 E-mail: csteward1@unl.edu.

STEWART, ALBERT ELISHA, safety engineer, industrial hygienist; b. Urbana, Mo., Dec. 20, 1927; s. Albert E. and Maurine (Lighter) S.; m. Elizabeth O. Tice, May 31, 1958 (div.); children: Sheryl E., Mical A. BA, U. Kans., 1949; MS, U. Mo., 1958, MBA, 1970; PhD, Western States U., 1984. Registered profl. engr., Calif., cert. safety engr., cert. indsl. hygenist. Sales engr. Kaiser Aluminum and Chem. Co., Toledo, 1949-56; tchr. Kansas City (Mo.) Pub. Schs., 1959-65; indsl. hygienist Bendix Corp., Kansas City, 1960-65; safety adminstr. Gulf R&D, Merriam, Kans., 1968-71; sr. indsl. hygienist USDOL-OSHA, Kansas City, 1971-77; pres. Stewart Indsl. Hygiene, 1977—. Adj. prof. Cen. Mo. State U. Mem. Boy Scouts Am. With U.S. Army, 1950-53. Mem. Am. Indsl. Hygiene Assn., Am. Chem. Soc., Am. Acad. Indsl. Hygiene, Am. Soc. Safety Engrs., Am. Welding Soc., Nat. Mgmt. Assn., Nat. Sci. Tchrs. Assn., Adminstrv. Govt. Soc., Am. Legion Post 596, DAV, ARC, Alpha Chi Sigma. Episcopalian. Avocations: fishing, golf, travel.

STEWART, ALEC THOMPSON, physicist, educator; b. Windthorst, Sask., Can., June 18, 1925; s. Arthur and Nelly Blye (Thompson) S.; m. Alta Aileen Kennedy, Aug. 4, 1960; children: A. James Kennedy, Hugh D., Duncan R. BSc, Dalhousie U., Halifax, N.S., Can., 1946, MSc, 1949, LLD, 1986; PhD, Cambridge U., Eng., 1952. Research officer Atomic Energy Can., Chalk River, Ont., Can., 1952-57; assoc. prof. Dalhousie U., Halifax, 1957-60; assoc. prof. to prof. U. N.C., Chapel Hill, 1960-68; head physics Queen's U., Kingston, Ont., 1968-74, prof. physics, 1968-90, prof. emeritus, 1990—. Vis. prof. various univs., Can., Europe, Japan, China, Hong Kong. Author 2 books; contbr. over 100 articles to profl. jours. Recipient CAP medal for achievement in physics, 1992, Canada 125 medal, 1992. Fellow Am. Phys. Soc., Royal Soc. Can. (pres. Acad. Sci. 1984-87), Japan Soc. for Promotion Sci.; mem. Can. Assn. Physicists (pres., other offices 1970-74). Achievements include research in solid state physics, behavior of phonons, electrons, positrons and postronium in crystals and liquids, public service: nuclear reactor safety, possible hazards of power frequency electric and magnetic fields, emergency measures following a nuclear accident. Office: Queens U Dept Physics Kingston ON Canada K7L 3N6

STEWART, ANNE WILLIAMS, historian, writer, researcher; b. New Haven, Oct. 13, 1933; d. Howard Dudley and Minnie Victoria (Rattelsdorfer) Williams; m. Kenneth Neal Stewart (div. Oct. 1985); children: Elizabeth Anne Stewart-Marshall, Kenneth Neal Stewart, Jr., David Bradley Stewart. BA, Allegheny Coll., Meadville, Pa., 1955. Coord. hist. sites survey Crawford County Planning, Meadville, 1976-80; chmn. hist. sites survey Meadville Redevel. Authority, 1980-83; program coord. Crawford County Hist. Soc., Meadville, 1981-88; bd. dirs. Meadville Bicentennial, 1986-88; dir. Academy Theater restoration Meadville Redevel. Authority, 1988-90; gen. reporter Meadville Tribune, 1990-92; grantsman Meadville Redevel. Authority, 1991—; adminstr. The Col. Inc., Drake Well Mus., Titusville, Pa., 1992-95. Historian, advisor Meadville Main St., 1986-90; historian Meadville Comprehensive Plan, 1992-93. Author: John A. Mather: Legacy of Pennsylvania's Oil Region Photographer, 1995, A Concise History of Meadville, 1995, 4th edit., 2002; author: (with Jonathan Miller Design) Meadville: Heart of the French Creek Valley, 1997; author: (with William B. Moore) Images of America, Meadville, 2001; editor: A Guide to City and County, 1972, Meadville:

Yesterday and Today, 1976, Gentle Giants: Stories of Ballooning, 1992, George Washington's French Creek Trip, 1999, The Oilfield Barker, 1993—96, Market Square Messenger, 1996—99, Crawford County History, 2001—; contbr. articles to mags. Planning commr. Crawford County, Meadville, 1971-95, City of Meadville, 2000—; bd. dirs. Meadville Area Meml., 1983-95; chmn. bd. dirs. Health Svcs. Inc., Crawford County, 1976-81; coord. Meadville Area Coalition; chair The Founders Forum, 1997—. Mem. Crawford County Hist. Soc., Woman's Lit. Club (lectr.), Pa. Planning Assn. (bd. dirs. 1974-80). Avocations: travel, research, textile crafts. Office: 443 Byllesby Ave Meadville PA 16335-1411 E-mail: byllesby@alltel.net.

STEWART, ARDEN RUTH, automotive aftermarket manufacturing executive; b. Wheeling, W.Va., Sept. 29, 1930; d. Oliver Shaw and Helen (Neitzel) Stewart; children: Mark, Todd. BA, Baldwin Wallace Coll., 1952. Trainee GM, Cleve., 1952-57; tchr. Elyria (Ohio) City Bd. Edn., 1967-85; pres., CEO AAR, Inc., Cleve., 1984—, also chmn. bd. dirs. Pres. Elyria Schs. PTA, 1967; treas. Homeowners Assn., North Ridgeville, Ohio, 1988-89; mem. adv. com. bus. and tech. Cuyahoga C.C. Recipient Weatherhead 100 award Case Western Res. U., 1990, 91, 92, 93, 94, 95. Republican. Episcopalian. Avocations: music, scuba diving, dancing. Home: 37 Princewood Ln PO Box 33599 Palm Beach Gardens FL 33420-3599 also: 37 Princewood Ln Palm Beach Gardens FL 33410 Office: AAR Inc 34999 Mills Rd North Ridgeville OH 44039-1366 E-mail: ardenstewart@aol.com.

STEWART, ARLENE JEAN GOLDEN, designer, stylist; b. Chgo., Nov. 26, 1943; d. Alexander Emerald and Nettie (Rosen) Golden; m. Randall Edward Stewart, Nov. 6, 1970; 1 child, Alexis Anne. BFA, Sch. of Art Inst. Chgo., 1966; postgrad., Ox Bow Summer Sch. Painting, Saugatuck, Mich., 1966. Designer, stylist Formica Corp., Cin., 1966-68; with Armstrong World Industries, Inc., Lancaster, Pa., 1968-96, interior furnishings analyst, 1974-76, internat. staff project stylist, 1976-78, sr. stylist Corlon flooring, 1979-80, sr. exptl. project stylist, 1980-89, sr. project stylist residential DIY flooring floor divsn., 1989-96, master stylist DIY residential tile, 1992-96; creative dir. Stewart Graphics, 1996—. Exhibited textiles Art Inst. Chgo., 1966, Ox-Bow Gallery, Saugatuck, Mich., 1966. Home and Office: 114 E Vine St Lancaster PA 17602-3550 E-mail: stewartgraphics@redrose.net.

STEWART, ARTHUR IRVING, III (ART STEWART), management consultant; b. Plainfield, N.J., Aug. 1, 1958; s. Arthur Irving Jr. and Audree Claire (Rollerson) S. BS in Mass Communication, Emerson Coll., 1982. Intern Sta. KYW Newsradio/TV, Phila., 1977; news anchorman, reporter Sta. WLBR-WUFM-FM, Lebanon, 1984; ops. mgr. Sta. WMSP-FM, Harrisburg, 1984-86; sr. account exec. mktg. and sales promotion Sta. WFCC-FM, Chatham, Mass., 1987-88; account mgr. Vizwiz Film-Video, Inc., Brookline, 1989-90; pub. rels. account exec. The Interface Group, Needham, 1991-92; sr. account exec. pub. rels. Mullen Advt., 1992-93; pres., sr. counsel Stewart Strategies Group, LLC, Wayne, Pa., 1993—. Dir. mktg. and pub. rels. Cape and Islands Chamber Music Festival, Cape Cod, Mass., 1988; asst. organist The United Parish, Brookline, 1982-84. Producer (radio concert broadcasts) Harrisburg Symphony Orch., 1984-86, documentary on U.S. debut tour of Westminster Cathedral Choir of London, 1985, investigative report on acid rain, 1985 (Excellence in Broadcasting award), documentary on Nat. Cathedral Washington, 1986 (Excellence in Broadcasting award). Editor OUTREACH newsletter Trinity Ch., Boston, 1990-94; staff media rels. 72d genl. conv. Episcopal Ch. U.S.A., 1997. Recipient Excellence in Broadcasting award Pa. Assn. Broadcasters. Mem. Internat. Assn. Bus. Communicators, Am. Guild Organists. Episcopalian. Avocations: running, bicycling, travel, the arts, politics. Fax: 610-407-0183. E-mail: results@stewartgrp.com.

STEWART, ARTHUR VAN, dental educator, geriatric health administrator; b. Buffalo, July 25, 1938; s. Arthur Sharpe and Doris (Simpson) S.; m. Jacqueline Fischer, June 5, 1965; children: Mark Van, Laura Kristin, Jeffrey Fischer. BS in Chemistry, U. Pitts., 1960, DMD, 1968, PhD, 1973. Clin. lic. Ky. USPHS postdoctoral fellow U. Pitts., 1968-70; chair, cmty. dentistry dept.; dean, student affairs Fairleigh Dickinson U. Dental Sch., Teaneck, N.J., 1970-75; dean for acad. affairs U. Louisville Dental Sch., 1975-88, asst. to provost, 1985-89, prof. dentistry, 1975—; dir., Ctr. on Aging U. Louisville Health Scis. Ctr., 1994-99. Cons. ADA, Chgo., OVAR: Geriatric Edn. Ctr., Lexington, Ky., Am. Dental Edn. Assn., Washington; dental cons. Baylor U., Dallas. Contbr. over 300 articles to profl. jours., chpts. to books, separately published monographs; presenter in field. Bd. mem. U. of Louisville Student Ctr., 1986-89, YMCA Camp Piomingo, Louisville, 1980-90; leader Cub Scout/Weblos, Boy Scouts of Am., Louisville, 1985-90. Recipient tchg. award Metroversity of Louisville, 1989, 90, 92; recipient over $2,000,000 in rsch. and tng. grants and awards. Mem. Ky. Dental Assn. (del. 1988-2001), Louisville Dental Soc. (chmn. 1994-95, Pres.'s award 1995), Ky. Assn. for Gerontology (pres. 1995-96), Quest for Excellence (dir. 1988-2000), OKU Honorary Soc. (pres. 1978-79), Delphi Honorary Soc. (pres. 1980-99, dir. U. Founder's Day Celebration 1995-98). Avocations: writing, photography, philately, travel. Office: Univ of Louisville Sch of Dentistry 501 S Preston St Louisville KY 40202-1701 E-mail: avstew01@gwise.lo.

STEWART, BARBARA DEAN, writer, musician, educational consultant; b. Rochester, N.Y., Sept. 17, 1941; d. George Adgate and Louise (Griswold) Dean; children: Allison, Whitney. AB, Cornell U., 1962; MS, Simmons Coll., 1964; diploma with honors in flute, Eastman Sch. Music., 1958; MFA in Playwriting, Columbia U., 1993; postgrad., Tuck Sch. Bus. Mgmt. Asst. law libr. Cornell U., Ithaca, N.Y., 1963-64; writer, performer Kazoophony, 1972-90; pub. rels. dir. Margaret Woodbury Strong Mus., 1978; pres. Stewart Assocs. Ednl. Sys. Group, Rochester, 1979-85; pres., CEO SWI, Fairport, N.Y., 1985—. Flutist La Jolla Civic Orch., 1966-68; exec. assoc. Tony Randall's Nat. Actors Theatre, N.Y.C., 1991, co. dramaturg, asst. to artistic dir., 1992-93. Author: How To Kazoo, Squash Raquets: Pro and Khan, From Camera to Finished Print; (plays) Sound Barriers, Platypus Rex. Founding chmn. jr. devel. U.S. Squash Racquets Assn.; pres. bd. dirs. Rochester Chamber Orch.; bd. dirs. Rochester chpt. English Spkg. Union, 1982-85; pole vault coach Pittsford (N.Y.) H.S., 1998; pres. Share Arts Found., 1989—; non-govtl. orgn. del. UN Human Rights Subcom., Geneva, 1998; mem. president's coun. on athletics Cornell U. Fellow Yale Sch. Drama, 1989-90; Recipient 68 nat. championships and 2 world championships in 20 different masters track and field events, holder 14 Am. and 6 world records, 5 MAC achievement awards Met. Athletics Congress, N.Y.C., 1986, 88, 90; 1st ofcl. world, U.S., Can. women's pole champion masters; Soviet women's pole vault record, 1990; named to Cornell U. Athletic Hall of Fame, Greater Rochester track Club Hall of Fame. Mem.: ASCAP, Nat. Tng. Sys. Assn., Nat. Def. Indsl. Assn., Nat. Classification Mgmt. Soc., Dramatist Guild, Am. Fedn. Musicians, N.Y. State Track Ofcls. Assn., U.S.A. Track and Field Ofcls., Ibsen Soc., Players Club (N.Y.C.), Yale Club N.Y.C. Office: 11 W Church St Ste 101 Fairport NY 14450-2111

STEWART, BARBARA DUNBAR, insurance consultant; b. Pitts., Mar. 29, 1943; d. John Charles and Ruth (Ryan) Dunbar. BS, Beaver Coll., Glenside, Pa., 1965. Econ. analyst Wood, Struthers & Winthrop, N.Y.C., 1965-72; systems analyst Bradford Computer, 1972-73; corp. economist Chubb Corp., 1973-81; pres. Stewart Econs., Inc., 1981—. Dir. Capital Re Corp., Ins. Svcs. Office, Inc., Nat. Grange Mut. Ins. Co. Author: The Profit Cycle in Property and Casualty Insurance, 1997, The Economic Impact of a Major Earthquake, 1989; co-author: Managing Insurer Insolvency, 1988, A Brief History of Underwriting Cycles, 1990, Insurance Insolvency Guarantees, 1990, Niche Insurance Companies, 1997, A Proposal to Modernize Insurance Agent Licensing, 1998. Named Ins. Woman of Yr., Assn. Profl. Ins. Women, 1987. Mem. Nat. Assn. Bus. Economists, Internat. Ins. Soc., Am. Econ. Assn., Am. Risk and Ins. Assn., Office: Ste 21A 2660 Peachtree Rd NW Atlanta GA 30305-3678

STEWART, B(OBBY) A(LTON), soil scientist, educator; b. Erick, Okla., Sept. 26, 1932; s. William David and Anna Maude (Howard) S.; m. Jane Ann Nelson; children: Steven Mark, Gregory Neal, Judith Ann Stewart Meadow. BS in Soils, Okla. State U., 1953, MS in Soils, 1957; PhD in Soil Sci., Colo. State U., 1961. Cert. soil scientist. Rsch. soil scientist Agrl. Rsch. Svc., USDA, Stillwater, Okla., 1953-57, Ft. Collins, Colo., 1957-68, dir. Conservation and Prodn. Rsch. Lab. Bushland, Tex., 1968-93; dir. Dryland Agr. Inst., disting. prof. West Tex. A&M U., Canyon, 1993—, interim head divsn. agr., 1998. Contbr. over 175 articles to profl. jours.; editor/co-editor over 50 books. Fellow Am. Soc. Agronomy (bd. dirs. 1979-82), Soil Sci. Soc. Am. (assoc. editor jour. 1967-72, chmn. soil and water divsn. 1971-72, bd. dirs. 1971-72, 75-82, editor-in-chief jour. 1975-79, pres. 1981-82, Profl. Svc. award 2000), Soil and Water Conservation Soc. (chmn. nat. meeting program com. 1972, chmn. waste mgmt. divsn. 1973, Pres.'s citation, 1972, Golden Spread Chpt. Achievement award 1975, Hugh Hammond Bennett award 1994); mem. Internat. Soil Sci. Soc. (vice chmn. divsn. soil conservation). Methodist. Office: West Tex A&M Univ 2402 N 3 Rd Ave Canyon TX 79016-0001 E-mail: bstewart@mail.wtamu.edu.

STEWART, BOBBY GENE, laboratory director; b. Jesse, W.Va., Apr. 18, 1940; s. Leonard Mart and Zeta Marie Stewart; m. Linda May Smith, Mar. 17, 1961; children: Barbara Lynn, Ramona Jean Stewart Pinkerman. Cert. in med. tech., Army Med. Svc. Sch., 1960; cert. blood banking specialist, 10th Med. Rsch. Lab., Landstuhl, Germany, 1961. Lic. nursing home adminstr. Mo., cert. clin. lab. scientist, bioanalytical lab. mgr. Med. and x-ray technologist Oceana (W.Va.) Med. Ctr., 1962-68; clin. mgr., med. technologist Sigourney (Iowa) Med. Clinic, 1968-69; staff med. and x-ray technologist Van Buren County Hosp., Keosauqua, Iowa, 1969; dir. lab. and x-ray svcs. Scotland County Hosp., Memphis, 1969-71; dir. lab. svcs. Keller Meml. Hosp., Fayette, 1971-95, Regional Med. Assocs., Fayette, 1995-97; med. technologist Boyce and Bynum Pathology Labs., 1998-99, Mo. Cancer Assocs., Columbia, 1999—. Mem. city coun. City of Fayette, 1977—85, mayor pro-tem, 1980—85, chmn. parks and recreation com., 1977—80, chmn. elec. dist. com., 1981—85. With U.S. Army, 1959—62. Mem.: Mo. State Soc. of AMT (legis. chmn. 1975—90, v.p. 1973—74, 1989—90, pres. 1975—76, Med. Technologist of Yr. 1977, Pres.'s award 2001), Am. Med. Technologists (dist. councillor 1977—81, 1988—93, nat. bd. dirs. 1993—, nat. treas. 1994—96, nat. v.p. 1996—97, nat. pres. 1997—99, 2001—02, Disting. Achievement award 1976, Exceptional Merit award 1981, Nat. Silver Svc. award 1997, Nat. Pillar award 1998, Nat. Order Golden Microscope award 2000). Avocations: tennis, golf, swimming. Home: 410 Cooper St Fayette MO 65248-9630 Office: Mo Cancer Assocs Keene St Columbia MO 65201 E-mail: bstewart@mcmsys.com.

STEWART, BURCH BYRON, laboratory director; b. Chattanooga, May 7, 1929; s. Burch Dayton and Mary Elizabeth (Hunnicutt) S.; m. Shirley Elizabeth Westervelt, June 18, 1967; children: Steven, Neal, Daryl. BS in Chemistry, U. Tenn., 1955, MS in Phys. Chemistry, 1957, PhD in Phys. Chemistry, 1959. Sr. engr. Western Electric, Princeton, N.J., 1959-60; rsch. chemist Allied Chem. Co., Morristown, 1960-68; mgr. Ciba-Geigy Co., Ardsley, N.Y., 1968-72; lab. dir. Applied Rsch. Labs., Miami, Fla., 1972-86; pres., tech. dir. Applied Consumer Svcs., Hialeah Garden, 1986—. Cons. All State Engring., Miami, 1986—, Worth Engring., 1986—. Contbr. articles to profl. jours. Treas. Miami Unitarian Ch., 1980-83, pres., 1984; fundraiser Askew for Pres, Miami, 1984. With USN, 1950-52. AEC grant, 1947; Westinghouse scholar, 1947. Mem. Am. Chem. Soc., Miami Mineralogy and Gem Soc., Am. Coun. Ind. Labs., Friends of Physics-U. Miami. Democrat. Achievements include patent for circular calculator, discovery of new type tin comlex using NMR. Avocations: writing, handwriting analysis. Office: 11890 NW 87th Ct Ste 8 Hialeah Gardens FL 33018-1984

STEWART, BURTON GLOYDEN, JR. retired banker; b. Clayton, N.C., Mar. 14, 1933; s. Burton Gloyden and Evelyn I. (Stallings) S.; m. Patricia Taylor, June 16, 1956; children: Burton Gloyden III, H. Taylor. AB, Duke U., 1955; grad., Sch. Banking of the south, 1970; exec. program, U. N.C., 1975. With Allstate Ins. Co., 1957-66, regional sales mgr. N.C., 1964-66; with Branch Banking and Trust Co., Wilson, 1966-98, sr. v.p., mgr. corp. planning and mktg. divsn., 1972-81, dir. investor rels., 1981-98, ret., 1998. Dir. Branch Corp., 1974-82; dir. N.C. Payments System, 1980-89, v.p., 1983-86, chmn. bd. 1986-89; bd. dirs., chmn. Electronic Fin. Svcs., Inc., 1988-90. Bd. dirs. Wilson Heart Assn., 1968; bd. dirs., treas. Wilson Arts Coun., 1969-71; bd. dirs. Wilson United Way, 1974-80, 86-89, campaign chmn., 1977, pres., 1979, chmn. strategic planning com., 1986-90; mem. N.C. Gov.'s Efficiency Study Commn., 1985, N.C. Goals and Policy Bd., 1985-93; mem. local com. Cypress Glen Retirement Cmty., 1991—, chmn., 1999-2001; mem. fin. com. United Meth. Ret. Homes, Inc., 1999—, trustee, 1999—, chmn., 2002-. Lt. USNR, 1955-57. Mem. Bank Investor Rels. Assn. (bd. dirs. 1984-98, v.p. 1984-87), Wilson Country Club, Dunes Club. Methodist. Address: 1107 Salem St NW Wilson NC 27893-2139

STEWART, CARL E. federal judge; b. 1950; BA magna cum laude, Dillard U., 1971; JD, Loyola U., New Orleans, 1974. Atty. Piper & Brown, Shreveport, La., 1977—78; staff atty. La. Atty. Gen. Office, 1978—79; asst. U.S. atty. Office U.S. Atty. (we. dist.) La., 1979—83; prin. Stewart & Dixon, 1983—85; spl. asst. dist. atty., asst. prosecutor City of Shreveport, 1983—85; judge La. Dist. Ct., 1985—91, La. Ct. Appeals (2d cir.), 1991—94, U.S. Ct. Appeals (5th cir.), 1994—. Adj. instr. dept. mgmt. and mktg. La. State U., Shreveport, 1982—85. Mem. chancellor's adv. bd. La. State U., Shreveport, 1983—89, chmn., 1988—89; mem. black achievers program steering com. YMCA, 1990. Capt. JAGC, 1974—77, Tex. Mem.: La. State Bar Assn. (bench/bar liaison com.), La. Conf. Ct. Appeal Judges, Black Lawyers Assn. Shreveport-Bossier, Am. Inns of Ct. (Harry Booth/Henry Politz chpt. Shreveport), Nat. Bar Assn., Omega Psi Rhi (Rho Omega chpt.). Office: US Ct Appeals 5th Cir 300 Fannin St Ste 2299 Shreveport LA 71101-3124

STEWART, CARLETON M. banker, corporate director; b. Chgo., 1921; s. Carleton Merrill and Margaret (Lyon) S.; m. Alicia Dewar (dec.); 3 children; m. Kathryn White. Student, Stanford U., 1939-42; grad. in indsl. adminstrn., Harvard U., 1943, MBA, 1947. With Citibank, 1947-76, v.p., 1960-67, sr. v.p. in charge of Asia Pacific area, 1967-69, sr. v.p. in charge of South Asia, Middle East and Africa, 1969-73, sr. officer London, 1973-76; dir. Grindlay's Bank Ltd., Banque Internat. pour L'Afrique Occidentale, Paris, 1973-76; chmn. bd., chief exec. officer Am. Security Corp. and Am. Security Bank, Washington, 1976-80; chmn. bd. Internat. Bank Miami, 1983-85; dir. Travelers Asset Mgmt. Internat. Corp., N.Y.C., 1985-87. Mayor Longboat Key, Fla., 1987-88, town commr., 1984-90, mem. ethics com., 1990--99, chmn. 1992-94; mem. Planning Commn., Sarasota County, Fla., 1990-92. Capt. AUS, 1943-46.

STEWART, CHARLES LESLIE, lawyer; b. Fayetteville, Ark., Aug. 12, 1919; s. Charles Leslie and Ruth (Want) S.; m. Edalee Esther Gastrock, Aug. 30, 1941; children: William Paul, Thomas Alan, Katherine Jean, Robert Edward. AB, U. Ill., 1940; MA, La. State U., 1941; student, George Washington U. Law Sch., 1944-45; JD, U. Chgo., 1947. Bar: Ill. 1948, U.S. Supreme Ct. 1954. Economist, Dept. Agr., 1941-42; adminstrv. asst. OPA, 1942-43, Bd. Econ. Warfare, 1943; exec. dir. Chgo. div. ACLU, 1946-47; practiced law Chgo., 1948-91, Glencoe, Ill., 1991-98; assoc. Mayer, Brown & Platt, Chgo., 1947-55, ptnr., 1956-67, 70-71, resident ptnr. charge European office, Paris, 1967-70; v.p., gen. counsel Hart Schaffner & Marx, 1971-73, v.p., sec., gen. counsel, 1974-83, Hartmarx Corp., Chgo., 1983-84, v.p., sec., sr. counsel, 1984, of counsel legal dept., 1985-89; arbitrator Mandatory Arbitration Program Cir. Ct., Cook County, Ill., 1990—. Mem. Am. Law Inst., 1983-90. Mem. Glencoe (Ill.) Bd. Edn., 1965-66; mem. planning com. Corp. Counsel Inst., Northwestern U. Sch. Law and Ill. Inst. Continuing Legal Edn., 1978-84, vice-chmn., 1983, chmn., 1984; mem. Glencoe Union Ch. Served with OSS, AUS, 1943-45. Mem. ABA, Ill. State Bar Assn., Chgo. Bar Assn. (com. devel. of law 1977-91, vice chmn. 1984-85, chmn. 1985-86, corp. law com. 1981-91, corp. law depts. com. 1981-83, sr. lawyers com. 1987-92), Am. Soc. Corp. Secs. (adv. com. Chgo. regional group 1978-83, vice chmn. 1979-80, chmn. 1980-81, nat. dir. 1981-84, exec. com. 1983-84, corp. practices com. 1982-87, assoc. mem. 1986-91), Skokie Country Club, Rotary, Delta Phi. Avocations: genealogy, history, bridge. Home: 2525 Mayapple Ct Northbrook IL 60062-6531

STEWART, CHARLES THORP, retired lawyer; b. Pitts., Feb. 14, 1918; s. William Denning and Margaret Boulton (Thorp) Stewart; m. Patricia Jane Carry, May 30, 1976. BA, Cornell U., 1940; JD, Yale U., 1943. Bar: N.Y. 1943, U.S. Supreme Ct. 1980. Assoc. Cravath, Swaine & Moore, 1943—45, 1946—55; asst. gen. atty., asst. sec. R.H. Macy & Co., Inc., 1955—56; sec., gen. counsel to sr. v.p., dir. pub. affairs J.C. Penney Co., Inc., 1960—78; counsel Winthrop, Stimson, Putnam & Roberts, N.Y.C., 1979—86; pvt. practice, 1986—92; ret., 1992. Adj. prof. law Cardozo Law Sch., 1978—80, NYU Law Sch., 1980—86. Chmn. YMCA Gtr. N.Y., 1983—86; vice chmn. Cornell U. Bd. Trustees, Ithaca, NY, 1978—83, chmn. exec. com.; bd. dirs. Legal Aid Soc., N.Y.C., 1979—85. Served with U.S. Army, 1945, served with USNR, 1945—46. Fellow: Am. Bar Found.; mem.: ABA, Am. Law Inst., Univ. Club (N.Y.C.), Ocean Club of Fla. (Ocean Ridge), Country Club of Fla. (Golf). Republican. Presbyterian. Home: 2613 N St Andrews Blvd Delray Beach FL 33483-7367

STEWART, CHARLES TODD, JR. economics educator; b. N.Y.C., May 13, 1922; s. Charles Todd and Leonor Pereira (de Magalhaes) S.; m. Nancy Thayer, Jan. 24, 1953; children: Eileen, David, Jocelyn. BA, George Washington U., 1946, MA, 1948, PhD, 1954. Asst. prof. econs. Utah State U., Logan, 1947-49; Sander teaching fellow George Washington U., Washington, 1949-51, rsch. assoc., 1951-52, rsch. prof. econs., 1963-65, prof. econs., 1965-92, emeritus prof., 1992—; sr. rsch. analyst Georgetown U., 1953-58; rsch. economist C. of C. U.S., 1958-62, dir. econ. rsch., 1962-63. Cons. Interam. Devel. Bank, Washington, 1978-79, NSF, Washington, 1970-71, 73-78, OAS, Washington, 1968-69, U.S.-P.R. Commn. on Status, San Juan, 1965-67, Litton Industries, 1965, Atlantic Rsch. Corp., 1967, NASA, 1969-70, Econ. Devel. Adminstrn., 1968-72, Nat. Bur. Stds., 1975-76. Author: Low Wage Worker in an Affluent, 1974, Air Pollution, Human Health, 1979, Technology Transfer and Human Factors, 1987 (Ohira award 1987), Healthy, Wealthy, or Wise, 1995, Inequality and Equity, 1998, Around the World in Eighty Years, 2000; co-author: From Basic Economics to Supply-Side, 1983; contbr. articles to profl. jours. With inf. U.S. Army, 1942-45. Mem. AAAS, Am. Econ. Assn. Avocations: painting, poetry.

STEWART, CONNIE WARD, academic administrator; b. Athens, Ga., Nov. 19, 1938; d. Fred Tendal and Elsie (Janes) Ward; m. D.G. Stewart, 1960 (div. 1967); 1 child, Sheri Lyn; m. Nick Vista, Apr. 16, 1982. AB in Journalism, U. Ga., 1959, MA, 1968; postgrad., George Washington U., 1979; cert. in ednl. mgmt., Harvard U., 1985. Cert. elem. and secondary tchr., Ga. Promotion-pub. rels. staff Sta. WSB-TV, Atlanta, 1959—61; assoc. dir. Ga. Scholarship Commn., 1967; faculty U. Ga. Journalism Sch., Athens, 1967—70; dir. orientation U. Ga., 1970—71; project mgr. Planned Mgmt. Corp., Tampa, Fla., 1976—77; dir. policy comm., mem., Carter-Mondale adminstrn. HEW, Washington, 1977—79; orgnl. staff U.S. Dept. Edn., 1979; v.p. Mich. State U., East Lansing, 1980—87; assoc. v.p. Emory U., Atlanta, 1987—93. Cons. in comm. svcs. and tng.; dir. Cmty. Forum on Children and Families Ga. State U., 1995; mil. acad. screening com. Office U.S. Senator Donald Riegle, Lansing, Mich., 1984-86. Editor, columnist Oconee Enterprise, 1971-72. Steering com. Carter for Pres. Campaign, Fla., 1975-76; mem. exec. com. Mich. Sesquicentennial Celebration, 1985-87; mem. Ga. Scholarship Commn., 1965-67, Ga. Motion Picture-TV Adv. Bd., 1972-76, Ga. Gov.'s Commn. on Edn., 1965-67, Mich. Film and TV Coun., 1984-86; bd. dirs. Olympic Acad., 1987-88, Atlanta Olympics Organizing Com. for Olympic Games, 1991-93; exec com. Comms. Coun., The Atlanta Project, 1992-94; vol. mentoring in pub. schs. Success-by-Six program, 1993-96; trainer United Way vols., 1993-96, Big Bros./Big Sisters Teach One program, 1997-99; docent Carter Presdl. Libr./Mus., 1998—. Recipient Outstanding Alumna award Henry W. Grady Coll. of Journalism and Mass Communications, U. Ga., 1993, hon. alumnus award Mich. State U., 1987; disting. svc. award Ga. Edn. Advancement Coun., 1990. Mem. Coun. for Advancement and Support Edn., Nat. Assn. State Univs. and Land Grant Colls. (univ. rels. coun. 1984-87), Atlanta C. of C. (Forward Atlanta 1989), Soc. Profl. Journalists, Nat. Press Club (Washington), Pub. Rels. Soc. Am., Phi Beta Kappa (v.p. Mich. State U. chpt. 1986, pres. 1987), Phi Kappa Phi, Sigma Delta Chi, Theta Sigma Phi, Di Gamma Kappa, Zeta Tau Alpha. Democrat. Avocations: travel, reading, writing poetry. Home: 2848 Warrington Close Tucker GA 30084-2598

STEWART, C(ORNELIUS) VAN LEUVEN, lawyer; b. Balt., Sept. 22, 1936; s. Charles Morton and Lillie Emerson (Van Leuven) S.; m. Clare Wright Horsley, June 18, 1960; children: Clare Winston, Lillie Elliotte, Jenett Ten Eyck (dec.). BA, Yale U., 1958; LLB, U. Va., 1961. Bar: Md. 1962, D.C. Bar 1982. Assoc. in law U. Calif. Law Sch., Berkeley, 1961-62; assoc. Venable, Baetjer & Howard, Balt., 1962-69, ptnr., 1970-91, Stewart, Plant & Blumenthal, LLC, Balt., 1991—. Bd. dirs., past pres. Irvine Natural Sci. Ctr.; past bd. overseers Balt. Sch. for the Arts; past bd. dirs. Pks. and People Found., Balt. Symphony Orch. Assn., Internat. Visitors Coun. of Balt., Roland Park Country Sch., Magic Me.; past pres. Md. Ballet Co., Met. Balt. Mental Health Assn. Mem. ABA, State Bar Assn., Balt. City Bar Assn., D.C. Bar Assn., Am. Coll. Trust and Estate Counsel (Md. chpt., past state chair), Internat. Acad. of Estate and Trust Law, Balt. Estate Planning Coun. (pres. 1987). Republican. Episcopalian. Office: 7 Saint Paul St Ste 910 Baltimore MD 21202-1672 E-mail: cvstewart@spblaw.com.

STEWART, D. JANE, nursing educator, researcher; b. Canton, Ohio, Nov. 7, 1948; d. Edward Hammond and Dorothy Elizabeth (Long) S. BSN, Ohio State U., Columbus, 1972. Staff nurse neurosurg. unit Duke Hosp., Durham, N.C., asst. head nurse neurosurg. unit, head nurse neurosurg. intermediate unit; staff nurse stroke acute care unit, researcher Duke U. Hosp.; asst. head nurse Fla. Hosp., Orlando, 1990-91; nurse mgr. orthopedics Orlando Regional Med. Ctr., 1992-94; mgr. patient care svcs. neurosci. George Washington U. Med. Ctr., Washington, 1994-96; nurse mgr. neurosci. unit Wake Med. Ctr., Raleigh, N.C., 1997-2000, ednl. resource specialist, 2000—. Mem. Am. Assn. Neurosci. Nurses, Alpha Tau Delta. Address: 4717 Hunt Manor Ct Raleigh NC 27616-5531

STEWART, DAVID MARSHALL, librarian; b. Nashville, Aug. 1, 1916; s. David and Mary (Marshall) S.; m. Gladys Carroll, June 9, 1947; 1 son, James Marshall. BA, Bethel Coll., 1938; BS in LS, George Peabody Coll., 1939. Circulation asst. Vanderbilt U. Library, 1938-39; county librarian Ark. Library Commn., 1939-40; Tenn. supr. WPA library service projects, 1940-42; librarian Memphis State U., 1942-46; spl. asst. to chief card div. Library of Congress, Washington, 1947; librarian CIA, 1948-60; chief librarian Nashville Pub. Library, 1960-85; Instr. Peabody Library Sch., 1966-80. Bd. dirs. Council Community Agys., Nashville, Middle-East Tenn. Arthritis Found. (v.p. 1965), Friends Chamber Music Nashville, Travelers Aid Nashville. Served to lt. comdr. USNR, 1942-46. Mem. ALA, Tenn. Library Assn. (chmn. legislative com. 1961-65, v.p. 1965, pres. 1966, Honor award, 1983), Southeastern Library Assn., Pub. Library Assn. Am. (chmn. standards com. 1964-65, pres. 1966-67), Alumni Assn. Bethel Coll. (dir., Disting. Alumni award 1992). Democrat. Mem. Ch. of Christ. Clubs: Kiwanian. (Nashville), Coffee House (Nashville). Home: 6342 Torrington Rd Nashville TN 37205-3157

STEWART, DAVID PENTLAND, lawyer, educator; b. Milw., Dec. 24, 1943; s. James Pentland and Frederica (Stockwell) S.; children from previous marriage: Jason, Jonathan; m. Jennifer Kilmer, June 21, 1986; children: Daniel, Mary Elizabeth. AB, Princeton U., 1966; JD, MA, Yale U., 1971; LLM, N.Y.U., 1975. Bar: N.Y. 1972, U.S. Dist. Ct. (ea. and so. dists.) N.Y. 1973, U.S. Ct. Appeals (2d cir.) 1973, D.C. 1976. Assoc. Donovan, Leisure, Newton & Irvine, N.Y.C., 1971-76; atty. adviser, office of legal adviser U.S. Dept. State, Washington, 1976-82, asst. legal adviser, 1982—. Adj. prof. law Georgetown U., Washington, 1984—, Am. U., Washington, 1985-86, Johns Hopkins U. Sch. Advanced Internat. Studies, 2000—; vis. lectr. Sch. Law U. Va., 1993-96, Nat. Law Ctr., George Washington U., 1993—. Contbr. articles to profl. jours.; also editorial adv. bds. Mem. dean's adv. coun. internat. law Am. U., 1984-88. Served to maj. USAR, 1970-87. Mem. ABA, Fed. Bar Assn., Am. Soc. Internat. Law., Internat. Law Assn. (adv. coun. procedural aspects internat. law inst.). Office: US Dept State Office Legal Adviser Washington DC 20520-6310 E-mail: stewartdp@ms.state.gov.

STEWART, DAVID WAYNE, marketing educator, psychologist, consultant; b. Baton Rouge, Oct. 23, 1951; s. Wesley A. Stewart, Jr. and Edith L. (Richhart) Moore; m. Lenora Francois, June 6, 1975; children: Sarah Elizabeth, Rachel Dawn. BA, N.E. La. U., 1972; MA, Baylor U., 1973, PhD, 1974. Rsch. psychologist HHS, La., 1974-76; rsch. mgr. Needham, Harper & Steers Advt., Chgo., 1976-78; assoc. prof. Jacksonville (Ala.) State U., 1978-80, Vanderbilt U., Nashville, 1980-86, sr. assoc. dean, 1984-86; prof. U. So. Calif., L.A., 1986-90, Ernest W. Hahn prof. mktg., 1990-91, Robert Brooker rsch. prof. mktg., 1991—, chmn. dept. mktg., 1995-99, dep. dean faculty, 1999-2001, dep. dean, 2001—. Mgmt. cons., 1978—. Author, co-author: Secondary Research: Sources and Methods, Effective Television Advertising: A Study of 1000 Commericals, Consumer Behavior and the Practice of Marketing, Focus Group: Theory and Practice, Attention, Attitude, and Affect in Repsonse to Advertising, Nonverbal Communication and Advertising; editor: Jour. of Mktg., 1999-02; contbr. articles to profl. jours.; editor: Jour. of Mktg.,

1999-2002; mem. edtl. bd. Jour. Mktg. Rsch., Jour. Consumer Mktg., Jour. Pub. Policy & Mktg., Jour. Mktg., Jour. Advt., Jour. Promotion Mgmt., Current Issues and Rsch. in Advt., Jour. Internat. Consumer Mktg., Jour. Managerial Issues, Jour. Promotion Mgmt.; past pres. policy bd. Jour. Consumer Rsch., Acad. Mgmt. Fellow APA (coun. rep.), Am. Psychol. Soc. (charter); mem. Soc. for Consumer Psychology (past pres.), Inst. Mgmt. Scis., Decision Sci. Inst., Am. Mktg. Assn. (pres. acad. coun. 1997-98, v.p. fin. 1998-99), Assn. for Consumer Rsch., Am. Statis. Assn. (chair sect. on stats. in mktg. 1997), Acad. of Mgmt. Republican. Baptist. Office: U So Calif Marshal Sch Bus Office Dep Dean HOH700B Los Angeles CA 90089-1426 E-mail: david.stewart@marshall.usc.edu.

STEWART, DAVID WITHERINGTON, aerospace engineer; b. Marion, Ind., Feb. 9, 1939; s. Edgar Allen Jr. and Faye Maxine (Cummings); m. Ruth Ada Valk, Aug. 26, 1961, (div.); m. Annette Louise Witherington, Dec. 17, 1962 (dec. Aug. 1999); children: Edna (dec.), Geoffrey. BS in Physics, U. Fla., Gainesville, 1959. Sr. engr. Atlas Gen. Dynamics/Convair, Cape Canaveral, Fla., 1959-63; lead engr. Gemini-Titan Martin Canaveral, 1963-66; lead engr. Sprint Martin-Orlando, Orlando, Fla., 1966-67; lead engr. Apollo Rockwell Internat., Kennedy Space Center, 1967-74, lead engr. avionics, 1975-78, prime system integ. engr. shuttle, 1978-79, supr. orbiter software, 1979-81; project mgr. software, 1982-84, project mgr. design, 1984-85, project mgr. adv. programs, 1985-89, mgr. adv. program, 1989-91, project mgr. adv. program and bus. devel., 1991-92, program devel. mgr. Fla. ops. space sys. divsn., 1992-96; pres. L&D Consulting, Titusville, 1996—. Pres. Rockwell Fla. Chpt. NMA, 1985-87. Author: Edie and the Gobie, 1966. Pres. North Brevard Environ. Action Com., Titusville, 1970-73; chmn. Marine Resources Coun. East Fla., 1996-97, 2000—; pres.-elect Space Coast Devel. Commn., 1995-96; sec. Space Coast Grant Profls. Network, 1997-99; pres. Brevard Adult Literacy Vols., Inc., 2000—. Mem. Inst. Cert. Prof. Mgrs. (cert. mgr.), Am. Cons. League (accredited profl. cons.). Republican. Unitarian Universalist. Home: PO Box 5869 Titusville FL 32783-5869 Office: Bus Devel Cons 609 Garden St Titusville FL 32796 Fax: 321-264-1885. E-mail: bizplnz@aol.com.

STEWART, DEBBIE ELAINE, librarian, artist; b. Bad Kreuznach, Germany, Sept. 24, 1962; d. Jesse Arthur and Rebecca Stewart; 1 child, Jesse. BA, Kent (Ohio) State U., 1984; MS in Libr. Sci., Drexel U., Phila., 1991. Cert. profl. librarian, Mich. Youth svcs. librarian Grand Rapids (Mich.) Pub. Library, 1994-99, youth svcs. specialist, 1999—. Reviewer: Sch. Library Jour., 2000—, one-woman shows include Franciscan Life Process Ctr., 2001, exhibitions include First United Meth. Ch., 2002. Active church choir Blessed Sacrament Ch., Grand Rapids, Mich., 1998—. Recipient juried art award Festival Regional Arts Exhbn., 1998, Franciscan Life Process Ctr., 1999, 2001, First United Meth. Ch., 2000, 2002. Mem. Soc. Children's Book Writers & Illustrators (assoc., adv, com. Mich. 1998—, Mich. illustrator coord. 1999-2001), Am. Library Assn. (life). Roman Catholic. Avocations: music, gardening, balloon animals. Office: Debbie's Home Studio 1218 Ridgeway St NE Grand Rapids MI 49505 E-mail: dstewart@grpl.org.

STEWART, DONALD GEORGE, musician, music industry executive, composer; b. Sterling, Ill., Jan. 8, 1935; s. Donald Balmer and Elinore Maud (Denison) S.; m. Susan Ann Trainer, June 13, 1963 (div. 1979); 1 child, Elizabeth Ann. MusB, Ind. U., 1960; postgrad., Manhattan Sch., 1960-62; student, Sch. of Jazz, 1958-60; studied with Roy Harris, Bernhard Heiden, Gunther Schuller. 2d clarinetist Birmingham (Ala.) Symphony, 1954-56, Fla. Symphony, Orlando, 1963; musician with numerous jazz groups including Ornette Coleman, David Baker, Sammy Davis, 1957-65; woodwind player Orch. USA, N.Y.C., 1963-65; libr. Harkness Ballet, 1967-72; founder, clarinetist Boehm Quintette, 1968-88; music asst. N.Y. State Coun. on the Arts, 1972-75; freelance copyist, 1958-88; founder, pres. Trillenium Music Co., 1986—, clarinetist, saxophonist, 1958—; pres. Opera North, Norwich, Vt., 1987-89. Founder, treas. Chamber Music Am., N.Y.C., 1977-81; panelist Vt. Coun. on the Arts, 1976-78. Composer Piccolo Concerto, 1973, August Lions for Youth Orch., 1978, Song of Arion, 1985 (2d prize Am. Harp Soc.), First Blue Symphony, 1988, Book of Sliding Things, 1989, Green Mountain Christmas Card (opera), 1995, Never Seek to Tell Thy Love (voice and ensemble), 1998, Duo for Violin and Cello, 1999; others; transcriber wind chamber music; composer, arranger for G. Schirmer, Boosey and Hawkes, Carl Fischer, Trillenium Music Co.; recs. for Columbia, Orion, New World, Margun and Marlboro, 1964—; participant Marlboro Festival, Vt., 1966-68, Berkshire Festival, Mass., summer 1965, 68. Vt. Coun. on the Arts fellow, 1985, Nat. Endowment for Arts grant, 1978—. Mem. ASCAP, Am. Fedn. Musicians, Am. Soc. Music Copyists (bd. dirs. 1970-87, treas. 1984-87), Am. Music Ctr., Music Pub.'s Assn. Democrat. Congregationalist. E-mail: don@trillenium.music@trillmusic.com; don@trillmusic.com. Office: Trillenium Music PO Box 88 Tunbridge VT 05077-0088

STEWART, DOROTHY K. educator, librarian; b. Bristol, Conn., Sept. 28, 1928; d. Robert and Anna Esther (Schwirtz) Konopask; m. David Benjamin Stewart, Sept. 27, 1952 (div. Nov. 1979); children: Douglas Neil, Diane Alison. BA in Romance Langs. and Lit. cum laude, Boston U., 1950; MSLS, Cath. U. Am., 1959. Children's libr. Brookline (Mass.) Pub. Libr., 1953-55, Takoma Park (Md.) Libr., 1955-57; reference libr. U.S. Geol. Survey, 1961; libr. Washington Internat. Sch., 1979-80, Office Sea Grant NOAA, Rockville, Md., 1980-82; info. specialist Life Ring, Inc., Silver Spring, 1983-84; pub. svc. libr. Urban Inst., Washington, 1984-85; user svcs. coord. ERIC Clearinghouse on Tchg. and Tchr. Edn., 1985-97; ret., 1997. Active, past pres. PTA, Rockville, Md., 1973-78; chmn., mem. com. Potomac (Md.) Libr. Adv. Com., 1975-85. Mem. Capital PC User Group, French lang. clubs, Phi Beta Kappa, Beta Phi Mu. Democrat. Avocations: travel, hiking, birding, microcomputers.

STEWART, E(DWARD) NICHOLSON, investment management executive; b. Bronxville, N.Y., Sept. 28, 1940; s. Edward Nicholson and Helen (Davis) S.; m. Mary Patricia Hunter, Aug. 8, 1964; children: Pamela S. Burke, Wendy S. Leary. Student, Hamilton Coll., 1959-62; BA, New Sch. Social Rsch., 1965. Dir. membership Investment Co. Inst., N.Y.C., 1968; v.p. Lord, Abbett & Co., 1969-74; pres. Trevor Stewart Burton & Jacobsen Inc., 1974-95, CEO, 1990—, chmn., 1995—. Pres., bd. dirs. Robert Hampton Tapp Found., 1993—. Co-founder, editor Hackley Rev., 1963-68. Trustee Hackley Sch., 1971-87, treas., 1972-87, v.p. 1980-87; pres. Hackley Alumni Assn., Inc., 1967-69. Mem. Am. Soc. Pension Actuaries (APM), USN League (Marine Corps com. N.Y. 1986—), Naval War Coll. Found. (life), Marine Corps Univ. Found. (assoc.), U.S. Naval Inst., Nat. Def. Indsl. Assn. (life), Union League Club (bd. govs. 1985-87, 95-97, vice chmn. 1987, pres. 1989-90), Pendennis Club (Louisville), Sleepy Hollow Country Club (bd. govs. 1993-96, sec. 1995, 2001—, asst. sec. 2000, Scarborough, N.Y.), Colony at Mountain Lake (Lake Wales, Fla.), Econ. Club N.Y., The 200 Club (Pinehurst, N.C.), Delta Kappa Epsilon. Republican. Office: 90 Park Ave New York NY 10016-1301

STEWART, FRANK MAURICE, JR. federal agency administrator; b. Okalona, Miss., Apr. 1, 1939; s. Frank Maurice Stewart and Henryne Annette (Walker) Goode; m. Regina Diane Mosley, Dec. 26, 1964; children: Lisa Ann, Dana Joy. BA, Wesleyan U., 1961, MA in Teaching, diploma further study, Wesleyan U., 1963; postgrad., Am. U., 1982-84. Dir. urban edn. corps N.J. State Dept. Edn., Trenton, 1969-70; dir. urban teaching intern program Sch. Edn. Rutgers U., New Brunswick, N.J., 1970-71; staff asst. White House Conf. on Aging, Washington, 1971-73; chief program devel. U.S. Office of Equal Edn. Opportunity, 1973-74; chief policy analysis U.S. Adminstrn. on Aging, 1974-75; asst. exec. sec. U.S. HEW, 1975-77; dir. govt. programs U.S. Dept. Energy, 1977-80, dir. instnl. conservation programs, 1980-84, dir. state and local assistance programs, 1984-90, dep. asst. sec. for tech. and fin. assistance, 1990-93; acting asst. sec. for energy efficiency and renewable energy, 1993-94; mgr. Golden (Colo.) Field Office, U.S. Dept. Energy, 1994—. Bd. dirs. Renewable Energy for African Devel., 1992-94; mem. U.S. Presdl. Del. on Sustainable Energy Devel. to South Africa, 1995, U.S. Del. to African-African-Am. Summit, Dakar, Senegal, 1995; bd. advisors Internat. Sustainable Tech. Bus. Ctr. Bd. dirs. Urban League of Met. Denver. Recipient Svc. Recognition award Assn. Phys. Plant Adminstrs., Washington, 1982, Svc. Appreciation award Nat. Assn. State Energy Officials, Washington, 1987, Midwest Rsch. Inst., 1996; named Energy Exec. of Yr. Assn. Energy Engrs., Atlanta, 1988. Mem. Sr. Execs. Assn., Nat. Assn. of Black Environmentalists (bd. dirs.), Am. Assn. of Blacks in Energy (bd. dirs. Denver chpt.), Denver Fed. Exec. Bd. Episcopalian. Home: 202 S Madison St Denver CO 80209-3010 Office: US Dept Energy Field Office 1617 Cole Blvd Golden CO 80401-3305 E-mail: frank_stewart@nrel.gov.

STEWART, GORDON CURRAN, insurance information association executive; b. Chgo., July 22, 1939; s. Henry Stewart and Evangeline (Williams) Bolton; m. Elizabeth Knorr, June 19, 1965 (div. 1968); m. Zanne Early, Dec. 20, 1995; 1 child Katarina Guadalupe Hadley. BA, Oberlin Coll., 1960; MA, U. Chgo., 1962; student, U. Vienna, Austria, 1963; MFA, Yale U., 1967. Instr. Amherst (Mass.) Coll., 1967-68; dir. Bus. Comm. for Arts, N.Y.C., 1969-71; exec. asst. Mayor of N.Y.C., 1971-73; dir., writer N.Y.C., L.A., U.K., 1973-78; dep. chief speechwriter President of U.S., Washington, 1978-81; instr. Bus. and Govt. Acad. forums, U.S. and fgn. countries, 1981-82; v.p. AMSE, N.Y.C., 1982-89; exec. v.p. Ins. Info. Inst., 1989-91, pres., 1991—. Cons. Am. Bus. Conf., Washington, 1982-89, Internat. Commn. for Ctrl. Am., Washington, 1986-88, Coun. on Competitiveness, Washington, 1987-88, Def. Sci. Bd., Washington, 1988-89. Writer films: The Store, 1978, Joey, 1978, Gallery, 1978; dir. (play) The Elephant Man (1st U.S. prodn.), 1977, Jesse, 1975, Cowboy Mouth, 1976, Sleep, 1977, (films) The Blazers, 1975; condr. Beggar's Opera, 1969, West Side Story, 1970. Dir. N.Y. Urban Coalition, N.Y.C., 1984-88; dir. policy Samuels for Gov., N.Y., 1974; speechwriter numerous dem. campaigns, 1974-81; mem. fin. coun. Dem. Nat. Com., 1984-88; mem. adv. coun. Dem. Leadership Coun., 1984-90. Woodrow Wilson fellow Woodrow Wilson Found., 1961. Mem. Writers Guild Am. (west), Judson Welliver Soc. of Chief Presdl. Speechwriters (sec.-treas.), Coun. Fgn. Rels., Century Assn., Phi Beta Kappa, Yale Club. Avocations: politics, music.

STEWART, GORDON MEAD, architect; b. Leonardtown, Md., May 18, 1959; s. William Nelson and Eileen Marie (Mead) S.; m. Jacqueline Joelle Le Moigne, Apr. 5, 1986; children: Gavin, Lauriane. BArch, BA in Urban Studies, U. Md., 1982. Registered architect, Md. Architect-intern sys. mgr. Wat & Assocs., Arlington, Va., 1981-84; architect prodn. mgr. RTKL, Balt., 1984-92; architect sys. mgr. MK Ferguson, Columbia, Md., 1992-93, CRSS Architects, Washington, 1993-94; architect project mgr., mem. tech. bd. HOK Inc., 1994-96, Jacob-Sverdrup/CRSS, Arlington, 1996—. Pres. bd. dirs. Bowie (Md.) Regional Arts Vision Assn., 1995—. Designer child care ctr. IRS, Martinsburg, W.Va., 1996; author (bus. plan) Vision 2000, 1997. Recipient 1st pl. residential design competition So. Homes Showcase, Balt., 1992, Olympic Design Competition award Bentley/Microstation, Atlanta, 1995. Mem.: Washington Area Microstation Cmty., Mid-Atlantic Region Intergraph LUG (sec., treas. 1983—95), AIA. Avocations: soccer, windsurfing, reading, photography. Home: 2830 Belair Dr Bowie MD 20715-2154 Office: Sverdrup-CRSS Jacobs Engring 1300 Wilson Blvd Ste 500 Arlington VA 22209-2307

STEWART, GREGORY WALLACE, physician; b. Balt., July 8, 1961; s. Don Milton and Martha (Davis) S.; divorced; 1 child, Lauren Elizabeth; m. Bonnie Marie Johnson, June 8, 1991; children: Tess Marie, Shaid Michael. BS in Biology, Chemistry and Para-Med. Sports Therapy, Houston Baptist U., 1982; MD, U. Tex. Med. Branch Sch. of Medicine, 1986. Diplomate Am. Bd. Physical Medicine and Rehab. Resident in physical medicine and rehab. La. State U./Charity Hosp. in New Orleans, 1986-90; instr. and asst. residency Sect. Phys. Medicine and Rehab. La. State U. Sch. Medicine in New Orleans, 1990-92; clin. asst. prof. Dept. Orthopaedics Tulane U. Sch. Medicine, 1990-95; asst. prof. and residency program dir. Sect. of Phys. Medicine La. State U. Sch. Medicine in New Orleans, 1992-95; assoc. prof. orthopedics Tulane U. Sch. Medicine, 1995—, chief divsn. phys. medicine and rehab., 1995—, med. dir. Tulane Ctrs. for Phys. Medicine and Rehab., 1996—, co-dir. Tulane Inst. Sports Medicine, 1995—. Team physician New Orleans Night Arena Football Team, 1991-92, Tulane U., 1990—, Hahnville H.S., 1987—; physician Ballet Hysell, New Orleans; coord. sports medicine St. Charles and Plaquemines Parish Sch. Dists.; assoc. coord. sports medicine St. Bernard and Orleans Parish Sch. Dists.; mem. adv. coun. La. Sports Medicine and Safety; mem. U.S. Olympic Track and Field Trials Sports Medicine Staff, 1992; mem. sports medicine organizing com. NCAA Track and Field Championships, 1993. Contbr. numerous articles to med. jours. Mem., chmn. task force on disabling violence La. Adv. Coun. on Disability Prevention, 1990-93, mem. com. on prevention of secondary disabilities; med. cons. Weiss Rehab. Ctr.; chmn. divsn. of rehab. svcs. head injury tech. assistance com. State of La.; mem. adv. com. for phys. therapy asst. program Delgado C.C.; reviewer Medicine and Sci. in Sports and Exercise Jour. of Orthopaedic and Sports Physical Therapy; abstract reviewer Nat. Head Injury Found.; grant reviewer Nat. Inst. Disability Rsch. and Rehab. Recipient Study of Personal Care Attendants for Indigent Quadriplegics grant Am. Assn. of Spinal Cord Injury Psychologists and Social Workers, 1991-93, Rehab. Long Term Tng. -Rehab. Medicine grant Rehab. Svcs. Adminstrn., 1993-95, La. Disability Prevention Program grant Sports Injury Surveillance in La., 1993-94; prin. investigator Inst. Disability and Rehab. Rsch., 1997-2001. Fellow Am. Coll. Sports Medicine; mem. AMA, Am. Acad. Phys. Medicine and Rehab., Am. Congress Rehab. Medicine, Nat. Athletic Trainers Assn., S.E. Athletic Trainers Assn., La. State Med. Soc., La. Athletic Trainers Assn., Orleans Parish Med. Soc., La. Sports Medicine Soc. (edn. chmn. 1994—). Avocations: gardening, genealogy. Home: 4905 Clearlake Dr Metairie LA 70006-1112 Office: Dept Orthopaedics SL32 1430 Tulane Ave New Orleans LA 70112-2699 E-mail: gstewart@tulane.edu.

STEWART, GUY HARRY, university dean emeritus, journalism educator; b. Keyser, W.Va., Feb. 12, 1924; s. Thomas R. and Martha (Mills) S.; m. Patricia Ann Groves, Dec. 27, 1948; children: Diane, Thomas, Jeffrey. BSJ., W.Va. U., 1948, MA, 1949; PhD, U. Ill., 1957. Reporter Cumberland (Md.) Evening Times, 1941-43, Mineral Daily News-Tribune, Keyser, 1941-43; asst. editor W.Va. U., Morgantown, 1949-50, dir. grad. studies and journalism, 1960-69, dean Sch. Journalism, 1969-89; dir. pub. rels., prof. Tenn. Tech. U., Cookeville, 1950-60. Author: A Touch of Charisma, 1969. Served as ensign USNR, 1944-46, PTO. Recipient P.I. Reed Achievement award W.Va. U. Journalism ALumni Assn., 1977; named to Keyser High Sch. Legion of Honor, 1991; Guy H. Stewart Journalism Endowment Fund named in his honor. Mem.: Assn. Edn. in Journalism and Mass Comms., W.Va. Press Assn. (life named endowed scholarship at W.Va. U. 2001), Rotary (dist. gov. 1983—84), Kappa Tau Alpha (nat. pres. 1980, Top Adviser award 1987). Democrat. Methodist. Home: 525 Pocahontas Ave Morgantown WV 26505-2274 E-mail: gnpstewart@earthlink.net.

STEWART, HAROLD BROWN, biochemist; b. Chatham, Ont., Can., Mar. 9, 1921; s. John Craig and Margaret Gertrude (Brown) S.; m. Audrey Pauline Blake, Oct. 14, 1950; 1 dau., Ann Margaret. MD, U. Toronto, 1944, PhD, 1950, Cambridge (Eng.) U., 1955. Prof. biochemistry U. Western Ont., London, 1956—; chmn. dept. biochemistry U. Western Ont., 1964-72, dean grad. studies, 1972-86, prof. emeritus, 1986—. Med. Research Council Can. vis. scientist dept. biochemistry U. Cambridge, Eng., 1971-72 Contbr. articles in biochemistry to sci. jours. Served with Royal Canadian Navy, 1945-46. Mem. Canadian, U.K. biochem. socs., Canadian Physiol. Soc., Am. Soc. Biochemistry and Molecular Biology, Coll. Physicians and Surgeons of Ont. Home: 118 Baseline Rd E London ON Canada N6C 2N8

STEWART, HAROLD SANFORD, real estate investment and supply executive; b. Cookeville, Tenn., Nov. 22, 1949; s. Willie Sanford and Margaret Eula (Wassom) S.; m. Diana Gail Law, May 3, 1968; children: Rhonda Gail, Scott Harold. Diploma, Nashville Vocat.-Tech. Sch., 1969. Cert. ACCA-EPIC instr., Air Conditioning Contractors of Am. Sales and part mgr. Scotsman Supply Co., Nashville, 1967-73; salesman Brock-McVey Supply Co., Bowling Green, Ky., 1973-76; pres., gen. mgr. Eds Supply Co., 1976-79, Nelsco Supply Co., Bowling Green, 1979-80; pres. Air Supply Co., Inc., 1980-88; sales mgr. One Stop Supply, Inc., 1988-89; pres. Bilt-Rite Constrn., Inc., 1989-92; sec., treas. K&H Enterprises, Inc., 1989-93; pres., gen. mgr. H.S. Properties, Ky., 1989—; pres., gen. mgr., stockholder Stewart Supply, Inc., 1993—. Chmn. Ky. State Vocat. HVAC Craft Com., Frankfort, 1987, Bowling Green Vocat. HVAC Craft Com., 1980-88; nat. adv. coun. Thermaflex Mfg. Co., Kansas City, Mo., 1986-87. City clk. and trustee City of Plum Springs, Ky., 1975-79; treas. Bowling Green Civitan Club, 1973-78; trustee Jackson Grove Bapt. Ch., Bowling Green, 1975-86. Named Civitan of Yr., Bowling Green Club, 1973-75, Col., Hon. Order of Ky. Cols. Mem. Masons, Optimist. Avocations: reading, computers, tennis, jogging. Home: 536 Detour Rd Bowling Green KY 42101-6501 Office: 300 W 6th St Bowling Green KY 42101-1878

STEWART, HAROLD T. social worker, consultant; b. Saratoga Springs, N.Y., May 22, 1958; s. David Andrew Stewart and Kathryn Ada Pratt; m. Jacqueline A. Newport-Stewart, June 10, 2000. AAS in Acctg., Hudson Valley C.C., Troy, N.Y., 1980; BA in Psychology, SUNY, Albany, 1996; MSW, U. New Eng., 1998. Retail acctg. program mgr. John L. English, Cohoes, NY, 1980—85; asst. compr. Lincoln Log Homes, Chestertown, 1985—87; asst. comptr. Citation Builders, Clifton Park, 1987—91; acct. Rosetti Assoc., Albany, 1992—93; substance abuse counselor York (Maine) Hosp., 1999—2000; crisis worker, cousnelor Counseling Svcs., Inc., Saco, 1999—2001; counselor, social worker Transitions Counseling, Standish, 2000—. Bd. dirs. Caring Unlimited, Sanford, Maine. Mem.: NASW. Avocations: sports, outdoor activities, fishing, camping, canoeing. Home: PO Box 64 East Parsonfield ME 04028-0064 Office: Adventure Counseling PO Box 91 171 Washington St Limerick ME 04048-0091

STEWART, HEATHER MERI, painter, sculptor; b. Appleton, Wis., Oct. 12, 1964; d. Paul James and Josephine Pauline (Smania) S. BA in Archaeol. Studies cum laude, BFA in Painting, Boston U., 1988; postgrad., Harvard U. Cert. tchr., Mass. Tchr., vol. arts and crafts The Hole in the Wall Gang Camp, Asford, Conn., 1995-97; cons., critic thesis revs. Boston Archtl. Ctr., 1998-99. One-woman shows include Curry Ctr. Art Gallery, Boston, 1999, Boston Archtl. Ctr. Atelier Gallery, 1999, exhibited in group shows at Colby Coll. Art Mus., Waterville, Maine, 1991, Boston Archtl. Ctr., 1994, Boston Mus. Sch., 1989, 1992, Boston Mus. Sch., 1995, Boston Mus. Sch., 2001, Bunting Inst. , Cambridge, Mass., 1998, 1999, Bunting Inst., 2000, Brickbottom Gallery , Somerville, Mass., 1998, 1999, 2000, 2001, The Discovery Mus., Bridgeport, Conn., 1999, Catherine Lorillard Wolfe Art Club , N.Y.C., 1999, 2000, 2001, Arlington Ctr. for the Arts, Heart of the Arts, 2000 (First prize, 2001, First prize, 2002), Harvard U., 2002, Stamford (Conn.) Art Assn., 2002, prin. works include paintings, sculptures, murals, and illustrations. Mem.: Internat. Registry Artists and Artwork, 96 Inc Writers/Artists Collaborative (bd. dirs. 1995—), Women's Caucus for Art (treas. steering com. 2000—). Avocations: fishing, hiking, cooking, martial arts.

STEWART, HOMER JOSEPH, engineering educator; b. Elba, Mich., Aug. 15, 1915; s. Earl Arthur and Alta Fern (Stanley) S.; m. Frieda Klassen, June 15, 1940; children— Robert Joseph, Katherine Stanley, Barbara Ellen. Student, U. Dubuque, 1932-33; B in Aero. Engring., U. Minn., 1936; PhD, Calif. Inst. Tech., 1940. Faculty Jet Propulsion Lab. Calif. Inst. Tech., Pasadena, 1938—, prof. aeros., 1949-80, prof. emeritus, 1980—, chief research analysis sect., 1945-56, chief Liquid Propulsion Systems div., 1956-58, spl. asst. to dir., 1960-62, chief Advanced Studies Office, 1963-67, advanced studies adviser, 1967-76. Dir. Sargent Industries, Inc., 1964-79, Office Program Planning and Evaluation, NASA, 1958-60; mem. tech. adv. bd. Aerojet-Gen. Corp., 1956-58, 61-70; mem. tech. evaluation group guided missile com. Research and Devel. Bd., 1948-50, chmn., 1951; mem. sci. adv. bd. USAF, 1949-56, 1959-64; mem. sci. adv. com. Ballistics Research Lab., 1959-69, 73-77. Author: Kinematics and Dynamics of Fluid Flow, sect. VI Handbook of Meteorology, 1945; Contbr. articles to tech. jours. Recipient Outstanding Achievement award U. Minn., 1954, NASA Exceptional Service medal, 1970, I.B. Laskowitz award N.Y. Acad. Scis., 1985 Fellow AIAA; mem. Am. Meteorol. Soc., Internat. Acad. Astronautics, Sigma Xi, Tau Beta Pi. Home: 2393 Tanoble Dr Altadena CA 91001-2729

STEWART, JACK, artist, educator, writer; b. Atlanta, Jan. 27, 1926; s. Jack Thomas and Lilly Ruth (Hemperley) S.; m. Margot S. Stewart (div.); 1 child, Brandon Burns; m. Regina Serniak, Dec. 10, 1976. BFA, Yale U., 1951; MA, NYU, 1975, PhD, 1989. Mem. faculty Columbia U. Grad. Sch. Art, N.Y.C., 1967-76; chmn. dept. art Cooper Union Sch. Art, 1971-74; v.p., provost R.I. Sch. Design, Providence, 1976-77. Exhibited at George Binet Gallery, N.Y.C., 1950, Pa. Acad. Phila., 1953, Grippi and Waddell Gallery, N.Y.C., 1963-64, Collegeo Raffaello, Urbino, Italy, 1973, La Scuola di Teodora, Venice, Italy, 1976, Sheldon Swope Gallery, Terre Haute, Ind., 1978, Broome St. Gallery, N.Y.C., 1990, 92, 96, 2001, Galeria Tonalli, Mexico City, 1997, Anita Shapolski Gallery, 1997, Silvermine Galleries, Conn., 1998, others; works include mosaic murals at Versaile Hotel, Miami Beach, Fla., mosaics on Grace Line's SS Santa Paula, 1957, Facade of Aruba (Netherlands Antilles) Carib Hotel, 1958, mosaic murals in Pub. Sch. 28, N.Y.C., 1958, stained glass Robin Internat. Cinarama, 1962, Cluett Shirt Group, Atlanta, 1990; editor: Modern Mosaic Techniques, 1967; author articles in encys. and mags; inventor laminated stained glass. Sgt. inf. U.S. Army, 1944-46, ETO. Mem. N.Y. Artists Equity Assn. (pres. 1987-89), Nat. Soc. Mural Painters (pres. 1996-2000), Fine Arts Fedn. NY (v.p. 2002). Baptist. Home: Stewart Studio 31 E 7th St New York NY 10003-8001

STEWART, JACK M. management consulting firm executive; b. Oneida, N.Y., Feb. 20, 1926; s. E. Jerome and Frieda Freeman (Holz) S.; m. Tudy Newman Stewart, June 26, 1955; children: Eileen Jan Guttman, Leslie Ann, Ralph Edward. BME, Syracuse U., 1946, MSIE, 1950. cert. mgmt. cons., cert. profl. material handling, cert. profl. material mgmt.; registered profl. engr. Rsch. engr. Martin-Marietta Co. (name now Lockheed-Martin), Balt., 1946-47; chief/indsl. engr. Syracuse (N.Y.) Ornamental Co., Inc., 1947-49; instr. Syracuse U., N.Y., 1949-50; asst. mgr. mfr. engring. General Electric Co., Syracuse & Auburn, 1950-53; v.p. Wheeler Associates, Inc., Cleve., 1953-57; pres. Research for Industry, Inc., 1960-88, Indsl. Technol. Assocs., Inc., Cleve., 1957--. Panel of Arbitrators Am. Arbitration Assoc., N.Y.C., 1986-2001. Contbr. numerous articles to profl. jours. Precinct Committeeman and mem. cen. com. Republican Party, Pepper Pike, Ohio, 1970-; pres. Pepper Pike Civic League, 1990-92. Mem. Internat. Material Mgmt. Soc., Am. Foundrymen's Soc., Am. Defense Preparedness Assoc., Solon (Ohio) C. of C., Chagrin Valley Shrine Club, Al Koran Temple, Interstate Scottish Rite 32 Club of Cleve. (pres. 1975-76), Ancient Accepted Scottish Rite, Forest City Lodge (Free & Accepted Masons), Am. Soc. Mech. Engrs., Inst. Packaging Profl., Inst. Mgmt. Cons. (pres.-N.E. Ohio, 1988-91), Coll. of Firm Prins., Syracuse U. Alumni Assn. (chmn. rep. program N.E. Ohio, Nat. v.p. 1964, Alumnus of Yr., 1973, Outstanding Alumni Rep. 1991). Republican. Avocations: organization work, gardening, biking, golf. Office: Indsl Tech Assocs 28326 Belcourt Rd Cleveland OH 44124-5622 E-mail: tns.jms@juno.com., ita12@juno.com.

STEWART, JAMES ANDREW, librarian; b. Oskaloosa, Iowa, June 5, 1949; s. William Warren (dec.) and Mary Helen (Merriam) S.; m. Fayette Mae Hamilton, Nov. 20, 1976; children: William Earl, Robert Andrew. Student, S.E. Iowa C.C., Burlington, 1968; BS, Iowa State U., 1972; MBA, S.W. Mo. State U., Springfield, 1982; MA in Libr. Sci., U. Iowa, Iowa City, 1987. Reference libr. C.L. Wilson Libr., U. Mo., Rolla, 1987-89, head reference, 1989-93, head collections, 1993—. Trustee Rolla Pub. Libr., 1998—. With U.S. Army, 1972-74, USAR, 1989—. Mem. Am. Soc. Engring. Edn. (sec.-treas. engring. librs. divsn. 1994-95, program chair 1995-96, chair 96-97), Univ. Orators Toastmasters (pres. 1994), CTM 1992. United Methodist. Avocations: bicyling, jogging, reading. Office: U Mo-Rolla Cl Wilson Libr Rolla MO 65409-0001

STEWART, JAMES BREWER, historian, writer, college administrator; b. Cleve., Aug. 8, 1940; s. Richard Henry and Marion Elizabeth (Brewer) S.; m. Dorothy Ann Carlson; children: Rebecca Ann, Jennifer Lynn. BA, Dartmouth Coll., 1962; PhD, Case Western Res. U., 1968. Asst. prof. history Carroll Coll., Waukesha, Wis., 1968-69, Macalester Coll., St. Paul, 1969-79, James Wallace prof. history, 1979—, provost, 1986-89. Cons. Am. Coun. of Learned Socs., N.Y.C., 1988-92. Author: Joshua R. Giddings & the Tactics of Radical Politics, 1970, Holy Warriors: Abolitionists & Slavery, 1976, rev. editon 1997, Liberty's Hero: Wendell Phillips, 1986 (Best Biography award, Soc. Midland Authors 1986), William Lloyd Garrison and the Challenge of Emmancipation, 1992, To Heal the Scourge of Prejudice: The Life and Writings of Hosea Easton, 1999, Race and the Construction of the Republican State, 2000. Rsch. fellow NEH, 1973, Am. Coun. Learned Socs., 1984. Mem. Am. Hist. Assn., Orgn. Am. Historians (nom. com. 1988-92), Soc. Historians of the Early Republic (exec. com. 1987-94, editl. bd. 1999—). Avocations: camping, gardening, furniture restoration. Home: 1924 Princeton Ave Saint Paul MN 55105-1523 Office: Macalester Coll Dept Of History Saint Paul MN 55105 E-mail: stewart@macalester.edu.

STEWART, JAMES CHARLES, II, insurance agent; b. Spartanburg, S.C., Jan. 2, 1952; s. James Charles Sr. and Thelma (Robertson) S.; m. Nancy Eleanor Bates, Dec. 23, 1973; children: James Ryan, Matthew Daniel, Megan

Eleanor. BS in Mktg., U. S.C., 1974; CLU, Am. Coll., Bryn Mawr, Pa., 1983. Mgr. I-26 Svc. Ctr., Woodruff, S.C., 1975; agt. Ind. Life Ins. Co., Jacksonville, Fla., 1975-84, N.Y. Life Ins. Co., N.Y.C., 1984—; pres. Ins. Group, Spartanburg, S.C., 1992—. Coach So. Spartanburg Youth Athletic Assn., Walnut Grove, S.C., 1984-88; treas. Roebuck (S.C.) Primary Sch. PTA, 1986-87, pres., 1987-88; asst. chief Hobbysville Vol. Fire Dept., Woodruff, 1978; treas. Cavins (S.C.) Dem. Precinct, 1978; v.p. Dorman H.S. (Spartanburg) All Sports Booster Club, 1995-96. Named Hon. Constable, S.C. Gov. Jim Edwards, 1975, S.C. Gov. R.W. Riley, 1979, S.C. Gov. Carrol A. Campbell, 1987, S.C. Gov. David Beasley, 1995, S.C. Gov. Jim Hodges, 1999; named Divsn. Co-winner, Grand Strand Fishing Rodeo, Myrtle Beach, S.C., 1987. Mem. Spartanburg Life Underwriters Assn. (pres. 1988-89, Underwriter of Yr. 1990), Soc. Fin. Svc. Profls., Nat. Assn. Ins. and Fin. Advisors, Gentlemen's Actuarial Soc. S.C. (charter), S.C. Assn. Life Underwriters (LUPIC chmn. 1989-92), U. S.C. Alumni Assn., Gamecock Club, Million Dollar Round Table (qualifying mem. 2000, 01), Masons (master chpt. 1983), Ruritan Club (charter, pres. 1988), Delta Sigma Pi, Sigma Pi Mu (various offices). Avocations: golf, reading, trout and surf fishing. Home: 8 Tims Creek Rd Roebuck SC 29376-3353 Office: NY Life Ins Co 251 Magnolia St Ste 5 Spartanburg SC 29306-2331

STEWART, JAMES GEORGE, producer, director, video executive; b. N.Y.C., Oct. 19, 1937; s. George I. and Margaret (Milo) S.; m. Linda Tower, July 12, 1980. Student, RCA Inst., N.Y.C., 1961-63, U. Md., 1957-58. With advt. dept. Pabst Brewing Co., Newark, 1958-62; lighting technician Shelle Prodns., N.Y.C., 1962-63; studio technician Sta. WTIC-TV, Hartford, Conn., 1963-66, producer, dir., 1966-74; prodn. mgr. Sta. WFSB-TV, 1974-77, exec. producer, 1978-81; sr. unit mgr. NBC, N.Y.C., 1977; freelance producer, dir. ESPN Network, Bristol, Conn., 1979—; dir. Cigna Creative Svcs., Cigna Corp., Hartford, 1981—, Sta. WTIC News at 10, 1989-96. Lighting technician: (TV show) Naked City, 1962-63; producer, dir.: Doubleplay Game Show (Regional Emmy award nomination 1976), NCAA Baseball, Basketball, Hockey, Soccer, Football telecasts, 1971—, NHL Hockey telecasts, 1971—, various news, spl. events telecasts, Conn., 1967-81; dir.: (TV series) Marlo and the Magic Movie Machine, 1976-80 (Emmy award nomination 1977, 78), Capt. Bob, 1970-74, (TV spl.) Kitty Hawk to the Stars. Served with USAF, 1955-58. Recipient regional Emmy nomination Acad. TV Arts and Scis., 1976, nat. Emmy nomination Nat. Acad. TV Arts and Scis., 1977, Hartford Advt. Fedn. award, 1977, 78. Mem. Internat. TV Assn., Air Force Assn., Comms. Media Mgrs. Assn., Conn. Radio Info. Svc., Comm. Media Mgrs. Assn., Soc. of Strategic Air Command. Roman Catholic. Avocations: photography, sports, music. Home: 39 Schoolhouse Crossing Wethersfield CT 06109-1341 Office: Cigna Comm Media Video Svcs # A-115 Hartford CT 06152

STEWART, JAMES IAN, agricultural water scientist, cropping system developer, consultant; b. San Diego, Jan. 9, 1928; s. Castle Elmore and Myrtle Catherine (Hasty) S.; m. Robbie Nell Oliver, Mar. 23, 1975; children: Virginia Lane Stewart Carton, Ian Castle Stewart, Kevin Scott Overby. BSc, U. Calif., Berkeley, 1950; PhD, U. Calif., Davis, 1972. Farm advisor Agrl. Extension Svc., U. Calif., Stockton and Merced, 1950-61; extension expert Irrigation, FAO UN, Nicosia, Cyprus, 1962-66; assoc. rsch. water scientist U. Calif., Davis, 1966-77; supervisory soil scientist USDA/Office for Internat. Cooperation and Devel., Nairobi, Kenya, 1977-83; team leader, agrometeorologist USAID/Kenya Mission, 1977-83; founder, pres. Found. for World Hunger Alleviation Through Response Farming (WHARF), Davis, 1984—. Cons. sustainable agrl. devel. and resource mgmt. for ecol. balance AID, USDA, World Bank, FAO/UNDP, 37 countries of Ams., Europe, Asia, Africa, Australia, 1965—; sci. convocations, 17 internat. countries, 1969—. Author: Response Farming in Rainfed Agriculture, 1988; creator (computer programs) Wharf, Wharfdat, 1993; contbr. numerous articles to profl. jours. Mem. Internat. Soil Sci. Soc., World Assn. Soil and Water Conservation, Internat. Com. for Irrigation and Drainage (life, U.S. com.), Indian Soc. Dryland Agr. (life), Sigma Xi, Phi Delta Theta. Achievements include pioneering research on soil water extraction by crops; crop water requirements; relations between crop yield and water evapotranspired; impacts of water deficits in different crop growth stages; relations between season rainfall behavior and season dates of onset. Developer of FAO world standard linear and weighted growth stage models for estimating crop yields from actual evapotranscription, and contributor to four-growth-period linear model for estimating crop water requirements. Developer of "response farming" methodology for design of dryland cropping systems based on historical rainfall behavior, and seasonal flexibility in their management based on realtime rainfall season date of onset, defined to meet crop establishment requirements. Home: 640 Portsmouth Ave Davis CA 95616-2738 Office: World Hunger Allev Through Response Farming PO Box 1158 Davis CA 95617-1158 E-mail: wharf@davis.com.

STEWART, JAMES KEVIN, judicial administrator, management technology consultant; b. Berkeley, Calif., Nov. 28, 1942; s. Berthold and Myrle (Minson) S.; m. Marise Rene Duff, Oct. 26, 1985; children: Daphne Brooks, Andrew MacLaren, James Kevin Spencer, Mary Elizabeth Ainsley. BS, U. Oreg., 1964; M.P.A., Calif. State U.-Hayward, 1977; grad. cert., U. Va., 1978; grad., FBI Nat. Acad., 1978. Cmmdr. criminal investigation div. Oakland Police Dept., 1976-81; instr. San Jose (Calif.) State U., 1978-81; spl. asst. atty. gen. Dept. Justice, Washington, 1981-82; dir. Nat. Inst. Justice, 1982-90, Booz, Allen & Hamilton, Inc., McLean, Va., 1990—. Guest lectr. U. Calif., Berkeley, Harvard, U.; steering com. global organized crime initiative Ctr. Strategic Internat. Studies, 1994; U.S. del. Couns. of Europe, Strasborg, France, 1984; advisor DOD/DOJ Ops. Other Than War and Law Enforcement, 1994; chmn. pun. safety conf. SPTE, 1992; advisor, chmn. Dept. Justice Nat. Conf. Law Enforcement Tech., 21st Century, Washington, 1993; bd. dirs. White House Fellows Found., 1990; mem. Internat. Law Enforcement Conf., Washington, 1995. Recipient O.W. Wilson award for outstanding contbns. to law enforcement, 1986, Ennis J. Olgiati award Nat. Assn. Pre-Trial Services Agys., 1987, Predl. citation AIA, 1987, Nat. Criminal Justice Service award Nat. Criminal Justice Assn., 1988, Outstanding Nat. Contbn. to Policing Spl. award Police Exec. Research Forum, 1988, August Vollmer award Am. Soc. Criminology, 1992; White House fellow, 1981-82. Mem. Internat. Assn. Chiefs of Police (dir. 1981-82), Police Mgmt. Assn. (founder, pres. 1979-81), White House Fellows Alumni, White House Fellows Found. (bd. dirs.), FBI Nat. Acad. Assn., Internat. Homicide Investigation Assn. (charter), Nat. Inst. Corrections (bd. dirs.), Soc. for Reform of Criminal Law (planning chmn. Police Powers and Citizens Rights Conf.), Coun. For Excellence In Govt. (prin.), Delta Upsilon. Clubs: University (Washington). Republican. Episcopalian. Home: 503 Roosevelt Blvd Apt A424 Falls Church VA 22044-3117 Office: Booz Allen & Hamilton Inc 8283 Greensboro Dr Ste 700 Mc Lean VA 22102-3838

STEWART, JAMES MALCOLM, lawyer; b. Aberdeen, Wash., May 8, 1915; s. Malcolm M. and Ethel Lucille (Hinman) S.; m. Dorothy Vera Gilardi, Sept. 16, 1945; children: Barbara Jane, Robert Bruce, William James. BA, U. Wash., 1939, JD, 1941. Bar: Wash., 1941, U.S. Dist. Ct. (we. dist.) Wash., 1948, U.S. Supreme Ct., 1998. Dep. prosecuting atty. Grays Harbor County, Wash., 1945-48; pvt. practice Montesano, 1952-99. Pres., dir. Gray Harbor Coll. Found., Aberdeen, 1955-95; bd. dirs. St. Joseph Hosp., Aberdeen, 1972-87; organizer Gray Harbor Cmty. Found., Aberdeen, 1993; scout leader Boy Scouts Am. Lt. USNR, 1942-45, PTO, admirality officer, 1945-46, lt. comdr., 1950-52, Korea, ret. Decorated 16 Battle Stars, 2 Silver Stars, Gold Star. Mem. Am. Judicature Soc., Wash. State Bar Assn. (50 Yr. award, 1991), Gray Harbor Bar Assn. (pres. 1953), Aberdeen Pioneers Assn. (pres., dir. 1948-98), Lions (Melvin Jones award 1997), Elks, Sigma Nu, Phi Delta Phi. Republican. Episcopalian. Avocations: tree farming, hiking, horseback riding, tennis. Home: 711 3rd St N # D Montesano WA 98563-1625

STEWART, JAMES MONTGOMERY, banker; b. Detroit, May 31, 1939; s. Albert Edwin and Dagny Winter (Jensen) S.; m. Kathleen Williams, Sept. 27, 1940; children— Laura, Wendy, Kathleen BBA, U. Mich., 1962, MBA, 1963. Asst. sec. Irving Trust Co., N.Y.C., 1966-68, asst. v.p., 1968-70, v.p., 1970-81, sr. v.p., 1981-86; regional gen. mgr. Copenhagen Handelsbank, 1986-90; gen. mgr. Danske Bank, N.Y.C., 1990—2001, sr. advisor, 2002—. Trustee, treas. Am. Scandinavian Found. Mem. Danish Am. C. of C. (bd. dirs., treas.), Anglers, Links Club, Racquet and Tennis Club, Country Club New Canaan. Republican. Avocations: trout fishing; golf; jazz; wine. Home: 130 Ramhorne Rd New Canaan CT 06840-3007 Office: Danske Bank 299 Park Ave New York NY 10171

STEWART, JANE, psychology educator; b. Ottawa, Ont., Can., Apr. 19, 1934; d. Daniel Wallace and Jessie Stewart; m. Dalbir Bindra, Aug. 5, 1959 (dec. 1981). BA with honours, Queen's U., Kingston, Ont., 1956; PhD, U. London, 1959; DSc (hon.), Queen's U., 1992. Sr. rsch. biologist Ayerst Labs., Montreal, Que., 1959-63; part-time instr. psychology Sir George, 1962-63; assoc. prof. psychology Williams U., 1963-69; prof., chmn. psychology SGW Univ. (now Concordia U.), 1969-75; prof. psychology Concordia U., 1975—. Dir. Ctr. for Studies in Behavioral Neurobiology, Concordia U., Montreal, 1990-97. Fellow AAAS, APA, Royal Soc. Can., Can. Psychol. Assn.; mem. Soc. for Neurosci., N.Y. Acad. Sci. Office: Concordia University 1455 de Maisonneuve Blvd W Montreal QC Canada H3G 1M8

STEWART, JANE, Canadian government minister; d. Robert Nixon; 2 sons. BS with honors, Trent U., 1978. Chair Nat. Liberal Caucus, 1994-96; Human Resources profl., to 1994; min. nat. revenue Govt. of Can., 1996-97, min. Indian Affairs and No. Devel., 1997-99; min. Human Resources devel. Govt. of Canada, 1999—. Can. del. to numerous confs.; chair Econ. Union, 2002—. Office: 14th Fl Human Resources Devel 2-5 Govt Canada 140 Promenade du Portage IV Hull QC Canada K1A OJ9 Fax: 819-994-5222. E-mail: stewaj@parl.gc.ca.

STEWART, JANICE MAE, judge; b. Medford, Oreg., Feb. 13, 1951; d. Glenn Logan and Eathel Mae (Jones) S.; m. F. Gordon Allen III, Aug. 10, 1975; children: Benjamin Stewart, Rebecca Mae. AB in Econs., Stanford U., 1972; JD, U. Chgo., 1975. Bar: Ill. 1976, Oreg. 1977, U.S. Dist. Ct. Oreg. 1977, U.S. Ct. Appeals (9th cir.) 1978. Assoc. Winston & Strawn, Chgo., 1975-76, McEwen, Gisvold, Rankin & Stewart, Portland, Oreg., 1976-81, ptnr., 1981-93; U.S. magistrate judge, 1993—. Mem. Multonomah County Profl. Responsbility Com., Portland, 1979-82, Oreg. Profl. Responsibility Bd., 1982-85, Oreg. State Bar Practice and Procedure Com., 1985-88, Profl. Liability Fund Def. Panel, Portland, 1985-93, Multnomah County Jud. Selection Com., 1985-88, Oreg. State Bar Professionalism Com., 1989-91, Oreg. State Bar Fed. Practice and Procedure Com., 1996-99, Coun. Ct. Procedures, 1991-93, lawyer rep. 9th Cir. Jud. Conf., 1990-93, Multnomah County Professionalism Com., 1997-2000. Mem. ABA, Am. Arbitration Assn. (arbitrator 1990-93), Oreg. Bar Assn., Multnomah County Bar Assn. (dir. 1990-93), Phi Beta Kappa. Democrat. Office: 1027 US Courthouse 1000 SW 3rd Ave Portland OR 97204-2930

STEWART, JEAN CATHERINE, critical care and neuroscience emergency trauma nurse, educator; b. Pitts., July 12, 1948; d. Frank E. and Bertha G. (Drawdy) Henry. BSN, Ariz. State U., 1971; MSN, U. Tex., Houston, 1988. Cert. neurosci. RN; cert. emergency nurse; cert. trauma nurse; cert. in clin. trials design and mgmt., San Diego; cert. clin. trials adminstr. Neurosurg. nursing cons. The Meth. Hosp., Houston, 1981-84; staff devel. instr. M.D. Anderson Hosp. and Tumor Inst., 1984-85; staff nurse Ben Taub Gen. Hosp. Emergency Ctr., 1985-87; continuing edn. instr. Ben Taub Gen. Hosp., 1987-91; clin. nurse specialist neurosci./orthopedics/trauma div. U. Calif. Med. Ctr., San Diego, 1991-96; surg clin. nurse specialist Kaiser Permanente, 1998-99; critical care internship program coord. San Diego Am. Assn. Critical Care Nurses, 1998—2000; clin. nursing coord. U. Calif. San Diego Mitochondrial & Metabolic Disease Ctr., 1999—. Announcer Dial A Shuttle program, Nat. Space Insts.; adj. clin. instr. ADN program Southwestern C.C., 2000—; trustee Neuroscience Nursing Found., 2001—; presenter meetings and confs. various profl. orgns. Mem. manuscript rev. bd. Jour. Neurosci. Nurses.; editorial rev. bd. Dimensions in Oncology Nursing. Trustee Neurosci. Nursing Found. Recipient Millie Fields Rsch. Assistance award U. Tex., 1987. Mem. AACN (Rsch. award 1987, rsch. grantee Houston Gulf Coast chpt.), Emergency Nurses Assn., Am. Assn. Neurosci. Nurses (founding mem., past treas. S.C. chpt., pres. and program dir. Houston chpt., bd. dirs. div. nursing affairs 1991-93), Am. Assn. Neurol. Surgeons, Harvey Cushing Soc. (assoc.), World Fedn. Neurosci. Nurses, Soc. Trauma Nursing, Nat. Assn. Clin. Nurse Specialists, Sigma Theta Tau. Home and Office: 1640 10th Ave # 103 San Diego CA 92101-2873

STEWART, JOANNE, secondary school educator; b. Vancouver, Wash., Mar. 10, 1944; d. Edward Charles and Claudine Marie Spencer; m. William Lemly Stewart, Sept. 2, 1966 (dec. June 1983); children: Amy Diane Stemple, Nicholas William. BS, Wash. State U., 1966, MA, 1973. Cert. tchr., Mont., Idaho, Wash., Calif. Tchr. foods Seaside High Sch., Monterey, Calif., 1966-67; tchr. home econs. Marysville (Wash.) High Sch., 1967-68, Palouse (Wash.) High Sch., 1968-73, Ennis (Mont.) High Sch., 1973-76, Genesee (Idaho) High Sch., 1976-77; instr. young family Missoula (Mont.) County High Sch., 1983-84; tchr. home econs. Woodman Sch., Lolo, Mont., 1985-86; travel cons. Travel Masters, Missoula, 1984-87; ticketing mgr. Blue Caboose Travel, 1987-91; tchr. family and consumer scis. Victor (Mont.) High Sch., 1991-2001; dir. Victor 21st Century Learning Ctr., 2001—, After Sch. Learning Ctr. Project dir. sch.-to-work implementation Victor Sch., 1996—2002, project dir. Op. Green Thumb, gender equity Carl Perkins grant, 1997—98. Co-pres. Lolo PTO, 1980-81; v.p. Lolo Community Ctr., 1981; sec. Lolo Mosquito Control Bd., 1988—; mem. telecommunications com. Conrad Burns & Gov. Racicot; sec. state supt. edn. task force on vocat. edn., 1995-96; coord. Health Rocks!, Nat. 4-H Program, 2000-01. Marysville Edn. Assn. scholar, 1962, Future Homemakers Am. scholar, 1962. Mem. AAUW (sec. 1986, program chmn. 1987), Forestry Triangle (pres. 1981, editor cookbook 1982), Washington State Future Homemakers Am. (hon. mem.), Am. Family and Consumer Scis. Assn., Mont. Family and Consumer Scis. Assn. (bylaws chair 1994, pres. elect 1995-96, pres. 1996-97, Profl. of Yr. 1997), Mont. Vocat. Tchrs. Assn. (returning Rookie of Yr. 1992, Am. Federated Tchrs., Mont. Vocat. Family and Consumer Scis. Tchrs. (v.p. 1993-94, pres. 1994-95, Tchr. of Yr. 1998). Republican. Methodist. Avocations: homemaking, swimming. Home: 1200 Lakeside Dr Lolo MT 59847-9705 Office: Victor High Sch ROPES 425 4th Ave Victor MT 59875-9468 E-mail: stewart@victor.k12.mt.us.

STEWART, JOHN HARGER, music educator; b. Cleve., Mar. 31, 1940; s. Cecil Tooker and Marian (Harger) S.; m. Julia Wallace, Aug. 14, 1977; children: Barbara, Cecily Bronwen. BA, Yale U., 1962; MA, Brown U., 1972; cert., New Eng. Conservatory, 1965. With various operas including Santa Fe Opera, N.Y.C. Opera, Met. Opera, U.S. and Europe, 1965—; lectr. Mt. Holyoke Coll., South Hadley, Mass., 1988-90; dir. vocal activities Washington U., St. Louis, 1990—; dir. Friends of Music. Office: Dept Music Washington U Campus Box 1032 One Brookings Dr Saint Louis MO 63130-4899

STEWART, JOHN LINCOLN, university administrator; b. Alton, Ill., Jan. 24, 1917; s. Frederick William and Hilda (Denovan) S.; m. Joan Elsdon Guthridge, Sept. 23 1939 (div. 1964); children: Leslie Cythera Stewart Chalmers, Ann Guthridge Stewart Nutt; m. Ruth Peabody Quinn, July 11, 1964; stepchildren: Geoffrey Cornelius Quinn, Andrew Dean Quinn. AB, Denison U., 1938, ArtsD (hon.), 1964; MA, Ohio State U., 1939, PhD, 1947. From tchg. asst. to instr. Ohio Sate U., Columbus, 1939-47; instr. UCLA, 1947-49; from asst. prof. to prof. English Dartmouth Coll., Hanover, N.H., 1949-64; prof. Lit. U. Calif., San Diego, 1964-87, provost John Muir Coll., 1965-87. Author: Exposition for Science and Technical Students, 1950, The Essay, 1952, John Crowe Ransom, 1962, The Burden of Time, 1965; (with others) Horizons Circled, 1974, Ernst Krenek, 1990; contbr. articles to profl. jours. Assoc. dir. Hopkins Ctr. for Arts, 1961-64; dir. Mandeville Ctr. for Arts, 1974-76; mem. Dartmouth Community Symphony Orch., 1949-58; trustee Kinhaven Music Sch., 1960-64, Fla. West Coast Symphony, 1958, Oakland Cmty. Orch., 1997—; bd. dirs. Theater and Arts Found. San Diego County, 1970; pres. La Jolla (Calif.) Friends Sch. Music, 1971-73, Friends of Music, U. Calif., San Diego. Served with Aus, 1942-45. Howard Found. fellow, 1953-54, Dartmouth Coll. fellow, 1962-63. Democrat. Avocation: performer with music ensembles. Home: 2361 E 29th St Oakland CA 94606-3511

STEWART, JOHN MURRAY, banker; b. Summit, N.J., Apr. 2, 1943; s. Robert John Stewart and Mary Catherine Yoder; m. Sandra Meyers Frazier, 1966 (div. 1997); children: Jennifer Bricar Crone, Catherine Dorothy Lochead; m. Rebecca Marie Mellen, July 10, 1998. BA, U. Va., 1965; MBA, NYU, 1983. Trust officer, v.p. Bankers Trust Co., N.Y.C., 1965-82, Morgan Guaranty Trust Co., N.Y.C., 1982-83; mgr., pres., dir. Morgan Trust Co. Fla., Palm Beach, 1983-89; pres., dir. Bankers Trust Co. Fla., 1989-93; founder, pres. pvt. capital group SunTrust Bank, Orlando, Fla., 1993-96; pres., dir. Harris Trust/Bank of Montreal, West Palm Beach, 1996—2001, Fla. Trust Co., Ft. Lauderdale, Fla., 2002—. Campaign chmn. Palm Beach Cmty. Chest, 1985, 1986; mem. exec. com. Palm Beach County Local Initiatives Support Corp.; vestryman Bethesda By the Sea Ch., Palm Beach, 1986—89, 1992—94, treas., 1986—87, Cathedral Ch. of St. Luke, Orlando, 1996; bd. dirs. Orlando Opera Co., 1994—96, Palm Beach Opera Co., 1996—2001. Mem. Fla. Bankers Assn. (chmn. trust bus. devel. com. 1989, planning commn., chmn. trust legis. com. 1990), N.Y. State Bankers Assn. (mem. trust bus. devel. com. 1978-82), N.Y. Yacht Club (N.Y.C.), Everglades Club (Palm Beach), Monmouth Boat Club (Red Bank, N.J.), Sailfish Club of Fla. (Palm Beach) (bd. govs. 1992-96), SAR (pres. Palm Beach chpt. 1997, 98). Office: 110 E Broward Blvd Fort Lauderdale FL 33301 E-mail: jstewart@floridatrustco.com.

STEWART, JOHN TODD, economist, consultant; AB, Stanford U., 1961; MA, Tufts U., 1962, MALD, 1970. With Am. Fgn. Svc., 1962-98; U.S. amb. to Republic of Moldova, 1995-98; dep. head U.S. diplomatic missions to Can., Costa Rica and Jamaica; dir. office maritime and land transport Dept. of State, Washington; dir. GATT affairs Pres.'s Spl. Rep. for Trade Negotiations; dep. dir. Inst. Internat. Econs., Washington, 1998—2002. Office: Inst Internat Econs 1750 Massachusetts Ave Washington DC 20036-1207 E-mail: stewartjt@aol.com.

STEWART, JOHN WRAY BLACK, college dean; b. Coleraine, Northern Ireland, Jan. 16, 1936; s. John Wray and Margaret Reid (Black) S.; m. Felicity Ann Patricia Poole, Aug. 7, 1965; children: J.W. Matthew, Hannah Louise. BSc with honors, Queen's U., Belfast, Northern Ireland, 1958, B.Agr. with honors, 1959, PhD, 1963, DSc, 1988. Registered profl. agrologist. Sci. officer chem. rsch. div. Ministry of Agr., Belfast, 1959-64; asst. prof. soil sci. dept. U. Sask., Saskatoon, Can., 1966-71, assoc. prof. Can., 1971-76, prof. Can., 1976-81, dir. Sask. Inst. Pedology, 1981-89, dean Coll. Agr., 1989-99, prof. emeritus, 1999—, dean emeritus, 1999—, interim dir. Inter-Am. Inst. for Global Change Rsch., 2002. Tech. expert, cons. FAO/IAEA, U.N.D.P., Vienna, Austria, 1971, 74-75; mem. program com. Can. Global Change , 1985—98; sec.-gen. Sci. Com. on Problems of Environ., Paris, 1988-92, pres., 1992-95, past pres., 1995-98, editor-in-chief, 1999- ; cons. UNESCO , Paris, 1990; trustee Internat. Inst. Tropical Agr. , Nigeria, 1991—97; chair sci. adv. com. Inter-Am. Inst. for Global Change Rsch. , 1994—2001. Contbr. articles to profl. publs., chapters to books. Fellow Can. Soc. Soil Sci., Berlin Inst. Advanced Study, Am. Soc. Agronomy, Soil Sci. Soc. Am., Agrl. Inst. Can.; mem. Brit. Soc. Soil Sci., Brazilian Soc. Soil Sci., Internat. Soc. Soil Sci. Avocations: squash, golf, tennis. E-mail: Jwbstew@island.net.

STEWART, JONATHAN TAYLOR, psychiatrist, educator; b. Bethpage, N.Y., Mar. 15, 1956; s. Allen Theodore and Vivian (Dreiblatt) S.; m. Linda Sue Irvin, Oct. 27, 1984; children: Jacob Zachary, Aaron Joshua. BA with honors, Rollins Coll., 1976; MD, U. South Fla., 1979. Diplomate Am. Bd. Psychiatry and Neurology, Geriatric Psychiatry, Nat. Bd. Med. Examiners. Resident in psychiatry U. Fla. Coll. Medicine, Gainesville, 1979-83, assoc. prof. psychiatry, 1983-94; asst. chief psychiatry VA Med. Ctr., 1987-94; prof. psychiatry U So. Fla. Coll. Medicine, 1994—; chief geropsychiatry sect. Bay Pines (Fla.) VA Med. Ctr., 1994—. Contbr. articles to profl. jours., 1985—. Mem. Head Injury Adv. Coun. State of Fla., 1985-90. Fellow: Am. Geriatrics Soc., Am. Psychiat. Assn.; mem.: Fla. Geriatrics Soc., Fla. Psychiat. Soc. Jewish. Avocations: cooking, cycling, skin diving, traveling. flying. Office: VA Med Ctr Psychiatry Service 116A Bay Pines FL 33744

STEWART, JOSEPH GRIER, lawyer; b. Tuscaloosa, Ala., July 24, 1941; s. Jesse Grier and Kyle Vann (Pruett) S.; m. Linda Louise Hogue, Mar. 2, 1963; children: Joseph Grier Jr., Robert Byars, James Vann. BS, U. Ala., Tuscaloosa, 1963, LLB, 1966. Bar: Ala. 1966, U.S. Dist. Ct. (no. dist.) Ala. 1968, U.S. Dist. Ct. (middle Dist.of Ala.), 1996, U.S. Tax Court. Ptnr. Burr & Forman LLP, Birmingham, Ala., 1968—. Mem. ABA, Ala. State Bar, Birmingham Bar Assn. (chmn. com. 1989-90), Ala. Law Inst., Kiwanis, Birmingham Tip Off Club (pres. 1988-89). Methodist. Avocation: tennis. Office: Burr & Forman LLP 3100 S Trust Tower 420 20th St N Birmingham AL 35203-5200

STEWART, JOSEPH TURNER, JR. retired pharmaceutical company executive; b. N.Y.C., Apr. 30, 1929; s. Joseph Turner and Edna (Pride) S.; m. Carol Graham, Aug. 7, 1954; children: Lisa D., Alison D. BS with honors, U.S. Mcht. Marine Acad., 1951; MBA, Harvard U., 1954. Systems analyst Warner Lambert Co., Morris Plains, N.J., 1954-56, budget dir. internat., 1956-60, asst. div. controller consumer products group, 1960-62, div. controller group, 1962-66; dir. adminstrn. and fin. Proprietary Drug div. Warner Lamber Co., 1966; dir. Lactona Products div. Warner Lamber Co., 1967; controller Beech-Nut subs. Squibb Corp., N.Y.C., 1968, v.p. fin., 1968-71, v.p. planning, corp. staff parent corp., 1971-79, v.p. fin. and planning parent co., 1979-82, sr. v.p. corporate affairs parent co., 1982-89; also bd. dirs.; cons. Johnson & Johnson, 1990-98. Bd. dirs. Gen. Am. Investment Corp., Liposome Co. Trustee Tax Found., 1985-89; commr. N.J. State Commn. on Income and Expenditures, 1985-88; mem. adv. com. Grad. Sch. Indsl. Adminstrn., Carnegie Mellon U., 1986-91; trustee New Sch. for Social Rsch., 1990-98, U. Medicine and Dentistry of N.J. Found., 1989—; bd. dirs. Liposome Co., 1995-2000; vis. coun. Marine Biol. Lab., 1995—. John Hay Whitney Opportunity fellow, 1952-54. Mem.: Harvard (N.Y.C.). E-mail: kingpin497@aol.com.

STEWART, KAREN MEYER, pediatrics nurse, nursing manager; b. Bryn Mawr, Pa., June 7, 1957; BSN, U. Mich., Ann Arbor, 1979; MS, U. Minn., 1994. Grad. nurse Pediatrics Mott Children's Hosp., Ann Arbor, Mich., 1979; staff nurse, charge nurse, pediatric ICU Saint Mary's Hosp., Rochester, Minn., 1979-84; asst. head nurse pediatric ICU, 1984-89; nurse mgr., pediatric ICU, pediatric transport team Mayo Clinic, Rochester, Minn., 1989—. Instr. pediat. Mayo Med. Sch., Rochester, Minn., 1994—. Mem. AACN, Minn. Nurses Assn., Minn. Orgn. Leaders in Nursing, Soc. Critical Care Medicine, Phi Kappa Phi, Sigma Theta Tau. Office: Mayo Eugenio Litta Children's Hosp Pediat ICU 1216 2nd St SW Rochester MN 55902-1906

STEWART, KATHERINE HEWITT, advanced practice nurse; BS in Statistics, BSN, U. Mich., 1988, MS in Med.-Surg. Nursing, 1991. Cert. specialist, med.-surg. nursing. Clin. nurse II med. ICU U. Mich. Med. Ctr., 1988-91; teaching asst. U. Mich. Sch. Nursing, 1990-91; clin. nurse specialist intermediate med. unit Henry Ford Hosp., Detroit, 1991-93; nurse practitioner Gen. Medicine, P.C., Plymouth, Mich., 1993—. Contbr. articles to profl. jours. Mem. nat. conf. Geronolog. Nurse Pracititoners. Dean's fellow U. Mich., 1989-90. Mem.: Nat. Assn. Clin. Nurse Specialists, Mich. Nurses Assn., Sigma Theta Tau. Office: Gen Medicine PC PO Box 6376 Plymouth MI 48170-0464 E-mail: khs@alienguppy.com.

STEWART, KAY BOONE, writer, retired educator and administrator; b. Amarillo, Tex., Feb. 2, 1934; d. Howard Taft and Olive Eugenia (Greer) Boone; m. Robert N. Alkire, July 22, 1952 (div. Aug. 1971); children: Shelley Kay Alkire, Kristin Lynne Alkire Porter; m. Elmer Donald Stewart, July 16, 1978. Student, Phoenix Coll., 1957-64, Glendale (Ariz.) C.C., 1967; BA in Elem. Edn. with distinction, Ariz. State U., 1969; postgrad., Seattle Pacific U., 1988-90. Cert. tchr. elem. edn., Ariz. Tchr. Glendale (Ariz.) Meth. Day Sch., 1960-63, Trinity Meth. Day Sch., Glendale, 1966-67, Ctrl. Meth. Day Sch., Phoenix, 1967-68, Catalina Elem. Sch., Phoenix, 1969-70, Valencia Elem. Sch., Phoenix, 1970-71, Palo Alto Pre-Sch., Tempe, Ariz., 1971-73; sales rep., ednl. program Western Pub., southwestern states, 1972-75; adminstr., program developer, thcr. Palo Alto and Glendale Meth. Day Sch. Adminstr. Skytech Cons., Inc., Elk Grove, Calif., 1999. Author: (novel) Chariots of Dawn, 1992, (poetry) Sunrise Over Galilee, 1993, Here's Help, A Management System for Chronic Fatigue Syndrome, 1996. (poetry) The Color Red, 1994; editor Writers Info. Network, 1986-99; creator line of frameable art note cards to benefit breast cancer rsch., 2001; composer and lyricist children's and adults' choir music. Mem. Am. Penwomen (pres. 1990-92), Writers Info. Network, Kappa Delta Phi. Republican. Presbyterian. Avocations: storytelling, singing, harp, directing children's choir. Home: 202 Rainbow Dr # 10261 Livingston TX 77399-2002 Office: Writers Info Network PO Box 11337 Bainbridge Island WA 98110 E-mail: kstew2234@aol.com., ksb@mymailstation.com.

STEWART, KENNETH MALCOLM, retired anthropologist, researcher; b. Tecumseh, Nebr., June 16, 1916; s. Kenneth Atwell and Alta Margaret S.; m. Mary Marguerite Reed, Jan. 7, 1942 (div. 1951); children: Kenneth Malcolm Jr., Geraldine Kay; m. Louise Garland Dyer, June 6, 1960. BA, U. Calif., 1938, MA, 1940, PhD, 1946. Asst. prof. Calif. State U., Fresno, 1946-47; prof. Ariz. State U., Tempe, Ariz., 1947-79, ret., 1979. Cons. Mohave Indian Tribe,

Needles, Calif., 1955-56, researcher Colo. River Reservation, 1970-71; tchr. Papago Indian Tribe, Sells, Ariz., 1946. Co-author: The Native Americans, 1965, 77, The Southwest, vol. 10, 1983. Fellow Am. Anthropol. Assn.; mem. AAUP, Soc. Am. Ethnology, Sigma Xi. Democrat. Avocations: musicology, travel. Home: 4353 Dowitcher Way Oceanside CA 92057-7515 E-mail: Kenji156@aol.com.

STEWART, KENT KALLAM, analytical biochemistry educator; b. Omaha, Sept. 5, 1934; s. George Franklin and Grace (Sledge) S.; m. Margaret Reiber, June 10, 1956; children: Elizabeth, Cynthia, Richard, Robert. Student, U. Chgo., 1951-53; AB, U. Calif., Berkeley, 1956; PhD, Fla. State U., 1965. Guest investigator Rockefeller U., N.Y.C., 1965-67, research assoc., 1967-68, asst. prof., 1968-69; research chemist U.S. Dept. Agr., Beltsville, Md., 1970-75, lab. chief Nutrient Composition Lab., 1975-82; prof., head dept. food sci. and tech. Va. Poly. Inst. and State U., Blacksburg, 1982-85, prof. biochemistry, anaerobic microbiology, food sci./tech., 1985-98; adj. prof. dept. chemistry and biochemistry U. Tex., Austin, 1996—. Editor Jour. Food Composition and Analysis, 1987-97, also 3 books; contbr. articles to profl. jours., co-author book; patentee in field. Capt. USMCR, 1956-59. Fellow Inst. Food Technologists, AAAS; mem. Am. Chem. Soc. Home: 3900 Glengarry Dr Austin TX 78731-3812 Office: Dept Chemistry and Biochemistry Mail Code A5300 U Tex Austin TX 78712 E-mail: kkstewart@mail.utexas.edu.

STEWART, KERRY, political scientist, educator; b. Toronto, Ontario, Can., Apr. 14, 1951; , permanent resident, U.S., 1953; s. William C. and Margaret M. Stewart. BA in History BA in Philosophy, U. Hawaii, Hilo, 1989; MA in History MA in Philosophy, Bowling Green (Ohio) State U., 1993; PhD in Polit. Sci., Ga. State U., Atlanta, 1999. Asst. prof. Polit. Sci. and Philosophy Ga. Southwestern State U., Americus, 1999—2000; asst. prof. Polit. Sci. and Philosophy Gainesville Coll., Oakwood, Ga., 2000—. Pub. policy cons. Gov.'s Coun. on Devel. Disabilities, Atlanta, 1995—96. Co-editor: (book) Ethics and Character: The Pursuit of Democratic Virtue, 1999; asst. editor (book) Cambridge History of Disease, 2000. Mem.: Am. Philos. Assn., Am. Polit. Sci. Assn., Forsyth C. of C. (mem. several coms. 2001—), Phi Alpha Theta. Libertarian. Avocations: hiking, literature, music, scuba diving. Home: 6535 Newcastle Way Cumming GA 30040 Office: Gainesville Coll Box 1353 Gainesville GA 30503

STEWART, KORDELL, professional football player; b. New Orleans, Oct. 16, 1972; , U. Colo. Quarterback Pitts. Steelers, 1995—. Achievements include playing in Super Bowl XXX, 1995, AFC championship game, 1995, 1997. Office: 300 Stadium St Pittsburgh PA 15204 also: Administrative Office 3400 South Water Street Pittsburgh PA 15203-2349 Mailing: P O Box 6763 Pittsburgh PA 15212*

STEWART, LESLIE MUELLER, editor, writer; b. Morristown, N.J., Oct. 25, 1942; d. Edward Arthur and Phyllis Virginia (Dohm) Mueller; m. James Alexander Stewart, Sept. 19, 1969; children: Alexander, Alison. BA in English Lit., Reed Coll., Portland, Oreg., 1964; postgrad., U. Calif., Berkeley, 1964-65. Libr. Golden Gate U., San Francisco, 1964-69, lectr., 1968-71; adminstrv. asst. Williams & Mocine, 1968-71; classroom aide Mt. Diablo Unified Sch. Dist., Concord, Calif., 1978-79, substitute libr., 1982-87; adminstrv. asst. Bay Area Monitor, Oakland and Lafayette, 1987-95, editor Lafayette, 1995—. Mem. adv. coun. U. Calif. Toxic Substances Rsch. and Tchg. Program, 1995—; prep. Decision Makers Directory, LWV Bay Area, Lafayette, 1987-95. Chair County Hazardous Materials Com., Contra Costa County, 1995—; bd. dirs. Contra Costa CAER Group, Inc., 1997—, Rainbow Cmty. Ctr., Concord, 2001—. Mem. LWV Calif. (bd. dirs., sec. 1993-95), LWV Diablo Valley (bd. dirs., program chair 1998—, pres. 1991-93). Avocations: word and crossword puzzles, mystery and science fiction books. Office: Bay Area Monitor 500 Saint Marys Rd Lafayette CA 94549-5431 E-mail: lesliestewart@lwvba-ca.org.

STEWART, LUCILLE MARIE, retired special education coordinator; b. Pitts., Feb. 24; d. William H. and Edna (Hoffman) S. BEd, Duquesne U.; MEd, U. Pitts.; postgrad., Columbia U., U. Calif., Calif. State U. Cert. elem. and secondary tchr., spl. edn. tchr., supr., adminstr. Tchr. mentally retarded Ednl. Alliance, N.Y.C., 1950—53; tchr. Lincoln (Ill.) State Sch., 1953; tchr., program leader, sec. Edn. Alliance, N.Y.C., 1954-58; tchr. mentally retarded Ramapo Ctrl. Sch. Dist., Spring Valley, N.Y., 1958-60, tchr. seriously emotionally disturbed, 1960-64, supr. presch. program for educationally disadvantaged, 1965-67; program dir. Pomona (N.Y.) Camp for Retarded, summers 1960-63; tchr. mentally retarded Stockton Sch., San Diego, 1964-65; tchr. mentally retarded sch. Cathedral City Sch. , 1967-78; program specialist spl. edn. Palm Springs (Calif.) Unified Sch. Dist. , 1978-95; prin. elem. summer schs. Palm Springs (Calif.) Unified Sch. Dist., 1971-72; tchr. elem. mentally retarded sch. Palm Springs (Calif.) Unified; prin.-tchr. Summer Extended Sch. for Spl. Students, summer 1979-99. Mem. exec. com. U. Calif. Extension area adv. com. Mem. NEA, AAUW, ASCD, Calif. Tchrs. Assn., Calif. Assn. Program Specialists, Calif. Adminstrs. of Spl. Edn. (desert cmty. mental health childrens com.), Coun. Exceptional Children (adminstrn. divsn., early childhood-learning handicap divsns.), Am. Assn. Childhood Edn., Autism Soc., Coachella Valley, Learning Disabilities Assn., Creative Desert, Desert Theater League, Alpha Kappa Alpha, Phi Delta Kappa, Delta Kappa Gamma.

STEWART, MAC A. educator; b. Forsyth, Ga., July 7, 1942; s. Alonzo and Zillia (Watson) S.; m. Tena Clemons, June 4, 1967; children: Bruce Kifle, Justin Che. BA, Morehouse Coll., 1963; MA, Atlanta U., 1965; PhD, Ohio State U., 1973. Lic. psychologist, Ohio. Tchr., counselor Jasper County Tng. Sch., Montivello, Ga., 1963-64; tchr. Crispus Attucks High Sch., Indpls., 1965-66; dir. student fin. aid Morehouse Coll., Atlanta, 1966-70, dir. upward bound, 1967-70; dir. residence hall Ohio State U., Columbus, 1970-71, grad. adminstrv. assoc. student fin. aid, 1971-73, asst. dean Univ. Coll., 1973-75, assoc. dean Univ. Coll., 1975-90, assoc. prof., 1991-98, assoc. provost for undergrad. studies, 1998—, dean Univ. Coll., 1998-2001, vice provost Minority Affairs, 2001—. Contbr. articles to profl. jours.; mem. editl. bd. The Negro Ednl. Rev., 1983—, editor-in-chief, 1999—. Bd. trustees The Columbus Acad., Gahanna, Ohio, 1990-96, Buckeye Boys Ranch, Grove City, Ohio, 1978-84, Mt. Carmel Coll. Nursing, 1998—, Internat. Found. Edn. & Self-Help, 1998—, Mt. Carmel Coll. Nursing, 1998—; mem. adv. coun. Internat. Found. Edn. and Self-Help, Phoenix, 1992—, bd. dirs., 1998—; bd. dirs. Urban Edn., Rsch. and Human Devel. Inst., Columbus, 1977-80. Mem. ASCD, Ohio Acad. Sci., Nat. Assn. Equal Opportunity in Health Edn., United Negro Coll. Fund, Phi Kappa Phi, Phi Beta Sigma, Sigma Pi Phi. Avocations: reading, collecting insulators, travel, jogging, weight lifting. Home: 930 Notchbrook Dr Delaware OH 43015-8996 Office: Ohio State U Bricker Columbus OH 43201-1806

STEWART, MARGARET MCBRIDE, biology educator, researcher; b. Guilford County, N.C., Feb. 6, 1927; d. David Henry and Mary Ellen (Morrow) S.; m. Paul C. Lemon, June 1962 (div. 1968); m. George Edward Martin, Dec. 19, 1969. AB, U. N.C.-Greensboro, 1948; MA, U. N.C.-Chapel Hill, 1951; PhD, Cornell U., 1956; DSc (hon.), U. P.R., Mayaquez, 1996. Instr. biology Greensboro Evening Coll. U. N.C., Greensboro, 1950-51; instr. biology Catawba Coll., Salisbury, N.C., 1951-53; extension botanist Cornell U., Ithaca, N.Y., 1954-56; asst. prof. biology SUNY, Albany, 1956-59, assoc. prof., 1959-65, prof. vertebrate biology, 1965-97, disting. tchg. prof., 1977—, disting. tchg. prof. emerita, 1997; dir. Program in Biodiversity Conservation and Policy, 1997-2000. Faculty rsch. participant Oak Ridge Assoc. Univs., 1983. Author: (with A.H. Benton) Keys to the Vertebrates of the Northeastern States, 1964, Amphibians of Malawi, 1967; contbr. numerous articles and revs. to profl. jours. Bd. dirs. E.N. Huyck Nature Preserve, Rensselaerville, N.Y., 1976-86; bd. dirs. Ea. N.Y. chpt. Nature Conservancy, 1983-88, 90-96, 97—, N.Y. State chpt., 1987-90; mem. Albany Pine Bush Commn., 1993—. Recipient Citizen Laureate award SUNY Found., 1987, Oak Leaf award Nature Conservancy, 1997; Am. Philos. Soc. rsch. grantee, 1975, 81, NSF grantee, 1978-80, Oak Ridge Assocs. Univs. grantee, 1983-97. Fellow Herpetologists League (bd. dirs. 1978-80); mem. Soc. for Study of Amphibians and Reptiles (pres. 1979), Am. Soc. Ichthyologists and Herpetologists (bd. govs. 1975-80, 87-90, 96—, herpetology editor 1983-85, pres. 1996, historian 1999—), Ecol. Soc. Am., Assn. for Tropical Biologists, Soc. Study of Evolution, III World Congress of Herpetology (mem. exec. com. 1995-01), Sigma Xi, Sigma Delta Epsilon, Phi Kappa Phi. Democrat. Presbyterian. Avocations: photography, gardening, reading, travel. Office: SUNY Dept Biol Scis 1400 Washington Ave Albany NY 12222-1000 E-mail: mstewart@csc.albany.edu.

STEWART, MARK THOMAS, compressed gas company executive; b. Butler, Pa., June 9, 1948; s. Paul William and Donna Ruth (Wonderly) S.; m. Judith Lynne Christie, Aug. 12, 1967; children: Andrew Paul, Elizabeth Christie. BA, Indiana U. Pa., 1969; MAT, Duquesne U., 1972; cert. in orthodox theology, St. Stephen Coll., 1996. Cert. tchr., Pa.; cert. master baloom artist Nat. Assn. Balloon Artists. Tchr. Butler (Pa.) Catholic Sch., 1970-74; acct. George F. Pott, CPA, Gibsonia, Pa., 1974-76; field rep. Republican State Com., Harrisburg, 1976; exec. dir. Harmony (Pa.) Mus., 1977-78; foreman Pullman Standard Co., Butler, 1978-82; mgr. P.W. Stewart Welding Supply, West Sunbury, Pa., 1982-84; v.p. Stewart & Stewart, Inc., 1984-87, pres., 1987—; balloon design cons., dir. Stewart and Stewart, Inc., 1984—. Originator balloon art techniques. Mem. campaign staff, writer, researcher various Rep. campaigns, Butler and Allegheny Counties, Pa., 1974-87; bd. dirs. Moniteau Sch. Dist., West Sunbury, 1982-85. Recipient 3d place award internat. design competition Nat. Assn. Balloon Artists, 1989. Mem. NRA (life), Nat. Fedn. Ind. Bus., Nat. Propane Gas Assn., Masons. Republican. Mem. Orthodox Ch. Avocations: reading, writing, hunting. Home: 1675 Oneida Valley Rd Chicora PA 16025-4123 Office: PO Box 248 West Sunbury PA 16061-0248

STEWART, MARLENE METZGER, financial planning practitioner, insurance agent; b. Portland, Oreg., Nov. 1, 1937; d. Eddie Charles and Helen M. (Grant) Metzger; m. Robert W. Stewart, Aug. 1, 1964 (dec. Jan. 1967); m. Melvin N. McBurney, Feb. 14, 1985. BA, U. Oreg., 1959; MA, U. Tex., El Paso, 1971. Exec. dir. Summer 72 Youth Com. Office of Mayor, Portland, 1972; registered rep. Mut. Life Ins. Co. N.Y., 1973-76, Prudential Life Ins. Co., Portland, 1976-77; ptnr. N.W. Fin. Planning, 1977-79; pres. Horizons Unltd. Fin. Planning, 1979-86; prin. EMR Fin. Adv. Svcs., Inc., 1986-89; registered rep. KMS Fin. Svcs., Inc., 1979—; owner Stewart Fin. Group, 1991—. Mem.-at-large nat. bd. YMCA's, 1971-73; bd. dirs. Met. YMCA, Portland, 1971-75; bd. dirs. YWCA, Portland, 1989-92, treas., 1990-92, chmn. investment com.; chmn. planned giving com. Arthritis Found., 1984-86. Bill Bottler scholar Portland chpt. CLU and Chartered Fin. Cons., 1981. Mem. Fin. Planning Assn., Oreg. Soc. Inst. CFP's (treas. 1985-86, Internat. Assn. Fin. Planners (pres. Oreg. chpt. 1987-88), Nat. Assn. Ins. & Fin. Adv., Soc. of Fin. Svc. Profls. and Portland Chpt. (treas. Portland chpt. 1985-86), Fin. Planning Assn., Assocs. Good Samaritan (steering com., chmn. 1991-92), Rotary (past chmn. World Cmty. Svc. com. 1998-2000). Republican. Presbyterian. Avocations: swimming, traveling, reading, knitting, sewing. Office: 5901 SW Macadam Ave Ste 135 Portland OR 97201 E-mail: stewfg@aol.com.

STEWART, MARVIN LEWIS, human resources professional; b. Fairmont, W.Va., June 30, 1953; s. Charles T. and Edna W. (Jones) S.; m. Phyllis A. Mitchell, July 7, 1973; children: Autumn Nicole, Kristen Leighann, Danielle Denise, Matthew Lewis. BS in Bus. Adminstrn., Fairmont State U., 1976; MS in Econs., W.Va. U., 1984. Preload supr. United Parcel Svc., western Pa., 1974-76, pers. supr. W.Va., 1976-82, packaging ctr. mgr., 1982-85, employment mgr., 1985-86, spl. assignment Ky., 1987, employment mgr., 1989, human resources div. mgr. Air Dist., Pa., 1989—. Loaned exec. United Way, Phila., 1989, dist. coord., 1990; chmn. activity bd. dirs. Marion Parks and Recreation, Fairmont, 1983-84; mem. Leadership Marion, Fairmont, 1984-85. Baptist. Avocations: tennis, golf, singing (gospel choir), travel. Office: United Parcel Svc 1 Hog Island Rd Philadelphia PA 19153-3996

STEWART, MAX DOUGLAS, economics educator, consultant; b. Edmonton, Alta., Can., June 6, 1919; s. Maurice Howard and Mary Penn (Ritchie) S. B.A., U. Alta., 1941, B.Com., 1942; M.A., U. Toronto, 1946; Ph.D., Mich. State U., 1960. Investment analyst Value Line Investment Survey, N.Y.C., 1949-50; registered rep. N.Y. Stock Exchange, Shuman, Agnew & Co., San Francisco, 1950-51; econ. affairs officer UN, N.Y.C., 1954; lectr. econs. Royal Mil. Coll., Kingston, Ont., Can., 1953-56; asst. prof. Waterloo Coll., Ont., 1956-59; Combines investigation officer Dept. Justice, Ottawa, Ont., 1959-61; prof. econs. Waterloo Luth. U., 1961-65; lectr. 15 sessions Banff Sch. Advanced Mgmt., Can., 1966-82; research officer Econ. Council of Can., Ottawa, 1967-68; prof. econs. U. Alta., Edmonton, 1965-74; prof. econs. Wilfrid Laurier U., Waterloo, Ont., 1974— , v.p. acad. affairs, 1982-83, dean bus. and econs., 1974-82; dir. Imtrex Commodities Inc., Oakville, Ont. Author: Concentration in Canadian Manufacturing and Mining, 1970; author monograph (with others) Report on Restrictive Business Practices in International Trade, 1955. Contbr. articles to profl. jours. Mem. Am. Econ. Assn., Can. Econ. Assn., Royal Econ. Assn., Fin. Execs. Inst., Delta Upsilon. Mem. United Ch. of Can. Clubs: Royal Commonwealth Soc. (London); Kitchener-Waterloo Gyro; Royal Can. Mil. Inst.; Westmount Golf and Country (Kitchener). Avocations: philately; photography; travel. Office: Wilfrid Laurier U, 75 University Ave West, Waterloo, ON Canada N2L 3C5

STEWART, MELINDA JANE, judge; b. Merced, Calif., Apr. 10, 1949; d. Donald Joel and Betty Yvonne (Santi) S.; m. Bruce G. Wilbur, Aug. 1998; children from previous marriage: Alexa Marie, Julienne Rose, Robert Patrick; stepchildren: Michelle, Keith, Kelly, Kevin. BA, Stanford U., 1972; JD, Golden Gate Law Sch., 1975. Bar: Calif. 1975, U.S. Dist. Ct. (no. dist.) Calif. 1975. Dep. dist. atty. Santa Clara County Dist. Atty., San Jose, Calif., 1976—80; atty. Miller & Hinkle Law Offices, 1980; pvt. practice Tondreau & Goodman, 1980—83; referee Santa Clara County Superior Ct., 1983—89, judge, 1989—2000; judge on assignment Superior Ct., 2001—. Faculty Calif. Ctr. for Jud. Edn. and Rsch., 1983—. Bd. dirs. Eastfield Ming Quong Childrens Ctr., 1993-98, pro bono project of Santa Clara County, 1992-95, YWCA Kids Connection, 1993-95, Hillbrook Sch., 1993-98. Named Calif. State Bar Assn. Family Law Judge of Yr., 1995; recipient Henry B. Collada Meml. award, 1995. Mem. Calif. Judges Assn., Assn. Family and Conciliation Cts. (Calif. chpt. bd. dirs.). Avocations: swimming, tennis, skiing. Office: Superior Ct Santa Clara County 191 N 1st St San Jose CA 95113-1001

STEWART, MICHAEL B. lawyer, mechanical and aerospace engineer; b. Royal Oak, Mich., Nov. 5, 1963; s. Colin M. and Jacqueline P. Stewart; m. Katherine Hewitt, May 1987; children: Elizabeth and Caitlin. BSME, BA in English, U. Mich, 1987, MS in Aerospace Engring., 1988, JD, 1991. Assoc. Dykema Gossett PLLC, Bloomfield Hills, Mich., 1991-96; mnging. ptnr. Rader, Fishman & Grauer PLLC, 1996—. Contbr. articles to profl. jours. Named 40 Under 40 Honoree Crain's Detroit Bus., 1998. Mem. ABA, Intellectual Property Law Assn., Mich. Patent Law Assn., Mich. Bar Assn., Oakland County Bar Assn. (chmn. continuing legal edn. subcom. for IP com. 1998), Optimists (bd. dirs. 1993-97), Delta Theta Phi (dean., bd. govs., Detroit alumni senate). Avocations: cycling, woodworking. Office: Rader Fishman & Grauer PLLC 39533 Woodward Ave Ste 140 Bloomfield Hills MI 48304-5098 E-mail: mbs@raderfishman.com.

STEWART, MICHAEL GLENN, medical educator, physician; b. Bowling Green, Ky., Sept. 17, 1962; s. Michael Joseph and Barbara (Weisser) S. B in Engring. summa cum laude, Vanderbilt U., 1984; MD, Johns Hopkins U., 1988; MPH, U. Tex., 1996; Gen. Surgery, Baylor Coll. Medicine, 1990, Otolaryngology, 1994. Diplomate Am. Bd. Otolaryngology. Asst. prof. Baylor Coll. Medicine, Houston, 1994-99, assoc. prof., 1999—, dir. residency edn. dept. otolaryngology, 1996—, asst. dean clin. affairs, 1998-2000, gen. dir. affil. med. svc., 1999—, assoc. dean clin. affairs, 2000—. Chief otolaryngology Ben Taub Gen. Hosp., 1994—; sci. cons. Surgeons' Outcomes Rsch. Coop., 1996—; chmn. med. bd. Harris County Hosp. Dist., Houston, 1999-2000. Rev. Head and Neck, 1994—, Archive Otolaryngology-Head and Neck, 1997—, Jour. Trauma, 1998—, Otolaryngology-Head and Neck Surgery, 1998—, Cancer, 2001—. Recipient Outstanding Clin. Rsch. award Kelsey-Seybold Found., 1992, 93. Fellow ACS, Am. Acad. Otolaryngology Head and Neck Surgery (chmn. outcomes rsch. subcom.), Am. Triological Soc., Am. Laryngol., Rhinol. and Otol. Soc.,Am. Rhinologic Soc. Office: Baylor Coll Medicine Dept Otolaryngology 1 Baylor Plz # Na102 Houston TX 77030-3411

STEWART, MICHAEL IAN, orthodontist; b. Yonkers, N.Y., May 22, 1955; s. William Bernard and Bernice Barbara (Friedman) S.; m. Vicki Lynn Sapperstein, Mar. 26, 1988. BA cum laude, U. Miami, 1978; DDS, Emory U., 1984; cert. in orthodontics, Yeshiva U., 1990. Cert. Nat. Bd. Dental Examiners; bd. eligible Am. Bd. Orthodontics. Pvt. practice gen. dentistry, Tampa, Clearwater, Fla., 1985; pvt. practice children's dentistry, Clearwater, New Port Richey, Plant City, Fla., 1985-88; fellow in orthodontics Montefiore Med. Ctr.-Albert Einstein Coll. Medicine, Bronx, N.Y., 1988-90; pvt. practice orthodontics, Clearwater, Plant City, New Port Richey, 1990—. Provider dental svcs. Fla. Dept. Health and Rehabilitative Svcs., Clearwater, New Port Richey, Plant City, 1985—, Head Start, Clearwater, New Port Richey, 1985-88; cons. Health South Rehab. Hosp., 1996—. Illustrator: Mandibular Surgery and Sleep Apnea, 1990. Cons. LaSertoma, New Port Richey, 1986—; vol. VA Med. Ctr., Miami, Fla., 1978; cons., lectr. Apple program Pasco County Assn. for Retarded Citizens, 1987. Rsch.grantee Northeastern Soc. Orthodontists, 1989. Mem. ADA, Am. Assn. Orthodontists, So. Assn. Orthodontists, Acad. 100, Fla. Dental Assn., West Coast Dental Assn., Upper Pinellas County Dental Assn., Am. Soc. Dentistry for Children, Ctrl. Fla. Orthodontic Study Club, Alpha Omega, Alpha Epsilon Delta. Avocations: automobiles and restoration, reading, sailing, landscaping, bicycling. Home: 2063 Swan Ln Palm Harbor FL 34683-6274 Office: 707 Druid Rd E Clearwater FL 33756-3913

STEWART, MICHAEL MCFADDEN, professional speaker; b. Eupora, Miss., Aug. 24, 1938; s. Judge Ernest and Billie Rivers (McFadden) S.; m. Barbara Ann Dickerson, June 2, 1962; children: Michael Jr., Mark Robert (dec. Dec. 1997). BS, La. State U., 1961. Cert. speaking profl. Nat. Spkrs. Assn., 1996. Cons. E.K. Williams & Co., Birmingham, Ala., 1964-66, br. mgr., 1966-68, Miami, Fla., 1968-69, Marcoin, Inc., Balt., 1969-73, dist. mgr. Falls Church, Va., 1973-74; v.p. Marcoin Western Ops., Inc., Houston, 1974-77; dir., v.p. Marcoin, Inc., Atlanta, 1977-85; ptnr. Cherokee/G & S Assocs., 1985-88; pres. Stewart & Stewart, Inc., Dunwoody, Ga., 1988—, The Sales Power Resource Group, Inc., Atlanta, 1991-95. Cons., speaker AMA, N.Y.C., 1989—, Duffy-Vinet Inst., Langhorne, Pa., 1987-92, The Sullivan Group, Guilford, Conn., 1990-92; guest speaker SBA, Bell South Success Symposium Series, 1990-91. Author: How to Get Started with a Small Business Computer, 1984, Quality Customer Service, 1990, Using Your Financial Statements to Boost Your Bottom Line Profits, 1990, Computerizing Your Business, 1991, The Magic of Customer Service, 1991, Bring Home the Bacon, 1992, Customer Service Excellence: How to Implement a Corporate-wide Program, 1992, Strategic Relationship Selling, 1992, Transition into Sales Management, 1992, Sales Managememt Call Reluctance Workshop, 1992, Negotiating with Style, 1992, Meeting Today's Competitive Challenges, 1992, Creative Management in Tough Economic Times, 1993, Relationship Empowered Technical Selling, 1993, Consultative Relationship Selling, 1993, Customer-Centered Sales Management Leadership, 1993, Customer Centered Selling, 1993, Being Different in a Niche Market, 1993, Moving, Shaking and Prospecting, 1993, 50/250 The Smart Way, 1993, Customer-Centered Relationship Selling, 1994, Working Sucessfully with Others, 1994, Fundamentals of Quality Customer Service, 1994, Sales Are The Life-Blood Service is the Heart Beat, 1994, Customer-Centered Value Selling, 1994, Customer-Centered Sales Management, 1994, Make the Number by Selling Value, 1995, Hiring Smart, 1995, Customer-Centered Sales Management, 1995, Live the Spirit, 1996, Sell Value, Not Price, 1996; contbg. author: Chicken Soup for the Soul at Work, 1996, Relationship Centered Value Selling, 1997, Professional Sales Skills, 1997, Sales Negotiation for Higher Profits, 1998; contbg. author: Reach for the Stars, 1998, Close More Sales!, 1999, Close More Sales With Premise, 2000, Developing A Productive Sales Orientation, 2000, Motivational Sales Management, 2000, Basic Sales Training Boot Camp, 2001, DNA of Sales Success: Hiring and Motivating Blue-Chip Sales Programs, 2002, Leading Explosive Growth-Encouraging Passionate Sales Performance, 2002, others; co-author: Embracing Change-Understanding and Managing Transitions in Life and Work, 2002; contbr. numerous articles to profl. jours. Fin. officer Atlanta Colts Youth Assn., 1979; vol. speaker Am. Cancer Soc., 1994—. Capt. U.S. Army, 1961-64. Recipient Silver award Carlson Learning Co., Mpls., 1990, numerous other awards. Mem. Ga. Speakers Assn. (past pres., past dir., Mem. of Yr. 1996), Nat. Spkrs. Assn. (cert. speaking profl.), Dunwoody Country Club, Dunwoody Gridiron Club (pres. 1981), Lambda Chi Alpha. Episcopalian. Avocation: golf. Home: 490 Tavern Cir Atlanta GA 30350-4455 E-mail: mike@mikestewartseminars.com.

STEWART, MILTON ROY, lawyer; b. Clovis, N.Mex., Dec. 16, 1945; s. Virgil Maurice and E. Marie (Collins) S. BA, Ind. U., 1968, JD summa cum laude, 1971. Bar: Oreg. 1971, U.S. Ct. Appeals (9th cir.) 1971, U.S. Dist. Ct. (no. dist.) Oreg. 1971. Assoc. firm Davies, Biggs et al, Portland, Oreg., 1971-75; v.p., gen. counsel U.S. Datacorp, 1975-77; pvt. practice, 1977-86; ptnr. Davis, Wright, Tremaine & predecessor firm, 1987—, mem. exec. com., past chmn. firmwide bus. group, 1990-98. Chmn. emeritus Oreg. chpt. Nat. Multisclerosis Soc., 1994—; mem. bd. dirs. Nat. Multiple Sclerosis Soc.; mem. bd. vis. Ind. U. Sch. Law. Capt. U.S. Army, 1968-78. State Farm Found. fellow, 1970; John H. Edwards fellow Ind. U. Found., 1971. Mem. Oreg. State Bar Assn., Multnomah Athletic Club, Astoria Golf and Country Club. Office: Davis Wright Tremaine 1300 SW 5th Ave Ste 2200 Portland OR 97201-5667 E-mail: miltstewart@dwt.com.

STEWART, MIRIAM, utilization review nurse; b. Afton, Wyo., Apr. 8, 1958; d. Howard William Vos and Carolyn Grace (Walker) Davis; children: Lesley, Vanessa. ADN, Indian Hills Community Coll., Ottumwa, Iowa, 1978. Cert. profl. in utilization review, Interqual. Staff nurse med./surg. St. Joseph Mercy Hosp., Clinton, Iowa, 1978-80; staff nurse surg. floor Wyo. Med. Ctr., Casper, 1980; staff nurse med./surg./ICU Meml. Hosp. Sheridan County, Wyo., 1981-82, with quality assurance/utilization rev., 1985-92; utilization rev. nurse Meml. Hosp. of Sheridan County, Wyo., 1992—.

STEWART, MURRAY BAKER, retired lawyer; b. Muskogee, Okla., May 16, 1931; s. Francis and Fannie Penelope (Murray) S.; m. Roseanna Furgason; children: Melinda, Jeffrey, Cheryl. BA, U. Okla., 1953, JD, 1955; postgrad., Georgetown U., 1958-59. Bar: Okla. 1955; CLU, ChFC. Judge adv. U.S. Army, 1955-59; ptnr. Stewart & Stewart, Tulsa and Muskogee, Okla., 1955, 62-72; asst. v.p. First Nat. Bank and Trust Co. of Tulsa, 1959-62, 77-78; mem. Hutchins, Stewart, Stewart & Elmore, Tulsa, 1972-77; atty. cons. advanced underwriting Metlife Ins. Co., N.Y.C., 1978-94; assoc. Metlife Securities, Inc., SEC Registered Investment Advisors, 1984-94; of counsel Brumley & Bishop, Tulsa, 1997-99; ret., 1999. Cons., lectr. in field. Contbr. articles to profl. and hist. jours.; prodr. texts and videos on history, investment and bus. Fellow Life Mgmt. Inst.; mem. Okla. Bar Assn., Okla. Indian Bar Assn., Sons Confederate Vets. (judge advocate Army of Trans-Mississippi 1998-2000). Office: PO Box 1000 Broken Arrow OK 74013-1000

STEWART, NANCY SUE SPURLOCK, educator; b. Phoenix, Dec. 31, 1933; d. Ernest Neal and Ethel Ora (Boothe) Spurlock; m. Biven Stewart, Dec. 31, 1953 (div. 1962); 1 child, Sally K. BA in Edn., Ariz. State U., 1961, MA in Edn., 1968, Reading Specialist Cert., 1970. Cert. tchr 1-12, Ariz. Elem. tchr., reading specialist Chandler (Ariz.) Pub. Schs. Dist. 80, 1961-92; instr. Greater Phoenix Area Writing Project Ariz. State U. and Chandler Unified Sch. Dist. 80, 1983—. Mem. AAUW, NEA, Chandler Edn. Assn., Ariz. Edn. Assn., Delta Kappa Gamma Soc. Internat., Kappa Delta. Mem. Ch. of Christ. Avocations: crafts, reading. Home: 750 W Detroit St Chandler AZ 85225-4413

STEWART, PAMELA L. lawyer; b. Bogalusa, La., Mar. 13, 1953; d. James Adrian and Patricia Lynn (Wood) Lloyd; m. Steven Bernard Stewart, Aug. 31, 1974 (div. July 1980); 1 child, Christopher. BA, U. New Orleans, 1986; JD, U. Houston, 1990. Intern La. Supreme Ct., New Orleans, 1984, Councilman Bryan Wagner, New Orleans, 1984-85; legal asst. Clann, Bell & Murphy, Houston, 1988-89, Tejas Gas Corp., Houston, 1989-90; atty. Law Offices of Pamela L. Stewart, Katy, Tex., 1991—. Bd. dirs. Alliance for Good Govt., New Orleans, 1983-84, Attention Deficit Hyperactivity Disorder Assn. Tex., 1989-90; vol. Houston Vol. Lawyers Program, Houston, 1992—; mem. Planned Giving Coun.; bd. dirs. West Lane Place Civic Assn., sec., 2001—; mem. com. Lawyers Against Waste, Habitat for Humanity; apptd. Harris County Appraisal Rev. Bd. Innsbruck scholar, U. New Orleans, 1985. Fellow Inst. Politics; mem. ABA, Tax Freedom Inst., Nat. Assn. Consumer Bankruptcy Attys., Nat. Assn. Elder Law Attys., Am. Networking Trust Planning Attys., Houston Bar Assn., Nat. Assn. of Chpt. 13 Trustees (assoc.), Katy Bar Assn. (3d v.p. 1997-98), Houston Assn. Debtors Attys. (pres. 1996-98), Upper Kirby Dist. Optimist Club (v.p. 2000-01, pres. 2001—), Planned Giving

Coun., Feng Shui Guild, Feng Shui Basics (pres.). Methodist. Avocations: music, cooking, swimming, politics. Home: 3326 Midlane St Houston TX 77027-5614 Office: 4265 San Felipe St Ste 1100 Houston TX 77027-2998 E-mail: plsatty@swbell.net.

STEWART, PATRICIA CANUP, vocal music and performing arts educator; b. Salisbury, N.C., July 15, 1944; d. Robert Lamont and Hazel Loretta (Heggie) Canup; (div.); children: Jeffrey Scott, J. Levi. BA, Greensboro (N.C.) Coll., 1966; cert. in teaching, U. N.C., 1969; MA, Appalachian State U., 1974; Cert. of Advanced Study, U. N.C., Greensboro, 1992; PhD, Am. State U., 1998. Buyer, mgr. music dept. Andrews Music Co., Charlotte, N.C., 1966-68; prof. Caldwell Community Coll., Lenoir, 1972-74; chmn. music dept. Charlotte Cath. High Sch., 1975-80, Catawba Sch., Rock Hill, S.C., 1983-86; dir. choral music Iredell/Statesville (N.C.) Schs., 1985-93, 98—, Balt. County Schs., Timonium, Md., 1993—98; choral and drama dir. Mooresville (NC) City Schs., 2000—. Choral dir. chs., 1964-88. Mem. ASCD, Am. Choral Dirs. Assn., Music Educators Nat. Conf., N.C. Music Educators, Pi Kappa Lambda. Home: 305 Windsor Dr Salisbury NC 28144-7725 Office: 659 E Center Ave Mooresville NC 28115

STEWART, PATRICIA CARRY, foundation administrator; b. Bklyn., May 19, 1928; d. William J. and Eleanor (Murphy) Carry; m. Charles Thorp Stewart, May 30, 1976. Student, U. Paris, 1948-49; BA, Cornell U., 1950. Fgn. corr. Irving Trust Co., N.Y.C., 1950-51; with Janeway Rsch. Co., 1951-60, sec., treas., 1955-60; with Buckner & Co. and successor firms, 1961-73, ptnr., 1962-70, v.p., treas., 1970-71, pres., treas., 1971-73, Knight, Carry, Bliss & Co., Inc., N.Y.C., 1971-73, G. Tsai & Co., Inc., 1973; v.p. Edna McConnell Clark Found. Inc., 1974-92. Dir. Cmty. Found. Palm Beach and Martin Counties, 1993—, chair, 1998, 2000; allied mem. N.Y. Stock Exch., 1962-73; past mem. nominating com. Am. Stock Exch., N.Y. Stock Exch., N.Y.C. Fin. Svcs. Corp.; dir. emeritus, past chmn. Investor Responsibility Rsch. Ctr. Trustee emerita, vice chair Cornell U., mem. bd. life overseers Cornell Med. Coll.; mem. vis. com. Grad. Sch Bus., Harvard U., 1974-80; bd. dirs. NOW Legal Def. and Edn. Fund, 1984-92, Women in Founds./Corp. Philanthropy, 1980-86; v.p. fin. com. Women's Forum, 1982-90; vice chmn. CUNY, 1976-80; bd. dirs. United Way of Tri-State, 1977-81, Inst. for Edn. and Rsch. on Women and Work; voting mem. Blue Cross and Blue Shield Greater N.Y., 1975-82; trustee N.Y. State 4-H Found., 1970-76, Internt. Inst. Rural Reconstrn., 1974-79; mem. N.Y.C. panel White House Fellows, 1976-78; mem. bus. adv. coun. The Hosp. Chaplaincy. Recipient Elizabeth Cutter Morrow award YWCA, 1977, Catalyst award Women Dirs. in Corps., 1978, Trustee medal CUNY, 1983, Aconplishment award Wings Club N.Y. 1984, Women's Funding Coalition Innovators for Women$hare award, 1986, Banking Industry Achievement award Nat. Assn. Bank Women, 1987, Cert. Disting. Accomplishments Barnard Coll., 1989; named to YWCA Acad. Women Achievers. Mem. Fin. Women's Assn. N.Y., Country Club of Fla. (bd. dirs.), Univ. Club (N.Y.C), Gullane Golf Club (Scotland), North Berwick Golf Club (Scotland), Dunbar Golf Club (Scotland), Phi Beta Phi. Home and Office: 2613 N Ocean Blvd Delray Beach FL 33483-7367 also: Halfland Barns North Berwick EH395PW Scotland E-mail: stewartpc@aol.com.

STEWART, PATRICIA RHODES, former clinical psychologist, researcher; b. Vallejo, Calif., Feb. 11, 1910; d. Butler Young Rhodes and Sarah Virginia (Ryan) Rhodes; m. John Kenneth Stewart (div.); children: John K., Nancy Rush. AB summa cum laude, Stanford U., 1930; MA, San Jose State U., 1959; PhD, U. London, 1963. Tchg. asst. San Jose State U., 1959-60; staff psychologist Napa State Hosp., 1964-77; pvt. practice in psychotherapy Berkeley, Calif., 1978-94; pvt. rsch. in adolescent deviance, 1979-85. Staff psychologist Westwood Mental Health Facility, Fremont, Calif., 1985-88. Author: Children in Distress: American and English Perspectives, 1976. Chair criminal justice com. No. Calif. region Am. Friends Svc. com., San Francisco, 1977-80, chair exec. com. 1970-74, 80-83, bd. dirs., 1980-83; bd. dirs. Friends Com. on Legis., Sacramento, 1985-88, No. Calif. Ecumenical Coun., Oakland, Calif., 1989-95. Mem. APA, AAAS, Phi Beta Kappa. Mem. Soc. Of Friends. Home: 1225 Monterey Ave Berkeley CA 94707-2718

STEWART, PAUL ARTHUR, pharmaceutical company executive; b. Greensburg, Ind., Sept. 28, 1955; s. John Arthur and Alberta Jeannette (Densford) S.; m. Susan Rhodes, Dec. 20, 1975; children: John Rhodes, Daniel Robbins. BS, Purdue U., 1976; MBA, Harvard U., 1987. Grad. asst. Purdue U., West Lafayette, Ind., 1977; asst. treas. Stewart Seeds Inc., Greensburg, 1997-82, sec., treas., 1982-84; cons. The Boston Cons. Group Inc., Chgo., 1986; founder, owner PASCO Group, mgmt. and computer cons., aircraft leasing, 1979-87; mgr. bus. planning agrichems. Eli Lilly & Co., Indpls., 1987-88, dist. sales mgr. agrichems., 1989-90, tech. acquisition mgr. med. devices and diagnostics divsn., 1990-92; dir. mktg. info. and bus. devel. IVAC Corp. subs. Eli Lilly & Co., 1992-94, advisor corp. fin. and investment banking, 1994-96; mgr. global bus. devel. (animal health) Eli Lilly & Co., 1996—. Mem. Greensburg-Decatur County Bd. Airport Commrs., 1980-85, pres., 1980, 81, 83; mem. Decatur County Data Processing Bd., 1982-85; deacon 2d Presbyn. Ch. Indpls., 1991-92, elder, 1996-99; bd. dirs. Friends of Nat. Inst. Nursing Rsch., NIH, 1995-98, Park Tudor Sch., Indpls., 1997—. Mem. Harvard Bus. Sch. Alumni Assn. (bd. dirs. 1999—, v.p. 2001—), Alpha Gamma Rho. Republican. Presbyterian. Office: Eli Lilly & Co Lilly Corp Ctr Indianapolis IN 46285-0001

STEWART, PETER BEAUFORT, retired beverage company executive; b. Montreal, Que., Can., Aug. 23, 1923; s. Harold Beaufort and Mary W. (Martin) S.; m. Yolande Winifred Powell, June 1955; children— Thomas B., Angus B. B.Comm., McGill U.; MBA, Harvard U. With Bldg. Products Ltd., Toronto, Ont., Can., 1947-62; dir., v.p. mktg. Molson Breweries Ltd., Montreal, 1962-66; pres. Molson Western Breweries Ltd., Calgary, Alta., Can., 1966-70; exec. v.p., pres. Molson Breweries Ltd., Montreal, 1970-75; exec. v.p. The Molson Cos. Ltd., Toronto, 1975-88.

STEWART, PETER J(EREMY), general surgery, trauma and critical care physician; b. Oxford, Eng., May 1, 1957; came to U.S., 1959; m. Huyen V. Cao; children: Daniel, Mai, Ian. BS, SUNY, Brockport, 1979; MD, U. Wis., 1983. Diplomate Am. Bd. Surgery. Intern in surgery St. Luke's-Roosevelt Hosp., N.Y.C., 1983-84, resident in surgery, 1984-88; trauma fellow U. Md. R. Adam Cowley Shock Trauma Ctr., 1988-89; attending surgeon SUNY Health Scis. Ctr., Bklyn., 1989-90; attending surgeon-trauma Kings County Hosp., 1989-90; dir. trauma svc. St. Luke's Roosevelt Hosp., N.Y.C., 1990-93; dir. trauma svc., dir. surg. critical care St. Joseph's Hosp. and Med. Ctr., Paterson, N.J., 1993—. Chair trauma com. St. Joseph's Hosp., 1993—, chair trauma quality assurance com., 1993—, chair critical care com., 1997—. Recipient award Eastman Kodak, Rochester, N.Y., 1978. Fellow ACS; mem. AMA, Am. Trauma Soc., Soc. Critical Care Medicine, Sigma Xi. Democrat. Roman Catholic. Office: St Joseph's Hosp and Med Ctr 703 Main St Paterson NJ 07503-2621

STEWART, PHILIP ROBERT, French language educator; b. Kansas City, Mo., May 21, 1940; s. Robert Nottingham and Lucile Elizabeth (Soule) Stewart; m. Joan Hinde, Jan. 31, 1970; children: Anna Faye, Justin. BA, Yale U., 1962; PhD, 1967. Asst. prof. Harvard U., Cambridge, Mass., 1968-72; assoc. prof. Duke U., Durham, N.C., 1972-80, prof., 1980—, Benjamin E. Powell prof. Romance studies, 2001—. Vis. prof. U. Grenoble (France), 1994, Sorbonne, Paris, 1997, U. S.C., Columbia, 2000. Author: Engraven Desire, 1992, Le Masque et la parole, 1973, Rousseau, Julie, 1997; mem. editl. bd. Studies on Voltaire, 1996—. Recipient Palmes académiques Govt. of France, 1991. Mem. Am. Assn. Tchrs. French (pres. 1986-88), Phi Beta Kappa. Office: Duke U Dept Romance Studies Durham NC 27708

STEWART, PRISCILLA ANN MABIE, art historian, educator; b. Iowa City, Sept. 21, 1926; d. Edward Charles and Grace Frances (Chase) Mabie; m. Thomas Wilson Stewart, Aug. 28, 1949 (dec. Mar. 1996). BA, U. Iowa, 1948; MA, U. South Fla., 1971; EdS, Fla. Atlantic U., 1983. Coord. elem. art Manatee County, Fla., 1953-59; prof. art history, intercultural humanities and photography Manatee C.C., Bradenton, 1959—. Organizer, dir. Pelican Perch Wild Bird Hosp., Bradenton, 1953-85; participant Women's Archives U. Iowa Librs. Apptd. charter mem. of adv. bd. to dean of Liberal Arts, U. Iowa, 1999. Mem. AAUP, Pres.'s Club U. Iowa, Fla. Assn. C.Cs., Sarasota-Manatee Phi Beta Kappa Assn. (pres. 1984-86), Phi Beta Kappa, Alpha Xi Delta, Phi Kappa Phi. Episcopalian. Home: 2705 Riverview Blvd Bradenton FL 34205-4335 Office: Manatee Community Coll Dept Art and Humanities 5840 26th St W Bradenton FL 34207-3522 E-mail: stewarp@aol.com., stewarp@mccfl.edu.

STEWART, RENÉE B. communications executive; b. Augusta, Ga., Feb. 14, 1961; d. Delmas and Patsy Bennett Busbee; m. Terry Lynn Stewart, Oct. 8, 1988. BA in Journalism, U. S.C., 1983, MA in Mass. Comm., 1989; postgrad., Regent U., 2001—. Advt. exec. Aiken (S.C.) Std., 1983-85; tech. editor, trainer Policy Mgmt. Sys., Columbia, S.C., 1985-87; student affairs grad. scholar U. S.C., 1987-88; tech. editor cons. Am. Computer Profls., 1988-89; bus. and strategic comm. program mgr. Westinghouse Savannah River Co., Aiken, 1990—. Pub. affairs profl. Tri-Devel. Ctr., Aiken, 1983-85; adminstr. advisor cons. Aiken County, 1985-86; v.p. mktg. pub. rels. S.C. Podiatry Assn., Columbia, 1987-88. Pub. rels. exec. United Way, Aiken, 1990—; music dir. Midland Valley Arts Coun., Graniteville, S.C., 2001—. Mem. Am. Mktg. Assn., Internat. Assn. Bus. Comm. Avocations: reading, art, tennis, music, horseback riding. E-mail: renee.stewart@srs.gov.

STEWART, RICHARD A. former mayor; m. Susan B. Stewart. Postgrad. Air War Coll.; BA, Calif. State U., 1965; MA, No. Mich. U., 1972; JD, Calif. So. Law Sch., 1982. Mayor City of Moreno Valley, Calif., 1996—2000; ptnr. Gellar Stewart and Foley, Riverside, 1995—; mem. Moreno Valley City Coun., 1990—. Active Res. Deputy Riverside County Sheriff's Dept., 1992—. Office: Law Offices of Gellar Stewart and Foley 6301 Day St Ste 106 Riverside CA 92507 : 3430 Bundy Ave Ste 107 March Air Force Base CA 92518 E-mail: richards@moval.org.*

STEWART, RICHARD ALFRED, business executive; b. Hartford, Conn., Nov. 2, 1945; s. Charles Alfred and Theresa (Procopio) S. BS, Valley Coll., 1967. Account exec. Bank Printing Inc., Los Angeles, 1967-70; pres. Carpet Closet Inc., 1970-73; western sales mgr. Josten's, 1973-84; pres. Western Internat. Premiums, 1984-87; dir. corp. sales Tiffany and Co., Beverly Hills, Calif., 1987-90, dir. major program sales, 1990-92, dir. regional sales N.Y.C., 1992-93, dir. major programs, 1992-93; v.p. sales mktg. and recognition divsn. Jostens, Memphis, 1993—; prin. The Stewart Group Sales & Mktg. Cons., 1994—. V.p. sales & mktg. Am. Gem Corp.; recognition cons. L.A. Olympic Com., 1983-84. Contbr. articles to profl. mags.; developer medals for 1984 summer Olympics. Chmn. bd. dirs. Athletes and Entertainers for Kids. Avocations: tennis, basketball, photography.

STEWART, RICHARD BURLESON, lawyer, educator; b. Cleve., Feb. 12, 1940; s. Richard Siegfreid and Ruth Dysert (Staten) S.; m. Alice Peck Fales, May 13, 1967; children: William, Paul, Elizabeth; m. Jane Laura Bloom, Sept. 20, 1992; children: Emily, Ian. AB, Yale U., 1961; MA (Rhodes scholar), Oxford (Eng.) U., 1963; LLB, Harvard U., 1966; D (hon.), Erasmus U., Rotterdam, 1993. Bar: D.C. 1968, U.S. Supreme Ct 1971. Law clk. to Justice Potter Stewart, U.S. Supreme Ct., 1966-67; assoc. Covington & Burling, Washington, 1967-71; asst. prof. law Harvard U., 1971-75, prof., 1975-82, Byrne prof. adminstrv. law, 1982-89, assoc. dean, 1984-86; asst. atty. gen. environment and natural resources div. Dept. Justice, Washington, 1989-91; prof. law NYU Law Sch., 1992-94, Emily Kempin prof. law, 1994—, univ. prof., 2002—; of counsel Sidley & Austin, 1992—. Spl. counsel U.S. Senate Watergate Com., 1974; vis. prof. law U. Calif., Berkeley Law Sch., 1979-80, U. Chgo. Law Sch., 1986-87, Georgetown U., 1991-92, European U. Inst., 1995; dir. Ctr. Environ. and Land Use Law, Health Effects Inst.; mem. adv. bd. Environ. Def. Author: (with P. Menell) Environmental Law and Policy, 1994, (with S. Breyer, C. Soustein and M. Spitzer) Administrative Law and Regulation, 1979, 5th edit., 2002, (with E. Rehbinder) Integration Through Law: Environmental Protection Policy, 1985, paper edit., 1987; editor: (with R. Revesz) Analyzing Superfund: Economics, Science, and Law, 1995, Markets v. Environment?, 1995. Fellow Am. Acad. Arts and Scis.; mem. ABA, Am. Law Inst. Office: NYU Law Sch 40 Washington Sq S New York NY 10012-1099 E-mail: stewartr@juris.law.nyu.edu.

STEWART, RICHARD DONALD, internist, educator, biographer; b. Lakeland, Fla., Dec. 26, 1926; s. LeRoy Hepburn and Zoa Irene (Hachet) S.; m. Mary Leeuw, June 14, 1952; children: R. Scot, Gregory D., Mary E. AB, U. Mich., 1951, MD, 1955, MPH, 1962; MA, U. Wis. Milw., 1979; PhD in English, U. Wis., Milw., 1997. Diplomate Am. Bd. Internal Medicine, Am. Bd. Med. Toxicology, Acad. Toxicol. Scis. Intern Saginaw (Mich.) Gen. Hosp., 1955-56; resident U. Mich. Med. Ctr., Ann Arbor, 1959-62; dir. med. rsch. sect. Dow Chem. Co., Midland, Mich., 1962-66; staff physician Midland Hosp., 1962-66; assoc. prof. preventive medicine Med. Coll. Wis., Milw., 1966-68, prof., chmn. dept. environ. medicine, 1969-78, adj. prof. dept. pharmacology and toxicology, 1978—. Cons. Children's Hosp. Wis., 1989-93, Internal Medicine St. Mary's Hosp., Racine, Wis., 1983-93; prof., dir. med. toxicology fellowship Dept. Emergency Medicine Milw. Regional Med. Ctr., 1989-91; sr. attending staff, 1967-90; staff Internal Medicine St. Luke's Hosp., Racine, 1983-93; med. dir. Poison Control Ctr. Southeastern Wis., 1989-93; corp. med. advisor S.C. Johnson & Son, Inc., Racine, 1971-78, corp. med. dir., 1978-89. Mem. adv. med. staff Milw. Fire Dept., 1975—. Cadet USAF, 1945-46. Fellow ACP, Am. Coll. Occuptl. Medicine, Am. Acad. Clin. Toxicology, Acad. Toxicological Scis.; mem. AMA, Soc. Toxicology, Wis. State Med. Soc., Racine Acad. Medicine, Rotary Internat., Phi Theta Kappa, Phi Kappa Phi, Sigma Tau Delta. Avocations: history of medicine, wilderness hiking, literature, creative writing, inventing medical devices, including hollow fiber artificial kidney. Home and Office: 5337 Wind Point Rd Racine WI 53402-2322

STEWART, RICHARD EDWIN, insurance consulting company executive; b. Washington, Nov. 4, 1933; s. Irvin and Florence Elsie (Dezendorf) S.; m. Barbara Lewis Dickson, Oct. 29, 1993. BA, W.Va. U., 1955; BA (Rhodes scholar), Oxford (Eng.) U., 1957, MA, 1961; JD, Harvard, 1959. Bar: N.Y. 1960. Assoc. Royall, Koegel & Rogers, N.Y.C., 1960-63; asst. counsel to Gov. of N.Y., 1963-64, 1st asst. counsel, 1965-66; supr. ins. N.Y. State Ins. Dept., 1967-70; sr. v.p., gen. counsel First Nat. City Bank, N.Y.C., 1971-72; sr. v.p., dir. Chubb & Son Inc., 1973-81; sr. v.p. Chubb Corp., 1973-81, chief fin. officer, 1974-81; gov. N.Y. Ins. Exchange, 1979-81; chmn. Stewart Econs., Inc., 1981-90, Chapel Hill, N.C., 1990—. Mem. adv. com. HUD, 1968-72; mem. Adminstrv. Conf. U.S., 1970-74; bd. dirs. Am. Arbitration Assn., 1970-80; mem. UN panel experts on Transnational Bank failure, 1991. Co-author: Automobile Insurance....For Whose Benefit?, 1970, Watergate: Implications for Responsible Government, 1974, Medical Malpractice, 1977, Managing Insurer Insolvency, 1988, Insurance Insolvency Quarentees, 1990, A Brief History of Underwriting Cycles, 1991, Niche Insurance Companies, 1997, Information Technology and Insurance Agent Licensing, 1998; author: Reason and Regulation, 1972, Insurance and Insurance Regulation, 1980. Trustee Coll. Ins., N.Y., 1970-78, Am. Coll. Life Underwriters, 1990-93; mem. Mayor's Com. on Taxi Regulation, 1979-82, ABA Com. to Improve Liability Ins. System, 1989; mem. panel experts on transnat. bank failure UN, 1991; mem. spl. panel U.S. Senate Com. on Presdl. Campaign Practice, 1974. Served with AUS, 1959. Mem. Nat. Acad. Pub. Adminstrn., Nat. Acad. Social Ins., Cosmos Club of Washington, Century Club of N.Y.C., Phi Beta Kappa Assn. Home and Office: 7600 Talbryn Way Chapel Hill NC 27516-7862

STEWART, RICHARD WILLIAMS, lawyer; b. Harrisburg, Pa., Aug. 21, 1948; s. Alexander H. and M. Winifred (Williams) S.; m. Mary A. Simmonds, June 7, 1975; 1 child, Anne W. AB cum laude, Franklin and Marshall Coll., 1970; JD, Duke U., 1973. Bar: Pa. 1973, U.S. Dist. Ct. (mid. dist.) Pa. 1975, U.S. Tax Ct. 1984. Assoc. Stone & Sajer, New Cumberland, Pa., 1973-77; ptnr. Stone, Sajer & Stewart, 1977-87, Johnson, Duffie, Stewart & Weidner, Lemoyne, Pa., 1987—. V.p. Secured Land Transfers, Inc., Camp Hill, Pa., 1985-2000, pres., 2000—; solicitor West Shore Sch. Dist., Lemoyne, Pa., 1977-93, No. York County Sch. Dist., Dillsburg, Pa., 1984—, Camp Hill Sch. Dist., 1986—, Fairview Twp., 1987-98; v.p. Cedar Cliff Abstract Agy., 1980-87. Chmn. Cumberland County Rep. Com., 1981-84; mem. Rep. State Com. Pa., 1990—. Mem. ABA, Pa. Bar Assn., Cumberland County Bar Assn., Supreme Ct. of Pa. (disciplinary bd. mem. 1998—), Ctrl. Pa. Estate Planning Coun. (bd. dirs. 1983-85), Pa. Sch. Solicitors Assn. (pres. 1995), Rotary (bd. dirs. West Shore). Presbyterian. Home: 1811 Warren St New Cumberland PA 17070-1148 Office: 301 Market St Lemoyne PA 17043-1628

STEWART, RITA JOAN, academic administrator; b. Muncie, Ind., June 6, 1945; d. John Marion and Crystalee Masterson; children: Jon Lewis, Robert Forrest. BS, Ball State U., 1967, MA, 1974. Tchr. Blue River H.S., Mt. Summit, Ind., 1968-69, Sunnyside Elem. Sch., New Castle, 1967-68; copywriter, announcer Sta. WTIM, Taylorville, Ill., 1974-75; dir. Kitselman Conf. Ctr. Ball State U., Muncie, Ind., 1978-2000, dir. conf. and spl. events, 2000—. Contbr. articles to profl. jours. Precinct committeewoman Henry County Dem. Party, New Castle, Ind., 1969-70; precinct chmn. March of Dimes, New Castle, Ind., 1974-75; chmn. edn. com. West Viwe Sch. Coun., Muncie, 1987-88; sec., bd. dirs. PAL Club, Muncie, 1988-93; pres., bd. dirs. Altrusa Club Found., Muncie, 1997-98, v.p., 2001-01, pres., 2002. Mem.: AAUW (v.p. 1984—85), Ind. Conf. Dirs. Assn., Assn. Collegiate Conf. and Event Dirs. Internat. (dir. region 8 1999—2000, internat. bd. dirs.), Altrusa Club of Muncie (pres. 2002—03), Kappa Delta Pi (Disting. Svc. award 1995). Methodist. Office: Ball State U Confs and Spl Events Muncie IN 47306 Home: # 1-203 4501 N Wheeling Ave Muncie IN 47304-1277 Fax: (765) 285-5457. E-mail: rstewart@bsu.edu.

STEWART, ROBERT GORDON, former museum curator; b. Balt., Mar. 5, 1931; s. Kenneth Elsworth and Ruth (Chambers) S. Student, Gilman Sch., 1946-49; B.F.A., U. Pa., 1954. Architect Ind. Nat. Hist. Park, Phila., 1954, Nat. Park Service, Phila., 1956-57; architect, curator Jefferson Barracks Hist. Park, St. Louis, 1958-61; dir. properties Nat. Trust for Historic Preservation, Washington, 1961-64; sr. curator Nat. Portrait Gallery, Smithsonian Instn., 1964-94, sr. curator emeritus, 1994—. Cons. Loyalist Homestead, St. John's, N.B., Can., 1960; vis. lectr. George Washington U., 1967-70 Author: Nucleus for a National Collection, 1965, Recent Acquisitions, 1966, A Nineteenth-Century Gallery of Distinguished Americans, 1969, Henry Benbridge (1743-1812): American Portrait Painter, 1971, Robert Edge Pine, A British Artist in America 1784-1788, 1979. Dir. Landmarks of St. Louis, 1959-61; adjudicator Jamaican Nat. Art Competition, 1971; cons. The Papers of George Washington, 1990-98; bd. dirs. Washington Studio Sch., 1997-99. Served with U.S. Army, 1954-56. Mem. Md., Dorchester County, Lewes hist. socs., Walpole Soc., Assn. of Historians of Am. Art, Zeta Psi. Episcopalian.

STEWART, ROBERT HENRY, oceanographer, educator; b. York, Pa., Dec. 26, 1941; s. Robert Henry and Mildred June (Smith) S.; m. Hedvig Susan Bagdy, June 26, 1966 (div. Dec. 1976); 1 child, Alethea Ildico Stewart; m. Tracy Ann Bertoluccci, July 19, 1986; children: Farrar Clee, Margaret Montgomery. BS, U. Tex., Arlington, 1963; PhD, U. Calif., San Diego, 1969. Asst. rsch. oceanographer Scripps Inst. Oceanography U. Calif., San Diego, 1969-78, assoc. rsch. oceanographer, 1978-79; assoc. rsch. oceanographer, assoc. adj. prof. Scripps Inst. Oceanography, U. Calif., 1979-83, rsch. oceanographer, adj. prof., 1983-89; mem. tech. staff Jet Propulsion Lab., Calif. Inst. Tech., Pasadena, 1979-80, rsch. scientist, 1980-83, sr. rsch. scientist, 1983-89; prof. oceanography Tex. A&M U., College Station, 1989—. Topex/Poseidon project scientist Jet Propulsion Lab., 1980-88; mem. many NASA coms.; mem. coms. of Nat. Rsch. Coun., Nat. Acad. Scis.; mem. various internat. scientific coms.; cons. Univ. Corp. for Atmospheric Rsch. Author: Methods of Satellite Oceanography, 1985; editor: Radio Oceanography, 1978; contbr. articles to profl. jours. Trustee San Juan Capistrano Inst. Co-recipient NASA Pub. Svc. medal, 1994; recipient William T. Pecora award Dept. Interior-NASA, 1999, Earth Sci. award for outstanding ednl. product NASA, 1999; U. Calif. Regents spl. fellow, 1963; NSF fellow, 1964. Mem. Am. Geophys. Union, Nat. Marine Educators Assn. Republican. Roman Catholic. Avocations: collect lepidoptera. Home: 8710 Appomattox Dr College Station TX 77845-5567 Office: Tex A&M U Oceanography College Station TX 77843-3146 E-mail: stewart@ocean.tamu.edu.

STEWART, ROBERT JACKSON, software development engineer, researcher; b. Beaumont, Tex., Feb. 1, 1958; s. Hester Reid and Donna Dea (Saxe) S.; m. Theresa Marie Goluszek, May 12, 1984. BA summa cum laude, U. Tex., 1980; MS, U. So. Calif., 1981. Mem. tech. staff AT&T Bell Labs., Naperville, Ill., 1980-88; staff engr. Tellabs, Inc., Lisle, 1988-91; systems engr. Compaq Computers, Houston, 1991—. Mem. Jaycees, Phi Beta Kappa. Office: Compaq Computer Corp 20555 S # H 249 Houston TX 77070

STEWART, ROBERT LEE, retired career officer, astronaut; b. Washington, Aug. 13, 1942; s. Lee Olin and Mildred Kathleen (Wann) S.; m. Mary Jane Murphy; children: Ragon Annette, Jennifer Lee. BS in Math., U. So. Miss., 1964; MS in Aerospace Engring., U. Tex., 1972; grad., U.S. Army Air Def. Sch., 1964, grad. advanced course, guided missile systems officers course, 1970. Commd. 2d lt. U.S. Army, 1964, advanced through grades to brig. gen., 1986, fire team leader armed helicopter platoon 101st Aviation Bn., instr. pilot Primary Helicopter Sch., 1967-69, bn. ops. officer, bn. exec. officer 309th Aviation Bn., Korea, 1972-73, exptl. test pilot Aviation Engring. Flight Activity Edwards AFB, Calif., 1974-78; astronaut candidate NASA, 1978, mission specialist Space Shuttle Mission 41-B, 1984; mission specialist STS-5IJ, 1985; dep. comdr. U.S. Army Strategic Def. Command, Huntsville, Ala., 1987-89; dir. of plans U.S. Space Command, 1989-92. Decorated D.S.M., (2) Legion of Merit, (4) DFC, (2) Purple Hearts, Bronze star, Def. Superior Svc. medal, others; recipient NASA Space Flight medal, 1984, 85, Fineburg Meml. award Am. Helicopter Soc., 1984, Herman Oberth award AIAA, 1990; named Army Aviator of Yr., 1984. Mem. Soc. Exptl. Test Pilots, Assn. U.S. Army, Army Aviation Assn. Am., Assn. Space Explorers. Avocations: photography, woodworking, skiing. Home and Office: 815 Sun Valley Dr Woodland Park CO 80863-7729

STEWART, ROGER CHARLES, consumer products executive; b. Indpls., Sept. 23, 1949; s. Charles Thomas and Mary Pearl Stewart. BS in Sci., Purdue, 1971, MS in Indsl. Admin., 1974. Staff disposable fin. analysis Procter Gamble, Cin., 1978-80, staff spl. assign analysis, 1980, assoc. dir. tissue, 1981-83, dir. soft drinks Lexington, Ky., 1983-85, dir. sys. RVI Wilton, Conn., 1986, dir. internat. treasury Cin., 1987-98, v.p. global treasury, 1998—. Lectr. Krannert Sch., Purdue U., West Lafayette, Ind., 1992—. Past pres. Cancer Family Care, 1978—; fundraiser local charities. Avocations: playing marimba, travel, biking. Home: 9829 Villageview Ct Cincinnati OH 45241-3802 E-mail: stewart.rc.@pg.com.

STEWART, ROSS, chemistry educator; b. Vancouver, B.C., Can., Mar. 16, 1924; s. David Methven and Jessie (Grant) S.; m. Greta Marie Morris, Sept. 7, 1946; children— Cameron, Ian BA, U. B.C., 1946, MA, 1948; PhD, U. Wash., 1954. Lectr. chemistry Royal Roads Coll., Victoria, B.C., 1949-52, asst. prof., 1952-54, assoc. prof., 1954-55; asst. prof. chemistry U. B.C., Vancouver, 1955-59, assoc. prof., 1959-62, prof., 1962-89, hon. prof., 1989—. Author: Oxidation Mechanisms, 1964, Investigation of Organic Reactions, 1966, The Proton: Applications to Organic Chemistry, 1985, (with J.D. Roberts & M.C. Caserio) Organic Chemistry, Methane to Macromolecules, 1970; contbr. numerous articles to profl. jours. Fellow Royal Soc. Can., Chem. Inst. Can.; mem. B.C. Thoroughbred Breeders Soc. (pres. 1972-74), Can. Thoroughbred Horse Soc. (v.p. 1974-75). Clubs: Point Grey Golf (Vancouver). Avocations: breeding and racing thoroughbred horses; golf; gardening. Home: 4855 Paton St Vancouver BC Canada V6L 2H9 Office: U B C Dept Chemistry Vancouver BC Canada V6T 1Z1

STEWART, RUTH ANN, public policy educator; b. Chgo., Apr. 4, 1942; d. Elmer Ashton and Ann (Mitchell) S.; m. David Levering Lewis; children: Allegra, Jason, Allison, Eric. Student, U. Chgo., 1960-61, Simmons Coll., 1963; BA, Wheaton Coll., Norton, Mass., 1963; MS, Columbia U., 1965; postgrad., Fisk U., 1970, Harvard U., 1976, John F. Kennedy Sch. Govt., 1987. Biol. scis. libr. Columbia U., N.Y.C., 1965-68; mktg. mgr. Macmillan Co., 1968-70; asst. chief Schomburg Ctr. Research in Black Culture, 1970-80; assoc. dir. for external svcs. N.Y. Pub. Libr., 1980-86; asst. Libr. of Congress for Nat. Programs, Washington, 1986-89; assoc. Dir. for Resource Devel., 1989-95; sr. policy analyst for arts, humanities & social legislation Congl. Rsch. Svc., 1989-97; rsch. prof. cultural policy Ctr. for Urban Policy Rsch. Bloustein Sch. Planning and Pub. Policy Rutgers U., New Brunswick, N.J., 1997—. Trustee, sec. Wheaton Coll., 1980-99; mem. libr. vis. com. Harvard U., 1975-88, MIT, 1986-90; bd. dirs. Nat. Park Found., Washington, 1978-84; bd. visitors Sch. Info. Sci., U. Pitts., 1987-95; bd. dirs. Fund for Folk Culture, Santa Fe, 1991—, The Lab. Sch. of Washington, 1992-94, Women's Fgn. Policy Group, 1995—, treas., 1999—, Bklyn. Bot. Garden, 2000—, Studio in a Sch., 2000—. Author: Portia, 1977; cons. editor Jour. Arts Mgmt., Law and Society, 1998—; founding co-editor Public Life of the Arts series Rutgers U. Press, 1998—. Mem. adv. com. Ctr. for Arts and Culture, Washington, 1997—,

The Ailey Sch., N.Y.C., 1998—, Parsons Sch. Design, N.Y.C., 2001—. Fellow Internat. Coun. Mus. Mem. Coun. Fgn. Rels., Friends Edn., Mus. Modern Art, ArtTable. Office: Rutgers U Ctr Urban Policy Rsch 33 Livingston Ave Ste 400 New Brunswick NJ 08901-1900

STEWART, SALLY, public relations practitioner; b. Phoenix, Mar. 1, 1955; d. Biven and Nancy Sue (Spurlock) S.; children: Padraic Haines, Colin Haines. BS in Broadcast Journalism, Ariz. State U., 1977, BA in Edn., 1980. Staff writer, media rep. Salt River Project, Phoenix, 1979-81; copy editor Mesa (Ariz.) Tribune, 1981-82; mktg. adminstrv. asst. Phoenix chpt. ARC, 1983; pub. info. asst. City of Scottsdale, Ariz., 1983-84; bus. editor, asst. city editor Scottsdale Progress Tribune, 1984-86; comms. mgr. Mesa Conv. and Visitors Bur., 1986-90; mgmt. asst. Neighborhood Improvement and Housing Dept., City of Phoenix, 1990-92, Pub. Info. Office, City of Phoenix, 1992-93; comm. cons. Ariz. Pub. Svc., Phoenix, 1993—. Mem. com. Fiesta Bowl, Phoenix, 1987-89; mem. pub. rels. com. Juvenile Diabetes Found., Phoenix, 1990; mem. pub. rels. com. Children's Garden Ground Breaking, Phoenix, 1993. Mem. Pub. Rels. Soc. Am. (accredited, bd. dirs. 1991-93, assembly del. 1993-95, pres. Valley of the Sun chpt. 1997). Avocations: travel, writing. Office: Ariz Pub Svc 2 Arizona Ctr 400 N 5th St Phoenix AZ 85004-3902

STEWART, SANDRA KAY, music educator; b. New Albany, Ind., Dec. 24, 1947; d. Dale F. and June V. (Martin) Byrne; m. William Lee Stewart, June 25, 1971. B Music Edn., Ind. U., 1969; MusM, Norfolk State U., 1992; D Mus. Arts, U. S.C., 1995. Cert. vocal music tchr., N.Y., Mo.; nat. cert., state cert. piano tchr. Vocal music tchr., choral dir. Ritenour Sch. Dist., St. Louis, 1969-75, Sch. Dist. # 54, Chgo., 1975-76, Waverly (N.Y.) Jr./Sr. H.S., 1977-78, Clarence (N.Y.) H.S., 1978-82; piano instr., show choir dir. Inst. Fine Arts, Reading, Pa., 1982-85; piano accompanist Berks Grand Opera Co., 1982-85, Va. Opera Co., Norfolk, 1986, U. S.C., Columbia, 1992-95, Jacksonville Masterworks Sr. Chorale, 1996-99, Bolles Sr. H.S., 1996-98, Pinewood Presbyn. Ch., 1996-98; piano and music theory instr. Acad. of Music, Virginia Beach, Va., 1986-91; piano instr., choral dir., vocal jazz dir., accompanist Jacksonville (Fla.) U., 1995—2000; chair vocal music dept. Douglas Anderson Sch. of Arts, 1998—2000; prof. music U. North Fla., Jacksonville, 2000—. Editor: Florida Music Teacher, 1999—; contbr. articles to profl. publs. Mem. Virginia Beach Pops Orch., 1989-91. Mem. AAUW (numerous offices 1975—), Am. Choral Dirs. Assn., Coll. Music Soc., Nat. Piano Found., Music Educators Nat. Conf., Nat. Guild Piano Tchrs., Music Tchrs. Nat. Assn., Delius Assn. Fla. (bd. dirs. 1997—), Phi Kappa Lambda, Mu Phi Epsilon, TRI-M Music Honor Soc. Home: 4782 Harpers Ferry Ln Jacksonville FL 32257-4544

STEWART, SANDRA L. investment/financial consultant; b. Bluefield, W.Va., May 8, 1940; m. James B. Stewart, Nov. 4, 1939 (div. 1994); children: Susan Wagner, Wendy Markey, Kristin Stewart. BS, Radford U. Pvt. practice tax cons., Reston, Va., 1978-84; v.p. investments Smith Barney, Pensacola, Fla., 1984—. Pres. Patomac Ballet Theater, Herndon, Va., 1989-96, Seashore Village Assn., Pensacola Beach, Fla., 1998. Mem. Assn. Profl. Investment Cons. Office: Smith Barney 13 W Garden St Pensacola FL 32501-5615

STEWART, SHEILA KAY, anthropologist, archaeologist; b. Fort Campbell, Ky., Aug. 18, 1954; d. James Doyle and Beulah Edna (Brasuel) Watts; m. John Felton Stewart, Mar. 25, 1978. AA with honors, St. Petersburg Jr. Coll., Fla., 1974; BA in Edn., U. South Fla., 1978, MA in Applied Anthropology, 1998. Cert. tchr. Fla., registered archaeologist. Tchr. gifted program Pinellas County Schs., St. Petersburg, 1979—93; field supr. USF Excavations at Sepphoris, Gallilee, Israel, 1992—93; field asst., lab. supr. Mackinac Island State Park Commn., Mich., 1995—96; archaeologist Panam. Cons., Inc., Tampa, Fla., 1999—2001; edn. dir. Ctr. for the Study of Rural Ireland, County Rascommon, 2000—01; Weedon Island Preserve cultral and natural his. ctr. dir. Pinellas County Dept. of Environ. Mgmt., Environ. Lands Divsn., St. Petersburg, 2001—. Curator Curse of the Black Legend: The Explorations of Narvaez, 1998—99. Adv. bd. ASAP Homeless Svcs., St. Petersburg, Fla., 1990—2002. Mem.: Fla. Anthropol. Soc. (2d v.p. 1999—2000, v.p. 2000—02, pres. 2002—, chair archaeology month com. 2000—02, Award for the Understanding and Preservation of Fla.'s Archaeol. and Anthropol. Heritage 2001), Ctrl. Gulf Coast Archaeol. Soc., Soc. for Am. Archaeology, Southeastern Archaeol. Conf., Fla. Archaeol. Coun., Soc. for Hist. Archaeology. Avocations: piano, flute, harp, swimming, snorkeling. Office: Weedon Island Preserve Cultral and Natural His Ctr 1800 Weedon Dr NE Saint Petersburg FL 33702

STEWART, SHIRLEY ANNE, educational administrator; b. Bridgeville, Del., June 8, 1957; d. James Elliott and Pearline (Jacobs) Stewart. BS in Spl. Edn., U. Del., 1979, MEd in Curriculum and Instrn., 2001; MEd in Spl. Edn., Temple U., 1981. Cert. tchr., Del. Spl. edn. tchr. Caesar Rodney Sch. Dist., Camden, Del., 1979, Indian River Sch. Dist., Frankford, 1980—; tchr. Frankford Elem. Sch., 1980-91, Sussex Ctrl. Mid. Sch., Millsboro, Del., 1991-94; asst. prin. Woodbridge Elem. Sch., Greenwood, 1994-96, Pleasantville Elem. Sch., New Castle, 1996-98, McCullough Elem. Sch., New Castle, 1998—2001; prin. Martin L. King Jr. Elem. Sch., Wilmington, Del., 2001—. Mem. Gov.'s Adv. Coun. for Exceptional Citizens, Dover, Del., 1986-91; mem. Coun. Exceptional Children, Dover, 1986—; mem. Statewide Multicultural Com., 1989-90; instr. Del. Tchr. Ctr., 1990; mem. mid. sch. adv. coun. State Del., 1990-91, adv. coun. on multicultural edn., 1991-92, Mid. Sch. Reading Com., 1992, Indian River Sch. Dist. Recruitment/Critical Shortage Com., 1992, instructional materials rev. com. 1993—; pres. Garden Cmty., Inc., 1999—. Mem. black recruitment com. U. Del., 1987; mem. Minority Action Com., Dover, 1985-87, chmn. Martin L. King Jr. Writing Contest, 1987-88, mem. exec. bd., 1988-89, chmn. black history com., 1986-87, sec. local minority action com., 1985-88; mem. attendance com. Indian River Sch. Dist., 1987-88, recruitment & retention com., 1992, mid. sch. reading com., 1992, mem. materials rev. com., 1993—; chmn. Del. State Edn. Minority Action Com., 1989-90; mem. strategic planning com. Del. State Edn. Assn., 1989-90, issues for the 90's com., 1991; active Dept. Pub. Instrn. Multicultural Inst. Tng., 1989; mem. middle sch. com. State of Del., 1991; mem. Statewide Multicultural Adv. Com., 1991—; vol. Saturday Sch. Com., 1992-93; mem. New Directions Com., 1992-93, Del. Prin.'s Leadership Acad., 1995-96; mem. tech. task force Colonial Sch. Dist., 1998-99; pres. Garden Cmty. Inc., 1999-2000. Recipient Instructional Profl. Devel. award Minority Action Com., 1987, Del. Tchr. Ctr. Svc. award, 1989, Instructional Profl. Devel. award Del. State Edn. Assn., 1990, Outstanding Black Woman award Nat. Polit. Congress of Black Women, Inc., 1997. Mem. NEA, NAACP, ASCD, Nat. Elem. Sch. Prins. Assn., Del. Assn. Sch. Adminstrs., Del. Elem. Sch. Prins. Assn., Del. State Edn. Assn. (chairperson minority action com. 1988-91, Instrnl. Profl. Devel. award 1991, Human and Civil Rights award 1992), Indian River Edn. Assn. (treas. 1989-91, chairperson minority action com. 1990-93), Adults and Children with Learning Disabilities. Democrat. Pentacostal/Apostolic. Avocations: reading, poetry. Home: 224 Becks Woods Dr Bear DE 19701-3831 E-mail: sstew63598@aol.com.

STEWART, SUE S. lawyer; b. Oct. 9, 1942; d. Fraizer McVale and Carolyn Eliabeth (Hunt) S.; m. Arthur L. Stern, III, July 31, 1965 (div.); m. children: Anne, Mark Alan; m. John A. Ciampa, Sept. 1, 1985 (div.); m. Stephen L. Raymond. BA, Wellesley Coll., 1964; postgrad., Harvard U. Law Sch., 1964-65; JD, Georgetown U., 1967. Bar: N.Y. 1968. Clk. to judges Juvenile Ct., Washington, 1967-68; mem. Nixon, Hargrave, Devans & Doyle (now Nixon Peabody LLP), Rochester, N.Y., 1968-74, ptnr. NY, 1975—2001, mng. ptnr., 1998—2001, ret., 2001. Lectr. in field; trustee Found. of Monroe County (N.Y.) Bar, 1976-78. Author: Charitable Giving and Solicitation. Sec., dir. United Cmty. Chest of Greater Rochester, 1973-87, 92—; trustee, sec. Internat. Mus. Photography at George Eastman House, Rochester, 1974-97, 2000-, Genesee Country Mus., Mumford, N.Y., 1976—; bd. dirs. Ctr. for Govtl. Rsch., 1990-97; trustee, chmn. United Neighborhood Ctr. of Greater Rochester Found., 1991—; trustee Nat. Ctr. Edn. and Economy, 1997—. Mem. ABA (chmn. task force on charitable giving, exempt orgns. com. tax sect. 1981—), N.Y. State Bar (exec. com. tax sect. 1974-76, chmn. com. exempt orgns. 1975-76), Monroe County Bar Assn. (trustee 1974-75), BNA Portfolio, Pvt. Found. Distbns. Office: Nixon Peabody LLP PO Box 31051 Clinton Sq Rochester NY 14603-1051

STEWART, SUSAN ELAINE, training director; b. Mar. 7, 1957; DVM, Colo. State U., 1982; M of Human Resources, Azusa Pacific U., 1996. Dir. L.Am. programs World Concern, Seattle, 1994-96; dir. tng. World Concern, Christian Vet. Mission, 1996—. Cons. in field. Office: World Concern 19303 Fremont Ave N Seattle WA 98133-3898

STEWART, TERESA ELIZABETH, elementary school educator; b. Cheverly, Md., Nov. 26, 1966; d. Richard Lynn and Sandra Lois (O'Neill) S. BS in Elem. Edn. cum laude, Bowie State U., 1988, MEd in Elem. Edn., 1996. Cert. elem. tchr., Md. Asst. tchr. Tom Thumb Day Care, Bowie, Md., 1989; elem. tchr. Berwyn Bapt. Sch., College Park, 1989-95, Berkshire Elem. Sch., Forestville, 1995-98, Paint Branch Elem. Sch., College Park, 1998-99, Berwyn Bapt. Sch., College Park, 1999—. Dir. vacation Bible sch., youth group leader Bowie United Meth. Ch., 1988-98, sec. adminstrv. coun., 1993-97, chairperson staff parish rels. com., 1996—, sec. membership com., 1993—, choir mem., 1980—, choir dir., 2000—; tchr. children's Bible class University Park Ch. of Brethren, 1990-94, Sun. sch. tchr., 1997-2000; instr., judge Belle-Aires Twirling Corp., Bowie, 1986—; pres. Md. Baton Coun., 1998—. Koonz, McKinney & Johnson Law Firm scholar, 1986-88. Mem. Kappa Delta Pi. Democrat. Avocations: camping, collecting postcards and teddy bears, twirling, choral singing. Home: 13202 11th St Bowie MD 20715-3707 Office: Berwyn Bapt Sch 4720 Cherokee St College Park MD 20740-1839 E-mail: tstwirl@aol.com.

STEWART, TERRY LEE, writer, human rights activist; b. Mar. 23, 1965; parents Theodore Mitchell and Yvonne Stewart. AA in Qaulity Assurance, Rock Island (Ill.) C.C., 1992. Sgt. USMC, Camp Pendleton, 1984—92; human rights advocate L.A. Human Rights. Assn., 1992—2000; group home supr. At Risk Children Program, L.A., 1992—. Counselor High Risk Children's Program, L.A., 1997—2001. Human rights spokesman Dem. Party, Palmdale, Calif., 2000—. Mem.: Masonic Lodge. Home and Office: 382020 Divsion St Palmdale CA 93550

STEWART, THOMAS CLIFFORD, trading and investment company executive; b. Portland, Oreg., Oct. 25, 1950; s. Jack Fry Stewart and Naomi June Gedney Cuyler; m. Susan Elizabeth Sample; children: Andrew, Tommy, MacKenzie, Cortny. Student, U. Gothenburg, Sweden, 1971; BS, U. Oreg., 1974; MBA, UCLA, 1982. Prin. Morgan Stanley & Co., N.Y.C., 1982-90; pres. Cort MacKenzie & Co., Eugene, Oreg., 1990-2000; dir. Acrymed, Lake Oswego, 1995-96, Morley Fin. Svcs., Lake Oswego, 1995-97. Dir. Oreg. Air and Space Mus., 2001—. Contbr. articles to profl. jours. Trustee U. Oreg. Found., 19945; chmn. U. Oreg. Pres.'s Assn., 1997-99; exec. com., Lundquist Coll. of Bus., Univ. Oregon, 1998-2001, bd. advisors Coll. Bus., U. Oreg., 1990—, Athletic Dept., Bd. Advisors, Univ. Oregon, 1998—; Oreg. State Commn. on Higher Bus. Edn., 1992-94; mem. leadership coun. U. Oreg., 1995-99; bd. dirs. Lake Oswego Sch. Found., 1996-2000; treas. adv. cabinet State of Oreg., 1993-94; adv. bd. Sec. of Navy Nat. Naval Res. Policy Bd., Washington, 1987-89. Comdr. USN, 1974-80, USNR, 1980-91. Decorated Air medal, Navy Commendation for Valor; Baker scholar, 1981. Mem. Naval Res. Assn. (Jr. Officer of Yr. 1988), U.S. Navy League, ROA, Am. Legion, VFW, Beta Gamma Sigma, Beta Alpha Psi, Alpha Mu Alpha, Skull & Dagger. Office: Cort MacKenzie 884 Park St Lebanon OR 97355-3204

STEWART, THOMAS TED, real estate developer, investment banker; b. St. Louis, July 17, 1940; s. Harold Mack and Lora Mae (Coil) S.; m. Susan Ann Schulte, Dec. 22, 1962; children: Thomas, Timothy. Grad., high sch., 1958. Restaurant owner and mgr., 1962-66; hotel owner and mgr., 1967-70; gen. ptnr. Sovereign Realty subs. Butcher & Co., Phila.; acquisition specialist E.G. Frances Realty; head of comml. real estate div. Sotheby Parke Bernet Internat. Realty Corp., N.Y.C., 1980s; ptnr., dir. Greenscape Devel. Corp., 1987—; pres. Stewart Capital Corp., Modesto, Calif., 1991—; prin. Thomas T. Stewart & Assocs., Jefferson City, Mo.; pres., owner, gen. mgr. Hotel DeVille. Cons. Gulf & We. Cos. in Ctrl. and S.Am.; site approval and acquisition for McDonald's Corp.; builder shopping ctrs. for Wetterau, Inc.; pres., gen. mgr. DeVille Hotel, Jefferson City, Mo., 1994—. Bd. dirs. Indsl. Devel. Commn., Jefferson City, 1986-89. With USMC, 1960-62. Mem. Harbor Club (bd. govs.), Seal Harbor Yacht Club (commodore 1986-88). Avocations: piano, flying, gardening.

STEWART, VERLINDSEY LAQUETTA, accounting educator; b. Birmingham, Ala., Dec. 27, 1965; d. Nathan Jr. and Shirley Ruth Brown; m. Kelvin Lorenzo Stewart I, June 22, 1991 (div. Feb. 1999); 1 child, Kelvin Lorenzo II. BS in Acctg., Ala. A&M U., 1988, MS in Bus. Edn., 1995, AA Cert. in Bus. Edn., 1997. Cert. tchr. bus. grades 7-12, Ala. Jr. acct. Childress Acctg., Huntsville, Ala., 1990-93; acctg. clk. Appeal Beauty Salon, 1988-94; receptionist Coop. Ext., Normal, Ala., 1992-94; grad. asst. Ala. A&M U., 1995; student tchr. J.O. Johnson H.S., Huntsville, Ala., 1995; acctg. instr. J.F. Drake State Tech., 1996—. Cons. Jr. Achievement, Huntsville, 1995-96. Post-reviewer: (book) College Accounting 9th, 1999 (Honorarium 1999). Vol. Habitat for Humanity, Huntsville, 1995-97; vol. asst. leader Girl Scouts North Ala., Huntsville, 1995-96. Recipient Adminstrv. Acad. award Rust Coll., 1999, Emerging Leaders Sch. award Ala. Edn. Assn., 1994, Ala. Master Tchr. Seminar, 2001. Mem. Nat. Bus. Edn., Ea. Star Mitzpah Ctr., Phi Beta Lambda (adviser 1998—), Delta Sigma Theta. Democrat. Baptist. Avocations: aerobics, weights, reading, listening to jazz music. Office: JF Drake State Tech Coll 3421 Meridian St N Huntsville AL 35811-1544 E-mail: vbdst28@aol.com.

STEWART, WARREN EARL, chemical engineer, educator; b. Whitewater, Wis., July 3, 1924; s. Earl Austin and Avis (Walker) S.; m. Jean Durham Potter, May 24, 1947; children— Marilyn, David, Douglas, Carol, Margaret, Mary Jean. BS in Chem. Engring, U. Wis., 1945, MS in Chem. Engring, 1947; Sc.D. in Chem. Engring, Mass. Inst. Tech., 1951. Project chem. engr. Sinclair Research Labs., Harvey, Ill., 1950-56, cons., 1956-83; asst. prof. chem. engring. dept. U. Wis., Madison, 1956-58, assoc. prof., 1958-61, prof., 1961—, chmn. dept., 1973-78, McFarland-Bascom prof., 1983-96, prof. emeritus, 1997—; pres. Stewart & Assoc. Engring. Software, Inc., 1998—. Cons. Engelhard Industries, Inc., Newark, 1956-58; instr. spl. courses transport phenomena Chemstrand Corp., Pensacola, Fla., 1962, Nat. U. La Plata, Argentina, 1962, Esso Rsch. & Engring. Co., 1963, 66, Phillips Petroleum Co., 1963, Am. Inst. Chem. Engrs., 1965, 68, 69, Inst. Tec. Celaya (Mex.), 1983, Univ. Autonoma de Mex., 1985; Reilly lectr. Notre Dame U., 1993. Author: (with R.B. Bird and E.N. Lightfoot) Transport Phenomena, 1960, 2d edit., 2002, Special Topics in Transport Phenomena, 1965, (with R.B. Bird, E.N. Lightfoot and T.W. Chapman) Lectures in Transport Phenomena, 1969; editorial advisor: Latin Am. Applied Rsch.; editorial advisor: Computers and Chem. Engring., 1977-2001. Recipient Benjamin Smith Reynolds teaching award, 1981, Byron Bird rsch. award, 1991. Fellow Am. Inst. Chem. Engrs. (Computing in Chem. Engring. award 1985); mem. NAE, Am. Chem. Soc. (Murphree award in indsl. and engring. chemistry 1989), Am. Soc. for Engring. Edn., (Chem. Engring. Lectureship award 1983), Phi Beta Kappa, Sigma Xi, Alpha Chi Sigma (research award 1981), Phi Eta Sigma, Tau Beta Pi, Phi Lambda Upsilon, Phi Kappa Phi. Conglist. (deacon, moderator). Home: 734 Huron Hill Madison WI 53711-2955 E-mail: Stewart@WISC.engr.edu.

STEWART, WHITNEY, children's book writer; b. Boston, Feb. 3, 1959; d. Richard Ramsdell Stewart and Carlin (Whitney) Scherer; m. Hans Christoph Andersson, Sept. 17, 1988. BA in Children's Lit. and Linguistics, Brown U., 1983. Puppeteer Le Theatre D'Avignon, France, 1977-78; children's libr., researcher Providence Athenaeum, Providence, 1981-82; travel agt., writer Parrish Travel Ctr., New Orleans, 1983-86; free lance writer, 1987—; editor Ctr. for Applied Linguistics, Washington, 1988-91; creative writing tchr. Fillmore Arts Ctr., 1991-92. Lectr. elem. and high schs.; dir. Tibetan sponsorship program, Washington, 1988-91. Author: To the Lion Throne, 1989, Clockwise Round the Stupa, 1989; author biographies of Dalai Lama of Tibet and Sir Edmund Hillary; former editor Tibet Today Newsletter, ERIC/CLL News Bull. Former sec. Capital Area Friends of Tibet, Washington, 1988-89. Mem. Soc. Children's Book Writers, Writer's Ctr., Asia Soc., Mongolia Soc. Avocations: bicycling, reading, travel, trekking.

STEWART, WILLIAM A. medical educator, neurosurgeon; b. Liberty Center, Ohio, Apr. 6, 1933; s. Cyrus Byron Stewart, Ardis Marjory Hicks; m. Nancy Newell Travis, June 18, 1960; children: Katherine, Elizabeth, Janet, Sarah, Heather, Alexandra. AB, Miami U., Oxford, Ohio, 1954; MD, Ohio State U., 1958. Diplomate Am. Bd. Neurosurgery. Resident in gen. surgery/neurosurgery SUNY-Upstate Med. Ctr., Syracuse, 1958—65, asst. prof. dept. neurosurgery, 1967—74, clin. prof., 1975—; dir. Project Hope team Project Hope, Ile Ife, Nigeria, 1974—75. Chmn. N.Y. State Dept. Health Bd. Profl. Med. Conduct, Albany, 1977—98, mem. adminstrv. rev. bd., 1992—98. Lt. comdr. M.C. USNR, 1965—67. Mem.: Coalition for Physician Enhancement. Presbyterian. Avocations: gardening, numismatics. Home: 7595 Hunt Ln Fayetteville NY 13066

STEWART, WILLIAM BARTLEY, software developer; b. Alexandria, La., June 13, 1962; s. William B. Sr. and Margaret Ellen (Robertson) S. BS in Computer Sci., La. Tech. U., 1985. System operator Procter & Gamble, Tioga, La., 1986; assoc. tech. specialist Computer Scis. Corp., Herndon, Va., 1987-90, programmer, analyst, 1990—. Nat. merit scholar Dresser Harbison-Walker Found., 1980. Mem. AAAS, Assn. for Computing Machinery (spl. interest group on artificial intelligence), Planetary Soc. Republican. Office: Computer Scis Corp 3001 Centreville Rd Herndon VA 20171-3709

STEWART, WILLIAM DOUGLAS, music educator; b. Columbus, Ohio, Mar. 31, 1963; s. William Glenn and Sandra Jane Stewart; m. Julie K. Kuhns, June 13, 2001; 1 child Natalie Elizabeth. MusB in Edn., U. Ky., 1987. Cert. 7-12 music Ohio. Dir. of bands Caverna H.S., Horse Cave-Cave City, Ky., 1987—89, Leonardtown (Md.) H.S., 1989—90, Parkside H.S., Salisbury, 1990—98; asst. dir. of bands Franklin Heights H.S., Columbus, Ohio, 1998—2000; dir. of bands Westerville South H.S., Westerville, 2000—. Dir. of bands: music edn./performance Ohio Gov.'s Meml. Day Celebration, 2002, dir. of bands: music edn./performance European tour, 1998, dir. of bands: music edn./performance Md.'s Gov. Inaugural Parade, 1995, dir. of bands: music edn./performance Can. tour, 1995; musician: (commd. original work for band) Ballad for Chris, 1996. Mem.: Internat. Trombone Assn., Tournament of Bands (Band Dir. award 1990, 1995, U. Ky. Marching Band Honor Bandsman 1985), Kappa Alpha Order (mem. honor coun.), Kappa Kappa Psi (v.p. 1985—86). Avocations: parenthood, Tae Kwon Do, ensemble performance, computers, reading. Home: 1927 Willoway Circle N Columbus OH 43220 Personal E-mail: wdstewart@aol.com.

STEWART, WILLIAM THOMAS, communications educator; b. Bryan, Tex., Sept. 29, 1934; s. Simeon Brooks and Bess Maude (McGee) S.; m. Roswitha Form Stewart, June 19, 1959; children: Terri M., Erin K. BA in History, U. Tex., Austin, 1957; MA in Speech and Drama, Calif. State U., Sacramento, 1969. Cert. tchr., Calif. Mgmt. trainee S.W. Bell Tel. Co., Houston, 1960—61; tchr. San Juan Unified Sch. Dist., Carmichael, Calif., 1962—99; instr. We. Career Coll., Sacramento, 1999—; student tchr. supr. Nat. U., 2000—, Chapman U., 2001—. Author: International Film Necrology, 1981, Ronald Reagan: A Biography, 1988; contbr. plays and poetry to profl. jours. With U.S. Army, 1957-63. Mem. NEA. Mem. Ch. Christ. Avocations: play directing and writing, reading, extra work in films. Home: 7101 Falcon Rd Fair Oaks CA 95628 E-mail: bvstew@pacbell.net.

STEWART-COUSINS, ANDREA ALICE, legislator; b. N.Y.C., Sept. 2, 1950; d. Robert Lucius and Beryl Agatha (Phipps); m. Tom Cousins, May 5, 1979; children: Kevin, Steven, Candice. BSc, Pace U., 1986. Cert. bus. edn. tchr., N.Y. Customer svc. rep. N.Y. Tel., 1970-78; market adminstr. AT&T, N.Y.C., 1979-83; journalist Gannett Westchester Newspapers, Yonkers, N.Y., 1986-88; tchr. Yonkers (N.Y.) Pub. Schs., 1988-89; pers. mgr. Career Blazers, White Plains, N.Y., 1989-92; dir. cmty. affairs Mayor's Office, Yonkers, 1992-95; legislator Westchester County Bd. Legislators, White Plains, 1996—, majority whip, 2001—. Sponsor Westchester County Human Rights Commn., N.Y., 1999—. Bd. dirs. Yonkers Gen. Hosp., 1999—; mem. Westchester County Dem. Com., 1998--, 1st vice chair, 1999--. Recipient Social Justice award Pace U., 1999, Legislator of Yr. award Westchester Black Women's Pol. Caucus, 2000, Racial justice award YWCA, White Plains, 2000, Civil Libertarian 2000 award Am. Civil Liberties Union, Weschester County, Trailblazer award N.Y. State Assn. of Human Rights Commn., 2000. Mem. NAACP (Legis. Excellence 2000), Westchester County Bd. Legislators (county legislator 1996—). Avocations: Sahaja yoga meditation, reading. Home: 293 N Broadway Yonkers NY 10701-2453 Office: Westchester County Bd Legislators 148 Martine Ave White Plains NY 10601-3311 Fax: 914-963-5831. E-mail: acyogi@aol.com., ac9@Westchester.gov.

STEWART-PÉREZ, RENICE ANN, technology writer, internal systems professional; b. Milw., Jan. 2, 1947; d. Fredrick and Lucia (Stewart) Fregin; children: Jennifer Jean, Whitney Susan; m. Robert Anthony Pérez, Dec. 21, 1995. BA, U. San Diego, 1989, MA, 1991. Pres. Chubby Bumpkins, Inc., Houston, 1980-82; contracts adminstr. Gulf States Computer Svcs., 1980-82; pres. RAM Prodns., 1981-82, Pizza Internat., Inc., Houston, 1982-84; contracts adminstr. First Alliance Corp., 1982-85; freelance pub. rels. cons. San Diego, 1985-97, Nortel Networks, Plano, Tex., 1997-98; mgr. mktg. comms. FirstWorld Comms., San Diego, 1998; web mgr. GERS Retail Sys., 1998-2000, Zama Networks, Seattle, 2000—01, Microsoft Corp., Redmond, 2001—. Tutor U. San Diego Writing Ctr., 1987-89; founder, dir. pub. rels.-tng. Montgomery County (Tex.) Crisis Action Line, Houston, 1979-84; founder, v.p., bd. dirs. Montgomery County Rape Crisis Coalition, 1982-84, speaker, 1982-84; speaker Rape Trauma Coalition, 1982-84; mem. prodn. com. Community Women Together, Montgomery County, 1980-82; pres. Living Arts Coun., Houston, 1980-81. Named Woman of Yr. YWCA, 1981, 82. Mem. Internat. Assn. Bus. Communicators, Am. Assn. Bus. Women (dir. activities Houston chpt. 1983-84), Bus. Women's Forum (bd. dir. community awareness Houston chpt. 1982-83), Assn. Women Bus. Owners, Lions (hon.), Phi Alpha Delta. E-mail: rstewart@zama.net.

STEWART-SMITH, DAVID, music educator, historian, researcher; b. N.Y.C., Nov. 13, 1951; s. Wentworth Smith and Helen Ridgely Ballantine; m. Karen Elizabeth Czajkowski, July 22, 1994; children: Daniel Stuart Smith, Brendan Strickland Smith. BA, Vt. Coll. of Norwich Univ., 1991; PhD, Union Inst., 1998. Mem. faculty Vt. Coll. Adult Degree Program, Brattleboro, 1994—; staff ethnohistorian and editor Sargent Mus. of Archaeology, Concord, NH, 1994—2001. Trustee NH Intertribal Coun., Lanconia, NH, 1992—. Editor: (local history) From the King's Plantation of Contoocook, 1997; contbr. articles to profl. jours. Mem.: Masons. Office: Vermont College of Union Institute 157 Old Guilford Rd Ste3 Brattleboro VT 05301-3669 Personal E-mail: pennacook@tds.net. E-mail: adp.dss@tds.net.

STEYTLER, C. ANNE WEBSTER, clinical social worker; b. Milw., Jan. 10, 1921; d. Royden Erastus and Jessie Emily (Beebe) Webster; m. Walter David Stimple, Dec. 31, 1941 (dec. May 1951); children: Jeanne Elizabeth Pitz, Alan Lee Steytler, Margaret Anne Rosenfield; m. Edmund John Steytler, Dec. 25, 1951 (dec. May 1998); 1 child, Carolyn Sue. BS, U. Wis., 1943, MA, 1945; MSSA, Western Res. U., Cleve., 1967. Lic. social work, Pa. Instr. U. Wis., Madison, Wis., 1946-47; pediatric aide Wis. Gen. Hosp., 1947-49; tchr. Blacksburg (Va.) High Sch., 1951-52; order clerk med. libr. U. N.C., Chapel Hill, 1953-55; caseworker children's svcs. Lake County Welfare Dept., Painesville, Ohio, 1964-65; psychiatric social worker Lake County MH-MR Ctr., Mentor, 1967-69; psychiatric unit dir. Southeastern MH-MR Ctr., Pitts., 1969-77; pvt. practice, 1974-95; staff therapist Persad Ctr., Inc., 1983-95; sex educator Family Health Coun., 1991—. In house therapist Dr. John Morocca, Sewickley, Pa., 1981-83; cons. Project Headstart, Pitts., 1980-83; cons., educator Parent and Child Guidance Ctr., Pitts., 1984-86; sex educator, Women's Health Svcs., Pitts., 1978-90. Co-founder Pub. Library, ad hoc com., Murray, Ky., 1962, Family Planning Svcs., Lake and Geauga Counties, Ohio, 1968, Women's Ctr. and Shelter, Pitts., 1974; lay leader Unitarian Universalist Ch. South Hills, Pitts., 1975-77; bd. dir., troop leader, day camp dir., Girl Scouts U.S., Murray, 1957; bd. dirs. Thomas Merton Ctr., Alliance for Progressive Action, 1995—. Mem. NASW (diplomate), Internat. Transactional Analysis Assn., Am. Assn. Marriage and Family Therapists. Democrat. Avocations: reading, theatre, camping, gardening. Home: 1001 Allegheny Ave # 2 Pittsburgh PA 15233

STHRESHLEY, CHARLES ARCHIE, sculptor; b. Brussels, Belgium, Oct. 14, 1954; s. Charles Arthur and Florence Temple (Moore) S.; m. Katherine McKee, Dec. 27, 1979. BA, Thomas Edison State Coll., Trenton, N.J., 1997. Propr. Sthreshley Studios, Ashland, Va., 1982—; exhibits specialist Nat. Mus. Am. History, Washington, 1996—. Exhibited sculpture in solo shows at Franz Bader Gallery, Washington, 1991, 92; exhibited in group shows at Ward-Nasse Gallery, N.Y.C., 1990, Peninsula Fine Arts Ctr., Newport News, Va., 1992, Flagler Mus., Palm Beach, Fla., 1995, Meredith Gallery, Balt., 1997, Smithsonian's Artists at Work, 2000, others; art pub. in Furniture Studio: The Heart of Functional Arts, 1999. Recipient Sculpure award Peninsula Fine Art Ctr., 1991 Home: 402 Duncan St Ashland VA 23005-1908 Office: Nat Mus Am History 14th St And Constitution NW Washington DC 20560-0001 E-mail: sthreshleyc@nmah.si.edu.

STIASSNY, MELANIE L.J. curator; BSc in Zoology with honors, U. London, 1976, PhD in Zoology , 1980. Fellow Rijksuniversiteit and Rijksmuseum, Leiden, Netherlands, 1980—83; asst. prof. dept organismic and evolutionary biology Harvard U., 1983—87; asst. curator dept. herpetology and ichthyology Am. Mus. Natural History, N.Y.C., 1987—92, assoc. curator dept. herpetology and ichthyology, 1992—97, Herbert R. and evelyn Axelrod rsch. curator, curator-in-charge dept. ichthyology, 1997—. Adj. prof. CUNY, 1992—, Ctr. for Environ. Rsch. and Conservation, NY, 1999—; sci. adv. World Wildlife Fund for Nature, Conservation Internat., World Resources Inst., Internat. Found. for Sci. Contbr. articles to profl. jours. Grantee, NSF, 1993—2001, Nat. Geog. Soc., 1997—98, Am. Mus. Natural History, 1997—99. Office: Am Mus Natural History Dept Ichthyology Central Park West at 79th St New York NY 10024*

STIBBE, AUSTIN JULE, accountant; b. St. Paul, Mar. 29, 1930; s. Austin Julius and Agnes Dorothea (Delaney) S.; m. Mary Elizabeth King, May 29, 1952; children: Anne Marie, Craig Jule, David King, Karen Lee. BSB in Acctg., U. Minn., 1952. CPA, Minn., Wis. Tax acct. Ernst & Ernst, Mpls., 1955-60; corp. tax mgr. EcoLab, Inc., St. Paul, 1960-65; audit mgr. Coopers & Lybrand, Mpls., 1965-74; v.p. Wilkerson, Guthmann & Johnson, Ltd., St. Paul, 1974-93, of counsel, 1993—. Exec. officer Twin Cities Squadron, U.S. Naval Sea Cadet Corps, Mpls., 1974-80; bd. dirs., treas., mem. Twin Cities coun. Navy League, 1970—, pres., 1979-81, treas., 1975-79, 81-91; mem. adv. coun. to dept. acctg. U. Minn., Mpls., 1983-86; bd. dirs., chmn. audit com. St. Paul Area Coun. Chs., 1985-87; mem. adv. bd. Headwaters Soc., 1987-88; mem. fin. reporting com. United Way St. Paul Area, 1981-93, mem. audit com., 1991-93; dist. commr. staff Indianhead coun. Boy Scouts Am., 1962-65. Lt. USN, 1952-55. Mem. Minn. Soc. CPAs (life), U.S. Naval Inst. (life), Belle Taine Lake Assn. (dir. 1995-2001, treas. 1996-2001), Hubbard County COLA Print Com., 1995-98, Friends of Heritage, 1996—, Hubbard County Works of Improvement (steering com. 2001). Presbyterian. Avocations: music, boating, history. Home: PO Box 41 Nevis MN 56467-0041

STICE, DWAYNE LEE, broadcasting company executive; b. Paducah, Ky., Aug. 10, 1956; s. Freeman D. and Dorris Olive (Lee) S. AA, Paducah Community Coll., 1976; BS, Murray State U., 1977; MS, Southern Ill. U., 1983. Lic. funeral dir., Ky. Dir. Johnson-Lambert Funeral Home, Calvert City, Ky., 1974-81; gen. mgr. Paducah Area Transit System, 1980-92; pres. Sta. WCCK-FM, Stice Comm., Inc., Calvert City, 1990—. Adj. bus. instr. Paducah Community Coll., 1979—, Lindsey Wilson Coll., Columbia, Ky., 1991; adj. reporter CBS Radio Network. Contbr. articles to profl. jours. Bd. dirs. Wesley Found., Murray State U., Calvert City United Fund; mem. Calvert Area Devel. Assn., purchase area development's dist. transp. com. Outstanding grantee Ky. Transp. Cabinet, 1985, 86. Mem. Ky. Pub. Transit Assn. (pres. 1988-91), Ky. Broadcasters Assn. (bd. dirs. 1997—), Marshall C. of C. (bd. dirs., vice chmn. govt. affairs 1998), Lyon County C. of C., Paducah C.C. Alumni Assn. (pres. 1983), Hon. Order Ky. Cols., Travelers Protective Assn. (pres. Paducah chpt. 1989-90), Lions, Masons (master Calvert City 1984), Shriners, Order Ea. Star, Phi Kappa Phi, Phi Theta Kappa. Methodist. Avocations: organist, travel, baseball. Home: 647 S Main St Calvert City KY 42029-8385 Office: Sta WCCK-FM 2 Aspen St Calvert City KY 42029-9304

STICH, JUNE JEACOMA, psychotherapist; b. Mineola, N.Y., June 27, 1939; d. John Daniel and Mercedes (Serrano) Jeacoma; m. William Thomas Lloyd, Sept. 16, 1961 (div. 1967); m. Edward Stich, July 6, 1974; 1 child, Edward John. AA, Nassau Community Coll., 1967; BS, Empire State Coll., 1981; MSW, Adelphi U., 1990; postgrad., Hunter Coll., Manhattan, N.Y., 1986-87. Cert. social worker. Welfare examiner I Dept. Social Svcs., Mineola, N.Y., 1971-74; pres., founder Happy Marriage League, Long Beach, 1974-81; asst. coord. St. Mary Roman Cath. Ch., 1980-82; social worker, case mgr. Cath. Charities, Lynbrook, 1985-87; social worker, counselor Peninsula Counseling Ctr., Woodmere, 1988-89, Jewish Assn. of Svcs. to Aged, Long Beach, 1989-90; social worker, psychotherapist Winter Park (Fla.) Home Health Care, 1991-92, Margaret Tietz Nursing Home, Jamaica, NY, 1992—94, Fla. Hosp. Ctr. Psychiatry, Orlando, 1995—96, Shands Homecare, Orlando, Fla., 1997—99, pvt. practice, Winter Park, 1998—2000, Mayfair Care Ctr., Hempstead, NY, 2001—, pvt. practice, Rockville Center, 2001—, New York City, 2002—. Held several bereavement groups & stress mngmt. groups, NY, 1999—. Narrator, writer audio tape: Think Thin, 1985. Coord. retreats L.I. Charismatic Renewal, 1985, 86. Recipient Silberman award Scholarship Com. of Hunter Coll., 1986; recipient 4 vol. svc. awards VA, 1988-89. Mem. Am. Assn. for Counseling and Devel., Nat. Assn. Social Workers, N.Am. Assn. of Christians in Social Wk. Roman Catholic. Avocations: painting, dancing, walking, gardening. Home: 111 West 71st St Apt 2B New York NY 10023

STICH, STEPHEN PETER, philosophy educator; b. N.Y.C., May 9, 1943; s. Samuel Joseph and Sylvia Lucille (Siegel) S.; m. Judith Ann Gagnon, Dec. 20, 1971; children: Jonathan Andrew, Rebecca Elizabeth. BA summa cum laude with distinction, U. Pa., 1964; PhD, Princeton U., 1968. Teaching asst. Princton U., 1965; asst. prof. U. Mich., 1968-73, assoc. prof., 1973-78, dir. grad. studies in philosophy, 1973-74, assoc. chmn. dept. philosophy, 1975-76; assoc. prof. U. Md., 1978-81, prof., 1981-86, dir. grad. studies in philosophy, 1982-83; prof. U. Calif., San Diego, 1986-89, dir. cognitive sci. program, 1988-89; prof. philosophy and cognitive sci. Rutgers U., New Brunswick, 1989—, acting chair dept. philosophy, 1992-93, dir. rsch. group on evolution and higher cognition, 1997—, bd. govs. prof., 1998—. Prof. Linguistic inst., Linguistic Soc. Am., summer 1982; dir. Summer Seminar for Coll. Tchrs. NEH, 1983, 89; vis. sr. lectr. U. Sydney, 1984-85; vis. fellow Australian Nat. U., 1992; Jemison prof. humanities U. Ala., Birmingham, 1993; adj. prof. CUNY Grad. Ctr., 1994-97; Erskine fellow Canterbury U., Christchurch, New Zealand, 1996; cons. Pres. Commn. for Nat. Priorities in the Eighties, Pres. Commn. on Ethics in Medicine and Biomed. and Behavioral Rsch.; mem. selection com. Mellon Fellowships in the Humanities, 1983-84; mem. Fulbright Selection Com., 1981-83, chair, 1983; vis. fellow Australian Nat. U., Rsch. Sch. Social Scis., 1992. Author: From Folk Psychology to Cognitive Science, 1983, The Fragmentation of Reason, 1990, Deconstructing the Mind, 1996; editor: Innate Ideas, 1975; (with others) The Recombinant DNA Debate, 1979, Philosophy and Connectionist Theory, 1991, Mental Representation, 1994; editor Evolution and Cognition Series; mem. editl. bd. Linguistics and Philosophy, 1984—, Mind and Language, 1985—, Cognitive Sci., 1990—, Minds and Machines, 1991—, Pragmatics and Cognition, 1991—, Philosophical Studies, 1992—, Philosophy of Sci., 1992—, Cognition, 1993—, Neural Network Modeling and Connectionism; mem. editl. adv. bd. Studies in Cognitive Sys.; contbr. articles to profl. jours., chpts. to books. Woodrow Wilson Nat. Fellowship Found. fellow, 1964-65, Woodrow Wilson dissertation fellow, 1967, Danforth grad. fellow, 1964-67, H.H. Ford fellow Princeton U., 1967, Coun. Philos. Studies Summer Inst. fellow, 1971, Am. Coun. Learned Socs. fellow, 1978-79, Rutgers U. competitive fellow, sch. liberal arts fellow U. Otago, Dunedin, New Zealand, 2001; recipient fellowships NEH, 1974, 83-84, 96, Ctr. for Advanced Study in Behavioral Scis., Stanford, Calif., 1983; Fulbright sr. rsch. scholar, Bristol (U.K.) U., 1978-79; grantee U.S.-Israel Ednl. Found., 1979, NRC and U.S. Nat. Com. for Internat. Union of History and Philosophy of Sci., Hannover, West Germany, 1979, NSF, 1981-82. Mem. Am. Philos. Assn., Soc. for Philosophy and Psychology (pres. 1982-83, exec. com. 1980-82, 83-84, chair program com. 1979-80), Philosophy of Sci. Assn., Brit. Soc. for Philosophy of Sci., Fulbright Alumni Assn. Office: Rutgers U Philosophy Dept Davison Hall Douglass Campus New Brunswick NJ 08901-2882 E-mail: stich@ruccs.rutgers.edu.

STICHT, J. PAUL, retired food products and tobacco company executive; b. Clairton, Pa., 1917; BA, Grove City Coll., 1939; postgrad., U. Pitts. With U.S. Steel Corp., 1939-44; pers. dir. Trans World Airlines, 1944-48; v.p. Campbell Soup Co., 1947-57, pres. internat., 1957-60; from exec. v.p. to pres. Federated Dept. Stores, Inc., 1960-72; chmn. exec. com., COO R.J. Reynolds Industries, Inc., Winston-Salem, N.C., 1972-73, pres., CEO, 1978-79, chmn. bd., 1979-85; chmn. RJR Nabisco, Inc., 1987-89, acting chmn., CEO, 1989; pres. Castle Springs, LLC, 1992—2002, chmn., 2002—. Pres. bd. trustees Grove City Coll.; trustee, former chmn. Caribbean/L.Am. Action; mem. bd. visitors Wake Forest U. Med. Sch., former chmn. bd. visitors; mem. bd. visitors Fuqua Sch. Bus. Duke U. Office: Castle Springs LLC 119 Brookstown Ave Winston Salem NC 27101-5245

STICK, ALYCE CUSHING, information systems consultant; b. N.J., July 13, 1944; d. George William and Adele Margaret (Wilderotter) Cushing; m. James McAlpin Easter, July, 1970 (div. Aug. 1986); m. T. Howard F. Stick, June, 1989. AA, Colby-Sawyer Coll., 1964; student, Boston U., 1964-65, Johns Hopkins U., 1972-74; cert., Control Data Inst. and Life Office Mgmt. Assn., 1976. Claims investigator Continental Casualty Co., Phila., 1967-69; data processing coord. Chesapeake Life Ins. Co., Balt., 1970-72; sr. systems analyst Comml. Credit Computer Corp., 1972-80; v.p. Shawmut Computer Systems, Inc., Owings Mills, Md., 1980-85; pres. Computer Relevance, Inc., Gladwyne, Pa., 1985—. Cons. Sinai Hosp., Balt., 1982-85, AT&T, Reading, Pa., 1987-88, Dun and Bradstreet, Allentown, Pa., 1988, Arco Chem. Co., Newtown Square, Pa., 1990-91, Rohm and Haas Co., Phila., 1992—. Designer/author: (computer software systems) Claim-Track, 1977, Property-Profiles, 1979, Stat-Model, 1989; co-designer/author: Patient-Profiles, 1983. Treas. Balt. Mus. Art, Sales and Rental Gallery, 1984. Mem. Assn. for Systems Mgmt., Data Processing Mgmt. Assn., Ind. Computer Cons. Assn., Merion Cricket Club (Haverford, Pa.). Republican. Avocations: Am. antiques, Chinese export porcelain dealer. Office: Computer Relevance Inc 1501 Monticello Dr Gladwyne PA 19035-1206

STICK, THOMAS HOWARD FITCHETT, corporate architect, construction litigation consultant; b. Balt., Feb. 28, 1938; s. Gordon M. F. and Anne Howard (Fitchett) S.; m. Rosalie Wade Reynolds, 1959 (div. 1982); children: H. Edward M., Alexander W., David F.; m. Joyce Yeargin Carr, 1982 (div. 1989); m. Alyce C. Cushing, 1989. BA in Psychology, Yale U., 1960; postgrad., Md. Inst., 1962, U. Pa. Grad. Sch. Arch., 1964. Registered arch., Pa., Md., Del., N.J., Va., Maine, N.Y., D.C., Mass., N.H., N.C., Vt., Tenn., Okla., Colo., Ind., Ga., Ill., Mich., Ky., Kans., Ohio, Peoples Republic of China; cert. recommendation Nat. Coun. Archtl. Registration Bds. Arch. Vincent G. Kling & Ptnrs., Phila., 1964-74, B.J. Hoffman & Assocs., Berwyn, 1974; ptnr. Grim & Stick, Ardmore, 1975-77; prin. Stick Assocs., Gladwyne, 1977-80; corp. arch. Gino's Inc., King of Prussia, 1980-81; mgr. constrn. adminstrn. Ballinger Co., Phila., 1981-83; sr. constrn. claims cons. MDC Sys. Corp., 1984-85; chief arch. Day & Zimmermann Inc., 1985—, discipline mgr., 1987—, corp. arch., 1995—; dir. Day & Zimmermann Internat. Corp., 2000—. V.p. F-S Found., 1986, also bd. dirs. One-man show in photography Ea. Camera Gallery, 1972. Named Arch. of Best Food Plant of Yr., Food Engring. Mag., 1992. Mem. AIA, Pa. Soc. Archs., Bldg. Ofcls. and Code Adminstrs. Internat., Internat. Conf. Bldg. Ofcls., So. Bldg. Code Congress Internat., Constrn. Specifications Inst., Nat. Fire Protection Assn., Soc. War of 1812 (sec. 1977-82), Soc. of Cincinnati, Soc. Colonial Wars, SR, Descs. of Lords of the Md. Manors, Mil. Order of Loyal Legion of U.S., Huguenot Soc., Am. Clan Gregor Soc., St. Andrew's Soc. of Balt., St. George's Soc. of Balt., Merion Cricket Club (Haverford, Pa.), Yale Club, Sovereign Mil. of Temple of Jerusalem (comdr.), Sovereign Order of St. John of Jerusalem (Knight of Justice), Knights Malta, Zeta Psi. Home: 1501 Monticello Dr Gladwyne PA 19035-1206 Office: Day & Zimmermann Internat 240 Continental Dr Newark DE 19713-4328

STICKEL, DELFORD LEFEW, retired general surgeon; b. Falling Waters, W.Va., Dec. 12, 1927; MD, Duke U., 1953. Diplomate Am. Bd. Surgery, Am. Bd. Thoracic Surgery. Intern Duke Hosp., Durham, N.C., 1953-55, resident, 1957-62; mem. staff Duke U. Hosp., 1962-97; ret., 1997; mem. staff, cons. VA Med. Ctr., Durham, 1962-83; chief resident Duke U. Sch. Medicine, 1961-62. Mem. AMA, ACS, Am. Soc. Transplant Surgeons, So. Surg. Assn. Home: 2 Chimney Top Ct Durham NC 27705-5442

STICKEL, FREDERICK A. publisher; b. Weehawken, N.J., Nov. 18, 1921; s. Fred and Eva (Madigan) S.; m. Margaret A. Dunne, Dec. 4, 1943; children—Fred A., Patrick F., Daisy E., Geoffrey M., James E., Bridget A. Student, Georgetown U., 1939-42; BS, St. Peter's Coll., 1943. Advt. salesperson Jersey Observer daily, Hoboken, N.J., 1945-51; retail advt. salesperson Jersey Jour., Jersey City, 1951-55, advt. dir., 1955-66, publisher, 1966-67; gen. mgr. Oregonian Pub. Co., Portland, Oreg., 1967-72, pres., 1972-86, publisher, 1975—. Bd. regents U. Portland; adv. bd. Portland State U., St. Vincent's Hosp.; bd. dirs. Portland Rose Festival Assn., United Way Oreg.; chmn. Portland Citizens Crime Commn. Capt. USMC, 1942-45. Mem. Assn. for Portland Progress (dir.), Portland C. of C. (dir.), Oreg. Newspaper Pubs. Assn. (past pres.), Pacific N.W. Newspaper Assn. (past pres.), Newspaper Assn. Am., University Club, Multnomah Athletic Waverley Country Club, Arlington Club, Rotary. Office: Oregonian Pub Co 1320 SW Broadway Portland OR 97201-3499

STICKEL, LISA MAYS, accountant; b. Nashville, June 9, 1969; d. Stanley Roger Mays and Linda Jean (Rickabaugh) Miller; m. Peter James Stickel, Aug. 8, 1992; children: Mayson James, Clayton Lee. BS, Western Ky. U., 1991. CPA, Tenn. Staff acct. Olson & Assocs., White House, Tenn., 1991-92, Ingersoll-Rand, White House, 1992-95; ptnr. Parker, Parker & Stickel, Goodlettsville, Tenn., 1995—; project chair JLN, 1998, 1999—2001, bd. dirs., treas., 2002—. Computer com., co-chair Jr. League of Nashville, 1996, 97, 98; bd. mem. White House Area C. of C., 1998—; asst. treas. Pky. Bapt. Ch., 2002—. Mem. AICPA, Tenn. Soc. CPAs, Beta Alpha Psi (Outstanding mem. 1990-91), Goodlettsville C. of C. (several coms.). Baptist. Avocations: running, skiing, reading, mountain bike riding, scrapbooking. Office: Parker Parker & Stickel 1000 Northchase Dr Ste 260 Goodlettsville TN 37072-2162

STICKEL, PATRICK FRANCIS, publishing executive, newspaper; b. Hoboken, N.J., Apr. 17, 1950; s. Fred A. and Margaret (Dunne) S.; m. Debra Isaak, May 10, 1986. Degree in bus. mgmt., U. Portland, 1975. With advt. dept. Jersey Jour., Jersey City, 1966-67; with Oregonian Pub. Co., Portland, 1967-68, 70-75, pressman, with retail advt. dept., 1975-77, with retail & circulation depts., 1980-86, adminstrv. asst., 1987-89, gen. mgr., 1990-94, pres., 1994—; project mgr. Times Picayune, New Orleans, 1986-87. Exec. com. Oreg. Forum, Portland. 1st lt. USMC, 1977-80. Mem. Pacific N.W. Newspapers Assn. (bd. dirs.), Waverley Country Club, Univ. Club, Multnomah Athletic Club. Avocation: golf. Office: The Oregonian 1320 SW Broadway Portland OR 97201-3499*

STICKELER, CARL ANN LOUISE, professional parliamentarian; b. Plant City, Fla., Dec. 26, 1930; d. Carl Ulysses and Marian Lucille (Churchill) Sangster; m. Nickolas Joseph Stickeler, May 14, 1949; children: Nickolas J., Juliann E., Carl A., John C., Katherine M. Profl. registered parliamentarian. Bus. mgr. Kendall Automobile Sales, Inc., Miami, 1967-82; parliamentarian Stickeler & Assocs., P.A., 1982-88, Ocala, Fla., 1988—. Editor: The Answer, 1983-89, 97—, The Florida Parliamentarian, 1983-87. Recipient Internat. Woman of Distinction Beta Sigma Phi Internat., 1980, Order of the Rose award Beta Sigma Phi Internat., 1969. Mem. Nat. Assn. Parliamentarians (bd. dirs. 1979-83, 91-93, 95-97, 99—, v.p. 1983-89, pres. 1989-91, parliamentarian 1997-99), Acad. Parliamentary Procedure and Law (bd. dirs. 1979—, pres. 1985-87), Gen. Fedn. Women's Clubs, Fla. Fedn. of Women's Clubs (parliamentarian 1992-98, 2000--), DAR (parliamentarian Fla. state soc. 1997-98), Beta Sigma Phi. Republican. Roman Catholic. Avocation: parliamentary research. Office: Stickeler & Assocs 102 Almond Rd Ocala FL 34472-8634 E-mail: CAStickeler@cs.com.

STICKLE, DAVID WALTER, microbiologist; b. Boston, Apr. 18, 1933; s. Harold Edwards and Lucille Margaret (Magee) S.; m. Mary Elizabeth DeLong, July 29, 1972. BS in Chemistry, Biology, Tufts U., 1955; MS in Pharmacy and Health, Northeastern U., Boston, 1968; MPH, U. N.C., 1969, DrPH, 1971. Bacteriologist Mass. Dept. Pub. Health, Boston, 1959-63, supr. immunology unit, 1963-68; UNC/CDC lab. dir.'s program Ctrs. for Disease Control, Atlanta, 1968-71; chief, clin. lab. improvement program Divsn. Med. Labs./Minn. Dept. Health, Mpls., 1971-82, acting dir., 1977-78, asst. dir., 1978-88. Ex-officio mem. Minn. Soc. Clin. Pathologists Exec. Com., Mpls., 1977-78; mem. Proficiency Testing Com., Minn. Acad. Family Physicians, Mpls., 1977-83; adj. asst. prof. U. Minn., Mpls., 1977-88; assoc. prof. emeritus, U. Minn., 1988—. Editor: Med. Lab. Forum periodical, 1973-88. Proctor Nat. Registry of Microbiology, Mpls. Examinations for Minn., 1987-92; instr. Edina Community Edn. Programs, Minn., 1992. With U.S. Army, 1955-57. Lab. tng. grantee Ctr. for Disease Control, HEW, Atlanta, 1977-78, 1978-80, 1979-81. Mem. Am. Soc. Microbiology, Phi Sigma, Sigma Xi. Achievements include serologic tests for systemic candidiasis which were in use for many years by the Ctrs. for Disease Control, U.S. Dept. of Health and Human Svcs.

STICKLER, DANIEL LEE, health care management consultant; b. Fairmont, W.Va., Jan. 4, 1938; s. Elmer Daniel and Ruby Lee (Ball) S.; m. Donna Lou Johnson, Apr. 16, 1960; children— Dwight Lorne, Dwayne Lee, Douglas Lynn BS in Civil Engring., W.Va. U., 1960; M.P.H. in Health Adminstrn., U. Pitts., 1970. Registered profl. engr., Tex. Asst. dir. Presbyn.-Univ. Hosp., Pitts., 1970-71, assoc. dir., 1971-72, adminstr., chief operating officer, 1972-76, exec. dir., chief exec. officer, 1976-83, pres., chief exec. officer, 1983-86; pres., CEO, The Cedars Med. Ctr., Miami, Fla., 1986-91; pres. DLS Assocs., Inc., 1991-95; sr. v.p. The Hunter Group, 1996—. Adj. assoc. prof. Grad. Sch. Pub. Health, U. Pitts., 1976-86. Fellow Am. Coll. Hosp. Adminstrn.; mem. Palmaire Country Club. Methodist. Avocations: golf, gardening. Home and Office: 5803 Fairwoods Cir Sarasota FL 34243-3821 E-mail: dstickle@tampabay.rr.com.

STICKNEY, JESSICA, former state legislator; b. Duluth, Minn., May 16, 1929; d. Ralph Emerson and Claudia Alice (Cox) Page; m. Edwin Levi Stickney, June 17, 1951; children: Claudia, Laura, Jeffrey. BA, Macalester Coll., St. Paul, Minn., 1951; PhD (hon), Rocky Mtn. Coll., Billings, Mont., 1986. Rep. State of Mont., 1989-92. Mem. Gov.'s Commn. on Post-Sec. Edn., Mont., 1973-75. Mem. Sch. Bd. Trustees, Miles City, Mont., 1968-74; mem., chmn. zoning bd., Miles City, 1975-89; mem. Govt. Study Commn., Miles City, 1974-76, United Ch. Christ Bd. Homeland Ministries, 1975-81; chmn., conf. moderator United Ch. Christ Bd. Mont.-Northern Wyo. Conf., 1980-82; chmn. Town Meeting on the Arts, Mont., 1980; mem., chmn. Miles Community Coll. Bd., 1975-89, chmn. 1978-80. Mem. Mont. Arts Coun. (chmn. 1982-85), Western States Arts Found. (vice chmn. 1984), Nat. Assembly State Arts Agys. (bd. dirs. 1982-88), AAUW (pres. 1964-66). Democrat. Avocations: writing, sewing, painting, reading.

STICKNEY, JOHN MOORE, lawyer; b. Cleve., Apr. 8, 1926; s. Isaac Moore and Alicia Margaret (Burns) S.; m. Elfriede von Rebenstock, Oct. 4, 1958; children: Michaela B., Alicia J., Thomas M. AB, Western Res. U., 1948, LLB, 1951. Bar: Ohio 1952. Sole practice, Cleve., 1952-79; ptnr. Burgess, Steck, Andrews & Stickney, Cleve., 1979-88; of counsel Weston, Hurd, Fallon, Paisley & Howley, Cleve., 1988-90, sole practice, 1990—; pres. Scranton-Averell, Inc., Cleve., 1979—. Trustee Cleve. Music Sch. Settlement, 1967—, Salzedo Sch. Harp, Cleve., 1962—, Bishop Brown Fund, Cleve., 1981—, Flats Oxbow Assn., Lake Erie Sci. & Nature Ctr., 1996—, also pres., 1970-72; co-trustee Margaret & Edwin Griffiths Trusts, Cleve., 1968—. Served with USNR, 1945-46. Mem. ABA, Ohio State Bar Assn., Cleve. Bar Assn., Hermit Club (Cleve.), Rowfant Club (Cleve.). Republican. Episcopalian.

STICKNEY, ROBERT ROY, fisheries educator; b. Mpls., July 2, 1941; s. Roy E. and Helen Doris (Nelson) S.; m. LuVerne C. Whiteley, Dec. 29, 1961; children: Robert Roy, Marolan Margaret. BS, U. Nebr., 1967; MA, U. Mo., 1968; PhD, Fla. State U., 1971. Cert. fisheries scientist. Research assoc. Skidaway Inst. Oceanography, Savannah, Ga., 1971-73, asst. prof., 1973-75, Texas A&M U., College Station, 1975-78, assoc. prof., 1978-83, prof., 1983-84; prof. zoology, dir. Fisheries Research Lab., So. Ill. U., Carbondale, 1984-85; dir. Sch. of Fisheries U. Wash., Seattle, 1985-91, prof., 1985-96; dir. Sea Grant Coll. program Tex. A&M U., College Station, 1996—. Chmn. S-168 com. So. Regional Coop. Research Project, 1981-84. Author: Principles of Warmwater Aquaculture, 1979, Estuarine Ecology of the Southeastern United States and Gulf of Mexico, 1984; editor: Culture of Non-Salmonid Freshwater Fishes, 1986, 1992, Flagship: A History of Fisheries at the University of Washington, 1989; co-editor: Fisheries: Harvesting Life from Water, 1989, 1995, Culture of Salmonid Fishes, 1992, Principles of Aquaculture, 1994, Fish Culture in the United States: A Historical Survey, 1996, Responsible Marine Aquaculture, 2002; editor: revs. in Fisheries Sci., Ency. of World Aquaculture; contbr. articles. Served with USAF, 1959-63. E-mail: rrstickney@aol.com., stickney@tamu.edu.

STIDHAM, SHALER, JR. operations research educator; b. Washington, Dec. 4, 1941; s. Shaler and Gladys (Ruddick) S.; m. Carolyn Jean Noble, Apr. 6, 1968; children: Christiane Wilson, Dana Claire, Ann-Elise. BA, Harvard U., l963; MS, Case Inst. Tech., 1964; PhD, Stanford U., l968. Asst. prof. dept. ops. rsch. Cornell U., Ithaca, N.Y., 1968-75; assoc. prof., prof. dept. indsl. engring. N.C. State U., Raleigh, 1975-86; prof. dept. ops. rsch. U. N.C., Chapel Hill, 1986—2002, chmn. dept. ops. rsch., 1990-95. Lectr. Aarhus (Denmark) U., 1971-72; guest prof. Tech. U., Denmark, Lyngby, 1976-77; vis. fellow Statis. Lab., Cambridge (Eng.) U., 1982-83; cons. Bell Telephone Labs., 1981; vis. scholar Stanford (Calif.) U., 1975, 79, Australian Nat. U., 2001; invited prof. Inst. Nat. Rsch. Informatique et en Automatique, Sophia Antipolis, France, 1991-92; keynote spkr. to profl. confs., The Netherlands, Germany, Poland, France and Japan, 1977—. Co-author (with M. El-Taha): Sample-Path Analysis of Queueing Systems, 1999 (Best Publ. award Applied Probability Soc. 1999). Bd. dirs. Friends of Coll., Raleigh, 1979-82, chmn. program com., 1981-82; bd. dirs. N.C. Symphony Found., Raleigh, 1990—, N.C. Mus. of Art Found, Raleigh, 1996—; bd. deacons Pullen Meml. Ch., 1995-98; mem. faculty coun. U. N.C., Chapel Hill, 1995-98. Overseas fellow Churchill Coll., Cambridge, l982—. Mem. Inst. for Ops. Rsch and Mgmt. Scis. (chmn. applied probability tech. sect. 1990-91, program co-chmn. internat. meeting Osaka, Japan 1989), Sigma Xi (Young Scientist Rsch. award 1978). Home: 10428 Whitestone Rd Raleigh NC 27615-1236 Office: U NC Dept Ops Rsch Cb 3180 Smith Bldg Chapel Hill NC 27599-0001

STIEBER, JACK, economist, educator, labor arbitrator; b. Mar. 27, 1919; BSS, CCNY, 1940; MA, U. Minn., 1948; PhD, Harvard U., 1956. Labor specialist Office of Housing Expeditor, Washington, 1946-47; rsch. asst., instr. in econs. Indsl. Rels. Ctr., U. Minn., 1947-48; rsch. assoc. United Steelworkers Am., CIO, Pitts., 1948-50; spl. asst. to dir. manpower Nat. Security Resources Bd., Washington, 1950-51; economist, exec. asst. labor mems. Wage Stblzn. Bd., 1951-52; rsch. assoc. Grad. Sch. Bus. Adminstrn., Harvard U., 1954-56; assoc. prof. dept. econs., assoc. dir. rsch. and planning Labor and Indsl. Rels. Ctr. Mich. State U., East Lansing, 1956-59, dir., prof. Sch. Labor and Indsl. Rels., 1959-85, prof. dept. econs. Sch. Labor and Indsl. Rels., 1985-89, prof. emeritus, 1989—. USIA lectr. in Japan, India, Iran, Israel, 1971, Japan, 1983; vis. prof. Indsl. Rels. Inst., U. Leuven (Belgium), 1971. Contbr. chpts. to books, articles to profl. jours. Mem. AAUP (pres. chpt. 1969-70), Am. Econ. Assn., Indsl. Rels. Rsch. Assn. (exec. bd. 1966-69, pres. 1983), Am. Arbitration Assn., Nat. Acad. Arbitrators (chmn. program com. 1969, chmn. com. on overseas corrs. 1976-81, bd. govs. 1987-90). Home: 231 Lexington Ave East Lansing MI 48823-4651

STIEBER, TAMAR, journalist; b. Bklyn., Sept. 15, 1955; d. Alfred and Florence (Spector) S. Student, Rockland C.C., 1972-75, West London (Eng.) Coll., 1973-74; BA in Film cum laude, U. Calif., Berkeley, 1985, postgrad. in comparative lit., 1985-86; grad. police res. acad. cum laude, Napa Valley Coll., 1988. Office mgr., confidential sec. AP, San Francisco, 1981-83; stringer Daily Californian, Berkeley, 1983-84; film rsch. tchg. asst. U. Calif., 1984—86; libr. and rsch. asst. Pacific Film Archive, 1984-86; intern San Francisco Examiner, 1984; reporter Sonoma (Calif.) Index-Tribune, 1987-88, Vallejo (Calif.) Times-Herald, 1988-89, Albuquerque Journal, 1989-94, freelancer, 1994—. Recipient Pulitzer prize for specialized reporting, 1990, first place pub. svc. divsn. N.Mex. Press Assn., 1990, pub. svc. award Albuquerque Press Club, 1990; first place newswriting N.Mex. Press Assn., 1991; honorable mention AP Managing Editors, 1994. Mem. AAUW, Phi Beta Kappa. Home: PO Box 9835 Santa Fe NM 87504-9835

STIEF, LOUIS JOHN, chemist; b. Pottsville, Pa., July 26, 1933; s. Louis Norman and Dorothy Elizabeth (Bassler) S.; m. Kathleen J. Talbot, Nov. 30, 1963 (div. 1980); children— Andrew, Lorraine. BA, La Salle Coll., 1955; PhD, Catholic U. Am., 1960. Nat. Acad. Scis.-NRC postdoctoral rsch. assoc. Nat. Bur. Standards, Washington, 1960-61; NATO postdoctoral fellow, ind. researcher chemistry dept. Sheffield (Eng.) U., 1961-63; sr. scientist, sr. chemist Melpar, Inc., Falls Church, Va., 1963-68; NAS-NRC sr. postdoctoral rsch. assoc. NASA/Goddard Space Flight Ctr., Greenbelt, Md., 1968-69, astrophysicist, 1969-76, head br. astrochemistry, 1976-90, sr. scientist, 1990—. Adj. prof. chemistry Cath. U. Am. Research: numerous publs., especially in Jour. Chem. Physics and Jour. Phys. Chemistry. Recipient

Alumni Achievement award Cath. U. Am., 1985; NASA fellow Queen Mary Coll., U. London, 1981-82 Fellow Washington Acad. Sci.; mem. Am. Chem. Soc. (Hillebrano prize Chem. Soc. Wash. 2002), Royal Soc. Chemistry, Am. Geophys. Union, Am. Astron. Soc. (div. planetary sci.), Sigma Xi. Office: NASA Goddard Space Flight Ctr Code 690 Ctr Greenbelt MD 20771-0001

STIEFEL, ETHAN, dancer; b. Tyroen, Pa. s. Alan and Mima Stiefel. Studies under Mikhail Baryshinikov, Sch. Classical Ballet, 1987; student, Fordham U., 1995—. From mem. to prin. dancer N.Y. City Ballet, 1989-95, prin. dancer, 1995-96, Am. Ballet Theatre, N.Y.C., 1997—. With Zurich Ballet, 1992-93; guest artist N.Y.C. Ballet, 1998-99, Atlanta Ballet, 1999, Royal Ballet, 1999, 2000, 2001, 2002. Dancer prin. roles include Le Corsaire, Romeo & Juliet, Giselle, Les Patineurs, Onegin, Swan Lake, Theme and Variations, Don Quixote, A Midsummer Night's Dream, La Bayadere, The Dream, The Four Temperaments, Apollo, Stars and Stripes, Harlequinade, Tarantella, Tchaikovsky Pas de Deux, Chaconne, Prodigal Son, La Fille Mal Gardee, The Nutcracker, Robbins' ballets Dances at a Gathering, West Side Story Suite, The Goldberg Variations, The Cage, Quiet City, Martins' ballets Fearful Symmetries, Ash, Thaikovsky Pas de Quatre, The Sleeping Beauty, others; appeard in PBS TV prodn. Le Corsaire, 1999, Born to be Wild, 2002; guest artist Teatro Colon, 1999, 2000, Kirov Ballet, 2001, also others; starring role: (film) Center Stage, 2000. Recipient Silver medal Prix de Lausanne, 1989, Statue award Princess Grace Found., 1999; emerging dance artist grantee Princess Grace Found. U.S.A., 1991-92 Office: care Peter S Diggins Assoc 133 W 71st St Ste 8-B New York NY 10023 E-mail: Festspiel@AOL.com.

STIEFEL, LEANNA, economics educator, education researcher; b. Maxton, N.C., Mar. 22, 1945; d. Donald Jack and Jane Leanna Stiefel; m. Melvyn Stuart Schoenfeld; children: Sara Schoenfeld, Daniel Schoenfeld. AB in French, U. Mich., 1967; MA in Econs., U. Wis., 1970, PhD in Econs., 1972; advanced profl. cert. in fin., NYU, 1984. Asst. prof. econs. Mich. State U., East Lansing, 1972-75; vis. prof. Sarah Lawrence Coll., Bronxville, N.Y., 1975; prof. econs. Wagner Sch., NYU, N.Y.C., 1976—. Cons. ACLU, N.Y.C., 1996, Campaign for Fiscal Equity, N.Y.C., 1997-2000; mem. tech. panning panel U.S. Dept. Edn., Washingtin. 1997—. Author: The Measurement of Equity in School Finance, 1984, Statistical Analysis for Public and Non-Profit Managers, 1990; contbr. articles to profl. jours. Recipient fellowship NSF, 1967-71, Joseph Wooley prize ASPA, 2000. Mem.: Nat. Tax Assn., Am. Econ. Assn., Am. Edn. Rsch. Assn., Assn. Policy Analysis and Mgmt. (rep. 1997—), Am. Edn. Fin. Assn. (bd. dirs. 1997—2000, pres. 2002), Phi Beta Kappa. Avocations: reading, tennis, bridge. Office: NYU Wagner Grad Sch 4 Washington Sq N 5-43 New York NY 10003 E-mail: leanna.stiefel@nyu.edu.

STIEFEL, LINDA SHIELDS, lawyer; b. Syracuse, N.Y., Nov. 14, 1948; d. Harold F. and Ellen (Brown) Shields; m. John L. Stiefel, Sept. 20, 1969; 1 child, John L. BS, Tusculum Coll., 1988; JD, Akron Sch. Law, 1991. Bar: Ohio 1992, D.C. 1993, N.Y. 1998, U.S. Dist. Ct. (no. dist.) Ohio 1993, U.S. Supreme Ct. 1997. Judicial law clk. Stark County Common Pleas, Canton, Ohio, 1991-94; pvt. practice Louisville, 1992-97, Cape Vincent, N.Y., 1998—. Trustee, mem. exec. com. Am. Handweaving Mus., 1997-2001. Mem. ABA, NOW, N.Y. State Bar Assn., Jefferson County Bar Assn. Methodist. Home and Office: 596 West Broadway Cape Vincent NY 13618

STIEFF, JOHN JOSEPH, legislative lawyer, educator; b. Indpls., Feb. 28, 1952; s. James Frederick and Mary Therese (Bisch) S.; m. Dusty Lee-Ann Warner, Apr. 21, 1989; stepchildren: Robert Franklin Russell, E.I. Annie Russell. BA with Distinction, Ind. U., 1973, JD, 1977. Bar: Ind. 1977. Sr. atty. Office of Bill Drafting & Rsch., Legislative Svcs. Agy., Indpls., 1977-86; dep. dir. and asst. revisor of statutes Office of Code Revision, Legislative Svcs. Agy., 1986-92, dir. and revisor of statutes, 1992—. Adj. prof. law Ind. Univ., Bloomington, 1985-86; instr. continuing legal edn. Ind. Gen. Assembly, Indpls., 1987-96; faculty mem. Nat. Conf. State Legislatures, Denver, Colo., 1988-89; supervising atty. program on law and state govt. Ind. U. Sch. Law, Indpls., 2001—; assoc commr. Nat. Conf. Commrs. on Uniform State Laws, Chgo., 1993—. Editor in chief: (books) The Acts of Indiana, 1986—, The Indiana Code, 1993—; ast. editor, The Indiana Code, 1986-92. Poetry instr. Gage Inst. for Gifted Children, Indpls., 1982-86. Named Hoosier Scholar, Indiana Commn. for Higher Edn., 1970-73. Mem. Writer's Ctr. of Indpls. (founding mem.), Ind. U. Varsity Club. Avocations: travel, photgraphy, writing poetry, Am. blues music. Home: 7707 Windy Hill Way Indianapolis IN 46239-8749 Office: Legislative Svcs Agy Office Code Revision 1 N Capitol Ave Ste 420 Indianapolis IN 46204-2097

STIEFVATER, PAMELA JEAN, chiropractor; b. Utica, N.Y., Oct. 16, 1956; d. Kenneth Carl and Henriette Ramona (Billick) S. BS cum laude, SUNY, Oswego, 1977; D of Chiropractic cum laude, Palmer Coll., 1984. Lic. chiropractor, N.Y., Mass.; diplomate Nat. Bd. Chiropractic Examiners. Sci. tchr. Altmar, Parish, Williamstown High Sch., Parish, N.Y., 1978-80; chiropractor, owner Bayside Chiropractic, South Dennis, Mass., 1986—. Mem. Am. Chiropractic Soc., Mass. Chiropractic Soc., Cape Cod Chiropractic Soc. Office: Bayside Chiropractic 430 Old Bass River Rd South Dennis MA 02660-2724

STIEGHORST, RANDALL ARTHUR, cultural organization administrator, consultant; b. LaCrosse, Wisc., June 2, 1971; s. Greg A Stieghorst, Dorothy J Willey, Lorin T Willey (Stepfather), Patricia Stieghorst (Stepmother). BA, Univ. of Wis., 1993; MBA, U. Chgo., 2002. Educator US Peace Corps., Ill., Latvia, 1996—99; ptnr. Lang. & Culture Worldwide, LLC, Chgo., 1999—. Office: Language & Culture Worldwide, LLC 1300 East 47th Street, #170 Chicago IL 60653 Personal E-mail: rstiegho@gsb.uchicago.edu. Business E-Mail: rstieghorst@languageandculture.com.

STIEGLITZ, PERRY JESSE, diplomat, journalist; b. Yonkers, N.Y., Apr. 18, 1920; s. Abraham Charles and Goldie (Klein) S.; m. Princess Moune Souvanna Phouma, Apr. 29, 1935; 1 child, Dara S.P. AB, NYU, 1941; postgrad., Harvard U., 1941-42, U. Lausanne, Switzerland, 1947-50. Lecturer, English Hunter Coll., N.Y.C, 1956-59; English teacher Hunter H.S., N.Y.C., 1956-59; Asst. cultural attache Am. Embassy, Paris, 1963-67, cultural attache Vientiane, Laos, 1967-68; Am. consul Am. Consulate, Marseille, France, 1968-70; cultural attache Am. Embassy, Bangkok, Thailand, 1973-76, Brussels, 1976-80; Washington Bureau chief The Bangkok Post, Thailand, 1984-85; Am. rep. Thomson Found. of Eng., London, 1986-88; dir. Gibraltar Info. Bur., Washington, 1988—. Author: In A Little Kingdom, 1990. Lt. USN, 1942-46. Fulbright grantee, Laos, 1959-60; recipient meritorious award USIA, 1967. Mem. Cercle Royal Gaulois de Bruxelles, Dacor House, Univ. Club of Washington. Office: Gibraltar Info Bureau 1156 15th St NW Washington DC 20005-1704

STIEGMAN, VICTOR KARL DANIEL, medical research volunteer, computer consultant; b. Chgo., July 25, 1977; s. Darryl Dean Carl and Arlene Mildred Stiegman. Student, Trinity Christian Coll., Palos Heights, Ill., 1995—96; degree in counseling psychology, Christian Heritage Coll., El Cajon, Calif., 1999. Care provider Redwood Sr. Homes and Svcs., Escondido, Calif., 1996—98; home health care svc. provider San Diego, 1998—2001; rsch. vol. Rev. J. Marvin Davis Meml., Valley Center, 2001—. Webmaster Stiegman.com, San Diego, 2000—. Computer Consultant / Technical Advisor: Remembering the Journey - The Robert Evan and Laura Jane Davis Family, 2000. Mem.: APA. Avocations: photography, hiking, writing, literature, travel. Business E-Mail: Victor@Stiegman.com.

STIEHM, E. RICHARD, pediatrician, educator; b. Milw., Jan. 22, 1933; s. Reuben Harold and Marie Dueno S.; m. Judith Hicks, July 12, 1958; children: Jamie Elizabeth, Carrie Eleanor, Meredith Ellen. BS, U. Wis., 1954, MD, 1957. Diplomate: Am. Bd. Pediatrics, Am. Bd. Allergy and Clin. Immunology (bd. dirs. 1977-83), Am. Bd. Diagnostic Lab. Immunology. Intern Phila. Gen. Hosp., 1957-58; fellow in physiol. chemistry U. Wis., 1959-61; med. officer USNR, Johnsville, Pa., 1961-63; resident in pediat. Babies Hosp., N.Y.C., 1963-65; rsch. fellow in pediat. immunology U. Calif., San Francisco, 1965-68; asst. prof. pediat. U. Wis., 1968-69, assoc. prof., 1969-72, UCLA, 1972-78, prof., 1978-87, chief div. immunology, allergy and rheumatology, 1972—, assoc. dir. Ctr. for Interdisciplinary Rsch. in Immunologic Diseases, 1981-82, co-dir. Cystic Fibrosis Ctr., 1988—, vice chair acad. affairs dept. pediatrics, 1989—; vis. scientist metabolism br. Nat. Cancer Inst., Bethesda, Md., 1982-88. Vis. prof. Yale U., Mayo Clinic, U. Cin., Great Ormond St. Hosp., U.K.; bd. sci. dirs. Immune Deficiency Found., 1981—, Eczema Found., 1988—, Pediat. AIDS Found., 1989-99; task force on pediat. allergy NIH, 1977; mem. gen. clin. rsch. ctr. study sect. NIH, 1978-82, 84-88; adv. com. Hartford Fellowship, 1984-88; co-dir. L.A. Pediat. AIDS Consortium, 1988—; commr. HHS adv. commn. on childhood vaccines, 1988-90. Editor: Immunologic Disorders in Infants and Children, 1972, 80, 89, 96; Am. editor: Pediatric Research, 1984-89; assoc. editor: Pediatrics Update, 1978-85; mem. editorial bd. Pediatrics, 1972-78, Pediatrics in Rev., 1978-81, Jour. Allergy and Clin. Immunology, 1976-80, Jour. Clin. Immunology, 1985-89, Jour. Asthma Pediatric Allergy and Immunology, 1987-91, Am. Jour. Diseases of Children, 1987-97, Contemporary Pediatrics, 1991-96, Am. Jour. Clin. Nutrition, 1992-97; contbr. articles to profl. jours. Mem. HHS Commn. on Childhood Vaccines, 1988-90; mem. clin. rsch. adv. com. Nat. Found. March of Dimes, 1992—. Recipient Career Devel. award Nat. Inst. Allergy and Infectious Diseases, 1967-69, E. Mead Johnson award for Pediat. Rsch., 1974, Alumni Citation award U. Wis. Med. Sch., 1988, Lifetime Achievement award Immune Deficiency Found., 1995, Med. Sci. award UCLA Med. Alumni, 1999, Disting. Alumni award Babies and Children's Hosp. Alumni Assn., N.Y., 1999; Markle scholar, 1967-72. Mem. AAAS, Am. Assn. Immunologists, Western Soc. Pediatric Research (coun. 1977-80, pres. 1983, Ross Rsch. award 1971), Soc. Pediatric Research, Am. Pediatric Soc., Am. Acad. Allergy and Clin. Immunology, Am. Acad. Pediatrics (infectious diseases com. 1971-77), Am. Soc. Clin. Investigation, Clin. Immunology Soc., Alpha Delta Phi, Phi Beta Kappa, Alpha Omega Alpha. Office: UCLA Dept Peds Divsn Immunology 10833 Le Conte Ave Los Angeles CA 90095-3075 E-mail: estiehm@mednet.ucla.edu.

STIEHM, JUDITH HICKS, university official, political science educator; b. Madison, Wis., Oct. 9, 1935; d. Stratton Elson and Eleanor Spencer (Kilbourn) Hicks; m. E. Richard Stiehm, July 12, 1958; children: Jamie Elizabeth, Carrie Eleanor, Meredith Ellen. Student, Oberlin Coll., 1953; BA in E. Asian Studies, U. Wis., 1957; MA in Am. History, Temple U., 1961; PhD in Polit. Theory, Columbia U., 1969. Dir. resident hons. program U. So. Calif., Los Angeles, 1970-73, asst. prof., 1970-74, assoc. prof., 1974-83, dir. program for study of women and men in soc., 1975-81, prof. polit. sci., 1983, vice provost, 1984-87; provost Fla. Internat. U., Miami, 1987-91, prof. polit. sci., 1987—. Vis. prof. U. Wis., 1994, U.S. Army Peacekeeping Inst., U.S. Army War Coll., 1995-96, U.S. Army Strategic Studies Inst., U.S. Army War Coll., 1996, U. So. Calif., 2002-; lectr. U. Wis., Madison, 1966-69, UCLA, 1969-70; vis. lectr. San Francisco State U., 1965-66; affiliate NAS Project, 1981-82; cons. UN Div. for the Advancement of Women, Calif. Elected Women, Dept. HEW, AAUW, LWV L.A., UN Lessons Learned Unit, Dept. Peacekeeping Ops. Author: Nonviolent Power: Active and Passive Resistance in America, 1972, Bring Me Men and Women..., 1981, Arms and the Enlisted Woman, 1989, The U.S. Army War College: Military Education in a Democracy, 2002; editor: The Frontiers of Knowledge, 1976, Women and Men's Wars, 1983, Women's Views of the Political World of Men, 1984, It's Our Military, Too!, 1996, The U.S. Army War College: Military Education in a Democracy, 2002; mem. editorial bd. Western Polit. Quar., 1972-75, Signs, 1981-84, Women and Politics, 1986-88, 2000-. Mem. Calif. Postsecondary Edn. Commn., 1978, Calif. Adv. Coun. on Vocat. Edn., 1978-82, Def. Adv. Com. on Women in Svcs., 1979-82; bd. dirs. So. Calif. and Miami chpts. ACLU. Named Woman of Yr., Santa Monica YWCA, 1981; recipient Outstanding Civilian Svc. medal U.S. Army, 1996. Mem. Am. Polit. Sci. Assn. (exec. coun. 1989, sec. 2000), Western Polit. Sci. Assn. (pres. 1986), Women's Caucus Polit. Sci. (pres. 1996-97), Nat. Council for Research on Women (exec. council 1982), Council on Fgn. Relations, Phi Beta Kappa, Phi Kappa Phi (Victoria Schuck Book award 1990). Avocations: tennis, skiing, stained glass. Home: 434 24th St Santa Monica CA 90402-3102 Office: Fla Internat U Dept Polit Sci Tamiami Trl Miami FL 33199-0001 E-mail: stiehmj@fiu.edu.

STIELOW-LEACH, FAY ANN, interior designer; b. Oostburg, Wis., Apr. 20, 1939; d. Arnold Lloyd and May Annette (Steenweg) Wykhuis; m. Curtis G. Stielow, June 16, 1961 (div. 1978); m. Harrison Langford Leach, July 11, 1987. Student, Carroll Coll., 1957-58; BS, U. Wis., 1961; postgrad., U. Calif., Long Beach, 1962-63. Tchr. Long Beach Jordan High Sch., 1961-64, Shoales Jr. High Sch., Milw., 1964-66, McPherson Jr. High Sch., Orange, Calif., 1966-69; realtor Myers and Hill, Vienna, 1971-74; sales rep. Ryland Homes, Manassas, 1974-76, Fairfield Homes, Woodbridge, 1976-79; v.p. Fairfield Design Studio, 1980-86, pres., 1986—. Mem. No. Va. Builders Assn., Prince William County C. of C. (com. chairperson 1984-87). Presbyterian. Avocations: sailing, reading.

STIENSTRA, STEPHANI ANN, editor; b. Baytown, Tex., Aug. 6, 1955; d. Herbert Howard and Janice Faye (Stowe) Cruickshank; m. George Keyston III, Oct. 8, 1983 (div. Mar. 1997); children: Jeremy George, Kristopher Samuel; m. Thomas Frank Stienstra, Dec. 4, 1998. AA with honors, Merced (Calif.) Coll., 1975; BA in Journalism with distinction, San Jose State U., 1976. Reporter Fresno (Calif.) Bee, 1974-75; reporter, photographer Merced (Calif.) Sun-Star, 1974-77; pub. info. officer Fresno City Coll., 1977-80; dir. comms. Aerojet Tactical Sys. Co., Sacramento, 1980-83; co-owner, v.p. Keyco Landscape Contractor Inc., Loomis, 1984-96; co-owner Tom Stienstra.com, 1999—. Author, editor (with Tom Stienstra): Northern California Cabins and Cottages, author, editor (with Tom Stienstra): Washington Camping. Co-coord. Aeroject United Way Campaign, 1981; Aerojet Tactical Sys. Co. coord. West Coast Nat. Derby Rallies, 1981-83; co-founder, pres. Calif. Lion Awareness. Mem. Internat. Assn. Bus. Communicators (dir. Sacramento chpt. 1983), Citrus Heights C. of C. (v.p. 1983). Republican. Office: Stephani Stienstra.com PO Box 151 Mount Shasta CA 96067-0151 E-mail: stienstra@jps.net.

STIER, MARY, publishing executive; m. Jeff Stier; 2 children. Grad. in comm., broadcasting, U. Iowa. Sr. group pres. Gannett Midwest Newspaper Group, 1982—; pres., pub., regional pres., sr. group pres. Reno Gazette-Jour., 1985; adv. mgr. Iowa City Press-Citizen, adv. dir., pres., pub., 1987; v.p. Ctrl. Region Newspaper Divsn. , 1990, pres. Midwest group, 1993; pres., pub., regional v.p., group pres. Rockford Register Star, 1991—2000; pres., pub. The Des Moines Register, 2000—; pres., pub., regional v.p. Binghamton (N.Y.) Press & Sun-Bulletin. Mem.: The Greater Des Moines Partnership, Am. Press Inst., Iowa Newspaper Assn., Newspaper Assn. Am., Phi Beta Kappa. Office: Des Moines Register PO Box 957 Des Moines IA 50304-0957 Address: 715 Locust St Des Moines IA 50309*

STIER, ROGER EDWIN, chemist, researcher; b. Hackensack, N.J., Dec. 23, 1946; s. Edwin Richard and Irmtraut Margaret Stier; m. Nancy Louise Stier, Oct. 5, 1969; children: David Roger, Brian Roger, Kathlean Ann. BS magna cum laude, Fairleigh Dickinson U., 1968. Technician Burroughs Wellcome Co., Tuckahoe, N.Y., 1968-70; analytical chemist Schering, Union, N.J., 1970-73; rsch. assoc. Beecham Products Rsch., Parsippany, 1973-97; sr. chemist Noville, South Hackensack, 1997—. Cons. Proctor & Gamble, Cin., 1999—, Smith Klein Beecham, Parsippany, 1997—, Diamond Products, Tampa, Fla., 1997—. Inventor in field. Asst. scout master Boy Scouts Am., Clifton, N.J., 1957-64; minister New Apostolic Ch., Clifton, 1967—. Named Outstanding Citizen, B'nai B'rith, 1968. Mem. AAAS, Am. Chem. Soc., Soc. Cosmetic Chemists, Internat. Assn. Dental Rsch., Sigma Xi, Phi Zeta Kappa, Phi Omega Epsilon. Republican. Avocations: playing and teaching organ, reading, writing poems. Home: 265 Washington Ave Clifton NJ 07011 Office: Noville 3 Empire Blvd South Hackensack NJ 07606 E-mail: rstier@noville.com.

STIER, WILLIAM FREDERICK, JR. academic administrator; b. Feb. 22, 1943; m. Veronica Ann Martin, 1965; children: Mark, Missy, Michael, Patrick, Willy III. BA, St. Ambrose Coll., 1965; MA, Temple U., 1966; EdD, U. S.D., 1972; postdoct., Marquette U., 1976-77, U. Wis., summer 1977. Grad. asst. Coll. Edn. Temple U., Phila., 1965-66; various faculty positions dept. health, phys. edn., recreation, 1968-74; pres., CEO Fla. Breeders, Inc., Largo and St. Petersburg, 1974-76; treas. Charolais of Fla., Inc., St. Petersburg and Ft. Myers, 1975-76; adminstrv. campus Cardinal Stritch Coll., Milw., 1976-80; chmn. dept. profl. health and phys. edn., athletic dir. Ohio No. U., Ada, 1980-83; chmn., prof. phys. edn. and sports dept. SUNY, Brockport, 1983-86, dir. intercollegiate athletics, 1983-90, grad. coord. sport mgmt., 1990—, pres. faculty senate, 1992-93, grad. coord., 1994—. Disting. Svc. prof. Pres., CEO Ednl. and Sport Mgmt. cons., N.Y. and Ohio, 1980—; chmn. bd. dirs. Kreative Kids Learning Ctrs., Inc., 1978—; bd. dirs. Cretive Children Child Care Ctrs.; cons. MacMIllan Pub. Co., Inc., 1981-83, Sport Fedn., Hong Kong, Singapore and Malaysia, 1987, 88, Nat. Coll. Sport Coaches, Mexico City, 1990; speaker numerous confs. and convs. Author of 16 books and contbr. to several compendiums in field; contbr. more than 250 articles to profl. jours.; mem. editl. bd. and reviewer profl. jours.; editor The Phys. Educator, 1998—, Internat. Jour. Sport Mgmt., 1999—. Active ARC, 1975-90, Boy Scouts Am., 1955-59; mem. greater Milw. REgional day Care adv. Com., 1979-81; adv. bd. Nat. Ctr. Exploration Human Petential, Del Mar, Calif., 1981-84; nat. basketball coach, St. Kitts-Nevis, 1984; cons. on basketball, Mex., 1982, 90. Brockport scholar, 1984-86, 92, 93, 94, 98, 99. Mem. AAHPERD (reviewer jour. 1984—), N.Y. Assn. Health, Phys. Edn., Recreation and Dance (higher edn. sect. 1983—, pres. 1985-86, 87-88), Nat. Assn. sport and Phys. Edn., Nat. Assn. Girls and Women's Sports, Nat. Assn. Phys. Edn. in Higher Edn., Nat. Assn. Phys. Edn. in Higher Edn., Nat. Assn. Athletic Mktg. and Devel. Dirs., Nat. Assn. Collegiate Dirs. Athletics, Internat. Soc. Comparative Phys. Edn. and Sports, N.Am. Sport Mgmt., Eta Sigma Gama, Phi Epsilon Kappa, Phi Kappa Phi, Phi Epsilon Omega. Office: SUNY-Brockport Dept Phys Edn and Sport Brockport NY 14420 E-mail: bstier@brockport.edu.

STIFEL, FREDERICK BENTON, pastor, biochemist, nutritionist; b. St. Louis, Jan. 30, 1940; s. Carl Gottfried and Alma J. (Clark) S.; m. Gail Joane Stewart, Aug. 10, 1963; children: Tim, Faith, Seth, Elizabeth. BS, Iowa State U., 1962, PhD, 1967; MDiv., Melodyland Sch. Theol., Anaheim, Calif., 1979. Ordained to ministry Evang. Presbyn. Ch., 1981. Lab. supr., research chemist U.S. Army Med. Research and Nutrition Lab., Denver, 1968-74, Letterman Army Inst. Research, San Francisco, 1974-76; intern pastor Melodyland Christian Ctr., Anaheim, 1979-80; assoc. pastor Faith Presbyn. Ch., Aurora, Colo., 1980—, moderator bd. deacons, 1997—; pastor Outreach and Missions, 1999—. Chmn. care of candidates com. Presbytery of West, Denver, 1985-88, 91-94; mem. Denver Seminary Commn., 1995-2002, mem. world outreach com., 1998-99; bd. dirs., v.p. Love Inc. of Metro Denver, 1987-90; regional coord. Nat. Assn. Single Adult Leaders, 1987-90, coord. Denver area, 1990-95; Colo. Pregnancy Ctrs., Inc., 1992-94, Rocky Mountain Prayer Network, 1994-96, Christian Family Svcs., 1990—; bd. dirs. St. James Bible Coll., 1995—, Slavic Christian Ministries, 2000-2002, Profile Publs.; mem. faculty St. James Bible Coll., Kiev, Ukraine; bd. dirs. Internat. Project Adv. Bd., 1997—. Contbr. clin. med. and nutritional articles to profl. jours. Del. Iowa and Colo. State Rep. Conv., Denver, 1984, 2002; mem. parent adv. coun. IMPACT drug intervention team Rangeview High Sch., Aurora, 1985-89, accountability com., 1989-96; mem. Friends of the Arts, 1992-96; Young Life leader Hinkley High Sch., Aurora, 1968-74; vice chmn. Young Life Com., Marin County, Calif., 1974-76. Capt. U.S. Army Med. Svc. Corps, 1967-70. Ralston Purina Rsch. fellow, 1962-63; Borden Agrl. scholar, 1962; recipient Sci. Achievement award U.S. Army Sci. Conf., West Point, N.Y., 1968, 70, Parents of the Yr. award Rangeview High Sch., 1992-93. Mem. Am. Soc. Nutritional Scis., Am. Soc. Clin. Nutrition, Am. Sci. Affiliation, Evang. Theol. Soc., Phi Eta Sigma, Phi Kappa Phi, Alpha Zeta, Gamma Sigma Delta, Kappa Sigma, Sigma Xi. Avocations: reading, hiking, swimming, writing poetry, gardening. Home: 3492 S Blackhawk Way Aurora CO 80014-3909 Office: Faith Presbyn Ch 11373 E Alameda Ave Aurora CO 80012-1023

STIFF, PATRICK JOSEPH, internist, hematologist, oncologist, educator; b. Toledo, Nov. 27, 1950; BS, U. Toledo, 1972; MD, Loyola U., 1975. Intern Cleve. Clinic, 1975-76, resident in medicine, 1976-78; fellow in hematology and oncology Meml. Sloan-Kettering Med. Ctr., N.Y.C., 1978-81; asst. prof. medicine Sch. Medicine So. Ill. U., 1981-86; asst. prof. medicine Loyola U. Med. Ctr., Maywood, Ill., 1986-92; assoc. prof. medicine Loyola U. Med. Ctr.-Stritch Sch. Medicine, 1992-96; prof. medicine and pathology Loyola U. Med. Ctr., 1996—. Chair transplant subcom. Ill. State Med. Adv. Com., 1999—. Mem. Internat. Soc. Exptl. Hematology, Internat. Soc. Hematotherapy and Graft Engrs., S.W. Oncology Group, Am. Soc. Clin. Oncology, Am. Soc. Hematology. Office: Loyola Univ Med Ctr 2160 S 1st Ave Maywood IL 60153-3304 E-mail: pstiff@lumc.edu.

STIFF, ROBERT HENRY, dentist, educator; b. Pitts., Apr. 23, 1923; s. Oliver R. and Ruth A. (Goucher) S.; m. Margaret J. Raley, Oct. 18, 1945; children— Barry, Dwight, Heather. BS, U. Pitts., 1940, D.D.S., 1945, M.Ed., 1953. Engaged in pvt. practice dentistry, Pitts., 1945-59; instr. U. Pitts., 1945-50, asst. prof., 1950-53, assoc. prof., 1954-65, prof., head dept. oral medicine and radiology, 1963-76, dir. clinics, 1976—; asst. dean U. Pitts. (Sch. Dental Medicine), 1979-81, assoc. dean, 1981-84. Cons. U. Garyounis, Benghazi, Libya, 1978—, Pa. Dept. Health, 1964, 66, Bd. Edn., City of Pitts. (dental asst. program 1983-86). Served to capt. Dental Corps AUS, 1946-48. Fellow Am. Coll. Dentists; mem. Am. Acad. Oral Pathology, ADA (pres. 1979-80), Orgn. Tchrs. Oral Diagnosis, Pa. Dental Assn., Sigma Xi, Omicron Kappa Upsilon. Home: 4601 Doverdell Dr Pittsburgh PA 15236-1824

STIFF, ROBERT MARTIN, newspaper editor; b. Detroit, Aug. 25, 1931; s. Martin L. and Gladys (Mathews) S.; m. Cindy Rose, Aug. 30, 1980; children: David Alan, Amy Anne, Kirsten Marie. BA in Radio and Journalism, Ohio State U., 1953. Reporter, bur. chief, city editor Painesville (Ohio) Telegraph, 1953-61; deskman, asst. city editor, sports editor, city editor, day editor, state editor, asst. mng. editor St. Petersburg (Fla.) Times, 1961-67; editor St. Petersburg Evening Ind., 1967-84; dir. St. Petersburg Times Pub. Co., 1969-84; exec. editor, v.p. Tallahassee Democrat, 1985-91; pres. Bob Stiff & Assocs., Tallahassee, 1991-95; exec. editor JMT Assocs., 1991—92, 1994—95; mng. editor About Florida, 1991-94; editor Lexington (N.C.) Dispatch, 1995—. Mem. Pulitzer Prize Jury, 1982-83; dir. devel. and pub. rels. Fla. Taxwatch Inc., 1992-94; bd. dirs. N.C. AP News Coun., 1995-2001, v.p., 1997-99, pres., 1999-2000; pres. Empty Stocking Fund, 1995—. Bd. dirs. Cancer Svcs. Davidson County, 1996—; pres. Capital Press Assn., 1998-2001, N.C. Daily Newspaper Assn., 1995—, v.p., 1998-99, pres., 1999-2000. Mem. AP Assn. Fla. (pres. 1970-71), Am. Soc. Newspaper Editors (dir. 1981-87), Am. Soc. Newspaper Editors Found. (bd. dirs., treas. 1986-90), Fla. Soc. Newspaper Editors (pres. 1975-76, dir. 1971-84, 90-93), Fla. Bar Found. (bd. dirs. 1990-92), AP Mng. Editors Assn., Sigma Delta Chi (pres. West Coast chpt. 1970-71, N.C. Press Assn. (bd. dirs. 1999-2000, 02–), Nat. Coun. Editl. Writers, Lexington Kiwanis (bd. dirs. 1996-2000). E-mail: bob.stiff@the-dispatch.com.

STIFFLER, JACK JUSTIN, electrical engineer; b. Mitchellville, Iowa, May 22, 1934; s. John Justin and Helen Irene (Roorda) S.; m. Ardis Ann Ackerman, Aug. 21, 1955; 1 child, Julia Alise; m. Sally Voris Burns, Apr. 20, 1989. AB magna cum laude in Physics, Harvard U., 1956; MS in E.E, Calif. Inst. Tech., 1957, PhD, 1962; postgrad., U. Paris, 1957-58. Engr. Hughes Aircraft Corp., Culver City, Calif., 1956-57; mem. tech. staff Jet Propulsion Lab., Pasadena, 1959-67; cons. scientist Raytheon Corp., Sudbury, Mass., 1967-81; exec. v.p. Sequoia Systems, Inc., Marlborough, 1981-97; cons., 1997—. Lectr. Calif. Inst. Tech., U. So. Calif., UCLA, Northeastern U. Author: Theory of Synchronous Communications, 1971; contbr. chpts. to books, articles to profl. jours. Fellow IEEE; mem. Phi Beta Kappa, Sigma Xi. E-mail: stiffler@capecod.net.

STIFLER, VENETIA CHAKOS, dancer, choreographer, dance educator; b. Chgo., Feb. 27, 1950; d. Theodore and Ruth (Pastirsky) Chakos; m. John G. Stifler, Jan. 28, 1972 (dec. 1977); m. Michael Hugos, 1994. BA, U. Ill., Chgo., 1983; MFA equivalency, Union Inst., Cin., 1987, PhD, 1992. Tchr. workshops Urban Gateways, Chgo., 1977; tchr. Chgo. Dance Ctr., 1971-78, Smith Coll., Northampton, Mass., 1975, Wilson Coll., Chambersburg, Pa., 1984; gusest tchr., artistic dir. composition/improvisation U. Wis., Madison, 1980-81, 85, 87; tchr. modern, jazz and ballet Venetia Stifler & Concert Dance, Inc., Chgo., 1978—; tchr. choreography workshop Bell Elem. Sch., 1987; tchr./artist in residence Mundelein Coll., 1982-90; asst. prof., chair dance program Northeastern Ill. U., 1987—; tchr. modern technique So. Ill. U., Carbondale, 1975. Lectr. Mundelein Coll., Chgo., 1983, 84, 85, 86, Mayor's Office of Spl. Events, Chgo., 1980program dir. and choreogrpaher spl. programs Chgo. Symphony Orch., 1985, 87; pres. bd. dirs. Chgo. Dance Arts Coalition, 1983-85; adv. dance panel Ill. Arts Coun., 1983-85, Chgo. Office of Fine Arts, 1983-86; guest speaker Chgo. Office of Fine Arts, 1987; choreographer Sears Fashion Files, BoMay Prodns., 1983, 84, 86; prodn. asst. Audio Visual Prodns., 1970-71; artistic dir. Ruth Page Dance Series, 1992—; centennial dir. Ruth Page Found. Centennial, 1999; exec. dir. Ruth Page Found., 2001. Choreographer Between Us, 1991, Magic Spaces, 1985, 86, Fugues, 1981, 82, Corporate Cases, 1988, Private places, 1987, Bell School Scrimmage, 1987, Blessings, 1986, Don't Dance with Your Back to the Moon, 1986, Imagery & Concept in the Dances of Venetia Stifler, 1985, Rhymes, 1984, Arriving at

Onion, 1984, Pulse, 1983, Haiku, 1982, Mundelein Madness, 1981, Solo Crane, 1981, Tales of a Winter's Night, 1980, Jackson Park-Howard, 1979, La Gaite Parisienne (opera), 1976, Chicago Sketches, 1995, Veils, 1996, Over Weight Over Wrought Over You, 1997, Three German Songs, 1999, Shenandoah. Recipient Ruth Page award; named for Outstanding Artistic Achievement, Chgo. Dance Coalition, 1985. Avocations: voice, film, art. Office: Northeastern Ill U 5500 N Saint Louis Ave Chicago IL 60625-4679 E-mail: venetia@ruth.

STIGALL, PHYLLIS GRAHAM, retired librarian; b. Ft. Wayne, Ind., Oct. 3, 1917; d. Edwin James and Mary Josephine (Palmer) Graham; m. Richard Patten Pooley, Apr. 4, 1943 (dec. Dec. 1950); 1 child Samuel Graham Pooley ; m. William Jasper Stigall Jr., Aug. 11, 1956 (dec. Sept. 2001). AA, Stephens Coll., 1937; AB, Northwestern U., 1939; MALS, U. Mich., 1952. Asst. counselor Stephens Coll., Columbia, Mo., 1939-42; asst. to dir. USO-YWCA Clubs, various locations, 1942-46; co-dir. U. Mich. Cmty. Ctr., Ann Arbor and Willow Run, 1946-47; libr., dean, instr. Lincoln (Ill.) Coll., 1952-66; mgr. publs. and librs. IBM Rsch. Ctr., Yorktown Heights, N.Y., 1966-88; ret. Author: Notes on 46 Women Writers, 1991, Journeys of the Brave, 1992, Ireland: Reader's Guide. Women, 1995; photographs exhibited, 1996. Mem. AAUW, LWV (chpt. bd. dirs., pres. 1947-66). Democrat. Episcopalian. Avocations: photography, research, biography, history, genealogy. Home: PO Box 211 Scarborough NY 10510

STIGALL, SCOTT OWEN, lawyer; b. Middletown, Ohio, Apr. 20, 1965; s. William Davis and Sharon Lee (Boyles) S. BA in Polit. Sci. summa cum laude, U. South Fla., 1987; JD with honors, U. Fla., 1990. Bar: Fla. 1990; U.S. Dist. Ct. (mid. dist.) Fla. 1990; U.S. Supreme Ct. 1995. Assoc. Barnett, Bolt, Kirkwood & Long, Tampa, Fla., 1990—. Adv. com. U. South Fla. Law, Tampa, 1991—; pupil William Glenn Terrell Am. Inn of Ct., 1992—. Recipient Order of Coif award, 1990. Mem. Hillsborough County Bar Assn. (dir. young lawyers divsn. 1994—). Home: 736 S Davis Blvd Tampa FL 33606-3914 Office: Barnett Bolt Kirkwood Long 601 Bayshore Blvd Ste 700 Tampa FL 33606-2763

STIGI, JOHN FRANCIS, federal agency administrator; b. Bklyn., Mar. 31, 1949; s. Dominic Louis and Susan (Morgello) S.; m. Olga Catherine Ratkowski, July 6, 1974; children: John Walter, Michael Anthony. BA, Hamline U., 1971; MS in Pub. Adminstrn., George Washington U., 1982. Cert. secondary tchr., N.Y. Investigator field office FDA, Bklyn., 1972-78, asst. to dir. office small mfrs. assistance Silver Spring, Md., 1978-81, dir. ops. office small mfrs. assistance, 1981-84, deputy dir. office small mfrs. assistance Rockville, 1984-90, dir. divsn. small mfrs. & internat. assistance, 1990—, chief negotiator U.S./European cmty. med. device, 1997-2001. Author: Regulation of Drug Delivery Devices, 1988, Documentation Basics That Support Quality Systems, 1990, International Perspectives on Health and Safety, 1994, Global Harmonization of Medical Device Premarket Review, 1998; editor: Regulatory Requirements for Medical Devices, 1985; contbr. articles to profl. jours. Activity coordinator Norbeck Meadows Civic Assn., 1986; mem. Minn. State Soc., Washington, 1988. Recipient Recognition award Ukranain Ministry of Health, 1988, Svc. Recognition award U.S. Pub. Health, 1994, Spl. Recognition award Taiwan Dept. Health, 1999. Fellow Nat. Law Enforcement Acad.; mem. Regulatory Affairs Profl. Soc. (Spl. Recognition award 1992), Am. Soc. Quality Control, Lambda Alpha (sec. treas. 1970). Clubs: Aspenhill Tennis. Avocations: travel, tennis, chess, carpentry. Home: 11145 Willowbrook Dr Potomac MD 20854-2588 Office: FDA 5600 Fishers Ln HFZ-220 Rockville MD 20857 E-mail: jfs@cdrh.fda.gov.

STIGLER, STEPHEN MACK, statistician, educator; b. Mpls., Aug. 10, 1941; s. George Joseph and Margaret (Mack) S.; m. Virginia Lee, June 27,1964; children: Andrew, Geoffrey, Margaret, Elizabeth. BA, Carleton Coll., 1963; PhD, U. Calif., Berkeley, 1967. Asst. prof. U. Wis., Madison, 1967-71, assoc. prof., 1971-75, prof., 1975-79, U. Chgo., 1979—; chmn. dept., 1986-92; Ernest DeWitt Burton Disting. Svc. prof. U. Chgo., 1992—. Trustee Ctr. for Advanced Study in the Behavioral Scis., Stanford, Calif., 1986-92, 93-99, 2000—, chmn., 1995-99, 2002--. Author: The History of Statistics, 1986, Statistics on the Table, 1999; contbr. articles to jours. in field. Guggenheim Found. fellow, 1976-77; Ctr. for Advanced Study in Behavioral Scis. fellow, 1978-79. Fellow AAAS, Am. Acad. Arts and Scis. (mem. coun. 1995-99), Inst. Math. Stats. (Neyman lectr. 1988, pres. 1993-94), Am. Statis. Assn. (editor Jour. 1979-82, Outstanding Statistician award Chgo. chpt. 1993), Royal Statis. Soc. (Fisher lectr. 1986); mem. Internat. Statis. Inst. (mem. coun. 1999—, pres.-elect 2001—), Statis. Soc. Can., Bernoulli Soc., History of Sci. Soc., Brit. Soc. for History Sci., Quadrangle Club, Sigma Xi, Phi Beta Kappa. Office: U Chgo Dept Statistics 5734 S University Ave Chicago IL 60637-1514

STIGLITZ, JOSEPH EUGENE, economist, educator; b. Gary, Ind., Feb. 9, 1943; s. Nathaniel David and Charlotte (Fishman) Stiglitz; children: Siobhan, Michael, Edward, Julia. BA, Amherst Coll., Mass, 1964; DHL, Amherst Coll., 1974; PhD in Econs., MIT, 1966; MA (hon.) , Yale U., 1970; D in Econs. (hon.) , U. Leuven, 1994. Prof. econs. Cowles Found., Yale U., New Haven, 1970—74; vis. fellow St. Catherine's Coll., Oxford, England, 1973—74; Joan Kenney professorship Stanford U., 1974—76, prof. of economics and senior fellow, Hoover Inst., 1988—2001; Oskar Morgenstern dist. fellow Inst. Advanced Studies Math., Princeton, NJ, 1978—79; Drummond prof. polit. economy Oxford U., England, 1976—79; prof. econs. Princeton U., 1979—88; sr. v.p., chief economist World Bank, Washington, 1995—2000; sr. fellow Brookings Inst., 2000; Stern visiting prof. Columbia U., 2000; prof. of economics and finance Columbia U. Grad. Sch. of Bus., Dept. of Econ. and Sch. of Internat. and Public Affairs, 2001—. Mem. Pres.'s Coun. Econ. Advisers, 1993—95, chmn. coun. econ. advisers, 1995—97, sr. v.p. devel. econs. and chief econs., exec. dir.; cons. World Bank, State of Alaska, Seneca Indian Nation, Bell Comm. Rsch. Editor: Jour. Econ. Perspectives, 1986—93; Am. editor: Rev. of Econ. Studies, 1968—76, assoc. editor: Am. Econ. Rev., 1968—76, assoc. editor: Energy Econs., Managerial and Decision Econs., mem. editl. bd.: World Bank Econ. Rev. Recipient John Bates Clark award, Am. Econ. Assn., 1979, Internat. prize, Accademia Lincei, 1988, Union des Assurances de Paris prize, 1989, The Nobel Prize in Economic Sciences, 2001, Rechtenwald Prize, Germany, 1998; fellow, Guggenheim, 1969—70; scholar guest, The Brookings Inst., Washington. Fellow: Inst. for Policy Rsch. (sr. 1991—93), Brit. Acad. (corr.); mem.: NAS (fellow, 1988), Econometric Soc., Am. Acad. Arts and Scis.(fellow, 1983), Am. Econ. Assn. (exec. com. 1982—84, v.p. 1985). Office: Columbia U Uris Hall Rm 814 Broadway and 116th St New York NY 10027*

STIGLITZ, MARTIN RICHARD, electrical engineer; b. Vienna, Austria, Mar. 24, 1920; came to U.S., 1939, naturalized, 1942; s. Georg Adolph and Maria (Brun) S.; BS, Northeastern U., 1957, MS in Electronics Engring., 1959; MBA in Mgmt., Western New Eng. Coll., 1977; m. Lenna Schoenberg, Dec. 10, 1950 (dec. Apr. 1991); m. Sachiko Sakimura, May 1, 1990. Mech. engr. S.A. Woods Machine Co., Boston, 1939-51; electronics engr., rsch. scientist Air Force Cambridge Rsch. Labs., Hanscom AFB, Bedford, Mass., 1945-75; rsch. electronics scientist Rome Air Devel. Command electromagnetic scis. div. U.S. Air Force, Bedford, Mass., 1985-88; tech. editor Horizon House-Microwave, Inc., Norwood, Mass., 1985-94; dir. Solar Energy Tech. Inc., Bedford. With U.S. Army, 1942-45. Mem. IEEE (life), N.Y. Acad. Scis., Sigma Xi. Patentee solid state devices, med. instruments; contbr. over 50 articles to sci. and profl. jours. Home: Lexington, Mass. Died Jan. 20, 2001.

STIGWOOD, ROBERT COLIN, theater, movie, television and record producer; b. Adelaide, Australia, Apr. 16, 1934; came to Eng., 1956; s. Gordon and Gwendolyn (Burrows) S. Student, Sacred Heart Coll., Adelaide. Worked as copywriter for advt. agy., Adelaide; held series of jobs, including mgr. provincial theater and halfway house for delinquents in Cambridge; opened talent agy. London, 1962; liquidated firm, 1965; became bus. mgr. for group Graham Bond Orgn.; became co-mng. dir. NEMS Enterprises, 1967; prin. Robert Stigwood Orgn., 1967; formed RSO Records, 1973; dir. Polygram, 1976; co-founder (with Rupert Murdoch) R&R Films, 1979. Founder Music for UNICEF. 1st ind. record producer in Eng. with release of single Johnny Remember Me; producer: films, including Jesus Christ Superstar, 1973, Bugsy Malone, Tommy, 1975, Survive, 1976, Saturday Night Fever, 1977, Grease I, 1978, Grease II, 1982, Moment By Moment, 1978, Sergeant Pepper's Lonely Hearts Club Band, The Fan, 1981, Times Square, 1980, Gallipoli, 1980, Staying Alive, 1983, Evita, 1996; stage musicals in Eng. and U.S., including Hair, Oh! Calcutta, The Dirtiest Show in Town, Sweeney Todd, Pippin, Jesus Christ Superstar, Evita, Grease, Saturday Night Fever; TV producer in Eng. and U.S.; prodns. include The Entertainer (dramatic spl.); All in the Family (series), The Prime of Miss Jean Brodie (dramatic series). Bd. dirs. Police Athletic League, N.Y.C.; patron Australian Nat. Art Gallery. Recipient Tony award for best musical (Evita); named Internat. Producer of Yr. ABC Interstate Theatres, Inc., 1976, Knight of St. John of Jerusalem, Malta, 1985. Mem. Royal Bermuda Yacht Club. Clubs: Royal Bermuda Yacht. Avocations: yachting, tennis. Home: Barton Manor East Cowes Isle of Wight England

STILES, DONALD ALAN, retired financial company executive; b. Waukegan, Ill., June 19, 1951; s. James Fuller and Helen Alma (Ferry) Stiles; m. Leslie Ann Herzog, June 24, 1978; children: Peter Alan, Thomas Joseph. BA, Carleton Coll., 1973; MBA, U. Minn., 1979. With Nat. Theatre Co., N.Y.C., 1973-74; corp. acct. Ministers Life Ins. Co., Mpls., 1974-81; sr. tax cons. Touche Ross & Co., 1981-83; mgr. tax planning Northwestern Nat. Life Ins. Co., 1983-86, dir. tax svcs., 1986-87; asst. v.p. corp. tax svcs. ING/ReliaStar, 1987-2000. Libr. treas. St. Stephen Luth. Ch., Bloomington, Minn., 1994—2001, bd. coun., 1998—, v.p., 2000, pres., 2001, treas., 2002—; bd. dirs. Minn. Opera, 1989—92. Mem.: Minn. Taxpayers Assn. (bd. dirs., treas. 2001—), Accountability Minn. (bd. dirs. 1987-96, pres. 1989-90), Tax Execs. Inst. (bd. dirs. Minn. chpt. 1987-92, 94-96, sec. 1988-89, v.p. 1989-91, pres. 1991-92, internat. bd. dirs. 1994-96). Avocation: Avocation: singing. E-mail: dolepeto@aol.com.

STILES, ELBIE SUSANNA, real estate broker; b. Middelburg, Transvaal, Republic of South Africa, Nov. 11, 1949; came to U.S., 1972; d. Jacobus Christoffel and Ella Magdalena (Joubert) Steenekamp; m. Henry Clary, Aug. 2, 1973 (div. Feb. 1983); m. Everett Stiles, Aug. 11, 1984; 1 child, Hardin Emory (dec.). Co-owner Afrikan-Am. Imports, Franklin, N.C., 1973-83; broker Sheffield Developers & Realty, 1982-83, Brownings Real Estate, Franklin, 1983-85; owner, broker Town Hill Realty, 1985-87; broker Lamplighter Realty, 1987—. Contbr. articles to profl. jours. Bd. dirs., sec. Nikwasi Found., Franklin, 1986—; chair Macon County March of Dimes, Franklin, 1987; bd. dirs. Southwestern Community Coll. Found., Sylva, N.C., 1987—; treas. Smoky Mountain Host of N.C., Franklin, 1987—. Mem. Franklin Bd. Realtors, Franklin Area C. of C. (bd. dirs., sec. treas. 1986—). Baptist. Avocations: hiking, canoeing, flying, loom weaving. Office: Lamplighter Realty PO Box 1252 Franklin NC 28744-1252

STILES, GARY LESTER, cardiologist, molecular pharmacologist, educator; b. N.Y.C., May 22, 1949; s. Robert L. and Vivian M. (Cano) S.; m. Alexis H. Stiles; children: Heather B., Wendy A. BS in Chemistry, St. Lawrence U., 1971; MD, Vanderbilt U., 1975. Diplomate Am. Bd. Internal Medicine, sub.-bd. Cardiovascular Medicine. Resident in internal medicine Vanderbilt U., Nashville, 1975-78; fellow in cardiology Duke U., Durham, N.C., 1978-81, mem. faculty, 1981—, assoc. prof., 1986-89, chief div. cardiology, 1989-99, prof. medicine, 1990—, prof. pharmacology, 1990—, Ursula Gellar prof. cardiology, 1999—; CMO, v.p. Duke Health Sys., 1999—. Mem. sci. adv. coun. Alta. Heritage Found., Edmonton, Can., 1990—; mem. pharmacology study sect. NIH, Bethesda, Md., 1988-91. Mem. editl. bd. Jour. Biol. Chemistry, 1990-95, Molecular Pharmacology, 1991-99. Recipient Katz prize Am. Heart Assn., 1983, award Am. Fedn. Clin. Rsch., 1989; grantee Am. Heart Assn., 1987-90. Fellow Am. Coll. Cardiology (award 1993); mem. Internat. Churchill Soc., Assn. Am. Physicians, Am. Soc. Clin. Investigation. Republican. Achievements include patent in field. Office: Duke U Med Ctr Divsn Cardiology PO Box 3681 Durham NC 27710-0001 E-mail: glsmd@duke.edu.

STILES, LA NELLE C. retired secondary school educator; b. Princeton, Fla., Jan. 13, 1940; d. Emory P. and Ethel P. Cowan; m. G. Edward Stiles, July 21, 1962; children: Christi Reed, Gregory. BA, Trevecca Nazarene U., 1962; MA, W.Va. U., 1974. Cert. profl. tchr. Tchr. DuPont H.S., Old Hickory, Tenn., 1962—66; tchr., dept. chair Waynesburg (Pa.) Ctrl. H.S., 1974—99; adj. instr. Brunswick C.C., Supply, NC, 2002. Inspirational spkr. clubs, chs., various orgns. Named All-Star Tchr., U. Pitts. and Pitts. Post-Gazette, 1996, 1998. Mem.: St. James Svc. Club, Phi Delta Lambda. Avocations: reading, writing, gardening, music, volunteer work. Home: 3224 Wexford Way Southport NC 28461

STILES, MARTHA BENNETT, writer; b. Manila, The Philippines, Mar. 30, 1933; came to U.S., 1934; d. Forrest Hampton Wells and Jane McClintock Bennett; m. Martin Stiles, Sept. 18, 1954. BS with high distinction, U. Mich., 1954. Tchr. creative writing U. Louisville, 1989, U. Ky., Lexington, 1989, 90. Author: One Among the Indians, 1962, The Strange House at Newburyport, 1963, Darkness Over the Land, 1966, Dougal Looks for Birds, 1972, James the Vine Puller, 1975, 2nd edit., 1992, Tana and the Useless Monkey, 1979, The Star in the Forest, 1979, Sarah the Dragon Lady, 1986, Kate of Still Waters, 1990, Lonesome Road, 1998, Island Magic, 1999. Recipient Fiction prize Frankfort Arts Found., 1984, 86, Profl. Assistance award Ky. Arts Coun., 1990; Al Smith fellow Ky. Arts Coun., 1992. Mem. Detroit Women Writers, U. Ky. Libr. Assocs. Episcopalian. Home: 861 Hume-Bedford Rd Paris KY 40361

STILES, MARY ANN, lawyer, author, lobbyist; b. Tampa, Fla., Nov. 16, 1944; d. Ralph A. and Bonnie (Smith) S.; m. Barry Smith. AA, Hills Community Coll., 1973; BS, Fla. State U., 1975; JD, Antioch Sch. Law, 1978. Bar: Fla. 1978. Legis. analyst Fla. Ho. of Reps., Tallahassee, 1973-74, 74-75; intern U.S. Senate, Washington, 1977; v.p., gen. counsel Associated Industries Fla., Tallahassee, 1978-81, gen. counsel, 1981-84, spl. counsel, 1986-97; assoc. Deschler, Reed & Crichfield, Boca Raton, 1980-81; founding ptnr. Stiles, Taylor, & Grace, P.A., Boca Raton, Tampa, Orlando, Jacksonville, Talahassee, and Miami, 1982—, shareholder, dir. Tampa; gen. counsel Associated Industries Ins. Co., Inc., 1996—, Associated Industries Fla., Inc., 1997—, Associated Industries Ins. Svcs., Inc., 1997—. Shareholder, dir. Six Stars Devel. Co. of Fla., Inc. Platnum Bank; dr. Eclipse, Inc.; owner, pres. Styles by Stiles; shareholder, pres. 42nd St., The Bistro; mem. Workers' Compensation Task Force, 2000-01. Author: Workers' Compensation Law Handbook, 1980-94 edit. Bd. dirs., sec. Hillsborough C.C. Found., Tampa, 1985-87, 94-96; bd. dirs. Hillsborough Area Regional Transit Authority, Tampa, 1986-89, Boys and Girls Club of Tampa, 1986—; The Spring, 1992-93, What's My Chance, 1992-94; mem. Gov.'s Oversite Bd. on Workers' Compensation, 1989-90, Workers' Compensation Rules Com., Fla. Bar, 1990-95, 2000—, Workers' Compensation Exec. Counsel Fla. Bar, 1990-95, Jud. Nominating Commn. for Workers' Compensation Cts., 1990-93, trustee Hillsborough Cmty. Coll., 1994-99, vice-chair, 1995-96, chair, 1996-97; bd. dirs. Seminole Boosters, Inc., Fla. State U., 1996—. Mem. ABA, Fla. Bar Assn., Hillsborough County Bar Assn., Hillsborough Assn. Women Lawyers, Fla. Assn. Women Lawyers, Fla. Women's Alliance, Hillsborough County Seminole Boosters (past pres.), Tiger Bay Club (Tampa, past. pres., sec.). Republican. Baptist. Avocations: boating, reading. Office: 315 S Plant Ave Tampa FL 33606-2325 also: 317 N Calhoun St Tallahassee FL 32301-7605 also: PO Box 310397 Miami FL 33231-0397 Address: PO Box 294349 Boca Raton FL 33429 also: PO Box 48190 Jacksonville FL 32247

STILES, RYAN, actor; b. Apr. 22, 1959; Actor (films) Rainbow War, 1985, Hot Shots!, 1991, Hot Shots! Part Deux, 1993, Courting Courtney, 1997, (tv series) Whose Line Is It Anyway, 1998—, The Drew Carey Show, 1995—; prodr.: Whose Line Is It Anyway?, 1998; tv guest appearances include: The Magic Hour, 1998, The Hitchhiker, 1983, Mad TV, 1995, The Beachcombers, 1971, Parker Lewis Can't Lose, 1990, The John Larroquette Show, 1993, Mad About You, 1992, Weird Science, 1994, Murphy Brown, 1988. Office: The Drew Carey Show 4000 Warner Blvd Burbank CA 91522-0001*

STILES, THOMAS BEVERIDGE, II, retired investment banking executive; b. Easton, Pa., Oct. 4, 1940; s. Ezra Martin and Vivien (de Fay) S.; m. Elaine Ann Patyk, July 2, 1966 (div. Oct. 1980); children— Thomas Beveridge III, Jonathan Ezra; m. Barbara Toll Alexander, Mar. 7, 1981. BA, Yale U., 1963; MBA, Harvard U., 1968. V.p. Laird, Inc., N.Y.C., 1968-73; sr. v.p., dir. Smith Barney Harris Upham and Co., Inc., 1973-82; exec. v.p., dir. E.F. Hutton & Co. Inc., 1982-87; chmn., CEO Shearson Lehman Advisors Asset Mgmt. Co., 1988-90, 99—, Bernstein Macaulay, N.Y.C., 1988-90; CEO, chmn. Greenwich Street Advisors, 1990-97; mng. dir. Smith, Barney, Inc., 1993-99, retired, 1999—. Bd. dirs., pres. Cedar Lawn Cemetery, Paterson, N.J., 1973—. Bd. dirs., mem. collections com., devel. com., fin. com., pers. com. Laguna Art Mus., Laguna Beach, Calif. 1st lt. M.I., U.S. Army, 1963-66. Fellow Fin. Analysts Fedn.; mem. N.Y. Soc. Security Analysts, Spring Lake Bath and Tennis Club (N.J.), El Niguel Country Club (Calif.). Republican. Presbyterian. Avocations: political science, tennis, swimming. E-mail: tom.stiles@cox.net.

STILES, WILLIAM A., JR. management consultant, consultant; s. William Alfred and Adell Jane Stiles; m. Margaret R. Mulholland, Sept. 23, 2000. BA in Sociology, Coll. William and Mary, 1971. Legis. asst. Congressman George E. Brown, Jr., Washington, 1976—82, adminstrv. asst., 1982—87; staff dir. House Agr. Subcom. on Dept. Obs., Rsch. and Fgn. Agr., 1983—91; legis. dir. House Com. on Sci. and Tech., 1991—98; exec. dir. Genetic Resources Comm. Sys., Inc., Bethesda, Md., 2000—01. Chair Neighborhood Reinvestment Project, Arlington, Va., 1998—99. Recipient Career Svc. award, Coun. on Govtl. Affairs, 1999. Mem.: AAAS (mem. com. on sci., engring., and pub. policy 2001—). Office: ABMI Consulting 1121 Graydon Ave Norfolk VA 23507

STILES, WILLIAM B. psychology educator; b. Seattle, Jan. 29, 1944; married. BA in Psychology, Oberlin Coll., 1966; MA in Psychology, UCLA, 1968, PhD, 1972. Lic. psychologist, N.C., Ohio. Instr. dept. psychology U. N.C., Chapel Hill, 1971-72, asst. prof., 1973-79; assoc. prof. Miami U., Oxford, Ohio, 1979-85, prof. psychology, 1985—, dir. psychology clinic, 1986-91. Hon. professorial rsch. fellow U. Leeds, U.K., summer 1996, 97, 2000; vis. scholar Massey U., Palmerston North, N.Z., 1982, 90, 99; vis. prof. U. Joensuu, Finland, 1997; vis. rschr. U. Sheffield, U.K., 1987, 89, 91, NIH Fogarty sr. internat. fellow, 1992-93, MRC/ESRC Social and Psychology Unit spl. appointment, 1995; advisory editor Psychotherapy Rsch., 1991-96, assoc. editor., 1996-98, N.Am. editor., 1999—; guest editor spl. issue Jour. Psychoterapy Integration; editl. bd. Jour. Lang. and Social Psychology; cons. editor Jour. Cons. Psychology; mem. editl. team Brit. Jour. Med. Psychology, 1995—; rschr. in field. Contbr. articles to profl. jours. Fellow Am. Psychol. Soc.; mem. APA, Soc. for Psychotherapy Rsch. (exec. coun. 1995-99, gen. v.p. 1995-96, pres.-elect, program chmn. 1996-97, pres. 1997-98), Midwestern Psychol. Assn., Person-Centered Assn., Soc. for Exploration of Psychotherapy Integration, Soc. for Personality and Social Psychology, Sigma Xi. Home: 200 W Withrow St Oxford OH 45056 Office: Miami U Dept Psychology Oxford OH 45056 E-mail: stileswb@muohio.edu.

STILL, CHARLES HENRY, SR. lawyer; b. Lubbock, Tex., Sept. 22, 1942; s. Charles Alphonso and Henri Sue S.; m. Frances Eugenia Odell, Apr. 29, 1967; children: Charles Henry Jr., Kathryn Elizabeth. BBA in Acctg., Tex. Tech. U., 1965; JD with honors, U. Tex., 1968. Bar: Tex. 1968. Assoc. Fulbright & Jaworski, Houston, 1968-75, ptnr., 1975—, head corp. dept., 1984-99, mem. exec. com., 1992-99. Speaker numerous confs. and meetings; bd. dirs. Oyo Geospace Corp., TrueTime Inc. Comment editor Tex. Law Rev., 1967-68. Bd. dirs. Alley Theatre, Houston, 1980-81, St. Luke's Episcopal Hosp., Houston, 1991—, Free Enterprise Inst., Houston, 1993—, Catalyst Found., Houston, 1992--; mem. vestry Christ Ch. Cathedral, Houston, 1981-84, sr. warden, 1983, chancellor, 1986-2002. Fellow Am. Bar Found., Tex. Bar Found., Houston Bar Found.; mem. ABA (bus. law sect. 1968—, corp. laws com. 1983-89, fed. regulation of securities com. 1976—, com. on legal opinions 1989—, adminstrv. law sect. 1981—, law firms com. 1990—, chmn. 1998-2000, ethics 2000 task force 1999-2002, multiple disciplinary practice task force 1998—, profl. conduct com. 2002--), Am. Law Inst., State Bar Tex. (chmn. bus. law sect. 1984-85, mem. coun. 1982-86, chmn. securities law com. 1981-83, com. on corp. laws 1985—), Forest Club, Petroleum Club, Order of Coif, Phi Delta Phi, Phi Kappa Phi, Gamma Phi Beta, Beta Alpha Psi, Phi Delta Theta, Phi Eta Sigma. Avocations: hunting, reading, photography. Home: 3734 Locke Ln Houston TX 77027-4006 Office: Fulbright & Jaworski 1301 Mckinney St Ste 5100 Houston TX 77010-3095

STILL, CHARLES NEAL, neurologist, consultant; b. Richmond, Va., Apr. 15, 1929; s. Charles Wright and Ruth (Kemp) S.; m. Dorothy Lee Varn, Dec. 27, 1958; children: Charles Herbert, Carl Nelson, Sara Alice. BS in Chemistry, Clemson U., 1949; MS in Biochemistry, Purdue U., 1951; MD, Med. U. S.C., 1959. Diplomate Am. Bd. Psychiatry and Neurology. Instr. chemistry Clemson (S.C.) U., 1951-52; rotating intern U. Chgo. Clinics, 1959-60; neurology fellow Sch. Medicine Johns Hopkins U., Balt., 1960-63; resident in neurology Johns Hopkins-Balt. City Hosp., 1960-63; NIH rsch. fellow Harvard U.-McLean Hosp., Belmont, Mass., 1963-65; chief neurology svcs. William S. Hall. Psychiat. Inst., Columbia, S.C., 1965-81, assoc. dir. gen. psychiatry and neurology, 1989-92; dir. C. M. Tucker Human Resources Ctr., 1981-88; clin. prof. neuropsychiatry USC Sch. Medicine, S.C., 1981-88, prof. neuropsychiatry, 1989—. Instr. chemistry U.S. Mil. Acad., West Point, N.Y., 1953-55; assoc. clin. prof. neurology Med. U. S.C., Charleston, 1973-92; assoc. prof. neuropsychiatry U. S.C. Sch. Medicine, Columbia, 1976-78, prof. neuropsychiatry, 1978-81. Author: (with others) Handbook of Clinical Neurology, 1976, Neurologic Clinics, 1984, Movement Disorders, 1986; editor The Recorder Columbia Med. Soc., 1991—; mem. editl. bd. Jour. S.C. Med. Assn., 1980—, Jour. Applied Gerontology, 1983-88; contbr. articles to profl. jours. Chmn. grants rev. bd. S.C. Dept. Mental Health, Columbia, 1973-78; mem. exec. bd. Alzheimer's Assn. Columbia, 1985-93, pres. Mid-State chpt. Alzheimer's Assn., 1991-92; med. dir. Alzheimer's Disease Registry, Columbia, 1989-92, Alzheimer's Daycare Ctr., Columbia, 1989-92; mem. Gov.'s Adv. Coun. to Alzheimer's Disease and Related Disorders Resource Coordination Ctr., 1995-99. 1st lt. U.S. Army, 1952-55. Fellow: Am. Geriatrics Soc., Am. Acad. Neurology, Gerontol. Soc. Am., Am. Inst. Chemists (life); mem.: AMA (life), Am. Chem. Soc. Baptist. Avocations: writing, photography. Home: 2 Culpepper Cir Columbia SC 29209-2234 Office: WJB Dorn VA Med Ctr Psychiatry Svc Columbia SC 29209-1639

STILL, IVAN HENRY, research scientist; b. Hastings, U.K., June 27, 1967; s. Roy ERic Reginald and Jean Lottie Anne Still. BS, U. Coll. London, 1988; PhD, U. Newcastle-upon-Tyne, U.K., 1992. Sr. postdoctoral rsch. asst. U. Durham, U.K., 1992-94; postdoctoral rsch. fellow Imperial Cancer Rsch. Fund, London, 1994-95, Cleve. Clinic Found., 1995-98, rsch. assoc. Lerner Rsch. Inst., 1998-2000; asst. mem. Roswell Park Cancer Inst., Buffalo, 2000—. Contbr. articles to profl. jours. Mem. Am. Asn. Cancer Rsch., Am. Soc. Cell Biology. Avocations: home improvement projects, computing, war gaming. Office: Elm And Carlton St Buffalo NY 14263-0001 E-mail: ivanstill@msn.com., ivanstill@roswellpark.org.

STILL, JAMES, adult education educator, writer; b. LaFayette, Ala., 1906; s. James Alexander and Lonie (Lindsey) S. AB, Lincoln Meml. U., 1929; MA, Vanderbilt U., 1930; BS in Libr. Sci., U. Ill., 1930; LittD (hon.), Berea Coll., 1973, Morehead State U., 1978, U. Ky., 1979; HLD (hon.), Lincoln Meml. U., 1974, Ky. Wesleyan U.; degree (hon.), Transylvania U., 1983, Cumberland Coll., 1996. Mem. staff Hindman (Ky.) Settlement Sch., 1932-39, 51-61; assoc. prof. Morehead (Ky.) State U., 1962-70; commentator Nat. Pub. Radio, Washington, 1980-83. Vis. prof. Appalachian Coll., 1987—. Author: (books) River of Earth, 1940, 2d edit., 1978, Sporty Creek, 1977, 2d edit., 1998, The Wolfpen Notebooks, 1991, (poetry) Hounds of the Mountain, 1937, 2d edit., 1968, (short stories) Pattern of a Man, On Troublesome Creek, 1977, The Run for the Elbertas, 1980, From the Valley, From the Mountain, 2001, (children's books), Way Down Yonder on Troublesome Creek, 1974, The Wolfpen Rusties, 1974, Jack and the Wonder Beans, 1977, 2d edit., 1996, An Appalachian Mother Goose, 1998. Sgt. U.S. Army, 1942-45. Recipient O. Henry Meml. prize for short story, 1939, So. Authors award, 1940, award Am. Acad. Arts and Letters and Nat. Inst. Arts and Letter, 1947, 79, Algernon Sydney Sullivan award Lincoln Meml. U., 1971, medal of hon. DAR, 1973, medallion for intellectual excellence U. Ky., 1994, Ednl. Svc. award to Appalachia Carson-Newman Coll., 1991, award Fellowship of So. Writers, 1997, award Appalachian Coll. Assn., 1998; Guggenheim fellow, 1941, 46; named Poet Laureate of Ky., 1995-96; James Still fellowship estab. U. Ky., 1989; James Still room dedicated Johnson-Camden Libr., Morehead State U., 1961. Mem. South Atlantic MLA, Phi Beta Kappa. Avocations: Mayan civilization, gardening, travel. Home: Hindman, Ky. Died May 5, 2002.

STILL, LISA STOTSBERY, lawyer; b. North Kingstown, R.I., Dec. 4, 1960; d. Lawrence Edward Stotsbery and Clarice Ann Dudley; m. July, 1992. BA with honors, U. West Fla., 1981; JD, U. Fla., 1985. Bar: Fla. 1986, U.S. Dist. Ct. (mid. dist.) Fla. 1986, U.S. Ct. Appeals (11th cir.) 1987, U.S. Tax Ct. 1987, U.S. Supreme Ct. 1993. Tax specialist Coopers & Lybrand, Miami, Fla., 1986, Jacksonville, 1986-87; pvt. practice, 1987; trial atty. SBA, 1987—; spl. asst. U.S. atty. Mid. Dist. Fla., 1990—. Mem. ABA (com. enforcement creditors rights and bankruptcy 1990), FBA (treas. Jacksonville chpt. 1990-92, v.p. membership 1993, v.p. programs 1994, pres.-elect 1995, pres. 1996, immediate past pres. 1997, nat. coun. 1996-99, chpt. activity fund 1997, editor of Fed. Career Svc. Divsn. newsletter 2001-), Fla. Bar (govt. lawyer com. 1990-91, voluntary bar liaison com. 1996-99, fed. practice com. 1998—, bus. law sect., issue editor Bankruptcy Casenotes 1996). Avocations: water skiing, fitness instruction, biking. Office: SBA 7825 Baymeadows Way Ste 100B Jacksonville FL 32256-7549

STILLER, JENNIFER ANNE, lawyer; b. Washington, May 4, 1948; d. Ralph Sophian and Joy (Dancis) S. AB in Econs. and History, U. Mich., 1970; JD, NYU, 1973. Bar: Pa. 1973, U.S. Dist. Ct. (mid. dist.) Pa. 1977, U.S. Supreme Ct. 1978, Ill. 1979, U.S. Dist. Ct. (no. dist.) Ill. 1979, U.S. Dist. Ct. (ea. dist.) Pa. 1983, U.S. Ct. Appeals (3rd cir.) 1983, U.S. Ct. Appeals (D.C. cir.), 1996. Dep. atty. gen. Pa. Dept. Justice, Harrisburg, 1973-75, Pa. Dept. Health, Harrisburg, 1975-78; sr. staff atty. Am. Hosp. Assn., Chgo., 1978-80, mgr., dept. fed. law, 1980-81; gen. counsel Ill. Health Fin. Authority, 1981-82; sr. assoc. Berriman & Schwartz, King of Prussia, Pa., 1983-85, Wolf, Block, Schorr & Solis-Cohen, Phila., 1985-88, Montgomery, McCracken, Walker & Rhoads, LLP, Phila., 1988-90; ptnr. Montgomery, McCracken, Walker & Rhoads, 1990-2000, chair health law group, 1991-2000; sr. counsel Tenet Healthcare Corp., 2000-2001; pvt. practice Haverford, Pa., 2001—. Contbr. health law articles to profl. jours. Mem. ABA (gov. com. Health Law Forum 1994-95), Am. Health Lawyers Assn. (bd. dirs. 1997—, exec. com. 2002—), Forum of Exec. Women, Pa. Soc. Healthcare Attys. (pres. 1995). Avocations: gardening, bicycling, hiking, music. Office: Law Office Jennifer A Stiller 625 Haydock Ln Haverford PA 19041-1207 E-mail: stiller@health-regs.com.

STILLER, JERRY, actor; b. N.Y.C., June 8, 1927; s. William and Bella S.; m. Anne Meara, Sept. 14, 1953; children: Amy, Benjamin. BS in Speech and Drama, Syracuse U., 1950. Actor with nat. co. of Peter Pan, 1951, also at Henry St. Playhouse, 1941, Cherry Lane Theatre, N.Y.C., 1947, Billy Barnes Showboat, Chgo., 1950, Erie (Pa.) Playhouse, 1951, 52, Memphis Arena Theatre, 1952, Phoenix Theatre, 1954, 55, 56, Shakespeare Festival Theatre, Stratford, Conn., 1955, Compass Players, 1959, mem. Shakespeare Co. in Central Park, N.Y.C., 1957, 71, Two Gentlemen, 1971, Much Ado, 1988; Broadway appearances include The Golden Apple, 1954, The Ritz, 1975, Unexpected Guests, 1977, Hurlyburly, 1985, Three Men on a Horse, 1993, What's Wrong With This Picture?, 1994, The Three Sisters, 1997; film appearances include The Taking of Pelham 1-2-3, 1974, Airport '75, 1975, The Ritz, 1976, Those Lips, Those Eyes, 1979, Nadine, 1986, That's Adequate, 1986, Hairspray, 1986, Shoeshine (Acad. award nomination, short subject 1989), A Pair of Jokers, 1990, The Pickle, 1992, Stag, 1996, Camp Stories, 1996, The Deli, 1997, Die Story Von Monty Spinnerratz, 1997, The Fish in the Bathtub, 1998, The Independent, 2001, On the Line, 2001, Serving Sara, 2002; Off-Broadway appearances include Boubouroche, 1971, Passione, 1980, Prairie du Chien, 1985, After-Play, 1995-96; mem. comedy team, Anne Meara, 1961—, Ed Sullivan Show 36 appearances; night club appearances include Compass Players, St. Louis, 1957, Happy Medium, Chgo., 1960, also Village Gate, Village Vanguard, Blue Angel, Bon Soir and, Phase Two, N.Y.C., Mr. Kelly's, Chgo., Hungry I, San Francisco, The Establishment, London, The Sands, Flamingo, Las Vegas, Harrah's, Reno and Lake Tahoe, Trump Plaza, QE II; co-star: daily TV series Take Five with Stiller and Meara, 1977-78; actor TV series Joe and Sons, 1975, Tattinger's, 1987, The Detective, The Sunset Gang, PBS, 1991, Seize the Day, 1990, The Hollow Boy, American Playhouse, 1991, Seinfeld, 1993-98, Subway Stories, Tales From the Underground, 1997, King of Queens, 1998—; commercials: Blue Nun, United Van Lines, Amalgamated Bank, Nike, AT&T, Glad Bags, Total Cereal; ESPN video (co-host with Anne Meara): So You Want to be an Actor?; animation: Teachers Pet "Pretty Boy", 2000-2002, Lion King III, 2003; author: (book) Married to Laughter (Grammy nomination for audio), 2000. Recipient Disting. Alumnus award Syracuse U., 1973, Voice of Imagery award, 1975, Arents Pioneer Medal, 1979, 1st Biffy award Balt. Internat. Film Festival, Entertainment Father of Yr. award, 1977, Syracuse Walk of Stars, 1994, Syracuse U. award for Achievement in the Arts, Am. Comedy award for role in Seinfeld, 1998; nominated Emmy award for role in Seinfeld, 1997, Ellis Island Medal of Honor, 2000.

STILLER, MATTHEW JAMES, dermatologist; b. N.Y.C., May 26, 1951; s. Jesse and Yetta (Weisfogel) S. BA, Pomona Coll., Claremont, Calif., 1973; MD, N.Y. Med. Coll., Valhalla, 1976. Diplomate Am. Bd. Dermatology. Pathology intern Mt. Sinai Hosp., N.Y.C., 1976; resident in dermatology N.Y. Med. Coll., 1977—80; assoc. dir. dermatopharmacology Univ. Hosp./NYU Sch. Medicine, N.Y.C., 1987-93; chief dermatology clin. investigations unit Mass. Gen. Hosp., Boston, 1993-97; dir. clin. pharmacology unit dept. dermatology Columbia U. Coll. Physicians and Surgeons, N.Y.C., 1997—. Contbg. editor: Yearbook of Dermatology, 1997. Recipient Conrad Jobst award N.Am. Congress of Phlebology, 1992. Fellow Am. Acad. Dermatology (chmn. dermatology rx task force 1991-93, computer tech. com. 1991-95, task force on databases 1992-96); mem. Soc. for Investigative Dermatology, Med. Mycology Soc. N.Y., Phi Beta Kappa, Alpha Omega Alpha. Office: New York-Presbyn Hosp Rm 1261 161 Ft Washington Ave New York NY 10032

STILLINGER, FRANK HENRY, chemist, educator; b. Boston, Aug. 15, 1934; s. Frank Henry and Gertrude (Metcalf) S.; m. Dorothea Anne Keller, Aug. 18, 1956; children: Constance Anne, Andrew Metcalf. BS, U. Rochester, 1955; PhD, Yale U., 1958. NSF postdoctoral fellow Yale U., 1958-59; with Bell Telephone Labs., Murray Hill, N.J., 1959-2001, head chem. physics dept., 1976-79; disting. mem. tech. staff Bell Labs., 1982-2001. Mem. evaluation panel Nat. Bur. Stds., 1975-78; mem. adv. com. for chemistry NSF, 1980-83, mem. adv. com. for advanced sci. computing, 1984-86, mem. adv. com. material and phys. sci. directorate, 1992-94; disting. lectr. chemistry U. Md., 1981; Karcher lectr. U. Okla., 1984; Trumbull lectr. Yale U., 1984; Washburn Meml. lectr. U. Nebr., 1986; Gucker lectr. Ind. U., 1987; W.A. Noyes lectr. U. Tex., 1988; Regents lectr. UCLA, 1990; Meek indsl. lectr. Ohio State U., 1990; McElvane lectr. U. Wis., 1992; Gomberg lectr. U. Mich., 1992; vis. faculty mem. Princeton U., 1996—, Norwegian U. Sci. & Tech., 2002. Assoc. editor Jour. Stat. Physics, Jour. Chem. Physics, Phys. Rev., Proceedings Nat. Acad. Scis.; contbr. articles to profl. jours. Recipient Elliott Cresson medal Franklin Inst., 1978, Hildebrand award Am. Chem. Soc., 1986, Peter J. Debye award Am. Chem. Soc., 1992, medal Norwegian U. Sci. & Tech., 2002; Welch Found. fellow, 1974 Fellow Am. Phys. Soc. (Langmuir award 1989); mem. AAAS, Nat. Acad. Scis. Clubs: Early Am. Coppers Inc. Home: 216 Noe Ave Chatham NJ 07928-1548 Office: Princeton U Chemistry Dept Princeton NJ 08544 E-mail: fhs@princeton.edu.

STILLINGS, DENNIS OTTO, research association administrator, consultant; b. Valley City, N.D., Oct. 30, 1942; s. Harlow Cecil and Ruth Alice (Wolff) S. BA, U. Minn., 1965. Tchr. Henry (S.D.) Pub. Schs., 1965-66, Darby (Mont.) Pub. Schs., 1966-68; tech. rsch. libr., then mgr. hist. dept. Medtronic, Inc., Mpls., 1968-79; instr. humanities U. Minn., 1970-72; founding dir., then curator Bakken Libr., 1976-80; ind. antiquarian hist. cons., 1979-81; sole proprietor Archaeus Project, Kamuela, Hawaii, 1981—; exec. dir. Five Mountain Med. Cmty., 1996-97, also bd. dirs., 1996—. Cons. Ctr. for Sci. Anomalies Rsch., Ann Arbor, Mich., 1993—; bd. dirs. Dan Carlson Enterprises, Mpls. Columnist Med. Progress Through Technology, 1974-76; columnist Med. Instrumentation, 1973-76, guest editor, 1975; editor: Cyberphysiology: The Science of Self-Regulation, 1988, Cyberbiological Studies of the Imaginal Component in the UFO Contact Experience, 1989, The Theology of Electricity: On the Encounter and Explanation of Theology and Science in the 17th and 18th Centuries, 1990, Project 2010: On the Current Crisis in Health and Its Implications of the Hospital for the Future, 1992; founding editor: (jours.) Artifex, 1981-93, Archaeus, 1982-84, Healing Island. Fellow Am. Inst. Stress; mem. Assn. Sci. Study Anomalous Phenomena, Bioelectromagnetics Soc., Soc. Sci. Exploration. Avocations: Jungian psychology, golf, fishing, travel. E-mail: dstillings@kohalacenter.org.

STILLINGS, IRENE ELLA GRACE CORDINER, foundation executive; b. Boston, Aug. 17, 1918; d. Matthew Wilson and Susan F. (Mason) Cordiner; m. Gordon A. Stillings, May 13, 1945; children: David Gordon, Susan Irene. Student, Radcliffe Coll., 1936-39; diploma, Burdett Coll., 1941. Sec., bookkeeper Boston Refrigerator Co., 1941-42; sec., tchr. Burdett Coll., 1942-44; sec., bookkeeper Gertrude Rittenburg, Boston, 1944-46. Town chmn. Heart Fund, Woodland, Maine, 1953-61; Brownie leader Girl Scouts U.S., 1954-58; pres. Woodland Woman's Club 1961-63; sec. PTA, 1961-62; chmn. Baileyville Superintending Sch. Com., 1962-64; chmn. women's activities Nat. Found., East Washington County, 1959-61; pres. Hosp. Aid, 1961-63; chmn. Newcomers Coll. group YWCA, 1965-66, chmn. theatre group, 1968-70, pres. Suburbanites, 1970-71; Stamford (Conn.) chmn. Expt. in Internat. Living, 1965-68; bd. dirs. YWCA of Stamford, 1969-78, chmn. antique show, 1960-77, chmn. devotion, 1970-92, ann. Antique Show benefit, 1970-77; pres. New Suburbanites, Stamford, 1994-95. Mem. Mass. Hort. Soc., St. Luke's Guild (treas. 1954-63), Radcliffe Club, Stamford Woman's Club (treas. 1975-79, program com., co-chmn. Am. home dept. 1974, 75, pres. 1981-83, bd. dirs. 1981—, 2d v.p. fin. 1979-81, 83-85, 87-89, chmn. bldg. investment 1979-81, parliamentarian 1990—. pres., newcomers/suburbanites, 1994-95), Theta Alpha Chi. Episcopalian. Home: 277 W Hill Rd Stamford CT 06902-1708

STILLMAN, ALFRED WILLIAM, JR. electrical engineer; b. Biloxi, Miss., Sept. 11, 1942; s. Alfred William and Marie Ann (Hengen) S.; children: Shannon Lynn, Laura Marie. AA, Am. River Coll., 1966; BSEE, BS in Applied Math., Calif. Poly. State U., 1970, MS in Applied Math., 1973; ME in Indsl. Engring., Tex. A&M U., 1976; postgrad. studies in Elec. Engring., N.J. Inst. Tech., 1977; PhD in Mgmt., Calif. Coast U., 1984. Cert. profl. logistician, instr. Calif. C.Cs. Engring. intern U.S. Army Material Command, Texarkana, Tex., 1973-75, electronic sys. staff maintenance engr. Fort Monmouth, N.J., 1975-77; mgr. mil. tactical data sys. integrated logistics support Office of Project Mgr. ARTADS, 1977-78; tactical ADP ILS mgr., ILS dir. CORADOM, 1978-79; engring. mgr. regional dist. office Office of Project Mgr. Firefinder Hughes Aircraft Co., Fullerton, Calif., 1979-80; prof. sys. acquisition mgmt. Dept. Def. Sys. Mgmt. Coll., Ft. Belvoir, Va., 1980-82; integrated logistics support engring. specialist advanced sys. divsn. Northrop Corp., Poco Rivera, Calif., 1982-83; program mgmt. rep. space sys. group Rockwell Internat., Downey, 1983-84; product assurance project engr. Space Sta. Sys. divsn. Rockwell Internat., 1984-85, mgr. product support, 1985-86; sr. mgr. ILS Amex Sys., Inc., Compton, Calif., 1986-88; dir. ILS NavCom Def. Electronics, Inc., Huntington Beach, 1988-91. Pres. AWS Assocs. Calif., Inc., El Monte, 1983—; corp. v.p., divsn. pres. HOPE Assocs., Inc., Huntington Beach, 1983—. With USAF, 1962-66. Mem. IEEE, Am. Mgmt. Assn., Am. Inst. Indsl. Engrs. (sr.), Soc. Logistics Engrs. (sr.), Am. Def. Preparedness Assn., Am. Security Coun., Acacia, Tau Beta Pi. Presbyterian. Home: 12020 226th St Unit B Hawaiian Gardens CA 90716-1379 Office: 7071 Warner Ave Ste F202 Huntington Beach CA 92647-5495 E-mail: aes@genesis1st.com., bill@stillman.cc.

STILLMAN, ELINOR HADLEY, retired lawyer; b. Kansas City, Mo., Oct. 12, 1938; d. Hugh Gordon and Freda (Brooks) Hadley; m. Richard C. Stillman, June 25, 1965 (div. Apr. 1975). BA, U. Kans., 1960; MA, Yale U., 1961; JD, George Washington U., 1972. Bar: D.C. 1973, U.S. Ct. Appeals (10th cir.) 1975, U.S. Ct. Appeals (9th cir.) 1976, U.S. Ct. Appeals (2d cir.) 1976, U.S. Ct. Appeals (5th cir.) 1983, U.S. Ct. Appeals (4th cir.) 1985, U.S. Supreme Ct. 1976. Lectr. in English CUNY, 1963-65; asst. editor Stanford (Calif.) U. Press., 1967-69; law clk. to judge U.S. Dist. Ct. D.C., Washington, 1972-73; appellate atty. NLRB, 1973-78; asst. to solicitor gen. U.S. Dept. Justice, 1978-82; supr. appellate atty. NLRB, 1982-86, chief counsel to mem. bd., 1986-88, 94-00, chief counsel to chmn. bd., 1988-94; ret., 2000. Mem.: D.C. Bar Assn., Order of Coif, Phi Beta Kappa. Democrat.

STILLMAN, JEANNE BETSOCK, public health administrator, consultant; b. Bethlehem, Pa., Dec. 15, 1942; d. Paul Thomas and Juliana Habera Betsock; m. David George Stillman, 1965; children: J. Alexander, Gregory D., Juliana E. C. BA, Am. U., 1964; MSPH, U. N.C., 1971; postgrad., Columbia U. Sch. Pub. Health, 1979-81. Assoc. dir. Quaker Svc./AFSC, Lome, Togo, 1969-70; from instr. to lectr. health adminstrn. Sch. Pub. Health U. N.C., Chapel Hill, 1971-74, rsch. assoc. Population Ctr., 1971-74; staff assoc., Tunisia project mgr. The Population Coun., N.Y.C., 1982-83; dir. N.Y. office Inst. for Devel. Tng., 1989-93; Nigeria project mgr. The Africa-Am. Inst., 1993-96; prin. Strategies for Devel., Inc., Hastings-on-Hudson, N.Y., 1998—; dep. dir. devel. The Children's Village, Dobbs Ferry, NY, 2002—. Cons. to numerous internat. and U.S. devel. orgns., including Africa-Am. Inst., CONGO, Acad. for Edn. Devel., IPPF, Cath. Relief Svcs., CTE, Inc., Austrian Relief Com., Columbia U. Ctr. for Population and Family Health, RONCO, Battelle Mem. Inst., Downstate Med. Ctr., UN Population Fund, UN, UNHCR, Ford Found., Hastings Ctr., 1970—; mem. NGO adv. com. UN Population Fund, N.Y.C., 1998. Assoc. editor, contbr. International Encyclopedia of Population, 2 vols., 1982; editor: (tng. manuals) Training Course in Women's Health, 2nd edit., 11 vols., 1993; editor, writer: UNHCR Manual for Health Services in Afghan Refugee Camps, 1985; project dir.: (video) Population and People of Faith, 1991 (N.Y. Internat. Film Festival Bronze medal 1992). Ch. coord. Habitat for Humanity, Hastings-on-Hudson, 1997—2000; vol. Internat. Microcredit Summit Meeting of Couns., N.Y.C., 1998; bd. sec. Greater Westchester Youth Orch. Assn., Valhalla, N.Y., 1997-99; parent fund vol. Phillips Exeter Acad., 1998-; mem. Ch. Vestry, 2001—. Mem. APHA, Westchester Assn. Devel. Officers, UN Assn. USA (Westchester chpt., bd. dir. 2002—), Am. Freedom Assn. Democrat. Episcopalian. Avocations: reading, theater, music. Office: Strategies for Development Inc 166 Edgars Ln Hastings On Hudson NY 10706-1108 Fax: (914) 478-7859. E-mail: jbs@stratdev.com.

STILLMAN, JOYCE L. artist, educator, writer, illustrator, consultant; b. N.Y.C., Jan. 19, 1943; d. Murray W. and Evelyn (Berger) Stillman. BA, NYU, 1964; student, Art Students League, 1965, Pratt Inst., 1972; MFA, L.I. U., 1975; postgrad., Calif. Inst. Integral Studies, 1994—. Tchr. N.Y.C. Pub. Schs., 1964-71; artist, 1974-76, Louis K. Meisel Gallery, N.Y.C., 1975-84, Tolarno Gallery, Melbourne, Australia, 1976—, Allan Stone Gallery, N.Y.C., 1990—; founder CoCreative Inst. Art, Fingerlakes Region, N.Y. Vis. assoc. prof. Towson State U., 1982; tchr. Tompkins Cortland C.C., 1988; lectr. Cornell U., 1990; founder Ithaca Women Artists Salon, Artistic Applications Decorative Arts Ctr. One-woman shows include Ctrl. Hall Gallery, Port Washington, 1975, Tolarno Gallery, Melbourne, 1976, Louis K. Meisel Gallery, N.Y.C., 1977, 1980—82, Heckscher Mus., Huntington, N.Y., 1980, Holtzman Gallery, Towson (Md.) State U., 1982, Roslyn Oxley Gallery, Sydney, 1976, 1982, Tomasulo Gallery, Union Coll., N.J., 1983, Stages Keuka Coll., Keuka Park, N.Y., 1985, New Visions, Ithaca, N.Y., 1989, Her-Chambliss, Hot Springs, Ark., 1990, Artist on the Lake, Hector, N.Y., 1992, Mus. Modern Art Christmas Card Collection, 1994, Arnot Mus., Elmira, N.Y., 2002, , over 75 group shows. Mem. Literacy Vols. Am. Recipient Flower Painting award, Artist's Mag., 1986, Distinctive Merit award, Art Dir.'s Club 58th Ann., 1979; grantee Pub. Svc., N.Y. State Creative Artist's, 1979. Mem.: AAUW, Nat. Assn. Women Artists. also: 203 S Genesse St Montour Falls NY 14865 Home: 112 Brooklyn Ter Odessa NY 14869-9786

STILLMAN, MARGARET D. library director; m. Peter R. Stillman; children: Lindsay H. and Walker H. Forehand. BA in Edn., U. Richmond, 1973; MA in Edn., Va. Commonwealth U., 1974; MLS, U. Md., 1977. Mem. staff to dir. Chesapeake (Va.) Pub. Libr. Sys., 1975-85, dir., 1985—. Chmn. State Adult Literacy Initiative, 1989-95; mem. Govs. Rural Econ. Devel. Task Force, 1990-92, U. Va. Continuing Edn. Ctr. Council, 1990-94; bd. dirs. United Way Hampton Rds., 1995—, Vol. Hampton Rds., 1996-98, Va. Stage Co., 1979-85 (v.p. 1981-82), Colonial Girl Scouts, 1993-95, Cultural Alliance, 1985-91, Tidewater Red Cross, 1980-83. Recipient Outstanding Young Career Woman of Va. award, 1978, Outstanding Profl. Woman, 1993. Mem. Pub. Libr. Assn. (bd. dirs. 1997-98, chmn. leadership dev. com. 1997), Libr. Va. Found. (bd. dirs. 1996—), WHRO Found. (bd. dirs. 1997—). Office: Chesapeake Public Library 298 Cedar Rd Chesapeake VA 23322-5598 Home: 3924 Oak Dr E Chesapeake VA 23321-5905

STILLMAN, MARTHA, interior designer; b. Chgo., Nov. 8, 1924; d. Frederick Arthur and Eva Mable (Ihle) Niestadt; m. Charles Harvey Stillman, Sept. 6, 1947; 1 child, Ann Elizabeth. Student, Beloit (Wis.) Coll., 1943-45; BS in Interior Design/Architecture, Northwestern U., 1947. Interior designer Interiors - Martha Stillman, New Canaan, Conn., 1961—. Cons. in field. Pres. Wilmette Jrs. Infant Welfare Soc., 1953-60; mem. women's bd. Chgo. Infant Welfare Soc., 1957-60, Women's Rep.; advisor Girl Scouts U.S.A. Mem. Assn. Interior Designers (sec., bd. govs. 1964-75), Am. Soc. Interior Designers, Phi Beta Phi. Republican. Mem. United Ch. of Christ. Clubs: Woodway Country (Darien, Conn.); Skytop (Pa.). Avocations: tennis, golf, fishing. Home and Office: 85 Blueberry Ln Concord MA 01742-4709

STILLMAN, MARTIN J. physical science research administrator, bioinorganic chemist; b. London, June 4, 1947; Can. citizen; BSc, U. East Anglia, 1969, MSc, 1970, PhD in Chemistry, 1973. Fellow in chemistry U. Alta., Edmonton, Can., 1973-75; from asst. prof. to assoc. prof. U. Western Ont., London, Can., 1975-86, prof. chemistry Can., 1986—, dir. Ctr. Chemistry and Physics Can., 1994—. Mem. Can. Inst. Chemistry, Am. Chem. Soc. Office: Univ Western ON Ctr Chem Phys P&A Bldg Rm 102 London ON Canada N6A 3K7 E-mail: stillman@uwo.ca.

STILLMAN, MICHAEL ALLEN, dermatologist; b. N.Y.C., Apr. 12, 1943; s. Aaron and Anne (Turansky) S.; m. Susan Fuchs, July 8, 1973; children: Julie, Jeremy. BA, Clark U., 1963; MD, SUNY, 1967. Diplomate Am. Acad. Dermatology. Med. intern Maimonides Hosp., Bklyn., 1967-68; dermatology resident NYU Med. Ctr. and Bellevue Hosp., N.Y.C., 1970-73; pvt. practice Mt. Kisco, N.Y., 1973—. Cons. in dermatology U.S. Mil. Acad., West Point, N.Y., 1973-75. Contbr. essays and articles to profl. jours. and newspapers. Bd. trustees South Salem (N.Y.) Libr., 1990-98; boys varsity tennis coach John Jay H.S., Katonah, N.Y., 1996. Capt. USAF, 1968-70, Vietnam. Decorated Combat Inf. badge. Fellow Am. Soc. Dermatol. Surgeons, Am. Acad. Dermatology; mem. N.Y. State Med. Soc., Noah Worcester Dermatology Soc. Avocations: tennis, jogging, writing. Home: 33 Mead St Waccabuc NY 10597-1107 Office: PO Box 268 Mount Kisco NY 10549-0268

STILLMAN, NINA GIDDEN, lawyer; b. N.Y.C., Apr. 3, 1948; d. Melvin and Joyce Audrey (Gidden) S. AB with distinction, Smith Coll., 1970; JD cum laude, Northwestern U., 1973. Bar: Ill. 1973, U.S. Dist. Ct. (no. dist.) Ill. 1973, U.S. Dist. Ct. (ea. dist.) Wis. 1979, U.S. Dist. Ct. (no. dist. trial bar) Ill. 1983, U.S. Ct. Appeals (7th cir.) 1974, U.S. Supreme Ct. 1981, U.S. Dist. Ct. (ctrl. dist.) Ill. 1994, U.S. Dist. Ct. (ea. dist.) Tex., 1996, U.S. Dist. Ct. (Colo.), 1999, U.S. Dist. Ct. (ND) 2002. Assoc. Vedder, Price, Kaufman & Kammholz, Chgo., 1973-79, ptnr., 1980—. Adv. bd. occupational health and safety tng. program U. Mich., Ann Arbor, 1980-83; adj. faculty Inst. Human Resources and Indsl. Rels., Loyola U., Chgo., 1983-86, bd. advisors, 1986—. Author: (with others) Women, Work, and Health: Challenge to Corporate Policy, 1979, Occupational Health Law: A Guide for Industry, 1981, Employment Discrimination, 1981, Personnel Management: Labor Relations, 1981, Occupational Safety and Health Law, 1988; contbg. author: Occupational Medicine: State of the Art Reviews, 1996; contbr. articles to profl. jours. Legal advisor, v.p. Planned Parenthood Assn. Chgo., 1979—81; sec. jr. governing bd. Chgo. Symphony Orch., 1983; trustee Merit Sch. Music, 2000—, vice chmn. bd. trustees, 2001—. Recipient Svc. award Northwestern U., 1994. Mem.: ABA (occupl. safety and health law com. 1978—), Human Resources Mgmt. Assn. Chgo. (bd. dirs. 1986—88, officer), Am. Inns of Ct. (v.p. Wigmore chpt. 1988—89), Chgo. Bar Assn. (chmn. labor and employment law com. 1986—87), Northwestern U. Sch. Law Alumni Assn. (pres. 1991—92), Univ. Club Chgo. (bd. dirs. 1988—2001, sec. 1999—2000, v.p. 2000—01), The Chgo. Com., Econ. Club Chgo., Lawyers Club, Smith Coll. Club Chgo. (pres. 1972). Avocations: travel, reading, the arts, collecting art. Office: Vedder Price Kaufman & Kammholz 222 N La Salle St Ste 2600 Chicago IL 60601-1100

STILLMAN, RICHARD JOSEPH, retired army officer, consultant, publisher writer; b. Lansing, Mich., Feb. 20, 1917; m. Darlene Slater, Nov. 15, 1941 (dec. Oct. 1992); children: Richard, Thomas, Ellen. BS, U. So. Calif., 1938; postgrad., Harvard U., 1938-39; MS, Syracuse U., 1950, PhD, 1955; postgrad., Command and Gen. Staff Sch., 1943, Army War Coll., 1959-60, NATO Def. Coll., 1960-61. Commd. 2d lt. U.S. Army, 1938, advanced through grades to col., 1955, ret., 1965; faculty mem. NATO Def. Coll., 1961-63; dir. Ctr. for Econ. Oppty. and Mgmt. Devel., Ohio U., Athens, 1965-67; prof. bus. adminstrn. Ohio U., 1965-67; prof. mgmt. U. New Orleans, 1967-82; pres. R.J. Stillman Co., New Orleans, 1982—. Author: (novels) U.S. Intantry: Queen of Battle, 1965, Do It Yourself Contracting to Build Your Own Home, 1974, Your Personal Financial Planner, 1981, Dow Jones Industrial Average: History and Role in an Investment Strategy, 1986, Small Business Management, 1981, General Patton's Timeless Leadership Principles, 1997—98, (video) , 1999, The Life and Times of Gen. George S. Patton, Jr., 2002, Guide to Personal finance, 5th edit., 1988; co-author (with J. Page): How to Use Your Personal Computer to Manage Your Personal Finances, 1987; co-author: (with M.F. Riggs) General Patton's Best Friend: The Story of G.S. Patton, Jr. and His Beloved Dog, Willie, 2001; contbr. articles. Mem. Mayor's Mill Adv. Com., New Orleans; apptd. spl. advisor on mil. affairs New Orleans region C. of C., 2001. Decorated Legion of Merit, Bronze star, Luxembourg Order of the Crown, Cross of Merit La. NG, 2001; named to Hon. Order Ky. Cols.; Maxwell scholar, 1949-50; recipient Paratrooper Badge, Plaque Nat. D-Day Mus., State Scouters award Boy Scouts Am., 1955, Stillman prize and professorship named in his honor U. New Orleans, two Gold and a Silver medal Louisiana State Sr. Olympics, 2000, Outstanding Tchr. award U. New Orleans, 2000, Gen. Patton award Gen. Patton Meml. Mus., 2001, honoree 60th Anniversary La. Maneuvers, 2001; jogging track named in his honor U. New Orleans, 2002. Mem. Army Navy C.C., Plimsoll Club of World Trade Ctr. Avocations: swimming, jogging, public speaking.

STILLMAN, ROBERT DONALD, government official; b. Chgo., Sept. 27, 1929; s. Arthur Joseph and Grace Ellen (McLean) S.; m. Joan Ellen Caspersen, 1963 (dec. May 1993); children: Nancy, Barbara, John. BE in Chem. Engring., Yale U., 1950; MBA, Harvard U., 1952. With orgn. planning dept. FMC Corp., San Jose, Calif., 1954-57; assoc. Payson & Trask, N.Y.C., 1957-62, gen. ptnr., 1962-72; exec. v.p., treas., dir. AEA Investors Inc., 1972-92; assoc. adminstr. for investment U.S. SBA, Washington, 1994-95; v.p. investment funds Overseas Pvt. Investment Corp., 1995—. Lt. USAF, 1952-54. Mem. Univ. Club (Washington and N.Y.C.), Yale Club (N.Y.C.), Tau Beta Pi, Sigma Xi, Alpha Chi Sigma. Office: Overseas Pvt Investment Corp 1100 New York Ave NW Washington DC 20527-0001

STILLWAGON, GARY BOULDIN, radiation oncologist; b. Memphis, Dec. 30, 1951; s. Jack Wright and Ida Jean (Bouldin) S.; m. Leta Fern Miller, Jan. 20, 1979. BS in Physics, Ga. Inst. Tech., 1974, MS in Nuclear Engring., 1975, PhD, 1978; MD, U. Tenn., 1983. Diplomate Nat. Bd. Med. Examiners, Am. Bd. Radiology in Radiation Oncology; cert. FLEX, 1983. Med. physicist Meth. Hosp., Memphis, 1974; rsch. asst. Ga. Inst. Tech., Atlanta, 1975-78; radiation safety officer, physicist VA Med. Ctr., Memphis, 1978-80, cons. radiation safety, 1980-83; fellow in radiation oncology Johns Hopkins U. and Hosp., Balt., 1983-87; asst. prof. oncology and radiology Johns Hopkins U. Sch. Medicine, 1987—. Vis. rschr. radiobiology lab. U. Utah, 1978; com. mem., site visitor, radiation therapy oncology group, coop. group Nat. Cancer Inst., 1989—; cons. in field. Contbr. articles to profl. jours. Active Boy Scouts Am., Bapt. Ch. Sunday Sch. Dept. of Energy fellow, 1976-78, Clin. fellow Am. Cancer Soc., 1986-87. Fellow Am. Coll. Radiology; mem. AAAS, AMA, Health Physics Soc., Am. Assn. Physicists in Medicine, Am. Nuclear Soc., Am. Soc. Therapeutic Radiology and Oncology, Am. Soc. Clin. Oncology, Sigma Xi. Republican. Home: 655 River Chase Rdg NW Atlanta GA 30328-3568 Office: 1136 Cleveland Ave Ste 119 Atlanta GA 30344-3618

STILLWAGON, WESLEY WILLIAM, corporate professional; b. Allentown, N.J., Sept. 16, 1940; s. Wesley L. and Catherine Cecilia (O'Malley) S.; children: Wesley William Jr., Matthew P., Beth Anne. AAS in Electronics Tech., USN Equivalency, 1961; BS in Psychology, Trenton State U., 1974. Cert. tchr., N.Y., N.J., NASA instr., signal corp instr. Quality control tech. RCA Astro, Princeton, N.J., 1962-68, tng. supr., 1968-74; mgr. skills tng. and quality control RCA G & CS, Camden, N.J., 1978-82; field engr. Rsch. Cottrell, Somerville, 1975-76; mgr. skills tng. Loral Electronic Systems, Yonkers and Bronx, N.Y., 1976-78; mgr. sales tng. Honeywell MicroSwitch, Freeport, Ill., 1982-83; mgr. job devel. and tng. Mainstream Access, N.Y.C., 1983-85; generation tng. mgr. Penelec/GPU, Johnstown, Pa., 1985-90; co-owner Wes Stillwagon Cons., Bus. Svcs., North Plainfield, N.J., 1990-94; internal cons. KPMG Peat Marwick, Montvale, 1994—; principal HallowQuest, Inc., 1997—, GnosTek, LLC, 2000—. Adj. faculty Hofstra U., Hempstead, Long Island, N.Y. Author: Human Factors Simulator Training Qualification, 1987, The Role of the Individual in Sound Process Control and Achieving Business Objectives, New Approach Speeds Simulator Design and Procurement, Improving the Competitive Edge Through Human Performance Engineering, The Comprehensive Performance Improvement Handbook; contbr. Cost Accounting for Training and Development Handbook, 4th edit.; contbr. articles to profl. jours., including Trustee mag. Am. Hosp. Assn. Vol. chief projectionist Union County Arts Ctr., Rahway, N.J. Mem. Pitts. Jung

Soc., Mid-Atlantic Fossil Utility Trainers Assn. (bd. dirs. 1989-90). Democrat. Episcopalian. Avocations: theatre organ, fishing, exploring, photography, analytical psychology. Home and Office: 80 Mali Dr North Plainfield NJ 07062 E-mail: wstillwagon@hallowquest.com.

STILLWELL, WALTER BROOKS, III, lawyer; b. Whitehall, Wis., July 30, 1946; s. Walter Brooks Jr. and Selpha T. (Everson) S.; m. Carolyn E. Laws, Dec. 20, 1992; children: Walter, Haviland. BA cum laude, Wake Forest U., 1968; JD, U. Ga., 1971. Bar: Ga. 1971, U.S. Dist. Ct. (so. dist.) Ga. 1971, U.S. Ct. Appeals (D.C. cir.) 1976, U.S. Ct. Appeals (11th cir.) 1981, U.S. Dist. Ct. (no. dist. 1996) Ga., U.S. Supreme Ct., 1977. Assoc. Hunter, Maclean, Exley & Dunn, P.C., Savannah, Ga., 1971-74, ptnr., 1974—; dir. First Nat. Bank, 2002—. Adv. dir. Century South Bank of Coastal Region, N.A., 1993-2001; v.p. and dir. W.E.T., Inc., 1991-96; adv. bd. Savannah Econ. Devel. Authority, 1996-2000. Alderman City of Savannah, 1974-92, mayor-pro-tem, 1990-92; chmn. Chatham County Bd. Elections, 1999—. Mem. State Bar of Ga. (real property sect., exec. com. 1986-93, chmn. 1992), Am. Coll. Real Estate Lawyers, Savannah Bar Assn. (pres. 1999-2000). Democrat. Baptist. Office: Hunter Maclean Exley & Dunn PC 200 E Saint Julian St Savannah GA 31401-2700 E-mail: BStillwell@HunterMaclean.com.

STILSON, WALTER LESLIE, radiologist, educator; b. Sioux Falls, S.D., Dec. 13, 1908; s. George Warren and Elizabeth Margaret (Zager) S.; m. Grace Beall Bramble, Aug. 15, 1933 (dec. June 1984); children: Carolyn G. Palmieri, Walter E., Judith A. Stirling; m. Lula Ann Birchell, June 30, 1985. BA, Columbia Union Coll., 1929; MD, Loma Linda U., 1934. Diplomate Am. Bd. Radiology, Nat. Bd. Med. Examiners. Intern White Meml. Hosp., Los Angeles, 1933-34; resident radiology Los Angeles County Gen. Hosp., 1934-36; instr. radiology Loma Linda (Calif.) U. Sch. Medicine, 1935-41, asst. prof., 1941-49, exec. sec. radiology, 1945-50, assoc. prof., 1949-55, head dept. radiology, 1950-55, prof. radiology, 1955-83, chmn. dept. radiology, 1955-69, emeritus prof., 1983—. Chief radiology service White Meml. Hosp., Los Angeles, 1941-65, Loma Linda U. Med. Ctr., 1966-69; chmn. dept. radiologic tech. Sch. Allied Health Professions, 1966-75, med. dir. dept. radiologic tech., 1975-83. Contbr. articles to health jours. Fellow Am. Coll. Radiology; mem. AAAS, Los Angeles Radiol. Soc. (sec. 1960-61, treas. 1961-62, pres. 1963-64), Radiol. Soc. N.Am., Am. Roentgen Ray Soc., N.Y. Acad. Sci., Inland Radiol. Soc. (pres. 1971), Alpha Omega Alpha. Republican. Adventist. Avocations: photography, classical music, travel. Home: 25045 Crestview Dr Loma Linda CA 92354-3414 Office: Loma Linda Radiol Med Group 11234 Anderson St Loma Linda CA 92354-2804

STILWELL, CHARLOTTE FINN, vocational counselor; b. San Francisco, Oct. 31, 1947; d. Frederick William and Helen Carolyn (Watson) Finn; Bobby Gene Stilwell, Dec. 17, 1937; children: Robert, Shelley, James, Joel. AA, St. Petersburg Jr. Coll., 1967; BS, Fla. State U., 1969; MA, U. South Fla., 1971; attended, U. S.C., 1972. Nat. cert. counselor; cert. sch. counselor. Dir. tutorial program Hillsborough County Schs., Tampa, Fla., 1971-72, tchr., counselor, 1972-73, h.s. counselor, 1973-77; vocat. counselor Pinellas County Schs., Clearwater, 1977—. Dist. coord. Counseling for High Skills Kans. State, 1992—. Vol. Suicide & Crisis Ctrs., Tampa, St. Vincent DePaul's Soup Kitchen, St. Petersburg, Fla., 1993, Toy Shop, 1994-95, Spl. Olympics, 1996. General Electric Found. fellow. Mem. Am. Counseling Assn., Am. Sch. Counselor Assn. (Am. Sch. Counselor of Yr. 1995), Fla. Counseling Assn., Fla. Sch. Counselor Assn. (v.p. post secondary 1993-95), Phi Delta Kappa (historian 1993—), Pinellas Sch. Counselor Assn. (pres. 1991-95). Republican. Avocations: oil painting, snow skiing, sports. Office: PTEC Clearwater 6100 154th Ave N Clearwater FL 33760-2140

STILWELL, WILLIAM EARLE, III, psychology educator, retired military officer; b. Cin., July 28, 1936; s. William Earle Jr. and Frances (Hunt) S. AB, Dartmouth Coll., 1958; MS, San Jose State U., 1966; PhD, Stanford U., 1969. Lic. counseling psychologist, Ky.; cert. psychologist Assn. State of Provincial Psychology Bds. Rsch. assoc. Am. Inst. Rsch., Palo Alto, Calif., 1967-69; prof. psychology U. Ky., Lexington, 1969—. V.p. Ednl. Skills Devel., Lexington, 1969-85. Author: Psychology for Teachers and Students, 1981; mem. editl. bd. Counsel Edn. and Supervision, 1980-87. Assigned to patron nine, USNR, 1960-63, active reserve in Wash. area, 1965-83, exec. ofcr., 1979-82. Recipient Natl. Defense Armed Forces Reserve with cluster, Teachers Who Make a Difference Awd., UK Coll. of Edn., 1998, Svc. award, Coun. Univ. Depts. Clin. Psychology, 1998, Study Web Academic Excellence Awd., 1999, Web Homework Spot award, 2000. Mem. APA, Coun. Counseling Psychology Tng. Programs (Svc. award 2001), Am. Assn. Advancement Profl. Psychology, Am. Ednl. Rsch. Assn. (v.p. 1980-82), Ky. Psychol. Assn., Ky. Sch. Counseling Assn. (v.p. 1979-80, 81-82), Ohio Soc. of the Colonial Wars, Res. Officers Assn. U.S. (life), Stanford Alumni Assn. (life). Avocations: hypertext mark up language, fishing in Ontario. Home: 1919 Williamsburg Rd Lexington KY 40504-3013 E-mail: westil3@uky.edu.

STILWILL, BELLE JEAN, record company executive, printing company owner; b. Mackay, Idaho, Oct. 27, 1955; d. Allen LeRoy Stilwill and Galia Vee (Larter) Stilwill Dodd. Student, Ricks Coll., 1974-79, Def. Language Inst., 1980. Quality control Best Foods, Hermiston, Oreg., 1972-73; leader dance band Ricks Coll., Rexburg, Idaho, 1975-77; reporter Standard Jour., 1976-77; news editor Chronicle-News, St. Anthony, 1978; editor-in-chief The Scroll Ricks Coll., 1979-80; exec. asst. Rapid Printers, Monterey, Calif., 1981-82; corp. acct. Color-Ad Printers, 1983-95, Bayshore Press, Scotts Valley, 1995—, v.p., 1995—; owner Stilwill & Hoover Group LLC. Author (record albums) 1st Step, 1988 (Sam Segal award 1988), Mixed Signals, 1989 (Sam Segal award 1990, Album of Month Sta. KOFE Radio Idaho), Lovin' Arms, 1990 (Sam Segal award 1991). Faculty scholar Ricks Coll., 1979-80. Mem. NAFE, NARAS, Nat. Assn. Ind. Record Distributors, Broadcast Music Industry. Home: 11611 Hidden Valley Rd Carmel Valley CA 93924-9241 Office: Bayshore Press 103 Whispering Pines Dr Ste E Santa Cruz CA 95066-4782

STIMMEL, BARRY, cardiologist, internist, educator, university dean; b. Bklyn., Oct. 8, 1939; s. Abraham and Mabel (Bovit) S.; m. Barbara Barovick, June 6, 1970; children: Alexander, Matthew. BS, Bklyn. Coll., 1960; MD, SUNY, Bklyn., 1964. Diplomate: Nat. Bd. Med. Examiners, Am. Bd. Internal Medicine. Resident Mt. Sinai Hosp., N.Y.C., 1964-65, 67-69; asst. dean admissions and student affairs Mt. Sinai Sch. Medicine, CUNY, 1970-71, assoc. dean, 1971-81, asst. prof. medicine, 1972-75, assoc. prof., 1975-83, prof. medicine and med. edn., 1984—, assoc. dean acad. affairs, 1975-81, assoc. attending physician, 1975-83, acting chmn. dept. med. edn., 1979-94, dean admissions, acad. affairs and student affairs, 1981-94, dean grad. med. edn., 1994—, attending physician, 1984—, Katherine and Clifford Goldsmith prof. medicine (cardiology), 1998—. Mem. com. planning, priorities and evaluation N.Y. Met. Regional Med. Program, 1971-73; adv. com. Nat. Ctr. Urban Problems CUNY, 1970-71; adv. com. methadone maintenance Office of Drug Abuse Svcs. State N.Y., 1976-79; sci. adv. bd. Nat. Coun. Drug Abuse, 1978-84, N.Y. State Bd. Profl. Med. Conduct, 1983-97; bd. dirs. Am. Soc. Addiction Medicine, N.Y. State Coun. on Grad. Med. Edn., Greater N.Y. Hosp. Assn. Task Force on Health Manpower. Author: Heroin Dependency: Medical Social and Economic Aspects, 1975, Cardiovascular Effects Mood Altering Drugs, 1979, Pain, Analgesia, Addiction, 1984, Ambulatory Care, 1983, The Facts about Drug Use, 1993, Drugs Abuse and Social Policy in America: The War That Must Be Won, 1996, Pain and Its Relief Without Addiction, 1997, Alcoholism, Drug Addiction and the Road to Recovery: Life on the Edge, 2002; editor Advances in Alcohol and Substance Abuse, 1980-91, Jour. Addictive Diseases, 1991—; assoc. editor Am. Jour. Drug and Alcohol Abuse, 1979-85; contbr. chpts. to books, articles to profl. jours. Served with M.C. USNR, 1965-67. Mem. AAUP, Am. Assn. Physicians Assts. (adv. bd. 1972-73), Am. Assn. Higher Edn., Soc. Study of Addiction to Alcohol and Other Drugs, Assn. Med. Edn. and Rsch. Substance Abuse, Inst. Study of Drug Addiction, Am., N.Y. heart assns., Am., N.Y. State socs. internal medicine, Soc. Internal Medicine County of N.Y. (dir.), Am. Coll. Cardiology, Greater N.Y. Coalition on Drug Abuse, NYS Coun. on Grad. Medical Edn., N.Y. Acad. Medicine, Nat. Coun. Alcoholism, Rsch. Soc. on Alcoholism, Am. Ednl. Research Assn., Am. Fedn. Clin. Rsch., Am. Soc. Addiction Medicine. Office: Mt Sinai Sch Med 5 E 98th St Fl 3 New York NY 10029-6501 E-mail: barry.stimmel@mssm.edu.

STIMPERT, MICHAEL ALAN, agricultural products company executive; b. Madisonville, La., Aug. 21, 1944; s. Warren Eugene and Louisa (Beale) S.; m. Kim Kathleen Agee, Apr. 17, 1970 (div. 1985); 1 child, Kelly Kathleen; m. Helen Marie Evans, June 27, 1987; children: Katherine Helen, Michael Adam. Student, Washburn U., 1962-64, U. Copenhagen, 1964; BA, Western Res. U., 1967; MBA, Harvard U., 1974. Asst. to group v.p. Gold Kist Inc., Atlanta, 1974, mgr. internat. div., 1975-80, dir. spl. markets and staff services, 1980-81, group v.p., 1982-86; v.p. ops. and govt. affairs Golden Peanut Co., 1986-89, exec. v.p., 1989-95; sr. v.p. Gold Kist Inc., 1996—. Chmn. bd. dirs. Sunpower, Inc., Athens, Ohio, Trade Network, Livermore, Calif., G.C. Properties, Atlanta, Agra Tech Seeds, Inc., Atlanta, G.K. Pecans, Atlanta, Luker Inc., Augusta, Ga., GKX Inc., Agana, Guam, Fundatropicos, Turrialba, Costa Rica; immediate past chmn. Global Health Action, Atlanta; chmn. Agra Trade Financing, Inc., Atlanta; bd. dirs. iTrade Network, Livermore, Calif.no Mem. adv. bd. dirs. Internat. Svc. Assn. for Health Devel. Edn. Project, 1982-91; bd. dirs. Global Health Action. Lt. (j.g.) USN, 1967-72, Vietnam. Mem. Assn. for Corp. Growth, Japan-Am. Soc. Ga., Harvard Bus. Sch. Club Atlanta, Cherokee Town and Country Club. Democrat. Roman Catholic. Office: Gold Kist Inc 244 Perimeter Center Pkwy NE Atlanta GA 30346-2397

STIMPSON, CATHARINE ROSLYN, English language educator, writer; b. Bellingham, Wash., June 4, 1936; d. Edward Keown and Catharine (Watts) S. AB, Bryn Mawr Coll., 1958; BA, MA, Cambridge U., Eng., 1960; PhD, Columbia U., 1967. Mem. faculty Barnard Coll., N.Y.C., 1963-80; prof. English, dean of grad. sch., vice provost grad. edn. Rutgers U., New Brunswick, N.J., 1980-92, Univ. prof., 1991—; chmn. bd. scholars Ms. Mag., N.Y.C., 1981-92; dir. fellows program MacArthur Found., 1994-97; Univ. prof., dean Grad. Sch. Arts and Sci. NYU, N.Y.C., 1998—. Author: Class Notes, 1979, Where the Meanings Are, 1988; founding editor: Signs: Jour. Women in Culture and Society, 1974-81; book series Women in Culture and Society, 1981; columnist Change Mag., 1992-93. Chmn. N.Y. Coun. Humanities, 1984-87, Nat. Coun. Rsch. on Women, 1984-89 ; bd. dirs. Stephens Coll., Columbia, Mo., 1982-85; trustee Bates Coll., 1990—; pres. Assn. of Grad. Schs., 2000-01. Hon. fellow Woodrow Wilson Found., 1958; Fulbright fellow, 1958-60; Nat. Humanities Inst. fellow New Haven, 1975-76; Rockefeller Humanities fellow, 1983-84 Mem. MLA (exec. coun., chmn. acad. freedom com., 1st v.p., pres. 1990), PEN, AAUP, NOW, PBS (bd. dirs. 1994-2000), Legal Def. and Edn. Fund (bd. dirs. 1991-96). Democrat. Home: 29 Washington Sq W Apt 15C New York NY 10011-9199 Office: NYU 6 Washington Sq N New York NY 10003-6668 E-mail: catharine.stimpson@nyu.edu.

STIMPSON, RITCHIE PLES, retired military officer; b. Black Mountain, N.C., Mar. 22, 1917; s. David Ples and Lydia Hinson Stimpson; m. Marjorie Spruce, May 3, 1942; children: Ritchie P. Jr., David Fleming. BS in Physics, Furman U., 1940. Commd. 2nd lt. USAF, 1941, advanced through grades to col., 1953; squadron comdr. 13th Tactical Reconnaissance Squadron, 1942-44; dir. ops. 24 Composite Wing, Borinquen Field, P.R., 1946-47; liaison officer Armed Forces Spl. Weapons Project to Strategic Air Command., Offutt AFB, Nebr., 1950-52; dir. plans and negotiations Joint U.S. Asst. Adv. Group, Madrid, 1957-59; staff officer Joint Chiefs of Staff, Washington, 1960-61, Weapons Sys. Evaluation Group/Office of Sec. of Def., 1964-67; comdt. Air Force ROTC detachment Auburn (Ala.) U., 1967-71; ret. USAF, 1971. Owner Ritch Stimpson Co., Inc., College Station, Tex., 1975-82; ind. writer, Dallas, 1982-93. Author: The Protestant Church and Bible Disregard the Truth, 1989, "Is It True?" Answers to Questions About the Bible, 1992. Decorated Commendation medals (2), Identification Badge, Outstanding Unit award. Mem. Air Force Assn., Greater Dallas Ret. Officers Assn., Greater Dallas Ret. Officers Assn. Investment Club, Oakridge Country Club, Furman U. Paladin Club. Republican. Methodist. Avocations: golf, travel, reading, bridge, gardening. Home: 2729 Laurel Oaks Dr Garland TX 75044-6939

STIMSON, EVELYN MARIE REINHEIMER, chemist; b. Callicoon, N.Y., Aug. 31, 1938; d. Clarence F. and Viola Emily (Weyrauch) Reinheimer; m. Thomas C. Stimson, Nov. 21, 1962 (dec. Oct. 1992). BA, Harpur Coll., 1960; MA, Brandeis U., 1962; PhD, SUNY, Binghamton, 1971. Tchg. asst. Brandeis U., Waltham, Mass., 1960-62; sr. lab. technician, NIH fellow, rsch. assoc. Cornell U., Ithaca, N.Y., 1963-67, 71-86; rsch. asst. SUNY, Binghamton, 1967-71; with First Nat. Bank N.J., Bridgewater, 1986-88; rsch. assoc. Harvard U. Med. Sch., Boston, 1989-97; sr. rsch. assoc. U. Cin. Coll. Medicine, 1997—. Owner ERS Technicorp, Groton, Mass., 1993—. Contbr. articles to profl. jours. Mem. AAAS, Am. Chem. Soc., Am. Protein Soc., Am. Peptide Soc., N.Y. Acad. Sci. Avocations: choral singing, backpacking, camping. Home: 4098 California Rd Okeana OH 45053-9650 Office: Dept Pharmacology UC Coll of Medicine 231 Bethesda Ave Cincinnati OH 45267-0001 E-mail: stimsoer@email.uc.edu.

STIMSON, PAUL GARY, pathologist; b. Ogden, Utah, Jan. 11, 1932; s. Margaret Georgia (Payne) S.; m. Ardell Elizabeth Quiser, June 27, 1958; children: Gregory, Louise, Janiece. DDS, Loyola U., Chgo., 1961; MS, U. Chgo., 1966. Diplomat Am. Bd. Forensic Odontology (pres. 1990-91), Am. Bd. Oral Pathology. From assoc. prof. to prof. U. Tex. Dental Br., Houston, 1965-97, emeritus prof., 1997—. Co-editor: Forensic Odontology, 1977, Forensic Dentistry, 1997. With USN, 1951-54, Korea. Fellow Am. Acad. Oral Pathology, Am. Acad. Forensic Scis.; mem. Masons (past master 1988-89, grand orator 1992), Omicron Kappa Upsilon. Presbyterian. Office: U Tex Dental Br PO Box 20068 Houston TX 77225-0068

STIMSON, RICHARD ALDEN, writer; b. Hamden, Conn., Jan. 18, 1923; s. Frank Giles and Susie Alden (Brown) S.; m. Joan D. Crabb, Apr. 19, 1947; 1 child, Richard Edgar Frank. BA, Yale U., 1943. Chief computer ops. U.S. Naval Hosp., Groton, Conn., 1985-90; asst. prof. fin. Conn. State U., Willmantic and Danbury, 1980-85; assoc. prof. U. New Haven (Conn.), 1980-82; nat. coord. U.S.A., Internat. Simultaneous Policy Orgn., 2001—. Author: Playing with the Numbers: How So-called Experts Mislead Us About the Economy, 1999, (e-book) Thirteen Generations in the New World: Life Styles of the Less Rich and Famous, 2001. Sgt. U.S. Army, 1943—46, maj. Res. ret. Office: c/o Westchester Press 2132-J Crossing Way High Point NC 27262 E-mail: westcpress@aol.com., stimso1@juno.com.

STINCHCOMB, ALBERT MONROE, producer, designer/realtor; b. Battle Creek, Mich., Apr. 6, 1944; s. Loid Monroe and Barbara Hough (Parks) S. Student, U. Mich., CUNY. Chmn. Stinchcomb and Monroe, Inc., N.Y.C., N.J., 1979—, Majestic Entertainment, Ltd., Jersey City, 1984—; pres. 275 Corp., 1983-95, Majestic Devel. Corp., Jersey City, 1989-95; exec. v.p. The Gyncyn Corp., 1994—, CJS Mgmt., 1996—. Owner Majestic Theatre, 1980-95. Appeared in numerous prodns. including Life With Father, 1954, Wizard of Oz, 1955, She Stoops to Conquer, 1985; produced numerous prodns. including Macbeth, 1986, Royal Shakespear Co., 1987, The Golden Handshake, 1987, Why Father Won't Come Home, 1987, Scarpa the Magician, Liberty, The Ballet, 1988, The Adams Letters, 1988. Pres. Liberty Ctr. for Performing Arts, Jersey City, 1984-94; bd. dirs. Fraunces Tavern Mus., 1977-94, Acad. of Art, 1987—, Ednl. Art Team, 1988-95; active Preservation N.J. Mem. Nat. Film Inst., Am. Soc. Interior Designers, Sons of Revolution, Soc. Colonial Wars, Saint Nicholas Soc., N.J. Assn. Realtors (Burgdorff Realtors Million Dollar Club). Home: Grove Cottage PO Box 487 Jersey City NJ 07303 E-mail: amsa@dellnet.com.

STINCHCOMB, AUDREY THOMPSON, respiratory care educator; b. Phila., May 2, 1944; d. Lewis and Theresa (Thompson) James; divorced; children: Davida, Dawn. ASc, Midlands Tech. Coll., 1976; BSc, U. S.C., 1991; MSc, So. Wesleyan U., 1997. Registered respiratory therapist. Therapist Baptist Med. Ctr., Columbia, S.C., 1976-78; supr. pulmonary lab. Dorn Med. Ctr., 1978-90; dept. head Orangeburg (S.C.)-Calhoun Tech. Coll., 1990—. Cons. Manor Care Nursing Home, Columbia, 1981-90. Mem. Am. Assn. Respiratory Care. Baptist. Avocations: exercise, sewing, reading. Office: Orangeburg Calhoun Tech Coll 3250 Saint Matthews Rd NE Orangeburg SC 29118-8299 E-mail: stinchcomba@org.tec.sc.us.

STINE, CATHERINE MORRIS, artist; b. Roanoke, Va., Jan. 12, 1953; d. Richard Dengler and Dorothy Geraldine (Cornog) S.; m. Norris Jewett Chumley, Oct. 22, 1983; children: Jack H.M., Nathaniel B. BFA, Mus. Sch. Fine Arts, Boston, 1975. Art dir. Ear Mag., N.Y.C., 1980-83; asst. art dir. Jacmel Jewelry, 1984-88; textile designer Style Coun., 1989-90, Ruvetta Designs, N.Y.C., 1990—; represented by Margaret Bodell Gallery, 1999—, Red Piano Gallery, Saint Helena, S.C. Curator Bratton Gallery, N.Y.C., 1989. One-woman shows include Plant Factory, Boston, 1974, Sixth Sense Gallery, N.Y.C., 1986, Pinnacle Awards/Am. Women in Radio and TV, N.Y.C., 1987, Limelight Club, N.Y.C., 1987, Parker-Bratton Gallery, N.Y.C., 1987, Bratton Gallery, N.Y.C., 1988, Carol Getz Gallery, Miami, Fla., 1990, Sunnen Gallery, N.Y.C., 1993, 94, Galley B.A.I., N.Y.C., 1996, Margaret Bodell Gallery, N.Y.C., 2000; group shows include Mus. Fine Arts Gallery, Boston, 1974, Williamsburg, Bklyn., 1982, ABC No Rio, N.Y.C., 1983, 85, City Without Walls Gallery, Newark, 1984, 85, Parsons Gallery, N.Y.C., 1985, author, illustrator: The Halcyon, 1984, Hudson Valley Exhbn., Poughkeepsie, 1985, Parker-Bratton Gallery, N.Y.C., 1986, Bratton Gallery, 1989, Neo Persona, N.Y.C., 1990, Tribeca 148, N.Y.C., 1991, Helio Gallery, N.Y.C., 1991, S. Bitter Larkin, N.Y.C., 1992, Sarah Rentschler Gallery, N.Y.C., 1992, Dooley-Le Cappellaine, N.Y.C., 1993, NYU Law Sch., 1994, Margaret Bodell Gallery, N.Y.C., 2001; reviewed by Art in Am., 2001; represented in permanent collections Art Mus. Western Va., Paramount Pictures, others; represented by Margaret Bodell Gall., N.Y.C.; author: Wild at Heart/Race to the Finish, 2002. Mem. Fifteenth St. Quaker Meeting, N.Y.C. Curatorial grantee Artist Space, N.Y.C., 1989. Mem. Soc. Childrens' Book Writers and Illustrators. Avocations: writing for young readers. Home: 214 E 17th St Apt 2 New York NY 10003-3647

STINE, EARLE JOHN, JR. radiologist; b. Feb. 21, 1932; s. Earle John and Ione Genevieve (Best) S.; m. Bernita Evelyn Emerson, Aug. 27, 1954; children: Renee Evelyn, Mark Earle, John Emerson. AB, Albion Coll., 1954; MD, Wayne State U., 1958. Diplomate Am. Bd. Radiology, Am. Bd. Nuclear Radiology. Intern Bon Secours Hosp., Grosse Pointe, Mich., 1958-59, gen. surgery resident, 1959-61; pvt. practice medicine Pigeon, 1961-62, Marcus, Iowa, 1962-65, Ida Grove, 1965-75; resident radiology U. Iowa, Iowa City, 1975-78; staff radiologist St. Joseph Med. Ctr., Ponca City, Okla., 1978-80; med. dir. radiology Jackson County Meml. Hosp., Altus, 1980-95; med. missions Karaganda, Kazakstan, 1995-98; locum tenens radiology, 1998—. Mem. AMA. Republican. Methodist. Avocations: loomweaving, oil painting. Office: Diagnostic Imaging Cons 1133 E Maple PO Box 679 Altus OK 73522-0679 E-mail: earle@stinesystems.com.

STINE, J(AMES) LARRY, lawyer; b. Birmingham, Ala., Dec. 18, 1950; s. James O. and Helen M. Stine; m. Kathryn Stokely, June 10, 1972; children: Kathryn Anne DeLoach, Laura Elizabeth Seybt, Amanda Leigh Franklin. BS cum laude, U. Ga., 1972, JD cum laude, 1975. Bar: Ga., U.S. Dist. Ct. (no. dist.) Ga. 1975, U.S. Dist. Ct. (mid. dist.) Ga. 1997, U.S. Ct. Appeals (11th cir.) 1992, U.S. Ct. Appeals (6th cir.) 1998, U.S. Dist. Ct. (ea. and we. dists.) Ark. 1999. Trial atty. U.S. Dept. of Labor, Atlanta, 1975-82, regional counsel, 1982-89; atty. Thompson, Mann & Hudson, 1989-92; of counsel Wimberly & Lawson, 1992-95; prin. Wimberly Lawson Steckel, 1995—. Bd. dirs. King's Bridge, Atlanta. Author: Wage and Hour Law: Compliance and Practice, 1995, Family and Medial Leave Act, 2001. Mem. Decatur Kiwanis (pres. 1988-89). Office: Wimberly Lawson & Steckel Ste #400 3400 Peachtree Rd NE Atlanta GA 30326-1107 E-mail: jls@wimlaw.com.

STINE, JEFFREY KIM, environmental historian, curator; b. San Diego, Feb. 25, 1953; s. Howard Henry and Dorothy (Graham) S.; m. Marcel Chotkowski LaFollette, July 28, 1986. BA, U. Calif., Santa Barbara, 1975, PhD, 1984. Cons. House Com. on Sci. and Tech., Washington, 1984-85; cons. U.S. Army Corps of Engrs., 1985-89; curator of engring. and environtl. history Smithsonian Inst., 1989—. Cons. Carnegie Commn. on Sci., Tech. and Govt., Washington, 1990, Libr. of Congress, 1995; commr. U.S., Can., Mex. Trilateral Com. on Environ. Edn., 1992-95. Editor: (series) Technology and the Environment, 1993-2001, (book reviews) Tech. and Culture, 1987-94; author: (Congl. report) A History of Science Policy in the United States, 1940-85, 1986; co-editor: Technology and Choice, 1991; author: Mixing the Waters: Environment, Politics, and the Building of the Tennessee-Tombigbee Waterway, 1993, Twenty Years of Science in the Public Interest, 1994; co-editor: Going Underground: Tunneling Past, Present, and Future, 1998. Trustee Pub. Works Hist. Soc., 1990-97, 99-2001, pres., 2002--; pres. Am. Soc. for Environ. History, 1999-01. Recipient Congl. fellow Am. Hist. Assn., 1984, Weyerhaeuser award Forest History Soc., 1984, James Madison prize Soc. for History in the Fed. Govt., 1992, Wesley Johnson prize Nat. Coun. Pub. History, 1993, Abel Wolman award Pub. Works Hist. Soc., 1994, Charles Thompson prize Soc. for History in the Fed. Govt., 1999. Mem. Am. Hist. Assn., Soc. for History of Tech., Am. Soc. for Environ. History, Forest History Soc., Pub. Works Hist. Soc., Nat. Coun. on Pub. History. Democrat. Office: Smithsonian Inst Nat Mus Am History Washington DC 20560-0629 E-mail: stine@si.edu.

STINE, ROBERT HOWARD, retired pediatrician; b. Nov. 1, 1929; s. Harry Raymond and Mabel Eva (Newhard) S.; m. Lois Elaine Kihlgren, Oct. 22, 1960; children: Robert E., Karen E., Jonathan N. BS in Biology, Moravian Coll., 1952. Diplomate Am. Bd. Pediatrics, Am. Subbd. Pediatric Allergy, Cojoint Bd. Allergy and Immunology. Intern St. Luke's Hosp., Bethlehem, Pa., 1960-61, resident in surgery, 1961-62; physician Jefferson Med. Coll., Phila., 1956-60; resident in pediatrics U. N.Y., Syracuse, 1962-64; resident in allergy Robert A. Cooke Inst. Allergy Roosevelt Hosp., N.Y.C., 1964-65; clin. instr. pediatrics U. Ill., Chgo., 1965-71; mem. courtesy staff Proctor Community Hosp., Peoria, 1966-77, mem. active staff, 1977—, chmn. dept. medicine, 1988—; pres. elect. med. staff, 1990-91; pres. med. staff, 1991-92; mem. teaching staff St. Francis Hosp., Peoria, 1969—; clin. instr. pediatrics Rush-Presbyn. St. Luke's Hosp., Chgo., 1971—2002; ret. Lt. (j.g.), USN, 1953-56. Fellow Am. Acad. Pediatrics, Am. Acad. Allergy Asthma and Immunology, Am. Coll. Allergy and Asthma, Am. Assn. Cert. Allergists; mem. Ill. Soc. Allergy and Clin. Immunology, Peoria Med. Soc. (pres.-elect 1993, pres. 1994), Christian Med. and Dental Soc. Home: 105 Hollands Grove Ln Washington IL 61571-9623

STINEHART, ROGER RAY, lawyer; b. Toledo, Jan. 27, 1945; s. Forrest William and Nettie May (Twyman) S.; m. Martha Jean Goodnight, Sept. 19, 1970; children: Amanda Jean, Brian Scott. BS, Bowling Green (Ohio) State U., 1968; JD, Ohio State U., 1972. Bar: Ohio 1972. Fin. analyst Gen. Electric, Detroit, 1968-69; assoc. Gingher & Christensen, Columbus, Ohio, 1972-76, ptnr., 1976-80; sr. v.p., gen. counsel, sec. G.D. Ritzy's, Inc., 1983-85; ptnr. Jones, Day, Reavis & Pogue, 1980-83, 85—. Adj. prof. law Capital U., Columbus, 1976-79; mem. adv. com. Ohio securities divsn. Dept. Commerce, Columbus, 1979—; fellow Columbus Bar Found., 1992—; adv. bd. The Entrepreneurship Inst., 1992-95. Contbr. Ohio State U. Coll. Law Jour., 1970-72. Gen. counsel, trustee Internat. Assn. Rsch. on Leukemia and Related Diseases, 1975—; v.p., trustee Hospice of Columbus, 1978-80; trustee Cen. Ohio chpt. Leukemia Soc. of Am., Columbus, 1983-93, v.p., 1985-87; trustee Ohio Cancer Rsch. Assocs., Columbus, 1983—, v.p., 1990—. With USMCR, 1963-68. Mem. ABA (bus. law com., franchise law com.), Ohio State Bar Assn. (corp. law com., franchise law com.), Columbus Bar Assn. (securities law com., chmn. 1981-83, bus. law com., franchise law com.), Rotary Club (Columbus), Sigma Tau Delta, Beta Gamma Sigma. Home: 2155 Waltham Rd Columbus OH 43221-4149 Office: Jones Day Reavis & Pogue 1900 Huntington Ctr Columbus OH 43215-6103

STINES, FRED, JR. publisher; b. Newton, Iowa, Mar. 16, 1925; s. Fred and Nella (Haun) S.; m. Dorothy G. McClanahan, Sept. 5, 1953 (dec.); children: Steven, Scott, Ann; m. Mary K. Devin, Sept. 12, 1989. B.C.S., U. Iowa, 1949. With Meredith Corp., Des Moines, 1949-90, sales promotion and mdse. mgr., 1955-63, advt. dir., 1963-66, pub., 1966-73, pub. dir. mag. div., 1973-76, v.p., gen. mgr. books and newspapers, 1976-83, sr. v.p., 1983-87, pres. book pub., 1986-90, corp. v.p. spl. projects, 1988-90; pres., prin. Concepts in Mktg., 1990—. Cert. instr. Dale Carnegie courses, 1958-63. Bd. dirs. Des Moines Ballet Assn., North Am. Outdoor Group, Mpls., 1992-95; bd. dirs., v.p. Jr. Achievement of Ctrl. Iowa. Served with AUS, 1946-49. Named Farm Marketing Man of Year, 1972 Mem. Future Farmers Am. Found. (nat. chmn. 1971), Rotary Internat., Des Moines Golf and Country Club, Phi Gamma Delta (sect. chief 1983, nat. bd. dirs. 1985-89), Alpha Kappa Psi, Alpha Delta Sigma. Clubs: Des Moines Golf and Country (dir., pres. 1981, pres. Ednl. Found.).

STING, (GORDON MATTHEW SUMNER), musician, songwriter, actor; b. Newcastle Upon Tyne, Eng., Oct. 2, 1951; s. Ernest Matthew and Audrey (Cowell) Sumner; m. Frances Eleanor Tomelty, May 1, 1976 (div. Mar. 1984); children: Joseph, Fuschia Katherine; m. Trudie Styler, Aug. 22, 1992; children: Brigette, Michael, Jake, Eliot, Paulina, Giacomo Luke. Grad., Warwick U.,

Coventry, Eng.; hon. doctorate, Northumbria U., 1992; hon. degree, Berklee Coll. Music, Boston, 1994. Schoolmaster, Newcastle Upon Tyne, Eng., 1975-77; songwriter, singer, bass player with rock group The Police, 1977-86; mng. dir. Kaliedescope Cameras, London, from 1982; singer, songwriter, 1986—. Albums recorded with The Police include Outlandos D'Amour, 1978, Reggatta De Blanc, 1979, Zenyatta Mondatta, 1980, Ghost in the Machine, 1981, Synchronicity, 1983, The Singles; Every Breath You Take, 1986; stage appearance: (Broadway) Three Penny Opera, 1989; solo albums include The Dream of the Blue Turtles, 1985, Bring On The Night, 1986, Nothing Like the Sun, 1987, The Soul Cages, 1991, Ten Summoner's Tales, 1993 (Grammy award, Best Long Form Music Video, 1994), Demolition Man (soundtrack), 1993, Mercury Falling, 1996, Brand New Day, 1999; appeared in films Quadrophenia, 1979, The Secret Policeman's Other Ball, 1981, Brimstone and Treacle, 1982, Dune, 1985, The Bride, 1985, Plenty, 1985, Julia and Julia, 1987, Stormy Monday, 1988, Resident Alien, 1990, The Grotesque, 1995, Lock, Stock and Two Smoking Barrels, 1998; voice artist tv series Captain Planet and the Planeteers, 1990-92; rec. soundtracks for films including Brimstone and Treacle, 1982, Party, Party, 1982, The Secret Policeman's Other Ball, 1982, The Emperor's New Groove, 2000. Recipient 16 Grammy awards with The Police and as solo artist, 13 BMI awards, 4 Brit awards; Downbeat mag. Readers' Poll Pop/Rock Musician of Yr. award, 1989, Downbeat mag. Readers' Poll Pop/Rock group award, 1989, Internat. Rock award for Video Legend, 1991, Star on the Hollywood Walk of Fame, 2000, Golden Globe award Kate and Leopold, 2001. Mem. Performing Rights Soc., Amnesty Internat., Rainforest Found. (co-founder). Office: Kathryn Schenker Assocs 12th Fl 1776 Broadway New York NY 10019 also: Firstars 3520 Hayden Ave Culver City CA 90232-2413 also: A & M Records Inc 70 Universal City Plz Universal City CA 91608-1011

STINGER, CHARLES LEWIS, history educator; b. Waverly, N.Y., Mar. 19, 1944; s. Gilbert B. and Helen Olmstead Stinger; m. Patricia Mary Freres, June 15, 1968; children: Owen A., Katherine L. BA, Hobart Coll., 1966; MA, Stanford U., 1967, PhD, 1971. Instr. dept. history Stanford (Calif.) U., 1970-72; asst. prof. dept. history SUNY, Buffalo, 1973-77, assoc. prof. dept. history, 1977-84, prof. dept. history, 1984—, assoc. dean faculty social scis., 1994-98, sr. assoc. dean Coll. Arts and Scis., 1998—2001, interim dean Coll. Arts and Scis., 2001—. Author: Humanism and the Church Fathers, 1977, The Renaissance in Rome, 1985 (Marraro prize Am. Hist. Assn. 1985). Fulbright fellow Italy, 1969-70, Villa I Tatti fellow Harvard U. Ctr. for Italian Renaissance Studies, Florence, Italy, 1972-73. Office: SUNY Buffalo Dept History Park Hall Buffalo NY 14260-4130 E-mail: stinger@acsu.buffalo.edu.

STINGER, HENRY J. engineer; b. Mpls., Nov. 22, 1920; s. Glen Arden and Ann Edna; m. Santhe Notaras, Aug. 30, 1922; children: Lawrence, David, Susan. BSEE, U. Minn., Mpls.; ME, Harvard U.; PhD, MIT. Reactor supr. Savannah River Atomic Energy Commn., Savannah, Ga.; rsch. assoc. Gen. Mills., Mpls., DuPont Epl. STN, Wilmington, Del.; cons. Wilmington and Devon , Pa. Lt. USN, 1943—46. Mem.: IEEE. Achievements include patents for 30 patents stratospher baloons, woven fabrics. Avocations: ham radio, ballooning, skiing, ice skating. Home: 119 Devonwood Ln Devon PA 19333

STINI, WILLIAM ARTHUR, anthropologist, educator; b. Oshkosh, Wis., Oct. 9, 1930; s. Louis Alois and Clara (Larsen) S.; m. Mary Ruth Kalous, Feb. 11, 1950; children— Patricia Laraine, Paulette Ann, Suzanne Kay. BBA, U. Wis., 1960, MS, 1967, PhD, 1969. Planner cost acct. Kimberly-Clark Corp., Niagara Falls, N.Y., 1960-62; from asst. prof. to assoc. prof. Cornell U., Ithaca, 1968-73; assoc. prof. U. Kans., Lawrence, 1973-76; prof. anthropology U. Ariz., Tucson, 1976—, prof. family and cmty. medicine, 1978—; panelist anthropology program NSF, 1976-78; cons. NIH, 1974—. Mem. Ariz. Cancer Ctr., 1995—; adj. prof. Nutritional Scis., 1997—; head dept. anthropology U. Ariz., 1980-89, prof. public health, 1998—; panelist NRC/NSF Grad. Fellowship Program, 1991-95. Author: Ecology and Human Adaptation, 1975, Nature, Culture and Human History - A Biocultural Introduction to Anthropology (with Davydd J. Greenwood), 1977, Physiological and Morphological Adaptation and Evolution, 1979 (with Frank E. Poirier and Kathy B. Wreden) In Search of Ourselves: An Introduction to Physical Anthropology, 1990, 5th edit., 1994; field editor phys. anthropology The Am. Anthropologist, 1980-83; editor-in-chief Am. Jour. Phys. Anthropology, 1983-89; assoc. editor Nutrition and Cancer, 1981-95; cons. editor Collegium Antropologicum, 1985—. Mem. Gov.'s Adv. Council on Aging, State of Ariz., 1980-83. Nat. Inst. Dental Rsch. tng. grantee, 1964-68; Clark Found. grantee, Cornell U., 1973; Nat. Dairy Coun. grantee, 1985-88; Wenner-Gren Found. grantee, 1991—; fellow Linacre Coll., Oxford, 1985; vis. fellow U. London, 1991. Fellow AAAS (steering group sect. H 1987-91), Am. Anthrop. Assn., N.Y. Acad. Scis.; mem. Am. Assn. Phys. Anthropologists (exec. com. 1978-81, pres. 1989-91), Human Biology Assn. (exec. com. 1978-81), Soc. for Study Social Biology, Am. Soc. Nutritional Scis., Am. Soc. on Aging, Sigma Xi. Home: 6240 N Camino Miraval Tucson AZ 85718-3025 Office: U Ariz Dept Anthropology Tucson AZ 85721-0001 E-mail: stini@u.arizona.edu.

STINNETT, JAMES LEBARON, psychiatrist; b. Washington, Aug. 1, 1938; s. Harry Caskie and Frances LeBaron S.; m. Deborah G., Dec. 23, 1963 (div. June 1988); children: Jonathan L., David A., Nathaniel C.; m. Carol Anderson, Nov. 1, 1991. AB, Princeton U., 1960; MD, U. Penn., 1965. Dir. cons. psychiatry Hosp. U. Penn., Phila., 1978—. Dir. clin. svcs. dept. psychiatry U. Penn., 1994-98, vice dean clin. affairs, 1991-92. Sr. trustee Episcopal Acad., Merion, Pa., 1980—. Major U.S. Army, 1970-72. Office: Hosp U Penn Philadelphia PA 19104 E-mail: stinnett@mail.med.upenn.edu.

STINNETT, MARK ALLAN, lawyer; b. Jackson, Miss., Sept. 15, 1955; s. Allan J. and Joan (Mouser) S.; m. Carol Fowler, Sept. 5, 1992; children: Michelle, Michael. BA in Polit. Sci. with honors, Tex. Tech U., 1977; JD with honors, U. Tex., 1980. Bar: Tex. 1980, U.S. Dist. Ct. (no. and ea. dists.) Tex. 1981, U.S. Ct. Appeals (5th cir.) 1993. Founding ptnr., mng. ptnr. Stinnett Thiebaud & Remington L.L.P., Dallas, 2000—; shareholder Cowles & Thompson, 1986—2000. Mem. Philmont Ranch com. Boy Scouts Am. Mem. ABA, Am. Bd. Trial Advocates, Am. Inns of Ct., Am. Coll. Legal Medicine, Am. Health Lawyers Assn., State Bar of Tex., Dallas Bar Assn., Tex. Assn. Def. Counsel, Dallas Assn. Def. Counsel, Def. Rsch. Inst., Inns Ct. (barrister Dallas chpt. 1988-91), Tex. Ctr. Legal Ethics and Professionalism, Nat. Eagle Scout Assn., Philmont Staff Assn. (pres. 1994-98). Avocations: backpacking, softball, military history. Home: 5541 Mallard Trce Frisco TX 75034-5058 Office: Stinnett Thiebaud & Remington LLP 1445 Ross Ave Ste 4800 Dallas TX 75202-2702 E-mail: mstinnett@strlaw.net.

STINSMUEHLEN-AMEND, SUSAN, artist; b. Balt., Nov. 5, 1948; d. William I. and Geraldine S. (Dodds) Hamilton; m. Richard E. Amend, Nov. 27, 1987; children: Jason Stinsmuehlen, Wyatt Amend. Student, Hood Coll., U. Tex. Designer, owner Renaissance Glass Co., Austin, 1973-87; artist dba. Impresa, Inc., L.A. and Ojai, Calif., 1987-2001. Mem. Art in Pub. Places Panel, Austin, 1986-87; cons. Nat. Endowment for the Arts, Washington, 1986, 87, Cmty. Redevel. Agy., L.A., 1990-92; artist trustee Am. Craft Coun., 1988-92; lectr., lead artist Hollywood Blvd. Streetscape Team, Hollywood, Calif., 1991-94; mem. Arts Commn., Ojai, Calif., 2000; mem. Hollywood Art and Design Adv. Panel, 1999—; educator in field. One-woman shows include Mattingly Baker Gallery, Dallas, 1984, Kurland Summers Gallery, L.A., 1985, 88, 90, 92, Traver Sutton Gallery, Seattle, 1986, Habatat Galleries, Detroit, 1991, The Nest Gallery, Ojai, Calif., 1997, The Glass Gallery, Bethesda, Md., 2000; exhibited in group shows at Whatcom Mus., Bellingham, Wash., 1992-94, Finegood Art Gallery, West Hills, Calif., 1993-94, Miller Gallery, N.Y.C., 1994, The Wignall Mus., Chaffey Coll., Rancho Cucamonga, Calif., 1995, Traver Gallery, Seattle, 1995, Smithsonian Inst. Travelling Exhbn., 1999, Muckenthaler Cultural Arts Ctr., Calif., 1999, Loveland (Colo.) Mus. Gallery, 1998, 99, Fresno Art Mus., 1998, SOFA Chgo., 1998, Santa Cruz Mus. Art and History, 1999, Smithsonian Inst., 1998-2000, L.A. County Mus. Art, 1999, Orange County Mus. Art, 1999, others; represented in permanent collection Am. Airlines, Dallas, Renwick Gallery Nat. Mus. Art, Washington, The Jewish Mus., N.Y.C., The Corning (N.Y.) Mus. Glass, Detroit Inst. Arts, Leigh Yawkey Woodson Mus., Wausau, Wis., Oakland (Calif.) Mus., Wagga Wagga City Art Gallery, NSW, Australia, Nishida Mus., Toyoma, Japan, Pilchuck Glass Ctr., Stanwood, Wash., Am. Craft Mus., N.Y.C., L.A. (Calif.) County Mus. Art, Radisson Hotel, Austin, AT&T, Dallas, AT&T, N.Y.C., Marshall Fields Corp. Collection, Chgo., City of L.A., Mus. Am. Art/Smithsonian Instn., others plus numerous pvt. collections. Nat. Endowment for the Arts grantee, Washington, 1982, 88; Hauberg fellow Pilchuck Glass Sch., 2001. Mem. Glass Art Soc. (hon. life; bd. dirs. 1982-86, pres. 1984-86), Mus. Contemporary Art (L.A.), L.A. County Mus. Avocations: gardening, swimming, walking, hiking.

STINSON, ANDREA MARIA, professional basketball player; b. Mooresville, N.C., Nov. 25, 1967; BA, N.C. State U., 1991. Guard Charlotte Sting, 1997—. Career highlights include being on All-ACC Tournament team, Kodak All-Am., 1990, 91, MVP of ACC Tournament, ACC Player of Yr., 1991, winning Gold medal with 1992 Jones Cup Team, Bronze medal 1991 Pan Am. Team, playing overseas for Thiene in Italy, 1996-97 and named to Italian League All-Star Team, named to the Eastern Conf. All-Star Team, 2001, lead scorer for Charlotte Sting for 1997-2001 season. Office: Charlotte Sting 100 Hive Dr Charlotte NC 28208-7707*

STINSON, DEANE BRIAN, mortgage broker, consultant; b. Ottawa, Ont., Can., Nov. 12, 1930; s. Earl Minto and Clara Edna (Acres) S.; m. Patricia Ann Paynter, Aug. 25, 1956; children: Steven Wayne, Brian Richard, Andrew Alan. Chartered acct. With Arthur A. Crawley & Co., Ottawa, 1949-58; staff chartered acct. KMPG, Sault Ste. Marie, Ont., 1958-59, audit ptnr., 1960-79, mng. ptnr., 1980-86, sr. exec. ptnr., 1986-88; mem. Ont. Regional Mgmt. Coun.; ptnr. in charge Grant Thornton, Sault Ste. Marie, 1988-93. Pres., CEO Tille Investments Ltd., Tolstar Mgmt. Inc., 985875 Ont. Ltd.; dir. No. Breweries Ltd.; chmn. Rapids Investment Inc., CGAN. Fellow Inst. Chartered Accts. Ont.; mem. Can. Inst. Chartered Accts. (pres. chpt. 1965), Rotary (pres. 1978). Progressive Conservative. Anglican. Home: 15 Atlas Ave Sault Ste Marie ON Canada P6A 4Z2 Office: Box 23110 Sault Ste Marie ON Canada P6A 6W6 Home: 6 White Lane Rd RR #1 Goulais River ON Canada

STINSON, MARION DENNIS, regional association administrator; b. Alton, Ill., Aug. 19, 1953; s. George Washington and Clara Alevia (Keene) S.; m. Shirley Joan Cartwright, Feb. 13, 1971; children: Casey René (dec.), Marion David. AA magna cum laude, Rogers State Coll., Claremore, Okla., 1992; BA summa cum laude, Northeastern State U., Tahlequah, Okla., 1997; postgrad., Oklahoma City U., 1998—. Leadman Stresscon Inc., Tulsa, 1971-74; crane operator Gardner-Denver, Pryor, Okla., 1974-79; laborer Lone Star Industries, 1979-88; owner, mgr. sml. bus., 1988-90; concrete finisher United Bridge Constrn., Joplin, Mo., 1990-91; sec. Grand Gateway Econ. Devel. Assn., Vinita, Okla., 1991-93; coord. cmty. devel. Grand Gateway Econd. Devel. Assn., 1993-94, dir. cmty. devel., 1994-95, dir. cmty./econ. devel. Big Cabin, 1995—, dep. exec. dir., 1999—. Com. chmn. MESTA, Pryor, 1995-98; citizen's adv. com. chmn. Mayes County Commrs., Pryor, 1997-98; mem. oversight com. Multiple Local Govts., Delaware/Adair County, Okla., 1995-99; mem. Salina (Okla.) Bd. Edn., 1995-98, v.p., 1996-97, pres., 1997-98; precinct chmn. Dem. Party, Salina, 1996; chmn. bd. N.E. Okla. Little League, Salina, 1994-96; bd. dirs. Pryor Sr. Citizens, Inc., 1996, Cmty. Devel. Soc., 1995—; com. mem. Okla. Dept. Commerce, 1994-96. Recipient Acad. Achievement award Northeastern State U., 1997, scholarship Okla. Scholar Leadership Enchancement Program, 1996, Cert. of Achievement, Okla. Mcpl. League, 1995, 96, 97, 98. Mem. Okla. Floodplain Mgmt. Assn. (cert. floodplain mgr., sec. com. 1996-98), Am. Planners Assn., Salina Area C. of C. (bd. dirs. 1996), Phi Theta Kappa, Alpha Chi. Democrat. Baptist. Avocations: boating, golf, movies, family time. Office: Grand Gateway Econ Devel Assn PO Drawer B 333 S Oak Big Cabin OK 74332 E-mail: mstinson@ggeda.com.

STINSON, MARY FLORENCE, retired nursing educator; b. Wheeling, W.Va., Feb. 11, 1931; d. Rolland Francis and Mary Angela (Voellinger) Kellogg; m. Charles Walter Stinson, Feb. 12, 1955; children: Kenneth Charles, Karen Marie, Kathryn Anne. BSN, Coll. Mt. St. Joseph, 1953, postgrad., 1983; MEd, Xavier U., Cin., 1967; postgrad., U. Cin., 1981. Staff nurse contagious disease ward Cin. Gen. Hosp., 1953-54, asst. head nurse med. and polio wards, 1955, acting head nurse, clin. instr., 1955-56; instr. St. Francis Hosp. Sch. Practical Nursing, Cin., 1956-57, Good Samaritan Hosp. Sch. Nursing, Cin., 1957-65; instr. refresher courses for nurses Cin. Bd.. Edn. and Ohio State Nurses Assn. Dist. 8, 1967-70; coord. sch. health office Coll. Mt. St. Joseph, Ohio, 1969-72, instr. dept. nursing, 1974-79, asst. prof., 1979-89; RN assessor Passport program Coun. on Aging Southwestern Ohio, 1989-90, quality assurance coord. Passport program, 1990-93; quality assurance supr. Passport and Elderly Svcs. Program, 1993-94; quality assurance mgr. Coun. Aging Southwestern Ohio, 1995-2000; ret., 2000. Staff nurse St. Francis/St. George Hosp., Cin., 1988-89. Charter mem. Adoptive Parents Assn. St. Joseph Infant and Maternity Home; women's com. for performing arts series Coll. Mt. St. Joseph; chmn. by-law com. Mt. St. Joseph Nursing Honor Soc., 1996—98; active St. Antoninus Rosary Altar and Sch. Soc., St. Antoninus Athletic Club, com. chmn., 1969—70; bd. dirs. Coll. Mt. St. Joseph Alumni Assn., 1982—84, sec., 1968—69, v.p., 1969—70, pres., 1970—71, chmn. revision of constn., 1976—77; homecoming chmn. Coll. Mt. St. Joseph, 1970, co-chmn., 1977, co-chair com. to celebrate 75 years of nursing edn., 2001—02; mem. com. to plan 50th ann. of graduation Coll. Mt. St. Joseph Alumni Assn. Democrat. Roman Catholic. Mem. River Squares Club (v.p. 1967), Sigma Theta Tau (charter Omicron Omicron chpt. 1998—). Home: 5549 Cleander Dr Cincinnati OH 45238-4266 E-mail: cstinson@fuse.net.

STINSON, RAYFORD H. arts educator; b. Dublin, Nov. 13, 1929; s. William and Robbie (Singleton) S.; m. Mary-Jane Mayer, Dec. 21, 1968 (dec. July 1997); 1 child, Rayford Andrew Lawrence. BA, U. Ga., 1956; MA, Northwestern U., 1960, U. Reading, 1969; PhD, Am. Coll., 1997. Capt. USAF, Alexandria, La., 1949-54; tchr. Richmond County Sch., Augusta, Ga., 1960-62; asst. headmaster Augusta Prep. Sch., 1962-67; chmn. dept. history Savannah County Day Sch., Savannah, Ga., 1967-76; v.p. Lawrence T. Mayer, Inc., 1976-86; assoc. headmaster St. Andrew's Sch., 1986-96; prof. liberal arts Savannah Coll. Art and Design, 1996—. Home: 121 White Pine Dr Durham NC 27705-7507

STINSON, RICHARD FLOYD, retired horticulturist, educator; b. Cleve., Feb. 4, 1921; s. Floyd Earl and Helen M. (Schiemann) S.; m. Lois D. Stinson; children: Leigh, Laurie, Glenn, Paul, Cathy. BS, Ohio State U., 1943, MS, 1947, PhD, 1952. Instr. floriculture SUNY, Alfred, 1947-48; asst. prof. floriculture U. Conn., Storrs, 1948-55; asst. prof. horticulture Mich. State U., East Lansing, 1955-59, assoc. prof. horticulture, 1959-67; assoc. prof. agrl. edn. and horticulture Pa. State U., University Park, 1967-73, prof., 1973-89, sr. faculty mem., 1979-89, prof. emeritus, 1990—. Cons. in field. Contbr. articles to profl. jours. Lt. (j.g.) USNR, 1943-46. Mem. Nat. Assn. Colls. and Tchrs. Agr. (E.B. Knight Jour. award 1992), Sigma Xi, Alpha Tau Alpha, Gamma Sigma Delta, Phi Delta Kappa. Office: Pa State U 323 Agrl Adminstrn Bldg University Park PA 16802-2601 E-mail: rfs5@psu.edu.

STINSON, STANLEY THOMAS, systems analyst; b. Dothan, Ala., Dec. 17, 1961; s. Leonis and Betty Lois (Harrison) S.; m. Sharin B. Clark, Aug. 25, 1984; children: Sarah Ashley, Amy Rebecca, Rachel Elizabeth, Thomas Clark. AS in Computer Sci., Enterprise State Jr. Coll., 1982; BSBA cum laude, Troy State U., 1984; MBA, Samford U., 1989. Fin. sys. engr. NCR Corp., Birmingham, Ala., 1984-87; sr. sys. specialist Systematics Inc., 1987-88, sys. engr., 1988-90, sr. sys. engr., 1990; consulting devel. analyst Systematics, Inc., Little Rock, 1990-92; sr. sys. engr. Systematics Fin. Svcs., Atlanta, 1992-93; sr. applications programmer/analyst Capital City Bank, Tallahassee, 1993-96; sys. cons. Consultec, Inc., 1996-98; ind. contractor, 1998—2002; founder DP Answers Inc., 1999, pres., 1999—2001; sr. systems analyst Deutsche Fin. Svcs., St. Louis, 2002—. Conservative. Baptist. Avocations: golf, personal computer. Home: 5998 Peachtree Dr Hillsboro MO 63050 Office: Deutsche Fin Svcs 655 Maryville Centre Dr Saint Louis MO 63141

STINSON, THOMAS FRANKLIN, economist, educator; b. Puyallup, Wash., July 17, 1942; s. John F. and Mildred F. (Thomas) S.; m. Susie Smith, Aug. 22, 1964. BA, Wash. State U., 1964; PhD, U. Minn., 1972. Economist econ. rsch. svc. USDA, Washington, 1965-69, St. Paul, 1970-85; full prof. econs. U. Minn., 1985—. With State of Minn. Economist, St. Paul, 1987—; cons. U.S. Senate Intergovtl. Rels. Subcom., Washington, 1986, Minn. Tax Study Commn., St. Paul, 1984; mem. econ. panel Pioneer Press, St. Paul, 1987—; mem. bd. economists Star-Tribune, Mpls., 1987—. Contbr. numerous articles to profl. jours. Mem. Am. Econ. Assn., Am. Agrl. Econs. Assn., Nat. Tax Assn., Minn. Econs. Assn. (pres. 1990).

STINSON, WESLEY R. museum director, archaeologist; b. Huntington, N.Y., Mar. 9, 1950; s. Richard and Elizabeth Ann Stinson; m. Bonnie Breitkopf, May 15, 1983; 1 child, Benjamin. BA, Clark U., 1973; postgrad., U. Conn., 1975-78. Project mgr. The Arctic Co., Inc., Fairfax, Va., 1978-79; br. mgr. Memphis, 1979-80; project mgr. Commonwealth Assocs., Jackson, Mich., 1980-82; project dir. Soil Sys., Inc., Marietta, Ga., 1982; cultural resources cons., Ann Arbor, Mich., 1983-87; asst. state archaeologist N.H. Divsn. Hist. Resources, Concord, 1987-95; pres. Sargent Mus. Archaeology, 1994—, dir., 1995—. Chmn. Milford (N.H.) Dem. Com., 1988-90, Concord Dem. Com., 1995-96; state chmn. Draft Cuomo for Pres., Concord, 1991-92; mem. fin. com. N.H. Dem. Com., Concord, 1995-96. Avocations: travel, photography, woodworking, writing. Office: Sargent Mus Archaeology 20 Central St Newport NH 03773 E-mail: sargentmuseum@mediaone.net., wstinson@mediaone.net.

STIPE, EDWIN, III, mechanical contracting company executive; b. Easton, Pa., Aug. 22, 1931; s. Edwin and Rose Mildred (Blackburn) S.; m. Jean Elizabeth Boyer, Aug. 14, 1954; children: Daniel McMichael, Kelly Jean. AAS, SUNY, Binghamton, 1958. Chief engr. Joseph E. Biro & Assocs., Easton, 1958-61; with ITT Nesbitt, 1961-72, br. mgr. N.Y., 1965-67, Boston, 1967-70, N.Y.C., 1970-72; v.p. Byko-Stipe Assocs., Morristown, N.J., 1972-77; pres. Edwin Stipe, Inc., Easton, 1973—, Thermogetics, Inc., Morristown, 1977-80. Bd. dirs. Easton Heights Cemetery, 1986—, Valley Health Employee Health Network, Valley Health Svcs. Served with USN, 1951-55. Mem. ASHRAE, Assn. Energy Engrs., Two Rivers Area C. of C. (chmn. small bus. coun. 1989-91, chmn. 1991-93), Pomfret Club, Harker's Hollow Golf Club, Kiwanis. Lutheran. Home: 1 Tanglewood Rd Easton PA 18042-1374 Office: 999 Conroy Pl Easton PA 18040-6646

STIPE, JOHN RYBURN, bank executive; b. Batesville, Ark., Oct. 14, 1930; s. Ryburn Irvin and Ethel (Martin) S.; m. Mary Ann Cato, Dec. 19, 1958; children: Richard M., Roger W. BS in Agrl., U. Ark., 1953. County agt. Ark. Corp. Extension Svc., Forrest City, 1954-58; credit officer Forrest City Prodn. Credit Assn., 1958-67, pres., 1967-86, Forrest City Bank N.A., 1986—. Mem. adv. coun. Ark. Gifted and Talented Children Assn., Little Rock, 1976-82; bd. dirs. Am. Inst. Coops., Washington, 1980-84, Ark. League Savs. Inst., Little Rock, 1988-92, vice chmn., 1994-95, chmn., 1995-96. Chmn. bd. trustees East Ark. C.C., Forrest City, 1990—, Ouachita Bapt. U., Arkedelphia, Ark., 1995—; deacon, treas. bd. deacons 1st Bapt. Ch., 1972—. Capt. U.S. Army, 1946-67. Mem. Rotary (bd. dirs. Forrest City chpt.), Jaycees (Ark chpt nat dir. 1964, pres. Forrest City chpt. 1963). Democrat. Avocations: skiing, golf, fishing, travel, music. Office: Forrest City Bank NA PO Box 1935 Forrest City AR 72336-1935

STIPE, ROBERT EDWIN, design educator; b. Easton, Pa., July 18, 1928; s. J. Norwood and Ethel M. Stipe; m. Josephine Davis Weedon, 1952; children: Daniel W. Stipe, Frederick Norwood Stipe. AB in Econ., Duke U., 1950, LLB, 1953; MRP, U. N.C., 1959. Urban planning cons. City and Town Planning Assocs., Chapel Hill, N.C., 1956-57; asst. dir., prof. pub. law and govt. U. N.C. Inst. Govt., 1957-74; sr. Fulbright rsch. fellow London U., 1968-69; dir. Divsn. Archives and History N.C. Dept. Cultural Resources, Raleigh, N.C., 1974-75; vis. prof. U. N.C., Chapel Hill, 1975-77; prof. design N.C. State U., Raleigh, 1976-89, emeritus prof. design, part time prof. design, 1989—. Lectr. Inst. Advanced Studies, Bratislava, Slovak Republic, 1992-95; bd. trustees U.S. com. Internat. Coun. on Monuments and Sites, Preservation Action, Nat. Coun. on Preservation Edn., Hist. Preservation Fund N.C., Alliance for Preservation Hist. Landscapes, Old Salem Inc., Stagville Ctr. for Preservation Tech.; trustee Nat. Trust for Hist. Preservation; bd. counsellors Conservation Trust for N.C., emeritus trustee, 2002; mem. bd. adv. Nat. Alliance Preservation Commn. Author, editor more than 150 articles and publs. in fields of historic preservation, landscape conservation, design, urban planning, and planning law. Mem. Chapel Hill Design Review Bd.; trustee Chapel Hill Preservation Soc.; founder, trustee Chapel Hill HIstorical Soc. Fellow U.S. Com. Internat. Coun. on Monuments and Sites, 1986; recipient Disting. Svc. award Ruth Coltrane Cannon award, N.C. Soc. for Preservation of Antiquities, 1973, Sec. of Interior's Disting. Conservation Svc. award, 1978, Spl. award outstanding contbns. to landscape architecture Am. Soc. Landscape Archiects, N.C. chpt., 1985, Louise DuPont Crowninshield award for Superlative Lifetime Achievement in Historic Preservation, Nat. Trust for Historic Preservation, 1988, Dist. Svc. and Profl. Leadership award Nat. Coun. for Preservation Edn., 1989. Mem. Cosmos Club (Washington), Sigma Pi Kappa (First Disting. mem. 1994), Sigma Lambda Alpha (disting. mem. 1996). Home: 100 Pine Ln Chapel Hill NC 27514-4331

STIRES, MIDGE, artist, painter; b. Orange, N.J., Apr. 10, 1943; d. Charles Rounsaville and Helen Louise (Tovey) S.; m. Stuart MacReynolds Wyeth, 1966 (div. 1969); m. Peter Daumants Schnore, 1969; children: Peter H., Emils. S. BFA, Syracuse U., 1966. Painter, 1966—. One-person shows include New Arts Program, Kutztown, Pa., 1992, Riverside Gallery, Pottersville, N.J., 1994; group exhbns. include Christopher Gallery, N.Y.C., 1975, 76, 77, Hennock Gallery, N.Y.C., 1983; included in Best of Landscape Painting, 2000. Grantee Pollock-Krasner Found. Inc., 1995, Elizabeth found. for Arts, n.Y.c., 1994; recipient prize Nat. Acad. Design, N.Y.C., 1978, Best of Show award Parrish Art Museum, Southampton, N.Y., 1977. Mem. Nat. Soc. Painters in Casein and Acrylic. Avocations: mountain biking, gardening. Home: 144 Red Oak Dr Boyertown PA 19512-8963

STIREWALT, JOHN NEWMAN, coal company executive; b. Springfield, Ill., July 14, 1931; s. Newman Claude and Genevieve (Henton) S.; m. Joan Marie McCarthy, Dec. 26, 1957; children: Genevieve, Janice, James, Christopher. AB, U. Miami, 1953; grad. execs. program, Carnegie Mellun U., 1978. Salesman Kaiser Aluminum, Indpls., 1957-63; dist. sales mgr. Consol. Coal, Detroit, 1963-67, Cleve., 1967-73, gen. sales mgr. Detroit, 1973-76, asst. v.p., 1976-79; v.p. mktg. Youghiogheny and Ohio Coal Co., St. Clairsville, 1979-81; v.p. mktg. Crown Coal and Coke Co. Pitts., 1981-85, Arch Mineral, 1985-90; sr. v.p. Crown Coal & Coke Co., 1990—. Exec. reservist U.S. Dept. Interior emergency solid fuels adminstrn., 1971, U.S. Energy Dept., 1991-97. Chmn. coun. Cub Scouts, Highland, Mich., 1976; mem. Mich. Energy Task Force, 1966; pres. bd. trustees Wheeling Country Day Sch., 1980-84; trustee Wheeling Symphony; bd. dirs. Teen Challenge for New Life Inc. Served with U.S. Army, 1954-56. Mem. Wheeling Country Club, Ft. Henry Club, Symposiarchs, Vinyard Christian Fellowship, Sigma Chi. Home: RR 5 Box 137B Wheeling WV 26003-9205 Office: Crown Coal and Coke Co Pittsburgh PA 15220

STIREWALT, RICHARD ERICK KURT, computer scientist, application developer; b. Atlanta, 1968; PhD, Ga. Inst. Tech., 1997. Mem. tech. staff MITRE Corp., McLean, Va., 1992—94; rsch. scientist Ga. Inst. Tech., Atlanta, 1995—97; asst. prof. Mich. State U., East Lansing, Mich., 1998—. Mem.: IEEE. Office: Mich State U Dept of Computer Sci and Engring East Lansing MI 48824

STIRLER, KAREN SUE, special education educator, adult education educator; b. Waterloo, Iowa, June 25, 1951; d. Walter Henry and Nadine Augusta (Boege) S. BS in Vocat. Home Econs., U. No. Iowa, 1973, MA in Spl. Edn., 1982. Tchr. vocat. home econs. and sci. Randolph (Nebr.) Pub. Schs., 1976-77; tchr. spl. edn. Highland Community Sch., Riverside, Iowa, 1978-82, New Hampton (Iowa) Schs., 1982-86, Roosevelt Mid. Schs., Cedar Rapids, Iowa, 1986-92, Kennedy High Sch., Cedar Rapids, 1992—. Tchr. adult basic edn. Kirkwood C.C., Cedar Rapids, 1987-99. Mem. NEA, Am. Home Econs. Assn., Coun. for Exceptional Children, Iowa Edn. Assn., Cedar Rapids Home Econs. Assn., Cedar Rapids Tchr. Edn. Assn. Lutheran. Avocations: sewing, crafts, antiques, sports. Office: Kennedy High Sch 4545 Wenig Rd NE Cedar Rapids IA 52402-2298

STIRLING, CLARK TILLMAN, lawyer; b. Washington, July 4, 1956; s. Edwin Tillman and Genevieve (Ruffner) S.; m. Linda Poumirau, May 30, 1986; children: Stephen Tillman, Grace Elizabeth. BS, Vanderbilt U., 1979; JD, George Washington U., 1983. Bar: D.C. 1984, Alaska 1984, Calif. 1987. Clk. to Judge Cutler, State of Alaska, Palmer, 1983-84, asst. dist. atty. Anchorage, 1984-87; assoc. Archbald & Spray, Santa Barbara, Calif., 1987-91; ptnr. Law Offices Kristofer Kallman, 1991-95; pvt. practice, 1996—2000; assoc. Snyder & Strozier, 2000; ptnr. Nye, Peabody & Stirling, LLP, Santa Barbara, 2001—. Bd. dirs. Childrens Creative Project, Santa Barbara, 1992-95, Wilderness Youth Project, 1999—; pres. bd. dirs. Transition House, Santa

Barbara, 1993—; mem. centennial com. All Sts.-By-Sea, Santa Barbara, 1996—. Mem. Calif. Bar Assn., Alaska Bar Assn., D.C. Bar Assn., Santa Barbara County Bar Assn. (co-chmn. litigation sect. 1996-97, conf. of dels. 1998—), Santa Barbara Inns Ct., Soc. of Cincinnati. Republican. Avocations: writing, reading, tennis. Office: 33 W Mission St Ste 201 Santa Barbara CA 93101

STIRLING, DOUGLAS BLEECKER, JR. minister, radio host; b. Kennett Square, Pa., Nov. 30, 1959; s. Douglas Bleecker and Katherine Parsons (Eaton) S.; m. Jo Lynn Kenes, July 18, 1981. BA in Sociology, Oral Roberts U., 1981; cert. basic mgmt., U. Tulsa, 1987; MBA, Okla. State U., 1993, Sr. Profl. Human Resources, 1994. Cert. temporary staffing specialist. Data analyst MPSI, Inc., Tulsa, 1981-82, quality control coord., 1982-84, tech. writer, 1984-89, adminstrn. mgr., 1989-90, corp. communications mgr., 1990-91; human resources mgr. StairMaster Sports/Medical Products, Inc., 1991-93; mgr. br. Maxwell Staffing of Bristow, Inc., Bristow, Okla., 1993-96; human resources mgr., cons. The Maxwell Cos., Tulsa, 1996-97; human resources cons. DecisionOne Corp., King of Prussia, Pa., 1997-2000; owner Stirling Comms., 1998—2002; acct. exec. WCOJ Radio Corp., Kennett Square, 2000—. Part-time computer graphics operator Mabee Ctr. Oral Roberts U., Tulsa, 1979-97; owner franchise Subway sandwich store; adj. instr. Tulsa Jr. Coll., 1993-96. Tchr. Jr. Achievement, Tulsa, 1987-88; coach basketball Tulsa Jr. Athletic Assn., 1987; sr. pastor Kennett Sq. Bible Meth. Ch., 1997—; mem. Kennett Square Sr. Men's Baseball League; mem. Borough Coun., Kennett Sq., 1998—, pres., 2002-. Mem. Soc. Human Resource Mgmt., Tulsa C. of C. (adopt-a-sch. com. 1989). Republican. Methodist. Avocation: reading. Home: 706 Meredith St Kennett Square PA 19348-3504 Office: 112 S Union St Kennett Square PA 19348-3504

STIRLING, JAMES PAULMAN, investment banker; b. Chgo., Mar. 30, 1941; s. Louis James and Beverly L. (Paulman) S.; m. Ellen Adair Foster, June 6, 1970; children— Elizabeth Ginevra, Diana Leslie, Alexandra Curtiss. AB, Princeton U., 1963; MBA, Stanford U., 1965. Chartered fin. analyst. Vice pres. corp. fin. Kidder, Peabody & Co. (now UBS Warburg PaineWebber), N.Y.C. and Chgo., 1965-71, 84-86, sr. v.p. corp. fin., 1987—; dir. internat. investments Sears Roebuck Co., Chgo. and London, 1971-75, 77-84; asst. to sec. U.S. Dept. Commerce, Washington, 1976-77. Chmn. bd. Northwestern Meml. Mgmt. Corp., Chgo., 1989—; trustee Northwestern Meml. Hosp., Chgo., 1985—. Pres. jr. bd. Chgo. Symphony, 1968—70; mem. exec. coun. Chgo. Metropolis 2020; trustee Chgo. Symphony, 1970—75, Tchrs. Acad. for Math. Sci., 1991—95. Mem. Investment Analysts Soc., Bond Club of Chgo., Nat. Econ. Hon. Soc. Clubs: Chicago, Racquet (Chgo.); Onwentsia (Lake Forest, Ill.). Office: UBS Tower 125 S Wacker Dr Ste 2500 Chicago IL 60606-4302

STIRLING, JO LYNN, special education educator; b. Harrisburg, Pa., July 6, 1960; d. Barry Lee and Audrey Rose (Shorter) Kenes; m. Douglas R. Bleecker Stirling, July 18, 1981. BS in Spl. Edn., Northeastern State U., Tahlequah, Okla., 1991. Technician MPSI Inc., Tulsa, 1981-91; trainable mentally handicapped tchr. Arrowhead Elem. Sch., Broken Arrow, 1991-93, Broken Arrow (Okla.) Sr. H.S., 1993-96; learning support tchr. Greenwood Elem. Sch., Kennett Square, Pa., 1998—. Camp counselor CEC Camp Mentally Retarded, Ft. Gibson, Okla., 1990; pre-intern I, Roy Clark Elem, Tulsa, 1988; pre-intern II, Union 7th Grade Ctr., Tulsa, 1990; intern tchr. Arrowhead Elem. Sch., North Intermediate High Sch., Broken Arrow, Okla., 1991. Part-owner Subway Sandwiches and Salads, Broken Arrow; corp. sec., treas. Treasure-Heart, Inc. Mem. Coun. Exceptional Children, Student Okla. Edn. Assn., Rho Theta Sigma. Republican. Methodist. Avocations: reading, walking, crafts, softball. Home: 706 Meredith St Kennett Square PA 19348-3504

STIRNWEIS, SHANNON, illustrator, painter; b. Portland, Oreg., Feb. 26, 1931; s. William Theodore and Daisy Dean (Daly) S.; m. Regina Catharine Bolivar, Sept. 6, 1958; children: Kevin, Kirk, Eric. B of Profl. Arts, Art Ctr. Coll. Design, L.A., 1954. Sketchman Compton Advt., N.Y.C., 1958-60; freelance illustrator Wilton, Conn., 1960—. Author: Painting of the Wild West, 1978; designer, illustrator: Dogs of the World, 1965 (Best Book of Yr., Dog Writers 1965); prin. works include painting Parks Svc. U.S. Dept. Interior, portrait Air Force Flanker Back-Sugar-Bowl, Air Force Acad.; exhibited in group shows at N.Y. Hist. Soc., Ann. Exhbn. of Am. Illustration, U.S. Army Hist. Mus., Air Force Acad.; represented in collections Leaning Tree, Rumley, Grumbacher, U. Wyho., U. Tex., El Paso. Cpl. U.S. Army, 1954-56. Mem. Soc. Illustrators (pres. 1972-74, chmn. adv. com. 1993—), Graphic Artists Guild (founding trustee, treas. 1970), Fairfield Watercolor Group, Sharon Arts Ctr. Home: 116 Perry Rd New Ipswich NH 03071-4019

STIRRAT, WILLIAM ALBERT, electronics engineer; b. Syracuse, N.Y., Nov. 5, 1919; s. Robert William and Doris (White) S.; m. Bernice Amelia Wilson, July 13, 1958; children: Valerie Lynne, Dorothy Grace, William Ellsworth. Student, Triuna (Yaddo) Arts of the Theatre Sch., 1936, Saratoga Eastman Sch Bus., 1936-37; BS in Physics, Rensselaer Poly. Inst., 1942, postgrad., 1949-50, Rutgers U., 1951-58, Fairleigh Dickinson U., 1971. Elecs. engr. GE, Schenectady, N.Y., 1941-44; instr. physics Clarkson Coll. Tech., 1947-49; electronic engr. rsch. and devel. U.S. Army, Fort Monmouth, N.J., 1950-87; prin. engr. Eagle Tech. Logicon, Inc., Northrop Grumman Corp., Eatontown, 1987-92; pres. Stirrat Arts & Scis., Freehold, 1992—. Author: (with Alex North) Unchained Melody, 1936 (Top song of Yr. 1955, ASCAP Song of Yr. 1990, a Top Song of the Century, Acad. award nomination 1955, Top ASCAP love song of the 50s decade), Why 3? (Army award 1985); assoc. editor IEEE Transactions on Electromagnetic Compatability, 1970-76; contbr. articles to profl. jours.; patentee in field. Chmn. pub. rels. Battleground dist. Monmouth coun. Boy Scouts Am., 1970-77; mem. Rep. Congl. Leadership Coun., 1989-91; mem. Rep. Campaign Coun., 1992-93, Rep. Nat. Com., 1992-99. Mem. SAR, IEEE (editor N.J. Coast sect. Scanner 1974-75), Internat. Songwriters Assn., Palgrave Soc., Internat. Platform Assn., Am. Soc. of Composers, Authors and Publishers. Episcopalian. Achievements include origination at Schnectady New York of "rock" in 1941; origination in 1964 of the binomial pulse, advancements in electromagnetic field theory, control of interference in design of SYNCOM 1 ground stations, deception control in Tactical Fire Control System. Home and Office: 218 Overbrook Dr Freehold NJ 07728-1525

STIRTON, CHARLES PAUL, lawyer; b. Cedar City, Utah, Mar. 24, 1950; s. John K. and Idonna G. (Gower) S. BS in Math., BS in Chemistry, U. Ariz., 1972, JD, 1975. Bar: Ariz. 1975, U.S. Dist. Ct. Ariz. 1975, U.S. Ct. Appeals (9th cir.) 1975. Assoc. Laber, Lovallo & Colarich, Tucson, 1975-77; ptnr. Lovallo & Stirton, 1977-84; sole practice, 1984—. Contbr. articles to newspapers. Mem. Big Brothers Tucson, 1973-80, adv. bd. Tucson Fitness Marathon, 1984-85, adv. bd. Wellness Council Tucson, 1986. Mem. Ariz. Bar Assn., Pima County Bar Assn. (ethics com. 1982-87), Phi Beta Kappa, Order of Coif. Democrat. Roman Catholic. Avocations: running, hiking, skiing, swimming, biking. Office: 1325 N Wilmot Rd Ste 310 Tucson AZ 85712-5168

STISHER, MICKEY D. music educator; b. Greencastle, Ind., Aug. 20, 1957; s. George W. and Charlotte J. Stisher; m. Teri L. Shonkwiler; children: Shauna, Lyndee. BS, Ball State U., 1979; MusM, La. State U., 1990. Assoc. dir. of bands Jefferson City H.S., Jefferson City, Mo., 1979—82; dir. of bands Yorktown H.S., Yorktown, Ind., 1982—87; grad. asst. & conducting intern La. State U. Bands, Baton Rouge, 1987—88; dir. of music LaPorte Cmty. Sch., LaPorte, Ind., 1988—. Contest dir. Midwest Color Guard Cir., Chgo., 2001—02; brass instr. Glassmen Drum & Bugle Corps, Toledo, 2000—02; dir. of tng. Drum Corps Midwest Judges Guild, Milw., 1997—99; dir. Ind. All-Star Marching Band, Indpls., 1988—2002; edn. adv. Intersections Jazz Festival, Indpls., 1999—2002. Mem.: Internat. Assn. of Jazz Educators, Music Educators Nat. Conf., Nat. Band Assn. (ind. state chmn. 1988—2002), Ind. State Sch. Music Assn. (pres. 1998—99), Phi Beta Mu. Home: 492 W. Curtis Dr. La Porte IN 46350

STITES, SUSAN KAY, human resources consultant; b. Colorado Springs, Colo., Sept. 20, 1952; d. William Wallace and Betty Jane (Kosley) Stites; m. Gerald Frederick Simon, Aug. 14, 1988. BA, Wichita State U., 1974; MA, Northwestern U., 1979. Benefits authorizer Social Security Adminstrn., Chgo., 1974-77; trainer Chgo. Urban Skills Inst., 1977-79; human resources mgr. Montgomery Ward, Chgo., 1979-83; mgr. tng. Lands' End, Dodgeville, Wis., 1983-87; dir. human resources Cen. Life Assurance, Madison, 1988-90; owner Mgmt. Allegories, 1987—. Author: Delegating for Results, 1992, Business Communications, 1992, Managing with a Quality Focus, 1994, Training and Orientation for the Small Business, 1994, Powerful Performance Management, 1994, Safety Management Techniques, 1995, Teaching First Aid and CPR, 1995, Alive at 25, 1995, Strategic Thinking and Planning, 1995, Teaching Alice at 25, 1996, Fundamentals of Industrial Hygiene, 1996, Recruiting, Developing and Retaining Volunteers, 1996, Creating a Credit Union University: An Administrator's Guide, 1997, 2d edit., 2001, Creating a Corporate University, 1997, Strategic Thinking for the Automotive Industry, 1997, Managing Sales and Service, 1997, Sales and Service Management in Credit Unions, 1997, Provide Training Without Straining Your Budget, 1997, Car America Sales Training manual, 1998, Introduction to Community Organizing, 1998, Car America Leader's Guide, 1998, Effective Loan Interviewing, 1999, Driven to Extremes, 2000, Safety Inspections, 2001, Job Safety Analysis, 2001, Incident Investigations, 2001; editor: Backstay, 1999-2001. Vol. tutor Japanese students in English, Evanston, Ill., 1977-80; reader to the blind Chgo. Coun. for the Blind, 1974-76. Named Outstanding Woman of the Yr. Wichita State U., 1974. Mem. ASTD (chpt. pres. 1988, v.p. membership 1986, region V awards chair 1992), Soc. Applied Learning Tech., Madison Area Quality Improvement Network, Assn. for Quality and Participation, Rotary (vol. fundraiser), Mendota Yacht Club (treas. 1990-94). Avocations: sailing, boardsailing, gardening, cooking, travel. Office: Mgmt Allegories 3788 Highridge Rd Madison WI 53718-6206

STITH, JAMES HERMAN, physics educator; b. Alberta, Va., July 17, 1941; s. Pierpont and Ruth (Stith) Morgan; m. Alberta Juanita Hill, Oct. 2, 1965; children: Adrienne, Andrea, Alyssa. BS, Va. State U., 1963, MS, 1964; DEd, Pa. State U., 1972; LHD, Va. State U., 1992. Instr. Va. State U., Petersburg, 1964-65; assoc. engr. RCA, Lancaster, Pa., 1967-69; commd. 2d lt. U.S. Army, 1965, advanced through grades to col., 1991; ret., 1993; assoc. prof. of physics U.S. Mil. Acad., West Point, N.Y., 1976-77, prof., 1991-93; vis. scientist USAF Acad., Colorado Springs, Colo., 1976-77; prof. physics Ohio State U., Columbus, 1993-98; vis. scientist Lawrence Livermore (Calif.) Nat. Lab., 1986-87; v.p. physics resources ctr. Am. Inst. Physics, 1998—. Contbr. articles to Jour. Applied Physics, Physics Tchr., Jour. Acoustical Soc. Am., Am. Jour. Physics. Chmn. West Point Sch. Bd., 1984-86. Recipient Archie L. Lacey award N.Y. Acad. Sci., 1994, Disting. Svc. citation Am. Assn. Physics Tchrs., 1995; NSF fellow, 1973. Fellow AAAS, Am. Phys. Soc.; mem. Am. Assn. Physics Tchrs. (v.p. 1990, pres.-elect 1991, pres. 1992), Am. Inst. Physics (governing bd. 1991-93), Nat. Soc. Black Physicists (chartered fellow 1992), Coun. Sci. Soc. Pres. (mem. exec. bd. 1992-96, treas. 1993-96), NAACP, Va. State U., ROTC Alumni Assn., Sigma Pi Sigma, Phi Kappa Phi, Alpha Phi Alpha (pres. 1980-82, Man of Yr. 1980, 83), Sigma Xi. Baptist. Home: 2013 Clearwood Dr Mitchellville MD 20721-2511 Office: Am Inst Physics One Physics Ellipse College Park MD 20740-3843 E-mail: jstith@aip.org.

STITH, JOSEPH, computer infosystems specialist, author; b. Ann Arbor, Mich., Sept. 1, 1962; s. Raymond Joseph and Rosemary Theresa (Babione) S.; m. Paula Campbell; children: Erin Peterson, Charles. BS in Computer Sci., Aurora (Ill.) Coll., 1983. Computer programmer, operator Aurora Coll., 1980-83; system programmer Moline Corp., St. Charles, Ill., 1983-84; mgr. system tech. Longman Group USA, Inc., Chgo., 1984-87; system mgr. tech. tracking Fermi Nat. Accelerator Lab., Batavia, Ill., 1987-94; sys. mgr., sys. support specialist Intel, Chandler, Ariz., 1994—. Mem. Digital Equipment Computer User's Soc., Alpha Chi. Avocations: running, biking, swimming, church activities. Home: 880 W Kroll Ave Gilbert AZ 85233-3754 *Personal philosophy: Church is more than a Sunday thing.*

STITH, LAURA DENVIR, judge; b. St. Louis, Oct. 30, 1953; BA magna cum laude, Tufts U., 1975; JD magna cum laude, Georgetown U., 1978. Law clk. to Hon. Robert E. Seiler, Mo. Supreme Ct., 1978—79; assoc. Shook, Hardy & Bacon, Kansas City, Mo., 1979—84, ptnr., 1984—94; judge. Mo. Ct. Appeals (we. dist.), 1994—2001; judge Supreme Ct. Mo., 2001—. Office: PO Box 150 Jefferson City MO 65102*

STITH, MARY BETH, marketing professional for graphic design; b. St. Louis, Jan. 19, 1945; d. William King and Ella Roe Barnett; 1 child, Elliot King. BA in Am. Studies, Grinnell Coll., 1966. Dir. spl. events March of Dimes, Chgo., 1982-86; dir. mktg. Gerhardt & Clemons, 1986-95, v.p., 1995—. Home: 2650 W Belden Ave Chicago IL 60647-3039 E-mail: rae@gerhardtclemons.com.

STITLEY, JAMES WALTER, JR. food manufacturing executive; b. York, Pa., May 23, 1944; s. James Walter and Geraldine Salome (Horn) S.; m. Tresa Rose Adkins, 1996. BS in Chemistry, Millersville U., 1970. Med. technician York Hosp., 1962-66; rsch. biochemist Carter-Wallace, Inc., Cranbury, N.J., 1970-75; mgr. Ward Labs. divsn. Ward Foods, East Orange, 1975-77; mgr. tech. svcs. Pepperidge Farms, Inc., Norwalk, Conn., 1977-86; dir. tech. devel. Am. Inst. Baking, Manhattan, Kans., 1986-88; dir. baking and cereal sci. rsch. and biscuit product devel. internat. Campbell Soup Co., Camden, N.J., 1988-90; nat. dir. rsch. and tech. Domino's Pizza, Inc., 1990-91, divsn. v.p. consumer and product rsch., 1992—; pres., CEO TechnoVation Network, Inc., 1992—; dir. new product innovation Weider Nutrition Internat., Salt Lake City, 1999—. Cons. biochemistry and toxicology. Contbr. articles to profl. jours.; patentee in field. Asst. scoutmaster Boy Scouts Am. Mem. AAAS, Am. Chem. Soc., Am. Mgmt. Assn., Am. Assn. Cereal Chemists, Am. Inst. Baking (edml. adv. com. 1978—), Instrument Soc. Am. (assoc. dir.-food industry liaison), Am. Astron. Rsch. Group, York Astron. Soc. (v.p. 1960). Home: 9295 S Vista West Dr West Jordan UT 84088-8842 Office: Weider Nutrition Internat 2002 S 5070 W Salt Lake City UT 84104 E-mail: gemini16usa@netscape.net.

STITT, DAVID TILLMAN, judge; b. St. Louis, Apr. 9, 1943; s. David Leander and Jane Wilkinson (Dupuy) S.; m. Elizabeth Celia Santino, Apr. 30, 1981; children: Rachel Elizabeth Botkin, Samuel Thornton. AB, Davidson Coll., 1964; JD, U. Tex., 1969. Assoc. Galland, Kharasch, Calkins & Brown, Washington, 1969-71; asst. corp. counsel D.C., 1971-73, asst. U.S. atty., 1973-74; asst. county atty. Fairfax County, Va., 1975-80, county atty., 1980-91; ptnr. Venable, Baetjer & Howard, McLean, Va., 1991-95; judge Cir. Ct. Fairfax County, 1995—. Lt. U.S. Army, 1964-66, Vietnam. Mem. Va. State Bar Coun. (exec. com. 1991-93), Local Govt. Attys. of Va. (pres. 1983-84, Disting. Svc. award 1991), Conf. of Local Bar Assn. (chmn. 1990-91), Fairfax Bar Assn. (pres. 1986-87). Presbyterian. Home: 6503 Smoot Dr Mc Lean VA 22101-4003 Office: Fairfax County Circuit Ct 4110 Chain Bridge Rd Fairfax VA 22030-4009

STITT, DOROTHY JEWETT, journalist; b. Houston, Sept. 4, 1914; d. Harry Berkey and Gladys (Norfleet) Jewett; m. James Wilson Stitt, Feb. 14, 1939; children: James Harry (dec. 1999), Thomas Paul. AB, Rice U., 1937; MS, Columbia U., 1938. Reporter Houston Post, 1936-38, asst. city editor, 1938; editor of publs. Jewett Family of Am., 1971-94, editor emeritus, 1994—. Spl. asst. to pub. Jewett Genealogy Vols. III and IV, 1995-97; Jewett family Dir.-for-Life, 1995—; gen. chair Jewett Family Reunion, 1996; exec. com. Jewett 2000 Millennium Reunion. Author, editor: The 100th Anniversary Yearbook and History of the George Taylor Chapter, DAR, 1895-1995, 1994, Easton Red Cross Fiftieth Anniversary Booklet and History—Fifty Years of Service, 1967. Adv. bd. Easton Salvation Army, pub. chmn., 1956—, chmn. bd. dirs., 1964, bd. treas., 1981; bd. dirs., pub. chmn. Easton chpt. ARC, 1952-67, vol. Lehigh Valley chpt., 1995-96, 98; founding chmn., pres. Easton JC Wives, 1950-53; mem. fin. com. Little Stone House Mus. Assn., 1974-76, 80, organizing bd. dirs. sec. and pub. chmn., 1974-91; bd. dirs. Easton United Cmty. Chest/United Way, 1957-60, publicity chmn. for 1st campaign, 1960; active Easton Civil Def. Comms., 1956-60; charter mem. bd. Montgomery County Pa. Girl Scouts USA, 1946-48, publicity chmn., initiator and editor county newsletter; den mother cub scouts Easton Boy Scouts Am., 1948-55; capt. renovation campaign area YWCA, 1956; mem. March Sch., Easton PTA, 1948-57, sec., 1952-54, v.p., 1954-56, bylaws chmn., 1953, Easton H.S., 1954-61, membership chmn., 1955-57, 59-60; bd. dirs. Easton Young Woman's Christian Assn., 1965-68, publicity chmn. Y-Teen com., 1953-68; sponsoring dir. Easton area H.S. Students weekly TV 30-minute news program, 1955-56; class agent 60th reunion Pulitzer Grad. Sch. Journalism Class of 1938 Columbia U., 1998. Recipient plaques Salvation Army, 1982, 91, Jewett Family of Am., 1993, cited for Outstanding Svcs., Easton chpt. ARC, 1967, cert. for Outstanding Svc. and Support, 1997, citation Hist. and Geneal. Soc. Northampton County for outstanding svc. in restoration and pub. of Little Stone House Mus., 1993, citation United Way of Easton, 1960, Molly Pitcher gold medal of appreciation SAR, 1980. Mem. AAUW (treas. Easton br. 1950-52, newsletter initiator and editor 1951-60, rep. of br. to UN N.Y.C. conf. 1961-68, internat. rels. chair 1960-68; Pa. achievement award 2000), UDC (Jefferson Davis chpt./Houston), DAR (George Taylor chpt. regent 1974-80, 89-95, vice regent 1980-83, historian 1971-74, 95—, pub. chair 1969—, Pa. state chair vol. svcs. 1995-98, DAR chmn. Kressler Meml. Garden, Easton, 1999—), DAR, PEO (chpt. AF Houston), Easton Tavern House Soc., World Affairs Coun. Phila., Woman's Club of Easton (pres. 1961-64, bd. dirs. 1957—, pub. chair 1952-68, 70-82, 92-96, parliamentarian 1984-92, 2000—, spl. fin. chair 1969-78, legis. chair 1982-84, internat. affairs chair 1996-2000, history update chair 1997—. Outstanding Woman of Yr. 1992, Gold Medal of Honor 1992), Pa. Northeastern Dist. Regents Club (pres. 1980-83, treas. 1997—), Northampton Country Club (Niners' Golf chair 1957-91), Women's Golf Assn. (constn. and bylaws chair, publicity chmn. 1957-92, parliamentarian 1960-92), Libr. of Congress Assn. (founding nat. mem., charter assoc.). Republican. Episcopalian. Avocations: antiques, historical research, golf, swimming, grandmothering. Home: 110 Upper Shawnee Ave Easton PA 18042-1377

STITT, IRENE CONSTANCE, music educator, writer; b. Ramsgate, Kent, Eng., Aug. 30, 1925; arrived in U.S., 1955; d. Percy Hugh and Gisele Constance Dannatt; m. Carroll E. Stitt, Jan. 9, 1955; children: Malcolm, Gwendolyn. LRAM, Royal Acad. Music, London, 1947. Pvt. violin, viola and piano tchr., Floral Park, NY, 1960—; music critic numerous newspapers, 1972—87; adjudicator NYSSMA, 1973—83; violin tchr. Queens Coll., CUNY, Flushing, 1983—. Author: Japanese Ceramics of the Last 100 Years, 1972. Mem.: Nassau Music Educators Assn., Music Educators Nat. Conf. Avocations: antiques, writing, gardening. Home: 15 Marshall Ave Floral Park NY 11001 Office: Queens Coll CUNY Kissena Blvd Flushing NY 11367

STITT, MARI LEIPPER, poet; b. Salem, Ohio, May 1, 1923; d. Robert and Myrtle (Cost) Leipper; m. Rodney Dean Stitt, Apr. 22, 1944; children: Dana Lovelace, Rodney D. Jr. BA in Music, San Diego State U., 1946; MA in Human Rels., Calif. Western U., 1966. Dir. religious edn. Cen. Congl. Ch., 1941-50; tchr. sociology San Diego Evening Coll., 1966-84; writer poetry, 1984—. Home: 7761 S Vivaldi Ct Tucson AZ 85747-9632 *Did we miss the point? Somehow the stories of the Garden of Eden, Cain and Abel, and the Tower of Babel seemed so simple—take only what you need, care for your brother, stay with your own kind. After all our pious ponderings, why don't we get it?.*

STITT, THOMAS PAUL, SR. lawyer; b. Sellersville, Pa., Oct. 2, 1943; s. James Wilson and Dorothy (Jewett) Stitt; m. Suzanne Ruth Reifsnyder, June 19, 1970 (div. Sept. 1982); children: Alicia Ann, Rebecca Jean; m. Melinda May Millheim, Aug. 20, 1983 (div. June 2000); children: Thomas Paul, Victoria Elizabeth, Andrew James; m. Donna L. Pum, Feb. 14, 2001. AB, Duke U., 1965; JD, So. Meth. U., 1968. Bar: Tex. 1968, Pa. 1969, U.S. Dist. Ct. (ea. dist.) Pa. 1971, U.S. Supreme Ct. 1986. Assoc. Coffin and DeRaymond, Easton, Pa., 1971-73; jr. ptnr. Coffin, DeRaymond, Shipman & Stitt, 1973-75; sr. ptnr. Coffin, DeRaymond, Shipman, Stitt, Lewis & Walters, 1975-87, Stitt and Cordts, Easton, 1987-94; pvt. practice, 1994-2000; ptnr. Stitt & Narlesky, 2001—. Sr. ptnr. Star Enterprises Partnerships, Lehigh Valley, Pa., 1986-2000; solicitor Borough of Stockertown, Pa., 1974-84, Easton Suburban Water Authority, 1987—; bd. dirs. Keystone Food Products, Inc., Easton, Premier Bank, Easton; bd. dirs., v.p. Jewett Family of Am., 1985-94, 96-99. Solicitor Lehigh Valley chpt. ARC, 1988-90, bd. dirs., 1990-96, chmn. 1994-96; trustee, elder First Presbyn. Ch., Easton, 1973-79, 80-86; pres. State Theater, Inc., Easton, 1988-91; bd. dirs. Easton Pub. Libr., 1973-78, pres., 1978. 1st lt. U.S. Army, 1969-71. Mem. ABA (Silver Key award 1968), Northampton Country Club (bd. dirs. 1987-96), AAA Northampton County (v.p., bd. dirs. 1973—), Masons, Shriners, Rotary. Republican. Avocations: reading, golf, tennis, swimming, travel. Office: Thomas P Stitt Sr Law Office 101 S 3rd St Easton PA 18042-4524

STIVANELLO, ROBERT ANTHONY, opera production company owner, director, designer, translator - opera productions; b. New York, NY, Aug. 4, 1958; s. Anthony Lionel Stivanello, Yolanda Rose Stivanello; m. Anne Elizabeth Riter; children: Victoria. BS - Magna Cum Laude, State University of New York at Albany, Albany, NY, 1976—80. President Stivanello Costume Co., Inc., Maspeth, NY, 1980—curr; Director & Lighting Designer New York Grand Opera, New York, 1983—curr; Partner Laboratori Scenografici Sormani, srl, Milano, Italy, 1985—curr; Producer & Director Intermountain Opera Association, Bozeman, MT, 1985—curr; Director of Opera Henry Street Settlement Music School, New York, NY, 1993—2000; Instructor of Histrionics Rosa Ponselle Foundation, Stevenson, MD, 1995—95. Dir.: (opera) 75 different productions, many; translator: (opera translation for projected titles) 20 different operas. Avocation: sailing, baseball. Home: 333 Ridge Road Little Neck NY 11363 Office: Stivanello Costume Co., Inc. 66-38 Clinton Avenue Maspeth NY 11378 Business E-Mail: stivanello@aol.com.

STIVENDER, DONALD LEWIS, mechanical engineering consultant; b. Chgo., May 8, 1932; s. Paul Macon and Grace (Larsen) S.; m. Margaret Ann Lourim, Apr. 14, 1956; children— Anne, Robert, Carole. BS in Engring, U.S. Coast Guard Acad., 1954; MS, U. Mich., 1959. Registered profl. engr., Mich. R & D engr. Rsch. Labs., GM Corp., Warren, Mich., 1959-92, sr. rsch. engr., 1968-92; owner, consulting engr. Stivender Engring. Assos., 1980—. Cons. engine, thermodynamics, emissions and systems engring. disciplines. Contbr. articles tech. jours. on diesel, gas turbine and spark ignition engine combustion, emission, constrn. and electronic control aspects. Engring. officer USCG, 1950-58. Fellow Soc. Automotive Engrs. (Arch T. Colwell award 1968, 69, 79, governing bd. 1971-73); mem. NAS (naval studies bd. 1990-92), ASME, NRC, Combustion Inst., Sigma Xi. Achievements include inventions of internal combustion engines and electronic control systems. Home: 1730 Hamilton Dr Bloomfield Hills MI 48302-0221 E-mail: stive@umich.edu.

STIVER, JAMES FREDERICK, pharmacist, health physicist, administrator, scientist; b. Elkhart, Ind., Jan. 27, 1943; s. Melvin Hugh and Pauline Anna (Schrock) S.; m. Joan Louise Trindle, Aug. 14, 1965; children: Gregory James, Richard Frederick, Kristin Louise, Elizabeth Ann. BS in Pharmacy and Pharm. Scis., Purdue U., 1966, MS, 1968, PhD, 1970. Lic. pharmacist, Ind., N.D. Asst. prof. N.D. State U., Fargo, 1969-73, radiol. safety officer, 1969-76, assoc. prof., 1973-76; radiation safety officer KMS Fusion Inc., Ann Arbor, Mich., 1976-80; mgr., pharmacist Kroger Sav-On Pharmacy Co., Elkhart, Ind., 1980-81; pharmacist Elkhrt Gen. Hosp., 1981; environ. regulatory affairs adminstr. Upjohn Co., Kalamazoo, 1981-88, patent liaison scientist, 1988-92, sr. patent liaison scientist, 1992-94; pharmacist, asst. mgr. Judd Drugs, Elkhart, 1994-95; pharmacist Meijer Pharmacy, Goshen, Ind., 1995-99; pharmacist, asst. mgr. Wal-Mart Pharmacy, Elkhart, 1999-2000, mgr., 2000, KMart Pharmacy, Elkhart, 2000—. Cons., lectr. Contbr. articles, abstracts to publs. Named to Hon. Order Ky. Cols. Fellow Am. Inst. Chemists; mem. AAAS, Am. Pharm. Assn., Am. Chem. Soc., Health Physics Soc., Internat. Radiation Protection Assn., Am. Biol. Safety Assn., Ind. Pharmacists Assn., N.D. Pharm. Assn., Order Ky. Cols., Kappa Psi, Rho Chi, Phi Lambda Upsilon, Sigma Xi. Home: 505 Skyview Dr Middlebury IN 46540-9427 Office: KMart Elkhart IN 46517

STIVER, WILLIAM EARL, retired government administrator; b. Madison, Ind., Mar. 30, 1921; s. John Virgil and Anna Lynne (Ryker) S.; m. Norma A. Cull, June 11, 1944; children: Vicki, Raymond, Gena, John. Student, Hanover Coll., 1947-49; BS, U. Calif., Berkeley, 1951, MBA, 1952. With Fed. Ser. Bur. Census, Commerce Dept., Suitland, Md., 1952-79, chief budget and finance div., 1963-73, dep. assoc. adminstr. Social and Econ. Stats. Adminstrn., 1973-75; spl. asst., assoc. dir. adminstrn. and field ops. Bur. of Census, 1975-77, electronic data processing staff coordinator, 1977-78, ret., 1979. Served with USA, 1942-45, 45-46. Recipient Silver medal Commerce Dept., 1969. Mem. Phi Beta Kappa, Beta Gamma Sigma. Home: 8104 Kerby Pky Ct Fort Washington MD 20744-4756

STIVERS, WILLIAM CHARLES, forest products company executive; b. Modesto, Calif., June 22, 1938; m. Karen L. Gaspar, Aug. 6, 1961; children: William, Gregory, Michael, Kristy, Kelly, John, Jeffrey. BA, Stanford, 1960; MBA, U. So. Calif., 1963; certificate, U. Wash., 1969; grad., Advanced Mgmt. Program, Harvard U., 1977. Asst. cashier, asst. v.p., v.p. First Interstate Bank, San Francisco and Los Angeles, 1962-70; finance mgr. treas. dept. Weyerhaeuser Co., Tacoma, 1970, asst. treas., 1971, treas., 1972—, v.p., 1980-91, sr.

v.p., chief fin. officer, 1991—, exec. v.p., CFO, 1991—. Treas. Weyerhaeuser Real Estate Co., 1970; bd. dirs., exec. com. mem. FM Global, Johnson, R.I.;bd. dirs., chmn., pres. S&S Land and Cattle Co. Mem. Financial Execs. Inst.

STIVES, WILLIAM ROBERT, pharmacist; b. Buffalo, Sept. 8, 1937; s. William Otto and Gertrude Evelyn Stives; m. Beverly Jean Barth, June 3, 1967; children: Michael William, Eric James. BS in Pharmacy, Ohio State U., 1960. Registered pharmacist, Ohio. Pharmacist, mgr. Cunningham Drugs, Sheffield Lake, Ohio, 1960-73; chief pharmacist Discount Drug Mart, Avon Lake, 1973—. Pharmacy intern trainer State of Ohio, Avon Lake, 1960—. Chmn. drug and alcohol abuse com. Avon Lake Cmty. Action Team; coach Avon Lake Youth Soccer; vol. Habitat for Humanity, Lorain County, Ohio; nation chief YMCA Indian Guides, Avon Lake; troop treas. Boy Scouts Am., Avon Lake; mem., host family AFS fgn. student exch., Avon Lake; mem. various coms. United Meth. Ch., Avon Lake. Named Outstanding Chain Pharmacist, Drug Topcs News Mag., 1998. Mem. Am. Pharm. Assn., Ohio Pharm. Assn., West Shore Pharm. Assn., Internat. Pharm. Students' Fedn., Ohio State Alumni Assn., Rho Chi, Phi Delta Chi. Republican. Avocations: gardening, camping, travel. Home: 31700 Electric Blvd Avon Lake OH 44012-2075 Office: Discount Drug Mart 33382 Walker Rd Avon Lake OH 44012-1495 E-mail: bstives@hotmail.com.

ST JOHN, RONALD, strategic planning manager; b. Peoria, Ill., May 22, 1943; s. Samuel Bishop and Francis Bailey St John; m. Carol Ann Vogel, Dec. 27, 1969; children: Alexander Ballard, Nathan Bailey. BA, Knox Coll., 1965; MA, U. Denver, 1969, PhD, 1970. Strategic planning mgr. Caterpillar, Inc., Peoria, Ill., 1973—2001; affiliate prof. Bradley U., 1980—. Legis. cons. Ill. Ho. of Reps., Springfield, 1971—73. Author: (novels) Foreign Policy of Peru, 1992, 1999, Historical Dictionary of Libya, 1998, Libya and the United States, 2002; adv. bd. dirs. (jours.) Jour. Libyan Studies, 2000—; contbr. articles to profl. jours. Bd. dirs. IMCI, Brussels, 1993—2001, Knox Coll., Galesburg, Ill., 1982—85, Ill. Stewardship Alliance, Rochester, 2000—. Capt. Mil. Intelligence U.S. Army, 1969—71, Vietnam. Avocations: climbing, hiking, running. Home: 1620 W Northedge Ct Dunlap IL 61525-9249 E-mail: bcstjohn@mtoo.com.

STOAKS, RALPH DUVAL, science administrator; b. Greenville, Miss., Apr. 8, 1935; s. Benjamin Duval and Joyce Fay (Neal) (div. 1968); 1 child, Kent Duval; m. Carolyn Jeanne Bush, Dec. 29, 1977. BA in Biology, McMurry Coll., Abilene, Tex., 1958; M of Natural Sci., U. Okla., 1967; PhD in Entomology, N.D. State U., 1975. Rsch. entomologist Bishop Mus. Natural History, Honolulu, 1978; urban entomologist, salesperson Orkin Pest Control, West Des Moines, Iowa, 1978-79; plant protection and quarantine officer USDA, Animal & Plant Health Inspection Svc., Plant Protection and Quarantine, San Diego, 1980—88, regional biotechnologist Sacramento, 1988—95, regional program mgr. biotech. and biol. control, 1996—. Contbr. numerous articles to profl. jours. and books. With U.S. Army N.G., 1959-64. Recipient Hammer award Vice Pres. Al Gore, 1997; NSF rsch. grantee U. Okla., 1960, 62, 66, N.D. State U., 1968; NIH rsch. fellow Bishop Mus., 1978. Mem. AAAS, Entomol. Soc. Am. (bd. cert. gen. entomologist), Am. Registry of Profl. Entomologists (bd. dirs. North Calif. br. 1989-91), N.D. Natural Sci. Soc. (life), N.Am. Bethnological Soc., Xerces Soc. Office: USDA Animal & Pland Health Inspection Svc 2150 Centre Ave Bldg B 3E10 Fort Collins CO 80526 Office Fax: 970-494-7501. E-mail: ralph.d.stoaks@aphis.usda.gov.

STOB, MARTIN, physiology educator; b. Chgo., Feb. 20, 1926; s. Cornelius and Theodora (Sluis) S. BS, Purdue U., 1949, MS, 1951, PhD, 1953. Mem. faculty Purdue U., Lafayette, Ind., 1953—, assoc. prof. animal scis., 1958-63, prof., 1963-92; ret., 1992—. Contbr. articles to profl. jours. Patentee prodn. of fermentation estrogen Served with USN, 1944-46; ETO, PTO Name Best Tchr. Sch. Agr., 1970, Best Counselor Sch. Agr., 1977, Best Counselor Purdue U., 1977 Fellow AAAS; mem. Am. Inst. Biol. Scis., Am. Soc. Animal Sci., Soc. Study of Reprodn., Soc. Study of Fertility Episcopalian. Home: 6218 W Rd 75 N West Lafayette IN 47906

STOBAUGH, ROBERT BLAIR, business educator, business executive; b. McGehee, Ark., Oct. 15, 1927; s. Robert B. and Helen (Parris) S.; m. Beverly Ann Parker, Oct. 18, 1947 (dec. 1990); children: Blair, Susan, William (dec.), Clay; m. June Gray Milton, Dec. 7, 1991. BS in Chem. Engring., La. State U., 1947; DBA, Harvard Bus. Sch., 1968. Refinery engr. Exxon Corp., Baton Rouge and Venezuela, 1947-52; engring. mgr. Caltex Oil Co., N.Y., Bahrain, London, 1952-59; mgr. econ. evaluation Monsanto Co., Houston, 1959-65; lectr. Harvard Bus. Sch., Boston, 1967-70, assoc. prof., 1970-71, prof., 1972-83, Charles E. Wilson prof., 1984-96, Charles E. Wilson prof. emeritus, 1996—, chmn. doctoral programs, 1984-89, dir. energy project, 1972-83, chmn. tech. and ops. mgmt. area, 1981-83. Bd. dirs. 11 cos. Co-author: Money in the Multinational Enterprise, 1973, Energy Future (best-seller list N.Y. Times and Time mag.), 1979, How To Build an Effective Small-Company Board, 1996; author: Nine Investments Abroad and Their Impact at Home, 1976, Innovation and Competition, 1988; co-editor: Technology Crossing Borders, 1984; contbr. articles on corp. governance to profl. publs. Mem. bd. advisors Instituto de Estudios Superiores de la Empresa, Barcelona, Spain, 1973-80; co-chmn. The Dumbarton Oaks Symposium on Energy Efficiency, Washington, 1979; bd. dirs. Alliance to Save Energy, Washington, 1979-94; expert testimony Congress; advisor to cabinet-level depts. of White House and UN; trustee French Libr. and Cultural Ctr., Boston, 1995—. Named to Hall of Distinction, La. State U., 1987. Fellow Acad. Internat. Bus. (pres. 1979-80), Council on Fgn. Relations, Am. Econ. Assn., Nat. Assn. Corp. Dirs. (bd. dirs. 1996—, Blue Ribbon commn. on dir. professionalism 1996, chair compensation 1995, co-chmn. role of bd. in corp. strategy 2000, vice chmn. 2002). Clubs: Belmont Hill (Mass.); Harvard (N.Y.), Forest (Houston). Episcopalian. Office: Harvard Bus Sch Soldiers Field Rd Boston MA 02163-1317 E-mail: rstobaugh@hbs.edu.

STOBER, WILLIAM JOHN, II, economics educator; b. Boston, Mar. 24, 1933; s. Ralph William and Marjorie Cairncross (Duthie) S.; m. Jeannine Lynn Defries, Sept. 10, 1955. B.Sc., Washington and Lee U., 1955; MA, Duke U., 1957, PhD, 1965. Instr., then asst. prof. econs. N.C. State U., Raleigh, 1959-65; asst. prof., then asso. prof. La. State U., 1965-69, acting head dept. econs., 1968-69; mem. faculty U. Ky., 1969—, prof. econs., 1974-97, chmn. dept., 1979-86, 90-95, dir. grad. studies, 1979-86, prof. emeritus, 1997—. Mem. Beta Gamma Sigma. Democrat. Home: 516 Mundys Lndg Versailles KY 40383-9468 E-mail: Stober@pop.uky.edu.

STOCK, ANITA See SCHERER, ANITA

STOCK, BEN, religious organization consultant; b. N.Y.C., June 27, 1948; BA, CUNY, 1975. Chmn. Religious Orgns. Computing Group, N.Y.C., 1989—; co-dir. Non-Profit Computing Inc., 1991—. Home: 277 Van Cortlandt Ave E Bronx NY 10467-3011 Office: Non-Profit Computing Inc 67 Wall St Ste 2411 New York NY 10005-3101

STOCK, DAVID EARL, mechanical engineering educator; b. Balt., Feb. 2, 1939; s. Walter E. and Minnie H. (Bauer) S.; m. Mary R. Wilford, Aug. 4, 1962; children: Joseph W., Katherine W. BS, Penn State U., 1961; MS, U. Conn., 1965; PhD, Oreg. State U., 1972. Test engr. Pratt & Whitney Aircraft, East Hartford, Conn., 1961-65; vol. Peace Corps, Ghana, 1965-68; prof. Wash. State U., Pullman, 1972—, chair faculty senate, 1997-98. Contbr. articles to profl. jours. Fellow ASME (chair multiphase flow com. 1988-90, Freeman scholar 1994, chair exec. com. fluid engring. divsn., 2000-01). Office: Wash State U Sch Mech Materials Engr PO Box 642920 Pullman WA 99164-2920 E-mail: stock@wsu.edu.

STOCK, GRACE EMMA, civic volunteer; b. Cleve., Dec. 26, 1914; d. Leonard Franklin and Clara Eve (Papcke) Uthe; m. Donald LaVern Stock, June 12, 1938 (dec. Aug. 1964); children: David, Janice, Joyce. Clk. Schwind & Son, Elyria, Ohio, 1934-40; owner, office mgr. Elyria Arts Co., 1940-62; sec. Elyria City Schs., 1962-77. Troop leader Girl Scouts Am., 1934-36, 59-75; publicity chair Waterfront Coun. St. Lucie County, Fort Pierce, Fla., 1993—; visions com. St. Lucie County, 1997-99; ednl. com. Heathcote Bot. Gardens, 1996-2000, St. Lucie Environ. Ctr., 1997-2001. Mem. Nat. Audubon Soc, Fla. Audubon Soc. (bd. dirs. 1990-99), St. Lucie Audubon Soc. (pres. 1984-86, 89-90, bd. dirs. 1990—), Elyria City Sch. Employees Retirement Assn. (pres. 1966-69, sec. 1972-74), N.E. Region Sch. Employees Retirement Ohio, Fla. Ornithol. Soc., Marine Resources Coun., LEAF, World Wildlife Fund, Conservation Alliance St. Lucie County Inc. (bd. dirs. 1989—, pres. 1998-2000, Conservationist of Yr. 2000), Manatee Observation and Edn. Ctr., St. Lucie Hist. Soc., Nat. Wildlife Fedn., Nature Conservancy. Avocations: traveling, hiking, birdwatching. Home: 274 Kingfisher Ave Fort Pierce FL 34982-6307

STOCK, GÜNTER, pharmaceutical company executive; b. Feb. 7, 1944; MD, U. Heidelberg, 1970, Habil., 1978; Dr h.c., Ludwig-Maximilians-Univ., Munich, 1999. Rschr. Inst. Physiology, U. Heidelberg, 1971, Inst. for Pharmacology, U. Gothenburg, Sweden, 1972-73; head cardiovascular pharmacology dept. Schering AG, Berlin, 1983-87, head Inst. Pharmacology, 1987-89, bd. exec. dirs., 1989—; extraordinary prof. Free U. Berlin, 1986. Mem. German Sci. Coun., 1992—; mem. senate and admin. coun. Max-Planck-Gesseschaft for Promotion of Scis., 1993, mem. com. for rsch. politics and rsch. planning, 1994—98, v.p., 2001; senator, mem. counsel German Rsch. Cmty., 2001—. Editor: (book) Current Topics in Neuroendocrinology "Sleep" series, 1982, Prostacyclin and Its Stable Analogue ILOPROST, 1987, Critical Leg Ischaemia, 1990, Ernst-Schering Foundation Workshops (series), 1990, Chemie und Geisteswissenschaften, 1992. Mem. country coun. Berlin/Brandenburg of Stifterverband fur die Deutsche Wissenschaft, 1994; mem. coun. Physikalisch-Technische Bundesanstalt, 1996; senator Deutsche Akademieder Naturforscher Leopoldina, 1999; mem German-Am. Acad. Coun., 1996—2000. Mem.: Berlin-Brandenburg Acad Scis (mem promotion comt 1995). Office: Schering Aktiengesellschaft Müllerstraße 178 13342 Berlin Germany E-mail: guenter.stock@schering.de.

STOCK, JEFFREY ALLEN, urologist, educator; b. Bronx, N.Y., May 24, 1962; MD, Mt. Sinai Sch. Medicine, 1988. Diplomate Am. Bd. Urology. Intern, resident gen. surgery, urology U. Medicine-Dentistry N.J.-U. Hosp., Newark, 1988-93; fellow U. Calif. San Diego-Children's Hosp., 1993-94; urologist West Orange, N.J., 1994—. Urologist St. Barnabas Med. Ctr., 1994—, Hackensack (N.J.) Med. Ctr., 1995—, Children's Hosp., N.J., 1994—, Newark Beth Israel Med. Ctr., 1994—, Morristown Meml. Hosp.; clin. asst. prof. U. Medicine-Dentistry N.J., 1995—. Fellow ACS, Am. Acad. Pediatrics, Soc. Pediatric Urology; mem. Am. Urol. Assn. Office: 101 Old Short Hills Rd Ste 203 West Orange NJ 07052-1023

STOCK, KIM H. dance studio owner, choreographer; b. Miami, Feb. 27, 1943; m. Edward S. Stock, Nov. 22, 1984; stepdau.: Salena M. Stock. Dance student, McKinley Acad. Dance, Miami, 1947-60, Luigi, 1961, Roland Duprée, Hollywood, Calif., 1962. Profl. dancer, various cities, 1959-84; dance tchr. Kennewick, Wash., 1993-96; owner Stock Ctr. Performing Arts, Nipomo, Calif., 1997—. Choreographer Richland (Wash.) Light Opera, 1994-95, Pacific Light Opera, Richland, 1995-96. Mem. Nipomo C. of C. (entertainment dir., Octoberfest com. 1998, 99, Kids Day Celebration, 1998, 99), Rotary Club of Nipomo. Avocations: sewing, gourmet cooking, gardening, puzzles. Office: Stock Ctr Performing Arts 330 W Tefft St Ste A Nipomo CA 93444-8876

STOCK, LAURI JANE, lawyer; b. Passaic, N.J., June 11, 1957; d. John Patterson and Marie (Lisbona) S. BA, U. Fla., 1979; JD, U. San Diego, 1988. Bar: Calif. 1988, U.S. Dist. Ct. (so. dist.) Calif. 1988. Lt. U.S. Navy, San Diego, 1981-87; prosecutor City Atty. of San Diego, 1988-90; ptnr. Malowney, Chialtas & Bishop, San Diego, 1990-92; sole practioner Law Office of Lauri Stock, 1992-99; ptnr. Lynn, Stock & Stephens, LLP, 1999—. Bd. dirs. Tom Homann Law Assn., 1997—, San Diego Police Chief's adv. bd., 2000—. Decorated Navy Commendation medal. Mem. San Diego Front Runners. Avocations: road racing, rock climbing, classical piano, reading. Office: Lynn Stock & Stephens LLP 2445 5th Ave Ste 330 San Diego CA 92101-1665 E-mail: lstock@lsslawfirm.com.

STOCK, NORMAN, librarian; b. Bklyn., July 14, 1940; s. Zvi Harry and Hadassah (Belenky) S.; m. Lydia Liang-Hwa Chang. BA, Bklyn. Coll., 1962; MLS, Rutgers U., 1967; MA in English, Hunter Coll., 1971. Reference libr. Monmouth Coll., West Long Beach, N.J., 1966-67, Queens Borough Pub. Libr., Jamaica, N.Y., 1967-73, Bklyn. Coll., 1973-76, Montclair State U., Upper Montclair, N.J., 1976-78, head collection devel/acquisition dept., 1978—. Author: Buying Breakfast for My Kamikaze Pilot, 1994 (Peregrine Smith contest 1993); contbr. poetry to mags. Recipient New Voice award in Poetry YMCA Writers Voice Program, 1984, Poetry prize Bennington Writing Workshops, 1988; Nat. Arts Club scholar in poetry Bread Load Writers Conf., 1985, Alan Collins fellow in poetry, 1994, Tanne Found. fellow, 1999; Tenn. Williams scholar poetry Sewanee Writers Conf., 1995. Mem. ALA, Poetry Soc. of Am., Acad. of Am. Poets. Democrat. Jewish. Home: 77-11 35th Apt 2P Jackson Heights NY 11372 Office: Harry Sprague Libr Montclair State U Upper Montclair NJ 07043 E-mail: stockn@mail.montclair.edu.

STOCK, PEGGY A(NN), college president, educator; b. Jan. 30, 1936; married; 5 children. BS in Psychology, St. Lawrence U., 1957; MA in Counseling, U. Ky., 1963, EdD, 1970. Lic. psychologist, Ohio. Instr., rsch. asst. dept. psychology and spl. edn. U. Ky., Lexington, 1958-59, 63-67, staff psychologist Med. Ctr., 1964-66; dir. edn. United Cerebral Palsy of the Bluegrass, 1962-64; exec. dir. Community Council for Physically Handicapped and Mentally Retarded, 1964-66; dir. clin. program No. Ky. Regional Cmty. Mental Health Ctr., Covington, 1969-71; pres. Midwest Inst. Tng. and Edn., Cin., 1971-75; assoc. prof., counseling psychologist Mont. State U., Bozeman, 1975-79, asst. dean Office of Student Affairs and Service, 1977-79; spl. asst. to pres. U. Hartford, Conn., 1979-80, assoc. prof. Coll. Edn., 1980-85, v.p. adminstrn., 1981-86; prof., pres. Colby-Sawyer Coll., New London, N.H., 1986-95; pres. Westminster Coll., Salt Lake City, 1995—. Mem. wild horse and burro adv. bd. Bur. Land Mgmt./Dept. Interior, 1997—2000; bd. dirs. BMW Bank of N.Am., Pacificorp, Fed. Res. Bank, Salt Lake City; trustee St. Mark's Hosp., 2000—. Contbr. chpts. to books, articles to profl. jours. Mem. adv. com. Rowland Hall-St. Mark's Sch., 1999—; chair Utah selection com. Rhodes Scholarships, 1995—; mem. program com. Coun. Ind. Coll., 1996—2000; bd. dirs. Utah Partnership for Edn. and Econ. Devel., 1996—; hon. bd. dirs. Big Bros./Big Sisters, 1999—. Recipient Disting. Alumna award, St. Lawrence U., 1989, Athena Pathfinder award, 2001; fellow, U. Ky., 1966—68, Am. Coun. Edn., 1979—80, United Jewish Com., 1981; grantee, George I. Alden Trust, Helene Fuld Health Trust, Surdna, Cogswell, U.S. Dept. Edn., numerous others. Mem. Am. Coun. on Edn., Am. Assn. for Higher Edn., Advancement Women in Higher Edn., Nat. Assn. Ind. Colls. and Univs. (bd. dirs. 1998—), Am. Assn. Pres.'s Ind. Colls. and Univs. (bd. dirs. 1996—), Salt Lake Area C. of C. (bd. govs. 1996-99), Utah Info. Techs. Assn. (trustee 1998-99). Avocations: breeding Arabian horses, reading, fishing. Office: Westminster Coll 1840 S 1300 E Salt Lake City UT 84105-3617

STOCK, STEPHEN MICHAEL, broadcast journalist; b. Colorado Springs, May 16, 1961; s. Ray Kesecker and Juanita Madeline (Keller) Stock; m. Lynn Victoria Peithman, July 20, 1985; 1 child Michael Stephen Ray. BA, U.N.C., 1983. From engring. tech. to gen. assignment reporter WDBJ-TV, Roanoke, Va., 1983-86; from investigative reporter to weekend anchor, producer WECT-TV, Wilmington, N.C., 1986-87; bur. chief Anderson, S.C. WYFF-TV, Greenville, S.C., 1987-91; investigative reporter-bur. chief Ocala, Fla. WESH-TV, Orlando, 1991—; standby SE corr. NBC NewsChannel, 1995—. Guest lecr. Marion County Sheriff's Office, Ocala, 1993—98, U. Fla. Press Club, Gainesville, 1993; participant Media Studies Initial Advanced Power Reporting Seminar The Poynter Inst., 1998, participant Getting Wired Seminar, 2001. Adv. bd. mem. Jack Eckerd Youth Camp E-Kel-Etu, Silver Springs, Fla., 1996—; founder Ocala/Marion County Town Mtg. on Violence, 1996; adv. bd. mem. Fla. Environthon, Ocala/Silver Springs, 1993; v.p., bd. dirs. Ocala Habitat for Humanity, 1996—99; elder First Presbyn. Ch., Ocala, 1996—99. Nominee Emmy, 2000; named TV Journalist of Yr., RTNDA of Carolinas, 1989; recipient TV Agrl. News Coverage award, S.C. Agr. Co., 1989, Fla. Media award, Fla. Emergency Mgmt. Assn., 1997. Mem.: Ctrl. Fla. Press Club (Best Gen. News 1994, Merit Recognition for Spot News 1995, Best Spot News award 1996, Merit Gen. News award 1996, Best Investigative Report award 1996), Investigative Reporters and Editors Assn., Soc. Profl. Journalists (Finalist Non-deadline News 1999, 1st pl. TV Investigations Market 1-100 Green Eyeshade award 2000, Fla. Sunshine State award for best investigative reporting 2000, Sunshine State award finalist 2001, RTNDA Communicator award of distinction). Avocation: Avocations: wine collecting, photography, sports, gardening, carpentry. Office: WESH-TV Bur Chief 7 E Silver Springs Blvd Ocala FL 34470-6634

STOCKAR, HELENA MARIE MAGDALENA, artist; b. Bratislava, Czechoslovakia, Mar. 22, 1933; came to the U.S., 1968; d. Arnost J. and Helen R. (Strakova) Kubasek; m. Ivo J. Stockar, Oct. 31, 1959; children: David, Laura Bates. Diploma, Graficka Skola, Prague, 1952, Music Conservatory, 1954. Piano tchr. Music Sch., Prague, 1954-68; company pianist State Ballet/Breacrest Sch., R.I., 1968-74; piano tchr. Music Tchr. Assn., 1968-86. One-woman shows include Warwick Mus., R.I., 1986, Brown U., Providence, 1987, Westerly Art Gallery, R.I., 1987, Westerly Art Gallery/Morin-Miller, 1988, 89, Galerie Horizon, Paris, 1989, Barnes & Noble, Warwick, 1999, 2000, Bohemian Gallery, N.Y.C., 1999, Hoxie Gallery, Westerly, R.I., 2000, Happy White Gallery, Barrington, R.I., 2000, C.C. R.I., Lincoln, 2000, Pittenween Art Festival, Scotland, 2001, Pawtucket Congrl. Ch., 2002; two-person shows at R.I. State Com. Nat. Mus. Women in the Arts, Triboro Studio, R.I., 1995, Bush Gallery, Bryce Studio, Providence, 2001, Monserat Gallery, Soho, 2002, Courthouse Ctr. for the Arts, West Kingston, R.I., 2002, De Blois Gallery, Newport, 2002, Stonington Vineyards Gallery, Conn., 2002; exhibited in group shows at World Congress Czechoslovak Soc. Art and Sci., Washington, 1988, Prague, 1992, Morin-Miller Internat., N.Y.C., 1989, Ariel Gallery, Soho, N.Y.C., 1989, Art Expo N.Y.C., 1989, New Eng. Internat. Art Expo, 1993, R.I. State Com. Nat. Mus. Women Arts, 1995, Providence Art Club, 1996-97, Sarah Doyle Gallery, Brown U., Providence, 1997, Visions, Newport, 2001; represented in permanent collections; featured on TV shows. Participant Art in Public Places: Convention Ctr., Providence, 1994. Recipient Second prize Nat. Competition of Children's Book Illustration, Prague, 1965; named finalist Internat. Art Competition, L.A., 1984. Mem.: Czechoslovak Soc. Art and Sci., Nat. Mus. Women in the Arts (R.I. state com.). Avocations: traveling, gardening.

STOCKARD, JAMES ALFRED, lawyer; b. Lake Dallas, Tex., Aug. 4, 1935; s. Clifford Raymond and Thelma Gladys (Gotcher) S.; m. Mary Sue Hogan, Aug. 17, 1956; children— Bruce Anthony, James Alfred, Paul Andrew. BA with honors, N. Tex. State U., Denton, 1956; LLB magna cum laude, So. Methodist U., 1959. Bar: Tex. 1959. Pvt. practice, Dallas, 1959-62; with Employers Casualty Co., 1962-65; v.p. Southland Life Ins. Co., 1965-77, sr. v.p., gen. counsel, dir., 1977-87; exec. v.p., gen. counsel, sec. Southland Fin. Corp., Dallas, 1978-87; dir. Tex. Life, Accident, Health and Hosp. Svc. Ins. Guaranty Assn., 1978-84, chmn. bd., 1980-84; ptnr. Butler & Binion, Dallas, 1987-2000; pvt. practice, 2000—; gen. counsel Employers Gen. Ins. Group, Inc., 1994—. Bd. dirs. Ins. Systems Am., Atlanta; pres., bd. dir. Dallas County Municipal Utility Dist. 1, Irving, Tex.; gen. counsel, bd. dirs. Lone Star Life Ins. Co., 1988-99. Contbr. legal jours. Mem. exec. com., precinct chmn. Dallas County Dem. Com., 1971. Mem. Am., Tex., Dallas Bar Assn., Assn. Life Ins. Counsel. Methodist. Home: 3607 Asbury St Dallas TX 75205-1848 Office: 7501 Inwood Rd Dallas TX 75209-4019 E-mail: astockard@i3s.net., jastockard2002@aol.com.

STOCKBAUER, ROGER LEWIS, physicist, educator; b. Victoria, Tex., Feb. 3, 1944; s. Fred Ferdinand and Elizabeth (Nitschman) S.; m. Catherine Pauline Jones, June 10, 1972; children: Robbin Renee, Kathryn Elizabeth, Marc Daniel. BA, Rice U., 1966; MS, U. Chgo., 1968, PhD, 1973. Rsch. assoc. U. Chgo., 1972-73; rsch. physicist Nat. Inst. Standards and Tech., Gaithersburg, Md., 1973-89; prof. physics La. State U., Baton Rouge, 1989—. Editor: High Tc Superconducting Thin Films, 1990; contbr. articles to profl. jours. Recipient Silver medal U.S. Dept. Commerce, 1983; NRC fellow, 1973-75. Fellow Am. Phys. Soc., Am. Vacuum Soc.; mem. AAAS, Materials Rsch. Soc., Sigma Xi. Office: La State U Dept Physics 202 Nicholson Hl Baton Rouge LA 70803-0001 E-mail: stockbauer@lsu.edu.

STOCKBURGER, JEAN DAWSON, lawyer; b. Scottsboro, Ala., Feb. 4, 1936; d. Joseph Mathis Scott and Mary Frances (Alley) Dawson; m. John Calvin Stockburger, Mar. 23, 1963; children: John Scott, Mary Staci, Christopher Sean. Student, Gulf Park Coll., 1954-55; BA, Auburn U., 1958; M in Social Work, Tulane U., 1962; JD, U. Ark., Little Rock, 1979. Bar: Ark. 1979, U.S. Dist. Ct. (ea. dist.) Ark. 1980. Assoc. Mitchell, Williams, Selig, Gates & Woodyard and predecessor, Little Rock, 1979-85, ptnr., 1985-94, of counsel, 1994—. Bd. dirs., sec. Cen. Ark. Estate Planning Council, Little Rock, 1984-85, 2d v.p., 1985-86; pres. Cen. Ark. Estate Council, 1987-88. Assoc. editor U. Ark. Law Rev., 1978-79. Sec. Little Rock Cmty. Mental Health Ctr., 1994—96, v.p., 1996—99, pres., 1999—2001; bd. dirs. Sr. Citizens Activities Today, Little Rock, 1983—88, treas., 1986—88; bd. dirs. Vol. Orgn. for Ctrl. Ark. Legal Svcs., 1986—91, sec., 1987—88, chmn., 1989—91, H.I.R.E. Inc., 1994—2001. Mem. ABA, Ark. Bar Assn. (chmn. probate and trust law sect. 1986-88), Pulaski County Bar Assn. (bd. dirs. 1994-97), Am. Coll. Trust and Estate Counsel. Democrat. Methodist. Office: Mitchell Williams Selig Gates & Woodyard 425 W Capitol Ave Ste 1800 Little Rock AR 72201-3525

STOCKDALE, JAMES BOND, writer, research scholar, retired naval officer; b. Abingdon, Ill., Dec. 23, 1923; s. Vernon Beard and Mabel Edith (Bond) S.; m. Sybil Elizabeth Bailey, June 28, 1947; children: James Bond, Sidney Bailey, Stanford Baker, Taylor Burr. BS, U.S. Naval Acad., 1946; MA, Stanford U., 1962; LLD (hon.), Brown U., 1979; LHD (hon.), U. R.I., 1980; 9 other hon. degrees. Commd. ensign USN, 1946, advanced through grades to vice admiral, served as naval aviator, test pilot sch. instr., squadron comdr. of supersonic fighters, air wing comdr.; prisoner of war (sr. naval service POW) North Vietnam, 1965-73; pres. Naval War Coll., Newport, R.I., 1976-79; retired USN, 1979; pres. The Citadel, Charleston, S.C., 1979-80; sr. research fellow The Hoover Instn., Stanford U., 1981-96, emeritus, 1996; independent candidate V.P. U.S. running mate of Ross Perot, 1992. Author: A Vietnam Experience, 1985 (Freedoms Found. at Valley Forge hon. prize 1985), (with Sybil Stockdale) In Love and War, 1984, Thoughts of a Philosophical Fighter Pilot, 1995 (Freedoms Found. Valley Forge George Washington honor medal). Mem. acad. adv. bd. U.S. Naval Acad., Annapolis, 1981-94. Decorated D.F.C. (2), D.S.M. (3), Silver Star (4), Medal of Honor; inducted Carrier Aviation Hall of Fame, 1993; enshrined U.S. Naval Aviation Hall of Honor, 1996. Fellow Soc. Exptl. Test Pilots (hon.); mem. Lincoln Acad. Ill. (laureate), Congl. Medal of Honor Soc., Soc. of Cincinnati, SAR, Bohemian Club (San Francisco). Episcopalian. Home: 547 A Ave Coronado CA 92118-1917

STOCKDALE, RUSSELL, information technology executive; BSc, Stanford U.; MBA, U. Pa. Mgr. Anderson Con.; from mgr. end-user mktg. to corp. v.p. Microsoft, Redmond, Wash., 1991, corp. v.p. knowledge worker solutions group. Office: One Microsoft Way Redmond WA 98052-6399*

STOCKDALE, SALLY BOYD, artist, realtor; b. Coral Gables, Fla., Apr. 20, 1941; d. Grant Stockdale and Alice Boyd (Magruder) Proudfoot; m. David Michael deWilde, Dec. 21, 1968 (div. 1978); children: Holland Stockdale, Christian duCroix; m. Mariano Eduardo Munoz-Lopez, Mar. 26, 1981. AA, Bennett Coll., Millbrook, N.Y., 1961; postgrad., Trinity Coll., Dublin, Ireland, 1962; B.F.A., Am. U., 1979; postgrad., Corcoran Sch. Art, Washington, 1980-93; grad., Realtor Inst., 1994. Lic. realtor, Washington, Md., Va. Realtor Pardoe Real Estate ERA, Washington, 1987—. One-woman shows include: Tahiti Gallery, Marbella, Spain, 1978, Dumbarton Series, Washington, 1982; commd. murals include Children's Hosp., Washington; represented Folger Library, Washington; portraits state and fed. legislators, others; illustrator Holiday Mag., 1963-68, Spanien Jour., 1979, The Dreadful Day, 1981, Patrick, 16 Centuries, 1983. Mem. Nat. Trust for Historic Preservation. Work featured in Washington Evening Star, Washington Post, New York Times; recipient Top Prodr. award Washington Assn. Realtors, 1987-99. Mem. Nat. Mus. Women in Arts, Capital Spkrs., Club Nautico de Altea. Home: 4719 Chesapeake St NW Washington DC 20016-4465

STOCKER, ARTHUR FREDERICK, classics educator; b. Bethlehem, Pa., Jan. 24, 1914; s. Harry Emilius and Alice (Stratton) S.; m. Marian West, July 16, 1968. AB summa cum laude, Williams Coll., 1934; A.M., Harvard U., 1935, PhD, 1939. Instr. Greek Bates Coll., 1941-42; asst. prof. classics U. Va., 1946-52, assoc. prof., 1952-60, prof., 1960-84, prof. emeritus, 1984—, chmn. dept., 1955-63, 68-78, assoc. dean Grad. Sch. Arts and Scis., 1962-66; vis. asst. prof. classics U. Chgo., summer 1951. Editor: (with others) Servianorum in Vergilii Carmina Commentariorum Editio Harvardiana, Vol. II, 1946, Vol. III, 1965; assoc. editor: Classical Outlook. Served with USAAF, 1942-46; col.

(ret.). Sheldon traveling fellow from Harvard, 1940-41 Mem. Va. Classical Assn. (pres. 1949-52), Mid. West and South Classical Assn. (pres. So. sect. 1960-62, pres. 1961-62), Am. Philol. Assn., Mediaeval Acad. Am., Poetry Soc. Va. (pres. 1966-69), Soc. Colonial Wars in the State of Va., S.A.R. (chpt. pres. 1972, 91), Huguenot Soc. Va. (pres. 1981-83), Raven Soc. (Raven award 1977), Phi Beta Kappa, Omicron Delta Kappa. Republican. Presbyterian (elder). Clubs: Masons, Red-Land (Charlottesville, Va.), Colonnade (Charlottesville, Va.), Farmington Country (Charlottesville, Va.), Commonwealth (Richmond, Va.), Williams (N.Y.C.), Army and Navy (Washington). Home: 250 Pantops Mountain Rd Charlottesville VA 22911-8694

STOCKER, JEFFREY DAVID, film acting coach; b. Barberton, Ohio, Apr. 20, 1954; s. John Edward and Rose Marie (Kruft) S. Owner, artistic dir. Film Acting Studio, N.Y.C., 1981—. Artistic dir. Theatre Workshop N.Y.C. Nat. Arts Club. Dir., filmacting coach. Mem. NATAS, Nat. Arts Club. Office: Film Acting Studio 90 Lexington Ave Apt 1H New York NY 10016-8912 E-mail: STUDIO-90-LEXS@prodigy.net.

STOCKER, JOYCE ARLENE, retired secondary school educator; b. West Wyoming, Pa., May 13, 1931; d. Donald Arthur and Elizabeth Mae (Gardner) Saunders; m. Robert Earl Stocker, Nov. 26, 1953; children: Desiree Lee Stocker Stackhouse, Rebecca Lois Stocker Genelow, Joyce Elizabeth Stocker Scrobola. Grad. cum laude, Coll. Misericordia, Dallas, 1953; Master's equivalency diploma, Pa. Dept. Edn., 1991. Cert. tchr., Pa. Tchr. music and lang. arts West Pittston (Pa.) Sch. Dist., 1953-60; tchr. music and choral Wyoming Area Sch. Dist., Exeter, Pa., 1970-78, tchr. English composition, 1978-93, chmn. lang. arts dept., 1982-90, dir. nat. history day activities, 1982-93. State cons. Nat. History Day, 1996—. Organist, choir dir. United Meth. Ch., Wyo., 1958—; dir. W. Wyo. Centennial Choir, 1998; mem. adminstrv. bd. West Wyo., 2000—; mem. worship com. United Meth. Ch. and Interch. Coun., Wyo. and West Wyo. Recipient DAR Tchr. of Yr. award, 1992-93, Wilkes U., 1990; named Outstanding Educator, Times Leader, 1993; honoree Wyo. United Meth. Ch. Choir, 1999. Mem. NEA, Pa. Edn. Assn., Wyo. Edn. Assn., N.E. Pa. Writing Coun., Nat. Coun. Tchrs. English, Women Educators Internat., Orgn. Am. History, Pa. Music Educators Assn., Music Educators Nat. Coun., Nat. Coun. Social Studies, Pa. Assn. Sch. Retirees (Vol. of Yr. 1998), Pa. Sch. Employees Retirement Sys. (social svcs. com.), Pa. Retired Pub. Sch. Employees Assn. (Luzerne-Wyoming counties chpt.), Pa. Coun. Social Studies, Delta Kappa Gamma (recording sec. 1991—, accompanist Pa. state chorus, 1999—, 2000—), Phi Mu Gamma. Methodist. Avocations: reading, writing, sewing, hunting, fishing. Office: Wyoming Area Sch Dist 20 Memorial St Exeter PA 18643-2659

STOCKER, MICHAEL A. health insurance company executive; Past exec. v.p., gen. mgr. N.Y. area market U.S. Healthcare; past pres. CIGNA Health Plans; pres., CEO Empire Blue Cross/Blue Shield, N.Y.C., 1994—. Office: Empire Blue Cross/Blue Shield 1 Rural Trade Ctr New York NY 10048*

STOCKGLAUSNER, WILLIAM GEORGE, accountant; b. St. Louis, Dec. 25, 1950; s. William George and Mary Virginia (Lopez) S.; m. Vickie Kay Mackler, Nov. 17, 1973 (div. Dec. 1999); children: Tyson Marshall, Jacob Cameron. BS summa cum laude, Columbia (Mo.) Coll., 1985. CPA, Mo. Staff acct. Wright-Price Inc., Jefferson City, Mo., 1974-77, Williams-Keepers CPAs, Columbia, 1977-81, supr. acctg. svc., 1981-85, auditor, 1985-86; acct. Don Landers & Co. CPAs, 1986-89, ptnr., 1990-99; founder, pres. William. G. Stockglausner CPA, PC, 1999—; ptnr. Ashland Manor Properties, 2001—. Coach Daniel Boone Little League, Columbia, 1986-90, 94-99, Diamond Coun., 1994-99, Columbia Soccer Club, 1988-90, 94-2000, divsn. coord., 1991-92; campaign vol. United Way, 1991-94, 97-98; fin. adv. com. City of Columbia, 1996—. Mem. AICPA, Mo. Soc. CPAs (tech. standards rev. com. 1989-90), Lions (sec. Columbia club 1983-85, bd. dirs. 1986-88). Republican. Roman Catholic. Avocations: fishing, photography, running, music/guitar, mem. Low-Water Crossing bluegrass band. Office: 601 W Nifong Blvd Ste 1E Columbia MO 65203-6804 E-mail: wstock139@att.net.

STOCKHAM, TOM, information technology executive; Bachelors, Dartmouth Coll.; MBA, Stanford U. Assoc. Boston Consulting Group; founder, pres. Sonic Innovations; gen. mgr. Citysearch office Ticketmaster, Utah, v.p. internat. devel., pres. online ticketing, pres. access and emerging markets; pres., CEO Myfamily.com, Provo, 2001—. Office: Myfamily.com 360 W 4800 N Provo UT 84604 Office Fax: 801-705-7001.*

STOCKING, GEORGE WARD, JR. anthropology educator; b. Berlin, Dec. 8, 1928; came to U.S., 1929; s. George Ward and Dorothé Amelia (Reichhard) S.; m. Wilhelmina Davis, Aug. 19, 1949 (div. 1965); children: Susan Hallowell, Rebecca, Rachel Louise, Melissa, Thomas Shepard; m. Carol Ann Bowman, Sept. 29, 1968. BA, Harvard U., 1949; PhD, U. Pa., 1960. From instr. to assoc. prof. history U. Calif., Berkeley, 1960-68; assoc. prof. anthropology and history U. Chgo., 1968-74, prof. anthropology, 1974—, Stein-Freiler Disting. Svc. prof., 1990—, prof. emeritus, 2000—, dir. Fishbein Ctr. for History Sci. and Medicine, 1981-92. Vis. prof. U. Minn., Mpls., 1974, Harvard U., Cambridge, Mass., 1977, Stanford U., Palo Alto, Calif., 1983, U. Ill., Urbana, 1999. Author: Race, Culture and Evolution, 1968, Victorian Anthropology, 1987, The Ethnographer's Magic, 1992, After Tylor, 1995, Delimiting Anthropology, 2001; author, editor: The Shaping of American Anthropology, 1974; editor History of Anthropology, 1983-97. Active labor union and radical polit. activity, 1949-56. Fellow Ctr. for Advanced Study in Behavioral Scis., 1976-77, John Simon Guggenheim Meml. Found., 1984-85, Inst. for Advanced Study, 1992-93; Getty Ctr. for History of Art and Humanities scholar, 1988-89, Dibner Inst., MIT, 1998. Fellow Am. Anthropol. Assn. (Franz Boas award 1998), Am. Acad. Arts and Scis.; mem. Royal Anthropol. Inst. (Huxley medal 1993), History Sci. Soc. Avocation: needlepoint. Office: Univ Chicago Dept Anthropology 1126 E 59th St Chicago IL 60637-1580 E-mail: g-stocking@uchicago.edu.

STOCKLIN, ALMA KATHERINE, retired public relations consultant; b. New London, Conn., May 9, 1926; d. Stephen Sullivan and Theresa Catherine (Flynn) Sheehan; m. Philip L. Stocklin, Jan. 28, 1950 (div. 1984); children: Brian, Christopher, Virginia Katherine, Walter, Stephen. Student, U. Conn., 1945-46, Conn. Coll., 1946; cert., Sch. Modern Photography, N.Y.C., 1948; AA, Charter Oak Coll., 1979; BA cum laude, Eastern Conn. State U., 1981. Advt. photographer GE, Bridgeport, Conn., 1948-49; chmn. Conn. PTA State Juvenile Protection, 1959; pub. rels. cons. Norwich and Groton, Conn., 1983-86; asst. to dean Ea. Conn. State U., Willimantic, 1984-91, ret., 1991, adminstr. br. office U.S. Submarine Base Groton, 1984-91; pub. rels. cons., 1994—. Coord. videotape courses for submarines, New London, 1984-91. Founder, chmn. bd. dirs. Newport (R.I.) Holiday for Sr. Citizens, 1972, Uncas on Thames Conn. State Hosp. Aux., 1978; mem. Norwich Harbor Day Com., 1982-83, Catchment Area coun. 11 S.E. Coun. Mental Health Bd., 1989-90, Norwich Regional Mental Health Adv. Bd., 1987-90, Norwich State Hosp. Adv. Bd., 1987-89; vice chair Ea. Conn. Regional Mental Health Bd., 1988-89; founder, chmn. Norwich Nuclear Freeze Com., 1982; bd. dirs. Ea. Conn. Symphony Orch., New London, 1984-87, Friend of the Symphony, 1987-90, Laurel Glen, Groton, 1984-91; co-founder, bd. dirs. Newport Ch. Cmty. Housing Corp., 1969-72; founder, chmn. Holiday for Sr. Citizens, Newport R.I., 1972; chair Conn. State PTA Juvenile Protection, 1957; founder, pres. Cath. Mother's Cir., Dorset, Eng., 1962; exec. sec. Overnight Shelter, Loughborough, Eng., 1973-74; founder, chair Bicycle Paths for Schoolchildren, Loughborough, 1974; bd. dirs. Friends of the Fairfield County Dist. Libr., Lancaster, Ohio, 1994-99, Fairfield Affordable Housing Bd.; mem. Fairfield County Literacy Coun., 1996—; bd. dirs. Fairfield Affordable Housing, 1999—; vol. ARC, 1991-. Recipient award for outstanding svc. in founding the Newport Holiday for Sr. Citizens, City Coun. of Newport, 1972, Outstanding Svc. award, Pres. of Conn. PTAs, 1967. Mem. Fairfield County (Conn.) Respiratory Disease and TB Assn. (bd. dirs. 1991-95), Friends of Libr. Assn. Fairfield County Dist. (bd. dirs. 1994-99), Nat. Alliance for the Mentally Ill, Phi Beta Phi, Conn. Alpha Pi Beta Phi. Democrat. Roman Catholic. E-mail: amyk5813@columbus.rr.com.

STOCKMAN, DAVID ALAN, former federal official, congressman, financier; b. Ft. Hood, Tex., Nov. 10, 1946; s. Allen and Carol (Bartz) S. BA in Am. History cum laude, Mich. State U., East Lansing, 1968; postgrad., Harvard U. Div. Sch., 1968-70; fellow, Inst. Politics, 1974. Spl. asst. to Congressman John Anderson, 1970-72; exec. dir. Republican Conf., Ho. of Reps., 1972-75; mem. 95th Congress from 4th Dist. Mich., Interstate and Fgn. Commerce Com., Adminstrn. Com.; chmn. Rep. Econ. Policy Task Force, 1977-81; dir. Office of Mgmt. and Budget, Washington, 1981-85; mng. dir. Salomon Bros., N.Y.C., 1985-88; sr. mng. dir. The Blackstone Group, 1988-99; founder Heartland Indsl. Ptnrs., 1999—. Mem. Nat. Commn. on Air Quality, 1978 Author: The Triumph of Politics: Why the Reagan Revolution Failed, 1986. Mem. Coun. on Fgn. Rels. Office: Heartland Indsl Ptnrs 55 Railroad Ave Greenwich CT 06830

STOCKMAN, JAMES ANTHONY, III, pediatrician; b. Phila., 1943; MD, Jefferson Med. Coll., 1969. Diplomate Am. Bd. Pediat. Intern Childrens Hosp. Pa., 1969—70, resident in pediat., 1970—72; fellow in pediatric hematology/oncology SUNY, Syracuse, 1972—74; now clin. prof. Duke U.; also with U. N.C., Chapel Hill; pres. Am. Bd. Pediat. Office: Office of the Pres Am Bd Pediatrics 111 Silver Cedar Ct Chapel Hill NC 27514-1512

STOCKMAN, ROBERT HAROLD, religious organization administrator, educator; b. Meriden, Conn., Oct. 6, 1953; s. Harold Herman and Margery (Fothergill) S.; m. Mana Derakhshani, 1992; 1 child, Lua Bahiyeh. BA in Geology and Archaeology, Wesleyan U., 1975; MSc in Geology, Brown U., 1977; MTS, Harvard U., 1984, ThD, 1990. Coord. Inst. for Bahai' Studies, 1990—. Grad. rsch. asst. geology dept., Brown U., Providence, 1975-77; instr. geology and oceanography, Cmty. Coll. R.I., Lincoln, 1977-80; instr. geology, Boston State Coll., 1980-82, U. Lowell, Mass., 1983-84; instr. geology and astronomy and operator of Astronomy Observatory, Bentley Coll., Waltham, Mass., 1983-90; teaching asst. Harvard U., 1986-89; instr. religion DePaul U., Chgo., 1990-95, 95-2002, vis. asst. prof. religions studies, 1995-96; spkr. on Baha'i Faith in America. Author: The Baha'i Faith in America, Vol. 1, Origins, 1892-1900, 1985, The Baha'i Faith in America, Vol. 2 Early Expansion, 1900-1912, 1995, Thornton Chase: First American Baha'i, 2002; mem. editl. bd. World Order, 1990—; contbr. articles to profl. jours. Mem. Am. Acad. Religion (mem. Baha'i studies unit 1984—, chairperson 1985-86, 89-90), Mid. East Studies Assn., Soc. Iranian Studies, Assn. Baha'i Studies (mem. Internat. Com. 1990-98, chair study of religions sect. 1989—). Home: 224 Swanson Cir South Bend IN 46615-2549 Office: Baha'i Nat Ctr Office Rsch Wilmette IL 60091 E-mail: rstockman@usbnc.org.

STOCKMAR, TED P. lawyer; b. Denver, May 9, 1921; s. Theodore Paul and Elda Marie (Robinson) S.; m. Suzanne Louise Harl, Feb. 14, 1947; children: Stephen Harl, John Brian, Anne Baldwin Stockmar Upton BS in Petroleum Engring., Colo. Sch. Mines, Golden, 1943; LLB, U. Denver, 1948. Bar: Colo. 1948. Ptnr. Holme Roberts & Owen Denver, 1951-91; of counsel, 1991—. Co-author: Law of Federal Oil and Gas Leases 1964, 1984; also articles Trustee Colo. Sch. Mines, Golden, 1948-82, bd. pres., 1970-80. 1st lt. USAF, 1943-45 Mem. Denver Bar Assn., Colo. Bar Assn., Rocky Mountain Oil and Gas Assn. (dir., exec. com. 1982-93, chmn. legal com. 1986-88), Denver Country Club, Univ. Club, Law Club. Republican. Avocations: bird watching, reading, gardening. Home: 2552 E Alameda Ave Apt 8 Denver CO 80209-3324 Office: Holme Roberts & Owen LLP 1700 Lincoln St Ste 4100 Denver CO 80203-4541

STOCKMAYER, WALTER H(UGO), chemistry educator; b. Rutherford, N.J., Apr. 7, 1914; s. Hugo Paul and Dagmar (Bostroem) Stockmayer; m. Sylvia Kleist Bergen, Aug. 12, 1938; children: Ralph, Hugh. SB, MIT, 1935, PhD, 1940; BSc (Rhodes scholar), Oxford U., 1937; DSc (hon.) , U. Louis-Pasteur, Strasbourg, France, 1972; LHD (hon.) , Dartmouth Coll., 1983; DSc (hon.) , U. Mass., 1996. Instr. MIT, 1939—41, asst. prof., 1943—46, assoc. prof., 1946—52, prof., 1952—61; prof. chemistry Dartmouth Coll., 1961—79, prof. emeritus, 1979—; instr. Columbia U., 1941—43. Cons. E.I. duPont de Nemours & Co., Inc., 1945—; vis. com. Nat. Bur. Stds., 1979—84. Author (with others): Polymer Phase Diagrams, 2001; contbr. articles on phys. and macromolecular chemistry to sci. jours. Recipient Nat. medal of Sci., 1987, MCA Coll. Chemistry Tchr. award, 1960, Hermann Staudinger prize, Soc. German Chemists, 2000; fellow Guggenheim, 1954—55, hon. Jesus Coll., Oxford (Eng.) U., 1976, Alexander von Humboldt, 1978—79. Fellow: Am. Phys. Soc . (Polymer Physics prize 1975), Am. Acad. Arts and Scis.; mem.: NAS, Soc. Plastics Engrs. (Internat. award 1991), Soc. Polymer Sci. Japan (hon.), Am. Chem. Soc. (assoc. editor Macromolecules 1968—74, 1976—94, chmn. polymer chem. divsn. 1968, Polymer Chemistry award 1965, Peter Debye award 1974, T.W. Richards medal 1988, polymer divsn. award 1988, Oesper award 1992), Appalachian Mountain Club, Sigma Xi (William Procter prize 1993). Office: Dartmouth Coll Chemistry Dept Dept Chemistry Hanover NH 03755 E-mail: walter.stockmayer@dartmouth.edu.

STOCKS, MARY LEE, social worker, administrator; b. Marietta, Ohio, Sept. 3, 1949; d. Graham Lee and Virginia Eleanor (Donaldson) S. BA, Marietta Coll., 1971; MSW, Ohio State U., 1985. Lic. ind. social worker, Ohio; diplomate Am. Psychotherapy Assn. Asst. supr. social worker Franklin County Welfare Dept., Columbus, Ohio, 1972-74; social worker Cen. Ohio Psychiat. Hosp., 1974-76; aftercare liaison Columbus Area Community Mental Health Ctr., 1976-77, North Cen. Mental Health Ctr., Columbus, 1977-80; aftercare specialist Worthington Community Counseling Svcs., 1980-81; social worker Cen. Ohio Psychiat. Hosp., Columbus, 1981-86; program specialist Ohio Dept. Mental Health, 1986-93, spl. projects coord. Office of Systems Devel. and Tng., 1993-97. Dir. Improve(e)-Ohio Mental Health Players, Columbus, 1986-97; mem. program com. Ohio Welfare Conf., Columbus, 1986-88; mem. W.E.C.A.R.E. Network, Cin., 1986—; mem. schizophrenia rsch. program adv. com. dept. psychiatry Ohio State U. Coll. Medicine, 1988; mental health rep. Ohio Devel. Disabilities Coun., 1990-93, Ohio State Use Com., 1991-94; pub. rels. chair ADA Bus. and Disability Tech. Assistance and Info. Ctr.; speaker, presenter in field. Co-author: Ohio's Curriculum for Case Managers, 1995; contbr. articles to self-help and profl. jours. and publs. Bd. dirs. Women's Outreach for Women, Columbus, 1991-92; mem. Ohio Com. on Women and Recovery, Ohio, 1986-89; mem. All-Ohio Youth Choir Alumni Assn., women's sustaining bd. Franklin Park Conservatory; mem. consumer adv. com. OHio Rehab. Svcs. Commn. Mem. NASW, Nat. Coun. on Alcoholism, Nat. Alliance for Mentally Ill, Mental Health Assn. Franklin County (trustee), Alliance for Mentally Ill Franklin County (bd. dirs., v.p.), Nat. Depressive and Manic Depression Assn., Am. Platform Assn., Mental Health Assn. Ohio (chmn. statewide task force on stigma and mental illness, bd. dirs.), Ohio Assn. Mental Adminstrs., Ohio Women with Disabilities (trustee, pres.), Disability Network Ohio Solidarity (trustee), Ohio Tech.-Related Assistance and Info. Network (state steering/adv. com.), Humane Soc. of U.S., Am. Legion Aux., Job's Daus., Order Ea. Star, Alpha Delta Mu, Gamma Sigma Sigma. Presbyterian. Avocations: camping, fishing, gardening, crafts, music.

STOCKS, WILLIAM L. federal judge; Bar: N.C. Chief bankruptcy judge for mid. dist. N.C. U.S. Bankruptcy Ct., Greensboro, 1993—. Office: US Bankruptcy Ct 101 S Edgeworth St Greensboro NC 27401-2219

STOCKTON, ANDERSON BERRIAN, electronics company executive, consultant, genealogist; b. Lithonia, Ga., Oct. 7, 1943; s. Berrian Henry and Mary Grace (Warbington) S.; m. Linda Arlene Milligan, June 9, 1963; 1 child, Christopher Lee. Cert. in cryptographic engring., USAF Acad., Wichita Falls, Tex., 1963. Supr. Western Union Telegraph Co., East Point, Ga., 1965-67; mgr. RCA Corp., Cherry Hill, N.J., 1967-72; v.p. Universal Tech., Inc., Verona, 1972-76; v.p. engring. Siemens Ag., Anaheim, Calif., 1976-84, Concorde, El Toro, 1984-85, Data Card Troy, Inc., Santa Ana, 1985-86; dir. laser engring. div. ITT, San Jose, 1986-87; v.p. S.T.A.R. Ricoh Corp., 1988-93; v.p. mktg. QMS, Inc., Mobile, Ala., 1993-94; mng. gen. dir. IDT, Inc., Santa Clara, Calif., 1994-98; gen. mgr. HDTV engring. Philips Semicondrs., Sunnyvale, 1998-99; COO. Mediagate Inc., Orlando, Fla., 1999—. Cons. Hutchinson (Minn.) Tech. Corp., 1984-87, Xerox, 1993, Hewlett Packard, 1993, NEC, 1997-98. Author: Polled Network Communications, 1976, A Quest for the Past, 1991; patentee in field. With USAF, 1961-65. Mem. IEEE, Am. Electronics Assn. Avocations: classic car collecting, genealogical and historical research, sword, coin and stamp collecting. Home: PO Box 1380 Flagler Beach FL 32136-1380 Office: Mediagate Inc Ste 300 PO Box 1380 Flagler Beach FL 32136-1380

STOCKTON, JOHN HOUSTON, professional basketball player; b. Spokane, Wash., Mar. 26, 1962; m. Nada Stepovich, Aug. 16, 1986; 1 child, John Houston. Grad., Gonzaga U., 1984. With Utah Jazz, Salt Lake City, 1984—. Mem. U.S. Olympic Basketball Team, 1992. Named to NBA All-Star team, 1989-94; holder NBA single season rec. most assists, 1991; NBA Assists leader, 1987-1992; NBA Steals leader, 1989, 92; named NBA All-Star Co-MVP, 1993, All-NBA First Team, 1994. Led NBA in most assists per game, 1988-93; led NBA with highest steals per game avg., 1989,1992; shares single-game playoff record for most assists, 24, 1988. Office: Utah Jazz 301 W South Temple Salt Lake City UT 84101-1216*

STOCKTON, KEVIN W. insurance and investment professional; b. Ariz., Oct. 1, 1967; m. Suzanne M. (Tadra), June 13, 1992; children: Reilly G., Paige R. BS magna cum laude, U. Colo., 1992. CLU; ChFC; CFP; registered health underwriter. Sales rep. Merck Human Hlth. Div., Warren, Mich., 1992-94; agent, registered rep. Northwestern Mutual Life/Baird Sec., Troy, 1994, Denver, 1995-98; dir. mktg. The Madison Group, Inc., 1998—. Fin. vice chmn., Boy Scouts of Am., Troy, Mich., 1992-94, U.S. Trnsplt. Games Steering Comm., Natl. Kidney Found., Ann Arbor, Mich, 1992-94, fin. comm., Denver, 1995, Distinguished Citizen Dinner Steering Comm., Boy Scouts of Am., Boulder, Colo., 1995-97, pres., chmn. bd. Gatsbys Cigar Merchants, Inc., Denver, 1996-97. Contrib. articles to profl. magazines, 1995. Cadet, Army, West Point, N.Y., 1985-87. Mem. Am. Soc. CLU's and ChFC, Internat. Assn. Fin. Planners, Nat. Assn. Life Underwriters, Inst. Cert. Fin. Planners, Million Dollar Round Table, Beta Gamma Sigma (life). Avocations: travel, fitness, family, music, reading. Office: The Madison Group Inc 4582 S Ulster St Ste 1300 Denver CO 80237-2639

STOCKWELL, LANCE, law educator; b. N.Y.C., Feb. 21, 1942; s. Eugene Lawrence Stockwell and Nelle (Dark) Stephens; children: David Christopher, Kelsey Dian; m. Susan Meschke, Mar. 10, 1962 (div. Mar. 28, 1994); m. Gail Provost, Dec. 16, 1996. BBA, Okla. U., 1965; MA, Okla. State U., 1996; JD, U. Tulsa, 1968. Bar: Okla. 1968, U.S. Dist. Ct. (no. dist.) Okla. 1968, U.S. Ct. Appeals (10th cir.) 1969, U.S. Ct. Appeals (9th cir.) 1972, U.S. Dist. Ct. (we. dist.) Okla. 1973, U.S. Dist. Ct. (ea. dist.) Okla. 1977, U.S. Supreme Ct. 1988, U.S. Ct. Appeals (fed. cir.) 1990, U.S. Ct. Appeals (8th cir.) 1993. Ptnr. Boesche McDermott & Eskridge, Tulsa, 1968—95; prof. law U. Tulsa, 1994—; freelance lectr. Tulsa, 1996—. Bd. dirs. Ctr. on Dispute Resolution, U. Tulsa, 1994—, developer, dep. dir. lawyering skills cert. program. Author: (seminar workshop) Secrets of Persuasion, 2000, Winning Communication, 1999. Named Outstanding Adj. Prof., 1996, 97. Fellow: Okla. Bar Found., Am. Coll. Trial Lawyers; mem.: Okla. Bar Assn., Am. Arbitration Assn. (arbitrator 1992—). Avocations: writing, sailing, skiing. Office: U Tulsa Coll Law 3120 E 4th Pl Tulsa OK 74104-2418

STOCKWELL, ROBERT PAUL, linguist, educator; b. Oklahoma City, June 12, 1925; s. Benjamin P. and Anna (Cunningham) S.; m. Lucy Louisa Floyd, Aug. 29, 1946; 1 child, Paul Witten. BA, U. Va., 1946, MA, 1949, PhD, 1952. Instr. English, Oklahoma City U., 1946-48; mem. linguistics staff Sch. Langs., Fgn. Service Inst., State Dept., 1952-56; mem. faculty UCLA, 1956-94, prof. English, 1962-66, prof. linguistics, 1986-94, chmn. dept., 1966-73, 80-84, prof. emeritus, 1994—. Mem. com. lang. programs Am. Council Learned Socs., 1965-69 Author: (with J.D. Bowen) Patterns of Spanish Pronunciation, 1960, Sounds of English and Spanish, 1965, (with J. D. Bowen, J.W. Martin) The Grammatical Structures of English and Spanish, 1965, The Major Syntactic Structures of English, 1973, (with P.M. Schachter, B.H. Partee) Foundations of Syntactic Theory, 1977, Workbook in Syntactic Theory and Analysis, 1977, (with Donka Minkova) English Words: History and Structure, 2001; also numerous articles.; editor: (with R.S.K. Macaulay) Linguistic Change and Generative Theory, 1972, ; assoc. editor: Lang., 1973-79, Festschrift: Rhetorica, Phonologica, Syntactica: A Festchrift for Robert P. Stockwell, 1989. Served with USNR, 1943-45. Am. Council Learned Socs. fellow, 1963-64 Mem. Linguistic Soc. Am. (exec. com. 1965-68), Philol. Assn. Great Britain. Home: 4000 Hayvenhurst Ave Encino CA 91436-3850 Office: UCLA Linguistics Dept Los Angeles CA 90025 E-mail: stockwel@ucla.edu.

STOCKWELL, WILLIAM F. fundraiser, management consultant; b. Belmont, Mass., Oct. 1, 1948; s. Fred F. and Marjorie (Werner) Stockwell; m. Sara Gray Stockwell, June 16, 1973; children: Quentin F., Carl W. BA, Rutgers U., 1971; MEd, Boston U., 1975. Dir. devel. Eaglebrook Sch., Deerfield, Mass., 1980-83, Hyde Sch., Bath, Maine, 1983-84, Western Regional Coun. on Alcoholism, Lewiston, 1992-94; dealer Target/1 Fundraiser, Auburn, 1985-95, Campagne Assn., Manchester, N.H., 1999—; cons. William F. Stockwell Fundraising and Nonprofit Mgmt. Cons., Waterford, Maine, 1984—. Dir. numerous workshops, presentations, retreats and studies including Arthur Griffin Ctr. for Photographic Art, Winchester, Mass., 1997, Shaw House, Bangor, Maine, 1998, Bear Mountain Learning Cmty., South Waterford, Maine, 1998, Cary Med. Ctr., Caribou, Maine, 1998, Deertrees Found., Ltd., Harrison, Maine, 1998, Calais Regional Hosp., 1998, Bridgton (Maine) Pub. Libr., 1998, Watershead Ctr. for Ceramic Arts, Nobleboro, Maine, 1999, Lincoln Home, Newcastle, Maine, 1999, Carriage and Driving Ctr., Skyline Farm, North Yarmouth, Maine, 1999, USM-Sr. Coll., Portland, Maine, 1999, Maine Bar Found., Augusta, 2000, Hyde Sch., Hardwick, Mass., 2001, Eagle Hill Sch., Hardwick, 2001, among others. Trustee Western Maine Health, Norway, Maine, 1990—; dir., pres. Oxford Hills Assn. Devel. Corp., Norway, 1985-94; corporator Norway Savs. Bank, 1986—, Maine HEalth, 1999—; mem. annual fund steering com., parent vol. Eagle Hill Sch., 1999—. Mem. Maine Hosp. Assn. (healthcare governance coun. 1991—), Kiwanis (dir. Norway-Paris chpt. 1986-88). Republican. Avocations: semi-precious gems, gardening. Home: PO Box 84 264 Passaconaway Rd Waterford ME 04088-0084 Office: PO Box 84 Waterford ME 04088 E-mail: fndrsr@megalink.net.

STOCKWELL, WILLIAM ROSS, atmospheric chemist; b. Findlay, Ohio, Feb. 20, 1953; s. Ross Weaver and Pauline Mae (Fry) S.; m. Jian Zhang, Apr. 21, 1992. BS, Bowling Green State U., 1975; MS, Ohio State U., 1977, PhD, 1981. Postdoctoral fellow Nat. Ctr. for Atmospheric Rsch., Boulder, Colo., 1982-83, scientist, 1984-86; sr. rsch. assoc. Atmospheric Sci. Rsch. Ctr./SUNY, Albany, 1987-90; sr. vis. scientist Forschangzentrum, Jülich, Germany, 1990; sr. project scientist Woodward-Clyde, Santa Ana, Calif., 1991-93; sr. scientist Fraunhofer Inst., Garmisch-Partenkirchen, Germany, 1993-98; assoc. rsch. prof. Desert Rsch. Inst., 1998—; chief scientist for air quality Nat. Oceanic and Atmospheric Admin. U.S. Dept. of Commerce, 2002—. Instr. U. Calif., Riverside, 1992-93; mem. doctoral jury U. Paris, 1994; contbr. to com. on aldehydes NAS, Washington, 1981; peer reviewer NSF, Washington, 1994; mem. panel NASA, Washington, 1993. Contbr. numerous articles to profl. jours.; peer reviewer Jour. Geophys. Rsch., 19839; assoc. editor: Jour. Geophys. Rsch., 19979. Mem. model working group South Coast Air Quality Mgmt. Dist., So. Calif., 1993-94; advisor Athens Olympic Bid Com., 1997. Grantee German Sci. Ministry, 1993, 94, 95, 96, 97, Forschungzentrum, 1992. Mem. Air and Waste Mgmt. Assn., Am. Geophys. Union, Am. Chem. Soc., Sigma Xi. Democrat. Methodist. Avocations: photography, music, hiking, bicycling, reading. Office: Desert Rsch Inst 215 Raggio Pkwy Reno NV 89512-1095

STODD, RICHARD LEE, music educator; b. Moline, Ill., May 14, 1949; s. Richard Edmund and Evelyn Stodd; m. Janet L McKelvey, May 27, 1972; children: Erin Kozakis, Katrina, Jennifer. MusB Edn., Augustana Coll., 1971; MA in Music Edn., Western Ill. U., 1995. Cert. tchr. Ill. Band dir. East Moline (Ill.) Pub. Schs., 1971—74; band/orch. dir. John Deere Jr. H.S., Moline, 1974—79; nat. dir. of devel. Leadership Mgmt., Inc., Waco, Tex., 1979—80; band dir. Alwood Comm. Schools, Woodhull, Ill., 1980—86, J.D. Darnall H.S., Geneseo, 1986—. Contest adjudicator, judge. Band dir. Bettendorf (Iowa) Park Band, 1974—79; musical dir. Qaud City Music Guild, Moline, 1974—76; band dir. Maple City Band, Geneseo, 1986—2002; choir dir. First Luth. Ch., 1995—2001. Mem.: Am. Sch. Band Dirs. Assn., Ill. Music Educators Assn. (bd. of directors 1993—96, dist. pres. 1993—), Music Educators Nat. Conf., Ill. Edn. Assn., Phi Mu Alpha Sinfonia (charter mem. Zzeta Beta chpt. 1971). Home: 319 West Pearl St Geneseo IL 61254-1530 Office: JD Darnall HS 700 North State St Geneseo IL 61254 Personal E-mail: gt_stodd@geneseo.net. E-mail: rstodd@dist228.org.

STODDARD, ALEXANDRA, designer, writer, lecturer; b. Weston, Mass., Nov. 8, 1941; d. Robert Powell and Barbara Rutledge (Green) Johns; m. Brandon Stoddard (div.); children: Alexandra Brandon, Brooke Goodwin; m. Peter Megargee Brown, May 18, 1974. Diploma in design, N.Y. Sch. Interior Design, 1961. Designer McMillen, Inc., N.Y.C., 1963-77; pres., CEO Alexandra Stoddard Inc., 1977—. Founder, pres. Design & Art Soc., Ltd., N.Y.C., 1987—. Author: Style for Living: How to Make Where You Live You, A Child's Place: How to Create a Living Environment for Your Child From Birth through Adolescence, Reflections on Beauty: Lectures and Notes on Interior

Design, The Postcard as Art: Bring the Museum Home (Cert. of Merit award 1986), Living a Beautiful Life: 500 Ways to Add Elegance, Order, Beauty and Joy To Every Day of Your Life, Alexandra Stoddard's Living Beautifully Together, Alexandra Stoddard's Book of Color, Gift of a Letter, Daring to be Yourself, Creating a Beautiful Home, Grace Notes, Making Choices, Alexandra Stoddard's Tea Celebrations, The Art of the Possible, Mothers: A Celebration, Gracious Living in a New World, The Decoration of Houses, Open Your Eyes - 1000 Simple Ways to Bring Beauty into Your Home and Life Each Day, Feeling at Home - Defining Who You are and How You Want to Live, Choosing Happiness: Keys to a Joyful Life; contbg. editor Country Antiques and Collectibles, Decorating with Americana; back page columnist Design Times - The Art of Interiors; columnist McCall's mag.; contbr. articles to profl mags. and jours. Founding mem., chmn. spiritual direction com. Ch. of Heavenly Rest, 1975-77; former mem. bd. regents Cathedral St. John the Divine; dame Am. Soc. of Order of St. John Hosp. of Jerusalem. Recipient Burlington prize, 1975, award for design Greenwich Arts Coun., 1985, Interior Design award Brandeis U., 1986, cert. of spl. merit Graphic Art Inst., Designer of Yr. award Kips Bay Boys and Girls Club, 1997, Disting. Womans' award Northwood U., 1999, Lit. Lion, 100th Anniversary prize 2000 Stonington (Conn.) Libr. Mem. English Speaking Union, Ch. Club, Decorators Club, Coral Beach and Tennis Club (Paget, Bermuda), New Eng. Soc. Republican. Episcopalian. Home: 1125 Park Ave New York NY 10128-1243 Office: John Rathbone House 87 Water St Stonington CT 06378-1432 also: 1125 Park Ave Ste 6A New York NY 10128-1243 Fax: 212-996.4625.

STODDARD, ELIZABETH JANE, physician assistant, artist; b. Buffalo, June 20, 1940; d. Robert Joseph and Marion Theresa (Lippert) Balk; m. Jerald Massy Stoddard, Sept. 10, 1960. AB, Bryant & Stratton Bus. Inst., 1959; AS, SUNY, Buffalo, 1961. Office mgr. Virgil H.J. Boeck, M.D., Buffalo, 1961-87; physician asst., office mgr. Thomas J. Cumbo, M.D., 1987—. Exhibited in group shows at Lewiston Art Festival, 1983-95, Allentown Village Soc. Outdoor Artfest, 1990-96, Adirondack Nat. Exhbn. Am. Watercolor, 1985, 2001, Springfield (Mass.) Nat. Show, 1990, Ga. Nat. Watercolor Show, 1992, 96, 2001, Midatlantic Watercolor Show, Balt., 1994, 96, Pa. Nat. Watercolor Show, 1995-2001, La. Internat. Watercolor Show, 1995-2001, Ala. Nat. Watercolor Show, 1995-97, Midwest Watercolor Soc. Nat. Show, 1996, Realism 97, Parkersburg, W.Va., 1997; contbr. articles to profl. jours. Vol. Amherst (N.Y.) Mus., 1990—, Millard Fillmore Healthcare Sys., Buffalo, 1980-84. Recipient 1st award Ala. Watercolor Soc., 1997, Meml. award North East Watercolor Soc., N.Y.C., 1997, Meml. Watercolor award Batavia (N.Y.) Art Soc., 1997, Best of Show award Batavia Nat. Show, Mo. Watercolor Show. Fellow Am. Artists Profl. League; mem. Nat. Watercolor Soc. (signature), Pa. Watercolor Soc. (signature), Ga. Watercolor Soc. (signature), Am. Pen Women (signature, west N.Y. chpt.), Catherine Lorillard Wolfe Art Club (signature), Niagara Frontier Watercolor Soc., Amherst Soc. Artists, Fine Arts League. Roman Catholic. Avocations: collecting folk art, antiques, gardening, tennis, golf. Home: 123 Wellingwood Dr East Amherst NY 14051-1746 Office: Dr T Cumbo 354 Lincoln Pkwy Buffalo NY 14216-3121 E-mail: jandjstoddard@aol.com.

STODDARD, FRANK, race car driver; Crew chief Busch North Series Team Dana Patten, 1986—90; crew chief Busch North Series, Stub Fadden, 1991—95; crew chief Roush Racing, Concord, NC, 1998—. Office: Roush Racing 7020 Aviation Blvd Concord NC 28027-8196

STODDARD, GEORGE EARL, investment company financial executive; b. Perry, Oreg., Jan. 7, 1917; s. G. Earl and Elthira (Thomas) S.; m. Elma Skelton, Feb. 4, 1942; children— Evan, Jean, Robert, Patricia. AB, Brigham Young U., 1937; MBA, Harvard U., 1939; LL.B., Fordham U., 1954. Investment analyst Central Hanover Bank & Trust Co., N.Y.C., 1939-42; v.p. investment ops. Equitable Life Assurance Soc. U.S., 1945-79; chmn. fin. com. W. P. Carey & Co., 1979—, also dir. Bd. dirs. United Fund of Bronxville-Eastchester, N.Y., 1960-61; pres. Home Sch. Assn., Eastchester, 1962. Served to lt. USNR, 1942-45. Mem.: Univ. Club (N.Y.C.), Harvard Bus. Sch. Club (N.Y.C.). Home: 11 Cedar Pl Eastchester NY 10709-5703 Office: 50 Rockefeller Plz New York NY 10020-1605

STODDARD, GLENN MCDONALD, lawyer; b. Washington, Feb. 18, 1958; s. Charles Hatch and Patricia (Coulter) S.; m. Sharon Lynn Stake, Aug. 22, 1981; children: Patrick M., Chloe F. BS, U. Wis., Stevens Point, 1980; MS, U. Wis., Madison, 1984, JD, 1994. Bar: Wis. 1995, U.S. Dist. Ct. (ea. and we. dists.) Wis. 1995. Assoc. code adminstr. Washburn County, Shell Lake, Wis., 1980-81; assoc. planner Manitowoc County, 1981-82; legis. aide Wis. Legis., Madison, 1983-85; asst. dir. Gov.'s Commn. on Agr., 1985; exec. dir. Wis. Land Cons. Assn., 1985-89; dir. govt. affairs Wis. Farmers Union, Chippewa Falls, 1989-92; law clk. U. Wis. Legal Asst. Program, Madison, summer 1993, Wis. Dept. Justice, Madison, summer 1994; ptnr./shareholder Garvey & Stoddard, S.C., 1995-99. Author: Essentials of Forestry, 4th edit., 1987. Chmn. Wis. Environ. Decade, Inc., Madison, 1991-92. Named Outstanding Citizen Adv., Ctr. for Pub. Rep., Madison, 1991. Mem.: ABA, ATLA, Wis. Acad. Trial Lawyers, State Bar Wis. Avocations: outdoor recreation, karate, Tai Chi, reading. Office: Garvey & Stoddard SC 634 W Main St Ste 101 Madison WI 53703-2687

STODDARD, M. ANITA, psychiatric nurse; b. Spartanburg, S.C., July 7, 1946; d. David Dupree and Maudie (Johnson) S. BSN, U. S.C., 1968; MSN, U. N.C., 1972. RN, S.C.; cert. clin. specialist in adult psychiatric and mental health nursing, lic. marriage and family therapist, S.C. Staff nurse in psychiatry S.C. Bapt. Hosp., Columbia, 1968; staff nurse Columbia Area Mental Health Ctr., 1968-70; dir. nursing Spartanburg Area Mental Health Ctr., 1972-87, asst. dir., 1987-2000, part-time spl. svcs. coord., 2001—. Mem. summer faculty U. S.C. Sch. Nursing, Columbia, 1971-72; adj. faculty Mary Black Sch. Nursing, U. S.C., Spartanburg, 1980-93; adv. bd. women's program Spartanburg Tech. Coll., 1987-2000; presenter at profl. meetings. Mem. Spartanburg Symphony/Festival Chorus, 1972—, Spartanburg County Emergency Preparedness, 1988-99. Mem. ANA (local bd. dirs. 1987-92, pres. 1974-76, Excellence in Practice award 1990), Am. Assn. Marriage and Family Therapy, Sigma Theta Tau. Methodist. Avocations: music, needlework, day trips, walking, reading.

STODDARD, PATRICIA FLORENCE COULTER, retired psychologist; b. Detroit, Oct. 13, 1923; d. Glenn Monroe and Doris Carlyle (McDonald) Coulter; m. Charles Hatch Stoddard, June 30, 1956 (div. 1991); children: Glenn, Jeffrey. BA, U. Mich., 1945; MA, George Washington U., 1953; MA in Gerontology, Coll. of Scholastica, Duluth, Minn., 1987. Asst. to dir. personnel Dewey & Almy Chem. Co., Cambridge, Mass., 1946-48; asst. dir. mgmt. tng. program Radcliffe Coll., 1948-49; tng. rep. Woodward Lothrop, Washington, 1949; personnel assoc. Hot Shoppes, Inc., 1950-53; placement officer George Washington U., 1953-58; placement asst. U. Minn., Duluth, 1967; psychiat. social worker Northwood Children's Home, 1968-80; coord. adult day svcs. Benedictine Health Ctr., 1980-98; ret. Adv. com. on aging Regional Area Redevel. Agy., Duluth, 1992—; apptd. State Commn. on Aging, Minn., 1997. Author: Wolf Springs 100 Years: A Century of Life on One Piece of Land, 1991; contbr. articles to profl. jours. Pres. Maple Crest Village Homeowners Assn., Duluth, 1997; vol. recruiter Am. Reads Project. Mem. LWV, Area Aging Network, Algonquin Club. Avocations: tennis, elderhostels, reading, aerobics. Home: 320 Wildwood Dr Duluth MN 55811-5203

STODDARD, PATRICK CLARE, retired military systems consultant, computer engineer; b. June 13, 1941; s. Frank Eudaly and Mary Clarann (Burns) Stoddard; m. Anneliese Barg, Sept. 18, 1963; children: Patrick Frank, Conni Maryann. Student, Cleve. Inst. Electronics, 1967—68, U. Md., 1961—63. Enlisted USAF, 1959, radar technician, 1959—67, resigned, 1967; asst. engr. Univac divsn. Sperry Rand, Minn., 1967—68, field engr., 1968; sys. engr. Hydrospace Challenger Rsch., Inc., Md., 1968—73; sr. engr. Control Data Corp., Arlington, Va., 1973—74, prin. engr. computer scis., 1974—78, mil. sys. cons., 1978—; ret., 2002. Contbr. numerous studies in support of mil. sys. devel. Recipient Bill Norris Shark Club award, Control Data Corp., 1978. Roman Catholic. Achievements include patents for electronic oil slick control. Home: 55 Mohegan Rd Groton CT 06340-5537 E-mail: thames1@mindspring.com.

STODDARD, PHILIP HENDRICK, foreign affairs analyst, writer; b. Iowa City, Apr. 30, 1929; s. George Dinsmore and Margaret (Trautwein) S.; m. Carol Cannon, Jan. 19, 1952 (div. 1959); children: Michele, Christopher, Eric; m. Doris Joyce Mills, Dec. 26, 1960; children: Leah, Evan. BA, U. Ill., 1950; MA, Princeton U., 1955, PhD, 1963. Asst. prof. SUNY New Paltz, 1958-60; analyst, 1963-80; with U.S. Dept. State, Washington, dep. asst. sec., 1980-83; exec. dir. Middle East Inst., 1983-87; cons. Nat. Intelligence Coun., 1988-90, dir., analytic group, 1990-94; ret., 1994; mem., dir. Ctrl. Intelligence's Sr. Rev. Panel, 1996-97. Author: Teskilat-i Mahsusa, 1993; editor: Change and the Muslim World, 1981; editor, co-translator: The Turkish Battle at Khaybar, 1997 (in English and Turkish); contbr. articles to profl. jours. State Dept. fellow Coun. Fgn. Rels., 1979-80. Sgt. USMC, 1951-53. Named Disting. Fed. Exec., U.S. Govt.; recipient Nat. Intelligence Disting. Svc. medal. Mem. Middle East Inst., Middle East Studies Assn., Turkish Studies Assn., Am. Fgn. Svc. Assn., Phi Beta Kappa, Sigma Chi. Home: 6000 Springfield Dr Bethesda MD 20816-1232 E-mail: phstoddard@aol.com.

STODDARD, ROBERT H. geography educator; b. Auburn, Nebr., Aug. 29, 1928; s. Hugh P. and Nainie L. (Robertson) S.; m. Sally E. Salisbury, Dec. 10, 1955; children: Martha, Andrew R., Hugh A. BA, Nebr. Wesleyan, Lincoln, 1950; MA, U. Nebr., 1960; PhD, U. Iowa, 1966. Instr. Nebr. Wesleyan, 1961-63, asst. prof., 1963-67, U. Nebr., Lincoln, 1967-71, assoc. prof., 1971-81, prof., 1981—2001. Vis. prof. Tribhuvan U., Kathmandu, Nepal, 1975-76, U. Columbo, Sri Lanka, 1986; inst. instr. Okla. State U., Stillwater, 1966; TV instr. Nebr. Ednl. TV Higher Edn., Lincoln, 1969; instr. Career Opportunity Program, Lincoln, 1973; dir. Geog. Edn. of Nebr., Lincoln, 1989-95. Author: Field Techniques, 1982; contbg. author: Human Geography, 2d edit., 1989; editor: Sacred Places, 1997. Mem. subcom. Lincoln-Lancaster Planning Com., 1974-78. Mem. Assn. Am. Geographers, Nat. Coun. for Geog. Edn. (Disting. Tchg. Achievement award 1992). Democrat. Unitarian Universalist. Office: U Nebr Dept Geography Lincoln NE 68588-0368

STODDARD, ROGER ELIOT, librarian; b. Boston, Dec. 2, 1935; s. Merton Edgar and Helen (Bonney) S.; m. Helen Louise Heckel, May 24, 1958; children— Alison Louise, Christopher Paine AB, Brown U., 1957. Asst. curator Harris Coll. Am. Poetry and Plays, Brown U., Providence, 1961-63, curator, 1963-65; asst. to librarian Harvard U. Houghton Library, Cambridge, Mass., 1958-61, asst. librarian, 1965-69, assoc. librarian, 1969-85; sr. curator, 1995—; curator rare books Harvard Coll. Library, Cambridge, Mass., 1985—; lectr. English Harvard U., 1984-86, sr. lectr., 1986—. Faculty mem. Columbia U. Rare Book Sch., N.Y.C., 1984-85; sec. Friends of Harvard Coll. Libr., Cambridge, Mass., 1983-98. Author: Catalogue of Books & Pamphlets Unrecorded in Wegelin's Early American Poetry, 1969, The Houghton Library 1942-82, 1982, Poet & PRinter in Colonial & Federal America, 1983, The Parkman Dexter Howe Library, part 1: Early New England Books, 1983, Marks in Books, Illustrated and Explained, 1985 (N.E. Book Show award, 1986, Am. Libr. Assn. award, 1987), Put a Resolute Hart to a Steep Hill: William Gowans Antiquary and Bookseller, 1990; editor: A Glance at Private Libraries, 1991, Edmond Jabès in Bibliography, 1998, 2nd ed., rev. and ednl., 2001, John Laurent, Maine Painter: An Annotated Register of Paintings, Prints and Drawings, 2000, Julian Offray de La Mettrie, 1709-1751: A Bibliographical Inventory, 2001, A Library-Keeper's Business: Essays, 2002; contbr. articles to profl. jours. Mem. Records and Archives Com., Concord, Mass., 1985-87; bd. dirs. Louisa May Alcott Meml. Assn., Concord, 1983— Huntington Library fellow, San Marino, Calif., 1978; W. F. Milton fellow Harvard U. Med. Sch., Boston, 1978-80; D.W. Bryant fellow Harvard U., 1992. Mem. Bibliog. Soc. Am. (coun. mem. 1982-88, Bibliography of Am. Lit. supervisory com. chmn. 1982-91, pres. 1996-2000), Am. Antiquarian Soc. (coun. mem. 1989-93), Assn. Internat. de Bibliophilie, Book Club Calif., Colonial Soc. Mass. (corr. sec. 1993-97), The Johnsonians, Bibliog. Soc. London (hon. sec. for Am. 1992—), Bibliog. Soc. Va., Grolier Club (N.Y.C.), Harvard Club (N.Y.C.), Odd Vols. Boston Club (exec. com. 1985-87). Home: 9 Birchwood Ln Lincoln MA 01773-4907 Office: Harvard Univ Houghton Library Harvard Yard Cambridge MA 02138-6502

STODDARD, SANDOL, freelance/self-employed writer; b. Birmingham, Ala., Dec. 16, 1927; d. Carlos French and Caroline (Harris) S.; m. Felix M. Warburg (div. 1966); children: Anthony, Peter, Gerald, Jason; m. Peter R. Goethals, May 1, 1984. BA magna cum laude, Bryn Mawr Coll., 1959. Author 26 books including: Growing Time, 1971, The Doubleday Children's Bible, 1983 (Lewis citation 1983), The Hospice Movement: Updated and Expanded Edition, 1992, Prayers, Praises and Thanksgivings, 1992. Bd. dirs., co-founder Hospice of Kona, Kailua-Kona, Hawaii, 1985; co-founder Kona Theol. Inst., 1990; bd. dirs. Choice in Dying, N.Y.C. Recipient Humanitarian Svc. award Forbes Health System, 1979, Notable Book award Am. Libr. Assn., 1964. Mem. AAUW, Nat. Writer's Guild, Cosmpolitan Club. Democrat. Episcopalian. Home and Office: 78-6646 Mamalahoa Hwy Holualoa HI 96725-9734

STODDARD, STEPHEN DAVIDSON, ceramic engineer, former state senator; b. Everett, Wash., Feb. 8, 1925; s. Albert and Mary Louise (Billings) S.; m. Joann Elizabeth Burt, June 18, 1949 (dec. Oct. 1993); children: Dorcas Ann, Stephanie Kay; m. Barbara L. Seitz, Feb. 18, 1995. Student, Tacoma Coll., 1944, Conn. Coll., 1946; BS, U. Ill., 1950. Asst. prodn. supr., asst. ceramic engr. Coors Porcelain Co., Golden, Colo., 1950-52; ceramics-powder metallurgy sect. leader Los Alamos (N.Mex.) Sci. Lab., U. Calif., 1952-82; pres., treas. Materials Tech. Assocs., Inc., 1978-94; cons. Ceramic Age Mag., 1958-60; Cons. Nuclear Applications for Ceramic Materials, 1958-60; Jury commr. Los Alamos County, 1969; justice of peace, 1956-62; mem. Los Alamos Sch. Adv. Council, 1966; mcpl. judge, 1976-77; chmn. Los Alamos Ordinance Rev. Com., 1958; Mem. Republican County and State Central Com., 1955—; county commr. Los Alamos, N.Mex., 1966-68; mem. Los Alamos County Planning Commn., 1962-63, N.Mex. Senate, 1980-92. Bd. dirs. Los Alamos Econ. Devel. Corp., U. N.Mex. Los Alamos Found. Patentee in field. Bd. dirs. Sangre de Cristo coun. Girl Scouts U.S.A., 1965—71; N.Mex. chpt. Nature Conservancy, 1988—97, v.p., 1993—94, disting. trustee, 2001; bd. dirs. Southwestern Assn. on Indian Affairs, Inc., 1987—91, chmn., 2000—02; bd. dirs. Los Alamos Vis. Nurses, 1995—2001; chmn. Gov.'s Commn. in Nat. and Cmty. Svc., 2001—, Los Alamos County 50th Anniversary Com., 1998—99; trustee Valles Caldera Nat. Preserve, 2000—; chair Los Alamos Vis. Nurses, 2000—; mem. Los Alamos Edn. Group, 1995—. With AUS, 1943—46. Decorated Bronze Star, Purple Heart, Combat Infantry Badge; recipient disting. alumni award U. Ill. Coll. Engring., 1986, Leopold Conservation award N.Mex. Nature Conservancy, 1988. Fellow Am. Inst. Chemists, Am. Ceramic Soc. (treas. 1972-74, pres. 1976-77, disting. life 1984); mem. Nat. Inst. Ceramic Engrs. (PACE award 1965, Greaves Walker award 1984), Am. Soc. Metals, N.Mex. Soc. Profl. Engrs. (Ingeniero Veterano de Nuevo Mejico award 1992), Los Alamos C. of C. (citizen of yr. award 1992), Masons, Shriners (pres. 1994-95), Elks (dist. dep. grand exalted ruler 1968-69), Los Alamos Golf Assn. (dir. 1964-66), Am. Legion (nat. legis. coun. 1992-94), Sigma Xi, Alpha Tau Omega. Episcopalian. Home: 4557 Trinity Dr Los Alamos NM 87544-1862 Fax: 505-662-2058. E-mail: stoddard@nmsu.edu.

STODDARD, WILLIAM BERT, JR. economist; b. Carbondale, Pa., Oct. 6, 1926; s. William Bert and Emily (Trautwein) S.; m. Carol Marie Swartz, Feb. 28, 1970; 1 child, Emily Coleman. Student, Lafayette Coll., 1944-45; BS, NYU, 1950, AM, 1952. Asst. chief acct., budget dir. Hendrick Mfg. Co., Carbondale, 1952-54, asst. dir. prodn., 1956-68, also dir.; credit corr. U.S. Gypsum Co., N.Y.C., 1954-56; investment counselor Carbondale, 1968-73, Ridgefield, Conn., 1973—. Dir. First Nat. Bank Carbondale, 1968-73; bd. dirs. Lackawanna County Mfrs. Assn., Scranton, Pa., 1960-73. Treas., trustee Aldrich Mus. Contemporary Art, Ridgefield, 1976-90; bd. dirs. Ridgefield Libr. and Hist. Assn., 1977-85, 87-93. With U.S. Army, 1946-47. Mem. Inst. Mgmt. Accts., Nat. Def. Indsl. Assn., NYU Club (N.Y.C.), Waccabuc (N.Y.) Country Club, Princeton Club (N.Y.C.), Phi Alpha kappa, Phi Delta Theta. Republican. Methodist. Home: 59 Bridle Trl Ridgefield CT 06877-1401 Office: 23 Catoonah St Ridgefield CT 06877-4431

STODDARD, WILLIAM LAWRENCE, civil engineer; b. Rockland, Maine, Apr. 28, 1950; s. Richard St. Clair and Virginia (Leach) S.; m. Diane Christine Poulin, Apr. 12, 1975; children: Mark, James. BSCE, U. Maine, 1973. Registered profl. engr., Maine. Structural engr. Harriman Assocs., Auburn, Maine, 1973-74; asst. engr., civil engr. Maine Dept. Environ. Protection, Augusta, 1975-82; constrn. engr. Maine Bur. Gen. Svcs., 1982—95, chief engr., 1995—2001; ret., 2001. Mem. State Contract Rev. Com., Augusta, 1990—. Author water quality status reports. Mem. ASCE, Constrn. Specifications Inst.

STODDERT, SANDRA SMITH, media director; b. Easton, Pa., Mar. 12, 1942; d. Harry James and Agnes (Krueger) Smith; m. D. Dale Kleppinger, Aug. 22, 1964 (div. Sept. 1981); children: Eric David, Deborah Ellen; m. Dorwin W. Stoddert, July 15, 1983 (dec. Feb. 1987); stepchildren: Joel Thomas, Jennifer Lea. BS in Edn., Bloomsburg U., 1964; MEd, Lehigh U., 1967. Tchr. Bethlehem (Pa.) Sch. Dist., 1964-67; permanent substitute South Burlington (Vt.) Sch. Dist., 1978-79, media ctr. dir., 1979—. Mem. LWV (pres. 1976-77), Nat. Coun. Social Studies (curriculum devel. com. 1986-88) Local Stds. Bd. (chmn. 1991-94), Vt. Ednl. Media Assn., Vt. State Tech. Coun., South Burlington Educators Assn. (bldg. rep. 1984-86, pres. 1987-90, negotiating team mem. 1988-91, grievance chair 1991-95). Republican. Lutheran. Avocations: cross stitch, sewing, reading. Office: Chamberlin Sch 262 White St South Burlington VT 05403

STODGHILL, RONALD, school system administrator; b. White Plains, N.Y., Dec. 21, 1939; s. Joseph and Marian (Wynn) Stodghill; children: Kimberly, Denise, Ronald. BS, Ea. Mich. U., 1961; MS, We. Mich. U., 1967; EdD, Wayne State U., 1981. Dir. edn. New Detroit, Detroit; deputy supt. St. Louis Pub. Schs., Mo.; supt. Wellston Pub. Schs. Mem. ASCD (exec.), Am. Assn. Advancement of Sci., Nat. Assn. Bilingual Edn. Home: 6574 Saint Louis Ave Saint Louis MO 63121-5725

STOEBNER, JOHN MARTIN, physician; b. Burlington, Tex., 1933; s. Alfred Walter Richard and Mary Evaleen (Martin) S.; m. Julia Bryan Fisher, Aug. 7, 1971; children: J. Eric, Richard, William Scott, Julia M., Kristin. BS, Loyola U., New Orleans, 1956; MD, U. Tex. Med. Br., Galveston, 1959. Intern Fitzsimons Gen. Hosp., Denver, 1959-60; resident Walter Reed Gen. Hosp., Washington, 1965-68; prof. Tex. A&M Coll. Medicine. Vice-chmn. radiology Scott & White Clin., Temple, Tex., 1986-92, chmn. 1992-96. Comdr. 94th Gen. Hosp. USAR, Dallas, 1972-82. Mem. Am. Coll. Radiology, Texas Radiol. Soc. Office: Scott & White Clin Radiology Temple TX 76508-0001

STOEBUCK, WILLIAM BREES, law educator; b. Wichita, Kans., Mar. 18, 1929; s. William Douglas and Donice Beth (Brees) S.; m. Mary Virginia Fields, Dec. 24, 1951; children: Elizabeth, Catherine, Caroline. BA, Wichita State U., 1951; MA, Ind. U., 1953; JD, U. Wash., 1959; SJD, Harvard U., 1973. Bar: Wash. 1959, U.S. Supreme Ct. 1967. Pvt. practice, Seattle, 1959-64; asst. prof. law U. Denver, 1964-67; assoc. prof. U. Wash., Seattle, 1967-70, prof., 1970-95, Judson Falknor prof., 1995—; of counsel Karr, Tuttle, Campbell, 1988—. Author: Washington Real Estate: Property Law, 1995, Washington Real Estate: Transactions, 1995, Basic Property Law, 1989, Law of Property, 1984, 3d edit., 2000, Nontrespassory Takings, 1977, Contemporary Property, 1996, 2d edit., 2002; contbr. articles to profl. jours. Bd. dirs. Cascade Symphony Orch., 1978-83, Forest Park Libr., 1975-80. 1st lt. USAF, 1951-56. Mem. Am. Coll. Real Estate Lawyers, Am. Coll. Mortgage Attys., Wash. State Bar Assn., Assn. Am. Law Schs., Order of Coif, Seattle Yacht Club. Home: 3515 NE 158th Pl Lk Forest Park WA 98155-6649 Office: U Wash Law Sch 1100 NE Campus Pkwy Seattle WA 98105-6605 E-mail: stoebuck@u.washington.edu.

STOECKER, DAVID THOMAS, banker; b. St. Louis, June 8, 1939; s. John Garth and Marie (Zahler) S.; m. Ann E. Conrad, Aug. 18, 1962; children— Lisa Ann, Susan Jane. BS, Ind. U., 1963. Sr. v.p. comml. loans Mercantile Trust Co. N.Am., St. Louis, 1965-80; pres. Gravois-Merc. Bank, 1980-87; pres., chief exec. officer Bank of South County, 1987-95; chmn. bd., pres., CEO Ctrl. West End Bank, 1996—. Served to 1st lt. AUS, 1963-65. Mem. Robert Morris Assos. (pres. St. Louis 1980) Clubs: Sunset Country. Methodist. Office: 415 Debaliviere Saint Louis MO 63112

STOECKER, RANDY REX, sociologist, educator; b. Waukesha, Wis., July 24, 1959; s. Rex and Joan Stoecker; m. Tammy J. Raduege, May 21, 1988; children: Haley. PhD, U. Minn., 1988. Prof. sociology U. Toledo, 1988—. Author: Defending Community, 1994. Mem.: Am. Sociol. Assn., Computer Profls. for Social Responsibility, Nat. Organizers Alliance, Midwest Sociol. Soc. (at-large dir. 1999—2001). Office: U Toledo Dept Sociology and Anthropology Toledo OH 43606 Office Fax: 419-530-8406. Business E-Mail: randy.stoecker@utoledo.edu.

STOECKL, SHELLEY JOAN, marketing professional; b. Buffalo, Feb. 24, 1951; d. Joseph T. and Joan (Carriere) S. AAS in Bus. Adminstrn., Bryant and Stratton, 1978; cert. in gen. banking, Am. Inst. Banking, 1982; cert. in pers. & human resource mgmt., Canisius Coll., 1983; postgrad., Empire State Coll. Cert. profl. sec. From sr. sec. to pers. mgr. Mfrs. Hanover Trust Co., Buffalo, 1974-87; acct. coord. Computer Task Group Direct Mktg. Svcs., 1987-89; project mgr. ANCOR Info. Mgmt., Inc., 1989-91; acct. mgr. IMPCO Integrated Mktg. Ptnrs., 1991-98; account mgr. Cathedral Corp., 1998-99; ops. mgr. Gajewski & Assocs., Williamsville, N.Y., 1999-2000; sr. account exec. The SKM Group (formerly Mktg. Resources of N.Y.), NY, 2000—. Co-author: (presentation) Go For the Gold: CPS, 1983—; coord.: 60 Minutes: A Look Inside the Inst. for Certifying Secs., 1991, Marketing Your Credentials to Management, 1992, In the Dark, 1993, Gain Without Pain: Recertification, 1993, Customer Service: Department or Philosophy?, 1995, Stressed at Work? Breathe it Away!, 1998, Winning Strategies in Event Planning, 1998. Co. coord. United Way, Buffalo, 1980-87; vol. Jack Kemp for Congress, Buffalo, 1970. Recipient scholastic award Buffalo Clearing House Assn., 1982. Fellow Cert. Profl. Secs. Acad. (cert.); mem. NAFE, Internat. Assn. Adminstrv. Profls. (bd. dirs. 1980-82, v.p. 1982-83, corr. sec. 1983-85, pres. 1986-87, intenrat. conv. coord. 1997), Cert. Profl. Secs. Soc. N.Y. State (pres. 1987-88), Inst. for Cert. (rep. N.E. dist. 1988-94). Conservative. Roman Catholic. Avocations: reading, theater, walking, yoga, public speaking. Home: 239 Wimbledon Ct Buffalo NY 14224-1955 Office: The SKM Group 5166 Main St Williamsville NY 14221

STOECKLIN, SISTER CAROL ANN, education educator; b. Detroit, July 20, 1953; d. Andrew Charles and Ernestine (Roselli) S. BA, Mercy Coll. of Detroit, 1974; M in theol. studies, St. John's Provincial Sem., 1986; MA, St. Louis U., 1991, PhD, 1993. Joined Religious Sisters of Mercy. Tchr. Bishop Borgess High Sch., Redford, Mich., spring 1976, St. Agatha High Sch., Detroit, 1976-79; adminstrv. asst., campus minister, religion dept. chair Muskegon (Mich.) Cath. Ctrl. High Sch., 1979-84; adminstrv. asst., dir. ministries Nouvel High Sch., Saginaw, Mich., 1984-85; acad. dean, counselor, tchr. St. Joseph's on the Rio Grande High Sch., Albuquerque, 1985-87; tchr. Holy Ghost Elem. Sch., 1988-89; grad. asst. edn. dept. St. Louis (Mo.) U., 1991-93; from asst. to assoc. prof. edn. U. Detroit Mercy, 1993—; project adminstr. Our Lady of Guadalupe Mid. Sch., Detroit, 1997-99; dir. cert. and field experiences U. Detroit Mercy, 1999—. Mem. edn. com. Sisters of Mercy, Farmington Hills, Mich., 1990-93; CHRPN, 1993-96; literacy program evaluator Macomb County Headstart, Mt. Clemens, Mich., 1990; curriculum cons. St. Mary's H.S., St. Louis, 1991. Co-author: Valuing Our Differences, 9-12, 1992, K-8, 1993. Mem. ASCD, Assn. Univ. Women, Mercy Secondary Edn. Assn., Mercy Elem. Edn. Network, Phi Delta Kappa, Pi Lambda Theta. Roman Catholic. Avocations: writing poetry, photography, calligraphy. E-mail: stoeckca@udmercy.edu.

STOEGER, JAMES ALAN, principal; b. Manitowoc, Wis., Aug. 4, 1946; s. Mark Joseph and Rose Mary (Morris) S. BA, Loyola U., 1970, MDiv, 1975; MEd, Harvard U., 1977; profl. diploma, Fordham U., 1978. Cert. in ednl. adminstrn. and supervision, Ind.; ordained Jesuit priest. Religion tchr. Loyola Acad., Wilmette, Ill., 1969-72; asst. headmaster Xavier H.S., N.Y.C., 1977-78; headmaster Gonzaga Coll. H.S., Washington, 1978-82; campus min. St. Xavier H.S., Cin., 1983-87; prin. Brebeuf Prep. Sch., Indpls., 1987—. Bd. dirs. Ind. Non-Pub. Edn. Assn., Indpls., Loyola Acad., Wilmette. Mem. Indpls. Athletic Club, Phi Delta Kappa. Roman Catholic. Office: Brebeuf Prep Sch 2801 W 86th St Indianapolis IN 46268-1925

STOEK, THOMAS, management and sales professional; b. Friedberg, Germany, Dec. 2, 1964; s. Norbert Leo and Elke Astrid Stoek; 1 child Robin. Degree in elect. engring., Darmstadt (Germany) U., 1992; IMD, Lausanne U. Cons. Interchip Unternehmensberatung, 1992-95; sr. cons. Softlab, Munich, 1995-96; sales mgr. Central Europe Seagate Software, Inc.; mng. dir. and mem. European Bd. Guardian iT (formerly debis Systemhaus Guardian), London, 1997-2000; exec. v.p. sales & mktg. Cybernet, Inc., Munich, 2001—. Bd. dirs. Novento AG, Multicale AG. Contbr. articles to profl. jours. Active

Bus. Angel Network Deutschland, Berlin, 2000—; chmn. McKinsey Social Projects. Served with German mil., 1984-85. Office: Cybernet Inc 81929 Munich Germany Fax: 49 8152 981372. E-mail: tstoek@t-online.de.

STOERMER, EUGENE FILMORE, biologist, educator; b. Webb, Iowa, Mar. 7, 1934; s. Edward Filmore and Agnes Elizabeth (Ekstrand) S.; m. Barbara Purves Ryder, Aug. 13, 1960; children: Eric Filmore, Karla Jean, Peter Emil. BS, Iowa State U., 1959, PhD, 1963. Assoc. rsch. scientist, rsch. scientist U. Mich., Ann Arbor, 1965-79, assoc. prof., 1979-85, prof., 1985—. Editl. advisor Jour. Paeleolimonology. Contbr. over 200 articles to profl. jours. Fellow Acad. Natural Scis., Phila., 1980; recipient Darbaker prize, Bot. Soc. Am., 1993. Mem. Phycological Soc. Am. (pres. 1988-89), Internat. Assn. for Diatom Rsch. (pres. 1992-94). Home: 4392 Dexter Ave Ann Arbor MI 48103-1636 Office: U Mich Ctr for Great Lakes Ann Arbor MI 48109 E-mail: stoermer@umich.edu.

STOESEN, ALEXANDER RUDOLPH, retired history educator; b. Austin, Tex., Apr. 9, 1932; s. Andrew Robert William and Laura Tomine (Thompson) S.; m. Carol Annette Cronk, Aug. 22, 1959 (dec. Feb. 1999); children: Robert Andrew, William Darden, Carolyn Anne. BA, The Citadel, 1954; MA, U. Rochester, 1958; PhD, U. N.C., 1965. Tchr. Washington Sq. Reading Ctr., N.Y.C., 1958-59; asst. prof. history Newberry (S.C.) Coll., 1964-66; from asst. to prof. history Guilford Coll., Greensboro, N.C., 1966-99, chmn. dept. history, 1972-77, 82-84, 90-91; Lilly fellow Duke U., Durham, 1976-77. Mem., past chair N.C. Hwy. Hist. Market Adv. Commn., Raleigh, 1986-91, 94-98, 2001—; v.p. So. Assn. Pre-Law Advisers, 1989-91, pres., 1991-93; mem. Pre-Law Advisers Nat. Coun., 1991-93, cons., 1993—. Author: Guilford College: On the Strength of 150 Years, 1987, Guilford County Since 1890, Part II of History of Guilford County, 1981, Guilford County: A Brief History, 1993; author: (with others) The North Carolina Experience, 1984, Encyclopedia of Southern History, 1979; contbr. articles to profl. jours. and reviews to newspapers. Mem. Greensboro Sit-Ins Twentieth Anniversary Com., 1979-80, 13th Anniversary Com., 1989-90, 40th Ann. Com., 1999-2000; chmn. bd. trustees Unitarian Ch. of Greensboro, 1979-81; trustee Greensboro Hist. Mus., 1997-99; vol. mission Habitat for Humanity, Zambia, 1991, New Zealand, 1992, London, 2000, Honduras, 2000-01, U.K., 2001, Hungary, 2001; vol. Quaker workteam in Ramallah, Palestine, 1999. 1st lt. U.S. Army, 1955-57, capt. USAR, 1969. 1st lt. USAR, 1955—57, capt. USAR, 1969. Recipient Congl. Leadership award Thomas Jefferson dist. Unitarian-Universalist Assn., 1995, Appreciation award Guilford County Bd. of Pub. Health, 2000, Christopher Crittenden award State N.C., 1990, 2000; grantee NEH, 1975, 82. Mem. Am. Hist. Assn., Hist. Soc. N.C. (coun. 1988-90, sec. 1990-96, v.p. 1997-98, pres. 1998-99, mem. Hugh T. Lefler undergrad. history award com. 1983, chmn. 1984), N.C. Lit. and Hist. Assn. (mem. Mayflower Cup book prize com. 1987, 91), Southern Hist. Assn., Orgn. Am. Historians (chmn. mem. com., 1991-96), Assn. of Citadel Men (life). Democrat. Avocations: bicycling, Bicentennial memorabilia collector, gardening, bird watching, whitewater rafting. E-mail: astoesen@aol.com.

STOESSINGER, JOHN GEORGE, political science educator; b. Vienna, Austria, Oct. 14, 1927; came to U.S., 1947; s. Oscar and Irene Stoessinger; m. Carolyn Stoessinger, 1966 (div. 1985); children: Richard Victor, Anna. BA, Grinnell Coll., 1950, LLB (hon.), 1970; MA, Harvard U., 1952, PhD, 1954; LLB (hon.), Am. Coll. in Switzerland, Leysin, 1981. Prof. polit. scis. CUNY, N.Y.C., 1957-83; dir. polit. affairs divsn. UN, 1967-74; disting. prof. internat. affairs Trinity U., San Antonio, 1983-2000; disting. prof. global diplomacy U. San Diego, 2000—. Teaching fellow Harvard U., Cambridge, Mass., 1952-54; asst. prof. polit. sci. Wellesley (Mass.) Coll., 1954-56; vis. prof. internat. affairs Columbia U., N.Y.C., 1963-67, Princeton (N.J.) U., 1978. Author: The Might of Nations, 1962, 10th edit., 2000 (Bancroft prize 1963), Nations at Dawn, 1979, 6th edit., 1996, Henry Kissinger, 1979, Why Nations Go To War, 1983, 8th edit., 2001 Mem. UNA-USA, N.Y., 1960—. Mem. Coun. on Fgn. Rels. (book rev. editor Fgn. Affairs 1968-78). Jewish. Avocation: classical music. Home: 418 Neptune Ave Encinitas CA 92024 Office: U San Diego 5998 Alcala Park San Diego CA 92110

STOFF, JEFFREY S. physician, educator; b. Oct. 20, 1942; BS, Hobart Coll., Geneva, N.Y., 1964; MD, SUNY, Buffalo, 1968. Dir. renal medicine U. Mass. Meml., Worcester, 1983—, dir. transplantation medicine, 1983—; prof. medicine/physiology U. Mass. Med. Sch., 1983—; assoc. prof. Harvard Med. Sch., Boston, 1982-83; asst. physician Beth Israel Hosp., 1974—. Editor: Jour. Intensive Care Medicine; editl. bd. Transplant Jour.; contbr. articles in profl. jours. Bd. trustees New England Organ Bank, 1996-98, councilor United Network Organ Sharing, Richmond, Va., 1998—. Office: Medicine Dept/Renal Medicine U Mass Meml 55 Lake Ave N Worcester MA 01655-0317 E-mail: stoffj@ummhc.org.

STOFFERSON, TERRY LEE, financial officer; b. Omaha, Apr. 22, 1957; s. Dale Leslie and Alma Rose (Flores) S. BSBA, U. Nebr., Omaha, 1980; MBA, DBA, Calif. Coast U., Santa Ana, 1998. Auditor Alexander Grant & Co., CPA's, Omaha, 1979-81; budget mgr. Archbishop Bergan Mercy Hosp., 1981-86; controller Lafayette (La.) Gen. Med. Ctr., 1986-87; chief fin. officer Opelousas (La.) Gen. Hosp., 1987-89; assoc. adminstr. fin. County of Fresno Valley (Calif.) Med. Ctr., 1989-94; v.p. fin. Trinity Med. Ctr., Minot, N.D., 1994-96; exec. v.p. St. Catherine Hosp., Garden City, Kans., 1996-2001; sr. v.p. Provena St. Joseph Hosp., Elgin, Ill., 2001—. Cons. in field. Mem. Healthcare Fin. Mgrs. Assn. (advanced), Nat. Assn. Accts. (contr.'s coun. 1988, 89), Am. Hosp. Assn., Am. Coll. Healthcare Execs Lodges: Optimist (pres. 1988). Republican. Presbyterian. Avocations: fishing, electronics, photography. E-mail: terrystofferson@provenahealth.com.

STOFFLE, CARLA JOY, university library dean; b. Pueblo, Colo., June 19, 1943; d. Samuel Bernard and Virginia Irene (Berry) Hayden; m. Richard William Stoffle, June 12, 1964; children: Brent William, Kami Ann. AA, So. Colo. State Coll., Pueblo, 1963; BA, U. Colo., 1965; MLS, U. Ky., 1969; postgrad., U. Wis., 1980. Head govt. publ. dept. John G. Crabbe Library, Eastern Ky. U., Richmond, 1969-72; head. pub. services U. Wis.-Parkside Library, Kenosha, 1972-76, exec. asst. to chancellor, 1978, asst. chancellor edn. services, 1979-85; assoc. dir. U. Mich. Library, Ann Arbor, 1985-91, dep. dir., 1986-91; mem. adv. commn. Sch. Libr. Sci. U. Mich., 1986-92; dean librs. U. Ariz., Tucson, 1991—, acting dir. Sch. Info. Resources and Libr. Sci., 1999—. Vol. Peace Corps, Barbados, W.I., 1965-67; mem. adv. bd. Bowker Libr., N.Y., 1985-90; mem. bd. advisors U. Ariz. Press, 1995-; mem. adv. coun. OCLC Rsch. Librs., 1995-; bd. dirs. Assn. for Rsch. Librs., 1997-, chair com. on stats. and measurement, 1999—, mem. steering com. scholarly pub. and acad. resource program, 1998-2002; mem. editl. bd. Internet and Higher Edn., 1998-99; bd. dirs. Ctr. for Rsch. Librs., 1999-, treas., 1999-2001, budget and fin. com., 1994; presenter in field. Co-author: Administration Government Documents Collection, 1974, Materials and Method for History Research, 1979, Materials and Methods for Political Science Research, 1979; assoc. editor Collection Building, 1986-91, editorial bd., 1986-95; mem. editl. bd. The Bottom Line, 1989-95; contbr. numerous articles to profl. jours. Recipient Most Outstanding Reference Quar. Article award Reference Svc. Press, 1986, Woman on the Move award Tucson Young Women's Christian Assn., 1992, Pres.'s award Ariz. Ednl. Media Assn., 1993, Student Honor Soc. Mortar Bd. award for Faculty Excellence, 1995; named Outstanding Alumnus, Coll. Libr. and Info. Sci., U. Ky., 1989, Libr. of Yr. Ariz. Libr. Assn., 2000. Mem. ALA (treas. 1988-92, exec. bd. dirs. 1985-92, councilor 1983-92, endowment trustee 2001—, Elizabeth Futas Catalyst for Change award 2002, com. accreditation 2002), Assn. Coll. Rsch. Librs. (pres. 1982-83, Bibliographic Instrn. Libr. of Yr. 1991, Acad. Rsch. Libr. of Yr. 1992, Excellence in Acad. award 2001). Office: U Arizona Main Libr 1510 E University Blvd Tucson AZ 85721-0005

STOFFLET, MARY KIRK, museum curator, writer; b. Long Branch, N.J., Dec. 23, 1942; d. Norman Kirk and Virginia (Birdsall) S. BA in Art History, Skidmore Coll., 1964; MA in Art History, NYU, 1969. Coord. intern program Fine Arts Museums of San Francisco, 1977-80; asst. curator San Francisco Internat. Airport, 1982-85; edn. curator San Diego Mus. Art, 1985-88, modern art curator, 1988-97; asst. dir. edn. and publs. San Francisco Airport Mus., 1998—. Editor newsletter Western Assn. Art Museums, Oakland, Calif., 1974-77; contbg. editor Artweek, Oakland, 1974-81, Images & Issues, L.A., 1980-85; author, coordinating editor (exhbn. catalog) California Cityscapes, 1991; essayist, coordinating editor (exhbn. catalog) Latin American Drawings Today, 1991; author (exhbn. catalogs) Dr. Seuss From Then to Now, 1987, Deborah Butterfield, 1996; editor (book) Correspondence Art, 1984. Rockefeller/NEA fellow in mus. edn., 1975-76; recipient Critic's Grant, NEA, 1981. Mem. MLA, Internat. Assn. Art Critics, Am. Assn. Museums, Coll. Art Assn., ArtTable. Avocation: writing mystery novels. Office: San Francisco Airport Mus 1766 El Camino Real Burlingame CA 94010-3206

STOGNER, WILLIAM LOUIS, pharmaceutical company executive; b. Las Vegas, Nev., Oct. 24, 1957; s. James Stogner and Mary Louise (Bierley) Alberts; m. Jennifer Dawn Pruitt, July 11, 1985; 1 child Dana DeAnne. Student, Niagara U., Niagara Falls, N.Y., 1976. Retail salesman, warehouse mgr. McGrath & Durk, Inc., Niagara Falls, 1973-77; retail salesman, S&R mgr. Gill's Plumbing Supply, Inc., 1977-79; prin. H.B. Contractors, 1979-81; sales supr. Parmed Pharms., Inc., 1981-82; sales cons. Republic Drug Co., Buffalo, 1982; sr. v.p. Ea. divsn. Major Pharms., Ormond Beach, Fla., 1982-92; ptnr. Suncoast Investors, 1988—; dir., v.p. Expert-Med, Inc., 1992—. Pres. Tuscany Trails Homeowners Assn., Inc., 1987-89; bd. dirs. The Trails Homeowners Assn., 1988-91, Hunters Ridge Homeowners Assn., 2001--. Named hon. mem. Ky. Colonials by Gov. Martha Layne Collins, 1985. Avocation: classic car restoration. Home: 8 Foxfords Chase Ormond Beach FL 32174-2426 E-mail: b.stogner@.att.net.

STOHL, ESTHER A. senior citizen advocate; b. Olympia, Wash., Apr. 13, 1919; d. James Vernon and Anna Marie (Rixe) Snodgrass; m. Edwin F. Crowell, Sept. 4, 1938 (div. Apr. 1958); children: John Steven Crowell, Charles Edwin Crowell; m. Donald L. Stohl, Oct. 16, 1960 (dec. 1983). Grad. high sch., Olympia. Asst. to sales mgr. Ga.-Pacific Plywood, Olympia, 1937-41, 46-54; adminstrv. asst. Wash. Fedn. State Employees, 1954-79; senate healthcare com. aide Wash. State Legislature, 1980; office mgr. Sr. Citizens Lobby, 1980-83, 84-89; office asst. Wash. State Ret. Tchrs. Assn., 1989-95. Pres. Srs. Educating Srs., Olympia, 1984-96; chmn. Area Agy. on Aging Adv. Coun., 1991-92. Author, editor Srs. Educating Srs. jour., 1984-96. Consumer advocate Wash. State Long Term Care Commn., Olympia, 1989-90. Mem. AFSCME (life), Wash. Fedn. State Employees (life), Am. Assn. Ret. Persons (lobbyist 1988-94), Sr. Citizens Lobby Wash., Ret. Pub. Employees Wash. Democrat. Lutheran. Avocations: reading, cooking, gardening, visiting in nursing homes. Home: 1347 Pear St NE Olympia WA 98506-3945

STOHLMAN, CONNIE SUZANNE, obstetrical gynecological nurse; b. Tucson, Sept. 27, 1960; d. Irvin Wendell and Betty Jo (Stewart) Holmes; m. Bruce R. Stohlman, Sept. 14, 1991. BSN, Bishop Clarkson Coll. Nursing, 1987; BA, U. Nebr., 1982; cert. med. asst., Omaha Coll. Health Careers, 1983. Primary nurse I U. Md. Med. System, Balt., 1987-90; staff nurse St. Joseph Hosp., Omaha, 1990—. Mem. quality assurance task force U. Md. Med. System, 1987-90; mem. quality assurance com. St. Joseph Hosp., 1992-96. Named to Outstanding Young Women of Am., 1986.

STOIA, DENNIS VASILE, industrial management educator; b. Aberdeen, S.D., Dec. 31, 1928; s. John and Seanna (Biliboca) S.; m. Margaret Ann Tyne, May 11, 1974; 1 child, Justin Michael. B of Indsl. Engring., Ohio State U., 1954; MBA, U. Chgo., 1962. Registered profl. engr., Ill. Indsl. engr. Sunbeam Corp., Chgo., 1953-64; v.p. mfg. Aerosol Rsch. Co., North Riverside, Ill., 1964-74; ops. mgr. Ethyl/VCA, Bridgeport, Conn., 1974-75; labor arbitrator Somonauk, Ill., 1975—; assoc. prof. No. Ill. U., DeKalb, 1978—, tech. dept. chmn., 1987-94, 96-98, acting assoc. dean, 1994-96. Arbitrator Fed. Mediation and Conciliation, Washington, 1981—, Ill. Local Labor Rels. Bd., Coal Arbitration Svc., Washington, 1987; hearing officer Ill. State Bbd. Edn., Springfield, 1980—. Author Arbitrator award, Bur. Nat. Affairs, 1995, 98, 2000, 2001, Commerce Clearing House, 1992. Bd. dirs. Somonauk Sch., sec., Sandwich Community Hosp., treas. Sgt. U.S. Army, 1946-48, Japan, 1950-51, Korea. Mem. Nat. Assn. for Indsl. Tech., Soc. Profls. in Dispute Resolution, Soc. Fed. Labor Rels. Profls., Am. Arbitration Assn., Am. Soc. for Engring. Edn., Theta Tau, Epsilon Pi Tau. Home: 13767 Chicago Rd Somonauk IL 60552-3013 Office: No Ill U Coll Engring and Engring Tech Dekalb IL 60115

STOIA, VIOREL G. life underwriter; b. Aberdeen, S.D., Feb. 13, 1924; s. John and Seana (Biliboca) S.; m. Donna Marie Maurseth Stoia, Sept. 10, 1949; children: Marsha Jo, Nancy Kay, Gregory Allen, Thomas John, James Vincent. BBA, U. Minn., 1949. CLU, ChFC, Am. Coll. Sr. agt. Northwestern Mutual Life, Milw., 1950—; broker Aetna Life Ins. Co., Hartford, Conn., 1960—, Principal Mutual Life, Des Moines, 1967—; with Reliastar, Mpls., 1971—. Co-founder, chmn. bd. Student Loan Fin. Corp., 1978—; ptnr. Aberdeen Real Estate, Ltd.; co-founder, mng. ptnr. Tel Serv, 1983—97; co-founder Northwest Regional Health and Fitness Ctr. Co-founder, pres. Northeastern Mental Health Ctr., 1957-59, North Plains Hospice, 1980-84; sec. Edn. Asst. Corp., 1978-97; bd. dirs. S.D. Crippled Children's Hosp.; trustee Aberdeen YMCA, 1969-73, St. Luke's Hosp., 1969-96; co-founder, trustee Northern State U. Found., 1972-99; bd. dirs. Avera Health Sys., 1996—; co-founder Great Plains Edn. Found., 1999—. With USN, 1942-46. Named Outstanding Civic Leader of Am., 1967; recipient, Jefferson award Nat. Inst. of Pub. Svc., Sioux Falls, 1980, George award Aberdeen C. of C., Aberdeen, 1979, 94, Gov.'s award for Excellence in Econ. Devel., 2000. Mem. Aberdeen Devel. Corp. (pres. 1972-87), Aberdeen Jr. C. of C. (pres. 1956), S.D. Jr. C. of C., Aberdeen C. of C., S.D. Soc. CLU's (co-founder, pres. 1958-59), Nat. Assn. Life Underwriters, Aberdeen Dist. Life Underwriters (pres. 1953-54), S.D. Assn. Life Underwriters (pres. 1959-60), Million Dollar Round Table (life), Moccasin Creek Country Club (v.p. 1969-75). Republican. Roman Catholic. Avocations: jogging, hunting, reading. Home: 1022 N Main St Aberdeen SD 57401-2426 Office: Stoia Kusler & Assoc PO Box 98 304 1/2 S Main St Aberdeen SD 57401-4146 E-mail: stoia@hdc.net.

STOIAN, CRISTINA, sales professional, real estate broker; b. Resita, Romania, Dec. 7, 1963; came to the U.S., 1993; d. Ion and Gina Nicu; m. Costin A. Stoian, Feb. 28, 1987; children: Andreea P., Raoul S. Mech. engr., Engring. Inst. Resita, 1987; quality contr., Constrn. Machinery Corp., Resita, 1989. Lic. real estate broker; registered investor svc. rep.; registered, lic. NASD. Engr. QQ bearings ICM, Resita, 1988-93; real estate broker Frontier Real Estate, Denver, 1994—; convenience store owner Lakewood, Colo., 1996-98; rental sales agt. Avis, Denver, 1998-00; registered rep. Janus, 2000—. Tax preparer Jackson Hewitt, 1999. Tennis coach Tennis Drs. Assn. Resita, 1980-83. 2nd Place winner Nat. Tennis Championship Costinesti-Romania, 1976-77. Mem. SEC, Assn. Realtors Jefferson. Avocations: painting, crafting, hiking, tennis, rock climbing. Home: 1434 W 103rd Pl Northglenn CO 80260-7116

STOIBER, CARLTON RAY, nuclear law consultant, retired federal official; b. Vallejo, Calif., July 5, 1942; s. Raymond F. and Grace (Fairhurst) S.; m. Susanne Alexander, Sept. 10, 1966. BA summa cum laude, U. Colo., 1964, LLB, 1969; diploma cum laude, Hague Acad. Internat. Law, 1975. Bar: Colo.1969, D.C.1970, U.S. Supreme Ct. 1973. Atty. U.S. Dept. Justice, Washington, 1969-71, dir. Office of Indian Rights, 1972-74; asst. gen. counsel U.S. NRC, 1975-80, U.S. Arms Control and Disarmament Agy., Washington, 1980-81; dir. Office Nuclear Export Control U.S. Dept. State, 1981-85, dir. Office Nuclear Non-Proliferation Policy, 1988-91, dir. Office Nuclear Tech. and Safeguards, 1991-93; counselor U.S. Mission to UN Agys., Vienna, Austria, 1985-88; dir. Internat. Programs Internat. Programs USNRC, 1993-99; cons. Sci. Applications Internat. Corp., 1999—. Rhodes scholar, 1964, Norlin award for disting. achievement U. Colo., 1994. Mem. Reform Club, Am. Soc. Internat. Law, Phi Beta Kappa. Avocations: cartooning and caricaturing, mountaineering, birding.

STOIBER, SUSANNE A. health science organization administrator; Degree in econs. and mgmt., U. Colo., London Sch. Econs. Dir. divsn. soc. and econ. studies NRC HHS, 1990-94, past adminstr. Clin. Rsch. Ctr. NIH, 1998, past sr. advisor to dep. dir. sci. NIH, past dir. health care reform Pub. Health Svc., past dep. asst. sec. health, dep. asst. sec. planning and evaluation/program sys., acting dep. asst. sec. health/disease prevention and health promotion; exec. dir. Inst. Medicine, 1998—. Contbr. articles to profl. jours. Recipient NIH Directors Award, 1985, Presidential Rank Award for lifetime achievement in Senior Exec. Service. Office: Inst of Med 500 5th St, NW Washington DC 20418-0007 Fax: 908-771-8618.*

STOICA, SUSANA, computer engineer, scientist, author, healer; b. Tirgu Muresh, Romania, Apr. 26, 1946; came to U.S., 1985; d. Andrei and Clara (Heisikovitsch) Gerson; m. Vladimir Stoica, Sept. 5, 1970; 1 child, Andrei. MS, Polytech. Inst., Bucharest, Romania, 1969, PhD, 1991. Reg. profl. engr., Ont., Can.; cert. healing touch practitioner, hypnotherapist. Jr. rsch. engr. Inst. Computer Rsch., Bucharest, 1969-72, sr. rsch. engr., 1972-77; engr. Ramzorei Siemens Industry Ltd., Tel Aviv, 1977-78; sr. elec. engr. Control Data Can. Ltd., Toronto, Ont., 1979-85, Control Data Corp., Mpls., 1985-86, cons., 1986-87, mgr. support, 1987-88; cons. very large scale integration/electronic computer aided design tech., 1988-90; chief scientist, mgr. advanced rsch. Delphax Systems, Toronto, 1990-92; sr. tech. specialist Advanced Vehicle Tech. Divsn. Ford Motor Co., Dearborn, Mich., 1993-96; sr. tech. specialist hardware and software test strategies Rsch. and Vehicle Tech. divsn. Ford Motor Co., 1996—. Contbr. articles to profl. jours.and confs.; inventor. Mem. IEEE, Internat. Med. and Dental Hypnotherapy Assn., Profl. Engrs. Ont., Healing Touch Internat. E-mail: SusanaStoica@aol.com., sstorica@ford.com.

STOICHEFF, BORIS PETER, physicist, educator; b. Bitol, Macedonia, June 1, 1924; s. Peter and Vasilka (Tonna) S.; m. Lillian Joan Ambridge, May 15, 1954; 1 child, Richard Peter. BSc, U. Toronto, 1947, MA, 1948, PhD, 1950, DSc (hon.), 1994, U. Skopje, Macedonia, 1981, York U., 1982, U. Windsor, 1989. McKee-Gilchrist postdoctoral fellow U. Toronto, Ont., Can., 1950-51; postdoctoral fellow NRC Can., 1951-53, sr. rsch. officer, 1954-64; vis. scientist MIT, 1963-64; prof. physics U. Toronto, 1964-89, univ prof., 1977-89, univ. prof. emeritus, 1989—, chmn. engring. sci., 1972-77, H.L. Welsh lectr., 1984; sr. fellow Massey Coll., 1979—; exec. dir. Ont. Laser and Lightwave Rsch. Ctr., 1988-91. Mem. NRC Can., 1977-83; govt. appointee to coun. Assn. Profl. Engrs. Ont., 1985-91; vis. sci. Stanford U., 1978; Walter E. Kaskan lectr. SUNY, Binghamton, 1980; Elizabeth Laird Meml. lectr. U. Western Ont., 1985; U.K./Can. Rutherford lectr., 1989; v.p. Internat. Union Pure and Applied Physics, 1994-96. Contbr. articles to profl. jours. Decorated officer Order of Can., 1982; I.W. Killam scholar, 1977-79; Geoffrey Frew fellow Australian Acad. Sci., 1980 Fellow Royal Soc. Can. (co-fgn. sec. 1995-2000, Henry Marshall Tory medal 1989), Royal Soc. London, Am. Phys. Soc., Optical Soc. Am. (pres. 1976, William F. Meggers award 1981, Frederic Ives medal 1983, Disting. Svc. award 2002), Indian Acad. Sci. (hon.), Macedonian Acad. Sci. and Arts (hon.), Am. Acad. Arts and Scis. (fgn. hon.); mem. Can. Assn. Physicists (pres. 1984, Gold medal 1974). Achievements include development of techniques for high resolution Raman spectroscopy of gases and determination of geometrical structures many molecules; use of lasers in spectroscopic investigations including Brillouin and Raman scattering and two photon absorption; observation of stimulated Raman absorption and stimulated Brillouin scattering resulting in generation of intense hypersonic waves in solids; use of Brillouin spectra to measure elastic constants of rare gas crystals; generation of tunable coherent VUV radiation for use in atomic and molecular spectroscopy. Home: 66 Collier St Apt 6B Toronto ON Canada M4W 1L9 Office: U Toronto Dept Physics Toronto ON Canada M5S 1A7

STOKELY, ERNEST M. biomedical engineer, educator, biomedical engineer, researcher; b. Greenwood, Miss., Mar. 26, 1937; s. Walter Tatum and Martha Bess Stokely; m. Joan E. Keagy; children: Ernest Mitchell Jr., Jennifer S. BSEE, Miss. State U., 1959; MS in Biomed. Engring., So. Meth. U., 1968, D in Elec. Engring., 1971. Registered profl. engr., Tex. Asst. sr. engr., mem. tech. staff Tex. Instruments, Inc., Dallas, 1959—69; asst. prof. radiology U. Tex. Southwestern Med. Ctr., 1972—77, 1978—80, assoc. prof. radiology, 1980—87; assoc. prof. computer sci. engring. U. Tex., Arlington, 1987—90; prof., chair biomed. engring. U. Ala., Birmingham, 1990—96, assoc. dean for rsch. Sch. Engring., 1996—2000, assoc. dean Sch. Engring., 2000—02, assoc. dean engring., interim chair dept. mech. engring., 2001—. Vis. adj. prof. computer sci. dept. U. Copenhagen, 1977—78; cons., proposal reviewer NIH, Washington, 1988—98, NSF, Washington, 1988—; cons. Whitaker Found., Washington, 1993—; cons., review acad. programs for various univs. Bd. dirs. Contact, Inc., Dallas, 1985—86, Birmingham Audubon Soc., 1999—2002. Fellow: IEEE (various positions Dallas sect. 1975—82, assoc. editor Trans. Med. Imaging 1975—82), Am. Inst. Med. and Biol. Engrs. (fin. com. chair 1999—2002); mem.: Assn. Computing Machinery, Soc. Mfg. Engrs. Office: Univ Ala 1530 3rd Ave South Birmingham AL 35294-4440

STOKELY, JAMES ROREX, III, benefits compensation administrator, consultant; b. Asheville, N.C., Aug. 6, 1951; s. James Rorex Jr. and Wilma (Dykeman) S.; m. Anne Davis Callison, Dec. 27, 1978; children: Elizabeth Dykeman, William Callison. BA, Yale U., 1972; MBA, Stanford U., 1984. Freelance writer, Newport, Tenn., 1972-78; dir. An Appalachian Experience Children's Mus. Oak Ridge, 1978-82; cons. Hay Mgmt. Cons., Atlanta, 1984-90; dir. compensation Brown-Forman Corp., Louisville, 1990—. Author: Constant Defender: the Story of Fort Moultrie, 1978, (poems) Mummy Truths, 1978 (Tenn. Arts Commn. publs. grant 1978); co-author: Highland Homeland: the People of the Great Smokies, 1978; editor: An Appalachian Studies Teachers Manual, 1981; co-editor: An Encyclopedia of East Tennessee, 1981. Co-chmn. adult edn. Cen. Presbyn. Ch., Atlanta, 1987, elder, 1988. Recipient Award of merit Tenn. Assn. Mus., 1982. Mem. Am. Compensation Assn. Clubs: Yale of Ga. (Atlanta). Avocations: jogging, reading, hiking, travel. Office: Brown Forman Corp 850 Dixie Hwy Louisville KY 40210-1091

STOKELY, MARY CURRY, marketing specialist; b. San Francisco, Jan. 15, 1950; m. Chesley Bernard Stokely Jr., Aug. 14, 1971; children: Brian Scott (dec.), Sharon Elizabeth. AA, Immaculata Coll., Washington, D.C., 1969. Lic. realtor, Fla., Md., mktg. cons. Claims processor Nat. Life Ins. Co. Vt., Washington, 1969-70; sec. Walker & Dunlop Inc., 1970-72, supr. word processing ctr., 1972-75; outreach worker Commn. on Aging, La Plata, Md., 1975-77, title III program dir., 1977-79; sales assoc. Long & Foster Real Estate Co., Waldorf, 1979-80; adminstrv. asst. Raleigh Homes, 1980-82; mgr. new homes sales L. K. Farrall Ltd., 1982-88; dir. mktg. and mgmt. svcs. Mil-Mar & Sons Builders Inc., La Plata, 1988-90; mktg. cons. L.K. Farrall, Ltd., 1990-91, ReMax 100, President's Club, Waldorf, 1991-96; founder, owner Motion Makers, Ltd., La Plata, 1997—; new home mktg. cons. builder svcs. Century 21 H.T. Brown Real Estate, Waldorf, 1997-2000, Lands End Properties, Steve Atkocius & Assoc., Waldorf, 2000—. Com. mem. Strategic Planning Women's Coun. Com. chair Bus. and Profl. Women's Club, Charles County, Md., 1978-80. Named Young Careerist Charles County Bus. and Profl. Women's Club, 1980. Mem. Nat. Assn. Realtors, Md. Assn. Realtors, So. Md. Assn. Realtors (bd. dirs. 1985-87, grievance com. 1993-95, strategic planning, 1987, women's coun. 1980-83, membership, 1993-95, new homes/builder, 1997—), Realtor Cmty. Rels. (chmn. 1995-97). Democrat. Roman Catholic. Avocations: writing, skiing, swimming, boating, dance. Office: Lands End Properties 2939 Old Washington Rd Waldorf MD 20601-

STOKEN, JACQUELINE MARIE, physician; b. Beaver Falls, Pa., Sept. 29, 1948; d. Jack Marc and Lillian Marie Stoken; m. John F. Edge, June 2, 1990; 1 child Randi Elizabeth Edge. Nursing diploma, Presbyn.-U. Hosp. Sch. Nursing, Pitts., 1970; BS in Biology with honors, Chatham Coll., Pitts., 1986; DO, U. Osteo. Med.-Health Scis., Des Moines, 1990. Cert. phys. medicine and rehab., holistic medicine. Home care staff nurse S. Hills Health Sys., Pitts., 1976-89; intern internal medicine Des Moines Gen. Hosp., 1990-91; resident physician dept. phys. medicine and rehab. U. Minn., Mpls., 1991-94; lectr. Internat. Rehab. Med. Assn., Des Moines, 1994—; physiatrist Iowa Orthop. Ctr., 1994-99; med. dir. Heartland Holistic Health Ctr., 1999—. Guest lectr. dept. phys. therapy U. Minn., Mpls., 1991—94, dept. occupl. therapy, 1991—94, chief resident dept. phys. medicien and rehab., 1992—93; guest lectr. Haceteppe U Tip Merkezi, Ankara, Turkey, 1998, Iowa Osteo. Family Practice Assn., 1996—, Am. Holistic Medicine Assn., Toronto, Canada, 2002; adj. prof. Des Moines U., 1997—, trustee, 1997—; mem. Iowa Gov.'s Task Force on Rural Health, 1989. Trustee Des Moines U., 1998—. Mem.: Am. Osteopathy Coll. Rehab. Medicine, Cranial Acad., Am. Acad. Osteopathy, Am. Holistic Med. Assn. (treas. 2000—, guest lectr. Toronto, Can. 2002), Iowa Osteo. Med. Assn. (student del. ho. of dels. 1987—88, student coun. rep. 1987—88), Am. Osteo. Assn. (sec. coun. student coun. pres. 1988—89), Am. Acad. Phys. Medicine and Rehab., Sigma Sigma Phi. Avocations: knitting, yoga, reading.

STOKES, ANGELA COHOON, pharmacist; b. Rocky Mount, N.C., June 22, 1970; d. William L. and Louvern Ann (Martin) C.; m. Robert Earl Stokes. PharmD, Campbell U., Buies Creek, N.C., 1994. Pharmacy mgr. Kerr Drugs, Wilson, N.C., 1994-96; clin. pharmacist Heritage Hosp., Tarboro, NC,

1996—2001; staff pharmacist, diabetes educator Almand's Drug Stores-Oakwood, Rocky Mount, 2001—. Office: Almands Drug Store Oakwood Plaza 127 Fairview Rd Rocky Mount NC 27801

STOKES, ARCH, lawyer, writer; b. Atlanta, Sept. 2, 1946; s. Mack B. and Rose Stokes; m. Maggie Mead; children: Jennifer Jean, Austin Christopher, Susannah Rose, Travis, Emmarose. BA, Emory U., 1967, JD, 1970. Bar: Ga. 1970, U.S. Dist. Ct. (no. dist.) Ga. 1970, U.S. Ct. Appeals (5th cir.) Ga. 1970, U.S. Ct. Mil. Appeals 1971, U.S. Ct. Appeals (9th cir.) Ga. 1980, (2d cir.) Ga. 1990, U.S. Supreme Ct. 1981, U.S. Dist. Ct. (no. dist.) Calif. 1981, U.S. Ct. Appeals (11th cir.) Calif. 1982, U.S. Ct. Appeals (7th cir.) Calif. 1986, U.S. Ct. Appeals (1st cir.) Calif. 1992, U.S. Ct. Appeals (8th cir.) Calif. 1991, U.S. Dist. Ct. (no. dist.) N.Y. 1991, U.S. Dist. Ct. (ea. dist.) Mich. 1986. Ptnr. Stokes Lazarus & Carmichael, Atlanta, 1972-92, Stokes & Murphy, Atlanta, 1992—, San Diego, Pitts., 1992—, Las Vegas, Ithaca, NY, 2001—. Author: The Wage & Hour Handbook, 1978, rev. edit., 2000, The Equal Employment Opportunity Handbook, 1979, The Collective Bargaining Handbook, 1981. Founding mem. adv. bd. William F. Harrah Hotel Coll., U. Nev., Las Vegas, also vis. spkr.; vis. spkr. Cornell U., Johnson and Wales U., U. Houston, Ga. State U. Recipient Hal Holbrook award Internat. Platform Assn., 1990. Mem. ABA, ATLA, Union Internat. des Avocats, Internat. Soc. Hospitality Cons., Confrérie de la Chaîne des Rôtisseurs, Am. Hotel and Lodging. Office: Stokes & Murphy PC 3593 Hemphill St College Park GA 30337-0468 E-mail: astokes@stokesmurphy.com.

STOKES, B. R. retired transportation consultant; b. Anadarko, Okla., Feb. 20, 1924; s. Robert Allan and Ethel Nan (James) S.; m. Joan Pringle, Oct. 22, 1950; children: Timothy, Leigh, Lindsey, Celia. Student, U. Okla., 1941-44; BA, U. Calif., Berkeley, 1947. Reporter, writer Oakland (Calif.) Tribune, 1946-58; dir. info. San Francisco Bay Area Rapid Transit Dist., 1958-61, asst. gen. mgr., 1961-63, gen. mgr., 1963-74; exec. v.p. Am. Public Transit Assn., Washington, 1974-80; sr. v.p. internat. ATE Mgmt. and Service Co., Inc., 1980-95. Dir. gen. Saudi Arabian Public Transport Co., 1980-81 Served with USNR, 1942-46. Recipient Salzberg medal Syracuse U., 1975; inductee Am. Pub. Transit Assn. Transit Hall of Fame, 1996; Reid Found. fellow, 1954. Office: 1911 Fort Myer Dr Arlington VA 22209-1603

STOKES, CATHERINE ANN, elementary education educator; b. N.Y.C., Jan. 26, 1951; d. Matthew John and Joanna Elizabeth (McEllen) Coffey; m. Edward Martin Stokes, Aug. 10, 1974; children: Matthew, Michael. AA, Suffolk Community Coll., 1970; BA, SUNY, Potsdam, 1972; MEd, SUNY, New Paltz, 1974; postgrad., L.I. U., 1988. Cert. elem. tchr., N.Y. 6th grade tchr. Rombout Sch., Beacon, N.Y., 1972-77; 5th grade tchr. S. Ave. Elem. Sch., 1978-91, elem. sci. coord., 1989-91; tchr. Rombout Mid. Sch., 1991—. Cub scout den mother, mem. com. Boy Scouts Am., 1985-87. Recipient award Nat. Energy Edn. Day Com., 1987, Outstanding Sci. Tchrs. award Sci. Tchrs. Assn. N.Y. State, 1987; NSF grantee, 1986-88. Mem. NEA, Nat. Sci. Tchrs. Assn. Avocations: science magic, reading, sports, crafts. Office: Rombout Mid Sch Mattewan Rd Beacon NY 12508

STOKES, CHARLES EUGENE, JR. wool merchant, textile executive; b. Temple, Tex., Oct. 11, 1926; s. Charles Eugene and Esther Annette (Lawlis) Stokes. BBA, U. Tex., 1948; MA, U. Tex., El Paso, 1968; PhD, Tulane U., 1974. Apprentice, then asst. wool buyer Conant & Co., Inc., Boston, 1946-48; wool buyer and dir. Stokes & Co., Ltd., Puno, Peru, 1949-55; pres., treas. Stokes Bros., Inc., New Braunfels, Tex., 1955-59; mng. ptnr. Stokes Bros. & Co., Peru, Uruguay and San Antonio, 1959-94; owner Merino Ranch, Ft. McKavett, Tex., 1994—, Stokes Bros. & Co., Ft. McKavett, 1994—; pres., treas. Stokeswool LLC. Wool mktg. and processing advisor Ministry Agr., La Paz, Bolivia, 1961—63. Author: (book) The Amazon Bubble: World Rubber Monopoly, 2000. Recipient Fulbright fellowship, Tulane U., Bolivia and Brazil, 1970—71. Mem.: Sons Rep. of Tex. (life), Phi Alpha Theta. Republican. Episcopalian. Avocations: sheep and cattle ranching, Latin American history. Home: Merino Ranch PO Box 7 Fort Mc Kavett TX 76841-0007 Office: Stokeswool LLC 7029 FM 864 at FM 1674 Fort Mc Kavett TX 76841

STOKES, HENRY ARTHUR, journalist; b. Jacksonville, Fla., Dec. 9, 1944; s. Henry Jasper and Waneta Marian (Lord) S.; m. Carolyn Elizabeth Morley, Aug. 6, 1966; children: Elizabeth, Virginia, Katherine. AA, St. Johns River Jr. Coll., Palatka, Fla., 1966; BS in Journalism with high honors, U. Fla., 1969. Reporter Daytona Beach (Fla.) News-Jour., 1966, Palatka (Fla.) Daily News, 1966-69, Fla. Times-Union, Jacksonville, 1969-71, night city editor, 1972; various editing positions Detroit News, 1972-88; asst. mng. editor Comml. Appeal, Memphis, 1988-92, mng. editor, 1992—. Mem. adv. bd. dept. econs. U. Memphis, 2002—. Mem. Memphis Literacy Coun., 1989-97, chmn., 1993, 94; bd. dirs. Friends Memphis/Shelby Co. Libr., 1991—, Memphis Rotary Club, 2002-; mem. pres. adv. coun. LeMoyne-Owen Coll., 1992-2000; bd. dirs. Memphis Downtown YMCA, 2001—; adv. bd. U. Memphis Dept. Econ., 2002-. Recipient Emig award Coll. Journalism U. Fla., 1970. Mem. AP Mng. Editors Assn. (bd. dirs. 1997—), Soc. Profl. Journalists, Investigative Reporters and Editors, The Egyptians, Rotary (bd. dirs. Memphis chpt. 2002-). Episcopalian. Avocations: ornithology, fly fishing. Office: Comml Appeal 495 Union Ave Memphis TN 38103-3221 E-mail: stokes@gomemphis.com.

STOKES, JAMES CHRISTOPHER, lawyer; b. Orange, N.J., Mar. 19, 1944; s. James Christopher and Margaret Mary (Groome) S.; m. Eileen Marie Brosnan, Sept. 7, 1968; children: Erin Margaret, Michael Colin, Courtney Dorothy. AB, Holy Cross Coll., 1966; JD, Boston Coll., 1975. Bar: Hawaii 1975, U.S. Ct. Appeals (1st and 9th cirs.) 1976, Mass. 1977, U.S. Ct. Internat. Trade 1988. Officer USMC, 1966-72; assoc. Carlsmith, Carlsmith, Wichman & Case, Honolulu, 1975-76, Bingham, Dana & Gould (now Bingham Dana LLP), Boston, 1976-82, ptnr. London, 1980-84, Boston, 1982—. Contbr. articles to profl. jours. Active personnel bd. Town of Wellesley, Mass., 1984-89, chmn. bd., 1988-89, town moderator, 1992-97. Capt. USMC, 1966-72, Vietnam. Mem. Hawaii Bar Assn., Mass. Bar Assn., Internat. Bar Assn., Boston Bar Assn., Traveller's Club (London), Union Club (Boston), Wellesley Club (bd. dirs.), German-Am. Bus. Club (Boston) (bd. dirs.). Roman Catholic. Office: Bingham Dana LLP 150 Federal St Boston MA 02110-1713 E-mail: jcstokes@bingham.com.

STOKES, JOELYNN TOWANDA, lawyer; b. Balt., May 28, 1961; d. Leslie M. and Mildred S. S. BA, Vanderbilt U., 1983; JD, Hofstra U., 1986. Assoc. Kitch Saurbier Drutchas Wagner & Kenney, Detroit, 1986-88, Harvey, Kruse, Westen & Milan, Detroit, 1988-90; ptnr. Hyatt Legal Svcs., Livonia, 1990-93; prin. atty. J.T. Stokes & Assocs., Farmington Hills, 1993-2000; dep. chief counsel Legal Aid and Defender Assn., Inc., Detroit, 2000—02; of counsel Sherbow & Mitchell, PC, 2002—. Adj. prof. Detroit Coll. Law, 1996-97. Mem. Delta Sigma Theta. Office: Sherbow & Mitchell 23880 Woodward Ave Pleasant Ridge MI 48069

STOKES, JOHN LEMACKS, II, clergyman, retired university official; b. Songdo, Korea, Aug. 23, 1908; s. Marion Boyd and Florence Pauline (Davis) S.; m. Alda Grey Beaman, June 20, 1933; children: John Lemacks III, Mary Anne (foster dau.). AB, Asbury Coll., 1930; postgrad., Asbury Theol. Sem., 1930-31; M.Div., Duke U., 1932; PhD, Yale U., 1936; LL.D., Pfeiffer Coll., 1975. Ordained to ministry Meth. Ch., 1931. Pastor Meth. chs., Randleman, Franklin and Elkin, N.C., 1936-45, Rock Hill, St. John's, S.C., 1945-50; sec. religion higher edn., div. ednl. instns. Bd. Edn. Meth. Ch., Nashville, 1950-53, del. jurisdictional conf., 1952, 60, 68; pres. Pfeiffer Coll., Misenheimer, N.C., 1953-68; exec. sec. Quadrennial Emphasis, United Meth. Ch., 1968-69; asso. dir. N.C. Bd. Higher Edn., Raleigh, 1969-71, acting dir., 1972; asso. v.p. U. N.C., Chapel Hill, 1972-75, spl. asst. in acad. affairs, 1976-93. Dir. numerous out-of-state programs in health professions, 1972-94; mem. Govs. Commn. Citizens for Better Schs. N.C., 1956-60, N.C. Com. on Nursing and Patient Care, 1956-64, N.C. Higher Edn. Facilities Edn., 1964-68, N.C. Com. on Drug Abuse, 1970-76, N.C. Com. on Aero. Edn., 1971-86; chmn. N.C. adv. com. Farmers Home Adminstrn., 1967-69, Marine Sci. Coun., 1969-72; dir. N.C. Inst. Undergrad. Curricular Reform, 1972-78; coordinator Fort Bragg-Pope Grad. Program, 1973-77; adv. com. Nat. Four-year Servicemens Opportunity Coll., 1973-78. Contbr. articles to religious publs. Bd. dirs. ARC, 1940-48, YMCA, 1946-50; vice chmn. Western N.C. Conf. Bd. Missions, 1960-64; trustee Asbury Coll., 1945-51. Recipient Outstanding Svc. award N.C. Optometric Assn., 1988, Merit award So. Coun. Optometrists, 1990. Mem. Aircraft Owners and Pilots Assn., U.S. Lawn Tennis Assn., Am. Assn. Higher Edn., So. Srs. Golf Assn., NEA, Nat. Christian Edn. Assn., So. Philos. Soc., Woman's Soc. Christian Service, Echo Farms Country Club, Masons, Shriners, Rotary, Civitan, Lions. Address: Barclay Place 2525 Costmary Ln Apt 3 Wilmington NC 28412

STOKES, KATHLEEN SARAH, dermatologist, educator; b. Springfield, Mass., Oct. 18, 1954; d. John Francis and Margaret Cecelia (MacDonnell) Stokes; m. William Walter Greaves; children: Ian R., Spenver W., Malcolm W. BS, U. Utah, 1978, MS, 1980; MD, Med. Coll. Wis., 1987. Diplomate Am. Bd. Dermatology. Intern in internal medicine Med. Coll. Wis., Milw., 1987-88, resident in dermatology, 1988-90, chief resident, 1990-91, asst. clin. prof. dermatology, 1991—; pvt. practice, 1991—. Contbr. articles to med. jours., including Critical Care Medicine, Jour. Pediatric Dermatology. Named A Top Physician, Milw. mag., 1996, 00. Fellow Am. Acad. Dermatology, Milw. Acad. Medicine; mem. AMA, Wis. Dermatol. Soc., Women's Dermatologic Soc., Tempo, Alpha Omega Alpha. Office: Affiliated Dermatologists 2300 N Mayfair Rd Milwaukee WI 53226-1505

STOKES, LOUIS, former congressman, lawyer; b. Cleveland, Ohio, Feb. 23, 1925; s. Charles and Louise (Stone) S.; m. Jeanette Francis, Aug. 21, 1960; children: Shelley, Louis C., Angela, Lorene. Student, Case Western Res. U., 1946-48; JD, Cleve. Marshall Law Sch., 1953; 26 hon. doctorate degrees, 1953-2001. Bar: Ohio 1953. Mem. 91st-105th Congresses from 11th (formerly 21st) Ohio dist., Washington, 1969-99; sr. counsel Squire, Sanders and Dempsey, 1999—. Former ranking minority mem. appropriations subcom. on Vets. Affairs, HUD & Ind. Agys.; sr. vis. scholar Mandel Sch. Applied Social Scis. Case Western Res. U., 1999—. Polit. analyst, WEWS TV, Cleve. Served with AUS, 1943-46. Recipient numerous awards for civic activities including Distinguished Service award Cleve. br. NAACP; Certificate of Appreciation U.S. Commn. on Civil Rights. Fellow Ohio State Bar Assn.; mem. Am., Cuyahoga County, Cleve. bar assns., Nat. Assn. Def. Lawyers Criminal Cases Fair Housing (dir.), Norman's Minor Bar Assn., Urban League, Citizens League, John Harlan Law Club, ACLU, Am. Legion, Kappa Alpha Psi. Clubs: Masons (Cleve.). Office: Squire Sanders & Dempsey 1201 Pennsylvania Ave Washington DC 20044-0407 Address: 127 Public Square Cleveland OH 44114-1304 E-mail: lstokes@ssd.com.

STOKES, MACK BOYD (MARION BOYD STOKES), bishop; b. Wonsan, Korea, Dec. 21, 1911; arrived in U.S., 1959; s. Marion Boyd and Florence Pauline (Davis) Stokes; m. Ada Rose Yow, June 19, 1942; children: Marion Boyd III, Arch Yow, Elsie Pauline. Student, Seoul Fgn. High Sch., Korea; AB, Asbury Coll., 1932; BD, Duke, 1935; postgrad., Boston U. Sch. Theol., 1935-37, Harvard, 1936-37; PhD, Boston U., 1940; LLD, Lambuth U., Jackson, Tenn., 1963; DD, Millsaps Coll., 1974. Resident fellow systematic theology Boston U., 1936-38, Bowne fellow in philosophy, 1938-39; ordained to ministry Meth. Ch., deacon, 1938, elder, 1940; vis. prof. philosophy and religion Ill. Wesleyan U., 1940-41; prof. Christian doctrine Candler Sch. Theology, Emory U., 1941-56, asso. dean, Parker prof. systematic theology, 1956-72, chmn. exec. com. div. of religion of grad. sch., 1956-72; acting dean Candler Sch. Theology, Emory U. (Candler Sch.), 1968-69; bishop-in-residence Peachtree Rd. United Meth. Ch. Atlanta, 1988—. Faculty mem. Inst. Theol. Studies Oxford U., 1958; del. Meth. Ecumenical Conf., 1947, 52, 61, 71, Holston, Gen. confs., S.E. Jurisdictional Conf., 1956, 60, 64, 68, 72; chmn. com. ministry Gen. Conf. Meth. Ch., 1960; nat. com. Nature Unity We Seek, 1956—; mem. gen. com. ecumenical affairs theol. study com. United Meth. Ch., 1968—72, com. on Cath.-Meth. rels., 1969—, bishop, 1972—. Author: (book) Major Methodist Beliefs, 1956, Major Methodist Beliefs, rev. 15th edit., 1990, The Evangelism of Jesus, 1960, The Epic of Revelation, 1961, Our Methodist Heritage, 1963, Crencas Fundamentals Dos Methodistas, 1964, Study Guide on the Teachings of Jesus, 1970, The Bible and Modern Doubt, 1970, Major United Methodist Beliefs, 1971, Major United Methodist Beliefs, Korean transl., 1977, Major United Methodist Beliefs, rev. with added study guide, 1998, The Holy Spirit and Christian Experience, 1975, The Holy Spirit and Christian Experience, Korean transl., 1985, Twelve Dialogues on John's Gospel, 1975, Jesus, The Master-Evangel, 1978, Can God See the Inside of an Apple?, 1979, Questions Asked by United Methodists, Philippine transl., 1980, The Bible in the Wesleyan Heritage, 1981, Respuestas A Preguntas Que Hacen Los Metodistas Unidos, 1983, The Holy Spirit in the Wesleyan Heritage, 1985, The Holy Spirit in the Wesleyan Heritage, Spanish transl., 1992, The Holy Spirit in the Wesleyan Heritage, Korean transl., 1992, Scriptural Holiness of the United Methodist Christian, 1988, Talking with God: A Guide of Prayer, 1989, Theology for Preaching, 1994, Questions and Answers about Life and Faith, 2000. Trustee Emory U., Millsaps Coll., Rust Coll., Wood Jr. Coll. Home: PO Box 497 Waynesville NC 28786 *Faith in God and basic trust in people. Knowing the direction in which to go, and moving with divine assistance toward it with persistence, resourcefulness, imagination and patience.*

STOKES, PAUL MASON, lawyer; b. Miami Beach, Fla., July 16, 1946; s. Walter Johnson and Juanita (Hemperley) S.; m. Carol Crocker, Sept. 12, 1970; children: Macon Lanford, Walter Ashley, Mary Juanita. BA, Duke U., 1968; JD, U. Chgo., 1971. Bar: Fla. 1971. Law clerk to hon. Milton Pollack U.S. Dist. Ct. (so. dist.) N.Y., N.Y.C., 1971-72; assoc. Smathers and Thompson, Miami, Fla., 1972-77, ptnr., 1977-88, Kelley Drye & Warren L.L.P., Miami, 1988-99, Stokes McMillan & Maracini, P.A., Miami, 1999—. Adj. prof. law U. Miami, Coral Gables, Fla., 1987-94; pub. defender City of Miami Springs, Fla., 1974, City of Hialeah, Fla., 1974-75. Mem. Code Enforcement Bd. Miami Springs, 1990-92; regent Trinity Internat. U., Deerfield, Ill., 1989-98; mem. Permanent Jud. Commn., Presbytery of Tropical Fla., 1997-2000; bd. dirs. Greater Miami Youth for Christ, 2000—. Fellow Am. Coll. Trust and Estate Coun.; mem. Dade County Bar Assn. (probate and guardianship ct. com. 1988—, bd. dirs. 1989-92, 94-97, 98-2000), Fla. Bar (cert. wills, trusts and estates), Phi Beta Kappa, Order of Coif. Democrat. Presbyterian. Office: Stokes McMillan & Marcini PA Ste 3750 Two S Biscayne Blvd Miami FL 33131-1808 E-mail: pstokes@smpalaw.com.

STOKES, RON, lawyer; b. Springfield, Mo., Dec. 2, 1950; s. Joe Alfred Stokes and MaryLee (Bennett) O'Rourke; m. Christine Monteleone, Nov. 9, 1986. BA, U. Ill., 1973; JD, St. John's U., Jamaica, N.Y., 1976. Bar: N.Y. 1977, U.S. Dist. Ct. (so. dist.) N.Y. 1987. Assoc. Francis J. Young, Hartsdale, N.Y., 1976-78; pvt. practice Rye Brook, 1979-95, Yorktown, 1995—. Mem. N.Y. State Dem. Com., 1976-95, Westchester County Dem. Exec. Com., White Plains, N.Y., 1976-95; mem. bd. mgrs. Rye Ridge Condominium, 1989-95. Mem. Westchester County Bar Assn. (sec. criminal justice sect. 1989-91, chair 1991-92), Sierra Club, Adirondack Mountain Club. Lutheran. Avocations: hiking, mountain climbing, sailing. Home and Office: 3224 S Shelly St Mohegan Lake NY 10547-1908

STOKES, SALLY RUTH SIMS, curator, architectural historian; b. Phila., Dec. 3, 1950; d. Eugene Kelly and Jean Ashby (Johnson) Sims; m. Samuel Newton Stokes, Nov. 5, 1988; 1 child, Thomas Wiatt. BA, Coll. William and Mary, 1972; MA, George Washington U., 1975; MSLS, Clarion U., 1982. Asst. dept. mgr. Strawbridge & Clothier, Phila., 1972-73; adminstrv. aide Fulbright program Coun. for Internat. Exch. of Scholars, Washington, 1975-78; archives technician Nixon Hist. Materials project Nat. Archives, 1978-79; dir. Northwestern Pa. Hist. Conservancy, Clarion, 1979-81; user edn. libr. Ohio State U., Columbus, 1983-87; curator Nat. Trust for Hist. Preservaton Libr. Collection U. Md., College Park, 1987—. Mem. U.S. com. Internat. Coun. on Monuments and Sites, 1990—; mem. steering com. Internat. Confedn. Archtl. Mus. N.Am., chair 2000; mem. Octagon com. Mus. Am. Archtl. Found.; curator, urban cartoonist U. Md. Gallery, 2001; prin. scholar travelling exhbn. Defining a Californian Style, 2001-02. Editor newsletter Com. for Preservation of Archtl. Records, Libr. of Congress, 1991-95; editor: Notes on Hampton Mansion, 2000; gen. editor NTLINDEX (Index to Hist. Preservation Periodicals), 1989—; contbg. author: Dress and Popular Culture, 1991; editl. advisor: Historic Preservation: Project Planning and Estimating, 2000; contbr. articles to profl. jour. Bd. dirs. Greenbelt (Md.) Mus., 1988-94, Washington Met. COPAR, 1992—. Grantee NEH, 1984, Ohio State U., 1985-86, Pa. Humanities Found., 1980. Mem. Nat. Trust for Hist. Preservation, Art Librs. Soc. Democrat. Episcopalian. Avocations: photography, local history studies. Office: Nat Trust Hist Preservation Libr Collection Hornbake Libr U Md College Park MD 20742-0001

STOKES, SAMUEL NEWTON, environmental conservationist; b. N.Y.C., Dec. 16, 1940; s. Isaac Newton Phelps and Barbara (Hoyt) S.; m. Sally Ruth Sims, Nov. 5, 1988; 1 child, Thomas Wiatt. BA, Yale U., 1963. Vol. Peace Corps, Côte D'Ivoire, 1963-65, ops. officer Washington, 1965-67, dir. Benin, 1967-70, chief career devel. and pvt. resources Washington, 1970-71; asst. dir. study com. Nat. Trust for Hist. Preservation, 1972-73; famine relief coord. Africare, West Africa, 1973; dep. program mgr. Smithsonian, Washington, 1974-75; dir. Mid-Atlantic regional office Nat. Trust for Hist. Preservation, 1976-81, dir. rural program, 1981-84; program mgr. Nat. Pk. Svc., 1990-91, chief rivers and trails program, 1991—. Adj. prof. U. Vt., Burlington, 1988-91; conservation cons., Washington, 1975-76, 84-90. Co-author: Saving America's Countryside: A Guide to Rural Conservation, 1989, 2d edit., 1997; contbg. author: Past Meets Future: Saving America's Historic Environments, 1992. Nat. Endowment for Arts fellow, 1985, Richard King Mellon fellow Yale U, 1983-84. Avocations: canoeing, skiing, sailing. E-mail: samstokes@aya.yale.edu.

STOKOWSKI, LEONARD JAMES, artist; b. Worcester, Mass., May 9, 1951; s. Leonard Walter and Ruth Bernice Stokowski. Student, Assumption Coll., 1969-71, Clark U., 1973-75. Exhibited in group shows at Yale Y., New Haven, 1972, Worcester (Mass.) Art Mus., 1972, Fitchburg (Mass.) Art Mus., 1982, Arts Worcester biennial, 1997, numerous others. Avocations: music, horticulture, writing, hiking, antiquing. Home and Office: 43 Hingham Rd North Grafton MA 01536-1281

STOLAR, HENRY SAMUEL, lawyer; b. St. Louis, Oct. 29, 1939; s. William Allen and Pearl Minnette (Schukar) S.; m. Mary Goldstein, Aug. 26, 1962 (dec. Nov. 1987); children: Daniel Bruce, Susan Eileen; m. Suzanne Chapman Jones, June 2, 1989. AB, Washington U., 1960; JD, Harvard U., 1963. Bar: Mo. 1963, U.S. Supreme Ct. 1972. Assoc. then ptnr. Hocker, Goodwin & MacGreevy, St. Louis, 1963-69; v.p., sec., gen. counsel LaBarge Inc., 1969-74; from v.p., assoc. gen. counsel then sr. exec. v.p., gen. counsel, sec. Maritz Inc., 1974—. Sec., bd. dirs. New City Sch. Inc., St. Louis, 1968-75, Ctrl. West End. Assn., 1993-2000; mem. St. Louis Bd. Aldermen, 1969-73, Bd. Freeholders City and County St. Louis, 1987-88; bd. dirs. Forest Park Forever, Inc., 1991—. Mem. ABA, Mo. Bar, Bar Assn. Met. St. Louis, Triple A Club, Phi Beta Kappa. Home: 59 Kingsbury Pl Saint Louis MO 63112-1824 Office: Maritz Inc 1375 N Highway Dr Fenton MO 63099-0001

STOLARIK, M. MARK, history educator; b. St. Martin, Slovak Republic, Apr. 22, 1943; s. Imrich and Margita (Vavro) S.; m. Anne Helene Ivanco, June 15, 1968; children: Roman Andrej, Matthew Mark. BA, U. Ottawa, 1965, MA, 1967; PhD, U. Minn., 1974. Ast. prof. history Cleve. State U., 1972-76; hist. rschr. Nat. Mus. of Man, Ottawa, Ont., Can., 1977-78; pres. Balch Inst. for Ethnic Studies, Phila., 1979-91; prof. history, chair dept. Slovak history and culture U. Ottawa, 1992—. Cons. Harvard Ency. Ethnic Groups, Cambridge, Mass., 1976-80; advisor State Hist. Records Bd., Harrisburg, Pa., 1982-91; cons. Ency. Canada's Ethnic Groups, 1991—. Author: film documentary Vianoce-Slovak Christmas, 1978 (2d prize 1979), Slovaks in Bethlehem, Pa., 1985, The Slovak Experience, 1870-1918, 1989. Mem. Pa. adv. com. to U.S. Commn. on Civil Rights, 1985-91. Lehigh U. fellow, 1976. Mem. 1st Cath. Slovak Union, Nat. Slovak Soc., Can. Slovak League (pres. 1994-99). Roman Catholic. E-mail: stolarik@uottawa.ca.

STOLER, MARK ALAN, history educator; b. N.Y.C., Mar. 2, 1945; s. Nathan and Anne Leah (Miller) S.; m. Jennie G. Versteeg, Nov. 22, 1975 (div. 1983); m. Diane Gabriel, Aug. 11, 1991; 1 child, Eben Cahan. BA, CCNY, N.Y.C., 1966; MA, U. Wis., 1967, PhD, 1971. Lectr. history dept. U. Wis., Milw., 1968-69; prof. history U. Vt., Burlington, 1970—. Vis. prof. strategy dept. U.S. Naval War Coll., Newport, R.I., 1981-82' Fulbright prof. history dept. U. Haifa, Israel, 1984-85; vis. prof. history U.S. Mil. Acad., West Point, N.Y., 1994-95. Author: Politics of the Second Front, 1977, George C. Marshall, 1989, Allies and Adversaries, 2000; co-author: Explorations in American History, 1987; editor microfiche Origins of the Cold War, 1982. Recipient Comdrs. Pub. Svc. award U.S. Army, 1995, Disting. Book award Soc. Mil. History, 2002. Mem. Am. Hist. Assn., Vt. Hist. Soc., Soc. for Historians of Am. Fgn. Rels. (coun. 2000—), Soc. Mil. History (trustee 2001—), WWII Studies Assn., Orgn. Am. Historians. Home: 43 Prospect Hl Burlington VT 05401-1615 Office: History Dept U Vt Burlington VT 05405-0001 E-mail: mstoler@zoo.uvm.edu.

STOLFI, THOMAS EDWARD, advertising executive; b. Bethpage, N.Y., July 30, 1963; s. John Michael and Catherine Rita (Reitano) S.; m. Jacqueline Laguardia, June 27, 1987; children: Jessica Marie, Thomas Patrick. BS summa cum laude, St. John's U. Assoc. media planning, acct. mgr. SFM Media Corp., N.Y.C., 1986, media planner, acct. mgr., 1987-88, sr. media planner, acct. mgr., 1988-90, acct. planning dir., rsch. dir., 1990-93, v.p., acct. planning dir., dir. planning rsch., 1993-98, sr. v.p., planning dir., dir. planning rsch., 1998—. Recipient Silver Effie for Advt. Effectiveness, Am. Mktg. Assn. Republican. Roman Catholic. Home: 267 Harbor Ln Massapequa Park NY 11762-4012 Office: SFM Media LLC Ste 2001 1180 Avenue Of The Americas Fl 10 New York NY 10036-8405

STOLGITIS, WILLIAM CHARLES, professional society executive; b. Ware, Mass., Jan. 9, 1941; s. Vincent Charles and Doris (Dansereau) S.; m. Helen Elizabeth Dermody, Apr. 18, 1969. BS, U.S. Naval Acad., 1962; MS, U.S. Naval Postgrad. Sch., 1969; JD, Georgetown U., 1977. Bar: N.J. 1977, D.C. 1977. Commd. ensign USN, 1962, officer, 1962-82; exec. dir. Soc. Tech. Comm., Arlington, Va., 1982—. Legal counsel Internat. Hydrofoil Assn., 1978—. Mem. D.C. Bar Assn., N.J. Bar Assn., Am. Soc. Assn. Execs., Am. Legion. Republican. Roman Catholic. Home: 3711 Military Rd Arlington VA 22207-4831 Office: Society for Tech Comm 901 N Stuart St Ste 904 Arlington VA 22203-1822 E-mail: bill@stc_va.org.

STOLINSKY, DAVID C. physician; b. Fargo, N.D., Nov. 19, 1934; s. Aaron and Rose Meblin S.; m. Stefanie Auerbach, May 17, 1966. AB (hons.), Univ. Calif., 1955, MD, 1958. Diplomate Am. Bd. Internal Medicine. Asst. rsch. physician Univ. Calif., San Francisco, 1965-66; asst. prof. medicine Univ. So. Calif., L.A., 1966-98; attending physician Univ. So. Calif. Medical Ctr., 1966-92. Contbr. articles to profl. jours. and internet. Assoc. investigator Nat. Cancer Inst., 1966-76. Fellow Am. Coll. Physicians; mem. Internat. Wound Ballistics Assn., Am. Assn. for Cancer Rsch., Am. Soc. Clinical Oncology, Phi Beta Kappa. Republican. Jewish. Avocation: history. Office: 420 S Beverly Dr Ste 100 Beverly Hills CA 90212-4410 E-mail: dcstolinsky@prodigy.net.

STOLL, HOWARD LESTER, JR. dermatologist; b. Buffalo, June 13, 1928; s. Howard L. and Margaret (Kahler) S.; m. Jacklyn Fay Straight, June, 1948; children— Shelley, Margaret, Amy, Howard III AB, Harvard U., 1948; MD, U. Pa., 1952. Diplomate Am. Bd. Dermatology. Intern E.J. Meyer Hosp., Buffalo, 1952, resident in dermatology, 1953-55; sr. cancer research surgeon Roswell Park Meml. Inst., Buffalo, 1958-59, assoc. cancer research dermatologist, 1959-67, chief, sect. dermatology, 1984-92; mem. courtesy staff Mercy Hosp., 1958-70; asst. in dermatology E.J. Meyer Meml. Hosp., 1962-72. Clin. assoc. prof. dermatology Sch. Medicine, SUNY-Buffalo, 1976-91, clin. prof., 1991—. Served to capt. U.S. Army, 1955-57 Mem. Am. Acad. Dermatology, Soc. Investigative Dermatology, Buffalo-Rochester Dermatologic Soc. Office: Roswell Park Meml Inst Elm & Carlto Sts 666 Elm St Buffalo NY 14263-0002

STOLL, NEAL RICHARD, lawyer; b. Phila., Nov. 7, 1948; s. Mervin Stoll and Goldie Louise (Serody) Stoll Wilf; m. Linda G. Seligman, May 25, 1972; children: Meredith Anne, Alexis Blythe. BA in History with distinction, Pa. State U., 1970; JD, Fordham U., 1973. Bar: N.Y. 1974, U.S. Dist. Ct. (ea. dist.) N.Y. 1974, U.S. Ct. Appeals (2d cir.) 1974, U.S. Ct. Appeals (11th cir.) 1982, U.S. Dist. Ct. (ea. dist.) Mich. 1983, U.S. Dist. Ct. (so. dist.) N.Y. 1974, U.S. Supreme Ct. 1986. Assoc. Skadden, Arps, Slate, Meagher & Flom, LLP, N.Y.C., 1973-81, mem., 1981—. Lectr. Practicing Law-Inst., N.Y.C. Author: (with others) Aquisitions Under the Hart Scott Rodino Antitrust Improvements Act, 1980; contbr. articles to profl. pubs. Mem. Assn. Bar City of N.Y. (mem. trade regulation com. 1983-85), ABA, N.Y. State Bar Assn. Democrat. Office: Skadden Arps Slate Four Times Sq New York NY 10036-6522 E-mail: nstoll@skadden.com.

STOLL, RICHARD EDMUND, retired manufacturing executive; b. Dayton, Ohio, Aug. 5, 1927; s. George Elmer and Mary Francis (Zimmerle) S.; m. Vera Mae Cohagen, Sept. 2, 1950; children: Richard Edmund, Linda Ann, Donna Gail. Student in mech. engring., MIT, 1945-47; MetE, Ohio State U., 1950. Registered profl. engr. Ill., Tex. Various staff and operating positions U.S. Steel Corp., Pitts., Chgo., Houston, 1952-78, gen. mgr. metall. services Pitts., 1978-84, dir. quality mgmt. program and tech., 1984-85; corp. chief metallurgist Wheeling-Pitts. Steel Corp., Wheeling, W.Va., 1985-86, v.p., gen. mgr. flat rolled steel, 1986-87, v.p., gen. mgr., interim chief ops. officer, 1987-89, exec. v.p., 1989-91, ret., 1991. Cons. McElrath & Assocs., Mpls., 1984. Contbr. articles to profl. jours.; patentee in field. Served with C.E., U.S. Army, 1950-52. Fellow Am. Soc. Metals (chmn. 1963); mem. Am. Iron and Steel Inst., Am. Inst. Mining and Metallurgy (Nat. Open Hearth award 1957, bd. dirs. 1961-68), Am. Inst. Steel Engrs., Am. Soc. Metals, Dolphin Head Golf Club. Republican. Roman Catholic. Avocation: golf. Home: 3 Kinglet Lagoon Hilton Head Island SC 29926-2548 E-mail: RStollhhi@aol.com.

STOLL, WILHELM, mathematics educator; b. Freiburg, Germany, Dec. 22, 1923; arrived in U.S., 1960; s. Heinrich and Doris (Eberle) S.; m. Marilyn Jane Kremser, June 11, 1955; children: Robert, Dieter, Elisabeth, Rebecca. PhD in Math, U. Tübingen, Fed. Republic Germany, 1953, habilitation, 1954. Asst. U. Tübingen, 1953-59, dozent, 1954-60, ausserplanmässiger prof., 1960; vis. lectr. U. Pa., 1954-55; temp. mem. Inst. Advanced Study, Princeton, 1957-59; prof. math. U. Notre Dame, 1960-88, Vincent J. Duncan and Annamarie Micus Duncan prof. math., 1988-94, prof. emeritus, 1994—, chmn. dept., 1966-68, co-dir. Ctr. for Applied Math., 1992. Vis. prof. Stanford U., 1968-69, Tulane U., 1973, U. Sci. and Tech., Hefei, Anhui, People's Republic of China, summer, 1986; adviser Clark Sch., South Bend, Ind., 1963-68; Japan Soc. Promotion Sci. fellow, vis. prof. Kyoto U., summer 1983. Publs. in field. Fellow: AAAS. Achievements include research complex analysis several variables. Home: 54763 Merrifield Dr Mishawaka IN 46545-1519 Office: U Notre Dame Dept Math Notre Dame IN 46556

STOLL, WILLIAM HERMANN, real estate company executive; b. Aug. 7, 1944; s. Gottfried Alois and Mary Elizabeth (Lochrie) Stoll; m. Elizabeth Anne Stoll, Aug. 5, 1967. BBA, U. Ark., Fayetteville, 1966; MA (grad. fellow), U. Tex., Austin, 1970. Budget examiner Tex. Gov.'s Office, 1967—71; fin. grants adminstr. City Mgrs. Office, Austin, 1971—73; dir. program devel. Tex. Dept. Cmty. Affairs, 1973—78; gen. mgr. AIS Data Sys., Inc., Austin, 1978—81; pres. Submariner, Inc., 1981—84; real estate agt. MK & Assocs., Inc., 1984—86; sales mgr. Better Homes & Gardens, 1986—97; sales counselor Standard Pacific Homes, 1997—. Chmn. Southwest Nat. Bank, Austin, 1980—82, also bd. dirs.; chmn. Austin Bd. Realtors, Austin, 1987. Author (digest): Texas Water Plan, 1967. Chmn. North Austin Mental Health/Mental Retardation Com., 1975—76; rep. Goals for Austin Tomorrow, 1974—75; chmn. Allandale Neighborhood Assn., 1975—76; mem. LBJ Library Found.; mem. selection com. Austin Most Worthy Citizen award, 1993—94; mem. pledge com. Muscular Dystrophy Ann. Campaign, Williamson County, 1999—2001; mem. fin. com. KLRO-TV PBS sta., 1994—95; presiding judge Travis County Election Commn., Austin, 1976—79; fin. chmn. Travis County Dem. Party, 1977—78; vice chmn. Austin Planning and Zoning Commn., 1976—80. Mem.: Austin Soc. Pub. Adminstrn., Austin C. of C., Exch. Park Toastmasters, U. Tex.-Austin Ex-students' Assn., Men's Polit Club Austin (co-founder), Young Men's Bus. Club, Kiwanis, Sigma Phi Epsilon (advisory dir. alumni assn. 1984—88). Roman Catholic. Home: 8704 Azalea Trl Austin TX 78759-7503

STOLLAR, BERNARD DAVID, biochemist, educator; b. Saskatoon, Sask., Can., Aug. 11, 1936; came to U.S., 1960; s. Percy and Rose (Direnfeld) S.; m. Carol A. Singer, Oct. 7, 1956; children: Lawrence, Michael, Suzanne. BA, U. Sask., Saskatoon, 1958; MD, U. Sask., 1959. Intern U. Sask. Hosp., 1959-60; postdoctoral fellow Brandeis U., Waltham, Mass., 1960-62; asst. prof. dept. pharmacology Tufts U. Schs. Medicine and Dental Medicine, Boston, 1964-67, asst. prof. dept. biochemistry, 1967-68, assoc. prof. biochemistry/pharmacology, 1968-74, prof., 1974—, acting chmn. dept. biochemistry and pharmacology, 1984-86, chmn. dept. biochemistry, 1986-2001. Vis. prof. internat. course in immunology and immunochemistry Mexico City, 1971; sr. fellow Weizmann Inst. Sci., Rehovot, Israel, 1971-72; vis. prof. chemistry Wellesley (Mass.) Coll., 1976, U. Tromsö, Norway, 1981; Dozor vis. prof. Ben-Gurion U. Sch. Medicine, Beer Sheva, Israel, 1986; cons. USAF Office Sci. Rsch., 1966-69, Seragen, Inc., 1983-88, Cetus, 1982-85, Gene-Trak, 1986-89, Alkermes, Inc., 1989-94, Catalytic Antibodies, Inc., 1993-98; 3d ann. alumni lectr. U. Sask. Coll. Medicine, 1989; mem. allergy/transplantation rsch. com. NIH/NIAID, 1990-94; mem. sci. vis. com. Okla. Med. Rsch. Found., 1996-98; mem. panel Israel Cancer Rsch. Found., 1996-2000. Contbr. over 200 articles to profl. jours., chpts. to books; exec. editl. bd. Analytical Biochemistry, 1988—; editl. bd. Jour. Immunology, 1981-85, Molecular Immunology, 1980-95, Arthritis and Rheumatism, 1986-89, Jour. Immunological Methods, 1988—. Mem. adult edn. com. Temple Reyim, Newton, Mass., v.p., 2001—. Capt. USAF, 1962-64. Recipient (with Carol Stollar) 2d Century award Jewish Theol. Sem. and Temple Reyim, 1997; rsch. grantee NSF, NIH, 1964—; sr. fellow Weizmann Inst. Sci., 1971-72. Mem. AAAS, Am. Assn. Immunologists, Am. Soc. Biochemistry and Molecular Biology, Am. Coll. Rheumatology, Clin. Immunology Soc., N.Y. Acad. Sci. Office: Tufts Univ Sch Medicine Dept Biochemistry 136 Harrison Ave Boston MA 02111-1800 E-mail: david.stollar@tufts.edu.

STOLLER, CLAUDE, architect; b. N.Y.C., Dec. 2, 1921; s. Max and Esther (Zisblatt) S.; m. Anna Maria Oldenburg, June 5, 1946 (div. Oct. 1972); children: Jacob, Dorothea, Elizabeth; m. Rosemary Raymond Lax, Sept. 22, 1978. Student, Black Mountain Coll., N.C., 1942; M.Arch., Harvard U., 1949. Architect Architects Collaborative, Cambridge, Mass., after 1949, Shepley, Bulfinch, Richardson & Abbot, Boston, 1951; co-founder, partner firm Marquis & Stoller, San Francisco, 1956; pvt. practice architecture N.Y.C. and San Francisco, 1974-78; founder, partner Stoller/Partners, Berkeley, Calif., 1978, Stoller, Knoerr Archs., 1988-95. Mem. faculty Washington U., St. Louis, 1955-56, U. Calif., Berkeley, 1957-91, prof. arch., 1968-92, acting chmn. dept., 1965-66, chair grad. studies, 1984-91; mem. Berkeley Campus Design Rev. Bd., 1985-91, chmn., 1992-93; commr. Calif. Bd. Archtl. Examiners, 1980-90, mem. exam. com., 1985-88; mem. diocesan commn. arch. Episcopal Diocese Calif., 1961-98; vis. arch. Nat. Design Inst., Ahmedabad, India, 1963; planning commr. City of Mill Valley, 1961-66, Marin County Planning Commn., 1966-67; mem. pub. adv. panel archtl. svcs. GSA, 1969-71; citizens urban design adv. com. City of Oakland, Calif., 1968; vis. com. nat. archtl. accrediting bd. U. Minn. and U. Wis., Milw., 1971; coun. Harvard Grad. Sch. Design Assn., 1976-77; mem. design rev. com. The Sea Ranch, Calif., 1990-2002. Prin. works include St. Francis Sq. Coop. Apts., San Francisco, 1961, Pub. Housing for Elderly, San Francisco, 1974, Learning Resources Bldg, U. Calif., Santa Barbara, 1975, Menorah Park Housing for Elderly, San Francisco, 1979, San Jose State U. Student Housing Project, 1984, Delta Airlines Terminal, San Francisco Internat. Airport, 1988. Served with AUS, 1943-46. Recipient numerous awards including AIA Honor awards, 1963, 64, AIA Bay Region Honor award, 1974, Concrete Reinforced Steel Inst. award, 1976, AIA award, 1976, CADA Site I Solar Housing award Sacramento, Calif., 1980, State of Calif. Affordable Housing award, 1981, PG&E Suntherm award, 1981, San Francisco Housing Authority award, 1983, Orchid award City of Oakland, 1989, Citation for achievement and svc. U. Calif., Berkeley, 1991, Design award Berkeley Design Advocates. Fellow AIA. Home: 2816 Derby St Berkeley CA 94705-1325 Office: Claude Stoller FAIA Arch 1818 Harmon St Berkeley CA 94703-2472 E-mail: stoller@uclink.berkeley.edu.

STOLLER, ELEANOR PALO, sociology educator; b. Chgo., June 13, 1946; d. Ernest Arthur and Helmi Sigrid (Nieminen) Palo; m. Michael Alan Stoller, June 8, 1968; children: Jeffrey Mark, Kirsten Elin. AB, Grinnell Coll., 1968; AM, Washington U., St. Louis, 1970, PhD, 1974. Asst. prof. sociology SUNY, Plattsburgh, 1973-78, assoc. prof., 1979-82, prof., 1982-95; disting. prof., 1990-95; prof. health policy U. Fla., Gainesville, 1995-97; Selah Chamberlain prof. Case Western Res U., Cleve., 1997—, assoc. dir. Ctr. Aging and Health. Mem. sci. rev. panels NIH, Bethesda, Md., 1992-96; master tchr. Assn. Gerontology in Higher Edn., 1996. Co-author: Worlds of Difference, 1994, 2d edit., 1997; mem. editl. bd. The Gerontologist, Jour. Gerontology, 1993-98, 2001—, Jour. Aging Studies, 1977-2002, Jour. Applied Gerontology, 1989—; contbr. articles to profl. jours., including Jour. Gerontology. Fellow Gerontol. Soc. Am.; mem. Am. Sociol. Assn. (sect. on aging 1998-2000, sec./treas. sect. on aging 2001—). Avocations: gardening, playing piano. Office: Case Western Res U 10900 Euclid Ave Cleveland OH 44106-7124 E-mail: eps3@po.cwru.edu.

STOLLER, PATRICIA SYPHER, structural engineer; b. Jackson Heights, N.Y., Dec. 16, 1947; d. Carleton Roy and Mildred Vivian (Ferron) Sypher; m. David A. Stoller Sr.; children: Stephanie Jean, Sheri Lynn. BSCE, Washington U., St. Louis, 1975; M in Mgmt., Northwestern U., 1989. R & D engr. Amcar divsn. ACF Industries, St. Charles, Mo., 1972-79; project engr. Truck Axle divsn. Rockwell Internat., Troy, Mich., 1979-81; sr. engr. ABB Impell, Norcross, Ga., 1981-83, supervising mgr., client mgr., divsn. mgr. Lincolnshire, Ill., 1983—; dir. bus. devel., v.p. VECTRA (formerly ABB Impell), 1991-94; pres., CEO ASC Svcs. Co., LLC, Chgo., 1994-97; CEO, pres. Beaumont Svcs. Co., LLC, Royal Oak, Mich., 1997—, ReSourcing Svcs. Co., LLC, Chicago, 1997—. Author computer program Quickpipe, 1983; patentee in field (numerous). Mem. ASCE, NAFE, Soc. Women Engrs., Am. Nuc. Soc. (mem. exec. bd. Chgo. sect. 1991-93), Chgo. Real Estate Women, World Pres. Orgn. Avocations: golf, music. Office: ReSourcing Svcs Co LLC Ste 1420 222 S Riverside Plz Chicago IL 60606-1720

STOLLERMAN, GENE HOWARD, physician, educator; b. N.Y.C., Dec. 6, 1920; s. Maurice William and Sarah Dorothy (Mezz) S.; m. Corynne Miller, Jan. 21, 1945 (dec. Mar. 1997); children: Lee Denise Stollerman Meyburg, Anne Barbara Stollerman DiZio, John Eliot; m. Vita Mark, Nov. 9, 1997. AB summa cum laude, Dartmouth Coll., 1941; MD, Columbia U., 1944. Diplomate Am. Bd. Internal Medicine. Clin. tng. Mt. Sinai Hosp., N.Y.C, 1944-46, chief med. resident, 1948; Dazian research fellow microbiology NYU Med. Sch., 1949-50, mem. dept. medicine, 1951-55; med. dir. Irvington House for Cardiac Children, 1951-55; prin. investigator Sackett Found. Research in Rheumatic Diseases, 1955-64; asst. prof. medicine Northwestern U., 1955-57, assoc. prof., 1957-61, prof. medicine, 1961-65; prof., chmn. dept. medicine U. Tenn., 1965-81, Goodman prof., 1977-81; physician-in-chief City of Memphis Hosps., 1965-81; prof. medicine Boston U. Sch. Medicine, 1981-95, prof. pub. health, 1991-95, prof. medicine and pub. health emeritus, 1996—. Chief sect. gen. internal medicine Univ. Hosp., Boston U. Med. Ctr., 1983-86; Disting. physician VA Med. Ctr., Bedford, Mass., 1986-89; assoc. chief of staff Geriatrics and Extended Care, 1989-92; clin. dir. Bedford div. Geriatric Rsch., Ednl. and Clin. Ctr., 1989-92; dir. VA Health Svcs. Rsch. Field, 1990-93; chmn. research career program com. NIAMD-NIH, 1967-70; mem. commn. streptococcal and staphylococcal diseases U.S. Armed Forces Epidemiol. Bd., 1956-74; adv. bd. immunization practices Center for Disease Control, 1968-71; expert adv. panel cardiovascular disease WHO, 1966—; mem. Am. Bd. Internal Medicine, 1967-73, chmn. cert. exam. com., 1969-73, mem. exec. com., 1971-73; chmn. Panel on Bacterial Vaccines, FDA, 1973-80; mem. nat. adv. council Nat. Inst. Allergy and Infectious Diseases, NIH, 1978-82; mem. Dept. Health & Human Services nat. vaccine adv. com.. Editor-in-chief Advances in Internal Medicine, 1968-93, Jour. Am. Geriatric Soc., 1984-88; co-editor Hosp. Practice, 1990—, editor, 1998—; contbr. chpts. to Braunwald's Textbook of Cardiology, Harrison's Textbook of Medicine, Cecil & Loeb Textbook of Medicine, others; contbr. articles to profl. jours. Served as capt. M.C., AUS, 1946-48. Recipient Bicentennial award in internal medicine Columbia U., 1967, Disting. Alumnus award Mt. Sinai Hosp., 1989, Thewlis award Am. Geriatric Soc., 1990. Master ACP (bd. regents 1978, v.p. 1984, Bruce medal for preventive medicine 1985), Am. Coll. Rheumatology; mem. Am. Heart Assn. (mem. exec. com., pres. coun. on rheumatic fever and congenital disease 1965-67), Am. Fedn. Clin. Rsch., Am. Rheumatism Assn., Am. Soc. Clin. Investigation, Cen. Soc. Clin. Rsch. (v.p. 1973-74, pres. 1974-75), Assn. Profs. Medicine (pres. 1975-76), Am. Assn. Immunologists, Assn. Am. Physicians, Infectious Disease Soc. Am. (coun. 1968-70), Phi Beta Kappa, Alpha Omega Alpha. E-mail: gstollerman@valley.net.

STOLLERY, ROBERT, construction company executive; b. Edmonton, Alta., Can., May 1, 1924; s. Willie Charles and Kate (Catlin) S.; m. Shirley Jean Hopper, June 11, 1947; children: Carol, Janet, Douglas. BSc English, U. Alta., 1949, LLD (hon.), 1985, Concordia U., Montreal, Que., 1986, St. Stevens Coll., 1999. Field engr. Poole Constrn. Ltd., Edmonton, 1949-54, project mgr., 1954-64, v.p., 1964-69, pres., 1969-81; chmn. bd. PCL Constrn. Group Inc., 1979-93; chmn. PCL Constrn. HOldings, 1993—. Bd. dirs. Melcor Devels. Ltd., Edmonton, Alta. Chmn. Edmonton Community Found. Recipient Exec. of Yr. award Inst. Cert. Mgmt. Cons. of Alta., 1988, Can. Businessman of Yr. award U. Alta., 1993. Fellow Can. Acad. Engring.; mem. Assn. Profl. Engrs. (Frank Spragins Meml. award 1981), Engring. Inst. Can. (Julian C. Smith medal 1990), Conf. Bd. Can. (vice chmn. 1980-82), Constrn. Assn. Edmonton (pres. 1972, Claude Alston Meml. award), Can. Constrn. Assn. (v.p. 1970, Can. Businessman of the Yr. award 1993, Order of Can. 2001). Conservative. Mem. United Ch. of Canada. Club: Mayfair Golf and Country (Edmonton). Office: PCL Constrn Group Inc 5410 99 St Edmonton AB Canada T6E 3P4

STOLLEY, ALEXANDER, advertising executive; b. Coethen Anhalt, Germany, May 12, 1922; came to U.S., 1923, naturalized, 1929; s. Mihail and Tatiana (Rainich) Stolarevsky; m. Patricia Martin, June 26, 1944 (dec. Aug. 1970); children: Christopher, Peter, Laura Stolley Smith, Annabel Stolley Hetzer, Megan Stolley Berry; m. Bette Scott Vogt, June 15, 1973. ME, U. Cin., 1948. With Cin. Milacron, Inc., 1941-50, dir. employee relations, 1948-50; with Northlich, Stolley, Inc., Cin., 1950-89, exec. v.p., 1959-67, pres., 1967-84; chmn. Northlich, Stolley, LaWarre, Inc. (formerly Northlich, Stolley, Inc.), 1984-89. Mem. exec. com. Cincinnatus Assn., 1968-73, sec., 1970-71, v.p., 1971-72, pres., 1972-73; mem. Cin. Council on World Affairs, 1969— ; chmn. Contemporary Arts Center, Cin., 1966-67; mem. exec. com. Cin. Conv. and Visitors Bur., 1975, chmn. long range planning com., 1983; trustee Cin. Symphony Orch., 1969-75. Served to 1st lt. AUS, 1943-46. Mem. Bus., Profl. Advt. Assn., Greater Cin. C. of C. (exec. com. 1982-83) Clubs: Cin. Country, Literary, Gasparilla Beach, Lemon Bay Golf, Boca Bay Pass. Home: 135 Garfield Pl Apt 514 Cincinnati OH 45202-5737 also: PO Box 1339 Boca Grande FL 33921-1339

STOLLEY, PAUL DAVID, medical educator, researcher; b. Pawling, N.Y., June 17, 1937; s. Herman and Rosalie (Chertock) Stolley; m. Jo Ann Goldenberg, June 13, 1959; children: Jonathan, Dorie, Anna. BA, Lafayette Coll., 1957; MD, Cornell U., 1962; MPH, Johns Hopkins U., 1968; MA (hon.), U. Pa., 1976. Diplomate Am. Coll. Preventive Medicine, Am. Coll. Epidemiology. Intern U. Wis. Med. Ctr., 1962—63, resident in medicine, 1963—64; med. officer USPHS, Washington, 1964—67; asst. prof. Johns Hopkins Sch. Pub. Health, Balt., 1968—71, assoc. prof., 1971—76; Herbert C. Rorer prof. medicine U. Pa. Sch. Medicine, Phila., 1976—91; prof. dept. epidemiology U. Md. Sch. Medicine, Balt., 1991—2002; staff epidemiologist Public Citizen Health Rsch. Group. Co-author: Foundations of Epidemiology, 3d edit., 1995, Epidemiology: Investigating Disease, 1995 (Am. Med. Writers Assn. award, 1996); contbg. author: Case-Control Studies, 1982, mem. editl. bd.: New Eng. Jour. Medicine, 1989—93, mem. editl. bd.: Millbank Quar., Health and Soc., 1986—, assoc. editor: Clin. Pharmacology and Therapeutics, 1987—93; contbr. articles to med. jours. Charter mem. Physicians for Social Responsibility, 1961—. Lt. comdr. USPHS, 1964—67. Fellow: ACP; mem.: Johns Hopkins Soc. Scholars, Internat. Epidemiol. Assn. (treas. 1982—84), Am. Epidemiol. Soc. (pres. 1994—), Soc. Epidemiol. Rsch. (pres. 1982—84), Inst. Medicine of NAS, Am. Coll. Epidemiology (pres. 1987—89). Home: 6424 Brass Knob Columbia MD 21044-4019 Office: Public Citizen 1600 20th St NW Washington DC 20009

STOLLEY, RICHARD BROCKWAY, journalist; b. Peoria, Ill., Oct. 3, 1928; s. George Brockway and Stella (Sherman) S.; m. Ann Elizabeth Shawber, Oct. 2, 1954 (div. 1981); children: Lisa Anne, Susan Hope, Melinda Ruth, Martha Brockway ; m. Lise Jane Hilboldt, 1997. BS in Journalism, Northwestern U., 1952, MS, 1953; LLD, Villa Maria Coll., 1976. Sports editor Pekin (Ill.) Daily Times, 1944-46; reporter Chgo. Sun-Times, 1953; mem. staff weekly Life mag., 1953-73, bur. chief, 1961-64, Washington, 1964-68, sr. editor Europe, 1968-70, asst. mng. editor, 1971-73; mng. editor monthly Life mag., 1982-86; founding mng. editor People mag., 1974-82, Picture Week mag., N.Y.C., 1985-86; dir. spl. projects Time Inc., 1987-89; editl. dir. Time Inc. Time Warner Inc., 1989-93, sr. editl. adviser, 1993—. Author: Sinatra: An Intimate Portrait of a Very Good Year, 2002; introd. to Leigh A. Wiener, Marilyn: A Hollywood Farewell: The Death and Funeral of Marilyn Monroe, 1990; editor People Celebrates People: The Best of 20 Unforgettable Years, 1994, rev. edit., 1996, Life: Our Century in Pictures, 1999, Life: Century of Change, America in Pictures, 1900-2000, 2000, LIFE: World War 2, 2001; exec. prodr. (TV show) Extra, 1995-96; editl. cons. Our American Century series Time-Life Books, 1998-99. Chmn. Twins Found., Providence; bd. govs. Nat. Parkinson Found., Miami, Fla.; mem. Child Care Action Campaign, N.Y.C.; trustee N.Y.C. Citizens Crime Commn. With USN, 1946-48. Recipient Alumni merit award Northwestern U., 1977, Alumni medal Northwestern U., 1994, Henry Johnson Fisher award for lifetime achievement in mag. pub., 1997, Mag. Profl. of Yr. award Assn. for Edn. in Journalism and Mass Comm., 2002; inducted into Am. Soc. Magazine Editors' Hall of Fame, 1996, Hall of Achievement Medill Sch. Journalism Northwestern U., 1997. Mem. Am. Soc. Mag. Editors (pres. 1982-84), Nat. Press Club, Overseas Press Club, Century Assn., Kappa Tau Alpha, Sigma Delta Chi.

STOLLMAN, ISRAEL, city planner; b. N.Y.C., Mar. 15, 1923; s. Philip and Yetta (Strelchik) S.; m. Mary Florence Callahan, Dec. 27, 1953; children—Susan Elisabeth, Katharine Rachel, Sarah Ellen. BS in Social Sci, CCNY, 1947; M. City Planning, MIT, 1948. Planner Cleve. Planning Commn., 1948-51; planning dir. Youngstown, Ohio, 1951-57; prof., chmn. div. city and regional planning Ohio State U., 1957-68; exec. dir. Am. Soc. Planning Ofcls., 1968-78, Am. Planning Assn., Washington, 1978-93, cons., 1994—. Lectr. Western Res. U., 1949-51, U. Chgo., 1968-69, U. Va., 1994—2002; pres. Assn. Collegiate Sch. Planning, 1966-67; chmn. Charles E. Merriam Center Pub. Adminstrn., 1977-93. Trustee Alfred Bettman Found.; bd. govs. Met. Housing and Planning Council Chgo., v.p., 1969-79. Served with USAAF, 1943-45. Fellow Am. Inst. Cert. Planners (exec. dir. emeritus), Internat. Fedn. Housing and Planning (bur. mem. 1988-98), Soc. for Am. City and Regional Planning History (trustee 1996—2001), Lambda Alpha. Avocation: stereoscopy. Home and Office: 1708 Swann St NW Washington DC 20009-5535

STOLOFF, DAVID L. education educator, department chairman; b. Bronx, N.Y., June 17, 1952; s. Martin and Florence (Rosen) S.; m. Deborah Leah Narotsky, Nov. 10, 1985; children: Nathan Benjamin, Charles Abraham, Daniel Harry, Florence Rose. BS in Biology, SUNY, Brockport, 1973; MA in Ednl. Tech., Concordia U., Montreal, 1977; PhD in Comparative and Internat. Edn., UCLA, 1982. Cert. life scis. tchr. N.Y., Tex., Calif. Sci., TEFL tchr. Peace Corp., Kinshasa, Chibambo, Zaire, 1973-75; tchr. Mollie Goodman Acad. H.S., Ashkelon, Israel, 1975-76; ednl. rschr. Dallas Indep. Sch. Dist., 1977-78; tchr. Long Beach (Calif.) Poly. H.S., 1982-84; asst. prof. SUNY, Plattsburgh, N.Y., 1984-86; assoc. prof. Calif. State U., L.A., 1986-90; prof. Sonoma State U., Rohnert Park, Calif., 1990-95; prof. edn., chmn. dept. East Conn. State U., Willimantic, 1995-97, 98—, interim dean Sch. Edn. and Profl. Studies, 1997-98. Co-prodr.: (video) Mosaic City, 1977; web page developer. Bd. dirs. Temple B'nai Israel, Willimantic, 1997-2001, Windham Hosp., Willimantic. Calif. Acad. Partnership Program grant Calif. State U., 1987-90; grant Conn. State U., 1997; fellow Bush Program Child Devel. and Social Policy, 1980-82. Mem. Conn. Distance Learning Consortium, Assn. State Tech. Using Tchr. Educators (pres. 1993-95), Calif. Faculty Assn. (Sonoma State chpt., pres. 1993-95), Phi Delta Kappa (v.p. program U. Conn. chpt. 2001—). Avocations: travel, gardening, science fiction. Home: 86 Pigeon Rd Willimantic CT 06226-1321 Office: Eastern Conn State U 83 Windham St Willimantic CT 06226-2211

STOLOFF, NORMAN STANLEY, materials engineering educator, researcher; b. Bklyn., Oct. 16, 1934; s. William F. and Lila (Dickman) S.; m. Helen Teresa Arcuri, May 15, 1971; children: Michael E., Linda M., David M., Stephen L. BMetE, NYU, 1955; MS, Columbia U., 1956, PhD, 1961. Metall. engr. Pratt & Whitney Aircraft, East Hartford, Conn., 1956-58; prin. rsch. scientist Ford Sci. Lab., Dearborn, Mich., 1961-65; asst. prof. materials engring. Rensselaer Polytechnic Inst., Troy, N.Y., 1965-68, assoc. prof., 1968-71, prof., 1971-97, prof. emeritus, 1997—. Cons. Electric Boat div. Gen. Dynamics, New London, Conn., 1987-89, Martin Marietta Rsch. Labs., Balt., 1990, Rockwell Internat., Thousand Oaks, Calif., 1989, Cummins Engine Co., Columbus, Ind., 1991. Editor: (with others) High Temperature Ordered Intermetallic Alloys, 1985, Superalloys II, 1987, Physical Metallurgy and Processing of Intermetallic Compounds, 1996, others; contbr. articles to profl. jours. Recipient Fulbright Rsch. award U.S. State Dept., 1968-69, DOE Fellowship Assoc. Western U., 1995. Fellow Am. Soc. Materials Internat.; mem. The Minerals, Metals and Materials Soc., Materials Rsch. Soc. Avocations: hiking, fishing, reading. Office: Rensselaer Polytechnic Inst Dept Materials Sci Engring MRC Bldg Troy NY 12180-3590 E-mail: stolon@rpi.edu.

STOLOV, JERRY FRANKLIN, healthcare executive; b. Kansas City, Mo., Jan. 31, 1946; s. I. Paul and Marion R. (Rothberg) Stolov. BA, Washington U., 1968; MPA, Roosevelt U., 1972. Adminstrv. asst. U. Ill. Chgo. Circle & Med. Sch. Campuses, Chgo., 1970-75; exec. dir. Hosp. Hill Health Svcs. Corp., Kansas City, Mo., 1976—, also bd. dirs., 1976—. Bd. dirs. Kansas City Psychoanalytic Found.; adv. dir. Mchts. Bank Corp., Kansas City, 1985-92. Leadership tng. C. of C., Kansas City, 1977-78. Mem. Assn. Am. Med. Colls. (group on faculty practice), Med. Group Mgmt. Assn., Internat. City Mgrs. Assn., Am. Soc. Pub. Health Adminstrs., Acad. Polit. Sci. (contbg. mem.). Office: Hosp Hill Health Svcs Corp 800 Hospital Hill Ctr 2310 Holmes St Kansas City MO 64108-2634

STOLOV, WALTER CHARLES, physician, rehabilitation educator, physiatrist; b. N.Y.C., Jan. 6, 1928; s. Arthur and Rose F. (Gordon) S.; m. Anita Carvel Noodelman, Aug. 9, 1953; children: Nancy, Amy, Lynne. BS in Physics, CCNY, 1948; MA in Physics, U. Minn., 1951, MD, 1956. Diplomate Am. Bd. Phys. Med. and Rehab., Am. Bd. Electrodiagnostic Medicine. Physicist U.S. Naval Gun Factory, Nat. Bur. Stds., Washington, 1948-49; teaching and rsch. asst. U. Minn., Mpls., 1950-54; from instr. to assoc. prof. U. Wash., Seattle, 1960-70, prof., 1970-99, prof. emeritus, 1999—, also chmn., 1987-99, prof. emeritus, 1999—. Editl. bd. Archives Phys. Medicine and Rehab., 1967-78, Muscle and Nerve, 1983-89, 92-95; cons. Social Security Adminstrn., Seattle, 1975—; sec. Am. Bd. Electrodiagnostic Medicine, 1995—. Co-editor: Handbook of Severe Disability, 1981; contbr. articles to profl. jours. Surgeon USPHS, 1956-57. Recipient Townsend Harris medal CCNY, 1990. Fellow: AAAS, Am. Heart Assn.; mem.: Am. Spinal Cord Injry Assn., Am. Assn. Electrodiagnostic Medicine (pres. 1987—88, Lifetime Achievement award 2001), Assn. Acad. Physiatrists, Am. Congress Rehab. Medicine (Essay award 1959), Am. Acad. Phys. Medicine and Rehab. (Disting. Clinician award 1987). Avocations: dancing, singing. Office: U Wash Box 356490 1959 NE Pacific St Seattle WA 98195-0001

STOLPER, EDWARD MANIN, secondary education educator; b. Boston, Dec. 16, 1952; s. Saul James and Frances A. (Liberman) S.; m. Lauren Beth Adoff, June 3, 1973; children: Jennifer Ann, Daniel Aaron. AB, Harvard U., 1974; M Philosophy, U. Edinburgh, Scotland, 1976; PhD, Harvard U., 1979. Asst. prof. geology Calif. Inst. Tech., Pasadena, 1979-82, assoc. prof. geology, 1982-83, prof. geology, 1983-90, William E. Leonhard prof. geology, 1990—, chmn. divsn. geol. and planetary sci., 1994—. Marshall scholar Marshall Aid Commemoration Commn., 1974-76, recipient Newcomb Cleve. prize AAAS, 1984, F.W. Clarke medal Geochem. Soc., 1985, Arthur Holmes medal European Union Geosci., 1997; Geochemistry fellow The Geochem. Soc. and The European Assn. for Geochemistry, 1997. Fellow Meteoritical Soc. (Nininger Meteorite award 1976), Am. Geophys. Union (James B. Macelwane award 1986), Mineral Soc. Am., Am. Acad. Arts and Scis.; mem. NAS, Geol. Soc. Am., Sigma Xi. Office: Calif Inst Tech Div Geol Planetary Sci Pasadena CA 91125-0001

STOLPER, PINCHAS ARYEH, religious organization executive, rabbi; b. Bklyn., Oct. 22, 1931; s. David Bernard and Nettie (Rosch) S.; m. Elaine Liebman, Nov. 22, 1955; children: Akiva Psachia, Michal Hadassah Cohen, Malka Tova Kaweblum. BA, Bklyn. Coll., 1952; MA, New Sch. for Social Rsch., 1971. Rabbinical ordination Chaim Berlin-Gur Aryeh Rabbinical Acad., 1956; dir. L.I. Zionist Youth Commn., 1956-57; dir. public relations, adminstrv. dean, adviser to English-speaking students Ponevez Yeshiva, Bnai Brak, Israel, 1957-59; also prin.; instr. English and Talmud Naehalim Bnai Akiva H.S., 1959-77; nat. dir. youth div. Union Orthodox Jewish Congregations Am., Nat. Conf. Synagogue Youth, N.Y.C., 1959-76, founder NCSY, Torah Fund, Ben Zakai Honor Soc., 1959-76; editor Jewish Youth Monthly, 1967—; exec. v.p. Union Orthodox Jewish Congregations Am., 1976-94, sr.

exec., 1994—. Adj. prof. Jewish studies Touro Coll., N.Y., 1975— ; mem. publs., Israel, campus commns., staff mem. responsible for edn., Talmud Torah, day sch. commns. Union Orthodox Jewish Congregations Am., 1965— ; del. White House Conf. on Children and Youth, 1961; cons. N. Am. Jewish Youth Conf., 1967— Author: Tested Teen Age Activities, 1961, rev. edit., 1964, Day of Delight, 1961, Tefilah, Text and Source Book, 1963, Revelation What Happened on Sinai, 1966, Prayer, The Proven Path, 1967, The Road to Responsible Jewish Adulthood, 1967, Jewish Alternatives in Love, Dating and Marriage, 1985, The Sacred Trust, Love, Dating and Marriage, The Jewish View, 1996, Beyond Belief, Revelation for the Modern Jew, 1996; contbr. numerous articles, plays, and revs. to Jewish publs.; columnist The Jewish Press, 1994. Nat. dir. Nat. Conf. Synagogue Youth, 1995-98; bd. dirs. Chaim Berlin Torah Schs.-Mesivta Rabbi Chaim Berlin-Rabbinical Acad., 1965—. Recipient Alumi Amudim award Mesivta Rabbi Chaim Berlin-Gur Aryeh Inst., 1967, award Assn. Orthodox Jewish Tchrs., 1975, citation Rabbinical Coun. Am., 1984, Jabotinsky medal, 1990, Alumnus of Yr. award Flatbush Yeshiva, 1989, Joseph K. Miller Achdut Yisrael award Shaalvim Yeshiva, 1993. Mem. Rabbinical Coun. Am. Home: 603 Twin Oaks Dr Lakewood NJ 08701-7147 Office: Union Orthodox Jewish Cong of Am 11 Broadway New York NY 10004-1303

STOLPIN, WILLIAM ROGER, artist, printmaker, retired engineer; b. Flint, Mich., June 25, 1942; s. William and Dorothy Florence (Mitchell) S.; m. Kathleen Diane Poyner, Aug. 14, 1970; children: Krishna Ann, James Mitchell. B of Mech. Engring., Kettering U., Flint, 1965; AA, Charles Stewart Mott C.C., Flint, 1978; postgrad., Ea. Mich. U., 1992. Jr. reliability engr. GM Corp., Flint, 1968-76, sr. reliability engr., 1976-80, quality control supr., 1980-83, product assurance mgr., 1983-89, asst. staff engr. Warren, Mich., 1990-93; printmaker, print pub. Flint, 1969-80; printmaker, print pub., co-founder DAS Print Co., Holly, Mich., 1980—. Resident artist Robert T. Longway Planetarium, Flint, 1975—. Printmaker: (lithograph) ...And the Santa Maria, 1969 (Smithsonian permanent collection 1973), (serigraph) One Giant Leap For Mankind, 1970 (Smithsonian permanent collection 1973), numerous published serigraphs, lithographs, intaglio prints and woodcuts, 1969—. Grant reviewer Greater Flint Arts Coun., 1989-90, 2000-01, v.p., 1973-74, programming and planning, 1988, mktg. and pub. rels., 1999—, bd. dirs., 1999—; pres. Buckham Fine Arts Project, Flint, 1993-94, bd. dirs., 1993-2000; bd. dirs. Whaley Hist. House, Flint, 1997-2000; adv. com. U. Mich. Flint Art Gallery, 1997-2000, Shiawassee Arts Coun., 1999-2000, Alma Coll., 1999-2001; mem. accessions and collections com. Flint Inst. Arts, 2000—. Recipient 1st in Graphics award Internat. Platform Assn., 1969, Koegler Meml. award Left Bank Gallery, 1991, 1st in Overall Attitude, Mich. Renaissance Festival, 1993, 98, 1st prize all media award Left Bank Gallery, 1998, purchase prize Saginaw Art Mus., 1994, 98 Mem. AAAS, AIAA, Internat. Assn. for Astron. Arts, Am. Soc. for Quality, Nat. Stereoscopic Assn., Soc. Automotive Engrs., Soc. Am. Graphic Artists, Flint Artist's Market, Left Bank Gallery, Detroit Artist's Market, Assn. Sci. Fiction and Fantasy Artists, Mich. Assn. Printmakers, Mich. Guild Artists and Artisans. Avocations: directing community theater, participant in Michigan Renaissance Festival, stereoscopic imaging. Studio: DAS Print Co 12201 Gage Rd Holly MI 48442-8339 E-mail: stolpin@ameritech.net.

STOLTE, LARRY GENE, marketing executive, former computer and publishing company executive; b. Cedar Rapids, Iowa, Sept. 17, 1945; s. Ed August and Emma Wilhelmina (Tank) S.; m. Rebecca Jane Tappmeyer, June 13, 1970; children: Scott Edward, Ryan Gene. BBA with highest distinction, U. Iowa, 1971; MBA, Trinity U., 2000. CPA Ill., Mo., Minn., Mich., Wis., Personal Fin. Specialist, Ill., Mo., Minn., Mich., Wis., CMA. Tax & auditing acct. McGladrey Pullen & Co., Cedar Rapids, 1971-73; v.p., gen. mgr. TLS Co. (subs. CCH Computax Inc.), 1973-92; re-engring. cons. CCH, Inc., Riverwoods, Ill., 1992-94; nat. dir. mktg. McGladrey & Pullen, Cedar Rapids, 1994-97; sr. v.p., mng. dir. Web Site Dynamics & Stolte Enterprises, 1997-2000; ins. agt. N.Y. Life Ins. Co. & N.Y.Life Securities, Inc., 2001—. Sgt. USMC, 1964-67. Mem. AICPA (CPA/PFS), Nat. Assn. Computerized Tax Processors (pres.), Am. Mgmt. Assn., Am. Mktg. Assn., Inst. Mgmt. Accts. (cert.), Nat. Bur. Profl. Mgmt. Cons. (cert.), Sales and Mktg. Execs. Internat. (cert. CME & CSE), Inst. of Cert. Mgmt. Cons. (cert.). Methodist. Address: 3000-A Towne House Dr NE PO Box 0489 Cedar Rapids IA 52406-0489 Office: NY Life Ins Co & NYLife Securities Inc 4250 Rivercenter Ct NE Cedar Rapids IA 52402 Fax: 319-378-0581. E-mail: lgstolte@ft.newyorklife.com.

STOLTENBERG, SCOTT FRANK, research scientist; b. Sioux Falls, S.D., Nov. 2, 1966; s. Bernard Dale and Joan Faye S.; m. Shelley Jennifer Creeger, Aug. 8, 1992. BS, Saint John's U., 1989; AM, U. Ill., 1992, PhD, 1995. Postdoctoral fellow U. Mich., Ann Arbor, 1996-99, asst. rsch. scientist, 1999—. Recipient Career Devel. award NIAAA, 2000—. Mem. Behavior Genetics Assn., Rsch. Soc. on Alcohol, Internat. Behavioural and Neurogenetics Soc. Office: U of Mich Addiction Rs Ctr Ste 2a 400 E Eisenhower Pkwy Ann Arbor MI 48108-3318 Fax: 734-615-6085. E-mail: sstolten@umich.edu.

STOLTZFUS, NATHAN A. history educator, documentary and film consultant; b. Harrington, Del., July 24, 1954; s. Llewellyn Roy and Anna Elizabeth Stoltzfus. BA, Goshen (Ind.) Coll., 1978; MDiv, Harvard U., 1984, AM, 1988, PhD, 1993. Prof. history Fla. State U., Tallahassee, 1994—. Cons. for documentary adaptations BBC, London, German TV, Berlin, 1992-93. Author: Resistance of the Heart, 1996; co-editor: Social Outsiders in Nazi Germany, 2001. H.F. Guggenheim scholar, 1993-94; Fulbright Commn. exch. scholar, Germany, 1984-86; Albert Einstein Inst. fellow, scholar in residence, 1985-87; IREX Exch. scholar, East Germany, 1987-88. Avocation: gardening. Home: 1551 Live Oak Dr Tallahassee FL 32301-4907 also: 1615 Kenyon St NW Apt 59 Washington DC 20010-2776

STOLTZMAN, RICHARD LESLIE, clarinetist; b. Omaha, July 12, 1942; s. Leslie Harvey and Dorothy Marilyn (Spohn) S.; m. Lucy Jean Chapman, June 6, 1976; children: Peter John, Margaret Anne. MusB summa cum laude, Ohio State U., 1964; MusM magna cum laude, Yale U., 1967; postgrad., Columbia U. Tchrs. Coll., 1967-70. Mem. faculty Calif. Inst. Arts, 1970-75, New Eng. Conservatory, 1996. Western regional dir. Young Audiences, Inc., 1972-74, mem. nat. bd. Appeared in concerts throughout U.S., Europe, Japan, Hong Kong, Australia, 1976—; rec. artist, 1974—; debut LaScala, Milan, 1981, Carnegie Hall, N.Y.C., 1982; appeared in world premiere of Einar Englund concerto Helsinki Festival, 1991, Toru Takemitsu concerto (Fantasma/Cantos) Wales BBC, 1991, U.S. premiere of Lukas Foss concerto L.A. Philharm. Orch., 1991, Copland concert, 1993 (Emmy award for best performing arts video 1993), world premiere of Leonard Bernstein sonata for clarinet and orch. Pacific Music Festival, Sapporo, Japan, 1994, world premiere of Steven Hartke concerto PBS, Tenn., 2001, world premiere of Thomas McKinley concerto 9 Shades of Lament, Boston Civic Orch., 2001, of Einohuhani Rautavaara Concerto, Nat. Symphony, Carnegie Hall, 2002. Recipient Horatio Parker award Yale U., 1966, Avery Fisher prize, 1977, Martha Baird Rockefeller award, 1973, Grammy award, 1983, 95, Avery Fisher artist award, 1986, Disting. Alumnus award Ohio State U., 1990. Home: 6 Lincolnshire Way Winchester MA 01890-3048 Office: 201 W 54th St Apt 4C New York NY 10019-5521 *Be mindful of the breath. It gives life to the sound which sends music to the soul.*

STOLWIJK, JAN ADRIANUS JOZEF, physiologist, biophysicist; b. Amsterdam, The Netherlands, Sept. 29, 1927; came to U.S., 1955, naturalized, 1962; s. Leonard and Cornelia Agnes (Van Der Bijl) S.; m. Deborah Rose, 1990. BS, Wageningen U., The Netherlands, 1948, MS, 1951, PhD, 1955. Biophysicist John B. Pierce Found., New Haven, 1957-61; assoc. fellow John B. Pierce Found. Lab., 1961-64, fellow, 1964, assoc. dir., 1974-89; instr. dept. physiology Yale U. Sch. Medicine, New Haven, 1962-63, asst. prof., 1964-68, asst. prof. epidemiology, 1968-69, assoc. prof., 1969-75, prof., 1975-99, dir. grad. studies, dept. epidemiology and public health, 1992-99, chmn. dept. epidemiology and pub. health, 1982-89; rsch. fellow Harvard U., 1955-56. Cons. divsn. disease prevention Conn. Health Dept., 1977-99; cons. vehicle inspection program Dept. Motor Vehicles, 1979-83; mem. sci. adv. bd. EPA, 1985-93; mem. tech. adv. bd. Dept. Commerce, 1972-77. Mem. Am. Physiol. Soc., Biophys. Soc., Aerospace Med. Soc., Am. Public Health Assn., AAAS, Internat. Biometeorol. Soc., Soc. Occupational and Environ. Health, Am. Conf. Govt. Indsl. Hygienists, ASHRAE, Conn. Acad. Sci. and Engring. Clubs: Cosmos. Home: 165 Dromara Rd Guilford CT 06437-2391 Office: PO Box 8034 60 College St New Haven CT 06510-3210 E-mail: stolwijk@prodigy.net.

STOLZ, ALAN JAY, youth camp executive; b. N.Y.C., May 7, 1931; s. Irving H. and Pearl (Maltz) S.; m. Sandra Stolz (div.); m. Gail C. Stolz; children: Maryann Stolz Ross, Gary M. AB, Wabash Coll., 1953; LHD (hon.), London Inst., 1973. Cert., lifetime camp dir. Colo. Outdoor Inst., state instr. emergency med. svc. Pres. Camp Cody, Inc., Freedom, N.H.; ptnr., prin. 72d St Assocs. Real Estate Corp., N.Y.C. Cons., profl. witness U.S. Senate and Ho. Reps., White House, Washington; cons. youth camp health various govtl. agys., Washington; guest speaker Am. Free Enterprise program, Moscow and St. Petersburg, Russia, 1993; speaker Internat. Youth Conf., Toronto, Ont., Can., 1994, Orlando, 1995; pres. Alanor, Inc., Fla., 1994—; apptd. consumer affairs specialist N.H. Atty. Gen. Office, Dept. of Justice, Fraud and Anti-Trust Bur. Author: National Camp Directors Guide, 1990; contbr. articles to profl. jours. Founding mem. USAF Mus. in Brit.; primary instr. Emergency Med. Svcs., Westport, Conn., v.p., 1996—, bd. dirs.; vol. staff lectr. Maritime Aquarium, Norwalk, Conn., 2000—; instr. trainer ARC, 1999, Conn. and N.H.; advisor explorer adv. coun. Boy Scouts Am.; justice of peace State of N.H., quorum mem.; bd. govs. Judaica Mus., Riverdale, N.Y., 1994—; vol. dist. coord. N.H. marine patrol Aux. State Dept. Safety, 1991—; mem. Am. Friends Brit. Mus., 1998—. Sgt. U.S. Army, 1955-57. Recipient honor award Emergency Med. Svcs., 1989, 97, 99, Environ. Youth Honors award White House-EPA, 1994, Citation for 55 yrs. svc. to Boy Scouts Am., Conn. State Legislature, 1994, Gov.'s Exec. Coun., N.H., 1995, Cold War Recognition cert. U.S. Dept. Def., 1999, numerous awards Boy Scouts Am., honored for safety patrol svc., 1996, White House Med. Corps Secret Svc. citation for svcs. on presdl. visit, 1999, Congressional Record Congratulations citation for 2 decades EMS vol. leadership, 1999, Congratulations citation from Conn. Gov., State Legislature and Town Mayor, 1999, Am. Red Cross Unsung Heroes award, 2000, EMS Vol. of Yr. award, 2000; named Conn. Vol. of Yr., Carosel Mag., 1990, Conn. Man of Yr., Spotlight Mag., 1991, EMS Vol. Yr., 2000, Disting. Svc. award EMS, Conn. State, 2001, 1st Pl. Nat. Gold award, EMS Vols., 2001. Mem. Am. Camp Assn. (life; nat. legislation chmn. 1970-86, nat. bd. dirs. 1972-84, nat. v.p. 1984-86), N.H. Camp Dir. Assn. (pres. 1974-76, state sec./hon. bd. mem. 1976—). Republican. Jewish. Avocations: archeology, photography, aviation, history, medical research. Home: 5 Lockwood Cir Westport CT 06880-1640 Office: 46 Gailan Rd Freedom NH 03836

STOLZ, BENJAMIN ARMOND, foreign language educator; b. Lansing, Mich., Mar. 28, 1934; s. Armond John and Mabel May (Smith) S.; m. Mona Eleanor Seelig, June 16, 1962; children: Elizabeth Mona, John Benjamin. AB, U. Mich., Ann Arbor, 1955; certificat, U. Libre de Bruxelles, Belgium, 1956; A.M., Harvard U., 1957, PhD, 1965. Mem. faculty U. Mich., 1964-2001, prof. Slavic langs. and lits., 1972-2001, chmn. dept., 1971-85, 89-91; prof. emeritus, 2001—. Cons. in field. Editor: Papers in Slavic Philology, 1977, Studies in Macedonian Language, Literature, and Culture, 1995; co-editor: Oral Literature and the Formula, 1976, Cross Currents, 1982-85, Language and Literary Theory, 1984, Mich. Slavic Publs., 1990—; co-editor, translator: (Konstantin Mihailovic): Memoirs of a Janissary, 1975; contbr. articles to profl. pubs. Served to lt. (j.g.) USNR, 1957-60. Recipient Orion E. Scott award humanities U. Mich., 1954, Fulbright scholar, 1955-56; Fgn. Area fellow Yugoslavia, 1963-64; Fulbright-Hays rsch. fellow Eng. and Yugoslavia, 1970-71; grantee Am. Coun. Learned Socs., 1968-70, 73, Internat. Rsch. and Exchs. Bd., 1985, 87, Woodrow Wilson Ctr., 1992. Mem. Am. Assn. Advancement Slavic Studies, Am. Assn. Tchrs. Slavic and East European Langs., Huron Valley Tennis Club, Phi Beta Kappa, Phi Kappa Phi, Delta Upsilon. Democrat. Home: 3423 Riverbend Dr Ann Arbor MI 48105 Office: Univ Mich 3040 MLB Ann Arbor MI 48109

STOLZ, RICHARD H. public policy administrator; b. Seoul, Republic of Korea, June 3, 1974; came to U.S., 1977; BA, Stanford U., 1996. Mickey Leland hunger fellow Congl. Hunger Ctr., Washington, 1996-97; dep. dir. for pub. policy Ctr. Cmty. Change, 1997—. Office: Ctr Cmty Change 1000 Wisconsin Ave NW Washington DC 20007 Fax: 202-342-1815. E-mail: rstolz@communitychange.org.

STOLZBERG, MARK ELLIOTT, psychologist; b. N.Y.C., Apr. 30, 1944; s. Seymour and Ruth (Petesky) S.; m. Marilyn Goldberg, Mar. 18, 1972; children: Susan Beth, David Jonathan, Daniel Jason. BA, Hofstra U., 1966, PhD, 1986; MA in Exptl. Psychology, C.W. Post Coll., 1970; postgrad. in clin. psychology, SUNY, Albany, 1973. Intern in clin. psychology Maimonides Hosp., Bklyn., 1972-73; pres. Stolzberg Rsch., LLC , Stony Brook, 1976—. Adj. lectr. Bklyn. Coll., 1973; mem. faculty Coll. Optometry, SUNY, 1985-86; cons. clin. psychologist to numerous nursing homes, 1994—. Contbr. articles to profl. jours. Co-pres. North Shore SEPTA, 1999—. Grad. fellow C.W. Post Coll., 1968-70, SUNY, Albany, 1970-72, N.Y. State War Svc. scholar; recipient Disting. Achievement award for Rsch., N.Y. State Optometric Assn., 1983. Mem. Ind. Practitioners of Geropsychology (co-founder, pres. 1999—). Home and Office: 3 Seabrook Ct Stony Brook NY 11790-3305 E-mail: mstolzbe@optonline.net.

STOLZENBERG, LISA ANN, education educator; b. Hollywood, Fla., July 15, 1963; d. Joel and Doris S.; m. Stewart John D'Alessio, July 16, 1999. PhD, Fla. State U., Tallahassee, 1993. Rsch. asst. Fla. State U., Tallahassee, 1985-86; rsch. analyst Fla. Sept. Corrections, 1986-88; program evaluator Fla. Dept. Health and Rehab. Svcs., 1988-90; social sci. analyst Westat Inc., Rockville, Md., 1990-91; rsch. assoc. Justice Rsch. and Statistics Assn., Washington, 1992-93; asst. prof. Fla. Internat. U., Miami, 1996—. Cons. Nat. Rsch. Coun. Washington, 1990, Westat, Inc., Rockville, Md., 1992-93, Ind. U.-Purdue U., Indpls., 1994-96. Author: Criminal Courts for the 21st Century, 1999, 2d edit., 2002; Contbr. articles to profl. jours. Grantee Ind. U., 1994, Ind. U.-Purdue U. Indpls., 1994, Purdue U., 1996, Nat. Inst. Justice, 1996, Fla. Dept. Children and Families, 2000. Mem. Am. Soc. Criminology, Acad. Criminal Justice Scis., Am. Sociol. Assn. Avocations: motorcycle riding. Office: Fla Internat U University Park ECS-435 Miami FL 33199 Fax: 305-348-5848. E-mail: stolzenb@fiu.edu.

STOLZENBERG, ROSS MARK, sociology educator; b. N.Y.C., Dec. 19, 1946; s. Seymour and Edith Richman Stolzenberg; m. Linda Joan Waite; children: Shana Anat, Nava Rachel. AB, Columbia U., 1968; MA, U. Mich., 1971, PhD, 1973. Asst. prof. sociology Harvard U., Cambridge, Mass., 1972-73; asst. prof. social rels. Johns Hopkins U., Balt., 1973-76, asst. prof. population dynamics, 1975-76; asst. prof., then assoc. prof. sociology U. Ill., Urbana, 1976-81, assoc. prof. program in applied stats., 1980-81; social scientist Rand Corp., Santa Monica, Calif., 1980-83; v.p. rsch. and test devel. Grad. Mgmt. Admission Coun., Santa Monica and L.A., 1983-91; prof. sociology U. Chgo., 1991—. Spl. agt., cons. U.S. Bur. Census, Washington, 1975-77, mem. adv. com. of profl. orgns., 1995-2001; cons. Rand Corp., 1983-2000; mem. editl. bd. sociol. Methodology, 1998-2001, Sociol. Methods and Rsch., 1974-80, 98—, Am. Jour. Sociology, 1990—, Social Forces, 1995-98, Rsch. on Social Stratification and Mobility, 1989-94; dep. editor Am. Sociol. Rev., 1977-79; mem. bd. cons. editors Am. Jour. Sociology, 1977-79; assoc. editor Social Sci. Rsch., 1974—. Contbr. articles to profl. jours.; author monographs in field. Trustee Sonia Shankman Orthogenic Sch., Chgo., 1997—, Hyde Park Sch. for Learning Disabled Children, Chgo., 1999—. Recipient citation for valor ARC, 1966, Rsch. Scientist Career Devel. award, NIMH, 1979; rsch. grantee U.S. Dept. Labor, 1971, NSF, 1978. Mem. Sociol. Rsch. Assn., Am. Sociol. Assn., Population Assn. Am. Democrat. Jewish. Home: 899 Kimball Rd Highland Park IL 60035 Office: U Chgo Dept Sociology 1123 E 57th St Chicago IL 60637 E-mail: r-stolzenberg@uchicago.edu.

STOLZER, LEO WILLIAM, bank executive; b. Kansas City, Mo., Oct. 14, 1934; s. Leo Joseph and Lennie Lucille (Hopp) S.; m. Eleanor Katherine Griffith, Aug. 17, 1957; children: Joan Ellen Stolzer Bolen, Mary Kevin Stolzer Giller. BS in Acctg., Kans. State U., 1957. Teller Union Nat. Bank & Trust Co., Manhattan, Kans., 1960-62, asst. cashier, 1962-63, asst. v.p., 1963-64, v.p., 1964-69, exec. v.p., 1969-72, pres., 1972-80, chmn., CEO, 1980-95; chmn., 1995—. Bd. dirs. Commerce Bankshares Inc., Commerce Bank-Manhattan; chmn., CEO Griffith Lumber Co., Cmty. Bancorporation of N.Mex., Inc. Trustee, past treas., past vice-chair Kans. State U. Found.; trustee Midwest Rsch. Inst.; chmn. Riley County Savs. Bond. Capt. USAF, 1957-60. Recipient Disting. Service award Manhattan Jr. C. of C., 1968, Kans. State U. Advancement award. Fellow Coll. Bus. Adminstrn. Alumni; mem. Am. Bankers Assn. (past treas., past exec. com., past bd. dirs.), Assn. U.S. Army (bd. dirs. Ft. Riley Ctl. Kans. chpt., past chair), Kans. U. Alumni Assn. (devel. com.), Newcomen Soc. in N.Am. (past Kans. chmn.), KC, Beta Theta Pi. Avocation: skiing. Office: Commerce Bank 727 Poyntz Ave Manhattan KS 66502-0118

STOMFAY-STITZ, ALINE MARIA, education educator; b. Newark; d. Adolph and Irene (Badowska) Wegrocki; m. Emery Stomfay-Stitz (dec.); children: Peter, John, Robert. BA, Barnard Coll.; MA, Case Western Reserve U.; EdD, No. Ill. U., 1984. Asst. prof. Coll. St Scholastica, Duluth, Minn., 1984-85, St. Leo (Fla.) Coll., 1985-87, Nicholls State U., Thibodaux, La., 1989-91; assoc. prof. edn. Christopher Newport U., Newport News, Va., 1991-96. Vis. prof., assoc. prof. edn. U. No. Fla., Jacksonville, 1996—; assoc. editor Joun. Early Childhood Tchr. Edn. *Aline M. Stomfay-Stitz has achieved distinction in the area of International Peace Education. She is active in the Am. Educ. Rsch. Assn., and Peace Educ. SIG as a past Chair and Online Newsletter Editor; Area SIG Exec. Comm., 2002-2004.* Author: Peace Education in America 1828-1990, 1993; author (book chpt.): Toward Education That is Multicultural, 1992, Multicultural Education for the 21st Century, 1993; contbr. articles to profl. jours. Mem.: Internat. Peace Rsch. Assn., Nat. Assn. for Early Childhood Tchrs. Educators, Am. Ednl. Rsch. Assn. (SIG exec. com.). Office: U No Fla 4567 Saint Johns Bluff Rd S Jacksonville FL 32224-2646 E-mail: astomfay@unf.edu.

STONE, ALAN ABRAHAM, law and psychiatry educator, psychiatrist; b. 1929; AB, Harvard U., 1950; MD, Yale U., 1955. Lectr. Harvard U., 1966-72, asst. prof. psychiatry, 1966-69, assoc. prof., 1969-72, prof. law, psychiatry, 1972—, Touroff-Glueck prof. law, psychiatry, 1982—. Adv. com. project mentally Ill Am. Bar Found., 1967-71; com. revision criminal code Mass. Gov., 1968-72; com. mentally disabled ABA, 1973-77; chmn. Mass. Com. Psychosurgery, 1974-75; Tanner lectr. Stanford U., 1982; mem. Justice Panel on Waco, 1993. Author: (with Onque) Longitudinal Studies of Child Behavior, 1961, Mental Health and Law: A System in Transition, 1975, Law, Psychiatry and Morality: Essays and Analysis, 1984; editor: (with Sue Stone) Abnormal Personality Through Literature, 1966. Capt. M.C., U.S. Army, 1959-61. Recipient Manfred S. Guttmacher award, Isaac Ray award, 1982; Ctr. Advanced Study Behavioral Sci. fellow Stanford U., 1980-81. Mem. Am. Psychiat. Assn. (trustee, v.p., pres., chmn. com. jud. action 1974-79), Group Advancement Psychiatry. Office: Harvard U Law Sch 1575 Massachusetts Ave Cambridge MA 02138-2801

STONE, ALAN JAY, retired college administrator; b. Ft. Dodge, Iowa, Oct. 15, 1942; s. Hubert H. and Bernice A. (Tilton) S.; m. Jonieta J. Smith; 1 child, Kirsten K. Stone Morlock. BA, Morningside Coll., 1964; MA, U. Iowa, 1966; MTh, U. Chgo., 1968, DMin, 1970; PhD (hon.), Kyonggi U., Korea, 1985; LLD, Stillman Coll., 1991, Sogong U., Korea, 1992, Alma Coll., 2001; HHD, Morningside Coll., 2001. Admissions counselor Morningside Coll., Sioux City, Iowa, 1964-66; dir. admissions, asso. prof. history George Williams Coll., Downers Grove, Ill., 1969-73; v.p. coll. relations Hood Coll., Frederick, Md., 1973-75; v.p. devel. and fin. affairs W.Va. Wesleyan Coll., Buckhannon, 1975-77; dir. devel. U. Maine, 1977-78; pres. Aurora (Ill.) U., 1978-88, Alma (Mich.) Coll., 1988-2000; pres., CEO Alzheimer's Assn., Chgo., 2001—02; ret., 2002. Home: 28897 N 94th Pl Scottsdale AZ 85262 E-mail: stone5613@earthlink.net.

STONE, ALAN JOHN, manufacturing company executive, real estate executive; b. Dansville, N.Y., Sept. 9, 1940; s. Guthrie Boyd and Doris Irene (Wolfanger) S.; m. Sandra Barber, Aug. 22, 1964; children: Teri, Timothy, Michael. BSME, Rochester Inst. Tech., 1963; MBA, U. Pitts., 1964. Engring. aide Xerox Corp., Webster, N.Y., 1960-63; gen. mgr. mech. component divsn. Stone Conveyor Co., Inc., Honeoye, 1964-67, v.p. sales, 1968; co-founder, CEO Stone Constrn. Equipment Inc., 1969-86, also cons., bd. dirs., 1969—; founder, pres. Canandaigua Apts. Inc., N.Y., 1968-83; pres. Wildtrak, Inc., 1983—; founder, gen. ptnr. Stone Properties, 1986—. Dir., co-founder Baker Rental Svc., Inc., 1973-75; met. adv. bd. Chase Lincoln Bank, 1981-84; co-founder, dir. Royal Lines Ltd., 1989-91; bd. dirs. Naples Biol. Rsch. Sta. Inc., v.p., 1996-98; bd. dirs. Canandaigua Nat. Bank & Trust Co., 1986—, chmn. 1994—. Patentee in field. Mem. Town of Richmond (N.Y.) Planning Bd., 1970-75, chmn., 1970-71; mem. Honeoye Ctrl. Sch. Bd. Edn., 1971-76, pres., 1974-75; com. chmn. pack 10 Boy Scouts Am., 1975-78; mem. Ontario County Overall Econ. Devel. Com., 1976-81; bd. dirs. F.F. Thompson Hosp., 1987-91; chmn. fin. com. United Meth. Ch., Allens Hill, 1995—; trustee Honeoye Pub. Libr., 1998—. Mem. Honeoye C. of C., Constrn. Industry Mfrs. Assn. (exec. mem. new bus. challenges coun. 1980-83), Honeoye Valley Assn. (dir. 1991-95, treas. 1993-95), Griswold and Cast Iron Collectors Assn. (treas. 1994-96, chmn. fin. com. 1996--), Honeoye Area Hist. Soc. (bicentennial com. 1989), Young Pres.'s Assn., Grand Slam Club, Safari Internat., Found N.Am. Wild Sheep. Methodist. Home and Office: Box 500 5170 County Road 33 Honeoye NY 14471-0500

STONE, ALAN WILLIAM, physician; b. N.Y., Sept. 18, 1940; s. Daniel and Ethel (Mandell) S.; m. Jerilyn Landry, June 27, 1969; 1 child, Phoebe Alice. BA cum laude, Harvard Coll., 1961; MD cum laude, Yale U., 1966. Diplomate Am. Bd. Internal Medicine, Nat. Bd. Medical Examiners. Rschr. in molecular biology Inst. Molecular Biology/U. Geneva, Switzerland, 1964-65; pathology intern Yale Med. Ctr., 1966-67; internship Peter Bent Brigham Hosp., Boston, 1967-68; asst. preventive med. officer Walter Reed Gen. Hosp., Washington, 1969-71; resident Georgetown U., 1973-75; clin. assoc. prof. medicine Georgetown U. Med. Ctr., 1975-80, program dir. primary care medicine, residency, 1980-88, assoc. prof., 1980-88; pvt. practice internal medicine, 1988—. Acting med. dir. George Washington U. Health Plan, 1980-82, dir. divsn. adult medicine, 1987-88; clin. assoc. prof. George Washington U., 1988-91, clin. prof., 1991—. Contbr. articles to profl. jours. With U.S. Army, 1968-71. Decorated Army Commendation medal; recipient Ferris prize in anatomy Yale U., 1962, Perkins Scholarship prize, 1963, Sternberg Meml. medal Walter Reed Army Inst. Rsch., 1969; James Hudson Brown Meml. Fund fellow, 1964. Fellow ACP; mem. AMA, Am. Soc. Internal Medicine, D.C. Med. Soc., Alpha Omega Alpha. Democrat. Avocations: piano, astronomy, sports. Office: 2021 K St NW Ste 404 Washington DC 20006-1003

STONE, ALEC J. healthcare lobbyist; b. San Antonio, Apr. 9, 1969; s. Gerald C. and Donna (Besser) S.; m. Lisa B. Stone; children: Aviva Kyra, Arianna Ruth, Ayden Meyer. BS in History, Memphis State U., 1992; MPA, So. Ill. U., 1994; MA in Polit. Sci., George Washington U., 1996. Polit. cons./strategist, Washington, 1990-98; nat. field coord. The Joint Steering Com. on Pub. Policy, Bethesda, Md., 1998-2000; dir. govt. affairs The Def. Rsch. Found., Washington, 2000—. Mem. Montgomery County Citizens Adv. Bd., Silver Spring, Md., 2000-2001; chair Grad. Sch. Polit. Mgmt. Alumni Steering Com., 1999-2000; pres. Young Israel of White Oak, 1997-99; mem. Nat. Jewish Dem. Coun., 1996—, Am. Diabetes Assn., 2000—. Recipient Shofar award Nat. Coun. of Young Israel, 1998. Mem. Nat. Hist. Preservation Soc.,Alpha Psi Omega. Democrat. Jewish. Avocations: golf, tennis, presidential history. Office: Nonprofit Mgmt Inc 1555 Connecticut Ave NW #200 Washington DC 20036

STONE, ALLAN DAVID, economics educator; b. Joliet, Ill., Jan. 9, 1937; s. William E. and Leona V. (Frieh) S.; m. Peggy J. Carter, Jan. 11, 1958; children: David, Richard. BA, Beloit Coll., 1961; MA, U. Okla., 1964, PhD, 1973. Asst. prof. econs. U. Tex., El Paso, 1963-65; instr. econs. Wartburg Coll., Waverly, Iowa, 1965-66; asst. prof. econs. Oklahoma City U., 1966-72; prof. econs. S.W. Mo. State U., Springfield, 1972—2001, dept. head, 1985-87, emeritus prof., 2001—. Served with U.S. Army, 1956-58. NSF grantee. Mem. Am. Econ. Assn., Mo. Coun. Econ. Edn. (bd. dirs. 1977-80), Phi Beta Kappa, Phi Kappa Phi. Home: 820 E Cherokee St Springfield MO 65807-2708

STONE, ANDREW GROVER, lawyer; b. L.A., Oct. 2, 1942; s. Frank B. and Meryl (Pickering) S.; divorced; 1 child, John Blair. BA, Yale U., 1965; JD, U. Mich., 1969. Bar: D.C. 1970, U.S. Dist. Ct. D.C. 1970, U.S. Ct. Appeals (D.C. cir.) 1972, Mass. 1981. Assoc. Rogers & Wells, Washington, 1969-71; atty. Bur. Competition, FTC, 1971-80; antitrust counsel Digital Equipment Corp., Maynard, Mass., 1980-83, mgr. N.E. law group, 1983-86, mgr. headquarters sales law group, 1986-88; asst. general counsel U.S. (acting), 1987, 88; corp counsel Washington, 1988-90; corp. counsel, pub. sect. mktg. Thinking Machines Corp., Cambridge, Mass., 1990-91, corp. counsel, 1992-95; pvt. practice on-site legal svcs. Marblehead, 1995—. Corp. mem. Tenacre Country Day Sch., Wellesley, Mass., 1981-88. Mem. ABA (bus. law sect.), Mass. Bar Assn. (internat. law steering com. 1993-94), Boston Bar Assn. (membership com. 1998-2000, chair corp. counsel com. 1995-98, gen. counsel forum 1995—), Am. Arbitration Assn. (comml. arbitrator), New Eng. Corp. Counsel Assn., Assn. Ind. Gen. Counsel.

STONE, ANN E.W. direct marketing company executive; BA in History and Comms., George Washington U.; postgrad., U. Pa. Founder, pres. The Stone Group, Inc., 1982—; chmn. Capstone Lists Inc. Spkr. in field. Bd. dirs. Nat. Women's History Mus., Assn. Direct Mktg. Agys., Washington Ctr., Rep. Liberty Caucus, Campagna Ctr., Make Women Count, others; past chmn. Alexandria br. Am. Heart Assn., Alexandria Seaport Found.; founder, chmn. Republicans for Choice, Alexandria, Va. Mem. Nat. Assn. Women Bus. Owners, Am. Assn. Polit. Cons. (bd. dirs.), Nat. Women's Hall of Fame, Direct Mktg. Club. Washington, Non-Profit Mailers Fedn., Nat. Trust for Historic Preservation, Alexandria Soc. for Preservation of Black Heritage, Animal Welfare League, Alexandria C. of C. (bd. dirs.), No. Va. Rep. Bus. Forum (bd. dirs.). Office: The Stone Group 2760 Eisenhower Ave Ste 250 Alexandria VA 22314-4553 E-mail: tsgrp@aol.com.

STONE, BEVERLY ANN, retired counselor; b. Detroit, Apr. 17, 1941; d. Russell E. and Esther Pauline (Bauman) Stewart; m. Roger George Stone, June 25, 1974. BA in French/Edn., U. Mich., 1963, MEd in Guidance/Counseling, 1966; EdS, Wayne State U., 1991. Cert. tchr., secondary sch. adminstr., counselor, Mich. Tchr. of French and English Lakeview Pub. Schs., St. Clair Shores, Mich., 1963-65; English tchr. South Lake Schs., 1966-67, secondary counselor, 1967-85, elem. counselor, 1985-96, mid. sch. counselor, 1996-2000. Mem. South Lake Counseling Adv. Bd., St. Clair Shores, 1991-94; mem. pub. rels. chmn. South Lake Edn. Assn., 1986-89. Mem. pub. policy and legis. com. Mich. Counseling Assn., 1992—; vol. Mother's March on Birth Defects, March of Dimes, Clinton Twp., Mich., 1990-95. Recipient scholarship/Nat. Def., U.S. Govt., Ann Arbor, Mich., 1965-66. Mem. Am. Counseling Assn., Mich. Sch. Counseling Assn., People to People Internat., Citizen Ambassador Program, Mich. Counseling Assn., Macomb Counselor Inst., Macomb County Counseling Assn. (pres. 1990-91). Lutheran. Avocations: extensive domestic and fgn. travel, fishing, cross-stitch, gardening, bridge. Home: 35194 Pappstein Dr Clinton Township MI 48035-2375

STONE, BRIAN A. urologist, surgeon, educator; b. Birmingham, Ala., Dec. 14, 1959; s. Alford and Bettie G. Stone; m. Laura F. Stone, May 29, 1989; childen: Antuan, Alyse, Brian, Alexandra. BA, Rutgers U., 1981; postgrad., Morehouse Sch. Medicine, Atlanta, 1981-83; MD, U. Ala., 1985. Diplomate Am. Bd. Urology. Gen. surgeon Montefiore Med. Ctr., N.Y.C., 1985-87, neuro urology fellow, 1987-89, impotence fellow, 1989-90, urology resident, 1990-94; dir. outpatient urology Harlem Hosp., 1994—; chief urology N. Gen. Hosp., 1995—; asst. prof. urology N.Y. Presbyn. Hosp., 1995—. Editor-in-chief Black Health Network, 1996—. Fellow Am. Coll. Surgeons, N.Y. Acad. Medicine. Office: 180 Fort Washington Ave New York NY 10032-3710

STONE, CAROLINE FLEMING, artist; b. N.Y.C., Mar. 26, 1936; d. Ralph Emerson and Elizabeth (Fleming) Stone; m. Oakleigh B. Thorne, June 1956 (div. 1969); children: Oakleigh, Henry; m. John Roderick Keating, July 2002. Student, Art Students' League, 1954-57, 71-72, Pratt Graphics, 1973-74. One-woman shows include Washington Art Assn., Conn., Ella Sharp Mus., Mich., 1980, San Diego Pub. Library, 1981, Trustman Gallery Simmons Coll., Boston, 1985, Mary Ryan Gallery, N.Y.C., 1989, Boston Pub. Libr., 1994, Messiah Coll., 1995; two-person shows include Mary Ryan Gallery, 1985, Katonah Gallery, N.Y., 1986, Davidson Gallery, Seattle, 1990, The Millbrook (N.Y.) Gallery, 1993; juried shows include Silvermine Nat. Printmaking, Conn., 1978, Print Club, Phila., 1981, Trenton State (Nat. Print Exhibn. Purchase award), 1982, Minot State Coll., N.D., 1985, Boston Printmakers (Jurors Commendation), 1986; group shows include Mus. N.Mex., 1984, De Cordova and Dana Mus., Nat. Acad. Art, N.Y.C., Boston Pub. Library, Mus. Contemporary Hispanic Art, N.Y.C., 1987, World Print Exhbn., San Francisco, Smith Coll. Gallery, Northampton, Mass., Mary Ryan Gallery, 1988, Virginia Lynch Gallery, R.I., 1989, 91, Accent on Paper, Lintas, N.Y., 1991, Women Printmaker's Nat. Touring Show, Boston Pub. Libr. 1991, The Tenth Anniversary Show Virginia Lynch Gallery, 1993; represented in permanent collections Art Inst. Chgo., Mid-West Mus. Am. Art, Ind., Mus. N.Mex., Nat. Mus. Am. Art, Boston Pub. Library, U. Chgo., U. Mich., The Portland Art Mus. Mem.: The Kitchen (bd. dirs.). Home and Office: C Stone Press 80 Wooster St New York NY 10012-4347

STONE, CHRISTOPHER JOHN, consulting executive, educator; b. Clacton, England, Aug. 13, 1960; s. Robert Edwin and Irene Winefride S. Lectr. Bournemouth (England) U., 1989-91; mng. cons. The ASH Consulting Group, Edinburgh, Scotland, 1991-92; sr. lectr. in tourism devel. and analysis Univ. Sunderland, Tyne & Wear, England, 1992—. Mem.: Instn. Environ. Scis., Tourism Soc., Internat. Assn. Sci. Experts in Tourism. Office: Univ Sunderland Green Terrace Sunderland Tyne & Wear SR1 3PZ England E-mail: chris.stone@sunderland.ac.uk.

STONE, CYNTHIA LAWSON, nursing educator; b. Rockford, Ill. d. Robert Edward and Marjorie Kathryn (Engberg) Lawson; m. Wayne R. Stone, May 28, 1977; children: Nicole, Lindsay. BSN, U. Mich., 1977; MSN, Wayne State U., 1982; DrPh, U. Pitts., 1995. Pub. health nurse Stark County Health Dept., Canton, Ohio, 1977-78, Visiting Nurses Svcs., Detroit, 1978-81; instr. Wayne State U., 1982-83; instr., supr. Allegheny Gen. Hosp., Pitts., 1983-91; instr. to clin. assoc. prof. Ind. U., Indpls., 1991—. Mem. ANA (cert. cmty. health nurse), APHA, Ind. Pub. Health Assn., Ind. Nurses Assn., Sigma Theta Tau. Office: Ind U 1111 Middle Dr/NU 463 Indianapolis IN 46202-5243 E-mail: cylstone@iupui.edu.

STONE, DAN N. educator; b. San Francisco, Nov. 18, 1955; s. Dan N. Stone, Norma J. Stone; m. Janis Carol Carter; children: Megan Laura. PhD, U. Tex., 1987. CPA 1981. Assoc. prof. U. Ill., Champaign, 1988—99; Gatton endowed chair U. Ky., Lexington, 2000—. Pres. Countryside Sch., Champaign, Ill., 1998—99. Avocations: building rock walls, reading, writing. Office: Univ Ky 355 Gatton B&E Bldg Lexington KY 40506 Office Fax: 859-257-3654. Business E-Mail: dstone@uky.edu.

STONE, DAVID M. career officer; m. Cynthia Faith Voth, 1977. Diploma, U.S. Naval Acad., 1974; MS in Nat. Security Affairs, U.S. Naval Postgrad. Sch., 1977; MA in Nat. Security/Strategic Studies, U.S. Naval War Coll., 1986; MS in Mgmt., Salve Regina Coll. Commd. ensign USN, 1974, advanced through ranks to rear adm., various assignments to comdr. Middle East Force and Destroyer Squadron 50, 1994-96; chief of staff U.S. Sixth Fleet, 1996-98; comdr. NATO's Standing Naval Force Mediterranean, 1998-99; deputy director surface warfare USN, 99-00, Nimitz battlegroup comm., 2000-01. Decorated Legion of Merit (3 times), Def. Meritorious Svc. medal (2 times), Meritorious Svc. medal (3 times), Navy Commendation medal (3 times), Navy Achievement medal, others. Address: 1027 N Edgewood St Arlington VA 22201-2119 Office: COMCRUDESGRU 5 Unit 25066 FPO AP 96601

STONE, DAVID MARK, plastic surgeon; b. Chgo., Jan. 11, 1956; MD, U. Ill., 1981. Diplomate Am. Bd. Otolaryngology, Am. Bd. Facial Plastic & Reconstructive Surgery. Intern U. Ill./Metro Group Hosps., Chgo., 1981-82, resident in gen. surgery, 1982-83; resident in otolaryngology, head and neck surgery Northwestern U., 1983-86; fellow in facial plastic surgery Am. Acad. Facial Plastic and Reconstructive Surgery, Birmingham, 1986-87; facial plastic surgeon Irvine (Calif.) Med. Soc.; asst. clin. prof. dept. otolaryngology/head and neck surgery U. Calif., Irvine. Fellow ACS; mem. AAOHNS, AMA, Am. Acad. Facial Plastic and Reconstructive Surgery. Office: Stone Creek Surg Svcs 33 Creek Rd Ste 240 Irvine CA 92604-7704

STONE, DAVID PHILIP, lawyer; b. N.Y.C., Sept. 11, 1944; s. Robert and Laura Stone; m. Arlene R. Stone, June 11, 1966; children: Aaron J., Rachel E. AB, Columbia U., 1967; JD, Harvard U., 1970. Bar: N.Y. 1971. Assoc. Cahill, Gordon & Reindel, N.Y.C., 1970-74, Baer & McGoldrick, N.Y.C., 1974-76, Weil, Gotshal & Manges, L.L.P., N.Y.C., 1976-79, ptnr., 1979—. Office: Weil Gotshal & Manges LLP 767 5th Ave Fl Concl New York NY 10153-0119 Business E-Mail: david.stone@weil.com.

STONE, DEE WALLACE, actress; b. Kansas City, Mo., Dec. 14, 1948; d. Robert Stanley and Maxine (Nichols) Bowers; m. Christopher Stone, June 28, 1980 (dec.); m. Skip Belyea. BA, U. Kans., 1971. Actress feature films The Christmas Visitor, Secret Admirer, Cujo, E.T., Jimmy the Kid, The Howling, 10; actress ABC movies of the week Eminent Domain, Hostage Flight, A Whale for a Killing; actress CBS movies of the week An Enemy Among Us, Sin of Innocence, The Sky is No Limit, Happy, Surprise, Surprise, The Five of Me, Young Love, First Love; actress NBC movies of the week Wait Til Your Mother Gets Home, Child Bride of Short Creek, Skeezer; actress CBS After School Special Dad's Out of a Job; actress ABC After School Special Run Don't Walk; actress CBS series Police Story, Together We Stand/Nothing is Easy, Lou Grant; actress stage prodns. including Annie Get Your Gun, Oklahoma, My Fair Lady, Applause, Butterflies are Free, Middle of the Night. Spkr. in field; mgr. DWS Acting Studio, Burbank, Calif. Appeared in films including Nevada, 1997, Mutual Needs, 1997, Black Circle Boys, 1997, Bad As I Wanna Be: The Dennis Rodman Story, 1998, Flamingo Dreams, 1998, To Love, Honor and Betray, 1999, Invisible Mom II, 1999, Pirates of the Plain, 1999, Out of the Black, A Month of Sundays, Dead Canaries, others. Fundraiser Actors and Others for Animals, L.A., 1980—, Amanda Found., L.A., 1986, 87; co-host, fundraiser Children's Hospital Telethon, Sta. KCET, L.A., 1985—; spokesperson Nat. Assn. of Children of Alcoholics, 1987—. Mem. Screen Actors Guild, Actors Equity, AFTRA. Methodist. Avocations: dancing, singing.

STONE, DIANNE ST. CHRISTINE, legal aid society executive; b. Jamaica, W.I., Mar. 12, 1964; came to U.S., 1980; d. Troy and Sonia (Roberts) S.; children: Jared Stone-Rigg, Kendra Stone-Rigg. BS, NYU, 1985. Asst. ops. mgr. Clark Boardman Co., Ltd., N.Y.C.; dir. adminstrn. Inspeco, 1990-93; adminstr. fed. defender's divsn. The Legal Aid Soc., Bklyn., 1993—. Avocations: African-American history, softball, tennis, reading. Office: Fed Defenders FDD 16 Court St Brooklyn NY 11241-0102 E-mail: Stonerigg1@aol.com.

STONE, DONALD DIAMOND, investment and sales executive; b. Chgo., June 25, 1924; s. Frank J. and Mary N. (Miller) Diamondstone; m. Catherine Mauro, Dec. 20, 1970; 1 child, Jeffrey. Student, U. Ill., 1942-43; BS, DePaul U., 1949. Pres. Poster Bros., Inc., Chgo., 1950-71, Revere Leather Goods, Inc., Chgo., 1953-71; owner Don Stone Enterprises, 1954—; v.p. Horton & Hubbard Mfg. Co. Inc. div. Brown Group, Nashua, N.H., 1969-71, Neevel Mfg. Co., Kansas City, Mo., 1969-71. Mem. adv. bd. San Diego Opera; founder Don Diego Meml. Scholarship Fund; mem. bd. overseers U. Calif., San Diego, chancellor's assoc.; mem. exec. bd. Chgo. Area council Boy Scouts of Am. Served with U.S. Army, 1943-46. Clubs: Bryn Mawr Country (Lincolnwood, Ill.) (dir.), Carlton, La Jolla Beach and Tennis, La Jolla Country, Del Mar Thoroughbred. Home: 8240 Caminito Maritimo La Jolla CA 92037-2204 E-mail: dstone1@san.rr.com.

STONE, DONALD JAMES, retired retail executive; b. Cleve., Mar. 5, 1929; s. Sidney S. and Beatrice (Edelman) S.; m. Norma Fay Karchmer, Oct. 26, 1952; children— Michael, Lisa, Angela. BBA, U. Tex., Austin, 1949. With Foley's, Houston, 1949-75, v.p., gen. mdse. mgr., 1960-75; chmn., chief exec. officer Sanger-Harris, Dallas, 1975-80; vice chmn. Federated Dept. Stores, Inc., Cin., 1980-88. Bd. dirs. M Corp., Fossil, Inc., Bloom Agy., Dallas, XTEC Corp., Cin. Pres. Dallas Symphony Soc., 1980-82, 88—, chmn. Found. bd., 1989—; chmn. exec. com. Dallas Ballet, 1979; bd. dirs. Dallas Mus. Fine Art, 1979-81; mem. adv. coun. Coll. Bus. Adminstrn. U. Tex., 1981—, chmn., 1990-92; bd. dirs. Cin. Ballet, 1982-87, Cin. Symphony, 1983-88, pres., 1987; bd. Cin. overseers, chmn., 1988-92; bd. govs. Hebrew Union Coll., 1988—; bd. dirs. Aspen Inst. Humanistic Studies, 1988-94. Mem. Dallas C. of C. (chmn. cultural com. 1979-81), Assoc. Mdse. Corp. (bd. dirs., exec. com.). Democrat. Jewish. Home: 3601 Turtle Creek Blvd Dallas TX 75219-5522

STONE, DONALD P. lawyer; b. Ironwood, Mich., July 31, 1937; s. Paul Clarence and Ethel (Moore) S.; m. Barbara Ann Schneider, Nov. 24, 1962 (dec.); children: Kimberly Ann, Paul Christian, Sandra Jane; m. Stephanie L. Brooks, Jan. 31, 1997. BA, Tchrs. cert., U. Mich., 1959, JD, 1962. Bar: Mich. 1962, U.S. Dist. Ct. (we. dist.) Mich. 1963. Ptnr. Stone, Campbell & Hoffelder, P.L.C., Niles, Mich., 1963—. Mem. ABA, Mich. Bar Assn., Berrien County Bar Assn. (pres. 1973-74), Elks. Presbyterian. Office: Stone Campbell & Hoffelder 223 N 4th St # 249 Niles MI 49120-2301

STONE, DONALD RAYMOND, lawyer; b. Madison, Wis., Mar. 6, 1938; s. Donald Meredith and June Dorothy (Graffenberger) S.; m. Dorothy Tetzlaff, June 23, 1962; children— Randall, Brian. BS in Physics, U. Wis., 1960, JD, 1963. Bar: Minn. 1963, D.C. 1987, U.S. Supreme Ct. 1987. Patent atty. Honeywell, Inc., Mpls., 1963-66; patent atty. firm Burd, MacEachron, Braddock, Bartz & Schwartz, 1966-68; with Medtronic, Inc., 1968-87, v.p., then sr. v.p. product assurance and regulation, 1973-77, sr. v.p., sec., gen. counsel, 1977-80, sr. v.p., 1980-85, v.p., 1985-87; ptnr., mem. Burditt, Bowles & Radzius, Chartered, Washington, 1987-90; ptnr. McKenna & Cuneo, L.L.P., 1990-2001, Kirkpatrick & Lockhart LLP, Washington, 2001—. Condr. seminars, 1974—. Contbr. articles to profl. jours. Bd. dirs., 1st v.p. East Side Neighborhood Services, Inc., Mpls., 1976-80; bd. dirs. Guthrie Theater Found., 1979-85; mem. allocations com. United Way Mpls., 1979-86, chmn. allocations com., 1985, bd. dirs. 1985-86; mem. Citizens League of Twin Cities, 1965-86. Mem. ABA, D.C. Bar Assn., Fed. Bar Assn., Hennepin County Bar Assn., Am. Soc. Quality, Am. Intellectual Property Law Assn., Advanced Med. Tech. Assn. (past chmn. legal and regulatory sect., standard sect., 1975-87), Nat. Elec. Mfrs. Assn. (past chmn. med. electronics sect., 1970-76), Assn. Advancement Med. Instrumentation, Minn. State Bar Assn., Minn. Intellectual Property Law Assn. (past sec.), Minn. Corp. Counsel Assn., Regulatory Affairs. Profls. Soc., Order of Coif, Phi Delta Phi, Kappa Sigma. Clubs: Mpls. Episcopalian. Office: Kirkpatrick & Lockhart LLP 2d Fl 1800 Massachusetts Ave NW Washington DC 20036 E-mail: dstone@kl.com.

STONE, DUANE SNYDER, school psychologist, clergyman; b. Turon, Kans., Nov. 10, 1935; s. Herman and Neva F. (Snyder) S.; m. Nancy R. Castillo, July 12, 1958; children: Patricia L. Stone Davis, Christopher D. AA, Graceland Coll., 1953; BA, San Jose State U., 1959, MA, 1961; EdS, Wichita State U., 1985. Ordained to ministry Reorganized LDS Ch., 1951. Tchr., adminstr., supt. Santa Clara County Schs., San Jose, Calif., 1959-63; commd. 2d lt. USAF, 1963, advanced through grades to maj., 1974, security police officer Okla., 1963-66, instr. Officer Tng. Sch. Lackland AFB, Tex., 1966-69, base def. officer 35 TRW Phan Rang Air Base, Vietnam, 1969-70; asst. prof. aerospace sci. Memphis State U. AFROTC, 1970-73; comdr. security police squadron USAF, Minot AFB, N.D., 1973-76; clin. psychologist 91st Regional Hosp. USAF, 1976-83; ret., 1983; sch. psychologist Wichita (Kans.) Pub. Schs., 1985-86, Butler County Sch. Bd., El Dorado, Kans., 1986—. Pres. Reality Theapy Assocs., Wichita, 1983—. Author: The Ministry of Health and Healing, 1986, Ministry to Persons with Debilitating Lifestyles, 1988. Treas. Springhaven, Andover, Kans., 1955—. Recipient award Reorganized LDS Ch., 1995. Mem. NASP (cert.), DAV, NRA, Ret. Officers Assn. Avocations: flying, photography. Home: 1112 S Kansas St Wichita KS 67211-2724 Office: Butler County Sch Bd 1518 W 6th Ave El Dorado KS 67042-1425

STONE, EDMUND CRISPEN, III, banker; b. Charleston, W.Va., Nov. 29, 1942; s. Edmund C. and Sallie Ragland (Thornhill); S.; m. Annette Margarethe Isaksen, Nov. 26, 1965 (div.); 1 child, Kristine Margarethe; m. Barbara J. Sarff, June 15, 2000. BS, U.S. Mil. Acad., 1964; MBA, U. Va., 1972. V.p. Wachovia Bank, Winston-Salem, N.C., 1972-81; exec. v.p. First Am. Corp., Nashville, from 1981; vice chmn. First Am. Nat. Bank Nashville, 1988; exec. v.p. Regions Fin. Corp. (formerly First Ala. Bancshares, Inc.), Birmingham, 1988—. Contbg. author: The International Banking Handbook, 1983. Mem. export policy task force U.S. C. of C., 1980-81. With inf. U.S. Army, 1964-70, Vietnam, Iran. Decorated Bronze Star (Valor) with oak leaf cluster, Vietnamese Cross of Gallantry, others; hon. mem. Imperial Iranian Spl. Forces, 1968. Mem. Assn. of Grads. U.S. Mil. Acad. (trustee 1992-93, 98-2001, 2001—). Republican. Avocations: golf, sailing, hunting, fishing. Office: Regions Fin Corp PO Box 10247 Birmingham AL 35202-0247

STONE, EDWARD CARROLL, physicist, educator; b. Knoxville, Iowa, Jan. 23, 1936; s. Edward Carroll and Ferne Elizabeth (Baber) Stone; m. Alice Trabue Wickliffe, Aug. 4, 1962; children: Susan, Janet. AA, Burlington Jr. Coll., 1956; MS, U. Chgo., 1959, PhD, 1964; DSc (hon.) , Washington U., Saint Louis, 1992, Harvard U., 1992, U. Chgo., 1992; BA (hon.) , U. So. Calif., 1998. From rsch. fellow in physics to v.p. Calif. Inst. Tech., Pasadena, Calif., 1964—91, v.p., dir. Jet Propulsion Lab., 1991—2001; Voyager project scientist, 1972—. Cons. Office of Space Scis., NASA, 1969—85, mem. adv. com. outer planets, 1972—73; mem. NASA Solar Sys. Exploration Com., 1983; mem. com. on space astronomy and astrophysics Space Sci. Bd., 1979—82; mem. NASA high energy astrophysics mgmt. oper. working group, 1976—84; mem. NASA Cosmic Ray Program Working Group, 1980—82; mem. Outer Planets Working Group, NASA Solar Sys. Exploration Com., 1981—82, Space Sci. Bd., NRC, 1982—85, NASA Univ. Rels. Study Group, 1983, steering group Space Sci. Bd. Study on Major Directions for Space Sci., 1984—85; mem. exec. com. Com. on Space Rsch. Interdisciplinary Sci. Commn., 1982—86; mem. commn. on phys. scis., math. and resources NRC, 1986—89; mem. adv. com. NASA/Jet Propulsion Labs. vis. sr. scientist program, 1986—90; mem. com. on space policy NAS/NAE, 1988—89; chmn. , chief sci. advisor The Astronomers, KCET, 1989—91; chmn. adv. panel NAS/WQED TV program "Sail on, Voyager!", 1989—90. Mem. editl. bd. Space Sci. Instrumentation, 1975—81, Space Sci. Rev., 1982—85, Astrophysics and Space Sci., 1982—, Sci. mag. Bd. dirs. W.M. Keck Found., 1993—. Named to Hall of Fame, Aviation Week and Space Tech., 1997; recipient medal for exceptional sci. achievement, NASA, 1980, Disting. Svc. medal, 1981, 1998, 2001, Disting. Pub. Svc. medal, 1985, Outstanding Leadership medal, 1986, 1995, Am. Edn. award, 1981, Dryden award, 1983, Aviation Week and Space Tech. Aerospace Laureate, 1989, Sci. Man of Yr. award, ARCS Found., 1991, Am. Acad. Achievement Golden Plate award, 1992, COSPAR award for outstanding contbn. to space sci., 1992, LeRoy Randle Grumman medal, 1992, Disting. Pub. Svc. award, Aviation/Space Writers Assn., 1993, Internat. von Karman Wings award, 1996, Alumni award, S.E. C.C., Burlington, Iowa, 1998, CEO of Yr. award, ARC, 1998, Carl Sagan award, Am. Astronautical Soc. and Planetary Soc., Allan D. Emil Meml. award, Internat. Astronautical Fedn., Asteroid named for Edward C. Stone, 1996, Von Karman lectureshp in astronautics, 1999, Nat. Medal of Sci., 1991; fellow Sloan Found., 1971—73. Fellow: AAAS (award 1993), AIAA (assoc. Space Sci. award 1984, von Karman lectureshp in astronautics 1999), Internat. Astron. Union, Am. Geophys. Union, Am. Phys. Soc. (exec. com. 1974—76, chmn. cosmic physics divsn. 1979—80); mem.: NAS, Calif. Coun. Sci. and Tech., Nat. Space Club (bd. govs., Sci. award 1990), Astron. Soc. Pacific (hon.), Calif. Assn. Rsch. in Astronomy (bd. dirs., vice chmn. 1986—88, chmn. 1988—91, bd. dirs., vice chmn. 1991—94, chmn. 1994—97, bd. dirs., vice chmn. 1997—2000, chmn. 2000—), Am. Philos. Soc. (Magellanic award 1992), Am. Astron. Soc. (divsn. planetary scis. com. 1981—84, Space Flight award 1997), Internat. Acad. Astronautics. Office: California Inst Tech Space Radiation Lab M/C 220-47 Pasadena CA 91125

STONE, EDWARD HARRIS, II, landscape architect; b. Lanesboro, Pa., Aug. 28, 1933; s. Frank Addison and Beth Lee (Brennan) S.; m. Diane Gertrude Berg, June 11, 1955; children: Randel Harris, Deborah Dee. BS, SUNY, 1955. Landscape architect Harmon, O'Donnell & Henninger, Denver, 1955-56, U.S. Forest Service, Colo., 1958-61; regional landscape architect Alaska, 1961-64, Colo., 1964-65; chief landscape architect U.S. Forest Service, U.S. Dept. Agr., Washington, 1966-79, asst. dir. for recreation, 1979-85; ret., 1985; with C-3 Co., Bowie, Md., 1986—. Served with AUS, 1956-57. Recipient Arthur S. Flemming award for outstanding fed. govt. service U.S. Jr. C. of C., 1969 Fellow Am. Soc. Landscape Architects (pres. 1975-76); mem. Sigma Lambda Alpha (hon.) Home and Office: 13200 Forest Dr Bowie MD 20715-4390

STONE, EDWARD HERMAN, lawyer; b. July 20, 1939; s. Sidney and Ruth Stone; m. Pamela G. Gray (dec. 1990); children: Andrew, Matthew; m. Elaine Ornitz, Dec. 22, 1995. BS in Acctg., U. Ill., 1961; JD, John Marshall Law Sch., 1967. Bar: Ill. 1967, Calif. 1970; cert. specialist Calif. probate, estate planning, and trust law. With IRS, 1963-71; assoc. Eilers, Baranger, Myers & Smith, 1971-72; pvt. practice Newport Beach, Calif., 1972-2001; mem. Davis, Samuelson, Goldberg & Blakely (formerly Cohen, Stokke & Davis), Santa Ana, 1984-88; pvt. practice, 1988-89; ptnr. Edward H. Stone A Law Corp., 1990—. Instr. income and estate taxes Western States U. Sch. Law, 1971-72, mem. CEB Joint Adv. Com., Estating Planning subcom.; judge pro tem, jud. arbitrator Orange County Superior Ct.; moderator, spkr. on probate and trust litigation; mediator for IRS ADR for tax cases in appeals, 2000—; moderator, spkr. Calif. Trust Probat Litigation CEB, 1999, 2001. Contbr. articles to profl. jours. Bd. dirs. Eastbluff Homeowners Comty. Assn., Newport Beach, 1980-82, pres., 1981-82; pres. Jewish Family Svcs. Orange County, 1975; v.p., bd. dirs. Orange County Jewish Fedn. of Orange County, 1985-88; bd. dirs. Heritage Points Orange County, 1992-95. Mem. Orange County Bar Assn. (vice-chmn. estate planning probate and trust law sect. 1976-77, chmn. sect. 1977-78, chairperson ADR com. 1996, instr. Probate Clinic 1980, spkr. in substansive law; dir. 1977-82, chmn. Profl. Ednl. Coun. 1980-82, past chmn. profl. edn. coun., chmn. Orange County Bar del. of real property and probate sect. for state bar conv. 1992—), Phi Alpha Delta (pres. alumni chpt. 1975-76).

STONE, EDWARD LUKE, private equity investor, realtor; b. Englewood, N.J., Jan. 18, 1937; s. James and Anna (Druskin) S.; m. Cassandra Reeve, Mar. 15, 1969. BA, Yale U., 1958; postgrad., Cambridge U., Eng., 1959; MBA, Harvard U., 1966. Dir. fin. planning Yale U., New Haven, 1966-69; pres. HDC, Inc., Boston, 1969-77; ptnr. Dane, Falb, Stone, 1977-81; exec. dir. White House Preservation Fund, Washington, 1981-90; trustee Newport Art Mus., 1991-94; chmn. Stone and Cranwell, Newport, R.I., 1995-99; pres. Hogan and Stone, 1996-99; broker, investor Benchmark Assocs., Middletown, RI, 1999—2001; chmn. Edward L. Stone Realty llc, Newport, 2002—. Cons. Booz Allen Hamilton, Bethesda, Md., 1987-88. Trustee Nat. Mus. of Women in the Arts, Washington, 1988-90, Tudor Pl. Found., Washington, 1988-95, The Washington Home, 1988-95, Touro Synagogue Friends, 1996—; gov. Newport Health Care Corp., 1997—; co-chmn. The Isaac Bell House, 1995—. Mem. Newport Reading Rm., Spouting Rock Beach Assn., Somerset Club, Elizabethan Club, Phi Beta Kappa. Avocations: early 19th Century American decorative arts. Home: The Poplars 12 Leroy Ave Newport RI 02840-4106 E-mail: estone3137@aol.com.

STONE, ELAINE MURRAY, author, composer, television producer; b. N.Y.C., Jan. 22, 1922; d. H. and Catherine Fairbanks Murray-Jacoby; m. F. Courtney Stone, May 30, 1944; children: Catherine Gustavson, Pamela Webb, Victoria Mattson. Student, Juilliard Sch., 1939-41; BA, N.Y. Coll. Music, 1943; licentiate in organ, Trinity Coll. Music, London, 1947; student, U. Miami, 1952, Fla. Inst. Tech., 1963; PhD (hon.), World U., 1985, Oxford (Eng.) U., 1998. Organist, choir dir. St. Ignatius Episc. Ch., 1940-44; accompanist Strawbridge Ballet on Tour, N.Y.C., 1944; organist All Saints Episc. Ch., Ft. Lauderdale, 1951-54, St. John's Episc. Ch., Melbourne, Fla., 1956-59, First Christian Ch., Melbourne, 1962-63, United Ch. Christ, Melbourne, 1963-65, piano studio, Melbourne, 1955-70; editor-in-chief Cass Inc., 1970-71; dir. continuity radio Sta. WTAI, AM-FM, Melbourne, 1971-74; mem. sales staff Engle Realty Inc., Indialantic, Fla., 1975-78; v.p. pub. relations Consol. Cybertronics Inc., Cocoa Beach, 1969-70; writer, producer Countdown News, Sta. KXTX-TV, Dallas, 1978-80; assoc. producer Focus News, 1980. Host producer TV show, Focus on History, 1982-94, Episc. Digest, 1984-90; judge Writer's Contest sponsored Brevard Cmty. Coll., 1987; v.p. Judges Fla. Space Coast Writer's Conf., 1985—, chmn., 1987. Author: The Taming of the Tongue, 1954, Love One Another, 1957, Menéndez de Avilés, 1968, Bedtime Bible Stories, Travel Fun, Sleepytime Tales, Improve Your Spelling for Better Grades, Improve Your Business Spelling, Tranquility Tapes, 1970, The Melbourne Bi-Centennial Book, 1976, Uganda: Fire and Blood, 1977, Tekla and the Lion, 1981 (1st Place award Nat. League Am. Pen Women), Brevard County: From Cape of the Canes to Space Coast, 1988, Kizito, Boy Saint of Uganda, 1989 (2nd Place award Nat. League Am. Pen Women 1990), Christopher Columbus: His World, His Faith., His Adventures, 1991 (1st Place award Nat. League Am. Pen Women 1992), Elizabeth Bayley Seton: An American Saint, 1993 (3d Place award Nat. League Am. Pen Women 1994), Dimples The Dolphin, 1994 (1st Place award Fla. Space Coast Writer's Guild, 1994), Brevard at The Edge of Sea and Space, 1995, The Widow's Might, 1996 (1st place award Space Coast Writer's Contest), Carter G. Woodson Father of Black History, 1997 (1st pl. Am. Heritage Contest of Nat. Soc. Daus. of Am. Revolution 1997), Maximilian Kolbe: Saint of Auschwitz, 1997 (Cath. Bestseller list 1997), Albert's Jungle Piano, 1997 (1st place Nat. League Am. Pen Women 1997, 2nd place, Nat. League of Am. Pen Women, 1999), Mother Teresa: A Life of Love, 1999, The Taming of the Tongue, 1999, C.S. Lewis: Creator of Narnia, 2001; composer: Christopher

Columbus Suite, 1992 (1st Place award Pen Women Music Awards 1992, 2d Place award 1993), Florida Suite for cello and piano, 1993, Two Crowns of St. Maximilian, 1998 (1st place in music Nat. League Am. Pen Women 1997), Pastorale, 2000 (1st Place award Nat. League Am. Pen Women, Washington, 2000), Anima Christi, 2000 (hon. mention Nat. League Am. Pen Women, Washington, 2000); contbr. articles to nat. mags., newspapers including N.Y. Herald Tribune, Living Church, Christian Life; space corr. Religious News Service, Kennedy Space Ctr., 1962-78. Mem. exec. bd. Women's Assn., Brevard Symphony, 1967—; mem. heritage com. Melbourne Bicentennial Commn.; mem. Evangelism Commn. Episc. Diocese Cen. Fla., 1985-94; v.p. churchwomen group Holy Trinity Episcopal Ch., Melbourne, 1988-89, Stephen minister, 1988—, pres. churchwomen group, 1989—; bd. dirs. Fla. Space Coast Council Internat. Visitors, Fla. Space Coast Philharm., 1989—, Aid for the Arts, 1994. Recipient 1st place for piano Ashley Hall, 1935-39, S.C. State Music Contest, 1939, 1st place for piano composition Colonial Suite, Constitution Hall, Washington 1987, 88, 89, 3d place for vocal composition, 1989, honorable mention for article, 1989, 2nd place for piano composition, 1989, award lit. contest Fla. AAUW, 1989, 1st place award Fla. State PEN Women, 1990, 1st Place award Nat. Black History Essay Contest, 1990, 2d place Nat. League Am. Pen Women, 1999, 2d place for music composition, 1999, named Woman of Achievement, 1999, Disting. Author of Yr. plaque Fla. Space Coast Writers Guild, 1992, 96, Woman of Achievement plaque AAUW, 1997; honoree Nat. Polish Alliance, 3d place award for essay "Remembering C.S. Lewis" Mount Dora Festival of Music and Literature, 2001. Mem. ASCAP, Nat. League Am. PEN Women (1st place awards Tex. 1979, 1st place award for duet, Washington, DC 2000, v.p. Dallas br. 1978-80, organizing pres. Cape Canaveral br. 1969, pres. 1988-90, 96—), Women Communications, DAR (Fla. state chmn. music 1962-63), Colonial Dames Am. (organizing pres. Melbourne chpt. 1994), Nat. Soc. DAR (organizing regent Rufus Fairbanks chpt. 1981-85, vice regent 1987—, historian 1989—, Fla. state chmn. Am. Heritage), Children Am. Revolution (past N.Y. state chaplain), Am. Guild Organists (organizing warden Ft. Lauderdale), Space Pioneers, Fla. Press, Aid for the Arts, Space Coast Writers Guild (past v.p.). Home: 1945 Pineapple Ave Melbourne FL 32935-7656

STONE, ELIZABETH CECILIA, anthropology educator; b. Oxford, Eng., Feb. 4, 1949; d. Lawrence and Jeanne Cecilia (Fawtier) S.; m. Paul Edmund Zimansky, Nov. 5, 1976. BA, U. Pa., 1971; MA, Harvard U., 1973; PhD, U. Chgo., 1979. Lectr. anthropology SUNY, Stony Brook, 1977-78, asst. prof., 1978-85, assoc. prof., 1985-95, prof., 1995—. Participated archaeol. in Eng., Iran, Iraq, Afghanistan; dir. archaeol. projects Ain Dara, Syria,, Tell Abu Duwari, Iraq, Ayanis Survey, Turkey. Author: Nippur Neighborhoods, 1987; co-author: (monograph) Old Babylonian Contracts from Nippur 1, 1976, Adoption in Old Babylonian Nippur and the Archive of Mannum-meshulissur, 1991, The Iron Age Settlement at Ain Dara, Syria, 1999; co-editor: The Cradle of Civilization Recent Archaeology in Iraq-Biblical Archaeologist, 1992, Velles Paraules: Ancient Near Eastern Studies in Honor of Miguel Civil on the Occasion of His 65th Birthday, 1991; mem. editl. bd. Bull. Am. Schs. Oriental Rsch., 1993-95, 99; contbr. articles to profl. jours. Assoc. trustee Am. Schs. of Oriental Rsch., 1983-90. Fulbright fellow, 1986-87; rsch. grantee Ford Found., 1974, Nat. Geog. Soc., 1983, 84, 88, 90, 97, 98, 99, Am. Schs. of Oriental Rsch., 1987, 88, NSF, 1989-92, 2000-02, NEH, 1989-93. Office: SUNY Dept Anthropology Stony Brook NY 11794-0001 E-mail: estone@notes.cc.sunysb.edu

STONE, ELIZABETH WENGER, retired dean; b. Dayton, Ohio, June 21, 1918; d. Ezra and Anna Bess (Markey) Wenger; m. Thomas A. Stone, Sept. 14, 1939 (dec. Feb. 1987); children: John Howard, Anne Elizabeth, James Alexander. AB, Stanford U., 1937, MA, 1938; MLS., Catholic U. Am., 1961; PhD, Am. U., 1968. Tchr. pub. schs., Fontana, Calif., 1938-39; asst. state statistician State of Conn., 1939-40; libr. New Haven Pub. Librs., 1940-42; dir. pub. relations, asst. to pres. U. Dubuque, Iowa, 1942-46; substitute libr. Pasadena (Calif. Pub. Libr. System), 1953-60; instr. Cath. U. Am., 1962-63, asst. prof., asst. to chmn. dept. libr. sci., 1963-67, assoc. prof., asst. to chmn., 1967-71, prof., asst. to chmn., 1971-72, prof., chmn. dept., 1972-80, dean Sch. Libr. and Info. Scis., 1981-83, prof. and dean emeritus, 1983—2002, lectr., 1990; libr. cons. U.S. Inst. of Peace, 1988-90; libr. Nat. Presbyn. Ch. and Ctr., Washington, 1991—2002, archivist, 1994—2002. Founder, exec. dir. Continuing Libr. Edn. Network and Exchange, 1975-79; founder Nat. Rehab. Info. Ctr., 1977, project mgr., 1977-83; co-chmn. 1st World Conf. on Continuing Edn. for the Libr. and Info. Sci. Professions, 1984-85, 2nd World Conf., Barcelona, 1993. Author: Factors Related to the Professional Development of Librarians, 1969, (with James J. Kortendick) Job Dimensions and Educational Needs in Librarianship, 1971, (with R. Patrick and B. Conroy) Continuing Library and Information Science Education, 1974, Continuing Library Education as Viewed in Relation to Other Continuing Professional Movements, 1975, (with F. Peterson and M. Chobot) Motivation: A Vital Force in the Organization, 1977, American Library Development 1600-1899, 1977, (with others) Model Continuing Education Recognition System in Library and Information Science, 1979, (with M.J. Young) A Program for Quality in Continuing Education for Information, Library and Media Personnel, 1980, (with others) Continuing Education for the Library Information Professions, 1985, The Growth of Continuing Education, 1986, Library Education: Continuing Professional Education, 1993, (with others) ALA World Encyclopedia of Library and Information Science, 3d edit., 1993; author, editor: Continuing Professional Education for Library and Information Science Personnel: Papers from Seminar at Matica Slovenska, Martin Czechoslovakia, 1989; editor: D.C. Libraries, 1964-66; contbr. articles to profl. jours. Mem. Pres.'s Com. on Employment of Handicapped, 1972-88, Establishment of Elizabeth W. Stone Annual Lectureship Cath. U. Am., 1990—; pres. D.C. chpt. Am. Mothers, Inc., 1984-86, nat. v.p., 1989-91. Recipient Presdl. award Cath. U. Am., 1982, Spl. Librs. Profl. award, 1988, DCLA Ainsworth Rand Spofford Pres.'s award, 1990, Hon. Life Mem. 1994, Alumni Achievement award in libr. and info. sci. Cath. U. Am., 1990, Outstanding Contbn. Congl. Librs. award Ch. and Synagogue Libr. Assn., 2001; named D.C. Mother of Yr., 1980. Mem. ALA (life; coun. 1976-83, v.p. 1980-81, pres. 1981-82, chmn. Nat. Libr. Week, 1983-85; founder ALA Nat. Ptnrs. for Librs. and Literacy 1984, Lippincott award 1986, Hon. Life award 1986, Nat. Advocacy Honor Roll 2000, Beta Phi Mu award 1998), Assn. Libr. Info. and Sci. Edn. (pres. 1974), Am. Soc. Assn. Execs., Am. Assn. Adult and Continuing Edn., Internat. Fedn. Libr. Assns. and Instns. (chmn. Continuing Profl. Edn. Roundtable 1986-93), D.C. Libr. Assn. (hon. life, pres. 1966-67, hon. chair centennial com. 1992-94, hon. life 1994), Spl. Librs. Assn. (hon. life, pres. D.C. chpt. 1973-74, Rose L. Vormelker award 1999-2000), Cath. Libr. Assn. (hon. life), Continuing Profl. Edn. Libr. and Info. Sci. Pers., Soc. Am. Archivists, Cosmos Club, Phi Sigma Alpha, Beta Phi Mu, Phi Lambda Theta. Presbyterian. Home: Washington, DC. Died Mar. 6, 2002.

STONE, F. L. PETER, lawyer; b. Wilmington, Del., Feb. 24, 1935; s. Linton and Lorinda (Hamlin) S.; m. Therese Louise Hannon, Apr. 7, 1969; 1 child, Lisa Judith. AB, Dartmouth Coll, 1957; LLB, Harvard U., 1960. Bar: Del. Supreme Ct. 1960, U.S. Ct. Appeals (3d cir.) 1964, U.S. Supreme Ct. 1965, U.S. Ct. Appeals (fed. cir.) 1983. Assoc. Connolly, Bove & Lodge, Wilmington, 1960-64; dep. atty. gen. State of Del., 1965-66; atty. Del. Gen. Assembly, Dover, 1967-68; counsel Gov. Del., 1969; U.S. atty. Dist. of Del., Wilmington, 1969-72; ptnr. Connolly, Bove, Lodge, & Hutz, 1972-97; counsel Trzuskowski, Kipp, Kelleher & Pearce, 1997-98, 2001—; dep. atty. gen., counsel to ins. dept. State of Del., 1998-2001. Mem. Del. Agy. to Reduce Crime, 1969-72, Del. Organized Crime Commn., 1970-72, State Drug Abuse Coun., 1990-93, State Judicial Nominating Commn., 1991-93, State Coun. Corrections, 1992-99; co-founder, adj. prof. criminal justice progra, West Chester (Pa.) U., 1975-79; chmn. Gov.'s Harness Racing Investigation Com., 1977, Del. Jai Alai Commn., 1977-78, Del. Govs. Corrections Task Force, 1986-88. Contbr. articles to profl. jours. Chmn. UN Day, Del., 1989; mem. Del. Gov.'s Task Force on Prison Security, 1994—95; trustee Leukemia Soc. Am., N.Y.C., 1972—74, Marywood Coll., Scranton, Pa., 1974—79, Ursuline Acad., Wilmington, 1974—80; bd. dirs. Boys and Girls Club Del., 1997—, Seamen's Ctr., Port of Wilmington, 2001—; Rep. candidate for atty. gen. Del., 1990; mem. Rep. exec. com. Wilmington region, 1991—2000; chmn. re-election campaign Del. Ins. Commr., 1996. Mem. Port of Wilmington Maritime Soc. (bd. dirs., chair 1998-2000), Wilmington Country Club, Lincoln Club Del. (pres. 1994), Wilmington Rotary (bd. dirs. 1995-97), Nat. Assn. Former U.S. Attys. (bd. dirs. 1995-98). Roman Catholic. Avocations: hiking/mountaineering, tennis, golf, music. Office: Box 429 1020 N Bancroft Pky Wilmington DE 19899 E-mail: pstone@tkkp.com. *My major accomplishment has been establishing and maintaining a close relationship with my family, first and foremost, regardless of what activities and accomplishments were pursued in my professional, political and community life.*

STONE, FLORENCE SMITH, film festival executive, consultant; b. Balt., June 15, 1938; d. Howard Chandler and Mary (Burnam) Smith; m. Roger David Stone; 1 child, Leslie Burnam. BA, Vassar Coll., 1960; cert. Inst. Arts Adminstrn., Harvard U., 1978. Asst. to v.p. for pub. rels. Transam. Corp., San Francisco, 1962-64; newsletter editor U.S. Embassy, Rio de Janeiro, 1964-66; coord. cmty. rels. Am. Mus. Natural History, N.Y.C., 1970-79, coord. spl. progrm, 1977-84; dir. Washington Office Earthwatch, Washington, 1985-90; ind. cons. to mus. and ednl. orgns., 1990—; coord., founder Environ. Film Festival, 1993—. Co-chmn. Margaret Mead Film Festival, 1977-84. Trustee The Textile Mus., Washington, 1994—, Laura Boulton Found., N.Y.C., 1980-99, Mus. of the Hudson Highlands, Cornwall-on-Hudson, N.Y., 1974-96; mem. adv. com. Margaret Mead Film Festival, N.Y.C., 1992—; chmn. Trees for Georgetown, Washington, 1996-2001. Mem.: Women in Film and Video, Ind. Film and Video Assn., Internat. Documentary Assn., Am. Anthropol. Assn., Am. Assn. Mus., Cosmos Club, Cosmopolitan Club, Georgetown Garden Club. Democrat. Avocations: textiles, film, trees, performing arts, outdoor activities. Office: Environ Film Festival 1228 1/2 31st St NW Washington DC 20007-3402 E-mail: flostonc@igc.org.

STONE, FRED LYNDON, retired human resources administrator; b. High Point, N.C., Mar. 30, 1941; s. Charlie Edward and Minnie (Killingsworth) S. AB, High Point U., 1963. Field epidemiologist USPHS, Raleigh, N.C., 1963-66; supr. tng. Manhattan Shirt Co., Lexington, 1966-68; mgr. tng. Manhattan Industries, Salisbury, Md., 1968-72; mgr. pers. Silver Springs Sportswear, Ocala, Fla., 1972-74; v.p. human resources Citrus Meml. Hosp., Inverness, 1974—2001; ret., 2001. Coord. nursing scholarships Ctrl. Fla. C.C., Ocala, 1974-96, Marion County Sch. Radiol. Tech., Ocala, 1985-99. Author: Heritage of Healing, 1995. Mem. Am. Soc. Healthcare Human Resources, Fla. Soc. Healthcare Human Resources, ACLU, Fla. Trust Hist. Preservation, Fla. Hist. Soc. Episcopalian. Home: 11471 W Dixie Shores Dr Crystal River FL 34429-5283

STONE, FRED MICHAEL, lawyer; b. Bklyn., Jan. 20, 1943; s. Nathan and Rose (Silverman) S.; m. Bonnie B. Dobkin, Aug. 14, 1965; children—Jonathan, Jennifer. AB cum laude, Bklyn. Coll., 1964; JD, Harvard U., 1967; LLM, NYU, 1971. Bar: N.Y. 1968. Assoc. Cadwalader, Wickersham & Taft, N.Y.C., 1967-69; asst. gen. counsel Standard & Poor's/Intercapital, Inc., 1969-71; v.p., gen. counsel Neuwirth Funds, 1971-73, Mocatta Metals Corp., N.Y.C., 1973-76; sr. v.p., gen. counsel Am. Stock Exchange, Inc., 1976-86; exec. v.p., gen. counsel Jamie Securities Co., Caronan Ptnrs., 1986-88; sr. v.p., gen. counsel, sec. M.D. Sass Assocs., Inc., 1989-2000; chmn. exec. com. Amex Commodities Exch., 1980-81; dir. Am. Gold Coin Exchange, Inc., 1981-85; exec. v.p., dir. Revere Copper and Brass, Inc., 1986-88; dir. Ea. Electric Motor Co., Inc., 1987-88, Chase & M.D. Sass Ptnrs., 1998-2000; gen. counsel Millennium Ptnrs., L.P., N.Y.C., 2000—. Ofcl. adv. Drafting Com. to Revise Uniform Securities Act of Nat. conf. Uniform State Law Commrs., 1981-85; chmn. options and futures regulation subcom. of fed. regulation of securities com. ABA, 1989-91, mem. task force on pvt. investment entities, 1994—; lectr. various legal seminars; sec. rules com. Investment Co. Inst., 1989-92; sec., treas. steering com. Taxable Mcpl. Bondholders Protective Com., 1990-95. Mem. Manalapan (N.J.) Twp. Zoning Bd. Adjustment, 1975—86, 2000—, chmn., 2001—02; mem. N.J. regional exec. com. Anti-Defamation League of B'nai B'rith, 1991—; vice chmn. Manalapan Dem. Com., 1988—96; Dem. candidate for Manalapan Twp. Com., 1989, 1993. Mem. ABA, Assn. Bar City N.Y. (mem. chorus), Harvard U. Law Sch. Assn., Am. Stock Exch., Inc. (arbitrator 1986—), Nat. Assn. Securities Dealers (arbitrator 1986—), Nat. Futures Assn. (nominating com. 1986-88) Democrat. Jewish. Home: 15 Kingsley Dr Manalapan NJ 07726-3134 E-mail: fstone@mlp.com.

STONE, GAIL ANN, elementary and secondary education educator; b. Chgo., Mar. 7, 1943; d. Leonard Oscar and Bernice L. (Grunwald) Johnson; m. Joe Thomas Stone, Dec. 28, 1963; children: Jason, Brandon. BS, U. Wash., 1968; MS, U. Rochester, 1988. Cert. math. educator K-12, spl. educator K-12. Math. paraprofessional, tchr. Pittsford (N.Y.) Schs., 1975-82; tchr. math. Norman Howard Schs., Rochester, N.Y., 1984—. Dir. coll. guidance Norman Howard Schs., 1985—; spkr. in field; core group tchr./writer NSF grant, 1992—. Dir. YWCA, Rochester, 1971-74; counselor CPT Housing, Rochester, 1969-75. Named Writer Computer Program NSF. Mem. Nat. Coun. Tchrs. Math., Assn. Math. Tchrs. N.Y. State, Coun. Exceptional Children. Avocations: gardening, hiking, cooking, swimming. Office: Norman Howard Sch 275 Pinnacle Rd Rochester NY 14623-4103 E-mail: gsswim@aol.com.

STONE, GEOFFREY RICHARD, law educator, lawyer; b. Nov. 20, 1946; s. Robert R. and Shirley (Weliky) S.; m. Nancy Spector, Oct. 8, 1977; children: Julie, Mollie. BS, U. Pa., 1968; JD, U. Chgo., 1971. Bar: N.Y. 1972. Law clk. to Hon. J.S. Kelly Wright U.S. Ct. Appeals (D.C. cir.), 1971-72; law clk. to Hon. William J. Brennan, Jr. U.S. Supreme Ct., 1972-73; asst. prof. U. Chgo., 1973-77, assoc. prof., 1977-79, prof., 1979-84, Harry Kalven Jr. disting. svc. prof., 1984—, dean Law Sch., 1987-93, provost, 1994—2002. Author: Constitutional Law, 1986, 4th edit., 2001, The Bill of Rights in the Modern State, 1992, The First Amendment, 1999, Eternally Vigilant: Free Speech in the Modern Era, 2001; editor The Supreme Ct. Rev., 1991—; contbr. articles to profl. jours. Bd. dirs. Ill. divsn. ACLU, 1978-84; bd. advisors Pub. Svc. Challenge, 1989; bd. govs. Argonne Nat. Lab., 1994—. Fellow AAAS; mem. Chgo. Coun. Lawyers (bd. govs. 1976-77), Assn. Am. Law Schs. (exec. com. 1990-93), Legal Aid Soc. (bd. dirs. 1988), Order of Coif. Office: U Chgo 1111 E 60th St Chicago IL 60637-5418

STONE, GEORGE, artist, art educator; BA, Calif. State U., Long Beach, 1972; MFA, R.I. Sch. Design, 1974. Instr. R.I. Sch. Design, Providence, 1972-74; instr. sculpture Portsmouth (R.I.) Abbey Sch., 1973-74, Wayne State U., Detroit, 1974-75; vis. lectr., sculpture dept. Ohio U., Athens, 1976-77; instr., found. dept. Otis/Parsons Sch. Design, L.A., 1982-83; vis. lectr., sculpture dept. UCLA, 1986; assoc. prof. fine arts Art Inst. So. Calif., Laguna Beach, 1989-93; assoc. prof. visual art U. La Verne, Calif., 1994-2000. Vis. artist Calif. State U. Long Beach, 1986, Crossroads H.S. for Arts and Sci., Santa Monica, 1987, Claremont (Calif.) Grad. Sch., 1987, 88, U. Calif. Santa Barbara, 1989, Art Ctr. Coll. Design, Pasadena, Calif., 1991, Yale U., New Haven, 1992, Chatham Coll., Pitts., 1992, Calif. State U. San Francisco, 1993; commd. artist City of West Hollywood, 1986, City of L.A. Cmty. Redevel. Agy., 1987, Metro Art L.A. County Met. Transp. Auth., 1990-97, City of L.A. Cultural Affairs Dept., 1995-97. Solo exhbns. include Forsythe Bldg., Detroit, 1975, Cline Bldg., Athens, Ohio, 1976, Lake Hope, Athens, 1977, Otis/Parsons Gallery, 1981, East Gallery Claremont Grad. Sch., 1985, Calif. State U. Long Beach Art Mus., 1986, Meyers/Bloom Gallery, Santa Monica, Calif., 1988, 91, Laguna Art Mus., Costa Mesa, Calif., 1990, Capp St. Project, 1991, New Langton Arts, San Francisco, 1991, Ruth Bloom Gallery, Santa Monica, 1993, Pitts. Ctr. Arts, 1994; 2-person exhbns. L.A. Contemporary Exhbns., 1985, Claremont Grad. Sch. Gallery, 1988; group exhbns. include Lehigh U. Art Gallery, Bethlemen, Pa., 1975, Wayne State U., 1975, U. Calif. Santa Cruz, 1978, Vanguard Gallery, L.A., 1979, L.A. Inst. Contemporary Art, 1979, NYU Art Gallery, N.Y.C., 1980, Charles Kobler and Assoc. Architects, L.A., 1983, Design Ctr. L.A., 1984, Univ. Art Mus. Calif. State U. Long Beach, 1985, IDM Corp. and Pub. Corp. Arts, Long Beach, 1985, CRA, L.A., 1987, Newport Harbor Art Mus., Newport Beach, Calif., 1988, Meyers/Bloom Gallery, 1989, Galerie Antoine Candeau, Paris, 1990, Sezon Mus. Art, Tokyo and Osaka, Japan, 1991, Muckenthaler Cultural Ctr., Fullerton, Calif., 1991, Contemporary Arts Ctr., New Orleans, 1993, Next Thread Waxing Space, N.Y.C., 1993, Contemporary Arts Forum, Santa Barbara, 1996, Armand Hammer Mus. Art and Cultural Ctr., UCLA, 1997, others; subject numerous catalogs, publs., and revs., 1984—. Home: 1815 Laurel Canyon Blvd Los Angeles CA 90046-2028 Fax: 323-654-3012.

STONE, GREGORY MICHAEL, law enforcement and public safety consultant; b. Hartford, Conn., July 31, 1959; s. George William Jr. and Patricia Gertrude (Fitton) S. BA in Polit. Sci., Loyola U., Chgo., 1982; MS, Pacific Western U., 1983, PhD, 1984. Dir. advanced projects Sachs/Freeman Assocs. Inc., Lake Bluff, Ill., 1980-88; dir. pub. safety, nat. security svcs. RJO Enterprises, Inc., Lanham, Md., 1988-89; sr. dir. Sci. & Tech. Analytics, Inc., Willow Grove, Pa., 1989-90; v.p. spl. projects Live Oaks Systems subs. Analytics, Inc., 1990—. Prin. Stone Industries, Inc., Mundelein, 1982-88; dir. systems engring. Airfone Inc., Oak Brook, Ill., 1983-84. Contbr. articles in field to profl. jours.; book reviewer John Wiley & Sons, N.Y.C., 1987—. Mem. Lake County Rep. Fedn., Waukegan, Ill., 1985—. Named to Hon. Order of Ky. Cols., 1988. Fellow Radio Club Am; mem. AAAS, IEEE (chmn. Chgo. sect. vehicular tech. soc. 1983-88, chmn. electromagnetic wave propagation com. 1990—), John Birch Soc., Am. Def. Preparedness Assn. (chmn. ops. security working group), Am. Soc. for Indsl. Security, Armed Forces Communications and Electronics Assn., Scientist's Inst. for Pub. Info., U.S. Naval Inst., SAR, Mayflower Soc., Internat. Assn. Chiefs Police (assoc.), Nat. Sheriffs Assn., Internat. Assn. Bomb Technicians and Investigators, Internat. Narcotic Enforcement Officers Assn., Internat. Carnahan Conf. Security Tech. (exec. com. crime countermeasures 1990—), Assn. of Former Intelligence Officers, Security Affairs Support Assn. Republican. Avocations: physics, cryptography, automobile racing, flying, photography. Office: Live Oaks System 3702 Pender Dr # 300 Fairfax VA 22030-6066

STONE, GWEN, visual artist; b. N.Y.C., Feb. 1, 1913; d. Hercule Sasso and Carlotta di Teresi; m. Karl Heinrich von Buchau, m. Oct. 10, 1937; children: Stephanie, Gregory. Student, Coll. of Marin, Kentfield, Calif., 1933-34, Calif. Sch. Fine Arts, 1936. Life drawing, painting and design tchg. cert., Calif. Instr. art Coll. of Marin, 1967-70, 75-79. Condr. workshops in collage, drawing and painting Sitka Art Ctr., Otis, Oreg., 1991, 93-96; lectr. on artists Highland Art Ctr., Weaverville, Calif., 1986—, Yreka (Calif.) Cmty. Ctr., 1988-96, 98, Redding (Calif.) Mus., 1988-94, 96, Coos Bay (Oreg.) Mus., 1994-96. Exhibited in group shows San Francisco Mus., 1959, Pratt Inst., N.Y., 1985, Redding Mus., 1987 (Best in Show award 1987); one-woman shows Palace of the Legion of Honor, San Francisco, 1966-67, Crocker Mus., Sacramento, 1966-67, 80; permanent collections include Redding Mus., San Francisco Art Commn., Coos Bay Mus. Oreg., U. Calif. Libr., Berkeley, Coll. of the Siskyous, City of Palo Alto, Std. Oil-Saudi Arabia, Lambert Pharms., Citibank. Bd. dirs. Siskiyou Arts Coun., Yreka, 1981-83. Recipient numerous awards from nat. and regional juried shows; Pollock-Krasner grantee, 1990-91, 2001. Mem. Nat. Mus. Women Artists, Rogue Gallery and Art Ctr. Avocations: reading, opera, live theatre. Home: 17530 Pilar Rd Montague CA 96064-9776

STONE, HARRY H. business executive; b. Cleve., May 21, 1917; s. Jacob and Jennie (Kantor) Sapirstein; m. Lucile Tabak, Aug. 10, 1960; children: Phillip, Allan, Laurie (Mrs. Parker), James Rose, Douglas Rose. Student, Cleve. Coll., 1935-36. With Am. Greetings Corp., Cleve., 1936—, v.p., 1944-58, exec. v.p., 1958-69, vice chmn. bd., chmn. finance com., chmn audit com., 1969-78, now dir., 1944—. Mem. Ofcl. U.S. Mission to India and Nepal, 1965; cons. U.S. Dept. Commerce, U.S. Dept. State; adviser U.S. del. 24th session UN Econ. Commn. for Asia and Far East, Canberra, Australia, 1968; cons. Nat. Endowment for Arts, Nat. Council on Arts. Treas. Criminal Justice Co-ordinating Council., 1968-82; trustee emeritus Brandeis U., also univ. fellow. Mem. Rotary (hon. pres.). Office: The Courtland Group Inc 1621 Euclid Ave Ste 1600 Cleveland OH 44115-2195

STONE, HAZEL ANNE DECKER, artist; b. Salt Lake City, Oct. 30, 1934; d. Carl Marcellus and Hazel Sheets (Van Cott) Decker; m. William Samuel Stone, July 20, 1956; children: Cynthia Anne Stone Barkanic, Lisa Marie. BS, RN, U. Utah, 1956; postgrad. in arts and humanities, Ariz. State U., 1979-81; studied with various artists, Ariz., N.Mex., 1985—. Nurse out-patient dept. Salt Lake County Hosp., 1956-57; instr. med.-surg. nursing U. Utah Coll. Nursing, 1957-59; watercolor fine artist. One-woman show Sun Cities Mus. of Art, Sun City, Ariz., 1997; exhibited in group show Chandler (Ariz.) Ctr. for the Arts, 1997; nat. juried exhbns. includes: Pikes Peak Watercolor Soc. exhbn., 2001, Az. Watercolor Assn. exhbn., 2000, Pa. Watercolor Soc., exhbn., 2000, 17th Annual Gallery '76, Wenatchee, 2000, Woodmere Art Gallery, 2000, Chandler Ctr. Arts, 1999, Watercolors Gallery, Pitts., 2000, Farmington Mus. at Gateway Park, Farmington, N.Mex., 1999 (regional exhbn.), Wenatchee (Wash.) Valley Coll., 1999, 2000, Tubac (Ariz.) Ctr. for Arts, 1999, Sangre de Cristo Arts Ctr., Pueblo, Colo., 1999, Watercolors Gallery, Pitts., 1999, 16th Annual Gallery '76, Wenatchee, Wash., 1999, Tubac Ctr. Arts, 1999, Sangre de Cristo Arts Ctr., 1999, West Valley Art Mus. (Ariz. juried exhbns.), Surprise, Ariz., 1999, Van Vechten-Lineberry Taos (N.Mex.) Art Mus., 1997, Wenatchee (Wash.) Valley Coll., 1997, Stables Gallery, Taos, 1996, Walton Arts Ctr., Fayetteville, Ark., 1995, Bareiss Gallery, Taos, 1995, Foothills Art Ctr., 1994, Golden, Colo., Tucson Mus. Art regional exhbn., 1988, Vision Gallery (2d Place award Chandler Ostrich Festival Fine Arts Print Contest 1998), others; one person exhbn. include Phoenix (Ariz.) 17 paintings, Sun Cities (Ariz.) Mus. Art, 1997; two person exhbns. include Gallery Nineteen, Phoenix, 1996, Ch. of the Beatitudes, Phoenix, 1995; Ariz. juried exhbn. include Vistas, 1989, 91, 93; commd. Chandler Ctr. Arts, 1999; TV interview includes Open My Album: A Collection of Watercolor Paintings and Stories Connecting Generations Channel 20 Ednl. TV Chandler Unified Sch. Dist., Ariz., 1997. Docent Phoenix Art Mus., 1979-80, master docent, 1989-96; mem. Ariz. Women's Caucus Art, 1988-91. Finalist annual art competition exptl. art category Artists Magazine, 1996. Mem. Ariz. Artists Guild (juried 1986—), Ariz. Watercolor Assn. (Award of Merit 1997, Merchant award 1994, bd. dirs. 1994—, co-chair nat. watercolor exhbn. 1999, chmn. nat. watercolor exhbn. 2000), Contemporary Watercolorists Ariz. (Merit award 1998, Award of Excellence 1997, 2000, chmn. spl. exhbns. 1998), Q Artists (chmn. exhbns. 1995-99), Waterworks Artists, Internat. Soc. Exptl. Artists, Nat. Watercolor Soc., Pa. Watercolor Soc., Phila. Watercolor Soc., Soc. Layerists in Multi-Media, La. Watercolor Soc. (assoc.), N.W. Watercolor Soc. (assoc.), San Diego Watercolor Soc. (assoc.), Taos Soc. Watercolorists (signature), Watercolor Art Soc. Houston, Watercolor West (assoc.), Western Colo. Watercolor Soc., Ariz. Watercolor Assn. (Coatimundi Honor Soc. 1995, juried 1988—, assoc.,1985-88, Merit award 1997, Merchant award 1994), Internat. Soc. Experimental Artists. Home: 3621 E Pasadena Ave Phoenix AZ 85018-1511

STONE, HERBERT ALLEN, management consultant; b. Washington, Sept. 14, 1934; s. Joseph and Marion (Solomon) S.; m. Marjorie Nelke Sterling, June 14, 1964; children: Joanna, Lisa. BSc, U. Mass., 1955, MSc, 1958; PhD, U. Calif., Davis, 1962. Specialist Exptl. Sta. U. Calif., Davis, 1961-62; food scientist SRI, Menlo Park, Calif., 1962-67, dir. food and plant sci., 1967-74; pres. Tragon Corp., Redwood City, 1974—. Mem. adv. bd. U. Mass. Food Sci., 1992—, Calif. Poly. U. Food Sci. and Nutrition , 1996—2001. Author: Sensory Evaluation Practices, 1985, Sensory Evaluation Practices, 2d edit., 1993; assoc. editor: Jour. Food Sci., 1977—80, assoc. editor: , 2000—02, chair editl. bd.: World of Food Sci.; contbr. sci. and tech. articles to profl. jours. Fellow Inst. Food Sci. & Tech., Inst. Food Exec. Com. (pres. S.E. divsn. 1977-78, exec. com., pres. mktg. and mgmt. divsn.), Inst. Food Sci. and Tech.; mem. AAAS, Inst. Food Technologists (nat. exec. com. 1994-97), Am. Soc. Enology, European Chemoreception Orgn., Ladera Oaks Club (Menlo Park, Calif.). Achievements include patents in field. Home: 990 San Mateo Dr Menlo Park CA 94025-5640 Office: Tragon Corp 365 Convention Way Redwood City CA 94063-1402 E-mail: hstone@tragon.com.

STONE, HERMAN HULL, internist; b. Noble, Ill., Dec. 12, 1915; s. Roy Edson and Carrie (Michels) S.; m. Marie Carlson Christensen; children, Patricia Marie Soln, Richard Allen. BS, U. Ill., 1937, MD, 1941. Resident in internal medicine U.S. VA Hosp., Hines, Ill., 1946-49; chief of medicine VA Hosp., Oklahoma City, 1949-50; with Riverside (Calif.) Med. Clinic, 1950-91; dir. Med. Libr., 1991—; clin. prof. medicine Loma Linda (Calif.) U., 1963—. Founder, dir. Patients' Info. Libr., Riverside, 1991—; pres. citizens univ. com. U. Calif. Riverside, 1979-81; trustee Calif. Blue Shield. Served to maj. M.C., AUS, 1942-46. Recipient Outstanding award Nat. Soc. Fund Raising Execs., 1996. Fellow ACP (life); mem. L.A. Acad. Medicine (trustee), Rotary Club. Avocations: golf, books, travel. Office: Patients Info Libr 3660 Arlington Ave Riverside CA 92506-3912 E-mail: rmfpil@aol.com.

STONE, HUBERT DEAN, editor, journalist; b. Maryville, Tenn., Sept. 23, 1924; s. Archie Hubert and Annie (Cupp) S.; student Maryville Coll., 1942-43; B.A., U. Okla., 1949; m. Agnes Shirley, Sept. 12, 1953 (dec. Mar. 1973); 1 son, Neal Anson. Sunday editor Maryville-Alcoa Daily Times, 1949; mng. editor Maryville-Alcoa Times, 1949-78, editor, 1978—; v.p. Maryville-Alcoa

Newspapers, Inc., 1960-90; pres. Stonecraft, 1954—. Photographer in field. Vice-chmn., chmn. Tenn. Great Smoky Mountains Park commn.; mem. State of Tenn. Hist. Commn.; co-chmn. 175th anniversary com. Maryville Coll.; mem. mayor's adv. com. City of Maryville; mem. air service adv. com. Knoxville Met. Airport Authority; bd. dirs. United Fund of Blount County, 1961-63, 74-76, vice chmn. campaign, 1971-72, chmn. campaign, 1973, v.p., 1974, pres., 1975; vice chmn. bd. dirs. Maryville Utilities Bd.; bd. dirs. Sam Houston Meml. Assn., Alcoa City Sch. Found., Blount County Hist. Trust, Nat. Hillbilly Homecoming Assn., Friendsville Acad., 1968-73, Alkiwan Crafts, Inc., 1970-73, Middle East Tenn. Regional Tourism Group; dir. Foothills Land Conservancy, Smoky Mountains Passion Play Assn., Blount County History Mus.; mem. adv. com. Blount County Alternative Center for Learning, Overlook Center, Inc., Sr. Citizens Home Assistance Svcs.; chmn. Blount County Long Range Planning for Sch. Facilities; mem. Blount County Bicentennial task force; mem. adv. bd. Harrison-Chilhowee Bapt. Acad, mem. Leadership Knoxville; co-founder, vice pres., pres. Leadership Blount County; founder, chmn. Townsend-in-the-Smokies Art Show/Sale, 1984—; mem. bd. govs. Maryville-Alcoa C.C. Orch. Soc; trustee, pres. bd. trustees, deacon, chmn. evangelism, fin. & pers. coms. Bapt. Ch.; mem. Blount County Bicentennial com., State of Tenn. Hist. commn. Served from pvt. to staff sgt. AUS, 1943-45. Decorated Bronze Star; named Outstanding Sr. Man of Blount County, 1970, 77, Hon. Order Ky. Cols., Commonwealth of Ky.; recipient Pride of Tenn. award for vol. work, 1993, Outstanding Leadership award Maryville Ch. of Christ, First Tourism Pioneer award Smoky Mount. Vis. Bur. and Blount C. of C., 1994; named Outstanding Alumnus U. Okla. Sch. Journalism, 1997. Mem. VFW, Profl. Photographers of Am., Internat. Post Card Distbrs. Assn., Great Smoky Mountains Natural History Assn., Ft. Loudoun Assn., Tenn. Jaycees (editor 1954-55, sec.-treas. 1955-56), Blount County Arts/ Crafts Guild, Jr. Chamber Internat. (senator) Maryville-Alcoa Jaycees (life mem., pres. 1953-54), Blount County C. of C. (v.p. 1971, 76, pres. 1977), Townsend C. of C. (dir. 1969-71, 83-85, pres. 1983), Tenn. AP News Execs. Assn. (v.p. 1973, pres. 1974), AP Mng. Editors Assn., Tenn. Profl. Photographers Assn., Am. Legion, Foothills Pkwy. Assn. (v.p., pres.), Chilhowee Bapt. Assn. (chmn. history com.) U. Okla. Alumni Assn. (life mem., pres. East Tenn. chpt. 1954-55), Sigma Delta Chi (life, dir. E. Tenn. chpt.), Mason, Kiwanian (pres. Alcoa 1969-70); Club: Green Meadow Country. Contbr. articles to profl. pubis. Home: 1510 Scenic Dr Maryville TN 37803-5634 Office: 307 W Harper Ave Maryville TN 37801-4723

STONE, IRA MICHAEL, internist, cardiologist; b. Bklyn., Nov. 8, 1946; s. Seymour Henry and Lucille Sybill (Daniels) S.; m. Christine Susan LePore, Feb. 25, 1984; children: Karen Amy, Jason Eli, Jessica Rachel, Jennifer Rebecca, Sarah LePore, Rebecca Danielle. BA, Johns Hopkins U., 1968; MD, U. Md., 1973. Diplomate Am. Bd. Internal Medicine, Am. Bd. Cardiovascular Diseases; lic in nuclear medicine. Resident internal medicine Mercy Hosp., Balt., 1973-75; cardiology fellow U. Miami, Fla., 1975-77; pvt. practice medicine specializing in cardiology Ocala, 1977—; mem. staff Ocala Regional Med. Ctr., 1977—; staff physician Munroe Regional Med. Ctr., Ocala, Fla., 1977—, chief medicine, 1987-89, dir. CCU, 1989-90. Contbr. articles to profl. jours. Fellow: Am. Coll. Chest Physicians, Am. Heart Assn., Am. Coll. Cardiology, Coun. Clin. Cardiology; mem.: ACP, AMA, Marion County Heart Assn. (pres. 1981—82), Fla. Med. Assn., Marion County Med. Soc. Republican. Jewish. Office: Ctrl Fla Heart Ctr 3310 SW 34th St Ocala FL 34474-7422

STONE, JAMES HOWARD, management consultant; b. Chgo., Mar. 4, 1939; s. Jerome H. and Evelyn Gertrude (Teitelbaum) S.; m. Carole Marlen David, Apr. 21, 1972; children: Margaret Elisa, Emily Anne, Phoebe Jane. AB cum laude, Harvard U., 1960, MBA, 1962. Cert. mgmt. cons., CMC, 1977. From staff analyst to exec. com. Stone Container Corp., Chgo., 1962—83, exec. com., 1983—96; founder, owner, CEO, pres. Stone Mgmt. Corp., 1969—2002; pres. Jemp, Inc., 2002—. Mem. strategic alliance Boston Cons. Group, 1990—; trustee, sec., exec. com. Roosevelt U., Chgo., 1983—, exec. com. edn. alliance, 1994—; co-chmn. commn. fgn. and domestic affairs Northwestern U., Evanston, Ill., 1981-85, bus. plan judge Kellogg Grad. Sch. Mgmt., 1994—; mem. vis. com. libr., lectr. U. Chgo., 1980—, The Chgo. Com., 1986—, Mid-Am. Com., Chgo., 1993-98; bd. overseers, lectr. IIT Stuart Sch. Bus., 1993—; bd. dirs. Cinema Chgo., Pilgrim Chamber Players. Mem. Chgo. Coun. Fgn. Rels., 1967, bd. dirs., 1974-78; bd. dirs., mem. exec. com. NCCJ, Chgo., 1985, presiding co-chmn., 1990-97; trustee Hadley Sch. Blind, Winnetka, Ill., 1985-96, chmn. planning com., 1989-96, Hadley life trustee, 1996—; vice chmn. fin. com. North Shore Congregation Israel, 1995-98; bd. dirs. Suzuki-Orff Sch., 1997—. Mem. Coun. Logistics Mgmt. (dir. Roundtable-Chgo. 1990-94), The Exec. Club Chgo., Econs. Club, Harvard Club Chgo. (dir. 1995—), Harvard Bus. Sch. Club Chgo. (dir. 1992—, pres. 1997-99), Traffic Club Chgo., Standard Club, Northmoor Country Club, Mid-Day Club, The Casino, Arts Club, Menttium 100, Juvenile Protective Assn. (trustee 1999—), The East Bank Club. Avocations: family-centered activities, reading, golf, travel. Office: Stone Mgmt Corp 208 S La Salle St Chicago IL 60604-1000

STONE, JAMES ROBERT, surgeon; b. Greeley, Colo., Jan. 8, 1948; s. Anthony Joseph and Dolores Concetta (Pietrafeso) S.; m. Kaye Janet Friedman, May 16, 1970; children: Jeffrey, Marisa. BA, U. Colo., 1970; MD, U. Guadalajara, Mex., 1976; MBA, Madison U., 2002. Diplomate Am. Bd. Surgery, Am. Bd. Surg. Critical Care, Am. Bd. Forensic Medicine. Intern Md. Gen. Hosp., Balt., 1978-79; resident in surgery St. Joseph Hosp., Denver, 1979-83; pvt. practice Grand Junction, 1983-87; staff surgeon, dir. critical care Va. Med. Ctr., 1987-88; dir. trauma surgery and critical care, chief surgery St. Francis Hosp., Colorado Springs, Colo., 1988-91; pvt. practice Kodiak, Alaska, 1991-92; with Summit Surg. Assocs., 1992-96; asst. dir. trauma Tristate Trauma System, Erie, Pa., 1996-99; med. dir. LifeStar Aeromed, 1997-99; dir. trauma, sr. assoc. physician, med. dir. emergency svcs. ISJ Mayo Health, 1999—2001; clin. prof. surgery U. Minn. Med. Sch., Mpls., 1999—2001, dir. trauma/EMS med. dir., sr. assoc.; gen., thoracic and vasc. surgery Caylor-Nickel Clinic, Bluffton, Ind., 2001—02, EMI, 2002—. Asst. clin. prof. surgery U. Colo. Health Sci. Ctr., Denver, 1984-96; pres. Stone Aire Cons., Grand Junction, 1988—; owner, operator Jjnka Ranch, Flourissant, Colo.; spl. advisor CAP, wing med. officer, 1992-96; advisor med. com. unit, 1990-92; advisor Colo. Ground Team Search and Rescue, 1994-96. Contbr. articles to profl. jours.; inventor in field. Bd. dirs. Mesa County Cancer Soc., 1988-89, Colo. Trauma Inst., 1988-91. Colo. Speaks out on Health grantee, 1988; recipient Bronze medal of Valor Civil Air Patrol. Fellow Denver Acad. Surgery, Southwestern Surg. Congress, Am. Coll. Chest Physicians, Am. Coll. Surgeons (trauma com. Colo. chpt.), Am. Coll. Critical Care; mem. Am. Coll. Physician Execs., Soc. Critical Care (task force 1988—), Assn. Air Med. Physicians. Roman Catholic. Avocations: horse breeding, hunting, fishing. Office: Caylor-Nickel Clinic 1 Caylor Nickel Sq Bluffton IN 46714

STONE, JEREMY JUDAH, public interest activist; b. N.Y.C., Nov. 23, 1935; s. I.F. and Esther (Roisman) S.; m. Betty Jane Yannet, June 16, 1957. BS magna cum laude, Swarthmore Coll., 1957, LL.D. (hon.), 1985; PhD, Stanford U., 1960. Research mathematician Stanford Research Inst., 1960-62; mem. profl. staff Hudson Inst., Croton-on-Hudson, 1962-64; research asso., arms control and disarmament Harvard Ctr. Internat. Affairs, 1964-66; asst. prof. math., lectr. polit. sci. Pomona Coll., Claremont, Calif., 1966-68; pres. Fedn. Am. Scientists, Washington, 1970-2000, Catalytic Diplomacy, 1999—. Author: Containing the Arms Race; Some Concrete Proposals, 1966, Strategic Persuasion, 1967, "Every Man Should Try." Adventures of a Public Interest Activist, 1999. Recipient award for pub. svc. Forum on Physics and Soc., Am. Phys. Soc., 1979, Fedn. of Am. Scientists Pub. Svc. award, 1994; Social Sci. Rsch. Coun. fellow in econs. Stanford U., 1968-69, Coun. Fgn. Rels. internat. affairs fellow, 1969-70. Mem. Coun. Fgn. Rels., Internat. Inst. Strategic Studies, Phi Beta Kappa. Home and Office: 5615 Warwick Pl Bethesda MD 20815-5503 E-mail: Jstone@catalyticdiplomacy.org.

STONE, JOHN FLOYD, soil physics researcher and educator; b. York, Nebr., Oct. 13, 1928; s. Harry Floyd and Anastasia (Klima) S.; m. Carol Ottilie Youngson, Aug. 2, 1953; children: Mary, Margaret, David, Jana. BS, U. Nebr., 1952; MS, Iowa State U., 1955, PhD, 1957. Lab. technician U. Nebr., 1944-53; from rsch. asst. to rsch. assoc. Iowa State U., 1953-57; from asst. to assoc. prof. Okla. State U., Stillwater, 1957-69, prof. soil physics, 1969-94; prof. emeritus, 1994—. Mem. adv. agrl. panel U.S. Dept. Def., 1977-78; mem. grant evaluation panel Water Quality Grant Program, USDA, 1989, Small. Bus. Initiative Rsch. Grant Program, 1990. Editor: Plant Modification for More Efficient Water Use, 1975, Plant Production and Management under Drought Conditions, 1983; contbr. chpts. to books, rsch. articles to profl. jours.; co-patentee apparatus for measuring water content of soil; co-discoverer Nova-Cygni, 1975. Commr. Stillwater City, 1974-75; mem. Stillwater Housing Appeals Bd., 1975-79; com. mem. troop 14 Boy Scouts Am., 1976-83, merit badge counselor, 1974—; del. to jurisdictional conf. United Meth. Ch., 1968, alt. del. to gen. conf., 1968. With USN, 1946-48 (WWII Victory medal). Grantee USDA, 1980, 83, 89, 90, 91, 92, NSF, 1961, U.S. Dept. Interior, 1968, 73, 79, 89, 91, Okla. Dept. Commerce, 1988, Okla. Coun. for Applied Sci. and Tech., Energy Efficient Irrigation, 1990. Fellow Am. Soc. Agronomy (editl. bd., assoc. editor Agronomy jour. 1982-85); mem. ASCE (com. on irrigation water requirements 1979-95, chmn. task com. on calibration and use of neutron moisture meters 1990-94, State-of-the-Art of Civil Engring. award 1992), Soil Sci. Soc. Am. (assoc. editor, mem. editl. bd. 1968-76 Soil Sci. Am. jour., com. on water resources 1964-73), Internat. Soil Sci. Soc., Am. Geophys. Union (vis. scientist lectr. 1972, mem. com. on the unsaturated zone of the hydrology sect. 1978-88, chmn. 1986-88), Sigma Xi, Am. Radio Relay League, Stillwater Amateur Radio Club. Democrat. Methodist. Avocations: photography, amateur astronomy, music, amateur radio.

STONE, JOHN MCWILLIAMS, JR. electronics executive; b. Chgo., Nov. 4, 1927; s. J. McWilliams and Marion (Jones) S.; m. Cheryl Johansen Cullison, Dec. 18, 1976; children: Jean Stone, Lee Stone Nelson, John III (dec.), Michael (dec.), Shannon Bergman, Tamra Stone. BA, Princeton U., 1950. Salesman A.B. Dick Co., Milw., 1950-51; prodn. supr. Dukane Corp., St. Charles, Ill., 1951-56, exec. v.p., 1956-62, pres., 1962-70, pres., chmn. bd., 1970—, chmn. bd., pres., CEO, 1991-97. Trustee The Elgin (Ill.) Acad. (recipient Elgin medal 1984, emeritus 1985—), Phillips Exeter (N.H.) Coun., 1985—, Three Rivers Coun. Boy Scouts Am., St. Charles; mem. Delnor Cmty. Hosp. Men's Found., St. Charles. Named Exec. of Yr. Valley chpt. Profl. Secs. Internat., Aurora, 1981. Mem. Commonwealth Club of Chgo., Econ. Club of Chgo., Princeton Club of Chgo., Execs. Club of Chgo., Dunham Woods Riding Club (pres. 1967-68, 78-79, 89-90). Republican. Episcopalian. Avocation: tennis. Home: PO Box 755 Wayne IL 60184-0755 Office: Dukane Corp 2900 Dukane Dr Saint Charles IL 60174-3395

STONE, JOHN TIMOTHY, JR. writer; b. Denver, July 13, 1933; s. John Timothy and Marie Elizabeth (Briggs) S.; m. Judith Bosworth Stone, June 22, 1955; children: John Timothy III, George Williams. Student, Amherst Coll., 1951-52, U. Mex., 1952; BA, postgrad., U. Miami, 1955, U. Colo., 1959-60. Sales mgr. Atlas Tag, Chgo., 1955-57; br. mgr. Household Fin. Corp., 1958-62; pres. Janeff Credit Corp., Madison, Wis., 1962-72, Recreation Internat., Mpls., 1972-74, Continental Royal Svcs., N.Y.C., 1973-74; dir. devel. The Heartlands Group/Tryon Mint, Toronto, Ont., Can., 1987-89; spl. cons. Creative Resources Internat., Madison, 1988-90, Pubs. Adv. Group, 1990—; spl. cons. art and antiques Treasure Hunt Assocs., 1994—. Bd. dirs. Madison Credit Bur., Wis. Lenders' Exch. Author: Mark, 1973, Going for Broke, 1976, The Minnesota Connection, 1978, Debby Boone So Far, 1980, (with John Dallas McPherson) He Calls Himself "An Ordinary Man", 1981, Satiacum, The Chief Who's Winning Back the West, 1981, Runaways, 1983, (with Robert E. Gard) Where the Green Bird Flies, 1984, The Insiders Guide to Buying Art, 1993, Anyone's Treasure Hunt, 1995; syndicated columnist The Great American Treasure Hunt, 1983-87. Served with CIC, U.S. Army, 1957-59. Mem. Minarani Club, African First Shotters Club, Sigma Alpha Epsilon. Presbyterian. Office: Pubs Adv Group 1009 Starlight Dr Madison WI 53711-2724

STONE, JOHN WARE, management consultant; b. Framingham, Mass., May 4, 1940; s. Henry Bowditch and Laura (Bement) S.; m. Sarah McClenny, Apr. 20, 1963 (div. 1979); m. Maribeth Kershaw, Oct. 10, 1981; children: Amy Elizabeth, Richard Taliaferro. BSBA, Charter Oak Coll., 1985. Mgmt. trainee Framingham Trust Co., 1963-65, mgr. data processing, 1964-65; asst. v.p. Essex County Bank, Lynn, Mass., 1965-68, v.p., 1968-71, Vt. Nat. Bank, Brattleboro, 1971-76, sr. v.p., 1976-78; dir. mktg. Fin. Industry Systems, Hartford, Conn., 1978-80; mgr. KPMG Peat Marwick, 1980-85, prin. NJ, 1980-85, ptnr. Boston, 1985-97; prin. Quest Worldwide, Saddle Brook, N.J., 1997-98; ptnr. Tower Group, Needham, Mass., 1998—99, ptnr.-in-charge consulting, 1999—2002; mng. ptnr. Internat. Adv. Svcs., 2002—. Contbg. editor: Bank Systems and Tech., 1983-90. Founder Brattleboro Hockey Assn., 1976; class corr. Northfield Mt. Hermon (Mass.) H.S., 1989-92. Mem. Data Processing Mgmt. Assn. (pres. 1969-70), Jaycees (pres. Greater Lynn chpt. 1970, founder Rowley, Mass. chpt. 1971), Holliston Newcomers (chmn. fund raising 1987-88). Avocations: sailing, golf, skiing. Office: Tower Group 2 Charles River Pl 63 Kendrick St Needham MA 02494-2708

STONE, KARL JOHNSON, genealogist, music composer; b. Petoskey, Mich., Feb. 7, 1935; s. Quinton Joseph and Mildred Haskins (Johnson) S.; m. Margaret Ann Brand, Aug. 14, 1965; children: Robert Quinton, Mary Catherine. BS, U. Mich., 1957, MS, 1959; PhD, U. Fla., 1969. Assoc. prof. Minot (N.D.) State Coll., 1969-72; bus. owner Wag In Tail Pet Grooming and Supplies, Minot, 1974-79, Parade of Pets, Boulder, Colo., 1979-81; salesman Fine Jewelers Guild Zale Corp., 1983-87, Evergreen Lawns, Denver, 1989-91; genealogist Longmont and Littleton, Colo., 1995—; cataloger Ames Framily Hist. Collection, 1997-2001. Author: (pamphlet) Arthropods of Florida, 1965; composer: (music for handbells) Revelation of Joy, 1987, (music for organ) Reclamare, 2001, (music for h.s. band) The M-K Music Box, 2001. Grantee Am. Philos. Soc., 1971, Spiders of N.D. Mem. Am. Mus. Natural History (life), Nat. Geneal. Soc., Colo. Geneal. Soc. (vol. coord. 1997-98), Foothills Geneal. Soc. (phone tree chmn. 1999-2001, award 2000, 2001). Avocation: stitchery. Home: 512 W Jamison Pl Littleton CO 80120-4265 E-mail: kjstone@infi.net.

STONE, LAWRENCE MAURICE, lawyer, educator; b. Malden, Mass., Mar. 25, 1931; s. Abraham Jacob and Pauline (Bernstein) S.; m. Anna Jane Clark, June 15, 1963; children: Abraham Dean, Ethan Goldthwaite, Katharine Elisheva. AB magna cum laude, Harvard U., 1953, JD magna cum laude, 1956. Bar: Mass. 1956, Calif. 1958. Rsch. asst. Am. Law Inst., Cambridge, Mass., 1956-57; assoc. Irell and Manella, L.A., 1957-61, ptnr., 1963, 79-96, of counsel, 1997—; internat. tax coordinator U.S. Treasury Dept., Washington, 1961-62, tax. legis. counsel, 1964-66; prof. law U. Calif., Berkeley, 1966-78. Vis. prof. law Yale U., New Haven, 1969, Hebrew U. Jerusalem, 1973-74, U. So. Calif., L.A., 1984; mem. adv. group to commr. IRS, Washington, 1973-74; mem. President's Adv. Commn. on Tax Ct. Appointments, Washington, 1976-80; tax advisory bd. Little Brown Co., 1994-96. Author: (with Doernberg) Federal Income Taxation of Corporations and Partnerships, (with Klein, Bankman and Bittker) Federal Income Taxation; bd. editors Harvard Law Rev., 1955-56. Fellow Am. Coll. Tax Counsel; mem. ABA, Am. Law Inst., Internat. Fiscal Inst., Am. Arbitration Assn., L.A. County Bar Assn. (recipient Dana Latham award 1995), Phi Beta Kappa. Office: Irell & Manella 1800 Avenue Of The Stars Los Angeles CA 90067-4276

STONE, LAWRENCE MYNATT, publishing executive; b. Balt., June 24, 1945; s. David G. and Clara Ruth (Coxey) S.; m. Lois V. Smith, June 10, 1967; children: Bradley Michael, Geoffrey David. BA, U. Iowa, 1968. Prof. Northeastern Bible Coll., Essex Fells, N.J., 1968-69; missionary Africa Evangelical Fellowship, Ndola, Zambia, 1969-71; asst. to production mgr. Am. Bible Soc., N.Y.C., 1971-72; book club mgr. Iversen-Norman Assocs., 1972-75; editl. v.p. Thomas Nelson Pubs., Nashville, 1976-85; pres. Rutledge Hill Press, 1985-99, pub., 1999—. Book and libr. adv. com. U.S. Info. Agency, Washington, 1984-88; editor in field; ghost writer. Office: Rutledge Hill Press PO Box 141000 Nashville TN 37214-1000 E-mail: larryrhp@aol.com, lstone@rutledgehillpress.com.

STONE, LELAND EDWARD, writer; b. Montebello, Calif., Aug. 16, 1962; s. Jimmy Lewis and Gloria Louise S.; m. Christine Lynette Phillips, Jan. 23, 1987 (div. July 1997); 1 child, Leland; m. Lynell Marie, Mar. 7, 1998. Blacksmith Leland Stone Horseshoeing, Covina, Calif., 1979-84; owner Leland Stone Wood & Ironworks, 1984-89; gen. contractor Leland Stone Fine Bldg. Col., Pomona, Calif., 1989-92, Leland Stone Fine Bldg. Co., Johannesburg, 1992-95; freelance writer Buena Park, 1998—. Mem. Constrn. Writers Assn. Republican. Avocations: Christian apologetics, antiques, magic, bonsai. Office: 14742 Beach Blvd # 102 La Mirada CA 90638-4259 Fax: (714) 994-9553. Personal E-mail: lelandedwardstone@earthlink.net.

STONE, LINDA D. organizational development and human resources consultant; b. Keene, N.H., Dec. 18, 1947; d. Gordon D. and Sophie B. (Blacker) S. BA in English, Hartwick Coll., 1969; cert. in pers. mgmt., NYU, 1978; MA in Human Resources, New Sch. for Social Rsch., 1985. Adminstrv. asst. Arlans Dept. Store, N.Y.C., 1969-72; pers./office svcs. mgr. ABC Leisure Mags., 1974-80; dir. pers. & adminstrn. Gruner and Jahr USA, 1980-82; dir. human resources & adminstrn. Warren, Gorham and Lamont, 1983; mgr. pers. adminstrn. John Wiley and Sons, Inc., 1984-88; dir. staffing Simon & Schuster, 1989-90; pres. Linda D. Stone Assocs., Inc., 1990—. Adj. prof. New Sch. for Social Rsch., N.Y.C., 1991—; adj. prof. NYU, N.Y.C., 1992—. Contbr. articles to profl. jours. Vol. N.Y.C. schs. Mem. AAUW, Applied Psychology (N.Y. chpt.), N.Y. Human Resource Planners, N.Y. Pers. Mgmt. Assn., Internat. Assn. Outplacement Profls., Assn. Psychol. Type, Soc. Human Resource Mgmt., Hartwick Coll. (alumni bd. 1983-91, class agt. 1984, founder N.Y.C. alumni chpt.). Office: Linda D Stone Assocs Inc 520 E 81st St New York NY 10028-7095

STONE, MARC J. lawyer; b. N.Y.C., Dec. 21, 1960; s. Lewis Michael and Wendy V. S.; children: Alexandra Paige, Justin Alexander. AB, Brown U., 1982; JD, U. Calif., Berkeley, 1985. Bar: N.Y., Fla. Assoc. corp. dept. Rubin Baum Levin Constant & Friedman, N.Y.C., 1985-87, Rubin Baum Levin Constant Friedman & Bilzin, Miami, Fla., 1987-92, ptnr., 1993-97; of counsel Bilzin Sumberg Dunn Baena Price & Axelrod, 1997—; v.p., gen. counsel, sec. TradeStation Group, Inc., 1997—. Mem.: ABA, Fla. Bar Assn., NY State Bar Assn. Avocations: theater , film, reading, team sports, tennis. Office: TradeStation Group Inc 8050 SW 10th St Plantation FL 33324 E-mail: mstone@tradestation.com.

STONE, MARTHA JANE, musician; b. Nashville, Nov. 10, 1919; d. Robert Burns and Ada Belle (Stewart) S. BA, Transylvania Coll., 1943; MA, U. Ky., 1949; student, Cin. Conservatory Music, 1950-51, '64-72. Organist New Union Christian Ch., Woodford County, Ky., 1938—; supr. music Garth Sch., Georgetown, 1943-45; cellist Lexington Civic Symphony, 1944-45; asst. prof. music Transylvania Coll., Lexington, Ky., 1947-80; pianist Chambers & Stone duo, various, 1953-65; cellist Lexington Symphony Orch., 1957-64, Lexington Philharmonic, 1966—. Music critic Lexington Herald, 1952-53. Author: The Genealogy and History of the Stewart Family, Vol. I, 1986, Vol. II, 1987, Life Is So Daily Cookbook, 1988, The Warren Family of Trigg County, Kentucky, 1990, A History of the Stone Family, Who Settled in the South and the Cherry Family of Tennessee, 1993, Glossary of Genealogical Terms, 1997, Red River Baptist Church, Robertson County, Tennessee, Members 1791-1818, 1999, The Goode Family of Virginia, Georgia and Kentucky, 2000. Martha Jane Stone scholarship to Lexington Philharmonic established 1984 by New Union Christian Ch. Mem. Daus. of the Confederacy, Order of Ea. Star. Home: 810 Cramer Ave Lexington KY 40502-1414 E-mail: majastone@peoplepc.com.

STONE, MARVIN JULES, physician, educator; b. Columbus, Ohio, Aug. 3, 1937; s. Roy J. and Lillian (Bedwinek) S.; m. Jill Feinstein, June 29, 1958; children: Nancy Lillian, Robert Howard. Student, Ohio State U., 1955-58; SM in Pathology, U. Chgo., 1962, MD with honors, 1963. Diplomate Am. Bd. Internal Medicine, (Hematology, Med. Oncology). Intern ward med. svc. Barnes Hosp., St. Louis, 1963-64, asst. resident, 1964-65; clin. assoc. arthritis and rheumatism br. Nat. Inst. Arthritis and Metabolic Diseases, NIH, Bethesda, Md., 1965-68; resident in medicine, ACP scholar Parkland Meml. Hosp., Dallas, 1968-69; fellow in hematology-oncology, dept. internal medicine U. Tex. Southwestern Med. Sch., 1969-70, instr. dept. internal medicine, 1970-71, asst. prof., 1971-73, assoc. prof., 1974-76, clin. prof., 1976—, chmn. bioethics com., 1979-81; mem. faculty and steering com. immunology grad. program, Grad. Sch. Biomed. Scis., U. Tex. Health Sci. Ctr., 1975, adj. mem., 1976—. Dir. Charles A. Sammons Cancer Ctr., chief oncology, dir. immunology, co-dir. divsn. hematology-oncology, attending physician Baylor U. Med. Ctr., Dallas, 1976—; v.p. med. staff Parkland Meml. Hosp., Dallas, 1982. Contbr. chpts. to books, articles to profl. jours. Chmn. com. patient-aid Greater Dallas/Ft. Worth chpt. Leukemia Soc. Am., 1971-76, chmn. med. adv. com., 1978-80, bd. dirs., 1971-80; mem. v.p. Dallas unit Am. Cancer Soc., 1977-78, pres., 1978—; mem. adv. bd. Baylor U. Med. Ctr. Found. With USPHS, 1965-68. Recipient Wings of Eagles award, Baylor Health Care Sys., 2001, Disting. Svc. award, U. Chgo., 2002. Master ACP (gov. No. Tex. 1993-97, laureate Tex. chpt. 2000); fellow Royal Soc. Medicine (London); mem. AMA, Am. Assn. Immunologists, Am. Soc. Hematology, Internat. Soc. Hematology, Coun. Thrombosis, Am. Heart Assn. (established investigator 1970-75), Am. Soc. Clin. Oncology, Am. Osler Soc. (bd. govs. 1997-2000, v.p. 2001-02), Am. Assn. for Cancer Rsch., So. Soc. Clin. Investigation, Tex. Med. Assn., Dallas County Med. Soc., Clin. Immunology Soc., Phi Beta Kappa, Sigma Xi, Alpha Omega Alpha. Office: Baylor U Med Ctr Charles A Sammons Cancer Ctr 3500 Gaston Ave Dallas TX 75246-2096 E-mail: marvins@baylorhealth.edu.

STONE, MARY ALICE, sales executive; b. Savannah, Ga., Oct. 27, 1940; d. Melvin Theodore and Alice May (Shaw) Pearson; m. Thomas Lanier Stone, Aug. 14, 1960; children: Mary Elizabeth (dec.), Thomas Lanier, Jr., Michael A., Vicki Lynn. Bookkeeper, Radix Microelectronics, Tustin, Calif., 1967-69; owner Smart Set Bookkeeping-Employment Agy., Santa Ana, Calif., 1969-72; cons. Princess House Products, Havelock, N.C., 1973-74, unit organizer, 1974-77, area organizer, New Bern, N.C. and Ga., 1977-82, sr. area organizer, Marietta, Ga., 1982-88, divisional organizer, 1989—. Philanthropic chmn. Cystic Fibrosis Found., Tustin, Calif., 1971-72; vol. Craven Cherry Point Child Devel. Ctr., Havelock, 1972, Spl. Olympics, Marietta, 1983-84; choir dir. Christ Episc. Ch., Havelock, 1973; cookie chmn. Craven Country Council Girl Scouts U.S.; active Mother's March of Dimes, 1989. Mem. NAFE, Am. Soc. Profl. Exec. Women, Beta Sigma Phi (Woman of Yr. Havelock chpt. 1973), Beta Sigma Phi Internat. (life, order of Rose Degree 1979). Avocations: Swimming; reading; dancing. Office: Princess House Products PO Box 965065 Marietta GA 30066-0002

STONE, MARY BETH See FISHTEIN, ELIZABETH

STONE, MARY ELIZABETH, artist; b. Columbus, Ohio, Feb. 5, 1928; d. Charles and Sarita Heenan Worley; m. Robert Samuel Stone, Aug. 14, 1949; children: Lael Anne. AB, Vassar Coll., 1948; MA, NYU, 1949. Mem. Nat. Watercolor Soc., Okla. Watercolor Soc., Kans. Watercolor Soc., Tex. Watercolor Soc., Soc. Layerists Multi-Media. Episcopalian. Home: 4756 Enchanted Oaks Dr College Station TX 77845-7649

STONE, MERRILL BRENT, lawyer; b. Jersey City, Aug. 16, 1951; s. Leonard and Claire (Orlean) S.; m. Geri Ellen Satkin, Nov. 24, 1976; children: Jacqueline Blair, Erica Lauren. AB summa cum laude, Rutgers U., 1973; JD, Columbia U., 1976. Bar: N.J. 1976, N.Y. 1977, Fla. 1981, U.S. Dist. Ct. N.J. 1976, U.S. Dist. Ct. (so. dist.) N.Y. 1977, U.S. Dist. Ct. (so. dist.) Fla. 1983. Assoc. Kelley Drye & Warren, N.Y.C., 1976-84, resident Miami, 1983-85, ptnr. N.Y.C., 1985-92, mng. ptnr., 1992--. Editor: (comments section) Columbia Human Rights Law Rev., N.Y.C., 1975-76. Trustee Greater Miami C. of C., 1984-85. Named Harlan Fiske Stone Scholar, Columbia Law Sch., N.Y.C., 1975-76. Mem. ABA (bus. bankruptcy com. sect. on bus. law, banking law com.), Am. Soc. Corp. Secs., Fla. Bar Assn., Club 101, Phi Beta Kappa, Pi Sigma Alpha. Office: Kelley Drye & Warren LLP 101 Park Ave New York NY 10178-0002 E-mail: mstone@kelleydrye.com.

STONE, MICHAEL DAVID, landscape architect; b. Moscow, Apr. 11, 1953; s. Frank Seymour Stone and Barbara Lu (Wahl) Stone/Schonthaller; m. Luann Dobaran, Aug. 12, 1978; children: Stephanie Nicole, David Michael. B in Landscape Architecture, U. Idaho, 1976; postgrad., Oreg. State U., 1986, Harvard U., 1990; MA in Orgnl. Leadership, Gonzaga U., 1990. Registered landscape architect, Wash., cert. park and recreation profl.Nat. Recreation and Park Assn. Landscape designer Robert L. Woerner, ASLA, Spokane, Wash., 1976—77; pk. planner Spokane County Pks. and Recreation, 1977—82; landscape architect City of Spokane Pks. and Recreation, 1982—84, asst. pks. mgr., 1984—86, golf and cmty. devel. mgr., 1986—95, co-dir., 1995—96, spl. ops. mgr., 1996—2000, interim dir., 2000—01, dir., 2001—. Cons. Lake Chelan (Wash.) Golf Course, 1988. Pres. Sacred Heart Parish Coun., Spokane, 1987-89; v.p. Cataldo Sch. Bd. Dirs., Spokane, 1987-89; pres. South Spokane Jaycees, 1977-86; active Leadership Spokane, 1989, Nat. Exec. Devel Sch., 1993. Named Outstanding Young Man Am., 1980, 85, Outstanding Knight, Intercollegiate Knights, 1972-73, Jaycee of the Yr., South Spokane Jaycees, 1981, Vet. of the Yr., South Spokane Jaycees, 1984-85; recipient Holy Grail award Intercollegiate Knights, 1972-73. Mem. Nat. Recreation and Pk. Assn. (bd. dirs. golf mgmt. sect. 1995-96), Am. Soc. Landscape Architects, Wash. Recreation and Pk. Assn., Nat. Inst. Golf Mgmt. (bd. dirs. 1995-98), Beta Chi, Delta Tau Delta. Roman Catholic. Avocations: golf, basketball, photography, travel. Home: 2007 E 55th Ave Spokane WA 99223-8212 Office: City of Spokane 808 W Spokane Falls Blvd Spokane WA 99256-0001

STONE, PETER, playwright, scenarist; b. Los Angeles, Feb. 27, 1930; s. John and Hilda (Hess) S.; m. Mary O'Hanley, Feb. 17, 1961. BA, Bard Coll., 1951, DLitt, 1971; MFA, Yale U., 1953. Ind. stage and screen writer, 1961—. Author: (musical comedies) Kean, 1961, Skyscraper, 1965, 1776, 1969 (Tony award Best Musical Book 1969, N.Y. Drama Critics Circle award 1969, London Plays and Players award 1969, Drama Desk award Best Musical Book writer 1969), Two by Two, 1970, Sugar, 1972, Woman of the Year, 1981 (Tony award Best Musical Book 1981), My One and Only, 1983, Grand Hotel, 1989, The Will Rogers Follies, 1991 (Tony award Best Musical 1991, N.Y. Drama Critics Circle award Best New Musical 1991, Grammy award 1991), Titanic, 1997 (Tony award Best Musical Book 1997), 1776 revival, 1997, Annie Get Your Gun, 1999 (Tony award Best Musical Revival 1999, Grammy award 1999), Finian's Rainbow, 2000, (play) Full Circle, 1973, (films) Charade, 1963 (Writers Guild award Best Comedy Film 1964, Mystery Writers Am. award Best Mystery Film 1964), Father Goose, 1964 (Acad. award Best Original Screenplay 1964), Mirage, 1965, Arabesque, 1966, Secret War of Harry Frigg, 1968, Sweet Charity 1969, Skin Game, 1971, 1776, 1972 (Christopher award for Best Film), Taking of Pelham 123, 1974, Silver Bears, 1978, Who is Killing the Great Chefs of Europe?, 1978, Why Would I Lie?, 1980, Just Cause, 1995, (TV spl.) Androcles and the Lion, 1968; (TV episodes) Studio One, 1956, Brenner, 1959, Witness, 1961, Asphalt Jungle, 1961, The Defenders, 1961-62 (Emmy award 1962), The Benefactors, 1962, Espionage, 1963, Adam's Rib, 1973-74, Ivan the Terrible, 1976, Baby on Board, 1988, Grand Larceny. Mem. Dramatists Guild (coun.), Authors League, Writers Guild Am., Motion Picture Acad. Home: 160 E 71st St New York NY 10021-5119 also: 68 Stony Hill Rd Amagansett NY 11930

STONE, RALPH KENNY, lawyer; b. Bainbridge, Ga., Aug. 7, 1952; s. Ralph Patrick and Joyce (Mitchell) S.; m. Julie Ann Waldren, Aug. 24, 1974; children: Laura Lee, Rebecca, Michael. BBA magna cum laude, U. Ga., 1974, JD cum laude, 1977. Bar: Ga. 1977, U.S. Dist. Ct. (so. dist.) Ga. 1977, U.S. Supreme Ct. 1980, U.S. Ct. Appeals (11th cir.) 1981. Staff acct. Price Waterhouse & Co., Columbia, S.C., 1974; assoc. Calhoun & Donaldson, Savannah, Ga., 1977; ptnr. Franklin & Stone, Statesboro, 1977-88, Edenfield, Stone & Cox, Statesboro, 1988-94; pres. R. Kenny Stone, P.C., 1994—. Instr. taxation Ga. So. Coll., Stateboro, 1979-80. Sect. chmn. United Way S.E. Ga., campaign chmn., 1989, pres. 1991; charter pres. Leadership Bulloch, Inc., 1984; chmn. Bulloch County Dem. Com., 1984-90, Bulloch 2000 Com., 1986-88; alt. del. Dem. Nat. Conv., 1988; sec. Ga. Assn. Dem. County Chairs, 1985-89, pres. 1989-91; dist. chmn. Boy Scouts Am., 1985; pres. Forward Bulloch Inc., 1986; participant Leadership Ga., 1986; mem. Ga. Bd. Industry Trade & Tourism, 1991-96. Mem. ABA, State Bar Ga., Bulloch County Bar Assn. (pres. 1982-83), Statesboro-Bulloch C. of C. (pres. 1986, chmn. bd. dirs. 1987, chmn. devel. authority Bulloch County 1991-2001), Rotary (Statesboro), Optimist Club (pres. 1980-81, dist. lt. gov. 1981-82), Phi Kappa Phi, Beta Alpha Psi. Baptist. Home: 319 Dogwood Trl Statesboro GA 30461-4253 Office: R Kenny Stone PC PO Box 681 Statesboro GA 30459-0681

STONE, RICHARD JAMES, lawyer; b. Apr. 30, 1945; s. Milton M. and Ruth Jean (Manaster) S.; m. Lee Lawrence, Sept. 1, 1979; children: Robert Allyn, Katherine Jenney, Grant Lawrence. BA in Econs., U. Chgo., 1967; JD, UCLA, 1970. Bar: Calif. 1971, Oreg. 1994, D.C., 2000. Assoc. O'Melveny & Myers, L.A., 1971-77; dep. asst. gen. counsel U.S. Dept. Def., Washington, 1978-79; asst. to sec. U.S. Dept. Energy, 1979-80; counsel Sidley & Austin, L.A., 1981, ptnr., 1982-88; ptnr., head litigation dept. Milbank, Tweed, Hadley & McCloy, 1988-94; mng. ptnr. Zelle & Larson, LLP, 1994-97; counsel Ball Janik LLP, Portland, Oreg., 1998—. Gen. counsel and staff dir. Study of L.A. Civil Disturbance for Bd. Police Commrs., 1992; adj. prof. law Lewis and Clark Northwestern Sch. Law, 1998-99; lawyer rep. 9th Cir. Jud. Conf., 1998-99; mem. legal ethics com. Oreg. State Bar, 2002-, com. on spl. rules, 2002-. Editor-in-chief: UCLA Law Rev., 1970. Mem. Pub. Sector Task Force, Calif., State Senate Select Com. on Long Range Policy Planning, 1985-86, U.S. del. Micronesian Polit. Status Negotiations, 1978-79; mem. adv. panel Coun. Energy Resource Tribes, 1981-85; mem. vestry St. Aidan's Episcopal Ch., 1990-93, 97-98, sr. warden, 1998; dir. Legal Aid Found. L.A., 1991-99, officer, 1994-98, pres., 1997-98; dir. Portland City United Soccer Club, 1999-2000; classic coach, 2002-. Recipient Amos Alonzo Stagg medal and Howell Murray Alumni medal U. Chgo., 1967; honoree Nat. Conf. Black Mayors, 1980; recipient spl. citation for outstanding performance Sec. Dept. Energy, 1981. Fellow Am. Bar Found.; mem. ABA, FBA, Calif. Bar Assn., Oreg. Bar Assn., L.A. County Bar Assn. (trustee 1986-88), Assn. Bus. Trial Lawyers, Multnomah County Bar Assn., Phi Gamma Delta. Home: 3675 NW Gordon St Portland OR 97210-1285 Office: Ball Janik LLP 101 SW Main St Portland OR 97204-3228 E-mail: rstone@bjllp.com.

STONE, ROGER DAVID, environmentalist; b. N.Y.C., Aug. 4, 1934; s. Patrick William and Kathleen Mary Stone; married; 1 child. BA in English, Yale U., 1955. Asst. to pub. Time Mag., 1959-61, corr., news bur. chief, 1961-68; asst. to pres. Time Inc., N.Y.C., 1968-70; v.p. internat. dept. Chase Manhattan Bank, 1970-74; pres. Ctr. for Inter-Am. Rels., 1975-82; v.p. World Wildlife Fund, 1982-86, sr. fellow, 1986-90; vis. fellow, cons. on environ. issues Coun. on Fgn. Rels., 1990-92; vice chmn. ECO Inc., Washington, 1992-96; pres. Sustainable Devel. Inst., 1993—. Vis. lectr. Yale Ctr. for Internat. and Area Studies, 1994-95. Author: Dreams of Amazonia, 1985, The Voyage of the Sanderling, 1990, Wildlands and Human Needs, 1991, The Nature of Development: Reports from the Rural Tropics on the Quest for Sustainable Economic Growth, 1992, Fair Tide: Sailing Toward Long Island's Future, 1996, Tropical Forests and the Human Spirit = Journeys to the Brink of Hope, 2001; contbr. chpts. to books; contbr. articles to Time, Life, Life en Espanol, Fgn. Affairs, N.Y. Times, Internat. Herald Tribune, Christian Sci. Monitor, Harvard Bus. Rev., USA Today Mag., Cruising World, Conservation Found. Letter, numerous others. Bd. dirs. Astrolabe, Inc., Caribbean Conservation Corp.; v.p. Armand G. Erpf Fund, Sotterley Found.; former bd. dirs. U. Andes Found.; former bd. dirs. and exec. com. World Wildlife Fund-U.S., Ctr. for Inter-Am. Rels., Ams. Found., Accion Internat., Arts Internat., others. Lt. (j.g.) USN, 1956-59. Mem.: Century Assn. Democrat. Episcopalian. Avocation: sailing. Home: 1527 30th St Nw # B-32 Washington DC 20007 Fax: 202-337-9639. E-mail: susdev@igc.org.

STONE, ROSS GLUCK, orthopedic surgeon; b. Pottsville, Pa., May 14, 1951; s. Jerome M. and Alma (Gluck) S.; m. Wendy E. Reiner, March 21, 1987; children: Melissa, Logan. BA in Philosophy, Yale U., 1973; MD, Columbia U., 1977. Diplomate Am. Bd. Orthopaedic Surgery. Intern, resident Harvard U., 1977-79; resident, vis. clin. fellow Columbia U., 1979-83; pvt. practice Atlantis, Fla., 1983—. Clin. fellow in surgery Harvard Med. Sch., 1978-79; expert med. advisor Fla. Dept. Labor & Employment, 1995-97, 97—; editl. adv. bd. Am. Jour. Pain Mgmt., 1992—; chmn. surg. rev. com. Palm Beach Regional Hosp., 1995, chmn. instnl. rev. com. John F. Kennedy Med. Ctr., 1995-02; chmn. divsn. ortho. surgery Columbia Hosp., 1994—; chmn. dept. surgery Palms West Hosp., 1998—. Contbr. chpt. to book and articles to profl. jours.; invented tension headache reliever device. Trustee Palms West Hosp., Loxahatchee, Fla., 1985-88. Recipient Physician's Choice award So. Med. Assn. 88th Assembly, 1994, Scientific Poster recognition So. Med. Assn. 88th Assembly, 1994, 89th Assembly, 1995, Sr. Resident award Eastern Ortho. Assn. 14th ann. meeting, 1983, Rsch. Manuscript award Assn. for the Advancement of Med. Instrumentation, 1996. Mem.: Palm Beach County (Fla.) Med. Soc. (emergency med. svc. and disaster relief plan coms. 1994—95, health and human svcs. com. 1994—95, pub. rels. com. 1995—98, legis. com. 1995—99, del. Fla. Med. Assn. 1995—2002, bd. dirs. 1995—, chmn. pub. rels. com. 1996—98, sec. 1998, 2d v.p. 1999, chmn. bd. censors and mediation 1999, sec. MEDPAC bd. dirs 1999, 1st v.p. 2000, treas. MEDPAC bd. dirs. 2000, chmn. membership 2000, pres.-elect 2001, pres. 2002, chmn. other coms.). Republican. Jewish. Avocations: weight lifting, aerobic conditioning, reading, tennis, golf. Office: 120 John F Kennedy Dr Ste 124 Lake Worth FL 33462-6623

STONE, RUSSELL A. sociology educator; b. Medicine Hat, Alta., Can., Feb. 8, 1944; came to U.S., 1966; s. Ben and Clara G. (Gibbs) S.; m. S. Rala Stollar, Aug. 18, 1965; children: Peter H., Mira Beth. BA, McGill U., Montreal, Que., Can., 1965; PhD, Princeton U., 1971. Asst. to assoc prof. sociology SUNY, Buffalo, 1970-84, prof., 1984-91, chmn. dept. sociology, 1985-88; prof. sociology Am. U., Washington, 1991—, assoc. dean for grad. affairs, 1991-96. Vis. rsch. assoc. Israel Inst. Applied Social Rsch., Jerusalem, 1977-78; vis. assoc. prof. Ben Gurion U. of the Negev, Beersheba, Israel, 1978; vis. prof. Hebrew U., Jerusalem, 1977-78. Author: Social Change in Israel: Attitudes and Events, 1982; co-author: Political Elites on Arab North Africa, 1982; editor: OPEC and the Middle East, 1977; co-editor: Change in Tunisia, 1976, Critical Essays on Israeli Social Issues and Scholarship, 1994; chmn. editorial bd. SUNY Press, 1987-90, series editor; contbr. articles to profl. jours. Mem. Am. Sociol. Assn., Middle East Studies Assn., Assn. for Israel Studies (sec., treas. 1989-93). Office: Am U Dept Sociology 4400 Massachusetts Ave NW Washington DC 20016-8003 E-mail: rstone@american.edu.

STONE, SAMUEL BECKNER, lawyer; b. Martinsville, Va., Feb. 4, 1934; s. Paul Raymond and Mildred (Beckner) S.; m. Shirley Ann Gregory, June 18, 1955; children: Paul Gregory, Daniel Taylor. BSEE, Va. Polytech. Inst. & State U., 1955; JD, George Wash. U., 1960. Bar: Md. 1960, Calif. 1963, Patent and Trademark Office. Patent examiner, 1955-58; patent adv. Naval Ordinance Lab., Silver Spring, Md., 1958-59; assoc. Thomas & Crickenberger, Washington, 1959-61, Beckman Instruments Inc., Fullerton, Calif., 1961-65, Lyon & Lyon, L.A., 1965-72, ptnr., 1972, mng. ptnr. Irvine, Calif., 1982-2000. Judge Disneyland Com. Svc. Awards, Anaheim, Calif., 1987. Mem. Orange County Bar Assn. (bd. dirs. 1988-91, travel seminar chair 1986-92), Orange County Patent Law Assn. (pres. 1987, bd. exec. com. 1987-90), Calif. Bar Assn. (intellectual property sect. bd. 1987-90), Am. Arbitration Assn. (intellectual property panel neutral arbitrators 1997-2000), Am. Electronics Assn. (lawyers com. 1988-99, co-chair 1996-97), Orange County Venture Group (dir. 1985-99, pres. 1996-97), Rams Booster Club (dir. 1984-90), Pacific Club (mem. legal adv. com., chair 1989-92, bd. dirs. 1999-2002). Republican. Avocations: tennis, waterskiing, music. Home: 1612 Antigua Way Newport Beach CA 92660-4344 Office: Lyon & Lyon 1900 Main St Fl 6 Irvine CA 92614-7317 E-mail: sbstone@lyonlyon.com.

STONE, SANDRA SMITH, sociologist, researcher; b. Chgo., Oct. 16, 1954; d. John Lawrence and Bernice (Pickett) Smith; m. Scott Lukens, 1973 (div. 1977)); m. Charles M. Huguley, Oct. 17, 1982 (div. 1988); 1 child, Bailey Anne; m. Anthony V. Stone, Aug. 4, 1990; 1 stepchild, Adam Maraman. BA, State U. West Ga., 1976, MA, 1978; PhD, Emory U., 1993. Cert. mediator. Social worker Carroll County Early Childhood Ctr., Carrollton, GA., 1977, Clayton Gen. Hosp., Riverdale, Ga., 1978-80; caseworker Fulton County Dept. Family and Children Svcs., Atlanta, 1981; caseworker prin. Cobb County Dept. Family and Children Svcs., Marietta, Ga., 1981-82; children's program supr. Coun. on Battered Women, Atlanta, 1982-83; sr. rsch. assoc. Ctrs. Disease Control/Ga. Dept. Human Resources, 1985-87; cons. Ctrs. Disease Control, 1987-88; rsch. assoc. Police Exec. Rsch. Forum, Washington, 1988-90; exec. dir. Rsch. Atlanta, 1990-91; sr. rsch. assoc. Emory U. Sch. Pub. Health, Atlanta, 1991-92; dir. planning & Rsch. Ga. Dept. Children & Youth Svcs., 1992-96; asst. prof. State U. West Ga., Carrollton, 1996—, now assoc. prof. Instr., Emory U., Atlanta, 1984-89; drug policy adviser Mayor's Office, City of Atlanta, 1989-90; grant application reviewer Nat. Ctr. Child Abuse and Neglect, Washington, Ga. Dept. Human Resources, Atlanta; cons. Coun. for Children, Atlanta, 1987. Contbr. articles, reports to profl. publs. Mem. DeKalb County Task Force on Child Care, Decatur, Ga., 1984, DeKalb County Task Force on Infant Mortality, Decatur, 1985-89, DeKalb County Task Force on AIDS, Decatur, 1987-88; assessor City of Atlanta Fire Chief Assessment Ctr., 1990; vol. United Way; mem. Criminal Justice Coord. Com., 1992-96; mem. statewide Task Force on Violence and Schs., 1993-95; profl. adv. coun. Mission New Hope, 1994-98; mem. nat. adv. bd. Juveniles Taken Into Custody Project, 1994-97; cons. statewide Family Connection Project, 1997—; chair adv. bd. Ga. Dept. Juvenile Justice, Carroll County Ct. Svcs. Office, 1999—. Mem. LWV, Ga. Coun. Child Abuse, Planned Parenthood, Am. Sociol. Assn., Am. Soc. Criminology, So. Sociol. Soc., Ga. Sociol. Assn., Am. Pub. Health Assn., Acad. Criminal Justice Scis., Am. Correctional Assn., Nat. Ctr. Women in Policing, AAUP, Coalition for Juvenile Justice, Sociol. Practice Assn., So. Criminal Justice Assn., Phi Kappa Phi, Alpha Kappa Delta. Democrat. Avocations: movies, theatre, concerts, crafts. Home: 2078 Amberwood Way NE Atlanta GA 30345-3904 Office: State U West Ga Dept Sociology Anthropol And Criminology Carrollton GA 30118-0001 E-mail: sstone@westga.edu.

STONE, STEPHEN PAUL, dermatologist; b. N.Y.C., Aug. 22, 1941; s. C. Sidney and Sylvia (Alpher) S.; m. Lisa Jane Wald, Mar. 1, 1969; children: Jason Harris, Erica Lauren, Charles David. AB cum laude, Tufts U., 1963; MD, NYU, 1967. Diplomate Am. Bd. Dermatology, Nat. Bd. Med. Examiners. Intern Lincoln Hosp., Bronx, N.Y., 1967-68, resident in internal medicine, 1968-69; fellow in dermatology Mayo Grad. Sch. Medicine, Rochester, Minn., 1971-74; pres. Dermatology Ctr. Ltd., Springfield, Ill., 1974-2000. Prof. clin. medicine, former chief dermatology So. Ill. U. Sch. Medicine, Springfield, 2000. Editor-in-chief: Dialogues in Dermatology, 1993-2001, assoc. editor, 1976-93, editl. cons., 2001—; mem. editl. bd. Clinics in Dermatology, 2000—, section editor, 2001—. Pres. Springfield Jewish Cmty. Rels. Coun., 1986-88, 90-91, 99-2000; mem. Nat. Jewish Cmty. Rels. Adv. Coun., vice chair, 1993-97, mem. exec. com., 1990-93; bd. dirs. Coun. of Jewish Fedns., 1981-83, 85-95, chmn. small cities nat. com., 1987-88, nat. com. leadership devel., 1981-87, v.p., 1988-91; bd. dirs. Springfield Jewish Fedn., 1976-96, 2000—, v.p., 1977-79, pres., 1980-83; bd. dirs. Springfield Jewish Fedn. Found., 1983-93, pres., 1984-85; bd. dirs. Jewish Coun. for Pub. Affairs, sec. 1999—, mem. exec. com., 1996—; bd. dirs. Springfield Zool. Soc., 1983-86, United Way of Greater Sangamon County, 1985-91, Planned Parenthood, Springfield area, 1979-80; trustee, bd. dirs. Temple B'rith Sholom, 1984-90, 98-2000, v.p. 2002—; trustee Lincoln Libr., 1991-99, v.p., 1993-94, pres., 1995-96; trustee Hope Sch., 1998—, treas. 1999-2000; mem. United Jewish Appeal, Nat. Young Leadership Cabinet, 1977-82, regional chmn., 1980-81, midwest regional cabinet, 1980-94, midwest Project Renewal cabinet, 1986-88, region II small cmtys. chmn., 1991-93; sec. B'nai Israel Synagogue, Rochester, Minn., 1973-74; bd. dirs. West Ctrl. Ill. Health Sys. Agy., 1978-83, exec. bd., 1978-84, v.p., 1982-84; mem., treas. Springfield Parks Found., 1992-95. Fellow: Am. Acad. Dermatology (bd. dirs., exec. com. 1997—2001); mem.: AMA, Ill. Bd. Med. Examiners, Calif. Bd. Med. Examiners, Minn. Bd. Med. Examiners, N.Y. Bd. Med. Examiners (cert.), Soc. for Investigative Dermatology, Sangamon County Med. Soc. (chmn. liaison com. 1985), Noah Worcester Dermatol. Soc. (continuing med. edn. com. 1982—83, trustee 1987—90, pres. 2001), Internat. Soc. Tropical Dermatology, Ill. State Med. Soc. (coun. on govtl. affairs 1983—86, alternate del. 1984—85), Ill. Dermatologic Soc. (sec.-treas. 1978—80, pres. 1981), Chgo. Dermatol. Soc. (plans and policy com. 1982—84), B'nai Brith Springfield (v.p. 1975—76, pres. 1976—77), Emes Lodge. Home: 2045 S Willemore Ave Springfield IL 62704-3341 Office: So Ill U Medicine PO Box 19644 751 N Rutledge St Rm 2300 Springfield IL 62794-9644 E-mail: sstone@siumed.edu., drspstone@aol.com.

STONE, SUSAN RIDGAWAY, marketing educator; b. Coronado, Calif., Oct. 30, 1950; d. Lester Jay and Marguerite Ridgaway (King) Stone; m. Martin Zachary Sipkoff, Oct. 27, 1984; 1 child, Benjamin. AB, Wilson Coll., 1977; MBA, Shippensburg U., 1980; DBA, George Washington U., 1992. Assoc. prof. mgmt. and mktg. Shippensburg (Pa.) U., 1983—; dir. mktg. VSP Wastewater Tech., Gettysburg, Pa., 1982; pres. Graham, Stone & Co. divsn. High Mark Internat., 1998—, Ridgaway Rose Internat., Inc., 1999—. Mktg. cons. Svcs. Unltd., Gettysburg, 1975—; lectr. in field. Author: (with Stephen J. Holoviak) Managing Human Productivity: People are Your Best Investment, 1987, 2nd printing 1991; contbr. articles to profl. jours. Recipient Excellence in tchg. award, Corning Found., 1993, Outstanding Svc. award, 1994, 2002, Sprint Tchg. Excellence award, 1998, Orrston Bank Tchg. Excellence award, 2001, Panhellenic Coun. Tchg. award, 1999; fellow John L. Grove Rsch. fellow, 2002. Mem.: DAR, NOW, Am. Mktg. Assn., Acad. Mktg. Sci., Mensa, Nat. Hist. Trust, Adams County Literacy Coun., Kappa Kappa Gamma, Beta Gamma Sigma. Democrat. Episcopalian. Avocations: gardening, writing, sailing. Office: Shippensburg Univ 1871 Old Main Dr Shippensburg PA 17257-2299 E-mail: srston@ship.edu.

STONE, THOMAS KENDALL, lawyer; b. Louisville, Dec. 15, 1956; s. Earle Victor and Mary Ann (French) S. BA, U. Ky., 1979; JD, U. Louisville, 1984. Bar: Ky., U.S. Dist. t. (we. dist.) Ky., U.ist. Ct. (ea. and so. dist.) Ind. Clk. U.S. Magistrate, Louisville, 1984-85; assoc. Boehl Stopher, Paducah, Ky., 1985; sole practice Louisville, 1985—. Mem.: Ky. Bar Assn., Louisville Bar Assn. Presbyterian. Avocations: gardening, boating, camping, hiking. Office: 7982 New Lagrange Rd Ste 3 Louisville KY 40222-4792 E-mail: tstonelaw@hotmail.com.

STONE, THOMAS RICHARDSON, cultural center president; b. Milw., Feb. 1, 1939; s. Thomas S. and Ann Louise (Taplin) S.; m. Cynthia White Hutchinson, July 20 1963; children: Sarah, Thomas. BS, U.S. Mil. Acad., 1961; MA, Rice U., 1971, PhD, 1974. Commd. 2d lt. field artillery U.S. Army, 1961, advanced through grades to col., 1988; v.p. medicare support svcs. Pa. Blue Shield, Camp Hill, 1988-90; dir. devel. and fin. Metro Arts of the Capital Region, Harrisburg, Pa., 1990-93; pres., CEO Whitaker Ctr. for Sci. & the Arts, 1993—2002; prin. The Franklin Cons. Group, 2002—. Author: The Second World War: Europe and the Mediterranean, Vol. II, 1980; contbr. articles to profl. publs. Deacon St. Paul's United Ch. Christ, Mechanicsburg, Pa., 1987-90, pres. of consistory, 1989-92, elder, 1990-92; mem. Pa. Heritage Soc.; mem. Cumberland-Perry Assn. for Retarded Citizens, 1980—, bd. dirs., 1980-82, 86-97, pres., 1984-86; mem. preservation com. Pa. Monuments at Gettysburg Battlefield, 1999-2000; bd. dirs. Capital Area Sch. for the Arts, 2000—, Cumberland Perry Assn. for Retarded Citizens; founding dir. Modern Transit Partnership, 2000—. Decorated Bronze Star, Legion of Merit; grantee Rice U., 1971-72; recipient Cmty. Svc. award, Am. Legion, Carlisle, Pa., 1987. Mem. Nat. Soc. Fund Raising Execs. (cert., bd. dirs. ctrl. Pa. chpt. 1994-2000, Outstanding Fund Raising Exec. Ctrl. Pa. chpt. award 1997), Assn. U.S. Army, Capital Fedn. Cosmopolitan Internat. Club (Cosmo of Yr. award 1981-82, pres. 1980-82, lt. gov. 1983-86, gov. elect 1986-87, gov. 1987-88, internat. 2d v.p. 1991-92, internat. 1st v.p. 1992-93, internat. pres.-elect 1993-94, internat. pres. 1994-95, Patrick J. Hodgins award 1999), Cosmopolitan Diabetes Found. (dir. 1988-91, 97-99, chmn. 1999—). Home: 6319 Stephens Xing Mechanicsburg PA 17050-2347 Office: The Franklin Cons Grp PO Box 414 Mechanicsburg PA 17055-0414 E-mail: tom.stone@ix.netcom.com.

STONE, VAN COURTRIGHT, professional society administrator; b. DeLand, Fla., June 22, 1946; s. Wilfred Arthur and Catherine Louise Stone; m. Nancy M. Stone, July 19, 1969 (div. 1989); 1 child, Edana A. Stone Neundorf; m. Lisa L. Stone, Dec. 22, 1990; children: Melisa A., Wesley Alan. BA, Wichita State U., 1968; JD, Washburn U., 1974. Exec. v.p., officer S.W. State Bank, Topeka, 1974-81; pres. Nat. Bank of Andover, 1985-87; corp. atty. various corps., 1987-91; COO Gerber Bus. Devel. Corp., Petaluma, Calif., 1991-94; exec. dir. Lions of Ill. Found., Sycamore, 1995—. Bd. dirs. Ill. Sch. for the Visually Impaired, Jacksonville, Ill. Eye Fund, Chgo., Lions of Ill. Endowment Fund, 1995—; pres., N.Am. Conf. of Lions Founds., 2000, 2001. Author: (newsletter) Lions Share, 1995—; contbr. articles to profl. jours. Capt. U.S. Army, 1968-71. Decorated 3 Bronze Stars; recipient Presl. medal of honor Ill. Coll. of Optimetry, 1999, Meritorious Svc. award Deicke Ctr., 1999; Lions of Ill. Found. fellow, 1995. Mem. VFW, No. Aurora Lions Club, Andover C. of C. (pres. 1986), Phi Sigma Rho, Tau Kappa Alpha, Phi Alpha Delta. Republican. Methodist. Avocations: golfing, running, bridge, writing, bowling. Office: Lions Ill Found 2814 Dekalb Ave Sycamore IL 60178-3117

STONE, WILLIAM EDWARD, academic administrator, consultant; b. Peoria, Ill., Aug. 13, 1945; s. Dean Proctor and Katherine (Jamison) S.; m. Deborah Ann Duncan; children: Jennifer, Allison, Molly. AB, Stanford U., 1967, MBA, 1969. Asst. dean Stanford U., 1969-71, asst. to pres., 1971-77; exec. dir. Stanford Alumni Assn., 1977-90, pres., CEO, 1990-98; pres., dir. Stanford Alumni Assn. divsn. Stanford U., 1998-2001, Stanford Sierra Programs LLC, South Lake Tahoe, Calif., 1998-2001, Alpine Chalet, Inc., Alpine Meadows, 1987-2001; pres.-emeritus Stanford Alumni Assn. Stanford U., 2001—, cons. in edn1. advancement, 2001—; prin. eAdvancement Consortium, 2001—. Dir. Coun. Alumni Assn. Execs., 1989-93, v.p., 1990-91, pres., 1991-92; trustee Coun. for Advancement and Support of Edn., 1988-91; bd. dirs. Univ. ProNet, Inc., chmn., 1990-92, sec. 1996-2000. Bd. dirs. North County YMCA, 1975-76; bd. dirs., chmn. nominating com. faculty club Stanford U., 1979-81; trustee Watkins Discretionary Fund, 1979-82; mem. cmty. adv. bd. Resource Ctr. for Women; dir. Stanford Hist. Soc., 2002--. Recipient K.M. Cuthbertson award Stanford U., 1987, Tribute award Coun. for Advancement and Support of Edn., 1991. Mem.: Stanford Assocs., Stanford Faculty Club. Home: 1061 Cathcart Way Stanford CA 94305-1048 Office: Stanford Alumni Assn Frances C Arrillaga Alumni Ctr Stanford CA 94305-6105 E-mail: westone@stanford.edu.

STONE, WILLIAM KENNETH, surgeon; b. Clarksville, Tenn., Dec. 13, 1948; BS, U. Tenn., 1970; MD, U. Tenn. Ctr. Health Scis., 1973. Diplomate Am. Bd. Surgery. Intern Memphis City Hosps., 1974; resident in surgery U. Calif. Davis Med. Ctr., Sacramento, 1976-80; fellow in vasc. surgery St. Mary's Hosp., Long Beach, Calif., 1980-81; surgeon Permanente Med. Group, 1981-88; staff surgeon Redding Med. Ctr., 1988—; chief surgery Mercy Hosp., Redding, Calif., 1995-97; staff surgeon Patients Hosp., 1995—. Mem. Am. Coll. Surgeons, Sacramento Surg. Soc., No. Calif. Vascular Soc. Office: No Calif Surg Group 2510 Airpark Dr Ste 301 Redding CA 96001-2462

STONE, WILLIAM ROSS, research and development company executive, physicist; b. Aug. 26, 1947; s. William Jack and Winifred (Beckcom) S.; m. Susan Letitia Lane, Aug. 8, 1970; 1 child, Ann Michele. AB in Earth Sci., U. Calif., San Diego, 1967, MS in Applied Physics, 1973, PhD in Applied Physics, 1978. Rsch. asst. U. Calif., San Diego, 1967-69; sr. physicist Gen. Atomic, La Jolla, Calif., 1969-72; sr. engr. engring. divsn. Gulf Gen. Atomic, 1972-73; sr. scientist Megatek Corp., San Diego, 1973-80; pres. stoneware, Ltd., La Jolla, 1976—; prin. physicist, inverse scattering group leader IRT Corp., San Diego, 1980-86, rsch. advisor, 1986-87; chief scientist McDonnell Douglas Techs., 1989-90, Expersoft Corp., 1990-91; exec. dir. Fund for Internat. Sci. Interchange, 1992-98. Dir., chmn. Samaritan Inst., San Diego, 1984-89. Editor: Vol. New Methods for Optical, Quasioptical, Acoustic and Electromatnetic Synthesis, 1981; contbr. articles to profl. jours. Recipient medal San Diego Soc. Tech. Writers and Pubs., 1962. Fellow IEEE (3d Millennium medal), Chinese Inst. Electronics; mem. NRC, NAS, AAUP, IEEE Antennas and Propagation Soc. (coord. profl. activities, 1980-83, editor-in-chief Ant. Prop Mag. 1984—), Internat. Radio Soc. Union (asst. sec. gen., publs. 2001—), Optical Soc. Am., Acoustical Soc. Am., Soc. Exploration Geophysics, Assn. Computing Machinery Soc. Indsl. and Applied Math., Soc. Photooptical Instrumentation Engrs., Phi Eta Sigma. Home: 1446 Vista Claridad La Jolla CA 92037-7839

STONEBRAKER, BARBARA J. telecommunications executive; b. Dayton, Ohio, Oct. 11, 1944; d. Paul E. and Betty J. (Swango) Andrews; m. David M. Stonebraker, Sept. 18, 1965; children: Nicholas, Stephen. AS in Retailing, U. Cin., 1965, BS in Mgmt., 1978, exec. program, 1987. Svc. rep. Cin. Bell Telephone, Cin., 1965, supr., 1966-74, dist. mgr., 1974-84, gen. acctg. mgr., 1984, sr. v.p., 1990—; v.p. Cin. Bell Telephone and Cin. Bell Inc., 1988-89; asst. v.p. Cin. Bell Inc., Cin., 1987, asst. to pres., 1988. Bd. dirs. U.S. Telephone Assn., Ohio Telephone Assn.; mem. adv. com. Inst. Pub. Utilities, Mich., 1989-93. Chmn. Cin. Bell PAC com., 1989-97; campaign cabinet United Way, Cin., 1996; bd. dirs. Cin. Nature Ctr., 1996-99. Recipient Disting. Alumni award U. Cin., 1996, Career Woman of Achievement award YWCA, Cin., 1992. Mem. Telephone Pioneers of Am., Leadership Cin., Jr. League, Commonwealth Club, Delta Delta Delta. Office: Cin Bell Telephone 201 E 4th St Rm 300 Cincinnati OH 45202-4122

STONEHAM, EDWARD BRYANT, technical company executive; b. Coronado, Calif., Oct. 13, 1946; s. Samuel Camp and Jennie Lynn (Reagor) S.; m. Haesook Nam, July 4, 1972; children: Anita Lynn, Trina Ann. AB, U. Calif., Berkeley, 1968; PhD, Stanford U., 1975. Devel. engr. Hewlett-Packard Corp., Palo Alto, Calif., 1971-75, project mgr. Santa Rosa, 1975-84; rsch. and devel. mgr. Microwave Tech., Inc., Fremont, 1984-89; engring. mgr. Pacific Monolithics, Inc., Sunnyvale, 1989-93; technology dir. Endwave Corp. (formerly Endgate Corp.), 1993—. Ptnr. Tamler-Stoneham Instruments, San Francisco, 1977-83; gen. mgr. Stoneham Innovations, Los Altos, 1980—. Patentee in field; contbr. articles to profl. jours. Co-pres. Palo Alto Chamber Orch., 1999-2001. Served with U.S. Army, 1969-71. Mem. IEEE (sr.), Sigma Xi, Phi Beta Kappa. Republican. Avocations: computer programming, music composition. E-mail: EStoneham@aol.com.

STONEHILL, ERIC, lawyer; b. Rochester, N.Y., Feb. 27, 1950; BA with distinction, Northwestern U., 1970; JD, Cornell U., 1973, MBA, cert. hosp. and health svc. adminstrn., Cornell U., 1981. Bar: N.Y. 1974, D.C. 1981, U.S. Dist. Ct. (we. dist.) N.Y. 1974, U.S. Dist. Ct. (no. dist.) N.Y. 1976. Assoc. Harris & Beach LLP, Rochester, 1973-81, ptnr., 1982—. Adj. instr. Rochester Inst. Tech., 1990-92. Contbr. articles to profl. jours. Bd. dirs. Rochester Eye and Human Parts Bank, 1983-91, 92-2001, pres., 1987-90. Mem. Am. Health Lawyers Assn., N.Y. State Bar Assn. (mem. health law sect.), D.C. Bar Assn., Monroe County Bar Assn., Sloan Alumni Assn., Phi Beta Kappa. Office: Harris & Beach LLP 99 Garnsey Rd Pittsford NY 14534

STONEHILL, LLOYD HERSCHEL, gas company executive, mechanical engineer; b. South Bend, Ind., May 20, 1927; s. Charles Myers and Louise Mary (Reed) S.; m. Jean Carole Herzer, Dec. 30, 1961; children: Mark, Bill, John, Rob. BSME, Purdue U., 1949. Registered profl. engr., La. Chief engr. Rothschild Boiler & Tank Works, Shreveport, La., 1949-54; chmn. bd. dirs. Frankfort (Ind.) Bottle Gas, Inc., 1956—. Patentee in field. Founding prs. Clinton County Hosp. Authority, Frankfort, 1974; membership chmn. Clinton County Hosp. Found., Frankfort, 1982-83, 89. With U.S. Army, 1954-56. Recipient Heroism award Elks Lodge, Frankfort, 1959. Mem. Nat. Propane Gas Assn. (mktg. awards 1986, 87), Am. Legion, Purdue Alumni Assn. (Clinton County Chpt. mem. pres.' coun.), Hudson Inst., Rotary (sec. 1963-65, Paul Harris fellow), Lambda Chi Alpha (sec. 1946-47). Republican. Mem. Christian Ch. Avocations: collecting old violins, sailing, reading. Home: 1258 Forest Dr Frankfort IN 46041-3230 Office: Frankfort Bottle Gas Inc 1555 McKinley Ave Frankfort IN 46041-1805

STONEHOUSE, JAMES ADAM, lawyer; b. Alameda, Calif., Nov. 10, 1937; s. Maurice Adam and Edna Sigrid (Thuesen) S.; m. Marilyn Jean Kotkas, Aug. 6, 1966; children: Julie Aileen, Stephen Adam. AB, U. Calif., Berkeley, 1961; JD, U. Calif., San Francisco, 1965. Bar: Calif. 1966; cert. specialist probate, estate planning and trust law. Assoc. Hall, Henry, Oliver & McReavy, San Francisco, 1966-71; ptnr. Whitney Hanson & Stonehouse, Alameda, 1971-77; pvt. practice, 1977-79; ptnr. Stonehouse & Silva, 1979—. Judge adv. Alameda coun. Navy League, 1978-98. Founding dir. Alameda Clara Barton Found., 1977-80; mem. Oakland (Calif.) Marathon-Exec. Com., 1979; mem. exec. bd. Alameda coun. Boy Scouts Am., 1979—, pres., 1986-88, endowment chair area III, 1996—; trustee Golden Gate Scouting, 1986-95, treas., 1989-91, v.p., 1991-92, pres., 1993-95, v.p. area III western region, 1990-95, bd. dirs. western region, 1991—; bd. dirs. Lincoln Child Ctr. Found., 1981-87, 94-98, pres., 1983-85; pres. Robert L. Lippert Found., 1990—; mem. sch. bd. St. Joseph Notre Dame, 1994-2000, pres., 1997-2000. Recipient Lord Baden-Powell Merit award Boy Scouts Am., 1988, Silver Beaver award, 1991, Silver Antelope award, 1999, Citizen of Yr. award City of Alameda, 1999; named Boss of Yr., Alameda Jaycees, 1977; Coro Found. fellow, 1961-62. Mem. ABA, Alameda County Bar Assn. (vice chmn. com. office econs. 1977-78), Commonwealth Club, Rotary (dir. 1976-78, trustee Alameda Rotary Found. 1991—, treas. 1994-98, pres. 1998-2000), Elks (past exalted ruler, all state officer 1975-76, all dist. officer 1975-77, 78-79). Republican. Roman Catholic. Home: 2990 Northwood Dr Alameda CA 94501-1606 Office: Stonehouse & Silva 512 Westline Dr Ste 300 Alameda CA 94501-5870

STONER, DAVID A. elementary school educator, consultant; b. Madison, Ind., Aug. 8, 1951; s. Gerald H. and Virginia E. Stoner; m. Judy C. Nesthus, June 20, 1955; children: Cory, Emy. BS in Edn., MS in Edn., Ind. U. S.E., 1976. Profl. tchg. lic. . Tchr. Madison Consol. Schs., Madison, Ind., 1973—. Ind. writing facilitator Educate Ind., Indpls., 1999—2002; writing coach, presenter, train/er State of Ind. Writing Initiative, 2002. Nominee Tchr. of the Yr., Disney Prodns., 1999, 2000; fellow Creativity, Lilly Found., 1992. Mem.: MTA, Internat. Reading Assn. (presenter 1992, 1994), Write Stuff, HTML Writer's Guild, Nat. Coun. Tchrs. English, Nat. Writing Project, Ind. Tchrs. Writing. Methodist. Avocations: reading, writing, web design, walking. Home: 315 Hillcrest Dr Madison IN 47250 Office: E O Muncie Elem Sch 800 Lanier Dr Madison IN 47250 Personal E-mail: starmax@venus.net. Business E-Mail: DStoner@madison.K12.in.us.

STONER, GERALD LEE, neurovirologist, medical researcher; b. Elizabethtown, Pa., Feb. 8, 1943; s. Andrew Kraybill and Esther (Longenecker) S.; m. Linda Elaine Buckwalter, Aug. 1, 1964 (dec. Oct. 1994); children: Anne Marie Stoner-Eby, Andrea E. AA, Hershey (Pa.) Jr. Coll., 1963; BA in Natural Sci., Eastern Mennonite Coll., Harrisonburg, Va., 1965; PhD in Biochemistry, Columbia U., 1974. Rsch. fellow Albert Einstein Coll. Medicine, Bronx, N.Y., 1974-76; rsch. scientist Armauer Hansen Rsch. Inst., Addis Ababa, Ethiopia, 1976-81; sr. staff fellow NIH, Bethesda, Md., 1981-88; chief neurotoxicology sect. Nat. Inst. Neurol. Disorders and Stroke, NIH, 1988—. Cons. WHO/IMMLEP Sci. Working Group, Geneva, 1977, 80, USPHS Hansen's Disease Rsch. Adv. Com., Carville, La., 1983-86. Co-editor: Human Polyomaviruses, 2001; mem. editl. bd. Jour. Neurovirology, 1994—; contbr. articles to profl. jours. Bd. dirs. Internat. Cmty. Sch., Addis Ababa, 1978-81, Mennonite Devel. Rehab. Bd., Addis Ababa, 1978-81, Am. Leprosy Missions, Greenville, S.C., 1987-93. Mem.: AAAS, Am. Soc. Virology. Mennonite. Avocations: book collecting, gardening, travel. Office: NIH Rm 4A 27 Bldg 36 Bethesda MD 20892-0001

STONER, JAMES LLOYD, retired foundation executive, clergyman; b. Point Marion, Pa., Apr. 23, 1920; s. Martin Clark and Bess (Hare) S.; m. Janice Faller Evans, Aug. 28, 1943; children: Thomas Clark, James Douglas and Geoffrey Lloyd (twins). BS, Bethany Coll., 1941, DD (hon.), 1958; BD, MA, Yale U., 1944. Ordained to ministry Christian Ch., 1943; minister in Hamden, Conn., 1942-44; assoc. exec. sec. U. Tex., YMCA, 1944-45; dir. Student Christian Fellowship, Bowling Green State U., 1945-47, Univ. Christian Mission, Fed. Council Ch. and Nat. Council Chs., 1947-56; minister North Christian Ch., Columbus, Ind., 1956-66; asst. gen. sec. for exec. operations Nat. Council Chs., 1966-72; sr. minister Central Christian Ch., Austin, Tex., 1972-80; dep. exec. dir. Found. for Christian Living, Pawling, N.Y., 1980-83, exec. dir., 1983-87. Chmn. com. recommendations Internat. Conv. Christian Chs., 1962-65; bd. mgrs. United Christian Missionary Soc., 1956-63; mem. adv. bd. Am. Bible Soc., 1966-72; life mem. coun. Christian Unity, Christian Ch.; a founder, 1st pres. LINK Award, Ridgewood, N.J., 1966-72; mem. Austin Conf. Chs., pres., 1973-75; rep. Tex. Conf. Chs., 1976-80; mem. goals com. Austin Tomorrow; mem. adv. bd. 1st Comml. Bank of Lakeway, Austin, Tex., 1990-95. Author: Down-to-Earth Meditations That Give You a Lift, 2000; contbr. articles to profl. publs. A founder, bd. dirs. Fellowship Christian Athletes, Kansas City, Mo., 1956-68; trustee Tougaloo (Miss.) Coll., 1968-74; trustee emeritus Lakeway Ch.; v.p., mem. exec. com. Ecumenical Ctr. Continuing Edn., Yale, 1966-72; mem. exec. com. Boy Scouts Am., Austin, 1980, Dutchess County council, 1981-82; bd. mgrs. New Milford Hosp., 1983-88; bd. dirs. Holiday Hills YMCA, 1983-87; com. mem. Town of Pawling 200th Anniversary, 1985-88, Lakeway Ecumenical Ch.; co-founder Holy Week Palm Observance, Lakeway,Tex. Mem. Pawling C. of C. (exec. com. 1984-87), Fellowship of Christian Athletes (nat. adv. bd. 1994—), Masons (32 degree), Pawling Rotary Club (pres. 1983-84, dist. gov.-elect 1991-92, dist. gov. 1992-93, Paul Harris fellow), Shriners, Austin Rotary Club (spl. lifetime mem.), Lake Travis/Lakeway Rotary Club (hon.), Alpha Psi Omega, Beta Theta Pi. Home: 1134 Challenger Austin TX 78734-3802 *Fill every day with rainbow colors, and punctuate life with a positive outlook... Even the Cross of Christ is a positive sign.*

STONER, JOHN RICHARD, federal government executive; b. Ypsilanti, Mich., May 11, 1958; s. Richard P. and Marjorie G. Stoner; m. Diane Leslie Snow. BA in Govt., B in Music Edn., Lawrence U., 1981. Staff asst. Senator Robert Kasten Jr., Washington, 1981-82; staff assoc. Wis. Office Fed.-State Rels., 1982-83; intergovtl. rels. officer U.S. Dept. Transp., 1983-86, congl. rels. officer, 1989-91; dir. Office of Program and Policy Support, Rsch. and Spl. Programs Adminstrn., Dept. Transp., 1991-93; exec. dir. Republican Nat. Lawyers Assn., 1993-97; rep. Primerica Fin. Svcs., 1993-97, mortgage banker, 1998—; state govt. rels. mgr. Am. Trucking Assns., Inc., Alexandria, Va., 1986-88; researcher George Bush for Pres. Com., 1988; staff asst. Office of Pres.-Elect, Washington, 1988-89; state dir. The Century Coun., 2000—. Admissions contact Washington area Lawrence U., 1986-87; softball team mgr. Montgomery County Recreation League. Recipient Eagle Scout award Boy Scouts Am., 1972; Mortar Bd. scholar, 1980; Senate Rep. Policy Com. Legis. fellow, 1993-96. Republican. Mem. Ch. of Christ, Scientist. Avocation: water skiing, organ. Home: 10409 Brunswick Ave Silver Spring MD 20902-4845 Office: The Century Coun 1310 G St NW Washington DC 20005-3000

STONER, LEONARD D. automotive parts company executive; b. Galion, Ohio, Feb. 19, 1950; s. Kenneth M. and Delores I. (Fix) S.; m. Katharine I. Wiese, Feb. 14, 1980; children: Elisha, Cameron, Aaron. AS in Electronics Engring. Tech., Bell Howell U., 1974-76; student, U. Nebr., 1976-80; BS of Bus. Adminstrn. in Tech. Svcs., Bellevue U., 1995. Maintenance stores Keeper Control Data Corp., Omaha, 1978-85; prodn. control mgr. Douglas and Lamason, Richmond, Mich., 1986-87; ops. mgr. Johnson Controls, Lapeer, 1987-89; project mgr. Dohrman Machine Prodn. Inc., Omaha, 1990-92; mgr. prodn. and inventory control Stuart Entertainment, Inc., Council Bluffs, Iowa, 1995-96; materials control mgr. Sears Mfg., Davenport, 1996-98; prodn. control mgr. Nishikawa Standard Co., Topeka, 1998-2000; materials mgr. RoMech, Red Oak, Iowa, 2000—. Assoc. cons. Internat. Purchasing Svc., Dearborn. With USAF, 1970-77. Mem. Am. Prodn. & Inventory Control Soc., Am. Radio Relay League. Avocations: ham radio, camping, boating, woodworking, car repair. Office: RoMech 2700 N Broadway Red Oak IA 51566 Home: 14884 320th St Council Bluffs IA 51503-3948 Fax: 712-487-3858. E-mail: LeonardStoner@email.msn.com., lstoner@romech.com.

STONESIFER, JOHN DEWITT, priest, educator; b. Alexandria, Va., May 26, 1958; s. Joseph Novak and Jean Ann (Fisher) Stonesifer; m. Susan Lee Meachum, June 2, 1984; children: Sarah Anne, John DeWitt. BA cum laude, Clemson U., 1980; MDiv, Va. Theol. Sem., 1984; MBA, Theol. Coll. of the Bahams, 1995. Ordained priest Episcopal ch. Asst. rector St. John's Episcopal Ch., Naples, Fla., 1984-86; rector St. Andrew's Episcopal Ch., Princess Anne, Md., 1986-88; assoc. rector St. Francis Episcopal Ch., Potomac, 1988-90; chaplain, dir. summer program Washington Episcopal Sch., Bethesda, 1990-97; chaplain, head religion dept. Trinity-Pawling (N.Y.) Sch., 1997-99; vicar Chapel of the Holy Spirit, Germantown, Md., 1999—. Ch. cons. Md. parishes, 1995—97. Co-author: (book) Children of Abraham; mem. editl. staff: Eastern Shore Churchman, 1984—86. Bd. dirs. Christmas in April, Montgomery County, 1989—92, Mental Health Assn., Collier County, Fla., 1984—86. Fellow Templeton, Theol. Coll., 1995. Mem.: Washington Episcopal Clergy Assn., Nat. Episcopal Clergy Assn., Nat. Assn. Episcopal Schs. Home and Office: 5 Ingleside Ct Rockville MD 20850-2944 E-mail: jdstone@bestweb.net.

STONG, DAVID HENRY, artist, computer graphic artist; b. Milw., Dec. 2, 1950; s. Roland Oliver and Irene Marie (Gerrits) S. BBA, U. Wis., Madison, 1980; MBA, U. Wis., 1985. Asst. mgr. Wis. Innovation Ctr., Whitewater, 1980-82; program assoc. Ctr. for Creative Leadership, Greensboro, N.C., 1982-85; owner Avatar Cons., 1985-87, Lightspeed GRAFX, Honolulu, 1987-92, 94-95, Glendale, Ariz., 1995—; creative dir. Computer-Aided Tech., Inc., Honolulu, 1992-94. Computer graphics adv. bd. Glendale C.C., 1998—; spkr. Rocky Mt. Inventors Congress Colo., 1984. Graphic designer AmeriVox Collectible Phone Card, Hawaii, 1994, Logo for 50th Anniversary of the End of World War II, 1995. Creative dir. The Future Within Youth Group, Phoenix, 1998—; vol. child care Marcus House, Phoenix, 1995—. Recipient Emmy cert. Nat. Acad. TV Arts and Scis., 1992-93, Mem. Corel Hawaii User Group (pres. 1995-96). Avocations: music, fiction writing, exercise. Home: 22615 N 71st Dr Glendale AZ 85310-5686

STONNINGTON, HENRY HERBERT, physician, medical executive, educator; b. Vienna, Austria, Feb. 12, 1927; came to U.S., 1969; m. Constance Mary Leigh Hamersley, Sept. 19, 1953. MB, BS, Melbourne U., Victoria, Australia, 1950; MS, U. Minn., 1972. Diplomate Am. Bd. Phys. Medicine and Rehab., 1973. Pvt. practice, Sydney, N.S.W., Australia, 1955-65; clin. tchr. U. N.S.W., 1965-69; resident in Phys. Medicine and Rehab. Mayo Clinic, Rochester, Minn., 1969-72, mem. staff, 1972-83; assoc. prof. Mayo Med. Sch., 1975-83; chmn. dept rehab. medicine Med. Coll. Va., Va. Commonwealth U., Richmond, 1983-88, prof. rehab. medicine, 1983-89, dir. rsch. tng. ctr., 1988-89; v.p. med. svcs. Sheltering Arms Hosp., 1985-92; prof. and chmn. dept. phys. medicine and rehab. U. Mo., Columbia, 1992-94; med. dir. Meml. Rehab. Ctr., Savannah, Ga., 1994-97; clin. prof. rehab. medicine Emory U., Atlanta, 1997—2000; clin. prof. medicine sect. phys. medicine and rehab. La. State U., 2001—. Med. dir. rehab. svcs. Meml. Hosp., Gulfport, Miss., 1998—; clin. prof. phys. med. and rehab. La. State U. Med. Sch., 2001—. Editor: Brain Injury, 1987—2001, Pediatric Rehabilitation, 1997—2000; contbr. articles to profl. jours. Recipient award Rsch. Tng. Ctr. Model Sys., Nat. Inst. Disability and Rehab. Rsch., Washington, 1987, 88. Fellow Australian Coll. Rehab. Medicine, Australasian Faculty Rehab. Medicine, Royal Coll. Physicians Edinburgh (Scotland), Am. Acad. Phys. Medicine and Rehab., Am. Coun. Rehab. Medicine, Am. Assn. Acad. Physiatrists; mem. Internat. Brain Injury Assn. (v.p. for sci. affairs 1998—, bd. govs.). E-mail: hencom2731@aol.com.

STOOKEY, GEORGE KENNETH, research institute administrator, dental educator; b. Waterloo, Ind., Nov. 6, 1935; s. Emra Gladison and Mary Catherine (Anglin) S.; m. Nola Jean Meek, Jan. 15, 1955; children: Lynda, Lisa, Laura, Kenneth. AB in Chemistry, Ind. U., 1957, MSD., 1962, PhD in Preventive Dentistry, 1971. Asst. dir. Preventive Dentistry Research Inst., U. Ind., Indpls., 1968-70; assoc. dir. Oral Health Research Inst., U. Ind., 1974-81, 99—, dir., 1981-99; assoc. prof. preventive dentistry Ind. U. Sch. Dentistry, 1973-78, prof., 1978-98, disting. prof., 1998—, assoc. dean rsch., 1987-97, 00-01, acting dean, 1996, assoc. dean acad. affairs, 1997-98, exec. assoc. dean, 1998-2000. Cons. USAF, San Antonio, 1973—, ADA, Chgo., 1972—, Nat. Inst. Dental Rsch., Bethesda, Md., 1978-82, 91-95. Author: (with others) Introduction to Oral Biology and Preventive Dentistry, 1971, Preventive Dentistry for the Dental Assistant and Dental Hygienist, 1977, Preventive Dentistry in Action, 1972ã 8ã (Meritorious award 1973); contbr. more than 245 articles to profl. jours. Mem. Internat. Assn. for Dental Research, European Orgn. Caries Research, Am. Assn. Lab. Animal Sci. Republican. Office: Oral Health Research Inst 719 Indiana Ave Indianapolis IN 46202-6100 E-mail: gstookey@iupui.edu.

STOOKEY, NOEL PAUL, folksinger, composer; b. Balt., Dec. 30, 1937; s. George William and Dorothea (St. Aubrey) S.; m. Mary Elizabeth Bannard, Sept. 4, 1963; children: Elizabeth Drake, Katherine Darby, Anna St. Aubrey. Student, Mich. State U., 1955-58; HHD (hon.), Husson Coll., 1978. Prodn. mgr. Cormac Chem. Corp., N.Y.C., 1959-60; artist in residence Northfield Mount Hermon Sch., 1999. Released album of songs Birds of Paradise, 1954; sang professionally, master ceremonies events, Mich. State U., 1955-58; profl. singer, Greenwich Village, N.Y.C., 1960-61; mem. folksinging group, Peter, Paul and Mary, 1961—; solo rec. artist for Warner Bros., 1971-74; producer folk albums for Scepter Records, Verve/Folkway Records; founder, Neworld Media, rec. studio Neworld Records, 1977-81; rec. artist: Paul And, 1971, One Night Stand, 1972, Real to Reel, 1976, Something New and Fresh, 1978, Band and Bodyworks, 1979, Wait'll You Hear This, 1982, There is Love, 1985, State of the Heart, 1985, In Love Beyond Our Lives, 1990; host Maine Pub. TV broadcasting series "E-Maine", 1997. Mem. AFTRA, Screen Actors Guild, ASCAP, Delta Upsilon. Clubs: St. Botolph's (Boston). Home and Office: Rt 175 Blue Hill Falls ME 04615 Personal E-mail: stook@celestat.com. Business E-Mail: neworld@celestat.com.

STOOKSBURY, WILLIAM CLAUDE, minister; b. Knoxville, Tenn., June 6, 1947; s. William Claude and Vera Faye (Hudman) S.; m. Mary Jayne Moyer, Mar. 21, 1970; 1 child, William David. BS, U. Tenn., Chattanooga, 1980; MDiv, Vanderbilt U., 1987; PhD, Pennington U., 2001. Ordained to ministry Bapt. Ch., 1978; ordinations transfered to Unithed Meth. Ch., 1988. Min. of visitation 1st Bapt. Ch., Chattanooga, 1975-78; pastor Beacon Bapt. Ch., Rossville, Ga., 1978-80; asst. min. Ea. Pkwy. Bapt. Ch., Louisville, 1980-81; pastor 1st Bapt. Ch., Fisherville, Ky., 1981-84, Baker's Grove Bapt. Ch., Mt. Juliet, Tenn., 1984-86, Fairgarden United Meth. Ch., Sevierville, 1988-92, Lonsdale United Meth. Ch., Knoxville, 1992-2000, St. Luke's United Meth. Ch., Knoxville, 2000—. Design team urban ministry Holston Conf., Meth. Ch., Knoxville, 1992. Mem. search com. dean of human svcs. U. Tenn., Chattanooga, 1980; co-chair area II, Campbellsville Coll. Fund-raising, Ky., 1983; mem. steering com. Tenn. Alliance Strong Cmtys., Nashville, 1989—; charter mem. Ams. for Change, Washignton, 1993—; mem. nat. steering com. Clinton/Gore '96 Campaign. Named one of Outstanding Young Men of Am., Outstanding Young Assn., 1982, Dyer scholarship Vanderbilt Div., 1986. Fellow Westar Inst.; mem. ACLU, Am. Acad. Religion, Long Run Bapt. Assn. (chair assn. message com. 1984, com. to study ordination 1982, exec. bd. dirs. 1981-84), People for the Am. Way, The Interfaith Alliance, Internat. Platform Assn. Democrat. Avocation: reading. Home: 2501 Pulaski Rd Knoxville TN 37914-2938 Office: St Luke's United Meth Ch 3839 Buffat Mill Rd Knoxville TN 37914-3398

STOOLMAN, HERBERT LEONARD, public relations executive; b. Newark, Apr. 6, 1917; s. Abe C. and Ida H. (Sinar) S.; AB, Catawba Coll., 1937; BS, Temple U., 1939; postgrad. Harvard U., 1938; m. Sarah Janice Cutler, Apr. 6, 1944; children: Cathy Lynn (Mrs. Richard Schwartz), Robert Henry. Pub., East Camden Newspapers, 1941-57; pres. Stoolman Assos., Camden, N.J., 1946—; dir. public relations Camden County, N.J., 1953-86. Mem. Camden County Econ. Devel. Commn., 1963—, Camden County Cultural and Heritage Commn., 1973—. With USAF, 1942-46. Recipient Nat. award Nat. Assn. Counties, 1969, 72, 78, 79; Nat. award Am. Indsl. Devel. Council, 1963. Mem. Am., N.J. hosps. public relations assns., S. Jersey, Phila. public relations assns., Am. Assn. County Public Relations Officers, N.J. Press Assn., Phila. Press Assn. Lodge: Lions (dir. pub. relations). Home and Office: 6 S Mansfield Ave Margate City NJ 08402-2514

STOOPLER, MARK BENJAMIN, physician; b. N.Y.C., Sept. 29, 1950; s. Alex and Blanche Sylvia (Kappel) S.; m. Lynn Sara Fruchter, Jan. 10, 1982; children: David Andrew, Emily Rachel, Jesse Bryan. BS, Tulane U., 1971; MD, Cornell U., 1975. Diplomate Am. Bd. Internal Medicine, Am. Bd. Oncology. Intern and resident in internal medicine North Shore U. Hosp., Manhasset, N.Y., 1975-78, Meml. Sloan-Kettering Cancer Ctr., N.Y.C., 1975-78, asst. chief resident in medicine, 1978, fellow in med. oncology, 1978-80; asst. attending physician Presbyn. Hosp., 1980-93, assoc. attending physician, 1993—; asst. clin. prof. medicine Columbia U. Coll. of Physicians and Surgeons, 1980-93; assoc. clin. prof. medicine, 1993—. Contbr. articles to profl. jours. Recipient U. scholar Tulane U., 1970-71. Fellow ACP; mem. Am. Soc. of Clin. Oncology, Am. Fedn. for Clin. Research, Internat. Assn. for the Study of Lung Cancer, Phi Beta Kappa. Office: Columbia-Presbyn Med Ctr 161 Fort Washington Ave New York NY 10032-3713

STOOPS, DANIEL J. lawyer; b. Wichita, Kans., May 27, 1934; s. Elmer F. and Margaret J. (Pickrell) S.; m. Kathryn Ann Piepmeier, Aug. 28, 1954; children: Sharon, Janet. BA, Washburn U., 1956, JD, 1958. Bar: Kans. 1958, Ariz. 1959, U.S. Dist. Ct. Kans. 1958, U.S. Dist. Ct. Ariz. 1960, U.S. Ct. Appeals (9th cir.) 1975, U.S. Supreme Ct. 1971. Assoc. Wilson, Compton, & Wilson, Flagstaff, Ariz., 1959-64; ptnr. Wilson, Compton & Stoops, 1964-67, Mangum, Wall & Stoops, Flagstaff, 1967-77, Mangum, Wall, Stoops & Warden, Flagstaff, 1977—. Editor Washburn Law Rev., 1958. Pres. Flagstaff Festival of the Arts, 1988-89, Flagstaff Sch. Bd., 1961-73, Ariz. Sch. Bd. Assn., 1971 Fellow Ariz. Bar Found., Am. Bar Found., Am. Coll. Trial Lawyers (state chmn. 1984-85), Internat. Soc. Barristers; mem. Ariz. Bar Assn. (pres. 1980-81), Masons. Republican. Methodist. Avocations: golf, political and historical reading and research. Office: Mangum Wall Stoops & Warden 100 N Elden St Flagstaff AZ 86001-5295 E-mail: mswattys@aol.com.

STOOPS, EMERY, writer, insurance agent; b. Pratt, Kans., Dec. 13, 1902; s. Eliakum and Mary Elizabeth (Brubaker) Stoops; m. Evelyn Ruth FitzSimmons, Sept. 6, 1929 (dec. Dec. 1936); children: Emelyn, Emerson, Eileen; m. Joyce King, July 3, 1968. AB, U. Colo., 1930; MA, U. So. Calif., L.A., 1934, EdD, 1943. Tchr., supt. Richfield Schs., Kans., 1934—35; tchr. Whittier Union H.S., Calif., 1934—35, Beverly Hills H.S., 1935—39; adult sch. prin. L.A. Sch. Dist., 1940—46; adminstrv. asst. L.A. County Supt. of Schs., L.A., 1946—53; prof. sch. adminstrn. U. So. Calif., 1953—70; life ins. agt. Aetna Life Ins. and Annuity Co., Hartford, Conn., 1972—96, Transamerica, Seal Beach, Calif., 1996—. Author: The Homesteaders, 1993, Psychology of Success, 2001; contbr. Elder, ch. bd. Christian Ch., Westwood, Calif. Recipient Hon. award, Mayor of L.A., 1970, Disting. Emeritus award, Pres. U. So. Calif., 1993. Mem.: Pacific Palisades Rotary (Sr. award 2002). Republican. Christian Ch. Home: 1634 Casale Rd Pacific Palisades CA 90272

STOORZA GILL, GAIL, corporate professional; b. Yoakum, Tex., Aug. 28, 1943; d. Roy Otto and Ruby Pauline (Ray) Blankenship; m. Larry Sttorza, Apr. 27, 1963 (div. 1968); m. Ian M. Gill, Apr. 24, 1981; 1 child, Alexandra Leigh. Student, N. Tex. State U., 1961-63, U. Tex., Arlington, 1963. Stewardess Cen. Airlines, Ft. Worth, 1963; advt. and acctg. exec. Phillips-Ramsey Advt., San Diego, 1963-68; dir. advt. Rancho Bernardo, 1968-72; dir. corp. communications Avco Community Developers, 1972-74; pres. Gail Stoorza Co., 1974—, Stoorza, Ziegaus & Metzger, San Diego, 1974—; CEO Stoorza, Ziegaust, Metzger, Inc., 1993—; chmn. Stoorza/Smith, San Diego, 1984-85, Stoorza Internat., San Diego, 1984-85; CEO ADC Stoorza, 1987—2001, Franklin Stoorza, San Diego, 1993—2001. Trustee San Diego Art Found.; bd. dirs. San Diego Found. for Performing Arts, San Diego Opera, Sunbelt Nursery Groups, Dallas. Names Small Bus. Person of Yr. Selest Com. on Small Bus., 1984, one of San Diego's Ten Outstanding Young Citizens San Diego Jaycees, 1979; recipient Woman of Achievement award Women in Communications Inc., 1985. Mem. Pubs. Soc. Am., Nat. Assn. Home Builders (residential mktg. com.), COMBO. Clubs: Chancellors Assn. U. Calif. (San Diego), Pub. Relations, San Diego Press. Methodist.*

STOPFORD, MICHAEL JOHN, university administrator; b. June 22, 1953; MA in English Lang. and Lit., Oxford (Eng.) U., 1975. With U.K. Diplomatic Svc., London, N.Y.C. and Vienna, 1975-79; sec. UN, N.Y.C. and Geneva, 1980-95, dir. Info. Ctr. Washington, 1992-95; chief media and pub. rels. Internat. Fin. Corp., 1996-97; sr. asst. to pres. Am. U., 1997—. Office: Am U 4400 Massachusetts Ave NW Washington DC 20016 E-mail: mjs@american.edu.

STOPHER, PETER ROBERT, civil and transportation engineering educator, consultant; b. Crowborough, Eng., Aug. 8, 1943; arrived in U.S., 1968,arrived in Australia, 2000; s. Harold Edward and Joan Constance (Salmon) S; m. Valerie Anne Alway, Apr. 11, 1964 (div. Feb. 1989); children: Helen Margaret Anne, Claire Elizabeth; m. Catherine Coville Jones July 7, 1990 (div. Apr. 1997); m. Carmen Louise Palermo, May 2, 1997. BSCE, U. Coll., London, 1964, PhD, 1967. Research officer Greater London Council, London, 1967-68; asst. prof. transp. planning, applied statistics, math. modeling Northwestern U., Evanston, Ill., 1968-70, from assoc. prof. to prof., 1973-79, vis. prof., 1980-81; asst. prof. McMaster U., Hamilton, Ontario, 1970-71; assoc. prof. Cornell U., Ithaca, N.Y., 1971-73; tech. v.p. Schimpeler Corradino Assoc., Miami, Fla., and Los Angeles, 1980-84, v.p., 1984-87; dir., CFO Evaluation and Tng. Inst., 1987-90; prin., co-founder Applied Mgmt. and Planning Group, 1988-90; prof. civil engring. La. State Univ., Baton Rouge, 1990-2000, dir. La. Transp. Rsch. Ctr., 1990-93; co-founder, ptnr. PlanTrans, 1994—; disting. prof. La. Land & Exploration Co., 1999-2000; prof. transport planning Inst. Transport Studies Univ. Sydney, 2001—. Spl. advisor Nat. Inst. Transp. and Rd. Research, Pretoria, S. Africa, 1976-77; vis. prof. U. Syracuse, N.Y., 1971-73, U. Louvain, Belgium, 1980, Inst. Transport Studies, U. Sydney, Australia, 1999; guest prof. U. für Bodenkultur, Vienna, 1998-99. Co-author Urban Transportation Planning and Modeling, 1974, Transportation Systems Evaluation, 1976, Survey Sampling and Multivariate Analysis, 1978; contbr. articles to profl. jours. Mem. Baton Rouge Symphony Chorus, 1996-99. Recipient Fred Burgraaf prize Hwy. Research Bd., 1968, Jules Dupuit prize World Conf. on Transp. Rsch., 1992, Joyce E. Yeager prize Transp. Rsch. Forum, 1994. Mem. ASCE, Am. Stats. Assn., Transp. Rsch. Bd. (com. chmn. 1970-77, 95-97, emeritus mem. 2002-), Transp. Rsch. Forum (Joyce E. Yaeger Intermodel Rsch. Paper award 1994), Inst. Transp. Engrs. Republican. Mem. Lds Ch. Avocations: gardening, photography, reading, classical music. Home: 3 Torrens Pl Cromer NSW 2099 Australia Office: U Sydney Inst Transport Studies C37 Sydney NSW 2006 Australia E-mail: peters@its.usyd.edu.au.

STOPP, DONALD L. retired educator, retired business owner; b. Allentown, PA, Mar. 15, 1928; s. Marcus Martin and Dorothy May; m. Jacklin Talmage Stopp, Dec. 22, 1967. AB, Duke Univ., Durham, NC, 1954; MBA courses, Univ. Buffalo, Buffalo, NY, 1973-74. Social Studies cert., East Stroudsburg Univ., East Stroudsburg, PA, 1957, Buffalo Univ., Buffalo, NY, 1972. Tchr. Kennett Square High School, KennettSquare, PA, 1957-58; social studies tchr. The Gow School, South Wales, NY, 1958-60; sales position Marquis Who's

Who, Chicago, IL, 1960-61; caseworker Erie County Dept. Social Svcs., Buffalo, 1961-63; driving instr. Three Buffalo Schs., 1964-66; rememdial math tchr. Buffalo Public Schs., 1966-70; owner, distr. Thesaurus Wholesale Maps, Lockport, 1975-91. Dept. head, Montgomery Ward, Springfield, IL, 1955-56, econs. instr., Leelanau Schs., Leelanau, Mich., 1965, sales, pub. rels., Goodwill Industries, Buffalo, NY, 1972-73, owner, founder, Pac-N-Ship, Buffalo, NY, 1980-84. Spkr. and lectr. in field. Mem. Kiwanis Club of Lockport (bd. dirs. 1997-01), Niagara County Hist. Soc., Canal Task Force C. of C. Avocations: history, past, present, future applications, The Cold War past and residual effects.

STOPPA, GERMAINE, community service executive; b. Alpena, Mich., Sept. 16, 1953; d. Eugene Stanley Stoppa and Pearl Ada Miller. HS, Alpena H.S., 1971. Office mgr. Real Estate One, Alpena, 1980-85, United Way of Northeast Mich., Alpena, 1985-95, assoc. dir., 1995-96, exec. dir., 1996—. Mem. Alpena Women's Bowling Assn. (treas. 1993—), Alpena Rotary Club (sec. 1999—). Roman Catholic. Avocations: bowling, camping, reading, biking. E-mail: rsomm@12k.net.

STORANDT, MARTHA, psychologist; b. Little Rock, June 2, 1938; d. Farris and Floy (Montgomery) Mobbs; m. Duane Storandt, Dec. 15, 1962; 1 child, Eric AB, Washington U., St. Louis, 1960, PhD, 1966. Lic. psychologist, Mo. Staff psychologist VA, Jefferson Barracks, Mo., 1967-68; asst. prof. to prof. Washington U., St. Louis, 1968—. Mem. nat. adv. council on aging Nat. Inst. on Aging, 1984-87; editor-in-chief Jour. Gerontology, 1981-86 Author: Counseling and Therapy with Older Adults, 1983; co-author: Memory, Related Functions and Age, 1974; co-editor: The Clinical Psychology of Aging, 1978, The Adult Years: Continuity and Change, 1989, Neuropsychological Assessment of Dementia and Depression in Older Adults: A Clinician's Guide, 1994. Recipient Disting. Service award Mo. Assn. Homes for the Aging, 1984. Fellow APA (pres. divsn. 20 1979-80, council rep. 1983-84, 86-88, Disting. Sci. Contbn. award divsn. adult devel. and aging 1988, Master Mentor award divsn. adult devel. and aging 2000, Disting. Contbns. to Clin. Geropsychology divsn. clin. psychology 2002), Gerontol. Soc. Am. Office: Washington U Dept Psychology Saint Louis MO 63130

STORB, JOHN WILLIAM, civil engineer, consultant; b. New Holland, Pa., Apr. 26, 1924; s. Lewis Mentzer and Elizabeth (Baumler) S.; m. m. Louise Catherine Williams, June 17, 1950; children: Audrey Louise, Diane Elaine, John William Jr., Nancy Suzanne. BS in Mil. Art and Engring., U.S. Mil. Acad., West Point, N.Y., 1945; MSCE, Ga. Inst. Tech., 1951. Registered profl. engr., D.C., 12 states. Commd. 2d lt. USAF, 1945, advanced through grades to capt., 1952, fighter pilot Japan, 1946-48, ops. officer Mitchel Field, N.Y., 1948-49; mem. radar outfit Pope AFB, N.C., 1951-52; civil engr. USAF Hqrs. Europe, 1952-54; engr. USAF Corps of Engrs Office, Boston, 1954-55; chief engr. mktg. Gulf Oil Corp., Phila., 1955-64; owner Storb Inc., Willow Grove, Pa., 1964—. Profl. engr. storage tank adv. com. Commonwealth of Pa., Harrisburg, 1992-96, mem. gov. com. to rev. fire marshal regulations, 1964-65. Mem. fundraising com. Holy Redeemer Hosp., Huntingdon Valley, Pa., 1998. Mem. NSPE, Nat. Fire Protection Assn. Avocations: golfing, fishing. Home: 2725 Brendan Cir Huntingdon Valley PA 19006-5524 Office: Storb Inc 410 Easton Rd Willow Grove PA 19090-2511

STORB, URSULA BEATE, molecular genetics and cell biology educator; b. Stuttgart, Germany; came to U.S., 1966; d. Walter M. Stemmer and Marianne M. (Kämmerer) Nowara. MD, U. Freiburg, Germany, 1960. Asst. prof. dept. microbiology U. Wash., Seattle, 1971-75, assoc. prof., 1975-81, prof., 1981-86, head. div. immunology, 1980-86; prof. dept. molecular genetics and cell biology U. Chgo., 1986—. Mem. editl. bd. Immunity, Current Opinion in Immunology, Internat. Immunology, Immunol. Revs.; contbr. articles to sci. jours. Grantee NIH, NSF, Am. Cancer Soc., 1973—. Fellow Am. Acad. Arts and Scis.; mem. AAAS, Assn. Women in Sci., Am. Assn. Immunologists. Office: U Chgo 920 E 58th St Chicago IL 60637-5415 E-mail: stor@midway.uchicago.edu.

STORBERG, ERIC PHILIP, financial planner; b. S.I., N.Y., Nov. 30, 1959; s. Arthur Lincoln Storberg and Donna Marie (Ford) Bertoldo; m. Joy Theresa Scaglione, June 16, 1984 (div. May 1996); children: Ryan, Kevin, Paul; m. Kristine Matarese, Oct. 27, 2000. BS in Econs., Coll. S.I., 1988. CFP. CFP Am. Express Fin. Advisors, S.I. Bd. mem. S.I. Cares Inc., 1993-2000, Rainbows Hope Inc., S.I., 1996-2001; chmn. bd. S.I. AIDS Task Force, 1996—. Mem. North Shore Dem. Club S.I., South Shore Rotary Club S.I. (treas. 1993-95, v.p. 1999, pres.-elect 2000, pres. 2001). Avocation: harness racing. Office: Am Express Fin Advs 900 South Ave Staten Island NY 10314-3425 Home: Apt 5I 50 Belair Rd Staten Island NY 10305-3055 E-mail: eric.p.storberg@aexp.com.

STORCH, ARTHUR, theater director; b. Bklyn., June 29, 1925; s. Sam and Bessie (Goldner) S.; children: Max Darrow, Alexander English, Bess Martin. BA, New Sch. Social Research, 1949. Actor in Broadway prodns. End as a Man, 1953, Time Limit, 1955, Girls of Summer, 1956, Look Homeward, Angel, 1957, Night Circus, 1958, The Long Dream, 1960, The Best Man, 1961; motion pictures The Strange One, 1956, Girls of the Night, 1959, The Exorcist, 1974; dir. off-Broadway Two by Saroyan, 1961, Three by Three, 1962, Talking to You (London debut), 1962, The Typists and the Tiger, 1963, The Owl and the Pussycat, 1964, The Impossible Years, 1965, The Local Stigmatic, 1970, Under the Weather, 1965, Golden Rainbow, 1967, The Chinese and Dr. Fish, 1969, Promenade All, 1970, 42 Seconds from Broadway, 1973, Tribute, 1978, Twice Around the Park, 1982, Clarence, 1986; Of Mice and Men, 1988; dir. nat. tour The King and I, 1989; dir. Syracuse Stage Waiting for Lefty, Noon, Of Mice and Men, 1974, 75, La Ronde, The Butterfingers Angel. Mornings at Seven, Dynamo, 1975-76, A Quality of Mercy, The Seagull, 1976-77, 1976-77, Love Letters on Blue Paper, End of the Beginning, 1977-78, Loved, 1978, Naked, 1979, The Comedy of Errors, 1980, The Impromptu of Outremont, 1982, The Double Bass, 1984, Arms and the Man, Handy Dandy, Cyrano de Bergerac, Romeo and Juliet, 1986, Of Mice and Men, N.Y.C., 1987, Fugue, 1988, Seven By Beckett, 1988, Look Homeward Angel, Wait Unitl Dark, Dangerous Corner, 1990, A Walk in the Woods, 1989, Finding Donis Ann, 1990, Androcles and the Lion, 1991; Lend Me a Tenor, 1992; Awake and Sing, 1993; dir., actor Love Letters, 1992. Founder, producing artistic dir. Syracuse Stage; chmn. drama dept. Syracuse U., 1974-92, Arthur Storch Theatre, 1992. Home: 148 Hommelville Rd Saugerties NY 12477-4204

STORCH, SUSAN BOROWSKI, lawyer; b. Jersey City, June 23, 1961; d. Raymond Edward and Clara Mary (Stryzek) Borowski; m. Michael John Storch, Feb. 9, 1985; children: Samantha Clare, Michael John Jr. BA, Rutgers U., 1983; JD, Seton Hall U., 1990. Bar: N.J. 1991. Corp. trust adminstr. Mfrs. Hanover Trust Co., N.Y.C., 1983-86; law clk. Congressman Dean Gallo, Washington, 1988, N.J. Supreme Ct. Com. on Complementary Dispute Resolution, Trenton, N.J., 1988; law clk. to asst. atty. gen. legis. affairs U.S. Dept. Justice, Washington, 1989; assoc. Rodino & Rodino, East Hanover, NJ, 1991—92; sr. assoc. Fragomen, Del Rey & Bernsen, Iselin, 1992—98, ptnr., 1998—2000; ptnr., chair corp. immigration practice group Sills Commis Radin Tischman Epstein & Gross, Newark, 2000—. Lectr. in field. Bd. dirs. Players Forum, N.Y.C., 1993-94; coord. Corp. Giving Coun., N.J. Women's Polit. Caucus, 1995; active various polit. fundraising campaigns. Recipient Commendation award Essex County Bd. Chosen Freeholders, N.J., 1990; Lyndon B. Johnson Congl. scholar, 1988. Mem.: ABA (labor and employment law sect. 1994—95), Exec. Women N.J. (nominations com.), Ctr. Study of Presidency, Psychology Assn. Am., Inst. Cont. Legal Edn. and Info. (N.J.), Coun. Internat. Personnel, Am. Immigration Lawyer Assn. (former press sec., former sec.), N.J. Bar Assn. (exec. bd. programs ctr. 1994—95). Democrat. Avocations: writing, sailing, golf. Office: Stills Cummis Radin Tischman Epstein & Gross PA One Riverfront Plaza Newark NJ 07102-5400

STORCK, THOMAS CHARLES JOLIFFE, author, librarian; b. Bklyn., Jan. 25, 1951; s. John Norman and Elizabeth Marian (Gabbert) S.; m. Martha Goddard Furman, May 11, 1974 (dec. July 1987); children: Michael Hector, Mary Gwyn, Clare Marie, Gabriel Charles; m. Inez Marie Fitzgerald, Dec. 12, 1987. BA, Kenyon Coll., 1973; MLS, La. State U., 1978; MA, St. John's Coll., Santa Fe, 1980. Documents libr. Okla. State U., Stillwater, 1979-81; libr. Christendom Coll., Front Royal, Va., 1981-85; philosophy instr. Mt. Aloysius Coll., Cresson, Pa., 1986; libr. Mount de Sales Acad., Catonsville, Md., 1986-88; lectr. philosophy Catonsville C.C., 1988; law libr. U.S. Treasury Dept. Libr., Washington, 1989—. Author: The Catholic Milieu, 1987, Foundations of a Catholic Politicl Order, 1998, Christendom and the West, 2000; contbr. numerous articles to profl. jours. and mags. Mem. K. Roman Catholic.

STORDALEN, DAVID JOHN, music educator; b. Fargo, N.D., July 17, 1968; s. Karlton B. and Emilie A. Stordalen; children: Anthony, Joshua. BS in Music Edn., N.D. State U., 1992. Cert. K-12 Instrumental, Vocal and Classroom Music Tchr. Minn., 2001. Band dir. Grand Forks Pub. Sch., Grand Forks, ND, 1997—99, St. James Pub. Sch., St. James, Minn., 1999—. Pres. Dist. 840 Found., St. James, 2001—. Sgt. U.S. Army, 1993—97. Mem.: Am. Legion. Lutheran. Avocations: music performance, reading, bicycling, weight-lifting, wrestling. Office: ISD 840 St James Public Schools 500 8th Ave S Saint James MN 56081 E-mail: dstordalen@stjames.k12.mn.us.

STORER, MARYRUTH, law librarian; b. Portland, Oreg., July 26, 1953; d. Joseph William and Carol Virginia (Pearson) Storer; m. David Bruce Bailey, 1981; children: Sarah, Allison. BA in History, Portland State U., 1974; JD, U. Oreg., 1977; M in Law Librarianship, U. Wash., 1978. Bar: Oreg. 1978. Assoc. law libr. U. Tenn., Knoxville, 1978-79; law libr. O'Melveny & Myers, L.A., 1979-88; dir. Orange County Pub. Law Libr., Santa Ana, Calif., 1988—. Mem. Am. Assn. Law Librs. (exec. bd. 1999-2002), So. Calif. Assn. Law Librs. (pres. 1986-87), Coun. Calif. County Law Librs. (sec.-treas. 1990-94, pres. 1994-96), Arroyo Seco Libr. Network (chair 2000—). Democrat. Episcopalian. Office: Orange County Public Law Library 515 N Flower St Santa Ana CA 92703-2304

STORER, NORMAN WILLIAM, sociology educator; b. Middletown, Conn., May 8, 1930; s. Norman Wyman and Mary Emily (House) S.; m. Ada Joan Van Valkenburg, Aug. 19, 1951; children: Martin Wilson, Thomas Wyman; m. Mary Ashton Pott Hiatt, Mar. 7, 1975. AB, U. Kans., 1952, MA, 1956; PhD, Cornell U., 1961. Lectr., asst. prof. Harvard U., Cambridge, Mass., 1960-66; staff assoc. Social Sci. Research Council, N.Y.C., 1966-70; prof. sociology CUNY-Baruch Coll., 1970-88, prof. emeritus, 1989—, dept. chmn., 1970-85, chmn. faculty senate, 1981-84. Author: The Social System of Science, 1966, Focus on Society, 1973, 2d edit., 1980, A Leer of Limericks, 1990, (with William Flores) Domestic Violence in Suburban San Diego, 1994; editor: The Sociology of Science, 1973; column editor San Diego Writers' Monthly, 1992-94. Vol. San Diego Sheriff's Dept., 1992—; mem. San Diego Hate Crimes Registry Mgmt. Team, 1993—. Sgt. AUS, 1953-55. Mem.: AAAS, Sigma Xi (sec. chpt. 2001—), Phi Beta Kappa. Democrat. Home: 1417 Van Buren Ave San Diego CA 92103-2339 E-mail: mwstorer@peoplepc.com.

STOREY, BOBBY EUGENE, JR. electrical engineer, engineering consultant; b. Bainbridge, Md., Jan. 26, 1958; s. Bobby E. Sr. and Rebecca J. (Seagraves) S.; m. Lynn M. Miller, May 24, 1976 (div. June 1988); 1 child, Christopher David; m. Mary H. Freeman, Feb. 14, 1992. AA in Math., Gordon Jr. Coll., 1986; BS in Applied Physics, Ga. Inst. Tech., 1988, M in Applied Physics, 1989; grad., N.Y. Inst. Photography, 1998. Engr. instrumentation and controls Va. Power Co., Mineral, 1982-85; engr. electro optics GEC Avionics, Norcross, Ga., 1988; v.p. EnerSci Inc., 1989-94; project engr. LXE, Inc., 1988-94; pres. E & H Enterprises, Inc., Duluth, Ga., 1994-96; mgr. engring. project office Sci. Atlanta, Inc., Norcross, 1995-96; dir. engring. project office Sci.-Atlanta Inc., 1996-98, dir. engring. Ga., 1998—. With USN, 1976-82. Mem. Internat. Orgn. Electrical and Electronic Engrs. Republican. Avocations: coins, woodworking, target shooting, photography. Home: 5311 Channel Dr Gillsville GA 30543-2800 Office: Sci Atlanta Inc 4386 Park Dr Norcross GA 30093-2906

STOREY, BRIT ALLAN, historian; b. Boulder, Colo., Dec. 10, 1941; s. Harold Albert and Gladys Roberta (Althouse) S.; m. Carol DeArman, Dec. 19, 1970; 1 child, Christine Roberta. AB, Adams State Coll., Alamosa, Colo., 1963; MA, U. Ky., 1965, PhD, 1968. Instr. history Auburn (Ala.) U., 1967-68, asst. prof., 1968-70; dep. state historian State Hist. Soc. Colo., Denver, 1970-71, acting state historian, 1971-72, rsch. historian, 1972-74; hist. preservation specialist Adv. Coun. on Hist. Preservation, Lakewood, Colo., 1974-88; sr. historian Bur. Reclamation, 1988—. Contbr. articles to profl. publs. Mem. Fed. Preservation Forum (pres. 1990-91), Naf. Coun. Pub. History (sec. 1987, pres.-elect 1990-91, pres. 1991-92), Orgn. Am. Historians (com. 1983-86, chmn. 1985-86), Victorian Soc. Am. (bd. dirs. 1977-79), Western History Assn. (chmn. com. 1982-86), Colo.-Wyo. Assn. Mus. (sec. 1974-76, pres. 1976-77), Cosmos Club (Washington). Avocation: birding. Home: 7264 W Otero Ave Littleton CO 80128-5639 Office: Bur Reclamation Denver Fed Ctr D 5300 Bldg 67 Denver CO 80225-0007

STOREY, CHARLES PORTER, lawyer; b. Austin, Tex., Dec. 4, 1922; s. Robert Gerald and Frances Hazel (Porter) S.; m. Helen Hanks Stephens, Oct. 14, 1950; children: Charles Porter, Harry Stephens, Frederick Schatz. BA, U. Tex., 1947, LLB, 1948; LLM, So. Methodist U., 1952. Bar: Tex. 1948. Pvt. practice law, Dallas, 1948—; sr. counsel Carrington Coleman Sloman & Blumenthal, LLP. Pres. Dallas Day Nursery Assn., 1958, Greater Dallas Coun. Chs., 1970-71; chmn. Internat. Com. YMCA, 1969-71; nat. bd. dirs. U.S. YMCA, 1964-75; pres. Children's Devel. Ctr., Dallas, 1959; trustee Baylor Coll. Dentistry, 1981-90, Hillcrest Found., 1994—; trustee emeritus Southwestern Legal Found., chmn. 1980-90; dir. Zale Lipsky U. Med. Ctr., 1999—. 1st lt., pilot USAAF, 1943-45, ETO. Decorated Air medal. Master Dallas Inn of Ct. (pres. 1991-93); fellow Am. Coll. Trial Lawyers, Am. Bar Found., Tex. Bar Found.; mem. ABA, Tex. Bar Assn. (bd. dirs. 1976-79), Dallas Bar Assn. (pres. 1975), Philos. Soc. Tex., Dallas Country Club, Crescent Club, Idlewild Club, Phi Delta Phi, Phi Delta Theta. Mem. Christian Ch. (Disciples Of Christ). Home: 5855 Farquhar Ln Dallas TX 75209 Office: 200 Crescent Ct Ste 1500 Dallas TX 75201-7839 Fax: 214-855-1333. E-mail: cstorey@ccsb.com.

STOREY, FRANCIS HAROLD, business consultant, retired bank executive; b. Calgary, Alberta, Can., June 20, 1933; s. Bertwyn Morrell and Hilda Josephine (Masters) S.; m. Willomae Saiter, Apr. 25, 1954; children: Daryl, Elizabeth, Brian, Shelley. Student, Gonzaga U., 1953, Pacific Coast Bankers Sch., 1974-76. Designated Certified Profl. Cons. Bank trainee Wash. Trust Bank, Spokane, 1950-56; owner Storey & Storey, 1956-64; agt. Bankers Life Nebr., 1964-67; sr. v.p. Old Nat. Bank, 1967-87, U.S. Bank of Wash., Spokane, 1987-90; pvt. practice cons., 1990—. Bd. dirs. Output Tech. Corp. Bd. dirs. Spokane Bus. Incubator, 1985-96, United Way of Spokane, 1987-95; bd. dirs., treas., fin. chair, gen. conv. dep. Episc. Diocese Spokane Dep., 1969-2001; trustee Spokane Symphony Soc., 1986-93, Spokane Area Econ. Devel. Coun., 1982-89; mem. adv. bd. Intercollegiate Ctr. Nursing Edn., 1990-96, chair, 1996; bd. dirs. Coalition for Women on Streets, treas., fin. chmn., 1999-2001. Mem. Acad. Profl. Cons. and Advisors, Inland N.W. Soc. Cons. Profls., Spokane Rotary, Spokane Country Club, Spokane Club. Episcopalian. Avocations: golf, reading, travel. Home: 214 E 13th Ave Spokane WA 99202-1115 E-mail: fhstorey@home.com.

STOREY, HARRY STEPHENS, lawyer; b. Dallas, June 24, 1955; s. Charles P. and Helen (Stephens) S.; m. Janet Brueggen, Aug. 20, 1983; children: William C., Christine A., Lisa M., Brooke A. BBA, U. Tex., Austin, 1978; JD, So. Meth. U., 1983; MS in Mgmt. and Adminstrv. Svcs., U. Tex., Dallas, 1986. Bar: Tex. 1984. Supr. United Techs.-Mostek, Carrollton, Tex., 1980-81; pres. Storey Corp., Dallas, 1983-89, Discount Realty Co., Dallas, 1984-89; exec. dir. Richards, Medlock & Andrews, 1989-96, Gallop, Johnson & Neuman, St. Louis, 1996-99; COO, Kostin, Ruffkess & Co., LLC, Hartford, Conn., 2000—. Mem. Assn. Legal Adminstrs. (pres. Dallas chpt. 1989-96). Office: Kostin Ruffkess & Co LLC 345 N Main St Ste 200 West Hartford CT 06117 E-mail: hss@kostin.com.

STOREY, JAMES MOORFIELD, lawyer; b. Boston, Apr. 12, 1931; s. Charles Moorfield and Susan Jameson (Sweetser) S.; m. Adair Miller, Aug. 28, 1954 (div. 1973); children: Barbara Sessums Storey McGrath, Mary Sweetser Storey Meley, Susan Adair Storey Frank, Eliza Allison Tebo Storey Anderson, Alice Leovy Storey Wille; m. Isabelle Helene Boeschenstein, May 17, 1973 AB, Harvard U., 1953, LL.B., 1956. Bar: Mass. 1956. Atty. SEC, Washington, 1956-57, legal asst. to chmn., 1957-59; assoc. Gaston, Snow, Motley & Holt, Boston, 1959-62; ptnr. Gaston, Snow, Motley & Holt (name changed to Gaston Snow & Ely Bartlett), 1962-87, Dechert Price & Rhoads, Boston, 1987-94, ret., 1994, profl. trustee, corp. dir., 1994—. Trustee Mt. Auburn Cemetery, Cambridge, Mass., 1980— Co-author: Mutual Fund Law Handbook, 1998, The Uneasy Chaperone, 2000. Mem. ABA, Boston Bar Assn., Tavern Club Boston (pres. 1985-87), Century Assn. of N.Y. Unitarian Universalist. Home: 89A Mt Vernon St Boston MA 02108-1330 Office: 5 Boylston Pl Boston MA 02116

STOREY, KENNETH BRUCE, biology educator; b. Taber, Alta., Can., Oct. 23, 1949; s. Arthur George and Madeleine Una (Mawhinney) S.; m. Janet Margaret Collicutt, June 6, 1975; children: Jennifer, Kathryn. BSc with honors, U. Calgary, Alta., 1971; PhD, U. B.C., Vancouver, Can., 1974. Asst. prof. Duke U., Durham, N.C., 1975-79; assoc. prof. Carleton U., Ottawa, Ont., Can., 1979-85, prof. Can., 1985—. Invited lectr. numerous confs., univs. Editor Cell and Molecular Responses to Stress; mem. editl. bd. Jour. Comparative Physiology, 1995—; contbr. over 400 articles to profl. jours. Recipient E.W.R. Steacie award Nat. Sci. and Engring. Rsch. Coun. Can., 1984-86, Killam sr. rsch. fellow, 1993-95. Fellow AAAS, Royal Soc. Can.; mem. Am. Soc. Biol. Chemists, Can. Biochem. Soc. (Ayerst award 1989), Can. Soc. Zoology, Soc. Cryobiology. Avocations: movies, music, Renaissance art. Office: Carleton U Dept Biology 1125 Colonel By Drive Ottawa ON Canada K1S 5B6 E-mail: kenneth_storey@carleton.ca.

STOREY, LEE A. lawyer; b. Ypsilanti, Mich., Nov. 28, 1959; d. Henry Perry Herold and Elsie Lorraine (Long) Wolf; m. William Storey; children: Jason Michael, Jenifer Lorraine. Student, U. Mich., 1977-79; BA, UCLA, 1982, MA, 1984; JD, U. Calif., Berkeley, 1987. Bar: Ariz. 1988, U.S. Dist. Ct. 1990. Circulations mgr. Inst. Archaeology UCLA, 1980-84; rsch. asst. John Muir Inst., Napa, Calif., 1985, Am. Indian Resources Inst., Oakland, 1985; assoc. editor Ecology Law Quarterly U. Calif., Berkeley, 1985-86; assoc. Evans, Kitchel & Jenckes, Phoenix, 1987-89, Gallagher & Kennedy, Phoenix, 1989-90, Meyer, Hendricks, Victor, Osborn & Maledon, Phoenix, 1991-95; ptnr. Meyer Hendricks Bivens & Moyes P.A., 1995-99; prin. ptnr. Moyes Storey, Ltd., 1999—. Guest lectr. water transfers Hydrological Soc. Symposium, Phoenix, 1989, environ. studies Ariz. State U., Tempe, 1990, water quality Soc. Mining Engrs., Denver, 1991, water transfers Wind River Assocs., Denver, 1991-92, Phoenix, 1992, Central Ariz. Project Utilization, Am. Water Resources Assn. Symposium, Tucson, 1992, Colo. River Basin Tribes, Coun. Energy Resource Tribes, Tucson, 1993, Indian Sovereignty, U.S. Dept. Interior, Bureau Reclamation, Phoenix, 1993; Indian Econ. Devel. Fed. Indian Bar Albuquerque, 1994, Water Rights, Ariz. Judicial Conf., Ariz. State Bar, Tucson, 1994, National Land Coun. sem., Water Rights, Rico Rico, Ariz., 1995, Ariz. Water Law, 2000; chair Ambs. for Change, 1996—; adj. prof. Indian water rights Sch. Law Ariz. State U., 1992, 97, mem. adv. com. on Indian law program Coll. of Law, 1999—, guest lectr. Flagstaff leadership program, 2000, 02. Co-author: Leasing Indian Water: Choices in Colorado River Basin, 1988; contbr. articles to profl. jours.; mem. Calif. Law Rev. U. Calif. Berkeley, 1985-87. Landlord tenant clinics Vols. Lawyers Program, Phoenix, 1988-89; mem. Ariz. Ctr. for Law-Related Edn., Ariz. Bar Found., Drug Awareness Program for Schs., 1990; chmn. bd. Ambs. for Change, 1996—; mem. Ariz. Town Hall, 1997, 2000. Scholar UCLA, 1980-84; recipient Am. Jurisprudence award Lawyers Coop., 1986. Mem. ABA, Ariz. State Bar Assn. (mem. com. on minorities and women in law 1993-97, chair-elect Indian law sect. 1997-98, chair 1998—, asst. editor Environ. and Natural Resources newsletter 1990-94, editor Indian law sect. Arrow newsletter 1996—), Ariz. Women Lawyers Assn., Maricopa County Bar Assn. Office: Moyes Storey 3003 N Central Ave Ste 1250 Phoenix AZ 85012-2923

STOREY, NORMAN C. lawyer; b. Miami, Fla., Oct. 11, 1943; BA cum laude, Loyola U., L.A., 1965; JD, U. Ariz., 1968. Bar: Ariz. 1968. Law clk. to Hon. James A. Walsh U.S. Dist. Ct. Ariz.; ptnr. Squire, Sanders & Dempsey, L.L.P., Phoenix. Mem. State Bar Ariz., Am. Arbitration Assn. (panelist). Office: 40 N Central Ave Ste 2700 Phoenix AZ 85004-4498

STORHOFF, DIANA CARMACK, research scientist; b. Anderson, Ind., Sept. 10, 1946; d. William Paul and Elsie Bernice (Wilson) Carmack; m. Bruce Norman Storhoff, July 25, 1970 (div. Mar. 1990); children: Damon Anthony, James Justin. BS, Ball State U., 1969, MS in Chemistry, 1973; MS, U. Fla., 1996; PhD, Northwestern U., 1999. Sec. Carmack's Inc., 1962; tchg. asst. Ball State U., Muncie, Ind., 1971-73, chemistry prof., 1981-82, 83-87; chemistry tchr. Delta H.S., 1982-83; rsch. scientist Boehringer Mannheim Corp., Indpls., 1987-98, Roche Diagnostics, 1999. Author: (poetry) Live Again, 1995, A Rose Upon The Mist, 1997, Where Eagles Dare Not Soar, 1998. Natural resources chair LWV, Muncie, 1981-97; chmn. conservation Audubon Soc., Muncie; bd. dirs. Mayors Task Force, Muncie. Named Internat. Poet of Merit. Mem. Am. Chem. Soc. Office: Roche Diagnostics 9115 Hague Rd Indianapolis IN 46256-1045 E-mail: donyasol@aol.com.

STORIN, MATTHEW VICTOR, retired newspaper editor; b. Springfield, Mass., Dec. 24, 1942; s. Harry Francis and Blanche Marie S.; m. Keiko Takita, Aug. 1, 1975; 1 child, Kenyatta; children by previous marriage: Karen, Aimee, Sean. BA, U. Notre Dame, 1964. Reporter Springfield Daily News, 1964-65, Griffin-Larrabee News Bur., Washington, 1965-69; Washington corr., city editor, Asian corr., nat. editor, asst. mng. editor, dep. mng. editor, mng. editor Boston Globe, 1969-85; dep. mng. editor U.S. News & World Report, Washington, 1985-86; editor, sr. v.p. Chgo. Sun-Times, 1986-87; editor The Maine Times, Topsham, 1988-89; mng. editor N.Y. Daily News, 1989-91, exec. editor, 1991-92, Boston Globe, 1992-93, editor, 1993—2001. Recipient Disting. Polit. Reporting award Am. Assn. Polit. Sci., 1969, Yankee Quill award New Eng. Chpt. Sigma Delta Chi, 1997. Home: 10 Hancock Rd Brookline MA 02445-4569 E-mail: storin@globe.com.*

STORING, PAUL EDWARD, retired foreign service officer; b. Ames, Iowa, Oct. 24, 1929; s. James Alvin and Edith Nora (Ryg) S.; children: Mimi Storing Harlan, Felice Storing Kite. Student, U Oslo, Norway, 1950-51; BA, Allegheny Coll., 1952; MA with honors, Colgate U., 1956; postgrad., U. Wis., Madison, 1955-59. Fgn. service officer Dept. State, Washington, Mex. and Scandinavia, 1960-80; spl. asst. U.S. Sect. Internat. Boundary and Water Commn. U.S. And Mex., 1980-99; ret. Contbr. articles to profl. jours. Served to cpl. U.S. Army, 1953-55 Fellow U. Wis., 1957-58; Fulbright fellow U. Oslo, 1959-60 Mem. Am. Fgn. Svc. Assn., Fulbright Assn., Phi Beta Kappa, Delta Tau Delta (pres. Alpha chpt. 1949-50). Baptist. Avocations: swimming; tennis; travel. Mailing: c/o Kite 6450 Steeple Chase Ln Manassas VA 20111 Home: Dar Es Salaam Tanzania E-mail: storingpe@netscape.net.

STORK, DONALD ARTHUR, advertising executive; b. Walsh, Ill., June 17, 1939; s. Arthur William and Katherine Frances (Young) S.; m. Joanna Gentry, June 9, 1962; 1 child, Brian Wesley. BS, So. Ill. U., 1961; postgrad., St. Louis U., 1968-69. With Naegele Outdoor Advtsg., Mpls. and St. Louis, 1961-63; acct. exec. Richard C. Lynch Advtsg., 1963-64; media exec. Gardner Advtsg. co., 1964-69; v.p. mktg. Advanswers Media/Programming, 1975-79; pres. Advanswers divsn. Wells/BDDP, N.Y.C., 1979-98; pres. Advanswers unit Omnicom, St. Louis, 1998—2002, pres. PHD unit, 2002—. Bd. dirs. Trailblazers, Inc.; corp. devel. St. Louis Art Mus., 1999. Pres. Signal Hill Sch. Assn. Parents Tchrs. Capt. Mo. Air N.G., 1961-67. Recipient Journalism Alumnus of Yr. award So. Ill. U., Alumni Achievement award. Mem. St. Louis Advtsg. Club, Mensa, Mo. Athletic Club, St. Clair Country Club (bd. dirs. 2001), Alpha Delta Sigma (Aid to Advtg. Edn. award). Home: 27 Symonds Dr Belleville IL 62223-1905 Office: PHD 10 S Broadway Saint Louis MO 63102-1712 E-mail: donstork@phdusa.com.

STORK, FRANK JAMES, lawyer; b. Boone, Iowa, June 28, 1952; s. Frank C. and Margaret E. (Ringsdorf) S.; m. Susan Karli Stork, Aug. 12, 1978; children: Abigail, Natalie, William, Michael. BA, Loras Coll., 1973; MA, JD, U. Iowa, 1977. Bar: Iowa 1977, U.S. Dist. Ct. Iowa 1977. Assoc. Gamble, Riepe, Burt, Webster & Fletcher, Des Moines, 1977-78; sec. Senate Iowa Gen. Assembly, 1978-80; asst. atty. gen. Iowa Dept. Justice, 1980-81; ptnr. McMahon, Cassel, McMahon, McEnroe & Stork, Algona, Iowa, 1981-83; dir. state rels., asst. to pres. U. Iowa, Iowa City, 1983-88; ptnr. Gamble & Davis, Des Moines, 1988-93, Dickinson, MacKaman, Tyler & Hagen, Des Moines, 1994-95; city atty. City of Windsor Heights, Iowa, 1989-94. Mediator Iowa Pub. Employment Rels. Bd., Des Moines, 1982—84, 1994—97; adj. faculty U. Iowa, Iowa City, 1986—88, interim dir. govt. rels., 1997—98; lectr. Drake U. Law Sch., Des Moines, 1989—97; exec. dir. Iowa Bd. Regents, Des Moines, 1998—2001; assoc. gen. counsel Wellmark Blue Cross Blue Shield, 2001—. Author: Lawmaking in Iowa, 1980; co-author: Iowa Gen. Assembly, 1980. Mem. Iowa Bd. Regents, Des Moines, 1983, Iowa Coll. Student Aid

Commn.; bd. dirs. Make-A-Wish Found. Ctrl. Iowa, Des Moines, 1990, Iowa Dollars for Scholars. Mem. ABA, Iowa Bar Assn. Avocations: reading, writing, farming, sports. Office: 636 Grand Ave Des Moines IA 50309

STORK, GILBERT, chemistry educator, investigator; b. Brussels, Belgium, Dec. 31, 1921; s. Jacques and Simone (Weil) Stork; m. Winifred Stewart, June 9, 1944 (dec. May 1992); children: Diana, Linda, Janet, Philip. BS, U. Fla., 1942; PhD, U. Wis., 1945; DSc (hon.) , Lawrence Coll., 1961, U. Paris, 1979, U. Rochester, 1982, Emory U., 1988, Columbia U., 1993, U. Wis., 1997. Sr. rsch. chemist Lakeside Labs., 1945—46; instr. chemistry Harvard U., 1946—48, asst. prof., 1948—53; assoc. prof. Columbia U., N.Y.C., 1953—55, prof., 1955—67, Eugene Higgins prof., 1967—92, prof. emeritus, 1992—, chmn. dept., 1973—76. Lectr. and cons. in field; chmn. Gordon Steroid Conf., 1958—59. Recipient Baekeland medal, 1961, Harrison Howe award, 1962, Edward Curtis Franklin Meml. award, Stanford, 1966, Gold medal, Synthetic Chems. Mfrs. Assn., 1971, Nebr. award, 1973, Roussel prize in steroid chemistry, 1978, Edgar Fahs Smith award, 1982, Nat. Medal of Sci., 1982, Linus Pauling award, 1983, Tetrahedron prize, 1985, Remsen award, 1986, Cliff S. Hamilton award, 1986, Mony Ferst award, Sigma Xi, 1987, George Kenner award, 1992, Robert Robinson award, 1992, Chem. Pioneer award, Am. Inst. Chemists, 1992, Welch Found. award in chemistry, 1993, Allan R. Day award, 1994, Wolf prize, 1996, Phila. Chemists Club award, 1998; fellow, Guggenheim, 1959. Fellow: NAS (award in chem. sci. 1982), Am. Philos. Soc., Am. Acad. Arts and Scis., Royal Soc., Royal Soc. Chemistry (Barton Gold medal 2002), French Acad. Scis.; mem.: Japanese Chem. Soc., Chem. Soc. Japan (hon.), Pharm. Soc. Japan (hon.), Am. Chem. Soc. (chmn. organic chemistry divsn. 1967, award in pure chemistry 1957, award for creative work in synthetic organic chemistry 1967, Nichols medal 1980, Arthur C. Cope award 1980, Willard Gibbs medal 1982, Roger Adams award in organic chemistry 1991), Chemists Club (hon.). Home: 188 Chestnut St Englewood Cliffs NJ 07632-1908 Office: Columbia U Dept Chemistry Chandler Hall New York NY 10027 E-mail: gjs8@columbia.edu.

STORK, SUSAN DIANA, musician, composer; b. Bryn Mawr, Pa., May 31, 1951; d. George Frederick and Mary Ernestine (Weber) S.; m. William Teed Rockwell, Mar. 22, 1987. BA, Colby Coll., 1974. Founder, dir. Festival of Harps concert series, 1990X, prodr., 1995X; dir. ednl. outreach program MultiCultural Music Fellowship and History of the Harp lectrs., 1995X; pvt. harp tchr. Harp performances include Grace Cathedral, San Francisco, Tlingit Tribal House, Haines, Alaska, Bremenale, Bremen, Germany Harp Fest, No. Italy, Morrison Planetarium, Acad. Scis., San Francisco, others; recs. include Harpestry, Herald of Spring, Harpdancing, Celtic Harpestry (also PBS spl.), Art of Harp, others; co-prodr. Harpestry series, 1997; composer over 100 compositions for Celtic-style harp and ensembles and 4 collections of original compositions for lever harp; contbr. articles to profl. jours. Pres. Bay Area Folk Harp Soc. 2-Terms, 1994-96, bd. dirs., 1997X. Mem. Internat. Soc. Folk Harpers (Bay Area Folk Harp Soc. chpt., newsletter editor 1984-88, pres. 1987-90, bd. dirs. 1997X, founder, dir. Harp Day for Kids 1993X, founder, dir. Summer Harp Camp 1997), Am. Harp Soc., Hist. Harp Soc. Avocations: studying Buddhist thought, poetry, painting, hiking, dance. Home and Office: Multi-Cultural Music Fellowship 2419A 10th St Berkeley CA 94710-2545

STORM, CARLYLE BELL, chemist; b. Balt., Mar. 2, 1935; s. Frederick Philip and Carol (Bell) S.; children: Carol, Michael, Christy. BA, Johns Hopkins U., 1961, PhD, 1965. Prof. chemistry Howard U., Washington, 1968-85; chief scientist explosives tech. divsn. Los Alamos (N.Mex.) Nat. Lab., 1985-93; dir. Gordon Rsch. Confs., 1993—. Office: Gordon Rsch Conf PO Box 984 West Kingston RI 02892-0984 E-mail: cbstorm@grc.org.

STORM, HARRIET NACHMAN, journalist, public relations consultant; b. Newport News, Va., Sept. 26, 1942; d. Abe and Isabel Reyner (Levy) Nachman; m. Charles Ray Storm, Feb. 16, 1967 (dec. May 1996); children: Lisa Ann Storm Hogge, Laura Elizabeth, Storm Wyatt. Student, U. Md., 1960-92; BA in English, Coll. William and Mary, 1964; grad., Am. Press Inst., 1974. Reporter, editor Daily Press, Newport News, 1964-74; freelance journalist, pub. rels. cons. Hampton, Va., 1974—. Contbr. articles to newspapers. Mem. adv. bd. Longwood Ctr. Visual Arts, Longwood Coll., Farmville, Va., 1994—; vice chairperson, then chairperson Va. Assn. Cmty. Svc. Bds., 1988-91; sec., chairperson, student affairs com., bd. visitors Coll. William and Mary, 1979-88; pres. William and Mary Cypher Soc., 1980—; trustee, bd. dirs., regional pres. William and Mary Athletic Ednl. Assn., 1979—; sec., treas., bd. dirs. Peninsula Legal Aid Ctr., Ea. Va., 1977—, pres. bd. trustees; chairperson bd. advisors Peninsula Fine Arts Ctr., 1990—; bd. dirs. Va. Symphony, 1995—; life mem., bd. dirs., past v.p., past pres. Nat. Coun. Jewish Women; mem. Living Interfaith Network, sec., 1991—; past chairperson, vice chairperson Hampton-Newport News Cmty. Svcs. Bd., 1979—; mem., vice chairperson, chairperson Hampton Clean City Commn., 1994—. Recipient Alumni medallion Coll. William and Mary, 1981, Commendation, Va. Gen. Assembly, 1992, Book of Golden Deeds award Exch. Club, Hampton, 1993, Humanitarian award NCCJ, 1996, Vol. award William and Mary Athletic Ednl. Assn., living Interfaith Network, 1996, Hampton Clean City Commn., 1996; named to Hall of Fame, Hampton-Newport News Cmty. Svcs. Bd., 1996. Mem. Va. Press Women's Assn. (sec., treas., conv. chairperson 1964-72, various awards), William and Mary Soc. Alumni (pres. 1978-79). Avocations: reading, watching sporting events, visiting art museums and symphonies. Home: 1454 Todds Ln Apt B41 Hampton VA 23666-2954

STORM, JACKIE, nutritionist, health education specialist; b. Halifax, N.S., Can., Sept. 20, 1943; d. Jack Charles Stone and Kathleen (Clow) Devisser. BA, NYU, 1979, MA, 1982, PhD, 1995. Cert. nutrition specialist. Nutrition educator N.Y. Health and Racquet Club, N.Y.C., 1973—; tchr. New Sch. Social Rsch., 1980-87. Adj. prof. Kingsborough C.C., Bklyn., 1987-2001, St. Francis Coll., Bklyn., 1987; tchr. Acad. Med. Sys., 2001-. Author: There's No Such Thing As A Fattening Food!, 1983. Mem. Am. Coll. Nutrition, Am. Nutraceutical Assn., Soc. nutrition Edn. Avocations: gardening, weight lifting. Office: 115 E 57th St New York NY 10022-2049 E-mail: jackiestorm@jackiestorm.com.

STORM, JANET S. psychiatric social worker; b. Indpls. d. Charles R. and Evelyn M. (Seitz) Howard; children: Beth A., Mary J. BSW with high distinction, Ind. U., 1982, MSW, 1984. Cert. ACSW. Pvt. indsl. social work therapist Supportive Systems Inc., Indpls.; med. social worker Wishard Meml. Hosp.; social work cons. State of Ind.; psychiat. sr. mental health clinician Community Hosp.; pscyhiat. social worker Adult and Child Mental Health Ctr.; psychiat. social worker St. Francis Counseing Ctr.; pvt. practice Indpls. Mem. NASW, Sigma Pi Alpha. Home: PO Box 47461 Indianapolis IN 46247-0461

STORM, ROBERT WARREN, lawyer; b. Battle Creek, Mich., June 3, 1951; s. Robert Warren and Patricia Ellen Knight (Klinck) S. AB in History, William and Mary Coll., 1973, JD, 1989; MA in History, Duke U., 1977. Bar: Conn., 1989; ordained elder Collinsville (Conn.) Congl. Ch., 1997. Historian, archivist U.S. Govt., Washington and Austin, Tex., 1977-85; cons. in info. mgmt. Arlington, Williamsburg, Va., 1985-88; assoc. Robinson & Cole, Hartford, 1989-92; pvt. practice West Hartford, 1993—. Gubernatorial appointee State Hist. Records Adv. Bd., Hartford, 1993—96; hon. advisor Ethiopian Cmty. Ctr., Conn., 1996—; bd. dirs. The Children's Home, Cromwell, 1993—99, v.p., 1995—96; bd. dirs. Conn. Coalition of Mut. Assistance Assns., 1997—, v.p., 1998—99, treas., 1999—2000; bd. dirs. Lea's Found. for Leukemia Rsch., 1998—. Mem.: ABA, Mil. Order Loyal Legion of U.S. (comdr. Conn. 2001—), Conn. Bar Assn., Soc. of the Cin. in the State of Conn., Soc. Colonial Wars in Conn. (treas. 2001—), Soc. Descs. of Founders of Hartford. Avocations: reading, writing, music, nature, the fine arts. Office: PO Box 271645 West Hartford CT 06127-1645

STORMER, BARBARA JEAN, artist; b. Knoxville, Tenn., Oct. 11, 1935; d. Paul Tingle and Mildred Elizabeth (Bridges) Bates; m. James Bob Stormer, Apr. 28, 1952; 1 child (dec.). Student pub. schs., Knoxville. Painter, tchr. Internat. China Painting Tchrs. Orgn., Dallas, 1965—. Baptist. Avocations: sweater designer, knitter, orchid grower, needlewoman. Home and Office: 107 Longview Dr La Follette TN 37766-3815

STÖRMER, HORST LUDWIG, physicist; b. Frankfurt-Main, Fed. Republic Germany, Apr. 6, 1949; arrived in U.S., 1977; s. Karl-Ludwig and Marie (Ihrig) S.; m. Dominique A. Parchet, 1982. PhD, U. Stuttgart, 1977. From tech. staff to dir. phys. rsch. lab. AT&T Bell Labs., Murray Hill, NJ, 1977—97; prof. physics and applied physics Columbia U., N.Y.C., 1998—. Adj. physics dir. Lucent Tech., 1997—. Decorated Officier de la Legion d'Honneur France, Grosses Verdienstkreuz Mit Stern Germany; recipient Otto Klung prize, 1985, Benjamin Franklin medal in physics, 1998, Nobel prize in Physics, 1998, N.Y.C. Mayor's award for excellence in sci. and tech., 2000; fellow Bell Labs., 1983. Fellow: NAS, Am. Acad. Arts and Scis., Am. Phys. Soc. (Buckley prize 1984). Office: Columbia U Dept Physics 538 W 120th St New York NY 10027-6601 also: Lucent Technologies 700 Mountain Ave New Providence NJ 07974-1208

STORMER, JOHN ANTHONY, minister emeritus, author, publisher; b. Altoona, Pa., Feb. 9, 1928; s. Regis Walter and Mary Ann (Forr) S.; m. Elizabeth Ruth Lewis, July 2, 1951; 1 child, Holly. BS in Journalism, San Jose (Calif.) State U., 1954; DLitt (hon.), Manahath Sch. Theology, Hollidaysburg, Pa., 1965; LittD (hon.), Shelton Coll., 1976. Ordained to ministry Bapt. Ch., 1968. Pastor Heritage Bapt. Ch., Florissant, Mo., 1968-86; supt. Faith Christian Acad., 1968—99; owner Liberty Bell Press, 1963—2002. Bd. dirs. Internat. Coun. Christian Chs., 1965-87; dir. I Chronicles 12:32 Ministry, Florissant, 1985-2002. *John Stormer's five books have sold over 10-million copies.* Author: None Dare Call It Treason, 1964, The Death of a Nation, 1968, Growing of God's Way, 1984, NDCIT—25 Years Later, 1990, None Dare Call It Education, 1999. Mem. rep. state com., state chmn. Mo. Young Reps., 1962-64, state del. Rep. Nat. Conv., San Francisco, 1964. With USAF, 1950-53. Mem. Coun. for Nat. Policy. Office: PO Box 32 Florissant MO 63033 *Through the resurrected life of the Lord Jesus Christ, individuals who have received Him have everything they need to be and do all that God the Father calls them to.*

STORMER, NANCY ROSE, lawyer; b. Traverse City, Mich., Mar. 7, 1950; d. Benjamin Voice and Frances Rose (Gold) S.; m. Michael Charles Bagge, Aug. 1, 1985; children: Sean, Kiernan. AA, Harriman (N.Y.) Coll., 1973; BA magna cum laude, Marist Coll., 1977; JD, Antioch Sch. Law, 1981. Bar: N.Y. 1983, U.S. Dist. Ct. (no. dist.) N.Y. 1983, U.S. Supreme Ct. 1989. Staff atty. Legal Aid Soc. Mid N.Y., Utica, 1983-95, sr. atty., 1990-95; atty. in pvt. practice, 1995—. Bd. dirs. Sister City Project, Utica, 1986-90, Salvation Army, Utica, 1988-89; mem. adv. coun. office for aging Oneida County Office for Aging, Utica, 1993-96; co-chairperson adv. coun. Hispanos Unidos, Utica, 1994. Named Profl. Woman of Yr. YWCA of Mohawk Valley, 1999. Mem. N.Y. State Bar Assn., Oneida County Bar Assn., Nat. Health Lawyers. Avocations: travel, reading, crafts. Home: 1314 Rutger St Utica NY 13501-2526 Office: Adirondack Bank Bldg 185 Genesee St Ste 1519 Utica NY 13501-2102

STORMES, JOHN MAX, instructional systems developer; b. Manila, Oct. 7, 1927; s. Max Clifford and Janet (Heldring) S.; m. Takako Sanae, July 29, 1955; children: Janet Kazuko Stormes-Pepper, Alan Osamu. *Father Max Stormes (1903-1942) was a U.S. Naval Academy graduate (1924) and fought in World War II as captain of USS Preston (DD379). He received the Navy Cross and Purple Heart posthumously, and a destroyer was named for him (USS Stormes, DD780). He had attained the rank of commander, USN.* BS, San Diego State U., 1950; BA, U. So. Calif., 1957, MA, 1967. Cert. secondary and community coll. tchr., sr. profl. human resources. Editing supr. Lockheed Propulsion Co., Redlands, Calif., 1957-61; proposals supr. Rockwell Internat., Downey, 1961-62; publs. dir. Arthur D. Little, Inc., Santa Monica, 1962-63; publs. coord. Rockwell Internat., Downey, 1963-68; project dir. Gen. Behavioral Systems, Inc., Torrance, Calif., 1969-73; tng. and comm. cons. Media Rsch. Assocs., Santa Cruz, 1973—; instrl. design supr. So. Calif. Gas Co., L.A., 1985-2001; adj. assoc. prof. Alliant U., Alhambra, Calif., 2001—. Lectr. Calif. State U., Northridge, 1991—; tng. cons. Nat. Ednl. Media, Chatsworth, Calif., 1966-81, comm. cons. Opinion Rsch. Calif., Long Beach, 1974—. Co-author: TV Communications Systems For Business and Industry, 1970; contbg. author: ASTD's In Action series of casebooks, 1996-99. Curriculum adv. bd. communications dept. Calif. State U., Fullerton, 1964-78. Sgt. U.S. Army, 1953-55, Japan. Mem. Soc. Tech. Communication (sr. mem., 2nd v.p. Orange County chpt. 1962-63), Internat. Soc. Performance and Instruction (v.p. L.A. chpt. 1989, pres. 1990). Democrat. Episcopal. Avocations: photography, sailing. Home and Office: 9201 Florence Ave Apt 102 Downey CA 90240-3578 E-mail: jmstormes@attbi.com.

STORMONT, RICHARD MANSFIELD, hotel executive; b. Chgo., Apr. 4, 1936; s. Daniel Lytle and E. Mildred (Milligan) S.; m. Virginia Louellen Walters, Nov. 21, 1959; children: Stacy Lee Freeman, Richard Mansfield, John Frederick. BS, Cornell U., 1958. Cert. hosp. adminstrn.; cert. hosps. industry profl. Food cost analyst, sales rep. Edgewater Beach Hotel, Chgo., 1957-58; asst. sales mgr. Marriott Hotels, Inc., Washington, 1962-64, dir. sales Atlanta, 1964-68, resident mgr., 1969-71; gen. mgr. Marriott Hotel, Dallas, 1971-73, Phila., 1973-74, Atlanta, 1974-79; pres. Hardin Mgmt. Co., 1979-80; v.p. Marriott Franchise div. Marriott Corp., Washington, 1980-83, v.p. ops. Courtyard by Marriott, 1981-83; pres. The Stormont Cos. Inc., Atlanta, 1984-92; chmn. bd. dirs. Stormont Trice Corp., 1993-2000; chmn. Stormont Hospitality Group, LLC, 2001—. Dir. Walters & Co. Cons. to Mgmt., 1975-82. Pres. Atlanta Conv. and Visitors Burs., 1975-76, chmn. bd., 1976-77, vice chmn., 1996-97, chmn. bd. exec. com., 1998-2000; trustee Young Harris Coll.; bd. dirs. Better Bus. Bur.; exec. com. Ctrl. Atlanta Progress, 1979-80; exec. coun. Boy Scouts Am.; bd. dirs., chmn. tourism divsn. Ga. Dept. Industry, Trade and Tourism, 1999-2001. Recipient Disting. Salesman of Yr. award Marriott, 1967, Obi T. Brewer award for Decade of Outstanding Svc., 1979. Mem. Sales and Mktg. Execs. (exec. v.p. 1969-70, pres. Atlanta 1970-71), Am. Hotel-Motel Assn. (exec. com., bd. dirs. 1993-95, Most Valuable Vol. Ga. 1999), Ga. Hospitality and Travel Assn. (founder 1975, bd. dir., pres. 1989-90, chmn. bd. 1991-92, Hotelier of Yr. award 1977, Hall of Fame 2001), Ga. Bus. and Industry Assn. (bd. dirs.), Atlanta Hotel Assn. (pres. 1976), So. Innkeepers Assn., Atlanta C. of C. (v.p. 1978-79), Gwinnett C. of C. (bd. dirs.), Cornell Soc. Hotelmen (pres. Ga. chpt. 1976, regional v.p. 1989-91), Rotary Club of Atlanta (chmn. program com. 1998, bd. dirs. 1999-2002). Home: 2980 Nancy Creek Rd NW Atlanta GA 30327-2000 Office: Riverside Ste 300 4401 Northside Pkwy NW Atlanta GA 30327-3065 E-mail: Richard.Stormont@StormontHospitality.com.

STORMS, CLIFFORD BEEKMAN, lawyer; b. Mount Vernon, N.Y., July 18, 1932; s. Harold Beekman and Gene (Pertak) S.; m. Barbara H. Grave, 1955 (div. 1975); m. Valeria N. Parker, July 12, 1975; children: Catherine Storms Fischer, Clifford Beekman. BA magna cum laude, Amherst Coll., 1954; LLB, Yale U., 1957. Bar: N.Y. 1957. Assoc. Breed, Abbott & Morgan, N.Y.C., 1957-64; with CPC Internat., Inc., Englewood Cliffs, N.J., 1964-97, v.p. legal affairs, 1973-75, v.p., gen. counsel, 1975-88, sr. v.p., gen. counsel, 1988-97, atty. alternate dispute resolution, corp. dir., 1997—; pvt. practice Greenwich, Conn., 1997—. Bd. dirs. Corn Products Internat., Inc., Atlantic Legal Found.; mem. Conn. Alternate Dispute Resolution panel Ctr. for Pub. Resources. Trustee emeritus Food and Drug Law Inst. Mem. ABA (com. of corp. gen. counsel), Am. Arbitration Assn. (panel arbitrators large complex case program), Assn. Gen. Counsel (pres. 1992-94), Assn. Bar City N.Y. (sec., com. on corp. law depts. 1979-81), Indian Harbor Yacht Club, Yale Law Sch. Assn. (exec. com.), Phi Beta Kappa. Home: 19 Burying Hill Rd Greenwich CT 06831-2604 Office: Ste 100 Two Sound View Dr Greenwich CT 06830 E-mail: cbstorms@aol.com.

STORMS, LESTER C. retired veterinarian; b. Camas, Wash., Oct. 13, 1920; s. Roy Lester and Helen Violet (Belshe) S.; m. Marjorie Louise Hudson, Apr. 10, 1943 (div.); children: Marjorie Maureen, Terry Jo, Sandra Diane. BS in Animal Husbandry, Wash. State U., 1951, DVM, 1952. Intern, Portland, 1952; gen. practice vet. medicine Camas, 1952-54; dr.'s asst. pvt. practice vet. office, Hollywood, Calif., 1954, L.A., 1954, Whittier, Calif., 1954, vet. in charge Artesia, 1955-56; owner, pvt. practice vet. medicine Buena Park, 1956-86; ret., 1986. Mem. adv. bd. Guide Dogs for Blind, San Rafael, Calif., 1957-58; mem. steering com. Children's Hosp., Fullerton, Calif., 1960-61. With USN, 1940-51, PTO. Decorated Air medal with 3 gold stars, DFC.; recipient Pappy Pedigoe Meml. Trophy Calif. Sports Car Racing Assn., 1965. Mem. NRA, So. Calif. Vet. Medicine Assn. (life), Am. Vet. Medicine Assn., Orange County Vet. Medicine Assn. (pres. 1958), Olde '78 Fraser's Highlanders (chief-of-staff), Explorer's Club, Adventurer's Club L.A. (sec. 1984, bd. dirs. 1980-82, 95-97), Long Beach Yacht Club, Rotary (Paul Harris fellow, pres. Buena Park chpt. 1963), Masons, Shriners (capt., pres. 1999—, Legion of Honor, capt. Legion of Honor Shrine). Avocations: race car driving, sailing, fishing, shooting. Home: 78th Frasers Highlanders 4316 Latona Ave Los Angeles CA 90031-1426

STORRER, WILLIAM ALLIN, consultant; b. Highland Park, Mich., Mar. 22, 1936; s. Fredrick Ray and Margaret Ann (Pitts) S.; m. Carol A. Tuthill, Nov. 6, 1964 (div. June 1969); 1 child, Kirsten; m. Patricia Alice Whalley, Dec. 30, 1976. Student, Albion Coll., 1954-56; AB in Engring. Scis., Harvard U., 1959; MFA in Theatre Arts, Boston U., 1962; PhD in Comparative Arts, Ohio U., 1968. Electronics engr. Raytheon Co., Wayland, Mass., 1958-60; tech. dir. small stage Boston Arts Festival, 1961, 62; dir. dramatics Melrose (Mass.) H.S., 1962-63; dir. playhouse and repertory theatre, instr. drama-speech Hofstra U., 1963-66, instr. opera, 1965; asst. prof. theatre, dir. univ. theatre, U. Toledo, 1968-69; assoc. prof. theatre and film, dir. Southampton Coll., L.I. U., 1969-73; asst. prof. cinema studies and still photography Ithaca (N.Y.) Coll., 1973-76; assoc. prof. media arts U. S.C., Columbia, 1976-82; pres. MINDaLIVE Creative Mind Enhancement, Newark, 1980—. Assoc. prof. theater and speech World Campus Afloat, Chapman Coll., 1972; edn. media specialist Newark Bd. Edn., 1990-94, Linden Bd. Edn., 1994-95, Harrison Bd. Edn., 1995-96, Rosa Parks Fine and Performing Arts H.S., Paterson, N.J., 1996, dir. Storrer/Storre/Storer Family Inst. Author: The Architecture of Frank Lloyd Wright, 1974, The Frank Lloyd Wright Companion, 1993; contbr. articles to popular mags. and profl. jours. Grantee Graham Found. for Advanced Studies in Fine Arts, 1987, 94. Home and Office: 289 Highland Ave Newark NJ 07104-1301 E-mail: mindalive@aol.com.

STORRS, BRUCE BRYSON, pediatric neurosurgeon; b. Syracuse, N.Y., Nov. 3, 1946; s. Bruce Dixson and Anna Margery (Bryson) S.; m. Kathleen Carrie Wiemold, Sept. 12, 1962; children: Anna, Alison. BA, U. N.Mex., 1968, MD, 1972. Diplomate Am. Bd. Neurosurgery, Am. Bd. Pediatric Neurosurgery. Resident in surgery Kaiser Hosp., Oakland, Calif., 1972-73, U. N.M., Albuquerque, 1973-74; resident in neurosurgery U. Utah, Salt Lake City, 1976-80; resident Hosp. for Sick Children, Toronto, Ont., Can., 1980-81; asst. prof. surgery and pediat. U. Utah, Salt Lake City, 1981-86, Northwestern U., Chgo., 1986-90; neurosurgeon Childrens Meml., 1990; prof. surgery and pediat. Med. U. S.C., Charleston, 1990-96; prof. surgery and pediatrics U. N.Mex., Albuquerque, 1996—. Safety and performance com. NIH. Mem. editl. bd. Pediat. Neurosurgery, 1994—. Fellow ACS, Am. Acad. Pediat.; mem. Am. Soc. Pediat. Neurosurgeons (sec. 1996—), Am. Assn. Neurol. Surgeons. Avocations: fishing, woodworking, shooting. Office: Children's Hosp N M 2211 Lomas Blvd NE Albuquerque NM 87106-2745

STORRS, ELEANOR EMERETT, research institute consultant; b. Cheshire, Conn., May 3, 1926; d. Benjamin Porter and Alta Hyde (Moss) S.; m. Harry Phineas Burchfield, Jr., Nov. 29, 1963; children: Sarah Storrs, Benjamin Hyde. BS with distinction in Botany, U. Conn., 1948; MS in Biology, NYU, 1958; PhD in Chemistry, U. Tex., 1967. Asst. biochemist Boyce Thompson Inst. for Plant Rsch., Yonkers, N.Y., 1948-62; rsch. scientist Clayton Found. Biochem. Inst., U. Tex., Austin, 1962-65; biochemist Pesticides Rsch. Lab., USPHS, Perrine, Fla., 1965-67; dir. dept. biochemistry Gulf South Rsch. Inst., New Iberia, La., 1967-77; adj. prof. chemistry U. Southwestern La., Lafayette, 1974-77; rsch. prof. biology Fla. Inst. Tech., Melbourne, 1977-94, cons. on leprosy-armadillo programs, 1975-94, mem. Faculty Senate, 1979-84, prof. emeritus, 1994—. Cons. in rehab. and prevention deformities leprosy Pan Am. Health Orgn., WHO, Venezuela, Argentina, Brazil, Mex., 1972-90; dep. v.p. Coll. Hansenology in Endemic Countries, 1980-85 Author: (with H.P. Burchfield) Biochemical Applications of Gas Chromatography, 1962, (with Burchfield, D.E. Johnson) Guide to the Analysis of Pesticide Residues, 2 vols, 1965; also articles, book chpts. Grantee NIH, 1968-88, CDC, 1969-73, WHO, 1973-93, Leprosy Program, 1978-93, German Leprosy Relief Assn., 1973-78, Nat. Coun. Episc. Ch., 1975-77, Brit. Leprosy Relief Assn., 1981-88; recipient plaque La. Health Dept., 1972, Disting. Alumni award U. Conn., 1975, Gold award Am. Coll. Pathologists and Am. Soc. Clin. Pathologists, 1974, Gerard B. Lambert award for spl. recognition, 1975. Fellow AAAS; mem. AAUW, Internat. Leprosy Assn., Am. Recorder Soc., Early Music Assn., Sigma Xi. Episcopalian (vestryman). Clubs: Appalachian (Boston); Green Mountain (Bear Mountain, N.Y.). Achievements include pioneering devel. leprosy in exptl. animal (armadillo) reproduction. Home: 72 Riverview Ter Melbourne FL 32903-4640 *Children display interests early in their lives, and in my life, this early interest - in animals, and the beauty of nature - is one which I have never lost, but one which seems to become more important now with the passing of years. Parents can help mold a child, but should mold the child in the child's interests as my parents did, not in a mold designed by them.*

STORRS, IMMI CASAGRANDE, sculptor; b. Aug. 2, 1945; d. Leo and Carla Maria Annie (Busch) Casagrande; m. Thomas Austin Storrs, Dec. 19, 1971 (div. 1983); 1 child, A. Maya. BA, U. Denver, 1968. Nessa Cohen grantee, 1981, 82, E.D. Found. grantee, 1989, 96; recipient Purchase award, Art Students League N.Y., Chaim Gross Found. award, 1989, Nat. Acad. Mus. Speyer prize, 1992. One-woman shows include Gallery 2, Woodstock, Vt., 1973, Fairwinds Gallery, Ferrisburg, Vt., 1974, Congress Hall, Timmendorferstrand, Germany, 1976, Amerika Haus, Hamburg, Germany, 1976, Cambridge Art Assn., Mass., 1978, Goethe Inst., Boston, 1980, 83, Sutton Gallery, N.Y.C., 1981, 82, 83, 86, Madison Gallery, 1987, Bologna-Landi Gallery, Easthampton, N.Y., 1987, 93, Vorpal Gallery, N.Y.C., 1989, 91, 92, La Posada, Santa Fe, 1989, Ruth Volid Gallery, Chgo., 1990, Bachelier-Cardonsky Gallery, Kent, Conn, 1996, Hurlbutt Gallery, Greenwich, Conn., 1997, Dillon Gallery, N.Y.C., 1997, 00; group shows include Fleming Mus., Burlington, Vt., 1973, ARtist Choice Mus., N.Y.C., 1983, Nat. Acad. Mus., N.Y.C., 1988, 92, 94, 95, 97, 99, Provincetown Art Assn. & Mus., Mass., 1988, Nat. Scultpure Soc., N.Y.C., 1989, 91, Elaine Benson Gallery, bridgehampton, N.Y., 1993, Sculptors Guild, Kyoto, Japan & Washington, 1993, N.Y.C., 1994, Cline Fine Art Gallery, Sante Fe, 1994, 95, Stamford Mus., Conn., 1996, Bachelier-Cardonsky Gallery, 1996, The White House, Washington, 1996, 97; represented in permanent collections at The Nat. Mus. Women in Arts, Washington, The Snite Mus., Nat. Acad. Mus., The Herbert Johnson Mus. at Cornell, numerous pvt. collections. Mem. Nat. Acad. Mus., Century Assn., Sculptors Guild. Avocations: skiing, tennis. Home: 169 E 78th St New York NY 10021-0485

STORY, ELLEN, state legislator; m. Ronald Story; 2 children. BA, U. Tex.; postgrad., U. Wis., SUNY, Stony Brook; MA, Cambridge Coll. County coord. Family Planning Coun. Western Mass., 1973, asst. exec. dir., 1981, assoc. exec. dir., 1984-92; mem. Mass. Ho. of Reps., Boston, 1992—. Founding mem. Hampshire County Human Svcs., Mass., 1974, past mem. prof. adv. com.; organizer Western Mass. Dems. and Independents for Frank Hatch for Gov., 1978; chmn. Barbara Griffith for Amherst Selectbd., 1982; coord. Evelyn Murphy for Lt. Gov., 1982; mem. Amherst Town Meeting, Mass.; pres., bd. dirs. Hampshire County Coun. Social Agencies, Mass.; bd. dirs. Hampshire Youth 2000 Coalition; charter mem. Friends of Amherst Recreation; co-founder, dir. Concerned Citizens for Quality Edn. Recipient Spl. Recognition award Hampshire County Coun. Social Agencies, 1991. Mem. Amherst Club, Rotary. Democrat. Office: Mass Ho of Reps State House Rm 167 Boston MA 02133

STORY, JOSEPH C. economist, consultant; b. Hillsboro, Ky., Aug. 31, 1931; s. Claude Leslie and Verna May Story; m. Grace N. Story, Apr. 13, 1957 (dec. Jan. 1999); 1 child, Sally. BS in Econs., Ind. U., 1954; MS in Econs., U. Ill., 1961. Intelligence officer CIA, Langley, Va., 1961-64; project dir. U.S. Agy. Internat. Devel., New Delhi, 1964-66; dep. project leader UN Devel. Program, Kunduz, Afghanistan, 1967-70; mgr. external econs. Nat. Iranian Oil Co., Tehran, 1970-74; br. chief U.S. Dept. Energy, Washington, 1973-76; mem. policy planning staff Arabian Am. Oil Co., Dharan, Saudi Arabia, 1976-79; pres. Gulf Consulting Svcs., McLean, Va., 1979-99, Policy and Planning Assocs., Flemingsburg, Ky., 1999—. Advisor State of Alaska, Anchorage, 1986-94, Directorate of Intelligence, Riyadh, Saudi Arabia, 1987-99; cons. Norsk Hydro, Oslo, Norway, 1986-93, Brit. Petroleum, London, 1987-94, Broken Hill Proprietary Petroleum, Melbourne, Australia, 1989-2002, Ashland Oil, Covington, Ky., 1999-2002, Shell Oil, Houston, 1988-2002, Pan Can. Petroleum, Calgary, Ont., 1998-2002. Author: The Economy of Iran, 1985. With U.S. Army, 1954-56. Office: Policy and Planning Assocs Southgate Estate Rt 2 Box 11A Flemingsburg KY 41041

STORY, MARTHA VANBEUREN, retired librarian; b. Morristown, N.J., Mar. 6, 1940; d. John Mohlman and Jane de Peyster vanB.; m. William Ferguson Story, Oct. 19, 1963; children: Jessica, Alexandra. BA, Wellesley Coll., 1962; MLS, U. Md., 1975. Libr. Dewberry & Davis, Fairfax, Va., 1976-77, 80-84, Ashley Hall, Charleston, S.C., 1977-80, 85-86; cataloger Norfolk (Va.) Pub. Libr., 1987-90; dir. Mathews (Va.) Meml. Libr., 1990-99. Publicity chmn. Mid. Peninsula Cmty. Concert Assoc., Gloucester, Va., 1993—2001, Concerts By the Bay, 2001—; mem. lay visitors com. Kingston Parish, Mathews, Va., 1996—, scholarship com., 1996—, mem. 350th Anniversary com., 2001—. Mem. Va. Libr. Assoc. Home: Holly Cove PO Box 117 Hudgins VA 23076-0117 E-mail: marthava88@yahoo.com.

STOSKUS, JOANNA JORZYSTA, computer information systems educator; b. Newark, Feb. 10, 1947; d. Joseph B. and Anna Mary (Stopa) Jorzysta; m. Joseph Thomas Stoskus, Jr., Oct. 25, 1969; 1 child, Caryn Judith. BA in Math., Kean Coll. N.J., 1968; MA in Computer Sci., Montclair State U., 1985. Programmer, analyst Prudential Ins. Co., Newark, 1968-70, Bell Labs., Murray Hill, N.J., 1970-72; adj. instr. Middlesex County Coll., Edison, 1974-77; prof. engring. tech. County Coll. of Morris, Randolph, NJ, 1977—. Avocation: golf. Office: County Coll Morris 214 Center Grove Rd Randolph NJ 07869-2007

STOSSEL, THOMAS PETER, medical educator, medical research director; b. Chgo., Sept. 10, 1941; m. Kerry Maguire, 1997. AB, Princeton U., 1963; MD, Harvard U., 1967; MD (hon.), U. Linkoping, Sweden, 1989. Diplomate Am. Bd. Internal Medicine. House staff medicine Mass. Gen. Hosp., Boston, 1967-69, chief hematology-oncology, 1976-90; staff assoc. NIH, Bethesda, Md., 1967-71; fellow to sr. assoc. Med. Ctr. Children's Hosp., Boston, 1971-76; prof. medicine Harvard Med. Sch., 1982—; chief divsn. exptl. medicine Brigham & Women's Hosp., 1991—; co-dir. hematology divsn. Brigham Women's Hosp., 1998—. Sci. bd. Biogen Corp., 1987-2002, Dyax Corp., 1996—; clin. rsch. prof. Am. Cancer Soc., 1987—; bd. dirs. Zymequest, Inc. Author: (with B. Babior) Hematology, A Pathophysiological Approach, 1984, 90, 94; contbr. articles to profl. jours.; editor: (with R. Handin & S. Lux) Blood, Principles & Practice of Hematology, 1995. 2d edit., 2002; holder 6 U.S. patents. Lt. comdr. USPHS, 1969-71. Mem. NAS, Inst. of Medicine, Am. Fedn. Clin. Rsch., Am. Soc. Clin. Investigation (pres. 1987), Am. Soc. Hematology (Damashek prize 1983, Thomas prize 1993, pres. 1997), Am. Soc. Cell Biology, Assn. Am. Physicians, Am. Acad. Arts and Scis. Office: Brigham & Womens Hosp 221 Longwood Ave Boston MA 02115-5804 E-mail: tstossel@rics.bwh.harvard.edu.

STOTLAR, CYNTHIA BYRD, human resources professional; b. Atlanta, Aug. 23, 1953; d. Jesse Lee and Elizabeth Evelyn (Daniell) Byrd; m. David Stotlar, Feb. 5, 1983; children: Eric David, Jason William. BS, Middle Tenn. State U., 1975; MEd, Cen. Mich. U., 1982; student, St. Thomas Sch. Med.Technology, 1975. Asst. dir. pathology St. Thomas Hosp., Nashville, 1975-83; asst. dir. orgnl. devel. St. Paul Med. Ctr., Dallas, 1983-87; assoc. dir. human resources Humana Health Care Plans Michael Reese, Chgo., 1989-92; human resources cons. Topeka, 1992—. Founder, prin. Creative Bus. Solutions. Mem. ASTD, Am. Mgmt. Assn., Soc. Human Resource Mgrs. Home: 6136 SW 38th St Topeka KS 66610-1308

STOTLER, ALICEMARIE HUBER, judge; b. Alhambra, Calif., May 29, 1942; d. James R. and Loretta M. Huber; m. James Allen Stotler, Sept. 11, 1971. BA, U. So. Calif., 1964, JD, 1967. Bar: Calif. 1967, U.S. Dist. Ct. (no. dist.) Calif. 1967, U.S. Dist. Ct. (cen. dist.) Calif. 1973, U.S. Supreme Ct. 1976; cert. criminal law specialist. Dep. Orange County Dist. Attys. Office, 1967-73; mem. Stotler & Stotler, Santa Ana, Calif., 1973-76, 83-84; judge Orange County Mcpl. Ct., 1976-78, Orange County Superior Ct., 1978-83, U.S. Dist. Ct. (cen. dist.) Calif., L.A., 1984—. Assoc. dean Calif. Trial Judges Coll., 1982; lectr., panelist, numerous orgns.; standing com. on rules of practice and procedure U.S. Jud. Conf., 1991-98, chair, 1993-98; mem. exec. com. 9th Cir. Jud. Conf., 1989-93, Fed. State Jud. Coun., 1989-98, jury com., 1990-92, planning com. for Nat. Conf. on Fed.-State Jud. Relationships, Orlando, 1991-92, planning com. for We. Regional Conf. on State-Fed. Jud. Relationships, Stevens, Wash., 1992-93; chair dist. ct. symposium and jury utilization Ctrl. Dist. Calif., 1985, chair atty. liaison, 1989-90, chair U.S. Constn. Bicentennial com., 1986-91, chair magistrate judge com., 1992-93; mem. State Adv. Group on Juvenile Justice and Delinquency Prevention, 1983-84, Bd. Legal Specializations Criminal Law Adv. Commn., 1983-84, victim/witness adv. com. Office Criminal Justice Planning, 1980-83, U. So. Calif. Bd. Councilors, 1993-01; active team in tng. Leukemia Soc. Am., 1993, 95, 97, 2000; legion lex bd. dirs. U. So. Calif. Sch. Law Support Group, 1981-83. Winner Hale Moot Ct. Competition, State of Calif., 1967; named Judge of Yr., Orange County Trial Lawyers Assn., 1978, Most Outstanding Judge, Orange County Bus. Litigation Sect., 1990; recipient Franklin G. West award Orange County Bar Assn., 1985. Mem. ABA (jud. adminstrn. divsn. and litigation sect. 1984—, nat. conf. fed. trial judges com. on legis. affairs 1990-91), Am. Law Inst., Am. Judicature Soc., Fed. Judges Assn. (bd. dirs. 1989-92), Nat. Assn. Women Judges, U.S. Supreme Ct. Hist. Soc., Ninth Cir. Dist. Judges Assn., Calif. Supreme Ct. Hist. Soc., Orange County Bar Assn. (mem. numerous com.s, Franklin G. West award 1984), Calif. Judges Assn. (mem. com. on jud. coll. 1978-80, com. on civil law and procedure 1980-82, Dean's coll. curriculum commn. 1981), Calif. Judges Found. Office: Ronald Reagan Fed Bldg & Courthouse 411 W 4th St Santa Ana CA 92701-4500

STOTLKES, EDITH ANN, retired grain company executive, financial planner; b. Champaign, Ill., Oct. 11, 1946; d. Kenneth Wagner and Mary (Odebrecht) S. Student, Mary Baldwin Coll., 1964-66; BA, U. Ill., 1968. Asst. v.p. Harris Trust and Savs. Bank, Chgo., 1969-83; mgr. Can. Imperial Bank of Commerce, 1983, sr. mgr., 1983-85, asst. gen. mgr. group head, 1985-88, v.p., dir. utilities, 1988-90; ptnr. Stotler Grain Co., Champaign, 1990—2002; pres. Homer Grain Co., 1990-2000; pres., bd. dirs. S&I Grain Co., 1990-2000, SEMCO Energy Inc., 1987—. Bd. dirs., mem. audit com., mem. and past chair fin. com. SEMCO Energy Inc. Past mem. investment com. 4th Presbyn. Ch.; past pres. liberal arts and scis. constituent bd. U. Ill., mem. pres.' coun.; bd. trustees Countryside Sch., 1997-2000, mem. fin. com.; mem. dean's bus. coun. and exec. coun. Coll. of Commerce, U. Ill., 1998—; bd. dirs. Champaign Country YMCA, 2000—, Champaign Pub. Libr. Found. Mem. U. Ill. Found., Champaign Country Club (mem. house com.), Art Club (past pres.), Libr. Bd. (mem. exec. com., treasurer, chair of budget com.). Avocations: needlepoint, reading, tennis, golf, cooking. Home: 900 N Lake Shore Dr Apt 2106 Chicago IL 60611-1522

STOTSENBERG, DOROTHY DANSKIN, free-lance journalist; b. Eau Claire, Wis., Feb. 4, 1914; d. John Silas Danskin and Clara Mary Bartz. AA, Chaffey Jr. Coll., Ontario, Calif., 1933; BA, U. Wash., 1936; MA, UCLA, 1954. Soc. page editor Yakima (Wash.) Daily Republic, 1936-38; women's sec. Washington Athletic Club, Seattle, 1940-46; dir. spl. events Jordan Marsh, Boston, 1946-47; program dir. Town & Country Club, Altadena, Calif., 1947-49; rep. from Calif. Saddle & Bridle, St. Louis, 1960-65; columnist The Evening Outlook, Santa Monica, Calif., 1960-80; hist. columnist Surfside News, Malibu, 1970—. V.p. for edn. Pepperdine Ctr. for the Arts Guild, Malibu, 1989-2001; coord. L.A. Philharm. Affiliates, 1989-2001.

STOTT, BRIAN, software company executive, consultant; b. Eccles, Eng., Aug. 5, 1941; came to U.S., 1983; s. Harold and Mary (Stephens) S.; m. Patricia Ann Farrar, Dec. 3, 1983. BSc, Manchester U., 1962, MSc, 1963, PhD, 1971. Asst. prof. Middle East Tech. U., Ankara, Turkey, 1965-68; lectr. Inst. Sci. and Tech., U. Manchester (Eng.), 1968-74; assoc. prof. U. Waterloo (Ont., Can.), 1974-76; cons. Electric Energy Rsch. Ctr. Brazil, Rio de Janeiro, 1976-83; prof. Ariz. State U., Tempe, 1983-84; chmn. Power Computer Applications Corp., Mesa, Ariz., 1984-2000. Cons. in field. Contbr. numerous articles to rsch. publs. Fellow IEEE (Millennium medal). Office: Stott Inc 36 E Bishop Dr Tempe AZ 85282 E-mail: brianstott@ieee.org.

STOTT, GRADY BERNELL, lawyer; b. Bailey, N.C., Sept. 19, 1921; s. William Willard and Zettie Harriett (Bissette) S.; m. Mays Beal, May 9, 1952; children: Sue J., Caroline Beal. AB, Duke U., 1947, JD, 1952. Bar: N.C. 1952. Dist. atty. 27th Jud. Dist., Gastonia, N.C., 1957-62; partner firm Stott, Hollowell, Palmer & Windham, 1960—. Served with USMC, 1943-48. Fellow Am. Bar Found., Am. Coll. Trial Lawyers; mem. N.C. State Bar (pres. 1978-79), Am. Bar Assn. (del. 1980), N.C. Bar Assn., Assn. Ins. Attys. Clubs: Masons. Democrat. Methodist. Office: 401 E Franklin Blvd Gastonia NC 28054-7152 E-mail: gbs@shpw.com.

STOTT, JAMES CHARLES, chemical company executive; b. Portland, Oreg., Sept. 5, 1945; s. Walter Joseph and Rellalee (Gray) S.; m. Caroline Loveriane Barnes, Dec. 7, 1973; children: William Joseph, Maryann Lee. BBA, Portland State U., 1969. Ops. mgr. Pacific States Express, Inc., Portland, 1970-73; bus. mgr. Mogul Corp., 1974-80; v.p. Market Transport, Ltd., 1980-85; pres., founder, chmn. bd. dirs. Chem. Corp. Am., 1985—, also bd. dirs. Chmn. bd. dirs. Carolina Industries, Portland. Mem. TAPPI. Clubs: University (Portland). Republican. Roman Catholic. Avocations: golf, outdoors. Office: Chem Corp Am 19535 SW 129th Ave Tualatin OR 97062-8076 Fax: 503-885-9701.

STOTT, PAUL EDWIN, chemist, research manager; b. Springfield, Mass., Jan. 18, 1948; s. Lyle Day and Shirley Ann (Fales) S.; m. Sharon Dowdle, Sept. 3, 1970 (div.); children: Melissa, Jason Allen, Gregory Robert; m. Mounira Gareeva, 1999. BS in Chemistry, Brigham Young U., 1971, PhD in Chemistry, 1979; MS in Chemistry, U. Mass., 1972. Gen. mgr. Parish Chem. Co., Orem, Utah, 1974-78; rsch. chemist Uniroyal Splty. Chems., Nagatuck, Conn., 1979-80, sr. group leader, 1980-82, rsch. mgr. Middlebury, 1985-92; tech. dir. Lubritex, Inc., Houston, 1982-83; v.p. tech. Am. Texmark, 1982-85; sci. rep. CIS Republics, 1992-97; mgr. external rsch. Uniroyal Chem. Co., 1997—, Crompton Corp., Middlebury, Conn., 1999—2001, head new tech. devel., 2001—. 1st lt. USAF, 1972-74. Mem. Comml. Devel. Assn. (vice chair internat. com.), Lic. Exec. Soc., Indsl. Rsch. Inst., External Rsch. Dirs. Network, Sigma Xi. Mem. Lds Ch. Achievements include patents for in fields of chemical blowing agents and polymerization inhibitors, controlled radical polymerization; development of joint research and licednsing programs with Former Soviet Research Centers in areas of polymers, polymer additives and crop protection chemicals. Office: Crompton Corp (2-2) Benson Rd Ofc Waterbury CT 06749-0001 E-mail: paul_stott@crompton.corp.com.

STOTT, PETER WALTER, forest products company executive; b. Spokane, Wash., May 26, 1944; s. Walter Joseph and Rellalee (Gray) S.; m. Julie L. Neupert, Oct. 12, 1996; 1 child, Preston. Student, Portland State U., 1962-63, 65-68, U. Americas, Mexico City, 1964-65. Founder, chmn. bd. dirs. Market Transport Ltd., Portland, Oreg., 1969—. Bd. dirs., pres., CEO, prin. Crown Pacific, Sunshine divsn.; bd. dirs. Liberty Northwest. Mem. pres.'s adv. bd. for athletics Portland State U.; trustee Lewis & Clark Coll.; mem. adv. bd. Cascade Pacific coun. Boy Scouts Am. With USAR, 1966-72. Mem. Nat. Football Found. and Hall of Fame, Oreg. Sports Hall of Fame (lifetime), Stop Oreg. Litter and Vandalism (founders' circle), Arlington Club, Mazamas Club, Multnomah Athletic Club, Portland Golf Club, The Racquet Club, Univ. Club, Waverly Country Club, Valley Club. Republican. Roman Catholic. Office: Crown Pacific 121 SW Morrison St Ste 1500 Portland OR 97204-3160

STOTT, THOMAS EDWARD, JR. retired engineering executive; b. Beverly, Mass., May 14, 1923; s. Thomas Edward and Mildred (Ayers) S.; m. Mary Elizabeth Authelet, Feb. 26, 1944; children: Pamela, Randi, Wendy, Thomas E., Diana. BS, Tufts U., 1945. Design engr. Bethlehem Steel, Quincy, Mass., 1956-59, project engr., 1959-64, sr. engr. basic ship design, 1960-63, project coordinator, 1963-64; pres. Stal-Laval, Inc., Elmsford, N.Y., 1964-84, Thomas Stott & Co., Cummaquid, Mass., 1984-88; ret., 1988. Bd. dirs. Friends of Prisoners, Inc.; deacon West Parish Barnstable, Mass., 1994-96, moderator, 1996-99. With USNR, 1944-46. Decorated (4) WWII medals with 5 combat stars, Combat ribbon. Fellow ASME (chmn. marine com., chmn. gas turbine div. exec. com., chmn. nat. nominating com., exec. sec. gas turbine div., Centennial medal 1980, R. Tom Sawyer award 1981, Dedicated Svc. award 1989), Soc. Naval Architects and Marine Engrs. Republican. Home: 51 Kates Path Yarmouth Port MA 02675-1448

STOTTER, HARRY SHELTON, banker, lawyer; b. N.Y.C., Aug. 28, 1928; s. Jack and Adele (Sgel) S.; m. Marilyn H. Knight, Nov. 7, 1954; children: Jeffrey Craig, Cheryl dee. Student, L.I. U., 1948-49; JD, St. John's U., 1952; postgrad., NYU Law Sch., 1956-57. Bar: N.Y. 1952, N.J. 1974, U.S. Supreme Ct. 1983. Pvt. practice in, N.Y.C., 1952-53, 54-56; atty. U.S. Dept. Def., 1953; with trust div. Bank of N.Y., 1956-63; exec. v.p., sr. mgmt. com. Summit Bank (now Fleet Boston Bank), NJ, 1963-84; exec. v.p. Chase Manhattan Bank, N.Y.C., 1984-94; dir., vice chmn. Chase Manhattan Trust Co. Fla., Palm Beach, Fla., 1984-87; pvt. trust and estates law practice N.J., 1974-2000; former mem. probate com. N.J. Supreme Ct. Jud. Conf. Mem. N.Y.C. and Bergen County estate planning couns.; former pres. Bergen County coun. Girl Scouts Am.; bd. dirs., pres., chief exec. officer Bergen County United Way; treas. 2d Century Fund, Hackensack Hosp.; bd. dirs. Holy Name Hosp., Teaneck, N.J. With USN, World War II; brig. gen. Army N.G. Mem. ABA (co-chmn. nat. conf. lawyers and corp. trustees 1991-93), Am. Bankers Assn. (chmn. trust counsel com. 1991-93), N.Y. Bar Assn., N.J. Bar Assn., N.Y. County Lawyers Assn., Bergen County Bar Assn. (former trustee, former chmn. probate and estate planning com.), Fed. Bar Assn., N.Y. Militia Assn.

STOTTER, JAMES, economist; b. Cleve., Feb. 13, 1941; s. Morton and Ruth (Biskind) S. BSBA, Miami U., Oxford, Ohio, 1965; MA in Econs., Case Western Res. U., 1972. Instr. Cleve. State U., 1966-72; bus. devel. coord. City of East Cleveland (Ohio), 1975-77; rsch. analyst Predicasts, Inc., Cleve., 1978; mgr. bus. devel. Greater Cleve. Growth Assn., 1979-81; econ. cons. Busimetrics, Cleve., 1981—. Mem. adj. faculty various local colls., Cleve., 1973-87. With U.S. Army, 1961-62. Mem. Nat. Assn. Bus. Economists (past pres. Cleve. chpt.), Am. Mktg. Assn., Coun. Smaller Enterprises (bd. dirs.), Cleve. C. of C., Soc. Competitive Intelligence Profls., World Future Soc. (profl. mem.). Home and Office: 5145 Chillicothe Rd Chagrin Falls OH 44022-4171

STOTTER, JAMES, II, lawyer, legal consultant; b. Cleve., Oct. 12, 1929; s. Raymond H. and Janet H. (Stern) S.; m. Hollie McGlohn, Oct. 31, 1954; children: Raymond Judd (dec.), Hillary Feidler, James Robin, Cameron Elizabeth. BA, Yale Coll., 1951; LLB, Yale U., 1954; M in Law Studies, U. So. Calif., 1961. Bar: Calif., U.S. Supreme Ct., U.S. Ct. Mil. Appeals. Asst. U.S. atty. U.S. Dept. Justice, L.A., 1957-59, 68-89, asst. chief civil div., chief drug forfeiture unit, 1980-89; pvt. practice L.A., Beverly Hills, Calif., 1960-67; instr., adj. prof. law U.S. Atty. Gen.'s Advocacy Inst. Calif. Coll. Law, U. West L.A., 1970-87; judge pro tem Mcpl. and Small Claims Ct., L.A., 1970-88; atty. at law Cambria, Calif., 1989—. Guide hist. monument Hearst Castle, San Simeon, Calif., 1991; active civic and vol. orgns., Cambria and San Luis Obispo, Calif. Capt. USAF, 1954-57. Mem. Am. Arbitration Assn. (mediator/arbitrator 1970—). Home and Office: 1595 Cardiff Dr 2d Flr Cambria CA 93428-5703

STOTTER, LAWRENCE HENRY, lawyer; b. Cleve., Sept. 24, 1929; s. Oscar and Bertha (Lieb) S.; m. Ruth Rapoport, June 30, 1957; children: Daniel, Jennifer, Steven. BBA, Ohio State U., 1956, LLB, 1958, JD, 1967. Bar: Calif. 1960, U.S. Supreme Ct. 1973, U.S. Tax Ct. 1976. Pvt. practice, San Francisco, 1963—; ptnr. Stotter and Coats, 1981-97; sole practitioner, 1997—; mem. faculty Nat. Judicial Coll.; mem. Calif. Family Law Adv. Commn., 1979-80. Editor in chief: Am. Bar Family Advocate mag, 1977-82; TV appearances on Phil Donahue Show, Good Morning America. Pres. Tamalpais Conservation Club, Marin County, Calif.; U.S. State Dept. del. Hague Conf. Pvt. Internat. Law, 1979-80; legal adv. White House Conf. on Families, 1980— . Served with AUS, 1950-53. Mem. ABA (past chmn. family law sect.), Am. Acad. Matrimonial Lawyers (past nat. v.p.), Calif. State Bar (past chmn. family law sect.), San Francisco Bar Assn. (past chmn. family law sect.), Calif. Trial Lawyers Assn. (past chmn. family law sect.) Home: 2244 Vistazo St E Belvedere Tiburon CA 94920-1970 Office: 1255 Columbus Ave # 200 San Francisco CA 94133-1326 E-mail: lhstotter@aol.com.

STOTTLEMYER, DAVID LEE, government official; b. Waynesboro, Pa., June 1, 1935; s. Omar Samuel and Miriam (Noll) S.; m. Jane Ann Hembree, Aug. 26, 1961; children: Todd Andrew, Kristen Elizabeth, Kathryn Ann. AB, Miami U., Oxford, Ohio, 1959; M. Pub. and Internat. Affairs (NDEA fellow), U. Pitts., 1964, also postgrad. Program and budget analyst Exec. Office of Pres., Office of Mgmt. and Budget, Washington, 1964-69; sr. mgmt. officer UN, N.Y.C., 1969-70; adviser internat. orgn. affairs U.S. Mission to UN, 1971-72, counsellor internat. orgn. affairs, 1973-75, counsellor UN resources mgmt., 1976-77; also mem. U.S. del. 26th-31st gen. assemblies, mem. UN Com. on Contbns., 1971; mem. UN Adv. Com. on Adminstrv. and Budgetary Questions, 1973-77; dir. policy mgmt. staff Bur. Internat. Orgn. Affairs, U.S. Dept. State, Washington, 1977-80, exec. asst. to asst. sec. of state for internat. orgn. affairs, 1980; mem. staff Office of Vice-Pres., Washington, 1981-83; dir. adminstrv. mgmt. service UN, N.Y.C., 1984-85; exec. asst., dir. Office of Under-Sec.-Gen. for Adminstrn. and Mgmt., UN, 1986-87; pvt. practice as cons., 1987-90; dir. industry rels. NASA, Washington, 1990-91, dir. office nat. svc., 1992-93; retired, 1993; cons. pvt. practice, 1993—. Served with AUS, 1953-56. Recipient Superior Honor award State Dept., 1975 Mem. Am. Fgn. Svc. Assn. Home and Office: 5920 Sherborn Ln Springfield VA 22152-1035 E-mail: dave.stot@verizon.net.

STOTZKY, GUENTHER, microbiologist, educator; b. Leipzig, Germany, May 24, 1931; came to U.S., 1939; s. Moritz Stotzky and Erna (Angres) Kester; m. Kayla Baker, Mar. 17, 1958; children: Jay, Martha, Deborah. BS, Calif. Poly. State U., 1952; MS, Ohio State U., 1954, PhD, 1956. Spl. sci. employee Argonne Nat. Lab. USAEC, Lemont, Ill., 1955; rsch. assoc. Dept. Botany U. Mich., Ann Arbor, 1956-58; head soil microbiology Cen. Rsch. Labs. United Fruit Co., Norwood, Mass., 1958-63; chmn., microbiologist Kitchawan Rsch. Labs. Bklyn. Botanic Garden, Ossining, N.Y., 1963-68; assoc. prof. Dept. Biology NYU, 1967-70, prof., 1970—, chmn., 1970-77. Editor: Soil Biochemistry, 1990-2000; series editor Marcel Dekker, Inc., 1986-92; contbr. over 275 articles to profl. jours. and chpts. to books. With USCG, 1957. Recipient Selman A. Waksman Hon. Lecture award Theobald Smith Soc., 1989, Honored Alumnus of Yr. award Calif. Poly. State U., 1992, fellowship Japanese Soc. for Promotion of Sci., 1996; named Disting. Vis. Scientist, U.S. EPA, 1986-89. Fellow AAAS, Am. Soc. Agronomy, Soil Sci. Soc. Am.; mem. Am. Acad. Microbiology, Am. Soc. Microbiology (Fisher Co. award for applied and environ. microbiology 1990, Excellence in Tchg. award N.Y.C. br. 1994). Jewish. Avocations: fishing, reading, music. Office: NYU Dept Biology 1009 Main New York NY 10003 E-mail: gs5@nyu.edu.

STOUCK, JERRY, lawyer; b. Washington, Mar. 24, 1955; s. Alex and Eileen Marion (Tepper) S.; m. Mindy A. Buren, Feb. 18, 1984; children: Danielle, David, Rachel. BA magna cum laude, Wesleyan U., 1977; JD, NYU, 1980. Bar: U.S. Dist. Ct. D.C. 1981, U.S. Ct. Fed. Claims 1981, D.C. Ct. Appeals, 1981, Md. Ct. Appeals 1983, U.S. Ct. Appeals (4th cir.) 1983, U.S. Dist. Ct. Md. 1985, U.S. Ct. Appeals (fed. cir.) 1992, U.S. Supreme Ct. 1993, U.S. Ct. Appeals (D.C. cir.) 1997. Law clk. to Hon. Pettine U.S. Dist. Ct. R.I., 1980-81; assoc. McKenna, Conner & Cuneo, Washington, 1981-83, Spriggs & Hollingsworth, Washington, 1983-84, 87-89, ptnr., 1989—; assoc. Shulman, Rogers, Gandel, Rockville, Md., 1984-87. Mem. Phi Beta Kappa. Office: Spriggs & Hollingsworth 1350 I St NW Ste 900 Washington DC 20005-3399 E-mail: jrstouck@spriggs.com.

STOUDENMIRE, WILLIAM WARD, minister; b. Charlotte, N.C., Apr. 8, 1944; s. Sterling F. and Betty Zane (Scott) S. BA in Polit. Sci., Furman U., 1966; JD, U. S.C., 1970; grad., Va. Theol. Sem., 1993. Bar: Ala. 1970, U.S. Dist. Ct. (s0. dist.) Ala. 1970, U.S. Ct. Appeals (5th cir.) 1971, U.S. Supreme Ct. 1973, U.S. Tax Ct., 1982, U.S. Ct. Appeals (11th cir.) 1982, U.S. Ct. Appeals (D.C. cir.) 1982, D.C. 1982; ordained to ministry Episcopal Ch. as deacon, 1993, as priest, 1994. Assoc. Pillans, Reams, Tappan, Wood, Roberts & Vollmer, 1970-74, jr. ptnr., 1974-78; sr. ptnr. Reams, Wood, Vollmer, Killion & Brooks, 1978-82; pvt. practice Mobile, Ala., 1982-90; legal rsch. asst. Select Com. on Crime U.S. Ho. of Reps., 1999. Mem. law day com. Ala. State Bar, 1975-78, chmn., 1978. Mem. Leadership Mobile Adv. Coun. on Govt., 1982; mem. transition adv. com. Ala. Gov.-Elect Guy Hunt, 1986; mem. Mobile County Rep. Exec. Com., 1976-90, vice chmn., 1976-81, chmn., 1979-86; mem. Ala. Rep. Exec. Com., 1979-86, platform com., 1976, 78, co-chmn., 1978, vice-chmn., 1985-89; bd. trustees Wilmer Hall Episc. Diocese Children's Home, 1987-90, sec., 1987, vice chmn., treas. 1988-90; sec. Diocese of Ctrl. Gulf Coast, 1994-99; deacon Holy Cross Episcopal Ch., 1993, asst. 1994; vicar St. Cyprians Episcopal Ch., 1994; rector St. Mary's Episcopal Ch., 1994-2001, Trinity Anglican Ch., 2001—. Served with USCGR, 1966-72. Mem. Mobile Bar Assn. (law day com. 1974-78, chmn. 1977, del. young lawyers sect. ABA conv. 1976, 77), ABA (internat. sect. human rights subcom. 1975—, chmn. 1976-79). Home: 4300 W Francisco Rd Apt 30 Pensacola FL 32504-9076 Office: Trinity Anglican Ch 4240 Hwy 90 Pace FL 32571

STOUDER, LINDA CHARMAINE, consultant to government and associations, economist, consultant; b. Richland, Wash., Dec. 12, 1950; d. Alvin Edward and Tess (Reeve) Smith; m. James Alan Mortensen, Oct. 12, 1969 (div. Aug. 1984); 1 child, Alan Stuart; m. Frederick Charles Stouder, Jan. 15, 1994. BA, Evergreen State Coll., 1988; MA, Antioch U. West, Seattle, 1990. Hosp. acct., Klamath Falls, Oreg., 1969-70; property acct. Weyerhaeuser, 1970-77; acct. Housing Authority, Sunnyside, Wash., 1978-80, exec. dir., 1980-83; housing coord. State of Wash., Olympia, 1983-85, mgr. Cmty. Devel. Block Grant, 1990-98; cons. to govt., non-profits and assns., 1998—. Chair Olympia Planning Commn., 1988-93; mem. Dem. precinct com. Olympia, 1988-90, del. Dem. state/county conv., 1988, Sonoma County Devel. com., chair, 1998-2002, cmty. devel. com.; counsellor Youth Exch. Mem.: LWV, Rotaplast Internat. (#3 treas., charter), Futurist Soc., Rotary (bd. dirs.). Home: 7400 Cathedral Oaks Rd Goleta CA 93117 Office: PO Box 4881 Petaluma CA 94955-4881 E-mail: charms4091@attbi.com.

STOUDT, HOWARD WEBSTER, biological anthropologist, human factors specialist, consultant; b. Pitts., May 13, 1925; s. Howard Webster and Harriet Catharine (Powers) S.; m. Jean Gorey Henderson, Feb. 14, 1953; children: Katharine Webster, Roberta Henderson. AB, Harvard Coll., 1949; MA, U. Pa., 1953, PhD, 1959; SM in Hygiene, Harvard U., 1963. Rsch. asst. Harvard Sch. Pub. Health, Boston, 1952-55; rsch. specialist Air U., U.S. Air Force, Montgomery, Ala., 1955-57; rsch. assoc. Harvard Sch. Pub. Health, Boston, 1957-66, asst. prof., 1966-73; prof. community medicine Mich. State U., East Lansing, 1973-88, chmn. dept., 1973-78, prof. emeritus, 1988—; cons. Stoudt Assocs., Bath, Maine, 1988—. Cons. U.S. Army, USAF, NASA, USPHS, VA, NRC, NAS, pvt. industry, 1952—. Author: Physical Anthropology of Ceylon, 1961; co-author: Human Body in Equipment Design, 1971; contbr. over 40 articles to profl. jours. Sgt. U.S. Army, 1943-46, Europe. Harrison fellow U. Pa., Phila., 1951-52, USPHS fellow, Boston, 1961-62. Fellow Human Biology Coun.; mem. AAAS, Am. Assn. Phys. Anthropologists, Human Factors and Ergonomics Soc. Democrat. Home and Office: 4 Schooner Ridge Rd Ste 4 Bath ME 04530-1662

STOUFFER, JOHN JACOB, retired music educator; b. Hagerstown, Md., May 5, 1938; s. Howard Horatio and Mildred Stouffer; m. Sandra Stetler, June 9, 1962; children: Steven, Sheri. BS, Lebanon Valley Coll., Annville, PA, 1956—60; MA Music, Univ. Mich., Ann Arbor, MI, 1962—63. Music educator Chester Sch. Dist., Chester, Pa., 1960—62, Cumberland Valley Sch. Dist., Mechanicsburg, 1963—69, Lowen Meaur Sch. Dist., Ardmore, 1969—96. Mem.: Diversified Real Estate Group. R-Conservative. Presbyterian. Home: 105 Mansion Drive Media PA 19063-1019 Office: PO Box 1270 Media PA 19063

STOUFFER, NANCY KATHLEEN, publishing company executive; b. Hershey, Pa., Feb. 14, 1951; d. William Lawrence Sweeny O'Brian and Edna Luttrell; m. David Joel Stouffer, July 19, 1980; children: Jennifer Belle, Vance David. Pres. Andé Pub. Co., Inc., Camp Hill, Pa., 1985-88; pres., chmn. B.C.I., 1988-90; v.p. R&D E.S.P. Inc., N.Y.C., 1989-90; v.p. corp. planning Nu-Tek Labs., Hershey, Pa.; exec. rschr. Assocs. in Law and Corp. Devel., Camp Hill, 1995—; owner RealMuggles.com and RealMuggles LLC. Exec. rschr Com. on Advanced Studies in Learning Disabilities Med. and Profl., SPECTRA. Author: Your Basic Guide to Creative Survival, 1991; contbr. articles on dyslexia and learning disabilities to popular mags.; author children's books; developer of Reading Genie, EZ read program, Real MUGGLES, LLC, RealMUGGLES.com Republican. E-mial. Address: 1619 S York St Mechanicsburg PA 17055 E-mail: alcdch@aol.com., chiefmuggle@aol.com., chiefmuggle@realmuggles.com.

STOUGH, LIZA BOYLE, government official; b. Homestead, Pa., Sept. 9, 1957; d. Eugene Francis and Elizabeth (Tester) Boyle. BA, U. Pitts., 1979. Adminstrv. svcs. divsn. FBI, Washington, 1981-86; facilities and adminstrv. positions Nat. Security Agy., Bedfordshire, Eng., 1986-91, travel officer Ft. Meade, Md., 1991-96, rsch. analyst, 1996—. Vol. Md. Pub. TV, ARC, 1994—,

Ctr. Stage, 1999—, ARC. Mem. Am. Mensa, Single Vols. Orgn. Balt., Annapolis, and Washington. Avocations: walking, travel, listening to music, wining, dining, antiquing. Home: 9054 Town And Country Blvd Ellicott City MD 21043-3209

STOUGHTON, HERBERT WARREN, geodetic engineer; b. Ann Arbor, Mich., Aug. 29, 1940; s. Herbert Baker and Theresa Agnes (Swab) S.; m. Catherine Wyman Dolan, May 15, 1970; 1 child, Sean Dolan. BSE in Civil Engring., U. Mich., 1963, MSE in Geodetic Engring., 1970, PhD in Civil Engring., 1980. Registered profl. engr., Colo., N.Y., Wyo.; lic. profl. land surveyor, Colo., Mich., N.Y., Ohio, Pa., Vt., W.Va., Wyo.; cert. photogrammetrist. Jr. civil engr. Atwell-Hicks, Inc., Ann Arbor, Mich., 1964; project surveyor O'Brien & Gere Cons. Engrs. and Surveyors, Syracuse, N.Y., 1965-66; jr. and asst. engr. Met. Water Dist. So. Calif., L.A., 1966-69; teaching asst., lectr. U. Mich., Ann Arbor, 1969-73; asst. prof. SUNY, Alfred, 1973-79; geodesist Dept. Def., Cheyenne, 1980—93; head surveying and mapping program Met. State Coll. of Denver, 1996—. Cons. geodetic engr., Ann Arbor, Almond, N.Y., Cheyenne, 1971—; lectr. geodetic engring. seminars, 1971—. Author 15 books; contbr. numerous articles and book revs. to profl. jours. Coach, referee Cheyenne Youth Soccer, 1981-88; vol. various civic orgns. NSF grantee, 1970, Ford Found. grantee, 1971. Mem. Am. Congress on Surveying and Mapping, Am. Soc. Photogrammetry and Remote Sensing, Can. Inst. Surveying, Am. Geophys. Union, Profl. Land Surveyors Wyo. (state pres. 1987-88), Tau Beta Pi, Chi Epsilon. Roman Catholic. Avocations: fishing, hunting, sightseeing, reading, music, refinishing antiques. Home: 2821 Carey Ave Cheyenne WY 82001-2756

STOUGHTON, W. VICKERY, healthcare executive; b. Peoria, Ill., Mar. 1, 1946; s. Warner Vickery and Mary Olive (McNamara) S.; m. Anne Stoughton; children: Zachary Benjamin, Samantha. BS, St. Louis U., 1968; MBA, U. Chgo., 1973. Asst. dir. Boston Hosp. for Women, 1973-74, Peter Bent Brigham Hosp., Boston, 1975-77, dir., 1978-80; pres. The Toronto Hosp., Ont., Can.; asst. prof. U. Toronto, 1982-90, assoc. prof., 1991; vice chancellor health affairs, chief exec. officer Duke U. Hosp., Durham, N.C., 1991-92; pres. Smithkline Beecham Clin. Labs., Collegeville, Pa., 1992-95, Smithkline Beecham Diagnostic Systems, King of Prussia, 1996; chmn., CEO Careside, Culver City, Calif., 1996—; dir. Biomira, 1988—. Bd. dirs. Sun Life Assurance Co. Bd. dirs. Toronto Symphony, 1983-86, Toronto United Way, 1988-91. Served to capt. AUS, 1969-72. Fellow Am. Coll. Hosp. Adminstrs. Home: 8820 Lookout Mountain Ave Los Angeles CA 90046-1820 Office: Careside 6100 Bristol Pkwy Culver City CA 90230-6604

STOUT, CHARLES BRIAN, anthropologist, webmaster; s. Ella Marie Petersen; m. Carol Knauss, Apr. 12, 1986; children: Corwin, Elliot. BA in Chemistry and Anthropology, MA in Anthropology, Western Mich. U.; PhD in Anthropology, U. Ill. Curator Mus. Natural History, Urbana, Ill., 1987—94; adj. asst. prof., field archaeologist Murray State U., Murray, Ky., 1994—95; contbg. cons. Wholonics Leadership Group, LLC/Quantum Muse LLC, Ann Arbor, Mich., 1995—98; ptnr. Wholonics Leadership Group, LLC, 1999; grant adminstr. Ann Arbor Hands-On Mus., 2000—01, media arts mgr., 2001—; dir., creative media developer CultureByDesign.com, Plymouth, 2001—02. Editor (author): (book) Mississippian Towns and Sacred Places, 1998; (dir., writer, prodr.): (educational music video) Solve-It Central News, 2001; composer, singer, musician, prodr.: albums American Artifacts, 2002, lyricist: musical comedy Jack and the Beanstalk, 2002. Mem.: Assn. Midwest Mus., Soc. Applied Anthropology. Avocations: walking, reading, exploring new technologies, movies. Office: Ann Arbor Hands On Mus 220 E Ann St Ann Arbor MI 48104 Personal E-mail: cstout@culturebydesign.com. E-mail: cstout@aahom.org.

STOUT, EDWARD IRVIN, medical manufacturing company executive; b. Washington, Mar. 2, 1939; s. George L. and M. Gladys (Gorsh) S.; m. Dixie Lee Farris (div.); children: Deborah Lee Stout Poole, Cathy Ann Stout Phillips, Angela Fay Stout McKessor; m. Marjorie Soria. BS, Iowa Wesleyan Coll., 1960; MS in Chemistry, Bradley U., 1968; PhD in Organic Chemistry, U. Ariz., 1973. Analytical chemist Lever Bros. Rsch., Edgewater, N.J., 1961-62; rsch. chemist USDA, Peoria, Ill., 1962-78; dir. rsch. Spenco Med. Corp., Waco, Tex., 1978-81; pres. S.W. Techs. Inc., Kansas City, Mo., 1981-96, chmn. bd., 1996—; dir. rsch. Chemstar Product Co., Mpls., 1982-86, cons., 1979-81. Cons. Stout Supply Co., Ainsworth, Iowa, 1985—; instr. Bradley U., Peoria, 1970-78. Contbr. articles to profl. jours.; patentee in field. Mem. Am. Chem. Soc., Inst. Food Technologists, Am. Assn. Cereal Chemists, Am. Burn Assn., Soc. Plastic Engrs., Mid-Am. Inventors Assn. (v.p. 1988), Wound Healing Soc. Avocation: tennis. Home: 10590 Haskins St Shawnee Mission KS 66215-4306 Office: SW Techs Inc 1746 E Levee St North Kansas City MO 64116-4404 E-mail: swtech@birch.net.

STOUT, ELIZABETH WEST, foundation administrator; b. San Francisco, Mar. 4, 1917; d. Claudius Wilson and Sarah (Henderson) West; m. Bruce Churchill McDonald, Mar. 19 1944 (dec. 1952); children: Douglas, Anne; m. Charles Holt Stout, Oct. 27, 1958 (dec. 1992); stepchildren: Richard, George (dec.), Martha Stout Gilweit. Student, U. Nev., 1934-37; grad., Imperial Valley Coll., 1990. Cashier, acct. N.Y. Underwriters, San Francisco, 1937-42; sec. supply and accounts USN, 1942-44. Contbr. articles to profl. jours. Mem. adv. bd. Anza-Borrego Desert, Natural History Assn., 1974-84; founder Stout Paleontology Lab., Borrego Springs, Calif., 1982; found. trustee Desert Rsch. Inst., Reno, 1989—; active Black Rock Desert Project, 1989, Washoe Med. Ctr. League, 1953—, St. Mary's Hosp. Guild, 1953—. Named Disting. Nevadan U. Nev., 1993. Mem. Anza-Borrego Desert Natural History Assn. (dir. emeritus 1984), Soc. Vertebrate Paleontology, De Anza Desert Country Club, Kappa Alpha Theta. Republican. Episcopalian. Avocations: travel, writing, reading, golf.

STOUT, GLENN EMANUEL, retired science administrator; b. Fostoria, Ohio, Mar. 23, 1920; AB, Findlay U., 1942, DSc, 1973. Sci. coord. NSF, 1969-71; asst. to chief Ill. State Water Survey, Champaign, 1971-74; prof. Inst. Environ. Studies, Urbana, Ill., 1973-94, dir. task force, 1975-79; dir. Water Resources Ctr. U. Ill., 1973-94; rsch. coord. Ill.-Ind. Sea Grant Program, 1987-94; emeritus, 1994—. Mem. Ill. Gov.'s Task Force on State Water Plan, 1980-94; bd. dirs. Univ. Coun. Water Resources, 1983-86, chmn. internat. affairs, 1989-92; mem. nomination com. for Stockholm Water Prize, 1994-96. Contbr. articles to profl. jours. Bd. govs. World Water Coun., 1996-98. Mem. Am. Water Resources Assn., Internat. Water Resources Assn. (sec. gen. 1985-91, v.p. 1992-94, exec. dir. 1984-95, pres. 1995-97), Am. Meteorol. Soc., Am. Geophys. Union, N.Am. Lake Mgmt. Soc., Ill. Lake Mgmt. Assn. (bd. dirs. 1985-88), Am. Water Works Assn., Kiwanis (pres. local club 1979-80, lt. gov. 1982-83), Sigma Xi (pres. U. Ill. chpt. 1985-86). Home: 920 W John St Champaign IL 61821-3907 Office: Intl Water Resource Assn 1101 W Peabody Dr Urbana IL 61801-4723 E-mail: g-stout@uiuc.edu.

STOUT, LANDON CLARKE, JR. pathologist, educator; b. Kansas City, Mo., Feb. 20, 1933; s. Landon Clarke and Mildred Ann (Buckner) S.; m. Martha Ann McKone, May 1, 1954 (div. Dec. 1975); children: Lynn, Clinton, Karen, Sally, Edward Halsted; m. Elaine Marie Farrell, Feb. 28, 1981. BS, U. Md., 1954, MD, 1957. Diplomate Am. Bd. Pathology. Rotating intern U. Okla., Oklahoma City, 1957-58, resident in internal medicine, 1958-61, resident in pathology, 1966-67, spl. fellow in pathology, 1967-68, asst. prof. medicine, 1963-72, asst. prof. pathology, 1968-71, assoc. prof., 1971-72, interim chmn. pathology, 1970-72; assoc. prof. pathology U. Tex. Med. Br., Galveston, 1972-74, prof., 1974—. Cons. Okla. Med. Rsch. Found., Oklahoma City, 1970-72. Contbr. articles on mitral valve disease and diabetic renal disease to profl. jours. Grantee NIH, John A. Hartford Found. Mem. Am. Heart Assn., ACP, Am. Gastroent. Assn., Am. Diabetes Assn., Am. Soc. Investigative Pathology, U.S. and Can. Acad. Pathology. Office: U Tex Dept Path 9th And Mechanic St Galveston TX 77555-0001

STOUT, LOWELL, lawyer; b. Tamaha, Okla., July 23, 1928; s. Charles W. and Rosetta (Easley) S.; m. Liliane Josue, Nov. 29, 1952; children: Georgianna, Mark Lowell. Student, Northeastern State Coll., Tahlequah, Okla., 1946-49, U. Okla., 1949-51; LLB, U. N.Mex., 1952. Bar: N.Mex. 1952. Ptnr. Easley, Quinn & Stout, Hobbs, N.Mex., 1954-58, Girand & Stout, Hobbs, 1958-60; pvt. practice, 1960-80; ptnr. Stout & Stout, 1980—. With U.S. Army, 1952-54. Perenially listed in Best Lawyers in America. Fellow Am. Coll. Trial Lawyers; mem. Assn. Trial Lawyers Am., State Bar N.Mex., N.Mex. Trial Lawyers Assn., Lea County Bar Assn. Home: 218 W Lea St Hobbs NM 88240-5110 Office: Stout & Stout PO Box 716 Hobbs NM 88241-0716

STOUT, MARY WEBB, education program specialist; b. Richmond, Va., Dec. 24, 1947; d. Frank Edmond Webb and Edith Diuguid (Harris) Webb Steger; m. Teddy Alvin Stout, July 8, 1972. BA, Mary Washington Coll., 1970; MEd, U. Va., Charlottesville, 1972; Edn. Specialist, Coll. William and Mary, 1991, EdD, 1995. Tchr. Harrisonburg (Va.) City Schs., 1970-71, Buckingham (Va.) County Schs., 1972-73; guidance counselor So. European Task Force U.S. Army, Vicenza, Italy, 1973-78, edn. specialist Quartermaster Sch. Ft. Lee, Va., 1978-80, edn. specialist Tng. Support Ctr. Ft. Eustis, 1980-82; edn. specialist Hqrs. Training, Doctrine Command, Ft. Monroe, 1982-83; edn. svcs. specialist Combined Arms Ctr., Ft. Leavenworth, Kans., 1983-88; instrnl. systems specialist Hqrs. TRADOC, Ft. Monroe, 1988-98; supervisory edn. svcs. specialist Hdqrs. U.S. Army Pers. Command, Alexandria, Va., 1998-2000; edn. program specialist OSD Office of Chancellor Edn. and Profl. Devel., Arlington, 2000—; online faculty U. Phoenix, 2002—. Legis. affairs rep. Running Man Homeowners Assn., Yorktown, Va., 1996—98; treas. Massanetta Springs Alumni Assn., Harrisonburg, 1988—2000, pres.-elect, 2002—; mem. devel. bd. Sch. Edn., Coll. William and Mary, 2002—; bd. dirs., membership chmn. Massanetta Springs Alumni Assn., Harrisonburg, 1998—, pres., 2002—; mem. devel. bd. Sch. of Edn. Coll. of William and Mary, 2002—. Recipient Alumni award Massanetta Springs Alumni Assn., 1996. Mem.: Am. Assn. for Advancement Adult and Continuing Edn., Mary Washington Coll. Alumni Assn., U. Va. Alumni Assn., Coll. William and Mary Alumni Assn., Assn. Advancement of Computing in Edn., Assn. Ednl. Comm. and Tech., Army Mgmt. Staff Coll. Alumni Assn., Am. Assn. Higher Edn., Assn. Study Higher Edn., Kappa Delta Pi. Presbyterian. Avocations: running, Red Cross water safety instructor. Home: 6006 River Dr Mason Neck VA 22079-4127 Office: Dept Def Chancellor Edn and Profl Devel 4040 Fairfax Dr Ste 200 Arlington VA 22203-1613 E-mail: STOUTMW@OSD.Pentagon.mil., MSTOUT8895@aol.com.

STOUT, MAYE ALMA, educator; b. Reliance, S.D., Mar. 3, 1920; d. Jesse Wilbur and Susie Maude (Fletcher) Moulton; m. Dennis William Stout, Jan. 6, 1943; children: Perry Wilbur, David Jay. BA, Dakota Wesleyan U., Mitchell, S.D., 1969. Tchr. Rural Lyman County Sch., Iona/Oacoma, S.D., 1939-42, Vivian (S.D.) Pub. Sch., 1942, Rural Lyman County Sch., Reliance, S.D., 1944-45, Reliance Cons. Dist., 1945-46, 49-51, Ft. Pierre (S.D.) Ind. Sch. Dist., 1954-67, Kadoka (S.D.) Ind. Sch., 1967-82; ret. Asst. editor: Jackson/Washabaugh County History 2, 1989; contbr. articles to publications. Pres. Kadoka Community Betterment Assn., 1987. Mem. Am. Legion Aux. (dist. pres. 1985-89, chmn. com. Dept. Fgn. Rels. 1990-91, dept. chmn. constitution and by-laws com. 1992-93). Republican. Methodist. Avocations: reading, crocheting, travel. Address: PO Box 231 Kadoka SD 57543-0231 E-mail: mastout@gwtc.net.

STOUT, ROBERT JOE, freelance journalist; b. Feb. 3, 1938; BA in Journalism/Creative Writing, Mexico City Coll. Freelance journalist and poet. Author: (poetry) They Still Play Baseball the Old Way, (novel) Miss Sally; contbr. articles to Chgo. Tribune Mag., Notre Dame Mag., Army Mag., Modern Maturity, Chic, American Way, Commonweal, Christian Social Action, For Men Only, Sunday Woman, The Nation, Christian Century. Address: PO Box 5074 Chico CA 95927-5074 also: Allende No 75 Dpto 5 La Paz Mexico 23000 E-mail: bobstout@journalist.com.

STOUT, THOMAS MELVILLE, control systems engineer; b. Ann Arbor, Mich., Nov. 26, 1925; s. Melville B. and Laura C. (Meisel) S.; m. Marilyn J. Koebnick, Dec. 27, 1947; children: Martha, Sharon, Carol, James, William, Kathryn. BSEE, Iowa State Coll., 1946; MSE, U. Mich., 1947, PhD, 1954. Registered profl. engr., Calif. Jr. engr. Emerson Electric Co., St. Louis, 1947-48; instr., then asst. prof. U. Wash., Seattle, 1948-54; rsch. engr. Schlumberger Instrument Co., Ridgefield, Conn., 1954-56; dept. mgr. TRW/Bunker-Ramo Corp., Canoga Park, Calif., 1956-65; pres. Profimatics, Inc., Thousand Oaks, 1965-83; pvt. practice cons. Northridge, 1984—. Active profl. engring. registration and certification; mem., bd. dirs. Accreditation Bd. for Engring. and Tech., 1995-2001. Contbr. articles, revs., papers to profl. publs., chpts. to books. Ens. USN, 1943-46. Fellow, hon. mem. Instrument Soc. Am.; mem. IEEE (sr. mem.), NSPE, AIChE, Am. Soc. for Engring. Edn., Calif. Soc. Profl. Engrs. Achievements include four patents in computer control of industrial processes; participant in early digital computer installations for industrial process control. Home and Office: 9927 Hallack Ave Northridge CA 91324-1120 E-mail: tomstoutpe@aol.com.

STOUTE, MARGUERITE ALLYN, nurse, educator, consultant; b. Bklyn., Aug. 27, 1949; d. Allan Humphrey and Ina Gertrude (Ricketts) S. B.A., Manhattanville Coll., 1973; B.S. in Nursing Edn., NYU-Washington Square, 1981, M.A. in Nursing Edn., 1983. R.N. Researcher Mt. Sinai Hosp., N.Y.C., 1973, Columbia U., N.Y.U., 1973-74; staff/in-charge nurse Kings County Hosp., Bklyn., 1983— ; coordinator nursing edn., inservice-staff devel., diabetes educator Bklyn. Hosp., 1986-88, supr., coord. med.-surg. Lincoln Med. Mental Health Ctr.; nursing educator Lincoln Hosp. Med. and Health Ctr., 1990—; cons. Ina Mag Assn., Bklyn., 1984— ; adj. prof. N.Y.C. Tech. Community Coll., 1985—, Lehman Coll., Bronx, 1990—. Pres. Scholarship Fund, Nazarene Ch., Bklyn., 1983— ; assoc. mem. Bedford Stuyvesant Alcoholic Treatment Ctr., Bedford, Monroe, Bklyn., 1980— ; class agt. class of '73, Manhattanville Coll. Served to capt. Nurse Corps USAR. Mem. Am. Nurses Assn., Assn. Diabetes Educators, Nat. Assn. Female Execs., Nat. Entrepreneur Assn., NYU Alumni Assn. Club: Manhattanville (Purchase, N.Y.). Avocations: writing; singing; speaking; teaching. Home: 1158 Bedford Ave Brooklyn NY 11216-1616

STOUTENBURG, JANE SUE WILLIAMSON, nurse practitioner, fund raiser, actress; b. Davenport, Iowa, Mar. 10, 1949; d. George Baker and Hazel Elaine (Kline) W.; m. Noel Wayne Stoutenburg, Aug. 25, 1979 (div. July 1996); 1 child, Karen Elaine. AS with honors, Black Hawk Jr. Coll., East Moline, Ill., 1970; BA, BS, Augustana Coll., 1973, 75; Cert. in Fire Sci. with honors, Harper Coll., Palatine, Ill., 1982; AS in Nursing with high honors, Elgin Community Coll., 1987. EMT; cert. paramedic; cert. tchr. Rsch. technologist Rush-Presbyn. St. Luke's Med. Ctr., Chgo., 1974-75; acct. supr., pvt. investigator Per Mar Security Inc., Davenport, Iowa, 1975-77; pre-trial release investigator 7th Jud. Ct. Dist., 1976-77; pharm. rep. Bristol Labs., Syracuse, N.Y., 1977-80; dir. safety tng. Zee Med., Irvine, Calif., 1981-83; tng. specialist ARC, Chgo., 1983-86, Lake County Fire Rescue, Barrington, Ill., 1981—; nurse practitioner Boy Scouts of Am., St. Charles, 1990—; nurse trainer Buehler YMCA, Palatine, 1990-94. Emergency med. svc. coord. Robbins (Ill.) Fire Dept., 1985—; bd. dirs. Barrington Area Devel. Coun., 1981-90; EMS coord. Lake Counte Fire Rescue, 1980—, owner, Snail's Pace Gifts, Barrington, IL, 1997—, pres. Karyn Etcetera Inc., 1997—. Author: Academy of Science, 1967, (poetry), 1970, actress: ER, 1997—, First Edition, 1998—, Backdraft, A Normal Life, Relic, My Best Friends Wedding. Troop leader Girl Scouts, Barrington, 1990-95; book fair chmn. Lines Sch. PTO, Barrington, 1991-94; camp nurse Boy Scouts Am., Camp Big Timber, Ill., YMCA Camp Duncan, Fox Lake, Ill.; pageant judge Miss Am. System, 1995—.bd. dirs. Elgin C.C., 1998—, NW Suburb Chgo. Vol. Bur., 1998—. Recipient Ill. EMT of the Yr. award, 1989-90, Disting. Svc. award ARC, 1989, Disting. Svc. key Alpha Phi Omega, 1989, Key, Phi Theta Kappa, 1989, Vol. of the Yr. award Chgo. Vol. Bur., 1993, J.C. Penney Golden Flame award, 1993. Mem. Am. Soc. Safety Engrs., Am. Trauma Soc., Am. Acad. Sci., Internat. Soc. Fire Sci. Instrs., Prehosp. Care Providers of Ill., Alpha Phi Omega (mem. bd. dirs. 1995—, publicity com.), P.E.O. Sisterhood. Episcopalian. Avocations: poetry, camping, firefighting, girl scouts, dixieland jazz. Office: Lake County Fire Rescue 618 W Northwest Hwy Ste 213 Barrington IL 60010-2730

STOVAL, LINDA, political party official; b. Wyo. m. Tony Stoval. Ran 2 campaigns former Dem. Gov. Mike Sullivan; owner Solutions, Wyo.; chairperson Wyo. Dem. Party, 2001—. Office: 737 Kirk Ave Casper WY 82601-3324 Business E-Mail: stoval@trib.com.*

STOVALL, CARLA JO, state attorney general; b. Hardner, Kans., Mar. 18, 1957; d. Carl E. and Juanita Joe (Ford) Stovall. BA, Pittsburg (Kans.) State U., 1979; JD, U. Kans., 1982, MPA , 1993. Bar: Kans. 1982, U.S. Dist. Ct. Kans. 1982. Pvt. practice, Pitts., 1982—85; atty. Crawford County, 1984—88; gov. Kans. Parole Bd., Topeka, 1988—94; atty. gen. State of Kans., 1995—. Lectr. law Pittsburg State U. , 1982—84; pres. Gilston Internat. Mktg., Inc., 1988—. Mem. bd. govs. U. Kans. Sch. Law; Nat. Ctr. Missing and Exploited Children; Am. Legacy Found.; Nat. Crime Prevention Coun.; Coun. State Govts.; mem. bd. govs. Kans. Children's Cabinet; pres. NAAG, 2001—02, chmn. exec. com. midwest region, sexually violent predator com., 1995—96; Bd. dirs., sec. Pittsburg Family YMCA, 1983—88. Named Outstanding Atty. Gen., Nat. Assn. Attys. Gen., 2001, Topeka Fraternal Order of Police's Amb. to Law Enforcement; recipient Champion award, Campaign Tobacco Free Kids, 2002, Adam Walsh Children's Fund Rainbow award, Nat. Ctr. Missing and Exploited Children, 2001, Kelley-Wyman award, Nat. Assn. Attys. Gen., 2001, Person of the Yr., Kans. Peace Officer Assn.'s Law Enforcement, Morton Baud Allied Profl. award, Nat. Orgn. Victim Assistance, Father Ken Czillinger award, Nat. Parents Murdered Children, Disting. Svc. to Kans. Children award, Kans. Children's Svc. League, Woman of Achievement award, Miss Kans. Pageant. Mem.: NAAG (pres. 2001—02), AAUW (bd. dirs. 1983—87), ABA, Bus. and Profl. Women Assn. (Young Careerist award 1984), Nat. Coll. Dist. Attys., Kans. County and Dist. Attys. Assn., Crawford County Bar Assn. (sec. 1984—85, v.p. 1985—86, pres. 1986—87), Kans. Bar Assn., Kans. Assn. Commerce and Industry (Leadership Kans. award 1983), Pittsburg Area C. of C. (bd. dirs. 1983—85, Leadership Pitts. award 1984), Pittsburg State U. Alumni Assn. (bd. dirs. 1983—88). Republican. Methodist. Avocations: travel, photography, tennis. Home: 3561 SW Mission Ave Topeka KS 66614-3637 Office: Atty Gen Office Meml Hall 120 SW 10th Ave Fl 2 Topeka KS 66612-1597*

STOVALL, JERRY (COLEMAN STOVALL), insurance company executive; b. Houston, July 31, 1936; s. Clifford Coleman and Maxine (Lands) S.; m. Elsie Hostetter, June 20, 1959; 1 child, Brent Allen. BBA, U. Houston, 1968. Adminstr. home office Am. Gen. Life, Houston, 1955-63, agt., agy. mgr., 1963-66, agy. mgr., regional dir. agys., regional v.p., 1969-74; sr. brokerage cons. Conn. Gen. Life, 1966-69; sr. v.p., dir. mktg. Capitol Life Inst. Co., Denver, 1974-78; v.p., dir. mktg. Integon Life Ins. Corp., Winston-Salem, N.C., 1978-81; pres. Life of Mid-Am. Ins. Co., Topeka, 1981-85, Victory Life Ins. Co., Topeka, 1981-85, chmn., pres., chief exec. officer, 1981-87; pres., retired chief exec officer Integon Life Ins. Co., Winston-Salem, N.C., 1987-91; pres. Lamar Life Ins. Co., 1992-95, ret., 1995; pres., CEO Am. Pub. Holding Inc., 1996-2000, ret., 2000. Bd. dirs., vice-chmn., Ga. Internat. Life; vice-chmn. Mktg. One Inc. Bd. dirs. Jr. Achievement Miss., Inc.; bd. trustees Miss. Bapt. Found. With U.S. Army, 1955-57. Mem. Nat. Assn. Life Cos., Nat. Assn. Life Underwriters, Am. Soc. CLUs (Gold Key soc.), Am. Coun. Life Ins., Exec. Round Table (chmn. 1995), The Country Club of Jackson. Home: 420 Saint Andrews Dr Jackson MS 39211-2511

STOVALL, RICHARD L. academic administrator; b. Springfield, Mo., Mar. 28, 1944; s. Wilbern Lee and Ernestine Patricia (Putman) S.; m. Susannah K. Young; children: Richard Christopher, Stacy Suzanne. BA, SW Mo. State U., 1966; MA, C.W. Post Coll. L.I. U., 1969; PhD, Ohio State U., 1975. Instr. SW Mo. State U., Springfield, 1969-72; asst. prof. U. S.C., Columbia, S.C., 1975-77; prof., asst. dept. head SW Mo. State U., Springfield, 1977—. Cons. Cedar Hills High Sch., Dallas, 1986, Andrews Ins. Agy., 1984, Mo. Cosmetology Assn., 1983-84, Springfield Pers. Assn., 1982, Syntex Corp. 1981-82; pub. rels. Halcyon of Dallas, 1988-96, Hawthorne Group of Washington, 1995-96, The Harrell Group, Dallas, 1999. Contbr. articles to profl. jours. Tabulation room coord. for MSHSAA Dist. Speech Festival; lectr. Springfield Pub. Schs., City Utilities Citizens Adv. Bd.; pres. Boy Scouts Am. With ES USNR-TAR, 1962-69. Mem. Pub. Rels. Soc. Am., Am. Forensics Assn., Speech Communication Assn. Am., So. Speech Communication Assn., Pub. Rels. of the Ozarks, Pub. Rels. Soc. Mid-Mo., Cen. States Speech Assn., Speech and Theatre Assn. Mo., Cherokee Homeowners Assn. (pres.). Episcopal. Home: 3 Whiterock Ln Kimberling City MO 65686 Office: SW Mo State U 901 S National Ave Springfield MO 65804-0088 E-mail: richardstovall@msn.c.

STOVALL, ROBERT H(ENRY), money management company executive; b. Louisville, 1926; s. Harold Samuel and Agnes C. (Hinkle) S.; m. Inger Bagger; children: Sten Torben, Harold Samuel II, Inger Benedikte, Robert Henry. BS in Econs., U. Pa., 1948; postgrad. in polit. economy, U. Copenhagen, 1948-49; MBA, N.Y. U., 1957. With E. F. Hutton & Co., 1953-67, mgr. dept. investment rsch., 1958-60, gen. ptnr. responsible for rsch., 1961-67, chmn. com. investment policy, 1966-68; rsch. dir. Nuveen Corp., 1968-69; ptnr. in mktg. and rsch. Reynolds & Co., 1969, dir. rsch., 1970-73; sr. v.p., dir. investment policy Dean Witter Reynolds Inc. (merger Reynolds & Co. and Dean Witter & Co., acquired by Sears, Roebuck and Co. 1981), N.Y.C., 1978-85, pub. comments on market column, 1961-85; pres. Stovall/Twenty-First Advisers, Inc., 1985-2000; sr. v.p. market strategist Prudential Securities Inc., 2000—. Lectr., tchr. in field; commentator Nat. Pub. Radio, 1982— ; prof. fin. NYU, 1985—; regular commentator CNN, 1981—, "This Morning's Business", CBS-TV, 1988-91, "Market Wrap", Sta. CNBC/FNN-TV; governing mem. Com. on Developing Am. Capitalism, Fairfield, Conn.; bd. dirs. Trust Cos. Am., Venice, Fla. Columnist Forbes, 1968-76, Fin. World, 1979-98, Sales and Mktg. Mgmt., 1995-99; contbr. articles to profl. publs.; panelist: Wall St. Week, Public Broadcasting System, 1977—, Hall of Fame, 1995. Bd. overseers Grad. Sch. Bus. Adminstrn. NYU, 1984-90, U. Pa. Librs., 1992-98; chmn. Security Industry Inst., 1986-88, life trustee, 1989—; chmn. Securities Industry Assn., Eco. Edn. Found., N.Y. and N.J., 1992-98; trustee St. Clare's-Riverside Health Care Ctr. Found., Denville, N.J., 1980-93, Wayne County (Pa.) Meml. Hosp.; mem. found. bd. 1989—; bd. overseers Seton Hall Prep. Sch., West Orange, N.J., 1985-93; bd. sponsors Loyola Coll. in Md. Schs. Bus., 1990-95, 1991—; dir. Sarasota Opera Assn., 1993—, Nat. Coun. Econ. Edun., 1998—. With U.S. Army, WWII, Italy. Mem. Inst. Chartered Fin. Analysts (CFA), N.Y. Soc. Security Analysts (past dir., vice chmn. program com.), Mensa, Sarasota Univ. Club, Penn Club N.Y., S.R., Kentuckians of N.Y. (pres. 1988-90), Sons of Confederate Vets., Pilgrims of N.Am., Beta Gamma Sigma. Home: 888 Blvd of Arts Sarasota FL 34236-4871 Office: Prudential Securities Inc 1 New York Plz Fl 16 New York NY 10292-0001 Fax: 212 778-7953. E-mail: robert_stovall@prusec.com.

STOVER, CARL FREDERICK, foundation executive; b. Pasadena, Calif., Sept. 29, 1930; s. Carl Joseph and Margarete (Müller) S.; m. Catherine Swanson, Sept. 3, 1954; children: Matthew Joseph, Mary Margaret Stover Marker, Claire Ellen Stover Herrell; m. Jacqueline Kast, Sept. 7, 1973. BA magna cum laude, Stanford U., 1951, MA, 1954. Instr. polit. sci. Stanford U., 1953-55; fiscal mgmt. officer Office Sec. Dept. Agr., 1955-57; assoc. dir. conf. program pub. affairs Brookings Instn., 1957-59, sr. staff govtl. studies, 1960; fellow Center Study Democratic Instns., Santa Barbara, Calif., 1960-62; asst. to chmn. bd. editors Ency. Brit., 1960-62; sr. polit. scientist Stanford Research Inst., 1962-64; dir. pub. affairs fellowship program Stanford U., 1962-64; pres. Nat. Inst. Pub. Affairs, Washington, 1964-70, Nat. Com. U.S.-China Relations, 1971-72; pres., dir. Federalism Seventy-Six, Washington, 1972-74; dir. cultural resources devel. Nat. Endowment Arts, 1974-78; pres., dir. Cultural Resources, Inc., Washington, 1978-85; bd. dirs. H.E.A.R. Found., 1976-86, treas., 1976-80, pres., 1980-86. Bd. dirs. Ctr. for World Lit., pres., 1987-90, chmn., 1990-92; pvt. profl. cons., 1970—; scholar-in-residence Nat. Acad. Pub. Adminstrn., 1980-82; cons. in field. Author: The Government of Science, 1962, The Technological Order, 1963; Founding editor: Jour. Law and Edn., 1971-73; pub. Delos mag., 1987-92. Treas. Nat. Com. U.S.-China Rels., 1966-71, 82-87, 89-94, bd. dirs., 1966-74, 79-98, dir. emeritus, 1998—; bd. dirs. Coord. Coun. Lit. Mags., 1966-68, H.E.A.R. Found., 1976-86, treas., 1976-80; trustee Inst. of Nations, 1972-76, Nat. Inst. Pub. Affairs, 1967-71, Kinesis Ltd., 1972-78; vol. Nat. Exec. Svc. Corps, 1984-89. Fellow AAAS, Phi Beta Kappa (hon. lectr. 1972-87); mem. Am. Soc. Pub. Adminstrn., Fedn. Am. Scientists, Soc. Internat. Devel., Jordan Soc. (dir. 1982-84), Nat. Acad. Pub. Adminstrn. (hon.), Md. U. Club, Internat. Soc. Panetics (pres. 1991-95, chmn. 1995-98, chmn. emeritus 1999—, bd. govs. 1991—, founding mem. 1991—). Democrat. Presbyterian. Home and Office: 4109 Metzerott Rd College Park MD 20740-2082 E-mail: carlfstover@aol.com.

STOVER, CAROLYN NADINE, middle school educator; b. Martinsburg, W.Va., May 30, 1950; d. Norman Robert and Garnet Agnes (Zombro) Whetzel; m. James Stenner Stover Sr., Nov. 20, 1971; children: Heather N., James S. Jr. BA in Home Econs., Shepherd Coll., 1972; cert. in advanced studies, W.Va. U., 1978; cert. in tchg. methods, Marshall U., 1973; cert. in spl. edn., Shippensburg Coll., 1972. Cert. tchr., W.Va., N.Mex.; reg. EMT.

Substitute tchr. Berkeley County Schs., Martinsburg, W.Va., 1972, adult edn. instr., 1972-77, home econs. instr., 1973-83; substitute tchr. Ruidoso (N.Mex.) Mcpl. Schs., 1984-90, child find coord. Region 9 edn. coop., 1990, life skills and at-risk educator, 1991—, coord. coun., 1991-93, mem. budget com., 1993. Elder First Presbyn. Ch., Ruidoso, 1984-90, 94-96, 2002--; sponsor Acad. Booster Club, Ruidoso, 1993—; instr. CPR, 1980. Named Outstanding Young Women of Am., 1981. Mem. NEA, Nat. Middle Sch. Assn., Ruidoso Edn. Assn. (reporter, membership chair), Ruidoso Bowling Assn. (sec. 1999-2001), Rotary (youth leadership councilor 1991—). Democrat. Avocations: cross-stitching, needlework, family, sports, youth. Home: Box 7837 PO Box 7837 Ruidoso NM 88355-7837 Office: Ruidoso Mid Sch 100 Reese Dr Ruidoso NM 88345-6016

STOVER, JAMES HOWARD, retired real estate executive; b. Forest Hill, W.Va., Oct. 20, 1911; s. Charles William and Zora (Goode) S.; m. May Simmons, Oct. 21, 1939 (dec.); children: Ann, Robert Bruce; m. Elizabeth J. Cobb, Dec. 27, 1977 (dec.). Student, Benjamin Franklin U., 1936-38; grad., Advanced Mgmt. Program, Harvard U., 1959, Exec. Devel. Program Ind. U., 1960, Inst. Mgmt. Northwestern U., 1960. Asst. purchasing agt. Woodward & Lothrop, Washington, 1932-35; asst. chief field supervision div., central accounts office Bur. Accounts Treasury Dept., 1935-41, asst. chief Treasury Budget sect., 1941-42, fiscal acct. Office Commr. Pub. Debt, 1946-51, chief treasury mgmt. analysis staff, 1951-63, dir. Office Mgmt. and Orgn., 1963-66, regional commr. customs Miami Region IV, 1966-72; real estate sales assoc., mgmt. cons., 1972-75; pres. Bay Realty of Fla., Inc., 1975-99; ret., 1999. Chmn. Inter-agy. Mgmt. Analysis Conf., 1958-59; mem. orgn. and mgmt. adv. com. Dept. Agr. Grad. Sch., 1956-63. Chmn. adv. coms. orgn. and procedure and legislative program Arlington (Va.) County Bd., 1958-63; pres. Tuckahoe Recreation Club, 1957; chmn. Greater Miami Fed. Exec. Coun., 1968-69; mem. exec. adv. coun. Coll. Bus. and Pub. Adminstrn., Fla. Atlantic U., 1969-80. 2d lt. to maj. AUS, 1942-46. Recipient Rockefeller Pub. Svc. award, 1959, Spl. Svc. award Treasury Dept., 1963, Exceptional Svc. award, 1965, other treasury awards, 1969, 70, 71, 72. Home: 707 Vilabella Ave Coral Gables FL 33146-1733

STOVER, JOHN FORD, railroad historian, educator; b. Manhattan, Kans., May 16, 1912; s. John William and Maud (Ford) S.; m. Marjorie Ellen Filley, Aug. 21, 1937; children: John Clyde, Robert Vernon (dec.), Charry Ellen Stover Olin. AB, U. Nebr., 1934, MA, 1937; PhD, U. Wis., 1951. Instr. social studies Arcadia (Nebr.) High Sch., 1936-37; instr. history and govt. Bergen (N.J.) Jr. Coll., 1937-41; grad. asst. history U. Wis., 1941-42, 46-47, Univ. fellow, 1946; from instr. to assoc. prof. Purdue U., Lafayette, Ind., 1947-59, prof. history, 1959-78, prof. emeritus, 1978—, Purdue Research Found. XL grantee, summer 1957, 59, fellow in Coll.-Bus. Exchange Program, I.C. R.R., summer 1962. Chmn. Pres.'s adv. coun. on retirement Purdue U., 1980-81. Author: The Railroads of the South, 1865-1900, 1955, American Railroads, 1961, rev. edit., 1997, A History of American Railroads, 1967, Turnpikes, Canals and Steamboats, 1969, The Life and Decline of the American Railroad, 1970, Transportation in American History, 1970, History of Illinois Central Railroad, 1975, Iron Road To The West, 1978, Sixty-Five Years of Kiwanis in Indiana, 1981, History of the Baltimore & Ohio Railroad, 1987, Seventy-Five Years of Kiwanis and Indiana, 1990, The Routledge Historical Atlas of the American Railroads, 1999; contbr. to hist. jours., books, numerous encys., including Americana and Academic Americana, and biog. works. Chmn. edn. com., mem. exec. com. Ind. Sesquicentennial Commn., 1962-67; hon. mem. Indiana Am. Revolution Bicentennial commn., 1972-82; mem. adv. council Centennial History of Ind. Gen. Assembly, 1979-83; pres. Lafayette Kiwanis Found., 1977-78. Served to capt. USAAF, 1942-46; Res., 1946-53, ret., 1953. George F. Hixson fellow, 1996; named Sagamore of the Wabash Gov. Ind., 1978; recipient Alumni Achievement award U. Nebr., 1985. Fellow Soc. Am. Historians; mem. Ind. Acad. Social Scis., Western History Assn., Bus. History Conf. (trustee 1973-76), Am. Hist. Assn., So. Ind. Hist. Assn. (com. on library 1975-91), Nebr. Hist. Assn., Tippecanoe County Hist. Assn. (pres. 1972-74), Lexington Group (r.r. historians), AAUP, Ind. History Tchrs. Assn. (pres. 1958-59), Orgn. Am. Historians, Newcomen Soc. N.Am., Ry. and Locomotive Hist. Soc. (editorial adv. bd. for Railroad History jour., 1970-94, Sr. Achievement R.R. History award 1983), Soc. Ind. Pioneers, Civil War Round Table of Nebr., Nat. Ry. Hist. Soc., Phi Beta Kappa (hon.), Phi Alpha Theta, Delta Sigma Rho. Clubs: Fortnightly, Lincoln Open Forum. Lodges: Kiwanis (local pres. 1973-74, disting. lt. gov. 1978-79, historian Ind. dist. 1980-81, 83-90, 91-92). Republican. Methodist. Avocations: golf, model railroading, stamps. Home: 2114 Heritage Pines Ct Lincoln NE 68506-2866

STOVER, LAURA ELKINS, artist; b. Exeter, N.H., Feb. 3, 1924; d. Ray Chase and Ina Laura (Nelson) Elkins; m. Alcot Haynes Stover, Nov. 23, 1944; children: Gregory Alcot Stover, Karyn Stover Lindsay, Andrew Nelson Stover. Grad. h.s., Hampton, N.H., 1942. Sec. War Prodn. Bd., Washington, 1942-43; asst. treas. Marjorie Webster Jr. Coll., Silver Springs, Md., 1943-44; sec. Dept. Agr., Washington, 1944-45; sec., asst. to curator Antique Sci. Instruments Harvard U., Cambridge, Mass., 1964-89. Founding mem. Saltbox Gallery, Topsfield, Mass., pres., 1998. Artist (books) Painting Flowers the Van Wyk Way, 2d edit., 1997, (Helen Van Wyk's) Successful Color Mixtures, rev. edit., Portraits in Oil, 1998. Mem. Topsfield Housing Authority, 1977-84. Mem. Newburyport Art Assn., Lynnfield Art Guild, Oil Painters of Am., Portrait Soc. Am., North Shore Arts Assn. (bd. dirs. 1979-87; Grumbacher Gold medal 1984, Marguerite S. Pearson Meml. award 1992, Emile A. Gruppe Meml. award 1996), Miniature Soc. Fla. (Third Place in oil Internat. Exhbn. 1996, First Place award Internat. Exhib., 2001). Avocations: braiding rugs, knitting, gardening, walking, hiking.

STOVER, LEON (EUGENE STOVER), anthropology educator, writer, critic; b. Lewistown, Pa., Apr. 9, 1929; s. George Franklin and Helen Elizabeth (Haines) S.; m. Takeko Kawai, Oct. 12, 1956. BA, Western Md. Coll., 1950, LittD (hon.), 1980; MA, Columbia U., 1952, PhD, 1962. Instr. Am. Museum Natural History, N.Y.C., 1955-57; asst. prof. Hobart and William Smith Colls., Geneva, 1957-63; vis. asst. prof. Tokyo U., 1963-65; assoc. prof. Ill. Inst. Tech., Chgo., 1966-74, prof. anthropology, 1974-94, prof. emeritus, 1995—. Founder, 1st chmn. John W. Campbell Meml. Award, 1972; guest lectr. Brit. Film Inst., 1986; humanities cons. Champaign (Ill.) Pub. Library H.G. Wells Traveling Exhbn., 1986; commd. as Robert A. Heinlein's authorized biographer, 1988. Author: La Science Fiction Americaine, 1972, The Cultural Ecology of Chinese Civilization, 1974, China: An Anthropological Perspective, 1976, The Shaving of Karl Marx, 1982, The Prophetic Soul: A Reading of H.G. Wells's "Things to Come", 1987, Robert A. Heinlein for Twayne's United States Authors Series, 1987, Harry Harrison for Twayne's United States Authors Series, 1990, The Annotated H.G. Wells: The Time Machine, 1996, The Annotated H.G. Wells: The Island of Docotor Moreau, 1996, The Annotated H.G. Wells: The Invisible Man, 1998, The Annotated H.G. Wells: The First Men in the Moon, 1998, The Annotated H.G. Wells: When the Sleeper Wakes, 2000, The Annotated H.G. Wells: The War of the Worlds, 2001, The Annotated H.G. Wells: The Sea Lady, 2001, Science Fiction from Wells to Heinlein, 2001; sr. author: Stonehenge: The Indo-European Heritage, 1979; co-author: Stonehenge: Where Atlantis Died, 1983; sr. editor: Apeman, Spaceman, 1968; co-editor: Above the Human Landscape, 1972; sci. editor: Amazing, Stories, 1967-69; cons. editor: Contemporary Authors, 1987. Recipient Chris award for best ednl. film, 1974; recipient Cine award Internat. Council Non-Theatrical Events, 1973; named Disting Faculty Lectr. Sigma Xi, 1978; honored with Stover Day Western Md. Coll., 1981 Mem. H.G. Wells Soc., Sci. Fiction Writers Am. Home: 3100 S Michigan Ave Apt 602 Chicago IL 60616-3825

STOVER, LOIS T. education educator, department chairman; b. West Chester, Pa., Aug. 5, 1955; d. D. Owen and Grace L. Thomas; m. Joseph M. Stover, June 23, 1979 (div. Dec. 31, 2001); 1 child Amanda Thomas. BA in English, Coll. of William and Mary, 1977; MAT in English and Edn., U. Vt., 1979; EdD in Curriculum and Instrn., U. Va., 1985. Cert. tchr. secondary English Md. Tchr. English Champlain Valley Union High, Hinesburg, Vt., 1978—79; tchr. English and drama Virginia Beach (Va.) City Schs., 1979—82; instr. English edn. U. Va., Charlottesville, 1982—85; asst. prof. edn. Wittenberg U., Springfield, Ohio, 1985—88; assoc. prof. secondary edn. Towson (Md.) U., 1988—96; prof. and chair edn. studies St. Mary's Coll. of Md., St. Mary's City, 1996—. Co-author: Creating Interactive Environments in Secondary Schools, 1993, Young Adult Literature: Heart of Middle School Curriculum, 1996, Presenting Phyllis Reynolds Nayla, 1996; editor: (young adult lit. column) English Jour., 1995—97. Recipient Exemplary Reading Program award, Md. Coun. Tchrs. of English, 1999; scholar, Fulbright Assn., Nicosia, Cyprus, 2000. Mem.: Nat. Coun. Tchrs. of English (pres. adolescent lit. assembly 1998—99, editor booklist for sr. h.s. students Books for You 1993—96), Phi Beta Kappa. Avocations: films, cooking, travel, singing. Office: St Mary's Coll of Md AA Hall 18952 E Fisher Rd Saint Marys City MD 20686 Fax: 240-895-4336. E-mail: ltstover@smcm.edu.

STOVER, LONNIE ALAN, music educator; b. Marietta, Ohio, Dec. 28, 1966; married. MusB, U. Cin., 1990. Dir. of bands Bklyn City Schools, Brooklyn, Ohio, 1993—95; asst. band dir. Forest Hills Local Schs.-Turpin H.S., Cin., 1990—93; dir. of bands Field Local Schs., Kent, 1995—97; band dir. Sycamore Cmty. Schs., Cin., 1997—. Freelance percussion arranger, 1990—. Named Local Tchr. Yr., Sam's Club, 2001; recipient Golden Apple Award, Sycamore Jr. H.S., 2002. Office: Sycamore Cmty Schs 4700 Cornell Rd Cincinnati OH 45242

STOVER, MARK EDWARD, economics educator; b. Elkins, W.Va., Jan. 14, 1955; s. Stanley O'Neil and Rosemary (Schauwecker) S.; m. Wendy Christine Osbourn, Aug. 9, 1989. BA, U. Ky., 1977; MS, Calif. Inst. Tech., 1980; PhD, Washington U., St. Louis, 1984. Economist Mo. Div. Budget and Planning, Jefferson City, 1983-84; vis. prof. Ill. State U., Normal, 1984-85; assoc. mgr. AT&T, Basking Ridge, N.J., 1985-86; asst. prof. econs. U. Mo., St. Louis, 1986—. Contbr. articles to profl. jours. Mem. Am. Econ. Assn., Regional Sci. Assn., Phi Beta Kappa. Office: U Mo Econ Dept 8001 Natural Bridge Rd Saint Louis MO 63121-4401 Home: Apt 1522 1400 E West Hwy Silver Spring MD 20910-3264

STOVER, MILES RONALD, manufacturing executive; b. Glendale, Calif., Dec. 23, 1948; s. Robert Miles and Alberta Mae (Walker) S.; m. Cynthia McNeil, Jan. 25, 1975; children: Christopher, Matthew. BS, U. So. Calif., 1974; MBA, Pepperdine U., 1979; D of Bus. Adminstrn., U.S. Internat. U., 1982. Cert. fraud examiner; cert. turnaround profl.; cert. profl. cons. V.p., gen. mgr., CFO Johnson Controls Inc., L.A., 1974-82; gen. mgr. MG Products Inc., San Diego, 1982-84; exec. v.p., gen. mgr. ICU Med. Inc., Mission Viejo, 1984-86; v.p., COO B.P. John Inc., Santa Ana, Calif., 1986-88; gen. mgr. MG Products Inc., San Diego, 1988-90; pres. Lucks Co., Kent, Wash., 1991-96, also bd. dirs.; pres. Turnaround Mgmt. Group, 1996—. Cons. Turnaround Mgmt. Assn., Tacoma, 1990; bd. dirs. Ansyr Tech., LaFarge & Egge, Inc. With USN, 1967-71. Recipient Gallantry Cross medal USN, 1971, Award for Productivity U.S. Senate, 1978. Mem. Inst. Mgmt. Cons. (cert. mgmt. cons.), Inst. Mgmt. Accts., Mensa. Republican. Methodist. Home: 3415 A St NW Gig Harbor WA 98335-7843

STOVSKY, MICHAEL DAVID, lawyer; b. Cleve., Mar. 10, 1964; s. Robert Leonard and Alyce Joan Stovsky; m. Jill Denise Simon, Oct. 31, 1993; children: Alexa, Matthew, Tyler. BA, Northwestern U., 1986; JD, U. Pa., 1991. Bar: Ohio 1991. Atty. Kahn, Kleinman, Yanowitz & Arnson Co., LPA, Cleve., 1991-96; ptnr. Ulmer & Berne LLP, 1996—. Chair Internet and e-commerce Group. Contbr. articles to profl. jours. Mem. steering com. Northwestern U. Dance Marathon for United Cerebral Palsy, Evanston, Ill., 1984-85. Zeta Beta Tau/Jack London scholar, Evanston, 1983. Mem. ABA (mem. bus. law sect. com. on the law of commerce in cyberspace 1996—, mem. planning com. and faculty Nat. Inst. on Representing High Tech. Cos. 1998), Cleve. Bar Assn. (chmn. securities inst. panel on electronic securities practice 1998, chmn. tech. com. 1998), Phi Delta Phi, Pi Sigma Alpha, Alpha Lambda Delta. Avocations: golf, skiing, squash, running. Office: Ulmer & Berne LLP 1300 E 9th St Ste 900 Cleveland OH 44114-1583 Fax: 216-621-7488.

STOWASSER, BARBARA R.F. foreign language and culture educator; MA, UCLA, 1959; PhD, U. Munster, Germany, 1961; hon. degree, Georgetown U., 1991. Asst. prof. dept. Arabic studies Georgetown U., Washington, 1976-83, assoc. prof., 1983-94, prof., 1994—, dir. Ctr. for Contemporary Arab Studies, 1993—. Author: Women in the Qur'an, 1994; editor: The Islamic Impulse, 1987. Mem. Mid. East Studies Assn. (pres. 1998-99), Am. Assn. Tchrs. Arabic (pres. 1986-87), Am. Coun. for Study of Islamic Studies (bd. dirs. 1983—). Office: Georgetown U Ctr Contemp Arab Studies Washington DC 20057-1020 E-mail: stowassb@georgetown.edu.

STOWE, ALEXIS MARIANI, accountant, consultant; b. Binghamton, N.Y., May 3, 1950; d. Albert Joseph and Gilda Ann (DiNardo) Mariani; m. Dennis James Stowe, June 3, 1972 (dec. Nov. 1988); children: Cort Andrew, Derek Anthony, Jilda Ann. Student, Le Moyne Coll., 1968-70; BS in Acctg., SUNY, Buffalo, 1972; MS in Acctg., SUNY, Albany, 1974; MS in Taxation, Southeastern U., 1980. CPA, N.Y., Va.; cert. fraud examiner; cert. govt. fin. mgr., cert. info. sys. auditor. In-charge acct. Ernst & Young, CPA's, Buffalo, 1973-74; sr. corp. acct. Moog, Inc., East Aurora, N.Y., 1974-76; auditor U.S. Gen. Acctg. Office, Washington, 1976-78, 79-80; tax law specialist IRS, 1978-79; pvt. practice CPA Woodbridge, Va., 1980-87; v.p., contr. M.T. Hall, Ltd., 1987-91; audit mgr. U.S. Dept. Health and Human Svcs., Washington, 1991-93; oversight mgr. Resolution Trust Corp., 1993-94; v.p., prin. Gardiner, Kamya, CPA's, 1994-97; v.p., ptnr. Leon Snead & Co., PC, Rockville, Md., 1998—. Trustee pension plan M.T. Hall, Ltd., Woodbridge, 1987-90; team leader CFO task force Pres.'s Coun. on Integrity and Efficiency, Washington, 1991-93; instr. Inspector Gen. Auditor Tng. Inst., Ft. Belvoir, Va., 1992—; mem. task force on grants Govtl. Acctg. Stds. Bd., Norwalk, Conn., 1992—; mem. faculty Assn. Cert. Fraud Examiners, 1995—. Contbr. articles to profl. jours. N.Y. Regents scholar, 1968-72. Mem. AICPA, Va. Soc. CPAs, Assn. Govt. Accts. (vice chair publs. 1994—, Author's award 1991), Assn. Cert. Fraud Examiners, Info. Sys. Audit Control Assn., Cath. Daus. of Am., Chi Omega, Beta Gamma Sigma. Roman Catholic. Home: 6013 Wheeler Ln Broad Run VA 20137-2201 Office: Leon Snead & Co PC 416 Hungerford Dr Ste 400 Rockville MD 20850-4127 E-mail: leonsnead.companypc@erols.com.

STOWE, CHARLES ROBINSON BEECHER, management consultant, educator, lawyer; b. Seattle, July 18, 1949; s. David Beecher and Edith Beecher (Andrade) S.; m. Laura Everett, Mar. 9, 1985. BA, Vanderbilt U., 1971; MBA, U. Dallas, 1975; JD, U. Houston, 1982; PhD, U. Warsaw, Poland, 1998. Bar: Tex. 1982, U.S. Dist. Ct. (so. dist.) Tex. 1984, U.S. Tax Ct. 1984. Acct. exec. Engleman Co., Dallas, 1974-75; instr. Richland Coll., 1976; acct. Arthur Andersen & Co., 1976-78; part-time pub. rels. cons.; dir. Productive Capital Assocs., 1975-81; pres. Stowe & Co., Dallas, 1978—; from asst. to prof. dept. gen. bus. and fin. Coll. Bus. Adminstrn., Sam Houston State U., 1982—, dir. Office Internat. Programs, 1997-2001. Dir. Office Free Enterprise and Entrepreneurship, 1983-86, Office Internat. programs, 2001—; adminstrv. intern asst. to pres., spring, 1985. Author: Bankruptcy I Micro-Mash Inc., 1989, rev. edit., 1995, The Implications of Foreign Financial Instutions on Poland's Emerging Entrepreneurial Economy, 1999; co-author: CPA rev.; co-editor: Knowledge Cafe for Intellect Product and Intellectual Entrepreneurship, 2001; editor Houston Jour. Internat. Law, 1981-82; contbr. articles to profl. jours. Trustee Stowe-Day Found., 1979-80; mem. nat. adv. bd. Young Am.'s Found., 1979—; vol. faculty State Bar Tex. Profl. Devel. Program, 1988—; vol., mediator Dispute Resolution Ctr. Montgomery County; mediator so. dist. U.S. Dist. Ct. Tex. 1993; team chief U.S. Mil. liaison Rep. Poland, 1994; pub. affairs officer George C. Marshall European Ctr. Security Studies, 1997. With USNR, 1971-74; capt. Res. Recipient Freedoms Found. award, Navy Achievement medal, Gold Star, Def. Meritorious Svc. medal with oak leaf cluster, Navy Meritorious Svc. award; Summer fellow Tex. Coordinating Bd., 1988, Prince-Babson fellow Entrepreneurship Symposium, 1991. Mem. ABA, Am. Arbitration Assn., State Bar Tex. (vol. faculty profl. devel. program 1988-90, vice chair profl. efficiency and econ. rsch. com. 1993, chair law office mgmt. com. 1993-94), Walker County Bar Assn. (pres. 1987-88), Pub. Rels. Soc. Am., Tex. Assn. Realtors, U.S. Navy League, Naval Res. Assn., Res. Officers Assn., Dallas Vanderbilt Club (pres. 1977-78). Office: PO Box 2144 Huntsville TX 77341-2144

STOWE, DAVID WARE, history educator, author; b. Newton, Mass., Nov. 13, 1960; s. David Metz and Virginia Ware Stowe; m. Linda Lou White, Aug. 6, 1989; children: Henry, Caroline. BA, Haverford Coll., 1983; MPhil, Yale U., 1990, PhD, 1993. Legis. aide U.S. Ho. of Reps., Washington, 1983-85; reporter, editor Thompson Pub., 1985-87; tchg. fellow Yale U., New Haven, 1988-93; asst. prof. Mich. State U., East Lansing, 1993-96, assoc. prof., 2000—; assoc. prof., dean Doshisha U., Kyoto, Japan, 1996-99. Cons. Folk Traditions, Inc., N.Y.C., 1995-96. Author: Swing Changes, 1994. Yale U. fellow, 1991-92; recipient Fireman prize Western History Assn., 1992. Mem. Am. Studies Assn., Orgn. Am. Historians, Phi Beta Kappa. Office: Mich State U 238 Bessey Hall East Lansing MI 48824

STOWE, MADELEINE, actress; b. L.A., Aug. 18, 1958; m. Brian Benben Films: Stakeout, 1987, Worth Winning, 1989, Revenge, 1990, The Two Jakes, 1990, Closetland, 1991, Unlawful Entry, 1992, The Last of the Mohicans, 1992, Another Stakeout, 1993, Short Cuts, 1993, China Moon, 1993, Blink, 1994, Bad Girls, 1994, Twelve Monkies, 1995, The Proposition, 1998, Playing By Heart, 1998, Dancing About Architecture, 1999, Imposter, 1999, The General's Daughter, 1999, We Were Soldiers, 2002, Avenging Angelo, 2002; TV movies: The Gangster Chronicles: An American Story, The Nativity, Beulah Land, Black Orchid (miniseries). Office: UTA care David Schiff 9560 Wilshire Blvd Ste 500 Beverly Hills CA 90212-2427

STOWE, ROBERT LEE, III, textile company executive; b. Charlotte, N.C., July 3, 1954; s. Robert Lee Jr. and Ruth Link (Harding) S.; m. Christine Ruth Edwards, Jan. 15, 1983; children: Christine Ruth, Lillian Rhyne. BA, Davidson (N.C.) Coll., 1976. Dir., mgmt. trainee R.L. Stowe Mills, Inc., Belmont, N.C., 1976-77, v.p., 1977-79, exec. v.p., 1979-84, chmn. bd., 1984—. Sec., treas. Lakeview Farms, Inc.; pres. Robrt Lee Stowe Jr. Found., Belmont, 1978—; bd. mgrs. Wachovia Bank of N.C., Gaston County; mem.-mgr. McAdams & Stowe, LLC. Trustee Belmont Abbey Coll., 1987-90, Mint Mus. Art, Charlotte, 1989-92, Crossnore (N.C.) Sch., 1987-98, Sci. Museums, Charlotte, 1989-91, Gaston Day Sch., 1994-97, Gaston County C. of C., 1992-95, Mis. of New South; trustee Daniel Jonathan Stowe Conservancy, 1990, pres., 1996-2000, vice-chmn., 2000; deacon, elder local Presbyn. Ch.; bd. dirs. Downtown Belmont, Inc., Gaston County Edn. Found., Gaston County YMCA; bd. trustees Presbyn. Hosp. Found., Charlotte, N.C. Named one of Outstanding Young Men Am., 1979. Mem. Am. Textile Mfrs. Inst. (bd. dirs. 1989-92), Newcomen Soc. U.S., N.C. Textile Found. (bd. dirs. 1986—), Met. Club N.Y., Charlotte Country Club, Gaston Country Club. Republican. Avocations: golf, boating, church activities. Home: 135 N Main St PO Box 232 Belmont NC 28012-0232 Office: RL Stowe Mills Inc 100 N Main St Belmont NC 28012-3104 E-mail: rlstowe@rlstowe.com.

STOWELL, CHRISTOPHER R. choreographer, retired dancer; b. N.Y.C., June 8, 1966; s. Kent and Francia (Russell) S. Student, Pacific N.W. Ballet Sch., 1979-84, Sch. Am. Ballet, 1984-85. Entered corps de ballet San Francisco Ballet, 1986, promoted to soloist, 1987, prin., 1990—2001; freelance choreographer for ballet and opera cos., 2001—; ballet master Balanchine Trust, 2001—. Guest artist Ballet Met, Ohio, Pacific N.W. Ballet, Seattle, and with Jean Charles Gil, Marseilles, France, Asami Maki Ballet, Tokyo. Created leading roles in Handel-A Celebration, Con Brio, The Sleeping Beauty, New Sleep, Connotations, Pulcinella, Meistens Mozart; other roles include Calcium Light Night, Rubies, The Sons of Horus, The Four Temperaments, Hearts, Tarantella, Flower Festival, La Fille Mal Garde, Haffner Symphony, Forgotten Land, The End, Agon, In the Middle Somewhat Elevated, Le Quattro Stagioni, Swan Lake, Job, Company B, Tchaikousky Pas de Deux, Maelstrom, Mercutio in Romeo and Juliet, The Dance House, Stars and Stripes, Ballo Della Regina, Drink to me Only With Thine Eyes, Pacific; performed in Reykjavik Arts Festival, Iceland, 1990, San Francisco Ballet at the Paris Opera Garnier, 1994, Bolshoi Theatre, Moscow, 1998. Avocations: cooking, reading, camping. Office: San Francisco Ballet 455 Franklin St San Francisco CA 94102-4471

STOWELL, EWELL ADDISON, botany educator, forestry consultant; b. Ashland, Ill., Sept. 2, 1922; s. Leslie Rockwell and Margaret Virginia (Flatt) S.; m. Barbara Joanne Edwards, June 21, 1953. BEd, Ill. State Normal U., Normal, 1943; MS in Botany, U. Wis., 1947, PhD, 1955. Instr. botany U. Wis., Milw., 1947-49, teaching asst. Madison, 1949-53; from instr. to assoc. prof. biology Albion (Mich.) Coll., 1953-65, prof., 1965-88, prof. emeritus, 1988—, chmn. dept., 1972-76. Vis. lectr. U. Wis., Madison, 1963; vis. prof. U. Mich., Ann Arbor, 1964. Co-author lab. manuals; contbr. articles to profl. jours. Cpl. U.S. Army, 1943-46, ETO. Stowell Arboretum at Albion Coll. named in his honor, 1988, Stowell Endowed Scholarship established 1996. Mem. Am. Inst. Biol. Sci., Mich. Acad. Sci., Arts and Letters (chmn. botany sect. 1970-71, 89-90), Mich. Bot. Club (v.p. 1981-85), Mycological Soc. Am., Nat. Audubon Soc., Sigma Xi (local pres. 1961, 73). Methodist. Avocations: birding, botanizing, gardening. Home: 1541 E Michigan Ave Albion MI 49224-9200 Office: Albion Coll 611 E Porter St Albion MI 49224-1831

STOWELL, PENELOPE MARY, nursing administrator, community health nurse; b. Warsaw, Aug. 17, 1941; d. Charles Edward and Leone Cecelia (Hawkins) Powers; children: Scott Edward Stowell, Holly Jean Stowell. Diploma in nursing, U. Rochester, 1962; BSN, Fla. So. Coll. Coord. community edn. Mid Fla. Home Health Svcs., Inc., Winter Haven, 1989-90; asst. dir. nursing Meridian Nursing Ctr., Lakeland, Fla., 1990-94, dir. nursing, 1995-96, Lakeland (Fla.) Hills Ctr., 1996-97; care mgr. Genesis Eldercare, Lakeland, 1997—.

STOWELL, ROBERT EUGENE, pathologist, retired educator; b. Cashmere, Wash., Dec. 25, 1914; s. Eugene Francis and Mary (Wilson) S.; m. Eva Mae Chambers, Dec. 1, 1945; children: Susan Jane, Robert Eugene Jr. Student, Whitman Coll., 1932-33; BA, Stanford U., 1936, MD, 1941; PhD, Washington U., 1944. Fellow in cytology Wash. U. Sch. Medicine, St. Louis, 1940-42; rsch. fellow Barnard Free Skin and Cancer Hosp., 1940-42, rsch. assoc., 1942-48; asst. resident in pathology Barnes, McMillan, St. Louis Children's Hosps., 1942-43, resident in pathology, 1943-44, asst. pathologist, 1944-48; instr. in pathology Washington U. Sch. Medicine, 1943-45, asst. prof. 1945-48, assoc. prof., 1948; advanced med. fellow Inst. for Cell Rsch., Stockholm, 1946-47; chmn. dept. oncology U. Kansas Med. Ctr., Kansas City, Kans., 1948-51, prof. pathology and oncology, dir. cancer rsch., 1948-59, chmn., 1951-59; sci. dir. Armed Forces Inst. Pathology, Washington, 1959-67; chmn. dept. pathology Sch. of Medicine U. Calif., Davis, 1967-69, asst. dean Sch. Medicine, 1967-72, prof. pathology Sch. Medicine, 1967-82, prof. emeritus, 1982—; dir. div. pathology Sacramento (Calif.) Med. Ctr., 1967-69. Vis. prof. U. Md. Sch. Medicine, Balt., 1960-67; acting dir. Nat. Ctr. for Primate Biology, U. Calif., Davis, 1968-69, dir., 1969-71; cons. U.S. Atomic Energy commn., Los Alamos, N.Mex., 1949-54, NIH, 1949-74, Cancer Control Div. USPHS, 1949-59, others; mem. adv. med. bd. Leonard Wood Meml. found., Washington, 1965-67, numerous univs.; prin. investigator, chmn. Expert Panel on Authentication Review of Selected Materials Submitted to the Food and Drug Administration Relative to Application of Searle Laboratories to Market Aspartame, 1977-78, Assessment of the Practical Risk to Human Health from Nitrilotriacetic Acid in Household Laundry Products, 1984-85. Contbr. 121 articles, 34 abstracts to jours. in field; editor 35 biomed. books, monographs and conf. reports, 1941-88; mem. editorial bd. Cancer Rsch., 1949-59, Lab. Investigation, 1952-71, editor, 1967-71. Recipient Meritorious Svc. award Dept. Army, 1963, Exceptional Civilian Svc. award Dept. Army, 1965, Disting. Svc. award U. Calif. Sch. Medicine, 1988, Robert E. Stowell ann. Med. Student award Outstanding Excellence in Pathology, 1981—; Robert E. Stowell ann. lectureship established U. Calif. Sch. Medicine, 1991 and Am. Registry of Pathology, Washington, 1991; endowed Robert E. Stowell professorship, 2002-. Mem. AMA, Am. Registry of Pathology (bd. dirs. 1976-83, exec. com. 1976-82, v.p. 1976-78, pres. 1978-79, Disting. Svc. award 1995), Am. Assn. Cancer Rsch., Am. Assn. Pathologists (Gold-headed Cane award 1990), Am. Assn. Pathologists and Bacteriologists (councilor 1965-72, v.p. 1969-70, pres. 1970-71), Am. Soc. Clin. Pathologists, Am. Soc. Exptl. Pathology (councilor 1962-66, v.p. 1963-64, pres. 1964-65), Calif. Med. Soc., Calif. Soc. Pathologists, Binford-Dammin Soc. Infectious Disease Pathologists, Coll. Am. Pathologists, Histochem. Soc., Internat. Acad. Pathology (councilor 1954-61, pres.-elect 1958-59, pres. 1995-60, Disting. Svc. award 1970, Diamond Jubilee award 1981, Stowell-Orbison award established 1982—), Soc. Cryobiology (bd. govs. 1968-71), Soc. Exptl. Biology and Medicine, U.S. and Can. Acad. Pathology, Yolo County Med. Soc., Assn. Mil. Surgeons U.S. (sustaining membership award 1965), Univs. Associated for Rsch. and Edn. in Path. (bd. dirs. 1975-90, sec.-treas. 1978-82, hon. dir. 1990—), Sigma Xi, Alpha Omega Alpha. Home: 44752 N El Macero Dr El Macero CA 95618-1040

STOWERS, CARLTON EUGENE, writer; b. Brownwood, Tex., Apr. 14, 1942; s. Ira Milton and Fay Eloise (Stephenson) S.; m. Patricia Ann Folks, Mar. 2, 1981; children: Anson, Ashley. Student, U. Tex., Austin, 1961-63.

Sportswriter Abilene (Tex.) Reporter News, 1963-64; sports editor Roswell (N.Mex.) Daily Record, 1964-65; sportswriter Lubbock (Tex.) Avalanche Jour., 1965-67; sports editor Amarillo (Tex.) Globe News, 1967-72; reporter, columnist Dallas Morning News, 1972-81; freelance writer Cedar Hill, Tex., 1981—. Editor Dallas Cowboys Weekly, 1985-89. Author: (non-fiction) The Randy Matson Story, 1971, Spirit, 1973, (with E.B. Hughes) Doc, 1976, (with Trent Jones) Where the Rainbows Wait, 1978, pub. softcover as Terlingua Teacher, 1982, (with Wilbur Evans) Champions, 1978, The Overcomers, 1978, (with Roy Rogers and Dale Evans) Happy Trails, 1979 (book clubs awards, Christian Herald Family Bookshelf main selection, selected for talking book program Nat. Library Svc. for Blind and Handicapped), The Unsinkable Titanic Thompson, 1982, softcover, 1988, Journey to Triumph, 1988 (also in Spanish), (with Steve Perkins and Greg Aiello) Dallas Cowboys Bluebook III, 1982 (Spanish lang. edit. 1982), Partners in Blue: The 100-Year History of the Dallas Police Department, 1983, Friday Night Heroes, 1983, Just One Kiss Baby, 1983, (with Greg Aiello) Dallas Cowboys Bluebook IV, 1983 (Spanish lang. edit. 1983), (with Billy Olson) Reaching Higher, 1984, The Dallas Cowboys: The First 25 Years, 1984, The Cowboy Chronicles, 1984, (ghosted for Ralph Carmichael) He's Everything To Me, 1986, (ghosted for Pam Lontos) Don't Tell Me It's Impossible Until I've Already Done It, 1988, Careless Whispers, 1986 (Edgar Allen Poe award Mystery Writers Am. 1986, Oppie award S.W. Booksellers Assn. 1986, other awards and included in talking book program), The Cotton Bowl: The First 50 Years, 1986, (with Jarret Bell) Dallas Cowboys Bluebook IX, 1988, (with William C. Dear) Please...Don't Kill Me: The True Story of the Milo Murder, 1989 (Literary Guild selection), (with Larry Wansley) The FBI Undercover: The True Story of Special Agent 'Mandrake', 1989, Innocence Lost, 1990, (childrens book) A Hero Named George, 1991, (childrens book) Hard Lessons, 1994, Open Secrets, 1994, Sins of the Son, 1995, Marcus (with Marcus Allen), 1997, To the Last Breath, 1998; gen. editor series 8 collections sports columns Sportswriters' Eye Series, 1988, 89; writer, producer 79-week, 30 minute news feature show Countdown to '84, official show of U.S. Olympic Com., documentary African Stars '84 for African Nat. TV., football halftime feature Greatest of the Great; writer cable TV show Polaroid's Sports Camera Internat.; co-producer TV show Texas by Land: The Story of the Sesquicentennial Wagon Train; script writer syndicated radio shows Faith Made Them Great, Inside the NFL Recipient Katie awards Dallas Press Club, 1985-92, Oppie award S.W. Booksellers, 1986, Edgar Allen Poe award for best fact crime book Mystery Writers Am., 1986, 99, Stephen Philben awards Dallas Bar Assn., 1987-92, other journalism awards Tex. Headliners Club, William Randolph Hearst Found., UPI, other; named Best Local Writer in the 1988's, reader's poll Dallas Observer. Home: 1015 Randy Rd Cedar Hill TX 75104-3035 Office: care Janet W Manus Lit Agy Inc 417 E 57th St Apt 5D New York NY 10022-3067 E-mail: cstowers@worldnet.att.net.

STOY, CHRISTOPHER JAMES, fundraising executive; b. Whittier, Calif., June 24, 1948; s. Donald Alford Stoy and Helen Keys Holt; m. Cynthia I. Ralphs, May 26, 1969. BA in Polit. Sci., Calif. State U., Fullerton, 1971; MPA, U. So. Calif., 1973, PhD, 1983. Sales, pub. rels. rep. Gen. Foods Corp., Anaheim, Calif., 1973; adminstrv. and mktg. asst. World Hockey Assn., Newport Beach, 1974; program officer Evening Coll. U. So. Calif., L.A., 1975-76, assoc. dir. divsn. acad. programs, 1976-80, dir. fin. affairs, 1980-82, asst. dean, 1982-83, assoc. dean, exec. dir. resource planning & adminstrv. svcs., 1983-85, exec. dir. univ. rels., 1985-89, asst. v.p. alumni rels., 1989-92, asst. v.p. univ. advancement, 1992-94, assoc. v.p. univ. advancement, 1994—. Mem. Nat. Univ. Continuing Edn. Assn. (sec., treas. region VI), Assn. Continuing Higher Edn. (chairperson region IX), Phi Kappa Phi. Episcopalian. Avocations: art, antiques, oriental rugs, wine, sports. Office: U So Calif Univ Pk Campus Adm 252 3551 Trousdale Pkwy Los Angeles CA 90089-0090

STOYAN, HORTENSIA RODRIGUEZ-SÁNCHEZ, library administrator; b. Yabucoa, P.R., June 9, 1917; d. Antonio and Juana (Sanchez) R.; m. Hector Aponte (dec.); children: Gloria, Jose. BA, U. P.R., Rio Piedras, 1943; MA, State Tchrs. Coll., 1946; MS, Columbia U., 1955. Cert. pub. librarian. Tchr. elem. and jr. H.S. Town of Juncos (P.R.) Dept. Edn., 1941-44; pub. libr. Bklyn. Pub. Library, Bklyn., 1954-58; head libr. John A. Howe Library, Albany, N.Y., 1958-65; asst. dir. Farmingdale (N.Y.) Pub. Library, 1967-77, ret., 1977. Author: History of Yabucoa, 1993; contbr. articles Cana Guarapo y Melao, 1995-98. Bd. dirs. Mentally Ill Assn., 1984-98. Mem. AAUW (bd. dirs. 1996, pres. Queens N.Y. br. 1999-2001). Avocation: writing poetry. Home: 43-01 208th St Bayside NY 11361

STRAATSMA, BRADLEY RALPH, ophthalmologist, educator; b. Grand Rapids, Mich., Dec. 29, 1927; s. Clarence Ralph and Lucretia Marie (Nicholson) S.; m. Ruth Campbell, June 16, 1951; children: Cary Ewing, Derek, Greer. Student, U. Mich., 1947; MD cum laude, Yale U., 1951; DSc (hon.), Columbia U., 1984. Diplomate Am. Bd. Ophthalmology (vice chmn. 1979, chmn. 1980). Intern New Haven Hosp., Yale U., 1951-52; resident in ophthalmology Columbia U., N.Y.C., 1955-58; spl. clin. trainee Nat. Inst. Neurol. Diseases and Blindness, Bethesda, Md., 1958-59; assoc. prof. surgery/ophthalmology UCLA Sch. Medicine, 1959-63, chief div. ophthalmology, dept. surgery, 1959-68, prof. surgery/ophthalmology, 1963-68, prof. ophthalmology, 1968—, dir. Jules Stein Eye Inst., 1964-94, chmn. dept. ophthalmology, 1968-94; ophthalmologist-in-chief UCLA Med. Ctr., 1968-94. Lectr. numerous univs. and profl. socs. 1971—; cons. to surgeon gen. USPHS, mem. Vision Research Tng. Com., Nat. Inst. Neurol. Diseases and Blindness, NIH, 1959-63, mem. neurol. and sensory disease program project com., 1964-68; chmn. Vision Research Program Planning Com., Nat. Adv. Eye Council, Nat. Eye Inst., NIH, 1973-75, 75-77, 85-89; mem. med. adv. bd. Internat. Eye Found., 1970-79; mem. adv. com. on basic clin. research Nat. Soc. to Prevent Blindness, 1971-87; mem. med. adv. com. Fight for Sight, 1960-83; bd. dirs. So. Calif. Soc. to Prevent Blindness, 1967-77, Ophthalmic Pub. Co., 1975-93, v.p. 1990-93, Pan-Am. Ophthalmol. Found., 1985-95; chmn. sci. adv. bd. Ctr. for Partially Sighted, 1984-87; mem. nat. adv. panel Found. for Eye Research, Inc., 1984-94; mem. cons. com. Palestra Oftalmologica Panamericana, 1976-81; coord. com. Nat. Eye Health Edn. Program, 1989; mem. sci. adv. bd. Rsch. to Prevent Blindness, Inc., 1993—; mem. Internat. Coun. Opthalmology, 1993—. Editor-in-chief Am. Jour. Ophthalmology, 1993—; mem. editorial bd. UCLA Forum in Med. Scis., 1974-82, Am. Jour. Ophthalmology, 1974-91, Am. Intra-Ocular Implant Soc. Jour., 1978-79, EYE-SAT Satellite-Relayed Profl. Edn. in Ophthalmology, 1982-86; mng. editor von Graefe's Archive for Clin. and Exptl. Ophthalmology, 1976-88; contbr. over 450 articles to med. jours. Trustee John Thomas Dye Sch., Los Angeles, 1967-72. Served to lt. USNR, 1952-54. Recipient William Warren Hoppin award N.Y. Acad. Medicine, 1956, Univ. Service award UCLA Alumni Assn., 1982, Miguel Aleman Found. medal, 1992, Benjamin Boyd Humanitarian award Pan Am. Assn. Ophthalmology, 1991, Lucian Howe medal, Am. Ophthalmological Soc., 1992, Internat. Gold Medal award 3rd Singapore Nat. Eye Ctr. Internat. Meeting and 11th Internat. Meeting on Cataract, Implant, Microsurgery and Refractive Keratoplasty, 1998. Fellow Royal Australian Coll. Ophthalmologists (hon.); mem. Academia Ophthalmologica Internationales (pres. 1998—), Am. Acad. Ophthalmology (bd. councillors 1981, Life Achievement award 1999), Found. of Am. Acad. Ophthalmology (trustee 1989, chmn. bd. trustees 1989-92), Am. Acad. Opthalmology and Otolaryngology (pres. 1977), Am. Soc. Cataract and Refractive Surgery, AMA (asst. sec. ophthalmology sect. 1962-63, sec. 1963-66, chmn. 1966-67, coun. 1970-74), Am. Ophthalmol. Soc. (coun. 1985-90, v.p. 1992, pres. 1993), Assn. Rsch. in Vision and Ophthalmology (Mildred Weisenfeld award 1991), Assn. U. Profs. of Ophthalmology (trustee 1969-75, pres.-elect 1973-74, pres. 1974-75), Assn. VA Ophthalmologists, Calif. Med. Assn. (mem. ophthalmology adv. panel 1972-94, chmn. 1974-79, sci. bd. 1973-79, ho. of dels. 1974, 77, 79), Chilean Soc. Ophthalmology (hon.), Columbian Soc. Ophthalmology (hon.), Glaucoma Soc. Internat. Congress of Ophthalmology (hon.), Heed Ophthalmic Found. (chmn., bd. dirs. 1990-98), Hellenic Ophthalmol. Soc. (hon.), Internat. Coun. Ophthalmology (bd. dirs. 1993—), Los Angeles County Med. Assn., Los Angeles Soc. Ophthalmology, The Macula Soc., Pan-Am. Assn. Ophthalmology (coun. 1972—, pres. elect 1985-87, pres. 1987-89), Peruvian Soc. Ophthalmology (hon.), Retina Soc., Barraquer Inst. Ophthalmology (pres. 1996—), The Jules Gonin Club, West Coast Retina Study Club. Republican. Presbyterian. Avocations: music, tennis, scuba diving. Home: 3031 Elvido Dr Los Angeles CA 90049-1107 Office: UCLA 100 Stein Plz Los Angeles CA 90095-7065

STRAAYER, CAROLE KATHLEEN, retired elementary education educator; b. Jackson, Mich., Jan. 4, 1934; d. Joseph and Maude Vivian (Whitney) Kerr; m. Richard Lee Straayer, Feb. 1, 1958; children: Steven Jay, Susan Kay Straayer Maxson. A, Jackson Community Coll., Mich., 1953; BS, Ea. Mich. u., 1957, MA, 1961. Cert. elem. tchr., Mich. Tchr. Napoleon (Mich.) Sch. Dist., 1954-56, Waterford (Mich.) Twp. Sch. Dist., 1957, Jackson (Mich.) Pub. Schs., 1957-98. Mem. choir 1st Presbyn. Ch., Jackson, 1983—. Jackson Citizen Patriot scholar, 1971. Mem. NEA, AAUW (group leader 1989-92, chmn. edn. com. 1998-2000, program v.p. 1999-2001), Mich. ASCD (region 3 rep. 1989-90), Mich. Edn. Assn. (ret.), Jackson Edn. Assn. (bldg. rep., chmn. tenure com. 1974-80, mem. negotiating team 1995, bd. dirs. 1996), Jackson/Hillsdale Profl. Devel. (rep. 1988-90), Delta Kappa Gamma (pres. Beta Beta chpt. 1986-88, 98—, mem. state nominating com. 2001—, state chmn. profl. affairs 2001). Avocations: playing bridge, giving parties, tutoring at school. Home: 2220 Pioneer Dr Jackson MI 49201-8900 E-mail: ckteacher@aol.com.

STRACHAN, GRAHAM, pharmaceutical company executive; b. Dundee, Scotland, Sept. 12, 1938; arrived in Can., 1968; s. Roualyn and Ellen Strachan. BSc, Glasgow U., 1961, MA, 1963. Registered patent and trade agt. Licensing officer Schering Inc., Switzerland, 1963-66; v.p. bus. devel. John Labatt Ltd., Can., 1967-82; pres., chief exec. officer Allelix Biopharms., Inc., Mississauga, Ont., Can., 1982—. Chmn. Nat. Biotech. Adv. Com.; dir. several biopharm. cos. Fellow Patent and Trademark Inst. Can.; mem. Am. Chem. Soc., Licensing Execs. Soc., Indsl. Biotech. Assn. Can. (bd. dirs.), Biotech. Indsl. Orgn. (bd. dirs. 1985—, past pres.), Can. Genetic Diseases Network (chmn.). Achievements include several patents relating to biotechnology. Home: 40 Deane Wood crescent Etobicoke ON Canada M9B 3B1 Office: Allelix Biopharmaceuticals Inc 6850 Goreway Dr Mississauga ON Canada L4V1P1

STRACHER, DOROTHY ALTMAN, education educator, consultant; b. N.Y.C., May 11, 1934; d. Joseph and Gussie (Newman) Altman; m. Alfred Stracher, July 4, 1954; children: Cameron Altman, Adam Reed, Erica Terri. BA, Bklyn. Coll., 1955; MA, Columbia U., 1957; postgrad., U. Copenhagen, 1958-59; acad. vis., Oxford (Eng.) U., 1973-74; PhD, Hofstra U., 1979. Cert. English and social sci. tchr., N.Y. Coordinator secondary reading Cen. Moriches (N.Y.) Sch. Dist., 1974-78; coordinator reading Ea. Williston (N.Y.) Sch. Dist., 1978-79; specialist reading and writing SUNY, Old Westbury, 1979-81; adj. prof. dept. reading Hofstra U., Hempstead, N.Y., 1979-82; asst. prof. edn. L.I. U., Bklyn., 1982-83, Coll. New Rochelle, N.Y., 1983-85; sr. learning diagnostic specialist child devel. div. L.I. Jewish Hosp., Bklyn., 1985-86; prof. Dowling Coll., Oakdale, N.Y., 1986—, acad. chair Sch. Edn., 1991-93, coord. elem. edn. dept., 2000-01, acad. chair Sch. Edn., 2001—; vis. prof. U. East London, London, 1994. Cons. Johnson & Johnson, Inc., Princeton, N.J., 1982—, Sanford (Fla.) Sch. Dist., 1983, Lawrence (N.Y.) Sch. Dist., 1984, Sch. Dist. 7, N.Y.C., 1984—. Author: (with others) First the Fundamentals, 1980, What Do You Call a Well-Behaved Martian?, A Manual For Thinkers' Parents, 1981, Integrating Assessment, 1982; editor: Differentiated Curricula, 1986, A Literature Based Integrated Curriculum: Grades Pre-K-, 1989, Successful Strategies for Learning Disabled College Students: Reading, Writing and Reasoning, 1991, Cognitive Development Through Literacy for Inner City Students: A Curriculum Staff Development Project in the South Bronx in Commitment to Excellence, 2002; contbr. articles to profl. jours. Bd. dirs. Roslyn (N.Y.) Sch. Dist., 1975-84, v.p., 1980-82, pres., 1982-84; mem. adv. bd. Children's Sch. Sci., Woods Hole, Mass., 1976-82. Mem. Coun. for Exceptional Children, Orton Soc., Internat. Reading Assn., Nat. Assn. for Gifted Edn., LWV (bd. dirs. 1961-70), NOW, Kappa Delta Pi. Avocations: reading, writing, traveling. E-mails. Home: 47 The Oaks Roslyn NY 11576-1704 E-mail: strached@dowling.edu., dastracher@cs.com.

STRACK, ALISON MERWIN, neurobiologist; b. Midland, Mich., Apr. 19, 1963; d. William James and Alice (Armstrong) S. BS, U. Mich., 1985; PhD, Washington U., St. Louis, 1990. Asst. rsch. physiologist U. Calif. Sch. Medicine, San Francisco, 1990-97; rsch. fellow Merck Pharms., Rahway, NJ, 1997—. Contbr. articles to profl. jours. Grantee Am. Heart Assn., Calif. affiliate, 1993. Mem. Soc. Neurosci. Office: Merck Rsch Labs Dept Pharmacology R80Y-145 PO Box 2000 Rahway NJ 07065

STRACK, HAROLD ARTHUR, retired electronics company executive, retired air force officer, planner, analyst, author, musician; b. San Francisco, Mar. 29, 1923; s. Harold Arthur and Catheryn Jenny (Johnsen) S.; m. Margaret Madeline Decker, July 31, 1945; children: Carolyn, Curtis, Tamara. Student, San Francisco Coll., 1941, Sacramento Coll., 1947, Sacramento State Coll., 1948, U. Md., 1962, Indsl. Coll. Armed Forces, 1963. Commd. 2d lt. USAAF, 1943; advanced through grades to brig. gen. USAF, 1970; comdr. 1st Radar Bomb Scoring Group Carswell AFB, Ft. Worth, 1956-59; vice comdr. 90th Strategic Missile Wing SAC Warren AFB, Cheyenne, Wyo., 1964; chief, strategic nuclear br., spl. studies group Joint Chiefs of Staff, 1965-67, dep. asst. to chmn. JCS for strategic arms negotiations, 1968; comdr. 90th Strategic Missile Wing SAC Warren AFB, Cheyenne, 1969-71; chief Studies, Analysis and Gaming Agy. Joint Chiefs Staff, Washington, 1972-74, ret., 1974; v.p., mgr. MX Peacekeeper Program v.p. strategic planning Northrop Electronics Divsn., Hawthorne, Calif., 1974-88; ret., 1988. 1st clarinetist, Cheyenne Symphony Orch., 1969-71. Mem. Cheyenne Frontier Days Com., 1970-71. Decorated D.S.M., Legion of Merit, D.F.C., Air medal, Purple Heart, Presdl. citation, Army, Air Force and Joint Svc. Commendation medals. Mem. Inst. Nav., Am. Def. Preparedness Assn., Air Force Assn., Aerospace Edn. Found., Am. Fedn. Musicians, Orde Pour le Merite, Cheyenne Frontier Days "Heels". Home: 707 James Ln Incline Village NV 89451-9612 *The precepts which have guided me recognize the dignity of the individual and human rights. I believe that living by the Golden Rule contributes to the quality of life by making us better and more useful citizens while favorably influencing others. Integrity, ideals, and high standards reinforce one's own character. While taking pride in accomplishment, show gratitude for opportunity and humility for success. Lead by example and always do your best. Service to humanity and country is the highest calling, and the satisfaction of a job well done, approbation, respect and true friendship are one's greatest rewards.*

STRACK, STEPHEN NAYLOR, psychologist; b. Rome, Nov. 13, 1955; s. Ralph and Grace (Naylor) S.; m. Leni Ferrero. BA, U. Calif., Berkeley, 1978; PhD, U. Miami, Fla., 1983. Psychologist L.A. County Dept. Mental Health, 1984-85; staff psychologist VA Outpatient Clinic, L.A., 1985—, dir. tng., 1992-97. Clin. assoc. U. So. Calif., L.A., 1986-95; adj. prof. Calif. Sch. Profl. Psychology, L.A., 1989—; clin. prof. Fuller Grad. Sch. Psychology, Pasadena, Calif., 1986—. Author (test): Personality Adjective Check List, 1987; co-author (book): Differentiating Normal and Abnormal Personality, 1994, Death and the Quest for Meaning, 1997, Essentials of Million Inventories Assessment, 1999, 2d edit., 2002; cons. editor Jour. Personality Disorders, N.Y.C., 1992—, Omega, 1997—, Jour. Personality Assessment, 1999—. U.S. Dept. VA grantee, 1986-93, 96-2000. Fellow APA, Soc. for Personality Assessment; mem. Internat. Soc. for the Study of Personality Disorders, Calif. Psychol. Assn., Soc. for Interpersonal Theory and Rsch., Soc. for Rsch. in Psychopathology, Western Psychol. Assn., Sigma Xi. Office: VA Outpatient Clinic 351 E Temple St Los Angeles CA 90012-3328 E-mail: snstrack@aol.com.

STRADER, JAMES DAVID, lawyer; b. Pitts., June 30, 1940; s. James Lowell and Tyra Fredrika (Bjorn) S.; m. Ann Wallace, Feb. 8, 1964; children: James Jacob, Robert Benjamin. BA, Mich. State U., 1962; JD, U. Pitts., 1965. Bar: Pa. 1966, U.S. Dist. Ct. (we. dist.) Pa. 1966, U.S. Dist. Ct. (ea. dist.) Pa. 1973, U.S. Dist. Ct. (mid. dist.) Pa. 1985, U.S. Ct. Appeals (4th and 5th cirs.) 1977, U.S. Ct. Appeals (3d and 11th cirs.) 1981, U.S. Supreme Ct. 1982, W.Va. 1996. Assoc. Peacock, Keller & Yohe, Washington, 1967-68; atty. U.S. Steel Corp., Pitts., 1968-77, gen. atty. worker's compensation, 1977-84; assoc. Caroselli, Spagnolli & Beachler, 1984-87; ptnr. Dickie, McCamey & Chilcote, 1987—. Bd. trustees Mt. Lebanon Pub. Libr., 2002—; del. Dem. Mid-Yr. Conv., 1974; mem. Dem. Nat. Platform Com., 1976; bd. dirs. Pa. Bar Inst., 2001—; commr. Mt. Lebanon Twp., Pa., 1974—78. Capt. U.S. Army, 1965—67. Mem. ABA (sr. vice-chmn. worker's compensation com. 1978-94), Pa. Bar Assn. (chmn. worker's compensation law sect. 1994-95), Pa. Bar Inst. (bd. dirs. 2001-),State Bar W.Va., Allegheny County Bar Assn., Valley Brook Country Club. Democrat. Presbyterian. Office: Dickie McCamey & Chilcote 2 PPG Pl Ste 400 Pittsburgh PA 15222-5491

STRADER, TIMOTHY RICHARDS, lawyer; b. Portland, Oreg., Jan. 17, 1956; s. Charles J. and Carol Jane (Dwyer) S.; m. Lisa M.K. Bartholomew, May 21, 1988; children: Kelly Meehan, Erin Dwyer. BBA in Mgmt., U. Notre Dame, 1978; JD, Willamette U., Salem, Oreg., 1981; LLM in Taxation, U. Fla., Gainesville, 1982. Bar: Oreg. 1981. Assoc. McEwen, Hanna, Gisvold & Rankin, Portland, 1982-85, Bullivant, Houser, Bailey, Hanna, Portland, 1985-87, Hanna, Urbigkeit, Jensen, et al., Portland, 1987-88, Hanna, Murphy, Jensen, Holloway, Portland, 1988-89; mem. Hanna Strader, P.C., 1989—. Mem. editorial bd. State Bar Estate Planning Newsletter, 1987—. Mem. alumni bd. Jesuit H.S., Portland, 1982-94, trustee, 1993-99; bd. dirs. Valley Cath. Sch., Beaverton, 1989-95; mem. Estate Planning Coun., Portland, 1990—, bd. dirs., 2000—. Mem. ABA, Multnomah Bar Assn., Multnomah Athletic Club, Waverley Country Club. Office: Hanna Strader PC 1300 SW 6th Ave Ste 300 Portland OR 97201-3461 E-mail: TRStrader@aol.com.

STRADLEY, RICHARD LEE, lawyer; b. Chula Vista, Calif., Sept. 10, 1951; s. George R. and Betty J. (Laughman) S.; m. Christine A. Crofts, Sept. 7, 1991; 1 child, Samuel Richard. BA, Coll. Santa Fe, 1972; JD, U. Miss., 1975. Bar: Miss. 1975, U.S. Dist. Ct. (no. dist.) Miss. 1975, U.S. Dist. Ct. Mont. 1980, U.S. Ct. Appeals (5th and 9th cirs.) 1980, U.S. Dist. Ct. (so. dist.) Miss. 1981, U.S. Ct. Appeals (10th and 11th cirs.) 1981, U.S. Tax Ct. 1981, U.S. Surpeme Ct. 1981, Mont. 1982, U.S. Dist. Ct. (we. dist.) Tenn. 1982, U.S. Dist. Ct. (no. dist.) Tex. 1984, Oreg. 1985, U.S. Dist. Ct. Oreg. 1986, U.S. Dist. Ct. Nebr. 1986, Wyo. 1994. Sole practice, 1975—; staff atty. East Miss. Legal Svcs., Forest, 1979. Mem. Christian Legal Soc. Avocations: chess, computers, woodworking. Office: PO Box 2541 Cody WY 82414-2541 E-mail: richard_l.stradley@bigfoot.com.

STRAEHLE, JOHN ROBERT, music educator; b. Phila., Apr. 21, 1966; s. Charles Leo and Diane Rose Straehle; m. Le Ann Elizbeth Malm, Sept. 3, 1994; 1 child Trenton. MusB, Wash. State U., 1990; MEd, Lesley Coll., 1996. Cert. tchr. Wash. Music tchr. Washtucna (Wash.) Sch. Dist., 1990—97, Kahlotus (Wash.) Sch. Dist., 1994—97, South Bend (Wash.) Sch. Dist., 1997—99, Highland Sch. Dist., Cowiche, 1999—; band dir. LaCrosse (Wash.) Sch. Dist., 1991—94. Mem.: Wash. Music Educators Assn. (small schs. curriculum officer 1996—), Music Educators Nat. Conf. Green Party. Avocations: music, travel. Office: Highland Sch Dist 17000 Summitview Rd Cowiche WA 98923 Office Fax: 509-678-4140. E-mail: jstraehle@highland.wednet.edu.

STRAHAN, JULIA CELESTINE, electronics company executive; b. Indpls., Feb. 10, 1938; d. Edgar Paul Pauley and Pauline Barbara (Myers) Shawver; m. Norman Strahan, Oct. 2, 1962 (div. 1982); children: Daniel Keven, Natalie Kay. Grad. high sch., Indpls. With Bechtel Nev./Lockheed Martin Nev. Techs., Las Vegas, 1967—; sect. head EG&G Co., 1979-83, mgr. electronics dept., 1984—. Recipient award Am. Legion, 1952, Excellence award, 1986. Mem. NAFE, Am. Nuclear Soc. (models and mentors), Internat. Platform Assn. Home: 5222 Stacey Ave Las Vegas NV 89108-3078 Office: EG&G PO Box 1912 Las Vegas NV 89125-1912 E-mail: jeweljcs@aol.com.

STRAHAN, MICHAEL, football player; b. Houston, Nov. 21, 1971; Student, Tex. State U. Defensive end N.Y. Giants, 1993—; game captain, 1998. Named NFC Defensive Player of Yr. Giants, 1997, NFL, 1998; recipient Defensive Game Ball coaching staff, 1998. Office: Giants Stadium East Rutherford NJ 07073*

STRAHILEVITZ, MEIR, inventor, researcher, psychiatry educator; b. Beirut, July 13, 1935; s. Jacob and Chana Strahilevitz; m. Aharona Nattiv, 1958; children: Michal, Lior. MD, Hadassah Hebrew U. Med. Sch., 1963. Diplomate Am. Bd. Psychiatry and Neurology, Royal Coll. Physicians and Surgeons Can. Asst. prof. Washington U. Med. Sch., St. Louis, 1971-74; assoc. prof. So. Ill. U., Springfield, 1974-77, U. Chgo., 1977, U. Tex. Med. Br., Galveston, 1978-81; chmn. dept. psychiatry Kaplan Hosp., Rehovot, Israel, 1987-88; clin. assoc. prof. U. Wash., Seattle, 1981-88; prof. U. Tex. Med. Sch., Houston, 1988-92. Contbr. articles to profl. jours. Fellow Am. Psychiat. Assn., Royal Coll. Physicians and Surgeons Can. Achievements include patents for immunological methods for removing species from the blood circulatory system, for treatment methods for psychoactive drug dependence; for immunological methods for treating psychoactive drug intoxication; methods of improved targeting of drugs and visualization ligands, particularly in the treatment and diagnosis of cancer; invention of use of antibodies to receptors and their fragments as drugs, of immunoadsorption treatment of hyperlipidemia, cancer, autoimmune disease, atherosclerosis and coronary artery disease; immunoassay methods for psychoactive drugs; discovery of the protective effects of Nitric Oxide (NO) on psychiatric patients. Office: PO Box 25008 Seattle WA 98125-1908

STRAHLER, ALAN H. geography educator, author, researcher; b. N.Y.C., Apr. 27, 1943; s. Arthur Newell and Margaret Elizabeth S.; m. Kristi Margaret Schrader, Feb. 4, 1967; 1 child, Amy Leona. BA, Johns Hopkins U., 1964, PhD, 1969; Doctorat scientarum/honoris causa, Cath. U. Louvain, Belgium, 2000. Asst. prof. U. Va., Charlottesville, 1969-74; asst. then assoc. prof. U. Calif., Santa Barbara, 1974-82; prof. Hunter Coll., N.Y.C., 1982-88, Boston U., 1988—. Mem. (selected) Moderate-Resolution Imaging Spectometer Sci. Team, NASA, 1989, Triana Sci. Team, 2000. Author, co-author phys. geography textbooks including 9 major titles in 17 edits.; contbr. numerous articles to profl. pubs. Recipient numerous grants NSF and NASA, 1978—, Outstanding Contbrs. to Remote Sensing medal Assn. Am. Geographers, 1993. Achievements include development of body of research on remote sensing of forests and vegetation emphasizing mathematical models of forest structure and viewing of forests by imaging instruments on space-borne platforms; production of global maps of land cover and surface reflectance using satellite data. Home: 225 Brattle St Cambridge MA 02138-4623 Office: Boston U Dept of Geography 675 Commonwealth Ave Boston MA 02215-1406

STRAHM, SAMUEL EDWARD, veterinarian; b. Fairview, Kans., Feb. 9, 1936; s. Silas Tobias and Martha Mary (Beyer) S.; m. Barbara Jean Wenger, June 1, 1958; children: Gregory Lee, Bryan Scott, Andrea Marie Enloe. BS, DVM, Kansas State U., 1959. Diplomate Nat. Acad. Practice. Owner Osage Animal Clinic Inc., Pawhuska, Okla., 1959—, pres., 1985—. Bd. 1st Nat. Bank, Pawhuska, Okla.; mem. bd. cons. Profl. Exam Svc., 1990-2000; mem. adv. bd. USDA Users, 1991-95; mem. adv. com. Pew Nat. Health Profession Vet. Medicine, 1991; mem. state adv. coun. Okla. Coop. Extension Svcs., 2000—, chmn.-elect, 2000-01, chmn., 2001-02 Mem. Okla. Sch. Bd. Assn., 1977--, 2d v.p., 1993, 1st v.p., 1994, pres., 1996; mem. Okla. All-State Sch. Bd., 1993; mem. Pawhuska Sch. Bd., 1974-98, 2001—, pres., 1991-98; mem. Pawhuska Planning Commn., 1965-70; mem. Okla. State U. Centennial Commn., Stillwater, 1986-91; bd. dirs. Nat. Sch. Bd. Assn., 1996-98, exec. com., 1997-99, western reg. chmn., 1996. Recipient Disting. Alumni award Coll. Vet. Medicine Kans. State U., 1994, Outstanding Svc. award Nat. Sch. Bds. Assn., 1997, Disting. Svc. award Nat. Bd. Exam. Com., 2000. Mem. AVMA (pres. elect 1988-89, pres. 1989-90, AVMA award 1986, Coun. on Govt. Affairs, 1992-98), Am. Vet. Med. Found. (chmn. 1995-98), Am. Assn. Theriogenealogy, Am. Assn. Bovine Practitioners, Am. Assn. Vet. State Bds., Am. Assn. Food Hygiene Vets. (bd. dirs. 2000—), Nat. Bd. Vet. Med. Examiners (Disting. Svc. award 2000), Okla. Vet. Med. Assn. (all offices from 1959, Veterinarian of Yr. 1990, Disting. Svc. award 1998), Kans. Vet. Med. Assn., Okla. Bd. Vet. Med. Examiners (pres.), Pawhuska C. of C. (pres. 1968), Pawhuska Jaycees (all offices 1959-69), Toastmasters Club. Republican. Baptist. Avocations: gardening, fishing, flying. Home: PO Box 1256 Pawhuska OK 74056-1256 Office: Osage Animal Clinic Inc PO Box 1209 Pawhuska OK 74056-1209

STRAIN, EDWARD RICHARD, psychologist; b. Indpls., Apr. 12, 1925; s. Edward Richard and Ernestine (Kidd) S.; m. Marsha Ellen Beeler, 1972; children: Chadwick Edward, Sarah Abigail, Zachary Richard. AB, Butler U., 1948; PhD, Duke U., 1952. Clin. psychologist Ohio State Med. Ctr., Columbus, 1952-53, Ind. U. Med. Ctr., Indpls., 1953-56; pvt. practice cons. psychology, 1956—. Lectr. dept. psychology Butler U., Indpls., 1958-68; pres. Marion County (Ind.) Mental Health Assn., 1967-69. Mem. 500 Festival Assocs., Indpls., 1961—; pres. Perry Twp. (Ind.) Rep. Club, 1968-69; founder Downtown Sr. Citizens Ctr., 1961; vestryman Episcopal Ch., 1975-77, 86-88, sr. warden, 1976-77. Recipient Disting. Tech. Alumni award Arsenal Tech. H.S., 1993, Hansen H. Anderson Cmty. Svc. Merit medal Arsenal Tech. H.S., 1994. Mem. Masons, Rotary, Indpls. Club, Athletic Club, Indpls. Press Club. E-mail: erstrain@aol.com.

STRAIN, JAMES ELLSWORTH, pediatrician, retired association administrator; b. Lincoln, Nebr., Apr. 23, 1923; s. Elmer Ellsworth and Tessa Elizabeth (Stevens) Strain; m. Ruby Lee Shepard; children: James A., John D., Janet M. Strain McKinney, Jeffrey Lee Phillips-Strain. AB, Phillips U., Enid, Okla., 1945; MD, U. Colo., Denver, 1947. Diplomate Am. Bd. Pediat. (examiner 1984-89, mem. 1989-93, emeritus mem. 1993—). Intern Mpls. Gen. Hosp., 1947—48; resident in pediat. Denver Children's Hosp., 1948—50, pres. med. staff, 1964, dir. genetic unit, 1982—86; pvt. practice specializing in pediat. Denver, 1950—86; exec. dir. Am. Acad. Pediat., Elk Grove Village, Ill., 1986—93, ret., 1993. Pres. med. bd. Colo. Gen. Hosp., 1969—70; clin. prof. pediat. U. Colo. Med. Ctr., 1969—86, 1993—, U. Chgo., 1987—93; mem. Colo. Med. Adv. Coun. for Title 19, 1968—75, chmn., 1968—71; mem. Task Force on Iowa Health Care Stds. Project, 1984—85; presenter numerous profl. confs. Editl. bd. Pediat. in Rev., reviewer Jour. Pediat.; contbr. articles to profl. publs. Mem. Colo. Commn. on Children and Youth, 1971—75; trustee Phillips U., 1974—. Capt. U.S. Army, 1953—55. Recipient Disting. Alumnus award, Phillips U., 1974, Florence Sabin award, U. Colo., 1984, Excellence in Pub. Svc. award, U.S. Surgeon Gen., 1988, Abraham Jacobi award, AMA and Am. Acad. Pediat., 1994, James E. Strain Child Advocacy award established in his name, Denver Children's Hosp., 1983. Fellow: Am. Acad. Pediat. (Clifford Grulee award 1985); mem.: AMA, APHA, Inst. Medicine NAS, Ambulatory Pediatric Assn., Can. Pediatric Soc., Denver Med. Soc., Colo. Med. Soc., Alpha Omega Alpha. Republican. Mem. Christian Ch. (Disciples Of Christ). Avocations: fishing, sports, reading.

STRAIN, JOHN ANDREW, mathematician, educator; b. Palo Alto, Calif., May 25, 1959; m. Nancy Chen. BA, U. Calif., Berkeley, 1984, PhD, 1988. Vis. mem. Courant Inst., N.Y. U., N.Y.C., 1988—90; mem. Inst. for Advanced Study, Princeton, NJ, 1991—92; asst. prof. math. Princeton U., 1990—92; prof. math. U. Calif., Berkeley, 2000—. Named Presdl. Young Investigator, NSF, 1992; recipient Bernard Friedman Meml. prize, U. Calif.-Berkeley, 1989; fellow Math. Scis. Postdoctoral Rsch. fellow, NSF, 1988—93. Office: Univ of Calif 970 Evans Hall #3840 Berkeley CA 94720-3840

STRAIN, LUCILLE BREWTON, education educator, researcher; b. Florence, S.C. d. William O. and Jurheutha (Gibbs) Brewton; m. Winston M. Strain (dec. 1984); 1 child, Rada Ruth Higgins. BA, Benedict Coll., 1943; MEd, Ohio State U., 1954, PhD, 1965. Cert. elem., secondary teaching, adminstrn., supervision. Tchr. Columbus (Ohio) Pub. Schs., 1950-62; prof. various U., 1965-79; policy analyst Nat. Ctr. Edn. Stats., Washington, 1979-83; from coord. to prof. and chmn. dept. edn. Bowie (Md.) State U., 1983-89, prof. edn., coord. grad. reading edn., 1989—. Nat. policy fellow Inst. Edn. Leadership, Washington, 1979-80; mem. adv. coun. edn. stats. Nat. Ctr. Edn. Stats., Washington, 1982-85. Author: Accountability in Reading Instruction, 1976; contbr. articles to profl. jours. Recipient grant U.S. Dept. Edn., Washington, 1989, Bowie State U., 1989. Mem. Internat. Reading Assn. (tchrs. rsch. com. 1991-93; chmn. internat. projects and activities com. State of Md. chpt.), Assn. Tchr. Educators (corp. by-laws com. 1990-93, meetings com. 1996—, disting. clinician com. 1996—). Home: 5508 Vantage Point Rd Columbia MD 21044-2632

STRAIN, MAC BURNS, civil engineer; b. Grand Junction, Colo., Jan. 5, 1925; s. Robert Louis and Allie Edith (Burns) S.; m. Audrey Fern Crider, June 6, 1948; 1 child, Duane Arnold. BS in Architectural Engring., U. Colo., 1948. Photogrammetric engr. Nat. Mapping div. U.S. Geol. Survey, Denver, 1951-59, chief tech. svcs. unit, 1959-67, chief tech. planning sec., 1967-72, chief br. photogrammetry, 1972-82, chief br. of cartometrics, 1982-85; ret., 1985; writer Lakewood, Colo., 1985—. Author, editor: (with others) Manual of Photogrammetry, 3rd rev. edit., 1966; author: The Earth's Shifting Axis: Clues to Nature's Most Perplexing Mysteries, 1977. Pres. Alameda Midget Football Assn., Lakewood, 1967; coach Jefferson County Boys Basketball, Lakewood, 1968; adv. com. Jefferson County R-1 Sch., Lakewood, 1972-75. Recipient Meritorious Svc. award, Sec. U.S. Dept. of Interior, 1977. Mem. AAAS, Am. Soc. Photogrammetry (pres. Rocky Mountain chpt., Denver, 1977-79, Denver Conv., Inc. Am. Congress of Surveying and Mapping, 1978-80, program chmn. 1980 ann. conv., Denver, 1977-80). Achievements include development of phototheodolite-numeric vertical control techniques and procedures, transvers low oblique aerial photography-long bar aerotriangulation, semi-analytical aerotriangulation, quadrangle centered aerial photography techniques and procedures, orthophotoquad mapping techniques and procedures. Home and Office: 480 S Nelson St Lakewood CO 80226-2634

STRAIT, PATRICIA BELLIN, organizational management educator; b. Cleve., Mar. 3, 1958; d. Charles David and Rosemary Knight Bellin; m. Chester Edwin Strait, July 6. PhD, Old Dominion U., 1993. Cert. air traffic contr. Air traffic contr. Dept. Def. (Navy), Norflk, Va., 1976-80; air ops. duty officer Dept. Def. (civil svc.), 1984-85; vis. prof. Va. Tech., Blacksburg, 1996-97; vis. prof. orgnl. mgmt., bus. ethics and human resources Old Dominion U., Norfolk, 1998—. Contbr. articles to profl. jours. Mem. U.S. Humane Soc., Wildlife Conservation Soc. Petty officer 2d class USN, 1976-80. Mem. Am. Soc. Pub. Adminstrn., Pi Alpha Alpha. Avocations: travel, tennis, reading. Home: 4628 Truman Ln Virginia Beach VA 23455 Office: Old Dominion U Hampton Blvd Norfolk VA 23511 E-mail: patriciastrait@yahoo.com.

STRAIT, VIOLA EDWINA WASHINGTON, librarian; b. El Paso, Tex., Aug. 29, 1925; d. Leroy Wentworth and Viola Edwina (Wright) Washington; m. Freeman Adams, Mar. 6, 1943; 1 child, Norma Jean (Mrs. Louis Lee James); m. Clifford Moody, Jan. 8, 1950; 1 child, Viola Edwina III (Mrs. Paul M. Cunningham); m. Amos O. Strait, Dec. 9, 1972. Bus. cert., Tillotson Coll., 1946, BA, 1948; MS in Libr. Sci., U. So. Calif., 1954. Substitute tchr. El Paso Pub. Schs., 1948; sec., bookkeeper U.S.O.-YWCA, El Paso, 1948-50; libr. asst. Spl. Svcs. Libr., Ft. Bliss, Tex., 1950-53, libr., 1954-71; equal employment opportunity officer, 1971-72; dep. equal employment opportunity officer Long Beach (Calif.) Naval Shipyard, 1972-85; with Temp. Job Mart, Torrance, Calif., 1986-87; substitute tchr. Ysleta Ind. Sch. Dist., 1988-89; profl. libr. Eastwood Hts. Elem. Sch., 1989-90; sec. Shiloh Bapt. Ch., El Paso, 1991-92; br. mgr. El Paso Pub. Libr., 1992-96, retired, 1996. Sec. Sunday sch. Bapt. Ch., 1956-66, 92-96, min. music, 1958-72, supr. young adult choir, 1966-72, pres. sr. choir, 1969-71; disc jockey Sta. KELP, El Paso, 1970-72; host radio show Sta. KTEP, U. Tex., El Paso, 1994—. Mem. ALA, Border Region Libr. Assn. (chmn. scholarship com. 1970), NAACP (sec. 1996), Alpha Kappa Alpha. Democrat. Baptist. Avocations: playing the piano and organ, public speaking, reading, ocean view dining. Home: 1667 Nancy Lopez Ln El Paso TX 79936-5410 E-mail: vstrait@aol.com.

STRAITON, T(HOMAS) HARMON, JR. librarian; b. Selma, Ala., June 28, 1941; s. Thomas Harmon and Marie (Khoeler) S. BS in Ornamental Horticulture, Auburn U., 1963; MLS, U. Ala., Tuscaloosa, 1979. Math. tchr. Tallassee (Ala.) City Schs., 1965-66, math., sci. tchr., 1966-68, head math. and sci. depts., 1968-78; head microforms and documents dept. Auburn (Ala.) U. Librs., 1980—, asst. dean info. svcs., 1998—2002, assoc. dean, 2002—. Adj. faculty Grad. Sch. Libr. Svc., U. Ala., 1988, 90, 95, 96—; chmn. Govt. Documents Roundtable, Southeastern Libr. Assn., 1986-88; condr. numerous workshops, seminars, presentations include 1992-93, 96 Notis Users Group meetings, Ala. Virtual Libr., 1997—; cons. Southeastern Libr. Network, 1997—. Contbr. numerous articles on microforms to fed. publs. and profl. jours. including The Ala. Librarian, Microform Rev.; pub.: Major Microform Sets Held by Alabama Libraries, 1988, Alabama's Major Microform Collections: The Enlarged and Revised Edition, 1991, Alabama's Major Microform Collections: The Electronic Edition, 1996. Group coord. United Way, 1981-83. Recipient Award of Excellence, Univ. Microfilm Internat., 1994, Eminent Librn. Ala. Lib. Assn., 1998. Mem. ALA (chmn. bylaws com. 1988-89, Govt. Documents Roundtable 1986-88, v.p. 1985-86, exec. coun. 1985-86, Eminent Libr. award 1998), Ala. Libr. Assn. (numerous editl. and ednl. coms., rep. 1991—, chmn. handbook com. 1986-90, chmn. awards com. 1995-96, bibliographic com. 1993—), Southeastern Libr. Assn. (Ala. rep., exec. bd. dirs., handbook com. 1995—, nominations com. 1995—), Alpha Zeta, Beta Phi Mu (Ala. chpt. Libr. of Yr. 1992), Gamma Sigma Delta, Pi Alpha Sigma. Democrat. Baptist. Avocations: gardening, reading. Home: PO Box 132 Auburn AL 36831-0132 Office: Assoc Dean Auburn U Librs Auburn AL 36849-5606 E-mail: strait@auburn.edu.

STRAJA, SORIN RADU, chemical engineer, mathematician, computer programmer; b. Bucharest, Romania; s. Radu and Sonica Straja; m. Mihaela Cirstea, Mar. 26, 1982. MS, Poly. Inst., Bucharest, 1979, PhD, 1987. Chem. engr. Plastics Processing, Bucharest, 1979-81; rsch. and devel. cons. Chem. and Biochem. Energetics Inst., 1982-89; cons., vol. USDA, Washington, 1991-92; chemist U. Md., Balt., 1992-93; dir. occupl. health and safety dept. Temple U., Phila., 1993—95, asst. prof. stats., 1994—2001; v.p. Inst. Regulatory Sci., Columbia, Md., 1996—. Cons. Montgomery Investment Tech., Radnor, 1995—. *Over twenty years experience working with the industry, academia, and government agencies in the United States and Europe. Proven expertise in mathematical modeling and software development applied in chemical and biochemical engineering, risk analysis, financial engineering, environmental and health sciences. Author of two books and over forty scientific papers published in internationally recognized and refereed journals. Editor of Environment International and contributing editor of Technology (formerly Jour. of the Franklin Institute). Received the "Nicolae Teclu" prize of the Romanian Academy of Sciences, a certificate of appreciation for teaching from Temple University and a certificate of appreciation from the United States Department of Agriculture for significant volunteer contributions.* Editor: Environmental International, 1993-99; contbg. editor: Technology, 1996—; contbr. numerous articles to profl. jours. Recipient Nicolae Teclu award Romanian Acad. Scis., 1983. Mem. AIChE, ACS, N.Y. Acad. Sci., Soc. Risk Analysis. Avocations: history, geography. Office: Inst Regulatory Sci Ste 200 5457 Twin Knolls Rd Columbia MD 21045-3297 E-mail: straja@nrsi.org.

STRAKA, LASZLO RICHARD, publishing consultant; b. Budapest, Hungary, June 22, 1934; came to U.S., 1950, naturalized, 1956; s. Richard J. and Elisabeth (Roeck) S.; m. Eva K. von Viczian, Jan. 20, 1962 (div. May 1981); children: Eva M., Monika E., Viktoria K. BA cum laude, NYU, 1959. Acct. Greatrex Ltd., N.Y.C., 1952-53; pres. Maxwell Macmillan Internat. Pub. Group, 1991-92; with Pergamon Press, Inc., Elmsford, N.Y., 1954-90, v.p., 1964-68, exec. v.p., treas., 1968-74, pres., 1974-75, 80-88, chmn. bd., 1975-77, 88-90, vice chmn. bd., 1977-80, 88-89, also dir.; vice chmn. bd. Pergamon Books Ltd., Oxford, Eng., 1986-88; group v.p. Macmillan Inc., N.Y.C., 1989-91; pub. cons., 1992—. Treas. Brit. Book Centre, Inc., N.Y.C., 1956-67; pres. Pergamon Holding Corp., 1981-86; chmn. bd. Microforms Internat., Inc., 1971-87. D. dirs., sec. Szechenyi Istvan Soc., N.Y.C., 1967-80, 89-93. Mem. Phi Beta Kappa. Home and Office: 80 Radnor Ave Croton On Hudson NY 10520-2610

STRAKA, MARTIN, professional hockey player; b. Pizen, Czech Republic, Sept. 3, 1972; Center Pitts. Penguins, 1992-95, 97—, Ottawa Hockey Team, 1994-96, N.Y. Islanders, 1995-96, Fla. Panthers, 1995-97. Mem. Czech Republic Olympic Team, Nagano, Japan, 1998. Office: Pittsburgh Penguins Mellon Arena 66 Mario Lemieux Place Pittsburgh PA 15219*

STRAKA, RONALD MORRIS, physicist; b. Reading, Pa., Apr. 22, 1935; s. Morris Richard and Irene (Gurtowski) S.; children: Erika Jane, Sonya Ellen. B of Engring. Sci., Johns Hopkins U., 1957, postgrad., 1957-58. Rsch. asst. Carnegie Instn., Washington, summer 1955, Astrophysics Lab., Johns Hopkins U., Balt., 1957-58; rsch. physicist Air Force Cambridge Rsch. Labs., Bedford, Mass., 1958-77; phys. scientist Air Force Sys. Command Hdqrs., Andrews AFB, Md., 1977-79; physicist Air Force Geophysics Lab., Bedford, 1979-91, ret., 1991. NATO fgn. sci. cons. U. Athens (Greece), 1964; sr. sci. cons. SENCOM Corp, Bedford, 1994-99. Photography exhbns. include Carl Siembab Gallery, Boston, DeCordova Mus., Lincoln, Mass., Boston Mus. Fine Arts, Mpls. Art Inst.; contbr. articles to profl. jours. Dir. photography Boston Ctr. Adult Edn., 1969-77; bd. dirs. Rockport Chamber Music Festival. Recipient Sci. Achievement award USAF, 1971, 84; NSF grantee, 1964. Mem. N.Y. Acad. Scis., Internat. Sci. Radio Union, Rockport Art Assn. (bd. trustees), North Shore Arts Assn. (pres. 1995-96, hon.), Acad. Arts Assn., Internat. Soc. Marine Painters, U.S. Senatorial Club, Air War Coll. Alumni Assn., U.S. Figure Skating Assn., Sigma Xi. Home: 40 Granite St Rockport MA 01966-1310 E-mail: straka@shore.net.

STRAKA, THOMAS JAMES, forester, educator; b. Chippewa Falls, Wis., Dec. 17, 1949; s. James Otto and Elieen Helen S.; m. Patricia Casciere, Feb. 14, 1976. BS, U. Wis., 1972, MS, 1973; MBA, U.S.C., 1978; PhD, Va. Tech. U., 1981. Registered forester, S.C., Miss. Porject forester Internat. Paper Co., Georgetown, S.C., 1974-78; grad. rsch. asst. Va. Tech. U., Blacksburg, 1978-81; assoc. prof. Miss. State U., Mississippi State, 1982-89; prof. Clemson U., S.C., 1989—. Mem. Appalachian Soc. Am. Foresters (chair 2000), Miss. Soc. Am. Foresters (chair 1987), Miss. Forestry Assn. (bd. dirs. 1984-89), Forest Products Soc., Lions, Kiwanis, Xi Sigma Pi, Sigma Xi. Republican. Episcopalian. Home: 130 Timber Trl Westminster SC 29693-5366 Office: Clemson U Dept Forest Resources PO Box 340331 Clemson SC 29634-0331

STRAKOWSKI, STEPHEN M. psychiatrist; b. Elkhart, Ind., Oct. 16, 1961; s. Richard A. and Marilyn R. (Houseman) S.; m. Stacy A. Davis, June 11, 1983; children: Lucas, Andrew. BS, U. Notre Dame, 1984; MD, Vanderbilt U., 1988. Intern, resident Harvard U./McLean Hosp., Belmont, Mass., 1992; clin. fellow Harvard U., Boston, 1988-92; from asst. prof. to assoc. prof. U. Cin., 1992—. Attending psychiatrist Univ. Hosp., Cin., 1992—. Mem. AMA, AAAS, APA, Am. Coll. Neuropsychopharmacology, Soc. Biol. Psychiatry. Office: U Cin Dept Psychiatry 231 Bethesda Ave # Po670559 Cincinnati OH 45229-2827

STRAMPEL, WILLIAM, dean, medical educator; B, Hope Coll. , 1970; DO, Chgo. Coll., 1976. Chief Quality Assurance Divsn., Dept. of Army, Office Surgeon Gen., 1991—94; dir. med. edn. Brooke Army Med. Ctr., 1994—96; comdr. Brooke Army Med. Ctr. and Great Plains Med. Command , 1996—97; dir. quality mgmt. Office Sec. Def.; chief med. officer Tricare Mgmt. Activity; spl. asst. to U.S. surgeon gen. ops. and readiness Mich. State U., Coll. Osteo. Medicine; leader Mich. State U. Health Team; sr. assoc. dean Mich. State U., Coll. Osteo. Medicine, 1999—, prof. internal medicine, acting dean, 2001—, dean, 2002—. Served with hosps. Colo., Kans., Korea. Office: A314 E Free Hall East Lansing MI 48824-1316*

STRAND, CURT ROBERT, hotel executive; b. Vienna, Austria, Nov. 13, 1920; naturalized Am. citizen, 1943; m. Fleur Lillian Emanuel, June 14, 1946; 1 child, Karen. BS, Cornell U., 1943. Supt. service Plaza, N.Y.C., 1947-49; asst. to v.p. Hilton Hotels Corp., 1949-53; v.p. Hilton Internat. Co., N.Y.C., 1953-64, exec. v.p., 1964-67, pres., chief exec. officer, 1967-86, chmn., 1986-87. Sr. v.p., dir. Trans World Air Lines, Inc.; lectr. Cornell U. Sch. Hotel Adminstrn., Ecole Superieure de Scis. Econs., Paris, NYU, Houston U.; sr. cons. Am. Express; mem. adv. panel com. Am. Hotel and Motel Assn.; dir. Sherry Netherland Corp. Mem. coun. Cornell U.; adv. bd. Aspen Found.; bd. govs. Snowmass Resort Assn., also pres.; fellow Aspen Inst. Mem. Cornell Soc. Hotelmen (Hotelier of Yr. 1986), Nat. Arts Club. Home: 340 E 64th St New York NY 10021-7503

STRAND, MARK, poet; b. Summerside, P.E.I., Can., Apr. 11, 1934; came to U.S., 1938. s. Robert Joseph and Sonia (Apter) S.; m. Antonia Ratensky, Sept. 14, 1961 (div. June 1973); 1 dau., Jessica; m. Julia Rumsey Garretson, Mar. 15, 1976; 1 son, Thomas Summerfield. BA, Antioch Coll., 1957; BFA, Yale, 1959; MA, U. Iowa, 1962. Instr. English U. Iowa, 1962-65; asst. prof. Mt. Holyoke Coll., 1967; assoc. prof. Bklyn. Coll., 1971-72; Bain-Swiggett lectr. Princeton, 1973; Hurst prof. poetry Brandeis U., 1974-75; prof. U. Utah, 1981-93; U.S. poet laureate Library of Congress, Washington, 1990-91; prof. Johns Hopkins U., 1994—97; Andrew MacLeish disting. svc. prof. U. Chgo., 1997—. Fulbright lectr. U. Brazil, Rio de Janeiro, 1965-66; adj. assoc. prof. Columbia U., 1969-72; vis. prof. U. Wash., 1968, 70, U. Va., 1977, Wesleyan U., 1979, Harvard U., 1980; vis. lectr. Yale, 1969-70, U. Va., 1976, Calif. State U., Fresno, 1977, U. Calif., Irvine, 1979. Author: Sleeping with One Eye Open, 1964, Reasons for Moving, 1968, Darker, 1970, The Story of Our Lives, 1973 (Edgar Allan Poe award Acad. Am. Poets 1974), The Sargeantville Notebook, 1974, The Monument, 1978, Elegy for My Father, 1978, The Late Hour, 1978, Selected Poems, 1980, The Planet of Lost Things, 1982, The Night Book, 1983, Mr. and Mrs. Baby and Other Stories, 1985, Rembrandt Takes a Walk, 1986, William Bailey, 1987, The Continuous Life, 1990, Dark Harbor, 1993, Hopper, 1994, Blizzard of One (Pulitzer Prize); Editor: The Contemporary American Poets, 1968, New Poetry of Mexico, 1970, 18 Poems from Quechua, 1971, The Owl's Insomnia, 1973, The Best American Poetry 1991, The Golden Ecco Anthology, 1994; co-author: 89 Clouds, 1999; co-editor: Another Republic: Seventeen European and South American Writers, 1976, The Art of the Real, 1983, Traveling in the Family, 1987; translator: Souvenir of the Ancient World, 1976. Recipient award Am. Acad. and Inst. Arts and Letters, 1975, Utah Gov.'s award in arts, 1992, Bobbitt Nat. prize for poetry, 1992, Bollingen prize for poetry Yale Univ. Libr., 1993; Fulbright scholar in Italy, 1960-61; Ingram Merrill Found. grantee, 1966; Nat. Endowment for Arts grantee, 1967-68, 78-79, 86-87; Rockefeller Found. grantee, 1968-69; Guggenheim fellow, 1975-76; Acad. Am. Poets fellow, 1979; MacArthur Found. fellow, 1987; Pulitzer Prize in Poetry, Blizzard of One, 1999. Fellow Acad. Am. Poets; mem. Am. Acad. and Inst. Arts and Letters.

STRAND, MELFORD LIEN, anesthesiologist; b. La Crosse, Wis., Aug. 15, 1940; BS in Pharm., U. Wis., 1963; MD, U. Iowa, 1967. Diplomate Am. Bd. Anesthesiology. Intern Sacramento County Hosp., 1967—68; resident U. Colo. Med. Ctr., Denver, 1970—72; asst. clin. prof. of Anesthesia U. Colo., 1972—76; pvt. practice, 1976—. Mem.: Colo. Med. Soc., Denver Med. Soc., Am. Soc. Anesthesiologists. Office: Met Denver Anesthesiology PO Box 481710 Denver CO 80248-1710

STRAND, MELVIN LEROY, English educator; b. Waseca, Minn., Mar. 15, 1936; s. Carl Morris and Dorothy Mae Augusta S. BS, Minn. State U., Mankato, 1961, MS in Edn., 1968; MS, Bemidji (Minn.) State U., 1972; EdD, U. S.D., 1976. Tchr. English Rockford (Ill.) Secondary Schs., 1960-61, Rochester (Minn.) Secondary Schs., 1961-63, Richfield (Minn.) Secondary Schs., 1963-82; asst. prof. English King Saud U., Abba, Saudi Arabia, 1982-92; prof. English Saudi Arabian Am. Oil Co., Dhahran, Saudi Arabia, 1994, Royal Saudi Navy, Dhahran, 1995-96, Ctrl. Tex. Coll., Killeene, 1996—. Author: The Basic Sentence, 1989, Sentence to Paragraph, 1990; subject of nat. Saudi Arabian telecast Guest of Kingdom, 1991; contbr. articles to jours. in field. Vol., instr. AARP 55-Alive. Served with USAF, 1955-59. Recipient, USAF Missile Badge, 1958. Mem. NEA, AARP, Minn. Edn. Assn., Nat. Coun. Tchrs. of English, Edn. Minn., Am. Fedn. of Tchrs., Ret. Educators Assn. of Minn., Edn. Minn., Sierra Club, World Wildlife Fund, Nature Conservancy, Childreach Plan Internat., Pi Delta Epsilon. Democrat. Lutheran. Avocations: world travel, reading, writing. Home: 13342 382nd Ave Waseca MN 56093

STRAND, ROGER GORDON, federal judge; b. Peekskill, N.Y., Apr. 28, 1934; s. Ernest Gordon Strand and Lisabeth Laurine (Phin) Steinmetz; m. Joan Williams, Nov. 25, 1961. AB, Hamilton Coll., 1955; LLB, Cornell U., 1961; grad., Nat. Coll. State Trial Judges, 1968. Bar: Ariz. 1961, U.S. Dist. Ct. Ariz. 1961, U.S. Supreme Ct. 1980. Assoc. Fennemore, Craig, Allen & McClennen, Phoenix, 1961-67; judge Ariz. Superior Ct., 1967-85, U.S. Dist. Ct. Ariz., Phoenix, 1985—. Assoc. presiding judge Ariz. Superior Ct., 1971-85; lectr. Nat. Jud. Coll., Reno, 1978-87; mem. jud. conf. U.S. com. on info. tech. Past pres. cen. Ariz. chpt. Arthritis Found. Lt. USN, 1955-61. Mem. ABA, Ariz. Bar Assn., Maricopa County Bar Assn., Nat. Conf. Fed. Trial Judges, Phi Delta Phi, Aircraft Owners and Pilots Assn. Lodges: Rotary. Avocations: computer applications, golf, fishing. Home: 5825 N 3rd Ave Phoenix AZ 85013-1537 Office: Sandra Day O'Connor US Courthouse SPC 57 401 W Washington Phoenix AZ 85003-2156

STRANDBERG, MALCOM WOODROW PERSHING, physicist; b. Box Elder, Mont., Mar. 9, 1919; s. Malcom and Ingeborg (Riestad) S.; m. Harriet Elisabeth Bennett, Aug. 2, 1947 (dec.); children— Josiah R.W., Susan Abby, Elisabeth G., Malcom B. S.B., Harvard Coll., 1941; PhD, M.I.T., 1948. Research asso. M.I.T., Cambridge, 1941-48, asst. prof. physics, 1948-53, asso. prof., 1953-60, prof., 1960-88, prof. emeritus, 1988—. Author: Microwave Spectroscopy, 1954; patentee in field. Fellow Am. Phys. Soc., Am. Acad. Arts and Scis., IEEE, AAAS; mem. Am. Assn. Physics Tchrs. Episcopalian. Home: 82 Larchwood Dr Cambridge MA 02138-4639 Office: Mass Inst Tech 26-351 Cambridge MA 02139

STRANDJORD, RONALD MILLARD, architect; b. Mason City, Iowa, May 22, 1932; s. Millard Ferdinand and Leone Marrietta (Smith) S.; m. Janet Esther Olson, Aug. 28, 1954; children: Karl Erik, Karen Christine Strandjord Anderson. BArch, U. Ill., 1956. Registered architect, Ind.; cert. Nat. Coun. Archtl. Registration Bds. Architect Reid, Quebe & Thompson, Indpls., 1962-66; prin. Ronald M. Strandjord, Architect, 1966-81; asst. prof. Purdue U., 1969-72, 78, 79; architect Wright Porteous & Lowe, 1982-84; prin. Strandjord Assocs., Architects, 1985—; assoc. Robson Lapina, Inc., 1995—. Cons. Met. Plan Commn., Indpls. Mem. vocat. adv. com. Indpls. Sch. Bd.; originator High Sch. Archtl. Competition, Indpls. Recipient 2d pl. award Beaux Inst. of Design. Mem. AIA (charter mem. Indpls. chpt., bd. dirs., treas.), Ind. AIA, Ind. Soc. Architects (treas.), Optimists (pres.).

STRANG, JOHN, association executive; b. Chgo. BfA, Wesleyan U., Middletown, Conn., 1950. Chmn. Huguenot Heritage/Musée de l'Héritage Huguenot, N.Y.C. Mem. coun., v.p. Huguenot Soc. Conn.; trustee, officer Huguenot Preservation Trust, N.Y.c.; officer, mem. coun. Huguenot Soc. Am., N.Y.C., 1989-98. Author: (film) A Poem of Life, 1954. Recipient Sylvania award for creative TV technique. Mem.: Decorative Arts Soc., N.Y. Silver Soc., N.Y. Acad. Scis., South Ctrl. Renaissance Conf., French-Am. Found., Netherland-Am. Found., Vieilles Maisons Francaises, New Eng. Hist. Soc., Omohundro Inst., N.Y. Geneal. & Biol. Soc., Furniture History Soc. (U.K.), Renaissance Soc., Decorative Arts Trust, Huguenot Soc. S.C., Great Britain Hist. Assn, Huguenot Soc. of Conn. (exec. bd., 1st v.p.), Renaissance Soc. Am., Coll. Art Assn. Office: Huguenot Heritage 35 Sutton Pl Ste 6 New York NY 10022-2464

STRANG, RUTH HANCOCK, pediatric educator, pediatric cardiologist, priest; b. Bridgeport, Conn., Mar. 11, 1923; d. Robert Hallock Wright and Ruth (Hancock) S. BA, Wellesley Coll., 1944, postgrad., 1944-45; MD, N.Y. Med. Coll., 1949; MDiv, Seabury Western Theol. Sem., 1993. Diplomate Am. Bd. Pediat.; ordained deacon Episc. Ch., 1993, priest, 1994. Intern Flower and Fifth Ave. Hosp., N.Y.C., 1949-50, resident in pediat., 1950-52; mem. faculty N.Y. Med. Coll., 1952-57; fellow cardiology Babies Hosp., 1956-57, Harriet Lane Cardiac Clinic, Johns Hopkins Hosp., Balt., 1957-59, Children's Hosp., Boston, 1959-62; mem. faculty U. Mich., Univ. Hosp., Ann Arbor, 1962-89, prof. pediatrics, 1970-89, prof. emeritus, 1989—; priest-in-charge St. Johns Episcopal Ch., Howell, Mich., 1994—. Dir. pediat. Wayne County Gen. Hosp., Westland, Mich., 1965-85; mem. staff U. Mich. Hosps.; mem. med. adv. com. Wayne County chpt. Nat. Cystic Fibrosis Rsch. Found., 1966-80, chmn. med. adv. com. nat. found., Detroit, 1971-78; cons. cardiology Plymouth (Mich.) State Home and Tng. Sch., 1970-81. Author: Clinical Aspects of Operable Heart Disease, 1968; contbr. numerous articles to profl. jours. Mem. citizen's adv. coun. Juvenile Ct., Ann Arbor, 1968—76; mem. med. adv. bd. Ann Arbor Continuing Edn. Dept., 1968—77; v.p. Am. Heart Assn. Mich. , 1989, pres., 1991; bd. dirs. Livingston Cmty. Hospice, 1995—99, Emrich Episcopal Conf. Ctr., 1998—; mem. Diocesan Com. for World Relief, Detroit, 1970—72; trustee Episcopal Med. Chaplaincy, Ann Arbor, 1971—96; mem. bishop's com. St. Aidan's Episc. Ch., 1966—69, sec., 1966—68, vestry, 1973—76, 1978—80, 1984—86, 1990—91, sr. warden, 1975—76, 1978, 1986, 1990; del. Episc. Diocesan Conv., 1980, 1991; mem. Congl. Life Circle Episcopal Diocese Mich., 1995—2001, mem. loans and grants com., 1995—99, mem. com. on reference ann. diocesan conv., 1995-98, chmn., 1996; mem. Diocese Mich. Clergy Family Project, 1996—98; co-dean Huron Valley area coun. Diocese Mich., 1998—2000; bd. trustees Ecumenical Theol. Sem., 1996—, chair acad. affairs com., 2000—; mem. Congl. Devel. Commn., 2001—. Mem. AMA, Am. Acad. Pediat., Am. Coll. Cardiology, Mich. Med. Soc., Washtenaw County Med. Soc., N.Y. Acad. Medicine, Am. Heart Assn., Women's Rsch. Club (membership sec. 1966-67), Ambulatory Pediat. Assn., Am. Assn. Child Care in Hosps., Am. Assn. Med. Colls., Assn. Faculties of Pediat. Nurse Assn./Practitioners Programs (pres. 1978-81, exec. com. 1981-84), Episc. Clergy Assn. Mich., Northside Assn. Ministries (pres. 1975, 76, 79-80). Home: 4500 E Huron River Dr Ann Arbor MI 48105-9335 E-mail: sjec@cac.net.

STRANG, SANDRA LEE, airline official; b. Greensboro, N.C., Apr. 22, 1936; d. Charles Edward and Lobelia Mae (Squires) S. BA in English, U. N.C., 1960; MBA, U. Dallas, 1970. With Am. Airlines, Inc., 1960—, mgr. career devel. for women, 1972-73, dir. selection and tng., 1974-75, sr. dir.

selection, tng. and affirmative action, 1975-79, sr. dir. compensation and benefits Dallas/Ft. Worth, 1979-84, dir. passenger sales tng. and devel., 1984—, regional sales mgr. Rocky Mt. region Denver, 1985—. Pres. The SLS Group, Inc., (DBAs) Sales Leadership Seminars, Inc., Sr. Leadership Svcs., Inc., Svc. Leadership Seminars, Inc., Speakers, Lectrs., and Seminars, Inc., 1988—. Mem. Am. Mgmt. Assn., Assn. Advancement of Women into Mgmt., Am. Soc. Tng. and Devel., Am. Compensation Assn., Internat. Platform Assn., AARP. Office: 3493 E Euclid Ave Littleton CO 80121-3663 E-mail: slstrang@compaq.net.

STRANG, STEPHEN EDWARD, magazine editor, publisher; b. Springfield, Mo., Jan. 31, 1951; s. A. Edward and Amy Alice (Farley) S.; m. Joy Darlene Ferrell, Aug. 19, 1972; children: Cameron Edward, Chandler Stephen. BS in Journalism, U. Fla., Gainesville, 1973; LittD (hon.), Lee Coll. (now Lee U.), Cleveland, Tenn., 1995. Reporter Orlando Sentinel Star, Fla., 1973-76; editor Charisma mag. Calvary Assembly, Winter Park, 1976-81; pres. Strang Comm. Co., Lake Mary, 1981—; owner Creation House Books, 1986, Christian Retailing mag., 1986, ChrismaLife Pubs., 1990—; founder, CEO Strang Comm. Co., Lake Mary, 1979—. Founding editor Charisma mag., 1975, also in Spanish, Vida Cristiana, 1996, Minist ries Today mag., 1983; founding pub. CharismaLife Learning Resources, 1990, New Man mag., 1994. Mem. steering com. N.Am. Renewal Svcs. Com., 1985—; trustee Internat. Charismatic Bible Ministries, 1986—; pres. Christian Life Missions, 1991—; bd. dirs. World Relief, 2001—. Recipient First Place award Nat. Writing Championship, William Randolph Hearst Found., 1973, Alumnus of Distinction award U. Fla. Coll. of Journalism and Comm., 1994, Industry of Yr. award for Seminole County, Fla., Econ. Devel. Commn. of Mid-Fla., 1994. Mem. Internat. Pentecostal Press Assn., Christian Booksellers Assn., Fla. Mag. Assn. (pres. 1979-80), Evang. Christian Pubs. Assn., Evang. Press Assn. Republican. Mem. Assemblies of God. Avocations: racquetball, golf. Office: Strang Comm Co 600 Rinehart Rd Lake Mary FL 32746-4898 E-mail: info@strang.com.

STRANG, WILLIAM GILBERT, mathematician, educator; b. Chgo., Nov. 27, 1934; s. William Dollin and Mary Catherine (Finlay) S.; m. Jillian Mary Shannon, July 26, 1958; children— David, John, Robert. SB, MIT, 1955; BA (Rhodes scholar), Oxford (Eng.) U., 1957; PhD (NSF fellow), UCLA, 1959. Asst. prof. mathematics MIT, 1959-63, assoc. prof., 1963-66, prof., 1966—. Pres. Wellesley-Cambridge Press; hon. prof. Xian Jiaotong U., People's Republic of China, 1980. Author: An Analysis of the Finite Element Method, 1973, Linear Algebra and Its Applications, 1976, Introduction to Applied Mathematics, 1986, Calculus, 1990, Introduction to Linear Algebra, 1993, Wavelets and Filter Banks, 1996, Linear Algebra, Geodesy, and GPS, 1997. Recipient Chauvenet prize Math. Assn. Am., 1977; Sloan fellow, 1966-67, Hon. fellow Balliol Coll., Oxford, 1999; Fairchild scholar, 1981. Mem. Soc. Indsl. and Applied Math. (pres. 1999-2000). Home: 7 Southgate Rd Wellesley MA 02482-6606 Office: MIT Math Dept Rm 2-240 Cambridge MA 02139 E-mail: gs@math.mit.edu.

STRANGE, DONALD ERNEST, health care company executive; b. Ann Arbor, Mich., Aug. 13, 1944; s. Carl Britton and Donna Ernestine (Tenney) Strange; m. Lyn Marie Purdy, Aug. 3, 1968 (div. Mar. 2001); children: Laurel Lyn, Chadwick Donald. BA, Mich. State U., 1966, MBA, 1968. Asst. dir. Holland (Mich.) City Hosp., 1968-72, assoc. dir., 1972-74; exec. dir. Bascom Palmer Eye Inst./Anne Bates Leach Eye Hosp., U. Miami, Fla., 1974-77; v.p. strategic planning and rsch. Hosp. Corp. Am., Nashville, 1977-80, group v.p. Boston, 1980-82, regional v.p., 1982-87; chmn., chief exec. officer HCA Healthcare Can., 1985-87; exec. v.p. Avon Products, Inc., 1987-89; chmn. Sigecom, Ltd., 1989-94, U.S. HomeCare Corp., 1990-91; exec. v.p., COO, dir. EPIC Healthcare Group, Dallas, 1991-93; chmn, CEO TransCare Corp., 1993-95; chmn., CEO First New Eng. Dental Ctrs., Inc., Boston, 1996-98; pres., CEO Behavorial Healthcare Ptnrs., Inc., Quincy, 2000; sr. v.p. Bon Secours Health Sys. Inc., 2001—. Author: Hospital Corporate Planning, 1981. Mem. Harvard Club (Boston), Nat. Arts Club (N.Y.). Episcopalian. Office: Bon Secours Health Sys Inc 1505 Marriottsville Rd Marriottsville MD 21104-1399

STRANGE, HENRY HAZEN, judge; b. Oleary, P.E.I., Can., July 26, 1939; s. Henry Hazen and Marion Yvonne (Copp) S.; m. Heather Susan Carson, July 30, 1966; children: Elizabeth Marion, Jennifer Jody. BBA, U. N.B., Fredericton, 1961, BA, 1963, B in Civil Laws, 1964. Pvt. practice barrister, solicitor, N.B., 1964-66; spl. asst. to dir. of pub. rels. Centennial Commn., Ottawa, Ont., Can., 1966-67; crown prosecutor Dept. Justice, Fredericton, N.B., 1967-71, dir. pub. prosecutions, 1971-81; judge Provincial Ct., 1981—, chief judge, 1987-97. Chmn. Can. Coun. Chief Judges, 1995. Apptd. as Queen's Counsel, N.B., 1977. Avocations: salmon fishing, sports. Home: 664 Woodstock Rd Fredericton NB Canada E3B 5N7 Office: Provincial Ct PO Box 6000 Fredericton NB Canada E3B 5H1

STRANIERE, ROBERT A. state legislator; b. N.Y.C., Mar. 28, 1941; m. Ruth Kaner; children: Geoffry, Pamela, Brett, Kenneth. Grad. cum laude, Wagner Coll.; LLM, NYU. Sr. ptnr. Staniere Law Firm; mem. N.Y. State Assembly, 1981—, asst. minority leader, mem. ways and means com., environ. conservation com., rules com. Recipient Torch of Liberty award Anti-Defamation League of B'nai B'rith, Negev award, Wagner Coll. Alumni Achievement award, N.Y. Ct. Officers Assn. award, Asian-Am. Coalition S.I. Cmty. Svc. award; named Man of Yr. A Very Spl. Pl. Address: 182 Rose Ave Staten Island NY 10306-2900 E-mail: stranir@assembly.state.ny.us.

STRAPP, NAOMI ANN, women's health nurse; b. Mt. Vernon, Ohio, Apr. 26, 1964; d. Harold Perry and Naomi Lysbeth (Houpt) D. AAS, Ctrl. Ohio Tech. Coll., 1984. Cert. neonatal resuscitation; cert. inpatient obstetric nursing Nat. Cert. Corp. Staff nurse med.-surg. Riverside Hosp., Columbus, Ohio, 1984-85; telemetry nurse intermediate care St. Ann's Hosp., Westerville, 1986-88, staff nurse labor and delivery, and high risk antepartum, 1988—. Office: St Ann's Hosp 500 S Cleveland Ave Westerville OH 43081-8998

STRAS, PENNY LYNN, director; b. Fergus Falls, Minn., Sept. 13, 1951; d. Orville James and Mildred Georgia Stras; m. Wade Elson Olson, Dec. 19, 1974 (div. Sept. 1977); 1 child J. D. Olson. AA, Yankton Coll., 1981, BA, 1982, U. Mont., 1991, MPA, 1993. From adminstrv. asst. to case mgr. Vietnam Vets. Childrens Asst. Program, Missoula, Mont., 1989—92; specialist Mont. Advocacy Program, Helena, 1992—93; child devel. specialist Comprehensive Devel. Ctr., Missoula, 1993—95; pvt. practice acct. Libby, 1995—99; asst. dir. Missoula Head Start, 1999—2000; bus. office coord. Ashby (Minn.) Care Ctr., 2001; dir. Grand Portage (Minn.) Head Start, Grand Portage, 2001—. Vol. Spl. Olympics, Yankton, SD, 1981—82, Missoula, 1991—93. Grantee Fed. grant, Dept. Health & Human Svcs., 2001. Avocations: refinishing furniture, latch hook rugs. Home: 30 Reservation River Rd Hovland MN 55606 Office: Grand Portage Head Start 42 Upper Rd Grand Portage MN 55605 E-mail: nvrtool8@yahoo.com.

STRASBAUGH, WAYNE RALPH, lawyer; b. Lancaster, Pa., July 20, 1948; s. Wayne Veily and Jane Irene (Marzolf) S.; m. Carol Lynne Taylor, June 8, 1974; children: Susan, Wayne T., Elizabeth. AB, Bowdoin Coll., 1970; AM, Harvard U., 1971, PhD, 1976, JD, 1979. Bar: Ohio 1979, Pa. 1983, U.S. Tax Ct. 1980, U.S. Ct. Fed. Claims 1980, U.S. Ct. Appeals (fed. cir.) 1982, U.S. Dist. Ct. (no. dist.) Ohio 1979, U.S. Dist. Ct. (ea. dist.) Pa. 1983. Assoc. Jones Day Reavis & Pogue, Cleve., 1979-82, Morgan Lewis & Bockius, Phila., 1982-84, Ballard Spahr Andrews & Ingersoll, LLP, Phila., 1984-88, ptnr., 1988—, chmn. tax group, 2001—. Mem. ABA (tax sect., chmn. com. 1992-94), Phila. Bar Assn. (tax sect., chmn. fed. tax com. 1992, coun. mem. 1995, sec.-treas. 1996, vice-chmn. 1997-98, chmn. 1999-2000). Episcopalian. Office: Ballard Spahr Andrews & Ingersoll LLP 1735 Market St Ste 5100 Philadelphia PA 19103-7599 E-mail: strasbaugh@ballardspahr.com.

STRASBURG, WILLIAM EDWARD, retired newspaper publisher; b. Lima, Ohio, June 8, 1927; s. Dewey Edward and Helen Mae Strasburg; m. Sylvia Schultz Schweiker, July 14, 1951; children: Bruce Edward, Scott Alan, Mark Douglas, Barbara Lee. BA, Ohio Wesleyan U., 1950; MA, Am. U., 1952; LittD (hon.), Lycoming Coll., 1970; LLD (hon.), Beaver Coll., 1979. Corr., Washington and Africa, 1950-52; pres., pub. Montgomery Pub. Co., Ft. Washington, Pa., 1952-90; v.p. Ind. Publs., Bryn Mawr, 1976-93; chmn. Meadowood Corp., Worcester, 1982-95; ret. Dir. exec. com., chmn. compensation com. Harleysville (Pa.) Ins. Cos., 1970-2000, ret.; assoc. dir. U.S. Info. Agy., Washington, 1969-70. Pres. Ambler Pub. Libr., 1960-62, Rotary Club, Ambler, Pa., 1960-61, YMCA, Phila., 1976-77, Pa. Newspaper Assn., Harrisburg, 1968-69; chmn. Found. Montgomery County C.C., Blue Bell, Pa., 1994-96. Recipient Amos award Nat. Newspaper Assn., 1970, Alumni award Ohio Wesleyan U., 1974, Dean Lesher award Suburban Newspapers Am., 1990, Leadership award Pa. News Assn., 1999. Mem. Soc. Profl. Journalists (chpt. pres. 1968), King of Prussia C. of C. (pres. 1978), Omicron Delta Kappa, Delta Sigma Rho, Phi Delta Epsilon, Phi Gamma Delta, Bonita Bay Club. Home: PO Box 419 Gwynedd Valley PA 19437-0419

STRASER, ERIK GREGORY, venture capitalist; b. Inglewood, Calif., Feb. 12, 1970; s. Valentine Paul and Rebecca Sue (Smith) S. BS, Harvey Mudd Coll., 1992; MS, Stanford U., 1993, PhD, 1998. Rschr. Los Alamos (N.Mex.) Nat. Lab., 1996-97; staff mem., cons. Interval Rsch. Corp, Palo Alto, Calif., 1997-98; assoc. Mohr, Davidow Ventures, Menlo Park, 1998-2000; gen. ptnr. Mohr Davidow Ventures, 2000—. Author (CD-ROM) Earthquake, 1994; patentee in field. Pres. Bus. Assn. Stanford Engrs., 1997-98. Office: 2775 Sand Hill Rd Ste 240 Menlo Park CA 94025 E-mail: estraser@straser.com.

STRASER, RICHARD ALAN, lawyer; b. Washington, Feb. 11, 1945; s. Woodward John and Nina Louise (Weaver) Straser; m. Beverly Jean Brickhouse, May 9, 1981; 1 child Whitney Marie. BA, George Washington U., 1971; JD, Wake Forest U., 1974. Bar: Pa. 1975, Va. 1977, U.S. Ct. Appeals (5th cir.) 1979, U.S. Supreme Ct. 1980. Mgmt. asst. NASA Hdqrs., Washington, 1972, 1973; primary trademark atty. U.S. Patent and Trademark Office, Crystal City, Arlington, Va., 1974—. Dep. dir. Herndon Cmty. Chorus, Va., 1981—82. Served with U.S. Army, 1963—64. Mem.: Phi Alpha Delta, Delta Phi Alpha. Democrat. Roman Catholic. Office: US Patent and Trademark Office Dept Of Commerce Washington DC 20230-0001 Business E-Mail: richard.straser@uspto.gov.

STRASFOGEL, IAN, stage director,playwright; b. N.Y.C., Apr. 5, 1940; s. Ignace and Alma (Lubin) S.; m. Judith Hirsch Norell, Feb. 15, 1973; children: Daniella Elizabeth, Gabrielle Sandra. BA, Harvard U., 1961. Adminstrv. asst. N.Y.C. Opera Co., 1962-64, stage dir., 1964—; tchr. music Julliard Sch. Music, N.Y.C., 1965-66, Augusta (Ga.) Coll., 1967-68; founder, previous artistic dir. Augusta Opera Co., from 1967; chmn. dept. opera New Eng. Conservatory, Boston, 1968-72; prof. opera U. Mich., Ann Arbor, 1980; freelance opera dir., playwright Rosenstone & Wander Agency, N.Y.C., 1982—. Stage dir. Balt. Civic Opera, Kansas City Lyric Theatre, Netherlands Opera Co., 1973—, N.Y.C. Opera, San Francisco Opera, Stuttgart Opera, Alte Oper Frankfurt, Edinburgh Festival, Aix-en-Provence Festival, Aspen Music Festival; dir. music theatre project Tanglewood Festival, Lenox, Mass., 1971-73; gen. dir. Opera Soc. Washington, 1972-75; artistic cons. Phila. Lyric Opera, 1973; dir. New Opera Theatre, Bklyn. Acad. Music, 1976-79. Author: Il Musico (music by Larry Grossman), 1990-91 The Caregiver (play), 1999, Jewish Ensemble Theatre, Detroit; editor: Ba-Ta-Clan, 1970. Served with AUS, 1966-68. Henry Russell Shaw travelling fellow, 1961-62; Ford Found. internship in performing arts, 1962-64; grantee: Internat. Inst. Edn., 1965, Berrillon Kerr Found., 1997 (for The Caregiver). Mem. Phi Beta Kappa. Home: 915 W End Ave New York NY 10025-3535

STRASSBERG, BARBARA ANN, sociology educator, researcher; b. Krakow, Poland, Aug. 22, 1945; came to U.S., 1984; d. Wincenty and Albina Smolak; m. (div.); children: Matthew, Peter. Student, Sorbonne U., Paris, 1973; PhD, Jagiellonian U., Krakow, 1975, postgrad., 1982, U. Chgo., 1977. Assoc. prof. Jagiellonian U., Krakow, 1975-84, Aurora (Ill.) U., 1991—. Vis. prof. U. Chgo., 1985-86; lectr. Triton Coll., Chgo., 1985-86, DePaul U., Chgo., 1987-88, Coll. of DuPage, Glen Ellyn, Ill., 1986—, Columbia Coll., Chgo., 1989-91; mem. Curriculum and Programs Bd., Aurora, 1994—; mem. Gen. Edn. and Diversity Task Groups, Aurora U., 1993—; interpreter Cosmopolitan, Chgo., 1986—. Author: Church and Assimilation, 1982 (Polish Acad. Sci. award 1982), Religiosity of France and Great Britain, 1977; author: (with others) World Catholicism in Transition, 1987; contbr. articles to profl. jours. U. Chgo. fellow, 1984-85; recipient F. Znaniecki award Polish Acad. Sci., 1982, A. Modrzewski award Polish Nat. Ch., 1983; Kosciuszko Found. grantee, 1977, Am. Coun. Learned Societies grantee, 1984. Mem. Am. Sociolog. Assn., Assn. for the Sociology Religion, Soc. for the Sci. Study Religion, Soc. for the Sci. Study Jewry, Soc. for Social Problems, Ill. Sociolog. Assn. Jewish. Avocations: travel, theater, music, art, reading. Office: Aurora Univ Aurora IL 60506

STRASSBERG, MARILYN, social worker; b. Paterson, N.J., July 25, 1943; m. Richard Strassberg, Aug. 14, 1966; children: Michael, Pamela. BA, Rutgers U., 1964; MSW, Columbia U., 1966. P-Cert. social worker, N.Y.; diplomate clin. social work. Sch. social worker DeKalb (Ill.) Community Unit Schs., 1966-67; social worker U. Colo. Med. Ctr., Denver, 1967-68, Family & Children's Svcs., Ithaca, N.Y., 1968-70; mem. med. rev. team N.Y. State Dept. Mental Health, Syracuse, 1979-81; aging svcs. specialist Tompkins County Office for the Aging, Ithaca, 1981-96; dir. resident svcs. Lonview/Ithacare Ctr., 1996—. Mem. NASW (diplomate), N.Y. State Social Workers, Phi Beta Kappa. Office: Longview/Ithacare Ctr 1 Bella Vista Dr Ithaca NY 14850-5792

STRASSER, ALEXANDER L(UDWIG), internist; b. Vienna, Austria, Mar. 6, 1934; s. Paul and Natalie (Kaufman) S.; m. Helga E. Buechele, June 30, 1963; 1 child, Stephen P. AB, Syracuse U., 1955; MD, U. Rochester, 1962, MS, 1967. Diplomate Am. Bd. Occupl. Medicine. Intern, resident Highland Hosp., Rochester, N.Y., 1962-65; resident in preventive medicine Strong Meml. Hosp., 1965-67; pvt. practice internal medicine, 1967—; med. dir. Electronics divsn. Gen. Dynamics, 1967-70, Stromberg-Carlson Corp., Rochester, 1970-77. Corp. cons. Gen. Dynamics, 1974-77, numerous other cos.; bd. dirs. Monroe Plan (HMO), Rochester. Co-editor The Bull., 1986—, N.Y. Soc. Internal Medicine Newsletter, 1982-85; asst. editor Occupl. Health and Safety; contbg. author: A Textbook of Family Practice. Bd. dirs. Finger lakes Reg. Occupl. Health Ctr., Rochester. Capt. USAF Res., 1967-69. Recipient Cert. of Merit Rochester Acad. Medicine, 1996. Fellow ACP, Am. Coll. Preventive Medicine, Am. Coll. Occupl. and Environ. Medicine, Rochester Acad. Medicine (bd. dirs.); mem. AMA, Am. Soc. Internal Medicine, N.Y. State Soc. Internal Medicine, Rochester Soc. Internal Medicine (past pres.), N.Y. State Med. Soc., Monroe County Med. Soc. (past pres., chmn. occupl. medicine com.). Avocations: golf, tennis. Home: 31 Hickory Ln Rochester NY 14625-1828 Office: 2479 Browncroft Blvd Rochester NY 14625-1431

STRASSER, GABOR, management consultant; b. Budapest, Hungary, May 22, 1929; s. Rezso and Theresa (Seiler) S.; m. Linda Casselman Pemble, Aug. 16, 1958 (div. 1976); children: Claire Margaret, Andrew John; m. Joka Verhoeff, Feb. 2, 1978; children: Steven Verhoeff, Tessa Christina. BCE, City Coll. N.Y., 1954; MS, U. Buffalo, 1959; PMD, Harvard, 1968; MDiv, Va. Theol. Sem., 1992. Research engr. Bell Aircraft Co., Buffalo, 1956-61; project leader Boeing Airplane Co., Seattle, 1961-62; dept. head Mitre Corp., Bedford, Mass., Washington, 1962-68; v.p. Urban Inst., Washington, 1968-69; tech. asst. to pres.'s sci. adviser White House, 1969-71, exec. sec. pres.'s sci. and tech. policy panel, 1970-71; dir. planning Battelle Meml. Inst., Columbus, Ohio, 1971-73; pres. Strasser Assocs., Inc., Washington, 1973-92. Author, editor: Science and Technology Policies-Yesterday, Today, Tomorrow, 1973; Contbr. articles to profl. jours. and theol. lit. Served to 1st lt., C.E. USAR. Recipient 1st nat. award Gravity Research Found., 1952 Mem. Am. Inst. Aeros. and Astronautics, AAAS (chmn. indsl. sci. sect. 1974), Sigma Xi. Clubs: Cosmos (Washington), Harvard (Washington).

STRASSER, JACK C. association professional; b. Hannibal, Mo., Aug. 4, 1934; s. Joseph Mast and Lois Elizabeth (Lucas) S.; m. Barbara Jean Patnoude, Apr. 21, 1957; children: Kimberly Ann and Karol Sue (twins). BA, Mich. State U., 1956; MA, Shippensburg U., Pa., 1975; grad., U.S. Army War Coll., 1975. Commd. pilot USAF; combat pilot S.E. Asia, 1966-67; advanced through grades to col. USAF, 1975; staff officer Hdqrs., Pacific Air Forces, Honolulu, 1967-71; spl. project officer Air Staff, Washington, 1971-73; staff officer Joint Chiefs of Staff, 1973-74; dir. mil. airlift command USAF, Scott AFB, Ill., 1975-80; adminstrv. mgr. Kassly, Bone, Becker, Dix & Tillery, Belleville, 1980-85; dir. adminstrn. Law, Snakard & Gambill, Fort Worth, Tex., 1985-89; assoc. dir. Tex. Workers Compensation Commn., 1990-95; pres. Metro Mgmt. Cons., Ft. Worth, 1995—. Decorated Legion of Merit, DFC, Bronze Star medal, Air Medals (9). Mem. U.S. Army War Coll. Found. (life), U.S. Army War Coll. Alumni Assn. (life), Ret. Officers Assn., Order of Daedalians, Lambda Chi Alpha. Presbyterian. Avocations: racehorses, boating, golf, travel. Home: 1021 N Shady River Ct Fort Worth TX 76126-2900

STRASSER, JOEL A. public relations executive, engineer, executive producer; b. N.Y.C., Aug. 8, 1938; s. Albert Gerson and Nellie (Singer) S.; children: Alison Debra, Andria Jocelyn, Jon Fredric. BS, CCNY, 1961. News editor Electronic Design mag., N.Y.C., 1962; space electronics editor Electronics mag. McGraw-Hill, 1963-65; account exec. Lescarboura Advt., Inc., Briarcliff Manor, N.Y., 1965-67; bur. chief Aerospace Tech. mag., N.Y.C., 1967-68; syndicated sci. columnist N.Am. Newspaper Alliance, 1974-80; sr. v.p., founding dir. indsl. and sci. communications svcs. Hill & Knowlton, Inc., 1968-83; exec. v.p. Thomas L. Richmond, Inc., 1983-85; sr. v.p., mng. dir. Dorf & Stanton Tech. Communications, 1985-91; pres. Joel A. Strasser & Assocs., 1991—; dir. corp. comms. People's Choice TV Corp., 1993-96; v.p. mktg. and corp. comms. Digital Broadcast Corp., 1996—; exec. prodr. WCN Radio, Worldwide Corp. Network, Inc., 1998-2000. Adj. asst. prof. NYU, 1988—; adj. instr. Marymount Coll., Tarrytown, N.Y., 1981—; course leader, guest lectr. Am. Mgmt. Assn., 1976—, Am. Med. Writers Assn., 1983—, Ecole Francais des Affaires Publique, 1988-90; speaker and program coord. in field. Transmitted 1st color photograph by communications satellite, 1963; conducted 1st press interview by communications satellite, 1963; regular columnist High-Tech Mktg., Atlantic Tech., O'Dwyer's PR Svcs. Report, The Counselor; contbr. numerous articles to profl. jours. V.p., Citizens of Ramapo, 1969-70, Jewish Temple, 1980-83. Fellow AIAA (assoc.), Pub. Rels. Soc. Am. (accredited, N.Y. chpt. pres., founding nat. chmn. tech. sect. 1985—, Silver Anvil award 1980, John W. Hill award 1989, Presdl. citations 1986, 87); mem. IEEE (sr.), Am. Astron. Soc., Nat. Assn. Sci. Writers, Internat. Solar Energy Soc., Internat. Assn. Bus. Communicators, Am. Med. Writers Assn. (guest lectr. 1983—). Office: PO Box 203 Tallman NY 10982-0203 E-mail: jjas888@aol.com.

STRASSER, SUSAN, historian, researcher, writer; b. Pitts., Mar. 27, 1948; d. Alexander and Maxine Harriet (Hochberg) S.; m. Robert Elliott Guldin, May 9, 1992. BA, Reed Coll., 1969; MA, SUNY, Stony Brook, 1971, PhD, 1977. Mem. faculty Evergreen State Coll., Olympia, Wash., 1975-88; lectr. Princeton (N.J.) U., 1989; dir. univ. honors program, assoc. prof. history George Washington U., Washington, 1990-92; rsch. fellow German Hist. Inst., 1993-95; vis. prof. Bard Grad. Ctr., N.Y.C., 1998-99; prof. history U. Del., Newark, 1999—. Cons. Smithsonian Instn., Washington. Author: Never Done, 1982 (Sierra award 1983), Satisfaction Guaranteed, 1988, Waste and Want, 1999 (Abel Wolman award 2000); editor: Getting and Spending, 1998, Social Justice Feminists in the United States and Germany, 1998; mem. bd. editors Am. Quar., 1993-95; also numerous articles. Fellow Woodrow Wilson Found., 1969-70, Smithsonian Instn., 1973-75, Am. Coun. Learned Socs., 1984-85, Bunting Inst., 1984-85, Harvard U. Bus. Sch., 1985-86, Guggenheim Found., 1992-93, Rockefeller Found. Bellagio Ctr., 1996. Mem. Am. Hist. Assn., Orgn. Am. Historians. Office: U Del Dept History Newark DE 19716 E-mail: strasser@udel.edu.

STRASSMANN, W. PAUL, economics educator; b. Berlin, July 26, 1926; s. Erwin Otto and Ilse (Wens) S.; m. Elizabeth Marsh Fanck, June 27, 1952; children— Joan, Diana, Beverly BA magna cum laude, U. Tex., Austin, 1949; MA, Columbia U., 1950; PhD, U. Md., 1956. Econ. analyst Dept. Commerce, 1950-52; instr. U. Md., 1955; mem. faculty Mich. State U., East Lansing, 1956—, assoc. prof. econs., 1959-63, prof., 1963—. Sr. research dir. ILO, Geneva, 1969-70, 73-74; cons. World Bank, AID Author: Risk and Technological Innovation, 1959, Technological Change and Economic Development, 1968, The Transformation of Housing, 1982, (with Jill Wells) The Global Construction Industry, 1988. Served with AUS, 1944-46 Mem. Am. Econ. Assn., Latin Am. Studies Assn., Am. Real Estate and Urban Econs. Assn., Assn. Evolutionary Econs., European Housing Rsch. Network, Phi Beta Kappa. Office: Mich State Univ Dept Econs East Lansing MI 48824 E-mail: strassma@msu.edu.

STRATAS, NICHOLAS EMANUEL, psychiatrist; b. Toronto, Aug. 9, 1932; came to U.S., 1957; s. Emanuel Nicholas and Argero (Terezakis) S.; m. Irene Printezi, Dec. 14, 1955; children: Nicholas Andrew, Byron Aristotle, Andrew James. BA, U. Toronto, 1953, MD, 1957. Diplomate Am. Bd. Psychiatry and Neurology, Internat. Acad. Behavioral Medicine, Fedn. State Med. Bds. U.S. Rotating intern Meml. hosp., Danville, Va., 1957-58; resident in psychiatry Ea. State Hosp., Williamsburg, 1958-60; chief resident in psychiatry Dorothea Dix Hosp., Raleigh, N.C., 1960-61, dir. residency tng., 1961-63; dir. profl. edn. and tng. State Dept. Mental Health, N.C., 1963-66, dir. research, 1965-66, dep. commr., 1966-73; asst. clin. prof. psychiatry U. N.C. Med. Sch., 1964-69, assoc. clin. prof. psychiatry, 1969-75, clin. prof., 1984—; assoc. cons. prof. Duke U. Med. Ctr., 1980—; pvt. practice clin. psychiatry, orgnl. mgmt. consultation, 1960—; sr. ptnr. Raleigh Psychiat. Assocs., 1977—. Lectr. William & Mary U., Williamsburg, Va., 1960, U. N.C. Sch. Pub. Health, 1964-65, U. W.Va. Med. Sch., Charleston, 1968, Vanderbilt U. Sch. Med., Nashville, 1970, U. N.C. Sch. Social Work, Chapel Hill, 1973, et. al.; organizer, pres. med. staff Ea. State Hosp., Williamsburg, 1958-59; cons. pvt. orgns. 1960—, Peace Corps, 1964-69, W. Va. State Dept. Mental Health state office program devel., 1968, Nationwide Ins. Co. mgmt. devel., 1970, Drug Action of Wake County mgmt. devel., 1970-74, The Human Ecology Inst., 1973-75, U.S. Fed. Ct. of N.C. ea. dist. expert witness, 1975-76, IBM personal devel. seminars, 1978—, Finley-Dillon Realty, 1983—, The Aviation, 1986; bd. dirs. Wake County Mental Health Assn., 1964-65; staff Wake Med. Ctr., 1973—, Rex Hosp., 1973—, Raleigh Community Hosp., 1978—; founder, med. dir. Holly Hill Hosp. 1978—, Raleigh Stress & Pain Clin., 1980-84, Cmty. Mental Health Clinic, 1996—. Author: N.C. Local Mental Health Programs-A Manual, 1968, A Multi-Discipline Approach to Consultation-Edn., 1969; contbr. articles to profl. and scholarly jours. Awards dir. Boy Scouts Am., Raleigh, N.C., Webelos coord., 1968; bd. trustees Holy Trinity Greek Orthodox Ch., 1971, Sunday sch. coord., 1975-77; mem. N.C. State Art Gallery, Raleigh Cultural Ctr., 1974. Recipient Gov. N.C. awards, 1968, 70, 84, Univ. Toronto award, 1957. Fellow AMA (life), APHA, Am. Acad. Pain Mgmt. (life), Am. Psychiat. Assn. (life; award 1970), Am. Soc. Clin. Hypnosis (life), Acad. Psychosomatic Medicine (life), Am. Coll. Forensic Psychiatry, Pan Am. Med. Assn. (life), Orthopsychiat. Assn., Acad. Pain Mgmt.; mem. AAAS, BiofeedbackInst. Am. (cert.), Wake County Med. Assn., N.C. Med. Assn., Soc. Gen. Sys. Rsch., N.Y. Acad. Scis., Am. Orthopsychiat. Assn., Orthodox Christian Profls., Bd. Med. Examiners of N.C. (pres. 1992-93). Home: 8717 Gleneagles Dr Raleigh NC 27613-5419 Office: Raleigh Psychiat Assocs PA 3900 Browning Pl Ste 201 Raleigh NC 27609-6508

STRATE, LANCE ADAM, communications educator; b. N.Y.C., Sept. 17, 1957; s. Benjamin and Betty (Bogomolny) S.; m. Barbara Deborah Gold, Dec. 29, 1991; children: Benjamin Lewis, Sarah Gabrielle. BS, Cornell U., 1978; MA, CUNY, Flushing, 1981; PhD, NYU, 1991. Adj. lectr. CUNY, Flushing, 1979—80, Adelphi U., Garden City, 1984—87, U. Conn., Stamford, 1985—88; instr. William Patterson U., Wayne, NJ, 1988—89; adj. prof. NYU, N.Y.C., 1988—94; from instr. to assoc. prof. Fordham U., Bronx, 1989—96, assoc. prof., 1996—, assoc. chair, 1996—98, chair dept. comm. media studies, 1998—2001. Bd. dirs. Donald McGannon Ctr. Comm. Rsch. Author (chpt.): Inter/Media, Interpersonal Communication a a Media World, 1982, 1986; author: Men, Masculinity, and the Media, 1992, A Rhetorical Analysis of Popular American Film, 1993, American Heroes in a Media Age, 1994, The Emerging Cyberculture, 2000; co-author: Academic American Ency., 1990, 2001, Grolier Multimedia Ency., 2000; co-editor: Communication and Cyberspace: Social Interaction in an Electronic Environment, 1996, Critical Studies in Media Commercialism, 2000, Explorations in Media Ecology, 2002; editor: Speech Comm. Annual, 2000, 2001; mem. editl. bd. N.J. Jour. Comm., 1995—, Media Ecology, 1996—, Interpersonal Computing Tech., 1996—, Qualitative Rsch. Reports, 1999—, Jour. Comm. Culture, 2001—; supervisory editor: Hampton Press, 1994—; reviewer Acad. Am. Ency., 1989, New Dimension Comm., 1992, Comm. Rsch., 1995, scriptwriter Area Arts, 1982; dir.: Area Arts, 1982; actor: , 1982; scriptwriter Adventures of Galaxy Rangers, 1985—86; contbr. articles. Advisor Mothers Onward Search for Autism Intervention and Cure, 1999—; bd. dirs. Temple Beth Elohim, Hasbrouck Heights, N.J., 1994-96, co-chair publ. com., co-editor newsletter. John F. Wilson fellow N.Y. State Comm. Assn., 1998; grantee Am. Automobile Assn. Found. Traffic Safety Rsch., 1987, Fordham U., 1996, 97, Can. Consulate, 1998—. Mem. Internat. Comm. Assn., Internat. Soc. Gen. Semantics, Nat. Comm. Assn. (nominating com., commn. comm. in future 1997-98, local arrangements com., chair conv. registration com. 1998), Am. Comm. Assn., Autism Soc. Am., Ctr. Outreach Svcs. Autistic Cmty., Ea. Comm. Assn.

(assoc. program contbr. 1999-2000), N.J. Comm. Assn. (bd. dirs. 1997-99), Media Ecology Assn. (founding pres. 1998—), N.Y. State Speech Comm. Assn. (v.p. 1997-98, pres. 1998-99), Kappa Delta Pi. Democrat. Jewish. Home: 519 Fourth St Palisades Park NJ 07650 Office: Dept Comm Media Studies Fordham U Bronx NY 10458 E-mail: strate@fordham.edu.

STRATECHUK, MICHAEL, musician, educator; b. New York, Ny, Apr. 12, 1961; s. Oleg Stratechukj and Ruth Stratechuk; m. Marie Celeste Leppanen, Oct. 20, 1984; children: Kurt Nicolas, Karl Emanuel. MFA, Queens Coll., CUNY, Flushing, Queens, 1985—87; BA, SUNY Purchase, Purchase, New York, 1980—84. Orchestral Studies Nat. Orchestral Assn., 1984. Tchr. Hunter Coll. Campus Schools, New York, NY, 1992—, Rudolf Steiner Sch., New York, 1988—92; condr. Queens Coll. Ctr. for Prep. Studies in Music, Flushing, 1988—99; instr. Bklyn Conservatory of Music, 1985—86. Violinist New Philharm. of NJ, Morristown, NJ, 1998—; freelance musician/ violin - condr. Local 802, New York, NY, 1984—. Musician (chamber music coach): (exhibition) Hernandez- Elegy (Artifaks - Scholastic, 2002); musician: (conductor) NA (Mr. Hollands Opus, 2000), (chamber music coach) (The Chamber Music Soc. of Lincoln Ctr. - Young Musicians Competition). Mem. Citizens Budgetary and Acctg. Commitee, Maplewood, NJ, 2001—02; vol. Arts Maplewood, 2000—02, 4th of July Commitee, Maplewood, 2001—02; dist. chmn. Rep. Party, 2000—02; vol. Our Lady of Sorrows, South Orange, 1999—2002; vice chair Profl. Staff Congress, New York, NY, 2001—02. R-Consevative. Roman Catholic. Avocations: travel, softball, soccer. Home: 3 Park Road Maplewood NJ 07040 Office: Hunter College Campus Schools 71 East 94th Stree New York NY 10128 Personal E-mail: mstratec@hchs.hunter.cuny.edu.

STRATHY, JANETTE HANSEN, obstetrician, gynecologist; b. Duluth, Minn., Apr. 25, 1956; m. Gregg M. Strathy, Oct. 6, 1979; 1 child, Bryan. BS in Chemistry, Hamline U., 1977; MD, Mayo Med. Sch., 1981. Resident in ob-gyn. Mayo Med. Sch., Rochester, Minn., 1985; ob-gyn. Park Nicollet Clinic, St. Louis Park, 1985—. Assoc. clin. prof. U. Minn., 1988—. Mem. Am. Coll. Ob-Gyn. (cert. 1987, re-cert. 1996). Lutheran.

STRATIGOS, WILLIAM NARGE, computer company executive; b. Huntington, N.Y., Mar. 14, 1946; s. Narge G. and Portia R. (Kleros) S.; m. Deborah Feller, Jan. 4, 1981; children: Stepahnie, Elena. BA in Biology cum laude, NYU, 1972, DDS, 1977. Lic. dentist, N.Y. Mgr. div. Med. Ctr. NYU, N.Y.C., 1966-74; mng. ptnr., dentist Stratigos Moses et al, 1978-88; pres. Sigma Imaging Systems Inc., 1988-95; v.p. Wang Software, N.Y., Inc., 1995-97, Eastman Software, Inc., N.Y.C., 1997, R2K, Inc., N.Y.C., 1997—, also bd. dirs. Bd. dirs. Sigma Imaging Systems Inc., N.Y.C., The Animal Med. Ctr., N.Y.C., 1997—, Comfidex Corp., N.Y.C., pres., 1998—. Author: Hot Spot, 1993; patents in field. Fellow NYU Acad. of Oral Rehab.; mem. Assn. for Image & Info. Mgmt. Internat. (bd. dirs., treas. exec. committee, chmn. accreditation committee), Dental Soc. of the State of N.Y., First Dist. Dental Soc., Omicron Kappa Upsilon. Greek Orthodox. Avocations: writing, chess, bowling. Office: R2K Inc 53 E 34th St New York NY 10016-4332 E-mail: wstratigos@aol.com.

STRATMAN, JOSEPH LEE, retired petroleum refining company executive, consultant, chemical engineer; b. Louisville, Oct. 15, 1924; s. Dominic Herman and Mary Ann (Wolf) S.; m. Elizabeth Jewell Doyle, July 1, 1950; children— Joseph Lee, Mary Elizabeth, Sharon Ann, Judith Ann BChemE, U. Louisville, 1947. Registered profl. engr., Tex. Chem. engr. Pan Am. Refining Corp., Texas City, Tex., 1947-55, operating supr., 1955-61; mgr. Texas City Refining, Inc., 1961-69, v.p., 1969-80, sr. v.p., 1980-88; pvt. practice, 1988-2001. Bd. dirs., exec. com., treas., chmn. Galveston County ARC, 1966-73; bd. dirs., exec. com., chmn. Texas City Jr. Achievement, 1966-73; treas. Texas City Refining Good Govt. Fund., 1983-88. With USNR, 1945-46. Mem. AIChE. Roman Catholic.

STRATMANN, HENRY GEORGE, cardiologist; b. Dec. 1, 1953; s. Henry George Sr. and Helen Catherine (Schrader) S.; m. Maryellen Amato, May 12, 1984; children: Henry, Joseph. BA in Chemistry, St. Louis U., 1974; MD, So. Ill. U., 1977. Diplomate Am. Bd. Internal Medicine and Cardiology. Intern St. Louis U. Group Hosps., 1977-78, resident in internal medicine, 1978-80; fellow in cardiology, 1980-82; staff John Cochran VA Hosp., St. Louis, 1982—; prof. medicine St. Louis U. Sch. Medicine, 1997—. Contbr. articles to profl. jours. Cardiology fellowship St. Louis U. Group Hosps., 1980-82. Fellow Am. Coll. Physicians, Am. Coll. Angiology, Am. Coll. Cardiology, Am. Coll. Chest Physicians. Office: 1900 S National Ste 3600 Springfield MO 65805 E-mail: hstratmann@aol.com.

STRATON, JOHN CHARLES, JR. investment banker; b. Warwick, N.Y., Apr. 18, 1932; s. John Charles and Helen (Sanford) S.; m. Sally M. Strawhand (div. Mar. 1970); children: John Charles III, Sara; m. Marion S. Holder, Feb. 18, 1974 (div. Mar. 1997); 1 child, Ashley Holder Straton; m. Donna S. DeCoursey, June 24, 1998. BA, U. Va., 1954. With Jas. H. Oliphant and Co., N.Y.C., 1956—, gen. ptnr., 1962—, 1st v.p., 1972-75; v.p. Spencer Trask & Co., Inc., N.Y.C., 1975-77, Hornblower, Weeks, Noyes & Trask, N.Y.C., 1977-78, Loeb Rhoades, Hornblower & Co., 1978-79, Shearson Loeb Rhoades, 1979-81; v.p., fin. cons. Shearson Lehman Bros., N.Y.C., 1981-93; sr. v.p. Smith Barney, 1993—, Saloman Smith Barney, N.Y.C., 1997—. Assessor Village of Tuxedo Park, 1963-70. Vestryman St. Mary's in Tuxedo. Served to maj. AUS, 1954-56; ret. Mem. U. Va. Alumni Assn. N.Y. (pres., treas. 1973-90), Mil. Order Fgn. Wars (comdr. 1981-86, treas. 1986—), Pilgrims of U.S., Tuxedo Pk. Club, Sigma Phi Epsilon. Home: Ledge Rd Tuxedo Park NY 10987 Office: 250 Park Ave New York NY 10177-0001

STRATT, RICHARD MARK, chemistry researcher, educator; b. Phila., Feb. 21, 1954; s. Stanford Lloyd and Florence Clair (Sussman) S. BS in Chemistry, MIT, 1975; PhD, U. Calif., Berkeley, 1979. Postdoctoral rsch. assoc. U. Ill., Champaign, 1979-80; NSF postdoctoral rsch. assoc., 1980; asst. prof. chemistry Brown U., Providence, 1981-85, assoc. prof., 1986-88, prof., 1988—, dept. chair, 1996—. Contbr. articles to profl. jours. Alfred P. Sloan fellow, 1985-89; Fulbright scholar Oxford U., 1981-82. Fellow Am. Phys. Soc.; mem. Am. Chem. Soc. (chmn.-elect theoretical chem. subdivsn. 1997-98, chair 1998-99), Sigma Xi, Phi Lambda Upsilon. Office: Brown U Dept Chemistry Providence RI 02912-0001

STRATTA, ROBERT J. surgeon; b. Chgo., Dec. 4, 1954; s. Peter J. and Lillian (Peretto) S.; children: Michael, Erin, David, Peter, Robert Jr. BS, U. Notre Dame, 1976; MD, U. Chgo., 1980. Diplomate Nat. Bd. Med. Examiners. Chief resident gen. surgery U. Utah Sch. Medicine, Salt Lake City, 1985-86; fellow clin. & rsch. transplant U. Wis., Madison, 1986-88; staff surgeon Bishop Clarkson Meml. Hosp., Omaha, 1988-96. Asst. prof. surgery U. Nebr. Med. Ctr., Omaha, 1988-91, instr. advance trauma life support program, 1988—, faculty supr. surg. residents seminar, 1992-96, assoc. prof. surgery, 1991-95, prof. surgery, 1995-96; dir. clin. pancreas transplant program U. Nebr. Med. Ctr.-Clarkson Hosp., 1989-96; prof. surgery U. Tenn., Memphis, 1997—. Edtl. bd. Chimera, 1991-94, Transplantation Sci., 1991-95, Transplantation, 1993—, Graft, 1998—; rev. jours. in field. Grantee NIH, Fujisawa Pharms. Co., Roche Labs., Sandoz Pharms., Sangstat Co., others. Fellow ACS; mem. AAAS, AMA, Transplantation Soc., Assn. for Acad. Surgery, Am. Assn. for Study of Liver Disease, Surg. Infection Soc., Am. Soc. Transplant Surgeons, Am. Soc. Transplant Physicians, Soc. Critical Care Medicine, Am. Diabetes Assn., Soc. Univ. Surgeons, Internat. Hepato-Biliary Pancreatic Assn., Soc. for Surgery of Alimentary Tract, Soc. for Organ Sharing, Southwestern Surg. Conf., Ctrl. Surg. Assn., Internat. Pancreas and Islet Transplantation Assn., Internat. Liver Transplantation Soc., Cell Transplant Soc., Am. Soc. Liver and Pancreas Surgery, European Soc. for Organ Transplantation. Roman Catholic. Avocations: baseball, jogging, golf, skiing, reading. Office: Wake Forest Univ Sch Medicine Dept Surgery Medical Ctr Blvd Winston Salem NC 27157-1095 Fax: 336-713-5055. E-mail: rstratta@wfubmc.edu.

STRATTON, BRUCE CORNWALL, writer, landscape photographer, publisher; b. San Francisco, Feb. 17, 1929; d, Ernest Kenneth and Dorothy Sinclair (Cornwall) S.; m. Isolde Helga Samovitch (div.). LLB, La Salle Coll., Chgo., 1960. With U.S. Dept. State, 1950-67; vice consul to Mex., 1964-67; educator "Center" (free sch.), Ibiza, Spain, 1975-87; landscape photographer San Miguel de Allende, Mex., 1987-91; author, publisher Fourth Dimension Press, Reno, 1991—. Author: (books) Yoni, 1992, The Last Boat to Barcelona, 1994; editor Works By Dr. Robert N. Spadaro, 1987—. Avocations: tournament bridge, gardening, skiing. Home: 2521 Carville Dr Reno NV 89512-2700

STRATTON, ELAINE AUDREY, small business owner, writer; b. Flint, Mich., Apr. 27, 1925; d. Victor William and Eva Jane (Moore) Miller; m. Olin W. Stratton, Dec. 25, 1946 (dec. Sept. 1991); children: Candace, Jeffrey, John. BS in Edn., So. Ill. U., 1946, MS, 1966; cert. in adminstrn., So. Ill. U., Edwardsville, 1976. Cert. sch. adminstrn. Tchr. Coulterville (Ill.) Sch., 1946-47; libr. Highland (Ill.) Cmty. Sch., 1948-80; dir. librs. Highland Cmty. Unit #5, 1970-80; dir. fed. elem. writing program WRITE ON, Highland, 1980-82; book reviewer KMOX, St. Louis, 1986; pub. Swiss Village Book Store, 1985-88, owner, 1978-94. Counselor Svc. Corps. Ret. Execs.-SCORE; cons. Libr. Book Selection Svc., Bloomington, Ill., 1975-82; oral historian, Ill. 1972-77; docent Landmarks, St. Louis; cons. in field. Author, editor, pub.: St. Louis and the River - a "Lite" History, 1988; editor, pub.: Illinois Sketches, 1985. Chmn. Bicentennial Rsch. and Dissemination Com. (developed and produced bicentennial calendar sent to Smithsonian), 1975-76; oral historian, 1975-77; mem. Friends of Louis Latzer Meml. Libr.; program dir., Sch. Vol. Program, 1978-82, Highland, Ill.; vol. St. Louis Visitors and Conv. Ctr., 1995; bd. dirs. Highland Hist. Assn.; sec. bd. dirs. Historyonics Theatre Co., St. Louis, 1992—. Recipient Ill. Bicentennial Com. award, 1976; grantee WRITE ON project, 1980-82. Mem. ALA (chair libr. media skills com. 1981-83), Nat. Assn. Women Bus. Owners, Am. Bookman's Assn. Address: 6 Evergreen Ln Glen Carbon IL 62034-1706

STRATTON, GREGORY ALEXANDER, computer specialist, administrator, mayor; b. Glendale, Calif., July 31, 1946; s. William Jaspar and Rita Phyllis (Smith) S.; m. Yolanda Margot Soler, 1967 (div. 1974); 1 child, Tiffany Schwarzer; m. Edith Carter, Sept. 27, 1975; stepchildren: Paul Henkell, D'Lorah Henkell Wismar. Student, Harvey Mudd Coll., 1964-65; BS in Physics, UCLA, 1968; MBA, Calif. Luth. U., 1977. Elec. engr. Naval Ship Weapon System Engring. Sta., Port Hueneme, Calif., 1968-73; sr. staff mem. Univac, Valencia, 1973-74; v.p. Digital Applications, Camarillo, 1974-75; cons. Grumman Aerospace, Point Mugu, 1975-76; F-14 software mgr. Pacific Missle Test Ctr., Pt. Mugu, 1976-84; software mgr. Teledyne Systems, Northridge, Calif., 1984-92, dir. engring. software dept., 1992-93; dep. dir. software engring. Teledyne Electronic Systems, 1993-94; software mgr. Litton Guidance and Controls, Woodland Hills, 1995-2001, Northrop/Grumman Nav. Sys., Woodland Hills, 2001—. Chmn. strategic planning Simi Valley Hosp. Mem. City Coun., City of Simi Valley, Calif., 1979-86, mayor, 1986-98; mem. Rep. County Cen. Com., Ventura County, 2000—; mem. Rep. State Cen. Com., Calif., 1990—; bd. dirs. Simi Valley Hosp., 1987-2001; pres. Simi Valley Cultural Arts Found., 1999—. Mem. Rotary (Paul Harris award Simi Sunrise chpt. 1989), Jaycees (pres. Simi Valley chpt. 1974-75, nat. bd. dirs. 1975-76, v.p. Calif. state 1976-77). Republican. Lutheran. Home: 2003 Tulip Ave Simi Valley CA 93063 Office: Northrop Grumman Navigation Sys 5500 Canoga Ave Woodland Hills CA 91367-6698 E-mail: gastratton@sbcglobal.net., greg.stratton@northropgrumman.com.

STRATTON, JAMES EDWARD, retired construction educator; b. Flushing, Ohio, Dec. 26, 1930; s. Stanley Willits and Marjorie Anna (Smith) S.; m. Eleanor Jean Koons, June 28 , 1952; children: Lisa Kay Stratton Yoder, Leslie Ann Stratton Norris. BArch, Miami U., Oxford, Ohio, 1958, M in City Design, 1961. Arch. draftsman Small & Wertz, Architects, Oxford, OH, 1958, Garriott & Becker, Architects., Cin., 1958-60; jr. planner City of Middletown, 1960; planning cons. Carroll Hill & Assocs., Columbus, 1961-67; planning cons., owner James E. Stratton Assocs., Worthington, 1967-77; facility mgr. Grace Brethren Ch., 1977-85; mem. faculty constrn. scis. dept. Columbus (Ohio) State C.C., 1985-2000, asst. prof., 1988-92, chmn. constrn. scis. dept., 1992-2000, assoc. prof., 1992-2000. Avocations: graphics, woodworking. Home: 5293 Ashford Rd Dublin OH 43017-8631 E-mail: jstratto@earthlink.net.

STRATTON, JOHN ALFRED, mechanical engineer, educator; b. Rochester, N.Y., Sept. 12, 1941; s. Burton Elbridge and Alice Adele (Howe) Stratton; m. Lois Averett; children: Thomas C., Linda S. Palmer, Ann-Marie Giannosa. AAS, Rochester Inst. Technology, 1962, BS, 1964; MSEE, Rensselaer Poly. Inst., Troy, N.Y., 1966. Profl. engr. Sys. planning engr. N.Y. State Elec. & Gas, Binghamton, 1966-69; asst. prof. Alfred (N.Y.) State Coll., 1969-71; from prof. elec. engring. tech. to chair dept., assoc. dean Rochester Inst. Technology, 1971-99, chair mfg. & mech. engring. technology, pckg. sci., 1999—. Cons. in field. Mem. IEEE, Inst. Power Engring. Soc., Am. Soc. Engring. Edn. Avocation: riding trains. Home: 43 Queensway Rd Rochester NY 14623-4627 Office: Rochester Inst Technology 78 Lomb Memorial Dr Rochester NY 14623-5604 E-mail: jasite@rit.edu.

STRATTON, JOSEPHINE MABEL, special education educator; b. Norwich, N.Y., July 5, 1926; d. Thomas A. and Ethel I. (Meeker) Kalicicki; m. Earl C. Stratton, Aug. 12, 1947 (dec. 1978); children: Elinor M Stratton Houston, Nancy Stratton Beith, Lois J. Stratton Kern. BEd, SUNY, Fredonia, 1947; MS in Spl. Edn., SUNY, Binghamton, 1981; EdM in Spl. Edn., Columbia U., 1989, EdD in Spl. Edn., 1991. Cert. tchr., spl. edn. tchr., tchr. of blind, N.Y. Tchr. Sherburne (N.Y.) Cen. Schs., 1954-55, Norwich City Schs., 1955-56, 62-73, resource tchr. for visually impaired and learning disabled, 1973-85; cons. blind and visually-impaired children Shield Sch., N.Y.C., 1986, Chenango/Delaware Bd. Coop. Ednl. Svcs., Norwich, 1990-2000. Tchr. Braille transcribing course for adults, Norwich, 1983; coord. office for disabled student svcs. Tchrs. Coll., Columbia U., N.Y.C., 1986-87; mem. Visually Impaired Infants Rsch. Consortium, N.Y.C., 1987-89; coll. tchr. lit. Braille course Tchrs. Coll., Columbia U., 1987-89; tchr. asessment of blind U. Nebr., 1991; cons., author Lit. Project for Young Blind and Visually Impaired Children, Am. Printing House for the Blind, Louisville, 1987-90; ind. cons. for children who are visually impaired; presenter in field. Contbr. articles to profl. publs. Mem. N.Y. State Com. for Literacy for Visually Impaird, 2000—. Recipient Virgil Zickel award, Am. Printing House for the Blind. Mem. Assn. Edn. and Rehab. of Blind and Visually Impaired (chair N.Y. State chpt. membership com. 1990-93, bd. dirs. N.Y. State chpt. 1991-94, 96—, Meritorious Achievement award 1992, Joyce M. Ogburn Nat. award 1998), Coun. Exceptional Children (chpt. pres. 1988-89, dir. divsn. visually handicapped 1990-92), Nat. Assn. Parents of Visually Handicapped, Nat. Braille Assn. (tactile graphics com. 1990-95, bd. dirs. 1993-95). Home and Office: 7 Willard Ct Norwich NY 13815-1315 E-mail: strat7@norwich.net.

STRATTON, JULIUS AUGUSTUS, psychologist, consultant; b. Norfolk, Va., July 9, 1924; s. Julius Augustus and Annie (Thornton) S. BS, Hampton U., Va., 1947; MEd, Cornell U., 1957; postgrad., Harvard U., 1966-67, U. Chgo., 1965. Instr., chmn. dept. counseling Roosevelt High Sch., Gary, Ind., 1952-68; assoc. faculty Ind. U. N.W., 1971-74; research dir. Gary Sch. Corp., 1968-76; v.p. Cornell Urban Cons., Chgo., 1976—. Author: Nonintellectual Factors Associated with Academic Achievement, 1957; contbr. articles to profl. jours. Mem. Nat. Coun. Tchrs. of Math., Assn. for Measurement and Evaluation in Counseling & Devel., Alpha Phi Alpha, Phi Delta Kappa, Sigma Gamma Mu. Democrat. Episcopalian. Avocations: opera, art, computer telecommunications.

STRATTON, KATHLEEN R. medical association administrator; PhD. Dir. divsn. health promotion and disease prevention Inst. Medicine NAS, sr. program officer, 1999—2002; study dir. Immunization Safety Rev. Comm., Inst. of Medicine, 2002—. Office: Inst Medicine Foundry Bldg 1055 Thomas Jefferson St NW Washington DC 20007-5259 also: 2101 Constitution Ave NW Washington DC 20418-0007*

STRATTON, MARIANN, retired naval nursing administrator; b. Houston, Apr. 6, 1945; d. Max Millard and Beatrice Agnes (Roemer) S.; m. Lawrence Mallory Stickney, nov. 15, 1977 (dec.). BSN, BA in English, Sacred Heart Dominican Coll., 1966; MA in Mgmt., Webster Coll., 1977; MSN, U. Va., 1981. Cert. adult nurse practitioner. Ensign USN, 1966, advanced through grades to rear adm., 1991; patient care coord. Naval Regional Med. Ctr., Charleston, S.C., 1981-83; nurse corps plans officer Naval Med. Command, Washington, 1983-86; dir. nursing svcs. U.S. Naval Hosp., Naples, Italy, 1986-89, Naval Hosp., San Diego, 1989-91; chief pers. mgmt. Bur. Medicine & Surgery, Washington, 1991-94; dir. USN Nurse Corps, 1991-94; ret. Oct. 1, 1994 USN, 1994. Decorated Disting. Svc. medal, Meritorious Svc. medal with two stars, Naval Achievement medal. Mem. Interagy. Inst. of Fed. Health Care Execs., Am. Volksporting Assn., Tex. Wanders, Fiber Artists of San Antonio, D'Vine Women.

STRATTON, ROBERT, financial company executive, physicist; b. Vienna, Austria, Aug. 14, 1928; came to U.S., 1959, naturalized, 1966; s. Kenneth Kurt and Eugenie (Schwatzer) S.; m. Elfriede Karlberger, Jan. 11, 1980; children: David Alexander, Valerie Pam. B.Sc. in Physics, Manchester U., 1949, PhD in Theoretical Physics, 1952. Rsch. physicist Met. Vickers Elec. Co., Manchester, Eng., 1952-59; with Tex. Instruments, Inc., Dallas, 1959-94, dir. physics rsch. lab., 1963-71, assoc. dir. cen. rsch. labs., 1971-72, dir. semiconductor R & D, 1972-75, dir. cen. rsch. labs., 1975-77, asst. v.p., dir. cen. rsch. labs., 1977-82, v.p. corp. staff, dir. cen. rsch. labs., 1982-94; dir. Indsl. Outreach Elec. Materials Sci. Tech. Ctr., dir. Engring. and Tech. Inst., U. Tex., Austin, 1994-96; co-founder, rsch. cons. Fin. Marketplace Group, Dallas, 1997—. Contbr. articles to profl. jours. Bd. dirs. Indsl. Rsch. Inst., 1985-88, Coun. on Superconductivity for Am. Competitiveness, 1987-90; adv. bd. dirs. Tex. Ctr. for Superconductivity, 1989-2000. Fellow IEEE, Inst. Physics (U.K.), Am. Phys. Soc.; mem. NAE. Office: Ste #266 500 N Ctrl Expressway Plano TX 75074 E-mail: bobstra@aol.com.

STRATTON, ROY FRANKLIN, retired electronics engineer; b. Memphis, July 23, 1929; s. Roy Franklin and Louisa (Ladenburger) Stratton; m. Pauline Woods, Sept. 7, 1963; 1 child James. BS in Physics, Rhodes Coll., 1951; MS in Physics, U. Tenn., 1953, PhD in Physics, 1957; MSEE, Ga. Inst. Tech., 1975. Registered profl engr, Ga. Teaching asst. U. Tenn., Knoxville, 1952-55, rsch. asst., 1955-57; physicist Oak Ridge (Tenn.) Nat. Lab., 1958-70; chmn. sci. divsn., prof. physics Pikeville (Ky.) Coll., 1970-73; teaching asst. Ga. Inst. Tech., Atlanta, 1973-75; electronic engr. Air Force Rsch. Lab, 1975-2001; ret, 2001. Contbr. articles to profl jours. Mem.: AAAS, IEEE, SE Sect Am Physics Soc. Achievements include patents in field. Avocations: fencing, reading, chess, Go. E-mail: pstratton@mindspring.com.

STRATTON, SHARON ELIZABETH SPAHN, mental and women's health nurse, nurse supervisor; b. Dubuque, Iowa, Oct. 11, 1956; d. Joseph and Shirley Spahn; div.; children: Chad and Todd Stratton, Tyler and Mallory Winter. Diploma, N.E. Iowa Tech. Inst., Peosta, 1984; ADN, N.E. Iowa Tech. Inst., 1985; BSN, U. Dubuque, 1988; grad. Critical Care Nursing, U. Tenn., Nashville, 1993. Charge nurse, skilled nursing Manor Care, Dubuque, 1985—88; charge and staff nurse, newborn nursery Broward Gen. Med. Ctr., Ft. Lauderdale, Fla., 1988—89, charge and staff nurse, locked psychiat. unit, 1989—90, staff nurse garden suites med.-surg. unit, 1990—91; agy. nurse Med. Pers. Pool, 1991; staff nurse med. unit Nashville Meml. Hosp., Madison, Tenn., 1991; nursing supr. Bapt. Hosp. Home Care Svcs., Nashville, 1992; emergency rm. staff nurse Nashville Meml. Hosp., Madison, 1993-94; emergency rm. staff-charge nurse St. Louis Regional Med. Ctr., 1994-95; emergency rm. staff nurse Barnes Hosp., St. Louis, 1994-95; staff devel. coord. Mary Mount Manor, Eureka, 1995-96; care team leader pediat. and family practice BJC Arnold (Mo.) Health Ctr., 1997-99; telephone triage nurse Magellan Health Svcs., St. Louis, 1998—; staff nurse St. Louis Correctional Med. Svcs., 2000-01; emergency rm. staff nurse St. Anthony's Med. Ctr., St. Louis, 2002—. Leader Brownie troop Girl Scouts U.S.A., 1994-95. Home: 5500 Duessel Ln Apt A Saint Louis MO 63128-5015

STRATTON, SONDRA KAY, primary school educator; b. Cin., Apr. 16, 1950; d. Robert C. and Marjorie (Cornetet) S. AA, Tri-County Acad. Ctr., 1970; BS in Elem. Edn., U. Cin., 1974; postgrad., U. Dayton, 1987—. Tchrs. aide Eastern Local Sch. Dist., Sardina, Ohio, 1968-69; tchr., jr. high sch. Ohio Valley Sch. Dist., Bentonville, 1970-71, tchr., primary West Union, 1971-74, Ea. Local Sch. Dist., Sardinia, 1974—2000; with Sardinia Elem Sch. Odyssey of the mind coach, Sardina, 1988. Mem. NEA, Ohio Edn. Assn., South Western Ohio Edn. Assn., Ea. Local Edn. Assn. (negotiating team 1989-91). Avocations: sewing, music, writing, crafts. Home: 7383 Staten Rd Sardinia OH 45171-9372 Office: Sardinia Elem Sch Coll Ave Sardinia OH 45171

STRATTON, WALTER LOVE, lawyer; b. Greenwich, Conn., Sept. 21, 1926; s. John McKee and June (Love) S.; children: John, Michael, Peter (dec.), Lucinda; m. DeAnna Weinheimer, Oct. 1, 1994. Student, Williams Coll., 1943; AB, Yale U., 1948; LL.B., Harvard U., 1951. Bar: N.Y. 1952. Assoc. Casey, Lane & Mittendorf, N.Y.C., 1951-53; assoc. Donovan, Leisure, Newton & Irvine, N.Y.C., 1956-63, ptnr., 1963-84, Gibson, Dunn & Crutcher, 1984-93, Andrews & Kurth, N.Y.C., 1993-95, of counsel, 1996—. Asst. U.S. atty. So. Dist. N.Y., N.Y.C., 1953-56; lectr. Practising Law Inst. Served with USNR, 1945-46. Fellow: Am. Coll. Trial Lawyers; mem.: ABA, N.Y. State Bar Assn., Fed. Bar Coun., Greenwich Riding and Trails Assn. (pres.), Colo. Arlberg Club, Indian Harbor Yacht Club. Home: 434 Round Hill Rd Greenwich CT 06831-2639 Office: Andrews & Kurth 805 3rd Ave New York NY 10022-7513 E-mail: walterstratton@akllp.com.

STRATTON-CROOKE, THOMAS EDWARD, financial consultant; b. N.Y.C., June 28, 1933; s. Harold and Jeanne Mildred (Stifft); children: Karen, John Ryland; m. Suzanne Williams, Oct. 21, 1989. Student, Hunter Coll., 1951-52; BS in Marine Engring. and Transp., U.S. Maritime Acad., 1952-56; student, Washington U., St. Louis, 1961; MBA in Internat. Mktg., Banking and Fin., NYU, 1967. Commd. ensign USN, 1956, advanced through grades to lt., 1957; with Goodyear Internat. Corp., Akron, Ohio, 1960-63, Esso Internat., N.Y.C., 1958-60; dir. market info. and devel. Hotel Corp. Am., Boston, 1964-68; with Continental Grain Co., N.Y.C., 1968-72; dir. charter contracts Conoco, Stamford, Conn., 1973-75; cons. A. T. Kearney, Cleve., 1976-81; investment banker E. F. Hutton, 1981-83, AG Edwards and Sons, Inc., Cleve., 1983-89; sr. fin. advisor, registered investment advisor, asst. v.p., sr. fin. cons. Merrill Lynch, 1989—. Chmn. Indsl. Devel. Resch. Coun., Atlanta, 1970, Indsl. Devel. Resch. Coun., Snow Mass, Colo., 1971; lectr. bus. U. R.I., Kingston, 1968-70, tchr. Bus. Coll. Internat., 1986-89. Contbr. articles to profl. jours. Mem. Findley Lake (N.Y.) Hist. Soc.; mem. Nat. Task Force Reps. for Pres. Reagan, Cleve., 1982—. Officer (ret.) USN. Mem. Naval Res. Officers Assn., Naval Res. Assn., Great Lakes Hist. Soc., Soc. Naval Architects/Engrs., Navy League, Civil War Roundtable, NYU Alumni Assn., U.S. Coast Guard Club (Cleve.), Univ. Club, Circumnavigators Club (life), Internat. Shipmasters Assn., Propeller Club, Army Club, Navy Club, French Creek Hist. Soc., Town Club (Jamestown, N.Y.), Masons, Shriners, Cleve. City Club, Kings Point Alumni Assn., Civil War Round Table, U.S. Merchant Marine Acad. Avocations: sailing, skiing, bird watching, gardening, sports car enthusiast. Office: Merrill Lynch One Cleveland Ctr 1375 E 9th St Cleveland OH 44114-1798 E-mail: tommyesc@aol.com.

STRAUB, CHESTER JOHN, judge; b. Bklyn., May 12, 1937; s. Chester and Ann (Majewski) Straub; m. Patricia Morrissey; children: Chester, Michael, Christopher, Robert. AB, St. Peter's Coll., 1958; JD, U. Va., 1961. Bar: N.Y. 1962, U.S. Dist. Ct. (so. and ea. dists.) N.Y. 1963, U.S. Ct. Appeals (2d cir.) 1967, U.S. Supreme Ct. 1978. Assoc. Willkie Farr & Gallagher, N.Y.C., 1963—71, ptnr., 1971—98; mem. N.Y. State Assembly, 1967—72, N.Y. State Senate, 1973—75, Dem. Nat. Com., 1976—80; judge U.S. Ct. Appeals (2d cir.), 1998—. Past mediator U.S. Dist. Ct. (so. dist.) N.Y.; neutral evaluator U.S. Dist. Ct. (ea. dist.) N.Y.; chmn. jud. screening com. State of N.Y., 1988—94, first dept. jud. screening com., 1983—94, Senator Moynihan's jud. selection com., 1976—98. Trustee Lenox Hill Hosp.; Cardinal's com. laity Cath. Charities, NY. With U.S. Army, 1961—63. Mem.: ABA, Assn. of Bar of City of N.Y.C., N.Y. State Bar Assn., Kosciuszko Found. Office: US Ct Appeals Second Circuit 500 Pearl St New York NY 10007-1316

STRAUB, LARRY GENE, business executive; b. Great Bend, Kans., Aug. 25, 1959; s. Walter Joseph and Barbara Jane (Schartz) S.; m. Julie Ann Miller, May 25, 1985; children: Hillary Ann, Brantley Joseph. BA, Ft. Hays State U., 1988, MS, 1990; MBA, Friends U., 1995. CEO Straub Internat., Great Bend, Kans., 1983—; v.p., CFO Celebrations Unlimited, Inc., 1984—. Trustee Barton County C.C., Great Bend, 1995—. Mem. Western Retailers Assn., Great Bend C. of C. (amb., pres.), Masons (32nd degree, bd. dirs.), Kiwanis, Pi Kappa Phi (v.p. recruitment). Republican. Roman Catholic. Avocations: tennis, book collecting, skiing, history. Home: 2813 Argonne Dr Salina KS 67401-1620

STRAUB, LINDA CATHERINE, poet; b. Tampa, Fla., Sept. 12, 1948; d. Martin James and Alvena Mae (Carwile) Estep; m. Robert E. Straub, May 23, 1970 (div. Mar. 1991); children: Robert Jeffrey, Amy Catherine, Kyle Martin. Cert. exec. sec., Lansdale (Pa.) Sch. Bus., 1968. Mgr. adminstrv. br. Navy Resale and Support Svcs., Mechanicsburg, Pa., 1987-90; exec. sec. A.Z. Ritzman Assocs., Harrisburg, 1990-95; adminstrv. asst. HealthAm. of Pa., 1996—. Contbr. poetry and short stories to lit. jours. and comml. mags. Mem. Acad. Am. Poets, IWWG, Pennwriters. Avocations: guitar, reading, photography.

STRAUB, PETER FRANCIS, novelist; b. Milw., Mar. 2, 1943; s. Gordon Anthony and Elvena (Nilsestuen) S.; m. Susan Bitker, Aug. 27, 1966; children: Benjamin Bitker, Emma Sydney Valli. BA, U. Wis., 1965; MA, Columbia U., 1966. English tchr. Univ. Sch., Milw., 1966-68. Author: Marriages, 1973, Julia, 1975, If You Could See Me Now, 1977, Ghost Story, 1979, Shadowland, 1980, Floating Dragon, 1983, Leeson Park and Belsize Square, 1984, Wild Animals, 1984, Blue Rose, 1985, Koko, 1988, Mystery, 1989, Houses Without Doors, 1990, Mrs. God, 1991, The Throat, 1993, The Hellfire Club, 1996, Mr. X, 1999, Pork Pie Hat, 1999, Magic Terror, 2000; (with Stephen King) The Talisman, 1984, Black House, 2001; editor: Peter Straub's Ghosts, 1995, Conjunctions #39, 2002. Recipient Brit. Fantasy award, August Derleth award, 1983, World Fantasy awards World Fantasy Conv., 1989, 93, World Horror Assn. awards, 1993, 98, 99, 2000, Grand Master award, World Horror Conv., 1997, award Internat. Horror Guild, 1999. Mem. PEN, Mystery Writers Am., Horror Writers Assn. Avocations: jazz, opera, classical music. E-mail: pstraub@nyc.rr.com.

STRAUB, PETER THORNTON, lawyer; b. St. Louis, Mar. 27, 1939; s. Ralph H. and Mary Louise (Thornton) S.; m. Wendy B. Cubbage, Dec. 29, 1964; children: Karl Thornton, Philip Hamilton, Ellen Elizabeth. AB, Washington and Lee U., 1961, LLB, 1964. Bar: Mo. 1964, Va. 1964, U.S. Dist. Ct. (ea. dist.) Mo. 1967, U.S. Circuit Ct. Appeals (8th cir.) 1969, U.S. Supreme Ct. 1970. U.S. Circuit Ct. Appeals (D.C. cir.) 1971, Ct. Mil. Appeals 1970, U.S. Tax Ct. 1971, U.S. Bankruptcy Ct. 1991. Assoc. Evans & Dixon, St. Louis, 1966-68; asst. pub. defender St. Louis County, 1968-69; asst. U.S. Atty., 1969-71; trial atty. internal security div. Dept. Justice, Washington, 1971-72, atty.-adviser office of dep. atty. gen., 1972-73, dir. office criminal justice, spl. asst. to atty. gen., 1974; minority counsel com. on judiciary U.S. Ho. of Reps., Washington, 1973-74; gen. counsel SSS, 1974-76; pvt. practice Law Offices of Peter T. Straub, Alexandria, Va., 1976—. Pres., gov. bd. Alexandria Cmty. Mental Health Ctr., 1982—95; mem. No. Va. Estate Planning Coun., 1981—; mem. pres.'s coun. Trinity Coll., Washington, 1980—87; mem. adv. bd. Am. Heart Assn., Alexandria, 1991—92, Salvation Army, Alexandria, 1991—, v.p., 1994—96, chmn., 1997—99, Alexandria Cmty. Shelter Adv. Bd., 1995—97; Va. escheat atty. City of Alexandria, 1994—; dist. chmn. Boy Scouts Am., 1998—2001; mem. adv. bd. Hospice No. Va., 2000—, Friends of the Washington and Old Dominion Trail; bd. dirs. Parc East Condominium, 1990—, sec., 1992—; bd. dirs. Sigma Nu Ednl. Found., Inc., 2000—. Recipient certificate of award Dept. Justice, 1970, certificate of appreciation Law Enforcement Assistance Adminstrn. Dept. Justice, 1974, Silver Beaver award Boy Scouts Am., Washington , 1987. Mem.: FBA, ABA, Va. Trial Lawyers Assn., Alexandria Bar Assn., Mo. Bar Assn., Bar Assn. Met. St. Louis, Va. Bar Assn., Optimists (bd. dirs., pres. Alexandria chpt. 1984, lt. gov. Nat. Capitol Va. Dist. 1987—89, treas. 1999—2001), Nat. Eagle Scout Assn., Nat. Lawyers Club, Sigma Nu. Republican. Congregationalist. Avocations: scouting, reading, bicycling. Office: 1225 Martha Custis Dr # 103 Alexandria VA 22302-2040 Fax: 703-820-8602. E-mail: straublaw@erols.com.

STRAUB, SUSAN MONICA, special education educator; b. Tampa, Fla., Jan. 31, 1954; d. Paul Ferdinand and Betty Hew (Wellacott) S. AA, Hillsborough Community Coll., 1975; BA, U. S. Fla., 1978. Lifeguard, swimming instr. Tampa Recreation Dept., 1970-74 summers, pool mgr., 1975-76 summers, office asst. sec., 1977-78 summers; tchr. Hillsborough Assn. Retarded Citizens, Tampa, 1978-79, Hillsborough County Sch. Bd., Tampa, 1979—, Sch. of Hope, 1979-81, Mango Elem. Sch., 1981-85, Lopez Elem Sch., Seffner, Fla., 1985-93, Wilson Elem. Sch., Plant City, 1993-98, Mann Mid. Sch., Brandon, 1998-2000, Armwood H.S., Seffner, 2000—. Coach Spl. Olympics, Tampa, 1980, 2000—, games ofcl., 1982, steering com., Hillsborough County, 1984-92. Sec., treas. Superstar Bowling League for Handicapped, Tampa, 1988-89, 1st v.p., 1989-91. Recipient Spl. Olympics award Hillsborough County, State of Fla., 1980; named Vol. of Yr. Mass. Mutual, 1982, Coach of Yr. Hillsborough County Spl. Olympics, 1982, Tchr. of Yr. U. So. Fla. Alumni Assn., 1990. Mem. Coun. Exceptional Children (hospitality chair, Dept. Exceptional Student Edn. Person of Yr. 1987-88, Chpt. Tchr. of Yr. 1990), Soroptimist Internat. (1st v.p., 2d v.p. 1990-91, Team Leader 1985-91, 92-93). Democrat. Roman Catholic. Avocations: soccer, swimming. Home: 4885 Puritan Cir Tampa FL 33617-8355 Office: Armwood H S 12000 Hwy 92 Seffner FL 33584-3418

STRAUBE, BARRY MAYNARD, physician executive; b. Montclair, N.J., Jan. 31, 1949; s. Harold M. and Mary Elsie (Amaral) S.; m. Patricia Lynn Roane, June 5, 1971; children: Christopher Roane, Jonathan Ramsey. AB magna cum laude, Princeton U., 1971; MD, U. Mich., 1975. Resident in internal medicine California Pacific Med. Ctr., San Francisco, 1975-78; fellow in nephrology Tufts-New Eng. Med. Ctr., Boston, 1980-82; nephrologist Calif. Pacific Med. Ctr., San Francisco, 1982-94; med. dir. quality mgmt. Found. Health Sys., Rancho Cordova, Calif., 1994-97; v.p. quality improvement, sr. med. dir. Health Net, Woodland Hills, 1997-99; chief med. officer region IX Ctrs for Medicare and Medicaid Svcs., San Francisco, 2000—. Capt. USAF, 1978-80. Mem. Am. Coll. Physician Execs., Phi Beta Kappa. Avocations: cycling, hiking, travel, art galleries, reading. Office: Ctrs for Medicare and Medicaid Svcs 75 Hawthorne St Ste 408 San Francisco CA 94105-3920 E-mail: bstraube@alumni.princeton.edu., bstraube@cms.hhs.gov.

STRAUCH, BERISH, plastic surgeon, hand and cosmetic surgeon; b. N.Y.C., Sept. 19, 1933; m. Rena Feuerstein, June 12, 1955; children: Robert, Laurie. BS, Columbia U., 1955, MD, 1959. Diplomate Am. Bd. Surgery, Am. Bd. Plastic Surgery, added qualification in hand surgery. Intern Bellevue Hosp., N.Y.C., 1959-60; resident gen. surgery Montefiore Med. Ctr., Bronx, 1960-63; hand surgery fellow Roosvelt Hosp., N.Y.C., 1961; resident plastic surgery Stanford U., Palo Alto, Calif., 1966-67, chief resident, 1967-68; asst. prof. plastic surgery Albert Einstein Coll. Medicine, Bronx, 1970-76, assoc. prof., 1976-81; chief plastic surgery svcs. Montefiore Med. Ctr. and Albert Einstein Coll. Medicine, 1978-87; prof. plastic surgery Albert Einstein Coll. Medicine and Montefiore Med. Ctr., N.Y., 1981—; acting chmn. dept. Montefiore Med. Ctr. and Albert Einstein Coll. Medicine, 1987-89, chmn., 1989—. Instr. Stanford U., 1967-68; vis. plastic surgeon Sing Sing (N.Y.) Prison, 1968-75. Co-author: (with others) Atlas of Microvascular Surgery: Anatomy and Operative Approaches, 1993 (Best Healt Sci. Book, Doody's Rating Svc. 1993); co-editor: (with A. Daniller) Textbook on Microsurgery, 1976, (with others) Grabb's Encyclopedia of Flaps, 3 vols., 1990, (Outstanding Publ. in Clin. Medicine, Assn. Am. Pubs. 1990), 2d edit. 1997; contbr. about 70 articles to profl. jours., and 20 chpts. to sci. books; assoc. editor Plastic and Reconstructive Surgery, 1982-88; founder, editor-in-chief Jour. Reconstructive Microsurgery, 1984—. Capt. Med. Corps. U.S. Army, 1964-66, Mem. AAAS, ACS, Am. Soc. for Reconstructive Microsurgery (founder, past sec., treas. pres., chmn. Founder's Lectr. 1988), Am. Assn. Plastic Surgeons, Internat. Soc. Reconstructive Microsurgery (chmn. founding coun. 1983-84, pres. 1984-85). Med. Soc. State of N.Y., Am. Trauma Soc. (founding mem.), N.Y. Acad. Sci., Am. Soc. for Peripheral Nerve Surgery (pres. 1993-94), and others. Office: Montefiore Med Park 1625 Poplar St Ste 200 Bronx NY 10461-2653 E-mail: bstrauch@montefiore.org.

STRAUCH, CARL EDWARD, physician; b. Canton, Ill., Aug. 8, 1953; m. Debra Jean Kumpf, Oct. 25, 1979; children: Christopher, Laura. BS, Purdue U., 1974; MS, No. Ill. U., 1975; MD, U. Ill., 1979. Diplomate Am. Bd. Internal Medicine, Am. Bd. Geriatrics. Intern, resident Butterworth Hosp., Grand Rapids, Mich., 1979-82; pvt. practice Galesburg, Ill., 1982—. Mem. Knox County Bd. Health, Galesburg, 1993-2001, Dist. 205 Bd. Edn., Galesburg, 1995—; elder 1st Presbyn. Ch., Galesburg, 1996-2001. Mem. ACP, Am. Geriatrics Soc., Rotary. Office: 834 N Seminary #303 Galesburg IL 61401-3726

STRAUCH, JOHN L. lawyer; b. Pitts., Apr. 16, 1939; s. Paul L. and Delilah M. (Madison) S.; m. Gail Lorraine Kohn, Dec. 5, 1991; children: Paul L., John M., Lisa E. BA summa cum laude, U. Pitts., 1960; JD magna cum laude, NYU Sch. Law, 1963. Law clk. to Judge Sterry Waterman U.S. Ct. Appeals (2d cir.), St. Johnsbury, Vt., 1963-64; assoc. Jones, Day, Reavis & Pogue, Cleve., 1964-70, ptnr., 1970—, mem. adv. com., partnership com., chmn. litigation group. Mem. Statutory Com. on Selecting Bankruptcy Judges, Cleve., 1985-88; mem. lawyers com. Nat. Ctr. for State Cts. Editor-in-chief: NYU Law Rev., 1962-63; contbr. chpt. to book. Pres., trustee Cleve. Task Force on Violent Crimes, 1985-88; trustee Legal Aid Soc., Cleve., 1978, Cleve. Greater Growth Assn., 1985-86, Citizens Mental Health Assembly, 1989-90, lawyers com. Nat. Ctr. for State Cts., 1989—. Fellow Am. Coll. Trial Lawyers (life); mem. ABA, Ohio Bar Assn., Cleve. Bar Assn. (trustee 1980-83, pres. 1985-86), Fed. Bar Assn. (trustee Cleve. chpt. 1978-79, v.p. Cleve. chpt. 1979-80), Sixth Fed. Jud. Conf. (life), Ohio Eighth Jud. Conf. (life), Order of Coif, Inns of Ct., Oakmont Country Club, The Country Club, Kiawah Island Club, Phi Beta Kappa. Home: 28149 N Woodland Rd Cleveland OH 44124-4522 Office: Jones Day Reavis & Pogue N Point 901 Lakeside Ave E Cleveland OH 44114-1190

STRAUCH, RICHARD C. music educator; b. Berkeley, Calif., June 22, 1964; s. Richard C. and Elvia N. Strauch; m. Sally S. Stewart, Nov. 23, 1991; children: Rachel E., Rebecca J. DMA, Yale U., New Haven, CT, 1988—91. Dir., whitworth wind symphony Whitworth Coll., Spokane, Wash., 1997—; dir. of instrumental activities Phillips U., Enid, Okla., 1993—97. Trombonist Spokane Symphony Orch., Spokane, Wash., 2001—. Mem.: Music Educators Nat. Conf., Internat. Trombone Assn., Coll. Band Directors Nat. Assn. Home: 709 E Brierwood Lane Spokane WA 99218 Office: Whitworth College 300 W Hawthorne Road MS 1701 Spokane WA 99218 Office Fax: 509-777-3739. Personal E-mail: rstrauch@whitworth.edu. E-mail: rstrauch@whitworth.edu.

STRAUGHAN, WILLIAM THOMAS, engineering educator; b. Shreveport, La., Aug. 2, 1936; s. William Eugene and Sara Chloetilde (Harrell) S.; m. Rubie Ann Barnes, Aug. 20, 1957; children: Donna Ann, Sara Arlene, Eugene Thomas. BS, MIT, 1959; MS, U. Tex., 1986; PhD, Tex. Tech. U., 1990. Registered profl. engr., Fla., Ill., Iowa., La., Tex., Wash. Project engr. Gen. Dynamics Corp., Chgo., 1959-60; chief project, design engr. Gen. Foods Corp., Kankakee, Ill., 1960-64; mgr. plant engring. Standard Brands Inc., Clinton, Iowa, 1964-66; regional mgr. Air Products & Chems., Inc., Creighton, Pa., 1966-68; gen. mgr. Skyline Corp., Harrisburg, N.C., 1968-70; cons. Charlotte, 1970-72; dir. engring. and Fla. ops. Zimmer Homes Corp., Pompano Beach, 1972-73; v.p. engring. and mfg. Nobility Homes, Inc., Ocala, Fla., 1973-78, Moduline Internat., Inc., Lacey, Wash., 1978-85; rsch. engr. U. Tex., Austin, 1985-86; lectr., rschr. Tex. Tech. U., Lubbock, 1987-90; assoc. prof. U. New Orleans, 1990-92; asst. prof. dept. civil engring. La. Tech. U., Ruston, 1992-98. Tchr. 26 different courses, 1987—; adj. prof. Coll. Engring., La. Tech. U., 2001--; cons. in field, Dubach, La., 1992—; condr. workshops in field; apptd. spokesman Mfrd. Housing Industry before U.S. Congress. Contbr. articles to profl. jours. Vol. engring. svcs. Lubbock Fire Safety House, 1990; judge sci. fair Ben Franklin H.S., New Orleans, 1990. Recipient T.L. James Svc. award La. Tech. U., 1994; grantee Urban Waste Mgmt. and Rsch. Ctr., New Orleans, 1991, Shell Devel. Co., 1993, La. Edn. Quality Support Fund, Insituform Techs., Inc., Trenchless Tech. Ctr., PABCO, Inc., InLiner USA, Inc., 1995, others; numerous grants in field. Mem. ASME (life), ASCE (Student chpt. Tchr. of Yr. award 1995, 98), NSPE, Am. Soc. Engring. Edn., Phi Kappa Phi, Sigma Xi, Chi Epsilon. Achievements include: designed, constructed and managed first plant for the prodn. of intermediate moisture pet food (Gainesburgers) in the world. Organized and directed all activities to allow Clinton, Iowa plant with a 1 mile shoreline to continue ops. during the greatest flood of the upper Miss. River in 1965. Avocations: flying, skiing, backpacking, golf, photography. Home: 199 Sellers Rd Dubach LA 71235-3218 E-mail: drtomstraughan@msn.com.

STRAULMAN, ANN THERESE, retired English language educator; b. Kansas City, Mo., Apr. 26, 1933; d. Francis Wilson and Theresa Irene (Greene) S. AB, Wellesley Coll., 1955; MA in English, U. Mo., Kansas City, 1962; PhD in English, U. Wis., 1968. Life cert. English tchr., Mo. Tchr. English Sunset Hill Sch., Kansas City, 1960-62; from asst. to assoc. prof. English U. Western Ont., London, Can., 1966-93, prof. emeritus Can., 1993—. Adv. editor restoration and 18th Century theatre rsch. Loyola U. Chgo., 1990—. Trustee, mem. mus. com. Liberty Meml., Kansas City, 1993—, treas. 1998—; bd. dirs., docent Union Cemetery Hist. Soc., Kansas City, 1996—; mem. Friends of Sacred Structures, Kansas City. Seven Coll. Conf. nat. scholar Wellesley Coll., 1951-55. Mem. MLA (life, mem. del. assembly 1975-77), Am. Soc. for 18th Century Studies (life), Samuel Johnson Soc. Ctrl. Region (v.p. 1976-77, pres. 1977-78), Jackson County Hist. Soc., Kemper Mus. Contemporary Art and Design, Archaeol. Inst. Am., Kansas City Wellesley Club. Avocations: local history, archaeology, world travel.

STRAUMANIS, JOHN JANIS, JR. psychiatry educator; b. Riga, Latvia, Apr. 22, 1935; came to U.S., 1950; s. Janis and Ella (Fredrichson) S.; m. Carol A. Sharar, Aug. 8, 1959; children: John, Susan. BA, U. Iowa, 1957, MD, 1960, MS, 1964. Intern Georgetown U. Hosp., Washington, 1960-61; resident U. Iowa, Iowa City, 1961-64; asst. prof. Temple U., Phila., 1966-71, assoc. prof., 1971-77, prof., 1977-85; prof. psychiatry La. State U., Shreveport, 1985-92; prof. psychiatry, dir. rsch. Tulane U. Med. Sch., New Orleans, 1992—. Cons. Camden County Hosp., Blackwood, N.J., 1967-85, VA Hosp., Shreveport, 1985-92, VA Hosp., New Orleans, 1992—. Contbr. articles to profl. jours. Lt. comdr. USN, 1964-65. Rsch. Career Devel. award NIMH, 1966. Fellow Am. Psychiat. Assn.; mem. ACP, Am. Psychopathol. Assn., Soc. Biol. Psychiatry, Am. EEG Assn., Phi Eta Sigma, Phi Beta Kappa, Alpha Omega Alpha. Avocations: travel, music, photography. Office: Tulane U Med Ctr Dept Psychiatry & Neurology 1430 Tulane Ave New Orleans LA 70112-2699

STRAUS, DAVID A. architectural firm executive; b. Medford, Oreg., 1943; m. Sherry Straus; 2 children. BArch, U. Oreg., 1967. Registered architect, Oreg. Founding ptnr. Skelton, Straus & Seibert, Medford, 1989—. Mem Oreg Transp Comn, Rogue Valley Area Comn Transp. Past pres Medford Arts Comn, Arts Coun Southern Oreg; coach Rogue Valley Soccer Asn; leader Boy Scouts Am; bd dirs, past pres Schneider Mus Art SOSC; bd dirs Medford YMCA, Rogue Valley Art Asn. Lt USNR, Vietnam. Mem.: AIA (past pres southern Oreg chpt), Archit Found Oreg (bd dirs), Medford/Jackson County CofC (bd dirs, Mem of the Yr 2000), Univ Oreg Alumni Asn, Oreg Club Southern Oreg (past pres), Univ Club Medford (past pres), Rotary. Office: Skelton Straus & Seibert Arch 26 Hawthorne St Medford OR 97504-7114 E-mail: dstraus@sssarchitects.com.

STRAUS, DONALD BLUN, retired company executive; b. Middletown, N.J., June 28, 1916; s. Percy S. and Edith (Abraham) S.; m. Elizabeth Allen, Sept. 7, 1940; children: David Allen, Robert Beckwith, Sara Elizabeth Byruck. AB, Harvard U., 1938, MBA, 1940. Exec. dir. labor relations panel AEC, 1948-53; v.p. Health Ins. Plan of Greater N.Y., 1953-61; pres. Am. Arbitration Assn., 1963-72, pres. research inst., 1972-81; cons. Internat. Inst. of Applied Systems Analysis, 1982-85. Mem. N.Y. State Bd. Mediation, 1956-59 Chmn. bd. Planned Parenthood Fedn. Am., 1962-65; emeritus bd. dirs. Internat. Council Comml. Arbitration, Population Resources Commn., Soc. Human Ecology; emeritus trustee Carnegie Endowment for Internat. Peace, Inst. Advanced Study, Princeton, Coll. of Atlantic. Mem. Coun. Fgn. Rels. Clubs: Century Assn., Knickerbocker, Pot and Kettle (Bar Harbor, Maine). Home: PO Box 59 Mount Desert ME 04660-0059 E-mail: don@dstraus.com.

STRAUS, FRANCIS HOWE, pathologist, educator; b. Chgo., Mar. 16, 1932; s. Francis Howe and Elizabeth (Kales) S.; m. Helen Lorna Puttkammer, June 11, 1955; children: Francis H., Helen E., Christopher M., Michael W. AB, Harvard Coll., 1953; MD, U. Chgo., 1957, MS, 1964. Intern U. Chgo. Hosp., 1957-58; resident Dept. Pathology U. Chgo., 1958-60, USPH fellowship, 1958-60, resident, 1960-62, chief resident, 1962-63, instr., 1962-65, asst. prof., 1965-71, assoc. prof., 1971-78, prof., 1978—. Author: Hyperparathyrodism, 1973, Essentials of Surgical Pathology, 1974. Chmn. profl. edn. com. Ill. divsn. Am. Cancer Soc., 1980-88, v.p., 1984-88, pres., 1988-90, nat. del., bd. dirs., 1988-92; mem. Inst. of Medicine of Chgo., 1969—, Ill. Coun. on Continuing Med. Edn.; bd. dirs. S.E. Chgo. Commn., Chgo., 1970—; pres. Beaumont Emergency Operating Rm. Bd., Mackinac Island, Mich., 1985—. Fellow Am. Cancer Soc., 1962-63, clin. fellow, 1965-68. Mem. Chgo. Pathology Soc., Am. Soc. for Investigative Pathology, Internat. Acad. Pathology, Am. Soc. Exptl. Pathologists, Chgo. Lit. Club, Cliffdwellers Club, Sigma Xi, Alpha Omega Alpha (hon.). Avocations: gardening, travel, boating, music apreciation, art appreciation. Office: U Chgo Dept Pathology 5841 S Maryland Ave Chicago IL 60637-1463

STRAUS, LAWRENCE GUY, anthropology educator, editor-in-chief; b. Ga., Oct. 17, 1948; s. David Albert and Clotilde (Magnant) S.; María del Carmen Rapado, July 12, 1975; 1 child, Eva Angela Rapado. AB, U. Chgo., 1971, AM, 1972, PhD, 1975. Asst. prof. U. N.Mex., Albuquerque, 1975-81, assoc. prof., 1981-87, prof., 1987—, archeology subfield chair, 1983-95, asst. dept. chair, 1987-93, Snead-Wertheim lectr. anthropology, history, 1990-91. Vis. prof. U. Buenos Aires, 1996, U. Zagreb, Croatia, 2002; supr. student fellowships, rsch. grants NSF, Leakey Found., Belgian-Am. Ednl. Found., Irene Levi-Sala Found., Fulbright Found., Am. Ctr. Oriental Rsch., U. N.Mex. Latin Am. and Iberian Inst. Author: El Solutrense Vasco-Cantábrico, 1983, Iberia Before the Iberians, 1992 (Choice/Am. Assn. U. and Rsch. Librs. award 1993); author, co-author, editor, or co-editor: La Riera Cave, 1986, The End of the Paleolithic in the Old World, 1986, A Quarter Century of Paleoanthropology, 1991, Les Derniers Chasseurs de Rennes du Monde Pyreneen: L'Abri Dufaure, 1995, Humans at the End of the Ice Age, 1996, Le Trou Magrite, 1996, La grotte du Bois Laiterie, 1997, As the World Warmed, 1998, L'Abri du Pape, 1999, An American in Stone Age Spain, 2000, La Station de l'Hermitage à Huccorgne, 2000, Out of Africa in the Pleistocene, 2001; editor-in-chief: Jour. Anthropol. Rsch., 1995—; contbr. more than 375 articles and revs. to profl. jours.; mem. editl. bd. Trabajos de Prehistoria, Jour. Iberian Archaelogy, Prehistoire Europeene. Fellow, grantee NSF, 1968, 71-74, 76-92, 99—; grantee Nat. Geog. Soc., 1979-80, 87-88, 90, 93-95, 97, L.S.B. Leakey Found., 1985, 87-88, 91-92, 94, 96, 97; travel grantee Am. Coun. Learned Socs., 1987, 96, Am. Geophys. Union, 1995, 99, Smithsonian Instn., 1994, Internat. Rsch. and Exchs. Bd., 1994, Fulbright Commn., 2002. Mem. Am. Anthropol. Assn., Soc. Am. Archeology, French Prehistoric Soc., Aranzadi Soc. Sci., S. African Archeol. Soc., Paleoanthropology Soc., Ariège-Pyrénées Prehistoric Soc., Internat. Union Quaternary Rsch. (sec. commn. paleontology early man 1992-95, chair working group archeology of the Pleistocene-Holocene transition 1992—, pres. commn. human evolution and paleontology 1996—, mem. U.S. nat. com.), Assn. for Improvement of Cooperation in Iberian Archaeology, Internat. Union Prehistoric and Protohistoric Sci. (commn. on Upper Paleolithic Europe, commn. on history of prehistory). Office: U NM Dept Anthropology Albuquerque NM 87131-0001

STRAUS, LEON STEPHAN, physicist; b. Takoma Park, Md., May 29, 1943; s. Sidney and Ruth Straus; m. Cheryl Sarran Straus, Apr. 4, 1970; children: Jonathan, Jennifer. BS in Physics, Antioch Coll., Yellow Springs, Ohio, 1965; M Physics, Georgetown U., 1970, PhD in Physics, 1971. Mem. rsch. staff Ctr. Naval Analyses, Alexandria, Va., 1973-75, field rep. CTF 69 Naples, Italy, 1975-77, project mgr. Alexandria, 1977-79, field rep. CTF 69 and CTF 66/67 Naples, Italy, 1979-82, assoc. dep. dir. Alexandria, 1982-85, field rep. CTF 72 Kamiseya, Japan, 1985-87, program mgr. Alexandria, 1987-90, field rep. COMSIXTHFLT Gaeta, Italy, 1990-92, project mgr. Alexandria, 1992-95, tech. dir. spl. projects, 1995-97, dep. dir. info. ops. warfare team, 1997-2000; pvt. contractor, 2001—. Asst. AEC, Germantown, Md., 1968-71. Contbr. articles to profl. jours. Vol. Jewish lay leader USN, Naples, 1975-77, 79-82. Recipient Fellowship Georgetown U., Washington, 1965-68. Mem. Acoustical Soc. Am., Navy Submarine League. Jewish. Achievements include planning, evaluating and documenting tests/exercises associated with U.S. Navy and joint strategy, tactics, comm. and tech. E-mail: strausie18@aol.com.

STRAUS, LORNA PUTTKAMMER, biology educator; b. Chgo., Feb. 15, 1933; d. Ernst Wilfred and Helen Louise (Monroe) Puttkammer; m. Francis Howe Straus II, June 11, 1955; children: Francis, Helen, Christopher, Michael. BA magna cum laude, Radcliffe Coll., 1955; MS, U. Chgo., 1960, PhD, 1962. Rsch. assoc. dept. anatomy U. Chgo., 1962-64, instr., 1964-67, asst. prof., 1967-73, assoc. prof., 1973-87, prof., 1987—, asst. dean, then dean students Coll., 1967-82, dean admissions Coll., 1975-80, univ. marshal, 1999—. Trustee Radcliffe Coll., Cambridge, Mass., 1973-83; chmn. Cmty. Found., Mackinac Island, Mich., 1994—. Recipient silver medal Coun. for Advancement and Support Edn., 1987. Mem.: North Ctrl. Assn. (commr. 1998—, pres.-elect 2001—), Harvard U. Alumni Assn. (bd. dirs. 1980—83), Phi Beta Kappa. Avocations: travel, gardening. Home: 5642 S Kimbark Ave Chicago IL 60637-1606 Office: U Chgo 5845 S Ellis Ave Chicago IL 60637-1476 E-mail: l-straus@uchicago.edu.

STRAUS, MARC JOSHUA, internist, oncologist, educator, poet; b. N.Y.C., 1943; married; 2 children. AB, Franklin and Marshall Coll., 1964; MD, SUNY, Bklyn., 1968. Straight medicine intern Kings County Hosp., Bklyn., 1968-69; staff assoc. Nat. Cancer Inst., NIH, Bethesda, Md., 1969-71; sr. cancer rsch. internist, head Cell Kinetics Lab. Barnes Hosp., 1972—74, resident in medicine St. Louis, 1971-72, fellow in hematology, 1974; chief sect. med. oncology Univ. Hosp., Boston, 1974-78; assoc. prof. medicine Boston U. Sch. Medicine, 1974-78; prof. medicine N.Y. Med. Coll., Valhalla, 1978—, chief divsn. neoplastic diseases, 1978-82; pvt. practice, White Plains, N.Y., 1982—. Rsch. pathologist Mallory Inst. Pathology, Boston, 1974-78; chief oncology Westchester County Med. Ctr., 1978-82; staff physician St. Agnes Hosp., White Plains, Yonkers (N.Y.) Gen. Hosp., St. Joseph's Hosp., Yonkers, Hudson Valley Hosp., Putnam Hosp., Carmel, N.Y., United Hosp., Portchester, N.Y. Recipient Robert Penn Warren award lectr. Yale U. Med. Sch., 1998; Yaddo fellow in poetry, 1993. Fellow ACP, ACPE; mem. Am. Assn. for Cancer Rsch., Am. Soc. Clin. Oncology. Office: 707 Westchester Ave Ste 110 White Plains NY 10604-3155 E-mail: mstraus@mdx-med.com.

STRAUS, OSCAR S., II, foundation executive; b. N.Y.C., Nov. 6, 1914; s. Roger Williams and Gladys (Guggenheim) S.; m. Marion Miller Straus, 1941 (div. 1982); 1 child, Oscar S. III.; m. Joan Sutton, 1982. AB, Princeton U., 1936; postgrad., U. Dijon, summer 1936, Sch. Bus. Adminstrn. Harvard U., 1938. Pvt. sec. Internat. Labor Office, Geneva, Switzerland, 1937-38; U.S. fgn. service officer, 1940-42; divisional asst. Dept. State, 1942-43, 44-45; treas., dir., v.p., chmn. finance com. Am. Smelting & Refining Co., 1945-59; partner Guggenheim Bros., 1959-83; pres., dir. Guggenheim Exploration Co., Inc., 1963-73; gen. ptnr. Straus Minerals, 1973-88; chmn., bd. dirs. Daniel and Florence Guggenheim Found., N.Y.C. Chmn., bd. dirs. Fred L. Lavanburg Found.; chmn., bd. dirs. Mutual of Omaha, Companion Life Ins. Co., United of Omaha. Trustee emeritus Am. Mus. Natural History, Mystic Seaport, Conn.; hon. chmn. Rensselaerville (N.Y.) Inst.; trustee Congregation Emanu-El. Mem. Coun. Fgn. Rels., Cruising Club Am., River Club, Megantic Fish and Game Club, Doubles Club, Knickerbocker Club, L.I. Wyandanch Club Inc. Jewish. Home: 345 E 57th St New York NY 10022 Office: Daniel & Florence Guggenheim Found 950 3rd Ave Fl 30 New York NY 10022-2705

STRAUS, ROBERT, behavioral sciences educator; b. New Haven, Jan. 9, 1923; s. Samuel Hirsh and Alma (Fleischner) Straus; m. Ruth Elisabeth Dawson, Sept. 8, 1945; children: Robert James, Carol Martin, Margaret Dawson, John William. BA, Yale U., 1943, MA, 1945, PhD, 1947. Asst. prof. Yale U., 1948—51, rsch. assoc. applied physiology, 1951—53; acting dir. Conn. Child Study and Treatment Home, New Haven, 1952—53; assoc. prof. preventive medicine SUNY Upstate Med. Ctr., 1953—56; prof. med. sociology U. Ky., Lexington, 1956—59, prof. dept. behavioral sci. Coll. Medicine, also chmn. dept., 1959—87; dir. for sci. devel. Med. Rsch. Inst. San Francisco, 1991—93. Vis. fellow Yale U., 1968—69; vis. prof. U. Calif., Berkeley, 1978, 86; sec. Com. Med. Sociology, 1955—57; chmn. Coop. Com. Study Alcoholism, 1961—63, Nat. Adv. Com. on Alcoholism, 1966—69; mem. Nat. Adv. Coun. on Alcohol Abuse and Alcoholism, 1984—87; trustee Med. Rsch. Inst. San Francisco, 1988—93; mem. Calif. Pacific Med. Ctr. Rsch. Coun., 1993. Author: Medical Care for Seamen, 1950; author: (with S.D. Bacon) Drinking in College, 1953; author: Alcohol and Society, 1973, Escape From Custody, 1974, A Medical School is Born, 1996; co-editor: Medicine and Society, 1963; mem. editl. bd.: Jour. Studies on Alcohol, 1950—2000. Pres. Bluegrass R.R. Mus., 1980. Mem.: Inst. Medicine NAS, Acad. Behavioral Medicine Rsch., Am. Pub. Health Assn. (lifetime achievement award sect. on alcohol, tobacco and other drugs 1993), Assn. Behavioral Scis. and Med. Edn. (pres. 1974), Am. Sociol. Assn. (chmn. med. sociology sect. 1967—68, Leo G. Reeder award Disting. Contbn. to Med. Sociology 1998), Sigma Xi, Phi Beta Kappa. Home: 656 Raintree Rd Lexington KY 40502-2874 E-mail: randrstraus@msn.com., rstraus@pop.uky.edu.

STRAUS, ROGER AUSTIN, marketing consultant, clinical sociologist; b. N.Y.C., Apr. 20, 1948; s. Siegbert and Trude (Salomon) S.; m. Diane E. Walker, May 6, 1967; children: Erica E., Amber C. BA, Humboldt State U., 1972, MA, 1975; PhD, U. Calif., 1977. Asst. prof. Alfred (N.Y.) U., 1983-86; dir. Ctr. Clin. Sociology, Sacramento, 1975-82; v.p. sales Straus-Artys Corp., Great Neck, N.Y., 1982-83; sr. study dir. Nat. Analysts, Phila., 1986-91; rsch. cons. Opinion Rsch. Corp., Princeton, N.J., 1991-93; exec. dir. TVG, Ft. Washington, Pa., 1993-96, v.p., 1996—. Author: Strategic Self-Hypnosis, 1982, rev. edit. 2000, Creative Self-Hypnosis, 2000, Spanish transl., 1991, Japanese transl. 1993, Using Sociology: an Introduction from the Clin. and Applied Perspectives, 1989, 3d edit., 2001; co-author: Marriage and Family Therapy: the Sociocognitive Approach, 1991; mem. editl. bd. Sociological Practice; also poetry; contbr. articles to profl. jours. Mem. Am. Sociol. Assn., Sect. Sociol. Practice (chmn. 1994-95), Sociol. Practice Assn. (co-founder, book editor, pres. 1991—, Disting. Contribution 1991), Soc. Study Symbolic Interaction. Avocations: writing, scuba, ballroom dancing. Home: 322 Portsmouth Rd Cherry Hill NJ 08034-3647 Office: TVG 520 Virginia Dr Fort Washington PA 19034-2707 E-mail: rogerstraus@earthlink.net.

STRAUS, STEPHEN EZRA, biomedical researcher; b. N.Y.C., Nov. 23, 1946; s. Samuel Lieb and Dora Beatrice (Drattel) S.; m. Barbara Ellen Portnoy, June 24, 1973; children: Kate, Julie, Benjamin. BS, MIT, 1968; MD, Columbia U., 1972. Diplomate Am. Bd. Internal Medicine with subspecialty Bds. in Infectious Diseases. Intern and resident in internal medicine Washington U., St. Louis, 1972-73, 75-76; chief Lab. Clin. Investigation Nat. Inst. Allergy and Infectious Diseases, Bethesda, Md., 1991—, head med. virology sect. Lab. Clin. Investigation, 1979-97; dir. Nat. Ctr. Complementary and Alternative Medicine, NIH, 1999-. Mem. recombinant DNA adv. com. NIH, Bethesda, 1993-96; mem. sci. adv. bd. Varicella Zoster Virus Rsch. Found., N.Y.C., 1991-02. Contbr. over 350 articles to profl. jours. Med. dir. USPHS, 1973-75, 79—. Recipient 4 medals USPHS, 1983, 87, 90, 98, 2000. Mem. Assn. Am. Physicians, Am. Soc. for Clin. Investigation, Infectious Diseases Soc. Am. Achievements include research and fundamental discovery on treatment and pathogenesis of human viral infections and immunological disorders. Office: Dept Health & Human Svcs/Nat Ctr Complementary and Alternative Medicine 31 Center Drive Bethesda MD 20892-0001

STRAUSE, RANDALL SCOTT, judge; b. Louisville, June 13, 1963; s. James L. and Charlotte Ray (Motherhead) S.; m. Rene Marie Ricci, Aug. 7, 1987; children: Randall Scott Jr., James Austin. BA, Ind. U., 1985; JD, U. Louisville, 1988. Bar: Ky. 1989, S.C. 1991, U.S. Dist. Ct. (ea. and we. dists.) Ky. 1992, U.S. Ct. Appeals (6th cir.) 1992. Atty. pvt. practice, Louisville, 1989-90; law clk. to Hon. Joseph M. Hood U.S. Dist. Ct. (ea. dist.) Ky., Pikeville, 1990-92; atty. Alagia, Day, Trautwein & Smith, Louisville, 1992-94; prin. asst. to commr. dept. medicaid svcs. Commonwealth of Ky., Frankfort, 1994-95, chief adminstrv. law judge cabinet health svcs., 1995-99. Dir. Strategic Mktg., Inc., Louisville, 1995-96. Bd. dirs. Louisville Tennis Assn., 1996-99, Kentuckiana Children's Ctr., 1998—. Rsch. grantee Tort & Litigation, 1987. Mem. ABA, Am. Health Lawyers Assn., Assn. Trial Lawyers Am., Nat. Assn. Adminstrv. Law Judges, Nat. Assn. Hearing Ofcls. (bd. dirs.), Ky. Bar Assn., S.C. Bar Assn., Nat. Assn. Securities Dealers (arbitrator 1998—), Ky. Real Estate Commn., Louisville Bar Assn., Kappa Sigma, Delta Theta Phi, Omicron Delta Kappa, Order of Ky. Cols. Republican. Episcopalian. Avocation: tennis. Home: 10107 Falling Tree Way Louisville KY 40223-3736 Office: One Riverfront Plz Ste 1400 Louisville KY 40202

STRAUSER, CAROL ANN, small business owner; b. Oak Ridge, Tenn., Sept. 3, 1947; d. Wilbur Arlen and Lois Irene (Carter) S. Student, U. Md. Salesperson Hecht Co., Bethesda, Md.; sec. Bricklayers, Washington, U.S. Govt., Rockville, Md. Mem. NOW, NAFE, AAUW, DAR, Mus. Women Arts. Avocations: reading, writing, painting, drawing. Home and Office: PO Box 144 Charleroi PA 15022-0144

STRAUSER, DAVID ROSS, healthcare educator; b. Sept. 4, 1968; m. Mary Ellen Chryst, Apr. 7, 1990; children: Matthew, David, John. MS, U. Wis., 1990, PhD, 1995. Asst. prof. U. Memphis, 1995-2001, dir. rehab. studies, 1998-2000, assoc. prof., 2001—. Dir. cmty. based job readiness program U. Memphis, 1997—2001; dir. Ctr. for Rehab. and Employment Rsch., 2000; presenter in field. Contbr. articles to nat. and internat. jours.; mem. editl. rev. bd.: leading jours. in field. Recipient New Faculty Rsch. award Nat. Coun. on Rehab. Edn. Mem. Am. Rehab. Counseling Assn. (com. on rsch. and knowledge), Am. Psychol. Assn. Roman Catholic. Office: University of Memphis Ctr for Rehab and Empl Rsch 123 Patterson Hall Memphis TN 38152-6010 E-mail: dstrausr@memphis.edu.

STRAUSER, JEFFREY ARTHUR, biologist, educator; b. Dunkirk, N.Y., May 24, 1947; s. Frederick Edward and Lucille Ruth (Mayott) S.; m. Sara Rollings Ritenburg, Aug. 12, 1972; children: Deborah Ann Patz, Frederick Jeffrey. BS, SUNY, Fredonia, 1972, MS, 1987; postgrad., Columbia Pacific U., 1994—, U. Sarasota, 2001—. Lt. univ. police SUNY, Fredonia, 1972—, instr. microbiology, 1990-91; dir. quality control NOG Inc., Dunkirk, 1978-83; instr. biology and food sci. Empire State Coll., Fredonia, 1995—. Cons. NOG Inc., 1983—, Jamestown (N.Y.) C.C., 1998—. Bd. dirs. PPD Sewer Dist., Mayville, N.Y., 1993—. With USNG, 1970-76. Mem. Nat. Assn. Scholars, AOAC Internat., Inst. Food Techs., Western Assn. Sanitarians, Torch Club, Chautauqua Leadership Network, Coun. for Agrl. Sci. and Tech. Avocations: enging building, auto racing, jet skiing, reading, walking. Home: 10243 Lakeside Boulevard Ext Dunkirk NY 14048-9683

STRAUSER, MATTHEW L. music educator; b. Fort Benning, Ga., Sept. 8, 1955; s. Glenn Dale Strauser; m. Naomi A. Strauser, Mar. 20, 1976; children: Hannah Karis, Kara Ann, Paul Joseph, Alethea Ann. MA, Wheaton Coll. Grad. Sch., Wheaton, Il, 1980—82; BA, BME, U. of Mont., Missoula, MT, 1976—80. K-12 State Teaching License Mont., 1980, Permanant Teaching Licence ACSI, 1999. Dir. of choral activities Western Bapt. Coll., Salem, Oreg., 1999—; min. of music West Hills Cmty. Ch., 2002—, First Bapt. Ch., Salem, 2000—01; tchr. Santiam Christian H.S., 1984—99; hydrologist Kennedy/Jenks, Reno, 1990—90; geologist Freeport McMoran, Elko, 1988—88. Church music NW Am. Choral Directors Assn. (ACDA), 2001—; ch. music Oreg. Am. Choral Directors Assn. (ACDA), Oreg., 1994—2000. Dir.: (choir and orchestra performance) Durufle Requiem. Mem.: Oreg. Music Educators Assn. (dist. choral chair 1996—99), Music Educators Nat. Conf., Am. Choral Directors Assn. (state bd. mem. 1994—2001), Am. Choral Directors Assn. (divisional bd. mem. 2001—02). Office: Western Baptist College 5000 Deer Park Drive SE Salem OR 97301 E-mail: mstrauser@wbc.edu.

STRAUSER, ROBERT WAYNE, lawyer; b. Little Rock, Aug. 28, 1943; s. Christopher Columbus and Opal (Orr) S.; m. Atha Maxine Tubbs, June 26, 1971 (div. 1991); children: Robert Benjamin, Ann Kathleen; m. Terri D. Seales, Oct. 17, 1998. BA, Davidson (N.C.) Coll., 1965; postgrad., Vanderbilt U., Nashville, 1965-66; LLB, U. Tex., 1968. Bar: Tex. 1968, U.S. Ct. Mil. Appeals 1971. Staff atty. Tex. Legis. Coun., Austin, 1969-71; counsel Jud. Com., Tex. Ho. of Reps., 1971-73; chief counsel Jud. Com., Tex. Constl. Conv., 1974; exec. v.p. and legis. counsel Tex. Assn. Taxpayers, 1974-85; assoc. Baker & Botts, 1985-87, ptnr., 1988—. Assoc. editor Tex. Internat. Law Jour., 1968. Mem. Tex. Ho. Speakers Econ. Devel. Com., Austin, 1986-87; assoc. dir. McDonald Obs. Bd. Visitors, 1988—; emeritus mem. adv. bd. Sch. Social Work, U. Tex. Lyceum Assn., 1980-81, 84-88; mem. bd. dirs. Tex. Assn. Bus. and C. of C., 2000-2002; mem. Dean's Roundtable, U. Tex. Law Sch.; bd. dirs. Austin Symphony Orch. Soc., 1985—, v.p., 1993-94, nominating com., 1998-. Capt. USNR, ret. Named Rising Star of Tex., Tex. Bus. Mag., 1983. Fellow Tex. Bar Found.; mem. State Bar of Tex. (coun. mem. tax sect.), Travis County Bar Assn., Headliners Club (Austin). Home: 3312 Gilbert St Austin TX 78703-2102 Office: Baker & Botts 1600 San Jacinto Blvd Austin TX 78701

STRAUSS, ALBERT JOHN, JR. pediatrician; b. Jersey City, July 16, 1938; s. Albert John and Marjorie Elizabeth (Boyd) S.; m. Mary Maddry, Oct. 12, 1963 (div. Jan. 1997); children: Alexandra, Stephanie, Albert III; m. Kelli Alisa Strauss, Jan. 31, 1997; 1 child, John Tylor. BA, Univ. Va., 1960, MD, 1964. Intern Duke Clinic, Durham, N.C., 1964-65; resident U. Va., Charlottesville, 1965-67; ptnr., owner The Children's Doctor, Hagerstown, Md., 1969—. Past vice chief of staff Washington County Hosp., Hagerstown. Bd. dirs. Dream Come True, Hagerstown, 1998—; co-founder Partners for Acad. and Creative Excellence, Hagerstown, 1985. Capt. USAF, 1967-69. Recipient holder Air Force Commendation Medal. Fellow Am. Acad. of Pediatrics; mem. AMA, Washington County Med. Soc. (pres. 1979), Med. and Chirigical Soc. of Md. (del., councillor 1975-85), Southern Med. Assn. Republican. Avocations: gardening, hunting, fishing, birding. Home: 18916 Geeting Rd Keedysville MD 21756-1476 Office: The Childrens Doctors 319 E Antietam St Hagerstown MD 21740-5701 E-mail: kidoc67@yahoo.com.

STRAUSS, CAROL KAHN, institute executive director, editor, consultant; b. N.Y.C., Sept. 21, 1944; d. Alfred and Lotte (Landau) K.; m. Peter Mathes, Dec. 1977 (div. 1980); m. Peter Strauss, June 1989. BS, Columbia U., 1970; MS, Hunter Coll., 1973. Asst. book editor Council on Fgn. Relations, N.Y.C., 1972-79; sr. editor, dir. pub. affairs Hudson Inst., Indpls., 1984-89; sr. editor, cons. 20th Century Fund, N.Y.C., 1990-94; exec. dir. Leo Baeck Inst., 1994—. Cons., writer, editor Ford Found., 20th Century Fund. Editor, co-author articles for profl. publs. Pres. Congregation Habonim, N.Y.C., 1984-92; trustee Self-Help, Inc., N.Y.C., 1986-93; v.p. Fedn. Jews from Ctrl. Europe, 1990—. Jewish. Office: Leo Baeck Inst 15 W 16th St New York NY 10011

STRAUSS, DOROTHY BRANDFON, marital, family, and sex therapist; b. Bklyn. d. Marcus and Beatrice Brandfon; widowed. BA, Bklyn. Coll., 1932; MA, NYU, 1937, PhD, 1963. Diplomate Am. Bd. Sexology, Am. Psychotherapy Assn. Instr. Hunter Coll./CUNY, 1960-63; prof. Kean U., 1963-77; pvt. practice Bklyn. and, N.J., 1970—. Clin. assoc. prof. psychiatry Downstate Med. Ctr., SUNY, Bklyn., 1974-88; assoc. dir. Ctr. for Human Sexuality, 1974-82; mem. NIMH rsch. team U. Pa., 1973-82; guest lectr. Menninger Clinic, 1990. Contbr. chpts. to Understanding Human Behavior in Health and Illness; contbr. articles to profl. jours. and self help and psychol. web mags. Fellow Am. Assn. Clin. Sexologists (founding); mem. APA, Am. Assn. for Marital and Family Therapy (clin. mem. 1971—, supr. 1981—, presenter nat. conf. 1998, accreditation site vis.), Am. Assn. Sex Therapists, Counselors and Educators (chair task force on supervision 1984-86, chair supr. cert. com. 1986-93, chair cert. steering com. 1992-98, Disting. Svc. award 1998), Soc. for Clin. and Exptl. Hypnosis, Kappa Delta Pi. Home and Office: 1401 Ocean Ave Apt 8D Brooklyn NY 11230-3971 E-mail: dbstrauss@aol.com.

STRAUSS, EDWARD ROBERT, carpet company executive; b. Jersey City, June 14, 1942; s. Abraham and Elsie Alice (Goldstein) S.; m. Martha Ann Patmore, Oct. 30, 1966; children: Jeffrey Aaron, Craig Michael. BSBA, Rutgers U., 1973. Dept. systems mgr. Port of N.Y. Authority, N.Y.C., 1961-68; account exec. Steiner Rouse & Co., 1968-70; purchasing mgr. N.Y. State Urban Devel. Corp., 1970-73; sales mgr. Siracco's, Staten Island, N.Y., 1973-76; carpet and TV buyer Hahnes Dept. Stores, Newark, 1976-80; sales mgr. Clodan Carpets, N.Y.C., 1980-83; regional mgr. Deans Carpets, Manchester, N.H., 1983-85; pres. Carpet Contractors Inc., N.Y.C., 1985—; v.p. contract sales Sher Land & Farrington, 1997-2000, Chelsea Floor Covering, N.Y.C., 2000—. Bd. dirs. Marlboro (N.J.) Little League, 1979-87, Marlboro Pop Warner Football, 1979-83. Mem. Free Sons of Israel (trustee, v.p.), Marlboro Mcpl. Swim Club (bd. dirs. 1989-91), Free and Accepted Masons (Menorah lodge # 249 1966—, master 1978). Jewish. Avocations: electric trains, sports. Office: Chelsea Floor Covering 139 W 139th St # 19 New York NY 10030-2204 E-mail: ed@strauss.com., carpetcontractors@hotmail.com.

STRAUSS, ELLEN LOUISE FELDMAN, lawyer; b. Worcester, Mass. d. William and Miriam (Jagodnik) Feldman; m. Douglas A. Strauss (div. May 1977). BA, Western Conn. State Coll., 1978; JD, Franklin Pierce Law Ctr., 1981. Bar: Conn. 1983, U.S. Dist. Ct., Conn., 1983, U.S. Dist. Ct., so. dist., N.Y., 1991, ea. dist., 1991. Self-employed Ellen L.F. Strauss, Esq., Weston, Conn., 1983—. Bd. dirs. Human Lactation Ctr., Fairfield, Conn., 1987—, Efficacy, Hartford, Conn., 1997—. Contbr. columns to local newspapers. Founder, mem. Keep Weston Rural, Conn., 1984—. Mem. Am. Trial Lawyers Assn., Conn. Trial Lawyers Assn. Avocation: travel. Office: Ellen LF Strauss Esq 88 Ladder Hill Rd N Weston CT 06883-1107 E-mail: elfs88law@aol.com.

STRAUSS, ELLIOTT BOWMAN, retired naval officer; b. Washington, Mar. 15, 1903; s. Joseph and Mary (Sweitzer) S.; m. Beatrice Phillips, Feb. 12, 1951; children by previous marriage: Elliott MacGregor, Armar Archbold, Lydia S. (Mme. Delaunay); 1 child, Christopher Joseph. BS, U.S. Naval Acad., 1923; student, Imperial Def. Coll., London, 1948. Commd. ensign USN, 1923, advanced through grades to rear adm., 1955; assigned ships at sea, 1923-30, 32-35; asst. naval attache London, 1935-37; staff comdr. Atlantic Squadron, 1937-40; spl. naval observer London, 1941; staff Chief Brit. Combined Ops., 1942-43; U.S. ops. officer Allied Naval Comdr.-in-Chief for Normandy Invasion, 1944; comdr. Attack Transport, Pacific, 1944-45; naval adviser 1st Gen. Assembly UN, staff Mil. Staff Com., UN, 1946; comdg. officer USS Fresno, 1946-47; staff div. strategic plans Office Chief Naval Ops., 1948-51; comdr. Destroyer Flotilla 6, 1951-52; dir. def. programs div. Office Spl. Rep. in Europe, Dept. Def. rep. econ. def., 1952-55; ret., 1955; dir. engring. Bucknell U., 1956-57; dir. U.S. ops. Mission to Tunisia, 1957-60; spl. asst. to dir. ICA, 1960; dir. AID Missions to Madagascar, 1961-63; pub. mem. Fgn. Service Inspection Corps, 1965; assoc. Laidlaw & Co., N.Y.C., 1963-66; econ. devel. cons. Gen. Electric Co., 1966-69; chmn. bd. Interplan Corp., 1969-81; rep. overseas of Interplan.; cons. Dept. State, 1970. Author profl. and newspaper articles. Bd. dirs. Am. Econ. Found.; chmn. Naval Hist. Found. Decorated Bronze Star; comdr. Order Brit. Empire; Croix de Guerre with palm France). Mem. U.S. Naval Inst., English Speaking Union (nat. bd. dirs.), Order of St. John of Jerusalem (assoc.). Mem. Ch. of England. Clubs: The Pilgrims; Army-Navy (Washington), Chevy Chase (Washington), Metropolitan (Washington); New York Yacht. Home: 2945 Garfield Ter NW Washington DC 20008-3507

STRAUSS, ELTON, orthopaedic surgeon; b. N.Y.C., Apr. 24, 1948; s. Carl and Shirley(Pinchuck) S.; m. Karen Louise Gustin, Jan. 2, 1971; children: Eric, Elisa. BA in Biology, C.W. Post Coll., 1970; MD, U. Autonoma, Guadalajara, Mexico, 1974. Intern Bronx-Lebanon Hosp./Albert Einstein Coll. Medicine, 1975-76; resident AECOM Bronx Lebanon, 1976-79; pvt. practice N.Y.C., 1979—; acad. pvt. practice; co-chief ortho-geriatric svc.; chief ortho trauma adult reconstn. Chief orthopaedic trauma Mt. Sinai Sch. Medicine, N.Y.C. Geriatric scholar Mt. Sinai Sch. Medicine, 1992. Fellow: ACS, Am. Bd. Orthop. Surgeons; mem.: Am. Acad. Orthop. Surgeons (chmn. com. on aging, com. mem.), Am. Geriatric Soc. (chmn. com. of aging), Orthop. Trauma Assn., N.Y. Med. Soc., Am. Fracture Soc., Am. Foot Soc. Avocation: tennis. Office: Mt Sinai Sch Medicine 5 E 98th St New York NY 10029-6501 E-mail: bonesdoc@optonline.net.

STRAUSS, ERIC JAMES, urban planning educator, lawyer, consultant; b. Chgo., Apr. 14, 1947; s. Harold Richard and Irene (Jacobson) S.; m. Emily Jane Fisher, July 3, 1971; children: Rebecca, Janet, Karen. BA, U. Wis., 1968, PhD, 1981; JD, Northwestern U., Chgo., 1971. Bar: Tex. 1971, Wis. 1972, Kans. 1987. Specialist U. Wis. Extension, Madison, 1971-78; prof. urban planning U. Kans., Lawrence, 1978—2001; prof. urban and regional planning Mich. State U., East Lansing, 2001—. Vis. lectr. Queen's U., Belfast, No. Ireland, 1983, U. Wis.-Madison, 1993—, Ind. U., Bloomington, 1995; cons. City of Eudora, Kans., 1988—, City of Hillsboro, Kans., 1992—; site vis. Planning Accrediation Bd., 1986—. Contbr. articles to profl. jours. Recipient Energy Ordinance award City of Lawrence, 1981, Govtl. Tng. award State of Kans., 1984, Profiles of Innovations award Am. Pub. Power Assn., 1986, Pub. Svc. award City Attys. Assn. of Kans., 1992. Mem. Am. Inst. Cert. Planners, Am. Planning Assn. (v.p. Kans. chpt. 1983-85). Democrat. Jewish. Avocations: arts and crafts fairs, gardening. Home: 5331 Starflower Dr Haslett MI 48840- Office: 101 UPLA Bldg East Lansing MI 48824- E-mail: strausse@msu.edu.

STRAUSS, ERIC L. retired materials scientist; b. Mainz, Germany, Dec. 13, 1923; arrived in U.S., 1938; s. Sigmund and Anna Strauss; m. Frances S. Simon, June 26, 1949; children: Stephen A., Andrea L. ME, Stevens Inst. Tech., 1949; MME, U. Va., 1953. Mech. engr. Nat. Adv. Com. Aeronautics, Hampton, Va., 1949—53; project engr. Taylor-Wharton Iron & Steel Co., Easton, Pa., 1953—54; rsch. and devel. scientist Martin Marietta Corp., Balt., 1954—67, dept. rsch. scientist, program mgr. Denver, 1967—92; cons. Lockheed Martin Space Sys. Co., New Orleans, 1998—99. Advisor thermal protection NRC, Washington, 1995; lectr. fibrous composites U. Wis., Madison, 1965; conf. program chair Balt.-Washington sect. Soc. Plastics Engrs., 1964. Contbr. chapters to books. Precinct election judge Arapahoe County Colorado, Littleton. Pvt. U.S. Army, 1943—45, ETO. Decorated Purple Heart; recipient IR 100 award, Indsl. Rsch. Mag., Balt., 1963. Mem.: Denver Mus. Nature and Sci., Denver Zool. Found., Denver Art Mus., AARP. Jewish. Achievements include patents for resin-impregnate ceramic heat shield and method of making, low density ablator compositions and thermoplastics exhibiting high viscosity at their decomposition. Avocations: travel, classical music, opera, art collection, historical non-fiction. Home: 5052 E Princeton Ave Englewood CO 80110

STRAUSS, GARY JOSEPH, lawyer; b. N.Y.C., July 6, 1953; s. Stanley Vinson and Frieda (Fischoff) S. BA magna cum laude, City Coll. of N.Y., 1974; JD, NYU, 1977. Bar: N.Y. 1978, Fla. 1980. Assoc. Finley, Kumble, Wagner, Heine & Underberg, N.Y.C., 1977-79; ptnr. Phillips, Nizer, Benjamin, Krim & Ballon, 1979-87, Gaston & Snow, N.Y.C., 1987-88; pvt. practice, 1988—. Mem. ABA (chmn. N.Y. com. current literature and real property law 1977), Fla. Bar Assn., N.Y. State Bar Assn. Home: 57 W 38th St Fl 9 New York NY 10018-5500

STRAUSS, H. WILLIAM, radiologist educator; b. Bklyn., Apr. 29, 1941; s. Morris and Stella (Selzer) S.; m. Judith F. Strauss, June 14, 1964; children: Cheryl, Marcy. MD, SUNY, Bklyn., 1965, Harvard U., 1988, MA (hon.); PhD (hon.), U. Autonoma de Barcelona, Spain, 1995. Cert. Am. Bd. Nuclear Medicine, 1972, 1998. Asst./assoc. prof. radiology Johns Hopkins Med. Inst., Balt., 1972-76; assoc. prof./prof. radiology Harvard Med. Sch., Cambridge, Mass., 1971-1992; v.p. diagnostic drug discovery Bristol-Meyers Squibb, Princeton, N.J., 1992-94; prof. radiology Stanford Med. Sch., Calif., 1994—2001, Weill Med. Coll. of Cornell U.2, 2001—; clin. dir. nuc. medicine Meml. Sloan-Kettering Cancer Ctr., N.Y.C., 2001—. Mem. sci. adv. bd. Berlex, Princeton, N.J., 1999—, Targesome, Palo Alto, Calif., 1998—. Contbr. to profl. jours. Named Life Mem. Am. Bd. Nuclear Medicine, 1993. Mem. Soc. Nuclear Medicine (pres. 1997-98). Home: 240 E 39th St Apt 45W New York NY 10016 Office: Meml Sloan Kettering Cancer Ctr 1275 York Ave Rm 5-212 New York NY 10021 E-mail: strauush@mskcc.org.

STRAUSS, HERBERT LEOPOLD, chemistry educator; b. Aachen, Germany, Mar. 26, 1936; came to U.S., 1940, naturalized, 1946; s. Charles and Joan (Goldschmidt) S.; m. Carolyn North Cooper, Apr. 24, 1960; children: Michael Abram, Rebecca Anne, Ethan Edward. AB, Columbia U., 1957, MA, 1958, PhD, 1960; postgrad, Oxford U., 1960-61. Mem. faculty U. Calif., Berkeley, 1961—, prof. chemistry, 1973—, vice chmn. dept. chemistry, 1975-81, 92-95, asst. dean. Coll. Chemistry, 1986-92, assoc. dean, 1995—. Vis. prof. Indian Inst. Tech., Kanpur, 1968-69, Fudan U., Shanghai, 1982, U. Tokyo, 1982, U. Paris du Nord, 1987; chmn. IUPAC Commn. I.1, 1994-99. Author: Quantum Mechanics, 1968; assoc. editor Ann. Rev. Phys. Chemistry, 1976-85, editor, 1985-2000. Recipient Bomen-Michaelson award Coblentz Soc., 1994, Ellis Lippincott award Optical Soc. Am., 1994; Alfred P. Sloan fellow, 1966-70. Fellow Am. Phys. Soc., AAAS; mem. Am. Chem. Soc., Sigma Xi, Phi Beta Kappa, Phi Lambda Upsilon. Achievements include research in elucidation of vibrational spectra associated with large amplitude molecular motion in gases, liquids and solids. Home: 2447 Prince St Berkeley CA 94705-2021 Office: U Calif Dept Chemistry Berkeley CA 94720-1420 E-mail: hls@cchem.berkeley.edu.

STRAUSS, JAMES LESTER, investment sales executive; b. Indpls., Aug. 24, 1944; s. Lester H. and Rosalie (Grossman) S. BS, Ind. U., 1966; MBA, Columbia U., 1968. CPA, Ohio. Acct. Deloitte & Touche, Dayton, Ohio, 1975-79, Main Hurdman, Cin., 1979-83; mng. exec. Royal Alliance Assocs., Inc., 1983—. Gen. securities prin. Nat. Assn. Securities Dealers; trustee Judah Touro Cemetary Assn.; speaker in field. With USAR, 1968-74. Mem. Am. Inst. CPA's, Ohio Soc. CPA's, Alliance Francaise, Mensa, Cin. Racquet Club. Republican. Home: 3435 Golden Ave # 604 Cincinnati OH 45226-2020 Office: Royal Alliance Assocs Inc 414 Walnut St Ste 502 Cincinnati OH 45202-3913

STRAUSS, JEFFREY LEWIS, healthcare executive; b. Balt., Aug. 16, 1963; s. Ronald Jay and Roberta Maude (Henriques) S.; m. Melissa Marie Nieding, Sept. 2, 1990. AA in Acctg., Purdue U., Westville, Ind., 1984, BA in Acctg., 1985. Staff acct. Bon Secour Hosp., Balt., 1986-88, Helix Health Systems/Franklin Sq. Hosp. Ctr., Balt., 1988-89; budget mgr., dir. provider svcs. Rush Prudential Health Plans, Chgo., 1989-93; dir. managed care fin. ops. West Suburban Hosp. Med. Ctr., Oak Park, Ill., 1993-94; dir. West Suburban Health Providers, Inc., 1995-97, Info Trust, Lake Forest, Ill., 1997; sr. cons. Ernst and Young, 1998-99; mgr. Cap Gemini Ernst & Young, 2000—. Mem. Antique Automobile Club Am. (life). Democrat. Jewish. Avocations: antique automobiles, sports, reading. Home: 2341 Haverton Dr Mundelein IL 60060-5389 Office: Cap Gemini Ernst & Young 233 S Wacker Dr Chicago IL 60606 E-mail: strau05@attglobal.net., jeffrey.strauss@us.cgeyc.com.

STRAUSS, JEROME FRANK, III, physician, educator; b. Chgo., May 2, 1947; s. Jerome Frank (Jr.) and Josephine (Newberger) Strauss; m. Catherine Blumlein, June 20, 1970; children: Jordan L., Elizabeth J. BA, Brown U., 1969; MD, U. Pa., 1974, PhD, 1975. Asst. prof. Sch. of Medicine U. Pa., Phila., 1976—83, assoc. prof. Sch. of Medicine, 1983—85, prof. Sch. of Medicine, 1985—, assoc. chair Sch. of Medicine, 1987—, assoc. dean Sch. of Medicine, 1990—; Luigi Mastroianni jr. prof. and founding dir. Ctr. Rsch. on Women's Health and Reproduction, 1990—94; prof. Inst. of Medicine NAS, 1994—. Mem. biochem. endocrinology study sect. NIH, 1983—87; mem., chair population rsch. com. Nat. Inst. Child Health and Human Devel., 1989—92; chair Reproductive Scientist of the Ams. Network, 1995—; dir. Ctr. Excellence in Women's Health, 1996—; co-chair Indo-U.S. Joint Workers Group on Reproductive Sci. and Contraceptive Tech., 1999—. Editor: Lipoprotein and Cholesterol Metabolism in Sterodogenic Tissues, 1985, Current Topics in Membrane Research, 1987, Uterine and Embryonic Factors in Early Pregnancy, 1991, New Achievements in Research of Ovarian Function, 1995, Cell Death in Reproductive Physiology, 1997, Molecular Biology in Reproductive Medicine, 1999, Ovarian Function Research: Present and Future, 1999, Steroids jour., 1993—; assoc. editor Ency. of Reproduction, 1998—, corr. editor Jour. Steroid Biochem. and Molecular Biology, 1990—99, assoc. editor, mem. editl. bd. Jour. Lipid Rsch., 1982—90, mem. editl. bd. Endocrinology, 1986—90, 1997—2000, Biology of Reprodn., 1986—90, 1999—, Jour. of Women's Health, 1991—, Jour. Soc. Gynecologic Investigation, 1993—, Placenta, 1995—98, Trends in Endocrinology and Metabolism, 1999, Reference en Gynecologie Obstetrique, 1999—, Seminars in Reproductive Endocrinology, 2000—, Jour. Endocrinology, 2000—, Human Reproduction Update, 2001—. Recipient Transatlantic medal, Brit. Endocrine Soc., 1998. Fellow: Internat. Acad. Human Reproduction; mem.: Perinatal Rsch. Soc., Am. Soc. for Reproductive Medicine, Soc. for Study of Reprodn. (bd. dirs. 1989—91, Rsch. award 1992), Endocrine Soc., Soc. Gynecologic Investigation (pres.-elect 2002, Pres.'s Achievement award 1990), Am. Physiol. Soc., Am. Assn. Pathologists. Office: U Pa Dept Ob/Gyn 415 Curie Blvd Philadelphia PA 19104-4218 E-mail: jfs3@mail.med.upenn.edu.

STRAUSS, JEROME MANFRED, lawyer, banker; b. Milw., Nov. 7, 1934; s. Emanuel and Loraine (Goetz) S.; m. Susan Jean Kauffman, Dec. 30, 1967; children: Martha Lynn, Jared Lee, David Aaron. BA with honors, Ind. U., 1956; JD, NYU, 1959. Bar: Ind. 1959, Fla. 1996, U.S. Dist. Ct. (so. dist.) Ind. 1959, U.S. Tax Ct. 1965, U.S. Ct. Appeals (7th cir.) 1969. Assoc. Ice Miller Donadio & Ryan, Indpls., 1959-69, ptnr., 1969-93; sr. v.p. and regional trust mgr. Merrill Lynch Trust Co., 1993-95; with Mershon, Sawyer, Johnston, Dunwody & Cole, Miami, Palm Beach, Naples, 1995-96; established Wollman, Strauss & Assocs., P.A., Pa., 1997—. Co-author: Marital Deduction Trusts, 1963, Real Estate in an Estate, 1963, Durable Powers of Attorney, 1993; contbr. articles to profl. jours. Bd. dirs. Orton Soc., Indpls., 1970-72, Indpls., 1970-72, Indpls. Hebrew Congregation, 1979-85, Planned Giving Group of Ind., Indpls., 1988-95, Ind. Continuing Legal Edn. Forum, 1989-94; devel. com. Collier County, Fla. Cmty. Found., 1995—; mem. Planned Giving Com. of Lee County, Fla., 1995—, Fla. Planned Giving Coun., 1995—. Fellow Am. Coll Trust and Estate Counsel (charitable com., estate and gift tax com. 1996-2001), Am. Coll. Tax Counsel; mem. ABA (vice-chmn. marital deductin com. real estate property, probate and trust sect. 1988-90), Internat. Acad. Estate and Trust Law (academician 1987—), Ind. State Bar Assn. (sec. 1979-80, chmn. probate, trust and real property sect. 1970-71), Ind. Estate

Planning Coun. (pres. 1970-71), Fla. State Bar Assn., Internat. Assn. of Fin. Planners of S.W. Fla., Collier County Bar Assn. Home: 1056 Diamond Lake Cir Naples FL 34114-9211 Office: 5129 Castello Dr Naples FL 34103-1926 E-mail: rv-atty@lawyer4u.com.

STRAUSS, JOHN STEINERT, dermatologist, educator; b. New Haven, July 15, 1926; s. Maurice Jacob and Carolyn Mina (Ullman) Strauss; m. Susan Thalheimer, Aug. 19, 1950; children: Joan Sue, Mary Lynn. BS, Yale U., 1946, MD, 1950. Intern U. Chgo., 1950-51; resident in dermatology U. Pa., Phila., 1951-52, 54-55, fellow in dermatology, 1955-57, instr., 1956-57; mem. faculty Boston U. Med. Sch., 1958-78, prof., 1966-78; head dept. dermatology U. Iowa, Iowa City, 1978-98, prof. dermatology, 1978-00, prof. emeritus, 2000—. Mem. editl. bd.: Archives of Dermatology, 1970—79, mem. editl. bd.: Jour. Am. Acad. Dermatology, 1979—89, mem. editl. bd.: Jour. Investigative Dermatology, 1977—82; contbr. articles to profl. jours. With USNR, 1952—54. Fellow James H. Brown Jr., 1947—48, USPHS, 1955—57; grantee. Fellow: Am. Acad. Dermatology (pres.); mem.: Internat. Com. Dermatology (pres. 1992—97), Internat. League Dermatol. Socs. (pres. 1992—97), 18th World Congress Dermatology (pres.), Am. Bd. Med. Spltys. (exec. com. 2001—), Coun. Med. Splty. Socs. (pres.), Am. Fedn. Clin. Rsch., Ctrl. Soc. Clin. Rsch., Assn. Am. Physicians, Am. Dermatol. Assn. (sec., pres.), Am. Bd. Dermatology (bd. dirs., assoc. exec. dir., pres., exec. cons.), Dermatology Found. (pres.), Soc. Investigative Dermatology (sec.-treas., pres.). Achievements include research in in sebaceous glands and pathogenesis of acne. Office: U Iowa Hosp & Clinics Dept of Dermatology 200 Hawkins Dr # BT2045-1 Iowa City IA 52242-1009

STRAUSS, JON CALVERT, academic administrator; b. Chgo., Jan. 17, 1940; s. Charles E. and Alice C. (Woods) S.; m. Joan Helen Bailey, Sept. 19, 1959 (div. 1985); children: Susan, Stephanie; m. Jean Anne Sacconaghi, June 14, 1985; children: Kristoffer, Jonathon. BSEE, U. Wis., 1959; MS in Physics, U. Pitts., 1962; PhD in E.E., Carnegie Inst. Tech., 1965; LLD (hon.), U. Mass., 1996. Assoc. prof. computer sci., elec. engring. Carnegie Mellon U., Pitts., 1966-70; dir. computer ctr., prof. computer sci. Tech. U. Norway, Trondheim, Norway, 1970; vis. assoc. prof. elec. engring. U. Mich., Ann Arbor, 1971; assoc. prof. computer sci. Washington U., St. Louis, 1971-74, dir. computing facilities, 1971-73; dir. computing activities U. Pa., Phila., 1974-76, faculty master Stouffer Coll. House, 1978-80, prof. computer, info. scis., prof. decision sci. Wharton Sch., 1974-81, exec. dir. Univ. Budget, 1975-78, v.p. for budget, fin., 1978-81; prof. elec. engring. U. So. Calif., Los Angeles, 1981-85, sr. v.p. adminstrn., 1981-85; pres. Worcester Poly. Inst., Mass., 1985-94; v.p., chief fin. officer Howard Hughes Med. Inst., Chevy Chase, Md., 1994-97; pres. Harvey Mudd Coll., Claremont, Calif., 1997—. Cons. Electronics Assocs., Inc., 1965, IBM Corp., 1960-64, Westinghouse Elec. Corp., 1959-60; bd. dirs. Transamerica Income Fund, Variable Ins. Fund, United Educators Ins. Contbr. articles on computer systems and university mgmt. to profl. jours.; co-holder patent. Bd. dirs. Presbyn.-U. Pa. Med. Ctr., Phila., 1980-81, U. So. Calif. Kenneth Norris Jr. Cancer Hosp., L.A., 1981-85, Med. Ctr. of Ctrl. Mass., 1986-94, Worcester Acad., 1986-91, Mass. Biotech. Rsch. Inst., 1985-94. Mem. New Eng. Assn. Schs. and Colls., Inc., Commn. on Instns. of Higher Edn., Nat. Collegiate Athletic Assn. (pres.'s commn. 1990-94). Avocations: rowing, running, sailing, swimming. Office: Harvey Mudd Coll 301 E 12th St Claremont CA 91711-5901

STRAUSS, LEWIS CARROLL, pharmaceutical executive, physician; b. Balt., Oct. 23, 1951; s. Lewis H. and Laurie S. (Zabin) S.; m. Karen Adelson Strauss, Dec. 27, 1981; children: Lewis, Jennifer, Andrea. AB, Harvard Coll., 1973; MD, Cornell U., 1977. Diplomate Am. Bd. Pediats., Am. Bd. Pediat. Hematology and Oncology. Intern./resident Johns Hopkins Med. Inst., 1977—80; mem. oncology staff Johns Hopkins U., Balt., 1980—91, Northwestern U., Chgo., 1991-97; v.p. clin. devel./ med. affairs Neopharm Inc., Lake Forest, 1998—. Office: Neopharm Inc 150 N Field Dr # 195 Lake Forest IL 60045-4847 E-mail: lstrauss@neophrm.com.

STRAUSS, RAYMOND BERNARD, otolaryngologist; b. N.Y.C., Mar. 25, 1930; s. Victor M. and Fannie (Price) S.; m. Lois Kelly, June 12, 1958; children: Steven Douglas, Keith Andrew. AB, Washington U., St. Louis, 1950; PhD, U. Fla., 1956; MD, Case We. Res. U., 1958. Diplomate Am. Bd. Otolarynology, Am. Bd. Cosmetic Plastic Surgery. Intern dept. medicine, asst. resident surgery U. Hosps., Cleve., 1958-60; resident otolaryngology Columbia-Presbyn. Med. Ctr., N.Y.C., 1960-63; pvt. practice otolaryngology and facial plastic surgery Englewood, N.J., 1963—. Attending otolaryngologist, past chief otolaryngology Englewood Hosp. and Med. Ctr.; assoc. attending otolaryngologist Vanderbilt Clinic and N.Y. Presbyn. Hosp.; past dir. facial plastic surgery clinic; assoc. prof. clin. otolaryngology Coll. Physicians and Surgeons, Columbia U. Dir., vice-chmn. bd. dirs. NVE Bank; past trustee Dwight-Englewood Sch.; past bd. dirs. No. Valley chpt. ARC; elder Presbyn. Ch., past clk. of session, past pres. bd. trustees. Recipient Coakley Meml. prize in otolaryngology Columbia U., 1958; Marie and Henry Heiner fellow in otolaryngology, 1961-62; decorated Army Commendation medal. Fellow ACS, Internat. Coll. Surgeons, Am. Acad. Facial Plastic and Reconstructive Surgery, Am. Acad. Cosmetic Surgery, Am. Acad. Otolaryngology and Head and Neck Surgery; mem. AMA, Royal Soc. Medicine, Am. Speech Lang. and Hearing Assn. (cert. clin. competence in speech pathology and audiology), Am. Acad. Audiology, N.Y. Laryngol. Soc. (past pres.), N.Y. Bronchoscopic Soc. (past pres.), N.Y. Otol. Soc. (past pres.), N.J. Soc. Cosmetic Surgery (trustee), N.J. Acad. Ophthalmology and Otolaryngology-Head and Neck Surgery (past pres.), N.J. Med. Soc., N.Y. County Med. Soc., Bergen County Med. Soc., Bergen County Soc. Otolaryngologists, Head and Neck Surgeons (past pres.), Englewood Surg. Soc. (past pres.), First Presbyn. Ch. Men's Assn. (past pres.), N.Y. Athletic Club, Englewood Club (past pres., Disting. Svc. award 1980), Knickerbocker Country Club, Rotary (dist. 7490 past pres., past gov.), Phi Beta Kappa, Alpha Omega Alpha, Nu Sigma Nu. Home: 436 Lewellyn Cir Englewood NJ 07631-2021 E-mail: raystrauss@msn.com.

STRAUSS, RICHARD JAY, surgeon; b. New York City, June 4, 1946; s. Michael and Anne (Sukman) S.; m. Pamela Kaufman, Jul. 4, 1970; children: Cindy, Jill. BA, N.Y.U., 1968; MD summa cum laude, Downstate Medical, 1972. Diplomate Am. Bd. Surgery, Diplomate Am. Bd. Colon and Rectal Surgery. Asst. resident in surgery L.I. Jewish Hillside Medical Ctr., New Hyde Park, N.Y., 1972-73, jr. resident in surgery, 1973-74, sr. resident in surgery, 1974-75, chief resident in surgery, 1975-76, fellow surg. rsch., 1976-77; spl. fellow colon and rectal surgery Cleve. Clin., 1977-78; assoc. prof. clin. surgery State Univ. N.Y., Stony Brook, 1985-90; assoc. clin. prof. surgery Albert Einstein Coll. Medicine, 1990—; instr. clin. surgery NYU Med. Sch., 1978—. Hosp. appointments L.I. Jewish Medical Ctr., North Shore Univ. Hosp., St. Francis Hosp. Contbr. numerous articles to profl. jours. Recipient First prize N.Y. Soc. Colon & Rectal Surgeons Residents, 1976, The Perdue Frederick fellowship award Am. Soc. Colon & Rectal Surgeons, 1977. Fellow ACS, N.Y. Soc. Colon & Rectal Surgeons; mem. Am. Soc. Colon & Rectal Surgeons, Am. Gastroent. Assn., Soc. Surgery of the Alimentary Tract, Rupert B. Turnbull Surg. Soc., N.Y. Surg. Soc., Nassau County Med. Soc., N.Y. State Med. Soc., L.I. Gastrointestinal Soc., Soc. Am. Gastrointestinal Endoscopic Surgeons. Office: 1000 Great Northern Blvd Great Neck NY 11021

STRAUSS, ROBERT PHILIP, economics educator; b. Cleve., May 11, 1944; s. Harry and Carrie S.; m. Celeste G. Meade, Jan. 11, 1980; children—Sarah Elizabeth, David Anthony, Elena Nicole AB in Econs., U. Mich., 1966; MA, U. Wis., 1968, PhD in Econs., 1970. Fellow Inst. Research on Poverty, 1968-69; asst. prof. econs. U. N.C., Chapel Hill, 1969-73, assoc. prof., 1973-79; econ. policy fellow Brookings Instn., Washington, 1971-72; economist U.S. Congress Joint Com. Taxation, 1975-78; prof. econs. and pub. policy Carnegie-Mellon U., Pitts., 1979—, assoc. dean Sch. Urban and Pub. Affairs, 1981-83, dir. Ctr. for Pub. Fin. Mgmt., 1984-91; dir. research Pa. Tax Commn., 1979-81. Vis. prof. econs. and pub. policy U. Rochester, 1992-94. Mem. Pa. Local Tax Reform Commn., 1987; sec. faculty Carnegie-Mellon U., 1991-92. Recipient Exceptional Service award U.S. Treasury, 1972, Disting. Service award Pitts. Tax Execs. Inst., 1987, Georgescun Roegen award, 1998; grantee NSF, U.S. Dept. Labor, U.S. Treasury, HUD, Social Security Adminstrn. Mem. Am. Econ. Assn., Econometric Soc., Nat. Tax Assn., Pub. Choice Soc., Assn. for Pub. Policy and Mgmt., Am. Soc. for Pub. Adminstrn., Nat. Tax Assn. (bd. dirs. 1995-98). Clubs: Cosmos. Home: 2307 Country Pl Export PA 15632-9059 Office: 5000 Forbes Ave Pittsburgh PA 15213-3890 E-mail: rpstrauss@att.net.

STRAUSS, ROBERT DAVID, lawyer; b. Cambridge, Mass., Oct. 20, 1951; s. Walter Adolf and Lilo (Teutsch) Strauss; m. Deborah Mackall, Feb. 15, 1986 (div. Dec. 1998); 1 child Benjamin Walter ; m. Ellen C. Handelsman, Apr. 6, 2002. BA, Emory U., 1973, JD, 1976. Bar: Ga. 1976. Assoc. Gambrell & Russell, Atlanta, 1976-81; ptnr. Smith, Gambrell & Russell, 1981-89, Trotter Smith & Jacobs, Atlanta, 1989-92, Troutman Sanders, Atlanta, 1992—. Contbr. articles to profl. jours. Mem. ABA (chmn. leasing subcom. 1988-94, uniform comml. code com.), State Bar of Ga., Equipment Leasing Assn. Am. Home: 729 Amsterdam Ave NE Atlanta GA 30306 Office: Troutman Sanders 5200 Bank of Am Plz 600 Peachtree St NE Atlanta GA 30308-2216 E-mail: bo.strauss@troutmansanders.com.

STRAUSS, SIMON WOLF, chemist, materials scientist; b. Bedzin, Keltz, Poland, Apr. 15, 1920; came to U.S., 1929; s. Israel Calvin and Anna (Hops) S.; m. Mary Jo Boehm, Dec. 27, 1957; children: Jack Calvin, Ruth Ann. BS in Chemistry, Polytech. Inst. of Bklyn., 1944, MS in Chemistry, 1947, PhD in Chemistry, 1950. Rsch. chemist Nat. Bur. Standards, Washington, 1951-55; from phys. chemist to head chem. metallurgy sect. Naval Rsch. Lab., 1955-63; sr. staff scientist Air Force Systems Command, 1963-80; ind. tech. cons., 1980—. Mem. bd. civil svc. examiners for sci. and tech. pers. U.S. Naval Dist. of Washington, 1959-63; mem. air force panel expert tech. reviewers patents for secrecy considerations Office Air Force Judge Advocate Gen., Washington, 1965-80; co-chair com. on career planning and appraisal of sci. and engrs. Air Force Sys. Command, Washington, 1966-67; air force mem. in-house com. mgmt. rev. tech. info. program, Dept. Def., 1967; chair rsch. steering com. Air Force Dir. of Sci. Tech., Washington, 1976-80; mem., chair editorial adv. com. Washington Acad. Jour., 1983-87, chair com. on scholarly activities, 1984-88. Author: Advanced Composites: An Historical Perspective, Retiring Presidential Lecture, 1987; prin. compiler 75 Years of Scientific Thought, 1987; mem. bd. reviewers Jour. Chem. Engring. Data, 1965-66; contbr. articles to profl. jours. Judge Internat. Sci. Engring. Fair, 1970, 72, 73; nat. evaluator space shuttle student involvement program Nat. Sci. Tchrs. Assn., NASA, Washington, 1984, 85. With U.S. Army, 1944-45. Recipient Air Force exceptional civilian svc. medal, 1980, first Disting. Career in Sci. award Wash. Acad. Scis., 1988, Disting. Svc. award, 1990. Fellow AAAS, Wash. Acad. Scis. (first Disting. Scholar-in-Residence 1984-89, pres.-elect 1985-86, pres. 1986-87, immediate past pres. 1987-88, life mem. fund trustee 1988—), Am. Inst. Chemists; mem. Math. Assn. Am., Air Force Assn., Cosmos Club, Air Force Materials Lab. (hon. life mem.), Sigma Pi Sigma, Phi Lambda Upsilon, Sigma Xi. Achievements include 3 patents for electrodeposition of Cadmium on high strength steel; research and development of advanced composites technology; the development of equations for the estimation of surface tensions, viscosities and densities of liquid metals as a function of temperature. Home: 4506 Cedell Pl Temple Hills MD 20748-3805 *Living a life not just for oneself contributes not only to the elevation of humankind, but also to the ennoblement and enrichment of one's own life.*

STRAUSS, STANLEY ROBERT, lawyer; b. N.Y.C., June 3, 1915; s. Maurice M. and Blanche Anna (Danciger) S.; m. Margaret Inglis Forbes, Mar. 13, 1944 (div. 1950); m. Helen Anne Cummings, Dec. 31, 1975 (dec. 1980). BA cum laude, Williams Coll., 1936; LLB, Columbia U., 1940. Bar: N.Y. 1941, D.C. 1964, U.S. Ct. Appeals (1st cir.) 1977, U.S. Ct. Appeals (3d cir.) 1986, U.S. Ct. Appeals (4th cir.) 1974, U.S. Ct. Appeals (5th cir.) 1970, U.S. Ct. Appeals (6th cir.) 1977, U.S. Ct. Appeals (8th cirs.) 1975, U.S. Supreme Ct. 1965. Assoc. Howard Henig, N.Y.C., 1940-41; atty. NLRB, Washington, 1946-52, supervising atty., 1953-59, chief counsel, 1959-63; assoc. Vedder, Price, Kaufman & Kammholz, 1963-65, ptnr., 1965-90; of counsel Ogletree, Deakins, Nash, Smoak & Stewart, 1990—. Co-author: Practice and Procedure Before the National Labor Relations Board, 3d edit., 1980, 4th edit., 1987, 5th edit., 1996. Officer U.S. Army, 1941-45, PTO. Decorated Bronze Star; Horn scholar Columbia U. Law Sch., 1937-40. Mem. ABA, Fed. Bar Assn., D.C. Bar Assn., Kenwood Country Club. Avocations: golf, tennis. Home: 4956 Sentinel Dr Bethesda MD 20816-3594 Office: Ogletree Deakins Nash 2400 N St NW Fl 5 Washington DC 20037-1154 E-mail: stanleystrauss@odense.com.

STRAUSS, ULRICH PAUL, chemist, educator; b. Frankfurt, Germany, Jan. 10, 1920; s. Richard and Marianne (Seligmann) S.; m. Esther Lipetz, June 20, 1943 (dec. Sept. 1949); children— Dorothy, David; m. Elaine Greenbaum, Nov. 23, 1950; children— Elizabeth, Evelyn. AB, Columbia U., 1941; PhD, Cornell U., 1944. Sterling fellow Yale U., 1946-48; faculty Rutgers U., New Brunswick, N.J., 1948—, prof. phys. chemistry, 1960-90, prof. emeritus, 1990—; also dir. Sch. Chemistry, 1965-71, chmn. dept. chemistry, 1974-80. Prof. emeritus Rutgers U., 1990—. Mem. editorial bd. Macromolecules, 1990-93; contbr. articles to profl. jours. Recipient Sci. achievement award Johnson Wax Co., 1986; NSF sr. fellow Nat. Center Sci. Research, Strasbourg, France, 1961-62; Guggenheim fellow U. Oxford, Eng., 1971-72 Fellow N.Y. Acad. Scis.; mem. Am. Chem. Soc. (chmn. phys. chemistry group N.J. sect. 1956, councillor 1961-72, honored by 1-day symposium at nat. meeting N.Y.C. 1986, Excellence in Edn. award N.J. sect. 1994). Home: 227 Lawrence Ave Highland Park NJ 08904-1837 Office: Rutgers U Dept Chemistry New Brunswick NJ 08903 E-mail: strauss@rci.rutgers.edu.

STRAUSS, WILLIAM VICTOR, lawyer; b. Cin., July 5, 1942; s. William Victor and Elsa (Lovitt) S.; m. Linda Leopold, Nov. 9, 1969; children: Nancy T., Katherine S. AB cum laude, Harvard U., 1964; JD, U. Pa., 1967. Bar: Ohio 1967. Pres. Security Title and Guaranty Agy., Inc., Cin., 1982—, Strauss & Troy, Cin., 1995—. Trustee Cin. Psychoanalytic Inst., 1990—, Cin. Contemporary Arts Ctr., 1997—. Mem. ABA, Nat. Assn. Office and Indsl. Parks, Ohio State Bar Assn., Cin. Bar Assn., Ohio Land Title Assn. Home: 40 Walnut Ave Wyoming OH 45215-4350 Office: Strauss & Troy Fed Res Bldg 150 E 4th St Fl 4 Cincinnati OH 45202-4018

STRAUTINS, VILNIS, flute educator, past symphony orchestra executive; b. Lubana, Madona, Latvia, Dec. 28, 1939; s. Fricis Strautins and Emma (Bundzis) Strautina; m. Dzidra Markevica, Dec. 31, 1964; children: Ineta, Peteris. MA, Latvian Music, Riga, 1965. Prin. flutist Latvian Nat. Symphony Orch., Riga, 1961-89, mng. dir., 1989-97; prof. flute Latvian Music Acad., 1971—. Mem.: Latvian Correspondence Chess Fedn. (pres. 2001—). Lutheran. Avocation: correspondence chess. Office: Latvian Music Acad Kr Barona 1 LV-1050 Riga Latvia E-mail: strautins@parks.lv.

STRAVALLE-SCHMIDT, ANN ROBERTA, lawyer; b. N.Y.C., Jan. 2, 1957; Grad. cum laude, Phillips Exeter Acad., 1975; student, Occidental Coll., 1975-78, Oxford Coll., Eng., 1976-77; BS cum laude, Boston Coll., 1980; JD, Boston U., 1987. Bar: Conn. 1987, U.S. Dist. Ct. Conn. 1988, U.S. Supreme Ct. 1993. Consulting staff Arthur Andersen, Boston, 1980-82; supr. CID ops. Aetna Life & Casualty, Hartford, Conn., 1982-84; summer intern U.S. Atty.'s Office, Boston, 1985; jud. clk. Hon. Judge Thayer III N.H. Supreme Ct., 1987-88; trial lawyer Day, Berry & Howard, Hartford, 1988-91; sr. lawyer comml. litigation and appellate practice Berman & Sable, 1991-96; dir. maj. case unit Travelers Property and Casualty Corp., 1996-98; sr. atty. Robinson & Cole, 1998-2000; gen. counsel Conn. Resources Recovery Authority, 2000—. Brief judge Nat. Appellate Advocacy Competition, 1996. Mem. editorial bd. Conn. Bar Jour., 1990—; contbr. articles to profl. jours. Mem. Hebron Dem. Town Com., Hebron Bd. Fin., 1995-99, Hebron Sch. Bldg. Com., 1997-99; justice of peace, 1997-99; apptd. mem. Hebron Bldg. Com., 1997-99. Hennessey scholar Boston U., 1987. Mem. ABA, Conn. Bar Assn. (founder, chair appellate practice com. litigation sect. 1994-96, mem. exec. com. litigation sect.). Home: 7 Don St Plainville CT 06062-1111 Office: Conn Resources Recovery Authority 100 Constitution Plz Ste 1700 Hartford CT 06103-1719 E-mail: astravalle@attbi.com.

STRAW, ELLEN KATRINA, English educator, writer; b. Covina, Calif., Sept. 9, 1965; d. Earl Wilson and Marie Ruth (Ulmer) S. AA in English, Mt. San Antonio Coll., 1985; BA in English, Calif. State Poly. U., Pomona, 1988, MA in English, 1991. Freelance writer, Covina, 1982—; freelance editor, 1988—; English tutor Calif. Poly. State U., Pomona, 1986—, instr. English, 1990-92, Citrus C.C., Glendora, Calif., 1992—, Mt. San Antonio Coll., Walnut, 2000—. Staff writer Write Away/Valley Writers, Covina, 1995-00. Author: Creative Writhing, 1993, (screenplays) Long Distance, 1996, The New Girl, 1996, Morning Person, 1998, Fred Plus Felix, 2000; editor: Hard Copies, 1988; co-editor: Litrus, 2000. Mem. Valley Writers (refreshments officer 1990—, pres., treas. 1999—). E-mail: vivalostwages@hotmail.com.

STRAWBRIDGE, MARY ELIZABETH, English educator; b. Chardon, Ohio, Mar. 13, 1949; d. Maurice McKinley and Mary Ruth (McGuire) S. BA, Case Western Res. U., 1971; MA, Edinboro U., 1984. Cert. tchr. secondary edn., English, Ohio. Liaison Case Western Res. U./Lancaster U., Cleve. and Lancaster, U.K., 1970-71; educator, dept. chmn. Conneaut (Ohio) Area City Schs., 1972-84, 86—; adminstr. Kent State U., Ashtabula, Ohio, 1985-86. Vice chair Local Profl. Devel. Com., Conneaut, 1998-2001; adv. bd. Kent State U., Ashtabula, 1985-86; curriculum cons. Conneaut Area City Schs., 1982, 87, Ashtabula County Schs., Jefferson, Ohio, 1997; cons./county rep. Northeast Regl. Profl. Devel. Ctr., Cleve. and Jefferson, 1993-95; co-chair curriculum and instruction com. Conneaut H.S., 1999. Bd. dirs. Community Counseling Ctr., Ashtabula, 1985-89; vol. March of Dimes, Heart Fund, Ashtabula, 1994-97, Nat. Diabetes Found., Ashtabula, 1994-97, 99; sec., negotiations rep. Conneaut Edn. Assn., 1980-84. Mem. AAUW, NEA, Nat. Coun. Tchrs. English, Conneaut Edn. Assn., Ohio Edn. Assn., U.S. Golf Assn., Delta Kappa Gamma, Chi Sigma Iota. Republican. Roman Catholic. Avocations: golf, writing, reading, gardening, painting. Home: 4311 Lake Rd W Ashtabula OH 44004-2017 Office: Conneaut Area City Schs 263 Liberty St Conneaut OH 44030-2705 E-mail: mimi@suite224.net.

STRAWDERMAN, WILLIAM E. statistics educator; b. Westerly, R.I., Apr. 25, 1941; s. Robert Lee and Alida Browning (Dow) S.; m. Susan Linda Grube; July 20, 1985; children: Robert Lee, William Edward, Heather Lynne. BS, U. R.I., 1963; MS, Cornell U., 1965, Rutgers U., 1967, PhD, 1969. Mem. tech. staff Bell Telephone Labs., Holmdel, N.J., 1965-67; prof. Stanford (Calif.) U., 1969-70; instr. Rutgers U., New Brunswick, N.J., 1967-69, prof. stats., 1970—. Contbr. more than 120 articles to profl. jours. Fellow Inst. Math. Stats., Am. Stats. Assn. Office: Rutgers U Statistics Dept Hill Ctr-Busch Campus New Brunswick NJ 08903 E-mail: straw@stat.rutgers.edu.

STRAWHECKER, PAUL JOSEPH, fundraising consultant; b. Oct. 31, 1947; s. John Leslie and Leone Francis (Kalamaja) S.; m. Margaret Ellen Baumann, Aug. 31, 1974; children: Risa Nicole, Ryan John. Student, St. Joseph's Sem., 1963-67, Blessed John Neumann Coll., 1968-68; BA, Creighton U., 1970, postgrad. Law Sch., 1971-73; MPA, U. Nebr., 1980. Advanced cert. fundraising exec. Assn. Fundraising Profls. Rsch. specialist mayor's office City of Omaha, 1970, spl. asst. to mayor, 1971, mgr. spl. programs, 1972-73; dir. spl. resources Father Flanagan's Boys Home, Boys Town, Nebr., 1974-81; v.p. for devel. Luth. Hosps. and Homes Soc. Am., Fargo, N.D., 1982-86; asst. adminstr. Sacred Heart Gen. Hosp., Eugene, Oreg., 1986-87; v.p. Northwood U., Midland, Mich., 1987-94; pres. Paul J. Strawhecker, Inc., Omaha, 1995—. Adj. prof. U. Nebr., Omaha, 1995—; treas. Credit Union, 1975; clk., treas., liaison officer Village of Boys Town, 1974-81; writer Am. Soc. Planning Ofcls.; past owner The Wooden Spoon Ltd., Omaha.; exec. com. Assn. Philanthropic Counsel. Author: Fund Raising, 1997, Capital Campaigns, 1998, Resource Development, 1999. Chmn. Met. Area Planning Agy. Coun. Ofcls. Goals Com. for Human Svcs., 1976; mem. Omaha/Douglas County Criminal Justice Commn., 1977-80; mem. adv. com. Douglas County Office on ChildrenYouth, Midland County Cmty. Corrections, 1991-92; bd. dirs. "Say Yes" to Youth, 1990-92; chmn. urban affairs com. Met. Area Planning Agy. Mem. Assn. Fundraising Profls. (cert., pres. N.D. area chpt., bd. dirs. 1994-95, pres. Mich. chpt. bd. dirs. 1987-90, pres. Nebr. chpt. bd. dirs. 1997-99, vice chair nat. bd. 1991, nat. found. bd. 2000—, bd. mem. Internat. Found.), Nat. Assn. Hosp. Devel. (spkr. 1983), Internat. City Mgmt. Assn. (spkr. 1971), Multi Hosp. Devel. Assn. (pres. 1986), Leadership Midland (alimni and steering com. 1990-92), Phi Kappa Psi. Roman Catholic. Home: 3424 N 129th Cir Omaha NE 68164-4240 Office: Paul J Strawhecker Inc 4913 Dodge St Omaha NE 68132-2917 E-mail: paul@pjstraw.com.

STRAWN, FRANCES FREELAND, real estate executive; b. Waynesville, N.C., Nov. 18, 1946; d. Thomas M. and Jimmie (Smith) Freeland; m. David Updegraff Strawn, Aug. 30, 1974; children: Trisha, Kirk, Laurel. AA, Brevard C.C., Cocoa, Fla., 1976; postgrad., U. Ctrl. Fla., 1976-77. Cert. real estate broker, cert. residential specialist; grad. Realtor Inst.; LTG. Realtor, broker, pres. Advance Am., Inc., Orlando, Fla., 1982-89; assoc. Ann Cross, Inc., Winter Park, 1988-99, Coldwell Banker, Winter Park, 1999—. Contbr. articles to Fla. Realtor, 1993, Communique, 1994. Co-chmn. fundraiser Black Tie Walk on the Wild Side, 1992; co-ticket chmn. Art and Arch. Orlando Regional Hosp.; mem. steering com. Fla. Heritage Homecoming, Orlando, 1987; sec. Mayor's Wife's Campaign Activities, 1986—87; chmn. Horizon Exec. Bd., 1989; rec. sec. Women's Bus. Edn. Coun., 1988, mem. adv. bd., 1987, bd. dirs., 1988—90; lectr. Jr. Achievement, 1988—93; mem. steering com. scholarship dinner Crummer Bus. Coll., Rollins Coll., 1992; mem. adv. bd. Ronald McDonald House, 2001—; active Planned Parenthood Bd., Orange County, Fla., 2001—; program chmn. Young Rep. Women, Orlando, 1983; coord. Congressman Bill Nelson's Washington Internship PRogram; bd. dirs. Vol. Ctr. Ctrl. Fla., rec. sec., 1989; bd. dirs. Ctrl. Fla. Zool. Pk., 1989—92, Women's Resource Ctr., 1989—90. Mem. Creative Bus. Ownership for Women (adv. bd. 1986-88, vice chair grievence com. 1989), Nat. Assn. Realtors. Orlando Bd. Realtors (lectr. Sucess Series 1988—), Women's Coun. Realtors (bd. dirs., program co-chair 1998), Women's Exec. Coun., Citrus Club (Orlando) (bd. dirs. 1990-95). Episcopalian. Avocations: travel, skiing, reading. Home: 1000 S Orlando Ave No A-7 Orlando FL 32751 Office: Coldwell Banker 400 S Park Ave Ste 210 Winter Park FL 32789-4320

STRAWN, JUDY C. public relations professional; b. Walla Walla, Wash., Oct. 8, 1950; d. Warren Clarence and Nora Melissa (Riley) S. BA in Pub. Communications, Columbia Union Coll., 1975; postgrad., UCLA, 1985—. Sec., editor Mitsubishi Bank of Calif., L.A., 1977-78; adminstrv. asst., bookkeeper Young & Rubicam West, 1978-80; advertising media coord. Thriftimart Inc (now SFI), 1980-82; dir. pub. rels. Phipps Racing Corp., Beverly Hills, Calif., 1985-86; coord. spl. projects Nat. Hot Rod Assn., Glendora, 1988-89; pvt. practice pub. rels. L.A., 1982—; legal sec. Morrison and Forester, 1989-93; legal sec. criminal def. firm Barry Tarlow, 1996-98, Trope and Trope, 1998-99. Founder and pres. Racers Who Care. Co-producer (play) Truth Be Told, 1989-90; contbr. articles to profl. jours.; author press releases. Pub. rels. and promotion for RWC Drug and Alcohol Abuse Program; organizer, founder So. Calif. Nat. Child's Day Celebration, 2000—. Mem. Amnesty Internat., Planetary Soc. Democrat. Avocations: photography, writing. Office: 7095 Hollywood Blvd PMB 769 Los Angeles CA 90028-8903

STRAYER, BARRY LEE, federal judge; b. Moose Jaw, Sask., Can., Aug. 13, 1932; s. Carl John and Nina Naomi Strayer; m. Eleanor Lorraine Staton, July 2, 1955; children: Allison Lee, Jonathan Mark, Colin James. BA, U. Sask., Can., 1953, LLB, 1955; BCL, Oxford U., Eng., 1957; SJD, Harvard U., 1966. Bar: Sask., 1959. Crown solicitor Gov. Sask., Regina, 1959-62; prof. law U. Sask., 1962-68; dir. constitutional rev. Gov. Can., Ottawa, 1968-72, dir. constitutional law, 1972-74, asst. dep. minister justice, 1974-83; judge trial divsn. Fed. Ct. Can., 1983-94; jud. mem. Competition Tribunal Can., 1986-93; judge Fed. Ct. Appeal of Can., 1994—; chief justice Ct. Martial Appeal Ct. of Can., 1994—. Sessional lectr. U. Ottawa, 1973-78; constitutional advisor Rep. Seychelles, 1979; adviser Hongkong Govt. Bill of Rights, 1989. Author: Judicial Review of Legislation, 1968, Canadian Constitution and the Courts, 1983, 3d edit., 1988; contbr. articles to profl. jours. Mem.: Commonwealth Lawyers Assn., Larrimac Golf Club, Rideau Club, Harvard Faculty Club. Office: Fed Ct Kent & Wellington Sts Ottawa ON Canada K1A 0H9

STRAZZELLA, JAMES ANTHONY, law educator, lawyer; b. Hanover, Pa., May 18, 1939; s. Anthony F. and Teresa Ann Strazzella; m. Judith A. Coppola, Oct. 9, 1965; children: Jill M., Steven A., Tracy Ann, Michael P. AB, Villanova U., 1961; JD, U. Pa., 1964. Bar: Pa. 1964, D.C., 1965, U.S. Dist. Ct. (ea. and mid. dist.) Pa. 1969, U.S. Ct. Appeals (3rd cir.) 1964, U.S. Ct. Appeals (D.C. cir.) 1965, U.S. Ct. Appeals (4th cir.) 1983, U.S. Supreme Ct. 1969. Law clk. to Hon. Samuel Roberts Pa. Supreme Ct., 1964-65; asst. U.S. atty. D.C., 1965-69; vice dean, asst. prof. law U. Pa., Phila., 1969-73; faculty Temple U., 1973—; James G. Schmidt chair in law, 1989—; acting dean, 1987-89. Chief counsel Kent State investigation Pres.'s Commn. Campus Unrest, 1970; chmn. Atty. Gen.'s Task Force on Family Violence, Pa., 1985-89; mem., chmn. justice ops. Mayor's Criminal Justice Coordinating Commn., Phila., 1983-85; Pa. Joint Coun. Criminal Justice, 1979-82; mem. Com. to Study Pa.'s Unified Jud. Sys., 1980-82; Jud. Coun. Pa., 1972-82; chmn. criminal procedural rules com. Pa. Supreme Ct., 1972-85; mem. task force on prison overcrowding, 1983-85, rsch. adv. com., 1988, Pa. Commn. on Crime and Delinquency; chmn. U.S. Magistrate Judge Merit Selection Com., 1991, mem., 1989, 90, 91;

co-chair Mayor's Transition Task Force on Pub. Safety, Phila., 1992; designate D.C. Com. on Adminstrn. of Justice Under Emergency Conditions, 1968; del. D.C. Jud. Conf., 1985, 95. Contbr. articles to profl. jours. and books. Mem. adv. bd. dirs., past pres. A Better Chance in Lower Merion; dir. Hist. Fire Mus., Phila., 1978—; bd. dirs., 1st v.p. Lower Merion Hist. Soc., 1998—2000; bd. dirs. Neighborhood Civic Assn., Bala-Cynwyd, Pa., 1984—87, Smith Meml. Playground in Fairmount Pk., 1997—, Coun. Legal Edn. Opportunity Bd., 1997—; bd. trustees Bala Cynwyd Pub. Libr., 1999—. Recipient award for disting. tchg. Linback Found., 1983, Advancement of Justice award Pa. Atty. Gen., 1989, Disting. Pub. Svc. award Assn. State and County Detectives, 1989, Spl. Merit award Pa. Assn. Police Chiefs, 1989, significant contbn. to legal scholarship and edn. Beccaria award Phila. Bar Assn. and Nat. IAB Assn., 1995. Fellow: Am. Bar Found.; mem.: St. Thomas More Soc. (pres. 1985—86, past dir. Phila. area, St. Thomas More award 1996), Phila. Bar Assn. (criminal justice sect., appellate cts. com.), Pa. Bar Assn. (commn. profl. stds. 1981—84, chmn. criminal law sect. 1986—88, Merit award 1987), FBA (Phila. crim. law com. adv. bd. 1988—93, chmn. nat. criminal law com. 1991—92), Am. Law Inst., ABA (faculty appellate judges seminars 1975—, various coms., acad. advisor appellate judges edn. com. 1993—, reporter task force on federalization criminal law 1998—99), Order of the Coif (exec. bd. U. Pa.). Roman Catholic. Home and Office: 100 Maple Ave Bala Cynwyd PA 19004-3017 Office: Temple U Law Sch 1719 N Broad St Philadelphia PA 19122-6002

STREAM, ARNOLD CRAGER, lawyer, writer; b. N.Y.C. s. Mervyn and Sophia (Hyams) S.; m. Barbara Bloom, Oct. 1, 1967; children by previous marriages: Jane, Abigail. BA, CCNY, 1936; LLD, St. Lawrence U., 1940. Bar: N.Y. 1940, D.C. 1942. Asst. U.S. Atty. N.Y.Dist., 1940-43; ptnr. Amen, Weisman & Butler, N.Y.C., 1948-55; exec. v.p., gen. counsel C & C TV Corp., 1955-60, Hazel Bishop, Inc., 1955-60; trial lawyer, 1960-91; sr. ptnr. Monasch, Chazen & Stream, N.Y.C., 1973-82, Blum, Gersen & Stream, N.Y.C., 1982-93; ret., 1993. Former trial counsel Gulfstream Aerospace Corp., Twentieth Century-Fox Film Corp., French Embassy, N.Y.C.; spl. counsel to TV industry; vis. lectr. Tauro Coll. Law; spkr. on lit. topics for Gt. Neck Libr.; archivist Palace of the Govs. and Mus. Fine Arts, Santa Fe; tutor lit. and bus. law Santa Fe C.C. Author: (novels) The Third Bullet, Until Proven Guilty, Nemo; (short story) Sudi, others; contbr. book revs., tax series, series on constl. law, articles to profl. jours. Served to lt. col. JAGD, AUS, 1943-46. Mem. Bar of Assn. of City of N.Y. *A lawyer standing in the courtroom provides the ultimate buffer against importunate government.*

STREAN, BERNARD M. retired naval officer; b. Big Cabin, Okla., Dec. 16, 1910; s. Ralph Lester and Maude (Hopkins) S.; m. Janet Lockey, June 12, 1935 (dec. 1978); children: Bernard M., Richard Lockey, Judy (Mrs. William S. Graves); m. Susan Noble Webb, 1978. BS, U.S. Naval Acad., 1933; grad., Armed Forces Staff Coll., 1949, Nat. War Coll., 1958. Commd. ensign USN, 1933, advanced through grades to vice adm., 1965, designated naval aviator, 1935, assigned USS Pennsylvania, 1933-35, assigned Naval Air Sta. Fla., 1935-36, assigned USS Saratoga, 1936-38, assigned San Diego Naval Sta., 1938-39, assigned Pearl Harbor Naval Air Sta. Hawaii, 1939-40, assigned Naval Air Sta. Fla., 1940-42, comdr. Fighter Squadron 1, USS Yorktown, 1943-44, comdr. Air Group 98, 1944-45, comdr. Air Group 75, 1945-46, head tech. tng. program sect. Office Chief Naval Ops., 1950-51, comdg. officer Air Transp. Squdaron 8, 1951-54, comdg. officer Pre-Flight Sch., 1954-56, comdg. officer USS Kenneth Whiting, 1956-57, comdg. officer USS Randolph, 1958-59, chief staff, aide to comdr. Naval Air Force, U.S. Atlantic Fleet, 1959-60, comdr. Fleet Air Whidbey, 1960-61, comdr. Patrol Force 7th Fleet, also U.S. Taiwan Patrol Force, 1961-62, asst. chief naval ops. for fleet ops. Operation Navy, High Command of Navy, Comdr. Naval ops., 1962-64, comdr. Carrier Div. 2, Atlantic Fleet, 1964-65, comdr. World's 1st All-Nuclear Naval Task Force, 1964, comdr. round the world cruise; dep. asst. chief for pers., Bur. Naval Pers. Dept. Navy, Washington, 1965-68, chief naval air tng. Naval Air Sta. Pensacola, Fla., 1968-71; ret., 1971; v.p. O.S.C. Franchise Devel. Corp., 1971-75; chmn. bd. Solaray Corp., 1975-80; v.p. Huet-Browning Corp., Washington. Bd. dirs. U.S. Olympic Com., 1965-68; trustee No. Va. Community Colls., 1978-82. Decorated Navy Cross, (2) D.F.C. with 2 gold stars, Air medal with 7 gold stars, Legion of Merit, D.S.M., numerous area and campaign ribbons; Disting. Svc. medal (Greece); medal of Pao-Ting (Republic of China). Mem. Mil. Order World Wars, Loyal Order Carabao, Early and Pioneer Naval Aviators Assn. (pres. 1977-79), Arlington County Tax Assn. (vice chmn. 1978-80), Md. Aviation Hist. Soc. (founder, bd. dirs. 1978-82), U.S. Naval Acad. Alumni Assn. (pres. Class 1933, 1973-88), Army Navy Club (Washington), N.Y. Yacht Club, Washington Golf and Country Club (Arlington), L.A. Country Club. Home: 6251 Old Dominion Dr Mc Lean VA 22101-4818

STREAR, JOSEPH D. public relations executive; b. N.Y.C., Nov. 5, 1933; s. Morris and Betty (Birenbaum) S. BA, CCNY, 1955. Pres. AC&R Pub. Relations, Inc., N.Y.C., 1972-82; mng. ptnr. Kanan, Corbin, Schupak & Aronow, Inc., 1982-84; pres. Strear, David & Mitchell, Inc., 1984-91; prin. Joseph Strear Pub. Rels., 1992—. 1st lt. U.S. Army, 1955-57. Mem. Pub. Relations Soc. Am. Avocation: sports. Office: 408 W 57th St New York NY 10019-3053

STREATOR, EDWARD, retired diplomat; b. N.Y.C., Dec. 12, 1930; s. Edward James and Ella (Stout) S.; m. Priscilla Craig Kenney, Feb. 16, 1957; children: Edward James, III, Elinor Craig Garcia, Abigail Merrill Squance. AB, Princeton U., 1952. Commd. fgn. service officer Dept. State, 1956; assigned ICA, 1956-58; 3d sec. embassy Addis Ababa, Ethiopia, 1958-60; 2d sec. embassy Lome Togo, 1960-62; intelligence research specialist Office Research and Analysis for Africa, Dept. State, Washington, 1962-63, staff asst. to sec. state, 1964-66, chief polit.-mil. affairs unit, 1966-67; dep. dir. polit.-mil. affairs, 1967-68; dep. dir. polit. affairs U.S. Mission to NATO, 1968-69; dep. dir. Office NATO and Atlantic Polit.-Mil. Affairs, Dept. State, 1969-73; dir. office, 1973-75; dep. U.S. permanent rep. to NATO, dep. chief U.S. Mission to NATO, 1975-77; minister, dep. chief of mission Am. embassy, London, 1975-84; ambassador, U.S. rep. OECD Paris, 1984-87. Bd. dirs. South Bank, 1991-99; chmn. New Atlantic Initiative, 1996—. U.S. dels. NATO and OECD Ministerial Meetings, 1964, 66, 69-75, 85-87; mem. 10th SEATO Coun. Min. Meeting, 1965; 2d spl. Inter-Am. Conf., 1965, Conf. Security and Coop., Europe, 1973; mem. Coun., Royal United Svcs. Inst., 1987-91, v. patron, 1991—; gov. com. The Pilgrims, 1988—, Internat. Inst. Strategic Studies, 1989-98; exec. com. Ditchley Found., 1988—, English Speaking Union, 1988-94; pres. Am. C. of C., U.K., 1988-94; chmn. European Coun. Am. C. of C., 1992-94; bd. dirs. Brit-Am. Arts Assn., 1987-98; dir. Brit. Mus. Natural History Internat. Found.; adv. bd. Inst. U.S. Studies-U. London, 1993-99; mem. coun. Oxford Inst. Am. Studies; adv. com. Fulbright Commn., 1995—. Recipient Presdl. Meritorious Svc. award, 1986, Wilbur Carr award Dept. of State, 1987, Benjamin Franklin medal Royal Soc. Arts, 1992. Mem. Met. Club (Washington), Beefsteak Club, Garrick Club, White's Club (London), Mill Reef Club (Antigua). Episcopalian. E-mail: edward. Address: Chateau de St Aignan 32480 La Romieu France E-mail: streator@cs.com.

STREB, PAUL GERARD, arbitrator; b. Balt., Dec. 8, 1945; s. Edwin and Marie (W.) S.; m. Mary Ament, Nov. 16, 1973. AB in Philosophy, Mount St. Mary's Coll., 1967; JD, U. Balt., 1973. Bar: Md. 1973, U.S. Ct. Appeals (Fed. cir.) 1986. Adminstrv. judge U.S. Civil Svc. Commn. and U.S. Merit Systems Protection Bd., Washington, 1973-83; atty. U.S. Merit Systems Protection Bd., 1983-90, dep. dir. regional ops., 1990-91; adminstrv. law judge U.S. Dept. HUD, 1991-94; chief adminstrv. law judge U.S. Merit Systems Protection Bd., 1994-2001; bd. dirs. fgn. svc. grievance bd. U.S. Dept. State, 2001—. Sec. Fed. Administrative Law Judges Conf., 1993-94; arbitrator Fed. Mediation and Conciliation Svc, 2002-. Vol. atty. for Homeless Persons Representation Project, Balt., 1990-91. Lt. U.S. Army, 1967-70, Vietnam. Decorated Purple Heart, U.S. Army; recipient Chmn.'s Legal Excellence award Merit Systems Protection Bd., 1987. Avocations: running, swimming, biking, travel, the arts. Office: Fgn Svc Grievance Bd 2201 C St SA-15 Washington DC 20522-1531

STRECK, FREDERICK LOUIS, III, lawyer; b. St. Louis, Nov. 6, 1960; s. Frederick Louis Jr. and Joan Kathrine (Faerber) S.; m. Michelle Renee Harding; children: Frederick IV, Robert Harding, Joseph Walter, Samuel Franklin. BBA, Tex. Christian U., 1983; JD, St. Mary's U., 1986. Bar: Tex. 1986, U.S. Dist. Ct. (no. dist.) Tex. 1987, U.S. Ct. Appeals (5th cir.) 1987; bd. cert. in personal injury trial law, civil trial advocacy; diplomate Am. Bd. of Trial Advocacy. Atty. Kugle, Stewart, Dent & Frederick, Ft. Worth, 1986-89, The Dent Law Firm, 1990—. State del. Dem. Party, Tex., 1988. Fellow Tex. State Bar Coll.; mem. ABA, ATLA, Am. Coll. Barristers (sr. counsel), Tex. Trial Lawyers Assn., Million Dollar Adv. Forum, Am. Coll. Barristers (sr. counsel). Democrat. Roman Catholic. Avocations: wine collecting, golf, fishing, scuba diving. Office: The Dent Law Firm 1120 Penn St Fort Worth TX 76102-3417 Fax: 817-332-5809. E-mail: fstreck3@yahoo.com.

STRECKER, DAVID EUGENE, lawyer; b. Carthage, Mo., Nov. 29, 1950; s. Eugene Albert and Erma Freida (Wood) S.; m. Katherine Ann Pugh; children: Charles David, Carrie Christina. BA, Westminster Coll., 1972; JD, Cornell U., 1975, M in Indsl. Labor Rels., 1976. Bar: N.Y. 1976, Okla. 1981, U.S. Dist. Ct. (no. dist.) N.Y. 1976, U.S. Dist. Ct. (ea. dist.) Okla. 1984, U.S. Dist. Ct. (we. dist.) Okla. 2000, U.S. Dist. Ct. (we. and ea. dists.) Ark. 2000, U.S. Ct. Appeals (no. dist.) Okla. 1981, U.S. Ct. Appeals (10th cir.) 1982, U.S. Ct. Appeals (6th cir.) 1990, U.S. Supreme Ct. 1991. Assoc. Conner & Winters, Tulsa, 1980-85, ptnr., 1985-91, Shipley, Inhofe & Strecker, Tulsa, 1991-95, Strecker & Assocs. P.C., Tulsa, 1995—. Instr. paralegal program Tulsa Jr. Coll., 1985—, mem. adv. com., 1986-91; mem. Cornell Secondary Schs. Com., Tulsa, 1985—; adj. instr. labor rels. Okla. State U., 1995—; master Am. Inns of Ct. Bd. dirs., v.p. Tulsa Sr. Svcs., 1988-91; mem. pers. com. Philbrook Art Mus. Capt. JAGC, U.S. Army, 1976-80. Mem. ABA, Okla. Bar Assn. (chmn. labor sect. 1990-91), Tulsa County Bar Assn. (continuing legal edn. com. 1981—), Soc. for Human Resource Mgmt., Tulsa Area Human Resources Assn. (gen. counsel 1989-2000, v.p. 1994-98, bd. dirs. family and children's svcs. 2000—), Kappa Alpha. Democrat. Episcopalian. Avocations: jogging, golf. Home: 5112 E 107th St Tulsa OK 74137-7238 Office: Midcontinent Tower 401 S Boston Ste 2150 Tulsa OK 74103-4009 E-mail: sandk@juno.com.

STREEB, GORDON LEE, diplomat, economist; b. Windsor, Colo., Dec. 24, 1935; s. Gerhard O. and Amelia (Martin) S.; m. Alice Junette Thomas, Aug. 11, 1962; children: Kurt, Kent, Kerry-Lynn. BSBA, BSChemE, U. Colo., 1959; PhD in Econs., U. Minn., 1978. Fgn. service officer U.S. Dept. State, Berlin, 1963-65; vice consul Am. Consulate, Guadalajara, Mex., 1965-67; instr. econs. U. Minn., 1968; examiner Bd. Examiners, 1972-73; internat. economist for trade policy Bur. Econ. and Bus. Affairs, Washington, 1973-77; econ. counselor U.S. mission European Office of the UN and other internat. orgns., Geneva, 1977-80; exec. asst. to undersec. of state on econ. affairs Washington, 1980-81; dep. asst. sec. state for econ. and social affairs Bur. Internat. Orgn. Affairs, 1981-84; dep. chief mission Am. Embassy, New Delhi, India, 1984-88; sr. inspector Dept. State, Washington, 1988-90; amb. to Zambia Am. Embassy, Lusaka, 1990-93; diplomat-in-residence The Carter Ctr., Atlanta, 1994-95, assoc. exec. dir. peace program, 1995—. Home: 2680 Churchwell Ln Tucker GA 30084-2402 Office: The Carter Ctr One Copenhill Atlanta GA 30307

STREEM, JAMES KENNETH, musician, educator; b. Cleve., Jan. 15, 1934; s. Irving Earl and Geraldine W. Streem; m. Prudence Vitale, July 4, 1968 (dec. June 29, 2000). BS, Juilliard, 1956, MS, 1959. Mem. piano faculty Cleve. Music Sch. Settlement, 1960—68; prof. piano Fla. State U., Tallahassee, 1968—; concert debut Carnegie Hall, N.Y.C., NY, 1966. Lectr. in field. Composer: (film score) Double Stop, 1967; author: 125 Pianists on the Legend of Vladimir Horowitz, 1996; performer: Steinway concert series, Kosciusko Found., Alice Tully Hall, numerous recitals throughout U.S. Trustee Temple Israel, Tallahassee, 1975—82, 1987—93. With U.S. Army, 1958—63. Home: 2604 Stonegate Dr Tallahassee FL 32308 E-mail: jks1115@aol.com.

STREEP, MERYL (MARY LOUISE STREEP), actress; b. Summit, N.J., June 22, 1949; d. Harry Jr. and Mary W. Streep; m. Donald J. Gummer, 1978. BA, Vassar Coll., 1971; MFA, Yale U., 1975, DFA (hon.), 1983, Dartmouth Coll., 1981. Co-founder Mothers & Others for a Livable Planet. Appeared with Green Mountain Guild, Woodstock, Vt.; Broadway debut in Trelawny of the Wells, Lincoln Center Beaumont Theater, 1975; N.Y.C. theatrical appearances include 27 Wagons Full of Cotton (Theatre World award), A Memory of Two Mondays, Henry V, Secret Service, The Taming of the Shrew, Measure for Measure, The Cherry Orchard, Happy End, Wonderland, Taken in Marriage, Alice in Concert (Obie award 1981); movie appearances include Julia, 1977, The Deer Hunter, 1978 (Best Supporting Actress award Nat. Soc. Film Critics, Acad. award nomination), Manhattan, 1979, The Seduction of Joe Tynan, 1979, Kramer vs. Kramer, 1979 (N.Y. Film Critics' award, Los Angeles Film Critics' award, both for best actress, Golden Globe award, Acad. award for best supporting actress), The French Lieutenant's Woman, 1981 (Los Angeles Film Critics award for best actress, Brit. Acad. award, Golden Globe award 1981, Acad. award nominiation), Sophie's Choice, 1982 (Acad. award for best actress, Los Angeles Film Critics award for best actress, Golden Globe award 1982), Still of the Night, 1982, Silkwood, 1983 (Acad. award nomination), Falling in Love, 1984, Plenty, 1985, Out of Africa, 1985 (Los Angeles Film Critics award for best actress 1985, Acad. award nomination), Heartburn, 1986, Ironweed, 1987 (Acad. award nomination), A Cry in the Dark, 1988 (named Best Actress N.Y. Film Critics' Circle, 1988, Best Actress Cannes Film Festival, 1989, Acad. award nomination), She-Devil, 1989, Postcards From the Edge, 1990, Defending Your Life, 1991, Death Becomes Her, 1992, The House of the Spirits,1994, The River Wild, 1994, The Bridges of Madison County, 1995 (Acad. award nominee for best actress 1996), Before and After, 1996, Marvin's Room, 1997, Dancing at Lugnasa, 1998, One True Thing, 1998, Music of the Heart, 1999 (Acad. award nominee for best actress), (voice) Artificial Intelligence, 2001, The Hours, 2002, Adaptation, 2002; TV film The Deadliest Season, 1977; TV mini-series Holocaust, 1978 (Emmy award); TV dramatic spls. Secret Service, 1977, Uncommon Women and Others, 1978, First Do No Harm, 1997; TV (narrator) The Velveteen Rabbit, 1985 (Emmy award Best Children's Rec.), A Vanishing Wilderness, 1990. Recipient Mademoiselle award, 1976, Woman of Yr. award B'nai Brith, 1979, Woman of Yr. award Hasty Pudding Soc., Harvard U., 1980, Best Supporting Actress award Nat. Bd. of Rev., 1979, Best Actress award Nat. Bd. of Rev., 1982, Star of Yr. award Nat. Assn. Theater Owners, 1983, People's Choice award, 1983, 85, 86, 87, 90, Women in Film Crystal Award, 1998, Gotham Award for Lifetime Achievement, 1999, Bette Davis Lifetime Achievement Award, 1999. Office: Creative Artists Agy 9830 Wilshire Blvd Beverly Hills CA 90212-1825*

STREET, DAVID HARGETT, investment company executive; b. Oklahoma City, Dec. 4, 1943; s. Bob Allen and Elizabeth Anne (Hargett) S.; m. Betty Ann Nichols, Oct. 1, 1966; children: Elizabeth Ann, Randall Hargett, Jeffrey David. BA in English, U. Okla., 1965; MBA in Fin., U. Pa., 1970. Vice pres. SEI Corp., 1970; v.p., prin. Street & Street, Inc., N.Y.C., 1970-74; v.p., mgr. San Francisco regional office First Nat. Bank Chicago, 1974-78; sr. v.p., CFO, treas. Bangor Punta Corp., Greenwich, Conn., 1978-84; v.p., treas. Penn Cen. Corp., 1984-86, v.p. fin., 1986-87, sr. v.p. fin. Cin., 1987-92; exec. v.p. Gen. Cable Corp., Highland Heights, Ky., 1992-94, also bd. dirs.; pres., CEO Street Capital Group, Duluth, Ga., 1994—. Mem. adv. bd. Mfrs. Hanover Trust Co., 1982-88. 1st lt. M.I. U.S. Army, 1966—67. Mem. St. Ives Country Club. Republican. Presbyterian. Home and Office: 103 Villamoura Way Duluth GA 30097-2068

STREET, DEBORRA LYNN, director of fine arts; b. Ft. Payne, Ala., Feb. 25, 1953; d. John M. and Mary (Adams) Long. B in Music Edn., Troy State U., 1976, MEd, 1982, EdS, 1994; student, Birmingham U. Sch. Law. Tchr. music S. Hall Jr. High Sch., Oakwood, Ga., 1976-77, Slocomb (Ala.), 1977-79, U.S. Collegiate Wind Bands European (summer) Tours, 1978-88, Judson Coll., Marion, Ala., 1980—, Marion Mil. Inst., 1980—, Marion Acad., 1987-88. Band camp instr. 22 U.S. Univs., 1968—; band judge U.S. music festivals, 1977—; asst. conductor U.S. Collegiate Wind Bands European Tours, 1979; sponsor Drama Soc., Marion, 1985—. Prodr.(over 30 musicals and plays):. Sunday sch. tchr. United Meth. Ch., Marion, 1987-88; chmn. Marion Mil. Inst. Fine Arts Coun., 1989-90; mem. steering com. Citizens for a Better Community, Marion, 1990-91; conductor Community Instrumental Ensemble, Marion, 1990—. Mem. Nat. Band Assn., Music Educators Nat. Conf., Women Band Dirs. Nat. Assn. (Indsl. chmn. 1988), DAR, Perry County Hist. Soc., Am. Legion Aux. (Americanism award 1971), Delta Kappa Gamma, Perry County Arts and Humanities Council, AAUW, Tau Beta Sigma, Kappa Kappa Psi, Delta Gamma. Avocations: music, drama, swimming. Home: 803 Washington St Marion AL 36756-3027 Office: Marion Mil Inst Washington St Marion AL 36756-1822

STREET, ERICA CATHERINE, lawyer; b. Lansing, Mich., July 5, 1958; d. Cassius English and Helen Joanna (Hoesman) S.; m. Robert John Pratte, Oct. 20, 1984; 1 child, Chelsea Nicole Pratte. BA, Hillsdale Coll., 1979; JD, U. Mich., 1981. Bar: Minn. 1982, U.S. Dist. Ct. Minn. 1982, U.S. Ct. Appeals (8th cir.) 1983. Assoc. Best & Flanagan, Mpls., 1981-85; sr. counsel Fingerhut Corp., Minnetonka, Minn., 1985-89, Target Stores, Mpls., 1989-97, asst. gen. counsel, 1997-99; pres. Dayton Hudson Brands Inc., 1999-2000, Target Brands, Inc., Mpls., 2000—. Office: Target Brands Inc 1000 Nicollet Mall Minneapolis MN 55403-3601 E-mail: erica.street@target.com.

STREET, JOHN CHARLES, linguistics educator; b. Chgo., Apr. 3, 1930; s. Charles Larrabee and Mary Louise (Rouse) S.; m. Eve Elizabeth Baker, June 4, 1975. BA, Yale, 1951, MA, 1952, PhD, 1955. Asst. prof. English Mich. State U., 1957-59; asst. prof. linguistics and Mongolian langs. Columbia, 1959-62; vis. asst. prof. linguistics U. Wash., 1962-63; assoc. prof. linguistics U. Wis., Madison, 1963-65, prof. linguistics, 1965-92, prof. emeritus, 1992—. Author: The Language of the Secret History of the Mongols, 1957, Khalkha Structure, 1963, The Journal of Oliver Rouse, 1983, An Ellis Family of Devon and Newfoundland, 1994. Research asso. Am. Council Learned Socs., 1959-62. Served with AUS, 1955-57.

STREET, JOHN F. mayor; b. Norristown, Pa., 1943; m. Naomi Street; children: Sharif, Rasida, Lateef, Akeem. BA, Oakwood Coll., 1966; JD, Temple U., 1975. City councilman City of Phila., 1979-98, coun. pres., 1992-98, past chmn. licenses and inspections, appropriations coms., chmn. Whole, Rules & Fiscal Stability, Intergovt. coop. com., 1992—; mem. Phila. Gas Commn., 1984-89, chmn., 1992—; mayor City of Phila., 2000—. Of counsel Ross & Goldstein.*

STREET, ROBERT LYNNWOOD, civil, mechanical and environmental engineer; b. Honolulu, Dec. 18, 1934; s. Evelyn Mansel and Dorothy Heather (Brook) S.; m. Norma Jeanette Ensminger, Feb. 6, 1959; children: Brian Clarke (dec.), Deborah Lynne, Kimberley Anne. Student, USN ROTC Program, 1952-57; MS, Stanford U., 1957, PhD (NSF grad. fellow 1960-62), 1963. Mem. faculty Sch. Engring. Stanford U., 1962—, prof. civil engring., assoc. chmn. dept. Sch. Engring., 1970-72, chmn. dept. Sch. Engring., 1972-80, 94-95, prof. fluid mechanics and applied math. Sch. Engring., 1972—, dir. environ. fluid mechanics lab. Sch. Engring., 1985-91, assoc. dean rsch. Sch. Engring., 1971-83, vice provost acad. computing and info. sys., 1983-85, vice provost, dean rsch. and acad. info. sys., 1985-87, v.p. for info. resources, 1987-90, acting provost, 1987, v.p. librs. and info. resources, 1990-92, vice provost, dean of librs. and info. resources, 1992-94, William Alden and Martha Campbell prof. Sch. Engring., 1997—. Vis. prof. U. Liverpool, Eng., 1970-71, Ctr. for Water Rsch., U. Western Australia, 1985; vis. prof. mech. engring. James Cook U., Australia, 1995; trustee Univ. Corp. Atmospheric Rsch., 1983-94, chmn. sci. programs evaluation com., 1981, treas. corp., 1985, vice chmn. bd., 1986, chmn. bd., 1987-91; bd. dirs., sec.-treas. UCAR Found., 1987-91; bd. govs. Rsch. Libr. Group, 1990-91; chmn. Com. Preservation Rsch. Libr. Materials, Assn. Rsch. Librs., 1993; mem. higher edn. adv. bds. computer corps., 1983-94; mem. basic energy sci. adv. com. U.S. Dept. Energy, 1993-96; bd. dirs. Stanford U. Bookstore, Inc., 1993-98. With C.E.C., USN, 1957-60. Sr. postdoctoral fellow Nat. Center Atmospheric Research, 1978-79; sr. Queen's fellow in marine sci., Australia, 1985; fellow N.E. Asia-U.S. Forum on Internat. Policy at Stanford U., 1985-89. Fellow AAAS; mem. ASCE (chmn. publs. com. hydraulics divsn. 1978-80, Walter Huber prize 1972, Hilgard Hydraulic prize 2002), ASME (R.T. Knapp award 1986), Am. Geophys. Union, Oceanographic Soc., Am. Meteorol. Soc., Phi Beta Kappa, Sigma Xi, Tau Beta Pi. Office: Stanford U Environ Fluid Mechs Lab Dept Civil/Environ Engring Stanford CA 94305-4020 E-mail: street@stanford.edu.

STREET, SUSAN LEE, elementary school educator; b. Kansas City, Kans., Aug. 4, 1955; d. Charley E. Taylor and Betty Lee Milum; m. Thomas D. Street, Dec. 20, 1980; children: Amanda Lee, Jordan Thomas. BS in Elem. Edn., Ark. Tech. U., 1977. Tchr. kindergarten Jasper (Ark.) Elem.; tchr. elem. Woodland Heights Sch., Harrison, Ark. Tchr. Bible Sch. Home: RR 6 Box 60K Harrison AR 72601-8808

STREET, TERRI EVANS, counselor, consultant; b. Marion, Va., Dec. 9, 1950; d. Edward Henry and Elizabeth (Burris) Evans; 1 child, Edward Brian Evans. BA in English and Edn., Emory and Henry Coll., 1972; MS in Edn. and Psychology, Radford Coll., 1977; MS in Counseling and Human Svcs., Radford U., 1992; cert. advanced grad. studies, Va. Poly. Inst. and State U., 1995, PhD in Counselor Edn., 1996. Nat. cert. counselor; cert. in secondary guidancce, speech, pub. speaking, English, grades 4-7, tchr. effectiveness and student achievement, Va. Tchr. social studies Austinville (Va.) Elem. Sch.cc, 1974-80; tchr. lang. arts Scott Meml. Elem. Sch., Wytheville, Va., 1980-85; tchr. English, speech and drama George Wythe H.S., 1985-91, counselor, 1991-94; grad. asst. Va. Poly. Inst. and State U. Coll. Edn., Blacksburg, 1995-96; counseling coord. Roanoke Valley Gov.'s Sch. for Sci. and Tech., Roanoke, Va., 1996—. Evening adminstr. Wytheville C.C., 1993; presenter in field, 1995—; mem. Wythe County Child Study Team, 1992-94; mem. steering com. Crossroads Tech. Prep. Consortium, 1991-94. Recipient presdl. citation U. Richmond Gov.'s Sch. for Visual and Performing Arts, 1990, 92. Mem. ACA, NEA, Nat. Assn. for Coll. Admission Counseling, Nat. Career Devel. Assn., Va. Edn. Assn. (resolutions com. 1983-85), Va. Career Devel. Assn., Va. Counselors Assn., Roanoke Edn. Assn., Roanoke Valley Counselors Assn., Wythe County Edn. Assn. (reporter 1976-77, 79-80, v.p. 1981-82, 92-93, treas. 1985-86), Chi Sigma Iota. Avocations: reading, spending time outdoors, theatre, dance. Home: 655 E Pine St Wytheville VA 24382-2019 Office: Roanoke Valley Gov's Sch for Sci and Tech 2104 Grandin Rd SW Roanoke VA 24015-3528

STREET, WILLIAM MAY, beverage company executive; b. Louisville, 1938; Grad., Princeton U., 1960; MBA, Harvard U., 1963. V.p. Brown-Forman Corp., Louisville, 1969, dir., mem. exec. com., 1971, sr. v.p., 1977, vice chmn., 1983, pres., 2000; pres., COO Brown-Forman Beverage Co. Divsn., 1986-94; pres., CEO Brown-Forman Beverages Worldwide Divsn., 1994—; pres. Brown-Forman Corp., 2001—. Office: Brown-Forman Beverages Worldwide 850 Dixie Hwy Louisville KY 40210-1038

STREETEN, BARBARA WIARD, ophthalmologist, medical educator; b. Candia, N.H., Mar. 3, 1925; d. Robert Campbell Wiard and Gertrude Sarah Matheson; m. David Henry Palmer Streeten, Aug. 2, 1952; children: Robert Duncan, Elizabeth Anne, John Palmer. AB magna cum laude, Tufts U., 1945, MD cum laude, 1950. Diplomate Am. Bd. Ophthalmology. Jr. resident in gen. pathology Mallory Inst., Boston City Hosp., 1951-52; fellow in ophthalmic pathology Mass. Eye and Ear Infirmary, Boston, 1952-53; resident in ophthalmology Wayne County Gen. Hosp., Eloise, Mich., 1953-56; from jr. to sr. clin. instr. ophthalmology U. Mich. Med. Sch., Ann Arbor, 1956-60; from asst. prof. to prof. ophthalmology SUNY Health Sci. Ctr. (now called SUNY Upstate Med. U.), Syracuse, 1964—, dir. eye pathology lab., 1966—; from asst. prof. to prof. pathology SUNY Health Sci. Ctr., 1968—. Contbr. articles. Mem. vision study sect. Nat. Eye Inst., NIH, Bethesda, Md., 1977-80, mem. bd. sci. counselors, 1982-86; mem. editl. bd., mem. editl. adv. com. Ophthalmology jour., 1982-94; gen. editor Investigative Ophthalmology and Visual Sci., 1979-82, mem. editl. bd., 1987-92. Recipient grant Nat. Eye Inst., NIH, 1975—. Mem. Am. Assn. Ophthalmic Pathologists (charter, past pres., bd. dirs., Zimmerman medal 1997), Am. Acad. Ophthalmology (honor award 1990), Verhoeff Ophthalmic Pathology Soc. (past pres.), Assn. for Rsch. in Vision and Ophthalmology (past sect. chmn.), Internat. Soc. Ophthalmic Pathology (co-v.p. N.Am. 1990-92), Phi Beta Kappa, Alpha Omega Alpha. Episcopalian. Achievements include establishment of elastic system nature of the suspensory ligament of the ocular lens; ultrastructural and immunopathologic contributions to diseases of the ocular connective tissue matrix, particularly those related to cataract and glaucoma. Home: 334 Berkley Dr Syracuse NY 13210-3000 Office: SUNY Upstate Med Univ WH Rm 2107 766 Irving Ave Syracuse NY 13210-1602 E-mail: streeteb@upstate.edu.

STREETER, JOHN WILLIS, information systems manager; b. Topeka, Sept. 3, 1947; s. Jack and Edith Bernice (Vowels) S.; m. Nancy Ann Buck, June 15, 1968 (div. 1985); children: Sarah Beth, Timothy Paine; m. Linda Lea Wenrich Weisbender, Sept. 13, 1986; stepchildren: Michael Leon Weisbender II, Debra Ann Weisbender Johnson, Dawn Marie Weisbender. BS in Computer Sci., Kans. State U., 1973, MBA in Mgmt., 1974; postgrad., Harvard U., 1992.

Computer programmer U.S.M.C., 1965-70, Kans. State U., Manhattan, 1970-74; cons., mgr., prin. Am. Mgmt. Systems, Inc., Arlington, Va., 1974-83; systems planning analyst Fed. Nat. Mortgage Assn., Washington, 1983-85; assoc. dir. computing and telecomm. Kans. State U., Manhattan, 1985-91, dir. info. systems, 1991—. Mem. State of Kans. Info. Tech. Adv. Bd., 1997-98. Author: Streeter Genealogy, 1985. Staff sgt. USMC, 1965-70. Recipient Navy Achievement medal in data processing Sec. Navy, 1971. Mem. IEEE, SR, KC, IEEE Computer Soc., Assn. for Computing Machinery, Am. Inst. Cert. Computer Profls., Educause, Inc. (Kans. State U. voting mem. rep. 1987—), Streeter Family Assn. (bd. dirs. 1988—, v.p. 1990-95), Am. Legion. Republican. Roman Catholic. Avocations: genealogy, history, book collecting. Home: 6765 Salzer Rd Wamego KS 66547-9636 Office: Kans State U Info Sys 2323 Anderson Ave Ste 215 Manhattan KS 66502-2912

STREETER, RICHARD EDWARD, retired lawyer; b. Mpls., Aug. 6, 1934; s. Donald Stivers and Beatrice Louise (Gibbs) S.; m. Charlotte Mae Tharp; children— Christopher A., Joanna G., Matthew J., Jonathan R. BA, Yale U., 1956; LL.B., Yale Law Sch., 1959. Bar: Ohio 1960, D.C. 1964, U.S. Supreme Ct. 1964. Assoc. Thompson Hine Flory LLP, Cleve., 1960-63, 65-68, ptnr., 1968-99; atty. State Dept. Legal Advisors Office, Washington, 1963, Justice Dept. Antitrust Div., Washington, 1964; asst. gen. counsel Senate Democratic Policy Com., 1964-65; ret. Contbr. article to profl. jour. Mem. Leadership Cleve., 1981; pres. Fedn. Commty. Planning, Cleve., 1980-82, Cleve. Legal Aid Soc., 1974-76, Plan of Action for Tomorrow's Housing, Cleve., 1987-88; chmn. Ctr. for Families and Children, 1990-93; trustee Center for Families and Children, 1987—, City Club, Cleve., 1987-91, St. Vincent Quadrangle Inc., 1991-96, Lake Erie Coll., 1993—, Youth Opportunities Unltd., Cleve., 1983—; bd. dirs. United Way Svcs. Cleve., 1992-96, Woodruff Found., 1993-94. Recipient Cleve. 10 Outstanding Young Men award Jr. C. of C., 1968 Mem. ABA, Bar Assn. Greater Cleve. (trustee 1971-74, chmn. securities law sect. 1979-80, chmn. corps. banking and bus. law sect. 1983-85), Ohio State Bar Assn. (corp. law com.). Home: 17420 Chagrin River Rd Chagrin Falls OH 44023-3414

STREETER, ROBERT DAVENPORT, electrical engineer, consultant; b. Springfield, Mass., Sept. 17, 1941; s. William Allen Streeter and Muriel Ethel Davenport; m. Carole Janet Riley; children: John Riley, Susan Elizabeth Billian. B in Elec. Engring., Ohio State U., 1964; MSEE, Purdue U., 1968. Registered profl. engr., Ind. Engr. WBNS Radio-TV, Columbus, Ohio, 1961—64, Ohio State U. Rsch. Found., Columbus, 1962—64, The Magnavox Co., Fort Wayne, Ind., 1965—82; pres. A M Stereo, Inc., 1982—; sr. prin. engr. Raytheon, 1985—. Contbr. articles to profl. jours. Mem.: IEEE, Eta Cappa Nu (life). Achievements include invention of AM stereo, microelectromechanical systems. Avocations: private pilot, amateur radio. Home: 6111 Eagle Creek Dr Fort Wayne IN 46814-3213 Office: Raytheon 1010 Production Rd Fort Wayne IN 46808 Personal E-mail: r.streeter@ieee.org.

STREETMAN, AUDREY JEAN, bank executive; b. Kosse, Tex., Dec. 16, 1940; d. Clyde Barclay and Reva Virginia (Pamplin) Williams; m. Byron Bates Oldham, July 10, 1960 (div. Sept. 10, 1970); children: Kristi Lynne, Kelly Diane, Kim Anne. Grad., Durham Bus. Sch., Waco, 1960; grad. Comml. Lending Sch., U. Okla., 1984; postgrad., U. Ctrl. Okla. V.p. Liberty Nat. Bank & Trust Co., Oklahoma City, 1973-97; sr. v.p. Bank One Okla. NA, 1997-2001, BancFirst, 2001—. Author: (poetry) The Train, 1991, A Gathering of Bones, 1995. Trustee Westminster Presbyn. Ch., Oklahoma City, 1999—, elder, 1991-93. Republican. Avocations: dancing, bridge, gardening, travel.

STREETMAN, BEN GARLAND, electrical engineering educator; b. Cooper, Tex., June 24, 1939; s. Richard E. and Bennie (Morrow) S.; m. Lenora Ann Music, Sept. 9, 1961; children: Paul, Scott. BS, U. Tex., 1961, MS, 1963, PhD, 1966. Fellow Oak Ridge Nat. Lab., 1964-66; asst. prof. elec. engring. U. Ill., 1966-70, assoc. prof., 1970-74, prof., 1974-82; rsch. prof. Coordinated Sci. Lab., 1970-82; prof. elec. engring. U. Tex., Austin, 1982—, dir. Microelectronics Rsch. Ctr., 1984—, Dula D. Cockrell Centennial chair engring., 1989-96, dean Coll. Engring., 1997—. Dir. Nat. Instruments, ZixIt. Author: Solid State Electronic Devices, 5th edit., 2000. Recipient Frederick Emmons Terman award Am. Soc. Engring. Edn., 1981, AT&T Found. award, 1987; named Disting. Alumnus, U. Tex. at Austin, 1998. Fellow IEEE (Edn. medal 1989), Electrochem. Soc.; mem. NAE, Am. Acad. Arts and Scis., Tau Beta Pi, Eta Kappa Nu, Sigma Xi. Office: Dean's Office Coll Engring ECJ 10.310/C2100 Austin TX 78712-1080

STREETMAN, JOHN WILLIAM, III, museum official; b. Marion, N.C., Jan. 19, 1941; s. John William, Jr. and Emily Elaine (Carver) S.; children: Katherine Drake, Leah Farrior, Burgin Eaves. BA in English and Theatre History, Western Carolina U., 1963; cert. in Shakespeare studies, Lincoln Coll., Oxford (Eng.) U., 1963. Founding dir. Jewett Creative Arts Ctr., Berwick Acad., South Berwick, Maine, 1964-70; exec. dir. Polk Mus. Art, Lakeland, Fla., 1970-75; dir. Mus. Arts and Sci., Evansville, Ind., 1975—; chmn. mus. adv. panel Ind. Arts Commn., 1977-78. Mem. Am. Assn. Museums, Assn. Ind. Museums (bd. dirs.) Episcopalian. Office: Evansville Mus Arts & Scis 411 SE Riverside Dr Evansville IN 47713-1037

STREETMAN, LEE GEORGE, sociology educator, criminology educator; b. Port Neches, Tex., Sept. 29, 1953; s. George Bernard and Roberta Valmeta (Fry) S. BA, U. Del., 1983, MA, 1985, PhD, 1995. Lectr. Ursinus Coll., Collegeville, Pa., 1990-92; asst. prof. Del. State U., Dover, Del., 1991-93, assoc. prof., 1996—; instr. Temple U., Phila., 1994; asst. prof. Cheyney (Pa.) U., 1994-96; assoc. prof. Del. State U., Dover, 1996—. Sr. rsch. analyst Admark, Inc., Horsham, Pa., 1986-88; rsch. specialist Del. Coun. Crime and Justice, Wilmington, Del., 1988-89. Author: Drugs, Delinquency, and Pregnancy, A Panel Study of Adolescent Problem Behavior, 1996, Crime Perception in Postmodern Society, 1997, Streetman Soldiers in the War of the Rebellion (1861-65), 2d edit., 2000; contbr. articles to profl. jours. Tutor Thresholds Inmate Pre-release Program, Smyrna, Del., 1995. Mem. Am. Sociol. Assn., Am. Soc. Criminology, Popular Am. Culture Soc., Pa. Sociol. Soc., Soc. Study Social Problems, Alliance Prevention Adolescent Pregnancy, Sons of Confederate Vets., Cherokee Nat. Hist. Soc., Living History Soc. of Del., Ctrl. Del. Civil War Round Table. Office: Dept Sociology and Criminal Justice Del State U Dover DE 19901

STREETMAN, PHILLIP ROGERS, music educator; b. Cordele, Ga., June 10, 1973; s. Phillip Arlen and Elizabeth Morgan Streetman. BS, Ga. Southwestern State U., 1998. Choral dir. Weaver Mid. Sch., Macon, Ga., 1998—2000, Columbia Mid. Sch., Grovetown, 2000—. Pianist, organist, instr. various ch., theater groups and music camps, 1991—. Musical dir.: Broadway musical Oliver (Best Musical award, 1998). Mem.: Ga. Music Educators Assn. Baptist. Avocations: singing, piano, reading. Home: 2787 Hillside Rd Appling GA 30802 Office: Columbia Mid Sch 6000 Columbia Rd Grovetown GA 30813 Personal E-mail: phillipstreet@comcast.net. Business E-Mail: phillip.streetman@ccboe.net.

STREETO, JOSEPH MICHAEL, catering company official; b. New Haven, Dec. 12, 1942; s. Pasquale Joseph and Marie Veronica (Matazzaro) S. BS, Quinnipiac U., Mt. Caramel, Conn., 1964. Mng. dir. spl. events divsn. Culinary Enterprises, Inc., Chgo., 1986-97; project dir. Blue Plate at Symphony Ctr., 1997—. Mem. com. DePaul U. Awards for Excellence in the Arts Gala, 1998. Co-chmn. telethon Muscular Dystrophy Assn., Chgo., 1989; Horizon Hospice, Chgo., 1988, vol., 1990, 96, chmn. annual benefit, 1999, Horizon Hospice Annual Benefit, 1999; co-chmn. gourmet dinner Blackstone benefit DePaul U.; bd. dirs. Horizon Hospice, 1995—; active Cooks by the Books/The Chgo. Fund on Aging, 1994-96. Home: 467 S Calle El Segundo Palm Springs CA 92262 E-mail: joestreeto@aol.com.

STREETT, WILLIAM BERNARD, retired university dean, engineering educator; b. Lake Village, Ark., Jan. 27, 1932; s. William Bernard and Marie Louise (Pfeffer) S.; m. Jackie Lou Heard, June 8, 1955 (dec. Jan. 14, 1999); children— Robert Stuart, David Alexander, Kathleen Ann, Michael Richard; m. Mary J. Sansalone, Oct. 23, 1999. BS, U.S. Mil. Acad., 1955; MS, U. Mich., 1961, PhD, 1963. Commd. 2d lt. U.S. Army, 1955; founder, first dir. Sci. Rsch. Lab., U.S. Mil. Acad., West Point, N.Y., 1968-78, asst. dean, 1968-78, ret. col., 1978; sr. rsch. assoc. Cornell U., Ithaca, 1978-81, prof. chem. engring., 1981-95, dean engring., 1984-93; v.p. Impact-Echo Cons., 1995; founder, pres. Impact-Echo Instruments, LLC, 1997—. Contbr. articles to profl. jours. Postdoctoral fellow NATO, 1966, Guggenheim fellow Oxford U., 1974 Mem. Am. Concrete Inst., Tau Beta Pi, Sigma Xi. Home: 105 Oak Hill Pl Ithaca NY 14850-2323 Office: Cornell U Coll Engring Hollister Hall Ithaca NY 14850 E-mail: wbs3@cornell.edu.

STREGE, KAREN, library director; State libr. Mont. State Libr., Helena, 1996—. Office: Mont State Library 1515 E 6th Ave PO Box 201800 Helena MT 59620*

STREIB, VICTOR LEE, dean; b. Marion, Ind., Oct. 8, 1941; s. Albert Wolfe and Melba Janice Streib; m. Lynn C. Sametz, Mar. 29, 1978; children: Noah, Jessi. BS in Indsl. Engring., Auburn U., 1966; JD, Ind. U., Bloomington, 1970. Bar: Ind. 1970, U.S. Supreme Ct. 1987. Rsch. assoc., scientist Inst. Rsch. Pub. Safety Ind. U., Bloomington, 1970-72, asst. to assoc. prof. dept. forensic studies, 1972-78; assoc. prof. law New Eng. Sch. Law, Boston, 1978-80; prof., assoc. dean coll. of law Cleve. State U., 1980-96; prof. law Ohio No. U., Ada, 1996—, dean, 1996—2000. Vis. prof. law U. San Diego, 1983-84, Mich. State U., 2001-02; vis. fellow Assn. Am. Law Schs., Washington, 1993-94, site evaluator, 1994—; mem. adv. bd. Ctr. Capital Punishment Studies U. Westminster, London, 1996—. Author: Juvenile Justice in America, 1978, Death Penalty for Juveniles, 1987, Death Penalty in a Nutshell, 2002; editor: Capital Punishment Anthology, 1993, Law Deanship Manual, 1993. Mem. ABA (site evaluator 1991-2000), North Ctrl. Assn. (cons. evaluator 1990-2001). Avocation: physical fitness. Office: Ohio No U Coll Law 525 S Main St Ada OH 45810-6000

STREIBEL, BRYCE, state senator; b. Fessenden, N.D., Nov. 19, 1922; s. Reinhold M. and Frieda I. (Broschat) S.; m. June P. Buckley, Mar. 23, 1947; 1 child, Kent. Attended U. N.D., Grand Forks; BS, San Francisco State Coll., 1947. Engr. U.S. Govt., Napa, Calif., 1943-46; dir. Martin Funeral Home, Stockton, 1946-55; owner Streibel Twin Oaks Farm, Fessenden, N.D., 1955—; state sen. State of N.D., Bismarck, 1981—; pres. pro tempore, 1995, state rep., 1957-75, majority leader, 1966-74. Author: Pathways Through LIfe, 1983. Chmn. N.D. Legis. Coun., Bismarck, 1969-75; councilman Town of Fessenden, 1976-84; former pres. 20-30 Internat. Group, Sacramento, trustee, 1952-54; dir. World Coun., Sacramento, 1951-53; bd. dirs. U. N.D. Fellows, Grand Forks, 1982-86; pres. Fessenden Airport Authority, 1980—; mem. N.D. Bd. Higher Edn., 1977-81; chmn. N.D. adv. commn. U.S. Commn. on Civil Rights, 1988-93. Recipient Sioux award U. N.D. Alumni Assn., 1976, Benefactor award U. N.D. Found., 1982, William Budge award, 1983, Outstanding Svc. award Jaycees, 1988, Nat. Barn Again Farm Heritage award, 1996; named Outstanding Alumnus Theta Chi, 1987. Mem. N.D. Centennial Farm, Commodore N.D. Mythical Navy, Masons (Master), Elks, Kiwanis, Shriners, Farm Bur. Republican. Baptist. Avocations: golf, philately. Home and Office: 226 2nd St N Fessenden ND 58438-7204 Office: PO Box 467 Fessenden ND 58438-0467

STREIBICH, RONALD LELAND, fundraising executive; b. Peoria, Ill., May 5, 1936; s. Leland Roy and Evelyn (Moffatt) S.; m. Donna Jane Matthews, Sept. 14, 1958 (div. Jan. 1980); children: John, James; m. Elinor Sue Gaines, Apr. 23, 1988. BA, Knox Coll., 1958. Regional pub. rels. dir. GE, Winston Salem, N.C., 1959-66; dir. devel. Northwestern U., Evanston, Ill., 1966-76; exec. v.p. Meth. Med. Found., Peoria, 1976-79; v.p. Knox Colll., Galesburg, 1979-82; exec. v.p. Meml. Hosp. Found., Houston, 1982-84; v.p. St. Louis Children's Hosp., 1984-88; asst. vice chancellor Tex. A&M U., College Station & Houston, 1988—. 1st lt. U.S. Army, 1958-59. Republican. Presbyterian. Avocation: golf. Office: Tex A&M U 2121 W Holcombe Blvd Ste 1107 Houston TX 77030-3303 Home: 4620 9th St Lubbock TX 79416-4720

STREICHER, JAMES FRANKLIN, lawyer; b. Ashtabula, Ohio, Dec. 6, 1940; s. Carl Jacob and Helen Marie (Dugan) S.; m. Sandra JoAnn Jennings, May 22, 1940; children: Cheryl Ann, Gregory Scott, Kerry Marie. BA, Ohio State U., 1962; JD, Case Western Res. U., 1966. Bar: Ohio 1966, U.S. Dist. Ct. (no. dist.) Ohio 1966. Assoc. Calfee, Halter & Griswold, Cleve., 1966-71, ptnr., 1972—. Bd. dirs. The Mariner Group Inc., Ft. Myers, Fla., Spectra-Tech Inc., Stamford, Conn., Mid Am. Consulting; mem. Divsn. Securities Adv. Bd., State of Ohio; lectr. Case Western Res. U., Cleve. State U.; mem. pvt. sector com. John Carroll U. Trustee Achievement Ctr. for Children, Western Reserve Hist. Soc., Make-A-Wish Found. Endowment. Mem. ABA, Fed. Bar Assn., Ohio State Bar Assn., Assn. for Corp. Growth, Ohio Venture Assn., Greater Cleve. Bar Assn. (founding chmn. corp., banking, bus. law sect.), Ohio State U. Alumni Assn., Case Western Res. U. Alumni Assn., Newcomen Soc., Bluecoats Club (Cleve.), Mayfield Country (bd. dirs. 1985-89), Union Club, The Pepper Pike Club, Beta Theta Pi, Phi Delta Phi. Roman Catholic. Republican. Fax: 216-241-0816. E-mail: j.streich@calfee.com.

STREIDL, ISABELLE ROBERTS SMILEY, economist; b. Glen Ridge, N.J., Nov. 7, 1913; d. Orton Ray and Louise Roberts (Speer) Smiley; m. Edward G. Streidl, Apr. 8, 1939 (dec. Sept. 1983); children: Nancy Louise, Linda Jeanne. BA cum laude, Mt. Holyoke Coll., 1935. Clk. VA, Washington, 1936; statis. clk. bur. of labor stats. U.S. Dept. Labor, 1936-39, sr. examining clk. children's bur., 1939-42, asst. child labor report analyst, 1942-45, child labor report analyst, 1945-46, labor economist women's bur., 1962-65, chief br. labor force rsch. women's bur., 1965-67, chief divsn. econ. status and opportunities, 1967-74. Mem. AAUW. Avocations: bridge, sewing, knitting. Home: 45 Strawberry Dr Carlisle PA 17013-4440

STREIFF, ARLYNE BASTUNAS, business owner, educator; b. Sacramento, Nov. 04; d. Peter James and Isabel (Gemnas) Bastunas; children: Peter Joshua, Joshua Gus. BS, U. Nev., 1965; postgrad., U. Calif., Davis, 1965-68, Calif. State U., Chico, 1968, 71. Cert. elem. tchr., Calif., Nev., cert. in English-specially designed lang. acad. instrn. devel. in English. Tchr. reading, lang. and kindergarten Enterprise Elem. Sch. Dist., Redding, Calif., 1965-98, tchr. kindergarten, 1988-98; owner, pres. Arlyne's Svcs., 1990—. Author: Niko and His Friends, 1989, Niko The Black Rottweiler, 1995, Color-Talk-Spell. Mem. Rep. Women, Five County Labor Coun., Redding, 1976-93, Calif. Labor Fedn., 1974-97, AFL-CIO, 1974-97. Named Tchr. of Yr., Enterprise Sch. Dist., 1969. Mem. AAUW, Am. Fedn. Tchrs., Calif. Tchrs. Assn. (bargaining spokesperson 1968-72, exec. bd. dirs.), United Tchrs. Enterprise (pres. 1979-80, chmn. lang. com.), Calif. Reading Assn., Enterprise Fedn. Tchrs. (pres. 1974, pres.-elect 1995-97), Calif. State Fedn. Tchrs. (v.p. 1974-75, exec. bd. 1995-97), Redding C. of C., Women of Moose, Elks. Avocations: home interior design, real estate, construction, creative writing, educational advancement. Office: Arlynes Svcs 1468 Benton Dr Redding CA 96003-3116

STREIKER, SUSAN L. law librarian; b. Phila., Dec. 11, 1959; d. Lowell Dean and Lois Suzanne Streiker. BA, Brigham Young U., 1981, MLS, 1983. Reference and media asst. Law Sch. Libr. Brigham Young U., Provo, Utah, 1981—83; instr. in legal rsch., reference and media libr. Sch. of Law Southwestern U., L.A., 1984—89; reference libr. Paul, Hastings, Janofsky & Walker, LLP, 1989—91, head law libr., 1991—. Fellow ABA; mem. Am. Assn. Law Librs., Southern Calif. Assn. Law Librs., Phi Alpha Theta. Avocations: music, traveling, painting, gardening, ballooning. Office: Paul Hastings Janofsky & Walker LLP 515 S Flower St Fl 25 Los Angeles CA 90071-2300

STREILEIN, J. WAYNE, research scientist; b. Johnstown, Pa., June 19, 1935; s. Jacob and Mina Alma (Krouse) S.; m. Joan Elaine Stein, June 15, 1957; children: Laura Anne, William Wayne, Robert Dietrich. BA in Chemistry, Gettysburg Coll., 1956; MD, U. Pa., 1960. Asst. prof., assoc. prof. genetics U. Pa. Sch. Medicine, Phila., 1965-71; prof. cell biology Southwestern Med. Sch., Dallas, 1971-84; prof., chair microbiology and immunology U. Miami, Fla., 1984-93; Charles L. Schepens prof. opthalmology, prof. dermatology Harvard Med. Sch., Boston, 1993—. Pres. Schepens Eye Rsch. Inst., Boston, 1993—. Capt. USAR, 1961-67. Recipient award Alcon Rsch. Inst., 1984, Merit award Nat. Eye Inst., 1990; Markle Found. scholar, 1967; named Outstanding Alumnus Gettysburg Coll., 2001. Mem. Assn. Rsch. in Vision and Ophthalmology (Procter award 1996), Am. Assn. Immunologists (chair pub. rels. 1988-93), Soc. Investigative Dermatology, Transplantation Soc. Achievements include elucidation of cellular and molecular basis of immune privilege in eye, genetic basis of effects of ultraviolet B light on cutaneous immunity, microenvironmental factor effects on tissue-restricted antigen presenting cells. Home: 44 Neptune St Beverly MA 01915-4751 Office: Schepens Eye Rsch Inst 20 Staniford St Boston MA 02114-2508 E-mail: waynes@vision.eri.harvard.edu.

STREISAND, BARBRA JOAN, singer, actress, director; b. Bklyn., Apr. 24, 1942; d. Emanuel and Diana (Rosen) S.; m. Elliott Gould, Mar. 1963 (div.); 1 son, Jason Emanuel; m. James Brolin, July 1, 1998. Grad. high sch., Bklyn.; student, Yeshiva of Bklyn. N.Y. theatre debut Another Evening with Harry Stoones, 1961; appeared in Broadway musicals I Can Get It for You Wholesale, 1962, Funny Girl, 1964-65; motion pictures include Funny Girl, 1968, Hello Dolly, 1969, On a Clear Day You Can See Forever, 1970, The Owl and the Pussy Cat, 1970, What's Up Doc?, 1972, Up the Sandbox, 1972, The Way We Were, 1973, For Pete's Sake, 1974, Funny Lady, 1975, The Main Event, 1979, All Night Long, 1981, Nuts, 1987; star, prodr. film A Star is Born, 1976; prodr., dir., star Yentl, 1983, The Prince of Tides, 1991, The Mirror Has Two Faces, 1996 (ASCAP Award for score, 1996) ; exec. prodr.: (TV movie) Serving in Silence: The Margarethe Cammermeyer Story, 1995; TV spls. include My Name is Barbra, 1965 (5 Emmy awards), Color Me Barbra, 1966; actress, prodr., dir. The Mirror Has Two Faces, 1996; rec. artist on Columbia Records; Gold record albums include People, 1965, My Name is Barbra, 1965, Color Me Barbra, 1966, Barbra Streisand: A Happening in Central Park, 1968, Barbra Streisand: One Voice, Stoney End, 1971, Barbra Joan Streisand, 1972, The Way We Were, 1974, A Star is Born, 1976, Superman, 1977, The Stars Salute Israel at 30, 1978, Wet, 1979, (with Barry Gibb) Guilty, 1980, Emotion, 1984, The Broadway Album, 1986, Til I Loved You, 1989; other albums include: A Collection: Greatest Hits, 1989, Just for the Record, 1991, Back to Broadway, 1993, Concert at the Forum, 1993, The Concert Recorded Live at Madison Square Garden, 1994, The Concert Highlights, 1995, Higher Ground, 1997, A Love Like Ours, 1999, Christmas Memories, 2001, The Essential Barbara Streisand, 2002. Recipient Emmy award, CBS-TV spl. (My Name Is Barbra), 1964, Acad. award as best actress (Funny Girl), 1968, Golden Globe award (Funny Girl), 1969, co-recipient Acad. award for best song (Evergreen), 1976, Georgie award AGVA 1977, Grammy awards for best female pop vocalist, 1963, 64, 65, 77, 86, for best song writer (with Paul Williams), 1977, 2 Grammy nominations for Back to Broadway, 1994; Nat. Acad. of Recording Arts & Sciences Lifetime Achievement Award, 1994, Cecil B. Demille Lifetime Achievement Award, 2000, Liberty & Justice Award, Rainbow/PUSH Coalition, 2001. Office: ICM c/o Jeff Berg 8942 Wilshire Blvd Beverly Hills CA 90211-1934*

STREIT, FRANCES NORRIS, artist; b. Macy, Ind., May 22, 1918; d. Elmer Lee and Faye Hume (Hammond) Norris; m. George B. Streit, Aug. 1, 1943 (dec. 1988); children: Robert William, Kathryn Louise Streit Hyatt. BFA, John Herron Art Sch., 1940; MFA, State U. Iowa, 1942; postgrad., Ind. U., 1940-42, Adelphi U., 1966. Cert. tchr., N.Y. Portrait painter, 1940—. Art tchr. Nassau Community Coll., Garden City, N.Y., 1965-66, Valley Stream (N.Y.) Cen. High Sch., 1967-73. Exhibited prin. works in numerous exhbns. including 3d Ann. Nat. Exhbn. Am. Art N.Y.C., Art League Long Island, Allied Artists Am., Country Art Gallery, Merrick Art Gallery, South Huntington Libr., Fine Arts Mus. Long Island, Camberwell Libr. Collection, Corcoran Gallery, Washington, Smithsonian Art Inst. Gallery, Washington, Carnegie Inst., Pitts.; commd. for numerous portraits including Gen. David M. Shoup, Gov. George N. Craig, Dr. Robert H. Wyatt, Dr. J. Dan Hull, many others; hist. murals include Bellmore, N.Y., Farmingdale, N.Y., West Hempstead, N.Y., Milleridge Inn, Jericho, N.Y., Recreation Ctr. Freeport, Roslyn Savs. Bank. Mem. Nat. Soc. Mural Painters, Mus. Women in Arts, DAR. Home and Office: 146 Labaugh Rd Hurleyville NY 12747-5109

STREIT, MICHAEL J. judge; b. Sheldon, Iowa; married; 1 child. BA, U. Iowa, 1972; grad., U. San Diego Sch. Law, 1975. Cert.: (U.S. Ct. Appeals) 1996. Asst. atty. Lucas County, atty.; dist. ct. judge, 1983; Supreme Ct. justice Iowa State Supreme Ct., 2001—. Mem.: Blackstone Inn of Ct., Supreme Ct. Jud. Tech. Com., Iowa Jud. Inst., Judges Assn. Edn. Com., Supreme Ct. Edn. Adv. Com. Office: State House Des Moines IA 50319*

STREITMAN, JEFFREY BRUCE, education administrator; b. Bronx, N.Y., Aug. 5, 1951; s. Milton and Marcia (Helfant) S.; m. Brenda Penny, July 4, 1974; 1 child, Jesse. BA cum laude, CUNY, 1974, MS, 1976; EdD, Fordham U., 1990. Guidance counselor Horizon Sch., Levitown, N.Y., 1976-80, asst. prin., 1980-84; guidance chmn. Lawrence (N.Y.) Pub. Schs., 1984-88, supr. student svcs., 1988-90; asst. supt. schs. Syosset (N.Y.) Cen. Sch. Dist., 1990-94; dep. supt. schs. Syosset Cen. Sch. Dist., 1994—. Mem. ASCD, N.Y. State Pers. Adminstrs., L.I. Pers. Adminstrs. Office: Syosset Cen Sch Dist Pell Ln Syosset NY 11791

STREITWIESER, ANDREW, JR. chemistry educator; b. Buffalo, June 23, 1927; s. Andrew and Sophie Streitwieser; m. Mary Ann Good, Aug. 19, 1950 (dec. May 1965); children: David Roy, Susan Ann; m. Suzanne Cope Beier, July 29, 1967. AB, Columbia U., 1949, MA, 1950, PhD, 1952; postgrad. (AEC fellow), MIT, 1951-52. Faculty U. Calif., Berkeley, 1952-92, prof. chemistry, 1963-92, prof. emeritus, 1993—. Researcher on organic reaction mechanisms, application molecular orbital theory to organic chemistry, effect chem. structure on carbon acidities; cons. to industry, 1957— Author: Molecular Orbital Theory for Organic Chemists, 1961, Solvolytic Displacement Reactions, 1962, (with J.I. Brauman) Supplemental Tables of Molecular Orbital Calculations, 1965, (with C.A. Coulson) Dictionary of Pi Electron Calculations, 1965, (with P.H. Owens) Orbital and Electron Density Diagrams, 1973, (with C.H. Heathcock and E.M. Kosower) Introduction to Organic Chemistry, 4th edit., 1992, A Lifetime of Synergy with Theory and Experiment, 1996; also numerous articles; co-editor: Progress in Physical Organic Chemistry, 11 vols., 1963-74. Recipient Humboldt Found. Sr. Scientist award, 1976, Humboldt medal, 1979, Berkeley citation, 1993. Fellow AAAS; mem. NAS, Am. Chem. Soc. (Calif. sect. award 1964, award in Petroleum Chemistry 1967, Norris award in phys. organic chemistry 1982, Cope scholar award 1989), Am. Acad. Arts and Scis., Bavarian Acad. Scis. (corr.), Phi Beta Kappa, Sigma Xi. Office: U Calif Dept Chemistry Berkeley CA 94720-1460 E-mail: astreit@socrates.berkeley.edu.

STREJAN, GILL HENRIC, immunologist, educator; b. Galati, Romania, Sept. 24, 1930; s. Henric S. and Rita (Kleiner) S.; m. Odette Isabella Fischer, May 30, 1963 MS, U. Bucharest, Romania, 1953; PhD, Hebrew U., Jerusalem, 1965. Postdoctoral fellow Calif. Inst. Tech., Pasadena, 1965-68; asst. prof. U. Western Ont., London, Can., 1968-73, assoc. prof. Can., 1973-80, prof. Can., 1980-96, prof. emeritus Can., 1996—; scientist J.P. Robarts Rsch. Inst., Can., 1994—. Author: (chpt.) Modern Concepts and Developments in Immediate Hypersensitivity, 1978; contbr. articles to profl. jours. Grantee Med. Rsch. Coun., Can., 1968-96, Multiple Sclerosis Soc. Can., 1981-2001. Mem. Am. Assn. Immunologists, Can. Soc. Immunology, Sigma Xi. Office: U Western Ont Dept Micro & Immun Health Sci Ctr London ON Canada N6A 5C1 E-mail: gstrejan@uwo.ca.

STREJCEK, ELIZABETH GEIERMAN, reading specialist, educator; b. Chgo., Dec. 7, 1948; d. Aloysius Herman and Lillian Elizabeth (Cowan) Geierman; m. George Joseph Strejcek, Jan. 27, 1971; children: James Edwin, Theodore Eliot. BA in History, U. Ill., Chgo., 1971, MA in Ednl. Leadership, 1981. Cert. reading specialist, Ill. Subs. tchr. pub. schs., Berwyn, Ill., 1972-74; tchr. reading grades 5-8 South Berwyn Pub. Sch., 1974-77; tchr. reading lab. grades 9-12 Bolinbrook (Ill.) High Sch., 1979-83; tchr. reading grades 7-8 Westview Mid. Sch., Romeoville, Ill., 1983-84, tchr. grades 6-8, 1984-85; chpt. I reading tchr. grades K-5 Northview Elem. Sch., Bolingbrook, 1985-91; tchr. grades 9-10 Morton East H.S., Cicero, 1991—, tchr. spl. program on attendance, chpt. I-title I tchr., 1991, 94, tchr. truancy and attendance program, 1993—, mem. various coms., 1991—. Presenter lectures, demonstrations on reading and writing and using technology in classroom, 1989—. Title I Summer Sch. Curriculum (reading and writing), 1997. Mem. AAUW, Internat. Reading Assn., Ill. Reading Coun. (bd. dirs. 1994-95), Ill. Computing Educators, Nat. Coun. Tchrs. English, Czech Cache, Secondary Reading League (pres. 1993-95, 99-2002), Ill. Title 1 Assn. (pres. 2001-2002). Avocations: pottery/ceramics, computer applications, reading, drawing. Office: 2423 S Austin Blvd Cicero IL 60804-2616

STREKOWSKI, LUCJAN, chemistry educator; b. Grabowo, Poland, June 21, 1945; came to U.S., 1981; s. Antoni and Janina (Chrapowicz) S.; m. Alewtina Smirnova, Oct. 14, 1967; children: Rafal, Anna. BS in Polymer Chemistry with distinction, Mendeleev Inst. Chemistry, Moscow, 1967; PhD in Organic Chemistry, Polish Acad. Scis., 1972; DSc in Chemistry, Adam Mickiewicz U., Poznan, Poland, 1976. Instr. organic chemistry Adam Mickiewicz U., Poznan, 1971-72, asst. prof. dept. chemistry, 1972-78, assoc. prof.

dept. chemistry, 1978-81; rsch. assoc. dept. chemistry U. Fla., Gainesville, 1981-84; asst. prof. dept. chemistry Ga. State U., Atlanta, 1984-89, assoc. prof. dept. chemistry, 1989-96, prof. dept. chem., 1996—. Vis. prof. U. Fla., Gainesville, 1979-80, 81, Australian Nat. U., 1980, U. Kans., Lawrence, 1972-73. Editor: Pyridine-Metal Complexes, Vol. 14, Part 6, 1985; N.Am. editor Heterocyclic Comms.; mem. editl. bd. Arkivoc; contbr. more than 200 articles to profl. jours.; patentee in field. Recipient award, Polish Ministry Sci., 1997, Polish Chem. Soc., 1973, Polish Acad. Scis., 1972, Ga. State U., 1993; grantee Am. Chem. Soc.-Petroleum Rsch. Fund, 1985—, Solvay Pharms., 1992—93, Nat. Diagnostics, 1991—93, NIAID/NIMH, 1988—89, Rohm and Hass Co., 1988, Am. Cancer Soc., 1987—89, Rsch. Corp., 1985—94, Milheim Found. Cancer Rsch., 1985—86, DuPont Co., 1996—2000, Small Bus. Innovation Rsch. Program, 2000—. Mem. Am. Chem. Soc., Internat. Soc. Heterocyclic Chemistry, Internat. Acad. Scis. of Nature and Soc. (mem. presidium). Avocation: classical music. Office: Ga State Univ Dept Chemistry Atlanta GA 30303 E-mail: lucjan@gsu.edu.

STRELAU, RENATE, historical researcher, artist; b. Berlin, Feb. 1, 1951; came to U.S., 1960; d. Werner Ernst and Gerda Gertrud (Bargel) S. BA, U. Calif., Berkeley, 1974; cert. Arabic lang. proficiency, Johns Hopkins U., 1976; MA, Am. U., 1985, MFA, 1991. Rsch. asst. Iranian Embassy, Washington, 1976-80. One-woman shows include Cafe Espresso, Berkeley, Calif., 1973, Riggs Bank, Arlington, Va., 1994-95; exhibited in group shows at Watkins Gallery, Washington, 1999; represented in permanent collections C. Law Watkins Meml. Collection, Am. U. Mem. Am. Hist. Assn., Orgn. Am. Historians, Soc. for Historians Am. Fgn. Rels. (life). Office: PO Box 12655 Arlington VA 22219-2655 E-mail: strelau@renatestrelau.com.

STRENA, ROBERT VICTOR, university research laboratory manager; b. Seattle, June 28, 1929; s. Robert Lafayette Peel and Mary Oliva (Holmes) S.; m. Rita Mae Brodovsky, Aug. 1957; children: Robert Victor, Adrienne Amelia. AB, Stanford U., 1952. Survey mathematician Hazen Engring., San Jose, Calif., 1952-53; field engr. Menlo Sanitary Dist., Menlo Park, 1954-55; ind. fin. reporter Los Altos, 1953-59; asst. dir. Hansen Labs. Stanford U., 1959-93, asst. dir. emeritus Ginzton Lab., 1993—. Ind. fin. cons., Los Altos, 1965—; mem. restoration adv. bd., Moffett Fed. Airfield, 1994—. Active Edn. System Politics, Los Altos, 1965-80, local Boy Scouts Am., 1968-80, Maj. USAR, 1948-70. Mem. AAAS, Mus. Soc., Big X (Los Altos), Cherry Chase Golf Club. Republican. Avocations: golf, sailing. Home: 735 Raymundo Ave Los Altos CA 94024-3139 Office: Stanford U Ginzton Lab Stanford CA 94305

STRENG, WILLIAM PAUL, lawyer, educator; b. Sterling, Ill., Oct. 17, 1937; s. William D. and Helen Marie (Conklen) S.; children: Sarah, John. BA, Wartburg Coll., 1959; JD, Northwestern U., 1962. Bar: Iowa 1962, Ill. 1962, Ohio 1964, Tex. 1975. Law clk. to U.S. circuit judge Lester L. Cecil, Cin., 1963-64; asso. firm Taft, Stettinius & Hollister, 1964-70; atty.-advisor Office Sec. Tax Policy, Office Tax Legis. Counsel, Dept. Treasury, Washington, 1970-71; dep. gen. counsel Export-Import Bank U.S., 1971-73; prof. law Sch. Law, So. Methodist U., Dallas, 1973-80; vis. prof. Coll. Law Ohio State U., Columbus, 1977; partner firm Bracewell & Patterson, Houston, 1980-85; Vinson & Elkins prof. of law U. Houston Law Ctr, 1985—. Vis. prof. Rice U., NYU Law Sch., 1990, U. Tex. Sch. Law, 2002; disting. vis. prof. U. Hong Kong Law Faculty, 1992; Fulbright prof. U. Stockholm Law Faculty, 1993; vis. fellow law faculty Victoria U., Wellington, New Zealand, 1996; vis. law lectr. U. Leiden, The Netherlands, 1997, The Netherlands, 98, The Netherlands, 2000; cons. Bracewell & Patterson, 1985—; lectr. various confs. Am. Law Inst., World Trade Inst., Practicing Law Inst., Internat. Fiscal Assn., ABA, Tex. State Bar. Author: International Business Transactions-Tax and Legal Handbook, 1978, Estate Planning, 1991, 2d edit., 1997, International Business Planning: Law and Taxation, 6 vols., 1982, 95, 96, 97, 98, 99, 2000, 01, 02, Tax Planning for Retirement, 2d edit., 2001, 02, Doing Business in China, 1990, 93, 94, 95, 96, Federal Income Taxation of Corporations and Shareholders--Forms, 1995, 96, 97, 98, 99, 2000, 01, 02, Choice of Entity, 1994, 99, U.S. International Estate Planning, 1996, 98, 99, 2000, 01; contbr. articles to profl. jours. Served with USMC, 1962. Lutheran. Home: 1903 Dunstan Rd Houston TX 77005-1619 Office: U Houston Law Ctr Houston TX 77204-6060 E-mail: wstreng@uh.edu.

STRENGTH, DANNA ELLIOTT, nursing educator; b. Texarkana, Ark., Aug. 20, 1937; d. Clyde Olin and Willie (Stephens) Elliott; m. Vernon E. Strength, Dec. 27, 1960; 1 child, Van E. BSN, Tex. Christian U., 1959; MSN, Washington U., 1968; DNSc, Cath. U. of Am., 1986. Instr. The Cath. Univ. of Am., Washington, 1976-84; asst. prof. Georgetown Univ., 1984-87; assoc. prof. Tex. Christian Univ., Fort Worth, 1987-2000. Edn. leader Profl. Seminars Internat.; edn. cons. Transcultural Edn. Corp.; med. com. Ft. Worth Sister Cities Internat., Budapest, Hungary, and Bandung, Indonesia. Contbr. articles to profl. jours. Recipient Edn. in a Global Soc. award to study health care in Indonesia and Scandinavia, 1992-94. Mem. ANA, Tex. Nurses' Assn., Am. Assn. for History of Nursing (chairperson nominating com., bylaws com.), Lucy Harris Linn Inst. (treas.), Sigma Theta Tau (Beta Alpha rsch. award). Home: 305 Birchwood Ln Fort Worth TX 76108-4601

STRENGTH, JANIS GRACE, management executive, educator; b. Ozark, Ala., Jan. 31, 1934; d. James Marion and Mary Belle (Riley) Grace; m. Robert Samuel Strength, Sept. 12, 1954; children: Stewart A., James Houston (dec.), Robert David (dec.), James Steven (dec.) BS in Home Econs. and Edn., Auburn U., 1956; MA in Edn., Washington U., St. Louis, 1978, MA in Adminstrn., 1980. Home economist Gulf Power Co., Pensacola, Fla., 1956-59; tchr. sci. Northside Jr. High Sch., Greenwood, S.C., 1961-68; tchrs. home econs. Greenwood High Sch., 1968-70; chairperson dept. sci. Parkway West Jr. High Sch., Chesterfield, Mo., 1975-82; tchr. sci. Parkway West High Sch., 1982-88; v.p.-sec. Product Safety Mgmt. Inc., Gulf Breeze, Fla., 1989—2001; ret., 2001. Chairperson dist. Phys. Scis. Curriculum Com., 1978-85, Sci. Fair Placement Com., 1978-82, Gifted Edn., 1983-84; leader Phys. Sci. Summer Workshops, Safety Sci. Lab. Workshop; sponsor Nat. Jr. Honor Soc., Parkway West Jr. Class. Supt. youth dept. Sunday sch. Greentrails Meth. Ch., sponsor summer camp; vol. fundraiser March of Dimes, Cerebral Palsy, Multiple Schlorosis, Cancer funds; judge Parkway/Monsanto/St. Louis Post Dispatch Sci. Fairs, 1978—; mem. citizens action com. Parkway Sch. Bd., 1980-84. Mem. NEA, Nat. Sci. Tchrs. Assn., Ladies Golf Assn. (sec. 1998-99), Santa Rosa Women's Club (pres. 1998-2000), Tiger Point Country Club (Gulf Breeze), Raintree Country Club (Hillsboro, Mo.). Republican. Methodist.

STRENSKI, JAMES B. retired communications executive; b. Jan. 2, 1930; m. Jane E.; 5 children. Grad., Marquette U. Pub. info. officer USN, NATO; with Pub. Communications Inc., Chgo.; chmn., chief exec. officer Pub. Communications Inc, Tampa, Fla. Cons. to nonprofit, health care and social agys., pub. and pvt. corps., fin. and acad. instns.; lectr. to industry groups, trade assns., bus. orgns. Contbr. more than 70 articles on pub. rels. to jours. in field. Mem. Tampa Jesuit High Sch. Found., Tampa Downtown Partnership Bd., Hillsborough County Affordable Housing Com., Bus. Adv. Coun., Coll. of Journalism of Marquette U.; bd. dirs. Chgo. Leadership Coun. for Met. Open Communities, Tampa Goodwill Industries-Suncoast; program chmn. Tampa Pkwy. Assn.; pub. rels. chmn. Paint Your Heart Out, Tampa, U. Tampa Bd. Fellows. Mem. Worldcom Group, Inc. (founder, exec. com.).*

STRETCH, JOHN JOSEPH, social work educator, management and evaluation consultant; b. St. Louis, Feb. 24, 1935; s. John Joseph and Theresa Carmelita (Fleming) S.; children: Paul, Leonmarie, Sylvan, Adrienne, Sharonalice; m. Barbara Ann Stewart, Mar. 16, 1985; children: Margaret, Thomas. AB, Maryknoll Coll., Glen Ellyn, Ill., 1957; MSW, Washington U., St. Louis, 1961; PhD, Tulane U., 1967; MBA, St. Louis U., 1980. Lic. clin. social worker, 1990. Instr. Tulane U., 1962-67, asst. prof., 1967-69; assoc. prof. social work St. Louis U., 1969-72, prof., 1972—87, asst. dean Sch. Social Service, 1976-87, dir. doctoral studies, 1976-94, dir. MSW. program, 1985-86, bd. dirs., mem. exec. com. Ctr. for Social Justice, mem. instnl. rev. bd. Sch. Social Svc., 1987—92; dir. rsch. Social Welfare Planning Coun. Met. New Orleans, 1962-69. Cons. to United Way Met. St. Louis, Cath. Charities of Archdiocese of St. Louis, Cath. Svcs. for Children and Youth, Full Achievement, Mo. Province of S.J., Cath. Commn. on Housing, Cath. Family Svcs., Youth Emergency Svcs., Mo. State Dept. Social Svcs., U. Mo. Extension Svc., St. Joseph's Home for Boys, Marian Hall Ctr. for Adolescent Girls, Boys Town-Girls Town of Mo., A World of Difference, Anti Defamation League of B'nai Brith, Prog. Youth Ctr., Foster Care Coalition of Greater St. Louis, Rankin-Jordan Children's Rehab. Hosp., 1999-2000, Old Man River; expert witness on homeless U.S. House Select Com. on Families, Children and Youth, 1987; mem. resource spl. task force on homeless Office of Sec. U.S. Dept. Housing and Urban Devel., 1989; survey design cons. U.S. Office of The Insp. Gen., 1990; methodology expert on homelessness U.S. Census Bur., 1989; expert homeless policy General Acctg. Office hearings, 1992; chair Mo. Assn. for Social Welfare Low Income Housing, 1982—; mem., chmn. St. Louis Low Income Housing Preservation Com., 1985—; mem. Comprehensive Housing Affordabiltiy Strategies (CHAS) Mo. Statewide Planning Group, Missouri Housing Devel. CHAS citizen's com., State of Mo. Affordable House Task Force, Mo. Housing Devel. Corp., 1998—, Mo. Inst. of Psychiatry, 1995, Univ. City sch. dist., 1990; mgmt. cons. People's Issues Task Force Agricultural div. Monsanto Chemical Inc., 1992, Nat. Conf. of Christians and Jews, regional office, 1990-92; vis. prof. Nat. Catholic U. of Am. Sch. of Soc. Svcs., 1991, 92, U. Bristol, England, 1992, U. Calif. Sch. of Pub. Health, Berkeley, 1990; cons. Mo. Speaker of the Ho. statewide legislative task force, 1990-92, Russian Am. Summer U., 2000; statewide grant project reviewer emergency shelter grant program Mo. Dept. Social Svcs., 1989—, chair, 2002; homeless svcs. grant reviewer City of St. Louis, 1996-97. Editl. bd. Social Work, 1968-74, Health Progress, 1988—01; manuscript referee Jour. Social Svc. Rsch., 1977-99; mgmt. and evaluation content referee Wadsworth Press, Human Svcs. Press, Allyn and Bacon Press; editor, contbr. books and profl. jours. and books. Bd. dirs. Beyond Housing, Inc. 1985—, pres. bd. dirs., 1993-95; bd. Housing Comes First, 1997—; mem. Mo. Assn. Social Welfare, 1980—, DuBourg Soc. of St. Louis U., 1988; bd. mem. St. Louis U. Ctr. for Social Justice, 1990—; mem. Salvation Army Family Haven, 1987, mem. adv. bd., 1988-92; chmn. United Way of Greater St. Louis venture grant com., 1988-91, mem. allocation com., 1985-95, mem. process and rev. com., 1991-93, inter-orgnl. priorities com., 1991-93; mem. leadership coun. Success By Six, 1990—; organizer Mo. State Nat. Coalition for the Homeless; appointee St. Louis U. Instl. Representation nat. Jesuits social Concern Group, 1993—; mem. exec. and support tng. group, St. Louis U., 1987—92; mem. instnl. rev. bd. Institutional Rev. Bd., St. Louis U. Med. Ctr., 1996-98. NIMH Career Leadership Devel. fellow, 1965-67, Fed. Ednl. grantee Ill. Sch. Sys., 2002; recipient Scholar of Yr. award Sch. Social Svc., St. Louis U., 1987; named Vol. of Yr. Ecumenical Housing Prodn. Corp., 1990; Presdl. scholar Sch. Social Svc., 1992. Mem. AAUP (St. Louis U. chpt. exec. com. 1990—, pres. 1994—), ACLU, Acad. Cert. Social Workers (charter mem.), Nat. Assn. Social Workers, Mo. Assn. for Social Welfare (bd. dirs., Outstanding State-Wide Mem. of Yr. 1987), Coun. on Social Work Edn., Common Cause, Amnesty Internat., Nat. Consumer's Union (com. on vital and health stats.), U.S. Census Bur. (subcom. on health stats. for minorities and other spl. populations of U.S. 1988—). Democrat. Roman Catholic. Home: 9100 Litzsinger Rd Saint Louis MO 63144-2214 Office: 3550 Lindell Blvd Saint Louis MO 63103-1021 *My entire professional life has been in the field of social work. My personal and professional values are derived from a dual commitment to empower the uniqueness of individuals and to enhance the development of caring communities. These goals have organized and directed my professional practice, teaching and writing. I believe that the profession of social work has a unique and singular mission in society. That mission is to advocate for and consciously bring about the social development of all people.*

STRETESKY, SUSAN M. pharmaceutical company executive; b. Newport News, Va., Dec. 2, 1969; d. Tony and Jeannie Stretesky. BFA, U. Okla., 1991. Sales rep. Merck & Co., Inc., Tulsa, Okla., 1992-95, sr. rep., 1996, sr. health scis. assoc. respiratory diseases, 1997, sr. HIV specialist, 1998-99, mgr. coronary syndrome specialists, 2000—01, mgr. human health, 2001—. Republican. Avocations: travel, outdoor activities, movies, arts.

STREU, RAYMOND OLIVER, financial planner, securities executive; b. Hereford, Tex., July 7, 1931; s. William Urlin and Yetta May (Hackworth) S.; m. Joan Eliz Hardwick, Nov. 24, 1953 (div. Oct. 1963); children: William Raymond, Ronald Hardwick, Russell Francis; m. Wanda Mae Daves, Sept. 2, 1964 (div. Sept. 1990); children: Randall Oliver; m. Doris Francis Wright, Mar. 6, 1993. BBA, Tex. Tech U., 1952. Cert. financial planner. Co-owner Streu Hardware Co., Hereford, 1948-60; agt., broker Justice Real Estate, 1960-62; pres. Mark IV Realtors, 1962-73; rep., div. mgr. Waddell & Reed, Inc., 1965-73, divsn. mgr., 1973-78; br. mgr. E.F. Hutton Fin. Svcs., Amarillo, Tex., 1978-83, Pvt. Ledger Fin. Svc., San Diego, 1983-85, Associated Planners Sec. Corp., L.A., 1985-87; pres. Asset Planning Group, Amarillo, Tex., 1983—; br. mgr. Sun Am. Securities Corp., Phoenix, 1987-98, United Planner Fin. Svcs. Am., Scottsdale, 1998—. Leadership chmn. Llano Estacado coun. Boy Scouts Am., 1972-73; dir. Amarillo chpt. Am. Heart Assn., 1993-98. Lt. comdr. USNR, 1952-66. Mem. Financial Planning Assn. (pres. local chpt. 1988-89), Inst. Cert. Fin. Planners, High Plains Eye Bank (life), Jaycees, Lions (pres. Amarillo chpt. 1975-76). Republican. Presbyterian. Avocations: sailing, dry fly fishing. Office: Asset Planning Group 1616 S Kentucky St Ste C-350 Amarillo TX 79102-2284 Business E-Mail: ostreu@moneydoctor.net.

STREVEY, GUY DONALD, insurance company executive; b. Norcatur, Kans., Mar. 8, 1932; s. Guy Ross Strevey and Maxine Elizabeth (Johnson) Gruse.; m. Irene Franklyn Corey Nov. 7, 1953; children: Richard A., Janet E. Bolte, Philip E., Melinda K. Halvorson. BS, Okla. A&M U., 1953. Cert. CFP, CLU, ChFC. Agt. Penn Mut. Life Ins. Co., Tulsa, 1955-62, regional mgr., 1958-62, gen. agt. Omaha, 1962-69, agt., 1969—; ptnr. Strevey and Assocs., 1979—; agt. Various Cos., 1979—; registered rep. Hornor, Townsend & Kent, Inc., 1985—. Bd. dirs. Citipower LLC: A Del. Corp.; cons. Appalachian Gas Assocs. I-XII; cons. Fortuna I Natural Gas Drilling Program. Deacon Hillcrest Bapt. Ch., Omaha, 1960, Westside Bapt. Ch., Omaha, 1978, chmn., 1979-81. 1st lt. U.S. Army, 1953-55. Mem. NAIFA (Nat. Quality award 1970-94), Soc. Fin. Svc. Profls., Nat. Assn. Ins. & Fin. Advisors, Million Dollar Roundtable (life), F.P.A. Assoc. (pres. 1997—, chmn. bd. 1998-99, named Mem. of Yr. 2002). Republican. Avocations: sports, traveling. Home: 3518 S 106th St Omaha NE 68124-3614 Office: Strevey & Assocs 11422 Miracle Hills Dr Ste 508 Omaha NE 68154-4420

STREVEY, TRACY ELMER, JR. army officer, surgeon, physician executive; b. Shorewood, Wis., Apr. 24, 1933; s. Tracy Elmer and Margaret (Rees) S.; m. Victoria Crowley (div.); children: Virginia Ann, Tracy Elmer III, Andrew Victor; m. Elizabeth Sommers; children: Stephanie Jean, James Sommers. Student, Pomona Coll., 1951-54; MD, U. So. Calif., 1958; student, Armed Forces Staff Coll., 1970-71, U.S. Army War Coll., 1977-78. Diplomate Am. Bd. Surgery, Am. Bd. Thoracic Surgery. Intern Los Angeles County Gen. Hosp., 1958-59; commd. officer U.S. Army, 1959, advanced through grades to maj. gen., 1983; resident in gen. surgery Letterman Gen. Hosp., San Francisco, 1962-66; resident in thoracic and cardiovascular surgery Walter Reed Gen. Hosp., Washington, 1968-70; comdg. officer 757 Med. Detachment OA, Ludwigsburg, Germany, 1959-61; ward officer orthopaedic svc. 75th Sta. Hosp., Stuttgart, Fed. Republic Germany, 1961-62; chief profl. svc., chief surgery 85th Evacuation Hosp., Qui Nhon, Vietnam, 1967; comdg. officer 3d Surg. Hosp., Dong Tam, Vietnam, 1967-68; asst. chief thoracic and cardiovascular surgery service Fitzsimons Army Med Ctr., Denver, 1971-73, chief thoracic and cardiovascular surgery service, 1973-75; asst. dir. med. activities and dir. Profl. Edn. Gorgas Hosp., Panama Canal Zone, 1975-77; chief dept. surgery Walter Reed Army Med. Ctr., Washington, 1978-81; comdr. Brooke Army Med. Ctr., Ft. Sam Houston, Tex., 1981-83, Tripler Army Med. Ctr., Hawaii, 1983-86, U.S. Army Health Svcs. Command, San Antonio, 1986-88; ret. U.S. Army, 1988; CEO Nassau County Med. Ctr., 1988-93; pres., CEO N.Y. Hosp Med. Ctr. Queens, N.Y.C., 1993-94; v.p. N.Y. Hosp. Care Network, 1994-95; v.p. for med. affairs Sisters of Mercy Health Sys., St. Louis, 1995-99; cons., 1999—. Asst. clin. prof. surgery U. Colo. Med. Ctr., Denver, 1973-75; prof. surgery Uniformed Services U. Health Scis., Bethesda, 1978— , vice chmn. dept. surgery, 1978-81 Contbr. articles to profl. jours. Mem. reg. bd. Am. Heart Assn. Decorated D.S.M., Legion of Merit with 2 oak leaf clusters, Meritorious Service medal with 2 oak leaf clusters, Purple Heart, Army Commendation Medal for Valor, Vietnam Cross of Gallantry with Palm; recipient Outstanding Service award U. So. Calif. Med. Alumni Assn., 1983 Fellow ACS, Am. Coll. Chest Physicians, Am. Coll. Cardiology, Am. Coll. Physician Execs. (disting.); mem. Assn. Mil. Surgeons U.S., Soc. Thoracic Surgeons, Western Thoracic Surg. Assn., Am. Assn. Thoracic Surgery, Masons. Avocations: ham radio; scuba diving; golf; computer science. Home and Office: 1509 Woodgate Dr Saint Louis MO 63131-4724

STRIBLIN, LORI ANN, critical care nurse, Medicare coordinator, nursing educator; b. Valley, Ala., Sept. 23, 1962; d. James Author and Dorothy Jane (Cole) Burt; m. Thomas Edward Striblin, Oct. 26, 1984; children: Natalie Nicole, Crystal Danielle. AAS in Nursing, So. Union State Jr. Coll., Valley, Ala., 1992. RN, Ala.; cert. ACLS, BLS, in fitness nutrition ICS. Surg. staff nurse East Ala. Med. Ctr., Opelika, 1992-93, surg. charge nurse, 1993-95, critical care ICU staff nurse, 1993-95; RN case mgr. East Ala. Home Care, 1995-96; staff devel. coord., medicare coord. Lanett (Ala.) Geriatric Ctr., 1996-97; case mgr. Lanier Home Health Svcs., Valley, Ala., 1996-97; med. advisor Nu Image Weight Loss Ctr., Opelika, 1996-97, nurse case mgr. weight loss ctr., counselor, diet educator, 1996-98; RN case mgr. Chattahoochie Hospice, Valley, 1998; case mgr. Chattahoochiee Hospice, 1998; critical care nurse cardiovasc. ICU and telementry unit East Ala. Med. Ctr., Opelika, 1999—2002; dialysis nurse Frecinus Dialysis Corp., Valley, Ala., 2002—. Clin. instr. educator So. Union C.C., Valley, 1994-97. Mem. AACN, Ala. State Nurses Assn. Baptist. Avocations: crafts, horseback riding, hiking, swimming, reading, arts. Home: PO Box 1103 Valley AL 36854 Office: FMC Dialysis Med Park Valley AL 36854

STRICK, SADIE ELAINE, psychologist; b. Masontown, Pa., May 5, 1929; d. Michael and Mary (Oziemblowski) Wierzbicki; m. John Mackovjak, Dec. 31, 1947 (dec. Mar. 1972); children: Deborah, Susan; m. Ellis Strick, Aug. 11, 1974. BSW, U. Pitts., 1975, MEd, 1977, PhD, 1981. Lic. psychologist; fellow, diplomate Am. Bd. Med. Psychotherapists. Psychologist I Mayview State Hosp., Bridgeville, Pa., 1984-87; owner Counseling & Behavior Specialists, P.C., Pitts., 1981—. Mem. C.G. Jung Ednl. Ctr., Pitts., 1980—; guest speaker Compassionate Friends, Pitts., 1986—, Womens Career Conv., Pitts., 1982. Bd. dirs. OAR/Allegheny, Pitts., 1981-82. Fellow Pa. Psychol. Assn.; mem. APA. Avocations: writing, walking, travel, gourmet cooking, reading. Home: 2160 Greentree Rd Apt 605W Pittsburgh PA 15220-1407 Office: Counseling and Behavior Specialists PC 429 Forbes Ave Ste 1614 Pittsburgh PA 15219-1604

STRICKER, LAWRENCE J. psychologist; b. Jamaica, N.Y., Aug. 19, 1933; s. Lawrence and Cora Irene Stricker; m. Brigitte M. Hammond, Dec. 29, 2000. BS, NYU, 1955, AM, 1957, PhD, 1961. Rsch. analyst Prudential Ins. Co., Newark, 1955-58; rsch. scientist Ednl. Testing Svc., Princeton, N.J., 1960—. Vis. prof. New Sch. for Social Rsch., N.Y.C., 1977, 79-98, CUNY, 1970-71, 75-76; vis. lectr. Princeton U., 1992. Contbr. articles to profl. jours.; assoc. editor Personality and Social Psychology Bull., 1977-81. Fellow APA (coun. reps. 1993-96), Am. Psychol. Soc. (charter); mem. Soc. Multivariate Exptl. Psychology (sec.-treas. 1976-80), Soc. Exptl. Social Psychology. Home: 37 W 12th St Apt 2A New York NY 10011 Office: Ednl Testing Svc Rosedale Rd Princeton NJ 08541 E-mail: lstricker@ets.org.

STRICKER, STEVE, golfer; b. Edgerton, Wis., Feb. 23, 1967; m. Nicki Stricker; 1 child Bobbi Maria. Student, U. Ill. Named winner, Kemper Open, 1996, Motorola Western Open, 1996, Victoria Open, Can., 1990, Can. PGA, 1993, WGC-Accenture Math Play Championship, 2001. Office: c/o PGA Tour 112 PGA Tour Blvd Ponte Vedra Beach FL 32082

STRICKHOLM, PETER WILLIAM, composer, environmentalist; b. Mpls., Jan. 3, 1958; BA magna cum laude, Colo. Coll., 1980; MusM in Composition, U. Colo., 1990; MA in Biology, Ind. U., 1995. Composer over 25 works for piano, chamber music, jazz, and orch. Mem. Nat. Alliance for the Mentally Ill, Ind. and Colo., 1988—. Mem. Nat. Speleological Soc., Sierra Club (program chair Uplands group Hoosier chpt. 1994-98), Phi Beta Kappa. Avocations: wilderness hiking, photography, jazz piano, ethnomusicology. Home: 351 S Madison St Bloomington IN 47403-2423

STRICKLAND, ARVARH EUNICE, history educator; b. Hattiesburg, Miss., July 6, 1930; s. Eunice and Clotiel (Marshall) S.; m. Willie Pearl Elmore, June 17, 1951; children: Duane Arvarh, Bruce Elmore. BA, Tougaloo Coll., 1951; MA, U. Ill., 1953, PhD, 1962. Tchr. Hattiesburg Schs., 1951-52; instr. Tuskegee Inst., 1955-56; prin. supr. Madison County Schs., Canton, Miss., 1956-59; asst. prof. history Chgo. State U., 1962-65, assoc. prof. history, 1965-68, prof., 1968-69, U. Mo., Columbia, 1969-96, prof. emeritus, 1996—, chmn. dept. history, 1980-83, interim dir. black studies program, 1994-96, sr. faculty assoc., Office of V.P. acad. affairs, 1987-88, assoc. v.p. acad. affairs, 1989-91. Author: History of the Chicago Urban League, 1966, reprint, 2001, (with Reich and Biller) Building the United States, 1971, (with Reich) The Black American Experience to 1877, 1974, The Black American Experience since 1877, 1974; editor: Working with Carter G. Woodson, (with Lorenzo J. Greene) The Father of Black History: A Diary, 1928-1930, 1989, Selling Black History for Carter G. Woodson: A Diary, 1930-33, 1996, (with Robert E. Weems) The African American Experience: A Historiographical and Bibliographical Guide, 2000. Commr. Planning and Zoning, Columbia, Mo., 1977-80, Boone County Home Rule Charter, 1982, Mo. Peace Officers Standards and Tng. Commn., 1988-89; co-chmn. Mayors Com. to Commemorate Contbns. of Black Columbians, Columbia, 1981; mem. exec. subcom. Mayor's Ad Hoc Election '82 Com., 1982; bd. dirs. Harry S. Truman Library Inst., 1987-96. Recipient Disting. Svc. award Ill. Hist. Soc., 1957, Byler Disting. Prof. award U. Mo., 1994, St. Louis Am.'s Educator of Yr. award, 1994, Disting. Faculty award U. Mo.-Columbia Alumni Assn., 1995, Tougaloo Coll. Alumni Hall of Fame, 1995, Alumni Achievement U. Ill. Coll. Liberal Arts and Scis., 1997, Disting. Svc. award State Hist. Soc. Mo., 1997. Mem. Orgn. Am. Historians, Am. Hist. Assn., Assn. Study Afro-Am. Life and History (Carter Godwin Woodson Scholars medallion 1999), So. Hist. Assn., State Hist. Soc. Mo. (Disting. Svc. award 1997), Boone County Hist. Soc. (bd. dirs. 1998—, 2d v.p. 1999), Kiwanis, Alpha Phi Alpha, Phi Alpha Theta (internat. v.p. 1991-93, pres. 1994-95, chair adv. bd. 1996-97, Disting. Svc. award 1997). Democrat. Methodist. E-mail: stricklanda@missouri.edu. Home: 4100 Defoe Dr Columbia MO 65203-0252 Office: U Mo Dept History 101 Read Hall Columbia MO 65211-7500

STRICKLAND, BONNIE RUTH, psychologist, educator; b. Louisville, Nov. 24, 1936; d. Roy E. and Billie P. (Whitfield) S. BS, Ala. Coll., 1958; MS, Ohio State U., 1960, PhD (USPHS fellow), 1962. Diplomate: clin. psychology Am. Bd. Examiners in Profl. Psychology. From asst. to asso. prof. psychology Emory U., Atlanta, 1962-73, dean of women, 1964-67; prof. psychology U. Mass., Amherst, 1973—, chmn. dept. psychology, 1976-77, 78-82, assoc. to chancellor, 1983-84. Mem. adv. coun. NIMH, 1984-87; Sigma Xi nat. lectr., 1991-93. Adv. editor numerous psychology jours., acad. pub. houses; contbg. author texts personality theory.; contbr. of numerous articles on social personality and clin. psychology to profl. jours.; contbg. author of two citation classics. Recipient Outstanding Faculty award Emory U., 1968-69; Chancellor's medal disting. service U. Mass., 1983. Fellow APA (pres. divsn. clin. psychology 1983, chmn. bd. profl. affairs 1980-83, chmn. policy and planning bd. 1983-85, pres. 1987, bd. dirs. 1986-87, Outstanding Leadership award 1992, Disting. Contbns. and Psychology in the Pub. Interest award 1999, Presdl. Citation 2001), Am. Psychol. Soc. (founder 1988, bd. dirs. 1989-93), Am. Assn. Applied and Preventive Psychology (founder 1990, bd. dirs. 1990-94, pres. 1992-94), Acad. Clin. Psychology, Coun. Grad. Depts. Psychology (chmn. 1982-83). Home: 558 Federal St Belchertown MA 01007-9754 Office: U Mass Dept Psychology Amherst MA 01003-7710

STRICKLAND, DOROTHY, education educator; BS, Newark State Coll.; MA, PhD, NYU. Elem. sch. tchr. N.J. pub. sch. sys., reading cons., learning disabilities specialist; prof. edn. Rutgers U., New Brunswick, NJ, 1985—; Prof. edn. Samuel Dewitt Proctor, 2002—. Active in numerous state and nat. adv. bds. Author: Language Literacy and the Child, Process Reading and Writing: A Literature Based Approach, The Administration and Supervision of Reading Programs, Educating Black Children: America's Challenge, Family Storybook Reading, Listen Children: An Anthology of Black Literature, Families: An Anthology of Poetry for Young Children, Teaching Phonics Today, 1998, Beginning Reading and Writing, 2000, Supporting Struggling Readers and Writers, 2002. Inducted into the Reading Hall of Fame, pres., 1997-98. Mem. Nat. Coun. Tchrs. English (Rewey Belle Inglis award for Outstanding Woman in English Education Annual Conv., rsch. award, Outstanding Educator in Lang. Arts award 1998), Internat. Reading Assn. (past pres., Outstanding Tchr. Educator of reading award). Home: 131 Coccio Dr West Orange NJ 07052-4121 Office: Rutgers U Dept Edn Grad Sch Edn New Brunswick NJ 08903

STRICKLAND, HUGH ALFRED, lawyer; b. Rockford, Ill., May 3, 1931; s. Hugh and Marie (Elmer) S.; m. Donna E. McDonald, Aug. 11, 1956; children: Amy Alice, Karen Ann. AB, Knox Coll., 1953; JD, Chgo. Kent Coll. Law, 1959. Bar: Ill. 1960. Partner firm McDonald, Strickland & Clough, Carrollton, Ill., 1961—; asst. atty. gen., 1960-67; spl. asst. gen., 1967-69; pres. McDonald Title Co. Mem. Greene County Welfare Svcs. Com., 1963—. Ill. Heart Assn., 1961-65; trustee Thomas H. Boyd Meml. Hosp., 1972-95. With AUS, 1953-55. Recipient award for meritorious service Am. Heart Assn., 1964 Fellow Ill. Bar Found. (charter); mem. ABA, Ill. Bar Assn., Greene County Bar Assn. (past pres.), Southwestern Bar Assn. (past pres.), Ill. Def. Counsel, Am. Judicature Soc., Def. Rsch. Inst., Elks Club, Westlake Country Club (v.p. 1968-70, dir.), Big Sand Lake Country Club, Phi Delta Theta, Phi Delta Phi. Methodist. Home: 827 7th St Carrollton IL 62016-1421 Office: 524 N Main St PO Box 71 Carrollton IL 62016-1027 Fax: 217-942-3178. E-mail: has3@irtc.net., lawyers@irtc.net.

STRICKLAND, JOHN ARTHUR VAN, minister; b. Detroit, Sept. 25, 1952; s. Maurice Alexander and Irma (Surovy) S.; m. Constance Fillmore, Dec. 24, 1976 (div. Aug. 1984); m. Brenda Cecile Bunch, Nov. 23, 1985. BA cum laude, Ga. State U., 1974; ministry program, Unity Ministerial Sch., 1974-76. Ordained to Assn. Unity Chs., 1976. Minister Unity Ch. Christianity, Santa Rosa, Calif., 1976-77, min. Jacksonville, Fla., 1978-79; dir. prayer ministry Unity Sch. Christianity, Unity Village, Mo., 1979-90, mem. task force, 1984-87, mem. adv. council, 1987—; min. Unity Ctr., N.Y.C., 1990-91, Unity Ch., Hawaii, 1991—. Trustee Assn. Unity Chs., 1994—, mem. exec. com., 1995—, chmn. bd., 1998—; coord. Internat. Youth of Unity, Unity Village, 1975-76; vol. chaplain Jackson County Jail, Kansas City, 1974-75. Contbr. articles to profl. jours. Trustee, Kans. Children's Mus.; vol. Unity Help Line, Unity Village, 1975-76. Named one of Outstanding Young Men Am., 1982. Mem. Rotary (youth svcs. com., chmn. invocation com. 1988-89, Paul Harris fellow). Avocations: running, physical fitness, hiking, music. Home: 1517 Makiki St Apt 1407 Honolulu HI 96822-4526 Office: Unity Ch Hawaii 3608 Diamond Head Cir Honolulu HI 96815-4430

STRICKLAND, KRISTY LYNN, accountant; b. St. Albans, Vt., Jan. 23, 1974; d. Robert Alfred and Paulette Jeanine Laroche; m. Samuel Roger Strickland Jr., Sept. 14, 1996. BS, Troy State U., 1995, MBA, 1996. CPA, Ga., 1998. Assoc., audit Coopers & Lybrand, Atlanta, 1996-98; assoc., tax Pricewaterhouse Coopers, 1998-99, sr. assoc., tax, 1999—2000; self employed tax profl., 2000—; with Sunburst Cons., LLC. Mem. AICPA, Ga. Soc. CPAs. Republican. Roman Catholic. Home: 3893 Scapa Rd Waycross GA 31503-0501 Office: 3178 Keen Dr Waycross GA 31503 E-mail: ks@sunburstllc.com.

STRICKLAND, ROBERT LOUIS, former retail company executive; b. Florence, S.C., Mar. 3, 1931; s. Franz M. and Hazel (Eaddy) S.; m. Elizabeth Ann Miller, Feb. 2, 1952; children: Cynthia Anne, Robert Edson. AB, U. N.C., 1952; MBA with distinction, Harvard U., 1957. Bd. dirs. Lowe's Cos., Inc., North Wilkesboro, N.C., 1961-2000, sr. v.p., 1970-76, exec. v.p., 1976-78, chmn. bd., 1978-98, chmn. exec. com., 1988-98, mem. office of pres., 1970-78, chmn. emeritus, 1999; founder Sterling Advt., Ltd., 1966. V.p., mem. adminstrv. com. Lowe's Profit-Sharing Trust, 1961-87, chmn. ops. com., 1972-78; mgmt. com. Lowe's ESOP Plan, 1978-97; bd. dirs. Krispy Kreme Corp., Winston-Salem; panelist investor rels. field, 1972-99; spkr., panelist employee stock ownership, 1978-2000; spkr. on investor rels., London, Edinburgh, Glasgow, Paris, Zurich, Frankfurt, Milan, Vienna, Singapore, Tokyo. Author: Lowe's Cybernetwork, 1969, Lowe's Living Legend, 1970, Ten Years of Growth, 1971, The Growth Continues, 1972, 73, 74, Lowe's Scoreboard, 1978; contbr. articles to profl. jours. Mem. N.C. Ho. of Reps., 1962-64, Rep. Senatorial Inner Circle, 1980-95; exec. com. N.C. Rep. Com., 1963-73; trustee U. N.C., Chapel Hill, 1987-95, chmn. bd., 1991-93; dir., dep. chmn. Fed. Res. Bank of Richmond, 1996-98; com. on bus. laws and the economy N.C., 1994-97; dir. U.S. Coun. Better Bus. Burs., 1981-85; bd. dirs., v.p. Nat. Home Improvement Coun., 1972-76; bd. dirs. N.C. Sch. Arts Found., 1975-79, N.C. Bd. Natural and Econ. Resources, 1975-76; bd. dirs., govt. affairs com. Home Ctr. Inst.; trustee, sec. bd. Wilkes C.C., 1964-73; chmn., pres. bd. dirs. Do-It-Yourself Rsch. Inst., 1981-89; pres. Hardware Home Improvement Coun. City of Hope Nat. Med. Ctr., L.A., 1987-89. With USN, 1952-55, lt. Res. 1955-62. Named Wilkes County N.C. Young Man of Yr., Wilkes Jr. C. of C., 1962; recipient Bronze Oscar of Industry award Fin. World, 1969-74, 76-79, Silver Oscar of Industry award, 1970, 72-74, 76-79, Gold Oscar of Industry award as best of all industry, 1972, 87, Excellence award in corp. reporting Fin. Analysts Fedn., 1970, 72, 74, 81-82, cert. of Distinction Brand Names Found., 1970, Retailer of Yr. award, 1971, 73, Disting. Mcht. award, 1972, Spirit of Life award City of Hope, 1983, Free Enterprise Legend award Students Free Enterprise, 1994; named to Home Ctr. Hall of Fame, 1985. Mem. Nat. Assn. Over-Counter Cos. (bd. advisers 1973-77), Newcomen Soc., Employee Stock Ownership Assn. (pres. 1983-85, chmn. 1985-87), James Madison Club, Federalist Soc., Forsyth Country Club, Piedmont City Club, Hound Ears Club (Blowing Rock, N.C.), Elk River Club (Banner Elk, N.C.), Roaring Gap Club (N.C.), Ponte Vedra Inn and Club (Fla.), Scabbard and Blade, Phi Beta Kappa, Pi Kappa Alpha. Home: 226 N Stratford Rd Winston Salem NC 27104-3132 Office: 2000 W 1st St Winston Salem NC 27104-4225

STRICKLAND, SYLVIA RAYE, social worker; b. Grand Prarie, Tex., Feb. 21, 1945; d. Nathaniel and Flora Evelyn Strickland; m. Julian B. Angel, Oct. 6, 1973 (div. Apr. 1983); 1 child, Sarah Renee. BSW, U. So. Colo., Pueblo, 1986; MSW, N.Mex. Highlands U., Las Vegas, N.Mex., 1987. Lic. social worker 93. Social worker Highland Park Nursing Home, Pueblo, 1988; social worker III El Paso County Social Svcs., Colorado Springs, Colo., 1988-89; resident svcs. coord. Villa Santa Maria, 1990-92, ballot initiative circulator, 1992; social worker Medalion Health Ctr. and Personal Care Unit, 1993—, activities dir., 1993—96. Vol. Hospice of the Comforter, 1994-96; sec. Social Work Action Team, U. So. Colo., 1984-85. Mem. Nat. Assn. Social Workers. Avocations: choir, hiking, quilting, water colors. Home: PO Box 3067 Colorado Springs CO 80934-3067

STRICKLAND, TED, congressman, clergyman, psychology educator, psychologist; b. Lucasville, Ohio, Aug. 4, 1941; m. Frances Smith. BA in History, Asbury Coll., 1963; MDiv, Asbury Seminary, 1967; PhD in Psychology, U. Ky., 1980. Clergyman; dir. social svcs. Ky. Meth. Home; consulting psychologist Southern Ohio Correctional Facility, 1985-92, 94-96; prof. psychology Shawnee State U., 1988-92, 94-96; mem. U.S. Congress from 6th Ohio dist., Washington, 1993-94, 97—; mem. energy and commerce com. Mem. numerous coms. in fields of: edn. and labor, post-secondary edn. and tng., labor standards, occupational health and safety, small bus., rural enterprise, exports and environ. Democrat. Office: US Ho of Reps 336 Cannon House Office Bldg Washington DC 20515-3506

STRICKLAND, WILLIAM BRADLEY, English educator; b. New Holland, Ga., Oct. 27, 1947; s. Silas Henry and Eavleen (Watkins) S.; m. Barbara Ann Justus, June 8, 1969; children: Jonathan Bradley, Amy Elizabeth. AB, U. Ga., 1969, MA, 1971, PhD, 1976. Lectr. English U. Ga., Athens, 1974-76; head dept. English Truett-McConnell Coll., Cleveland, Ga., 1976-85; head secondary English dept. Lakeview Acad., Gainesville, 1985-87; assoc. prof. English, dir. student publs. Gainesville Coll., 1987—. Dir. communicative arts Ga. Gov.'s Honors Program, 1981-85. Author: (novels) To Stand Beneath the Sun, 1986, Moon Dreams, 1988, Shadowshow, 1988, Nul's Quest, 1989, Wizard's Mole, 1990, Dragon's Plunder, 1992, The Ghost in the Mirror, 1993; also short stories; contbr. articles to profl. jours. NDEA fellow, 1980. Mem. MLA, South Atlantic Modern Lang. Assn., Sci. Fiction Writers Am. Baptist. Avocations: photography, travel. Office: Gainesville Coll PO Box 1358 Gainesville GA 30503-1358

STRICKLAND, WILLIAM JESSE, lawyer; b. Newport News, Va., Mar. 21, 1942; BSBA, U. Richmond, 1964, JD, 1970. Bar: Va. 1969, U.S. Dist. Ct. (ea. and we. dists.) Va., U.S. Ct. Claims, U.S. Tax Ct., U.S. Ct. Appeals (4th cir.). Exec. com. coord. dept., mng. ptnr. McGuire Woods LLP, Richmond, Va., 1969—. Bd. dirs. Cableform Inc., Zion Crossroads, Va., Eimeldingen Corp., Indpls. Bd. dirs. Va. Found. Rsch. & Econ. Edn., Inc. Capt. USMC 1964-67, Vietnam. Mem. ABA, Va. Bar Assn., Richmond Bar Assn., Nat. Assn. Bond Lawyers, Va. Govt. Fin. Officers Assn., Local Govt. Attys. Assn., Va. Bond Club. Office: McGuire Woods LLP 901 E Cary St Richmond VA 23219-4057

STRICKLAND, WILTON L. lawyer; b. Ft. Myers, July 1, 1942; s. Lorenzo Strickland and Mary Voncille Singletary; m. Barbara Hathaway Lahna (div. July 1984); children: Amy Beth Strickland-Quattlebaum, Wilton Hathaway Strickland. BA, U. Fla., 1964; JD, Stetson U., 1969. Bar: Fla. 1969, U.S. Dist. Ct. (so. dist.) Fla. 1969, Trial Bar (so. dist.) Fla. 1983, U.S. Dist. Ct. (mid. dist.) Fla. 1988, U.S. Ct. Appeals (5th cir.) 1978, U.S. Ct. Appeals (11th cir.) 1981, U.S. Supreme Ct. 1977. Ptnr. Howell, Kirby, Montgomery et al, Ft. Lauderdale, Fla., 1969-73, Ferrero, Middlebrooks & Houston, Ft. Lauderdale, 1974-77, Ferrero, Middlebrooks & Strickland, Ft. Lauderdale, 1977-91, Strickland & Seidule, Ft. Lauderdale, 1991-98; pvt. practice Wilton L. Strickland, P.A., 1998—. Chmn. bd. Hospice Care Broward County, Inc.; bd. dirs. Salvation Army Broward County; mem. Helping Abandoned and Dependent Youth. Mem. ABA, ATLA, Fla. Bar (mem. ethics com.), Acad. Fla. Trial Lawyers (dir. 1980-84), Broward County Trial Lawyers Assn. (past pres. 1981), Broward County Bar Assn., Am. Bd. Trial Advs. (founder Broward County chpt.), Million Dollar Advocates Forum, The Bar Register of Preeminent Lawyers, Phi Alpha Delta (former pres. Brewer chpt.). Democrat. Presbyterian. Avocations: winter skiing, reading, hiking, boating, white water rafting. Home: 2897 NE 25th St Fort Lauderdale FL 33305-1722 Office: # 303 1401 E Broward Blvd Ste 303 Fort Lauderdale FL 33301-2100

STRICKLER, HOWARD MARTIN, physician; b. New Haven, Oct. 26, 1950; s. Thomas David and Mildred Laing (Martin) S.; m. Susan Hunter, May 2, 1982; children: Hunter Gregory, Howard Martin Jr. BA, Berea Coll., 1975; MD, Univ. Louisville, 1979. Diplomate Am. Bd. Family Practice, Am. Bd. Forensic Medicine, Am. Bd. Forensic Examiners. Resident Anniston (Ala.) Family Practice Residency, 1979-82; pvt. practice Monteagle, Tenn., 1982-85; fellow in addictive diseases Willingway Hosp., Statesboro, Ga., 1985-86; faculty devel. fellow Univ. N.C., Chapel Hill, 1985-86; pvt. practice Birmingham, Ala., 1986-90; pres. Employers Drug Program Mgmt., Inc., 1990—; med. dir. Am. Health Svcs., Inc., 1993—. Med. dir. Bradford Facilities, Birmingham, 1987-90, New Life Clinic, Bessemer, ala., Physicians Smoke Free Clinic, Birmingham, 1988-90, Am. Health Svcs., Inc., 1993—; chmn. dept. family practice and emergency medicine Bessemer Carraway Med. Ctr., 1993-95. Mem. tennis anti-doping appeals com. ATP Tour, Inc., 1997; bd. dirs. Ala. Vets. Meml. Found. With U.S. Army, 1969-72, Vietnam. Decorated Bronze Star, 1971, Vietnam Campaign medal, Vietnam Svc. medal 3 Stars, 1971. Fellow Am. Acad. Family Physicians, Am. Acad. Disability Evaluating Physicians; mem. Am. Soc. Addiction Medicine (cert.), Am. Coll. Occupl. and Environ. Medicine, Am. Assn. Med. Rev. Officers (cert.), Med. Assn. State of Ala., Phi Kappa Phi. Methodist. Avocations: flying, tennis, golf. Home: 868 Tulip Poplar Dr Birmingham AL 35244-1633 Office: 616 9th St S Birmingham AL 35233-1113 E-mail: HowHunMarS@aol.com.

STRICKLER, IVAN K. dairy farmer; b. Carlyle, Kans., Oct. 23, 1921; s. Elmer E. and Edna Louise (James) S.; m. Madge Lee Marshall, Aug. 7, 1949; children— Steven Mark, Thomas Scott, Douglas Lee. BS, Kans. State U., 1947. Owner, mgr. dairy farm, Iola, Kans., 1947—; tchr. farm tng. to vets. World War II, 1947-54; judge 1st and 2d Nat. Holstein Show, Brazil, 1969-70, Internat. Holstein Show, Buenos Aires, 1972, Nat. Holstein Show, Ecuador, 1978, 10th Nat. Holstein Show, Brazil, 1980, Holstein Show, Australia, Mex. and Argentina, 1981, Lang Lang, 1984, Adelaide (Australia) Royal Show, 1987; pres Mid-America Dairymen, Inc., Springfield, MO, 1981—. Appointed chmn. Nat. Dairy Bd., 1985-90; dairy leader 4-H Club, 1962-75; dir. Iola State Bank; rep. U.S. Internat. Dairy Symposium, 1994, Belo Horinzote, Brazil. Author: Wholly Cow We Did It, 1996 (Centennia Honor roll 1997). Trustee Allen County Community Jr. Coll.; mem. agr. edn. and rsch. com. Kans. State U. (recipient Medallion-highest honor, 2000), U.S. Agrl. Trade and Devel. Mission, Algeria and Tunisia, 1989. With USN, 1942-46, PTO. Recipient Silver award Holstein Friesian Assn. Brazil, 1969, Top Dairy Farm Efficiency award Ford Found., 1971, Master Farmer award Kans. State U. and Kans. Assn. Commerce and Industry, 1972, Gold award Holstein Friesian Assn. Argentina, 1972, Richard Lynng award Nat. Dairy Bd., 1990, award of merit Gamma Sigma Delta, 1987, Alumni medallion Kans. State U., 1999; named Man of Yr. World Dairy Exposition, 1978; portrait in Dairy Hall of Fame Kans. State U., 1974; Guest of Hon. Nat. Dairy Shrine, 1985; selected First Dairy Leader of Yr., 1996; inductee Kans. Co-op Hall of Fame, 1999. Mem. Mid Am. Dairymen (sec. corporate bd. 1971-81, pres. 1981-95), Holstein Friesian Assn. Am. (nat. dir. 1964-72), Dairy Shrine (nat. dir. 1971-81), United Dairy Industry Assn. (dir. 1971-79), Nat. Holstein Assn. Am. (pres. 1979-80), Alpha Gamma Rho (highest honor 1989, Hall of Fame 1998). Mem. Christian Ch. (elder, bd. dirs.). Club: Nat. Dairy Shrine (pres. 1978). Home: PO Box 365 Iola KS 66749-0365 Office: Mid America Dairymen Inc 3253 E Chestnut Expy Springfield MO 65802-2584

STRICKLER, JEFFREY HAROLD, pediatrician; b. Mpls., Oct. 14, 1943; s. Jacob Harold and Helen Cecelia (Mitchell) S.; m. Karen Anne Stewart, June 18, 1966; children: Hans Stewart, Liesl Ann. BA, Carleton Coll., 1965; MD, U. Minn., 1969. Diplomate Am. Bd. Pediatrics. Resident in pediatrics Stanford (Calif.) U., 1969-73; pvt. practice Helena, Mont., 1975—; chief staff Shodair Children's Hosp., 1984-86. Dir. maternal-child health Lewis and Clark County, Helena, 1978-88; chief of staff St. Peters Hosp., Helena, 1994-96; bd.chmn. Helena Health Alliance, 1996-99. Mem. Mont. Gov.'s Task Force on Child Abuse, 1978-79; mem. steering com. Region VIII Child Abuse Prevention, Denver, 1979-82; bd. dirs. Helena Dist. 1 Sch. Bd., 1982-88, vice chmn., 1985-87. Maj. M.C., USAF, 1973-75. Fellow: Am. Acad. Pediatrics (vice chmn. Mont. chpt. 1981—84, chmn. 1984—87, mem. nat. nominating com. 1987—90, chmn. 1989—90, coun. on govt. affairs 1990—96, future of pediatric edn. II 1996—2000, Wyeth award 1987); mem.: Am. Bd. Pediatrics (PMCP-G practice performance com. 2001—), Rotary (youth exch. chmn. dist. 539 1984—88, pres. Helena 1988—89, polio plus chair dist. 5390 1996—, asst. gov. dist. 5390 2002—). Avocations: skiing, hiking. Office: Helena Pediatric Clinic 1122 N Montana Ave Helena MT 59601-3513 E-mail: drjeff@mt.net.

STRICKLER, MATTHEW M. lawyer; b. Bryn Mawr, Pa., June 27, 1940; s. Charles S and Mary Webster (Cornman) S.; m. Margaret Renshaw, Sept. 3, 1966; children: Matthew David, Andrew Kellogg, Timothy Webster, Edward Charles. AB, Haverford Coll., 1962; JD, Harvard U., 1965. Bar: Pa. 1965, U.S. Supreme Ct. 1975. Assoc. Ballard, Spahr, Andrews & Ingersoll, Phila., 1965-74, ptnr., 1974—. Adj. prof. Temple U. Sch. Law, Phila., 1993—. Editor: Representing Health Care Facilities, 1981. Bd. dirs. Phila. chpt. Girl Scouts Am., 1978-96, v.p., 1984-90, 94-96; bd. dirs. Kardon Inst. Arts, 2000—. Mem. Union League Phila. Office: Ballard Spahr Andrews & Ingersoll 1735 Market St Fl 51 Philadelphia PA 19103-7599

STRICKLIN, HUT, race car driver; b. June 24, 1961; m. Pam Stricklin; children: Taylor, Tabitha. Racecar driver NASCAR, 1982—84, Bobby Allison, 1990—95, Stavola Bros. Racing, 1996—98; crew chief Triad Motorsports team, 1998—99; racecar driver SBII Motorsports, 1999, Junie Donlavey Racing, 2000—01, Bill Davis Racing, 2002—. Named champion, Ala. Ltd. Sportsman, 1978—79, Winston Cup Racing Series, 1982, 1984, Dash Series, 1986, Most Popular Driver, All Am. Challenge Series, 1984, Bud Pole winner, 1995, BGN Bud Pole winner, 1999—2000; recipient 2d pl., Southern 500, 1991, 1996, Rockingham, 1995, 14th pl., Brickyard 400, 2000, 11th pl., NAPA 500, 2001, 6th pl., Kmart 400, 2001. Office: c/o Bill Davis Racing 300 Old Thomasville Rd High Point NC 27620-8190*

STRICKON, HARVEY ALAN, lawyer; b. Bklyn., Nov. 9, 1947; s. Milton and Norma (Goodhartz) S.; m. Linda Carol Meltzer, July 2, 1972; children: Joshua Andrew, Meredith Cindy, Erica Stacey. BBA, CCNY, 1968; JD, NYU, 1971. Bar: N.Y. 1972, U.S. Dist. Ct. (so. and ea. dists.) N.Y. 1973, U.S. Ct. Appeals (2d cir.) 1973, U.S. Supreme Ct. 1975, U.S. Dist. Ct. (no. dist.) N.Y. 1980, U.S. Dist. Ct. (we. dist.) N.Y. 1981, U.S. Dist. Ct. Ariz. 1991, U.S. Dist. Ct. Conn., 1996. Law clk. U.S. Dist. Ct. (ea. dist.) N.Y., Bklyn., 1971-73; assoc. Moses & Singer, N.Y.C., 1973-80; from assoc. to ptnr. Kaye, Scholer, Fierman, Hays & Handler, 1980-91; from ptnr. to counsel Paul, Hastings, Janofsky & Walker LLP, 1991—. Mem. complaint mediation panel, departmental disciplinary com. appellate div., 1st dept. Supreme Ct. State N.Y.; mem. mediation panel U.S. Dist. Ct. (ea. dist.) N.Y.; mem. mediation register U.S. Bankruptcy Ct. (so. dist.) N.Y. Co-author: Enforcing Judgments and Collecting Debts in New York, 1996. Mem. Nassau County Rep. Com., Great Neck, N.Y., 1982—; chmn. bd. dirs. Flushing Community Vol. Ambulance Corps. Inc., N.Y., 1981-86, vice chmn., 1987-92. Mem. ABA, N.Y. State Bar Assn., Assn. Bar City N.Y. (chmn. complaint mediation panel com. on profl. discipline), Am. Judicature Soc., Assn. Comml. Fin. Attys., N.Y. Law Inst., Bankruptcy Lawyers Bar Assn., (bd. govs. 1987-89, corr. sec. 1989—), Am. Bankruptcy Inst. Republican. Jewish. Home: 11 West Brook Rd Great Neck NY 11024-1219 Office: Paul Hastings Janofsky & Walker LLP 75 E 55th St New York NY 10022-3205 E-mail: harveystrickon@paulhastings.com., hastrick@optonline.net.

STRICKSTEIN, HERBERT JERRY, lawyer; b. Detroit, Sept. 4, 1932; s. Samuel and Leah (Freedman) S.; m. Elaine Frances Cohen, Aug. 22, 1963; children: Jaynee Esther, Jill Rose. AA, UCLA, 1952; BS in Law, U. So. Calif., 1954, JD, 1956. Dep. judge adv. USAF, 1957-60; dep. city atty. L.A., 1960-61; assoc. Axelrad, Seville & Ross, 1961-65; ptnr. Iliff & Strickstein, 1965-72; pvt. practice Herbert J. Strickstein Law Corp., L.A., 1972—. Contbr. numerous articles to profl. jours. Commr. Small Craft Harbor Comm., Marina del Rey, Calif., 1983-2000. Mem. State Bar Calif. Assn. (real property sec.), Beverly Hills Bar Assn., El Caballero Country Club, Del Rey Yacht Club, Mission Hills Country Club. Avocations: racquetball, golf, tennis, sailing. Office: Ste 1420 1801 Avenue Of The Stars Los Angeles CA 90067-5899

STRIDER, MARJORIE VIRGINIA, artist, educator; b. Guthrie, Okla. d. Clifford R. and Marjorie E. (Schley) S. BFA, Kansas City Art Inst., 1962. Faculty Sch. Visual Arts, N.Y.C., 1970-2001; artist-in-residence City U. Grad. Ctr. Mall, 1976, Fabric Workshop, Phila., 1978, Grassi Palace, Venice, Italy, 1978. One-woman shows of sculpture, drawings and/or prints include Pace Gallery, N.Y.C., 1963-64, Nancy Hoffman Gallery, N.Y.C., 1973-74, Weather Spoon Mus., U.N.C., Chapel Hill, 1974, City U. Grad. Center Mall, 1976, Clocktower, N.Y.C., 1976, Sculpture Center, N.Y.C., 1983, Steinbaum Gallery, N.Y.C., 1983, 84, Andre Zarre Gallery, 1993, 95, Outdoor Installation, N.Y.C., 1997, Selby Gallery, Ringling Sch. of Art, Sarasota, Fla., 1998, Neuherzer Mus., Purchase, N.Y., 1999; exhibited in group shows at The Sculpture Center, N.Y.C., 1981, Drawing Biennale, Lisbon, Portugal, 1981, Newark Mus., 1984, William Rockhill Nelson Mus., Kansas City, 1985, Danforth Mus., Framingham, Mass., 1987, Delahoyd Gallery, N.Y.C., 1992; represented in permanent collections Guggenheim Mus., N.Y.C., U. Colo., Boulder, Albright-Knox Mus., Buffalo, Des Moines Art Center, Storm King (N.Y.) Art Center, Larry Aldrich Mus., Ridgefield, Conn., City U. Grad. Center, N.Y.C., Hirschhorn Mus. and Sculpture Garden, Washington, Santa Fe (N. Mex.) Mus. of Art, also pvt. collections. Nat. Endowment for Arts grantee, 1973, 80, Longview Found. grantee, 1974, Pollock-Krasner Found. grantee, 1990, Florsheim Art Fund grantee, 1998; Va. Ctr. for Creative Arts fellow, 1974, 92, Millay Colony for Arts fellow, 1992, Yaddo Colony, 1996, 97. E-mail: mstrider@msn.com.

STRIDIRON, IVER ALLISON, attorney general; m. Priscilla Blyden; 4 children. BA Lincoln U., 1969; JD, Howard U. Sch. of Law, 1974. Atty. U.S. Nuclear Regulatory Commn., U.S. Commn. on Civil Rights, Washington, 1974—77; pvt. practice St. Thomas, 1977—99; mem. V.I. Legis., 1981—83, 1985—89; atty. gen. V.I., 1999—. Office: Dept Justice 48B-50C Kronprindsens Gade GERS Bldg 2nd fl Charlotte Amalie VI 00802*

STRIDSBERG, ALBERT BORDEN, advertising consultant, educator, editor; b. Wyoming, Ohio, July 22, 1929; s. Carl Alexander Herbert and Edith Vivian (Farley) S. BA with honors, Yale U., 1950; Diplome D'Etudes Franc., U. of Poitiers, Tours, France, 1951; postgrad., Am. U. Beirut, Lebanon, 1953-54; diploma, Direct Mktg. Inst., 1986. Copywriter Howard Swink Advt., Inc., Marion, Ohio, 1955-58; acct. supr. McCann-Erickson, Co., Brussels, 1958-60, J. Walter Thompson Co., Amsterdam, The Netherlands, 1960-63, asst. to internat. exec. v.p. N.Y.C., 1963-67, internat. cons. spl. projects, acquisitions and diversifications, 1969-73; cons., coord. Internat. Markets Advt. Agy., Inc., N.Y., London, 1967-69; editor-in-chief Advt. World mag., N.Y.C., 1975-77; lectr. in mktg. NYU, 1978-84; lectr. in advt. Marist Coll., Poughkeepsie, N.Y., 1984-94; U.S. features editor Media Internat. Mag., London, 1984-90. Assoc. prof. NYU, 1966-78; ind. cons., freelance writer on advt. and mktg. issues, N.Y.C., 1972—; seminar leader, Lagos, Nigeria, 1991. Author: Effective Advertising Self-Regulation, 1974, Progress Toward Advertising Self Regulation, 1976, Controversy Advertising, 1977, Advertising Self-Regulation, 1980, also articles, memoirs and papers contb. to Hartman Collection, Duke U. Libr. With U.S. Army, 1951-53. Fulbright fellow U. Poitiers, 1950-51, Ford. Found. fellow Beirut U., 1953-54. Mem. Internat. Advt. Assn. (cons., project coord. 1974-80), Alcoholics Anonymous, Elizabethan Club New Haven. Democrat. Episcopalian. Office: Box 1846 South Rd PO Poughkeepsie NY 12601-0846 E-mail: realtoads@webtv.net.

STRIEDER, LEON F. priest, theology studies educator; b. Sealy, Tex., Mar. 10, 1950; s. Frank and Ora Dell Strieder. BA in Classics, U. St. Thomas, Houston, 1972; B in Sacred Theology, Gregorian U., Rome, 1975; lic. in Sacred Liturgy, Pontifical Liturgical Inst., San Anselmo, Rome, 1980, PhD in Sacred Liturgy, 1994. Parish priest Diocese of Austin, Tex., 1976—82; dir. campus ministry Tex. A&M U., College Station, 1982—90; seminary formation dir. St. Mary's Seminary, Houston, 1990—2002, vice rector, 1998—2002; asst. prof. liturgy and sacrements St. Thomas Sch. Theology, 2002—. Adj. prof. liturgy and sacraments U. St. Thomas Sch. Theology, Houston, 1991—2002; chair liturgical commn. Diocese Austin, 1977—, dir. campus ministries, 1998—; bd. dirs. S.W. Liturgical Conf. Author: The Promise of Obedience, 2001. Mem.: Nat. Assn. Diocesan Dirs. Campus Ministry (exec. bd. 1998—). Home and Office: 9845 Memorial Dr Houston TX 77024

STRIEFEL, SEBASTIAN, psychologist, educator; b. Orrin, N.D., May 18, 1941; s. Anton and Pauline (Wentz) S.; m. Janet L. Hager, June 19, 1965 (div. 1975); children: Marnie R., Seth R. BS, S.D. State U., 1964; MA, U. S.D., 1966; PhD, U. Kans., 1968. Diplomate Am. Bd. Adminstrv. Psychology; diplomate in neurofeedback. Rsch. assoc., adj. asst. prof. U. Kans., Parsons, 1970-74; pvt. practice psychology, 1972-74, Logan, Utah, 1974—; asst. prof. psychology Utah State U., 1974-76, dir. div. svcs., 1975—, assoc. prof. psychology, 1976-80, prof. psychology, 1980—. Cons. in field; vis. scientist U. S. Fla. Mental Health Inst., Tampa, 1987-88; vis. prof. U. Tex., 1994-95. Author: (with others): Functional Integration for Success: Preschool Intervention, 1991, (with M.J. Cadez) The program Assessment and Planning Guide for Developmentally Disabled and Preschool Children, 1983; author: How to Teach Through Modeling and Imitation, 1981, 98, 2d edit., 1997, others; contbr. numerous articles to profl. jours. Mem. adv. bd. sys. change Utah Office Edn., Salt Lake City, 1989-90; mem. select com. Div. Svcs. for Handicapped, 1990; mem. Legis. Task Force, State of Utah, 1989-90; mem. Cache County Human Resource Com., 1979—, others. Capt. U.S. Army, 1968-70. Recipient Shiela Adler Syc. award, Assn. Applied Psychophysiology/Biofeedback, 1988, Individual Merit award, Mt. Plains Resource Ctr. for Deaf/Blind, 1983; numerous grants, 1970—. Fellow Am. Assn. Mental Deficiency, Am. Bd. Med. Psychotherapists; mem. APA, Utah Bd. Mental Health (chmn. 1989-91), Assn. Applied Psychophysiology and Biofeedback (treas. 1989-95, pres. 1997—, pres. EEG divsn. 2000—, cert. neurotherapist 1995—), Soc. for Neuronal Resolution (bd. dirs. 1999-2000). Roman catholic. Avocations: skiing, photography, fishing, diving. Office: Ctr for Persons Disabilities Utah State U 6800 Old Main Hill Logan UT 84322-6800 E-mail: sebst@msn.com.

STRIEFSKY, LINDA A(NN), lawyer; b. Carbondale, Pa., Apr. 27, 1952; d. Leo James and Antoinette Marie (Carachilo) S.; m. James Richard Carlson, Nov. 3, 1984; children: David Carlson, Paul Carlson, Daniel Carlson. BA summa cum laude, Marywood Coll., 1974; JD, Georgetown U., 1977. Bar: Ohio 1977. Assoc. Thompson Hine LLP (formerly Thompson, Hine & Flory), Cleve., 1977-85, ptnr., 1985—. Loaned exec. United Way N.E. Ohio, Cleve., 1978; trustee Cleve. Pub. Radio. Mem. ABA (real estate fin. com. 1980-87, vice chmn. leader liability com. 1993-97, mem. non-traditional real estate fin. com. 1987—), Am. Bar Found., Am. Coll. Real Estate Lawyers (bd. govs. 1994-98, treas. 1999), Internat. Coun. Shopping Ctrs., Nat. Assn. Office and Indsl. Parks, Urban Land Inst. (chmn. Cleve. dist. coun. 1996-2000), Cleve. Real Estate Women, Ohio Bar Assn. (bd. govs. real property sect. 1985-97), Greater Cleve. Bar Assn. (chmn. bar applicants com. 1983-84, exec. coun. young lawyers sect. 1982-85, chmn. 1984-85, mem. exec. coun. real property sect. 1980-84, Merit Svc. award 1983, 85), Pi Gamma Mu. Democrat. Roman Catholic. Home: 2222 Delamere Dr Cleveland OH 44106-3204 Office: Thompson Hine LLP 3900 Key Ctr 127 Public Square Cleveland OH 44114-1216 E-mail: linda.striefsky@thompsonhine.com.

STRIER, KAREN BARBARA, anthropologist, educator; b. Summit, N.J., May 22, 1959; d. Murray Paul and Arlene Strier. BA, Swarthmore Coll., 1980; MA, Harvard U., 1981, PhD, 1986. Lectr. anthropology Harvard U., Cambridge, Mass., 1986-87; asst. prof. Beloit (Wis.) Coll., 1987-89, U. Wis., Madison, 1989-92, assoc. prof., 1992-95, prof., 1995—, dept. chair, 1994-96. Panel mem. U.S. Dept. Edn., Washington, 1989—92. Author: (book) Faces in the Forest, 1999, Primate Behavioral Ecology, 2000; co-author: Planning, Purposing, and Presenting Science Effectively; mem. editl. bd.: Internat. Jour. Primatology, 1990—, mem. editl. bd.: Primates, 1991—, mem. editl. bd.: Yearbook of Phys. Anthropology. Recipient Presdl. Young Investigator award, NSF, 1989—94. Fellow: Am. Anthropol. Assn.; mem.: AAAS (coun. del. anthropology sect. 1998—2000), Animal Behavior Soc., Internat. Primatological Soc., Am. Assn. Phys. Anthropologists. Office: U Wis Dept Anthropology 5403 Social Sci Bldg 1180 Observatory Dr Madison WI 53706-1320 E-mail: kbstrier@facstaff.wisc.edu.

STRIKER, CECIL LEOPOLD, archaeologist, educator; b. Cin., July 15, 1932; s. Cecil and Delia (Workum) S.; m. Ute Stephan, Apr. 27, 1968. BA, Oberlin Coll., 1956; MA, NYU, 1960, PhD, 1968; MA (hon.), U. Pa., 1972. From instr. to asst. prof. Vassar Coll., 1962-68; assoc. prof. U. Pa., Phila., 1968-78, prof. history of art, 1978—, chmn. dept. history of art, 1980-87; field archaeologist Dumbarton Oaks Center for Byzantine Studies, 1966-80, fellow, 1972-73. Adj. prof. Sabanci U., 1999—; dir. survey and excavation, Myrelaion, Istanbul, 1965-66; co-dir. Kalenderhane Archaeol. Project, Istanbul, 1966-78, Aegean Dendrochronology Project, 1977-88; gen. archaeol. cons. Istanbul Metro and Bosphorus Tunnel Project, 1985-87; dir. Archtl. Dendrochronology Project, 1988—; cons. Integrated Study of Hagia Sophia Structure, 1991-95. Mem. editorial bd. Architectura: Zeitschrift für Geschichte der Architektur, 1986—. Adv. bd. Ctr. for Advanced Study in the Visual Arts, 1986-88, Samuel H. Kress Found. Art History Fellowship Program, 1986-87. With U.S. Army, 1954-57. Fulbright grant in Germany, 1960-62, NEH grant, 1985-86; art historian in residence Am. Acad. in Rome, 1973. Mem. Archaeol. Inst. Am., Coll. Art Assn., Am. Rsch. Inst. in Turkey (fellow 1965-66, pres. 1978-84, hon. dir. 2002), Coun. Am. Overseas Rsch. Ctr. (chmn. 1980-84), Soc. Archtl. Historians, Turkish Studies Assn., U.S. Nat. Com. for Byzantine Studies, Koldewey Gesellschaft, German Archaeol. Inst. (corr.). E-mail: cstriker@sas.upenn.edu.

STRILER, RAY, distance education consultant; b. Crystal City, Mo., Dec. 21, 1938; BS in Edn., S.W. Mo. U., 1961; MS, Peabody Coll., Vanderbilt U., 1978; MA, Rider U., 1984; EdD, U.S. Internat. U., 1989. Prof., dept. chmn. Rider U., N.J.; tchr. coll. prep., Carlsbad, Calif.; dir. acad. programs and v.p. mil. programs Inst. for Profl. Devel., Phoenix; tech. cons. Voltek Inc., Belleville, Ill. Pres. Edn. 2020 Inc. Alumni bd. dirs. U.S. Internat. U. Lt. col. U.S. Army, 1962-86.

STRIMBAN, ROBERT, graphic designer; b. N.Y.C., Aug. 18, 1923; s. Max and Yetta (Spencer) S.; m. Irma Ferguson, Aug. 1, 1959. Diploma, Pratt Inst., 1942. Ptnr., designer Strimban Design, N.Y.C., 1946-59, designer, self-employed, 1959-90; sculptor N.Y.C. and Cutchogue, N.Y., 1959—. Designer: (book jacket) The Sea Around Us, 1970s (Art Dir.'s Club award 1970s), The Golden Bough, 1970s (Aiga award 1970s); designer/illustrator: (mag. covers) Forbes, 1980s (Art Dir.'s Club award 1980s), N.Y. Times, 1970s-80s; group exhbns. include Springs Invitational Show, Elaine Benson Gallery, Bridgehampton, 1995-96, Jimmy Ernst Springs Invitational, 1995, 97, 98, Greenport Internat. Outdoor Sculpture Exhibit, 1997, Artist's Woods, Amagansett, L.I., 2001 ; commd. sculptures Greenway Plaza Indsl. Park, Farmingdale, 1999. With USAF, 1942-45, China, Burma, India. Home: 1925 Eugenesro Cutchogue NY 11935

STRIMBU, VICTOR, JR. lawyer; b. New Philadelphia, Ohio, Nov. 25, 1932; s. Victor and Veda (Stancu) S.; m. Kathryn May Schrote, Apr. 9, 1955 (dec. 1995); children: Victor Paul, Michael, Julie, Sue; m. Marjorie Bichsel, Oct. 23, 1999. BA, Heidelberg Coll., 1954; postgrad., Western Res. U., 1956-57; JD, COlumbia U., 1960. Bar: Ohio 1960, U.S. Supreme Ct. 1972. With Baker & Hostetler LLP, Cleve., 1960—, ptnr., 1970—. Bd. dirs. North Coast Health Ministry; mem. Bay Village (Ohio) Bd. Edn., 1976-84, pres., 1978-82; mem. indsl. rels. adv. com. Cleve. State U., 1979—, chmn., 1982, 98; mem. Bay Village Planning Commn., 1967-69; life mem. Ohio PTA; mem. Greater Cleve. Growth Assn.; trustee New Cleve. Campaign, 1987-94—, North Coast Health Ministry, 1989-2001, Heidelberg Coll., 1996—; mem. indsl. rels. adv. com. Cleve. State U., 1979—, chmn., 1982,1999, vice chmn., 1998. With AUS, 1955-56. Mem. ABA, Ohio Bar Assn., Greater Cleve. Bar Assn., Ohio Newspaper Assn. (minority affairs com. 1987-90), Ct. of Nisi Prius Club, Cleve. Athletic Club, The Club at Soc. Ctr. Republican. Presbyterian. Office: Baker & Hostetler LLP 3200 National City Ctr 1900 E 9th St Ste 3200 Cleveland OH 44114-3475

STRINE, HARRY CORNELIUS, III, communications educator; b. Danville, Pa., Jan. 18, 1943; s. Harry C. Jr. and Helen Elizabeth (Barron) S.; m. Mry Ann Bolig, June14, 1969; children: harry C. Strine IV, Sean Bolig Strine. BA, Susquehanna U., 1964; MA, Ohio U., 1969. Cert. H.S. tchr., Pa. Tchg. grad. asst. U. Md., College Park, 1964-66; tchr. speech, English Shamokin (Pa.) Area H.S., 1966-70; instr., asst., assoc. prof., dir. forensics Bloomsburg (Pa.) U., 1970—. Home: 250 Sunnyside Ave Bloomsburg PA 17815-8238 Office: Bloomsburg U 400 E 2d St Bloomsburg PA 17815-1399 E-mail: hmstrine@digital-link.net.

STRINER, HERBERT EDWARD, economics educator; b. Jersey City, Aug. 16, 1922; s. Harry and Pearl (Strynar) S.; m. Erma Steinert, Dec. 9, 1943 (div. 1970); children: Richard Alan, Deborah Jane; m. Iona V. Meredith. AB, Rutgers U., 1947, MA, 1948; PhD (Maxwell fellow 1949-50), Syracuse U., 1951. Asst. prof. Syracuse U., 1951; economist Interior Dept., 1951-54; program dir. NSF, 1954-55, Nat. Planning Assn., 1955-57; sr. analyst Operations Research Office, Johns Hopkins, 1957-59; program dir. Brookings Inst., 1959-61, Stanford Research Inst., 1961-62; program devel. dir. Upjohn Inst., Washington, 1962-69; dean Coll. Continuing Edn. Am. U., 1969-72, dean Coll. Bus., 1974-81, prof. econs. and mgmt., 1981-89; cons. Los Alamos Nat. Lab., 1990-91; chief planning and policy NIH, 1972-73; pres. U. Research Corp., 1973-74; assoc. faculty mem. Johns Hopkins U., 1997. Chmn. bd. dirs. Nettalon Corp., 2002—. Author: Toward a Fundamental Program for the Training, Employment and Economic Equality of the American Indian, 1968, Continuing Education as a National Capital Investment, 1972, Regaining The Lead: Policies for Economic Growth, 1984; co-author: Local Impact of Foreign Trade, 1960, Civil Rights, Employment and the Social Status of American Negros, 1966; Contbr. profl. jours. Mem. rev. panel Pres.'s Cabinet Com. Juv. Delinquency, 1961-63, D.C. Youth Employment Com., 1963, Pres.'s Task Force Am. Indians, 1967, White House Conf. Aging, 1971; bd. dirs. Opportunities Industrialization Ctr., NAACP, Washington. Officer inf. U.S. Army, 1943-46. Decorated Breast Order of Yun Hui with Ribbon, World War II Govt. China. Home: 4979 Battery Ln Bethesda MD 20814-4986

STRINGER, EDWARD CHARLES, state supreme court justice; b. St. Paul, Feb. 13, 1935; s. Philip and Anne (Driscoll) S.; m. Mary Lucille Lange, June 19, 1957 (div. Mar. 1991); children: Philip, Lucille, Charles, Carolyn; m. Virginia L. Ward, Sept. 10, 1993. BA, Amherst Coll., 1957; LLD, U. Minn., 1960. Bar: Minn. Ptnr. Stringer, Donnelly & Sharood, St. Paul, 1960-69, Briggs & Morgan, St. Paul, 1969-79; sr. v.p., gen. counsel Pillsbury Co., Mpls., 1980-82, exec. v.p., gen. counsel, 1982-83, exec. v.p., gen. counsel, chief adminstrv. officer, 1983-89; gen. counsel U.S. Dept. Edn., Washington, 1989-91; chief of staff Minn. Gov. Arne H. Carlson, 1992-94; assoc. justice Minn. Supreme Ct., St. Paul, 1994—. Mem. ABA, Minn. State Bar Assn., Ramsey County Bar Assn. (sec. 1977-80), Order of Coif, Mpls. Club. Congregationalist. Home: 712 Linwood Ave Saint Paul MN 55105-3513 Office: Minn Judicial Center 25 Constitution Ave Saint Paul MN 55155-1500

STRINGER, GAIL GRIFFIN, information systems consultant; b. Montgomery, Ala., July 31, 1941; d. Leonard and Margaret (Wade) G.; m. Orum David Stringer, Jan. 25, 1964; 1 child, Odessa. BFA, U. Fla., 1963; MLS, Pratt Inst., 1968; M of City Planning, U. Pa., 1976; PhD in Info. Sys., Drexel U., 1998. Sect. adminstr. Fla. State Libr., Tallahassee, 1969-73; exec. dir. Germantown Homes, Inc., Phila., 1977-80; community devel. specialist II Office Housing/Comm Devel. City of Phila., 1981-82; coord. computer svcs. Ctr. for Social Policy/Comm. Devel. Temple U., Phila., 1982-87; divsn. dir. accts. receivable/client infosystems John F. Kennedy Comm. Mental Health/Mental Retardation Ctr., 1987-96; project mgr. Prudential Healthcare, 1997; info. sys. cons., project mgr. Burger, Carroll & Assocs., Santa Fe, 1998—. Editor: Introduction to Computers: A Manual for Social Service Agencies, 1984; head start data mgr. (software package) User Manual, 1986; contbr. articles and papers to profl. jours. Mem. AAUW, Network of Women in Computer Tech. (bd. dirs. 1990-92), World Future Soc. (pres. Phila. chpt. 1981-82, editor newsletter Phila. chpt. 1981-82), Bus. and Profl. Women's Club (chair past legis. com.). Avocations: music, women's issues, reading, entertaining. Home: 1109 Gloria Ln Yardley PA 19067-4711 Office: Burger Carroll & Assoc 1421 Luisa St Ste A Santa Fe NM 87505-4073

STRINGER, HOWARD, media executive; b. Cardiff, Wales, U.K., Feb. 19, 1942; came to U.S., 1965, naturalized, 1985; s. Harry and Marjorie Mary (Pook) S.; m. Jennifer Kinmond Patterson, July 29, 1978; children: David, Ridley, Harriet, Kinmond. BA, MA, Oxford (Eng.) U., 1964. Prodr., dir. CBS News, N.Y.C., 1973-76; exec. prodr. CBS Reports, 1976-81, Evening News, 1981-84; exec. v.p., 1984-86; pres. CBS News, 1986-88, CBS Broadcast Group, 1988-95; chmn., CEO Tele-TV, 1995-97, Sony Corp. Am., 1998. Bd. dirs. Applied Graphics, Sony Corp. Chmn. Am. Film Inst.; bd. dirs. Am. Theatre Wing; trustee NY Presbyn. Hosp., Mus. Radio and TV. Sgt. U.S. Army, 1965—67, Vietnam. Created knight bachelor; recipient Emmy awards Nat. Assn. TV Arts and Scis., 1973, 79 (2), 81 (2), 83 (4), Columbia Dupont award Columbia Journalism Sch., 1979, 81, Overseas Press Club awards, 1974, 79, 82, IRTS Found. award, 1994, First Amendment Leadership award Radio & TV News Dirs. Found., 1996; inductee to Broadcasting and Cable Hall of Fame, 1996, Royal TV Soc. Wales, 1999; hon. fellow Merton Coll., Oxford, 2000, Welsh Coll. Music and Drama, 2001 Presbyterian. Office: Sony Corp of Am 550 Madison Ave New York NY 10022-3211

STRINGER, L.E. (DEAN STRINGER), retired lawyer; b. Sayre, Okla., June 22, 1936; s. Rex Herman and Bessie (Morris) S.; m. Carol Ann Woodson, Aug. 31, 1963; children: Craig Woodson, Laura DeAnn. BA, Okla. State U., 1958; LLB, Harvard U., 1961. Bar: Okla. 1961, U.S. Ct. Appeals (10th cir.) 1962, U.S. Dist. Ct. (we. dist.) 1963, U.S. Supreme Ct. 1972. Assoc. Crowe, Boxley, et al (now Crowe & Dunlevy), Oklahoma City, 1961-68, mem., dir., 1968-2000, chmn. bd., 1999-2000; ret., 2000. Pres. Crowe & Dunlevy, P.C., 1979-81, chmn. litigation dept., 1987-2000. Pres. Okla. State U. Alumni Assn., 1972-73; bd. regents Okla. State U. and A&M Colls., Stillwater, 1986-94, vice chmn., 1989-90, chmn., 1990-91; chmn. Okla. State U. Found., Stillwater, 1982-85; pres. Friends of the Libr., Okla. State U., 2000—; dir. Okla. Heritage Assn., 1995-2000; mem. provost adv. com. Okla. State U./OKC, 1998—, chmn., 2000—; mem. Regents Edn. Adv. Com., Okla. State Regents for Higher Edn., 1995—2001; bd. trustees Youth Svcs. Okla. County, Inc., 2001—(vice chmn. 2002). Maj. Okla. N.G., 1961-71. Recipient Disting. Alumnus award Okla. State U., 1979; inducted Hall of Fame Okla. State U. Alumni Assn, 1998. Fellow Am. Bar Found. (adv. rsch. com. 1996-2000); mem. Okla. Bar Assn. Democrat. Methodist. Home: 325 NW 17th St Oklahoma City OK 73103-3424

STRINGER, LORRIE STEEN, pianist, educator; b. Pascagoula, Miss., July 12, 1966; d. George E. and Nora Loraine (King) S.; m. Stephen Ray Stringer, Aug. 9, 1996. MusB, William Carey Coll., 1989; M of Music Edn., U. So. Miss., 1998, postgrad., 1998—. Nat. cert. tchr. music. Pvt. piano tchr., Pascagoula, Miss., 1989-96, Hattiesburg, 1996—; instr. piano U. So. Miss., 1997—, William Carey Coll., 1999—. Pianist, children's choir coord. FBC Hattiesburg, 2001—; divsn. dir. Miss. Boychoir, 2001—. Mem.: Jones County Music Tchrs. Assn., Miss. Music Educators Assn. (advisor for spl. learners 2001—), Music Educators Nat. Conf., Hattiesburg Music Tchrs. League (pre-coll. co-chair 1995—98, pres. 2000—02), Music Tchrs. Nat. Assn., Miss. Music Tchrs. Assn. (cert. chair 1994—98, pre-coll. activities asst. 1998—99). Home: 909 Bailey Ave Ellisville MS 39437-2094

STRINGER, MARY EVELYN, art historian, educator; b. Huntsville, Mo., July 31, 1921; d. William Madison and Charity (Rogers) S. AB, U. Mo., 1942; AM, U. N.C., Chapel Hill, 1955; PhD (Danforth scholar), Harvard U., 1973. From asst. prof. art to prof. Miss. State Coll. for Women (now Miss. U. for Women), Columbus, 1947-91, prof. emeritus, 1991—. Regional dir. for Miss., Census of Stained Glass Windows in Am., 1840-1940. Bd. dirs. Mississippians for Ednl. Broadcasting; mem. Miss. com. Save Outdoor Sculpture, 1992-93. Fulbright scholar W.Ger., 1955-56; Harvard U. travel grant, 1966-67; NEH summer seminar grant, 1980. Mem. AAUW, Coll. Art Assn., Southeastern Coll. Art Conf. (dir. 1975-80, 83-89, Disting. Svc. award 1992, Miss. Hist. Soc. (Merit award 1995), Internat. Ctr. Medieval Art, Am. Birding Assn., Audubon Soc., The Nature Conservancy, Sierra Club, Phi Beta Kappa, Phi Kappa Phi. Democrat. Episcopalian.

STRINGER, NANETTE SCHULZE, lawyer; b. Stuttgart, Germany, May 29, 1952; came to U.S., 1952; d. Herbert Charles and Marie-Jeanne (Raphael) Schulze; m. James Cooper Stringer, Oct. 9, 1982; children: David, Sarah, Amy. BA, Harvard U., 1974; JD, Stanford U., 1978. Bar: Calif. 1978, U.S. Dist. Ct. (no. dist.) Calif. 1978. Atty. Keogh, Marer & Flicker, Palo Alto, Calif., 1979-81, Carr, McClellan, Burlingame, 1981-83, Lakin-Spears, Palo Alto, 1983-89, Law Ofc. of John Miller, Palo Alto, 1991-93; atty., owner Nanette S. Stringer, Atty. at Law, 1993—. Sec., bd. mem. Palo Alto Little League, 1995—. Mem. Palo Alto Bar Assn. (lawyer referral svc. com.), Calif. State Bar (cert specialist family law bd. specialization, 1994—). Roman Catholic. Avocations: masters' swimming, running, gardening. Office: 375 Forest Ave Palo Alto CA 94301-2521

STRINGER, PAMELA MARY, retired headmistress; b. Birmingham, Eng., Aug. 30, 1928; d. Edwin Allen and Margherita Mary (Holland) S. MA, Oxford U., 1950. Asst. classics mistress Sherborne Sch. for Girls, 1950-59; head of classics Pate's Grammar Sch. for Girls, Cheltenham, 1959-64, dep. headmistress, 1963-64; headmistress Clifton H.S. for Girls, 1965-85. Mem. Secondary HEADS Assn., Girls Schs. Assn. Roman Catholic. Avocations: travel in Tuscany and Umbria, reading, cooking, Italian art and culture. Home: 36 Henleaze Gardens Bristol BS9 4HJ England

STRINGER, RONALD E. lawyer, educator; b. N.Y.C., Feb. 23, 1934; s. Irving and Mary Stringer; m. Sandra Deutsch, Oct. 30, 1986; children from previous marriage: Scott, David. AB, CCNY, 1954; LLB, Bklyn. Law Sch., 1957, JD, 1968. Bar: N.Y. 1958, U.S. Dist. Ct. (so. and ea. dists.) N.Y., U.S. Supreme Ct. Law sect. to comptroller City of N.Y., 1971-73, counsel to mayor, 1974-77; counsel Balsam Felber & Goldfield, 1977—; asst. prof. John Jay Coll. Criminal Justice, N.Y.C., 1992-99. Hon. consul Dominican Republic, N.Y.C., 1972-74. Recipient Svc. award Alianza Hispano-Am., 1975. Democrat. Office: Balsam Felber & Goldfield 99 Wall St New York NY 10005-4301

STRINGER, WILLIAM JEREMY, university official; b. Oakland, Calif., Nov. 8, 1944; s. William Duane and Mildred May (Andrus) S.; m. Susan Lee Hildebrand; children: Shannon Lee, Kelly Erin, Courtney Elizabeth. BA in English, So. Meth. U., 1966; MA in English, U. Wis., 1968, PhD in Ednl. Adminstrn., 1973. Dir. men's housing Southwestern U., Georgetown, Tex., 1968-69; asst. dir. housing U. Wis., Madison, 1969-73; dir. residential life, assoc. dean student life, adj. prof. Pacific Luth., Tacoma, 1973-78; dir. residential life U. So. Calif., 1978-79, asst. v.p., 1979-84, asst. prof. higher and post-secondary edn., 1980-84; v.p. student life Seattle U., 1984-89, v.p. student devel., 1989-92, assoc. provost, 1989-95, assoc. prof. edn., 1990—, chair ednl. leadership, 1994—. Author: How to Survive as a Single Student, 1972, The Role of the Assistant in Higher Education, 1973. Bd. dirs. N.W. Area LUth. Social Svcs. of Wash. and Idaho, pres.-elect, 1989, pres., 1990-91; bd. dirs. Seattle Coalition Ednl. Equity. Danforth Found. grantee, 1976-77. Mem. AAUP, Assn. Higher Edn., Nat. Assn. Student Pers. Adminstrs. (bd. dirs. region V 1985—, mem. editl. bd. Jour. 1995—), Am. Coll. Pers. Assn., Phi Eta Sigma, Sigma Tau Delta, Phi Alpha Theta. Lutheran. Home: 4553 169th Ave SE Bellevue WA 98006-6505 Office: Seattle U Dept Edn Seattle WA 98122 E-mail: stringer@seattleu.edu.

STRINGFELLOW, GERALD B. engineering educator; b. Salt Lake City, Apr. 26, 1942; s. Paul Bennion and Jean (Barton) S.; m. Barbara Farr, June 9, 1962; children: Anne, Heather, Michael. BS, U. Utah, 1964; PhD, Stanford U., 1968. Staff scientist Hewlett Packard Labs., Palo Alto, Calif., 1967-70, group mgr., 1970-80; disting. prof. elec. engring., materials sci. U. Utah, Salt Lake City, 1980—, chmn., 1994-98, adj. prof. physics, 1988—, dean Coll. of Engring., 1998—. Cons. Tex. Instruments, Dallas, 1995-97, AT&T-Bell Labs., Holmdel, N.J., 1986-90, Brit. Telecom., London, 1989-92; editor-in-chief Phase Diagrams for Ceramics, Vol. IX. Author: Organometallic Vapor Phase Epitaxy, 1989, 2d edit., 1999; editor: Metal Organic Vapor Phase Epitaxy, 1986, American Crystal Growth, 1987, Alloy Semiconductor Physics and Electronics, 1989, Phase Equilibria Diagrams-Semiconductors and Chalcogenides, 1991, High Brightness LEDs, 1997; prin. editor Jour. Crystal Growth; letters editor Jour. Electronic Materials, 1992-99; contbr. over 360 articles to profl. jours. Recipient U.S. Sr. Scientist award Alexander von Humboldt Soc., Bonn, Germany, 1979, Gov.'s Sci. Tech. medal State of Utah, 1997; guest fellow Royal Soc., London, 1990. Fellow IEEE, Japan Soc. Promotion of Sci.; mem. Am. Phys. Soc., Electronic Materials Com. (pres. 1985-87), Nat. Acad. Engring. Achievements include pioneering development of organometallic vapor phase epitaxy, development of theories of thermodynamic properties of alloy semiconductors; discovery of phenomenon of compositional latching in alloy semiconductor layers grown by epitaxial techniques. Office: U Utah Coll Engring 1495 E 100 S Salt Lake City UT 84112-1109 E-mail: stringfellow@coe.utah.edu.

STRINGFIELD, HEZZ, JR. contractor, financial consultant; b. Heiskell, Tenn., Oct. 4, 1921; s. Hezz and Cecil Willie (Williams) S.; m. Helen Louise Hinton, Mar. 20, 1939; children— Carolyn Mae Joyce (Mrs. James M. Corum), Don Wayne, Gail Louise (Mrs. John D. Gamble), Debra June (Mrs. Patrick T. Cassidy). Grad. bus. adminstr., Draughon Coll., 1939; student finance and bus., U. Tenn. Fin. and bus. adminstrn. exec. Clinton Engr. Works, E.I. duPont de Nemours & Co., 1943-44; Manhattan Dist. metall. project U. Chgo., 1944-45, Monsanto Chem. Co., 1945-48; nuclear div. Union Carbide Corp., 1948-77; ind. bldg. contractor, real estate developer, 1946—; cons. gen. bus., real estate financing, 1946—; pres. FBF, Inc., 1977—2002; with U.S. AID Mission to Middle East. Cons. with industry, govt. and edn. in developing nations, 1965; bd. dirs. Found. Mgmt. Edn., Advanced Mgmt. Council, Council for Internat. Progress in Mgmt., Inc., Found. for Internat. Progress in Mgmt.; mem. Adv. Council Univs. and Colls. Fellow Soc. Advancement Mgmt. (Profl. Mgr. citation 1963, v.p. 1958-62, exec. v.p. 1962-63, pres. 1963-64, chmn. bd. 1964-65); mem. Am. Mgmt. Assn., Am. Inst. Accountants Baptist. Home: 5314 Ball Rd Knoxville TN 37931-3501

STRINGHAM, LUTHER WINTERS, economist, administrator; b. Colorado Springs, Colo., Dec. 14, 1915; s. Luther Wilson and Fern (Van Duyn) S.; m. Margret Ann Pringle, Dec. 1, 1942 (dec. May 1998); 1 child, Susan Jean; m. Kathryn Cochran Baehr, June 19, 1999. BA summa cum laude, U. Colo., 1938, MA in Econs, 1939; Rockefeller fellow pub. adminstrn., U. Minn., 1939-40, Nat. Inst. Pub. Affairs, 1940-41. Economist Dept. Commerce, also OPA, 1941-43; intelligence officer Def. Dept., 1946-55; program analysis officer Office of the Sec. HEW, 1956-63, chmn. sec.'s com. mental retardation, 1961-63; exec. dir. Nat. Assn. for Retarded Children, 1963-68; intergovtl. relations officer HEW, 1968-77; planning dir. Central Va. Health Systems Agy., 1977-83. Dir. TV series Healthy Virginians, 1981-83. Mem. Pres.'s Com. Employment Handicapped, 1963-68; pres. Music for People, Inc., 1971-74; lectr. CUNY, 1971-76; mem. nat. coun. Boy Scouts Am., 1963-83; co-founder Older Virginians for Action, 1983-84; bd. dirs. Capital Area Agy. Aging, 1984-87; Midlothian Dist. rep. Keep Chesterfield Clean Corp. Capt. AUS, 1943-46; lt. col. USAFR, 1946-56. Mem. Am. Econ. Assn., Greater Richmond C. of C. (mem. quality coun. 1993-94), Phi Beta Kappa, Pi Gamma Mu, Delta Sigma Rho, Va. Hist. Soc., 2001—. Home: 3101 Mount Hill Dr Midlothian VA 23113-3932

STRINGHAM, RENÉE, physician; b. Mpls., July 16, 1940; d. Clifford Leonard and Helen Pearl (Marcineak) Heinrich; children: Lars Eric, Leif Erik, Lance Devon. BS, St. Lawrence U., 1962; MD, U. Ky., 1972. Diplomate Am. Bd. Family Practice. Intern U. Fla., Gainesville, 1972-73; physician Lee County Coop. Clinic, Marianna, Ark., 1973-74; pvt. practice Coastal Health Practitioners, Lincoln City, Oreg., 1975-84; county med. officer Lincoln County Health Dept., Newport, 1986-90; pvt. practice, 1984-90; student health Miami U., Oxford, Ohio, 1991-93; pvt. practice Macadam Clin., Portland, 1994; cons. student health Willamette U., 1994-95; contract physician West Salem Clinic, 1995-97; med. dir. Capital Manor, 1997-99; locum tenens, 1999—. Trustee Coast Home Nursing, Lincoln County, 1984-86; expert witness EPA, 1980. Facilitator Exceptional Living, 1984-86. Fellow Am. Acad. Family Practice; mem. Lincoln County Med. Soc. (pres. 1984), Oreg. Med. Assn. Avocations: spontaneous music, folk dancing, sailing.

STRINGILE, MARIE ELIZABETH, educational administrator; b. Bayonne, N.J., May 13, 1954; d. Orlando Salvatore and Amelia Mary (Prisco) S. BA in edn., Jersey State Coll., 1976; MA in adminstrn., St. Peter's Coll., 1988; PhD in Edn. Adminstrn., 1976. Cert. elem. tchr., prin./supr., sch. adminstr., N.J. Tchr. St. James Sch., Newark, 1976-79; remedial math tchr. Ind. Child Study Teams, Jersey City, 1979-88, assoc. dir., 1988-90, adminstr., 1990—97, dir. ednl. programs, rsch. and evaluation mgr., 1997—2000; edn. program devel. specialist N.J. Dept. Edn., 2000—. Data documentation monitor Ind. Child Study Teams, Jersey City, 1990—, testing and curriculum specialist, 1990—, staff inservices, 1990—, data collection on all eligible remedial students, 1990—; cons. Devel. Remedial Math. Curriculum, 1993, resource room, 1985-88. Bd. dirs. O.L. Assumption Sch. Bd., 1991-93. Mem. ASCD, Sisters of St. Joseph of Peace (assoc.), Nat. Coun. Tchrs. Math., Internat. Reading Assn., Disabled Vets. Am., Medic Alert Found., Handyman Club Am., Black Seal Boiler Operator, Phi Delta Kappa. Avocations: carpentry, gardening, reading, mechanics, educational research. Home: 133 W 25th St Bayonne NJ 07002-1715 Office: NJ State Dept Edn Program Improvement 240 S Harrison St South Orange NJ

STRINKO, THOMAS EDWARD, medical services administrator; b. Middletown, Ohio, June 20, 1943; s. Thomas John and Mary Earlene (Taylor) S.; m. Vanna Om Strinko, Dec. 23, 1978; 1 child, Sontha Sue. Student, U. So. Calif., 1961-63; BS in Edn., Bowling Green State U., 1965; MA, Antioch U., 1968. Vol. Peace Corps, Nepal, 1965-67; fgn. svc. officer U.S. Dept. State, Vietnam, Peru and Washington, 1969-74; dir. Peace Corps, Micronesia, 1976-79; state dir. Action, Columbus, Ohio, 1979-87; child care coord. U.S. Army, European Divsn., Germany, 1987-94; program adminstr. Children's Med. Svcs., Miami, 1994—. Prodr. (record) The Bloody Boys at Phnom Penh, 1974. Founder Cambodian Mut. Assistance Assn., Columbus, Ohio, 1980; bd. dirs. Patches, Miami, Me Boun Found., Palm Beach, Fla., Wings of Valor, Miami, Vietnam Vets. Am., Dayton, 1974-75; cand. for U.S. Congress, 8th dist. Ohio, 1974, cand. for Miami-Dade County Commr., 1998. Mem. Longan and Lychee Growers of Miami-Dade, Human Svc. Coalition of Miami-Dade, State of Fla. Health Adminstrs., Early Intervention Coalition, Phi Alpha Theta, Phi Kappa Pi. Democrat. Avocations: philately, Cambodian stamp collecting, gardening, sports, travel, languages. Home: 8120 SW 178th St Miami FL 33157 Office: Childrens Med Svcs 1500 NW 12th Ave Miami FL 33136 E-mail: tesvos@aol.com.

STRIP, CAROL ANN, gifted education specialist, educator; b. Jackson, Mich., July 3, 1945; d. Harold Don and Marion Estelle (Diemer) Gillespie; m. Asriel Strip, June 15, 1978 (div. Dec. 1992). BS, Western Mich. U., 1966, MA, 1969; PhD, Ohio State U, 1994. Cert. elem. prin., Mich.; cert. supr., ednl. specialist, Ohio. Kindergarten tchr. Kalamazoo (Mich.) Pub. Schs., 1967-74, primary tchr., 1974-75, 76-78, title 1-B adminstr., 1975-76; 4th grade tchr. Westerville (Ohio) City Schs., 1978-83; enrichment specialist Dublin (Ohio) City Schs., 1983-88, gifted edn. coord., 1988-94, gifted edn. specialist, 1988-94, gifted edn. specialist, tchr., 1994—; tchr. edn. Ohio State U., 1999—. Adv. bd. mem. Ohio Wesleyan Jr. League, Delaware, 1987—, Dublin Arts Coun., 1989—; workshop presenter, spkr. in field; adj. prof. Ohio State U., Ashley U. Pub. Roeper Rev. Instr. Jour.; author: Helping Gifted Children Soar, 2000; contbr. articles to profl. jours. Bd. dirs. Friends of the Libr., Columbus, 1978-83; com. mem. Ohio State Fair Orphans Day Com., Columbus, 1983-90. Recipient Master of Comms. award Ednl. Facilities Ctr., 1975, Golden Apple Achiever award Ashland Oil, 1993, Silver Anvil award AMA, 1972; named Ctrl. Mich. Tchr. of Yr., 1976. Fellow ASCD, Ohio Assn. Supervision Curriculum Devel., Sch. Study Coun. of Ohio, Ctrl. Ohio Coord. of Gifted, Alpha Chi Omega; mem. NEA, Ohio Ednl. Assn., Nat. Ret. Tchrs. Assn., Ohio Assn. of Gifted Children (regional rep. 1994, Outstanding Educator of Yr. 1994), Gifted Coord. of Ctrl. Ohio (pres. 1992-93), Alpha Delta Kappa.

Republican. Avocations: reading, travel, music, theatre, museums. Home: 8929 Turin Hill Ct N Dublin OH 43017-9414 Office: Arrowhead Elem Sch 2385 Hollenback Rd Lewis Center OH 43035-9043 Fax: (740) 549-1756. E-mail: docCaroloh@aol.com.

STRIPLING, BETTY KEITH, artist, medical/surgical nurse; b. Stephenville, Tex., Aug. 22, 1930; d. Fred Lancaster and Myrtle Ethel (Patton) Keith; m. Warren Lee Stripling, Mar. 22, 1952 (div. 1961); children: Keith, Kelley, David(dec.). Student, John Tarleton Agrl. Coll., 1948-50, Tarleton State U., 1980-85. LVN, Tex. Clk.-typist Kimbell-Food Products Co., Ft. Worth, 1950-52; LVN Stephenville Hosp. and Clinic, 1963, LVN floor duty, 1963-64, LVN surgery, 1964-66, Ft. Worth Osteo. Hosp., 1966-68; LVN, charge nurse Sunset Nursing Home, Stephenville, 1968-80, LVN, DON, 1973-78; LVN, charge nurse Cmty. Nursing Home, 1980-86, 89-94, pvt. duty nurse, 1986-89, cmty. nursing home LVN, 1998-99; freelance painter, 1999—2002. Democrat. E-mail: bjstrip@ont.com., bjkstrip@yahoo.com.

STRIPPOLI, WILLIAM PETER, academic administrator; b. Camden, N.J., June 15, 1952; s. Frank and Rose Mildred (DiCarmine) S. BS, Rutgers U., 1975; MBA, Drexel U., 1977; MS, U. Pa., 1990. CPA, N.J. Sr. loan clk. Heritage Bank N.A., Camden, 1972-75; sr. acct. Moss Rehab. Hosp., Phila., 1975-76; instr. acctg. Rider U., Lawenceville, N.J., 1976-79; instr. of acctg. Ocean County Coll., Toms River, 1979-81; mgr. of budgeting and fin. analysis Thomas Jefferson U., Phila., 1981-86, dir. of budgeting and fin. analysis, 1986-87, exec. assoc., 1988-90; sr. adminstrv. officer U. So. Calif., L.A., 1990—. Project adminstr.: The NAMES Project AIDS Meml. Quilt, displayed at U. So. Calif., 1992 (Display Excellence award 1993). Democrat. Avocations: writing, bicycling, travel, performing comedy. Home: 2031 W Pacific Ave Burbank CA 91506-1036 Office: U So Calif Bovard Adminstrn Bldg Los Angeles CA 90089-0001 E-mail: strippol@usc.edu.

STROBBE, STEPHEN, psychiatric nurse practitioner; b. Port Huron, Mich., Aug. 19, 1955; s. Ronald A. and Jessie Kelley Strobbe; m. Lynn Marie Haeussler, Oct. 4, 1992; children: Joseph, David. AA, St. Clair County C.C., Port Huron, 1979; BSN, Ea. Mich. U., 1989; MS in Psychiat.-Mental Health Nursing, U. Mich., 1998. Cert. clin. specialist in adult psychiat. and mental health nursing Am. Nurses Credentialing Ctr. Psychiat. aide Ctr. for Mental Health and Chem. Dependency, Ann Arbor, Mich., 1983-89, RN, clin. nurse I, II, III, 1989-91, nursing supr., 1991-94; nurse mgr., coord. Chelsea Arbor Treatment Ctr., 1994-99, nurse practitioner, 1999-2000; clin. cons. substance-related disorders dept. psychiatry U. Mich., 1999-2001; co-investigator, study coord. U. Mich., Addiction Rsch. Ctr., 2000—. Dean's Merit scholar U. Mich., Ann Arbor, 1996. Mem. ANA, Internat. Nurses Soc. on Addictions, Sigma Theta Tau. Office: U Mich Alcohol Rsch Ctr Ste 2A 400 E Eisenhower Pkwy Ann Arbor MI 48108-3318 E-mail: strobbe@med.umich.edu.

STROBECK, CHARLES LEROY, real estate executive; b. Chgo., June 27, 1928; s. Roy Alfred and Alice Rebecca (Stenberg) S.; m. Janet Louise Halverson, June 2, 1951; children: Carol Louise, Nancy Faith, Beth Ann, Jane Alison, Jean Marie. BA, Wheaton (Ill.) Coll., 1949. Mgr. Sudler & Co., Chgo., 1949-50, ptnr., 1951-63; chmn. bd. Strobeck, Reiss & Co., 1964-82; pres. Strobeck Real Estate, 1983-94, chmn. bd. dirs., 1994—. Bd. dirs. Am. Slide-Chart Corp., Carol Stream, 1971—. Bd. dirs. YMCA, Ill. Humane Soc., 1982—; pres. Chgo. Youth Ctrs., 1981-83, bd. dirs., 1985—; trustee Wheaton Sanitary Dist., 1976-91. Mem. Inst. Real Estate Mgmt. (pres. 1970-71), Am. Soc. Real Estate Counselors, Mental Health Assocs. Greater Chgo. (bd. dirs.), Am. Arbitration Assn., Chgo. Club, Chgo. Golf Club (bd. dirs. 1984-86), Union League Club (pres. 1975-76), Mid-Am. Club, Laurel Oak Country Club, Long Boat Key Club, Mill Creek Club, Lambda Alpha. Republican. Home: 642 Maplewood Dr Wheaton IL 60187-8067 Office: 104 S Michigan Ave Chicago IL 60603-5902

STROBER, MYRA HOFFENBERG, education educator, consultant; b. N.Y.C., Mar. 28, 1941; d. Julius William Hoffenberg and Regina Scharer; m. Samuel Strober, June 23, 1963 (div. Dec. 1983); children: Jason M., Elizabeth A.; m. Jay M. Jackman, Oct. 21, 1990. BS in Indsl. Rels., Cornell U., 1962; MA in Econs., Tufts U., 1965; PhD in Econs., MIT, 1969. Lectr., asst. prof. dept. econs. U. Md., College Park, 1967-70; lectr. U. Calif., Berkeley, 1970-72; asst. prof. grad. sch. bus. Stanford (Calif.) U., 1972-86, assoc. prof. sch. edn., 1979-90, prof. edn., 1990—, assoc. dean acad. affairs, 1993-95, interim dean, 1994; program officer in higher edn. Atlantic Philanthropic Svcs., Ithaca, N.Y., 1998-2000. Organizer Stanford Bus. Conf. Women Mgmt., 1974; founding dir. ctr. rsch. women Stanford U., 1974-76, 79-84, dir. edn. policy inst., 1984-86, dean alumni coll., 1992, mem. policy and planning bd., 1992-93, chair program edn. adminstrn. and policy analysis, 1991-93, chair provost's com. recruitment and retention women faculty, 1992-93, chair faculty senate com. on coms., 1992-93; mem. adv. bd. State of Calif. Office Econ. Policy Planning and Rsch., 1978-80; mem. Coll. Bd. Com. Develop Advanced Placement Exam. Econs., 1987-88; faculty advisor Rutgers Women's Leadership Program, 1991-93. Author: (with others) Industrial Relations, 1972, 1990, Sex, Discrimination and the Division of Labor, 1975, Changing Roles of Men and Women, 1976, Women in the Labor Market, 1979, Educational Policy and Management: Sex Differentials, 1981, Women in the Workplace, 1982, Sex Segregation in the Workplace: Trends, Explanations, Remedies, 1984, The New Palgrave: A Dictionary of Economic Theory and Doctrine, 1987, Computer Chips and Paper Clips: Technology and Women's Employment, Vol. II, 1987, Gender in the Workplace, 1987, Challenge to Human Capital Theory: Implications for the HR Manager, American Economic Review, 1995, Rethinking Economics Through a Feminist Lens, Feminist Economics, 1995, Making and Correcting Errors in Economic Analyses: An Examination of Videotapes, (with Agnes M.K. Chan) The Road Winds Uphill All the Way: Gender, Work, and Family in the U.S. and Japan, 1999; editor (with Francine E. Gordon) Bringing Women Into Management, 1975, (with others) Women and Poverty, 1986, Industrial Relations, 1990, Challenges to Human Capitol Theory: Implications for HR Managers, 1995, (with Sanford M. Dornbusch) Feminism, Children and the New Families, 1988, Rethinking Economics Through a Feminist Lens, 1995, (with Agnes M.K. Chan) The Road Winds Uphill All The Way: Gender, Work and Family in the U.S. and Japan, 1999; mem. bd. editors Signs: Jour. Women Culture and Soc., 1975-89, assoc. editor, 1980-85; mem. bd. editors Sage Ann. Rev. Women and Work, 1984—; mem. editorial adv. bd. U.S.-Japan Women's Jour., 1991—; assoc. editor Jour. Econ. Edn., 1991—; contbr. chpt. to book, articles to profl. jours. Mem. rsch. adv. task force YWCA, 1989—; chair exec. bd. Stanford Hillel, 1990-92; bd. dirs. Resource Ctr. Women, Palo Alto, Calif., 1983-84; pres. bd. dirs. Kaider Found., Mountain View, Calif., 1990-96. Fellow Stanford U., 1975-77, Schiff House Resident fellow, 85-87. Mem.: NOW (bd. dirs. legal def. and edn. fund 1993—98), Ctr. Gender Equality (bd. dirs. 2000—), Internat. Assn. Feminist Econs. (assoc. editor Feminist Econs. 1994—, pres. 1997), Indsl. Rels. Rsch. Assn., Am. Ednl. Rsch. Assn., Am. Econ. Assn. (mem. com. status of women in profession 1972—75). Office: Stanford U School Edn Stanford CA 94305 E-mail: myra.strober@stanford.edu.

STROBER, SAMUEL, immunologist, educator; b. N.Y.C., May 8, 1940; s. Julius and Lee (Lander) S.; m. Linda Carol Higgins, July 6, 1991; children: William, Jesse; children from a previous marriage: Jason, Elizabeth. AB in Liberal Arts, Columbia U., 1961; MD magna cum laude, Harvard U., 1966. Intern Mass. Gen. Hosp., Boston, 1966-67; resident in internal medicine Stanford U. Hosp., Calif., 1970-71; rsch. fellow Peter Bent Brigham Hosp., Boston, 1962-63, 65-66, Oxford U., Eng., 1963-64; rsch. assoc. Lab. Cell Biology Nat. Cancer Inst. NIH, Bethesda, Md., 1967-70; instr. medicine Stanford U., 1971-72, asst. prof., 1972-78, assoc. prof. medicine, 1978-82, prof. medicine, 1982—, Diane Goldstone Meml. lectr., 1978-97, John Putnam Merrill Meml. lectr., chief div. immunology & rheumatology, 1978-97. Investigator Howard Hughes Med. Inst., Miami, Fla., 1976-81; bd. dirs. La Jolla Inst. for Allergy and Immunology; founder Dendreon, Inc. Assoc. editor: Jour. Immunology, 1981-84, Transplantation, 1981-85, 99—, Internat. Jour. Immunotherapy, 1985—, Transplant Immunology, 1992—, Biol. Bone Marrow Transplantation, 1999—; contbr. articles to profl. jours. Served with USPHS, 1967-70. Recipient Leon Reznick Meml. Rsch. prize Harvard U., 1966. Mem. Am. Assn. Immunology, Am. Soc. Clin. Investigation, Am. Coll. Rheumatology, Transplantation Soc. (councilor 1986-89), Am. Soc. Tranplantation Physicians, Western Soc. Medicine, Am. Assn. Physicians, Clin. Immunology Soc. (pres. 1996), Alpha Omega. Home: 405 Minoca Rd Portola Valley CA 94028-7740 Office: Stanford U Sch Medicine 300 Pasteur Dr Palo Alto CA 94304-2203

STROBLE-THOMPSON, COLETTE MARY HOULE, plastering and stucco company executive; b. Manchester, N.H., Aug. 10, 1947; d. George Albert and Mary Agnes (Sala) Houle; children: B.J., Danielle, Alden; m. Dennis W. Thompson. Student, CAP Regional Staff Coll. Tex., 1985, 86. Lic. real estate agt., stucco/plasterer. Switchboard operator Leavitt's Dept. Store, Manchester, N.H., 1965-66, with credit office, 1966-67, merchandizer, advertiser, 1966-69; advt. marketer Ariz. wide K-Mart, Mesa; owner, mgr. Colette's Boutique, 1980-82; co-founder, CEO, pres. Stroble Plastering, Gilbert, Ariz., 1977—. Cons. area wide constrn. firms, Phoenix, 1979—; contractor plastering and stucco, Phoenix, 1987-90; realtor personal real estate property, Phoenix, 1988-90. Author, editor Wing Tips, 1985-86; co-inventor, electronic locator transmitter. Maj., squadron leader, fin. officer, personnel officer CAP, Mesa, 1990; active Dept. Disabled/Disadvantaged, Phoenix, 2000. Recipient Humanitarian award Dept. Econ. Security, Mesa, 1989, Letters of Appreciation, Leper Colony, Mexico, 1989. Mem. Nat. Assn. Search and Rescue (life), World Wing Kung Fu Assn., Rosicrucian Order Amorc (dep. master, master). Avocations: collector of masks & fetishes of all cultures, fishing, traveling, real estate, boating. Office: Stroble Plastering & Stucco 721 N Monterey St Ste 103 Gilbert AZ 85233-3835

STROCK, DAVID RANDOLPH, brokerage house executive; b. Salt Lake City, Jan. 31, 1944; s. Clarence Randolph and Francis (Hornibrook) S.; m. Phyllis A. Tingley, Dec. 13, 1945 (div. June 15, 1982); children: Sarah, Heidi. AA, San Mateo Coll., 1967; BS, San Jose State U., 1970. Investment exec. Paine Webber, San Jose, Calif., 1970-78, corp. trainer N.Y.C., 1978-79, rsch. coord., 1979-82, br. mgr. Northbrook, Ill., 1982-84, Palos Verdes, Calif., 1984-89, Napa, 1989-90, investment exec., 1990—. Contbr. articles to profl. jours. Mem. San Jose Jr. C. of C. (chmn. 1977, v.p. 1978), North Napa Rotary (past pres.), Moose. Republican. Avocations: reading, Indy car racing, formula one racing, biking, whitewater rafting. Home: 3324 Homestead Ct Napa CA 94558-4275 Office: Paine Webber 703 Trancas St Napa CA 94558-3014 E-mail: David.Strock@wbspw.com.

STROCK, HERBERT LEONARD, motion picture producer, director, editor, writer; b. Boston, Jan. 13, 1918; s. Maurice and Charlotte Ruth (Nesselroth) S.; m. Geraldine Polinger, Dec. 25, 1941; children: Leslie Carol, Genoa Ellen, Candice Dell. BA, U. So. Calif., 1941, MA, 1942. Asst. editor Metro-Goldwyn-Mayer, Culver City, Calif., 1941-42; prodr., dir. IMPPRO, 1946-51; dir., film editor Hal Roach Studios, 1951-53, Ivan Tors Prodns., Culver City, 1951-58; prodr., dir. ZIV Prodns., Hollywood, Calif., 1956-61; dir. Warner Bros., Burbank, 1958-63; ind. dir., pres. Herbert L. Strock Prodns., Hollywood, 1963—. Pres., chmn. bd. Hollywood World Films Inc., lectr. U. So. Calif. Producer, dir.: I Led Three Lives, Mr. District Attorney, Favorite Story, Corliss Archer, Science Fiction Theater, Highway Patrol, Dr. Christian, Man Called X, Harbor Command, 1954; dir. Battle Taxi; assoc. producer, dir.: Tom Swift series,(TV shows) Mann of Action, Red Light and Siren Sky King; Maverick, Alaskans, Colt 45, Bronco, Cheyenne, 77 Sunset Strip, Bonanza, Hans Brinker Spl., Decisions-Decisions, (feature pictures) Perfect World of Rodney Brewster, I Was a Teenage Frankenstein, Blood of Dracula, How to Make a Monster, Rider on a Dead Horse, Strike Me Deadly, Search the Wild Wind, Magnetic Monster, Riders to the Stars, Gog - Storm Over Tibet; editor, dir.: The Crawling Hand, One Hour of Hell; editorial supr. Shark; writer, dir. Brother on the Run; editor: So Evil My Sister, Chamber-Mades; co-producer Small Miracle; editor, dir. (documentary) They Search for Survival; supervising film editor Hunger Telethon; editor (spl.) The Making of America, co-writer, film editor Hurray for Betty Boop; dir., chief prodn. coordinator for Miss World, 1976; editor (documentary) UFO Journals, UFO Syndrome, Legends, all 1979, Neighborhood Watch; co-dir., film editor Witches Brew, 1979; writer, film editor (TV series) Flipper, 1981. Editor post prodn. services: China--Mao to Now, Eucatastrophe, Tibet, El Papa, Night Screams, King Kung Fu; dir., editor Deadly Presence; producer, writer, dir. (med. documentary) A New Lease on Life; editor Snooze You Lose, Olympic Legacy, Water You Can Trust, Distance, Fish Outta Water; dir., editor Gramma's Gold; co-editor Infinity, Peaceful Sabbath; producer, writer, dir. (fund raising documentary) Combined Federal Campaign; co-dir., editor Detour; editor (experimental film) This Old Man..., Sidewalk Motel; author: Picture Perfect, 2000. Served with U.S. Army, 1940-41. Mem. Acad. Motion Picture Arts and Scis., Dirs. Guild Am., Am. Cinema Editors (dir., bd. mem. 1984-85), Motion Picture Editors Guild, Delta Kappa Alpha (pres. 1941-65), Editors Guild. Democrat. Avocation: photography. E-mail: herbstrock@earthlink.net.

STROCK, JAMES MARTIN, management consultant, writer, mediator; b. Austin, Tex., Aug. 19, 1956; s. James Martin Strock Sr. and Augusta (Tenney) Mullins. AB, Harvard U., 1977, JD, 1981; postgrad, New Coll. Oxford U., 1981-82. Bar: Colo. 1983. Tchg. asst. Harvard U., 1980-81; spl. cons. to majority leader U.S. Senate, Washington, 1982-83; spl. asst. to adminstr. EPA, 1983-85, asst. adminstr. for enforcement, 1989-91; spl. counsel U.S. Senate Com. on Environment and Pub. Works, 1985-86; atty. Davis, Graham & Stubbs, Denver, 1986-88; acting dir., gen. counsel U.S. Office Pers. Mgmt., Washington, 1988-89; sec. for environ. protection State of Calif., Sacramento, 1991-97; prin. jamesstrock.com. inc., San Francisco, 1997—. Adj. prof. U. So. Calif., 1996-97, mem. adv. bd. Global Nature Fund 1998—; mem. Intergovtl. Policy Adv. Com., rep. U.S. Trade, 1991-97; mem. Calif. State Pers. Bd., 1998; guest prof. U. Konstanz, 1998; bd. dir. Raoul Wallenberg com. of the U.S. Author: Reagan on Leadership, 1998, Theodore Roosevelt on Leadership, 2001; contbr. articles to profl. jours. Capt. JAGC USAR, 1987—96. Recipient Ross Essay award ABA, 1985, Environ. Leadership award Calif. Environ. Bus. Coun., 1994, Fed. Republic Germany Friendship award, 1996; Environ. Soc. India fellow, 1997, commendation Calif. Dist. Attys. Assn., 1997; Rotary Internat. scholar, 1981-82. Mem. Coun. Fgn. Rels., Pacific Coun. on Internat. Policy, Nat. Spkrs. Assn., Am. Arbitration Assn., Authors' Guild, Phi Beta Kappa. Republican. Office: 400 Spear St Ste 107 San Francisco CA 94105-1691 E-mail: jms@jamesstrock.com.

STRODE, JOSEPH ARLIN, lawyer; b. DeWitt, Ark., Mar. 5, 1946; s. Thomas Joseph and Nora (Richardson) S.; m. Carolyn Taylor, Feb. 9, 1969; children: Tanya Briana, William Joseph. BSEE with honors, U. Ark., 1969; JD, So. Meth. U., 1972. Bar: Ark. 1972. Design engr. Tex. Instruments Inc., Dallas, 1969-70; patent agent Tex. Instruments, 1970—72; assoc. Bridges, Young, Matthews, Drake, Pine Bluff, Ark., 1972-74, ptnr., 1975—. Chmn. Pine Bluff Airport Commn., 1993; bd. dirs. United Way Jefferson County, Pine Bluff, 1975-77, campaign chmn., 1983, pres., 1986, exec. com., 1983-87; bd. dirs. Leadership Pine Bluff, 1983-85. Mem. Ark. Bar Assn., Jefferson County Bar Assn. (pres. 1995), Pine Bluff C. of C. (dir. 1981, 84, 94, 97), Ark. Wildlife Fed. (dir. 1979-81), Jefferson County Wildlife Assn. (dir. 1973-80, pres. 1974-76), Kiwanis (lt. gov. Mo.-Ark. divsn. 1983-84, chmn. lt. govs. 1983-84), Order of Coif, Tau Beta Pi, Eta Kappa Nu. Home: 7600 Jay Lynn Ln Pine Bluff AR 71603-9387 Office: 315 E 8th Ave Pine Bluff AR 71601-5005 E-mail: joestrode@bridgesplc.com.

STRODE, STEVEN WAYNE, physician; b. Dallas, Jan. 4, 1949; s. Royall Maurice and Maida (Somerville) S.; m. Peggy Lee O'Neill, Sept. 21, 1974; children: Sean Wayne, Colleen Leigh. BS, So. Meth. U., 1969; MD, U. Tex. Southwestern Med. Sch., 1974; MEd, U. Ark., Little Rock, 1996. Diplomate Am. Bd. Family Practice. Intern U. Ark. for Med. Scis., Little Rock, 1974-75, resident in family practice, 1974-77, chief resident in family medicine, 1976-77, assoc. prof. dept. family and cmty. medicine, 1978—. Med. dir. Regional Program; dir. Telemedicine Programs; teaching fellow in family medicine U. Western Ont., London, Can., 1977; pvt. practice family medicine, Jacksonville, Ark., 1977, Sherwood, Ark., 1980-84. Fellow: Am. Acad. Family Physicians; mem.: Ark. Acad. Family Physicians (v.p., pres.), Pulaski County Med. Soc. (v.p.), Accreditation Coun. for Continuing Med. Edn. Com. for Rev. and Recognition, Ark. Med. Soc. (del.), Am. Assn. for Cancer Edn., Soc. Tchrs. Family Medicine, Beta Beta Beta, Phi Eta Sigma, Phi Beta Kappa. Methodist. Home: 104 Charter Ct Sherwood AR 72120-5049 Office: U Ark Med Scis 4301 W Markham St # 599A Little Rock AR 72205-7101 E-mail: strodestevenw@uams.edu.

STRODE, WALTER STERLING, urologist; b. Honolulu, May 5, 1925; s. Joseph Emerson and Pauline Elizabeth Strode; m. Nancy Weller, Nov. 5, 1948 (div. Sept. 1980); children: Margaret, Mardi, Mary, Cay; m. Molly Melcher, Nov. 17, 1985; children: Michael, David. BA, Williams Coll., 1946; MD, Washington U., St. Louis, 1948. Diplomate Am. Bd. Urology. Intern Queen's Med. Ctr., Honolulu, 1948-49; fellow in urology Ochsner Clinic, New Orleans, 1949-52; resident in urology Charity Hosp., 1954-55; urologist Straub Clinic, Honolulu, 1955—. Chief urologist Queen's Med. Ctr., Honolulu, 1960-70, Straub Clinic, 1984—. Contbr. articles to profl. jours. Capt. U.S. Army, 1952-54, Korea. Mem. Am. Urol. Assn., Panpacific Surg. Assn., Endourol. Assn., Hawaii Med. Assn., Honolulu County Med. Assn. Office: Straub Clinic 888 S King St Honolulu HI 96813-3083

STRODE, WILLIAM HALL, III, photojournalist, publisher; b. Louisville, Aug. 6, 1937; s. William Hall and Margaret (Diehl) S.; m. Elizabeth Ann Wheeler, Nov. 26, 1960 (div. 1973); children: Alissa Michelle, Erin Hall; m. Hope Powel Alexander, Nov. 12, 1977 (div. 1997); children: Hope Ives, Charlotte Alexander. BS, Western Ky. U., 1959. News photographer Courier Jour. and Louisville Times, 1960-64, asst. dir. photography, 1968-75; photographer Courier Jour. mag., 1964-77; formed William Strode Assocs., photog. and pub. co., Louisville, 1978—, Harmony House pubs., 1984—. Author 21 books; exhbns. include Fine Arts III, 1961, Profile in Poverty, Smithsonian Instn., 1966, Documerica, in Corcoran Gallery, Washington, 1972, 73, Picture of the Year Travelling Exhibits; one man show includes Speed Mus. Active local Boy Scouts Am.; founder Nat. Press Photographers Found., 1975. Served with AUS, 1959. Recipient Headliners best photojournalism award, 1965; award for excellence for best mag. photog. reporting Overseas Press Club, 1967; co-recipient Pulitzer Prize for pub. service Courier Jour., 1967, for feature photography, 1976; Art Dirs. Gold medal, 1980, World Press Photog. Arts and Scis. award, 1985 Mem. Nat. Press Photographers Assn. (nat. ednl. chmn. 1966-68, v.p. 1973, pres. 1974, Photographer of Yr. 1966, Newspaper Mag. Picture Editor of Yr. 1968), Am. Soc. Mag. Photographers, Soc. Profl. Journalists, Sigma Chi, Kappa Alpha Mu. Methodist. E-mail: harmonypub.a-ol.com. Home and Office: 1008 Kent Rd Goshen KY 40026-9768

STRODEL, ROBERT CARL, lawyer; b. Evanston, Ill., Aug. 12, 1930; s. Carl Frederick and Imogene (Board) S.; m. Mary Alice Shonkwiler, June 17, 1956; children: Julie Ann, Linda Lee, Sally Payson. BS, Northwestern U., 1952; JD, U. Mich., 1955. Bar: Ill. 1955, U.S. Supreme Ct. 1970; diplomate Am. Bd. Profl. Liability Attys.; cert. civil trial specialist Am. Bd. Trial Advocacy. Mem. firm Davis, Morgan & Witherell, Peoria, Ill., 1957-59; pvt. practice, 1959-69; prin. Strodel, Kingery & Durree Assoc., Ill., 1969-92, Law Offices of Robert C. Strodel, Ltd., Peoria, 1992—; asst. state's atty., 1960-61; instr. bus. law Bradley U., 1961-62; lectr. Belli seminars, 1969-87. Mem. U.S. Presdl. Commn. German-Am. Tricentennial, 1983; lectr. in trial practice and med.-legal litigation. Author: Securing and Using Medical Evidence in Personal Injury and Health-Care Cases, 1988; contbr. articles to profl. jours. Gov. appointee Ill. Dangerous Drugs Adv. Coun., 1970-71; gen. chmn. Peoria-Tazewell Easter Seals, 1963, Cancer Crusade, 1970; pres. Peoria Civic Ballet, 1969-70; mem. Mayor's Commn. on Human Rels., 1962-64; chmn. City of Peoria Campaign Ethics Bd., 1975; chmn., builder City of Peoria Mil. Svcs. Meml. Plaza Project, 1998; Peoria County Rep. Sec., 1970-74; campaign chmn. Gov. Richard Ogilvie, Peoria County, 1972, Sen. Ralph Smith, 1970; treas. Michel for Congress, 1977-94, campaign coord., 1982; bd. dirs. Crippled Children's Ctr., 1964-65, Peoria Symphony Orch., 1964-68. Served with AUS, 1956-64. Decorated Officer's Cross of Order of Merit (Fed. Republic Germany), 1984; named Outstanding Young Man Peoria Peoria Jr. C. of C., 1963. Mem. ATLA (bd. govs. 1987-96), ABA, Ill. Trial Lawyers Assn. (bd. mgrs. 1985—), Ill. Bar Assn. (Lincoln awards for legal writing 1961, 63, 65), Am. Inns of Ct. (charter master of bench, Lincoln Inn-Peoria, Ill.), Civil Justice Found. (pres., charter founder, trustee 1986-2002. Clubs: Mason, Scottish Rite. Office: 927 Commerce Bank Peoria IL 61602 E-mail: stro927@aol.com. *The pursuit of professional excellence has been a lifetime goal, coupled with contributions to public, political and civic affairs. He who takes from his community must also contribute to it.*

STRODEL, WILLIAM EDWARD, surgeon, medical educator; b. Sturgis, Mich., Sept. 16, 1947; s. William Edward and Margaret (Tate) S.; m. Melanie Lou Lobdell, Aug. 10, 1990; children: Amy, Matthew, Joshua, William, Forrest. BA, U. Mich., 1969, MD, 1973. Diplomate Am. Bd. Surgery (assoc. examiner 1994, 97-99, 2001--); lic. physician, Mich., Ky., Tex. Intern U. Mich. Affiliate Hosps., Ann Arbor, 1973-74, asst. resident, then resident, 1974-76, sr. resident, 1977-78, chief surg. resident, 1978-79; instr. sect. gen. surgery dept. surgery Med. Sch. U. Mich., 1979-81, asst. prof., 1981-84, assoc. prof., 1984-87; staff surgeon U. Mich. Med. Ctr., 1979-87, U.S. VA Hosp., Ann Arbor, 1979-87; prof., chief divsn. gen. surgery, assoc. chmn. dept. surgery U. Ky. Med. Ctr., Lexington, 1987-96, staff surgeon, 1987-96, W.O. Griffen endowed chair dept. surgery, 1991-967; Dr. Witten B. Russ prof., chmn. dept. surgery U. Tex. Health Scis. Ctr., San Antonio, 1996—2001. Cons. surgeon U. Mich. Health Svc., 1979-82, Wayne County Gen. Hosp., Westland, Mich., 1979-85, U.S. VA Med. Ctr., San Antonio, 1996—; vis. prof. Temple U., Phila., 1984, Abington (Pa.) Meml. Hosp., 1984, 94, Loyola U., Maywood, Ill., 1987, U. Louisville, 1988, Shandong Med. U., Jinan, China, 1990, Mich. State U., Grand Rapids, 1990, Henry Ford Hosp., Detroit, 1991, Good Samaritan Hosp., Cin., 1991, Dartmouth-Hitchcock Med. Ctr., Hanover, N.H., 1991, Tripler Army Hosp., Honolulu, 1996, U. Hawaii, 1996, U. Tenn., Chattanooga, 1996, Sch. Medicine Dartmouth Coll., 1996; mem., then chmn. promotions com. U. Ky., 1988-92; mem. pathology rev. com., chmn. radiation medicine rev. U. Ky. Med. Ctr., 1987-88, mem. ICU com., mem. grad. edn. com., mem., then chmn. oper. rm. com., 1987-96; mem. physician's liaison coun. U. Mich., 1985-87, mem. coms., 1984-87; chmn. spl. study group/ambulatory surg. svcs. VA Med. Ctr., Ann Arbor, 1983, mem. various coms., 1980-84, co-dir. surg. ICU, 1980-82; preceptor U. Mich., 1979-87, mem. coms., 1979-87, participant faculty conf. on edn., 1982, dir. grad. surg. edn., 1983-87; mem. subcom. on practice guidelines for colorectal cancer screening Health Policy Bd. State of Ky., 1995; presenter numerous profl. confs. and symposia, most recently U. Hawaii, 1996, U. Tenn., Chattanooga, 1996, U. Tenn., 1996, Assn. Program Dirs. in Surgery, Phoenix, 1996, Dartmouth-Hitchcock Med. Ctr., 1996, Pan-Pacific Surg. Assn., Honolulu, 1996; presenter videotape ACS, 1982, 83, Southea. Surg. Congress, 1989. Co-author: Surgical Endoscopy, 1985, Surgical Education, 1986; contbr. more than 30 articles to books; reviewer Gastrointestinal Endoscopy, Digestive Disease Scis., Jour. Surg. Endoscopy, NIH, Jour. Surg. Rsch., Am. Jour. Gastroenterology, Surgery; contbr. more than 150 articles to profl. publs. Rsch. grantee or co-grantee various instns., most recently Markey Ctr., 1994, NIH, 1994-96. Fellow ACS (pres. Ky. chpt. 1995-96, mem. coun. 1993); mem. AMA, AAAS, Am. Surg. Assn., Am. Assn. Endocrine Surgeons, Am. Coll. Gastroenterology, Am. Gastroenterology Assn. (mem. abstract selection com. esophageal, gastric and duodenal disorders sect. 1990-91), Am. Soc. Gastrointestinal Endoscopy, Assn. for Acad. Surgery, Soc. Am. Gastrointestinal Endoscopic Surgeons (bd. dirs. 1984-87), Assn. VA Surgeons, Soc. Critical Care Medicine, Soc. Univ. Surgeons, Ctrl. Surg. Assn. (mem. program com. 1991-94, chmn. 1993), Midwest Surg. Assn., Pancreas Club, Frederick A. Coller Surg. Soc. (mem. coun. 1987-90, mem. acad. fellowship com. 1993, scholar 1978), Pan-Pacific Surg. Assn., Ky. Soc. Gastrointestinal Endoscopy (pres. 1991-92), N.Y. Acad. Scis., Western Surg. Assn. (program com. 1995—), Soc. Surgery Alimentary Tract. Home: 118 Box Oak San Antonio TX 78230-5626 Office: U Tex Health Sci Ctr Mail Code 7840 7703 Floyd Curl Dr San Antonio TX 78229-3901

STROER, ROSEMARY ANN, real estate broker; b. N.Y.C., Oct. 1, 1934; d. Joseph and Rose Ann (Maguire) McBrien; m. Charles Stroer, Dec. 6, 1961 (dec. 1976). BA in English, CUNY, 1958, MA in English, 1973; MA, NYU, 1976. Dir. pub. relations PepsiCo, Purchase, N.Y., 1960-70; dir. student services and publs. N.Y.C. Bd. Edn., 1970-82; cons. pub. relations numerous orgns. including Ford Found., Architects for Social Responsibility, Cathedral St. John the Divine, Hampton Day Sch., Local TV, Inc., N.Y.C., 1975—; real estate broker, consultant Equity Analysis Internat. Inc., IT Properties, Inc., 1986—. Author: Work as You Like It, 1979; editor: Holocaust: A Study in Genocide, 1977, Minimum Teaching Essentials, 1980. Spl. rep. Mayor's Task Force on Immunization, N.Y.C., 1982-83; spl. Dem. asst. campaign for Ho. of Reps., N.Y.C., 1972. Recipient Order of the Sun award govt. of Peru, 1964, numerous pub. service awards. Mem. Hunter Coll. Alumni Assn., Mus.

Modern Art, UNICEF. Roman Catholic. Avocations: running, writing, landscaping. Home: 315 E 68th St New York NY 10021-5692 Office: 575 Lexington Ave Ste 505 New York NY 10022-6102

STROH, GUY WESTON, philosophy educator; b. Elizabeth, N.J., Mar. 28, 1931; s. Galusha Amos and Hanna Isabel Stroh; m. Marion Lorraine Kopec, Aug. 13, 1966. AB, Princeton U., 1953, AM, 1955, PhD, 1957. Asst. prof. philosophy Rider U., Lawrenceville, N.J., 1956-63, assoc. prof. philosophy, 1963-66, prof. philosophy, 1966—. Author: Plato and Aristotle, 1964, American Philosophy Edwards to Dewey, 1968, American Ethical Thought, 1979, American Ethics: A Source Book, 2000. Recipient Disting. Tchg. award Lindback Found., 1966. Mem. AAUP (pres. N.J. state conf. 1969-71). Avocation: tennis. Home: 501 Parkway Ave Trenton NJ 08618-2542 Office: Rider U 2083 Lawrenceville Rd Lawrenceville NJ 08648-3099

STROH, RAYMOND EUGENE, retired personnel executive; b. Bloomington, Ill., Aug. 13, 1942; s. Harry William and Felcie Cleo (Weaver) S.; m. Peggy Jane Whitacre, June 12, 1966; children: Rebecca Jane, David Ray. BA, So. Ill. U., 1966, U. Ill., 1977. Pers. technician Ill. Dept. Mental Health, Springfield, Ill., 1966-67; pers. officer Andrew McFarland Mental Health Ctr., 1967-68, Manteno (Ill.) State Hosp., 1968-69; chief pers. officer Ill. Dept. Law Enforcement, Springfield, 1969-75, Ill. Dept. Revenue, Springfield, 1975-81, Ill. Dept. Mental Health, Springfield, 1981-82; pers. exec. Ill. Dept. Cen. Mgmt. Svcs., 1982-2001; ret. State govt. chmn. U.S. Savs. Bond Campaign, Springfield, 1978-82. Bd. dirs. Consumer Credit Counseling Svc., Springfield, 1988-94, sec., 1994; coun. exec. bd. Boy Scouts Am., Springfield, 1987—, v.p., 1987-99, dist. commr., 1979-86, unit commr., 1970-79; bd. dirs. Ill. State Employees Credit Union, 1984-85. Recipient Patriotic Svc. awards U.S. Treasury Dept., 1979-82, Silver Beaver award Boy Scouts Am., 1987, Dist. award of merit, 1981, Area Pres. awards, 1985, 86, Scouters Key award, 1976, Order of the Arrow Vigil Honor, 1998, James E. West Fellowship award, 1998. Mem. NRA, U. Ill. Alumni Assn., So. Ill. U. Alumni Assn., Exptl. Aircraft Assn., Aircraft Owners and Pilots Assn., Ponce De Leon Inlet Lighthouse Assn., Nat. Geog. Soc., Cornell U. Lab. of Ornithology, Abraham Lincoln Gun Club, Appalachian Trail Conf., Union County (Tenn.) Hist. Soc., Bass Anglers Sportsman Soc., Lionel Railroader Club, Wabash R.R. Hist. Soc., Theta Delta Chi. Republican. Lutheran. Avocations: aviation, hunting, fishing, bird watching, model railroading. Home: 2111 Warwick Dr Springfield IL 62704-4147

STROHBEHN, EDWARD ALLEN, investment company executive; b. Madison, Wis., Nov. 13, 1952; s. Bernhard Edward and Helen Lorraine (Evans) S. BS, Bob Jones U., 1974; postgrad., Clemson U., 1974-77. Instr. math. Bob Jones U., Greenville, S.C., 1974-77; rsch. dir. PCA Internat., Charlotte, N.C., 1977-81; v.p. Merrill Lynch, Pierce, Fenner & Smith, Inc., N.Y.C., 1981-91; mgr. Riyad (Saudi Arabia) Bank, 1987-89; sr. v.p. Oppenheimer & Co., Inc., N.Y.C., 1991-92; pres. Strohbehn & Co., Inc., 1992—; v.p. product devel. officer Coutts & Co. Inc., 1996-98. Mem. C. of C. Baptist. Avocations: golf, cello. Home: 245 96th St Apt B9 Brooklyn NY 11209-6843

STROHECKER, LEON HARRY, JR. orthodontist; b. Schuylkill Haven, Pa., Aug. 14, 1932; s. Leon Harry and Anna (Fabian) S.; m. Juanita Mary Puyoou, Apr. 13, 1957; children: Sandra Lee Strohecker Beckett, Leon Harry III. Student, U. Pa., 1950-53, DDS, 1957, orthodontic cert., 1960. Bd. cert. Am. Bd. Orthodontics. Pres., pvt. practice, Lansdale, Pa., 1961—; dir. Face Head & Neck Pain and Trauma Ctr., 1987-99. Bd. dirs. Artman Home Retirement Ctr., Ambler; treas., bd. dirs. Valley Ctr. Mental Health Clinic, Lansdale, 1984—2002; guest lectr. in field. Pres. Lansdale Rotary Club, 1967-68; coun. mem. Trinity Luth. Ch., Lansdale, 1977-85, chmn. fin. com., 1980-85. Lt. (j.g.) USN, 1957-59. Recipient Widsom award of Honor, Best Orthodontist vote, 2 Landsdale area newspapers, One Thousand Great Ams. award, Internat. Biographical Ctr., 2001, 2002. Mem. ADA, Internat. Acad. Head, Neck and Facial Pain, Internat. Coll. Cranio-Mandibular Orthopedics, Am. Acad. Pain Mgmt. (diplomate), Am. Assn. for Functional Orthodontics, Am. Profl. Practice Assn., Am. Soc. Dentistry for Children, Am. Acad. Oral Medicine, Am. Assn. Orthodontists, Am. Assn. Stomatologists, Am. Acad. Oral Medicine, Middle Atlantic Orthodontic Soc., Pa. Orthod ontic Soc., Phila. Orthodontic Soc., Pa. Dental Assn., Second Dist. Dental Assn., Montgomery-Bucks Dental Soc., Alpha Omega, Omicron Kappa Epsilon. Avocations: tennis, travel, bridge, water sports. Bus. Home: 1512 Cedar Hill Rd Ambler PA 19002-1406 Office: 456 E Hancock St Lansdale PA 19446-3803 E-mail: braces4u@erols.com., juanitas@erols.com.

STROHKIRCH, CAROLYN SUE, communication educator; b. Gladwin, Mich., Aug. 11, 1952; d. Lewis and Elsie Wanda (Endert) S. BA, U. Mich., Ann Arbor, 1974; MA, Ctrl. Mich. U., Mt. Pleasant, 1980; PhD, U. Washington, Seattle, 1988. Cert secondary tchr., Mich. Dir. forensics U. Texas, El Paso, 1980-82, McMurry U., Abilene, Tex., 1982-84; grad. tchg. asst. U. Washington, Seattle, 1984-87; asst. prof. Ill. State U., Normal, 1987-94; basic course dir., assoc. prof. Fort Hays (Kans.) State U., 1994—. Co-author: Fundamentals of Oral Communication, 2d edit., 1997; editl. bd. Ill. Speech and Theatre Assn. Jourl, 1992-95, Kans. Speech Jour., 1996—; contbr. articles to profl. jours. Adv. bd. Human Soc. High Plains, Hays, Kans., 1996—; exec. bd. Sunflower Coun. Girl Scouts Am., Hays, 1998—. Mem. Nat. Comm. Assn., We. Speech Comm. Assn., Ctrl. States Comm. Assn. (officer interest group 2000—), Kans. Speech Comm. Assn., Tex. Speech Comm. Assn. Home: 115 E 18th St Hays KS 67601 Office: Fort Hays State U Dept Comm 600 Park St Hays KS 67601 E-mail: sstrohki@fhsu.edu.

STROHMEIER, GREGG ROBERT, research scientist; b. Alamoso, Colo., Nov. 18, 1964; s. Robert Charles and Betty Jean (Siney) S. BS, U. Rochester, 1987; PhD, Boston U., 1992. Clin. lab. technician Boston (Mass.) U., 1989-91; post-doctoral fellow Brigham and Women's Hosp./Harvard Univ, Boston, 1992—. Contbr. articles to profl. jours. NIH Tng. grantee NRSA, NIH/NIDDK, Harvard U., 1994—. Mem. AAAS, Am. Soc. for Cell Biology. Avocations: gardening, traveling. Office: Brigham & Womens Hosp Harvard Univ 20 Shattuck St # 1433 Boston MA 02115-6024

STROHMEYER, JOHN, writer, former editor; b. Cascade, Wis., June 26, 1924; s. Louis A. and Anna Rose (Saladunas) S.; m. Nancy Jordan, Aug. 20, 1949; children: Mark, John, Sarah. Student, Moravian Coll., 1941-43; AB, Muhlenberg Coll., 1947; MA in Journalism, Columbia, 1948; L.H.D. (hon.), Lehigh U., 1983. With Nazareth Item, 1940-41; night reporter Bethlehem (Pa.) Globe-Times, 1941-43, 45-47; investigative reporter Providence Jour.-Bull., 1949-56; editor Bethlehem Globe-Times, 1956-84, v.p., 1961-84, dir., 1963-84. African-Am. journalism tchr. in Nairobi, Freetown, 1964; Atwood prof. journalism U. Alaska Anchorage, 1987-88, writer-in-residence, 1989—; Clendinen Prof., U. S. Fla., 2001. Author: Crisis in Bethlehem: Big Steel's Struggle to Survive, 1986, Extreme Conditions: Big Oil and The Transformation of Alaska, 1993, Historic Anchorage, 2001. Lt. (j.g.) USNR, 1943-45. Pulitzer Traveling fellow, 1948; Nieman fellow, 1952-53; recipient Comenius award Moravian Coll., 1971; Pulitzer prize for editorial writing, 1972; Alicia Patterson Found. fellow, 1984, 85. Mem. Am. Soc. Newspaper Editors, Pa. Soc. Newspaper Editors (pres. 1964-66), Anchorage Racquet Club. Home: 6633 Lunar Dr Anchorage AK 99504-4550 E-mail: jstroh@gci.net.

STROIK, DUNCAN GREGORY, architect, architectural design educator; b. Phila., Jan. 14, 1962; s. John Stephen and Mary Eugenia (Dorsey) S.; m. Ruth Valeira Engelhardt, Aug. 29, 1987; children: Gabrielle Marie, Raffaella Maria, Giovanni Battista, Pietro Francesco. BS in Architecture, U. Va., 1984; MArch, Yale U., 1987. Registered arch., Ill., Ind., Conn., Ariz., Ala., Ga., Wis., Minn. Tchg. asst. Yale U. Sch. Architecture, New Haven, 1985-87; arch. Allan Greenberg, Arch., Washington, 1987-90; assoc. prof. U. Notre Dame (Ind.) Sch. Architecture, 1990—; arch. Duncan Stroik, Arch., South Bend, Ind., 1990—. Chmn. lectr. com. U. Notre Dame, Ind., 1990—, mem. undergrad. com., 1992—, com. on internat. studies, 1993-94; chmn. jury Ind. Concrete Masonry Assn., Ind., 1994. Arch., author Building Classical, 1993;exhibitions include U. Steubenville, 1995, N.Y. Acad. of Art, 1994, Yale U. Sch. Architecture, 1995, Chgo. Cultural Ctr., 1995, others; editor: Sacred Arch. Mag., Reconquering Sacred Space, 2000; contbr. articles to profl. jours.; appeared on Bob Vila's In Search of Palladio, 1998. With East Rock Pavilion-Design and Constrn., Yale U. Sch. Architecture, New Haven, 1985; active Habitat for Humanity, New Haven, 1987, U. Notre Dame chpt. faculty adv.; mem. faculty senate U. Notre Dame, 1998—. Palladio and Vitruvius grantee Graham Found. for Advanced Studies, 1991, Student Rsch. grantee Promote Women and Minorities Grad. Studies, U. Notre, Dame, 1993; C.L.V. Meeks Meml. scholar Yale U., New Haven, 1987; Sacred Architecure grantee Homeland Found., 1996; recipient Ind. award, AIA, 1998. Mem.: Inst. for Classical Architecture, Assn. Collegiate Schs. Architecture, Nat. Trust for Hist. Preservation, Classical Am. Roman Catholic. Avocations: classical music, philosophy, travel, painting. Home: 52488 Briarcliff Ln South Bend IN 46635-1104 Office: Univ Notre Dame Sch Architecture Notre Dame IN 46556

STROJNIK, TADEJ, neurosurgeon, researcher; b. Ljubljana, Slovenia, July 11, 1963; s. Franc and Marija (Petrič) S.; m. Irena Šurca, June 6, 1987; children: Tom, Maša. MD, U. Ljubljana, 1989, MSc, 1994, PhD, 1998. Physician Health Ctr., Ptuj, Slovenia, 1989-90; resident in neurosurgery Univ. Clinic Neurosurgery, Ljubljana, 1995-96, Tchg. Hosp., Maribor, Slovenia, 1990-95, neurosurgeon Slovenia, 1996—. Aitken Clin. Rsch. fellow, 1998-99. Mem. Med. Chamber Slovenia, Slovene Med. Soc., Slovenian Neurosurg. Soc. (sec. 1997-2001), European Assn. Neurosurgeons, Ctrl. European Neurosurg. Soc. (bd. dirs.). Roman Catholic. Avocations: photography, fishing, reading. Office: Tchg Hosp Dept Neurosurgery Ljubljanska 5 2000 Maribor Slovenia E-mail: tadej.strojnik@siol.net., tadej.strojnik@sb-mb.si.

STROJNY, NORMAN, analytical chemist; b. Edwardsville, Pa., June 14, 1943; s. John M. and Brunislawa (Stawarz) S. BS in Chemistry, Wilkes Coll., 1966; MS in Chemistry, Montclair State Coll., 1974; PhD in Analyt. Chemistry, Rutgers U., 1980, MBA in Mgmt., 1985. From jr. chemist to sr. chemist Hoffmann LaRoche, Nutley, N.J., 1965-85; from sr. chemist to mgr. Danbury Pharmacal, Carmel, N.Y., 1985-99; drug industry cons. Washington, 1999—. Contbr. articles to profl. jours. Mem. Am. Assn. Pharm. Scientists, Am. Chem. Soc., Am. Inst. Chemistry, Soc. Applied Spectroscopy (local chmn. 1983-84, Ea. Analytical Symposium bd. dirs. 1983-84). Achievements include research in analytical methods for pharmaceuticals. Office: 16 Cook St Washington CT 06794

STROKE, HINKO HENRY, physicist, educator; b. Zagreb, Croatia, June 16, 1927; came to U.S., 1943, naturalized, 1949; s. Elias and Edith (Mechner) S.; m. Norma Bilchick, Jan. 14, 1956; children: Ilana Lucy, Marija Tamar. BEE, N.J. Inst. Tech., 1949; MS, MIT, 1952, PhD, 1955. From rsch. asst. to rsch. assoc. Princeton (N.J.) U., 1954-57; rsch. staff lab. electronics, lectr. dept. physics MIT, 1957-63; assoc. prof. physics NYU, N.Y.C., 1963-68, prof., 1968—. Dept. chmn. NYU, 1988-91; prof. associé. U. Paris, 1969-70, Ecole Normale Supérieure, 1976; vis. scientist Max Planck Inst. für Quantenoptik, Garching, U. Munich, 1977-78, 81-82, 93; cons. Atomic Instrument Co., MIT Sci. Translation Svc., Tech. Rsch. Group, Cambridge Air Force Rsch. Ctr., Am. Optical Corp., ITT Fed. Labs., NASA, others; mem. com. on line spectra of elements NAS-NRC, 1976-82; sci. assoc. CERN, Geneva, 1983—. Contbg. author: Nuclear Physics, 1963, Atomic Physics, 1969, Hyperfine Interactions in Excited Nuclei, 1971, Francis Bitter: Selected Papers, 1969, Atomic Physics 3, 1973, Nuclear Moments and Nuclear Structure, 1973, A Perspective of Physics, Vol. 1, 1977, Atomic Physics 8, 1983, Lasers in Atomic, Molecular, and Nuclear Physics, 1989—, Symposium on Probing Luminous and Dark Matter, 2000; editor: Comments on Atomic and Molecular Physics, The Physical Review-The First Hundred Years. Mem. Chorus Pro Musica, 1951—54, 1957—63, Münchener Bach-Chor, Munich, 1977—82, 1992; Choeur pro Arte Lausanne, 1983—; mem. Collegiate Chorale, NY, 1964—94, Dessoff Choirs, 1994—2001, Westchester Oratorio Soc., 2001—. Recipient Sr. U.S. Scientist award Alexander von Humboldt Found., 1977; NATO sr. fellow in sci., 1975 Fellow Am. Phys. Soc. (publs. oversight com. 1991-93), Optical Soc. Am., AAAS; mem. IEEE, European Phys. Soc., Soc. Fraçaise de Physique, Sigma Xi, Tau Beta Pi, Omicron Delta Kappa. Office: NYU Dept Physics 4 Washington Pl New York NY 10003-6621 E-mail: henry.stroke@nyu.edu.

STROM, BRIAN LESLIE, internist, educator; b. N.Y.C., N.Y., Dec. 8, 1949; s. Martin and Edith (Singer) S.; m. Elaine Marilyn Moskowitz, June 4, 1978; children: Shayna Lee, Jordan Blair. BS, Yale U., 1971; MD, Johns Hopkins U., 1975; MPH, U. Calif., Berkeley, 1980. Diplomate Am. Bd. Internal Medicine, Am. Bd. Epidemiology. Intern in medicine U. Calif., San Francisco, 1975-76, resident in medicine, 1976-78, research fellow in clinical pharmacology, 1978-80; from asst. prof. to assoc. prof. medicine and pharmacology U. Pa., Phila., 1980-93, prof. medicine, 1993—, prof. biostatistics & epidemiology, 1995—. Adj. asst. prof. clin. pharmacy Phila. Coll. of Pharmacy and Sci., 1981-90, adj. assoc. prof., 1990-93, adj. prof., 1993—; mem. U. Pa. Cancer Ctr., 1981—; attending staff Hosp. U. Pa., 1980—, co-dir Clin. Epidemiology Unit, 1980-91, dir., 1991—; dir. Clin. Pharmacology Cons. Svc., 1981-82; dir. Ctr. for Clin. Epidemiology and Biostats., 1993—, chair dept. biostats. and epidemiology, 1995—; lectr. in field; cons. CDC, 1981, Coun. for Internat. Orgn. of Med. Scis., Geneva, Switzerland, 1981-83, Office of Tech. Assessment, Congress of U.S., 1980-81, Aging Rev. Com., Nat. Inst. Aging, 1982, Ministry of Pub. Health, State of Kuwait, 1982, Royal Tropical Inst., Amsterdam, 1983, others. Editl. cons. Johns Hopkins U. Press, J.B. Lippincott; referee Annals of Internal Medicine, Archives of Internal Medicine, Clin. Pharmacology and Therapeutics, Digestive Diseases and Sci., Internat. Jour. Cardiology, Internat. Jour. Epidemiology, Jour. AMA, Jour. Gen. Internal Medicine, Med. Care, Primary Care Tech., Sci.; editor Pharmaepidemiology and Drug Safety; assoc. editor Jour. Gen. Internal Medicine; mem. editl. bd. 7 jours.; contbr. numerous articles to profl. jours. Nat. Acad. Scis. grantee, Rockefeller Found. grantee, NIH grantee, many others. Fellow ACP, Am. Coll. Epidemiology, Am. Epidemiology Soc.; mem. Am. Fedn. Clin. Rsch., Am. Pub. Health Assn., Am. Soc. Clin. Pharmacology and Therapeutics, Am. Soc. Clin. Investigation, Am. Assn. Physicians, Internat. Soc. Pharmacoepidemiology, Internat. Epideliol. Assn., Soc. for Epidemiologic Rsch., Soc. Gen. Internal Medicine. Democrat. Jewish. Avocations: hiking, biking, camping, skiing. Home: 332 Hidden River Rd Narberth PA 19072-1111

STROM, J. PRESTON, JR. lawyer; b. May 21, 1959; s. Grace and J.P. Sr. S.; m. Donna Savoca, Oct. 5, 1985; children: Margaret, Caroline. BA, U. S.C., 1981, JD, 1984. Bar: S.C. 1984, U.S. Dist. Ct. S.C., 1984, U.S. Ct. Appeals (4th cir.) 1984. Asst. solicitor 5th Jud. Cir., S.C., 1985-86; ptnr. Leventis, Strom & Wicker, 1986-88, Harpootlian & Strom, 1988-90, Bolt, Popowski, McCulloch & Strom, 1990-93; acting U.S. atty. Office U.S. Atty., S.C., 1993, U.S. atty., 1993-96; atty. Strom Law Firm, LLC, Columbia, 1996—. Chmn. Law Enforcement Coord. Com.; chmn. juvenile justice and child support enforcement subcom. U.S. Dept. Justice; active Atty. Gen. Adv. Com. Mem. S.C. Bar, S.C. Trial Lawyers Assn., Richland County Bar Assn. (chmn. criminal law sect.). Office: Strom Law Firm LLC 1201 Hampton St Ste 3A Columbia SC 29201-2865

STROM, KRISTINA CHASE, writer, consultant; b. Schenectady, Ny, Dec. 28, 1948; d. Raymond Olaf and Lois Moulton Strom; children: Kia Strom Kuresman, Kamala Strom Kuresman, Kimberly Strom Kuresman, Kara Strom Kuresman. PhD, Universal Life Sem. Lic. Insurance OH; Ordained Clergy OH. Asst. buyer, buyer Hess's Dept. Store, Allentown, Pa., 1968—69; educator Xavier U. New Orleans, New Orleans, 1970; columnist Denver Free Press, Denver, 1972; co-founder, owner New World Ctr. Bookshop and Foodshop, 1973—74; tchr. Beth Adam Religious Sch., 1981—88, art dir. Ohio, 1987—89; editor Beth Adam Newsletter, 1982—86; prin. Beth Adam Religious Sch., 1988—89; designer Del Favero Enterprises, 1984—90; store mgr. B. Dalton Books, 1990—91; systems operator TriStateOnline Greater Cin. Consortium Colleges and Universities, 1999, adminstr. Cincinatti, 1999; pvt. practice Glendale, 1968—; freelance artist, 1970—; design and bus. cons., 1985—. Columnist, staff writer Silent Sessages, Cincinnati, Ohio, 1996—99; moderator Wells List, 1995—; owner, mgr. CelestialPerspectives.com, Cincinnati, Ohio, 1999—. Designer and co-creator (fiber art, four innovative torah covers); fiber wall hanging; author: (book) Denim and Lace, An historical mystery of first love, timeless love; co-editor and contributor (book) From Eulogy to Joy, A Heartfelt Anthology; contbr. articles to professional journals, poems to journals. Pres. Kindervelt #17 Cin. Children's Hosp. aux., Cincinnati, Ohio, 1983—85. Mem.: Smithsonian Nat. Mus. Am. Indian, The Nature Conservancy, Nat. Audubon Soc., The Nat. Ctr. for the Preservation of Medicinal Herbs, Am. Quilter's Soc., Sierra Club, The Twilight Club Ctr. Evolutionary Ethics. Avocations: gardening, genealogy, book collecting, archeology, archeology. Home: 171 West Sharon Road Glendale OH 45246-4334 Personal E-mail: kristinastrom@celestialperspectives.com.

STROM, LYLE ELMER, federal judge; b. Omaha, Jan. 6, 1925; s. Elmer T. and Eda (Hanisch) Strom; m. Regina Ann Kelly, July 31, 1950 (dec.); children: Mary Bess, Susan Frances(dec.) , Amy Claire, Cassie A., David Kelly, Margaret Mary, Bryan Thomas. Student, U. Nebr., 1946-47; AB, Creighton U., 1950, JD cum laude, 1953. Bar: Nebr. 1953. Assoc. Fitzgerald, Brown, Leahy, Strom, Schorr & Barmettler and predecessor firm, Omaha, 1953-60, ptnr., 1960-63, gen. trial ptnr., 1963-85; judge U.S. Dist. Ct. Nebr., 1985-87, chief judge, 1987-94, sr. judge, 1995—. Adj. prof. law Creighton U., 1959-95, clinical prof., 1996—; mem. com. pattern jury instrns. and practice and proc. Nebr. Supreme Ct., 1965-91; spl. legal counsel Omaha Charter Rev. Commn., 1973; chair gender fairness task force U.S. Ct. Appeals (8th cir.), 1993-97. Exec. com. Covered Wagon Coun. Boy Scouts Am., 1953—57, bd. trustees, exec. com. Mid-Am. Coun., 1988—; chmn. bd. trustees Marian H.S., 1969—71; mem. pres. coun. Creighton U., 1990—. With U.S. Maritime Svc., 1943—46. Fellow Am. Coll. Trial Lawyers, Internat. Acad. Trial Lawyers; mem. Nebr. Bar Assn. (ho. of dels. 1978-81, exec. coun. 1981-87, pres. 1989-90), Nebr. Bar Found. (bd. trustees 1998—), Omaha Bar Assn. (pres. 1980-81), Am. Judicature Soc., Midwestern Assn. Amateur Athletic Union (pres. 1976-78), Rotary (pres. 1993-94), Alpha Sigma Nu (pres. alumni chpt. 1970-71). Republican. Roman Catholic. Office: US Dist Ct Roman Hruska Courthouse 111 S 18th Plz Ste 3190 Omaha NE 68102

STROM, MILTON GARY, lawyer; b. Rochester, N.Y., Dec. 5, 1942; s. Harold and Dolly (Isaacson) S.; m. Barbara A. Simon, Jan. 18, 1975; children: Carolyn, Michael, Jonathan. BS in Econ., U. Pa., 1964; JD, Cornell U., 1967. Bar: N.Y. 1968, U.S. Dist. Ct. (W. dist.) N.Y. 1968, U.S. Ct. Claims 1969, U.S. Ct. Mil. Appeals 1969, U.S. Ct. Appeals (D.C. cir.) 1970, U.S. Supreme Ct. 1972, U.S. Dist. Ct. (so. dist.) N.Y. 1975. Atty. SEC, Washington, 1968-71; assoc. Skadden, Arps, Slate, Meagher & Flom, N.Y.C., 1971-76, ptnr., 1977—. Served with USCGR, 1967-73. Mem. ABA, N.Y. State Bar Assn. (corp. law sect.), Assn. of Bar of City of N.Y., Internat. Bar Assn., Beach Point Club. Republican. Jewish. Avocations: tennis, skiing, golf. Office: Skadden Arps Slate Meagher & Flom 4 Times Sq Fl 42 New York NY 10036-6522 E-mail: mstrom@skadden.com.

STROM, ROBERT DUANE, psychologist, educator; b. Chgo., Jan. 21, 1935; m. Shirley Mills; children: Steven, Paris. BS, Macalester Coll., 1958; MA, U. Minn., 1959; PhD, U. Mich., 1962. Prof. U. Conn., Storrs, Conn., 1962—64, Ohio State U., Columbus, Ohio, 1964—69, Ariz. State U., Tempe, Ariz., 1969—. Author: Teaching In The Slum School, 1965, Mental Health And Achievement, 1965, The Inner-City Classroom, 1966, Psychology For The Classroom, 1969, Expreiences In Educational Psychology, 1970, Values And Human Development, 1972, Education For Affective Achievement, 1973, Parent And Child In Fiction, 1977, Parent And Child Development, 1978, Growing Through Play, 1981, Eductional Psychology, 1982, Human Development And Learning, 1989, Grandparent Education, 1991, Becoming A Better Grandparent, 1991, Achieving Grandparent Potential, 1992, (measurement instruments) Grandparent Strengths and Needs Inventory, 1993, Parent As a Teacher Inventory, 1995, Parent Success Indicator, 1998, Interpersonal Intelligence Inventory, 2002. Scholar, Fulbright Found., 1975, 1976, 1985. Home: 6017 East Cambridge Ave Scottsdale AZ 85257 Office: Coll Education Arizona State Univ Tempe AZ 85287-0611 Fax: 480-994-1834. E-mail: bob.strom@asu.edu.

STROMBERG, BERT E. veterinary medicine educator; b. Trenton, N.J., May 19, 1944; s. Bert E. and R. Evelyn Stromberg; m. JoAnn Earling Stromberg, June 22, 1968; children: B. Erik, Kristin L. BA, Lafayette Coll., 1966; MA, U. Mass., 1968; PhD, U. Pa., 1973. Instr. Trenton State Coll., Ewing, NJ, 1968—70; asst. prof. U. Pa., Phila., 1973—79; assoc. prof. U. Minn. Coll. Vet. Med., St. Paul, 1979—86, prof., 1986—, assoc. dean rsch., 2000—. Adj. prof. Inst. Agronomique at Vet. Hassan II, Morocco, 1985—. Contbr. articles to profl. jours.; mem. editl. bd. (jours.) Experimental Parasitology, 1984—, Veterinary Parasitology, 1995—, Animal Health Rsch. Revs. and Veterinary Therapeutics, 1999—. Mem.: Conf. Rsch. Workers in Animal Disease (pres. 1996—97), Am. Assn. Vet. Parasitologists (pres. 1989—90). Office: U Minn Coll Vet Med 1365 Gartner Ave Saint Paul MN 55108 Business E-Mail: b-stro@umn.edu.

STROMBERG, BEVERLY A. certified public accountant; b. Des Moines, Nov. 1, 1946; d. Kenneth and Neola E. Atkinsol; m. David A. Stromberg, June 22, 1968; children: Kristin E., Kevin D. BS in Acctg., Drake U., 1968. CPA, Iowa. Staff acct. Peat, Marwick, Mitchell, CPAS, Des Moines, 1968-70; revenue agt. IRS, 1971-76; acctg. instr. Des Moines Area C.C., Ankeny, Iowa, 1976-80; tax and risk mgr. Des Moines Register & Tribune, Des Moines, 1980—; revenue agt. IRS. Author: (tng. course) IRS-Pension Law Tng. Course, 1974, IRS-Partnership Law Tng. Course, 1976, IRS-Managers EEO Tng. Course, 1990. Mentor, evaluator 4-H, Des Moines, 1990-97; tchr., Church, Des moines, 1969—; support Amateur Ice Hockey, Des Moines, 1993—. Recipient One of the First Five Women To Become CPA in Iowa award, 1969, numerous IRS awards. Mem. Iowa Soc. CPAs. Avocations: swimming, ice skating, travel, costume design, music.

STROMBERG, CLIFFORD DOUGLAS, lawyer; b. N.Y.C., June 1, 1949; s. George M. and Greta (Netzow) S.; m. Ava S. Feiner, June 25, 1972; children: Kimberly, Eric. BA summa cum laude, Yale U., 1971; JD, Harvard U., 1974. Bar: N.Y. 1975, D.C. 1975, U.S. Dist. Ct. (so. and ea. dists.) N.Y. 1975, U.S. Ct. Appeals (D.C. cir.) 1975, U.S. Ct. Appeals (2nd cir.) 1975, U.S. Supreme Ct. 1980. Law clk. to judge U.S. Dist. Ct. (ea. dist.) N.Y., 1974-75; assoc. Arnold & Porter, Washington, 1975-78, 80-83; dep. exec. sec. HHS, 1978-80; cons. FTC, 1980; ptnr. Dorsey & Whitney, 1983-84, Hogan & Hartson, Washington, 1984—. Adj. asst. prof. emergency medicine George Washington U. Sch. Medicine, 1991-97. Co-author: Mental Health and Law: A System in Transition, 1975, Alternatives to the Hospital: Ambulatory Surgery Centers and Emergicenters, 1984, Entrepreneurial Health Care: How to Structure Successful New Ventures, 1985, The Psychologist's Legal Handbook, 1988, Access to Hospital Information: Problems and Strategies: 4 Frontiers of Health Services Management 3-33, 1987, Healthcare Provider Networks: Antitrust Issues and Practical Considerations in Devels. in Antitrust Law, 1990, Healthcare Credentialing: Implications for Academic Medical Centers, 1991; mem. editl. bd. Harvard Law Rev., 1972-73; editor in chief Healthspan: The Report of Health Business and Law, 1984-87; cons. editor: Managed Care Law Strategist, 1999-2002; contbr. articles to profl. jours. Bd. dirs. Nat. Children's Eye Care Found., Washington, 1985-87. Teaching fellow in govt. Harvard U., 1973-74. Fellow Am. Bar Found.; mem. ABA (chair working group health care reform 1993-96, state membership chmn. 1984, forum com. health law 1987-90, adv. com. govt. affairs 1993-98, governing bd., individual rights and responsibilities sect., exec. coun., 1980-90, sec. 1984-87, chair-elect 1987-88, chair 1988-89, legal aid and indigent defendants com. 1982-87), Am. Health Lawyers Assn., Nat. Assn. Coll. and Univ. Attys., Phi Beta Kappa. Office: Hogan & Hartson 555 13th St NW Washington DC 20004-1161 E-mail: cdstromberg@hh.law.com.

STROMBERG, GREGORY, printing ink company executive; b. Milw., Feb. 10, 1948; s. Clifford Norman and Margaret Betty (Hoover) S.; m. Gail Elizabeth Steinbach, Aug. 22, 1970; children: Christopehr, Brian, Ellen. BS, Marquette U., Milw., 1970. Office contact salesman Continental Can Co., Milw., 1970-78; sales rep. Sun Chem. Co., 1978-82; v.p., gen. mgr. Acme Printing Ink Co., 1982—; exec. v.p. Can. ops. Acme Printing Ink Can. Ltd., 1985—, pres., 1990—, v.p. sales/mktg. metal divsn., 2000—. Bd. dirs. Can. Ops. Acme Inks of Can.; pres. Toobee Internat., Inc., Milw., 1981—; v.p., dir. mktg. and internat. sales INX Internat. Ink Co., 1991—. Author: Toobee Air Force Flight Training Manual, 1983. Advisor Milw. Jr. Achievement, 1974; sponsor Muscular Dystrophy, 1983; asst. mem. com. toys for Tots, Children's Hosp., Milw., 1983; active United Meth. Men. Mem. Am. Mktg. Assn., Sales and Mktg. Execs. of Milw., Am. Mgmt. Assn., Am. Soc. Quality Control, Nat. Metal Decorators Assn., Nat. Assn. Printers and Lithographers, Nat. Assn. Printing Equipment and Suppliers. Home: N69w23448 Donna Dr Sussex WI 53089-3245 E-mail: mitze@execpc.com.

STROMBERG, JEAN WILBUR GLEASON, lawyer; b. St. Louis, Oct. 31, 1943; d. Ray Lyman and Martha (Bugbee) W.; m. Gerald Kermit Gleason, Aug. 28, 1966 (div. 1987); children: C. Blake, Peter Wilbur; m. Kurt Stromberg, Jan. 3, 1993; 1 child, Kristoffer Stromberg. BA, Wellesley Coll., 1965; LLB cum laude, Harvard U., 1968. Bar: Calif. 1969, D.C. 1978. Assoc.

Brobeck, Phleger & Harrison, San Francisco, 1969-72; spl. counsel to dir. div. corp. fin. SEC, Washington, 1972-76, assoc. dir. div. investment mgmt., 1976-78; of counsel Fulbright & Jaworski, 1978-80, ptnr., 1980-96; dir. fin. instns. and market issues GAO, 1996-97; cons., 1997—. Mem. adv. panel on legal issues GAO, 1992—96; mem. NASD select com. on NASDAQ, 1994—96; trustee AARP Intestment Program and AARP Scudder Mut. Funds, 1997—2000; bd. dirs. Scudder Mut. Funds., Svc. Source, Inc., Mut. Fund Dirs. Forum. Dir. William and Flora Hewlett Found., 2000—. Mem. ABA (chmn. subcom. on securities and banks, corp. laws com., bus. sect. 1982-93), D.C. Bar Assn. (chmn. steering com. bus. sect. 1982-84), FBA (chair exec. coun., securities com. 1993-95), Am. Bar Retirement Assn. (bd. dirs. 1986-90, 94-96), Phi Beta Kappa. Home and Office: 3816 Military Rd NW Washington DC 20015-2704

STROMBERG, LISEN HOEM, fundraiser, consultant; b. Palo Alto, Calif., Aug. 9, 1962; d. Jackson Clafflin and Elizabeth (Hoem) S. B.A. in Poli. Sci., Dartmouth Coll., 1984. Mktg. rep. Outline, Inc., N.Y.C., 1984-85; coordinator planning and devel. NOW Legal Def. and Edn. Fund, N.Y.C., 1985— ; cons. Planned Parenthood Fedn. of Am., N.Y.C., 1984-85. Chmn. jr. com. of friends Ensemble Studio Theatre, N.Y.C., 1985— . Clubs: Meadowwood (Napa, Calif.); Mill Valley Tennis (Calif.). Democrat. Avocations: skiing; tennis; running. Office: NOW Legal Def and Edn Fund Now Legal Def Fund # 99 New York NY 10013

STROMBERG, ROSS ERNEST, lawyer; b. Arcata, Calif., May 5, 1940; s. Noah Anders and Anne Laura (Noyes) S.; m. Toni Nicholas, Dec. 16, 1961; m. Margaret Telonicher, Oct. 3, 1965; children: Kristin, Matthew, Gretchen, Erik. BS, Humboldt State U., 1962; JD, U. Calif., Berkeley, 1965. Bar: Calif. 1966, U.S. Dist. Ct. (no. dist.) Calif. 1966, U.S. Ct. Appeals (9th cir.) 1966. Assoc. Hanson Bridgett, San Francisco, 1965-70, ptnr., 1970-85, Epstein Becker Stromberg & Green, San Francisco, 1985-90, Jones Day Reavis & Pogue, L.A., 1990—. Chmn. Jones Day's Healthcare Specialized Industry Practice; pres. Shyster Creek Vineyards, Healdsburg, Calif., 2002—. Author: Economic Joint Venturing, 1985, Acquisition and Enhancement of Physician Practices, 1988. Bd. dirs. Sutter Med. Ctr., Santa Rosa, 2001—; pres. Am. Acad. Hosp. Attys. of Am. Host. Assn., Chgo., 1978, East Bay AHEC, Oakland, Calif., 1984—87; bd. dirs. Am. Cancer Soc., 1984—95, Wildflowers Inst., San Francisco. Mem. Am. Health Lawyers Assn. Democrat. Office: Jones Day Reavis & Pogue 555 W 5th St Ste 4600 Los Angeles CA 90013-1025

STROMBERG, WALTER JAMES, radio personality; b. Brooklyn, Ny, July 8, 1944; s. Everett Clinton and Edna Lillian Stromberg; m. Wetona Clark Stromberg, Mar. 2, 1984; m. Joan Rita Stromberg, Aug. 12, 1967 (div. Jan. 30, 1980); children: Robin Angela, Susan Justine, Gary Walter, Lawrence Everett. MBA, Rutgers U., Newark, New Jersey, 1975; BA, Windham Coll., Putnay, Vermont, 1967. Newsman WFAS and WKO Radio, Hartsdale and Nanuet, NY, 1967—; trust and estate acct. Joel E. Mitchell and Company, 1962—67; rschr. Self-employed, Aquebogue, NJ, 2000—; telemarketer Various Cities, South Kearny and Newark, 1980—94; editor NJ Bell Tel. Co., Newark and Madison, 1975—80; acct. AT&T Technologies, South Kearney and Newark, 1969—75. Treas. West Hudson Jaycees, Kearney, NJ, 1973. Airman basic USAF, 1962, San Antonio, Texas. Recipient Outstanding Young Men of Am., Outstanding Young Men of Am., 1974, Writing Award, NJ Assn. of Bus. Comm., 1976. Methodist. Avocation: music. Home: PO Box 711 Jamesport NY 11947-0711

STROMBOM, CATHY JEAN, transportation planner, consultant; b. Bremerton, Wash., Nov. 4, 1949; d. Paul D. and Carolyn (Snitman) Powers; m. David Glen Strombom, June 17, 1972; 1 child, Paul Davis. BA summa cum laude, Whitman Coll., 1972; M in City and Regional Planning, Harvard U., 1977; postgrad., U. Wash., 1982-84. Urban planner Harvard Inst. for Internat. Devel., Tehran, Iran, 1977; sr. transp. planner Puget Sound Coun. Govts., Seattle, 1978-84; asst. v.p., mgr. transp. planning/prin. profl. assoc. Parsons Brinckerhoff Quade and Douglas, Inc., 1984—. V.p. Women's Transp. Seminar, Seattle, 1988-90 (Woman of Yr. 1989). Contbr. articles to profl. jours. Vol. U.S. Peace Corps, Marrakech, Morocco, 1973-75. Mem. Am. Inst. Cert. Planners (cert.), Am. Planning Assn., Inst. Transp. Engrs.,Leadership Tomorrow, Phi Beta Kappa. Home: 2580 W Viewmont Way W Seattle WA 98199-3660 Office: Parsons Brinckerhoff Quade and Douglas Inc 999 3rd Ave Ste 2200 Seattle WA 98104-4044

STROMBOM, DAVID GLEN, designer; b. Pullman, Wash., Apr. 18, 1951; s. Donald A. and Dona S. (Bell) S.; m. Cathy J. Powers, June l7, 1972; l child, Paul Davis. Student, Whitman Coll., l968-70; BS in Architecture, Wash. State U., 1973; MArch, Harvard U., 1977. Registered arch., Wash. Vol. U.S. Peace Corps, Marrakech, Morocco, 1973-75; designer Seattle, 1978-82; prin. The Strombom Architects, 1982-91; dir. David Roberts Bowman, Ltd., 1991—; assoc. Internat. Devel. Bus. Cons., Washington, 1996—, Islamabad, Pakistan, 1996, Port au Prince, Haiti, 1997-99, Bali, Indonesia, 1999, Chiang Mai, Thailand, 1999. Fulbright scholar Ahmedabad, India, 1977-78; vis. prof. Ahmedabad Sch. Architecture; designer Ctr. Devel. Studies and Activities, Pune, India. Reg. Architect, State of Washington.

STROME, MARSHALL, otolaryngologist, educator; b. Lynn, Mass., Apr. 27, 1940; s. David and Rose (Cantor) S.; m. Deena Lazarov, Sept. 23, 1962; children: Scott Eric, Randall Alan. Degree, U. Mich., 1960, MD, 1964, MS, 1970. Resident in otolaryngology U. Mich., Ann Arbor, 1966-70; asst. prof. U. Conn., Hartford, 1971, Beth Israel-Harvard, Boston, 1972-77, chief otolaryngology, 1977-93; prof., chmn. otolaryngology Cleve. Clinic Found., 1993—. Sr. surgeon Brigham & Women's Hosp., Boston, 1982-93; assoc. prof. harvard Med. Sch., Boston, 1989-93, Longwood ORL coord., 1982-90; mem. cons. bd. Xomed Treace Corp., Jacksonville, Fla., 1987-90; advisor SLT Laser Corp., Oaks, Pa., 1994—; dir. Great Comebacks, Gresham, Oreg.; prof. otolaryngology Cleve. Clinic Found. Health Scis. Ctr. Ohio State U., 1994; hon. guest, prin. spkr. Turkish Otolaryngol. Soc., 1997; Qgura lectr., 2000; mem. sci. adv. bd. Somnus Corp. Mem. editl. bd. Harvard Health News Letter, 1976-85; author: Differential Diagnoses in Pediatric ORL, 1975; editor: Manual of Otolaryngology, 1985, Complications of Laser Surgery of the Head and Neck, 1986; transplanted 1st total human larynx, 1998. Mem. fund raising com. Belmont Hill (Mass.) Sch., 1984. Capt. U.S. Army, 1965-71. Recipient Medal, City of Paris, 1987, Sword of Saudi Arabia, 1991, Cert. of Appreciation, Ministry of Health-Singapore, 1995, Presdl. citation Coll. Physicians and Surgeons of Pakistan, Classic Telly award, 1999; named One of Best Doctors in Cleve., Cleve. Mag., 1995—, One of Best Drs. in Am., 1996—, Outstanding People of 20th Century, 1999, Medical Hero Guiness Book of World Records, 2000. Mem.: Triological Soc. (v.p. 1990—91), Cartesian Soc. (pres. 1999), Soc. U. Otolaryngologists (pres.-elect), Am. Soc. Head and Neck Surgery, Am. Acad. Otolaryngology (Honor award 1987, one of nine recognized for conbtn. to medicine in last 250 years 1999), Am. Acad. Facial Plastic Reconstructive Surgery (Medallion of Honor 1989), U. Mich. Med. Ctr. Alumni Soc. (coord. New Eng. Fund. Raising 1992, chair bd. govs. 1992—93, Cleve. Clinic tchr. of yr. 2002, Internat. Scientist of Yr. 2002). Avocations: cycling, skiing, sculling, sea kyacking, tennis. Office: Cleve Clinic Found 9500 Euclid Ave Cleveland OH 44195-0001

STROME, STEPHEN, distribution company executive; b. Lynn, Mass., June 20, 1945; s. David and Rose (Cantor) S.; m. Phyllis Ruth Fields, Jan. 14, 1967; children: Michael, Rochelle. BA, Hillsdale (Mich.) Coll., 1967; MBA, Wayne State U., 1968. Trainee KMart Corp., Detroit, 1968-69, mgr. work measurement Troy, Mich., 1970-73; mgr. tng., edn. Fruehauf Corp., Detroit, 1974-76, regional mgr. labor relations, 1976-78; dir. ops. Handleman Co., Clawson, Mich., 1978-80, account exec., 1980-82, v.p. computer software div. Troy, 1983-85, pres. computer software/video div., 1986-87, exec. v.p., 1987-89, exec. v.p., chief oper. officer, 1990, pres., CEO, 1991-2001, chmn., CEO, 2001—. Home: 4597 Kiftsgate Bnd Bloomfield Hills MI 48302-2331 Office: Handleman Co 500 Kirts Blvd Troy MI 48084-4142

STROMME, GARY L. law librarian; b. Willmar, Minn., July 8, 1939; s. William A. and Edla A. (Soderberg) S.; m. Suzanne Readman, July 21, 1990. BA, Pacific Luth. U., 1965; BLS, U. B.C., Vancouver, Can., 1967; JD, U. Calif., San Francisco, 1973. Bar: Calif. 1973, U.S. Supreme Ct. 1977. Serials libr. U. Minn. St. Paul. Campus Libr., 1967-69; asst. libr. McCutchen, Doyle, Brown and Enerson, San Francisco, 1970-71, Graham & James, San Francisco, 1971-73, ind. contracting atty., 1973-74; law libr. Pacific Gas and Electric Co., 1974-95; cons., 1995—. Lectr. in field. Author: An Introduction to the use of the Law Library, 1974, 76, Basic Legal Research Techniques, 1979. With USAF, 1959-63. Mem. ABA (chmn. libr. com. of sect. econs. of law practice 1978-82), Am. Assn. Law Librs. (chmn. com. on indexing of legal periodicals 1986-88), Western Pacific Assn. Law Librs., No. Calif. Assn. Law Librs., Pvt. Law Librs., Corp. Law Librs. Home: 6106 Ocean View Dr Oakland CA 94618-1841 E-mail: stromme1@earthlink.net.

STROMMEN, MERTON PETER, research psychologist, clergyman; b. Calumet, Mich., Mar. 31, 1919; s. Peter Andrew and Nellie (Framstad) S.; m. Irene Anna Huglen, June 23, 1944; children: Peter, Timothy, James, John, David. BA, Augsburg Coll., Mpls., 1942; BTh, Augsburg Theol. Sem., Mpls., 1944; MA, U. Minn., 1956, PhD, 1960. Ordained to ministry Luth. Ch., 1944; cert. cons. psychologist, Minn. Nat. youth dir. Luth. Free Ch., Mpls., 1944-58; parish pastor Calvary Luth. Ch., Mora, Minn., 1943-47; campus pastor Augsburg Coll., 1947-58; exec. dir. Search Inst., Mpls., 1958-85, Augsburg Inst., Mpls., 1986-90; rsch. psychologist, 1990—. Author: Profiles of Church Youth, 1963, Bridging the Gap, 1973, Five Cries of Youth, 1988, The Innovative Church, 1997; co-author: A Study of Generations, 1972, Ministry in America, 1980, How Church Related Are Church-Related Colleges?, 1980, Five Shaping Forces, 1982, Ten Faces of Ministry, 1979, Five Cries of Parents, 1985, Five Cries of Grief, 1990; editor: Research on Religious Development: A Comprehensive Handbook, 1971, Passing on the Faith, 2000, Transformational Youth Ministry, 2000, The Church and Homosexuality: Searching for Middle Ground, 2001. Mem. bd. regents Augsburg Coll., 1980-88; mem. Richfield (Minn.) Sch. Bd., 1970-80. Recipient Preus award Luth. Brotherhood, Mpls., 1956; named Disting. Alumnus, Augsburg Coll., 1970. Fellow APA (William James award 1983). Democrat. Avocations: piano, choral directing, reading, hiking, sports. Home: 7005 Garfield Ave Minneapolis MN 55423-3057

STROMMER, ANNE ELIZABETH RIVARD, librarian; b. Columbus, Ohio, Dec. 24, 1940; d. Edwin Kenneth Rivard and Alda Nathan (Olin) Rivard Willis; m. Mathias Adolf Strommer, Jan. 3, 1965; children: Elisabeth Anne, Mathias Edwin. BA, Kent (Ohio) State U., 1962; MA in Libr. Sci., U. MIch., 1964. Reference libr. Detroit Pub. Libr., 1962-65, Ft. Knox (Ky.) Mil. Libr., 1968-69, Houston Pub. Libr., 1978-80, branch mgr., 1980-81; tech. svcs. libr. North Harris County Coll., Houston, 1981-85, coord. tech. svcs., 1985-89, coord. tech. and automation svcs., 1990-93, coord. automated libr. svcs., 1993-96; dir. automated libr. svcs., 1996—. Mem. ALA, Tex. Libr. Assn., Freedom to Read Found. Home: 20718 Greymoss Ln Houston TX 77073-3108 Office: N Harris Montgomery CC Dist 250 N Sam Houston Pkwy E Houston TX 77060-2000

STROMQUIST, KENNETH J., JR. pilot, retired military officer; m. Edna Dyrud; children: Virginia, Paul. BBA, U. Minn., 1968; grad., USMC Weapons, Tactics Instrn., 1969, Air Command Staff Coll., 1979, Air War Coll., 1993. Commd. 2d lt. USAF, 1968, forward air controller Vietnam, 1969-70; pilot instr. T-41, T-33 USAF Acad. Aerospace Defense Command, Peterson AFB, Colo., 1970-73; pilot, flight comdr., unit plans officer, officer in charge of alert forces Duluth (Minn.) Air Nat. Guard, 1973-90; comdr. detachment 1, 148 Fighter Wing USAF, Tyndall AFB, Fla., 1990-93; advisor Air Nat. Guard NORAD/USSPACECOM, Peterson AFN, Colo.; air comdr. 148 fighter wing Duluth Air Nat. Guard Base, 1995-98, wing comdr. 148 fighter wing, 1997-98; vice comdr. First Air Force USAF, Tyndall AFB, Fla., 1998-99, ret.; pilot Frontier Airlines, Denver. Past Minn. State pres. Nat. Guard Assn. U.S. Decorated Letion of Merit, Disting. Flying Cross, Purple Heart, Air medal, Meritorious Svc. medal.

STROMSWOLD, DOROTHY, retired secondary educator, book reviewer; b. Mankato, Minn., Jan. 13, 1920; d. Andrew August and Mary Angela (Wachter) Farm; m. Stanley Andrew Stromswold, Oct. 30, 1942 (dec. Apr. 1998); 1 child, Carol. BS, Mankato State U., 1941; student, Mankato Comml. Coll., 1942. Cert. tchr., Minn. Tchr. high sch., Waldorf, Minn., 1942-43, 51-52, Worthington, 1945-46, Mankato Comml. Coll., 1942-45, 46-47; placement officer Sch. Journalism, U. Minn., Mpls., 1947-49; patent sec. Clark Equipment Co., Buchanan, Mich., 1952-59; book reviewer South Bend (Ind.) Tribune, 1978-93. Spkr. on travel and on the Supreme Ct. Elder, deacon Presbyn. Ch., Buchanan, 1974-81, 98—. Democrat. Avocations: Supreme Court, reading, giving informal talks. Home: PO Box 27 Buchanan MI 49107-0027

STRONACH, BELINDA, retail executive; m. Johann Olav Koss; 2 children. With Magna Internat. Inc., Aurora, Canada, 1985—, vice chmn. Canada, 1995—, pres., CEO Canada, 2001—. Office: Magna Internat Inc 337 Magna Dr Aurora ON Canada

STRONACH, CAREY ELLIOTT, physicist, educator; b. Boston, Aug. 8, 1940; s. Ralph Howard and Frances Burns (Maynard) S.; m. Joan Alice Louise Venner, Aug. 20, 1966; children: John Maynard, Howard Stanley. BS, U. Richmond, Va., 1961; MS, U. Va., 1963; PhD, Coll. William and Mary, 1976. Instr. physics Va. State U., Petersburg, 1965-66, asst. prof., 1966-71, 72-76, assoc. prof., 1976-78, 79-80, prof., 1980—. Dir. Muon Spin Rotation Rsch. Program, 1977—; dir. Solid State Physics Rsch. Inst., 1983-87, radiation safety officer, 1983-87, dir. Superconducting Materials Rsch. Program, 1988-97, Nanostructured Materials Rsch. Program, 1997—, Galactic Cosmic Radiation Rsch. Program, 1993-97, U.S.-France Joint Muon Spin Rotation Rsch. Program, 1985-91, Magnetic Materials Lab. Devel. Program, 1999-2001, dir. Ctr. Interactive Micromagnetics, 2001—; vis. assoc. prof. U. Alta, 1978-79; guest scientist Brookhaven Nat. Lab.; mem. organizing com. Internat. Symposium on the Electronic Structure and Properties of Hydrogen in Metals, 1982, Internat. Symposium on the Physics and Chemistry of Small Clusters, 1986, From Clusters to Crystals, 1991, The Sci. and Tech. of Atomically Engineered Materials, 1995, Internat. Symposium on Cluster and Nanostructure Interfaces, 1999; mem. Internat. Adv. Com. Eighth Internat. Conf. on Muon Spin Rotation, 1996-99; mem. sci. adv. com. European Workshop on the Spectroscopy of Subatomic Species in Non-Metallic Solids, 1985, govs. com. on Superconducting Supercollider, 1987; TV physics lectr., 1991-94; chair internat. adv. com. Ninth Internat. Conf. on Muon Spin Rotation, 1999-2002, founding mem. Internat. Soc. on Muon Spectroscopy. Contbr. numerous articles to publs. in field; playwright. Pres. Petersburg area chpt. Va. Coun. Human Rels., 1965—67; mem. Petersburg Commn. Cmty. Rels. Affairs, 1974—77; mem. long-range transp. adv. com. City of Petersburg, 1994—98; mem. steering com. Gilmore for Gov., 1997; mem. Dramatists Guild; mem., sec. adv. coun. bds. and commns. Commonwealth Coun., 1998—2000; mem. Richmond Playwrights Forum, 1999—, Virginians for Warner, 2001; corr. sec. Petersburg Dem. Com., 1974—77, mem., 1972—78, 1979—85, vice chmn., 1981—85. Fellow duPont Corp., 1961-63, NSF, 1971-72, NASA, 1976. Mem.: AAUP (chpt. pres. 1968—70), AAAS, Sci. Netlinks Adv. Bd., N.Y. Acad. Scis., The Planetary Soc., High Speed Rail/Maglev Assn. (govt. rels. com. 1992—97, Maglev task force 1994—97), Va. Assn. Scholars (bd. govs. 1999—), Southeastern Univs. Rsch. Assn. (site sel. com. 1980—81, materials sci. com. 1983—86, trustee 1983—98, sci. and tech. com. 1986—88, rules com. 1988—92, edn. com. 1992—94, new projects com. 1994—95, Jefferson Lab. com. 1995—98), Va. Acad. Sci. (sec. astronomy, math. and physics sect 1983—84, chmn. 1984—85), Nat. Assn. Scholars, Am. Assn. Physics Tchrs., Am. Phys. Soc., Tri-univ. Meson Facility Users Group, Coun. Secular Humanism (assoc.), Richmond Area Free Thinkers, Pi Mu Epsilon, Sigma Pi Sigma, Sigma Xi (chpt. sec. 1977—78, chpt. pres. 1980—84, 1987—88), Phi Beta Kappa. Achievements include devel. (with others) of low-energy muon beam line at the AGS of Brookhaven Nat. Lab.; rsch. in pion-nucleus interactions, heavy-ion reactions, muon spin rotation studies of high-temperature superconductors and related materials, fullerenes, heavy-fermion materials, ferromagnetic metals, metal hydrides, fatigue in metals and other materials; participation in the establishment of the Southeastern Universities Research Association and the Thomas Jefferson Nat. Accelerator Facility; discovery of formation of muonium and muonated radicals in Buckminsterfullerene; devel. of TV lecture series on physics; discovery of simultaneous high-temp. superconductivity and magnetic ordering in strontium yttrium ruthenate. Home: 2241 Buckner St Petersburg VA 23805-2207 Office: Va State U PO Box 9325 Petersburg VA 23806-0001 E-mail: cstronac@vsu.edu.

STRONG, ANN LOUISE, planning educator; b. Amsterdam, N.Y., Apr. 26, 1930; d. Gustav Ernst and Helen (Davis) Schulz; m. Michael L. Strong; children: Mark L., Christopher D. BA, Vassar Coll., 1951; JD, Yale U., 1954; MA (hon.), U. Pa. Bar: Fla. 1954, N.Y. 1956, Pa. 1959. Pvt. practice, Tampa, Fla., Syracuse, N.Y. and New Haven, 1954-58; with Urban Renewal Adminstrn., Washington, 1961-63, U. Pa., Phila., 1959-61, 63—, prof. dept. city and regional planning, 1968-95, chmn. dept., 1978-82, 83-84, assoc. dean Grad. Sch. Fine Arts, 1985-91, dir. Inst. for Environ. Studies Grad. Sch. Fine Arts, 1968-72, prof. emeritus, 1995—. Mellon vis. lectr. Sch. Forestry and Environ. Studies, Yale U., 1978-79; prof. Salzburg Seminar in Am. Studies, 1968; vis. prof. Australian Nat. U., 1995, U. Auckland, 1997, 98. Author: Open Space for Urban America, 1965, Planned Urban Environments: Sweden, Finland, Israel, The Netherlands, France, 1971, Private Property and the Public Interest: The Brandywine Experience, 1975, Land Banking: European Reality, American Prospect, 1979; co-author: The Plan and Program for the Brandywine, 1968, (with G.E. Thomas) The Book of the School, 1990, (with T.A. Reiner and J. Szyrmer) Transitions in Land and Housing: Bulgaria, The Czech Republic and Poland, 1996; mem. editorial bd. Jour. Planning Lit., 1984-98; contbr. articles to profl. jours. Chmn. Housing Authority County of Chester, 1963-66, vice chmn., 1966-82; mem. adv. coun. Princeton U. Sch. Architecture and Urban Planning, 1977-82; mem. legal adv. com. Coun. on Environ. Quality, 1970-72; mem. forest rsch. adv. com. USDA Forestry Svc., 1967-69; mem. Pa. State Planning Bd., 1973-80, Easttown Twp. Planning Commn., 1969-75; bd. dirs. Environ. Def. Fund, 1972-82, mem. exec. com., 1972-79; bd. dirs. Environ. Law Inst., 1980-86; mem. exec. com. Greenspace Alliance, 1999—. Sr. fellow NEH, 1973-74; named Disting. Planning Educator, Assn. Collegiate Schs. of Planning, 1993. Mem. Fla. Bar Assn., Pa. Bar Assn., N.Y. State Bar Assn., Am. Planning Assn., Am. Inst. Cert. Planners, Merion Cricket Club (Haverford, Pa.). Democrat. Office: Univ Pa 127 Meyerson Hall Philadelphia PA 19104 E-mail: strong@pobox.upenn.edu.

STRONG, CAROL JOAN, communication disorders educator, researcher; b. Portland, Oreg., Dec. 26, 1942; d. Orval I. and Marian T. (Lewis) Dunlap; m. William J. Strong, Oct. 20, 1961; children: Kristin, Eric. BS, Utah State U., 1971, EdD, 1989; MA, U. Ill., 1972. Clinician Champaign (Ill.) Sch. Dist., 1972-73; trustee prof. and assoc. dean for rsch. Utah State U., Logan, 1973—. Rsch. dir. Ski*Hi Inst., Logan, 1989-92. Utah State U. fellow, 1983; ASHA Found. grantee, 1989. Mem. AAUW (State of Utah Emerging scholar 1991), Am. Speech, Lang. and Hearing Assn., Coun. for Exceptional Children, Nat. Assn. Edn. of Young Children, Utah Speech, Lang. and Hearing Assn., Internat. Reading Assn., Nat. Coun. Tchrs. of English. Avocations: gardening, sailing, motorcycling, walking, reading.

STRONG, CARTER, lawyer; b. Bronxville, N.Y., July 17, 1947; s. Shirley Carter and Hélène Strong; m. Helen Anne Marvel, May 17, 1980; children: Winslow C., Hilary H. BA in History, Ithaca Coll., 1969; JD, U. Miami, 1972. Bar: Fla. 1972, D.C. 1973. Assoc. Arent, Fox, Kintner, Plotkin & Kahn, PLLC, Washington, 1972-80, ptnr., 1981—. Mem. Chevy Chase Club, Siasconset Casino Assn. Avocations: tennis, golf, reading, travel. Office: Arent Fox Kintner Plotkin & Kahn PLLC 1050 Connecticut Ave NW Washington DC 20036-5339

STRONG, DOROTHY SWEARENGEN, educational administrator; b. Feb. 3, 1934; d. John Harrison and Willie Beatrice (Hawkins) Swearengen; m. Joseph Nathaniel Strong, Mar. 19, 1953; 1 child, Joronda Ramette Crawford. BS in Edn., Chgo. State U., 1958, MA in Math. Edn., 1964; EdD, Nova U., 1985. Elem. and secondary tchr. Chgo. Pub. Schs., 1958-65, dir. math., 1976-94; co-prin. investigator Access 2000, 1991-93; dir. NSF Urban Systemic Initiative, 1993-94, regional coord., 1994-96; dir. Bimathematics Project, 1996—. Cons. math., 1965-76; dir. Pre-Algebra Devel. Ctrs., 1967-84; dir. BiMath. Curriculum Devel. project 1996—; instr. Chgo. State U., 1969-71; mem. Commn. on Tchr. Edn., Task Force on Math. in Urban Ctrs., Ill. Basic Skills Adv. Coun., Nat. Inst. Edn. Conf. on Basic Skills; mem. coun. acad. affairs Coll. Bd., v.p., 1983-86; bd. dirs. Allendale Sch. for Boys, 1974—, mem. com. educating tchrs. math., 1974-77, in-svc. handbook com., chmn. exhibits, 1972, ann. meeting ann. regional meetings, 1977-84. Author: Modern Mathematics Structure and Use-Spirit Masters, 1977, Pre-Algebra Unit Packs: Ratios and Proportions, Fractions, Decimals, Percent, Measurements, Chgo. Pub. Schs. curriculum materials; co-author: Bible Mathematics, Book I, 1995; contbg. author: Algebra for Everyone; contbr. articles to profl. jours. Co-leader People-to-People South African Amb. team, 2000; pres. United Pentecostal Coun. of the Assemblies of God, midwest dir, dir. Christian edn. Home: 2820 Paris Rd Olympia Fields IL 60461-1826 Office: 3300 S Indiana Chicago IL 60616

STRONG, ELLIOT WILSON, retired surgeon, educator; b. Concord, Mass., Aug. 7, 1930; s. Lawrence Leroy and Helen Storey (Cole) S.; m. Marjorie Edith Linn, July 2, 1954; children: Scott Christian, Keith Raymond, Karen Linn. BS, Tufts U., 1952, MD, 1956. Diplomate Am. Bd. Surgery. Intern in surgery Hartford (Conn.) Hosp., 1956-57, resident in surgery, 1957-61; fellow in surg. oncology Meml. Sloan-Kettering Cancer Ctr., N.Y.C., 1961-63, clin. asst. surgeon, 1963-67, asst. attending, 1967-69, chief head and neck svc. dept. surgery, 1969-92, attending surgeon, 1969-99, emeritus, 1999—; prof. surgery Cornell U. Med. Coll., 1976-99; ret., 1999. Cons. Norwalk (Conn.) Hosp., 1975—, Temple U. Dental Sch., Phila., 1980-83. Contbr. numerous articles to med. jours., chpts. to books. Pres. bd. trustees Huguenot Meml. Ch., Pelham Manor, N.Y., 1976, ruling elder, 1977-83, 98—, clk. of session, 1998—. Fellow ACS (bd. govs. 1989-94); mem. Soc. Head and Neck Surgeons (sec. 1977, v.p. 1978, pres. 1979-80, Martin lectr. 1987), Am. Radium Soc. (v.p. 1975, sec. 1986-89, pres. 1989-90, Janeway lectr. 1983), N.Y. Head and Neck Soc. (pres. 1979-81), Phi Beta Kappa, Alpha Omega Alpha. Presbyterian. Avocations: photography, fishing, stamp collecting. E-mail: ewsmd30@aol.com.

STRONG, FRANKLIN WALLACE, JR. lawyer; b. Iowa City, Oct. 26, 1949; s. Franklin Wallace and Rosemary (Nielsen) S.; m. Ann Grant Walter, Mar. 20, 1976 (div. Nov. 1997); 1 child: Franklin Wallace Strong III; m. Barbara Jean Reynolds, Feb. 14, 2001. AB, U. Mich., Ann Arbor, 1971; JD, U. Mich. Law Sch., Ann Arbor, 1974; MBA, U. Dallas, 1993. Bar: Iowa 1974, S.C. 1991, Tex. 1992. Judge advocate U.S. Navy, Washington, 1974-91; gen. counsel ProSearch Assocs., Inc., Fort Worth, 1993; staff atty., supr. Office of Hearings & Appeals, Columbia, S.C., 1996—. Lt. Cmdr. U.S. Navy, 1974-91. Mem. Phi Delta Legal Fraternity. Office: Office Hearings & Appeals 1927 Thurmond Mall Ste 200 Columbia SC 29201-2375

STRONG, GARY EUGENE, librarian; b. Moscow, June 26, 1944; s. Authur Dwight and Cleora Anna (Nirk) S.; m. Carolyn Jean Roetker, Mar. 14, 1970; children: Christopher Eric, Jennifer Rebecca. BS in Edn., U. Idaho, 1966; AMLS, U. Mich., 1967. Adminstrv. and reference asst. U. Idaho, 1963-66; extension librarian Latah County Free Library, Moscow, 1966; head librarian Markeley Residence Library, U. Mich., 1966-67; library dir. Lake Oswego (Oreg.) Public Library, 1967-73, Everett (Wash.) Public Library, 1973-76; asso. dir. services Wash. State Library, Olympia, 1976-79, dep. state librarian, 1979-80; state librarian Calif. State Library, Sacramento, 1980-94; dir. Queens Borough Pub. Libr., Jamaica, 1994—; dir. emeritus Calif. State Library Found., 1994—. Adj. prof. Queens Coll. Grad. Sch. of Libr. and Info. Scis., 2000—; chief exec. Calif. Libr. Svcs. Bd., 1980-94; founder, bd. dirs. Calif. State Libr. Found., 1982-94, Calif. Literary Campaign, 1984-94, Calif. Rsch. Bur., 1992; bd. dirs. No. Regional Libr. Bd., 1983-94, Queens Libr. Found., 1994—; mem. adv. bd. Ctr. for Book in Libr. of Congress, 1983-86; mem. nat. adv. com. Libr. of Congress, 1987-89; chmn. adv. bd. Calif. Libr. Constrn. and Renovation Bond Act Bd., 1989-94; vis. lectr. Marylhurst Coll., Oreg., 1968, Oreg. Divsn. Continuing Edn., 1972, San Jose State U. Sch. Libr. Svc., 1990; mem. N.Y. State Adv. Coun. Librs., 1996-97; mem. chancellor's task froce ednl. tech. and librs. CUNY, 1996-97; convenor Archons of the Colophan, 1997-98; regents adv. coun. librs. N.Y. State, 1999—; lectr. and cons. in field. Host, producer: cable TV Signatures Program, 1974-76, nationwide videoconfs. on illiteracy, censorship, 1985; author: On Reading-in the Year of the Reader, 1987; editor Calif. State Library Found. Bull., 1982-94 (H.W. Wilson Periodical award 1988), Western Americana in the Calif. State Library, 1986, On Reading-In the Year of the Reader, 1987, Chinatown Photographer: Louis J. Stellman, 1989, Local History Genealogical Resources, 1990, Literate America Emerging, 1991; curator Queens Libr. Gallery, 1998; contbr. articles to profl. jours.; editor, designer and pub. of various books. Bd. dirs., v.p. Pacific N.W. Bibliog. Ctr., 1977-80; bd. dirs. Thurston Mason County Mental Health Ctr., 1977-80, pres., 1979-80; bd. dirs. Coop. Library Agy. for Sys. and Svcs., 1980-94, vice chmn., 1981-84; bd. dirs. Sr. Svcs. Snohomish County,

1973-76, HISPANEX (Calif. Spanish lang. database), 1983-86; bd. govs. Snohomish County Hist. Assn., 1974-76; mem. psychiat. task force St. Peters Hosp., Olympia, 1979-80; co-founder Calif. Ctr. for the Book, bd. dirs., 1987-94; mem. adv. bd. Calif. State PTA, 1981-86, Gov.'s Tech. Conf., 1993-94; mem. adv. com. Sch. Libr. Sci., UCLA, 1991-94, Sch. Libr. and Info. Studies, U. Calif., Berkeley, 1991-94, Libr. Sch. Queens Coll., 1996—, libr. sch. St. John's U., 1996-98; mem. Oreg. Coun. Pub. Broadcasting, 1969-73, Calif. Adult Edn. Steering Com., 1988-94, N.Y. State Adv. Coun. on Librs., 1996-97; chmn. collaborative coun. Calif. State Literacy Resource Ctr., 1993-94; bd. dirs. Queens coun. Boy Scouts of Am., 1994—; mem. Chancellor's Task Force on Ednl. Tech. and Librs., CUNY, 1996-97; participant N.Y. Pub. Libr. Conf. of World Libr. Leaders, 1996; trustee Flushing Cemetary, 1998—; mem. com. on intellectual property rights and the engring. info. infrastructure Nat. Rsch. Coun., 1998-2000; chair organizing com. China-U.S. Libr. Conf., 2001. Oreg. Libr. scholar, 1966; recipient Disting. Alumnus award U. Mich., 1984, Disting. Svc. award Calif. Literacy Inc., 1985, Spl. Achievement award Literacy Action, 1988, Assn. Specialized and Coop. Libr. Agys. Exceptional Achievement award 1992, Gov.'s award of Achievement Govt. Tech. Conf., 1994, Advancement of Literacy award Pub. Libr. Assn., 1994, John Cotton Dana award Libr. Adminstrn. and Mgmt. Assn., 1994; named Libr. of Yr. Calif. Assn. Libr. Trustees and Commrs., 1994, Disting. Svc. award Chinese Am. Libr. Assn., 1996. Mem.: Assn. Specialized and Coop. Libr. Agys., Western Coun. State Librs. (pres. 1989—91), Chief Officers of State Libr. Agys. (pres. 1984—86), Calif. Libr. Assn. (govt. rels.com. 1980—94), Pacific N.W. Libr. Assn. (hon. life mem., pres. 1978—79), Oreg. Libr. Assn. (hon. life mem., pres. 1970—71), N.Y. Libr. Assn., Libr. Adminstrn. and Mgmt. Assn. (bd. dis. 1980—88, pres. 1984—85), Am. Printing History Assn., ALA (legis. com. 1980—82, Commn. on Freedom and Equality of Access to Info. 1983—86, legis. com. 1995—97, chair intellectual property subcom. 1995—98, chmn. conf. librs. Beijing 1996, rep. Internat. Fedn. of Libr. Assn. nat. organizing com. 1996—2001, intellectual property com. 1998—2001), METRO (bd. dirs. 1994—, 1st v.p. 1999—2001, treas. 1996—99), Queens County C. of C. (bd. dirs. 1996—), Jamaica Devel. Corp., Everett Area C. of C. (bd. dirs. 1974—76), The Typophiles, Guild of Book Workers, Grolier Club, The Book Collectors Club of L.A., Roxburghe Club, Sacramento Book Collectors Club, Book Club of Calif. Office: Queens Borough Pub Libr 89-11 Merrick Blvd Jamaica NY 11432-5200 E-mail: gstrong@queenslibrary.org.

STRONG, GEORGE GORDON, JR. litigation and management consultant; b. Toledo, Apr. 19, 1947; s. George Gordon and Jean Boyd (McDougall) S.; m. Annsley Palmer Chapman, Nov. 30, 1974; children: George III, Courtney, Meredith, Alexis. BA, Yale U., 1969; MBA, Harvard U., 1971; JD, U. San Diego, 1974. Bar: Calif. 1974, U.S. Dist. Ct. (cen. dist.) Calif. 1974; CPA, Calif., Hawaii, cert. mgmt. cons. Contr. Vitredent Corp., Beverly Hills, Calif., 1974-76; sr. mgr. Price Waterhouse, L.A., 1976-82, ptnr., 1987—2001, mng. ptnr. west region dispute analysis and corp. recovery, 1993-98, mem. policy bd., bd. dirs., 1995-98, combination bd., 1997-98; bd. ptnrs., prin Pricewaterhouse Coopers LLP, 1998-2001; ret., 2002; global oversight bd. Pricewaterhouse Coopers, 1998-2001; exec. v.p., COO Internat. Customs Service, Long Beach, Calif., 1982-84; CFO Uniform Software Systems, Santa Monica, 1984-85; exec. v.p., COO Cipherlink Corp., 1986; pres. Woodleigh Lane, Inc., Flintridge, Calif., 1985-87. Chmn. bd. dirs. L.A. SPCA; bd. dirs. So. Calif. Humane Soc. Mem. ABA, AICPA, Calif. State Bar, Calif. Soc. CPAs, Andover Abbott Alumni So. Calif. (bd. dirs., treas.), Inst. Mgmt. Cons., Harvard Bus. Sch. Alumni Assn. (bd. dirs. 1996-99), Harvard Bus. Sch. Assn. So. Calif. (chmn. bd. trustees scholarship fund 1992—, pres. 1988-89, dir. 1996-99, 2001—), Harvard Club N.Y., Yale Club N.Y., Lincoln Club, Calif. Club, Jonathan Club, Flint Canyon Tennis Club, Olympic Club, Annandale Golf Club, Coral Beach and Tennis Club, Mid Ocean Golf Club, Royal Bermuda Yacht Club, Valley Hunt Club. Republican. Presbyterian. Avocations: golf, tennis, bridge. Home and Office: 5455 Castle Knoll Rd La Canada Flintridge CA 91011-1319 E-mail: george.strong@gstrong.net.

STRONG, GEORGE HOTHAM, private investor, consultant; b. Johnstown, Pa., July 15, 1926; s. George Hite and Mary Elizabeth (Hotham) S.; m. Mary Louise Lyon, Sept. 19, 1953; children: Cynthia Strong Hibbard, Dexter, Sarah Strong Bornstein. AB magna cum laude, Allegheny Coll, 1949; MBA, Harvard U., 1951. V.p. Smith Barney & Co., N.Y.C. & Boston, 1951-67, Norlin Corp., N.Y.C., 1967-73, Am. Medicorp, Bala-Cynwyd, Pa., 1974-78; cons. A.D. Little, Cambridge, Mass., 1973-74; sr. v.p., dir. Universal Health Services, King of Prussia, Pa., 1978-84; pvt. practice investor N.Y.C., 1985—. Bd. dirs. Health South Rehab., Birmingham, Ala.; bd. advisers The Directorship Group, N.Y.C. Served to sgt. U.S. Army, 1944-46, Italy. Mem. Phi Beta Kappa. Clubs: Harvard (N.Y.C.); Union League (Phila.); Seabright (N.J.) Lawn Tennis, Seabright Beach, Rumson Country (N.J.). Republican. Episcopalian. Home: 946 Navesink River Rd Rumson NJ 07760-2330

STRONG, GEORGE WALTER, political consultant; b. Rapid City, S.D., June 8, 1937; s. Wesley Milo and Mariel Brown (Loomis) S. BS, S.D. State U., 1959; M in Pub. Adminstrn., U. Denver, 1963. Labor relations specialist AEC, Washington, 1963-69; asst. dir. Southwest Ctr. for Urban Research, Houston, 1969-73; exec. asst. Office of the Mayor, 1973-75; asst. to pres. for pub. policy Houston Natural Gas Corp., 1975-81; owner George Strong & Assocs., Houston, 1981—. Lobbyist Sunrise Housing, City of Houston, 1986—; gulf coast mgr. Al Gore for Pres., 1987-88; state coord. Paul Tsongas for Pres., 1992; advisor Clinton Gore Campaign, Houston, 1992; campaign cons. Mike Andrews for U.S. Senate, 1994, Ken Bentsen for Congress, 1994, 96, 98, 00, Chris Bell for Congress, 2002; campaign cons., media cons. for Mayor of Houston, 1997, 99, 2001, mayor, 1997, 99, 2001, and over 80 Tex. polit. candidates. Maj. USAR, 1959-73. Mem. Houston C. of C. Methodist. Home and Office: 2242 Bartlett St Houston TX 77098-5202

STRONG, HENRY, foundation executive; b. Rochester, N.Y., Oct. 6, 1923; s. L. Corrin and Alice (Trowbridge) S.; m. Malan Swing, June 30, 1951; children: Sigrid Anne, Barbara Kirk, Dana Elizabeth, Henry Lockwood. AB, Williams Coll., 1949; LHD, Mt. Vernon Coll., 1999. Joined Fgn. Service, 1950; with State Dept., 1950-51; vice consul The Hague, 1951-54, Washington, 1954-55; 2d sec. U.S. Embassy, Copenhagen, 1955-58, State Dept., 1958-62, Djakarta, Indonesia, 1962-64; resigned, 1968; chmn. bd., pres. Hattie M. Strong Found., 1968—. Mem. D.C. Commn. Arts, 1968-75; mem. D.C. Bd. Higher Edn., 1973-76; vice chmn. bd. trustees J.F. Kennedy Ctr. for Performing Arts, 1975-90, hon. trustee, 1991—; bd. dirs. Nat. Symphony Orch., Pomfret Sch., M.M. Post Found. D.C., Community Found. of Greater Washington, 1974-91, Mt. Vernon Coll., 1969-88, 91-98, Nat. Capital chpt. ARC, 1994—. Lt. (j.g.) USN, 1943-46. Mem.: Chevy Chase; Metropolitan (Washington); Gibson Island (Md.). Republican. Episcopalian. Home: 5039 Overlook Rd NW Washington DC 20016-1911 Office: Hattie M Strong Found 1620 I St NW Ste 700 Washington DC 20006-4005

STRONG, JAMES ALAN, architect; b. Louisville, May 29, 1960; s. Lummy Merill and Rubye (Edwards) S.; m. Anita Christine Tremarche, June 19, 1993. BAS, U. Ky., 1983. Prin. Strong Design Assoc., Manchester, Conn., 1990—; project architect Jeter, Cook & Jepson Architects, Inc., Hartford, 1995-98, The S/L/A/M Collaborative Architects, Glastonbury, 1998-2001, DeCarlo & Doll, Inc. Architects, Hamden, 2001—. Mem. AIA, Nat. Trust for Historic Preservation. Home: 20 Clover Ln Manchester CT 06040-6770 Office: DeCarlo & Doll Inc 1952 Whitney Ave Hamden CT 06517

STRONG, JAMES THOMPSON, management, security, human resources consultant; b. Boca Raton, Fla., Oct. 26, 1945; s. Earl William and Mary Joe (Thompson) S.; m. Lenore Jean Stager, Feb. 2, 1974; 1 child, Daria Nicole. BA in Polit. Sci., U. Calif., Riverside, 1973; MS in Strategic Intelligence, Def. Intelligence Coll., Washington, 1982. Factoring specialist. Commd. USAF, 1968, advanced through grades to maj., ret., 1990; faculty Def. Intelligence Coll., Washington, 1982-86; dir. translations USAF, 1986-88, dir. info. svcs., 1988-90; proprietary security mgr. McDonnell-Douglas Technologies, San Diego, 1990-92; owner Employment Svcs. for Bus., 1995-97. Adj. prof. internat. rels. U.S. Internat. U., 1996—, internat. bus. Palomar Coll., 1997—. Author: The Basic Industrial Counter-Espionage Cookbook, 1993, The Government Contractor's OPSEC Cookbook, 1993; co-author: The Military Intelligence Community, 1985; mem. editl. bd. Internat. Jour. Intelligence and Counterintelligence, 1986—; contbr. articles to profl. jours. Recipient Disting. EEO award USAF, 1987, Def. Meritorious Svc. medal 1986, Meritorious Svc. medal, 1981, 90, Joint Svc. Commendation medal Def. Intelligence Agy./NATO, 1982, 85. Mem. Nat. Mil. Intelligence Assn. (bd. dirs. 1984—, chpt. pres. 1989, 94), Ops. Security Profls. Soc. (chpt. chair 1993, 94-96), Nat. Cargo Security Coun., San Diego Roundtable (exec. coord. 1994, 95), Assn. Former Intelligence Officers (nat. scholarship adminstr. 1994—), Am. Soc. for Indsl. Security, Air Force Assn., San Diego Soc. for Human Resource Mgmt. Republican. Avocations: bridge, golf, reading. Home and Office: 1142 Miramonte Gln Escondido CA 92026-1724 E-mail: afiosdc4jt@aol.com.

STRONG, JOHN DAVID, insurance company executive; b. Cortland, N.Y., Apr. 12, 1936; s. Harold A. and Helen H. Strong; m. Carolyn Dimmick, Oct. 26, 1957; children: John David, Suzanne. BS, Syracuse U., 1957; postgrad., Columbia U., 1980. With Kemper Group, 1957-90, Kemper Corp., 1990-96, Empire sales divsn. mgr., 1972-74, CEO, 1988-93, chmn. bd., 1989-93; vice chmn. Millikin Assocs., 1993-96, chmn., 1996; exec. v.p., dir. Facilitators, Inc., 1995-98. Mem. adv. coun. Sch. Bus., Millikin U., 1975-79, 84—; bd. dirs. United Way of Decatur and Macon County, Ill., 1976-83, campaign chmn., 1978-79, pres. bd. dirs., 1979-81; pres. United Way of Ill., 1981-83; bd. dirs. DMH Commn. Svcs. Corp., 1985-97, chmn., 1988-90; bd. dirs. Decatur-Macon County Econ. Devel. Found., 1983-88, DMH Health Systems, 1987-94, Richland C.C. Found., 1987-90, Symphony Orch. Guild of Decatur, 1992-96, DMH Found., 1988-97; bd. dirs. Ill. Ednl. Devel. Found., 1983-90, pres., 1986-87; bd. dirs. Decatur Meml. Hosp., 1985-94, vice chmn., 1988, chmn., 1990-92; bd. dirs. Ctrl. Ill. Health Assocs., Inc., 1994, vice chmn., 1994-96; mem. steering com. Decatur Advantage, 1981-93, pres., 1988-93. Capt. USAR, 1958-69. Mem. Metro Decatur C. of C. (bd. dirs. 1977-80, chmn. 1983-84), Decatur Club (bd. dirs. 19080-83, pres. 1983), Country Club of Decatur (bd. dirs. 1993-99, pres. bd. 1995-97), Alpha Kappa Psi. E-mail: jack@strongs.net.

STRONG, JOHN SCOTT, finance educator; b. Phila., Aug. 28, 1956; s. John S. and Thelma J. (Willard) S. BS, Washington & Lee U., 1978; M of Pub. Policy, Harvard U., 1981, PhD in Bus. Econs., 1986. Rsch. fellow Harvard U., Cambridge, Mass., 1983-85, 89-90, 93, vis. asst. prof. econs., 1989-90; prof. fin. Coll. William and Mary, Williamsburg, Va., 1985—. Cons. on econs. and fin. Republic of Indonesia, 1987—, MITI, Japan, 1988-89, European Bank for Reconstruction and Devel., 1993-95, Govt. of Bolivia, 1994, Govt. of Russia, 1996, Govts. of Brazil, Argentina and Uruguay, 1997, Govt. of Peru, 1998, World Bank, 1997—. Author: Why Airplanes Crash: Aviation Safety in a Changing World, 1992, Moving to Market: Restructuring Transport in the Former Soviet Union, 1996; co-author 2 books on airline deregulation; contbr. articles to profl. jours. Fulbright scholar, 1978-79; grad. fellow NSF, 1979-82. Office: Coll William & Mary Sch Bus Williamsburg VA 23187

STRONG, JOHN WILLIAM, lawyer, educator; b. Iowa City, Aug. 18, 1935; s. Frank Ransom and Gertrude Elizabeth (Way) S.; m. Margaret Waite Cleary, June 16, 1962; children— Frank Ransom, Benjamin Waite. BA, Yale U., 1957; JD, U. Ill., 1962; postgrad U. N.C., 1966-67. Bar: Ill. 1963, Oreg. 1976. Assoc. firm LeForgee, Samuels, Miller, Schroeder & Jackson, Decatur, Ill., 1963-64; asst. prof. law U. Kans., 1964-66; assoc. prof. Duke U., 1966-69; prof. U. Oreg., 1969-75; legal counsel Oreg. Task Force on Med. Malpractice, 1976; prof. U. Nebr., 1977-84, dean, 1977-82, vice chancellor for acad. affairs, 1981-84; Rosenstiel Disting. prof. law U. Ariz., 1984-98, prof. emeritus, 1998—. Nat. sec.-treas. Order of the Coif, 1992-98; cons. Nat. Judicial Coll. Author: (with others) Handbook on Evidence, 5th edit., 1999. Served with U.S. Army, 1957-59. Mem. Ill. Bar Assn., Oreg. Bar Assn., ABA, Am. Law Inst., Phi Delta Phi. Independent. Congregationalist. Home: 3220 E 3rd St Tucson AZ 85716-4233 Office: U Ariz Coll Law Tucson AZ 85721-0001 E-mail: strong@nt.law.arizona.edu.

STRONG, JUDITH ANN, chemist, educator; b. Van Hornesville, N.Y., June 19, 1941; d. Philip Furnald and Hilda Bernice (Hulbert) S.; B.S. cum laude (N.Y. State regents scholar), SUNY, Albany, 1963; M.A., Brandeis U., 1966, Ph.D., 1970. Asst. prof. chemistry Moorhead State U. (Minn.), 1969-73, acting chmn. chemistry dept., 1976, assoc. prof., 1973-81, prof., 1981— , chmn. dept., 1984-86, dean social and natural scis., 1986—97; assoc. v.p. acad. affairs, 1997—. Recipient Tietzen Meml. award SUNY, Albany, 1963; NSF fellow, 1965-67. Mem. Am. Chem. Soc., Assn. Women in Science, Soroptomist Internat. (gov.-elect N. Ctrl. region 2000—02, gov. 2002—), Minn. Acad. Sci., Sigma Xi. Home: 1209 12th St S Moorhead MN 56560-3707 Office: Minn State U Moorhead Academic Affairs Moorhead MN 56563-0001

STRONG, KARIN HJORT, artist, educator; b. N.Y.C., Jan. 30, 1956; d. Corrin Peter and Mette Hjort (Matthiesen) S. BA, Boston U., 1981; AA, Pratt U., 1985. Art tutor Hampshire Coll., Amherst, Mass., 1977; co-founder, mgr., tchr. Poland Springs (Maine) Cmty. Program, 1977-79; tchr. Southampton Cultural Ctr., 1989-96; tchg. asst. master workshop on art L.I. Univ., Southampton, N.Y., 1990. Bd. mem. Catharine Lorillard Wolfe Art Club, Inc., N.Y.C., 1989-96; painting judge Pen and Brush Club, Inc., N.Y.C., 1995; art show judge J.L.C. Art Ctr., Inc., Stony Brook, N.Y., 1995. Artist represented by Gallery East, Images Gallery, Lizan Tops Gallery, others. Vol. coord. Appalachian Mountain Club, Boston, 1981; monkey trainer to aid quadreplegics Boston U., 1981; spkr., event M.C. CLWAC, Nat. Arts Club, N.Y.C., 1992-95; spkr., lectr. Jimmy Ernst Artist Alliance, East Hampton, N.Y., 1993, Southampton Artists, 1994. Mem. Soc. Animal Artists, Southampton Artists (bd. mem., exhbn. chair, publicity com. 1988-90), Catharine Lorillard Wolfe Art Club, Inc. (pres. 1992-95). Avocations: music, playing guitar, flute and dulcimer, sports, writing.

STRONG, LINDA LOUISE, music educator; b. Rice Lake, Wis., Apr. 26, 1948; d. Jess Willard and Lorraine H. (Scheidecker) Knutson; m. Charles William Strong, Jan. 31, 1970; children: Kirsten Anne, Michael Allan. BA, U. Wis., 1970; MAT, Northwestern U., 1971; MusB, U. Wis., Stevens Point, 1985. Pvt. piano and violin tchr., various locations, Wis., 1973—; tchr., dir. Suzuki Talent Assn. of Eau Claire, 1989—. Dir. Suzuki Kids on Tour, Eau Claire, 1991—. 1st violinist Chippewa Valley Symphony, Eau Claire, 1988—, Red Cedar Symphony, 2001—; internat. coord. Aspect Found. fgn. exch. program, 1998—. Mem.: Suzuki Assn. of the Ams., Chippewa Valley Music Tchrs. Assn. (v.p., program chair 1993—99, newsletter editor 1999—2001), Wis. Music Tchrs. Assn. (rec. sec. 1994—2000, co-chair Eau Claire dist. 2001—). Democrat. Methodist. Avocations: reading murder mysteries, swimming, singing. Home and Office: 1018 Yorkshire Ave Rice Lake WI 54868-1062 E-mail: lstrong@discover-net.net.

STRONG, RICHARD S. investment company executive; married; 1 child. Master's degree, U. Wis. CEO Advisor Strong Funds, Menomonee Falls, Wis., 1974—, dir. Advisor, 1981—, security analyst, portfolio mgr. Advisor, 1985—, chmn. Advisor, 1991—, chief investment officer, 1996—, dir., chmn. bd. Office: Strong Funds 100 Heritage Res Menomonee Falls WI 53051

STRONG, ROBERT THOMAS, former mayor, middle school educator; b. N.Y.C., June 16, 1936; s. Joseph A. and Pauline R. (Manger) S.; m. Evelyn Ann Repasky, Aug. 23, 1958; children: Robyn, Robert Jr. BS, SUNY, Oswego, 1958; MLS, SUNY, Stony Brook, 1976. Social studies tchr. South Country Sch. Dist., Bellport, N.Y., 1958-66, asst. prin. middle sch., 1966-72, tchr., chmn. social studies dept., 1972-91. Student coun. adviser Bellport Middle Sch., 1968-91; prin. Infant Jesus Religious Sch., Port Jefferson, 1966-68. Trustee Village of Port Jefferson, 1991-95, code commr., 1991-99, dep. mayor, 1993-95, mayor, 1995-99; mem., chmn. Zoning Bd. Appeals, Port Jefferson, 1978-91; liaison to pub. safety adv. bd. Village of Port Jefferson, 1991-95; charter mem. Friends of St. Charles Hospice; grad. Suffolk County Citizens Police Acad.; 2d v.p. Suffolk County Village Ofcls., 1998-99; mem. Port Jefferson Harbor Complex Harbor Mgmt. Group; founder, pres. Suffolk County Citizens Police Alumni Assn.; chmn. Village of Port Jefferson Harbor Front Com.; bd. dirs. Port Jefferson Civic Assn. Mem. N.Y. State Tchrs. Assn., Bellport Tchrs. Assn. (treas. 1974-76, bldg. rep. 1989-91), L.I. Coun. for Social Studies, Moose, Kiwanis, S.C.C. Pa. Alumni Assn. (pres.). Roman Catholic. Avocations: skiing, travel, ice skating. Home: 8 Shady Tree Ln Port Jefferson NY 11777

STRONG, SARA DOUGHERTY, psychologist, marriage and family therapist, mediator; b. Phila., May 30, 1927; d. Augustus Joseph and Orpha Elizabeth (Dock) Dougherty; m. David Mather Strong, Dec. 21, 1954. BA in Psychology, Pa. State U., 1949; MA in Clin. Psychology, Temple U., 1960, postgrad., 1968-72; cert. in family therapy, Family Inst. Phila., 1978. Lic. psychologist, Pa. Med. br. psychologist Family Ct. Phila., 1960-85, asst. chief psychologist, 1985-88, chief psychologist, 1988-92; ret., 1992; pvt. practice Phila., 1992—. Cons. St. Joseph's Home for Girls, Phila., 1963-84, Daughters of Charity of St. Vincent De Paul, Albany, N.Y., 1965-90 Mem. APA (assoc.), Am. Assn. Marriage and Family Therapists, Pa. Psychol. Assn., Nat. Register of Health Svc. Providers in Psychology, Family Inst. Phila. Democrat. Avocations: reading, dramatic productions, writing, Yoga, dance.

STRONG, SELDEN RICE, advocate; b. Hartford, Conn., Jan. 24, 1927; s. Edward Winslow and Maude Emily (Foster) S.; m. Dorothy May Lewis, July 4, 1947 (div. July 1981); children: Thor M., Nathan B., Jill P., Amanda C. BA, U. N.H., 1954; postgrad., U. Va. Child welfare worker State of N.H., Dover, 1954-56; buyer II Concord, 1963-64; dep. purchasing agts. aide L.A. County, 1956-61; purchasing agent Imperial Co., El Centro, Calif., 1961-62; contract splst. D.C. Gov., Washington, 1964-71; owner, mgr. Bikers' and Hikers' Retail, Woodbridge, Va., 1972-77. Social worker Elder Svc. of Merval, Lawrence, Mass., 1989-91, ret. 1991. Founder Relevance, Reality, Reason & Peace, 1999. Avocations: writing, walking, bicycling, camping. Home: 464 Suncook Valley Hwy Unit D5 Epsom NH 03234-4351 E-mail: strongsr1@juno.com.

STRONG, STEPHEN ANDREW, lawyer; b. Longview, Tex., June 13, 1960; s. Jack B. and Rose N. (Otts) S.; m. LeAnn Troop, Aug. 6, 1983; children: Mark Andrew, Lindsey Michelle. BBA, Baylor U., 1983, JD, 1984. Bar: Tex. 1984. Assoc. Boyd, Veigel & Hance, Dallas, 1984-87, Liddell, Sapp, Zivley, Hill & LaBoon, Dallas, 1987-90; v.p., sr. counsel AmWest Savs. Assn., 1990-94; sr. v.p., sr. counsel 1st Am. Bank Tex., SSB, Bryan, 1994—. Adv. dir. Briarcrest Ins. Agy., Inc., Bryan, Tex., 1991-97, SALSCO, Inc., Bryan, 1990-97; adv. Rutherford Inst., Dallas, 1991—. Co-author: Southern Methodist U.—Mortgages in Depth, 1991. Adv. dir. Internat. Crusades Found., Inc., Dallas, 1988—; chmn. policy com. Brazos Christian Sch., 1997-98; chmn. Carrollton (Tex.)/Farmers Br. Christian Network, 1990-94; bd. dirs., fin. chmn. Concerned Parents Tex., Inc., Dallas, 1991—; deacon, dir. Sunday schs., Ctrl. Baptist Bryan; chmn. Pub. Sch. Awareness com. Citizens for Excellence in Edn., 1992—. Mem. Tex. Bar Assn., Baylor Bear Found., Tex. Eagle Forum. Avocations: family, church, golf, tennis. Office: 1st Am Bank Tex SSB 2800 S Texas Ave Bryan TX 77802-5343

STRONG, SUSAN CLANCEY, writer, communication consultant, editor; b. Cin., Nov. 10, 1939; d. William Power and Elizabeth (Browne) Clancey; m. Oliver Swigert, 1957 (div. 1972); children: Silvia, David Mack; m. Richard Devon Strong, 1977. BA, Northwestern U., 1965; MA, U. Calif., Berkeley, 1972, PhD, 1979. Tchr. Helen Bush Parkside Sch., Seattle, 1965-66, Taipei (Taiwan) Lang. Inst., 1967-68; acting instr. U. Calif., Berkeley, 1972-78, teaching fellow, 1979, lectr., 1979-84, St. Mary's Coll., Moraga, Calif., 1982-85; pvt. practice Orinda, 1985-90, 97—; sr. rsch. assoc. Ctr. for Econ. Conversion, 1990-96. Mem. Contra Costa County Conflict Resolution Panels, Calif., 1987-90; affiliate Support Ctr./CTD, San Francisco, 1987-90; del. UN Conf. on Econ. Conversion, Moscow, 1990; co-founder "The Who's Counting?" Project, 1996; founder The Metaphor Project, 1997. Author: The GDP Myth: How It Harms Our Quality of Life, and What Communities are Doing About It, 1995; editor Deficit Delirium, 1993, Shaping A New Conversion Agenda, 1995; author poetry; columnist, book reviewer, film reviewer. Mem. Bay Area Global Tomorrow Com., 1986; co-founder Peace Economy Working Group, 1988; co-founder Peace Economy Campaign, 1988; mem. Peace Action Nat. Strategy Com., 1989-95, co-chair strategy com., 1992-93; conf. co-chmn. Nat. Sane/Freeze Congress, 1989-90, rep. nat. bd. advisors Nat. Peace Action, Washington, 1989-95; mem. bd. advisors Peace and Environ. Project, San Francisco, 1986-88; chmn. No. Calif. Sane Freeze, San Francisco, 1985-89; co-convenor The Natural Step Open Space Com. Conf., San Francisco, 1997. Mem. Phi Beta Kappa. Democrat. Episcopalian. Avocation: music, gardening. Fax: 925-254-3304. E-mail: sstrong@metaphorproject.org.

STRONG, VIRGINIA WILKERSON, freelance writer, former educator; b. Vernal, Utah, Mar. 19, 1935; d. Arbun C. and Mildred (Wyman) Wilkerson; m. David Smith, Oct. 6, 1950 (div. Jan. 1960); children: Anna Smith Blyton, Dorothy Smith Wolf, Wendell Lee, Ava Smith Eatman, Karen Smith Ritter; m. Lawrence D. Strong, June 1961 (div. May 1973); children: Lawrence D. Jr., Jeffrey A. BA, U. Miss., 1970, MEd, 1972; PhD, Ohio U., 1985. Cert. elem. edn. tchr., spl. edn. K-12 tchr., ednl. adminstrn. Rsch. asst. U. Miss., University, 1968-70, Utah State U., Logan, 1974-78; tchr. spl. edn. various schs., nr. Oxford, Miss., 1969-74; instr. spl. edn., project coord., rsch. asst. Ohio U., Athens, 1978-82; supr. spl. edn. Meigs County Bd. Edn., Pomeroy, Ohio, 1982-84; tchr. spl. edn., dept. chmn. L.A. Unified Sch. Dist., 1986-93, co-facilitator alcohol drug abuse, 1990-93; freelance writer, owner, mgr. Fenix Devel., Long Beach, Calif., 1990—. Early childhood adv. Utah Bd. Edn., Salt Lake City, 1976, evaluator edn. programs, Salt Lake City and Logan, 1976-77; acting dir. edn., cons. North Miss. Retardation ctr., Oxford, 1993-94; curriclum developer Meigs County, 1982-84; dir. gifted edn. workshop Ohio U., 1980. Author: The Role of the Special Education Supervisor, 1985, (screenplays) To See the Elephant, Dark Encounters; contbr. articles. Elector Dem. Party, Logan, 1976; religious instr. LDS Ch., various locations, 1953-97. U.S. Dept. Edn. grantee Utah Stat U., 1976. Mem. ASCD, Kappa Delta Pi, Phi Delta Kappa. Avocations: genealogy, gemology, photography, history buff, travel.

STRONG, WINIFRED HEKKER, educational counselor, consultant; b. Passaic, N.J., May 16, 1923; d. Frank T. and Wilhelmine (Bohack) Hekker; divorced; 1 child, Frank R. Bush; m. Fred N. Strong, June 21, 1969. BA, Marymount Coll., 1945; MA, NYU, N.Y.C., 1948; postgrad. counseling, Calif. State U., Long Beach, 1958-62, 72, 73. Cert. counselor U.S., Calif. State Bd. Edn. Tchr. Marymount Acad., Tarrytown, N.Y., 1945-46; instr. Fairleigh Dickinson U., Rutherford, N.J., 1950-57; tchr. Long Beach Unified Sch. Dist., 1957-60, sch. counselor, 1960-80, cons. counseling svcs., 1980-90; cons. Calif. Acad. Math. and Sci., Dominguez Hills, 1990-93; pvt. practice Laguna Hills, Calif., 1990-95. Mem. profl. adv. bd. Learning Disabilities Assn. Calif., San Leandro, 1990—; part-time instr. U. La Verne, Calif., 1991-92; chair profl. devel. com. Calif. Assn. for Counseling and Devel., Fullerton, Calif., 1993-95, co-chair, 1995-96. Author: (elem. career awareness program) Color Me Successful, 1988; contbr. handbook Caution - Crisis Ahead, 1994. Mem. League Women Voters, Long Beach, 1982—. Recipient Counseling Program award L.A. County Office Edn., 1988, Adminstr. Recognition award Calif. Sch. Counselor Assn., 1990, Cmty. Contbn. citation Delta Kappa Gamma, 1990; co-recipient Morgan Vail Profl. Devel. award, 1996. Mem. AAUW (com. edn. found. 1993—), Am. Assn. Adult Devel. and Aging (exec. coun. 1993-96), Am. Counseling Assn., Nat. Learning Disabilities Assn., Learning Disabilities Assn. Calif., Calif. Assn. Counseling & Devel. (Clarion Modell award 1990), Calif. Assn. for Adult Devel. & Aging (pres. 1991-92), Long Beach C. of C. (bd. dirs. women's coun. 1987-89), Nat. Bd. Cert. Counselors. Avocations: travel, reading, needlework, swimming. Home and Office: 5216 Elvira Laguna Hills CA 92653-1817

STRONGIN, BONNIE LYNN, English language educator; b. Chgo., Sept. 27, 1943; d. Arthur Caroll and Jennie Grace (Coffler) Bondy; m. Barry Michael Woldman, Jan. 27, 1965 (div. Aug. 1979); children: Scott, Erika, Jonathan; m. Stuart Jeffrey Strongin, Jan. 26, 1992. BA, Roosevelt U., 1964; MA, Concordia U., 1990. Cert. sec. English tchr., Ill. Core tchr. Dist. 15, Rolling Meadows, Ill., 1964-65, 79—; English tchr., chair freshman level Leyden Twp. H.S., Franklin Park, 1965-69. Ednl. cons. French Internat. Sch. of Chgo., 1995; spkr. in field. Contbg. editor Collage Mag., 1980-82; contbr. articles to Collage Mag., Chgo. Tribune; guest Phil Donahue Show, 1984. Recipient Golden Apple State finalist award Golden Apple Found., Chgo., 1993, Excellence in English award English Speaking Union, Chgo., 1994, Tchrs. Who Care Enough to Challenge award Ill. Math. and Sci. Acad., 2002. Fellow: Internat. Biographical Assn.; mem.: Ill. Assn. Tchrs. English, Ill. Edn. Assn., ASCD, NOW, NEA. Avocations: theater, opera, travel, film, art. Office: Plum Grove Jr HS 2600 Plum Grove Rd Rolling Meadows IL 60008-2042

STRONGIN, JONATHAN DAVID, physician; b. Kingston, N.Y., June 19, 1951; s. Jack and Thelma (Kaufman) S.; m. Ellen Wells Seely, June 11, 1983; children: Jessica, Matthew. BA, Columbia Coll., 1973; PhD, MD, Columbia U., 1982. Diplomate Am. Bd. Internal Medicine, Am. Bd. Pulmonary Disease, Am. Bd. Critical Care Medicine. Intern, resident Cambridge (Mass.) Hosp., 1982-84; med. resident Beth Israel Hosp., Boston, 1984-85; pulmonary fellow Mass. Gen. Hosp., 1985-97; physician Pulmonary Assocs. of Greater Boston,

1987—. Pres. med. staff Whidden Meml. Hosp., Everett, Mass., 1995-97; trustee Melrose Wakefield Health Care Corp., 1996—; med. dir. respiratory care Cambridge Health Alliance. Chmn. Bd. of Health, Everett. Fulbright scholar, 1976-77. Fellow Am. Coll. Physicians, Am. Coll. Chest Physicians. Avocation: running.

STRONG-TIDMAN, VIRGINIA ADELE, marketing and advertising executive; b. July 26, 1947; d. Alan Ballentine and Virginia Leona (Harris) Strong; m. John Fletcher Tidman, Sept. 23, 1978. BS, Albright Coll., Reading, Pa., 1969; postgrad., U. Pitts., 1970-73, U. Louisville, 1975-76. Exec. trainee Pomeroy's divsn. Allied Stores, Reading, 1969-70; mktg. rsch. analyst Heinz U.S.A., Pitts., 1970-74; new products mktg. mgr. Ky. Fried Chicken, Louisville, 1974-76; dir. Pitts. office M/A/R/C, 1976-79; assoc. rsch. dir. Henderson Advt., Inc., Greenville, S.C., 1979-81; sr. v.p., dir. rsch. Bozell, Jacobs, Kenyon & Eckhardt, Inc., Dallas, 1981-86, 1981-86, sr. v.p., dir. rsch. and strategic planning Atlanta, 1986-88; sr. v.p., dir. mktg. svcs. Bozell, Inc., 1988-91; sr. v.p., mng. ptnr. Henderson Adv., Inc., 1991-95; prin. Ender-Ptnr., Inc., 1995-96; v.p. mktg. Booth Rsch. Svcs., Inc., 1996-98; COO Moore & Symons, Inc., 1998—. Cons. mktg. rsch. Greenville Zool. Soc., 1981; adj. prof. So. Meth. U., 1984-85. Mem. Am. Mktg. Assn. (Effie award N.Y. chpt. 1982). Republican. Episcopalian. Home: 11 Revival St Roswell GA 30075-4801

STROOBANDT, DIRK RUDY, research scientist; b. Oost-Vlaanderen, Belgium, Jan. 21, 1972; s. Roger F. and Brigitta (DeClercq) S.; m. Mieke Marleen Roelens, May 12; 1995. Electrotechnical Engr., U. Gent, 1994, PhD in Applied Scis., 1998. Rsch. asst. Fund Scientific Rsch.-Flanders/U. Gent, 1994-98, postdoct. fellow, 1998—. Contbr. article to profl. jour. Office: Veldstraat 41 Deinze Oost-Vlaanderen B-9800 Belgium Fax: 32 9 264.35.94. E-mail: dstr@elis.rug.ac.be.

STROOCK, MARK EDWIN, II, public relations company executive; b. N.Y.C., Nov. 6, 1922; s. Irving Sylvan and Blanche (Loeb) S.; m. Hanna Marks Eiseman, June 24, 1945; children— Mark E., Carolyn E. BA, Bard Coll., 1947. Reporter The New York Journal of Commerce, 1947-50; writer Barrons, N.Y.C., 1950-51; mng. editor Fairchild Publ., 1952-53; bus. editor World Mag., 1953-54; contbg. editor Time Mag., 1954-56; with Young & Rubicam Inc., 1956-87, sr. v.p., dir. corp. rels., cons., 1987—. Bd. trustee N.Y. Urban League, 1971-78, Alvin Ailey Dance Theatre, N.Y.C., 1977-84, Friends of the Theatre Mus. City N.Y., 1977-85, Arts Horizons, N.Y.C., 1998—; vice-chmn. Covenant House, N.Y.C., 1978-90; exec. com., mktg. and communications com., assoc. nat. commr. Anti-Defamation League, 1992—. With U.S. Army, 1943-46. Democrat. Jewish. Home: 50 Park Ave Apt 11B New York NY 10016-3075 Office: Young & Rubicam Inc 285 Madison Ave New York NY 10017-6486

STROOCK, THOMAS FRANK, oil and gas company executive; b. N.Y.C., Oct. 10, 1925; s. Samuel and Dorothy (Frank) S.; m. Marta Freyre de Andrade, June 19, 1949; children: Margaret, Sandra, Elizabeth, Anne. BA in Econs., Yale U., 1948; LLB (hon.) , U. Wyo., 1995; PhD (hon.) , Universidad del Valle, Guatemala, 2001. Landman Stanolind Oil & Gas Co., Tulsa, 1948-52; pres. Stroock Leasing Corp., Casper, Wyo., 1952-89, Alpha Exploration, Inc., 1980-89; ptnr. Stroock, Rogers & Dymond, Casper, 1960-82; dir. First Wyo. Bank, 1967-89; mem. Wyo. Senate, 1969-89, chmn. appropriations com., 1983-89, co-chmn. joint appropriations com., 1983-89, mem. mgmt. and audit com., pres., 1988-89; mem. steering com. Edn. Commn. of States; amb. to Guatemala Govt. of U.S., 1989-93; pres. Alpha Devel. Corp., 1992—; prof. pub. diplomacy U. Wyo., Laramie, 1993—. Dir. Wyo. Med. Ctr., 1996—. Rep. precinct committeeman, 1960-68; pres. Natrona County Sch. Bd., 1969; pres. Wyo. State Sch. Bds. Assn., 1965-66; chmn. Casper Cmty. Recreation, 1955-60; chmn. Natrona County United Fund, 1963-64; chmn. Wyo. State Rep. Com., 1975-78, exec. com. 1954-60; del. Rep. Nat. Conv., 1956-76; regional coord. campaign George Bush for pres., 1979-80, 87-88; chmn. Western States Rep. Chmn. Assn., 1977-78; chmn. Wyo. Higher Edn. Commn., 1969-71; mem. Nat. Petroleum Coun., 1972-77; chmn. trustees Sierra Madre Found. for Geol. Rsch., New Haven; chmn. Wyo. Nat. Gas Pipline Authority, 1987-88; bd. dirs. Ucross Found., Denver; mem. Nat. Pub. Lands Adv. Coun., 1981-85; chmn. Wyo. Health Reform Commn., 1993-95; trustee Nature Conservancy, 1993—; chmn. Universidad del Valle Found., Guatemala City, 1995-2000. Sgt. USMC, 1943-46. Mem. Rocky Mountain Oil and Gas Assn., Petroleum Assn. Wyo., Kiwanis, Casper Country Club, Casper Petroleum Club, Yale Club N.Y. Republican. Unitarian Universalist. Home and Office: PO Box 2875 Casper WY 82602-2875

STROOPE, KAY, mathematician, educator; b. Odessa, Tex., Mar. 28, 1947; d. Cecil Clyde and Maurita Rosa Stroope. BS, Henderson U., 1970; MS in Edn., Delta State U., 1989; postgrad., U. Ark., 1987-88. Instr. math. Miller Jr. H.S., Helena-West Helena, Ark., 1970-79, Ctrl. H.S., Helena-West Helena, 1979-87, Benton (Ark.) Mid. Sch., 1987-89, Phillips C.C. U. Ark., Helena, 1989—. Basketball coach Miller Jr. H.S., 1977-81, Ctrl. H.S., 1981-86; math crusade trainer Dept. Higher Edn., Little Rock, 1993—, CMP trainer, 1995—. Co-author (handbook) Metrifacation for Teachers, 1975. Vol. Easter Seal, Helena, 1981-86, March of Dimes, 1987-95, Am. Cancer Soc., 1987—. Named Outstanding Young Educator Helena Jaycees, 1979. Mem. Nat. Coun. Tchrs. Ark., Ark. Coun. Tchrs. Math., Am. Assn. Two-Yr. Colls. Baptist. Home: 600 Galloway West Helena AR 72390-3223 Office: Phillips CC Univ Ark Campus Dr Helena AR 72342

STROPPEL, BETTY MACNAIR, artist, educator; b. Woodbridge, N.J., Feb. 26, 1927; d. S. Herbert and Alice Rebecca (Hoagland) MacN.; m. Aug 27, 1947 (div. July 1970); children: Margaret Alison, David Perry. BFA, Miami U., 1948. Instr. Union County Coll., Cranford, N.J., 1974-86; pvt. instr. North Plainfield, 1977—. Instr. du Cret Sch. Arts, Plainfield, 1979-80, adult schs., art orgns., 1970—; artist-in-residence Severnside Travel, Landing, N.J., 1990. Vol. Longview State Hosp. for Mentally Ill, Cin., 1952-69. N.J. State Coun. Arts fellow, 1977; recipient Cotswold award Phila. Watercolor Soc., 1998, Dana award Phila. Watercolor Soc., 1997, Dunn award Garden State Watercolor Soc., 1999, award of excellence Perkins Art Inst., 1999, Dr. Bowe award Ridgewood Art Inst., 2001, Pauline Wick award Am. Artists Profl. League, 2001. Mem. Am. Artists Profl. League (11 awards), Am. Watercolor Soc. (signature mem.), N.J. Watercolor Soc. (medal of honor 1979, 11 awards, including Henry Gasser Meml. award 1994, Grumbacher medal 1995, Nick Reale Meml. award 1996), Hudson Valley Art Assn. (Mrs. John C. Newington award 1990), Catharine Lorillard Wolfe Club (2 awards), Audubon Artists (2 awards). Republican. Avocation: travel. Home: 115 Sweetbriar Ln North Plainfield NJ 07060-3939

STROSCIO, MICHAEL ANTHONY, physicist, educator; b. Winston-Salem, N.C., June 1, 1949; s. Anthony and Norma Lee (Sidbury) S.; children: Elizabeth de Clare, Charles Marshall Sidbury, Gautam Dutta. BS, U. N.C., 1970; MPhil in Physics, Yale U., 1972, PhD in Physics, 1974. Physicist Los Alamos Sci. Lab., N.Mex., 1975-78; sr. staff mem. Johns Hopkins U. Applied Physics Lab., Laurel, Md., 1978-80; prof. mgr. for electromagnetic research Air Force Office of Sci. Research, Washington, 1980-83; spl. asst. to research dir. Office of Under Sec. Def., 1982-83; policy analyst White House Office of Sci. and Tech. Policy, 1983-85; prof. dir. for microelectrons, prin. scientist U.S. Army Research Office, Research Triangle Park, NC, 1985—2001; adj. prof. depts. physics and elec. and computer engring. N.C. State U., Raleigh, 1985—; prof. depts. bioengring. and elec. computer engring. U. Ill., Chgo., 2001—. Adj. prof. depts. elec. engring. and physics Duke U., Durham, 1986—; vis. prof. dept. of elec. engring. U. Va., Charlottesville, 1990-95, U. Md., College Park, 1996-97; mem. Congrl. Coun., 1989-91; lectr. UCLA, 1987, U. Mich., 1988; cons. U.S. Dept. Energy, Washington, 1985-90; vice-chmn. White House Panel on Sci. Communication, Washington, 1983-84; chmn. Dept. Def. Rsch. Instrumentation Com., Washington, 1982; assoc. mem. Adv. Group on Electron Devices, 1985-91, liaison Nat. Laser Users Facility, Rochester, N.Y., 1984; liaison Panel on Sci. Comm. and Nat. Security, NAS, 1982, Panel on Materials for High-Density Electron Packaging, 1987-90; U.S. Army liaison to JASON, 1991—; mem. U.S. Govt. coord. com. on Semiconductor Rsch. Corp., 1992—. Author: Positronium: A Review of the Theory, 1975, Onslow Families, 1977, Quantum Heterostructures: Microelectronics and Optoelectronics, 1999, Phonons in Nanostructures, 2001; editor: Quantum-Based Electronic Devices and Systems, 1998, Advanced Semiconductor Lasers and Applications to Optoelectronics, 2000; reviewer: Army Rsch. Office, reviewer: NSF, reviewer: Office of Naval Rsch., reviewer: Dept. Commerce and the Natural Scis., reviewer: Engring. Rsch. Coun. Can., 1981—, referee jours.: ; contbr. articles to profl. jours. Capt. USAF, 1974-75. Los Alamos Sci. Lab. grant, 1977. Fellow AAAS, IEEE (exec. com. for plasma sci. 1983—, Harry Diamond Meml. award 1998), Yale Sci. and Engring. Assn. (exec. bd. dirs. 1983—), Army Rsch. Lab.; mem. Am. Phys. Soc., Phi Beta Kappa, Nat. Geneal. Soc. Achievements include patents in field. Home: 2045 Central Ave Wilmette IL 60091-2383 Office: U Ill Dept Elec and Computer Engring MC154 851 S Morgan St Chicago IL 60607 E-mail: stroscio@uic.edu., m.stroscio@gte.net.

STROSS, JEOFFREY KNIGHT, physician, educator; b. Detroit, May 2, 1941; s. Julius Knight and Molly Ellen (Fishman) S.; m. Ellen Nora Schwartz, May 22, 1965; children: Wendy, Jonathan. BS in Pharmacy, U. Mich., 1962, MD, 1967. Diplomate Am. Bd. Internal Medicine. Intern Univ. Mich. Hosp., Ann Arbor, 1967-68, resident in internal medicine, 1971-73; instr. internal medicine U. Mich., 1973-74, asst. prof., 1974-79, assoc. prof., 1979-87, prof., 1987—. Cons. Merck Sharp Dohme Co., West Point, Pa., 1982—, U.S. Dept. State, Washington, 1976—. Contbr. numerous articles to med. jours. Served to maj. USAF, 1969-71. Nat. Heart, Lung and Blood Inst. grantee, 1975—. Fellow ACP; mem. Soc. for Gen. Internal Medicine (regional chmn. 1984-86). Jewish. Home: 824 Asa Gray Dr Ann Arbor MI 48105-2853 Office: U Mich Med Sch 3119 Taubman Ann Arbor MI 48109-0376 E-mail: jstross@umich.edu.

STROSSEN, NADINE, law educator, human rights activist; b. Jersey City, Aug. 18, 1950; d. Woodrow John and Sylvia (Simicich) S.; m. Eli Michael Noam, Apr. 25, 1980. AB, Harvard U., 1972, JD magna cum laude, 1975; LHD (hon.) , U. Vt., 1992, U. R.I., 1992; JD (hon.) , San Joaquin Coll. Law, 1996; LHD (hon.) , Rpcky Mountain Coll., 1996, Mass. Sch. Law, 2000. Jud. clk. Minn. Supreme Ct., St. Paul, 1975-76; assoc. Lindquist & Vennum, Mpls., 1976-78, Sullivan & Cromwell, N.Y.C., 1978-83; prof. clin. law, supervising atty. Civil Rights Clinic, Sch. Law, NYU, 1984-88; prof. law N.Y. Law Sch., N.Y.C., 1988—. Editor Harvard Law Rev., 1975; contbr. book chpts., articles to profl. jours.; author: In Defense of Pornography: Free Speech and the Fight for Women's Rights, 1995. Mem. Coun. Fgn. Rels., 1994—. Recipient Outstanding Young Person award Jaycees Internat., 1986; named one of Ten Outstanding Young Ams., U.S. Jaycees, 1986; adj. fellow Yale U. Calhoun Coll., 1997-. Mem. ACLU (pres. 1991—), Nat. Coalition Against Censorship (bd. dirs. 1988—), Human Rights Watch (exec. com. 1989-91), Harvard Club (N.Y.C.). Avocations: travel, skiing, singing. Home: 450 Riverside Dr # 51 New York NY 10027-6801 also: Sedgewood Club RR 12 Carmel NY 10512-9812 Office: NY Law Sch 57 Worth St New York NY 10013-2959

STROTE, JOEL RICHARD, lawyer; b. N.Y.C., Apr. 19, 1939; s. Jack and Fortuna (Benezera) S.; children: Jared, Noah, Sebastian; m. Elisa Ballestas, Dec. 14, 1991. BA, U. Mich., 1960; JD, Northwestern U., 1963. Bar: N.Y. 1964, D.C. 1965, Calif. 1967, U.S. Dist. Ct. (cen. dist.) Calif. 1967, U.S. Supreme Ct. 1971. Assoc. Damman, Blank, Hirsh & Heming, N.Y.C., 1964-65, ICC, Washington, 1965-66, Capitol Records, Hollywood, Calif., 1966-67; ptnr. Strote & Whitehouse, Beverly Hills, 1967-89; of counsel Selvin, Weiner & Ruben, 1989-94; ptnr. with Cohen, Strote & Young, 1992-94; sole practice law, 1994—. Judge pro tem L.A. County Mcpl. Ct., 1973—; probation monitor Calif. State Bar Ct., L.A., 1985—; pres. Liberace Found., Las Vegas, Nev., 1987—; bd. chmn. Tuesday's Child, L.A., 1989-91. Mem. Thousand Oaks Arts Commn., 1997-99. Cpl. USMC, 1963-64. Mem. Calif. State Bar Assn., L.A. County Bar Assn., L.A. Copyright Soc., Beverly Hills Bar Assn., Assn. Internat. Entertainment Lawyers, Internat. Fedn. of Festival Orgns. Democrat. Jewish. Avocations: swimming, bicycling, hiking, opera, travel. Office: Strote and Levinson 21700 Oxnard St Ste 340 Woodland Hills CA 91367-7560 E-mail: Strote@attglobal.net.

STROTHER, ALLEN, biochemical pharmacologist, researcher; b. Nolan County, Tex., Feb. 20, 1928; s. Henry Allen and Minnie Etta (Taylor) S.; m. Julia Ann Gutch, Feb. 7, 1957; children: Wesley Allen, Lori Ann. BS, Tex. Tech U., 1955; MS, U. Calif., 1957; PhD, Tex. A&M U., 1963. Rsch. asst. Tex. A&M, Coll. Sta., 1959-63; rsch. biochemist FDA, Washington, 1963-65; asst. prof. pharmacology Loma Linda (Calif.) U., 1965-70, assoc. prof., 1970-75, prof., 1975-95, retired, vol. faculty, 1995—, prof. emeritus Physiology and Pharmacology, 1997—. Cons. WHO, Geneva, 1982-86. Contbr. numerous articles to profl. jours.; chpt. to WHO Bull. Pilot CAP/USAF Search and Rescue San Bernardino, Calif., 1967-95; pilot examiner CAP Air Force Aux., Norton AFB, 1970-86. Named Investigator of Yr. Walter E. McPherson Soc., Loma Linda U., 1984, Basic Sci. Fellow of Yr., 1986, Outstanding Faculty Rschr. of Yr. award, 1997. Mem. Am. Soc. Pharmacology and Exptl. Therapeutics, Am. Chem. Soc., Xzenobiotic Soc. Avocations: flying, golf. Home: 74448 Nevada Cir E Palm Desert CA 92260-2269 Office: Loma Linda U Sch Medicine Loma Linda CA 92354

STROTHMAN, JAMES EDWARD, editor; b. Pitts., Mar. 27, 1939; s. Edward Charles and Harriet Hope (Jones) S.; m. Eleanor Shawfield Jacobs, Sept. 9, 1961; children— Joseph, Jill, Stuart BA in Journalism, Pa. State U., 1961. Asst. city editor, city hall reporter Williamsport Grit, Pa., 1961-64; with Miami Herald, Fla., 1964-67; aerospace writer AP, Cape Kennedy, 1967-69; reporter Los Angeles bur. Electronic News, 1969-71, sr. editor computer news sect., 1971-73, mng. editor, 1973; sr. info. rep. corp. hdqrs., then program adminstr. data processing div. hdqrs. IBM Corp., 1973-77, mgr. eastern area communications data processing div., 1977-79, field communications mgr. data processing div., 1979-81, mgr. communications research div., 1981; free-lance writer and cons. Strothman Assocs., 1981-82; editor-in-chief MIS Week, N.Y.C., 1982-88; free-lance writer, cons., 1988-89; editor-in-chief Computer Pictures, Chappaqua, N.Y., 1989-94; news editor ISA On Line Instrument Soc. Am. (ISA), Research Triangle Park, N.C., 1994-2000. Online editor, eCommerce Bus. Mag., 2000-01; assoc. editor InTech Mag., 2001—. Episcopalian. E-mail: jstrothman@mindspring.com.

STROTHMAN, JOHN HENRY, lawyer; b. Mpls., July 10, 1939; s. Maurice Henry and Anne Healy Strothman; m. Barbara Joan Palmen, Sept. 22, 1972; children: David, Peter. BA, Yale U., 1961; JD, U. Minn., 1964. Bar: Minn. 1964. Law clk. to chief justice Oscar Knutson Minn. Supreme Ct., 1964-65; sr. ptnr. Lindquist & Vennum, Mpls., 1965—. Dir., cons. in field. Office: Lindquist & Vennum 4200 IDS Ctr Minneapolis MN 55402 E-mail: jstrothman@lindquist.com.

STROUD, BETSY DILLARD, artist; b. Roanoke, Va., Aug. 12, 1940; d. Peter Hairston Dillard and Alice Elizabeth (Fitch) Madden; m. Ethan Beden Stroud, Dec. 29, 1979 (div. Mar. 1986); 1 child, John Hatcher Ferguson, III. BA, Radford Coll., 1968; MA, U. Va., 1970. Assoc. editor Internat. Artist mag., Scottsdale, Ariz., 1998-2001; profl. artist. Tchr. workshops throughout U.S.; judge art shows including those in Farmington, N.Mex., 1999, The Adirondacks Nat. Watermedia Exhbn., Old Forge, N.Y., 1996, Contemporary Watercolorists of Ariz., 1998, others. Contbr. articles to Am. Artist mag., 1987— and other profl. jours. Mem. S.W. Watercolor Soc. (pres. 1988-89, Edgar A. Whitney award 1989), Am. Watercolor Soc. (High Winds medal 1992, Artist Mag. award 1995), Nat. Watercolor Soc., Rocky Mountain Nat. Honor Soc. (Brass Cheque award 1992), Knickerbocker Artists, Ariz. Watercolor Soc. Avocations: piano, bridge, scrabble, movies. E-mail: betsydillart@uswest.net.

STROUD, HERSCHEL LEON, retired dentist; b. Peabody, Kans., Sept. 21, 1930; Student, U. Kans., 1948-50; BS, U. Mo., Kansas City, 1952; OD cum laude, Ill. Inst. Tech., 1954; DDS magna cum laude, U. Mo., Kansas City, 1961. Diplomate Nat. Dental Bd. Officer, founder Topeka Dental Lab., Inc., 1971; ptnr. Gage Ctr. Dental Group, P.A., Topeka, 1979-98. Pres., bd. dirs. Delta Dental Ins. of Kans. Corp., 1974-92; mem. dental staff St. Francis Hosp. and Med. Ctr., Topeka, 1963—, C.F. Menninger Meml. Hosp., Topeka, 1964—; cons., lectr. civil war medicine. Contbr. articles to profl. publs.; co-partner Kings of Swing Big Band. Vesteryman St. David's Episcopal Ch., 1966-68, composer/dir. Jubilee Mass, dir. Rejoice folk mass, 1967-74, mem. choir; dir. music for blessing of animals Friends of Topeka Zoo, 1983—; mem. U. Kans. Alumni Marching Band; founder/dir. Kans. U. Pep Band, Topeka Club; re-enactor surgeon Maj. Frontier Brigade, 1st Fed. Divsn., Union Army, Civil War, officer Kans. City Civil War Round Table. With USNR, 1950-54; capt. USAF, 1954-57, USAR, 1957-70. Fellow Am. Coll. Dentists, Internat. Coll. Dentists; mem. Soc. Preservation Oral Health (bd. dirs. 1965, exec. sec.-treas. 1966-70), Kans. State Dental Assn. (chmn. coun. on dental care plans 1972-76, state peer rev. com. 1974-76), Am. Dental Assn., Chgo. Dental Soc., Midwest Soc. Peridontology, Am. Prosthodontic Soc., Am. Equilibration Soc., Acad. Gen. Dentistry, Am. Pain Soc., Soc. for Preservation Barbership Quartet Singing Am. (chorus dir.), Rip Chords babershop quartet, Shawnee Yacht Club, Masons, Shriner, Associated Club Spkrs of Am., Knife and Fork Club Inc., Tau Kappa Epsilon, Tau Kappa Nu, Xi Psi Phi. Avocations: scuba diving, snow skiing, sailboat racing, marching band. Home: 3640 SW Drury Ln Topeka KS 66604-2550

STROUD, JACQUELINE LUCILLE, medical supply company executive; b. Carthage, Mo., Jan. 5, 1932; m. Herschel L. Stroud; children: Susan K. Stroud Milash, John L. Student, U. Mo., Kansas City, 1949-50, Sarachon Hooley Sec. Sch., 1950-51; BA in Spanish magna cum laude, Washburn U., Topeka, 1980. Pvt. sec. Recordak Corp., Chgo., 1951-54, Vance AFB, Okla., 1954-57, Hallmark Cards, Kansas City, Mo., 1957-61; adminstrv. asst., translator, export mgr. Munns Med. Supply (now MedVentures Internat. Inc.), Topeka, 1980—. Hist. lectr. Mid-19th Century Women, Civil War Medicine, U.S. San. Commn., recreation of Civil War era personages, 1995—; lectr. Associated Club Spkrs. Am., Knife and Fork Club, Inc. Officer, bd. mem. Internat. Ctr. Topeka, 1980's; bd. dirs. Girls' Club Topeka, 1980's; panelist Panel of Am. Women, 1967-75; Spanish translator Topeka Police Dept., 1981—; choir mem. St. David's Episcopal Ch., 1961—; participant, co-organizer Rejoice, Jubilee and Godspell folk masses, Blessing of the Animals at Topeka Zoo, 1968-96; columnist Westboro Neighborhood newsletter, 1975-98; mem. St. Francis Hosp. Aux. Recipient Outstanding Vol. award Jr. League Topeka, 1973, 1st pl. Mother-Dau. Nat. Equitable Ski Challenge, Keystone, Colo., 1972-73 Mem. ADA, Nat. Mus. Civil War Medicine, Am. Soc. Civil War Surgeons, Frontier Brigade of the 1st Western Divsn., Kans. Dental Auxs., Topeka Knife and Fork Club (pres. 1989-90), Minerva Lit. and Music Club (treas. 1999-2000), Kans. State Hist. Soc., Topeka Hist. Soc., Shawnee County Hist. Soc., N.E. Kans. Civil War Round Table, Kansas City Round Table (officer), Victorian Carthage. Avocations: hostess for Kings of Swing big band, snow skiing, Spanish conversation classes, scuba diving, photography, Civil War reenacments, church choir. Address: 3640 SW Drury Ln Topeka KS 66604-2550

STROUD, JAMES STANLEY, retired lawyer; b. Wimbledon, N.D., Jan. 26, 1915; s. Herbert Montgomery and Amanda Getchell (Longfellow) S.; m. Marjorie Marsh Hovey, Sept. 11, 1940; children: Jay Stanley, Steven Hovey. AB, Jamestown Coll., 1936; JD, U. Chgo., 1939. Bar: Ill. 1939, U.S. Supreme Ct. 1945, D.C. 1972. Counsel Ill. Mcpl. Code Commn., Chgo., 1939-40; bill drafter Ill. Legis. Ref. Bur., Springfield, 1941; from assoc. to ptnr. Mayer, Brown & Platt, Chgo., 1941-71, ptnr.-in-charge Washington, 1972-80, ret., 1982. Bd. dirs. Chgo. Community Renewal Found., 1962-70; mem. adminstrv. bd. Nat. United Meth. Ch., Washington, 1982-84; coord. Extended Family Program, 1981-82. Capt. AUS, 1943-46. Home: Cottage 304 3300 Darby Rd Haverford PA 19041-1063

STROUD, JOHN FRED, JR. judge; b. Hope, Ark., Oct. 3, 1931; s. John Fred and Clarine (Steel) S.; m. Marietta Kimball, June 1, 1958; children: John Fred III, Ann Kimball, Tracy Steel. Student, Hendrix Coll., 1949-51; BA, U. Ark., 1959, LLB, 1960. Bar: Ark. 1959, Tex. 1988, U.S. Supreme Ct. 1963. Ptnr. Stroud & McClerkin, 1959-62; city atty. City of Texarkana (Ark.), 1961; legis. asst. to U.S. Senator John L. McClellan, 1962-63; ptnr. Smith, Stroud, McClerkin, Dunn & Nutter, 1963-79, 81-95; assoc. justice Ark. Supreme Ct., Little Rock, 1980; judge Ark. Ct. Appeals, 1996—2001, chief judge, 2001—. Chmn. Texarkana Airport Authority, 1966-67, Texarkana United Way Campaign, 1988; pres. Caddo area coun. Boy Scouts Am., 1971-73; former trustee Ark. Nature Conservancy; former bd. dirs. Ark. Cmty. Found.; former pres. Red River Valley Assn.; former commr. Red River Compact Commn.; past vice chmn. Ark. Water Code Study Commn.; chmn. bd., chmn. coun. ministries Meth. Ch. Lt. col. USAF, 1951-56, Res. ret. Recipient award of exceptional accomplishment Ark. State C. of C., 1972, 86, Silver Beaver and Disting. Eagle awards Boy Scouts Am.; named Outstanding Young Man of Texarkana, 1966, One of Five Outstanding Young Men of Ark., 1967, Outstanding Alumnus of U. Ark. Law Sch., 1980. Fellow Am. Bar Foun.; mem. ABA, Ark. Bar Assn. (chmn. exec. coun. 1979-80, pres. 1987-88, Presdl. award of excellence and Charles L. Carpenter Meml. award 1997-98), Four States Area Estate Planning Coun. (past chmn.), State Bar Tex., Miller County Bar Assn. (past pres.), Texarkana Bar Assn. (pres. 1982-83), Ark. Bar Found. (chmn. 1974-75), Am. Coll. Trust and Estate Counsel (chmn. Ark. chpt. 1986-91), S.W. Ark. Bar Assn., Texarkana C. of C. (pres. 1969, C.E. Palmer award 1979), Texarkana Country Club (pres. 1990-92), Rotary (pres. Texarkana 1965-66). Avocations: tennis, golf, hunting, fishing. Office: Ark Ct Appeals 625 Marshall St Little Rock AR 72201-1075

STROUD, PATRICIA TYSON, writer; b. Phila., Dec. 22, 1932; d. George Peterson and Jane (Chapman) Huber; m. Noel J. Tyson, Sept. 8, 1956 (dec. July 1982); children: John Tyson II, Peter H. Tyson, Lisa Tyson Ennis; m. Morris Wistar Stroud III, Mar. 11, 1989 (dec. Apr. 1990); m. Alexander McCurdy III, Nov. 16, 1991. AB, Smith Coll., Northampton, Mass., 1955. Writer, pub. rels. releases First Pa. Bank, Phila., 1968-69; editor, Frontiers Acad. Natural Scis., 1979-82; writer pvt. practice, 1982—. Author: Thomas Say: New World Naturalist, 1992, The Emperor of Nature: Chares Lucien Bonaparte and His World, 2000. Pres. bd. dirs. Ga. Farm Found., 1990—; bd. dirs. Hist. Bartram's Garden, 1992-98, U. Pa. Press, 1999—. Avocations: reading, gardening, tennis, piano. E-mail: fdaza@earthlink.net.

STROUD, RHODA M. elementary education educator; Tchr. Webster Magnet Elem. Sch., St. Paul. Apptd. mem. Minn. Bd. Edn. for State of Minn. Recipient State Tchr. of Yr. Elem. award Minn., 1992. Office: Webster Magnet Elem Sch 707 Holly Ave Saint Paul MN 55104-7126

STROUD, RICHARD HAMILTON, aquatic biologist, scientist, consultant; b. Dedham, Mass., Apr. 24, 1918; s. Percy Valentine and Elizabeth Lillian (Kimpton) S.; m. Genevieve Cecelia DePol, Dec. 20, 1943; children: William DePol, Jennifer Celia Trivett. BS, Bowdoin Coll., 1939; MS, U. N.H., 1942; postgrad., Yale U., 1947-48, Boston U. Sch. Edn., 1948-49. Asst. aquatic biologist N.H. Fish and Game Dept., Concord, 1940-41; jr. aquatic biologist TVA, Norris, Tenn., 1942, asst. aquatic biologist, 1946-47; chief aquatic biologist Mass. Div. Fisheries and Game, Boston, 1948-53; asst. exec. v.p. Sport Fishing Inst., Washington, 1953-55, exec. v.p., 1955-81, editor monthly bull.; sr. scientist Aquatic Ecosystems Analysts, Fayetteville, Ark., 1983-88. Del. Rio Conf. of Plenipotentiaries on Conservation of Tuna and Tuna-Like Fishes, 1966; founder., mng. v.p., trustee Sport Fishery Rsch. Found., Washington, 1967-88; cns. aquatic resources, 1981-89, cons. editor fish sci. publs., 1982-95; rsch. adv. bd. Sport Fishing Inst. Fund, 1988-94; Pentelow lectr. U. Liverpool, England, 1975; mem. Marine Fisheries adv. com. Dept. of Commerce; fishery expert advisor to Senate select com. on govt. ops.; fishery advisor Calif. Fish and Game Dept. 1965-66, Ark. Game and Fish Commn., 1969, Iowa Cons. Commn., 1970-71, Tenn. Valley Authority, 1972; guest lectr. Japan Sport Fishing Found., 1976. Author Fisheries Report for Massachusetts Lakes, Ponds, and Reservoirs, 1955; editor (ann. series) Marine Recreational Fisheries Symposia, 1982-95, Nat. Leaders of American Conservation, 1985, World Angling Resources and Challenges, 1985, Fish Culture in Fisheries Management, 1986, Multi-Jurisdictional Management of Marine Fisheries, 1986, Management of Atlantic Salmon, 1988, Planning the Future of Billfishes, Part 1, 1989, Part 2, 1990, Stemming The Tide of Coastal Fish Habitat Loss, 1991, Fisheries Management and Watershed Development, 1992, Conserving America's Fisheries, 1994; co-editor The Biological Significance of Estuaries, 1971, Black Bass Biology and Management, 1975, Predator Prey Systems in Fisheries Management, 1979, N. Am. Jour. of Fisheries Mgmt., 1980—; contbr. articles to profl. jours. Bd. dirs. Nat. Coalition Marine Conservation, 1977-96; treas. Natural Resources Coun. Am., 1961-68, chmn., 1969-71, hon. mem., 1981— . Served with U.S. Army, 1942-46. Decorated Croix de Guerre with cluster.; recipient Conservation Achievement award Nat. Wildlife Fedn., 1975, 81, SOAR award Boy Scouts Am., 1972; named to Nat. Fishing Hall of Fame, 1984 Fellow Am. Inst. Fishery Research Biologists (emeritus, Outstanding Achievement award 1981), Am. Fisheries Soc. (pres. 1979-80, hon. life, emeritus, Outstanding Achievement award 1990, initiated

N. Am. Jour. Fisheries Mgmt.); mem. Internat. Fish and Wildlife Agys., Freshwater Biol. Assn. (U.K.), Fisheries Soc. Brit. Isles. Achievements include being a nationally recognized exponent of catch-and-release philosophy of recreational fisheries management.

STROUD, ROBERT ARLEN, medical equipment company executive; b. Lake Charles, Ill., Nov. 26, 1937; s. Grover Cleveland Stroud and Dolly Lucille (Mericle) S.; m. Mary Erin Coge, Oct. 1, 1965; children: Shannon Dene Stroud Dowden, Robert Arlen II. BS, La. State U., 1962. Sales rep. Chemetron Corp. Nat. Cylinder Gas, Inc., New Orleans, 1962-64; SE regional mgr. Orthopedic Equipment Corp., 1964; dist. mgr. Ohio Med. Products, Inc. Airco, 1964-75; v.p. sales and mktg. Med. Equipment Co. Inc., 1975-76, pres., CEO, 1976—. Pres., CEO Clin. Svcs. Inc., New Orleans, 1983-99. Contbr. papers to profl. jours. Chmn. bd. dirs. New Eng. Presch. Acad., Windsor Locks, Conn., 1992-99; chmn. bd. civil svc. bd. City of Slidell, La., 1977-97; state bd. adv. coun. La. Dept. Edn., Baton Rouge, 1977-82; adv. bd., small bus. coun. La. Assn. Bus. and Industry, Baton Rouge, 1985-96. Mem. Internat. Camellia Soc. (bd. dirs. 2000—), Am. Camellia Soc. (bd. dirs. 1989-99, dir.-at-large 1991-96, v.p. 1997-99, endowment bd. 1993-99, pres. 2002—), Gulf Coast Camellia Soc. (pres., v.p., treas. 1985-99, Dedication award 1996), Camellia Club (pres., v.p. 1992-99, Dedication award 1996). Republican. Avocation: camellia hobbyist. Home: 2 Oak Grove Way Slidell LA 70458-5328 E-mail: bobcamelia@aol.com.

STROUD, ROBERT EDWARD, lawyer; b. Chester, S.C., July 24, 1934; s. Coy Franklin and Leila (Caldwell) S.; m. Katherine C. Stroud, Apr. 8, 1961; children: Robert Gordon, Margaret Lathan. AB, Washington and Lee U., 1956, LLB, 1958. Bar: Va. 1959, U.S. Ct. Appeals (4th cir.) 1967, U.S. Tax Ct. 1959. Assoc. McGuire Woods, LLP, Charlottesville, Va., 1959-64; ptnr. McGuire Woods, LLP, 1964—2002, exec. com., 1978-89. Lectr. math. Washington and Lee U., 1957-59; lectr. bus. tax Grad. Bus. Sch., U. Va., Charlottesville, 1969-87, lectr. corp. taxation law sch., 1985-91; lectr. to legal edn. insts., lectr. in corp. law Washington and Lee Law Sch., Lexington Va., 1984. Co-author: Buying, Selling and Merging Businesses, 1975; editor-in-chief Washington and Lee Law Rev., 1959; editor: Advising Small Business Clients, Vol. 1, 1978, 4th edit., 1994, Vol. 2, 1980, 3d edit., 1990; contbr. articles to profl. jours. Pres. Charlottesville Housing Found., 1968-73; mem. mgmt. coun. Montreat Conf. Ct., N.C., 1974-77; trustee Presbyn. Found., 1972-73, Union Theol. Sem., Va., 1983-91; bd. dirs. Presbyn. Outlook Found., 1968-2002, pres., 1985-88; mem. governing coun. Presbyn. Synod of the Virginias, 1973-78, moderator of coun., 1977-78, moderator of Synod, 1977-78; trustee, v.p. Va. Tax Found., 1984-95; adv. bd. Westminster Orgn. Concert Series, 1989-93; bd. dirs. Shannon Found. for Excellence in Pub. Edn., Charlottesville, 1996—; adv. bd. Ashlawn-Highland Summer Festival, 1989—, pres., 1994-2000; gov. coun. Presbyn. Presbytery of the James, 1993-96, moderator of coun., 1995-96; moderator of presbytery, 1997. Capt. inf. U.S. Army, 1958, with res. 1958-70. Fellow Am. Bar Found., Va. Law Found.; mem. ABA, Va. State Bar, Va. Bar Assn., Nat. Tax Inst., Am. Judicature Soc., Washington and Lee Law Sch. Assn. (governing coun. 1974-80, pres. 1979-80), Redland Club, Bull and Bear Club, Phi Delta Sigma, Omicron Delta Kappa, Phi Delta Phi. Democrat. Home: 345 Terrell Ct Charlottesville VA 22901-2171 Office: McGuire Woods LLP PO Box 1288 Charlottesville VA 22902-1288 E-mail: rstroud@mcguirewoods.com.

STROUD, TED WILLIAM, lawyer; b. Lansing, Mich., Nov. 13, 1952; BS (hons.), Mich. State Univ., 1976; JD cum laude, Cooley Law Sch., 1979. Bar: Mich. 1979, U.S. Dist Ct. (ea. dist., we. dist.) Mich. 1980. Assoc. McNeal & Oade, East Lansing, Mich., 1979-83; ptnr. Oade & Stroud, 1983-89, Oade, Stroud & Kleiman, East Lansing, 1989—. Office: Oade Stroud & Kleiman 200 Woodland Pass East Lansing MI 48823-2000

STROUGO, ROBERT ISAAC, lawyer; b. N.Y.C., May 23, 1943; s. Victor and Mary Strougo; m. Barbara Lieb, June 27, 1976; children: Debra, David. BA, CCNY, 1965; JD, N.Y. Law Sch., 1970. Bar: N.Y. 1971, U.S. Dist. Ct. (so. and ea. dists.) N.Y. 1975. Pvt. practice, N.Y.C., 1971—; owner NYC Realty; also investment and fin. adviser; arbitrator Civil Ct. of N.Y. Active Rep. Nat. Com.; mem. Nat. Rep. Senatorial Com., Rep. Campaign Coun.; mem. N.Y. Rep. County Com. Adv. Bd. Recipient certs. of recognition Nat. Rep. Congl. Com.; honoree Eisenhower Commn. Rep. Nat. Com., 1997. Mem. ABA, Kings County Bar Assn., N.Y. State Legis. Com., Nat. Defenders Assn., N.Y. State Com. on Trial Cts., Bklyn. Bar Assn., Am. Judges Assn., Am. Arbitration Assn. (arbitrator civil ct.), Am. Registry of Arbitrators. E-mial. Home: 305 E 86th St # 17ne New York NY 10028-4702 Office: 21 E 40th St Ste 1800 New York NY 10016-0501 E-mail: strougo@aol.com., atty.nyc@aol.com.

STROUP, KALA MAYS, educational alliance administrator, former state higher education commissioner; BA in Speech and Drama, U. Kans., 1959, MS in Psychology, 1964, PhD in Speech Comm. and Human Rels., 1974; EdD (hon.), Mo. Western State Coll., 1996; LHD (hon.), Harris-Stowe State Coll., 2000. V.p. acad. affairs Emporia (Kans.) State U., 1978-83; pres. Murray State U., Ky., 1983-90, S.E. Mo. State U., Cape Girardeau, 1990-95; commr. higher edn., mem. gov.'s cabinet State of Mo., Jefferson City, 1995—2002; pres. Am. Humanics, Kansas City, Mo., 2002—. Pres. Mo. Coun. on Pub. Higher Edn.; mem. pres.'s commn. NCAA; cons. Edn. Commn. of States Task Force on State Policy and Ind. Higher Edn.; adv. bd. NSF Directorate for Sci. Edn. Evaluation; adv. com. Dept. Health, Edn. and Welfare, chair edn. com.; citizen's adv. coun. on state of Women U. S. Dept. Labor, 1974-76. Mem. nat. exec. bd. Boy Scouts Am., nat. exploring com., former chair profl. devel. com., mem. profl. devel. com., exploring com., Young Am. awards com., 1986-87, north ctrl. region strategic planning com., bd. trustees, nat. mus. chair; mem. Gov.'s Coun. on Workforce Quality, State of Mo.; bd. dirs. Midwestern Higher Edn. Commn.; chair ACE Leadership Commn.; mem. bd. visitors Air U.; v.p. Missourians for Higher Edn.; mem. bd. St. Francis Med. Ctr. Found., 1990-95, Cape Girardeau C. of C., 1990-95, U. Kans. Alumni Assn.; pres. Forum on Excellence, Carnegie Found.; adv. bd. World Trade Ctr., St. Louis, Svc. Mems. Opty. Colls., 1997—; mem. Mo. Higher Edn. Loan Authority, 1995—, depts. econ. devel. & agrl. Mo. Global Partnership, 1995—, Mo. Tng. & Employment Coun., 1995—, Concordia U. Sys. Advancement Cabinet, State Higher Edn. Exec. Officers, 1995—, mem. com. workforce edn. and tng., 1996; bd. govs. Heartland's Alliance Minority Participation, 1995—; chair, mem. workforce devel. com. NPEC coun. U.S. Office of Edn., 1997—; bd. dirs. Midwestern Higher Edn. Com. Distributed Learning Workshop, 1998—, Dept. Natural Resources Minority Scholarship Adv. Bd.; chair Show Me Results sub-cabinet Educated Missourians; mem. Pub. Policy Initiative Stakeholder Com., 1999—; mem. Coun. Higher Edn. transfer and pub. interest com.; mem. access/diversity com. State Higher Edn. Exec. Officers; trustee, mem. adv. coun. Assn. Governing Bds. of Univs. and Colls. Ctr. for Pub. Edn., 2000—. ACE fellow; recipient Alumni Honor Citation award U. Kans., Award Distinction Profl. Black Men's Club, S.E. Mo., 1990, Dist. Svc. to Edn. award Harris-Stowe State Coll., 1996; named to U. Kans. Womans Hall of Fame, Ohio Valley Conf. Hall of Fame, 1997. Mem. Am. Assn. State Colls. and Univs. (past bd. dirs., mem. Pres.'s Commn. on Tchr. Edn., Task Force on Labor Force Issues and Implications for the Curriculum), Mortar Board, Phi Beta Kappa, Omicron Delta Kappa, Phi Kappa Phi, Rotary (found. Ednl. awards com.). Office: Am Humanics 4601 Madison Ave Kansas City MO 64112

STROUP, RICHARD LYNDELL, economics educator, writer; b. Sunnyside, Wash., Jan. 3, 1943; s. Edgar Ivan and Inez Louise (Kellet) S.; m. Sandra Lee Price, Sept. 13, 1962 (div. Sept. 1981); children— Michael, Craig; m. Jane Bartlett Steidemann Shaw, Jan. 1, 1985; 1 child, David. Student, MIT, 1961-62; BA, MA, U. Wash., 1966, PhD in Econs., 1970. Asst. prof. econs. Mont. State U., Bozeman, 1969-74, assoc. prof. econs., 1974-78; dir. Office Policy Analysis, Dept. Interior, Washington, 1982-84; prof. econs. Mont. State U., 1978—, asst. dept. head, 2000—. Vis. assoc. prof. Fla. State U., Tallahassee, 1977-78; sr. assoc. Polit. Economy Research Ctr., Bozeman, 1980—/lectr. summer univ., U. Aix (France), 1985— Co-author: Natural Resources, 1983, Economics: Private and Public Choice, 10th edit., 2002, Basic Economics, 1993, What Everyone Should Know About Economics and Prosperity, 1993; editor: Cutting Green Tape, 2000; also articles, 1972—; mem. editorial bd. Regulation, 1993—. Adj. scholar Cato Inst., 1993—. Mem. Am. Econ. Assn., Western Econ. Assn., So. Econ. Assn., Mont Pelerin Soc., Phila. Soc., Pub. Choice Soc., Assn. of Pvt. Enterprise Edn. (dir.). Episcopalian. Home: 9 W Arnold St Bozeman MT 59715-6127 Office: PERC 502 N 19th Ave Ste 211 Bozeman MT 59718-3124 E-mail: rstroup@montana.edu.

STROUP, SALLY, federal agency administrator; b. Harrisburg, Pa. Grad., Ind. U. Pa., Loyola U. From staff atty. to sr. v.p. legal svcs. and chief counsel Pa. Higher Edn. Agy.; mem. profl. staff com. on edn. and the workforce U.S. Ho. of Reps., 1993—2001; dir. industry and govt. affairs Apollo Group Inc./U. Phoenix; asst. sec. postsecondary edn. Dept. Edn., Washington, 2001—. Office: Dept Edn Office Postsecondary Edn 1990 K St NW Washington DC 20006*

STROUP, STANLEY STEPHENSON, lawyer, educator; b. Los Angeles, Mar. 7, 1944; s. Francis Edwin and Marjory (Weimer) S.; m. Sylvia Douglass, June 15, 1968; children: Stacie, Stephen, Sarah. AB, U. Ill., 1966; JD, U. Mich., 1969. Bar: Ill. 1969, Calif. 1981, Minn. 1984. Atty. First Nat. Bank Chgo., 1969-78, asst. gen. counsel, 1978-80, v.p., 1980; sr. v.p., chief legal officer Bank of Calif., San Francisco, 1980-84; sr. v.p., gen. counsel Norwest Corp., Mpls., 1984-93, exec. v.p., gen. counsel, 1993-98, Wells Fargo & Co., San Francisco, 1998—. Mem. adj. faculty Coll. Law, William Mitchell Coll., St. Paul, 1985-98; mem. Regulatory Affairs Coun., Bank Adminstrn. Inst., 1996—. Bd. dirs. San Francisco Zool. Soc., 2000—, Legal Aid Soc. San Francisco, 1999—. Mem. ABA, Ill. Bar Assn., State Bar Calif., Minn. Bar Assn., Bar Assn. San Francisco (bd. dirs. 2000—), Fin. Svcs. Roundtable. Office: Wells Fargo & Co 633 Folsom St San Francisco CA 94107-3600 E-mail: stroup@wellsfargo.com.

STROUS, ALLEN, poet; b. Circleville, Ohio, Jan. 12, 1959; ss. Ned A. and Donna (Ralston) S. AB in English and Creative Writing, Ohio U., 1981, MA in English and Creative Writing, 1984. Contbr. poetry to lit. publs., including Ohio Rev., Blue Unicorn, Kans. Quar. Artist fellowship Ohio Arts Coun., 2000. Home: 11339 Spangler Rd Circleville OH 43113-9439

STROUSE, JEAN, writer; b. L.A., Sept. 10, 1945; d. Carl David and Louise (Friedberg) S. BA, Radcliffe Coll., 1967. Editl. asst. N.Y. Rev. of Books, 1967-69; freelance writer N.Y.C., 1969-72; editor Pantheon Books, 1972-75; freelance writer, 1975-79; book critic Newsweek Mag., 1979-83; freelance writer, 1983—. Selection com. J.S. Guggenheim Found., N.Y.C., 1995-97, trustee, 1987-94, 2001—, fellow, 1977, 86; exec. coun. Authors Guild; Ferris prof. journalism Princeton U., 1998. Author: Alice James, A Biography, 1980, Morgan American Financier, 1999; editor: Women and Analysis: Dialogues on Psychoanalytic Views of Femininity, 1974. Fellow NEH, 1976, 92, John D. and Catherine T. MacArthur Found., 2002—; recipient Bancroft prize Columbia U., 1981. Mem. Soc. Am. Historians (pres. 2001-02), Phi Beta Kappa (vis. scholar 1996-97).

STROUSE, WAYNE STEVEN, physician; b. Phila., Nov. 11, 1954; s. Albert and Selma (Friedman) s.; m. Janet Lisa Lewis, June 1, 1986; 1 child, Kelsey Lynn. BA cum laude, U. PA., 1976; MD, Med. Coll. Va., 1986. Diplomate Am. Bd. Family Practice. Intern Charleston (S.C.) Naval Hosp., 1986-87; resident Kingsport (Tenn.) Family Practice, Holston Valley Hosp., Kingsport, Tenn., 1992-94, attending physician, 1994-95, Soldiers and Sailors Meml. Hosp., Penn Yan, NY, 1995—; asst. prof. East Tenn. State U., Johnson City, 1994-95, U. Rochester, 1995-96, asst. clin. prof., 1997—. Recipient Mead-Johnson award. Fellow: Am. Bd. Family Practice; mem.: AMA, Am. Acad. Family Physicians. Democrat. Jewish. Office: Main St Family Health 108 Kimble Ave Penn Yan NY 14527 E-mail: pennyandoc@medscape.com.

STROUTH, BARON HOWARD STEVEN, geologist, mining engineer; b. Frankfurt, Germany, Sept. 28, 1919; arrived in U.S., 1941; s. Baron Karl Siegfried and Ida (Morck) von Strauss; m. Penelope Ann Creamer-Osteen, Nov. 3, 1951. BSc, U. Sorbonne, 1939; PhD in Engring., Bretton Woods U., 1965; PhD in Engring. (hon.), Rochedale U., Can., 1970. Asst. mgr. Drexel Bros. Ltd., N.Y.C., 1941-43; pres. Std. Mining, 1951-58, Stanleigh Uranium Mine, Toronto, Can., 1954-61; mng. dir. Norsul Oil and Mining Quito, Ecuador, 1961-71; dir., officer Mining and Oil Cos., various locations; founder, operator Stanleigh Uranium and Norsul Oil. Sr. trustee Weingueter Baron K. S. von Strauss, Erben Trust, Vaduz, 1954—. Translator: The Cornet (Rilke), 1950; author: A Window to the Morrow, 1963, A Sonata for Frankfurt, 1987, Cities of the Break of Dawn, 1988, Beauty is Forever, 1996; patentee in mining and oil porcesses. Maj. USAR, 1943-69, ret. Recipient Conspicuous Svc. Cross, Gov. Dewey, 1947, French, Czech, Cambodian decorations. Fellow Explorers Club; mem. Can. Inst. Mining Engrs. (life), Am. Inst. Mining Engrs. (sr.), St. James Club (London), Ontario Club Toronto. Avocations: collector, antique books, pre-Colombian art, antique maps.

STROYD, ARTHUR HEISTER, lawyer; b. Pitts., Sept. 5, 1945; 1 child, Elizabeth. AB, Kenyon Coll., 1967; JD, U. Pitts., 1972. Bar: Pa. 1972, U.S. Dist. Ct. (we. dist.) Pa. 1972, U.S. Ct. Appeals (3d cir.) 1972. Law clk. to judge U.S. Ct. Appeals (3d cir.), Phila., 1972—75; with Reed, Smith, LLP, Pitts., 1975—, mng. ptnr., Allegheny Region, 1997—2001. Mem. Nat. Adv. Council on Child Nutrition, U.S. Dept. Agriculture, 1984-85. Treas. Mt. Lebanon Zoning Hearing Bd., 1978-81; pres. bd. dirs. Mt. Lebanon Sch. dist., 1981-87; solicitor Allegheny County Rep. Com., 1988-95; pres. bd. dirs. Ctr. for Theatre Arts, Pitts., 1984-93; grad. Leadership Pitts., 1991-92; chair bd. dirs. Mt. Lebanon Hosp. Authority, 1993-2001; bd. dirs. U. Pitts. Cancer Inst., 1993—; mem. alumni coun. Kenyon Coll., 1996-2000; bd. dirs. Edn. Policy and Issues Ctr., 2000—. Lt. USNR, 1969-71. Mem. ABA, Pa. Bar Assn., Allegheny County Bar Assn. (pres.-elect, bd. govs., past chair civil litigation sect., past chmn. judiciary com.), Acad. Trial Lawyers (treas., bd. govs.), Duquesne Club, Pitts. Golf Club, Western Pa. Hist. Soc. (bd. dirs. 1999—). Episcopalian. Avocations: skiing. Office: Reed Smith LLP 435 6th Ave Ste 2 Pittsburgh PA 15219-1886 E-mail: astroyd@reedsmith.com.

STROZESKI, MICHAEL WAYNE, director research; b. McKinney, Tex., Aug. 19, 1944; s. Edwin Guy and Margaret K. (Orr) Parchman; m. Sandra Samples, June 9, 1967. BS, U. North Tex., 1966, MEd, 1970, PhD, 1980. Cert. tchr. sci. secondary, prin., supt. Tchr. sci. Grapevine (Tex.) Ind. Sch. Dist., 1966-70; tchr. physics and biology Ft. Worth Country Day Sch., 1970-78; tchg. fellow U. North Tex., Denton, 1978-79; evaluator, exec. dir. planning, research and evaluation Garland (Tex.) Ind. Sch. Dist., 1979—. Adv. mem. grad. program U. North Tex., Denton, 1985—99; dir., CEO Strozeski Enterprises Consulting, Garland, 1985—. LEA rep. Nat. Ctr. for Ednl. Stats., Washington, 1998—; bd. dirs. Garland YMCA; pres. Tex. Statewide Network of Assessment Profls., 2001—. Mem.: Nat. Assn. Test Dirs. (pres. 1988), Nat. Coun. on Measurement in Edn., Am. Assn. Sch. Adminstrs., Am. Edn. Rsch. Assn., Am. evaluation Assn. (charter), Garland Rotary Club (pres. 1993-94, Paul Harris fellow 1994). Avocation: Avocations: camping, climbing, snowmobiling, reading, computers. Home: PO Box 462306 Garland TX 75046-2306 Office: Garland Ind Sch Dist 870 W Buckingham Rd Garland TX 75040-4616

STRUBBE, THOMAS R. insurance industry executive; b. Ft. Wayne, Ind., Mar. 30, 1940; s. Rudolph C. and Maverne E. (Wagoner) S.; children: Tracy Lynn, Patrick Thomas, Christina Lee. BS, Ind. U., 1962; JD, Tulane U., 1965. Bar: Ind. 1965, Ill. 1969. Atty. Lincoln Nat. Life Ins. Co., Ft. Wayne, Ind., 1965-66, asst. counsel, 1967-68; with Washington Nat. Corp., Evanston, Ill., 1968-90, counsel, 1968-73, gen. counsel, 1973-79, corp. sec., 1970-84, v.p., 1975-79, sr. v.p., 1979-83, exec. v.p., 1983-84, pres., 1984-90, also bd. dirs., mem. exec. com.; pres., CEO Osborn Labs. Inc., Olathe, Kans., 1990-98, Guarantee Res. Life Ins. Co., Chgo., 1998-99, also bd. dirs., ret., 2000. V.p., bd. dirs., exec. com. Chgo. chpt. Epilepsy Found. Am., 1975—79; trustee Glencoe (Ill.) Union Ch., 1984—87; bd. dirs. Assn. Retarded Citizens Ill., 1985—89, Northlight Theater, 1984—89. Lt. USNR, 1965—71. Lincoln Found. grantee, 1964 Mem. ABA, Assn. Life Ins. Counsel, Nat. Investor Rels. Inst., Am. Soc. Corp. Secs., Home Office Life Underwriters Assn., Ind. Bar Assn., Ill. Bar Assn., Skokie Country Club (Ill.), Shadow Glen Golf Club (Kans.), Hideaway Beach Club (Fla.). Home (Summer): 9210 Oak Valley Dr De Soto KS 66018-7994 E-mail: thomstruble@aol.com.

STRUBE, CHRISTOPHER WILLIAM, pastor; b. Clinton, Iowa, Nov. 4, 1963; s. LeRoy Henry Strube and Becky Jane (Hansen) Emerson; m. Ruth Effie Kaufman, Apr. 27, 1985; children: Elizabeth, Anna, Aimee, Jonathan. AA, World Harvest Bible Coll., South Bend, Ind., 1985; BA, World Harvest Bible Coll., 1986; MA, Ind. Christian U., 1991. Ordained minister. Founder, pastor Good Samaritan Ch. Inc., Centerville, Iowa, 1990—. Founder, pres. Tower Ministries, Inc., Centerville, Iowa, 1986—; founder Good Samaritan Ctr., Centerville, 1993—; owner Good Samaritan Constrn. Co., Inc., Truck Heaven, Inc. Developer Valley View Subdivsn., Walnut Grove Subdivisn.; vol. builder log homes, Lake Rathbun, Iowa. Mem. Internat. Conf. Faith Ministries (area rep. 1991—), LeSea Ministers Network. Republican. Avocations: photography, missionary travel, humanitarian aid, hunting and fishing, collecting antique Buick automobiles. Office: Good Samaritan Ch Inc 19793 Hwy 5 Centerville IA 52544-1839

STRUBEL, ELLA DOYLE, advertising and public relations executive; b. Chgo., Mar. 14, 1940; d. George Floyd and Myrtle (McKnight) D.; m. Richard Craig G'sell, Apr. 26, 1969 (div. 1973); m. Richard Perry Strubel, Oct. 23, 1976; stepchildren: Douglas Arthur, Craig Tollerton. BA magna cum laude, U. Memphis, 1962; MA, U. Ill., 1963. Staff asst. Corinthian Broadcasting Co., N.Y.C., 1963-65; dir. advt. and pub. rels. WANE-TV, Ft. Wayne, Ind., 1965-66; asst. dir. advt. WBBM-TV, Chgo., 1966-67, mgr. sales promotion, 1967-69, dir. advt. sales promotion and info. svcs., 1969-70; dir. pub. rels. Walthaw Watch Co., 1973-74; mgr. advt. promotion and pub. rels. WMAQ-TV, 1974-76; v.p. corp. rels. Kraft, Inc., Glenview, 1985-87; sr. v.p. corp. affairs Leo Burnett Co., Inc., Chgo., 1987-92, exec. v.p., 1992-98; mng. dir. EllaQuent Designs, 2002—. Mem. vis. com. U. Chgo. Harris Sch. Pub. Policy; pres. women's bd. Rehab. Inst. Chgo., 1982—84; chair Chgo. Network, 1994—95, Rehab. Inst. Chgo., 1998—2001; bd. dirs. Chgo. Pub. Libr. Found., Athena Found. Named Outstanding Woman in Comms. in Chgo., YWCA, 1995, one of 100 Most Influential Women in Chgo., Crain's Chgo. Bus., 1996, Who's Who in Chgo. Bus., 2002. Mem. Casino Club, Econ. Club. Democrat. Presyterian. Home: 55 W Goethe St Chicago IL 60610-7406 Office: 737 N Michigan Ave Ste 1405 Chicago IL 60611-6654 E-mail: estrubel@aol.com.

STRUBEL, RICHARD PERRY, company executive; b. Evanston, Ill., Aug. 10, 1939; s. Arthur Raymond and Martha (Smith) S.; m. Linda Jane Freeman, Aug. 25, 1961 (div. 1974); children: Douglas Arthur, Craig Tollerton; m. Ella Doyle G'sell, Oct. 23, 1976. BA, Williams Coll., 1962; MBA, Harvard U., 1964. Assoc. Fry Cons., Chgo., 1964-66, mng. prin., 1966-68; with N.W. Industries, Inc., 1968-83, v.p. corp. devel., 1969-73, group v.p., 1973-79, exec. v.p., 1979-83, pres., 1983; chmn. bd., pres. Buckingham Corp., N.Y.C., 1972-73; pres., chief exec. officer Microdot Inc., Chgo., 1983-94; mng. dir. Tandem Ptnrs. Inc., 1990-99; pres., COO, dir. UNext Inc., Deerfield, 1999—. Trustee Mut. Funds of The No. Trust Co., Chgo., and various mutual funds of Goldman Sachs Asset Mgmt., N.Y.C.; bd. dirs. Gildan Activewear, Inc., Montreal, Que., Can. Trustee U. Chgo.; bd. dirs. Children's Meml. Hosp., Children's Meml. Med. Ctr.; chair vis. com. Divinity Sch., U. Chgo.; adv. bd. Martin Marty Ctr. Mem. Casino Club, Chicago Club, Comml. Club, Racquet Club of Chicago, Commonwealth Club, Econ. Club. Presbyterian. Office: UNext Inc Ste 150 500 Lake Cook Rd Deerfield IL 60015

STRUBLE, GEORGE WARING, computer science educator; b. Phila., July 6, 1932; s. George Goodell and Lillie O. (Strand) S.; m. Elsa Laura Bennett, June 18, 1955; children: Andrew, Jennifer, Laura. BA with honors, Swarthmore Coll., 1954; MS, U. Wis., 1957, PhD, 1961. From asst. to assoc. prof. U. oreg., Eugene, 1961-82, research assoc., dir. computer ctr., 1961-74; prof. computer sci. Willamette U., Salem, Oreg., 1982—. Author: Assembler Language Programming, 3d rev. edit. 1984, Business Information Processing with Basic, 1979; contbr. articles to profl. jours. Musician Amateur Chamber Music Players. With U.S. Army, 1954-56. Mem. Am. Helvetia Philatelic Soc., Oreg. Cello Soc. Mem. Unitarian Ch. Clubs: Chemeketans (Salem). Avocation: chamber music. Home: 210 18th St NE Salem OR 97301-4316 E-mail: gstruble@willamette.edu.

STRUBLE, JOHN WARTHEN, historian, educator; b. Washington, Apr. 4, 1952; s. John Brenton and Margaret Lillian (Warthen) Struble. BA, Ind. U., 1974; MA, U. Calif., San Diego, 1978; postgrad., Calif. State U., 1980. Chair fine arts dept. Aquinas H.S., San Bernardino, 1978—84; founding dir. Wolfeboro (N.H.) Acad. Music, 1985—. Author: (book) The History of American Classical Music, 1995; author, editor: music anthology Classic American Folk Music, 1996, mem. editl. bd.: Am. Music Tchr. Mag., 1999—2001. Mem. Conservation Commn., Wolfeboro, 1997—; Bd. dirs. Inland Empire Symphony, San Bernardino, 1979—81. Named 1st Commd. Composer, State of N.H., 1987; recipient Spl. award, ASCAP, 1996—2001; fellow Regents fellow in music, U. Calif., San Diego, 1974, individual artist fellow, N.H. State Coun. on Arts, 1992. Mem.: Music Tchr.'s Nat. Assn. (N.H. state sec. 1999—2002). Democrat.

STRUBLE, SUSAN C. artist, volunteer art therapist; b. N.Y.C., Jan. 4, 1939; d. Calvert Horton and Catherine (Snell) Crary; m. Robert Musser Struble, Mar. 30, 1985. BA, Carleton Coll., 1960. Art therapist Skills Inc., State College, Pa., 1995—, Adult Day Activities Ctr., State College, 1995—, adv. com., 2001—. Vol. art therapist Centre County Youth Ctr., Pa., 1990-93, Laurelton State Sch. and Hosp., 1973-74. Artist: works include Reclining Figure (1st prize Art Alliance Ctrl. Pa.), 1999. Asst. English tchr. Internat. Hospitality Coun., State Coll., 1995—; bd. dirs. friends Palmer Mus. of Art, Pa. State U., 1999—, sec., 2000—. Named Vol. of Yr. Ctrl. Counties Youth Ctr., 1993, Internat. Hospitality Coun., 1999, Adult Day Activities Ctr., 1999. Mem. Am. Art Therapy Assn., State Coll. Woman's Club (sec. art dept. 1998-99), Antique Automobile Club Am. Republican. Presbyterian. Avocations: art, music. E-mail: rmstruble@webtv.net.

STRUCHTEMEYER, CAROL SUE, middle school educator; b. Kansas City, Mo., Apr. 21, 1954; d. Olin Carl and Anna Christine (Skou) Brookshier; m. Leland Leonard Struchtemeyer, May 26, 1973; children: Rhonda Sue, Thomas Leland. BS in Edn., Ctrl. Mo. State U., 1975, MS in Edn., 1981; ednl. resource tchr. tng., U. Mo., 1977. Cert. elem. tchr., spl. edn. tchr., Md.; cert. mid. sch. math. tchr., Md. Tchr. elem. Mayview (Mo.) R-7 Sch. Dist., 1975-76; tchr. learning disabilities Odessa (Mo.) R-5 Sch. Dist., 1976-78; tchr. 5th grade Lexington (Mo.) R-5 Sch. Dist., 1978-96, tchr. 7th and 8th grade math, 1997—. Sec. Leslie Bell Intervention Team, Lexington, 1992-94. Mem. Trinity United Ch. of Christ, Lexington, 1990—, Lexington Athletic Boosters, 1992—, Lexington Fine Arts Club, 1992—. Mem. NEA, Nat. Coun. Tchrs. Math., Mo. Edn. Assn., Mo. Coun. Tchrs. Math., Lexington Cmty. Tchrs. Assn. (sec. 1983-84, treas. 1985-86). Avocations: reading, sewing, gardening, walking. Home: PO Box 58 Lexington MO 64067-0058

STRUCK, NORMA JOHANSEN, artist; b. West Englewood, N.J., Feb. 17, 1929; d. Hans Christian and Amanda (Solberg) Johansen; m. H. Walter Struck, Aug. 21, 1955; children: Steven, Laurie. Student, N.Y. Phoenix Sch. Design, 1946-50, Art Students' League, N.Y.C., 1976-77. Staff artist Norcross, Inc., N.Y.C., 1950-60, free-lance artist, 1967-75; artist portraits, prints Scafa-Tornabene, Nyack, N.Y., 1976—; artist portraits, paintings U.S.N., U.S. Coast Guard, Washington, 1976—. Com. bd. mem. Navy Art Coop. Liaison, N.Y.C., 1976-80, Coast Guard Art Program, N.Y.C., 1980--. One-woman shows include Nabisco Co., Fairlawn, N.J., 1987; exhibited in group shows Navy Hist. Mus., Washington, 1976, Navy Combat Art Gallery, Washington, World Trade Ctr., 1979, USCG, New Eng. Air Mus., Windsor Locks, Conn., 1984, Fed. Hall, N.Y.C., 1986, 93, 94, 95, 96, 97, Salmagundi Club, N.Y.C., Officers Club, Governor's Island, Hudson Valley Show, White Plains, N.Y., Intrepid Mus., N.Y.C., Alexander Hamilton U.S. Custom House; represented in permanent collections U.S. Pentagon, Washington, Henie-Onstad Mus., Oslo, World Figure Skating Hall of Fame and Mus., Colorado Springs, Alexander Hamilton custom House, N.Y.C. Recipient Louis E. Seley award, Navy Art Program, 1979; Grumbacher award, Catherine Lorillard Wolfe, Nat. Arts Club, N.Y.C., 1978; George Gray award Coast Guard Art Program, Governors Island, N.Y., 1983, 89. Fellow Am. Artists Profl. League (pres.'s award 1979); mem. Portrait Soc. Am., Art Students League (life), Hudson Valley Assn. (bd. dirs. 1985-88, M. Dole award 1980), Soc. Illustrators, Salmagundi Club, Portrait Soc. Am., Inc. Avocations: antique collecting, gourmet cooking. Home: 910 Midland Rd Oradell NJ 07649-1904 E-mail: njstruck99@cs.com.

STRUCK, ROBERT FREDERICK, cancer research scientist; b. Pensacola, Fla., Jan. 9, 1932; s. Carl Herman and Hilda (Ropke) S.; m. Ruby Richardson, June 8, 1963; children: Lesley Dianne, Bert Richardson. BS, Auburn U., 1953, MS, 1957, PhD, 1961. Assoc. scientist So. Rsch. Inst., Brimingham, Ala., 1957-58, rsch. scientist Birmingham, 1961-64, sr. rsch. scientist, 1964-81, head metabolism sect., 1981-88, head biol. chemistry div. Brimingham, 1988-93, dir. biochemistry and molecular biology, 1994—. Mem. exptl.

therapeutics study sect. NIH, Bethesda, Md., 1983-86, mem. exptl. therapeutics 2 study sect., 1996—. Contbr. articles on cancer rsch. to profl. jours., chpts. to books; patentee in field. 1st lt. USAF, 1954-56. Grantee NIH, 1979—. Mem. Am. Assn. Cancer Rsch. Democrat. Presbyterian. Home: 3533 Laurel View Ln Birmingham AL 35216-3859 Office: So Rsch Inst 2000 9th Ave S Birmingham AL 35205-2708 E-mail: struck@sri.org.

STRUDWICK, IVAN H. archaeologist; b. Santa Monica, Calif., Apr. 8, 1959; s. Peter Hugh and Barbara June Strudwick; m. Diane Valko, July 4, 1987. BA in Anthropology, Calif. State U., Long Beach, 1981, MA in Anthropology, 1986. Registered profl. archaeologist Calif. Field dir. Chambers Group, Inc., Irvine, Calif., 1990—91; project archaeologist Gallegos & Assocs., Carlsbad, 1991—94; assoc. LSA Assocs., Inc., Irvine, 1994—. Spkr. in field. Mem.: Soc. Calif. Archaeology, Soc. Am. Archaeology, Calif. State U. Long Beach Anthropol. Alumni Assn. (exec. com. 1999—). Republican. Achievements include identification of circular fishhook style associated with preshistoric culture group for coastal Southern California. Avocation: surfing. Home: 235 S Beach Blvd # 93 Anaheim CA 92804 Fax: 949-553-8076. E-mail: ivan.strudwick@lsa-assoc.com.

STRUGGLES, JOHN EDWARD, management consultant; b. Wilmette, Ill., Nov. 29, 1913; s. William George and Sarah Adell (Chambers) S.; m. Dorothy Eloise Goetz, Oct. 23, 1937; 1 child, John Kirk. Student, Miami U., Oxford, Ohio, 1932-34. Supt. Consol. Biscuit Co., Chgo., 1934-37; sales rep. Pillsbury Mills, 1937-41; various personnel and operating positions Montgomery Ward & Co., Chgo., Kansas City, Denver, 1941-50, v.p. personnel, 1950-53; co-founder, co-chmn. Heidrick & Struggles, Inc., Chgo., 1953—. With USNR, World War II. Republican. Home: 505 Sheridan Rd Winnetka IL 60093-2639 Office: Heidrick Struggles Inc 233 S Wacker Dr Chicago IL 60606-6306

STRUHL, STANLEY FREDERICK, real estate developer; b. Bklyn., Oct. 10, 1939; s. Isidore and Yvette (Miller) S.; BS with honors in Engring., UCLA, 1961, MBA in Data Processing, 1963; m. Patricia Joyce Wald, Feb. 26, 1966; children: Marc Howard, Lisa Lynn. Mem. tech. staff Hughes Aircraft Co., Fullerton, Calif., 1963-65; sr. asso. Planning Research Corp., Los Angeles, 1965-70; mgr. corporate info. systems Logicon, Inc., Torrance, Calif., 1970-73; mgr. operations analysis System Devel. Corp., Santa Monica, Calif., 1973-77; gen. partner TST Developers, Canyon Country, Calif., 1977-81; pres. Struhl Enterprises, Inc., Northridge, Calif., 1977-85; owner Struhl Properties, Northridge, 1979— . Mem. planning sub. com. 12th council dist., L.A., 1986-98. Lic. real estate broker, Calif. Mem. San Fernando Valley Bd. Realtors, Trail Dusters, Tau Beta Pi, Beta Gamma Sigma, Alpha Phi Omega. Home: 7309 Easthaven Ln West Hills CA 91307-1257 *Personal philosophy: Word(s) to live by: "Think"!.*

STRUHL, THEODORE ROOSEVELT, surgeon; b. N.Y.C., Jan. 5, 1917; s. Samuel and Florence (Kossoy) S.; m. Ruth Brand, Oct. 19, 1941; children: Karsten, Wendy. BA, NYU, 1936; MS, 1938; MD, NY Med. Coll., 1942; MS in Surg., 1947; grad., Juliard Conservatory of Music, 1933. Dipl. Am. Bd. Abdominal Surg., Am. Bd. Surg.; spl. expert Agy. Health Care Adminstrn., Bd. Medicine, Fla. Int. Queens Gen. Hosp., Jamaica, NY, 1942-43; res. VA Hosp., Newington, CT, 1947-48, Cumberland Med. Ctr., Brooklyn, NY, 1948-51; prac. med. specializing in surg. Miami, FL, 1951—; staff mem. Mt. Sinai Med. Ctr., Miami Beach, Jackson Meml. Hosp., Cedars of Lebanon Health Care Ctr., Variety Chldrns. Hosp., South Shore Hosp., Miami Beach, FL, Victoria Hosp.; former instr. in anatomy L.I. Coll. Med., NY; instr. in surg., instr. in anatomy and surg. anatomy U. Miami; instr. in surg. anatomy and surg. Mt. Sinai Med. Ctr. Mem. adv. ARC of Dade County, Fla.; chief med. examiner Miami Beach Boxing Commn.; med. adv. World Martial Arts, Judo and Karate; mem. Am. Bd. Quality Assurance and Utilization Rev. Physicians; formerly instr. in diving med. Underwater Demolition Team Sch., U.S. Navy, Key West, Fla.; spl. expert Bd. of Medicine of the State of Fla. ; lectr., instr. in scuba diving, diving med. ; lectr. med. and surg., cancer, artificial respiration, anatomy, hypnosis, boxing, weight lifting, judo, skin and scuba diving, swimming, water skiing; spl. expert AHCA Bd. Medicine, State of Fla., Agy. for Health Care Adminstrn. Contbr. articles to profl. jours. Active ARC, 1936—, now bd. dirs., chmn. safety svcs. ARC of Dade County, bd. trustees; instr./trainer in CPR, instr. in advanced cardiac life support Am. Heart Assn.; former mem. N.Y. div. Olympic Wrestling Com. Served to maj. M.C., U.S. Army, World War II; ETO. Fellow ACS, Internat. Coll. of Surgeons (vice-regent Fla.), Am. Coll. Angiology, Internat. Acad. Proctology; mem. AMA, So. Med. Assn., Fla. Med. Assn., Dade County Med. Assn., Israeli Med. Assn., Fla. Assn. Gen. Surgeons (charter), Med. Hypnosis Assn. Dade County Med. Assn., Israeli Med. Assn., Fla. Assn. Gen. Surgeons (charter), Med. Hypnosis Assn. Dade County (past pres.), Am. Coll. Angiology, Pan Am. Med. Assn., Am. Soc. Abdominal Surgeons, Am. Soc. Contemporary Med. and Surg., Med. Aspects of Atomic Explosion, Assn. Mil. Surgeons U.S., Am. Coll. Sports Med., Fla. Bar Ass. (appointed bd. govs. 1990-94, mem. unlicensed practice of law 1997—, mem. pub. info. com. 1997—, grievance com.), Dade County Bar Assn. (mem. grievance com. 1987-90, 94-97), Commodore Longfellow Soc., Miami Beach Power Squadron (charter), Am. Canoe Assn., Am. White Water Assn., Underwater Med. Soc., Photog. Soc. Am., Contin. Hon. Soc. of N.Y. Med. Coll., Phi Delta Epsilon (past pres. chpt.). Democrat. Jewish. Avocations: judo (3rd degree black belt), karate (black belt, 4th degree). Home: 44 Star Island Dr Miami FL 33139-5146 Office: 1444 Biscayne Blvd Ste 304 Miami FL 33132-1423

STRUHS, RHODA JEANETTE, civic and political worker; b. Fresno, Calif., Aug. 31, 1953; d. Edward Stanley and Mary Juanita (Pate) De Vere; m. Parry Leon Struhs, July 3, 1971; children: Jason, Lanisa. Grad. high sch., Fresno. Office mgr. Gunn McKay for U.S. Congress, Ogden, Utah, 1986; saleswoman Realty World-Simplified, 1987-89; spl. edn. aide, substitute tchr. Weber Sch. Dist., 1989-92; human svcs. aide Weber County Mental Health, 1991; No. Utah field dir., office mgr. Pat Shea for Gov., 1992; office adminstr. SHARE, INC., 1993-97; mgr. cmty. resource-vol. ctr. Your Cmty. Connection, 1997-99; Dem. adminstrv. asst. Utah Ho. of Reps., Salt Lake City, 1999—. Block leader Am. Heart Assn., March of Dimes, Easter Sales, 1979-93; troop leader, com. mem. Boy Scouts Am., Girl Scouts U.S.A., 1982-89; bd. dirs. Riverdale Elem. Sch. PTA, 1985-89, pres., 1987-88; bd. dirs. Women's Legis. Coun., 1989-91; conv. del. Weber County. Utah and Nat. Dem. Coms., 1981—; state sec. Utah Dem. Com., 1989-93; pres. Women's Legis. Coun. Weber County, 1993-95, parliamentarian, 1999-01; bd. dirs. Women's State Legis. Coun., 1993-97; vol. ctr. adv. com. Davis County United Way, 1989-99, Nat. Conf. State Legislatures, 1999—, Coun. State Govts., 1999—. Named Weber County Young Dem. of Yr., 1984, Dem. Vol. of Yr., 1986; recipient Extra Mile award Bonneville Coun. PTA, 1986, Disting. Svc. award Utah Dem. Com., 1993. Mem. Altrusa (pres. Ogden 1995-96, dist. membership chmn. 1997-99, dir. 1998-2002, Internat. Dist. Ten dir., 2001—). Avocations: handicrafts, camping, reading, travel. Home: 4312 S 700 W Ogden UT 84405-3404 Office: Utah Ho of Reps 318 State Capitol Salt Lake City UT 84114

STRUKOFF, RUDOLF STEPHEN, retired music educator; b. Rostov, Don, Russia, July 18, 1935; came to U.S., 1951; s. Stephen and Olga (Flemming) S.; m. Donna Lee Hill, May 31, 1959; children: Rudolf Stephen, Jr., Robbin Stanley, Regan Stuart. B Music Edn., Andrews U., 1960; MusM, Mich. State U., 1964, PhD in Music, 1970. Instr. music Mich. State U., East Lansing, 1963-65; asst. prof. Ind. State U., Terre Haute, 1966-69; assoc. prof. Andrews U., Berrien Springs, Mich., 1969-76; prof. music Gov's. State U., Univ. Park, Ill., 1977-97. Chorus master Ill. Philharm. Chorus, Park Forest, Ill., 1982-84; music dir. Univ. Cmty. Chorale, Univ. Park, Ill., 1978-96, Chamber Orch., Univ. Park, 1978-96. Composer: The Greatest of These, 1970, Childhood Sketches, 1973; singer (opera) Attila by Verdi, 1979; condr. Christmas Oratorio by Saint-Saens, 1986, Stabat Mater by Rossini, 1988, German Requiem by Brahms, 1989, Requiem by Mozart, 1990, Mass in C by Beethoven, 1991, Mass in E Flat by Schubert, 1992, Requiem in C Minor by Cherubini, 1993, Cathedral Series, Joliet, Ill., Mass in B Flat by Haydn, St. Liborius, Steger, Ill., 1994, Symphony #2 (Hymn of Praise), Temple Anshe Sholom, 1994, Olympia Fields, Ill., Requiem by Mozart, St. Liborius, Steger, Ill., 1995, Messiah by Handel, Ctr. for Performing Arts, University Park, Ill., 1995, Concert Overture and Requiem by Cherubini, 1996. Lectr. Lyric Opera, Chgo., 1979-89, Libr. Lectr. Series, Park Forest, 1982, Career Days, Chgo., 1982-97, Symposium on Soviet Russia, Univ. Park, 1985, Ill. Philharmonic Workshop Series, 1991-96. Mem. ASCAP, Chgo. Singing Tchrs. Guild (pres. 1984-86, 91-93, bd. dirs. 1986-96), Am. Choral Dirs. Assn., Nat. Assn. Tchrs. Singing, Nat. Assn. Schs. Music, Pi Kappa Lambda. Avocations: antiques, golf, reading.

STRULL, GENE, technology consultant, retired electrical manufacturing company executive; b. Chgo., May 15, 1929; s. Albert and Helen (Wolf) S.; m. Joyce Landsbaum, July 6, 1952; children— David Jay, Brian Lee. BSEE, Purdue U., 1951; MS, Northwestern U., 1952, PhD in Elec. Engring, 1954. With Westinghouse Electric Corp., Pitts., later Balt., 1954-93, supervisory engr., adv. engr., mgr. solid state tech.-aerospace, 1958-68, mgr. sci. and tech. systems devel. div., mgr. advanced tech. labs., 1968-78, dep. gen. mgr. systems devel. div., 1979-81, gen. mgr. advanced tech. div., 1981-93, exec. dir. tech., 1987-93. Cons. Army Sci. Bd., 1979-83, NRC-NAS, 1980-82, Def. Sci. Bd., 1981-83, NSF, 1992—; cons. NASA, 1967-87, com. chmn., 1976-78; adv. com. panel USNR, 1989. Contbg. author: Integrated Electronic Systems, 1970, Integrated Circuit Technology, 1967; contbr. articles to profl. jours.; patentee in field. Gene Strull Tech. Ctr. at Westinghouse Electric Corp. Advanced Tech. Labs. named in his honor, Balt., 1993; named Outstanding Elec. Engr. award Purdue U., 1994. Fellow IEEE (life, Govt. Industry Svc. award 1987, Frederik Philips award 1991); mem. Md. Acad. Scis. (chmn. 1978-80). Home: One Gristmill Ct # 606 Baltimore MD 21208

STRUM, BRIAN J. real estate executive; b. Bklyn., Nov. 27, 1939; s. Max J. and Beatrix (Galitzky) S.; m. Mickey Weiss, Nov. 19, 1966; children: Ira, Howard, Beth. BA, Bklyn. Coll., 1960; LLB, NYU, 1963. Bar: N.Y. 1964, N.J. 1969; CLU; counselor of real estate. Atty. Gilbert, Segall and Young, N.Y.C., 1963-65; assoc. res. atty. Prudential Ins. Co. Am., 1965-67, various positions, law dept., 1967-75, v.p. real estate investments, 1975-86; chmn. Prudential Property Co., Newark, 1986—94; CEO Prudential Realty Group, 1992-94; Silverstein chair of real estate devel. NYU, 1995-98. Pres., trustee Prudential Realty Trust, 1985-94; mem. adv. bd. Chgo. Title & Trust Co., N.Y.C., 1982-96. Editor: Financing Real Estate in the Inflationary Eighties, 1981; contbr. articles to profl. jours. With USAR, 1963-69. Recipient Disting. Cmty. Svc. award Brandeis U., 1983, Urban Leadership award NYU, 1990, Good Scout award N.Y.C. coun. Boy Scouts Am., 1991, Nat. Achievement awrd D.A.R.E. Am., 1993. Fellow Anglo Am. Real Property Inst. (charter); mem. ABA (chmn. real property, probate and trust law sects. 1984-85), N.Y. State Bar Assn. (chmn. real property sect. 1975-76), Urban Land Inst. (coun. mem.), Am. Coll. Real Estate Lawyers (charter), Am. Soc. Real Estate Counselors. Home: 435 Pine Ln Haworth NJ 07641-1308 E-mail: mstrum77@aol.com.

STRUNA, NANCY L. social historian and American studies educator; b. Painesville, Ohio, May 24, 1950; d. Edward A. and Betty J. (Hoffacker) S. BS, U. Wis., 1972; PhD, U. Md., 1979. Social studies tchr. The Andrews Sch., Willoughby, Ohio, 1972-74; grad. asst. U. Md., College Park, 1974-76; tchr. 1-8 grades St. Mark's Elem., Adelphi, Md., 1976-78; instr. U. Md., College Park, 1978-80; asst. prof. U. Minn., Mpls., 1980-82; prof. dept. Am. Studies U. Md., College Park, 1982-2001, acting chair, 2001. Spl. asst. to pres. women's issues U. Md., 1998-2000, fellow Acad. Affairs, 1998-99, campus legis. liaison, 1999. Author: People of Prowess, Sport, Leisure and Labor in Early America, 1996; contbr. articles to profl. jours., chpts. to books. Chair Pres. Commn. on Women's Issues U. Md., 1996—98; mem. Omohundro Inst. for Early Am. History, Culture and Soc. Named Disting. scholar Nat. Assn. Phys. Edn. in Higher Edn., 1993. Fellow Am. Acad. Kinesiology, N.Am. Soc. Sport History (pres. 1995-97). Orgn. Am. Historians, Am. Hist. Assn., Am. Studies Assn., U.S. Capitol Hist. Assn. Office: U Md 1102 Holzapfel Hall Coll College Park MD 20742-5620

STRUNK, BETSY ANN WHITENIGHT, education educator; b. Bloomsburg, Pa., May 28, 1942; d. Mathias Clarence and Marianna (Naunas) Whitenight; children: Robert J. Jr., Geoffrey M. BS in Edn., Bloomsburg U., 1964; MEd, West Chester U., 1969; cert. mentally/physically handicapped, Pa. State U., 1981; postgrad., Wilkes U., St. Joseph's U., Drexel U., Western Md. Coll. Cert. elem. edn., spl. edn., single engine pvt. pilot. Tchr. Faust Sch., Bensalem (Pa.) Twp., 1964, Eddystone (Pa.) Elem. Sch., 1964-66, Lima Elem. Sch., Rose Tree Media Sch. Dist., 1966-69, Rose Tree Media (Pa.) Sch. Dist., 1977—; adj. prof. Wilkes Coll., Wilkes-Barre, Pa., 1981-86; instr. Delaware C.C., Media, 1986; instr., dir. ground sch. edn. Brandywine Airport, West Chester, Pa., 1986-88; instr. Drexel U., Phila., 1989—2001, Performance Learning Systems, Inc., Emerson, N.J. and Nevada City, Calif., 1981—2001; rep. FAA, Phila., 1986-88. Spl. edn. resource rm. specialist, tchr. cons. Media Elem. Sch.; spl. edn. supervisory selection com. Rose Tree Media Sch. Dist., spl. edn. resource rm. specialist, tchr. cons.; curriculum designer pvt. pilot ground sch.; instr. and course designer introduction to flying and pilot companion course; chairperson profl. devel. com. Rose Tree Media Sch. Dist., 1992; mem. Insvc. Coun. Delaware County, 1992—2002; mem. educator's adv. com. Phila. Franklin Inst., 1990—92, 1995—; cons. ednl. programs, 1988—; owner, designer Betsy's Belts, Del., N.J., Pa., 1970—74; mem. gov. bd. Southeastern Tchr. Leadership Ctr. West Chester U., Pa.; learning support specialist Glenwood Elem. Sch., Media, Pa., 1994—; educator liaison between sr. citizens and learning support students Lima Estates Retirement Home and Glenwood Elem. Sch., 1994—; tchr. academically gifted program Indian Ln. and Glenwood Elem. Schs., 1998—99; presenter State Pa. Lead Tchr. Conf., 1994, Ind. Sch. Tchrs. Assn., 1995; project dir. video documentary Performance Learning Sys., Calif., 1994; ptnr., owner Whitenight Homestead Partnership, Bloomsburg, Pa. (program dir. video documentaries including): Learning Through Live Events and Teaching Skills for the 21st Century, 1995; contbr. articles to profl. jours. Mem. Middletown Free Libr. Bd., 1977—79; officer Riddlewood Aux. to Riddle Meml. Hosp., Media, 1973—76; chairperson Lima Christian Nursery Sch., Pa., 1973, March of Dimes, Middletown, 1973; pres. Roosevelt PTG (Elem. Sch.), Media, 1982; capt. March of Dimes, 1987—91, Diabetes Assn., Media, 1989—91; vol. Tyler Arboretum, Middletown Twp., 1980—82; mem. cmty. rels. com. Deerfield Knoll Homeowner's Assn., 1998—, v.p., bd. dirs., 1999—2002; mem. Wilmington Opera House, Dupont Theatre; com. person, v.p. Middletown Twp. Dem. Com., 1974; mem.Vietnamese refugees com. Media Presbyn. Ch., 1975; assoc. mem. Skidaway Presbyn. Ch., Savannah, Ga. Recipient 1st pl. color divsn. Photography award, Pa. Colonial Plantation, 1st pl. color divsn. in Photography, Bloomsburg State Fair, 1994; grantee Fine Arts in Spl. Edn., Pa. Dept. Edn., 1993—94. Mem.: NEA, Media Soc. Performing Arts, Aircraft Owners and Pilots Assn., Nat. Staff Devel. Coun., Pa. State Edn. Assn., Rose Tree Media Edn. Assn. (profl. devel. com. chairperson 1992—93, profl. devel. com. rep. 1990—93, Exceptional Svc. award), Longwood Gardens, Chester County Hist. Soc., Phila. Zoo, Tyler Arboretum. Democrat. Avocations: reading, writing, interior decorating, nature walking, gardening. Home: Willistown Twp 203 Cohasset Ln West Chester PA 19380-6507 Office: Rose Tree Media Sch Dist Glenwood Elem Sch Pennell Rd Media PA 19063 also: The Landings on Skidaway Island 7 Franklin Creek Rd South Savannah GA 31411

STRUNK, ROBERT CHARLES, physician; b. Evanston, Ill., May 29, 1942; s. Norman Wesley and Marion Mildred (Ree) S.; m. Juanita; children: Christopher Robert, Alix Elizabeth. BA in Chemistry, Northwestern U., 1964, MS in Biochemistry, MD, Northwestern U., 1968. Lic. MD, Ariz., Colo., Mass., Mo. Resident in pediatrics Cin. Children's Hosp., 1968-70; pediatrician Newport (R.I.) Naval Hosp., 1970-72; rsch. fellow in pediatrics Harvard Med. Sch., Boston, 1972-74; asst. prof. pediatrics U. Ariz. Health Sci. Ctr., Tucson, 1974-78; dir. clin. svcs. Nat. Jewish Ctr. for Immunology and Respiratory Med., Denver, 1978-87; sabbatical leave Boston Children's Hosp., 1984-85; dir. divsn. allergy and pulmonary medicine Children's Hosp., St. Louis, 1987-98; pediatrician Barnes and Allied Hosp., 1987—; prof. pediatrics Washington U. Sch. Medicine, 1987—. Recipient Allergic Disease Acad. award Nat. Inst. Allergy and Infectious Disease of NIH. Mem. Am. Acad. Allergy and Immunology, Am. Thoracic Soc. Office: Washington U Sch Med Dept Pediatrics 1 Childrens Pl Saint Louis MO 63110-1002

STRUNZ, KIM C. career officer; b. Caro, Mich., May 3, 1954; d. Herbert James and Geraldine (Elliott) S. AAS with honors, Delta Coll., 1974; BS with honors, Alma Coll., 1980; postgrad., Ctrl. Mich. U., 1978-80; MPA, U. Okla., 1989. Commd. 2d lt. U.S. Army, 1980, advanced through grades to lt. col., telecomms. ctr. specialist 178th signal co. Germany, 1974-77, chief plans, ops., tng. and security med. dept. activity Bremerhaven, Germany, 1980-82, ambulance platoon leader Co. C 47th med. bn. Furth, Germany, 1982-83, exec. officer dental activity Ft. Lee, Va., 1983-85, adjutant Kenner Army Cmty. Hosp., 1985, comdr. med. co. 47th Field Hosp. Ft. Sill, Okla., 1986-88, chief pers. svcs. divsn. 121st Evac. Hosp. 18th med. command Seoul, Korea, 1988-89; chief mil. pers. br. William Beaumont Army Med. Ctr., El Paso, Tex., 1990-92, comdr. troop command, 1992-93; career planning officer U.S. Total Army Personnel Command, Alexandria, Va., 1993-95; pers. policy analyst Office of the Army Surgeon Gen., Falls Church, 1995-97; exec. asst. health affairs Office of Asst. Sec. of Def., Pentagon, 1997-98; dir. pers. and adminstrn. Tricare Mgmt. Acty., Falls Church, 1998-99; dep. cmdr. for adminstrn. Weed Army Cmty. Hosp., Ft. Irwin, Calif., 1999-2001; dep. comdr. for adminstrn. Ireland Army Cmty. Hosp., Ft. Knox, Ky., 2001—. Contbr. rsch. articles to profl. jours. Vol. Therapeutic Horsemanship Assn., El Paso, Alexandria Hosp.; vol Alexandria Tutoring Consortium; mem. Highland Presbyn. Ch. Softball Team, El Paso; mem. First Presbyn. Ch., Caro, Mich.; affiliate mem. Fairlington Presbyn. Ch., Alexandria, Va. Fellow Am. Coll. Healthcare Execs., Am. Legion, Assn. Mil. Surgeons U.S., Am. Soc. Pub. Adminstrn., Assn. U.S. Army, Army Women's Profl. Assn., Order Mil. Med. Merit. Presbyterian. Avocations: horseback riding, fishing, skiing, hiking. Home: PO Box 584 Fort Knox KY 40121

STRUPP, HANS HERMANN, psychologist, educator; b. Frankfurt am Main, Germany, Aug. 25, 1921; came to U.S., 1939, naturalized, 1945; s. Josef and Anna (Metzger) S.; m. Lottie Metzger, Aug. 19, 1951; children: Karen, Barbara, John. AB with distinction, George Washington U., 1945, AM, 1947, PhD, 1954; MD (hon.), U. Ulm, Fed. Republic of Germany, 1986. Diplomate in clin. psychology Am. Bd. Profl. Psychology; lic. clin. psychologist, Tenn. Research psychologist Human Factors Ops. Research Labs., Dept. Air Force, Washington, 1949-54; supervisory research psychologist, personnel research br. Adj. Gen.'s Office, Dept. of Army, 1954-55; dir. psychotherapy research project Sch. Medicine, George Washington U., 1955-57; dir. psychol. services, dept. psychiatry U. N.C. Sch. Medicine, Chapel Hill, 1957-64, asso. prof. psychology, 1957-62, prof., 1962-66; prof. dept. psychology Vanderbilt U., Nashville, 1966-76, dir. clin. tng., dept. psychology, 1967-76, disting. prof., 1976-94, Harvie Branscomb disting. prof., 1985-86; disting. prof. emeritus, 1994—. Mem. editorial adv. bd. Psychotherapy: Theory, Research and Practice, 1963-97, Jour. Cons. and Clin. Psychology, 1964— , Jour. Nervous and Mental Disease, 1965— , Jour. Am. Acad. Psychoanalysis, 1972— , Jour. Contemporary Psychotherapy, 1972-86, Psychiatry Research, 1979-86, Jour. Profl. Psychology, 1976-89; founding editor Psychotherapy Rsch., 1990-95; others; contbr. chpts. to books, articles and revs. to profl. jours. Recipient Helen Sargent meml. prize Menninger Found., 1963; Alumni Achievement award George Washington U., 1972; Disting. Profl. Achievement award Am. Bd. Profl. Psychology, 1976, Disting. Profl. Contbns. to Knowledge award Am. Psychol. Assn., 1987; others Fellow Am. Psychol. Assn. (mem. exec. council 1964, exec. bd. 1969-72, council of reps. 1970-73, chmn. com. on fellows div. psychotherapy 1970-74, pres. div. clin. psychology 1974-75, recipient Disting. Profl. Psychologist award 1973, Disting. Scientist award 1979), Tenn. Psychol. Assn., AAAS; mem. Eastern Psychol. Assn., Southeastern Psychol. Assn., Am. Psychopathol. Assn., Am. Psychoanalytic Assn. (hon.), Soc. for Psychotherapy Research (pres. 1972-73, Career Contbr. award 1986), Psychologists Interested in Advancement of Psychoanalysis, Phi Beta Kappa, Sigma Xi. Home: 4117 Dorman Dr Nashville TN 37215-2404 *As a refugee from Nazi Germany, I remain deeply grateful for the opportunities my adopted country has provided me.*

STRUTHERS, MARGO S. lawyer; BA, Carleton Coll., 1972; JD cum laude, U. Minn., 1976. Atty., shareholder Moss & Barnett, P.A. and predecessor firms, Mpls., 1976-93; ptnr. Oppenheimer Wolff & Donnelly, LLP, 1993—. Mem. Am. Health Lawyers Assn., Minn. State Bar Assn (bus. law sect., former chair nonprofit com., former chair and former mem. governing coun. health law sect.). Office: Oppenheimer Wolff & Donnelly LLP Plaza VII 45 S 7th St Ste 3300 Minneapolis MN 55402-1614 E-mail: mstruthers@oppenheimer.com.

STRUTIN, KENNARD REGAN, lawyer, educator, legal information consultant; b. Bklyn., Dec. 1, 1961; s. Fred and Estelle (Brodzansky) S. BA summa cum laude, St. John's U., Jamaica, N.Y., 1981; JD, Temple U. Sch. Law, Phila., 1984; MLS, St. John's U., 1994. Bar: N.Y. 1986, U.S. Dist. Ct. (ea. and so. dists.) N.Y. 1990, U.S. Dist. Ct. (no. and we. dists.) N.Y. 1991, U.S. Ct. Appeals (2d cir.) 1990, U.S. Ct. Appeals (fed. cir.) 1991, U.S. Tax Ct. 1991, U.S. Ct. Mil. Appeals 1991, U.S. Supreme Ct. 1990. Atty. pvt. practice, West Hempstead, N.Y., 1986; trial atty. Nassau County Legal Aid Soc., Hempstead, 1987-88, Orange County Legal Aid Soc., Goshen, 1988-90; atty. pvt. practice, West Hempstead, 1990-91; staff atty. N.Y. State Defenders Assn., Albany, 1991-93; adj. asst. prof. St. John's U., Jamaica, 1993-96; small claims tax assessment hearing officer Supreme Ct., Nassau, Suffolk, 1993-96; law libr. Syracuse U. Coll. Law, 1996-98; legal info. cons., 1998—. Spkr. lawyer in classroom Nassau County Bar Assn., Mineola, N.Y., 1987-94; spkr. pre-release program Correctional Facilities, Lower Hudson Valley, N.Y., 1989-94. Author: ALI-ABA's Checklist Manual on Representing Criminal Defendants, 1998, Insider's Guide: Criminal Justice Resources on the Web, 2002; co-author: (computer-assisted, interactive instrnl. program) Legal Research Methodology, 1997; contbr. articles to profl. jours. Recipient Orange County Exec. Recognition award, 1990, 93, 2nd place winner libr. divsn. Donald Trautman Ctr. for Computer-Assisted Legal Instrn. Lesson Writing Competition, 1996-97. Mem. Beta Phi Mu.

STRUTTON, LARRY D. former newspaper executive; b. Colorado Springs, Colo., Sept. 12, 1940; s. Merril and Gladys (Sheldon) S.; m. Carolyn Ann Croak, Dec. 3, 1960; children— Gregory L., Kristen AA in Electronics Engring., Emily Griffith Electronics Sch., 1968; BS in Bus. Mgmt. and Systems Mgmt., Met. State Coll., 1971; diploma in Advanced Mgmt. Program, Harvard U., 1988. Printer Gazette Telegraph, Colorado Springs, Colo., 1961-64; prodn. dir. Rocky Mountain News, Denver, 1964-80, pres., 1990, pres. and CEO, 1991—2001; exec. v.p. ops. and advt. Detroit Free Press, 1981-83; v.p. ops. Los Angeles Times, 1983-85, exec. v.p. ops., 1986-90; former pub. Rocky Mountain News, Denver. Mem. adv. com. Rochester Inst. Tech., 1984—. Mem. Am. Newspaper Pubs. Assn. (chmn. 1987, chmn. TEC com. 1985-86), R&E Council (research and engring. council of the Graphic Arts Industry Inc.). Clubs: Lakeside Golf (Los Angeles).*

STRUTZ, WILLIAM A. lawyer; b. Bismarck, N.D., May 13, 1934; s. Alvin C. and Ina Vee (Minor) S.; m. Marilyn Seagly, Aug. 31, 1957; children: Heidi Jane Mitchell, Colin Christopher, Nathaniel Paul. Student, Drake U., 1952-53; BA, North Ctrl. Coll., 1956; postgrad., Washington and Lee U., 1956-57; JD, U. N.D., 1959. Bar: N.D. 1959, U.S. Dist. Ct. N.D. 1959, U.S. Ct. Appeals (8th cir.) 1961. Atty., pres. Fleck, Mather & Strutz, Ltd., Bismarck, N.D., 1959—. Mem. grievance com. N.D. Supreme Ct., Bismarck, 1974-77, chmn. supreme ct. svcs. com., 1979—. Bd. dirs. Vets. Meml. Pub. Libr., Bismarck, Shiloh Christian Sch., Bismarck, 1978—; pres. student body North Ctrl. Coll., 1956. Recipient Herbert Harley award Am. Judicature Soc., 1991. Mem. ABA, Am. Bd. Trial Advs. (adv.), Lions Club. Methodist. Avocations: reading, rare book collecting, music, sports. Home: 1238 W Highland Acres Rd Bismarck ND 58501-1259 Office: Fleck Mather Strutz Ltd 400 E Broadway Ave Bismarck ND 58501-4038

STRUTZEL, J(OD) C(HRISTOPHER), escrow company executive; b. L.A., Sept. 20, 1947; s. James Rudolph and Charlotte Elizabeth (Weiss) S.; m. Christine Melba Kemp, Dec. 28, 1969; children: Jason James, Jess Warren. BS in Bus. Mgmt., Calif. State U., Long Beach, 1970. Bellman Edgewater Hyatt House Hotel, Long Beach, 1970, night auditor, 1970-71; asst. mgr. Sands Resort Hotel, Palm Springs, Calif., 1971-72, gen. mgr., 1972-73; sales coordinator Bendix Home Systems, Santa Fe Springs, Calif., 1973-74; loan rep. J.E. Wells Fin. Co., L.A., 1974-75; v.p. Express Escrow Co., Huntington Beach, Calif., 1976-78, pres., chmn. bd. bd. dirs., 1978—. Pres., chmn. bd., bd. dirs. Elsinore (Calif.) Escrow, Inc., 1977-79; bd. dirs. Sorrell Devel., Redondo Beach, Calif.; expert witness on escrow, litigation and cons., 1982—; chmn. liability reduction com. Escrow Agts. Fidelity Corp., 1983-84, legis. chmn., 1985-86, 87-90, 95-97, vice-chmn. bd., 1989-90, 94-95, treas., 1992-93; bd. dirs., sec. Discovery Escrow Co., 1989-94; drafted sections of Calif. Fin. Code, Health and Safety Code, Calif. Adminstrv. Code. Contbr. articles to trade publs. Bd. dirs. publicity chmn. Fountain Valley (Calif.) Youth Baseball, 1986-87; AD HOC com. on Escrow Regulations Dept. Housing and Cmty. Devel., 1980; escrow adv. com. Dept. Corps., 1990-93. Recipient J.E. Wells Meml. award, 1988, Chmn.'s award, Pres.'s award Calif. Mfrs. Housing

Inst. Mem. Escrow Agts. Fidelity Corp. (bd. dirs. 1983-90, 91-97), Escrow Inst. of Calif. (bd. dirs. 1991), Calif. Manufactured Housing Assn. (treas., bd. dirs. 1984-86), Calif. Manufactured Housing Inst. (bd. dirs. 1986—, treas. 1986-87, legis. chmn. 1993—, Polit. Action Com. Man of Yr. award 1988, Orange County chpt. Man of Yr. award 1988, Chmn.'s award 1997, Pres. award 1999). Avocations: golf, war games, athletic coaching. Office: Express Escrow Co 7812 Edinger Ave Ste 300 Huntington Beach CA 92647-3727

STRUVE, GUY MILLER, lawyer; b. Wilmington, Del., Jan. 5, 1943; s. William Scott and Elizabeth Bliss (Miller) S.; m. Marcia Mayo Hill, Sept. 20, 1986; children: Andrew Hardenbrook, Catherine Tolstoy, Frank Leroy Hill, Guy Miller, Beverly Marcia Wise Hill (dec.), Elena Wise Struve-Hill. AB summa cum laude, Yale U., 1963; LLB magna cum laude, Harvard U., 1966. Bar: N.Y. 1967, D.C. 1986, U.S. Dist. Ct. (so. dist.) N.Y. 1970, U.S. Dist. Ct. (ea. dist.) N.Y. 1973, U.S. Dist. Ct. (no. dist.) Calif. 1979, U.S. Dist. Ct. D.C. 1987, U.S. Dist. Ct. (no. dist.) N.Y. 2000, U.S. Ct. Appeals (2d cir.) 1969, U.S. Ct. Appeals (D.C. cir.) 1973, U.S. Ct. Appeals (8th cir.) 1976, U.S. Ct. Appeals (9th cir.) 1979, U.S. Supreme Ct. 1971, U.S. Dist. Ct. (we. dist.) N.Y. 1991. Law clk. Hon. J. Edward Lumbard, Chief Judge United States Ct. Appeals for 2d Circuit, 1966-67; assoc. Davis Polk & Wardwell, N.Y.C., 1967-72, ptnr., 1973—, Ind. Counsel's Office, 1987-94. Mem. ABA, N.Y. State Bar Assn., Assn. of Bar of City of N.Y. (chmn. com. antitrust and trade regulation, 1983-86, chmn. com. fed. cts. 1998-2001), Am. Law Inst. Home: 116 E 63rd St New York NY 10021-7325 Office: Davis Polk & Wardwell 450 Lexington Ave Fl 31 New York NY 10017-3982

STRUYK, ROBERT JOHN, lawyer; b. Sanborn, Iowa, May 17, 1932; s. Arie Peter and Adriana (VerHoef) S.; m. Barbara Damon, Sept. 7, 1963; children: Arie Franklin, Damon Nicholas, Elizabeth Snow. BA, Hope Coll., 1954; MA, Columbia U., 1957; LLB, U. Minn., 1961. Bar: Minn., U.S. Dist. Ct. Minn. Secondary tchr. Indianola (Iowa) Pub. Schs., 1957-58; assoc., then ptnr. Dorsey & Whitney, Mpls., 1961—. Mem.: Mpls., Minikahda. Episcopalian. Office: Dorsey & Whitney 220 S 6th St Ste 2200 Minneapolis MN 55402-1498

STRYCKER, STEVE LYNN, accountant; b. Mishawaka, Ind., June 2, 1962; s. Bill Dean and Mardell Jean (Anthony) S.; m. Jaynee Clark; 1 child, Anthony. BS, Ind. U., South Bend, 1985. CPA, Ind. Bookkeeper Elcona Country Club, Elkhart, Ind., 1986; contr. Continental Stamping, Wakarusa, 1986-88; supr. gen. acctg. Utilimaster Corp., 1988-90; gen. acct. Crown Internat., Elkhart, 1990; treas. Home Lumber & Supply Co., Inc., Goshen, Ind., 1990-92; dir. acctg. Free Meth. Ch., Indpls., 1992—. Fundraiser, sidewalker Morning Dove Therapeutic Riding, 2000—; treas. Wakarusa Missionary Ch., 1991; mem. John Wesley Free Meth. Ch. Mem.: Ind. CPA Soc. (not-for-profit com. 1995—99, vice chair 1999), Chapel Bend Assn. (bd. dirs. 1995—2001, sec. 1999—2001), Phi Eta Sigma. Avocations: health club, tennis, swimming. Office: Free Meth Ch NA 770 N High School Rd Indianapolis IN 46214-3688 E-mail: steves@fmcna.org.

STRYK, ROBERT ANTHONY, software engineer; b. St. Paul, Mar. 10, 1937; s. Michael and Mabel (Mitchell) S.; m. Lorraine Helen Hadlich, Aug. 31, 1957 (dec. Mar. 1966); children: Steven Robert, William Michael; m. Marilyn Roettger, May 10, 1969 (div. Jan. 1978); 1 child, Susan Margaret; m. Roberta Sophia Wick, Sept. 12, 1981 (wid. Nov. 1995). MS in Physics, U. Minn., 1963, PhD in Physics, 1967. Rsch. scientist Honeywell Corp. Rsch., Mpls., 1967-78; devel. engr. Honeywell Corp. Computer Ops., 1978-82; software engr. Honeywell Defense Systems, 1982-90, Alliant Techsystems, Mpls., 1990—. Mem. Am. Phys. Soc., Assn. for Computing Machinery, Sigma Xi, Tau Beta Pi. Achievements include patent (with others) for smoke detector. Home: 5441 Halifax Ln Edina MN 55424-1438

STRYKER, AMY, actress; b. Greenville, S.C., June 26, 1949; d. Richard Jay and Margaret Sprague Irwin; m. Randolph Ray Mathena; children: Ivan Randolph Mathena, Margaret Amelia Mathena. BFA, U. N.C., Winston Salem, 1976. Cert. one year study acting London. Author: And Counting..., 1992, Almost to the Point, 2001; actor: (films) A Wedding, 1976, Long Riders, 1979, Impulse, 1988. Mem. Christ Ch. Episcopal, Greenville, 1950—2002. Mem.: AFTRA, SAG. Episcopalian.

STRYKER, DANIEL RAY, adult education educator; b. Ruslip, Eng., July 15, 1957; came to U.S., 1959; s. Theodore Ray and Nina Margaret (Bryant) S. BS, Sam Houston State, 1980; MEd, U. Houston, 1988, EdD, 1996. Pulmonary functions technician St. Joseph Hosp., Houston, 1981; rschr. U. Tex. Med. Br., 1981-82; taxpayer svc. rep. IRS, 1982-85; substitute tchr. Conroe (Tex.) Schs., 1986-88, 91-95; tchr. Aldine Schs., Houston, 1988-90; instr. U. Houston, 1995-96, Western Carolina U., Cullowhee, 1997-98; instr. dept. history and geography Houston C.C., 1998—; instr. dept. history N. Harris Coll., Houston, 1998—. Author: A Cognitive Approach to Teaching History, 1994, Twilight in the City, 1996, Nowhere in the Shadow, 1996, Mirror of Dreams, 1996. Precinct judge Klein Schs., Houston, 1992-96. Athletic scholar Sam Houston State, Huntsville, 1976. Avocations: reading, writing, camping, mountain climbing. Home: 4135 Swinden Dr Houston TX 77066-3511 Office: Houston CC Dept History and Geography 1550 Foxlake Dr Dept And Houston TX 77084-6029 also: N Harris Coll Dept History 2700 W W Thorne Blvd Houston TX 77073-3410 E-mail: dstryker@nhmccd.com.

STRYKER, JAMES WILLIAM, automotive executive, former military officer; b. Grand Rapids, Mich., Apr. 20, 1940; s. John Alvin and Marian (Anderson) S.; m. Eleanor Marie Finger, Sept. 26, 1964; children: James William II, Marian Marie Jenkins, Kathryn Alison Greenbauer. BS, U.S. Mil. Acad., 1963; MA, U. Mich., 1972; postgrad., U.S. Army Command and Gen. Staff Coll., 1978. Commd. 2d lt. U.S. Army, 1963, battery exec. officer 6th/20th field arty. Colo., 1964-65, advisor Vietnam, 1965-66, battery comdr. 4th/3d field arty. Tex., 1967-68, advisor Thailand, 1969-70; S-3 ops. officer 1st/7th F.A., Ft. Riley, Kans., 1972-73; assoc. prof. history U.S. Mil. Acad., West Point, N.Y., 1973-77; chief nuclear ops. Ctrl. Army Group NATO, Heidelberg, Germany, 1978-81; dir., project mgr. tank-automotive command U.S. Army, Warren, Mich., 1981-86, ret., 1986; program mgr. military vehicles operation GMC Truck, Pontiac, Mich., 1987-95; cross brand portfolio mgr. Pontiac-GMC Divsn. GM Corp., Detroit, 1996-98, asst. brand mgr. product full size and mid size vans, 1999-2001, asst. brand mgr. product alternative fuel and mobility, 2001—, product mgr. alternative fuels and mobility, 2002—. Author: (with others) Encyclopedia of Southern History, 1977; co-author: Early American Wars, 1978. Torch bearer Olympic Winter Games, Salt Lake City, 2002. Decorated Legion of Merit, Bronze Star medal, Def. Meritorious Svc. medal, Meritorious Svc. medal with oakleaf cluster, Army Commendation medal with oakleaf cluster, U.S. Army/Vietnamese Cross of Gallantry with palm and gold star; Olympic torchbearer Winter Olympics, 2002. Mem.: NRA (dir. Detroit chpt. 1994—97, endowment), Nat. Def. Indsl. Assn. (dir. Detroit chpt. 1991—92, 2d v.p. 1995, 1st v.p. 1995—96, pres. 1996—97, adv. 1997—2000), Trout Unltd., Ruffed Grouse Soc. (banquet com. Detroit 1998—2002, 2002), Assn. U.S. Army (dir. Detroit chpt. 1990—95), Nodrog Setter Club Mich., Gordon Setter Club Am. Avocations: hunting, skeet shooting, trout fishing, field training English and Gordon Setters. Home: 168 First St Romeo MI 48065-5000 Office: GM Fleet & Comml Orgn MC 482-A20-B36 PO Box 100 100 Renaissance Ctr Detroit MI 48243-1001 E-mail: bill.stryker@gm.com.

STRYKER, SHELDON, sociologist, educator; b. St. Paul, May 26, 1924; s. Max and Rose (Moskevitz) S.; m. Alyce Shirley Agranoff, Sept. 7, 1947; children: Robin Sue, Jeffrey, David, Michael, Mark. BA summa cum laude, U. Minn., 1948, MA, 1950, PhD, 1955. Mem. faculty Ind. U., 1951—, prof. sociology, 1964—, disting. prof. sociology, 1985—2002, disting. prof. emeritus, 2002—; dir. Inst. Social Research, 1965-70, 89-94, chmn. dept. sociology, 1969-75; co-dir. Ctr. for Social Rsch., 1989-94. Cons. in field; mem. social scis. research rev. com. NIMH, 1974-79, chmn., 1976-79, mem. research scientist devel. award com., 1981-85 Editor: Sociometry, 1966-69, Rose Monograph Series of Am. Sociol. Assn., 1971-73, Am. Sociol. Rev., 1982-85; assoc. editor: Social Problems, 1957-59; author books, monographs, articles, chpts. in books. Served with AUS, 1943-46. Fellow Social Sci. Research Council, 1959-60, Ctr. Advanced Behavioral Scis., 1986-87; Fulbright research scholar Italy, 1966-67. Mem. Am. Sociol. Assn. (nat. coun. 1965-67, 80-81, chmn. social psychology sect. 1978-79, chmn. publs. com. 1991-93, Cooley-Mead award), Soc. for the Study of Symbolic Interaction (George Herbert Mead award for lifetime scholarship 2000), Ohio Valley Sociol. Soc. (coun. 1965-67), North Ctrl. Sociol. Assn. (pres. 1978-79), Sociol. Rsch. Assn. (coun. 1978-84, pres. 1983-84), Phi Beta Kappa. Home: 3710 Saint Remy Dr Bloomington IN 47401-2418

STRYKER, STEVEN CHARLES, lawyer; b. Omaha, Oct. 26, 1944; s. James M. and Jean G. (Grannis) S.; m. Bryna Dee Litwin, Oct. 20, 1972; children: Ryan, Kevin, Gerrit, Courtney. BS, U. Iowa, 1967, JD with distinction, 1969; postgrad. studies, Northwestern U. Grad. Sch. Bus, 1969-70, DePaul U., 1971. Bar: Iowa 1969, Tex. 1986; CPA Ill., Iowa. Sr. tax acct. Arthur Young & Co., Chgo., 1969-72; fed. tax mgr. Massey Ferguson, Des Moines, 1972-74; fed., state tax mgr. FMC Corp., Chgo., 1974-78; gen. tax atty. Shell Oil Co., Houston, 1978-81, asst. gen. tax counsel, 1981-83, gen. mgr., 1983-86, v.p., gen. tax counsel, 1986—. Mem. ABA, AICPA, Tex. Bar Assn., Iowa Bar Assn., Ill. Soc. CPAs, Iowa Soc. CPAs, Tax Execs. Inst., Am. Petroleum Inst. Home: 2121 Kirby Dr Unit 124 Houston TX 77019-6068 Office: Shell Oil Co 1 Shell Plz Ste 4570 Houston TX 77001

STRYKER, TERENCE WAYNE, secondary school educator; b. Daytona Beach, Fla., Nov. 21, 1956; s. Judson Phillip and Irene Lillian Stryker; m. Lynn Lyda. B in Music Edn., Fla. State U., 1980; M in M in Music Edn., PhD in Music Edn., Trinity Coll., 2001. Cert. network engr. ; music tchr. grades K-12 Fla. Choral dir. Port St. Joe (Fla.) H.S., Port St. Joe, 1985—89; band dir. Wewahitchka (Fla.) H.S., 1989—. Named All USA Tchr. Team, USA Today, 1999, Tchr. of Yr., Gulf County Schs., 2000. Mem.: Fla. League Arts Tchrs., Fla. League Tchrs., Music Educator's Nat. Conf., Fla. Music Educator's Assn., Fla. Bandmaster's Assn. Baptist. Avocations: numismatics, auto restoration, woodworking, technology. Home: 4801 Sunset Dr Panama City FL 32404 Office: Wewahitchka HS One Gator Circle Wewahitchka FL 32465 Office Fax: 850-639-5394. Personal E-mail: stryker_t@firn.edu. Business E-Mail: tstryker@wewahigh.com.

STRYKER, WENDY ELLISON, nurse; b. Cedar Rapids, Iowa, Aug. 5, 1951; d. Lloyd William and Mary Jean (Hurd) Ellison; m. David A. Stryker, July 21, 1973 (div. Aug. 1980). BS in Nursing, U. Iowa, 1973. Staff nurse Luth. Med. Ctr., Omaha, 1973-74, charge nurse, 1974; staff nurse U. Iowa Hosps., Iowa City, 1974-75; head nurse Oaknoll Retirement Residence, 1975-76; staff nurse Christian Hosp., St. Louis, 1976, head nurse, 1976, MBSA, St. Louis, 1976-80; charge nurse No. Va. Dr. Hosp., Arlington, Va., 1980-81, asst. head nurse, 1981-88; nurse mgr. REACH program, 1988-89, case mgr., 1989-90, clin. case mgr. LSC, 1990-91; home health cons. Vis. Nurses Assn. No. Va., 1991-97; supr. clin. access and liaisons dept. Inova VNA Home Health, Springfield, Va., 1997-98; continuing care coord. Inova Alexandria Hosp., 1998-99; fin. case mgr. The Hospices Nat. Capital Area, 1999—2002, mgr. reimbursement dept. fin. case mgmt., 2002—. Mem. NAFE, Am. Nursing Assn., Nat. League for Nursing, Assn. Rehab. Nurses, U. Iowa Coll. Nursing Constituent Soc., Va. Assn. Rehab. Nurses (past v.p., past and current treas.), Alpha Phi. Avocations: sports, reading, dogs. Home: 12760 Gazebo Ct Woodbridge VA 22192-2411 Office: Hospices of the Nat Capital Area 9300 Lee Hwy Ste 500 Fairfax VA 22031 Business E-Mail: wstryker@thehospices.org.

STRYSICK, MICHAEL OTTO, terrestrial ecologist, physicist, microbiologist; b. Sheboygan, Wis., Jan. 13, 1931; s. Michael Sr. and Agnes (Czaja) S.; m. Carol Ann Greiner, June 25, 1955 (dec. July 1992); children: Peter Michael, Mary Susan. Terrestrial ecologist, rschr., Sheboygan, Wis., 1954—. Cons. Master Gardner program U. Wis. Ext. Svcs., Sheboygan Falls, Wis., 1988—; rschr. Neem Oil Margosan-O, 1992. Cubmaster to commr. Boy Scouts Am.; treas. Cath. Com. Scouting, Sheboygan, 1970-97. With U.S. Army, 1952-54, Korea. Recipent St. George medal Boy Scouts Am., 1984. Mem. AAAS, Korean War Vets. Assn., VFW, Am. Legion. Achievements include Neem Oil development in the 1980s and field studies; Hanta Virus verification in Ams. as med. problem, 1990—; researcher in Myology 2000, a post-genome 30 protein complex of the nucleus of human cells; Krebs/Calvincycle phenomena citric TNF alpha beta gamma omega role of un P un Ca polarity to transfat and uric acid lactic acidosis in human diabetes; symbiotic GUT thermobacteria excess citric acid as source of H3 and of NH3 and to NO and excess uric acid and E. coli or salmonella muntation, or UVB radiation induced cancers; including all life forms cycle of reproduction avoidance of overpopulation and evolutionary adaptation; and use of woodchip mulch, adverse effects in anerobic conditions in 1970-80. Avocation: travel to gain information on interrelationships of life forms and symbiotic associations required for survival. Home and Office: 1002 N 16th St Sheboygan WI 53081-3825 Office Fax: 920-458-2690.

STRZALKA, DIANA LYNN, journalist; b. Chgo., Nov. 3, 1959; d. Antoni Strzalka and Lottie Ciesla; children: Emily Delogu, Julia Delogu, Russell Delogu. AA, Thornton C.C., S. Holland, Ill., 1981; BA, Columbia Coll., 1985. Reporter The Daily Calumet, Chgo., 1985—86; reporter, editor Daily Southtown-The Star, 1987—91; freelance journalist Chgo. Tribune, 1991—2000, staff reporter, 2000—01, freelance journalist, 2001—, Todo-s.com, Houston, 1998—2000; tchr. Kosciuszko Found., N.Y.C., 2000. Mem.: Guild Complex, S.W. Polish Soc., Assn. Women Journalists, Soc. Profl. Journalists. Avocations: travel, bike riding, writing poetry, playing piano. Personal E-mail: dstrzalka@mindspring.com.

STUART, ALICE MELISSA, lawyer; b. N.Y.C., Apr. 7, 1957; d. John Marberger and Marjorie Louise (Browne) S. BA, Ohio State U., 1977; JD, U. Chgo., 1980; LLM, NYU, 1982. Bar: N.Y. 1981, Ohio 1982, N.Y. 1982, Fla. 1994, U.S. Dist. Ct. (so. dist.) Ohio, 1983, U.S. Dist. Ct. (so. and ea. dists.) N.Y. 1985. Assoc. Schwartz, Shapiro, Kelm & Warren, Columbus, Ohio, 1982-84, Paul, Weiss, Rifkind, Wharton & Garrison, N.Y.C., 1984-85, Kassel, Neuwirth & Geiger, N.Y.C., 1985-86, Phillips, Nizer, Benjamin, Krim & Ballon, N.Y.C., 1987—92; pvt. practice, 1992—98; atty. LeBoeuf, Lamb, Greene & MacRae, 1998—. Adj. prof. So. Coll., Orlando, Fla., 1997-98. Surrogate Speakers' Bur. Reagan-Bush Campaign, N.Y.C., 1984; mem. Lawyers for Bush-Quayle Campaign, N.Y.C., 1988; bd. dirs. Mayflower Soc. in State of NY, 1998-, counsellor, 2002-. Mem. ABA, N.Y. State Bar Assn., Winston Churchill Meml. Library Soc., Jr. League, Soc. Mayflower Descs. in State of N.Y. (bd. dirs. 1999–, counselor 2002–), Phi Beta Kappa, Phi Kappa Phi, Alpha Lambda Delta. Republican. Office: LeBoeuf Lamb Greene & MacRae 125 W 55th St New York NY 10019-5369

STUART, ANDREW MICHAEL, educator; b. Fredericton, Can., Aug. 14, 1957; s. Roy Graham and Jean Mary S.; m. Naomi Joy Shaw, Oct. 25, 1997; 1 child, Joshua Graham. BS, Dalhousie U., Halifax, Can., 1978, MS, 1986, PhD, 1996. Audiologist Children's Hosp. Ea. Ont., Ottawa, Can., 1986-89; rsch. asst. Dalhousie U., Halifax, Can., 1989-92; assoc. prof. East Carolina U., Greenville, N.C., 1996—. Audiology cons. Soc. Card of Handicapped in Gaza Strip, 1994-95. Contbr. articles to profl. jours.; assoc. editor Jour. Speech-Lang.-Pathology and Audiology, 1996-2000; patentee in field. Recipient D.O. Hebb Postgrad. prize, Dalhousie U., 1992; postdoctoral fellow Dalhousie U., 1996; Izaak Walton Killam Meml. Hon. scholar, Dalhousie U., 1992-96. Mem. Am. Speech-Lang.-Hearing Assn., Am. Auditory Soc., Can. Speech-Lang Pathologists and Audiologists. Office: East Carolina U Dept Comm Scis & Disorders Greenville NC 27834

STUART, CAROLE, publishing executive; b. N.Y.C., Feb. 22, 1941; d. Frank and Sally (Stern) Rose: m. Lyle Stuart, Feb. 4, 1982; 1 child, Jennifer Susan Livingston. Student, Bklyn. Coll. Pub. Lyle Stuart, Inc., Secaucus, N.J.; assoc. pub. Carol Pub. Group, N.Y.C.; pub. Barricade Books, Inc. Author: Why Was I Adopted?, To Turn You On, 39 Sex Fantasies for Women, (with Claire Ciliotta), Why Am I Going to the Hospital?, I'll Never Be Fat Again, How To Lose 5 Pounds Fast, The Thank You Book. Mem. Authors Guild, Women's Media Group, Wine and Food Soc. N.Y.. Home: 1530 Palisade Ave Apt 6L Fort Lee NJ 07024-5402 Office: Barricade Books Ste 308A 185 Bridge Plz N Fort Lee NJ 02024

STUART, CHARLES EDWARD, electrical engineer, oceanographer; b. Durham, N.C., Feb. 9, 1942; s. Charles Edward and Wilma Kelly Stuart; m. Margaret Ann Robinson, Jan. 9, 1982; children: Marjorie Kelly, Heather Alison. BSEE, Duke U., 1963. Engr. Westinghouse Electric Corp., Balt., 1963-65; sr. engr. Booz Allen Hamilton, Chevy Chase, Md., 1966-68; rsch. dir. B-K Dynamics Inc., Huntsville, Ala., 1969-78; oceanographer Office of Naval Rsch., Arlington, Va., 1979-84; dir. Maritime System Office Advanced Rsch. Projects Agy., 1985-98; with def. programs U.S. Dept. Energy, Washington, 1998-99; pres. Competitive Enterprise Solutions, LLC, Arlington, 2000—. Contbr. 12 papers on ocean acoustics, unmanned systems and maritime tech. to profl. jours. Recipient Am. Def. Preparedness Assn. award, Bushnell award for career contbns. to undersea warfare, 1996. Mem. IEEE (sr., ad. com. 1991-93), Assn. Unmanned Vehicle Systems (trustee 1989-93). Methodist. Achievements include leading work in antisubmarine warfare and development of unmanned undersea vehicle technology. Office: Competitive Enterprise Solutions LLC 4718 17th St N Arlington VA 22207-2031

STUART, CYNTHIA MORGAN, university administrator; b. Harrisburg, Pa., June 29, 1949; d. Paul William and Bernice Leona (Boyer) M.; m. David Edward Stuart, June 14, 1971. Student, Elizabethtown (Pa.) Coll., 1967-69; BA, U. N.Mex., 1971, MPA, 1982, postgrad., 2001—. Admissions counselor U. N.Mex., Albuquerque, 1974-77, asst. dir. admissions, 1977-80, assoc. dir. admissions, 1980-83, dir. admissions, 1983—, univ. articulation officer, 1989—, dir. student outreach svcs. (secondary appointment), 1991-95, enrollment mgmt. team mem., 1998—. Mem. N.Mex. Coordinating Coun. Secondary Schs. and Colls., 1983-92; chair Coun. for Common Concerns, Albuquerque, 1987-95; mem. N.Mex. Articulation Com., Santa Fe, 1983-95; mem. adv. bd. Albuquerque Tech. Vocat. Inst., 1991—. Compiler, editor Statewide Statistical Profile Report, N.Mex. H.Ss., 1983-90; cover photographer Prehistoric New Mexico, 2d edit., 1994, Glimpses of the Ancient Southwest, 1995. Coord. United Way, Albuquerque, 1980-81; elected del. N.Mex. Dem. Conv., 1982; mem. issues and advocacy com. Albuquerque Bus. Edn. Compact, 1991-93; mem. Am. Indian Edn. Initiative, Albuquerque, 1992—; Coll. Bd. del., 1991—. Recipient sys. devel. grant Commn. on Higher Edn., Santa Fe, 1995. Mem. Am. Assn. Collegiate Registrars and Admissions Officers (reporting officer of transfer credit N.Mex. 1979—), Rocky Mountain Assn. Collegiate Registrars and Admissions Officers (v.p. 1979-81, pres. 1983-84), N.Mex. Assn. Collegiate Registrars and Admissions Officers (sec.-treas. 1978-82, pres. 1991-92, Outstanding Svc. award 1990), N.Mex. Am. Coll. Testing Coun. (chair 1996-97, state rep. 1997—, trustee Am. Coll. Testing 1999—, del. to Coll. Bd. 1991—). Democrat. Avocations: photography, travel, drawing, music. Home: 423 Tulane Dr SE Albuquerque NM 87106-1417 Office: Univ New Mex Office of Admissions Student Svcs Ctr Albuquerque NM 87131-0001 E-mail: cstuart@unm.edu.

STUART, DABNEY, poet, author, English language educator; b. Richmond, Va., Nov. 4, 1937; s. Walker Dabney Jr. and Martha (vonSchilling) S.; m. Sandra Westcott, Jan. 20, 1983; children: Martha, Nathan vonSchilling, Darren Wynne AB, Davidson Coll., 1960; AM, Harvard U., 1962. Instr. Coll. William and Mary, Williamsburg, Va., 1961-65; prof. English Washington and Lee U., Lexington, 1965—2002, S. Blount Mason Jr. prof. English, 1991—2002. Vis. prof. Middlebury (Vt.) Coll., 1968-69, Ohio U., Athens, 1975, U. Va., Charlottesville, 1981-83. Author: The Diving Bell, 1966, A Particular Place, 1969, The Other Hand, 1974, Friends of Yours, Friends of Mine, 1974, Round and Round, 1976, Nabokov: The Dimensions of Parody, 1978, Rockbridge Poems, 1981, Common Ground, 1982, Don't Look Back, 1987, Narcissus Dreaming, 1990, Sweet Lucy Wine, 1992, Light Years: New and Selected Poems, 1994, Second Sight: Poems for Paintings by Carroll Cloar, 1996, Long Gone, 1996, The Way to Cobbs Creek, 1997, Settlers, 1999, Strains of the Old Man, 1999, No Visible Means of Support, 2001, The Man Who Loved Cezanne, 2003. Recipient Dylan Thomas prize Poetry Soc. Am., 1965, Gov.'s award State of Va., 1979; Nat. Endowment for Arts lit. fellow, 1975, 82, Guggenheim fellow, 1987-88, Individual Artist fellow Va. Commn. for Arts, 1995, Resident fellow Rockefeller Study and Conf. Ctr., Bellagio, Italy, 2000. Mem. Authors Guild Am., Acad. Am. Poets. Avocations: food, travel, painting. Home: 30 Edmondson Ave Lexington VA 24450-1904

STUART, DAVID EDWARD, anthropologist, writer, educator; b. Calhoun County, Ala., Jan. 9, 1945; s. Edward George and Avis Elsie (Densmore) S.; m. Cynthia K. Morgan, June 14, 1971. BA , W.Va. Wesleyan Coll., 1967; MA in Anthropology, U. N.Mex., 1970, PhD, 1972, postdoctoral student, 1975-76; LHD, W.Va Wesleyan Coll., 2001. Rsch. assoc. Andean Center, Quito, Ecuador, 1970; continuing edn. instr. anthropology U. N.Mex., 1971-72; asst. prof. Eckerd Coll., St. Petersburg, Fla., 1972-74; rsch. archeologist Office Contract Archeology U. N.Mex., 1974; rsch. coord., 1974-77, asst. prof. anthropology, 1975-77, assoc. prof. anthropology, 1984-99, prof. anthropology, 1999—, asst. v.p. acad. affairs, 1987-95, assoc. v.p. acad. affairs, 1995-99, assoc. provost, 1999—, prof. architecture and planning, 2001—. Cons. archeologist right-of-way divsn. Pub. Svc. Co. N.Mex., Albuquerque, 1977-78; cons. anthropologist Bur. Indian Affairs, Albuquerque, 1978, Historic Preservation Bur. N.Mex., Santa Fe, 1978-81, Nat. Park Svcs., 1980, Albuquerque Mus., 1981; sr. rsch. assoc. Human Sys. rsch., Inc., 1981-83, Quivira Rsch. Ctr., Albuquerque, 1984-86; bd. dirs. Table Ind. Scholar, 1979-83, pres., bd. dirs. Rio Grande Heritage Found., Albuquerque and Las Cruces, 1985-87; advisor Human Sys. Rsch., Ind., Tularosa, N.Mex., 1978-80, Albuquerque Commn. on Hist. Preservation, 1984-86. Co-author: Archeological Survey: 4 Corners to Ambrosia, N.Mex., 1976, A Proposed Project Design for the timber Management Archeological Surveys, 1978, Ethnoarcheological Investigations of Shepherding in the Pueblo of Laguna, 1983; author: Prehistoric New Mexico, 1981, 2d edit., 1984, 3rd edit., 1989, Glimpses of the Ancient Southwest, 1985, The Magic of Bandelier National Monument, 1989, Power and Efficiency in Eastern Anasazi Architecture, 1994, Anasazi America, 2000, others; columnist New Mexico's Heritage, 1983-87, others; editor: Archeological Reports, No. 1, 1975, No. 2, 1982. Grantee Eckerd Coll., 1973, Historic Preservation Bur., 1978-80; recipient Essayist award N.Mex. Humanities Coun., 1986. Mem. Am. Anthrop. Assn., N.Mex. Archeol. Coun., Albuquerque Archeol. Soc. (pres. 1986-88), Descs. Signers Declaration Independence, Sigma Xi, Phi Kappa Phi. Office: U NMex Dane Smith Hall Rm 220 Albuquerque NM 87131-0001 E-mail: dstuart@unm.edu. *Personal philosophy: In academics, as in life, reliabilty, integrity, and compassion are far more precious than mere intellectual brilliance.*

STUART, DOROTHY MAE, artist; b. Fresno, Calif., Jan. 8, 1933; d. Robert Wesley Williams and Maria Theresa (Gad) Tressler; m. Reginald Ross Stuart, May 18, 1952; children: Doris Lynne Stuart Willis, Darlene Mae Stuart Cavalletto, Sue Anne Stuart Peters. Student, Calif. State U., Fresno, 1951-52, Fresno City Coll., 1962-64. Artist, art judge, presenter demonstrations at schs., fairs and art orgns., Calif., 1962—. Editor, art dir. Fresno High School Centennial 1889-1989, 1989; art advisor Portrait of Fresno, 1885-1985; contbg. artist Heritage Fresno, 1975; exhibited in group shows, including M.H. De Young Mus., San Francisco, 1971, Charles and Emma Frye Mus., Seattle, 1971, Calif. State U.-Fresno tour of China, 1974. Mem. adv. Ctrl. Calif. Women's Conf., 1989—, Patrons for Cultural Arts, Fresno, 1987-92, bd. dirs., 1991-92. Recipient 53 art awards, 1966-84; nominated Woman of the Yr., Bus./Profl. of Fresno, 1990. Mem. Soc. Western Artists (bd. dirs. 1968-74, v.p. 1968-70), Fresno Womens Trade Club (bd. dirs. 1986-93, pres. 1988-90), Fresno Art Mus., Fresno Met. Mus., Native Daus. Golden West Fresno. Republican. Avocations: world travel, photography, collecting art and dolls of different cultures. Home and Office: 326 S Linda Ln Fresno CA 93727-5737 *Personal philosophy: Dedication to yourself, your work and to your community.*

STUART, FRANK ADELL, county official; b. Tahoka, Tex., Dec. 18, 1928; s. John Franklin and Mary Elizabeth (Reed) S.; m. Mary Louise Wheat Crelia, Feb. 2, 1962; children: Rita, Donna, Franklin, Burce, Susan, Mary, Chris. BBA, Tex. Tech U., 1979. Asst. cashier Am. State Bank, Lubbock, Tex., 1949-52, Citizen Nat. Bank, Lubbock, 1953-59; acct. in pvt. practice, 1960-63; asst. mgr. Gibson Discount Ctr., 1964-77; tax. assessor and collector Lubbock County, 1979-94, ret., 1994. Served to col. Tex. State Guard, 1988-98. Mem. Tax Assessor-Collectors Assn. Tex., Lubbock C. of C., Masons, YorkRite, Scottish Rite, Shriners, Yellow House Lodge, Daylight Lodge. Baptist. Home: 2704 57th St Lubbock TX 79413-5605 E-mail: stuart2704@aol.

STUART, GARY MILLER, financial executive; m. Sylvia Georgeades, 1965; children: David, Peter, Paul, Michael. BS, MIT, 1962; MA, Harvard U., 1965. With Ford Motor Co., Dearborn, Mich., 1965-74, Gen. Foods Corp., White Plains, N.Y., 1974-81; dir. operational rsch. Union Pacific Corp., 1981-83, asst. treas., 1983-87, treas., 1987-89, v.p., treas., 1990-98, exec. v.p., CFO, 1998-99; CFO Optimum Logistics, Stamford, Conn., 2000—01. Bd. dirs. ACE Ltd., Union Pacific Resources Group; adj. faculty Fairfield U., 2000;

exec. in residence Pace U., 2000; adv. bd. Sch. of Bus., Fairfield U., 2000—. Bd. govs. Lehigh Valley Cmty. Found., 1993-97; bd. dirs. Sta. WLVT-TV/Lehigh Valley Pub. TV, 1992-94. NSF fellow, 1962-65, Hon. Woodrow Wilson fellow, 1962. Mem. Fin. Execs. Internat., Assn. Am. Railroads (chmn. treas. div. 1992-93).

STUART, GERARD WILLIAM, JR. investment company executive, city official; b. Yuba City, Calif., July 28, 1939; s. Gerard William and Geneva Bernice (Stuke) S.; m. Lenore Frances Lorona, 1981. Student, Yuba Jr. Coll., 1957-59, Chico State Coll., 1959-60; AB, U. Calif., Davis, 1962; MLS, U. Calif., Berkeley, 1963. Rare book libr. Cornell U., 1964-68; bibliographer scholarly collections Huntington Libr., San Marino, Calif., 1968-73, head acquisitions libr., 1973-75; sec.-treas., dir. Ravenstree Corp., 1969-80, pres, chmn. bd., 1980—, William Penn Ltd., 1981—. Councilman City of Yuma, 1992-96, deputy mayor, 1995; bd. dirs Ariz. Humanities Coun., 1993-99, Yuma Libr. Found., 1997, chmn., 1997-98, 99-2001. Lilly fellow Ind. U., 1964-63. Mem. Bibliog. Soc. Am., Rolls-Royce Owners Club, Grolier Club (N.Y.C.), Zamorano Club (L.A.), Phi Beta Kappa, Alpha Gamma Sigma, Phi Kappa Phi.

STUART, HAROLD CUTLIFF, lawyer, business executive; b. Oklahoma City, July 4, 1912; s. Royal Cutliff and Alice (Bramlitt) S.; m. Joan Skelly, June 6, 1938 (dec. 1994); children: Randi Stuart Wightman, Jon Rolf; m. Frances Langford, Nov. 18, 1994. JD, U. Va., 1936. Bar: Okla. 1936, D.C. 1952. Ptnr. Stuart, Biolchini, Turner & Givray, Tulsa; judge Common Pleas Ct., 1941-42; asst. sec. U.S. Air Force, 1949-51; chmn. bd. 1st Stuart Corp., radio, oil, real estate and investments, Tulsa; dir. Lowrance Electronics, Inc. Spl. cons. to sec. Air Force, 1961-63; mem. Okla. Hwy. Commn., 1959-63; bd. dirs. Great Empire Broadcasting Inc., Wichita, Kans. Trustee emeritus Lovelace Found., Albuquerque; trustee N.Am. Wildlife Fedn; mem. Nat. Eagle Scout Coun. Boy Scouts Am., Disting. Eagle Scout; past pres. Air Force Acad. Found., chmn. bd. Served from 1st lt. to col. USAAF, 1942-46, ETO. Decorated Bronze Star (U.S.) and 6 battle stars; comdr. Order of St. Olav; King Haakon 7th Victory medal; medal of Liberation (Norway); Croix de Guerre (Luxembourg); named to Okla. Aviation and Space Hall of Fame, Okla. Hall of Fame Mem. Am., Okla., D.C. bar assns., Air Force Assn. (dir., nat. pres., chmn. bd. 1951-52), Tulsa C. of C., Tulsa Headliner, Falcon Found. (vice chmn.), Ducks Unltd. (trustee), Delta Kappa Epsilon. Clubs: Southern Hills Country, The Boston (Tulsa); Burning Tree (Washington), Willoughby Golf, The Amb. (Stuart, Fla.). Democrat. Home: PO Box 96 2460 Palmer St Jensen Beach FL 34958-0096 also: Ste 600 2431 E 61st St Tulsa OK 74136-1235

STUART, JAMES, banker, broadcaster; b. Lincoln, Nebr., Apr. 11, 1917; s. Charles and Marie (Talbot) S.; m. Helen Catherine Davis, July 24, 1940; children: Catherine, James, William Scott. BA, BS, U. Nebr., 1940, HHD (hon.), HHD (hon.), DHL (hon.), U. Nebr., 1990. Chmn. bd. Stuart Mgmt. Co.; mng. ptnr. Stuart Enterprises; chmn. exec. com., bd. dirs. Nat. Bank Commerce, Lincoln; pres. Stuart Found. Founder, trustee Nebr. Human Resources Rsch. Found., 1948—; trustee Bryan Meml. Hosp., 1952-58, U. Nebr. Found., 1956—, Nebr. U. Endowment Fund for Disting. Tchrs.; mem. Lincoln Found., 1955—, Lincoln Sch. Bd., 1961-64, pres., 1964; chmn. bd. trustees 1st Plymouth Ch., Lincoln, 1956; pres. Lincoln Community Chest, 1960. With AUS, 1942-45. Recipient Disting. Svc. award U. Nebr., 1961, Alumni Achievement award, 1980, Kiwanis Disting. Svc. award, 2002; named Nebraskan of Yr., Lincoln Rotary Club, 1997. Mem. U. Nebr. Alumni Assn. (past pres.), Lincoln U. Club, Country Club of Lincoln, Gitchigami Club (Duluth, Minn.), Sunrise Country Club (Rancho Mirage, Calif.), Thunderbird Country Club. Home: 3500 Faulkner Dr Lincoln NE 68516 Office: 1248 O St Ste 852 Lincoln NE 68508

STUART, JAMES DAVIES, analytical and environmental chemist, educator; b. Elizabeth, N.J., Sept. 30, 1941; s. Norman Fisher and Madeleine Davies (Harris) S.; m. Carol Ann Morrison, June 14, 1964; children: James Edward, Jean Ann. BS in Chemistry, Lafayette Coll., 1963; PhD in Analytical Chemistry, Lehigh U., 1969. Instr. Lafayette Coll., Easton, Pa., 1967-69; asst. prof. U. Conn., Storrs, 1969-75, assoc. prof., 1975-98, prof., 1998—, dir. marine environ. analysis lab. Avery Point, 1990-92. Vis. lectr. U. Ga., Atlanta, 1976; vis. fellow Yale U., New Haven, 1983; mem. adv. bd. dept. health Water Supply Sect., State of Conn., Hartford, 1977-78; cons. IBM Instruments, Danbury, Conn., 1983-85, HNU Sys., Inc., Newton, Mass., 1991-95, Tekmar-Dohrman Co., Cin., 1994-97; past co-chmn. Town of Coventry (Conn.) Solid Waste Mgmt. Com. Contbr. more than 60 articles to sci. jours. Co-prin. investigator methods for measuring sub-surface gasoline pollution EPA, 1987-94. Mem. New Eng. Chromatography Coun. (exec. com. 1990-96, pres. 1996-2002).

STUART, JESSICA JANE, writer, poet; b. Aug. 20, 1942; BA, Western Res. U., 1964; MA, Ind. U., 1967, 69, PhD, 1971. Tchr. U. Fla., Gainesville, Santa Fe C.C., Gainesville, St. John's River C.C., St. Augustine, Fla., Flagler Coll., St. Augustine. Author: Yellowhawk, 1973, Passerman's Hollow, 1974, Land of the Fox, 1976; (short stories, poems) Whalebone and Stars (Winner chapbook contest 1998); (poems) Journeys, 1998, Sestinas, 2000, The Heart Shaped Moon, 2002, Finding Tents, 2002, A Tiny Xmas Tree, 2002, The Candle Lady, 2002 Mem. Soc. Am. Poets, W.Va. Poetry Soc., Ohio Poetry Assn., Ga. Poety Soc., Acad. Am. Poets, Poets Roundtable (Ark. chpt.), Soc. of Am. Poets, Miss. Poetry Soc., Phi Beta Kappa, Eta Sigma Phi. Home: 1000 W Hollow Rd Greenup KY 41144-1248

STUART, JOSEPH MARTIN, Dt museum administrator; b. Seminole, Okla., Nov. 9, 1932; s. Arch William and Lillian (Lindsey) S.; BFA in Art, U. N.Mex., 1959, MA in Art, 1962; m. Signe Margaret Nelson, June 18, 1960; 1 dau., Lise Nelson Stuart. Dir., Roswell (N.Mex.) Museum and Art Center, 1960-62; curator U. Oreg. Mus. Art, 1962-63; dir. Boise (Idaho) Gallery Art, 1964-68, Salt Lake (City) Art Ctr., 1968-71, S.D. Art Mus., Brookings, 1971-93; prof. art S.D. State U., 1971-93; represented in permanent collections: Civic Fine Arts Ctr., Sioux Falls, S.D., Coll. Idaho, Eureka Coll., Salt Lake Art Ctr., Sioux City (Iowa) Art Ctr., U. N.Mex. Art Mus., West Tex. State U.. With USN, 1951-55. Mem. Phi Kappa Phi. Unitarian. Author: Index of South Dakota Artists, 1974; Art of South Dakota, 1974, Harvey Dunn: Son of the Middle border, 1984, Art for a New Century, 1989; The Legacy of South Dakota Art, 1990; author numerous exhbn. catalogs.

STUART, LILLIAN MARY, writer, raconteur; b. Chgo., Nov. 7, 1914; d. Ira and Katherine (Tries) Daugherty; m. Robert Graham Stuart, Aug. 7, 1936 (dec. Sept. 1969); 1 child, Mary Leone. Asst. to pres. Weisberger Bros., South Bend, 1933-42; head TWX distbn. Davis-Monthan AFB, Tucson, 1946-48; artist and music tchr., 1945-55; interviewer-counselor Ariz. State Employment Commn., Tucson, 1955-70; residence dir. YWCA, 1970-71; tax preparer, 1971-72; U.S. census taker U.S. Govt., N.Mex., 1976, 80; mng. Luna County Rep. Party, Deming, 1976; tchr. YWCA, Tucson, 1969, El Paso Coll. Bus., 1972; tutor math, English, 1981. Travel lectr. various civic groups and clubs; radio reader Lighthouse for the Blind, El Paso, 1983—89; spkr. Internat. Women's Day Celebration, 1996, Lovington Rotary Internat., 1999, Kiwanis Internat., Lovington, 1999, Lovington Internat. Lions Club, 1999, Women's Club, Lovington, 2000, schs. in Lovington, 2002. Contbr. stories to The Quarterly; author: The Avestan, 1997; (series of biographies) Lighthouse for the Blind; actress Studebaker Players, South Bend, 1936-42, South Bend Theatre, 1936-42, (film) Extreme Prejudice, 1986; writer Centennial Mus. at U. Tex., El Paso, 1992-95; actress in commls., 1996-97. Counselor, vol. Crisis Ctr., Deming, 1975-77. Recipient plaques and prizes for various pieces of writing. Mem. Mensa, Rosicrucians. Avocations: travel, art. Address: 212 W Avenue A Lovington NM 88260-4120

STUART, LYLE, publishing company executive; b. N.Y.C., Aug. 11, 1922; s. Alfred and Theresa (Cohen) Stuart; m. Mary Louise Strawn, Sept. 26, 1946; children: Sandra Lee Strawn, Rory John Strawn; m. Carole Livingston, Feb. 4, 1982; 1 child Jennifer Susan. Student pub. schs., N.Y.C.; PhD (hon.), State of Calif. Reporter Internat. News Service, 1945, Variety, 1945-46; script writer Dept. State, Voice of Am., 1946; editor Music Bus. mag., 1946-48; founder Expose, 1951; pub. The Independent, 1951-75; bus. mgr. MAD mag., 1952-54; pres. Citadel Press, 1970-89; founder Lyle Stuart, Inc., 1956; pres. University Books, Inc., 1983—, Hot News, 1983, Barricade Books, 1990—. Founder North Bergen (N.J.) Pub. Library. Prodr. Chinese Festival of Music, 1952-62; author: God Wears A Bowtie, 1949, The Secret Life of Walter Winchell, 1953, Mary Louise, 1970, Casino Gambling for the Winner, 1978, Lyle Stuart on Baccarat, 1983, 2d edit., 1997, Winning at Casino Gambling, 1995. Served with AUS, 1942-44. Mem.: Silurians, Nat. Acad. TV Arts and Scis., Soc. Ky. Cols., NY Zool. Soc. Home: 1530 Palisade Ave Apt 6L Fort Lee NJ 07024-5402 Office: Barricade Books Inc 185 Bridge Plaza N Fort Lee NJ 07024

STUART, NANCY RUBIN (NANCY ZIMMAN STETSON), journalist, author, writer, producer; b. Boston, Nov. 25, 1944; d. Stuart Wendell and Ethel (Rabinovitz) Zimman; m. William W. Stetson, Apr. 28, 2001; children: Elisabeth, Jessica. BA, Tufts U., 1966; MA in Teaching, Brown U., 1967; PhD (hon.), Mt. Vernon Coll., 1995. Playwright, dir. Equity Library Theatre, Roundabout, Joseph Jefferson and St. Clement's theaters, N.Y.C., 1971-74; freelance reporter Westchester-Gannett newspapers and mags., 1975-77, N.Y. Times, N.Y.C., 1977—. Faculty affiliate Bush Ctr. in Child Devel., Yale U., New Haven, 1981-86; mem. Westchester County Women's Adv. Bd., chair, 1988; mem. faculty SUNY, Purchase, 1994-95, Fordham U., N.Y.C., 1996-99. Author: The New Suburban Women, Beyond Myth and Motherhood, 1982, The Mother Mirror: How a Generation of Women is Changing Motherhood in America, 1984, Isabella of Castile: The First Renaissance Queen, 1991, American Empress: The Life and Times of Marjorie Merriweather Post, 1995, Club Dance: The Show, The Steps, The Spirit of Country, 1998; writer, assoc. prodr: TV series America's Castles for A&E Network, 1996—99 (Telly award , 1999, Telly award (3), 2001, Writing Communicator award , 1999), writer, assoc. prodr: The Gold Coast for The Grand Tour A & E TV, 1997, writer prodr., prodr. : TV series Restore America, 1999, writer/assoc. prodr. : TV series Eccentrics, 1999 (Crystal award, Telly award), writer/assoc. prodr. : The N.Y. Times, 1997—2001, contbg. editor: Parents mag., 1987—91, contbg. editor: McCalls, contbg. editor: Savvy, contbg. editor: Travel & Leisure, contbg. editor: Ladies Home Jour., 1980—92; (theater critic): Stamford Advocate, 1994—96. Recipient Washington Irving award Westchester Libr. Assn., 1993, Telly award finalist, 2001; Time, Inc.-Bread Loaf Writers' Colony scholar, 1979. Fellow MacDowell Colony; mem. Author's Guild, Am. Soc. Journalists and Authors (Author of Yr. award 1992), PEN, Nat. Arts Club. Avocations: skiing, sailing, ballet and jazz dancing, classical music.

STUART, PAMELA BRUCE, lawyer; b. N.Y.C., Feb. 13, 1949; d. J. Raymond and Marion Grace (Cotins) S. AB with distinction, Mt. Holyoke Coll., 1970; JD cum laude, U. Mich., 1973. Bar: N.Y. 1974, D.C. 1975, U.S. Dist. Ct. D.C. 1979, U.S. Ct. Appeals (D.C. cir.) 1980, U.S. Supreme Ct. 1980, U.S. Dist. Ct. Md. 1989, Md. 1992, Va. 1993, U.S. Ct. Appeals (4th cir.) 1993, Fla. 1994, U.S. Dist. Ct. (ea. dist.) Va. 1994, U.S. Dist. Ct. (no. dist.) N.Y. 1996, U.S. Dist. Ct. (so. dist.) Fla. 1998, U.S. Dist. Ct. (so. dist.) N.Y. 1999, U.S. Dist. Ct. (ea. dist.) N.Y. 1999, U.S. Dist. Ct. (mid. dist.) Fla. 2001. Trial atty., deputy asst. dir. Bur. of Consumer Protection, FTC, Washington, 1973-79; asst. U.S. atty. U.S. Atty's Office, 1979-85; sr. trial atty. Office of Internat. Affairs, U.S. Dept. Justice, 1985-87; atty. Ross, Dixon & Masback, 1987-89; mem. Lobel, Novins, Lamont & Flug, 1989-92; pvt. practice, 1992—. Instr. Nat. Inst. for Trial Advocacy, Atty. Gen.'s Advocacy Inst., Legal Edn. Inst., Fed. Practice Inst.; mem. Jud. Conf. D.C., 1985-88, 91-98; mem. Jud. Conf., D.C. Cir., 1996, 98, 2000; assoc. mem. Consular Corps Washington; legal analyst CNN, MSNBC, Fox News, other TV networks. Author: The Federal Trade Commission, 1991; contbr. articles to profl. jours. Bd. dirs. Anacostia Econ. Devel. Corp., 1993—, Anacostia Holding Co., Inc., Anacostia Mgmt. Co., Inc., 1997—. Mem. ABA (internat. criminal law com., chmn., 1993-96, chmn. fed. crime rules subcom. white collar crime com. sect. criminal justice 1997-99), Bar Assn. D.C. (bd. dirs. 1995-2001), Asst. U.S. Attys. Assn. D.C. (exec. coun. 1993-99, pres. 1998-99), Assn. Trial Lawyers Am., Women's Bar Assn. D.C., Fla. Bar (exec. coun. real property probate and trust law sect. 1999—), Alumnae Assn. Mt. Holyoke Coll. (bd. dirs. 1986-89, 92-95, Alumnae medal of honor 1990), Edward Bennett Williams Inn of Ct. (master of bench), Fed. City Club (bd. govs. 1992—), Cosmos Club. Avocations: writing, interior design, investments, piano. Home: 5115 Yuma St NW Washington DC 20016-4336 Office: The Stuart Bldg 1750 N Street NW Washington DC 20036 also: 111 Johns Island Dr Apt 7 Vero Beach FL 32963-3274 E-mail: pamstuart@aol.com.

STUART, ROBERT, container manufacturing executive; b. Oak Park, Ill., Aug. 3, 1921; s. Robert S. and Marie (Vavra) Solinsky; m. Lillian C. Kondelik, Dec. 5, 1962 (dec. May 1978); m. Lila Winterhoff Peters, May 21, 1982. BS, U. Ill., 1943; LLD, U. Ill., Chgo., 1982. Sec.-treas., gen. mgr. Warren Metal Decorating Co., 1947-49; asst. to gen. mgr. Cans, Inc., 1950-52; asst. to v.p., then v.p. Nat. Can Corp., Chgo., 1953-59, exec. v.p., 1959-63, pres., 1963-69, chief exec., 1966-69, chmn. bd., chief exec. officer, 1969-73, chmn. bd., 1973-83, chmn. fin. com., 1983, mem. corp. devel. com., until 1986, chmn. emeritus, 1986—. Past pres., bd. dirs. Corp. Responsibility Group of Greater Chgo. Past pres., bd. dirs. Chgo. Crime Commn.; dir. Nat. Crime Prevention Coun.; founding chmn. Nat. Minority Supplier Devel. Coun., 1972-73, Lloyd Morey Scholarship Fund: Freedoms Found. at Valley Forge, trustee; bd. assocs. Chgo. Theol. Sem.; life trustee Ill. Masonic Med. Ctr.; mem. adv. bd. Salvation Army, Broader Urban Involvement and Leadership Devel.; chmn. emeritus World Federalist Assn.; past pres., trustee Cen. Ch. Chgo. Congregationalist; chmn. emeritus Assn. to Unite the Democracies; numerous other civic activities. Capt. AUS, 1943-46. Mem. Chgo. Club, Comml. Club, Yacht Club, Little Ship Club (London), Mason (32 degree, Red Cross of Constantine), Rotary (past pres. Chgo. club, past dist. gov.), Alpha Kappa Lambda (past nat. pres.). Office: 233 SW 43d Ter Cape Coral FL 33914

STUART, ROBERT KENNETH, internist, oncologist, hematologist, educator; b. Baton Rouge, July 6, 1948; s. Walter Bynum and Rita Bess (Kleinpeter) S.; m. Gail Elaine Wiscarz, June 12, 1971 (div. Dec. 1988); children: R. Morgan, Elaine C.; m. F. Charlene Gates, Nov. 2, 1991. BS, Georgetown U., 1970; MD, Johns Hopkins U., Balt., 1974. Diplomate Am. Bd. Internal Medicine. Resident in medicine Johns Hopkins Hosp., Balt., 1974-76, oncology fellow Oncology Ctr., 1976-78; rsch. fellow Sloan-Kettering Inst., N.Y.C., 1978-79; asst. prof. Johns Hopkins U., Balt., 1979-84, assoc. prof., 1984-85; prof. medicine Med. U. S.C., Charleston, 1985—; assoc. dir. Hollings Cancer Ctr., 1993-97; chmn. dept. oncology King Faisal Specialist Hosp and Rsch. Ctr., Riyadh, Saudi Arabia, 1997-2001; prof. medicine Med.U. S.C., Charleston, 2001—. Bd. dirs. Aplastic Anemia Found., Balt., 1982-93, med. adv. bd., 1993—. Democrat. Roman Catholic. Office: Medical Univ of South Carolina 171 Ashley Ave Charleston SC 29425-0100 E-mail: stuartrk@musc.edu.

STUART, SANDRA JOYCE, computer information scientist; b. Wheatland, Mo., Aug. 15, 1950; d. Asa Maxville and Inez Irene (Wilson) Friedley; m. John Kendall Stuart, Apr. 17, 1971; 1 child, Whitney Renee. Student, Cen. Mo. State U., 1968-69; AA (hon.), Johnson County C.C., 1980; BSBA cum laude, Avila Coll., 1992. Cert. Cert. Info. Systems Security Profl. Statis. asst. Fed. Crop Ins. Corp., Kansas City, Mo., 1978-83; mgr. Fed. Women's Program, 1979-80; mgmt. asst. Marine Corps Fin. Ctr., 1983-85, analyst computer systems, 1985-88; computer programmer analyst Corps. of Engrs., 1988-91; regional program mgr. FAA, 1991—. Author: The Samuel Walker History, 1983. Asst. supt. Sunday sch. Overland Park (Kansas) Christian Ch., 1979-80, supt., 1980-82. Mem. Wheatland H.S. Alumni Assn. (pres. 1990-91), Mo-Kan High Tech. Crime Investigation Assn. (charter, 2d v.p. 1998-99, 1st v.p. 1999-2000, pres. 2000-2001), Kansas City Security Coalition. Avocations: needlework, genealogy, reading, travel.

STUART, SIGNE MARGARET, artist; b. New London, Conn., Dec. 3, 1937; d. Carl Einar and Anna Louise (Gustafson) Nelson; m. Joseph Martin Stuart; 1 child, Lise Nelson Stuart. Student, Yale-Norfolk Art Sch., 1959; BA, U. Conn., 1959; MA, U. N.Mex., 1961. Prof. of art S.D. State U., Brookings, 1970-94; ind. artist Santa Fe, 1994—. One-woman shows included in Sheldon Meml. Art Gallery, Lincoln, 1972, Montgomery Mus. Art, Ala., 1977, Plains Art Mus., Fargo, N.D., 1990, S.D. Art Mus., 1995; muralist: Landwave, 1977, Dakota Loft, 1985; juror Manitoba, Can., Arts Coun., 1992, 93, WESTAF, Santa Fe, 1996. NEA painting fellow, 1976; artist fellowship S.D. Arts Coun., 1986; artist residency U-Cross Found., 1990, Kans. State U., 1991.

STUART, SPENCER RAYMOND, management consultant; b. Balt., Sept. 25, 1922; s. William Moore Stuart and Helen Lenore Raymond; m. Eugenia Presler Birdsall, Sept. 24, 1949; children: Spencer Raymond Stuart Jr., Cooper B., Eugenia Anne. BS, Haverford Coll., 1947. Mgr. mktg. and advt. Martin Senour Paint Co., Chgo., 1947—52; cons. Booz Allen and Hamilton, 1952—55; prin. Heidrick and Struggles, 1955; founder, CEO Spencer Stuart, Exec. Search Consultants, 1956—74, founder, chmn. N.Y.C., 1974—, Dean Witter Coun. of Mgmt. Advisors, N.Y.C., 1990—92; mgmt. cons., corp. dir. Palm City, Fla., 1974—2001. Dir., chmn. compensation and mgmt. succession com., chmn. corp. governance com. Enhance Fin. Svcs. Group, N.Y.C., 1986—2001; dir., chmn. audit com., mem. compensation stock option and mgmt. succession com. UST, Inc., Greenwich, Conn., 1977—97; dir., mem. audit and compensation com. U.S. Timberlands Co., L.P., N.Y.C., 1997; dir., mem. exec. com., chmn. compensation and mgmt. succession com. Western Airlines, L.A., 1984—87; dir., chmn. compensation and corp. strategy coms. Allegheny Internat., Pitts., 1984—89; panelist Am. Mgmt. Assn., Presidents Assn., N.Y.C., 1960—72; exec. compensation Blue Ribbon com. Nat. Assn. Corp. Dirs., Washington, 1974—97; past dir. Assn. Exec. Recruiting Consultants, N.Y.C.; dir. Mass. Co./Keystone Custodian Funds, Boston, 1982—97. Contbr. articles to newspapers and profl. jours. Reception com. Econ. Club. Chgo., 1956—65; chmn. exploring divsn. Boy Scouts Am., Stamford, Conn., 1974—86, founder, chmn. corp. adv. bd. Fairfield County, 1975—86; trustee, pres. Silvermine Guild of Artists, New Canaan, 1972—79; trustee Green Mountain Coll., Poultney, Vt., 1980—84; chmn. fundraising dinner com., athlete of decade program Am. Cancer Soc., N.Y.C., 1977—82; panelist Aspen (Colo.) Inst. Humanistic Studies, 1948—58; mem. Conf. Christians and Jews, Conn., 1960—68. 1st lt. AUS, 1943—46, ETO. Decorated Bronze Star, Purple Heart; recipient Wm. H. Splurgen III award for disting. svc., Nat. Exploring Coun., Boy Scouts Am., 1978, Profl. Leadership award, Newcomen Soc. Am., 1981, Heidrick award, Assn. Exec. Search Consultants, 1995. Mem.: Hassayampa Golf Club, The Sky Club, Eldorado Country Club, Univ. Club N.Y.C. Avocations: golf, fitness, writing, computers, art. Address: 948 Winding Spruce Way Prescott AZ 86303-6912 Home: 1725 NW Buttonbush Cir Palm City FL 34990

STUART, SPENCER RAYMOND, JR. real estate development company executive; b. Evanston, Ill., Sept. 10, 1950; s. Spencer R. and Eugenia B. Stuart; children: Spencer III, Hillary. BFA, U. Conn., 1974. Sr. acct. rep. Xerox Corp., Dallas, 1978-81; sector exec. InveQuest Inc., 1981-90; v.p. Anderson Capital Advisors, 1990-92, Walden Residential Properties, Dallas, 1992-95; COO, exec. v.p. Palladium USA Internat. Inc., 1995—. Mem. adv. bd. Signature Athletic Club, Dallas, 1996-99. Recipient Best Comml. Sign award Tex. Sign Assn., 1999. Mem. Nat. Assn. Home Builders (Pillars of the Industry award 1999), Urban Land Assn. (assoc.), Nat. Multi Housing Coun. (adv. bd.), Real Estate Fin. Execs. Assn. (chief tech. officer 1999—). Avocations: golf, snow skiing, tennis. Office: Palladium USA Internat Inc 13455 Noel Rd Ste 1000 Dallas TX 75240-6602

STUART, TARA, management consultant; b. Passaic, N.J., Aug. 2, 1966; d. Stanton and Carol Stuart. BA in Polit. Sci., Kean U., 1988; M Internat. Rels. and Diplomacy, Schiller Internat. U., Paris, 1989; M Econs. and Social Studies, Inst. Etudes Econ. et Sociales, Paris, 1995; PhD in Bus. Adminstrn., Harrington U., London, 1999. Sr. cons. internat. bus. devel. Palco Group Ltd., London, 1989-98; exec. mgr. western Europe UPI, Paris, 1994-97; mgr. profiling desk, office of chmn. Deloitte & Touche LLP, N.Y.C., 1999—. Country chmn. France, Republicans Abroad Internat., Washington, 1997-2000. Mem.: NAFE, UN Assn. U.S.A., Fgn. Policy Assn., Acad. Polit. Sci., Soc. Competitive Intelligence Profls. Home: 108 E 38th St Ste 18B New York NY 10016 Office: Deloitte & Touche LLP 2 World Financial Ctr New York NY 10281

STUART, WALTER BYNUM, III, banker; b. Baton Rouge, Oct. 5, 1922; s. Walter Bynum and Rosa (Gauthreaux) S.; m. Rita Kleinpeter, May 20, 1944; children— Walter Bynum IV, Robert, Douglas, Ronald, Scott. BS, La. State U., 1943. Adminstrv. mgr. Kaiser Aluminum & Chem. Corp., 1946-63; v.p. First Nat. Bank Commerce, New Orleans, 1963-65, sr. v.p., 1965, exec. v.p., 1965-73; vice chmn. bd., dir. 1st Nat. Bank Commerce, 1973-78; exec. v.p. 1st Commerce Corp., 1972-73, pres., 1973-75, vice-chmn. bd., 1975-78, dir., 1973-78; pres. Am. Bank & Trust Co., Lafayette, La., 1978-86, cons. Assoc. dir., mem. faculty Sch. Banking La. State U., 1973-75, dir., 1975-78; mem. Faculty Assemblies for Bank Dirs. Campaign group chmn. industry com., mem. United Fund for Greater New Orleans Area, 1974; mem. research com. Pub. Affairs Research Council La., 1973-76, v.p., trustee, 1973-76; bd. dirs. Bur. Govtl. Research, 1973-77, Council Better La., 1975— ; pres. New Orleans Indsl. Devel. Bd., 1973-75. Served to lt. (j.g.) USNR, 1943-46. Mem. C. of C. of Greater New Orleans Area (v.p. 1973-75, bd. dirs.), Am. Bankers Assn., La. Bankers Assn. (pres. 1977), Am. Mgmt. Assn., Kappa Alpha, Delta Sigma Pi, Beta Gamma Sigma. Democrat. Roman Catholic. Office: Jefferson at Lee Lafayette LA 70501 *Recognizing that life is the experiencing of reality, and that reality is simply a continuing series of problems, I long ago decided that I would treat a problem as an opportunity. Every incident of difficulty has always invited my intense interest as a challenge, and my thoughts have been immediately marshalled for positive effort. My life has been most rewarding because I believe that "a problem is an opportunity!".*

STUART, WILLIAM CORWIN, federal judge; b. Knoxville, Iowa, Apr. 28, 1920; s. George Corwin and Edith (Abram) S.; m. Mary Elgin Cleaver, Oct. 20, 1946; children: William Corwin II, Robert Cullen, Melanie Rae, Valerie Jo. BA, State U. Iowa, 1941, JD, 1942. Bar: Iowa 1942. Pvt. practice, Chariton, 1946-62; city atty., 1947-49; mem. Iowa Senate from, Lucas-Wayne Counties, 1951-61; justice Supreme Ct. Iowa, 1962-71; judge U.S. Dist. Ct., So. Dist. of Iowa, Des Moines, 1971-86, sr. judge, 1986—. With USNR, 1943-45. Recipient Outstanding Svc. award Iowa Acad. Trial lawyer, 1987, Iowa Trial Lawyers Assn., 1988, Spl. award Iowa State Bar Assn., 1987, Disting. Alumni, U. Iowa Coll. Law, 1987. Mem. ABA, Iowa Bar Assn., Am. Legion, All For Iowa, Order of Coif, Omicron Delta Kappa, Phi Kappa Psi, Phi Delta Phi. Clubs: Mason (Shriner). Presbyterian. Home: 216 S Grand St Chariton IA 50049-2139

STUBBE, RAY WILLIAM, minister, writer; b. Milw., Aug. 15, 1938; s. Clarence Arnold and Ruby Otillie (Mueller) Stubbe. *Grandfather, Julius F. Mueller, emigrated in 1889 from Germany at age 4. Although schooled only through 8th grade and loosing both his parents, his subsequent employment in a cast iron foundry saw him eventually rise to become superintendent of that foundry. In later years, his innovative techniques drew inquires from numerous foreign foundry men and, upon retirement, he traveled to Sao Paulo, Brazil where he successfully modernized a foundry. His boundless energy and value on education saw him flying bi-planes in the 1920's, building a reflecting telescope in the 1930's, singing in a civic male chorus, and visiting by car every state as well as Canada and Mexico on vacations.* BA, St. Olaf Coll., 1962; MDiv, Northwestern Luth. Theol. Sem., 1965; postgrad., U. Chgo., 1967. Ordained to ministry Evang. Luth. Ch. Am., 1965. Mission devel. bd. Am. missions Luth Ch. in Am., Oak Creek, Wis., 1965-66; organizer, pastor All Saints Luth Ch., 1966-67; enlisted USN, 1955; commd. ensign USNR, 1963, advanced through grades to lt., comdr. chaplain corps, 1971; augmented to USN, 1971; chaplain, 1967-85; ret. USN, 1985; asst. pastor Evang. Luth. Ch. of Redeemer, Milw., 1985—. Interviews on national televised programs. *Subject of numerous nationally televised programs, including: "Vietnam: A Soldier's Story" aired on The Learning Channel, Sep 6, 1998, " War Stories with Oliver North: Khe Sanh," Aired on Fox News, Oct 28, 2001, "Atmospheres: War and Weather," aired on The Weather Channel, Mar 3, 2002.* Author: (book) Inside Force Recon, 1989, Khe Sanh Chaplain, 1970, Paddles, Parachutes, Patrols, 1979, Aarugha, 1989, Valley of Decision, 1991, The Final Formation, 1995, Psalms of the Revised Common Lectionary Pericope System, 1998; editor: Khe Sanh Veteran/Red Clay, 1996—98; contbr. articles and poems to profl. jours. and books. Founder, pres. emeritus Khe Sanh Vets., Inc., 1988—; chaplain Wis. Vietnam Vets., Milw., 1984—, 3d Marine Divsn. Assn., 1988. Decorated Bronze Star with combat V; recipient Legion of Honor award, Chapel Four Chaplains. Mem.: DAV (life), VFW (life), Am. Assn. Rel., Wis. Acad. Scis., Arts and Letters (life), Spl. Ops. Assn. (life), 3d Marine Divsn. Assn. (life), Spl. Forces Assn. (life), Force Reconnaissance Assn. (life), Soc. Bibl. Lit., Vietnam Vets. Am. (life), Marine Corps Hist. Found. (life), Ret. Officers Assn. (life), Wis. Vietnam Vets., Pi Kappa Delta. Home: 8766 Parkview Ct Milwaukee WI 53226-2729 Office: Redeemer Luth Church 631 N 19th St Milwaukee WI 53233-2152 *The most powerful Words of God have always been communicated to me by the occasional people encountered in life's pathways. These are the quiet ones whose very being reflect possibilities of being the image of God we all are; living Words of God who make us know* *we are free, forgiven, loved, blessed with value and future; heroes, who at great risk and pain to themselves, transform negatives into positives; great, good people who empty themselves into servants and incarnate love into all human conditions. When the vision they offer becomes life's task of who to become, all of life becomes a gift of everdeepening wells which nourish everything living with the deep underground stream, which is God.*

STUBBEN, DOLUS JANE (D. J. STUBBEN), advertising executive; b. Clovis, N.Mex., Sept. 12, 1951; d. Joseph P. Harmon and Maurine Yvonne (Simmons) McDonald; m. Ronald Patrick Day, Apr. 11, 1970 (div.); m. John David Stubben, Sept. 23, 1979 (div.); 1 child, Patricia Joan. Student, West Tex. State U., 1969-70. Instr. Amarillo (Tex.) Coll., 1971-73; advt. cons. Amarillo, 1976-78; advt. mgr. Montgomery Ward, 1978-80; musician Furr's Cafeteria, 1978-80; piano bar musician, comedienne Quigley's Restaurant, Eugene, Oreg., 1980-81, Jolly's Comedy Club, Amarillo, 1986-88, Sheraton Towers Amarillo, 1988-89. Owner, mgr. Welcome Pardner!, Amarillo, 1981—; arbitrator Better Bus. Bur., Amarillo, 1978-79 Author: #555 Death Row, 1981 (Nat. Press Women 2nd place award 1982), Dog Pause..., 1981 (Nat. Press Women 2nd place award 1982, Hon. Mention award 1987), It's a Secret, I Can't Tell You, 1984, poems; songwriter. Media chmn. Am. Cancer Soc., Amarillo, 1978-79; media dir. Bralley's 45h of July Picnic, Amarillo, 1977-78; mem. media rels. com. St. Jude's Hosp. Tex. Com., Amarillo, 1983; publicity chmn. Miss Amarillo Area, 1993—; mem. nominating com. Tex. plains Girl Scouts U.S.A., 1999. Top 10 Winner Am. Mktg. Awards, 1996; recipient Rookie award 1989, Entrepreneur award Center City BPW, 1999, BPW Achievement of the Decade award, 1999. Mem.: Tex. Panhandle Broadcasters Assn. (treas. 1998—99), Tex. Press Women (v.p. 1982, state treas. 1986, membership chmn. 1986, First Pl. (2) awards 1988), Lions Club (chmn. pub. rels. com. 1990—, Rookie of Yr. Downtown 1989—90, fellow 1999). Office: Welcome Pardner PO Box 30926 Amarillo TX 79120-0926 E-mail: stubben@amaonline.com.

STUBBERUD, ALLEN ROGER, electrical engineering educator; b. Glendive, Mont., Aug. 14, 1934; s. Oscar Adolph and Alice Marie (LeBlanc) S.; m. May B. Tragus, Nov. 19, 1961; children: Peter A., Stephen C. BS in Elec. Engring, U. Idaho, 1956; MS in Engring, UCLA, 1958, PhD, 1962. From asst. prof. to assoc. prof. engring. UCLA, 1962-69; prof. elec. engring. U. Calif., Irvine, 1969—, assoc. dean engring., 1972-78, dean engring., 1978-83, chair elec. and computer engring., 1993-98, interim dean engring., 1994-96; chief scientist U.S. Air Force, 1983-85. Dir. Elec. Communications and Systems Engring. divsn. NSF, 1987-88. Author: Analysis and Synthesis of Linear Time Variable Systems, 1964, (with others) Feedback and Control Systems, 2d edit., 1990, (with others) Digital Control System Design, 2d edit., 1994; contbr. articles to profl. jours. Recipient Exceptional Civilian Svc. medal USAF, 1985, 90, Meritorious Civilian Svc. medal, 1996. Fellow IEEE (Centennial medal 1984, Millennium medal 2000), AIAA, AAAS, NYAS; mem. INFORMS, Sigma Xi, Sigma Tau, Tau Beta Pi, Eta Kappa Nu. Office: U Calif Dept Ece Irvine CA 92697-0001 E-mail: arstubbe@uci.edu.

STUBBINS, HUGH A(SHER), JR. architect; b. Birmingham, Ala., Jan. 11, 1912; s. Hugh Asher and Lucile (Matthews) S.; m. Diana Hamilton Moore, Mar. 3, 1938 (div. 1960); children: Patricia, Peter, Hugh Asher III, Michael; m. Colette Fadeuilhe, Sept. 1960 (dec. 1992); m. June M. Kootz, 1994 (dec. July, 2001). BS in Architecture, Ga. Inst. Tech., 1933; MArch, Harvard U., 1935. Pvt. practice, Boston, 1935-38, 41—; formed partnership, 1938-40; pvt. practice Birmingham, 1940; assoc. prof. Grad. Sch. Design Harvard U., 1946-52, chmn. dept. architecture, 1953, mem. vis. com. Grad. Sch. Design, 1958-72; pres. Hugh Stubbins & Assocs., Inc., 1957-83, also chmn. bd. dirs., 1983-92. Vis. critic-in-residence, Yale U., 1948-49, U. Oreg., 1950; sec. Rotch travelling Scholarship, 1971-80; Thomas Jefferson prof. architecture U. Va., 1979; mem. adv. coun. Sch. Architecture, Princeton U., 1962-65; mem. Harleston Parker Medal Com., 1973. Designer Berlin Congress Hall, 1957, Countway Libr. Medicine, Harvard U., Fed. Res. Bank, Boston, U. Va. Law Sch., Citicorp Ctr., N.Y.C., St. Peter's Ch., N.Y.C., Fifth Ave. Pl., Pitts., 1988, Bank One, Indpls., 1989, Landmark Tower, Minoto-Mirai 21, Yokohama, Japan, 1989, Ronald Reagan Presdl. Libr., 1990, numerous other bldgs.; exec. architect Phila. Stadium; one-man show Norton Sculpture Gallery, West Palm Beach, 1997-98. Hon. mem. Boston Archtl. Ctr.; chmn. design adv. com. Boston Redevel. Authority, 1964-76; mem. design rev. panel Worcester Redevel. Authority, 1966-70; mem. adv. com. Office Fgn. Bldgs. Ops., U.S. Dept. State, 1979-82; bd. dirs. Benjamin Franklin Found.; mem. arts and archtl. com. Kennedy Meml. Libr.; mem. Fgn. Bus. Coun., Commonwealth of Mass., 1978-79; mem. nat. adv. bd. Ga. Inst. Tech., 1978-81; trustee Tabor Acad., 1974-78; mem. adv. bd. Whitney Libr. Design, 1976-78. Recipient Alpha Rho Chi medal, 1933, 3d prize at competition Nat. Smithsonian Gallery of Art, 1939, Progressive Architecture 1st Design award, 1954, Arcadia Achievement award, 1957, Rodgers and Hammerstein award, 1961, award Am. Inst. Steel Constrn., 1970, award Archtl. Record, 1971, award Prestressed Concrete Inst., 1971, award of merit Inst. So. Affairs and So. Acad. Letters, Am. Acad. Arts and Scis., 1973, citation Am. Assn. Sch. Adminstrs., 1974, award for environ. design, 1975, award of merit Libr. Bldgs. award for Nathan Marsh Pusey Libr., Harvard U./AIA/ALA, 1976, Spl. Energy award for Shiraz Tech. Inst., Am. Assn. Sch. Adminstrs./AIA, N.E. Regional Coun. award Fed. Res. Bank, 1979, Thomas Jefferson Meml. medal U. Va., 1979, R.S. Reynolds Meml. award Citicorp, 1981, numerous other awards. Fellow AIA (v.p. 1964-65, jury fellows 1974-75, chmn. Nat. Honor award com. 1966, 79, 80, award of merit 1970, honor award 1979, firm award 1967), Mexican Soc. Archs. (hon.), AAAS; mem. NAD (academician), Mass. Assn. Archs., Boston Soc. Archs. (pres. 1969-70, award of honor 1988), Archl. League N.Y. (silver medal 1958), Harvard Club, Laurel Brook Club, Malapan Yacht Club, The Little Club (Gulf Stream, Fla.), Century Club (N.Y.C.), Soc. Four Arts (Palm Beach), Beta Theta Pi, Omicron Delta Kappa. Home: 6110 N Ocean Blvd Boynton Beach FL 33435-5248 also: 199 Brattle St Cambridge MA 02138-3345

STUBBLEFIELD, JERRY MASON, religious educator, minister; b. Paducah, Ky., May 15, 1936; s. Bobbie and Lorene (Fleming) S.; m. Joanne McCaffrey, June 28, 1957; children: Robert, Mason, Alice. BA, Belmont U., 1957; MA, Vanderbilt U., 1958; BD, So. Bapt. Theol. Sem., 1961, MRE, 1962, PhD, 1967. Ordained to ministry So. Bapt. Conv., 1955. Pastor Victory Bapt. Ch., Shepherdsville, Ky., 1958-65; spl. instr. religious edn. Southeastern Bapt. Sem., Wake Forest, N.C., 1965-66; prof. religion Norman Coll., Norman Park, Ga., 1966-70; min. edn. First Bapt. Ch., Greenville, S.C., 1970-75; dir. ch. community ministry Greenville Bapt. Assn., 1975-77; assoc. prof. religious edn. Golden Gate Bapt. Theol. Sem., Mill Valley, Calif., 1977-83, prof., 1983—2002, J.M. Frost Sunday sch. bd. chair Christian edn., 1988—. Mem. various acad. coms. Golden Gate Bapt. Theol. Sem., Mill Valley; min. edn. Tiburion (Calif.) Bapt. Ch., 1978-81; trustee Calif. Bapt. Coll., 1984-88. Editor, contbg. author: A Church Ministering to Adults, 1986; contbg. author: Christian Education Handbook, 1981, 96; author: The Effective Minister of Education, 1993; contbr. articles to religious jours. Mem. Western Bapt. Religious Edn. Assn. (pres. 1983-84), Bapt. Assn. of Chritian Educators (pres. 1988-89), North Am. Profs. Christian Edn. Avocations: golf, running, reading, travel, sports. Office: 175 Grevilla Dr Petaluma CA 94952 E-mail: jerrylazarus@worldnet.att.net. *It is my desire to live each day at my best and enable those around to live life at their best. I hope that the world will be a better place because of the quality of life that I have lived.*

STUBBLEFIELD, J(OSEPH) STEPHEN, lawyer; b. Jackson, Miss., Mar. 28, 1947; s. Joseph Murat and Mary Alice (Ragland) S.; m. Mary Margaret McRae, Mar. 7, 1970; children: Mary Lindsay, David Stephen. BS, Miss. State U., 1969; JD, U. Miss., 1974. Bar: Miss. 1974. Estate tax atty. IRS, Jackson, 1974-78; assoc. Peterson, Harper & Bellan, 1978-82; ptnr. Wells, Moore, Simmons, Stubblefield & Neeld, 1982-91, Stubblefield & Assocs., Jackson, 1991-97, Stubblefield Harvey & Shivers, PLLC, Jackson, 1997—. Mem., pres. Fiduciary Mgmt. Co., LLC, Jackson, 1995—. Mem. Belhaven Estate Planning Council, 2000—, Miss. State U. Planned Gifts Council, 1999—; mem. bd. regents Miss. Bapt. Health Sys. Trust, 1998—. 1st lt. U.S. Army, 1970-72. Mem. Fin. Planning Assn. (sec., treas. 1992-94), Nat. Lawyers Assn., Miss. Coll. Estate Planning Coun. (exec. bd.), Miss. Estate Planning Counsel, Belhaven Coll. Estate Planning Counsel, Miss. State Bar Assn., Phi Delta Phi (past officer). Republican. Baptist. Avocations: fishing, hunting, hiking, boating. Home: 340 Sherborne Pl Jackson MS 39232 Office: 3900 Lakeland Dr Ste 401 PO Box 320399 Jackson MS 39232 E-mail: srj0201@aol.com.

STUBBLEFIELD, PAGE KINDRED, banker; b. Bloomington, Tex., Aug. 28, 1914; s. Edwin Page and Vinnye L. (Kindred) S.; m. Dorothea Mock, July 7, 1940; children— Edwin Mark, Bob Lynn. Student, Southwestern U., Georgetown, Tex., 1931; BBA, U. Tex., Austin, 1936. Mgr. Page Stubblefield Gen. Mdse., 1936-42; owner-operation P.K. Stubblefield Ins. Agy., 1946-51; asst. v.p. pub. relations Victoria (Tex.) Bank & Trust Co., 1951-52, v.p., 1952-58, sr. v.p., 1958-69, pres., 1969-81, chmn. bd., from 1977, chmn. bd. dirs., 1984-88; pres. Victoria Bankshares, Inc., 1974-84. Past chmn. bd. dirs. Victoria Bankshares, Inc.; past chmn. bd. dirs. Victoria Bank and Trust Co. Hon. mem. U. Tex. Centennial Commn. With fin. dept. USAAF, 1942-45. Mem.: Victoria Country Club, Plz. Club. Home: 2402 N De Leon St Victoria TX 77901-4814 Office: 1 Oconnor Plz Ste 501 Victoria TX 77901-6502

STUBBLEFIELD, THOMAS MASON, agricultural economist, educator; b. Taxhoma, Okla., Apr. 16, 1922; s. Temple Roscoe and Martha Lacy (Acree) S.; BS, N.Mex. State Coll., 1948; MS, A. and M. Coll. Tex., 1951, PhD, 1956; postgrad. U. Ariz., 1954; m. Martha Lee Miller, Mar. 7, 1943; children: Ellen (Mrs. Richard Damron), Paula (Mrs. James T. Culbertson), Thommye (Mrs. Gary D. Zingsheim). Specialist cotton mktg. N.Mex. State Coll., 1948; extension economist, then asst. agrl. economist U. Ariz., Tucson, 1951-58, from assoc. prof. to prof., 1958-64, prof. and agrl. economist, 1964-83, emeritus prof., 1983—, acting asst. dir. agrl. expt. sta., 1966-68, asst. to dir. sta., 1973-74, chief party Brazil contract, 1968-70. Mem. Pima Council Aging, 1974-77, 80-90; chmn. adv. com. Ret. Sr. Vol. Program, Pima County, 1974-77, 80-90, mem. 1974—. Chmn. bd. Saguaro Home Found., 1980-85. With AUS, 1942-45. Author bulls. in field. Adv. bd. Unified Cmty., 1994—. Home: 810 W Calle Milu Tucson AZ 85706-3925

STUBBS, DONALD CLARK, secondary education educator; b. Providence, Mar. 6, 1935; s. Edward J. and Margaret Eleanor (Clark) S.; m. Lorraine Alice Thivierge, Apr. 3, 1969 (dec. Jan. 1986); 1 child, Derek C.; m. Sarah E. Andrews, Apr. 23, 1999. AB, Cath. U. Am., Washington, 1959, MS, 1966; postgrad., St. John's U., N.Y.C., 1960. Tchr. Bishop Loughlin Meml. High Sch., Bklyn., 1959-61, Bishop Bradley High Sch., Manchester, N.H., 1961-66; tchr., sci. dept. chair LaSalle Mil. Acad., Oakdale, N.Y., 1966-69, Ponaganset Regional High Sch., Glocester, R.I., 1969-2000; ret., 2000. Home: 35 Shove St Woonsocket RI 02895-5741 E-mail: naddad@aol.com.

STUBBS, GERALD, biochemist, educator; b. Hobart, Australia, May 9, 1947; came to the U.S., 1976; m. Rebecca Lynn Harris; children: Andrew, Tamsin, Anneliese, Rachel. BSc, Australian Nat. U., 1968; DPhil, Oxford U., 1972. Sci. asst. Max Planck Inst., Heidelberg, Fed. Republic of Germany, 1973-76; rsch. assoc. Brandeis U., Waltham, Mass., 1976-83; asst. prof. Vanderbilt U., Nashville, 1983-87, assoc. prof., 1987-90, prof., 1990—. Contbr. articles to profl. jours. Achievements include determination of molecular structure of tobacco mosaic virus. Office: PO Box 1634 Nashville TN 37202-1634 E-mail: gerald.stubbs@vanderbilt.edu.

STUBBS, JOHN HOWELL, architectural educator, preservationist; b. Monroe, La., Apr. 26, 1950; s. William King and Sue (Graves) S.; m. Jane Kelley, Dec. 30, 1983 (div. Aug. 1998); m. Linda Karsteter, Apr. 9, 1999. BS in Archtl. Tech., La. State U., 1972; MS in Arch., Preservation and Planning, Columbia U., 1974; cert., Internat. Ctr. Conservation of Cultural Property, Rome, 1977. Asst. prof. La. State U. Sch. Architecture, 1974-77; hist. arch. Tech. Preservation Svcs. U.S. Nat. Park Svc., Washington, 1977-78; pres. Stubbs Books and Prints Inc., N.Y.C., 1978-98; assoc. Beyer Blinder Belle Archs., 1979-89; assoc. prof. Columbia U., 1989—; v.p. programs World Monuments Fund, 1989—. Advisor Abagail Adams Smith House, N.Y.C., 1983-95; advisor gallery coun. N.Y. Sch. Interior Design, 1988-91; mem. adv. coun. U. Fla. Sch. Landscape Architecture, 1997-98. Contbg. author: Conservation on Archaeological Sites, 1984, 93, Five Centuries of Great Architectural Books, 1997; editor: Architecture of W.K. Stubbs, 1994; also articles. Trustee Met. Hist. Structures Assn., 1990-94, James Marston Fitch Charitable Trust, 1992, Archaeol. Inst. Am., Boston, 1999—. UNESCO fellow, Rome, 1977, fellow Salzburg (Austria) Seminar, 1990, travel fellow S.H. Kress Found., Sri Lanka, 1993. Mem. Internat. Coun. on Monuments and Sites, Coll. Art Assn., Columbia U. Preservation Alumni Assn. (pres. 1981-82), Century Club, Nat. Trust Hist. Pres. Forum. Avocations: books, rare books, antiques, travel. Office: World Monuments Fund 95 Madison Ave New York NY 10016-7801 E-mail: wmf@wmf.org.

STUBBS, KENDON LEE, librarian; b. Washington, Apr. 6, 1938; s. Donald Harrison and Rosalee Adelia (Brown) S.; m. Patricia Townsend, June 3, 1961; children— Christopher, Peter, Timothy. BA, St. John's Coll., Annapolis, Md., 1960; MA, U. Va., 1964; MS, Columbia U., 1965. Sr. asst. in manuscripts U. Va. Libr., Charlottesville, 1965, reference libr., 1966-76, acting acquisitions libr., 1967-68, assoc. univ. libr., 1976-87, assoc. univ. libr. for pub. svcs., 1987-92, acting univ. libr., 1993, assoc. univ. libr., 1994-98, dep. univ. libr., 1998—. Cons. U.S. Dept. Edn., Washington, 1982-84. Author: Quantitative Criteria for Academic Research Libraries, 1984; editor: Cumulated Assn. Research Libraries Statistics, 1981, Rsch. Libr. Statistics, 1990, ARL Statistics, 1992-95, Japanese Text Initiative on World Wide Web, 1995—; contbr. articles on library stats., rsch. to profl. publs., Internet. Mem. Assn. of Rsch. Librs. (mem. stats. com., vis. program officer 1995-97), Bibliog. Soc. U. Va. (pres. 1975-78, v.p. 1978-99). Office: Alderman Libr U Va Charlottesville VA 22904-4114 E-mail: kls9h@virginia.edu.

STUBBS, MARILYN KAY, education administrator; b. Great Bend, Kans., Mar. 21, 1950; d. John Calvin and Rosanna (Edler) Rapp; m. Stephen Richard Stubbs, Apr. 4, 1970; children: Adam Richard, Anna Elizabeth. BA in English, Kans. State U., 1972. Asst. instr. Kans. State U., Manhattan, 1972; educator All Saints Sch., Kansas City, Kans., 1973-74, Archdiocese of Kansas City, Mo., 1975-78; adminstrv. asst. Sherwood Ctr. for the Exceptional Child, Kansas City, 1979-89, assoc. dir., 1989—. Cons., trainer NW Mo. Autism Consortium, 1993—98; NW Mo. dist. team leader Positive Behavior Support, Kansas City, 1996—, Team Tng. Project, Kansas City, 1995—96; trainer Jackson County Bd. Svcs., Kansas City, 1995—. Author (newsletter): Sherwood Chronicle, 1980—86; editor, 1986—; editor: Families Addressing Auditory Integration Tng., 1993—95, Bridges, 1997—98. Mem Employment Task Force, 1995—98; spkrs. bur. United Way, Kansas City, 1982—; mem. Assn. United Way Execs., 1989—; adv. com. mem. Nat. Coun. Devel. Disabilities, 1990—94. Named Parent of Yr., Sherwood Parents Assn., 1985. Mem.: TASH (Mo. state bd. dirs.), Am. Assn. on Mental Retardation, Autism Soc. Am. (sec. We. Mo. chpt. 1999, conf. com. mem. 1999), Divers Alert Network, Astron. Soc. Kansas City. Avocations: horseback riding, astronomy, scuba diving, skiing, hunting. Office: Sherwood Center 7938 Chestnut Ave Kansas City MO 64132-3698

STUBBS, ROY HARRINGTON, music educator; b. Aberdeen, N.C., Apr. 8, 1944; BA, Allen U., Columbia, S.C., 1967. Cert. tchr. 7-12 vocal music Iowa. K-12 vocal and instrumental music Walthill (Nebr.) Pub. Sch., 1998—2000; dir. of choral music Wapsie Valley H.S., Fairbank, Iowa, 2000—. Musician. Mem.: NEA, ASCD, Nat. Fedn. Interscholastic Music Assn., Am. Choral Dirs. Assn., Music Educators Nat. Conf. Democrat. Presbyterian. Home: 1133 Hawthorne Ave Waterloo IA 50702 Office: Wapsie Valley H S 2535 Viking Ave Fairbank IA 50629 Home Fax: 319-638-7061; Office Fax: 319-638-7061. Personal E-mail: harrington@mchsi.com. E-mail: rstubbs@wapsie-valley.k12.ia.us.

STUBBS, SUSAN CONKLIN, statistician; b. Washington, July 26, 1935; d. Maxwell Robertson and Marcia (Nye) Conklin; m. LeRoy Carter Hostetter, May 20, 1975 (div. 1988); m. Joel Richard Stubbs, Sept. 20, 1992. BA, Pa. State U., 1957. Economist Bur. of Census, Suitland, Md., 1973-74, Bur. of Labor Statistics, Washington, 1974-78, supervisory economist, 1978-84; statistician IRS, 1984-95, chief rschr. stats. of income divsn., 1989-92, coord. for indsl. classification, 1994-95; ret., 1995. Cons. joint com. on taxation U.S. Congress, 1992-94; OPM legis. fellow, 1988. Contbr. articles to profl. jours.; editor govtl. statis. publs. Leader, del., bd. dirs., v.p., chmn. nominating com. Nation's Capital coun. Girl Scouts U.S., 1968—; sec.-treas. Middlesex Beach Assn. , Bethany, Del., 1991—94; jobs. editor Caucus for Women in Stats. , Washington, 1992—95; mentor Mentors Inc., 1992—94; treas. Smith Point Sea Rescue, 1997—; chmn. Christmas on Cockrell's Creek Reedville Fisherman's Mus., 2001—02, docent, 1997—; active Boy Scouts Am. Campaign for Family Values; tutor and mentor People Helping People; treas. Region II, Episc. Diocese of Va., 1999—; bd. dirs. Rice's Hotel/Hughlett's Tavern Found., 1998—2000, Rappahannock C.C. Found., 2002—. Mem.: Am. Statis. Assn., Bus. and Profl. Women Essex County and No. Neck (sec. 1999—2001), Va. Federated Woman's Clubs (pres Ea. area Lee dist. 1998—2000), Rivers Bend Assn. (v.p., bd. dirs. 1996—98, 2001—, chair bylaws com., chair long range planning com., chair budget com. 1998—2001), Woman's Club Northumberland County (pres. 1996—98, treas. 1998). Avocations: sailing, swimming, gardening, reading. Home: 776 Riverview Ln Heathsville VA 22473-4011

STUBBS, THOMAS HUBERT, company executive; b. Americus, Ga., Aug. 16, 1944; s. Hubert F. and Elizabeth (Askew) S.; m. Mary Louise Quarles, Mar. 19, 1965; children: Thomas C., Chad P. BS, Auburn U., 1966. CPA, Ala., Ga., Miss. Sr. acct. Peat, Marwick, Mithcell and Co., Birmingham, Ala., 1966-72; supr. L. Paul Kassauf and Co., CPA's, 1972-73; staff mem. Snow, Stewart and Bradford, 1973-75; v.p. Cen. Computer Svcs., Inc., 1975-79, Cen. Bancshares of the South, Birmingham, 1979-81; ptnr. Bradford and Co., CPA's, Gulf Shore, Ala., 1981-82; v.p., trust officer Deposit Guaranty Nat. Bank, Jackson, Miss., 1983; treas. Data Supplies, Inc., Norcross, Ga., 1983-88, Stevens Graphics, Inc., Atlanta, 1988-89, v.p., 1989-90, pres. bus. products div., 1990-93, v.p., CFO, 1994—2002; fin. cons. LPL Fin. Svcs., Buford, 2002—. Served with USNG, 1966-72. Mem. Am. Inst. CPA's, Ala. Soc. CPA's, Ga. Soc. CPA's, Miss. Soc. CPA's. Republican. Presbyterian. Avocations: tennis, jogging, golf. Home: 2875 Towne Village Dr Duluth GA 30097-7616 Office: 2760 Chiraquapin Ct Buford GA 30519 E-mail: mlq3020@becgrowth.net.

STUBBS, WILL, JR. pharmaceutical company manager; b. Birmingham, Ala., Feb. 26, 1955; s. Will, Sr. and Elizabeth S.; 1 child, Will III. BS in Mgmt. and Econs. cum laude, Fisk U., 1977. Sys. engr. Procter & Gamble, Jackson, Tenn., 1977-78, prodn. team mgr., 1978-80; large parenterals labeling/packaging supr. Abbott Labs., Rocky Mount, N.C., 1980-81, large parenterals terminal sterile filling supr., 1981-85, aseptic sterilization supr., 1985-88, small parenterals terminal sterile fill supr., 1988-90, aseptic filling supr., 1990-93, sr. prodn. supr., 1993-95, pharm. prodn. mgr., 1995-2001, terminal sterile filling prodn. mgr., 2001—. Contbr. poetry to Fisk Herald. Mem. econ. growth task force Rocky Mount City Coun., 1992-94; bd. dirs. Nash Edgecombe Econ. Devel. Inc., Rocky Mount, 1994-99, vice chmn. bd. dirs., 1998, chmn., 1999; mem. Adult Basic Edn. Bd., 1980-84; pres. Rocky Mount Pan Hellenic Coun., 1991-93. Named to Outstanding Young Men of Am., Jayucees, 1983, 5th Dist. Scholar of the Yr., Omega Psi Phi, 1977; recipient internship Mobil Oil Corp. Mem. Omega Psi Phi (Vice-Basileus grad. chap. 1989-91). Democrat. Baptist. Avocations: community service, travel, music, swimming, jogging. Home: 1028 Niblick Dr Rocky Mount NC 27804-9655 Office: 4285 N Wesleyan Blvd Rocky Mount NC 27804-8612

STUBENBORD, WILLIAM T. surgeon; b. N.Y., July 4, 1936; MD, Cornell Univ., 1962. Intern N.Y. Hosp., 1962-63, resident, 1963-68, staff; prof. surgery Cornell Univ. Fellow Am. Coll. Surgeons.

STUBER, CHARLES WILLIAM, genetics educator, researcher; b. St. Michael, Nebr., Sept. 19, 1931; s. Harvey John and Minnie Augusta (Wilks) S.; m. Marilyn Martha Cook, May 28, 1953; 1 child, Charles William Jr. BS, U. Nebr., 1952, MS, 1961; PhD, N.C. State U., 1965. Vet., agrl. instr. Broken Bow (Nebr.) H. S., 1956-59; research asst. U. Nebr., Lincoln, 1959-61; research geneticist Agrl. Rsch. Svc., USDA, Raleigh, N.C., 1962-75, supervisory research geneticist, research leader, 1975-98, collaborator, 1998—; prof. genetics & crop sci. N.C. State U., 1975-98, prof. emeritus, 1998—. Assoc. editor Crop Sci. Jour., 1979-82, tech. editor, 1984-86, editor, 1987-89; contbr. over 200 articles to profl. jours., chpts. to books. Chmn. coun. on ministries and numerous offices Highland United Meth Ch., Raleigh. Lt. USN, 1952-56. Named Outstanding Scientist of Yr., USDA-ARS, 1989; recipient Genetics and Plant Breeding award Nat. Coun. Comml. Plant Breeders, 1995, Award of Merit, U. Nebr. Alumni Assn., 1997; inductee USDA-Agrl. Rsch. Svc. Sci. Hall of Fame, 1999; Vol. 45 of MAYDICA dedicated to Charles W. Stuber, 2000. Fellow: Crop Sci. Soc. Am. (editor-in-chief 1987—91, pres. 1992—93, Crop Sci. Rsch. award 1995, DeKalb Genetics Crop Sci. Disting. Career award 1999), Am. Soc. Agronomy (pres. 2002); mem.: AAAS, Am. Genetic Assn. (sec. 1984—86), Genetics Soc. Am., Phi Kappa Phi, Sigma Xi. Avocations: windsurfing, water skiing, sailing. Home: 1800 Manuel St Raleigh NC 27612-5510 Office: USDA-ARS NC State U Dept Genetics PO Box 7614 Raleigh NC 27695-0001 E-mail: cstuber@ncsu.edu.

STUBER-MCEWEN, DONNA, psychology educator; b. Kansas City, Mo., Dec. 12, 1954; d. Richard L. Stuber and Nadine Stuber; m. Michael J. McEwen, Nov. 16, 1951. BS in Psychology, Mo. Western State Coll., 1985; MS in Gen./Exptl. Psychology, Emporia State U., 1987; PhD in Student Counseling & Pers. Svcs., Kansas State U., 1992. Instr., dept. chmn. North Ctrl. Mo. Coll., Trenton, 1991-96; prof., vice chmn. Friends U., Wichita, Kans., 1996—. Author: How to Host a Psychology Conference at Your College, 1999, Internet Psychology: Web Site Based Exercises, 2001; contbr. articles to profl. jours. Mem. APA, Assn. for Psychol. and Ednl. Rsch. in kans. (sec. 1997-2000, pres.-elect 2001-02, pres. 2002—), Coun. Undergrad. Tchrs. of Psychology, Great Plains Behavioral Rsch. Assn., Midwestern Psychol. Assn. Democrat. Mem. United Ch. of Christ. Avocation: web design. Office: Friends U 2100 W University Wichita KS 67213 E-mail: mcewen@friends.edu.

STUBERT, HARALD GUNNAR, management consultant; b. Malmo, Sweden, Jan. 4, 1948; s. Sven and Anna (Petersson) S. BA, U. Lund, Sweden, 1973. Tng. officer SAAB Scania, Sodertalje, Sweden, 1974-75; cons. Stats. Cons., Stockholm, 1976-81; sr. cons. Bohlin & Stromberg Mgmt., 1982-83; pres. Bohlin & Stromberg Search, 1984, Esselte Cinema Internat., Stockholm, 1985-90, Bohlin & Strömberg, Stockholm, 1990-95; mgr. process mgmt. Ericsson Radio, Wideband Radio Networks, 1995—. Author: Stockholm Restaurants, yearly; contbr. articles to profl. jours. Mem.: Sallskapet. Home: Roslagsgatan 15 11355 Stockholm Sweden Office: Ericsson Radio Systems Wideband Radio Networks S-16480 Stockholm Sweden E-mail: harald.stubert@ericsson.com.

STUCK, ROGER DEAN, electrical engineering educator; b. Ventura, Calif., Nov. 6, 1924; s. William Henry and Marian Grace (Ready) S.; m. Opal Christine Phillips, July 25, 1948; children: Dean, Phyllis, Sandra. BSEE, Calif. Inst. Tech., 1947; MSEE, N.C. State U., 1957. Elec. engr. Warren Wilson Coll., Swannanoa, N.C., 1947—, instr. elec. engring. physics, 1948-69, dean students, 1969-72, instr. physics, elec. engr., 1972-86. Author: (charts) The Periodic Table of Physical Concepts, 1977, The Periodic Table of Physical Concepts with Economic Concepts, 1980; (book) The Periodic Table of Physical Concepts Book of Definitions, 1980. Lt. (j.g.) USNR, 1942-46. Mem. Sigma Xi. Republican. Presbyterian. Achievements include identification of gravitational inductance, capacitance and splendor (MVVV) and energy-spread (hc) as a fundamental initial concept of physical creation relating mass and charge which is fundamental to any Grand Unification Theory; the statement of a quantized conservation law for energy-spread to establish an internal and external structure for neutrons, protons, electrons and neutrinos. Home: 65 Green Forest Rd Swannanoa NC 28778-2246

STUCK, WANDA MARIE, special education educator; b. Schoolcraft, Mich. d. Glen Robert and Luella Shearer; m. Paul Stuck; children: Pamela, Lauri, Jeffrey. BS, MA, Western Mich. U. Tchr. spl. edn.; tchr. adult edn. sewing Cunningham Fabrics, Vicksburg, Mich.; tchr. adult edn. computers Edwardsburg (Mich.) Sch., tchr. spl. edn., home econs. Prof. seamstress, Schoolcrest, Mich.; clk. Fields Fabric, Kalamazoo. Bd. dirs. Meth. Ch., Schoolcraft, 1994—; mem. Ladies Libr., Schoolcraft. Mem. AAUW, Coun. Exceptional Children, Learning Disabilities Assn. Mich., Order of Ea. Star. Methodist. Avocations: sewing, reading, quilting.

STUCKEY, HELENJEAN LAUTERBACH, counselor educator; b. Bushnell, Ill., May 17, 1929; d. Edward George and Frances Helen (Simpson) Lauterbach; m. James Dale Stuckey, Sept. 30, 1951; children: Randy Lee, Charles Edward, Beth Ellen. BFA, Ill. Wesleyan U., 1951; MEd, U. Ill., 1969. Cert. art tchr., guidance, psychology instr.; lic. clin. profl. counselor, Ill. Display designer Saks Fifth Ave., Chgo., 1951; interior designer Piper City, Ill., 1953-63; tchr. art Forrest (Ill.)-Strawn-Wing Schs., 1967-68; tchr., counselor Piper City Schs., 1969-74; counselor, tchr. art Ford Cen. Schs., Piper City, 1974-85; psychiat. counselor Community Resource Counseling Ctr.,

Ford County, Ill., 1985-87; tchr. history, counselor Iroquois West H.S., Gilman, 1987-88; spl. needs coord. Livingston County Vocat., Pontiac, 1988-93; ret., 1993; clin. profl. counselor, pvt. practice Piper City, 1995—. Substitute tchr., 1993—. Mem. ACA, Ill. Counseling Assn., Ill. Mental Health Counselors Assn., Ill. Ret. Tchrs. (membership chmn.), Delta Kappa Gamma (v.p., sec., program chmn., pres.). Presbyterian. Avocations: skiing, reading, travel, sewing, playing flute. Personal E-mail: hjstuckey@bwsys.net.

STUCKEY, JAMES P. real estate company executive; b. Bklyn., Feb. 15, 1954; s. John McRae and Ethel Lilian Stuckey; m. Deborah Marie Stuckey, Apr. 6, 1974; children: Nicole Marie, James P. Jr., Danielle Antionette. BS, St. John's U., 1975, MA, 1977. Various Office Econ. Devel., 1977-80, N.Y.C. Pub. Devel. Corp., 1980-86, pres., CEO, 1986-89, also bd. dirs.; mng. dir. Gronich & Co., Inc., 1990-93; exec. v.p., dir. comml. devel. Forest City Ratner Cos., S.I., N.Y., 1994—. Lectr. Columbia U., Yale U., St. John's U., NYU, John Jay Coll., Pratt Inst. Mem. Westside Task Force, N.Y.C. Mcpl. Water Fin. Authority, Ctr. Family Life, Ctr. Elimination Violence Family, Nat. Trust Historic Preservation; vice chmn. Cmty. Bd. 2, S.I. Mem. Nat. Assn. Corp. Real Estate Execs., Urban Land Inst., Coun. Urban Econ. Devel., Inst. Urban Design (mem. regional adv. coun.). Avocations: music, bicycling, racquetball, golf. Office: Forest City Ratner Corp 1 Metrotech Center Brooklyn NY 11201-3831 E-mail: jstuckey@fcrs.com.

STUCKEY, SUSAN JANE, perioperative nurse, consultant; Diploma in nursing, The Polyclinic Med. Ctr., 1971; BBA in Health Care Adminstrn., Pa. State U., 1985; cert., Del. County C.C., Media, Pa., 1988; MBA, Kutztown U., 1996. RN, Pa.; cert. operating rm. nurse; cert. RN first asst. Charge nurse Nightingale Nursing Home, Camp Hill, Pa., 1971-72; clin. educator oper. rm. svcs., staff nurse Harrisburg (Pa.) Hosp., 1972-80; adminstr., nursing coord. Hillcrest Women's Med. Ctr., Harrisburg, 1978-81; office mgr., pvt. scrub nurse Office Dr. Henry Train, 1979-82; with Kimberly Nurses Med Temps, Cleve., 1982-84; sr. splty. nurse oper. rm. Harrisburg Hosp., 1984-86, splty. supr. surg. svcs. dept., 1986-90; 1st asst. laser/abdominal endoscopy Women's Med. Assocs. P.C., Harrisburg, 1990-96; 1st asst., cons. C.B. Laser Assocs. Inc., Camp Hill, Pa., 1990—96; 1st asst., cons., propr. Peri Operative Care Assocs., Harrisburg, 1996-98; clin. nurse Morton Plant Mease, Dunedin, Fla., 1998-99; clin. nurse, eastern regional clin. specialist mgr. Medtronic Neurol., 1999—. Mem. faculty Pa. Jr. Coll. Med. Arts. Contbr. articles to profl. jours. Mem. Assn. Oper. Rm. Nurses, Am. Assn. Gynecol. Laparoscopists, Am. Soc. for Laser Medicine and Surgery. Office: 301 Lindenwood Dr Ste 217 Malvern PA 19355-1758

STUCKWISCH, CLARENCE GEORGE, retired university administrator; b. Seymour, Ind., Oct. 13, 1916; s. William Henry and Clara Sophia (Benter) S.; m. Esther Elizabeth Ebert, Dec. 19, 1942; children: William, Stephen, David, Deborah, Stephanie. BA magna cum laude, Ind. U., 1939; PhD, Iowa State U., 1943. Mem. faculty U. Wichita, Kans., 1943-60, prof. chemistry, 1958-60; prof., chmn. dept. N.Mex. Highlands U., Las Vegas, 1960-64; prof., exec. officer dept. chemistry SUNY, Buffalo, 1964-68; prof., chmn. dept. U. Miami, Coral Gables, Fla., 1968-72, assoc. v.p. advanced studies and research, dean Grad. Sch., 1972-81, exec. v.p., provost, 1981-82; ret. Mem. council Oak Ridge Assn. Univs. Contbr. articles to profl. jours.; patentee in chem. intermediates and pharms. Mem. AAAS, Am. Chem. Soc., Lions, Phi Beta Kappa, Sigma Xi, Phi Kappa Phi. Democrat. Lutheran.

STUCKY, JEAN SEIBERT, lawyer; b. Berkeley, Calif., Feb. 9, 1951; d. Edward Raymond and Frances Selma (Berg) S.; m. Scott Wallace Stucky, Aug. 18, 1973; children: Mary-Clare, Joseph. BA in Econs., Wellesley (Mass.) Coll., 1973; JD, Cornell U., 1978; MA in Econs., Trinity U., San Antonio, 1980; postgrad., George Washington U., Washington, 1991—. Bar: D.C. 1978. Atty.-advisor Adminstrv. Conf. U.S., Washington, 1978-79, Divsn. Advice, NLRB, Washington, 1979-94; contractor labor counsel U.S. Dept. Energy, Office Gen. Counsel, 1994—. Mem. Washington Cathedral Altar Guild, 1988—. Mem. D.C. Bar, Dames of Loyal Legion of U.S., Washington Wellesley Club (pres. 1992-94), Wellesley Coll. Alumnae Assn. (regional chmn. 1995-97). Republican. Episcopalian. Avocations: gardening, flower arranging. Home: 11004 Homeplace Ln Potomac MD 20854-1406 Office: US Dept Energy Office Gen Counsel 1000 Independence Ave SW Washington DC 20585-0001

STUCKY, SCOTT WALLACE, lawyer; b. Hutchinson, Kans., Jan. 11, 1948; s. Joe Edward and Emma Clara (Graber) S.; m. Jean Elsie Seibert, Aug. 18, 1973; children: Mary-Clare, Joseph. BA summa cum laude, Wichita State U., 1970; JD, Harvard U., 1973; MA, Trinity U., 1980; LLM with high honors, George Washington U., 1983; postgrad., Nat. War Coll., 1993. Bar: Kans. 1973, U.S. Dist. Ct. Kans. 1973, U.S. Ct. Appeals (10th cir.) 1973, U.S. Ct. Mil. Appeals 1974, U.S. Supreme Ct. 1976, D.C. 1979, U.S. Ct. Appeals (D.C. cir.) 1979. Assoc. Ginsburg, Feldman & Bress, Washington, 1978-82; chief docketing and svc. br. Nuclear Regulatory Commn., 1982-83; legis. counsel U.S. Air Force USAF, 1983-96, gen. counsel sen. com. on armed svcs., 1996—2001, principal minority counsel, 2001—. Lectr. bus. law Maria Regina Coll., Syracuse, N.Y., 1977; congrl. fellow Office Senator John Warner, 1986; res. judge adv. USAF Res., Washington, 1982—; col. Appellate Mil. Judge, USAF Ct. Criminal Appeals, 1991-95, 97-98, 2001—; sr. reservist USAF Judiciary, 1995-97, Air Res. Personnel Ctr., 1998-99, Air Force Legal Svcs. Agy., 19990-01. Contbr. articles to profl. jours. Capt. USAF, 1973-78. Decorated Air Force Meritorious Svc. medal with two oak leaf cluster. Mem. Fed. Bar Assn., Judge Advs. Assn. (bd. dirs. 1984-88), Res. Officers Assn., Wichita State U. Alumni Assn. (pres. chpt. 1981-86, nat. bd. dirs. 1986-92), Adoption Svc. Info. Agy. (bd. dirs. 1998—), Army and Navy Club (Washington), Mil. Order of Loyal Legion U.S. (state comdr. and recorder 1984-92, nat. treas. 1987-89, nat. vice comdr. 1989-93, nat. comdr.-in-chief 1993-95), Sons of Union Vets Civil War (chpt. vice-comdr 1986-88), Phi Delta Phi, Phi Alpha Theta, Phi Kappa Phi, Omicron Delta Kappa, Sigma Phi Epsilon. Republican. Episcopalian. Home: 11004 Homeplace Ln Potomac MD 20854-1406 Office: Sen Armed Svcs Com 228 Senate Office Bldg Washington DC 20510-0001

STUCKY, STEVEN (STEVEN EDWARD STUCKY), composer, conductor; b. Hutchinson, Kans., Nov. 7, 1949; s. Victor Eugene and Louise Doris (Trautwein) S.; m. Melissa Jane Whitehead, Aug. 22, 1970; children: Maura Catharine, Matthew Steven. MusB, Baylor U., 1971; MFA, Cornell U., 1973, DMA, 1978. Vis. asst. prof. Lawrence U., Appleton, Wis., 1978-80; prof. Cornell U., Ithaca, N.Y., 1980—, chmn. dept. music, 1992-97. Composer-in-residence L.A. Philharm. Orch., 1988— Author: Lutoslawski and His Music, 1981 (Deems Taylor award ASCAP 1982); composer: Sappho Fragments, 1982, Voyages, 1984, Boston Fancies, 1985, Dreamwaltzes, 1986, Concerto for orch., 1987, Son et Lumière, 1988, Angelus, 1990, Impromptus, 1991, Four Poems of A.R. Ammons, 1992, Ancora, 1994, Double Flute Cto., 1994, Fanfares and Arias, 1994, Pinturas de Tamayo, 1995, Music for Saxophones and Strings, 1996, Cradle Songs, 1997, Concerto Mediterraneo, 1998, Ad Parnassum, 1998, American Muse, 1999, Nell'ombra, nella luce, 1999, Etudes, 2000, Pastorale-Partita, after J.S.B., 2000, Concerto for Percussion and Wind Orchestra, 2001, Skylarks, 2001, Colburn Variations, 2002, Whispers, 2002; received commn. from Nat. Endowment for Arts, 1982, Koussevitzky Found., 1991, Meet the Composer, 1995. Bd. advisors Barlow Endowment, 1993-97; bd. dirs. MacDowell Colony, 1993-95. Fellow Guggenheim Found., Nat. Endowment for the Arts, Bogliasco Found. Mem.: Am. Acad. Arts and Letters. Office: Theodore Presser Co care One Presser Pl Bryn Mawr PA 19010 E-mail: ses6@cornell.edu.

STUDEBAKER, GLENN WAYNE, steel company executive; b. Jefferson City, Mo., Oct. 12, 1939; s. Glenn Noble and Dora Mabel (Scrivner) S.; m. Regina Louise O'Kane, Jan. 28, 1961 (div. 1977); children: Glenn Wayne, Ted William, John Christopher, Patrick O'Kane; m. Harriet Jean Hansen, Aug. 7, 1978; stepchildren: Scott Robert Jundt, Jill Michelle Jundt. BSCE, U. Mo., 1962. Bridge design engr. Mo. Hwy. Dept., Jefferson City, 1962-66; sales engr. Vulcraft div. Nucor corp., Norfolk, Nebr., 1966-67, engring. mgr., 1967-70, mgr. rsch., 1970-78; mgr. rsch. and devel. Nucor Corp., 1978-82, gen. mgr. rsch. and devel., 1982—. Chmn. rsch. com. Steel Joist Inst., Myrtle Beach, S.C., 1972—; rsch. overseer Iowa State U., Okla. U., U. Minn., Va. Poly., Washington U., U. Wis., 1970—. Adv. dir. Faith Regional Hosp., Norfolk, 1985-98; trustee York (Nebr.) Coll., 1989—; elder Ch. of Christ, 1996—; dir. N.E. C.C. Found., 1999—. Mem. NSPE, Am. Welding Soc., Am. Soc. Metals, Wire Assn. Internat., Soc. Mfg. Engrs., Structural Stability Rsch. Coun., Norfolk Country Club (bd. dirs. 1987-89), Kiwanis, Chi Epsilon. Republican. Avocations: investing, golf, archeology, architecture, travel. E-mail: wstudebaker@nucor-rd.com.

STUDEBAKER, IRVING GLEN, mining engineering consultant; b. Ellensburg, Wash., July 22, 1931; s. Clement Glen and Ruth (Krause) S.; (widowed); children: Ruth, Betty, Raymond, Karl, Donna. BS in Geol. Engring., U. Ariz., 1957, MS in Geology, 1959, PhD in Geol. Engring., 1977. Registered profl. engr., Wash., Nev., Ariz., Colo., Mont. Geophys. engr. Mobil, 1959-61; civil engr. City of Yakima, Wash., 1964-66; instr. Yakima Valley Coll., 1962-67; sr. rsch. geologist Roan Selection Trust, Kalulushi, Zambia, 1967-72; sr. mining engr. Occidental Oil Shale, Grand Junction, Colo., 1974-81; prof. Mont. Coll. Mining Sch., Butte, 1982-96; prof. emeritus, 1996—. Cons. in field. Sgt. U.S. Army, 1951-54, Korea. Mem. N.W. Mining Assn., Geol. Soc. Am., Soc. for Mining and Metall. Engring., Soc. Econ. Geologists, Sigma Xi (pres. Mont. tech. chpt. 1990-91). Avocations: golf, travel. Home and Office: 34222 1st Pl S Apt C Federal Way WA 98003-6537

STUDEBAKER, JOHN MILTON, utilities engineer, consultant, educator; b. Springfield, Ohio, Mar. 31, 1935; s. Frank Milton and Monaruth (Beatty) S.; m. Virginia Ann Van Pelt, Mar. 12, 1960; 1 child, Jacqueline Ann Allcorn. BS in Law, LaSalle U., Chgo., 1969; MS and PhD in Indsl. Engring., Columbia Pacific U., San Rafael, Calif., 1984. Cert. plant engr. Am. Inst. Plant Engrs., profl. cons. Acad. Profl. Cons. & Advisors. Indsl engr. Internat. Harvest Co., 1957-60, supr. indsl. engring., 1960-66, gen. supr. body assembly, 1967-68, mgr. indsl. engring., 1968-70; mgr. manufacturing engring. Lamb Electric Co., 1970-72, Cascade Corp., 1972-78; engring. mgr. Bundy Tubing Corp., Winchester and Cynthia, Ky., 1978—98; chmn. The Studebaker Group, Inc., Alexandria, Va., 1998—; pres. Studebaker Energy Cons., LLC, 1989—. Instr. numerous univs. including Boston U., Clemson U., Cornell U., Harvard U., Duquesne U., U. Ala., U. Ill., U. Wis., Ga. State U., James Madison U., Tex. Tech. U., U. Calif., Calif. State U., Columbia U., Fairleigh Dickinson U., San Francisco State U.; instr. Am. Mgmt. Assn., Rochester Inst. Tech., Ctr. for Profl. Advancement. Author: Slashing Utility Costs Handbook, 1992, Natural Gas Purchasing Handbook, 1994, Electricity Retail Wheeling Handbook, 1995, Electricity Purchasing Handbook, 1996, Utility Negotiation Handbook, 2001, ESCO Handbook, 2001, CPT Utility/Energy Cost Reduction Strategies Handbook, 2002. Mem. NSPE, Am. Inst. Plant Engrs. (cert.), Assn. Energy Engrs. (instr.), Doctorate Assn. N.Y. Educators. Republican. Office: PO Box 708 Winchester KY 40392-0708 E-mail: jstudebaker@studebakerenergy.net.

STUDEBAKER, WILLIAM VERN, sports and literature educator, writer; b. Salmon, Idaho, May 21, 1947; s. Robert Rolland Studebaker and Betty L. Silbaugh; m. Judy Kay Infanger, Aug. 23, 1969; children: Tona Rae, Robert Vern, Elizabeth Tyler, Eric James. B of History, Idaho State U., 1970, M of English, 1972. Tchg. asst. Idaho State U., Pocatello, 1970-72; educator English and lit. Coll. So. Idaho, Twin Falls, 1972-95, adminstr. honors program, 1990-98, mktg. coord. Herrett Ctr. for Arts & Sci., 1995-99; educator lit. Idaho State U., 1994—; dir. outdoor programs Coll. So. Idaho, 1998—. Idaho River guide Idaho Guide Svc., Twin Falls, 1997—; bd. dirs. Idaho Writers Connection, Twin Falls; commr. Idaho Commn. on Arts, Boise, 1981-86; counselor Idaho Humanities Coun., Boise, 1997—. Author: (memoir) Short of a Good Promise, 1999, (poetry books) Travelers in an Antique Land, 1997, River Religion, 1997; editor: (book) Where the Morning Light's Still Blue, 1992, others. Baseball coach Twin Falls Park and Recreation, Twin Falls, 1982-90, Twin Falls Babe Ruth, 1987-93. Ethel E. Redfield scholar Idaho State U., 1970. Mem. Am. Canoe Assn. (cert. kayak instr.), Idaho Rivers United, Idaho Whitewater Assn., Log Cabin Lit. Ctr. Avocations: high desert hiking, whitewater photography, sporting dog trainer, carpentry, kayaking. Home: 2616 E 4000 N Twin Falls ID 83301-0123 Office: ASCSI Outdoor Program 315 Falls Ave W Twin Falls ID 83301-3119 E-mail: bstude@earthlink.net.

STUDENT, JOHN MICHAEL, secondary school educator; b. Astoria, N.Y. s. John Michael Student and Marcella Imaculata Spielman; m. Christine Ann Mouland, Sept. 14, 1952; 1 child Matthew Stephen. BA, Pembroke State U., 1974; MFA, Villanova U., 1976; MEd, Neumann Coll., 2002. Gen. contractor Jim Student Assocs., Drexel Hill, Pa., 1976—95; instr. Haverford/Bryn Mawr (Pa.) Colls., 1988—89, U. Pa., Phila., 1990—91; tchr. Monsignor Bonner H.S., Drexel Hill, 1996—. Named All State soccer player, N.J., 1971, All South Coll. soccer player, 1974. Mem.: Internat. Alliance Theatrical and Stage Employes. Avocations: varsity soccer coach, freshman baseball coach. Office: Monsignor Bonner H S 403 N Landsdowne Ave Drexel Hill PA 19026-1196

STUDENY, RICHARD ALAN, music educator, musician; b. New Britain, Conn., June 29, 1944; s. Richard Frank and Jeanette Irene Studeny; m. Gladys Irene Wesson, Nov. 19, 2000; children: Scott Chase, Winston Mignott; m. Gale Sakaris, Feb. 14, 1970 (div. Mar. 13, 1995); children: Gretchen, Jared. BM, Boston U., Boston, MA, 1962—66; MM, U. of Mass., Amherst, MA, 1968—72. Music instr./band dir. Northhampton Pub. Schools, Northhampton, Mass., 1966—72; tubist Springfield Symphony Orch., Springfield, 1966—80; music instr./band dir. East Longmeadow Pub. Schools, East Longmeadow, 1972—80; tubist Clarion Brass Quintet, Springfield, 1976—; music instr./band dir. Wilbraham Pub. Schools, Wilbraham, 1980—; tubist Pioneer Valley Symphony, Greenfield, 1994—99. Manager-band, orch. Mass. Music Educators Adminstrn., Western Massachusetts, Mass., 1967—78; music curriculum com. Wilbraham Pub. Schools, Wilbraham, Mass., 1998—2000; music tutor, Springfield, Mass., 1972—2001. Composer: (music) Suite for Unaccompanied Tuba ; organizer (small music ensembles) The Tuba Workshop. Mem. Kawanis, Northhampton, Mass., 1968—71. Mem.: Tubist Universal Brotherhood Assn. (regional clinician 1968—98), Quabbin Valley Music Educators Assn., Music Educators Nat. Conf. Democrat-Npl. Avocations: tennis, walking, hiking, photography.

STUDER, CAROL A. creative director, graphic designer, consultant; b. Joliet, Ill. BA in Design with honors and distinction, U. Ill., Chgo., 1975. Photographer Motorola Inc., Schaumburg, Ill., 1977-78; photographer, designer Revell/MONOGRAM, Morton Grove, 1978-80; sr. graphic designer Bank of Am., Chgo., 1980-88; graphic design mgr. Strombecker Corp./TOOTSIETOY, 1988-98. Pvt. practice design cons. Carol Studer Design, Oak Park, Ill., 1987—. Inventor (children's toy) Mr. Bubbles, Finger Wands, 1991. Democrat. Avocations: downhill skiing, gardening, international child welfare issues, the arts. E-mail: Stu206n@aol.com.

STUDER, JAMES EDWARD, geological engineer; b. Aurora, Colo., Sept. 1, 1961; s. Fredrick Ernest and Patricia Dora (McWilliams) S.; m. Anita Louise Palmer, Apr. 19, 1986; 1 child, Matthew Bernard. BS in Geol. Engring., U. Mo., Rolla, 1984, MS in Geol. Engring., 1985. Registered profl. engr., Kans., Fla., Tex., N.Mex., Okla., Ariz.; registered geologist, Ky. (inactive). Engring. aide engring. divsn. pub. works City of Kansas City, Mo., 1981-83; civil engr. tech. U.S. Army Corps Engrs., Kansas City, 1984; staff engr. Woodward-Clyde Cons., St. Louis, 1985, staff to asst. project engr. Overland Park, Kans., 1986-89, project engr., 1989-90; grad. teaching asst. U. Mo., Rolla, 1985; sr. project engr. Coastal Remediation Co., Norman, Okla., 1990-92; program dir. Hall Southwest Corp., Austin, Tex., 1992-93; S.W. region program mgr. Envirogen, Inc., 1993-94; sr. engr. Duke Engrg. and Svcs., Albuquerque, 1995-98, sect. mgr., 1998-2000; founder, prin. Cons. and Funding Resources LLC, 1997—. Lectr. grad. sch. seminars, 1987-96, Nat. Seminar on RCRA Corrective Action, 1990, Internat. Symposium on Bioremediation, 1995, 97, 99, Superfund Conf., 1996, U.S. EPA Tech. Transfer Conf., 1996, 98, Internat. Symposium on Chlorinated and Recalcitrant Compounds, 1998, 2000; adv. bd. Albuquerque Tech.-Vocational Inst., 1995-99; youth soccer coach, 1997-2001. Contbr. articles on environ. sci. and engring. to profl. jours. and books. Environ. adv. bd. City of Round Rock, Tex., 1993. Eagle Scout Boy Scouts Am. Mem. ASCE, Waste Edn. and Rsch. Consortium, Am. Cash Flow Assn., Assn. Ground Water Scientists and Engrs., N.Mex. Optics Industry Assn., Coronado Venture Forum, N.Mex. Entrepreneurs Assn., N.Mex. Biotech. and Biomed. Assn., Sigma Gamma Epsilon (W.A. Tarr award 1984). Roman Catholic. Achievements include leading first full-scale vadose zone partitioning interwell tracer test for in-situ quantification of dense non-aqueous phase liquid (DNAPL); leading design of first US EPA-permitted arid-land final cap for hazardous waste landfill; on team that discovered and mapped previously unrecorded cave in Missouri; devel. of innovative technologies for characterization and restoration of hazardous waste sites and water resources. Avocations: winter quadrathlons. Office: Cons and Funding Resources LLC 9900 Lorelei Ln NE Albuquerque NM 87111-1246 E-mail: funding_resource@msn.com.

STUDER, LOUIS, priest, religious organization administrator; b. Algona, Iowa, Oct. 24, 1949; s. Paul Otto and Marcella Bertha (West) Studer. BA in Sociology, Lewis U., 1971; MDiv in Theology, Weston Coll. Sch. Theology, 1975; MS in Edn. Adminstrn. and Supervision, So. Ill. U., 1979; PhD in Philosophy of Edn., St. Louis U., 1984. Assoc. pastor St. Patrick's Parish, McCook, Nebr., 1976—77; prin. St. Henry's Seminary, Belleville, Ill., 1977—84; dir. campus ministry U. Minn., Duluth, Minn., 1984—86; dir. Pre-Novitiate Program, Omaha, 1986—89, St. Louis, 1989—91; vocation dir. Oblate House Theology, Chgo., 1991—96; sabbatical program Jerusalem, Israel, Cambridge, Mass., 1996—97; dir. Shrine of Our Lady of the Snows & Missionary Assn. of Mary Immaculate, Belleville, 1997—. Provincial coun. mem. Oblates of Mary Immaculate, St. Paul, 1990—99. Author: (book) The High School Seminary in U.S. Today, 1984. Bd. dirs. Bethany Place, Belleville, 1998—. Home: 442 S De Mazenod Dr Belleville IL 62223 Office: Nat Shrine of Our Lady of the Snows 442 S DeMazenod Dr Belleville IL 62223

STUDER, PATRICIA S. psychologist; b. Ft. Scott, Kans., Sept. 3, 1942; d. Herb E. Studer and Mary Edith (McElroy) Cook; children: Mary Paige, Catherine Ann. BS, Cen. Mo. State U., Warrensburg, 1964; MS, Pittsburg (Kans.) State U., 1975; PsyD, U. Minn., 1999. Lic. psychologist, N.Y.; cert. elem. tchr., Mo. Supervisory tchr. Cen. Mo. State U., 1966; tchr. Consolidated Sch. Dist. 1, Hickman Mills, Mo., 1964-68; clin. psychologist Nevada (Mo.) State Hosp., 1977-80, chief unit psychologist, 1980-83; dir. psychology dept., staff psychologist Raphael Ctr. Hosp., Nevada, 1982-83; exec. dir., psychologist Nevada Counseling Ctr., 1983-91; adj. med. staff Nevada Regional Med. Ctr., 1983-99; exec. dir. Ctr. for Human Devel., Nevada, Mo., 1992-95. Practicum supr. Pittsburg State U., 1980-95; clin. supr. Cmty. Counseling Cons., Cinton, Mo., 1987-88; cons. psychologist Barton County Meml. Hosp., 1993-95, Heartland Hosp., Nevada, 1995, South Oaks Hosp., L.I., 1999-2000, Clin. PsychAssocs., N.Y.C., 2000—; mem. Com. for Drug Free Schs., Nevada, 1988-95, cons. psychologist, 1988-90; cons. psychotherapist Nevada Child Abuse Coun., 1981-82; pvt. practice, Long Island, N.Y., 2001.. Mem. The Nelson-Adkins Mus. Art; mem. Mo. Regional Adv. Coun. on Alcohol and Drug Abuse, 1985-94, v.p., 1988, 92; bd. dirs. Mental Health Adv. Bd., 1993-95, Sch. Health Adv. Com., 1994-95. Mem. APA (assoc.)., Mo. Psychol. Assn., Soroptimist Internat. of Nevada (pres. 1992-93), Rotary Internat., Nevada Vernon County C. of C. Avocations: gardening, interior decorating, environmental issues. Office: 328 Ocean Ave Amityville NY 11701

STUDER, WILLIAM ALLEN, county official; b. Chgo., July 27, 1939; s. William Gotlieb and Annette Elizabeth (Bruzek) S.; m. Donna Barnes Bray, Dec. 26, 1961; children: Scott, Shannon. BS in Indsl. Mgmt., Ga. Inst. Tech., 1961; MS in Guidance and Counseling, Troy State U., 1975, MS in Mgmt., 1978; student, Air War Coll., Maxwell AFB, Ala., 1980-81. Commd. 2d lt. USAF, 1961, advanced through grades to maj. gen., 1989; legis. liaison U.S. Senate, Washington, 1981-83; dir. fighter ops./tng. USAF Hdqrs. Europe, Ramstein AB, Fed. Republic Germany, 1983-84; vice comdr. 10th Tactical Reconnaissance Wing RAF USAF, Alconbury, Eng., 1984-85, comdr. 10th Tactical Reconnaissance Wing RAF Eng., 1985-86, cmdr. 81st Tactical Fighter Wing RAF Bentwaters, Eng., 1986-87, comdr. 316th Air Div/Kaiserslautern Ramstein AB, Fed. Republic Germany, 1987-88, vice comdr. 12th Air Force/U.S. So. Command Bergstrom AFB, Tex., 1988-90, comdr. 13th Air Force Clark AFB, The Philippines, 1990-91; dir. ops. CENTCOM/J-3, MacDill AFB, Fla., 1992-94; ret. USAF, 1994; dir. pub. safety dept. Hillsborough County, Tampa, Fla., 1994—. Decorated D.S.M., Legion of Merit with oak leaf cluster, DFC with three oak leaf clusters, Bronze Star, Air medal with 35 oak leaf clusters; Legion of Honor, Bronze Cross medal (The Philippines). Mem. Daedalians, Quiet Birdmen, Rotary. Avocations: golf, reading. Home: 3301 Bayshore Blvd #1801 Tampa FL 33629-8845 Office: Hillsborough County Pub Safety Dept Tampa FL 33601 E-mail: studerw@hillsboroughcounty.org., studerdm@aol.com.

STUDER, WILLIAM JOSEPH, library educator; b. Whiting, Ind., Oct. 1, 1936; s. Victor E. and Sarah G. (Hammersley) S.; m. Rosemary Lippie, Aug. 31, 1957; children: Joshua E., Rachel Marie. BA, Ind. U., 1958, MA, 1960, PhD (Univ. fellow), 1968. Grad. asst. divsn. libr. sci. Ind. U., 1959-60, reference asst., 1960-61; spl. intern Libr. of Congress, 1961-62, reference libr., sr. bibliographer, 1962-65; dir. regional campus librs. Ind. U., Bloomington, 1968-73, assoc. dean univ. librs., 1973-77; dir. librs. Ohio State U., Columbus, 1977-2000, prof. emeritus libr. sci., 2000—, coord. univ. oral history program, 2001—. Mem. Libr. Svcs. and Constrn. Act Adv. Com. of Ind., 1971-76, Adv. Coun. on Fed. Libr. Programs in Ohio, 1977-85, chmn., 1980-81; adv. coun. Libr. Svcs. and Tech. Act, 1997-99; mem. ARL Office Mgmt. Studies Adv. Com., 1977-81, ARL Task Force on Nat. Libr. Network Devel., 1978-83, chmn., 1981-83, com. on preservation, 1985-88, vice-chmn., 1989-90, chmn., 1991-92, task force on scholarly comm., 1983-87, com. stats. and measurement, 1993-99, chmn., 1997-98; network adv. com. Libr. of Congress, 1981-88; libr. study com. Ohio Bd. Regents, 1986-87; steering com. Ohio Libr. and Info. Network (Ohio Link), 1987-90; vice-chmn. Ctr. Rsch. Librs., 1993-94, chmn., 1994-95, sec., chmn. membership com., 1990-93; adv. coun. Ohio Link Libr., 1990-2000, chmn., 1991-92, policy adv. coun., governing bd., 1991-92. Contbr. articles to profl. jours. Trustee On Line Computer Libr. Ctr. Inc., 1977-78; del. On Line Computer Libr. Ctr. Users Coun., 1983-91; rsch. librs. adv. com. OnLine Computer Libr. Ctr., 1989-95, vice-chmn., chmn.-elect, 1993-94, chmn., 1994-95; bd. dirs. Ohio Network of Librs. Ohionet, 1977-87, chmn., 1980-82, 86-87, treas., 1983-86; mem. Columbia U. Sch. Library Svc. Conservation Programs, vis. com., 1987-90; nat. adv. coun. to commn. on preservation and access, 1989-92; treas. Monroe County (Ind.) Mental Health Assn., 1968-76; budget rev. com. United Way, 1975-77; bd. dirs. Mental Health Assn. Recipient citation for participation MARC Insts., 1968-69; Louise Maxwell award Ind. U., 1978 Mem. ALA, Ohio Libr. Assn. (bd. dirs. 1980-83), Assn. Coll. and Rsch. Librs. (bd. dirs. 1977-81, com. on activities model for 1990, 1981-82, chmn. libr. sch. curriculum task force 1988-89), Acad. Libr. Assn. Ohio, Torch Club (pres. 1993-94), Phi Kappa Phi (pub. rels. officer 1982-83, sec. 1983-85), Phi Eta Sigma, Alpha Epsilon Delta, Beta Phi Mu. Home: 724 Olde Settler Pl Columbus OH 43214-2924 Office: Ohio State U William Oxley Thompson Meml Libr 1858 Neil Ave Columbus OH 43210-1286 E-mail: studer.2@osu.edu.

STUDLEY, JAMIENNE SHAYNE, academic administrator, lawyer; b. N.Y.C., Apr. 30, 1951; d. Jack Hill and Joy (Cosor) Studley; m. Gary J. Smith, July 14, 1984. BA magna cum laude, Barnard Coll., 1972; JD, Harvard U., 1975. Bar: DC 1975, U.S. Dist. Ct. DC 1978. Assoc. Bergson, Borkland, Margolis & Adler, Washington, 1976—80; spl. asst., sec. U.S. HHS, 1980—81; assoc. Weil, Gotshal & Manges, Washington, 1981—83; assoc. dean law sch. Yale U., New Haven, 1983—87; lectr. law, 1984—87; syndicated columnist Am. Lawyer Media, 1990—91; exec. dir. Nat. Assn. for Law Placement, Washington, 1987—90, Calif. Abortion Rights Action League, 1992—93; dep. gen. counsel U.S. Dept. Edn., 1993—99, acting gen. counsel, 1997—99; pres. Skidmore Coll., Saratoga Springs, NY, 1999—. Vis. scholar adj. faculty U. Calif., Berkeley Law Sch., 1992; vis. com. Harvard Law Sch.; bd. dirs. Adirondack Trust Co.; vice chair for program, chair-elect The Annapolis Group, 2001—. Pres. Conn. Women's Ednl. and Legal Fund, Hartford, 1986—87; co-founder Washington Area Women's Found., 1997; founding bd. dirs. Wood Art Collectors; Jacob Javits fellowship bd. U.S. Dept. Edn. Mem.: ABA (commn. on women in the profession 1991—94, chair editl. bd. Perspectives 1991—99, chair coord. coun. legal edn. 1996—97, com. on loan repayment and forgiveness 2001—02), Assn. Colls. and Univs. (bd. dirs.), Nat. Assn. for Ind. Colls. and Univs. (accountability com.), DC Bar Assn., Barnard in Washington (pres. 1977—78), Assn. Alumnae Barnard Coll. (bd. dirs. 1978—81), Phi Beta Kappa. Office: Skidmore Coll 815 N Broadway Saratoga Springs NY 12866-1631

STUDNESS, CHARLES MICHAEL, economist; b. Mpls., Nov. 2, 1935; s. Leo C. and Alma (Mehus) S.; m. Harriet Leah Katz, Oct. 27, 1968; children: Erica, Lisa, Roy. BA, U. Minn., 1957, MA, 1958; PhD in Econs., Columbia U., 1963. Lectr. CCNY, 1961-64, U. Minn., Mpls., 1964-65; economist Fed. Res. Bank N.Y., N.Y.C., 1965-67, N.Y. Stock Exchange, N.Y.C., 1967-68,

Eastern Airlines, N.Y.C., 1968-70, Baker Weeks, N.Y.C., 1970-76, E.F. Hutton, N.Y.C., 1976-79; pres. Studness Rsch., Manhasset, N.Y., 1979—; lectr. Baruch Coll., N.Y.C., 1968-74. Contbg. editor Public Utilities Fortnightly, 1990—. Columnist, Pub. Utilities Fortnightly, 1979—. E-mail: studness@optonline.net.

STUDWELL, WILLIAM EMMETT, librarian, writer; b. Stamford, Conn., Mar. 18, 1936; s. Alfred Theodore and Mary Alice (Baker) S.; m. Ann Marie Stroia, Aug. 28, 1965; 1 child, Laura Ann. BA, U. Conn., 1958, MA, 1959; MLS, Cath. U. Am., 1967. Tech. abstracter Libr. Congress, Washington, 1963-66, asst. editor decimal classification office, 1966-68; head libr. Kirtland C.C., Roscommon, Mich., 1968-70; head/prin. cataloger No. Ill. U., DeKalb, 1970-2000; freelance writer, editor, 2001—. Mem. U.S. Adv. Com. to Chemistry Sects., Universal Decimal Classification, 1968-72; chmn. adv. group Libr. Rsch. Ctr., Urbana, Ill., 1982-84. Author: Chaikovskii, Delibes, Stravinskii, 1977, Christmas Carols, 1985, Adolphe Adam and Leo Delibes, 1987, Ballet Plot Index, 1987 (named One of Outstanding Acad. Books by Choice Mag. 1988-89), Cataloging Books, 1989, Library of Congress Subject Headings, 1990, Opera Plot Index, 1990, Christmas Card Songbook, 1991, Subject Access to Films and Videos, 1992, Popular Song Reader, 1994, Christmas Carol Reader, 1995, National and Religious Song Reader, 1996, Americana Song Reader, 1997, Minor Ballet Composers, 1997, State Songs of the United States, 1997, Publishing Glad Tidings, 1998, College Fight Songs, 1998, Barbershops, Bullets, and Ballads, 1999, Circus Songs, 1999, The End of the Year, 1999, The Classic Rock and Roll Reader, 1999, They Also Wrote, 2000, The Big Band Reader, 2000, The Clandestine Classical Music Reader, 2000, Forward! Forward! Is the Word, 2000, College Fight Songs II, 2001, Cataloging for the New Millennium, 2001, Lest We Forget, 2001, A Fable, A Fantasy, and a Farewell, 2002, The French Violin School, 2002; asst. editor Western Assn. of Map Librs. Info. Bull., 1989-94; editor Music Reference Svcs. Quarterly, 1991-99, Resources in Music History Book Series, 1999—; text editor (Christmas music) The Millennia Collection, 2000—; contbg. editor Technicalities, 1996—; contbr. over 370 articles to profl. jours.; over 540 radio, TV and print media appearances. U.S. expert on Christmas Carols; internat. recognized expert on Am. Coll. fight songs; internat. leader to devel. standardization code for libr. congress subject headings; leading internat. proponent multinat., multicultural and multilingual subject access sys. Named most productive author among librs. in U.S., Coll. and Rsch. Librs. Mag., 1983-87, 93-97, Outstanding Alumnus, Sch. Libr. and Info. Sci., Cath. U. Am., 2002. Mem. Ill. Assn. Coll. and Rsch. Librs. (exec. bd. 1980-85, newsletter editor 1980-85, lifetime achievement award 1992), Ill. Libr. Assn., Librs. for Social Responsibility (editor newsletter 1986-87, bd. dirs. 1986-94). Home: 612 S SR 446 #1B Bloomington IN 47401-5569

STUEBE, DAVID CHARLES, steel products manufacturing company executive; b. Racine, Wis., May 29, 1940; s. Edwin C. Stuebe and Henrietta (Dryanski) Stuebe Tunnell; m. Joy L. Laughlin, Aug. 23, 1986; children: David C., Kelly Ann, Ginger, Kelly Catherine, Jon. BBA, U. Notre Dame, 1962. C.P.A., Ill. Audit mgr. Arthur Andersen, Chgo., 1962-75; v.p.-fin. School Products div. Schering Plough Inc., 1975-76, 80; pres. Arno Adhesives div. Schering Plough Inc., 1976-79; v.p. fin.-adminstrn. Carpetland, Merrillville, Ind., 1980-81; v.p. fin. MSL Industries, Inc., Lincolnwood, Ill., 1981-84, chmn. Oak Brook, 1982—, pres., chief exec. officer, 1984-87, also bd. dirs.; chmn., chief exec. officer Laughlin & Flynn, Inc., Barrington, 1987-88; pres., chief exec. officer Auto Specialties Mfg. Co., Benton Harbor, Mich., 1988—. Vice pres., bd. dirs. Ill. Assn. Retarded Citizens, Chgo., 1971-75 Mem. Ill. Soc. CPA's, Am. Inst. CPA's, Turnabout Mgmt. Assn. Clubs: Met. (Chgo.). Office: Hon Industries Inc 414 E 3rd St PO Box 1109 Muscatine IA 52761-7109 Home: 22620 Forest Ridge Dr Lakeville MN 55044-8004

STUEBING, EDWARD WILLIS, research scientist; b. Cin., Sept. 9, 1942; s. Edward Norman and Ruth Marcella (Glass) S.; m. Mary Ann Brown (div. 1980); children: Barbara Jean, Jennifer Jane. BS with high honors, U. Cin., 1965; PhD, Johns Hopkins U., Balt., 1970. Rsch. scientist U.S. Army Frankford Arsenal, Phila., 1971-1977, U.S. Army, Edgewood R&D Ctr., Aberdeen Proving Ground, Md., 1977—; joint svcs. bus. area mgr. CB Def. Supporting Sci. and Tech., chief scientist for physical scis., team leader aerosol sci. Adj. prof. Drexel U., Phila., 1973-1976. Contbr. articles to profl. jours. Dir. Civic Assn., Kingsville, Md., 1989-92; pres. Gunpowder Valley Conservancy, Md., 1990-94, treas., 1995—; elder Presbyn. Ch., Franklinville, Md., 1993—. Capt. U.S. Army, 1970-71. Recipient Army R&D Achievement award, 1974, 85, medal for Meritorious Civilian Svc., 1984, The Outstanding Fed. Profl. of 1984 award Fed. Exec. Bd., 1984, William H. Walker award, 1989. Mem. Am. Assn. for Aerosol Rsch. (chmn. nat. meeting 1983, dir. 1998—2001), Am. Chem. Soc., Am. Phys. Soc., Phi Beta Kappa, Sigma Xi. Avocations: trombone, sailing. Home: PO Box 233 Aberdeen Proving Ground MD 21010-0233 Office: Attn AMSSB RRT TA Bldg E5951 5183 Blackhawk Rd Aberdeen Proving Ground MD 21010-5424

STUEBNER, ERWIN AUGUST, JR. internist; b. Phila., Oct. 9, 1944; s. Erwin August and Frances Badge (Quinn) S.; m. Jane Sigrid Christensen, Sept. 21, 1968; children: Eric Jay, Andrew Todd, Scott August. AB, Dartmouth Coll., 1966; MD, Northwestern U., Chgo., 1970. Diplomate Am. Bd. Internal Medicine. Intern, resident U. Mich., Ann Arbor, 1970-74; physician Williamstown (Mass.) Med. Assocs., 1976—; chmn. dept. medicine North Adams (Mass.) Regional Hosp., 1991—. Corporator North Adams Regional Hosp., 1992—; bd. dirs. Med. Profl. Mut. Ins. Co., Boston. Fundraising chmn. Campaign for New Athletic Field, Williamstown, Mass., 1995-96. Maj. U.S. Army, 1974-76; trustee No. Berkshire Health Sys., 2002—. Mem. ACP, Am. Heart Assn. (exec. com. 1978-94), Mass. Med. Soc. (trustee 1988-90, 2000—, alt. trustee 1994-2000), Berkshire Dist. Med. Soc. (pres. 1984-86, exec. com. 1982—). Avocations: classical music, hiking, tennis, adventure vacation. Office: Williamstown Med Assn 197 Adams Rd Williamstown MA 01267-2930

STUEBNER, JAMES CLOYD, real estate developer, contractor; b. Phila., Dec. 15, 1931; s. Erwin A. and Frances (Quinn) Stuebner; children: Kathleen, Stephen, James, Susan, Elizabeth. BA, Dartmouth Coll., 1953. Sales engr. Rohm & Haas Co., Phila., 1956-69; pres. Structural Plastics Corp., Mpls., 1961-69; pres., gen. ptnr. Stuebner Properties, 1969—; pres. Northland Inn and Exec. Conf. Ctr., 1988—; CEO Five Star Realty and Devel. Co., Mpls., 1992—, Boone 94 Properties (Sleep Inn Hotel), 1998. Mem. Minn. Conv. Ctr. Commn., St. Paul, 1988; commr. Minn. Econ. Devel. Commn., St. Paul, 1985; bd. dirs. Bach Soc. of Minn., Mpls., 1986—, Minn. Orchestral Assn., Mpls., 1988-91. Sgt. U.S. Army, 1953-55. Mem. Nat. Assn. Office and Indsl. Parks (bd. dirs. Minn. chpt. 1976-85, 81-90, pres. 1978-80, 92-93, nat. pres. 1983-84, v.p. 1981-81, Developer of Yr. award 1987, Minn. Bus. Person of Yr. award 1990, vice chmn. indsl. devel. forum 1996, chmn. 1997). Avocations: sailing, running, singing. Office: Five Star Realty and Devel Co 7000 Northland Dr N Minneapolis MN 55428-1502

STUECK, MAURITA ESTES, civic volunteer, elementary science and ecology educator; b. St. Louis, Aug. 18, 1922; d. Wellborn and Fay (Ostner) Estes; m. Cornelius Frederick Stueck, Oct. 18, 1946 (dec. 1992); children: Linda, Lawrence, Katherine, Sara; m. Joseph E. Burch, 2000. AA, Lindenwood Coll., 1941; AB, Wash. U., St. Louis, 1943. Field dir. Girl Scouts of Kanawha County, Charleston, W.Va., 1943-46; tchr. Springboard to Learning, 1970-77; vol. instr. edn. divsn. Mo. Botanical Gardens, Saint Louis, 1977-2000. Vol. instr. Girl Scouts U.S., St. Louis, 1948-96, leader, dist. chmn. program svcs.; bd. dirs. Springboard to Learning Conf. on Edn., Girl Scouts of Greater St. Louis, Lindenwood U., St. Charles, Mo., 1987-95, Epworth Children's Home, St. Louis, 1983-87, Thompson Ctr., 1993, Maria Ctr., 1980-86, Webster Child Care Ctr., 1996-99, Interfaith Housing Help, Gifted Resource Coun., 1993-97, coord. vol. devel. program, 1985-88; instr. Mo. Bot. Garden, 1976-2000, garden guide, 1975-2001, chmn. guides, 1976-78, chmn., vol. instr., 1990-93; mem. Lindenwood U. bd. dirs., 1983-92, Leadership Ctr. of St. Louis; coord. children's ministries St. Louis so. dist. United Meth. Ch., 1970- 80; trustee St. Paul Sch. Theology, Kansas City, 1996-2002. Recipient Spl. Recognition, Mo. Bot. Garden, 1987, Disting. Alumni Merit award Lindenwood Coll., 1990, Thanks badge Girl Scouts USA, 1976, God and Svc. award United Meth. Ch. Com. for Ch. and Youth Agy. Relationships, 1993, Gold Laurel award Girl Scouts Greater St. Louis, 1995; named Vol. of Yr., Mo. Bot. Garden, 1979. Mem. AAUW (pres. Kirkwood-Webster Groves br. 1975-78, bd. dirs. 1990-94), Wednesday Club of St. Louis, Pi Beta Phi. Avocations: hiking, travel. E-mail: mes73ww@aol.com.

STUEHRENBERG, PAUL FREDERICK, librarian; b. Breckenridge, Minn., Mar. 14, 1947; s. Henry Ernest Frederick and Marian Violet (Sandberg) S.; m. Suzanne Elaine Draper, June 14, 1969 (div. Apr. 1982); m. Carole Lee DeVore, Aug. 1, 1983. BA, Concordia Sr. Coll., 1968; MDiv, Concordia Sem., 1972; STM, Christ Sem., 1974; MA, U. Minn., 1978, PhD, 1988. Asst. libr. U. Minn., Mpls., 1974-82; monographs libr. Yale Divinity Libr., New Haven, 1982-91, div. libr., 1991—; adj. assoc. prof. in theol. lit. Yale Divinity Sch., 1993—. Asst. pastor Christ Meml. Luth. Ch., Plymouth, Minn., 1974-82; adj. pastor Bethesda Luth. Ch., New Haven, 1984—; sec. Luth. Student Found., Mpls., 1978-81. Contbr. articles to profl. jours. Sec. North Haven (Conn.) Libr. Bd., 1989—. Mem. Am. Theol. Libr. Assn., Soc. Bibl. Lit., Am. Acad. Religion, North Haven Meml. Libr. Assn. Home: 280 Bayard Ave North Haven CT 06473-4307 Office: Yale U Div Sch Libr 409 Prospect St New Haven CT 06511-2167 E-mail: paul.stuehrenberg@yale.edu.

STUEMPFLE, ARTHUR KARL, physical science manager; b. Williamsport, Pa., Jan. 5, 1940; s. Arthur Carl and Jeanette Esther (Jacobs) S.; m. Linda Jean Campbell, Mar. 30, 1961; children: Jeffrey, Karl. BS in Physics, Drexel U., 1962; MS in Physics, Johns Hopkins U., 1971. Chief, test/measurement br. U.S. Army Chem. Sch., Ft. McClellan, Ala., 1962-64; physicist Edgewood Arsenal, Aberdeen Proving Ground, Md., 1964-71; rsch. physicist Chem. Systems Lab., 1971-78; chief operational sci. br., rsch. dir. Chem. Rsch., Devel. and Engring. Ctr., 1978-85, chief, physics div. rsch. dir., 1985-92; chief test methodology and program integration, rsch. & tech. dir. Edgewood Rsch., Devel. and Engring. Ctr., 1992-94; dir. ops. rsch. simulation, R & T dir. Edgewood Rsch., Devel., & Engring. Ctr., 1994-95; sr. scientist Optimetrics, Inc., Bel Air, Md., 1996—. U.S. mem. aerosol tech. The Tech. Coop. Program U.S./U.K./Can./Australia, Washington, 1982-95; U.S. chmn. Indsl. Chems. Task Force, Can./U.S./U.K. Coop. Program, Washington, 1994-95; cons. phys. property subcom. Nat. Spray Drift Task Force, Wilmington, Del., 1990; tri-nat. chmn. Can./U.S./U.K. Task Force on Chem-Bio Simulants, 1987-88. Contbr. articles to profl. jours.; patentee in field. Organizing mem. Edgewood Meadows Civic and Improvement Assn., 1990; lay reader, com. chair, cantor, choir mem. Lord of Life Luth. Ch., Edgewood, 1979—; bus. mgr. LC Sewing Sch., Edgewood, 1971-75. Recipient R&D Achievement award U.S. Army, Washington, 1977, Meritorious Civilian Svc. award Dept. Army, Washington, 1986, Meritorious Civilian Svc. with oak leaf cluster award Dept. Army, Washington, 1996, AMC Spl. Features award Army Materiel Command, 1989; W.H. Walker Tech. Leadership award Chem. Rsch., Devel. and Engring. Ctr., 1987, Internat. Tech. Devel. award U.S./U.K./Can. Dept. Def., 1990. Republican. Achievements include research on aerosol and spray dissemination and characterization, on chemical warfare and chemical biological defense technology, mathematical modeling and operations research analyses, on aerosol transport, deposition and environmental fate, on evaporation and persistency, on powder technology, on simulants and simulation, on NBC survivability technology, on domestic preparedness, vulnerability assessment, homeland def. and force protection for CB terrorism incidents, on management of basic and applied research. Home: 2300 Perry Ave Edgewood MD 21040-2808 Office: Optimetrics Inc Ste 209 2107 Laurel Bush Rd Bel Air MD 21015-5203

STUFANO, THOMAS JOSEPH, criminologist, author, inventor; b. Newport, R.I., July 23, 1955; s. Thomas and Zoe Anne (Halsey) S.; 1 child, Christine Anne; m. Rene Ellen Goldfarb, Nov. 10, 1994. BSc in Criminal Justice, Pacific Western U., 1988; PhD in Criminal Justice, Clayton U., 1992; disting. grad., U.S. Air U., 2000; postgrad., Eurotech. Rsch. U., 1997; MBA in Mil. Scis., Touro U., 2001. Legis. rschr. R.I. Ho. of Reps., Providence, 1978-79; sub com. investigator U.S. Ho. of Reps., Washington, 1979-81; law enforcement staff rschr. State of Fla., 1981-88; intelligence officer, cons. U.S. Govt., Washington, 1988-96; CEO, dir. Diversified Intelligence Group, Inc., Coral Springs, Fla., 1989—; exec. dir. Diversified Technologies and System Inc., 1989—. Cons. crime commn. State of Fla., 1986-87, U.S. Govt., Washington, 1990-92, State of R.I., 1979-80; mem. Pres.' Commn. on Aviation Security and Terrorism. Author: Human Element in Business, 1992, Combating Terrorism, 1994, Investigators Pretext Investigation Manual, 1998, BEA Training Manual, 1998; Applied Impact Theory patentee, 1999; contbr. articles to profl. jours. Mem. Rep. Senatorial Inner Circle, Washington, 1992—; instr. ARC, Fla., 1994—; mem. adv. bd. Nat. Civil Def., Washington, 1988—; mem. Presdl. Round Table. Recipient Presdl. Commendation Pres. of U.S., 1988, 91, 94, Commendation U.S. Ho. of Reps. and Senate, 1982, 91, 94, commendation Prime Minister Lady Margaret Thatcher, 1991, Citation R.I. Ho. of Reps., 1980, Gov. of Mass., 1980, Tenn., Fla., Ky., 1990, Commendation U.S. Dept. of State, 1992, Min. Intelligence Security, Eng., 1996, Meritorious Achievement award for global antiterrorism, 1997, 20th Century Achievement award ABI, 1998, Millennium Hall of Fame award, 1998, 500 Leaders of Influence award IBI, 1998. Mem. Air Force Assn., Internat. Narcotic Enforcement Officers Assn., Res. Officers Assn., World Assn. of Investigators, Internat. Assn. Counter Terrorism and Security Profls., USAF/SARCAP (instr. search/rescue command pilot), Aircraft Owners and Pilots Assn., Profl. Assn. of Diving Instrs. (instr., Platnuim Diving award 1989), Am. Shorin Kempo Karate Assn. (5th degree blackbelt), Order of Ky. Cols. Roman Catholic. Avocations: scuba diving, airplane pilot, parachuting, bicycling, karate. E-mail: Intel6Dig@aol.com.

STUFFLEBEAM, DANIEL LEROY, education educator; b. Waverly, Iowa, Sept. 19, 1936; s. LeRoy and Melva Stufflebeam; m. Carolyn T. Joseph; children: Kevin D., Tracy Smith, Joseph. BA, State U. Iowa, 1958; MS, Purdue U., 1962, PhD, 1964; postgrad., U. Wis., 1965. Prof., dir. Ohio State U. Evaluation Ctr., Columbus, 1963-73; prof. edn. Western Mich. U. Evaluation Ctr., Kalamazoo, 1973-99, dir., 1973—; Beula McKee prof. edn. Western Mich. U., 1997—2002, disting. univ. prof., 2002—. Author monographs and 15 books; contbr. chpts. to books, articles to profl. jours. Served with U.S. Army, 1960. Recipient Paul Lazersfeld award Evaluation Rsch. Soc., 1985, Jason Millman award Consortium for Rsch. on Ednl. Accountability and Tchr. Evaluation, 1999. Mem.: Am. Evaluation Assn. Baptist. Office: Western Michigan Univ The Evaluation Ctr Kalamazoo MI 49008-5237 Fax: 616-387-5923. E-mail: daniel-stufflebeam@umich.edu.

STUFFT, WILLIAM DAVID, music educator; b. Somerset, Pa., Oct. 26, 1947; s. William Denton Stufft, Freda Mildred (Daniels) Stufft; m. June Carol Gestine, June 12, 1971; 1 child Carolyn Joy. BS in Music Edn., Indiana U. Pa., 1969, MEd, 1978; postgrad., Alliance Theol. Sem., 1978, U. Pitts., 1979—80. Tchr. band Meyersdale Sch. Dist., Meyersdale, Pa., 1969—78; min. music Tellmadge Alliance Ch., Tallmadge, Ohio, 1978—82; pastor Oakhill Alliance Ch., Warrendlae, Pa., 1982—85; prof. music Toccoa Falls Coll., Toccoa Falls, Ga., 1985—. Musical dir. Toccoa Symphony Orch., Toccoa, Ga., 2001—, player trumpet and aux. percussion, 1989—2001; dir. concert band Toccoa Falls Coll., Toccoa Falls, 1985—. Contbr. Spec 4 U.S. Army, 1970—72. Mem.: Ga. Music Educators Assn., Pa. Music Educators Assn. (pres., pres.-elect 1970—77), Music Educators Nat. Conf. Avocations: woodworking, writing, playing trumpet, composing music. Home: 927 Skyline Dr Toccoa GA 30577 Office: Toccoa Falls College Falls Rd Toccoa Falls GA 30598

STUHAN, RICHARD GEORGE, lawyer; b. Braddock, Pa., July 1, 1951; s. George and Pauline Madeline (Pavlocik) S.; m. Mary Ann Cipriano, Aug. 23, 1975; children: Brendan George, Sara Katherine, Brian Christopher, Caitlin Emily. BA summa cum laude, Duquesne U., 1973; JD, U. Va., 1976. Bar: Va. 1976, D.C. 1977, U.S. Ct. Appeals (D.C. cir.) 1977, U.S. Ct. Appeals (4th cir.) 1977, U.S. Claims Ct. 1979, U.S. Supreme Ct. 1980, U.S. Ct. Appeals (3d cir.) 1981, U.S. Ct. Appeals (11th cir.) 1982, U.S. Dist. Ct. (no. dist.) Ohio 1985, Ohio 1986. Assoc. Arnold & Porter, Washington, 1976-84; of counsel Jones, Day, Reavis & Pogue, Cleve., 1984-86, ptnr., 1987—. Mem. Va. Law Review, 1974-76. Recipient Gold Medal for Gen. Excellence, Duquesne U., 1973, Mem. Order of Coif. Democrat. Roman Catholic. Avocations: tennis, swimming, basketball, home repair. Home: 2865 Falmouth Rd Shaker Heights OH 44122-2838 Office: Jones Day Reavis & Pogue 901 Lakeside Ave Cleveland OH 44114-1190 E-mail: RGSTUHAN@JONESDAY.COM.

STUHL, OSKAR PAUL, scientific and regulatory consultant; b. Dec. 23, 1949; s. Johannes Alexander and Johanna Wilhelmine (Hoelling) S. S. Dipl. Chem., U. Duesseldorf, 1976, Dr.rer.nat., 1978. Tutor Inst. Organische Chemie U. Duesseldorf, 1975-76, sci. assoc., 1976-79; mgr. product devel. Drugofa GmbH, Cologne, Fed. Republic of Germany, 1980; mgr. sci. rels. RJRN, 1981-88, mgr. sci. svcs., 1989-94; co-founder, co-owner WRKM Internat., 1996—. Cons. in field, 1995—. Mem. editl. bd. Beitraege zur Tabakforschung Internat., 1986-96; contbr. articles to profl. jours.; patentee in field. Mem. Duesseldorf Mus. Verein, Verein der Freunde des Hetjens-Museums, Verein der Freunde des Stadtmuseums Duesseldorf, Met. Mus. Art, N.Y.C., Friends Royal Acad. Arts, London, Friends of Tate Gallery, London, Art Soc. of Rheinlande and Westfalen, Gesellschaft der Freunde der Kunstammlung NRW, Gesellschaft der Freunde und Foerderer der Univ. Duesseldorf, Zuercher Kunstgesellschaft, Freundeskreis Theatermuseum, Duesseldorf, Foerderverein NRW-Stiftung, Forum fuer Film, Duesseldorf, Freunde und Foerder der Akademie fuer Kommunikations Design, Duesseldorf, Deutsch-Japanische-Gesellschaft. Mem. AAAS, Gesellschaft Deutscher Chemiker, Gesellschaft Deutscher Naturforscher und Aerzte, Max-Planck-Gesellschaft, Deutsche Gesellschaft fuer Arbeits hygiene, Am. Chem. Soc. (including various divsns.), Chem. Soc. Japan, N.Y. Acad. Scis., Royal Soc. Chemistry, Am. Pharm. Assn., Acad. Pharm. Rsch. and Sci., Internat. Union Pure and Applied Chemistry, Am. Soc. Pharmacognosy, Fedn. Internat. Pharmaceutic, Christlich Demokratische Union, Vereinigung AC Club Duesseldorf, PCL Club (London), KDStV Burgundia-Leipzig Club, Golf Club Velbert. CDU-Mittelstands und Wirtschaftsvereinigung. Roman Catholic. Office: PO Box 140544 D-40075 Düsseldorf Germany

STUHLINGER, ERNST, physicist; b. Niederrimbach, Germany, Dec. 19, 1913; came to U.S., 1946, naturalized, 1955. s. Ernst and Pauline (Werner) S.; m. Irmgard Lotze, Aug. 1, 1950; children: Susanne, Tilman, Hans Christoph. PhD, U. Tuebingen, Germany, 1936. Asst. prof. Technische Hochschule, Berlin, Germany, 1936-41; guidance and control equipment rocket Devel. Center, Peenemuende, Germany, 1943-45; with Guided Missile Devel. Office, Ft. Bliss, Tex., 1946-50; physicist Ordnance Missile Labs., Huntsville, Ala., 1950-56, Army Ballistic Missile Agy., 1956-60; dir. Space Scis. Lab., George C. Marshall Space Flight Center, NASA, Huntsville, Ala., 1960-68; assoc. dir. for sci. George C. Marshall Space Flight Center, NASA, 1968-76; sr. research scientist, adj. prof. U. Ala. at Huntsville, 1976-84; sr. research assoc. Teledyne Brown Engring. Corp., Huntsville, 1984-88; cons. aerospace cos. Vis. scientist Tech. U. Munich, W. Germany, 1978, Max Planck Inst. Nuclear Physics, Heidelberg, 1983-85; cons. Teledyne-Brown Engring., 1984-90. Author: Ion Propulsion for Space Flight, 1964; co-author: Skylab, A Guidebook, 1973, Project Viking, 1976, Aufbruch in Den Weltraum, 1992, Wernher von Braun, Crusader for Space, 1994. Served with German Army, 1941-43, Russian Campaign. Recipient Humboldt prize Tech. U. Munich, 1978, Rainer Bauer award Ala.-Germany Partnership, 2002; induction Ala. Aviation Hall of Fame, 2001. Fellow Am. Astronautical Soc., Am. Rocket Soc. (dir.), AIAA (tech. dir.), Brit. Interplanetary Soc.; mem. Internat. Acad. Astronautics, Von Braun Astron. Soc. (dir.), Austrian Astron. Soc. (hon.), Am. Optical Soc., Deutsche Roentgengesellschaft (hon.), Deutsche Physikalische Gesellschaft, Deutsche Gesellschaft Fuer Luft und Raumfahrt (hon.), Hermann Oberth Gesellschaft (hon.), Sigma Xi. Rsch. cosmic rays, nuclear physics, 1934-41, electric space propulsion, 1947—, studies on manned missions to Mars, 1954—. Home: 3106 Rowe Dr SE Huntsville AL 35801-6151

STUHR, DAVID PAUL, business educator, consultant; b. Ridgewood, N.J., Oct. 10, 1938; s. Edward Philip and Theresa Alma (Cherny) S. B Engring., Yale U., 1960; MS, Rensselaer Poly. Inst., 1962; PhD, NYU, 1972. Research fellow Fed. Res. Bank of N.Y., N.Y.C., 1968-69, cons. economist, 1969-92; assoc. in bus. Columbia U. Grad. Sch. Bus. Adminstrn., 1969-72, asst. prof. fin., 1972-73; assoc. prof. fin. Rutgers U. Grad. Sch. Bus. Adminstrn., Newark, 1973-77, Fordham U., Faculty of Bus., N.Y.C., 1977—, acting dean faculty, 1984-85; assoc. dean Fordham U. Coll. Bus. Adminstrn., Bronx, N.Y., 1980-83, dean, 1983-87; pres. faculty senate Fordham U., 1994-95, assoc. v.p. for acad. affairs, 1995—. Mem. bus. faculty com. Regents Coll., Albany, 1987-97. Contbr. articles to profl. jours. Mem. Exec. bd. Bergen coun. Boy Scouts Am., 1979-95; mcpl. chmn. Ho-Ho-Kus (N.J.) Rep. Com., 1968—; chair fin. com. St. Gabriel the Archangel Ch., Saddle River, N.J., 1986—, trustee Notre Dame School, N.Y.C., 1998—. Mem. Am. Econ. Assn. (life), Am. Fin. Assn. (life), Fin. Mgmt. Assn., Phila. Soc. (founding mem., trustee 1977-80, treas. 1979—). Republican. Roman Catholic. Avocations: backpacking, camping, skiing. Office: Fordham Univ Office of Academic Affairs Bronx NY 10458 E-mail: stuhr@fordham.edu.

STUHR, ELAINE RUTH, state legislator; b. Polk County, Nebr., June 19, 1936; m. Boyd E. Stuhr, 1956; children: Cynthia (Stuhr) Zluticky, Teresa (Stuhr) Robbins, Boyd E., Jr. BS, U. Nebr. Tchr. jr. and sr. vocat. h.s. Nebr. schs.; senator Nebr. Unicameral, Lincoln, 1994—; farmer Bradshaw, Nebr. Former asst. instr. U. Nebr., Lincoln; participant farmer to farmer assignment to Russia with Winrock, Internat., 1993, to Lithuania with Vol. Overseas Coop. Asistance, 1993; former pres. Agrl. Womens Leadership Network; former mem. bd. dirs. Feed Grains Coun., Nebr. Corn Bd.; agrl. adv. com. for Congressman Doug Bereuter. Past pres., bd. dirs. Found. for Agrl. Edn. and Devel.; former mem. exec. com. and bd. dirs. Agrl. Coun. Am.; nat. pres. Women Involved in Farm Econs., state pres.; mem. adv. com. Nebr. Extension Sv.; bd. dirs. Nebr. Family Comty. Leadership Program; past chmn. Nebr. Agrl. Leadership Coun. Office: Nebr State Capitol Dist # 24 Lincoln NE 68509 E-mail: estuhr@unicam.state.ne.us.

STULC, JAROSLAV PETER, surgeon, educator; b. Teplitz, Czechoslovakia, Sept. 14, 1947; came to U.S., 1948; s. Jaroslav Pavel and Emilie Vanca Stulc; m. Diana Susan Minassian, Dec. 27, 189; children: Alexan Christopher, Evan Thomas. BA, Cornell Coll., Mt. Vernon, Iowa, 1969; MD, U. Iowa, 1973; student, U.S. Naval War Coll., Newport, R.I., 1997-98. Diplomate Am. Bd. Surgery. Intern SUNY, Syracuse, 1973-75; resident in surgery Georgetown U., Washington, 1975-80, instr. surgery, 1979-80; instr. surgery, fellow transplant surgery Loyola U., Chgo., 1980-83; fellow surg. oncology Roswell Park Cancer Inst., Buffalo, 1983-85, attending surgeon, 1985-90; asst. prof. surgery SUNY, 1988-91; chief surgery VA Hosp., 1990-91; attending surgeon Trover Clinic Found., Madisonville, Ky., 1991—. Clin. faculty U. Louisville, 1991—; co-dir. Mahr Cancer Ctr., Madisonville, 1992—. Editor Ky. Med. Jour., Physician Focus; contbr. articles and abstracts to publs. Vis. lectr. outreach program Am. Cancer Soc., bd. dirs. Ky. chpt., 1993—. Capt. USNR. Fellow Naval War Coll., R.I., 1997, 98. Fellow ACS (cert. advanced trauma life support), Internat. Coll. Surgeons; mem. AMA, AAAS, Am. Soc. Gastrointestinal Endoscopy, Am. Soc. Abdominal Surgeons, Am. Soc. Clin. Oncology, Soc. Am. Gastrointestinal Surgeons, Nat. Surg. Adjuvant Breast and Bowel Protocl, Ea. Coop. Oncology Group, Iowa Jr. Acad. Sci., Chgo. Assn. Immunologists, Roswell Park Surg. Soc., Buffalo Surg. Soc., Acad. Surg. Rsch., Assn. Acad. Surgery, Adrian Kantrowitz Surg. Rsch. Soc., VFW, Tri Beta. Presbyterian. Home: 1200 College Dr Madisonville KY 42431-9182 Office: Trover Clinic Found 435 N Kentucky Ave Madisonville KY 42431-1768

STULL, DANIEL RICHARD, retired research thermochemist, educator, consultant; b. Columbus, Ohio, May 28, 1911; s. Lucius Walter and Irene Mabel (Haldeman) S.; m. Ruth Louise Keck, Sept. 26, 1936 (dec. 1982); children: Louise Irene Stull Hassman, Richard Walter; m. Mary Morton Lowe, Apr. 28, 1984. BS in Chemistry, Math., Baldwin-Wallace Coll., 1933; PhD in Chemistry, Johns Hopkins U., 1937. Asst. prof. chemistry East Carolina U., Greenville, N.C., 1937-40; rsch. crew leader Dow Chem. Co., Midland, Mich., 1940-50, rsch. tech. expert, 1950-60, dir. thermal lab., 1960-69, rsch. scientist, 1969-76, cons., 1976-77; ret., 1976. Rsch. adv. com. Mfg. Chemists Assn., Washington, 1958-65, NRC rev. bd. Nat. Bur. Stds., Washington, 1959-70; rsch. mem., commr. Internat. Union Pure and Applied Chemistry, 1963-72; printer Hobby Print Shop, Alembic Press, 1954-92; plenary spkr. 50th Calorimetry Conf., Washington, 1995. Author: Fundamentals of Fire and Explosion, 1976; author, editor books Joint Army Navy Airforce Rocket Propulsion Group, 1958-76; co-author: Chemical Thermodynamics of Organic Compounds, 1948-69; contbr. to more than 70 sci. rsch. publs. Fin. chmn. 1st United Meth. Ch., Midland, 1946-56; mem. Cosmos Club, Washington, 1967-72; mem. ch. choir various cmtys., 1928-2002. Recipient Hugh Huffman Meml. award Calorimetry Conf., Ames, Iowa, 1965, Alumni Merit award Baldwin-Wallace Coll., Berea, Ohio, 1968, Book award Rsch. Soc. Am., 1969.

Fellow Am. Inst. Chemists; mem. AAAS, Am. Chem. Soc. (local sect. award 1980), Sigma Xi, Phi Beta Kappa, Phi Lambda Upsilon. Achievements include extensive compilation of vapor pressure data, development of automatic strip chart recorder for platinum resistance thermometry, 1st automatic recording low temperature calorimeter, computer program to calculate thermodynamic functions, thermal equilibria. Home: 441 S Main St Apt 14 Manchester CT 06040-7043

STULL, EVALYN MARIE, artist; b. Hays, Kans., June 7, 1949; d. Harold Kenneth Gossett and Helen Marie Loreg; m. Dennis Eugene Kincaid, Dec. 4, 1967 (div. 1968); children: Pamela Sue Kincaid, Mark Allen Kincaid; m. Kenneth Eugene Stull, Dec. 4, 1973 (div. 1983); children: Daniel Eugene, Carl Andrew. AGS Degree, Morgan C.C., Fort Morgan, Colo. Owner Stull's Kinder Day Care, Fort Morgan, Colo., 1994, Paintings by Evalyn Stull, Chase, Kans., 2001—02. Home: 201 Cedar/PO Box 134 Chase KS 67524

STULL, FRANK WALTER, elementary school educator; b. Easton, Pa., June 4, 1935; s. George Washington and Minnie Elizabeth S.; m. Darlene Joy Hunsicker, Aug. 2, 1958; children: James, Ronald, Wendy. BS, East Stroudsburg State Coll., 1956; MEd, Lehigh U., 1966. Cert. tchr., N.J. Tchr. Korea Heung-Up Bank, Seoul, Korea, 1957-58, Howell Twp. Elem. Sch., Freehold, N.J., 1958-59, Holland Twp. Elem. Sch., Milford, 1959-91. Bd. dirs., sec., treas., mgr. Hunterdon County Sch. Employees Fed. Credit Union, Phillipsburg, N.J., 1969-87, mem. adv. com., 1995; merit badge counselor Boy Scouts Am., 1970-84, cubmaster, 1971-72; treas., mem. Hist. Preservation Commn. Holland Twp., 1993—; bd. govs. Riegel Ridge Cmty. Ctr., 1997-2000; trustee, scholarship coord. C&E Found., 1997—. Recipient Meritorious Svc. award N.J. Credit Union League, 1988, Tchr. Recognition award State N.J. Gov., 1987, Disting. Achievement award for rsch. and preservation of history of Holland Twp. and surrounding areas; named Outstanding Elem. Tchr. Am., 1972; Experienced Tchr. in Geography fellow Pa. State U., 1967. Mem. NEA, Holland Twp. Edn. Assn., Hunterdon County Edn. Assn., N.J. Edn. Assn., Phi Delta Kappa (chartered mem. Zeta Gamma chpt.). Avocations: photography, travel. Home and Office: 806 Rugby Rd Phillipsburg NJ 08865-2033

STULL, SCOTT D. archaeologist; s. Robert Louis and Carol G Stull; m. Laurie C. Hemmings, June 1, 2002. PhD, Binghamton U., 2002—02; degree in mus. studies, Harvard U., 2001. Sr. hist. archeologist Hartgen Archeol. Assoc., Rensselaer, NY, 2000—. Office: Hartgen Archeological Assoc Inc 1744 Washington Ave Ext Rensselaer NY 12144 E-mail: scott@hartgen.com.

STULTS, WALTER BLACK, management consultant, former trade organization executive; b. Hightstown, N.J., Oct. 25, 1921; s. C. Stanley and Nettie M. (Black) S.; m. Ann D. Haynes, June 28, 1947; children: Andrew Haynes, Thomas Stanley. BA, Williams Coll., 1943; MA (Woodrow Wilson fellow), Princeton U., 1949. Teaching asst. Princeton (N.J.) U., 1946-49; legis. asst. to U.S. Senator Robert Hendrickson, Washington, 1949-50; staff dir. U.S. Senate Small Bus. Com., 1950-61; pres. Nat. Assn. Small Bus. Investment Cos., 1961-86; prin. W.B. Stults, Cons., Chapel Hill, N.C., 1979-99. Dir. Pardee & Curtin Lumber Co., Pardee Resources Co., Phila.; chmn. Coun. Small and Ind. Bus. Assns., 1976-81. Pres. Carol Woods Residents Assn.; dir. Carol Woods Retirement Comty., 1995-97, 2001—. With USAAF, 1943-46. Mem. Am. Soc. Assn. Execs., The Exchequer Club, Masons. Congregationalist.

STULTZ, KATHERINE DIANE, genealogical society administrator; b. Bladensburg, Md., Feb. 7, 1945; d. Irvin Ellsworth Hawthorne and Beulah Isabella (Perry) McGaha; m. Franklin Eugene Stultz, Dec. 10, 1977. With SEC, Washington, 1963-85. Compiler: Gleanings from the Records of the Francis Gasch's Sons Funeral Home Prince George's County Maryland 1860-1940, 1996. Records chmn. Prince George's County Geneal Soc., Inc., Bowie, Md., 1990-99, spl. publs. chmn., 1996-99, publs. chmn., 1999; mem. Prince George's County Hist. Soc., Riverdale, Md., St. Mary's County Geneal. Soc., Inc., Leonardtown, Md., Mid-Atlantic Germanic Soc., Kensington, Md., Ind. Hist. Soc., Indpls., Kosciusko County Hist. Soc., Warsaw, Ind., Clarion County Hist. Soc., Clarion, Pa., Clan Donald USA Mid-East Region, Bowie Family Hist. Soc., Abbeville, S.C. Recipient Jane Rousch McCafferty, C.G. award of excellence Prince George's County Geneal. Soc., Inc., 1996, St. George's Day award Prince George's County Hist. Soc., 1997. Republican. Lutheran. Avocations: music, leather craft, genealogy, miscellaneous crafts. Office: Prince Georges County Geneal Soc PO Box 819 Bowie MD 20718-0819

STULTZ, NEWELL MAYNARD, political science educator; b. Boston, June 13, 1933; s. Irving Washburn and Marjorie May (MacEachern) S.; m. Elizabeth Petronella Olckers, Apr. 6, 1958; children: Elliot Andries, Amy Elizabeth. AB, Dartmouth Coll., 1955; MA, Boston U., 1960, PhD, 1965; MA hon., Brown U., 1968. Fulbright exchange scholar U. Pretoria, South Africa, 1955-56; asst. prof. polit. sci. Northwestern U., Evanston, Ill., 1964-65; asst. prof. to prof. polit. sci. Brown U., Providence, 1965—, assoc. grad. dean, 1970-74, assoc. dean of faculty, 1993-98, assoc. provost, 1998-2000. Vis. fellow Yale U.-South African Research Program, 1977; vis. prof. U. South Africa, Pretoria, 1980; James Gathings lectr. Bucknell U., Lewisburg, Pa., 1980 Author: Afrikaner Politics in South Africa, 1974, Who Goes to Parliament?, 1975, Transkei's Half Loaf, 1979, (bibliography) South Africa, 1989, 2d edit., 1993; co-author: South Africa's Transkei, 1967; co-editor: Governing in Black Africa, 1970, 2d edit., 1986 V.p. World Affairs Council R.I., 1983. Served as lt. (j.g.) USN, 1956-59. Fulbright fellow, 1955-56; NDEA grantee, 1959-62; Ford Found. fellow, 1962-64; Rockefeller Found. fellow, 1976-77 Unitarian Universalist. Home: 371 New Meadow Rd Barrington RI 02806-3729 Office: Brown U Dept Polit Sci PO Box 1844 Providence RI 02912-1844 E-mail: newell_stultz@brown.edu.

STUMAN-JONES, DOROTHY LUCILLE, civic leader; b. Marianna, Fla., Mar. 30, 1924; d. Thomas Otto and Shandora (Tharpe) Temples; m. Robert B. Stuman Jr., June 17, 1944 (dec. 1980); children: Barbara Ann, Robert B., Cathy Amanda; m. J. Arthur Jones, Aug. 22, 1987 (dec. May 1988). Student, Massey Bus. Coll., 1945-47, Alverson Bus. Coll., 1947-48, Jefferson State Jr. Coll., 1967-68. Dept. head R.P. McDavid & Co., Birmingham, Ala., 1944-45; sec. to pres. Armour & Co., 1945-49; free-lance interior decorator, 1950—; exec. sec. CLP Corp., doing bus. as McDonald's, 1973—. Contbr. short stories to Nat. Clubwoman, (best in category award for Life of Modern Woman). Active Women's Com. Ala. Symphony Orch.; program chmn. Camelia Scholarship Luncheon; pub. chmn. Birmingham Beautification Bd., 1986-87, plant dig chmn., garden club chmn., litter chmn., 1980-88, chmn., 1988—; vol. East End Hosp.; supt. jr. dept. Sunday sch.; membership chmn. Decorator Showhouse Com.; pres. Women's Missionary Union, 1961-65. Mem. Bus. and Profl. Women's Orgn. (dist. dir. 1985-86, pres. Huffman chpt.,1987—), Women's C. of C. (1st v.p. 1987—, pres. 1988—), VFW, LWV, Iris Soc. Thalian Lit. Club. Clubs: Floradora Garden (pres. 1987—). Lodges: Shriners, Order of Eastern Star (grand chpt. com. mem., worthy matron two terms). Republican. Avocations: china painting, flower arranging, interior decorating. Home: 245 Roebuck Dr Birmingham AL 35215-7752 Office: CLP Corp 124 Summit Pky Birmingham AL 35209-4708

STUMBLES, JAMES RUBIDGE WASHINGTON, multinational service company executive; b. Harare, Zimbabwe, Aug. 13, 1939; came to U.S., 1980; s. Albert R.W. and Mary Dallas (Atherstone) S.; m. Vyvienne Clare Shaw, Dec. 19, 1964; children: Christopher, Timothy, Jonathan. BA, U. Cape Town, Republic of South Africa, 1960, LLB, 1962. Adv. Supreme Ct. of S. Africa. Mng. dir. Rennies Confirming & Fin. Pty. Ltd., Johannesburg, 1971-72; group mng. dir., chmn. subsidiaries Pritchard Svcs. Group South Africa, Pty., Ltd., 1972-80; dir. security, pres. subs. Pritchard Svcs. Group Am., Columbus, Ohio, 1980-83; exec. v.p., pres. subs. Mayne Nickless/ Loomis Corp., Seattle, 1984-87; v.p. N.W. Protective Svc. Inc., 1987-91, pres., CEO, 1991—, N.W. Protective Svc.-Imprimis, Inc., Spokane, 1991—, Northwest Protective Svc. Inc.-Oreg., Portland, 1992—. Chmn. Clarington Inc., 1996—, Washington Law Enforcement Exec. Forum, 1999-2001. Sec. Boy Scouts, Johannesburg, 1978-80. Mem. Rand Club, Rainier Club, Rotary, Kiwanis, Round Table (officer 1969-80). Avocations: tennis, boating, fishing. Office: NW Protective Svc Inc 2700 Elliott Ave Seattle WA 98121-1189 *Personal philosophy: Love thy God, love thy neighbor, and be true unto thyself.*

STUMBO, JANET LYNN, state supreme court justice; b. Prestonsburg, Ky. d. Charles and Doris Stanley Stumbo; m. Ned Pillersdorf; children: Sarah, Nancee, Samantha. BA, Morehead State U., 1976; JD, U. Ky., 1980. Bar: Ky. 1980, W.Va. 1982. Staff atty. to Judge Harris S. Howard Ky. Ct. Appeals, 1980—82; asst. county atty. Floyd County, 1982—85; ptnr. Turner, Hall & Stumbo, P.S.C., 1982—88; prosecutor Floyd Dist. Ct. and Juvenile Ct.; ptnr. Stumbo, DeRossett & Pillersdorf, 1989; judge Ct. Appeals, Ky., 1989—93, Supreme Ct. of Ky., 1993—. Named to Morehead State U. Alumni Assn. Hall of Fame, 1990, U. Ky. Coll. Law Alumni Hall of Fame, 1999; recipient Justice award, Ky. Women Advocates, 1991, Outstanding Just award, 1995, Bull's Eye award, Women in State Govt. Network, 1995. also: 311 N Arnold Ave Ste 502 Prestonsburg KY 41653-1279

STUMM, BRIAN J. mechanical engineer, researcher; b. Freeport, N.Y., Dec. 19, 1968; s. Hugo and Therese Stumm; m. Janet W. Shazer, Aug. 29, 1998. BS in Mech. Engring., Rochester Inst. Tech., 1992, MS in Mech. Engring., 1993. Devel. engr. project AMP, Harrisburg, Pa., 1993-97, mgr. tech., 1997-98; dir. tech. AMP/Tyco, 1998-99; mgr. tech. Tyco Electronics, 1999-2000; dir. product rsch. ETCO, Inc., Sarasota, Fla., 2000—. Trustee Lymphoma and Leukemia Soc., Harrisburg, 1999-2000, Tampa, Fla., 2000—. Mem. ASME, IEEE, NSPE, Internat. Inst. Connecter and Interconnection Tech., Fla. Engring. Soc., N.Y. Acad. Sci., Kappa Delta Rho. Republican. Lutheran. Achievements include inventor/patentee Scrap Handly in Blanky Die. Avocations: golf, sailing, reading, model railroads. Office: ETCO Inc Ste 12 6300 Tower Ln Sarasota FL 34240

STUMP, ANN LOUISE B. nurse; b. Rochester, Minn., Feb. 24, 1952; d. Andrew Owen and Barbara Carol (Kolden) Balerud; m. Brian William Stump, Dec. 28, 1973; children: Kevin, Julia. BSN, Pacific Luth. U., 1974. RN, Tex.; cert. BLS, ACLS. Critical care staff nurse, relief supr., head nurse Providence/Summitt Hosp., Oakland, Calif., 1974-79; critical care staff, charge nurse St. Joseph Hosp., Albuquerque, 1979-81; labor and delivery staff nurse Presbyn. Hosp., 1981-83; thoracic, medical and surgical ICU staff, charge nurse Presbyn. Hosp. of Dallas; clin. nurse III, preceptor Presbyn. Hosp., Dallas, 1983-93; staff nurse, critical care nurse Los Alamos (N.Mex.) Med. Ctr., 1993-97, relief care coord., discharge planner, 1996; staff nurse, relief charge nurse, neuro M/S ICU Presbyn. Hosp., Dallas, 1997—. Mem. documentation com., Presbyn. Hosp., Dallas, preceptor, 2001—. Home: 1605 Pembroke Ln Mc Kinney TX 75070-4279 Office: 8200 Walnut Hill Ln Dallas TX 75231-4426 E-mail: stump1@attbi.com.

STUMP, BOB, congressman; b. Phoenix, Apr. 4, 1927; s. Jesse Patrick and Floy Bethany (Fields) S.; children: Karen, Bob, Bruce. BS in Agronomy, Ariz. State U., 1951. Mem. Ariz. State Ho. of Reps., 1957-67, Ariz. State Senate, 1967-76, pres., 1975-76; mem. U.S. Congress from 3d Ariz. dist., Washington, 1977—; vice chmn. nat. security com.; chmn. vets. affairs com. With USN, 1943-46. Mem. Am. Legion, Ariz. Farm Bur. Republican. Seventh-day Adventist. Office: Ho of Reps 211 Canon HOB Washington DC 20515-0001 : 401 West Washington St. Suite 280 SPC 9 Phoenix AZ 85003*

STUMP, CHRISTINE JO, daycare provider; b. Warsaw, Mar. 11, 1966; d. Robert Cecil Stump Jr. and Linda Kay (Alexander) Harris. Cert. food store security, Cornell U., 1985; student, Ind. U., 1991, 92. Mgr. frozen foods Marsh Supermarket, Warsaw, 1984-90; daycare provider, 1991—. Author: The Kitten Who Couldn't Grow, 1994, The Christmas Spider, 1996, Gilbert the Goose, 1996, Murphy the Magical Digger, 1999. Mem.: Internat. Bank Note Soc., Soc. of Paper Money Collectors, Sierra Club, Elkhart Coin Collectors, Am. Forests, Am. Numis. Assn., Ind. Farm Bur., U.S. Humane Soc., Internat. Myeloma Found., World Wildlife Fund. Republican. Avocations: travel, reading, pets, home repairing, fishing. Home and Office: 2041 S Blue Spruce Ct Warsaw IN 46580-7344 E-mail: erohrer@kconline.com.

STUMP, D. MICHAEL, librarian; b. Santa Monica, Calif., Dec. 22, 1947; s. H. Walter and Margaret June (Stetler) S. BA in History, Pasadena Coll., 1971; MLS, U. So. Calif., 1977. Library asst. Calif. Inst. Tech., Pasadena, 1970-74; librarian 1st Bapt. Ch. of Van Nuys, Calif., 1974-81, 82-87, Laurence/2000, Van Nuys, 1981-82, Van Nuys Christian Coll., 1975-76, Hillcrest Christian Sch., Granada Hills, Calif., 1987—. Asst. scoutmaster San Fernando coun. Boy Scouts Am., 1970-73. Named to Outstanding Young Men Am., U.S. Jaycees, 1976. Mem. ALA, Am. Assn. Sch. Librs., Evang. Ch. Libr. Assn. (So. Calif. chpt.). Republican. Baptist. Office: Hillcrest Christian Sch 17531 Rinaldi St Granada Hills CA 91344-3399 E-mail: mstump@hillcrestchristianschool.org.

STUMP, E. GORDON, association administrator; m. Marie Stump; children: Scott, Traci Wills. B of Mech. Engring., U. Akron. V.p. automotive engring. Michelin Tire Corp., ret.; commd. 2d lt. USAF, 1965, advanced through grades to, 1969; with Ohio Air N.G., 1970—73, Wolverine State's N.G., Mich., 1973—91, adj. gen., 1991—; v.p. air N.G. Assn. U.S., 1996—98, pres., 1998—. Office: NG Assn of US 1 Massachusetts Ave NW Washington DC 20001*

STUMP, EARL SPENCER, psychologist; b. Parkersburg, W.Va., Dec. 12, 1943; s. Amos Earl Stump and Harriet Gertrude (White) Stiff; m. Ann Chadwick, Sept. 30, 1967 (div. 1985); 1 child, Andrea Renee; m. Joan Irene Croft, Sept. 28, 1985. BA, Ohio State U., 1966; MS in Corrections, Xavier U., 1971; PhD, Ohio U., 2000. Lic. psychologist, Ohio, profl. clin. counselor; cert. rehab. counselor. Psychiat. aide Harding Hosp., Worthington, Ohio, 1965-67; psychology trainee Athens (Ohio) State Hosp., 1966-67; psychologist Ohio Dept. Rehab. and Correction, Columbus, 1967-97; supr. psychology and clin. dir. Chillicothe (Ohio) Correctional Inst., 1977-97. Pvt. practice psychology Columbus Mental Health Clinic, Columbus, 1976-77; instr. psychology Hocking Tech. Coll., Chillicothe, 1973-78; adj. prof. Ohio U., Athens, 2001; psychologist Scioto Point Valley Mental Health Ctr., Chillicothe; instr. clin. pathology, Athens, Ohio, 2001. Mem.: ACA, APA, Nat. Rehab. Assn., Ohio Assn. for Treatment Sexual Abusers. Home: 15 N May Ave Athens OH 45701-1817 E-mail: estump@eurekanet.com.

STUMP, JOHN EDWARD, veterinary anatomy educator, ethologist; b. Galion, Ohio, June 3, 1934; s. Clarence Willard and Mabel Katherine (Pfeifer) S.; m. Patricia Anne Auer, Aug. 7, 1955; children— Karen, James. D.V.M. summa cum laude (Borden award for acad. excellence 1958), Ohio State U., 1958; PhD, Purdue U., 1966. Pvt. practice vet. medicine, Bucyrus, Ohio, 1958-61; mem. faculty Purdue U., West Lafayette, Ind., 1961-91, prof. vet. anatomy, 1976-91, prof. emeritus vet. anatomy, 1991; vis. prof. dept. physiol. scis. Sch. Vet. Medicine, U. Calif.-Davis, fall 1980; vis. prof. Coll. Vet. Medicine, Tex. A&M U., spring 1981. Recipient Autotutorial Excellence award Student AVMA, 1974, Amoco Found.-Purdue undergrad. teaching award, 1979, Outstanding Tchr. award Purdue U. Alumni Found., 1978, Norden Disting. Tchr. award Purdue U., 1977; named Outstanding Tchr. Freshman Vet. Students, Purdue U., 1987. Mem. AVMA, Ind. Vet. Med. Assn., World Assn. Vet. Anatomists, Am. Assn. Vet. Anatomists (pres. 1977-78), Am. Assn. Anatomists, Am. Vet. Soc. Animal Behavior, Ind. Acad. Sci., Sigma Xi, Phi Zeta, Gamma Sigma Delta. Clubs: Tecumseh Kiwanis (pres. 1973). Republican. Presbyterian.

STUMP, JOHN SUTTON, retired lawyer; b. Clarksburg, W.Va., Aug. 7, 1929; s. John Sutton and Helen (Mannix) S.; m. Elaine Claire Scammahorn, Sept. 14, 1968; children— John Sutton IV, James Felix. Student, Washington and Lee U., 1946-47, LL.B., 1957; BS in Commerce, U. N.C., 1951. Bar: W.Va. 1957, Va. 1957, D.C. 1983. Assoc. Jackson, Kelly, Holt & O'Farrell, Charleston, W.Va., 1957-58, Boothe, Dudley, Koontz & Boothe, Alexandria, Va., 1958-61, Boothe, Dudley, Koontz & Blankingship, Fairfax and Alexandria, 1962-63; ptnr. Boothe, Dudley, Koontz, Blankingship & Stump, 1963-71, Boothe, Prichard & Dudley, 1971-87, McGuire, Woods, Battle & Boothe LLP, 1987-99. Served to lt. comdr. USNR, 1951-54, 61-62. Fellow Am. Coll. Trial Lawyers; mem. Am. Law Inst. Home: 8329 Weller Ave Mc Lean VA 22102-1717 Office: 1750 Tysons Blvd Mc Lean VA 22102-4208

STUMP, M. PAMELA, sculptor; b. Detroit, July 8, 1928; d. Clarence Homer S. and Gladys Greening Bogue; m. David Everet Walsh, Aug. 1950 (div. 1975); children: Kimberly Klaerr, Sara Greening Walsh Munro, John Klaerr II; m. Richard Taylor White, March, 1989. B of Design, U. Mich., 1950, M of Design, 1951. Educator Ann Arbor (Mich.) Adult Edn., 1950-51, Saginaw (Mich.) Mus. Sch., 1963-68, Birmingham (Mich.) Bloomfield Art Assn., 1969, Washtenaw C.C., Ypsilanti, Mich., 1968-69, Cranbrook Ednl. Cmty., Bloomfield Hills, 1969-90. One-woman shows include Cranbrook Kingswood, Bloomfield Hills, 1969-90, Mich. Women's Hist. Ctr. & Hall of Fame, Lansing, 1994, Swann Gallery, Detroit, 1997; exhibited in group shows at Cranbrook Kingswood, 1950, 70, 87, City Art Mus., St. Louis, 1951, Terry Art Inst., Miami, Fla., 1951, Temple Israel, Detroit, 1951, 58, Ceceile Gallery, N.Y.C. (3rd prize), 1956, Pa. Acad. Fine Arts, Phila., 1958, Horace H. Rackham Sch. Grad. Studies, Detroit, 1960, Detroit Artists Market, 1961, R and R Robinson Gallery, Naples, Fla., 1962, Rubiner Gallery, West Bloomfield, Mich., 1963, Mich. Fine Arts Competition (Juror's award), 1983, 87, Slusser Gallery, U. Mich., 1989, Outdoor Sculpture II, III, Southfield, Mich., 1990, 91, N.Y. Acad. Scis., N.Y.C., 1991, Oakland U., 1991-92, Urban Park, Detroit, 1991, 92, Arc Gallery, Chgo., 1992, 1 Heritage Place, Southgate, Mich., 1993, Art Ctr., Sarasota, Fla.; prin. works include courtyard sculpture Kingswood Sch., steel sculpture Sister City, Tokushima, Japan, 10 bronze sculptures for Cranbrook Schs., Bloomfield Hills, Civic Ctr., Saginaw, bronze fountain at Presbyn. Ch., Grosse Ile, Mich, bronze sculpture of history of U. of Mich. Women, Ann Arbor, Mich. Bell Telephone Co., Saginaw, bronze sculpture at Providence Hosp., Southfield, meml. for poet T. Roethke Saginaw Valley State U., bronze sculpture at First Presbyn. Ch., Pompano Beach, Fla., Rochester Hills Libr., Saginaw Mus., Western Mich. U., Kalamazoo, numerous others. Mem. Emily's List, Planned Parenthood. Mem. ACLU, NOW, LWV, Nat. Assn. Women Artists, Nat. Mus. Women in Arts (charter), Detroit Artist Market, Detroit Inst. Arts Founders Soc., Internat. Sculptors. Avocations: reading, writing. Home: 19629 Parke Ln Grosse Ile MI 48138-1024 E-mail: mpamelastump@gatecom.com.

STUMP, PAMELA FERRIS, music educator; b. Roanoke, Va., May 1, 1955; d. Leo George and Virginia Belle (Garst) Ferris; m. John Gregg Stump, Sept. 20, 1975; children: John Jr., Matthew Todd, Carrie Michelle. BA in Music, Hollins Coll., 1991, MA, 1996. Cert. music tchr., Va. Pvt. piano tchr., Fincastle, Va., 1976. Organist Wheatland Luth. Ch., Buchanan, Va., 1981—, coun. mem., 1996-97, dir. children's choir, 1993—; pres., part-owner Tinkerview Swim Club Inc., Daleville, Va., 1992—; sec., part-owner Fincastle Motors Inc., 1996—, Fincastle Mulch and Stone, 1996—; instr. in music history Dabney Lancaster C.C., Clifton Forge, Va., 1997—; substitute music tchr. William Clark Middle Sch., Fincastle, 1996. Chmn. Va. Fedn. Music Clubs Festival, Roanoke, 1992-97; bd. dirs. Va. Luth. Homes Aux./Brandon Oaks, Roanoke, 1990-96; chapel and music vol. Brandon Oaks Health Ctr., Roanoke, 1990-96; chmn. ways and means Troutville (Va.) Elem. Sch. PTA, 1994-95. Anne Jett Rogers scholar Roanoke Symphony Assn., 1990, Dorminy Music scholar Hollins Coll., 1990. Mem. Roanoke Valley Music Tchrs. Assn. (pres. 1987-90), Va. Music Tchrs. Assn. (chmn. high sch. concerto 1990-92), Music Tchrs. Nat. Assn., Thursday Morning Music Club, Order Eastern Star. Avocations: swimming, computers, music. Home: 310 Blue Bird Ln Fincastle VA 24090-3201 Office: Dabney Lancaster CC Clifton Forge VA 24422

STUMP, PETER LEE, environmental engineer; b. Cleve., Mar. 26, 1947; s. Alvin H. and Velma M. S.; m. Margaret A. Stump, May 25, 1968; 1 child, Megan D. Stump. AAS in Machine Design, Joliet (Ind.) Jr. Coll., 1967; BS in Environ. Engring., U. Ill., Chgo., 1985. Registered profl. engr., Ill., Ga. Draftsman, designer Argonne (Ill.) Nat. Lab., 1967-72; environ. engr. Environ. Tech. Assessment Inc., Oak Brook, Ill., 1973-77, RJN Environ. Assocs., Wheaton, 1977-80, ETA Engring., Westmont, 1981-83; evaluator Inst. Nuc. Power Operations, Atlanta, 1984-94; mgr., support svcs. Cobb County Water Sys., Marietta, Ga., 1995-96; mgr. br. office RJN Group, Norcross, 1997—. Bd. dirs. Capital City Ballet, Roswell, Ga., 1996—, pres., 1997-98; mem. Atlanta Ballet Guild, 1988-96. With U.S. Army, 1968-70. Mem. Ga. Water and Pollution Control Assn. (chmn. scholarship com.). Avocations: sailing, model ship building, sports cars, computers.

STUMP, RICHARD CARL, environmental services administrator, consultant; b. Reading, Pa., Aug. 14, 1952; s. Richard Carl Stump and Jean Alice Peters; m. Brenda Lee Roughton, Jan. 11, 1974; children: Richard, Nathan, Jonathan. Grad. high sch., Muhlenberg, Pa. Cert. radon testing specialist. Lab. dir. Suburban Water Testing Labs., Temple, Pa., 1978—; pres. Suburban Property Inspections, Inc., 1996—. Cons. to various news media and pubs. of books and mags. on drinking water issues; expert witness. Mem. Am. Water Works Assn., Am. Assn. Radon Scientists and Technologists, Pa. Assn. Accreditation Environ. Labs., Am. Chem. Soc., Aircraft Owners and Pilots Assn. Avocations: amateur radio, aviation, private pilot. Office: Suburban Water Testing Labs 4600 Kutztown Rd Temple PA 19560-1548

STUMPE, WARREN ROBERT, county official, retired scientific, engineering and technical services company executive; b. Bronx, N.Y., July 15, 1925; s. William A. and Emma J. (Mann) S.; children: Jeffrey, Kathy, William. BS, U.S. Mil. Acad., 1945; MS, Cornell U., 1949; MS in Indsl. Engring, N.Y. U., 1965; grad., Command and Gen. Staff Coll., 1972, Army War Coll., 1976; PhD (hon.), Milw. Sch. Engring., 1982. Registered profl. engr., N.Y., Fla., Wis. Commd. 2d lt., C.E. U.S. Army, 1945, advanced through grades to capt., 1954; with (65th Engr. Bn.), 1945-48; asst. prof. mechanics U.S. Mil. Acad., 1951-54; resigned, 1954; from capt. to col. Res., 1958-79; dep. gen. mgr., gen. engring. div. AMF, Stamford, Conn., 1954-63; exec. v.p. Dortech, Inc., 1963-69; dir. systems mgmt. group Mathews Conveyor div. REX, Darien, Conn., 1969-71; dir. research and devel. Rexnord, Inc., Milw., 1971-73, v.p. corp. research and tech., from 1973, v.p. bus. devel. sector, 1981-83, v.p., chief tech. officer, 1983-86; pres. Rexnord Techs., 1986-87; v.p. Radian Corp., 1987—90; civilian aide to sec. army for State of Wis., 1981-85; alderman City of Mequon, 1994—97, pres. coun., 1996—97, county supr., 1998—. Mem. adv. bd. technology transfer program U. Wis.-Whitewater. Contbr. articles to profl. jours. Founder, pres. No. Little League, Stamford, 1965-69; pres. Turn of River Jr. High Sh. PTA, 1967-68; vice chmn. for Wis. Dept. Def., Nat. Com. Employer Support Guard and Res.; bd. regents Milw. Sch. Engring.; mem. liaison coun. Coll. Engring., U. Wis., also mem. indsl. adv. coun.; mem. adv. coun. Marquette U.; mem. Wis. Gov.'s Task Force on Energy, Coun. Great Lakes Govs.' Regional Econ. Devel. Commn., 1987-88; bd. dirs. MRA-Inst. Mgmt., Inc. Mem. Am. Water Pollution Control Fedn., Indsl. Rsch. Inst. (pres., dir.), Wis. Assn. Rsch. Mgrs. (founder), West Point Soc. Wis., Tau Beta Pi, Phi Kappa Phi. Clubs: Wis., Ozaukee Country.

STUMPF, BERNHARD JOSEF, physicist; b. Neustadt der Weinstrasse, Rhineland, Germany, Sept. 21, 1948; came to U.S., 1981; s. Josef and Katharina (Cervinka) S. Diploma physics, Saarland U., Saarbrucken, West Germany, 1975, Dr.rer.nat., 1981. Rsch. asst. physics dept. Saarland U., Saarbrucken, 1976-81; rsch. assoc. Joint Inst. Lab. Astrophysics, U. Colo., Boulder, 1981-84; instr. physics, physics dept. NYU, N.Y.C., 1984-86, asst. rsch. scientist Atomic Beams Lab., 1984-85, assoc. rsch. scientist Atomic Beams Lab., 1985-86; vis. assoc. prof. physics dept. U. Windsor (Ont., Can.), 1986-88; assoc. prof. physics dept. U. Idaho, Moscow, 1988—. Chmn. Conf. on Atomic and Molecular Collisions in Excited States, Moscow, 1990. Contbr. articles to profl. jours. German Sci. Found. postdoctoral fellow U. Colo., 1981-83. Mem. AAUP, German Phys. Soc., Am. Phys. Soc., Am. Chem. Soc., Optical Soc. Am. Home: 825 W C St Moscow ID 83843-2108 Office: U Idaho Dept Physics Moscow ID 83844-0903 E-mail: bjstumpf@uidaho.edu.

STUMPF, DAVID ALLEN, pediatric neurologist; b. L.A., May 8, 1945; s. Herman A. and Dorothy F. (Davis) S.; children: Jennifer F., Kaitrin E.; m. Elizabeth Dusenbery, Feb. 2, 1989; children: Todd Coleman, Shilo Walker. BA, Lewis and Clark Coll., 1966; MD cum laude, PhD, U. Colo., 1972. Pediatric intern Strong Meml. Hosp., Rochester, N.Y., 1972-73, resident, 1973-74; resident in neurology Harvard Med. Sch., Boston, 1974-77; dir. pediatric neurology U. Colo. Health Sci. Ctr., Denver, 1977-85; chief neurology Children's Meml. Hosp., Chgo., 1985-89; chmn. neurology, Benjamin and Virginia T. Boshes prof. Northwestern U., 1989-98, prof. neurology and pediatrics, 1999—; pres. and CEO Oyxis, LLC, 1999—. Mem. sci. adv. com. Muscular Dystrophy Assn., 1981-87; bd. dirs. North-Western Meml. Corp., Chgo. Mem. editl. bd. Neurology, 1982-87; contbr. articles to sci. jours. Recipient Lewis and Clark Coll. Disting. Alumni award, 1991; NIH grantee, 1979-84; Muscular Dystrophy Assn. grantee, 1977-89; March of Dimes grantee, 1983-85. Fellow Am. Acad. Neurology; mem. Child Neurology Soc. (counsellor 1982-84, pres. 1985-87), Am. Neurol. Assn., Am. Pediatric Soc., Soc. Pediatric Rsch., Internat. Child Neurology Assn. (v.p. 1998—). Presbyterian. Office: 540 Judson Ave Evanston IL 60202-3084 Mailing: Northwestern U Dept Neurology Abbott Hall 710 N Lakeshore Dr Chicago IL 60611-3006 Office Fax: 800-701-9821. E-mail: david@stumpf.org.

STUMPF, EARLWAYNE SCHWARZE, actor, advertising executive; b. Red Bud, Ill., Dec. 7, 1951; s. Earl William and Ardell Hulda (Schwarze) S.; m. Jane Ellen Flath, Sept. 21, 1990; 1 child, Ethan Wayne. BA in Speech and Mass Communications, So. Ill. U., Edwardsville, 1973. Film editor Sta. KMOX-TV, St. Louis, 1973-75, producer, program host, 1973-86, news writer, video editor, 1975-77; writer Gardner Advt., 1977, Kenrick Advt., St. Louis, 1978-83; pres., comml. actor ESSINC Communications, 1983—. Consumer media cons. St. Louis Dist. Dairy Council, 1980-87. Writer, dir.: (TV info. comml.) Salute to American Agriculture, 1982 (Emmy award 1982), (radio comml. series) Banvel Players, 1983 (Nat. Agri-Mktg. Assn award 1983); writer, producer (radio comml. series) Land O' Lakes Players, 1983. Mem. NATAS, St. louis-Nat. Agri-mktg. Assn. (pres. 1983), St. Louis Agri-Bus. Club (bd. dirs., pres. 1995-96), Sports Car Club Am. (bd. dirs.), Porsche Club Am. (bd. dirs.). Republican. Lutheran. Avocation: sports car construction and racing. Office: ESSINC Communications PO Box 510109 Saint Louis MO 63151-0109 E-mail: essescom@aol.com.

STUMPF, HEINRICH J. psychometrician, research consultant; b. Cologne, Germany, Dec. 10, 1951; came to U.S., 1991; s. Friedrich Hubert and Johanna Luise (Bauer) Stumpf; m. Doris Elisabeth Hoffmann, May 10, 1990. Diploma in Psychology, U. Bonn, Germany, 1975, PhD, 1978. Sci. employee German Nat. Scholarship Found., Bonn, Germany, 1978-91; sr. rsch. assoc. Ctr. for Talented Youth, Johns Hopkins U., Balt., 1991-95; rsch. cons. Ctr. for Talented Youth Johns Hopkins U., 1996—. Contbr. to German Encyclopedia of Psychology. Mem. German Psychol. Assn., Am. Psychol. Soc., N.Y. Acad. Scis. Achievements include: sr. author of the Cube Perspective Test of Spatial Ability, 1983, the German Personality Research Form, 1985 and the Spatial Test Battery of the Ctr. for Talented Youth; contbr. to German Ency. Psychology; contbr. about 50 scientific publications. Office: Ctr for Talented Youth 2701 N Charles St Baltimore MD 21218-4351 E-mail: StumpfHJ@aol.com.

STUMPF, MARY RITA, administrator, executive director; b. Bklyn., Apr. 15, 1951; d. George Valentine and Rita Josephine (Kunz) S. Nursing Diploma, St. Mary's Hosp. Sch. Nursing, 1971; BSN, SUNY, Albany, 1980; MSN, Hunter Coll., 1982; PhD in Health Adminstrn., LaSalle U., 1995. RN, N.Y.; cert. nurse adminstr. advanced. Staff nurse St. Mary's Hosp., Bklyn., 1971-73, head nurse, 1973-78; clin. nurse II Meml. Sloan Kettering Inst., N.Y.C., 1978-82; adminstrv. supr. St. Mary's Hosp., Bklyn., 1983-85, assoc. dir. nursing, 1985-94; exec. dir. CMC Profl. Registry, Inc., Queens, N.Y., 1994-2001; asst. v.p. New Island Hosp., Bethpage, 2001—. Proctor, advisor St. Joseph's Coll., Windham, Maine, 1990-94; advisor SUNY, Albany, 1995—. Mem. Soc. for Nurse Execs., N.Y. State Nurses Assn., St. Mary's Hosp. Alumni Assn. Roman Catholic.

STUMPF, PAUL KARL, biochemistry educator emeritus; b. N.Y.C., Feb. 23, 1919; s. Karl and Annette (Schreyer) S.; m. Ruth Rodenbeck, June 1947; children: Ann Carol, Kathryn Lee, Margaret Ruth, David Karl, Richard Frederic. AB, Harvard Coll., 1941; PhD, Columbia U., 1945. Instr. pub. health U. Mich., Ann Arbor, 1946-48; faculty U. Calif., Berkeley, 1948-58, prof., 1956-58, Davis, 1958-84, prof. emeritus, 1984—. Chief scientist Competitive Rsch. Grants Office USDA, Washington, 1988-91; cons. Palm Oil Rsch. Inst., Kuala Lumpur, Malaysia, 1982-92; mem. sci. adv. bd. Calgene, Inc., Davis, 1990-93; mem. sci. adv. panel Md. Biotech. Inst., 1990-92; Inaugural lectr. Tan Sri Dato'Seri B. Bek-Nielsen Found., Kuala Lumpur, 1996. Co-author: Outlines of Enzyme Chemistry, 1955, Outlines of Biochemistry, 5th edit., 1987; co-editor-in-chief Biochemistry of Plants, 1980; exec. editor Archives of Biochemistry/Biophysics, 1965-88; contbr. over 250 articles to profl. jours. Planning commn. City of Davis, 1966-68. Guggenheim fellow, 1962, 69; recipient Lipid Chemistry award Am. Oil Chemists Soc., 1974, Sr. Scientist award Alexander von Humboldt Found., 1976, Superior Svc. Group award USDA, 1992, Award of Excellence, Calif. Aggie Alumni Found., 1996. Fellow AAAS; mem. NAS, Royal Danish Acad. Scis., Am. Soc. Plant Physiologists (pres. 1979-80, chmn. bd. trustees 1986-90, Stephen Hales award 1974, Charles Reid Barnes Life Membership award 1992). Avocation: golf. Home: 764 Elmwood Dr Davis CA 95616-3517 Office: U Calif Molecular & Cellular Biology Davis CA 95616 E-mail: pkstumpf@ucdavis.edu.

STUMPF, SUZANNE ELIZABETH, classical musician; b. Syracuse, N.Y. d. Norman and Dorothy Carol (Boone) S.; m. Daniel Robert Ryan, June 10, 1990. BA, Wellesley (Mass.) Coll., 1980; postgrad, Mozarteum, Salzburg, Austria. Chamber music coach Wellesley Coll., 1985—, concert mgr., 1985-2000; flute instr. New England Conservatory Ext. Divsn., Boston, 1989—; prof. of flute Clark U., Worcester, Mass., 1985-89, Coll. of Holy Cross, Worcester, 1985-88. Artistic dir. Musicians of the Old Post Road, Boston, 1989—; freelance flutist Boston Baroque, The N.Y. Bach Ensemble, Handel and Haydn Soc., 1982—. Flutist: (compact disc) The Virtuoso Double Bass, 1994, Trios and Scottish Song Settings of J.N. Hummel, 1999, Galant with an Attitude-Music of Juan and José Pla for flutes, strings and continno, 2000. Recipient Noah Greenberg award Am. Musicol. Soc., 1998; Mary Elvira Stevens Travelling fellow Wellesley Coll., 1984-85; rsch. grantee Coll. of the Holy Cross, 1986. Mem. Boston Musicians Assn.

STUMPF, WALTER ERICH, cell biology educator, researcher; b. Oelsnitz, Sachsen, Germany, Jan. 10, 1927; came to U.S., 1963; m. Ursula Emily Schwinge, May 20, 1961; children: Andrea, Martin, Carolin, Silva. MD summa cum laude, Humboldt U., Berlin, 1952; PhD in Pharmacology, U. Chgo., 1967; D in Biol. Humanities (hon.), U. Ulm, Germany, 1987. Resident in neurology and psychiatry Humboldt U., Berlin, 1954-57, U. Marburg, 1957-61, resident in radiobiology, 1961-62; rsch. assoc. U. Chgo., 1963-67, asst. prof., 1967-70; assoc. prof. U. N.C., Chapel Hill, 1970-73, prof., 1973-95, mem. labs. for reproductive biology and neurobiology program, mem. Cancer Rsch. Ctr., Carolina Population Ctr., mem. curriculum in toxicology. Vis. psychiatrist Maudsley Hosp., London, 1959; vis. prof. Max-Planck Inst. for Cell Biology, Wilhelmshaven, Germany, 1975, U. Ulm, 1981, U. Sao Paulo, Brazil, 2000-02; rsch. advisor Chugai Pharm. Co., Ltd., Tokyo, 1992-95; lectr. U. São Paulo, 1997, 2000, Ain Shams U., Cairo, 1998; cons. Harris Mfg. Co., North Billerica, Mass., Rsch. Triangle Inst., Chemistry and Life Scis. Divsn., Rsch. Triangle Park, N.C., Merck Sharp and Dome , Westpoint, Pa., Glaxo Wellcome, Rsch. Triangle Park; exec. com. NRC, Inst. of Lab. Animal Resources, Nat. Acad. Scis., 1979-81, coun. Inst. of Lab. Animal Res., 1978-81, com. Soc. for Exptl. Biology and Medicine, 1987-92, founder Internat. Inst. Drug Distbn. Cytopharmacology and Cytoxicology, Chapel Hill, N.C., 1995—. Editor: Autoradiography of Diffusible Substances, 1969, Anatomical Neuroendocrinology, 1975, Autoradiography and Correlative Imaging, 1995; mem. editl. bd. Neuroendocrinology Letters, 1979-87, Exptl. Aging Rsch., 1975-85, Jour. Histochemistry and Cytochemistry, 1982-90, Cell and Tissue Rsch., 1982-88, Molecular and Cellular Neurosci., 1989-94, Biomed. Rsch., 1991-94, Histochemistry, 1992-96; contbr. numerous articles to profl. jours. Recipient Humboldt Found. award, 1989. Mem. AAAS, Am. Assn. Anatomists, N.Y. Acad. Scis., Soc. for Exptl. Biology and Medicine, Soc. for Neurosci., Endocrine Soc., Internat. Brain Rsch. Orgn., Am. Soc. Zoologists, Histochem. Soc. (coun. 1977-81), Histochem. Gesellschaft (Feulgen lectureship 1982), Internat. Soc. Xenobiotics (charter), Internat. Inst. Drug Distbn. Cytopharmacology and Cytotoxicology (founder). Home: U NC Sch Medicine 2612 Damascus Church Rd Chapel Hill NC 27516-8043 Office: Internat Inst Drug Distribution Cytopharmacology & Cytotoxicology Chapel Hill NC 27516

STUMPFF, ROBERT THOMAS, academic administrator; b. Lewistown, Pa., June 25, 1945; s. Harry Clarence and Marjorie Louise (Bossinger) S.; m. Sylvia Simmons, Apr. 22, 1972; children: Robert Dale, Cherie Lynn Stumpff Zimmer. BS, U. Md., 1968; cert., U. Ky., 1978. Asst. dir. athletics U. Md., College Park, 1968-69, asst. dir. Md. student union, 1969-72, assoc. dir. Md. student union, 1974-80, acting dir. Md. student union, 1974-75, bus. mgr. athletics, 1980-81, asst. athletic dir., 1982-88, coord. gen. svcs., facilities mgmt., 1988—. Cons. U.S. Naval Acad. Athletic Assn., Annapolis, Md., 1984; assisting minister St. Paul's Luth. Ch., Fulton, Md., 1996—. Author, editor: Maryland Wrestling, 1964-65, 68-69 (Nation's Best award); asst. editor: Maryland Football Guide, 1965-69, Maryland Basketball, 1964-65, 68-69. Mem. ch. coun. Abiding Savior Lutheran Ch., Columbia, Md., 1986-87; mem. Lutheran campus ministry bd. U. Md., 1995—. Mem. Am. Pub. Works Assn., Solid Waste Assn. N.Am. (cert. mcpl. solid waste mgr., bd. dirs. Mid-Atlantic chpt. 1992-94), Nat. Solid Wastes Mgmt. Assn. Md.-Del. Solid Waste Assn., Md. Recyclers Coalition (bd. dirs. 1997—), Nat. Recycling Coalition, Coll. and U. Recycling Coun., Assn. Phys. Plant Adminstrs., U. Md. Alumni Assn. (life), U. Md. Terrapin Club, U. Md. M Club Found. (life, bd. dirs. 1970—, past pres.), Omicron Delta Kappa (Sigma Chpt. faculty sec.-treas. 1972-76, faculty adviser 1976-91, faculty coord. 1991—). Avocations: reading, sightseeing. Home: 8206 Bubbling Spring Laurel MD 20723-1079 Office: Univ Md Facilities Mgmt Dept Bldg & Landscape Svcs 1300 Service Building College Park MD 20742-6055 E-mail: rs76@umail.umd.edu.

STUNKARD, ALBERT JAMES, psychiatrist, educator; b. N.Y.C., Feb. 7, 1922; s. Horace Wesley and Frances (Klank) Stunkard. BS, Yale U., 1943; MD, Columbia U., 1945, U. Edinburgh, 1992. Intern in medicine Mass. Gen. Hosp., Boston, 1945—46; resident physician psychiatry Johns Hopkins Hosp., 1948—51, rsch. fellow psychiatry, 1951—52; 1rsch. fellow medicine Columbia U. Svc., Goldwater Meml. Hosp., N.Y.C., 1952—53; Commonwealth rsch. fellow, then asst. prof. medicine Cornell U. Med. Coll., 1953—57; mem. faculty U. Pa., 1957—73, 1976—, prof. psychiatry, 1962—73, 1976—, Kenneth Appel prof. psychiatry, 1968—73, chmn. dept., 1962—73; prof. psychiatry Med. Sch., Stanford U., 1973—76. Contbr. articles on psychol., physiol., sociol., therapeutic and genetic aspects of obesity to profl. jours. Capt. M.C. U.S. Army, 1946—48. Recipient Disting. Svc. award, Am. Psychiat. Assn., 1994, Goldberger award, AMA, 1990, Willendorf award for clin. rsch., Internat. Assn. for Study of Obesity, 1998; fellow, Ctr. for Advanced Study in Behavioral Scis., 1971—72. Mem.: Soc. Behavioral Medicine (past pres.), Assn. Rsch. in Nervous and Mental Diseases (past pres.), Am. Psychosomatic Soc. (past pres.), Acad. Behavioral Medicine Rsch. (past pres.), Am. Assn. of Chmn. of Depts. of Psychiatry (past pres.), Inst. of Medicine of NAS. Achievements include contributions to the behavioral and pharmacological treatment of obesity and to understanding of sociological, physiological, psychological and genetic aspects of the disorder; contributions also to nosology and treatment of the eating disorders. Office: U Pa Sch Medicine Dept Psychiatry 3535 Market St 3rd Flr Philadelphia PA 19104-2641 E-mail: stunkard@mail.med.upenn.edu.

STUNTEBECK, CLINTON A. lawyer; b. Hibbing, Minn., May 25, 1938; s. Robert F. and S. Mary Stuntebeck; m. Mary Joan Carmody; children: Robin, M. Alison, Susan, John, William. BA in Psychology, U. Minn., 1960; LLB, U. Maine, 1968. Bar: Pa. 1969, U.S. Dist. Ct. (ea. dist.) Pa. 1969. Ptnr., chmn. corp. fin. and securities, mem. exec. com. Schnader, Harrison, Segal & Lewis, Phila. Bd. dirs. Markel Corp., Greater Phila. First Partnership for Econ. Devel.; lectr. corp. and securities law. Contbr. articles to profl. jours. Pres. Radnor (Pa.) Twp. Bd. Commn., 1981-83, 92-99; bd. visitors U. Maine Sch. Law; trustee Cabrini Coll.; bd. dirs. Am. Heart Assn. Capt. USAF, 1960-68. Mem. ABA, Am. Law Inst., Pa. Bar Assn., Phila. Bar Assn., Securities Industry Assn. (law and compliance com.), U. Maine Law Alumni Assn. (pres. 1974-76), Union League Phila., Phila. Country Club, Sunday Breakfast Club, Corinthian Yacht Club. Avocations: sailing, skiing, golf, tennis. Office: Schnader Harrison Segal 1600 Market St Ste 3600 Philadelphia PA 19103-7287 E-mail: cstuntebeck@schnader.com.

STUNZ, JOHN HENRY, JR. retired physician; b. Freeland, Pa., May 20, 1921; s. John Henry and Anna Amelia (Gross) S.; m. Geraldine Kutz, July 2, 1944; children: Beverly A. Stunz Boyd, Geri Stunz Konstantin. BA, U. Pa., 1943, MD, 1946. Diplomate Am. Bd. Occupational Medicine. Intern U.S. Naval Hosp., Saint Albans, N.Y., 1946-47; pvt. practice Freeland, 1949-50; plant physician Harrison Radiator div. Gen. Motors Corp., Lockport, N.Y., 1950-52, med. dir., 1952-78, Cadillac Motor Car div. Gen. Motors Corp., Detroit, 1978-86; occupational medicine cons. Preferred Med. Assocs., Southfield, Mich., 1987-98, ret., 1998. Pres. Niagara County (N.Y.) Bd. Health, 1966; acting commr. health Niagara County, 1972-73. Lt. (j.g.) M.C., USNR, 1946-49. Fellow Am. Coll. Occupl. and Environ. Medicine; mem. Mich. State Med. Soc., Oakland County Med. Soc. (environ. health com. 1988), Mich. Occupl. and Environ. Med. Assn. (bd. dirs. 1985-88), Detroit Occupl. Physicians Assn. Republican. Presbyterian. Avocations: philately, boating, golf. Home: 735 Ardmoor Dr Bloomfield Hills MI 48301-2417

STUPAK, BART T. congressman, lawyer; b. Feb. 29, 1952; m. Laurie Ann Olsen; children: Ken, Bart Jr. (dec.). AA in Criminal Justice, Northwestern Mich. C.C., Traverse City, 1972; BS in Criminal Justice, Saginaw Valley State Coll., 1977; JD, Thomas M. Cooley Law Sch., 1981. Patrolman Escanaba City Police Dept., 1972-73; state trooper Mich. Dept. State Police, 1973-84; instr. State Police Tng. Acad., 1980-82; atty., 1981-84, Hansley, Neiman, Peterson, Beauchamp, Stupak, Bergman P.C., 1984-85; ptnr. Stupak, Bergman, Stupak P.C., 1985-88; mem. Mich. Ho. of Reps., 1989-90; prin. Bart T. Stupak P.C., 1991—; mem. 103rd-106th Congresses from 1st Mich. dist., 1993—. Mem. commerce subcom. on health & environment. Nat. committeeman Boy Scouts Am., coach Menominee Youth Baseball Assn., Little League; active Wildlife Unltd., Menominee Woods and Streams Assn., Menominee County Hist. Soc.; adv. com. Bay Pines Juv. Detection Ctr. Mem. Nat. Rifle Assn., Sons of the Am. Legion, Knights of Columbus, Elks Club, State Employees Retirees Assn., fin. com. Holy Spirit Catholic Ch. Democrat. Office: US Ho of Reps 2348 Rayburn Ho Office Bldg Washington DC 20515-2201 E-mail: stupak@mail.house.gov.*

STUPIN, SUSAN LEE, investment banker; b. L.A., Sept. 14, 1954; d. Paul Alex and Elizabeth Lee (Williams) S.; m. Theodore Robert Gamble Jr., Mar. 3, 1984. AB cum laude, Princeton U., 1975; MBA, Harvard U., 1979. Rep. corp. bond sales Paine, Webber, Jackson & Curtis, N.Y.C., 1975-77; assoc. instl. fin. Eastdil Realty Inc., 1979-83; assoc. real estate dept. Goldman, Sachs & Co., 1983-85, v.p. real estate dept., 1985-88; prin. The Prescott Group Inc., 1988—; mng. dir. Transwestern Comml. Svcs., LLC, 1999—. Fellow Morgan Library; Bryant fellow Met. Mus. Art; exec. com., fund raiser Princeton Class of 1975. Mem. Urban Land Inst. (exec. group Urban Devel. and Mixed Use Coun.), Real Estate Bd. N.Y., Internat. Coun. Shopping Ctrs., Internat. Assn. Corp. Real Estate Execs., Young Mortgage Bankers Assn., Am. Soc. Order St. John of Jerusalem, N.Y. Jr. League, Doubles Club, Colony Club, River Club, Harvard Club (N.Y.C., Boston), Coral Beach and Tennis Club (Bermuda). Republican. Episcopalian. Home: 860 United Nations Plz New York NY 10017-1810 Office: The Prescott Group Inc 445 Park Ave 9th Fl New York NY 10022 Office Fax: 917-322-2422. Personal E-mail: slstupin@msn.com. Business E-Mail: slstupin@prescott_group.com.

STURCKOW, FREDERICK W. (RICK), astronaut; b. La Mesa, Calif., Aug. 11, 1961; s. Karl H. and Janette R. Sturckow; m. Michele A. Street. BS in Mech. Engring., Calif. Poly. State U., 1984. Commd. 2d lt. USMC, 1984, advanced through grades to lt. col.; with MCAS, Beaufort, SC, Sheik Isa Air Base, Bahrain; mission comdr. Operation Desert Storm; with Naval Air Warfare Ctr.-Aircraft Divsn., Patuxent River, Md.; astronaut NASA, Houston, 1994—, with Vehicle Systems and Ops. Br. Decorated Single Mission Air medal with combat "V", 4 Strike/Flight Air medals. Mem.: Marine Corps Assn. Achievements include logged 4,000 flight hours in over 50 different aircraft; logged 568 hours in space; pilot STS-88 Endeavour (1998) and STS-105 Discovery (2001). Avocations: flying, physical training. Office: Astronaut Office/CB NASA Johnson Space Ctr Houston TX 77058*

STURDEVANT, WAYNE ALAN, executive management consultant; b. Portland, Oreg., Apr. 3, 1946; s. Hervey Sturdevant and Georgia Bright; m. Helen F. Radbury, Sept. 24, 1976; children: Wayne Jr., Stephen, John, Brian, Daniel. BS in Edn., So. Ill. U., 1980. With USAF, 1964—85, chief on-job-tng. ops., 1982-85; lead engr. McDonnell Douglas Corp., 1985-88; br. mgr. Southeastern Computer Cons., Inc., 1988-2000; pres., COO Apollo Software/eSaba Systems, 2000-01; CEO Sturdevant Assocs., Austin, 2001—. Developed advanced concepts in tech. mgmt., program and media design, and formal quality systems; published articles on mgmt., ops. and tng. innovations in the work place. Bishop LDS Ch., 1983-84, 98-2002, stake presidency, 1990-96; exec. bd. Boy Scouts Am., 1986—. Recognized for leadership in multi-nat. programs; recipient Citation of Honor Air Force Assn., 1980, Silver Beaver award Boy Scouts Am., 1998; named Internat. Man of Yr., Internat. Biog. Ctr., 1992. Republican. Avocations: reading, camping. Home: 9214 Independence Loop Austin TX 78748-6312 E-mail: sturde1@ev1.net.

STURE, STEIN, civil engineering educator; b. Oslo, Norway, Nov. 12, 1947; came to U.S., 1970; s. Alf and Gunnvor (Een) S.; m. Karen J. Marley, June 3, 1989. Student, Schous Inst. Tech., Oslo, 1970; BSCE, U. Colo., 1971, MSCE, 1973, PhD, 1976. Asst. prof. Va. Polytechnic Inst., Blacksburg, 1976-80; rsch. scientist Marshall Space Flight Ctr. NASA, Huntsville, Ala., 1979; from asst. prof. to prof. civil engring. U. Colo., Boulder, 1980—, acting chmn. dept. civil engring., 1990-91, chmn. dept. civil engring., 1994—98, assoc. dean, 2002—. Sr. vis. dept. engring. sci. U. Oxford, Eng., 1985; vis. prof. Norway Inst. Tech., Trondheim, 1985-86. Editor Jour. Engring. Mechanics. Jenkin fellow, 1986. Mem. Am. Soc. Civil Engrs. (pres. Colo. sect. 1990-91, jour. editor, Walter Huber Civil Engring. Rsch. prize 1990, Richard Torrens award 2000), Am. Assn. Advancement Sci., Am. Geophys. Union, Am. Soc. Engring. Edn., NASA Ctr. Space Construction, Internat. Soc. Soil Mech. Found. Engrs., U.S. Nat. Comm./Theoretical and Applied Mechanics. Avocations: skiing, sailing, cross-country skiing, hiking. Home: 1077 Diamond Ct Boulder CO 80303-3244 Office: Univ Colo Dept Civil Engring Boulder CO 80309-0001

STURGE, MICHAEL DUDLEY, physicist, educator; b. Bristol, Eng., May 25, 1931; came to U.S., 1961, naturalized 1991; s. Paul Dudley and Rachel (Graham) S.; m. Mary Balk, Aug. 21, 1956; children: David Mark, Thomas Graham, Peter Daniel, Benedict Paul. BA in Engring. and Physics, Gonville and Caius Coll., Cambridge, Eng., 1952; PhD in Physics, Cambridge U., 1957. Staff Mullard Rsch. Lab. (now Philips), Redhill, Eng., 1956-58; sr. rsch. fellow Royal Radar Establishment, Malvern, Eng., 1958-61; tech. staff Bell Labs., Murray Hill, N.J., 1961-83, Bellcore, Red Bank, 1984-86; prof. dept. physics Dartmouth Coll., Hanover, N.H., 1986-98, prof. emeritus, 1999—. Rsch. assoc. Stanford U., 1965, U. B.C., Vancouver, Can., 1969; vis. prof. Technion, Haifa, Israel, 1972, 76, 81, 85, Williams Coll., Williamstown, Mass., 1982, 84, Trinity Coll., Dublin, 1989, 93, 96, U. Fourier, Grenoble, France, 1989, 91, Hong Kong U. Sci. and Tech., 1999; exch. scientist Philips Rsch. Lab., Eindhoven, The Netherlands, 1973-74; vis. scholar U. Sheffield, Eng., 1996. Contbr. over 130 papers in solid state physics to profl. publs.; co-editor: Excitons, 1982; editor Jour. of Luminescence, 1984-90. Fellow Am. Phys. Soc.; mem. Am. Assn. Physics Tchrs. Office: Dartmouth Coll Dept Physics Wilder Lab Hanover NH 03755-3528 E-mail: m.sturge@dartmouth.edu.

STURGEON, EDWIN L. music educator, director; b. Tulsa, Okla., May 13, 1966; s. Richard L. and Ruth A. Sturgeon; m. Katrina L. Hillhouse; children: Michael Richey, Kaylee, Taylor, Allison, Brittany. MusM in Edn., U. of Ctrl. Okla. Cert. K-12 Instrumental/Vocal Music Edn. 1989, Secondary Prin. (6-12) 2001. Band dir. Pawnee Pub. Schools, Pawnee, Okla., 1990—95; dir. of instrumental music studies Coffeyville C.C., Coffeyville, Kans., 1995—2000; band dir. Tulsa Will Rogers H.S., Tulsa, Okla., 2000—. Mem.: NEA, Okla. Edn. Assn., Okla. Music Educators Assn., Music Educators Nat. Conf. Home: 5926 E 24th St Tulsa OK 74114 Office: Tulsa Will Rogers High School 3909 E 5th Place Tulsa OK 74112 Personal E-mail: elsturgeon@aol.com. Business E-Mail: sturged@tulsaschools.org.

STURGEON, JOHN ASHLEY, insurance company executive; b. Alliance, Alaska; B degree, Midland Luth. Coll., 1962. Ptnr. Arthur Andersen & Co., 1962—82; exec. v.p., gen. comptroller The Mutual of Omaha Ins. Cos., Omaha, 1982—97, pres., 1997—98, pres., COO, 1998—; pres. United World Life Ins. Co., 1997—. Bd. dirs. Kirkpatrick, Pettis, Smith, Polian Inc., 1983—, Companion Life Ins. Co., 1984—, United World Life Ins. Co., 1990—, The Omaha Indemnity Co., 1993—, Mut. of Omaha Structured Settlement Co., 1995—, KFS Corp., 1996—, Mut. of Omaha Holdings, Inc., 1997—, Mut. of Omaha Ins. Co., 1997—, Mut. of Omaha Life Ins. Co., 1997—, Health Ins. Assn. Am., 1998—, Creighton U., 2000—, Mut. of Omaha Investor Svcs., Inc., 2000—; chmn. Omaha Property and Casualty Ins. Co., 1996—, Innowave Inc., 1998—. Consultation com. U.S. Strategic Command; bd. trustees Mid-Am. Coun. Boy Scouts Am. Mem.: Nebr. Soc. CPA's, Am. Inst. CPA's. Office: The Mutual of Omaha Ins Co Mutual of Omaha Plz Omaha NE 68175

STURGES, JOHN SIEBRAND, management consultant; b. Greenwich, Conn., Feb. 12, 1939; s. Harry Wilton and Elizabeth Helen Sturges; m. Anastasia Daphne Sturges, May 6, 1967; children: Christina Aurora, Elizabeth Athena. AB, Harvard U., 1960; MBA, U. So. Calif., 1965; postgrad., NYU, 1972, U. Mich., 1982; PhD, Columbia U., 1997; ThD, Am. Coll., 1997, PhD, 2000. Cert. profl. mgmt. cons., sr. profl. in human resources; cert. mgmt. cons.; cert. profl. cons. to mgmt. With Equitable Life Assurance Soc. U.S., N.Y.C., 1965-79, mgr. sys. devel., 1965-70, dir. compensation and benefits, 1971-75, v.p. pers. and adminstrv. svcs., 1975-79; sr. v.p. pers. Nat. Westminster Bank U.S.A., 1979-82; corp. sr. v.p. adminstrn. and human resources Willis-Corroon Corp., 1982-84; mng. dir. human resources Marine Midland Bank, 1984-87; mng. dir. Siebrand-Wilton Assocs., 1986-87, pres., 1987—. Lay reader, Stephen minister St. Peters Episcopal Ch., Freehold, N.J., 1972—. Lt. USNR, 1960-65. Fellow Am. Coll.; mem. Internat. Found. Employee Benefit Plans, Strategic Leadership Forum, Commerce Assocs., Soc. for Human Resource Mgmt. (dir. 1979—), Am. Compensation Assn., Human Resource Planning Soc., Inst. Mgmt. Cons. (bd. dirs. 1992-2001), Cons. Bur., Harvard Club (N.Y.C., Boston, Princeton; dir. 1991-97), Nassau Club, Monmouth Boat Club, Beta Gamma Sigma (dir. N.Y. 1978—), Phi Kappa Phi. Republican.

STURGES, SIDNEY JAMES, pharmacist, educator, investment and development company executive; b. Kansas City, Mo., Sept. 29, 1936; s. Sidney Alexander and Lenore Caroline (Lemley) S.; m. Martha Grace Leonard, Nov. 29, 1957 (div. 1979); 1 child, Grace Caroline; m. Gloria June Kitch, Sept. 17, 1983. BS in Pharmacy, U. Mo., 1957, post grad.; MBA in Pharmacy Adminstrn., U. Kans., 1980; PhD in Bus. Adminstrn., Pacific Western U., 1980; cert. in Gerentology, Avila Coll., 1986. Registered pharmacist, Mo., Kans.; registered nursing home adminstr., Mo.; cert. vocat. tchr., Mo. Pharmacist, mgr. Crown Drugs, Kansas City, Mo., 1957-60; pharmacist, owner Sav-On-Drugs and Pharmacy, Kansas City, 1960-62; ptnr. Sam's Bargain Town Drugs, Raytown, Mo., 1961-62; pharmacist, owner Sturges Drugs DBA Barnard Pharmacy, Independence, Mo., 1962—; pres., owner Sturges Med. Corp., Independence, Mo., 1967-1977, Sturgess Investment Corp., Independence, 1967-1978, Sturwood Investment Corp., Independence, 1968—, Sturges Agri-Bus. Co., Independence, 1977—, Sturges Devel. Co., 1984—; bd. dirs. Comprehensive Mental Health Corp., Truman Med. Ctr., 1992; instr. pharmacology Penn Valley C.C., 1976-92; instr., lectr. various clubs and groups. Contbr. articles to profl. jours. Bd. dirs. Independence House, 1981-83; mem. Criminal Justice Adv. Commn., Independence, 1982—. Recipient Outstanding award Kans. City Alcohol and Drug Abuse Council, 1982. Mem. Mo. Sheriffs Assn., Mo. Pharm. Assn. (pharmacy dr. 1981, Pharmacists Against Drug Abuse award 1989), Mo. Found. Pharm. Care, U. Mo. Alumni Assn. Home and Office: Sturges Co 16805 E Cogan Rd Ste B Independence MO 64055-2815

STURLEY, MICHAEL F. law educator; b. Syracuse, N.Y., Feb. 14, 1955; s. Richard Avern and Helen Elizabeth (Fisher) S.; m. Michele Y. Deitch, July 2, 1989; children: Jennifer Diane, Elizabeth Claire. BA, Yale U., 1977, JD, 1981; BA in Jurisprudence, Oxford U., 1980, MA, 1985. Bar: N.Y. 1984, U.S. Dist. Ct. (so. and ea. dists.) N.Y. 1984, U.S. Supreme Ct. 1987. Law clk. to Judge Amalya L. Kearse, U.S. Ct. Appeals for 2d Cir., N.Y.C., 1981-82; law clk. to Justice Lewis F. Powell, Jr. U.S. Supreme Ct., Washington, 1982-83; assoc. Sullivan & Cromwell, N.Y.C., 1983-84; asst. prof. law U. Tex. Law Sch., Austin, 1984-88, prof., 1988—. Vis. prof. Queen Mary and Westfield Coll., U. London, 1990, advisor Restatement (3d) of Property (servitudes), 1989-2000. Author: (with David W. Robertson and Steven F. Friedell) Admiralty and Maritime Law in the United States, 2001; compiler, editor: The Legislative History of the Carriage of Goods by Sea Act and the Travaux Préparatoires of The Hague Rules, 3 vols., 1990; mem. editl. bd. Jour. Maritime Law and Commerce, 1989—, book rev. editor, 1993—; contbg. author: Benedict on Admiralty, 1990—; contbr. articles to legal jours. Mem. Am. Law Inst., Maritime Law Assn. (proctor), Comité Maritime Internat. (titulary) Office: U Tex Sch Law 727 E Dean Keeton St Austin TX 78705-3224 E-mail: msturley@mail.law.utexas.edu.

STURM, CONNIE ARRAU, music and music education educator; b. Jackson Heights, N.Y., Mar. 7, 1957; d. Raymond Victor and Clara (Rosenthal) Arrau; m. Ronald Lee Sturm, Dec. 10, 1990. B of Music Edn., Northwestern U., 1978; MA, Ohio State U., 1980; PhD, U. Okla., 1990. Nat. cert. tchr. music. Lectr. class piano Western Ill. U., Macomb, 1980-82; instr. class piano and pedagogy U. Minn., Mpls., 1982-85; prof. class piano and pedagogy W.Va. U., Morgantown, 1986—, instr., 1986—. Mem. adv. com. nat. D.H. Baldwin Fellowship program Baldwin Piano Co., 1985-87; mem. adminstrn./pedagogy liaison com. Nat. Conf. on Piano Pedagogy, 1986-87; music clinician Morgantown Early Learning Facility and North Elem. Sch.;

spokesperson for Nat. Piano Found., 1991. Contbr. articles to profl. jours. Adjudicator for more than 50 music competitions, auditions and festivals at local, state and regional levels; local organizer, promoter and host of 3 nationally broadcast Keyboard Tchrs. Videoconfs., Morgantown. Phi Delta Kappa Competitive Rsch. grantee; W.Va. U. faculty travel grantee. Mem. Music Tchrs. Nat. Assn. (nat. chair for student chpts. 1999—), World Piano Pedagogy Conf. (chair hist. perspectives com. 1996—). Office: WVa U Coll Creative Arts PO Box 6111 Morgantown WV 26506-6111 E-mail: u1a00906@wvnvm.wvnet.edu.

STURM, WILLIAM CHARLES, lawyer; b. Milw., Aug. 4, 1941; s. Charles William and Helen Ann (Niesen) S.; m. Kay F. Sturm, June 10, 1967; children: Patricia, Elizabeth, Katherine, William, Susan. BS in Bus. Adminstrn., Marquette U., 1963; JD, 1966. Bar: Wis. 1966, U.S. Dist. Ct. (ea. dist.) Wis. 1966, U.S. Supreme Ct. 1980. Sole practice, Milw., 1966-78; ptnr. Rausch, Hamell, Ehrle & Sturm, S.C., 1978-81, Rausch, Hamell, Ehrle, Sturm & Blom, Milw., 1981-83, Rausch, Hamell, Ehrle & Sturm, 1983-95, Rausch, Hamell, Sturm & Israel S.C., 1995-98, Rausch, Sturm, Israel & Hornik, S.C., 1999—. Asst. prof. Marquette U., 1982-91; lectr. U. Wis., Milw., 1991-97, sr. lectr. 1997-2002. Contbr. articles to profl. jours. Mem. adv. bd. Pallotine Order, 1985—. Recipient Editors award Wis. Med. Credit Assn., 1980. Mem. ABA, Wis. Bar Assn., Comml. Law League Am. (exec. council midwestern dist. 1981-83, 86-88, chmn. state membership com. 1981-88, nat. nominating council 1984-86, 1988-89, sec., 2d v.p. midwestern dist. 1989-90, 1st v.p. midwestern dist. 1990-91, chmn. 1991-92, nat. bd. govs. 1997-99, pres. 2001-02), Nat. Spkrs. Assn., Am. Bus. Law Assn., Midwest Bus. Law Assn. (sec. 1988-89, v.p. 1989-90, pres. 1990-91), Wis. Profl. Speakers Assn., Healthcare Fin. Mgmt. Assn., Beta Alpha Psi (faculty v.p. Psi chpt. 1985-88, Eta Theta chpt. 1992-99), Midwest Bus. And Health Assn. (v.p. procs. 1987-88, v.p. program 1988-89, pres. 1989-90). Clubs: Westmoor Country (Milw.); Kiwanis (pres. 1979, lt. gov. div. 5, 1980) (Wauwatosa, Wis.). Office: 1233 N Mayfair Rd Milwaukee WI 53226-3255 E-mail: wsturm@wiscollect.com.

STURTEVANT, BRERETON, retired lawyer, former government official; b. Washington, Nov. 24, 1921; d. Charles Lyon and Grace (Brereton) S. BA, Wellesley Coll., 1942; JD, Temple U., 1949; postgrad., U. Del., 1969-71. Bar: D.C. 1949, Del. 1950. Research chemist E.I. duPont DeNemours & Co., 1942-50; law clk. Del. Supreme Ct., 1950; gen. practice law Wilmington, Del., 1950-57; partner Connolly, Bove & Lodge, 1957-71; examiner-in-chief U.S. Patent and Trademark Office Bd. Appeals, Washington, 1971-88. Adj. prof. law Georgetown U., 1974-79 Trustee Holton-Arms Sch., Bethesda, Md., 1977-96, chmn. or mem. all coms., trustee emerita, 1997—. Mem. ABA, Exec. Women in Govt. (charter mem., chmn. 1978-79) Clubs: Wellesley College, Washington-Wellesley (pres. 1982-84). Episcopalian. Home: 1227 Morningside Ln Alexandria VA 22308-1042

STURTEVANT, PETER MANN, JR. television news executive; b. Northampton, Mass., Feb. 27, 1943; s. Peter Mann and Katharine Bryan (Hobson) S.; m. Anne Elizabeth Fitzpatrick, July 12, 1969 (div. Dec. 1984); 1 child, Amanda Hadden; m. Toni E. Siegel, Apr. 14, 1985; 1 child, Gillian Lee. BA, Wilmington Coll., 1965; MA, U. Iowa, 1967. Assoc. prodr. CBS News, Washington, 1967-71, bur. chief Viet Nam Saigon, 1971-73, nat. news editor N.Y.C., 1974-80, asst. v.p. spl. events, 1981-83, producer 60 Minutes, 1984-85; exec. bus. news editor CNN, 1985-86; prodr. Today's Bus. Buena Vista TV, 1987; dir. news coverage CNBC, Fort Lee, N.J., 1988-90, v.p., mng. editor Ft. Lee, 1991-94; sr. v.p. Internat. Bus. News NBC, 1994-98; disaster relief, instr. Am. Red Cross, 1999—. Tutor, mentor Children's Aid Soc., 2001—; trustee Wilmington coll., 2000—. Named Disting. Alumnus, Wilmington Coll., 1975, 97; named to Journalism Hall of Fame, U. Iowa Sch. Journalism, 1988; named to Wilmington Coll. Sports Hall of Fame, 1997. Mem. Nat. Acad. Cable Programming (nominated ACE award 1992, 93, 94), Soc. Profl. Journalists, Deadline Club N.Y., The Asia Soc., Overseas Press Club (bd. dirs.). Episcopalian. Avocations: racquet sports, landscaping, travelling, philately, parenting. Home: 90 Riverside Dr New York NY 10024-5306

STURTEVANT, RUTHANN PATTERSON, anatomy educator; b. Rockford, Ill., Feb. 7, 1927; d. Joseph Hyelmun and Virginia (Wharton) P.; m. Frank Milton Sturtevant Jr., Mar. 18, 1950; children: Barbara (dec.), Jill Sturtevant Rovani, Jan Sturtevant Cassidy. BS, Northwestern U., 1949, MS, 1950; PhD, U. Ark., 1972. Instr. life scis. Ind. State U., Evansville, Ind., 1965-72, asst. prof., 1972-74; asst. prof. anatomy Ind. U. Sch. Medicine, Evansville, 1972-74, U. Evansville, 1972-74; lectr. anatomy Northwestern U., Chgo., 1974-75; asst. prof. anatomy and surgery Loyola U., Maywood, 1975-81; assoc. prof. Loyola U. Sch. Medicine, 1981-88, prof., 1988-90, prof. emerita, 1990—. Contbr. articles to profl. jours.; editorial bd. Chronobiology Internat., 1988-90; reviewer numerous profl. jours. Mem. Mayor's Task Force on High Tech. Devel., Chgo., 1983-85; exec. bd. Anatomical Gifts Assn. Ill., Chgo., 1978-89. Grantee, Pott's Found., NIH, others, 1978-88. Mem. Am. Assn. Anatomists, So. Soc. Anatomists (councillor 1978-80), Internat. Soc. Chronobiologists, Am. Soc. Pharmacology and Exptl. Therapeutics, Soc. for Exptl. Biology and Medicine, Am. Assn. Clin. Anatomists, League of Underwater Photographers, Sarasota Scuba Club, Sigma Xi. Avocations: underwater photography, scuba diving, flying. Address: 5760 Midnight Pass Rd Unit 610-D Sarasota FL 34242 E-mail: patty.dives@verizon.net.

STURTEVANT, WILLIAM T. fundraising executive, consultant; b. Balt., Feb. 2, 1947; s. Charles N. and Mary Jane (Thomson) S.; m. Teresa L. Woollen Sturtevant, Apr. 8, 1988; children: Stephanie A., Robert E., Melissa N. BBA, Western Mich. U., Kalamazoo, 1969; MBA, Wayne State U., Detroit, 1971. Cert. Fin. Planner. Devel. officer WTVS, Detroit, 1969-71; legis. aide Mich. House of Reps., 1971-73; pres. Portage Rubber Co., Kalamazoo, 1973-76; sr. devel. officer Western Mich. U., 1976-79; v.p. devel. Lake Erie Coll., Painesville, Ohio, 1979-80; dir. planned giving U. Ill. Found., Urbana, 1980—. Bd. dirs. Sirazi Found., Chgo., 1997— Jagdish N. Sheth Found., Urbana, Ill., 1991—, The Lauritsen Family Found., Urbana, 1994—, Strategic Capital Bank Corp., Champaign, Ill., 1999—; cons. pvt. practice, Mahomet, Ill., 1990—; pres. Inst. for Charitable Giving, Chgo., 1990—. Author: The Artful Journey: Cultivating and Soliciting the Major Gifts, 1997, The Continuing Journey, 2000. Mem. Union League Club, Chgo., 1990—. Named Planned Giving Prof. of Yr., Planned Giving Today, 1995. Mem. Nat. Soc. Fundraising Execs., Coun. for Advancement and Support of Edn. Avocations: reading, tennis, travel. Home: 1305 Cross Creek Rd Mahomet IL 61853-3723 Office: U Ill Found Harker Hall MC-386 1305 W Green St Urbana IL 61801-2945 E-mail: sturtevant@uif.uillinois.edu., wtstls@aol.com.

STURTZ, DONALD LEE, physician, educator, naval officer; b. Coshocton, Ohio, Apr. 18, 1933; s. Walter Raymond and Helene Josephine (Kubic) S.; m. Alice Marie McGuire, June 11, 1955; children: Jimalee, Janel. BS, U.S. Naval Acad., Annapolis, Md., 1955; MD, U. Pa., 1965; diploma med. care catastrophe, Soc. Apothecaries London, 1996. Diplomate Am. Bd. Surgery. Surg. resident USN, Phila., 1965-70, ship's surgeon, 1970-71; staff surgeon Bethesda Naval Hosp., USN, 1971-80; chief of surgery San Diego Naval Hosp., USN, 1980-84; exec. officer Oakland (Calif.) Naval Hosp., USN, 1984-85; prof. clin. surgery USN, Bethesda, Md., 1985-87, commd. Naval Med. Command, 1987-88, fleet surgeon Va., 1989-91; prof. surgery USUHS, Bethesda, Md., 1991—. Contbr. articles to profl. jours. Recipient B.D. Larrey award for Surgical Execellence, Surgical Dept. USUHS, Bethesda, 1988, Exceptional Svc. medal Uniformed Svcs. U., 1998. Fellow ACS (gov. 1985-88); mem. Am. Assn. for Surgery of Trauma, Assn. Mil. Surgeons, USN Inst. Republican. Presbyterian. Avocations: travel, gardening, antiquing, music, reading. Office: USUHS Dept Surgery 4301 Jones Bridge Rd Bethesda MD 20814-4799

STURTZ, WILLIAM ROSENBERG, retired judge; b. Albert Lea, Minn., Apr. 7, 1925; s. William and Gladys (Rosenberg) S.; m. Helen Hedwig Schlotter, July 23, 1949; children: William, Richard (dec.), Robert, John. LLB, U. Mich., 1948, JD, 1951. Atty. Sturtz, Peterson, Sturtz & Butler, Albert Lea, Minn., 1951-69; probate & juvenile judge Freeborn County, 1969-72, county ct. judge, 1972-86; dist. judge State of Minn., 1986-91. Faculty Lea Coll., Albert Lea, 1967-71. Mem. Am. Contract Bridge League, Shriners, Masons, Rotary. Republican. Avocations: travel, duplicate bridge, golf, cooking, theatre (actor, director, playwright). Home: 209 Ridge Rd Albert Lea MN 56007-1442 E-mail: bill@sturtz.org.

STURTZ-DAVIS, SHIRLEY ZAMPELLI, artist, retired arts administrator/educator, fashion archivist; b. Lewistown, Pa., Apr. 1, 1937; d. Frank Paul and Helen L. (Barnes) Zampelli; m. William Sturtz (dec.); children: Kraig, Steffany; m. William D. Davis, Dec. 29, 1984; stepchildren: Kimberly, Bryan, Mark. BS, Pa. State U., 1959, MA, 1961. Instr. Frostburg (Md.) State U., 1961-62, Pa. State, University Park, 1962-76, cons., instr., 1962-86; dir. arts in edn. program Central Intermediate Unit 10, Pa. State U., 1976-89; exec. dir. Pa. Alliance for Arts Edn., Shippensburg, Pa., 1988-89; dir. fashion archives Shippensburg U., 1989-96, adj. prof. dept. art, 1990-94, adj. prof., 1996-98. Author: (handbook) Exploring My World, 1981; artist juried nat. exhibits at mus. galleries, works in numerous collections, 1959—; contbr. articles to profl. jours. Chair Central Pa. Festival of the Arts, State Coll., Pa., 1966-76; bd. chair for youth Palmer Mus. Art, 1979-86. Recipient Gold Sable Brush award for excellence in watercolor, Images CPFA, 2001. Mem. North East Watercolor Soc. (signature mem.), Midwest Watercolor Soc., Watercolor U.S.A. Honor Soc. (signature mem., bd. dirs.), Pa. Watercolor Soc. (signature mem.), Ga. Watercolor Soc. (signature mem.), Tex. Watercolor Soc. (purple sage brush, signature mem.), Phila. Water Color Soc. (signature mem.), Balt. Watercolor Soc. (signature mem.), La. Watercolor Soc. (signature mem.), Niagara Frontier Watercolor Soc. (signature mem.), Ala. Watercolor Soc. (signature mem.), Kappa Delta Gamma, Phi Delta Kappa, Phi Kappa Phi. Avocations: bonsai, antique collecting, gardening. Home: 265 Newville Rd Shippensburg PA 17257-9523

STURWOLD, SISTER RITA MARY, educational administrator; b. Dayton, Ohio; d. Bernard Theodore and Christene (Huwer) S. BA in Latin, Our Lady of Cin., 1965; MA in English, Northwestern U., 1973; Cert. in Adminstrn., Ohio State U., 1983. Joined Sisters of Notre Dame de Namur, 1960; cert. fundraising profl.; cert. tchr., secondary adminstr., Ohio. Tchr. Mt. Notre Dame H.S., Cin., 1970-75; chair English dept. Notre Dame H.S., Chgo., 1975-82, dir. devel., 1982-90; dir. Cath. Inner City Schs. Ednl. Fund Archdiocese of Cin., 1995-97, asst. supt. for devel., 1990-97; sabbatical St. Stephen Priory, Dover, Mass., 1997-98; dir. Mission Advancement Rsch. Srs. of Notre Dame, Ipswich, 1998-2000; dir. Holy Cross Fund Coll. of the Holy Cross, Worcester, 2000—02. Asst. provincial Sisters of Notre Dame, Cin., 1988-94. Grad. Leadership Cin., 1994-95, mem. steering com., 1995-97, mem. alumni bd., 1997. Mem. Assn. Fundraising Profls. Roman Catholic. Avocations: public speaking, reading, theater, holistic health. Home: 137 Cohasset St #1 Worcester MA 01604-3238 E-mail: sturwoldsnd@aol.com.

STUTMAN, LEONARD JAY, research scientist, cardiologist; b. Boston, Apr. 8, 1928; s. Herbert Hyman and Nellie (Wiener) S.; BS, MIT, 1948; MA, Boston U., 1949; MD, U. Rochester, 1953; m. Jeanne Ann Soblen, Dec. 23, 1951; children: Peter, David, Marc, Robin. Intern, resident medicine Bellevue Hosp., 1953-57; chief, med. services br. WPAFB, Dayton, Ohio, 1957-59; spl. advanced research fellow NIH, Nat. Heart Inst. 1959-61; instr. in clin. medicine N.Y. U. Coll. Medicine, 1956-61, asst. prof. pathology, 1961-65; assoc. prof. clin. medicine N.Y. Med. Coll., 1980—; head coagulation research lab. St. Vincent's Hosp. and Med. Center, N.Y., 1965—; attending physician St. Vincent's Hosp.; sr. attending physician medicine, sr. cardiologist Nyack (N.Y.) Hosp.; med. dir. Presdl. Life Ins. Co., Nyack; bd. dirs. Metriplex, Inc. Cambridge, Mass., 1992—. Contbr. articles to profl. jours. Dir. cardiac epidemiology study Ford Found. Vera Inst.; mem. Internat. Com. on Thrombosis and Hemostasis. Capt. USAF, 1957-59. Fellow Am. Coll. Cardiology, ACP, N.Y. Acad. Medicine; mem. Am. Soc. Hematology, N.Y. Med. Soc., Sigma Xi. Home: 250 Townline Rd West Nyack NY 10994-2824 Office: 153 W 11th St New York NY 10011-8305

STUTTERHEIM, BEVERLY J. music teacher; b. Hays, Kans., July 2, 1938; d. Dallas Franklin and Inez Ruth (Gillman) Powers; m. Robert Eugene Stutterheim, Aug. 10, 1958; children: Monte, Tony, Michael. BS in Music Edn., Ft. Hays State U., 1960, MS in Music Edn., 1989. Cert. tchr.; cert. in piano and voice. Music tchr. LaCrosse (Kans.) Schs., 1960-62, WaKeeney (Kans.) Schs., 1962-68, Wichita (Kans.) Schs., 1969-72, Phillipsburg (Kans.) Schs., 1975-78, No. Valley Kans. Schs., Alemena-Long Island, 1979-88, Hays Schs., 1989—98, chmn. music dept., 1995-98; ret., 1998; pvt. music tchr., 1998—. Dir. cmty. chorus, Phillipsburg; dir. Children's Coll. Choir, Hays, 1996-98. Mem. Kans. Music Tchrs. Assn., Kans. Music Edn. Assn., ACDA, PEO, Orf. Avocations: golf, gardening, grandchildren, teaching church clubs. Home: 1198 W Navajo Rd Prairie View KS 67664-9723

STUTTS, GARY THOMAS, clinical analyst; b. Dyersburg, Tenn., Feb. 13, 1957; s. Wiley Thomas and Betty Jane (Weeks) S.; m. Amy Ayers, June 19, 1993; children: Andrew Thomas, Emily Lynn, Joseph Wayne, Allison Claire. AS, Austin Peay State U., Clarksville, Tenn., 1982; BS, Coll. St. Francis, Joliet, Ill., 1991; Paralegal, Blackstone Sch. Law, Dallas, 2000. RN Tenn., cert. managed care nurse, Am. Assn. Managed Care Nurses, 2001. Organ donor coord. Nashville Regional Organ Procurement Agy., 1984-85; staff nurse emergency unit Jesse Holman Jones Hosp., Springfield, Tenn., 1982-83; mem. nursing staff emergency dept. Jackson-Madison County Gen. Hosp., Jackson, 1983-94; nursing instr. Tenn. Tech. Ctr. at Jackson, 1994-95; geriat. liaison psychiat. unit Bolivar (Tenn.) Gen. Hosp., 1995-96; clin. nurse analyst, clin. svcs. evaluation and edn. dept. Blue Cross Blue Shield of Tenn., 1996—. Nurse preceptor Genentech, Inc.; mem. nursing practice adv. com. Tenn. Bd. Nursing. Home: 225 Us Highway 412 E Jackson TN 38305-9140 E-mail: Gary_Stutts@BCBST.com.

STUTTS, WILLIAM FLOYD, JR. lawyer, educator; b. El Dorado, Ark., Nov. 8, 1952; s. William Floyd and Marilyn Martin Stutts; m. Susan P. Campbell, May 16, 1992. BA, U. Tex., 1973; JD, U. Va., 1976. Bar: Tex. 1976, U.S. Dist. Ct. (we. dist.) Tex. 1992. Law clk. U.S. Ct. Appeals (5th cir.), Austin, 1976-77; assoc. Baker & Botts, Houston, 1978-85; ptnr. Baker Botts, Austin, 1987—, Clark, Thomas, Winters, Austin, 1985-87. Adj. prof. U. Tex. Law Sch., Austin, 1997—; instr., cons. Internat. Law Inst., Washington, 1998, 2001. Bd. dirs. Ballet Austin, 1988-96, Austin Oita Sister City Com., 1990—, Travis County Bar Assn., 1995-96, Capital Area Coun. Boy Scouts Am., Austin, 1996—. Fellow Am. Coll. Investment Counsel, Tex. Bar Found. (life); mem. ABA, Am. Bankruptcy Inst., Comml. Law League of Am. Lutheran. Home: 1405 Hardouin Ave Austin TX 78703 Office: Baker Botts 98 San Jacinto Blvd # 1500 Austin TX 78701

STUTZ, PEARL HEWLETT, retired photojournalist; b. Rochester, N.Y., Apr. 28, 1927; d. Herbert Henry Hewlett and Carolyn Amanda Brockmann; m. Peter Swan Stutz, May 23, 1953 (dec. July 1988); children: Eric Edward, Carolyn Edith Stutz Kourofsky. BA in Journalism, Ohio State U., 1949; MLS, SUNY, Geneseo, 1971. Cert. profl. libr. and media specialist, N.Y. Reporter Pampa (Tex.) Daily News, 1949, Great Falls (Mont.) Tribune, 1950; staff photographer Democrat and Chronicle, Rochester, 1950-56; libr. dir. Irondequoit Pub. Libr., 1976-91; ret., 1991. Libr. cons. Cancer Action, Inc., Rochester, 1992-01. Named Disting. Communicator, Women in Comms., 1996. Achievements include first woman press photographer for large-city newspaper.

STUTZENBERGER, LINDA PRUITT, music educator; b. Louisville, Mar. 17, 1944; d. Henry Edward and Margaret (Smith) Pruitt; m. David Ray Stutzenberger, Aug. 29, 1965; 1 child, Daniel Pruitt. MusB, U. Ky., Lexington, 1964; MusM, George Peabody Coll., Nashville, 1965; DMA, U. Md., College Park, 1979. Instr. Okaloosa-Walton Jr. Coll., Niceville, Fla., 1966-68; asst. prof., chmn. keyboard divsn. Shenandoah U., Winchester, Va., 1968-82; interim instr. Carson-Newman Coll., Jefferson City, Tenn., 1989, 97-98; vis. prof. U. Tenn., Knoxville, 1991-92; organist First Christian Ch., 1985—; program coord. music Pellissippi State Tech. C.C., 1989—. Coach, accompanist U. Tenn., Knoxville, 1983-89, 92-97. Recipient Outstanding Tchr. award Tenn. Gov.'s Sch. for Arts, 1993. Mem. Nat. Guild Piano Tchrs. (adjudicator), Am. Guild Organists, Knoxville Music Tchrs. Assn. (scholarship chair 1983—, Tchr. of Yr. 1999), Pi Kappa Lambda. Mem. Christian Ch. (Disciples Of Christ). Avocations: book club, antiques, gardening. E-mail: lstutzenberg@pstcc.edu.

STUTZMAN, L. LEE, pastor; b. Clinton, Okla., June 13, 1953; s. Clamens L. Stutzman and Viola Darlene (Waters) Bonn; m. Connie R. Stutzman, June 3, 1972; children: Elizabeth, Jonathan, Rebecca. BA in Theology, MS in Theol. Studies, D in Ministry, Vision Christian U. With traveling ministry, 1972-78; founder Liberty Temple, Lima, Ohio, 1978-88, Liberty Christian Cathedral, 1988—; with nat. traveling ministry; apostle Liberty Network of Chs., Dayton, Ohio, 1986—. Author: From the Ground Up, 1987; producer (TV show) Foundation for Faith, 1985—; motivational spkr., Sci. of Empowered Living Forum. Author: From the Ground Up, 1987, Order Out of Chaos, 1995, Spiritual Gifts, 1992; prodr. (TV show) Life Without Limit, 1985—. Republican. Office: Christ Cathedral 295 E Salem St Clayton OH 45315-9719 *The greatest key to Godly success: you've got to start where you're at to get where you're going.*

STUTZMAN, SANDRA LOUISE, advanced nurse practitioner; b. Ashland, Pa., Nov. 10, 1953; d. Kenneth Robert and Mary (Tersavige) S. Diploma, Sacred Heart Hosp. Sch., Norristown, Pa., 1979; LPN, Pottstown Meml. Med. Ctr.; diploma, St. Joseph Sch. Nursing, Reading, Pa., 1983; BSN, Pa. State U., Reading, 1991; MS, U. South Fla., 1994. Advanced RN practitioner. Advanced RN practitioner Infectious Disease Ctr., Tampa (Fla.) Gen. Hosp.; staff nurse Pottstown Meml. Med. Ctr.; advanced RN practitioner EverCare, Tampa, Fla., 1998-99, Sergio H. Vallejo, M.D., Lakeland, 1999—. Mem. Am. Acad. Nurse Practitioners, Fla. Nurses Assn., Sigma Theta Tau.

STUTZMAN, THOMAS CHASE, SR. lawyer; b. Portland, Oreg., Aug. 1, 1950; s. Leon H. and Mary L. (Chase) S.; m. Wendy Jeanne Craig, June 6, 1976; children: Sarah Ann, Thomas Chase Jr. BA with high honors, U. Calif., Santa Barbara, 1972; JD cum laude, Santa Clara U., 1975. Bar: Calif. 1976; cert. family law specialist. Pvt. practice, San Jose, Calif., 1976-79; pres., sec., CFO Thomas Chase Stutzman, PC, 1979—. Legal counsel DMJ Pro Care, Inc., Sparacino's Foods, Tax Firm, Inc., United Charities, Marina Assocs. Inc., E.M.I. Oil Filtration Systems, Inc., Creative Pacifica, Inc., Am. First Tech., Excel-Law Video, Inc., First Am. Real Estate Financing Co., Hoffman Industries, Inc., Info. Scan Tech., Inc., PRD Construction Mgmt. Svcs., Marine Biogenic Pharm. USA, Inc., Mi Pueblo Mt. View, Inc., others; instr. San Jose State U., 1977-78. Bd. dirs. Santa Cruz Campfire, 1978-80, Happy Hollow Park, 1978-80, 83-86, Pacific Neighbors, pres., 1991-92. Mem. Calif. Bar Assn., Santa Clara County Bar Assn. (chmn. environ. law com. 1976-78, exec. com. family law), Assn. Cert. Law Specialists, San Jose Jaycees (Dir. of Yr. 1976-77), Rotary, Lions (dir. 1979-81, 2d v.p. 1982-83, 1st v.p. 1983-84, pres. 1984-85), Scottish Rite, Masons, Phi Beta Kappa. Congregationalist. Office: 1625 The Alameda Ste 626 San Jose CA 95126-2207 E-mail: stutzman@tomstutzman.com.

STUTZMAN, WARREN LEE, electrical engineer, educator; b. Elgin, Ill., Oct. 22, 1941; s. James Earl and Christina Louise (Steidinger) S.; m. Claudia Janeanne Morris, Dec. 20, 1964; children: Darren Morris, Dana Lynn. BEE, AB in Math., U.Ill., 1964; MEE, Ohio State U., 1965, PhD in Elec. Engring., 1969. Asst. prof. Va. Poly. Inst. and State U., Blacksburg, 1969-74, assoc. prof., 1974-79, prof., 1979—, Thomas Phillips prof. engring., 1992—. Author: (with G. Thiele) Antenna Theory and Design, 1981, 2d edit., 1998, Polarization in Electromagnetic Systems, 1993. Fellow IEEE. Office: Va Poly Inst & State U Elec Engring Dept Blacksburg VA 24061-0111 E-mail: stutzman@vt.edu.

STUVER, FRANCIS EDWARD, former railway car company executive; b. Greenville, Pa., Aug. 22, 1912; s. Willard Seeley and Anna Katherine (Henry) S.; m. Jessie Lucile Bright, Jan. 26, 1938; children: Robert Edward, Nancy (Mrs. Randolph Patrick Mutdosch). Grad. high sch. With Greenville Steel Car Co. (subsidiary Pitts. Forgings Co.), 1937—, chief accountant, 1944-46, asst. treas., 1946-54, asst. sec., 1948-56, treas., 1956-61, v.p., 1956-61, exec. v.p., 1961-75, ret., 1975; pres. Greenville Savs. & Loan Assn., 1977-83, dir., 1949-83, Greenville Steel Car Co., 1961-74, Pitts. Forgings Co., 1975-80. Bd. dirs. Municipal Authority Borough Greenville, 1946-74, treas., 1946-73; bd. dirs., mem. exec. com. Mercer County br. Pa. Economy League, 1949-64; bd. dirs., treas., chmn. finance com. Greenville Hosp., 1953-59. Mem. Am. Ry. Car Inst. (dir. 1964-75) Clubs: Masons, Elks, Moose, KP, Greenville Country. Home: 46 Chambers Ave Greenville PA 16125-1856

STUVINSKI, B. C. See FELKER, WILLIAM H.

STWALLEY, BRIAN DAVID, pharmacist; b. Greencastle, Ind., Aug. 1, 1972; s. David Earl and Norma Jean Stwalley; m. Diane Marie Stwalley, Oct. 21, 1995; children: Andrew, Lauren. BS in Pharmacy, PharmD, Phila. Coll. Pharmacy Sci., 1996. Cert. geriatric pharmacist. Pharmacy mgr. Managed Care Rx, Lemoyne, Pa., 1996-98; v.p. clin. svcs. Continuing Care Rx, Camp Hill, 1998—. Fellow: Am. Soc. Cons. Pharmacists (pres. Pa. chpt. 2002); mem.: Am. Med. Dirs. Assn. Avocations: musician, reading, golfing. Home: 6 N Alydar Blvd Dillsburg PA 17019 Office: Continuing Care Rx 5775 Allentown Blvd Ste 202 Harrisburg PA 17112 E-mail: bdsrph@adelphia.net.

STWALLEY, WILLIAM CALVIN, physics and chemistry educator; b. Glendale, Calif., Oct. 7, 1942; s. Calvin Murdoch and Diette Clarice (Hanson) S.; m. Mauricette Lucille Frisius, June 14, 1963; children: Kenneth William, Steven Edward BS, Calif. Inst. Tech., 1964; PhD, Harvard U., 1968. Asst. prof. U. Iowa, Iowa City, 1968-72, assoc. prof., 1972-75, prof. dept. chemistry, 1975-93, prof. dept. physics and astronomy, 1977-93, dir. Iowa Laser Facility, 1979-93, dir. Ctr. for Laser Sci. and Engring., 1987-89, George Glockler prof. physical scis., 1988-93; program dir. NSF, Washington, 1975-76 (leave of absence); prof. and head dept. physics, prof. chemistry U. Conn., Storrs, 1993—, bd. trustees disting. prof., 2002—. Program chmn. Internat. Laser Sci. Conf., 1985, co-chmn., 1986, chmn., 1987; lectr. Chinese Acad. Scis., 1986. Editor books in field; contbr. numerous articles to profl. publs. Japan Soc. for Promotion of Sci. fellow, 1982; Sloan fellow, 1970-72; numerous grants in field, 1970—. Fellow Am. Phys. Soc. (sec.-treas. divsn. chem. physics 1984-90, vice chair/chair/past chair Topical Group on Laser Sci. 1989-92), Optical Soc. Am. (William F. Meggers award 1998); mem. AAAS, Am. Chem. Soc. Democrat. Avocations: comic books and cartoons, philately. Home: 21 Britony Dr Mansfield Center CT 06250-1647 Office: U Conn Unit 3046 Dept Physics Storrs Mansfield CT 06269 E-mail: w.stwalley@uconn.edu.

STYBEL, LAURENCE JAMES, business executive; b. N.Y.C., Aug. 16, 1947; s. Leo and Irene (Hirschman) S.; m. Maryanne Peabody, May 20, 1991; 1 child, Jennifer. BA cum laude, CCNY, 1969; MA in Clin./Cmty. Psychology, U. Tex., 1973; D of Adminstrn., Planning, Social Policy, Harvard U., 1978. Lic. psychologist, Mass. Staff psychologist Dallas County Mental Health Ctrs., 1972-74; sr. assoc. Hay Assocs., 1978-80; asst. prof. mgmt. Babson Coll., Wellesley, Mass., 1980-84; pres. Stybel, Peabody & Assocs., Inc., a Lincolnshire Internat Co., Waltham, 1980—, Lincolnshire Internat., 1999—; bd. dirs., CEO Interactive, Inc.; co-founder, bd. dirs. Boardoptions.com. Bd. dirs. Lincolnshire Internat. Co., Web000; cons. to fin. svcs., mfg., profl. svcs., health and ins., internet and utilities; presenter in field. Columnist Hosp. News, 1993-95. Corporator New England Bapt. Hosp. Mem. Nat. Assn. Corp. Dirs. (bd. dirs.) Avocations: golf, skiing. Home: 27 Bayfield Rd Wayland MA 01778-4205 Office: Sixty State St S 700 Boston MA 02109 E-mail: lstyble@stybelpeabody@com.

STYBLO, CLARENCE JOHN, retired surgeon; b. Cleve., Jan. 9, 1919; MD, St. Louis U., 1944. Diplomate Am. Bd. Surgery. Intern St. Mary's Group Hosps., St. Louis, 1944-45; resident in surgery Elyria (Ohio) Meml. Hosp., 1947-48, Jefferson Barracks VA Hosp., St. Louis, 1949-53; sugeon U.S. Vet. Hosp., Spokane, Wash., 1955-59; pvt. practice, 1959-86; ret., 1986. Officer in Med. Corps U.S. Army, 1945-47, 53-55. Mem. AMA, Calif. Med. Assn., Soc. Critical Care Medicine.

STYCOS, JOSEPH MAYONE, retired demographer, educator; b. Saugerties, N.Y., Mar. 27, 1927; s. Stravos and Clotilda (Mayone) S.; m. Maria Nowakowska, Nov. 25, 1964; children: Steven Andrew, Christina Mayone (by previous marriage), Marek. AB, Princeton U., 1947; PhD, Columbia U., 1954. WithBur. Applied Social Rsch. Columbia U., 1948-50, lectr. sociology, 1951-52; project co-dir. U. P.R., 1952-53; postgrad. PC fellow U. N.C., 1954-55; assoc. prof. sociology St. Lawrence U., 1955-57; faculty Cornell U., Ithaca, N.Y., 1957-2000, prof. emeritus, 2000, prof. sociology N.Y., 1963—, chmn. dept., 1966-70, dir. Latin Am. program, 1962-66, dir. internat. population program, 1962-88, prof. rural sociology, 1987-2001, dir. population and devel. program, 1988-92. Fulbright-Hayes Disting. prof. U. Warsaw, Poland, 1979; external examiner U. Ife, Nigeria, 1973; Cons. AID, 1962-64; sr. cons. Population Council, 1963-74, 77-79; cons. Airlie Found., 1972-73, Inst. for Research in Social Behavior, 1974, Clapp & Mayne, Inc., 1974, Ford-Rockefeller Population Program, 1977, Nat. U. Costa Rica, 1979, U. P.R.,

1979; trustee Population Reference Bur., 1964-68, cons., 1968-74; mem. exec. com. Internat. Planned Parenthood Fedn., West Hemmis, 1965-71, cons., 1971-77; adv. com. population and devel. OAS, 1968-70; mem. bd. Population Assn. Am., 1968-71, editorial cons. demography, 1965-69; adv. panel population Nat. Inst. Child Health and Human Devel., Dept. Health, Edn. and Welfare, 1969; co-chmn. population task force U.S. Nat. Commn. for UNESCO, 1972-73; adv. council, interdisciplinary communications program Smithsonian Instn., 1974-76; cons. Pan Am. Health Orgn., WHO, 1975; cons. steering com., acceptability task force WHO, 1978-85; cons. UNESCO, 1978-79, UN Fund for Population Activities, 1979-82, WHO, 1987-90; co-dir. Spanish family life project U. Complutense de Madrid, 1978-80; internat. adv. coun. Internat. Ctr. Photography, 1979-95; Fulbright-Hays prof. Nat. U. Costa Rica, spring 1986; chmn. U.S. Census Adv. Com. on Population Stats., 1983-84; mem. Fulbright-Hays program Nat. Screening Com. Cen. Am., 1989-92; population rsch. team Environ. & Natural Resources Policy & Tng. Project, 1992-96; planning com. Global Omnibus Environ. Survey (GOES) Human Dimensions of Global Environ. Change Program, 1993—, chair, 1996-97. Author: (with Hussein Abdel Aziz Sayed, Roger Avery and Samuel Firdman) Community Development and Family Planning: An Egyptian Experiment, 1988; mem. editl. bd. Human Orgn., 1962-64; editor: Demography as an Interdiscipline, 1989. Mem. council Cornell U., 1969-70. Mem. Rural Sociological Soc., Am. Sociological Assn., Population Assn. of Am., Internat. Union for the Scientific Study of Population. Home: 28 Twin Glens Rd Ithaca NY 14850-1041 Office: Cornell U Population & Devel Program Warren Hall Ithaca NY 14853-7801

STYER, OSCAR HARRY, machinist; b. West Chester, Pa., Oct. 13, 1940; s. Jonathan Penrose and Virginia Reese S.; m. Joan Harding, Dec. 23, 1967; children; Nancy, Kevin (dec.). BA, Lexington Bapt. Coll., 1971. Machinist varius cos., N.J., 1972-79; machinist, leadman Flinchbaugh Products, Red Lion, Pa., 1979-81; shop foreman Pneu-Hydro Products, Wharton, N.J., 1981-82; toolmaker Gen. Wire, Randolph, 1983-85; machinist Strahman Valves, Florham Park, 1986—. With USN, 1961-65. Republican. Avocations: carpentry, running, golf, investing, photography. Home and Office: 358 Willow Grove St Hackettstown NJ 07840 E-mail: harrys1@mindspring.com.

STYLE, CHRISTINE L. art educator, curator; b. Mar. 21, 1952; BS, U. Wis., Madison, 1974; MFA, U. Wis., Milw., 1986. V.p. Print Forum/Milw. Art Mus., 1997-98, pres., 1998-2000; asst. to the curator U. Wis., Green Bay, 1987-93, assoc. prof., 1993—. Office: 2731 Bay Settlement Rd Green Bay WI 54311-7360 E-mail: stylec@uwgb.edu.

STYLER, ANDA JASAMINE, artist, educator; b. Norfolk, Va., Sept. 25, 1952; d. Franklin Merritt Brown and Edith Kathrine Knox; m. Richard James Barbera, Aug. 13, 1978 (div. Dec. 18, 1992); children: Melonie Ann Carroll. Student, Western State U., 1979-80; BFA, Parsons Sch. Design, 1983. Asst. art dir. Altamount Advtg., N.Y.C., 1983-84, Bell Yellow Pages, Elmsford, N.Y., 1984-86; art dir. Dellwood Pub., N.Y.C., 1986-93; freelance artist Wire Focus, Danbuy, Conn., 1994-98; tchr. various workshops, 1992—. Judge art work, show Watertown Art League, Conn., 1999, Soc. Creative Artists, Newtown, Conn., 2000, Memphis Art League, Tenn., 2000; tchr. The Art Ctr., Danbury, Conn. 1990; selected artist Gibson Card Co., 1994, 97; designer artwork Accent on Home, 1994; cover designer Women's Forum Mag. Using Quilts, 1993. One woman show at Bay State Med. Ctr., Springfield, Mass., 1995; exhibited in group shows at Nat. Congress Art Show, 1988, Art Horizons Show, 1989 (cert. excellence), Houstatonic Art League Show , 1989 (1st pl. award), Bethel Art League Show, 1989, 90, 91 (1st pl. award 1989, 91, 2d pl. award 1990), Richter Assn. Arts Show, 1989, 90, Housatonic Art League Summer Show, 1989, The Gallery Card, Kent, Conn., 1989, Ariel Gallery, N.Y.C., 1989, Soc. Creative Artisits Newton, 1990 (2d pl. award), Kent Gallery, Paris, N.Y., 1990, Hartford Architecture Conservancy, 1991, Conn. Capital Bldg., 1991, Aetna Gallery, Hartford, Conn., 1991, Gallery 7, Danbury, 1991 (featured painting), Christi Gallery, Washington, 1992, The Artist Son Gallery, Boston, 1993, The Madison Ave. Art Gallery, Memphis, 1995, Beaux Art Gallery, Southbury, Conn., 1996, The Birchstone Gallery, Egg Harbor, Wis., 1996, Springfield Mus. Fine Art, 1997, Birchstone Gallery & Studio, Egg Harbor, 1997, 98, 2000, Beaux Arts, Woodbury, 1998, 99, Food for Thought Gallery, New Milford, 2000; represented in permanent collections Morales Art Gallery, Nags Head, N.C., Beaux Art Gallery, Woodbury, Conn., Peel Gallery, Danby, Vt., Fleck Worner Fine Art, West Palm Beach, Fla., Barn Gallery, New Fairfield, Conn., Bay State Hosp., Springfield, Mass., St. Frances Hosp., Hartford, Conn., St. Vincents Hosp., Bridgeport, Conn., GTE Corp., Stamford, Conn., Bank Boston, Dean Witter, West Palm Beach. Recipient Honor award The Artist Mag., 1995. Mem. Husdon Valley Art Assn. (hon. mention award 1989), Richter Assn. Arts (bd. dirs. 1989, 91, two 2d pl. award 1989, 1st pl. acrylics award 1990, judge 1990, 91, 1st pl. award 1992), Avocations: quilting, gardening, collecting salt glaze pottery, cooking.

STYLES, ANGELA B. federal agency administrator; BA with distinction, U. Va.; JD with honors, U. Tex. Legis. aide Congressman Joe Barton , Washington; counsel Miller & Chevalier; wigh gen. svcs. adminstrn. Office Govt.-Wide Policy and Pub. Bldgs. Svcs., 2001; counselor to the dir. Office Mgmt. and Budget; adminstr. for fed. procurement policy Exec. Office of the Pres., Washington, 2001—. Articles editor: Am. Jour. Criminal Law. Mem.: ABA (chair legis. coordinating com. sect. pub. contract law, vice chair acctg., cost and pricing com.), Order of the Coif. Office: Exec Office of the Pres Fed Procurement Policy EEOB 17th & Pennsylvania Ave NW Washington DC 20503*

STYLES, BEVERLY, entertainer; b. Richmond, Va., June 6, 1923; d. John Harry Kenealy and Juanita Russell (Robins) Carpenter; m. Wilbur Cox, Mar. 14, 1942 (div.); m. Robert Marascia, Oct. 5, 1951 (div. Apr. 1964). Studies with Ike Carpenter, Hollywood, Calif., 1965—98; student, Am. Nat. Theatre Acad., 1968—69; studies with Paula Raymond, Hollywood, 1969—70; diploma, Masterplan Inst., Anaheim, Calif., 1970. Freelance performer, musician, 1947-81; owner Beverly Styles Music, Joshua Tree, Calif., 1971—. V.p. spl. programs Lawrence Program of Calif., Yucca Valley, Calif.; talent coord., co-founder Quiet Place Studio, Yucca Valley, 1994; mem. exec. bd., awards dir. Am. chpt. Diogenes Process Group, 1996—. Composer, lyricist: (songs) Joshua Tree, 1975, Wow, Wow, Wow, 1986, World of Dreams, 1996, Thank You God, 1996, (music for songs) I'm Thankful, 1978, The Whispering, 1994; piano arrangements include Colour Chords and Moods, 1995, Desert Nocturne, 1996; records include The Perpetual Styles of Beverly, 1978; albums include The Primitive Styles of Beverly, 1977; tape cassettes include Gospel Diamonds, 1996; author: A Special Plan to Think Upon, The Truth as Seen by a Composer, 1978, A Special Prayer to Think Upon, 1983. Mem. ASCAP (Gold Pin award), Profl. Musicians Local 47 (life), Internat. Platform Assn. Republican. Avocation: creating abstract art. Home and Office: 7839 Aster Ave Yucca Valley CA 92284-4130

STYLES, TERESA JO, producer, educator; b. Atlanta, Oct. 19, 1950; d. Julian English and Jennie Marine (Sims) S. BA, Spelman Coll., 1972; MA, Northwestern U., 1973; PhD, U. N.C., Chapel Hill, 1998. Rschr. CBS News, N.Y.C., 1975-80, prodr., 1980-85; instr. mass comms. and English Savannah (Ga.) State Coll., 1985-89, asst. prof. English, 1990; asst. prof. mass comm. and women studies dir. Bennett Coll., Greensboro, N.C., 1990-93; assoc. prof. mass comm. N.C. A&T State U., 1993—, interim chair speech and comm., 2001—. Researcher documentary CBS Reports: Teddy, 1979 (Emmy cert.); assoc. producer documentaries for CBS Reports: Blacks: America, 1979 (Columbia Dupont cert. 1979), What Shall We Do About Mother?, 1980 (Emmy cert.), The Defense of the U.S., 1980 (Columbia Dupont cert.). Adv. bd. Greensboro Hist. Mus., Eastern Music Festival, Women's Short Film Project. Mem. Writers Guild Am. (bd. dirs. east 1991-95), Dirs. Guild Am. (bd. dirs. east 1991-95), African Am. Atelier (Greensboro, N.C. bd. dirs.), Eastern Music Festival (bd. dirs.). Avocation: swimming. Home: 4400 Suffolk Trl Greensboro NC 27407-7842 E-mail: teresaj@ncat.edu.

STYNE, DENNIS MICHAEL, physician, educator; b. Chgo., July 31, 1947; s. Irving and Bernice (Coopersmith) S.; m. Donna Petre, Sept. 5, 1971; children: Rachel, Jonathan, Juliana, Aaron. BS, Northwestern U., 1969, MD, 1971. Diplomate Am. Bd. Pediats. Intern in pediatrics U. Calif., San Diego, 1971-72, resident in pediatrics, 1972-73, Yale U., New Haven, 1973-74; fellow in pediatric endocrinology U. Calif., San Francisco, 1974-77, asst. prof. pediatrics, 1977-83, assoc. prof. Davis, 1983-90, prof., 1990—, chair pediatrics, 1989-97; now prof., sect. chief pediatric endocrinology U. Calif. Davis Med. Ctr., Sacramento. Author numerous book chpts., contbr. articles to profl. jours. Mem. Endocrine Soc., Soc. Pediat. Rsch., Am. Pediat. Soc., Am. Acad. Pediats., Lawson Wilkins Soc. for Pediat. Endocrinology, Western Assn. of Physicians. Avocations: sailing, music. Office: UC Davis Med Ctr Dept Pediat 2516 Stockton Blvd Fl 3 Sacramento CA 95817-2208

STYNE, MARLYS MARSHALL, retired English educator; b. Whitewater, Wis., Oct. 12, 1932; d. Clifford William and Violet Marie (Uhl) Marshall; m. Robert Carter Clark, Feb. 14, 1959 (div. Sept. 1964); m. Julian Harold Styne, June 27, 1970 (dec. Mar. 2000). BA, Luther Coll., 1954; MA, U. Minn., 1957; postgrad., U. Wis., 1958-59. Instr. English W.Va. U., Morgantown, 1956-58; tchg. asst. U. Wis., Madison, 1958-59; instr. English Wilbur Wright Coll., Chgo., 1959-65, asst. prof., 1965-76, assoc. prof., 1976-87, prof. English, 1987-99, chair. dept. English, 1993-99; ret., 1999. Adj. faculty dept. English, Wilbur Wright Coll., Chgo., 2000—. Contbr. articles to profl. jours. Recipient Outstanding C.C. Faculty award Ill. C.C. Trustees Assn., 1996, Excellence award Nat. Inst. Staff and Orgnl. Devel., Austin, Tex., 1996. Avocations: travel, opera, classical music, writing. E-mail: mstyne@aol.com.

STYNES, STANLEY KENNETH, retired chemical engineer, educator; b. Detroit, Jan. 18, 1932; s. Stanley Kenneth and Bessie Myrtle (Casey) S.; m. Marcia Ann Meyers, Aug. 27, 1955; children: Peter Casey, Pamela Kay, Suzanne Elizabeth. BS, Wayne State U., 1955, MS, 1958; PhD, Purdue U., 1963. Lab. asst. U. Chgo., 1951; instr. Purdue U., 1960-63; asst. prof. chem. engring. Wayne State U., Detroit, 1963-64, assoc. prof., 1964-71, prof., 1971-92, dean engring., 1972-85, prof. emeritus, 1992—. Dir. Energy Conversion Devices, Inc., Troy, Mich., MacMedia; cons. Schwayder Chem. Metallurgy Co., 1965, chemistry dept. Wayne State U., 1965—66, Claude B. Schneible Co., Holly, Mich., 1968. Contbr. engring. articles to profl. jours. Mem. coun. on environ. strategy S.E. Mich. Coun. Govts., 1976—81; sec.-treas. Mich. Ednl. Rsch. Info. Triad; trustee Sci. Ctr. Met. Detroit, 1980—92; mem. ops. com. MACTV, 2000; bd. dirs. Program for Minorities in S.E. Mich., Sci. and Engring. Fair of Met. Detroit, pres., 1983; bd. dirs. Midwest Program for Minorities in Engring., Friends of Herrick Dist. Libr. Ford Found. fellow, 1959-63; DuPont fellow, 1962-63; Wayne State U. faculty research fellow, 1964-65 Fellow: AIChE (past chmn. Detroit sect.), Mich. Soc. Profl. Engrs. (pres. 1987—88), Engring. Soc. Detroit (past bd. dirs.); mem.: Adult Learning Inst. (bd. dirs. 1994—99), Engring. Sci. Devel. Found. (pres. 1992—94), Am. Chem. Soc., Phi Lambda Upsilon, Omicron Delta Kappa, Tau Beta Pi, Sigma Xi. Presbyterian. Home: 145 Columbia #609 Holland MI 49423-2980 E-mail: stynes@macatawa.org.

STYPULKOWSKI, JACEK BOGDAN, geotechnical engineer; b. Wroclaw, Poland, Jan. 27, 1959; s. Bogdan Daniel and Krystyna Stypulkowski; m. Bogda Kolt, Feb. 16, 1993; children: Anna Monica, Luke Jacek. DSc, Wroclaw U. Tech., Poland, 1999, MSc, 1983; MEng, McMaster U., Hamilton, Ont., Canada, 1987. Profl. Engrs. , Ont., 1992, engring. lic., Poland, 1998, Profl. Engrs., Tex. State Bd. Profl. Engrs., 2002. Student trainee Civil Engring. Bur., Rovaniemi , Finland, 1980; tchg. asst., rsch. asst. Geotechnical Inst., Wroclaw, Poland, 1983—85, Civil Engring. and Engring. Mechanics Dept., McMaster U., Hamilton, Canada, 1985—87; geotechnical engr. Sarafinchin Assocs. Ltd., Toronto, Canada, 1987—88, Acres Internat. Ltd., Niagara Falls, Canada, 1988—93; sr. geotechnical engr. Toronto Transit Commn., Toronto, Canada, 1994—98; lead geotechnical engr. Parsons Brinckerhoff Quade & Douglas, Inc. , N.Y.C., 1998—. Contbr. articles to profl. jours. Internat. v.p. Independed Student Orgn., Wroclaw, Poland, 1980—82. Mem.: ASCE, European Fedn. Nat. Engring. Assns., Internat. Soc. Soil Mechanics and Found. Engring., Internat. Soc. Rock Mechanics, Internat. Tunnelling Assn., Polish Assn. Civil Engrs. and Technologists, Tunneling Assn. Canada, Canadian Geotechnical Soc., Am. Underground Cons. Assn. Home: 11 Loret Ln East Northport NY 11731 Office: PBQD Inc One Penn Plz New York NY 10119 Office Fax: 212-465-5592. Personal E-mail: jstypulk@optonline.net. Business E-Mail: stypulkowski@pbworld.com.

STYRON, ROSE, human rights activist, poet, journalist; b. Balt., Apr. 4, 1928; d. Benjamin Bernei and Selma (Kann) Burgunder; m. William Styron, May 4, 1953; children: Susanna, Polly, Thomas, Alexandra. BA, Wellesley Coll., 1950; MA, Johns Hopkins U., 1952; LHD (hon.), Briarcliff Coll., 1976, SUNY, Purchase, 1991, Trinity Coll., 2000. Bd. dirs. Amnesty Internat., USA, N.Y.C., 1973-83, chair nat. adv. coun., 1984-94. Author: (poems) From Summer to Summer, 1965, Thieves' Afternoon, 1973, By Vineyard Light, 1995; co-author, translator: Modern Russian Poetry, 1972; contbr. editorials, profiles, articles, book revs. and poetry to maj. newspapers and mags. Chair, judge Robert F. Kennedy Meml. Human Rights Award, 1983—; mem. adv. bd. Reebok Found. for Human Rights, 1987—; mem. exec. bd. Human Rights Watch, N.Y.C., 1975-94; bd. dirs. Acad. of Am. Poets, 1995—, Equality Now, 1993—; chmn. adv. coun. Roxbury (Conn.) Libr., 1990-92; bd. dirs. N.Y. Found. for Arts, N.Y.C., 1986-94, Lawyers Com. for Human Rights, N.Y.C., 1981—, Rainforest Found., 1989-95, Assn. to Benefit Children, 1993—, Folger Shakespeare Libr., 1994-00; bd. overseers NYU Faculty of Arts and Scis., 1994—. Mem. P.E.N. (chair freedom-to-write com. 1983-89, bd. dirs. 1983-93), Coun. Fgn. Rels., Vineyard Haven Yacht Club. Democrat. Home: 12 Rucum Rd Roxbury CT 06783-1906

STYRON, WILLIAM, writer; b. Newport News, Va., June 11, 1925; s. William Clark and Pauline Margaret (Abraham) S.; m. Rose Burgunder, May 4, 1953; children: Susanna Margaret, Paola Clark, Thomas, Claire Alexandra. Student, Christchurch Sch., Davidson Coll.; Litt.D., Davidson Coll., 1986; AB, Duke U., 1947, Litt.D., 1968. Fellow Am. Acad. Arts and Letters at Am. Acad. in Rome, 1953; fellow Silliman Coll., Yale, 1964-99. Jury pres. Cannes Film Festival, 1983. Author: novels Lie Down in Darkness, 1951, The Long March, 1953, Set This House on Fire, 1960, The Confessions of Nat Turner, 1967 (Pulitzer prize 1968, Howells medal Am. Acad. Arts and Letters 1970), Sophie's Choice, 1979 (Am. Book award 1980), In the Clap Shack (play), 1972, This Quiet Dust, 1982, Darkness Visible, 1990, A Tidewater Morning, 1993; also articles, essays, revs.; editor: Best Stories from the Paris Rev., 1959; adv. editor: Paris Rev., 1953— ; mem. editorial bd. The Am. Scholar, 1970-76. Decorated Commandeur de l'Ordre des Arts et des Lettres, Commandeur Legion d'Honneur (France); recipient Duke U. Disting. Alumni award, 1984, Conn. Arts award, 1984, Prix Mondial del Duca, 1985, Elmer Holmes Bobst award for fiction, 1989, Edward MacDowell medal for excellence in the arts, 1988, Nat. Mag. award, 1990, Nat. medal of Arts, 1993, Medal of Honor, Nat. Arts Club, 1995, Common Wealth award, 1995, F. Scott Fitzgerald award, 1996. Mem. Am. Acad. Arts and Scis., Am. Acad. Arts and Letters, Soc. Am. Historians, Signet Soc., Harvard, Académie Goncourt, Phi Beta Kappa. Democrat.

STYSLINGER, LEE JOSEPH, JR. manufacturing company executive; b. Birmingham, Ala., June 28, 1933; s. Lee Joseph and Margaret Mary (McFarl) S.; m. Catherine Patricia Smith, Apr. 30, 1960; children— Lee Joseph III, Jon Cecil, Mark Joseph. Student, U. Ala., 1952. Pres., chief exec. officer Altec Industries, Inc. and predecessors, truck equipment mfrs., Birmingham, 1956-89, chief exec. officer, chmn. bd., 1989-92, chmn., 1992—. Bd. dirs. MeadWestvaco Corp., Jemison Investment Co., Birmingham, Ala., Electronic Healthcare Systems, Advanced Labelworx. Bd. dirs. St. Vincent's Hosp. Mem. Country Club Birmingham, Mountain Brook Club, Shoal Creek Club, Willow Point Golf and Country Club, Jupiter Island Club (Hobe Sound, Fla.), Rotary. Roman Catholic. Home: 3260 E Briarcliff Rd Birmingham AL 35223-1305 Office: 210 Inverness Center Dr Birmingham AL 35242-4834

STYVE, ORLOFF WENDALL, JR. electrical engineer; b. Winnebago, Minn., Feb. 1, 1936; s. Orloff Wendall and Katharine (Drake) S.; m. Jane Carol Meister, Feb. 25, 1961 (div. 1981); children: Elizabeth Anne, David John, Robert Peter, Susan Katharine; m. Beverly Ann Cauwels, Sept. 5, 1997; stepchildren: Nicole Marie, Trevor Ray, Travis John. BEE, U. Minn., 1959. Registered profl. engr., Wis. Dist. distbn. engr. Wis. Electric Power Co., Menomonee Falls, 1959-69, divsn. distbn. engr., then svc. ctr. engring. supr. West Bend, 1969-73, planning engr. Milw., 1973-76, sr. underground dist. engr., 1976-84, elec. engr. underground dist., 1984-94; cons. elect. distbn. engr Slinger (Wis.) Utilities, 1995-96, utility mgr., 1996; dir. WPPI, 1996, sr. engr., cons. engring., 1996-2000. Mem. elec. bd., West Bend, 1972-94. Mem. IEEE (voting mem. 1993, insulated conductors com. 1991—, balloting com. 1998—), Assn. of Edison Illuminating Cos. (cable engring. sect. 1991-94), Am. Nat. Stds. Inst. (distbn. transformer stds. com. 1985-88), Masons, Scottish Rite (chmn. stage properties and elec. effects com. 1986-2000, stage dir. 1998-2000, Wis. Player's award Valley of Wis. 1989, Svc. award 1991), Shriners (potentate's aide emeritus Tripoli Shrine 1986), Nat. Honor Soc. Avocations: amateur theater, camping. Office: PO Box 67016 Saint Petersburg FL 33736-7016 E-mail: styve@juno.com.

SU, DONGWEI, economist, educator; b. Xiamen, Fujian, People's Republic China, Dec. 12, 1970; s. Jinyu Su and Yuande Lin; m. Nan Chi. BA, Xiamen U., 1992; MA, Ohio State U., 1993, PhD, 1997. Asst. prof. U. Akron, 1997—. Expert Inst. of Fin. Rsch. and Edn., McGill U., Montreal, Can., 1997—. Contbr. articles to profl. jours. Dir. Chinese Fin. Assn. in Am., Columbia U., 1996. Rsch. fellow Sandra-Ann Morsillis Pacific-Basin Capital Markets Rsch. Ctr., 1997—. Avocations: biking, cooking, reading, movies, classical music. Office: Univ of Akron Dept Econs Akron OH 44325-0001 Home: 330 Union Pl Akron OH 44304-1315 E-mail: su@uakron.edu.

SU, GEORGE SHENGHUI (SHENG-HUI SU), medicinal chemist, researcher; b. Shanghai, Mar. 9, 1941; came to U.S., 1992; s. Cheng-Ye and Zao-Fu (Hwang) S.; m. Qi Qi Zhang, Mar. 8, 1967; 1 child, Junjie. BS in Pharmacy, Shanghai Med. U., 1962, PhD in Med. Chemistry, 1966. Vis. rsch. fellow Inst. Microbial Chemistry, Tokyo, 1981-83; v.p., R & D dir. Shanghai Inst. Pharm. Industry, 1983-89, rsch. prof., 1989-92; rsch. scientist BioGenex Labs., San Ramon, Calif., 1992-95, sr. rsch. scientist, mgr. R & D, 1995-99, dir. R & D, 2000—. Guest prof. Shanghai Inst. Pharm. Industry, 1993—. Contbr. articles to profl. jours. Mem. AAAS, Am. Chem. Soc., Chinese Am. Chem. Soc. Achievements include patents in field; development of novel synthetic process for antibiotics Amikacin, Tobramycin, cephalosporins and penicillins; invention and development of novel technology for DNA synthesis applied in oligonucleotide labeling and signal amplification. Home: 2 Craydon Ct San Ramon CA 94583-3906 Office: BioGenex Labs 4600 Norris Canyon Rd San Ramon CA 94583-1320 E-mail: geoshsu@hotmail.com., georges@biogenex.com.

SU, JEN-HOUNE HANNSEN, mechanical engineer; b. Taipei, Taiwan, Aug. 31, 1954; came to U.S. 1978; BS, Nat. Cen. U., Chung-Li, Taiwan, 1977; MS, Ohio State U., 1979, PhD, 1982. Rsch. asst. Ohio State U., Dept. Engring. Mechanics, Columbus, 1978-82; project engr. Structural Mechanics Consultants Corp., Warren, Mich., 1982-84; sr. rsch. engr. Goodyear Rsch. Div., Akron, Ohio, 1984-89; sr. rsch. engr., program mgr. Carderock div. Naval Surface Warfare Ctr., West Bethesda, Md., 1989—. Contbr. articles to profl. jours.; patentee (2) in field. Pres. Taiwanese Assn. of Akron, 1988, N. Am. Tiwanese Profs. Assn., 2001. Mem. AIAA (sr. mem.), ASME, SAE, Am. Soc. for Composites, Acoustical Soc. Am., Phi Kappa Phi. Avocations: dance, golf, basketball. Home: 14123 Rock Canyon Dr Centreville VA 20121-3861 Office: Naval Surface Warfare Ctr Code 722 9500 Macarthur Blvd West Bethesda MD 20817-5701 E-mail: suj@asme.org.

SU, JULIE, legal association administrator; BA, Stanford U., 1991; JD, Harvard U., 1994. With Asian Am. Legal Ctr., L.A., 1994—, dir. litig. Recipient Reebok Internat. Human Rights award, 1996, Individual Award of Achievement, State Bar Calif., 1996, Am. Spirit award, Changing Images in Am., 1997, Adv. award, Nat. Asian Women's Health Orgn., 1998, Achievement award for pub. svc., YWCA, 1998; fellow Skadden fellow, 1994—96. Office: Asian Pacific Am Legal Ctr 1145 Wilshire Blvd Fl 2 Los Angeles CA 90017*

SU, KENDALL LING-CHIAO, engineering educator; b. Fujian, China, July 10, 1926; came to U.S., 1948; s. Ru-chen and Sui-hsiong (Wang) S.; m. Jennifer Gee-tsone Chang, Sept. 10, 1960; children: Adrienne, Jonathan. BEE, Xiamen U., Peoples Republic China, 1947; MEE, Ga. Inst. Tech, 1949; PhD, Ga. Inst. Tech., 1954. Jr. engr. Taiwan Power Co., Taipei, Republic China, 1947-48; asst. prof. Ga. Inst. Tech., Atlanta, 1954-59, assoc. prof., 1959-65, prof., 1965-70, Regents prof., 1970-94, Regents' prof. emeritus, 1994—. Mem. tech. staff Bell Labs., Murray Hill, N.J., 1957. Author: Active Network Synthesis, 1965, Time-Domain Synthesis of Linear Networks, 1969, Fundamentals of Circuits, Electronics, and Signal Analysis, 1978, Handbook of Tables for Elliptic-Function Filters, 1990, Fundamentals of Circuit Analysis, 1993, Analog Filters, 1996; mem. sci. adv. com. Newton Graphic Sci. mag., 1987—. Fellow IEEE (life); mem. Sigma Xi (pres. Ga. Inst. Tech. chpt. 1968-69, 72-73, Faculty Rsch. award 1957), Phi Kappa Phi, Eta Kappa Nu. Methodist. Office: Ga Inst Tech Sch Elec & Comp Engring Atlanta GA 30332-0250 E-mail: ksu@ece.gatech.edu.

SU, TSUNG-CHOW JOE, engineering educator; b. Taipei, Taiwan, Republic of China, July 9, 1947; came to U.S., 1969; s. Chin-shui and Chen-ling (Shih) S.; m. Hui-Fang Angie Huang, Dec. 26, 1976; children: Julius Tsu-Li, Jonathan Tsu-Wei, Judith Tsu-Te, Jessica Tsu-Yun. BS, Nat. Taiwan U., 1968; MS in Aeronautics, Calif. Inst. Technology, 1970, AE, 1973; EngScD, Columbia U., 1974. Registered profl. engr., Fla., Tex. Rsch. teaching asst. Calif. Inst. Technology, Pasadena, 197-72; rsch. asst. Columbia U., N.Y.C., 1972-73; naval architect John J. McMullen Assoc., Inc., 1974-75; asst. prof. civil engring. Tex. A&M U., College Station, Tex., 1976-82; assoc. prof. ocean engring. Fla. Atlantic U., Boca Raton, 1982-87, prof. ocean engring, 1987-92, prof. mech. engring., 1992—. Contbr. over 80 articles to profl. jours.; assoc. editor Jour. Engring. Mechs., 1991-94. Coord. Calif. Tech. Alumni Fund, South Fla. area, 1987-88. 2d lt. Chinese Army, 1968-69. Grantee in field. Fellow AIAA (assoc.); mem. ASME, ASCE (chmn. fluids com. 1992-94), Am. Acad. Mechanics, Calif. Tech. Alumni Assn., Royal Palm Improvement Assn. Home: 2150 Areca Palm Rd Boca Raton FL 33432-7994 Office: Fla Atlantic U Dept Mech Engring Boca Raton FL 33431 E-mail: su@fau.edu.

SUAREZ, GEORGE MICHAEL, urologist; b. Havana, Cuba, Apr. 21, 1955; came to U.S., 1955; s. Miguel Angel and Elena (Sanchez) S. BA, Heideberg U., 1976; MD, U. Dominica, Portsmouth, 1980, Rutgers U., 1980. Diplomate Am. Bd. Urology; lic. physician, Ind., Fla., La. Intern straight gen. surgery Columbus-Cuneo-Cabrini Med. Ctr., Northwestern U. Med. Sch., Chgo., 1980-81, resident gen. surgery, 1981-82; urology rsch. fellow Tulane U. Sch. Medicine and Delta Regional Primate Ctr., New Orleans, 1982-83; resident, chief resident urology Tulane U. Sch. Medicine, 1983-87; attending urologist, dir. urodynamics lab. spinal cord unit VA Med. Ctr., Miami, Fla., 1987-90; attending urologist U. Miami Hosp. and Clinics, 1987-90, dir. Urodynamics Lab., Jackson Meml. Med. Ctr., 1987-90, dir. urology rehab. rsch. program Bantle Rehab. Rsch. Ctr., 1987—; attending urologist Jackson Meml. Hosp., Miami, 1987—; asst. prof. dept. urology U. Miami Sch. Medicine, 1987-90. Cons. Sylvester Comprehensive Cancer Ctr., Miami, 1987—, Childrens Med. Svcs., Miami, 1987—, Avalon Technologies, Indpls., Mentor Corp., Santa Barbara, Calif., Cook Urol., Spence, Ind., Teknar Ultrasound, Inc., Santa Barbara, Schering Labs. N.J., Rorer Pharms., Ft. Washington, Pa.; attending urologist Doctors Hosp., Bat. Hosp., Childrens Hosp., South Miami Hosp., Larkin Hosp., Mercy Hosp., Victoria Hosp., West Gables Hosp., Cedars Med. Ctr., Kidney Stone Ctr. Contbr. articles to profl. jours. Founder, pres. For the Love of Life Found. Recipient Urology Rsch. award Touro Infirmary Hosp., New Orleans, 1983-84, award of excellence Video Urology, 1989. Mem. ACS, AMA, Am. Acad. Pediatrics, Am. Fertility Soc., Am. Med. Polit. Action Com., Am. Soc. Andrology,. Am. Urol. Assn., Colegio Interam. de Medicos y Cirujanos, Am. Confederation Urology, Cuban Am. Urol. Soc., Dade County Med. Assn., European Urologic Soc., Fla. Med. Assn., Fla. Urol. Soc., Internat. Continence Soc., Greater Miami Urol. Soc., N.Y. Acad. Scis., So. Med. Assn., World Med. Assn., Urodynamics Soc., Surg. Aid to Children of the World, Internat. Soc. Urology. Office: Miami Urologic Inst PO Box 143167 Coral Gables FL 33114-3167

SUAREZ, MICHAEL ANTHONY, civil engineer, consultant; b. Havana, Cuba, Dec. 14, 1948; came to U.S., 1961, naturalized, 1973; s. Miguel Angel and Elena Felicia (Sanchez) Suarez. BS in Civil Engring., U. Miami, 1973, postgrad., 1974. Registered profl. engr., Fla.; lic. gen. contractor, Fla. Civil engr. Bert Saul Cons. Engr., Miami, 1969-72, De-Zarraga & Donnell Cons. Engrs., Coral Gables, Fla., 1972-76; spl. cons. Cadillac Fairview-Southeastern Fla. Properties, Miami, 1976-80; pres., dir. Michael A. Suarez & Assocs., Inc. Cons. Engrs., 1980—. Pres. Summa Devel. Corp., Real Devel. Corp., United Capital Group, Inc.; spl. cons. to chmn. of the bd. Ashland Oil Co.; pres. Gulfstream Petroleum Co., Brit. Oil Refining Co., Ltd. Mem. nat. adv. bd. Am. Security Coun.; chmn.'s adviser U.S. Congl. Adv. Bd.; mem. Rep. Presdl. Task Force, Rep. Nat. Com., Fgn. Affairs Coun. Recipient Presdl. Achievement award. Mem. NSPE, ASCE, Fla. Engring. Soc., Constrn. Specifications Inst., Am. Concrete Inst., Pre-Stressed Concrete Inst., Nat. Engring. and Physics Honor Socs. Republican. Roman Catholic.

SUAREZ, PATRICK JOSEPH, technology company executive; b. Canton, Ohio, Mar. 17, 1948; s. Benjamin and Mary Suzanne (DeBord) S.; m. Nola Jean Pencil, Apr. 29, 1972; children: Gregory Edmund, Justin Gabriel. BA in Polit. Sci., Wright State U., 1975; MS in Adminstrn., Cen. Mich. U., 1989. Contract specialist Aero. Systems div. Wright-Patterson AFB, Ohio, 1976-83; contract adminstr. Northrop Corp., Hawthorne, Calif., 1983-84; sr. contract adminstr. Gould Navcom Systems div., El Monte, 1984; sr. buyer EG&G Mound Applied Technologies, Miamisburg, Ohio, 1984-92, sr. tng. analyst, 1992-95; owner Suarez Assocs., Springfield, 1990—. Adj. prof. Urbana (Ohio) U., 1990—; adj. instr. Wright State U., OHio, 1994—. Author: (software) The Beginner's Introduction to the Personal Computer, 1992, The Beginner's Guide to the Internet (Windows, DOS, Mac), 1993—; author: (books) The Beginner's Guide to the Internet, 1995, The Beginner's Guide to the Internet for Mac Users, 1995. Bd. founders Sta. WDPR-FM, Dayton, 1980; founder Radio Broadcasts of the Springfield Symphony Orch., 1973. With USAF, 1968-72. Avocations: computers, music, politics, cinema, reading. Home: 3703 Marbella Ave Springfield OH 45502-9443 Office: Knowledgelink Inc 3020 S Tech Blvd Miamisburg OH 45342-4860

SUAREZ-MURIAS, MARGUERITE C. retired language and literature educator; b. Havana, Cuba, Mar. 23, 1921; came to U.S., 1935, naturalized, 1959; d. Eduardo R. and Marguerite (Vendel) S.-M. AB, Bryn Mawr Coll., 1942; MA, Columbia U., 1953, PhD, 1957. Lectr. in Spanish Columbia U., 1954-56; pub. rels. officer med. divsn. Johns Hopkins U., 1957-58; asst. prof. Spanish and French Sweet Briar Coll., 1958-59, Hood Coll., 1960-61; lectr. Cath. U., 1960-63, asst. prof., summers 1960-62, assoc. prof., summers 1964-66; asst. prof. dept. langs. and linguistics Am. U., 1961-63, assoc. prof., 1963-66; prof. dept. classical and modern langs. Marquette U., Milw., 1966-68; prof. Spanish and Portuguese U. Wis., 1968—83, chmn., 1972-75. Guest prof. U. South Africa, Pretoria, 1980 Author: La Novela Romántica en Hispanoamérica, 1963, Antología Estilística de la Prosa Moderna Española, 1968, Essays on Hispanic Literature/Ensayos de Literatura Hispana, 1982; contbr. articles to profl. jours.; editor: Gironella's Los Cipreses Creen en Dios, 1969; designed built homes, 1987-93. Mem. Nat. Trust for Historic Preservation. Roman Catholic. Home: 1315 Cold Bottom Rd Sparks MD 21152-9518

SUAZO, MIGUEL, civil engineer, consultant; b. Lima, Peru, Apr. 4, 1940; s. Fernando Suazo and Isolina Giovannini; m. Luisa Bellacci, Oct. 20, 1965; children: Verónica, Virna, José-Antonio, Rodrigo. Degree in civil engring., Nat. U. Engring., Lima, 1963; degree in hydroelec. power plant and water supply, Poly. Milan, 1964; cert. specialist in dams, ACTIM, Paris, 1972. Project engr. ELC-Electroconsult, Milan, 1963-67, Corp. Energía Eléctrica del Mantaro, Lima, 1967-69, project divsn. chief, 1969-72; dep. dir. civil engring. Inst. Investigaciones Energéticas y Servicios de Ingenieria Electrica, 1973-76, dir., 1976-78; gen. mgr. S&Z Consultores Asociados S.A., Lima, 1978—, pres., 1979—. Hydraulic designer Majes Irrigation Project, Arequipa, Peru, 1964-67; chief of design Mantaro Project, Lima, 1967-72; engr., dir. Inst. Investigaciones Energéticas y Servicios de Ingeniería Eléctrica, 1973-78. Author: Underwater Drainage of Lake Paron, 1984; co-author: Old Spanish Dam in Peru, 1986; contbr. articles to profl. jours. Mem. Coll. Ingenieros del Peru (Consejo Departamental de Lima rep. to assembly 1994-97, bd. dirs. 1997—, dir. nat. coun. 1998-99, nat. treasure 2000-01), Com. Peruano de Grandes Presas (pres. 1992—), Interam. Nat. Com. Large Dams (bd. dirs. 1999—). Roman Catholic. Avocations: water sports, diving, swimming, sailing. Home: Av Arequipa 2912 Lima 27 Lima Peru Office: S&Z Consultores Assoc SA Av Del Parque Norte 1174 Lima 41 Lima Peru Fax: 051-1-4754270. E-mail: migsuazo@millicom.com.pe, syzmsjs@millicom.com.pe.

SUBA, STEVEN ANTONIO, obstetrician, gynecologist; b. Columbia, Mo., July 4, 1957; s. Antonio Ronquillo and Sylvia Marie (Karl) S.; m. Brenda Charlene Crosby, Aug. 9, 1986; children: Bethany Caroline, Sarah Marie. BA in Biology, St. Mary's U., San Antonio, 1979; MD, Tex. Tech U., 1984. Diplomate Am. Bd. Ob.-Gyn. Resident ob-gyn. Tex. Tech. U., Lubbock, Tex., 1984-87; chief resident ob-gyn. John Peter Smith Hosp., Ft. Worth, 1987-88; pvt. practice ob-gyn., 1988—. Fellow Am. Coll. Ob.-Gyn., mem. AMA, Tex. Med. Assn. Office: 6100 Harris Pky Ste 245 Fort Worth TX 76132-4107

SUBACH, JAMES ALAN, information systems company executive, consultant; b. Lawrence, Mass., Mar. 24, 1948; s. Anthony John and Bernice Ruth (Pekarski) S. m. Marilyn Butler, Feb. 16, 1980. BS with distinction, U. Maine, 1970; MS, U. Ariz., 1975, PhD, 1979. Vis. scientist NASA Johnson Space Ctr., Houston, 1977-79; rsch. assoc. Baylor Coll. Medicine, 1977-79; pres. Subach Ventures, Inc., San Antonio, 1980-84, JAS & Assocs., Inc., Phoenix, 1984—, C.I.O. Inc., 1987-90; v.p. PTIMS, Inc., Phoenix, 1992-96; faculty assoc. Ariz. State U., Tempe, 1992-93; v.p. Multipoint Tax Systems, Scottsdale, Ariz., 1996-97; chief info. officer Multipoint Nat. Property Tax Info., 1997-98. Co-founder Bridge Alliance LLC, Phoenix, 1998. Assoc. editor Jour. Applied Photog. Engring., 1973-78; author software Gen. Acctg. System, 1987; bus. computing columnist, 1987. Pres. Forest Trails Homeowners Assn., Phoenix, 1987-88. Mem. Phoenix C. of C. (Pres.'s Roundtable, Technology Roundtable), Toastmasters (treas. Phoenix chpt. 1984), Ariz. Progress Users Group (co-founder, pres. 1997), Tau Beta Pi, Sigma Pi Sigma. Republican. Avocations: public speaking, cross-country skiing, photography, golf. Office: JAS & Assoc Inc 13236 N 7th St # 4-276 Phoenix AZ 85022-5343 E-mail: dr.jim.subach@worldnet.att.net. *Personal philosophy: Go with your strengths and buttress your weaknesses.*

SUBAK, JOHN THOMAS, lawyer; b. Trebic, Czechoslovakia, Apr. 19, 1929; came to U.S., 1941, naturalized, 1946; s. William John and Gerda Maria (Subakova) S.; m. Mary Corcoran, June 4, 1955; children: Jane Kennedy, Kate, Thomas, Michael. BA summa cum laude, Yale U., 1950, LLB, 1956. Bar: Pa. 1956. From assoc. to ptnr. Dechert, Price & Rhoads, Phila., 1956-76, v.p., gen. counsel, dir., 1976-77; group v.p., gen. counsel, dir. Rohm and Haas Co., 1977-93; counsel Dechert Price & Rhoads, 1994—. Bd. dirs. Newport Corp. Editor: The Bus. Lawyer, 1982-83. Bd. dirs. Am. Cancer Soc., 1982-95; trustee Smith Coll., 1991-2001; pres. Gasparilla Island Conservation and Improvement Assn., 1991-2001. Lt. (j.g.) USN, 1950-53. Mem. ABA (chmn. corp. and bus. law sect. 1984-85), Am. Law Inst. (coun. mem.), Defender Assn. of Phila. (v.p., bd. dirs. 1982-95), Gasparilla Island Conservation and Improvement Assn. (pres.), Merion Cricket Club, Lemon Bay Club. Democrat. Roman Catholic. Office: Dechert Price & Rhoads 4000 Bell Atlantic Tower Philadelphia PA 19102-2793 E-mail: johnsubak@aol.com.

SUBAK-SHARPE, GERALD EMIL, electrical engineer, educator; b. Vienna, Austria, June 15, 1925; came to U.S., 1959, naturalized, 1967; s. Robert and Nelly (Brull) S.; m. Genell Jackson, Nov. 23, 1963; children: David, Sarah and Hope (twins). BS with 1st class honors, Univ. Coll., London, 1951; PhD, U. London, 1965; ScD, Columbia U., 1969. Rsch. engr. Brit. Telecommunications Rsch., Taplow, Eng., 1951-58; mem. tech. staff Bell Labs., Murray Hill, N.J., 1959-64, cons., 1977-78; assoc. prof. elec. engring. Manhattan Coll., Bronx, N.Y., 1966-68; prof. elec. engring. CCNY, N.Y.C., 1968—; v.p. G.S. Sharpe Communications Inc., 1981—. Author: (with A.B. Glaser) Integrated Circuit Engineering, 1978; contbr. articles on network structure and semicondr. theory to profl. jours. Served as lt. Royal Warwickshire Regt., 1944-47. Recipient Prof. of Yr. award Eta Kappa Nu/CCNY, 1985-86. Fellow Instn. Elec. Engrs. (London); mem. IEEE (sr.), N.Y. Acad. Scis., Nat. Trust for Historic Preservation Home: 606 W 116th St Apt 71 New York NY 10027-7024 Office: CCNY Dept Elec Engring Convent Ave New York NY 10027 also: Knollcroft East Chatham NY 12060

SUBER, ROBIN HALL, former medical and surgical nurse; b. Bethlehem, Pa., Mar. 14, 1952; d. Arthur Albert and Sarah Virginia (Smith) Hall; m. David A. Suber, July 28, 1979; 1 child, Benjamin A. BSN, Ohio State U., 1974. RN, Ariz., Ohio. Formerly staff nurse Desert Samaritan Hosp., Mesa, Ariz. Lt. USN, 1974-80. Mem. ANA, Sigma Theta Tau.

SUBHASH, GHATU, engineering educator; PhD, U. Calif., San Diego, 1991. Postdoctoral rsch. fellow Calif. Inst. Tech., Pasadena, 1992—93; asst. prof. Mich. Technol. U., Houghton, 1993—97. Named Disting. Faculty Mem. of Mich., Mich. Assn. Governing Bds. of State Univs., 1995, Outstanding New Mechanics Educator, Am. Soc. Engring. Edn., 1996; recipient cert. of recognition, Mich. Gov. and Mich. Legis., 1995, Ralph R. Teetor Ednl. award, Soc. Automotive Engrs., 2000. Mem.: ASME, Soc. Mfg. Engrs. Office: Mich Technol U ME-EM Dept Houghton MI 49931

SUBIN, ELI HAROLD, lawyer; b. Phila., June 25, 1935; s. Benjamin and Freda (Kalen) S.; m. Suzon Bette Rosenbluth, Oct. 21, 1962; children: Andrea Beth Craig, Ben William. BA, U. Pa., 1957; LLB, U. Miami, Coral Gables, Fla., 1961. Bar: Fla., 1961, U.S. Dist. Ct. (mid. dist.) Fla., 1961, U.S. Supreme Ct., 1964, U.S. Ct. Appeals (5th, 11th cirs.), 1966. Trial atty. antitrust divsn. U.S. Dept. Justice, Phila., 1962-63; rsch. aide Dist. Ct. Appeal (1st dist.) Fla., Tallahassee, 1963-64; atty. Roth Segal & Levine, Orlando, Fla., 1964-72, Subin Shams, et. al. P.A., Orlando, 1972-96; city atty. City of Orlando, 1980-82; atty. Maguire, Voorhis & Wells, P.A., Orlando, 1997-98, Holland & Knight LLP, Orlando, 1998—. Referee Supreme Ct. Fla., Tallahassee, 1975; mem. Fla. Bd. Bar Examiners, 1982-87, chmn., 1986-87. Mem. exec. com. Seminole County Dems., Sanford, Fla., 1970-74; mem. jud. nominating com. 9th cir. Fla., 1976-79; dir. Fla. Bar Found., Orlando, 1992-00. 1st lt. USAR, 1957-64. Mem. Am. Law Inst., Am. Bd. Trial Advs. (assoc.), Orange County Bar Assn. (dir. 1968-71). Jewish. Office: Holland & Knight LLP PO Box 1526 Orlando FL 32802-1526 E-mail: escbin@hkluw.com.

SUBIN, FLORENCE, retired lawyer; b. N.Y.C., June 5, 1935; d. George and Beatrice (Rodam) Katroser; m. Bert W. Subin, June 6, 1953 (dec.); children: Glen D., Beth Subin Ambler. BA, Herbert H. Lehman Coll., 1972; JD magna cum laude, Bklyn. Law Sch., 1975. Bar: N.Y. 1976, U.S. Dist. Ct. (so. and ea. dists.) N.Y. 1976. Pvt. practice, N.Y.C. and Scarsdale, N.Y., 1976-99; retired. Trustee Bklyn. Law Sch., 1998—. Mem. Assn. Trial Lawyers City of N.Y. (bd. dirs. 1982-86), Met. Women's Bar Assn. (pres. 1979-81, bd. dirs. 1981—), Bronx Women's Bar Assn. (pres. 1983-85), Bklyn. Law Sch. Alumni Assn. (pres. 1992-94), Phi Beta Kappa.

SUBKOWSKY, ELIZABETH, insurance company executive; b. New London, Conn., Feb. 17, 1949; d. Thomas and Matilda (Mastroianni) Logan; m. Robert A. Subkowsky, June 9, 1972. BA with honors and dist., U. Conn., 1971; MBA, DePaul U., Chgo., 1977. Asst. v.p. info. tech. CNA Ins., Chgo., 1973—2002; sr. cons. CHS Holdings Inc., 2002—. Mem. Highland Park (Ill.) Housing Commn., 1997-98; bd. dirs. Highland Park Hist. Soc., 1991-96, 1st v.p., 1993-96. Recipient De Paul U. Disting. Alumni award, 1999. Mem. Fin. Women's Assn. Avocations: golf, bridge. E-mail: esubkowsky@prodigy.net.

SUBLER, EDWARD PIERRE, advertising executive; b. Shelby, Ohio, Mar. 24, 1927; s. Leo John and Dorotha (Armstrong) S.; m. Alice Ellen Carpenter, Sept. 8, 1956; children: Leo, Scott, Dorotha. BA, Denison U., 1950; grad. advanced mgmt. course, Emory U. Mgr. product advt. Westinghouse Electric Co., Mansfield, Ohio, 1950-65; mgr. advt. and sales promotion Bell & Howell Co., Chgo., 1965-69; v.p. mdsg. Westinghouse Consumer Products Co., 1969-76; sr. v.p. Ketchum Advt., Pitts., 1976-92, ret., 1992; v.p., sec. Pacific Garden Co., Millheim, Pa., 1998—, also bd. dirs. Trustee BCB Anglers, Baie Jeanne Assn., Tanglewood Assn. Served with USN, 1945-46. Mem. Am. Mktg. Assn., Am. Assn. Advt. Agencies (regional chmn.), Catawba Island Club, Bus./Profl. Adv. Assn. (Pitts. Advt. Exec. of Yr. 1988), U.S. Power Squadron, Baie Jeanne Assn. (bd. dirs.). Presbyterian. Home: 2465 Circleville Rd Unit 122 State College PA 16803-3390 E-mail: esubler@yahoo.com.

SUBLETT, CARL CECIL, artist, educator; b. Johnson County, Ky., Feb. 4, 1919; s. Tandy and Beulah (Fitzpatrick) S.; m. Helen C. Davis, Aug. 20, 1942; children: Carol, Eric. Student, Western Ky. U., 1938-40, Univ. Center, Florence, Italy, 1945, U. Tenn., 1955-56. Indsl. engr., draftsman Enterprise Wheel & Car Corp., Bristol, Va., 1946-49; staff artist Bristol, Va.-Tennesean & Herald Courier, 1950-52; artist, asst. mgr. Bristol Art Engravers, 1952-54; art dir. Advt., Knoxville, Tenn., 1954-65; prof. art U. Tenn., 1966-82; juror Watercolor Soc. Ala., Birmingham, 1979, Jacksonville U. Ann., 1980. Juror Bristol Art Guild 8th ann. juried exhbn., 1993. Artist prize-winning watercolors, 1964, drawing Soc. Nat. Exhbn., 1965, Artists U.S.A., 1971-72, 73-74, 74-75; one-man shows in oil and watercolors, 1995—; numerous exhbns. art in embassies program, 1964—; numerous exhbns. featured in publs. Taipei Fine Arts Inst. including Allied Publs. Inc.; numerous exhbns. in catalogs Tenn. State Mus., Nashville, Artist U.S.A., others; retrospective exhbn. Knoxville Mus. Art, 1991, Ewing Gallery, U. Tenn., 2000; invitational show Hampton III Gallery, Ltd., Taylors, S.C., 1992, Union U., Jackson, Tenn., 1991, Collector's Gallery, Nashville, 1960, 93, 96, 2000, Bennett Galleries, Knoxville, 1992-93, 95; featured in Watercolor Impressions, 1999. Hon. mem. Oak Ridge Tenn.Community Art Ctr. Served with U.S. Army, 1943-45. Recipient Purchase Mead Corp. Painting of Yr., Atlanta, 1963, Grumbacher Washington Watercolor Club, 1964, Rudolph Leach Am. Watercolor Soc., N.Y.C., 1972, Purchase Watercolor U.S.A., Springfield, Mo., 1975, Lifetime Achievement award Knoxville Arts Coun. and Knoxville Mus. of Art, 1994, Disting. Alumni award U. Tenn. and Cmty. Adv. Bd., 2000. Mem. NAD (Alfred Easton poor prize 1995), Bristol Art Guild (treas. 1951-54), Tenn. Watercolor Soc. (gold medal 1973, award of merit 1974, 75, 77, 78, 81, 84, 85), Knoxville Watercolor Soc., Port Clyde (Maine) Arts and Crafts Soc., Watercolor USA Soc., Knoxville Mus. Art. Methodist. Home: 2104 Lake Ave Knoxville TN 37916-2802 *We are creatures of history; credit your helpers, share your successes, and the future will reward your time.*

SUBLETTE, JULIA WRIGHT, music educator, performer, adjudicator; b. Natural Bridge, Va., Sept. 13, 1929; d. Paul Thomas and Annie Belle (Watkins) Wright; m. Richard Ashmore Sublette, Oct. 18, 1952; children: C. Mark, Carey P., Sylvia S. Bennett, Wright D. BA in Music, Furman U., 1951; MusM, Cin. Conservatory, 1954; postgrad., Chautauga Inst., N.Y., 1951-52; PhD, Fla. State U., 1993. Ind. piano tchr., 1953—; instr. music and humanities Okaloosa-Walton C.C., Niceville, Fla., 1978—. Panelist Music Tchr. Nat. Conv., Milw., 1992; instr. art humanities Troy State U., Ala.; featured performer N.W. Fla. Symphony Orch. Editor Fla. Music Tchr., 1991-99; contbr. articles to profl. music jours. Mem. AAUW, Music Tchrs. Nat. Assn. (cert., chmn. so. divsn. jr. high sch. piano/instrumental contests 1986-88), Fla. State Music Tchrs. Assn., So. Assn. Women Historians, Southeastern Hist. Keyboard Soc., Friday Morning Music Club, Colonial Dames of 17th Century Am., Pi Kappa Lambda. Avocations: reading, travel, folk music, herb gardening. Home: 217 Country Club Rd Shalimar FL 32579-2203

SUBRAMANIAM, SURESH, electrical engineering educator; b. Bhadravati, Karnataka, India, Mar. 14, 1968; m. Deepa Venkataraman, July 15, 1994; 1 child, Ashwin. B Engring., Anna U., Madras, India, 1988; MS, Tulane U., 1993; PhD, U. Wash., 1997. Staff mem. MIT Lincoln Lab., Lexington, Mass., 1996; asst. prof. George Washington U., Washington, 1997—. Editor: Optical WDM Networks: Principles and Practice, 2000; contbr. articles to profl. jours., chpt. to book. J. Watamull scholar, 1994-96; rsch. grantee NSF, 1999—, Nat. Security Agy., 1999—, Def. Advanced Rsch. Projects Agy., 2000— Mem. IEEE, Eta Kappa Nu. Office: George Washington U T-612 Phillips Hall 801 22d St NW Washington DC 20052 Fax: (202) 994-0227. E-mail: suresh@seas.gwu.edu.

SUBRAMANIAN, MANI, communications educator, consultant; b. Chennai, Tamil Nadu, India, Jan. 11, 1934; s. Pavur R and Kalyani Mahadevan; m. Ruth Pressler, June 6, 1960; children: Ravi, Meera. BS, U. Madras, Madras, India, 1953; Dip MIT, Madras Inst. Tech., Madras, India, 1956; MSEE, Purdue U., West Lafayette, IN, 1962, PhD, 1964. Asst. prof. Purdue U., West Lafayette, Ind., 1964—66; dist. mgr. Bell Labs/Bellcore, Piscataway, NJ, 1966—87; v.p. engring Racal-Milco Info Systems, Atlanta, 1987—91; v.p. advanced product devel. Verilink Corp, San Jose, Calif., 1991—92; pres. engring and ops. Melita Internat., Atlanta, 1992—93; pres. tech. Cadnet Corp, 1994—96; adj. rsch. prof. Ga. Inst. Tech., 1996—; founder, ceo ChanneLogics, 2000—01. Tech dir., bd. trustee OSI Network Mgmt. Forum, Holmdel, NJ, 1989—90. Contbr. articles Lasers, Optics, Network Management; author: (textbook) Network Management: Principles and Practice. Recipient Bellcore's Best, Bellcore, 1985. Mem.: IEEE (life). Democrat-Npl. Unitarian Universalist. Achievements include patents for 5 For Co-Inventions In Telecommunications; discovery of DC polarization in non-linear crystals; patents pending for 8 In Telecommunications. Avocations: running, tennis, music. Home: 1652 Harts Mill Rd Atlanta GA 30319-1821 Office: Ga Institute Tech-College Computing Atlantic Ave Atlanta GA 30332 Personal E-mail: manis@bellsouth.net.

SUBRAMANIAN, R. SHANKAR, chemical engineering educator; b. Madras, India, Aug. 10, 1947; arrived U.S., 1968, naturalized, 1977; s. R. K. Rama and Sita (Lakshmi) S.; m. Jane M. Gatta, Nov. 24, 1973; children: Laura S., Erin S. BTech. in Chem. Engring., U. Madras (India), 1968; MS, Clarkson U., 1969, PhD, 1972. Part-time instr. SUNY, Buffalo, 1972-73; asst. prof. chem. engring. Clarkson U., Potsdam, N.Y., 1973-79, assoc. prof., 1979-82, prof., 1982— , chmn. dept., 1986—; mem. tech. staff Jet Propulsion Lab. and vis. assoc. dept. chem. engring. Calif. Inst. Tech., Pasadena, 1979-80; assoc. dir. Inst. Colloid and Surface Sci., Clarkson U., 1981-87; prin. investigator NASA Space Shuttle Expts. on low gravity fluid mechanics. Editorial adv. bd. Jour. Colloid and Interface Sci., 1984-86; contbr. articles to profl., tech. jours. Recipient Graham Rsch. award Clarkson U., 1978, Dow Outstanding Young Faculty award, 1980; Disting. Teaching award Clarkson U. 1981. Fellow AAAS; mem. Am. Inst. Chem. Engrs., Am. Soc. Engring. Edn., Am. Ceramic Soc., Sigma Xi.

SUBRAMANIAN, RAVI, electrical engineer; b. Geneva, Switzerland, Oct. 22, 1965; came to U.S., 1983; BSEE with honors, Calif. Inst. Tech., 1987; PhDEE and Computer Sci., U. Calif., Berkeley, 1991. From assoc. engr. to co. scientist Teknekron Comm. Sys., Inc., Berkeley, Calif., 1988-91; mem. tech. staff AT&T Bell Labs., Holmdel, N.J., 1991-95; tech. mgr. Synopsys, Inc., Mountain View, Calif., 1995-96, dir., 1997-98; founder, dir., v.p. Morphics Tech. Inc., San Jose, 1999—. Invited spkr. in field. Assoc. editor IEEE Transactions on Circuits & Sys., 1995-97; contbr. articles to profl. jours.; patentee in digital comms. U. Calif. fellow, 1988-89. Mem. AAAS, IEEE (chmn. 1996 workshop on VLSI Comms.), N.Y. Acad. Scis. Avocations: soccer, mountain biking, traveling. E-mail: r.subramanian@att.net.

SUBRAMANYA, SHIVA, aerospace systems engineer; b. Hole-Narasipur, India, Apr. 8, 1933; s. S.T. Srikantaiah; m. Lee. S. Silva, Mar. 3, 1967; children: Paul Kailas, Kevin Shankar. BSc, Mysore U., Bangalore, India, 1956; MSc, Karnatak U., Dharwar, India, 1962; postgrad., Clark U., 1963; MBA, Calif. State U., Dominguez Hills, 1973; D in Bus. Adminstrn., PhD in Bus. Adminstrn., Nova Southeastern U., 1986. Sr. scientific officer AEC, Bombay, India, 1961-63; chief engr. TEI, Newport, R.I., 1964-67; prin. engr. Gen. Dynamics Corp., San Diego, 1967-73; asst. project mgr. def. and systems group TRW, Colorado Springs, Colo., 1973-87, asst. project mgr. space and def. group Redondo Beach, Calif., 1987-98; cons. aerospace industry Cerritos, 1998—. Cons. Contbr. over 150 articles to profl. jours. V.p. VHP of Am., Berlin, Conn., 1984-88; pres. IPF of Am., Redondo Beach, 1981-88; appointed by Pres. of India to Atomic Energy Commn., India. Winner of dozens of awards and commendations from U.S. Dept. of Defense and the Aerospace Industry. Mem. Armed Forces Comm. and Electronics Assn. (v.p.-elect Rocky Mountain chpt. 1986—, Meritorious Svc. award 1985, Merit medal 1990), Am. Acad. Mgmt. Hindu. Avocation: social service. Home and Office: 12546 Inglenook Ln Cerritos CA 90703-7837

SUCCOP, PAUL ALLAN, biostatistics educator, consultant; b. Buffalo, Aug. 4, 1951; s. Walter Edwin and Lillian Agnes Succop; m. Christine Anne Orlando, Nov. 23, 1972. BA, SUNY, Buffalo, 1975, PhD, 1988. Rsch. asst. SUNY, Buffalo, 1975-79; rsch. assoc. U. Cin., 1979-88, prof., 1988—. Biostat. cons. Stat Solutions, Cin., 1996—. Contbr. articles to profl. jours. Mentor Cin. Youth Collaborative, Cin., 1998—. N.Y. State Bd. Regents scholar, 1969; grantee Nat. Inst. Occupational Safety and Health U. Cin., 1998, Cystic Fibrosis Found., 1999. Mem. Am. Stat. Assn., The Psychometric Soc. Avocations: creative writing, music, model trains. Home: 2809 Cyclorama Dr Cincinnati OH 45211-8318 Office: U Cin Med Ctr 3223 Eden Ave Cincinnati OH 45267-0001

SUCHENEK, MAREK ANDRZEJ, computer science educator; b. Warsaw, Poland, May 2, 1949; came to U.S., 1986, naturalized, 1999; s. Tadeusz Aleksander and Barbara Krystyna (Zych) Suchenek; m. Ewa Aleksandra Czerny, July 30, 1974 (div. 1991); m. Cynthia M. Vincent, July 6, 2001. MSc in Math. Engring., Warsaw Tech. U., 1973, PhD in Tech. Scis. with distinction, 1979. Instr. Warsaw Tech. U., 1973-79, asst. prof., 1979-88; assoc. Nat. Inst. for Aviation Rsch., Wichita, 1987-90; vis. asst. prof. Wichita (Kans.) State U., 1986-88, assoc. prof., 1988-89, assoc. prof., chair, 1989-90; prof. Calif. State U.-Dominguez Hills, Carson, 1990—, co-chair, 1996—97, chair, 1997-98, 2001—. Adj. prof. Pepperdine U., Malibu, Calif., 1999; mem. organizing com. Internat. Symposium on Methodologies for Intelligent Sys., 1989-90; program com. Ann. Ulam Math. Conf., 1990-91, Internat. Conf. on Computing and Info., 1992-94; referee NSF, 1990-92, Annals of Math. and Artificial Intelligence, 1992-93, Jour. Logic Programming, 1992-94; presenter in field. Author: (with Jan Bielecki) ANS FORTRAN, 1980, (with Jan Bielecki) FORTRAN for Advanced Programmers, 1981, 2nd edit., 1983, 3rd edit., 1988 (Minister of Sci. Higher Edn. and Techs. prize 1982); reviewer Zentralblatt fur Mathematik, 1980-89, Math. Revs., 1989-91, Jour. Symbolic Logic, 1998—; mem. editl. bd. Ulam Quar., 1990—; contbr. articles to profl. jours. Rsch. grantee Polish Govt., 1974-76, 85-86, FAA, 1988-90, NASA, 1997. Mem. AAUP, The Assn. for Logic Programming, Computer Soc. IEEE, Assn. Symbolic Logic, Sigma Xi. Avocations: cats, collectibles, swimming, target shooting. Office: Calif State U Dominguez Hills 1000 E Victoria St Carson CA 90747-0001 Home: 5461 Cynthia Cir Cypress CA 90630-4522 E-mail: suchenek@csudh.edu.

SUCHMAN, MARK CHARLES, sociologist, educator, law educator; b. N.Y.C., Dec. 17, 1960; s. Edward Allen and Elaine Markley Suchman; m. Nina Tannenwald, June 24, 2001. BA, Harvard U., 1983; JD, Yale U., 1989; PhD, Stanford U., 1994. Bar: Conn. 1990. Asst. prof. U. Wis., Madison, 1993—98, assoc. prof., 1998—. Grantee faculty early career devel. grantee, NSF, 1998—. Mem.: Acad. Mgmt., Law and Soc. Assn. (membership com. chair 2000—01), Am. Sociol. Assn. Office: U Wis Madison 1180 Observatory Dr Madison WI 53706

SUCHY, SUSANNE N. nursing educator; b. Windsor, Ont., Can., Sept. 20, 1945; d. Hartley Joseph and Helen Viola (Derrick) King; m. Richard Andrew Suchy, June 24, 1967; children: Helen Marie, Hartley Andrew, Michael Derrick. Diploma, St. Joseph Sch. Nursing, Flint, Mich., 1966; BSN, Wayne State U., 1969, MSN, 1971. RN, Mich. Afternoon supr., staff nurse oper. and recovery rm. St. John Hosp., Detroit, 1966-70; nursing instr. Henry Ford Community Coll., Dearborn, Mich., 1972—, on leave 1988-90; CNS/case mgr. surg. nursing Harper Hosp., Detroit, 1988-89; CNS case mgr. oncology, 1989—. Mem. Detroit Demonstration Site Team for defining and differentiating ADN/BSN competencies, 1983-87. Contbr. articles to profl. jours. Past bd. dirs., pres. St. Pius Sch. Mem. ANA, AACH, N.Am. Nursing Diagnosis Assn. (by-law com. chmn. 1992-98), Mich. Nursing Diagnosis Assn. (pres. 1987-90, elected by-law chmn. 1991-92, treas. 1993—), NLN, Mich. Nurses Assn. (cabinet nursing practice 1996-98, conv. com. 1996-98), Detroit Dist. Nurses Assn. (past chmn. nominating com., legis. com., sec. 1994-96), Oncology Nursing Soc. (gov. rels. chmn. 1992—, presenter abstract conf. 1991, 95, poster presentations ann. conf. 1991-93, 95, 96, dicussion presenter 1998), Daus. of Isabella (internat. dir. 1992-96, local auditor 1995—, state vice regent 1997—, cir. auditor 1995-97), Wayne State U. Alumni Assn., Sigma Theta Tau (nominating com. 1991-93). Roman Catholic. Home: 12666 Irene St Southgate MI 48195-1765 Office: Henry Ford CC 5101 Evergreen Rd Dearborn MI 48128-2407

SUCHYTA, CASIMIR JOHN, III, computer analyst, researcher; b. Trenton, Mich., Aug. 15, 1959; s. Casimir John Jr. and Monica Ann S.; m. Monica Lee Wawrzyniec, June 5, 1982; children: Scott Allen, Eric Daniel. BS in Physics, U. Mich., Dearborn, 1981; PhD in Physics, U. Wis., 1987. Am. Phys. Soc. indsl. summer intern Gen. Tire and Rubber Co., Akron, Ohio, 1981; rsch. asst. U. Wis., Madison, 1984-87; rsch. assoc. Wayne State U., Detroit, 1987-89; computer analyst Boeing Computer Svcs., Auburn, Ala., 1989-91, Cray Rsch., Inc., Dayton, Ohio, 1991-93, Eagan, Minn., 1993-96, Silicon Graphics, Inc., Dayton, 1996—. Rsch. cons. Wayne State U., Detroit, 1989-94. Contbr. articles to profl. jours. Names James B. Angell scholar U. Mich., 1978, 81; Wisc. Alumni Rsch. Found. fellow U. Wisc., 1981, 84; recipient Hon. Mention award NSF, 1981. Mem. AAUP, Am. Phys. Soc.

SUCICH, DIANA CATHERINE, school psychologist, counselor; b. N.Y.C., Apr. 23, 1948; d. Nicholas and Mildred (Bobich) S. MEd, Springfield (Mass.) Coll., 1973, cert. counseling, 1974; PhD, U.S. Internat. U., 1975. Cert. trainer, educator and practioner in psychodrama, sociometry and group psychotherapy; cert. sch. crisis response. Dean of women Anderson Sch., Staatsburg,

N.Y., 1971; cons. human devel. dept. YMCA, San Diego, 1975-77; postdoctoral resident Navy Alcohol Rehab. and Tng. Ctr., 1975-77; instr. Chapman Coll., Orange, Calif., 1977-79; pvt. practice cons.; cons., instr. Moreno Acad. Psychodrama, Beacon, N.Y., 1982-83; cons. sch. psychologist Millbrook Ctrl. Sch. Dist., 1983-84; sch. psychologist Rhinebeck (N.Y.) Cen. Sch. Dist., 1984-86, Beacon City Sch. Dist., 1986-87, Wappingers Cen. Sch. Dist., Wappingers Falls, N.Y., 1987-92, Orange-Ulsta BOCES, 1992-93, Wallkill Ctrl. Sch. Dist., Wappingers Falls, N.Y., 1993-94; Wappingers Ctrl. Sch. Dist., 1994—. AIDS dist. com. and sexual abuse prevention program trainer.; sch. psychologist, cons. N.Y. State mandated course on child abuse reporting and suicide prevention, devel. of abduction prevention program, supt. search com., dist. psychologists adv. com., Crisis Team VWJHS; security adv. com. Wappingers Ctrl. Sch. Dist. Mem. APA, Psychologists in Marital and Family Therapy, Fedn. Trainers and Tng. Programs in Psychodrama, Am. Bd. Examiners Psychodramas, Diplomat The Am. Acad. Experts inTraumatic Stress, Psi Chi. Home: Stony Brook Estate 237 Old Hopewell Rd Wappingers Falls NY 12590-4428 Office: Stony Brook Estate Wappingers Falls NY 12590 E-mail: dsucich@aol.com.

SUCKIEL, ELLEN KAPPY, philosophy educator; b. June 15, 1943; d. Jack and Lilyan Kappy; m. Joseph Suckiel, June 22, 1973 AB, Douglass Coll., 1965; MA in Philosophy, U. Wis., 1969, PhD in Philosophy, 1972. Lectr. philosophy U. Wis., Madison, 1969-71; asst. prof. philosophy Fla. State U., Tallahassee, 1972-73, U. Calif., Santa Cruz, 1973-80, assoc. prof., 1980-95, prof., 1995—, provost Kresge Coll., 1983-89. Author: The Pragmatic Philosophy of William James, 1982, Heaven's Champion: William James's Philosophy of Religion, 1996, also articles, book introductions and chpts. Mem. Am. Philos. Assn., Soc. for Advancement Am. Philosophy Office: U Calif Stevenson Coll Santa Cruz CA 95064

SUD, YOGESH C. climate studies scientist, researcher; b. Amritsar, Punjab, India, Dec. 20, 1938; B in Engring., 1960; PhD, Birmingham U., Eng., 1971. Mem. faculty mech. engring. IIT Delhi, New Delhi, 1963—73; sr. rsch. scientist NASA/Goddard Space Flight Ctr., Greenbelt, Md., 1973—. Program mgr. modeling and analysis NASA-HQ, Washington, 2001—. Contbr. articles to profl. jours. Recipient Earth Sci. Achievement award, Goddard Space Flight Ctr., 2001. Office Fax: 301-614-6307 301-614-6307. Business E-Mail: sud@climate.gsfc.nasa.gov.

SUDA, TATSUYA, computer science educator; b. Fukushima, Japan, Aug. 20, 1953; came to U.S., 1982; s. Tatsuo and Toshiko (Koshlishi) S.; children: Kentaro, Shotaro. BS, Kyoto U., 1977, MS, 1979, PhD, 1982. Rsch. assoc. Columbia U., N.Y.C., 1982-84; asst. prof. computer science U. Calif., Irvine, 1984-89, assoc. prof., 1990—, prof., 1994—. Program dir. networking rsch. NSF, 1997-99. Fellow IEEE; mem. Assn. Computing Machinery.Fell E-mail: suda@ics.uci.edu.

SUDAK, HOWARD STANLEY, physician, psychiatry educator; b. Cleve., Nov. 13, 1932; s. Sol and Leona (Simms) S.; m. Diane M. Ressler, Dec. 25, 1955 (dec.); children: Ellen, Nancy, Janet, David; m. Donna M. Miller, Mar. 25, 1995. AB in Chemistry magna cum laude, Case Western Res. U., 1954, MD, 1958. Diplomate Am. Bd. Psychiatry and Neurology (sr. examiner 1991—). Intern in medicine Univ. Hosps. Cleve., 1958-59, resident in psychiatry, 1959-62; clin. assoc. NIMH, Bethesda, Md., 1962-64; chief psychiatry Cleve. VA Med. Ctr., 1964-84; asst. prof. psychiatry Case Western Res. U., Cleve., 1964-74, assoc. prof., 1974-82, prof., 1982—, vice dean Med. Sch., 1985-92; chmn. dept. psychiatry The Pa. Hosp., Phila., 1992-2001; psychiatrist-in-chief Inst. of Pa. Hosp., 1992-96; clin. prof. psychiatry U. Pa. Sch. Medicine, 1993-94, 97—; prof. psychiatry, vice chmn. psychiatry/human behavior Thomas Jefferson U., Phila., 1994-96. Mem. profl. adv. coun. Youth Suicide Nat. Ctr., Washington, 1986—; com. mem. Ctrs. for Disease Control, Atlanta, 1990-91. Editor: Suicide in the Young, 1984, Clinical Psychiatry, 1985; cons. editor Suicide and Life Threatening Behavior, 1988—; contbr. numerous articles to profl. jours., chpt. to books. Dir. Inst. for Urban Health, Cleve., 1990-92. Grantee NIMH, 1972-73, 83-86. Fellow Am. Psychiat. Assn., Am. Coll. Psychiatrists, Am. Coll. Psychoanalysts; mem. Am. Assn. Suicidology (trustee 1988-90), Am. Suicide Found. (trustee 1987—, pres. 1989-91), Phi Beta Kappa, Alpha Omega Alpha. Avocations: biking, sailing, reading, skiing, jazz and classical music. Home: 321 S Lawrence Ct Philadelphia PA 19106-4220 Office: Mezzanine Fl 210 W Washington Sq Philadelphia PA 19106-3514 E-mail: hosuda@pahosp.com.

SUDANOWICZ, ELAINE MARIE, government executive; b. Dorchester, Mass., Aug. 3, 1956; d. John Anthony and Helen Mary Sudanowicz. Student, Fontbonne Acad., Milton, Mass., 1974; BA, Boston State Coll., 1978; MPA, Suffolk U., Boston, 1986; grad. Exec. Leadership Devel. Program, Dept. of Def., 1993. Cert. level 2 contractor, level 3 in program mgmt., Mass. Pub. rels. office mgr. MacDonald & Evans Inc. Litho., Dorchester, 1974-78; rsch. asst. Nat. Commn. Neighborhoods, Washington, 1978; polit. cons. various nat., state and local polit. campaigns, 1974-86; telephonist supr., cons. ARC, Boston, 1980-81; adminstrv. asst. Suffolk County Courthouse Commn., 1981-82; exec. asst. sheriff Suffolk County Sheriff's Office, 1982-86; presdl. mgmt. intern ESD/PK Air Force Systems Command, Hanscom AFB, Mass., 1986-89, advanced copper CAP Andrews AFB, Md., 1989-90; contract negotiatior Hdqrs., Electronic Systems divsn. Joint STARS Program, Hanscom AFB, Mass., 1990-92; program mgr. Hdqrs., Electronic Sys. Ctr., EN-1, 1992-95; asst. program dir. bus. acquisition re-engring. Elec. Sys. Ctr., 1994-95; dep. commr. for transp. City of Boston, 1995—. Mayor's interagency liaison Boston Emergency Mgmt. Agy., 1995—; guest spkr. Amred Forces Comm. and Elecs. Assn., 2000-; guest lectr. Suffolk U., Sawyer Sch. Mgmt., 2001-. Author: Constitutional Vignette, Separation of Powers and Contracting in the Bureaucrat, 1987; contbr. PMInformer, 1989—; also articles; agt., cons Theatre Arts-Play 1988—. Vol., cons. City & State Pub. Agys.-Pub. Sector, Boston; literacy vol., 1988-89; task force Transp. Rsch. Bd. on Critical Transp. Infrastructure Security, 1999—. Recipient Spl. Achievement award U.S. Dept. Transp., 1989, Outstanding Alumnus award Suffolk U., 1990 Mem. Am. Soc. Pub. Adminstrn. (coun. mem. 1996—, mem. exec. bd. emergency and crisis mgmt. sect. 1999—), Nat. Contract Mgmt. Assn. (bd. dirs. 1996—, photographer No. Va. chpt. 1989-90, cert. profl. contracts mgr., nat. chair program mgmt. spl. topics com.), Presdl. Mgmt. Alumni Group (nat. bd. dirs. 1989-90, N.E. field bd. dirs. 1990—. Outstanding Alumnus award 1990), Trustees of Reservations Mass., Dept. Def. Sr. Profl. Women's Assn., Boston Network for Women in Govt. and Politics, Pi Alpha Alpha (pres. Suffolk U. chpt.). Democrat. Roman Catholic. Avocations: art, cross country and downhill skiing, hiking, outdoors, gardening. Home: 108 Alban St Dorchester MA 02124-3711 Office: Boston Emergency Mgmt Agy Boston Fire Alarm 59 The Fenway Boston MA 02115-3700 E-mail: elaines.bfd@ci.boston.ma.us.

SUDARSKY, JERRY M. industrialist; b. Russia, June 12, 1918; s. Selig and Sara (Ars) S.; m. Mildred Axelrod, Aug. 31, 1947; children: Deborah, Donna (dec.). Student, U. Iowa, 1936-39; BS in Chem. Engrging., Poly. U. Bklyn., 1942; DSc (hon.), Poly. U. N.Y., 1976; PhD Hebrew U. Jerusalem (hon.) , 2002. Founder, CEO Bioferm Corp., Wasco, Calif., 1946-66; cons. to Govt. of Israel, 1966-67; founder, chmn. Israel Chems., Ltd., Tel Aviv, 1967-72; chmn. I.C. Internat. Cons., 1971-73; vice chmn., bd. dirs. Daylin, Inc., L.A., 1972-76; pres., chmn. J.M.S. Assocs., 1976—f; vice chmn. bd. dirs. Jacobs Engring. Group Inc., Pasadena, Calif., 1982-94; chmn., CEO Health Sci. Prop. Holding Corp., 1994-97; chmn. Alexandria Real Estate Equities Inc., Pasadena, 1997—. Patentee in field of indsl. microbiology. Bd. govs. Hebrew U., Jerusalem; trustee Polytechnic U. N.Y., 1976—; bd. dirs. Mgmt. Edn. Assn., UCLA, 1990-99. Served with USNR, 1943-46. Mem. AAAS, Am. Chem. Soc., Brentwood Country Club, Sigma Xi. Office: 2220 Ave of Stars Los Angeles CA 90067-5656 E-mail: jmsudarsky@aol.com.

SUDBECK, ROBERT FRANCIS, music educator, philosophy educator; b. Sioux City, Iowa, May 14, 1955; s. Gorman Francis and Lois Mae (Lawless) S.; m. Lorraine Suzanne Delgadillo, June 27, 1987; children: John Robert, Patrick Michael. MusB, Cath. U. Am., 1977, MusM, MusM, Cath. U. Am., 1979; MA in Philosophy, Calif. State U., Long Beach, 1989, MA in Edn., 1994. music, philosophy, ednl. admin., Calif. Sch. Leadership Acad. Music educator Santa Ana (Calif.) Sch. Dist., 1981—; adjunct prof. Calif. State U., 1991-92; elem. dir. Santa Ana Edn. Assn., 1993—. Calif. mentor tchr., Santa Ana Sch. Dist., 1989-90, mentor tchr. selection com., 1994—, fine arts com., 1998; adv. bd., edl. admin. dept., Calif. State U., 1994—. Mem. Santa Ana Edn. Assn. (bd. mem. 1993—, co-chair human rights 1995-97, polit. action comm. mem. 1996-98), Calif. Tchrs. Assn. (state del. to State Coun. of Edn., mem. state rights and responsibilities com., TA governing rep., Burlingame, Calif. 1996—). Avocations: piano, hiking, foreign travel, reading. Home: 1145 Salvador St Costa Mesa CA 92626-5566 Office: Santa Ana Unified Sch. Dist 1601 E Chestnut Ave Santa Ana CA 92701-6322

SUDBRINK, JANE MARIE, sales and marketing executive; b. Sandusky, Ohio, Jan. 14, 1942; niece of Arthur and Lydia Sudbrink. BS, Bowling Green State U., 1964; postgrad. in cytogenetics, Kinderspital-Zurich, Switzerland, 1965. Field rep. Random House and Alfred A. Knopf Inc., Mpls., 1969-72, Ann Arbor, Mich., 1973, regional mgr. Midwest and Can., 1974-79, Can. rep., mgr., 1980-81; psychology and ednl. psychology adminstrv. editor Charles E. Merrill Pub. Co. div. Bell & Howell Corp., Columbus, Ohio, 1982-84; sales and mktg. mgr. trade products Wilson Learning Corp., Eden Prairie, Minn., 1984-85; fin. cons. Merrill Lynch Pierce Fenner & Smith, Edina, 1986-88; sr. editor Gorsuch Scarisbrick Pubs., Scottsdale, Ariz., 1988-89; regional mgr. Worth Publs., Inc. - von Holtzbrinck Pub. Grp., N.Y.C., 1988-97; mktg. assoc. Harcourt Brace Coll. Pubs., Northbrook, Ill., 1997-98, cons. midatlantic region, 1998—; mktg. assoc. W.W. Norton & Co., Ill., Ind., Ohio, 1998—. Lutheran. Home and Office: 3801 Mission Hills Rd Northbrook IL 60062-5729 E-mail: jsudbrink@wwnorton.com.

SUDBURY, JOHN DEAN, religious foundation executive, petroleum chemist; b. Natchitoches, La., July 29, 1925; s. Herbert J. and Mary Flora S.; m. Jean Elizabeth Jung, July 18, 1947; children: John Byron, James Vernon (dec.), Linda Gail. BS, U. Tex., Austin, 1943, MA, 1947, PhD, 1949. Registered profl. engr., Okla. With Conoco Inc., various locations, 1949-83, asst. to v.p. tech. N.Y.C., 1970-72, v.p. coal research Conoco Coal Devel. Co. subs. Pitts., 1972-83; pres. Ea. European Mission and Bible Found., Houston, 1983-98, pres. emeritus, 1999—. Author: Oil Well Corrosion, 1956; contbr. articles to profl. jours.; patentee in energy field. Mem. Ponca City (Okla.) Sch. Bd., 1965-67; trustee Okla. Christian U., 1968— . Served with USN, 1943-45. Recipient Frank Newman Speller award Nat. Assn. Corrosion Engrs., 1967 Mem. Am. Chem. Soc., N.Y. Acad. Scis., AAAS, Sigma Xi. Republican. Mem. Ch. of Christ. Home and Office: 3 Devon Mill Pl The Woodlands TX 77382-5304 Fax: (281) 440-1955. E-mail: jejs@evi.net.

SUDBURY, JULIA C. ethnic studies educator, writer; b. Edinburgh, Scotland, May 30, 1967; d. George C. and Mary Sudbury, Sonny Oparah. BA in Modern and Medieval Langs., Cambridge (Eng.) U., 1989; postgrad. diploma in cmty. practice, Luton (Eng.) U., 1991; MA in Race and Ethnic studies, U. Warwick, Coventry, Eng., 1994, PhD, 1997. Lectr. cmty. studies U. Calif., Santa Cruz, Calif.; cmty. devel. officer Cambridge City Coun., 1989—91; dir. Nat. Devel. Agy. for Black Non Profit Sector, London, 1994—96; coord. Osaba Women's Ctr., Coventry, 1991—94; asst. prof. ethnic studies Mills Coll., Oakland, Calif., 1998—2001, assoc. prof., chair ethnic studies, 2001—. Author: (book) Other Kinds of Dreams: Black Women's Organizations and the Politics of Transformation, 1998; contbr. book. Co-founder Nat. Black Alliance, London, 1993—95, 1993—95; Nat. bd. dirs. Critical Resistance, Oakland, 1997—, Incite: Women of Color Against Violence, Santa Cruz, 2001—, Prison Activist Resource Ctr., Oakland, 2001—; bd. dirs. Nat. Coun. for Vol. Orgns., London, 1994—95, Black Health Found., London, 1993—95, Vol. Orgns. Liaison Coun. for Under 5S, London, 1992—94. Recipient Seachange award, Gaea Found., 2002, Grad. Studies award, European Social Rsch. Coun., 1994—97; fellow Rockefeller Humanities felow, U. Ariz., 2002; grantee, Flora Found., 2001, multicultural devel. grantee, Irvine Found., 1999—2000, devel. grantee, Vanguard Pub. Found., 1998—99, Meg Quigley Women's Studies rsch. grantee, Mills Coll., 1998—99. Mem.: AAUP, Am. Sociol. Assn. Office: Mills Coll Ethics Studies 5000 MacArthur Blvd Oakland CA 94613 Home Fax: 510-430-2067; Office Fax: 510-430-2067.

SUDDARTH, ROSCOE SELDON, diplomat; b. Louisville, Aug. 5, 1935; s. George Seldon and Anna (Urfer) S.; m. Michele Regine Lebas, Mar. 15, 1963; children: Anne, Mark. BA, Yale U., 1956, Oxford (Eng.) U., 1958, MA, 1961; MS, MIT, 1972; cert. Arabic lang. and area specialist program, Fgn. Service Inst., Beirut, 1965. Fgn. service officer Am. Embassy, Mali, Lebanon, Yemen Arab Republic, Libya, 1961-69, dep. chief-of-mission Jordan, 1974-79; exec. asst. to undersec. of State for Polit. Affairs U.S. Dept. State, Washington, 1979-81; dep. chief-of-mission Am. Embassy, Riyadh, Saudi Arabia, 1982-85; dep. asst. Sec. of State for Near Ea. and South Asian Affairs U.S. Dept. State, Washington, 1985-87; U.S. ambassador to Jordan, 1987-90; dep. inspector gen. U.S. State Dept., Washington, 1991-94; internat. affairs adv. Naval War Coll., Newport, R.I., 1994-95; pres. Mid. East Inst., Washington, 1995-2001. Ind. dir. Merrill Lynch Mutual Funds, 2000—. Co-author: Tales of the Foreign Service, 1971. With USAFNG, 1958-61 Scholar Keasbey Found., Oxford U., 1956-58. Mem. Am. Acad. Diplomacy, Cosmos Club (Washington), Phi Beta Kappa, Delta Kappa Epsilon. Episcopalian. Avocations: tennis, modern jazz, classical music.

SUDDOCK, FRANCES SUTER THORSON, grief educator, writer; b. Estelline, S.D., Oct. 23, 1914; d. William Henry and Anna Mary (Oakland) Suter; m. Carl Edwin Thorson, July 6, 1941 (dec. Apr. 1976); children: Sarah Thorson Little, Mary Frances Thorson; m. Edwin Matthew Suddock, Aug. 7, 1982 (dec. Sept. 1986). BA, Iowa State Tchrs. Coll., 1936; postgrad., Syracuse U., 1940-41, U. Iowa, 1946; MA, Antioch U., San Francisco, 1981. Cert. tchr. Tchr. various high schs., Correctionville and Eagle Grove, Iowa, 1936-38, 38-40, 41-43, 45-47; chief clk. War Price and Rationing Bd., Eagle Grove, 1943-45; instr. (part time) Eagle Grove Jr. Coll., 1953-61; adminstr. Eagle Grove Pub. Library, 1961-77; facilitator Will Schutz Assocs., Muir Beach, Calif., 1987-88. Author: Whither the Widow, 1981. Vol. Nat. Trainer Widowed Persons Svc. Am. Assn. Retired Persons, 1989—, ret. sr. vol. program, Anchorage, 1988—; pres., bd. dirs. Anchorage Widowed Persons Svc., 1992-94; bd. dirs. North Iowa Mental Health Ctr., Mason City, Iowa, 1959-76, Eagle Grove Cmty. Chest, 1960, Help Line, Inc., Ft. Dodge, Iowa, 1976-77; chmn. Cmty. Mental Health Fund, Eagle Grove, 1966-73; charter pres. Eagle Grove Concerned, Inc., 1973-77; active various civic orgns. Mem. AAUW (charter pres. Eagle Grove br. 1973-75), Alaska Assn. Gerontology (treas. 1992-94), Anchorage Woman's Club, P.E.O., Kappa Delta Pi. Home: 333 M St Apt 404 Anchorage AK 99501-1902

SUDHIVORASETH, NIPHON, pediatrician, allergist, immunologist; b. Bangkok, Thailand, 1940; MD, Chulalongkorn Hosp. U., Bangkok, 1966. Diplomate Am. Bd. Pediatrics, Am. Bd. Allergy and Immunology. Intern Ch. Home Hosp., Balt., 1967-68; resident in pediatrics St. Lukes Hosp., N.Y.C., 1968-69, Beth Israel Hosp., N.Y.C., 1969-70; fellow in allergy Metro Hosp., N.Y. Med. Coll., 1970-72; staff Marshall Meml. Hosp., Tex., 1978—; pvt. practice. Mem. AMA, Am. Acad. Allergy, Asthma, and Immunology, Am. Acad. Pediats., Am. Coll. Allergy and Immunology. Office: PO Box 2087 705 S Grove St Marshall TX 75670-5220

SUDHOFF, VIRGINIA RAE, retired elementary education educator; b. Saginaw, Mich., Jan. 12, 1937; d. Clarence R. and Thelma V. (Lakin) Curtindale; m. Harold J. Sudhoff, Nov. 17, 1962; children: Cynthia R., Candice K. BS, Ea. Mich. U., 1959; MA, Saginaw Valley State U., 1981. Cert. elem. tchr., Mich. Classroom tchr. St. Stephen's Cath. Sch., Saginaw, Mich., 1965-67; classroom tchr. Saginaw City Pub. Schs., 1959-65, Swan Valley Sch. Dist., Saginaw, 1967-93, mem. innovative coun. Chair sch. improvement and accreditation teams R.B. Havens Sch., Saginaw; tutor St. Helen Sch., Saginaw. Lay minister. Mem. NEA-Retired, Mich. Edn. Assn.-Retired, Saginaw County Assn. Retired Personnel. Home: 3358 Dale Rd Saginaw MI 48603-3122

SUDOL, WALTER EDWARD, lawyer; b. Passaic, N.J., Jan. 13, 1942; s. Walter and Ann (Kopec) S.; m. June Ann Jancio, Oct. 14, 1967; children: Karen Ann, Alyson Anne. BA, Tulane U., 1963; JD, Seton Hall U., 1975. Bar: N.J. 1975, U.S. Dist. Ct. N.J. 1975, N.Y. 1985. Indsl. engr. Westinghouse Electric Co., Jersey City, 1969-72, indsl. relations mgr., 1972-75, atty., mgr. contracts Millburn, N.J., 1975-80; gen. counsel, sec. Internat. Computers Ltd., East Brunswick, 1980-81, Belco Pollution Control Corp., Parsippany, 1981-85; v.p., gen. counsel, sec. H-R Internat., Inc., Edison, 1985-94; assoc. counsel Louis Berger Internat., Inc., East Orange, 1997—. Cons. constrn. claims Westinghouse Electric Co., Washington, 1977-79, Foster Wheeler Energy Corp., Livingston, N.J., 1983-84. Pres. St. Andrew's Parish Council, Clifton, N.J., 1980. Served to capt. USNR, 1963-91, Vietnam. Mem. ABA, N.J. Bar Assn., Passaic County Bar Assn., Nat. Constructors Assn. (chmn. gen. counsels com. 1985-86), Am. Legion, VFW. Lodges: Masons. Republican. Roman Catholic. Avocations: sailing, tennis. Home: 67 Village Rd Clifton NJ 07013-3436

SUDOR, CYNTHIA ANN, sales and marketing professional; b. Hershey, Pa., June 11, 1952; d. Milan and Mary (Strahosky) Sudor. BS in Design, Drexel U., 1974. Various mktg. positions in advt., promotion and publicity Hersheypark, Hershey, Pa., 1975-85, dir. sales and mktg., 1985-90; dir. destination mktg. Hershey Entertainment and Resort Co., 1990-91, dir. corp. sponsorship, 1991; owner Cynthia A. Sudor Enterprises, Grantville, Pa., 1992—, mktg., strategic planning, corp. sponsorship consulting, 1992—; v.p. sales, mktg. and IMAX Whitaker Ctr. for Sci. and the Arts, Harrisburg, 1998—2001. Freelance writer, spkr., seminar presenter. Contbr. to Apprise Mag., Harrisburg, Pa., 1994-95, Funworld Mag., Alexandria, Va., 1987-90. Bd. dirs., v.p., mktg. chair Profiles In Excellence, Inc., Harrisburg, 1993-99, Energy Entertainment, 1998-99. Recipient Best Seminar award Internat. Assn. Amusement Parks and Attractions (IAAPA), Dallas, 1988. Mem.: Pa. Arabian Horse Assn., Internat. Arabian Horse Assn. Avocations: travel, writing, Ukrainian egg decorating, reading, horseback riding. Office: Cynthia A Sudor Enterprises 1205 Ridge Rd Grantville PA 17028-9135 E-mail: csudor@ezonline.com.

SUDOW, THOMAS NISAN, marketing services company executive, broadcaster, chamber of commerce executive; b. Stevens Point, Wis., Nov. 7, 1952; s. Noah and Gertrude (Fein) S.; m. Michele Ross, Aug. 8, 1976; children: Erin, Noah, Nathaniel. Student, U. Wis., 1971, Jerusalem Inst., Israel, 1972; BA, Kent State U., 1976; MSW, Yeshiva U., N.Y.C., 1980. Tchr. Akron (Ohio) Hebrew High Sch., 1976-78; sr. assoc. Jewish Cmty. Fed. of Cleve., 1978-85; exec. dir. Am. Friends of Hebrew U., Beachwood, Ohio, 1986-88; v.p. Cleve. Coll. of Jewish Studies, 1988-93, Solid Sound Rec. Studio, Chgo., 1980-99; pres. T.N.S. and Assocs., 1993—; exec. producer, host Sports Talk for Kids Radio Network, Cleve., 1993—; exec. dir. Beechwood (Ohio) C. of C., 2002—. Instr. Kent (Ohio) State U., 1976-78; radio host Cleve. Hockey Jour. on the Air, Tonight in Baseball, Play by Play, H.S. Hockey Game of the Week; instr. fund raising course Mandel Sch. for Applied Social Sci., Case Western Res. U. Columnist Family Recreation mag., The Cleve. Hockey Jour.; editor Torchlight; host The Cleve. Crunch Coaches Show and playoff, pre-game and half-time shows. Exec. bd. dirs. Kent Sunday Sch., 1976-78; bd. dirs. Park Synagogue, Cleveland Heights, Ohio, 1986-97, pres. Men's Club, 1989-91; bd. dirs. Cleve. Pops Orch.; regional program chair FJMC Conv., v.p. Gt. Lake region, 1992-2000, pres. cabinet, 1995-97 chmn. Cleve. region, 1995-98, internat. exec. com., 1997-99, internat. sec., 1999-2001, internat. v.p. 2001—; founding dir. Congregation Cmty. Inst. Adult Jewish Studies, 1988-93; hon. dir. Bejing Ctr. for Jewish Studies, 1993—; trustee Beachwood C. of C., 1993—, v.p., 1995-99, pres., 1999-2001; exec. com. Beachwood Area Transp. Orgn. Mgmt.; vice chair No. Ohio Assn. Chambers Commerce. Lt. col. M.C. USAF. Recipient Young Leadership award, United Jewish Appeal, N.Y.C., 1976, No. Ohio Live award of Achievement Media, 1996; named Man of the Yr. Park Synagogue, Cleveland Heights, 1986; Sherman fellow Brandeis U., Waltham, Mass., 1986. Mem. NASW, Conf. Jewish Communal Svc. Workers (chmn. 1986-93), Assn. Jewish Communal Orgn. Profs. (regional chmn. 1981-85), Conf. Alternatives in Jewish Edn., Glass Inst. (chmn. 1986-87), Wahoo Club (pres. 1993-95), Cleve. Indians Heavy Hitters, Nat. Soc. Fundraising Exec., Ohio Fundraising Exec. Coun., Cleve. Cavs Reboudersn (bd. dirs., v.p 2000, pres. 2001), Sports Media and Mktg. Assn. Ohio, Crohn's and Colts Found. of No. Ohio. Avocations: sports, photography, family, humor. Office: TNS and Assocs 3665 Tolland Rd Cleveland OH 44122-5140

SUE, ALAN KWAI KEONG, dentist; b. Honolulu, Apr. 26, 1946; s. Henry Tin Yee and Chiyoko (Ohata) S.; m. Ginger Kazue Fukushima, Mar. 19, 1972; 1 child, Dawn Marie. BS in Chemistry with honors, U. Hawaii, 1968; BS, DDS, U. Calif., San Francisco, 1972. Film editor, photographer Sta. KHVH-TV ABC, Honolulu, 1964-71; staff dentist Strong-Carter Dental Clinic, 1972-73; dentist Waianae Dental Clinic, 1972-73; pvt. practice Pearl City, Hawaii, 1973—; chief exec. officer Dental Image Specialists, 1975—; dental dir. Hawaii Dental Health Plan, Honolulu, 1987—; dental cons. Calif. Dental Health Plan, Tustin, 1987—, Pacific Group Med. Assn., The Queen's Health Care Plan, Honolulu, 1993—. Dental cons. Pacific Group Med. Assn., 1994—; cons. Hawaii Mgmt. Alliance Assn., 1996—; bd. dirs. Kula Bay Tropical Clothing Co., Hawaiian Ind. Dental Alliance; mem. exec. bd. St. Francis Hosp., Honolulu, 1976-78, chief dept. dentistry, 1976-78; mem. expert med. panel Am. Internat. Claim Svc., 1995—. Mem. adv. bd. Health Svcs. for Sr. Citizens, 1976—; mem. West Honolulu Sub-Area Health Planning Coun., 1981-84; mem. dental task force Hawaii Statewide Health Coordinating Coun., 1980, mem. plan devel. com., 1981-84; vol. oral cancer screening program Am. Cancer Soc.; v.p. Pearl City Shopping Ctr. Merchants Assn., 1975-84, 92-93, pres., 1994—. Regents' scholar U. Calif., San Francisco, 1968-72. Fellow Pierre Fauchard Acad., Acad. Gen. Dentistry; mem. ADA, Acad. Implants and Transplants, Am. Acad. Implant Dentistry, Hawaii Dental Assn. (trustee 1978-80), Honolulu County Dental Soc. (pres. 1982), Am. Acad. and Bd. Head, Facial, Neck Pain and TMJ Orthopedics, Intertel, Internat. Platform Assn., Mensa, Porsche Club, Pantera Owners Club, Mercedes Benz Club. Democrat. Avocations: cars, tennis, photography, gardening. Office: Dental Image Specialists 850 Kam Hwy Ste 116 Pearl City HI 96782-2691

SUEDFELD, PETER, psychologist, educator; b. Budapest, Hungary, Aug. 30, 1935; emigrated to U.S., 1948, naturalized, 1952; s. Leslie John and Jolan (Eichenbaum) Field; m. Gabrielle Debra Guterman, June 11, 1961 (div. 1980); children: Michael Thomas, Joanne Ruth, David Lee; m. Phyllis Jean Johnson, Oct. 19, 1991. Student, U. Philippines, 1956-57; BA, Queens Coll., 1960; MA, Princeton U., 1962, PhD, 1963. Research assoc. Princeton U.; lectr. Trenton State Coll., 1963-64; vis. asst. prof. psychology U. Ill., 1964-65; asst. prof. psychology Univ. Coll. Rutgers U., 1965-67, assoc. prof., 1967-71, prof., 1971-72, chmn. dept., 1967-72; prof. psychology U. B.C., Vancouver, 1972-2001, head dept., 1972-84, dean faculty grad. studies, 1984-90, disting. scholar-in-residence, P. Wall Inst. Adv. Studies, 2000, dean and prof. emeritus, 2001—. Disting. vis. scholar Ohio State U., 2000—; cons. in field; chmn. Can. Antarctic Rsch. Program, 1994-98. Author: Restricted Environmental Stimulation: Research and Clinical Applications, 1980; editor: Attitude Change: The Competing Views, 1971, Personality Theory and Information Processing, 1971, The Behavioral Basis of Design, 1976, Psychology and Torture, 1990, Restricted Environmental Stimulation: Theoretical and Empirical Developments in Flotation REST, 1990, Psychology and Social Policy, 1991, Light from the Ashes, 2001; editor Jour. Applied Social Psychology, 1975-82 ;assoc. editor Environment and Behavior, 1992—; contbr. articles to profl. jours. Served with U.S. Army, 1955-58. Recipient Antarctica svc. medal, 1994, Donald O. Hebb award, 1996, Zachor award, 2000, Harold D. Lasswell award, 2001; grantee NIMH, 1970-72, Can. Coun., 1973—, Soc. Sci. Rsch. Coun. Can., 1973—, Nat. Rsch. Coun. Can., 1973-90, NIH, 1980-84; named Weinmann lectr. U.S. Holocaust Meml. Mus., 2002. Fellow Royal Soc. Can., Can. Psychol. Assn. (pres. 1998-99), APA, Am. Psychol. Soc., Acad. Behavioral Medicine Resch., Soc. Behavioral Medicine, N.Y. Acad. Scis.; mem. Internat. Soc. Polit. Psychol. (v.p. 1999-2001), Soc. Exptl. Social Psychology, Phi Beta Kappa, Sigma Xi. Office: U BC Dept Psychology Vancouver BC Canada V6T 1Z4

SUELTO, CONSUELO QUILAO, retired nursing educator; b. The Philippines, June 27, 1924; d. Catalina Pamplona; m. Anacleto T. Suelto, Apr. 28, 1952; children: Ramona, Anacleto Q. Jr. Diploma, U. Philippines Sch. Nursing, Manila, 1949; BS in Nursing Edn., Philippine Women's U., Manila, 1955, EdD, 1983; MA in Nursing, U. Philippines, Quezon City, 1960; EdD, P.W. U., 1983. Staff nurse U. Philippines-Philippine Gen. Hosp., 1949-50, instr. Sch. Nursing, 1950-61; adminstrv. officer, asst. dean Philippine Women's U., 1961-68; prin. St. Jude Sch. Nursing, Manila, 1968-73, Lipa City (The Philippines Sch. Nursing, 1976-80; dean Lipa City Coll. Nursing, 1980-84, Golden Gate Coll. Coll. Nursing, Batangas City, The Philippines, 1980-84; coord., instr. St. James Mercy Hosp. Sch. Nursing, Hornell, N.Y., 1973-75, 84-94. Mem. adv. bd. PNA of Fla., 1995. Mem. Philippines Nurses Assn. (life, bd. dirs.), Nurses Assn. of the Am. Assn. of Ob-Gyn. Home: 1623 19th St NE Rochester MN 55906-4339

SUEN, CHING YEE, computer scientist and educator, researcher; b. Chung Shan, Kwang Tung, China, Oct. 14, 1942; s. Stephen and Sin (Kan) S; m. Sheung Ling Chan, May 12, 1970; children: Karwa, Karnon. BSc in Engring., U. Hong Kong, 1966, MSc in Engring., 1968; MASc., U. B.C., 1970, PhD, 1972. Asst. prof. computer sci. Concordia U., Montreal, Can., 1972-76, assoc. prof. Can., 1976-79, prof. Can., 1979—, chmn. Can., 1980-84, dir. Centre for Pattern Recognition and Machine Intelligence Can., 1988—, assoc. dean faculty engring. and computer sci. Can., 1993-97, chair artificial intelligence and pattern recognition, 2001—. Vis. scientist Rsch. Lab. of Electronics, MIT, Cambridge, 1975, 76, 78-79; invited prof. Ecole Polytechnique Fédérale de Lausanne, Switzerland, 1979, Institut de Recherche d'Informatique et d'Automatique, Rocquencourt, France, 1976, 78, 79, founder, Vision Interface, 1986; founder, co-chmn. Internat. Conf. on Document Analysis and Recognition, St.-Malo, France, 1991, Tsukuba Sci. City, Japan, 1993, chmn., Montreal, Can., 1995; founder, chmn. Internat. Workshop on Frontiers 2, gen. chair Internat. Conf. on Pattern Recognition, Quebec City, Canada, 2002; organizer numerous confs. Author: Computational Analysis of Mandarin, 1979, Computational Studies of the Most Frequent Chinese Words and Sounds, 1986, (with Z.C. Li, T.D. Bui, Y.Y. Tang) Computer Transformation of Digital Images and Patterns, 1989; editor: (with R. De Mori) Computer Analysis and Perception Vol. 1, Visual Signals, 1982, Computer Analysis and Perception Vol. 2, Auditory Signals, 1982, (with R. De Mori) New Systems and Architectures for Automatic Speech Recognition and Synthesis, 1985, (with R. Plamondon and M.L. Simner) Computer Recognition and Human Production of Handwriting, 1989, Frontiers in Handwriting Recognition, 1990, Operating Expert System Applications in Canada, 1992, (with P.S.P. Wang) Thinning Methodologies for Pattern Recognition, 1994; assoc. editor Signal Processing, 1979—, Pattern Recognition Letters, 1982—, Pattern Recognition, 1983—, IEEE Transactions on Pattern Analysis and Machine Intelligence, 1986-89, Internat. Jour. Pattern Recognition and Artificial Intelligence, 1986—, Pattern Analysis and Applications, 1998—, Internat. Jour. on Document Analysis and Applications, 1998—; founder, editor-in-chief Computer Processing of Chinese and Oriental Langs., 1982-93; adviser IEEE Transactions on Pattern Analysis and Machine Intelligence, 1989-92; author more than 300 publs.; patentee in field. Recipient award Fedn. Chinese Can. Profls., 1988; rsch. fellow Concordia U., 1998; Swire scholar U. Hong Kong, 1967, ITAC/NSERC award Info. Tech. Assn. Can. and Natural Scis. and Engring. Rsch. Coun. Can., 1992. Fellow IEEE (advisor Computer Soc.), Royal Soc. Can., Internat. Assn. for Pattern Recognition; mem. Chinese Lang. Computer Soc. (v.p. 1987-90, pres. 1990-93, award 1988), Can. Image Processing and Pattern Recognition Soc. (pres. 1984-90, award 1997). Office: Concordia U Dept Computer Sci 1455 Maisonneuve W Ste GM-606 Montreal QC Canada H3G 1M8

SUEN, JAMES YEE, otolaryngologist, educator; b. Dermott, Ark., Oct. 9, 1940; s. Yee Gow and Mary (Chaing) S.; m. Karen Hannahs; children: Brent, Tiffany, Bradley, Brennan. BA in Zoology, U. Tex., 1962; BS, MD, U. Ark., 1966. Diplomate Am. Bd. Otolaryngology. Rotating intern San Francisco Gen. Hosp., 1966-67; resident in gen. surgery U. Ark. Med. Ctr., Little Rock, 1969-70, resident in otolaryngology, 1970-73; advanced sr. fellow M.D. Anderson Hosp. and Tumor Inst., Houston, 1973-74, faculty assoc., 1974; asst. prof. U. Ark. Coll. Medicine, Little Rock, 1974-76, assoc. prof., 1976-78, prof. otolaryngology, 1978—, chief div. otolaryngology, 1974-78, chmn. dept. otolaryngology and head and neck surgery, 1978—; dir. Ark. Cancer Rsch. Ctr., 2001—. Author, editor: Cancer of the Head and Neck, 1981, 3d edit., 1996, Emergencies in Otolaryngology, 1986; co-author: Hemangiomas and Vascular Malformations of the Head and Neck, 1999. Capt. USAF, 1967-69. Recipient Disting. Alumnus award U. Tex., M.D. Anderson Cancer Ctr., 1995; named Chinese Man of Yr., Chinese Soc. Ark., 1983, Disting. Citizen of Yr. Gov. Ark., 1991. Fellow ACS, Am. Acad. Otolaryngology and Head and Neck Surgery, Am. Soc. Head and Neck Surgery (pres. 1993-94, coun. 1988-92); mem. Soc. Univ. Otolaryngologists. Methodist. Office: U Ark Coll Medicine 4301 W Markham St Little Rock AR 72205-7101

SUEN, TZENG-JIUEQ, chemical enginner, researcher; b. Hangzhou, China, June 7, 1912; s. Zu-Huan and Zhang-Shi Suen; m. Ming-Tung Chang, Jan. 1, 1944; children: Caroline Vera, Theodore Michael. BS, Tsing Hua U., Beijing, 1933; MS, MIT, 1935, DSc, 1937, postdoc., 1937-38. Prof. chem. engring. Chongqing (China) U., 1938-39; dir. rsch. Tung Li Oil Works, Chongqing, 1939-44; mem. staff MIT Radiation Lab., Cambridge, 1944-45; dir. rsch. Am. Cyanamid Co., Stamford, Conn., 1945-77. Cons. indsl. and rsch. orgns., U.S., China, France, 1977—. Contbr. articles to profl. jours.; 57 patents in field of polymers and resins. Pres. Chinese Assn. Fairfield County, 1976-80, Tsing Hua Alumni Assn., Inc., N.Y.C., 1978-82. Mem. AAAS, Am. Chem. Soc. Home: 349 Mariomi Rd New Canaan CT 06840 E-mail: TJSuen@aol.com.

SUER, MARVIN DAVID, architecture, consultant; b. Phila., Apr. 4, 1923; m. Gertrude Litvin, 1947; children: Marsha Suer Clark, Sharon, Deborah Suer Berman. BArch, U. Pa., 1950. Registered architect, N.J., Pa. Ptnr. Suer & Livingston, 1961-62, Suer, Livingston & Demas, 1962-69; dir. tech. prodn. Eshbach, Pullinger, Stevens & Bruder, Phila., 1969-74; assoc. Ballinger, 1974-79, Bartley Long Mirenda, Phila., 1979-85, S.T. Hudson Internat., Phila., 1986-95; archtl. cons., 1996—. Archtl. works include State Hosp. for Crippled Children addition, 1964, Huey Elem. Sch., Phila., 1964, Dist. No. 4 Health Ctr., Phila., 1967, Stephen Smith Towers, 1969, Foxchase Br. Libr., 1969. Chmn. bd. trustees Phila. Found. for Architecture, 1980-81. With C.E., AUS, 1943-46. Fellow AIA (pres. Phila. chpt. 1968, 125th Yr. citation 1982); mem. Tau Sigma Delta. Home: 305 Overlook Ave Willow Grove PA 19090-2806

SUESS, JAMES FRANCIS, retired psychiatry educator; b. Rock Island, Ill., Nov. 27, 1919; s. Joseph John and Elizabeth Ida (Dalton) S.; m. Rae Love Miller, Mar. 24, 1946; children: Rae Anne, James Francis, John Randall. B Med. Sci., Northwestern U., 1950, MD, 1952; postgrad., Coll. Physicians and Surgeons, Columbia U. and N.Y. Psychiat. Inst., 1958. Diplomate Am. Bd. Psychiatry and Neurology (examiner various times). Intern USPHS Hosp., New Orleans, 1952-53; resident in psychiatry Warren (Pa.) State Hosp., 1953-56, clin. dir., 1956-62; asst. prof. psychiatry U. Miss. Med. Sch., Jackson, 1962-65, assoc. prof., 1965-69, prof., 1969-82; prof. emeritus, 1982—; chmn. dept., 1967-69, 73-75; asst. dean, 1978-82. Assoc. chief staff for edn. VA Med. Ctr., Jackson, 1978-82; vis. prof. Inst. Psychiatry, London, 1977, 83; referee editl. bd. Am. Jour. Psychiatry, Washington. Contbr. articles to med. jours., including Am. Jour. Psychiatry, Jour. Med. Edn., chpts. to books. Capt. U.S. Army, 1941-45. Fellow Am. Psychiat. Assn., So. Psychiat. Assn. (edn. com. 1973-77), Miss. Psychiat. Assn. (pres. 1968-69); mem. Am. Assn. Dirs. Psychiat. Tng. (a founder, exec. bd. 1969-71). Avocations: piano, organ, golf, duplicate bridge. Home: 1415 Radcliffe St Jackson MS 39211-4824 E-mail: jamespsychman@cs.com.

SUESS, JAMES FRANCIS, clinical psychologist; b. Evanston, Ill., Aug. 8, 1950; s. James Francis and Rae Love (Miller) S.; m. Linda Grace Powell, July 31, 1976; 1 child, Misty Lynne. BS, U. So. Miss., 1974, MS, 1978, PhD, 1982. Lic. psychologist, N.Y., Ala.; diplomate Am. Bd. Profl. Psychology, Am. Bd. Med. Psychotherapists, Profl. Assn. Custody Evaluators, Am. Coll. Forensic Examiners, Am. Bd. Forensic Medicine. Assoc. psychologist State of Miss., Ellisville, 1978-80; clin. psychologist SUNY Med. Sch./Erie County Med. Ctr., Buffalo, 1982-84, supervising clin. psychologist, 1984-87, assoc. dir., 1987—; prof. dept. psychology U. South Ala., 2001—. Dir. practica SUNY Med. Sch., 1982-90, faculty counsel, 1988—; cons. Buffalo Dept. Social Svcs., 1985—; mem. spkrs. bur. Erie Alliance for Mentally Ill, 1986—; vis. prof. U. Guadalajara Sch. Medicine, 1985—; clin. dir. Stickney Adolescent Ctr. Mobile Met. Hosp. Ctr., 1993-97; chmn., dir. Physicians' Psychiat. Clinic, 1997—; CEO Stillwood Clin. Group, 1998—; adj. prof. dept. psychology U. South Ala., 2000—; dur. aminstrn. Mc Collough Inst. of Rejuvenology. Author: Annotated Bibliography of Sex Roles, 1972, Personality Disorder and Self Psychology, 1991; contbr. articles to refereed jours. including Perceptual and Motor Skills, Jour. Clin. and Consulting Psychology, Am. Annals of Deaf. With USAR, 1969-76. Fellow Am. Orthopsychiat. Assn., Soc. Personality Assessment; mem. Am. Psychol. Assn., Ala. Lic. Psychol. (pres.), Mobile Assn. Psychol. (pres.). Home: 507 Evergreen Rd Mobile AL 36608-3845 Office: The Stillwood Clin Grp 717 Executive Park Dr Ste B Mobile AL 36606-2843 Fax: 251-479-8172. E-mail: drjfsuess@cs.com.

SUFLETA, ZBIGNIEW JOZEF, computer systems designer, software consultant; b. Lodz, Poland, Nov. 7, 1953; came to U.S., 1987; s. Jozef and Zofia (Kuc) S.; m. Urszula Jolanta Dreglewska, Dec. 24, 1976; children: Magdalena, Tomasz. MS, Tech. U. Worcklaw (Poland), 1976, PhD, 1979. Asst. prof. Tech. U. Wroclaw, 1979-86, Mich. Technol. U., Houghton, 1987-88; sr. software engr. Prog. Computing, Inc., Glen Ellyn, Ill., 1987-90, cons., 1987—; sr. programmer-analyst Reuters Info. Svcs., Inc., Chgo., 1988-91; project leader rsch. and devel. Progressive Computing, Inc., Oak Brook, Ill., 1991-94; mgr. software devel. Network Gen. Corp., Menlo Park, Calif., 1994-98, Network Assocs., Inc., Santa Clara, 1997-2000; founder, dir. sys. design Transparent Networks Inc., 2000—. Software cons. Computer Systems Ctr. Elwro, Wroclaw, 1983-86. Contbr. articles to profl. jours. Mem. IEEE. Roman Catholic. Home: 7159 Brisbane Ct San Jose CA 95129-4648 Office: Transparent Networks Inc 471B El Camino Real Santa Clara CA 95050 E-mail: zsufleta@pacbell.net., zsufleta@transparentoptical.com.

SUGA, STEVEN HIDENORI, neurologist; b. Apr. 24, 1942; came to U.S., 1971, naturalized, 1987; Bachelor's degree, Tohoku U., Sendai, Japan, 1963, MD, 1967. Cert. Am. Bd. Psychiatry and Neurology, 1978, Am. Assoc. EMG and electrodiagnosis, 1979, Am. Bd. Electrodiagnostic Med., 1989. Intern Bronx-Lebanon Hosp., 1971-72; resident in neurology Baylor Coll. Medicine, 1972-75; fellow in neuropathology Upstate Med. Ctr., 1975-76; fellow in neuromusular disease U. Colo. Med. Ctr., 1976-77; fellow in EEG Sepulveda VA Hosp. (UCLA affiliated), 1977-78; fellow in EMG U. Calif., San Diego, 1978-79; pvt. practice L.A., 1979-83; group practice Affiliated Med. Ctr., 1983-90; neurologist Solano Regional Med. Group, Vacaville, Calif., 1991—. Office: 770 Mason St Vacaville CA 95688 Fax: 707-454-5952. E-mail: ssuga218@ipninet.com.

SUGAHARA, BYRON MASAHIKO, transportation company executive; b. Jan. 22, 1940; s. Kay and Yone (Kuwahara) S.; m. Nancy Shaw Hall, June 5, 1977; children: Christopher, Abigail, Alexandra. BA, Harvard Coll., 1962. From v.p. to pres. Gt. Am. Lines, Roseland, N.J., 1985—. Mem. Am. Bur. of Shipping. Bd. dirs. The Peck Sch., Morristown, N.J., 1993-95. 1st Lt. U.S. Army, 1963-65, Korea. Mem. Henryville Conservation Club, Tokyo Club. Avocations: fly fishing, golf. Home: Blue Mill Rd Morristown NJ 07960 Office: Great American Lines 5 Becker Farm Rd Ste 4 Roseland NJ 07068-1779

SUGAR, ROBERT JOSEPH, software engineer, physicist; b. Steubenville, Ohio, Aug. 31, 1949; s. Joseph and Anne (Rock) S.; m. Martha Francis Hahn, Apr. 5, 1975; children: Mary Francis, Robin Ann. BS in Physics, Kent State U., 1971; MS in Physics, Ohio U., 1974, MS in Systems Engring., 1977. Instr. Hocking Tech. Coll., Nelsonville, Ohio, 1974-77; sr. engr. Kaiser Aluminum Co., Ravenswood, W.Va., 1977-79, Allen-Bradley Co., Highland Heights, Ohio, 1979-81, B.F. Goodrich Chem. Co., Independence, 1981-82, Fairfield Engring. Co., Marion, 1982-83, Picker Internat., Highland Heights, 1983-85, Keithley Instruments, Solon, Ohio, 1985-93. Mem. IEEE. Home: 10867 Ravenna Rd Twinsburg OH 44087-1015 Office: Allen Bradley Co Div Rockwell Internat 1 Allen Bradley Dr Mayfield Hts OH 44124-6107

SUGARBAKER, EVERETT VAN DYKE, surgical oncologist; b. N.Y.C., Aug. 6, 1940; s. Everett Dornbush and Geneva Irene (Van Dyke) S.; m. Myriam Rodriguez, Nov. 2000; children: Everett Mongiello, Kathryn Anna. BS in Chemistry, Wheaton (Ill.) Coll., 1962; MD, Cornell U., 1966. Diplomate Am. Bd. Surgery, Am. Bd. Thoracic Surgery. Resident Mass. Gen. Hosp., Boston, 1966-68, 70-73, chief resident, 1974; clin. assoc. NIH, Bethesda, Md., 1966-68; sr. fellow in surg. oncology M.D. Anderson Hosp., Houston, 1975; assoc. prof. surgery U. Miami, Fla., 1975-80; staff surgeon Cedars Med. Ctr., Miami, 1980—, co-dir. oncology lab., 1984-99; pres., dir. surg. oncology Miami Cancer Inst., 1980—. Pres. Surg. Oncology Assocs., Miami, 1981—; dir. Women's Ctr.; dir. surg. oncology, pres. Miami Cancer Inst., 1985—. Contbr. chpts. to books, more than 200 articles to profl. jours. Lt. comdr. USPHS, 1968-70. Mem. Surg. Oncology Assn. (pres.) Avocations: bicycling, inline skating. Office: Surg Oncology Assocs 1500 Brickell Ave Miami FL 33129-1210 E-mail: docsug@aol.com.

SUGARBAKER, STEPHEN PHILIP, surgeon, educator; b. Jefferson City, Mo., Mar. 13, 1956; s. Everett Dornbush and Geneva Irene (Van Dyke) S.; m. Clera Jane Perdue, June 24, 1995; 1 child, Stephen James. BS in Biology cum laude, Wheaton Coll., 1978; MD, Cornell U., 1982. Cert. in surgery, specialty in surg. critical care. Intern Vanderbilt U. Med. Ctr., Nashville, 1982-83, resident in gen. surgery, 1983-84, 86-87, Kaiser Found. Hosp., San Francisco, 1988-91; fellow Brigham and Women's Hosp., Boston, 1984-86; clin. fellow in nutrition Dana Farber Cancer Ctr., 1985-86. Asst. prof. surgery U. Mo.-Columbia Sch. Medicine, 1991-94, clin. asst. prof. surgery, 1994-97; mem. tumor bd., cancer com., critical care com. Capitol Region Med. Ctr., Jefferson City, 1994-98. Fellow: ACS; mem.: AMA, Cole County Med. Soc., Mo. State Med. Soc., Southwestern Surg. Congress, Soc. Critical Care Medicine. Southern Baptist. Office: Sugarbaker Surg Assocs 503 E High St Jefferson City MO 65101-3216

SUGARMAN, ALAN WILLIAM, education administrator; b. Boston, Sept. 26, 1924; s. Henry and Dorothy (Adams) S.; m. Alice Mulhall, 1974; children: Michael, Susan, Ellen, William, Jane, James. BS, Boston U., 1948; MA, Columbia U., 1949, EdD, 1967; postgrad., SUNY, Albany, 1954-56. Entrance examiner Boston U., 1947-48; tchr. Public Schs. Hudson, N.Y., 1950-54, prin. jr. high sch., 1954-56, prin. sr. high sch., 1956-61; prin. Spring Valley (N.Y.) Sr. High Sch., 1961-67; dir. secondary edn. Ramapo Central Sch. Dist. No. 2, Spring Valley, 1967-69, asst. supt. instrn., 1969-73; prin. Ramapo Sr. High Sch., Spring Valley, 1969; supt. schs. Connetquot Central Sch. Dist. Islip, Bohemia, N.Y., 1973-80, Ft. Lee (N.J.) Sch. Dist., 1980—2000; nat. spkr., cons., 2000—. Adj. prof. N.Y. U., N.Y.C., U. P.R., Rio Piedras, Hofstra U., 1967— ; prof. Fordham U., N.Y.C., 1969 Athletic dir. East River Day Camp, N.Y.C., summer 1949; group worker St. John's Guild, summer 1950; asst. dir. Tenn. Work Camp, Unitarian Service Com., summer 1951; dir. spl. activities Hudson Youth Bur., Hudson, N.Y., summer 1952; exec. dir. Jewish Community Center, Hudson, 1953-56; chmn. vis. coms. Middle States Commn. Colls. and Secondary Schs., 1958-76; chmn. county leadership tng. com., mem. Rockland County exec. council Boy Scouts Am., 1956; bd. dirs. Bergen County Red Cross; corr. sec. Rockland County Negro Scholarship Fund, Inc.; pres. Spring Valley Youth Activities Com., 1956-58; bd. dirs., past campaign co-chmn. Greater Hudson Community Chest; bd. dirs., 2d v.p. Hudson Youth Recreation Center, 1958-61; bd. dirs. Rockland County br. Am. Cancer Soc., 1958-61, Columbia Meml. Hosp., 1959-61; chmn. Town of Islip Health Usage Com., 1973; bd. dirs. Am. Heart Assn. N.J. affiliate, 1993—. Served with AUS, 1944-46, ETO. Recipient Disting. Svc. award Hudson Jr. C. of C., 1960, Ft. Lee Citizen of Yr. award VFW, Bergen County Citizen of Yr. award VFW, 1989, N.J. State Elks Alcohol and Drug Prevention award, 1989, St. Michael's award, 1992, PBA Silver Life Card award, 1993, EIA award Greek Orthodox Archdiocese, 1993; named Adminstr. of Yr., Fordham U., 1990, B'nai Brith Man of Yr., 1995. Mem. Nat. Honor Soc. Secondary Schs. (hon.), Nat. PTA (hon. life), Am. Assn. Sch. Adminstrs., Assn. Supervision and Curriculum Devel., Nat. Sch. Public Relations Assn., Assn. Sch. Bus. Ofcls., Nat. Soc. Study Edn., DAV, VFW, Jewish War Vets., Rotary (bd. dirs.), Phi Delta Kappa (Adminstr. of Yr. award 1990), Kappa Delta Pi, Pi Gamma Mu. Home: South Pointe Harbor Club 75 Broadway Apt 116 Somers Point NJ 08244-1147 Office: 75 Broadway Somers Point NJ 08244 also: 401 Park Place Fort Lee NJ 07024 E-mail: amwsintac@msn.com.

SUGARMAN, BAHIRA, clinical social worker; b. Apr. 8, 1945; d. Seymour Harvey and Gladys (Packer) S.; m. Sheldon Robert Isenberg. BA, Conn. Coll., 1967; MS, Columbia U., 1972. Lic. clin. social worker, marriage and family therapist, Fla; registered in clin. social work Nat. Registry Health Care Workers; diplomate in clin. social work Nat. Bd. Examiners, Inst. Acad. Behavioral Medicine, Counseling and Psychotherapy; ordained spiritual guide, 1996. Psychiat. social worker Clifford Beers Child Guidance Ctr., New Haven, 1972-73; instr. social work psychiatry children's mental health unit U. Fla. Med. Sch. Dept. Psychiatry, Gainesville, 1973-79; clin. social worker, pvt. practice psychotherapy, 1979—; faculty, co-founder Traditional Healing Arts Assocs., Gainesville, 1984-96; ptnr. Living Tree Assocs., 1987—. Instr. Arica Inst., 1978—; apprentice instr. Sch. Taichi Chuan, 1981-; sr. faculty Spiritual Eldering Inst., Traditional Reiki Master tchr. 1994—. Contbr. articles to profl. jours. Fellow Am. Orthopsychiat. Assn., Arica Inst., Fla. Soc. for Clin. Social Workers; mem. NASW (treas. Gainesville chpt. 1980-89, cert.), Acad. Cert. Social Workers, Nat. Registry of Health Care Providers in Clin. Social Work, Am. Assn. Marriage and Family Therapists, Assn. Transpersonal Psychology. Office: 115 NE 7th Ave Gainesville FL 32601-4391

SUGARMAN, HELEN LYNNE, English educator, researcher; b. Springfield, Mass., Mar. 22, 1967; d. Edward David and Lois-Marie Loucks S. BA, Colby Coll., 1989; MA, Cath. U. of Am., 1993; PhD, La. State U., 2000. English instr. Northwestern State U., Natchitoches, La., 1999—, La. Sch. for Math, Sci. and the Arts, Natchitoches, 2001—. Mem. MLA, South Ctrl. MLA. Avocations: photography, tennis, dogs. E-mail: helensugarman@yahoo.com.

SUGARMAN, IRWIN J. lawyer; b. Dayton, Ohio, June 17, 1943; s. Nathan and Esther (Goldstein) S.; 1 child, Alexander David Sugarman. BA, Rutgers U., New Brunswick, N.J., 1965; JD, Rutgers U., Newark, 1968. Bar: N.Y. 1968. Law clk. to Judge Edmund Palmieri U.S. Dist. Ct. for So. Dist. N.Y., N.Y.C., 1968-69; assoc. Debevoise Plimpton Lyons & Gates, 1969-79; ptnr. Schulte Roth & Zabel, 1979—. Bd. dirs. Santa Fe Opera, 1989-94. Office: Schulte Roth & Zabel 919 3rd Ave Fl 23 New York NY 10022-4774 E-mail: irwin.sugarman@srz.com.

SUGARMAN, JULE MEYER, children's services consultant, former public administrator; b. Cin., Sept. 23, 1927; s. Melville Harty and Rachel Wolf (Meyer) S.; m. Sheila Mary Shanley, May 20, 1956 (dec.); children: Christopher, Maryanne, Jason, James; m. Candace Sullivan, Apr. 2, 1989. Student, Western Res. U., 1945-46; AB with highest distinction, Am. U., 1951. Dir. Head Start, 1965-69; adminstr. Human Resources Adminstrn., N.Y.C., 1970-73; chief adminstrv. officer City of Atlanta, 1974-76; vice chmn. CSC, Washington, 1977-78; dep. dir. Office Personnel Mgmt., 1979-81; mng. dir. Human Service Info. Ctr., 1981-83; v.p. Hahnemann U., 1983-86; sec. Wash. State Dept. Social and Health Services, 1986-89; exec. dir. Spl. Olympics Internat., Washington, 1989-91; chmn. Ctr. on Effective Svcs. for Children, 1991—. Cons. Delotte & Touch, 1997-98. Program dir. AmeriCorps, Calvert County, 2000; vice chmn. Boys and Girls Clubs So. Md., 2000-. Served with U.S. Army, 1946-48. Recipient Meritorious Service award Dept. State, 1963, Alumni Service award Am. U., 1977, Disting. Pub. Svc. award Nat. Acad. Pub. Adminstrn., 1988, Gov.'s Volunteer of Yr. award, 2001. Home and Office: 4023 Evergreen Rd Port Republic MD 20676 E-mail: sullsugar@chesapeake.net.

SUGARMAN, MICHAEL, physician, rheumatologist; b. Galveston, Tex., May 26, 1945; s. Harold and Amelia Sugarman; m. Hilda Roberta Krug, Aug. 26, 1967; children: Jason, Steven. BS, U. Calif., Berkeley, 1966; MD, U. Calif., San Francisco, 1970. Diplomate Am. Coll. Physicians, Am. Coll. Rheumatology. Rheumatologist Fullerton (Calif.) Internal Medicine Ctr., Fullerton, Calif., 1976-94. Pres. St. Jude Heritage Med. Group, 1996—. Bd. trustees St. Jude Hosp. Fellow Am. Coll. Rheumatology, Orange County Rheumatism Soc.; mem. AMA, Orange County Med. Assn. Office: St Jude Heritage Med Group 433 W Bastanchury Rd Fullerton CA 92835-3404

SUGARMAN, MYRON GEORGE, lawyer; b. San Francisco, Nov. 7, 1942; s. Irving Carden and Jane Hortense (Weingarten) S.; m. Cheryl Ann Struble, June 8, 1968 (div. 1993); children: Andrew, Amy, Adam; m. Cynthia Wilson Woods, Apr. 16, 1994. BS, U. Calif., Berkeley, 1964, JD, 1967. Assoc. Cooley Godward LLP, San Francisco, 1972-77, ptnr., 1977—. Served to capt. U.S. Army, 1968-71. Fellow Am. Coll. Trust and Estate Counsel, Am. Coll. Tax Counsel, Am. Bar Found.; mem. U. Calif. Alumni Assn. (bd. dirs. 1985-88), San Francisco Tax Club (pres. 1990), San Francisco Grid Club, Order of Coif, Phi Beta Kappa, Beta Gamma Sigma. Avocations: skiing, tennis. Office: Cooley Godward LLP 1 Maritime Plz San Francisco CA 94111-3404

SUGARMAN, PAUL RONALD, lawyer, educator, academic administrator; b. Boston, Dec. 14, 1931; m. Susan J. Sugarman; children: Amy J., Ellen L. AA, Boston U., 1951, JD cum laude (Law Week award 1954, asso. editor law rev. 1952-54), 1954; LLD (hon.), Suffolk U., 1989. Bar: Mass. 1954, U.S. Supreme Ct. 1965. Ptnr. Sugarman & Sugarman, Boston, 1967-90, 94—; prof. law, dean Suffolk U. Law Sch., 1990-94. Mem. Atty. Gen. Mass. Hwy. Law Study Commn., 1965, Mass. Gov.'s Select Com. on Jud. Needs, 1976; bd. bar overseers Supreme Jud. Ct., 1984-88, chmn., 1985-88; advocate Am. Bd. Trial Advocates; spl. master, commr. Boston Mcpl. Ct. Report Supreme Jud. Ct. of Mass., 1990. Trustee Mass. Bar Found., 1980-81. Served as officer AUS, 1955-58. Recipient Courageous Adv. award, Mass. Acad. Trial Attys., 1984, William O. Douglas First Amendment Freedom award, Anti-Defamation League, 1986, Silver Shingle award for svc. to legal profession Boston U. Sch. Law, 1989, Jurisprudence award Am. Orgn. for Rehab. through Tng. Fedn., 1991, Civil Justice award Am. Bd. trial Adv., 1993. Fellow: Internat. Soc. Barristers, Mass. Bar Found., Am. Coll. Trial Lawyers, Am. Bar Found.; mem.: ATLA (gov. 1966—68, pres. Mass. chpt. 1968—70), ABA, Boston U. Sch. Law Alumni Assn. (pres. 1979—80), Boston Bar Assn., Mass. Bar Assn. (pres. 1976—77, chmn. com. on recall of ret. judges 1982—86, chmn. Jud. Adminstrn. Sect. Coun., chmn. 2000—01, Task Force on Jud. Conduct Commn., Gold Medal award 1991). Office: Sugarman and Sugarman PC One Beacon St Boston MA 02108

SUGARMAN, ROBERT GARY, lawyer; b. Bronx, N.Y., Sept. 3, 1939; s. Eugene Leonard and Frances (Solomon) S.; m. Brenda Harrison, Sept. 8, 1963 (div. 1984); children: Dana, Alison; m. Surie Rudoff, June 16, 1985; children: Amanda, Jason. BA, Yale U., 1960, LLB, 1963. Bar: N.Y. 1963, Fla. 1963, U.S. Supreme Ct. 1971, U.S. Dist. Ct. (so. dist.) N.Y. 1966, U.S. Dist. Ct. (ea. dist.) N.Y. 1982, U.S. Ct. Appeals (2d cir.) 1970, U.S. Ct. Appeals (10th cir.) 1971. Assoc. Sugarman, Kuttner & Fuss, N.Y.C., 1966, Sullivan & Cromwell, N.Y.C., 1966-72, Weil, Gotshal & Manges, N.Y.C., 1972-75, ptnr., 1975—. Author: (with others) Litigation Strategy and Tactics , 1979, Deposition Strategy Law and Forms, 1980, Masters of Trial Practice, 1988; contbr. articles on intellectual property law to profl. jours. Assoc. counsel N.Y. State Constl. Conv., Albany, N.Y., 1967; pres. Hillel of N.Y., 1986-88. Served to capt. U.S. Army, 1963-65. Fellow Am. Coll. Trial Lawyers; mem. Assn. of Bar of City of N.Y. (chmn. comm. and media law com. 1989-92, mem. copyright com. 1996—), B'nai Brith (internat. bd. govs. 1975-85), Anti-Defamation League (nat. commn. 1981—, vice chmn. 1997—, nat. exec. com. 1988—, vice chmn. 1990-92, chmn. intergroup rels. com. 1992-94, chmn. civil rights com. 1994-97). Democrat. Jewish. Office: Weil Gotshal & Manges 767 5th Ave Fl Conc1 New York NY 10153-0119

SUGAWARA, TAKU, neurosurgeon, researcher; b. Kamaishi, Japan, Oct. 12, 1963; s. Kazuro and Noriko Sugawara; m. Mikiko Ishikawa, Oct. 12, 1996. MD, Akita (Japan) U., 1989, PhD, 1995. Japanese Bd. Cert. Neurosurgeon, 1996. Neurosurgery resident Akita U., 1989-95, asst. prof. neurosurgery, 1996—. Rsch. scholar, Med. Coll. Pa., Phila., 1992-94, Stanford U., 1998—; vis. cons. neurosurgery, Kiev Neurosurg. Inst., Ukraine, 1993. Author: Maturation Phenomenon in Cerebral Ischemia, 2001; contbr. articles to profl. jours. Rsch. grantee Japanese Ministry Edn., 1996—. Mem: Soc. Neurosci., Japanese Congress Neurol. Surgeons, Japanese Neurosurg. Soc. Office: Stanford U MSLS # P 355 1201 Welch Rd Stanford CA 94305 Fax: (650) 498-4551. E-mail: taku@stanford.edu.

SUGDEN, RICHARD LEE, pastor; b. Compton, Calif., Apr. 13, 1959; s. L. Fred Sugden and Nancy Jane (Motherwell) Coulter; m. Rebecca Lynn Travis, June 1981; children: Richard Lee II, Ryan Leon, Rachel Lynn, Lawrence Fred, Nicole Irene. BA, Pensacola (Fla.) Christian Coll., 1981. Ordained pastor, 1985. Assoc. pastor Chippewa Lake Bapt. Ch., Medina, Ohio, 1981-84; dir., evangelist Victory Acres Christian Camp, Warren, 1985; asst. pastor Bible Bapt. Temple, Campbell, 1985-93; missionary evangelist Sugden Evang. Ministries, Struthers, 1993—. Del. pastors' sch. 1st Bapt. Ch., Hammond, Ind., 1982—. Author: Philippians on Your Level, 1990, James on Your Level, 1991, I Timothy On Your Level, 1991. Founder, dir. Penn-Ohio Bapt. Youth Fellowship. Mem. Christian Law Assn., Buckeye Ind. Bapt. Fellowship. Republican. Avocations: gardening, home improvements. Home and Office: Sugden Evang Ministries 71 Harvey St Struthers OH 44471-1538 E-mail: ricsugden@juno.com. *Purpose is found in life when you are involved in the work of God. Jesus said, "This is the work of God, that ye believe in Him whom He hath sent." Trusting and following Jesus is what life is all about.*

SUGERMAN, ABRAHAM ARTHUR, psychiatrist, educator; b. Dublin, Ireland, Jan. 20, 1929; came to U.S., 1958, naturalized, 1963; s. Hyman and Anne (Goldstone) S.; m. Ruth Nerissa Alexander, June 5, 1960; children: Jeremy, Michael, Adam, Rebecca. BA, Trinity Coll., Dublin, 1950, MB, BChir, BA in Obstetrics, 1952; DSc, SUNY, Bklyn., 1962. Diplomate Am. Bd. Psychiatry and Neurology. House officer Meath Hosp., Dublin, 1952-53, St. Nicholas Hosp., London, 1953-54; sr. house physician Brook Gen. Hosp., 1954; registrar in psychiatry Kingsway Hosp. Derby and Kings Coll. Med. Sch., Newcastle, Eng., 1955-58; clin. psychiatrist Trenton (N.J.) Psychiat. Hosp., 1958-59; cons. psychiatry, 1964-80; rsch. fellow Downstate Med. Ctr., Bklyn., 1959-61; chief investigative psychiatry sect. N.J. Bur. Rsch., Princeton, 1961-73; cons. rsch., assoc. psychiatrist Carrier Clinic, Belle Mead, N.J., 1968-72, 78-90, dir. outpatient svcs., 1972-74, 77-78, med. dir., 1974-77; dir. rsch. Carrier Found., 1972-79; med. dir. addiction recovery svcs. Cmty. Mental Health Ctr., U. Medicine and Dentistry of N.J., Piscataway, 1990-93; cons. psychiatry Med. Ctr., Princeton, N.J., 1972—; clin. assoc. prof. psychiatry Rutgers Med. Sch. (now Robert Wood Johnson Med. Sch.), New Brunswick, 1972-78, clin. prof., 1978—. Vis. prof. Rutgers Ctr. for Alcohol Studies, 1977-83, Hahnemann Med. Coll., Phila., 1978-93; contbg. faculty Grad. Sch. Applied and Profl. Psychology, Rutgers U., 1974-78. Editor: (with Ralph E. Tarter) Alcoholism: Interdisciplinary Approaches to an Enduring Problem, 1976, Expanding Dimensions of Consciousness, 1978; contbr. articles to profl. jours. Bd. dirs. N.J. Mental Health R & D Fund, Princeton, 1968-74; v.p. Jewish Family Svc., Trenton, 1972-78; 1st v.p. Trenton Hebrew Acad., 1972-75. Fellow AAAS, Am. Psychiat. Assn., Am. Coll. Neuropsychopharmacology, Am. Coll. Clin. Pharmacology, Am. Coll. Psychiatrists, Royal Coll. Psychiatrists; mem. AMA, Soc. Biol. Psychiatry, Assn. Rsch. Nervous and Mental Diseases. Office: 256 Bunn Dr Princeton NJ 08540-2859

SUGERMAN, HARVEY JAY, surgery educator; b. Pitts., Apr. 13, 1938; s. Samuel J. and Rose M. (Margolis) S.; m. Elizabeth Levine, Sept. 1, 1968; children: Kathryn, Andrew, David, Elizabeth. BS, Johns Hopkins U., 1959; MS, Thomas Jefferson U., 1962, MD, 1966. Intern medicine Hosp. U. Pa., Phila., 1966-67, resident surgery, 1967-72; pvt. practice surgery Allentown, Pa., 1975-78; asst. prof. surgery Med. Coll. Va., Va. Commonwealth U., Richmond, 1978-81; assoc. prof. surgery Med. Coll. Va., VCU, 1981-85, prof. surgery, 1985—, David Hume professorship, 1989—, vice chmn. dept. surgery, 1991-98, 99—, chief divsn. gen. trauma surgery, 1998-99, interim chmn. dept. surgery, 1998—. Co-editor: (textbook) Current Practice Surgery, 1993; contbr. numerous articles to profl. jours. Lt. col. U.S. Army, 1972-75. Mem. Am. Surg. Assn., So. Surg. Assn., Soc. Univ. Surgeons, Surg. Infection Soc., Am. Assn. Surgery Trauma. Avocation: skiing. Office: Va Commonwealth Univ PO Box 980519 Richmond VA 23298-0519

SUGG, ROBERT PERKINS, former state supreme court justice; b. Eupora, Miss., Feb. 21, 1916; s. Amos Watson and Virgie Christian (Cooper) S.; m. Elizabeth Lorraine Carroll, June 23, 1940; children: Robert Perkins, Charles William, John David. Student, Wood Jr. Coll., 1933-34, Miss. State U., 1935-37, Jackson Sch. Law, 1939-40. Bar: Miss. Practice law, 1940-51; chancery judge, 1951-71; asso. justice Miss. Supreme Ct., 1971-83; county pros. atty. Webster County, Miss., 1949-50; spl. chancery judge Hinds, Scott and Jasper counties, 1989; sr. judge, 1990-2000. Mem. adv. council Nat. Ctr. for State Cts., 1973-79. Bd. govs. Miss. Jud. Coll., 1973-80; literacy missions assoc. Home Mission Bd. of So. Bapt. Conv., 1983—; tchr. internat. class First Bapt. Ch., Jackson, Miss., 1980--, tchr. adult Bible class, 1973-2002, mem. fin. com. 1995-98, vision com. 1996-97, legal com. 1998-2001, missions com., 1997-2001. Named Outstanding Citizen, Eupora Jr. C. of C., 1970, Alumnus of Year, Wood Jr. Coll., 1973; recipient Service to Humanity award Miss. Coll., 1976, Literacy Missions Svc. award Home Mission Bd. of So. Bapt. Conv., 1995. Mem. Miss. State Bar, Am. Judicature Soc., CAP (Miss. Wing, squadron comdr. 1974-76), Am. Legion (post comdr. 1950) Democrat. Baptist (chmn. bd. deacons 1964). Home: 1067 Meadow Heights Dr Jackson MS 39206-6021

SUGGARS, CANDICE LOUISE, special education educator; b. Pitts., Jan. 16, 1949; d. Albert Abraham and Patricia Louise (Stepp) S. BS in Elem. Edn., W.Va. U., 1972; MS in Spl. Edn., Johns Hopkins U., 1979, Cert. Advanced Studies, 1986. Clin. supr./head tchr. The Kennedy Kreiger Inst., Balt., 1974-80, inpatient coord., 1980-83, ednl. evaluator, 1980-85, spl. educator/pediatric rehab. team, 1985-86; spl. edn. cons. Charleston County (S.C.) Sch. Dist., 1986-90, spl. edn. pre-sch. tchr., 1990-95; pvt. tutor & cons. children with spl. needs and disabilities Charleston, 1995—; spl. needs cons. U. S.C., 1996—. Mem. adv. bd. S.C. Accelerated Schs. Project, Charleston, 1994-95; parenting instr. Internat. Network of Children and Families, 1999. Contbg. author: Disadvantaged Pre-School Child, 1979, Leisure Education for the Handicapped Curriculum, 1984. Exhibitor ann. conv. S.C. State Sch. Bd. Assn., 1994. Mem. Coun. for Exceptional Children (hospitality chair 1987-89, publicity chair 1989-90), Nat. Assn. for Edn. of Young Children. Avocations: singing, reading, travel, tennis. Home: 29 Savage St Charleston SC 29401-2409

SUGGS, MICHAEL EDWARD, lawyer; b. Conway, S.C., Nov. 9, 1962; s. Edward and Rebecca S. BSBA, U. S.C., 1985, JD, 1992. Bar: S.C. 1992, U.S. Dist. Ct., S.C., 1995. Asst. pub. defender Def. Corp. Horry County, Conway, S.C., 1993—. Troop 847 com. Boy Scouts Am., Loris, S.C., 1985—; coun. City of Loris, 1994—, mayor pro-tem, 1998-00. Recipient Eagle Scout award Boy Scouts Am., 1976. Mem. S.C. Assn. Criminal Def. Lawyers, Horry County Bar Assn., Loris C. of C. Methodist. Home: 4932 Circle Dr Loris SC 29569-3146 Office: Def Corp Horry County PO Box 1666 114 Laurel St Conway SC 29526-5134

SUGHRUE, ROBERT NORMAN, financial analyst; b. N.Y.C., June 20, 1949; s. Henry Gordon and Ann Catherine (Klein) S.; m. Beverly K. Kachurik, Jan. 21, 1977; children: Shannon S., Valerie L. BSBA, Duquesne U., 1971. Staff acct. LTV Steel Corp., Pitts., 1973-76, staff auditor, 1976-78, Blue Cross Western Pa., Pitts., 1979-81, sr. auditor, 1981-84, mgr. payroll svcs., 1984-86; mgr. fiscal affairs Pitts. Rsch. Inst., 1986-95; grants adminstr. Duquesne U., Pitts., 1995—. Cons. in field, Pitts., 1986—; pub. arbitrator Nat. Assn. Securities Dealers, N.Y.C., 1990—. Co-author: Qualifying as a Nonprofit Tax-Exempt Organization, 1991. Pres. Allegheny County Transit Coun., Pitts., 1989-91, v.p., 1988-89. Mem. Inst. Mgmt. Accts. Republican. Roman Catholic. Avocations: camping, reading, volunteering for community work. Home: 837 Fredericka Dr Bethel Park PA 15102-3736

SUGIHARA, KENZI, publishing executive; b. Kearny, N.J., Oct. 4, 1940; s. Kyuichi and Shinobuko (Yamaguchi) S.; m. Roslyn Forbes, Dec. 1966 (div. Mar. 1981); children: Kenichi, Takeo, Akira, Fumio; m. Nancy Elizabeth Kirsh, June 8, 1981; 1 child, Toshiro. BA, NYU, 1963. Supr. McGraw Hill, Inc., N.Y.C., 1965-67; assoc. dir. coll. product dept. Harcourt Brace Jovanovich Inc., 1978-82, dir. electronic pub., 1982-83; v.p., pub. Bantam Electronic Pub. div., pub. Bantam Reference Books, Bantam Profl. Books, Bantam Doubleday Dell, 1983-93; v.p., pub. Random House Reference & Electronic Pub. (Random House Inc.), 1993-95; pres. Sugihara and Rose, 1995—; pres., pub. ToExcel divsn. Kaleidoscope Software Corp., 1998—2001; CEO, pres. SelectBooks, Inc., 2001—. Pub. 1Universe.com. Democrat. Presbyterian. Home: 585 West End Ave Apt 15D New York NY 10024-1715 Office: SelectBooks Inc 405 Park Ave New York NY 10022

SUGIKI, SHIGEMI, ophthalmologist, educator; b. Wailuku, Hawaii, May 12, 1936; s. Sentaro and Kameno (Matoba) S.; m. Bernice T. Murakami, Dec. 28, 1958; children: Kevin S., Boyd R. AB, Washington U., St. Louis, 1957; MD, Washington U., 1961. Intern St. Luke's Hosp., St. Louis, 1961-62; resident ophthalmology Washington U., 1962-65; chmn. dept. ophthalmology Straub Clinic, Honolulu, 1965-70, Queens Med. Ctr., Honolulu, 1970-73, 80-83, 88-90, 93-2000; clin. prof. ophthalmology Sch. Medicine U. Hawaii, 1997. Maj. M.C., AUS, 1968-70. Decorated Hawaiian NG Commendation medal, 1968. Fellow ACS; mem. Am., Hawaii med. assns., Honolulu County Med. Soc., Am. Acad. Ophthalmology, Contact Lens Assn. Opthalmologists, Pacific Coast Oto-Ophthal. Soc., Pan-Pacific Surg. Assn., Am. Soc. Cataract and Refractive Surgery, Am. Glaucoma Soc., Internat. Assn. Ocular Surgeons, Am. Soc. Contemporary Ophthalmology, Washington U. Eye Alumni Assn., Hawaii Ophthal. Soc., Rsch. To Prevent Blindness. Home: 2398 Aina Lani Pl Honolulu HI 96822-2024 Office: 1380 Lusitana St Ste 714 Honolulu HI 96813-2443

SUGINTAS, NORA MARIA, veterinarian, scientist, medical company executive, performing arts dancer, photographer; b. Evergreen Park, Ill., Mar. 12, 1956; d. George and Mary (Navickas) S. BS in Biol. Scis. with highest distinction, U. Ill., Chgo., 1978; DVM, U. Ill., 1982. Lic. veterinarian, Ill. Profl. hosp. specialist Abbott Labs., Detroit, 1983-87; anes./crit. care patient monitoring equipment acct. exec. Shiley, Inc., 1987-91; anesthesia and critical care monitoring equipment sales exec. and cons. Ohmeda, 1991-94; regional mgr. Criticare Systems, 1994-95, nat. acct. dir., 1995-96; dir. corp. accounts Isolyser Health Care, 1996-98; cons. healthcare industry, 1998—2000; v.p. HealthCare Partnerships Healthgrades, Inc. , Detroit, 2000—. Journalist The Lithuanian World-Wide Daily Newspaper, 1975; author: The Production of S-Adenosylmethionine by Saccharomyces cerevisiae and Candida utilis. Troop leader Girl Scouts Lithuanian, Chgo., 1972-77, camp dir., 1977; mem. Mirage Middle Eastern Dance Ensemble. Recipient Louis Pasteur award for Academic Excellence in the Biol. Scis. and Ind. Rsch. U. Ill., 1978. Mem. Internat. Platform Assn., Mich. Orchid Soc., Econ. Club Detroit, Kirk Garden Guild, Phi Beta Kappa. Republican. Avocations: hiking, nature preservation, photography, internat. politics.

SUGIOKA, KENNETH, anesthesiologist educator; b. Hollister, Calif., Apr. 19, 1920; s. Seigiro and Kameno (Takeda) S.; m. Mary Trabue Hinternhoff, June 18, 1966; children— Stephanie, Colin, Kimi (by previous marriage), Nathan, Brian. BS, U. Denver, 1945; MD, Washington U., St. Louis, 1949. Intern, resident U. Iowa, 1949-52, instr. anesthesiology, 1952; asst. prof. surgery N.C. Meml. Hosp., Chapel Hill, 1954-62, assoc. prof. surgery, 1962-64; prof. surgery, chmn. div. anesthesiology U. N.C., 1964-69, prof., chmn. dept. anesthesiology, 1969-83; prof. anesthesiology and physiology Duke U., 1985—. Vis. prof. Physiol. Inst., U. Göttingen, Fed. Republic of Germany, 1963, Kings Coll. Med. Sch., London, Max-Planck Inst. Physiology, Dortmund, Fed. Republic of Germany, 1976-77; vis. prof. Royal Coll. Surgeons, Eng., 1983-84; dir. Morgan Creek Land Co.; mem. adv. com. on anesthetic and life support drugs FDA; bd. alumni U. Denver. Author textbook of clin. anesthesiology; contbr. articles to profl. jours. Pres. Triangle Opera Theater. Served to capt., M.C. USAF, 1952-54. Recipient spl. research fellowship NIH, 1961-62 Fellow Faculty Anaesthesiologists Royal Coll. Surgeons (Eng.) (hon.); mem. Soc. Acad. Anesthesia Chairmen (past pres.) Home: 319 Bayberry Dr Chapel Hill NC 27517-9116

SUGIYAMA, KAZUNORI, music producer; b. Tokyo, Aug. 18, 1950; came to U.S., 1976; s. Hiroshi and Michiko (Maeda) S.; m. Emi Fukui, Aug. 11, 1981. BS, Waseda U., 1974, postgrad., 1974-75; MA, Boston U., 1977. Jr. adminstrv. officer Japanese Mission to UN, N.Y.C., 1978-88; rep. N.Y. Toshiba EMI Records, Jazz Div., Tokyo, 1990-93; rep. U.S., exec. producer DIW/Avant Records, 1991—; exec. producer Tzadik Records, N.Y.C., 1995—; mem. adv. bd. The New Grove Dictionary of Jazz, 1997—. Corr. Jazz Life, Tokyo, 1980-88; columnist OCS News, N.Y.C., 1982-90; columnist Asahi Newspaper, 1998-99. Rec. engr. (album) Bud and Bird/Gil Evans, 1988 (Grammy); prodr. V/Ralph Peterson, 1990 (Jazz Album of Yr.); co-prodr. The Nurturer/Geri Allen, 1991 (2d pl. Jazz Album of Yr.), Big Band & Quartet/David Murray, 1992 (Best Prodn. Jazz Album of Yr.), Picasso/David Murray, 1993 (3d pl. Jazz Album of Yr.); translator Autobiography of Miles Davis, 1989. Mem. NARAS, USTA. Avocations: tennis, travel. Office: 93 Mercer St Apt 3W New York NY 10012-4452 E-mail: tzadik@tzadik.com.

SUGIYAMA, TOKU MARY, retired school administrator; b. Sacramento, Sept. 6, 1921; d. Sakae and Kuniko (Kosaka) Koda; m. Yone J. Sugiyama, Apr. 5, 1952; m. George Y. Morishita, Mar. 23, 1942 (dec. Mar. 1949); children: Maeona, Carolyn, George. Jr. cert., U. Claif., Berkeley, 1941; BA, Towson State U., 1980, MA, 1984. Tchr. Poston Relocation Ctr., Ariz., 1941-44; purchasing agt. U.S. Dept. Def., Tokyo Ordnance Depot, 1952-56; instr. Ikebana Sogetsu Sch., Tokyo, 1956-67; exec. dir. Sogetsu USA, sch. Japanese flower arrangement, 1967-93; ret., 1993. Author: Sogetsu Ikebana Notes, 1997. Recipient Mohan Sho, Sogetsu Sch., 1960, Sofu Sho, 1967, Flower Arranger of Yr. award Nat. Coun. State Garden Clubs, 1979, 1st Sofu Teshigahara Meml. award, 1991. Mem. Md. Fedn. Garden Clubs, Ikebana Internat. (charter), Balt.-Kawasaki Sister City Cultural Com. Home: 959 Ellendale Dr Baltimore MD 21286-1511 E-mail: msugiy8305@aol.com.

SUGIYAMA, TORU TOM, automotive executive; b. Hiratsuka, Japan, Aug. 15, 1956; s. Tadatsugu and Hatsue S. MBA, Calif. State U., 1994, MS in Acctg., 1997; MS in Engring., Oakland U., 1997. Mgr. Denny's Japan Co., Ltd., Tokyo, 1979-80; indsl. engr. NHk Spring Co., Ltd., Yokohama, Japan, 1980-82, acct. mgr. Japan, 1983-89; mgr. NHK Internat. Corp., Southfield, Mich., 1992-96, corp. sec., treas., 1996-2001; treas. Gen. Seating of Can., 2001—; bd. dirs. Gen. Seating Am., 2001—; pres., CEO NHK Internat. Corp., Wixom, Mich., 2001—. Lectr. Oakland U., Rochester, Mich., 1998—; bd. dirs. New Mather Metals Inc., NHK Associated Spring Suspension Components Inc., Gen. Seating Am., Inc. Avocations: golf, tennis, swimming. Office: NHK Internat Corp 50706 Varsity Ct Wixom MI 48393

SUGNET, LINDA A'BRUNZO, elementary education educator; b. Elmira, N.Y., Aug. 6, 1949; d. Louis N. and C. Elizabeth (Smith) A'Brunzo. BE, SUNY, Geneseo, 1971; MEd, Elmira Coll., 1976; postgrad., SUNY, Cortland, L.I. U. Cert. elem. tchr., N.Y., Fla. Dir. Gerber Children's Ctr., Jacksonville, Fla., 1980-81; elem. tchr. Monroe County Sch. Bd., Key West, 1987-88, South Seneca Cen. Sch., Interlaken, N.Y., 1971—. Adj. instr., cons. N.Y. State United Tchrs.; with L.I. U., Albany, Coll. of St. Rose, Albany, Performance Learning Sys., Inc., Nevada City, Calif., 1984—; tchr., mentor, 1995—; mem. Elem. Shared Decision Making Team, 1994-96, mem. curriculum coun., 1996-2000. Recipient Early Childhood Preventive Curriculum grant. Mem. ASCD, Am. Fedn. Tchrs., N.Y. State United Tchrs., South Seneca Tchrs. Assn. (co-pres. 1992-94), Internat. Assn. for the Study of Coop. in Edn., Delta Kappa Gamma. E-mail: lsugnet@southseneca.k12.ny.us.

SUGRUE, DENNIS PATRICK, clinical psychologist; b. Detroit, Oct. 28, 1949; s. Francis Michael and Diane (Reckinger) S.; m. Bernadette Tomasik, June 11, 1976; children: Dennis Patrick II, Sean Michael Francis. BA magna cum laude, Sacred Heart Sem., 1971; MA, U. Detroit, 1976; MS, Ea. Mich. U., 1976; PhD, U. Windsor, Ont., Can., 1981. Sr. staff psychologist Henry Ford Hosp., Detroit, 1979-85; clin. instr. psychiatry Med. Sch. U. Mich., 1985-92; founder, dir. Henry Ford Ctr. Human Sexuality, Farmington Hills, Mich., 1986-95; asst. clin. prof. psychiatry Med. Sch. U. Mich., Ann Arbor, 1992-93; regional clin. dir. dept. psychiatry Henry Ford Hosp., West Bloomfield, Mich., 1993-95; asoc. divsn. head outpatient psychiatry Henry Ford Health Sys., Detroit, 1995-98; pvt. practice Bloomfield Hills, Mich., 1998—. Asst. adj. prof. psychiatry Coll. Human Medicine Mich. State U., 1991; lectr. on human sexuality; cons. U. Mich. Comprehensive Gender Svcs. Program, 1994—; clin. assoc. prof. psychiatry Med. Sch. U. Mich., Ann Arbor, 1999—. Co-author: Sex Matters for Women, 2002; contbr. chpts. to books, articles to profl. jours. Den leader Farmington Hills Boy Scouts Am., 1988-91; coach South Farmington Little League Baseball, Farmington Hills, 1990-96. Mem. Am. Psychol. Assn., Harry Benjamin Internat. Gender Dysphoria Assn., Internat. Coun. Psychologists (chair counseling and psychotherapy), Internat. Soc. for Study of Women's Sexual Health, Soc. Sci. Study Sex, Am. Assn. Sex Educators, Counselors and Therapists (Mich. chair, profl. edn. chair, bd. dirs., cert. sex therapist, pres.), Phi Kappa Phi. Roman Catholic. Avocations: golf, bridge, tae kwon do (1st degree black belt). Office: Affil Psychologists Mich 74 W Long Lake Ste 104 Bloomfield Hills MI 48304-2770

SUGRUE, MICHAEL JOSEPH, humanities educator; b. N.Y.C., Feb. 1, 1957; s. Michael Joseph Sugrue and Margaret Mary Clancy; m. Seana Carole McGuire, June 6, 1996; children: Thalia Elizabeth, Pamela Emily. BA, U. Chgo., 1979; MA, MPhil, PhD, Columbia U. Fellow in history Johns Hopkins U., Balt., 1992—94; lectr. humanities Princeton (N.J.) U., 1994—. Lectr. in field. Active Renaissance Inst., Hilton Head, SC, 1996—. Fellow fellow, Huntington Libr., San Marino, Calif., 1994. Avocations: chess, sportfishing. Home: 70 Winchester Dr Hightstown NJ 08520-2609 Office: Coun for the Humanities Princeton U Princeton NJ 08544 Business E-Mail: sugrue@princeton.edu.

SUH, DAE-SOOK, political science educator; b. Hoeryong, Korea, Nov. 22, 1931; came to U.S., 1952; s. Chang-Hee and Chong-Hee (Paek) S.; m. Yun-Ok Park, Oct. 29, 1960; children: Maurice, Kevin. BA, Tex. Christian U., 1956; MA, Ind. U., 1958; PhD, Columbia U., 1964. Asst. prof. U. Houston, 1965-67, assoc. prof., 1968-71; prof. polit. sci., dir. Ctr. for Korean Studies, U. Hawaii, Honolulu, 1972-95, Korea Found. prof. policy studies, 1994-99; George L. Paik prof. Yonsei U., 1999; prof. polit. sci. U. Hawaii, Manoa, Hawaii, 1972—. Author: The Korean Communist Movement, 1967, Documents of Korean Communism, 1970, Korean Communism, 1980, Kim Il Sung, 1988, Kim Il Sung and Kim Jong Il, 1996. Mem. Conv. Ctr. Authority, Honolulu, 1989-94. Grantee Social Sci. Rsch. Coun.-Am. Coun. Learned Socs., 1963, East-/West Ctr., Columbia U., 1971, The Wilson Ctr. for Scholars, 1985, Fulbright, 1988. Mem. Am. Polit. Sci. Assn. (life), Assn. for Asian Studies. Avocations: tennis, golf. Home: 7122 Niumalu Loop Honolulu HI 96825-1635 Office: U Hawaii Manoa Dept Political Sci 2424 Maile Way Honolulu HI 96822-2223 E-mail: daesook@hawaii.edu.

SUH, DONG-CHURL, pharmaceutical economics educator; b. Kimcheon, Korea, June 27, 1956; s. Nam and Ok S.; m. Kumsil Suh, Dec. 3, 1983; children: Kangho, David. BS, Chung-Ang U., Seoul, Korea, 1979, MS, 1984; MBA, SUNY, Buffalo, 1988; PhD, U. Minn., 1993. Registered pharmacist. Assoc. dir. Yonsei U. Severance Hosp., Seoul, Korea, 1979-82; asst. to market rsch. mgr. Pfizer Korea Co., 1982-84; rsch. assoc. U. Minn., Mpls., 1993-94; asst. prof. Rutgers U., Piscataway, N.J., 1994-2001, assoc. prof., 2001—; asst./assoc. prof. Sch. Pub. Health U. Medicine and Dentistry N.J., 1996—. Faculty rep. Nat. Assn. Chain Drug Stores, Washington, 1995—; bd. dirs. N.J. Joint Bd. C.C.P., Trenton, 1995—; mem. adv. panel Garden State Pharmacy Owners Providers Corp., 1996—. Mem. editl. bd. Jour. Health Care Mktg., 1994, Jour. Am. Pharm. Assn., 1999—, Disease Mgmt. and Clin. Outcomes, 1999—; reviewer: Social and Behavior Aspects of Pharmaceutical Care, 1996. Recipient Cert. of Appreciation, Am. Soc. Cons. Pharmacists, 1996, Outcomes Rsch. award Am. Coll. Clin. Pharmacy, 1999. Mem. Am. Assn. Colls. Pharmacy (New Investigator award 1998), Am. Pharm. Assn., Internat. Quality of Life Assessment Group (rep. Korea), Internat. Health Econs. Assn., Internat. Soc. Technical Assessment in Health, European Orgn. Rsch. and Treatment of Cancer (rep. Korea), Rho Chi (faculty advisor 1995—). Presbyterian. Avocations: golf, tennis. Office: Rutgers U Coll Pharmacy 160 Frelinghuysen Rd Piscataway NJ 08854

SUH, NAM PYO, mechanical engineering educator; b. Seoul, Apr. 22, 1936; came to U.S., 1954, naturalized, 1963; s. Doo Soo and Joon Joo (Lee) S.; m. Young Ja Surh; children: Mary M., Helen H., Grace J., Caroline Y. SB, MIT, 1959, SM, 1961; PhD, Carnegie-Mellon U., 1964; D of Engring. (hon.), Worcester Poly. Inst., 1986; LHD (hon.), U. Mass., Lowell, 1988; Dr.Tech. (hon.), Royal Inst. Tech., Sweden. Devel. engr. Guild Plastics Inc., Cambridge, Mass., 1958-60; sr. research engr., project mgr. USM Corp., Beverly, 1961-65; asst. prof. U. S.C., Columbia, 1965-68, assoc. prof., 1968-69; assoc. prof. mech. engring. MIT, Cambridge, 1970-75, prof., 1975—, Ralph E. and Eloise F. Cross prof., 1989—, dir. Lab. Mfg. and Productivity, 1977-84, dir. industry polymer processing program, 1973-84, dir. Mfg. Inst., 1989—, Cross prof., dept. head mech. engring., 1991-2001; presdl. appointee asst. dir. for engring. NSF, Washington, 1984-88. Bd. dirs. Trexell, Inc. (formerly Axiomatics Corp.), Woburn, Mass., SVG Industries, SVG, Inc., Axiomatic Design Software, Inc., Internat. Circuit Sys., Inc., AMT, Inc., Newton, Mass.; former chmn. bd. Sutek Corp., Hudson, Mass.; tech. advisor Daewoo Group; cons. Lawrence Livermore Nat. Lab.; advisor Korea Elec. Power Rsch. Inst.; former mem. sci. and tech. rev. bd. Idaho Nat. Engring. Lab.; mem. NRC rev. panel Nat. Engring. Lab., 1986-90; mem. vis. com. (statutory) Nat. Inst. Stds. and Tech., 1990-94; mem. tech. adv. com. Alcan Aluminum Corp., 1989-90; editor advanced mfg. series Oxford U. Press. Author: (with A.P.L. Turner) Mechanical Behavior of Solids, 1975, Tribophysics, 1986, The Principles of Design, 1990, (with others) Manufacturing Engineering, 1990; editor: (with N. Saka) Fundamentals of Tribology, 1980, (with N. Sung) Science and Technology of Polymer Procs., 1979, The Delamination Theory of Wear, 1977, (with B.M. Kramer) University: Industry Cooperation, 1982, Axiomatic Design: Advances and Applications, 2001; former co-editor-in-chief Robotics and Computer Aided Mfg.; contbr. over 250 articles to profl. jours.; holder 45 U.S. patents. Former chmn. bd. Korean-Am. Soc. New Eng., 1979. USM Corp. fellow, 1962-63; recipient Best Paper award Soc. Plastics Engrs., 1981, citation Classic Inst. for Sci. Info., 1981, F.W. Taylor Research award Soc. Mfg. Engrs., 1986, Disting. Svc. award NSF, 1988, Mainstream Am. award, 1991, scholarly award Korea Broadcasting Svsc., 1994, The Mensforth Internat. Gold Medal, U.K. Instn. of Elec. Engrs., 2000; named Fed. Engr. of Yr., NSF/NSPE, 1987. Fellow ASME (Gustus L. Larson Meml. award 1976, Blackall award 1982, W.T. Ennor Mfg. Tech. award 1993, Best Tribology Paper award 1993, Ho-Am. prize for Engring. Ho.-Am. com. 1997); mem. AAAS, Am. Soc. for Engring. Edn. (Centennial medal 1993), Internat. Instn. for Prodn. Engring., Royal Swedish Acad. Engring. Sci. (fgn.), Korean Acad. Sci. and Engring., Sigma Xi, Pi Tau Sigma, Phi Kappa Phi. Office: MIT Rm 35-237 Dept Mech Engring Cambridge MA 02139

SUH, YUNG DOUG, physical chemist; b. Seoul, Republic of Korea, Oct. 26, 1967; s. Dong Hyuk Suh and Jae Soon Byun; m. Hye Jeong Cho, June 27, 1992; children: Jeong In, Jeong Hye. BS, Seoul Nat. U., 1991, MS, 1993, PhD, 1999. Post doctoral fellow Swiss Fed. Inst. Tech., Zurich, 1999-2000; rsch. asst. prof. Pohang U. Sci. and Tech., Republic of Korea, 2000-01; rsch. assoc. Pacific N.W. Nat. Lab. EMSL, Richland, Wash., 2001—. Contbr. articles to profl. jours. Alumni Assn. fellow dept. chemistry Seoul Nat. U., 1990; fellow Blue House, 1984-85; recipient Young Investigator award Korea Rsch. Found., 1993, Young Vacuum Scientist award Korean Vacuum Soc., 1996. Mem. Am. Chem. Soc. Presbyterian. Achievements include research in C60 solution fluorescence and the invention of tip-enhanced Raman spectroscopy in nanometer scale. Avocations: travel, music, cooking. Office: Pacific NW Nat Lab EMSL MSIN K8-88 3335 Q Ave PO Box 999 Richland WA 99352 Fax: 509-376-6066. E-mail: ydougsuh@yahoo.com., suh@pnl.gov.

SUHM, BERNHARD, scientist; b. Gengenbach, Germany, Mar. 14, 1968; s. Albert Franz and Elisabeth Berndes. MS in Computer Sci., Fridericiana U., Karlsruhe, Germany, 1993, PhD in Computer Sci., 1998. Rsch. asst. Fridericiana U., Karlsruhe, Germany, 1995-96; rsch. programmer Carnegie Mellon U., Pitts., 1993-95, 96-98; sr. scientist BBN Techs., Cambridge, Mass., 1999—. Contbr. chpt. to book. Mem. Assn. Computing Machinery, Sigma Chi. Episcopalian. Avocations: piano, sports, travel, outdoors. Home: 45 Norris St # 3 Cambridge MA 02140-1814 Office: BBN Techs/GTE Internetworking 70 Fawcett St Cambridge MA 02138-1110

SUHR, GERALDINE M. medical/surgical nurse; b. Sumner, Iowa, Mar. 16, 1960; d. Marvin Edward and Peggy Marie (Reiser) S. Diploma, Allen Meml. Luth. Sch. Nursing, Waterloo, Iowa, 1982; student, U. No. Iowa, Cedar Falls, 1979, U. Tenn., 1995. Cert. legal nurse cons. Sr. ship's nurse Carnival Cruise Lines, Miami, Fla.; emergency room and ICU/CCU nurse New Hampton (Iowa) Community Hosp.; charge nurse Trav Corps, Malden, Mass., Flying Nurses, Dallas, Hosp. Staffing Inc., Fla.; telemetry med./surg. charge nurse, critical care nurse So. Hills Hosp., Nashville; emergency nurse, intensive care Ft. Sanders Sevier Med. Ctr., Sevierville.

SUHR, J. NICHOLAS, lawyer; b. N.Y.C., Nov. 14, 1942; s. Heinrich P. and Anna H. (Isenschmid) S.; m. Anne Aylett Stone, July 6, 1965; children: John Nicholas Jr., Erika Christl Efthymiou. BA, U. Va., 1964; JD, Am. U., 1967. Bar: N.Y. 1967, N.J. 1969, U.S. Supreme Ct. 1989; cert. civil trial atty. Assoc., ptnr. Topken & Farley, N.Y.C., 1967-73, Conboy, Hewitt, O'Brien & Boardman, N.Y.C., 1973-86; counsel Hunton & Williams, 1986-87, Quinn, Cohen, Shields & Bock, N.Y.C., 1987-88; ptnr. Quinn & Suhr, White Plains, N.Y., 1988-95, Herzfeld & Rubin, P.C., N.Y.C., 1995-2000, Chase, Kurshan, Suhr, Weidenfeld, Herzfeld & Rubin, LLC, Newark, 1995-2000; pvt. practice N.Y.C., Holmdel, N.J., 2000—. Arbitrator U.S. Dist. Ct. N.J., Trenton, 1985—, Am. Arbitration Assn., N.Y.C., 1976—; qualified mediator N.J. Superior Ct., 2000—. Contbr. articles to profl. jours.; commentator Ct. TV network. 1st v.p. Liederkranz Found. Inc., N.Y.C., 2000—. Mem. ABA, N.Y. State Bar Assn., N.J. State Bar Assn., U.S. Supreme Ct. Bar, Internat. Law Soc., Consular Law Soc., Def. Rsch. Inst., German Soc. of N.Y.C. (v.p., treas., trustee 1976—), German-Am. Sch. Assn. (v.p., trustee 1986—), German Seamen's Mission N.Y. (pres., dir. 1972—). Lutheran. Avocations: fishing, woodworking. Office: 15 Glenn Way Holmdel NJ 07733 E-mail: jnsuhr@aol.com.

SUHR, PAUL AUGUSTINE, lawyer; b. Sonwunri, Chonbuk, Korea, Jan. 20, 1940; came to U.S. 1966; s. Chong-ju and Oksuk (Pang) So; m. Angeline M. Kang Suhr; 1 child, Christopher. BA, Campbell Coll., Buies Creek, N.C.,

1968; MA, U. N.C., Greensboro, 1970; MS, U. N.C., Chapel Hill, 1975; JD, N.C. Cen. U., 1988. Bar: N.C. 1989, U.S. Dist. Ct. (ea. and mid. dist.) N.C. 1989, U.S. Ct. Appeals D.C. 1990, U.S. Ct. Appeals (4th cir.) 1992. Bibliographer N.C. Div. of State Libr., Raleigh, 1975-78; dir. Pender County Pub. Libr., Burgaw, N.C., 1978-80; libr. Tob. Lit. Svc., N.C. State U., Raleigh, 1980-85; pvt. practice law Law Offices of Paul A. Suhr, PLLC, Raleigh and Fayetteville, N.C., 1989—. Author short stories and novelettes various lit. mags., jours. and revs. Mem. Human Resources and Human Rels. Adv. Commn., City of Raleigh, 1990-95, chmn., 1994-95. N.C. Humanities Com. grantee, 1979-80; recipient Presdl. award President of Korea, 1992. Mem. ABA, ATLA, Am. Immigration Lawyers Assn., N.C. Bar Assn., N.C. Trial Lawyers Assn., Wake County Bar Assn. (bd. dirs. 1996-97), D.C. Bar Assn. Democrat. Roman Catholic. Avocations: gardening, fishing, writing. Office: 1110 Navaho Dr Ste 502 Raleigh NC 27609-7322 E-mail: paulsuhr@bellsouth.net.

SUHRE, EDITH LAVONNE, adult education educator; b. North Vernon, Ind., Mar. 20, 1941; d. Raymond L. and Virginia Ruth (Yeager) S.; m. Michael Lee Commons, Aug. 12, 1963 (div. Sept. 1997); children: Ruth Ellen Commons Cherry. BA in Edn., Ball State U., 1963, MA in Edn., 1971. Cert. tchr., Ind. Tchr. Jennings County Sch. Corp., North Vernon, Ind., 1963-64, Madison-Grant Sch. Corp., Fowlerton, 1964-65, Lewisville (Ind.) Sch. Corp., 1965-66; prin., tchr. Bur. Indian Affairs, Bethel, Alaska, 1966-69; tchr. Ripley County Schs., Holton, Ind., 1970, Bartholomew Sch. Corp., Columbus, 1970-71; substitute tchr. South Knox, North Knox, Knox County Schs., Vincennes, 1976-77; pastry chef Exec. Inn, 1976-81; tchr., prof. Ind. Bus. Coll., 1985-87; tchr. Gary (Ind.) Sch. Corp., 1987-93; tchr. English, writing Lakeshore Employment and Tng., Gary, 1994-96; tchr., edn. coord. workforce devel. svcs. divsn. Ivy Tech. State Coll., East Chgo., 1996—. Salesperson, trainer Avon, Vincennes, Ind., 1982-87; vol., leader Reading Is Fundamental, Vincennes and Gary, 1977-93. Leader, cons. Girl Scouts Am., Vincennes, Ind., 1979-86; co. team leader AHA, East Chgo., Gary, Crown Point and Hammond, 1997—. State scholar Ind., 1959. Mem. NAFE. Democrat. Methodist. Avocations: quilting, crocheting rag rugs, embroidery, sewing. Office: WorkOne Express Workforce Devel Svcs Ivy Tech State Coll 420 W Chicago Ave East Chicago IN 46312-3544 E-mail: esuhre@ivy.tec.in.us.

SUHRE, WALTER ANTHONY, JR. retired lawyer and brewery executive; b. Cin., Jan. 17, 1933; s. Walter A. and Elizabeth V. (Heimbuch) S. BS in Bus. Adminstrn., Northwestern U., 1956; LL.B. with honors, U. Cin., 1962. Bar: Ohio 1962, Mo. 1982. Assoc. Taft, Stettinius & Hollister, Cin., 1962-65; with Eagle-Picher Industries, Inc., 1965-82, v.p., gen. counsel, 1970-82; v.p., gen. counsel Anheuser-Busch Cos., Inc., St. Louis, 1982-93; ret., 1994. Served with USMC, 1956-59. Republican. Presbyterian. Home: 48 Woodcliffe Rd Saint Louis MO 63124-1336 E-mail: suhre@prodigy.net.

SUHRHEINRICH, RICHARD FRED, judge; b. 1936; BS, Wayne State U., 1960; JD cum laude, Detroit Coll. Law, 1963, LLM, 1992, U. Va., 1990. Bar: Mich. Assoc. Moll, Desenberg, Purdy, Glover & Bayer, 1963—67; asst. prosecutor Macomb County, 1967; ptnr. Rogensues, Richard & Suhrheinrich, 1967; assoc. Moll, Desenberg, Purdy, Glover & Bayer, 1967—68; ptnr. Kitch, Suhrheinrich, Saurbier & Drutchas, 1968—84; judge U.S. Dist. Ct. (ea. dist.) Mich., Detroit, 1984—90, U.S. Ct. Appeals (6th Cir.), Lansing, 1990—. Mem.: Ingham County Bar Assn., State Bar Mich. Office: US Ct Appeals 6th Cir USPO & Fed Bldg 315 W Allegan St Rm 241 Lansing MI 48933-1514

SUIB, STEVEN LAWRENCE, chemist; b. Olean, N.Y., May 1, 1953; s. Sidney Lincoln and Shirley Anne (Moyer) S. BS, SUNY, Fredonia, 1975; PhD, U. Ill., 1979. Asst. prof. chemistry U. Conn., Storrs, 1980-86, prof., 1986—, bd. trustees, disting. prof., 2001. Chemistry educator; b. Olean, N.Y., May 1, 1953; s. Sidney Lincoln and Shirley Anne (Moyer) S. B.S., SUNY-Fredonia, 1975; Ph.D., U. Ill., 1979. Asst. prof. chemistry U. Conn., Storrs, 1980-86, prof., 1986—. Mem. Am. Chem. Soc. (Exxon Faculty fellow 1983). Mem. Am. Chem. Soc. (Exxon Faculty fellow 1983). Office: U Conn Unite 3060 55 N Eagleville Rd Storrs Mansfield CT 06269-3060 E-mail: suib@uconnvm.uconn.edu.

SUINN, RICHARD MICHAEL, psychologist; b. Honolulu, May 8, 1933; s. Maurice and Edith (Wong) S.; m. Grace D. Toy, July 26, 1958; children: Susan, Randall, Staci, Bradley. Student, U. Hawaii, 1951-53; BA summa cum laude, Ohio State U., 1955; MA in Clin. Psychology, Stanford U., 1957, PhD in Clin. Psychology, 1959; PhD (hon.), Calif. Sch. Profl. Psychology, 1999. Lic. psychologist, Colo.; diplomate Am. Bd. Profl. Psychology. Counselor Stanford (Calif.) U., 1958-59, rsch. assoc. Med. Sch., 1964-66; asst. prof. psychology Whitman Coll., Walla Walla, Wash., 1959-64; assoc. prof. U. Hawaii, Honolulu, 1966-68; prof. Colo. State U., Ft. Collins, 1968-99, head dept. psychology, 1972-93, emeritus prof., 2000—. Cons. in field; psychologist U.S. Ski Teams, 1976, Olympic Games, U.S. Women's Track and Field, 1980 Olympic Games, U.S. Ski Jumping Team, 1988, U.S. Shooting Team, 1994; mem. sports psychology adv. com. U.S. Olympic Com., 1983-89; reviewer NIMH, 1977-80, 94-98. Author: The Predictive Validity of Projective Measures, 1969, Fundamentals of Behavior Pathology, 1970, The Innovative Psychological Therapies, 1975, The Innovative Medical-Psychiatric Therapies, 1976, Psychology in Sport: Methods and Applications, 1980, Fundamentals of Abnormal Psychology, 1984, 88, Seven Steps to Peak Performance, 1986, Anxiety Management Training, 1990; editorial bd.: Jour. Cons. and Clin. Psychology, 1973-86, Jour. Counseling Psychology, 1974-91, Behavior Therapy, 1977-80, Behavior Modification, 1977-78, Jour. Behavioral Medicine, 1978-83, Behavior Counseling Quar., 1979-83, Jour. Sports Psychology, 1980-91, Clin. Psychology: Science and Practice, 1994-97, Professional Psychology, 1994-97; author: tests Math. Anxiety Rating Scale, Suinn Test Anxiety Behavior Scale, Suinn-Lew Asian Self-identity Acculturation Scale. Mem. City Council, Ft. Collins, 1975-79, mayor, 1978-79; mem. Gov.'s Mental Health Adv. Council, 1983, Colo. Bd. Psychologist Examiners, 1983-86. Recipient cert. merit U.S. Ski Team, 1976, APA Career Contbn. to Edn. award, 1995; NIMH grantee, 1963-64; Office Edn. grantee, 1970-71. Fellow APA (chmn. bd. ethnic minority affairs 1982-83, chmn. edn. and tng. bd. 1986-87, policy and planning bd. 1987-89, publs. bd. 1993-97, bd. dirs. 1990-93, pres.-elect 1998, pres. 1999), Behavior Therapy and Rsch. Soc. (charter); mem. Am. Psychol. Found. (trustee 2000—), Assn. for Advancement Psychology (trustee 1983-86), Assn. for Advancement Behavior Therapy (sec.-treas. 1986-89, pres. 1992-93), Asian Am. Psychol. Assn. (bd. dirs. 1983-88), Am. Bd. Behavior Therapy (bd. dirs. 1987-2000), Phi Beta Kappa, Sigma Xi. Home: 808 Cheyenne Dr Fort Collins CO 80525-1560 Office: Colo State U Dept Psychology Fort Collins CO 80523-0001

SUITER, JOHN WILLIAM, industrial engineering consultant; b. Pasadena, Calif., Feb. 16, 1926; s. John Walter and Ethel May (Acton) S.; BS in Aero. Sci., Embry Riddle U., 1964; m. Joyce England, Dec. 3, 1952; children: Steven A., Carol A. Cons. indsl. engr., Boynton Beach, Fla., 1955— . Instr. U. S.C. Tech. Edn. Ctr., Charleston, 1967-69. Pilot USAF, 1944-46. Registered profl. engr., Fla. Mem. Am. Inst. Indsl. Engrs., Soc. Mfg. Engrs. (sr.), Computer and Automated Sys. Assn., Methods-Time Measurement Assn. (assoc.), Soc. Quality Control. Home: PO Box 360821 Melbourne FL 32936-0821

SUITS, ALICE-MAE, retired school social worker; b. Portland, Oreg., Sept. 18, 1932; d. Scire Dexter and Blanche Gertrude (McDonald) Buell; m. Thomas Allan Suits, Sept. 10, 1955; children: Elizabeth Suits Kaufman, William Andrew. BA, Bucknell U., 1954; MSW, Columbia U., 1966. Lic. clin. social worker, Conn.; cert. tchr., sch. social worker, Conn. Social worker ARC, Newark, 1954-55; case aide Yale-New Haven Hosp., 1955-58; case worker Dept. Child Welfare, White Plains, N.Y., 1958-59; psychiat. social worker Children's Village, Dobbs Ferry, 1965-66; social worker Child and Family Svcs., Manchester, Conn., 1966-68; social work cons. Project ASK, Mansfield, 1968-70; sch. social worker Stafford Bd. Edn., Stafford Springs, 1970-99; surrogate parent Conn. State Bd. Edn., 1999—. Vol. counselor Rape Crisis Ctr., Willimantic, Conn., 1989-90. Mem. NEA, Conn. Edn. Assn., Stafford Edn. Assn., Conn. Assn. Sch. Social Workers, NASW (com. on inquiry for Conn. 1980-86), Acad. Cert. Social Workers (cert.). Home: 12 Hillyndale Rd Storrs Mansfield CT 06268-1802

SUITS, BERNARD HERBERT, philosophy educator; b. Detroit, Nov. 25, 1925; s. Herbert Arthur and Helen Dorothy (Carlin) S.; m. Nancy Ruth Berr, July 3, 1952; children— Mark, Constance; m. Cheryl Ann Ballantyne, June 14, 1996. BA, U. Chgo., 1944, MA, 1950; PhD, U. Ill., 1958. Investigator venereal disease USPHS, 1950-51; personnel officer Detroit Civil Service Commn., 1952-54; instr. philosophy U. Ill., Urbana, 1958-59; asst. prof. Purdue U., 1959-66; asso. prof. U. Waterloo, Ont., 1966-72, prof. philosophy, chmn. dept., 1971-74, asso. dean arts for grad. affairs, 1981-84. Vis. prof. U. Lethbridge, Alta., Can., 1980, U. Bristol, Eng., 1980, disting. prof. emeritus U. Waterloo, 1995. Author: The Grasshopper: Games, Life, and Utopia, 1978, paper, 1990; contbr. to profl. jours. and books; featured guest on seven-week TV Ontario series The Academy of Moral Philosophy, 1982. Served with USNR, 1944-46. Recipient Disting. Tchg. award U. Waterloo, 1983. Mem. Am. Philos. Assn. (pres. 1976). Office: U Waterloo Dept Philosophy Waterloo ON Canada E-mail: bsuits@sprint.ca.

SUJANSKY, EVA BORSKA, pediatrician, geneticist, educator; b. Bratislava, Slovak Republic, Feb. 14, 1936; d. Stefan and Terezia (Kaiserova) Borsky; m. Eduard Sujansky, Apr. 2, 1960 (dec. Sept. 1979); children: Paul, Walter. MD, Comenius U., Bratislava, Czechoslovakia, 1959. Diplomate Am. Bd. Pediats., Am. Bd. Med. Genetics. Resident in pediats. U. Iowa, Iowa City, 1969-71; fellow in human genetics Mt. Sinai Sch. Medicine, N.Y.C., 1971-73; clin. geneticist Beth Israel Hosp., 1973-74; dir. clin. genetics Sch. Medicine, U. Colo., Denver, 1974-90, assoc. prof. pediats., biochemistry, biophysics and genetics, 1981—; co-dir. divsn. genetic svcs. The Children's Hosp., U. Colo., 1990—. Contbr. articles to profl. jours. Fellow Am. Acad. Pediats., Am. Soc. Human Genetics, Am. Coll. Med. Genetics (founding fellow). Avocations: fine arts, reading, travel. Office: U Colo Med Ctr 1056 E 19th Ave Denver CO 80218-1007

SUK, JIN HONG, pathologist; b. Seoul, Sept. 11, 1937; came to U.S., 1965; s. Il Keun and Soon Ae (Lee) S.; m. Soon Ja Lee, June 7, 1967; children: Peter, Mary. MD, Yonsei U., Seoul, 1962. Diplomate Am. Bd. Pathology. Staff pathologist Franklin (Pa.) Hosp., 1970-71; dir. lab. Grove City (Pa.) Hosp., 1971-75; staff pathologist U. Pa. Med. Ctr. Northwest, Franklin, Pa., 1975—. Lt. USN, 1962-65. Mem. AMA, Am. Soc. Clin. Pathologist, Am. Soc. Cytology, Pa. Med. Soc., Internat. Acad. Pathology (U.S. and Can. div.). Democrat. Roman Catholic. Avocation: golf. Office: NW Med Ctr 1 Spruce St Franklin PA 16323-2544

SUKHAREV, VALERIY Y. engineer, consultant; b. Murmansk, Russia, Oct. 26, 1952; s. Yakov N. Raykhman and Irina V. (Durakova) Demina; m. Margarita I. Sukharev, Dec. 20, 1975; children: Jeffrey, Michael. MS, Moscow Inst. Elec. Engring., 1976; PhD, Karpov Inst. Phys. Chemistry, 1983. Rsch. asst. Karpov Inst. Phys. Chemistry, Moscow, 1977-78, rsch. assoc., 1978-83, mem. tech. staff, 1983-87, sr. mem. tech. staff, 1987-92; prin. process devel. engr. LSI Logic Corp., Santa Clara, Calif., 1995—. Guest rschr. Nat. Inst. Std. and Tech., Dept. Commerce, Gaithersburg, Md., 1993; vis. prof. chemistry Brown U., Providence, 1993-95; cons. Phys. Sci. Inc., Andover, Mass. 1994-95, Nat. Inst. Stds. and Tech., Gaithersburg, 1994-95, Alpha and Omega, Inc., Cumberland, R.I., 1993-95. Author: Semiconductor Sensors in Physico-chemical Studies, 1996; contbr. more than 40 articles to profl. jours.; patentee in field. Sgt. USSR Paratroopers, 1976-77. Mem. Am. Chem. Soc., Am. Vacuum Soc., Electrochemica Soc. Avocations: travel, art, theaters, classical and jazz music, dogs. Home: 11476 Garden Terrace Dr Cupertino CA 95014-5073 Office: LSI Logic Corp 3115 Alfred St Santa Clara CA 95054-3326 E-mail: vsukhare@lsil.com.

SUKO, LONNY RAY, judge; b. Spokane, Wash., Oct. 12, 1943; s. Ray R. and Leila B. (Snyder) S.; m. Marcia A. Michaelsen, Aug. 26, 1967; children: Jolynn R., David M. BA, Wash. State U., 1965; JD, U. Idaho, 1968. Bar: Wash. 1968, U.S. Dist. Ct. (ea. dist.) Wash. 1969, U.S. Dist. Ct. (we. dist.) Wash. 1978, U.S. Ct. Appeals (9th cir.) 1978. Law clk. U.S. Dist. Ct. Ea. Dist. Wash., 1968-69; assoc. Lyon, Beaulaurier & Aaron, Yakima, Wash., 1969-72; ptnr. Lyon, Beaulaurier, Weigand, Suko & Gustafson, Yakima, 1972-91, Lyon, Weigand, Suko & Gustafson, P.S., 1991-95; U.S. magistrate judge, Yakima, 1971-91, 95—. Mem. Phi Beta Kappa, Phi Kappa Phi. Office: PO Box 2726 Yakima WA 98907-2726

SUKOPP, KARL MARTIN, sculptor, painter, graphic artist; b. Mannersdorf, Austria, Nov. 4, 1928; s. Karl and Magdalena (Rossner) S.; m. Margaretha Anna Meidl, Feb. 21, 1953; children: Krl, peter, paul, Margaretha, Barbara, Do-Hee Kim. Student graphic arts and design, Vienna, 1946-50; diploma in scultpure, Acad. Applied Arts, Vienna, 1959; MA, Acad. Applied Arts, 1984. Free-lance artist, Schwechat, Austria, 1953-74, 79—. Artistic collaborator workshops of Pub. theatre Union, Vienna, 1974-79. One man shows include Gallery ZB, Austria, 1966, Galeria Galeria de Arte, Naharro, Zaragoza, 1971, The Austria-Days, Kiev, 1974, Salzburger Kunstverein, 1980; group shows include The New Hagenbund, Warsaw, 1968, La Chaux de Fonds, 1969, House of Artists, vienna, 1973, Salzburg, 1977, Vienna, 1983, Paris, 1983, Schwechat Anniv. Exposition, 1988, Gladbeck, 1992, Schwechat Anniv. Exposition, 1998, Europe '99, Neustadt; represented in permanent collections including State Govt. Lower Austria, Fed. Ministry of Edn., Bldg. Soc. Vienna, nat. and internat. assns.; prin. works include Vietcong/resistance (Biennale Rzezby with Metalu Warzawa 1968), 1964, 3 sculptures in bronze (House of Arts prize 1973), 1969, 70, 73, dep. chmn. of the new hagenbund, Vienna, 1957, others. Recipient prize Union f Arts, 1967, Vienna Festival, 1983, Chapel of St. Laurentius' Home, 1984, 85, badge of honour in gold, 1998, ring of honor Schwechat, 1998, badge of honour in gold, 1998. Mem. House of Arts Salzburg, Union of Artists of Austria, Union of Artists. Mem. Social Dem. Party. Roman Catholic.

SUKOV, RICHARD JOEL, radiologist; b. Mpls., Nov. 13, 1944; s. Marvin and Annette Sukov; m. Susan Judith Grossman, Aug. 11, 1968; children: Stacy Faye, Jessica Erin. BA, BS, U. Minn., 1967, MD, 1970; student, U. Calif.-Berkeley, 1962-64. Diplomate Am. Bd. Radiology; lic. physician, Calif. Intern pediatrics U. Minn., Mpls., 1970-71; resident radiology UCLA Ctr. for Health Sci., 1973-76; fellow in ultrasound and computed tomography UCLA, 1976-77; staff radiologist Centinela Hosp. Med. Ctr., Inglewood, Calif., 1977-85, Daniel Freeman Meml. Hosp., Inglewood, 1977—, dir. radiology, 1988-90, chmn. dept. medicine, 2000—. Med. dir. dept. radiology Daniel Freeman Meml. Hosp., 1998—; asst. clin. prof. radiology UCLA Ctr. for Health Scis., 1977-83; adv. bd. Aerobics and Fitness Assn. Am., 1983—. Contbr. articles to profl. jours. Vol. Venice Family Clinic, 1985—. Lt. comdr. USPHS, 1970-72. U. Minn. fellow, 1964-65, 66, 70. Mem.: Am. Coll. Radiology (alt. councilor 2001—), LA Ultrasound Soc., LA Radiol. Soc. (contg. edn. com. 1990—, mgmt. com. 1996—, sec. 1997—98, treas. 1998—, pres.-elect 1999—2000, pres. 2000—), Calif. Med. Assn. Radiol. Soc. N.Am., LA County Med. Assn., Soc. Radiologists in Ultrasound (charter), Minn. Med. Alumni Assn. Avocations: bicycling, skiing. Office: Ingelwood Radiology 323 N Prairie Ave Ste 160 Inglewood CA 90301-4503

SUKYS, PAUL ANDREW, law educator, lawyer, consultant; b. Cleve., Feb. 7, 1948; s. Vitus John and Catherine Louise (Corsi) S.; m. Brenda Dee Stitzlein, Sept. 16, 1983. B.A., John Carroll U., 1970, M.A., 1972; J.D., Cleve. State U., 1980. Bar: Ohio 1980. Instr. John Carroll U., Cleve., 1970-72, Fairmount Ctr. Creative and Performing Arts, 1971-72; asst. prof. English, North Central Tech. Coll., Mansfield, Ohio, 1972-80, assoc. prof. law, 1980-84, prof. law, 1984— ; newspaper cons., 1972-76, lit. cons., 1973-77, pub. relations coordinator, 1984— . Campaign mgr. Johns for Councilman Com., Mansfield, 1973. Recipient Am. Jurisprudence award Bancroft Whitney Co., 1978, 79, William K. Gardner award Cleve. State U., 1979, Sidney A. Levine award Cleve. State U., 1979. Mem. AAUP (com. chmn. Ohio Conf. 1974-75, v.p. local chpt. 1974-75), Am. Bus. Law Assn., Associated Writing Program. Home: PO Box 47 Gambier OH 43022-0047 Office: North Central Tech Coll 2441 Kenwood Cir Mansfield OH 44906-1546

SUL, YI CHUL, neurologist; b. Seoul, Korea, May 5, 1947; came to U.S., 1976; s. Tae Woon Sul and Jung Sook Suh; m. Kyu Won, Nov. 21, 1976; children: Caroline, Douglas, Joseph. MD, Yonsei U., Seoul, 1972. Bd. cert. in neurology Am. Bd. Psychiatry and Neurology, subspecialty clin. neurophysiology. Clin. instr. Vanderbilt U., Nashville, 1981-82; v.p. Rim and Sul, M.D., P.C., Grosse Pointe Woods, Mich., 1985—; asst. clin. prof. Mich. State U., Lansing, 1995—; chief neurology sect. St. John Northeast Cmty. Hosp., Detroit, 2002—. Adj. clin. asst. prof. U. Osteo. Medicine and Health Sci., 1998-99; clin. asst. prof. Coll. Osteo. Medicine U. Health Sci., 2000—. Chairperson adminstrv. bd. Korean United Meth. Ch., Detroit, 1997-98, chairperson bd. trustees, 2001; sec. Christian Assn. for Med. Mission, Detroit, 1991-95. Capt. Korean Army, 1972-75, Korea. Grantee Muscular Dystrophy Assn., 1981-82. Fellow Am. Assn. Electrodiagnostic Medicine; mem. AMA, Am. Acad. Neurology, Am. Clin. Neurophysiology Soc., Mich. State Med. Soc., Christian Assn. for Med. Mission (pres. 1999-2001). Home: 20720 Green Ct Grosse Pointe Woods MI 48236-1459 Office: Rim and Sul MP PC 20867 Mack Ave Ste 6 Grosse Pointe Woods MI 48236-1356

SULAK, LAWRENCE RICHARD, physicist; b. Columbus, Ohio, Aug. 29, 1944; s. John Matthew and Helen Rose (Labons) S.; m. Elizabeth Sulak, Sept. 7, 1970; children: Camilla, Lawrence. BS, Carnegie-Mellon U., 1966; AM, Princeton U., 1968, PhD, 1970. Ctr. Nuclear Rsch. assoc. scientist, charge de recherche U. Geneva, 1970-71; asst. assoc. prof. physics Harvard U., Cambridge, Mass., 1971-79, vis. scholar, 1979-81, vis. prof. physics, 1984-85; guest/assoc. physicist Fermilab., Batavia, Ill., 1972—, Brookhaven Nat. Lab., Upton, N.Y., 1974—; assoc. prof. physics U. Mich., Ann Arbor, 1979-84, prof., 1984-86; prof., head dept. physics Boston U., 1985—, David M. Myers disting. prof., 1990—. Vis. scientist Superconducting Super Collider Lab., Dallas, 1990—; mem. U.S. Dept. Energy High Energy Physics Adv. Panel, Washington, 1987-91; mem. sci. program com. Gran Sasso Lab., Italy, 1984—. Contbr. articles to profl. jours. Recipient Outstanding Young Scientist award Sci. Digest, 1984, Rossi prize Am. Astrological Assn., 1989; NSF fellow Princeton U., 1966-70. Fellow Am. Phys. Soc. (exec. com. 1984-86). Achievements include patent for exponentially retrograded hybrid photodiode; measurement of K-K mass difference; discovery of neutral currents, space-time form of neutral currents, anti-neutrino and neutrino-proton elastic scattering; first observation of neutrinos from a supernova; best limits on proton lifetime and Grand Unified Theories. Home: 111 Carlton St Brookline MA 02446-4008 Office: Boston U Dept Physics 590 Commonwealth Ave Boston MA 02215-2521

SULC, JEAN LUENA (JEAN L. MESTRES), lobbyist, consultant; b. Worcester, Mass., Mar. 17, 1939; d. Emilio Beija and Julia Luena; m. Lee Gwynne Mestres, Oct. 9, 1965 (div. Dec. 1973); m. Lawrence Bradley Sulc, Nov. 4, 1983. BS in Psychology, Tufts U., 1961; M in Urban and Regional Planning, U. Colo., 1976. Lic. real estate, Va.; lic. pvt. pilot. Mem. staff U.S. fgn. svc. Dept. State, Washington, 1962-65; intern Adams County Planning Dept., Brighton, Colo., 1974-75; cons. office policy analysis City and County of Denver, 1976; program dir. Coun. Internat. Urban Liaison, Washington, 1976-79; asst., dir. internat. Cities Svc. Oil & Gas Corp., 1980-81; govt. affairs rep. Cities Svc., OXY USA Inc., 1982-89; mgr. fed. rels. OXY USA Inc., 1990-95; pres. EdgeSystem.XXI, 1996—. Chmn. govt. affairs com. L.P. Gas Clean Fuel Coalition, Irvine, Calif., 1990-92. Author, editor: (newsletter) Dayton Climate Project, 1979-80; contbr. articles to newsletters. Vol. Reagan/Bush and Bush/Quayle Presdl. Campaigns and Inaugural Coms., Washington, 1984-89; pres. Hale Found., Nathan Hale Inst., Washington, 1984-85; mem. nat. panel consumer arbitrators Better Bus. Burs., Va., 1991—. Recipient Presdl. citation Nat. Propane Gas Assn., 1992; Minority Intern grantee Denver Regional Coun. Govts., 1974-76. Mem. ASTD, ABA (assoc., arbitration sect.), Am. League Lobbyists (bd. dirs. 1994-97, 2nd v.p. 1996-97, emeritus 1999—), Assn. Image Cons. Internat. (ea. regional adv. 1998—), Greater Beaufort C. of C., Psi Chi. Episcopalian. Avocations: skiing, sports shooting.

SULCER, FREDERICK DURHAM, advertising executive; b. Chgo., Aug. 28, 1932; s. Henry Durham and Charlotte (Thearle) S.; m. Dorothy Wright, May 2, 1953; children— Thomas W., Ginna M., David T. BA, U. Chgo., 1949, MBA, 1963. Reporter UP Assn., Chgo., 1945-46; reporter AP, 1947; with Needham, Harper & Steers Advt., Chgo., 1947-78, dir., 1965-78, sr. account dir., 1965-66, mem. exec. com., 1966-78, exec. v.p., 1967, dir. N.Y. div., 1967-78, pres. N.Y. div., 1974-75; chmn. bd. NH & S Internat., 1975-76; pres. Sulcer Communication Co., Inc., 1977-78; group exec., dir. Benton & Bowles (advt.), 1978-85; dir. bus. devel. D'Arcy Masius Benton & Bowles, advt., N.Y.C., 1985-90; vice-chmn. DDB Needham Worldwide, 1990-95; founder, prin. The Persuasion Group, 1995—. Schering-Plough disting. vis. prof. corp. comm. Fairleigh Dickinson U., Madison, N.J., 1993—. Served to capt. C.E. AUS, 1950-53. Mem. Am. Assn. Advt. Agys. (bd. govs. N.Y. chpt.), Internat. Advertisers Assn., Alpha Delta Phi. Home and Office: The Persuasion Group 350 W 50th St Ph 1-d New York NY 10019-6679 E-mail: sandy.sulcer@ny.ddb.com.

SULEIMAN, MICHAEL WADIE, humanities educator; b. Tiberias, Palestine, Feb. 26, 1934; s. Wadie Mikhail Suleiman and Jameeleh Khalil Ailabouni; m. Penelope Ann Powers, Aug. 31, 1963; children: Suad Evans, Gibran. BA, Bradley U., 1960. Asst. prof. Kans. State U., Manhattan, 1965-68, assoc. prof., 1968-72, head dept. polit. sci., 1975-82, prof., 1972—90, Univ. Disting. prof., 1990—. Vis. scholar U. Calif., Berkeley, 1979, U. London, 1969-70; h.s. tchr. Abbotsholme Sch., Rocester, England, 1955-56, The Bishop's Sch., Amman, Jordan, 1953-55. Author: U.S. Policy On Palestine From Wilson to Clinton, 1995, The Arabs in the Mind of America, 1988, American Images of Middle East Peoples, 1977, Political Parties in Lebanon: The Challenge of a Fragmented Political Culture, 1967; author, editor: Arabs in American: Building a New Future, 1999, Arab Americans: Continuity and Change, 1989; mem. editl. bd. dirs. Jour. Arab Affairs, 1980-93, Arab Jour. Internat. Studies, Internat. Jour. Middle East Studies, 1982-88, Arab Studies Quar., 1979-86, Maghreb Rev., 1988—; contbr. articles to profl. jours., chpts. to books. Pres. Assn. Arab Am. Univ. Grads., Detroit, 1977; scholar, advisor Pub. Affairs TV, Inc., N.Y.C., 1991; bd. dirs. Arab Sociological Assn., Tunis, Tunisia, 1996-97; bd. govs. Am. Rsch. Ctr. in Egypt, N.Y.C., 1991-97; mem. adv. bd. Arab World and Islamic Resources, Berkeley, Calif. Recipient Rsch. fellowship Am. Rsch. Ctr., Cairo, 1972-73, Ford Found., 1969-70, U. Wis., 1963-64; Faculty Rsch. Abroad Program fellowship Fulbright-Hayes, 1983-84, Rsch. grant Nat. Endowment for Humanities, 1989-91, Islamic Civilization grant Ctr. for Internat. Exch. Scholars, 1984. Mem. Am. Polit. Sci. Assn., Middle East Studies Assn. N.Am. (bd. dirs. 1980-82, mem. ethics com. 1992-98), Am. Inst. Maghribi Studies (bd. dirs. 1985-88). Avocations: chess, travel. Office: Kans State U Waters Hall Manhattan KS 66506-4030 Fax: 785-532-2339. E-mail: suleiman@ksu.edu.

SULEIMAN, SUSAN RUBIN, romance literature educator, writer; b. Budapest, Hungary, July 18, 1939; came to U.S., 1950; d. Michael N. and Lillian (Stern) Rubin; m. Ezra N. Suleiman, Feb. 1966 (div. 1985); children: Michael, Daniel. BA magna cum laude, Barnard Coll., 1960; cert. Inst. Phonétique, U. Paris, 1961; MA, Harvard U., 1964, PhD, 1969. Teaching fellow in romance langs. and lits. Harvard U., 1962-65, assoc. prof. romance langs. and lits., 1981-83, John L. Loeb assoc. prof. humanities, 1983-84, prof. romance langs. and lits., 1984-85, prof. romance and comparative lits., 1985-97, C. Douglas Dillon prof. of civilization of France, 1997—, prof. comparative lit., 1997—; instr. French Columbia U., 1966-68, asst. prof. French, 1969-76; from asst. to assoc. prof. French Occidental Coll., 1976-81. Vis. asst. prof. dept. classics UCLA, 1976; mem. faculty coun. Harvard U., 1985-88, mem. exec. com., dir. seminar on politics, lit. and arts Ctr. for Lit. and Cultural Studies, 1986—, dir. Summer Inst. on Approaches to Study Avant-Gardes: The 20th Century, 1987, placement advisor dept. comparative lit., 1987-91, dir. grad. studies in French, 1989-93, co-dir. Summer Inst. on Future Avant-Garde in Postmodern Culture, 1989, head French sect., 1991-93, chair dept. romance lang. & lits., 1997-00. Author: Authoritarian Fictions: The Ideological Novel as a Literary Genre, 1983, (with new preface 1993), Subversive Intent: Gender, Politics, and the Avant-Garde, 1990, Risking Who One Is: Encounters with Contemporary Art and Literature, 1994, Budapest Diary: In Search of the Motherbook, 1996; editor, prefacer: Pour une Nouvelle Culture, 1971; co-editor: The Reader in the Text: Essays on Audience and Interpretation, 1980; editor: The Female Body in Western Culture: Semiotic Perspectives, 1985, The Female Body in Western Culture: Contemporary Perspectives, 1986; Exile and Creativity: Signposts, Travelers, Outsiders, Backward Glances, 1998; contbr. chpts. to books and articles to profl. jours. Decorated officer Ordre des Palmes Académiques (France), 1992; recipient Grad. medal Radcliffe Coll., 1990; Woodrow Wilson fellow, 1961-62, Travel fellow Harvard U., 1965-66, Chamberlain fellow Columbia U., 1973, NEH fellow, 1980, Rockefeller Found. Humanities, 1984, Guggenheim fellow, 1988-89, invited fellow Collegium Budapest, 1993, fellow Ctr. for Judaic Studies, U. Pa., 2001; grantee Columbia U. Coun. Rsch. in Humanities, 1972-74, NEH, 1977, Am. Coun. Learned Socs., 1977-78, Mellon Faculty Rsch. Fund, 1977-78, Fulbright grantee, 1983. Mem. MLA (exec. com. divsn. on lit. criticism 1984-88, chmn. 1987 conv., nominating com. 1990-91, exec. com. divsn. on 20th century French lit. 1992, exec. coun.

nat. election 1993-96), Internat. Comparative Lit. Assn. (com. on lit. theory 1985-92), Camargo Found. (acad. selection com. 1992-98), Am. Comparative Lit. Assn. (adv. bd. nat. election 1983-86, v.p. 1995-97, pres. 1997-99), Phi Beta Kappa. Office: Harvard Univ Dept Romance Langs and Lits Cambridge MA 02138 E-mail: suleiman@fas.harvard.edu.

SULFARO, JOYCE A. alternative high school principal; b. Bklyn., Oct. 23, 1948; d. John Joseph and Mildred Ann (Credidio) Carvelli; m. Guy Sulfaro, Aug. 1, 1971; children: Jacqueline Amber, Kristin Lynn. BA, Molloy Coll., 1970; postgrad., Fla. Atlantic U., 1979-80; MS in Adminstrn. and Supervision, Nova U., 1982. Tutor reading Our Lady of Loretto, Rockville Centre, N.Y., 1969-70; tchr. lang. arts and math. Resurrection Sch., Bklyn., 1970-73; tchr. Annunciation Sch., Holllywood, Fla., 1976-80, prin., 1980-84; tchr. St. Thomas More Sch., 1984-88; dropout prevention dir. NASH-Rocky Mount Sch. Sys. Writer English curriculum, Jr. High for Archdiocese of Miami, 1979. Author: (with M. Sue Timmins) The Basket, 1980. Travel coord./sec. Rego Park (N.Y.) Met. Youth Orgn., 1969-70. Mem. ASTD, Nat. Coun. Tchrs. Math., Fla. League Mid. Schs., Cath. Educators Guild Archdiocese of Miami, Nat. Cath. Ednl. Assn. (chair Sch.-based com. 1988-91), Am. Mus. Natural History, Rocky Mt. Mental Health Assn. (bd. dirs. 1988-90), IBS Adv. Coun., Prins. and Asst. Prins. Assn. (sec. 1990-91, adminstr. vocat. adv. com. 1990-93, adminstr. media adv. com. 1990-94, sec. 1991-94), Nat. Assn. Secondary Sch. Prins. Home: 104 Granite Falls Ct Rocky Mount NC 27804-4652

SULG, MADIS, corporation executive; b. Tallinn, Estonia, May 25, 1943; came to U.S., 1950; s. Hand Eduard and Erika (Turk) S.; m. Mary Diane Detellis, Dec. 30, 1967; children: Danielle Marie, Michaella Erika. SB in Engring. Mgmt., MIT, 1965, SM in Mgmt., 1967. Cons. Barss, Reitzel & Assocs., Cambridge, Mass., 1970-71; mgr. planning and research Converse Rubber Co., Wilmington, 1971-75; dir. bus. planning and devel. AMF, Inc., Stamford, Conn., 1975-79; sr. v.p. planning and devel. Bandag, Inc., Muscatine, Iowa, 1978-88; pres. Prime Investments, 1988—, Muscatine Natural Resources Corp., 1981-88; chmn., chief exec. officer Sieg Auto Parts, Davenport, Iowa, 1989-93; COO Hammer's Plastic Recycling, Iowa Falls, 1994, Purethane, Inc., West Branch, 1994-98; COO, Bytec, Inc., Clinton Township, Mich., 1999-2001; prin. M&D Mgmt. Assocs., 1989—. With U.S. Army, 1968-70. Presbyterian. Avocations: bridge, jogging, swimming. Home: 11238 Home Place Lane Charlotte NC 28227 E-mail: madissulg@aol.com.

SULICK, JOSEPH EDWARD, information technology professional; b. Columbus, Ohio, July 31, 1945; m. Mary Kathleen Kleeberg; children: Scott, Shawn, Sandra, Joseph Jr. BS in Edn., Ohio State U., 1967; grad., USAF Squadron Officer Sch., 1971; MBA, St. Edward's U., 1973; grad., Air Command and Staff Coll., 1974, Air War Coll., 1987; MS in Nat. Resource Strategy, Nat. Def. U., 1996; graduate, Information Resources Mgmt. Coll., 2000. Comm. officer USAF, Keesler AFB, Miss., 1968; radar officer 689th Radar Squadron, Mt. Hebo, Oreg., 1968—71; spl. electronics officer Lowry AFB, Colo., 1971—72; comm. officer Bergstrom AFB, Tex., 1972-74; combat ops. specialist Dover AFB, Del., 1974-76; comm. officer Holloman AFB, N.Mex., 1976-79; combat sys. requirements office staff Langley AFB, Va., 1979-82; chief of frequency assignments, exec. officer USAF Frequency Mgmt. Ctr., Washington, 1982-88; ret., 1988. Mem. Frequency Assignment subcom., US Mil. Comms.-Electronics Bd. Frequency Panel, 1994—2001; dir. Plans and Programs, USAF Frequency Mgmt. Agy., Alexandria, Va., 1994—, chief info. officer, 1994—. Mem. Air Force Assn. (life), Air War Coll. (life), N.Y. Acad. Scis. Home: 2025 Harbour Gates Dr Apt 269 Annapolis MD 21401 Office: USAF Frequency Mgmt Agy 2461 Eisenhower Ave Alexandria VA 22331-1500 E-mail: JoeSulick@msn.com.

SULICK, ROBERT JOHN, general contractor; b. Columbus, Ohio, Jan. 2, 1947; s. Edward Joseph and Elizabeth Jane (Winters) S.; m. Patricia J. Taylor, Dec. 2, 1965 (div. 1989); children: Roberta Michelle (dec.), Melissa Marie; m. Christine Heidy Morton, Oct. 29, 1994. AD in Architecture, Columbus Coll., 1966; photography student, Ohio U., Lancaster, 1987. Elec. engr. Metzger and Blackburn, Columbus, Ohio, 1965-67; archtl. draftsman Van Buren and Firestone, 1967-69; asst. ops. mgr. Capp Homes, 1969-76; plant mgr. Parsons Floors and Cabinet Co., 1976-81; gen. contractor, photographer R.J. Co., Lancaster, Ohio, 1981—. Part-time photography bus. Mayor Village of Brice, Ohio, 1974-79; project coord. Habitat for Humanity Fairfield County, 2001—. Democrat. Roman Catholic. Avocations: stock market, reading, radio controlled models, black and white photography. Home and Office: 547 Tarkiln Rd SE Lancaster OH 43130-9653 E-mail: sulick@buckeyeinternet.com.

SULKOWICZ, KERRY J. psychiatrist, psychoanalyst, management consultant; b. Dallas, Dec. 9, 1958; s. Adam and Helen S.; m. Sandra Susan Leong, Sept. 22, 1990; children: Emma Claire, Olivia Leong. AB, Harvard U., 1981; MD, U. Tex., Galveston, 1985. Diplomate Am. Bd. Psychiatry and Neurology; cert. psychoanalyst, N.Y. Resident, chief resident in psychiatry NYU Med. Ctr., Bellevue Hosp. Ctr., N.Y.C., 1985-89; unit chief, inpatient psychiatry Tisch Hosp./NYU Med. Ctr., 1989-90; pvt. practice, 1989—; attending psychiatrist Tisch Hosp./NYU Med. Ctr., 1990—, Lenox Hill Hosp., N.Y.C., 1998—; pres. The Boswell Group, LLC. Co-dir. NYU Psychodynamic Psychotherapy Tng. Program, NYU Psychoanalytic Inst., 1995-97, faculty, 1992—; clin. instr. psychiatry NYU Sch. Medicine, 1988-96, clin. asst. prof., 1996-98, clin. assoc. prof., 1998—. Mem. Am. Psychoanalytic Assn., Psychoanalytic Assn. of N.Y., NYU/Bellevue Psychiat. Soc. Office: 151 E 80th St Ofc 1B New York NY 10021-0442

SULLAM, BRIAN ELIOT, journalist; b. Pitts., Sept. 8, 1949; s. Edward and Fredda (Reich) S.; m. Susan Fisher, Apr. 1, 1978; children: Jennifer M., Karen E. BA, Johns Hopkins U., 1971; postgrad., Sch Advanced Internat. Studies, 1971-72. Assoc. editor Hawaii Observer, Honolulu, 1973-76; reporter Jour. of Commerce, Washington, 1977-79, Balt. Sun, 1979-92, editl. writer, 1992-01; web editor T. Rowe Price, 2001—. Freedom Forum fellow U. Hawaii, 1990-91. Mem. Nat. Press Club. Office: 100 E Pratt St Baltimore MD 21202 E-mail: brian_sullam@troweprice.com.

SULLEBARGER, JOHN THOMPSON, internist, cardiologist, educator; b. Plainfield, N.J., May 2, 1957; s. Franklyn Jackson and Joanne Abbott (Aspinall) S.; m. Lorrie Jeanne Miller, June 14, 1980; children: Jeffrey Franklyn, Melissa Jeanne. Student, U. Mainz, 1977; AB, Dartmouth Coll., 1979; MD, Johns Hopkins U., 1983. Intern U. Rochester, N.Y., 1983-84, resident in medicine, 1984-86, fellow in cardiology, 1986-89, from sr. instr. to asst. prof., 1989-92; asst. prof. U. South Fla., Tampa, 1992-96, assoc. prof., 1997-99; dir. CCU Tampa Gen. Hosp., 1997—; dir. interventional cardiology Fla. Cardiovascular Inst., 1999—. Dir. Cardiac Catheterization Lab. James Haley VA Hosp., Tampa, 1992—99; dir. interventional cardiology U. South Fla., 1994—99; attending physician Strong Meml. Hosp., Rochester, 1989—92. Author: (with others) book chapters; contrb. articles to profl. jours. Chmn. Bd. Christian Svc., 1st Bapt. Ch., Rochester, 1991-92. Fellow ACP, 1992, Am. Coll. of Cardiology, 1991, Counc. on Clin. Cardiology of Am. Heart Assn., 1991, N.Y. Cardiological Soc., 1992. Fellow ACP, Soc. Cardiac Angiography and Interventions, Am. Coll. Cardiology, N.Y. Cardiol. Soc.; mem. Am. Heart Assn. (fellow coun. on clin. cardiology). Avocations: music. Office: 508 S Habana Ave Ste 340 Tampa FL 33609-4191

SULLENBERGER, ARA BROOCKS, mathematics educator; b. Amarillo, Tex., Jan. 3, 1933; d. Carl Clarence and Ara Frances (Broocks) Cox; m. Hal Joseph Sullenberger, Nov. 2, 1952; children: Hal Joseph Jr., Ara Broocks Sullenberger Switzer. Student, Randolph-Macon Woman's Coll., 1951-52, So. Meth. U., 1952, U. Tex., Arlington, 1953, Amarillo Coll., 1953-54; BA in Math., Tex. Tech. U., 1955, MA, 1958; postgrad., Tex. Christian U., 1963-67, U. N. Tex., 1969-80, Tarrant County Coll., Fort Worth, Tex., 1972-83. Cert. tchr., Tex. Math. tchr. Tom S. Lubbock (Tex.) High Sch., 1955-56; instr. math. Tex. Tech U., Lubbock, 1956-63; teaching fellow math. Tex. Christian U., Ft. Worth, 1963-64; chmn. dept. math. Ft. Worth Country Day Sch., 1964-67; instr. math. Tarrant County Coll.-South, Ft. Worth, 1967-70, asst. prof. math., 1970-74, assoc. prof. math., 1974-95; prof. emeritus, 1995—; ret., 1995. Cons. Project Change, Ft. Worth, 1967-68; math. scis. advisor Coll. Bd., Princeton, N.J., 1979-83; math. book reviewer for various pub. cos. including Prentice-Hall, McGraw Hill, D.C. Heath, Prindle, Weber & Schmidt, MacMillan, Harcourt, Brace Jovanovich, West, Worth, Saunders, Wadsworth; adj. prof. math. Tex. Christian U., fall 1996. Contbr. article, book revs. to profl. publs.; author book supplement to Intermediate Algebra, 1990. Active mem. Jr. League of Ft. Worth, 1954-73, sustaining mem., 1973—; editor newsletter Crestwood Assn., Ft. Worth, 1984, 86, 91, membership sec., 1985, 90, 91, 95, 99, pres., 1988-89, 98-99, crime patrol capt., 1993, 2000-01, v.p., 1993, treas., 1987, 96, sec., 1997-98, crime patrol sec., 1999, crime patrol sec.-treas., 2001—. Recipient award for excellence in teaching Gen. Dynamics, 1968. Mem. Math. Assn. Am. (life), Nat. Coun. Tchrs. Math. (life), Am. Math. Assn. Two-Yr. Colls. (life), Tex. Math. Assn. Two-Yr. Colls. (charter, v.p. 1997-99), Tex. Jr. Coll. Tchrs. Assn., Ft. Worth League Neighborhood Assn. (v.p. 1999-2000), Pi Beta Phi. Republican. Episcopalian. Avocations: grandchildren, reading, pets, walking, writing. Home: 600 Eastwood Ave Fort Worth TX 76107-1020 E-mail: halandara@aol.com., halara@juno.com.

SULLENTRUP, MICHAEL GERARD, structural engineer, consultant; b. Washington, May 15, 1958; s. William J. III and Ruth M. (Eckelkamp) S.; m. Glenda S. Brinker, Aug. 2, 1980; children: Jeremy M., Jane M. BSCE, U. Mo., 1980, MSCE, 1981. Rsch. asst. U. Mo., Columbia, 1979-80, rsch. specialist, 1980-81, teaching asst., 1981; quality control insp. Quinn Concrete Co., Marshall, Mo., 1980; engr. McDonnell Aircraft Co., St. Louis, 1982-85, sr. engr., 1987-89, lead engr., 1990-97, recruiter, 1986—, product quality integrator, 1993-94; with Technical Integrator, 1994-96; principal tech. spec. fatigue and fracture mechanics, 1998—. Contbr. articles to profl. jours.; author personal computer software. Tchr. Roman Cath. Ch., Hazelwood, Mo., 1986—, mem. parish coun., 1992—; leader Boy Scouts Am., Hazelwood, 1989—. Mem. AIAA (sr.), ASTM, Digital Equipment Corp. User Soc., KC (officer, bd. dirs. Hazelwood, 1984—). Achievements include expertise in development and maintenance of engineering database management systems, and in automation of structural engineering analysis methods. Home: 7494 Naples Dr Hazelwood MO 63042-1369 Office: McDonnell Douglas Aerospace MC2704240 PO Box 516 Saint Louis MO 63166-0516

SULLIVAN, ADDIE LOUISE, trade association project assistance administrator; b. Chgo., July 7, 1942; d. Fred and Jimmie Sophie (Lacey) S. AA, Kennedy-King Coll., Chgo., 1973. Waitress Moon's Restaurant, Chgo., 1962; sec. Zenith Corp., 1963-65; sec., collector Household Fin., 1965-68; sec. temporary agencies, 1968-70, Chgo. Housing Authority, 1973-75, 78-80, Cook County Hosp., Chgo., 1975-80; libr., membership rep. U. Chgo., 1980—. Steward Internat. Brotherhood Teamsters Local 743, Chgo., 1984—, counselor Local743, Chgo., 1993—. Mem. Teamster Black Caucus, Washington, 1990, Coalition of Black Unionists, Chgo., 1991, Labor Party Advs., Chgo., 1995. Named Steward of Yr., Internat. Brotherhood Teamsters, 1989, Alpha Lambda chpt. ETA Phi Beta, 1994. Mem. Order of Ea. Star, Prince Hall Affiliation (past matron 1986, 89). Apostolic. Home: 11941 S Wallace St Chicago IL 60628-5923

SULLIVAN, ANNE DOROTHY HEVNER, artist; b. Boston, Mar. 17, 1929; m. James Leo Sullivan, Jan. 20, 1951; children: Maura, Mark, Lianne, Christopher. Student, Northeastern U., 1973-75; BA, U. Mass., Lowell, 1977; postgrad., De Cordova Mus., Lincoln, Mass., 1978-81. Art dir., instr. Whistler House Mus., Lowell, Mass., 1971-73, 96; art instr., dir. alternatives for individual devel. program U. Mass., 1976-84; incorporator Depot Square Artists Gallery, Lexington, Mass., 1981-84; dir., art cons. Abbey Art Gallery, Boston, 1987-88; juried artist Emerson Umbrella Ctr. for Arts, Concord, Mass., 1989-92, Brush with History Gallery, Lowell, 1992-96, instr., 1996. Juror, lectr., demonstrator, tchr. to art groups and assns., 1971—. Exhibited in nat. juried group shows at Fed. Res. Gallery, Boston, 1990, 92, 94, 96, 98, Brush With History Gallery, 1990-96, Midwest Mus. of Am. Art, Elkhardt, Ind., 1991, Cahoon Mus., Cotuit, Mass., 1991, Sumner Mus., Washington, 1992, Whistler Mus., 1992, 95, 96, Duxbury Mus., 1992, Attleboro (Mass.) Mus., 1992, C.L. Wolfe Art Club, N.Y.C., 1992, 96, N.E. Ctr.-U. N.H., 1992, Emerson Umbrella at Fed. Res. Boston, 1993, Bentley Coll., Waltham, Mass., 1993, Fitchburg (Mass.) Mus., 1994, U. Mass. Med. Sch., Worcester, 1994, Whistler Mus. Invitational Exhibit of Paintings, Lowell, 1995, Fuller Mus.-Printmakers' Monotype Exhibit, Brockton, Mass., 1995, Nat. Assn. Women Artists 107th Ann., N.Y.C., 1996, N.Am. Open Competition, Boston, 1996, 98, Lowell Urban Nat. Pk., 1996, Charlotte Art Assn. Nat. Open Competition, Punta Gorda, Fla., 1998, 2000, Nat. Assn. Am. Pen Women Biennial-U. Tampa, Fla., 1998, Arlington, Va., 2000, Nat. Open Biennial Competitions, Fed. Res. Gallery, Boston, 1992, 94, 96, 98, Internat. Soc. Exptl. Artists Exhbn., 1998-99, others; represented in permanent collections at Neil Sulier Art Collection, Lexington, Ky., The New Eng. Bank, Shawmut Bank, Bay Banks, Concord Nat. Bank, Amoskeag Banks, N.H., 1st Capital Bank of Concord, N.H., Sheraton Corp., Boston, Calif., New Orleans; publs. of paintings include Best of Abstract Watercolors, 1996, Best of Watercolors 2, Painting Compositions, 1997. Bd. dirs. Human Svcs. Corp., Lowell, 1971-72; v.p. Whistler Mus. Art, 1972-73; chmn. Lowell Arts Coun., 1980-81; mem. Mass. Arts Advocacy Coun., Boston, 1982. Recipient Catharine Lorillard Wolfe Art Club, Inc. award, 1992, Catharine L. Wolfe Art Club, N.Y., Am. Artist Mag. award, 1996, Fitchburg Mus. 59th Ann., 1994, 2d prize watercolor Cahoon Mus., Cotuit, Mass., 1991, Best of Show award Women's Caucus for Art Exhibit, Longboat Key, Fla., 1997, M.M. Rines award for Outstanding Contemporary Painting, 1994, M.Hoarty and C.Grimm Meml. award 1996, others. Mem. Internat. Soc. Exptl. Artists (Merit award 1998), Nat. Assn. Women Artists (Martha Reed Meml. award 1988, Leila Sawyer Meml. award 1994), Women Contemporary Artists (Sarasota, Fla. Best of Show award 1997), New Eng. Watercolor Soc. (bd. dirs. 1984-92, Escort prize Shannon Exhibit 1997) Nat. Open Biennial Competitions, 1992, 94, 96, 98 (M.M. Rines award for Outstanding contemporary painting, 1994, M. Hoarty and C. Grimm Meml. award, 1996, New England Open comp. hon. mention, 1989, Campion award, 1997, Signature exhibit award of merit, 1997), Monotype Guild New Eng. (pres. 1992-93), Nat. League Am. Penwomen (award of excellence 1990, award of merit nat. biennial exhibit 2000), Copley Soc. (Copley Artist award), Sarasota Visual Arts Ctr., Internat. Soc. Exptl. Artists (hon. mention 7th annual exhibit 1998), Fla. Artist Group, Inc. Home: 28 Rindo Park Dr Lowell MA 01851-3413 E-mail: jls1225@aol.com.

SULLIVAN, AUSTIN PADRAIC, JR. diversified food company executive; b. Washington, June 26, 1940; s. Austin P. and Janet Lay (Patterson) Sullivan; m. Judith Ann Raab, June 1, 1968 (dec. Jan. 1995); children: Austin P. Sullivan III, Amanda, Alexander; m. Marie Elise de Golian, Aug. 1, 1997; children: Lauren Gibbons, Georgia Gibbons, Samuel Gibbons. AB cum laude, Princeton U., 1964. Spl. asst. to dep. dir. N.J. Office Econ. Opportunity, Trenton, 1965-66; prof. staff mem. Com. on Edn. and Labor, U.S. Ho. of Reps., Washington, 1967-71, legis. dir., 1971-76; dir. govt. relations Gen. Mills, Inc., Mpls., 1976-78, v.p., corp. dir. govt. relations, 1978-79, v.p. pub. affairs, 1979-93, v.p. corp. comms. and pub. affairs, 1993-94, sr. v.p. corp. rels., 1994—. Lectr. fed. labor market policies Harvard U., 1972—76, Boston U., 1972—76. Bd. dirs., exec. com. Guthrie Theatre, Mpls., 1978—84, Minn. Citizens for the Arts, 1980—83, Urban Coalition Mpls., 1978—80; chmn. Pub. Affairs Coun., 1993—94, Gov.'s Coun. on Employment and Tng., 1976—82; mem. Nat. Commn. on Employment and Tng., 1979—81; co-chmn. Gov.'s Commn. on Dislocated Workers, 1988—89; trustee Minn. Pub. Radio, 1999—; bd. advisors Min. C. of C., bd. dirs., 1993—99; mem. U.S. Sec. Agr. Adv. Com. on Agrl. Biotech., 2000—; bd. advisors Dem. Leadership Coun., 1996—. With1959 USMC, 1957. Fellow Eleanor Roosevelt fellow in interracial rels., 1964—65. Mem.: Grocery Mfrs. Assn. (govt. affairs coun. 1991—, chmn. biotech. task force 1999—, co-chmn. bus. roundtable fiscal policy coord. com. 2001—), Coun. of Pub. Affairs Execs. (chmn. 1989—90), Conf. Bd., Medica (bd. dirs. 2001—), GreaterMpls. C. of C. (exec. com. 1980—86, 1990—93, bd. dirs.), Mpls. Club (bd. govs. 2001—). Home: 17830 County Rd 6 Minneapolis MN 55447-2905 Office: Gen Mills Inc One Gen Mills Blvd Minneapolis MN 55426

SULLIVAN, BARBARA ANN, attorney, rehabilitation services professional; b. Haverhill, Mass., Mar. 20, 1952; d. Vincent R. and Helen (Lane) S. Diploma in nursing, Lynn Hosp. Sch. Nursing, 1979; MEd in Rehab. Adminstrn. magna cum laude, Northeastern U., 1988; postgrad., Mass. Gen. Hosp., 1987-89; JD, Mass. Law Sch., 1994. RN, Mass.; lic. rehab. counselor; cert. case mgr. Nurse various hosps., 1979-84; liaison, health care mktg. rep. Cambridge (Mass.) Vis. Nurse Assn., 1984-87; med./vocat. rehab. specialist Comprehensive Rehab. Assocs., Inc., North Andover, Mass., 1987-88; rehab. adminstrn. intern Class, Inc., Lawrence, 1988; rehab. cons., med. claims reviewer Am. Internat. Health and Rehab. Svcs., Boston, 1988-89; ind. contractor, home health care nurse Community Health Network, Cambridge, 1989-90; rehab. mgr. Commonwealth of Mass. Pub. Employee Retirement Adminstrn., Boston, 1990-91; nurse cons. risk mgmt., case mgmt., disability, workers comp, 1991-95; nurse cons. U.S. Dept. Labor, Boston, 1992—. Mem. Am. Assn. Nurse Attys., Nat. Rehab. Assn., Northeastern U. Alumni Assn., Mass. Nurses Assn. (co-chmn. pub. rels. com. 1986-88), Kappa Delta Pi. Home: 30 Emily St Haverhill MA 01832-3031

SULLIVAN, BARBARA BOYLE, management consultant; b. Scranton, Pa., Apr. 12, 1937; d. Edmund F. and Mary R. (O'Connell) Boyle; m. John L. Sullivan Jr. BS in Bus. Adminstrn., Drexel U., 1958; PhD (hon.), Newton Coll., 1975, Gwynedd Mercy Coll., 1975. With IBM, 1959-72, systems engring. mgr. Ea. and Cen. Europe Austria, 1967-70, mgmt. devel. mgr., 1970, mgr. spl. programs, 1970-71, sales mgr., asst. br. mgr., 1971-72; pres. Boyle/Kirkman Assocs., N.Y.C., 1972-88; mng. ptnr. Innovation Assocs., Framingham, Mass., 1988-92. Bd. dirs. Ams. Fostering Latino Edn. and Culture; chair compensation com. Equitable Resources, Inc 1989-92, nominating com., 1991, mem. audit, pension trust, and compensation com.; cons. major corps. on human resource devl. programs, organizational change programs, changing work force; condr. exec. leadership and visionary and strategic planning awareness seminars Harvard Bus. Sch., Internat. Mgmt. Conf. Trustee Drexel U.; mem. Pres.'s adv. com. Gwynedd Mercy Coll., adv. com. Drexel U. Coll. Bus. Adminstrn.; vice chmn. bd. trustee Marymount Manhattan Coll., N.Y., bd. regents Mt. St. Mary's Coll., L.A., 1982-88; bd. dirs. Mary House Day Care Ctr.; chair Tour of Homes Christ Ch. Featured in numerous mags., books, radio and TV programs, including CBS 60 Minutes; named Bus. Person of Yr. St. Johns U., 1973, One of 50 Leaders for Future, Time mag., 1979. Mem. AAUW, Women's Forum, Weston Womens' League, Rotary Womens Aux. (v.p.), Boston Club, Newcomers Club (bd. dirs.). Home: 264 Saint Andrews Saint Simons GA 31522-2465

SULLIVAN, BARBARA JEAN, artist; b. Indpls., Jan. 7, 1935; d. Charles Arthur and Melida Mae Minnick; m. Charles Ray Poindexter, Dec. 31, 1990; children: Joseph Ruggless, Pamela Ruggless-Consoli, Diana Ruggless-Larsen, Milo Ballan. Fine artist, 1978—. Author (paperback cover illustrations): Winter Rage, 1991, The Horsemen, 1992, limited edit. giclee prints, 1999—;one-woman shows include Artists' Gallery, Las Vegas, 1983; exhibited in group shows U.S. Fed. Bldg. Exhbn., Las Vegas, 1982, George Phippen Meml. Invitational We. Art Show, Prescott, Ariz., 1984, Burk Gallery, Boulder City, Nev., 1983, 6th Ann. Kalispell (Mont.) Art Show and Auction, 1983, 16th Ann. C.M. Russell Auction of Original We. Art, Great Falls, Mont., 1983 (Silver medal), 7th Ann. We. Art Show and Sale, Burk Gallery, 1984, guest artist Women Artists of Am. West, Pa-Jo's Gallery, Pinedale, Wyo., 1985, C.M. Russell Mus. Artist Invitational Exhibit, 1986, 10th Ann. We. Art Show and Sale, Burk Gallery, 1987, Far We. Art Assn. Show, Caesar's Palace, Las Vegas, 1987, Braithwaite Fine Arts Gallery, Cedar City, Utah, 1999, Bosque Conservatory of Art, Clifton, Tex., 2001 (Gold medal); Represented in permanent collections Nev. Nat. Bank, Virgin River Hotel and Casino, White House, Washington; contbr. poem to anthology, 2001. Bd. dirs. Charles Arthur Minnick Sunset Meml. Park Found., Las Vegas, Nev., 1992-95; adv. bd. Las Vegas, 1992-95. Recipient 1st Place award, Jaycee State Fair, 1976, 1977, 5 Painting of Month awards, Las Vegas Art Mus., 1978, Popular award, San Gabriel Fine Arts Assn. Invitational, 1978, Reserve Grand Championship, Las Vegas State Fair, 1981, 1st Place Oils, Caliente Profl. Invitational, 1982, award of Excellence, Am. Mothers State Competition, 1982, 1983, Best of Show award, Las Vegas Art Mus., 1994, Judges Choice award, 1995, juried award, Canyon Country Fine Arts Competition, Braithwaite Fine Arts Gallery, 1999, Gold medal award for Best Oil, Bosque Conservatory of Art, Tex., 2001, Quick Draw award, Mont. Gov. Ted Schwinden and C.M. Russell Auction of Original Western Art, 1983. Mem. Las Vegas Art Mus., 1977—, juried mem. Am . Inst. Fine Art, 1984. Avocations: traveling, photography, horseback riding, subject research, visiting art galleries. Office: PO Box 81056 Las Vegas NV 89180-1056

SULLIVAN, BARRY, lawyer; b. Newburyport, Mass., Jan. 11, 1949; s. George Arnold and Dorothy Bennett (Furbush) S.; m. Winnifred Mary Fallers, June 14, 1975; children: George Arnold, Lloyd Ashton. AB cum laude, Middlebury Coll., 1970; JD, U. Chgo., 1974. Bar: Mass. 1975, Ill. 1975, Va. 1995, U.S. Dist. Ct. (no. dist.) Ill. 1976, U.S. Ct. Appeals (7th cir.) 1976, U.S. Ct. Appeals (10th cir.) 1977, U.S. Ct. Appeals (11th cir.) 1986, U.S. Ct. Appeals (5th and 9th cirs.) 1987, U.S. Ct. Appeals (fed. cir.) 1993, U.S. Ct. Appeals (DC cir.) 1994, U.S. Ct. Appeals (4th cir.) 1997, U.S. Supreme Ct. 1978. Law clk. to judge John Minor Wisdom U.S. Ct. Appeals (5th cir.), New Orleans, 1974-75; assoc. Jenner & Block, Chgo., 1975-80; asst. to solicitor gen. of U.S. U.S. Dept. of Justice, Washington, 1980-81; ptnr. Jenner & Block, Chgo., 1981-94, 2001—; prof. law Washington and Lee U., Lexington, Va., 1994-2001, dean, 1994-99, v.p., 1998-99; Fulbright prof. U. Warsaw, Poland, 2000—01; lectr. in law U. Chgo., 2001—. Vis. fellow Queen Mary and Westfield Coll., U. London, 2001; spl. asst. atty. gen. State of Ill., 1989—90; lectr. in law Loyola U., Chgo., 1978—79; adj. prof. law Northwestern U., Chgo., 1990—92, Chgo., 1993—94, vis. prof., 1992—93; Jessica Swift Meml. lectr. in constnl. law Middlebury Coll., 1991. Assoc. editor U. Chgo. Law Rev., 1973-74; contbr. articles to profl. jours. Trustee Cath. Theol. Union at Chgo., 1993—; mem. vis. com. Irving B. Harris Grad. Sch. Public Policy Studies U., Chgo., 2001—; mem. vis. com. U. Chgo. Divinity Sch., 1987—2001; mem. adv. panel Fulbright Sr. Specialist Program, 2001—. Yeats Soc. scholar, 1968; Woodrow Wilson fellow, Woodrow Wilson Found., 1970. Mem. ABA (chmn. coord. com. on AIDS 1988-94, mem. standing com. on amicus curiae briefs 1990-97, mem. coun. of sect. of individual rights and responsibilities 1993-98, mem. sect. of legal edn. com. on law sch. adminstrn. 1994-98, chair sect. legal edn. com. on professionalism 1999-2000), Va. Bar Assn., Va. State Bar (chair sect. on edn. of lawyers 1998-99), Bar Assn. 7th Fed. Cir. (vice chmn. adminstrv. justice com. 1985-86), Am. Law Inst., Chgo. Bar Assn., Ill. State Bar Assn., Lawyers Club Chgo., Phi Beta Kappa. Democrat. Roman Catholic. Home: 5555 S Everett Apt A1-2 Chicago IL 60637 Office: Jenner & Block One IBM Plz Chicago IL 60611 E-mail: bsullivan@jenner.com.

SULLIVAN, BEN FRANK, JR. real estate broker, rancher; b. Brookesmith, Tex., Aug. 10, 1919; s. Ben Frank and Vera Scott (Hennigan) S.; m. Frances Louise Levisay, Dec. 28, 1946; children: Thomas James, Ben Charles, Harold Lyndon. Student, Tarleton State U., 1937-39; BS, Tex. A&M U., 1941. Commd. 2d lt. U.S. Army, 1942, advanced through grades to capt., 1943-46; capt. U.S. Army Res., 1946-53, ret., 1953; sales/mktg. Armour & Co., Ft. Worth, 1946; owner Grocery Bus., Bangs, Tex., 1946-48; postmaster U.S. Postal Svc., 1947-66, rural mail carrier, 1966-75; owner/broker Sullivan Real Estate, 1963—. Owner Sullivan Ranch, Bangs, 1962—; owner oper. Oil & Gas Prodn. on Ranch, Bangs, 1974—; owner, mgr. Home Bldg. & Sales, Bangs, 1965-94. Sunday sch. tchr., ch. supt., chmn. ofcl. bd. Bangs United Meth. Ch.; trustee Brownwood Dist. Ctrl. Tex. Conf. United Meth. Ch., 1983—, also chmn. bd.; committeeman Meth. Home, Waco, 1982-83, 98, 2000, 2001; mem. steering com. to form Brookesmith Water Corp., Brown County, Tex., 1971, bd. dirs., 1971-73. With U.S. Army, 1941-46, WWII. Decorated 4 bronze stars, WWII victory medal. Mem. Brown County C. of C. (bd. dirs. 1993-95), Am. Legion (comdr. post # 308 1949), Masons, Order of Ea. Star, Shriners, Lions (pres. 1963-64). Methodist. Avocations: hunting, fishing, boating, sports, travel, reading.

SULLIVAN, BERNARD JAMES, accountant; b. Chgo., June 25, 1927; s. Bernard Hugh and Therese Sarah (Condon) S.; m. Joan Lois Costello, June 9, 1951; children: Therese Lynn Scanlan, Bernard J., Geralyn M. Snyder. BSC, Loyola U., Chgo., 1950. CPA, Ill. Staff Bansley and Kiener, Chgo., 1950-66, ptnr., 1966-82, mng. ptnr., 1982—. Bd. dirs. Associated Acctg. Firms, Internat.; exec. com. Moore Stephens and Co., U.S.A., 1984—, Arbitrator Nat. Assn. Security Dealers. Served with USN, 1945-46. Mem. Am. Inst. CPA's, Ill. Soc. CPA's, Govt. Fin. Officer Assn., Internat. Found. Employee Benefit Plans, Delta Sigma Pi. Clubs: Beverly Country (Chgo.), Metropolitan (Chgo.). Lodges: Elks, K.C. Avocations: golf, sports, travel. Home: 9636 S Kolmar Ave Oak Lawn IL 60453-3214 Office: Bansley & Kiener 125 S Wacker Dr Ste 1200 Chicago IL 60606-4496 E-mail: bsullivan@bk-cpa.com.

SULLIVAN, BRENDAN PAUL, state official, communications educator; b. Boston, Apr. 20, 1949; s. Francis Joseph and Margaret Rita (McDonough) S.; m. Debra Marie Fitzgerald, Feb. 11, 1988; children: Erin, Patrick. BS, Boston State Coll., 1970; MA in Comms., Fairfield U., 1976; MBA, Boston Coll., 1995. Tchr. Boston Pub. Schs., 1970-81; mgr. adminstrn. Mass. State Lottery,

Braintree, 1981-91; asst. clk.-magistrate Commonwealth of Mass. Superior Ct., Brockton, 1993—. Adj. prof. Massasoit C.C., Brockton, 1996—, mem. mediation adv. bd., 1999—. Mem. Plymouth County Dem. League, Abington, Mass., 2000—. Mem. Furnace Brook Golf Club (past gov. 1976—). Democrat. Roman Catholic. Avocations: golf, fishing, coaching baseball. Home: 220 Plymouth Ave Quincy MA 02169 Office: 72 Belmont St Brockton MA 02301-5248 E-mail: brendeb@attbi.com.

SULLIVAN, BRENDAN V., JR. lawyer; b. Providence, Mar. 11, 1942; AB, Georgetown U., 1964, JD, 1967. Bar: R.I. 1967, D.C. 1970, U.S. Dist. Ct. D.C. 1970, U.S. Ct. Appeals (D.C. cir.) 1970, U.S. Supreme Ct. 1972, U.S. Dist. Ct. Md. 1974, U.S. Ct. Appeals (4th cir.) 1981, U.S. Ct. Appeals (3d cir.) 1979, U.S. Ct. Appeals (6th cir.) 1991, U.S. Ct. Appeals (9th cir.) 1996, U.S. Ct. Fed. Claims 1998. Mem. Williams & Connolly, Washington. Lectr. Practicing Law Inst., 1981—, Md. Inst. for Continuing Profl. Edn. of Lawyers, Inc., 1979—, D.C. Criminal Practice Inst., 1975-81. Author: Grand Jury Proceedings, 1981, Techniques for Dealing with Pending Criminal Charges or Criminal Investigations, 1983, White Collar Criminal Practice Grand Jury, 1985. Fellow Am. Coll. Trial Lawyers; mem. ABA, R.I. Bar Assn., D.C. Bar. Office: Williams & Connolly 725 12th St NW Washington DC 20005-5901

SULLIVAN, CHARLES, university dean, educator, author; b. Boston, May 27, 1933; s. Charles Thomas and Marion Veronica (Donahue) S.; divorced; children: Charles Fulford, John Driscoll, Catherine Page; m. Shirley Ross Davis, Sept. 6, 1997. BA in English, Swarthmore Coll., 1955; MA, NYU, 1968, PhD in Social Psychology, 1973; MPA, Pa. State U., 1978. Predoctoral fellow NYU, 1964-68; postdoctoral fellow Ednl. Testing Svc., Princeton, N.J., 1973-74; asst. prof. psychology Ursinus Coll., Collegeville, Pa., 1973-78; mgmt. cons., 1978-86; adj. prof. Pa. State U., Radnor, Pa., 1978-80; prof., head dept. pub. adminstrn., dir. student svcs. Southeastern U., Washington, 1986-89; asst. dean Grad. Sch. Arts and Scis. Georgetown U., 1989-92, assoc. dean Grad. Sch. Arts and Scis., 1992-97, professorial lectr., dept. psychology, 1994-95; exec. dir. Doylestown Found., Doylestown, Pa., 1958-73; assoc. dean, prof. Coll. Profl. Studies U. San Francisco, 1997-98. Adj. prof. social and behavioral scis. U. Md., 1984-96; lectr., spkr. on lit. and art Cooper-Hewitt Mus., N.Y.C., Nat. Soc. Arts and Letters, Washington, Martin Luther King Jr. Libr., Washington, Met. Mus. Art, N.Y.C., Smithsonian Instn., Washington, Children's Book Fair, N.Y.C., Nat. Mus. Women in Arts, Lombardi Cancer Rsch. Ctr., Georgetown U., Arts Club of Washington, Phillips Collection, Corcoran Gallery of Art, U. San Francisco Multicultural Lit. Program, Nat. Mus. Am. History, New Coll. of Calif., others. Author: Alphabet Animals, 1991, The Lover in Winter, 1991, Numbers at Play, 1992, Circus, 1992, Cowboys, 1993, A Woman of A Certain Age, 1994, Out of Love, 1996, American Folk, 1998, In a Certain Place, 1999, The Lovers' Companion, 2002; editor: America in Poetry, 1988, 2d edit., 1992, 3d edit., 1996, Imaginary Gardens, 1989, Ireland in Poetry, 1990, Children of Promise, 1991, 2d edit., 2001, Loving, 1992, American Beauties, 1993, Here Is My Kingdom, 1994, Fathers and Children, 1995, Imaginary Animals, 1996, Dancing in the Wind, 2002. Trustee Folger Poetry Bd., 1988-92; Nat. Soc. Arts and Letters, 1992-94, Am. Acad. Liberal Edn., 1995—, San Francisco Art Inst., 2000—; pres. Am. Found. Arts, 1995—; mem. collectors com. Nat. Gallery Art, Washington, 1998-2002; mem. Dir.'s Cir., San Francisco Mus. Modern Art, 1998—. Recipient Best Books for Young Adults award Young Adult Libr. Svcs. Assn., 1992, 98, Best Books for Teens award N.Y. Pub. Libr., 1992, 93. Mem. Am. Poetry Soc., Acad. Am. Poets, Cosmos Club, The Family. E-mail: artsfound@earthlink.net.

SULLIVAN, CHARLES R. engineering educator; b. Princeton, N.J., Dec. 1, 1964; s. Roger D. and Margaret Peplow Sullivan. BS with highest honors, Princeton U., 1987; PhD, U. Calif., Berkeley, 1996. Design and devel. engr. Lutron Electronics, Coopersburg, Pa., 1987-90; asst. prof. engring. Dartmouth Coll., Hanover, NH, 1996—2002, assoc. prof. engring., 2002—. Cons. Volterra, Fremont, Calif. Assoc. editor IEEE Transactions on Power Electronics; contbr. articles to profl. jours. Recipient Ross N. Tucker Electronic Materials award Am. Inst. Mining, Metallurgical & Petroleum Engrs., 1995, Career award NSF, 1999, Prize paper award IEEE Power Electronics Soc., 2000. Mem.: IEEE, Am. Soc. for Engring. Edn. Achievements include patent for circuit and method for improved dimming of gas discharge lamps. Avocations: bicycling, music. Home: 4 Burton Rd Hanover NH 03755 Fax: 603-646-3856. E-mail: charles.r.sullivan@dartmouth.edu.

SULLIVAN, COLLEEN ANNE, physician, educator; b. Lucknow, India, Feb. 11, 1937; came to U.S., 1961; d. Douglas George and Nancy Irene (MacLeod) S.; m. Alexander Walter Gotta, July 17, 1965; 1 child, Nancy Colleen. MB, ChB, U. St. Andrews, Scotland, 1961. Diplomate Am. Bd. Anesthesiology, Am. Coll. Anesthesiologists. Rotating intern Nassau Hosp. (now Winthrop U. Hosp.), Mineola, N.Y., 1961-62; clin. instr. Cornell U., N.Y.C., 1962-64; resident in anesthesiology N.Y. Hosp./Cornell U., 1962-64; fellow in anesthesiology Meml. Sloan-Kettering Cancer Ctr., N.Y.C., 1964-67, asst. prof. Cornell U. Med. Coll., 1978-79; assoc. dir. anesthesia St. Mary's Hosp.-Cath. Med. Ctr., Bklyn., 1968-78; clin. assoc. prof. SUNY, 1979-90, clin. dir. anesthesia, 1990-93, clin. prof. anesthesiology, 1990-97. Clin. dir. anesthesia Kings County Hosp., Bklyn., 1983-90, med. dir. ambulatory surg. unit, 1993-97. Author numerous chpt. in anesthesiology textbooks; contbr. articles to profl. jours. Mem. N.Y. State Soc. Anesthesiologists (mem. ho. dels. 1983-97, asst. editor Sphere 1990-95, mem. com. sci. program 1990-97), Woman's Club of Great Neck. Republican. Roman Catholic. Avocations: reading, cooking.

SULLIVAN, CONNIE CASTLEBERRY, artist, photographer; b. Cin., Jan. 8, 1934; d. John Porter and Constance (Alf) Castleberry; m. John J. Sullivan, June 6, 1959; children: Deirdre Kelly, Margaret Graham. BA, Manhattanville Coll., 1957. Spl. lectr. Cin. Contemporary Art Ctr., 1984, Toledo Friends of Photography, 1991, U. Ky. Art Mus., 1993, Dennison U. Sch. Art, 1993, El Instituto de Estudios Norte Americanos, Barcelona, 1994, Ctr. for Photography, Bombay, India, 1997, Miami U. Art Mus., Oxford, Ohio, 1998, Alice and Harris K. Weston Gallery, Aronoff Ctr. for the Arts, Cin., 2000. One-woman shows include Contemporary Art Ctr. Cleve., 1982, Cin. Contemporary Arts Ctr., 1983, Fogg Art Mus., Cambridge, Mass., 1983, 90, Neikrug Gallery, N.Y.C., 1984, Camden Arts Ctr., London, 1987, Evanston Art Ctr., Chgo., 1987, Silver Image Gallery Ohio State U., Columbus, 1988, Jean-Pierre Lambert Galerie, Paris, 1988, 96, David Winton Bell Gallery, Brown U., Providence, 1989, Toni Burckhead Gallery, Cin., 1989, Rochester Inst. Tech., 1991, Fotomus. im Münchner Stadtmus., Munich, 1992, U. Ky. Art Mus., Lexington, 1993, Internat. Photography Hall, Kirkpatrick Mus. complex, Oklahoma City, 1993, Institut d'Estudios Fotografics de Catalunya, Barcelona, Spain, 1994, Cheekwood Art Mus., Nashville, 1994, Museo Damy di Fotografia Contemporanea, Brescia, Italy, 1995, Photography Gallery U. Notre Dame, Ind., 1995, Louisville Visual Art Assoc., Watertower, Louisville, KY, 1995, Jean-Pierre Lambert Galarie, 1996, Museo Damy, Milan, 1997, Ctr. for Photography, Bombay, India, 1997, Miami U. Art Mus., Oxford, Ohio, 1998, Aronoff Ctr. for the Arts, Cin., 2000, Vine St. Studios, Houston, 2000, Columbus Mus. Art, 2001, Visual Studies Worshop Gall. Rochester, NY, 2000, NuNatte Duo Centre Photography, OP Photo Gall., Hong Kong, 2000, FotoFest, 2000; exhibited in numerous group shows including Robert Klein Gallery, Boston, 1981, Cin. Art Mus., 1981, 84, 85, 93, Witkin Gallery, N.Y.C., 1984, Milw. Art Mus., 1986, Dayton (Ohio) Art Inst., 1987, J.B. Speed Art Mus., Louisville, 1988, Trisolini Gallery Ohio U., 1989, Ohio U., Athens, 1989, Centre Nat. Photographie, Paris, 1989, Cleve. Ctr. for Contemporary Art, 1991, Tampa Mus. Art, 1991, 93, Images Gallery, 1991, Dayton Art Inst./Mus. Contemporary Art Wright State U., Dayton, 1992, Bowling Green State U. Sch Art, 1992, Carnegie Arts Ctr., Covington, Ky., 1993, POLK Mus. Art, Lakeland, Fla., 1993, Tampa (Fla.) Mus. Art, 1993, Adams Landing Fine Art Ctr., Cin., 1995, Checkwood Mus. Art, Nashville, 1995, Photo Forum Gallery, 1995, 96, Jean-Pierre Galerie, 1996, Soros Ctr. Contemporary Art, Kiev, Ukraine, 1996, Dom Khudozhnikiv, Kharkiv, Ukraine, 1996, Wolf Photographic Galleries, Cin., 1996, Columbus Mus. Art, 1996, Mus. fine Arts, St. Petersburg, Fla., 1997, Louisville Visual Art Assn., Water Tower, 1997, Mus. Damy di Fotografia Contemporanea, Brescia, Italy, 1998, Kharkiv Mcpl. Art Gallery, Kharkiv, Ukraine, 1999, Jean-Pierre Lambert Gallery, Paris, 1999, Huntington (W.Va.) Mus. Art, 2000, Centre Socio-Cultural Galerie Pierre Tal Coat, Hunnebont, France, 2000; represented in numerous permanent collections Tampa Mus. of Art, Münchner Stadt Mus., Munich, Germany, Museo Damy, Brescia, Italy, Ctr. Creative Photography, Tucson, Detroit Inst. Arts, Biblioteque National, Paris, Internat. Photography Hall of Fame and Mus., Kirkpatrick Ctr. Mus. Complex, Okla. City, Nelson Gallery-Atkins Mus., Kansas City, Ctr. for Photography, Bombay, Milw. Art Mus., Mus. Photography Arts, San Diego, Musee Nat. D'Art Modern, Cin. Art Mus., High Mus., Atlanta, Mus. Fine Arts, St. Petersburg, Fla., Centre Georges Pompidou, Paris, Denver Art Mus., Boston Mus. Fine Arts, Stanford U. Mus. Art, Palo Alto, Indpls. Art Mus., New Orleans Mus. Art, Fogg Mus., Cambridge, Mass., numerous others; also pvt. collections; author: Petroglyphs of the Heart, Photographs by Connie Sullivan, 1983; work represented in numerous publs. Trustee Images Ctr. for Fine Photography, Cin., 1986-94. Named Hyde Park Living Person of Yr., 1996; recipient Juried Show, Toledo Friends Photography, 1986, Best of show, 1988, Images Gallery, 1986, Pres.'s Coun. for Arts award, Manhattanville Coll., 1991, Treasure of the Month award, Mus. Fine Arts St. Petersburg, Fla., 1995; fellow Arts Midwest fellow, NEA, 1989—90; grantee Aid to Individual Artists grantee, Summerfair, 1987, travel grantee, Ohio Arts Coun., 1995, 1997, 2000, Artist Projects, 1999. Mem. McDowell Soc. Avocations: travel, reading, gardening, music. Home: 1950 Mount Vernon Dr Fort Wright KY 41011 Fax: 513-871-6931.

SULLIVAN, DANIEL EDMOND, fundraising executive; b. Alexandria, La., Jan. 22, 1946; s. Edmond James and Ruth (Morris) S.; m. Camille Lafleur Broussand, June 13, 1970; children: Daniel Edmond Jr., Parish Coughlin. Student, La. State U., 1964-67; BS, Northwestern State U., Natchitoches, La., 1968. Field underwriter N.Y. Life Ins. Co., New Orleans, 1968-70; asst. dir. Tulane U. Alumni Fund, 1970-71; assoc. dir. La. Civil Svc. League, 1971-73, exec. v.p., 1973—, also bd. govs., 1973—; bd. of gov. La. Orgn. for Jud. Excellence, 1992—, v.p., 1995—. Mem. com. La. Joint Legis. Com., 1982—; mem. pub. adminstrn. tng. adv. com. U. New Orleans, 1983-90. Bd. dirs. Young Audiences New Orleans, 1974-78. Named Hon. Alumnus Tulane U., 1977. Mem. Nat. Soc. Fund Raising Execs. (cert.), Am. Arbitration Assn. (panel of arbitrators), Royal Soc. St. George, Northwestern State U. Alumni Assn. (bd. dirs. 1974-84), New Orleans Lawn Tennis Club (bd. govs. 1978-80), Stratford Club. Republican. Roman Catholic. Home: 919 Short St New Orleans LA 70118-2730 Office: La Civil Svc League 810 Union St Ste 305 New Orleans LA 70112-1426

SULLIVAN, DANIEL JOSEPH, theater critic; b. Worcester, Mass., Oct. 22, 1935; s. John Daniel and Irene Ann (Flagg) S.; m. Helen Faith Scheid, 1965; children: Margaret Ann, Benjamin, Kathleen. AB, Holy Cross Coll., 1957; postgrad., U. Minn., 1957-59, U. So. Calif., 1964-65, Stanford U., 1978-79. Reporter Worcester Telegram, Mass., 1957, Red Wing Republican Eagle, Minn., 1959, St. Paul Pioneer Press, 1959-61; music and theater critic Mpls. Tribune, 1962-64; comedy writer Dudley Riggs' Brave New Workshop, 1961-64; arts reporter/theater reviewer N.Y. Times, 1965-68; theater critic L.A. Times, 1969-90. Dramaturg Eugene O'Neill Theatre Ctr., Waterford, Conn., 1972-73, 93-98; instr. O'Neill Critics Inst., Waterford, 1977-92, assoc. dir., 1993-98, dir., 1999—; adj. prof. U. Minn., Mpls., 1990—; juror theater panel Nat. Endowment for Arts, 1983; juror Pulitzer Prize for Drama, 1985, 89, 92; pres. L.A. Drama Critics Circle, 1970-71, Ctr. for Arts Criticism, St. Paul, 1992-95. Mem. Am. Theater Critics Assn. (founding).

SULLIVAN, DANIEL MADDEN, business executive; b. Sparta, Wis., Apr. 19, 1924; s. Daniel Casper and Kathryn (Madden) Sullivan; m. Doris Cureau, Apr. 6, 1957; 1 child, Jane Madden Sullivan. BS, U. Wis., 1948; MBA, Harvard U., 1955. Sales engr. No. Engring., Sparta, 1948-53; mem. pres.'s staff W.R. Grace, N.Y.C., 1955-57, ITT, N.Y.C., 1958-61; founder, CEO, Frost & Sullivan, Inc., 1958—87. Chmn. bd. dirs. J.L.M. Couture, Inc., N.Y.C.; bd. dirs. Bliss Gouveneur, N.Y.C., Std. Comml., Wilson, N.C.; trustee Engring. Info., N.Y.C. Pub. Frost & Sullivan Reports; contbr. articles to profl. jours. 2d lt. USAAF, 1943-45. Mem. Union Club, Dorset Field Club, Harvard Club, Downtown Assn. Avocations: tennis, skiing. Home: 305 E 72d St New York NY 10021

SULLIVAN, DAVID BRYAN, lawyer; b. Cleve., Nov. 28, 1962; s. John Keeley and Mary Lane (Bryan) S.; m. Deana Racine Jordan, June 19, 1999. BA, Yale Coll., 1985; MA in Law & Diplomacy, Fletcher Sch. Law & Diplomacy, 1995; JD, Yale U., 1995. Bar: N.Y. 1997, D.C. 1998. Vol. Crossroads Africa, Kenya, 1985; systems engr. IBM, Bethesda, Md., 1985-89; vol. (computer specialist) U.S. Peace Corps, Swaziland, 1989-91; law clk. to Hon. Dana Fabe, Hon. Dan Moore Supreme Ct. of Alaska, Anchorage, 1995-96; assoc. White & Case, N.Y.C., 1996-97; honors atty. U.S. Dept. Treasury, Washington, 1997-98; atty.-adviser U.S. Dept. State, 1998—. Contbr. book revs., articles to profl. jours. Office: U S Dept State 2201 C St NW Washington DC 20520

SULLIVAN, DONAL D. federal bankruptcy judge; b. 1931; Attended, Loyola U., Chgo., 1949-50, Ill. Inst. Tech., 1952-54; LLB, De Paul U., 1957. Bar: Oreg. 1957, Ill. 1958. 1st asst. U.S. atty. for Oreg., Portland, 1962-65; clk. U.S. Dist. Ct. Oreg., 1966-69, bankruptcy judge, 1969—98; ret., 1998; recalled, 1998—. Office: US Bankruptcy Ct 900 Bank of Am Plz 1001 SW 5th Ave Portland OR 97204-1147 E-mail: dds@teleport.com.

SULLIVAN, DOROTHY RONA, state official; b. Boston, Jan. 7, 1941; d. Lewis Robert and Dorothy (Hopkins) S.; B.A., Boston U., 1963; M.Ed., State Coll. Boston, 1966; C.A.G.S., Boston U., 1972; postgrad. Northeastern U., 1970-71, Boston Coll., 1974-78, U. Mass., 1980. Rsch. asst. Boston Lying-in Hosp., 1963-64; employment counselor Mass. Div. Employment Security, Boston, 1964-66, sr. employment counselor, 1966-67, prin. employment counselor, 1967-70, employment office mgr., 1970-75, supr., 1975-78, chief rsch. dept., 1978-88, dir. def. employment analysis, 1985-87; chief rsch. dept. Mass. Divsn. Employment and Tng., 1989-98, chief rsch. dept., 1998—. Supr. community counselor interns and rehab. adminstrn. interns Northeastern U. Grad. Sch. Edn., 1968-74; supr. public adminstrn. interns Suffolk U., 1976; supr. econ. interns Boston U., 1979, Regis Coll., 1984, U. Mass.-Boston, 1998; presenter in field. Recorder Gov.'s Conf. on Rehab., 1970, mem. Gov.'s Commn. Employment of Handicapped, 1972-78, Pres.'s Com. Employment of Handicapped, 1975-78; exec. bd. Greater Boston council Camp Fire Girls, 1971-73; R.S.V.P. adv. bd. Boston Commn. Affairs of the Elderly, 1977-78; mem. adv. com. equal employment opportunity practices Dept. Personnel Adminstrn., 1984-85; mem. adv. group Mass. Occupl. Info. Coordinating Com., 1991-98. Recipient Recognition award Nat. Occupl. Info. Coordinating Com., 1994. Mem. ACA (recorder), AACD, ASPA, APGA (nat. recorder conf. 1968), Nat. Career Devel. Assn., Nat. Rehab. Assn. (Mass. sec. 1971-72, exec. bd. 1972-74, v.p. 1974-75, pres. 1976-77), Am. Fedn. State, County and Mcpl. Employees (exec. bd. local 164 1972-73, 74-76), Am. Acad. Polit. and Social Sci., Rockport Art Assn. (patron), Am. Econ. Assn., Am. Bus. Women's Assn. (del. nat. conv. 1980, 83, pres. Boston chpt. 1982, Woman of Yr., Boston chpt. 1983), Am. Soc. Pub. Adminstrn. (life, region I-II liaison, sect. women in pub. adminstrn. 1988-90, Mass. chtp. coun. mem., officer, treas. 1997, sec. 1998, v.p. 1998—, pres. elect 1999, pres. 2000, nat coun. mem. campaign for internat. rels.), Boston Ctr. for Internat. Visitors, Charitable Irish Soc., Chatham Swim Club. Author: Boston Employment Service Guide, 1969, Careers and Training in the Allied Health Field, 1989, Higher Skills, Higher Wages and Higher Achievement, 1997, Career Families and Career Paths, 1997, Massachusetts Cities and Towns, 1978-82, Outplacement Program, 1993, Presentation and Performance Portfolio, 1998; editor Mass. Trends, 1978-82; contbr. articles to profl. jours. Home: 33 Morey Rd Roslindale MA 02131-1037 also: Eldredge Sq Chatham MA 02633 Office: 19 Staniford St Charles F Hurley Bldg Boston MA 02114

SULLIVAN, EARL LE ROY, political science educator, academic administrator; b. Anaconda, Mont., Aug. 11, 1942; s. Earl Richard Sullivan and Margaret Jones; m. Jean Ann Wendell, Aug. 10, 1963; children: Mark, Erin, Colin. BA in Polit. Sci., Seattle U., 1964; PhD in Internat. Rels., Claremont Grad. U., 1970. Asst. prof. U. Portland, Oreg., 1967-73, chair social sci., 1970-73; from asst. to full prof. Am. U., Cairo, 1973-99, chair polit. sci., 1994-97, provost, 1998—. Vis. scholar Von Grunebaum Ctr., UCLA, 1984-85, U. Utah, Salt Lake City, 1991-92. Author: Women in Egyptian Public Life, 1986, Social Background and Bureaucratic Behavior in Egypt, 1990; editor: Contemporary Study of the Arab World, 1991, Multilateral Diplomacy and the United Nations Today, 1999; chair editl. bd. Cairo Papers in Social Sci., 1982-84, 87-88. Mem. bd. trustees Cairo Am. Coll., 1974-84, chair bd. trustees, 1974-79. Mem. Am. Soc. Internat. Law, Middle East Studies Assn. Avocations: reading, hiking, camping, fishing, music. Office: Am Univ Cairo 113 Kasr el Aini Cairo Egypt E-mail: tims@aucegypt.edu.

SULLIVAN, EDWARD JOSEPH, lawyer, educator; b. Bklyn., Apr. 24, 1945; s. Edward Joseph and Bridget (Duffy) S.; m. Patte Hancock, Aug. 7, 1982; children: Amy Brase, Molly Elsasser, Mary Christine. BA, St. John's U., 1966; JD, Willamette U., 1969; MA, cert. Urban Studies, Portland State U., 1974; LLM, Univ. Coll., London, 1978; diploma in law, Univ. Coll., Oxford, 1984; MA, U. Durham, 1999. Bar: Oreg. 1969, D.C. 1978, Wash. 2001, U.S. Dist. Ct. Oreg. 1970, U.S. Ct. Appeals (9th cir.) 1970, U.S. Supreme Ct. 1972. Counsel Washington County, Hillsboro, Oreg., 1969-75; legal counsel Gov. of Oreg., Salem, 1975-77; ptnr. O'Donnell, Sullivan & Ramis, Portland, Oreg., 1978-84, Sullivan, Josselson, Roberts, Johnson & Kloos, Portland, Salem and Eugene, 1984-86, Mitchell, Lang & Smith, Portland, 1986-90, Preston Gates & Ellis, Portland, 1990—. Bd. dirs., pres. Oreg. Law Inst. Contbr. numerous articles to profl. jours. Chmn. Capitol Planning Commn., Salem, 1975-77, 78-81. Mem. ABA (local govt. sect., com. on planning and zoning, adminstrv. law sect.) Oreg. State Bar Assn., D.C. Bar Assn., Wash. State Bar Assn., Am. Judicature Soc., Am. Polit. Sci. Assn. Democrat. Roman Catholic. Office: Preston Gates & Ellis 222 SW Columbia Ste 1400 Portland OR 97201-6632 Business E-Mail: esulliva@prestongates.com.

SULLIVAN, EDWARD LAWRENCE, lawyer; b. Boston, May 8, 1955; s. Edward L. and Dorothy L. (Gregory) S.; m. Susan M. Griffin, Dec. 2, 1983; children: Erica A., Brittany M. BA in Polit. Sci., St. Anselm Coll., 1977; JD, St. Louis U., 1980. Bar: Mo. 1980, Mass. 1981, Ill. 1981, D.C. 1986. Atty., Ill. divsn. Peabody Coal Co., Fairview Heights, 1980-85; legis. counsel Peabody Holding Co., Washington, 1985-88; dir., legal and pub. affairs, western divsn. Peabody Coal Co., Flagstaff, Ariz., 1988-90; sr. counsel Peabody Holding Co., St. Louis, 1990-94; gen. counsel Powder River Coal Co., Gillette, Wyo., 1994-95; gen. counsel, western region Peabody Holding Co., St. Louis, 1995—2000, sr. counsel, 2000—. Industry rep. (alt.) royalty policy com. U.S. Dept. Interior, Washington, 1995—. Mem. Bar Assn. Met. St. Louis. Office: Peabody Holding Co Inc 701 Market St Ste 700 Saint Louis MO 63101-1895

SULLIVAN, EDWARD MICHAEL, lawyer; b. Boston, June 2, 1929; s. Edward M. and Isabelle C. (Cassidy) S. BA, Dartmouth Coll., 1949; LLB, Harvard Coll., 1952. Bar: N.Y. 1952, Mass. 1953. Assoc. Wickes, Riddell, et al, N.Y.C., 1952-55; asst. counsel Boston & Maine R.R., 1955-57; pvt. practice Boston, 1957—. Avocations: reading, travel, squash. Office: Edward M Sullivan 28 Exeter St Boston MA 02116-2841

SULLIVAN, ERNEST LEE, human resources director; b. Columbus, Ohio, Dec. 17, 1952; s. Robert Lee and Emma Jane (Phillips) S. BA, Capital U., Columbus, 1980. Cert. profl. in human resources. Mgmt. trainee Bank One Corp., Columbus, 1971-73, personnel generalist, 1973-77, profl. recruiter, 1977-79, employment mgr., 1979-81, v.p. employment mgr., 1981-87; mgr. staffing, employee rels. and labor rels. Rockwell Internat., 1988-96; v.p. of exec. selection, regional human resources dir. Banc One Corp., nat. staffing mgr., 1997—, sr. v.p. human resources. Personnel cons. Martin Luther King Ctr., Columbus, 1989—, bd. dirs.; advisor United Negro Coll. Fund, Columbus, 1983—; bus. adv. bd. Cen. State U., Wilberforce, Ohio, 1989—. Pres. bd. Jobs for Columbus Grads., 1995—, Urban Scouting Bd., 2000; pres. bd. dirs. St. Stephen's Cmty. House. Named to Hall of Fame Columbus Met. Housing, 1989-92; recipient Outstanding Bus. and Profl. award, 1993—, Pinnacle award, Eagle award, 1995, Lazarus award, 1997, Cultural Diversity Leadership award, 1998, Roosevelt Carter Cmty. Svc. award, 1999. Mem. Soc. Human Resources and Mgmt., Employment Mgrs. Assn., Personnel Soc. Columbus. Avocations: swimming, flag football, travel, japanese lang. study. Office: Bank One Corp 800 Brookedge Blvd Columbus OH 43271-0001

SULLIVAN, EUGENE JOHN JOSEPH, manufacturing company executive; b. N.Y.C., Nov. 28, 1920; s. Cornelius and Margaret (Smith) S.; m. Gloria Roesch, Aug. 25, 1943; children: Eugene John Joseph, Edward J., Robert C., Elizabeth Ann Hansler. BS, St. John's U., 1942, D in Commerce, 1973; MBA, NYU, 1948. With chem. divsn. Borden, Inc., N.Y.C., 1946—, beginning as salesman, successively asst. sales, 1957-58, exec. v.p., 1958-64; pres. Borden Chem. Co. divsn. Borden, Inc.; v.p. Borden, Inc., 1964-67, exec. v.p., 1967-73, pres., COO, 1973-79, chmn., pres., CEO, 1979-86; former adj. prof., prof. St. John's U., 1987—. Bd. dirs. W.R. Grace & Co.; chmn. bd. dirs. Hamilton Fund; trustee Atlantic Mut. Ins. Co. Trustee, vice chmn., past sec. St. John's U., chmn. bd. dirs., 1999—; trustee N.Y. Med. Coll., Cath. Health Assn., Cath. Charities U.S.A., 1999—; chmn. Commn. on Cath. Health Care. Served as lt. USNR, 1942-46; lt. Res. Mem. Coun. Fgn. Rels., Knights of Malta, Knights of Holy Sepulchre, Knights of St. Gregory, Univ. Club, Plandome Country Club, Westhampton Country Club.

SULLIVAN, EUGENE RAYMOND, federal judge; b. St. Louis, Aug. 2, 1941; s. Raymond Vincent and Rosemary (Kiely) S.; m. Lis Urup Johansen, June 18, 1966; children— Kim, Eugene II. BS, U.S. Mil. Acad., 1964; JD, Georgetown U., 1971. Bar: Mo. 1972, D.C. 1972. Law clk. to judge U.S. Ct. Appeals (8th cir.), St. Louis, 1971-72; assoc. Patton Boggs & Blow, Washington, 1972-74; asst. spl. counsel The White House, 1974; trial counsel U.S. Dept. of Justice, 1974-82; dep. gen. counsel U.S. Air Force, 1982-84, gen. counsel, 1984-86; gov. Wake Island, 1984-86; judge U.S. Ct. Appeals (Armed Forces), Washington, 1986-90, 95—, chief judge, 1990-95. Mem. Fed. Commn. To Study Honor Code at West Point, 1989-90. Trustee U.S. Mil. Acad., 1989—. With US Army, 1964-69. Decorated Bronze Star, Air medal, airborne badge, ranger badge, others. Republican. Roman Catholic. Home: 6307 Massachusetts Ave Bethesda MD 20816-1139 Office: US Ct Appeals (Armed Forces) 450 E St NW Washington DC 20442-0001

SULLIVAN, EVELIN ELISABETH, writer, educator; b. Munich, Mar. 20, 1947; came to the U.S., 1965; d. Harmon Edward Fennell and Irmgard Jones; m. Michael Kenneth Sullivan, Aug. 1, 1976. BA in Physics, U. Calif. San Diego, La Jolla, 1974, MS in Physics, 1976, PhD in English and Am. Lit., 1981. Writing tutor, cons. Stanford U., Sch. Engring., Calif., 1985—2002, lectr., 2002—. Author: The Dead Magician, 1989, The Correspondence, 1993, Games of the Blind, 1994, Four of Fools, 1995, The Concise Book of Lying, 2001. Mem. PEN, PEN Ctr. USA West, Authors Guild, Dalkey Archive Press (bd. mem., sec. 1994-2000). Avocations: running, hiking. E-mail: EvelinSull@aol.com.

SULLIVAN, FRANCIS ALFRED, priest, educator; b. Boston, May 21, 1922; s. George Bernard Sullivan and Bessie Henrietta Peterson. MA in Philosophy, Boston Coll., 1945; MA in Classics, Fordham U., 1948; STD in Theology, Gregorian U., Rome, 1956. Prof. Gregorian U., Rome, 1956-92, dean, faculty of theology, 1964-70; adj. prof. Boston Coll., Newton, Mass., 1992—. Author: Magisterium, 1983, Salvation Outside Church, 1992, Church We Believe In, 1988, Creative Fidelity, 1996. Mem. Cath. Theol. Soc. of Am. (John C. Murray award 1994). Home: 140 Commonwealth Ave Newton MA 02467 E-mail: sullivft@bc.edu.

SULLIVAN, G. CRAIG, household products executive; b. 1940; BS, Boston Coll., 1964. With Procter & Gamble Co., 1964-69, Am. Express Co., 1969-70; regional sales mgr. Clorox Co., Oakland, Calif., 1971-76, v.p. mktg., 1976-78, mgr. food svc. sales devel., mgr. bus. devel., 1978-79, gen. mgr. food svc. products divsn., 1979-81, v.p. food svc. products divsn., 1981, v.p. household products, 1981-89, group v.p. household products, 1989-92, chmn. bd., pres., CEO, 1992-99, chmn. bd., CEO, 1999—. Office: The Clorox Co 1221 Broadway Oakland CA 94612-1888*

SULLIVAN, GEORGE EDWARD, author; b. Lowell, Mass., Aug. 11, 1927; s. Timothy Joseph and Cecilia Mary (Shea) S.; m. Muriel Agnes Moran, May 24, 1952; 1 son, Timothy. BS, Fordham U., 1952. Pub. relations mgr. Popular Library, N.Y.C., 1952-55; pub. relations dir. AMF, 1955-63. Adj. prof. Fordham U. Author: numerous books including: Work When You Want to Work, 1985, The Thunderbirds, 1986, Work Smart, Not Hard, 1987, How the White House Really Works, 1988, Mikhail Gorbachev, 1988, The Day Man Walked on the Moon, 1989, All About Basketball, 1990, The Day They Bombed Pearl Harbor, 1991, Racing Indy Cars, 1992, Mathew Brady, His Life and Photographs, 1993, The Day Women Got the Vote, 1994, Black Artists in Photography, 1995, Alamo!, 1996, Not Guilty, 1997, Portraits of War, Civil War Photographers and Their Work, 1998, One Hundred Years in Photographs,

1999, Picturing Lincoln, 2000, The Civil War at Sea, 2001, Power Football, 2001, In Their Own Words: The Wright Brothers, 2002.. Served with USN, 1945-48. Mem. PEN, Authors Guild, Am. Soc. Journalists and Authors Roman Catholic. E-mail: gjsbooks@aol.com.

SULLIVAN, GEORGE MURRAY, transportation consultant, former mayor; b. Portland, Oreg., Mar. 31, 1922; s. Harvey Patrick and Viola (Murray) S.; m. Margaret Eagan, Dec. 30, 1947; children: Timothy M., Harvey P. (dec. July 1996), Daniel A., Kevin Shane, Colleen Marie, George Murray, Michael J., Shannon Margaret, Casey Eagan. Student pub. schs.; D.P.A. (hon.), U. Alaska, 1981. Line driver Alaska Freight Lines, Inc., Valdez-Fairbanks, 1942-44; U.S. dep. marshal Alaska Dist., Nenana, 1946-52; mgr. Alaska Freight Lines, 1952-56; Alaska gen. mgr. Consol. Freightways Corp. of Del., Anchorage, 1956-67; mayor of, 1967-82; exec. mgr. Alaska Bus. Council, 1968; sr. cons. to pres. Western Air Lines Inc., 1982-87; former legis. liaison for Gov. of Alaska; now cons. Past mem. Nat. Adv. Com. on Oceans and Atmosphere, Joint Fed.-State Land Use Planning Commn.; past chmn. 4-state region 10 adv. com. OEO; mem. Fairbanks City Council, 1955-59, Anchorage City Council, 1965-67, Greater Anchorage Borough Assembly, 1965-67, Alaska Ho. of Reps., 1964-65. Trustee U. Alaska Found.; chmn. Anchorage Conv. and Visitors Bur.; bd. dirs. Western council Boy Scouts Am., 1958-59. Served with U.S. Army, 1944-46. Mem. Nat. Def. Transp. Assn. (life mem., pres. 1962-63), Nat. League Cities (dir.), Pioneers of Alaska, Alaska Mcpl. League (past pres.), Anchorage C. of C. (exec. com. 1963-65, treas. 1965-66, dir.), Alaska Carriers Assn. (exec. com.), Alaska Transp. Conf. (chmn.), U.S. Conf. Mayors (exec. com.), VFW (comdr. Alaska 1952) Clubs: Elks. Home and Office: George M Sullivan Co 1345 W 12th Ave Anchorage AK 99501-4252 *America is truly the land of opportunity, and I feel that the success with which God has blessed my life attests to this fact. I have been blessed four times. Not only was I born in America, but I have lived my life in Alaska. My other two blessings are my wonderful and supportive wife and our eight healthy children.*

SULLIVAN, GREGORY PATRICK, research engineer; b. Boston, Aug. 10, 1963; s. Paul David and Thomasina Sullivan; m. Alisa Dean Sullivan, Aug. 19, 1989; children: Benjamin Patrick, Margaret Marie, Aidan Thomas. BS in Physics, U. Oreg., 1987; BSME, Oreg. State U., 1991; MS in Bldg. Engring., MIT, 1995. Market analyst Applied Strategies, Inc., Natick, Mass., 1985-91; sr. rsch. engr. Pacific N.W. Nat. Lab., Richland, Wash., 1991—. Contbr. articles to profl. jours. V.p., bd. dirs. Benton Affordable Housing Assn., Richland, Wash., 1999—; soccer coach Tri-City Youth Soccer Assn., Richland, 1998—. Mem. ASME, Am. Soc. Heating, Ventilation and Air Conditioning Engrs., Assn. Energy Engrs. Avocations: ice hockey, skiing, ultimate frisbee.

SULLIVAN, HARRY TRUMAN, research scientist; b. Camden, Ala., Mar. 21, 1952; s. Ernest Curley and Luticia Ann (Aaron) B.; m. Sandra Carol Jackson, Nov. 13, 1976; 1 child, Asha Nicole. AA, So. Tech. Inst., Marietta, Ga., 1976; BS in Computer Sci., Ga. State U., 1989. Instrumentation technician Ga. Power Co., Baxley, 1976-78; electronic technician Micromeritics Instrument Corp., Atlanta, 1978-80, GEC Avionics, Inc., Atlanta, 1980-82; electronic technician II Ga. Inst. of Tech., 1982—. Mem. IEEE, Assn. for Computing Machinery. Avocation: Tang Soo Do.

SULLIVAN, JAMES LEO, organization executive; b. Somerville, Mass., Dec. 11, 1925; s. James Christopher and Anna Agnes (Kilmartin) S.; m. Anne Dorothy Hevner, Jan. 20, 1951; children: Maura, Mark, Lianne, Christopher. BS in History and Govt. cum laude, Boston Coll., 1950, MEd in Adminstrn. and Fin., 1958; DCS (hon.), Suffolk U., 1990. Asst. town mgr., Arlington, Mass., 1957-62; town mgr. Watertown, Conn., 1962-65; chief adminstrv. officer Town of Milton, Mass., 1965-68; city mgr. Cambridge, 1968-70, 74-81, Lowell, 1970-74; sr. research asst. MIT, 1970-71; pres. Greater Boston C. of C., 1981-91, H.M.S. Mktg., Boston, 1991—. Chmn. Mass. Gov.'s Local Govt. Adv. Com., 1978; del. to Orgn. Econ. and Cooperative Devel., Paris, 1979; chmn. New Eng.-Can. Bus. Coun., 1983; pres. Careers for Later YEars, 1983; bd. dirs. Input-Output Computer Svcs., Imugen Inc., Mass. Bus. Devel. Corp. Trustee Emerson Coll., 1984-88, mem. fin. and investment com., 1985-88; bd. dirs. Bunker Hill Community Coll. Found., 1988—; mem. Adv. Com. on Reorgn. of Mass. Ct. System, 1991—, chmn. budget subcom. 1991—; bd. overseers Univ. Hosp. Boston. With USN, 1943-46. Mem. Mass. League of Cities and Towns (pres. 1978), Mass. Mayors Assn., Internat. City Mgmt. Assn., Nat. League Cities, Am. C. of C. Execs. (bd. dirs. 1988—). Clubs: World Trade (bd. govs. 1986—). Office: HMS Mktg 65 Franklin St Boston MA 02110-1303

SULLIVAN, JAMES EDWARD, poet; b. Cohasset, Mass., July 11, 1928; s. James J. Jr. and E. Louise (Hyland) S.; m. Frances Elizabeth Lynch, Aug. 11, 1963 (dec. Oct. 1976); children: Julia Marietta, John Franklin Joseph. AB, Boston Coll., 1948, MA, 1950. Dir. Woods Meml. Libr., Barre, Mass., 1967-94; ptnr. Crisis and Climax, 1989—. Lectr. in history, Boston Coll., 1962-63. Author: American Town: Barre, Mass., 1774-1994, 1974, In Order of Appearance: 400 Poems, 1988; numerous poems, plays. Selectman, Town of Barre, 1986-92, bd. chmn., 1988-92. Sergeant U.S. Army, 1950-52. Democrat. Roman Catholic. Home: PO Box 451 Barre MA 01005-0451

SULLIVAN, JAMES F. physicist, educator; b. Cin., Mar. 7, 1943; s. James E. and Alma L. (Lienesch) S.; m. Sylvia J. Kasselmann, Aug. 16, 1969; 1 child, Robert L. BS, Xavier U., 1965, MS, 1969. Instr. physics Brebeuf Prep. Sch., Indpls., 1965-67, OMI Coll. Applied Sci., U. Cin., 1968-71, asst. prof. physics, 1971-77, assoc. prof. physics, 1977-88, prof. physics, 1988—; dept. head math., physics, computing tech. U. Cin. OMI Coll. of Applied Sci., 2002. Summer faculty researcher Solar Energy Rsch. Inst., Golden, Colo., 1980; mem. high sch. evaluation team N. Ctrl. Assn., Cin., 1983-85; vis. prof. Arcada Polytechnic Inst., Finland, (Jan-May, 2001). Author: Technical Physics, 1988; Co-author: Laboratory Manual for General Physics, 1973, 83, 90, 92, Physics for Technology Laboratory Manual, 1995, 97. Organizer of events St. Xavier H.S. Alumni, Cin., 1983—; vol. examiner Am. Radio Relay League for U.S. Fed. Comm. Commn., Newington, Conn., 1984—; judge physics category Ohio State Sci. Fair, Delaware, Ohio, 1986—; chief negotiator faculty and librs. U. Cin., 1995. Received John B. Hart award (disting. svc. to Southern Ohio sect. of Am. Assn. of Physics Tchrs.), 2001; named Faculty Mem. of Yr., Gamma Alpha chpt. Tau Alpha Phi, 1983. Fellow Ohio Acad. Sci.; mem. AAUP (v.p. U. Cin. chpt. 1994-96), Am. Assn. Physics Tchrs. (founder, past pres., assoc. sec. So. Ohio sect. 1993—, com. on instrnl. media 1994-98, chief organizer and presenter Fundamentals of Radio workshop Toronto 1985, Columbus, Ohio 1986, Bozeman, Mont. 1987, Orono, Maine 1992, Boise, Idaho 1993, South Bend, Ind. 1994, College Park, Md. 1996, Denver, 1997, com. on metric measurements, 2000-03), Ohio Valley Amateur Radio Assn. (pres. 1997—), Am. Soc. Engring. Edn. Achievements include supervising successful attempt of OMI Coll. Applied Sci. contact of shuttle Challenger during STS-51F mission, 1985. Office: Univ Cin 2220 Victory Pkwy Cincinnati OH 45206-2822

SULLIVAN, JAMES GERALD, business owner, postal letter carrier; b. Bad Axe, Mich., Sept. 13, 1935; s. John Thomas and Frances Eugena (O'Henley) S.; m. Florence Marie Tack, Sept. 12, 1959; children: Kevin Michael, Kathleen Marie. Student. U. Detroit, 1957-58, Highland Park Coll., 1959-60. Owner Jerry's Barber Shop, Kinde, Bad Axe, Mich., 1963-66, 79—; purchasing agt. Thumb Elec. Coop., Ubly, 1966-79, Walbro Corp., Cass City, 1979-80; sales rep. Thumb Blanket, Bad Axe, 1980-81, Sta. WLEW, Bad Axe, 1981-82; regional mgr. Pri Am. Fin. Svcs., 1985—; treas. Colfax Twp., 1979-90; rural letter carrier U.S. Postal Svc., 1982-98, ret., 1998. Loss clk., Toplis & Harding Wagner & Gliddon, Detroit, 1959-61; inventory control clk., Carrick Products Co., Royal Oak, Mich., 1957-59. Pres., Huron County (Mich.) Twp. Assn., 1988-90; leader Boy Scouts Am., Bad Axe,1975-77. Served in U.S. Army, 1954-56. Mem. Huron County Rural Letter Carriers Assn. (pres. 1990—), Armed Forces Vets. Club of the Nat. Rural Letter Carriers Assn. (Mich. divsn., state sec. 1999—), Am. Legion, 4-H Club (pres. 1948-50), Lions (pres. 1979-80), Cmty. Club (pres. 1976-77), KC (mem. coun. #1546), Ushers Club Sacred Heart Ch. Republican. Roman Catholic. Avocations: gardening, golf, swimming, snowmobiling, fishing. Home: 122 W Richardson Rd Bad Axe MI 48413-9108

SULLIVAN, JAMES KIRK, management consultant; b. Greenwood, S.C., Aug. 25, 1935; s. Daniel Jones and Addie (Brown) S.; m. Elizabeth Miller, June 18, 1960; children: Hal N., Kim J. BS in Chemistry, Clemson U., 1957, MS, 1964, PhD, 1966; postgrad. program for sr. execs., MIT, 1975; DSc (hon.), U. Idaho, 1990. Prodn. supr. FMC Corp., South Charleston, W.Va., 1957-62, tech. supt. Pocatello, Idaho, 1966-69, mktg. mgr. N.Y.C., 1969-70; v.p. govtl. and environ. affairs Boise (Idaho) Cascade Corp., 1970-98; pres., CEO Veritas Advisors, LLP, 1999—; exec. com., chmn. trust and investment com., dist. bd. dirs. Key Bank of Idaho, 1983—90. Bd. dirs., chmn. audit com. Key Trust Co. of the West; chmn. adv. bd. U. Idaho Coll. Engring., 1966-70, 80-87, centennial campaign, 1987-89, rsch. found., 1980-82; mem. Accreditation Bd. Engring. and Tech., Inc., 1994-99; bd. dirs. Pub. Employees Retirement Sys. of Idaho, St. Al's Regional Med. Ctr. Contbr. articles to profl. jours.; patentee in field. Mem. Coll. of Forest and Recreation Resources com. Clemson U., Idaho Found. for Pvt. Enterprise and Econ. Edn., Idaho Rsch. Found., Inc., Idaho Task Force on Higher Edn.; bd. dirs. Idaho Found. for Excellence in Higher Edn., Exptl. Program to Stimulate Competitive Rsch. NSF, N.W. Nazarene Coll., 1988-90, Boise Philharm., 1996-99, mem. Len B. Jordan Pub Affairs Symposium; trustee Idaho Children's Emergency Fund, 1984-90; trustee Bishop Kelly H.S., 1987-89; chmn. adv. bd. U. Idaho Coll. Engring., Am. Forest and Paper Assn., Govtl. Affairs Com., Environ. Com., Options Adv. Group; bd. dirs. Boise Master Chorale, 1995-98; pres. Ore-Ida coun. Boy Scouts Am., St. Al's Found.; bd. trustees The Heard Mus., 2000—. 1st lt. U.S. Army, 1958-59. Recipient Presdl. Citation U. Idaho, 1990. Mem. AIChE, Am. Chem. Soc., Bus. Week Found. (chmn. Bus. Week 1980), Am. Forest and Paper Assn. (environ. and health coun., product and tech. com., solid waste task force), Bus. Roundtable (environ. com.), Idaho Assn. Commerce and Industry (past chmn. bd. dirs.), C. of C. of U.S. (pub. affairs com.). Republican. Home: 5206 Sorrento Cir Boise ID 83704-2347 Office: Veritas Advisors LLP 802 W Bannock St Ste 401 Boise ID 83702-5841 E-mail: j.kirksullivan@worldnet.att.net., kirk@veritasadvisor.com.

SULLIVAN, JAMES LENOX, clergyman; b. Silver Creek, Miss., Mar. 12, 1910; s. James Washington and Mary Ellen (Dampeer) S.; m. Velma Scott, Oct. 22, 1935; children: Mary Beth (Mrs. Bob R. Taylor), Martha Lynn (Mrs. James M. Porch, Jr.), James David. BA, Miss. Coll., 1932, D.D., 1948; Th.M., So. Bapt. Theol. Sem., 1935. Ordained to ministry of Bapt. Ch., 1930, pastor, 1932-33, Beaver Dam, 1933-38, Ripley, Tenn., 1938-40, Clinton, Miss., 1940-42, First Bapt. Ch., Brookhaven, 1942-46, Belmont Heights, Nashville, 1946-50, Abilene, Tex., 1950-53; exec. sec., treas. Bapt. Sunday Sch. Bd., Nashville, 1953-73, pres., 1973-75; with Broadman Press, 1953-75; exec. sec. Convention Press, 1955-75; pres. So. Bapt. Conv., 1977. Author: Your Life and Your Church, 1950, John's Witness of Jesus, Memos for Christian Living, Reach Out, Rope of Sand with Strength of Steel, God Is My Record, Baptist Polity As I See It, Southern Baptist Polity at Work in a Church; also articles and manuals. Trustee Union U., Cumberland U., So. Bapt. Theol. Sem., Hardin-Simmons U., Midstate (Tenn.) Bapt. Hosp., Hendrick Meml. Hosp., Tex.; chmn. long-range planning com. City of Nashville. Recipient E.Y. Mullins Denominational Service award, 1973; named Miss. Bapt. Clergyman of Century Mem. Baptist World Alliance (exec. com. 1953-80, v.p. 1970-75). Clubs: Rotary (Ripley, Tenn.); Lions (Brookhaven, Miss.); Kiwanis (Abilene, Tex.).

SULLIVAN, JAMES NELSON, physician; b. Greenville, S.C., Dec. 19, 1946; s. Edgar Nelson and Henrietta Barnwell Sullivan; m. Margaret E. Sullivan, June 10, 1989; children: Frank, Lily, Emma, Julia. BA, U. of the South, 1965; MD, Vanderbilt U., 1974. Med. resident Vanderbilt Hosp., Nashville, 1974—76, 1979—81; endocrinology fellow NIH, 1976—79; instr. in medicine Vanderbilt U., Nashville, 1980-83, clin. assoc. prof. medicine, 1985—; clin. instr. Meharry Med. Coll., 1998—, U. Tenn., Nashville, 1983—. Chair ethics com. Bapt. Hosp., 1994-99. Dir. Living Will Project, Nashville, 1997-99; founder Soc. for the Preservation of the Book of Common Prayer, Nashville, 1970-74. Fellow ACP; mem. The Endocrine Soc. (comms. com. 1990-98), Nashville Acad. Medicine (bd. dirs. 1999-2002), Alpha Omega Alpha. Avocations: fishing, reading. Office: Nashville Med Group # 700 300 20th Ave N Ste 700 Nashville TN 37203-2117 E-mail: jsullivan@pol.net.

SULLIVAN, JAMES STEPHEN, retired bishop; b. Kalamazoo, July 23, 1929; s. Stephen James and Dorothy Marie (Bernier) S. Student, St. Joseph Sem.; BA, Sacred Heart Sem.; postgrad., St. John Provincial Sem. Ordained priest, Roman Cath. Ch., 1955, consecrated bishop, 1972. Assoc. pastor St. Luke Ch., Flint, Mich., 1955-58, St. Mary Cathedral, Lansing, 1958-60, sec. to bishop, 1960-61; assoc. pastor St. Joseph (Mich.) Ch., 1961-65, sec. to bishop, 1965-69; assoc. pastor Lansing, 1965; vice chancellor, 1969-72; aux. bishop, vicar gen. Diocese of Lansing, 1972-85, diocesan consultor, 1971-85; bishop Fargo, ND, 1985—2002; ret., 2002. Pres. World Apostolate Fatima; episc. liaison Cath. Mktg. Network; nat. episcopal liaison to the Cath. Cursillo Movement. Mem. U.S. Conf. Cath. Bishops. Office: Church of the Holy Spirit 1420 7th St N Fargo ND 58102

SULLIVAN, JERRY STEPHEN, electronics company executive; b. Havre, Mont., July 17, 1945; s. Patrick Joseph and Evangeline (O'Neil) S.; m. Sharon Lee Horton, June 17, 1967; children: Garrett, Mindy, Darren. BS, U. Colo., 1967, MS, 1969, PhD, 1970; advanced mgmt. program, Harvard U. Bus. Sch., 1986. Tech. mgr. N.V. Philips Co., Eindhoven, The Netherlands, 1971-75; group dir. N.Am. Philips Corp., Briarcliff Manor, N.Y., 1975-80; dir. Tektronix, Beaverton, Oreg., 1981-83, div. gen. mgr., 1983-85, corp. dir., 1985-88; v.p. Microelectronics & Computer Tech. Corp., Austin, Tex., 1988-92; pres., CEO, Design Techs. Inc., 1992—. Chmn. bd. MBA Techs., Inc., Phoenix; bd. dirs. Sherpa Corp., San Jose, Calif., Ontos, Inc. Boston, MBA Tech. Inc., Phoenix; mem. adv. bd. Ctr. Integrated Sys., Stanford U., Palo Alto, Calif., 1982—. Mem. adv. com. Coll. Engring., U. Tex., Austin, 1989—, bd. dirs. Edn. Found., 1990—. Mem. IEEE, Am. Phys. Soc., Assn. Computing Machinery, Am. Mgmt. Assn., Nat. Assn. Corp. Dirs. Avocations: scuba diving, golf, chess, sailing. Office: Design Techs Inc 107 Ranch Rd 620 S Austin TX 78734-3942

SULLIVAN, JERRY WARNER, educator, physician; b. Madisonville, Ky., Sept. 26, 1942; s. Henry Warner and Elsie (Lutz) S.; m. Judith Allen, June 13, 1964 (div. May 1988); children: Suzanne Robin, John Christopher. BS, Georgetown Coll., 1964; MD, U. Louisville, 1968. Intern San Diego Naval Hosp., 1968-69; resident in surgery Med. Sch. Tulane U., New Orleans, 1971-72, resident in urology Med. Sch., 1972-76; fellow in urology Sloan Kettering Meml. Hosp., N.Y.C., 1976-77; instr. in urology Med. Sch. La. State U., New Orleans, 1977-78, asst. prof., 1978-82, assoc. prof., 1982-87, chmn. dept. urology, 1984—, prof., 1987—. Sec. La. Lithotripter, Inc., New Orleans, 1987-91; sec.-treas. med. staff Hotel Dieu Hosp., New Orleans, 1985-90, pres. med. staff, 1991-92, bd. dirs., 1990. Bd. dirs. YMCA, New Orleans, 1980—; bd. dirs. La. State U. Clinic, 1987-95, chmn., 1990-92. Mem. AMA, ACS, Am. Urologic Assn., Soc. Surg. Oncologists, Southeastern Sect. Am. Urologic Assn., Southwest Oncology Group, Am. Soc. Clin. Oncology. Avocations: jogging, weight lifting, swimming, biking. Office: La State U Med Sch Dept of Urology 1542 Tulane Ave New Orleans LA 70112-2825 Home: 1750 St Charles Ave # 420 New Orleans LA 70130

SULLIVAN, JIM, artist; b. Providence, Apr. 1, 1939; s. James Henry, Jr. and Frances Winifred (Welch) S.; m. Marie-Louise Paulson. BFA, R.I. Sch. Design, 1961; postgrad., Stanford U., 1962-63. Prof. emeritus art Bard Coll., Annandale-on-Hudson, N.Y., 1966-95, prof. emeritus, 1995—. Pres. bd. dirs. Schoharie Land Trust; juror Fulbright Fellowship Program, 1998. One-man shows Paley and Lowe Gallery, N.Y.C., 1971, 73, Henri Gallery, Washington, 1974, Fischback Gallery, N.Y.C., 1974, Willard Gallery, N.Y.C., 1978, Nancy Hoffman Gallery, N.Y.C., 1980, 82, 84, 86, 88, Foker Skulima Gallery, Berlin, Germany, Anne Jaffe Gallery Bay Harbor Islands, Fla. 1990; exhibited in group shows including, Whitney Mus., Mus. Modern Art, Columbus Gallery Fine Arts, Worcester Art Mus., Corcoran Gallery Art, Washington; pub. collections including Met. Mus., Whitney Mus., Albany State Mus., Wadsworth Atheneum, Philip Morris INc., Owens Corning Coll., Amerada Hess. Fulbright Nomination juror, 1998, 99, 2000. Recipient Hinda and Richard Rosenthal award Am. Acad. Arts and Letters, 1973; Stanford grantee, 1962-63; R.I. Sch. Design European Honors program Rome, 1960-61; Fulbright fellow, Paris; Fulbright fellow, 1961-62; Guggenheim fellow, 1972-73; grantee Nat. Endowment for Arts, 1982. Home: 59 Wooster St New York NY 10012-4349 also: Box 212 Rum Hill Rd Jefferson NY 12093

SULLIVAN, JOHN A. congressman; b. Tulsa, Okla. m. Judy Beck; children: Tommy Beck, Meredith Beck, Sydney Beck. BBA, Northeastern Okla. State U. Congressman Okla. Dist., 2002—. Republican. Achievements include working with civic officials at Okalhoma State University and the University of Oklahoma to create Okla. State U., Tulsa sponsoring the largest tax cut in state history; fighting to eliminate the state sales tax on groceries and over-the-counter drugs; passing the Parental Notification Bill for minors seeking abortions. Office: Congress 106 Cannon Ho HOB Washington DC 20515 Office Fax: 202-225-9187.*

SULLIVAN, JOHN CORNELIUS, JR. lawyer; b. Erie, Pa., Oct. 23, 1927; s. John Cornelius and Catherine J. (Carney) S.; m. Helen E. Kennedy, Feb. 3, 1951; children: John III, Timi Ann, Michael, Elizabeth. BA in Econs., Allegheny Coll., 1953; LLB, Dickinson Sch. Law, 1959. Bar: Pa. 1960, U.S. Supreme Ct. 1976. Sales rep. IBM Corp., 1953-56; mem. firm Nissley, Clecker & Fearen, Harrisburg, Pa., 1959-63; ptnr. Nauman, Smith, Shissler & Hall, 1964—. Asst. city solicitor City of Harrisburg, 1964-68, city solicitor, 1968-70; gen. counsel Harrisburg Redevel. Authority, 1964-68, Harrisburg Mcpl. Authority, 1964-87; solicitor Silver-Spring Twp., 1970-81; dir. accounts and fin. City of Harrisburg, 1963; mem. Pa. House of Reps., 1963-64. Assoc. editor Dickinson Law Rev., 1958-59; editor Dauphin County Reporter, 1961-63. Chmn. bd. dirs. Harrisburg Pub. Library, 1965-73; bd. dirs., sec. Harrisburg Hosp.; bd. dirs. Harrisburg Hosp. Found., 1975-89. Mem. ABA, Pa. Bar Assn., Dauphin County Bar Assn. (past. dir.), The Pa. Soc. (N.Y.C.), Phi Gamma Delta. Home: 107 Sample Bridge Rd Mechanicsburg PA 17050-1940 Office: 200 N 3rd St Fl D18 Harrisburg PA 17101-1518

SULLIVAN, JOHN LOUIS, JR. retired search company executive; b. Macon, Ga., Aug. 27, 1928; s. John Louis and Elizabeth (Macken) S.; m. Barbara Boyle, Aug. 17, 1974; children: John, Katherine, Betsy, Ted. AB in Econs., Duke U., 1950; MBA, U. Pa., 1957; postgrad. Advance Mgmt. Program, Harvard U., 1975. Br. mgr. IBM, Phila., 1962-63, mgr. edn. Endicott, N.Y., 1963-64; asst. to pres. Data Procesing Div. IBM, White Plains, 1965-67; dist. mgr. Data Processing Div. IBM, Washington, 1967-69; mgr. eastern and fed. regions Memorex Corp., 1969-71; v.p. mktg. Infonet div. Computer Sci. Corp., El Segundo, Calif., 1971-75; exec. v.p. Fin. Service Group-ADP Inc., Clifton, N.J., 1975-77; sr. v.p. Heidrick & Struggles Inc., San Francisco and Los Angeles, 1977-82, dir., 1977-82, office mgr., 1979-82; v.p., mng. dir. Korn-Ferry Internat., Los Angeles, 1982-87, v.p., mng. ptnr. Boston, 1987-94; ret., 1994. Bd. dirs., mem. exec. com. March of Dimes, Los Angeles County; bd. regents Mount St. Mary's Coll., Los Angeles. Served to lt. (j.g.) USN, 1950-53. Mem. Harvard U. Bus. Sch. Alumni Assn. (dir.). Clubs: Regency (Los Angeles), Bankers (San Francisco), Atheneum (Pasadena), Mission Hills (Rancho Mirage), Calif. Yacht (Los Angeles), Harvard (Boston), Newcomers (pres.), Rotary (bd. dirs.). Democrat.

SULLIVAN, JOHN MATTHEW, mathematician, educator; b. Princeton, N.J., Feb. 25, 1963; s. Roger D. and Margaret Gummere (Peplow) S. AB summa cum laude, Harvard U., 1985; cert. of advanced studies in math., Cambridge (Eng.) U., 1986; PhD, Princeton (N.J.) U., 1990. Software cons. Marble Assocs., Waltham, Mass., 1984-91; asst. prof. math. U. Minn., Mpls., 1991-97, U. Ill., Urbana, 1977-2000, assoc. prof. math., 2000—. Contbr. articles to profl. jours. Recipient Arnold O. Beckman rsch. award, 1997-99; Henry Cambridge U. fellow, 1985-86, NSF grad. fellow, 1986-89, Alfred P. Sloan doctoral dissertation fellow, 1989-90, Geometry Computing Group postdoctoral fellow, 1990-93, Math. Scis. Rsch. Inst. postdoctoral fellow, 1993-94. Mem. Am. Math. Soc., Math. Assn. Am. Achievements include research in minimal surfaces, knot theory and computational and optimal geometry. Office: U Ill Dept Math 250 Altgeld Hall 1409 W Green St Urbana IL 61801-2943 E-mail: jms@uiuc.edu.

SULLIVAN, JOSEPH PETER, risk and insurance management consultant; b. Boston, Sept. 8, 1939; s. Joseph Francis and Mary Anna S.; m. Rachael Anne Cullen, Dec. 22, 1974; children: Philip, Sandra, Susan, Frederick. B Gen. Studies, U. Nebr., 1968; MA, U. No. Colo., 1973, Cen. Mich. U., 1976. Sr. acct. exec. Arkwright Ins., Greenwich, Conn., 1977-83; v.p. Frenkel & Co., N.Y.C., 1983-84; sr. account exec. Republic Hogg Robinson, 1984-85; v.p. Alexander & Alexander, 1985-92, Hugh Wood Inc., N.Y.C., 1992-93, Crawford-THG, N.Y.C., 1993-98; sr. v.p. Frontline Ins. Mgrs., Tampa, Fla., 1998—. Assoc. Miller-Heiman Internat., 1986-92; instr. Dale Carnegie and Assocs., 1980-87; ajd. prof. ins. The Coll. of Ins., N.Y.C., 1991-98. Mem. membership com. Met. Rep. Club; bd. advisors The Salvation Army. With U.S. Army, 1956-77, ETO, Korea and Vietnam. With U.S. Army, 1956—77, with ETO, Korea and Vietnam. Decorated Bronze Star. Mem. Soc. Human Resource Mgmt., Assn. Former Intelligence Officers (life), Ret. Officers Assn. (bd. dirs. Knickerbocker chpt.), Soc. CPCU's, Am. Soc. CLU's, Nat. Assn. Health Underwriters, Profl. Liability Underwriting Soc., N.Y. Soc. Security Analysts, Soc. Competitive Intelligence Profls., Toastmasters, N.Y. Athletic Club, Rotary, Masons, Shriners. Republican. Roman Catholic. Avocations: American history, photography, collecting old photographic prints and antique photographic equipment. Home: 15920 Dawson Ridge Dr Tampa FL 33647-1324 Office: Frontline Ins Mgrs 8875 Hidden River Pkwy Ste 300 Tampa FL 33637-2087

SULLIVAN, JUDITH PATRICE, social worker; b. Texarkana, Ark., Jan. 28, 1945; d. Joseph and Agnes (Wilson) Eldridge; m. J.P. Sullivan, Apr. 4, 1966 (div. 1972). BA, U. Tex., 1966; MSW, SUNY, Buffalo, 1972; cert. legal asst., VTI Inst., Dallas, 1987. Diplomate Nat. Assn. Social Work; licensed master social work, advanced clin. practitioner. Counseling supr. Erie Med. Ctr., Buffalo, 1972-74; prog. dir. child psychiatry Buffalo Children's Hosp., 1974-80; clin. assoc. prof. psychiatry, pediat. SUNY Sch. of Medicine, Buffalo, 1974-80; pvt. practice, 1980-86, Dallas, 1988—; social worker Adoption Advisory, Inc., 1988-90, Dallas County Mental Health/MR, Dallas, 1990-91; pvt. practice DeSoto, Tex., 1991—. Home: 4719 Cole Ave Apt 124 Dallas TX 75205-3558

SULLIVAN, KAREN LAU, real estate company executive, campaign consultant, federal commissioner; b. Honolulu, Jan. 21, 1948; d. Ralph Karn Yee and Beatrice (Loo) Lau; m. Paul Dennis Sullivan, Apr. 24, 1976. BA, Whittier Coll., 1970; MA, U. Hawaii, 1987. Staff asst. to Congresswoman Patsy Mink U.S. Ho. Reps., Washington, 1974, staff asst. subcom. mines and mining, 1975-77, legis. asst. to Congressman Cec. Heftel, 1977-79; spl. asst. to asst. to Pres. for policy and women's affairs The White House, 1979; spl. asst. office of sec. of transp. U.S. Dept. Transp., 1979-81; regional dir. mid-Atlantic states Mondale-Ferraro Presdl. Campaign, 1984; dep. nat. field dir. Paul Simon Presdl. Campaign, 1987-88; Ill. dir. forum inst. Martin & Glantz Polit. Cons., San Francisco, 1988; regional dir. western states Clinton-Gore Presdl. Campaign, Little Rock, 1992; dep. dir. for pub. outreach Office of Pres.-Elect Bill Clinton, Little Rock/Washington, 1992-93; v.p. Hoaloha Ventures, Inc., Honolulu, 1981—. U.S. alt. rep. South Pacific Commn., 1995-99, U.S. rep. Pacific Cmty., 1999-2001. Mem. Carter/Mondale Alumni Fund, The Carter Ctr. Avocations: downhill skiing, auto racing. Home and Office: 149 Kaimoani Way Kailua HI 96734-1600

SULLIVAN, KATHLEEN N. political organization administrator, lawyer; b. Manchester, N.H., June 21, 1954; Student, Georgetown U.; BA cum laude, Coll. Holy Cross, 1976; JD, Cornell U., 1981. Bar: N.H. 1981. Chair N.H. Dem. Party, Concord. Bd. dirs. Fed. Home Loan Bank of Boston. Trustee Manchester Pub. Lib.; former mem. Mancester charter commn. N.H. Juvenile Parole Bd.; past. treas., dir. N.H. Women's Lobby; past dir. YWCA, Manchester. Mem. N.H. Bar Assn. Office: 192 S Mammoth Rd Manchester NH 03109-4908 also: 43 Centre St Concord NH 03301*

SULLIVAN, KATHRYN ANN, librarian, educator; b. Elmhurst, Ill., Jan. 22, 1954; d. Joseph Terrence and Rose Marie (Wright) S. Student, Triton Jr. Coll., 1972-73; BA, No. Ill. U., 1975, MLS, 1977; D of Sci. in Info. Sci., Nova U., 1991. Chief periodicals clk. No. Ill. U., Dekalb, 1976-77; periodicals librarian West Chgo. (Ill.) Pub. Library, 1977-78, Winona (Minn.) State U., 1978-99, distance learning libr., 2000—. Contbr. articles and short stories to profl. publs. Grantee Winona State U., 1986, 88, 92, 94. Mem.: ALA, Electronically Published Internet Connections, Minn. Libr. Assn. Avocation: writing. Home: 670 Winona St Winona MN 55987-3353

SULLIVAN, KENNETH W. engineer; b. N.Y.C., Apr. 15, 1957; s. William A. and Helen J. Sullivan; m. Christina A. Eastwood, Sept. 10, 1983 (div. Apr. 1997); children: Daniel, Sarah. AAS, SUNY, Farmingdale, 1978, student, 1998—. Draftsman, jr. designer Cosentini Assocs., N.Y.C., NY; sr. designer Syska & Hennessy Engrs.; project engr. Sikorski Engring. Assn., Jericho, Lehr

Assocs., N.Y.C., Sear Brown, Melville. Prin. works include Am. Sch. and Univ. Archtl. Portfolio, 1997. Assoc. Nat. Trust for Hist. Preservation, Washington, 1998. Mem.: Am. Soc. Heating, Refrigerating and Air Conditioning Engrs. Roman Catholic. Avocations: reading, history, music, running. Home: 21 Ferney St Hicksville NY 11801-5147 Office: Sear Brown Group Ste 301 201 Old Country Rd Melville NY 11747

SULLIVAN, KEVIN B. state legislator; b. Hartford, Conn., Aug. 20, 1949; s. John (dec.) and Gwendolyn Price (Bancroft) S.; m. Carolyn Thornberry, 1985. AB, Trinity Coll., 1971; JD, U. Conn., 1982. Polit. cons. in pvt. practice, West Hartford, Conn., 1973-74; adminstrv. clk. edn. com. Conn. Ho. of Reps., Hartford, 1974-76; legis. asst. State Commr. Edn., 1976-81; atty. Byrn Slater Sandler Shulman & Rouse, Hartford, 1981—; councilman Town of West Hartford, 1981-86, mayor, 1983-85, dep. mayor, 1985-86; mem. Dist. 5 Conn. Senate, Hartford, 1986—, Pro Tempore, 1997—. Chmn. edn. com., mem. internship and transp. coms., dep. minority leader Conn. State Senate. Mem. ABA, Hartford Bar Assn., Greater Hartford Jaycees (Man of Yr. 1983), Pi Gamma Mu. Founded State Capitol Vietnam Veterens Meml. Democrat. Office: Conn State Senate Rm 3300 Legislative Office Bldg Hartford CT 06106 E-mail: kevin.b.sullivan@po.state.ct.us.*

SULLIVAN, KEVIN PATRICK, lawyer; b. Waterbury, Conn., June 9, 1953; s. John Holian Sullivan and Frances (McGrath) Coon; m. Peggy Hardy, June 13, 1975 (div. Jan. 1985); m. Jarnine Welker, Feb. 15, 1985; children: S. Craig Lemmon, Michael Scott Lemmon, Lindsay Michelle Lemmon. BS in Polit. Sci., BS in Police Sci. cum laude, Weber State Coll., 1979; JD, Pepperdine U., 1982. Bar: Utah 1982, U.S. Dist. Ct. Utah 1982, U.S. Ct. Appeals (10th cir.) 1986, U.S. Supreme Ct. 1986. Assoc. Farr, Kaufman & Hamilton, Ogden, Utah, 1982-87; ptnr. Farr, Kaufman, Hamilton, Sulivan, Gorman & Perkins, 1987-91, Farr, Kaufman, Sullivan, Gorman & Perkins, Ogden, 1991—. Judge pro tem Utah 2d Cir. Ct.; city prosecutor of South Ogden, 1990-92. Mem. Eccles Community Art Ctr., Victim's Rights Com. of 2d Jud. Dist. Mem. ABA (criminal justice sect., litigation sect., justice and edn. fund lawyers' coun.), ACLU, ATLA, Utah Bar Assn. (criminal law, young lawyer, litigation sects., unauthorized practice law com.), Utah Trial Lawyers Assn., Utah Assn. Criminal Def. Lawyers, Weber County Bar Assn. (criminal law sect., pres.-elect 1993, pres. 1994), Weber County Pub. Defenders Assn. (assoc. dir. 1987), Weber State Coll. Alumni Assn., Amicus Pepperdine, Elks, Kiwanis, Phi Kappa Phi. Mem. Lds Ch. Avocations: skiing, golf, tennis, fishing. Home: 2731 E 6425 S Ogden UT 84403-5461 Office: Farr Kaufman Sullivan Gorman & Perkins 205 26th St Ste 34 Ogden UT 84401-3109 E-mail: KevinSullivan@qwest.net.

SULLIVAN, LARRY EDWARD, librarian; b. Chgo., June 6, 1944; s. George A. and Veronica B. (Cibulka) S.; children: Mara, Alene and Elena. BA, DePaul U., 1966; Fulbright fellow, U. Poitiers, France, 1966-67; MA, Johns Hopkins U., 1970, PhD, 1975. Asst. prof. history Western Md. Coll., Westminster, 1975-76; libr. dir. Md. State Penitentiary, Balt., 1977-78; head libr. Md. Hist. Soc., 1978-80, N.Y. Hist. Soc., N.Y.C., 1980-84; prof., chief libr. Lehman Coll., CUNY, Bronx, N.Y., 1984-89; chief Rare Book and Spl. Collections div. Libr. of Congress, Washington, 1989-95, chief rare book and spl. collections divsn., 1989-95; prof., chief librarian John Jay Coll. of Criminal Justice, N.Y., 1995—; prof. criminal justice Grad. Sch. and Univ. Ctr. CUNY. Mem. editl. bd. Book History, Ency. of Crime and Punishment, Crime and Justice in New York City; editor-in-chief Ency. Law Enforcement; author/co-editor: Guide to the Research Collections of the Maryland Historical Soc., 1981, The Prison Reform Movement: Forlorn Hope, Boston, 1990, rev. edit., 2002, Library of Congress Rare Books and Special Collections: An Illustrated Guide, 1992, Pioneers, Passionate Ladies and Private Eyes: Dime Novels, Series Books and Paperbacks, 1996; contbr. articles to profl. jours., chpts. to books in field. Fellowship NDEA, 1967-71; grantee George N. Shuster Publs., 1989. Mem. ALA, Am. Hist. Assn., Medieval Acad. Am., Am. Soc. Criminology, Am. Printing History Assn., Assn. Internat. de Bibliophilie, Grolier Club, Cosmos Club, Century Assn. Office: Sealy Libr John Jay Coll CUNY 899 10th Ave New York NY 10019-1069 E-mail: lsullivan@jjay.cuny.edu.

SULLIVAN, LORETTA ROSEANN, elementary education educator; b. Pitts., Jan. 24, 1949; d. Stephen Francis and Loretta (Walz) S. BA, Marymount Coll., Tarrytown, N.Y., 1970; MEd, Duquesne U., 1972. Cert. psychology, elem. edn. and elem. sch. guidance tchr., Pa. Tchr. Colfax Sch., Pitts., 1970—, primary instrnl. team leader, 1997—. Project dir. Common Knowledge, 1997—; math. resource person Pitts. Free Learning Environ. Program, 1972-74. Mem. ednl. task force Pitts. Opera, 2000; reading coach Literacy Plus, 2001. Frick Commn. fellow, Pitts., 1972; Tri-State area mini-grantee U. Pitts., 1973; mini-grantee Allegheny Conf. on Community Devel., Pitts., 1980-90; named one of Outstanding Elem. Tchrs. Am., 1974; Pitts. Coun. on Pub. Edn. grantee, 1999. Office: Colfax Sch 2332 Beechwood Blvd Pittsburgh PA 15217-1818

SULLIVAN, MARCIA WAITE, lawyer; b. Chgo., Nov. 30, 1950; d. Robert Macke and Jacqueline (Northrop) S.; m. Steven Donald Jansen, Dec. 20, 1975; children: Eric Spurlock, Laura Macke, Brian Northrop. BA, DePauw U., 1972; JD, Ind. U., 1975. Assoc. Arnstein, Gluck, Weitzenfeld & Minow, Chgo., 1975-76; ptnr. Greenberger and Kaufmann, 1976-86, Katten Muchin Zavis Rosenman, Chgo., 1986—. Adj. prof. Kent Coll. Law, Ill. Inst. Tech., Chgo., 1991—94; pres. Chgo. Real Estate Exec. Women, 2000—01. Mem. ABA, Chgo. Bar Assn., Am. Land Title Assn. (lender's coun.). Avocations: bicycling, cross country skiing, gardening, camping. Office: Katten Muchin Zavis Rosenman 525 W Monroe St Ste 1600 Chicago IL 60661-3693

SULLIVAN, MARY JANE, elementary school educator; b. Mason City, Iowa, Nov. 23, 1947; d. Lawrence Wesly and Elizabeth Barbara (Steinbach) Kohler; m. Mark Jay Sullivan, June 26, 1993. BS, Mankato (Minn.) State U., 1970; MS, Iowa State U., 1982. Cert. tchr. K-9, coach K-12, Iowa. Tchr. 5th grade Keokuk (Iowa) Cmty. Sch., 1970-77, West Bend (Iowa) Cmty. Sch., 1977-80; tchr. 6th grade North Mahaska Cmty. Sch., New Sharon, Iowa, 1980—. Author: (poetry teaching book) Poetry Pals, 1982. Mem. Regional telecomms. Coun., Des Moines, 1994—; mem. Iowa Pub. TV, Des Moines, Iowa Heritage Assn., Des Moines. Recipient Excellence in Elem. Sci. award Iowa Acad. Sci., 1998; named County Sci. Tchr. of Yr., Mahaska County Conservation Bd., Oskaloosa, Iowa, 1992; sci. grantee Ctrl. Coll., Iowa Dept. Edn. Mem. NEA, ASCD, Iowa State Edn. Assn. (exec. bd. negotiations), Nat. Staff Devel. Coun. (mem. 1st acad.), Kappa Delta Pi, Phi Delta Kappa (v.p. 1990-91). Roman Catholic. Avocations: reading, cross stitch, walking, gardening. Office: N Mahaska Elem Sch 2163 135th St New Sharon IA 50207-8108

SULLIVAN, MARY JEAN, elementary school educator; b. Cambridge, Mass., May 13, 1956; d. Joseph Leo and Jean Marie (Isaac) S. BA, Flagler Coll., 1978; postgrad., U. No. Fla., 1980—, Fla. State U., 1992, Okla. State U., 1992, U. Fla., 1998, 99. Cert. elem. educator, Fla. Tchr. grade 2 St. Agnes Sch., St. Augustine, Fla., 1978-79; tchr. grades 1 through 5 Evelyn Hamblen Elem. Sch., 1979-91; tchr. grade 5 Osceola Elem. Sch., 1991—, chair math./ sci. Adv. Sci. Club; chairperson, St. John's County Tchr. Edn. Coun., 1985—, SACS Evaluation Team, Duval County Schs., 1988, 89, 90; rep. tchr. edn. coun.; sch. improvement co-chair, 1994-95; trainer coll. intern students; mem. St. John's County Accomplished Practices Acad., 1995, 96; mem. Staff Devel. Coun. for St. John's County, 1997—; state facilitator Project WET; mem. Tchr. Evaluation Renewal Com.; amb. Jet Propulsion Lab., 1999—; amb. Jet Propulsion Ctr., 1999—. Developer tchr. edn. coun. tng. handbook for State of Fla. Active PTO, past pres.; active Cub Scouts Am.; coord. summer recreation Evelyn Hamblen Sch., St. Augustine, 1987—90; dir. tournament Pam Driskell Meml. Paddle Tennis Scholarship Fund, 1986, 1987, 1988, 1989; vol. United Way Olympic Torch Run, summer, 1996, World Golf Hall of Fame, 1998—, Liberty Mut. Legends of Golf, 1998—, First Tee, 2000, Fan Fest, 2000, 2001, Mark Brunell Charity Softball Game, Channel 7 Auction, Let Us Play, Family First, 1999—, 1st Family, 1999, 2000, Joel Smengee Found.; past asst. program dir. Cathedral-Basilica Ch., United Child Care After Sch. Program, 1988—89; mem. Jacksonville Jaguars Booster Club, 1999—; most valuable people fan, 2000. Jacksonville Jaguars; escort Tournament Players Championship, 1993—, co-capt., 2001; chmn. spl. events. Liberty Mut. Legends of Golf, 2001. Grantee Fla. Coun. Elem. Edn., 1981-82, Summer Enhancement, 1988-89, Fla. Inst. Oceanography, 1994, St. John's County Horizon award mini-grantee, 1994, 96, 98, Fla. Assn. for Computer Edn., 1994, Fla. Humanities Coun., 1995, Project ARIES, summer 1998; recipient Human Rels. award State of Fla., 1992, NEWEST award, 1992, award Geography Summer Inst., 1992; named Kiwanis Tchr. of Month, 1993, Evelyn Hamblen Elem. Tchr. of the Yr., 1990, Osceola Elem. Tchr. of the Yr., 1996-97. Mem. NEA, NSTA, Fla. Tchg. Profession, Fla. Assn. Staff Devel. (planning com.), Fla. Geographic Alliance, Fla. Assn. Computer Edn., St. John's Educator Assn., Fla. Assn. for Sci. Tchrs., Solar Sys. Ambs., Jacksonville Jaguars Booster Club (historian, bd. dirs. 2000—). Office: Osceola Elem Sch 1605 Osceola Elem Sch Rd Saint Augustine FL 32095

SULLIVAN, MARY ROSE, English language educator; b. Boston, May 13, 1931; d. John Joseph and Elinor Mary (Crotty) Sullivan BA, Emmanuel Coll., Boston, 1952; MA, Cath. U. Am., 1957; PhD, Boston U., 1964. Tchr. Woburn Pub. Schs., Mass., 1957-60; faculty Emmanuel Coll., Boston, 1960-66; prof. English U. Colo., Denver, 1966-96. Book reviewing staff San Diego Mag., 1980-90. Author: Browning's Voices in the Ring and the Book, 1969; co-editor: (3 vols.) letters of E.B. Browning to M.R. Mitford, 1836-54, 1983, Women of Letters: Selected Letters of E.B. Browning to M.R. Mitford, 1987, Crime Classics, 1990, Elizabeth Barrett Browning: Selected Poetry and Prose, 1993; editl. bd. English Lang. Notes, 1970-96. Served to capt. USNR, 1952-83. Am. Council Learned Socs. fellow, 1973. Mem. MLA, Boston Browning Soc., Mystery Writers of Am.

SULLIVAN, MICHAEL JOACHIM, financial executive; b. Offenbach, Germany, Apr. 30, 1954; s. Donald and Eleanor (Denver) S.; m. Marianne Murphy, July 7, 1990. BA, LeMoyne Coll., 1976; MS, Syracuse U., 1980, MBA, 1993. Counselor County of Onondaga, Syracuse, N.Y., 1976-79, rsch. tech. 1, 1979, rsch. tech. 2, 1980-81, adminstrv. planning and funding coord., 1982-85, budget analyst 3, 1985, budget analyst 4, 1985-86, dep. dir. mgmt. and budget, 1986-87, dir. mgmt. and budget, 1988-92, commr. of fin., CFO, 1992-95; chief fiscal officer Loretto, Inc., 1995—. Bd. dirs. Lourdes Camp, Inc., Syracuse, 1980—, Syracuse Opera, 1994-97, Light on the Hill, 1995-2001; trustee, sec., fin. com. chmn. Onondaga C.C., 1998-2001; mem. fin. com. Interreligious Coun., Syracuse, 1993-97; mem. Thursday morning roundtable Univ. Coll., Syracuse, 1991-2000; mem. adminstrv. com., trustee, chmn. fin./budget com. Immaculate Conception Cathedral Ch., 1997—; trustee, mem. fin. com. Syracuse Cmty. Health Ctr., 2002--. Mem. N.Y. State Govt. Fin. Officers Assn. (chmn. ctrl. region 1993-95, bd. dirs. 1993-95), Govt. Fin. Officers Assn. (Disting. Budget award 1988-92), Beta Gamma Sigma. Roman Catholic. Avocations: gardening, reading, cultural arts, cooking. Home: 4644 Bloomsbury Dr Syracuse NY 13215-2326 Office: Loretto Inc 700 E Brighton Ave Syracuse NY 13205-2298 E-mail: sullmi@lorettosystem.org.

SULLIVAN, MICHAEL D. lawyer; b. Chgo., Feb. 16, 1940; s. John J. and Tillie (Babel) S.; m. Irene A. Brandt. BBA cum laude, U. Notre Dame, 1962, JD, 1965. Bar: Ill. 1965, U.S. Dist. Ct. (no. dist.) Ill. 1966, U.S. Ct. Appeals (7th cir.) 1966, U.S. Tax Ct. 1967. Law clk. to judge U.S. Ct. Appeals (7th cir.), Chgo., 1965-66; assoc. Jenner & Block, 1967-73; gen. atty. CMC & Chgo., Milw. R.R., 1974-78; gen. solicitor, corp. trustee property Chgo., Milw. R.R., Chgo., 1978-85; gen. solicitor Soo Line R.R., 1985-86; pvt. practice River Forest, Ill.; atty. The Sullivan Firm, Ltd., Rolling Meadows, 1985—. Counsel, bd. dirs. various orgns., Chgo., 1980-85. Mem. ABA, Ill. Bar Assn., Chgo. Bar Assn., N.W. Suburban Bar Assn. Home: 739 Park Ave River Forest IL 60305-1705 Office: The Sullivan Firm Ltd 2550 Golf Rd Rolling Meadows IL 60008-4051 E-mail: thesullivanfirm@aol.com.

SULLIVAN, MICHAEL EVAN, investment and management company executive; b. Phila., Dec. 30, 1940; s. Albert and Ruth (Liebert) S. BS, N.Mex. State U., 1966, MA, 1967; BS, U. Tex., 1969; MBA, U. Houston, 1974; MS, U. So. Calif., 1976, MPA, 1977, PhD in Adminstrn., 1983; BS in Acctg., U. La Verne, 1981. Sr. adminstrv. and tech. analyst Houston Lighting & Power Co., 1969-74; electronics engr. U.S. Govt., Point Mugu, Calif., 1974-77; mem. tech. staff Hughes Aircraft Co., El Segundo, 1977-78; staff program adminstr. Ventura divsn. Northrop Corp., Newbury Park, 1978-79; divsn. head engring. Navastrogru, Point Mugu, 1979-82; br. head, divsn. head spl. programs head operational sys. Pacific Missile Test Ctr., Calif., 1983-90, head tech. devel. office, head capability devel., 1993-98; far west regional coord., exec. com., exec. bd. Fed. Lab. Consortium, 1998—. CNO, dir. rsch., devel. and acquisiiton The Pentagon, Washington, 1987-88, dir. rsch. devel. test and evaluation and tech., 1990-93; pres., chmn. bd. Diversified Mgmt. Sys., Inc., Camarillo, Calif., 1978—. Author: The Management of Research, Develoopment, Test and Evaluation Orgainzations; Organization Behavior Characteristics of Supervisors-Public versus Private Sectors; Self-Actualization in RDT & E Organizations: Self-Actualization in a Health Care Agency; others. V.p., bd. dirs. Ventura County Master Chorale and Opera Assn.; bd. dirs. So. Calif. Assn. of Pub. Adminstrn. (also mem. fin. com., programs com., student aid com., exec. bd., exec. com. fed. lab. consortium). Served with U.S. Army, 1958-62. Ednl. Rsch. Info. Clearing House fellow, 1965-67, Ednl. Rsch. Tng. Program fellow N.Mex. State U., 1967. Mem. IEEE, Am. Math. Soc., Math. Assn. Am., Am. Statis. Assn., IEEE Engring. Mgmt. Soc., Am. Soc. Pub. Adminstrn., So. Calif. Assn. Pub. Adminstrn. (bd. dirs., various coms.), Assn. Fedn. Tech. Transfer Execs., Fed. Mgrs. Assn., Am. Assn. Individual Investors, Mcpl. Mgmt. Assts. So. Calif., Acad. Polit. Sci., Internat. Soc. for the Sys. Scis., Assn. MBA Execs., Tech. Transfer Soc., Internat. Fedn. for Sys. Rsch., Phi Kappa Phi, Pi Gama Mu. Home: PO Box 273 Port Hueneme CA 93044-0273 Office: PO Box 447 Camarillo CA 93011-0447

SULLIVAN, MICHAEL FRANCIS, III, executive; b. DuBois, Pa., Mar. 11, 1948; s. Michael F. and Mary Jane (Borger) S.; m. Janice Marie Calame, May 30, 1969 (dec.); children: Courtney, Shannon, Michael IV; m. Rosa Leigh Gillespie, Aug. 16, 1997. BS in English & Speech, Bowling Green State U., 1969; MEd in Curriculum Devel., Wright State U., 1971; EdD in Instructional Technology, Va. Polytech Inst. & State U., 1976. Specialist in instructional design Md. State Dept. Edn., Balt., 1974-80, asst. state supt. in instructional technology, 1980-86; sr. edn. cons. UNISYS Corp., Bluebell, Pa., 1986-87, product mktg. mgr., 1987-88, dir. strategic planning and devel., 1988-90; exec. dir. Agy. for Instructional Technology, Bloomington, Ind., 1990—. Contbr. articles to profl. jours. Office: Agency for Instructional Tech Box A Bloomington IN 47402

SULLIVAN, MICHAEL JOHN, ambassador, former governor; b. Omaha, Sept. 22, 1939; s. Joseph Byrne and Margaret (Hamilton) S.; m. Jane Metzler, Sept. 2, 1961; children: Michelle, Patrick, Theresa. BS in Petroleum Engring., U. Wyo., 1961, JD, 1964. Bar: Wyo. 1964, U.S. Ct. Appeals (10th cir.) 1968, U.S. Supreme Ct. 1980. Assoc. Brown, Drew, Apostolos, Barton & Massey, Casper, Wyo., 1964-67; ptnr. Brown, Drew, Apostolos, Massey & Sullivan, 1967-86, 95-98; gov. State of Wyo., Cheyenne, 1987-95; amb. to Ireland Dublin, 1998-2001; spl. counsel Rothgerber, Johnson & Lyons, LLP, Casper, Wyo., 2001—. Trustee St. Joseph's Children's Home, Torrington, Wyo., 1986-87; bd. dirs. Natrona County Meml. Hosp., Casper, 1976-86. Mem. ABA, ATLA, Wyo. Bar Assn., Wyo. Trial Lawyers Assn., Rotary (pres. Casper club). Democrat. Roman Catholic. Avocations: fly fishing, golf, tennis, jogging. Office: Casper Bus Ctr 123 W 1st St Ste 200 Casper WY 82601 E-mail: guvsuv@aol.com.

SULLIVAN, MICHAEL PATRICK, food service executive; b. Dec. 5, 1934; s. Michael Francis and Susan Ellen (Doran) S.; m. Marilyn Emmer, June 27, 1964; children: Katherine, Michael, Maureen, Bridget, Daniel, Thomas. BS, Marquette U., 1956; JD, U. Minn., 1962. Bar: Minn. 1962, U.S. Dist. Ct. Minn. 1962, U.S. Supreme Ct. 1975, U.S. Ct. Appeals (8th cir.) 1978. Assoc. Gray, Plant, Mooty, Mooty & Bennett, Mpls., 1962-67, ptnr., 1968-87, mng. ptnr., 1976-87; pres., CEO Internat. Dairy Queen, Inc., 1987-2001, chmn. bd., 2001—. Bd. dirs. The Valspar Corp., Allianz Life Ins. Co. N.Am., Opus Corp.; instr. U. Minn. Law Sch., 1962-67; lectr. continuing legal edn.; spl. counsel to atty. gen. Minn., 1971-79, 82-84; bd. dirs. Met. Mpls.YMCA, chmn. bd. dirs., 1997-99; pres. Uniform Law Commn., 1987-89. Contbr. articles to profl. jours. Bd. regents St. John's U., 2000; bd. dirs. YMCA Met. Mpls.; bd. trustees St. Paul Sem. Served with USN, 1956-59. Mem. ABA (ho. of dels., 1984-89), Minn. Bar Assn. (gov. 1974-86), Hennepin County Bar Assn. (pres. 1978-89), Am. Bar Found., Am. Law Inst., Am. Arbitration Assn. (bd. dirs.), Order of Coif. Roman Catholic. Office: Internat Dairy Queen 7505 Metro Blvd Minneapolis MN 55439-3020

SULLIVAN, MITZI, accountant; b. Chattanooga, Feb. 6, 1948; d. James Warren and Maysell Lucille Sullivan; m. Hassan Zayed, Sept. 27, 1975 (div. Oct. 1983); 1 child Janine Amira Zayed. BA Liberal Arts, U. Tenn., 1971; MS Mgmt., Fla. Internat. U., 1977. French and English tchr. Hamilton County Dept. Edn., Chattanooga, 1971—75; social worker Divsn. Retardation, Miami, 1975—78; employment specialist City of Wichita, Kans., 1985—98, accountant, 1998—; owner Internat. Dairy Queen, Kingman, 1998—2000. Bd. dirs., 1st v.p. City of Wichita Deferred Compensation Bd., 1998—. Mem.: Wichita Irish Assn. (membership chmn. 1989—92), Wichita Hispanic Assn. (v.p. 1988—90). Buddhist. Avocations: writing, gardening, quilting, cooking, reading. Home: 942 S Longfellow St Wichita KS 67207-2737 Office: City Wichita Career Devel Office 444 E Wiliam Wichita KS 67202 Personal E-mail: mitzigsullivan@hotmail.com.

SULLIVAN, MORTIMER ALLEN, JR. lawyer; b. Buffalo, Sept. 19, 1930; s. Mortimer Allen Sr. and Gertrude (Hinkley) S.; m. Maryanne Calella, Nov. 20, 1965; children: Mark Allen, Michael John. BA, U. Buffalo, 1954. Bar: N.Y. 1964, U.S. Dist. Ct. (we. dist.) N.Y. 1966, U.S. Dist. Ct. (no. dist.) N.Y. 1967, U.S. Supreme Ct. 1970. Counsel liability claims Interstate Motor Freight System, Grand Rapids, Mich., 1964-82. V.p. J.P.M. Sullivan, Inc., Elmira, N.Y., 1959-67; govt. appeal agt. U.S. Selective Service System, 1967-71; dep. sci. div. Erie County (N.Y.) Sheriff's Office, 1971—, lt., 1986—. Inventor (with others) in field; creator, dir. video depiction JudiVision, 1969; composer High Flight, 1983. Chmn. com. on Constn. and Canons Episcopal Diocese of Western N.Y., 1975-96; bd. dirs. Erie County Law Enforcement Found., Inc., 1987—; bd. dirs. Orchard Park (N.Y.) Symphony Orch., 1975-97, v.p., 1977-79, 91-94. With USAF, 1954-57; spl. agt. Air Force Office of Spl. Investigations, 1972-87, col. res. ret. Decorated Legion of Merit. Mem. Erie County Bar Assn. (chmn. law and tech. com., 1970-81), Transp. Lawyers Assn., Kappa Alpha Soc. Clubs: Saturn (Buffalo); Wanakah (N.Y.) Country. Republican. Avocation: aviation. Home: 19 Knob Hill Rd Orchard Park NY 14127-3917 Office: 88 S Davis St PO Box 1003 Orchard Park NY 14127-8003 E-mail: masulaw@aol.com.

SULLIVAN, NEIL MAXWELL, oil and gas company executive; b. May 25, 1942; s. Thomas James and Jane Mason (Ginn) S.; m. Holly Abolt; children: Margaret Blair, Mason Pedrick. BS, Dickinson Coll., 1970; MS, Tulane U., 1994; postgrad., U. S.C., 1992—. Exploration geologist Bass Enterprises, Midland, Tex., 1976-77; dist. geologist ATAPCO, 1977-78; div. geologist Anadarko Prodn. Co., 1978-79, chief geologist, 1979-80, v.p. exploration, regional mgr. Houston, 1980-82; exploration ops. mgr. Valero Producing Co., San Antonio, 1982-85, v.p. exploration New Orleans, 1985-87; pres. Bluebonnet Petroleum Co., New Orleans, Eastover, S.C., 1987-97; v.p. exploration Forcenergy, Inc., Houston, 1997-98; pres. GAPCO Energy, 1998—2001; COO Tex. Keystone, Inc., Pitts., 2002—. Mem. Dept. Interior Outer Continental Shelf Com. adv. bd., 1985-87. Editor: Petroleum Exploration in Thrust Belts and Their Adjacent Forelands, 1976, Ancient Carbonate Reservoirs and Their Modern Analogs, 1977, Guadalupian Delaware Mountain Group of West Texas and Southeast New Mexico, 1979, Deep Water Sands in the Gulf Coast Region, 1988, Offshore Louisiana Geology: An Onshore Exploration Model, 1988, Risk: Evaluation and Management, 1989, Volga-Ural Basin Analysis, 1993, Northern Marginal Zone of the Pricaspian Basin, 1996. Bd. dirs. Permian Basin Grad. Ctr., Midland, 1979; com. chmn. Mus. of S.W., Midland, 1978. Served with USAF, 1964-68. Mem. Geol. Soc. Am., A. assn. Petroleum Geologists (cert. petroleum geologist), Houston Geol. Soc., New Orleans Geol. Soc. (chmn. continuing edn. com. 1987-89), South Tex. Geol. soc. (nominating com. chmn. 1985), Soc. Econ. Paleontologists and Mineralogists (pres. Permian Basin sect. 1979), Am. Inst. Profl. Geologists (cert. profl. geologist). Lodges: Elks. Home: 421 Forest Highlands Dr Pittsburgh PA 15238-1340 Business E-Mail: nsullivan@texasKeystone.com.

SULLIVAN, NELL INKLEBARGER, administrative official, counselor; b. Charleston, Ark., Jan. 27, 1932; d. Hubert Huel and Maybelle (Heather) Inklebarger; m. J.W. Miller, June 10, 1950 (div. 1973); children: Allan Evan Miller, Sandy Miller Hays-Lusted, Elizabeth Kay Nicholes, Judith Lynelle Bartholomew. AA in Journalism, U. Ark., Ft. Smith, 1986; BA in Journalism, U. Ark., 1987. Clk. U.S. Postal Svc., Lavaca, Ark., 1959-73; co-owner, operator, photographer Nell Miller Studio, 1960-75; office supr. U.S. Postal Svc., Ft. Smith, 1972-75; computer specialist Westark Coll., 1984-86; adminstrv. asst. BDM, Inc., Ft. Chaffee, Ark., 1987-89; rehab. counselor Ark. Rehab. Svc., Ft. Smith, 1990-99; ret., 1999. Journalism scholar U. Ark., Ft. Smith, 1984-86. Mem. YWCA (bd. dirs. Ft. Smith 1986-93), Nat. Rehab. Assn., Ark. State Employees Assn., Nat. Assn. Rehab. Secs., 4-H Alumni Assn. (life), Phi Beta Lambda. Avocations: reading, painting, photography, travel.

SULLIVAN, NICHOLAS G. science educator, speleologist; b. Phila., Dec. 20, 1927; s. Edward James and Florence (Delaney) S. BS, Cath. U. Am., 1950; MSc, U. Pitts., 1954; PhD, U. Notre Dame, 1961. Asst. prof. U. Notre Dame (Ind.), 1961-63; asst. prof., assoc. prof., prof. La Salle Coll., Phila., 1963-78, asst. to pres., 1972-74; prof. sci. Manhattan Coll., Riverdale, N.Y., 1979—. Vis. prof. U. Alaska, Anchorage, 1961, U. NSW, Sydney, Australia, 1963; chmn. U.S. Deep Caving Team. Author: Speleology, the Study of Caves, 1962; contbr. over 200 articles on speleology to profl. jours. Trustee Gwynedd (Pa.) Mercy Coll., 1963-75, Nat. Speleological Found., Washington, 1978-84, Charles Lindbergh Found., 1989—. Fellow Nat. Speleological Soc. (hon. life, trustee 1955-79, pres. 1957-63), Royal Geog. Soc., AAAS, N.Y. Acad. Scis., Explorers Club (pres. 1989-92, trustee 1968—, Explorer's medal Phila. chpt. 1978, Sweeney medal 1979); mem. Sydney Speleological Soc. (hon. life), South African Speleological Soc. (hon. life), Rittenhouse Club, Bankstown Sports Club (Sydney).

SULLIVAN, PATRICIA W. (TERRY SULLIVAN), real estate trainer; b. Hempstead, N.Y., July 25, 1936; d. Gilbert Hudson and Vera (Morgan) Wehmann; m. Richard J. Sullivan, June 8, 1957 (div. Apr. 1982); children: Katherine Sullivan-Irwin, Gillian Stewart, Adam W. BS, Skidmore Coll., 1958; MS, Syracuse U., 1965. Mgr. Purtell & Wigdale, Inc., Cedarburg, Wis., Merrill Lynch Real Estate, Cedarburg; office mgr. Coldwell Banker Real Estate; sales mgr. Coldwell Banker Residential Brokerage, Mequon, WI; owner, trainer, cons. Terry Sullivan Tng. and Seminars, Belgium, Wis., 1991—; sales mgr. Coldwell Banker, Mequon. Contbr. articles to profl. jours. Named Wis. Cert. Real Estate Brokerage Mgr. of Yr., 1990. Mem. Nat. Assn. Realtors (bd. dirs. 1989-90, Omega Tau Rho award 1983, Outstanding Educator of the Year award for medium states, 1989), Nat. Women's Coun. Realtors (pres. 1990), Women's Coun. Realtors (pres. Milw. chpt. 1982, bd. dirs. 1983-90, named WCR of Yr. 1983, LTG 1985), Ozaukee Bd. Realtors (pres. 1979, bd. dirs. 1977-79, Realtor of Yr. 1979), Realtors Nat. Mktg. Inst. (dir. RS coun. 1983-86, CRS 1978, CRB 1981), Wis. Realtors Assn. (v.p. 1982-83, bd. dirs. 1983-86, Instr. of Yr. 1988, Disting. Svc. award 1992, GRI 1975), Wis. Cert. Residential Specialists (cert.; pres. 1982, Cert. Residential Specialist of Yr. 1983), Wis. Cert. Residential Brokers (cert.; pres. 1988). Address: Terry Sullivan Tng & Seminars 5342 Sandy Beach Ln Belgium WI 53004-9731

SULLIVAN, PATRICIA A. academic administrator; b. S.I. m. Charles Sullivan. Grad., St. John's U.; MS in Biology, PhD in Biology, NYU. Tchg. fellow, NIH pre-doctoral fellow NYU; post-doctoral fellow in cell biology Upstate Med. Ctr., Syracuse, N.Y.; vis. fellow Cornell U., 1976; tchr. Wells Coll., N.Y.; dir. biology honors program Tex. Woman's U., 1979-81; dean Salem Coll., Winston-Salem, 1981-87; v.p. acad. affairs Tex. Woman's U., 1987-94, interim pres., 1993-94; chancellor U. N.C., Greensboro, 1995—. Pres. Assn. Tex. Colls. and Univs. Acad. Affairs Officers, Assn. So. Colls. for Women, N.C. Assn. Chief Acad. Officers; active numerous coms. Tex. Higher Edn. Coordinating Bd.; lectr. in field. Contbr. articles to profl. jours. Office: U NC at Greensboro Office of Chancellor PO Box 26170 Greensboro NC 27402-6170

SULLIVAN, PATRICIA G. maternal, child and women's health nursing educator; b. Denver, June 26, 1948; d. Dale F. and Wilma (Fritz) Greb; m. Michael T. Sullivan, Sept. 10, 1971; children: Nicholas O., Matthew Alexander, Adam Michael. BS, Loretto Heights Coll., 1971; MS, U. Colo., 1976. Cert. bereavement svcs. counselor. Clin. instr. Loretto Hts. Coll., 1977-81; instr. pathophysiology U. Denver, summers 1983, 84; coord. women's health edn. Swedish Med. Ctr., Englewood, Colo., 1985-86; coord. childbirth edn. Med. Ctr. Hosp., Odessa, Tex., 1986-88; instr. nursing Midland (Tex.) Coll.,

1990—; cons. Mosby's Med. Nursing & Allied Health Dictionary. Reviewer: Basic Nursing and Practice, 3d edit., 1995, reviewer: Women's Health During The Childbearing Years, 2001. Counselor RTS Bereavement Svcs., 1996. Recipient medal for exceptional performance N.I.O.S.D., 2001. Mem. AWHONN, Tex. Nurses Assn., Tex. C.C. Tchrs. Assn., Assn. Reproductive Health Profls., Internat. Soc. Nurses in Genetics, Sigma Theta Tau. Home: 2803 Douglas Ave Midland TX 79701-3831 Office: Midland Coll 3600 N Garfield St # 216 Midland TX 79705-6329 E-mail: psull@midland.cc.tx., durangokid@earthlink.net.

SULLIVAN, PATRICK HENRY, assistant chancellor; b. N.Y.C., May 6, 1938; s. Patrick Henry II and Elinor Regina (Smith) S.; children: Christine E., Suzanne P., Patrick H. IV. BS in gen. engring., U.S. Navel Acad., 1960; MS in R & D mgmt., Fla. State Univ., 1969, DBA in mgmt., 1972. Rsch. engr. The Boeing Co., Cape Canaveral, Fla., 1966-69; chief fin. planning officer Fla. State Univ., Tallahassee, 1970-73; fellow, adv. to vice-chancellor Univ. Calif. Berkeley, 1973-74; asst. chancellor Univ. Calif. Santa Cruz, 1974-78; prin. cons. SRI Internat., 1973-84; v.p. MAC Group, 1984-88; pres. Sullivan & Assocs., 1998-93; chief oper. officer Law & Econs. Cons. Group, 1994; ptnr. ICM Co., 1995—. Author: Value Driven Intellectual Capital, 2000; co-editor: (book) Technology Licensing, 1996; editor: (book) Profiting From Intellectual Capital, 1998. U.S. naval officer USN, 1960-66. Mem. Licensing Executives Soc. Avocations: biking, scuba, walking. Home: 250 Meadow Rd Santa Cruz CA 95060-2040 Office: ICM Group 2465 E Bayshore Rd Ste 403 Palo Alto CA 94303-3228 E-mail: psullivan@icmgroup.com.

SULLIVAN, PAUL ANDREW, retired research electrical engineer; b. Sterling, Colo., June 22, 1944; m. Joan Leslie Rasmussen, May 22, 1965 (div. May 1971); children: Kimberly Lynne Amontree, Heather Paige Lyijynen; m. Gerry Wood, Aug. 1, 1980. BS in Elec. Engring., Colo. State U., 1966; MS in Elec. Engring., U. So. Calif., 1968, PhD in Materials Sci., 1975. Mem. tech. staff surface sci. Hughes Rsch. Labs., Malibu, Calif., 1967-71, head micropattern replication, 1971-77, assoc. program mgr. Dept. Defense very high speed integrated circuits program, 1978-80; guest scientist Max Planck Inst. Solid State Rsch., Stuttgart, Germany, 1977-78; mgr. advanced devel. NCR Microelectronics, Ft. Collins, Colo., 1980-84, dir. digital signal processing, 1984-86; dir. engring. personal computer div. NCR, Clemson, S.C., 1987-89; dir. systems engring. CAD program Microelectronics and Computer Tech. Corp., Austin, Tex., 1989-91; dept. head electronic packaging rsch. Bell Labs Lucent Technologies (formerly AT&T), Murray Hill, N.J., 1992-99. Contbr. articles to profl. jours. Recipient Industrial Rsch. and Devel. 100 award Rsch. & Devel. Found., Chgo., 1985. Mem. IEEE (sr.), Sigma Xi, Eta Kappa Nu, Phi Kappa Phi. Achievements include patents for Apparatus Synchronizing an Opaque Video Tape with a Video Display, Strip Exposure Apparatus for Nucleation Medium, Alignment System and Method with Micromovement Stage, Hard X-Ray and Fluorescent X-Ray Detection of Alignment Marks for Precision Mask Alignment, Method and Apparatus for Mask-to-Wafer Gap Control in X-Ray Lithography, Process for Channeling Ion Beams, Method of Making CMOS by Twin-Tub Process Integrated with a Vertical Bipolar Transistor, Process for Fabricating a Bipolar Transistor with a Thin Base and an Abrupt Base-Collector Junction, Use of Selectively Deposited Tungsten for Contact Formation and Shunting Metallization, High Density, Low Power, Merged Vertical Fuse/Bipolar Transistor Device and Method of Fabrication. E-mail: p7sullivan@earthlink.net.

SULLIVAN, PAUL WILLIAM, communications specialist; b. Brockton, Mass., Dec. 7, 1939; s. Augustus Henry and Pearl Irene (Chisholm) S.; children: Todd Andrew, Geoffrey Scott, Dustin Raymond; m. Frances Tina Brown, Jan. 23, 1989. BA cum laude, Yale U., 1961; MA, U. Fla., 1971; PhD, So. Ill. U., 1977. Gen. mgr. Chronicle Pub. Co., Stoughton, Mass., 1962-67; editor Easton Bull., N. Easton, 1963-70; pub., editor Associated Weekly Newspapers, Stoughton, 1967-70; instr. dept. mass comm. Moorhead (Minn.) State U., 1971-73; assoc. prof., chmn. dept. comm. U. Evansville, Ind., 1973-78; prof., chmn. dept. journalism Temple U., Phila., 1978-87; pvt. practice comm. cons., sales tng. cons. Indian Rocks Beach, Fla., 1986-92; pvt. practice comm. and fin. cons. Sullivan Comms., 1992—; mng. gen. ptnr. Atlantis Adventure Ltd. Partnership, Largo, Fla., 1996—. Mem. rev. panel Harry S Truman Scholarship Found., 1981-86. Author: The Modern Free Press Fair Trial Precedent, 1987, monograph News Piracy, 1978; co-author, editor: The Teaching of Graphic Arts, 1977, The Art of Consulting, 1989; contbr. articles to profl. jours. Mem. Gov.'s Commn. for Pa. Lottery, 1981. Mem. Assn. for Edn. in Journalism and Mass Communications, Soc. Profl. Journalists, Pa. Soc. Newspaper Editors (bd. dirs. 1980-87), Phila. Bar Assn. (media rels. com. 1982-87), ACLU. Avocations: photographer, landscape gardening. Office: PO Box 1049 Indian Rocks Beach FL 33785-1049 *Never underestimate the power of a liberal education to keep opening doors into the future. That education coupled with what I learned from my father and keep learning from my wife has made all the difference.*

SULLIVAN, PEGGY (PEGGY ANNE SULLIVAN), librarian, consultant; b. Kansas City, Mo., Aug. 12, 1929; d. Michael C. and Ella (O'Donnell) S. AB, Clarke Coll., 1950; MS in L.S., Cath. U. Am., 1953; PhD (Tangley Oaks fellow, Higher Edn. Act Title II fellow), U. Chgo., 1972. Children's public librarian, Mo., Md., Va., 1952-61; sch. library specialist Montgomery County (Md.) public schs., 1961-63; dir. Knapp Sch. Libraries Project, ALA, 1963-68, Jr. Coll. Library Info. Ctr., 1968-69; asst. prof. U. Pitts., 1971-73; dir. Office for Library Personnel Resources, ALA, Chgo., 1973-74; dean of students, assoc. prof. Grad. Library Sch., U. Chgo., 1974-77; asst. commr. for extension services Chgo. Public Library, 1977-81; dean Coll. Profl. Studies, No. Ill. U., DeKalb, 1981-90; dir. univ. librs. No. Ill. U., 1990-92; exec. dir. ALA, 1992-94; assoc. Tuft & Assocs., 1995-98; dean Grad. Sch. Libr. and Info. Sci. Rosary Coll., 1995-97. Instr. grad. libr. edn. programs, 1958-73, UNESCO cons. on sch. librs., Australia, 1970; trustee Clarke Coll., 1969-72; sr. ptnr. Able Cons., 1987-92; cons. in field. Author: The O'Donnells, 1956, Many Names for Eileen, 1969, Problems in School Media Management, 1971, Carl H. Milam and the American Library Association, 1976, Opportunities in Library and Information Science, 1977, Realization: The Final Report of the Knapp School Libraries Project, 1968; co-author: Public Libraries: smart Practices in Personnel, 1982. Mem.: ALA, Assn. for Libr. and Info., Ill. Libr. Assn., Cath. Libr. Assn., Carlton Club. Roman Catholic. Home and Office: 2800 N Lake Shore Dr Apt 816 Chicago IL 60657-6202 E-mail: sullivanp@ioptener.net., sullivanp2@mindspring.com. *Opportunities to use my abilities in a variety of public services have enriched my life, as I hope the results have enriched and empowered others.*

SULLIVAN, PENELOPE DIETZ, computer software development company executive; b. Roanoke, Va., Dec. 29, 1939; d. Joseph Budding and Katherine Dietz; m. Thomas F. Sullivan, Sept. 7, 1963 (div. Mar. 1975); children: Courtney, Todd; m. Paul B. Hill, Mar. 31, 1990. BA, Colby Coll., 1961. Claims examiner Blue Cross/Blue Shield of D.C., Washington, 1961-66; self employed maker slipcovers and upholstery Springfield, Va., 1966-75; ins. sales Met. Life Ins. Co., Arlington, 1975-76, Med. Pers. Pool Inc., Alexandria, 1976-77; mktg. rep. IBM Corp., Washington, 1977-88, program mgr. Advanced Workstations Somers, N.Y., 1988-92; sales cons. IBM Open Sys., Washington, 1992-93; co-founder Open Sys. Assocs., Inc., Reston, Va., 1993—; v.p. bus. devel., co-founder Guru Networks Inc., 2001—. Avocations: golf, skiing, gardening, renovating houses. Office: Guru Networks Inc 4100 Lafayette Ctr Chantilly VA 20151 E-mail: penny@gurunet.net.

SULLIVAN, PETER THOMAS, III, lawyer; b. Jersey City, Aug. 6, 1950; s. Peter T. Jr. and Daisy (Stallard) S.; m. Brenda J. Stanley, July 1, 1972 (div. 1980); children: Patrick, Margaret McGaw-Sullivan. BA, So. Ill. U., 1972; JD, DePaul U., 1976. Bar: Ill. 1976, U.S. Dist. Ct. (no. dist.) Ill. 1976, U.S. Ct. Appeals (7th cir.) 1982. Assoc. Thomas, Kostantacos & Traum, Rockford, Ill., 1976-77; atty. Pub. Defender's Office, 1977-82; ptnr. Sreenan, Cain & Sullivan, 1982-89; pvt. practice Pete Sullivan & Assocs., 1989—. Mem. Assn. Trial Lawyers Am., Ill. Bar Assn., Ill. Trial Lawyers Assn. Democrat. Roman Catholic. Office: Pete Sullivan & Assoc PC 134 N Main St Rockford IL 61101-1169

SULLIVAN, PHILIP G. retired obstetrician-gynecologist; b. Boston, 1932; s. Francis Albert and Catherine A. (Clark) S.; m. Valerie Lee Wood, Apr. 29, 1960; children: Deirdre, John, Maura, Kathleen. AB, Providence Coll., 1954; MD, Tufts U., 1958; MPH, Harvard U., 1971. Diplomate Am. Bd. Ob-Gyn. Intern New Eng. Ctr. Hosps., Boston, 1958-59, resident in surgery, 1959-61, resident in ob-gyn., 1961-64, med. adminstr.; clin.asst. prof. ob-gyn. Tufts U., 1972—. Fellow ACS, ACOG; mem. Mass. Med. Soc., Alpha Omega Alpha. Office: 489 Shore Rd Monument Beach MA 02553 E-mail: pgsull@aol.com.

SULLIVAN, RENEE SHEVONNE, composer, writer; b. Chgo., Sept. 16, 1971; d. Gable René Maxwell and Deborah Ann Berry; m. Brian Keith Sullivan, Oct. 26, 1990 (div. Feb. 1999); 1 child Brianna Renee. Pers. mgr. U.S. Army, Fort Sheridan, Ill., 1990—91, promotions clk. Stuttgart, Germany, 1991, clk. med. recs. Fort Knox, Ky., 1992—93. Author: The Jazz Cat, 2001; composer (arranger), 1999; composer: Over the Rainbow, 1999, I Lived My Life, 1999. Mem.: DAV. Avocation: Avocations: writing songs, writing children's books. Home: 2501 Waverly Dr Gary IN 46404-1237

SULLIVAN, ROBERT EDWARD, lawyer; b. San Francisco, May 18, 1936; s. Edward C. S. and Mary Jane (Sullivan); m. Maureen Lois Miles, June 14, 1958 (dec. 1972); children: Teresa Ann, Andrew Edward, Edward Braddock. BS, U. San Francisco, 1958; LLB, U. Calif-Berkeley, 1961. Bar: Calif. 1962. Assoc. Pillsbury, Madison & Sutro, San Francisco, 1963-70, ptnr., 1971—2000, Pillsbury, Winthrop, LLP, 2001—. Lectr. bus. law Calif. Continuing Edn. Bar and Practicing Law Inst.; v.p., treas., dir. MPC Ins., Ltd., 1986-93. Contbr. articles to profl. jours. Bd. dirs., exec. com. mem., sec. San Francisco Opera Assn., 1993—. 1st lt. U.S. Army, 1961-63. Mem. ABA, State Bar Calif. (com. corps. 1979-82, chmn. 1981-82, mem. exec. com. bus. law sect. 1982-85, vice chmn. 1983-84, chmn. 1984-85, advisor 1985-86, mem. partnership com. 1990-92, chmn. ltd. liability co. drafting com. 1992-93), San Francisco Bar Assn., Bankers Club San Francisco (bd. dirs., sec., treas.). Democrat. Roman Catholic. Office: Pillsbury Winthrop LLP 50 Fremont St San Francisco CA 94105-2228

SULLIVAN, ROBERT EMMET, JR. lawyer; b. Detroit, Oct. 2, 1955; s. Robert Emmett Sr. and Gloria Marie (Lamb) S. BA in Polit. Sci. and Sociology, Wayne State U., 1977; M Urban Planning, U. Mich., 1979; JD, U. Detroit, 1983; postgrad., Oxford (Eng.) U., 1981. Bar: Mich. 1984, U.S. Dist. Ct. (we. dist.) Mich. 1984, U.S. Dist. Ct. (ea. dist.) Mich. 1984, U.S. Ct. Appeals (6th cir.) 1984, U.S. Ct. Appeal (D.C. cir.) 1984, U.S. Tax Ct. 1984, D.C. 1985, U.S. Supreme Ct. 1987. Planning commr. City of Detroit, 1982-85; shareholder Sullivan, Ward, Bone, Tyler & Asher, P.C., Detroit, 1984—; v.p., bd. dirs. Internat. Inst. Metro. Detroit. Bd. dirs. Internat. Inst. of Met. Detroit. Contbr. articles to profl. jours. Active St. Scholastica Parish Ch., North Rosedale Park Civic Assn., Detroit Hist. Soc. Moffitt scholar, 1982, 83. Mem. AIA, Detroit Bar Assn., Am. Planning Assn., Am. Inst. Cert. Planners. Roman Catholic. Home: 7464 Wilshire West Bloomfield MI 48322-2875 Office: Sullivan Ward Bone Tyler & Asher 25800 Northwestern Hwy Southfield MI 48075-1000 E-mail: rsullivanjr@swbta.com.

SULLIVAN, SHIRLEY ROSS (SHIRLEY ROSS DAVIS), art collector; b. Berkeley, Calif. d. Edwin M. Ross; m. George Freeborn (dec.); children: George, Tita, Nelly, Mary; m. Thomas Davis (dec.); m. Charles Sullivan, Sept. 6, 1997. Interior designer, Woodside, Calif., 1963-90. Tchr., lectr., Woodside, 1965-70; art collector, Woodside and San Francisco, 1968—. Trustee San Francisco Mus. Modern Art, 1986—; pres. Collectors' Art Forum, San Francisco, 1983-85; mem. collectors' com. Nat. Gallery Art, 1998—. Office: ICMS 790 Laurel St San Carlos CA 94070-3164

SULLIVAN, STEPHEN FRANCIS, systems analyst; b. Newport, R.I., June 9, 1964; s. Allan Francis Sullivan and Sally (Rosaria) Rizzo; m. Cynthia Ann Spain, May 23, 1987; children: Ashley Marie, Stephen Francis II. A degree, N.H. Tech. Inst., Concord, 1985; student, Franklin Pierce Coll., 1989—. Computer operator State of N.H., Concord, 1985-86, programmer trainee, 1986-87, systems analyst, 1989—; mem. capacity planning staff Wang Labs., Lowell, Mass., 1987-89. Republican. Roman Catholic. Avocations: golf, cooking, spending free time with family. Office: State of NH Gen Ct 107 N Main St Rm 35 Concord NH 03301-4951

SULLIVAN, STEPHEN GENE, psychiatrist, pharmacologist, administrator; b. Manchester, N.H., Feb. 27, 1947; BS, Georgetown U., 1970; MS, NYU, 1976, PhD, 1977, MD, 1984. Assoc. research scientist NYU Sch. Med., 1978-81, rsch. asst. prof. pharmacology, 1981-82, adj. asst. prof. pharmacology, 1984-91; intern Beth Israel Med. Ctr., N.Y.C., 1984, resident in psychiatry, 1984-88, physician-in-charge Clin. Psychopharmacology Lab., 1988-90; sci. dir. The Corp. for Clin. Psychopharmacology Research, 1988-99; pvt. practice, 1986—. Instr. psychiatry Mt. Sinai Sch. Med. CUNY, 1986-88, asst. clin. prof. psychiatry, 1988-90. Author, adminstr.: (Web site) speciesaccounts.org, 2001—; contbr. numerous articles to profl. jours., author ten book chpts., 1976—. Med. scientist tng. program fellow NIH, 1970-76, 82-83, postdoctoral fellow, 1976-77. Mem. AAAS, AMA, Am. Psychiat. Assn., N.Y. Acad. Sciences. Avocation: composing music. Office: 533 E 13th St New York NY 10009-3508

SULLIVAN, STUART FRANCIS, anesthesiologist, educator; b. Buffalo, July 15, 1928; s. Charles S. and Kathryn (Duggan) S.; m. Dorothy Elizabeth Faytol, Apr. 18, 1959; children: John, Irene, Paul, Kathryn. BS, Canisius Coll., 1950; MD, SUNY, Syracuse, 1955. Diplomate Am. Bd. Anesthesiology. Intern Ohio State Univ. Hosp., Columbus, 1955—85; resident Columbia Presbyn. Med. Ctr., 1958—60; fellow Columbia-Bellevue Hosp. Ctr., 1960—61; instr. anesthesiology Columbia U. Coll. Physicians and Surgeons, 1961—62, assoc., 1962—64, asst. prof., 1964—69, assoc. prof., 1969—73; prof. dept. anesthesiology UCLA, 1973—91, vice chair anesthesiology, 1974—77, exec. vice chair, 1977—90, acting chmn., 1983—84, 1987—88, 1990—91, prof. emeritus, 1991—. Capt. M.C., USAR, 1956-58. Fellow NIH, 1960-61; recipient research career devel. award NIH, 1966-69. Mem. Assn. Univ. Anesthetists, Am. Physiol. Soc., Am. Soc. Anesthesiologists. Home: 101 Foxtail Dr Santa Monica CA 90402-2047 Office: UCLA Sch Medicine Dept Anesthesiology Los Angeles CA 90095-0001

SULLIVAN, SULLINS GRENFELL, former surgeon, consultant; b. Stonewall, Okla., Oct. 6, 1912; s. Bedford Forrest and Jessie Eulalia (Lyles) S.; m. Alyce Idella Thomas, Oct. 6, 1937; 1 child, Thomas Joseph. BS in Medicine, U. Okla., 1933, MD, 1935. Diplomate Am. Bd. Surgery. Intern St. Joseph Hosp., Balt., 1935-36, resident in medicine, 1936-37, resident in surgery, 1937-39; chief resident in surgery Bon Secours Hosp., 1939-40, chief of surgery, 1955-76, St. Joseph Hosp., Balt., 1976-83. With U.S. Army, 1942-46. Fellow ACS; mem. Med. Chirurg. Faculty of Md., (founder) Balt. Acad. of Surgery, Porsche Club Am. Avocation: sports cars. Home: 419 Oak Ln Baltimore MD 21286-7329

SULLIVAN, TERESA ANN, law and sociology educator, academic administrator; b. Kewanee, Ill., July 9, 1949; d. Gordon Hager and Mary Elizabeth (Finnegan) S.; m. H. Douglas Laycock, June 14, 1971; children: Joseph Peter, John Patrick. BA, Mich. State U., 1970; MA, U. Chgo., 1972, PhD, 1975. Asst. prof. sociology U. Tex., Austin, 1975-76, assoc. prof. sociology, 1981-87, dir. women's studies, 1985-87, prof. sociology, 1987—, prof. law, 1988—, assoc. dean grad. sch., 1989-90, 1992-95, chair dept. sociology, 1990-92, vice provost, 1994-95, v.p., grad. dean, 1995—; asst. prof. sociology U. Chgo., 1977-81. Pres. Southwestern Sociol. Assn., 1988-89; mem. faculty adv. bd. Hogg Found. Mental Health, 1989-92; mem. sociology panel NSF, 1983-85. Author: Marginal Workers Marginal Jobs, 1978; co-author: As We Forgive Our Debtors, 1989 (Silver Gavel 1990), Social Organization of Work, 1990, 2d edit. 1995; co-author: The Fragile Middle Class, 2000; contbr. articles and chpts. to profl. jours. Bd. dirs. Calvert Found., Chgo., 1978, CARA, Inc., Washington, 1985; mem. U.S. Census Bur. Adv. Com., 1989-95, chmn., 1991-92; mem. sociology panel NSF, 1983-85; trustee St. Michael's Acad., 1996-2001. Leadership Tex. 1994. Fellow AAAS (liaison to Population Assn. Am. 1989-91, chair sect. K 1996), Sociol. Rsch. Assn., Am. Sociol. Assn. (sec. 1995—, editor Rose Monograph Series 1988-92), Philos. Soc. Tex., Soc. Study of Social Problems (chair fin. com. 1986-87), Population Assn. Am. (bd. dirs. 1989-91, chair fin. com. 1990-91), Assn. Grad. Schs. (pres. 2001-2002). Roman Catholic. Avocations: volkssporting, sci. fiction. Office: U Tex Office Grad Studies Main Bldg 101 Austin TX 78712

SULLIVAN, TERRANCE CHARLES, lawyer; b. Neptune, N.J., Mar. 23, 1950; s. John Joseph and Marilyn Anne (DiBlasi) S.; m. Kathy Lavonne Collett, June 21, 1980; children: Jennifer Collett, Michael Charles, Cynthia Grace, Philip Gregory. BA, U. Ga., 1972; JD, U. Va., 1975. Bar: Ga. 1975. Assoc. Swift, Currie, McGhee & Hiers, Atlanta, 1975-77; assoc., ptnr. Phillips, Hart & Mozley, 1977-82; sr. ptnr. Hart & Sullivan, P.C., 1982-89, Sullivan, Hall, Booth & Smith, P.C., Atlanta, 1989-98, Butler, Wooten, Overby, Fryhofer, Daughtery and Sullivan, Atlanta, 1998—. Bd. dirs. Atlanta Coun. Younger Lawyers, 1975-77. Contbr. articles on legal edn. to profl. jours. Bd. dirs. Murphey Candler Little League, 1997—; assoc. mem. deans coun. U. Va. Law Sch., 1993—. Capt. USAF Res., 1972-80. Fellow Am. Coll. Trial Lawyers, Am. Bd. Trial Advocate's; mem. ABA, State Bar Ga., Atlanta Bar Assn., Nat. Inst. Trial Advocacy, Atlanta Inst. Trial Advocacy (co-dir. 1986-88), Atlanta Lawyers Club, Trial Lawyers Assn. Am. (conf. speaker 1988), U. Ga. Nat. Alumni Assn. (bd. dirs. 1998—), Dekalb Med. Ctr., Medallion Soc. Roman Catholic. Home: 3986 Fernway Ct NE Atlanta GA 30319-1667 Office: Butler Wooten Overby Fryhofer Daughtery and Sullivan 2719 Buford Hwy NE Atlanta GA 30324-3207 Fax: 404-321-1713.

SULLIVAN, THOMAS CHRISTOPHER, coatings company executive; b. Cleve., July 8, 1937; s. Frank Charles and Margaret Mary (Wilhelmy) S.; m. Sandra Simmons, Mar. 12, 1960; children: Frank, Sean, Tommy, Danny, Kathleen, Julie. BS, Miami U., Oxford, Ohio, 1959. Div. sales mgr. Republic Powdered Metals, Cleve., 1961-65, exec. v.p., 1965-70; pres., chmn. bd. RPM, Inc., Medina, Ohio, 1971-78, chmn. bd. and CEO, 1978—. Bd. dirs. Pioneer Standard Electronics, Inc., Cleve., Nat. City Bank, Cleve., Cleve. Clinic Found., Huffy Corp., Dayton, Ohio, Kaydon Corp., Ann Arbor, Mich. Trustee emeritus Culver (Ind.) Ednl. Found.; trustee Cleve. Tomorrow; bd. advisors Urban Cmty. Sch., Cleve., Malachi House, Cleve.; trustee City Year Cleve. Lt. (j.g.) USNR, 1959-60. Mem.: Nat. Assn. Securities Dealers (bd. govs. 1986—88, long-range strategic planning com.), Nat. Paint and Coatings Assn. (chmn. bd., CEO). Roman Catholic. Office: RPM Inc 2628 Pearl Rd Medina OH 44256-7623

SULLIVAN, THOMAS JAMES, retired manufacturing company executive; b. Franklin, N.H., Mar. 26, 1923; s. James J. and Helen (Mullin) S.; m. Anne Clark, Aug. 31, 1963. AB, Holy Cross Coll., 1947; JD, Harvard U., 1949. With Gen. Dynamics Corp., 1949-61, asst. div. mgr., 1959-61; sr. assoc. Harbridge House, Cambridge, Mass., 1961-63; with Hydraulic Research & Mfg. Co., Valencia, Calif., 1963-71, v.p., 1964-68, exec. v.p., 1968-69, pres., 1969-71; v.p. Textron, Inc., Providence, 1971-73; pres. Walker/Parkersburg (W. Va.) Co., 1973-81, Sprague Meter, Bridgeport, Conn., 1981-84, Dimetrics Inc., Diamond Springs, Calif., 1984-86. Served with USAAF, 1943-46. Fellow Nat. Contract Mgmt. Assn. Home: 2186 Augusta Ct San Luis Obispo CA 93401-4500 E-mail: tsullivan0323@aol.com.

SULLIVAN, THOMAS M. federal agency administrator; BA English, Boston Coll., 1989, MA, 1993; JD, Suffolk U. Bar: U.S. Ct. Appeals (D.C. cir.), Mass. Exec. dir. Nat. Dedn. Ind. Bus. Legal Found.; chief counsel advocacy Small Bus. Adminstrn., Washington, 2002—. Office: Small Bus Adminstrn 409 3d St SW Washington DC 20416*

SULLIVAN, THOMAS PATRICK, lawyer; b. Evanston, Ill., Mar. 23, 1930; s. Clarence M. and Pauline (DeHaye) S.; children: Margaret Mary, Timothy Joseph, Elizabeth Ann; m. Anne Landau. Student, Loras Coll., Dubuque, Iowa, 1947-49; LL.B. cum laude, Loyola U., Chgo., 1952. Bar: Ill. 1952, Calif. 1982, N.Mex., 1997. Asso. firm Jenner & Block, Chgo., 1954-62, partner, 1963-77, 81—; U.S. atty. for No. Dist. Ill., Chgo., 1977-81. Contbr. articles to profl. jours. Served with U.S. Army, 1952-54. Decorated Bronze Star.; Recipient medal of excellence Loyola U. Law Sch., 1965; Ill. Pub. Defender Assn. award, 1972, Justice John Paul Stevens award, 2000. Fellow Am. Coll. Trial Lawyers; mem. Am., Ill., Fed. Seventh Circuit, Chgo. bar assns., Fed. Bar Assn., Am. Law Inst., Am. Judicature Soc., Chgo. Council Lawyers. Office: Jenner & Block 1 Ibm Plz Fl 4100 Chicago IL 60611-5697 E-mail: tsullivan@jenner.com.

SULLIVAN, THOMAS PATRICK, academic administrator; b. Detroit, July 8, 1947; s. Walter James and Helen Rose (Polosky) S.; m. Barbara Jean Fournier, Aug. 9, 1968; children: Colleen, Brendan. BA in English, U. Dayton, 1969; M. Edn. and Adminstrn., Kent State U., 1971; postgrad., U. Mich., 1988. Tchr. Resurection Elem. Sch., Dayton, Ohio, 1968-69; adminstr. residence hall Kent (Ohio) State U., 1969-71; program mgr. residence hall Ea. Mich. U., Ypsilanti, 1971-73, adminstrv. assoc., 1973-76, dir. housing, 1976-83; assoc. provost Wayne County Community Coll., Belleville, Mich., 1983-84, dir. budget and mgmt. devel. Detroit, 1984-85, sr. v.p. acad. affairs, acting provost, 1985-86, acting exec. dean Belleville, 1986-88, dir. budget and mgmt. devel. Detroit, 1988-89; pres. Cleary Coll., Ypsilanti, 1989—. Part-time instr. English and math. Schoolcraft Coll., Livonia, Mich., 1980-90. Home: 9835 Whisperwood Ln Brighton MI 48116-8859 Office: Cleary Coll 3601 Plymouth Rd Ann Arbor MI 48105-2659

SULLIVAN, TIMOTHY, lawyer; b. Detroit, May 16, 1948; s. Paul Gilmary and Virginia (Rosier) S.; m. Marsha Rosenberg Sullivan, June 19, 1971; children: Eileen A., Hugh V. BA Journalism, U. Mich., 1970; JD, Georgetown U., 1975. Bar: Va. 1975, D.C. 1976. Contract negotiator CIA, Washington, 1973-75; assoc. Fried, Frank, Harris, Shriver & Kampelman, 1975-78; ptnr. Capell, Howard, Knabe & Cobbs P.A., 1978-83, Dykema Gossett, Washington, 1983-95, Adduci, Mastriani & Schaumberg, LLP, 1995—2001. Lectr. in field. Narrator (audio cassette) How to Negotiate Government Contracts, 1986. Citizen mem. Alexandria Commn. Persons with Disabilities, Va., 1992-99, vice-chmn. 1997-98, 98-99. Sgt. U.S. Army, 1970-73. Mem. ABA, Nat. Contract Mgmt. Assn., Univ. Club Washington (bd. govs.), Congl. Country Club (v.p. 1998-99, bd. govs. 1995-2000, pres. 1999-2000). Roman Catholic. Avocations: reading, sports. Office: Thompson Coburn LLP 1909 K St NW 6th Fl Washington DC 20006-1167

SULLIVAN, TIMOTHY JACKSON, law educator, academic administrator; b. Ravenna, Ohio, Apr. 15, 1944; s. Ernest Tulio and Margaret Elizabeth (Caris) Sullivan; m. Anne Doubet Klare, Jan. 21, 1973. AB, Coll. William and Mary, 1966; JD, Harvard U., 1969; LLD (hon.) , U. Aberdeen, Scotland, 1993. Asst. prof. law Coll. William and Mary, Williamsburg, Va., 1972—75, assoc. prof., 1975—78, prof., 1978—85, Bryan prof. law, dean, 1985—92, pres., 1992—; exec. asst. for policy Office of Gov. Charles S. Robb, Richmond, 1982—85; atty. Freeman, Drapers' Co., London, 1992. Vis. prof. law U. Va., Charlottesville, 1981; exec. dir. Gov.'s Commn. on Va.'s Future, Richmond, 1982—84; vice-chmn. Gov.'s Commn. on Fed. Spending, Richmond, 1986; mem. Gov.'s Fellows Selection Com., 1985—90, Gov.'s Commn. on Sexual Assault and Substance Abuse on the Coll. Campus (chmn. enforcement subcom.), 1991—92; counsel Commn. on Future of Va.'s Jud. Sys., 1987—89. Mem. Va. State Bd. Edn., Richmond, 1987—92; chair Gov.'s Task Force on Intercollegiate Athletics, 1992—93. Decorated Bronze Star; named Outstanding Virginian, Va. 4-H Found., 1999. Fellow: Va. Bar Fedn., Am. Bar Fedn.; mem.: ABA, Va. Bar Assn., Va. State Bar, Am. Arbitration Assn. (bd. dirs. 2000—), Cosmos Club, Univ. Club (N.Y.C., Washington), Bull and Bear Club, Omicron Delta Kappa, Phi Beta Kappa. Democrat. Avocations: wine, swimming, reading, golf. Home: Pres House Williamsburg VA 23185 Office: Coll William & Mary PO Box 8795 Williamsburg VA 23187-8795

SULLIVAN, TIMOTHY PATRICK, telecommunications company executive; b. Springfield, Ill., Mar. 4, 1942; s. Jeremiah Joseph and Genevieve Anastasia (Stapleton) S.; m. Kathleen Veronica Logue, May 4, 1974; children: Timothy Patrick Jr., Michael Sean, Shannon Kathleen, Jennifer Hillary, Thomas Brendan. BSEE, U. Notre Dame, 1964; postgrad., Syracuse U., 1966-67. Tech. mgr. IBM Corp., Poughkeepsie, NY, 1964—68, Hursley, England, 1968—69, middle mgr. Poughkeepsie, San Jose, 1969—77, sr. mgr. Research Triangle Park, NC, 1977—81, corp. cons. Armonk, NY, 1981—83, product mgr. Research Triange Park, NC, 1983—85; v.p., officer No. Telecom, Richardson, Tex., 1985—92; pres., CEO Connectware, Inc., 1993—97; CEO Com World, Inc., 1997—98; pres. Optical Networking, SBU, Lucent Techs., Richardson, Tex., 1998—2000; pres. optical networking group Lucent Techs., 2001—. Bd. dirs., chmn. Corp. for Open Systems, McLean, Va., 1992; exec. adv. coun. Nat. Communications Forum, Chgo., 1989-90; chmn. bd. Osinet Corp., 1991. Inventor storage subsystems in field, 1969-71; author: Captain, 1974; contbr. articles to profl. jours. Adv. bd. Dallas Mus. of Art, 1988-92; mem. North Tex. Commn., Dallas, 1988-91. Republican. Roman Catholic. Avocations: creative writing, chess, golf. Home: 5221 Corinthian Bay Dr Plano TX 75093-4028 Office: Lucent Tech 101 Crawfords Corner Rd Holmdel NJ 07733

SULLIVAN, WARREN GERALD, business executive, lawyer; b. Chgo., Sept. 8, 1923; s. Gerald Joseph and Marie (Fairrington) S.; m. Helen Ruth Young, Aug. 21, 1948 (div.); children: Janet M., Douglas W., William C.; m. Helen Louise Curtis. BA, U. Ill., Urbana, 1947; JD, Northwestern U., 1950. Bar: Ill. 1950, Conn. 1971, Mo. 1981, U.S. Ct. Appeals (7th cir.) 1955, U.S. Ct. Appeals (DC cir.) 1964, U.S. Ct. Appeals (6th cir.) 1966, U.S. Ct. Appeals (2nd cir.) 1974, U.S. Supreme Ct. 1968. Atty Ill. Dept. Revenue, Chgo., 1950-52; from assoc. to ptnr. Naphin, Sullivan & Banta and predecessors, 1952-69; v.p. personnel Avco Corp., Greenwich, Conn., 1969-75; v.p. indsl. rels. Gen. Dynamics Corp., St. Louis, 1975-84; mgmt. cons., 1984—. Author: Contbr. Articles to Profl. Jours. Bd. dirs. YMCA Greater St. Louis. 1st lt. Mil. Intelligence Svc., 1942-45; mil. govt. USAR, 1949-54. Fellow Col. Labor and Employment Lawyers; mem. ABA, Conn. Bar Assn., Mo. Bar Assn., Bellerive Country (Creve Coeur, Mo.), Delta Tau Delta, Phi Delta Phi. Office: 400 S 14th St #1102-03 Saint Louis MO 63103 E-mail: wgsulli@attglobal.net.

SULLIVAN, WILLIAM FRANCIS, lawyer; b. San Francisco, May 6, 1952; s. Francis Michael and Jane Frances (Walsh) S.; children: Matthew, Meghan, Kathleen; m. Kait Sullivan. AB, U. Calif., Berkeley, 1974; JD, UCLA, 1977. Bar: Calif. 1977, U.S. Dist. Ct. (no. dist.) Calif. 1977, U.S. Ct. Appeals (9th cir.) 1977, U.S. Dist. Ct. (ea. dist.) Calif. 1978, U.S. Ct. Appeals (D.C. cir.) 1979, U.S. Ct. Appeals (fed. cir.) 1985, U.S. Dist. Ct. (so. dist.) Calif. 1986, U.S. Dist. Ct. (cen. dist.) Calif. 1990, U.S. Supreme Ct. 1986. Assoc. Chickering & Gregory, San Francisco and Washington, 1977-81, Brobeck, Phleger & Harrison, San Diego and San Francisco, 1981-84, ptnr., 1984—, mng. ptnr. San Diego, 1992-96, 2001—, securitie litigation group leader, 2002—, firmwide mng. ptnr., 1996-98. Panelist Calif. Continuing Edn. Bar; instr. Fed. Practice Program, U.S. No. Dist., chair Litigation sect., 1992, U.S. Dist. Ct. (no. dist.) Calif., 1980; instr. Coll. of Advocacy, Hastings Law Sch.; adv. bd. AMICUS Info. Svcs. Mem. ABA, Assn. Bus. Trial Lawyers (bd. govs. San Diego chpt. 1993-95), Calif. Bar Assn. (litigation sect.), San Francisco Bar Assn., San Diego Bar Assn., Barristers Club San Francisco (bd. dirs. 1984-86, pres. 1985), Calif. Young Lawyers Assn. (bd. dirs. 1986-89, sec. 1987-99, 1st v.p. 1988-89). Democrat. Roman Catholic. Office: Brobeck Phleger & Harrison 12390 El Camino Real San Diego CA 92130-2081 E-mail: wsullivan@BroBeck.com.

SULLIVAN, WILLIAM JOHN, osteopath; b. Pittsburg, Kans., Nov. 5, 1963; s. William Leroy and Joan Elizabeth (Prete) S.; m. Shelly Renee Lotterer, Oct. 24, 1992; 1 child, Lauren Marie. BS in Biology, Pittsburg (Kans.) State U., 1986; DO, U. Health Scis., Kansas City, Mo., 1990. Diplomate Nat. Bd. Osteo. Med. Examiners, Am. Bd. Internal Medicine, Am. Assn. Med. Rev. Officers. Intern Riverside Hosp., Wichita, Kans., 1990-91; resident Deaconess Hosp., St. Louis, 1991-94; pvt. practice Pittsburg Internal Medicine P.A., 1994—; active staff Mt. Carmel Med. Ctr., Pittsburg, 1994—, med. dir. occupl. health, med. dir. employee health, 1995—2002, med. dir. cardiomyopathy clinic, 1997—, chief medicine, 1998—, chief-of-staff-elect, 1999—, pres. med. staff, 2001—. Med. staff sec. Mt. Carmel Med. Ctr., Pitts., 1999; clin. instr. Pitts. State U. Sch. Nursing; clin. adv. Pitts. State U. Pre-Med Club; participating physician Pitts. Free Clinic; alumni bd. dirs. Pitts. State U.; mem. health occupations adv. bd. Unified Sch. Dist. # 250; adv. bd. of dir. Cmty. Nat. Bank, Pitts., Kans. Mem. exec. bd. dirs. Pitts. Family YMCA. Lt. col. Kans. Army N.G., 1988—, chief internal medicine, 1995—; bd. dirs. Pitts. State U. Alumni Assn. Mem. ACP, Kans. Med. Soc., Am. Assn. Med. Rev. Officers, N.G. Assn. U.S., KC., Crawford County Med. Soc. (pres.), Am. Legion, Sigma Chi (life loyal Sig program). Republican. Roman Catholic. Avocations: music, golf, stamp collecting. Home: 2606 Knollview St Pittsburg KS 66762-6514 Office: Pittsburg Internal Med PA 2401 S Tucker Pittsburg KS 66762-6601

SULLOWAY, FRANK JONES, psychologist, historian; b. Concord, N.H., Feb. 2, 1947; s. Alvah Woodbury and Alison (Green) S.; 1 child, Ryan. AB summa cum laude, Harvard U., 1969, AM in History of Sci., 1971, PhD History of Sci., 1978. Jr. fellow Harvard U. Soc. Fellows, 1974-77; mem. Sch. Social Sci. Inst. for Advanced Study, Princeton, N.J., 1977-78; rsch. fellow Miller Inst. for Basic Rsch. in Sci., U. Calif., Berkeley, 1978-80, MIT, Cambridge, 1980-81, vis. scholar, 1989-98; postdoctoral fellow Harvard U., 1981-82, vis. scholar, 1984-89; rsch. fellow Univ. Coll., London, 1982-84; Vernon prof. biography Dartmouth Coll., Hanover, N.H., 1986; vis. Miller rsch. prof. U. Calif., Berkeley, 1999—, vis. prof., 2000—. Author: Freud, Biologist of the Mind, 1979 (Pfizer award History Sci. Soc. 1980), Born to Rebel, 1996; contbr. numerous articles on Charles Darwin, Sigmund Freud, and personality devel. to profl. jours. Fellow NEH, 1980-81, NSF, 1981-82, John Simon Guggenheim Meml. Found., 1982-83, MacArthur Found., 1984-89, Dibner Inst., MIT, 1993-94, Ctr. for Advanced Study in Behavioral Scis., Stanford, Calif., 1998-99; recipient Randi award Skeptics Soc., 1997, Golden Plate award Am. Acad. Achievement, 1997. Fellow AAAS (mem. electorate nominating com. sect. L 1988-91, 94-97), Linnean Soc. London; mem. Am. Psychol. Soc., Human Behavior and Evolution Soc., History of Sci. Soc. (fin. com. 1987-92, com. on devel. 1988-92). Home: 1709 Shattuck Ave Apt 205 Berkeley CA 94709-1753 Office: U Calif Dept Psychology IPSR 4125 Tolman Hall Berkeley CA 94720-1603 E-mail: sulloway@uclink.berkeley.edu.

SULS, JERRY M. psychologist, educator; b. Washington, Jan. 9, 1947; s. Abraham Issac and Leah Suls; m. Suzzanne Bendt, Sept. 6, 1968 (div Nov. 1993); m. Rene Elizabeth Martin, May 6, 1994; 1 son, Robert. BA, Temple U., Phila., 1968, MA, 1971, PhD in Social Psychology, 1973. Asst. prof. Georgetown U., Washington, 1972-75, SUNY, Albany, 1975-78, assoc. prof., 1978-87, prof., 1987-90; prof. dept. psychology U. Iowa, Iowa City, 1990—. Mem. behavioral medicine panel NIH, Bethesda, Md., 1983-86; mem. adv. panel NSF, Washington, 1992-95. Editor: Social Comparison Processes, 1977, Social Comparison, 1991, Handbook of Social Comparison, 2000; assoc. editor Jour. Personality and Social Psychology, 1990-96; editor Personality and Social Psychology Bull., 1998—; contbr. articles to profl. jours., chpts. to books. Grantee NIH, 1988-90, 90-94, NSF, 1996-99, Am. Heart Assn., 1996-98, NSF, 2000—. Avocations: jazz, jazz piano. Office: U Iowa Dept Psychology E-11 SSH Iowa City IA 52242 E-mail: jerry-suls@uiowa.edu.

SULT, JEFFERY SCOT, performing company executive, playwright, director, actor; b. Washington, Dec. 29, 1956; s. Elmer Ray Sult and Elizabeth Bush (DeVary) La Barbera. AA, Fla. C.C., Jacksonville, 1979; BFA, U. Fla., 1981; MA, NYU, 1982, cert. in film and video, 1990; cert., Royal Acad. Dramatic Art, London, 1995; MFA, City U. N.Y., 1999. Artistic dir. Acme Prodns., N.Y.C., 1983—. Writer, dir.: (plays) Relationship, 1983, Trialogue #1, 1983, Letter, 1984, Party, 1984, Trialogue #2, 1984, Marines, 1984, Thinking, 1984, Horseshoe, 1985, Anniversary, 1985, Trialogue #3, 1985, Wedding, 1985, Quagmire, 1985, Reunion, 1986, (teleplays) Call-In, 1987, Dialogue #1, 1988, Enigma, 1989, Maze, 1990, A Map of the City, 1991, dir. The Comedy of Errors, 1998, 99, Troilus and Cressida, 1998, Twelfth Night, 1998, Hamlet, 1999, The Comedy of Errors, 1998, Macbeth, 2000; appeared in stage prodns. Richard II, A Midsummer Night's Dream, Richard III, Henry VI-Part 1, Philoctetes, Macbeth, Orestes, La Boheme, The Tempest, The Taming of the Shrew, Twelfth Night, Troilus and Cressida, Hamlet, Romeo and Juliet. Sgt. USMC, 1975-77. Mem. AFTRA, Soc. Am. Fight Dirs., Internat. Brotherhood Electrical Workers. Avocations: football, theater, films. Home: 4489 Broadway Apt 3G New York NY 10040-2406 Office: Acme Prodns 4489 Broadway Apt 3G New York NY 10040-2406 E-mail: jssult@aol.com.

SULTAN, JAMES LEHMAN, lawyer; b. New Haven, Oct. 10, 1953; s. Stanley Ezra Sultan and Florence Lehman Nichols. BA, Yale U., 1974; JD, Harvard U., 1980. Bar: Mass. 1980, U.S. Dist. Ct. Mass. 1981, U.S. Ct. Appeals (1st cir.) 1981, U.S. Supreme Ct. 1989. Legis. asst. U.S. Rep. Robert F. Drinan, Washington, 1974-77; law clk. to William Wayne Justice U.S. Dist. Ct., Tyler, Tex., 1980-81; assoc. Silvergate, Shapiro & Gertner, Boston, 1981-82; pvt. practice, 1982-86; ptnr. Rankin & Sultan, 1986—. Lectr. profl. seminars, 1987—. Contbr. (book) Massachusetts Criminal Law, 1990. Mem. Nat. Assn. Criminal Def. Lawyers. Office: Rankin & Sultan 1 Comml Wharf North Boston MA 02110 E-mail: jsultan@rankin-sultan.com.

SULTANIK, JEFFREY TED, lawyer; b. N.Y.C., July 26, 1954; s. Solomon and Anna (Tiger) S.; m. Judith Ann Clyman, Nov. 14, 1981; children: Evan A., Sara A. BA cum laude, U. Pa., Phila., 1976; JD, Hofstra U., 1979. Bar: Pa. 1979, Fla. 1980, U.S. Dist. Ct. (ea. dist.) Pa., U.S. Ct. Appeals (3d cir.). Ptnr. Fox, Rothschild, O'Brien & Frankel, L.L.P., Lansdale, Pa., 1979-81; solicitor Upper Merion Sch. Dist., 1995—. Solicitor Boyertown (Pa.) Area Sch. Dist., 1981—, North Montco Vocat.-Tech. Sch., Lansdale, 1981—, Souderton (Pa.) Area Sch. Dist., 1989—, Wallingford-Swarthmore Sch. Dist., 1999—; spl. counsel Penn Delco Sch. Dist., Aston , Pa., Coun. Rock Sch. Dist., Newtown, Pa., 1998, Kennett Consolidated Sch. Dist., 1999—, Norristown Sch. Dist., 1999—, Coun. Rock Sch. Dist., 2000—; co-chair pers. com., mktg./admissions com., sec. bd. trustees Germantown Acad., Ft. Washington, Pa., 1991—; presenter in field. Regular columnist Your School and the Law, 1992. Mem. Nat. Sch. Bds. Assn., 2001. Mem. Nat. Assn. Sch. and Coll. Attys., Nat. Sch. Bds. Assn., Pa. Sch. Bds. Assn., Inc., Pa. Assn. Sch. Bus. Ofcls. (cert. of appreciation 1991), Pa. Bar Assn. (labor and edn. sects.), Montgomery County Bar Assn. (mcpl. law com. 1983—), Lehigh U. Law Forums, Assn. Del. Valley Ind. Schs. Republican. Jewish. Avocations: automobiles, travel. Home: 3229 Barley Ln Lansdale PA 19446-5114 Office: Fox Rothschild O'Brien & Frankel LLP 1250 S Broad St Ste 1000 Lansdale PA 19446-5343 E-mail: jsultanik@frof.com.

SULTON, ANNE THOMAS, lawyer, criminologist; b. Racine, Wis., Oct. 24, 1952; d. William Henry and Esther (Phillips) Thomas; m. James E. Sulton Jr., Aug. 1, 1981; children: James E. III, William Francis, Patrice Amandla. BA in Psychology, Wash. State U., 1973; MA in Criminal Justice, SUNY, 1975; PhD in Criminal Justice, U. Md., 1984; JD, U. Wis., 1985. Bar: Wis. 1985, U.S. Dist. Ct. (we. dist.) Wis. 1985, Colo. 1993, U.S. Dist. Ct. Colo. 1994, U.S. Ct. Appeals (7th cir.) 1995, U.S. Ct. Appeals (10th cir.) 1996. Instr. criminal justice and criminology Spelman Coll., Atlanta, 1976-78; rsch. assoc. Nat. Orgn. Black Law Enforcement Execs., Balt., 1978-80; lectr. criminal justice and criminology Howard U., Washington, 1980-84; asst. prof. criminal justice U. Wis., Oshkosh, 1984-85; project dir. Police Found., Washington, 1985-87; pvt. practice law Madison, Wis., 1985—, Englewood, Colo., 1993—. Dir. grad. criminal justice program U. Balt.; former instr. Atlanta U., Atlanta Fed. Penitentiary, Md. State Penitentiary, Balt. City Police Tng. Acad., Inst. Criminal Justice and Criminology, U. Md., Taycheeda Correctional Instn. for Women, Century 21 Sch. Real Estate; presenter, spkr., facilitator in field; numerous TV and radio appearances; assoc. prof. criminal justice N.J. City Univ., 2000—. Contbr. articles to various publs., poetry to books, mags. and newspapers. Bd. dirs. Washington Halfway Home for Women, 1983; pres. bd. dirs. Willard Thomas Scholarship Found., Inc., Racine, Wis., 1973—, South Madison Neighborhood Ctr., 1987-88; mem. allocations panel on un-and underemployment United Way Dane County, 1987-88; spokesperson Coalition African-Am. Orgns., Madison, 1987-88, legal counsel NAACP Madison chpt., 1989-90, Denver chpt., 1994-99. Recipient cert. Atlanta Commr. Pub. Safety, 1977, Outsdanding Citizen award Fulton County Commr.'s Office, 1977, cert. of appreciation Atlanta Crime Analysis Team, 1978; named to Washington Park High Sch. Hall of Fame, 1986; recipient Spl. Friend award Atlanta Fed. Penitentiary Bd., NAACP, 1978. Mem. NAACP, ABA, ATLA, Acad. Criminal Justice Scis., Wis. Bar Assn., Nat. African-Am. Braintrust on Criminal Justice and Criminology, Police Exec. Rsch. Forum. Avocation: flying small aircraft.

SULTZER, BARNET MARTIN, microbiology and immunology researcher; b. Union City, N.J., Mar. 24, 1929; s. Moses Joseph and Florence Gertrude (Fischer) S.; m. Judith Ray Moreinis, Aug. 26, 1956; 1 child, Steven Bennett. BS, Rutgers U., 1950; MS, Mich. State U., 1951, PhD, 1958. Rsch. assoc. Princeton (N.J.) Labs., Inc., 1958-64; from asst. prof. to prof. microbiology SUNY, Bklyn., 1964-94, prof. emeritus, 1994—, interim chmn. dept. microbiology, 1980-82. Vis. scientist Karolinska Inst., Stockholm, 1971-72; vis. prof. Pasteur Inst., Paris, 1979-80; adj. prof. Fels Inst. of Cancer Rsch. and Molecular Biology, Temple U., Phila., 1995—; v.p. rsch. Stem Cell Therapeutics, King of Prussia, Pa., 1995-2000. Assoc. editor Jour. of Immunology, 1983-86; contbr. book chpts. and over 60 articles to profl. jours. on microbiology and immunology; mem. editl. bd. Infection and Immunity, 1980-94. Pres. Tenants Assn. Gateway Plz., Manhattan, N.Y., 1990-92; mem. Cmty. Bd. #1, Manhattan, 1989-94. 1st lt. USMC, 1952-55. Pres.'s fellow Am. Soc. Microbiology, 1957; grantee USPHS, NIH, Office of Naval Rsch., 1967-94. Mem. AAAS, Am. Soc. Microbiology, Am. Assn. Immunologists, N.Y. Acad. Sci., Harvey Soc., Internat. Endotoxin Soc., Reticuloendothelial Soc., Sigma Xi. Achievements include patent for chemical detoxification of endotoxins and discovery of the genetic basis for mammalian responses to endotoxins including immunological and pathophysiological effects; co-discoverer of a signal transduction gene controlling mammalian cellular responses to lipopolysaccharide endotoxin; developed first commercial immunological pregnancy test. Office: 375-8M South End Ave New York NY 10280 E-mail: bsultzer@aol.com.

SULZBACH, CHRISTI ROCOVICH, lawyer; b. L.A. BA, U. So. Calif., 1976; JD, Loyola U., 1979. Bar: Calif., 1980. Various to assoc. gen. counsel Tenet Healthcare Corp., Santa Barbara, 1983-99, exec. v.p., gen. counsel Calif., 1999—. Bd. dirs. Nat. Health Found., L.A. Mem. State Bar of Calif., ABA (exec. v.p., gen. counsel), FBA (bd. dirs. L.A. chpt.), Fedn. Am. Health Sys. (bd. dirs.). Office: Tenet Healthcare Corp Corporate Office 3820 State St Santa Barbara CA 93105-3112 E-mail: christi.sulzbach@tenethealth.com.

SULZBERGER, ARTHUR OCHS, JR. newspaper publisher; b. Mt. Kisco, N.Y., Sept. 22, 1951; s. Arthur Ochs Sulzberger and Barbara Winslow Grant; m. Gail Gregg, May 24, 1975; children: Arthur Gregg, Ann Alden. BA, Tufts U., 1974; postgrad., Harvard U. Bus. Sch., 1985. Reporter The Raleigh (N.C.) Times, 1974-76; corr. AP, London, 1976-78; Washington corr. N.Y. Times, 1978-81, city hall reporter, 1981, asst. metro editor, 1981-82, group mgr. advt. dept., 1983-84, sr. analyst corp. planning, 1985, prodn. coordinator, 1985-87, asst. pub., 1987-88, dep. pub., 1988-92, pub., 1992—97; chmn. bd. dirs. N.Y. Times Co., 1997—. Mem. Newspaper Assn. of Am. Office: The NY Times 229 W 43rd St New York NY 10036-3959

SULZER-AZAROFF, BETH, psychology educator; BS in Edn., MA, CCNY; postgrad., Columbia U.; PhD, U. Minn., 1966. Elem. sch. tchr. various pub. schs., N.Y.C., Washington; assoc. prof. of guidance and ednl. psychology So. Ill. U., 1966-72; psychol. tng. cons., part time Mansfield Tng. Sch., 1972-73; rsch. asoc. U. Conn. Health Ctr., 1972-73; prof. psychology, prof. edn. U. Mass., 1973-92, prof. emeritus, 1992—; prin. The Browns Group. Vis. fellow Western Australian Inst. Tech., Perth, 1981; trustee Cambridge Ctr. for Behavioral Studies; mem. adv. bd. May Inst. for Autistic Children, The Groden Ctr.; workshop presenter, lectr. and cons. in field. Assoc. editor: Journal of Applied Behavior Analysis, 1974-76; editorial bd. mem.: including Safety Sci., Behavioral Assessment, Behavior Therapy, Spl. Svcs. in the Schs.; guest reviewer: including Am. Psychologist, Rev. of Ednl. Rsch.; co-author of various textbooks and monographs; contbr. chpts. to books and articles to profl. jours. Recipient numerous grants Univ. Mass., 1973—. Fellow APA (pres. divsn. 25), Am. Psychol. Soc., Am. Acad. Behavioral Medicine; mem. Soc. for Exptl. Analysis Behavior (v.p. 1978-79), Assn. for Behavior Analysis (pres. 1981-82), Conn. Acad. Sci. and Engring., Berkshire Assn. for Behavior Analysis and Therapy (v.p. 1981-82, pres. 1982-83), Am. Edn. Rsch. Assn., Assn. for Advancement of Behavior Therapy, Acad. Behavioral Medicine Rsch., Am. Soc. for Quality Control.

SUMANTH, DAVID JONNAKOTY, industrial engineer, educator; b. Machilipatnam, India, Jan. 28, 1946; arrived in U.S., 1972; s. John Devraj and Nancy (David) Jonnakoty; m. Chaya J. Victor, June 26, 1974; children: John J., Paul J. BME, Osmania U., India, 1967, MME, 1969; MS in Indsl. Engring., Ill. Inst. Tech., 1974, PhD in Indsl. Engring., 1979. Tchg./rsch. asst. Ill. Inst. Tech., Chgo., 1973-78, instr., 1979; asst. prof. indsl. engring. U. Miami, Coral Gables, Fla., 1979-83, founding dir. productivity research group, 1979—, dir. grad. studies, 1980-83, assoc. prof. indsl. engring., 1983-88, Coll. Engring. coordinator MBA/MSIE, 1984-93, prof. indsl. engring., 1988—. Chmn. 1st and 2d Internat. Conf. on Productivity Rsch., 3d, 4th, 5th Internat. Conf. on Productivity and Quality Rsch. Author: Productivity Engineering and Management, 1984, internat. student edit., 1985, Spanish edit., 1990, Indian edit., 1990, coll. custom series edit., 1994, also instrs. manual, (script) Total Productivity Management, 1985; editor: Productivity Management Frontiers-I, 1987, II, 1989, Productivity and Quality Management Frontiers III, 1991, IV, 1993, V, 1995, VI, 1997, VII, 1998, Total Productivity Management, 1998. Recipient over 60 honors, awards and recognitions including YMCA Edn. Gold medal, 1969, Freedoms Found., 1987;, Alexander Orr award of Tchg. Excellence, U. Miami, 2000; fellow U. Miami Eaton Honors Coll., 1986, fellow World Acad. Productivity Sci., 1989; gov.'s appointee as sr. judge Fla. Sterling award, 1992-93, judge, 1993-98. Mem. Am. Inst. Indsl. Engrs. (sr. mem., pres. Miami chpt. 1982-83, bd. dirs. 1983-84, nat. asst. dir. productivity mgmt. 1984—, chairperson rsch. com. 1987, Outstanding Indsl. Engr. of Yr. Miami chpt. 1983, 84); Productivity Ctr. (trustee 1985-89), Internat. Soc. for Productivity and Quality Rsch. (founder 1993, founding pres. 1993-95, chmn. 1995-97). Republican. Baptist. Avocations: reading, writing, people. Office: U Miami Productivity Rsch Group Coral Gables FL 33124

SUMARSAM, music educator; b. Bojonegoro, East Java, Indonesia, July 27, 1944; came to U.S., 1972; s. Samidi and Diwati Partoredjo; m. Urip Sri Maeny; children: Tistha, Dwi. Teaching diploma, Indonesian Nat. Music Conserv., Surakarta, 1964; BA, Indonesian Nat. Acad. Music, Surakarta, 1968; MA, Wesleyan U., Middletown, Conn., 1976; PhD, Cornell U., 1992. Tchr. Indonesian Nat. Conservatory of Music, Surakarta, 1966-71; vis. artist dept. music Wesleyan U., Middletown, Conn., 1972-76, artist in residence, 1976-90, adj. assoc. prof. music, 1990-92, adj. prof. music, 1992—. Instr. Gamelan, Kasatriyan Jr. High Sch., Surakarta, 1965-69; Indonesian Embassy, Canberra, Australia, 1971-72; asst. lectr. Indonesian Nat. Acad. of Music, Surakarta, 1967-71; 1977 (summer) dir. U. Wis. Gamelan Ensemble, Madison, 1977, 1979; vis. instr. Javanese music, Brown U.; co-dir. Cornell U. Gamelan Ensemble, 1983-84, dir, (spring) 84; vis. instr. Javanese music, Winter Study Program, Williams Coll., Williamstown, Mass., 1991; cons. Art of Indonesia: Tales from Shadow World, 1990, others. Author: Gamelan: Cultural Interaction and Musical Development in Central Java, 1995; composer: Ladrang Panggayuh, 1968, Gendhing Wulan Sih, 1968, Pambuka and Panutup, 1969, Swimming, 1974, Celebration, 1982, Gendhing Hayu Rahayu, 1982, Contemplation, 1987; musician and puppeteer since 1952, performing in Indonesia, Japan, Australia and in many ednl. instns. in U.S.; contbr. numerous articles to profl. jours. Recipient scholarships Cornell U., 1983-87. Mem. Soc. for Ethnomusicology, Koninklijk Inst. voor Taal-Land-en Volkenkunde, Soc. for Asian Music, Assn. for Asian Studies, Masyarakat Seni Pertunjukan Indonesia, Internat. Coun. Traditional Music. Home: 576 Millbrook Rd Middletown CT 06457-5520 Office: Wesleyan U Dept Music Middletown CT 06459-0001

SUMBERG, ALFRED DONALD, professional association executive; b. Utica, N.Y., Nov. 22, 1928; s. Samuel M. and Rachel Frances (Silverstein) S.; m. Dolly Primakow, June 26, 1955; children: Susan Diane Beldon, Laurie Darlene Sumberg. Student, Utica Coll., 1946-48, Hebrew Union Coll., 1948-50; AB, U. Cin., 1950, MA, 1951; PhD, U. Wis., 1960; LHD (hon.), U. Cin., 1994. Exec. dir., founding dir. Am. Jewish Tercentenary Com. Wis. Wis. Jewish Archives, 1954-55; instr. history U. Wis., Parkside, 1955-56; prof. history and econs. East Stroudsburg (Pa.) U., 1956-67; vis. prof. history U. Cin., Cin., 1954, 58, 67; assoc. gen. sec., dir. govt. rels. AAUP, Washington, 1967-94. Founding pres. N.E. Pa. Sch. Employees Fed. Credit Union, 1960-67; mem. exec. com. educator's ad hoc com. on copyright law, 1976-94, co-chair ad hoc com. for the creation of a cabinet-level dept. of edn., 1978-80, com. for edn. funding v.p.-treas., 1980-82, pres., 1982; bd. dirs. The Tuition Exch., 1988-96. Contbr. chapters to books, articles to profl. jours. Bd. dirs., chair edn. com. The Hist. Found. of Pa., 1961-67; pres. The Hist. Assn. Northeastern Pa., 1963-67, Monroe County (Pa.) Hist. Soc., 1965-67; edn. coord. Mondale-Ferraro campaign, 1984; vol. Nat. Exec. Svc. Corps, 1994-96. Mem. AAUP, Am. Hist. Assn., Nat. Trust for Hist. Preservation, U.S. Capitol Hist. Soc., Am. Econs. Assn., Nat. Economists Club, Nat. Dem. Club, Libr. of Congress Assocs., U. Cin. Alumni Assn. (life, pres. Washington chpt. 1972-74), U. Wis. Alumni Assn. (life, pres. Washington chpt. 1978-80), Phi Alpha Theta, Kappa Delta Pi, Utica Coll. Alumni Assn. Democrat. Jewish. Home and Office: 1309 Fallsmead Way Rockville MD 20854-5523

SUMBERG, THEODORE A. retired economist; b. N.Y.C., Oct. 1, 1916; s. Nathan I. and Ray (Levy) S.; m. Miriam Buttrick, Nov. 7, 1948; 1 child, Judith Sumberg Giuricich. BS in Social Sci., CCNY, 1939; PhD, New Sch. for Social Rsch., 1955. Economist Centro de Estudios Monetarios Latinoamericanos, Mex., 1955-58, Orgn. for Econ. Coop. and Devel., Paris, 1962, U.S. Govt. Economic advisor to ctrl. banks and govts. Guatemala, Burma, Nicaragua, Ecuador, Laos, Vietnam, Togo, Taiwan, UN, N.Y.C. Author: Foreign Aid as Moral Obligation, 1973, Political Literature of Europe, 1993; contbr. articles to profl. publs. Social Sci. Rsch. Coun. fellow, 1953. Home: 5802 Wilmett Rd Bethesda MD 20817-2521

SUMER, B. MUTLU, civil engineer, educator, researcher, consultant; b. Malatya, Turkey, Nov. 15, 1945; arrived in Denmark, 1984; s. Sait and Muserref (Metan) S.; m. Tijen Erkolencik, Nov. 27, 1970; children: Kaan, Ufuk. MSCE, Tech. U. Istanbul, Turkey, 1967, PhD in Hydraulics, 1970. Asst. prof. Tech. U. Istanbul, 1970—71, 1973—75, from assoc. prof. to prof., 1975—84; rsch. engr. U. Cambridge, England, 1971—73; assoc. prof. Tech. U. Denmark, Lyngby, 1984—2002, prof., 2002—. Vis. scholar U. So. Calif., L.A., 1983; chmn., organizer Euromech Colloquium on Sediment Transport, Istanbul, 1982; cons. Hydraulic Engring., 1976—, Marine Civil Engring. and Petroleum Industry, 1987—; guest rschr. Tech. U. Denmark, Lyngby, 1977, guest prof., 1979; coord. EU rsch. program Scour Around Coastal Structures, 1997-2000, EU rsch. program Liquefaction Around Marine Structures, 2001—. Co-editor: Mechanics of Sediment Transport, 1983; sr. author: Hydrodynamics Around Cylindrical Structures, 1997; sr. author The Mechanics of Scour in the Marine Environment, 2002; assoc. editor: Jour. of Waterway, Port, Coastal and Ocean Engring. of ASCE, 2001—, assoc. editor: Internat. Jour. Offshore and Polar Engring., 1996—; contbr. articles. Recipient Hydraulic Structures award, Turkish Soc. Civil Engring., 1971; NATO postdoctoral fellow Sci. and Tech. Rsch. Coun. Turkey, U. Cambridge, 1971-72, Support award, 1976, Sci. award, 1991. Mem. Internat. Soc. Offshore and Polar Engring. Home: Lyngby Rosenvaenge 9 2800 Lyngby Denmark Office: Tech U Denmark MEK Coastal and River Engring Sect DK 2800 Lyngby Denmark E-mail: sumer@isva.dtu.dk.

SUMERS, ANNE RICKS, ophthalmologist, museum director; b. Beverly, Mass., May 8, 1957; d. David Frank and Anne Russell (Russell) Ricks; m. Elliott H. Sumers, May 31, 1983; children: Ben, Ted. BA in English Lit. with honors, U. Mich., 1979; MD, U. Cin., 1983. Diplomate Am. Bd. Ophthalmology. Intern in internal medicine Mt. Auburn Hosp., Cambridge, Mass., 1984; resident in ophthalmology NYU/Bellevue Hosp., 1984-87; ptnr. Ridgewood (N.J.) Ophthalmology, PC, 1990—; dir. N.J. Childrens Mus., Paramus, N.J., 1992—; co-owner Saddle River (N.J.) Market, 1995—. Team ophthalmologist N.Y. Giants Football Team, 1994—, N.J. Nets, 1999—; state coord. N.J. Turn Off Your TV Week, 1994, 95, 96; spkr. in field. Author: The Offical M.D. Handbook, 1983, Be A Better Mother—Today!, 1999; writer, host Channel 11/WPIX Wonder Zone, 1993; interviewed on Good Morning Am., Am.'s Talking, CBS This Morning, NJN Discover N.J., Comcast Cablevision, Cablevision, Fox Channel 5 Good Day N.Y., 1992—, NBC Nightly News, numerous radio shows; writer (essays) Newsweek, USA Today. Named one of 10 N.J. Women of Yr., N.J. Woman Mag., 1993; profiled in AMA News, Med. Econs., The N.Y. Times, Star Ledger, Argus and other newspapers and mags. Fellow Am. Acad. Ophthalmology (media spokesperson, media info. com.); mem. AMA, Assn. Youth Museums, N.J. Acad. Ophtholmology (bd. govs. 1997), Alpha Omega Alpha. Office: Ridgewood Ophthalmology PC 1200 E Ridgewood Ave Ridgewood NJ 07450-3937

SUMERS, REBECCA ANN, interior designer; b. Marengo, Iowa, Sept. 9, 1947; d. Russell Dean and Arvena Maxine (Seaton) S. BFA, Drake U., 1969; postgrad., Venezia Isola di Studies, Venice, Italy, 1969-71. Lic. interior designer, Tex. Arts advisor Office of the Mayor, Washington, 1971-73; apparel mgr. Apogee Internat., Boston, 1973-75; dir. World Fine Arts Ctr., Atlanta, 1975-77; arts advisor Dept. Human Resources, San Antonio, 1977-79; interior designer/buyer Leonard's Furniture, 1979-95; interior designer Coles Drexel Heritage, Fairfax, Va., 1995-98, Colony House, Arlington, 1998—. Lectr. in field. Mem. San Antonio Artists Alliance. Mem. Am. Soc. Interior Designers, Alpha Xi Delta.

SUMIDA, GERALD AQUINAS, lawyer; b. Hilo, Hawaii, June 19, 1944; s. Sadamy and Kimiyo (Miyahara) S. AB summa cum laude, Princeton U., 1966; JD, Yale U., 1969. Bar: Hawaii 1970, U.S. Dist. Ct. Hawaii 1970, U.S. Ct. Appeals (9th cir.) 1970, U.S. Supreme Ct. 1981. Rsch. assoc. Ctr. Internat. Studies, Princeton U., 1969; assoc. Carlsmith, Ball, Honolulu, 1970-76, ptnr., 1976-99; gen. counsel Asian Devel. Bank, 1999—. Mem. cameras in courtroom evaluation com. Hawaii Supreme Ct., 1984-86. Co-author: (with others) Legal, Instutional and Financial Aspects of An Inter-Island Electrical Transmission Cable, 1984, Alternative Approaches to the Legal, Instutional and Financial Aspects of Developing an Inter-Island, Electrical Transmission

Cable System, 1986; editor Hawaii Bar News, 1972-73; contbr. chpts. to books. Mem. sci. and statis. com. Western Pacific Fishery Mgmt. Coun., 1979-99; mem. study group on law of armed conflict and the law of the sea Comdr. in Chief Pacific, USN, 1979-82; chmn. Pacific and Asian Affairs Coun. Hawaii, 1991, pres., 1982-91, bd. govs., 1976-96; bd. govs. ARC, 1994-2000, mem. exec. com., 1996-2000, chmn. human resources com., 1996-2000, chmn. Hawaii chpt., 1983-99, bd. dirs., 1983-99, vice chmn., 1990; chmn. Hawaii C. of C., 1997-98, bd. dirs., 1990-99; vice chmn. Honolulu Com. Fgn. Rels., 1983—; pres., dir., founding mem. Hawaii Ocean Law Assn., 1978—; mem. Hawaii Adv. Group for Law of Sea Inst., 1977-85; pres. Hawaii Inst. Continuing Legal Edn., 1979-83, dir., 1976-87; pres., founding mem. Hawaii Coun. Legal Edn. Youth, 1980-83, dir., 1983-88; chmn. Hawaii Commn. Yr. 2000, 1976-79; mem. Honolulu Cmty. Media Coun., 1976-99, exec. com., 1976-84, legal coun., 1979-83; bd. dirs. Hawaii Imin Centennial Corp., 1983-90, Hawaii Pub. Radio, 1983-88, Legal Aid Soc. Hawaii, 1984; founding gov., exec. v.p., chmn. rules and procedures Ctr. Internat. Comml. Dispute Resolution, 1987—; exec. com. Pacific Aerospace Mus., 1991—; exec. com. Pacific Islands Assn., 1988—; exec. com. Asia-Pacific Ctr. Res. Internat. Bus. Disputes, 1991-95; mem. Coun. Asia-Pacific Dispute Rsch. Ctrs., 1991-95; bd. dirs. U.S. C. of C., 1998—; mem. Pacific Basin Econ. Coun., 1993—; mem. mgmt. com. PBEC-U.S. Nat. Com., 1994-99. Recipient cert. of appreciation Gov. of Hawaii, 1979, resolutions of appreciation Hawaii Senate and Ho. of Reps., 1979; grantee Japan Found., 1979. Mem. ABA, Hawaii Bar Assn. (pres. young lawyers sect. 1974, v.p. 1984), Japan-Hawaii Lawyers Assn., Am. Soc. Internat. Law, Internat. Bar Assn., Am. Judicature Soc., Inter-Pacific Bar Assn., Internat. Law Assn., Plaza Club (Honolulu), Colonial Club (Princeton). Democrat. Office: Office Gen Coun Asian Devel Bank 6 ADB Ave 0401 Metro Manila Mandaluyong Philippines also: Gen Coun Asian Devel Bank PO Box 789 0980 Manila Philippines E-mail: gsumida@adb.org.

SUMIDA, GREGORY ZIO, artist, photographer, musician, astronomer; b. L.A. Grad., Alhambra H.S. One-man shows include Palm Springs Desert Mus., 1973, Desert S.W. Art Gallery, 1974, Pioneer Mus. and Haggin Art Gallery, 1975, Potlatch Art Gallery, 1976, Maxwell Galleries, San Francisco, 1977, Smith Gallery, N.Y.C., Troy's Gallery, Ariz., 1984, 86, 88, Zantman Galleries, Palm Desert, Calif., 1990, Legacy Gallery, 1991, 2002; group shows include Americana Gallery, Carmel, Calif., 1978, Fireside Gallery, Carmel, Calif., 1979, De Colores Gallery, Denver, 1979, Stremmel Galleries, Reno, 1980, Period Gallery West, Scottsdale, Ariz., 1981, Artist Union Gallery, 1982, 84, 85, Smith Gallery, N.Y.C., 1983, Artist Union Gallery, 1982, 84, 85, Hunter Art Gallery, San Francisco, 1984, For Art Lovers Only, Denver, 1984, Classic-Am. Show, 1988, 89, Legacy Gallery, Scottsdale, 1990, 2000, Zantman Galleries, Carmel, Calif., 1996, Urubamba Gallery, Paris, 1996, Artist FocusShow Legacy Gallery, Scottsdale, 2000, winter 2001, Eiteljorg Mus., 2002; represented in numerous pub. and pvt. collections; included in numerous publs. including S.W. Art, 1977, Contemporary We. Artists, 1982, We. Art Digest, 1986, Palm Springs Desert Life, 1987, Calif. Rev., 1989, Palm Springs Life, 1991, Am. Reference, 1991, Le Peintre Sumida, 1991, Internat. Fine Art Collector, 1992, Art West, 1999, Cowboys and Indians, 2001, Jour. Pharm. Medicine, 2001. Office: PO Box 9210 Stockton CA 95208-1210 E-mail: ziogregory@hotmail.com.

SUMIDA, KEVIN P.H. lawyer; b. Honolulu, Feb. 14, 1954; s. William H. and Dorothy A. Sumida. BA in Philosphy, Case Western Res. U., 1976; JD, U. Pa., 1979. Bar: Hawaii 1979, U.S. Ct. Appeals (9th cir.) 1981. Assoc. Fong & Miho, Honolulu, 1979-81; law clk. to hon. judge Harold M. Fong U.S. Dist. Ct., 1981-82; assoc. Matsui & Chung, 1982-89; ptnr. Matsui Chung Sumida & Tsuchiyama, 1989—. Bd. dirs., officer Farrington Alumni and Community Found., Honolulu, 1980—. Mem. ABA (litigation sect., tort and ins. practice sect.), Hawaii Bar Assn. Avocation: music. Office: Matsui Chung Sumida & Tsuchiyama 737 Bishop St Ste 1400 Honolulu HI 96813-3205

SUMIYOSHI, TOMIKI, psychiatrist, researcher; b. Tokyo, Dec. 18, 1964; s. Hiroshi and Fusako (Naganuma) S.; m. Sawako Suemasa, Apr. 4, 1993. MB, MD, Kanazawa U., Japan, 1989, PhD, 1993. Med. diplomate. Resident Fukui Prefectural Psychiat. Hosp., Japan, 1990; ward adminstr., dir. neurochemistry rsch. Kanazawa U. Hosp., Japan, 1991-93; rsch. assoc. dept. psychiatry Case Western Res. U., Cleve., 1993-95; asst. prof. dept. psychiatry, dir. psychopharmacology rsch. Saitama Med. Sch., Japan, 1995-96; asst. prof. dept. neuropsychiatry, dir. neurochemistry rsch. Toyama Med. and Pharmaceutical U., Japan, 1996—, assoc. prof. dept. neuropsychiatry Japan, 2000—; apptd. psychiatrist Health and Welfare Ministry Japan, 1996—. Cons. Jansson, Inc., Tokyo, 1993—, Fujisawa, Inc., 1999—; vis. prof. dept. psychiatry Verderbilt U., Nashville, 2000—02. Author: Clinical Perspective of the New Antipsychotic Drugs, 2001, Relapse in Schizophrenia, 2002; contbr. articles to profl. jours. Rep. athlete The Nat. Athletic Meeting, Hachinohe, Japan, 1993. Recipient psychiat rsch. awsard, Saburo Matsubara Meml. Fund, Kanazawa, Japan, 1993, young investigator award, Nat. Alliance for Rsch. on Schizophrenia and Depression, Chgo., 1995, N.Y., 2001—02, rsch. prize, Japanese Soc. Biol. Psychiatry, Tokyo, 1996, Meml. Travel award, Am. Coll. Neuropsychopharmacology, 2001; fellow rsch. fellow, Min. Edn. and Sci., Japan, 2000—02; scholar, Rotary, 1994—95. Mem. Soc. Neurosci., N.Y. Acad. Scis., World Fedn. Socs. Biol. Psychiatry, Japanese Soc. Psychiatry and Neurology, Japanese Soc. Biol. Psychiatry, Japanese Soc. Neuropsychopharmacology, Japanese Soc. Clin. Neuropsychopharmacology, Am. Soc. Neuropsychopharmacology. Avocations: foreign languages, classical music, figure skating, foreign travel. Home: 420 Elmington Ave # 1026 Nashville TN 37205 Office: Toyama Med & Pharm U Dept Neuropsychiatry 2630 Sugitani Toyama 930-0194 Japan E-mail: sumiyo@ms.toyama-mpu.ac.jp.

SUMMA, PHILIP WAYNE, medical/surgical nurse, political organization worker; b. San Diego, May 1, 1965; s. John DAvid and Mary Ethel Summa; m. Mary Claire Watson, Oct. 6, 2000; children: Brett Lopez, Micca Thomas. BS in Cultural Anthropology, Bapt. Bible Coll., 1986; LPN, Boone State U., 1990. LPN State of Idaho, Nampa, 1990—92; charge nurse Sunny Ridge Care, 1992—93, LPN supr., 1993—96, Tresem Valley Manor, Boise, 1996—99; LPN charge Cascade Care, Caldwell, 1999—. Author: Campaign Management Plans, 1992, A Summa Family History, 1999; editor: (newsletter) The Haywood, 1998—. State committeeman Idaho Dem. Party, Boise, 1992—96, state platform chmn., 1996—98; state chmn. Communist Party USA, Nampa, 1998—; candidate for state rep. Dem. Party, 1990, 1992. Named Organizer of Yr., Communist Party, 1998—; recipient Best Actor, Knockem Dead Prodns., 1995. Mem.: Earth First. Avocations: guitar, singing, politics. Home: 614 Astor Ave Nampa ID 83651 Office: Communist Party of Idaho 614 Astor Ave Nampa ID 83651

SUMMERFIELD, JOHN ROBERT, textile curator; b. St. Paul, Feb. 21, 1917; s. Isaac and Irene (Longini) S.; m. Anne Benson, July 14, 1945. SB in Mech. Engring., MIT, 1938; MBA, U. Calif., Berkeley, 1947, PhD in Econs., 1954. Asst. prof. Sloan Sch. Mgmt., MIT, 1952-54; br. chief CIA, Washington, 1954-56; project leader The Rand Corp., Santa Monica, Calif., 1956—62; corp. economist Douglas Aircraft Co., 1962—66; v.p. econ. planning Western Airlines, L.A., 1966-70; staff v.p. econ. planning Pan Am. Airways, N.Y.C., 1970-71; pres. Summerfield Assocs., Pacific Palisades, Calif., 1972-92; vis. curator Fowler Mus. Cultural History, UCLA, 1993—. Co-curator exhbns. of antique Minangkabau ceremonial textiles from West Sumatra, Textile Mus., Washington, 1990-91, Santa Barbara (Calif.) Mus. Art, 1991, Bellevue (Wash.) Art Mus., 1992, Utah Mus. Fine Art, 1992, Fowler Mus. of Cultural History, UCLA, 1999. Served to lt. USNR, 1942-45. E-mail: summerf@ucla.edu.

SUMMERFORD, BEN LONG, retired artist, educator; b. Montgomery, Ala., Feb. 3, 1924; s. Ben Long and Ollie Jo (Gilchrist) S.; m. Christene Morris, Jan. 30, 1951 (dec.); children: Jeffrey (dec.), Rebecca, James. Student, Birmingham-Southern Coll., 1942-43; BA, Am. U., 1948, MA, 1954; student, Ecole des Beaux Arts., Paris., 1949-50. Staff art dept. Am. U., 1950-88, chmn. dept., 1957-66, 70-86, prof., 1960-88; prof. emeritus, 1988—; artist in residence Dartmouth Coll., 1993. One-man shows include, Balt. Mus. Art, Goucher Coll., Franz Bader Gallery, Washington, Jefferson Place Gallery, Washington; one-man show include Phillips Collection, Washington; represented in permanent collection, Watkins Gallery, Phillips Gallery Art, Corcoran Gallery Art, all Washington, numerous group shows of paintings. Served to ensign USNR, 1943-46. Fulbright fellow, France, 1949-50; J. Paul Getty scholar, Phillips Collection, 1990-91. Home: 2029 Ashley Dr Shepherdstown WV 25443 Office: Am U Dept Art Washington DC 20016

SUMMERLIN, GLENN WOOD, retired advertising executive; b. Dallas, Apr. 1, 1934; m. Anne Valley, Oct. 16, 1971; 1 child Wade Hampton ;children from previous marriage: Glenn Wood III, Edward Lee. Student, Ga. Inst. Tech., 1951-52; BBA, Ga. State U., 1956, MBA, 1967. Prodn. mgr. Fred Worrill Advt., Atlanta, 1956-65; v.p. sales Grizzard, 1965-74, pres., 1974-94, vice chmn., 1994-99; retired, 1999. Vice chmn. Polaris dist. Boy Scouts Am., 1967, Ga. State U. Found., 1974; chmn. distributive edn. adv. com. DeKalb Coll., 1974—76; bd. founders Geo. M. Sparks Scholarship Fund; bd. dirs. Atlanta Humane Soc., 1971—, treas., 1973, 1981—82, 1984—86, asst. treas. for capital devel., 1987—99, pres., 2000—02, investment com., 1996—; mem. steering com. to honor Hank Aaron, 1982; lay rep. animal care com. Emory U., 1984—85; mem. adv. bd. Families in Action, 1985—86; bd. dirs. Travelers Aid Metro, Atlanta, 1989—90; mem. adv. bd. Emmaus Ho., 2000—; chmn.'s coun., mem. mktg. adv. com. Crow Canyon Archaeol. Ctr., 1993—95. Recipient C.S. Bolen award Soc. Coun. Indsl. Editors, 1967; named Outstanding Young Man in DeKalb County, DeKalb Jaycees, 1967, Alumnus of Yr., Ga. State U., 1973; recipient Direct Mail Spokesman award Direct Mktg. Assn., 1973. Mem. Nat. Soc. Fund Raising Execs. (bd. dirs. Ga. chpt. 1984, cert. 1983-99), Ga. Assn. Bus. Communicators (pres. 1966-67), Ga. State Alumni Assn. (pres. 1971-72, dir. 1966-78), Sales and Mktg. Execs. Atlanta (dir. 1969-71), Ga. Bus. and Industry Assn. (bd. govs. 1976-76), Ga. Arms Collectors Assn. (dir. 1974-76, Pres.'s award 1973), Southeastern Antique Arms Collectors (charter, bd. dirs. 1978—, v.p. 1999—), Assn. Am. Sword Collectors (charter), Mid-Am. Antique Arms Soc. (charter), Mensa, Soc. Animal Welfare Adminstrs. (Disting Svc. award 2000), Travelers Aid of Atlanta (bd. dirs. 1989-90), Omicron Delta Kappa. Home: 1133 Ragley Hall Rd NE Atlanta GA 30319-2511

SUMMEROUR, DARLENE ANN, director of music; b. Leavenworth, Knas., Jan. 2, 1951; d. Francis Simon and LaVern Matilda (Fry) Frederick; m. David Andrew Summerour, May 29, 1981; children: Eric, Shelly. MusB in Edn., St. Mary Coll., Leavenworth, 1973. Vocal music dir. Palmer Jr. High Sch., Independence, Mo., 1973-81, Indian Trail Jr. High Sch., Olathe, Kans., 1982—. Mem. Am. Choral Dirs. Assn., Mo. Music Educators Assn., Kans. Music Educators Assn. (vocal chairperson dist. I 1987-89), Nat. Music Educators Conf. (registered music educator). Roman Catholic. Avocations: gardening, walking, sewing, cooking. Office: Indian Trail Jr High Sch 1440 E 151st St Olathe KS 66062-2855 Home: 10195 Monticello Rd Shawnee Mission KS 66227-4514

SUMMERS, ANITA ARROW, public policy and management educator; b. N.Y.C., Sept. 9, 1925; d. Harry I. and Lillian (Greenberg) Arrow; m. Robert Summers, Mar. 29, 1953; children: Lawrence H., Richard F., John S. BA, Hunter Coll., 1945, DHL (hon.), 1995; MA, U. Chgo., 1947. Sr. econ. analyst Standard Oil Co. N.J., N.Y.C., 1947-54; asst. in econs. Yale U., New Haven, 1956-59; lectr. dept. econs. Swarthmore (Pa.) Coll., 1965-71; sr. economist Fed. Res. Bank Phila., 1971-75, research officer, 1975-79; adj. prof. pub. policy U. Pa., Phila., 1979-82, prof. pub. policy and mgmt., 1982—, dept. chair, 1983-88, univ. ombudsman, 2001—, co-dir Wharton Urban Decentralization Project, 1987-97, sr. scholar Nat. Ctr. on the Edn. Quality of the Workforce, 1991—96. Expert witness schs. fin. Md., Mass., Va., 1980-85, Md., Va., 1996, bd. dirs. William Penn Found., Phila., 1993-98; chair bd. dirs. Mathematica Policy Rsch., Inc., Princeton, N.J., 1993—. Author: Economic Report on the Philadelphia Metropolitan Area, 1985, Economic Development within the Philadelphia Metropolitan Area, 1986, Local Fiscal Issues in the Philadelphia Metropolitan Area, 1987; editor: Urban Change in the United States and Western Europe, 1992, 99; contbr. articles to profl. jours. Chair econ. subcom. Pa. Three Mile Island Commn., Harrisburg, 1979; pres. Lower Merion (Pa.) LWV, 1963-65; mem. Mayor's Econ. Roundtable, Phila., 1984-88; mem. policy coun., 1992-94, Com. for Econ. Devel. Rockefeller Found. resident scholar, Bellagio, Italy, 1986. Mem. Am. Econ. Assn., Assn. for Pub. Policy and Mgmt. (policy coun. 1986), Phi Beta Kappa. Avocations: needlepoint, cooking. Home: 641 Revere Rd Merion Station PA 19066-1007 Office: U Pa Wharton Sch Dept Pub Policy and Mgmt Philadelphia PA 19104 E-mail: summers@wharton.upenn.edu.

SUMMERS, BARBARA JUNE, artist; b. Syracuse, N.Y., June 18, 1960; d. Stanley Edward Grabowski and Judith Dawn (Yager) Austen. BFA, U. Tex., 1996. Served in USAF, Vandenburg AFB, Calif., 1981-82, Lakenheath AFB, U.K., 1982-84, Lackland AFB, Tex., 1984-85, Civil Svc., San Antonio, 1986-89. Freelance artist and tchr. Democrat. Home: 6811 Maple Lake St San Antonio TX 78244-1723 E-mail: BarbaraSummers@msn.com.

SUMMERS, CAROL, artist; b. Kingston, N.Y., Dec. 26, 1925; s. Ivan Franklin and Theresa (Jones) S.; m. Elaine Smithers, Oct. 2, 1954 (div. Aug. 1967); 1 son, Kyle; m. Joan Ward, May 6, 1974. BA, Bard Coll., 1951, DFA (hon.), 1974. Tchr. Hunter Coll., Sch. Visual Arts, Haystack Mountain Sch. Crafts, Bklyn. Mus. Art Sch., Pratt Graphic Art Ctr., Chelterham Twp. Art Ctr., Valley Stream Community Art Ctr., U. Pa., Columbia Coll., U. Calif., Santa Cruz, San Francisco Art Inst., U. Utah, Logan, Art Study Abroad, Paris, Casa de Espiritus Alegres Marfil, Mex., USIS workshop tour, India, 1974, 79; folk art and textiles tour leader to Rajasthan, India, winters 1995-2002. Represented in permanent collections at, Mus. Modern Art, Bklyn. Mus., N.Y. Pub. Libr., Libr. of Congress, Nat. Gallery, Victoria and Albert Mus., London, Bibliotheque Nationale, Paris, Kinstmuseum, Basil, Lugan (Switzerland) Art Mus. Grenchen (Switzerland) Art Mus., Malmo (Sweden) Mus., Los Angeles County Mus., Phila. Mus., Balt. Mus., Seattle Mus., Boston Mus., Art Inst. Chgo., Am. embassies in Russia, Can., India, Thailand, Fed. Republic Germany and Eng.; traveling exhibit, Mus. Modern Art, 1964-66; retrospective exhbn. Brooklyn Mus., 1977, Nassau County Mus. Art, 1990, Belles Artes, San Miquel de Allende, Mex., 1992, Miami U. Art Mus., Oxford, Ohio, 1995, Egon Schiele Centrum Česky Krumlov, Czech Republic, 1997-98; 50-yr. retrospective at Mus. Art and History, Santa Cruz, 1999, Woodstock (N.Y.) Artists Assn., 1999, San Francisco Mus. Modern Art Rental Gallery, 2000. Served with USMCR, 1944-48, PTO. Named Artist of Yr., Santa Cruz County Arts Commn., 2001; Louis Comfort Tiffany Found. fellow, 1955, 60, John Simon Guggenheim Found. fellow, 1959, Fulbright fellow, Italy, 1961; Italian govt. study grantee, 1954-55, Coun. for Internat. Exch. Scholars rsch. grantee, India, 1993-94. Mem. NAD, Calif. Soc. Printmakers. Address: 2817 Smith Grade Santa Cruz CA 95060-9764

SUMMERS, CLYDE WILSON, law educator; b. Grass Range, Mont., Nov. 21, 1918; s. Carl Douglas and Anna Lois (Yontz) S.; m. Evelyn Marie Wahlgren, Aug. 30, 1947; children: Mark, Erica, Craig, Lisa. BS, U. Ill., 1939, JD, 1942, LLD, 1998; LLM, Columbia U., 1946, JSD, 1952; LL.D., U. Leuven, Belgium, 1967, U. Stockholm, 1978, U. Ill., 1998. Bar: N.Y. 1951. Mem. law faculty U. Toledo, 1942-49, U. Buffalo, 1949-56; prof. law Yale U., New Haven, 1956-66, Garver prof. law, 1966-75; Jefferson B. Fordham prof. law U. Pa., 1975-90, prof. emeritus, 1990—. Hearing examiner Conn. Commn. on Civil Rights, 1963-71 Co-author: Labor Cases and Material, 1968, 2d edit., 1982, Rights of Union Members, 1979, Legal Protection for the Individual Employee, 1989, 2d edit., 1995; co-editor: Labor Relations and the Law, 1953, Employment Relations and the Law, 1959, Comparative Labor Law Jour., 1984-97. Chmn. Gov.'s Com. on Improper Union Mgmt. Practices N.Y. State, 1957-58; chmn. Conn. Adv. Council on Unemployment Ins. and Employment Service, 1960-72; mem. Conn. Labor Relations Bd., 1966-70, Conn. Bd. Mediation and Arbitration, 1964-72. Guggenheim fellow, 1955-56; Ford fellow, 1963-64; German-Marshall fellow, 1977-78; NEH fellow, 1977-78, Fullbright fellow, 1984-85. Mem. Nat. Acad. Arbitrators (nat. chmn.), Internat. Soc. Labor Law and Social Legislation. Congregationalist. Home: 753 N 26th St Philadelphia PA 19130-2429 Office: U Pa Sch Law 3400 Chestnut St Philadelphia PA 19104-6204 E-mail: csummers@law.upenn.edu.

SUMMERS, DAVID STEWART, neurologist, consultant; b. Canton, Ohio, Feb. 16, 1932; s. William Edward and Stewart (Jordan) Summers; m. Ada Ernestine Cumber, Nov. 30, 1957; children: David Stewart II, Timothy C. *Wife "Tean" (Ernestine) Cumber Summers, graduate of N.C. A & T State Univ., former Elementary School teacher, now volunteers at Immanuel Lutheran Church & makes dolls as a hobby. Son, David S. Summers, II, has a B.S. in computer science & a Masters in teaching English as a second Language, both from PA State University, University Park at State College, PA; he has taught at Pa. State Univ., University Park at State College. Son, Timothy C. Summers, also has a B.S. in computer science from PA State University, University Park, and is a Computer Programmer at University Park, State College, PA.* BS, Va. State U., 1954; MD, U. Va., 1959. Diplomate Am. Acad. Pain Mgmt. Resident in neurology SUNY, Syracuse, 1960-63; asst. prof. neurology U. Rochester, N.Y., 1968-72, U. Utah Coll. Medicine, Salt Lake City, 1972-76; staff neurologist St. Vincent Health Ctr., Erie, Pa., 1976-91, Meadville (Pa.) Med. Ctr., 1991-93; neurologist Warren (Pa.) State Hosp., 1993-2000; investor, 2000—. Cons. Reflex Sympathetic Dystrophy Assn., Erie, 1988-97; mem. adv. coun. Health and Human Svcs., Washington, 1974-77. *Devoted to "the supremacy of reason", scientific progress, & humanism, Dr. Summers also supports women's rights including their right to choose abortion, their voting right & ERA as prime methods of saving Democracy & protecting First Amendment right. He also supports the Free Inquiry Inst. Amherst, NY, The Robert Green Ingersoll the Thomas Paine National Foundation, Police & Veterans causes, research in Monument cancer, diabetes, traumatic spinal-cord paralysis, chronic pain, the Public Citizen Health Research Group, etc, and regularly contributes to National Public Radio (WQLN), AM. Red Cross, the free thought Society of Greater Phil, The Wilson Ctr, the Americans Legion, and United Negro College Fund.* Contbr. articles to profl. publs. Supporter City Mission, Erie, 1991—, Am. United Separation Ch. and State, Am. Assn. Advancement Sci., Am. Assn. Univ. Women, Washington, 1997, NOW, ACLU, Am. Humanist Assn., People for the Am. Way, Ctr. Reproductive Law & Policy, Planned Parenthood, others; life mem. NAACP, Balt., 1976—; adv. to gov. Coun. on Black Affairs, Salt Lake City, 1975; mem. Human Rights Campaign, Zero Population Growth. A.A. Rockefeller scholar, Williamsburg, Va., 1951-54; grantee Nat. Med. Fellowships, 1956-59. Mem. Am. Acad. Neurology, Nat. Med. Assn., Am. Epilepsy Soc., U. Va. Alumni Assn., Menninger Soc., N.Y. Acad. Scis. Democrat. Avocations: reading, cycling, skiing. E-mail: dssmd@erie.net.

SUMMERS, FRANK WILLIAM, retired librarian; b. Jacksonville, Fla., Feb. 8, 1933; s. Frank Wesley and Kathleen (Gilreath) S.; 1 son, William Wesley. BA, Fla. State U., 1955; MA, Rutgers U., 1959, PhD, 1973. Libr. Jacksonville Pub. Libr., 1955, 57; sr. libr. Linden (N.J.) Pub. Libr., 1958-59; dir. Cocoa (Fla.) Pub. Libr., 1959-61; assoc. libr. Providence Pub. Libr., 1961-65; libr. Fla. State Libr., 1965-69; rsch. fellow Rutgers U., New Brunswick, N.J., 1969-70; asst. dean, prof. Coll. Librarianship, U. S.C., 1971-76, dean, 1976-85; dean Sch. Libr. and Info. Studies Fla. State U., Tallahassee, 1985-94, prof., 1994-99, dir. of librs., 2000-01. Lectr. Libr. Sch. U. R.I., 1964-95; libr. surveys in Fla., Ohio, N.Y., S.C., N.C., Ky., Tex. Contbr. profl. jours. Mem. R.I. Bd. Library Commrs., 1964-65. Served to lt. (j.g.) USNR, 1955-57. Mem. ALA (exec. bd., v.p., pres.-elect 1987-88, pres. 1988-89, Joseph W. Lippincot award 1996), R.I. Libr. Assn. (pres.), S.C. Libr. Assn. (pres.), Assn. Am. Libr. Schs. (pres.), Beta Phi Mu (exec. dir. 1996-99). Home: 505 Live Oak Plantation Rd Tallahassee FL 32312-2335 E-mail: summers@lis.fsu.edu.

SUMMERS, HARDY, state supreme court justice; b. Muskogee, Okla., July 15, 1933; s. Cleon A. and Fern H. Summers; m. Marilyn, Mar. 16, 1963; children: Julia Clare, Andrew Murray. BA, U. Okla., 1955, LLB, 1957. Asst. county atty. Muskogee County, 1960-62; pvt. practice law Muskogee, 1962-76; dist. judge 15th dist. Okla. Dist. Ct., 1976-85; justice Okla. Supreme Ct., Oklahoma City, 1985—, chief justice, 1999-2000. Sec. Muskogee County Election Bd., 1965-72. Capt. JAGC, USAF, 1957-62. Recipient Disting. Alumnus award, U. Okla. Coll. Law, 2000. Mem. ABA, Okla. Bar Assn., Okla. Jud. Conf. (pres. 1984). Avocations: outdoor sports, music. Office: Okla Supreme Ct Rm 202 State Capital Bldg Oklahoma City OK 73105

SUMMERS, JAMES IRVIN, retired advertising executive; b. Lexington, Mo., July 10, 1921; s. William E. and Elizabeth (Hoeflicker) S.; m. Priscilla Barstow West, Jan. 15, 1948 (div. 1985); children: Susanne Cornelia, Elizabeth Barstow, James Irvin, Daniel Edward; m. Jane Browning Beckwith, Oct. 4, 1986 (div. Feb. 1996). With Harold Cabot & Co. Inc., Boston, 1946-86, exec. v.p., 1960-77, pres., chief exec. officer, dir., chmn. exec. com., 1977-86; mem. editorial bd. Sta. WEEI, 1985-90, also bd. dirs. Mem. exec. com., bd. dirs., v.p., chmn. Pub. Info. Com., Mass. Bay United Way, 1979-84; chmn. Swampscott Rep. Fin. Com., 1964-75; trustee, bd. mgrs., exec. com. Mass. Eye & Ear Infirmary; trustee Family Svc. Assn. Greater Boston, 1952-62; bd. dirs. Mass. Taxpayers Com., 1984-87; pres. Lit. Vols. Mass., 1987-88; pub. rels. bd. USS Constn. Mus., 1988-91. With USAAF, 1941-45. Decorated Bronze Star. Mem. Greater Boston Advt. Club (bd. dirs. 1984-86), Internat. Fedn. Advt. Agys. (bd. dirs. 1985-86), Am. Assn. Advt. Agys. (bd. dirs., treas. 1985-86), New. Eng. Broadcasters Assn. (bd. dirs. 1985-86), Bay Club, Madison Square Garden Club, Tedesco Country Club, Boca Raton Resort and Club. Home: Boca Highlands 4748 S Ocean Blvd PH 3 Highland Beach FL 33487

SUMMERS, JANIS LEE, lawyer, consultant; b. La Porte, Ind., Apr. 13, 1954; d. Erle T. and Donna E. Summers. BA, Ind. U., 1975, JD, 1978. Bar: Ind. 1978, U.S. Supreme Ct. 1984. Assoc. Merrillville (Ind.) Legal Clinic, 1978-79; dep. attorney gen. State of Ind., Indpls., 1979-81; atty.-advisor U.S. Internat. Trade Commn., Washington, 1981—. Author: government reports, bills, proclamations on trade and tarrif matters. Elder, deacon, choir mem., organist Darnestown Presbyn. Ch., 1985—. Avocations: music, travel, reading, walking, pets. Office: US Internat Trade Commn 500 E St SW Washington DC 20436-0001 E-mail: jsummers@usitc.gov.

SUMMERS, JOSEPH FRANK, author, publisher; b. Newnan, Ga., June 26, 1914; s. John Dawson and Anne (Blalock) S.; BA in Math., U. Houston, 1942; profl. cert. meteorology, UCLA, 1943, U. Chgo., 1943; postgrad., U. P.R., 1943-44; MA in Math., U. Tex. at Austin, 1947; postgrad. Rice U., 1947-49; m. Evie Margaret Mott, July 8, 1939 (dec. May 1989); children: John Randolph, Thomas Franklin, James Mott. With Texaco Inc., Houston, 1933-42, 49-79, mgr. data processing, 1957-67, asst. gen. mgr. computer svcs. dept., 1967-79, automation cons., 1979-83; pres. Word Lab Inc., Houston, 1983—; instr. math. AAC, Ellington Field, Tex., 1941-42, U. Tex. at Austin, 1946-47. Pres. Houston Esperanto Assn., 1934-39; vol. tutor Thousand Points of Light, 1991—. Capt. AAC, 1942-46. Rice U. fellow, 1947-49. Mem. Assn. Computing Machinery (pres. 1956-58), Nat. Assn. Accts. (past bd. dir.), Am. Petroleum Inst. (mem. data processing and computing com. 1955-59), Rice U. Hist. Soc., Rice U. Assocs., Esperanto League N.Am., Universal Esperanto Assn. Author: Mathematics for Bombadiers and Navigators, 1942, Wholly Holey Holy, An Adult American Spelling Book, 1984. Contbg. author: American Petroleum Institute Drilling and Production Practices. Home and Office: 10150 Metronome Dr Houston TX 77080-6312

SUMMERS, KATHY "JOY" COUSER, evangelist; b. Winston-Salem, N.C., Aug. 20, 1952; d. Leroy Jack and Normallee Nevada Couser; m. Hershal Lamont Summers, Mar. 14, 1980 (div. Mar. 4, 1999); children: Latasha, Lewis, Vernee. Environ. tech. I & II N.C. Bapt. Hosp., Winston-Salem, 1975—81, OR phys. asst. II, 1981—83. Choir directress Upper Room Ch. of God in Christ, Winston-Salem, 1983—89; min. in song directress Love in Action Outreach Ministry, Winston-Salem, 1992—95; Evangelist, min. in song, dir. Love In Action Outreach Ministry, Winston-Salem, 1999—; supt./surolay sch. and tchr. True Faith Tabernacle, Winston-Salem, 1997—99. Author poetry. Avocations: reading, writing, nature exploring, traveling, computers. Home: 2860 Millbrook Dr #A Winston Salem NC 27105

SUMMERS, KYLE, biologist, educator; b. N.Y.C., Nov. 30, 1958; s. Carol Summers, Elaine Summers; life ptnr. Susan Barbara McRae; 1 child Anita Wren. PhD, U. Mich., 1990; grad., U. Calif., 1984. Fellow Smithsonian Tropical Rsch. Inst., Panama City, Panama, 1991—92; NSF NATO fellow Queen's U., Kingston, Canada, 1992—93, Cambridge U., England, 1993—95; asst. prof. biology East Carolina U., 1996—2002, assoc. prof. biology, 2002—. Field rschr. Smithsonian Tropical Rsch. Inst., Bocas del Toro, Bocas del Toro, Panama, 1998—98. Contbr. articles to profl. jours. Recipient Vice Chancellor's Rsch. award, East Carolina U., 1998; fellow, Smithsonian Instn., 1986, 1987, Rackham Sch. Grad. Studies, U. Mich., 1988, Donald W. Tinkle Meml. Fund, U. Mich., 1990; grantee, Smithsonian Instn., 1985, Sigma Xi, 1986, 1987, Explorer's Club, 1986, 1987, Hinsdale Fund, U. Mich., 1987, Nat. Geog. Soc., 1993, 2000, 2002, East Carolina U., 1997, 2000, NSF, 2002.

Mem.: Internat. Soc. Behavioral Ecologists, Herpetologist's League. Avocation: bicycling. Office: East Carolina Univ 10th St Greenville NC 27858 Office Fax: 252-328-4178. Business E-Mail: summersk@mail.ecu.edu.

SUMMERS, LAWRENCE, former government official, academic administrator; b. New Haven, 1954; m. Victoria Summers; 2 daughters (twins), 1 son. SB, MIT, 1975; PhD, Harvard U., 1982. Mem. faculty MIT, 1979-82; domestic policy economist Pres'. Coun. Econ. Advisors, 1982-83; v.p. devel. econs., chief economist World Bank, 1991-93; prof. econs. Harvard U., Cambridge, Mass., 1983-93, Nathaniel Ropes prof. polit. economy, 1987, pres., 2001—; under sec. for internat. affairs U.S. Dept. Treasury, Washington, 1993-95, dep. sec., 1995-99, sec., 1999-2001. Author Understanding Unemployment; co-author Reform in Eastern Europe; editor series Tax Policy and the Economy; contbr. numerous articles to profl. jours. Recipient John Bates Clark medal, 1993, Alan Waterman award NSF, 1987, disting. achievement award Boys' & Girls' Club Greater Washington, 2000, disting. svc. award Golden Slipper Club & Charities 2000, economic patriot award Concord Coalition, 2000, Stephen P. Guggan award Inst. Internat. Edn., 2000. Fellow Econometric Soc., Am. Acad. Arts and Scis. Office: Harvard U Office of the President Massachusetts Hall Cambridge MA 02138 E-mail: lawrencesummers@harvard.edu.*

SUMMERS, LORRAINE DEY SCHAEFFER, librarian; b. Phila., Dec. 14, 1946; d. Joseph William and Hilda Lorraine (Ritchey) Dey; m. F. William Summers, Jan. 28, 1984. BA, Fla. State U., 1968, MS, 1969. Ext. dir. Santa Fe Regional Libr., Gainesville, 1969-71; pub. libr. cons. State Libr. of Fla., Tallahassee, 1971-78, asst. state libr., 1978-84; dir. adminstrv. svcs. Nat. Assn. for Campus Activities, Columbia, S.C., 1984-85; asst. state libr. State Libr. of Fla., Tallahassee, 1985—2001. Bd. dirs., sec. Southeastern Libr. Network, Inc.; cons. in field. Contbr. articles to profl. jours. Del. Pres.'s Com. on Mental Retardation Regional Forum, Atlanta, 1975; del. Fla. Gov.'s Conf. on Libr. and Info. Svcs., 1978, 90. Mem. ALA (orgn. com. 1979-83, coun. 1982-84, 93-97, resolutions com. 1983-85, mem. legislation com. 1993-95, nominating com. 1996, awards com. 1998-99, Spectrum awards jury 1999-2000), Assn. Specialized and Coop. Libr. Agys. (dir. 1976-82, chmn. planning and orgn. com. 1976-80, chmn. nominating com. 1980-81, chmn. by laws com. 1985-86, exec. bd. state libr. agy. sect. 1983-86, pres. 1987-88, chmn. stds. rev. com. 1990-92), Southeastern Libr. Assn. (exec. bd. 1976-80, v.p., pres.-elect 1994-96, pres. 1996-98, past pres. 1998-2000, nominating com. 2000-02), Fla. Libr. Assn. (sec. 1978-79, dir. 1976-80, nominating com. 1995-96), Zonta (dir. 1992-95, sec. 1999-2001). Democrat. Methodist. E-mail: lorsummers@worldnet.att.net.

SUMMERS, PAUL, state attorney general; b. Somerville, Tenn., Mar. 28, 1950; BS, Miss. State U.; JD, U. Tenn. Dist. atty. gen. 25th Jud. Dist., Somerville, Tenn., 1982—90; judge Ct. of Criminal Appeals, Nashville, 1990—99; atty. gen. State of Tenn., 1999—. Adj. prof. law U. Memphis; former adj. faculty Cumberland U.; pres. elect Tenn. Dist. Atty.'s Gen. Conf.; mem. Ct. Criminal Appeals, 1990—99; lectr. in field. Former mem. Tenn. Sentencing Commn.; col. Tenn. Army N.G. With USAF. Mem.: Tenn. Dist. Attys. Gen. Conf. (pres.), Tenn. Bar Assn. (former gov.). Avocations: racquetball, rollerblading, Karate (black belt). Office: Office of the Attorney General 500 Charlotte Ave Nashville TN 37243-1401*

SUMMERS, RENEE ANN, clinical social worker; b. Chgo., Mar. 23, 1952; d. Jerry and Selma (Putterman) Schaffner; m. Frank L. Summers, Aug. 15, 1981; children: Nicole, Todd. BA, Ind. U., 1973; MSW, U. Mich., 1975; cert. in child and adolescent psychotherapy, Chgo. Inst. for Psychoanalysis, 1989. Diplomate Acad. Cert. Social Workers; lic. clin. social worker. Sch. social worker Palatine (Ill.) Sch. Dist. 15, 1975-79; psychiat. social worker Infant Welfare, Chgo., 1980-85; clin. social worker Irene Josselyn Clinic, Northfield, Ill., 1985-88; pvt. practice clin. social work Chgo. and Evanston, 1980—. Mem. Assn. Child Psychotherapists, Ill. Soc. for Clin. Social Work. Avocations: reading, running, cooking. Office: 708 Church Ste 229 Evanston IL 60201

SUMMERS, RICHARD HENRY, music educator, musician; b. Wheeling, W.Va., Sept. 18, 1952; s. Earl Francis and Mary Summers; m. Karen Sue Wode, June 19, 1973; children: Stephen. MusB, Juilliard Sch., 1975, MusM, 1979. Cert. tchr. NJ. Clarinetist and saxophonist U.S. Mil. Acad. Band, West Point, NY, 1972—75; instrumental music tchr. Kinnelon (NJ) H.S., 1981—85; band dir. William Paterson Coll., Wayne, 1992—96; clarinet prof., woodwind and orchestral methods William Paterson Coll. and U., 1996—2000; dir. of bands and music chmn. Pequannock Twp. H.S., Pompton Plains, 1985—. Prin. clarinetist, soloist, and asst. condr. Ridgewood Concert Band, 1988—; 2nd clarinetist NJ Pops Orch., Livingston, 1997—. With U.S. Army, 1972—75. Mem.: Nat. Band Assn., NJ Music Educators Assn. (Condr. NJ Jr. Region Band 1992), North Jersey Area Band (pres. 1989—93, Condr. North Jersey Area Concert Band 1988).

SUMMERS, ROBERT, economics educator; b. Gary, Ind., June 20, 1922; s. Frank and Ella (Lipton) Samuelson; m. Anita Arrow, Mar. 29, 1953; children: Lawrence Henry, Richard Fredric, John Steven. BS, U. Chgo., 1943; PhD, Stanford, 1956; postgrad. (Social Sci. Research Council fellow), King's Coll., U. Cambridge, Eng., 1951-52. Instr. Stanford, 1949-50; mem. faculty Yale, 1952-59, asst. prof., 1956-59; staff mem. Cowles Found., 1955-59; economist RAND Corp., Santa Monica, Calif., 1959-60, cons., 1960-80. Mem. faculty U. Pa. Wharton Sch., 1959— , prof., 1967— , chmn. grad. group in econs., 1967-70, 73-76 Author: (with Lawrence R. Klein) The Wharton Index of Capacity Utilization, 1966, (with others) Strategies for Research and Development, 1967, (with others) A System of International Comparisons of Gross Product and Purchasing Power, 1975, International Comparisons of Real Product and Purchasing Power, 1978, (with others) World Product and Income, 1982; contbr. articles to profl. jours. Served with AUS, 1944-46. Ford Found. faculty rsch. fellow London Sch. Econs., 1966-67; NSF grantee 1957-59, 63-66, 80-82, 86-90, 92-94, 95-97, 97-2000, 2000—; resident scholar Rockefeller Found. Study Ctr., 1986. Fellow Econometric Soc., Am. Econs. Assn. (disting. fellow), Am. Acad. Arts and Scis. Home: 641 Revere Rd Merion Station PA 19066-1007 Office: U Pa Dept Econ Philadelphia PA 19104-6297

SUMMERS, SANDRA LEE, nursing educator; b. Lamar, Colo., Oct. 20, 1958; d. John William and Velma Bernadine Jackson; m. Ronald Lee Summers, July, 2, 1977; children: Jeremy Keith, Jerrod Ray, Sarah Jean. MSc in Nursing, MSN, U. Colo., 1997. RN, Colo. Dir. Sonshine Presch., Wiley, Colo., 1988-90; staff nurse Ft. Lyon (Colo.) VA Med. Ctr., 1990-93; dir. nursing program Lamar (Colo.) Cmty. Coll., 1993—. Chair Wellness Conf. com., 1997—; bd. dirs. High Plains Cmty. Health Ctr., Lamar. Recipient Masonic Excellence in Edn. award Masonic Temple, Lamar, 1997, Tchr. of Yr. award Cmty. Colls. Colo., 1997. Republican. Mem. Ch. of Christ. Avocations: camping, reading. Office: Lamar Community Coll 2401 S Main St Lamar CO 81052-3912 E-mail: sandy.summers@lcc.cccoes.edu.

SUMMERS, THOMAS CAREY, lawyer; b. Frederick, Md., Feb. 9, 1956; s. Harold Thomas and Doris Jean (Culler) S.; m. Robin Ann Stalnaker, May 12, 1990; children: Kristin, Heather, Lindsay. BA, Dickinson Coll., 1978; JD, U. Balt., 1981. Bar: Md. 1981, U.S. Dist. Ct. Md. 1981, D.C. 1986. Assoc. Ellin & Baker, Balt., 1979-89, Peter G. Angelos, Balt., 1989—. Adj. prof. law U. Balt. Sch. of Law. Mem. ABA, Md. State Bar Assn., Md. Trial Lawyers Assn. Democrat. Lutheran. Avocation: golf. Office: Law Offices of P G Angelos One Charles Ctr Baltimore MD 21201

SUMMERS, WILLIAM COFIELD, science educator; b. Janesville, Wis., Apr. 17, 1939; s. Crosby Hungerford and Rebecca Delores (Cofield) S.; m. Wilma Jean Poos, July 24, 1965; 1 child, Emily Alexandra. BS, U. Wis., 1961, MS, 1963, Phd, MD, 1967; MA, Yale U., 1977. Post-doctoral fellow MIT, Cambridge, Mass., 1967-68; asst. prof. Yale U., New Haven, 1968-70, assoc. prof., 1970-77, prof., 1977—. Cons. NIH, Bethesda, Md., 1976—. Editor Nucleic Acids Research Jour., 1977-79, Gene jour., 1984-91; contbr. articles to profl. jours. Cons. Anna Fuller Fund, New Haven, 1973-88, Searle Scholars Program, Chgo., 1980-84; trustee Leukemia Soc. Am., N.Y.C., 1981-85, Yale-China Assn., New Haven, 1982-88, 94-98. Mem. Am. Soc. for Microbiology, History Sci. Soc., Am. Assn. History of Medicine. Office: Yale U Sch Medicine 333 Cedar St New Haven CT 06520-8040 E-mail: william.summers@yale.edu.

SUMMERS, WILLIAM KOOPMANS, neuropsychiatrist, researcher; b. Jefferson City, Mo., Apr. 14, 1944; s. Joseph S. and Amy Lydia (Koopmans) S.; m. Angela Forbes McGonigle, Oct. 2, 1972 (div. Apr. 1985); children: Elisabeth Stuart, Wilhelmina Derek. Student, Westminster Coll., Fulton, Mo., 1962-64; BS, U. Mo., 1966; MD, Washington U., St. Louis, 1971. Internal medicine intern Barnes Hosp-Washington U., St. Louis, 1971-72; resident in internal medicine Jewish Hosp., 1972-73; resident in psychiatry Rsch. Hosp., 1973-76; asst. prof. U. Pitts., 1976-78, U. So. Calif., L.A., 1978-82; asst. clin. prof. rsch. UCLA, 1982-88; rschr. Arcadia, Calif., 1988-92, Albuquerque, 1992—; pres., CEO Alzheimers Corp., 1999—. Patentee in field. Mem. AMA, ACP, Am. Psychiat. Assn., Soc. Neurosci., N.Y. Acad. Scis., Am. Fedn. Clin. Rsch. Episcopalian. Avocation: gardening. Office: Alzheimers Corp 5th Fl Ste 530 2400 Louisiana NE Albuquerque NM 87110-4303 Fax: 505-878-0211.

SUMMERS-BAIR, LINDY JEAN, rehabilitation physician; b. Pendleton, Oreg., Aug. 1, 1954; m. Allen Charles Summers-Bair; 1 child, Kate Elizabeth. MD, Loma Linda U., 1980. Med. cons. Calif. State Dept. Rehab., San Diego, 1990—. Office: Calif State Dept Rehab Ste 107 7575 Metropolitan Way San Diego CA 92108

SUMMERSELL, FRANCES SHARPLEY, organization worker; b. Birmingham, Ala. Student, U. Montevallo, Peabody Coll.; LHD (hon.), U. Ala., 1996. Ptnr., artist, writer Assoc. Educators, 1959—. Home: 1411 Caplewood Dr Tuscaloosa AL 35401-1131

SUMMERS-POWELL, ALAN, lawyer; BA, Yale Coll., 1985; JD, U. Pa., 1988. Bar: N.Y. 1989, N.J. 1989, U.S. Dist. Ct. (fed. dist.) N.J. 1989, D.C. 1990, Fla. 1993, U.S. Dist. Ct. (mid. dist.) Fla. 1996, U.S. Ct. Appeals (11th cir.) 1996, U.S. Tax Ct. 1997, U.S. Dist. Ct. (so. dist.) Fla. 2001. Pvt. practice, Palm Harbor, Fla. Chmn. David Leasing and Devel., Inc. Office: PO Box 6043 Palm Harbor FL 34684-0643

SUMMERTREE, KATONAH See WINDSOR, PATRICIA

SUMMERVILLE, RICHARD M. mathematician, academic administrator; Provost Christopher Newport U. Office: Christopher Newport U Office of the Provost 1 University Pl Newport News VA 23606-2998 E-mail: rsummer@cnu.edu.

SUMMEY, STEVEN MICHAEL, advertising company executive; b. Abingdon, Va., Jan. 26, 1946; s. Lee Roy Summey and Jacqueline Forest (Tomlinson) Kiser; m. Linda Sue Rasnake, June 27, 1965 (div. 1977); 1 child, Steven Michael II; m. Linda Lee Hoff, July 29, 1978; children: Jason Lee, Matthew Lawrence. Student, Western Carolina U., 1964, U. N.C. Lab technician Northrop Corp., Asheville, N.C., 1965-67; pres. Summey Outdoor Advt., 1967-97, Concepts-N-Edn. Inc., Asheville, 1997—. Co-founder Ind. Advt. Coun., Washington, 1986. Designer outdoor advt. package; inventor in field. Spl. dep. Buncombe County Sheriffs Dept., Asheville, 1964—; mem. Peaks Soc. United Way; grad. Leadership Asheville Program. Mem. Nat. Assn. Realtors, Nat. Spkrs. Assn., Carolina Spkrs. Assn. (pres. 1998-99, Mem. of Yr. award 2000), N.C. Assn. Realtors, Asheville Bd. Realtors, Asheville Sales and Mktg. Execs., N.C. Outdoor Advt. Assn. (pres. 1986-88), Asheville C. of C., Coun. Ind. Bus. Owners (found., pres. 1987-91). Avocations: hunting, fishing, golf, bowling, flying. Office: Concepts-N-Education Inc PO Box 16648 Asheville NC 28816-0648 E-mail: mikesummey@aol.com.

SUMMITT, APRIL, history educator; b. Knoxville, Tenn., Apr. 2, 1964; d. Ted E. and Connie L. (Westerberg) Summitt. BA in History, BA in English, Newbold Coll., Bracknell, Eng., 1987; MA in History, Andrews U., Berrien Springs, Mich., 1993; postgrad., Western Mich. U., Kalamazoo, 1993—. Adj. instr. Jordan Jr. Coll., Benton Harbor, Mich., 1988-93, Andrews U., 1990-92, asst. prof., 1996—. Doctoral assoc., lectr. Western Mich. U., 1993-96. Sec., bd. dirs. Berrien County Hist. Assn., 1997—. John F. Kennedy Libr. rsch. fellow, 1998. Mem. Am. Hist. Assn., Orgn. Am. Historians, Soc. for Historians of Am. Fgn. Rels., Phi Alpha Theta. Avocations: sailing, poetry, drama, cross-country skiing, piano. Office: Andrews U Dept History And Polit Sci Berrien Springs MI 49104-0001 Home: Apt 11 9766 Rosehill Rd Berrien Sprgs MI 49103-1287

SUMMITT, ROBERT (WILLIAM SUMMITT), chemist, educator; b. Flint, Mich., Dec. 6, 1935; s. William Fletcher and Jessie Louise (Tilson) S.; m. Nancy Jo Holland, Apr. 2, 1956; children: Elizabeth Louise, David Stanley. A.S., Flint Jr. Coll., 1955; BS in Chemistry, U. Mich., 1957; PhD, Purdue U., 1961. Research asso., instr. chemistry Mich. State U., 1961-62, asst. prof. metallurgy, mechs. and materials, 1965-68, asso. prof., 1968-73, chmn. dept. metallurgy mechs. and materials sci., 1972-78, prof., 1973-92, prof. emeritus, 1992. Research chemist Corning Glass Works, 1962-65; cons. in field. NRC Sr. Research asso. Air Force Materials Lab., Fairborn, Ohio, 1974-75 Research, publs. in corrosion, failure analysis, optical properties of materials, spectroscopy, and color sci. Mem. Am. Chem. Soc., Am. Phys. Soc., Am. Soc. Metals, Sigma Xi. Home: 8535 Clough Dr Grayling MI 49738-8438 Office: Dept Materials Sci & Mechs Michigan State Univ East Lansing MI 48824

SUMMITT, ROBERT LAYMAN, JR. obstetrician, gynecologist; b. Pensacola, Fla., Nov. 13, 1957; s. Robert Layman and Joyce (Sharp) S.; m. Margaret Anne Zavada, Oct. 12, 1985; children: Elizabeth Anna, Olivia Grace. BS, Rhodes Coll., 1979; MD, U. Tenn., 1983. Diplomate Am. Bd. Ob-Gyn. Intern U. Tenn., Memphis, 1983-84, resident in ob-gyn., 1984-87, obstetrician, 1988—, assoc. prof., 1988-99, residency program dir. Dept. Ob-Gyn., 1996—, prof., 1999—. Fellow in urogynecology and reconstsructive pelvic surgery U. Calif., Irvine, 1987-88. Mem. AMA, Am. Coll. Ob-Gyn., Am. Assn. Gynecol. Laproscopy, Am. Coll. Surgeons, Am. Urologic Gynecol. Soc. (chair edn. com. 1995—), Ctrl. Assn. Obstetricians and Gynecologists. Office: 853 Jefferson Ave Ste E102 Memphis TN 38103-2807 also: 7945 Wolf River Blvd Germantown TN 38138

SUMMONTE, JOSEPH F., JR. lawyer; b. Long Branch, N.J. BS in Polit. Sci., Monmouth U., 1994; JD, Stetson U., 1997. Bar: Fla. 1997, U.S. Dist. Ct. (mid. dist. Fla.) 1998. Atty. Straughn, Straughn & Turner, P.A., Winter Haven, Fla., 1997-99, Walters Levine Brown Klingensmith & Thomison, P.A., Sarasota, 1999—. Vol. atty. Manasota Legal Svcs., Sarasota, 1999. Mem. ABA, Fla. Bar, Sarasota County Bar Assn. Office: Walters Levine Brown Klingensmith & Thomison PA 1515 Ringling Blvd Ste 900 Sarasota FL 34236-6762 Fax: 941-361-3023. E-mail: jsummonte@walterslevine.com.

SUMNER, CHRISTINE MARIE, counselor; b. Pitts., Mar. 13, 1975; d. Edward Anthony and Susan Marie Hollo. BS, U. Pitts., 1997; MA, EdS, James Madison U., 2000. Nat. cert. counselor Nat. Bd. for Cert. Counselors, Inc. Waitress Lincoln Hills Country Club, North Huntingdon, Pa., 1993-97; yoga tchr. James Madison U., Harrisonburg, Va., 1997, grad. asst. office of sexual assault and substance abuse, 1998-99, rsch. specialist Mine Action Info. Ctr., 1997-99; counseling intern Latrobe (Pa.) Area Hosp., 1999-2000; mobile therapist Pressley Ridge Schs., 2000—; consulting assoc. Select Internat., 2000-01; adult outpatient therapist Diversified Human Svcs., Inc., Monessen, Pa., 2001—02; Cmty. Connections Imperative caseworker YWCA, Greensburg, 2002. Yoga tchr. Westmoreland C.C., Yungwood, Pa., 2002; contract employee Select Internat., 2002. Scholar U. Pitts., 1996-97. Mem. Am. Counseling Assn., Pa. Counseling Assn., U. Pitts. Alumni Assn., Chi Sigma Iota (v.p. 1998-99), Psi Chi (pres. 1996-97). Lutheran. Avocations: yoga, painting, jewelry making, reading, gardening. Home and Office: 139 Morey Pl Greensburg PA 15601-2923

SUMNER, DANIEL ALAN, economist, educator; b. Fairfield, Calif., Dec. 5, 1950; BS in Agrl. Mgmt., Calif. State Poly. U., 1971; MA in Econs., Mich. State U., 1973, U. Chgo., 1977, PhD, 1978. Post-doctoral fellow, labor and population group, econ. dept., Rand Corp., Santa Monica, Calif., 1977-78; asst. prof. N.C. State U., Raleigh, 1978-83, assoc. prof., 1983-87, prof., 1987-92; resident fellow Resources for the Future, Washington, 1986-87; sr. economist Pres.'s Council of Econ. Advisers, 1987-88; dep. asst. sec. for econs. USDA, 1990-91, asst. sec. for econs., 1992-93; Frank H. Buck Jr. prof. dept. agrl. econs. U. Calif., Davis, 1993—. Dir. U. Calif. Agrl. Issues Ctr., 1997—; chair Internat. Agrl. Trade Rsch. Consortium, 1997-99. Author and editor books and monographs; contbr. chpts. to books, articles in profl. jours. Named Alumnus of Yr., Calif. State Poly. U., 1991; recipient Quality of Rsch. Contbn. award Am. Agrl. Econ. Assn., 1996, Policy Contbrn., 1995, fellow, 1999. Mem. Am. Econ. Assn., Econometric Soc., Am. Agrl. Econs. Assn., Internat. Assn. Agrl. Economists. Office: U Calif Davis Dept Agrl Econ Davis CA 95616 E-mail: dasumner@ucdavis.edu.

SUMNER, DAVID SPURGEON, surgery educator; b. Asheboro, N.C., Feb. 20, 1933; s. George Herbert and Velna Elizabeth (Welborn) S.; m. Martha Eileen Sypher, July 25, 1959; children: David Vance, Mary Elizabeth, John Franklin. BA, U. N.C., 1954; MD, Johns Hopkins U., 1958. Diplomate Am. Bd. Surgery; cert. spl. qualification gen. vascular surgery. Intern Johns Hopkins Hosp., Balt., 1958-59, resident in gen. surgery, 1960-61, U. Wash. Sch. Medicine, Seattle, 1961-66; clin. investigator in vascular surgery VA Hosp., 1967, 70-73; asst. surgery U. Wash. Sch. Medicine, 1961-66, instr. surgery, 1966-70, asst. prof. surgery, 1970-72, assoc. prof. surgery, 1972-75; prof. surgery, chief sect. peripheral vascular surgery So. Ill. U. Sch. Medicine., Springfield, 1975-84, Disting. prof. surgery, chief sect. peripheral vascular surgery, 1984-98, disting. prof. emeritus, 1998. Staff surgeon Seattle VA Hosp., 1973-75, Univ. Hosp., Seattle, 1973-75, St. John's Hosp., Springfield, 1975-98, Meml. Med. Ctr., Springfield, 1975-98; mem. VA Merit Review Bd. Surgery, 1975-78; mem. vascular surgery rsch. award com. The Liebig Found., 1990-95, chmn., 1994; bd. dirs. Am. Venous Forum Found., 1993-95; vis. prof. Cook County Hosp., Chgo., 1971, Washington U., St. Louis, 1976, U. Tex., San Antonio, 1978, Wayne State U., Detroit, 1978, U. Ind., Indpls., 1979, Ea. Va. Med. Sch., Norfolk, 1979, Case-Western Res. U., Cleve., 1980, U. Chgo., 1981, U. Manitoba, Winnipeg, Can., 1983, others; dist. lectr. Yale U., 1982; guest examiner Am. Bd. Surgery, St. Louis, 1982, assoc. examiner, 1989; lectr. in field. Author: (with D.E. Strandness Jr.) Ultrasonic Techniques in Angiology, 1975, Hemodynamics for Surgeons, 1975; (with R.B. Rutherford, V. Bernhard, F. Maddison, W.S. Moore, M.O. Perry) Vascular Surgery, 1977; (with J.B. Russell) Ultrasonic Arteriography, 1980; (with F.B. Hershey, R.W. Barnes) Noninvasive Diagnosis of Vascular Disease, 1984; (with R.B. Rutherford, G. Johnson Jr., R.F. Kempczinski, W.S. Moore, M.O. Perry, G.W. Smith) Vascular Surgery, 3d edit., 1989; (with A.N. Nicolaides) Investigation of Patients With Deep Vein Thrombosis and Chronic Venous Insufficiency, 1991; (with R.B. Rutherford, G. Johnson, K.W. Johnston, R.F. Kempczinski, W.C. Krupski, W.S. Moore, M.O. Perry, A.J. Comerota, R.H. Dean, P. Gloviczki, K.H. Johansen, T.S. Riles, L.M. Taylor Jr.) Vascular Surgery, 4th edit., 1995; (with K.A. Myers, A.N. Nicolaides Lower Limb Ischaemia, 1997; author 150 chpts. to books; mem. editl. bd. Vascular Diagnosis and Therapy, 1980-84, Appleton Davies, Inc., 1983—, Jour. Soc. of Non-Invasive Vascular Tech., 1987—, Jour. Vascular Surgery, 1987-97; series editor Introduction to Vascular Tech., 1990—; mem. exec. editl. com. Phlebology, 1987-91; mem. Internat. Editl. Adv. Bd., 1991-2000; mem. editl. com. Internat. Angiology, 1992—; contbr. over 150 articles to profl. jours. Lt. col. U.S. Army, 1967-70. Fellow in surg. rsch. Johns Hopkins U. Sch. Medicine, 1959-60, Am. Cancer Soc., Inc. fellow, 1965-66; Appleton-Century Crofts scholar, 1956, Mosby scholar, 1958. Fellow Am. Coll. Surgeons (Wash. chpt. 1971-75, Ill. chpt. counselor 1981-83), Cyprus Vascular Soc. (hon.); mem. AMA, Soc. Univ. Surgeons, Soc. Vascular Surgery (constn. and by-laws com. 1983, Wiley Fellowship com. 1990), Internat. Soc. Cardiovascular Surgery (N.Am. chpt. program com. 1985-88), Am. Surg. Assn., Am. Heart Assn. (stroke coun., cardiovascular surgery coun. 1978), Soc. Noninvasive Vascular Tech. (hon.), Vascular Surgery Biology Club, Am. Venous Forum (organizing com. 1987, founding mem. 1988, chmn. membership com. 1988-91, treas. 1992-95, pres. elect 1998, pres. 1999-2000), Cardiovascular Sys. Dynamics Soc., Internat. Soc. Surgery, Vascular Soc. So. Africa (hon.), North Pacific Surg. Assn., Ctrl. Surg. Assn., Midwestern Vascular Surg. Soc. (counselor 1977-79, pres.-elect 1980-81, pres. 1981-82), So. Assn. for Vascular Surgery, Ill. Heart Assn., Ill. Med. Soc., Ill. Surg. Soc., Chgo. Surg. Soc., Seattle Surg. Soc., Sangamon County Med. Soc., Henry N. Harkins Surg. Soc., Harbinger Soc., Phi Eta Sigma, Phi Beta Kappa, Sigma Xi, Alpha Omega Alpha. Presbyterian. Achievements include research in surgical hemodynamics and noninvasive methods for diagnosing peripheral vascular disease. Avocations: painting, sailing, history, computers. Home: 2324 W Lake Shore Dr Springfield IL 62707-9521 Office: So Ill U Sch Medicine Dept Surgery 701 N 1st St Ste D346 Springfield IL 62702 E-mail: dsumner1@aol.com.

SUMNER, DELORES TITCHYWY, school librarian, educator; b. Lawton, Okla., May 11, 1931; d. George Wallace and Blanche Titchywy; m. Rex Lee Sumner; children: Rodney Wayne, Larry Dean, DeeAnn Dickerson, Rosemary Wempen. BS in Edn., Northeastern State U., Okla., 1964, M, 1967; M in Libr. Sci., U. Okla., 1981. Cert. tchr. 1978, libr. 1978. Spl. collections libr. Northeastern State U. , Tahlequah, Okla., 1982—, historian, 1982—. Resource coord. Northeastern State U., United States, 1982—. Author: (book) Numu-Nu: The Fort Sill Indian School Experience, 1979, Descendents of Wis-Sis-Che, 2000, Descendents of Titchywy, 2000. Mem.: Am. Indian Engring. and Sci. Soc. (faculty sponsor 1985—2002, Certificate of Exemplary Service 1999), N.Am. Indian Women's Assn. (pres. 1985—95), Delta Kappa Gamma (rsch. com. chair 1984—2002). Baptist. Home: 405 N Bliss Tahlequah OK 74464 Office: Northeastern State Univ 612 N Grand Tahlequah OK 74464 Home Fax: 918-458-2197; Office Fax: 918-458-2197. Business E-Mail: sumner@nsuok.edu.

SUMNER, GORDON, JR. retired military officer; b. Albuquerque, July 23, 1924; s. Gordon and Esstella (Berry) S.; m. Frances Fernandes, May, 1991; children: Ward T., Holly Rose. AS, N.Mex. Mil. Inst., 1943; BA, La. State U., 1955; MA, U. Md., 1963. Commd. 2d. lt. U.S. Army, 1944, advanced through grades to lt. gen., 1975, ret., 1978; founder, chmn. Cypress Internat., 1978-96; chmn. La Mancha Co., Inc., 1981-89, Sumner Assoc. Cons. U.S. Depts. State and Def; amabassador at large for Latin Am.; spl. advisor U.S. Dept. State; nat. security advisor Pres.' Bi-Partisan Commn. Cen. Am.; cons. Los Alamos Nat. Lab. Contbr. articles to profl. jours. Decorated D.S.M., Silver Star, Legion of Merit with three oak leaf clusters, Disting. Flying Cross with 13 oak leaf clusters, Bronze Star, Army Commendation medal with oak leaf cluster, Purple Heart. Mem. Phi Kappa Phi, Pi Sigma Alpha. Office: La Mancha Co 100 Cienega St Ste D Santa Fe NM 87501-2003

SUMNER, GORDON MATTHEW See STING

SUMNER, JAMES DUPRE, JR. lawyer, educator; b. Spartanburg, S.C., Nov. 30, 1919; s. James DuPre and Frances Grace (Harris) S.; m. Evvie Lucille Beach, Apr. 1, 1945 (dec.); children: Chery Erline (Mrs. Horacek), James DuPre III; m. Doris Kaiser Malloy, Oct. 20, 1972; children: John L. Malloy III, Mary Margaret Malloy, Kenneth S. Malloy, James M. Malloy. AB, Wofford Coll., 1941; LLB, U. Va., 1949; LLM, Yale U., 1952, JSD, 1955. Bar: Va. 1948, Calif. 1957. Practice law, Los Angeles, 1957—; instr. law U. S.C., 1949-52; assoc. prof. UCLA, 1952-55, prof., 1955—. Distinguished vis. prof. Instituto Luigi Sturzo, Rome, 1959; vis. prof. U. Tex., 1962, U. So. Calif., 1971; lectr. Calif. Bar Rev. Co-author: An Anatomy of Legal Education; contbr. articles to profl. jours. Lt. col. inf. AUS, 1941-46, ETO. Decorated Silver Star, Purple Heart with oak leaf cluster. Mem.: Bel Air Assn. (bd. dirs.), Rotary (pres. Westwood Village chpt.), Westwood Village Bar Assn. (pres.), Va. Bar Assn., Calif. Bar Assn., Sertoma (pres.), Westwood Village Sertome Club (pres.), Braemar Country Club, L.A. Country Club. Republican. Methodist. Home: 10513 Rocca Pl Los Angeles CA 90077-2904

SUMNER, MARGARET ELIZABETH, elementary school educator; b. Clarksdale, Miss., Mar. 17, 1952; d. John Franklin and Julia Myrtle (Hopson) Sullivan; m. David Edwin Sumner, June 3, 1972; children: Julia Dawn, Oakley Raymond. BS in Edn., Delta State U., 1974. Cert. elem. tchr., Miss. Bridal cons. Hancock Fabric, Tupelo, Miss., 1974; mem. prodn. staff Arvin Inc., Verona, 1976; kindergarten tchr. Bissell (Miss.) Day Care, 1976-77; sec. Borden's Inc., Tupelo, 1977-79; tchr. 3rd grade Verona Jr. High Sch., 1979-80, kindergarten tchr., 1991, tchr. chpt. I remedial reading and math. Miss., 1991—; 4th grade tchr. Presbyn. Day Sch., Clarksdale, 1981-83; 1st grade tchr. Clarksdale Pub. Sch., 1984-90, Tupelo Pub. Sch., 1990, 9th-12th grade tchr. specific learning disability, 1992-93; tchr. developmentally disabled class West Amory (Miss.) Elem. Sch., 1991-92; home econ., computer tchr. Jumpertown Sch. and Wheeler Attendance Ctr., 1993-94; math, lang. arts spl. edn. tchr. Guntown (Miss.) Mid. Sch., 1994-95; tchr. spl. edn. for TMR, developmentally disabled DD, traumatic brain injury, TBI, severe/profound, SP Noxapater (Miss.) Sch., 1995—. Presenter to workshops in field; evaluator Miss. Tchr. Assessment Instrument, 1986—. Mem. Miss. Prof. Educators, Miss. Assn. Children Under Six. Baptist. Home: PO Box 100 Noxapater MS 39346-0100

SUMNER, MELANIE, writer, educator; b. Middletown, Ohio, Dec. 30, 1963; d. Joseph Roger and Mary Ruth (Page) S.; m. David William Marr, Mar. 31, 1996; children, Zoe Page, Sumner Rider. Student, Darlington Sch., Rome, Ga., 1982; BA, U. N.C., 1986; MA, Boston U., 1987. Instr. ESL US Peace Corps, Dakar, Senegal, West AFrica, 1988-90; instr. Cape Fear Cmty. Coll., Wilmington, N.C., 1990-93, Santa Fe Cmty. Coll., 1998-99, U. N.Mex., Taos, 1999—2001; assoc. prof. English, Shorter Coll., Rome, 2002—. Vis. lectr. U. N.C., Chapel Hill, 1995-96, assoc. prof., Shorter Coll, Rome, Ga. Author: Polite Society, 1995, The School of Beauty and Charm, 2001; contbr. articles, short stories to publs. including The New Yorker, N.Y. Times, others. Fellow Yaddo, 1992, Fine Arts Work Cetr., 1993-95; recipient Whiting award, 1996, Maria Thomas award for best Peace Corps novel, 1995. Avocations: quilting, hiking, skiing. Home: 12 Sagewood Dr Rome GA 30165

SUMNER, STACEY LYNN (STACEY MUCK), lawyer; b. Toledo, Feb. 25, 1966; d. Thomas Jude and Rebecca Jean (Heilman) M.; m. Kevin D. Sumner; 1 child, Christopher D. BA, Fla. So. Coll., 1988; JD, Thomas M. Cooley Law Sch., Lansing, Mich., 1992. Bar: Fla. 1992, U.S. Dist. Ct. (mid. dist.) Fla. 1993, U.S. Ct. Appeals (11th cir.) 1993. Asst. state atty. 6th Jud. Cir. Office of State Atty., Clearwater, Fla., 1992—. Avocations: golf, tennis, gardening. Home: PO Box 144 San Antonio FL 33576-0144 Office: Office State Atty 6th Jud Cir 38053 Live Oak Ave Rm 204 Dade City FL 33523

SUM-PING, SAM THIO, anesthesiologist, hospital administrator; b. Pt. Louis, Mauritius, Sept. 11, 1952; came to U.S., 1986; s. Maxime and Mui (Fock) S-P.; m. Lynal Law Chin Yung, Feb. 18, 1978; children: Joanne, Oliver. MB BChir, U. Manchester, Eng., 1978. Diplomate Am. Bd. Anesthesiology. House officer Manchester Hosps., 1978-79, sr. house officer, 1979-82, registrar, 1982-84, sr. registrar, 1984-86; lectr. U. Manchester, 1985-86; vis. asst. prof. U. Iowa, Iowa City, 1986-90, asst. prof., 1990-94, assoc. prof., 1994-98; dir. surg. ICU U. Iowa Hosps. and Clinics, 1994-98; assoc. prof. Duke U. Med. Ctr., 1998—; dir. surg. ICU Durham VA Med. Ctr. Author: Memory and Awareness in Anesthesia, 1990, Principles and Practice of Anesthesia, 1994; contbr. articles to jours. Anesthesia and Analgesia, Anesthesiology. Fellow Royal Coll. Anesthesiologists; mem. Internat. Anesthesia Rsch. Soc., Am. Soc. Anesthesiologists. Office: Duke U Med Ctr Dept Anesthesiology Dumc 3094 Durham NC 27710-0001

SUMRALL, LINDA, geophysicist; b. Baton Rouge, Feb. 1, 1954; d. Lindsey and Katherine Moreau; m. Willie Sumrall, July 21, 1984; children: Lindsey, Joanna. BS in Geology, La. State U., 1976. Geophysicist Gulf Oil, Houston, 1976-80; sr. geophysicist UTPC, 1980-90; divsn. geophysicist EDC, 1990-96; sr. staff geophysicist Burlington Resources, 1996—2002, Moreau-Sumrall Geophys. Svcs., Houston, 2002—.

SUMSION, JOHN WALBRIDGE, information scientist; b. Gloucester, Eng., Aug. 16, 1928; s. Herbert Whitton and Alice Hartley (Garlichs) S.; m. Annette Dorothea Wilson (div. 1979); children: Bridget, Christopher, Michael, Kate; m. Hazel Mary Jones, 1979. BA in Modern History, Cambridge (Eng.) U., 1952, MA, 1981; MA in Econs., Yale U., 1953. Prodn. mgr. K Shoemakers, Kendal, Eng., 1954-62, dir. Eng., 1962-81; registrar Pub. Lending Right, Eng., 1981-91; dir. libr. and info. stats. unit Loughborough (Eng.) U., 1991-96, sr. fellow dept. info. scis., 1996—. Mem. Copyright Tribunal, Eng., 1990-93; non-exec. dir. TeleOrdering Ltd., Alton, Eng., 1992-94;mem. Libr. & Info. Svcs. Coun., Eng., 1992-95. Author: PLR in Practice, 1st edit., 1988, 2d edit., 1991; joint author: Perspectives of Public Library Use, 1995, Library Performance Indicators and Library Management tools, 1995; contbr. articles to profl. jours. Decorated Order Brit. Empire. Fellow Libr. Assn.; mem. Internat. Fedn. Libr. Assns. (hon. chmn. stats. sect. 1995-99). Liberal Democrat. Anglican. Avocations: singing, flute, walking. Home: The Granary, 29 Main St Rotherby, Melton Mowbray Leicestershire LE14 2LP England Office: Loughborough U Dept Info Sci Loughborough LE11 3TU England E-mail: j.w.sumsion@lboro.ac.uk.

SUMWALT, ROBERT LLEWELLYN, JR. retired construction company executive; b. Columbia, S.C., Dec. 29, 1927; s. Robert Llewellyn and Caroline M. (Causey) S.; m. Mary Joyce Mills, Mar. 8, 1952; children: Elizabeth Ladson, Robert Llewellyn III. BSCE, U. S.C., 1949; MSCE, MIT, 1950. Registered profl. engr., S.C. Area engr. E.I. duPont de Nemours & Co., Camden, S.C., 1950-52; constrn. engr. Columbia City Sch. Sys., 1952-58; sr. v.p., dir. McCrory-Sumwalt Constrn. Co., Inc., Columbia, 1958-77; chmn. bd., treas., dir. Sumwalt-Mashburn Engring. & Constrn. Co., Inc., 1977-79; chmn. bd., pres., dir., CEO Sumwalt Constrn. Co., Inc., 1979-98; ret. Bd. dirs. Columbia City Wachovia Nat. Bank. Pres. Richland County unit Am. Cancer Soc., 1956, bd. dirs. S.C. chpt., 1957; chmn. Carolina Carillon Ball, 1963; sect. chmn. United Cmty. Svcs., 1957; divsn. chmn. constrn. divsn. United Way, 1973; bd. dirs. Richland County unit ARC, 1955-56; mem. adv. bd. Salvation Army, 1982-84; mem. Bicentennial Commn. U. S.C., 1998-2001, pres. Coll. Engring. Partnership Bd., 1999—. Served to comdr. C.E.C., USNR. Named Young Man of Yr., Columbia Jr. C. of C., 1958; recipient Disting. Alumnus award Coll. engring., 2001. Mem. Carolinas Assn. Gen. Contractors Am. (chmn. bldg. divsn., dir. Carolinas br. 1977, v.p. 1986, sr. v.p. 1987, pres. Carolinas AGC 1988, nat. dir. AGC of Am. 1989, 90, pub. rels. com.), Columbia Contractors Assn. (pres. 1969), S.C. Soc. Engrs., S.C. Soc. Profl. Engrs., Assn. U.S. Army, U. S.C. Assocs. (v.p. 1997, pres. 1998), U. S.C. Alumni Assn. (circuit v.p. 1956), Prison Fellowship Ministries, Kiwanis (pres. 1962), Forest Lake Country Club, Tip Off Club (pres. 1981-82), Dreher H.S. Found. (pres. 1994-96), Tarantilla Club, Columbia Ball Club, Centurion Club (Columbia), Litchfield Country Club (Litchfield Beach, S.C.), Springdale Hall Club (Camden), Phi Beta Kappa, Omicron Delta Kappa, Tau Beta Pi, Sigma Alpha Epsilon (chmn. S.C. Delta Housing Corp. 1999-2001). Presbyterian (chmn. bd. deacons 1968, elder, chmn. adminstrn. com. 1987, 88, adv. bd. Heathwood Hall Sch. 1995-98). Home: 445 Alexander Way Columbia SC 29206-4974 Office: PO Box 6576 Columbia SC 29260-6576

SUN, ALBERT YUNG-KWANG, biochemistry and neurochemistry educator; b. Amoy, Fukien, Peoples Republic of China, Oct. 13, 1932; came to U.S., 1959, naturalized, 1972; s. Pehcheng and SuiHo Kuo Wu; m. Grace Yen-Chi Cheung Sun, May 9, 1964; 1 child, Aggie Yee-Chun. BS in Agrl. Chemistry, Nat. Taiwan U., Taipei, 1957; PhD in Biochemistry, Oreg. State U., 1967. Postdoctoral research assoc. Case-Western Res. U., Cleve., 1967-68; sr. research scientist Cleve. Psychiat. Inst., 1968-74; project dir. Ohio Mental Health Research Ctr., Cleve., 1972-74, research prof./assoc. prof. pharmacology, 1989-91, prof. pharmacology, 1991—. Mem. adv. panel NSF, Washington, 1984-85. Editor: Neural Membranes, 1983, Molecular Mechanism of Alcohol, 1989. Advisor Chinese Christian Fellowship Group, Columbia, 1974—. Grantee Nat. Inst. Alcohol Abuse and Alcoholism, 1974-78, 82-98, Nat. Inst. Neurol. Com. Disease and Stroke, 1975-79, Nat. Cancer Inst., 1979-83, EPA, 2000—. Mem. Research Soc. Alcoholism, Am. Soc. Neurochemistry, Am. Soc. Neurosci., Am. Soc. Biol. Chemists, Am. Chem. Soc. Current work: Structure-functional relationship of neural membranes using biochemical and biophysical approaches, study on the biochem.mechanism of aging and Alzheimer's Disease in the brain. Subspecialies: Biochemistry (medicine); Neurochemistry. Home: 2908 Shoreside Dr Columbia MO 65203-0941 E-mail: suna@missouri.edu.

SUN, BILL KAUO-HWA, energy consulting company executive, electric power industry executive; b. Shanghai, China, Oct. 11, 1944; came to U.S., 1967; s. Pao-Fa and Wen-Gin (Chen) S.; m. Meiling Tang, Aug. 10, 1969; children: Jennifer, Christine, Valerie. BS, Nat. Taiwan U., 1966; MS, U. Ky., 1969; PhD, U. Calif., Berkeley, 1973. Registered profl. engr. Tech. leader, sr. engr. GE Co., San Jose, Calif., 1972-77; program & project mgr. Elec. Power Rsch. Inst., Palo Alto, 1977-94; pres. Sunutech, Inc., Los Altos, 1994-2000. Advisor ROC Overseas Affairs Commn.; advisor to chmn. Rep. of China Atomic Energy Coun., Taipei, 1995—; com. chmn. Internat. Atomic Energy Agy., Vienna, Austria, 1990—. Contbr. articles to profl. jours. Bd. dirs. Sister City Com., Los Altos, 1996—; angel investor in high-tech. start-up cos. Mem. ASME, Am. Nuclear Soc. (life), N.Am. Taiwanese Engrs. Assn., Chinese Am. Econ. & Tech. Devel. Assn. (pres. 1993-94, bd. dirs.), Chinese Inst. Engrs. (pres., chmn. bd. dirs. 1989-90). Avocations: classic opera, classical music, golf, computer. Home: 12444 Robleda Rd Los Altos Hills CA 94022-3420 Office: Sunutech Inc PO Box 978 Los Altos CA 94023-0978 E-mail: Billsun@aol.com.

SUN, DONGCHU, statistics educator; b. Shanghai, People's Republic of China; s. Zenze Sun and Yun Chen; m. Zhuoqiong He, May 5, 1987; children: Abby P., Tony K. BS in Math., East China Normal U., 1982; MS in Statistics, Ohio State U., 1988; Phd in Statistics, Purdue U., 1991. Lectr. East China Normal U., Shanghai, 1985-87; fellow Ohio State U., Columbus, 1987-88; tchg. asst., fellow Purdue U., West Lafeyette, Ind., 1988-91; vis. asst. prof. U. Mich., Ann Arbor, 1991-92; asst. prof. U. Mo., Columbia, 1992-98, assoc. prof., 1998—2002, prof., 2002—. Rsch. fellow Nat. Inst. of Statis. Scis., Research Triangle Park, N.C., 1998-99. Contbr. articles to profl. jours. Grantee NSF, 1999—, Nat. Inst. of Statis. Sci., 1996-99; fellow U. Calif., Berkeley, 1987; recipient I.W. Burr award Purdue U., 1991, Albert Winemiller Prizes for Outstanding Rsch. in Psychological Stats., Univ. of Mo., 2002, Chancellor's Award for Outstanding Rsch, and Creative Activity in Physical and Math. Sci., Univ. of Mo.Columbia, 2002. Mem. Am. Statis. Assn., Inst. of Statis. Scis., Intrnat. Chinese Statis. Assn., Internat. Statis. Inst. Avocations: stamp collecting, exercise. Office: U Mo Dept Stats 316 Math Scis Bldg Columbia MO 65211-0001

SUN, HAIYIN, optical engineer, educator; b. Kunming, Yunnan, China, July 27, 1958; came to the U.S., 1990; s. Qiyuan Sun and Shouzheng Wang; m. Nan Yang, Oct. 3, 1987; children: Tobias Y., Christina N. BS in Physics, Shanghai (China) Tchrs. U., 1982; MS in Photonics, Shanghai (China) Inst. Optics, and Fine Mechanics, 1985; PhD in Photonics, U. Ark., 1994. Instr. Shanghai Tchr.'s U., 1982; asst. prof. Shanghai Inst. Optics and Fine Mechanics, 1986-88; vis. scientist Telecom. Network Rsch. Ctr. of Germany's Post, Darmstadt, 1988-90; optical engr. Power Tech., Inc., Little Rock, 1994-96; sr. optical engr. Coherent Inc., Auburn, Calif., 1996—. Adj. prof. U. Ark., Little Rock, 1996—; prin. investigator various projects; editor Jour. Optical Comm. Contbr. chpt. to book and numerous articles to profl. jours.; inventor several optical devices. Named Outstanding Rschr., The Justice Dept. USA Govt., 1995; rsch. grantee Ark. Sci. & Engring. Authority, 1993. Avocations: classical music, watching TV movies and sports, cooking. Home: 1801 Eureka Rd # 62 Roseville CA 95661

SUN, HONGWEI, mechanical engineer; b. Liaoyang, China, Sept. 17, 1962; d. Dingxian Sun and Suzhi Zheng; m. Shaofu Wu, Dec. 30, 1985; children: Jenny Wu, Kevin Wu. BS, Beijing U. Aeronautics, 1982, MS, 1984; PhD, U. Ill., Chgo., 1991. Profl. engr., Tex. Rsch. engr. Aurora (Ill.) Pump, 1991-94; lead design engr., sr. engr. Flow Products, Inc., Brookshire, Tex., 1994—. Patentee in field; contbr. articles to profl. jours. Mem. ASME (assoc.), Tau Beta Pi. Avocations: singalong, swimming. Office: Flow Products Inc 800 Koomey Rd Brookshire TX 77423-8202 Fax: 281-934-6056. E-mail: HSUN@flow-products.com.

SUN, HUN H. electrical engineering and biomedical engineering educator; b. Shanghai, China, Mar. 27, 1925; s. Yu F.and Tuk F. Sun; m. Nancy Liu, Jan. 30, 1951; 1 child, Elizabeth A. BSEE, Chiao-Tung U., Shanghai, 1946; MSEE, U. Wash., 1950; PhD, Cornell U., 1955. Asst. prof. elect. engring. Drexel U., Phila., 1953-56, assoc. prof., 1956-59, prof., 1959—, dir. Biomed. Engring. and Scis. Inst., 1964-74, chmn. elec. engring. dept., 1973-78, E.O. Lange prof., 1978-95, prof. Emeritus, 1995—; NIH spl. fellow MIT, Cambridge, Mass., 1963-64. Cons. Wright-Patterson AFB, Dayton, Ohio, 1963-65; mem. study com. NIH, Bethesda, Md., 1981-85; mem. adv. com. NSF, Washington, 1985-88; adj. prof. Temple U. Dept. Physiology, 1971-91. Author: Synthesis of R. C. Networks, 1967; editor in chief Annals of Biomed. Engring., 1984-94; mem. editl. bd. Automatica (London), 1974-90, Critical Rev. in Bioengring, 1978-81; cons. editor Elec. Engring. Monograph Series, 1964-67; contbr. chpts. to books, articles to profl. jours. Mem. Com. on Art and Sci. Franklin Inst., 1969-82. Recipient 1st Rsch. Achievement award Drexel U., 1973. Fellow IEEE (editor in chief Trans. Biomed. Engring. 1972-78); mem. Biomed. Engring. Soc. (founding), Sigma Xi (life). Home: 939 Hedgerow Ct Blue Bell PA 19422-2408 Office: Drexel Univ Dept Elec Engring Philadelphia PA 19104

SUN, JEFFREY C. legal educator; b. San Francisco, 1971; s. Gary and Ruth Sun. BBA, Loyola Marymount U., L.A., 1993, MBA, 1994; JD, Ohio State U., 1998; postgrad., Columbia U., 1998—. Bar: Ohio 1998. Dir. student activities Santa Monica (Calif.) Cath., 1993-95, dir. mktg. and admissions, 1993-95; assoc. Thompson, Hine & Flory, Columbus, Ohio, 1995; rsch. asst. Ohio State U., 1997, rsch. assoc., 1998; rsch. asst. to pres. Tchrs. Coll. Columbia U., N.Y.C., 1998, instr., 1999—. Mem. adv. bd. St. Monica Cath., Ohio Ctr. for Law Related Edn.; adj. asst. prof. NYU, N.Y.C., 1998—. Mem. Ohio State Bar Assn., Coun. on Law and Higher Edn., Edn. Law Assn. Office: Tchrs Coll Columbia U 585 W 120th St Box 175 New York NY 10027 E-mail: jcs81@columbia.edu.

SUN, JI, research scientist; b. Changsha, Hunan, China, Dec. 4, 1971; s. Ming and Hong-Yan (Zhou) S. BS cum laude, Morningside Coll., 1991; PhD, U. Md., 1997. Rsch. scientist Hunan Med. U., Changsha, 1989-91; rsch. scientist chemistry dept. Morningside Coll., Sioux City, Iowa, 1991; tchg. asst. biology dept. U. Md., Balt., 1992-96, rsch. asst., 1992—; rsch. asst. biology dept. U. Tex., Dallas, 1996; rsch. scientist Columbia U. Coll. Physicians and Surgeons, N.Y.C., 1997—. Mem. editl. bd. Chinese Jour. Modern Medicine, 1996—; contbr. articles to profl. jours. Chmn. Student Govt., Hunan Med. U., 1989-91. Recipient Sci. and Technol. Progress award Chinese Nat. Health Dept., 1994; Travel grantee NSF, 1996. Mem. AAAS, Am. Philatelic Soc. Office: Divsn Cardiol Dept Medicine 630 W 168th St New York NY 10032-3702

SUN, LI-TEH, economics educator; b. Hong Kong, Dec. 5, 1939; s. Beh-Yu and Ruey-Jeng (Wang) S.; m. Ping Zhong, June 1, 1991. BA in Econs., Chung Hsing U., Taipei, Taiwan, 1962; MS in Econs., Okla. State U., 1968, PhD in Econs., 1972. Rsch. assoc. U. Mont., Missoula, 1969-70; lectr. Humboldt State U., Arcata, Calif., 1972-75; acad. resource specialist Chancelor's Office Calif. State U. and Colls., Long Beach, 1975-77; assoc. prof., prof. econs. Nat. Chung Hsing U., Taipei, 1977-81, chair dept. pub. fin., 1978-82; prof. econs. Moorhead (Minn.) State U., 1982-96. Coord. China programs Moorhead State U., 1987-89. Contbr. articles to profl. jours. Mem. adv. bd. Centre of Humanomics, 1985-96; mem. Mid-Am. Cons. Internat., 1993—. Named Prof. of Yr., Humboldt State U., Arcata, Calif., 1974. Mem. Moorhead Cen. Lions (newsletter editor 1990-93, bd. dirs. 1983-96, pres. 1987-88, Lion of Yr. 1984, 85, 90, 91). Avocations: walking, karaoke, travel. Home: 7312 Charlesborough Ct Lorton VA 22079-1538

SUN, MINGHE, business educator; b. Shouguang, China, Mar. 11, 1954; s. Fulu Sun and Meiying Wang; m. Xingqi Sun, July 10, 1954; children: Shining, Andrew. BS, Northeastern U., Shenyang, China, 1982; MBA, Chinese U. Hong Kong, 1997; PhD, U. Ga., 1992. Asst. prof. U. Tex., San Antonio, 1992-98, assoc. prof., 1998—. Contbr. articles to profl. jours. Recipient Outstanding Dissertation award Decisoin Scis. Inst., 1993, Outstanding Paper award So. Mgmt. Assn., 1998, Outstanding Tchg. award U. Tex. Sys., 1999, Outstanding Svc. as the Local Arrangements Chair award Prodn. Ops. Soc., 2000. Mem. Inst. Ops. Rsch. and Mgmt. Scis. Home: 14107 Soapberry Cove San Antonio TX 78249 Office: U Tex Coll Bus San Antonio TX 78249 Home Fax: 210-558-7861; Office Fax: 210-458-5783. E-mail: msun@utsa.edu.

SUN, NE-ZHENG, mathematics and environmental engineering educator; b. Qingdao, China, Dec. 5, 1937; came to U.S., 1988; s. Hi-Peng and Xin-Ru (Wang) S.; m. Fang Luo, Nov. 4, 1967; children: Yixing, Alexander Yishan. BS, Shandong U., Jinan, China, 1959, MS and PhD, 1965. Asst. prof. Shandong U., 1965-79, assoc. prof., 1979-85, prof. applied math. and environ. engring., 1985-88; assoc. rschr. UCLA, 1982-84, rschr., 1988-95, adj. prof. applied math. and environ. engring., 1995—. Cons. Bur. Geology and Minerals, Beijing, China, 1974-88, MWD, So. Calif., L.A., 1991-94. Author: Inverse Problems in Groundwater Modeling, 1994, Mathematical Modeling of Groundwater Pollution, 1996; contbr. articles to profl. jours. Recipient Excellent Result award Nat. Sci. Com., Beijing, 1978, Sci. and Tech. Developing award Nat. Edn. Com., Beijing, 1986, 95. Mem. ASCE, Am. Geophys. Union. Achievements include being first groundwater modeler of China, leading a team that developed models for more than 20 groundwater basins in China in 1970s and 1980s; contribution of new concepts and methods for groundwater modeling such as the multiple cell balance method, management equivalent identifiability, model structure identification, others. Office: Dept Civil and Environ Engring UCLA 405 Hilgard Ave Los Angeles CA 90095-9000 E-mail: nezheng@ucla.edu.

SUN, NORA CHI-JUN, pathologist; b. Shanghai, China, June 16, 1937; came to U.S., 1966; d. K.F. and S.W. Sun; m. David T. Sung; children: Thomas C.K. Lee, Anthony D. Sung. MD, Shanghai 2d Med. Coll., 1960; MS in Pathology, U. Minn., 1973. Demonstrator U. Hong Kong, 1964-66; rsch. biologist A.H. Robins Co., Richmond, Va., 1966-67; clin. teaching asst. Boston U. Sch. Medicine, 1968-70; asst. prof. pathology U. So. Calif., L.A., 1973-76; staff pathologist John Wesley Hosp., 1973-76; asst. prof. UCLA Sch. Medicine, 1976-82; staff pathologist, head hematopathology Harbor-UCLA Med. Ctr., Torrance, Calif., 1976—; assoc. prof. UCLA Sch. Medicine, L.A., 1982-88, prof. pathology, 1988—. Recipient Women Achievement award Delta Kappa Gamma, Rochester, Minn., 1972. Mem. Internat. Assn. Chinese Pathologists (pres.-elect 1991-93, pres. 1993-95), Harbor-UCLA Med. Ctr. Faculty Soc. (pres.-elect 1990-91, pres. 1991-92). Office: Harbor UCLA Med Ctr 1000 W Carson St Torrance CA 90502-2004 E-mail: nejsun@ucla.edu.

SUN, OSBERT JIANXIN, ecophysiologist, researcher; b. Denkou, Inner Mongolia, China, May 1, 1961; s. Qiaoxiu Qu and He Sun; m. Xiao Zhang, Jan. 29, 1972; children: June. PhD, U. Canterbury, Christchurch, New Zealand, 1993. Asst. lectr. Inner Mongolia Agrl. U., Huhhot, China, 1982—86; scientist New Zealand Forest Rsch. Inst., Christchurch, New Zealand, 1994—99; rsch. assoc. Oreg. State U., Corvallis, Oreg., 2001—. Author: (research articles) Tree Physiology, 1995, (research article) , 1999, Trees - Structure and Function, 2001, New Phytologist, 1999, Plant and Soil, 2000. Recipient Sci. and Tech. Achievement award, Ministry of Forestry, China, 1987; scholar BNZ scholar, Bank of New Zealand, 1989, T.W. Adams scholar, U. Canterbury, 1989. Mem.: AGU, N.W. Forest Soils Coun. Office: Oreg State Univ Corvallis OR 97331 Office Fax: 541-737-1393. Business E-Mail: osbert.sun@orst.edu.

SUN, PETER P. neurosurgeon; b. Taipei, Taiwan, China, Oct. 6, 1965; s. Yeng C. and Yueh Y. Sun; m. Mindy Lin, Jan. 18, 1992; children: Austin, Jason. MD, Columbia U., 1991. Resident Yale U.; attending neurosurgeon Children's Hosp. of Phila., 1997-2000; dir. neurosurgery Children's Hosp. Oakland, Calif., 2000—. Asst. prof. U. Pa., Phila., 1997-2000. Contbr.: (books) Neurological Surgery, 1996, Principles and Practice of Pediatric Neurosurgery, 1999, Atlas of Pediatric Neurosurgery, The Unborn Patient: The Art and Science of Fetal Therapy, 2001; contbr. articles to profl. jours. NIH Rsch. Svc. awardee, 1990. Mem. Congress of Neurol. Surgeons. Office: Children's Hospital Oakland 747 52d St Oakland CA 94609 Office Fax: (510) 597-7034. E-mail: psun@mail.cho.org.

SUN, ROBERT ZU JEI, manufacturing company executive, inventor; b. Shanghai, July 5, 1948; s. David C.H. and Evelyn (Lee) S.; m. Nan Jennifer Ronis, Sept. 20, 1986; children: Matthew Nyland, Michael Elias. BS in Elec. Engring., U. Pa., 1970. Sr. project engr. Drexelbrook Engring. Co., Horsham, Pa., 1970-78; pres., chmn. bd. Suntex Internat., Inc., Easton, 1981—. Inventor 24 Math Game, Mhing Card Game; 5 patents in field. Pres. Coalition of Religious and Civic Orgns., Easton, 1979-81; mem. transition team Pa. Gov.-elect Tom Ridge, 1994; apptd. by Gov. Ridge to Pa. State Bd. Edn., 1995, Team Pa. Amb. Coun., 1999. Recipient 2 Excellence awards for Mhing pkg. Nat. Paperbox and Pkg. Assn., 1984-85. Office: 118 N 3rd St Easton PA 18042-1804

SUN, RON, computer scientist, cognitive scientist; b. Shanghai, Oct. 8, 1960; BS, Fudan U., Shanghai, 1983; MS, Clarkson U., Potsdam, N.Y., 1986; PhD, Brandeis U., Waltham, Mass., 1991. Rsch. engr. SRIEA, 1983-85; asst. prof. computer sci., psychology U. Ala., Tuscaloosa, 1992-98, assoc. prof. computer sci., psychology, 1998-99; assoc. prof. computer engring. and sci. U. Mo., Columbia, 1999—2002, prof. computer engring. and sci., 2002—. Spkr. in field. Author: Integrating Rules and Connectionism for Robust Commonsense Reasoning, 1994, Duality of the Mind, 2001, Neural Networks for High Level Knowledge Representation and Inference, Artificial Intelligence and Neural Networks: Steps Towards Principled Integration, vol. 1, 1994, Progress in Neural Networks, vol. 5, 1995; co-author: Neural and Intelligent Systems Integration, 1991, Neural Network Perspectives on Cognition and Adaptive Robotics, 1997, A Companion to Cognitive Science, 1999, Deep Fusion of Computational and Symbolic Processing, 1999, others; co-editor: Computational Architectures Integrating Neural and Symbolic Processes, 1994, Hybrid Neural Systems, 2000, Sequence Learning, 2000; editor-in-chief: Cognitive Sys. Rsch.; editor: Neural Computing Surveys, 1997—, Applied Intelligence, 1997—, Connection Sci., 1995—; contbr. articles to profl. jours. including; reviewer MIT Press, John Wiley and Sons, Kluwer Acad. Pubs., Blackwell Pubs., World Sci. Lawrence Erlbaum Assocs., Acad. Press, Oxford U. Press. Grantee Office Naval Rsch., 1994, U. Ala., 1993, Army Rsch. Inst., 2000. Mem. IEEE (sr. mem.), Cognitive Sci. Soc. (David Marr award 1991), Am. Assn. Artificial Intelligence, Internat. Neural Network Soc., Assn. Computing Machinery, Soc. Psychology Philosophy, Upsilon Pi Epsilon. Address: CECS Dept Univ of Missouri 201 Engineering Building W Columbia MO 65211-2060 E-mail: rsun@cecs.missouri.edu.

SUN, RONGQI, organic chemistry educator, researcher; b. Zhen Jiang City, Jiangsu, China, Jan. 23, 1960; s. Sun Shoukang and Li Lansheng; m. Yangsheng Wang, Aug. 14, 1987; 1 child, Jie. BSc, Lanzhou (China) U., 1982, MSc, 1985, PhD, 1988. Asst. prof. Shanghai Inst. Pharm. Industry, 1988-90; assoc. prof. organic chemistry East China U. Sci. and Tech., Shanghai, 1991-96, prof., 1996-99, dean dept. fine chem. tech., 1992-99, v.p. Coll. Pharm. Tech., 1996-99. Vis. scholar Rutgers U., N.J., 1999—. Contbr. articles to sci. jours., including Phytochemistry, Planta Medica, Chinese Sci. Bull., Chinese Jour. Organic Chemistry. Recipient Shanghai edn. prize City of Shanghai, 1997. Mem. Chinese Pharm. Assn. Avocations: sports, travel. Office: East China U Sci and Tech 130 Meilong Rd Shanghai 200237 China

SUN, SIAO FANG, chemistry educator; b. Shaoshing, China, Feb. 19, 1922; came to U.S., 1949; s. Yuan and Yu C. Sun; m. M. Emily Chao, June 23, 1951; children: Patricia Viane, Caroline Marie, Diana Kate. MA, U. Utah, 1950; MS, Loyola U., 1956; PhD, U. Chgo., 1958, U. Ill., 1962. Prof. math. Northland Coll., Ashland, Wis., 1960-64; asst. prof. chemistry St. John's U., Jamaica, N.Y., 1964-70, assoc. prof. chemistry, 1970-75, prof. chemistry, 1975-92, adj. prof., 1992—. Vis. scientist Nat. Ctr. Sci. Rsch., Strasbourg and Meudon-Bellevue, France, 1975-78, Carlsberg Lab., Copenhagen, 1981; staff scientist Max Planck Inst. Biophysical Chemistry, Gottingen, Germany, 1976. Contbr. articles to profl. jours. Office: St John's Univ Dept Chemistry Jamaica NY 11439-0001 E-mail: suns@stjohns.edu.

SUN, TUNG-TIEN, medical science educator; b. Chung King, Szechuan, People's Republic of China, Feb. 20, 1947; s. Chung-Yu and Wen (Lin) S.; m. Brenda Shih-Ying Bao, Aug. 14, 1971; children: I-Hsing, I-Fong. BS in Agrl. Chemistry, Nat. Taiwan U., Taipei, 1967; PhD in Biochemistry, U. Calif., Davis, 1974. Rsch. assoc. dept. biology MIT, Cambridge, 1974-78; asst. prof. depts. dermatology, cell biology and anatomy Johns Hopkins Med. Sch., Balt., 1978-81, assoc. prof. depts. cell biology and anatomy, dermatology, ophthalmology, 1981-82; assoc. prof. depts. dermatology and pharmacology NYU Med. Sch., N.Y.C., 1982-86, prof., 1986-90, Rudolf L. Baer prof., 1990—, prof. dept. urology, 1996—, assoc. dir. Skin Disease Rsch. Ctr., 1989-93, dean's lectr., 2000. Mem. cell biology study sect. NIH, 1984-88; adj. prof. dept. dermatology U. Pa. Med. Sch., Phila., 1992—; chair Gordon Conf. Keratinization & Epithelial Differentiation, 1995; Angus lectr. U. Toronto, 1986, Pinkus lectr. Am. Acad. Dermatopathologists, 1986, Liu lectr. Stanford Med. Sch., 1987, Susan Swerling lectr. Harvard Med. Sch., 1991, Kihei Tanioku Meml. lectr. Japanese Soc. Investigative Dermatology, 1998, dean's lectr. N.Y.U. Med. Sch., 2000, William W. Scott Meml. lectr. Johns Hopkins Med. Sch., 2001—; adj. prof. Coll. Life Sci. Peking U., 1998—; hon. prof. Third Mil. Med. U., Chung King, China, 1998—. Mem. editl. bd. Differentiation, 1984—, Epithelial Cell Biology, 1990-93; assoc. editor Jour. Investigative Dermatology, 1990—, Jour. Dermatol. Sci., 1992—; U.S. mng. editor Molecular Biology Report, 1994-96. Recipient Career Devel. award Nat. Eye Inst., 1978-82, Monique Neill-Caulier Career Scientist award, 1984-89, Alcon award in vision rsch., 1993, Wu Jieping Urololgy Found. award Chinese Med. Assn., 1998. Fellow AAAS; mem. Academia Sinica, Am. Soc. Biol. Chemists, Am. Soc. for Cell Biology, Internat. Soc. Differentiation (bd. dirs. 1985-88), Nat. Inst. Arthiritis and Musculoskeletal and Skin Diseases (bd. sci. counselors), Soc. Investigative Dermatology (Montagna lectr. 1989, bd. dirs. 1993-98), Assn. Rsch. in Vision Sci. and Ophthalmology. Office: NYU Med Sch Dept Dermatology 560 1st Ave New York NY 10016-6402 E-mail: sunt01@med.nyu.edu.

SUN, WEI, computer scientist, educator; b. Benbu, Anhui, China, May 8, 1957; s. Shangyun Sun and Tongfang Song; m. Ming Song, May 5, 1983; children: Serena Xiling, Selina Yuling. PhD, Drexel U., 1992. Asst. prof. Drexel U., Phila., 1998—. Dir. Rapid Product Devel. Ctr. - Drexel, Phila., 1994—; guest rschr. U.S. Army Rsch. Lab., Aberdeen Proving Ground, Md., 2001—02. Contbr. articles to profl. jours. Grantee, NSF, 1999, U.S. Army Rsch. Lab., 2001, FAA, 2002. Mem.: AAUP, ASME, Am. Acad. of Mechanics, Am. Soc. of Mfg., Am. Soc. of Composites. Office: Drexel University 32nd & Chestnut Street Philadelphia PA 19104

SUN, WEI YUE, internist; b. Guangzhou, China, Nov. 9, 1959; came to U.S., 1990; s. Chu Yin Sun and Wei Huang; m. Xiao Jing Li, Dec. 24, 1994. MD, Sun Yat-sen U. Med. Scis., Guangzhou, 1988; MPH, U. Wis., La Crosse, 1992; M of Health Sci. Edn., U. Fla., 1995; postgrad., Columbia U., 1998—. Resident dept. medicine Sun Yat-sen U. Med. Scis. Med. Ctr., 1988-90; pub. health advisor, educator Am. Cancer Soc., La Crosse, 1990-92; rsch. and tchg. scholar dept. health sci. edn. U. Fla., Gainesville, 1995; clin./pub. health epidemiologist divsn. family health svcs. Rsch. and Devel. Unit, N.Y.C. Dept. Health, 1995-98; rsch. scholar dept. health and behavior studies Columbia U., 1998—; extendship dept. medicine Brookdale U. Hosp. and Med. Ctr., Bklyn., 1998—, resident dept. medicine, 1998—; clin. fellow in nephrology, dept. nephrology and hypertension Brookdale U. Hosp. and Med. Ctr., 2002—. Adj. asst. prof. dept. health, phys. edn. and wellness Bronx C.C. of CUNY, 1996-98; presenter in field. Author: (with W. W. Chen) Tai Chi Chuan—The Gentle Workout for Mind and Body, 1995, (with X. J. Li) Chi Kung—Increase Your Energy, Improve Your Health, 1997, New-Style Tai Chi Chuan—The Official Chinese System, 1999; contbr. articles to profl. jours. C.A. Boyd Grad. scholar U. Fla., 1994-95. Mem. AMA, APHA, Am. Sch. Health Assn., Am. Assn. Chinese Physicians. Avocations: reading, tennis, table tennis. Home: 7 Hegeman Ave Apt 14B Brooklyn NY 11212-4744 Office: Brookdale Univ Hosp and Med Ctr 1 Brookdale Plz Brooklyn NY 11212-3139 E-mail: weiyuesun@yahoo.com.

SUN, YANYI, research scientist; b. Beijing, June 14, 1944; came to U.S., 1986; d. Yufeng Sun and YiQing Li; m. Rirong Cheng, Sept. 30, 1972; children: Cheng. BS, U. Sci. and Tech. of China, 1967. Engr. Yan Shan Petrochemical Plant, Beijing, 1968-80; instr. Beijing (China) Indsl. U., 1980-83; lectr. Ctrl. Radio and TV U. of China, Beijing, 1984-86; rschr. Tex. Ctr. for Superconductivity U. Houston, 1986—. Contbr. articles to Phys. Rev. Letters, Nature, Physica C. Mem. Am. Phys. Soc. Office: U Houston Tex Ctr Superconductin Houston TX 77004

SUN, YONGJIAN (ERIC SUN), process engineer, researcher; b. Rudong, Jiangsu, China, Dec. 25, 1967; came to U.S., 1994; parents Wei Sun and Shuyun Zhang; m. Suning Zhang. BS, Shanghai Jiaotong U., China, 1989, MS, 1992; PhD, U. Cin., 1998. Project mgr. China Jiangsu Tech. Import and Export Corp., Nanjing, China, 1992—94; rsch. assoc. Northwestern U., Evanston, Ill., 1998—2000; process devel. engr./scientist IBM Corp., San Jose, Calif., 2001—. Contbr. book chpt. Advance in Materials Science and Applications, 1999. Recipient A.E. Focke Graduate award U. Cin., 1998. Mem. Am. Ceramic Soc., Am. Soc. of Metals, Materials Rsch. Soc. Home: 1855 Bexley Landing San Jose CA 95132 Office: IBM Corp 1560 Cottle Rd 201E/14 San Jose CA 95193

SUN, ZHUO, material scientist, researcher; b. Gulang, Gansu, China, Nov. 7, 1967; m. Suxia Liu, Mar. 28, 1995. PhD, Lanzhou (China) U., 1995. Postdoctoral fellow Nanyang Technol. U., Sinapore, 1996-97, rsch. fellow, 1997—. Contbr. over 100 articles to profl. publs. Mem. Soc. of Info. Display. Achievements include research on materials synthesis and applications, specializing in carbon-based materials. Office: EEE Nanyang Technol U Nanyang Ave Singapore Singapore Fax: 65-7933318. E-mail: ezsun@ntu.edu.sg.

SUNAGAWA, MASANORI, physiologist, researcher; b. Hirara, Okinawa, Japan, Dec. 14, 1966; s. Shotoku and Emiko Sunagawa; m. Noriko Sunagawa, Feb. 28, 1992; children: Ayano, Masataka. MD, U. Ryukyus, Nishihara, Okinawa, Japan, 1992, PhD, 1996. Tchg. asst. U. Ryukyus, Nishihara, 1994-96, asst. prof., 1996. Vis. scientist U. Cin., 1996—. Contbr. articles to profl. jours. including Jour. Vasc. Rsch., Jour. Cardiovasc. Pharmacol., Toxicon, among others. Avocations: basketball, skin diving, skating, skiing. Home: 72-3 Kakeboku Nishihara, Okinawa 903-0101 Japan Office: U Cin 231 Bethesda Ave Cincinnati OH 45267-0001

SUNAMI, JOHN SOICHI, designer; b. N.Y.C., June 10, 1949; s. Soichi and Suyeko (Matsushima) S.; m. Marialyce Norman, Apr. 21, 1973; children: Christopher Andrew-Soichi, Jennifer Kiyoko. BA, CCNY, 1969. Cert. Gemological Inst. Am. Vol. Peace Corps, Jamaica, W.I., 1969-71; jeweler N.Y.C. and Columbus, Ohio, 1971-82; dir. mktg. Knight's Inn/Cardinal Industries, Columbus, 1982; founder, exec. designer Nimbus, 1983—. Designer/sculptor pub. artwork IntroCenter, 1990; designer logo identities for various cos.; exhibited paintings and sculpture; author poems and essays. Bd. dirs. William H. Thomas Gallery, Columbus, 1992-93; v.p., bd. dirs. South Side Settlement House, Columbus, 1982-93; mem. cultural diversity outreach com. United Way of Franklin County, 1993-01. Recipient 1st prize Macworld Gallery/Macworld Mag., 1985. Mem.: Ctrl. Ohio Machine Knitters. Avocations: music, travel. Home: 408 Fairwood Ave Columbus OH 43205-2244 Office: Nimbus 413 Fairwood Ave Columbus OH 43205-2202 E-mail: design@nimbus-art.com.

SUND, JEFFREY OWEN, retired publishing company executive; b. Bklyn., June 19, 1940; children: Catherine, Meredith. BA, Dartmouth Coll., 1962. Sales rep. Prentice-Hall, Englewood Cliffs, N.J., 1967-73, Houghton Mifflin, Boston, 1973-74, coll. div. editor, 1974-77, editor-in-chief, 1977-86, v.p., editorial dir., 1986-89; pres., chief exec. officer Richard D. Irwin, Burr Ridge, Ill., 1989-96; pres. McGraw-Hill Higher Edn., 1996-2000; ret. Lt. USN, 1962-66.

SUNDARAM, RAMAKRISHNAN, engineering educator; b. New Delhi, India, Oct. 12, 1959; came to US, 1982; s. Ramakrishnan and Rajeswari S. B. Tech., Indian Inst. Tech., New Delhi, 1982; degree in elec. engring., MIT, 1985, MS, 1987; PhD, Purdue U., 1994. Scientist Tektronix Inc., Beaverton, Oreg., 1985, 1987; tech. staff AT&T Bell Labs., Holmdel, N.J., 1987-88; rsch. cons. Info. Sys. Inc., West Lafayette, Ind., 1994-95, designer fast computing architectures T, 1995-2000; asst. prof. ECE dept. Gannon U., Erie, Pa., 2000—. Contbr. articles to profl. jours. Mem. IEEE, Optical Soc. Am., SPIE. Avocations: classical music, tennis, reading. E-mail: sundaram001@gannon.edu.

SUNDARAM, SHANMUGAVELAYUTHAM KAMAKSHI, materials scientist, consultant; b. Vaigai, Tamilnadu, India, Apr. 30, 1958; came to U.S., 1990; s. S. and Saraswathy Velayutham; m. T.M. Nalini, Mar. 11, 1987; 1 child, Sudhandra. A.I.I. Ceramics, Indian Inst. Ceramics, Calcutta, 1983; M.Tech., Indian Inst. Tech., Kharagpur, 1986; PhD, Ga. Inst. Tech., 1994. Tradesman B Reactor Rsch. Ctr., Kalpakkam, India, 1977-79; tech. asst. Indian Inst. Tech., Kharagpur, 1979-87; rsch. engr. Tata Rsch. Devel. and Design Ctr., Pune, India, 1987-90; rsch. asst. Alfred (N.Y.) U., 1990-92; tchg./rsch. asst. Ga. Inst. Tech., Atlanta, 1992-94; postdoctoral fellow dept. energy Assoc. Western U., Richland, Wash., 1994-96; sr. rsch. scientist Pacific N.W. Nat. Lab., 1996—. Vis. scientist MIT, 1998—; adj. faculty Wash. State U., 1997—; guest lectr. Ga. Inst. Tech., 1995—; literacy tutor Wash. State Literacy Program, 1995; vis. scholar Harvard Univ.; participant Frontiers of Engring. NAE; lectr. in field. Contbr. articles to profl. jours. Vol. elder care Benton-Franklin Counties, Wash., 1995—; spkr. Nat. Engrs. Week, 1995—. Recipient Ganpule award Indian Ceramic Soc., Calcutta, 1985, 86; AMIC Industries Ltd. award, Calcutta, 1983. Mem.: AAAS, Materials Rsch. Soc., Nat. Inst. Ceramic Engrs., Am. Ceramic Soc. (phase diagrams editor 1992—94, abstractor 1992—94), N.Y. Acad. Scis., Instit. of Mechanics, Soc. of Glass Tech., Keramos, Battelle Spkrs. Bur. Avocations: writing, reading, museums, religions, international art film. Office: Pacific Northwest National Lab PO Box 999 MSIN: K6-24 Richland WA 99352-0999 E-mail: sk.sundaram@pal.gov.

SUNDARAPANDIAN, VAIDYANATHAN, mathematics educator, researcher; b. Uttamapalayam, Tamil Nadu, India, July 15, 1967; s. Viswanathan and Gomathi Vaidyanathan; m. Vidya Ramamurthi; 1 child Laxmi Sundar. BS in Math., S.N. Coll. Madurai Kamaraj U., India, 1984—87; MS in Math., IIT/Kanpur, India, 1987—89; DSc in Sys. Sci. and Math., Washington U., St. Louis, 1989—96. Vis. asst. prof. SSM Dept. Wash. U., St. Louis, 1996—99, asst. prof., 1999—2000, Math. Dept., IIT/Kanpur, India, 2000—. Author: (conf. paper) Nonlinear Observer Design for Bifurcating Systems, 2001 (Best Theory Paper award 25th Nat. Systems Conference Sys. Soc. India, 2001); contbr. articles. Mem.: Systems Soc. of India (life).

SUNDARESAN, MOSUR KALYANARAMAN, physics educator; b. Madras, India, Sept. 2, 1929; parents Mosur Ramanathan and Kanakavalli Kalyanaraman; m. Bharathy Sundaresan, June 7, 1957; children: Sudhir, Sujata. BSc with honors, Delhi U., 1947, MSc, 1949; PhD, Cornell U., 1955. With Atomic Energy Establishment, Bombay, 1955-57; postdoctoral fellow NRC, Can., 1957-59; reader in physics Punjab U., Chandigarh, India, 1959-61; prof. physics Carleton U., Ottawa, Can., Can., 1961-95, hon. disting. rsch. prof. physics, 1995—, prof. emeritus, 1999—. Mem. Can. Assn. Physicists, Am. Phys. Soc., Am. Assn. Physics Tchrs., Inst. Particle Physics Can.

SUNDARESAN, P. RAMNATHAN, research chemist, consultant; b. Madras, India, Aug. 11, 1930; came to U.S., 1961; s. Peruvemba A. and Saraswathi Subramanian Ramnathan; m. Gloria Marquez Sundaresan, Dec. 23, 1970; children: Sita, Ramesh. BS, U. Banaras, Banaras, India, 1950, MS, 1953; PhD, Indian Inst. Sci., Bangalore, 1958. Rsch. assoc. Radiocarbon Lab., U. Ill., Urbana, 1961-62, Dept. Nutrition and Food Sci., MIT, Cambridge, Mass., 1962-64; vis. scientist, rsch. assoc. U.S. Army Rsch. Inst. Environ. Medicine, Natick, 1964-66, rsch. biochemist, 1966-68; chief Lipids Lab., Rsch. Inst. St. Joseph Hosp., Lancaster, Pa., 1968-77; rsch. chemist FDA, Washington, 1977-98; divsn. rsch. and applied tech. Office Nutritional Products Labelling & Dietary Supplements, 1998—2001, College Park, Md., 2002. Cons. Millersville (Pa.) U., 1972-77, VA Med. Ctr., Washington, 1973-77, 84—; panel mem. source evaluation group Nat. Cancer Inst. Contbr. articles to nat. and internat. profl. jours. Coun. Sci. and Indsl. Rsch. sr. rsch. fellowship, New Delhi, India, 1959-61; NIH rsch. grantee, 1970-77. Fellow Am. Inst. Chemists; mem. Am. Soc. Biochemistry and Molecular Biology, Am. Coll. Toxicology, Internat. Soc. for Nutrition and Cancer, Assn. Ofcl. Analytical Chemists Internat., Am. Soc. Nutritional Sci., Sigma Xi. Office: FDA 200 C St SW Washington DC 20204-0001 E-mail: PSundare@CFSAN.FDA.gov.

SUNDARESAN, SANKARAN, engineering educator, consultant; b. Madural, India, June 9, 1955; s. Gurumoorthy and Sarojini Sankaran; m. Latha Subramanian Sundaresan, June 17, 1982; children: Hema G., Neereja M. B in Chem. Engring., Indian Inst. Tech., Madras, India, 1976; MS in Chem. Engring., U. Houston, 1978, PhD in Chem. Engring., 1980. Asst. prof. chem. engring. Princeton (N.J.) U., 1980-87, assoc. prof. chem. engring., 1987-92, assoc. dean for acad. affairs SEAS, 1997—, prof. chem. engring., 1992—. Cons. Mobil Tech. Co., Paulsboro, N.J., 1990-96, Exxon Rsch. & Engring. Co., Florham Park, N.J., 1997-01, ExxonMobil Rsch. & Engring. Co., Fairfax, Va., 2001—. Co-inventor, patentee Precious metal catalysts with oxygen-ion conducting support, 1994, Vanadium/phosphorus oxide oxidation catalyst, 1995, catalytic process for production of maleic anhydride, 1996; assoc. editor: Chem. Engring. Jour., 1997—2000; contbr. scientific papers. Mem. K-12 Curriculum Com., Hamilton Twp., N.J., 1995-96. Recipient Disting. Alumnus award Indian Inst. Tech. Madras, 2000. Mem. AIChE (vice chair catalysis and reaction engring. divsn. 1999-00, chair, 2001, RH Wilhelm award, 1999). Hindu. Avocations: squash, racquetball, table tennis, bridge. E-mail address. Office: Dept Chem Engring Princeton University Princeton NJ 08544-0001 Fax: 609-258-0211. E-mail: sundar@princeton.edu.

SUNDBERG, CARL-ERIK WILHELM, telecommunications executive, researcher; b. Karlskrona, Sweden, July 7, 1943; came to U.S., 1984; s. Erik Wilhelm and Martha Maria (Snaar) S. MEE, U. Lund, Sweden, 1966, PhD, 1975. Tchr., rsch. asst., lectr. U. Lund, 1966-75, rsch. prof. (docent), 1977-84; rsch. fellow European Space Agy., Nordwijk, The Netherlands, 1975-76; disting. mem. tech. staff AT&T Bell Labs., Murray Hill, N.J., 1984-96, Lucent Technologies, Bell Labs., 1997-2000; with media signal processing rsch. dept. Agere Sys., 2000—01, iBiquity Digital, Warren, NJ, 2002—. Cons. L.M. Ericsson, Gothenburg, Sweden, 1976-77, Bell Labs., Crawford Hill, N.J., 1981-82; instr. Carl Cranz Gesellschaft, Oberpfaffenhofen, Fed. Republic Germany, 1990-93. Co-author: Digital Phase Modulation, 1986, Source-Matched Mobile Communications, 1995; contbr. articles to profl. jours.; patentee in field. Served in Swedish Navy, 1968. Fellow IEEE (Best Paper award 1986, guest editor Jour. on Selected Areas in Comm. 1988-89), IEE Marconi Premium (Best Paper award 1989); mem. Swedish Union Radio-Scientifique Internationale. Lutheran. Avocations: travel, history, photography. Home: 25 Hickory Pl Apt A11 Chatham NJ 07928-1465 Office: iBiquity Digital Corp 20 Independence Blvd Warren NJ 07059

SUNDBERG, CYNTHIA JEAN, telecommunications professional; b. Mpls., Oct. 11, 1954; d. Sherwin Stauffer and Margaret Jean (Park) Plummer; m. Richard Paul Sundberg, Oct. 20, 1984. BS in Cmty. Svc., Bemidji State U., 1981; MS in Telecomm., Saint Mary's U., Mpls., 1998. Telecom. PBX operator Vail (Colo.) Assocs., Inc., 1982-83, telecom. records clk., 1983-85, telecom. adminstrv. supr., 1985-89; telecom. mgr. U. St. Thomas, St. Paul, 1989—. Sec.-treas. 1989 World Alpine Ski Championships, Vail, 1988-89; telecom. coord. 1991 Spl. Olympics, Mpls. and St. Paul, 1990-91. Mem. Assn. Coll. and Univs. Telecom. Adminstrs., Minn. Telecom. Assn. Methodist. Avocations: skiing, camping, reading, needlepointing. Home: 7455 Bittersweet Dr Eden Prairie MN 55344-5714 Office: Univ St Thomas 2115 Summit Ave # Aqu16 Saint Paul MN 55105-1048

SUNDBERG, JOHAN EMIL FREDRIK, music educator, researcher; b. Stockholm, Mar. 25, 1936; s. Halvar G.F. and Margit F.K. (Hammarberg) S.; m. Agneta Sundberg, 1968 (div.); 1 child, Susanna; m. Ulla E.M. Ahlesten, Dec. 3, 1983; children: Martin, Erik. Degree filosofie kandidat, Uppsala U., 1961, degree filosofie licentiat in musicology, 1963, degree filosofie doktor, docent in musicology, 1966; D (honoris causa), U. York (Great Britain), 1996. Guest researcher Royal Inst. Tech., Stockholm, 1962-66, rsch. scientist, 1967-79, prof. music acoustics, 1979—2001. Author: The Science of the Singing Voice, 1987, The Science of Musical Sounds, 1991; editor Harmony and Tonality, 1987, Gluing Tones, 1992; contbr. more than 150 articles to scientific jours. Mem. Stockholm Bach Choir, 1964-79, pres. 1973-79. Fellow Acoustical Soc. Am.; mem. Swedish Royal Acad. Music, Swedish Acoustical Soc. (pres. 1976-81). Avocation: singing. Office: KTH Royal Inst Tech SE 10044 Stockholm Sweden

SUNDBERG, MARSHALL DAVID, biology educator; b. Apr. 18, 1949; m. Sara Jane Brooks, Aug. 1, 1977; children: Marshall Isaac, Adam, Emma. BA in Biology, Carleton Coll., 1971; MA in Botany, U. Minn., 1973, PhD in Botany, 1978. Lab. technician Carleton Coll., Minn., 1973-74; teaching asst. U. Minn., Mpls., 1974-76, rsch. asst., 1976-77; adj. asst. prof. Biology U. Wis., Eau Claire, 1978-85, mem. faculty summer sci. inst., 1982-85; instr. La. State U., Baton Rouge, 1985-88, asst. prof. Biology, 1988-91, coord. dept. Biology, 1988-93, assoc. prof. Biology, 1991-97; prof., chair divsn. biol. scis. Emporia State U., 1997—. Author: General Botany Laboratory Workbook, 5th revision, 1984, General Botany 1001 Laboratory Manual, 1986, General Botany 1002 Laboratory Manual, 1987, Biology 1002 Correspondence Study Guide, 1987, Boty 1202: General Botany Laboratory Manual, 1988, Biol 1208: Biology for Science Majors Laboratory Manual, 1988, 2d edit., 1989, Instructor's Manual for J. Mauseth, Introductory Botany, 1991; contbr. articles to profl. jours. Judge sci. fairs, La. schs., 1985—; coach Baton Rouge Soccer Assn., 1991-96; asst. scoutmaster Boy Scouts Am., 1991-97, scoutmaster, 1998—. Brand fellow U. Minn., 1976-77, Faculty Grants scholar U. Wis., 1984-85. Fellow Linnaean Soc. London; mem. NSTA, AAAS, Am. Inst. Biol. Scis. (coun. mem. at large 1992-95, edn. com. 1994-95, 98—), Assn. Biology Lab. Edn., Bot. Soc. Am. (chmn. teaching sect. 1985-86, workshop com. teaching sect. 1983-84, slide exchange/lab. exchange teaching sect. 1980-89, edn. com. 1991, 92, Charles H. Bessey award 1992, editor Plant Sci. Bull. 2000—), Internat. Soc. Plant Morphologists, Nat. Assn. Biology Tchrs. (Outstanding 4-Yr. Coll. Tchr. award 1997), Soc. Econ. Botany, The Nature Conservancy, Sigma Xi (sec. 1982-84, 93-95, v.p. 1984-85, 96-97). Home: 1912 Briarcliff Ln Emporia KS 66801-5404 Office: Emporia State U Divsn Biol Scis 1200 Commercial St Emporia KS 66801-5087

SUNDBERG, RICHARD JAY, chemistry educator; b. Sioux Rapids, Iowa, Jan. 6, 1938; 2 children— Kelly, Jennifer. BS, U. Iowa, 1959; PhD, U. Minn., 1962. Faculty dept. chemistry U. Va., Charlottesville, 1964-74, prof., 1974—. Author (with F. A. Carey) Advanced Organic Chemistry, 4th edit., 2000. Served to 1st lt. U.S. Army, 1962-64 Mem. Am. Chem. Soc., Internat. Soc. Heterocyclic Chemistry Lutheran. Home: 2001 Greenbrier Dr Charlottesville VA 22901-2916 Office: U Va Dept Chemistry Box 400319 Charlottesville VA 22904-4319

SUNDBORG, STEPHEN V. academic administrator; s. George and Mary Sundborg. Ordained Jesuit, 1974. Tchr. religion and Latin Gonzaga Prep. Sch., Spokane, Wash., Jesuit High, Portland, Oreg.; tchr. theology Seattle U.; rector Seattle U. Jewish Cmty., 1986-90; provincial Oreg. Province, 1990-97; pres. Seattle U., 1997—. Office: Admin Bldg 109 900 Broadway Seattle WA 98122-4340*

SUNDBY, CONNIE L. paralegal; b. Minot, N.D., Oct. 4, 1955; d. Christ and Geraldine Schatz; m. Ed Sundby, Oct. 26, 1974; children: Ty J., Cody L. Student, Nat. Coll., Rapid City, S.D., 1973-74. Legal asst. Winkjer Law Firm, Williston, N.D., 1974-93, Schmitz Law Firm, Williston, 1993-95, McGee Hankla Backes & Dobrovolny, P.C., Minot, N.D., 1995—. Bd. dirs. N.D. Legal Assts. Task Force, 1994-96. Mem. ATLA (Paralegal divsn.), Nat. Assn. Legal Assts. (cert. legal asst., Affiliates award 1998), Western Dakota Assn. Legal Assts. (pres. 1994-96). Lutheran. Avocations: riding motorcycles, gardening, cooking, rodeo. Office: McGee Hankla Backes & Dobrovolny 15 2d Ave SW #305 Minot ND 58702 Home: 2417 8th St SW Minot ND 58701-7062

SUNDBY, SCOTT EDWIN, law educator; b. Aurora, Ill., Oct. 24, 1958; s. Elmer Arthur and Marilyn Edruth (Koeller) S.; m. Katie Louise Rees, June 15, 1980; children: Russell Taylor, Christopher Scott, Kelsey Kathleen. BA, Vanderbilt U., 1980; JD, Cornell U., 1983. Bar: Calif. 1985, U.S. Dist. Ct. (no. dist.) Calif. 1985. Law clk. to judge U.S. Ct. Appeals for 11th Cir., Savannah, Ga., 1983-84; prof. law U. Calif. Hastings Coll. Law, San Francisco, 1984-92; prof. Washington and Lee U., Lexington, Va., 1992—; spl. asst. U.S. Atty. (so. dist.), Fla., 1994-95. Editor-in-chief Cornell Law Rev., 1982-83. Mem. Order of Coif, Phi Beta Kappa. Office: Washington and Lee Univ Sch Law Lexington VA 24450

SUNDE, DOUGLAS, plastic surgeon; b. Evanston, Ill., May 18, 1960; s. Edward Albert and Marilyn S.; m. Linda Neff, 1989; children: Samuel, Joseph. AB, Stanford U., 1982; MD, U. Calif., San Francisco, 1986. Diplomate Am. Bd. Plastic Surgery. Resident in plastic surgery Stanford (Calif.) U., 1986-92, clin. instr., 1992; fellow in aesthetic surgery Manhattan Eye Ear and Throat Hosp., N.Y.C., 1990; fellow in hand, microsurgery Davies Med. Ctr., San Francisco, 1993; pvt. practice Monterey, Calif., 1994—. Clin. asst. prof. Stanford Med. Ctr., 1998—. Contbr. articles to profl. jours. Named Nat. Merit scholar 1977. Fellow ACS; mem. Am. Bd. Plastic Surgery, Am. Soc. Plastic Reconstructive Surgery, Calif. Soc. Plastic Surgery, Alpha Omega Alpha. Office: 856 Munras Ave Monterey CA 93940-3112

SUNDE, MILTON LESTER, retired poultry science educator; b. Volga, S.D., Jan. 7, 1921; s. Andrew Carl and Clara Josephine (Mehl) S.; m. Genevieve C. Larson, Dec. 29, 1946; children: Roger, Scott, Robert. BS in Poultry Sci., S.D. State Coll., 1947; MS in Biochemistry, U. Wis., 1949, PhD in Nutrition, 1950. Instr. in poultry sci. U. Wis., Madison, 1949-51, asst. prof., 1951-55, assoc. prof., 1955-57, prof., 1957-64, 66-71, prof., chmn. dept. poultry sci., 1964-66, 71-85, prof. emeritus, 1987—. Mem. nutrition adv. bd. Nat. Rsch. Coun., Washington, 1970-78; cons. Min. of Agriculture Govt. of Venezuela, 1964, FAO, India, 1977; poultry scientist Rockefeller Found., 1960. Patentee Vitamin D compounds; assoc. editor: Poultry Sci. Jour., 1964-72, 77-83; contbr. articles to profl. jours. and chpts. to books. Inducted into Am. Poultry Hall of Fame, 1992; recipient Award Am. Poultry Hist. Soc., 1996. Fellow Poultry Sci. Assn. (pres. 1967-68, v.p. 1965-67, Hist. award 1996), World Poultry Sci. Assn. (coun. 1970—, chmn. nutrition program com. 1974, chmn. scientific papers 1981-84, v.p. U.S. br. 1979-84, pres. 1984-89, v.p. 1988-96), Am. Soc. Nutritional Scis. Lutheran. Avocations: consulting with Cage Bird people. Office: U Wis Poultry Sci Dept Madison WI 53706

SUNDEL, HARVEY H. marketing research analyst, consultant; b. Bronx, N.Y., July 24, 1944; s. Louis and Pauline (Brotman) S. BBA, St. Mary's U., San Antonio, 1969, MBA, 1970; PhD, St. Louis U., 1974. Asst. dir. research Lone Star Brewery, San Antonio, 1970-71; cons. Tri-Mark, Inc., 1972-73; asst. prof. mktg. Lewis and Clark Coll., Godfrey, Ill., 1973-74, Met. State Coll., Denver, 1974-77, chmn., prof. mktg., 1977-86; pres. Sundel Rsch., Inc., 1976—. Cons. Frederick Ross Co., Denver, 1979-84, U.S. West Direct, Denver, 1986—, Monsanto Chems. Co., St. Louis, 1985-97, Mountain Bell, Denver, 1979-88, U.S. West Comm., Denver, 1988—, AT&T, 1986-91, Melco Industries, 1987-90, Norwest Banks, 1990-94, PACE Membership Warehouse, 1992-93, U.S. Meat Export Fedn., 1992—, G.D. Searle, 1996-98, Nextel Comms., 1996-2000, Solutia, 1997—, Ethyl Corp., 2000—, Watlow Electric Mfg. Co., 2000—; expert witness in legal cases. Contbr. papers and proceedings to profl. jours. Com. mem. Mile High United Way, Denver, 1975-80, Allied Jewish Fedn. Cmty. Rels. Action Com., 1995—, Hewlett Packard, 1998—, Agilent Techs., 1999—, Encore Media, 2000—. Jewish. Avocation: handball. Home: 1616 Glen Bar Dr Lakewood CO 80215-3014 Office: Sundel Rsch Inc 1150 Delaware St Denver CO 80204-3608 E-mail: sundel@rm.incc.net.

SUNDEL, MARTIN, psychologist, educator, management consultant; b. Bronx, N.Y., Sept. 22, 1940; s. Louis and Pauline (Brotman) S.; m. Sandra Stone, Aug. 22, 1971; children: Adam Daniel, Jenny Rebecca, Ariel Pauline. BA cum laude, St. Mary's U., 1961; MSW., Our Lady of the Lake Univ., 1963; MA, PhD, U. Mich., 1968. Social group work supr. Valley Cities Jewish Community Ctr., Van Nuys, Calif., 1963-65; asst. prof. U. Mich. Sch. Social Work, Ann Arbor, 1968-71; postdoctoral fellow Harvard U. Lab. Community Psychiatry, Boston, 1971-72; dir. research and evaluation River Region Mental Health-Mental Retardation Bd., Louisville, 1972-77; adj. prof. Kent. Sch. Social Work-U Louisville, 1972-77, assoc. clin. prof. dept. psychiatry and behavioral scis., 1974-77, assoc. in psychology, 1975-77; sr. research assoc. The Urban Inst., Washington, 1977-80; pvt. practice psychology Dallas, 1980-95; Dulak Disting. prof. U. Tex., Arlington, 1980-89, prof., 1980-95, Fla. Internat. U., Miami, Fla., 1995-2000; faculty assoc. S.E. Fla. Ctr. on Aging, 1996-2000; pres. Sundel Cons. Group, 2000—. Mental health cons. UN High Commn. for Refugees in Cyprus, 1993-95; profl. adv. coun. Dallas Geriatric Rsch. Inst., 1980-89; long-range planning com. Dallas Jewish Coalition for the Homeless, 1986-95; coordinating com. Arlington Human Svcs. Project, 1981-90, Mayor's Forum on Human Svc. Needs Assessment, Ft. Worth, 1983-86; vis. prof. U. So. Calif. Sch. Social Work, spring 1985. Author: (with Sandra Stone Sundel) Behavior Modification in the Human Services, 1975, 4th edit., 1999; Be Assertive, 1980; co-author: Midlife Women, 2002; co-editor: Assessing Health and Human Service Needs, 1983, Individual Change Through Small Groups, 2d edit., 1985, Midlife Myths, 1989; mem. editorial bds. and cons. to profl. jours. Fellow Sr. Rsch. Sortium fellow, Def. Manpoewr Data Ctr., Dept. Def., 1996—99. Fellow Prescribing Psychologists Register (diplomate), Internat. Coun. Prescribing Psychology (diplomate in psychopharmacology); mem. APA, NASW (mem. futures commn. 1979-85), Behavior Therapy and Rsch. Soc. (charter clin. fellow), Acad. Cert. Social Workers, Coun. Social Work Edn., Internat. Soc. for the Sys. Scis. Home: 3804 Barbados Ave Hollywood FL 33026-4659

SUNDEL, SANDRA STONE, social worker; b. Chgo., Oct. 8, 1948; d. Harry Bernard and Lillian (Kantor) Stone; m. Martin Sundel, Aug. 22, 1971; children: Adam Daniel, Jenny Rebecca, Ariel Pauline. BA with distinction, U. Mich., 1970; MSW, U. Louisville, 1973; PhD, U. Tex., Arlington, 1990. Lic. clin. social worker. Pvt. practice, Louisville, Ky., Bethesda, Md., 1974-80, Dallas, 1980-85; dir. Jewish Social Svc. Agy., Ft. Worth, 1982-84; exec. dir.

Community Homes for Adults, Inc., Dallas, 1986-95; asst. prof. Fla. Atlantic U., 1995-97; exec. dir. Jewish Family Svc. Broward County, Plantation, Fla., 1997—. Co-author: Behavior Modification in Human Services, 1975, 2d rev. edit., 1982, 3rd rev. edit., 1993, Be Assertive, 1980, Behavior Change in the Human Services, 4th edit., 1999. Mem. NASW, Assn. for Advancement Behavior Therapy, Nat. Coun. Jewish Women, Hadassah. Office: Jewish Family Svc 100 S Pine Island Rd Ste 130 Fort Lauderdale FL 33324-2664 E-mail: sundel@aol.com.

SUNDELIUS, HAROLD W. geology educator; b. Escanaba, Mich., July 6, 1930; s. Herbert A. and Caroline (Johnson) S.; m. Charlene P. Swanson, May 21, 1955; children: Karin, Kristine. AB, Augustana Coll., Rock Island, Ill., 1952; MS, U. Wis., 1957, PhD, 1959. Geologist U.S. Geol. Survey, Washington, 1959-65; asst. prof. geology Wittenberg U., Springfield, Ohio, 1965-67, assoc. prof., 1967-74, prof., 1974-75, assoc. dean Coll., 1971-75; v.p., dean Coll., Augustana Coll., 1975-88, prof. geology, 1988-95, ret., 1995. Cons. Dow Chem. Co., Midland, Mich., 1957, minerals dept. Exxon, Houston, 1968-75. Contbr. articles to geol. jours., chpt. to book. Bd. dirs. Luth. Hosp., Moline, Ill., 1984-89, Swenson Swedish Immigration Rsch. Ctr., Rock Island, 1984—. With U.S. Army, 1953-55, Korea. Fulbright fellow, Oslo, 1952-53, C.K. Leith fellow, 1955-57, Univ. fellow, 1957-58; recipient Sweden's Order of the Polar Star, Outstanding Svc. award Augustana Alumni Assn., 1997. Fellow Soc. Econ. Geologists, Geol. Soc. Am.; mem. Nat. Assn. Geology Tchrs., Rock Island C. of C. (bd. dirs.), Augustana Hist. Soc. (bd. dirs. 1995—, pres. 1995-2000), Am.-Scandinavian Assn. (bd. dirs. 1997—), Rotary (bd. dirs. Rock Island chpt.), Phi Beta Kappa, Sigma Xi. Lutheran. Home: 2512 1st Ct Moline IL 61265 Office: Augustana College 600 38th St Rock Island IL 61201 E-mail: hwsundelius@qconline.com.

SUNDEM, GARY LEWIS, accounting educator; b. Montevideo, Minn., Nov. 8, 1944; s. Clifford Leroy and Sylvia Edna (Larson) Sundem; children: Garth Clifford, Jens Lewis. BA, Carleton Coll., 1967; MBA, Stanford U., 1969, PhD, 1971. Asst. prof. U. Wash., Seattle, 1971—74, assoc. prof., 1974—80, prof., 1980—, acctg. dept. chmn., 1978—82, 1988—89, 1996—99, assoc. dean, 1992—95, 1999—2002. Vis. prof. Norwegian Sch. Econs., Bergen, 1974—75; vis. assoc. prof. Cornell U., Ithaca, NY, 1977—78; vis. prof. INSEAD, Fontainebleau, France, 1987; exec. dir. Acctg. Edn. Change Commn., 1989—91; cons. in field. Author: Introduction to Financial Accounting, 1987, 8th edit., 2002, Introduction to Management Accounting, 1987, 12th edit., 2002; editor: The Acctg. Rev., 1982—86; contbr. articles to profl. jours. Mem.: Nat. Assn. Accts. (nat. bd. dirs. 1986—88, 1999—2002), Fin. Execs. Inst., Am. Acctg. Assn. (exec. com. 1982—85, dist. internat. lectr. 1989, pres. 1991—92). Home: 489 39th Ave E Seattle WA 98112 Office: Sch Bus Adminstrn Univ Wash PO Box 353200 Seattle WA 98195-3200 E-mail: glsundem@u.washington.edu.

SUNDERLAND, ELDON KENNETH, physician; b. Quill Lake, Can., Sept. 12, 1946; came to U.S., 1996; s. Edeth Lemuel and Norma Ellen (Whelen) S.; m. Doreen Grace Petry Sunderland, May 20, 1967; children: Kenneth Eldon, Sheri Doreen Mcnamara-Sunderland. BS, U. Alta., 1967, MD, 1970. Diplomate Am. Bd. Otolaryngology. Practice otolaryngology, 1975—. Office: Wichita Clinic 3311 E Murdock St Wichita KS 67208-3079 E-mail: esunderland@kscable.com.

SUNDERLAND, JACKLYN GILES, former alumni affairs director; b. Corpus Christi, Tex., Oct. 21, 1937; d. Elbert Jackson and Mary Kathryn (Garrett) Giles; m. Joseph Alan MacInnis, Nov. 24, 1963 (div. Feb. 1982); children: Mary Kendall, Jackson Alan; m. Lane Von Sunderland, June 12, 1988. BA, U. Tex., Austin, 1960. Editor's asst. House & Garden mag., N.Y.C., 1962; reporter Corpus Christi Caller-Times, 1960, 69, Home Furnishings Daily, Fairchild Publs., N.Y.C., 1961, Houston Post, 1963; writer, rschr. Saudi Press Agy., Washington, 1980; writer/rschr. for V.P. U.S. White House, 1982-84; dir. pub. affairs President's Com. on Mental Retardation, 1984-85; dir. speakers bur. Commn. on Bicentennial U.S. Constn., 1985-87; speech-writer Sec. of HHS, 1987-88, U.S. Sec. of Labor, Washington, 1989; dir. alumni affairs Knox Coll., Galesburg, Ill., 1990-92. Campaign chmn. Am. Cancer Soc., Corpus Christi, 1961; liaison Am. Embassy, Copenhagen, 1965-68; docent, tchr. art Nat. Gallery and Smithsonian Mus., Washington, 1970-73; vestrywoman Grace Episcopal Ch., Galesburg, 1991; mem. Jr. League Washington, 1963—; vol. Hospice, 1996-97. Recipient Continental Marine citation for community svc., Camp Pendleton, Calif., 1977. Republican. Home: 185 Park Ln Galesburg IL 61401

SUNDERLAND, NORMAN RAY (NORM SUNDERLAND), health physicist, nuclear engineer educator; b. Lone Wolf, Okla., Aug. 1, 1933; s. Alva Franklin and Octava Pearl (Purcell) S.; m. Marilyn NMN Stanworth, Aug. 27, 1970; children: Melody, Larry, Derreck, Toni, James, Jo Lynn, Stacie, Thomas. BS, Okla. State U., 1960; MEd, U. Nev., Las Vegas, 1973; PhD, Columbia-Pacific U., 1985. Registered radiation protection technologist. Asst. dir. environ. sci. REECO (Nev. Test Site), Mercury, Nev., 1966-77; univ. sys. radiation safety officer U. Mo., Columbus, 1977-80; prof. N.E. Mo. State, Kirksville, 1978-84; dir. environ. health, safety U. Mo., Columbia, 1980-82; nuc. power cons. AWC, Inc., Cedar Rapids, Iowa, 1982-85; asst. dir. nuc. assessment divsn. EPA, Las Vegas, 1985-91; dir. environ. health, safety Utah State U., Logan, 1991-98; dir. Envirocare of Tex., Andrews, 1998—. Chair radiation control, Utah, 1987-1992; EPA rep. to Ea. Europe (Poland, Russia), 1989-96; cons. French AEC. Author: Bio-Physics of Radiation, 1997; co-author: Rad Emergency Response Operations, 1968, (Jour.) Transfer of Radiocesium to Grass, 1993, Transfer of Radiocesium to Soil, 1994; patentee in field. Pres. Mo. Higher Ednl. Assoc., Columbia, 1980-81; bishop LDS Ch., Cedar Rapids, Iowa, 1982-85. With combat engring. U.S. Army, 1953-56, Alaska. Fellow Nat. Health Physics Soc. (pres. MidAm. chpt. 1981-82, Lake Mead chpt. 1988-89, Great Salt Lake chpt. 1994-95, chmn. bd., mem. membership com. 1998—), Nat. Registry Radiation Protection Technicians (sec., mem. nat. bd. 1975-98, emeritus 1992, Arthur Humm Jr. Meml. award 1998); mem. Jaycees. Republican, Democrat. Mem. LDS Ch. Achievements include TRUclean process patent which removes radioactive material from soil (now owned by Lockeed Internat.). Home: 1851 N 1600 E North Logan UT 84341-2114

SUNDERLIN, CHARLES EUGENE, consultant; b. Reliance, S.D., Sept. 28, 1911; s. Glen Eugene and Frances (Smith) S; m. Sylvia Alice Sweetman, July 8, 1936; children: Ann Elizabeth, Mary Cornelia, Katherine Patricia, William Dana. AB, U. Mont., 1933; BA, MA (Rhodes scholar), Oxford U., Eng., 1936; PhD, U. Rochester, 1939. Instr. chemistry Union Coll., 1938-41; instr., asst. prof. U.S. Naval Acad., Annapolis, Md., 1941-43, 45-46; sci. liason officer U.S. Office Naval Rsch., London, 1946-47, dep. sci. dir., 1948-49, sci. dir., 1949-51; dep. dir. NSF, Washington, 1951-57, Union Carbide European Rsch. Assocs., 1957-62; rsch. mgr. def. and space systems Union Carbide Corp., 1962-65; spl. asst. to pres. Nat. Acad. Scis., Washington, 1965-69; v.p., sec. Rockefeller U., N.Y.C., 1969-76; spl. asst. Nat. Sci. Bd., Washington, 1976-78; exec. sec., staff dir. Com. on 10th Nat. Sci. Bd. Report, 1976-78. U.S. del. 6th and 7th Gen. Assemblies Internat Coun. Sci. Unions, Amsterdam, 1952, Oslo, 1955; mem. working party on Establishment of Internat. Adv. Com. on Sci. Rsch., Paris, 1953; Meeting of Dirs. Nat. Rsch. Ctrs., Milan, 1955, Symposium on Orgn. and Adminstrn., Applied Rsch., Vienna, 1956; mem. Com. Experts on Scientists' Rights, Paris, 1953, Nat. Acad. Scis. Workshop on Indsl. Devel. Taiwan, Rep. of China, 1968; chmn. AIAA/ASME 9th Structures, Structural Dynamics and Materials Conf., 1968; treas., bd. dirs. Engrs. and Scientists Com., Inc., People to People Program. Lt. USNR, 1943-45. Fellow AAAS, Chem. Soc. (London); mem. AIAA, Am. Chem. Soc., Faraday Soc., Royal Instn. Gt. Britain, Soc. Chem. Industry, N.Y. Acad. Scis., Wadham Assn. U.S., United Oxford and Cambridge Univ. Club, Internat. Club, Sigma Alpha Epsilon. Episcopalian. Home: 3036 P St NW Washington DC 20007-3052 also: 137 E Main St Cambridge NY 12816-1208

SUNDERMAN, DEBORAH ANN, wellness consultant, fashion and business educator, real estate agent; b. Detroit, Feb. 21, 1955; d. Eugene Wayne Sunderman and Nancy May (Reams) Sunderman-Elert. BS magna cum laude, No. Mich. U., 1978. Ordained min. Universal Life Ch., 1995; cert. ind. Reiki master, 1995. Design instr. Newbury Coll., Boston, 1978-82, 92-93; asst. to designers Clothware, 1978-82; designer, ptnr. Toute Nue Swimwear, 1982; designer Mast Industries, The Limited, Woburn, 1982-83; designer, founder Deborah Mann & Co., Boston, 1983-98; instr. fashion Mt. Ida Coll., Newton, 1991, 2001—02; owner, designer, buyer Deborah Mann Atelier, 1997-00; owner Alchemy, 2000—. Fashion instr. Framingham State Coll., 2001, Lasell Coll., Newton, Mass., 2001, Sch. Fashion Design, Boston, 2001, Mass. Coll. Art, Boston, 2001, Mt. Ida Coll., 2001—. Designer garment The Fiberarts Design Book, 1980. Organizer Neighborhood Crime Watch Group, Rossmore Rd., Boston, 1989-90. Recipient 2d Pl. award Peter White Art Exhibit, Marquette, Mich., 1978, Fresh Start award Self Mag., Washington, 1985; named one of Boston's Most Interesting Women, Boston Woman Mag., 1990. Mem. Harvard Sq. Bus. Assn. (past bd. dirs.). Avocations: swimming, reading, walking, music, travel. E-mail: Sunderwoman@worldnet.att.net.

SUNDERMAN, DUANE NEUMAN, chemist, research institute executive; b. Wadsworth, Ohio, July 14, 1928; s. Richard Benjamin and Carolyn (Neuman) S.; m. Joan Catherine Hoffman, Jan. 31, 1953; children: David, Christine, Richard. BA, U. Mich., 1949, MS, 1954, PhD in Chemistry, 1956. Researcher Battelle Meml. Inst., Columbus, Ohio, 1956-59, mgr., 1959-69, assoc. dir., 1969-79, dir. internat. programs, 1979-84; sr. v.p. Midwest Rsch. Inst., Kansas City, Mo., 1984-90, exec. v.p., 1990-94, Golden, Colo., 1990-94. Dir. Nat. Renewable Energy Lab., Golden, Colo., 1990-94, dir. emeritus, 1994—. Contbr. numerous articles to profl. jours. Bd. dirs. Mid-Ohio chpt. ARC, 1982-83, U. Kansas City, 1985-90, Mo. Corp. for Sci. and Tech., Jefferson City, 1986-90, Colo. Energy Sci. Ctr., 2000. Mem. Am. Chem. Soc. Republican. Presbyterian. Avocation: computers. E-mail: dsunderm@columbus.rr.com.

SUNDERMAN, FREDERICK WILLIAM, SR. physician, educator, author, musician; b. Altoona, Pa., Oct. 23, 1898; s. William August and Elizabeth Catherine (Lehr) S.; m. Clara Louise Baily, June 2, 1925 (dec. 1972); children: Louise (dec.), F. William, Joel B. (dec.); m. Martha-Lee Taggart, May 3, 1980 (dec. Sept. 1998). BS, Gettysburg Coll., 1919, ScD (hon.), 1952; MD, U. Pa., 1923, MS, 1927, PhD, 1929; LittD, Beaver Coll., 2000. Diplomate Am. Bd. Internal Medicine, Am. Bd. Pathology (v.p. 1944-50 life trustee 1950—), Nat. Bd. Med. Examiners. Intern, then resident Pa. Hosp., 1923-25; assoc. rsch. med. U. Pa., Phila., 1925-48; assoc. in chem. divsn. William Pepper Lab. U. Pa. Hosp., 1929-48, physician, 1929-48; med. dir. Office of Sci. R & D, 1943-46; physician, hon. pathologist Pa. Hosp., 1988—; mem. faculty U. Pa. Sch. Medicine, Phila., 1925-47, assoc. prof. research medicine, also lectr.; acting head med. dept. Brookhaven Nat. Lab., Upton, N.Y., 1947-48; chief chem. div. William Pepper Lab. Clin. Medicine, U. Pa. Med. Sch., 1933-47; prof. clin. pathology, dir. Temple U. Lab. Clin. Medicine, 1947-48; med. dir. govt. explosives lab. Carnegie Inst. Tech. and Bur. Mines, 1943-46; head dept. clin. pathology Cleve. Clinic Found., 1948-49; dir. clin. research M.D. Anderson Hosp. Cancer Research, Houston, 1949-50; dir. clin. labs. Grady Meml. Hosp., Atlanta, 1949-51; prof. clin. medicine Emory U. Sch. Medicine, 1949-51; chief clin. pathology Communicable Disease Center, USPHS, 1950-51; med. adviser Rohm & Haas Co., 1947-71; med. cons. Redstone Arsenal, U.S. Army Ordnance Dept., Huntsville, Ala., 1947-49; cons. clin. pathology St. Joseph's Hosp., Tampa, Fla., 1965-66; attending physician Jefferson Hosp., Phila., 1951—, dir. div. metabolic research, clin. prof. medicine, 1951-67, clin. prof. medicine, 1951-74, hon. clin. prof. medicine, 1975—; dir. Inst. Clin. Sci., 1965—; prof. pathology Hahnemann U. Med. Coll., 1970—, co-chmn. dept. lab. medicine, 1970-75, prof. emeritus, 1989. Med. adviser and cons. bus. and industry, 1947— ; dir. internat. seminars on clin. chemistry and pathology, 1947—; guest lectr. Beijing (People's Republic of China) Med. U., 1989. Author, editor 44 books on clin. chemistry and pathology; author: Our Madeira Heritage, 1979, Musical Notes of a Physician, 1982, Painting with Light, 1993, A Time to Remember, 1998; editor-in-chief Annals Clin. Lab. Sci., 1970—; mem. editl. bd. Am. Jour. Clin. Pathology, 1939-87, Am. Jour. Indsl. Medicine, 1979-85; cons. editor Am. Jour. Occupl. Medicine, 1979-85; also over 350 articles. Trustee Gettysburg Coll., 1967-89, chmn. bd. trustees, 1972-74, hon. life trustee, 1986—; bd. dirs. Mus. Fund Soc. Phila., 1938—, hon. life bd. dirs., 1993—; bd. dirs. Dwight D. Eisenhower Soc., 1984—, German Soc. Pa., 1986—, Geog. Soc. Phila., 1995; violin soloist Chautauqua Summer Series, Ea. U.S., 1919-20; guest soloist Concerto Soloists Pa., 1979, 83, 84, Pa. String Tchrs. Assn., Gettysburg, 1959, Westchester, 1962, 63, 67, 68, Trenton (N.J.) Tchrs. Coll. Orch., 1965; Internat. String Conf. soloist World Congress on Arts and Medicine, Carnegie Hall, N.Y.C., 1992; trustee Bermuda Biol. Sta. for Rsch., 1960, life trustee 1984. Recipient Naval Ordnance Devel. award, 1946, cert. appreciation War Dept., 1947, Honor medal Armed Forces Inst. Pathology, 1964; recipient Meritorious Svc. award, 1979, Honor award Latin Am. Assn. Clin. Biochemistry, 1976, Disting. Svc. award Am. Soc. Clin. Pathology-Coll. Am. Pathologists, 1988, Life-time Achievement award in clin. chemistry Joint Congresses of IX Congresso Nacional de la Sociedad Espanola de Quimica Clin., 2d Internat. Congress Therapeutic Drug Monitoring and Toxicology, and 4th Internat. Congress on Automation and New Tech., Spain, 1990, John Gunther Reinhold award Phila. Sect. Am. Assn. for Clin. Chemistry, 1991, Cert. of Honor N.J. sect., 1998, Jacob Ehrenzeller award Res. Assn. Pa. Hosp., 1993, Letter of Appreciation 100th Birthday Celebration Gettysburg Coll., 1998; named Disting. Alumnus Gettysburg Coll., 1963; Sunderman Seminar Rm. dedicated at Bermuda Biol. Sta. for Rsch., 1992, Letter of Appreciation from Bd. of Trustees for 100th Birthday, 1998, Little D. award Beaver Coll., 2000; 1st ann. F. William Sunderman award for Disting. Community Svc. and Excellence in a Chosen Field of Endeavor established by Rho Deuteron chpt. Phi Sigma Kappa, Gettysburg Coll; recipient Nat. Phi Sigma Kappa Disting. Alumnus award, 1995, Prime Time award Green Thumb, Inc., 1998, Union League Phila. Gold medal, 1998. Fellow ACP (life), Royal Soc. Medicine (hon., life), Royal Soc. Health Great Britain (life); mem. Am. Assn. History Medicine, Am. Diabetes Assn., AMA, Am. Soc. Clin. Investigation, Royal Soc. Health, AAUP, Endocrine Soc., Am. Assn. Biol. Chemistry, AAAS, Am. Chem. Soc., Internat. Union Pure and Applied Chemistry (nickel subcom. Commn. on Toxicology), Inst. Occupational Health (Finland), Outokumpu Oy (Finland), Am. Assn. Clin. Chemists (award for outstanding efforts in edn. and tng. 1981, John Gunther Reinhold award 1991), Coll. Am. Pathologists (founding gov., Pathologist of Yr. award 1962, Pres.'s Honor award 1984, Dist. Svc. award 1988, 50th Anniversary award 1997), Coll. Physicians (70 Yr. award 2000), Am. Soc. Clin. Pathology (pres. 1951, archives com. 1977—, intersoc. pathology coun. 1976—, interpathology soc. coun. 1976—, Ward Burdick award 1975, Continuing Edn. Distinguished Service award 1976), Assn. Clin. Scientists (pres. 1957-59, dir. edn. 1959—, diploma honor 1960, ann. goblet award 1964, Gold-headed cane 1974), Coll. Physicians of Phila. (sec. 1946-48, hon. pres. arts medicine sect. 1995, Disting. Service award 1980, 85, 90, 95), Knight of Order of St. Vincent of Portugal, Order of Merit (disting. svc. cross 1985), German Soc. Pa. (Bronze medal 1988, hon. dir. 1998), Am. Indsl. Hygiene Assn., Am. Occupational Medicine Assn., Med. Soc. Pa., Nat. Soc. Med. Research, Nat. Acad. Clin. Biochemistry, Pan Am. Med. Assn., Pa. Assn. Clin. Pathology (honors award 1997), Philadelphia County Med. Soc., Mus. Fund Soc. Phila. (hon. life), Soc. Toxicology, Brit. Assn. Clin. Biochemists (hon.), Soc. Pharm. and Environ. Pathologists (hon.), Internat. Union Pure and Applied Chemistry, Inst. Occupational Health Finland (nickel subcom. commn. toxicology), Phi Beta Kappa, Pa. Assn. Pathologists (Recognition award more than 50 yrs. contbns. to medicine and practice of pathology), Sigma Xi, Alpha Omega Alpha, Phi Sigma Kappa (1st annual F. William Sunderman award for Cmty. Svc Rho Deuteron chpt. Gettysburg Coll. 1995, Nat. Disting. Alumnus award grand chpt. 1995). Lutheran. Achievements include spl. symposium given in honor for lifetime achievement, Internat. Union Pure and Applied Chemistry, Finland, 1988. Home: 1833 Delancey Pl Philadelphia PA 19103-6606 Office: Pa Hosp Inst for Clin Sci 301 S 8th St Duncan Bldg 3A Philadelphia PA 19106-4014

SUNDERMAN, ROBERT ALLEN, artist, set designer; b. Clarinda, Iowa, Nov. 11, 1956; s. Lavern Charles and Jenny Lee Sunderman; m. Michele Ann Dunne, Jan. 15, 1983. BFA, U. Iowa, 1979, MA, 1981, MFA, 1982. Artist, scenic designer Sunderman Enterprises, Des Moines, 1982—; scenic designer Iowa Pub. TV, Johnston, 1984-2000; art instr. Des Moines Art Ctr., 1986—; asst. prof. tech. and design theatre Iowa State U., Ames, Iowa, 2000—. Asst. sculptor to Chungi Choo, 1982-96; scenic designer, painter World Food Prize, Hoyt Sherman Theatre, Des Moines, 1999; scenic designer in residency Grinnell Coll., Iowa, 1999, 2001; scenic designer Aspen Music Festival/Theatre Opera, 2002. Prin. works include Meml. Wall, Iowa Luth. Hosp., Des Moines, Ceremonial Mace, Mercy Coll., Des Moines, Little Boxes, Iowa Pub. TV, Johnston, Iowa. Recipient Jury award Sedona Art Assn., 1992, Best in Metal award Two Rivers Art Assn., 1997, Windsor Newton award 6th Nat. Art Exhbn. Northern Colo. Art Assn., 1997, Excellence award Iowa Film Assn., 1998, Merit award Iowa Film Assn., 1998, Kennedy Ctr. Regional Merit award Twelfth Night Set Design, 2001. Mem. U.S. Inst. Theatre Tech., Soc. Am. Silversmiths, Des Moines Art Ctr., Iowa Craft Assn., Kansas City Artists Coalition, Arts Iowa City. Avocations: hiking, biking, traveling, skiing, volleyball. Office: Iowa State U 210 Pearson Hall Ames IA 50311 also: Sunderman Enterprises 1134 46th St Des Moines IA 50311-3310 E-mail: rsunde7511@aol.com., rsunder@iastate.edu.

SUNDERMEYER, MICHAEL S. lawyer; b. Kansas City, Mo., Feb. 8, 1951; s. Edgar W. and Ruth (Shobe) S.; m. Susan Talarico; children: Kim Marie, Mark Shobe. BA, U. Kans., 1973; JD, U. Va., 1976. Bar: D.C., Md., Va., U.S. Dist. Ct. D.C., U.S. Dist. Ct. Md., U.S. Dist. Ct. (ea. dist.) Va., U.S. Dist. Ct. (no. dist.) Okla., U.S. Ct. Appeals (D.C. cir.), U.S. Ct. Appeals (4th cir.), U.S. Ct. Appeals (5th cir.), U.S. Ct. Appeals (3d cir.). Law clk. to Hon. John Minor Wisdom U.S. Ct. Appeals (5th cir.), New Orleans, 1976-77; law clk. to Hon. Harry A. Blackmun U.S. Supreme Ct., Washington, 1977-78; assoc. Williams & Connolly, 1978-84, ptnr., 1985—. Editor-in-chief Va. Law Rev., 1975-76. Mem. ABA. Office: Williams & Connolly LLP 725 12th St NW Washington DC 20005-5901 E-mail: msundermeyer@wc.com.

SUNDGAARD, ARNOLD OLAF, playwright; b. St. Paul, Oct. 31, 1909; s. Olaf Johannes Sundgaard and Borghild Marie Pehrson; m. Margaret Christianson, Jan. 3, 1929 (div.); children: Joy, Jill; m. Marge Kane, Jan. 17, 1940; children: Stephen, Jeremy. Student, Yale U., 1932-35; BA, U. Wis., 1935. Resident playwright U. Tex., 1945; lectr. Columbia U., N.Y.C., 1946-49; head drama dept. Bennington (Vt.) Coll., Vt., 1949-51; staff Tanglewood, 1950. Mem. Chgo. Fed. Theatre, 1936-38, Barter Theatre, 1938, Group Theatre, 1939, Theatre Inc., 1945 (founding), Chekhov Theatre Studio, 1941, Actors Studio, 1963; playwright, lectr., assoc. prof. U. Ill., 1949; vis. lectr. in playwriting SUNY Stony Brook, 1967-68; occupied John Cranford Adams Chair in Lit., Hofstra U., 1970-71; U.S. Exchange Lectr., Trinity Coll., Dublin, 1958-59. Playwright: Spirochete, 1938, Everywhere I Roam, 1938, The First Crocus, 1941, Virginia Overture, 1946, The Great Campaign, 1947, The Kilgo Run, 1952, Forest of the Night, 1963, Of Love Remembered, 1967, (musicals) Rhapsody, 1944, Promised Valley, 1947, The Wind Blows Free, 1950, Nobody's Earnest, 1973, Winnie, 1988; librettist: (operas) Down in The Valley, 1948, Giants in the Earth, 1951, The Lowland Sea, 1952, Cumberland Fair, 1954, Gallantry, 1958, The Opening, 1970, The Truth About Windmills, Mosaic, 1988, (TV scripts) Village Incident, India, (with Leonard Bernstein) Beethoven's Fifth, Jack Be Normal, Four Flags of the Confederacy; narration, continuity (TV) Festival of Music; contbr. stories, poetry, articles to popular mags.; writer (children's books) Jethro's Difficult Dinosaur, 1977, The Lamb and the Butterfly, 1988, Jack Appleknocker, 1988, The Bear Who Loved Puccini, 1990, Ching Ching, and the Seven Golden Nightingales, 1991; (children's album with Bing Crosby) An Axe, An Apple, and A Buckskin Jacket, 1957; rec. songs include Where Do You Go, Baggage Room Blues, Douglas Mountain, Brack's Song, Sweet Lorena, Long John. Rockefeller Fellow, 1935, Dramatists Guild Fellow, 1939, Guggenheim Fellow, 1951. Mem. ASCAP, Dramatists Guild, Songwriters Guild, Authors Guild, Pen West. Clubs: Century (N.Y.). Home: 7831 Park Ln Apt 67B Dallas TX 75225-2039

SUNDICK, SHERRY SMALL, author, journalist, poet; b. Washington, July 17, 1946; d. Charles Haskell and Ruth (Behrend) Small; B.A., Am. U., 1970; m. Gary Norman Sundick, Aug. 3, 1969; children— Amy Beth, Suzanne Faye. Columnist, Today Newspapers, Rockville, Md., 1973-75; journalist The Jour. Newspapers, Chevy Chase, Md., 1975— , The Potomac Almanac, 1976-80. Recipient N.Am. Mentor Mag. Ann. Mentor Poetry award, 1973. Mem. Nat. League Am. Pen Women, Writers Center, World Poetry Soc. Jewish. Author: Celebration, 1977; (with Ruth Small) Potpourri, 1978; contbr. articles to various mags. and jours. including Md. Mag., No. Va. Mag. Design, Maine Life, Feelings, Smile, The Pen Women, Haiku Headlines, others. Address: 11809 Hunting Ridge Ct Potomac MD 20854-2152

SUNDIN, MATS JOHAN, professional hockey player; b. Sollentuna, Sweden, Feb. 13, 1971; Selected 1st round NHL entry draft Que. Nordiques, 1989; traded Toronto Maple Leafs, 1994, right wing, 1994—. Played in Europe during 1994-95 NHL lockout; named to Swedish League All-Star Team 1990-91, 91-92; selected NHL All-Star Game, 1996. Office: Toronto Maple Leafs Air Canada Ctr 40 Bay St Ste 300 Toronto ON Canada M5J 2X2*

SUNDINE, MICHAEL JAMES, plastic surgeon; b. Cut Bank, Mont., Sept. 29, 1960; s. James Edward and Beverly Elaine Sundine; m. Kay Antionette Otero, June 22, 1991; children; Candace Marie, Lauren Nicole. BA, U. Colo., 1983; MD, St. Louis U., 1987. Diplomate Am. Bd. Surgery, Am. Bd. Plastic Surgery. Gen. surg. intern U. Calif.-Irvine, Orange, 1987-88, resident in gen. surgery, 1988-92; resident in plastic surgery Duke U., Durham, N.C., 1992-95; fellow in craniofacial surgery Hosp. for Sick Children, Toronto, 1998; asst. clin. prof. plastic surgery U. Calif., Irvine, 2001—. Mem. Phi Beta Kappa. Avocations: snowboarding, squash, weightlifting. Office: U Calif-Irvine Divsn Plastic Surgery 101 The City Dr Orange CA 92868 Home: 2019 Los Trancos Dr Apt F Irvine CA 92612-4020 Fax: 714-456-7718. E-mail: msundine@uc.edu.

SUNDLOF, STEPHEN FREDERICK, veterinary administrator; DVM, PhD in Toxicology, U. Ill., 1980. Diplomate Am. Bd. Vet. Toxicology. From instr. to prof. U. Fla. Coll. Vet. Medicine, 1980-94; dir. Ctr. for Vet. Medicine, FDA, Washington, 1994—. Chmn. WHO/FAO Codex Alimentarius Com.; presenter in field. Contbr. articles to profl. jours. Recipient Presidential Rank Award, 2000. Mem. Am. Acad. Vet. Pharmacology and Therapeutics (past pres.). Office: Ctr Vet Medicine Office of Dir 7500 Standish Pl Rockville MD 20855-2764 Fax: 301-827-4401.*

SUNDLUN, BRUCE, former governor; b. Providence, Jan. 19, 1920; s. Walter I. and Jan Z. (Colitz) Sundlun; m. Susan Garvin Dittelman, Jan. 1, 2000; stepchildren: Heather Conover, Max Dittelman. BA, Williams Coll., 1946; LLB, Harvard U., 1949; student, Air Command and Staff Sch., 1948; DSBA (hon.), Bryant Coll., 1980; DBA (hon.), Roger Williams Coll., 1980; LLD (hon.), Johnson and Wales U., 1993, Williams Coll., 1993; WD (hon.), U. R.I., 1998. Bar: R.I. and D.C. 1949. Asst. U.S. atty., Washington, 1949-51; spl. asst. to U.S. atty. gen., 1951-54; ptnr. Amram, Hahn & Sundlun, Sundlun, Tirana & Scher, Washington and Providence, R.I., 1954-76; v.p., gen. counsel, dir. Outlet Co., Providence, 1960-76, pres., CEO, 1976-84, chmn. bd., CEO, 1984-88. Pres. Exec. Jet Aviation, Inc., Columbus, Ohio, 1970—76; apptd. by Pres. Kennedy incorporator, bd. dirs. Comms. Satellite Corp., 1962—92; bd. dirs. Round Hill Devel. Ltd. Mem. adv. group Nat. Aviation Goals, 1961; chmn. Inaugural Medal Com., Washington, 1961, 65; vice chmn. Inaugural Parade Com., 1961; appointed by Pres. Carter bd. visitors USAF Acad., 1978-80; mem. R.I. Capital Center Commn., 1980, R.I. Legis. Pay Commn., 1980; vice chmn. Providence Rev. Com., 1981, chmn., 1982-85; mem. Providence Sch. Bd., 1985-90; mem. Providence Housing Authority, 1987, chmn. 1987-90; elected del. Dem. Nat. Conv. 1964, 68, 80, 88, 92, 2000 R.I. Constl. Conv., 1985; Dem. candidate for gov. R.I., 1986, 88, 90, 92; gov. R.I., 1990-92, 1992-95; mem. exec. com. Dem. Gov. Assn., 1990-94; vice chmn. CONEG, 1992-94, chmn., 1994, chmn., vice chmn. Com. on Economy Nat. Gov. Assn., 1992-94, chmn. N.E. Gov. Assn., 1994; pres. Washington Internat. Horse Show, 1970-75, trustee, 1975-90; pres. Providence Performing Arts Ctr., 1978-90; bd. dirs. Friends Touro Synagogue, Newport, R.I., 1979—, Miriam Hosp., 1985-90; bd. dirs. Temple Beth El, Providence, 1979-84, v.p., 1984-88, pres., 1988-91; bd. dirs. Trinity Repertory Theater, 1980-89, chmn., 1984-89; trustee R.I. Philharm. Orch., 1981-90; trustee Providence Preservation Soc., 1981-90, v.p., 1987-90; trustee Newport Art Mus., 1985, pres., 1987-91; pres. Providence Found., 1985-86; pres. R.I. C. of C. Fedn., 1981-84, bd. dirs., 1977-81; pres. Greater Providence C. of C., 1978-81, bd. dirs. 1976-85; bd. dirs. New Eng. Coun., 1978, vice chmn., 1980-81, chmn., 1981-83; trustee Bryant Coll., 1989-98; gov.-in-residence U. R.I., 1995—; appointed by Pres. Clinton dir. Nat. Security Edn. Bd., 2000—. Capt. USAAF, 1942-45; col. USAFR, ret., 1980. Decorated D.F.C., Air medal with oak leaf cluster, Purple Heart; chevalier Legion d'Honneur (France); Prime Minister's medal (Israel). Mem.: Aurora Assn., Saratoga Reading Assn., Spouting Rock Beach Assn., Clambake Club, Hope Club, Delta Upsilon. Home: 257 Walmsley Ln Saunderstown RI 02874-3617 Office: Univ RI 216 University Libr Kingston RI 02881

SUNDQUIST, DON, governor, former congressman, sales corporation executive; b. Moline, Ill., Mar. 15, 1936; s. Kenneth M. and Louise (Rohren) S.; m. Martha Swanson, Oct. 3, 1959; children: Tania, Andrea, Donald Kenneth. BA, Augustana Coll., 1957. Div. mgr. Josten's, Inc., 1961-72; exec. v.p. Graphic Sales of Am., Memphis, 1972, pres., 1973-82; mem. 98th-103rd Congresses from 7th Tenn. dist., Washington, 1983-94; gov. State of Tenn., Nashville, 1995—. Vice chmn. bd. Bank of Germantown, Tenn. Past mem. White House Commn. Presdl. Scholars; past chmn. Jobs for High Sch. Grads. of Memphis; chmn. Congl. Steering Com. George Bush for Pres., 1988, 92; nat. campaign mgr. Howard Baker for Pres., 1979; dir. com. ops., alt. del. Republican Nat. Conv., 1980; chmn. Shelby County Rep. Party, 1975-77; alt. del. Rep. Nat. Conv., 1976; exec. com. Rep. Nat. Com., 1971-73; nat. chmn. Young Rep. Nat. Fedn., 1971-73; sec. Bedford County Election Commn., 1968-70; chmn. Tenn. Young Rep. Fedn., 1969-70; dir. Mid-South Coliseum, Am. Council Young Polit. Leaders, 1972-74, U.S. Youth Council, 1972-75; bd. govs. Charles Edison Meml. Youth Fund; nat. adv. bd. Distributive Edn. Clubs Am.; mem. U.S. del. study tour, People's Republic of China, 1978, study tour, USSR, 1975. Served with USN, 1957-59. Mem. Kiwanis. Lutheran. Office: Office of Gov State Capitol Bldg Nashville TN 37243-0001*

SUNDQUIST, ERIC JOHN, American studies educator; b. McPherson, Kans., Aug. 21, 1952; s. Laurence A. and Frances J. (Halene) S.; m. Tatiana Kreinine, Aug. 14, 1982; children: Alexandra, Joanna, Ariane. BA, U. Kans., 1974; MA, Johns Hopkins U., 1976, PhD, 1978. Asst. prof. English Johns Hopkins U., Balt., 1978-80, U. Calif., Berkeley, 1980-82, assoc. prof., 1982-86, prof. English, 1986-89, UCLA, 1989-97, chair dept. English, 1994-97; dean Judd A. and Marjorie Weinberg Coll. Arts and Scis. Northwestern U., Evanston, Ill., 1997—. Vis. scholar U. Kans., 1985, dir. Holmes grad. seminar, 1993; dir. NEH Summer Seminar for Coll. Tchrs., U. Calif., Berkeley, 1986, 90, UCLA, 1994; cons. Calif. Coun. for Humanities, 1986-87; prof. Bread Loaf Sch. English, Middlebury (Vt.) Coll., 1987, 89, Sante Fe, 95; mem. fellowship com. Newberry Libr., 1987, 88, 92; dir. NEH Summer Seminar for Secondary Sch. Tchrs., Berkeley, 1988; vis. prof. UCLA, 1988; Andrew Hilen vis. prof. U. Wash., 1990; Lamar Meml. lectr. in so. states Mercer U., 1991; Gertrude Conaway Vanderbilt prof. English Vanderbilt U., Nashville, 1992-93; mem. fellowship cons. Nat. Humanities Ctr., 1992, 93; acad. specialist in Am. studies Tel Aviv U., 1994; mem. adv. bd. Colloquium for the Study of Am. Culture, Claremont (Calif.) Grad. Sch. & Huntington Libr., 1994—. Author: Home as Found: Authority and Genealogy in Nineteenth-Century American Literature, 1979 (Gustave Arlt award Coun. Grad. Schs. in U.S. 1980), Faulkner: The House Divided, 1983, The Hammers of Creation: Folk Culture in Modern African-American Fiction, 1992, To Take the Nations: Race in the Making of American Literature, 1993 (Christian Gauss award Phi Beta Kappa 1993, James Russell Lowell award MLA 1993, Choice Outstanding Acad. Book 1994); co-author: Cambridge History of American Literature, Vol. II, 1995; editor: American Realism: New Essays, 1982, New Essays on Uncle Tom's Cabin, 1986, Frederick Douglass: New Literary and Historical Essays, 1990, Mark Twain: A Collection of Critical Essays, 1994, Cultural Contexts for Ralph Ellison's Invisible Man, 1995, Oxford W.E.B. DuBois Reader, 1996; mem. adv. bd. Studies in Am. Lit. and Culture, 1987-90, gen. editor, 1991-97; mem. editl. bd. Am. Lit. History, 1987—, Ariz. Quar., 1987—; assoc. editor Am. Nat. Biography, 1990—; cons. The Libr. of Am., 1992—; consulting reader African-Am. Rev., 1992—; contbr. articles to profl. jours. Am. Coun. Learned Socs. fellow, 1981, NEH fellow, 1989-90, Guggemheim fellow, 1993-94 (declined). Mem. MLA (chair adv. coun. Am. lit. sect. 1994, mem. exec. com. divsn. 19th Century Am. lit. 1994-97), Am. Studies Assn. (chair John Hope Franklin Prize com. 1993, mem. nat. coun. 1994-97, mem. fin. com. 1995-97, and other coms.), Am. Lit. Assn., Orgn. Am. Historians, So. Hist. Assn., So. Am. Studies Assn. (mem. exec. com. 1993-97), Phi Beta Kappa. Office: Northwestern U Coll Arts and Scis 1918 Sheridan Rd Evanston IL 60208-0847

SUNDQUIST, JAMES LLOYD, retired political scientist; b. West Point, Utah, Oct. 16, 1915; s. Frank Victor and Freda (Carlson) S.; m. Beth Ritchie, Dec. 25, 1937 (dec. 1982); children: Erik L., Mark L., James K.; m. Geraldine Coote, Dec. 3, 1983. Student, Weber Coll., 1932-34, HHD (hon.), 1990; student, Northwestern U., 1934-35; BS, U. Utah, 1939; MS in Pub. Adminstrn, Syracuse U., 1941; DDS (hon.)., Carthage Coll., 1987. Reporter Salt Lake Tribune, 1935-39; adminstrv. analyst U.S. Bur. Budget, 1941-47, 49-51; reports and statistics officer Office Def. Moblzn., 1951-53; dir. mgmt. control European Command, U.S. Army, Berlin, 1947-49; asst. to chmn. Democratic Nat. Com., 1953-54; asst. sec. to gov. N.Y. State, 1955-56; asst. to U.S. Senator Clark, 1957-62; dep. under sec. agr., 1963-65; sr. fellow Brookings Instn., 1965-85, emeritus, 1985—, dir. govtl. studies, 1976-78; adj. prof. Smith Coll., 1975-78. Sec. platform com. Dem. Nat. Conv., 1960, 68 Author: Politics and Policy: The Eisenhower, Kennedy and Johnson Years, 1968, Making Federalism Work, 1969 (Louis Brownlow award for best pub. adminstrn. book), Dynamics of the Party System, 1973, 2d edit., 1983, Dispersing Population: What America Can Learn form Europe, 1975, The Decline and Resurgence of Congress, 1981 (Hardeman prize for best book on Congress), Constitutional Reform and Effective Government, 1986, 2d edit., 1992; editor: Internat. Rev. Adminstrv. Scis., 1980—89, Beyond Gridlock?, 1993, Back to Gridlock?, 1995. Mem. Gov.'s Commn. on Va.'s Future, 1983-84 Recipient Exceptional Civilian Service award War Dept., 1945, Lifetime Achievement award Maxwell Sch. (Syracuse U.) Alumni Assn., 1994; sr. Research fellow U. Glasgow, Scotland, 1972-73. Mem. Nat. Acad. Pub. Adminstrn., Am. Soc. Pub. Adminstrn., Am. Polit. Sci. Assn. (treas. 1980, Charles E. Merriam award 1985, Eldersweld award 1994), Am. Acad. Arts and Scis. Home: 900 N Taylor St Unit 2117 Arlington VA 22203

SUNDRAM, MIRIAM ANNE, social worker; b. Bombay, Nov. 1, 1958; came to U.S., 1966, naturalized, 1976; d. Joseph D. and Husnara H. Sundram. BSW, Niagara U., 1980; MS in Social Work, U. Tex., 1986. Cert. social worker, Tex., advanced clin. practitioner. Social worker Assn. for Retarded Citizens, Niagara Falls, N.Y., 1980-82; mental health specialist Austin (Tex.) State Hosp., 1982-84; child care supr. Jr. Helping Hand, Austin, 1984-86; unit dir. San Marcos (Tex.) Treatment Ctr., 1986-89; program dir. The Oaks Treatment Ctr., Austin, 1989—; cons. Jr. Helping Hand, 1988; CEO, pres. Integrated Mental Health, 2001, Tejas Behavioral Health, 2001. Mem. NASW. Avocations: professional musician, weightlifting, reading.

SUNDSTROM, HAROLD WALTER, public relations executive; b. Chgo., Jan. 26, 1929; s. Elmer A. and Rosalind Lillian (Busse) S.; m. Mary Olin, Oct. 1, 1955; children: Geoffrey Lee, Lori Lynn, Deborah Barron. AA, Wright Jr. Coll., 1949; BA, Mich. State U., 1952, MA, 1954. Fgn. svc. info. officer USIA, Tokyo, Jakarta, Seoul, 1955-61; sr. pub. rels. assoc. Eli Lilly and Co., Indpls., 1962-66; v.p., dir. pub. rels. Eisenhower People to People Program, Kansas City, Mo., and Copenhagen, 1966-68; govt. and pub. affairs rep. North Ctrl. States Automobile Mfrs. Assn., Kansas City, 1968-69; speechwriter, pub. rels. cons. Commdr.-in-Chief U.S. Pacific Forces, Aiea, 1969-75; pres. No. Ariz. Comm., Inc., Flagstaff, 1975-79; asst. sec., dir. pub. affairs U.S. Internat. Trade Commn., Washington, 1977-87; v.p. pub. affairs and publs. Export-Import Bank U.S., 1987-89; pres. Halamar, Inc., Manassas, Va. and Easley, S.C., 1983—, Silver Springs, Fla., 1983-98. Mem. Pres.'s Consumer Affairs Couns., 1977-89; freelance writer and poet. Author: The American West, 1956, Garuda, Introducing Indonesia, 1957, Politics and Nationalism in Indonesia, 1962, Faces of Asia: Korea, 1965, The Northern Arizona Scene, 1976, American Collie Champions, Vol. I, 1979, Vol. II, 1980, Vol. III, 1987, Collies - A Complete Pet Owners Manual, 1994; editor, pub. Hawaiian Dog Rev., The Alaska Cir., The Arizona Cir., Internat. Lhasa Apso Rev., Sandwich Isles Dog Gazette, 1972-76, Collie Cues, 1983-86, Travel Writer, Honolulu Sun Press, 1972-76. Active Civil War Trust Colonial Williamsburg, Nat. Trust for Hist. Preservation, Habitat for Humanity, Hist. Mount Vernon, Va. Recipient People to People Disting. Svc. award, 1967, George Washington Honor medal Freedom Found., 1968, Silver Beaver award Boy Scouts Am., 1975. Fellow Japan Soc. N.Y.; mem. Pub. Rels. Soc. Am. (past pres. Hawaii chpt., Silver Anvil award 1973), Dog Writers Assn. Am. (pres. 1984-92, Disting. Svc. award 1993), Dog Writers Ednl. Trust (vice chmn., chmn. 1999—), Collie Club Am. (pres. 1984-86), Collie Club Am. Found. (life, pres. 1990-92), Am. Kennel Club (del. 1986—), Pi Sigma Alpha, Phi Kappa Sigma. Republican. Avocations: pure-bred dog breeding and showing, travel, photography, conservation, preservation of historic properties. Home and Office: 11245 NW 17th Court Rd Ocala FL 34475-1339

SUNDT, HARRY WILSON, construction company executive; b. Woodbury, N.J., July 5, 1932; s. Thoralf Mauritz and Elinor (Stout) S.; m. Dorothy Van Gilder, June 26, 1954; children: Thomas D., Perri Lee Sundt Touche, Gerald W. BS in Bus. Adminstrn., U. Ariz., 1954, postgrad., 1957-59. Salesman ins. VanGilder Agys., Denver, 1956-57; apprentice carpenter M.M. Sundt Constrn. Co., Tucson, 1957-58, estimator, 1958-59, adminstrv. asst. Vandenberg AFB, 1959-62, sr. estimator Tucson, 1962-64, div. mgr., 1964-65, exec. v.p., gen. mgr., 1965-75, pres., chmn., 1975-79; chmn. Sundt Corp., 1980-83, chmn., chief exec. officer, 1983-98; ret., 1999. Bd. dirs.Tucson Electric Power Co.; bd. dirs. Schu7ff Steel Co., Unisource Energy Co., Millenium Energy Co. Pres. Tucson Airport Authority, 1982; bd. dirs. U. Ariz. Found. 1981. 1st lt. U.S. Army, 1954-56. Recipient Disting. Citizen award U. Ariz., 1982, Centennial Medallion award, 1989, Founders award Tucson C. of C., 2000. Mem. Tucson Country Club. Republican. Episcopalian. Avocation: tennis. Home: 6002 E San Leandro Tucson AZ 85715-3014

SUNDY, GEORGE JOSEPH, JR. retired engineering executive; b. Nanticoke, Pa., Apr. 22, 1936; s. George Joseph Sr. and Stella Mary (Bodurka) S.; m. Stella Pauline Miechur, May 21, 1966; children: Sharon Ann, George Joseph III. BS, Pa. State U., 1958. Rsch. engr. Bethlehem (Pa.) Steel Corp., 1959-85; reliability engr. Flo-Con Systems, Inc. (name now Vesuvius USA), Champaign, Ill., 1985-90, reliability mgr., 1990-96, slide gate product line specialist, 1996—2001. Patentee in field. Mem. Am. Ceramics Soc., Iron and Steel Soc., AIME, Keramos, Sigma Tau. Democrat. Roman Catholic. Home: 604 E South Mahomet Rd Mahomet IL 61853-3602 E-mail: gsundy@mahonline.com.

SUNELL, ROBERT JOHN, retired army officer; b. Astoria, Oreg., June 5, 1929; s. Ernest and Grace L. S.; m. JoAnn L. Toikka, Dec. 29, 1951; children— Perry Sunell Peterson, Patti Sunell Sigl, Robert P. Student, U. Oreg., 1949-53; B.E., U. Nebr., 1963; MS, Shippensburg State Coll., 1973. Commd. U.S. Army, 1953, advanced through grades to maj. gen., 1983, ret., 1987, exec. officer 1st Brigade, 4th Inf. div. Vietnam, 1966-67, comdr. 2d Bn., 8th Inf., 4th Inf. div. Vietnam, 1969-70, chief Bn. and Brigade Tactical Ops. div. Armor Sch. Ky., 1973-74, dep. dir. Armored Reconnaissance Scout Vehicle Task Force, 1974-76, dep. program mgr. XM1 Tank Systems Warren, Mich., 1976-78, comdr. 11th Armored Cav. Regt. Germany, 1978-79, comdr. Army Tng. Support Ctr. Ft. Eustis, Va, 1980-83, program mgr. Tank Systems Warren, Mich., 1983-86; dir. Armored Family of Vehicles Task Force, Fort Eustis, Va., 1986-87. Apptd. adv. bd. dirs. Land Combat Com., Assn. of U.S. Army, 1995; cons. U.S. Army Sci. Bd.; founder Suonperra, Inc., 1987. Decorated Silver Star, Legion of Merit, Bronze Star, Meritorious Service award, Disting. Service medal. Mem. Saab Sci. Coun., U.S. Army Assn., Armor Assn. Republican. E-mail: rj2933@aol.com.

SUNIA, TAUESE, governor; BA in Polit. Sci., U. Nebr.; M in Ednl. Adminstrn., U. Hawaii; DHL, Golden Gate U. Formerly lt. gov. Ter. of Am. Samoa, Pago Pago, now gov. Office: Office of the Gov Am Samoa Govt Pago Pago AS 96799

SUNIL, RANGAPPA, research scientist, physician; b. Bancalore, India, Nov. 25, 1971; s. Rangappa and Mallika Sunil. MBBS, Bancalore Med. Coll., India, 1995; MS, Nat. U. Singapore, 2001. Post doctoral fellow MCP Hahnemann U., 2001—; rsch. fellow Nat. U. Singapore, 1999—2001; med. officer Inst. Aviation Medicine , Bangalore , India, 1998—99, Wockhardt Hosp. & Heart Inst., 1998—99, Bangaldre Heart Inst., 1998—99. Contbr. articles. Organizer Unicef, India, 1996—97. Mem.: AMSRO, ASAIO. Office: MCP Hahnemann U 245 N 15 St Philadelphia PA 19102

SUNIL, SAIGAL, civil engineering educator; b. Karnal, India, July 13, 1957; came to U.S., 1980; s. Jagjit Singh and Surrinder (Bhandari) S. BSC in Civil Engring., Punjab Engring. Coll., 1978; MS in Structures, Indian Inst. Sci., l980; PhD in Aerospace Engring., Purdue U., 1985. Postdoctoral rsch. asst. Purdue U., West Lafayette, Ind., 1986; asst. prof. mech. engring. Worcester (Mass.) Poly. Inst., 1986-89; asst. prof. civil engring. Carnegie-Mellon U., Pitts., 1989-91; assoc. prof. Carnegie Mellon U., 1991—95, prof., 1995—2002; dept. chair U. South Fla., Tampa, 2003—. Program mgr. NSF, 1996—98. Contbr. articles to profl. jours. Recipient Adm. Ralph Earle medal Worcester Engring. Soc., 1987, Ralph R. Teetor award Soc. Automotive Engrs., 1988, Presdl. Young Investigator award NSF, 1990, George Tallman Ladd rsch. award Carnegie Mellon U., 1990. Mem. ASME (assoc.), AIAA (assoc.), ASCE. Avocations: jogging, biking, racquetball. Home: 1201 Richmond St Pittsburgh PA 15218-1016 Office: Carnegie-Mellon U Dept Civil Engring Pittsburgh PA 15213

SUNLEY, EMIL MCKEE, economist; b. Morgantown, W.Va., July 30, 1942; s. Emil McKee and Nelle Berniece (Traer) S.; m. Judith Evelyn Steere, Dec. 23, 1966; children: Rachel Anne, Gillian Traer, Neil Steere. BA, Amherst Coll., 1964; MA, U. Mich., 1965, PhD, 1968. Economist office tax analysis Dept. Treasury, Washington, 1968-73, assoc. dir. office tax analysis, 1973-75, dep. asst. sec. for tax policy, 1977-81; sr. fellow Brookings Instn., Washington, 1975-77; dir. tax analysis Deloitte & Touche, 1981-92; asst. dir. fiscal affairs dept. Internat. Monetary Fund, 1992—. Mem. editl. bd. Nat. Tax Jour., 1992-95. Mem. Commn. on RR Retirement Reform, 1987-90. Mem. Am. Econ. Assn., Nat. Tax Assn. (pres. 1995-96), Tax Analysts (bd. dirs. 1982-93). Episcopalian. Office: Internat Monetary Fund Fiscal Affairs Dept Washington DC 20431-0001 E-mail: esunley@imf.org.

SUNUNU, JOHN E. congressman; m. Kitty Sununu; children: John Hayes, Grace. B in Mech. Engring., M in Mech. Engring., Mass. Inst. Tech.; MBA, Harvard Grad. Sch. Bus. Design engr. Remec, Inc., 1987-90; mgr., ops. specialist Pittiglio, Rabin, Todd & McGrath, 1990-92; chief fin. officer, dir. ops. Teletrol Sys. Inc.; cons. JHS Assocs., Ltd.; mem. U.S. Congress from 1st N.H. dist., 1997—. Mem. appropriations com., budget com.; previous mem. natural resources working group, house govt. reform and oversight com., house small bus. com.; vice-chmn. Nat. Econ. Growth, Natural Resources and Regulatory Affairs sub-com.; mem. Rep. Policy com. Active N.H. C. of C., N.H. Bus. and Industry Assn., N.H. High Tech Coun. Roman Catholic. Office: Office Congressman 316 Cannon Hob Washington DC 20515-0001*

SUNWARD, JUSTIN HUGO, artist, writer; b. Chgo., Feb. 20, 1939; s. Arthur Peter and Dorothy Irene Johnsen. Student, Sch. of Art Inst. of Chgo., 1951-52; diploma with honors, Frances Harrington Profl. Sch. Interior Decoration, Chgo., 1958. Represented in permanent collections Mus. Modern Art, N.Y.C., Met. Mus. Art, N.Y.C., Whitney Mus. Am. Art, N.Y.C., Mus. Contemporary Modern Art, Uuskila, Finland, others; contbr. art revs. to publs. Recipient numerous nat. art competition awards. Mem. Chgo. Art Critics Assn. (founding mem.). Avocations: cooking, gardening, history, architecture, traveling.

SUOTMAA, JUHA OLAVI, training manager, journalist, lecturer; b. Turku, Finland, Sept. 22, 1963; s. Jukka Urho Olavi and Marita Johanna (Lindström) S.; m. Shu-Ming Linda Su, Sept. 5, 1986 (div. Feb. 1999); children: Jessica Johanna, Josephine Jennifer. Student, Paasikivi Coll., Turku, 1983-84; BA, U.S. Internat. U., San Diego, 1988; postgrad., London Sch. Econs., 1989-90; MA in Polit. Sci., Turku U., 1994. Money exchange asst. OKOBANK Turku Finland, 1985-86, fgn. payments asst., 1986-88, fgn. payments advisor, 1988-89, 90-91; v.p. Hubertus Oy, Turku, 1988-96; translator Turku Sch. Econs. and Bus. Adminstrn., 1990-91; asst. to sport sect. Turun Sanomat, 1991—; tng. mgr. Ctr. Maritime Studies U. Turku, 1994—. Vis. lectr. Paasikivi Coll., Turku, 1991-93, Loimaa Evangel. Inst., 1996-2001. Contbr. essays to profl. jours. Mem. San Diego World Affairs Coun., 1986-88, Kaarinan (Finland) Ristiritarit (Boy Scouts), 1982-90. With Finnish mil., 1983. Recipient award for Excellent Svc. Coast-Arty. Guild, Turku, 1983. Mem. U.S. Internat. Rels. Club (treas. 1987-88), U.S. Internat. Univ. Table Tennis Club, Order of St. Lazarus, Order of St. John, Order of St. Andrew, Turun Pöytätennisseura ry (pres. 1991-94, 96-98, sec. 1999—). Nat. Coalition Party. Lutheran. Home: Laivurinkatu 2 B 42 20810 Turku Finland E-mail: juha.suotmaa@utu.fi.

SUP, STUART ALLEN See ALLEN, STUART

SUPANICH, BARBARA ANN, family practice physician; b. Detroit, Sept. 24, 1952; d. Donald George and Mildred Mary (Stanovich) S. BS in Chemistry, Mercy Coll. of Detroit, 1974; MD, Mich. State U., 1980. Joined Sisters of Mercy, 1973; diplomate Am. Bd. Family Practice; lic. physician, Mich. Resident in family practice Creighton U. Affiliated Hosps., Omaha, 1980-83; family physician in pvt. practice, Eaton Rapids, Mich., 1983-86, Houghton Lake, 1986-92; fellow in clin. ethics Ctr. for Ethics, Mich. State U., East Lansing, 1992-93; asst. prof. family practice Mich. State U., 1993-97, assoc. chair clin. svcs., dept. family practice, 1995-99, assoc. prof., 1998, assoc. residency dir. family practice residency Munson, 1999—. Cons. Mich. Dept. Cmty. Health, Lansing, 1996-99. Contbr. chpts. to books, articles to profl. jours. Fellow Am. Acad. Family Physicians (bd. dirs., regional dir. 2000—); mem. Am. Coll. Physician Execs., Mich. Acad. Family Physicians, Am. Med. Women's Assn., Mich. State Med. Soc. Roman Catholic. Avocations: swimming, bicycling, mystery and science fiction novels. Home: 3525 La Casita Ave Apt 202 Traverse City MI 49684-4336 Office: Mich State U Munson Family Practice Ctr 1400 Medical Campus Dr Traverse City MI 49684-7823 E-mail: bsupanic@mhc.net, barbrsm@earthlink.net.

SUPERNEAU, DUANE WILLIAM, geneticist, physician; b. Ogden, Utah, Dec. 31, 1950; s. Richard Edwin and Mary Ellen Superneau; m. Connie A. Saltalamacchia, Apr. 21, 1978; children: Adam, Ashley, Allison. BA, Carroll Coll., 1973; MD, U. Wash., 1977. Diplomate Am. Bd. Pediat., Am. Bd. Med. Genetics. Asst. prof. dept. med. genetics U. So. Ala., Mobile, 1982-87, assoc. prof. dept. med. genetics, 1987-91; chief sect. med. genetics Ochsner Clinic, New Orleans, 1991—; clin. asst. prof. dept. biometry and genetics La. State U., 1992—, clin. asst. prof. dept. pediatrics, 1994—. Bd. dirs. The Arc Greater New Orleans, 1991—, pres. 1994-96; bd. dirs. Arc of La., 1994—, Jefferson Parish Human Svcs. Authority, Jefferson Parish, La., 1992-99. Roman Catholic. Office: Ochsner Clinic Depts Pediatrics 1514 Jefferson Hwy New Orleans LA 70121-2429 E-mail: DSuperneau@ochsner.org.

SUPINO, ANTHONY MARTIN, lawyer; b. Weehawken, N.J., Oct. 1, 1962; s. Anthony Edward and Gloria (DeBari) S. BA, Rutgers U., 1984, postgrad., 1984-85, JD, 1988. Bar: N.J. 1988, U.S. Dist. Ct. N.J. 1988, N.Y. 1989, U.S. Dist. Ct. (so. dist.) N.Y. 1990, U.S. Ct. Appeals (3d cir.) 1991. Law sec. to the Hon. Marie L. Garibaldi Supreme Ct. of N.J., Jersey City, 1988-89; litigation assoc. Cravath, Swaine & Moore, N.Y.C., 1989-92; spl. litigation assoc. Chadbourne & Parke, 1992-93; ptnr. Arkin, Schaffer & Supino, 1994-96; pvt. practice Supino, Jacobs & Rudy, N.Y.C., West Orange, N.J., 1996—. Community organizer Human Serve Fund, New Brunswick, N.J., 1984. Democrat. Avocations: coin collecting, sports, weightlifting. Home: 30 Quimby Pl West Orange NJ 07052-5208 Office: Anthony M Supino & Assocs 475 5th Ave New York NY 10017-6220

SUPPES, PATRICK, philosophy, statistics, psychology educator and education; b. Tulsa, Mar. 17, 1922; s. George Biddle and Ann (Costello) Suppes; m. Joan Farmer, Apr. 16, 1946 (div. 1970); children: Patricia, Deborah, John Biddle; m. Joan Sieber, Mar. 29, 1970 (div. 1973); m. Christine Johnson, May 26, 1979; children: Alexandra Christine, Michael Patrick. BS, U. Chgo., 1943; PhD (Wendell T. Bush fellow), Columbia U., 1950; LLD, U. Nijmegen, Netherlands, 1979; Dr. honoris causa (hon.) , U. Rene Descartes, Paris, 1982, U. Regensburg, Germany, 1999, U. Bologna, Italy, 1999. Instr., Stanford U., 1950—52, asst. prof., 1952—55, assoc. prof., 1955—59, prof. philosophy, statistics, psychology and edn., 1959—92, prof. emeritus. Founder, CEO Computer Curriculum Corp., 1967—90. Author: Introduction to Logic, 1957, Axiomatic Set Theory, 1960, Sets and Numbers, books 1-6, 1966, Studies in the Methodology and Foundations of Science, 1969, A Probabilistic Theory of Causality, 1970, Logique du Probable, 1981, Probabilistic Metaphysics, 1984, Estudios de Filosofia y Metodologí de la Ciencia, 1988, Language for Humans and Robots, 1991, Models and Methods in the Philosophy of Science, 1993, Representation and Invariance of Scientific Structures, 2002; author: (with Davidson and Siegel) Decision Making, 1957; author: (with Richard C. Atkinson) Markov Learning Models for Multiperson Interactions, 1960; author: (with Shirley Hill) First Course in Mathematical Logic, 1964; author: (with Edward J. Crothers) Experiments on Second-Language Learning, 1967; author: (with Max Jerman and Dow Brian) Computer-assisted Instruction, 1965—66, Stanford Arithmetic Program, 1968; author: (with D. Krantz, R.D. Luce and A. Tversky) Foundations of Measurement, Vol. 1, 1971, Vol. 2, 1989, Vol. 3, 1990; author: (with M. Morningstar) Computer-Assisted Instruction at Stanford, 1966-68, 1972; author: (with B. Searle and J. Friend) The Radio Mathematics Project: Nicaragua, 1974-75, 1976; author: (with Colleen Crangle) Language and Learning for Robots, 1994; author: (with Mario Zanotti) Foundations of Probability with Applications, 1996. Served to capt. USAAF, 1942-46. Recipient Nicholas Murray Butler Silver medal, Columbia U., 1965, Disting. Sci. Contbr. award, APA, 1972, Tchrs. Coll. medal for disting. svc., 1978, Nat. medal Sci., NSF, 1990; fellow, Ctr. for Advanced Study Behavioral Scis., 1955—56, NSF, 1957—58. Fellow: APA, AAAS, Assn. Computing Machinery, Am. Acad. Arts and Scis.; mem.: NAS, Chilean Acad. Scis., European Acad. Scis. and Arts, Norwegian Acad. Sci. and Letters (fgn.), Russian Acad. Edn. (fgn.), Am. Ednl. Rsch. Assn. (pres. 1973—74), Internat. Union History and Philosophy of Sci. (pres. divsn. logic, methodology and philosophy of sci. 1975—79), Finnish Acad. Sci. and Letters, Internat. Inst. Philosophy, Nat. Acad. Edn. (pres. 1973—77), Croatian Acad. Scis. (corr.), Acad. Internat. de Philosophie des Scis. (titular), Am. Math. Soc., Assn. Symbolic Logic, Am. Philos. Soc., Am. Philos. Assn., Psychometric Soc., Math. Assn. Am., Sigma Xi. E-mail: psuppes@cstanford.edu.

SUPPLE, DIANE MARIE, computer information scientist; b. Pasadena, Calif., Oct. 20, 1956; d. John Robert and Shirley Ann (Remy) S. AA, Pasadena City Coll., 1977; BS, Calif. Poly. State U. San Luis Obispo, 1980; MBA, Loyola Marymount, Westchester, Calif., 1984. Systems rep. Info. Internat., Inc., Culver City, Calif., 1980-83; jr. programmer analyst Xerox Corp., El Segundo, 1983-86, sr. programmer analyst, 1986-89, software computer tester, 1989—. Author: Online Computers Hyphenation and Justification, 1980. Republican. Roman Catholic. Avocations: swimming, instr. at the local YMCA. Home: 2040 Carolwood Dr Arcadia CA 91006-1513

SUPRUN, HARRY ZVI, pathologist; b. San Antonio, Aug. 19, 1924; arrived in Israel, 1934; s. Joseph Jacob and Bertha Batya (Payes) S.; m. Hedva Storch-Chassidi, Mar. 26, 1950; children: Ilana Sarah, Leora Oli. BA in Medicine, Am. U. Beirut, 1948; MD, cert. med. studies, U. Lausanne, Switzerland, 1952. Rotating intern Beilinson Med. Ctr., Petah Tikvah, Israel, 1953-54; gen. practice, Affuleh, Israel, 1954-55; resident in pathology Ctrl. Emek Hosp. and Med. Ctr., 1955-58; resident and chief resident in anatomic pathology Tel Aviv U.-Mcpl. Tchg. Med. Ctrs., 1958-62, specialist in anatomic pathology, assoc. attending, 1961; tng. in cytopathology, rsch. fellow Sloan-Kettering Inst., N.Y.C., 1962-63; instr., asst. pathologist Ohio State U. Med. Coll., Columbus, 1963-64; instr. Tel Aviv U. Med. Sch. Tchg. Hosps., 1964-65; dir., founder dept. pathology and cytology Regional Med. Ctr. West Galilee, Nahariyya, Israel, 1965-91; lectr. gynecologic, gastrointestinal, fine needle aspiration cytology and urol. cytopathology Tel Aviv U. Postgrad. Med. Sch., 1987-92; lectr. anatomic pathology, U.S. students Tel Aviv U., 1990-92. Lectr. normal histology Technion Med. Sch., Haifa, Israel, 1977-82; mem. Internat. Bd. Cytopathology, 1986-92; head orgn. com. Israel Soc. Cytology, 1971; fellow Internat. Acad. Cytology, 1971-73. Nat. editor Acta Cytologica, 1971-93, mem. European rev. bd., 1982-93; assoc. editor The Cervix and Lower Female Genital Tract, 1987-90, mem. editl. bd., 1989-91; mem. N.Am. rev. bd. Acta Cytol, 1997-; contbr. more than 100 articles to profl. publs. Rsch. fellow Israel Cancer Rsch. Fund, 1979-82. Fellow Internat. Acad. Cytology (continuing edn. and quality assurance com. 1992—), Israel Soc. Cervical Pathology and Colposcopy (pres. 1986). Achievements include correlative study on incidence of pulmonary cancer and other lung diseases associated with squamous metaplasia of bronchial epithelium. Avocations: visiting European countries, languages, art and cultures, music, ballet, walking.

SUPUT, RAY RADOSLAV, librarian; b. Columbus, Ohio, May 13, 1922; s. Elias and Darinka (Balac) S.; m. Mary Grace Hansen, May 23, 1953 (dec. Nov. 1980); children: David Ray, Dorothy Mary; m. Milana Preradov, July 12, 1986. BA, Ohio State U., 1950; MSL.S., Case Western Res. U., 1951, PhD, 1972; MA, U. Chgo., 1955. Librarian Northwestern U., Evanston, Ill., 1951-52; reference and circulation librarian Law Library, U. Chgo., 1952-54, cataloger, 1954-57; asso. librarian Garrett-Evang. Theol. Sem., Evanston, 1957-58, head librarian, 1958-64; asst. dir. libraries and adj. lectr. dept. Slavic and E. European langs. Sch. Library Sci. Case Western Res. U., Cleve., 1964-67, acting dir. libraries, 1967-68; adj. instr. Case Western Res. U. (Sch. Library Sci.), 1965-69; librarian Case Western Res. U. (Freiberger Library), 1968-69; dir. univ. library, head dept. and prof. library sci. Ball State U.,

Muncie, Ind., 1969-78, univ. librarian, head dept. and prof. library service, 1978-81, prof. library service, also adj. prof. library sci., 1981-82, chmn. dept. library and info. sci., prof. library sci., 1982-87, prof. library sci., info. sci. emeritus, 1987—. Contbr. articles to profl. jours. Nat. Endowment for Humanities and Council on Library Resources Inc. grantee. Mem. ALA, AAUP, African Violet Soc. Am., Am. Theol. Libr. Assn., Serb Nat. Fedn., Ohio Hist. Soc. Eastern Orthodox. E-mail: rsuput@infinet.com.

SUR, WILLIAM KENNETH, executive search consultant; b. Toledo, Apr. 6, 1932; m. Margaret C. Sur, Oct. 6, 1956; 4 children. BS in Econs., Villanova (Pa.) U., 1954. Sales rep. Olin Ma Thieson Chem. Corp., N.Y.C., 1958-61; sr. fin. analyst Merck & Co., Inc., Rahway, N.J., 1961-66; sr. v.p., dir. Spencer-Stuart, N.Y.C., 1966-82; pres. Sollis, Sur & Assocs., 1982-89, Stricker, Sur & Assocs., N.Y.C., 1989-91; sr. v.p., dir. Canny, Bowen Inc., 1991-98; mng. dir. Conboy, Sur & Assocs., 1998—. Lt. j.g. USN, 1954-58. Office: Conboy Sur & Assocs 545 5th Ave Rm 630 New York NY 10017-3620

SURACI, CHARLES XAVIER, JR. retired federal agency administrator, aerospace education consultant; b. Washington, Feb. 10, 1933; s. Charles Xavier and June Celcia (Hunter) Suraci; m. Florence Patricia De Mino, May 23, 1970. Cadet, Penn Mil. Coll. (now Widener U.), 1951-53; grad., Nat. Acad. Broadcasting Sch., Washington, 1959; student, Columbia Union Coll., 1962-63, 72, Catholic U., 1969; grad. extension course, CAP Staff Coll., 1974; BA, HHD (hon.), Calif. Christian Coll., 1977; grad., USAF Inspectors Gen. Sch., Eglin AFB, Fla., 1982; also grad. numerous other govt. schs. and courses. Served with USAF, 1953-57; enlisted CAP, 1957, commd. 1st lt., 1961; advanced through ranks to Col. CAP USAF Aux, 1974; co-founder Wheaton-Silver Spring Cadet Squadron; comdr. Nat. Capital Wing, 1973-76; dep. chief of staff cadet activities Middle East region, 1977-79, dir. cadet tng., 1979-82, insp. gen., 1982—. With Henry Diamond Lab. U.S. Army, Adelphi, Md., 1963—, materials publs. asst. Harry Diamond Lab., 1963—68, later asst. to motor transp. officer, now supply specialist, logistics sect.; bd. dirs. Centro Tepeyac Crisis Pregnancy Ctr., Silver Springs, Md. Mem. youth com. YMCA, Silver Spring, 1962—69, mem. bd. mgmt., 1967—; bd. dirs. Am. Youth Com.; mem. Commn. on Children and Youth Bd., Montgomery County, Md., Montgomery County Juvenile Ct. Com., 1978—86; co-chmn. Right to Life com. KC-Rosensteel Coun.; bd. dirs. Pregnancy Aid Ctr., College Park, Md.; choir mem. Blessed Sacrament Cath. Ch., Washington. Nominee Pres.'s Vol. Action award, Pres. of U.S., 1988, 1991; named Air Man of Month, USAF, 1956, Grand Marshall Meml. Day Parade, Rockville, Md., 1971, Man of Yr. State of Md., Air Force Assn., 1993; recipient Leader and Svc. award, YMCA Silver Spring, 1968, 1969, CAP Meritorious Svc. award, Dept. Def., 1969, 1977, Cert. of Commendation, Pres. Richard Nixon, 1970, CAP Exceptional Svc. award, Congressman Lester Wolff of N.Y., 1972, award, Montgomery County C. of C., 1973, Commendation, Gov. of Tenn., 1975, Letter of Commendation, Washington Mayor Walter Washington, 1977, Outstanding Patriotic Civilian Svc. award, Dept. Def., 1977, Md. Vol. Cmty. honor award, Montgomery County, 1981, Vol. Activist award, 1984, George Washington honor medal, Valley Forge Freedom Found., 1995, Patrick Henry medal for Patriotic Achievement, Mil. Order of World Wars, 1995, Honor, Md. Ho. Dels., 1974, D.C. Govt., 1977, numerous AF and CAP ribbons and medals, Dept. of Army Spl. Act or Svc. award, Dept. of Army Superior Performance award, 1987, Cmty. Svc. award, Wheaton-Kensington News, Bethesda Chevy Chase Current, Montgomery County Press Assn., 1990, Outstanding Support Aviation Career Day Tuskegee Airmen and Commdg. Gen. of D.C., Air Nat. Guard, 1992, Spl. award for tng. over 1000 youth cadets in CAP in 31 yrs., State of Md., 1986, Plaque Name Displayed at U.S. Army-Harry Diamond Lab., Pro-Life award, KC-Rosensteel Coun., 1992, Frank G. Brewer Meml. Aerospace award-CAP Mid. East Region HQ, 1984, 1991, 1992, CAP-USAF Aux. Meritorious Svc. award, Mid. East Region HQ, 1993, Cert. Appreciation Aerospace Edn. of Md., Air Force Assn., 1993—95, Exceptional Svc. award, USAF Aux., 1994—95, Sr. Officer of Yr. Mid East Region, USAF Aux.-CAP, 1998. Mem.: Md. Pvt. Industry Coun. (bd. dirs. Opportunity Skyway program), Md. Press. Assn. Montgomery County, Nat. Officers Assn., Mil. Order of World Wars (jr. vice comdr. Bethesda chpt. 1996—), Tuskegee Airmen Inc., Fed. Ret. Employees Assn., Army Aviation Assn., Navy League, Nat. Aerospace Assn., Air Force Assn. (bd. dirs., v.p. aerospace edn. Thomas W. Anthony chpt. 1996—, pres. Thomas W. Anthony chpt. 1998—, Medal of Merit 1990, Exceptional Svc. award 1991, 1994, Commd. Officer of Yr. 1995, Spl. Cert. Appreciation 1996, Disting. Svc. as Inspector Gen. 1991, Member of Distinction Thomas W. Anthony chpt.), Alumni Assn. Widener U., Andrews AFB Officers Club, KC (chmn. Pro-Life Father Rosensteel coun., Outstanding Leadership Pro-Life activities 1990—91, Outstanding Svc. award 1993—94, Honored Guest of Yr. 1996—97), Chester Lodge. Democrat. Achievements include 2 plaques in his name displayed at Columbia Union Coll., Takoma Park, Md., Widener U. (formerly Pa. Mil. Coll.), Chester. Home: Rock Creek Hills 9817 La Duke Dr Kensington MD 20895-3156 Office: USAF Aux CAP Mid East Region Hdqrs Office of Insp Gen 9817 La Duke Dr Kensington MD 20895-3156

SURACI, PATRICK JOSEPH, clinical psychologist; b. Rochester, N.Y., May 31, 1936; s. Frank and Josephine Rosalie (Marino) S. PhD in Psychology, New. Sch. for Social Rsch., N.Y.C., 1981. Cert. clin. psychologist, N.Y. Intern in clin. psychology Morrisania Neighborhood Family Care Ctr., Montefiore Hosp., N.Y.C., 1979-80; staff psychologist N.Y. Police Dept., 1981-83; pvt. practice N.Y.C., 1982—. Adj. lectr. N.Y. Inst. Tech., N.Y.C., 1975-78, John Jay Coll. Criminal Justice, CUNY, 1973-81; adj. asst. prof. Baruch Coll. Psychology Dept., CUNY, 1983-92; vol. Manhattan Ctr. for Living, 1994-96. Author: Male Sexual Armor. Erotic Fantasies and Sexual Realities of the Cop on the Beat and the Man in the Street, 1992. Mem. The Nat. Arts Club. With U.S. Army, 1959-62. Mem. APA, N.Y. State Psychol. Assn. (task force on AIDS), Actors Equity. Office: 8 Gramercy Park S New York NY 10003-1718 E-mail: DrSuraci@aol.com.

SURAWICZ, BORYS, physician, educator; b. Moscow, Russia, Feb. 11, 1917; came to U.S., 1951, naturalized, 1956; s. Josef and Mathilda (Solowieczyk) S.; m. Frida G. Van Klaveren, July 19, 1946; children: Christina M., Nina M., Tanya S., Serge J. MD, Stefan Batory U., Wilno, Poland, 1939. Mem. staffs hosps., Germany, Norway, 1945-49; staff De Goesbriand Meml. Hosp., Burlington, Vt., 1951-53, Phila. Gen. Hosp., 1953-55; instr. cardiology U. Pa., Phila., 1954-55; instr. U. Vt., Burlington, 1955-57, asst. prof. clin. and exptl. medicine, 1957-62; chief div. cardiology U. Ky. Coll. Medicine, Lexington, 1962-81, asso. prof. medicine, 1962-66, prof., 1966-81; prof. medicine Ind. U. Sch. Medicine, Indpls., 1981—. Cons. VA Hosp., Indpls. Editor: (with E.D. Pellegrino) Sudden Cardiac Death, 1964, (with C. Fisch) Digitalis, 1969; (with E. Prystowsky, C.P. Reddy) Tachycardias, 1985, Electrophysiologic Basis of ECG and Cardiac Arrhythmics, 1995, Chou's Electrocardiography in Clinical Practice, 2001; mem. editl. bds. profl. jours. Mem. AMA, ACP, Am. Heart Assn., Assn. Univ. Cardiologists (pres. 1978), Am. Coll. Cardiology (pres. 1979), Am. Physiol. Soc., Sigma Xi. Home: 4310 E Onyx Ave Phoenix AZ 85028-4518 Office: 8333 Naab Rd Ste 400 Indianapolis IN 46260-1919 E-mail: b.surawicz@worldnet.att.net., tscott@thecaregroup.com.

SURBAUGH, DOLORES SAYAS, accountant, educator; b. Taumuning, Sept. 9, 1953; d. Feliciano Barsaga and Francisca San Nicolas Sayas. BBA Acctg./Bus. Adminstrn. magna cum laude, Chaminade U. Honolulu, 1982, MBA, 1984. CPA Tex. Tax, acct. and fin. supervisory positions Mobil Oil, Dallas, 1995-2001; nat. bank mgr. Exxon Mobil Corp., Lenexa, Kans., 1994—2002; instr. acctg. and profl. devel. Wright Bus. Sch., Overland Park, 2002—. Dir. MCFC Nat. Bank, Lenexa, 1995-2001, cmty. devel., 1995-2001; dir. Mobil Oil Credit Corp., Lenexa, 1999—. Art instr. for physically and mentally challenged Johnson County Devel. Support, Olathe, Kans., 1999-2001. Recipient Cert. of Recognition, Safehome, 1999, Recognition at Fund Raiser, Met. Luth. Ministry, 2000. Mem. AICPA. Roman Catholic. Avocations: fine art, camping, jogging. Office: Wright Bus Sch Lenexa KS E-mail: loli_surbaugh@hotmail.com.

SURBER, JOE ROBERT, assistant superintendent of schools; b. Pawhuska, Okla., Apr. 11, 1942; s. Hugh Richard and Odema (Harris) S.; m. Jo Del Novak; children: Robert Brian, Karrie Jo. BA in Edn., Northeastern State U., 1964; MS in Edn., Okla. State U., 1969, EdD, 1974. Cert. supt., sch. psychologist, sch. counselor. High sch. prin. Unity Bd. Govs., Ponca City, Okla., 1970-71; sch. psychologist Bi-State Mental Health Found., 1971-74; adj. prof. Okla. State U., 1976-84; asst. supt. Ponca City Pub. Schs., 1984—. Pub. The Blue Book of Counseling: Concrete Tools and Techniques, 1976. Past dir. ARC, Ponca City Crime Stoppers, Kay County Youth Shelter, Okla. Assn. Schs. with Impacted Svcs. Staff sgt. USAR, 1966-72. Named One of 3 Outstanding Oklahomans, 1976; recipient Disting. Svc. award, 1973, Outstanding Educator award, 1972. Pres. Okla. Dirs. Spl. Svcs. (past pres.), Okla. Sch. Psychol. Assn. (v.p.). Home: 1308 Desoto Ponca City OK 74604 E-mail: surbej@poncacity.K12.ok.us.

SURDAM, ROBERT MCCLELLAN, retired banker; b. Albany, N.Y., Oct. 28, 1917; s. Burke and LeMoyne (McClellan) S.; m. Mary Caroline Buhl, July 8, 1946; children— Peter Buhl, Robert McClellan, Mary Caroline. BA cum laude, Williams Coll., 1939. With Nat. Bank Detroit, 1947-88, exec. v.p., 1964-66, pres., 1966-72, chmn. bd., 1972-82, also bd. dirs., 1966-88. Served to lt. comdr. USNR, 1941-46. Recipient, Navy and Marine Corps. medal. Mem. Detroit Club, Country Club of Detroit, Yondotega Club, Jupiter Island Club (Hobe Sound, Fla.), Jupiter Hills Club (Tequesta, Fla.), Little Traverse Yacht Club (Harbor Springs, Mich.), Rolling Rock Club (Ligonier, Pa.), Hobe Sound Yacht Club, Little Harbor Club (Harbor Springs, Mich.). Home: 396 Provencal Rd Grosse Pointe Farms MI 48236-2959

SURFACE, CAROL PRICE, artist, educator; b. Akron, Ohio, May 10, 1955; d. Thomas Lee and Mary Anita (Stahl) Price; m. Henry E. Surface Jr., Feb. 15, 1981. BA summa cum laude, U. Ctrl. Fla., 1986. Materiels mgr. Haris Corp., Melbourne, Fla., 1973-79; purchasing agent Fujitsu Am., 1980-81; artist self-employed, Venice and Redondo Beach, Calif., 1988—; art tchr. Palos Verdes (Calif.) Art Ctr., 1988-96; faculty mem. art dept. Santa Monica Coll., 2000—02; model, actress Christensen Group, Orlando, Fla., 1985-88; arts writer Orlando Sentinel, 1986-88. V.p. Women Painters West, L.A., 1995—96; artist Venice Art Walk Studio Artists' Tour, 2001; artistic cons. Film Industry; cons. Various painting orgs., Calif. Recipient First Place award Henry Hopkins of UCLA Armand Hammer Mus., 1995, Mayor's award City Beverly Hills, Calif., 1996, Best of Show award Art Inst. So. Calif., Laguna Beach, Calif., 1995-96. Mem. San Diego Watercolor Soc. Avocations: sewing, interior decorating, writing poetry. Home: 822 Avenue A Redondo Beach CA 90277-4814

SURFACE, JAMES LOUIS, SR. trust officer, lawyer; b. Roanoke, Va., May 20, 1941; s. Thomas James and Elizabeth (Abbott) S.; m. Judith Marcia Woodford, Aug. 11, 1962; children: Susanna Elizabeth, James Louis Jr. BA cum laude, Washington & Lee U., 1963, JD cum laude, 1965. Bar: W.Va. Assoc. Spilman, Thomas, Battle & Klostermeyer, Charleston, W.Va., 1965-71; trust officer Kanawha Valley Bank, N.A., 1971-77; v.p., trust counsel Liberty Nat. Bank & Trust Co., Louisville, 1977-84; v.p., trust officer United Va. Bank, Richmond, 1984-85; v.p., sr. trust officer First Citizens Nat. Bank, Dyersburg, Tenn., 1985-93; sr. v.p., sr. trust officer SunTrust Bank East Tenn., Johnson City, 1993—. Mem. adminstrv. bd. First United Meth. Ch., Dyersburg, 1988-90, pres., bd. dirs. Cmty. Concert Assn., Dyersburg, 1988-93; treas., bd. dirs. Louisville-Jefferson County Youth Orch., Louisville, 1980-84; pres., bd. dirs. W.Va. Opera Theater, Inc., Charleston, 1972-77; elder First Presbyn. Ch., Johnson City, 1998-2000; bd. dirs. Tipton-Haynes Hist. Site, 2001—. Mem. ABA (chmn. subcom. on duties and responsibilities of successor trustee real property, probate and trust sect., Charleston 1974-75), W.Va. Bar Assn., Tenn. Bankers Assn. (treas. trust divsn. Nashville chpt. 1988-89, sec. 1989-90, v.p. 1990-91, pres. 1991-92), W.Va. Bankers Assn. (chmn. trust divsn. Charleston chpt. 1974-75), Rotary (bd. dirs. Dyersburg chpt. 1987-88), East Tenn. State U. Friends of Music (bd. dirs. 1994-99, 2000—). Democrat. Avocations: tennis, racquetball, photography, reading. Home: 2 Queens Ct Johnson City TN 37604-3641

SURFACE, STEPHEN WALTER, water treatment chemist, environmental protection specialist; b. Dayton, Ohio, Feb. 25, 1943; s. Lorin Wilfred and Virginia (Marsh) S.; m. Suzanne MacDonald, Aug. 29, 1964 (div.); 1 child, Jennifer Nalani; m. Sinfrosa Garay, Sept. 16, 1978; children: Maria Lourdes, Stephanie Alcantara. BS, Otterbein Coll., 1965; MA, U. So. Calif., 1970; postgrad., U. Hawaii, 1971. Cert. profl. chemist. Tchr. Hawaii State Dept. Edn., Honolulu, 1970-71; staff chemist Del Monte Corp., 1971; head chemist USNPearl Harbor, 1971-76; staff chemist USN Pearl Harbor, 1976-90; chief office installation svcs., environ. protection Def. Logistics Agy., Camp Smith, Hawaii, 1990-98, dir. adminstrv. support ctr. Pacific, 1998—. Contbr. articles to profl. jours. Recipient DuPont Teaching award, U. So. Calif., 1966. Fellow Am. Inst. Chemists; mem. Am. Chem. Soc., Am. Def. Preparedness Assn., N.Y. Acad. Scis., Nat. Def. Indsl. Assn. (life), Sigma Xeta, Phi Lambda Upsilon. Democrat. Methodist. Avocations: traveling, artifact collecting, landscaping. Office: Def Logistics Agy DASC FP Camp H M Smith HI 96861-4110 Home: 17610 Deweys Run Ln Dumfries VA 22026-4546

SURGI, MARION RENE, chemist; b. New Orleans, Dec. 19, 1956; s. George Edward and Barbara Ruth (Pearce) S.; m. Elizabeth Benson, May 22, 1981; children: Reneé Elizabeth, Sara Elizabeth. BS, U. New Orleans, 1979; PhD, La. State U., 1981-84. Gen mgr. Superior Amusement Co., New Orleans, 1975-80; rsch. assoc. U. New Orleans, 1980-81; grad. asst. La. State U., Baton Rouge, 1981-84; sr. rsch. chemist Signal Cos., Des Plaines, Ill., 1984-86; rsch. specialist Allied Signal Corp, 1986-90; rsch. mgr. in math. simulation sci. AlliedSignal Corp, 1990-94; pres. Analytical and Environ. Svcs., Inc., Chgo., 1994—. Contbr. articles to profl. jours. Patentee in field. Mem.: Am. Chem. Soc., Phi Lambda Upsilon. Republican. Episcopalian. Avocations: bicycle racing, real estate renovation, business and real estate acquisitions. Office: 503 Oakdale Ave Glencoe IL 60022-2180 E-mail: renesurgi@aol.com.

SURI, DEEPIKA, nephrologist, internist; b. Chandigarh, UT, India, June 1, 1964; d. Lalit Mohan and Usha Suri. MBBS, Panjab U., Punjab, India, 1988. Diplomate Am. Bd. Internal Medicine, Am. Bd. Nephrology. Intern, resident Good Samaritan Hosp./Johns Hopkins, 1991-94; fellow Stanford U. Med. Ctr., 1994-97; assoc. H.A. Rodiles, Inc., El Centro, Calif., 1997-99; house physician Alpena (Mich.) Gen. Hosp., 1999-2000; med. dir. Alpena Dialysis Unit, 2000—. Mem. ACP, Am. Soc. Nephrology. Office: Alpena Gen Hosp 1501 W Chisholm St Alpena MI 49707-1498

SURI, JASJIT S. research scientist; BS in Computer Engrng., Regional Engrng. Coll., Bhopal, India, 1988; MS, U. Ill., Chgo., 1991; PhD in Elec. Engrng., U. Wash., 1997. Lectr. dept. electronic and computer engrng. Regional Engrng. Coll., Bhopal, 1988-89; rsch. asst. biomed. visualization dept. U. Ill., Chgo., 1989-90; rsch. programmer image sci. group IBM Palo Alto (Calif.) Sci. Ctr., summer 1990-91; rsch. assoc. U. Wash., Seattle, 1992-97; rsch. software engr. radiation treatment planning group Siemens Med. Sys., Calif., 1991-92; rsch. scientist Gammex Inc., Middleton, Wis., 1997, Sch. Medicine, U. Wis., Madison, 1997; rsch. scientist software devel. TSI, N.Y., 1997; rsch. staff scientist image guided surgery dept. Image Processing and Computer Graphics Picker Internat., Cleve., 1999—. With Bharat Heavy Elec. Ltd., Bhopal, summer 1986, Larson & Tubro Ltd., Bombay, India, summer 1987, Nat. Info. Tech. Ltd., Bhopal, summer 1987; presenter in field; mem. Mayo Clinic Procs., Rochester, Minn.; mem. rev. com. Internat. Conf. in Pattern Analysis and Applications, Plymouth, Eng., 1998. Author: (with others) Model Based Segmentation, 2d. rev. edit., 2000; mem. rev. bd. bd. Radiology, Jour. Computer Assisted Tomography, Internat. Jour. Pattern Analysis and Applications, Internat. Conf. Pattern Analysis and Applications; contbr. more than 75 articles. to profl. jours.; patentee in field. Scholar Regional Engrng. Coll., 1985-88 Mem. IEEE, Assn. Computing Machinery, Artificial Intelligence, Optical Engrng. Soc. Am., Engrng. in Medicine and Biology Soc. (mem. editl. bd.), Am. Assn. Artificial Int., USENIX-Tcl/Tk. Office: Marconi Med Sys MR Clin Sci Rsch Divsn 595 Minor Rd Cleveland OH 44143 E-mail: jsuri@mr.marcoimed.com.

SURIAN, ELVIDIO, music educator; b. Lussingrande, Istria, Italy, Jan. 10, 1940; s. Santo and Dobrilla (Ballarin) S.; m. Eugenia Venturi, Nov. 6, 1971; 1 child, Laura. BS, CUNY, 1962, MA, 1964; postgrad., NYU, 1965-70. Instr. music SUNY, Stony Brook, 1970; lectr. Lehman Coll., CUNY, N.Y.C., 1970-72; music librarian G. Rossini Music Conservatory, Pesaro, Italy, 1973-76, prof. music history Italy, 1976—, mem. adminstrn. bd. Italy, 1986-89. Coordinator Repertoire Internat. Sources Musicales Group, Italy, 1975-83. Author: A Checklist of Writings on 18th Century French and Italian Opera, 1970; editor: D. Cimarosa, Orazi e Curiazi, 1986, Storia della Musica in Venezia, 1987, Manuale di storia della musica, 4 vols., 1991-95; contbr. articles to music jours. Mem. Internat. Musicological Soc., Am. Musicological Soc., Italian Soc. Musicology (mem. exec. council 1976-79, 82-85). Roman Catholic. Avocation: collecting stamps. Home: Via dell'iride 5 61020 Candelara (Pesaro) Italy Office: G Rossini Conservatorio Musica Piazza Olivieri 61100 Pesaro Italy E-mail: elv.surian@libero.it.

SURIANI, RAYMOND JOSEPH, music educator; b. Hornell, NY, Sept. 3, 1960; s. Francis and Laura Suriani. BME in Music Edn., Mansfield (Pa.) U., 1982; MS in Music, Mansfield U., 1987. Cert. N.Y. Dept. Edn. Music 1987. Tchr., instrumental music Warsaw (N.Y.) H.S., 1982—. Dir. of dramatic activities, dir. of fine arts Warsaw (N.Y.) H.S. Dir., musician Geneseo Cmty. Players, Leroy Rotary Club, Genesee CC; dir., condr. Siena, Italy music festival, Italy, 1990—93. Recipient U. of Rochester Excellence in Secondary Tchg., U. of Rochester, Rochester Cmty. Savs. Bank, 1997. Mem.: Music Educators Nat. Conf., NY State Sch. Music Assn. Avocation: travel. Home: 16 Jacqueline Way Geneseo NY 14454 Office: Warsaw Ctrl HS 153 West Buffalo St Warsaw NY 14569 Personal E-mail: rsuriani@bigplanet.com.

SURKIN, ELLIOT MARK, lawyer; b. Phila., Apr. 22, 1942; s. Hersh M. and Minnie (Shore) S.; m. Carol E. Foley, May 26, 1973; 1 child, Jennifer Dykema. AB, Princeton U., 1964; LLB, Harvard U., 1967. Bar: Mass. 1967. Assoc. Hill & Barlow, P.C., Boston, 1967-73, mem., 1973—, chmn. mgmt. com., 1988-92, chmn. real estate dept., 1996-2001; mem. mgmt. com., 1980-84, 2001—. Lectr. law Harvard U., 1975-96, MIT, Ctr. for Real Estate, 1996—. Chmn. bd. Boston Ctr. Arts, 1972-81, dir., mem. exec. com., 1981-83, hon. dir., 1983—; clk., trustee, mem. exec. com. Wang Ctr. for Performing Arts, Boston, 1980—, mem. fin. com., 1995—, vice chmn. bd., 1997—; clk., mem. New Eng. com. Legal Def. Fund NAACP, 1976-93; chmn. standing com. Trustees of Reservations, 1997—, chmn. Chappaquiddick local com. 1986-97, trustee 1985—, mem. standing com. 1994—, mem. exec. com. 1996—; dir. Sheriff's Meadow Found., 1994-97. Mem. ABA, Am. Law Inst., Am. Coll. Real Estate Lawyers, Mass. Bar Assn., Boston Bar Assn., St. Botolph Club, Harvard Club of Boston, Edgartown Yacht Club, Country Club of Brookline, Mass. Home: 1784 Beacon St Waban MA 02468-1434 Office: Hill & Barlow PC One International Place Boston MA 02110-2600 E-mail: esurkin@hillbarlow.com.

SURKS, MARTIN I. medical educator, endocrinologist; b. N.Y.C., May 21, 1934; AB, Columbia U., 1956; MD, NYU, 1960. Diplomate Nat. Bd. Med. Examiners, Am. Bd. Internal Medicine, Am. Bd. Endocrinology and Metabolism; lic. physician, N.Y. State. Intern Montefiore Hosp., N.Y.C., 1960-61, jr. asst. resident in medicine, 1961-62; sr. asst. resident VA Hosp., Bronx, 1962-63; postdoctoral rsch. fellow Nat. Inst. Arthritis and Metabolic Diseases, 1963-64; assoc. in medicine Albert Einstein Coll. Medicine, Bronx, 1967-69, asst. prof. medicine, 1969-72, assoc. prof., 1972-78, prof., 1978—, assoc. prof. lab. medicine, 1978-85, prof., 1985—, prof. pathology, 1994—. Co-dir. endocrine rsch. lab. Montefiore Hosp., Bronx, 1969—76, head divsn. endocrinology and metabolism, 1976—96, dir. program divsn. endocrinology & metabolism, 1996—; attending N. Ctrl. Bronx Hosp., 1976—98, 2000—. Mem. editl. bd.: Endocrinology, 1974—78, mem. editl. bd.: Endocrine Rsch. Comm., 1974—, mem. editl. bd.: Am. Jour. Physiology: Endocrinology and MEtabolism, 1982—85, mem. editl. bd.: Jour. Clin. Endocrinal Metabolism, 1991—95, mem. editl. bd.: Thyroid, 2000—, assoc. editor: Endocrinology, 1986—87; contbr. articles to profl. jours. Capt. M.C., U.S. Army, 1964-66. Grantee U.S. Army, Am. Cancer Soc., USPHS, Nat. Cancer Inst.; Schering fellow, 1968. Fellow: ACP; mem.: AAAS, Am. Assn. Clin. Endocrinologists, Assn. Program Dirs. Endocrinology, Diabetes and Metabolism (coun. 1995—97, pres. 1997—99), Am. Soc. Cell Biology, Assn. Am. Physicians, Am. Soc. Clin. Investigation, Am. Physiology Soc., Harvey Soc., Am. Bd. Internal Medicine (sect. of endocrinology and metabolism 1987—95, chmn. 1991—95, bd. dirs. 1991—95), Am. Fedn. Clin. Rsch., N.Y. Zool. Soc., Endocrine Soc. (manpower liaison com. 1983—86, fin. com. 1994—, chmn. 1998—, internat. endocrine congress com. 1995—2000, mem. steering com. self-assessment program, editor endocrine self-assessment program 1997—), Am. Thyroid Assn. (program com. 1975—77, 2d v.p. 1976—77, chair membership com. 1977—78, 1980—81, dir. 1982—83, nominating com. 1982—85, chair awards and prizes com. 1983—84, dir. 1987—90, 1988—92, sec. 1993—98, pres.-elect 1998—99, pres. 1999—2000, past pres. 2000—01, chair pubs. com. 2001—, internat. coord. com. 2001—. Van Meter prize 1973), European Thyroid Assn. (corr.), Interurban Clin. Club (councilor 1987—89), Alpha Omega Alpha, Phi Beta Kappa. Office: Montefiore Med Ctr 111 E 210th St Bronx NY 10467-2401 E-mail: msurks@westnet.com.

SURLES, CAROL D. academic administrator; b. Pensacola, Fla., Oct. 7, 1946; d. Elza Allen and Versy Lee Smith; divorced; children: Lisa Surles, Philip Surles. BA, Fisk U., 1968; MA, Chapman Coll., 1971; PhD, U. Mich., 1978. Personnel rep. U. Mich., Ann Arbor, 1973-78, vice-chancellor-adminstrn. Flint, 1987-89; exec. asst. to pres., assoc. v.p. for human resources U. Ctrl. Fla., Orlando, 1978-87; v.p. acad. affairs Jackson State U., Miss., 1989-92; v.p. adminstrn. and bus. Calif. State U., Hayward, 1992-94; pres. Tex. Woman's U., Denton, 1994-99, Ea. Ill. U., Charleston, 1999—. Trustee Pub. Broadcasting Ch. 24, Orlando, 1985-87; bd. dirs. First State Bank, Denton, Tex., Tex.-N.Mex. Power Co., TNP-Enterprise. Recipient Outstanding Scholar's award Delta Tau Kappa, 1983. Mem. AAUW, Am. Assn. Colls. and Univs., Golden Key Honor Soc., Mortar Bd. Soc., Dallas Citizens' Coun., Dallas Women's Found., Coun. of Pres. (Austin, Tex.), Phi Kappa Phi, Alpha Kappa Alpha. Methodist. Avocation: playing piano and oboe. Office: Ea Ill U 600 Lincoln Ave Charleston IL 61920-3011

SURLES, RICHARD HURLBUT, JR. retired law librarian; b. Norfolk, Va., Mar. 28, 1943; s. Richard H. and Elda Florine (Belvin) S.; m. Judith Louise Coffin, May 29, 1964; children— Stephanie Anne, Richard H. BA, Tex. A&M U., 1963; JD, U.Houston, 1967; M.L.L., U.Wash., 1969. Bar: Colo. 1971. Asst. to law librarian U. Houston, 1966-68; asst. to law librarian King county Law Library, Seattle, 1968-69; dir. of law library, prof. law U. Denver, 1969-71, U. Tenn., Knoxville, 1971-76, U. Oreg., Eugene, 1976-81, U. Ill., Champaign, 1981-99, prof. libr. adminstrn., 1991; ret., 1998. Author: Legal Periodical Management Data, 1977 Mem. Am. Assn. Law Libraries Republican.

SURMAN, OWEN STANLEY, psychiatrist; b. Boston, Apr. 21, 1943; s. Aaron Harry and Edith Anne (Silver) S.; m. Lezlie Anne Humber, July 19, 1969 (dec. Nov. 5, 1994); children: Craig Bruce Hackett, Kathleen Bridget Lezlie. BSc with honors, McGill U., 1964, MD, CM, 1968. Diplomate Am. Bd. Psychiatry and Neurology. Intern Balt. City Hosp., 1968-69; clin. fellow in medicine Johns Hopkins U., Balt., 1968-69; resident in psychiatry Mass. Gen. Hosp., Boston, 1969-72; clin. fellow in psychiatry Harvard Med. Sch., 1969-72; clin. asst. in psychiatry Mass. Gen. Hosp., 1975-76, asst. in psychiatry, 1977-80, asst. psychiatrist, 1980-86, assoc. psychiatrist, 1986-89, psychiatrist, 1990—; instr. psychiatry Harvard U. Med. Sch., 1975-80, asst. prof., 1980-90, assoc. prof., 1990—. Psychiat. cons. Boston Ctr. Heart Transplant, 1988-94; mem. ethics com. Mass. Ctr. Organ Transplantation, 1988—; mem. subcom. Human Studies, Mass. Gen. Hosp., 1982—, acting chmn., 1996-97, co-vice-chmn., 1999-2001, cons. transplant unit, 1975—, vice-chmn. xenotransplant adv. com., 1997-98, living related partial liver donor oversight com., 2000—; mem. Inst. for Study of Smoking Behavior and Policy, John F. Kennedy Sch. Govt., 1982-89; vis. prof. Tokyo U., 2001; mem. N.Y. State Com. on Quality Improvement in Living Liver Donation, 2002. Contbr. articles and letters to profl. jours., chpts. to books. Bd. dirs. Unitarian-Universalist Area Ch., Sherborn, Mass., 1983-86, 93-96; advancement officer troop 1 Boy Scouts Am., Sherborn, 1983-91. Lt. comdr. M.C., USNR, 1972-75. Grantee Milton Fund, 1969-70, Upjohn Corp., 1982-84, Burroughs Wellcome Co., 1984-85, Eli Lily Corp., 1989, 90-92. Fellow Am. Psychiat. Assn., Am. Acad. Psychosomatic Medicine (ethics com., awards com. 1994-97); mem. AAAS, Mass. Med. Soc., Boston Bar Assn., N.Y. Acad. Scis., Johns Hopkins Med. and Surg. Soc., Mass. ACLU, Libr. of Boston Athenaeum, Ford Hall Forum, New Eng. Poetry Club. Republican. Avocation: creative writing. Office: Mass Gen Hosp Wang ACC 815 15 Parkman St Boston MA 02114 E-mail: osurman@partners.org.

SUROVELL, EDWARD DAVID, real estate company executive; b. Washington, Mar. 20, 1940; s. Samuel and Florence Deborah (Starfield) S.; m. Barbara Ann Bartelmes, Apr. 26, 1958 (div. Jan. 1974); children: David Alexander, Claire Katherine; m. Natalie A. Sallade, June 3, 1999. BA, Columbia U., 1962; postgrad., U. Mich., 1968-71. Lic. real estate broker, Mich. Copy editor Harcourt, Brace & World, Inc., N.Y.C., 1963-65; editor

Princeton (N.J.) U. Press, 1965-67, Scott, Foresman Co., Glenview, Ill., 1967-68, U. Mich., Ann Arbor, 1968-72; real estate agt. Fletcher & Klein, Inc., 1973-75; sales mgr. Charles Reinhart Co., 1975-82; pres. Edward Surovell Realtors, 1982—. Mem. Ann Arbor City Planning Commn., 1988-91, 95-98, Downtown Devel. Authority, Ann Arbor, 1991-95; trustee Ann Arbor Dist. Libr., 1996—; bd. dirs. Mich. Shakespeare Festival, 1999—, Jackson Symphony Orch., 2000—; mem. Mich. Bd. Profl. Cmty. Planners, 1988-92. Mem. Nat. Assn. Realtors, Hist. Soc. Mich. (trustee 1992—, v.p. 1996-97), Ann Arbor Area Bd. Realtors (v.p. 1984, pres. 1985, Realtor of Yr. 1990), Univ. Mus. Soc. (bd. dirs. 1992-98, trustee Mich. Ctr. for the Book 1998—). Avocations: book collecting, arts philanthropy. Home: 1000 Forest Rd Ann Arbor MI 48105-1047 Office: Edward Surovell Realtors 1884 W Stadium Blvd Ann Arbor MI 48103-4504 E-mail: esurovell@surovellrealtors.com.

SUROWIEC, ANDREW JULIUS, biophysicist, researcher; b. Lwów, Poland, Apr. 13, 1940; came to U.S., 1986; s. Jan Jakub and Maria (Knobloch) S.; m. Irene Regina Baranowski, Apr. 27, 1977; 1 child, Caroline Maria. Engr., Tech. U., Gliwice, Poland, 1962, MS, 1964; PhD, Silesian U., Katowice, Poland, 1972. Cert. elec. engring. Asst. prof. Silesien Sch. Medicine, Katowice, 1964-82; postdoctoral fellow Ctr. d'Etude L'Energie Nucleaire, Mol, Belgium, 1973-74; disting. vis. scientist U. Ottawa, Ont., Can., 1983-87; asst. prof. Bowman U. Sch. Medicine, Winston-Salem, N.C., 1987-88, U. So. Calif., L.A., 1988-93; sr. physicist Centennial Med. Ctr., Nashville, 1993—. Peer reviewer: Cancer, Internat. Jour. Am. Cancer Soc., 1993; contbr. articles to Physics in Medicine and Biology, Bioelectromagnetics, IEEE Transactions Biomed., Internat. Jour. Hyperthermia, Biopolymers, Jour. Chem. Soc. Faraday Transactions. Grantee Nat. Sci. and Engring. Rsch. Coun., 1985. Fellow Radiation Rsch. Soc.; mem. Internat. Clin. Hyperthermia Soc., N.Y. Acad. Scis. Achievements include patent for recording system for rotating viscometer; finding of simulated materials for electromagnetic studies and cancer treatment; findings of dielectric spectroscopy of normal and cancer tissues; finding of dielectric and hydrodynamic properties of DNA. Avocations: music, modern history, swimming. Home: 8209 Londonberry Rd Nashville TN 37221-4640 Office: Centennial Med Ctr Radiation Therapy 2300 Patterson St Nashville TN 37203-1528 E-mail: andsur@aol.com.

SURPLUS, ROBERT WILBUR, retired music educator; b. Scranton, Pa., Sept. 1, 1923; s. Willard K. and Olive T. (Wrightson) S.; m. Jean Craig, June 25, 1976; children: Amy, Melanie. BS, Susquehanna U., 1945; MA, Columbia U., 1947, EdD, 1968. Music tchr., Mineola, N.Y., 1945-46, Butler, N.J., 1946-47; music supr. Red Lion, Pa., 1947-56; assoc. prof. Shippensburg (Pa.) State U., 1956-58; music tchr. Fox Lane Sch., Bedford, N.Y., 1958-59; instr. Columbia U., N.Y.C., 1959-61; asst. prof. U. Minn., Mpls., 1961-65; prof. music Ea. Ky. U., Richmond, 1965-94; ret., 1994. Rsch. chmn., So. Div., Music Educators Nat. Conf., 1974-80, rsch. coun. mem., 1974-80; cons. Nat. Assn. Jr. Colls., 1973-75. Author: Follow the Leader, 1962, The Alphabet of Music, 1963, The Beat of the Drum, 1963, The Story of Musical Organizations, 1963; editor: A Guidebook for State Music Education Associations, 1985, Beyond the Classroom: Informing Others, 1987; contbr. articles to profl. jours. Bd. dirs. Ky. Citizens for Arts. Mem. Music Educators Nat. Conf. (pres. so. divsn. 1982-84), Ky. Music Educators Assn. (bd. dirs., pres. 1971-73, Disting. Svc. award 1983), Ky. Alliance for Arts Edn. (pres. 1974-82).

SURPRISE, JUANEE, chiropractor, nutrition consultant; b. Gary, Ind., Apr. 28, 1944; d. Glenn Mark and Willia Ross (Vasser) Surprise; m. Peter E. Coakley, Feb. 12, 1966 (div. Jan. 1976); children: Thaddeus, Mariah, Darius; m. Robert T.Howell, Feb. 24, 1984. RN, Phila. Gen. Hosp. Sch. Nursing, 1965; DrChiropractic summa cum laude, Life Chiropractic Coll, Marietta, Ga., 1981. Diplomate Nat. Bd. Chiropractic Examiners, Am. Chiropractic Bd. Nutrition, Am. Acad. Pain Mgmt.; bd. cert. naturopathic med. doctor; diplomate Am. Acad. Pain Mgmt.; cert. clin. nutritionist; cert. in acupuncture, Thompson technique, Nimmo receptor tonus technique. Staff nurse Children's Hosp., Balt., 1966-67; charge nurse Melrose (Mass.)-Wakefield Hosp., 1967-68; hosp. adminstr. Animal Hosp. of Wakefield, Mass., 1967-79; chiropractor Chiropractic Clinic of Greenville, N.C., 1982-84, Family Med.-Chiropractic Clinic, Denton, Tex., 1984—; dean Sch. Nutrition Quantum-Veritis Interant. Univ. Sys.; dir. Ctr. Clin. Sci., Parker Coll. Chiropractic, Dallas, 1996-97, dir. diplomate and certification programs, 1997-2000. Mem. postgrad. faculty Tex. Chriopractic Coll., Northwestern U. Health Scis. Mem., chmn. Cmty. Planning Commn., North Reading, Mass., 1976-79; chmn. bldg. com. Immaculate Conception Ch., Denton, 1987-90, parish coun., 1990-92; v.p. Property Owners Assn., 2000-02. Fellow Am. Chiropractic Coll. Nutrition; mem. Am. Assn. Pain Mgmt., Am. Chiropractic Assn., Am. Coun. on Nutrition (pres.), Am. Chiropractic Bd. on Nutrition (past pres.), Tex. Chiropractic Assn. (chair nutrition coms.), Pi Tau Delta. Republican. Roman Catholic. Avocations: maine coon cat breeding, health education, camping. Office: Family Med and Chiropractic Rehab Clinic 1100 Dallas Dr Denton TX 76205-5121 E-mail: doctormunda@hotmail.com.

SURRATT, JOHN RICHARD, lawyer; b. Winston-Salem, N.C., Aug. 7, 1928; s. Wade Talmage and Julia (Efird) S.; m. Estella Eason, Dec. 2, 1961; children: Margaret Virginia, Estella Elizabeth, Susan Efird. BS in Commerce, U. N.C., 1948; JD, Duke U., 1951. Bar: N.C. 1951. Pvt. practice, Winston-Salem, 1951—. Judge Mcpl. Ct. Winston-Salem; lectr. law Wake Forest U., Winston-Salem, 1976-80. Mayor City of Winston-Salem 1961-63, chmn. city planning bd., 1972-78; sec., mem. Forsyth County Dem. Exec. Com., N.C.; mem. bar candidate com. N.C. Bd. Law Examiners. Served to capt. USAR, 1951-53, Korea. Mem. ABA, N.C. Bar Assn., Forsyth County Bar Assn. (pres. 1984, exec. com. 1986), Rotary (pres. local chpt. 1983), Old Town Club, Twin City Club. Clubs: Old Town, Twin City. Lodges: Rotary (pres. local chpt. 1983). E-mail: jsurratt@surrattpa.com.

SURRENCY, GARY LAWRENCE, military officer; b. Blackshear, Ga., Jan. 14, 1953; s. Alfred Moses and Margaret Elizabeth Surrency; m. Millie Elizabeth Edwards-Rodriguez, June 5, 1993; children: Krystal, Brandon Witt-Surrency, Hosie Witt; m. Annette Wheeler, June 3, 1975 (div. Mar. 5, 1983); children: Gary L. Jr., James. Student, several instns., Hawaii, Fla., Alaska and Tex., 1976—94. Cert. drug and alcohol counselor. field recruiter U.S. Army, equal opportunity counselor, logistical specialist. Sgt. 1st class U.S. Army, Orlando, Fla., 1978—81, sta. comdr. Orange Pk., 1981—88, logistical support/ peace keeper Camp David accord Sinai, Israel, 1990—91. Vol. for disabled vets. rights, Jacksonville, Fla., N/A, 1994—2002. Co-author: (book) Fatal Friendship, 2002. Mentor for at risk youth, Jacksonville, 1994—2002; drug and alcohol counselor for youth, 1994—2002. Mem.: Am. Legion. Baptist. Avocations: travel, cooking. Office: 12469 Del Rio Dr Jacksonville FL 32258

SURREY, MILT, artist; b. N.Y.C., Mar. 18, 1922; s. Leopold and Pauline Schleifer; m. Eleanor Gallant, Sept. 15, 1946; children— Elaine, Robert, David. Student, Coll. City N.Y., 1939-42. Represented in permanent collections, Allentown (Pa.) Art Mus., Butler Inst. Am. Art, Youngstown, Ohio, Cin. Art Mus., Coll. Mus., Hampton (Va.) Inst., Columbia (S.C.) Mus. Art, Davenport (Iowa) Mus., Detroit Inst. Arts, Evansville (Ind.) Mus. Art, Hickory (N.C.) Mus. Art, Jacksonville (Fla.) Art Mus., Lowe Art Center, Syracuse (N.Y.) U., Massillon (Ohio) Mus., Miami (Fla.) Mus. Modern Art, Springfield (Mo.) Art Mus., Telfair Acad. Arts and Scis., Savannah, Ga., Holyoke (Mass.) Mus. Natural History, Theodore Lyman Wright Art Center, Beloit (Wis.) Coll., Treat Gallery, Bates Coll., Lewiston, Maine. Served with AUS, 1942-45. Mem. Am. Fedn. Arts. Home: 425 E 58th St New York NY 10022-2300

SURRIDGE, STEPHEN ZEHRING, lawyer, writer; b. N.Y.C., Dec. 12, 1940; s. Robert George and Florence Elizabeth (Zehring) S.; m. Helen Frances McKenna, Mar. 15, 1969; children: Christopher S., Jonathan R., Matthew W., Martha H. BA magna cum laude, Yale U., 1962; MBA (with distinction), JD, U. Mich., 1969. Bar: Wis. 1969, Mich. 1969. Assoc. Quarles & Brady, Milw., 1969-76, ptnr., 1977-89; freelance writer, tchr., 1990—. Author: (monograph) Seven Thunders of Revelation, 1985, Revelation Revisited, 1995. 1st lt. U.S. Army, 1963-65. Mem. Phi Beta Kappa. Mem. Christian Ch. Home: 4480 N Ardmore Ave Milwaukee WI 53211-1418

SURSO, JOHN MICHAEL, physician; b. Cleve., June 28, 1953; s. John J. and Julia S.; m. Mary Sue S., June 3, 1978; children: John Matthew, Jaclyn Michelle. BA in Bioilogy, Case Western Res. U., 1974; MD, Ohio State U., 1977. Intern, resident in family medicine Akron City Hosp., 1977—80; pvt. practice, Medina, Ohio, 1980—; chief of staff Medina Gen. Hosp., 1987-90; ptnr. Med. Cons. Bus., Medina, 1990—. Clin. asst. prof. family medicine N.E. Ohio U., Rootstown, 1990—; bd. dirs. Century Bank; lectr. in field. Trustee Medina Gen. Hosp., 1990-92; mem. bd. edn. Medina City Sch., 1993—, past pres. Fellow Am. Acad. Family Physicians, Ohio State Med. Assn. Republican. Byzantine Catholic. Avocations: computers, photography. Office: Family Medicine Assocs Medina 970 E Washington St Medina OH 44256 E-mail: jmsunso@aol.com.

SURVANT, JOE, English language educator, poet; b. Owensboro, Ky., Oct. 9, 1942; s. Joseph Wilbur Survant and Martha Elizabeth Magruder; m. Jeannie Ashley Survant, Sept. 4, 1965; children: Anastasia Ashley, Alexandra Durham. PhD, U. Del., 1970. Instr. English dept. U. Ky., Lexington, 1967-69; prof. English dept. Western Ky. U., Bowling Green, 1970—. Author: (poetry collections) We Will All Be Changed, 1995 (State St. Press Poetry Competition 1995), Anne & Alpheus, 1842-1882, 1996 (Ark. poetry award 1995), The Presence of Snow in the Tropics, 2001, Rafting Rise, 2002. Avocations: running, backpacking, fishing. Home: 762 Minnie Way Bowling Green KY 42101 Office: Western Ky U English Dept Bowling Green KY 42101 E-mail: joe.survant@wku.edu.

SURVILO, FRANCINE MARION, painter, sculptor; b. Toms River, N.J., Dec. 30, 1955; d. Victor and Marion Francis (Beardsley) S.; 1 child, Matthew. BFA, San Jose State U., 1998. Exhibited in group shows at Rosicrusian Mus., San Jose, Calif., 1989, Villa Montavlo, Saratoga, Calif., 1990, Pacific Art League, Palo Alto, Calif., 1996, Coos Art Mus., Coos Bay, Oreg., 1998. Home: 957 Webster St Palo Alto CA 94301

SURWIT, RICHARD SAMUEL, psychology educator; b. Bklyn., Oct. 7, 1946; s. David and Ethel S.; m. Sandra E. Cummings, May 23, 1982; children: Daniel Alan, Sarah Jeanne. AB, Earlham Coll., 1968; PhD, McGill U., Montreal, Que., Can., 1972; postgrad., Harvard U., Boston. Postdoctoral fellow Harvard Med. Sch., 1972-74, instr., 1974-76, asst. prof., 1976-77; assoc. prof. psychiatry Duke U. Med. Ctr., Durham, N.C., 1977-83, prof., 1980, 83—, vice chmn., 1993—; chief divsn. med. psychology Duke U., 1997, prof. psychology, 1991—; CEO ZyCare Inc. (formerly Healthware Corp.), Chapel Hill, 1983—. Author: Fear and Learning to Cope, 1978, Behavioral Approaches to Cardiovascular Diseases, 1982. Recipient rsch. devel. award NIMH, 1980, rsch. scientist award NIMH, 1993. Fellow APA, Soc. Behavioral Medicine (pres. 1994), Acad. Behavioral Medicine Rsch. Achievements include co-discovery in 1997, of UCP2, a novel gene related and diabetes and immunity; co-developer of the Diacare diabetes disease management system, Coag-Care anticoagulation management system. Home: 3804 Sweeten Creek Rd Chapel Hill NC 27514-9706 Office: Duke U Med Ctr PO Box 3842 Durham NC 27702-3842 E-mail: richard.surwit@duke.edu.

SURYANARAYANA, CHALLAPALLI, materials scientist, educator; b. Pedana, Andhra Pradesh, India, Mar. 20, 1945; s. Ramabrahmam and Kameswari; m. C. Meenakshi. BE in Metallurgy, Indian Inst. Sci., Bangalore, 1965; MS in Metall. Engring., Banaras Hindu U., Varanasi, India, 1967, PhD in Metall. Engring., 1970. Prof. metallurgy Banaras Hindu U., Varanasi, 1967—87; assoc. prof. materials U. Ctrl. Fla., Orlando, 2001—. Presenter in field. Author: (Operas) (textbook) X-Ray Diffraction: A Practical Approach, 1998; editor: (book) Non-equilibrium Processing of Materials, 1999; contbr. articles to profl. jours. Recipient Young Scientist medal, Indian Nat. Sci. Acad., 1975, National Metallurgists' Day award, Govt. India, 1983, Best Technical Paper award, Steel Authority India Ltd., 1993. Fellow: Inst. Materials London, Am. Soc. Materials Internat. (chmn. materials synthesis and processing com. 2000—); mem.: Minerals, Metals and Materials Soc. (sec. powder materials com. 2001—), Indian Inst. Metals (life Pandya Meml. medal 1973). Office: U Ctrl Fla Mech Materials & Aerospace Engring Orlando FL 32816-2450 Office Fax: 407-823-0208. Business E-Mail: csuryana@mail.ucf.edu.

SURYANARAYANAN, RAJ GOPALAN, researcher, consultant, educator; b. Cuddalore, Tamil Nadu, India, Apr. 19, 1955; came to U.S., 1985; s. Natesan and Pushpa (Subramanian) Rajagopalan; m. Shanti Venkateswaran, Nov. 24, 1985; children: Priya Mallika Sury, Meera Sindu Sury. B in Pharmacy, Banaras Hindu U., Varanasi, India, 1976, M in Pharmacy, 1978; MS, U. BC, Vancouver, Can., 1981, PhD, 1985. Mgmt. trainee Indian Drugs and Pharms. Ltd., Rishikesh, India, 1978; supr. Roche Products, Bombay, India, 1979; tchg. asst. U. B.C., Vancouver, Can., 1979, 82-83; asst. prof. pharmaceutics U. Minn., Mpls., 1985-92, assoc. prof., 1992-99, prof., 1999—, dir. grad. studies, 1994-98. Cons. numerous pharm. cos. in U.S., 1987—. Contbr. articles to profl. jours.; patentee quantitative analysis of intact tablets. Recipient numerous grants for rsch., U.S., 1985—. Mem. Am. Assn. Pharm. Scientists, Am. Assn. Colls. Pharmacy. Hindu. Avocations: Tamil literature, sports. Home: 1861 Moore St Saint Paul MN 55113-5530 Office: U Minn Coll of Pharmacy 308 Harvard St SE Minneapolis MN 55455-0353 E-mail: surya001@tc.umn.edu.

SUSAN, DONALD FRANCIS, materials scientist, researcher; b. Pottsville, Pa., Mar. 8, 1971; s. Frank D. and Dorothy J. (Cickavage) S. BA, Lehigh U., 1993, MS, 1995, PhD, 1999. Tech. staff Sandia Nat. Lab. Mem. Am. Soc. Materials, Sigma Xi. Roman Catholic. Avocations: softball, music, reading. Home: 11005 Kaibab Rd SE Albuquerque NM 87123 E-mail: dfsusan@sandia.gov.

SUSANKA, SARAH HILLS, architect; b. Bromley, Kent, England, Mar. 21, 1957; d. Brian and Margaret (Hampson) Hills; m. Lawrence A. Susanka, July 4, 1980 (div. May 1984); m. James Robert Larson, Sept. 4, 1988 (div. Jan. 2000); m. Alfred B. Urzi, May 7, 2001. BArch, U. Oreg., 1978; MArch, U. Minn., 1983. Registered architect. Founding prin. Mulfinger, Susanka, Mahady & Ptnrs., Mpls., 1983-99; founder Susanka Studios, Raleigh, NC, 1999—. Author: The Not So Big House, 1998, Creating the Not So Big House, 2000, Not So Big Solutions for Your Home, 2002; columnist Fine Homebuilding mag. Mem. AIA. Office: 2600 Salisbury Pln Raleigh NC 27613-4331 E-mail: ssusanka@notsobighouse.com.

SUSCOVICH, DAVID J. neuropsychologist, marriage and family therapist; b. Mt. Pleasant, Pa., Sept. 20, 1952; s. Joseph Anthony and Helen G. Suscovich; m. Edith P. Suscovich, May 23, 1980 (dir. Sept. 15, 2001); children: Joseph Alfred, John David, Mark Andrew. BS/BA in Psychology and Sociology, U. Pitts., 1973, postgrad., 1974; MA in Marriage and Family Therapy, U. Conn., 1977; PsyD in Clin. Psychology, Antioch New Eng., 1997. Cert. marriage family therapist AAMFT, Conn., diplomate Am. Coll. Forensic Examiners, Nat. Bd. Addiction Examiners. Psychiat. clinician psychiatry dept. Waterby (Conn.) Hosp., 1974—80; pvt. practice individual and marriage and family therapy Naugatuck, 1987—. Clin. cons. Waterby Youth Svcs., Inc., 1988—, Salvation Army Youth Shelter, Waterby, 1995—; clin. neuropsychology examiner Conn. Resource Group, LLC, Waterby, 1988—, Conn. Edn. Svcs., Middletown, 2001—; mental health cons. Danby (Conn.) Head Start, Conn., 1994—97; adj. faculty So. Conn. State U., New Haven, 1992—, Yale U., New Haven, 2002—; full adj. prof., adj. Ctrl. Conn. State U., New Britain, Conn., 1994—; presenter in field. Weeblos Cub Scout leader Boy Scouts Am. Pack 110, Naugatuck, 1989—98; troop com. mem. Boy Scouts Am. Troop 109, 1997—. Mem.: Conn. Assn. Marriage and Family Therapy (chair state election com. 2002—), Phi Kappa Phi. Democrat. Roman Catholic. Achievements include research in negative neurophysiological effects of stress on children and teens delaying development of executive brain functions; neurofeed back training for brain disorders. Avocations: camping, canoeing, fishing, woodworking, music. Home: 23 May St Naugatuck CT 06770 Office: 16 Orchard St Naugatuck CT 06770

SUSI, ANTHONY J, music educator, composer; b. Meriden, Conn., Jan. 11, 1963; s. Enio John and Constance Felicia Susi; m. Susan Eve Rubinstein, June 25, 1988; children: Nicholas Andrew, Jeremy Alan. BM, U. Hartford, West Hartford, CT, 1985; MM, U. Conn., Storrs, CT, 1990. Cert. Beginning Educator Support and Training CT State Dept Edn., 1993. Band dir. Region Dist. #17, Higganum, Conn., 1985—86, Bennet Jr High/Mid. Sch., Manchester, 1986—97; dir. and instr. Manchester Summer Music Camp, 1987—97; jazz band dir. Somers H.S., Somers, 1995—96; jr jazz band dir. Manchester CC, Manchester, 1995—; dir. and instr. Coventry Summer Music Camp, Coventry, 1998—2001; band dir. Coventry H.S., 1997—. Festival chmn. Conn. Music Edn. Assn., Eastern Region, Conn., 1994—96; adjudicator Colchester Mid. Sch. Jazz Fest, Colchester, Conn., 1997—99; composer, pub. Susi Music Co., Vernon, Conn., 1999—. Contbr. articles to profl. jour. Recipient Disting. Band Dir., Am. Sch. Band Directors Assn., 1997, Up and Coming Music Tchr., Music Educators Nat. Conf., 2000. Mem.: Conn. Songwriters Assn., Am. Sch. Band Directors Assn., Phi Beta Mu Band Masters Frat. Roman Catholic. Avocations: backpacking, graphic art. Home: 51 Hillside Ave Vernon Rockville CT 06066 Office Fax: 860-742-4591.

SUSKIND, SIGMUND RICHARD, microbiology educator; b. N.Y.C., June 19, 1926; s. Seymour and Nina Phillips S.; m. Ann Parker, July 1, 1951; children: Richard, Mark, Steven. AB, NYU, 1948; PhD, Yale U., 1954. Research asst. biology div. Oak Ridge Nat. Lab., 1948-50; USPHS fellow NYU Med. Sch., N.Y.C., 1954-56; mem. faculty Johns Hopkins U., Balt., 1956—, prof. biology, 1965-96, univ. prof., 1983-96, prof. emeritus, 1996—, Univ. ombudsman, 1988-91, dean grad. and undergrad. studies, 1971-78, dean Sch. Arts and Scis., 1978-83. Head molecular biology sect. NSF, 1970-71; cons. NIH, 1966-70, Coun. Grad. Schs., Mid States Assn. Colls. and Secondary Schs., 1973—, NSF, 1986; vis. scientist Weizmann Inst. of Sci., Israel, 1985; trustee Balt. Hebrew U., 1985-93; mem. adv. bd. La. Geriatric Ctr., 1990—. Author: (with P.E. Hartman) Gene Action, 1964, 69, (with P.E. Hartman and T. Wright) Principles of Genetics Laboratory Manual, 1965; editor: (with P.E. Hartman) Foundations of Modern Genetics series, 1964, 69; mem. sci. editorial bd. Johns Hopkins U. Press, 1973-76, 88-91. With USNR, 1944-46. NIH grantee, 1957-76 Fellow AAAS; mem. Am. Soc. Microbiology, Genetics Soc. Am., Am. Assn. Immunology, Am. Soc. Biol. Chemistry and Molecular Biology, Coun. Grad Schs., Assn. Grad. Schs., Northeastern Assn. Grad. Schs. (exec. com. 1975-76, pres. 1977-78). Avocations: research in microbial biochemical genetics and immunogenetics. Office: Johns Hopkins U Dept Biology and McCollum-Pratt Inst 34th and Charles Sts Baltimore MD 21218

SUSKO, CAROL LYNNE, lawyer, accountant; b. Washington, Dec. 5, 1955; d. Frank and Helen Louise (Davis) S. BS in Econs. and Acctg., George Mason U., 1979; JD, Cath. U., 1982; LLM in Taxation, Georgetown U., 1992. Bar: Pa. 1989, D.C. 1990; CPA, Va., Md. Tax acct. Reznick Fedder & Silverman, P.C., Bethesda, Md., 1984-85; sr. tax acct. Pannell Kerr Forster, Alexandria, Va., 1985; tax specialist Coopers & Lybrand, Washington, 1985-87; supervisory tax sr. Frank & Co., McLean, Va., 1987-88; mem. editl. staff Tax Notes Mag., Arlington, 1989-90; adj. faculty Am. U., Washington, 1989—; tax atty. Marriott Corp., 1993-94; sr. tax mgr. Host Marriott Inc., 1994-99, KPMG LLP, McLean, Va., 1999—. Mem. ABA, AICPAs, Va. Soc. CPAs, D.C. Soc. CPAs, D.C. Bar Assn. Office: KPMG LLP Ste 3064 1660 International Dr Mc Lean VA 22102-4832 E-mail: csusko@kpmg.com.

SUSLA, JEFFREY JONATHAN, English language educator; b. Bridgeport, Conn., Oct. 30, 1958; s. Nicholas Jonathan and Betty Irene (Stavnitzky) S.; m. Patricia Anne Plumb, June 25, 1995. BA in English and History, Wesleyan U., 1982; MALS, Dartmouth Coll., 1991. English tchr. U.S Peace Corps, Illassit, Kenya, 1988-89, Woodstock (Conn.) Acad., 1993—. Co-advisor Woodstock Acad. Student Coun., 1995—; dir. Woodstock Acad. Theatre, 1994, 96; mem. supt. search com. Town of Woodstock, 1995. Fellowship Conn. Writing Project U. Conn., 1994, Nat. Endowment for the Humanities, 1996, Fulbright Meml. Fund., Japan, 1997, Tchg. Excellence award, Kazakhstan, 1998; named Educator of Yr. 21st Century Newspaper, 1996. Avocations: reading, travel. Home: PO Box 27 Woodstock CT 06281-0027 E-mail: jsusla@snet.net.

SUSLICK, KENNETH SANDERS, chemistry educator; b. Chgo., Sept. 16, 1952; s. Alvin and Edith Suslick. BS with honors, Calif. Inst. Tech., 1974; PhD, Stanford U., 1978. Rsch., teaching asst. Stanford (Calif.) U., 1974-78; chemist Lawrence Livermore (Calif.) Lab., 1974-75; asst. prof. U. Ill., Urbana, 1978-84, assoc. prof., 1984-88, prof. of chemistry, 1988—, Alumni Rsch. Scholar prof., 1995-97; prof. Beckman Inst. for Advanced Sci. and Tech., 1989-92; prof. of materials sci. and engring. U. Ill., 1993—, William H. and Janet Lycan prof. chemistry, 1997—; founder, CEO ChemSensing, Inc., 2001—. Vis. fellow Balliol Coll., Inorganic Chemistry Lab., Oxford (Eng.) U., 1986; cons. in field. Editor: High Energy Processes in Organometallic Chemistry, 1987, Ultrasound: Its Chemical, Physical and Biological Effects, 1988, Comprehensive Supramolecular Chemistry, vol. 5, 1996; co-editor: Sonochemistry and Sonoluminescence, 1999; editl. bd. Ultrasonics, 1992-96, Ultrasonic Sonochemistry, 1996—; patentee isotope separation by photochromatography, protein microspheres, drug delivery, blood substitutes, smell-seeing, artificial olfaction; contbr. articles to profl. jours. Fellow DuPont Found., 1979-80, Sloan Found., 1985-87; recipient Rsch. Career Devel. award NIH, 1985-90, NSF Spl. Creativity award 1992-94, Material Rsch. Soc. medal, 1994. Fellow AAAS, Am. Acoustical Soc. Royal Soc. Arts, Mfrs. and Commerce (Silver medal 1974); mem. Am. Chem. Soc. (chmn. sect. 1987-89, Nobel Laureate Signature award 1994). Avocations: sculpting, folk music. Office: U Ill Dept Chemistry 600 S Mathews Ave Urbana IL 61801-3602 E-mail: ksuslick@uiuc.edu.

SUSLICK, RANDALL HUGH, family practice physician; b. San Diego, May 14, 1947; s. Alphonse Donald and Claire Edith (Smith) S. BA, U. Va., 1969; MD, Med. Coll. Va., 1973. Ptnr. physician Dominion Health Med. Assocs., Chase City, Va., 1980-81, ptnr., 1981—, lab. dir., 1990—96; assoc. prof. dept. family practice VCU, MCV, 2002. Bd. dirs. Southside AHEC, Farmville, Va., 1993-98. Served with U.S. Navy, 1973-80. Mem. AMA, Med. Soc. Va., Southside Va. Med. Soc. (pres. 1988), Am. Acad. Family Physicians, Va. Acad. Family Physicians, Southside Va. Acad. Family Physicians (pres. 1994), Lions Club Chase City (pres. 1995-96, 98-99). Baptist. Avocations: snow skiing, water sports, white-water canoeing, wood working, hunting. Office: Dominion Health Med Assocs. PO Box 579 Chase City VA 23924-0579

SUSLOW, VALERIE YVONNE, economist, educator; b. San Francisco, Feb. 22, 1958; d. Sidney and Adele (Wasserstein) S. BA with cert. of distinction, U. Calif., Berkeley, 1979; PhD, Stanford U., 1984. Vis. asst. prof. Dept. Econs. Brown U., Providence, 1984; asst. prof. Sch. Bus. U. Mich., Ann Arbor, 1984-92; prof. sch. bus. U. Mich., 1992—. Faculty rsch. fellow Nat. Bur. Econ. Rsch., 1991—; co-investigator market rsch. Warner-Lambert, Inc., 1990-91. Contbr. articles and reviews to profl. jours. Mem. Commn. for Status of Women in Econs. Profession. Named John M. Olin Nat. fellow Hoover Instn., Stanford U., 1987-88. Mem. Am. Econ. Assn.

SUSMAN, MILLARD, geneticist, educator; b. St. Louis, Sept. 1, 1934; s. Albert and Patsy Ruth S.; m. Barbara Beth Fretwell, Aug. 18, 1957; children: Michael K., David L. AB, Washington U., St. Louis, 1956; PhD, Calif. Inst. Tech., 1962. With microbial genetics research unit Hammersmith Hosp., London, 1961-62; asst. prof. genetics U. Wis., Madison, 1962-66, assoc. prof., 1966-72, prof., 1972—2002, prof. emeritus, 2002—, chmn. lab. genetics, 1971-75, 77-86, assoc. dean med. sch., 1986-95, acting dean Sch. Allied Health Professions, 1988-90, vice dean med. sch., 1994-95, spl. advisor to the dean med. sch., 1995; dir. Ctr. for Biology Edn., Madison, 1996—2002. Phage course instr., Cold Spring Harbor, N.Y., 1965; v.p. scis., Wis. Acad. Scis., Arts and Letters, 2000—. Co-author: Life on Earth, 2d edit., 1978, Human Chromosomes: Structure, Behavior, Effects, 3d edit., 1992; contbr. articles to sci. jours. Mem Genetics Soc. Am., AAAS, Sigma Xi, Phi Beta Kappa, Phi Eta Sigma, Omicron Delta Kapp. Home: 2707 Colgate Rd Madison WI 53705-2234 Office: 507 Genetics Blvd Madison WI 53706 E-mail: msusman@factstaff.wisc.edu.

SUSMAN, MORTON LEE, lawyer; b. Aug. 6, 1934; m. Nina Meyers, May 1, 1958; 1 child, Mark Lee. BBA, So. Meth. U., 1956, JD, 1958. Bar: Tex. 1958, U.S. Dist. Ct. (so. dist.) Tex. 1961, U.S. Ct. Appeals (5th cir.) 1961, U.S. Supreme Ct. 1961, U.S. Ct. Appeals (11th cir) 1981, D.C. 1988, U.S. Ct. Appeals (D.C. cir.) 1988, N.Y. 1990, Colo. 1996. Asst. U.S. atty., Houston, 1961-64; 1st asst. U.S. atty., 1965-66; U.S. atty., 1966-69; ptnr. Weil, Gotshal & Manges and predecessor firm Susman & Kessler, Houston, 1969-97; ret., 1998. Lt. USNR, 1958-61. Fellow Am. Coll. Trial Lawyers, Tex. Bar Found.; mem. ABA, FBA (dir., Younger Fed. Lawyer award 1968), Tex. Bar Assn. Democrat. Home: 1000 Uptown Park Blvd Ste 151 Houston TX 77056-3247

SUSMAN, ROBERT M(ARK), lawyer; b. St. Louis, Jan. 15, 1951; s. Bernard and Lorraine (Abramson) S.; m. Shelby Zarick; children: Jane, Stephanie. BA, Ind. U., 1973; JD, St. Louis U., 1976. Bar: Mo. 1976, U.S. Dist. Ct. (ea. dist.) Mo. 1976, U.S. Supreme 1994. Ptnr. Goffstein, Raskas, Pomerantz, Kraus, Sherman, L.L.C., St. Louis, 1976—. Mem. ATLA (basic course trial advocacy Nat. Coll. Advocacy 1983), Mo. Assn. Trial Attys., Lawyers Assn. St. Louis (pres. 1988-89), Met. Bar Assn. St. Louis. Office: 7701 Clayton Rd Saint Louis MO 63117-1301

SUSMAN, STEPHEN DAILY, lawyer; b. Houston, Jan. 20, 1941; m. Ellen Spencer, 1999; children: Stacy, Harry. BA magna cum laude, Yale U., 1962; LL.B. summa cum laude, U. Tex. Austin, 1965. Bar: Tex. 1965, D.C. 1999, U.S. Supreme Ct. 1960. Law clk. U.S. Ct. Appeals (5th cir.), New Orleans, 1965-66, U.S.Supreme Ct., Washington, 1966-67; ptnr. Fulbright & Jaworski, 1966-75; spl. counsel to atty. gen. Austin, Tex., 1975, Mandell & Wright, 1975-80; sr. ptnr. Susman Godfrey, Houston, 1980—. Vis. prof. law U. Tex., Austin, 1975; chmn. adv. com. on discovery Tex. Supreme Ct. Contbr. articles to profl. jours. Bd. dirs. Contemporary Arts Mus., 1988-94, 98—, Yale Art Gallery, 1998—, Yale Devel. Fund, Southwest Legal Found., Inns of Ct., Houston Grand Opera, 1998—, Phoenix House, Lawyers Com. for Human Rights, 1998—; mem. U.S. Holocaust Meml. Coun., 2000— (devel. comm.), Million Dollar Advocates Forum, (life), 2000—; others. Recipient ADL Jurisprudence award, 1995; named one of Best Trial Lawyers in Am., Nat. Law Jour., 1989; named Best Litigator in World, Comml. Litigation. Mem. ABA (antitrust sect., mem. coun. litigation sect., chmn. task force on fast track litigation), Houston Bar Assn., Dallas Bar Assn., State Bar Tex., Am. Law Inst., Assn. Trial Lawyers Am., Am. Bar Trial Advocates, Houston Bar Assn., Southwestern Legal Found. Rsch. Fellows, Yale Club (Houston, N.Y.C.), Houston Trial Lawyers Assn. (dir.), Tex. Assn. Civil Trial and Appellate Specialists (former pres., dir.), Houston Club, Houstonian Club, Petroleum Club (Dallas), Quinnipiac Club (New Haven), Order of the Coif, Friars, Phi Delta Phi. Avocations: jogging, hiking. Office: Ste 5100 1000 Louisiana St Houston TX 77002-5091

SUSSBERG, MILTON JOEL, marketing professional; b. New Rochelle, N.Y., Oct. 5, 1949; s. Darwin Ralph and Carol G Sussberg; m. Linda Aland, June 27, 1971; children: Matthew H, Jordan A. BBA with distinction, U. Wis., Madison, 1971; MBA, Columbia U., 1973. Car. mktg. & sales Pearl-Wick Corp., Long Island City, N.Y., 1973-76; v.p. M. Ware Assocs., N.Y.C., 1976-79, Meteor/SKelly, Inc., Stamford, Conn., 1979-84; pres. Robot-Coupe Internat., Norwalk, 1984-86; CEO, founder Sussberg & Co., Inc., White Plains, N.Y., 1986—; owner Savannah (Ga.) Sand Gnats Baseball Club, 1991—; pres. Pearl-Wick LLC, Wallingford, Conn., 2000—. Adj. prof. mktg. Fordham U., Bronx, NY, 1996—99; mem. adv. coun. Thermoscan, San Diego, 1991—95, Sonicare Inc, Seattle, 1996—98. Mem.: Trump Nat. Golf Club, Phi Kappa Phi. Avocations: golf, skiing. Office: Sussberg & Co Inc Ste 308W 701 Westchester Ave White Plains NY 10604

SUSSE, SANDRA SLONE, lawyer; b. Medford, Ma., June 1, 1943; d. James Robert and Georgie Coffin (Bradshaw) Slone; m. Peter Susse, May 10, 1969 (div. May 1993); 1 child, Toby. BA, U. Mass., 1981; JD, Vt. Law Sch., 1986. Bar: Mass. 1986, U.S. Dist. Ct. Mass. 1988, U.S. Ct. Appeals (1st cir.) 1995. Staff atty. Western Mass. Legal Svcs., Springfield, 1986—. Mem. ABA, Women's Bar Assn. Mass. Avocations: hiking, German literature, films, skating. Address: Western Mass Legal Serv 127 State St Fl 4 Springfield MA 01103-1905 E-mail: ssusse@wmls.org.

SUSSKIND, CHARLES, engineering educator, writer, publishing executive; b. Prague, Czech Republic; came to U.S., 1945, naturalized, 1946; s. Bruno Bronislav and Gertruda (Seger) S.; m. Teresa Gabriel, May 1, 1945; children: Pamela Susskind Pettler, Peter Gabriel, Amanda Frances. Student, City U., London, 1939-40; BS, Calif. Inst. Tech., 1948; M in Engring., Yale U., 1949, PhD, 1951. Rsch. asst. Yale U., 1949-51; rsch. assoc. Stanford U., 1951-55, lectr., asst. dir. microwave lab., 1953-55; faculty U. Calif., Berkeley, 1955—, prof., 1964-91, prof. emeritus, 1991—; asst. dean U. Calif. Coll. Engring., 1964-68; statewide adminstr. U. Calif., 1969-74. Vis. prof. U. London, 1961-62, U. Geneva, Switzerland, 1968-69; cons. EPA Sci. Adv. Bd., 1982-92; bd. dirs. San Francisco Press, Inc. Author: (with M. Chodorow) Fundamentals of Microwave Electronics, 1964; (with L. Schell) Exporting Technical Education, 1968, Understanding Technology, 1973, 74, 85 (transl. into Dutch, French, Italian, Korean, Spanish, Indian edit. in English), Twenty-Five Engineers and Inventors, 1976; (with F. Kurylo) Ferdinand Braun, 1981; (with M.E. Rowbottom) Electricity and Medicine: History of their Interaction, 1984, Janáček and Brod, 1985, Heinrich Hertz: A Short Life, 1995; editor: (with M. Hertz) Heinrich Hertz: Memoirs, Letters, Diaries, bilingual edit., 1977; editor-in-chief Ency. Electronics, 1962. With USAAF, 1942-45. Named to Hon. Order Ky. Cols. Fellow IEEE; mem. AAAS, Histor of Sci. Soc., Soc. for History of Tech., Instn. Elec. Engrs. (London), Sigma Xi (pres. Berkeley chpt. 1972-73), Tau Beta Pi. Office: U Calif Coll Engring Berkeley CA 94720-0001

SUSSKIND, LAWRENCE ELLIOTT, urban and environmental planner, educator, mediator; b. N.Y.C., Jan. 12, 1947; s. David J. and Marjorie H. (Friedman) S.; m. Miriam Mason, June 8, 1968 (div. Dec. 1982); m. Leslie Webster Tuttle, Dec. 12, 1982; children: Noah Gates, Lily Webster. AB in Sociology, Columbia U., 1968; M.C.P., MIT, 1970, PhD in Urban Planning, 1973. Asst. prof. urban and environ. planning MIT, Cambridge, 1971-74, assoc. prof., 1974-82, prof., 1982-95, Ford prof., 1995—, head dept., 1978-82, dir. MIT-Harvard Pub. Disputes Program, 1980—; exec. dir. program on negotiation Harvard U. Law Sch., 1984-87; visiting prof. law Harvard Law Sch., 2001—. Pres. Consensus Bldg. Inst., 1993—. Author: Paternalism, Conflict and Co-Production, 1983, Proposition 1 1/2; Its Impact on Massachusetts, 1983, Resolving Environmental Regulatory Disputes, 1983, Breaking the Impasse, 1987, Environmental Diplomacy, 1994, Reinventing Congress for the 21st Century, 1995, Dealing With an Angry Public, 1996, Consensus Building Handbook, 1999, Negotiating on Behalf of Others, 1999, Negotiating Environmental Agreements, 1999, Better Environmental Policy Studies, 2001, Transboundary Environmental Negotiation, 2002; sr. editor, founder Environ. Impact Assessment Rev., 1980-96; editl. policy bd. Negotiation Jour., 1984—. Mem. Am. Inst. Cert. Planners, Assn. for Conflict Resolution. Jewish. Home: 32 Jericho Hill Rd Southborough MA 01772-1007 Office: MIT 9-330 Cambridge MA 02139 E-mail: susskind@mit.edu.

SUSSKIND, TERESA GABRIEL, publishing executive; b. Watford, Eng., Aug. 15, 1921; came to U.S., 1945; d. Aaron and Betty (Fox) Gabriel; m. Charles Susskind, May 1, 1945; children: Pamela Pettler, Peter Gabriel, Amanda. Ed., U. London, 1938-40. Profl. libr. Calif. Inst. Tech., Pasadena, 1946-48, Yale U., New Haven, 1948-51, Stanford (Calif.) U., 1951-52, SRI Internat., Menlo Park, Calif., 1953; founder, pres. San Francisco Press, Inc., 1959—. Active in cultural affairs; bd. govs. San Francisco Symphony, 1986-89. With Women's Royal Naval Svc., 1943-45. With Women's Royal Naval Svc., 1943-45. Mem. Town and Gown Club (Berkeley, Calif.; pres. 1984-85). Office: PO Box 426800 San Francisco CA 94142-6800

SUSSMAN, ALEXANDER RALPH, lawyer; b. Bronx, N.Y., Sept. 24, 1946; s. Herman R. and Claire (Blumenson) S.; m. Edna Rubin, Mar. 24, 1973; children: Jason, Carl, Matthew, Eric. AB cum laude, Princeton U., 1968; JD, Yale U., 1972. Bar: N.Y. 1973, U.S. Dist. Ct. (so. and ea. dists) N.Y. 1974, U.S. Ct. Appeals (2d, 3d, 5th, 6th, 8th and 10th cirs.) 1983, U.S. Supreme Ct. Law clk. to Hon. Constance Baker Motley U.S. Dist. Ct., N.Y.C., 1972-73; assoc. Cravath, Swaine & Moore, 1974-76, Fried, Frank, Harris, Shriver & Jacobson, N.Y.C., 1977-79, ptnr., 1979—. Author: (with A. Fleischer, Jr.) Responses to Takeover Bids, 2000, Takeover Defense, 2 vols., 2002; editor Yale Law Jour., 1971-72. Mem. N.Y. Lawyers for Pub. Interest, 1983—, mem. exec. com., bd. dirs., 1983—; bd. dirs., mem. exec. com. Legal Aid Soc., 1987-93. Fulbright scholar U. Bordeaux, 1969. Mem. ABA, Am. Law Inst., N.Y. State Bar Assn., Assn. of Bar of City of N.Y. (fed. cts. com. 1984-87, jud. com. 1987-90, chmn. legal assistance com. 1988-91, Marden lectr. com. 1991-94, chmn. mergers and acquisitions com. 1995-99). Home: 20 Oak Ln Scarsdale NY 10583-1627 Office: Fried Frank Harris Shriver & Jacobson 1 New York Plz Fl 25 New York NY 10004-1980 E-mail: Alex.Sussman@ffhsj.com.

SUSSMAN, ARTHUR MELVIN, law educator, foundation administrator; b. Bklyn., Nov. 17, 1942; m. Rita Padnick; children: Eric, Johanna. BS, Cornell U., 1963; JD magna cum laude, Harvard U., 1966. Bar: N.Y. 1967, Ill. 1970. Assoc. atty. Cahill, Gordon, Reindel & Ohl, N.Y.C., 1966-67; from assoc. atty. to ptnr. Jenner & Block, Chgo., 1970-77; legal counsel So. Ill. U., Carbondale, 1977-79; gen. counsel, v.p. U. Chgo., 1979-84, gen. counsel, v.p. adminstrn., 1984-2001, lectr. law Grad. Sch. Bus., 1986-94, master Broadview Hall, 1986-87, resident master Woodward Ct., 1987-92, bd. dirs. Lab. Schs., 1985-01; law school lecturer, 1998—; v.p. & sec. John D and Catherine T MacArthur Found., 2001—. Exec. dir. Borman Commn., U.S. Mil. Acad., 1976; chmn., bd. dirs. Ency. Brit., Inc., 1995-96; presenter in field. Contr. articles to profl. jours. Mem. Ill. Sec. of State's Com. on Not-for-Profit Corp. Act, 1984-85; chair regional selection panel Harry S. Truman Scholarship Found.; bd. dirs. Chapin Hall for Children, 1986—. Capt. JAGC, U.S. Army, 1967-70. Fulbright fellow, London, 1987. Mem. Nat. Assn. Coll. and Univ. Attys., Am. Coun. Edn. Office: The MacArthur Foundation 140 S Dearborn St Chicago IL 60603 E-mail: asussman@macfound.org.

SUSSMAN, BARRY, author, public opinion analyst and pollster, journalist; b. N.Y.C., July 10, 1934; s. Samuel and Esther (Rosen) S.; m. Peggy Earhart, Jan. 20, 1962; children: Seena, Shari. BA, Bklyn. Coll., 1956. Reporter Herald Courier, Bristol, Va., 1960-62, mng. editor, 1962-65; editor Washington Post, 1965-69, city editor, 1970-73, spl. Watergate editor, 1972-74, pollster, pub. opinion analyst, 1975-87; co-founder, co-dir. Washington Post-ABC News poll, 1981-87; columnist Washington Post Nat. Weekly, 1983-87; mng. editor nat. affairs UPI, Washington, 1987; ind. pub. opinion analyst and pollster, 1988—. Adv. bd. Innovation news media cons. group, 1994—. Author: The Great Coverup: Nixon and the Scandal of Watergate, 1974, What Americans Really Think, 1988, (with Lowell P. Weicker, Jr.) Maverick, 1995; editor: (with J.A. Giner) Innovations in Newspapers: The 1999 Global Report, 1999, The 2000 Global Report, 2000, The 2001 Global Report, 2001, 2002. Recipient Drew Pearson award for Nat. Reporting, 1972, 1st Prize award Washington Newspaper Guild, 1973, Editor of Yr. award Washington Newspaper Guild, 1973. Mem. Am. Assn. for Pub. Opinion Rsch. (exec. coun. 1985-87). Jewish. Avocation: chess. E-mail: bsussman@his.com.

SUSSMAN, BRIAN JAY, meteorologist, weather broadcaster; b. L.A., Apr. 3, 1956; s. Alan E. and Beverly A. (Carlson) S.; m. Sue Ann Rittenhouse, June 18, 1978; chilren: Elisa, Samuel, Benjamin. BS, U. Mo., 1978. Reporter, anchor Sta. KCBJ-TV, Columbia, Mo., 1977-80; weather anchor Sta. KOLO-TV, Reno, 1980-83; on-air meteorologist Sta. KNTV-TV, San Jose, Calif., 1983-87, Sta. KDKA-TV, Pitts., 1987-89; substitute weatherman CBS This Morning, N.Y.C., 1988-93; on-air meteorologist Sta. KPIX-TV, San Francisco, 1989—. Co-author: (textbook) For Spacious Skies, 1987, rev. edit., 1989. Recipient Best Weathercast award Radio-TV News Dirs. Assn., 1987, 90-95, 97-99, AP, 1989, 90-99, Advancement of Learning Through Broadcasting award NEA, 1989. Mem. Am. Meteorol. Soc. (Seal of Approval cert.). Avocations: pub. speaking, adult ice-hockey. Office: Sta KPIX-TV 855 Battery St San Francisco CA 94111-1503

SUSSMAN, DEBORAH EVELYN, designer, company executive; b. N.Y.C., May 26, 1931; d. Irving and Ruth (Golomb) S.; m. Paul Prejza, June 28, 1972. Student, Bard Coll., 1948-50, DHL (hon.), 1998; student, Inst. Design, Chgo., 1950-53, Black Mountain Coll., 1950, Hochschule für Gestaltung Ulm, Germany, 1957-58. Art dir. Office of Charles and Ray Eames, Venice, Calif., 1953-57, 61-67; graphic designer Galeries Lafayette, Paris, 1959-60; prin. Deborah Sussman and Co., Santa Monica, Calif., 1968-80; founder, pres. Sussman-Prejza and Co., Inc., 1980-90, Culver City, 1990—. Spkr., lectr. UCLA Sch. Arch., Archtl. League N.Y.C., Smithsonian Inst., Stanford Conf. on Design, Am. Inst. Graphic Arts Nat. Conf. at MIT, Design Mgmt. Inst. Conf., Mass.; spl. guest Internat. Design Conf., Aspen, Colo.; Fulbright lectr., India, 1976; spkr. NEA Adv. Coun., 1985, Internat. Coun. Shopping Ctrs., 1986, USIA Design in Am. seminar, Budapest, Hungary, 1988. One-woman shows include Visual Arts Mus. Sch. Visual Arts, N.Y.C., 1995; participant exhbn., Moscow, 1989, Walker Art Ctr., Mpls., 1989; mem. editl. adv. bd. Arts and Arch. Mag., 1981-85, Calif. Mag., Arch. Calif. Fulbright grantee Hochschule für Gestaltung Ulm, 1957-58; recipient numerous awards AIA Nat. Inst. Honors, 1985, 88, Am. Inst. Graphic Arts, Calif. Coun. AIA (hon. mem., 1988), Comms. Arts Soc., L.A. County Bd. Suprs., Vesta award Women's Bldg. L.A. Fellow Soc. Environ. Graphic Design; mem. AIA (hon.), Am. Inst. Graphic Arts (bd. dirs. 1982-85, founder L.A. chpt., chmn. 1983-84, numerous awards), Am. Ctr. Design (hon.), L.A. Art Dirs. Club (bd. dirs., numerous awards), Alliance Graphique Internat. (elect. mem.), Archs., Designers, and Planners Social Responsibility. Calif. Women in Environ. Design (adv. d.), Trusteeship (affiliate Internat. Women's Forum, chmn.'s cir. Town Hall). Democrat. Jewish. Avocation: photography. Office: Sussman/Prejza & Co Inc 8520 Warner Dr Culver City CA 90232-2431 E-mail: dsussman@sussmanprejza.com.

SUSSMAN, GERALD, publishing company executive; b. Balt., Feb. 21, 1934; s. Hyman Jacob and Sylvia (Applebaum) S.; m. Arla Ilene Ellison, Aug. 25, 1963; children: Daniel Leonard, Andrew Louis. BA, U. Md., 1956. Co-founder, prin. Investors Service of Md., Balt., 1956-60; coll. traveller Oxford U. Press, Inc., N.Y.C., 1961-62, coll. sales mgr., 1962-69, gen. advt. mgr., 1970-73, v.p., dir. mktg., 1974-79, sr. v.p., dir. mktg., 1979-83, sr. v.p., dir. adminstrn. and planning, 1983—. Mem. Assn. Am. Pubs. (chmn. mktg. com.), Assn. Am. Univ. Presses (chmn. mktg. com. 1980-81), Pubs. Advt. Club, Phi Alpha Theta. Democrat. Jewish. Home: 10424 City Lights Dr NE Albuquerque NM 87111-7536 Office: Oxford U Press Inc 198 Madison Ave Fl 9 New York NY 10016-4341

SUSSMAN, HOWARD S(IVIN), lawyer; b. N.Y.C., Feb. 12, 1938; s. Joseph and Dora (Sivin) S. AB cum laude, Princeton U., 1958; LLB, Columbia U., 1962. Bar: N.Y. 1964, U.S. Dist. Ct. (so. and ea. dists.) N.Y. 1967, U.S. Ct. Appeals (2d cir.) 1967, U.S. Tax Ct. 1969, U.S. Dist. Ct. (no. dist.) N.Y. 1970, U.S. Supreme Ct. 1970, Tex. 1979, U.S. Ct. Appeals (5th cir.) 1982. Assoc. Chadbourne, Parke, Whiteside & Wolff, N.Y.C., 1963-71; asst. U.S. atty. So. Dist. N.Y., 1971-77; assoc. prof. law U. Houston, 1977-82; of counsel Wood, Lucksinger & Epstein, Houston, 1982-83; pvt. practice, N.Y.C., 1983-94; ptnr. Sussman Sollis Ebin Tweedy & Wood, LLP, 1995—. Instr. continuing legal edn. U. Houston, Nat. Inst. for Trial Advocacy. Editor Columbia U. Law Rev., 1960-62; contbr. articles to profl. jours. Harlan Fiske Stone scholar, 1959-61, Edvard Cassels Stiftelse vis. scholar, Stockholm, 1962-63; travelling fellow Parker Sch. Fgn. and Comparative Law Columbia U., 1962-63. Mem. ABA, N.Y. State Bar Assn., Assn. Bar City N.Y. (com. adminstrv. law 1974-76, profl. conf. 1979, com. fed. legis. 1984-87, com. criminal law 1987-90, com. lectr. and continuing edn. 1990-93, com. fgn. and comparative law 1993-96, arbitration com. 2002—), Fed. Bar Coun., Swedish Am. C. of C. (dir. N.Y. chpt. 1996—). Clubs: Princeton N.Y. E-mail: sstwsussman@msn.com.

SUSSMAN, JEFFREY BRUCE, public relations and marketing executive; b. N.Y.C., Mar. 15, 1943; m. Suzy Hirschland-Prudden, 1964 (div. 1981); 1 child, Robert; m. Barbara Ramsay, 1984. BA in English, NYU, 1969. Pres. Suzy Prudden Studios, N.Y.C., 1975-81; v.p. Zachary and Front, 1981-88; pres. Jeffrey Sussman, Inc., 1988—. Instr. mktg. The New Sch. U., N.Y.C. Author: Creative Fitness for Baby and Child, 1972, Suzy Prudden's Family Fitness Book, 1975, Fit for Life, 1977, See How They Run, 1978, Suzy Prudden's Spot Reducing Program, 1979, Suzy Prudden's Pregnancy and Back-To-Shape Exercise Program, 1980, I Can Exercise Anywhere, 1981, How to Sleep Without Drugs, 1986, Power Promoting: How to Market Your Business to the Top!, 1997; book rev. editor The Manhattan Tribune, 1969-75; contbr. book revs. to N.Y. Times Book Rev., 1974; bi-monthly columnist Weight Watchers Mag., 1977-79; monthly columnist Fortune Small Business, 2000—; contbr. articles to profl. jours. including Bottom Line Bus., Independent Bus., Small Bus. Report, N.Y. Real Estate Jour., East Hampton Star, M World mag. Press sec. N.Y.C. Coun.-Henry Stern, 1981. Avocations: photography, writing, music, painting, drawing. Home and Office: 249 E 48th St New York NY 10017-1526 E-mail: marketingpro@aol.com.

SUSSMAN, LAUREEN GLICKLIN, junior high school educator; b. N.Y.C., Mar. 21, 1953; d. Harry and Ruth (Goldstein) G.; m. Alan Neil Sussman, May 30, 1977; children: David Efrem, Adam Jacob, Daniel Joshua. BA, Bklyn. Coll., 1974; MS, MSc, Hofstra U., 1998. Cert. tchr. nursery-6, spl. edn. tchr. all grades. Sec. McCann-Erickson, Inc., N.Y.C., 1974-75; adminstrv. asst., tour operator EasTours divsn. Fgn. Tours, 1975-78; adminstrv. asst. Alan N. Sussman, CPA, Woodmere, N.Y., 1978-96; kindergarten tchr. Hebrew Acad. Long Beach (N.Y.), 1996-97; elem., jr. high sch. tchr. Torah Acad. Girls, Far Rockaway, N.Y., 1997—. Participant Instrumental Enrichment/IRI Skylight, N.Y., 1995, 98, Dynamic Assessment project Touro Coll., N.Y.C., 1996; CSE parent rep., adv. Lawrence (N.Y.) Pub. Schs., 1992-97. Contbr. articles to profl. jours. Mem. Spl. Edn. PTA Lawrence Schs., 1986—, Sisterhood Congregation Bais Tefilah, 1990—; mem. Sisterhood East Meadow Jewish Ctr., chairperson social action, Israel affairs, 1979-81; mem. steering com. Kulanu of the South Shore of Nassau County, 2000—. Mem.: AMIT Women (Masada chpt.), OTSAR (founder Nassau County chpt. 1987—, nat. bd. dirs., pres. Nassau chpt. 1987—2002). Democrat. Avocations: Israeli and simcha dancing, walking, reading, needlepoint. Office: Torah Acad Girls 444 Beach 6 St Far Rockaway NY 11691 E-mail: lauglick@aol.com.

SUSSMAN, LEONARD RICHARD, foundation executive; b. N.Y.C., Nov. 26, 1920; s. Jacob and Carrie (Marks) S.; m. Frances Rukeyser, May 9, 1942 (div. 1958); m. Marianne Rita Gutmann, May 28, 1958; children: Lynne, David William, Mark Jacob. AB, NYU, 1940; MS in Journalism, Columbia U., 1941. Copy editor N.Y. Morning Telegraph, news editor radio sta. WQXR, 1941; cable editor San Juan (P.R.) World Jour., also corr. Business Week mag., 1941-42; editor fgn. broadcast intelligence svc. FCC, 1942; press sec. to Gov. of P.R., 1942-43; dir. info. in N.Y. for Govt. of P.R., 1946-49; regional dir., then nat. exec. dir. Am. Coun. Judaism, 1949-66; cons. pub. affairs cons. Nationwide Ins. Cos. (and indsl. subs.), 1955-57; mem. editorial com. Coun. Liberal Chs., 1956-59; exec. dir. Freedom House, 1967-88, 96, sr. scholar in internat. communications, 1988—; evaluator Fulbright Program Bd. Fgn. Scholarships, 1990-92; exec. dir. Willkie Meml., 1970-88. Adj. prof. journalism and mass communication NYU, N.Y.C., 1990-99; adj. prof. Sch. for Internat. and Pub. Affairs, Columbia U., 2000-01; organizer, dir. Freedom House/Books USA, 1968-85; editor Freedom at Issue, bimonthly, 1970-81; mem. U.S. Dels. to Conf. World Communicaiton Yr./83, 1982-83; organizer acad. confs.; participant Internat. Conf. on Press Freedom, Venice, Italy, 1976, 77, Cairo, 1978, Talloires, 1981, 83, San Jose, Costa Rica, Johannnesburg, and Santiago Chile, 1987, also others; mem. panel competition in space Congl. Office Tech. Assessment, 1982-83. Author: American Press-Under Siege?, 1973, Mass News Media and The Third World Challenge, 1977, Glossary for International Communications: Warning of a Bloodless Dialect, 1983, Spanish version, 1987, Power, The Press and the Technology of Freedom: The Coming of Age of ISDN, 1990, The Culture of Freedom: The Small World of Fulbright Scholars, 1992, Good News Bad News, 1994, Can A Free Press Be Responsible? To Whom?, 1995, The Press: Pressed and Oppressed, 1995, The Journalist as Pariah: Press Freedom, 1996, The Global Airscape, 1996, Democracy, Yes; Press Freedom, Maybe, 1997, Press Law Epidemic: Press Freedom, 1997, Global Warning: Press Controls Fuel the Asian Debacle, 1998, The News of the Century, 1999, Censor Dot Gov: The Internet and Press Freedom, 2000, Press Freedom in Our Genes, A Human Need, 2001, How Free? The Web and the Press, 2001, Democracy's Advocate: The Story of Freedom House, 2002, The Press at War: Marksman and Target, 2002, repub. in Freedom and Responsibility Yearbook, 2001-2002; editor: Three Years at the East-West Divide, 1983, Today's American: How Free?, 1986; contbr. sects. to books, articles to profl. jours. and newspapers; project dir.: Big Story-How the American Press and Television Reported and Interpreted the Crisis of Tet-1968 in Vietnam and Washington, 1977; editor: textbook series, also quar. mag. Issues, 1953-66; editl. bd. Polit. Comm. and Persuasion. Trustee Internat. Coun. on Future of Univ., 1973-84; bd. dirs. World Press Freedom Com., 1977—; chmn. Friends of Survey Mag. Charitable Trust, London, 1978-92; mem. U.S. Nat. Commn. for UNESCO, 1979-85, vice chmn., 1983-85; mem. U.S. dels. to internat. conf. on space, African Aid, UNESCO, London Info. Forum; mem. Internat. Freedom of Expression Exch., 1995—, mem. coun., 1997-99. 2001-2002. Decorated Legion of Merit; recipient Ann. First Amendment award N.Y. br. Soc. Profl. Journalists, 1988. Mem. Internat. Inst. Comm., Internat. Press Inst., Internat. Assn. Mass Comm. Rsch., Century Club. Home: 215 E 73d St New York NY 10021-3653 Office: 120 Wall St Fl 26 New York NY 10005-3904 E-mail: sussman@freedomhouse.org.

SUSSMAN, MARTIN VICTOR, chemical engineering educator, inventor, consultant; b. N.Y.C. s. Samuel and Selma (Bagno) S.; m. Jeanne Fowler, Aug. 22, 1953; children: M. Ann Edmunds, Eve Leslie, David Fowler. BS, CCNY; MS, Columbia U., PhD, 1958. Registered profl. engr. Mass.; lic. marine engr. Instr., research assoc. chem. dept. Fordham U., N.Y.C., 1949-50; research fellow chem. engring. dept. Columbia U., 1951-53; sr. engr., research engr. Pioneering Lab., DuPont, Del., 1953-58; co-founder, 1st dept. chem. engring in Turkey Robert Coll., Istanbul, Turkey, 1958-61; prof. chem. engring. dept. Tufts U., Medford, Mass., 1961-98, prof. emeritus, 1998, dept. chmn., established PhD and MS programs, 1961-71. Cons. engring. edn. US AID, Brazil and Uruguay, 1963, Ethiopia, 1965; cons. engring. edn. Ford Found., India, 1971, 72, 73, 74, 79; coord. engring. edn. NSF, New Delhi, 1967-68; vis. prof. MIT, 1976, U. Capetown, Republic South Africa, 1990; Disting. vis. scholar Va. Poly. Inst., 1980; vis. scholar chem. engring. dept. U. Cambridge, Eng., 1996-97; hon. rsch. fellow U. Exeter, 1990; co-founder chem. engring. dept. Robert Coll., Turkey. Author: Elementary General Thermodynamics, 1972, 89, Availability (Exergy) Analysis, 1980; patentee in field. Mem. Town Meeting, Lexington, Mass., 1971-78. Served with U.S. Maritime Service, 1945-47, U.S. Coast Guard. NIH Spl. Research fellow, 1968; AEC fellow, 1951; Fulbright Hays lectr., 1977; Erskine fellow U. Canterbury (N.Z.), 1983; Meyerhoff fellow Weizman Inst. Sci., 1984-85 Fellow Am. Inst. Chem. Engrs., Am. Inst. Chemists; mem. Am. Chem. Soc., Sigma Xi, Tau Beta Pi (eminent engr. 1974) Achievements include invention of "Incremental Draw Process" for synthetic fiber manufacture now in use by industry, "Fibra-Cel" tissue culture matrix, "Vertigon" 3-D printed text, establishment of first modern chemical engineering department in a Turkish university, introduced graduate degree in chem. engring. program at Tufts U. Office: 1361 Massachusetts Ave Lexington MA 02420-3800 E-mail: vertigon2@juno.com.

SUSSMAN, NEIL A. lawyer; b. N.Y.C., Jan. 26, 1956; s. Herbert and Ruth S.; m. Suzanne R. Thompson, Aug. 31, 1990; children: Annabelle, Franklin. BS in Econs., U. Pa., 1978; JD, U. Wash., 1982. Bar: Wash. 1982. Pvt. practice, Seattle, 1982—. Mem. Wash. State Bar Assn., King County Bar Assn. Office: 10727 Interlake Ave N Seattle WA 98133-8907 E-mail: neilsussman@mindspring.com.

SUSSMAN, NEIL M(ARK), neurologist; b. Oct. 28, 1945; BA in Biology, Hofstra U., 1967; MD, N.Y. Med. Coll., 1972. Diplomate Am. Bd. Psychiatry and Neurology. Intern in medicine Nassau County Med. Ctr., East Meadow, N.Y., 1972-73; resident in medicine Hartford (Conn.) Hosp., 1973-74; resident in neurology Thomas Jefferson U. Hosp., Phila., 1974-77; instr. dept. neurology Boston U. Sch. Medicine, 1977-78; fellow in epilepsy, electroencephalography, instr. neurology U. Minn., 1978-79; fellow in neurology U. Pa., Phila., 1979-80, clin. asst. prof. neurology, 1981-85; mem. staff Grad. Hosp., 1979-87, assoc. med. dir. comprehensive epilepsy ctr., 1981-85; assoc. prof. neurology Med. Coll. Pa., 1985-89; mem. staff Phila. Geriat. Ctr., 1988-89, West Haven (Conn.) VA Hosp., 1995-2000; clin. faculty neurology Yale U. Sch. Medicine, New Haven, 1995-2000, clin. assoc. prof. neurology, 1997—. Med. dir. Mid-Atlantic Regional Epilepsy Ctr., Med. Coll. Pa., Phila., 1985-88, dir. med. rsch., 1988-89; project dir. dept. clin. rsch. Merrell Dow Rsch. Inst., Cin., 1989-90; dir. dept. clin. rsch. Marion Merrell Dow Inc., Cin., 1990-92, sr. product team leader, 1992-93; venture head neurotherapeutics Abbott Labs., Abbott park, Ill., 1993-94; dir. Ctrl. Nervous Sys. (CNS) clin. rsch. Bristol-Myers Squibb Pharm. Rsch. Inst., Wallingford, Conn., 1995-99; dir. CNS clin. rsch. Forest Labs., N.Y.C., 1999-2000; dir. med. affairs Pharm. Rsch. Assocs. Internat., 2000—; lectr. in field. Author: (chpt.) Textbook of Medicine, 2nd edit., 1990, Basic Pharmacology in Medicine, 3rd edit., 1990, New Antiepileptic Drug Development: Preclinical and Clinical Aspects, 1993, Antiepileptic Drug Development, 1998; Co-author: (chpt.) Positron Emmission Tomography, 1984, Intensive Care Unlimited, 1988, Expert Opinions on Investigational Drugs, 1994; contbr. articles to profl. jours.; patentee Nefazodone for migraine prophylaxis. With USPHS, 1977-78. Grantee, Lorex, 1984—85, Merck/Sharp and Dohme Rsch. Labs., 1985, Burroughs-Wellcome, 1988—89, 1989—90, McNeil Pharm., 1988—89, Wallace Labs., 1989—90, NIH, 1991. Fellow Am. Acad. Neurology; mem. Internat. Soc. Quality Life Rsch., Royal Coll. Physicians, Am. EEG Soc., Am. Epilepsy Soc., Am. Assn. Pharm. Physicians, Am. Soc. Exptl. NeuroTherapeutics (founding bd. dirs.), New England Pain Assn., Epilepsy Found. Phila. (bd. dirs. 1979-88, sec. 1982-84, pres. 1984-87, profl. adv. bd. 1987-89). Home: 1563 Grouse Ln Mountainside NJ 07092-1340 E-mail: sussmanneil@praintl.com.

SUSSMAN, PETER ALAN, entertainment company executive; b. Toronto, Ont., Can., July 16, 1958; came to U.S., 1992; s. Murray Sussman and Norma Weisfeld; m. Heather Ann Hartt, Sept. 30, 1993; children: Scott Oliver, Jack Elliott. BA, York U., 1979; LLB, Osgoode Hall, 1982. CEO Alliance Atlantis Entertainment Group, 1986—. Exec. prodr.: (TV miniseries) Joan of Arc, 1999

(TV Critics Best Movie or Miniseries, 13 Emmy and 4 Golden Globe nominations and 1 Emmy award), Nuremberg, 2000 (4 Emmy and Golden Globe nominations and 1 Emmy award), Life with Judy Garland: Me and My Shadows, 2001 (TV Critics Best Movie or Miniseries, 13 Emmy and 3 Golden Globe nominations, 5 Emmy awards and 1 Golden Globe award, Broadcast Film Critics Assn. award for Best Picture made for TV), more than 50 other movies and TV series. Mem., Alliance Atlantis Comms. c. (bd. dirs. 1989—). Avocations: sports, the arts. Office: Alliance Atlantis 3d Fl 808 Wilshire Blvd Fl 3D Santa Monica CA 90401-1889 E-mail: peter.sussman@allianceatlantis.com.

SUSSMAN, WENDY RODRIGUEZ, artist, educator; b. N.Y.C., June 3, 1949; BA, Empire State Coll., 1978; MFA, Bklyn. Coll., 1980. Lectr. Touro Coll., N.Y.C., 1985-86, Pratt Inst., Bklyn., 1987-89; asst. prof. U. Calif., Berkeley, 1989-96, assoc. prof., 1996—. One-woman shows include Bowery Gallery, N.Y.C., 1982, 87, John Bergruen Gallery, San Francisco, 1992, D.P. Fong Gallery, San Jose, Calif., 1994, Platt Gallery U. Judaism, L.A., 1995, Jan Baum Gallery, L.A., 1996, The Jewish Mus., San Francisco, 1996; group shows include Bowery Gallery, 1980-88, Munson-Williams-Proctor Inst. Mus. Art, 1982, Reading (Pa.) Pub. Mus. and Art Gallery, 1983, Queens Mus., N.Y.C., 1983, Colby Coll. Mus. Art, Waterville, Maine, 1983, Butler Inst. Am. Art, Youngstown, Ohio, 1983, Bklyn. Coll., 1983, Am. Acad. Inst. Arts and Letters, N.Y.C., 1984, Am. Acad. in Rome, 1987, John Berggruen Gallery, San Francisco, 1992, San Francisco Arts Commn. Gallery, 1992, 94, D.P. Fong Gallery, 1994, Boulder Mus. Art, 1995, Gallery Paule Anglin, San Francisco, 1996, 98, Jan Baum Gallery, L.A., 1996, U. Calif. San Diego Art Gallery, 1997. Rome Prize fellow in painting Am. Acad. in Rome, 1986-87, Visual Arts fellow NEA, 1989, Guggenheim fellow, 1998; Pollock-Krasner grantee Pollock-Krasner Found., 1988; recipient Max and Sophie Adler award Jewish Mus., Judah Magners Mus., 1996. Office: U Calif Berkeley Dept Art Berkeley CA 94720-0001

SUSSNA, EDWARD, economist, educator; b. Phila., Nov. 26, 1926; s. Louis and Manya (Prytzycka) S.; m. Sylvia Fishman, Mar. 8, 1953; children: Audrey Francine, Ellen Sondra. BA, Bklyn. Coll., 1950; MA, U. Ill., 1952, PhD, 1954. Instr. U. Ill., 1952-54; asst. prof. Lehigh U., 1956-57; prof. bus. adminstrn. and econs. U. Pitts., 1957—; dir. ctr. for exec. edn. Grad. Sch. Bus. U. Pitts., 1983-89; dir. mgmt. program for execs. Center for Econ. Edn., Grad. Sch. Bus., acad. dir. study program in Hong Kong and Peoples Republic China, spring 1989, 95; inaugural prof. MBA program Bratislava Sch. Econs., Slovakia, 1996. Vis. Fulbright prof. U. Tehran, Iran, adviser, 1972-73; cons. Bur. of Budget, Dept. HEW, Dept. Transp., UN Indsl. Devel. Orgn., Bell Telephone Co., Alcoa, Westinghouse Corp., NSF, Pitts. Nat. Bank, Japanese Regional Bankers Assn., others; vis. prof. UCLA, 1970, Ecole Superieure des Scis. Economiques et Commerciales, Paris, 1976-77, U. East Asia, Hong Kong and Macau, winter 1986; vis. scholar Internat. Inst. Mgmt., Berlin, spring 1982 Contbr. articles to profl. jours. Served with U.S. Mcht. Marine, 1944-47; Served with AUS, 1954-56. Vis. prof. under Ford Found. fellowship Harvard, 1960-61; guest scholar under Ford Found. fellowship Brookings Instn., Washington, 1962-63 Mem. Am. Econ. Assn., Am. Fin. Assn., Strategic Mgmt. Inst., Beta Gamma Sigma, Omicron Delta. Home: 1538 S Negley Ave Pittsburgh PA 15217-1420 E-mail: Sussna@pitt.edu.

SUSTAR, T. DAVID, evangelism and home missions administrator; Pres. East Coast Bible Coll., Ch. of God, Charlotte, N.C., 1996-99; evangelism and home missions dir. Western N.C. Ch. of God, 1999—2002. Office: 8724 University City Blvd Charlotte NC 28213-3558 E-mail: tdsustar@aol.com.

SUSTENDAL, DIANE, media executive; b. New Orleans, Aug. 30, 1944; d. George and Mary (Anderson) S. Student, La. State U., 1963-64. With Times-Picayune, New Orleans, 1966-68, Fairchild Publs., N.Y.C., 1986—. With Men's Fashions of the Times, N.Y. Times, N.Y.C.; fashion and interior design editor N.Y. Daily News; freelance writer, editor. Bd. dirs. New Orleans Ballet, 1971-73. Recipient award La. Press Anns., 1972, Aldo award Men's Fashion Assn. Am., 1985. E-mail: sustendal@hotmail.com.

SUSTER, ZELJAN, business educator, dean; b. Split, Yugoslavia, Nov. 18, 1958; came to the U.S., 1989; s. Emil and Olga (Jelenkovic) S.; m. Sanja Grubacic, Dec. 3, 1988. BA in Econs. and Fin., U. Belgrade, Yugoslavia, 1981, MA in Econs., 1984, PhD in Econs., 1988. Rsch. assoc. Inst. Econ. Scis., Belgrade, 1983-89; assoc. prof. U. New Haven, West Haven, Conn., 1990—, chair dept. econs. and fin., 1996-97, assoc. dean Sch. Bus., 1997—. Vis. fellow Mellon Found., Yale U., 1990-91; rsch. assoc. U. Ill., Champaign-Urbana, 1995-96; sr. analyst Analytic Resources, Woodbridge, Conn., 1995—; mem. adv. bd. Charter Oak State Coll., Newington, Conn., 1996—. Author: Historical Dictionary of FR of Yugoslavia, 1999; mem. editl. bd. Serbian Studies, 1993—, Dialogue, 1998—, New Serbian Political Thought, 1998—; contbr. articles to profl. jours. Mem. N.Am. Soc. for Serbian Studies (mem. governing bd. 1993—, v.p. 1998—, pres. 1999—), Ea. Econ. Assn., Atlantic Econ. Soc., Multinational Fin. Soc., Internat. Soc. for Intercomm. of New Ideas, Am. Assn. for the Advancement of Slavic Studies, Kiwanis Internat. Avocation: chess. Office: U New Haven Sch Bus 300 Orange Ave West Haven CT 06516-1916

SUTCLIFFE, ERIC, lawyer; b. Calif., Jan. 10, 1909; s. Thomas and Annie (Beare) S.; m. Joan Basché, Aug. 7, 1937; children: Victoria, Marcia, Thomas; m. Marie C. Paige, Nov. 1, 1975. AB, U. Calif., Berkeley, 1929, LLB, 1932. Bar: Calif. 1932. Mem. firm Orrick, Herrington & Sutcliffe, San Francisco, 1943-85, mng. ptnr., 1947-78. Trustee, treas., v.p. San Francisco Law Libr., 1974-88; founding fellow The Oakland Mus. of Calif.; bd. dirs. Merritt Peralta Found., 1988; past bd. dirs. Hong Kong Bank of Calif., Friends of U. Calif. Bot. Garden, sec. Fellow Am. Bar Found (life); mem. ABA (chmn state regulation securities com. 1960-65), San Francisco Bar Assn. (chmn. corp. law com., 1964-65), San Francisco C. of C. (past treas., dir.), State Bar Calif., Pacific Union Club, Bohemian Club, Phi Gamma Delta, Phi Delta Phi, Order of Coif. Home: 260 King Ave Oakland CA 94610-1231 Office: Old Fed Reserve Bank Bldg 400 Sansome St San Francisco CA 94111-3304

SUTCLIFFE, MARION SHEA, real estate developer, writer, artist; b. Washington, July 29, 1918; d. James William and Ida (Hewitt) Shea; m. James Montgomery Sutcliffe, Aug. 23, 1941; 1 child, Jill Marion. BMus, Boston Conservatory Music, 1956-60; EdM, Boston State Coll., 1969. Cert. music, English, psychology and reading tchr., Mass. Tchr. Milford (Mass.) Pub. Schs., 1966-70; tchr. music Worcester (Mass.) Pub. Schs., 1970-71; reading tchr. Natick and Newton (Mass.) Pub. Schs., 1971-73; real estate developer Sutcliffe Family Trust, South Dennis, Mass., 1969—; developer Delray Beach Club, Dennisport; mfr. A&A Assocs., South Dennis, 1989—. Dir., sec. bd. mgrs. The Soundings Resort, Dennisport, Mass., 1990-2000. Songwriter Diablo, 1954. Founder, mgr. Boston Women's Symphony, 1962-66. Fuller grantee New England Conservatory, 1957, grantee State Mass., 1957. Mem.: AAUW, Organ-Aires, Ea. Mass. Am. Theatre Organ Soc. (bd. dirs. 1989—92), Nat. Am. Theatre Organ Soc., The Questers, Inc. (Yankee Pedlar chpt. #811), Sounding's Assn., Amateur Organists Assn. Internat., West Dennis Garden Club. Episcopalian. Avocations: painting, playing the organ, swimming, gardening, walking. Home: 145 Cove Rd South Dennis MA 02660-3515 Office: 60 Macarthur Rd Natick MA 01760-2938

SUTER, ALBERT EDWARD, manufacturing company executive; b. East Orange, N.J., Sept. 18, 1935; s. Joseph Vincent and Catherine (Clay) S.; m. Michaela Sams Suter, May 28, 1966; children: Christian C., Bradley J., Allison A. BME, Cornell U., 1957, MBA, 1959. Pres., chief exec. officer L.B. Knight & Assocs., Chgo., 1959-79; v.p. internat. Emerson Electric Co., St. Louis, 1979-80, pres. motor div., 1980-87, group v.p., 1981-83, exec. v.p., 1983-87, vice chmn., 1987; pres., chief operating officer, dir. Firestone Tire & Rubber Co., Akron, Ohio, 1987-88; pres., chief operating officer Whirlpool Corp., Benton Harbor, Mich., from 1988; exec. v.p. Emerson Electric Co., St. Louis, until 1990, pres., COO, 1990-92, sr. vice chmn., COO, 1992-97; CAO, 1999—2001; ret. sr. advisor, COO Emerson Electric Co., St. Louis, 2001. Bd. dirs. Furniture Brands Internat. Bd. dirs. Jr. Achievement Nat. Bd., Colorado Springs, Colo., Jr. Achievement Miss. Valley, St. Louis Sci. Ctr. Bd.; chmn. Torch div. St. Louis chpt. United Way, 1982-86. Mem. Glenview (Ill.) Country Club, St. Louis Club, Old Warson Country Club , Log Cabin Club. Republican. Episcopalian. Office: Emerson Electric Co PO Box 4100 Saint Louis MO 63136-8506

SUTER, CAROL J. non-profit organization executive, lawyer; b. Highland Park, Mich., Mar. 5, 1949; d. Francis and Doris (Weis) Salucci; m. Eugene W. Suter, Mar. 21, 1970; children: Leanne M., Tracy L. BSc in Edn., Bowling Green State U., 1971; JD, Ohio No. U., 1981. Bar: Ohio 1981. Law clk. Schroeder, Schroeder and O'Malley, Ottawa, Ohio, 1979-81; assoc. Schroeder, Schrock and O'Malley, 1981-85; devel. dir. Gen. Conf. Mennonite Ch., Newton, Kans., 1984-87; dir. external affairs Ohio No. U., Ada, 1987-90; assoc. Benson Law Offices, Lima, Ohio, 1990-93; owner CS Resources, Kansas City, Mo., 1993-95; v.p., counsel Mennonite Econ. Devel. Assocs., 1995-98; exec. dir. Ctr. Mgmt. Assistance, 1999—. Dir. Mennonite Mut. Aid Assn., Goshen, 1995—. Chmn. bd. dirs. Pandora (Ohio)-Gilboa Sch. Found., 1987-83, Appleseed Ridge Girl Scout Coun., Lima, 1984-90. Fellow Am. Bar Found.; mem. ABA, Ohio State Bar Assn. (del. 1992-93, Ohio Supreme Ct. task force on gender fairness 1991-93). Office: Ctr Mgmt Assistance 600 Broadway Ste 170 Kansas City MO 64105

SUTER, JON MICHAEL, academic library director, educator; b. Holdenville, Okla., Oct. 30, 1941; s. Franklin Hyatt and Erma (Abee) S. BA cum laude, East Cen. State Coll., 1963; MLS, U. Okla., 1964; PhD, Ind. U., 1973. Asst. libr. East Cen. State Coll., Ada, Okla., 1964-76; assoc. libr. East Cen. U., 1976-84; dir. librs. Houston Bapt. U., 1984—. Chmn. Libr. Edn. Div. Okla. Libr. Assn., 1981, Coll. Rsch. Libr. Div., Okla., 1982. Contbr. articles to profl. jours. Pres. Ada Camp Gideons Internat., 1980-82. Higher Edn. Act fellow Ind. U., 1969-71. Mem. Popular Culture Assn., Richard III Socl., Med. Acad., Renaissance Soc., Patristics Soc. Republican. Baptist. Avocations: comic books, medieval history. Home: 8271 Wednesbury Ln Houston TX 77074-2918 Office: Houston Bapt U - Moody Libr 7502 Fondren Rd Houston TX 77074-3204 E-mail: jsuter@hbu.edu.

SUTER, KENNETH HARRIS, personal investments consultant; b. Cin., Aug. 31, 1919; s. Herbert Wallace Sr. and Edith Marie (Harris) S.; m. Margaret Anne Benninghofen, Jan. 3, 1948; children: H.W. II, A.M. Suter Mueller, S.A. Grad. high sch., 1938. Printing apprentice V.S. Lithographing Co., Cin., 1940-41; paper mfg. apprentice Champion Paper & Fiber Co., Hamilton, Ohio, 1941, 46; paper salesman Whitaker Paper Co., Detroit, 1946-74; v.p. various cos., 1946-74; personal investments cons. Birmingham, Mich., 1974—. Capt. U.S. Army, 1941-46. Mem. Oakland Hills Country Club, Hunters Creek Club, Ad Craft Club Detroit. Republican. Methodist. Avocations: golf, bowling, fishing, hunting, card playing. Home: 807 Yarmouth Rd Bloomfield Hills MI 48301-2630 Office: 1100 Woodward Ave Ste 122 Bloomfield Hills MI 48304-3970

SUTER, PEGGY JEAN, library director; b. Wilburton, Okla., July 18, 1937; d. Henry Paul and Violet Jessie Eads; m. James William Suter, May 15, 1954; children: Pauline Jeanette Owens, Jo Lavonne Ahlm. Grad., Hartshorne (Okla.) H.S., 1955. Cert. grade I libr., N.Mex. Piano tchr., Lovington, N.Mex., 1968-72, Eunice, 1973-88; kindergarten music tchr. First Meth. Ch., Lovington, 1970-73; substitute sch. tchr. Eunice Pub. Schs., 1978-81; libr. dir. Eunice Pub. Libr., 1981—. Organist First Meth. Ch., Eunice, 1982—. Mem. Am. Libr. Assn., N.Mex. Libr. Assn. (community Svc. award 1992), Lea County Libr. Assn. (v.p. 1982, pres. 1983, treas. 1984). Democrat. Methodist. Avocations: playing piano, singing, crochet. Office: Eunice Pub Libr Corner of 10th and Ave Eunice NM 88231

SUTER, SUSAN VIRGINIA, social worker; b. Grand Island, Nebr., Oct. 23, 1942; d. David Chester and Virginia Artell (Hueneke) Jones; m. Gene H. Suter (div. 1977). BA, U. Nebr., 1964; MSW, Tulane U., 1969. Lic. clin. social worker, Oreg. Group worker St. Marks Community Ctr., New Orleans, 1964-65; caseworker La. Dept. Pub. Welfare, 1965-68; social worker Fairview Hosp. & Tng. Ctr., Salem, Oreg., 1969-72; social worker Children's Svc. div. State of Oreg., Portland, 1972—, adoption com. Children's Svc. div., 1984-86. Field instr. Portland State U., 1989-90; pvt. practice, 1990—. Co-author: Post Adoption Family Therapy: A Practice Manual, 1990. Recipient Profls. in Human Svcs. award Am. Acad. Human Svcs., Chgo., 1974-75. Mem. NASW (membership com.), Acad. Cert. Social Workers. Office: Children Svc Div 815 NE Davis St Portland OR 97232-2987

SUTERA, SALVATORE PHILIP, mechanical engineering educator; b. Balt., Jan. 12, 1933; s. Philip and Ann (D'Amico) S.; m. Celia Ann Fielden, June 21, 1958; children: Marie-Anne, Annette Nicole, Michelle Cecile. BS in Mech. Engring, Johns Hopkins, 1954; postgrad., U. Paris, 1955-56; MS, Calif. Inst. Tech., 1955; PhD, Cal. Inst. Tech., 1960; MA (hon.), Brown U., 1965. Asst. prof. mech. engring. Brown U., Providence, 1960-65, assoc. prof., 1965-68, exec. officer div. engring., 1966-68; prof. dept. mech. engring. Washington U., St. Louis, 1968-97, chmn. dept., 1968-82, 86-97, Spencer T. Olin prof. engring. and applied sci., 1997—, prof. biomed. engring., 1997—. Vis. prof. U. Paris VI, 1973. Assoc. editor: Jour. Biomech. Engring., 1993-97; mem. editorial bd. Circulation Rsch., 1975-82. Pres. St. Louis-Lyon Sister Cities, Inc., 2000—. Fulbright fellow Paris, 1955; recipient Nat. Marconi Sci. award UNICO, 1999. Fellow ASME, Am. Inst. of Med and Biol. Engring. (founding); mem. Biomed. Engring. Soc. (bd. dirs. 1997-2000), Internat. Soc. Biorheology, N.Am. Soc. Biorheology (pres.-elect 1986-89, pres. 1989-90), Am. Soc. Artificial Internal Organs, Am. Soc. Engring. Edn., AAAS (Lindbergh award St. Louis sect. 1988), AIAA, European Acad. Sci., Tau Beta Pi, Pi Tau Sigma. Republican. Roman Catholic. Achievements include research in fluid mechanics, heat transfer, blood flow, rheology of suspensions. Home: 830 S Meramec Ave Saint Louis MO 63105-2539 E-mail: sps@biomed.wustl.edu.

SUTHAHARAN, SHANMUGATHASAN, computer science educator, researcher; b. Batticaloa, Sri Lanka, Oct. 26, 1958; s. Subramaniam and Jeiyaluckshmi (Sivasubramaniam) Shanmugathasan; m. Manimehala Suthaharan, Sept. 15, 1985; children: Lovepriya, Praveen, Prattheeba. BSc, U. Jaffna, Sri Lanka, 1980, BSc with honors, 1981; MSc, Dundee (Scotland) U., 1988; PhD, Monash U., Melbourne, Australia, 1995. Asst. lectr. U. Jaffna, 1981-85; lectr. Middlesex U., London, 1988-90; computer courseware developer CompuTeach Coll., Melbourne, 1990; sr. instr., UNIX adminstr. Computer Power Tng. Inst., 1991-96; from rsch. fellow to lectr. Monash U., 1995—98; dept. head, prof. computer sci. Tenn. State U., Nashville, 1999—; prof. computer sci. U. N.C., Greensboro, NC, 2001—. Adj. prof. Ctr. Excellence in Info. Sys. Engring. and Mgmt., Tenn. State U., Nashville, 1997-98; chief investigator Monash U., 1997-98; vis. prof. U. Tex., Arlington, 1997-98; rschr., presenter in field. Editor Real-Time Imaging, 1998-99; contbr. articles to profl. jours., chpts. to books. Grantee FIT, 1995-96, Australian Rsch. Coun., 1998, Monash U., 1997-98. Mem. IEEE (sr. mem., tech. com. 1997-98).

SUTHERLAND, ALAN ROY, business educator; b. N.Y.C., Jan. 15, 1944; s. Arthur Abbott and Margaret Louise (Schweitzer) S. BFA, Pratt Inst., Bklyn., 1964; MPA, NYU, 1969, PhD, 1984. Personnel dir. Manhattan Psychiat. Ctr., N.Y.C., 1966-72; dep. dir. Rockland Children's Psychiat. Ctr., Orangeburg, N.Y., 1972-74, L.I. Devel. Ctr., Melville, 1974-78, dir., 1978-80; program dir. Vols. Am., N.Y.C., 1983-86; sr. staff officer Nat. Acad. Scis., Washington, 1986-88; dep. dir. U.S. Interagy. Coun. on Homeless, 1988-89; exec. dir. Travelers Aid Internat., 1989-91, AIDS Ctr. of Queens County, Rego Park, N.Y., 1992-96; chair dept. mgmt. studies Southeastern U., Washington, 1998-99. Prof. U. Md., College Park, 1998—. Editor: Homlessness, Health and Human Service Needs. Recipient citation N.Y.C. Coun., 1986. Mem. ASPA, World Futurist Soc. Lutheran. Avocation: weightlifting. Home: 1617 15th St NW Washington DC 20009-3801 Office: Univ of Maryland 3501 University Blvd E Adelphi MD 20783-7998 E-mail: arslitplas@aol.com.

SUTHERLAND, DIANA WESTLAKE, visual artist; b. Martins Ferry, Ohio, Apr. 15, 1931; d. Melvin Jones and Dorothy Virginia (Pickens) Westlake; m. James Frederick Sutherland, Aug. 2, 1951; children: Laurie Giudice, Jan Hundley, Eve Curtis. Student, Carnegie Mellon U., Pitts., 1949-51. Sec. Minn. Region 2 Arts Coun., Bemidji, 1981-82. Recipient 24 awards including Revington Arthur Found. award Stamford (Conn.) Mus., 1996, Purchase award Sunrise Art Mus, Charleston, W.Va., 1975, Butler Inst. Am. Art, Youngstown, Ohio, 1973, Huntington (W.Va.) Mus. Art, 1972. Avocations: piano, organ, harpsichord, recorders. Home: 2459 S Orchard View Dr Green Valley AZ 85614-1440

SUTHERLAND, DONALD, actor; b. St. John, N.B., Can., July 17, 1935; m. Lois Hardwick; m. 2d, Shirley Douglas; children: Kiefer, Rachel; m. 3d, Francine Racette; children: Roeg, Rossif, Angus. Grad., U. Toronto, 1958. Actor: London Acad. Music and Dramatic Art, Perth Repertory Theatre, Scotland, also Nottingham, Chesterfield, Bronley, Sheffield, (plays) The Spoon River Anthology, The Male Animal, The Tempest, August for People (London debut), On a Clear Day You Can See Canterbury, The Shewing Up a Blanco Posnet, Enigma Variations, 2000, Ten Unknowns, 2001 (films) The World Ten Times Over, 1963, The Castle of the Living Dead, 1964, Dr. Terror's House of Horrors, 1965, Fanatic, 1965, The Bedford Incident, 1965, Promise Her Anything, 1966, The Dirty Dozen, 1967, Sebastian, 1968, Oedipus the King, 1968, Interlude, 1968, Joanna, 1968, The Split, 1968, Start the Revolution Without Me, 1969, The Act of the Heart, 1970, M*A*S*H, 1970, Kelly's Heroes, 1970, Little Murders, 1970, Alex in Wonderland, 1971, Klute, 1971, Johnny Got His Gun, 1971, Steelyard Blues, 1972, Lady Ice, 1972, Alien Thunder, 1973, Don't Look Now, 1973, S*P*Y*S, 1974, The Day of the Locust, 1975, End of the Game, 1976, Casanova, 1976, 1900, 1976, The Eagle Has Landed, 1977, Animal House, 1978, Invasion of the Body Snatchers, 1978, The Great Train Robbery, 1979, The Kentucky Fried Movie, 1978, Murder by Decree, 1979, Bear Island, 1979, A Man, A Woman and a Bank, 1980, Nothing Personal, 1980, Ordinary People, 1980, Eye of the Needle, 1981, Gas, 1981, The Disappearance, Blood Relative, Threshold, 1983, Max Dugan Returns, 1983, Crackers, 1984, Heaven Help Us, 1985, Revolution, 1985, The Trouble with Spies, 1987, The Wolf at the Door, 1987, Apprentice to Murder, 1988, The Rosary Murders, 1988, Lock Up, 1989, Lost Angels, 1989, A Dry White Season, 1989, Backdraft, 1991, JFK, 1991, Eminent Domain, 1991, Buffy the Vampire Slayer, 1992, Younger and Younger, 1993, Shadow of the Wolf, 1993, Six Degrees of Separation, 1993, The Puppet Masters, 1994, Quicksand, Disclosure, 1994, Outbreak, 1995, Bethune: The Making of a Hero, FTA, The Shadow Conspiracy, 1997, The Assignment, 1997, Fallen, 1997, Without Limits, 1998, Free Money, 1998, Toscano, 1999, CSS Hunley, 1999, Virus, 1999, Instinct, 1999; TV shows and movies include Marching to the Sea, The Death of Bessie Smith, Hamlet at Elsinore, The Saint, The Avengers, Gideon's Way, The Champions, The Winter of Our Discontent, 1984, Ordeal By Innocence, 1985, Buster's Bedroom, Citizen X, 1995 (Emmy award), The Big Heist, 2001. Decorated officier dans l'Ordre des Artes et des Lettres (France); officer Order of Can. Office: c/o CAA Katherine Olin 9830 Wilshire Blvd Beverly Hills CA 90212-1804*

SUTHERLAND, DONALD GRAY, retired lawyer; b. Houston, Jan. 19, 1929; s. Robert Gray and Elizabeth (Cunningham) S.; m. Mary Reynolds Moodey, July 23, 1955; children: Stuart Gray, Elizabeth Dana. BS, Purdue U., 1954; LLB, Ind. U., Bloomington, 1954. Bar: Ind. 1954, U.S. Dist. Ct. (so. dist.) Ind. 1954, U.S. Tax Ct. 1956, U.S. Ct. Claims 1957, U.S. Ct. Appeals (7th cir.) 1981, U.S. Ct. Appeals (3d cir.) 1984, U.S. Ct. Internat. Trade 1987, U.S. Supreme Ct. 1987. Assoc. IceMiller, Indpls., 1954-64, ptnr., 1965-98, ret., 1998. Practitioner in residence Ind. U. Sch. of Law, Bloomington, 1987; trustee, pres. Pegasus Funds, Detroit, 1992-99; trustee, chmn. bd. dirs., pres. Bison Money Market Fund., Indpls., 1982-92. Contbr. articles to numerous profl. jours. Bd. dirs., v.p. Japan-Am. Soc. of Ind., Inc., Indpls., 1988-97; bd. dirs. Conner Prairie Inc., Fishers, Ind., 1988-97, v.p., 1989-90, chmn. bd., 1990-93; tennis ceremonies 10th Pan-Am. Games, Indpls., 1987; bd. dirs. The Children's Bur. Indpls., 1962-73, v.p., 1968-70, pres., 1970-72; bd. dirs. Orchard Country Day Sch., Indpls., 1970-73, Episc. Cmty. Svcs., Indpls., 1965-73, v.p., 1968, pres., 1969; trustee United Episc. Charities, Indpls., 1970-71, pres., 1971. With USMC, 1946-48. Mem.: Econ. Club (bd. dirs. Ind. chpt. 1988—94), Contemporary Club, Woodstock Club. Republican. Avocations: golf, tennis, opera. Office: Ice Miller Donadio & Ryan 1 American Sq Indianapolis IN 46282-0020

SUTHERLAND, DONALD WOOD, cardiologist; b. Kansas City, Mo., July 29, 1932; s. Donald Redeker and Mary Frances (Wood) S.; m. Margaret Sutherland, Sept. 11, 1954 (div. 1994); children: Kathleen Massar, Ellen Baltus, Richard, Ann, Julia McMurchie; m. Roslyn Ruggiero Elms, Mar. 31, 1995. BA, Amherst Coll., 1953; MD, Harvard U., 1957. Intern, resident Mass. Gen. Hosp., Boston, 1957-60; fellow in cardiology U. Oreg., Portland, 1961-63; pvt. practice, 1963—. Assoc. clin. prof. medicine Oreg. Health Sci. U., Portland, 1967—; chief of staff St. Vincent Hosp. and Med. Ctr., Portland, 1971-72. Contbr. articles to profl. jours. Fellow Am. Heart Assn., Am. Coll. Cardiology (pres. Oreg. chpt. 1972); mem. Multnomah Athletic Club, North Pacific Soc. Internal Medicine (pres. 1985), Pacific Interurban Clin. Club (pres. 2000). Avocations: flying private planes, scuba diving. Home: 4405 SW Council Crest Dr Portland OR 97239 Office: Columbia Cardiology Assocs 9155 SW Barnes Rd Ste 233 Portland OR 97225-6629

SUTHERLAND, FRANK, publishing executive, editor; b. Mt. Juliet, Tenn., May 31, 1945; s. Ernest Franklin and Fontelle (Moore) S.; m. Natilee Duning; children: Kate, Daniel. BA, Vanderbilt U., 1970. Reporter The Tennessean, Nashville, 1963-77, zone editor, 1977-78, city editor, 1978-82, v.p. news, editor, 1989-99, sr. v.p., 1999—; editor The Shreveport (La.) Times, 1988-89; mng. editor The Hattiesburg (Miss.) Am., 1982-86; exec. editor The Jackson (Tenn.) Sun, 1986-88. Mem. Soc. Profl. Journalists (middle Tenn. chpt. pres. 1974-81, nat. bd. dirs. 1974, nat. treas. 1981, sec. 1982, pres.-elect 1983, pres. 1984-85), Am. Soc. Newspaper Editors (mem. steering com., reporters com. for freedom of press 1979-82). Office: The Tennessean 1100 Broadway Nashville TN 37203-3134*

SUTHERLAND, GAIL RUSSELL, retired industrial equipment manufacturing company executive; b. Rush Lake, Wis., Dec. 20, 1923; s. Gail Marion and Edith (Grueb) S.; m. Leone Marie Witkowski, Mar. 10, 1945; children: Keith Allan, Glenn Elliott. BS in Agr., U. Wis., Madison, 1947, BSME, 1948, MS in Agrl. Engring., 1949. Div. engr. Deere & Co., Ottumwa, Iowa, 1949-63, mgr. product engring. Des Moines, 1963-77, dir. product planning Moline, Ill., 1977-80, dir. product engring. planning, 1980-83, dir. product engring., 1983-84, v.p. engring., 1984-86, v.p. engring. and tech., 1986-87. Mem. editorial adv. bd. Mfg. Engring. Mag., 1987; inventor: cotton harvester blower discharge, combine soybean header, beet harvester flail feeder, pasture renovator cutter. Bd. dirs. Bella Vista Property Owners Assn., 1992-98. Served as ensign USN, 1943-46 Mem. Nat. Acad. Engring., Am. Soc. Agrl. Engrs. (Engr. of Yr. 1980, Disting. Engr. of Yr. 1983), Soc. Automotive Engrs., Am. Nat. Standards Inst. (bd. dirs. 1984-86) Republican. Home and Office: 5109 Mueller Rd Mariposa CA 95338-9500 E-mail: gruss@sierratel.com.

SUTHERLAND, GEORGE LESLIE, retired chemical company executive; b. Dallas, Aug. 13, 1922; s. Leslie and Madge Alice (Henderson) S.; m. Mary Gail Hamilton, Sept. 9, 1961 (dec. Mar. 1984); children: Janet Leslie, Gail Irene, Elizabeth Hamilton; m. Carol Brenda Kaplan, Feb. 19, 1986 BA, U. Tex., Austin, 1943, MA, 1947, PhD, 1950. With Am. Cyanamid Co., various locations, 1951-87; asst. dir. research and devel. Princeton, N.J., 1969-70; dir. research and devel., agr. div., 1970-73; v.p. med. research and devel. Pearl River, N.Y., 1973-86; dir. med. research div., 1978-86; dir. chem. research div., 1980-81; v.p. corp. research tech., 1986-87. Served with USN, 1944-46. Mem. Assn. Research Dirs. (pres. 1975-76), AAAS, Am. Chem. Soc. Home: 42 Sky Meadow Rd Suffern NY 10901-2519

SUTHERLAND, DAME JOAN, retired soprano; b. Sydney, Australia, Nov. 7, 1926; d. McDonald S.; m. Richard Bonynge, 1954; 1 son. Student, Royal Coll. Music, London, 1951. Appeared concert and oratorio performances, Australia; appeared in: opera Judith, Syndey Conservatory of Music; debut Covent Garden in Magic Flute, 1952; Italian debut in Handel's Alcina, Teatro la Fenice, Venice, 1960, Bellini's Puritani, Glyndebourne Festival, Sussex, Eng., 1960, Bellini's Beatrice di Tenda, La Scala, 1961, Rossini's Semiramide, La Scala, 1962, Meyerbeer's Les Huguenots, La Scala, 1962, N.Y. debut, Carnegie Hall, 1961; Opera debut Lucia, 1961; opened Sutherland-Williamson Opera Co. tour, Australia, 1965; appeared: Handel's Julius Caesar, Hamburg Opera, 1969, Bellini's Norma, Met Opera, 1970, opened, Lyric Opera Chgo. with, Semiramide, 1971, San Francisco Opera with, Norma, 1972, San Francisco Opera with, Trovatore, 1975, Met. Opera with, I Puritani, 1976, Vancouver Opera with, Le Roi de Lahore, 1977; premiered new prodn., Met. Opera in, Tales of Hoffmann, 1973; 1st prodn. in Am. in 80 years Esclarmonde, Massenet, San Francisco Opera, 1974; author: (with Richard Bonynge) The Joan Sutherland Album, 1986, A Prima Donna's Progress, 1997. Decorated Order of Merit, comdr. and dame comdr. Order Brit. Empire, 1991; Companion, Order Australia, 1991; recipient Grammy award for best classical vocal soloist, 1981. Fellow Royal Coll. Music. Office: care Colbert Artist Mgmt 111 W 57th St New York NY 10019-2211

SUTHERLAND, JOHN BENNETT, chemical engineer; b. Burlingame, Kans., Feb. 21, 1918; s. Earl Wilbur and Edith May (Hartshorn) S.; m. Maxine Louise Turvey, Oct. 13, 1935; children: John Walter, Max Earl, Lynn Ann Sutherland Bradshaw. BS in Chem. Engring., Kans. State U., 1939, MS in Chem. Engring., 1940; PhD in Chem. Engring., U. Pitts., 1946. Rsch. engr. Texaco, Port Arthur, Tex., 1940-41; rsch. asst. Mellon Inst., Pitts., 1941-43; asst. prof. Northwestern U., Evanston, Ill., 1943-46; pres. Sutherland-Becker Lab., Burlingame, Kans., 1946-62; exec. dir. Kans State Indsl. Devel. Commn. State of Kans., Topeka, 1953-56; dir. planning and rsch. Butler Mfg. Co., Kansas City, Mo., 1956-65; dir. indsl. rsch. and ext. U. Mo. System, Columbia, 1966-80; exec. dir., v.p. Master Practitioners, Inc., Sedalia, Mo., 1983-84; prof. emeritus U. Mo., Columbia, 1980—. Cons. Kans. Indsl. Devel. Commn., 1946-53; dept. dir. econ. devel. Office Indsl. Devel. Studies Report Series, 1966; mem. Sci. Adv. Commn., Kansas City, Mo., 1962. Mem. Gov.'s Energy Adv. Com., State of Mo., 1970; treas. Pub. Sch. Dist., Burlingame, Kans., 1948. Mem. AIChE, Am. Chem. Soc., Rotary Club (pres. 1949-50). Achievements include development of new state-wide technology transfer system coordinating field specialists serving manufacturers backed by a referral system, campus experts and a technical library. Avocations: gardening, fishing, reading. Home: 3021 SW Burlingame Rd Topeka KS 66611-2003

SUTHERLAND, JOHN CAMPBELL, pathologist, educator; b. Tamingfu, Hopei, People's Republic of China, Oct. 28, 1921; came to U.S., 1926; s. Francis Campbell and Ann Findlay (Bowman) S.; m. Eunice Lucille Kindschi, June 16, 1950; 1 child, John Mark. AB, N.W. Nazarene Coll., 1941; MD, Med. Coll. Wis., 1946. Intern Milw. Hosp., 1946-47; resident in pathology St. Francis Hosp., Wichita, Kans., 1950-52, Barnes Hosp., St. Louis, 1952-54, Stanford (Calif.) Med. Ctr., 1967-68; gen. practitioner Mangum Clinic, Nampa, Idaho, 1949-50; gen. med. officer Raleigh Fitkin Meml. Hosp., Manzini, Swaziland, 1955-56, Ethel Lucas Meml. Hosp., Acornhoek, South Africa, 1956-61, 62-67; acting head biology dept. N.W. Nazarene Coll., Nampa, 1961-62; head rsch. pathology dept. Balt. Cancer Rsch. Ctr., 1968-74; asst. prof. dept. pathology U. Md., Balt., 1974-76, assoc. prof., 1976-84, mem. grad. faculty, 1982-84; vis. assoc. prof. dept. surgery U. Ariz., Tucson, 1984-96; dep. med. examiner Mohave County, 1996—2000. Co-author: Guinea Pig Doctors, 1984, Behind the Silence, 1999; contbr. articles to sci. jours. Capt. USAF, 1947-49. Mem. Alumni Assn. of N.W. Nazarene Coll. (Profl. Achievement award 1984), Toastmasters, Gideons. Republican. Mem. Nazarene Ch. Avocations: reading, bird watching, speaking. Address: PO Box 737 Atkinson NE 68713-0737 Home: 408 W Central Atkinson NE 68713-0737

SUTHERLAND, KIEFER, actor; b. London, Eng., Dec. 21, 1966; s. Donald and Shirley Douglas S.; m. Camelia Kath, Sept. 12, 1986 (div.), m. Kelly Winn (div.); children: Sarah. Appearances include (theater) debut in Throne of Straw, 1977, (films) Max Dugan Returns, 1983, The Bay Boy, 1984 (Genie award nominee 1984), At Close Range, 1986, Crazy Moon, 1986, Stand By Me, 1986, The Lost Boys, 1987, The Killing Time, 1987, Promised Land, 1987, 1969, 1988, Bright Lights, Big City, 1988, Young Guns, 1988, Renegades, 1989, Chicago Joe and the Showgirl, 1990, Flashback, 1990, Flatliners, 1990, The Nutcracker Prince (voice), 1990, Young Guns II, 1990, Article 99, 1991, Twin Peaks: Fire Walk With Me, 1992, A Few Good Men, 1992, The Vanishing, 1993, The Three Musketeers, 1993, The Cowboy Way, 1994, Eye for an Eye, 1995, A Time to Kill, 1996, The Last Days of Frankie the Fly, 1996, Freeway, 1996, Truth or Consequences N.M, 1997, Dark City, 1997, Sweetheart of the Song Tra Bong, 1998, Ground Control, 1998, (voice) Dinosaur, 1998, The Breakup, 1998, Dark City, 1998, Woman Wanted, 1999, The Red Dove, 1999, Hearts and Bones, 1999, Beat, 2000, Picking Up the Pieces, 2000, Ring of Fire, 2000, The Royal Way, 2000, The Right Temptation, 2000, To End All Wars, 2001, Paradise Found, 2001, Desert Saints, 2002, Dead Heat, 2002, Behind the Red Door, 2002; (TV movies) Trapped in Silence, 1986, Brotherhood of Justice, 1986, Last Light, 1993; (TV series) 24, 2001— (Best Performance by Actor in TV Series Drama Golden Globe award 2002, Best Performance by Actor in a Drama Series Golden Satellite award 2002, nominee Outstanding Lead Actor in Drama Series Emmy award 2002). Office: William Morris Agency attn: Steve Dontanville 151 El Camino Dr Beverly Hills CA 90212*

SUTHERLAND, MALCOLM READ, JR. clergyman, educator; b. Detroit, Nov. 11, 1916; s. Malcolm Read and Edith Ione (Osborne) S.; m. Mary Anne Beaumont, Dec. 23, 1943; children: Malcolm Read III, Maryanne B. AB, Miami (Ohio) U., 1938; MS, Western Res. U., 1941; BD, Fed. Theol. Faculty U. Chgo., 1945; LLD, Emerson Coll., 1963; LHD, Meadville-Lombard Theol. Sch., 1975. Ordained to ministry Unitarian Universalist Assn., 1945. Dir. boys work Goodrich Social Settlement, Cleve., 1938-40; housing mgr. Cleve. Met. Housing Authority, 1940-41; regional housing supr. Farm Security Adminstrn., 1941-42; housing mgmt. supr. FPHA, 1942-43; pastor in Ill., Va., Mass., 1944-94; exec. v.p. Am. Unitarian Assn., 1959-61; Robert Collier prof. ch. and soc., pres., dean faculty Meadville Theol. Sch. of Lombard Coll., Chgo., 1960-75; minister Harvard (Mass.) Unitarian Ch., 1975-94, min. emeritus, 1994—; minister emeritus Thomas Jefferson Meml. Ch., Charlottesville, Va., 1985—. Adj. prof. dept. ministry Andover Newton Theol. Sch., 1992—; exec. dir. U.S. Com. World Conf. on Religion and Peace, N.Y.C., 1980-83, internat. coun., 1984—, also v.p. U.S. exec. coun.; bd. dirs. Unitarian Universalist Svc. Com., Beacon Press; chmn. editl. adv. com. bd. Christian Register, 1955-60; field rep. Unitarian Svc. Com., Mex., 1950-51; mem. sr. secretariat World Conf. Religion and Peace, Kyoto, 1970 and del. to Louvain, 1974, Princeton, 1979, Nairobi, 1984, Melbourne, Australia, 1989, Reva del Garda, Italy, 1994, hon. pres., 1994—; cons. Niwano Peace Found., Tokyo, 1982-96; lectr., del. Japan-U.S. consultation on peace Internat. Assn. for Religious Freedom, 1970; v.p. and trustee Dana McLean Greeley Found. for Peace and Justice, 1986-94, trustee emeritus, 1994—; Thomas Minns lectr., Boston, 1955, Charlottesville, Va., 1978, Berry St. lectr., Boston, 1956; Harvard chair lectr. Warner Free Lectrs., 1985, 93; chmn. common. coun. Chgo. Cluster of Theol. Schs., inc., 1970-74; pres. Inst. on Religion in an Age of Sci., 1969, 75-77, hon. v.p., 1980—, acad. fellow, 1988—; bd. dirs., sec. Ctr. for Advanced Study Religion and Sci., Chgo., 1965—. Author: Personal Faith, 1955, Creators of the Dawn, 1979, Star Light, Star Bright, 1993; co-chmn. pubs. bd. jour. religion and sci. Zygon, 1964—; also articles. Bd. govs. Harris Manchester Coll., Oxford U., 1968—, hon. fellow, 1974—. Recipient Disting. Svc. award Charlottesville (Va.) Jr. C. of C., 1949, Disting. Svc. award Internat. Assn. Religious Freedom, 1975, Disting. Svc.award Konko Kyo Chs. Am., 1975 Mem. Unitarian Universalist Ministers Assn., Phi Delta Theta, Phi Mu Alpha, Alpha Kappa Delta, Omicron Delta Kappa. Clubs: Bucks Harbor Yacht (Maine) (commodore 1979-81). Home: 21 Woodside Rd Harvard MA 01451-1616 also: Timothys Ln Brooksville ME 04617

SUTHERLAND, MELANIE JAN, theatre director and producer; b. Johnson City, N.Y., Jan. 17, 1957; d. Rudolph Blake and Diane Thomas Sutherland. AB in Theatre, Kirkland-Hamilton Coll., 1979. Lic. massage therapist, N.Y. Resident and artistic dir. AAI Prodns., N.Y.C., 1986—; resident dir. Circle Rep Theatre, 1992-95, Rattlestick Prodns., N.Y.C., 1995—, Circle East, N.Y.C., 1995—. Freelance dir., 1979—; judge Joseph A. Callaway Award, N.Y.C., 1992—, Susan Smith Blackburn Award, N.Y.C., 1993—; program dir. Directors Nite Out, 1991-2001; artistic assoc. Women's Project and Prodns., N.Y.C.; prodr. Blatant Self-Interest Networking Event, N.Y.C. Dir. Easter in an Alley, The Love of the Nightingale, The Misanthrope, A Pirate's Lullaby, Doves on a Lark, H'r Story. Bd. dirs. Coalition, co-pres., 1994—. Recipient John Golden award for directing, 1990. Avocations: running, hiking, raising border collie, travel. Fax: 775-522-0617. E-mail: msuther766@aol.com.

SUTHERLAND, MICHAEL CRUISE, librarian; b. Morgantown, W.Va., Aug. 29, 1938; s. Charles Fish and Mildred (Haymond) S. BA in English, San Fernando Valley State U., 1967, postgrad., 1968-69, UCLA, 1967, MLS, 1970. Office asst., clk. Lindsey & Hall, L.A., 1959-60; libr. asst. I, bindery clk. Biomed. Libr. UCLA, 1961-65; jr. adminstrv. asst. Dept. Pub. Works City of L.A., 1967; intermediate clk. typist San Fernando Valley State U., Northridge, Calif., 1967-69; libr. I, tchg. asst. Grad. Sch. Libr. and Info. Sci. UCLA, 1970; spl. collections libr. Occidental Coll., L.A., 1970—. Attendee numerous workshops and seminars; organizer Western Books Exhbn. at various librs. throughout the Western U.S., 1992, 96; judging organizer, 1993. Author numerous exhbn. catalog booklets; author: (with others) Encyclopedia of Library and Information Sciences, 1979, Western Books Exhibition Catalog, 1986, Striking Research Gold: Distinguished Collections in California Independent Academic Libraries, 1988; contbr. articles to profl. jours. Active Neighborhood Watch, AIDS Quilt Program. Mem. Rounce and Coffin Club (sec., treas.), Robinson Jeffers Assn., Tor House Found., Zamorano Club, Book Club Calif. Office: Occidental Coll Mary Norton Clapp Libr 1600 Campus Rd Los Angeles CA 90041-3314 E-mail: bun@oxy.edu.

SUTHERLAND, ROBERT DONALD, writer; b. Blytheville, Ark., Nov. 4, 1937; s. Donald Charles and Opal G. S.; m. Marilyn F. Neufeldt, July 25, 1959; children: David, Allan. BA, Wichita State U., 1959; MA, U. Iowa, 1961, PhD, 1964. Prof. English Ill. State U., Normal, 1964-92; editor, publ. The Pikestaff Press, 1977—. Author: Language and Lewis Carroll, 1970, Sticklewort and Feverfew, 1980. Recipient Dr. Martin Luther King Jr. Human Rels. award, 1998. Avocations: drawing, painting, travel, reading, walking, classical music. Home: 501 E Willow St Normal IL 61761

SUTHERLAND, WILLIAM OWEN SHEPPARD, English language educator; b. Wilmington, N.C., Jan. 19, 1921; s. William Owen Sheppard and Mary Owen (Green) S.; m. Madeline Ethel Cooley, Sept. 12, 1947; children: Madeline, William, John, Thomas. AB in English with honors, U. N.C., 1942, MA, 1947, PhD, 1950. Instr. English. U. N.C., Chapel Hill, 1950-51, Northwestern U., Evanston, Ill., 1951-54; asst. prof. U. Tex., Austin, 1954-58, assoc. prof., 1958-65, prof., 1965-98, Robert A.-Thomas H. Law Centennial prof. humanities emeritus, 1998—, chmn. dept., 1983-90, faculty humanist rep. Deans of Humanities of S.W. Conf., 1980; cons. Ednl. Testing Svc. and Coll. Bd., Princeton, N.J., 1965-72, NEH, Washington, 1978—; prof. emeritus U. Tex., 1998. Author: Art of the Satirist, 1965; co-editor: The Reader, 1960, Six Contemporary Novels, 1961, An Index to 18th Century Periodicals, 1800, 1956. Served to capt. C.E. U.S. Army, 1942-45. Recipient Scarborough Excellence in Tchg. award U. Tex. Austin, 1959, Liberal Arts Pro Bene Meritis award, 1996, Pres. Assocs. Tchg. award, 1982; NEH grantee, 1978-79. Mem. MLA, South Central MLA (exec. com. 1967-69), AAUP (state v.p. 1970-71), Nat. Council Tchrs. English (dir. 1974-78) Democrat. Episcopalian. Home: 3610 Highland View Dr Austin TX 78731-4033 Office: U Tex Dept English Austin TX 78712 E-mail: woss@utxums.cc.utexas.edu.

SUTHERS, HANNAH LOUISE BONSEY, biologist; b. Lorain, Ohio, Oct. 4, 1931; d. William Edwin and Hannah Elisabeth Bonell B.; m. Derwent Albert Suthers, June 20, 1953 (div. Oct. 1968); children: Daniel Derwent, Hannah Marie Suthers McCabe, Edwin Bonsey. BA, Oberlin Coll., 1953, MS equivalent in biology, MA equivalent in theology, Oberlin Coll., 1998. Master permitee Bird Banding, USGS, Migratory Bird Mgmt.; cert. avian rehabilitator USDI Fish and Wildlife Svc. Sec./clk. Union Theol. Seminary, N.Y.C., 1953-54; nursery sch. tchr. Berkeley (Calif.) Unified Sch. Dist., 1954-55; sec./clk. Ch. Divinity Sch. of Pacific, Berkeley, 1955; nursery sch. tchr. Edgewood People's Ch., East Lansing, Mich., 1964-65; overseas missionary Protestant Episcopal Ch., Brazil, 1965-68; lab. tech. Princeton (N.J.) Labs., Inc., 1968; profl. rsch. staff Princeton U., 1968-89, profl. tech. staff, 1989-96. Reviewer Am. Jour. Botany, 1971—73, 1983, N.Am. Bird Bander, 1977—2002; area rep. Princeton U., 1978—80, 1982—89; coord. com. Princeton U. Women's Orgn., 1982—89; cons. Bracco Rsch. USA, Inc., Princeton, 1996—, Williams Transcontinental Gas Pipeline Corp., Lawrenceville, NJ, 1996—, FMC Corp., Princeton, 1997—2001, Allelix Neurosci., Inc., Cranbury, NJ, 1997—99, Johnson & Johnson Consumer Products, Inc., Skillman, NJ, 1998—, Purdue Bio Pharma LP, Princeton, 1999—. Contbr. articles to profl. jours. Bird bander U.S. Geol. Survey, 1953—; leader Bits and Boots 4-H Horse Club, Mercer County, NJ, 1969—75; county coach Mercer County 4-H Competitive Trail Ride and Mercer County 4-H Horse Judging Team, 1973—75; rep. Mercer County Horse Coun., 1970—75; mem. Migratory Bird Rehab. Policy and Permit Rev. Com., , 1988—90, others; participant N.J. Audubon Breeding Bird Atlas, 1980—85, 1991—95; trainer N.Am. Banding Coun., 1998—; vol. cons. Woodrow Wilson Nat. Fellowship Found., Princeton, 1997; vol. State of N.J. Wildlife Conservation Corps, 2000—. Recipient Outstanding Layperson award Diocese of Mich. Bishop's award 1955, Frank M. Chapman Meml. award Am. Mus. of Natural History, 1986, Paul A. Stewart award Wilson Ornithol. Soc., 1986, 87, Small Grants, Audubon/Washington Crossing Chpt., 1986-88, 94—, others. Mem. Sigma Xi. Democrat. Episcopalian. Achievements include the discovery of day-length sensitivity of Xanthium seedlings, allowing aseptic culture of sprouts for plant hormone bioassays; developed aseptic culture techniques of Xanthium hypocotyl tissue for bioassays; teammate in discovery of the chemoattractant in the cellular slime mold Polysphondylium violaceum and in the discovery of the role of ammonia in chemotaxis; discovered the transcontinental tranport of cellular slime molds (Dictyostelids) by migratory songbirds.

SUTIN, NORMAN, chemistry educator, scientist; b. Ceres, Republic of South Africa; came to U.S., 1956; s. Louis and Clara (Goldberg) S.; m. Bonita Sakowski, June 29, 1958; children: Lewis Anthony, Cara Ruth. B.Sc., U. Cape Town (S. Africa), 1948, M.Sc., 1950; PhD, Cambridge U. (Eng.), 1953. Research fellow Durham U. (Eng.), 1954-55; research assoc. Brookhaven Nat. Lab., Upton, N.Y., 1956-57, assoc. chemist, 1958-61, chemist, 1961-66, sr. chemist, 1966—2001, dept. chmn., 1988-95; affiliate Rockefeller U., N.Y.C., 1958-62; vis. fellow Weizmann Inst., Rehovoth, Israel, 1965; vis. prof. SUNY-Stony Brook, 1968, Columbia U., N.Y.C., 1968-69, Tel Aviv U., Israel, 1973-74, U. Calif.-Irvine, 1977, U. Tex. Austin, 1979; disting. prof. Rutgers U., 1999—2001; ret., 2001. Editor: Comments on Inorganic Chemistry Jour., 1980-87; mem. editorial bd. Jour. Am. Chem. Soc., 1985-89, Inorganic Chem., 1986-89, Jour. Phys. Chem., 1987-92; contbr. articles to profl. jours. Mem. NAS, Am. Acad. Arts and Scis., Am. Chem. Soc. (recipient award for disting. svc. in advancement of inorganic chemistry 1983). Office: Brookhaven Nat Lab Dept Chemistry Upton NY 11973

SUTLIN, VIVIAN, advertising executive; b. Chgo. d. Samuel E. and Doris (Weinberg) S. BA, Roosevelt U. V.p. creative group head Grey North Advt., Inc., Chgo.; v.p. creative dir., founder Pilot Products, Inc.; TV writer, producer Grey Advt., Inc., NY; sr. writer Young and Rubicam, Inc., NY; v.p. creative dir. Dodge and Delano, NY; pres. Vivian Sutlin Advt., new products and consumer packaged goods specialist with full svc. TV and print, domestic and internat. ops.; creative supr. William Douglas McAdams, Inc., NY, Grey Med. Advt., Inc.; pres. Vivian Sutlin Comm. Cons. Consumer and Med./Pharm. Advt.; pres. Signature Products East, N.Y.C., Internat. Packaging, Printing and Promotional Products Co. Co-author: Industry Women Speak Out. Recipient Chgo. Fedn. Advt. Clubs award, Am. TV Commls. Festival award, TV award Art Dirs. Club Chgo., Triangle award Med. Advt. Print, Internat. Broadcasting award, Best of Decade award RX Club, Guacaipuro TV award. Avocations: jogging, aerobics, tennis, art.

SUTMAN, FRANCIS XAVIER, university dean; b. Newark, Dec. 20, 1927; s. Joseph L. and Ella (Joyce) S.; m. Mabel Ranagan, Apr. 1, 1956; children: Frank J., Catherine J., Elizabeth A. AB, Montclair State U., 1949, MA, 1952; EdD, Columbia U., 1956. Tchr. pub. secondary schs., N.J., 1949-55; instr. chemistry Upsala Coll., 1953-55; asst. prof. Wm. Paterson Coll., 1955-57; chmn., assoc. prof. natural scis. Inter-Am. U. P.R., 1957-58; prof. gen. edn., chmn. SUNY, Buffalo, 1958-62; prof. sci. edn., chmn. dept. secondary edn., dir. Merit Bilingual Center Temple U., Phila., 1962-82; dean Coll. Edn., Fairleigh Dickinson U., 1982-88. Tech. rsch. staff Exxon Engring. & Rsch. Lab., Linden, N.J., 1955; vis. lectr. Rutgers U.; cons. India AID Project; vis. prof., scientist Hebrew U., Israel; sr. scholar Temple U., 1988—; vis. sci. educator, program dir. edn. and human resources NSF, 1989-93; exec. dir. curriculum devel. coun., Rowan U., N.J.; vis. scientist Morgan State U.; del. OAS Coun. Sci. Edn. and Culture, 1971; co-dir. Environ. Edn. Conf. Environ. Protection Svc., Jerusalem, 1975; cons. fed., state, local sch. dists.; dir. sci. tech. project Huazhong U., China, 1980-87; co-dir. chem. edn. conf. Tianjin Normal U., 1984. Author: Concepts in Chemistry, 1962, 2d edit., 1968, What Kind of Environment Will Our Children Have?, 1971, Chemistry in Today's Environment (U.S. and Israel), 1977, Educating Personnel for Bilingual Settings: Today and Beyond, 1979, Teaching English Through Science, 1985, Improving Learning in Science and Basic Skills Among Diverse Student Populations, 1995. Active Haddonfield (N.J.) Bd. Edn., 1976-79; v.p. alumni bd. Montclair State U., 1982-88. Recipient Air Force Assn. award, 1968, N.J. Gov.'s Albert Einstein Edn. award, 1987, award Hispanic Congress of Pa., 1980, Alumni Citation Montclair State U., 1988. Fellow AAAS; mem. NSTA, Am. Chem. Soc., Am. Assn. Colls. Tchr. Edn. (chief instnl. rep. 1968-87), Nat. Assn. Rsch. Sci. Tchg. (pres.), N.J. Gov.'s Acad., Sigma Xi, Phi Delta Kappa (pres. Temple U. chpt. 2000-02), Coun. Sci. Soc. Presidents. Home: 311 W Royal Ave Linwood NJ 08221-1458 also: Rowan U Curriculum Devel Coun Glassboro NJ 08028 E-mail: fmsutman@msn.com. *Professional success comes after one accepts the paradoxes of human activity and accepts conflict and criticism, and gives of one's self for a cause. With all of this, timing is critical.*

SUTNICK, ALTON IVAN, dean, educator, researcher, physician; b. Trenton, N.J., July 6, 1928; s. Michael and Rose (Horwitz) S.; m. Mona Reidenberg, Aug. 17, 1958; children: Amy Sutnick Plotch, Gary Benjamin Sutnick. AB, U. Pa., 1950, MD, 1954; student in Biomed. Math., Drexel Inst. Tech., 1961—62; student in Biometrics, Temple U., 1969—70. Diplomate Am. Bd. Internal Medicine. Rotating intern Hosp. U. Pa., 1954-55, resident in anesthesiology, 1955-56, resident in medicine, 1956, USPHS postdoctoral research fellow, 1956-57; asst. instr. anesthesiology, then asst. instr. medicine U. Pa. Sch. Medicine, 1955-57; resident in medicine Wishard Meml. Hosp., Indpls., 1957-58, chief resident in medicine, 1960-61; resident instr. medicine Ind. U. Sch. Medicine, Indpls., 1957-58; USPHS postdoctoral research fellow Temple U. Hosp., 1961-63; instr., then assoc. in medicine Temple U. Sch. Medicine, 1962-65; mem. faculty U. Pa. Sch. Medicine, 1965-75, assoc. prof. medicine, 1971-75; clin. asst. physician Pa. Hosp., 1966-71; research physician, then assoc. dir. Inst. Cancer Research (now Fox Chase Cancer Ctr.), Phila., 1965-75; vis. prof. medicine Med. Coll. Pa., 1971-74; prof. medicine Drexel U. Coll. Medicine, 1975—; dean Med. Coll. Pa., 1975-89, sr. v.p., 1976-89; v.p. Ednl. Commn. Fgn. Med. Grads, 1989-95; dir. internat. med. edn. Carelift Internat., 1997—. Dir. clin. devel. Am. Oncologic Hosp., Phila., 1973-75; attending physician Phila. VA Hosp., 1967-89, Allegheny U. Hosps., 1971-95; cons. in field; mem. U.S. nat. com. Internat. Union Against Cancer, 1969-72; mem. Nat. Conf. Cancer Prevention and Detection, 1973, Nat. Cancer Control Planning Conf., 1973; vice chmn. Gov. Pa. Task Force Cancer Control, 1974-76, chmn. com. cancer detection, 1974-76; mem. health rsch. adv. bd. State of Pa., 1976-78; mem. diagnostic rsch. adv. group Nat. Cancer Inst., 1974-78; chmn. coord. com., comprehensive cancer ctr. program Fox Chase Cancer Ctr., U. Pa. Cancer Ctr., 1975; cons. WHO, Govt. of India, 1979, Govt. of Indonesia, 1980, entire S.E. Asia region, 1981, U. Zimbabwe, 1989, Minister of Health of Poland, 1992, Israel Sci. Coun., 1992, U. Autonoma de Guadalajara, Mex., 1993, Generalitat de Catalunya, Spain, 1993, Ministry of Health Russian Fedn., 1993; mem. Inst. de Pos-Graduacae Medica Carlos Chagas, 1993, Fondazione Smith Kline, Italy, 1995, Assn. Med. Schs. Europe, 1995-99, U. Jordan, 1995, U.S.-China Ednl. Inst., 1996, Georgian Postgrad. Med. Found., 1996, Instituto Universitario de Ciencias Biomedicas, Argentina, 1996, faculty of medicine, U. Saarland, Germany, 1996, Ctr. for Med. Edn., Ben Gurion U., Israel, 1996—, Hungarian Nat. Health Ins. Fund, 1996, Carelift Internat., 1997, Intercoll., Cyprus, 1997, Open Soc. Inst., 1997-99, Moldova State Med. and Pharm. U., 1997—, Aieti Med. Sch., Ga., 1997-2001, Tartu U., Estonia, 1998-99, WHO European Office, 1998, Vilnius U. and Kaunas Med. U., Lithuania, 1998-99, U. Zagreb, Croatia, 1998-99, Larnaca Hosp., Cyprus, 1998, Netherlands and Russian med. schs., others ; rep. for internat. med. and health scis. edn. MCP Hahnemann U. of the Health Scis., 1996-99; mem. adv. com. Open Soc. Inst. Muskie Fellowship Program, 1997, working group on implementation of presdl. policy on internat. edn., 2000, selection comm. Internat. Consortium for the Advancement of Medical Education, 2001—. Author numerous articles in field.; Asst. editor: Annals Internal Medicine, 1972-75; editorial bd. other med. jours. Bd. dirs. Israel Cancer Rsch. Fund, 1975—95, Am. Assocs. for Democracy in Ga., 2000—; nat. bd. dirs. Am. Assocs. Ben Gurion U., 1991—; bd. Internat. Med. Scholar Program, 1988—89, Sight Savers Internat., 1988—91; adv. commn. Internat. Participation Phila. '76, 1973—76; bd. dirs. Phila. Coun. Internat. Visitors, 1972—77; nat. bd. dirs. Phila. divsn. Am. Assocs. Ben Gurion U., 1986—99, assoc. chair, 1993—95, 2000—. Capt. M.C. U.S. Army, 1958—60. Recipient Arnold and Marie Schwartz award in medicine AMA, 1976, Torch of Learning award Am. Friends of Hebrew U., 1981, medal Ben Gurion U. of Negev, Israel, 1985, medal U. Cath. de Lille, France, 1987, medal U. Belgrade, Yugoslavia, 1988, Founder's award and medal Med. Coll. Pa., 1989, St. Thomas Aquinas award Santo Tomas U. Med. Alumni Assn., The Philippines, 1989, medal Kiev Med. Inst., Ukraine, 1991, Benjamin Albagli medal Inst. de Pos-Graduacao Medica Carlos Chagas, Brazil, 1993, shield Coll. Physicians and Surgeons, Pakistan, 1993, medal Ukrainian State Med. U., 1994, medal Universidad de Cantabria, Spain, 1999, medal Hadassah-Hebrew U. Dental Sch., 1999, Negev award Am. Assocs., Ben Gurion U., 2000. Fellow ACP (internat. adv. network), Coll. Physicians Phila. (censor 1977-86 , councillor 1977-86); mem. AMA, AAAS, Am. Fedn. Clin. Research (pres. Temple U. chpt. 1964-65), Am. Assn. Cancer Research, Am. Soc. Clin. Oncology, Am. Dermatoglyphics Assn., Assn. Am. Cancer Insts., Assn. Am. Med. Colls., Northeast Consortium on Med. Edn. (treas. 1983-89, chmn. 1986-87), Council of Deans of Pvt. Free-Standing Med. Schs. (co-founder, nat. chmn. 1983-85), Pa. Council Deans (chmn. 1987-89), Am. Cancer Soc. (vice chmn. service com. Phila. div. 1974-76, bd. dirs. 1974-80, chmn. awards com. 1976), Am. Lung Assn., Am. Heart Assn., NAFSA-Assn. Internat. Educators, Pan Am. Med. Assn., Phila. Coop. Cancer Assn., N.Y. Acad. Scis., Pa. Heart Assn., Heart Assn. Southeastern Pa., Pa. Med. Soc., Phila. County Med. Soc. (chmn. com. internat. med. affairs 1964-72), Pa. Lung Assn., Phila. Assn. for Clin. Trials (bd. dirs. 1980-81), Health Systems Agy. Southeastern Pa. (gov. bd., exec. com. 1983-87, sec. 1985-87), Am. Assn. Ben Gurion U. (bd. dirs. 1986—), Soc. des Medecins Militaires Français, Assn. Med. Edn. in Europe, Soc. Española de Educacion Medica, Internat. Med. Sch. Affiliates Consortium (co-founder, vice chmn. 1985-87), Phi Beta Kappa, Sigma Xi, Alpha Omega Alpha (councillor 1963-65) Achievements include discovery of association of hepatitis B surface antigen with hepatitis; performed 1st studies of pulmonary surfactant in adult human lung disease; developed cancer screening system based on risk status; pioneer in describing non-A non-B hepatitis C, pioneer in showing relationship of body iron stores to cancer susceptibility and life expectancy; organized first symposium on problems of foreign medical graduates; coined word "ergasteric" for lab.-contracted disease; responsible for advances in assessment of clinical competence. Office: Carelift Internat GSB Bldg Ste 425 One Belmont Ave Bala Cynwyd PA 19004 E-mail: alsutnick@carelift.org.

SUTO, DARLENE ANNE, not-for-profit developer; b. Troy, NY, Apr. 10, 1948; d. Lloyd Templeton and Gladys Butler Viall; m. Andrew Anthony Suto, Aug. 23, 1969 (div. Apr. 1992); 1 child Drew Bentley. AA, Harcum Jr. Coll., Bryn Mawr, Pa., 1968; BA, SUNY, Albany, 1991. Mng. dir. Cmty. Exptl. Repertory Theatre Inc., Poughkeepsie, NY, 1974—80; adminstrv. asst. Rensselaer County Hist. Soc., Troy, 1985—92; coord. devel. St. Anne Inst., Albany, 1992—94; dir. devel. Hudson Valley Girl Scout Coun., Delmar, 1994—98, Commn. on Econ. Opportunity, Troy, 1998—. Bd. dirs., chair Samaritan Counseling, Albany, 1997—99; treas., bd. dirs. Women in Devel., Albany, 1998—; mem. legis. com. NY State Cmty. Action Assn., 1999—. Recipient Spl. Mission Recognition, Embury Dist. United Meth. Women, 2001. Mem.: Bus. and Profl. Women (v.p. Latham chpt. 1992—97, mem. Greater Capital Region br. 1997—). Republican. Methodist. Avocations: reading, theater , concerts. Home: 862 Tamarac Rd Troy NY 12180 E-mail: dviall51@aol.com.

SUTOWSKI, THOR BRIAN, choreographer, educator; b. Trenton, N.J., Jan. 27, 1945; s. Walter X. and Kathryn (Tang) S.; m. Sonia Arova, Mar. 11, 1965; 1 child, Ariane. Student, San Diego Ballet, 1958-63, San Francisco Ballet, 1963-64, Nat. Ballet, 1964. Cert. solo dancer Genossenschaft Deutscher Buhnen-Angehorigen, Germany. Soloist Norwegian State Opera, Oslo, 1965-70; 1st soloist Hamburgische Staatsoper, Hamburg, Germany, 1970-71; dir. San Diego Ballet, 1971-76, Ballet Ala., Birmingham, 1978-81, State of Ala. Ballet, Birmingham, 1982-83; chmn. Ala. Sch. Fine Arts, 1976-96; assoc. dir. Calif. Ballet Co., San Diego, 1996-98; artistic prodr. San Diego Ballet Co., 1998-2000. Artistic advisor, choreographer Asami Maki Ballet, Toyko, 1976-79; choreographer Atlanta Ballet, 1980-87, resident choreographer Atlanta Ballet Co., 1987-93; dance advisor Ala. State Arts Council, Montgomery, 1977-78; advisor Tenn. Ballet Co.; dance advisor Miss. Arts Council; choreographer Ballet South and State of Ala. Ballet; mem. City of Atlanta Mayor's Review Fellowship panel, 1987; adj. prof. choreography U. Ala., Tuscaloosa, 1988—; prof. U. Calif., San Diego, 1998—; commd. choreographer Bavarian State Ballet-State Opera, Munich, 1994; Am. Masters choreographer Sacramento Ballet, 2001. Recipient Pub. TV Emmy award, 1976, Obelisk award for choreography, 1977, 78, 79, 80; grantee Ford Found., 1964, Nat. Endowment for Arts, 1973-74. Mem. Am. Guild. Mus. Artists. Republican. Lutheran.

SUTPHEN, HAROLD AMERMAN, JR. retired paper company executive; b. Verona, N.J., Feb. 13, 1926; s. Harold Amerman and Marion Esther (Mason) S.; m. Greta May Peterson, June 24, 1950; children— Judith Amerman, Peter Lehmann, Pamela Torrance. Grad., Phillips Exeter Acad., 1944; BS in Mech. Engring, Princeton, 1950. With Universal Oil Products Co., Chgo., 1950-51, Texaco, Inc., 1951-52; bus. research analyst Arthur D. Little, Inc., 1952-56; asst. div. mgr. adminstrn., fine papers div. W.Va. Pulp and Paper Co. (name now changed to Westvaco Corp.), 1956-60, v.p., 1967-80, sr. v.p., 1980-88, mgr. fine papers div., 1974-88, dir., 1975-88. V.p., treas. U.S. Envelope Co., Springfield, Mass., 1960-62, pres., CEO, 1962-67, chmn. bd., 1967-74; bd. dirs. Assessment Appeals, Fairfield, Conn., 1993-97, chmn., 1996-97. Served with AUS, 1944-46. Mem. Holland Soc. N.Y., Phi Beta Kappa. Clubs: Country of Fairfield (Conn.); Weston (Conn.) Gun. Home: 33 Hill Brook Ln Fairfield CT 06430-7169

SUTPHIN, JOHN E. ophthalmologist, educator; b. Atlanta, Dec. 14, 1948; s. John Everett and Elsie Eubank Sutphin; m. Emily Anne Mitchell, Aug. 29, 1970; children: Amanda, Rhett, John G. MD, Vanderbilt U., 1974. Diplomate Am. Bd. Ophthalmology. Commd. ensign USN, 1971, advanced through grades to capt., 1988; ret., 1993; intern Naval Regional Med. Ctr., San Diego, 1974-75, resident in ophthalmology, 1976-79, comprehensive ophthalmologist Orlando, Fla., 1979-82; clin. instr. Baylor Coll. Medicine, Houston, 1982-84; dir. cornea svcs. Naval Med. Ctr., San Diego, 1984-86, chmn. dept. ophthalmology, 1986-93; prof. ophthalmology U. Iowa, Iowa City, 1993—. Past advisor Surgeon Gen. of Navy, Bur. Medicine and Surgery, Washington. Fellow Am. Acad. Ophthalmology (com. chmn. 2000—, Honor award 1996). Presbyterian. Avocations: reading, hiking, biking, woodworking. Office: U Iowa Hosps and Clinics 200 Hawkins Dr Iowa City IA 52242-1091 Fax: (319) 353-7996. E-mail: john-sutphin@uiowa.edu.

SUTPHIN, WILLIAM TAYLOR, lawyer; s. William Halstead and Catharine (Bonner) S.; m. Alissa L. Kramer, June 21, 1958. AB in History, Princeton U., 1957; LLB, U. Pa., 1960. Bar: N.J. 1960; U.S. Ct. Appeals (3d cir.) 1964, U.S. Supreme Ct. 1965. Assoc. Stryker, Tams & Dill, Newark, 1960-67, ptnr., 1967-73; sole practice Princeton, N.J., 1973—. Coadj. faculty mem. Rutgers U. Govt. Svcs. Tng. Program, 1973—; assoc. counsel N.J. Planning Ofcls., 1975—. Mem. Princeton Twp. Planning Bd., 1967-72, Regional Planning Bd. Princeton, 1970-74; atty. Green Brook Twp. Planning Bd., 1972-2001, Millstone Twp. Bd. Adjustment, 1978-98, Del. Twp. Bd. Adjustment, 1982—, Princeton Borough Bd. Adjustment, 1983—; committeeman Twp. Princeton, 1973-75, police commr., 1974-75; treas. Youth Employment Svc. Princeton Inc., 1981-84. Served with U.S. Army, 1953-56, capt. JAGC Ret. Mem. N.J. Bar Assn. (chmn. ins. com. 1979-81), Princeton Bar Assn. (pres. 1981-82), N.J. Inst. Mcpl. Attys. Home: 501 Jefferson Rd Princeton NJ 08540-3418 Office: Law Offices of William T Sutphin 34 Chambers St Princeton NJ 08542-3700 E-mail: william.t.sutphin@verizon.net.

SUTRADHAR, SANTOSH CHANDRA, research scientist; s. Gopal Chandra and Suniti Sutradhar; m. Joyasree Sutradhar, Jan. 16, 2001. Ph. D., U. of Md., Baltimore County, USA, 1998—2001; M. Sc., Meml. U. of Nfld., St. John's, Canada, 1996—98, U. of Dhaka, Dhaka, Bangladesh, 1991—93. Rsch. trainee Internat. Centre for Diarrhoeal Disease Rsch., Dhaka, Bangladesh, 1994—95, statistician Bangladesh, 1995—96; lectr. U. of Dhaka, Bangladesh, 1995—96; tchg. asst./instr. Meml. U. of Nfld., St. John's, Canada, 1996—98; tchg./rsch. asst. U. of Md., Baltimore, Md., 1998—2001; biometrician Merck & Co., Inc., Blue Bell, Pa., 2001—. Author: (journals) Communication in Statistics, (presentation) Graduate Student Research Day (Monetory award for best presented paper, 1999). Recipient Fellow of the Sch. of Grad. Studies, Grad. Sch. of Meml. U. of Nfld., 1998, Hon. Medal, Loin's Club, Dhaka Bangladesh, 1991, Books, Internat. Soc. for Krishna Conciousness, 1992; scholar Gen. Merit Scholarship, U. of Dhaka, Bangladesh, 1991-1993, Bd. of Edn., Commila, Bangladesh, 1983-1991. Mem.: Amercian Statistician Assn.

SUTTA, STUART, accountant; b. New Haven, Apr. 29, 1947; s. Martin Sutta and Marion (Slachter) Seligman; m. Patricia Sutta, Aug. 18, 1983; children: Michael, David, Jessica, Derek, Shawn. BS, Fla. State U., 1967. CPA, Fla. Pres. Stuart Sutta, Miami, Fla., 1977—. Chief YMCA Indian Guides, Miami, Fla., 1982-83; mem. various coms. Jaycees, Tallahassee, Fla., 1977-80. Mem. Lions. Avocations: golf, travel. Office: Stuart Sutta & Co PA Ste 210 770 Ponce De Leon Blvd Coral Gables FL 33134-2066

SUTTER, BARTON E. education educator, writer; b. Mpls., Dec. 15, 1949; s. Harold Edwin and Virginia Mae (Eastman) Sutter; m. Dorothea Stowell Diver, Aug. 28, 1994; children: Liselotte D. Stuecher, Bettina J. Stuecher; m. Annette Marie Atkins, 1981 (div. 1991). BA, S.W. State U., Marshall, Minn., 1972; MA, Syracuse U., 1975. Typesetter Composing Rm. New Eng., Boston, 1972—73, Typographic Arts, Mpls., 1976—85; lectr. U. Minn., 1986—90, Duluth, 1988—98; from lectr. to sr. lectr. U. Wis., Superior, 1998—. Bd. dirs. Spirit Lake Poetry Series, Duluth. Author: My Father's War, 1991, The Book of Names, 1993, Cold Comfort, 1999. Recipient Minn. Book award for fiction, 1992, Minn. Book award for poetry, 1994, Minn. Book award for creative non-fiction, 1999. Mem.: Assn. Univ. Wis. Profls., Acad. Am. Poets (assoc.). Democrat. Mem. Soc. Of Friends. Avocations: canoeing, fishing, camping, cross country skiing. Home: 1321 E 8th St Duluth MN 55805 Office: Univ Wis Belknap & Catlin Superior WI 54880

SUTTER, DARRYL JOHN, professional hockey coach; Player Chgo. Blackhawks, 1980-86, asst. coach, 1987-88, assoc. coach, 1991-92, head coach, 1992-95, cons., 1995-97; head coach San Jose Sharks, 1997—. Office: San Jose Sharks 525 W Santa Clara St San Jose CA 95113-1500*

SUTTER, ELEANOR BLY, diplomat; b. N.Y.C., Oct. 21, 1945; d. Samuel M. and Sylvia Gertrude Bly; children: Deborah Nelson, Willis. BA, Swarthmore Coll., 1966; MA, Am. U., 1978; diploma in strategic studies, U.S. Army War Coll., 1997. Instr. English Thammasat U., Bangkok and Udornthani Tchr. Tng. Coll., 1967-71, Lomonosov State U., Moscow, 1973-74; rschr. Kennan Inst. for Advanced Russian Studies, 1977-79; fgn. svc. officer Office Soviet Internal Affairs, Dept. of State, 1979-80, U.S. Embassy, Kinshasa, 1980-82, London, 1982-85, Office of Strategic Nuclear Policy, Dept. of State, 1986-88, Office of Soviet Union Affairs, Dept. of State, 1988-90, U.S. Embassy, Moscow, 1990-92, charge d'affaires ad interim Bratislava, 1993, dep. prin. officer, 1993-95, dep. chief of mission, 1995-96; office dir. Dept. of State, Washington, 1997-99, sr. inspector Office Inspector Gen., 1999-2001, dir. Office of Proliferation Threat Reduction, 2001—. Exec. dir., exec. sec., advisor U.S. Del. to Nuclear and Space Talks, Geneva, 1987-91; teaching fellow Russian lit. The Am. U., 1976-77; escort interpreter and translator Dept. of State, 1976. Co-author: Final Report of the Kennan Institute's Soviet Research Institutes Project, 1981. Founder Camp Wocsom, Moscow, 1974. Mem. Am. Fgn. Svc. Assn. Avocations: music, folk dance.

SUTTER, ELIZABETH HENBY (MRS. RICHARD A. SUTTER), civic leader; b. St. Louis, May 15, 1912; d. William Hastings and Alvina (Steinbreder) Henby; m. Richard A. Sutter, June 15, 1935; children: John Richard, Jane Elizabeth, Judith Ann. AB, Washington U., 1931. Sec.-treas. Sutter Mgt. Co., St. Louis, until 1985. Chmn. com. on mental health AMA Aux., 1960-62, v.p., 1962-63, 63-64, pres. 1965-66, editor Direct Line newsletter, 1964-74; assoc. editor MD's Wife, 1973-80; mem. adv. bd. Deaconess Hosp. Sch. of Nursing, st. Louis; trustee John Burroughs Sch., 1958-61, v.p. 1959, devel. commn., 1960-61; mem. Hist. Bldgs. Commn. St. Louis County, 1957-91, chmn., 1973-91; bd. dirs. Gamma Phi Beta House Corp. Washington U., St. Louis, 1989-93; chmn. Com. for Preservation Children's Teeth; mem. planning bd. Health, Hosp. Health, Welfare Coun. Met. St. Louis, 1955-64; pres. Aux. Cen. States Soc. Indsl. Medicine and Surgery, 1960-61; pres. St. County Med. Soc. Aux., 1949, 52-53; pres. Mo. State Medical Aux., 1952; pres. Am. Medical Assn Aux., 1965-66; sec. St. Louis County Health and Hosp. Bd., 1956-61; chmn., 1961; bd. dirs. Am. Lung Assn. Eastern Mo., exec. com., 1956-85, v.p., 1960-61; pres. Tb and Health Soc. of St. Louis, 1962-65; adv. coun. vol. svcs. Nat. Assn. Mental Health, 1962-64; bd. dirs. Am. Cancer Soc., St. Louis, exec. com., 1954-64; bd. dirs. Mental Health Assn. St. Louis, 1960-61; mem. Practical Nursing Edn. Coun., chmn. exec. com., 1959-60; mem. AMA Coun. on Mental Health Planning for Nat. Conf. on Mental Health, 1961; mem. adv. com. on women in svcs. Dept. Def., 1969-72, vice chmn., 1971; participant 24th ann. global strategy discussion U.S. Naval War Coll., 1972; bd. govs. Washington U. Alumni, 1970-71, 75—, vice chmn. 1979-80, chmn., 1980-81; trustee Washington U., 1979-81; pres. Washington U. Arts and Scis. Century Club, 1970-71; bd. dirs. St. Louis Conv. and Tourist Bur., 1975-83, sec., 1980-82; bd. dirs. Health Svcs. Agy., 1975-82; mem. East West Gateway Coordinating Coun. Task Force on Hist. Preservation, 1975-81, U. City Hist. Preservation Commn., 1977-85; bd. dirs. Whitney Beach III Assn., Longboat Key, Fla., 1984-87, 91-94; del. Mo. Rep. Conv., 1972, 76, 80, 84, 88, 92, del. Nat. Rep. Conv., 1984. Hon. grand marshall commencement parade Washington U., 2001. Named 1 of 10 Women of Achievement in good citizen category St. Louis Globe-Democrat, 1961, hon. Grand Marshall Washington Univ. Reunion Parade Class of 1931, 2001; Alumna of Yr., Gamma Phi Beta, St. Louis, 1966; recipient St. Louis County Me. Soc. award of merit, 1964, Disting. Alumni citation Wash. U., 1968, Disting. Alumni Svc. citation, 1977, Life Style award Eastern Mo. chpt. Am. Lung Assn., 1982, Lifetime Svc. award, 1997, Meritorious Svc. award Am. Park and Recreation Soc., 1985, U. City High Sch. Hall of Fame Celebration of the Century, 1999; Endowed Richard A. and Elizabeth H. Sutter Visiting Professorship Wash. U., 1981; Endowed chair Richard A. and Elizabeth H. Sutter chair in Occpl., Indsl. and Environ. Med., 1993. Mem. Mo. Hist. Soc. St. Louis Symphony Soc., AMA Aux. (hon. life), Mo. Med. Aux. (hon. life), Met. St. Louis Med. Aux. (hon. life), Gamma Phi Beta (bd. found. St. Louis chpt. 1989). Mem. Ladue Chapel. Address: # 3 McKnight Pl Saint Louis MO 63130 Home: 6701 Gulf Of Mexico Dr Apt 321 Longboat Key FL 34228-1323

SUTTER, JANE ELIZABETH, science educator, writer, conservationist; b. St. Louis, Nov. 27, 1939; d. Richard A. and Elizabeth Henby Sutter. AB in Sociology and English, Vassar Coll., 1961; MA in Health Facilities Mgmt., Webster Coll., St. Louis, 1979. Healthcare analyst, Chgo. and St. Louis, 1966-83; asst. dir. radio, TV and motion picture dept. AMA, Chgo., 1966-67; staff coord., rsch. assoc. Chgo. water quality study and environ. health study Inst. of Medicine of Chgo., 1967-69; dir. environ. health planning Comprehensive Health Planning, Inc., Chgo., 1969-73; planning assoc., spl. asst. to med. dir. Sutter Clinic, Inc., St. Louis, 1975-84; vol. activist, educator; founder, dir. Wild Birds for the 21st Century, 1994—; dir., corr. www.wild-birds.org, 1999—. Chmn. Opera Theatre of St. Louis Newsletter, Recitative, Vol. 1, No. 1, 1980, Vol. 1, No. 2, 1980; co-founder, com. mem. 1st Internat. Alewife Festival of Chgo., Chgo. Yacht Club, summer 1968; appointee Gov.'s Com. for Pure Air and Water, Chgo., 1968; spl. advocate N.Am. Migratory Birds particularly hummingbirds; mem. Ladue Chapel. Mem. Nat. Garden Clubs, Inc., Federated Garden Clubs of Mo., Inc., Clayton Garden Assn., Mo. Bot. Garden, St. Louis Artists' Guild (mem. artists' sect. 1992-95, portraitist), Inst. Religion in an Age of Sci., Univ. Club, Neotropical Bird Club (U.K.). Avocations: artist, music, landscaping for birds. Home: 7376 Pershing Blvd Saint Louis MO 63130-4206 E-mail: jesutteri@aol.com.

SUTTER, JEAN, sculptor; b. Chgo., Aug. 9, 1934; d. John H. and Lulu Kennedy Sutter; m. Paul W. Berg, Jan. 1, 1953 (dec. Mar. 1968); children: Mark, Julie, Karen;. B Visual Arts, Ga. State U., 1974, M Visual Arts, 1978. One-woman shows include: Lowe Gallery, Atlanta, 1989, U. Okla., Norman, 1984, Quinlan Art Ctr., Gainesville, Ga., 1981, Ga. State U., Atlanta, 1979, Auburn U., Ala., 1978; group shows include: Arts Connection, Atlanta, 1990, Jubilee-So. Festival of the Arts, Atlanta, 1987, Heath Gallery, Atlanta, 1985, Atlanta Arts Festival, 1980, 82, 84, Sculptural Arts Mus., 1982, Columbia Mus., S.C., 1982, Mus. of Touch, Atlanta, 1981, Am. Art Inc., Atlanta, 1981, Temple U., Phila., 1980, Cedar Crest Coll., Allentown, Pa., 1980-81, High Mus. Art, Atlanta, 1979, 78, others; collections include Ga. State U., New Life Covenant Ch., Atlanta, Macon (Ga.) State Coll., numerous pvt. parties. Home and Office: 18 Padsett Ct # 20334 Jasper GA 30143-7217

SUTTER, JOHN RICHARD, manufacturer, investor; b. St. Louis, Jan. 18, 1937; s. Richard Anthony and Elizabeth Ann (Henby) S.; children: John Henby, Mary Elizabeth, Sarah Katherine S. Glazar; m. Madeline Ann Traugott Stribling, June 5, 1984; 1 stepchild, William Stribling. BA, Princeton U., 1958; MBA, Columbia U., 1964. CPA, N.Y., Mo. Mgr. Price Waterhouse, N.Y.C., 1964-71; pres. John Sutter and Co., Inc., St. Louis, 1972-86, Handlan-Buck Co., St. Louis, 1975-88; investor, 1988—; pres. Pamlico Jack Group, Oriental, N.C., 1989—. Pres. Sutter Mgmt. Corp., St. Louis, 1972-79. Mem. Chpt. Christ Ch. Cathedral, 1987-88. Lt. (j.g.) USNR, 1959-63. Mem. AICPAs, Mo. Soc. CPAs, Neuse Sailing Assn., Sailing Club of Oriental. Clubs: Princeton, Oriental Dinghy. Episcopalian. Avocations: painting, sailboat racing, ocean cruising, ceramic arts. Home and Office: PO Box 481 Oriental NC 28571-0481

SUTTER, JOSEPH F. aeronautical engineer, consultant, retired aircraft company executive; b. Seattle, Mar. 21, 1921; m. Nancy Ann French, June 14, 1943. BA, U. Wash., 1943. Various engring. positions Boeing Comml. Airplane Co., Seattle, 1946—65, dir. engring. for Boeing 747, 1965—71, v.p., gen. mgr. 747 div., 1971—74, v.p. program ops., 1974—76, v.p. ops. and product devel., 1976—81, exec. v.p., 1981—86, cons., 1986—87, 1987—. Chmn. aerospace safety adv. panel NASA, 1986; mem. Challenger Accident Commn., 1986. Served to lt. j.g. USN, 1943—45. Named Joseph F. Sutter professorship established in his honor, U. Wash., Boeing Co., 1992; named to, Interant. Air Cargo Assn. Hall of Fame; recipient Master Design award, Product Engring. mag., 1965, Franklin W. Kolk Air Transp. Progress award, Soc. Aero. Aerospace Coun., 1980, Elmer A. Sperry award, 1980, Nuts & Bolts award, Transport Assn., 1983, Nat. Medal Tech., U.S. Pres. Reagan, 1985, Sir Kingsford Smith award, Royal Aero. Soc. in Sydney, 1980, Wright Bros. Meml. Trophy, 1986, Alumnus Summa Laude Dignatus award, U. Wash., 2001. Fellow: AIAA (Daniel Guggenheim award 1990), Royal Aero Soc. (hon.); mem.: Internat. Fedn. Airworthiness (pres. 1989). Address: Boeing 7755 E Marginal Way S Seattle WA 98108-4002

SUTTER, LAURENCE BRENER, lawyer; b. N.Y.C., Feb. 5, 1944; s. Meyer and Beatrice Sutter; m. Betty A. Satterwhite, June 9, 1979. AB, Columbia Coll., 1965; JD, N.Y.U., 1976. Bar: N.Y. 1977, U.S. Dist. Ct. (so. and ea. dists.) N.Y. 1977. Assoc. Shea & Gould, N.Y.C., 1976-80, Meyer, Suozzi, English & Klein P.C., Mineola, N.Y., 1980-82; assoc. counsel publs. Gen. Media Internat., Inc., N.Y.C., 1982-96, sr. v.p., gen. counsel, 1997—. With N.Y. Army N.G., 1966-72. Mem. Assn. of Bar of City of N.Y. (mem. com. on civil rights 1986-89, mem. com. on comm. and media law 1989-92, mem. com. on copyright and lit. property 1994-97), First Amendment Lawyers Assn., Nat. Arts Club, Orient (N.Y.) Yacht Club (dir. 1997-2000, sec. 2000-2001). Democrat. Jewish. Avocations: music, sailing. Office: Gen Media Comm Inc 11 Penn Plz 12th Fl New York NY 10001-0006

SUTTER, MADELINE ANN, landscape architect; b. Chgo., Oct. 13, 1941; d. William Charles Matthew Traugott and Antonette Florence Geller; m. Gray Carroll Stribling Jr., June 3, 1967 (div. Aug. 1982); 1 child, William Charles Matthew Stribling; m. John Richard Sutter, June 1984. BA, U. Wis., 1965; A of Horticulture, Meramec Coll., 1982; M of Landscape Arch. with honors, N.C. State U., 1999. Sys. analyst McDonnell-Douglas Corp., St. Louis, 1965-67; mem. faculty Washington U., 1967-70; pres. Inside/Outside, Inc., 1971-89; v.p. Handlan-Buck Co., 1983-88; pres. Madeline Sutter, ASLA, Oriental, N.C., 1989—. Lectr. Pamlico C.C., Grantsboro, N.C., 1990-94; cons. Hist. Beaufort (N.C.) Preservation, 1992-95, Coalition for Cmty. Conservation, Raleigh, N.C., 1995—. Author: Trees for Small Towns, 1999, Ma: An Investigation Into the Making of Exterior Meditative Physical and Sequential Space, 1999; creator: (urban forest program) Trees for Oriental, 1992-96 (Tree City U.S.A. award 1996). Chmn. Tree Bd. of Oriental, 1992-96; mem. phys. environment com., campus planning and design N.C. State U. Named Disting. Woman of N.C., N.C. Coun. for Women, 1996; grantee Trees for Oriental Phase I, II and II Am. the Beautiful, 1992, 94, 95, Phase III Small Bus. Adminstrn., 1995, Trees for Small Towns Urban and Comty. Forestry Grant Program, 1996. Mem. Am. Soc. Landscape Archs. (chmn. P.I. Group Residential Landscape Design), Herb Soc. Am. (mem.-at-large 1971—), N.C. Soc. Landscape Archs., N.C. League Landscape Archs., St. Louis Herb Soc. (pres., all offices 1967—), N.C. Urban Forest Coun. (mem. exec. bd., treas. 1992—), St. Pete Mad Dog Triathlon Club, Tau Sigma Delta Natl. Honor Soc. for Architecture and the Allied Arts, Neuse Sailing Assn., Sailing Club Oriental. Avocations: sailboat racing, offshore and coastal cruising, harpsichord, kayaking, painting. Home and Office: PO Box 481 Oriental NC 28571-0481

SUTTER, MORLEY CARMAN, medical scientist; b. Redvers, Sask., Can., May 18, 1933; s. Christian Benjamin and Amelia (Duke) S.; m. Virginia Frances Mary Laidlaw, June 29, 1957; children— Gregory Robert, F. Michelle, Brent Morley. MD, B.Sc., U. Man., 1957, PhD, 1963. Intern Winnipeg (Man.) Gen. Hosp., 1956-57, resident, 1958-59; teaching fellow pharmacology U. Man., 1959-63; supr. Downing Coll., Cambridge U., 1963-65; asst. prof. pharmacology U. Toronto, 1965-66, U. B.C., 1966-68, asso. prof., 1968-71, prof., 1971-98, retired prof. emeritus, 1998—, head dept. pharmacology, 1971-87. Former mem. staff Vancouver (B.C.) Hosp. & Health Sci. Ctr., St. Paul's Hosp.; mem. Minister of Health's Adv. Com. on Drugs, Province of B.C., 1971-87. Contbr. articles to sci. jours. Recipient Gov. Gen. medal, 1950; Med. Research Council of Can. fellow, 1959-63; Wellcome Found. Travelling fellow, 1963; Imperial Chem. Industries fellow, 1963-65; Med. Research Council scholar, 1966-71 Mem. British Pharmacol. Soc., Am. Soc. Pharmacology and Exptl. Therapeutics. Office: U BC Faculty Medicine Therapeutics 2176 Health Scis Mall Dept Pharmacology Vancouver BC Canada V6T 1Z3 E-mail: mcsutter@interchange.ubc.ca.

SUTTER, WILLIAM PAUL, lawyer; b. Chgo., Jan. 15, 1924; s. Harry Blair and Elsie (Paul) S.; m. Helen Yvonne Stebbins, Nov. 13, 1954; children: William Paul, Helen Blair Sutter Doppelheuer. AB, Yale U., 1947; JD, U. Mich., 1950. Bar: Ill. 1950, Fla. 1977, U.S. Supreme Ct. 1981. Assoc. Hopkins & Sutter (and predecessors), Chgo., 1950-57, ptnr., 1957-89, of counsel, 1989—2001. Mem. Ill. Supreme Ct. Atty. Registration Commn., 1975-81 Contbr. articles on estate planning and taxation to profl. jours. Chmn. Winnetka Caucus Com., 1966-67; pres., trustee Lucille P. Markey Charitable Trust, 1983-98; precinct capt. New Trier Twp. (Ill.) Rep. party, 1960-68; asst. area chmn. New Trier Rep. Orgn., 1968-72; trustee Gads Hill Center, pres., 1962-70, chmn., 1971-80; trustee Northwestern Meml. Hosp., 1983-98, life trustee, 1998—; bd. dirs. Chgo. Hort. Soc., 1982—; mem. dean's coun. Sch. Medicine, Yale U., 1991—; bd. visitors Waisman Ctr., U. Wis., 1996-2002; corr. sec. Yale U. Class of 1945, 1990—. Served to 1st lt. AUS, 1943-46. Fellow Am. Bar Found., Am. Coll. Trust and Estate Counsel (bd. regents 1977-83, exec. com. 1981-83); mem. ABA (ho. dels. 1972-81, chmn. com. on income estates and trusts, taxation sect. 1973-75), Ill. Bar Assn. (bd. govs. 1964-75, pres. 1973-74), Chgo. Bar Assn. (chmn. probate practice com. 1963-64), Am. Law Inst., Internat. Acad. Estate and Trust Law, Am. Judicature Soc., Ill. LAWPAC (pres. 1977-83), Order of Coif, Phi Beta Kappa, Phi Delta Phi, Chi Psi, Mid-Day Club, Indian Hill Club, Gulf Stream Golf Club, Country Club Fla., Ocean Club (Fla.) (bd. govs. 1993-99, sec. 1993-97, pres. 1997-99), Lawyers Club Chgo. Episcopalian. also: Two Par Club Cir Village of Golf 96 Woodley Rd Winnetka IL 60093 Office: Foley & Lardner 3 First Nat Pl Chicago IL 60602 E-mail: wpsutter@aol.com.

SUTTERBY, LARRY QUENTIN, internist; b. North Kansas City, Mo., Sept. 11, 1950; s. John Albert and Wilma Elizabeth (Henry) Sutterby; m. Luciana Risos Magpuri, July 5, 1980; children: Leah Lourdes, Liza Bernadette. BA in Chemistry, William Jewell Coll., 1972; MD, U. Mo., Kans. City, 1976. Diplomate with qualifications in geriatric medicine Am. Bd. Internal Medicine. Resident in internal medicine Mt. Sinai Hosp., Chgo., 1976-79; physician Mojave Desert Health Svc., Barstow, Calif., 1979-86; pvt. practice, 1986-2001; med. cons. State of Calif., L.A., 2001—. Med dir Mojave Valley Hospice, 1983—2001, VNA Hospice, Barstow, 1994—2001, Optioncare Home Health Servs, 1995—2001. Recipient Loving Care Award, Vis Nurse Asn Inland Counties, 1988. Fellow: ACP; mem.: Am. Soc. Internal Medicine, Am. Numismatic Assn. Democrat. Roman Catholic. Avocation: astronomy. Office: 311 S Spring St Ste 700 Los Angeles CA 90013

SUTTERLIN, JAMES SMYRL, political science educator, researcher; b. Frankfort, Ky., Mar. 15, 1922; s. Frederick J. and Agnes (Douglas) S.; m. Betty C. Berven, June 24, 1950 (dec. Jan. 1989); children: Rose E., Sabrina, Jamie Ann, James E.; m. Renate Craine, Dec. 27, 1997. BA, Haverford Coll., 1943; postgrad., Harvard U., 1949, 67; hon. degree in jurisprudence, Kyung Hee U., Seoul, Korea, 1973. Vice-consul U.S. Fgn. Svc., Berlin, 1946-48; polit. officer U.S. Mission, 1951-54; 1st sec. U.S. Embassy, Tel Aviv, 1954-56; desk officer U.S. State Dept., Washington, 1956-60; 1st sec. U.S. Embassy, Tokyo, 1960-63, counselor Bonn, 1963-68; dir. U.S. Dept. State, Washington, 1969-72, insp.-gen., 1972-74; dir. UN, N.Y.C., 1974-87; dir. rsch. L.I. U., Bklyn., 1985-87, adj. prof., 1985—; fellow/lectr. Yale U., New Haven, 1988—. Author: Berlin—Symbol of Confrontation, 1989, UN and the Maintenance of Security, 1995, The United Nations in Iraq: Defanging the Viper, 2002. Elder Presbyn. Ch., Port Chester, N.Y., 1976-96; chmn. Samaritan House, White Plains, N.Y., 1990-95; pres. Wainwright House, Rye, 1995-96; chmn. acad. coun. on the UN Brown U., 1995-97. 1st lt. U.S. Army, 1945-46. Recipient Grosse Verdienstkreuz, Fed. Republic of Germany, 1974. Mem. UN Assn. of U.S.A., Am. Coun. on Germany, Coun. Fgn. Rels., Phi Beta Kappa. Avocation: gardening. Home: 17 N Chatsworth Ave Apt 6k-l Larchmont NY 10538-2126 Office: Yale U 34 Hillhouse Ave New Haven CT 06511-3704 E-mail: jsutter729@aol.com.

SUTTIE, JOHN WESTON, biochemist; b. La Crosse, Wis., Aug. 25, 1934; married; 2 children. BS, U. Wis., 1957, MS, 1958, PhD, 1960. Fellow biochemist Nat. Inst. Med. Rsch, England, 1960-61; asst. prof. to assoc. prof. U. Wis., Madison, 1961-69, prof., 1969—2001, prof. nutrition sci., 1988-97, Bd. agrl. Nat. Rsch. Ctr., 1996—2001. Assoc. editor Jour Nutrition, 1991-97; editor Jour. Nutrition, 1997—. Mem. NAS, Am. Soc. Expl. Biology and Medicine, Am. Soc. Biochemistry and Biology, Am. Soc. for Nutrition Scis. (Osborne and Mendel award award 1980, Mead Johns award 1974), Internat. Soc. Thrombosis and Hemostasis (Hemostasis Career award 1989), Am. Soc. Clin. Nutrition. Office: U Wis Dept Biochemistry Madison WI 53706-1544 E-mail: suttie@biochem.wisc.edu.

SUTTLE, HELEN JAYSON, retired education educator; b. Plattsburgh, N.Y., Dec. 13, 1925; d. Harold Lincoln Jayson and Blanche Rabideau Jayson Woods; widowed, 1993; 1 child, Adolphia Helen Suttle Blanton. BA in Edn., Limestone Coll., 1961; MA in Edn., Winthrop U., 1973. Cert. tchr., S.C. Tchr. Madden Elem. Sch., Spartanburg, S.C., 1961-71, West Jr. High Sch., Gaffney, 1971-81, L.L. Vaughn Elem. Sch., Gaffney, 1981-88; substitute tchr. Gaffney Dis. 1, 1988—. Vol. SC Budget Control Bd., Upstate Carolina Med. Ctr., Meals on Wheels, Literacy Assn., local soup kitchen; chmn. Cherokee County Rep. Com.; v.p. Ch. Women's Guild, pres., 1998—; dir. religious edn. Sacred Heart Ch., 2001—; pres. Sacred Heart Sr. Citizens Club; treas. ch. com. Greenville Deanery; pres.-elect Piedmont Deanery, 2002—; Eucharistic min., lector; mem. exec. bd. SC Coun. Cath. Ch. Women, 1998—, chair family commn., 1998—; trustee Limestone Coll. Named woman of Yr., S.C. Coun. Cath. Women Greenville Deanery, 1996. Fellow Internat. Biog. Assn. (life, dep. gov. Am. chpt.), Limestone Coll. Alumni Assn. (pres., chpt. pres.), Fountain Club (charter mem.), Kalosophia Honor Soc. Roman Catholic. Avocations: writing, art, gardening, crafts. Home: 201 Trenton Rd Gaffney SC 29340-3626

SUTTLE, STEPHEN HUNGATE, lawyer; b. Uvalde, Tex., Mar. 17, 1940; s. Dorwin Wallace and Ann Elizabeth (Barrett) Suttle; m. Rosemary Williams Davison, Aug. 3, 1963; children: Michael Barrett, David Paull, John Stewart. BA, Washington and Lee U., 1962; LLB, U. Tex., 1965. Bar: Tex. 1965, U.S. Dist. Ct. (no. and we. dists.) Tex. 1965, U.S. Ct. Appeals (5th cir.) 1967, U.S. Supreme Ct. 1970. Law clk. to Hon. Leo Brewster U.S. Dist. Ct. , Ft. Worth, 1965-67; ptnr. McMahon, Surovik, Suttle, Buhrmann, Hicks & Gill, P.C., Abilene, 1970—. Pres. Abilene Boys Clubs, Inc., 1975—76; bd. dirs. Abilene Cmty. Theater, 1979—80, Abilene Fine Arts Mus., 1977—78. Fellow: State Bar Tex. (dir. 1999—2002), Tex. Bar Found., Am. Bd. Trial Advocates (pres. Tex. 2003—), Am. Coll. Trial Lawyers; mem.: ABA (chmn. young lawyers sect. award of merit 1976), Tex. Bar Assn. (dir. 1999—2002), Abilene Bar Assn. (pres. 1987—88), Am. Judicature Soc. (bd. dirs. 1981—84), Tex. Young Lawyers Assn. (chmn. bd. dirs. 1976), Def. Rsch. Inst., Tex. Assn. Def. Counsel, Assn. Def. Trial Attys., Abilene Country Club. Episcopalian. Home: 1405 Woodland Trl Abilene TX 79605-4705 Office: McMahon Surovik Suttle Buhrmann Hicks & Gill PC PO Box 3679 Abilene TX 79604-3679 E-mail: ssuttle@mcmahonlawtx.com.

SUTTLES, DAVID CLYDE, educator; b. Harriman, Tenn., June 14, 1948; s. Clyde and Virginia (Stewart) S.; m. Barbara Chambers, June 3, 1968; children: Julia Kay, Robert David. BS in Bus. Adminstrn., U. Tenn., 1972, MS, 1975, MEd, 1998. Assoc. prof. Cleve. State Coll., Tenn., 1975—; news dir. WTNB-TV, 1998—99; counselor Pine Ridge Treatment Ctr., 2001—. Adj. faculty Tenn. Wesleyan Coll., 1987—; crisis intervention specialist Vol. Behavioral, 2000—01; counselor Pine Ridge Treatment Ctr., 2001. Active Cmty. Devel. Citizens Adv. Com., Cleveland, 1981; active Gov.'s Com. Employment of Handicapped, 1984; mem. Tenn. Com. on Persons with Disabilities, 1991—; lay dir. Diocese East Tenn. Episc. Cursillo Secretariat; eucharistic min. St. Luke's Episc. Ch.; bd. dirs. Friends of Libr., Cleve., 1984, Habitat for Humanity. Recipient Aciever award Gov. Tenn., 1976; cert. of appreciation Mayor of Cleveland, 1980. Mem. Coll. Media Advisors, Mensa, Phi Theta Kappa. Democrat. Office: Cleveland State Community Coll PO Box 3570 Cleveland TN 37320-3570 E-mail: sudsy1948@aol.com.

SUTTLES, DONALD ROLAND, retired academic administrator, business educator; b. Coldsprings, Ky., Nov. 14, 1929; s. Noah Elseworth and Bertha Viola (Seward) S.; m. Phyllis JoAnn McMullen, Dec. 12, 1952; children: Daniel, Ruth, Jonathan, Donna, Joanna, Stephen. Student, U. Md., 1949-50, U.S. Naval Acad., 1951-52; BBA, U. Cin., 1959; MBA, Xavier U., 1966; EdD, U. N.C.-Greensboro, 1977. Cert. mgmt. acct., internal auditor. With Procter & Gamble Co., Cin., 1952-73, supr., 1959-60, indsl. engr., 1960-63, cost engr., 1963-64, mgr. prodn. planning, 1965-68, asst. security coord., 1968-70, dept. mgr., 1970-73; dir. bus. affairs Piedmont Bible Coll., Winston-Salem, N.C., 1973-80, v.p. adminstrn., faculty, 1990-98; ret., 1998; assoc. prof. bus. Winston-Salem State U., 1978-87; prof. acctg. Catawba Coll., Salisbury, N.C., 1987-91. Bus. cons. Deacon, trustee, tchr. Bible sch. Salem Bapt. Ch.; vol. chaplain, Forsyth Med. Ctr. Served with USAF, 1948-51. Mem.: Gideons Internat. Home: 2300 Denise Ln Winston Salem NC 27127-8764

SUTTLES, VIRGINIA GRANT, advertising executive; b. Urbana, Ill., June 13, 1931; d. William Henry and Lenora (Fitzsimmons) Grant; m. John Henry Suttles, Sept. 24, 1977 (dec. July 1996); step-children: Linda, Peggy, Pamela Suttles Diaz, Randall. Grad. pub. schs., Mahomet, Ill. Media estimator and Procter & Gamble budget control Tatham-Laird, Inc., Chgo., 1955-60; media planner, supr. Tracy-Locke Co., Inc., Dallas and Denver, 1961-68; media dir., account exec. Lorie-Lotito, Inc., 1968-72; v.p., media dir. Sam Lusky Assocs., Inc., Denver, 1972-86; ind. media buyer, 1984-89; mktg. asst. mktg. dept. Del E. Webb Communities, Inc., Sun City West, Ariz., 1985-88, with telemktg. dept., 1989-90, homeowner coord., 1993-97; mktg. coord. asst./media buyer Del Webb Corp., Phoenix, 1990-93. Lectr. sr. journalism class U. Colo., Boulder, 1975-80; condr. class in media sems. Denver Advt. Fedn., 1974, 77; Colo. State U. panelist Broadcast Day, 1978, High Sch. Inst., 1979, 80, 81, 82, 83. Founder Del E. Webb Meml. Hosp. Found.; patron founder Tree of Life Nat. Kidney Found. Colo.-Rockies Snow Mountain YMCA Ranch, Winter Park, Colo., Sun Health Found. Sun Cities, Ariz. State U. Found. Sundome Performing Arts Ctr. Mem. Denver Advt. Fedn. (bd. dirs. 1973-75, program chmn. 1974-76, 80-82, exec. bd., v.p. ops. 1980-81, chmn. Alfie awards com. 1980-81, Advt. Profl. of Yr. 1981-82), Denver Advt. Golf Assn. (v.p. 1976-77, pres. 1977-78), Colo. Broadcasters Assn., Sun City West Bowling Assn. (bd. dirs. 1987-88), Am. Legion Aux. (historian, pub. chmn. 1998-2000, sec. 1999-2002, at large bd. mem. 2002--), VFW Aux. (life), Air Force Sgt.'s Assn. Aux., Sun Health Aux. (life), West Valley Art Mus. Women's League (treas. 1999-2000). Republican. Congregationalist. Home: 20002 N Greenview Dr Sun City West AZ 85375-5579 *Personal philosophy: Over the years has been to work your full day, volunteer to help young people coming up in their profession, so they will be able to do their tasks properly and volunteer your services to help in any way you can to make this a good world to live in.*

SUTTON, BETTY SHERIFF, elementary education educator; b. Orangeburg, S.C., Jan. 16, 1933; d. Luther Doyle and Mattie (White) Sheriff; m. William Bryan Nunn, June 19, 1954; 1 child, Lisbeth Sheriff Nunn (Mrs. William Reid Clark); m. James Carlton Sutton, Dec. 28, 1979 (dec., 1998). Student, Columbia Coll., 1949-52; BS, U. S.C., 1953. Tchr. grade 4 State of S.C. Pub. Sch., Blackville, 1953-54; tchr. grade 2 Dream Lake Elem. Sch., Apopka, Fla., 1954-64; tchr. spl. edn. Leon County Sch., Tallahassee, 1965-66; page mother Fla. Ho. Reps., 1966-67; tchr. grade 3 Timberlane Elem. Sch./Leon County Schs., 1967-71; tchr. grades 3 and 4 Golfview Elem. Sch./Brevard County Schs., Rockledge, Fla., 1972-86; tchr. grade 1 Cambridge Elem. Sch./Brevard County Schs., Cocoa, 1987-98; ret., 1998. Pres. Bits of Brevard, Inc., Rockledge. Chmn. Democrats for Conner, 1988, Keep Brevard Beautiful, 1990; active Brevard Symphony Orch. Guild, Brevard Mus. Guild, 1973—, Brevard Heritage Coun., Inc., Episcopal, St. Marks Guild. Recipient S.C. Forestry award State of S.C. Forestry Commn., 1977; ART grantee J. Paul Getty Ctr. for Edn. in the Arts, 1990. Mem. AAUW (pres. 1968-70), Apopka Woman's Club (pres. 1960-62), Apopka Garden Club, Brevard Reading Coun. (v.p. 1980-82), Am. Mothers, Inc., Columbia Coll. Column Club, Columbia Coll. Alumni Club. Ctrl. Fla., U. S.C. Alumni Club (life), Country Club of Rockledge, Delta Kappa Gamma (pres. 1992-94). Avocations: volunteering, reading, swimming, travel, farming. Home: 2201 Royal Oaks Dr Rockledge FL 32955-5440

SUTTON, BRIAN DALE, lawyer; b. Wichita Falls, Tex., Sept. 22, 1961; s. Emmett and Susan (Spindler) S.; m. Fern V. Jacobs. BS, Tex. A&M U., 1984; JD, St. Mary's U., 1987. Bar: Tex. 1987, U.S. Dist. Ct. (ea. dist.) Tex. 1988. Assoc. Weller, Wheelus & Green, Beaumont, Tex., 1987-89, Dryden, Grossheim & Sutton, LLP, Beaumont, 1987—2002, Sutton & Jacobs LLP, Beaumont, 2002—. Bd. dirs. Humane Soc. S.E. Tex., Beaumont, 1991—, pres., 1993-94. Mem. ABA, Assn. Trial Lawyers Am., Tex. Trial Lawyers Assn., S.E. Trial Lawyers Assn., Tex. State Bar. Office: Sutton & Jacobs LLP 850Park St O Beaumont TX 77706

SUTTON, DANA FERRIN, classics educator; b. White Plains, N.Y., Oct. 10, 1942; s. Joseph Guy Jr. and Eleanor Sutton; m. Kathryn A. Sinkovich, Aug. 16, 1975. BA, The New Sch. for Social Rsch., N.Y.C., 1965; MA, U. Wis., 1966, PhD, 1970. Lectr. Herbert Lehman Coll., CUNY, 1969-72; postdoctoral rsch. Darwin Coll., Cambridge, Eng., 1972-74, U. Auckland, New Zealand, 1974-75; asst. prof. U. Ill., Urbana, 1975-79; prof. U. Calif., Irvine, 1979—, dept. chair., 1986-94. Author: The Greek Satyr Play, 1975, numerous other books and monographs; editor: William Gager: The Complete Works, 1994, The Complete Works of Thomas Watson (1556-1592), 1995, The Complete Latin Poetry of Walter Savage Landor, 1999; contbr. articles to profl. jours. John Guggenheim fellow, 1975-76. Mem. Am. Philol. Assn., Calif. Classical Assn. Office: U Calif Dept Classics 120 Hob Ii Irvine CA 92697-0001 E-mail: danasutton@mac.com.

SUTTON, DOLORES, actress, writer; b. N.Y.C. BA in Philosophy, NYU. Appeared in broadway plays including Man With the Golden Arm, 1956, Career, 1958, Machinal, 1960, Rhinoceros, Liliom, She Stoops to Conquer, Hedda Gabler, Anna Karenina, Eccentricities of a Nightingale, Brecht on Brecht, Young Gifted and Black, Luv, The Friends, The Web and the Rock, The Seagull, Saturday, Sunday, Monday, The Little Foxes, What's Wrong With This Picture, The Cocktail Hour, My Fair Lady (Broadway revival), 1994, My Fair Lady (nat. tour), 1993-94; films include The Trouble With Angels, Where Angels Go, Trouble Follows, Crossing Delancey, Crimes and Misdeameanors, Tales of the Darkside; TV appearances include Studio One, Hallmark Hall of Fame Prodn. An Wilderness, Theatre Guild of the Air: Danger, Suspense, Gunsmoke, Valiant Lady, General Hospital, From These Roots, As the World Turns, Edge of Night, F. Scott Fitzgerald in Hollywood, Patty Hearst Story, All in the Family, Bob Newhart Show, All My Children, others, (TV drama) Lady Somebody, 1999; TV writer Lady Doc, The Secret Storm, Loving; playwright: Down at the Old Bull and Bush, The Web and the Rock, Company Comin', Born Yesterday, 1995, A Perfect Ganesh, 1995, Detail of a Larger Work, 1995, The Front Page, 1996, The Exact Center of the Universe, 1997, A Drop in the Bucket, 1997, Spring Storm (newly discovered Tennessee Williams play), 1997, Signs and Wonders, 1998, It Gives Me Great Pleasure, 2001; prodns. Free Ascent, 2001, Burial Society, 2001, The Find, 2002. Mem. League of Profl. Theatre Women (bd. dirs.), Ensemble Studio Theatre (bd. dirs.).

SUTTON, DONALD DUNSMORE, science educator, consultant; b. Oakland, Calif., June 8, 1927; s. Ben Bryan and Mabel Dunsmore Sutton; m. Treva Tose Sudhalter Dye, Dec. 24, 1981; children: Alice K., Peggy A. Kluthe, Donald C. AB (Bactelocogy), U. Calif., Berkeley, 1951—51; MA (Microbiology), U. Calif., Davis, 1954—54, PHD (Microbiology), 1957—57. Rsch. asst. U. Calif., Davis, Calif., 1953—55, natl sci fdn predoct, 1955—57; microbiology educator asst. Ind. U. Med. Ctr., Indianpolis, Ind., 1957—59; merak-walrman postdsc Insto Microbiology, Rutgers U., New Brunswick, NJ, 1959—60; biology educator Calif. State U., Fullerton, Calif., 1965—70; appl. microbiology vis. educator Tokyo U., Tokyo, Japan, 1970—71; microbiology educator Calif. State U., Fullerton, Calif., 1960—2002. Cons. Environa associates, Enoinitas, Calif., 1982—2002. Contbr. articles to profl. jours. Electronic technician USN Res., 1945—46, Pto. Mem.: Audubon Soc., Am. Soc. for Microbiology, Mycrological Soc. Am. Achievements include research in Bacterial diseases of orchids; Taxonomy of Genus Erwinia. Home: 231 La Veta Ave Encinitas CA 92024 Office: California State University 800 N State College Fullerton CA 92834

SUTTON, DOUGLAS HOYT, nurse; b. McHenry, Ill., Oct. 27, 1962; s. Hoyt Douglas Sutton and Barbara (Sutton) Hensley. Cert. in emergency med. tech., Polk Community Coll., Winter Haven, Fla., 1985; ADN, SUNY, Albany, 1990, BS in Nursing, 1991, BS in Psychology, 1993; MSN, U. Fla., 1995; MPA, Troy State U., 1997; EdD, master's cert., Fla. Intenrat. U., 2000. Cert. adv. nursing adminstrn., Post Master's Cert. Adult Health Nurse Practitioner, Fla. Internat. U., 2000. Paramedic Polk County Emergency Med. Svcs., Bartow, Fla., 1984-88; edn. cons. Moore Pubs., 1990-94; mgr. orthopedics and skilled care programs Columbia Healthcare, Inc., Gainesville, 1995-97; dir. med. surg. nursing U. Cmty. Hosp., Tampa, 1997-98; dir. patient svcs. Bethesda (Fla.) Meml. Hosp., 1998-2000; asst. prof. nursing Broward C.C., Ft. Lauderdale, Fla., 2000—02, Barry U., Miami, 2002—. Mem. Fla. Orgn. Nurse Execs., Am. Coll. Healthcare Execs., Sigma Theta Tau. Home: 1747 NE 45 St Fort Lauderdale FL 33334 E-mail: dsutton@mail.barry.edu.

SUTTON, ERNEST SHAW, chemical engineer; b. Burlington, N.J., May 22, 1922; s. Ernest Shaw Sr. and Elizabeth Bauer (Sholl) S.; m. Janet Gilbertson, July 1, 1950 (dec. Mar. 1974); children: Jane M., Douglas S., Andrea L.; m. Lois Williams, June 12, 1975. BSChemE, U. Pa., 1943. Analytical chemist Nat. Synthetic Rubber Corp., Louisville, 1943-44; polymer chemist Hewitt Robins, Inc., Buffalo, 1946-48, United Aircraft, Inc., Hartford, Conn., 1948-50, Thermoid Rubber Co., Trenton, N.J., 1950-53; propellant chemist Thiokol Corp., Elkton, Md., 1953-54, head R&D labs., 1954-84; head preliminary design Morton-Thiokol, Inc., 1984-86, dir. mktg., 1986-87, v.p., gen. mgr., 1987-88; pvt. practice aerospace cons. West Grove, Pa., 1988—. Bd. dirs. Cecon, Inc., Wilmington, Del., So. Chester County Med. Ctr., West Grove. Author: History of Thiokol and Rockets, 1996. Pres. residents coun. Jenners Pond Retirement Cmty., West Grove, 1996—. With U.S. Army, 1944-46. Mem. AAAS, AIAA, Am. Chem. Soc., Planetary Soc. Achievements include 8 patents in solid rocket propellants and rocket motor componants. Avocations: skiing, community theater, gardening, computers, investing. Home: 252 Azalea Ln West Grove PA 19390-9479 Office: Cecon Inc 242 N James St Wilmington DE 19804-3168 E-mail: esutton@kennett.net.

SUTTON, FRANCES HAMMER, computer science educator; b. Hillsboro, Md., Sept. 28, 1941; d. Arthur Walter and Mary Catherine (Coulby) Hammer; m. Thomas Townsend Sutton, July 14, 1962 (dec. June 1987); children: Thomas Arthur, Steven John, Michael David. AAS in Data Processing, Coll. of Albermarle, 1984; BS in Computer Sci., Elizabeth City State U., 1987. Sec./procurement asst. CIA, Washington, 1959-62; sec. Aeros. div. Mpls. Honeywell, St. Petersburg, Fla., 1962-63; cons. data base mgmt. system Watermark Assn. Artisans, Elizabeth City, N.C., 1986-87; instr. computer sci. Coll. of Albemarle, 1987—. Computer analyst U.S. Coast Guard, 1990—. Vol. campaign worker Winnie Wood for state senate, 1982. Cummings scholar, 1983, Chancellor's achievement scholar, 1984. Mem. Phi Theta Kappa, Alpha Kappa Mu. Roman Catholic. Avocations: reading, needlework, designing clothing. Home: 106 Holly Dr Elizabeth City NC 27909-3216 Office: Coll of Albemarle PO Box 2327 Elizabeth City NC 27906-2327

SUTTON, FRANCIS XAVIER, social scientist, consultant; b. Oneida, Pa., July 7, 1917; s. Frank James and Rose Marie (Burns) S.; m. Ruth Jacqueline Young, Aug. 24, 1948 (dec. July 2002); children: Peter, Sean, Philip, Elizabeth. BS, Temple U., 1938; MA, Princeton U., 1940, Harvard U., 1941, PhD, 1950. Jr. fellow, Soc. Fellows Harvard U., Cambridge, Mass., 1946-49, asst. prof., lectr., 1949-54; program officer, overseas rep. Ford Found., N.Y.C., 1954-67, dep. v.p., acting v.p., 1968-83; cons. Ford Found. and Harvard U., 1983-85; acting pres. Social Sci. Rsch. Coun., N.Y.C., 1985-86, also bd. dirs., chmn., 1985-92; cons. Rockefeller Found, U.S. Agy. for Internat. Devel. and World Bank, N.Y.C. and Washington, 1987-92; acting dir. Rockefeller Study and Conf. Ctr., Bellagio, Italy, 1990-92; cons. Aga Khan U., 1992—. Author: The American Business Creed, 1956; editor: A World to Make/Development in Perspective, 1989; contbr. articles to profl. jours. and chpts. to books. Pres. Am. Found. for Intellectual Coop. with Europe, N.Y.C., 1987-93; mem. bd. fgn. scholarships Dept. State, Washington, 1961-63; bd. dirs. Nat. Ctr. on Adult Literacy, U. Pa., Phila., 1990-97; mem. adv. bd. Ctr. on Philanthropy, City Univ., N.Y.C., 1988—. Capt. U.S. Army Air Corps, 1941-45. Fellow AAAS; mem. Council on Fgn. Relations, Assn. for Asian Studies (Disting. Service award 1984). Clubs: Century Assn. (N.Y.C.). Democrat. Avocations: piano playing, dancing, snorkeling. Home: 80 Bellair Dr Dobbs Ferry NY 10522-3504 E-mail: fxsutton@aol.com.

SUTTON, GARY L. music educator; b. Warsaw, June 20, 1953; s. Keith and Joan Sutton; m. Janie Marie Fisher; children: Julie. BME, Mars Hill Coll., 1975; MA, Furman U., 1984. Cert. Tchr. S.C., Orff Level 1 1983. Band dir. Carolina H.S., Greenville, SC, 1975—85; music tchr. Cone, Alexander, Sue Cleve., Sirrine Elem. Sch., 1980—87, Fountain Inn Elem., Fountain Inn, 1987—. Music camp tchr. First Bapt. Ch., Greer, SC, 1999; tchr. Arts in Edn. Camp, Greenville, SC, 2001—02; all county band clarinet, sax audition judge Sch. Dist. of Greenville County, Greenville; honors choir audition com. mem. SC. Music Educators Conf., SC, 2001; spring sing audition com. Sch. Dist. of Greenville County, Greenville, 2001. Mem. Furman U. Summer Band, Greenville, SC, 2001; hand bells First Bapt. Ch., Greer, 1998—2002, mem. adult choir orch., 1994—2002, co-dir. children's choir, 1999—2001. Nominee First Fed. Arts Educator of Yr., First Fed. Bank, 1999, 2000; grantee, State Dept. of Edn., 1999. Mem.: SC. Music Edn. Conf., Menc, Foothills ASOA (historian 1998—2002), Greer H.S. Band Booster Club (co. pres. 1999—2000), Phi Mu Alpha (life). Avocations: gardening, swimming. Home: 310 Roscoe Drive Greer SC 29651 Office: Fountain Inn Elementary School 608 Fairview Street Fountain Inn SC 29644

SUTTON, GEORGE PAUL, rocket propulsion engineer, writer, educator; b. Sept. 5, 1920; s. Fred Charles and Augusta Amalie (Landegger) S.; m. Kathleen M. Sutton, July 1944 (dec. July 1952); m. Yvonne B. Sutton, Apr. 1954 (dec. Dec. 1992); children: Christine, Marilyn. BS in Mech. Engring., Calif. Inst. Tech., 1942, MS, 1943, postgrad., 1943-46. Registered profl. engr., Calif. Devel. engr. Aerojet Corp., Pasadena/Asuza, Calif., 1943-46; asst. to pres., exec. dir. engring. Rocketdyne (now The Boeing Co.), Canoga Park, 1946-69; chief scientist Advanced Rsch. Project Agy., Dept. Def., Pentagon, Washington, 1959-60; v.p. Envirotech Corp., Menlo Park, 1969-74, Johnston Pump Co., Glendora, 1975-77; lab. assoc., program leader, asst. divsn. leader Lawrence Livermore Nat. Lab., Livermore, 1977-88, part time, 1988-00. Pres., v.p., bd. dirs. Am. Rocket Soc., 1955-59; instr. mech. engring. Calif. Inst. Tech., Pasadena, 1943-46; Hunsaker prof. aero. engring. MIT, Cambridge, 1958-59; exec. v.p. Sumitomo Jukikai Envirotech, Tokyo, 1971-74. Author: Rocket Propulsion Elements, 1949, 7th edit., 2000; contbr. over 40 articles to profl. jours. Mem. Sci. Adv. Bd. USAF, 1960-71. Fellow AIAA (past pres., Pendray award 2002); mem. ASME, Soc. Mfg. Engrs. Achievements include several patents related to rocket propulsion.

SUTTON, GEORGE WALTER, research laboratory executive, mechanical engineer, physicist; b. Bklyn., Aug. 3, 1927; s. Jack and Pauline (Aaron) S.; m. Evelyn D. Kunnes, Dec. 25, 1952; children: James E., Charles S., Richard E., Stewart A. BSME with honors, Cornell U., 1952; MS, Calif. Inst. Tech., 1953, PhD Engring. & Physics magna cum laude, 1955. Rsch. scientist Lockheed Missile Co., 1955; rsch. engr. Space Sci. Lab. GE, 1955-61, mgr. magneto-hydrodynamic power generation, 1962-63; vis. Ford prof. MIT, 1961-62; sci. adviser Hdqrs. USAF, 1963-65; with Avco Rsch. Lab., 1965-83, dir. laser devel., 1971-82, v.p., 1972-82, v.p., tech. dir. Helionetics Laser div., 1983-85; v.p. JAYCOR, San Diego, 1985-90; dir. E-O rsch. Kaman Aerospace Corp., Tucson, 1990-92; chief scientist Aero Thermal Tech., Inc., Arlington, Va., 1993-96; prin. engr. ANSER, 1996—. Cons. Energy Agy., 1977-79, Arms Control Agy., 1986; lectr. magnetohydrodynamics U. Pa., 1960-63, Stanford, 1964; developer of ablation heat protection for ICBM and high energy lasers, pioneer aero-optics, missile interceptor tech.; judge Intel Sci. Talent Search. Author: (with A. Sherman) Engineering Magnetohydrodynamics, 1965, Direct Energy Conversion, 1966; editor-in-chief Jour. AIAA, 1967-96; editor-in-chief emeritus, 1997—; editor various procs.; contbr. over 95 articles to profl. jours. With USAAF, 1945-47. Recipient Arthur Flemming award for outstanding govt. service, 1965 Fellow AIAA (chmn. plasmadynamics tech. com., Thermophysics award 1980, Disting. Svc. award 1988), ASME, AAAS, Nat. Acad. Engrng. (aerospace sect. sec., peer com.), Nat. Rsch. Coun. (coms. on shuttle upgrades, aging avionics, thermionics). Avocations: tennis, travel, sailing. Office: Ste 800 2900 S Quincy Dr Arlington VA 22206 *I have been blessed with certain abilities and I strain to utilize and sharpen them to the maximum. But I do the right thing - always. Love of my family and my desire to do best for them have led to situations where my values could have been compromised. I still did the right thing. It has usually worked out best for my family and myself, and preserved my honor and integrity.*

SUTTON, GREGORY PAUL, obstetrician, gynecologist; b. Tokyo, Dec. 12, 1948; (parents Am. citizens); s. Vernon S. And Vonna Lou (Streeter) S.; m. Judith Craigie Holt, June 26, 1977; children: Anne Craigie, James Streeter. BS in Chemistry with honors, Ind. U., 1970; MD, U. Mich., 1976. Diplomate Am. Bd. of Ob/Gyn. Prof. gynecol. oncology Ind. U. Sch. Medicine, Indpls., 1986-97; Mary Fendrich Hulman prof. Gynecologic Oncology Ind. U. Sch. Med., 1997-2000; prof. gynecologic oncology St. Vincent Hosp. and Health Svcs., 2000—01. Cancer Clin. fellow Am. Cancer Soc., Phila., 1981-83; recipient Career Devel. award Am. Cancer Soc., 1986-89. Fellow: Am. Coll. Obstetrics and Gynecology (chair Ind. sect.); mem.: Hoosier Oncology Group, Soc. of Gynecologic Oncologists, Bayard Carter Soc., Ind. State Med. Soc., Marion County Med. Soc., Gynecologic Oncology Group (cert. Spl. Competence in Gynecologic Oncology 1985). Avocations: swimming, cycling, woodworking, sailing. Office: 2001 W 86th St Indianapolis IN 46260-1902 Fax: (317) 338-4312. E-mail: gsutton@stvincent.org.

SUTTON, HARRY ELDON, geneticist, educator; b. Cameron, Tex., Mar. 5, 1927; s. Grant Edwin and Myrtle Dovie (Fowler) S.; m. Beverly Earlene Jewell, July 7, 1962; children: Susan Elaine, Caroline Virginia. BS in Chemistry, U. Tex., Austin, 1948, MA, 1949; PhD in Biochemistry, U. Tex., 1953. Biologist U. Mich., 1952-56, instr., 1956-57, asst. prof. human genetics, 1957-60; assoc. prof. zoology U. Tex., Austin, 1960-64, prof., 1964-99, chmn. dept. zoology, 1970-73, asso. dean Grad. Sch., 1967-70, 73-75, v.p. for research, 1975-79, prof. molecular genetics and microbiology, 1999—. Mem. adv. council Nat. Inst. Environ. Health Scis., 1968-72, council sci. advs., 1972-76; mem. various coms. Nat. Acad. Scis.-NRC; cons. in field; bd. dirs. Associated Univs. for Research in Astronomy, 1975-79, Argonne Univs. Assn., 1975-79, Univ. Corp. for Atmospheric Research, 1975-79, Associated Western Univs., 1978-79 Author: Genes, Enzymes, and Inherited Disease, 1961, An Introduction to Human Genetics, 1988, Genetics: A Human Concern, 1985; editor: First Macy Conference on Genetics, 1960, Mutagenic Effects of Environmental Contaminants, 1972, Am. Jour. Human Genetics, 1964-69. Trustee S.W. Tex. Corp. Public Broadcasting, 1977-80, sec., 1979-80; bd. dirs. Ballet Austin, 1978-84, 98—; mem. Austin Arts Commn., 1991-95. Served with U.S. Army, 1945-46. Mem. AAAS, Am. Soc. Human Genetics (dir. 1961-69, pres. 1979), Genetics Soc. Am., Am. Soc. Biochem. and Molecular Biology, Am. Chem. Soc., Tex. Genetics Soc. (pres. 1979), Am. Genetic Assn., Headliners Club (Austin), Town and Gown Club. Achievements include research and publications in human genetics. Home: 1103 Gaston Ave Austin TX 78703-2507 Office: Univ Tex Sect Molecular Genetics & Microbiology Austin TX 78712 E-mail: eldon.sutton@mail.utexas.edu.

SUTTON, HOWARD G. publishing executive; m. Kimberly G. P. Sutton; 1 child, H. J. Degree in history, Notre Dame U., 1972; MBA, Providence Coll., 1978; grad. PMD program, Harvard U., 1984. Various mgmt. positions Providence Jour. Co., 1973—, pub., pres., CEO, 1997—. V.p. devel. R.I. Philharm.; past chmn. Christmas in Apr., Providence; chmn. R.I. Acad. Decathlon, NCAA Hockey 2000; bd. dirs. Nat. Conf., Leadership R.I., Women and Infants' Hosp., Providence Coll. Pres. Coun., United Way, WaterFire Providence, First Night, The Bus. Edn. Roundtable, World Scholar Games. Mem. Greater Providence C. of C. (exec. bd.), R.I. Commodores, Hope Club, Univ. Club, R.I. Country Club, Notre Dame Club of R.I. (past pres., Man of Yr. 1993). Office: Providence Jour 75 Fountain St Providence RI 02902-0050*

SUTTON, JAMES HERCULES, poet, former educational association administrator; b. Boston, Jan. 8, 1943; s. Hercules James and Paras (Zingovas) S.; m. Nancy Mona Kohrt, June 8, 1982; children: Michael, Raphael, Robert, Thessaly, Athena, Thalia. Cert. des solfèges, South End Music Ctr., Boston, 1958; BA, Brown U., 1964; MFA, U. Iowa Writers Workshop, 1968; PhD, U. Iowa, 1988. Lic. C.C. teaching, regional supt. and evaluator, Iowa. Asst. to dir. Textual Ctr., U. Iowa, Iowa City, 1966-68; labor organizer Iowa Higher Edn. Assn., Des Moines, 1971-73, exec. dir., 1973-74; lobbyist Iowa State Edn. Assn., 1974-80, dir. profl. devel., 1980-83, state agy. liaison, 1983-87, sr. policy analyst, 1987-94; orgn. specialist profl. issues, 1994—2002. Licensure cons. NEA, Washington, 1989. Author: Sonnets for Athena, 1991, Prometheus, 1995, Harry's Gloom, 1997, Harry's Gloomsday Dictionary, 1997, The Last Samurai, 1997 (Mellen Poetry prize best long poem in Great Britain and U.S., 1997), Harry's Love--150 Sonnets, 2001. Fax: 515-471-8017. E-mail: JamesSutton@Juno.com.

SUTTON, JOHN EWING, lawyer; b. San Angelo, Oct. 7, 1950; s. John F. Jr. and Nancy (Ewing) S.; 1 son, Joshua Ewing; 1 stepson, Michael Brandon Ducote. BBA, U. Tex., 1973, JD, 1976. Bar: Tex. 1976, U.S. Tax Ct. 1977, U.S. Ct. Claims 1977, U.S. Ct. Appeals (5th cir.) 1978, U.S. Dist. Ct. (we. dist.) Tex. 1979, U.S. Supreme Ct. 1980; CPA, Tex. Tax specialist Peat, Marwick, Mitchell & Co., CPAs, Dallas, 1976-77; ptnr. Shannon, Porter, Johnson, Sutton and Greendyke Attys. at Law, San Angelo, Tex., 1977-87; judge 119th Dist. Ct. of Tex., 1987-99; pvt. practice Law Offices of John E. Sutton, 1999—. Treas. Good Shepherd Episcopal Ch., San Angelo, 1979-81; co-chmn. profl. divsn. United Way, San Angelo, 1980-82; trustee Angelo State U. Found., 1987-99, pres., 1988-91, 95-97, v.p., 1992-94, 98-99, sec.-treas., 1991-92. Fellow Tex. Bar Found.; mem. ABA, Tex. Bar Assn., Tex. Criminal Def. Lawyers Assn., Tom Green County Bar Assn. (sec.-treas. young lawyers 1977-78), AICPAs, Tex. Soc. CPAs (bd. dirs. 1980-87, pres. San Angelo chpt. 1980-81, mem. state exec. com. 1981-82, 86-87, state sec. 1986-87, chmn. profl. ethics com. 1985-86, Young CPA of Yr. 1984-85), Concho Valley Estate Planning Coun. (v.p. 1979-80, also dir.). Office: Law Office of John E Sutton 117 S Irving St San Angelo TX 76903-6419

SUTTON, JOHN F., JR. law educator, dean, lawyer; b. Alpine, Tex., Jan. 26, 1918; s. John F. and Pauline Irene (Elam) S.; m. Nancy Ewing, June 1, 1940; children: Joan Sutton Parr, John Ewing. JD, U. Tex., 1941. Bar: Tex. 1941, U.S. Dist. Ct. (we. dist.) Tex. 1947, U.S. Ct. Appeals (5th cir.) 1951, U.S. Supreme Ct. 1960. Assoc. Brooks, Napier, Brown & Matthews, San Antonio, 1941-42; spl. agt. FBI, Washington, 1942-45; assoc. Matthews, Nowlin, Macfarlane & Barrett, San Antonio, 1945-48; ptnr. Kerr, Gayer & Sutton, San Angelo, Tex., 1948-50, Sutton, Steib & Barr, San Angelo, 1951-57; prof. U. Tex.-Austin, 1957-65, William Stamps Farish prof., 1965-84, A.W. Walker centennial chair, 1984-88, emeritus, 1988—, dean Sch. Law, 1979-84. Editor: (with Wellborn) Materials on Evidence, 8th edit., 1996, (with Dzienkowski) Cases and Materials on Professional Responsibility of Lawyers, 1989, (with Schuwerk) Guideline to the Texas Disciplinary Rules of Professional Conduct, 1990, (with Dzienkowski) Cases and Materials on Professional Conduct, 2d edit., 2002; contbr. articles to profl. jours. Served to 1st lt. JAGC USAR, 1948-54. Fellow Am. Bar Found. (life), Tex. Bar Found. (life); mem. ABA (com. on ethics 1970-76), State Bar Tex. (com. on rules of profl. conduct, com. adminstrn. rules of evidence), Philos. Soc. Tex., Order of Coif, U. Tex. Club, Phi Delta Phi, San Angelo Country Club, North Austin Rotary (pres. 1969). Presbyterian. Home: 3830 Sunset Dr San Angelo TX 76904-5956 Office: U Tex Sch Law 727 E Dean Keeton St Austin TX 78705-3224

SUTTON, JOHN PAUL, lawyer; b. Youngstown, Ohio, July 24, 1934; m. Jane Williamson, Aug. 20, 1958; children— Julia, Susan, Elizabeth. BA, U. Va., 1956; JD, George Washington U., 1963. Bar: Calif. 1965. Patent examiner

U.S. Patent Office, Washington, 1956, 59-62; law clk. U.S. Ct. Customs and Patent Appeals, 1962-64; assoc. Flehr, Hohbach, Test, Albritton & Herbert, San Francisco, 1964-68; ptnr. Limbach, Limbach & Sutton, 1969-91; spl. counsel Heller, Ehrman, White & McAuliffe, 1992-95; of counsel Medlin & Carroll, 1995, Bryan, Hinshaw & Barnet, San Francisco, 1996-99; sole practice, 2000—. Adj. instr. Practicing Law Inst., 1968-69; continuing edn. program Calif. State Bar, 1972, 75, U. Calif. Law Sch., Berkeley, 1975, 84. Contbr. articles to legal jours. Served with USNR, 1956-59. Mem. Calif. Patent Law Assn. (pres. 1975), San Francisco Patent Law Assn. (pres. 1976), State Bar Calif. (exec. com. patent sect. 1975-77), Am. Chem. Soc. Democrat. Episcopalian. Home and Office: 2421 Pierce St San Francisco CA 94115-1131

SUTTON, JOHN SCHUHMANN, JR. retired purchasing consultant; b. Louisville, July 12, 1931; s. John Schuhmann and Ruth Evelyn (Roby) S.; m. Doris Jean Hornung, Dec. 12, 1953; children: Deborah Ann, Francis Eugene, Thomas Gerard. BA in Zoology, U. Louisville, 1953, MA in Math., 1965. Cert. purchasing mgr. Quality control technician Brown-Forman Corp., Louisville, 1956-64, mgr. quality control, 1964-80, purchasing mgr., asst. dir. purchasing, 1980—83, dir. purchasing, 1983-85, asst. v.p. purchasing, 1985-88, v.p. purchasing, 1988-91; cons. in field, 1991-95; ret., 1995. Cons. in field. Author poems. With U.S. Army, 1953-55. Mem. Am. Soc. Quality Control, Nat. Assn. Purchasing Mgrs., Purchasing Mgrs. Assn. Louisville, Jefferson Club. Democrat. Roman Catholic. Avocations: thoroughbred racing, fishing, poetry, writing. Home: 8628 Birch Ct Louisville KY 40242-3461 E-mail: suttonjss@aol.com.

SUTTON, JOYCE ELAINE, medical records director; b. Chillicothe, Mo., Aug. 28, 1946; d. William Stanley and Helen Louise (Ashlock) Henderson; m. Ferold Rodrick Vermilyea, Jr., Feb. 7, 1964 (div. Aug. 1973); m. Ronald Eldon Sutton, Jan. 15, 1978; children: Sherra Wood, Janae Nezerka, Michael, Brian, Marcia Wright. Accredited record technician. Ward clk. Heartland West Hosp. (formerly Meth. Med. Ctr.), St. Joseph, Mo., 1970-73; ward clk. Hedrick Med. Ctr., Chillicothe, 1973-74, med. records clk., 1974-75, accredited record tech. trainee, 1975-77, med. transcriber, 1977-82, asst. supr., 1982-85, med. records supr., 1985-89, med. records dir., 1989—, quality assurance cons., 1989-92, also med. staff sec., treas., coord.; dir. med. records Pershing Meml. Hosp., Pershing Regional Hosp., Brookfield, Mo., 1992—, dir. admissions dept.; dir. performance improvement Pershing Meml. Hosp., 2000—. Chair mgmt. of info. com. Pershing Meml. Hosp., 1997, chair Y2K readiness, 1998; cons. Brookfield Nursing Ctr., 1987—, Excelsior Springs (Mo.) City Hosp., 1988—; dir. outpatient program, Hedrick Med. Ctr., Chillicothe, 1987—, dir. quality assurance/risk mgmt., 1988—. Mem. local civic orgns., Chillicothe, 1987—. Mem. Hedrick Med. Ctr. Aux. (life), Am. Health Info. Mgmt. Assn., Mo. Med. Records Assn., Kansas City Area Health Info. Assn. Republican. Baptist. Avocations: camping, fishing, walking, reading. Home: PO Box 114 Meadville MO 64659-0114 Office: Pershing Meml Hosp 130 E Lockling St Brookfield MO 64628-2337 E-mail: rnesutn@grm.net.

SUTTON, JULIA SUMBERG, musicologist, dance historian; b. Toronto, July 20, 1928; d. Samuel L. and Anne R. (Rubin) Sumberg. AB summa cum laude, Cornell U., 1949; MA, Colo. Coll., 1952; PhD, U. Rochester, 1962. Instr. music history New Sch. for Social Research, 1962-63; instr. music Queens Coll., CUNY, 1963-66; chmn. dept. music history and musicology New Eng. Conservatory Music, 1971-90, chmn. faculty senate, 1971-73; prof. emerita New England Conservatory Music, 1992. Vis. asst. prof. George Peabody Coll. for Tchrs., 1966-67; instr. NYU, summers 1963, 64; pvt. tchr. piano, 1949-65; lectr., rsch. dir. in musicology, music as related to the dance; presenter numerous workshops and summer insts. on Renaissance dance. Dance dir. N.Y. Pro Musica prodn. An Entertainment for Elizabeth, Caramoor, N.Y., Saratoga, N.Y., U. Ariz., Stanford U., UCLA, 1969, ann. nationwide tours, 1970-1973; dance dir. Descent of Rhythm and Harmony, Colorado Springs, Colo., 1970, Renaissance Revisited, Phila., 1972, An Evening of Renaissance Music and Dance, York U., Toronto, 1974; author: Jean Baptiste Besard's Novus Partus 1617, 1962; editor: Thoinot Arbeau: Orchesography 1588, 1967; translator, editor: Fabritio Caroso: Nobiltà di dame 1600, 1986, reprinted 1995; producer, co-dir. (tng. video) Il Ballarino, 1991; contbr. numerous articles to profl. jours. and Internat. Ency. of Dance, New Grove Dictionary of Music and Musicians 2d edit., Die Musik in Geschichte und Gegenwart, 2 edit. Mem. Am. Musicological Soc., Soc. of Dance History Scholars, Phi Beta Kappa.

SUTTON, KAREN E. administrator; b. New Brunswick, N.J., Aug. 26, 1952; d. Alfred Michael and Carmen (Collado) Sutton; children: Sloane, Brooke, Devon, Megan, Christopher. BA, Hofstra U., 1974; postgrad., NYU, 1987-89. Asst. to dir. Mus. Am. Folk Art, N.Y.C., 1975-76, acting dir., 1976-77, bd. dirs., exec. com. officer, 1980-88, gallery dir., 1989-92, dir. ops., 1992-94, dep. dir. planning and adminstrn., 1994-95; v.p. Sotheby's, 1995-96, sr. v.p. adminstrn., 1996-2001, sr. v.p. worldwide mktg., 2001—. Bd. dirs. Family Dynamics, N.Y.C., 1976-80. Mem. Cosmopolitan Club (younger members chmn). Democrat. Episcopalian. Home: 4 Sutton Pl New York NY 10022 Office: Sotheby's 1334 York Ave New York NY 10021-4806

SUTTON, L. PAUL, criminal justice educator; b. Munich, Aug. 16, 1948; s. William L. Sutton and Paulette Mikkelson. BS in Polit. Sci. and History, U. Kans., 1970; MA in Criminal Justice, SUNY, Albany, 1971, PhD in Criminal Justice, 1975. Asst. prof. sociology U. N.Mex., Albuquerque, 1976-78; rsch. assoc. Hindelang Criminal Justice Rsch. Ctr., Albany, N.Y., 1974-76; prof. criminal justice San Diego State U., 1981—; sr. rsch. assoc. Nat. Ctr. for State Cts., Williamsburg, Va., 1978-81. Ind. filmmaker, N.Mex., Calif., 1982-92; cons. State of Calif. Dept. of Corrections, 1997-98; commr. cmty.-based punishment planning com., San Diego, 1996-97; bd. dirs. Nat. Forum on Criminal Justice, Springfield, Ill., 1980-81; expert witness on sentencing reform Nat. Acad. Scis., Washington, 1981. Producer documentary film Doing Time: Ten Years Later, 1991, Doing Time, 1979; co-author: The Search Warrant Process, 1984, Sentencing by Mathematics, 1982. Grantee Calif. State Dept. Corrections, 1997, NEH, 1979. Mem. AAUP, Am. Soc. Criminology-,Acad. Criminal Justice Scis., Western Soc. Criminology, Phi Beta Kappa. Avocations: filmmaking, sailing, jogging. Office: San Diego State U Dept Criminal Justice San Diego CA 92182-4505 E-mail: psutton@mail.sdsu.edu.

SUTTON, LOUISE NIXON, retired mathematics educator; b. Hertford, N.C., Nov. 4, 1925; d. John Calhoun and Annie Mariah (McNair) Nixon. BS, N.C. A&T State U., 1946; MA, NYU, 1951, PhD, 1962. Cert. tchr. sci. and math., N.C. Tchr. math./sci. Willis Hare H.S., Pendleton, N.C., summer 1946; tchr. math. Dudley High Sch., Greensboro, 1946-47; instr. math. N.C. A&T State U., 1947-57; asst. prof. math. Del. State U., Dover, 1957-62; assoc. prof. to prof. and dept. head math. Elizabeth City (N.C.) State U., 1962-87, prof. emeritus, 1987—. Adv. com. math. cert. Del. State Bd. Edn., Dover, 1961-62, adv. com. cert. in math. and sci., 1959-61. NAACP rep. adv. com. N.C. Bd. Social Svcs., Raleigh, 1969—71; mem. fin. bd. Pearson St. YWCA, Greensboro, 1954—56; AME Zion rep. com. on Christian edn. of exceptional persons Nat. Coun. Chs., N.Y.C., 1963—65; rep. 150th Anniversary Advance, Am Bible Soc., 1964—66; trustee St. Paul AME Zion Ch., 1972—73, ch. treas., 1997—98; bd. dirs. Perquimans County Indsl. Devel. Corp., Hertford, 1967—72; bd. dirs. divsn. higher edn. N.C. Assn. Educators, 1969—72. Recipient Disting. Tchr. award Elizabeth City (N.C.) State U. Gen. Alumni Assn., 1974, Tchr. of Yr., 1980, Woman of Yr. award NAUW, 1976, Plaque St. Paul AME Zion Ch., 1999; honoree Daughter of Isis, Arabia Ct. # 23, 1998, Elizabeth City State U. Gen. Alumni Assn., 1997. Mem. NAUW (pres. 1974-80, regional dir. 1976-80), NAACP (life), Nat. Coun. Tchrs. Math. (life), N.C. Coun. Tchrs. Math. (v.p. colls. 1979-80), Order Ea. Star (grand assoc. dean 1993-95, worthy matron 1994-97), George Washington Carver Floral Club (pres. 1991-99), Daus. of Isis, Delta Sigma Theta (life, pres. Dover, Del. and Elizabeth City Alumnae chpts.). Republican. Avocations: mini-golf, bowling, quilting, crochet, fishing. Home: 109 Driftwood Rd Hertford NC 27944-9684

SUTTON, MARCELLA FRENCH, interior designer; b. Prague, Czechoslovakia, Sept. 4, 1946; came to U.S., 1952, naturalized, 1956; d. Eugen E. and Frances V. (Pruchovia) French; m. Michael D. Sutton, Feb. 11, 1978; 1 child, Kevin Christopher. BS in Profl. Arts, Woodbury U., 1971. Mgr. design dept. W. & J. Sloane, Beverly Hills, Calif., 1972-76; project dir. Milton I. Swimmer, 1977-78; owner, interior designer Marcella French Designs, Woodland Hills and La Crescenta, Calif., 1969-94, owner, designer, project mgr., constrn. and design, 1994—; prin. designer. Property mgmt. coord., interior designer Home Savs. and Loan., State of Calif., L.A., 1979-82; regional premises officer, asst. v.p. regional hdqrs. Bank Am., L.A., 1981-86; v.p. M.D. Sutton Ins. Agy.; cons. pvt. residences, comml. bldgs., office and banks. Project mgr., 1st v.p. fundraising Shephard of the Valley Sch., 1989-90, enrichment chmn., 1990-91, mem. enrichment program pub. sch. calendar, 1991; active Young Reps., Vinyard Ch.; treas. West Hills Baseball Aux., 1989-93; arcades coord. Theatre Arts Festival for Youth, Agoura, 1992-94, co-chmn. ways and means RTRWF, 1992-94, 1st v.p., 1995-97, program chmn., 1996-97, pres. 1998-99, chmn. Caring for Am.; judge Sci. Fair, 1993-95; treas. Taxpayers United for Fairness, 1994-99; co-organizer 9th and 10th Grade Parent Network Orgn. & Found., Chaminade, 1994-95; pres., area chmn. Paul Jhin, 1998—, del. C.R.A., alt. Los Angeles County ctrl. com., 1998-99, 2000-2001; Mamie Eisenhower chmn. for book donations LACRFW, 1999—, chmn. Caring for Am., conv. chmn., historian so. divsn., 2002-; issues chmn. higher edn. CFRW, 2000-2002, so. divsn. historian, 2000-2002; 41stad Ctrl. Com. ofcl. Recipient various scholarships. E-mail: marcella@ix.netcom.com.

SUTTON, NIGEL JAMES, aeronautical engineer, test flight officer; b. Kingston, Jamaica, W.I., June 19, 1963; came to U.S., 1982; s. Harold James and Sheila Claire (Murray) S.; m. Gail Ann Burris, Sept. 5, 1998. BS in Computer Sci., Park Coll., 1987; MS in Indsl. Engring., U. Tenn., 1995; MS in Aero. Engring., Naval Postgrad. Sch., 1998; MBA, Fla. Inst. of Tech., 2000. Enlisted USAF, 1983—87; commd. ensign USN, 1987; advanced through grades to comdr.; student flight officer VT-10/VAW-110, San Diego, 1988—89; mission comdr. VAW-114, 1989—92; flight instr. VAW-110, 1992; test naval flight officer Navy Test Pilot Sch., Patuxent River, Md., 1993—94, Force Aircraft Test Squadron, Patuxent River, 1994—96, chief test project leader, 1998—, acquisition profl., aerospace engr. duty officer, 1998—2000, asst. program mgr. test and evaluation, 1998—2000; aide to the comdr. Navairsyscom, 2000—02; mgr. deputy program F/A-18 Office, 2002—. Contbr. articles to profl. jours. Finalist NASA Astronaut finalist, 1995; named Navy Test Flight Officer of Yr., 1994; recipient Officer of Yr. award for leadership, USN, 1994; fellow White House fellow, Region Finalist, 2001. Mem. AIAA (tech. com. on aircraft survivability, def. subcom.), Soc. Flight Test Engrs., Toastmasters Internat. (v.p. membership 1996-98, Best Spkr. award 1997), Nat. Naval Officer Assn. Republican. Roman Catholic. Achievements include research in radar discrimination between moving objects and free floating objects in UHF band; in critical component identification and combat kill modes of the JSF. E-mail: suttonnj@navair.navy.mil.

SUTTON, PHILIP D(IETRICH), psychologist, educator; b. June 20, 1952; s. Clifton C. and Ida-Lois (Dietrich) S.; m. Kathleen E. Duffy, June 17, 1973; children: Heather, Shivonne. BA, So. Ill. U., 1974; MA, U. Chgo., 1975; PhD, U. Utah, 1979. Lic. psychologist, Colo. Psychologist VA Hosp., Salt Lake City, 1975-76; psychology intern Salt Lake Cmty. Mental Health Ctr., 1976-78; counselor, instr. Counseling Ctr., U. Utah, 1976-78; counselor, acting dir. spl. svcs. program Met. State Coll., Denver, 1978-80; pvt. practice psychology Boulder (Colo.) Med. Ctr., 1983-2001. Cons. spl. program for disacvantaged students in higher edn. Hew, 1980; staff psychologist Kaiser-Permanente Health Plan, Denver, 1980-83; adj. prof. U. Colo., 1979-83. Mem. APA, Biofeedback Soc., Am. Soc. Behavioral Medicine. Office: Box 1781 Nederland CO 80466 E-mail: pdsphd@aol.com.

SUTTON, ROBERT EDWARD, investment company executive; b. Burlington, Vt., July 3, 1943; s. Rollin Robert and Blanche Margaret (Deforge) S.; m. Julie Robin Levine, Feb. 1, 1975; children: Katherine Vanessa, David Robert. BA in Econs., St. Michaels Coll., 1962-66. V.p. Compretic, Inc., Beverly Hills, Calif., 1967-70; brokerage cons. Conn. Gen. Life Ins. Co., Denver, 1970-74; pres. The Core Corp., 1975-80; mng. dir. Willshire Investments & Holding Co., 1981-91; pres., chmn. Gen. Capital, Inc., 1991-93; pres, CEO WK Capital Advisors, Inc., 1994—. Dir. NAt. Assn. Indep. Contr., Denver. 1991—, Nat. Endowment Trust, Denver, 1990—, Tri Corp, Denver, 1980-89, Nat. Acceptance Corp., L.A., 1991—, Nat. Investment Holdings, L.A., 1990—; chmn. Centrix Findmiol, LLC, 1998—, EIF, Inc., 1998—. Mem. Nat. Rep. Eagles, Washington, 1986-90, Inner Circle, Washington, 1985-90, Denver Ctr. Performing Arts, 1976-86. Mem. Am. Cancer League, Glenmoor Country Club. Home: 57 Glenmoor Cir Cherry Hills Village CO 80110-7121

SUTTON, SHARON EGRETTA, architect, educator, artist, musician; b. Cin., Feb. 18, 1941; d. Booker and Egretta (Sutton) Johnson. Student, Manhattan Sch. Music, 1959-62; MusB, U. Hartford, Conn., 1963; postgrad., Parson's Sch. Design, N.Y.C., 1967-69; MArch, Columbia U., 1973; PhM, CUNY, 1981, MA, PhD in Psychology, 1982. Registered architect, N.Y. Pvt. practice, N.Y.C. and Dexter, Mich., 1976-97. Vis. asst. prof. Pratt Inst., Bklyn., 1975-81; adj. asst. prof. Columbia U., N.Y.C., 1981-82; asst. prof. U. Cin., 1982-84; assoc. prof. U. Mich., Ann Arbor, 1984-94, prof., 1994-97; prof., dir. ctr. environment, edn., and design studies U. Wash., Seattle, 1998—; architect-in-residence NEA, N.Y.C., 1978-82; keynote spkr., lectr. colls. and profl. meetings. One-woman shows include Nat. Urban League, N.Y.C., 1980, Your Heritage House, Detroit, 1986, June Kelly Gallery, N.Y.C., 1987, exhibited in group shows at Studio Mus., 1979, U. Mich. Mus. Art, Ann Arbor, 1988, Art-in-Gen. Gallery, Soho, N.Y.C., 1990, Represented in permanent collections Mint Mus., Charlotte, N.C., Wadsworth Atheneum, Hartford, Conn., Balt. Mus. Art; author: Learning Through the Built Environment, 1985, Weaving a Tapestry of Resistance, 1996; mem. editl. bd.: Jour. Archtl. Edn., 1984—87; contbr. articles to profl. jours.; musician: Man of La Mancha original cast and album, 1967—69; musician: (performed with) orchs. of Bolshoi, Leningrad, and Moiseiye, Ballt Cos., Man of La Mancha original cast and album, New World Symphony, Music Makers, Phoenix Woodwind quintet, others. Coord. The Urban Network-an urban design program for youth funded by NEA Design Cities Program Kellogg Found., U. Mich., 1988-97; mem. Seattle Design Commn. 2000—. Recipient Postbaccalaureate award Danforth Found., 1977-81, Design Rsch. award NEA, 1983, Edn. award Am. Planning Assn., 1991, Regents award for disting. pub. svc. U. Mich., 1992, Mich. Humanities award, 1995, Disting. Prof. award Assn. Collegiate Schs. Architecture, 1996, Life Achievement award Mich. Women's Hall of Fame, 1997; grantee NEA, 1988-90; W.K. Kellogg Found. fellow, 1986-89. Fellow AIA (mem. nat. ethics coun. 2000—); mem. Am. Psychol. Assn., Am. Ednl. Rsch. Assn., Nat. Archtl. Accreditation Bd. (bd. dirs. 1995-98, pres. 1997-98). Democrat. Home: 1017 Minor Ave Apt 504 Seattle WA 98104-1304 Office: Dept Architecture Box 355720 U Wash Seattle WA 98195-5720 E-mail: sesut@u.washington.edu.

SUTTON, THOMAS C. insurance company executive; b. Atlanta, June 2, 1942; m. Marilyn Sutton; children: Stephen, Paul, Matthew, Meagan. BS in Math. and Physics, U. Toronto, 1965; postgrad., Harvard U., 1982. With Pacific Mut. Life Ins. Co., Newport Beach, Calif., 1963—, actuarial asst., 1966-69, successively asst. actuary, assoc. actuary, asst. v.p., 2d v.p., v.p. individual ins., 1969-80, successively v.p. individual fin., sr. v.p. corp. devel., exec. v.p. individual ins., 1980-87, pres., from 1987; now chmn. bd., CEO Pacific Life Corp.; also bd. dirs. Pacific Mut. Life Ins. Co. Mem. affiliates adv. bd. U. Calif. Irvine Grad. Sch. Mgmt. Trustee South Coast Repertory; bd. dirs. Ind. Colls. So. Calif. Fellow Soc. of Actuaries (mem. numerous coms.); mem. Am. Acad. Actuaries (com. on dividend prins. and practices, 1978), Pacific States Actuarial Club, L.A. Actuarial Club (sec. 1974-75, pres. 1978-79). Office: Pacific Mut Life Ins Co 700 Newport Center Dr Newport Beach CA 92660-6307*

SUTTON, WILLIAM DWIGHT, lawyer; b. Butler, Pa., Oct. 22, 1916; s. James S. Sutton and Ada Elizabeth Emrick; m. Mary Ella Newsome, Dec. 4, 1943; children: Ann, Melissa. BA, Washington & Jefferson, 1938; JD, U. Mich., 1941. Bar: Pa. 1946, U.S. Ct. Appeals (3d cir.) 1946, U.S. Supreme Ct. 1946. Assoc. atty. Donovan, Leisure, Newton & Irvine, N.Y.C., 1941-42; ptnr. Thorp Reed & Armstrong, Pitts., 1952-90, sr. ptnr., 1991—2001; ret., 2001. Major U.S. Army, 1942-46, PTO. Decorated Bronze Star, 1944. Mem. ABA, Pa. Bar Assn., Allegheny County Bar Assn. Home: 605 Scenic View Dr Pittsburgh PA 15241-3999

SUTTON, WILLIS ANDERSON, JR. sociology educator; b. Atlanta, July 18, 1917; s. Willis Anderson and Louneal (Walton) S.; m. Dorothy Rebecca Drake, Dec. 22, 1941; children: Willis Anderson III, Franklin Drake, Sarah Sutton Haggard. Student, Young Harris Jr. Coll., 1934-36; BA, U. N.C., 1939, MA, 1941, PhD, 1952. Project dir. WPA, Ga., 1940-41; instr. Emory U., Atlanta, 1948-52; asst. prof. U. Ky., Lexington, 1952-58, asso. prof., 1959-68, prof. sociology, 1968-82, chmn. dept., 1976-82. Author: Village Level Workers and Their Work, 1962. Served to 2d lt. U.S. Army, 1941-45. Ford Found. fellow India, 1959-60 Mem. Am. Sociol. Assn., Soc. Study Social Problems, Soc. Study Symbolic Interaction, So. Sociol. Soc., North Central Sociol. Soc. Democrat. Presbyterian.

SUTTON-STRAUS, JOAN M. journalist; b. Mimico, Ont., Can., Nov. 30, 1932; d. Frederick Edward and Anna May (Taylor) Treble; m. Walter J. Sutton, Feb. 1955 (div. 1979); children: Walter John, Deborah Anne.; m. Oscar S. Straus, Mar. 1982. Fashion editor Toronto Telegram, 1972; lifestyle editor, daily columnist Sutton's Place, Toronto Sun, 1972-79; daily commentator Sta. CFRB, Toronto, 1974-77; columnist Toronto Star, 1979; agt. gen. to U.S. Ont., 1990-91; columnist Toronto, Calgary, Edmonton and Ottawa Sun. Fin. Post, 1992-94. Author: Lovers and Others, 1974, Once More with Love, 1975, Clothing and Culture, 1975, Lovelines, 1979, All Men are not Alike, 1980, A Legacy of Caring, 1996. Former mem. adv. bd. Peggy Guggenheim Mus.; former trustee Am. Acad. Dramatic Arts; nat. gov. The Shaw Festival; trustee Am. Friends of Can., The Banff Ctr.; dir. Citizens Com. for N.Y.C. Decorated Canada medal; recipient Judy award Garment Salesmen Ont., 1964; named Can. Woman of Yr., N.Y.C., 1990; honored with Freedom of City of London. Home: 345 E 57th St Apt 14C New York NY 10022

SUTUSKY, JOHN CHARLES, higher education educator; b. Altoona, Pa., Dec. 25, 1947; s. J.C. and Mary M. (Kitko) S.; m. Kathryn Fay, Apr.5, 1975 (div.); children: Stephen C., Sarah C.; m. Rebecca Steedly, Oct. 17, 1998. BA, St. Francis Coll., 1969; MS, W.Va. U., 1972; PhD, Fla. State U., 1979. Asst. to the pres. So. W.Va. C.C., Logan, 1973-74, interim pres., 1974-75, dean learning resources, 1974-77; rsch. assoc. Fla. Dept. Edn., Tallahassee, 1977-79; coord. health affairs S.C. Commn. on Higher Edn., Columbia, 1979-82, asst. dir. health affairs, 1982-85, asst. dir. acad. affairs, 1985-88, assoc. commr., 1988-95; dir. planning Med. U. S.C., Charleston, 1995—. Cons. in field. Recipient Kellogg fellow Fla. State U., Tallahassee, 1977. Mem. Am. Assn. for Higher Edn., Soc. for Coll. and Univ. Planning (pub. com. 1996-97, bd. dirs. 1998—). Home: 302 Ayers Cir Summerville SC 29485-3306 Office: Med U SC 141 Ashley Ave Charleston SC 29403-5808

SUUBERG, ERIC MICHAEL, chemical engineering educator; b. N.Y.C., Nov. 23, 1951; s. Michael and Aino (Berg) S.; m. Ina Inara Vatvars, Apr. 26, 1987; 1 child, Alessandra Anna. BSChemE, MSChemE, BS in Bus. Mgmt., MIT, 1974, MS in Bus. Mgmt., 1976, ScD in Chem. Engring., 1978. Asst. prof. chem. engring. Carnegie-Mellon U., Pitts., 1977-81; asst. prof. engring. Brown U., Providence, 1981-84, assoc. prof. engring., 1984-90, prof. engring., 1990—, rep. exec. com. fluids, thermal and chem. processes group, 1991—. Vis. scientist Centre National de la Recherche Scientifique, Mulhouse, France, 1988; invited lectr. Ministry Edn., Monbusho, Japan, 1991, 93; vis. prof. Tallinn Tech. U., 2001. Mem. internat. editl. bd. Fuel, 1988—, mem. editl. adv. bd. Energy and Fuels, 1990—93, 1998—2000, Americas editor Fuel, 2000—, contbr. over 100 articles to profl. jours. Elected mem. Estonian Am. Nat. Coun., N.Y.C., 1984-99, v.p. 1996-99. Vice Chancellor's Rsch. Best Practice fellow U. Newcastle, Australia, 1995; Fulbright scholar, 2000-01. Mem. AIChE, Combustion Inst., Am. Chem. Soc. (chmn. divsn. fuel chemistry 1991, bd. dirs.-at-large 1995-97, H.H. Storch award in fuel chemistry Am. Chem. Soc.. 1999). Office: Brown Univ Divsn Engring Box D Providence RI 02912 E-mail: eric_suuberg@brown.edu.

SUYCOTT, MARK LELAND, systems engineer, retired naval flight officer; b. Riverside, Calif., Oct. 3, 1956; s. Morgan L. Suycott and Dixie L. (Drury) Bobbitt; m. Lisa Lyn Brammer, Oct. 1, 1983. BSCE, U. Mo., 1979; MS in Aero. Engring., Naval Postgrad. Sch., Monterey, Calif., 1987; test flight officer, U.S. Naval Test Pilot Sch., Patuxent River, Md., 1987; student, Def. Sys. Mgmt. Coll., Ft. Belvoir, Va., 1994. Commd. ensign USN, 1979, advanced through grades to comdr., 1995; aviation armament divsn. officer Fighter Squadron Thirty Three, Virginia Beach, Va., 1981-84; flight test project officer Pacific Missile Test Ctr., Point Mugu, Calif., 1987-89; air ops. officer Comdr. U.S. 7th Fleet, Yokosuka/Manama, Japan/Bahrain, 1989-91; ops./maintenance officer Fighter Squadron 11, San Diego, 1992-93; dep. asst. program mgr. Naval Air Sys. Command, Arlington, Va., 1994-97; prof. Def. System Mgmt. Coll., Fort Belvoir, 1997-99; sr. sys. engr. SAIC Space and Def. Group, San Diego, 2000-01, program mgr., 2001—. Asst. dist. commr. Boy Scouts Am.; eagle scout, Order of the Arrow, Woodbadge. Decorated Def. Meritorious Svc. medal, Meritorious Svc. medal (2), Navy Commendation medal (2), Navy Achievement medal; named Outstanding Grad. U.S. Naval Test Pilot Sch.; recipient Woodbadge and Commr.'s Key awards, Boy Scouts Am. Mem. AIAA (sr.), Internat. Test and Evaluation Assn., Soc. Flight Test Engrs., Assn. Naval Aviation, Tailhook Assn., Nat. Eagle Scout Assn., Masons (master mason, 32d degree Scottish Rite, Al Bahr Shrine), Inst. of Navigation, Assn. Old Crows, Omicron Delta Kappa, Tau Beta Pi, Chi Epsilon, Alpha Phi Omega (life). Avocations: running, bicycling, sailing, skiing. Address: SAIC 10260 Campus Point Dr # Msx2 San Diego CA 92121-1522

SUZIEDELIS, VYTAUTAS A. engineering corporation executive; b. Kaunas, Lithuania, June 22, 1930; s. Simas and Antanina S. BS, Northeastern U., 1954; MS, N.Y. U., 1955. With Stone & Webster Engring. Corp., Boston, 1956-90, chief power engr., 1972-74, v.p., 1974-76, sr. v.p., 1976-79, exec. v.p., 1979-87, dir., 1975-87, cons., 1987-90; pres. Vasair Corp., Brockton, Mass., 1977-91. Mem. ASME, Aircraft Owners and Pilots Assn., Pi Tau Sigma (hon.). Republican. Roman Catholic. Home: 6849 Grenadier Blvd Ph 5 Naples FL 34108-7223 E-mail: vasuziedelis@cs.com.

SUZUKI, HIDETARO, violinist; b. Tokyo, June 1, 1937; came to U.S., 1956; s. Hidezo and Humi (Sakai) S.; m. Zeyda Ruga, May 16, 1962; children: Kenneth Hideo, Nantel Hiroshi, Elina Humi. Diploma, Toho Sch. Music, Tokyo, 1956, Curtis Inst. Music, 1963. Prof. violin Conservatory Province Que., Quebec, 1963-79, Laval U., Quebec, 1971-77, Butler U., Indpls., 1979—. Concertmaster Que. Symphony Orch., 1963-78, Indpls. Symphony Orch., 1978—; performed as concert violinist Can., U.S., Ea. and Western Europe, Cuba, Japan, S.E. Asia, India, USSR 1951-; guest condr. orchs. in numerous concerts, broadcasts, 1968—; mem. jury Mont. Internat. Competition, 1979, Internat. Violin Competition, 1979, Internat. Violin Competition of Indpls., 1982, 86, 90, 94; artistic dir. Suzuki and Friends chamber music series, 1980—; rec. artist. Office: Indpls Symphony Orch 45 Monument Cir Indianapolis IN 46204-2907

SUZUKI, HOWARD KAZURO, retired anatomist, educator; b. Ketchikan, Alaska, Apr. 3, 1927; s. Goerge K. and Tsuya S.; m. Tetsuko Fujita, Sept. 12, 1952; children: Georganne, Joan, James, Stanley. BS, Marquette U., 1949, MS, 1951; PhD, Tulane U., 1955. Instr. anatomy Yale U. Sch. Medicine, 1955-58; asst. prof. anatomy U. Ark. Med. Center, Little Rock, 1958-62, asso. prof., 1962-67, prof., 1967-70; prof. anatomy, assoc. dean health related professions U. Fla., Gainesville, 1970-71; prof. anatomy U. Fla. (Coll. Medicine), 1970-71; dean U. Fla. (Coll. Health Related Professions), 1971-79; prof. anatomy U. Fla. (Coll. Medicine and Health Related Professions), 1979-90, ret., 1990. Cons. NIH, VA, NASA; vis. research prof. U. Utah Sch. Medicine, 1962 Contbr. articles to profl. jours. Bd. dirs. Civitan Regional Blood Bank, 1977— ; regional v.p. Fla. Retarded Citizens Assn., 1974-76; mem. Fla. Adv. Council on Vocat. Edn., 1978-86, chmn., 1981; active United Way. Fellow AAAS; mem. Soc. Exptl. Biol. Medicine, Am. Assn. Anatomists, Am. Soc. Allied Health Professions, Am. Soc. Marine Artists, Sigma Xi. Episcopalian. Home: 4331 NW 20th Pl Gainesville FL 32605-3436 E-mail: hksuzuki@aol.com.

SUZUKI, ISAMU, microbiology educator, researcher; b. Tokyo, Aug. 4, 1930; emigrated to Can., 1962; s. Jisaku and Michie (Baba) S.; m. Yumiko Kanehira, May 16, 1962; children: Kenji, Miyo, Kohji. B.Sc.Agr., U. Tokyo, 1953; PhD, Iowa State U., 1958. NIH postdoctoral fellow Western Res. U., 1958-60; instr. Inst. Applied Microbiology, U. Toyko, 1960-62; asst. prof. mcirobiology U. Man., Winnipeg, Canada, 1964—66, assoc. prof., 1966—69, prof., 1969—99, head. dept., 1972—85, sr. scholar, 1999—2000, prof. emeritus, 2000—. Contbr. articles on sulfur-oxidizing bacteria, chemoautotrophic bacteria, mechanism of inorganic oxidation to sci. jours. NRC of Can. postdoctoral fellow, 1962-64. Mem. AAAS, Can. Soc. Microbiologists, Am. Soc. Microbiology, Can. Soc. Biochem. and Molecular Cell Biology, Sigma Xi Office: U Manitoba Dept Microbiology Winnipeg MB Canada R3T 2N2 E-mail: isuzuki@cc.umanitoba.ca.

SUZUKI, JON BYRON, assoc. dean, periodontist, educator; b. San Antonio, July 22, 1946; s. George K. and Ruby (Kenaya) S. BA in Biology, Ill. Wesleyan U., 1968; PhD in Microbiology magna cum laude, Ill. Inst. Tech., 1971; DDS magna cum laude, Loyola U., 1978. Med. technologist Ill. Masonic Hosp. and Med. Ctr., Chgo., 1966-67; instr. lab. in histology and parasitology Ill. Wesleyan U., Bloomington, 1967-68; med. technologist Augustana Hosp., Chgo., 1968-69; rsch. assoc., instr. microbiology Ill. Inst. Tech., 1968-71; clin. rsch. assoc. U. Chgo. Hosps., 1970-71; clin. microbiologist St. Luke's Hosp., Columbia Coll., Physicians and Surgeons, N.Y.C., 1971-73; assoc. med. dir. Paramed Tng. and Registry, Vancouver, B.C., Can., 1973-74; dir. clin. labs. Registry of Hawaii, 1973-74; chmn. clin. labs. edn. Kapiolany Cmty. Coll., U. Hawaii, Honolulu, 1974; lectr. periodontics, oral pathology Loyola U. Med. Ctr., Maywood, Ill., 1974-90; lectr. stomatology Northwestern U. Dental Sch., Chgo., 1982-90; HIH rsch. fellow depts. pathology and periodontics Ctr. for Rsch. in Oral Biology, U. Wash., Seattle, 1978-80; prof. dept. periodontics and microbiology U. Md. Coll. Dental Surgery, Balt., 1980-90; mem. attending faculty divsn. dentistry and oral and maxillofacial surgery The Johns Hopkins Med. Inst., 1985—; practice specializing in periodontics Balt. and Pitts.; dean Sch. Dental Medicine U. Pitts., 1989—. Cons. Dentsply Internat., York, Pa., U.S. Army, Walter Reed Med. Ctr., Washington, U.S. Army, Ft. Gordon, Ga., USN, Nat. Naval Med. Command, Bethesda, The NutraSweet Col, Deerfield, Ill., FDA, Rockville, Md.; mem. Biology/Medicine Study Sect. NIH, Bethesda, 1985-90; mem. nat. adv. dental rsch. coun. NIH/NIDR, Bethesda, 1994—; vis. scientist Moscow State U., USSR, 1972, NASA, Houston, 1976-92; lectr. Internat. Congress allergology, Tokyo, 1973; lab. dir. Hawaii Dept. Health. Author: Clinical Laboratory Methods for the Medical Assistant, 1974; mem. editl. bd. Am. Health Mag.; contbr. articles on rsch. in microbiology, immunology and dentistry to sci. jours. Instr. water safety ARC, Honolulu, 1973-90. Recipient Pres.'s medallion Loyola U., Chgo., 1977; named Alumnus of Yr., Ill. Wesleyan U., 1977. Fellow Acad. Dentistry Internat., Am. Coll. Dentists, Internat. Coll. Dentists, Am. Coll. Stomatognathic Surgeons; mem. AAAS, ADA (vice chair coun. sci. affairs), AAUP, ADA (vice chair coun. sci. affairs), AAUP, Am. Acad. Periodontology (diplomate), Am. Inst. Biol. Scis., Internat. Soc. Biophysics, Internat. Soc. Endocrinologists, Ill. Acad. Sci., Am. Internat. Assn. Dental Rsch. (pres. Md. chpt.), Am. Acad. Microbiology (diplomate, examiner), N.Y. Acad. Scis., Sigma Xi, Omicron Kappa Upsilon (past nat. pres., exec. sec.), Beta Beta Beta Hon. Soc. Home: 3501 Terrace St Pittsburgh PA 15213-2523 Office: U Pitts Sch Dental Medicine B100 Salk Hall Pittsburgh PA 15261

SUZUKI, KUNIHIKO, biomedical educator, researcher; b. Tokyo, Japan, Feb. 5, 1932; arrived in U.S., 1960; s. Nobuo and Teiko (Suzuki) Suzuki; m. Kinuko Ikeda, Dec. 20, 1960; 1 child Jun. BA in History and Philosophy of Sci., Tokyo U., 1955, MD, 1959; MA (hon.), U. Pa., 1971. Diplomate Nat. Bd. Med. Licensure Japan. Rotating intern USAF Hosp. Tachikawa, Tokyo, Japan, 1959-60; asst. resident in neurology Bronx (N.Y.) Mcpl. Hosp. Ctr.-Albert Einstein Coll. Medicine, 1960-61, resident in neurology, 1961-62, clin. fellow in neurology, 1962-64; instr. in neurology Albert Einstein Coll. Medicine, Bronx, 1964, asst. prof., 1965-68; assoc. prof. U. Pa. Sch. Medicine, Phila., 1969-71; prof. neurology and pediatrics, 1971-72; prof. neurology Albert Einstein Coll. Medicine, 1972-86, prof. neurosci., 1974-86; prof. neurology and psychiatry, faculty curriculum in neurobiology U. N.C. Sch. Medicine, Chapel Hill, 1986—; dir. UNC Neurosci. Ctr., 1986-99, dir. emeritus, 1999—. Staff dept. neuropsychiatry Tokyo U. Faculty Medicine, 1960, U. Pa. Inst. Neurol. Scis., 1969—72; attending physician Bronx Mcpl. Hosp. Ctr., 1976—86, Hosp. Albert Einstein Coll. Medicine, 1977—86; vis. prof. fellowship Japan Soc. for Promotion Sci., 1980, Yamada Sci. Found., 1981; mem. neurology B study sect. NIH, 1971—75, guest scientist, 1984—85, program com. mental retardation and devel. disabilities, 1989—92; mem. basic neurosci. task force Nat. Inst. Neurol. and Communicative Disorders and Stroke, 1978, adv. panel directions and opportunities for future rsch., 83; bd. sci. counselors NIH, 1980—84; mem. adv. com. on fellowships Nat. Multiple Sclerosis Soc., 1974—77; jury St. Vincent Internat. award for Med. Sci., 1979; mem. adv. com. Eunice Kennedy Shriver Ctr., Waltham, Mass., 1974—84; mem. adv. bd. Children's Assn. for Rsch. on Mucolipidosis Type IV, 1983—; mem. U.S. Nat. Com. for Internat. Brain Rsch. Orgn., 1985—89. Editor: Ganglioside Structure and Function, 1984; editor: (chief) Jour. Neurochemistry, 1977—82; contbr. Mem. Nat. Adv. Commn. on Multiple Sclerosis, 1973—74; mem. med. adv. bd. United Leukodystrophy Found., 1982—86, 1997—, Nat. Tay-Sachs and Allied Diseases Assn., 1971—, Canavan Found., 1992—. Recipient A. Weil award, Am. Assn. Neuropathologists, 1970, Saul R. Korey Lectureship, 1993, M. Moore award, 1975, Jacob K. Javits Neurosci. Investigator award, NIH, 1985, 1992, Humboldt Sr. Rsch. award, Humboldt Found., 1990, Eminent Scientist award, Inst. Phys. Chem. Rsch., Japan, 1995, Japan Acad. prize, 2002. Mem.: AAAS, Japan Soc. Inherited Metabolic Disease (hon.), Am. Soc. Human Genetics, Internat. Brain Rsch. Orgn., Japanese Neurochem. Soc., Japanese Med. Soc. Am. (Disting. Scientist award 1985), Am. Acad. Neurology, Am. Soc. Biochemistry and Molecular Biology, Soc. for Neurosci., Internat. Soc. for Neurochemistry (coun. 1987—89, treas. 1989—93, pres. 1993—95), Am. Soc. for Neurochemistry (pres. 1985—87, coun. 1973—77, 1987—91, Basic Neurochemistry Lectureship 1995), Inst. Medicine NAS. Avocations: piano, photography, birdwatching, skiing. Office: U NC Chapel Hill Neurosci Ctr PO Box 7250 Chapel Hill NC 27599-0001

SUZUKI, NOBUTAKA, chemistry educator; b. Nishio, Aichi, Japan, Nov. 8, 1942; s. Kihachiro and Masayo (Miwa) S.; m. Fumiko Sato, Mar. 21, 1971; children: Mina, Kumi. B of Chemistry, Nagoya U., Japan, 1966, D of Chemistry, 1972. Asst. prof. dept. chemistry Mie U., Tsu, Japan, 1971-88, assoc. prof. Japan, 1988; sr. rsch. Biophoton project JRDC, Sendai, Japan, 1988-90; assoc. prof. Shimonoseki (Japan) Nat. U. Fisheries, 1990-92, prof., 1993—. Postdoctoral staff Johns Hopkins U., Balt., 1977-79. Author: Natural Products Chemistry, 1975, 2d rev. edit., 1983, Bioluminescence of Chemiluminescence, Current Status, 1991, Oxygen Radicals, 1992, Chemistry of Functional Dyes, Vol. 2, 1993, Bioluminescence and Chemiluminescence, status report, 1993, Bioluminescence and Chemiluminescence: Fundamentals and Applied Aspects, 1994, Maillard Reactions in Chemicals, Food, and Health, 1994, Food Factors: Chemistry and Cancer Prevention, 1997, Bioluminescence and Chemiluminescence, Molecular Reporting and Photons, 1997, Food Factors for Cancer Prevention, 1997, The Maillard Reaction in Foods and Medicine, 1998, Recent Research Developments in Agricultural and Biological Chemistry, Vol. 2, 1998, Advances in Shrimp Biotechnology, 1998, Dictionary of Biochemistry, 3d edit., 1998, Bioluminescence and Chemiluminescence: Perspectives for the 21st Century, 1999, Recent Development of Food Factors for the Aging Prevention, 1999, Agricultural and Biological Chemistry, Vol. 3, 1999; editor: (book) The Roles of Oxygen in Chemistry and Biochemistry, 1988, (book/tape) Scientific English in Fisheries, 1992, English for Science and Technological Experiments, 1994, English for Pharmacy and Medical Science, 1995, English for International Conference, 1995, Future in Fisheries Science, 1999, Food Sciences, 2001; mem. editl. bd. ITE Letters on Batteries, New Techs. and Medicine, 2000—, award com. chmn., 2000. Recipient Rsch. award Internat. Battery Material Assn., 1997, Spl. award Internat. Tech. Exch. Soc.-Internat. Battery Material Assn., 1998; grantee Naito Meml. Found., 1977, Tokai Sci. Rsch. Found., 1986, Agrl. Biol. Chemistry Japan, 1990, Kiei-Kai Sci. Rsch. Found., 1991-96, Skylark Rsch. Found., 1992, The Sci. and Tech. Agy., Japan, 1994-96, Internat. Tech. Exch. K-Found., 1996-97, Internat. Battery Material Assn., 1998—, Nakatani Electronic Measuring Tech. Assn. Japan, 1998-99; grant-in-aid Sci. and Tech. Agy. of Japan, 1998-99, 99—, Rsch. Devel. Corp. Japan, 1998, Small Bus. Promotion Corp., Japan, 2000. Mem. Am. Chem. Soc., Am. Soc. for Photobiology, Agrl. Biol. Soc. Japan, Chem. Soc. Japan, Japan Soc. Sci. Fisheries, Internat. Tech. Exch. Soc. (award 1995, bd. dirs. 1995—, v.p. 2000—, grantee 1998—, ITE-IBA Spl. award 1998). Office: Shimonoseki U Fisheries Yoshimi Shimonoseki Yamaguchi 7596595 Japan Fax: 81-832-86-7434. E-mail: suzukin@fish-u.ac.jp.

SUZUKI, NORMAN HITOSHI, lawyer; b. Honolulu, Dec. 5, 1935; s. Hajime and Mildred (Fujimoto) S.; m. Lois A. Tatsuguchi, Aug. 19, 1962; children: Grant T., Brandon A. BA, U. Mich., 1957; LLB, Harvard U., 1960. Bar: Hawaii 1960, U.S. Dist. Ct. Hawaii 1960, U.S. Ct. Appeals (9th cir.) 1962, U.S. Supreme Ct. 1974. Sole practice, Honolulu, 1960—; pres. Suzuki & Lee, Attys., 1990-93, Suzuki & Goo, Attys., Honolulu, 1993—. Served to capt. USAR, 1960-66. Mem. ABA, Hawaii Bar Assn. Home: 3517 Kahawalu Dr Honolulu HI 96817-1029 Office: Suzuki & Goo 1188 Bishop St Century Sq Suite 1805 Honolulu HI 96813

SUZUKI, YASUHIKO, law educator; b. Mishima, Japan, Sept. 6, 1936; arrived in U.S., 68; s. Heijo and Hiro Suzuki; m. Kyoko Teraizumi Suzuki, May 14, 1961; children: Iori, Anri, Claude. LLB, Chuo U., Tokyo, 1960; LLM, Georgetown U., 1972. V.p. Nissan Motor Corp., Gardena, Calif., 1968—85; chmn. bd. dirs. Pacific Trade & Investment Corp., Washington, 1985—90; prof. U. Va., Charlottesville, 1991—93, Showa Joshi U., Tokyo, 1994—96, George Mason U., Fairfax, Va., 1996—. Vice chmn. Automobile Importers Am., Washington, 1975—85. Author: Washington Lobby, 1990, The American Nation, 1999, The Constitution of the United States - The Evolving Constitution, 2000. Bd. dirs. Japanese C. of C., N.Y.C., 1978—85, Washington, 1979—85. Named to Automotive Hall of Fame, 1984; recipient cert. of recognition for outstanding contbns. and efforts, Humane Soc. of Washington, DC, 1980, Youth for Understanding, 1981. Mem.: Internat. Law Inst. Japan, Acad. Polit. Sci. Home: 31242 Avenida Terramar San Juan Capistrano CA 92675 Office: George Mason U 4400 University Dr Fairfax VA 22030-4444

SVADLENAK, JEAN HAYDEN, museum consultant; b. Wilmington, Del., Mar. 4, 1955; d. Marion M. and Ida Jean (Calcagni) Hayden; m. Steven R. Svadlenak, May 26, 1979. BS in Textiles and Clothing, U. Del., 1977; MA in History Mus. Studies, SUNY, Oneonta, 1982; postgrad., U. Calif., Berkeley, 1982. Curatorial asst. The Hagley Mus., Wilmington, 1976-77; curator of costumes and textiles The Kansas City (Mo.) Mus., 1978-82, chief curator, 1982-84, assoc. exec. dir. for collection and exhibits mgmt., 1984-86, interim pres., 1986-87, pres., 1987-89. Researcher, guest curator N.Y. State Hist. Assn., Cooperstown, 1980; grant reviewer Inst. for Mus. Svcs., 1985-89; ad hoc faculty U. Kans., 1991—, U. Mo., Kansas City, 1992—. Mem. Am. Assn. Mus. (surveyor mus. assessment program 1985-89, mem. accreditation vis. com. 1990—), Am. Assn. State and Local History, Costume Soc. Am., Heritage League Kansas City (bd. dirs. 1987-89), Midwest Mus. Conf. (coun. 1992-94), Mo. Mus. Assocs. (pres. 1992-94), Com. on Mus. Profl. Tng. (2d v.p. 1994-96, at-large rep. 1997-2000). Avocations: music, photography, cooking. Home: 624 Romany Rd Kansas City MO 64113-2037

SVAHN, JOHN ALFRED, government official; b. New London, Conn., May 13, 1943; s. Albert Russell and Esther Marilu (Caffero) S.; m. Jill Weber, July 12, 1977; children: Kirsten Marie, John Alfred III. BA in Polit. Sci, U. Wash., 1966; postgrad., U. Pacific, 1970-73, Georgetown U., 1973-74. Spl. asst. to dir. Calif. Dept. Public Works, 1968-70; chief dep. dir. Calif. Dept. Social Welfare, 1971-73, dir., 1973; acting commr. Community Services Adminstrn., HEW, Washington, 1973-74; commr. Assistance Payments Adminstrn., 1973-76; dep. adminstr. Social and Rehab. Service, 1974-75; adminstr. Social and Rehab. Svcs., 1975-76; mgr. Haskins and Sells, 1976-79; pres. John A. Svahn, Inc., Annapolis, Md., 1979-81; U.S. commr. social security Balt., 1981-83; undersec. HHS, Washington, 1983-84; asst. to Pres. for policy devel., 1984-86; chmn. Maximus Inc., 1988-94; U.S. commr. Commn. for Study of Alternatives for Panama Canal, 1987-92; exec. v.p. The Wexler Group, Washington, 1995—; chmn. Captial Assocs., Inc., 1994—; bd. dirs. Logisticare, Inc., 2000—, EpicEdge, Inc., 2001—. Mem. Nat. Devel. Disability Adv. Council, 1975-76, Pres.'s Transition Team, 1980-81, Calif. Health Care Commn., 1972, pub. affairs com. United Way Am., 1987—; chmn. Govs. Commn. on Corrections Health Care, Md., 1990—; assoc. mem. Calif. Republican State Cen. Com., 1970-72; bd. dirs. Nat. Aquarium, Balt.; bd. dirs. Health Care Svcs. NAS Inst. Medicine, 1987-92; bd. dirs. Logisticare, Inc., 2001-; bd. dirs. Epic Edge, Inc., 2001-; mem. Gov.'s Privatization Coun., 1992—. Served to lt. USAF, 1966-68. Named Outstanding Young Man in HEW, 1974; recipient Sec.'s citation, 1975, Adminstr.'s spl. citation, 1975 Mem. Phi Delta Phi, Zeta Psi. Clubs: Annapolis Yacht, Sailing of the Chesapeake. Republican. Office: 4790 Caughlin Pkwy #201 Reno NV 89509

SVALYA, PHILLIP GORDON, lawyer; b. Ferndale, Mich., June 28, 1943; s. John Michael and Ann Marie (Peters) S.; m. Lois Faith Wallace, Aug. 15, 1969; children: Daniel Gordon, Karina Renee. BS, U.S. Naval Acad., Annapolis, Md., 1966; JD, U. Santa Clara, Calif., 1973. Bar: Calif. 1974, U.S. Dist. Ct. (no. dist.) Calif. 1974. Pvt. practice, Sunnyvale, Mountain View, Calif., 1974-81, Cupertino, 1981—. Officer, bd. dirs. Albanian Health Fund. Lt. USN, 1966-70, capt. USNR SEAL ret., 1970-91. Mem. ATLA, Calif. Bar Assn., Consumer Attys. of Calif., Santa Clara County Bar Assn., Sunnyvale/Cupertino Bar Assn., Underwater Demolition Team-SEAL Assn., Million Dollar Advocates Forum. Roscoe Pound Inst. Republican. Avocations: hiking, gardening. Office: Phillip G Svalya Inc 10455 Torre Ave Cupertino CA 95014-3203

SVÄRD, N. TRYGVE, electrical engineer; b. Gothenburg, Sweden; came to U.S., 1973; s. Owe V. and Berit S. (Heden) S.; children: Michael, Stefan. BEE, Gothenburg U., Sweden, 1966. Registered profl. engr. Engr. Volvo Car Div., Gothenburg, 1969-73; from project engr., sr. sect. engr. to program mgr. Honeywell Inc., Mpls., 1973-90; sr. program mgr., internat. programs Alliant Techsystems, Inc., 1990-99; ret., 1999. Pres. Nord Mark Inc., Mpls, 1986-- Sgt. Swedish Coast Arty., 1967-68. Mem. Am. Swedish Inst. Republican. Home and Office: 12075 48th Ave N Minneapolis MN 55442-2129

SVARLIEN, DIANE ARNSON, verse translator, classics educator; b. N.Y.C., Feb. 5, 1960; d. Alan and Nancy (Matthews) Arnson; m. John E. Svarlien, Nov. 27, 1987; children: Aaron, Corinna. BA, U. Va., 1983; MA, U. Tex., 1985, PhD, 1991. Vis. assoc. prof. Georgetown (Ky.) Coll., 1994—. Mem. Am. Philol. Assn., Am. Literary Translators Assn., Classical Assn. Midwest & South, Archaeol. Inst. Am., SERVAS Internat.

SVEC, HARRY JOHN, chemist, educator; b. Cleve., June 24, 1918; s. Ralph Joseph and Lilian Josephine (Pekarek) S.; m. Edna Mary Bruno, Oct. 27, 1943; children— Mary, Peter, Katherine, Jan, Thomas, Jeanne, Benjamin, Daniel, Lillian. BS, John Carroll U., 1941; PhD in Phys. Chemistry, Iowa State U., 1949. Asst. chemist Iowa State U., 1941-43; rsch. assoc. Inst. Atomic Rsch., 1946-50, asst. prof. chemistry, 1950-55, assoc. prof., 1955-60, prof., 1960-83, emeritus prof. chemistry, 1983—, Disting. prof. in scis. and humanities emeritus, 1978—; assoc. chemist Ames Lab., 1950-55; chemist Ames Lab., Dept. Energy, 1955-60, sr. chemist, 1960-85, program dir., 1974-85, assoc. scientist, 1983—. Jr. chemist Manhattan Project, Iowa State Coll., 1943-46; cons., lectr. in field. Author lab. manual in phys. chemistry; contbr. numerous articles to profl. publs.; founding editor: Internat. Jour. Mass Spectrometry and Ion Processes, 1968-86. NSF grantee, 1972-82; EPA grantee, 1974-81; AEC grantee, 1950-74; ERDA grantee, 1974-77; Dept. Energy grantee, 1977-87; Am. Water Works Assn. grantee, 1977-79 Fellow: AAAS, The Chem. Soc.; mem.: ASTM, Am. Soc. Mass Spectroscopy (charter, v.p. 1972—74, pres. 1974—76), Geochem. Soc., Am. Chem. Soc. (emeritus), Alpha Chi Sigma (cons. 1985—), Phi Lambda Upsilon, Alpha Signa Nu, Sigma Xi. Roman Catholic. Home: 2427 Hamilton Dr Ames IA 50014-8203 Office: Iowa State U 1605 Gilman Hall Ames IA 50014-8203 *Success in anything we choose to do requires a commitment. The degree of one's success depends directly on the kind of commitment that is made.*

SVENDSBYE, LLOYD AUGUST, college president, clergyman, educator; b. Hamlet, N.D., May 26, 1930; s. Anders A. and Gudrun J. (Birkelo) S.; m. Annelotte Frieda Erika Moertelmeyer, Dec. 20, 1958. BA, Concordia Coll., Moorhead, Minn., 1951, DD (hon.), 1983; BTh, Luther Theol.Sem., 1954; postgrad, U. Erlangen, Germany, 1954-55, Columbia U., 1959-60; ThD, Union Theol. Sem., 1966; LLD (hon.), Gettysburg Coll., 1977; LHD (hon.), Kilian C.C., 1992. Ordained to ministry, 1955; asst. pastor Our Saviours Luth. Ch., Mpls., 1955-56; adminstrv. asst. to dir. 3d Assembly Luth. World Fedn., 1956-57; asst. prof. religion Concordia Coll., 1957-59; asst. pastor Trinity Lutheran Ch., Bklyn., 1959-61; chmn. dept. religion Concordia Coll., 1962-66; editor in chief Augsburg Publ. House, Mpls., 1966-71; v.p., dean St. Olaf Coll., 1971-74; pres., prof. ch. history Luther Theol. Sem., St. Paul, 1974-82; pres. Northwestern Luth. Theol. Sem., 1976-82, Luther Northwestern Theol. Sem., 1982-87, prof. ch. history, 1982-87; pres. Augustana Coll., Sioux Falls, S.D., 1987-92. V.p. Am. Luth. Ch., 1981-87; Mem. Am. Luth. Ch.-Luth. Ch. Am. coop. com., 1974-78; Luth. World Fedn. Com. on Info. Services, 1971-76; mem. Com. on Luth. Unity, 1978-82, Commn. To Form a New Luth. Ch., 1982-86. Chmn. senate dist. 49A, Dem. Farm Labor Com., 1970-71; bd. dirs. Luth. Brotherhood, 1970-95, Luth. Gen. and Health Care Sys., Park Ridge, Ill., 1981-87; trustee Luth. Deaconess Hosp., Mpls., 1970-71, Fairview-Southdale Hosp., 1975-87, Fairview Cmty. Hosps., 1979-87. Recipient Alumni Achievement award Concordia Coll., 1974 Mem. Phi Beta Kappa. Home: 2500 Quentin Ct Minneapolis MN 55416-1900

SVENDSEN, ALF, artist, art educator; b. Bklyn., Mar. 24, 1930; s. Alf and Anna Thordina (Fjeldberg) S. BFA cum laude, Syracuse U., 1955; MFA summa cum laude, U. Notre Dame, 1965. Asst. sculptor Ivan Mestrovic, Notre Dame, Ind., 1955-56; sculptor Hall of African Man Am. Mus. Natural History, N.Y.C., 1966-68; tchr. art Mt. Anthony H.S., Bennington, Vt., 1969-71; prof. Delaware County C.C., Media, Pa., 1971-89. Exhibited work at New Sch. Social Rsch., N.Y.C., 1958, N.Y. Six Gallery, 1962, Berkshire (Mass.) Mus., 1970, Gallery 14 Sculptors, N.Y.C., 1974, Darmouth (N.H.) Coll., 1978, Deshong Mus., Chester, Pa., 1981, Art Sutton, Que., 1998, Mary Bryan Gallery, Jeffersonville, Vt., 1999. With USN, 1948-52. Home: 465 Daigle Dr Enosburg Falls VT 05450-5088

SVENGALIS, KENDALL FRAYNE, law librarian; b. Gary, Ind., May 16, 1947; s. Frank Anthony and Alvida Linnea (Matheus) S.; children: Hillary Linnea, Andrew Kendall; m. Ellen Christine Haffling, June 16, 2001. BA, Purdue U., 1970, MA, 1973; MLS, U. R.I., 1975. Reference librarian Roger Williams Coll., Bristol, R.I., 1975, Providence (R.I.) Coll., 1975-77; asst. law librarian R.I. State Law Library, Providence, 1976-82, state law librarian, 1982—. Adj. prof. libr. and info. studies U. R.I., 1987—. Author: The Legal Information Buyer's Guide and Reference Manual, 1996 (Best Legal Reference Book of 1996), 1997—98, 1998—99, 2000, 2001, 2002; editor: The Criv Sheet, 1988—94; contbr. articles to profl. jours. Chmn. jud. branch United Way Com. R.I., 1980. Recipient AALL Joseph L. Andrews Bibliographical awd. Mem. Am. Assn Law Librs. (state, ct. and county libr. spl. interest sect., recipient Connie E. Bolden significant publ. award 1993, 99, bd. dirs. 1986-88, 96-99), Law Librs. New Eng. (treas. 1983-85, v.p. 1985-86, pres. 1986-87), Com. on Rels. with Info. Vendors (editor 1988-94), New Eng. Law Libr. Consortium (v.p. 1990-92, pres. 1992-94). Republican. Lutheran. Home: 204 Wyassup Rd North Stonington CT 06359 Office: RI State Law Libr Frank Licht Jud Complex 250 Benefit St Providence RI 02903-2719 E-mail: ksven@ids.net., rilawpress@ids.net.

SVENSON, CHARLES OSCAR, investment banker; b. Worcester, Mass., June 28, 1939; s. Sven Oscar and Edahjane (Castner) S.; m. Sara Ellen Simpson, Nov. 15, 1968; children: Alicia Lindall, Tait Oscar. AB, Hamilton Coll., 1961; LL.B., Harvard U., 1964; LL.M., Bklyn. Law Sch., 1965. Bar: N.Y. 1965, U.S. Dist. Ct. (so. dist.) N.Y. 1965, U.S. Ct. Appeals (2d. cir.) 1965. Atty. Dewey, Ballantine, Bushby, Palmer & Wood, N.Y.C., 1964-68; v.p. Goldman Sachs & Co., 1968-75; sr. v.p. Donaldson, Lufkin & Jenrette, N.Y.C, 1975-89, mng. dir., 1989-2000. Trustee Kirkland Coll., Clinton, N.Y., 1976-78; trustee Hamilton Coll., Clinton, 1979-83, 90—. Mem. ABA, N.Y. State Bar Assn., Assn. of Bar of City of N.Y. Clubs: Tuxedo (Tuxedo Park, N.Y.); Harvard (N.Y.C.). Home: 1185 Park Ave New York NY 10128-1308 Office: Donaldson Lufkin & Jenrette Securities Corp 277 Park Ave 16th Fl New York NY 10172-3400

SVENSSON, LARS GEORG, cardiovascular and thoracic surgeon; b. Barbeton, Republic South Africa, Aug. 11, 1955; came to U.S., 1986; s. Karl-Georg and Marianne S.; m. Marion Frances Robinson, June 14, 1986. MB, BCh, U. Witwatersrand, Johannesburg, South Africa, 1978, MSc (Med.), 1983, PhD, 1986. Diplomate Gen., Vascular and Cardiothoracic Surgery. Resident in surgery Johannesburg Hosp., 1981-86; fellow cardiovascular surgery Cleve. Clinic Found., 1986-87, Baylor Coll. of Medicine, Houston, 1987-89, resident cardiothoracic surgery, 1989-91; attending surgeon Meth. Hosp., VA Med. Ctr., 1991-92, Lahey Clinic, Burlington, Mass., 1993—2001, dir. Aortic Surgery Ctr. and Marfan Syndrome Clinic, 1993—2001; dir. Cleve. Clinic Found., 2001—, dir. Aorta Ctr. and Marfan Syndrome Clinic, 2001—. Spkr. in field. Contbr. numerous articles to profl. jours. including Jour. Vascular Surgery, Chest, Ann. Thoracic Surgery, Jour. Thoracic, Cardiovascular Surgery and Anesthesia.; mem. editorial bd. Annals of Thoracic Surgery, Annals of Cardiovasc. and Thoracic Surgery. Recipient Good Fellowship award Treverton Coll., 1970, Cert. of Merit South African Sugar Assn., 1972, Robert Niven award 1974-76, DeBakey Heart Fund Rsch. award 1988, 89, 90, 91, V.A. Rag Rsch. Fund award 1992; Dana Fund Rsch. fellowship, 1994, David Lurie Rsch. fellowship 1985; Davis and Geck Surg. Rsch. scholarship, 1985. Fellow Am. Coll. Surgeons, Royal Coll. Surgeons, Coll. Surgeons and Physicians of South Africa, Royal Coll. Surgeons in Can. in Vascular and Cardiothoracic Surgery, Am. Coll. Cardiology; mem. AMA, Soc. Thoracic Surgeons. Achievements include animal research to find methods of intraoperatively locating the spinal cord blood supply and methods to prevent paraplegia after aortic surgery; investigation of methods to protect the brain, spinal cord and kidneys; study of hydrogen injection to localize spinal cord supply in humans, study of intrathecal papaveine in patients undergoing aortic surgery, minimizing use of homologous blood for major aortic surgery, particularly of the ascending and aortic arch; novel operations for ascending and aortic arch surgery; first reported replacement of the entire aorta from the heart to the aortic bifurcation during a single operation; pioneered a technique for doing minimal access "keyhole" heart surgery; (with E. Stanley Crawford) wrote the first definitive textbook on the aorta entitled Cardiovascular and Vascular Disease of the Aorta; devel. an approach for minimal access to the heart for heart operations.

SVENSSON, SVEN EILIF, civil engineer, consultant; b. Copenhagen, Dec. 15, 1945; s. Palle and Agnes Svensson; m. Dorte Merete Ahlbom, Aug. 10, 1968; children: Trine, Rikke, Jakob. MSc, Tech. U. Denmark, 1970, PhD, 1973; postgrad., Univ. Coll., London. Civil engring. Ramboel & Hannemann, Copenhagen, 1974-85, dir., 1985-90, ES Cons. Ltd., Copenhagen, 1990—. Cons. Great Belt Link Brige, Copenhagen, 1990—, Oresund Link Bridge, Copenhagen, 1993—; vis. prof. U. Coll., London, 1997—. Contbr. articles to profl. jours. Mem. ASCE, Nat. Acad. of Tech. Scis. Denmark. Avocations: music, tennis. Home: Bistrupvej 92B Birkeroed 3460 Denmark Office: ES-Consult Staktoften 20 Vedbaek DK 2950 Denmark E-mail: eilif@es-consult.dk.

SVERDLIK, SAMUEL SIMON, physiatrist, physician; b. N.Y.C., July 22, 1916; s. Simon and Fannie (Kaufman) S.; m. Norma Siegelman, June 13, 1943; children: Judy, Steven, William. BS, Alfred (N.Y.) U., 1938; MD, Hahnemann Med. Coll., Phila., 1942. Intern Jewish Hosp., Bklyn., 1942-43; residency Bellevue Hosp., N.Y.C., 1947-49; dir. rehab. medicine St. Vinent's Hosp. Med. Ctr., 1949-89, emeritus dir., 1989—; clinical prof. N.Y.U. Coll. Medicine, 1989—. Capt. U.S. Army, 1943-45, ETO. Decorated Bronze Star, 4 Battle Stars; Baruch fellow MIT, Cambridge, 1947. Fellow Am. Acad. Phys. Medicine and Rehab., N.Y. Acad. Medicine (chmn. sect. physical medicine rehabilitation 1965). Republican. Jewish. Office: St Vincents Hosp & Med Ctr 130 W 12th St New York NY 10011-8271

SVETLOVA, MARINA, ballerina, choreographer, educator; b. Paris, May 3, 1922; came to U.S. from Australia, 1940; d. Max and Tamara (Andreieff) Hartman. Studies with Vera Trefilova, Paris, 1930-36, studies with L. Egorova and M. Kschessinska, 1936-39; studies with A. Vilzak, N.Y.C., 1940-57; D honoris causa, Fedn. Francaise de Danse, 1988. Ballet dir. So. Vt. Art Ctr., 1959-64; dir. Svetlova Dance Ctr., Dorset, Vt., 1965-95; prof. ballet dept. Ind. U., Bloomington, 1969-92, prof. emeritus, 1992—, chmn. dept., 1969-78. Choreographer Dallas Civic Opera, 1964-67, Ft. Worth Opera, 1967-83, San Antonio Opera, 1983, Seattle Opera, Houston Opera, Kansas City Performing Arts Found. Ballerina original Ballet Russe de Monte Carlo, 1939-41; guest ballerina Ballet Theatre, 1942, London's Festival Ballet, Teatro dell Opera, Rome, Nat. Opera, Stockholm, Sweden, Suomi Opera, Helsinki, Finland, Het Nederland Ballet, Holland, Cork Irish Ballet, Paris Opera Comique, London Palladium, Teatro Colon, Buenos Aires, others; prima ballerina Met. Opera, 1943-50, N.Y.C. Opera, 1950-52; choreographer: (ballet sequences) The Fairy Queen, 1966, L'Histoire du Soldat, 1968; tours in Far East, Middle East, Europe, S.Am., U.S.; performer various classical ballets Graduation Ball; contbr. articles to Debut, Paris Opera. Mem. Am. Guild Mus. Artists (bd. dirs.), Conf. on Ballet in Higher Edn., Nat. Soc. Arts and Letters (nat. dance chmn.) Office: 2100 E Maxwell Ln Bloomington IN 47401-6119

SVEUM, RICHARD JAMES, allergist; b. Mpls., July 7, 1953; s. Arthur Byron and Mary Lucille (Vukelich) S.; m. Jennifer Mainquist Olson, June 28, 1975; children: Mara, Kari, Eric, Adam. BA, St. Olaf Coll., 1975; MD, U.

Minn., 1979. Resident U. Wis., Madison, 1979-83; cons. Park Nicollet Clinic, Mpls., 1986—. Clin. prof. medicine and pediatrics U. Minn., Mpls., 1995—. NIH fellow, Bethesda, Md., 1983-86. Fellow Am. Acad. Pediatrics, Am. Acad. Allergy, Asthma & Immunology, Am. Coll. Asthma, Allergy & Immunology; mem. Am. Thoracic Soc. Avocations: Sherlockian, bibliophile, running. Home: 2700 Sylvan Rd S Minnetonka MN 55305-2820 Office: Park Nicollet Clinic Allergy Dept 3800 Park Nicollet Blvd Minneapolis MN 55416-2527 E-mail: sveumr@parknicollet.com.

SVEUM, STEVEN JOHN, secondary school educator; b. St. Louis, Oct. 27; B in Music Edn., U. Wis., Eau Claire, 1985; M in Music Edn., U. Wis., Madison, 1992. High sch. band dir. Sun Prairie (Wis.) Area Sch. Dist., Wis., 1985—. Named Jazz Personality of the yr., Isthmus Jazz Festival, Madison, 2001, Top Notch Tchr., WISC-TV, Madison, 2002. Mem.: Internat. Assn. for Jazz Edn. (pres. Wis. chpt. 2001—03). Achievements include jazz ensemble selected to perform with internationally-prominent jazz artists such as Richard Davis, Winton Marsalis, Arturo Sandoval, and Ed Thigpen at various state and nat. music convs. Avocation: baseball, Civil War history, jazz history. Office: Sun Prairie High Sch 220 Kroncke Dr Sun Prairie WI 53590

SVIGGUM, STEVEN ARTHUR, farmer, state representative; b. Minn., Sept. 15, 1951; m. Debra Beegh; children: Hans, Erik, Marit. BA in Math., St. Olaf Coll., 1973. Tchr. math., coach Belgrade (Minn.) High Sch., 1973-77, West Concord (Minn.) High Sch., 1977-78; farmer, 1973—; state rep. State of Minn., 1992—, speaker of the ho., 1999—. Bd. dirs. Riverview Manor, Inc., Wanamingo, Minn.; Rep. caucus leader Minn. Ho. of Reps., St. Paul, 1992—. Recipient Hutchinson award Am. Assn. for Mentally Retarded, 1991, Recognition of Disting. Svc. award Minn. Assn. Rehab. Facilities and Minn. Devel. Achievement Ctr. Assn., 1991, Champion of Small Bus. award Nat. Fedn. Ind. Bus. Minn., 1991; named Legislator of Yr., Assn. Retarded Citizens, 1986. Mem. Kenyon (Minn.) Lions, Kenyon Sportsmen's Club. Lutheran. Avocations: baseball, basketball, coaching. Home: 42490 60th Ave Kenyon MN 55946-3224 Office: 463 State Office Bldg Saint Paul MN 55155-0001 E-mail: rep.steve.sviggum@house.leg.state.mn.us.*

SVIKHART, EDWIN GLADDIN, investment banker; b. Chgo., July 12, 1930; s. Edwin Gabriel and Mildred Charlotte (Slapnicka) S.; m. Joann Barbara Frisk, Aug. 22, 1954; children: David E., Robert E. BA, Beloit (Wis.) Coll., 1952; postgrad., Bradley U., 1957-59. With Caterpillar Tractor Co., Peoria, Ill., 1956-66; chief fin. officer Berglund Inc., Napa, Calif., 1966-71; chief fin. officer, treas. Galion (Ohio) Mfg. Co., 1971-77; chief operating officer constrn. equip. internat. div. Dresser Industries, Inc., Columbus, Ohio, 1977-81; chief operating officer Rocky Mountain Machinery Co., Salt Lake City, 1981-87; chief oper. officer Custom Equipment Corp., 1989-92; ptnr. Travis Capital Mkts., 1992—. Served to lt. (j.g.) USN, 1952-56.

SVIKLA, ALIUS JULIUS, pharmacist; b. Merbeck, Germany, Jan. 12, 1947; came to U.S., 1949; s. Julius and Brone (Maksimavich) S. BS in Pharmacy, Northeastern U., Boston, 1973. Pharmacist Osco Drug, Cambridge, Mass., 1973-75; profl. sales rep. Pfizer Labs., N.Y.C., 1976-77; pharmacist, mgr. CVS Pharmacy, South Dennis, Mass., 1977—. Drug abuse cons. Healthcare Assn., Boston, First Group of Boston, 1979-87; liason Kaunas Med. Acad., Lithuania. Served with USMC, 1965-74. Decorated Purple Heart. Mem. Am. Pharm. Assn., Internat. Pharm. Fedn., Mass. Pub. Health Assn., Mass. State Pharm. Assn., Lithuanian Am. Pharm. Assn., Mil. Order of Purple Heart (life), Fleet Res. Assn. Republican. Roman Catholic. Avocations: golf, sailing, tennis, fitness. Home: 9 Seagrove Rd South Dennis MA 02660-2737 Office: PO Box 715 South Dennis MA 02660-0715

SVINKELSTIN, ABRAHAM JOSHUA, information technology executive; b. Stuttgart, Germany, Nov. 14, 1948; came to U.S., 1950; s. Emanuel and Sabina (Lederman) S.; m. Janet Mostel, Nov. 7, 1976; children: Jeremy David, Rachel Sabina, Ilana Michelle. BS in Aerospace Engring., Poly. U. N.Y., 1970; MS in Ops. Rsch. and Engring. Math., Columbia U., N.Y.C., 1971; MS in Computer Sci., SUNY, Stony Brook, 1972. Programmer/analyst Bank Leumi, Tel Aviv, Israel, 1973-74; assoc., cons. Monchik Weber Assocs., N.Y.C., 1974-79; ptnr., cons. Computer Programming Assocs., 1979-84; project leader Shearson Lehman Bros., 1984-87; asst. v.p. Warner Ins. Svcs., Fair Lawn, N.J., 1988-92; v.p. software devel. Everlink Corp., N.Y.C., 1992-94; project mgr. Am. Internat. Group, 1994-97; prin. cons. CAP GEMINI, 1997—. Pres. Seminole Condominiums, Forest Hills, N.Y., 1979-86; Cub Scout den leader Boy Scouts Am. Mem. Data Processing Mgmt. Assn., MIS Network Assocs. (v.p. adminstrn./fin. 1992-94), Sigma Gamma Tau. Libertarian. Jewish. Home: 13-61 Finn Ter Fair Lawn NJ 07410-5135 Office: CAP GEMINI 1114 Ave of Americas New York NY 10036 E-mail: asvink@rocketmail.com.

SVIRSKY, MARIO ALFREDO, biomedical engineer; b. Montevideo, Uruguay, July 5, 1959; came to U.S., 1984; s. Ruben and Dora (Gilbert) S.; m. Elizabeth Fanny Sosenke, Mar. 19, 1982; children: Pablo, Daniel, Nina. B Engring., U. De La Republica, Montevideo, 1981, Engr., 1983; PhD, Tulane U., 1988. Lab. instr. U. De La Republica, Montevideo, 1981, instrumentation engr., 1983-84; asst. engr. UTE, Montevideo, 1982-83, engr., 1983-84; rsch. fellow Kresge Lab./La. State U. Med. Ctr., New Orleans, 1986-88; postdoctoral assoc. MIT, Cambridge, Mass., 1988-91, rsch. scientist, 1991-95; assoc. prof. dept. otolaryngology Ind. U. Sch. Medicine, 1995—; assoc. prof. dept. biomed. engring. Purdue U., 2000—. Cons. La. State U. Med. Ctr., New Orleans, 1990-92, ATR, Japan, 1990-91, Haskins Labs., New Haven, 1990-91, Sensimetrics, Cambridge, 1991; radio commentator as Capt. Figolo Sta. WRCA 1330 AM, Cambridge, 1991-92. Reviewer Jour. Acoustical Soc. Am., 1991—, Ear and Hearing Jour., 1992—; assoc. editor for cochlear implants and aural rehab. Ear and Hearing, 1997-2001; grant reviewer Neural Protheses Program, House Ear Inst., Ohio State U.; editor in chief Ear and Hearing, 2001—. Rsch. grantee NIH, 1992-94, 92-95, 99-04, Deafness Rsch. Found., Motorola, Nat. Orgn. Hearing Rsch., others. Mem.: IEEE, Collegium Oto-Rhino-Laryngologicum Amicitiae Sacrum, Am. Auditory Soc., Engring. in Medicine and Biology Soc., Am. Speech-Hearing-Lang. Assn., Acoustical Soc. Am. Achievements include development of EMMA (electromagnetic midsagittal articulometer), math models of speech perception by users of cochlear implants, studies on the effect of cochlear implantation on speech production, studies of speech perception by cochlear implant users, studies of speech and language development in children with cochlear implants; establishing the first cochlear implant program in Uruguay, South America. Home: 5315 E 72nd Pl Indianapolis IN 46250-2657 Office: DeVault Otologic Rsch Lab Ind Univ Rm 044 702 Barnhill Dr Indianapolis IN 46202-5128 E-mail: msvirsky@iupui.edu.

SVOBODA, ALBERT CARL, JR. gastroenterologist; AB, U. Chgo., 1951, BS in Zoology, 1955, MD, 1958; MS in Physiology, U. So. Calif., 1955. Diplomate Nat. Bd. Med. Examiners, Am. Bd. Internatl Medicine, subspecialty gastroenterology; lic. physician, Ill., Calif. Rotating intern Univ. Hosp., Ann Arbor, Mich., 1958-59, asst. resident-resident, jr. clinic instr. internal medicine, 1959-62, fellow dept. gastroenterology, 1962-63; assoc. div. gastroenterology Scripps Clinic and Rsch. Found., La Jolla, Calif., 1963; mem. staff dept. gastroenterology Sansum Med. Clinic, Santa Barbara, 1966-96; sr. scientist Sansum Med. Rsch. Inst., 1996—. Mem. physician payment rev. commn. panel of expert witnesses; cons. gastroenterology and endoscopy San Diego County Hosp., 1963; bd. trustees Sansum Med. Rsch. Found., 1972-75, 96—. Master: Am. Coll. Gastroenterology; fellow: ACS, Am. Soc. Gastrointestinal Endoscopy; mem.: AMA, Santa Barbara Soc. Internal Medicine (past pres.), Santa Barbara County Med. Soc., Calif. Fedn. Digestive Disease Socs. (rep. 1979—80, 1981), So. Calif. Soc. Gastrointestinal Endoscopy (past pres.), So. Calif. Soc. Gastroenterology (past pres.), Calif. Med. Assn., Internat. Bockus Soc., Am. Fedn. Clin. Rsch., Am. Pancreatic Assn., Am. Soc. Tropical Medicine and Hygiene, Am. Gastroenterol. Assn., Cymbidium Soc. Am. (pres. 2002—), Nu Sigma Nu (past pres.,). Home: 231 Middle Rd Santa Barbara CA 93108-2449 Office: 2219 Bath St Santa Barbara CA 93105 Fax: (805) 682-3332. E-mail: asvoboda@sansum.org.

SVOBODA, DONNA LEE, neonatal nurse; b. St. Clair County, Ill., Aug. 28, 1951; d. James F. Sr. and Pat Lee (Souchek) Durer; m. John R. Svoboda, July 25, 1970; 1 child, Jennifer Lynn. BS in Edn., So. Ill. U., 1973; BSN, So. Ill. U., Edwardsville, 1987. Neonatal staff nurse, parenting skills coord. and educator Anderson Hosp., Maryville, Ill. Recipient Esther Ott Estes award in nursing, 1987, Outstanding Nurse Recognition award March of Dimes Birth Defects Found., 1995. Mem. Nat. Assn. Neonatal Nurses, Sigma Theta Tau (Granting Body Esther Ott Estes award Epsilon Eta chpt.), Phi Kappa Phi. Home: 106 Dunlap Cove Ct S Edwardsville IL 62025-2491 E-mail: cybernurse@charter-il.com.

SVOBODA, GEORGE JIRI, historian, librarian; b. Bratislava, Slovak Republic, Mar. 28, 1933; s. Vaclav and Marie Svoboda; m. Yanna A. Verunacova, Dec. 21, 1963; 1 child, John. PhD, Charles U., Prague, 1956. Asst. prof. Charles U., Prague, 1957-68; head Slavic libr. U. Calif., Berkeley, 1980-93, cons., 1993-94. Sec. Czechoslovak Hist. Conf., 1986-90. Author: Social Movements in Bohemia in the 18th Century, 1967. Avocation: travel. Home: 5811 Sierra Ave Richmond CA 94805-2020

SVOBODA, JANICE JUNE, nurse; b. Dorchester, Wis., June 13, 1933; d. Alfred A. and Jessie (Boor) Hinke; m. Glenn R. Svoboda, July 20, 1957; children: Melora, Kevin, Craig. Diploma, Luther Hosp., 1954; cert., U. Wis., 1955; student, U. Wis., Madison; BS in Health Edn. cum laude, U. Wis., Milw., 1980; student, Alverno Coll., 1991-92. Cert. Holistic nursing, Mass., 1999. Pub. health nurse Ozaukee County, Wis., 1979, 86; asst. instr. nursing Milw. Area Tech. Coll., 1979-83; instr. seminar Cardinal Stritch Coll., Milw., 1985-87; nutritional counselor Nutri-Sys., Grafton, Wis., 1987-90. Instr. seminar Milw. Area Tech. Coll., 1983, 90, health seminars Alverno Coll., Milw., 1991-95, designed and implemented alternative health and healing seminar, Alverno Coll., 1994-97; pvt. practice holistic nurse cons., nutrition and herbal therapy, 1997--. Mem. Am. Holistic Nurses Assn. (grad. certification program 1999--), N.Am. Nutrition Preventive Medicine Assn., Ctr. for Sci. in the Pub. Interest.

SVOBODA, JOANNE DZITKO, artist, educator; b. Dec. 24, 1948; d. John Richard and Joanna Frances (Rygiel) Dzitko; m. Peter W. Svoboda, Sept. 3, 1972; children: Kimberly Anne, Lauren Anne. Student, Parsons Sch. Design, 1966, Kean Coll., 1970; BA, Jersey City State Coll., 1970, MA, 1975; postgrad., Tchrs. Coll., Columbia U., 1972, Chubb Inst., 1983-84. Art tchr., Jersey City, 1966-70, Henry Snyder H.S., 1970-80; tng. specialist Johnson & Johnson Baby Products, Skillman, N.J., 1984-89; cons., 1989—; pres. Mgmt. Strategies Internat., 1991—. Computer instr. Raritan Valley C.C., 1999—. Exhibited Courtney Gallery, Jersey City State Coll., 1970, 74, Long Valley, 1979-80; contbr. articles in field to various publs. Trustee Jersey City Mus. Assn., 1973-79, chmn. fine arts dept., 1972-79; mem. curriculum revision com. Jersey City Bd. Edn., 1976; mem. Washington Twp. Shade Tree Commn., 1979-81, chmn., 1981; mem. Washington Twp. Hist. Heritage Commn., 1981-85; active encouraging establishment of hist. zone Long Valley, landmarks, Jersey City and Washington Twp. Grantee N.J. State Dept. Edn., 1973; recipient awards N.J. Fedn. Jr. Woman's Clubs: black and white photography, 1979, crafts, 1979, 1st pl. color photography, 1980, free form, 1981. Mem. Am. H.S. Assn. (asst. exec. dir. 1997-99, 2000-), Inst. Raritan Valley CC. (2000-). Office: PO Box 336 Oldwick NJ 08858-0336

SVOBODA, MARY BETH, health physicist, environmental science educator; d. Arthur Earl and Rosemary Irene S.. Grad. with honors, III Corps Nuclear, Biol. and Chem. Warfare Sch., 1986; BS, U. Ariz., Tucson, AZ, 1993. Radiation safety officer Oakland U., Rochester, Mich., 1998—2001; health physicist Wayne State U., Detroit, 2001—. Adj. faculty environ. health sci. Wayne State U., Detroit, 2001—. Sgt. U.S. Army, 1984—87. Mem.: AAHP (assoc.), Phi Theta Kappa, Golden Key. Home: PO Box 70543 Rochester Hills MI 48307 Office: Wayne State U 5425 Woodward Ave Ste 300 Detroit MI 48202 Office Fax: 313-993-4079. E-mail: aj8368@wayne.edu.

SVRCEK, DEBBIE M. English educator; b. Waco, Tex., Mar. 17, 1951; d. William and Eilleen (Webb) S. AA, McLennan C.C., 1971; BA, Baylor U., 1973. Payroll clk. Wolfe Mfg., Waco, 1973-74; English tchr. St. Louis Catholic Sch., 1974—. Mem. Nat. Assn. Student Activity Advisers, Nat. Coun. Tchrs. English. Republic. Roman Catholic.

SVRLUGA, RICHARD CHARLES, entrepreneur; b. Berwyn, Ill., Feb. 6, 1949; s. William J. and Ruth E. (Crowell) S.; m. Donna M. Hanson, Aug. 11, 1978; children: Sara M. Sullivan, Krista A. Wachter. BA in Math. and History, U. Dubuque, 1971; MS in Edn., Ind. U., 1973; MBA, Boston U., 1978. Asst. to v.p. overseas program, Boston U., Heidelberg, Germany, 1978-81, asst. dean Coll. Liberal Arts and Grad. Sch. Boston, 1981-85; co-founder, exec. v.p., bd. dirs. Summit Tech., Inc., Waltham, Mass., 1985-90; pres., bd. dirs. Seragen, Inc., Hopkinton, 1988-94. Co-founder, bd. dirs. GreenPages, Inc., Kittery, Maine; co-founder, CEO, bd. dirs. Zentox Corp., Boston, 1996—. Co-patentee catalytic process for degradation of organic materials to produce environmentally compatible products. Bd. dirs. United Way Metrowest, Framingham, Mass., 1992-94, Arthritis Found. Mass., Newton, 1992-95, U. Dubuque, Iowa, 1994—, Svrluga Found., 1995—. Home: 16 Croftdale Rd Newton MA 02459-2009 E-mail: rsvrluga@worldnet.att.net.

SWACKER, FRANK WARREN, lawyer; b. N.Y.C., May 18, 1922; m. Irene Maloney Michael; children: Carolyn, Frances, Michele, Ruth. BA, Union Coll., Schnectady, 1947; JD, U. Va., 1949; LLM in Internat. Law, NYU, 1961. Bar: Va. 1948, N.Y. 1950, Ohio 1962, Wis. 1969, D.C. 1977, Fla. 1991, U.S. Ct. Internat. Trade 1978, U.S. Supreme Ct. 1952. Pvt. practice, N.Y.C., 1949-54, 64-68, Washington, 1977-84, Clearwater, Fla., 1984-89, St. Petersburg, 1994—; atty. Caltex Petroleum Corp., N.Y.C., 1955-60, Marathon Oil Co., Ohio, 1961-63; internat. counsel Allis-Chalmers Corp., Milw., 1968-78; sr. mem. Swacker & Assocs., P.C., Springfield, Va., 1980=84, chmn., pres. firm, sr. mem. Largo, Fla., 1989-93; dir. ATM CardPay, 1993-94; vice chmn. Lasergate Sys., Inc., 1995-99. Spl. asst. dep. atty. gen. State of N.Y., 1950; govtl. adviser U.S., P.I., Algeria; lectr. Ohio No. U., 1962, N.Y. World Trade Inst., 1976; adj. prof. Stetson U. Coll. Law, St. Petersburg, Fla., 1996-2000, LLM internat. adv. coun., 1997—. Author: Business International Guide for Going Global, 1999; co-author: World Trade Without Barriers: World Trade Organization and Dispute Resolution, 1995, vol. 2, 1996; co-editor, contbr. Bus. and Legal Aspects of Latin American Trade and Investment, 1977, Reference Manual on Doing Business with Latin America, 1979; contbr. articles to legal jours. Mem. internat. bus. adv. bd. U. So. Fla., 1993-94. Lt. (j.g.) USN, 1943-46, WWII. Mem. ABA (lectr. 1978, internat. comml. arbitration com. 1991—), Nat. Law Inst., Am. Arbitration Assn. (panel experts), World Intellectual Property Orgn. (arbitration panel). E-mail: integra10@aol.com.

SWAFFORD, DOUGLAS RICHARD, corporate credit executive; b. Chattanooga, Aug. 19, 1951; s. Herbert Harding and Helen Margaret (Smith) S.; m. Lynn Romaine Wudarcki, Aug. 18, 1973 (div. Aug. 1977); 1 child, Douglas Richard Jr.; m. Carole P. Farmer, Oct. 6, 1989 (div. Apr. 1992); m. Kimberly A. Armstrong, Nov. 8, 1997. BSBA, U. Tenn., Chattanooga, 1982; postgrad., Stanford U., 1994. Asst. credit mgr. Hart's Automotive Parts Co., Chattanooga, 1972-74; dir. corp. credit Brock Candy Co., 1974-95; credit mgr. Brentwood Svc. Group, Inc., 1995-96; corp. credit mgr. Arnold Palmer Golf Co., Ooltewah, Tenn., 1996-97; cons., project specialist Creditek Corp., 1998; credit mgr. ADC Telecomm. Systems Ingetration Divsn., Chickamanga, Ga., 1998-2001; credit and collections mgr. U.S. Xpress, 2001—. Chmn. Nat. Food, Allied Lines & Meat Packers Credit Group, Nashville, 1989. Pres. Citizens Taxpayers Assn., 1989; mem. Leadership Chattanooga, Friends of the Libr., Chattanooga Nature Ctr., Hunter Mus. Art, Allied Arts Chattanooga; bd. dis. Chattanooga Regional History Mus.; mem. U. Tenn. at Chattanooga Alumni Coun. Mem. Nat. Assn. Credit Mgmt. (chmn. S.E. unit 1991-92, Credit Mgr. of Yr. award 1994), Chattanooga C. of C. (chmn. fed. issues com. 1988-89), Chattanooga Track Club, Civitans (pres. Chattanooga 1986, bd. dirs. Appalachian dist. 1988-90). Republican. Avocations: running, travel, politics, physical fitness. Home: 1219 Woodsage Dr Soddy Daisy TN 37379-8936

SWAFFORD, LESLIE EUGENE, physician assistant, consultant; b. Long Beach, Calif., Aug. 31, 1950; s. Leslie Eugene Swafford, Sr. and Kathryn Shirley (Gros) Jarvis; children: Jayson Patrick, Jonathan Allyn, Jude Christopher, Joshua Douglas; m. Cheryl Kaleen Killman, Apr. 10, 1993; 1 child, Lesli Tayte. BS in Allied Health, physician asst. degree of completion, George Washington U., 1978; postgrad. in Occupl. Medicine, U. Cin., 1994-95; M. in Physician Asst. Studies, U. Nebr., 2001. Cert. physician's asst. NCCPA, ACLS, PALS, CDC AIDS Counselor, EBT (Alco-Sensor IV), EBT (EC/IR) QAP, TTT, lic. JBORPA. Chief EEG technologist Group Health Assn., Washington, 1974-76; physician asst. Pediat. Assocs., Frederick, Md., 1978-81, Heart Inst. for Care, Amarillo, Tex., 1981-84, Maricopa County Medicine Assocs., Avondale-Goodyear, Ariz., 1984-89; mgr. Samarital Occupl. Health Svcs. Samaritan Health System, Phoenix, 1989-98; dir. employee health/occupl. medicine, worker's comp program Maryvale Hosp. Med. Ctr., 1998, MRO asst., dir. adminstr. respiratory protection program, 1998-2001; Emergency Assocs. Ariz. St. Joseph's Emergency Rm. and Trauma Ctr., 2001—. Med. edn. and policy cons. Occupl. Health and Med. Edn. Consultants; adminstr. drug test program Samaritan Health Svcs., Phoenix, 1991—95; mem. com. Ariz. Rural Health Conf., 1992—96; adj. asst. prof. physician asst. tng. program Kirksville Coll. of Osteo. Medicine, Phoenix, 1995—; instr. Calif. Tech. Contbr. articles to profl. jours. Chmn. sex edn. com. North Ctrl. Accreditation-Aqua Fria H.S., Avondale, Ariz., 1991; physician asst. Camp Geronimo (Boy Scouts of Am.), Phoenix, 1989-94; team mem. Young People's Beginning Experience Grief Recovery Program for Children, Phoenix, 1989-93; mem. com. Ariz. Dept. Health Svcs.-Robert Wood Johnson Application, Phoenix, 1992-93. With USN, 1969-74. Recipient scholarship NIH, 1976, Squibb Pharm. Rural Physician Asst. of Yr. award honorable mention Am. Acad. Physician Assts., 1987, Dr. Paul L. Singer award for disting. cmty. svc. Samaritan Found., 1991. Fellow Ariz. State Assn. Physician Assts. (pres.-elect 1990-91, pres. 1991-92, chmn. Ariz. physician asst. tng. program task force 1990-94); mem. Am. Coll. Forensic Examiners. Republican. Roman Catholic. Avocations: fishing, hiking, softball, basketball, golfing. Home: 17723 Cactus Flower Dr Goodyear AZ 85338-5232 Office: St Joseph's Hosp & Med Ctr ER 350 W Thomas Rd Phoenix AZ 85013

SWAIM, C. HALL, lawyer; b. Delta, Colo., Dec. 31, 1939; s. H. Albert and Janet (Hall) S.; m. Patricia Fahey, Oct. 9, 1976; children: Caitlin Fahey, Bryan Hall. Grad. Geophys. Engr., Colo. Sch. Mines, 1961; JD, NYU, 1964. Asst. counsel Tex. Instruments Inc., Dallas, 1964-71; assoc. Hale & Dorr LLP, Boston, 1971-74, ptnr., 1974—. Served to capt. U.S. Army, 1965-67, Vietnam. Mem. ABA, Mass. Bar Assn., Boston Bar Assn., Comml. Law League Am. Office: Hale and Dorr LLP 60 State St Boston MA 02109-1816 E-mail: hall.swaim@haledorr.com.

SWAIM, JOHN FRANKLIN, physician, health care executive; b. Bloomingdale, Ind., Dec. 24, 1935; s. Max DeBaun and Edna Marie (Whitely) S.; m. Joan Dooley, Sept. 19, 1957 (div. Apr. 1979); children: John Franklin, Parke Allen, Pamela Ann; m. Peggy Lou Sankey, May 30, 1979; one child, Anne-Marie. BS cum laude, Ind. State U., 1959; MD, Ind. U., Indpls., 1963. Diplomate Am. Bd. Family Practice with added cert. in geriatrics; Lic. Health Facility Admin. Med. dir. Newport (Ind.) Chem. Depot, 1968—, Parke Clinic, Rockville, Ind., 1969—, Rockville Correctional Facility, 1970—; pres. Parke Investments Inc., Rockville, 1972—, Vermillion Health Care Corp., Clinton, Ind., 1977—, Parke County Coroner, 1980, Swaim Farm Corp., 1998—, Parke County Health Officer, 1999—. Med. dir. Lee Alan Bryant Health Facility, med. dir. Parke County Jail and Vermillion County Jail. Author: One Year and Eternity, 1978; contbr. articles to profl. jours. Coroner, Parke County, Ind., 1972-82. Capt. USAF, 1963-67, Vietnam. Decorated Bronze Star. Mem. Am. Acad. Family Physicians, AMA, Ind. Med. Assn. (dist. pres. 1986—), Hoosiers Assocs. Club, Elks, Masons, Shriners. Republican. Avocations: reading and investing. Home and Office: Parke Clinic PO Box 185 Rockville IN 47872-0185

SWAIM, MARK WENDELL, hepatologist, molecular biologist, gastroenterologist, educator, photographer; b. Winston-Salem, N.C., Dec. 4, 1960; s. Donnie Lee and Bernice Earline (Brown) S. BA summa cum laude, U. N.C., 1983; MD, PhD with honors, Duke U., 1990. Diplomate Am. Bd of Internal Medicine, Am. Bd. Gastroenterology and Hepatology. Resident Dept. of Med. Duke U. Med. Ctr., Durham, N.C., 1990-93, fellow gastroenterology, 1993-97, clin. med. instr., 1994-2000, fellow in advanced hepatology and endoscopy, 1997-98, attending physician, 1998-2000, Durham VA Med. Ctr., 1998-2000; asst. prof. medicine Gastrointestinal Ctr., U. Tex.-M.D. Anderson Cancer Ctr., Houston, 2000—. Assoc. Dept. of Medicine Duke U., 1998-2000; instr. clin. medicine Duke U. Sch. Medicine, 1994-2000, mem. admissions com.; asst. prof. medicine Gastrointestinal Ctr., U. Tex. M.D. Anderson Cancer Ctr., Houston; vis. med. resident Nat. Taiwan U., Taipei, 1991, 92; vis. physician Saratov (Russia) Med. U., 1995; faculty senator U. Tex. M.D. Anderson Cancer Ctr., 2000—; book rev. panelist The Pharos of Alpha Omega Alpha; consulting physician Al-Jazeira Hosp., Abu Dhabi, United Arab Emirates. Contbr. articles to profl. jours., Ency. Brit. Great Ideas Today, 1996; photography pub. in Am. Photo. Recipient Brody award for history of medicine, 1998, Davison award for tchg. excellence, 2000; NIH Med. Sci. Tng. Program fellow, 1983-90, ACP fellow, 2002, numerous acad. scholarships. Fellow: ACP (winner assocs. competition 1994); mem.: Houston Acad. Medicine, Tex. Med. Assn., Am. Liver Found. (bd. dirs. Tex. Chpt.), Engel Soc., Am. Coll. Forensic Examiners, Reticuloendothelial Soc., Am. Assn. for Study Liver Diseases, Am. Soc. for Gastrointestinal Endoscopy, Am. Coll. Gastroenterology, Sigma Pi Sigma, Phi Lambda Upsilon, Sigma Xi, Phi Beta Kappa, Alpha Omega Alpha (pres. Duke chpt. 1989). Avocations: photography, traveling, chamber music. Home: 6301 Almeda Rd Apt 116 Houston TX 77021-1056 Office: Dept Gastroenterology Box 78 Holcombe Blvd Houston TX 77030 E-mail: mwswaim@netscape.net.

SWAIM, MICHAEL E. mayor; BA, UCLA, 1967, MA, 1968, JD, 1971. Lawyer Simon, McKinsey & Miller, 1971-78; pvt. practice, 1978—; mayor City of Salem, Oreg., 1997—. Office: City Hall 555 Libert St Rm 220 Salem OR 97301 E-mail: mswaim@open.org.*

SWAIM, ROBERT LEE, engineering educator; b. Rensselaer, Ind., Aug. 7, 1935; s. Maurice Lee and Viola Nina (Houston) S.; m. Wanda Charlene Wasson, Feb. 13, 1960; children: Gregory, Suzanne, Deborah. BS in Aero. Engring., Purdue U., 1957, MS in Aero. Engring., 1959; PhD in Elec. Engring., Ohio State U., 1966. Registered profl. engr., Okla. Sr. research engr. Air Force Flight Dynamics Lab., Wright-Patterson AFB, Ohio, 1962-67; assoc. prof. aero. and astronautical engring. Purdue U., West Lafayette, Ind., 1967-75, prof. aero. and astronautics, 1975-78; assoc. dean Okla. State U., Stillwater, 1978-87, prof. mech. and aerospace engring., 1978-92, prof., assoc. dean emeritus, 1992—; pres. RLS Products and Svcs., Inc., 1992—. Contbr. articles to profl. jours. Bd. dirs. Payne County United Way, Stillwater, 1983-86. Served to 1st lt. USAF, 1959-62. Recipient Outstanding Achievement award City of Dayton, 1966; NASA grantee, 1975-79. Fellow AIAA (assoc.); mem. Am. Soc. Engring. Edn. (chmn. midwest sect. 1987-88). Republican. Avocations: flying, fishing. Home: 5105 Woodland Dr Stillwater OK 74074-1349 E-mail: srobert@ceat.okstate.edu.

SWAIMAN, KENNETH FRED, pediatric neurologist, educator; b. St. Paul, Nov. 19, 1931; s. Lester J. and Shirley (Ryan) S.; m. Phyllis Kammerman Sher, Oct. 1985; children: Lisa, Jerrold, Barbara, Dana. BA magna cum laude, U. Minn., 1952, BS, 1953, MD, 1955; postgrad., 1956-58. Diplomate Am. Bd. Psychiatry and Neurology, Am. Bd. Pediatrics, Am. Bd. Psychiatry and Neurology with Spl. Competence in Child Neurology. Intern Mpls. Gen. Hosp., 1955-56; resident in pediatrics, fellow in pediatrics to chief resident U. Minn. Hosp., 1956-58, spl. fellow in pediatric neurology, 1960-63, dir. pediatric neurology tng. program, 1968-94, various to interim head dept. neurology, 1994-96; chief pediatrics U.S. Army Hosp., Ft. McPherson, Ga., 1958-60; asst. prof. pediatrics, neurology U. Minn. Med. Sch., Mpls., 1963-66, prof., dir. pediatric neurology, 1969-96, mem. internship adv. coun. exec. faculty, 1966-70, interim head dept. neurology, 1994-96; postgrad. fellow pediatric neurology Nat. Inst. Neurologic Diseases and Blindness, 1960-63, assoc. prof., 1966-69. Cons. pediatric neurology Hennepin County Gen. Hosp., 1963—, Mpls., St. Paul-Ramsey Hosp., St. Paul Children's Hosp., Mpls. Children's Hosp.; vis. prof. numerous univs. including Loyola U., 1982, U. N.Mex., 1982, U. Ind. Med. Sch., 1983, U. Kyushu, Shiga, Nagoya, Tokyo, 1985, Driscoll Children's Hosp., Corpus Christi, Tex., 1986, Inst. Nacional de Pediatria, Mexico City, 1986, U. de Concepion, Chile, 1989, Beijing U. Med. Sch., 1989, Xian Med. U., China, 1989, Children's Hosp. of Mich., Detroit, 1990, Hong Kong Child Neurology Soc., 1995, Tartu, Estonia, 1997, Krem, Austria, 1997, Santiago, Chile, 1997, Kaunas, Lithuania, 1998, ICNA Ednl. Seminar, Tartu, 1998, Montevideo, Uruguay, 1999, others; lectr. in field; guest worker NIH, NICHD, Bethesda, Md., 1978-79, 79-81. Author: (with Francis S. Wright) Neuromuscular Diseases in Infancy and Childhood, 1969, Pediatric Neuromuscular Diseases, 1979, (with Stephen Ashwal) Pediatric Neurology Case Studies, 1978, 2d edit., 1984, Pediatric Neurology: Practice and Principles, 1989, 3d edit., 1999; editor: (with John A. Anderson) Phenylketonuria and Allied Metabolic Diseases, 1966, (with Francis S. Wright) Practice

Pediatric Neurology, 1975, 2d edit., 1982; mem. editorial bd.: Annals of Neurology, 1977-83, Neurology Update, 1977-82, Pediatric Update, 1977-85, Brain and Devel. (Jour. Japanese Soc. Child Neurology), 1980—, Neuropediatrics (Stuttgart), 1982-92; editor-in-chief: Pediatric Neurology, 1984—; contbr. articles to sci. jours. Chmn. Minn. Gov.'s Bd. for Handicapped, Exceptional and Gifted Children, 1972-76; mem. human devel. study sect. NIH, 1976-79, guest worker, 1978-81. Served to capt. M.C. U.S. Army, 1958-60. Fellow Am. Acad. Pediatrics, Am. Acad. Neurology (rep. to nat. coun. Nat. Soc. Med. Rsch.); mem. Soc. Pediatric Rsch., Ctrl. Soc. Clin. Rsch., Ctrl. Soc. Neurol. Rsch., Internat. Soc. Neurochemistry, Am. Neurol. Assn., Minn. Neurol. Soc., AAAS, Midwest Pediatric Soc., Am. Soc. Neurochemistry, Child Neurology Soc. (1st pres. 1972-73, Hower award 1981, Founder's award 1996, chmn. internat. affairs com., 1991-96, mem. long range planning com. 1991-97, chmn. fin. com. 1995—), Internat. Assn. Child Neurologists (exec. com. 1975-79, chmn. global edn. com. 1996-99), Profs. of Child Neurology (1st pres. 1978-80, mem. nominating com. 1986-92), Japanese Child Neurology Soc. (Segawa award 1986, mem. nominating com. 1986-92, chair internat. affairs com. 1991—, mem. long range planning com. 1991-98), Soc. de Psiquiatria y Neurología de la Infancia y Adolescencia, Internat. Child Neurology Assn. (chair internat. edn. com. 1996-99), Lithuanian Child Neurology Soc. (hon., pres. 2000—), Child Neurology Found. (pres. 2000—), Phi Beta Kappa, Sigma Xi. Office: U Minn Med Sch Dept Pediatric Neurology 1821 University Ave W Saint Paul MN 55104-2801 also: UMHC Box 486 420 Delaware St SE Minneapolis MN 55455-0374 E-mail: pncomm@uswet.net.

SWAIN, DONALD CHRISTIE, retired university president, history educator; b. Des Moines, Oct. 14, 1931; s. G. Christie and Irene L. (Alsop) S.; m. Lavinia Kathryn Lesh, Mar. 5, 1955; children: Alan Christie, Cynthia Catherine. BA, U. Dubuque, 1953; MA in History, U. Calif., Berkeley, 1958, PhD, 1961; D (hon.), U. Louisville, 1995, Bellarmine Coll., 1995. Asst. rsch. historian U. Calif., Berkeley, 1961-63, mem. faculty Davis, 1963-81, prof. history, 1970-81, acad. asst. to chancellor, 1967-68, asst. vice chancellor acad. affairs, 1971, vice chancellor acad. affairs, 1972-75; acad. v.p. U. Calif. System, Berkeley, 1975-81; pres. U. Louisville, 1981-95, pres. emeritus, 1995—, prof. history, 1981-95; ret., 1995. Chmn. bd. dirs. Lincoln Found. Author: Federal Conservation Policy, 1921-33, 1963, Wilderness Defender: Horace M. Albright and Conservation, 1970; co-editor: The Politics of American Science 1939 to the Present, 1965. Recipient William B. Hellestine award Wis. State Hist. Soc., 1967, Disting. Tchg. award U. Calif., Davis, 1972, Wilson Wyatt award U. Louisville Alumni Assn., 1995; named Louisvillian of Yr., 1995. Democrat. Presbyterian. Office: U Louisville Alumni Ctr Louisville KY 40292-0001 E-mail: dcsandlls@aol.com.

SWAIN, LAURA TAYLOR, judge; b. Bklyn., 1958; d. Justus E. and Madeline V. (Allgood) Taylor; m. Andrew J. Swain, 1991. AB, Harvard U., 1979, JD, 1982. Bar: Mass. 1982, N.Y. 1983, U.S. Dist. Ct. (so. and ea. dists.) N.Y. 1983. Law clk to chief judge U.S. Dist. Ct. (so. dist.) N.Y., 1982-83; assoc. Debevoise & Plimpton, N.Y.C., 1983-95, counsel, 1995-96; U.S. bankruptcy judge U.S. Bankruptcy Ct., Bklyn., 1996-2000; U.S. dist. judge U.S. Dist. Ct. (so. dist.) N.Y., N.Y.C., 2000—. Mem. N.Y. State Bd. Law Examiners, Albany, 1986-96; mem. multistate bar exam. com. Nat. Conf. Bar Examiners, 1987-99, mem. testing, R&D devel. com., 1990-94, mem. long range planning com., 1994-96; cons. N.Y. Profl. Edn. Project, 1995-96. Co-contbr. articles on employee benefits, employee stock ownership plans, acctg. and bankruptcy to profl. publs.; contbg. author: New York Insurance Law, 1991. Trustee Diocese of N.Y. (Episcopal), 1991-92; mem. Dessoff Choirs, N.Y.C., 1984-92; bd. dirs. Episcopal Charities, Inc., 1996—, Coalition Consumer Bankruptcy Debtor Edn., 1998—. Mem. ABA, Assn. of Bar of City of N.Y., Met. Black Bar Assn., N.Y. State Bar Assn., Nat. Conf. Bankruptcy Judges, Nat. Assn. Women Judges. Episcopalian. Avocation: music. Office: US Dist Ct So Dist NY 40 Foley Sq New York NY 10007

SWAIN, MARY ANN PRICE, university official; b. Chardon, Ohio, Apr. 20, 1941; d. A. David and Mary A. Price; m. Donald B. Swain, June 27, 1964; children: Judy, Brenda Swain. BA in Psychology, DePauw U., Greencastle, Ind., 1963; MA in Psychology, U. Mich., 1964, PhD in Psychology, 1969. Dir. Sch. Nursing Doctoral Program U. Mich., Ann Arbor, 1975-76, chmn. dept. nursing rsch., 1977-82, assoc. v.p. acad. affairs, 1983-93, interim co-dir. pers., 1986-88, interim dir. affirmative action, 1988-89, interim v.p. student svcs., 1990-92; provost and v.p. acad. affairs SUNY, Binghamton, 1993—. Evaluation site visitor U. Balt. Sch Law, 1996-97, Tex. Wesleyan U., 1998-99, U. Va. Sch. Nursing, Charlottesville, 1994-95; chmn. coun. on acad. affairs Nat. Assn. State Univs. and Land Grant Colls., 1998-99. Co-author: (with H. Erickson and E. Tomlin) Modeling and Role-modeling: A Theory and Paradigm for Nursing, 1983. Chmn. campaign United Way of Broome County, Binghamton, 1998-99; pres. bd. dirs. Vis. Nurses Assn. of Huron Valley, Ann Arbor, 1989-92. Woodrow Wilson fellow, 1963. Mem. Am. Soc. Quality Control, Am. Assn. Higher Edn., Am. Psychol. Soc., Golden Key, Phi Beta Kappa, Sigma Theta Tau. Office: SUNY PO Box 6000 Binghamton NY 13902-6000 E-mail: mswain@binghamton.edu.

SWAIN, MARY MARGARET, editor, marketing consultant; b. Dec. 31, 1967; BS summa cum laude, U. N.C., Wilmington, 1989. Asst. gen. mgr. Comfort Inn, Laurinburg, N.C., 1989-90; internat. account mgr. AVX Corp., Myrtle Beach, S.C., 1991-93; prodn. mgr., editl. asst. The First Word Bulletin, Madrid, 1998-2000; pres., owner Profl. Data Svcs./M.M.H. Swain Agy., Wilmington, N.C., 1993—. Home and Office: 913 Deer Spring Ln Wilmington NC 28409-3122 E-mail: D-MSwain@juno.com.

SWAIN, PHILIP C., JR. lawyer, mechanical engineer; b. Akron, Ohio, Dec. 10, 1957; s. Philip C. Sr. and Shirley I. (Tessier) S.; m. Roseanne K. Vita, May 5, 1990; children: Kimberly A., Jennifer R. BA and BSME, Tufts U., 1981; JD, Northwestern U., 1984. Bar: Ill. 1984, Mass. 1985, D.C. 1988, Calif. 1990. Acting asst. dean Sch. of Law Northwestern U., Chgo., 1984; law clk. U.S. Ct. Appeals (federal cir.), Washington, 1985-86; from assoc. to ptnr. Kirkland & Ellis, Chicago and L.A., 1986-97; ptnr. Foley, Hoag & Eliot, Boston, 1997—. Adj. prof. Suffolk U. Sch. Law, 1998—. Mem. Fed. Cir. Bar Assn. (pres. 2000-01), Internat. Assn. for Protection of Intellectual Property (exec. com.), Fed. Cir. Hist. Soc. (pres. 2002—). Avocations: running, ice hockey. Home: 114 Pine Hill Ln Concord MA 01742-4414 Office: Foley Hoag LLP 155 Seaport Blvd Boston MA 02210-

SWAIN, ROBERT, artist; b. Austin, Tex., Dec. 7, 1940; s. Robert O. and Beth (Brower) S.; m. Annette Carol Leibel, Oct. 4, 1969. BA, Am.U., 1964. Prof. fine arts Hunter Coll.; vis. artist to various schs., univs., including Bklyn. Mus. Art Sch., 1975, 77, 78; dept. architecture Harvard U. Grad. Sch. Design, 1977 One-man shows, Thenan Gallery, N.Y.C., 1965, Fischbach Gallery, N.Y.C., 1968-69, Everson Art Museum, N.Y.C., 1974, Susan Galdwell Gallery, N.Y.C., 1974, 75, 78, Tex. Gallery, Houston, 1975, Columbus (Ohio) Gallery Fine Arts, 1976, Nina Freundenhein Gallery, Buffalo, 1978, group shows include, Mus. Modern Art, N.Y.C., 1968, Grand Palais, Paris, 1968, Kunsthaus, Zurich, Switzerland, 1969, Tate Gallery, London, 1969, Corcoran Gallery Art, Washington, 1969, Whitney Mus. Am. Art, N.Y.C., 1971, Albright-Knox Gallery, Buffalo, 1971, Mus. Modern Art Internat. Circulating Exhbn.-Latin Am., 1974-75; represented in permanent collections, Corcoran Gallery Art, Walker Art Center, Mpls., Va. Mus. Fine Arts, Richmond, Everson Art Mus., Columbus Gallery Fine Arts, Detroit Inst. Art, Albright-Knox Mus., works include archtl. installations, Am. Republic Ins. Co., Des Moines, 1969, N.K. Winston Corp., N.Y.C., 1969, Schering Labs., Bloomfield, N.J., 1970, Skidmore, Owings and Merrill, N.Y.C., 1970, Kahn & Mallis Assos., N.Y.C., 1972, Harris Bank, Chgo., 1977, Powell/Kleinschmidt Chgo., 1977, Travenol Labs., Deerfield, Ill., 1977, Skidmore, Owings and Merrill, Chgo., 1977. John Simon Guggenheim Meml. Found. fellow, 1969; Nat Endowment for Arts grantee, 1976 Home and Office: 57 Leonard St Fl 4 New York NY 10013-2919

SWAIN, ROGER B. editor, writer, television host; b. Cambridge, Mass., Feb. 5, 1949; s. Charles Gardner and Marguerite Stay Swain; m. Elisabeth Ward Mahnke, July 21, 1979; children: Robert Mahnke, Benjamin Mahnke, Asa. BA, Harvard U., 1971, MA, 1972, PhD, 1977. Sci. editor Horticulture Mag., Boston, 1978—; host The Victory Garden WGBH-TV & PBS Affiliates, 1987—. Mem. vis. com. Arnold Arboretum Harvard U., 1998—; adv. bd. Natick Cmty. Organic Farm, Natick, Mass., 2002. Author: Earthly Pleasures, 1981, Saving Graces, 1991, Groundwork, 1994. Recipient Writing award, Am. Hort. Soc., 1992, Gold medal, Mass. Hort. Soc., 1996. Mem.: Cambridge Entomological Club (pres. 1975), Garden Writers of Am., Phi Beta Kappa. Home: 20 Columbus St Newton Highlands MA 02461

SWAIN, SUSAN MARIE, communications executive; b. Phila., Dec. 23, 1954; d. Samuel B. Swain and Marie (Baeder) Paget. BA in Comms. magna cum laude, U. Scranton, Pa., 1976, Doctorate (hon.) , 2000. Reporter Sta. WDAU-TV, Scranton, 1975-76; pub. relations staff Up With People, Inc., Tuscon, 1976-78; supr. Raytheon Service Co., Cambridge, Mass., 1978-80; research assoc. Nat. Counsel Assocs., Washington, 1980-82; producer C-SPAN Cable Network, 1982-83, dir. pub. relations, 1983-87, v.p. corp. communications, mem. exec. mgmt. com., 1987-89, sr. v.p., 1989—, exec. v.p., co-chief oper. officer; also creator & host "American Writers", C-SPAN. Speaker in field. Moderator (TV program) C-SPAN Viewer Call-In, 1982—. Trustee U. Scranton, 1992—2000. Recipient Alumni award U. Scranton, 1976, Disting. Achievement award, 1991. Mem. Cable TV Pub. Affairs Assn. (bd. dirs. 1986-90, sec. 1988-89), Washington Cable Club, Alpha Sigma Nu. Roman Catholic. Avocations: sailing, biking. Office: C-SPAN 400 N Capitol St NW Ste 650 Washington DC 20001-1550*

SWAIN, VIRGINIA M. executive mentor, conflict resolution, reconciliation and peace education consultant, educator; b. Buffalo, June 8, 1943; d. Robert Burrough and Joan (Wood) S.; m. Thomas Edward Cone III, May 20, 1964 (div. 1974); 1 child, Thomas Edward Cone IV; m. Joseph Preston Baratta, Jan. 1, 1995. AA, Colby Sawyer Coll., New London, N.H., 1963; MA in Cmty. Bldg. in Orgns., Lesley U., 1993. Tchr. U.S. Peace Corps, West Africa, 1964-66; personnel mgr. Pepperidge Farm Mail Order Co., Clinton, Conn., 1975-81; sales coord. Internat. Salt, Essex, 1981-84; dir. mktg. Mercy Ctr., Madison, 1984-86; dir. pub. rels., mktg. Wainwright House, Rye, N.Y., 1986; ind. cons. internat. peacemaking and conflict resolution Old Lyme, Conn., 1986—; co-founder Ctr. for Global Cmty. & World Law, 1993—. Rep. non-govtl. orgn. to UN, N.Y.C., 1991, Global Mediation and Reconciliation Svc., 1992—; mem. Comms. Coord com., Congress for a More Dem. UN, 1991; del. Earth Summit, UN Conf. on Environ. and Devel., Rio de Janeiro, 1992; rep. Assn. World Citizens at the UN; del. UN World Social Summit, Copenhagen, 1995; founder, pres. Ctr. Reconciliation Leadership, 2001—. Co-author: The Gift of Peace, 1989. Facilitator, cons. Am. Cancer Soc., New London, Conn., 1991; mem. exec. com. Coalition for Strong UN, Boston, 1993-98. Mem. ACA, Inst. for Global Leadership, 2000, Transcend Network Internat. Peace Rsch. Assn., Women in Foreign Policy, Peace Studies Assn., NY Orgnl. Devel. Network, New Eng. Holistic Counselors Assn. Episcopalian. Quaker. Avocations: tennis, walking, travel, reading, bicycling.

SWAIN, WILLIAM GRANT, landscape architect; b. Covington, Ky., Sept. 5, 1923; s. George Wellington and Emma Grant (Holmes) S.; m. Sybil Yvonne Harris, Mar. 30, 1946 (div. 1954); 1 son, Grant Marc; m. Marjorie Page Reno, Dec. 21, 1957; children: Margaret Page, Jill Holmes. B.Arch., Carnegie-Mellon U., 1952. Registered landscape architect, Pa. Ptnr. Griswold, Winters, Swain & Mullin, Pitts., 1957-75; pres. GWSM Inc., 1975-83, chmn. bd., 1983—. Chmn. Interprofl. Council on Environ. Design, Washington, 1974 Author: (with Ralph E. Griswold) Opportunities in Landscape Architecture, 1978. Mem. Mayor's Com. on Community Improvement, Monroeville, Pa.; 1965; bd. dirs. W. Pa. Conservancy, Pitts., 1970— , Rachel Carson Homestead Assn., Springdale, Pa., 1976— ; mem. Pa. State Art Commn., Harrisburg, 1977-84, chmn., 1981-84. Served as 1st lt. U.S. Army, 1943-46, ETO. Decorated Purple Heart; recipient Service award Carnegie-Mellon U. Alumni Fedn., 1963 Fellow Am. Soc. Landscape Architects (pres. 1973-74 recipient medals), Phi Kappa Phi Clubs: University (dir.) (1976-82). Republican. Episcopalian. Home: 413 Harper Dr Monroeville PA 15146-1235 Office: GWSM Landscape Architects 1101 Greenfield Ave Pittsburgh PA 15217-2930 *The central thread of my life is a sense of loyalty to those for whom I have worked or served in professional capacities. I have been motivated to do my best for all who depend on me. It remains my belief that volunteer service to one's community is an obligation.*

SWAINE, HOWARD RALPH, economist, educator, economist, consultant; b. Des Moines, Dec. 21, 1928; s. Alvin Ralph and Sarah (Underhill) S.; m. Suzanne Elise Terrell, Oct. 8, 1952; children: Abigail Ann, Edward Terrell. BA, U. Iowa, 1952, MA, 1956; PhD, UCLA, 1965. Economist Rand Corp., Santa Monica, Calif., 1959-66, Omaha, 1960-61, Washington, 1961-63, Paris, 1965-66; prof. No. Mich. U., Marquette, 1966—, dept. head, 1969—97. Cons. Rand Corp., Santa Monica, 1966-70, CAB, Washington, 1971-72, NSF, Washington, 1975-77. Co-author: (monograph) Navy Cost Model, 1963. Commr. City of Marquette, 1976-81, mayor, 1977-78; bd. dirs. Light & Power Bd., Marquette, 1984-90, Econ. Devel. Bd., Marquette, 1984—. 1st lt. U.S. Army, 1952-54, Korea. 1st lt. U.S. Army, 1952—54, Korea. Mem. Am. Econ. Assn. Republican. Presbyterian. Home: 1506 Garfield Ave Marquette MI 49855-1633

SWAISGOOD, HAROLD EVERETT, biochemist, educator; b. Ashland, Ohio, Jan. 19, 1936; s. Ray Weaver and Jennie (Morr) S.; m. Janet Cromwell, Sept. 15, 1956; children: Mark Harold, Ronald Ray. BS, Ohio State U., 1958; PhD in Chemistry (NIH fellow), Mich. State U., 1963. Reserach asst. Mich. State U., 1958-63; postdoctoral research asso. NIH, 1963-64; asst. prof. food sci. and biochemistry N.C. State U., 1964-67, assoc. prof., 1967-72, prof., 1972-84, William Neal Reynolds prof., 1984—2001, prof. emeritus William Neal Reynolds, 2001—, Alumni Disting. Grad. Rsch. prof., 1997. Vis. prof. U. Lund, Sweden, 1974, chmn. biotech. program, 1986-92.. Editor for Ams., Comments on Agr. and Food Chemistry; assoc. editor Jour. Food Biochemistry, 1983-2000; mem. editl. bd. Jour. Dairy Sci, 1975-85, Jour. Food Sci. 1978-83; regional editor Nahrung-Food, 1995-2002; contbr. articles, chpts. to profl. publs. USPHS fellow, 1963-64; recipient Holladay medal for excellence, 1999. Fellow Am. Chem. Soc. (agriculture food chem. divsn., award advancement of application of agrl. and food chemistry sponsored by IFF 1994), Am. Dairy Sci. Assn. (pres. 1999-2000, Borden awardee 1987); mem. Am. Inst. Nutrition, Am. Soc. Biochemists and Molecular Biologists, AAAS, Inst. Food Technologists, Sigma Xi, Phi Kappa Phi, Gamma Sigma Delta. Democrat. Methodist. Achievements include research in protein structure, interactions, and functionality; characteristics and applications of immobilized enzymes; patents in field. Office: NC State U Dept Food Sci Raleigh NC 27695-0001 E-mail: harold_swaisgood@ncsu.edu.

SWALIN, RICHARD ARTHUR, scientist, company executive; b. Mpls., Mar. 18, 1929; s. Arthur and Mae (Hurley) S.; m. Helen Marguerite Van Wagenen, June 28, 1952; children: Karen, Kent, Kristin. BS with distinction, U. Minn., 1951, PhD, 1954. Rsch. assoc. GE, 1954-56; mem. faculty U. Minn., Mpls., 1956-77, prof., head Sch. Mineral and Metall Engring., 1962-68, assoc. dean Inst. Tech., 1968-71, dean Inst. Tech., 1971-77; acting dir. Space Sci. Center, 1965; v.p. tech. Eltra Corp., N.Y.C., 1977-80; v.p. R & D Allied-Signal Corp., Morristown, N.J., 1980-84; dean Coll. Engring. and Mines U. Ariz., Tucson, 1984-87, prof., 1984-94; pres. Ariz. Tech. Devel. Corp., 1987; prof. emeritus U. Ariz., 1995—. Guest scientist Max Planck Inst. für Phys. Chemie, Göttingen, Fed. Republic Germany, 1963, Lawrence Radiation Lab., Livermore, Calif., 1967; cons. to govt. and industry; bd. dirs. emeritus Medtronic Corp., BMC Industries; corp. adv. bd. AMP Inc., 1990-93. Author: Thermodynamics of Solids, 2d edit, 1972; Contbr. articles to profl. jours. Dir. div. indsl. coop. U. Ariz. Found., 1985-86; trustee Midwest Research Inst., 1975-78, Sci. Mus. Minn., 1973-77, Nat. Tech. U., 1983-90. Recipient Disting. Teaching award Inst. Tech., U. Minn., 1967, Leadership award U. Minn. Alumni, 1993; NATO sr. fellow in sci., 1971. Mem. Sigma Xi, Tau Beta Pi, Phi Delta Theta, Gamma Alpha. Home: PO Box 65454 Port Ludlow WA 98365-0454 Office: 4705 N Via De La Granja Tucson AZ 85718-7404 E-mail: raswalin@earthlink.net.

SWALLEY, ROBERT FARRELL, structural engineer, consultant; b. Ponca City, Okla., June 1, 1930; s. Robert Arthur and Jeannette Dean (Edwards) S.; children: Arthur Gentry, Susanne Evelyn. BS with distinction, U.S. Naval Acad., 1952; BSCE, U. Mo., 1958; MS, Stanford U., 1959. Registered profl. engr., structural engr. Sr. rsch. engr. USN Civil Engring. Lab., Port Hueneme, Calif., 1959-63; structural engr. Benham Blair & Affiliates, Oklahoma City, 1967-69; sr. project engr. AMF Inc., Advanced System Lab., Santa Barbara, Calif., 1969-73; structural engr. Penfield & Smith Engrs. Inc., 1973-77; structural engr., prin. engr., CEO Swalley Engring. Inc., 1978-93; cons., structural engr., 1993—. Contbr. tech. reports on Small Buried Arches, Design of a Cast in Place Personnel Shelter, Behavior of Buried Model Arch Structures, Loadings on Drydock Gates from Nuclear Explosions. Mem. ASCE (pres. 1976-77, v.p. 1983-84), NSPE (pres. 1978-84), Structural Engrs. Assn. Calif. Achievements include patent for Ventilator Blast Closure. Home: 3724 Monterey Pines St Apt C102 Santa Barbara CA 93105-3271 Office: 500 E Montecito St Santa Barbara CA 93103-3245 E-mail: rfs314@earthlnik.net.

SWALLOW, JOHN, mathematician, educator; BA, U. of the South, Sewanee, Tenn., 1989; MS, MPhil, Yale U., 1991, PhD, 1994. Asst. prof. math. Davidson Coll., NC, 1994—2000, Macarthur asst. prof. math., 1995—97, John T. Kimbrough asst. prof. math., 1998—2000; maitre de conferences invite U. de Lille I, Lille, France, 1997—97; vis. scientist Technion-Israel Inst. Tech., Haifa, Israel, 1998—99. Trustee U. of the South, Sewanee, 2001—. Fellow Internat. Rsch. fellow, NSF, 1998—99; grantee Career grantee, 1995—99, Young Investigator grantee, Nat. Security Agy., 2001—. Mem.: Math. Assn. Am., Am. Math. Soc. Episcopalian. Office: Davidson Coll Box 7046 Davidson NC 28035 Office Fax: 704-894-2005.

SWALLOW, KRISTINA LOUISE, civil engineer; b. Newport News, Va., Dec. 9, 1972; d. Edwin John and Cynthia Louise (Earle) Konrath; m. David Christopher Swallow, May 30, 1998. BSCE, U. Ariz., 1994. Sr. hydrologist E.S.I., Las Vegas, 1994-96; svc. mgr. Hunsaker & Assocs., 1996-97; dir. engring. ops. CRS Cons. Engrs., 1997-2000; adm. v.p. JLLV, 2000—; mgr. land devel. Poggemeyer Design Group, 2000—. Project mem.-at-large Jr. League of Las Vegas, 1998-99, fin. v.p. 1999—. Mem. ASCE (bd. dirs. 1998—, pres. younger mem. group 1996-97, Young Engr. of Yr. 1997-98, 150th anniversary steering com.), Pi Beta Phi (pres. 1996-99). Home: PO Box 27808 Las Vegas NV 89126-1808 E-mail: kswallow@pdg-lv.com.

SWALLUM, MARYANN, musician, music educator; b. L.A., Sept. 6, 1944; d. Robert James and Alice Agasteen S. BM, Immaculate Heart Coll., L.A., 1966; MM, Northwestern U., 1972. Registered tchr., trainer Suzuki piano. Dir. piano program Our Lady of the Holy Rosary Sch., Sun City, Calif., 1964-66; music dir. N.W. Suburban Aide for Retarded Adults, Park Ridge, Ill., 1970-72; piano instr. Elmhurst (Ill.) Coll., 1972-79; founder, dir. Swallum Music Sch., Wilmette, Ill., 1974-79; music dir. Montessori sch., Park Ridge, 1975-79; music dir. Suzuki piano Dunbarton Sch., Hamilton, Bermuda, 1993-94; chair, instr. prep. dept. Coll. St. Scholastica, Duluth, Minn., 1994—. Piano instr., clinician Suzuki Inst. U. Wis., Stevens Point, 1978-82, U. We. Ont., London, 1980-82; dist. chair Am. Music Scholarship Competition, Cin., 1976-78; founder, dir. piano workshop for children; piano judge Ill. State Music Tchrs. Assn., Winnetka, 1977-78, Minn. State Music Tchrs., Duluth, 1980-92. Presdl. scholar The White House Commn., 1985; grantee to study with Daniel Pollack Steinway Recording Artist, 1989. Mem. Music Tchrs. Nat. Assn., Cecilian Soc. (sec. 1991-92, founder, dir. 1998), Suzuki Assn. Am. Avocations: hiking, snow skiing, snow shoeing.

SWALM, THOMAS STERLING, aerospace executive, retired military officer; b. San Diego, Sept. 28, 1931; s. Calvin D. and Margaret A. (Rynning) S.; m. Charlene La Vern Garner, June 26, 1954; children: Edward Steven, Lori Ann. BS, U. Oreg., 1954; MS in Pub. Adminstrn., George Washington U., 1964; grad., Air Command and Staff Coll., 1964, Nat. War Coll., 1974. Commd. USAF, 1954, advanced through grades to maj. gen., 1982, instr. fighter-interceptor weapons sch. Fla., 1956, pilot 434th Fighter-Day Squadron George AFB, Calif., 1957-58, engring. test pilot and flight examiner 50th Tactical Fighter Wing, 10th Tactical Fighter Squadron Toul-Rosieres AFB, France, and Hahn AFB, Fed. Republic Germany, 1958-61, hdqrs. 12th Waco, Tex., 1961-64, instr. pilot, flight examiner 4453d Combat Crew Tng. Wing Davis-Monthan AFB, Ariz., 1965-66, flight comdr. 12th Tactical Fighter Wing Cam Ranh Bay AFB, Republic Vietnam, 1966-67; comdr. air-to-air flight, instr. and chief R&D/OT&E sect. Fighter Weapons Sch., Nellis AFB, Nev., 1967-70; comdr., leader Thunderbirds USAF, 1970-73, chief fighter attack directorate N.Mex., 1974-75, dep. dir. test and evaluation, 1975-76, from vice comdr. to comdr. 8th Tactical Fighter Wing Kunsan AFB, Republic of Korea, 1976-78, comdr. 3d Tactical Fighter Wing Clark AFB, Philippines, 1978-79, comdr. 57th Fighter Weapons Wing, comdr. fighter weapons sch. Nellis AFB, Nev., 1979-80, comdr. 833d air div. Holloman AFB, N.Mex., 1980-81, comdr. tactical air warfare ctr. Eglin AFB, Fla., 1981-86, ret., 1986; pres. T. Swalm and Assocs., Ft. Walton Beach, Fla., 1986-91; v.p. Melbourne Systems Div. Grumman Corp., 1991-95; pres. T. Swaim and Assocs., Melbourne, Fla., 1995—. V.p. Applications Group Internat., Inc. , Atlanta, 1986—89; bd. dirs. Nat. Correlation Working Group. Mem. editorial bd. Jour. Electronic Def., 1983-86; contbr. articles to profl. jours. Hon. chmn. Heart Assn., Las Vegas, Nev., 1972; exec. dir. Boy Scouts Am., Las Vegas and Alamagordo, N.Mex., 1970-81; chmn. AFA Scholarship Found., 1989-91; active Fla. Govs. Coun. for TQM, 1992-94; bd. dirs. Jr. Achievement, Ctrl. Fla., 1992-94; mem. USAF scientific adv. bd., 1994-98. Decorated D.S.M., Legion of Merit with two oak leaf clusters, DFC, Air medal with 14 oak leaf clusters, Vietnam Service medal with three service stars, Republic Vietnam Campaign medal; recipient R.V. Jones Trophy Electronic Security Command, 1984, Exceptional Civilian Svc. award USAF, 1999. Mem. Air Force Assn. (exec. advisor, Jerome Waterman award 1985, Jimmy Doolittle fellow 1986), Thunderbirds Pilots Assn., Old Mission Beach Athletic Club (founder), Assn. Old Crows (editl. bd. R.V. Jones trophy 1984), Order of Daedalians (flight capt.), Melbourne C of C. (trustee 1993-95), Sigma Nu. Republican. Presbyterian. Avocations: golf, tennis, sailing.

SWALM, WILLIAM KELLER, investment advisor; b. Williamsburg (Newport News) , Va., May 13, 1953; s. William Henry Swalm, Carolyn Keller Swalm, Anne Cornell Swalm (Stepmother). BA summa cum laude, U. Pa., 1977, MBA, 1981. Portfolio mgr. GE Co.(G.E. Capital) , Fairfield, Conn., 1981—88; investment banker Oppenheimer & Co., N.Y.C., 1988—91, Lehman Bros., N.Y.C., 1991—97; dir. mktg. Rubenstein Assocs., 1997—. Mem.: SAR, The St. Andrews Soc., The St. George's Soc., The Sons of the Revolution, The Huguenot Soc. (Vice President 1995—97), The New Eng. Soc. (Stuarts Committee 1994—Pres), The Soc. of Colonial Wars, The Union League Club, Phi Beta Kappa, The Order of St. Catherine (Knighthood), The Sovereign Order of the Knights Hospitaller of St.John (Knighthood), The Sovereign Mil. Order of the Knights Templars (Knighthood - Knight Commander). Republican. Presbyterian. Avocations: sailing, squash, English literature, studying biographies of statesmen and world leaders, collecting historical autographs of world leaders and statesmen. Home: 780 Madison Ave New York NY 10021

SWAMIDASS, PAUL M(UTHUKUMAR), technology management educator; b. Tamilnadu, India, Jan. 25, 1945; s. Jacob M. and Gnanam Swamidass; m. Nimmi Swamidass; children: Vijay, Jay. BEME, Osmania U., 1966; MBA, Wash. State U., 1975; PhD, U. Wash., 1983. Asst. supt. BHEL, Tiruchi; asst. prof. Ill. State U., Normal; vis. asst. prof. Ind. U., Bloomington; assoc. prof. U. Mo., Columbia; prof. ops. mgmt., assoc. dir. Thomas Walter Ctr. for Technology Mgmt., Auburn (Ala.) Univ.; cons. UNIDO, 1997-98. Reviewer U.S. Dept. of Edn. 1994, U.S. Dept. of Energy, 1993, speaker, facilitator workshop. Assoc. editor Jour. of Ops. Mgmt., 1988-92; editor Technology and Innovation Newsletter, 1994-97, Encyclopedia of Production and Manfucturing Management, 1999; author: (book) Cross-Functional Management of Technology, 1996. Mem. Acad. of Mgmt. (Best Paper award 1992), Inst. of Mgmt. Sci., Am. Prodn. and Inventory Control Soc. (assoc. editor JOM 1984-92), Decision Scis. Inst. Achievements include research on the benchmarking of manufacturing technology use in the U.S., Manufacturing Institute; manufacturing technology and strategy. Office: Thomas Walter Ctr for Technology Mgmt 104 Tiger Dr Auburn AL 36849

SWAMIDOSS, STEPHENSON, pathologist, health facility administrator; b. Tanjore, Tamil Nadu, India, Apr. 11, 1946; Came to U.S., 1973; s. Asirwatham and Alice Flora; m. Premila M.K., Jan. 15, 1973; children: Cynthia, Philip. Asst. pathologist Holy Spirit Hosp., Camp Hill, Pa., 1978-82, assoc. pathologist, 1983-96, med. dir. lab. medicine, 1997—; clin. asst. prof. pathology Penn State U. Hershey Med. Ctr., Hershey, 1995—. Organizer, dir. implementation of thin prep PAP test Holy Spirit Hosp., 1997. Fellow: Internat. Acad. Cytologists, Am. Soc. Clin. Pathologists, Coll. Am. Pathologists; mem.: AMA, Nat. Soc. for Histotechnology, Dauphin County Med. Soc., Pa. Assn.

Pathologists, Pa. Med. Soc., Am. Soc. Cytology, Am. Soc. Cytopathologists. Lutheran. Avocations: photography, gardening. Home: 13 Northwatch Ln Mechanicsburg PA 17050-1775 Office: Holy Spirit Hosp-Lab 503 N 21st St Camp Hill PA 17011-2204

SWAMINATHAN, JAYASHANKAR M. finance educator, consultant; B Tech in Computer Sci., Indian Inst. Tech., New Delhi, 1992; MS, Carnegie Mellon U., 1994, Doctorate, 1996. Asst. prof. Haas Sch. Bus. U. Calif., Berkeley, 1996—2001; assoc. prof. Kenan-Flagler Bus. Sch. U. N.C., Chapel Hill, 2000—. Cons. IBM, Yorktown Heights. Recipient George Nicholson prize, INFORMS, 1996, Career award, NSF, 2000. Office: U NC 4717 McColl Bldg Chapel Hill NC 27599-3490 Business E-Mail: msj@unc.edu.

SWAMY, PONNUSWAMY T. plastic surgeon; b. Pollachi, Tamilnadu, India, June 15, 1942; came to U.S., 1967; s. Ponnu and Uthami Swamy; m. Sara Swamy, June 29, 1967; children: Ravi, Priya, Nithya. MD, U. Madras, India, 1966. Pres. Plastic Surgery Ctr., Sherman, Tex., 1976—. Chief of surgery Cmty. Med. Ctr., Sherman, 1999. Fellow ACS. Avocations: reading, gardening, travel. Office: Plastic Surgery Ctr 3400 Loy Lake Rd Sherman TX 75090-1739

SWAN, CHARLES E. not-for-profit organizations consultant; b. Rochester, N.Y., May 11, 1935; s. Edwin M. and Florence E. (Doescher) S.; m. Mary Lawrence, June 17, 1961 (div. 1994); children: Gregory C., Tracy A., Amy L. AB in Polit. Sci., U. Rochester, 1957, EdM in Adminstrn., 1963; cert. in urban policy, Brookings Instn., Washington, 1973. Cert. leisure profl. Purchasing agt. Rochester Germicide Co., 1957-60; dir. admissions Rochester Inst. Tech., 1960-63; U.S. sales mgr. C.H. Stuart & Co., Rochester, 1964; sales cons., 1965-69; exec. dir. North East Area Devel., 1969-71; research cons. Ford Found./U.S. Catholic Conf., 1973-74; community program specialist N.Y. State Div. for Youth, 1974-94; now pvt. cons., 1995—. Author: Careers in Business, 1963. Chmn. City Planning Commn., Rochester, 1970-73; vice chmn. City Charter Commn., Rochester, 1973; commr. Monroe County Planning Bd., Rochester, 1973, Regional Planning Bd., Rochester, 1973. Recipient Nat. citation Nat. Ctr./Vol. Action, Washington, 1973, County citation Monroe County Planning Coun., 1973, County award Wayne County, Lyons, N.Y., 1988, Dirs. award N.Y. State Div. for Youth, 1981, Svc. to Youth award Seneca County Youth Bd., 1988, Assn. N.Y.C. Youth Burs. award 1994, Genesee Valley Parks and Recreation Soc. award, 1994, Livingston County award, 1994, Town of Gates award, 1994. Republican. Avocations: music, photography, travel, reading.

SWAN, GEORGE STEVEN, law educator; b. St. Louis; BA, Ohio State U., 1970; JD, U. Notre Dame, 1974; LLM, U. Toronto, 1976, SJD, 1983. Bar: Ohio 1974, U.S. Dist. Ct. (so. dist.) Ohio 1975, U.S. Supreme Ct. 1987, U.S. Ct. Appeals (6th and 11th cirs.) 1993, U.S. Ct. Appeals (10th cir.) 1994, D.C. 1997, Ga. 1997, U.S. Dist. Ct. (no. dist.) Ga. 1997, Fla. 1997, Minn. 1998, Nebr. 1998, N.D. 1998, U.S. Ct. Appeals (7th cir.) 1998, La. 1999, Mass. 1999; ChFC, CLU, CFP. Asst. atty. gen. State of Ohio, Columbus, 1974-75; jud. clk. Supreme Ct. Ohio, 1976-78; asst. prof. Del. Law Sch., Wilmington, 1980-83, assoc. prof., 1983-84; prof. law St. Thomas U. Law Sch., Miami, Fla., 1984-88; jud. clk. U.S. Ct. Appeals (7th cir.), Chgo., 1988-89; assoc. prof. N.C. Agrl. & Tech. State U., Greensboro, 1989—. Vis. prof. John Marshall Law Sch., Atlanta, 1996—97, 2000—01. Contbr. articles to law jours. Mem. Ohio State Bar Assn., D.C. Bar, State Bar Ga., Fla. Bar, Mass. Bar Assn., Nebr. State Bar Assn., La. State Bar Assn., N.D. State Bar Assn., Soc. of Fin. Svc. Profls., Fin. Planning Assn., Am. Polit. Sci. Assn. Office: Merrick Hall 1601 E Market St Greensboro NC 27411

SWAN, HENRY, forester, consultant; b. Barre, Mass., Jan. 15, 1935; m. Freda Theopold, June 26, 1960. BS in Forestry, U. Maine, Orono, 1957; MBA, Harvard U., 1963. Registered profl. forester. Asst. dist. ranger U.S. Forest Svc., Laconia, N.H., 1957-61; investment officer John Hancock Ins. Co., Boston, 1963-68; v.p. Keystone Funds Inc., 1968-76, Legg Mason & Co., Washington, 1976-77; pres. Wagner Woodlands, Inc., Lyme, N.H., 1977-96; chmn. Wagner Forest Investments, Inc., 1981-97; gen. ptnr. Wagner Woodlands & Co., 1981—99; chmn., pres. Wagner Forest Mgmt. Ltd., 1992-98, chmn., 1998—. Mem. adv. com. White Mountain Nat. Forest, Laconia, 1989—; bd. dirs. New Eng. Forestry Cons., Inc. Commr. Conn. River Valley Resource Com., Charleston, NH, 1988—; advisor Lake Baikal Watershed Program, Ulan Ude, Buryat, 1991—92, No. Forest Lands, Concord, NH, 1989—91; pres. Friends of Tuckerman Ravine, 2000—; bd. dirs. New Eng. Forestry Found.; dir. Henry's Fork Found., 2001—. Recipient Outstanding Mgmt. of Natural Resources award Northeastern Loggers Assn., 1986. Mem.: Upper Valley Land Trust, Nature Conservancy N.H. (trustee 1997—), Forest Soc. Maine (bd. dirs. 1984—2000), Soc. for Protection of N.H. Forests (chmn. 1984—86, chmn. emeritus 1988—), Soc. Am. Foresters (Outstanding Svc. award N.Y. chpt. 1991), Harvard Club Boston, Harvard Club N.Y., Nat. Economists Club, Trout Unltd. Republican. Episcopalian. Avocations: skiing, boating, fly fishing, woodworking. Home: 133 Breck Hill Rd Lyme NH 03768-3022 Office: Wagner Forest Mgmt Ltd PO Box 160 Lyme NH 03768-0160 Office Fax: 603-795-4631. E-mail: hank@wagnerforest.com.

SWAN, KENNETH CARL, surgeon; b. Kansas City, Mo., Jan. 1, 1912; s. Carl E. and Blanche (Peters) S.; m. Virginia Grone, Feb. 5, 1938; children: Steven Carl, Kenneth, Susan. AB, U. Oreg., 1933, MD, 1936. Diplomate: Am. Bd. Ophthalmology (chmn. 1960-61). Intern U. Wis., 1936-37; resident in ophthalmology State U. Iowa, 1937-40; practice medicine specializing in ophthalmology Portland, Oreg., 1945—; staff Good Samaritan Hosp.; asst. prof. ophthalmology State U. Iowa, Iowa City, 1941-44; asso. prof. U. Oreg. Med. Sch., Portland, 1944-45, prof. and head dept. ophthalmology, 1945-78. Chmn. sensory diseases study sect. NIH; mem. adv. council Nat. Eye Inst.; also adv. council Nat. Inst. Neurol. Diseases and Blindness. Contbr. articles on ophthalmic subjects to med. publs. Recipient Proctor Rsch. medal, 1953, Disting. Svc. award U. Oreg., 1963, Meritorious Achievement award U. Oreg. Med. Sch., 1968, Howe Ophthalmology medal, 1977, Aubrey Watzek Pioneer award Lewis and Clark Coll., 1979, Disting. Alumnus award Oreg. Health Scis. U. Alumni Assn., 1988, Disting. Svc. award, 1988, Mentor award Oreg. Health Scis. Found., 1996; named Oreg. Scientist of Yr. Oreg. Mus. Sci. and Industry, 1959. Mem. Assn. Research in Ophthalmology, Am. Acad. Ophthalmology (v.p. 1978, historian), Soc. Exptl. Biology and Medicine, AAAS, AMA, Am. Ophthal. Soc. (Howe medal for distinguished service 1977), Oreg. Med. Soc., Sigma Xi, Sigma Chi (Significant Sig award 1977) Home: 4645 SW Fairview Blvd Portland OR 97221-2624 Office: Oreg Health Scis U Ophthalmology Dept Portland OR 97201

SWAN, PATRICIA BRINTNALL, research administrator; b. Hickory, N.C., Oct. 21, 1937; d. Philip Earle and Mary Lucille (Farmer) Brintnall; m. James Byron Swan, Apr. 23, 1962; children: Kathryn Ann, Deborah Lee. BS, U. N.C., 1959; MS, U. Wis., 1961, PhD, 1964. Rsch. assoc. U. Wis., Madison, 1963-64, U. Minn., St. Paul, 1964-65, asst. prof., 1965-68, assoc. prof., 1968-73, prof., 1973-89; assoc. dean U. Minn. Grad. Sch., Mpls., 1987-89; prof. Iowa State U., Ames, 1989—2001, prof. emeritus, 2002—, vice provost, dean, 1989-91, 92-99, interim provost, 1991-92. Program coord. SEA-USDA, Washington, 1979-80; bd. dirs. Fedn. of Am. Socs. for Exptl. Biology, Bethesda, Md., 1988-91; mem. Bd. Agr., NRC, Washington, 1992-94; mem. Grad. Rsch. Examination Bd., 1994—. Contbr. over 80 tech. articles to profl. jours. Pres. U. Minn. Faculty Polit. Action Com., Mpls., 1984-87; bd. dirs. Ames Econ. Devel. Commn., 1991-99. Recipient Disting. Alumni award U. Wis., 1994. Mem. Am. Inst. Nutrition (sec. 1981-84), Nat. Agrl. Biotechnology Coun. (chair 1996-97), Rsch. Coun. of Iowa (pres. 1994-96). Avocation: history of nutrition sci. in U.S. Home: 1301 Crest Ridge Ct Nashville TN 37221-4336 E-mail: pswan@iastate.edu.

SWAN, PEER ALDEN, public utility executive; b. Beverly, Mass., June 16, 1944; s. E.M. and Stella Swan; m. Nancy Carol Mosier, Jan. 24, 1969; children: Michael, Ashley. AA, Orange Coast Coll., Costa Mesa, Calif., 1966; BA, Calif. State U., Fullerton, 1973. Fin. analyst Brunswick, Costa Mesa, 1974-76; asst. treas. Pacific Sci. Co., Newport Beach, Calif., 1977-84, treas., 1984-98. Dir. SC Bancorp, Downey, Calif., 1992-97, Met. Water Dist. of So. Calif., 1999-2002. Dir. Irvine (Calif.) Ranch Water Dist., 1979—, Orange County Sanitation Dist., Fountain Valley, Calif., 1985—2001, So. Calif. Water Com., Irvine, 1984—92, Nat. Water Rsch. Inst., Fountain Valley, 1991—2001. Capt. U.S. Army, 1966—71, Vietnam. Avocations: sailing, hiking. Home: 7 Terraza Dr Newport Coast CA 92657-1510

SWAN, RALPH EDWARD, education educator; b. Harrisburg, Pa., May 2, 1946; s. Ralph C. and D. Grace (Cox) S.; m. Anne Marie Young. BS, Edinboro (Pa.) State Coll., 1969; MEd, Lehigh U., 1971; PhD, U. Pa., 1997. Cert. tchr., Pa. Tchr. Marple Newtown Sch. Dist., Newtown Square, Pa., 1969-99; instr. U. Pa., Phila., 1984-89; adj. prof. Chestnut Hill Coll., 1987—. Assoc. adj. prof., Drexel U., 2001—; adj. prof. Widener U., 1999-2001. Mem. Phi Delta Kappa. Avocations: hiking, camping, book discussion, cycling. Home: 165 Dowlin Forge Rd Downingtown PA 19335-1426 Office: Chestnut Hill Coll 9601 Germantown Ave Philadelphia PA 19118-2643 E-mail: rralphswan@cs.com.

SWAN, RICHARD GORDON, retired mathematics educator; b. N.Y.C., Dec. 21, 1933; s. A. Gordon and Rose (Nespor) S.; m. Erdmuthe J.D.B. Plesch-Ritz, Mar. 18, 1963; children— Adrian Alexander, Irit Alexandra AB, Princeton U., N.J., 1954, PhD, 1957. From instr. to prof. U. Chgo., 1958-96, ret., 1996. Author: Theory of Sheaves, 1964, Algebraic K-Theory, 1968, K-Theory of Finite Groups and Orders, 1970; editor Am. Jour. Math., 1977-83, Jour. Algebra, 1981-95; contbr. articles to profl. jours. Alfred P. Sloan fellow, 1961-65; recipient Cole prize in Algebra Am. Math. Soc., 1970 Fellow AAAS; mem. Nat. Acad. Scis., Am. Math. Soc., Math. Assn. Am., Sigma Xi. Avocation: music. Home: 700 Melrose Ave Apt M3 Winter Park FL 32789-5610

SWAN, SUSAN LINDA, history educator; b. Everett, Wash., May 31, 1943; d. Joseph William Franckevitch and Doris Aline (Doolittle) Berry; m. Victor LaMarr Swan, June 19, 1965 (div. Apr. 1994); 1 child, Kerrigan Aline. BA in History, BA in English, U. Wash., 1965; MA in History, Western Wash. U., 1969; PhD in History, Wash. State U., 1976. Employment interviewer Wash. State Employment Security, Tacoma, 1971-72; asst. prof. history Wash. State U., Pullman, 1977-82, student affairs officer III, 1984-94, assoc. prof. gen. edn. program, 1994—; rsch. assoc. Nat. Coord. Spl. Hist. Projects, Mex., 1991-92. Co-author: Breve Historia de las Sequias en Mexico, 1995; adaption editor: Study Guide for the Heritage of World Civilizations; contbg. editor: Reading About the World, I, II, 3d edit., 1999; contbr. articles to profl. publs. Mem. student affairs com., mem., chair acad. advising and reinstatement subcom., mus. adv. subcom. Wash. State U., chpt. advisor Alpha Phi Omega, 1995-99; vol. Pullman Meml. Hosp. Aux., 1983-92; group leader Sacajawea coun. Camp Fire, Pullman, 1984-90; adv. Sikh Student Assn., 2002—. Recipient Faculty award, Wash. State U. Multicultural Student Svcs., 2002. Mem. AAUP, AAAS, World History Assn., Am. Mus. Women in the Arts, Seattle Art Mus., Assn. Faculty Women (treas. 1998-99), Phi Alpha Theta (pres. 1974-75), Phi Kappa Phi. Avocations: watercolors, gardening. Home: PO Box 3195 Pullman WA 99165-3195 Office: Wash State U Dept History Pullman WA 99164-0001

SWAN, WALLACE KENT, public administrator; b. Kearney, Nebr., June 13, 1942; s. Kenneth Dean and Regina Joy Swan. MA in Pub. Adminstrn., Humphrey Inst. Pub. Affairs, 1969; MPA, Nova U., 1978, D Pub. Adminstrn., 1979. Intern City of Edina, Minn., 1966; rsch. fellow Humphrey Inst., Mpls., 1967; adminstrv. analyst Minn. Dept. Pub. Welfare, St. Paul, 1969-72, planner office regional devel., 1972-74, dir. office regional devel., 1974-75; program analysis mgr., prin. mgmt. analyst Hennepin County Govt., Mpls., 1975-85, sr. planning analyst, 1985—. Cmty. faculty mem. Met. State U., Mpls., 1979-95; adj. asst. prof. polit. sci. U. St. Thomas, St. Paul, 1979-86; dir. external doctorate program Nova U., Roseville, Minn., 1979-81; mem. humanities seminar for pub. adminstrs. NEH, 1976. Editor: Breaking the Silence, 1995 (book award Myers Ctr. for study of human rights in N.Am.), Gay/Lesbian/Bisexual/Transgender Public Policy Issues: A Citizen's and Administrator's Guide to the New Cultural Struggle, 1997. Pres. Mpls. Bd. Estimate and Taxation, 2000, 01, v.p. 1998-99; chair Mpls. Dem. Farmer Labor Fin. Com., 1999; candidate devel. dir. Stonewall Dem. Farmer Labor Caucus, 2000, 01. Ford Found. grantee, 1989. Mem. ASPA (pres. Minn. chpt. 1976-77, 78, nat. coun. 1993-97, co-chair "ASPA 2000" 1998-99), Govt. Fin. Officers Assn., First Unitarian Soc. (bd. chair 1993-95, found. bd. vice chair 2001, pres. 2002). Mem. Dem. Farmer Labor Party. Unitarian Universalist. Avocation: politics. Home: Towers A-420 15 S 1st St Minneapolis MN 55401 E-mail: swanx009@tc.umn.edu.

SWAN, WILLIAM, actor; b. Buffalo, Feb. 6, 1932; s. Earl B. and Irene (Hall) S. Student, Geller Workshop, L.A. Appeared in films, including Lady in a Cage, Hotel, The Parallax View, Bombers B-52; more than 200 TV guest appearances including Streets of San Francisco, Quincy, Perry Mason, Felony Squad, Twilight Zone, Have Gun Will Travel, Cannon, Barnaby Jones; appeared in off-Broadway plays, including Anne of a Thousand Days, Night Fishing in Beverly Hills; appeared in regional theatre prodns. of A Delicate Balance, The Rehearsal, The Cocktail Hour, California Suite, The Middle Ages, Stained Glass, What the Butler Saw, The Price, Golf with Alan Shepard, Moby-Dick-Rehearsed, and others; continuing role of Walter Hines on TV daytime drama All My Children, 1982-2000. Trustee Berkshire Theatre Festival, Stockbridge, Mass., 1984—. Sgt. U.S. Army, 1948-49, ETO. Mem. Acad. TV, Arts and Scis., The Players, The Yale Club. Democrat. Avocation: tennis. Home: 141 E 55th St Apt 12B New York NY 10022-4034 also: Barberry Close Monterey MA 01245

SWAN, WILLIAM IRVING, nutritionist; b. Ames, Iowa, July 18, 1948; BS, Iowa State U., 1970; BS in Home Econs., U. Mo., 1982. Lic. dietitian, Md. Consulting dietitian St. Joseph's Mercy Hosp., Mason City, Iowa, 1982-83, Manor Care, Cedar Rapids, 1983-84, food svc. dir. Wilmington, Del., 1984-85, Meridian Healthcare, Voorhees, N.J., 1985-90; pvt. practice, 1989-93; clin. dietitian Anne Arundel Med. Ctr., Annapolis, Md., 1990-2000, nutrition case mgr., 2000—. Vol. Chase Brexton Health Svcs., Balt. Mem. Am. Dietetic Assn. (registered dietitian), Am. Soc. Parenteral and Enteral Nutrition (Cert. Nutrition Support Dietitian), Dietitians in Nutrition Support. Office: 2001 Med Pky Annapolis MD 21401-3019 E-mail: bswan@aahs.org.

SWANBERG, NEIL RALPH, scientist, educator; b. Oakland, Calif., June 14, 1951; s. Ralph Norman and Marian Arlene (Dorsey) S.; m. Inger Maria Lindström, June 24, 1989; children: Kevin Andreas, Carl Anton. BS, U. Calif., Davis, 1974; PhD, MIT, 1979. Postdoctoral rschr. Columbia U., Palisades, N.Y., 1980; rsch. assoc. Lamont-Doherty Geol. Obs., 1981-87; rsch. sci. U. Bergen, Norway, 1987-92; assoc. program mgr. NSF, Washington, 1992-93; rschr. Royal Swedish Acad. Sci., Stockholm, 1993-2000; dir. arctic natural scis. program U.S. NSF, Arlington, Va., 2000—. Vis. asst. prof. Dartmouth Coll., Hanover, NH, 1980; adj. assoc. sci. Lamont-Doherty Earth Obs., Palisades, 1987—96; adj. asst. prof. CCNY, 1992—; vis. investigator Woods Hole (Mass.) Oceanographic Inst., 1992—93; dep. exec.-dir. Internat.-Geosphere-Biosphere Programme, Stockholm, 1993—2000; dir. Artic Natural Scis. Program NSF, 2000—. Contbr. articles to profl. jours. Scholar Norwegian Marshall Fund, 1982, 83, Exch. scholar NAS, 1986. Avocations: classical music, travel, family. Office: US NSF Office of Polar Programs/Nat Sci Found Arlington VA 22230

SWANEK, SUSAN ANN, quality assurance professional; b. Pittston, Pa., Oct. 21, 1955; d. William Stanley and Dorothy Lena (Siglin) S. AS in Med. Lab. Technology, City Univ., Bellevue, Wash., 1993; BS in Health Care Adminstrn., City Univ., 1994, Grad. Cert. in Total Quality Mgmt., 1995, MBA, 1996. Cert. lab. asst. Med. technologist Nesbitt Meml. Hosp., Kingston, Pa., 1974-79; from med. technologist to quality improvement coord. Pa. State-Geisinger Wyo. Valley Med. Ctr., Wilkes-Barre, 1979-96; tech. specialist quality improvement Geisinger Wyo. Valley Med. Ctr., 1996—. Recipient Technologist of Yr. award Pa. State Soc. Am. Med. Technologists, 1988, Fisher Sci. award, 1985, 96, 97, Infolab Tech. Writing award, 1988, 89, 94, Instrumental Lab. award, 1990, 91, 92. Mem. Am. Med. Technologists (state sec. 1993-94, state v.p. 1996-2000, state editor 2000—, Tech. Writing award 1987, Disting. Achievement award 1991, Exceptional Merit award 1994, Scholarship award 1994, Editor award 2000, 01). Avocations: covered bridging, needlework, travel, photography. Office: Geisinger Wyo Valley Med Ctr 1000 E Mountain Dr Wilkes Barre PA 18711-0001 E-mail: sswanek@geisinger.edu.

SWANER-SMOOT, PAULA MARGETTS, clinical psychologist; b. Salt Lake City, Nov. 23, 1927; d. Sumner Gray and Pauline (Moyle) Margetts; m. Leland Scowcroft, May 22, 1951; children: Leland S., Jr., Sumner Margetts, Paula June Swaner-Sargetakis; m. Stephen P. Smoot, Sept. 25, 1997. BA in Eng. Lit., U. Utah, 1949, MA in Eng. Lit., 1972, MS in Ednl. Psychology, 1978, PhD in Clin. Psychology, 1986; postgrad., Washington Sch. Psychiatry, 1991, Mill Valley Calif. Acad., 1990. Lic. clin. psychologist, Utah. Psychotherapist Granite Mental Health Ctr., Salt Lake City, 1978-80; intern Mental Health Unit, Juvenile Ct., 1984-87; pvt. practice, 1986—. CEO Evergreen Coalition, 1993—2002; faculty Internat. Inst. Object Rels. Therapy, Chevy Chase, Md., 1996—. dir., Salt Lake City, 1996, founder, dir. infant observation teleconferencing satellite program, 2000; established IIORT Videoconf. Supervision and Clin. Application Program, 2001. Chair Swaner Nature Preserve Found., 1993-2002. Mem. APA, Utah Psychol. Assn. Democrat. Avocations: hiking, cross-country skiing, swimming.

SWANGER, DANIEL A.I. artist; b. Council Bluffs, Iowa, Aug. 10, 1954; s. Harry LaVerne Swanger and Elisabeth Patermann. BFA in Painting, Sch. of the Art Inst., Chgo., 1982; student, U. Ill., Harper Jr. Coll., No. Ill. U.; postgrad., Am. Acad. Art, Chgo. Dealer art videos Side Track nightclub, Chgo., 1980-82; instr. Richard J. Daley Coll., Chgo., 1981-82; guest lectr. Sch. of Art Inst. Chgo., 1982; curator children's exhibit, co-curator Lithuania: Reflections in Time, Balzekas Mus. Lithuanian Culture, Chgo., 1981-82. One man shows include the Book Nook, Mt. Prospect, Ill., 1969, Humanities Ctr., Elk Grove (Ill.) H.S., 1971, Bird of Paradise, Chgo., 1983-89, Ontario (Wis.) Libr., 1990-96; group exhibits include Gallery 200, DeKalb, Ill., 1976, Neptune Hall exhibits, No. Ill. U., 1976, North Wing Sculpture Gallery, Sch. of Art Inst. Chgo., 1981, Randolph St. Gallery, Chgo., 1980, 81, West Hubbard Gallery, Chgo., 1981, Body Politic Theater Gallery, Chgo., 1982, The Magic Show, Santa Barbara, Calif., 1982, Columbus Dr. Gallery, Sch. of Art Inst. Chgo., 1982, Excalibur, Chgo., 1988, Postal Workers' Union, Caspar, Wyo., 1989, Brick City Ctr. for the Arts, Ocala, Fla., 1997, Cooper Seeman Fine Art, N.Y.C., 1988-93 (now Laurie Seeman Fine Art), Willoughby Tower gallery, Chgo., 1980-81, Inn at Wildcat Mountain, 1996—, Assn. Visual Artists Mem. Exhibits, Chattanooga, 1997—, Austin-Palmer Galleries, Chattanooga, 1998, Invitational Mail and Book Art Exhibit, Noriguchi City, Japan, 1984, Mail Art, Centre Georges Pompidou, Paris, 1985, Decalomania Gallery, Chgo., 1980, others; mural Euterpe, Muse of Lyric Poetry installed Elk Grove H.S., 1972, Episcopal Found., U. Ill., Champaign, 1973, North Wing Sculpture Gallery, Sch. of Art Inst. Chgo., 1981, others; works include church altarpieces at St. Mary of the Lake, Chgo., St. Joseph's Ch., Kendall, Wis., Our Lady of the Springs, Ocala, Fla.; author: Classical Sonnets with Lyric Poems, 1971-97, Postmodern Essays on Religion and Society, 1981-93. Grantee Ill. Arts. Coun., Chgo. Cmty. Trust, 1981-82. Mem. SAR, Fraunces Tavern Mus. (N.Y.), Hunter Mus. (Chattanooga), Blue Army of Fatima (Washington, N.J.). Avocations: writing, opera, horseback riding. Home: 2007 Merlin Dr Chattanooga TN 37421-2600

SWANGER, STERLING ORVILLE, appliance manufacturing company executive; b. Jan. 5, 1922; s. Orville M. and Alma Louise Swanger; m. Maxine O. Hindman, July 2, 1950; 1 child Eric. BS, Iowa State U., 1947; postgrad., U. Va., 1965. Registered profl. engr., Iowa. Indsl. engr. Maytag Co., Newton, Iowa, 1947—52, methods engr., 1952—54, asst. chief methods engr., 1954—57, chief methods engr., 1957—68, mgr. prodn. engring., 1968—71, mgr. engring., 1971—74, asst. v.p. mfg., 1974—75, v.p. mfg., 1975—86, sr. v.p. and chief mkg. officer, 1986—87, also dir., cons., 1987—. Mem. Newton Pllanning and Zoning Commn., 1966—70; trustee Newton Skiff Hosp., 1970—85, chmn., 1982—85; trustee Progress Industries, 1987—90, chmn., 1991. With AUS, 1943—46. Mem.: NSPE, A. Ordnance Assn., Am. Mgmt. Assn., Nat. Mgmt. Assn., Iowa Engring. Soc., Newton Country Club, Elks. Republican. Presbyterian.

SWANK, ANNETTE MARIE, software designer; b. Lynn, Mass., Nov. 9, 1953; d. Roland Paterson and Rita Mary (Edwards) S. BSEE and Computer Sci., Vanderbilt U., 1975; postgrad., Pa. State U., 1992—. Lead programmer GE, Phila., 1975-80; system analyst SEI Corp., Wayne, 1980-82; mgr., designer Premier Systems, Inc., 1982-85, dir., 1985-88, tech. advisor, 1988-90, tech. architect, 1990-92, Funds Assocs. Ltd., Wayne, 1992-99; sr. bus. analyst First Data Investor Svcs. Group, Berwyn, Pa., 1999; prin. bus. analyst PFPC Global Fund Svcs., 1999-2000, v.p., mng. dir. SURPAS bus. unit, 2000—. Designer: (programming lang. and data dictionary) Vision, 1985. Treas. Master Singers, Plymouth Meeting, Pa., 1987-88. Mem. Assn. for Computing Machinery, Gamma Phi Beta (com. chmn. alumna Phila. 1986-87). Avocations: singing, dancing, bowling, bridge, wine tasting. Home: 136 Pinecrest Ln King Of Prussia PA 19406-2368 Office: PFPC Global Fund Svcs 100 Berwyn Park Berwyn PA 19312-2701

SWANK, DAMON RAYNARD, lawyer; b. Boulder, Colo., Sept. 14, 1940; s. Raynard Coe and Ethel Louise (Mershon) S.; m. Susan M. Heigl, June 13, 1970; children: Stephen Carl, Lauren Marie. BA, Coll. of Wooster, 1962; JD, U. Calif., Berkeley, 1965. Bar: Calif. 1965, U.S. Dist. Ct. (no. dist.) Calif. 1965, U.S. Ct. Appeals (9th cir.) 1965, U.S. Dist. Ct. (cen. dist.) Calif. 1969, Minn. 1977. Dep. pub. defender Pub. Defender Office County of Los Angeles, L.A., 1965-84; pvt. practice Long Beach, Calif., 1984—. Judge pro tem L.A. Superior Ct., 1996—. Mem. Long Beach Bar Assn. (bd. govs. 1993-94). Avocation: offshore sailing. Office: 7 Chaparral Ln Rancho Palos Verdes CA 90275-5167 E-mail: damonswank@cox.com.

SWANK, WILLIAM GEORGE, historian, writer; b. Chgo., June 17, 1940; s. William George and Estelle Jensen Swank; m. Jeri Lynne Bessie; 1 child William Corey ; children: Eric William, Karen Estelle. BS, San Diego State Coll., 1962. Cert. tchr. c.c. Calif. . Supervising probation officer County of San Diego, San Diego, 1963—94; historian, lectr., writer, 1994—. Baseball historian San Diego Hall of Champions, 1988—2003, San Diego Hist. Soc., 1994—2003; chmn. Gavy Cravath Hall of Fame Com., Escondido, 1995—2003; cons. Calif. Hist. Soc., San Francisco, 1999—2003, Pacific Coast League, Colorado Springs, 2001—03. Editor: (newsletter) Echoes from Lane Field, 1995; author: (book) The Lane Field Padres (Two Volumes), 1997, (newspaper) San Diego Union-Tribune, 1998, (book) Echoes from Lane Field, 1999 (San Diego Press Club and San Diego Book Awards, 1999), (newspaper) Tombstone Independent, 2000, (program) Ted Williams Museum, 2000; contbr. Coach youth soccer, baseball, basketball, San Diego, 1975—93; judge Greater San Diego Science and Engring. Fair, 1992—2003. Officer candidate USMC, 1962. Mem.: Soc. for Am. Baseball Rsch. (mem. dead ball era com. 1998—2003), Pacific Coast League Hist. Soc. (coord.San Diego reunion 1995—2003). Avocations: scale model of Lane Field, baseball scrapbooks, photo albums. Home: 3474 Via Beltran San Diego CA 92117-5729

SWANKIN, DAVID ARNOLD, lawyer, consumer advocate; b. Boston, Jan. 18, 1934; s. Max and Anne (Rotefsky) S.; m. Jeanne Phyllis Herrick; 1 dau., Sheryl. AB, Brandeis U., 1954; MS, U. Wis., 1957; JD, George Washington U., 1962. Mgmt. intern U.S. Dept. Labor, Washington, 1957-60, spl. asst. to asst. sec. labor, 1961-63, dep. asst. sec. labor, 1967; dir. Bur. Labor Standards, 1967-68; exec. sec. Pres.'s Consumer Adv. Council, Washington, 1964; exec. dir. Pres's Com. on Consumer Interests, 1965-66; Washington rep. Consumer's Union, 1969-71; exec. dir. Consumer Interests Found., 1971-73; sr. partner Swankin & Turner, 1973—. Pres. Citizen Advocacy Ctr. 1994—; cons. U.S. Dept. Labor; pres. Citizen Advocacy Ctr., 1994—. Mem. president's coun. Brandeis U., 1968-69; mem. PEW Health Profls. Commn., 1997-98. Served with AUS., 1954-56. Recipient Jump award U.S. Govt., 1969 Home: 300 N Cherry St Falls Church VA 22046-3522 Office: 1400 16th St NW Washington DC 20036-2217 Business E-Mail: davidswankin@cacenter.org.

SWANN, BARBARA, lawyer; b. N.Y., Sept. 15, 1950; d. George Arthur. BA summa cum laude, Montclair State U., 1988; JD, Rutgers Law, 1992. Bar: N.J. 1992, D.C. 1994, N.Y. 1995, U.S. Dist. Ct. N.J. 1992, U.S. Ct. Appeals (3rd cir.) 1994, U.S. Dist. Ct. N.Y. 1996, Calif. 2000. Correspondent The Associate Press, Newark, 1974-80; reporter, bureau chief The Hudson Dispatch, Union City, 1973-80; editorial page editor The Paterson (N.J.) News, 1980-81; v.p., acct. supr. Gerald Freeman, Inc., Clifton, N.J., 1981-86; pres. LePore Assoc., Inc., West Caldwell, 1986-89; law clk. to Hon. Robert N. Wilentz N.J. Supreme Ct., 1992-93; law clk. to Hon. Leonard I. Garth U.S. Ct. Appeals (3rd cir.), 1993-94; assoc. Cahill, Gordon & Reindel, N.Y., 1994-97; liaison Republic of Ga. ABA Cen. and East European Law Initiative, 1997-98, media law specialist, 1998-2000; exec. dir. Internat. Sr. Lawyers Project, N.Y.C., 2000—. Editor-in-chief: Rutgers Computer & Technology Law Jour., 1991-92. Founding trustee Ctr. for Children's Advocacy, Riverdale, N.J. 1994—. Mem. ABA, Assn. of the Bar of the City of New York, N.J. State Bar Assn., N.Y. County Lawyers' Assn. Am. Inn of Ct., D.C. Bar Assn., State Bar Calif. E-mail: swann2002@email.msn.com.

SWANN, BRIAN, writer, humanities educator; b. Wallsend, Northumberland, Eng., Aug. 13, 1940; came to U.S., 1963, naturalized, 1980; s. Stanley Frank and Lilyan Mary (Booth) S.; m. Roberta Metz. BA, Queens Coll., Cambridge U., 1962, MA, 1965; PhD, Princeton U., 1970. Instr. Princeton U., 1964-65, lectr., 1968-70, asst. prof., 1970-72; instr. Rutgers U., 1965-66; asst. prof. humanities Cooper Union for Advancement Sci. and Art, N.Y.C., 1972-75, assoc. prof., 1975-80, prof., 1980—, acting dean, 1990-91. Dir. Bennington Writing Workshops, 1988-91. Author: (poetry) The Middle of the Journey, 1982, Song of The Sky: Versions of Native American Song-Poems, 1993, Wearing the Morning Star: Native American Song-Poems, 1996, (children's books) A Basket Full of White Eggs, 1988, The House With No Door, 1998, other books of fiction, translations: editor: Smoothing The Ground: Essays of Native American Oral Literature, 1983; (with Arnold Krupat) Recovering the Word, 1987, I Tell You Now: Autobiographical Essays by Native American Writers, 1987, Coming to Light: Contemporary Translations of the Native American Literatures, 1992, (with Krupat) Here First: Autobiographical Essays by Contemporary Native American Writers, 2000; editor The Smithsonian Series of Essays on Native American Literatures, 1990-98. NEA fellow, 1981; Creative Arts in Pub. Service grantee, 1982. Office: Cooper Union Adv Sci & Art Faculty Humanities & Social Sci Cooper Sq New York NY 10003

SWANN, ERIC JERROD, professional football player; b. Pinehurst, N.C., Aug. 16, 1970; Student, Wake Tech. Coll. Defensive tackle Ariz. Cardinals, Phoenix, 1991—. Selected to Pro Bowl, 1995. Office: Arizona Cardinals PO Box 888 Phoenix AZ 85001-0888

SWANN, LOIS LORRAINE, writer, editor, educator; b. N.Y.C., Nov. 17, 1944; d. Peter J. and Edith M. (De Rose) Riso; m. Terrence Garth Swann, Aug. 15, 1964 (div. 1979); children: Peter Burgess, Polly Lorraine Swann; m. Kenneth E. Arndt, Sept. 3, 1988. BA, Marquette U., 1966. Editor Peat, Marwick, Mitchell & Co., N.Y.C., 1980-81; publs. cons. Mfrs. Hanover Trust, 1981-88. Cons. bus. writing, 1988—; tchr. West H.E.L.P., Mt. Vernon, N.Y., 1991; tchr. nontraditional age students of writing; founder, reader Calliope's Chamber, 1995—. Author: (novels) The Mists of Manittoo, 1976 (Ohiona Libr. award for 1st novel 1976), Torn Covenants, 1981; contbr. articles to mags. Election inspector Dem. Party, Bronxville, N.Y., 1990—. Mem. Authors Guild, poets and writers. Avocations: gardening, interior design. Home and Office: 168 Ellison Ave Bronxville NY 10708-2725

SWANN, MELISSA LYNNE, psychologist; b. Albuquerque, Aug. 25, 1962; d. Jimmie Gleen and Medgie (Nix) Swann. AA, Hinds C.C., Raymond, Miss., 1986; BA, Belhaven Coll., Jackson, Miss., 1989; MEd, Miss. Coll., Clinton, 1992; PhD, Southwest U., Kenner, La., 2000. Cert. emergency med. technician; lic. psychometrist. Youth counselor Cath. Charities, Jackson, 1991-92; psychologist Miss. State Hosp., Whitfield, 1992—. With Miss. Air N.G., 1985—. Named to Outstanding Young Women of Am., 1997. Mem. VFW, Am. Legion. Office: Miss State Hosp Psychology Dept Whitfield MS 39193

SWANN, NAT HENDERSON, JR. physician; b. Danville, Va., Nov. 2, 1927; s. Nat Henderson, Sr. and Mary Stokes S.; m. Sarah Hayes, Aug. 7, 1952; children: Nat H. III, Wayland Hayes. AB in Chemistry, U. N.C., 1950, MD, 1954. Fellow Royal Soc. Medicine/London. Resident in internal medicine Med. Coll., Va., 1954-56, Boston VA Hosp., 1956-57, Cleve. VA (Crile) Hosp., 1957-58; specialist internal medicine Chattanooga, 1958—. Med. dir. Chattem, Inc., Chattanooga, 1960—; cons. rheumatic heart clin. Children's Hosp., Chattanooga, 1959-63; chief of staff Downtown Gen. Hosp., Chattanooga, 1986-90. Contbr. articles to profl. jours. Dir. Physician's Giving, United Way, Chattanooga, 1980; mem. Chattanooga Met. Coun., 1961; bd. spkr. Air Pollution Control Bd., Chattanooga, 1962; bd. dirs. The Salvation Army. With U.S. Army Med. Corps, 1946-47. Recipient Disting. Achievement award Am. Heart Assn. Fellow: Royal Soc. Medicine, Am. Coll. Angiology, Am. Coll. Chest Physicians (assoc.); mem.: AMA, Am. Cardiology, ACP, Athenians Club (Chattanooga), Torch Club (Chattanooga), Mountain City Club (bd. dir.), Rotary (bd. dir.). Avocations: short story writer, golf, tennis. Home: 412 Brady Point Rd Signal Mountain TN 37377-2206 E-mail: natswann@mindspring.com.

SWANNER, BARBARA MELSON, artist; b. Balt., Aug. 23, 1951; d. Everett and Mary M.; m. William C. Swanner, Jr., July 1, 1978; 1 child, Rebecca. BS, U. Md., 1976; BFA, Coll. Art and Design, Detroit, 1999. Trust officer, stock trader Md. Nat. Bank, Balt., 1971-73, Equitable Trust Co., Balt., 1978-79; corp. cash mgr. Alexander & Alexander, Towson, Md., 1979-81; program mgr. Bus. Enterprise Devel. Ctr., Troy, Mich., 1994-95; artist, 1996-99. Artist ink wash drawing (Young Artist of Yr. award, Best of Show 1969), Hallmark card (Best Graphic Divsn. 1969). Chmn. bd. Furniture Resource Ctr., Pontiac, Mich., 1993-95; treas. Coun. Troy Homeowners, 1993-95; co-chair Kaleidoscope and class mother Cranbrook Sch., Bloomfield Hills, Mich., 1989-90; bd. dirs. Windridge Pk. Homeowner's Assn., Troy, 1993-98. Recipient Homeowner Assn. Vol. of Yr. award Coun. Troy Homeowner Assns., 1995, Golden Rule Cert. of Appreciation, J.C. Penney, 1995. Mem. Mich. Silversmiths Guild, Detroit Artist Market, Oakland County Master Gardener Soc. Republican. Lutheran. Avocations: golf, reading, gardening.

SWANSBOURNE, CLIVE RICHARD, music educator, musician; b. Worthing, Sussex, Eng., Sept. 17, 1954; s. John Francis Causton and Jean Ailsa Swansbourne; m. Lydia Orias Swansbourne, Apr. 1979 (div. 1981); m. Sophie Elizabeth Westphal, June 30, 1995. MusB, Royal Coll. Music, London, 1976; D in Musical Arts, Yale U., 1982. Artist in residence Mo. So. State Coll., Joplin, Mo., 1986—88; assoc. prof. piano Idaho State U., Pocatello, 1990—99; coord. piano studies Sam Houston State U., Huntsville, Tex., 1999—. Concert pianist Western Arts Fedn., 1992—95, over 500 concerts nationwide, 1982—; instr. clinics and master classes over 40 U.S. univs. and colls. Performer: CD Piano Recital, 1999; contbr. articles to profl. jours.; recital: Concerts Atlantiques, 1990. Fellow, Idaho Commn. Arts, 2000; grantee, Sam Houston State U., 2002. Mem.: Music Tchrs. Nat. Assn. Achievements include U.S. city premiere of Tippett's Fourth Sonata; recitals in New York, London, Frankfurt, Geneva, Boston, Chicago, San Francisco, L.A., Cheltenham International Festival and more. Avocations: literature, theater , tennis.

SWANSBURG, RUSSELL CHESTER, medical administrator educator; b. Cambridge, Mass., Aug. 6, 1928; s. William W. and Mary A. (Pierce) S.; m. Laurel Clark, Sept. 1951; children: Philip Wayne, Michael Gary, Richard Jeffrey. Diploma, N.S. Hosp. Sch. Nursing, 1950; BSN, Western Res. U., 1952; MA in Nursing Edn., Columbia U., 1961; PhD, U. Miss., 1984. CNAA. Asst. adminstr. U. of S. Ala. Med. Ctr., Mobile; v.p. U. South Ala.; prof. Auburn U., Montgomery, Ala., Med. Coll. of Ga., Augusta. Mil. cons. USAF Surgeon Gen., 1972; sr. med. svc. cons., 1973-76; nurse cons. VA Med. Ctr., Tuskegee, Ala., 1987-88; mem. editl. adv. bd. Nursing Adminstrn. Manual. Author: Team Nursing: A Programmed Learning Experience, 1968, Inservice Education, 1968, The Measurement of Vital Signs, 1970, The Team Plan, 1971, Management of Patient Care Services, 1976, Strategic Career Planning and Development, 1984, The Nurse Manager's Guide to Financial Management, 1988, Management and Leadership for Nurse Managers, 1990 (Book of Yr. Selection, Am. Jour. Nursing 1990), 3d edit. 2002, Introductory Management and Leadership for Clinical Nurses, 1993, 2d edit., 1999 (Book of the Yr. Selection, Am. Jour. Nursing 1999), Staff Development: A Component of Human Resource Development, 1994, Budgeting and Financial Management for Nurse Managers, 1997, (audiovisual course) Nurses & Patients: An Introduction to Nursing Management, 1980; contbr. articles to profl. publs. Bd. dirs. Air Force Village Found., Alzheimer's Care and Research Found. Col. USAF, 1956-76. Decorated Air medal with oak leaf clusters, Legion of Merit; recipient award for outstanding work in hosp. adminstrn. Ala. State Nurses' Assn., 1985, Outstanding Nursing Svc. Adminstrn. award, 1981, Outstanding Nurse Rschr. 1984, Disting. Svc. award Air Force Village Found., 1999. Fellow AONE, Ala. Orgn. Nurse Exec's. (past state pres.); mem. Council Grad. Edn. Adminstrn. in Nursing (sec.), Ala. Acad. Sci., Sigma Xi, Phi Kappa Phi, Sigma Theta Tau. Home and Office: 4917 Ravenswood Dr Apt 1711 San Antonio TX 78227-4356

SWANSEN, DONNA MALONEY, landscape designer, consultant; b. Green Bay, Wis., July 8, 1931; d. Arthur Anthony and Ella Marie Rose (Warner) Maloney; m. Samuel Theodore Swansen, June 27, 1959; children: Jessica Swansen Bonelli, Theodor Arthur Swansen, Christopher Currie Swansen. AS in Integrated Liberal Studies, U. Wis., 1956; AS in Landscape Design, Temple U., 1982. Bridal cons. Richard W. Burnham's, Green Bay, 1951-54, 57-58; asst. buyer Shreve Crump & Low, Boston, 1958-59; buyer Harry S. Manchester, Madison, Wis., 1959-62; ptnr. Corson Borie & Swansen, Ambler, Pa., 1976, Swansen & Borie, Ambler, 1977-82; owner, operator Donna Swansen/Design, 1983—. V.p. Energy Islands Internat. Inc., East Troy, Wis., 1963-94. Editor: Internat. Directory Landscape Designers, 1993; judge Del. Valley Coll., 2002, Assn. of Profl. Landscape Design, 2002. Co-founder Friends of Rising Sun, Ambler, Ambler Area Arts Alliance, 1975—76; founder, 1st pres. Plant Ambler, 1973—83, 1997—; chair Do It, Dig It exhibit Temple U. , 1987; judge Temple U., 2002, Bucks County Beautiful Flowers Show, 2002; Dem. candidate for judge elections, 1988; mem. Gwynedd (Pa.) Monthly Meeting of Friends (Quakers), 1974—; mem. search com. for chair dept. landscape arch. and horticulture Temple U., 1987, mem. curriculum rev. com., 1993; mem. adv. com. Green Bay Bot. Garden, 1993—, Del. Valley Coll., Doylestown, Pa., 2000—, mem. adv. bd., 2000—. Recipient Key to the Borough, Borough of Ambler, 1972; winner urban beautification project Roadside Coun. Am., Ambler, 1975, Athena award Wissahickon Valley C. of C., 1996. Mem. Assn. Profl. Landscape Designers (cert., co-founder, 1st pres. 1989-91, bd. dirs. 1989-95, 1st pres. Landscape Design Network Phila. 1978-85, Distinction award 1996, judge internat. design competition 2002), Sigma Lambda Alpha. Democrat. Avocations: putting people and plants together, encouraging women, travel, gardening. Home and Office: 221 Morris Rd Ambler PA 19002-5202 E-mail: donna@donnaswansendesign.com

SWANSEN, SAMUEL THEODORE, lawyer; b. Milw., June 6, 1937; s. Theodore Lawrence and Clarinda Dingwall (Crittenden) S.; m. Donna Rae Elizabeth Maloney, June 27, 1959; children: Jessica Swansen Bonelli, Theodor Arthur, Christopher Currie. AB, Dartmouth Coll., 1959; LLB, U. Wis., 1962. Bar: Wis. 1962, Pa. 1964, U.S. Supreme Ct. 1969, accredited estate planner: Nat. Assn. Estate Planners & Couns. 1995. Law clk. to presiding justice Wis. Supreme Ct., Madison, 1962-63; assoc. Dechert, Price & Rhoads, Phila., 1963-68, 70-73, ptnr., 1973-93; asst. dist. atty. City of Phila. Dist. Atty.'s Office, 1968-70, chief frauds div., 1969; pvt. practice Phila., 1963—, Blue Bell, Pa., 1994—. Adj. prof. law Temple U., Phila., 1970-80; lectr. Pa. Bar Inst., Nat. Bus. Inst., Ctr. Profl. Edn., 1985—. Editor, author U. Wis. Law Rev., 1960-62. Corp. mem. Anna T. Jeanes Found., Fox Chase, Phila, 1985—93, Associated Svcs. for the Blind, Phila, 1974—91, Bach Festival of Phila., 1989—, pres., 1993—97; founding dir. Global Bach Cmty., 2000—, pres., 2001—, 2001—; bd. dirs. Friends Rehab. Program, Inc., Phila., 1966—73, 1985—, Franklin Found., Phila., 1969—; v.p., sec., bd. dirs. Foulkeways at Gwynedd, 1979—, pres., 1986—97; chmn. bd. dirs. Friends Life Care at Home, Inc., 1990—, bd. dirs., 1985—, Friends Retirement Concepts, Inc., Gwynedd, sec. bd. dirs., 1985—96; hon. bd. dirs. Friends Neighborhood Guild, Greater Phila. Fedn. Settlements; dir., sec. Energy Islands Internat., Inc., 1963—; mem. Nat. Network of Estate Planning Attys., 1993—; violinist, trombonist North Penn Symphony Orch., 1977—; mem. Gwynedd Monthly Meeting of Friends, 1974—. Fellow Esperti Peterson Inst. Wealth Strategies Planning, 1996—. Mem. ABA, Pa. Bar Assn., Phila. Bar Assn., Dartmouth Club Phila., Delta Upsilon, Phi Delta Phi. Republican. Mem. Soc. Of Friends. Home: 221 Morris Rd Ambler PA 19002-5202 Office: 640 Sentry Pky Ste 104 Blue Bell PA 19422-2317 E-mail: sam@samswansen.com.

SWANSON, ARTHUR DEAN, lawyer; b. Onida, S.D., Apr. 19, 1934; s. Obert W. and Mary I. (Barnum) S.; m. Paula Swanson, Aug. 22, 1965 (div. Feb. 1984); children: Shelby, Dean, Sherry; m. Ann Swanson, Aug. 21, 1989. BA, Wash. State U., 1956; JD, U. Wash., 1963. Bar: Wash. 1963. Dep. prosecutor King County, Seattle, 1964-65; ct. commr. Renton and Issaquah Dist. Cts., Wash., 1966-68; pvt. practice law Renton, 1965—. Lectr. various orgns.; former counsel Wash. State Law Enforcement Assn., Wash. State Dep. Sheriff's Assn. Served with Fin. Corps, U.S. Army, 1956-58. Named one of Best Lawyers Am., 1991-92, 93-94, 95-96, 97-98, 99-2000, 2001—. Fellow Am. Coll. Trial Lawyers; mem. Wash. State Bar Assn. (past sec. trial sect.), Seattle-King County Bar Assn. (bd. trustees 1977-80), Assn. Trial Lawyers Am., Wash. State Trial Lawyers Assn. (past pres.), Am. Bd. Trial Advs. (bd. dirs., pres. Wash. state chpt. 1995-96), Damage Attys. Roundtable (pres. 1998-99). Democrat. Avocation: tennis. Office: 4512 Talbot Rd S Renton WA 98055-6216 E-mail: adswanson@aol.com.

SWANSON, AUGUST GEORGE, physician, retired association executive; b. Kearney, Nebr., Aug. 25, 1925; s. Oscar Valderman and Elnora Wilhelmina Emma (Block) Swanson; m. Ellyn Constance Weinel, June 28, 1947; children: Eric, Rebecca, Margaret, Emilie, Jennifer, August. BA, Westminster Coll., Fulton, Mo., 1951; MD, Harvard U., 1949; DSc (hon.) , U. Nebr., 1979. Intern King County Hosp., Seattle, 1949—50; resident in internal medicine U. Wash. Affiliated Hosp., 1953—55, neurology, 1955—57; resident in neurology Boston City Hosp., 1958; dir. pediatric neurology, then dir. divsn. neurology U. Wash. Med. Sch., Seattle, 1958—67, assoc. dean acad. affairs, 1967—71; v.p. acad. affairs Assn. Am. Med. Colls., Washington, 1971—89, v.p. grad. med. edn., exec. dir. nat. resident matching program, 1989—91; ret., 1991. Vis. fellow physiology Oxford (Eng.) U., 1963—64; cons. in field. Contbr. articles to profl. jours. With USNR, 1943—46, with USNR, 1950—53. Recipient Abraham Flexner award for distinguished svc. to medical edn., Assn. of Am. Medical Coll., 1992; scholar Markle scholar medicine, 1959—64. Mem.: Am. Neurol. Assn., Inst. Medicine NAS. Achievements include research in brain function, physician edn., med. manpower. Home: 3146 Portage Bay Pl E Apt H Seattle WA 98102-3847 E-mail: gusellyn@home.com.

SWANSON, BARRY ERNEST, securities company executive; b. Buffalo, June 23, 1940; BS, St. Lawrence U., 1962; lang. cert., U. Heidelberg, 1969. Registered investor-advisor; CFP. V.p. Intervest Internat. Corp., Heidelberg, Germany, 1980-86; pres., chief exec. officer Integrated FIn. Planning Corp., 1986—. Contbr. articles to newspapers and mags. Lt. col. U.S. Army. Mem. NAACP Europe, Fin. Planning Assn. Europe (pres. 1991-92), Internat. Bd. Cert. Fin. Planners (cons. 1988—, cert.), Heidelberg Internat. Ski Club (pres. 1974-76), Heidelberg Internat. Toastmasters Club (pres. 1990-91), Am./German Bus. Club (pres. 1997—). Home: 510 Postal Det Unit 29234 Box 96 APO AE 09102 Office: Integrated Fin Planning Svc Karl Strasse 20 69117 Heidelberg Germany

SWANSON, CAROLYN RAE, news reporter, counselor; b. Riverton, Wyo., Nov. 10, 1937; d. Leonard Rae Swanson and Ruby Francis Mulholland Laliberte; m. William Glenn (dec. 1959); children: Donald, Rocky, Laurel; m. Larry T. Hess, Nov. 23, 1962; children: Lance Hess, Aaron Hess. AA, West Valley Coll., Saratoga, Calif., 1970; BA, San Jose State U., 1975. Cert. substance abuse counselor. Counselor, program dir. Carson Regional Coun., Carson City, Nev., 1977-82; Women's Internat. News Gathering Svc. news reporter Radio for Peace Internat., Costa Rica, 1988-89; reporter Nevada City, Calif., 1990-97; dir. Innovative Voices, Paradise, 1990—. Mem. adv. bd. UN U. of Peace, Costa Rica, 1988-89; bd. dirs. No. Nev. Lang. Bank, 1978-80; cons. Intertribal Coun., Nev.-No. Calif., 1977-80; mem. exec. bd. Grandparent State Coun., Calif., 1992-96. Coord. shelter for battered women, Carson City, 1979; U.S. del. Soviet-Am. dialog, Washington, 1988; N.Am. del. Peace Conf., Costa Rica, 1989; leader Fellowship of Reconciliation, Chico-Paradise area, 1991-92; Butte County contact Green Party, 1991—; Humboldt County coord. Postcorporate World, 1999—. Recipient Promoting Arts award Villa Montalvo Theatre, Saratoga, Calif., 1975, award Nat. Inst. on Drug Abuse, Utah, 1978. Avocations: reading, travel, hiking, theatre, writing. Home: 2255 Alliance Rd Apt 2 Arcata CA 95521-5180

SWANSON, CHERYL ANN, small business owner, nurse; b. L.A., Feb. 17, 1967; d. Donald Herbert Cox and Mary Rosalie (Bowlds) Hook; m. Timothy Howard Swanson, Feb. 28, 1982 (div. Sept. 1987); 1 child, Christopher Michael. BSN magna cum laude, U. Ariz., 1995. RN, Ariz.; CCRN. Sales mgr. Double M Gem, Pocatello, Idaho, 1987-89, Desert Gem, Tucson, 1990-93; owner, mgr. AAA Loan & Jewelry, 1993—; critical care nurse St. Joseph's Hosp., 1995. Scholar Idaho State U., 1988-89, M.B. and C.J. O'Connel scholar U. Ariz., 1995. Mem. ANA, Nat. League for Nursing, Golden Key, Sigma Theta Tau, Phi Kappa Phi. Democrat. Roman Catholic. Avocations: travel, writing, reading. Office: AAA Loan & Jewelry 1902 S Craycroft Rd Tucson AZ 85711-6621

SWANSON, DAVID ELMER, editor; b. June 26, 1940; married; three children. Student, Bethel Coll., 1958-61; BS in Journalism, U. Colo., 1968. Asst. editor The Typographical Jour., 1968-71; head sect. comm. Mayo Clinic, Rochester, Minn., 1971-85, editor Mayovox, 1971-77, dir. News Media Rels., 1977-81, editor The Mayo Alumnus, 1978-82, mem. Mayo Med. Ventures, 1985—2001, founding mng. editor Mayo Clinic Health Letter, 1983-88, 90-93, sr. editor, 1988-93; editl. dir. Mayo Clinic Family Health Book, 1990-96; editor-at-large Mayo Clinic, Rochester, Minn., 1993-2001; editor Mayo Clinic Complete Book of Pregnancy and Baby's First Year, 1994—. Speaker, panelist in field; participant in numerous continuing edn./profl. confs. and workshops. Mng. editor: Mayo Clinic on Arthritis, Mayo Clinic Guide to Self-Care, 3d edit., Mayo Clinic Heart Book, 2d edit., May Roots: Profiling the Origins of Mayo Clinic, Perspectives on Mayo: Pen and Ink Renderings of the Mayo Heritage, Mayo Clinic on Healthy Weight, Mayo Clinic on Healthy Aging. Pres. United Way Olmsted County, 1987, Rochester Covenant Ch., chair congregation, 1999. U.S. Army Med. Svc. Corps, 1962-64; bd. dirs. Am. Cancer Soc., Olmsted County chpt. Youth Employment Project, Rochester. Named Outstanding Grad. in Journalism, U. Colo., Soc. Profl. Journalists, Paul Harris fellow Rotary Found. Internat. Mem. Nat. Assn. Sci. Writers, Am. Med. Writers Assn., Soc. Profl. Journalists, Internat. Assn. Bus. Communicators (accredited, Gold Quill award Mayovox Readership Survey, Dist. Four Award of Excellence, the Mayo Alumnus, Northstar chpt.), Rotary (Rochester), Rochester Area C. of C., Toastmaster Internat. E-mail: deswanson@charter.net.

SWANSON, DAVID HEATH, agricultural company executive; b. Aurora, Ill., Nov. 3, 1942; s. Neil H. and Helen J. (McKendry) S.; m. Carolyn Breitinger; children: Benjamin Heath, Matthew Banford. BA, Harvard U., 1964; MA, U. Chgo., 1969. Account exec. 1st Nat. Bank Chgo., 1967-69; dep. mgr. Brown Bros. Harriman & Co., N.Y.C., 1969-72; treas. Borden, Inc. Internat., 1972-75; v.p., treas. Continental Grain Co., 1975-77, v.p., CFO, 1977-79, gen. mgr. European div., 1979-81, exec. v.p. and gen. mgr. World Grain div., 1981-83, corp. sr. v.p., chief fin. and adminstrv. officer, 1983-86, group pres., 1985-86; pres., CEO Cen. Soya, Ft. Wayne, Ind., 1986-93; chmn., CEO Explorer Nutrition Group, N.Y.C., 1994-96; pres., CEO, Countrymark, Inc., Indpls., 1996-98. Mem. adv. bd. U.S. Export-Import Bank, 1985-86; bd. dirs. Fiduciary Trust Internat., Conrail. Founding bd. dirs. Internat. Policy Coun. on Agr. and Trade; mem. adv. bd. Purdue U. Agr. Sch.; mem. Gov.'s Econ. Devel. Ind. Bd.; bd. govs. Exec. Coun. on Fgn. Diplomats and U.S. Agr. Libr.; gov. Found. for U.S. Constn. Mem. Coun. Fgn. Rels., Nat. Assn. Mfrs. (bd. dirs.), Ind. C. of C. (bd. dirs.), Am. Alpine Club (bd. dirs.), Links Club, Racquet and Tennis Club, Explorers Club (bd. dirs., sec., pres.), Millbrook Golf and Tennis. Republican. Congregationalist. Office: PO Box 609 Bangall NY 12506-0609 also: PO Box 1418 Millbrook NY 12545

SWANSON, DAVID H(ENRY), consultant, retired economist, educator; b. Anoka, Minn., Nov. 1, 1930; s. Henry Otto and Louise Isabell (Holiday) S.; m. Suzanne Nash, Jan. 19, 1952 (dec. Sept. 1990); children: Matthew David, Christopher James; m. Joanne Perkins, Feb. 1, 1991. BA, St. Cloud State U., 1953; MA, U. Minn., 1955; PhD, Iowa State U., 1987. CPCU. Econ. area devel. dept. No. State Power Co., Mpls., 1955-56, staff asst., v.p. sales, 1956-57, economist indsl. devel. dept., 1957-63; dir. area devel. dept. Iowa So. Utilities Co., Centerville, 1963-67, dir. econ. R&D, 1967-70; dir. New Orleans Econ. Devel. Coun., 1970-72; divsn. mgr. Kaiser Aetna Tex., New Orleans, 1972-73; dir. corp. rsch. United Svcs. Automobile Assn., San Antonio, 1973-76; pres. Lantern Corp., 1974-79; adminstr. bus. devel. State of Wis., Madison, 1976-78; dir. Ctr. Indsl. Rsch. and Svc. Iowa State U., Ames, 1978-89, mem. mktg. faculty Coll. Bus. Adminstrn., 1979-85; prin. rshch assoc., econ. devel. Insts. Ga. Insts. Tech., Atlanta, 1996-99, ret. Ames, 1999. Cons. Indsl. Modernization and Univ. Ext., Mexico, 1997—2000, Tech. Tng. and Indsl. Ext., Poland, 1998—2000, Mendes England & Assocs. Polish Project, 1998—2000; dir. Iowa Devel. Commn., 1982—83; mem. adv. bd. Iowa Venture Capital Fund, 1985—88; dir. Applied Strategies Internat. Ltd., 1983—88; dir. econ. devel. lab. Ga. Inst. Tech., Atlanta, 1989—93; mem. adv. bd. Nat. Tech. Transfer Ctr, 1992—96; exec. on loan Nat. Inst. Stds. and Tech., 1993—96; chmn. owa Curriculum Assistance Sys., 1984—85; cons. Ctr. for Indsl. Rsch., Iowa State U., 1998—2001; award evaluator Fed. Lab. Consortium, 1999—. Mem. Iowa Airport Planning Coun., 1968-70; mem. adv. coun. Office Comprehensive Health Planning, 1967-70; mem. adv. coun. Ctr. Indsl. Rsch. and Svc., 1967-70, New Orleans Met. Area Com., 1972-73; mem. Iowa Dist. Export Coun., 1977-88; mem. Atlanta Dist. Export Coun., 1989-96; mem. region 7 adv. coun. SBA, 1978-88; dir. Mid-Continent R&D Coun., 1980-84; chmn. Iowa del. White House Conf. on Small Bus., 1980; chmn. Gov.'s Task Force on High Tech., 1982-83; chmn. Iowa High Tech. Coun., 1983-86; mem. adv. com. U. New Orleans, 1971-73; county fin. chmn. Rep. Party, 1966-67; bd. dirs. Greater New Orleans Urban League, 1970-73, Indsl. Policy Coun., 1984-88, Suwanee Crossroads Inc., 2001--; mem. Iowa Gov.'s Export Coun., 1984-89; v.p. Iowa Sister State Friendship Com., 1985-87, pres., 1988; chmn. nat. adv. coun. Fed. Lab. Consortium, 1985-98, chmn., 1993-96, mem., 1985, award reviewer, 1998—; mem. Ga. Tech. Faculty Assembly, 1990-92; pres. Chattahoochee Run Homeowners Assn., 1997-99; mem. planning com. Internat. Tech. Transfer Conf., 1997; mem. adv. com. Ga. Oglethorpe Quality Award, 1997-99, quality examiner, 1998-99, Georgians Mfg., 1997-99; mem. Suwanee Planning and Zoning Bd. Appeals, 1999, chair, 2000—; vice chmn. econ. devel. com. Suwanee Cmty. Betterment Program, 1999-2000; chmn. transition com. Chattahoochee Run Neighborhood Assn., 2000; chair Suwanee Day Festival, 2001-02; bd. dirs. Suwanee Crossroads Inc., 2001--. With USAF, 1951-52. Mem. Am. Indsl. Ext. Alliance (pres. 1992-96, editor 1998-2000), Nat. Assn. Mgmt. Tech. Assistance Ctrs. (pres. 1985, bd. dirs. 1982-86), Tech. Transfer Soc. (bd. dirs. 1984-94, v.p. 1987-90, pres.-elect 1991-92, pres. 1992-93), Oak Ridge Assoc. Univs. (tech. transfer adv. coun. 1992-95), Ga. Fin. Developers Assn., Ga. 2000, Profl. Developers Assn., Nat. Univ. Continuing Edn. Assn., Internat. Coun. Small Bus., Rotary (bd. dirs. 1986-88), Toastmasters (past pres.). Episcopalian. Home: 1415 Chattahoochee Run Dr Suwanee GA 30024-3808 E-mail: swansondh@mindspring.com.

SWANSON, DAVID PAUL, accountant; b. Everett, Wash., Nov. 27, 1945; s. Lloyd E. and Electa A. (McFarland) S.; m. Barbara J. Clough, Feb. 25, 1968 (div. Sept. 1977); children: Elizabeth, Devin; m. Linda Diane Westby, Dec. 4, 1995. BA, Western Wash. U., 1968; MBA, City U., Seattle, 1984. CPA, Wash. With Everett Trust Bank, 1968-70, Security Bank, Portland, Oreg., 1970-71; mgr. Herfys, Seattle, 1971-73, Chuckwagon Restaurant, Seattle, Aberdeen, Wash., 1973-74, Yukon Jacks, Seattle, 1974-76; acctg. specialist Data I/O, Bellevue, Wash., 1977-83; acctg. and tax mgr. Balance Sheet Acctg. Svcs. Inc., Lynnwood, 1983—; pres. Delta Pacific Securites Inc., Everett, 1989—. Instr. City U., 1986-90; treas., bd. dirs. Log C Corp., Everett, 1987—; pres., bd. dirs. Delta Pacific Securities, Everett, 1989—; corp. contr. Black Mountain Escrow, San Diego, 1990—. Bd. dirs. Everett Drug Abuse Coun., 1984-87, J-Bird Ranch, Everett, 1991—; bd. dirs., pres. Evergreen Manor, 1987—; bd. dirs., treas. Big Bros. and Big Sisters, Everett, 1988-92. Mem. Nat. Fedn. Ind. Bus., Inst. Bus. Appraisers, Wash. State Soc. CPA's, Sons of Norway, South Snohomish County Chamber, Northshore C. of C. Avocations: bowling, hiking, reading, travel, biking. Office: Delta Pacific Securities Inc PO Box 2543 Everett WA 98203-0543

SWANSON, DIANE L. finance educator, researcher; b. Manhattan, Kans., Oct. 6, 1950; d. Harold Albin Swanson and Betty Jo Lusby; m. Michael Dale Scott, Aug. 5, 1970 (dec. July 19, 1975); 1 child Christopher William Scott. BS in Mgmt. and Fin., Avila, Kansas City, Mo., 1980; MA in Econs., U. Mo., Kansas City, 1982; PhD in Bus. Adminstrn., U. Pitts., 1996. Instr. econs., interim dir. Inst. Mgmt. Old Dominion U., Norfolk, Va., 1984—86; asst. prof. fin. Hampton (Va.) U., 1987—88; asst. prof. bus. econs. U. Pitts., 1988—89; assoc. prof. mgmt. Robert Morris Coll., 1989—97; assoc. prof. mgmt., faculty fellow Kans. State U., Manhattan, 1997—. Mem. Pres.'s Commn. on Women Kans. State U., 2000—01, mentor Developing Scholars Program for Minority Students, 2000—01; spkr., presenter confs. in field. Contbr. articles to profl. jours.; book rev. editor, consulting editor: Internat. Jour. Orgnl. Analysis, 1994—; contbg. editor: Managing Ego Energy , 1994—. Bd. dirs. Women's Intercultural Network, San Francisco, 1994—, People's Coop., Manhattan, 1998—2000. Recipient nat. award for tchg. excellence, Bell and Howell, 1982, award for entrepreneurial leadership, Advances in Mgmt. Conf., 1996, Best Article on Bus. and Soc. award, Internat. Assn. for Bus. and Soc. and

Calif. Mgmt. Rev., 1999; fellow, David Berg Family Found. in Bus. Ethics, 1994; grantee, Beard Ctr. for Ethics, Duquesne U., 2000, Australian Grad. Sch. Mgmt., 2001—02. Mem.: Nat. Acad. Mgmt. (governing bd. Social Issues in Mgmt. 1998—), Beta Gamma Sigma. Democrat. Avocations: yoga, travel, gardening. Office: Kans State U 101 Calvin Hall Manhattan KS 66506

SWANSON, DOLORES, special education educator, musician; b. Omaha, Sept. 5, 1931; d. Oswald Adelord Albert Hawkins and Mary Margaret Franckewicz; m. Emory Wilkins Bridgeford (div. July 1970), children: Emory Wilkins Jr., Lenora, Joseph, Mary, Irwin, Peter, Jeannette, Patrick, Mark, Gerard; m. Conrad John Swanson, Oct. 15, 1970 (div.). B Music Edn., U. Nev., Reno, 1985. Cert. spl. edn. tchr., generalist resource, Nev. Sec. Natelson's Women's Apparel, Omaha, 1949-50; sec.-stenographer U.S. Army Chem. Corps, Denver, 1952-54; singer, entertainer in midwest and western U.S., 1964-79; co-founder, instr. adult basic edn. Truckee Meadows C.C., Reno, 1989-91, 93-95; tchr. music Washoe County Sch. Dist., 1986-87, tchr. spl. edn., 1991—. Bd. dirs. No. Nev. Bus. Inst., Reno, 1971-72; choir dir. Our Lady of Wisdom Newman Ctr., Reno, 1996—. Recipient Fred and Anna Stadtmuller Meml. award U. Nev., 1987; Command scholar U. Nev., 1983-84. Mem. NEA, Coun. for Exceptional Children, Nev. Tchrs. Assn., Washoe County Tchrs. Assn. Democrat. Roman Catholic. Avocations: sewing, crafting, ceramics, crocheting, gardening. Office: Marvin Picollo Sch 900 Foothill Rd Reno NV 89511-9427

SWANSON, DON RICHARD, university dean; b. L.A., Oct. 10, 1924; s. Harry Windfield and Grace Clara (Sandstrom) S.; m. Patricia Elizabeth Klick, Aug. 22, 1976; children— Douglas Alan, Richard Brian, Judith Ann. BS, Calif. Inst. Tech., 1945; MA, Rice U., 1947; PhD, U. Calif., Berkeley, 1952. Physicist U. Calif. Radiation Lab., Berkeley, 1947-52, Hughes Research and devel. Labs., Culver City, Calif., 1952-55; research scientist TRW, Inc., Canoga Park, 1955-63; prof. Grad. Library Sch., U. Chgo., 1963-92, dean, 1963-72, 77-79, 86-90, prof. bio-sci. coll. divsn. and divsn. humanities, 1992-96, prof. emeritus, 1996—. Mem. Sci. Info. Council, NSF, 1960-65; mem. toxicology info. panel Pres.'s Sci. Advisory Com., 1964-66; mem. library vis. com. Mass. Inst. Tech., 1966-71; mem. com. on sci. and tech. communication Nat. Acad. Scis., 1966-69 Editor: The Intellectual Founds. of Library Education, 1965, The Role of Libraries in the Growth of Knowledge, 1980; co-editor: Operations Research: Implications for Libraries, 1972, Management Education: Implications for Libraries and Library Schools, 1974; mem. editorial bd.: Library Quarterly, 1963-93; contbr.: chpt. to Ency. Brit, 1968—; sci. articles to profl. jours. Trustee Nat. Opinion Research Center, 1964-73; Research fellow Chgo. Inst. for Psychoanalysis, 1972-76. Served with USNR, 1943-46. Recipient Award of Merit Am. Soc. for Info. Sci. and Tech., 2000. Mem. Am. Soc. for Info. Sci., Am. Assn. Artificial Intelligence. Home: 5468 S Ingleside Ave Chicago IL 60615-5062 Office: U Chgo Divsn Humanities 1010 E 59th St Chicago IL 60637-1512 E-mail: d-swanson@uchicago.edu.

SWANSON, DONALD ALAN, geologist; b. Tacoma, July 25, 1938; s. Leonard Walter and Edith Christine (Bowers) S.; m. Barbara Joan White, May 25, 1974. BS in Geology, Wash. State U., 1960; PhD in Geology, Johns Hopkins U., 1964. Geologist U.S. Geol. Survey, Menlo Park, Calif., 1965-68, 71-80, Hawaii National Park, 1968-71, sr. geologist Cascades Volcano Obs. Vancouver, Wash., 1980-90, rsch. scientist-in-charge, 1986-89, sr. geologist Seattle, 1990-96; assoc. dir. Volcano Systems Ctr. U. Wash., 1993-96; scientist-in-charge Hawaiian Volcano Obs., 1997—. Affiliate prof. U. Wash., 1992—; adj. prof. U. Hawaii, 2002--; cons. U.S. Dept. Energy, Richland, Wash., 1979-83; volcanologist New Zealand Geol. Survey, Taupo, 1984; advisor Colombian Volcano Obs., Manizales, 1986. Assoc. editor Jour. Volcanology and Geothermal Rsch., 1976—, Jour. Geophys. Rsch., 1992-94; editor Bull. of Volcanology, 1985-90, exec. editor, 1995-99; contbr. numerous articles to profl. jours. Recipient Superior Service award U.S. Geol. Survey, 1980, Meritorious Service award U.S. Dept. Interior, 1985; postdoctoral fellow NATO, 1964-65. Fellow Geol. Soc. Am., Am. Geophys. Union, AAAS; mem. Sigma Xi. Avocation: hiking. Home: 417 Linaka St Hilo HI 96720-5927 Office: US Geol Survey Hawaiian Volcano Obs PO Box 51 Hawaii National Park HI 96718-0051 E-mail: donswan@usgs.gov.

SWANSON, DONALD FREDERICK, retired food company executive; b. Mpls., Aug. 6, 1927; s. Clayton A. and Irma (Baiocchi) S.; m. Virginia Clare Hannah, Dec. 17, 1948; children— Donald Frederick, Cynthia Hannah Lindgren, Janet Clare Webster. BA, U. Minn., 1948. With Gen. Mills, Inc., 1949-85, div. v.p., dir. marketing flour, dessert and baking mixes, 1964-65, v.p., gen. mgr. grocery products div., 1965-68, v.p., corporate adminstrn. officer consumer foods group, fashion div., transp. and purchasing depts., advt. and marketing services, 1969, exec. v.p. craft, game and toy group, fashion group, direct marketing group, travel group, dir., 1968-76, sr. exec. v.p. consumer non-foods, 1976-85, chief financial officer, 1977-79, sr. exec. v.p. restaurants and consumer non-foods, 1980-81, vice chmn. restaurants and consumer non-foods, 1981-85. Ret. chmn. bd. Soo Line Corp. Served with AUS, 1946-47. Mem. Lafayette Club, Mpls. Club, Wayzata Country Club, Royal Poinciana Golf Club, Phi Kappa Psi. Home: 2171 Gulf Shore Blvd N Apt 504 Naples FL 34102-4685 Office: 641 Lake St E Wayzata MN 55391-1760

SWANSON, ERIK CHRISTIAN, museum director; b. Breckenridge, Colo., June 17, 1940; s. Glen Leonard and Eveitte Leona (Snell) S.; m. Elizabeth Jane Thompson, Aug. 22, 1976; children: Johannah Elizabeth, Nils Christian. Student, Royal U., Lund, Sweden, 1960-64; BA in History, German Lang., tchg. cert., U. No. Colo. Curator South Pk. City Mus., Fairplay, Colo., 1974-89; dir. Alma (Colo.) Fire House Mus., 1976-82; exec. dir. Cripple Creek (Colo.) Dist. Mus., 1988—. Chief of police Alma, Colo., 1977-80. With U.S. Army, 1966-68. Mem. Odd Fellows (past grand South Park Lodge # 10, Fairplay, Colo.), Masons (sr. warden Cripple Creek chpt. 1995), Elks. Republican. Home: PO Box 27 Alma CO 80420-0027 Office: Cripple Creek Dist Mus PO Box 1210 Cripple Creek CO 80813-1210

SWANSON, FERN ROSE, retired elementary education educator; b. Kalmar Twp., Minn.; d. Henry E. and Susie (Hastings) Rose; student Winona (Minn.) Normal Coll., 1918-20; BS, St. Cloud (Minn.) State Coll., 1955, MS, 1958; m. Walter E. Swanson, June 24, 1928. Tchr. high sch. English, Latin, Eyota, Minn., 1920-21; tchr. jr. high sch. English, Appleton, Minn., 1921-22; tchr. elem. schs., Harmony, Minn., 1922-23; tchr. high sch. English, Latin, Augusta, Wis., 1923-24, South Haven, Minn., 1924-26; tchr. elem. and high sch. dramatics, Waterville, 1926-27; tchr. elem. schs., South Haven, 1927-41, 43-51, Silver Creek, Minn., 1941-43; tchr. elem. schs., Annandale, Minn., 1951-53, prin., 1953-67; tchr. elem. reading, Belgrade, Minn., 1967-71. Organizer, South Haven coun. Girl Scouts U.S., 1927, leader, 1927-30. Mem. Minn. Elem. Sch. Prins. Assn. (charter mem. 25 Year Club), Ret. Educators Assn. Minn., Minn. Edn. Assn., Cen. Minn. Reading Coun. (past dir.), DAR (charter 50 Yr. Club), Ladies of Grand Army Rep. (registrar Lookout Circle, dept. pres. Minn. 1974-77, Betsy Ross Club (nat. pres. 1978, nat. historian 1980-89), nat. patriotic instr. 1981-84, nat. jr. v.p. 1984-85, nat. coun. adminstrn. 1985-88), Rebekah, Delta Kappa Gamma (past chpt. pres., Minn. Woman of Achievement award 1982). Episcopalian and Lutheran. Home: 200 Park Ln Buffalo MN 55313-1336

SWANSON, FLORINE MARY, foundation administrator; b. Cedar Rapids, Iowa, Sept. 26, 1942; d. Bernard Charles and Sylvia Jane (Brockshink) Schulte; m. Ronald Edwin Swanson, Sept. 5, 1964; children: Kendell Joseph, Stuart John, Steven Arthur. BS, Iowa State U., 1964; postgrad., U. Iowa, 1965. Librarian high sch. Clarion (Iowa) Community Schs., 1965-66; adminstr., tchr. Clarion Nursery Schs., 1971-73; conf. planner women's ctr. Iowa State U., Ames, 1986-87; exec. dir. Iowa 4-H Found., 1987—. Adv. bd. Coll. Agr., Iowa State U., 1979—81, Coll. Home Econs., Iowa State U., 1983—86; mem. 4-H sect. Nat. and Iowa Ext. Assn., 1987—, mem. 4-H youth exch. to Germany; chmn. Iowa Farm City Coun., Inc., 1986—91; mem. Nat. 4-H Strategic Design Team, 1999—2002; cons. Armenia Youth Program, 2002—. Chmn. Iowa Product Devel. Corp., 1983—89; mem. Dist. II B Jud. Commn., Iowa, 1982—88, Consumer Advs. Bd., 1987; sec. Mid-Iowa Planned Giving Coun., 1993—2002; 2d v.p., convenor of grants com. Virginia Gildersleeve Internat. Fund, 1995—2001; nat. rsch. and project com. Nat. AAUW Ednl. Found., 1989—95; dir. religious edn. St. John's Cath. Ch., Clarion, lay min., 1990—; bd. dirs. Nat. AAUW Ednl. Found., 1995—99. Mem. AAUW (past pres. Iowa chpt. 1965—), Women in Sci. and Engring. (com. Iowa State U. chpt. 1988-90), Assn. Fund Raising Profls. (past v.p. pub. rels. Ctrl. Iowa chpt.). Home: 2796 290th St Galt IA 50101-7507 Office: Iowa 4H Found 32 Curtiss Ames IA 50010 E-mail: fswanson@ia.state.edu.

SWANSON, FRED A. retired communications designer, former councilman; b. Pitts., July 22, 1946; s. Earl F. and Irene F. (McQuaide) S.; m. Leticia Garcia; children: Thomas R., Melissa A., Todd A. Student, Robert Morris Coll., 1964-65, 75-78. Laborer Equitable Gas Co., Pitts., 1965; technician AT&T Long Lines, 1970-78; tech. designer AT&T, 1978-98, ret., 1998. Baseball coach Brentwood (Pa.) Athletic Assn.; football coach Brentwood Dukes; founding mem. The Am. Air Mus. Staff sgt. USAF, 1965-70. Mem. Libr. of Congress (assoc.), Am. Mus. Natural History, Smithsonian Assocs., Non-Commd. Officers Assn., Am. Legion (past vice comdr.). Democrat. Roman Catholic. Avocations: golf, coaching football. Home: 4023 Lawnview Ave Brentwood PA 15227-3235

SWANSON, GALE ALDEN, accountant, educator; b. Lemmon, SD, Jan. 12, 1939; s. George Harry Alden Swanson and Freda (Wolff) Swanson; m. Treasure Gaylene Moore, Jan. 1, 1959 (div. 1990); children: Connie Scheid, George, Nolan. BS, Lee U., Cleveland, TN, 1969; MA in Coll. Tchg., U. of Tenn., Knoxville, 1971; PhD, Ga. State U., Atlanta, 1982; DLitt (hon.) , Oxford Grad. Sch., Dayton, TN. CPA Tenn., 1979. Asst. prof. Lee U., Cleveland, Tenn., 1975—77, SW State U., Marshall, Minn., 1977—78, West Ga. Coll., Carrollton, Ga., 1978—82; asst., assoc., prof., and dept. chair Tenn. Technol. U., Cookeville, Tenn., 1982—2002. Author: (book) Measurement and Interpretation in Accounting - A Living Systems Theory Approach, 1989, Internal Auditing Theory - A Systems View, 1991, Management Observation and Communications Theory, 1992, Macro Accounting and Modern Money Supplies, 1993. Master: Oxford Soc. of Scholars (bd. of govs. 1987—2002); mem.: Internat. Fedn. Systems Rsch. (bd. dirs.), Internat. Soc. for the Systems Scis. (life; pres., v.p adminstrn., coun. 1997—2000), Tenn. Soc. for Acctg. Educators (co-founder, 1st pres. 1984), TSCPA Ednl. Found. (life), Delta Pi Epsilon (life), Beta Gamma Sigma (life). Office: Tenn Tech Univ Campus Box 5024 Cookeville TN 38505 Office Fax: 931-372-6249. Business E-Mail: GASwanson@tntech.edu.

SWANSON, GEORGIA MAY, retired speech communication educator; b. Ashland, Ohio, Oct. 12, 1934; d. Franklin R. and Arline I. (Mason) Koontz; m. Allan V. Swanson, June 26, 1955; children: Devora, Douglas, Caryn. BA, Baldwin-Wallace Coll., Berea, Ohio, 1956; MA, Kent State U., 1972; PhD, Bowling Green (Ohio) State U., 1982. Tchr. Berea City Schs., 1958-65; instr. speech communication Baldwin-Wallace Coll., 1967-99, chmn. dept., 1983-85, chmn. faculty, 1985-88; ret., 1999. Resource person for community projects, tng. local bus. people. Chmn. Commn. on Status and Role of Women, Berea United Meth. Ch., 1980—; pub. speaker, 1st person characterization of famous Am. women presenter to civic and religious orgns., Ohio. Recipient Exemplary Tchg. award Gen. Bd. Higher Edn. and Ministry, United Meth. Ch., 1999; named Faculty Woman of Yr., Baldwin-Wallace Coll., 1990. Mem. Speech Comm. Assn. (presenter 1987, 89, 90, 92), Ohio Speech Comm. Assn. (presenter 1986, 88, 90-92, Ohio Outstanding Coll. Speech Tchr. award 1990), Omicron Delta Kappa. Avocations: acting in little theatre, sewing, arts and crafts. E-mail: talk2@en.com.

SWANSON, GERALD CARL, chemistry educator; b. Chgo., Oct. 13, 1941; s. Eric Arthur Wilhelm and Marie S.; m. JoAnne Ligeri Swanson, Aug. 1, 1988. BS, Ill. Inst. Tech., 1964; MS, Mich. State U., 1968; PhD, Fla. State U., 1977. Prof. Daytona Beach (Fla.) C.C., 1977—. Pres. United Faculty of Fla., Daytona Beach, 1998—. Author: Intro Chem Lab Manuals, 1997. Mem. ACS, AAAS. Avocation: raquetball. Office: Daytona Beach CC 104-222 1200 Internation Spdwy Blvd Daytona Beach FL 32114

SWANSON, GORDON IRA, former educational administrator; b. Zimmerman, Minn., Aug. 7, 1920; s. Charles Henry and Alma Hermenia (Collins) S.; m. Dorothy Evangeline Hanson, Jan. 13, 1946; children: Dale Gordon, Dean Edward, Janet Marie, Charles Alan. BS, U. Minn., 1942, MS, 1949, PhD, 1954. Secondary sch. tchr. Alexandria (Minn.) Pub. Schs., 1942-43, 46-49; prof. vocat. edn. U. Minn., St. Paul, 1951-92; program officer UNESCO, Paris, 1959-61; assoc. dir. Nat. Ctr. for Rsch. in Vocat. Edn., Berkeley, Calif., 1989-92; ret., 1992. Spkr., cons. in field, 1965-92. Author: Old Breed News - The High Road, 1993, Memorial Day - Its Meaning, 1993; contbr. articles to profl. jours. Cub master Boy Scouts Am., St. Paul; moderator St. Anthony Park United Ch. of Christ, St. Paul, 1968-69; pres. Am. Swedish Inst., Mpls.; mem. White House Conf. on Edn., Children and Youth. Maj. USMC, 1942-46. Recipient Prosser award Dunwoody Inst., 1992, Outstanding Educator award U. Minn. Coll. Edn., 1994; hon. mem. Ret. Officers Assn. Ireland, 1978. Mem. AAAS, Am. Vocat. Assn. (pres. 1978—), Rural Edn. Assn. (pres.), VFW (life), Svenska Sallskapet, Royal Order of North Star, Phi Delta Kappa (pres. 1964-65). Avocations: writing, collecting and repairing clocks, woodworking. Home: 1440 Raymond Ave Saint Paul MN 55108-1428

SWANSON, HARRY FREDERICK, artist; b. Hartford, Conn., June 5, 1931; s. Harry Bernard and Anna Maria (Glansholm) S.; m. Marion Louise Rydberg, Apr. 30, 1955; children: Alan Mark, Anne Louise. Cert., Art Instrn. Inc., Mpls., 1948-50; student, Hartford Art Sch., 1953, Practical Art Sch., Boston, 1955. Machinist, draftsman Pratt & Whitney Aircraft, East Hartford, Conn., 1950-55; draftsman MIT, Cambridge, Mass., 1955-56; tech. illustrator The Purnell Co., Boston, 1956-59; illustrator and graphics designer Itek Corp., Lexington, Mass., 1959-72; artist, illustrator Studio & Fine Art Gallery, Newbury, 1972-89, Fine Art Gallery, Lincolnville, Maine, 1988—. Exhibited in group shows inlcuding Nat. Exhibit Ellsworth Gallery, 1973; also nat. and internat. pvt. and corp. collections including MBNA and Key Bank. Recipient awards art assns. Mem. Copley Soc. Boston. Unitarian-Universalist. Avocations: writing, running, cross country skiing, gen. sports, crossword puzzles. Home: Gallery: US Rte 1 PO Box 60 Lincolnville ME 04849-0060

SWANSON, JENNIE ELIZABETH WILLIAMS, healthcare administrator, mentor, volunteer; b. Atlanta, Aug. 5, 1932; d. Chester Arthur and Cleo Annie Williams; m. Richard Edward Swanson, Apr. 24, 1954; children: Laurel Dee, Jeffrey Richard, Scott Edward. BS, Northwestern U., 1954; MS, No. Ill. U., 1972, EdD, 1976. Pub. sch. tchr., 1954-69; psycho-ednl. diagnostician, 1969-72; faculty Loyola U., Chgo., 1976-82, asst. prof. ob-gyn and pediat., 1979-82; dir. pre-start project depts. ob-gyn and pediat. Stritch Sch. Medicine, 1978-82; dir. spl. svcs. Cmty. Unit Sch. Dist. 220, 1982-92. Hospice bereavement vol., 1997—; coun. mem., mentor Cong. Unitarian Ch.; antique dealer; mem. Gov. Ill. Com. Preventive Svcs., 1979-80; chair B-3 subcom. First Chance Consortium, 1978-80; chair INTER-ACT, 1979-80; cons. in field. Author: (with others) Partners in Child Development, 1978. Active Opera House Commn., 2001—. Grantee HEW, 1973-76, 78-82. Mem. Coun. Exceptional Children, Assn. Maternal and Child Health, Nat. Perinatal Assn., Nat. Acad. Neuropsychology, Nat. Assn. Edn. Young Child, Northwestern U. Alumni Assn., Delta Delta Delta, Delta Kappa Gamma (scholar 1974). Unitarian Universalist.

SWANSON, JERRY WILLIAM, neurologist; b. Peoria, Ill., Dec. 15, 1950; s. Clarence William and Joanne Krull S.; m. Kristine Kay Haugen, Dec. 28, 1974; children: Elizabeth, Rachel. BA, Wartburg Coll., 1973; MD, Northwestern U. Med. Sch., Chgo., 1977. Diplomate Am. Bd. Psychiatry and Neurology. Cons. in neurology Mayo Clinic, Rochester, Minn., 1982—; from assoc. prof. to prof. neurology Mayo Med. Sch., 1992—; vice-chmn. edn., dept. neurology Mayo Clinic, 1996-98, residency program dir. dept. neurology, 1996-98, chmn. headache divsn., dept. neurology, 1996—, chair headache sect., dept. neurology, 1998—; prof. of neurology Mayo Med. Sch., 2002—. Co-editor: (book) Mayo Clinic Examinations in Neurology, 7th edit., 1998; contbr. more than 40 articles to profl. jours. and publs. Recipient Faculty Svc. award, Mayo Med. Sch., 2001. Fellow Am. Acad. Neurology (chair A.B. Baker sect. of neurologic edn. 2002); mem. Am. Neurol. Assn., Minn. Soc. Neurol. Scis., Am. Headache Soc. (ann. scientific mtg. co-chair 1999—), Internat. Headache Congress (sci. program com. 2001). Lutheran. Avocations: canoeing, Nordic skiing, hiking. Office: Dept Neurology/Mayo Clin 200 1st St SW Rochester MN 55905-0001

SWANSON, KARIN, hospital administrator, consultant; b. New Britain, Conn., Dec. 8, 1942; d. Oake F. and Ingrid Lauren Swanson; m. B. William Dorsey, June 26, 1965 (div. 1974); children: Matthew W., Julie I., Alison K.; m. Sanford H. Low, Oct. 14, 1989. BA in Biology, Middlebury Coll., 1964; MPH, Yale U., 1981. Biology tchr. Kents Hill (Maine) Sch., 1964-66; laboratory instr. Bates Coll., Lewiston, Maine, 1974-78; asst. to gen. dir. Mass. Eye and Ear Infirmary, Boston, 1979-80; v.p. profl. services Portsmouth (N.H.) Hosp., 1981-83; v.p. Health Strategy Assn. Ltd., Chestnut Hill, Mass., 1983-85; v.p. med. affairs Cen. Maine Med. Ctr., Lewiston, 1986-89; health care mgmt. cons. Cambridge, Mass., 1989-91; CEO Hahnemann Hosp., Brighton, 1991-94; adminstr. Vencor Hosp., Boston, 1994-95; pres., CEO The Laser Inst. New Eng., Newton, 1996-97; health care mgmt./real estate devel. cons. Newcastle, Maine, 1997—. Mem. Phi Beta Kappa. Avocations: reading, gardening, walking. Home and Office: PO Box 1281 Damariscotta ME 04543-1281

SWANSON, KEITH EDWIN, music educator, conductor; b. Duluth, Minn., Apr. 14, 1951; s. Leslie E. Swanson and Helen Marie Hammerbeck; m. Jackie Dee Brown, Sept. 10, 1990; children: Sam, Mack, Ted. BS in Music, U. Minn., Duluth, 1973; MA in Edn., U. Wis., Superior, 1988. Tchr. Duluth East H.S., 1973—77, Hermantown H.S., 1977—; condr., music dir. Itasca Symphony Orch., Grand Rapids, 1991—, Northland Opera Theater, Duluth, 1991—; prof. Lake Superior Coll., 1994—; condr. orch. U. Minn., 1999—2000. Mem.: Minn. Music Educators Assn. Democrat. Avocation: tennis. Home: PO Box 529 Carlton MN 55718

SWANSON, LAUREN A. consultant, entrepreneur, educator, researcher; b. Apr. 17, 1951; BS, U. Wyo., 1973; MS, 1974; postgrad., Wheaton Coll., 1977; PhD, U. Ga., 1983. Instr. mktg. U. Wyo., Laramie, 1974-76; grad. instr. mktg., mgmt. sci. U. Ga., Athens, 1978-79; vis. prof. mktg. Grad. Sch. Bus. Adminstrn. Atlanta U., 1980-81; asst. prof. mktg. U. Mass., Boston, 1981-86; rsch. cons. Hill-Holliday-Connors-Cosmopulos Inc., 1983-86; assoc. in rsch. Fairbank Ctr. for East Asian Rsch. Harvard U., Cambridge, Mass., 1986—; fgn. expert, prof. mktg. and econs. U. Internat. Bus. and Econs., Beijing, 1986-87; assoc. prof. mktg. Chinese U. Hong Kong, 1987-98, assoc. dir. MBA programs, 1991-96; v.p. Dalton (Nebr.) Telecom, 1998-99; cons. in mktg. and telecomms. Dalton, 1999—. Cons. to industry; examiner Hong Kong Quality Award, 1991-95. Guest editor: Internat. Jour. Advtsg.; contbr. numerous articles to profl. jours.

SWANSON, LEALAN ANDERSON NUNN, art historian, artist; b. Paterson, N.J., Jan. 9, 1942; d. Leonard Robert Nunn and Eva Kathryn Cook; m. Jon Cloyd Swanson, (div. 1986); children: Gunnar Kristian, Catherine Christine; m. Lance Carl Richards, June, 1996. BA, U. N.C., Greensboro, 1964; MA, U. Iowa, 1966; PhD, Ohio State U., 1997. Elem. art tchr. Muhammad Ali Othman Sch., Taizz, Yemen, 1974-75; instr. Wayne State U., Detroit, 1970-73, 76-79; asst. dir. S.E. Dearborn (Mich.) Cmty. Coun., 1979-82; resident dir. Am. Inst. Yemeni Studies, San'a, Yemen, 1982-84; instr. N.C. Ctrl. U., Durham, 1985-86, 88-89; illustrations editor Am. Schs. Oriental Rsch., N.C., 1987-88; assoc. prof. Jackson (Miss.) State U., 1990—. African art condition reporter Tougaloo Coll. Art, Jackson, 1999, archives cons., 2000. One-woman shows include Eudora Welty Libr., Jackson, Miss., 1997, exhibitions include Ctr. Gallery, Carrboro, N.C., 1985, Vend-Art Project, N.Y. and Durham, N.C., 1986, Ann. Faculty shows, Jackson State U., 1990—, Treasures of the Queen of Sheba, Jackson State U., 1993—; contbr. Mem. edn. com. Miss. Mus. Art, 1998-2000; judge archtl. models Tech. Students Assn., Jackson, 1999-2001. Recipient Faculty Rsch. award, NEH, 2000—01, Tchg. Excellence award, Miss. Humanities Coun., 2001; grantee Career Devel. grantee, AAUW, 1994, Rsch. grantee, Am. Inst. Maghribi Studies, Morocco, 1998. Mem.: S.E. Regional Mid. East and Islamic Studies Seminar, Southeastern Coll. Art Conf., Am. Inst. Yemeni Studies, Coll. Art Assn., Phi Kappa Phi. Unitarian Universalist. Avocations: gardening, kayaking, reading. Office: Jackson State U Dept Art 1400 John R Lynch St Jackson MS 39217 E-mail: leaswan@aol.com.

SWANSON, LESLIE KEATING, financial services executive; b. Wilmington, Del., Sept. 27, 1952; BS, U. Del., 1974, postgrad., 1980-83. Registered securities broker and ins. broker. Registered securities broker Merrill Lynch Pierce Fenner & Smith, Wilmington, 1984-89; fin. advisor, rule 144 specialist Morgan Stanley Dean Witter, Phila., 1989—. Avocations: golf, photography, skiing, tennis. Home: PO Box 4046 Wilmington DE 19807-0046 Office: Morgan Stanley Dean Witter Two Logan Sq 18th And Arch Sts Philadelphia PA 19103-1199 Fax: 215 963-3925.

SWANSON, LESLIE MARTIN, JR. lawyer; b. Yakima, Wash., May 16, 1940; s. Leslie Martin and Eleanor Louise (Morris) S.; children: Mark, Carl, Todd. BA, Augustana Coll., Rock Island, Ill., 1961; MA, Claremont Grad. U., Calif., 1964; JD, U. Oreg., 1966. Bar: Oreg. 1966, Wash. 1993, U.S. Dist. Ct. Oreg. 1966, U.S. Ct. Appeals (9th cir.) 1969, U.S. Supreme Ct. 1978. Ptnr. Harrang, Swanson, Long & Watkinson, Eugene, Oreg., 1966-85; pres., shareholder Swanson & Walters, 1985-92; pvt. practice Les Swanson Jr., Atty. at Law, Portland, Oreg., 1992—. Assoc. prof. and adj. prof. law U. Oreg., Eugene; prof. humanities Portland State U.; consul for Iceland, 2001—. Mem. Oreg. State Bd. Higher Edn., 1989-97, pres., 1994-96; mem. Oreg. Arts Commn., 1980-83; v.p. bd. visitors U. Oreg. Sch. Law, 1987-89; mem. bd. visitors arts and humanities Claremont Grad. U. Mem. Lane County Bar Assn. (pres. 1983-84), Am. Law Inst. Office: 808 SW 3rd Ave Ste 400 Portland OR 97204-2439 E-mail: lesswan@portland.quik.com.

SWANSON, LINDA ARLENE, programmer/analyst; b. Rheinfelden, Germany, June 8, 1967; came to U.S., 1985; d. Lawrence Everett and Evelyn Ruth (Tanner) S. AS in Computer Sci.-Tech., Lansing C.C., 1988, Oakland C.C., 1998. Hotel & restaurant operator Mission Point Resort, Mackinac Island, Mich., 1988; media auditor, asst. program coord. Advt. Audit Svc., Farmington Hills, 1988-92; computer lab. aide Oakland C.C., 1991; computer operator PMH Caramanning, Inc., 1992-93; recycling coord. Payroll, Inc., Royal Oak, 1994-96, programmer/analyst, 1993-96, Sanwa Leasing Corp., Troy, 1996-97; software developer Integral Solutions, Inc., Royal Oak, 1997-98; web programmer, software developer Sigmalo Interactive Media, Inc., Detroit, 1998—. Mem. Detroit Inst. Arts Founders Soc. Avocations: gardening, photography, skiing, mountain climbing, genealogy. Home: 517 W Lincoln Ave Royal Oak MI 48067-3133

SWANSON, MARY CATHERINE, educational reform program administrator; b. Kingsburg, Calif., Sept. 3, 1944; d. Edwin Elmore and Corrine (Miller) Jacobs; m. Thomas Edward Swanson, Aug. 27, 1966; 1 child, Thomas Jacobs. BA in English and Journalism, Calif. State U., San Francisco, 1966; standard teaching credential in secondary edn., U. Calif., 1966; MA in Edn., U. Redlands, 1977; DHL (hon.) , U. San Diego, 2002. Svc. adminstrv. credential, Calif.; specialist learning handicapped, Calif.; gifted cert., Calif. Tchr. English and journalism Woodland (Calif.) High Sch., 1966-67, Armijo High Sch., Fairfield, Calif., 1967-69, Moreno Valley High Sch., Sunnymead, 1969-70, Clairemont High Sch., San Diego, 1970-86; coord. San Diego County Office Edn., 1986-90, dir. AVID project, 1990-92; founder, exec. dir. AVID Ctr., 1992—. Newspaper and yearbook advisor Moreno Valley High Sch., Moreno Valley Sch. Dist., 1969-70; reading program coord. Clairemont High Sch., 1974-80, project English coord. and site plan coord., 1975-80, English dept. chairperson, 1978-86, coord. Advancement Via Individual Determination and WASC accreditation, 1980-86, in-sch. resource tchr., 1982-86; mem. numerous positions and coms. San Diego City Schs., 1974-91; mem. com. univ. and coll. opportunities commn. Calif. State Dept. Edn., 1981-82; mem. adv. com. tchr. edn. program Pt. Loma Coll., 1982-83, tchr. English methods course for tchrs. secondary edn., 1986-87; mem. accreditation vis. com. WASC, 1983, integration monitoring team Crawford High Sch., 1984, adv. com. San Diego Area Writing Project, 1987—; developer numerous curricular programs, 1967—. Community leader Olivenhain Valley 4-H Club, 1981-90; founder Olivenhain Valley Soccer Club, 1982; coord. Clairemont High Sch./Sea World Adopt-A-Sch., 1982-84. Named Headliner of Yr.-Edn./Creative Tchg., San Diego Press Club, 1991, Headline of Yr.-Cmty. Activist, 2002, Woman of Vision, LWV-San Diego, 1992, Nat. Educator of Yr., McGraw Hill, 2001, America's Best Tchr., Time Mag. and CNN, 2001; named to Pres.'s Forum on Tchg. as a Profession, Am. Assn. Higher Edn., 1991; recipient EXCEL award for excellence in tchg., 1985, Exemplary Program award, Nat. Coun. States on Insvc. Edn., 1990, Pioneering Achievement in Edn. award, Charles A. Dana Found., 1991; grantee, BankAmerica Found., 1980, UCSD Acad. Support Svcs., 1980, San Diego Gas and Elec. Found., 1984. Mem. Nat. Coun. Tchrs. English (Nat. Ctr. Excellence award 1985-87), Calif. Coun. Tchrs. English,

Calif. Assn. Gifted Edn., Golden Key Nat. Honor Soc. (hon. mem.), Phi Kappa Phi. Office: San Diego County Office Edn 6401 Linda Vista Rd Rm 623 San Diego CA 92111-7319 Also: AVID Ctr 5353 Mission Center Rd Ste 222 San Diego CA 92108-1305 E-mail: mcswanson@avidcenter.org.

SWANSON, NORMA FRANCES, federal agency administrator; b. Blue Island, Ill., Oct. 24, 1923; d. Arnold Raymond and Bessie Oween (Bewley) Brown; m. George Clair Swanson, Mar. 18, 1948; 1 child, Dane Craig. AB, Asbury Coll., 1946; BS cum laude, Eastern Nazarene Coll., Wollaston, Mass., 1970; MA cum laude, Ind. Christian U., 1986. Confidential asst. dep. undersec. interagy. intergovt. affairs U.S. Dept. Edn., Washington, 1981—; pres. Window to the World, Inc., Schroon Lake, N.Y., 1985—; asst. dir. edn. Commn. Bicentennial U.S. Constn., Washington, 1987—; dir. Horizons Plus Values Program Hampton Roads Va. Detention Homes; dir. Project Fresh Start Washington D.C. Pub. Sch., 1993-96. Cons. Conf. Industrialized Nations, Williamsburg, Va., 1982, Nellie Thomas Inst. Learning, Monterey, Calif., 1981-82. Author: Dear Teenager, A Teen's Guide to Correct Social Behavior, 1987, A Constitution is Born, A Teacher's Guide to Resource Materials, 1987, Sunlights and More, Bright Beginnings, 1993, Vols. I, II, 1996, The Ones that Count and Other Stories with Values to Live By, 1994, A Think and Write Journal Sunlights and More Vols. I, II, 1993 (story album) The Ones that Count and Other Stories with Virtues to Live By, 1996, Keeping Christmas: A Family Sampler of Best-Loved Stories and Hymns plus Our Christmas Heritage, Then and Now, 1998; editor: (anthology) Horizons Plus; developer ednl. materials; theorem artist Early Life mag., 1974. Bd. regents Ind. Christian U., 1986—; program dir. Tidewater (Va.) Outreach, 1992; dir. project Fresh Start, Washington Pub. Sch., 1993-94; dir. youth outreach with values program U.S. Dept. Juvenile Justice, 1992-93. Recipient J.C. Penney award for volunteerism, 1993, Precision Tune awrd for svc. tto Washington Inner-City Schs. Republican. Baptist. Avocation: theorem painting. Address: 5501 Woodlyn Rd Frederick MD 21703-6965 E-mail: norma@netstorm.com.

SWANSON, NORMAN RASMUS, social sciences educator; b. Deep River, Ont., Can., Feb. 9, 1964; s. Max Lynn and Gudrun Swanson; m. Christine Anne Forker, Aug. 29, 1963; children: Rachel, Joshua, Justin. BA, U. Waterloo, Ont., 1988; MA, U. Calif., San Diego, 1990, PhD, 1994. Asst. prof. econs. Pa. State U., State College, 1994-99, Tex. A&M U., College Station, 1999-2001. Purdue U., West Lafayette, Ind., 2001—02, Rutgers U., New Brunswick, NJ, 2002—. Cons. DFA Capital Mgmt., Inc., Purchase, N.Y., 1999—. Contbr. articles to profl. jours., including Jour. Bus. and Econ. Stats., Jour. Econometrics, Jour. Monetary Econs., others. Recipient Young Rschr. award NSF, 1999. Mem. Am. Stats. Assn., Econometrics Soc., Royal Stats. Assn. Avocations: running, biking, hiking. Office: Rutgers U Dept Econs 75 Hamilton St New Brunswick NJ 08901-1248 E-mail: nrasmus@yahoo.com.

SWANSON, PATRICIA E. engineer; b. Hudson, N.Y., Oct. 19, 1955; d. John Francis and Margaret Bixby Kearney; m. Richard Charles Swanson, July 13, 1985. BS in Mech. Engring., U. N.Mex., 1978; JD, Columbia Pacific U., 1991. Weapons sys. engr. Naval Weapons Evaluation Facility, Kirtland AFB, N.Mex., 1979-82; nuc. effects engr. Air Force Weapons Lab., 1982-92; chem. laser facility mgr., engr. Phillips Lab., Air Force, 1992-95; gen. engr. Air Force Rsch. Lab., 1995—. Addv. bd. chem. warfare conv. Phillips Lab. Air Force Rsch. Lab., Kirtland AFB, 1996-99. Contbr. articles to profl. jours. Participant Albuquerque Internat. Balloon Fiesta, 1982—. Mem. ASME. Roman Catholic. Avocations: horseback riding, piloting hot air balloon, flying fixed-wing aircraft.

SWANSON, PEGGY EUBANKS, finance educator; b. Ivanhoe, Tex., Dec. 29, 1936; d. Leslie Samuel and Mary Lee (Reid) Eubanks; m. B. Marc Sommers, Nov. 10, 1993. BBA, U. North Tex., 1957, M. Bus. Edn., 1965; MA in Econs., So. Meth. U., 1967, PhD in Econs., 1978. Instr. El Centro Coll., Dallas, 1967-69, 71-78, bus. div. chmn., 1969-71; asst. prof. econs. U. Tex., Arlington, 1978-79, asst. prof. fin., 1979-84, assoc. prof., 1984-86, chmn. dept. fin. and real estate, 1986-88, prof. fin., 1987—, interim dean Coll. Bus. Adminstrn., 1999—. Expert witness various law firms, primarily Tex. and Calif., 1978—; cons. Internat. Edn. Program, 1992-99; curriculum cons. U. Monterrey, Mexico, 1995, New Saudi Arabia U., 1999. Contbr. articles to acad. profl. jours. Vol. Am. Cancer Soc., Dallas, Arlington, 1981—, Meals on Wheels, Arlington, 1989—; mem. adv. bd. Ryan/Reilly Ctr. for Urban Land Utilization, Arlington, 1986-88. Mem. Fin. Exec. Inst. (chmn. acad. rels. 1987-88), Internat. Bus. Steering Com. (chmn. 1989-91), Am. Fin. Assn., Am. Econ. Assn., Fin. Mgmt. Assn. (hon. faculty mem. Nat. Honor Soc. 1985-86, program com. 1998-99), Southwestern Fin. Assn. (program com. 1987-88, 96), Midwest Fin. Assn. (program com. 1997-98, 98-99), Acad. of Internat. Bus. (program com. 1992-95), Acad. Disting. Tchrs., Phi Beta Delta (membership com. 1987-89). Republican. Episcopalian. Avocations: tennis, gardening. Home: 4921 Bridgewater Dr Arlington TX 76017-2729 Office: U Tex at Arlington PO Box 19449 Arlington TX 76019-0001 E-mail: swanson@uta.edu.

SWANSON, PHILLIP DEAN, neurologist; b. Seattle, Oct. 1, 1932; s. William Dean and Kathryn C. (Peterson) S.; m. Sheila N. Joardar, Apr. 20, 1957; children: Stephen, Jennifer, Kathryn, Rebecca, Sara. BS, Yale U., 1954; student, U. Heidelberg, 1952-53; MD, Johns Hopkins U., 1958; PhD in Biochemistry, U. London, 1964. Intern Harvard med. svc. Boston City Hosp., 1958-59; resident in neurology Johns Hopkins Hosp., Balt. City Hosp., 1959-62; asst. prof. U. Wash. Sch. Medicine, Seattle, 1964-68, assoc. prof., 1968-73, prof., 1973—, head divsn. neurology, 1967-95. Mem. med. adv. bd. Puget Sound chpt. Nat. Multiple Sclerosis Soc., 1967-97, chmn., 1970-74; mem. com. to combat Huntington's Disease Nat. Sci. Council, 1975-84. Author: (with others) Introduction to Clinical Neurology, 1976; editor: Signs and Symptoms in Neurology, 1984; contbr. articles to profl. jours. NIH spl. fellow, 1962-64; NIH grantee. Fellow Am. Acad. Neurology; mem. Am. Neurol. Assn., Assn. Univ. Profs. Neurology (pres. 1975-76), Am. Heart Assn., Am. Soc. Neurochemistry, Internat. Soc. Neurochemistry, Biochem. Soc. (London), Am. Soc. Clin. Investigation (emeritus) Home: 6537 29th Ave NE Seattle WA 98115-7234 Office: U Wash Sch Medicine Dept Neurology PO Box 356465 Seattle WA 98195-6465 E-mail: swansonp@u.washington.edu.

SWANSON, RALPH WILLIAM, aerospace executive, consultant, engineer; b. Mpls. m. Virginia May Peoples (dec.); children: John W., Timothy R.; m. Patricia Anne Smith. BS in Aero. Engring., U. Minn., 1947; MS in Nuclear Engring., N.C. State U., 1954; PhD in Engring., Kennedy-Western U., 1989. Design engr. Los Alamos (N.Mex.) Sci. Lab., 1948-52; asst. prof. physics Air Force Inst. Tech., Wright Patterson AFB, Ohio, 1954-56; chief radiation div. armed forces spl. weapons project Pentagon, Washington, 1957-61; dep. chief staff plans and programs Air Force Eastern Test Range, Patrick AFB, Fla., 1961-64; dep. for programs and requirements Air Force Nat. Range Div., 1964-65; mgr. advanced programs IBM Corp., Kennedy Space Center, 1965-75; chief engr. Planning Rsch. Corp., 1975-79, dep. project mgr., gen. mgr., 1979-87; project mgr. Bamsi, Inc., 1987-93. Freelance cons., Cocoa Beach, Fla., 1987—; pres. R&A Cons. Corp., Cocoa Beach. Bd. dirs. Brevard Achievement Ctr., Rockledge, Fla., 1970—. Col. USAF, 1941-65, ETO and Korea, ret. Mem. Air Force Assn., Assn. AFIT Grads., Masons, Shriners, Sigma Xi, Sigma Pi Sigma. Republican. Avocations: scuba diving, under water photography, jogging.

SWANSON, RICHARD WILLIAM, retired statistician; b. July 26, 1934; s. Richard ( ) and Erma Marie (Herman) Swanson; m. Laura Yoko Arai, Dec. 30, 1970. BS, Iowa State U., 1958, MS, 1964. Ops. analyst Stanford Rsch. Inst., Monterey, Calif., 1958—62; statistician ARINC Rsch. Corp., Washington, 1964—65; sr. scientist Booz-Allen Applied Rsch., Vietnam, 1965—67, L.A., 1967—68; sr. ops. analyst Control Data Corp., Honolulu, 1968—70; mgmt. cons., 1970—73; exec. v.p. SEQUEL Corp., 1973—75; bus. cons. Hawaii Dept. Planning and Econ. Devel., Honlulu, 1975—77; tax rsch. and planning offider Dept. Taxation, 1977—82; ops. rsch. analyst U.S. Govt., 1982—89, shipyard statistician, 1989—97; ret., 1997. Mem.: Hawaiian Acad. Sci., Sigma Xi. Home: 583 Kamoku St Apt 3505 Honolulu HI 96826-5241

SWANSON, ROBERT LAWRENCE, oceanographer, academic program administrator; b. Balt., Oct. 11, 1938; s. Lawrence Wilbur and Hazel Ruth Swanson; m. Dana Lamont, Sept. 12, 1963; children: Lawrence Daniel, Michael Nathan. BSCE, Lehigh U., 1960; MS in Oceanography, Oreg. State U., 1965, PhD in Oceanography, 1971. Cert. hydrographer. Commd. ensign U.S. Coast and Geodetic Survey (now NOAA), 1960, advanced through grades to capt., 1978; ops. officer U.S. Pathfinder, 1965; comdg. officer U.S. Marmer, 1966; chief oceanographic divsn. Nat. Ocean Survey, NOAA, Rockville, Md., 1969-72; mgr. Marine Ecosys. Analysis, N.Y. Bight project, Stony Brook, 1973-78; dir. Office Marine Pollution Assessment NOAA, Rockville, 1978-83, rsch. assoc. Sea Grant Stony Brook, 1983-84; comdg. officer U.S. Researcher, Miami, 1984-86; chief internat. activities group NOAA, Rockville, 1986, exed. dir. Office Oceanic and Atmospheric Rsch., 1986-87; dir. Waste Reduction and Mgmt. Inst. SUNY, Stony Brook, 1987—. Adj. prof. Marine Scis. Rsch. Ctr., SUNY, Stony Brook, 1976—; mem. Suffolk County Coun. Environ. Quality, 1988—, vice chair, 1996—; mem. N.Y. State Oversight Com. on Brookhaven Nat. Lab., 1996—; mem. Coastal Mgmt. Commn. Villages Head-of-the-Harbor and Nissequogue, 1994—2002; chmn. Coastal Mgmt. Commn. Villages Head Harbor and Nissequogue, 1995—97, 1999—2001; trustee Three Village Hist. Soc., 1994—2002; co-chair L.I. Environ. Econ. Roundtable, 1995—; adv. bd. Evan L. Lit Meml. Fund, 1998—; cons. in field; trustee Village of Head-of-the-Harbor, 2002—. Co-author, co-editor: Oxygen Depletion and Associated Benthic Mortalities in N.Y. Bight, 1979; co-editor: Floatable Wastes and the Region's Beaches; mem. editl. bd. N.Y. Bight Monograph Series, 1973-81, Chemistry and Ecology, 1995—; co-pub. Waste Mgmt. Rsch. Report, 1988-95; mem. adv. bd. L.I. Hist. Jour., 1995—. Recipient Karo award Am. Soc. Mil. Engrs., 1972; Silver medal Dept. Commerce, 1973; Program and Adminstrn. Mgmt. award NOAA, 1975, Unit citation, 1981; sr. exec. fellow John F. Kennedy Sch. Govt., Harvard U., 1983, Spl. Achievement award, 1987, NOAA Corps. Commendations, 1987; named Man of Yr. for environment Three Village Times, 1998. Mem. Am. Mil. Engrs., N.Y. Acad. Scis., ASCE (chmn. hydrography and oceanography com. 1972-74), AAAS, Am. Geophys. Union, Marine Tech. Soc. (chmn. marine pollution com. 1982-92), Cosmos Club, Sigma Xi (pres. SUNYSB chpt. 1998—). Presbyterian. Home: 46 Harbor Hill Rd Saint James NY 11780-1217 Office: SUNY Waste Reduction And Mgmt Ins Stony Brook NY 11794-5000 Office Fax: 631-632-8064. E-mail: lswanson@notes.cc.sunysb.edu.

SWANSON, ROBERT DRAPER, college president; b. Sioux City, Iowa, Aug. 6, 1915; s. Alfred and Tida Ruth (Draper) S.; m. Roberta B. Clements, May 5, 1941 (dec. Oct. 1975); children: Sara Louise, Mark Robert; m. Dorothy B. Howe, Aug. 4, 1979. AB, Park Coll., 1937; student, U. Iowa, 1937; B.D., McCormick Theol. Sem., 1941; D.D., James Millikin U., 1950; L.H.D., Tusculum Coll., 1966, Olivet Coll., 1971, Central Mich. U., 1979, Alma Coll., 1981; LL.D., Hillsdale Coll., 1968, Hope Coll., 1981. Dir. athletics, phys. edn. Park Coll., 1937-38; ordained to ministry Presbyn. Ch., 1941; pastor Second Presbyn. Ch., Tulsa, 1941-45; dean of students McCormick Sem., 1946-47, v.p., prof. preaching, 1948-56; pres. Alma Coll., 1956-80, pres. emeritus, 1980—. Dir. Gen. Telephone Co. Mich. Served as lt. (j.g.), Chaplain's Corps USNR, 1945-46. Recipient Disting. Alumni award Park Coll., 1971, Disting. Alumnus award McCormick Theol. Sem., 1981. Mem. Phi Beta Kappa. Clubs: Rotary (Alma). Home: 4105 Riverview Dr Alma MI 48801-9563 E-mail: swanson@alma.edu.

SWANSON, ROBERT H. JR. electronics executive; BS Indsl. Engring., Northeastern U. V.p., gen. mgr. Nat. Semiconductor, 1968—81; founder, pres., CEO, dir. Linear Tech. Corp., Milpitas, Calif., 1981, chmn. bd. dirs., CEO, 1999—. Office: Linear Tech Corp 1630 Mccarthy Blvd Milpitas CA 95035-7417*

SWANSON, ROBERT KILLEN, management consultant; b. Deadwood, S.D., Aug. 11, 1932; s. Robert Claude and Marie Elizabeth (Kersten) S.; m. Nancy Anne Oyaas, July 19, 1958; children: Cathryn Lynn, Robert Stuart, Bart Killen. BA, U. S.D., 1954; postgrad., U. Melbourne, Australia, 1955. With Gen. Mills, Inc., Mpls., 1955-58, 71-79, v.p., 1971-73, group v.p., 1973-77, exec. v.p., 1977-79; with Marathon Oil Co., Findlay, Ohio, 1958-60; sr. v.p., dir. Needham, Harper & Steers, Inc., Chgo., 1961-69; joint mng. dir. S. H. Benson (Holdings) Ltd., Eng., 1969-71; pres., chief operating officer Greyhound Corp., Phoenix, 1980; chmn., chief exec. officer Del E. Webb Corp., 1981-87; chmn. RKS Inc., 1987—. Bd. dirs. Am. S.W. Concepts Inc., ST Internat. Ltd., Granite Dells LLP. 2d lt. U.S. Army, 1955. Fulbright scholar, 1954-55; Woodrow Wilson scholar. Mem. U.K. Dirs. Inst., U.S. Internat. Scholars Assn., English Speaking Union, Phoenix Country Club. Episcopalian. Office: RKS Inc 5600 N Palo Cristi Rd Scottsdale AZ 85253-7543

SWANSON, ROBERT LEE, lawyer; b. Fond du Lac, Wis., July 15, 1942; s. Walfred S. and Edna F. (Kamp) S.; m. Mary Ruth Francis, Aug. 19, 1967; children: Leigh Alexandra, Mitchell Pearson. BS, U. Wis., 1964; JD, Valparaiso U., 1970; LLM, Boston U., 1979. Bar: Wis. 1970, U.S. Dist. Ct. (ea. dist.) Wis. 1970, U.S. Dist. Ct. (we. dist.) Wis. 1974, U.S. Dist. Ct. (we. dist.) Okla. 2002, U.S. Tax Ct. 1981, U.S. Dist. Ct. (cen.) Ill. 1988, Okla. 1999, U.S. Ct. Appeals (7th cir.) 1999. Atty. Kasdorf, Dahl, Lewis & Swietlik, Milw., 1970-73; atty., ptnr. Wartman, Wartman & Swanson, Ashland, 1973-80; city atty. City of Ashland, 1976-80; atty., ptnr. DeMark, Kolbe & Brodek, Racine, 1980-95; ptnr. Hartig, Bjelajac, Swanson & Koenen, 1995-99; contract atty. Okla. Indigent Def. Sys., Lincoln County, 2000—02. Lectr. civil rights and discrimination laws, 1980—; lectr.bus. law Cardinal Strich U., 1996—99, U. Wis.-Parkside, 1997—99; participating atty. Alliance Def. Fund, 2000—; legal columnist Burlington Std. Press, 1991—95, Wis. Restaurant Assn. Mag., 1986. Chmn. Ashland County Rep. Party, 1976—79; v.p., bd. dirs. Meml. Med. Ctr., Ashland, 1975—80; bd. trustees Kendrick Mcpl. Authority, Okla., 2001—; vice comdr. USCG Aux. Bayfield (Wis.) Flotilla, 1975—81; vol. atty. ACLU Wis., 1975—90. 1st lt. U.S. Army, 1964—66. Named one of Outstanding Young Men of Am., Jaycees, 1978; recipient Disting. Achievement in Art and Sci. of Advocacy award Internat. Acad. Trial Lawyers, 1970. Mem. Racine County Bar Assn. (bd. dirs. 1986-89), Wis. Acad. Trial Lawyers, Def. Rsch. Inst., Am. Hockey Assn. U.S. (coach, referee 1983-90), Am. Legion, Okla. Limousine Assn. (parliamentarian, 2002—). Avocations: softball, volleyball, hockey. Home: RR 1 Box 478 Stroud OK 74079-9723 E-mail: rswanson@brightok.net.

SWANSON, ROY ARTHUR, classicist, educator; b. St. Paul, Apr. 7, 1925; s. Roy Benjamin and Gertrude (Larson) S.; m. Vivian May Vitous, Mar. 30, 1946; children: Lynn Marie (Mrs. Gerald A. Snider), Robin Lillian, Robert Roy (dec.), Dyack Tyler, Dana Miriam (Mrs. Jon Butts). BA, U. Minn., 1948, BS, 1949, MA, 1951; PhD, U. Ill., 1954. Prin. Maplewood Elementary Sch., St. Paul, 1949-51; instr. U. Ill., 1952-53, Ind. U., 1954-57; asst. prof. U. Minn., Mpls., 1957-61, assoc. prof., 1961-64, acting chmn. classics, 1963-64, prof. classics, chmn. comparative lit., 1964-65; prof. English Macalester Coll., St. Paul, 1965-67, coord. humanities program, 1966-67; prof. comparative lit. and classics U. Wis.-Milw., 1967—, prof. English, 1990-96, chmn. classics dept., 1967-70, 86-89, chmn. comparative lit., 1970-73, 76-83, coord. Scandinavian studies program, 1982-96. Cons. St. Paul Tchrs. Sr. High Sch. English, 1964 Author: Odi et Amo: The Complete Poetry of Catullus, 1959, Heart of Reason: Introductory Essays in Modern-World Humanities, 1963, Pindar's Odes, 1974, Greek and Latin Word Elements, 1981, The Love Songs of the Carmina Burana, 1987, Pär Lagerkvist: Five Early Works, 1989; editor Minn. Rev., 1963-67; Classical Jour., 1966-72; contbr. articles to profl. jours. With AUS, 1944-46. Decorated Bronze Star; recipient Disting. Teaching award U. Minn., 1962, Disting. Teaching award U. Wis.-Milw., 1974, 91, 99. Mem. Am. Philol. Assn., Am. Comparative Lit. Assn., Modern Lang. Assn., Soc. for Advancement Scandinavian Study, Phi Beta Kappa (pres. chpt. 1975-76). Home: 11618 N Bobolink Ln Mequon WI 53092-2804 Office: U Wis French/Italian/Comp Lit PO Box 413 Milwaukee WI 53201-0413 E-mail: rexroy333@aol.com., rexcy@uwm.edu.

SWANSON, SHIRLEY JUNE, registered nurse, travel nurse, adult education educator; b. Dade City, Fla., Feb. 26, 1942; d. Alan John and Ollie Mae (Jackson) S.; m. James A. Whatley, 1960 (div. 1962); 1 child, Marsha L. Glunt; m. Jerald Ward Steen, Sr., June 7, 1963; children: Linda A. Stanley, Jerald Ward, Jr., Jerald Wagner. AA, Hillsborough C.C., 1974; BA, U. South Fla., 1975; AS, Gupton-Jones Coll., 1992, No. Maine Tech. Coll., 1996; postgrad., St. Joseph's Coll., Windham, Maine, 2001—. RN; cert. in elem. and adult edn. scis., Maine; mortician. Personal life underwriter Home Ins. Co., N.Y.C., 1979-82; with L.L. Bean, Freeport, Maine, 1988-90; tchr. biology Caribou (Maine) Adult Edn., 1994-96. Owner Alan's Dau.'s Place, 1988—, Angel Quilts, 1996—; spkr. in field. Author, editor Coffee Break, 1963-64. Ofcl. spinner Fla. State Fair, Tampa, 1984-85; spinner East Animal Farm/Westshore Mall, Tampa, 1984-85; guest spinner Town of Westfield (Maine) Jubilee Days, 1995; hospice vol. Vis. Nurses of Aroostook County, Caribou, 1995—. Billerica, Mass. O.E.S. scholar, 1975, Am. Bd. Funeral Svc. Edn. scholar, 1992, Caribou Adult Edn. Sys. scholar, 1995. Mem. Phi Theta Kappa, Pi Sigma Eta. Roman Catholic. Avocations: wool spinning, commision quilting, tutoring, weaving, amateur radio W4EFM. Home: 1584 Woodland Ctr Rd Perham ME 04766-3314 Office: Caribou Adult Edn Ctr Sweden St Caribou ME 04736

SWANSON, STEPHEN OLNEY, minister, retired English educator; b. Mpls., Aug. 31, 1932; s. Carl R. and Dorothy Olney Swanson; m. Judith Seleen Swanson, June 10, 1956; children: Scott, Shelley, Noel, Kim, Brian. BA, St. Olaf Coll., 1954; grad. in theology, Luther Theol. Sem., St. Paul, 1958, BD, 1960; MA, U. Oreg., 1964, ArtsD, 1970. Ordained to ministry Evang. Luth. Ch. Am., 1958. Instr. theology Augustana Coll., Sioux Falls, S.D., 1957; instr. writing U. Oreg., Eugene, 1964-66; asst. prof. English and writing Tex. Luth. Coll., Seguin, 1966-70; assoc. prof. English and writing Camrose (Alta.) Univ. Coll., 1970-73; prof. writing St. Olaf Coll., Northfield, Minn., 1976-99. Parish pastor Luth. congregations, Minn., 1958-61, Oreg., 1962-65, Sask., 1973-74; interim pastor 31 congregations, Minn., Iowa, Wis., Alta., Sask., 1956—; dir. creative writing Tex. Luth. Coll., 1966-70, Camrose Univ. Coll., 1970-73; coach wrestling, football, volleyball, hockey, Tex., Can., Minn.; co-owner Nine-Ten Press, Northfield, 1997—. Author 26 books for adults, teens and children, including Is There Life After High Sch., 1991, The Earthkeeper Mystery Series, 4 vols., 1994, Moving Out on Your Own, 1995, The First Fall: Ytterboe Hall, 1946, 1997; playwright 6 plays; contbr. articles to jours.; columnist Now and Then, 1998-99; metal sculpture exhbns. include Luth. Brotherhood Corp. Gallery, Mpls., 1992, 94, 98, Waldorf Coll., Forest City, Iowa, 1999, Luther Coll., Decorah, Iowa, 2002. Recipient award Minn. Arts Bd., 1987, Blandin Found., Grand Rapids, Minn., 1988-89; fellow NDEA, Washington, 1968-69. Avocations: metal sculpture, fishing, volvo repair. Home: 910 St Olaf Ave Northfield MN 55057

SWANSON, STEVEN R. astronaut; b. Syracuse, NY, Dec. 3, 1960; s. Stanley and June Swanson; m. Mary Drake Young; 3 children. BS in Engring. Physics, U. Colo., 1983; MAS in Computer Sys., Fla. Atlantic U., 1986; PhD in Computer Sci., Tex. A&M U., 1998. Software engr. GTE; sys. engr. aircraft ops. divsn. NASA, Johnson Space Ctr., Houston, 1987—89, flight simulation engr. for shuttle tng. aircraft, 1989—98, astronaut, mission specialist candidate, 1998—. Mem.: Phi Kappa Phi. Avocations: mountain biking, basketball, skiing, weightlifting, running. Office: Astronaut Office/CB NASA Johnson Space Ctr Houston TX 77058*

SWANSON, WALLACE MARTIN, lawyer, investor; b. Fergus Falls, Minn., Aug. 22, 1941; s. Marvin Walter and Mary Louise (Lindsey) S.; children: Kristen Lindsey, Eric Munger. BA with honors, U. Minn., 1962; LL.B. with honors, So. Methodist U., 1965. Bar: Tex. 1965. Assoc. Coke & Coke, Dallas, 1965-70; ptnr. firm Johnson & Swanson, 1970-88; prin. Wallace M. Swanson, P.C., Rice, 1988—; chmn., CEO Ace Cash Express Inc., Irving, 1987-88, State St. Capital Corp., 1990—. Served with USNR, 1960-65. Mem. Tex. Bar Found., State Bar Tex. (securities com. 1972-86, chmn. 1978-80, coun. bus. law sect. 1980-86), Crescent Club. Methodist. Address: 6234 FM 879 Ennis TX 75119

SWANSON, WILLIAM FREDIN, III, manufacturing executive; b. Pitts., Mar. 6, 1960; s. William Fredin Jr. and Marjorie Beatrice (Davis) S.; m. Jane Anne Crosby, June 30, 1990; children: Elisabeth Anne, William Fredin IV. BSME, U. Va., 1982; M in Mgmt., Northwestern U., 1985. Asst. to v.p. mfg. Bridgestone/Firestone, Inc., Akron, Ohio, 1985-87, project mgr. Decatur, Ill., 1987-89, operating mgr., 1989-92; plant mgr. Am. Roller Co., Walkerton, Ind., 1992-95, mfg. mgr. Union Grove, Wis., 1995—2002; gen. mgr. Diamond Holding Corp., Marietta, Ga., 2002—. Mem. alumni admissions orgn. Kellogg Grad. Sch. Mgmt., Northwestern U., Evanston, Ill., 1986-97; long range planning com. chmn. Antioch (Ill.) United Meth. Ch., 1997-98, chmn. adminstrv. coun., 2000-02, lay leader, 2001-02. Avocations: golf, spectator sports, reading. Home: 1701 Kenbrook Ct Acworth GA 30101 Office: Diamond Holding Corp 150 Marr Ave Marietta GA 30060 E-mail: wfswaniii@prodigy.net., bills@diamondroller.com.

SWANSON-SCHONES, KRIS MARGIT, developmental adapted physical education educator; b. Mpls., Mar. 22, 1950; d. Donald Theodore Swanson and Alice Alida (Swanson) Suhl; m. Gary Wallace Suhl, Apr. 6, 1974 (div. Aug. 1985); m. Gregory Edward Schones, Dec. 30, 1989. BA, Augsburg Coll., 1972. Cert. devel. adapted phys. edn. tchr., phys. edn. tchr., health tchr., coach/corrective therapist. Devel. adapted phys. edn. tchr. St. Paul Schs., 1972—, adapted athletic dir., 1989—. Mem. adapted athletics adv. bd. Minn. State H.S. League, 1992—. Author: On the Move, 1979. Chmn. hospitality Tanbark Club, Lakeville, Minn., 1992—, mem. show cmty., 1991—; mem. outreach com. Spl. Olympics, Minn., 1989-94. Recipient Nutrition Edn. grant Fed. Govt., 1978-79, Christmas Album grant Spl. Olympics, 1989, Internat. Spl. Olympics Coach award Minn. Spl. Olympics, 1991. Mem. NEA, AAHPERD, Minn. Edn. Assn., Minn. Assn. Adapted Athletics (exec. bd. 1989—, sec. exec. bd. 1990—, Outstanding Svc. award Minn. State H.S. League 2001). Avocations: showing horses and dogs, gardening, fishing. Home: 16280 Webster Cir Prior Lake MN 55372-9772 Office: Humboldt Jr High Sch 640 Humboldt Ave Saint Paul MN 55107-2996

SWANSTROM, THOMAS EVAN, economist; b. Green Bay, Wis., May 17, 1939; s. Alfred Enoch and Elizabeth Nan (Thomas) S.; m. Nancy Anne Roche; children: Amy, Scott. Student. U. Notre Dame, 1957-59; BA, U. Wis., 1962, MA, 1963; postgrad., Am. U., 1963-66. Economist, U.S. Bur. Labor Statistics, Washington, 1963-66. Dir. research Population Ref. Bur., Washington, 1966-68; economist Sears, Roebuck & Co., Chgo., 1968-70, market analyst, 1970-72, mgr. catalog research, 1972-75, asst. mgr. econ. research, 1974-80, chief economist, 1980-90; pres. Consumer Econs., Chgo., 1991—; mem. bus. research adv. council Bur. Labor Stats.; adj. prof. Lake Forest Grad. Sch. Mgmt. Contbr. articles to industry publs. Mem. Nat. Assn. Bus. Economists, Conf. Bus. Economists. E-mail: tevanswan@aol.com.

SWANTON, SUSAN IRENE, library director; b. Rochester, N.Y., Nov. 29, 1941; d. Walter Frederick and Irene Wray S.; m. Wayne Holman, Apr. 12, 1969 (div. June 1973); 1 child, Michael; ptnr. James Donald Lathrop; children: Kathryn, Kristin. AB, Harvard U., 1963; MLS, Columbia U., 1965. Libr. dir. Warsaw (N.Y.) Pub. Libr., 1963-64, Gates Pub. Libr., Rochester, N.Y., 1965—. Pres. Drug and Alcohol Coun., Rochester, 1985-91, mem. adv. coun., 1992-94; bd. dirs., co-chair info. svcs. Rochester Freenet, 1995—; sec. Gates Hist. Preservation Commn., 2000—. Mem. Gates Historical Soc. (pres. 1998—), Gates-Chili Coun. Rochester Met. C. of C. (pres. 1982, sec. 1990-94, Citizen of Yr. 1995), Harvard Club of Rochester (mem. adv. bd.). Office: Gates Pub Libr 1605 Buffalo Rd Rochester NY 14624-1637 E-mail: sswanton@ggw.org., sswanton@gateslibrary.org.

SWANTON, VIRGINIA LEE, writer, publisher, bookseller; b. Oak Park, Ill., Feb. 6, 1933; d. Milton Wesley and Eleanor Louise (Linnell) S. BA, Lake Forest (Ill.) Coll., 1954; MA in English Lit., Northwestern U., 1955; cert. in acctg., Coll. of Lake County, Ill., 1984. Editorial asst. Publs. Office, Northwestern U., Evanston, Ill., 1955-58; reporter Lake Forester, Lake Forest, 1959; editor Scott, Foresman & Co., Glenview, Ill., 1959-84; copy editor, travel coord. McDougal Littell/Houghton Mifflin, Evanston, 1985-94; sr. bookseller B. Dalton Bookseller, Lake Forest, Ill., 1985—; author, pub. Gold Star Publ. Svcs., 1994—. Contbr. articles to profl. jours.; pub. local interest, poetry and ref. works. Mem. bd. deacons First Presbyn. Ch. of Lake Forest; former sec. bd. dirs., newsletter editor Career Resource Ctr., Inc., Lake Forest; current events discusssion vol. Lake Forest/Lake Bluff Sr. Ctr. Mem. Deerpath Art League, Chgo. Women in Pub., Lake Forest/Lake Bluff Hist. Soc. Presbyterian. Avocation: gardening. Office: Gold Star Publ Svcs PO Box 125 Lake Forest IL 60045-1333

SWART, BONNIE BLOUNT, artist; b. Shreveport, La., May 19, 1939; d. Jonathan Prescott and Alice Florence (Crawford) Blount; m. Carter Eaton Swart; children: Kathleen Anne, Nancy Laurie, Sherry Colleen. Student, U. Calif., Davis, Ventura Coll., 1984-88. Exhibited in group exhbns. at Am. Acad. Equine Art, 1989, 92, 93, 94, 96, 97, 2000, 01, Nat. Mus. of the Horse, Lexington, Ky., Pastel Soc. of West Coast, Sacramento, 1995, 96, 97, Ann. Exhbn. on Animals in Art, La. State U., Baton Rouge, 1995, 96, Art at the Dog Show, Wichita, Kans., 1995, Harness Tracks of Am., Lexington, 1994, 96, Am. Acad. of Equine Art, Louisville, 1992, 93, 96, Arabian Jockey Club Art

Auction, Delaware Park, Del., 1991, Equine Rsch. Benefit, Morvin Park, Leesburg, 1991, Arabian Horse Trust Art Auction, Scottsdale, 1990, 97-98, Women Artist's of the West, Biloxi, Miss., 1989, 97, 98, Internat. Arabian Horse Assn., Ky. Horse Park, Louisville, 1989, Arabian Horse Trust Mus. Exhibit, Westminster, Colo., 1987-89, Oil Painters of Am., Taos, N.Mex., 1997, Nat. Sporting Libr., Middleburg, Va., 2001; represented in pvt. collections. Mem. Am. Acad. Equine Art (assoc.), Knickerbocker Artists (signature mem.), Pastel Soc. West Coast (signature mem.). Home: 160 Lakeside Loop Crescent City CA 95531 E-mail: cswart@earthlink.net.

SWART, JANICE LYNN, accountant, consultant; b. Colby, Kans., July 9, 1964; d. Robert Dean and Alma Kay S. BBA in Fin., Fort Hays State U., Kans., 1986. Acctg. supr. U. Kans. Sch. of Medicine, Wichita, 1987-91; auditor Fourth Fin. Corp., 1991-94, project support analyst, 1994-95; support cons. NxTrend Tech., Colorado Springs, Colo., 1995-97, support cons. ptnr., 1997-98, bus. cons., 1998—. Office: NxTrend Tech Inc 5555 Tech Center Dr Ste 300 Colorado Springs CO 80919-2372

SWART, SARAH LELGARDE, director, librarian; b. Jackson, Mich., July 9, 1947; m. Kenneth Dale Swart. BA in Secondary Edn., Western Mich. U., 1969; M Bus. Mgmt.-Mktg., Aquinas Coll., 1989; M in Libr. and Info. Sci., Wayne State U., 1996. Cert. in spirituality. Info. scientist GM, Pontiac, Mich., 1996—98, Ford Motor Co., Dearborn, 1998—2000; dir. instrnl. tech. U. Detroit Mercy, 2001—. Contbr. articles to profl. jours. Mem.: ALA, Spiritual Dirs. Internat., Am. Assn. for Higher Edn. Avocations: knitting, reading, spirituality. Home: 651 Laprairie Ferndale MI 48220 Office: Univ Detroit Mercy PO Box 19900 Detroit MI 48219 Home Fax: 313-993-6195; Office Fax: 313-993-6195. Personal E-mail: swartclan@earthlink.net. Business E-Mail: swartsa@udmercy.edu.

SWARTHWORTH, SHARON T. military officer; b. Providence, Nov. 8, 1959; Enlisted U.S. Army, 1977; pers. adminstrn. specialist 50th Signal Bn., Ft. Bragg, NC, 304th Signal Bn., Republic of Korea; legal specialist 16th Signal Bn., Ft. Hood, Tex., 1981—82; legal specialist/ct. reporter 110th JAG Detachment, Ft. Carson, Colo., 1st Army, Ft. Meade, Md., sgt. 1st class; legal adminstr. Judge Advocate Gen.'s Corps, 1984; tng., advising and counseling officer Warrant Office Cand. Sch., Ft. McCoy, Wis.; IMA legal adminstr. Spl. Forces Command, Ft. Bragg, NC; legal adminstr. Legal Assistance Task Force/Desert Storm, Office of Judge Advocate Gen., Washington, Legal Svc. Study Group, Office of Gen. Counsel, Washington, Presidio of San Francisco, U.S. Army Litigation Ctr., Arlington, Va., U.S. Army Legal Svcs. Agy.; dir. ops. for legal tech. Office of Judge Advocate, Arlington, Va.; warrant officer Judge Advocate Gen.'s Corps, 1999—. Decorated Meritorious Svc. medal with 3 oak leaf clusters, Army Commendation medal with 6 oak leaf clusters, Army Achievement medal, numerous others. Office: Office of Judge Advocate General US Pentagon Washington DC 20310-1500*

SWARTOUT, HANK B. gas industry executive; m. Carol Swartout; 4 children. Grad. in Petroleum Engring., U. Wyo., 1976. Pres. Cypress Drilling, 1985; chmn., pres., CEO Precision Drilling Corp., Calgary, Canada. Office: Precision Drilling Corp 4200 150-6th Ave SW T2P 3Y7 Calgary AB Canada*

SWARTOUT, TORIN SHERWIN ROBERTS, logistics executive, transportation consultant; b. Brockport, N.Y., Mar. 14, 1952; s. Sherwin George and Eileen May (Tavenner) S.; m. Anne Elizabeth Washington, July 21, 1978; children: Jesse, Jason, Katherine Lynne, Joseph. BA in Philosophy, Antioch Coll., 1972; cert. custom house broker, World Trade Inst., 1978, cert. of chartering, 1979. Lic. customhouse brokers. European sales mgr. Antioch Bookplate Co., Yellow Springs, Ohio, 1971; pres. Alternative Living, Inc., Brockport, N.Y., 1972-76; import mgr. Spies Shipping Corp., N.Y.C., 1976-77; equipment control mgr. Hansen and Tidemann, 1977-78; intermodal ops. mgr. Star Shipping of N.Y., Inc., 1979-81, mgr. container svcs., 1981-85; dist. mgr. midwest Star Shipping, Inc., Des Plaines, Ill., 1985-86, 87-89, v.p. sales Tokyo, 1986-87, trade mgr. U.S. gulf Stamford, Conn., 1989-91; gen. traffic mgr. Atlantic Trades, 1991-96; pres. Viking Homes, Hempstead, N.Y., 1981-85. Bd. dirs. Alternative Living, Inc., Brockport, 1977-91, Viking Homes, Ridgefield, Conn.; custom house broker T. Swartout CHB, Chgo., 1978—; cons. TransNat. Shipping Corp., N.Y.C., 1981-88; owners' rep. Spliethoff's, 1996—; mng. dir. Ocean Transport Svcs., Ridgefield, Conn., 1996—. Vice pres. N.W. Civic Assn., Hempstead, 1983, Georgetown Manor Homeowners Assn., Arlington Heights, 1987; cubmaster pack 74 Cub Scouts, Ridgefield, Conn. Mem. Midwest Fgn. Commerce Club, Ocean Freight Agts. Assn., Norwegian-Am. C. of C., Japanese C. of C. (affiliate), Holland Soc., Sons of Norway (v.p. 1981-82, 90-91, pres. 1983-84), Conn. Maritime Assn., Internat. Forest Products Transport Assn., Railway Industrial Clearance Assn. Congregationalist. Avocations: hiking, farming, travel, cooking, Norwegian language. Office: Ocean Transport Svcs 68 Great Hill Rd Ridgefield CT 06877-2629 E-mail: otsusa@aol.com.

SWARTWOUT, JOSEPH RODOLPH, obstetrics and gynecology educator, administrator; b. Pascagoula, Miss., June 17, 1925; s. Thomas Roswell and Marshall (Coleman) S.; m. Brandon C. Leftwich, Jan. 23, 1989. Student, Miss. Coll., 1943-44; MD, Tulane U., 1951. Intern Touro Infirmary, New Orleans, 1951-52; asst. in obstetrics and medicine Tulane U., 1952-53, instr., 1955-60; Nat. Found. fellow Harvard U., 1953-55; asst. in medicine Peter Bent Brigham Hosp., Boston, 1953-55; assoc. in obstetric rsch. Boston Lying-In-Hosp., 1953-55; asst. prof. U. Pitts., 1960-61; assoc. prof. Emory U., Atlanta, 1961-66; assoc. prof. ob-gyn. U. Chgo., 1967-80; chief ob-gyn. at Prime Health, also clin. assoc. prof. U. Kans. Sch. Medicine, 1978-80; prof. dept. ob-gyn. Mercer U. Sch. Medicine, Macon, Ga., 1980-95, prof. emeritus, 1995; dist. health dir. Dist. 5-2, 1996—; dist. dir. Ga. Divsn. Pub. Health, 1996—. Fellow Am. Coll. Obstetricians and Gynecologists, Am. Heart Assn. (coun. clin. cardiology), Am. Acad. Reproductive Medicine; mem. AMA, APHA, Med. Assn. Ga., Bibb County Med. Soc. Home: 4384 Peach Pkwy Fort Valley GA 31030-8155

SWARTZ, ALAN E. music educator; s. Russell F. Swartz; m. Laura H. Hughes, Aug. 13, 1983; 1 child Meghan. B of Music Edn., Baylor U., 1982; MA, U. Tex., 1996. Music faculty U. Tex., Tyler, 1992—, Tyler (Tex.) Jr. Coll., 1995—2001; instr. pvt. music studio, 1983—2001. Reviewer: book Advanced Harmony, Robert Ottman, 1999, musician regional orch. performances, regional choral performances. Mem.: Soc. for Music Theory, Tex. Music Educators Assn., Music Educators Nat. Conf., Internat. Trombone Assn., Gamma Beta Phi, Pi Kappa Lambda. Avocations: photography, computers, gas engines. Office: U Tex 3900 University Blvd Tyler TX 75799

SWARTZ, ALLAN JOEL, hospital administrator; b. July 2, 1935; s. Milton and Rosalie Swartz; m. Roslyn Thelma Holt, June 2, 1963. AB, Ctrl. H.S., 1955; PharmD, U. So. Calif., 1958; postgrad., Loyola U. Sch. Law, 1964—66; MA in Edn., Pepperdine U., 1976. Asst. dir. pharmacy City of Hope Nat. Med. Ctr., Duarte, Calif., 1966—69, dir. pharm. svcs., 1969—78, Encino Hosp., 1978—93, quality assurance coord., 1986—93, hazardous materials officer, 1986—93, risk and safety mgr., 1987—93; asst. clin. prof. pharmacy U. So. Calif., 1971—82, 1987—; asst. clin. prof. U. Pacific, 1978—86, regional coord. externship program, 1982—86; dir. pharm. svcs. Century City Hosp., 1994—96, Santa Monica/UCLA Med. Ctr., 1996—98. Chmn. pharm. group purchasing com. Hosp. Coun. So. Calif., 1978—82; mem. prof. edn. com. Am. Cancer Soc., 1970—78. Feature editor: Pharmaceutics Cancer Nursing, 1977—81, mem. editl. bd.: , 1983—98, cons. editor: Am. Jour. Hosp. Pharmacy, 1978—83, mem. editl. bd.: , 2001—04. Founder L.A. Music Ctr.; bd. dirs. Vis. Nurses Assn., L.A., 1983—93; chmn. bd. dirs, Vis. Nurse Home Svc., Inc., 1986—88; bd. dir. H.O.P.E. Unit Found., 1980—83; founder Gold Circle, Frat. Friends, L.A. County Mus. Art, W. Ctr. at UCLA; mem. Royo Ctr. Circle. With U.S. Army, 1958—59. Recipient Order of Golden Sword award, Calif. divsn. Am. Cancer Soc., 1974, cert. merit, 1978, award of recognition, U. So. Calif. Comprehensive Cancer Ctr., 1983. Mem.: AAAS, Am. Med. Writers Assn., So. Calif. Soc. Health-Systems Pharmacists (pres. 1972), Calif. Soc. Health-Systems Pharmacists (pres. 1976), Am. Soc. Health-Systems Pharmacists (commendation 1976). Address: PO Box 241866 Los Angeles CA 90024

SWARTZ, B(ENJAMIN) K(INSELL), JR. archaeologist, educator; b. L.A., June 23, 1931; s. Benjamin Kinsell and Maxine Marietta (Pearce) S.; m. Cyrilla Casillas, Oct. 23, 1966; children: Benjamin Kinsell III, Frank Casillas. AA summa cum laude, L.A. City Coll., 1952; BA, UCLA, 1954, MA, 1958; PhD, U. Ariz., 1964. Curator Klamath County Mus., Oreg., 1959-61, rsch. assoc., 1961-62; asst. prof. anthropology Ball State U., Muncie, Ind., 1964-68, assoc. prof., 1968-72, prof., 1972-2001, prof. emeritus, 2001—. Vis. sr. lectr. U. Ghana, 1970-71; exch. prof. U. Yaounde, Cameroon, 1984-85; field rschr. N.Am. and West Africa; mem. exec. bd., pres. Am. Com. to Advance the Study of Petroglyphs and Pictographs; rep. to Internat. Fedn. Rock Art Orgns.; bd. dirs. Coun. Conservation Ind. Archaeology; mem. adv. bd. Am. Com. for Preservation of Archaeol. Collections. Contbr. revs. and articles to profl. jours.; author books, monographs in field, including: West African Culture Dynamics, 1980, Indiana's Prehistoric Past, 1981, Rock Art and Posterity, 1991, Procs. of Ist Internat. South African Rock Art Assn. Conf., 1991. Klamath County chmn. Oreg. Statehood Centennial, 1959. With USN, 1954-56. Fellow AAAS, Ind. Acad. Sci.; mem. Current Anthropology (assoc.), Soc. Am. Archaeology, Internat. Com. Rock Art, Sigma Xi, Lambda Alpha (nat. coun., exec. sec.). Home: 805 W Charles St Muncie IN 47305-2235 E-mail: 01bkswartz@bsuvc.bsu.edu.

SWARTZ, BETH AMES, artist; b. N.Y.C., Feb. 5, 1936; BS, Cornell U., 1957; MA, NYU, 1960. Co-founder Internat. Friends of Transformative Art, Phoenix; exec. dir. Culture Care, 1994; visual artist N.Y.C..Scottsdale/Phoenix, 1965—. Exhibited in solo shows at Ariz. State U, Phoenix, 1970, Rosenzweig Ctr. Gallery, Phoenix, 1970, Galleria Janna, Mexico City, 1971, Pavilion Gallery, Scottsdale, 1975, Springfield (Mo.) Art Mus., 1979, Frank Marino Gallery, N.Y.C., 1979, 81, Art Resources Gallery, Denver, 1983, U. Calif., Irvine, 1983, ACA Galleries, N.Y.C., 1985, Elaine Horwitch Galleries, Palm Springs, Calif., Scottsdale, Ariz., Salt Lake Art Ctr., Univ. Art Mus./U. Ariz., Tempe, Holtzman Art Gallery/Towson State U., 1990, Joy Tash Gallery, Scottsdale, Hermann Hesse Mus., Montqgnola, Switzerland; group shows in Scottsdale, Provincetown, Mass., Lake Forest, Ill., Gainesville, Fla., N.Y.C., Salt Lake City, Palm Springs, L.A., Spokane, St. Louis, Knoxville, Atlanta, Colorado Springs, Tucson, Reno, San Francisco, others; represented in collections at Albuquerque Mus. Art, Bklyn. Mus. ARt, Denver Art Mus., The Jewish Mus., N.Y.C., San Francisco Mus. Modern Art, skirball Mus./Hebrew Union Coll., U. Ariz. Mus. Art, Yuma Art Ctr., Ariz. Bank, Canyon Ranch, Home Petroleum, Nat. Bank Ariz., Phelps Dodge Corp., Subaru Corp., United Bank, numerous others; subject of numerous articles. Home: 5346 E Sapphire Ln Paradise Valley AZ 85253-2531

SWARTZ, BURTON EUGENE, artist, actor, director, writer, educator; b. Mpls. MA, Columbia U. Cert. tchr. English, drama, N.Y.C. Dir. Ensemble Studio Theatre, N.Y.C., 2000; performer Mono-Loggers Orfinmagic Prod, Prodrs Club, 2000, performer Don't Tell Mama, 2001—. Author, prodr.: (dramas) Once Upon a Deal, The Hidden, Eastside Roulette, Grasshoppers; contbr. theater revs., articles to various publs. Winner essay competition WLIB Radio, N.Y.C., nat. art competition 1st St. Gallery, N.Y.C., 1992, play contest atheatre Co., N.Y.C., 1995; artist residency fellow Millay Colony, Austerlitz, N.Y., 1993. Mem. Poets and Writers, Inc., Actors Equity, Dramatists Guild. Office: Cathedral Sta PO Box 292 New York NY 10025

SWARTZ, CONRAD MELTON, psychiatrist; b. Bklyn., Nov. 22, 1946; s. Louis Jules and Frances (Shaw) S.; m. Cynthia Anne Heise, June 22, 1975; children: Meryle, Sandor. B Engring., Cooper Union, 1966; MS, Calif. Inst. Tech., 1968; PhD in Chem. Engring., U. Minn., 1972, MD, 1974. Diplomate Am. Bd. Psychiatry and Neurology. Intern Northwestern Hosp., Mpls., 1974-75; resident in psychiatry U. Iowa Hosps. and Clinics, Iowa City, 1975-78, asst. prof. psychiatry, 1978-82, U. Health Scis./Chgo. Med. Sch., North Chicago, Ill., 1982-83, assoc. prof. psychiatry and pharmacology, 1983-87, prof. psychiatry, 1987-91; assoc. chief of staff for edn. VA Med. Ctr., 1987-91; prof. psychiatry med. sch. U. Okla., Oklahoma City, 1991-92; prof. psychiatry East Carolina U., Greenville, N.C., 1992-96; dir. rsch., prof. psychiatry East Tenn. State U., Johnson City, Tenn., 1996-98; prof. psychiatry St. Louis U., 1998—99; prof. psychiatry, chief psychiat. rsch. So. Ill. U., Springfield, 1999—. Cons. Somatics, Inc., Lake Bluff, Ill., 1984—. Contbr. articles on adverse health effects of male hypogonadism, hormone kinetics theory to profl. publs. Recipient clin. rsch. award Am. Acad. Clin. Psychiatrists, 1989, 90. Fellow Am. Psychiat. Assn., Am. Coll. Clin. Pharmacology; mem. Assn. Convulsive Therapy (pres. 1990-92), Soc. Biol. Psychiatry, Tau Beta Pi. Achievements include 8 patents on instrumentation and methods for electroconvulsive therapy; discovery of low levels of male sex hormone testosterone imply substantial risk for myocardial infarction, ECT emergence agitation is induced by the products of muscle metabolism and is thereby similar to chemically-induced panic disorder; rsch. on graphical methods that exactly state drug dose prediction according to 1-compartment pharmacokinetics. Home: PO Box 581 Chatham IL 62629-0581 Office: Dept Psychiatry So Ill U PO Box 19642 Springfield IL 62794-9642

SWARTZ, DONALD EVERETT, television executive; b. Mpls., Mar. 7, 1916; s. Albert L. and Sara (Shore) S.; m. Helen Gordon, Mar. 24, 1940; children: Stuart, Lawrence, Gary. Grad. high sch. Owner Ind. Film Distbrs., 1940-53, Tele-Film Assocs., 1953-57; pres., gen. mgr. KMSP-TV, Mpls., 1957-79; pres. United TV, Inc. (subs. 20th Century Fox Film Corp. until 1981); operating KMSP-TV, KTV4, Salt Lake City, KBHK-TV, San Francisco KMOL-TV, San Antonio; CEO United Television, Inc., Mpls., 1979-85; cons. KMOL-TV, 1985—; founder Tele-Video Assocs., 1985—, Tele-Video Entertainment, 1985—; owner/mgr. Donald Investment Co., 1989—. Vice pres. Twin City Broadcast Skills Bank (scholarship program), St. Paul Arts and Sci. Inst.; pres. U. Minn. Heart Hosp.; mem. Gov.'s Commn. Bicentennial; bd. dirs. Mpls. United Jewish Fund and Council; Mem. Mpls. Inst. Arts, Mpls., St. Paul chambers commerce, Minn. Orch. Assn., Citizens League. Named Minn. Pioneer Broadcaster of Yr., 1992, charter mem. Hall of Fame, Panck Mus. of Broadcasting, 2001; recipient Silver Circle award, St. Paul chpt. NATAS., 2000. Mem.U. Minn Alumni Assn., Press Club (Mpls.), Advt. Standard Club (Mpls.), Hillcrest Country Club (St. Paul), Variety Club, Mission Hills Country Club (Rancho Mirage, Calif.), Oak Ridge Country Club (Mpls.), B'nai B'rith. Jewish (pres. temple). Home: 2221 Youngman Ave Saint Paul MN 55116-3055 Office: Ste 224 10505 Wayzata Blvd Minnetonka MN 55305 Fax: (763) 952-0661.

SWARTZ, DONALD PERCY, physician; b. Preston, Ont., Can., Sept. 12, 1921; s. Simon Wingham and Lydia Ethel Swartz; m. Norma Mae Woolner, June 24, 1944 (dec. May 1980); children: Ian Donald, Rhonda Swartz Peterson; m. Isabelle Liz Dales, Apr. 21, 1984. BA, MD cum laude, U. Western Ont., 1951, M.Sc. cum laude, 1953. Intern Victoria Hosp., London, 1951-52; asst. resident Westminster Hosp., 1953-54; resident Johns Hopkins U., Balt., 1954-58; asst. prof. ob-gyn. U. Western Ont., London, 1958-62; prof. Columbia U., N.Y.C., 1962-72; dir. ob-gyn. Harlem Hosp.; prof. dept. ob-gyn. Albany (N.Y.) Med. Coll., 1972-99, prof. emeritus, 2000—, chmn., 1972-79, chief sect. gen. gynecology, 1982-88, head. div. gen. gynecology, 1988—, acting chmn., 1992. Vis. prof. dept. Ob-Gyn. U. Rochester, N.Y., 1981 Assoc. editor: Advances in Planned Parenthood. Vice pres., pres. Assn. Planned Parenthood Physicians, 1972-74. Served with RCAF, 1942-45. NRC Can. fellow, 1952-53; Am. Cancer Soc. fellow, 1956-57; Markle scholar, 1958-63 Fellow ACOG, Royal Coll. Surgeons Can., Am. Gynecologic Soc., Am. Gyn-Ob Soc., Am. Fertility Soc., Royal Soc. Health, Soc. Gynecologic Surgeons. Home: 24 Devon Rd Delmar NY 12054-3534 Office: Albany Med Coll 47 New Scotland Ave Albany NY 12208-3412 E-mail: swartzd@mail.amc.edu. *It has been a privilege and a challenge to participate in the forefront of the revolutionary changes in the health care of women during the past five decades. Acceptance, initiation and implementation of positive change have been guidelines for gratifying action.*

SWARTZ, JACK, chamber of commerce executive; b. Nov. 24, 1932; s. John Ralph and Fern (Cave) S.; m. Nadine Ann Langlois, Aug. 4, 1956; children: Dana, Shawn, Tim, Jay. AA, Dodge City C.C., 1953; student, St. Mary of Plains Coll., 1953-55, 58; BBA, Washburn U., 1973, BA in Econs., 1974. V.p. D.C. Terminal Elevator Co., Dodge City, Kans., 1957-65; exec. v.p. Kans. Jaycees, Hutchinson, 1965-68, Kans. C. of C. and Industry, Topeka, 1968-82; pres. Nebr. C. of C. and Industry, Lincoln, 1982—. Past chmn., bd. regents U.S. C. of C. Inst. U. Colo. With U.S. Army, 1955-57. Named Outstanding Local Pres. in State, Kans. Jaycees, 1961, Outstanding Young Man of Yr., Dodge City Jaycees, 1961, Outstanding State V.P., U.S. Jaycees, 1962, Outstanding Nat. Dir., 1963, Nebr. Bus. Hall of Fame, Sublette H.S. Wall of Honor. Mem. Am. Soc. Assn. Execs. (cert.), Am. Chamber Commerce Execs. (bd. dirs., cert.), Nebr. Chamber Commerce Execs. (sec.-treas.), Nebr. Soc. Assn. Execs. (past pres.), Nebr. Fedn. Bus. Assns. (pres. 1986-88), Nebr. Thoroughbred Breeders Assn. (bd. dirs.), Washburn U. Alum. (bd. dirs.), Rotary. Republican. Roman Catholic. Home: 625 W Gibraltar Ln Phoenix AZ 85023-5243

SWARTZ, JON DAVID, psychologist, educator; b. Houston, Dec. 28, 1934; s. Orville Elmo and Nina June (Baker) S.; m. Carol Joseph Hampton, Oct. 20, 1966; children: Eric Jason McFarland, Sally Katherine Baker, Edward Joseph Bryson. BA, U. Tex., Austin, 1956, MA, 1961, PhD, 1969, postgrad., 1973-74. Rsch. and tng. asst. dept. psychology U. Tex., 1956-62, asst. prof. dept. ednl. psychology, 1969-72; assoc. prof. psychology, chmn. U. Tex.-Permian Basin, 1974-78, chmn. anthropology and sociology, 1975-78, field dir., 1962-65; asst. dir. Austin Longitudinal Rsch. project, 1965-69, co-dir., 1969-74; research scientist Hogg Found. for Mental Health, 1972-74; prof. edn. and psychology Southwestern U., Georgetown, Tex., 1978-90, vis. prof. psychology, 1991, dir. testing and guidance, 1978-81, holder Brown vis. chair, 1978-82, assoc. dean for librs. and learning resources, 1981-90; coord., adminstrv. head Killeen office Cen. Counties Ctr. for MHMR Svcs., Temple, Tex., 1990-91; chief psychol. svcs., 1991-99; pvt. practice, 2000—. Lectr. Nat. U., Mexico, 1962, U. Ctrl. Tex., 1994, Temple Coll., 1994. Author: (with W.H. Holtzman) Inkblot Perception and Personality, 1961, (with C.C. Cleland) Mental Retardation: Approaches to Institutional Change, 1969, Administrative Issues in Institutions for the Mentally Retarded, 1972, Exceptionalities Through the Lifespan: An Introduction, 1982, Multihandicapped Mentally Retarded, 1973, (with W.H. Holtzman, R. Diaz-Guerrero) Personality Development in Two Cultures, 1975; editor: (with C.C. Cleland, L.W. Talkington) Profoundly Mentally Retarded, 1976, (with R.K. Eyman, C.C. Cleland) Research with the Profoundly Retarded, 1978, Holtzman Inkblot Technique: An Annotated Bibliography (supplement), 1988, (with R.C. Reinehr, W.H. Holtzman) Holtzman Inkblot Technique: An Annotated Bibliography 1956-1982, 1983, SW U. Bibliographic Series, 1986-90, (with R.C. Reinehr) Handbook of Old-Time Radio, 1993, Holtzman Inkblot Technique: Research Guide and Bibliography, 1999; contbr.: Handbook of Texas, 1996; editl. assoc. Current Anthropology, 1971-77; assoc. editor: Am. Corrective Therapy Jour., 1971-81, Exceptional Children, 1982-84; mem. editl. bd. Tex. Psychologist, 1979-83 , Phi Kappa Phi Jour./Nat. Forum, 1976-80; editl. cons. Mental Retardation, 1972-77; book rev. editor Jour. Biol. Psychology, 1972-80; book rev. editor for English lang. publs. Revista Interamericana de Psicologia, 1983-89; reviewer Sci. Books, Films, 1978—; cons. editor Jour. Personality Assessment, 1981-90; contbr. over 500 articles to profl. jours. Mem. Mayor's Drug Abuse Panel, Odessa, Tex., 1975-78; chmn. adv. bd. Human Potentials Ctr., Permian Basin Cmty. Ctrs. for Mental Health and Mental Retardation, Odessa and Midland, Tex., 1975-78; bd. govs. Mood-Heritage Mus., 1984-90. U.S. Office Edn. fellow, 1964-66, U. Tex. fellow, 1973-74; recipient Franklin Gilliam prize Humanities Rsch. Ctr. U. Tex., 1965, Spencer Rsch. award Nat. Acad. Edn., 1972, Faculty Fellowship award Southwestern U., 1981 Fellow AAAS, Am. Psychol. Soc., Soc. Personality Assessment (life); mem. Western Rsch. Conf. on Mental Retardation, Am. Acad. Mental Retardation, Southwestern Psychol. Assn., Bell County Psychol. Assn., Sigma Xi, Psi Chi, Mu Alpha Nu, Delta Tau Kappa, Phi Kappa Phi, Phi Delta Kappa. E-mail: jon_swartz@hotmail.com. *All my life I have had teachers, in school and out, who challenged me to do more than I thought I was capable of doing. Any success I have achieved, I owe to them and their efforts in my behalf.*

SWARTZ, MARC JEROME, anthropologist, educator; b. Omaha, Oct. 31, 1931; s. Samuel and Esther (Brown) Swartz; m. Audrey Marcia Rosenbaum, July 10, 1952; children: William, Matthew, Robert. BA, Washington U., St. Louis, 1952; MA, Washington U., 1954; PhD, Havard U., 1958. Instr. U. Mass., Amherst, 1957, asst. prof., 1958—59, U. Chgo., 1958—64; assoc. prof. Mich. State U., East Lansing, 1964—67; prof. U. Calif. San Diego, La Jolla, 1969—. Vis. prof. Cornell U., Ithaca, NY, 1967—68; chmn. dept. anthropology U. Calif. San Diego, La Jolla, 1970—76, chmn. social sci. divsn., 1973—76; conf. organizer Werner -Gren Found. for Anthrop. Rsch., 1975; rsch. dir. society study NIH (Swahali Rsch), 1975—79; chmn. Muir Coll. faculty U. Calif. San Diego, 1986—88; external examiner U. Nairobi, Kenya, 1987—89. Author and editor): (book) Political Anthropology, 1966, Local Level Politics, 1968; author: The Way the World Is: Swahali (Life), 1991. Mem. exec. com. La Jolla Shores Heights Arch. Com., Calif., 1988—89. Fellow, John Simn Guggenheim Found., 1975—76. Fellow: Am. Anthrop. Assn. (exec. bd. 1991—92, ethics com. 1972—73); mem.: Assn. for Polit. and Legal Anthropology (pres. 1991—92). Achievements include first to cultural anthropologist to study the WaBena of southwestern Tanzania and the first to carry out intensive fieldwork with the Mombasa Swahili Community. The study began in 1975 and is continuing. Avocations: travel, reading, media. Office: Anthrop Dept UCSD 9500 Gillman Dr La Jolla CA 92037 Office Fax: 858-534-5946.

SWARTZ, MARK EVAN, archivist; b. Boston, June 5, 1958; s. Hyman and Helen Shirley S. BA, Harvard U., 1980; MA, NYU, 1983, PhD, 1996. Monitor Grey Art Gallery, NYU, N.Y.C., 1981—84; reference asst. Bobst Libr., NYU, 1984—88; archivist Shubert Archive, 1988—. Asst. reading room supr. Harvard Theatre Collection, Cambridge, Mass., 1978-80, supr., 1980; bibliographer Am. Trust for British Libr., Cambridge, 1986. Author: Oz Before the Rainbow: L. Frank Baum's "The Wonderful Wizard of Oz" on Stage & Screen to 1939, 2000; co-author: The Shuberts Present: 100 Years of American Theater, 2001; editor The Passing Show, 1988—. Mem. Am. Soc. Theatre Rsch., Soc. Am. Archivists, Archivists Roundtable N.Y. Home: 40 Waterside Plaza # 21 H New York NY 10010 Office: Shubert Archive 149 W 45th St New York NY 10036 E-mail: markes@shubertarchive.org.

SWARTZ, MARK LEE, lawyer; b. Amesbury, Mass., May 17, 1954; s. Bernard Jerome and Evelyn Vivian Swartz. BS, U. Mass., 1976; JD, Case Western U., 1979. Bar: Mass. 1979, Ohio 1979, U.S. Dist. Ct. Mass. 1980, U.S. Ct. Appeals (1st cir.) 1980. Pub. defender Essex County, Mass., 1980-83; pvt. practice Amesbury, 1980—. Atty. Amesbury Housing Rehab. Program, 1980-81, Merrimac Housing Authority, Merrimac, 1980-86, Amesbury Housing Authority, 1980-86. Mem. Mass. Bar Assn., Phi Beta Kappa, Phi Kappa Phi. Republican. Avocations: reading, dancing, travel, chess, walking. Home: PO Box 185 Amesbury MA 01913-0004 Office: 1 School St Amesbury MA 01913-2812

SWARTZ, MELVIN JAY, lawyer, writer; b. Boston, July 21, 1930; s. Jack M. and Rose (Rosenberg) S.; children: Julianne, Jonathan Samuel. BA, Syracuse U., 1953; LLB, Boston U., 1957. Bar: N.Y. 1959, Ariz. 1961. Assoc. Alfred S. Julian, N.Y.C., 1957-59; ptnr. Finks & Swartz, Youngtown, Sun City, Phoenix, 1961-70, Swartz & Jeckel, P.C., Sun City, Youngtown, Scottsdale, 1971-82; exec. v.p. APPPRO, Inc. Author: Don't Die Broke, A Guide to Secure Retirement, 1974, rev. edit., 2000, (book and cassettes) Keep What You Own, 1989, rev. edit., 2000, Retire Without Fear, 1995; columnist News-Sun, Sun City, 1979-83; author column Swartz on Aging. Bd. dirs. Valley of the Sun Sch. for Retarded Children, 1975-79. Mem. ABA, Ariz. Bar Assn., N.Y. Bar Assn., Maricopa County Bar Assn., Scottsdale Bar Assn., Ctrl. Ariz. Estate Planning Coun., Masons (Phoenix). Jewish. Office: 3416 N 44th St Unit 22 Phoenix AZ 85018-6044 E-mail: swartzmj@worldnet.att.net.

SWARTZ, MORTON NORMAN, medical educator, educator; b. Boston, Nov. 11, 1923; s. Jacob H. and Janet (Heller) W.; m. Cesia Rosenberg, Sept. 18, 1956; children: Mark David, Caroline Joan. BA, Harvard Coll., 1945; MD, Harvard U., 1947; MD (hon.), U. Geneva, Switzerland, 1988. Diplomate Am. Bd. Internal Medicine (subsplty. exam. com. 1971-76, bd. govs. 1979-85). Med. intern and resident Mass. Gen. Hosp., Boston, 1947-50, chief resident in medicine, 1953-54; USPHS postdoctoral rsch. fellow Johns Hopkins U., McCollum-Pratt Inst. Enzymology, Balt., 1954-56; chief infectious disease unit Mass. Gen. Hosp., Boston, 1956-90, chief James Jackson Firm, med. svcs., 1990—; assoc. prof. medicine Harvard Med. Sch., 1967-73, prof., 1973—. Vis. assoc. prof. biochemistry, Stanford Med. Sch., Palo Alto, Calif., 1969-70. Author: (with others) Osteomyelitis, 1971; editor: Current Clinical Topics in Infectious Diseases, 1980—; assoc. editor New Eng. Jour. Medicine, 1981—; contbr. articles to profl. jours. 1st lt. U.S. Army, 1950-52. Sir MacFarlane Burnett lectr. Australasian Soc. Infectious Disease, 1981, Fellow ACP (master 1988, Disting. Tchr. award 1989); mem. Am. Soc. Biochemistry and Molecular Biology, Am. Soc. for Clin. Investigation, Assn. Am. Physicians, Infectious Diseases Soc. Am. (Bristol award 1984, Feldman award 1989), Inst. Medicine, Nat. Inst. Child Health and Devel. (bd. sci. counselors

1992—, chmn. 1995-97). Jewish. Avocations: biology, bird watching, cosmology. Home: 54 Shaw Rd Chestnut Hill MA 02467-3122 Office: Mass Gen Hosp Dept Medicine Bulfinch Bldg #127 Boston MA 02114-2696 E-mail: mswartz@partners.org.

SWARTZ, PATTI CAPEL, literature educator; b. Salem, Ohio; d. Roy Stephen and Edith Lucile (Hively) Capel; children: Ralph Morris, George Harry, Edith Lucille. BA, Kent State U., 1966; BS in Edn., Youngstown State U., 1987, MA in English, 1991; PhD, Claremont Grad. U., 1996. Caseworker, adoption recruiter Children Svcs., Warren, Ohio, 1988-90; asst. prof. Ga. So. U., Statesboro, Ga., 1993-94, Morehead (Ky.) State U., 1994-99, Kent State U., East Liverpool, Ohio, 1999—. Author: When We See Together, 1999, short story; contbr. articles to profl. jours. Fellow Cleve. Play House, 1966, 67. Mem. AAUP, Nat. Coun. Tchrs. of English, MLA, Constance Fenimore Woolson Soc. Office: Kent State U 400 E 4th St East Liverpool OH 43920 E-mail: pswartz@eliv.kent.edu.

SWARTZ, PAUL FREDERICK, clergyman; b. New Philadelphia, Ohio, Mar. 2, 1943; s. Luther Franklin and Dorothy Mae (Keppler) S.; m. Betty Lou Lacina, Apr. 24, 1965; children: Aaron Joel, Lynnea Renee. Student, Bowling Green State U., 1963-64; BA, Wittenberg U., 1965; BD, Trinity Luth. Sem., 1968, MDiv, 1976. Ordained to ministry Luth. Ch. in Am., 1968. Pastor Trinity Luth. Ch., Sebring, Ohio, 1968-72; mission developer Christ the Redeemer Luth. Ch., Brecksville, 1972-73, pastor, 1973-75; asst. to bishop, mem. exec. bd. Ohio Synod, Luth. Ch. in Am., Columbus, 1975-88; sr. pastor St. Matthew's Luth. Ch., Urbana, Ill., 1989-99, King of Glory Luth. Ch., Carmel, Ind., 1999—. Mem. Ohio Synod, Luth. Ch. in Am., 1965-88; cons. Profl. Leadership, Columbus, 1981-87; treas., bd. dirs. Midwest Career Devel. Svcs., Columbus and Chgo., 1981-87; del. Luth. Ch. in Am. Conf., Toronto, Ont., Can., 1984, mem. Cen. So. Ill. Synod, 1989-99; dean E. Cen. Conf. Cen./So. Ill. Synod Coun., Evang. Luth. Ch. Am., 1990; news corr. The Luth., 1970-75; mem. Ind.-Ky. Synod, 1999—. Contbr. articles to religious publs., chpt. to book. Vice pres. Community Action Ctr., Sebring, 1969-72; bd. dirs. Luth. Children's Aid and Family Svcs., Cleve., 1973-75, Luth. Social Svcs. N.E. Ohio, 1980-84, Luth. Metro Ministries, Cleve., 1980-85, Wittenberg U., Springfield, Ohio, 2000—; mem. Goals for Greater Akron (Ohio), 1982; cons. Greater Cleve. East Strategy, 1984-87, Greater Akron Strategy, 1985-87. Bowling Green State U. President's scholar, 1962-64; Nat. Luth. Coun. European study grantee, 1963. Avocations: U.S. stamps, Luther and Reformation stamps, model railroading, sailing, 1933 Plymouth. E-mial. Office: King of Glory Luth Ch 2201 E 106th St Carmel IN 46032-4011 E-mail: paul.swartz@kogcarmel.com. *To accomplish great things one must not only act, but also dream; not only plan, but also believe!.*

SWARTZ, ROSLYN HOLT, real estate executive; b. Los Angeles, Dec. 9, 1940; d. Abe Jack and Helen (Canter) Holt; m. Allan Joel Swartz, June 2, 1963. AA, Santa Monica (Calif.) Coll., 1970; BA summa cum laude, UCLA, 1975; MA, Pepperdine U., 1976. Cert. community coll. instr., student-personnel worker, Calif. Mgr. pub. relations Leader Holdings, Inc., L.A., 1968-75, pres., 1991—, sec., treas. North Hollywood, Calif., 1975-81, pres., 1981-91; chief exec. officer Beverly Stanley Investments, L.A., 1979—. Pres. Leader Properties, Inc., The Leader Fairfax, Inc., Leader 358, Inc., Leader 359, Inc., Leader Ventura, Inc., 1996—. Condr. An Oral History of the Elderly Jewish Community of Venice, Calif. at Los Angeles County Planning Dept. Library, 1974. Founder Pres.'s Cir. L.A. County Mus. Art; mem. The Blue Ribbon, Club 100, Ctr. Dance Assn., Music Ctr. L.A. County; founder West Alumni Ctr., UCLA; capital patron Simon Wiesenthal Ctr.; past trustee Odyssey Theatre Ensemble; assoc. House Ear Inst.; founder Gold Circle; hon. bd. dirs. West L.A. Symphony. Mem.: NAFE, Comml. Real Estate Women, Am. Pharm. Assn., Nat. Mus. of Women in the Arts (So. Calif. coun.), Women of L.A., Las Donas, Friends of Robinson Gardens, Women's Guild Cedars-Sinai Med. Ctr., Friends of Fox, Town Hall (life), UCLA Alumni Assn. (life), Santa Monica Coll. Alumni Assn. (life), UCLA Chancellor's Assocs., Fashion Circle of Costume Coun., UCLA Prytanean Alumnae Assn., Women of L.A., KCET Women's Coun., KCET Women's Coun., Order Eastern Stara, Phrateres Internat., Phi Beta Kappa (Bicentennial fellow), Pi Lambda Theta, Pi Gamma Mu, Phi Delta Kappa, Alpha Kappa Delta, Alpha Gamma Sigma, Phi Alpha Theta. Avocation: horticulture. Office: PO Box 241866 Los Angeles CA 90024-9666

SWARTZ, STEPHEN ARTHUR, corporate financial executive; b. Boston, Oct. 7, 1941; s. Norman and Frances S.; m. Karen M. McLoughlin, Aug. 18, 1992; children: Marti Anne, Nanci Beth, Lori Ellen, Stephen Arthur, Jr., Kerry Anne. BA in Polit. Sci., U. Mass., 1963; LLB, Boston U., 1966; postgrad. in fin. and mgmt, Boston Coll., 1968-70. Bar: Mass. 1967, N.Y. 1971. Asst. counsel Fed. Res. Bank Boston., 1968-70, Irving Trust Co., N.Y.C., 1970-74; counsel, asst. sec. Charter N.Y. Corp., 1974-77, v.p., asst. dir. investor communications, 1977-79; v.p., dir. investor communications Irving Bank Corp., N.Y.C., 1979-86; v.p. investor relations Seamen's Corp., 1986-88, sr. v.p., corp. sec., 1990; sr. v.p. investor rels. H.F. Ahmanson & Co., L.A., 1990-98; exec. v.p. IndyMac Mortgage and Holdings, Inc., 1998-99; v.p. investor rels. The St. Joe Co., Jacksonville, Fla., 1999—. Served to capt. AUS, 1966-68, Vietnam. Decorated Bronze Star (2), Army Commendation medal (2), Air medal (2); Vietnamese Honor medal 1st class. Mem. ABA, Mass. Bar Assn., N.Y. State Bar Assn., Nat. Investor Rels. Inst. (former bd. dirs., treas., pres. L.A. chpt.), Bank Investor Rels. Assn. (founder, former pres., bd. dirs., dir.). Home: 187 Bridle Way Ponte Vedra Beach FL 32082-1901 Office: The St Joe Co 1650 Prudential Dr Ste 400 Jacksonville FL 32207-8168 E-mail: sswartz@joe.com.

SWARTZ, THOMAS R. economist, educator; b. Phila., Aug. 31, 1937; s. Henry Jr. and Elizabeth (Thomas) S.; m. Jeanne Marie Jourdan, Aug. 12, 1961; children: Mary Butler, Karen Miller, Jennifer, Anne, Rebecca. BA, LaSalle U., 1960; MA, Ohio U., 1962; PhD, Ind. U., 1965. Asst. prof. U. Notre Dame, Ind., 1965-70, assoc. dept. chair, 1968-70, assoc. prof., 1970-78, acting dir. grad. studies, 1977-78, prof. econs., 1978—82, dir. program econ. policy, 1982-85; resident dir. U. Notre Dame London Program, 1990-91, U. Notre Dame Austraulia Program, Fremantle, 1996. Vis. prof. U. Notre Dame London Program 1982, 85, 90-91, 2001; dir. London Summer Program, 2001--; fiscal cons. Ind. Commn. State Tax, Indpls., 1965-68, also spl. tax cons., 1971-81, City of South Bend, Ind., 1972-75. Co-editor: The Supply Side, 1983, Changing Face of Fiscal Federalism, 1990, Urban Finance Under Siege, 1993, Taking Sides, 10th edit., 2002, America's Working Poor, 1995; contbr. articles to profl. jours. Bd. dirs. Forever Learning Inst., South Bend, Ind., 1988-93; mem. steering com. Mayor's Housing Forum, South Bend, 1989-95; chair Com. Svcs. Block Grant, South Bend, 1985-90, Econ. Devel. Task Force, South Bend, 1985. Rsch. fellow Nat. Ctr. Urban Ethnic Affairs, 1979-85; recipient Danforth Assoc. award Danforth Found., 1972-86, Tchg. award Kanzajian Found., 1974; rsch. grantee Mellon Found., 1998—. Fellow Inst. Ednl. Initiatives. Democrat. Roman Catholic. Avocation: racquetball. Office: U Notre Dame Dept Econs 414 Decio Hall Notre Dame IN 46556-5644 E-mail: swartz.i@nd.edu.

SWARTZ, WILLIAM JOHN, retired transportation resources company executive; b. Hutchinson, Kans., Nov. 6, 1934; s. George Glen and Helen Mae (Prather) S.; m. Dorothy Jean Parshall, June 5, 1956; children: John Christopher, Jeffrey Michael. BSME, Duke U., 1956; JD, George Washington U., 1961; MS in Mgmt. (Alfred P. Sloan fellow), MIT, 1967. With AT & SF Ry., 1961-78, 79—, asst. v.p. exec. dept., 1973-77, v.p. adminstrn., 1977-78, exec. v.p., 1979-83, Santa Fe Industries, Chgo., 1978-79, pres., 1983-90; vice chmn. Santa Fe So. Pacific, 1983-90; pres. AT & SF Ry., 1986-89. Past bd. dirs. Chgo. Mus. Sci. and Industry; mem. Dean's Coun. Duke U. Sch. Engring; mem. regent's cir. Mus. N.Mex., 1996—; mem. Coun. on Internat. Rels., 1996—; bd. dirs. U.S. Def. Orientation Conf. Assn., 1998—, N.Mex. Mus. Natural History and Sci., 1999-2001, Santa Fe Desert Chorale, 1999—; N.Mex. commr. Cubres & Toltec Scenic Rd., 2000—; bd. dirs. Santa Fe Coun. Internat. Rels., 2001—. Mem. Assn. Am. R.R. (past bd. dirs.). Methodist. Home: 1201 Ojo Verde Santa Fe NM 87501-8870

SWARTZ, WILMA JEANNE, music educator; b. Marshfield, Oreg., Mar. 8, 1926; d. Henry Dewey Sr. and Gladys Kathleen Wilson; m. Allan Ernest Swartz, Sept. 2, 1950 (dec. Mar. 1996); children: Ted A., Dawn K., Timothy W., Bonnie S. Villaire Courtright. BA in Music, U. Oreg., 1948; MusM in Piano, U. Mich., 1950. Nat. cert. music tchr. Pvt. practice, Muskegon, Mich., 1951—. Active Reach for Recovery Am. Cancer Soc., Muskegon, 1998-99; women's pres. Forest Park Covenant Ch., diaconate, 1996-99, ch. bd. sec. Named Music Tchr. of Yr. Greater Muskegon Music T. Assn., 1990, 97. Mem.: PEO Sisterhood (sec., treas., chaplain), Mich. Fedn. of Music Clubs (jr. club counselor 1951—). Republican. Avocations: sewing, photography, travel. Home: 3070 Sherwood Ct Muskegon MI 49441-1158

SWARTZBAUGH, MARC L. lawyer; b. Urbana, Ohio, Jan. 3, 1937; s. Merrill L. and Lillian K. (Hill) S.; m. Marjory Anne Emhardt, Aug. 16, 1958 (deceased May 20, 2000); children: Marc Charles, Kathleen Marie, Laura Kay. BA magna cum laude, Wittenberg Coll., 1958; LLB magna cum laude, U. Pa., 1961. Bar: Ohio 1961, U.S. Dist. Ct. (no. dist.) Ohio 1962, U.S. Claims Ct. 1991, U.S. Ct. Appeals (6th cir.) 1970, U.S. Ct. Appeals (3d cir.) 1985, U.S. Ct. Appeals (Fed. cir.) 1995, U.S. Supreme Ct. 1973. Law clk. to judge U.S. Ct. Appeals (3d cir.), Phila., 1961-62; assoc. Jones, Day, Reavis & Pogue, Cleve., 1962-69, ptnr., 1970-98; ret., 1998; cons., 1998—. Note editor U. Pa. Law Rev., 1960-61; co-author: Ohio Legal Ethics, 2001. Co-chmn. Suburban Citizens for Open Housing, Shaker Heights, Ohio, 1966; v.p. Lomond Assn., Shaker Heights, 1965-68; trustee The Dance Ctr., Cleve., 1980-83; amb. People to People Internat., 1986; chmn. legal divsn. Cleve. campaign United Negro Coll. Fund, 1989-96. Mem. ABA (litigation sect., sr. lawyers divsn.), Fed. Bar Assn., Ohio Bar Assn., Cleve. Bar Assn., Order of Coif, Beta Theta Pi. Democrat. Avocations: poetry, painting, music, skiing, photography. Office: Jones Day Reavis & Pogue N Point 901 Lakeside Ave E Cleveland OH 44114-1190

SWARTZENDRUBER, DALE, soil physicist, educator; b. Parnell, Iowa, July 6, 1925; s. Urie and Norma (Kinsinger) S.; m. Kathleen Jeanette Yoder, June 26, 1949; children: Karl Grant, Myra Mae, John Keith, David Mark. BS, Iowa State U., 1950, MS, 1952, PhD, 1954. Instr. sci. Goshen (Ind.) Coll., 1953-54; asst. soil scientist U. Calif., Los Angeles, 1955-56; assoc. prof. soil physics Purdue U., West Lafayette, Ind., 1956-63, prof., 1963-77; prof. soil physics U. Nebr., Lincoln, 1977-98, prof. emeritus soil physics, 1998—. Vis. prof. Iowa State U., 1959, Ga. Inst. Tech., 1968, Hebrew U. Jerusalem at Rehovot, 1971, Griffith U., Brisbane, Australia, 1989-90, Centre for Environ. Mechanics, CSIRO, Canberra, Australia, 1990; vis. scholar Cambridge (Eng.) U., 1971. Contbr. articles on soil physics to profl. jours.; assoc. editor: Soil Sci. Soc. Am. Proc., 1965-70; mem. editorial bd. Geoderma (Amsterdam), 1975-93; editor: Soil Sci., 1976-98. Fellow Soil Sci. Soc. Am. (Soil Sci. award 1975, Editors' citation for excellence in manuscript rev. 1993, Soil Sci. Disting. Svc. award 2001), Am. Soc. Agronomy; mem. Am. Geophys. Union, Internat. Union Soil Sci., Am. Sci. Affiliation, Sigma Xi, Phi Kappa Phi, Gamma Sigma Delta. Mennonite. Achievements include research in water infiltration into soil, validity of Darcy's equation for water flow in soils, measurement of water and solid content in soils, mathematical solutions to problems of water flow in saturated and unsaturated soils. Home: 1400 N 37th St Lincoln NE 68503-2016 Office: U Nebr E Campus Dept Agronomy and Horticulture 246 Keim Hall Lincoln NE 68583 E-mail: agrohort@unl.edu. *Along with complete dedication and honesty in spirit and action, bring to each task a new thought, or ask the implications, should the customary or conventional wisdom not hold.*

SWARTZLANDER, EARL EUGENE, JR. engineering educator, former electronics company executive; b. San Antonio, Feb. 1, 1945; s. Earl Eugene and Jane (Nicholas) S.; m. Joan Vickery, June 9, 1968. BSEE, Purdue U., 1967; MSEE, U. Colo., 1969; PhD, U. So. Calif., 1972. Registered profl. engr., Ala., Calif., Colo., Tex. Devel. engr. Ball Bros. Rsch. Corp., Boulder, Colo., 1967-69; Hughes fellow, mem. tech. staff Hughes Aircraft Co., Culver City, Calif., 1969-73; mem. rsch. staff Tech. Svc. Co., Santa Monica, 1973-74; chief engr. Geophys. Systems Corp., Pasadena, 1974-75, staff engr. to sr. staff engr., 1975-79, project mgr., 1979-84, lab. mgr., 1985-87; dir. ind. R&D TRW Inc., Redondo Beach, 1987-90; Schlumberger Centennial prof. engring. dept. elec. and computer engring. U. Tex., Austin, 1990—. Gen. chmn. Internat. Conf. Wafer Scale Integration, 1989, Internat. Conf. Application Specific Array Processors, 1990, 94, 11th Internat. Symposium on Computer Arithmetic, 1992, 31st Ann. Asilomar Conf. on Signals, Sys., and Computers, 1997, others; chmn. 3d Internat. Conf. Parallel and Distributed Sys., Taiwan, 1993, 12th Internat. Conf. on Application-Specific Systems, Architectures and Processors, 2000. Author: VLSI Signal Processing Systems, 1986; editor: Computer Design Development, 1976, Systolic Signal Processing Systems, 1987, Wafer Scale Integration, 1989, Computer Arithmetic Vol. 1 and 2, 1990, Application Specific Processors, 1996; editor-in-chief Jour. of VLSI Signal Processing, 1989-95, IEEE Transactions on Computers, 1991-94, IEEE Transactions on Signal Processing, 1995; editor: IEEE Transactions on Computers, 1982-86, IEEE Transactions on Parallel and Distributed Systems, 1989-90; hardware area editor ACM Computing Revs., 1985—; assoc. editor: IEEE Jour. Solid-State Circuits, 1984-88; contbr. more than 200 articles to profl. jours. and tech. conf. procs. Bd. dirs. Casiano Estates Homeowners Assn., Bel Air, Calif., 1976-78, pres., 1978-80; bd. dirs. Benedict Hills Estates Homeowners Assn., Beverly Hills, Calif., 1984—, pres., 1990-95. Recipient Disting. Engring. Alumnus award Purdue U., 1989, U. Colo., 1997, Outstanding Elec. Engr. award Purdue U., 1992, knight Imperial Russian Order St. John of Jerusalem (Knights of Malta), 1993. Fellow: IEEE (3d Millennium medal 2000); mem.: IEEE Solid-State Cirs. Coun. (sec. 1992—93, treas. 1994—97), IEEE Signal Proc. Soc. (bd. govs. 1992—94), IEEE Computer Soc. (bd. govs. 1987—91, Golden Core award 1996), Omicron Delta Kappa, Sigma Tau, Eta Kappa Nu. Office: U Tex Austin Dept Elec Computer Engring Austin TX 78712

SWARZ, JEFFREY ROBERT, securities analyst, neuroscientist; b. Nov. 9, 1949; s. Irvin Brad and Blanche S. (Marcus) S.; m. Kathy Helen Kafer, June 20, 1976. BS with hons., U. Calif., Irvine, 1971; PhD, U. Rochester, 1976. Postdoctoral fellow in neurovirology Johns Hopkins U. Sch. Medicine, Balt., 1976-79; staff fellow infectious diseases NIH, Bethesda, 1979-80; dir. biotech. group Teknekron Rsch. Inc., McLean, Va., 1980-81; pres. AgroBiotics, Inc., Balt., 1981-82; from sr. scientist to dir. mktg. and sales Pall Corp., Glen Cove, N.Y., 1982-85, dir. mktg. and sales, 1985-86; biotech./healthcare analyst Goldman Sachs & Co., 1986-92; dir. CS First Boston, N.Y.C., 1992-99; ptnr. Partner-Eagle Ptnrs., 1999—; prodr. Shadow Prodns.; mng. dir. Life Sci. Group, 2001—; pres. Eldersupplies.com, 1999—. Cons. U.S. Senate Subcom. on Sci., Tech. and Space, 1979-80; prodr. Shadow Prodns., 1998—. Author: (with others) Genetic Engineering: Issues and Trends, 1982; contbr. articles to profl. jours. Recipient Rsch. award Bank of Am., 1970-71, Nat. Rsch. Svc. award 1976-79; NIH fellow 1975-76. Mem. U. Club, N.Y. Athletic Club, Neptune Boat Club. Democrat. Jewish. Office: Life Sci Group 1 Lafayette Pl Greenwich CT 06830-5449

SWARZ, SAHL, sculptor; b. N.Y.C., May 4, 1912; s. Samuel and Ida (Fass) S.; m. Naoco Kumasaka, May 1978. Student, Clay Club, N.Y.C., 1928-34, Art Students League, 1930-31. Assoc. dir. Clay Club (now Sculpture Center), 1938-54; creative sculpture Italy, 1951-63; residence Am. Acad., Rome, 1955-57; lectr. sculpture Columbia U., N.Y.C., 1966-68, asst. prof., 1969-78. Instr. Pratt Inst., Bklyn., 1964; instr. New Sch. for Social Rsch., 1965, 66; vis. lectr. art U. Wis., 1966; trustee Mus. Contemporary Sculpture, Tokyo; lectr. art dept. Nippon U., Tokyo, 1997. Author, illustrator: Blueprint for the Future of American Sculpture, 1943, also monograph.; one man exhbns. Sculpture Ctr., 1954, 57, 60, 62, 66, 71, 74, 78, Art Alliance, Phila., 1958, Fairweather-Hardin Gallery, Chgo., 1963, Brandeis U., Waltham, Mass., 1964, (retrospective exhbn.) Fair Lawn (N.J.) Pub. Library, 1977, Saikaya Gallery, Fujisawa, Japan, 1983, Mus. Contemporary Sculpture, Tokyo, 1985, Shonan Gallery, Fujisawa, Japan, 1985, 90, 93, 2001 (retrospective exhbn.) Toni de Rossi Gallery, Verona, Italy, 1983, 87, 91, Takashimaya Gallery, Yokohama, Japan, 1984, Atagoyama Gallery, Tokyo, 1988, 91, 94, 99, 1st exhibition of painting Toni de Rossi Gallery, Verona, Italy, 1992, 96, Move Gallery Chigasaki, Japan, 1993; group shows include Fairmont Park Internat., Phila., 1948, Whitney Mus. Am. Art, 1948, 58, 60, 62, 64, Pa. Acad., 1948, 52, 54, 57, 60, 62, 66, Bklyn Mus., 1935, Detroit Inst. Fine Arts, 1957, San Francisco Mus., 1955, U. Ill., 1960, 62, others; represented in permanent collections Norfolk (Va.) Mus., Whitney Mus. Am. Art, Ball State Tchrs. Coll., Williams Coll. Mus., Ford Found., Mpls. Inst. Fine Arts, Va. Mus. Fine Arts, Richmond, Newark Mus., N.J. State Mus. at Trenton, Vatican Mus. Collection Modern Religious Art, Rose Art Mus., Brandeis U., Stamford (Conn.) Mus., Columbia U., Tokyo Mus. Contemporary Sculpture, others; bronze group The Guardian at Brookgreen (S.C.), Gardens Mus.; terra cotta wall sculpture, Linden, (N.J.), Post Office, sculptural designs, Fed. Courthouse, Statesville, N.C.; equestrian monument Gen. Bidwell, Buffalo; fountain commn., Spruce Run State Park, N.J.; mall sculpture, Pittsfield, Mass.; monument to Demeter in stainless steel, Fujisawa, Japan; subject of biography: Fifty Years of Sculpture by Sahl Swarz. Chmn. sculpture panel N.J. Coun. on Arts. With AUS, 1941-45. Grantee Am. Acad. Arts and Letters, 1955; Guggenheim fellow, 1955, 58 Address: Kumasaka-Swarz Via Strettoia 43 55040 Ripa Italy *The essence of creativity is in the searching after the form. Search leads to revelation, understanding, knowledge. Realization of one's ignorance is the first step to the attainment of wisdom. A wise man makes a work of art out of life itself.*

SWARZMAN, HERBERT GEORGE, real estate investment executive; b. N.Y.C., May 29, 1937; s. Herman and Mollie (Mosberg) S.; m. Abby Levingson, Jan. 29, 1961 (div. May 1971); 1 child, David; m. Joyce Burick, Feb. 12, 1976; 1 child, Elizabeth Barbara. BA, Dartmouth Coll., 1958; LLB, Bklyn. Law Sch., 1960. Sales and mgmt. Dempsey-Tegeler Co., N.Y.C., 1961-62; with A.G. Becker & Co., N.Y.C., 1963-68; founder, mng. ptnr. Dryfoos & Co., N.Y.C., 1969-73; cons. security firms, 1974-75; founder, pres. Gulfcoast Cons. and Investors Corp., Tampa, Fla., 1976—; pres. Herand Inc., Real Estate Investments, Tampa, 1978-95; chmn. N.Am. Steel Corp., Lakeland, Fla., 1979-82; pres. Gulf Coast Realty Investors, Inc., 1981—. West Coast Realty Mgmt. Inc., Tampa. Mem. fin. com. Horace Mann Elem. Sch., N.Y.C., 1971-72; chmn. N.Y.C. interviewing com. for applications for admission Dartmouth, 1965-75, dist. dir. enrollment for N.Y.C., 1974-75, chmn. reunion fund, 1974, pres. Class of 1958, 1974-79; co-chmn. basic gifts Tampa Jewish Fedn., 1977-78; treas. Dem. Com., N.Y.C., 1971-73; co-chmn. fin. Fla. for Reagan Campaign, 1980; del. Rep. Nat. Conv., 1980; spl. advisor on Jewish interests Rep. Party Fl., 1981-84; mem. adv. council SBA of Fla., 1981—; bd. dirs. Univ. Settlement, 1966-68; bd. dirs., treas. Tampa Jewish Fedn., v.p., 1984—; mem. ethics com. Fla. Bar Assn., 1983-87, ethics com. Meml. Hosp., Tampa, 1985-90; bd. dirs. Menorah Home, 1987—, Anti-Defamation League, 1987-90, Tampa Holocaust, 1991-94; chmn. Fla.-Israel Inst., 1990—, apptd. by gov. to Fla.- Israel Cooperation Com., 1996—. Mem. Am.-Israel Pub. Affairs Com. (exec. com. 1981—), Dartmouth Alumni Assn. N.Y.C. (founder, pres. 1975-76). Clubs: Dartmouth (dir., bd. govs. 1974-75), Lawyers (N.Y.C.); Carrollwood Village Golf and Tennis. Home: 4214 Fairway Run Tampa FL 33624-4642

SWASEY, MARTHA GRACY, school administrator; b. Dayton, Tenn., Apr. 3, 1917; d. Brainerd Bradshaw and Emma Belle (Adkerson) Gracy; m. Allan Vincent Swasey, July 16, 1937; children: Patricia Belle, Allan Vincent Jr., Dorothy Alice. BS, George Peabody Coll., 1936, MA, 1937; postgrad., Mid. Tenn. State U., 1975. Lic. tchr. Tenn., Fla. Chmn. phys. edn. dept. Tenn. Coll. for Women, Murfreesboro, 1941-43; asst. prof. Duke U., Durham, N.C., 1944-49; tchr. phys. edn. Durham Children's Mus., 1946-48; dir. health, tchr. phys. edn. Oak Ridge (Tenn.) H.S., 1952-70; assoc. prof., coach men's and women's gymnastic team U. Tenn., Chattanooga, 1970-72; assoc. phys. dir. Ctrl. YMCA, 1972-74; dir. women's athletics U. of the South, Sewanee, Tenn., 1974-79; founder, dir. Signal Sch. of Phys. Edn., Signal Mountain, Jasper, 1979—. Dir. gymnastics promotion tour to Venezuela for Ptnrs. of the Ams., 1979; spl. tchr. gymnastics, Coll. of Sports and Phys. Ednn. for Orgn. of Am. States, Spanish Town, Jamaica, 1984, 85, 86, 87; clinic dir. for gymnastics for Hawaii Phys. Edn. Dept., Oahu, 1988, 89; gymnastics clinic dir., Nassau (Bahamas) Athletic Assn., 1990, Edu Deportes, San Juan, P.R., 1992, 93; dir. fencing, trampolining, gymnastics clinics U. P.R., Mayuez, 1994, 95, 96, tennis clinic U. P.R., 1999. Vol. Tenn. Aquarium, Chattanooga, 1993-95; v.p. Oak Ridge Parks Assn., 1967-69. Recipient gold medal in racquetball, Nat. Sr. Olympic Games, Tucson, 1997, silver medal in racquetball and archery, Nat. Sr. Olympic Games, Orlando, 1999, Gold medal in archery, silver medal in racquetball, Nat. Sr. Olympic Games, Baton Rouge, 2001. Mem. U.S. Gymnastics Assn. (state chmn. 1963-65), U.S. Fencing Assn., Ptnrs. of the Ams. (chmn. outreach com. 1994), Kiwanis (pres. Signal Mountain chpt. 1992-94, internat. del. 1994, 2000). Avocations: boating, SCUBA diving, horseback riding, antiques, travel. Home and Office: Signal Sch of Phys Edn 107 Golf Dr Signal Mountain TN 37377-1846

SWATEK, FRANK EDWARD, microbiology educator; b. Oklahoma City, June 4, 1929; s. Clarence Michael and Bessie (Doubek) S.; m. Mary Frances Over, Jan. 28, 1951; children: Frank Edward, Lorraine Beth Butcher, Martha Lynn Bradshaw, Susan Ann, Cheryl Lee. BS in Zoology, San Diego State Coll., 1951; MA in Microbiology, UCLA, 1955, PhD, 1956. Mem. faculty Calif. State U. at Long Beach, 1956-93, prof. microbiology, 1962-82, chmn. dept., 1960-82. Cons. to industry, 1953—; cons. dept. dermatology Long Beach VA Hosp., 1956—; lectr. postgrad. medicine U. So. Calif., 1958—; adj. prof. clin. med. U. Calif., Irvine, 1980—; mem. fuel sect. Coordinating Research Council, 1961—. Author: Textbook of Microbiology, 1967, Laboratory Manual and Workbook for General Microbiology, 1969; also articles. Fellow Royal Soc. Health, Am. Acad. Microbiology; mem. Am. Soc. Microbiology (chmn. bd. edn. and tng. 1980-85, Carski Found. Disting. Teaching award 1974), Internat. Platform Assn., Sigma Xi, Lambda Xi Alpha, Phi Kappa Phi. Clubs: Long Beach Aquatic (pres. 1963-65). Achievements include research on med. mycology. Home: 812 Stevely Ave Long Beach CA 90815-5022

SWATERS, CHERIE LYNN BUTLER, nurse; b. Warrenton, Mo., Aug. 17, 1954; d. Thomas Pershing and Dorothy Fredrika (Wulff) Butler; m. James Louis Swaters, Jr., July, 20, 1974; children: Bradley Thomas, Rebecca Lynn. Diploma, St. Luke's Hosp. Sch. Nursing, Kansas City, Mo., 1979; BSN, Webster U., 1988. RN; cert. neonatal advanced life support. Staff nurse St. Luke's of Kansas City (Mo.), 1979-80, Menorah Med. Ctr., Kansas City, 1985-87, 87-89, North Kansas City (Mo.) Meml. Hosp., 1987, Liberty (Mo.) Hosp., 1989-96; perinatal continuing edn. program coord. Liberty Hosp., 1994-96, staff nurse, 2000—02; sch. RN North Kansas City Sch. Dist., 1996-97; staff nurse ICN Children's Mercy Hosp. of Kansas City, Mo., 2002—. Sch. vol. PTA for Davidson Elem. Sch., Kansas City, 1985-92; sch. vol. Liberty (Mo.) Mid. Sch., Ridgeview Elem. Sch., Liberty, 1992-93; former co-dir. Stephen Ministry and facilitator grief recovery; facilitator Alzheimer's support groups for Liberty United Meth. Ch. Methodist. Avocations: reading, sewing, embroidery.

SWATOS, WILLIAM HENRY, JR. priest, sociologist; b. Paterson, N.J., Sept. 25, 1946; s. William H. Sr. and Lucille (MacNab) S.; m. Priscilla Lampman, June 16, 1969; children: Giles S., Eric B. AB, Transylvania U., 1966; MDiv summa cum laude, Episc. Theol. Sem., Lexington, Ky., 1969; MA, U. Ky., 1969, PhD, 1973. Ordained to ministry Episcopal Ch., 1969. Mem. sociology faculty King Coll., Bristol, Tenn., 1973-80; vicar St. Mark's Episc. Ch., Silvis, Ill., 1980-94; mem. sociology faculty No. Ill. U., 1984-88; chair dept. edn. Diocese of Quincy, 1988-90, 93-96. Mem. faculty Black Hawk and Scott Community Coll., Moline, Ill., Bettendorf, Iowa, 1988-96. Editor: Time, Place and Circumstance, 1990, Religious Politics in Global and Comparative Perspective, 1989, Religious Sociology, 1987; editor Sociol. Analysis/Sociology of Religion, 1989-94; editor-in-chief The Encyclopedia of Religion and Society, 1998; contbr. articles to profl. jours. Full grantee World Soc. Found., Zurich, Switzerland, 1987, grantee NEH, 1974, 79, 85, 89, rsch. grantee Soc. for the Sci. Study of Religion, 1984-85, 91-92; named Disting. Alumnus Dept. of Sociology, U. Ky., Lexington, 1990. Fellow Soc. Sci. Study of Religion; mem. Assn. for the Sociology of Religion (editor 1989-94, book rev. editor 1986-88, exec. coun. 1984-86, exec. officer 1996—), Religious Rsch. Assn. (sec. 1990-91, bd. dirs. 1986-89, exec. officer 1994—). Home and Office: 3520 Wiltshire Dr Holiday FL 34691-1239 E-mail: swatos@microd.com.

SWATT, STEPHEN BENTON, communications executive, consultant; b. L.A., June 26, 1944; s. Maurice I. and Lucille E. (Sternberger) S.; m. Susan Ruth Edelstein, Sept. 7, 1968; 1 child, Jeffrey Michael. BSBA, U. Calif., 1966, M in Journalism, 1967. Writer San Francisco Examiner, 1967; reporter United Press Internat., L.A., 1968-69; producer news Sta. KCRA-TV, Sacramento, 1969-70, reporter news, 1970-79, chief polit. and capitol corres., 1979-92; mng. ptnr. NCG Porter Novelli, 1992—. Adj. prof., guest lectr. Calif. State U., Sacramento. Contbr. articles to profl. jours. With USCG, 1966. Recipient No. Calif. Emmy NATAS, 1976-77, Pub. Svc. award Calif. State Bar, 1977, Exceptional Achievement Coun. advancement and Support of Edn., 1976, Nat. Health Journalism award Am. Chiropractic Assn., 1978. Mem. Soc. Profl.

Journalists (8 awards), Capitol Corres. Assn., U. Calif. Alumni Assn., Sacramento Press Club. Avocations: hiking, jogging, fishing. Office: Porter Novelli 1215 K St # 2100 Sacramento CA 95814 E-mail: sswatt@ncgpn.com.

SWATZELL, MARILYN LOUISE, nurse; b. Johnson City, Tenn., July 31, 1942; d. Dallas Fred and Minnie Thelma (Clark) S. BS cum laude, East Tenn. State U., 1966, MS, 1967; BSN, U. Tenn., 1974. Chmn. pediatric nursing Meth. Hosp. Sch. Nursing, Memphis, 1978-80; head nurse Le Bonheur Children's Med. Ctr., 1981-83; dir. maternal child nursing Jackson (Tenn.) Madison County Gen. Hosp., 1985-88; staff nurse Vanderbilt U. Hosp., Nashville, 1988-90; supr. Meth. Hosp. Lexington, Tenn., 1990—. Contbr. articles on care plans to profl. jours. Mem. ANA, Tenn. Nurses Assn., Tenn. Orgn. Nurse Execs. Home: 231 Law Ln Lexington TN 38351-6048

SWAUGER, TERRY ALLEN, lawyer; b. Warren, Ohio, Apr. 14, 1969; s. Byron M. and Dorothy Ellen Swauger; m. Kellee Marie O'Dell, Oct. 7, 1995; 1 child, Jillian Paige. BA, Ohio State U., 1992; JD, Capital U., 1995. Bar: Ohio 1995, U.S. Dist. Ct. (no. dist.) Ohio 1998. Assoc. Tackett Zapka & Leuchtag, Warren, Ohio, 1995-97, Law Offices of Dennis W. Tackett, Warren, 1997—. Baptist. Avocations: sports, golf, Bocce. Office: Law Offices Dennis W Tackett 106 E Market St Ste 308 Warren OH 44481-1151 Home: 1480 Butterfield Cir Niles OH 44446-3576

SWAZEY, JUDITH POUND, academic administrator, sociomedical science educator; b. Bronxville, N.Y., Apr. 21, 1939; d. Robert Earl and Louise Titus (Hanson) Pound; m. Peter Woodman Swazey, Nov. 28, 1964; children: Elizabeth, Peter. AB, Wellesley Coll., 1961; PhD, Harvard U., 1966. Rsch. assoc. Harvard U., 1966-71, lectr., 1969-71, rsch. fellow, 1971-72; cons. com. brain scis. NRC, 1971-73; staff scientist neuroscis. rsch. program MIT, Cambridge, 1973-74; assoc. prof. dept. socio-med. scis. and cmty. medicine Boston U., 1974-77, prof., 1977-80, adj. prof. Schs. Medicine and Pub. Health, 1980—; exec. dir. Medicine in the Pub. Interest, Inc., Boston and Washington, 1979-82, 89-93; pres. Coll. of the Atlantic, Bar Harbor, Maine, 1982-84, Acadia Inst., Bar Harbor, 1984-2001, founding pres., sr. scholar, 2001—. Mem. Army Sci. Bd., 1987-92. Author: Reflexes and Motor Integration, the Development of Sherrington's Integrative Action Concept, 1969, (with others) Human Aspects of Biomedical Innovation, 1971, (with R.C. Fox) The Courage to Fail, a Social View of Organ Transplants and Hemodialysis, 1975, rev. edit., 1978 (hon. mention Am. Med. Writers Assn., C. Wright Mills award Am. Sociol. Assn.), Chlorpromazine in Psychiatry, a Study of Therapeutic Innovation, 1974, (with K. Reeds) Today's Medicine, Tomorrow's Science, Essays on Paths of Discovery in the Biomedical Sciences, 1978; editor: (with C. Wong) Dilemmas of Dying, Policies and Procedures for Decisions Not to Treat, 1981, (with F. Worden and G. Adelman) The Neurosciences: Paths of Discovery, 1975, (with R.C. Fox) Spare Parts, Organ Replacement in American Society, 1992, (with C. Messikomer and A. Glicksman) Society and Medicine. Essays in Honor of Renée Fox, 2002; assoc. editor IRB: A Jour. of Human Subjects Rsch., 1979-2000; mem. editl. bd. Sci. and Engring. Ethics, 1994—; contbr. articles to profl. jours. Mem. Maine Dept. Human Svcs. Bioethics Adv. Com. (chair 1991-94); mem. Commn. on Rsch. Integrity, 1994-95; bd. dirs. Maine Bioethics Network, 1994-99. Wellesley Coll. scholar, 1961; Wellesley Coll. Alumnae fellow Harvard U., 1966, NIH predoctoral fellow, 1966. Radcliffe Coll. Coll. grad. fellow, 1966. Fellow AAAS (sci. freedom and responsibility com. 1986-89), Inst. Medicine NAS (mem. health scis. policy bd. 1986-89), Grad. Record Exam. (bd. dirs. 1987-91), Phi Beta Kappa, Sigma Xi. Office: Acadia Inst PO Box 243 Bar Harbor ME 04609-0243

SWEARER, WILLIAM BROOKS, lawyer; b. Hays, Kans. Grad., Princeton U., 1951; law degree, U. Kans., 1955. Bar: Kans. 1955. Pvt. practice, Hutchinson, Kans., 1955—; ptnr. Martindell, Swearer & Shaffer, LLP, 1955—. Mem. Kans. Bd. Discipline for Attys., 1979-92, chmn., 1987-92. With U.S. Army, 1952-53, Korea. Mem. ABA (ho. of dels. 1995-2000), Am. Bar Found. (state chair 1998—), Kans. Bar Assn. (pres. 1992-93, various offices, mem. coms.), Kans. Assn. Sch. Attys. (pres. 1989-90), Reno County Bar Assn. Office: PO Box 1907 Hutchinson KS 67504-1907 E-mail: wbs@martindell-law.com.

SWEARINGEN, KARL DAVID, music educator; b. Colorado Springs, Colo., Nov. 26, 1958; s. David Robert Swearingen and Stephanie Carol Bazley. BA, Western State Coll., Gunnison, CO, 1976—80; MM, U. of So. Calif., Los angeles, CA, 1989—80, Ph. D, 1990—93. Music educator Olathe H.S., Olathe, Colo., 1981—84, Indio H.S., Indio, Calif., 1984—90; asst. prof. Ithaca Coll., Ithaca, NY, 1994—97; assoc. band dir. U. of So. Calif., Los Angeles, Calif., 1997—, music educator, 1997—. Bd. mem. CMEA, Calif.; artist clinician Yamaha Corp., Calif. Contbr. articles to profl. jour. R-Consevative. Episcopalian. Achievements include teaching partnership with a school in Sevastopol, Ukraine; first American to tour with Russian Black Sea Fleet Band; first American to play in Ukrainian Navy Band. Home: 2514 Grant Avenue #7 Redondo Beach CA 90278 Office: University of Southern California University Park Los Angeles CA 90089 E-mail: kds@usc.edu.

SWEATLOCK, JOSEPH ANDREW, research scientist; b. Emerson, N.J., Aug. 12, 1955; s. Joseph Francis and Susann Sweatlock; m. Susan Leigh Sweatlock, May 28, 1978; children: Joseph F., Keith P., Johanna L. BA in Chemistry, Susquehanna U., 1977; PhD in Med. Chemistry, SUNY, Buffalo, 1983. Diplomate Am. Bd. Toxicology. Rsch. scientist N.J. Dept. Health and Sr. Svcs., Trenton, 1986—; adj. prof. Bucks County C.C., Newtown, Pa., 1992—. Mem. AAAS, APHA, Am. Chem. Soc., N.Y. Acad. Scis., Mid-Atlantic Soc. Toxicology.

SWECKER, JOHN H. secondary school educator; b. Clarkston, Wash., May 18, 1956; s. Johnnie J. and Janette M. Swecker; m. Robin A. Swecker; children: Sophie, Barbara. AA, Highline Coll., Midway, Wash., 1976; BA in Edn., Western Wash. U., 1978, MMus, 1990. Tchr. Raymond Jr.-Sr. H.S., Wash., 1978—85; tchr., dept. chair music Mark Morris H.S., Longview, 1985—. Mem.: Internat. Jazz Educators Assn., Wash. Music Educator Assn., Music Educators Nat. Conf. Avocations: bicycling, archery, motorcycling, woodworking.

SWEDA, EDWARD LEON, JR. lawyer; b. Boston, Dec. 31, 1955; s. Edward Leon and Lucy (Daniszewski) S. BA, Boston Coll., 1977; JD, Suffolk Law Sch., Boston, 1980. Pvt. practice, Boston, 1981—. Lobbyist Group Against Smoking Pollution, Boston, 1980-93. Vol. Common Cause, Boston, 1977-83. Recipient Appreciation award, Am. Lung Assn. Mass., Boston, 1989. Democrat. Roman Catholic. Home: 172 Boston St Dorchester MA 02125-1142 Office: GASP Kenmore Sta PO Box 15463 Boston MA 02215-0008 E-mail: esweda@lynx.neu.edu.

SWEDLOW, JUDITH MEYER, volunteer; b. Cin., May 7, 1940; d. Joseph Samuel and Hazel (Gordon) Meyer; m. Gerald Howard Swedlow, Mar. 19, 1961; children: Tracy Ellen, Pamela Jean, Deborah Jane. BFA, Ohio State U., 1990. Acct. exec. Columbus (Ohio) Monthly Mag., 1977-80; owner, v.p. Elja, Unltd., Columbus, 1980-82; mktg. dir. Mentor Techs., 1983-85; sales mgr. Target Pub., 1986-87. Exec. com. Am. Israel Pub. Affairs Com., Washington; bd. dirs. Wexner Heritage Village and its Found.; nat. bd. dirs. women's divsn. United Jewish Appeal, N.Y.C., 1978—94; nat. exec. com., nat. women's campaign chmn. Network of Ind. United Jewish Cmtys.; bd. dirs. Jewish Telegraphic Agy., N.Y.C., 1985—; exec. com., bd. dirs. Columbus (Ohio) Jewish Fedn., 1974—; bd. dirs. Columbus Jewish Found. Recipient Therese Stern Kahn Young Leadership award Columbus Jewish Fedn., 1974, Leadership Recognition award Columbus Jewish Cmty. Ctr., 1976, United Jewish Cmtys. Endowment Achievement award, 1999, Columbus AIPAC Zacks Leadership award, 2001. Avocations: computers, treadmill, travel.

SWEED, PHYLLIS, publishing executive; b. N.Y.C., Dec. 6, 1931; d. Paul and Frances (Spitzer) S.; m. Leonard Bogdanoff (dec. Oct. 1975); children: Patricia Romano (dec. June 1994), James Alan. BA, NYU, 1950. Asst. buyer Nat. Bellas Hess, N.Y.C., 1950; assoc. editor Fox-Shulman Pub., 1951-57; products editor McGraw-Hill Pub., 1957-61; mng. editor Haire Pub., 1962-66; editor Gifts & Decorative Accessories Mag., 1966-78; sr. v.p. Geyer-McAllister Pub., N.Y.C., 1978-98, editor, co-pub., 1978-95, editor-in-chief, co-pub., 1995-98; dir. editl. devel. Gifts & Decorative Accessories, 1998-99; prin. P.S. Consulting & Mktg., 1999—; editor-in-chief, pub. Gift Executive, 1999—. Bd. dirs. Frances Hook Scholarship Fund, 1989-96. Recipient Editorial Excellence award Indsl. Mktg., 1964, Nat. Assn. Ltd. Edit. Dealers award, 1993, 96, MagWeek Excellence award, 1992, Dallas Mkt. Ctr. award, 1969, 80, 82. Mem. Nat. Assn. Ltd. Ed. Dealers (assoc.), Internat. Furnishings and Design Assn. Avocations: gardening, collecting antique Belleek. Office: 505 Laguardia Pl Ste 17D New York NY 10012-2004

SWEEDLER, BARRY MARTIN, transportation safety consultant; b. Bklyn., Mar. 11, 1937; s. Louis and Sadie (Sweedler; m. Kathryn Grace Stewart, June 26, 1988; children by previous marriage: Ian, Elizabeth. BME, CCNY, 1960; MBA, CUNY, 1966. Registered profl. engr., N.Y. From asst. and jr. engr. to sr. gas engr. N.Y. State Pub. Svc. Commn., N.Y.C., 1960-69; chief pipeline safety divsn. Nat. Transp. Safety Bd., Washington, 1969-74, dep. dir. bur. surface transp. safety, 1974-76, dep. dir., acting dir. Bur. plans and programs, 1976-79, dep. dir. bur. tech., 1979-82, dir. bur. safety programs, 1982-90, dir. office safety recommendations, 1999-2000; ptnr. Safety and Policy Analysis Internat., Lafayette, Calif., 2000—. Guest lectr. Inst. Gas Tech., 1973, U. Md., 1974, U. Calif., San Diego, 1986, 88-89, U. N.Mex., 1987, U. Calgary, 1988; participant Internat. Workshop on High Alcohol Consumers and Traffic, Paris, 1988; presenter on alcohol and drug abuse in transp.; co-editor proc., chmn. alcohol, drugs and traffic safety program 35th Internat. Congress on Alcoholism and Drug Dependencies, Oslo, Norway, 1988, the Internat. Conf. on Alcohol, Drugs and Traffic Safety, Cologne, 1992, Internat. Inst. on Prevention and Treatment of Alcoholism, Stockholm, 1991, World Congress of Internat. Assn. Accident and Traffic Medicine, 1992, Internat. Conf. on Alcohol, Drugs and Traffic Safety, Adelaide, Australia, 1995, Annecy, France, 1997. Author: (with others) Gas Engineers Handbook, 1985, Alcohol - Minimizing the Harm, 1997; contbr. articles on transp. safety to jours.; mem. editorial bd. Jour. Traffic Medicine, 1989-95; TV and print media interviews. Bd. dirs. Great Falls (Va.) Citizens Assn., 1980-85, Tysons Manor Home Owners Assn., Vienna, Va., 1973-77; mem. Fairfax County (Va.) oversight com. on drinking and driving, 1984—, chmn., 1986-88. Recipient Presdl. Rank of Meritorious Exec. award, 1987. Mem. ASME, Transp. Rsch. Bd. NAS (chmn. com. on alcohol, other drugs and transp. 1991-97, com. on transp. of hazardous materials 1972-78, chmn. users and vehicle sect. 1998—) Internat. Coun. Alcohol and Addictions (co-chmn. sect. on traffic safety 1988—), Internat. Coun. Alcohol, Drugs and Traffic Safety (sec. 1992-97, pres. 2000—, co-editor coun. newsletter ICADTS Reporter 1990—), Am. Acad. Forensic Scis. (adv. mem. drugs and driving com. 1988—), Operation Lifesaver (program devel. coun. 1987-98), Nat. Safety Coun. (motor vehicle occupant protection com. 1983—), Am. Pub. Works Assn. (exec. com. utility location and coordination coun. 1980-87, hon. life mem.), Internat. Transp. Safety Assn. (founding editor assn. newsletter ITSA Report 1994—). Jewish. Avocations: travel, hiking, bicycling. E-mail: sweedlb@home.com.

SWEELEY, MICHAEL MARLIN, foundation executive, public relations executive; b. Twin Falls, Idaho, Aug. 19, 1924; s. Everett Marlin and Hazel Jay (Browne) S. BS in Music, Juilliard Sch. Music, N.Y., 1949, MS in Music, 1950. With press rels. S. Hurok Attractions, N.Y., 1951-69; pres. exec. dir. Caramoor Ctr. for Arts, Katonah, N.Y., 1955-88, pres. emeritus, 1988—; chmn. Marian Anderson Award, Danbury, Conn., 1988-2000. Contbr. articles to jours. in field. Bd. dirs. Little Hill A. Lodge, Blairstown, N.J., 1984-91, Caramoor Ctr. for the Arts, Katonah, N.Y., 1957-94. With USAF, 1943-45. Mem. N.Y. Athletic Club, Union of Theatrical Press Agents. Avocations: travel, swimming, music, art. Home: 91 Central Park W # 13-c New York NY 10023-4600 also: 6060 Pelican Bay Blvd Naples FL 34108-7127

SWEEM, BILLY DON, minister; b. Bartlesville, Okla., Aug. 7, 1942; s. Verl D. and Viola (Benner) S.; m. Roberta Marie Hawthorn, Dec. 26, 1990; children: Mark A. Bradburn. Dipl., Internat. Bible Inst. & Sem., Portsmount, Fla.; ThD. Magna Cum Laude, Bethel Full Gospel Seminary, Okla. Ordained to ministry Gospel Mins. and Chs. Internat., 1991, Ind. Assemblies Fellowship, 1991. Evangelist Lighthouse Temple, Colorado Springs, Colo., 1977-80, Tulsa, 1980-85; youth pastor Echoes of Faith, Las Vegas, Nev., 1985-89; exec. dir. Billy Sweem Gospel Ministries, Tulsa, 1990—. Evangelist United Meth. Coop. Ministries, Tulsa, 1990—. Special interest in mission works with "Throw Away and Troubled Teens", Pine Meadows Boys Ranch Found. Home: PO Box 2171 Bartlesville OK 74005-2171 Address: PO Box 2171 Bartlesville OK 74005-2171

SWEENEY, ASHER WILLIAM, state supreme court justice; b. Canfield, Ohio, Dec. 11, 1920; s. Walter William and Jessie Joan (Kidd) S.; m. Bertha M. Englert, May 21, 1945; children: Randall W., Ronald R., Garland A., Karen M. Student, Youngstown U., 1939-42; LL.B., Duke U., 1948. Bar: Ohio 1949. Practiced law, Youngstown, Ohio, 1949-51; judge adv. gen. Dept. Def., Washington, 1951-65; chief Fed. Contracting Agy., Cin., 1965-68; corp. law, 1968-77; justice Ohio Supreme Ct., Columbus, 1977—. Democratic candidate for Sec. of State Ohio, 1958. Served with U.S. Army, 1942-46; col. Res. 1951-68. Decorated Legion of Merit, Bronze Star; named to Army Hall of Fame Ft. Benning, Ga., 1981 Mem. Ohio Bar Assn., Phi Delta Phi. Democrat. Home: 6690 Drake Rd Cincinnati OH 45243-2706 Office: Ohio Supreme Ct 30 E Broad St Fl 3D Columbus OH 43215-3414

SWEENEY, CHRISTOPHER JOHN, psychology educator, consultant; b. Boston, May 22, 1940; s. John James Sweeney and Adelaide Boomhower; m. Nancy Carol Symmes, Aug. 29, 1964; children: Christopher, Daniel, Rachel. AB cum laude, Boston Coll., 1964; MEd, Northeastern U., Boston, 1966; PhD, U. Okla., 1968. Lic. psychologist, Ohio. Assoc. prof. psychology Youngstown (Ohio) State U., 1968-75, prof., 1975—. Contbr. articles to profl. jours. Bd. dirs. Potential Devel. Ctr., Youngstown, 1975-90, Child and Adult Mental health Ctr., Youngstown, 1977-84. Recipient, Disting. Prof. Awd., Youngstown State U., 1979. Mem. Am. Assn. Applied and Preventive Psychology, NDEA fell., U. Oklahoma, 1967-68. Avocations: reading, racquetball. Home: 405 Garden Gate Dr Youngstown OH 44512-5805 Office: Youngstown State U Psychology Dept 1 University Plz Youngstown OH 44555-0002 E-mail: csweeney@cc.ysu.edu.

SWEENEY, CHRISTOPHER ROBERT, music educator, researcher; b. Pottsville, Pa., Dec. 29, 1966; s. James Thomas and Mary Louise Sweeney. BS in Music Edn. magna cum laude, BS in Music Therapy suma cum laude, Duquesne U., 1989; MusM with honors, U. Miami, Coral Gables, FL, 1998; PhD, U. Miami, Coral Gables, Fla., 2002. Registered music therapist Am. Music Therapy Assn. Music tchr. Gallup-McKinley County Pub. Schs., Thoreau, N.Mex., 1990—95, Miami-Dade County Pub. Schs., Miami, 2000—01; asst. prof. Limestone Coll., Gaffney, SC, 2001—. Low brass instr. Charles W. Flanagan HS, Pembroke Pines, Fla., 1996—2001; adj. prof. U. S.C., Union, 2002—. Mem.: S.C. Music Edn. Assn., Coll. Band Dirs. Nat. Assn., Music Educators Nat. Conf. Home: 1022 W Buford St #1107 Gaffney SC 29341 Office: Limestone Coll 1115 College Dr Gaffney SC 29340 Home Fax: 864-488-4511; Office Fax: 864-488-4511. E-mail: csweeney@saint.limestone.edu.

SWEENEY, CLAYTON ANTHONY, lawyer, business executive; b. Pitts., Oct. 20, 1931; s. Denis Regis and Grace Frances (Roche) S.; m. Sally Dimond, Oct. 4, 1958; children: Sharon, Lorrie, Maureen, Clayton Anthony, Tara, Megan. BS, Duquesne U., 1957, LLB, 1962. Bar: Pa. 1962, U.S. Supreme Ct. 1968. Supr. transp. claims H.J. Heinz Co., Pitts., 1955-57; mgr. market research Murray Corp. Am., 1957-62; ptnr. Buchanan, Ingersoll, Rodewald, Kyle and Buerger, 1962-78; sr. v.p. Allegheny Ludlum Industries, Inc., 1978-81; exec. v.p., chief adminstrv. officer Allegheny Internat., Inc., 1981-84, vice chmn., 1984-85; ptnr., mng. dir. Dickie, McCamey & Chilcote, 1986-98, also bd. dirs.; pres. Sweeney Metz Fox McGrann & Schermer, 1998-2000; with Schnader Harrison Segal & Lewis, LLP, Pitts., 2000—. Bd. dirs. Wilkinson Sword Group Ltd., U.K., Landmark Savs. and Loan Assn., Liquid Air N.Am., Halbouty Energy Co., Koppers Holding Corp., Koppers Industries, Inc., Schaefer Mfg., Inc., Schaefer Marine, Inc., Schaefer Equipment, Inc.; adj. prof. Duquesne U. Sch. Law; lectr. Pa. Bar Inst.; mem. procedural rules com. Supreme Ct. Pa. Named Disting. Alumnus Sch. Law Duquesne U., 1997. Bd. dirs. Met. Pitts. Pub. Broadcasting, Inc., Diocesan Sch. Bd., Roman Cath. Diocese Pitts., Toner Inst., Christian Assocs. of Southwestern Pa., Wesley Inst., Inc., Jr. Achievement S.W. Pa., YMCA Western Pa.; chmn. Seton Hill Coll.; mem. St. Thomas More Sch. Bd., Bethel Park, Pa.; chmn. St. Francis Med. Ctr., St. Francis Health System; chmn. bd. DePaul Inst. With U.S. Army, 1953-55. Named one of 100 Most Disting. Living Alumni Duquesne U. Century Club, 1978 Mem. Acad. Trial Lawyers Allegheny County, ABA, Pa. Bar Assn., St. Thomas More Soc. Home: 232 Thornberry Cir Pittsburgh PA 15234-1025 Office: Schnader Harrison Segal & Lewis LLP Ste 2700 Fifth Ave Pl 120 Fifth Ave Pittsburgh PA 15222-3010 E-mail: csweeney@schnader.com.

SWEENEY, CLAYTON ANTHONY, JR. lawyer; b. Pitts., Jan. 2, 1964; s. Clayton Anthony and Sally (Dimond) S. BA in Econs. with honors, McGill U., 1987; JD, U. Pitts., 1991. Bar: Pa. 1992, Del. 1995, U.S. Dist. Ct. Del. 1995, U.S. Dist. Ct. (we. dist.) Pa. 1991, U.S. Dist. Ct. (eas. dist.) Pa. 1997, U.S. Ct. Appeals (3d cir.) 1992, U.S. Supreme Ct. 2002. Assoc. Burns, White & Hickton, Pitts., 1991-92; law clk. Hon. Donald J. Lee U.S. Dist. Ct. (we. dist.) Pa., 1992-94; assoc. Skadden, Arps, Slate, Meagher & Flom, Wilmington, Del., 1994-96; sole practitioner Phila., 1997—. Vol. atty. Vols. for the Indigent Program, Phila., 1997—, Del. Vol. Legal Svcs., Wilmington, 1995. Mem. Fed. Bar Assn. (criminal law com.), Phila. Bar Assn., Allegheny County Bar Assn., Del. State Bar Assn., Pa. Assn. Criminal Def. Lawyers. Republican. Avocations: guitar, dance. Office: PO Box 55441 Philadelphia PA 19127-5441

SWEENEY, DALE M. (DALE LYNN), college administrator; b. N.Y., Apr. 25, 1953; d. Ralph Michael Esposito and Lucy Mele; m. Dennis R. Sweeney, Nov. 2, 1996. BA, Fairfield (Conn.) U., 1974; MA, MEd, Tchr's. Coll. Columbia U., N.Y.C., 1976. Coord. women's programs Manhattan Coll., Riverdale, N.Y., 1976-78; career devel. secialist Springfield (Mass.) Tech. C.C., 1978-80; counselor Alvin (Tex.) C.C., 1980-84, chair coop. edn., dir. coop. edn. program, 1984-87; asst. dir. admissions and advising Grad. Sch. Bus., NYU, 1987-89; coord. supported edn. program Kennedy Ctr., Bridgeport, Conn., 1989-90, psychosocial rehab. coord., 1990-91; dir. admissions and recruitment Grad. Sch. Health Scis., N.Y. Med. Coll., Valhalla, N.Y., 1991-98. Adj. prof. psychology Alvin C.C., 1984-87, Housatonic C.C., Bridgeport, 1990-91, Westchester C.C., Valhalla, 1992-96; adj. prof. psychology and mgmt. Manhattanville Coll., Purchase, N.Y., 1996; mem. subcom. on student recruitment, strategic planning N.Y. Med. Coll., Valhalla, 1994-96; mem. subcom. on student recruitment Middle States Accreditation, N.Y. Med. Coll., Valhalla, 1994-98, job evaluation com., 1994-98. Contbr. articles to profl. jours. V.p. bd. dirs. Forest Square Condo Assn., Stamford, 1994-97; mem. aux. com. Stamford Mus., 1995-96; mem. Exec. Women's Golf League, 1994—. Recipient Young Woman Am. award, 1984. Mem. APA, AAUW, Am. Assn. Collegiate Registrars and Admissions Officers, Nat. Assn. Grad. Admissions Profls., Nat. Assn. Fgn. Student Advisors, Am. Coun. Edn., Nat. Identification Program, Women Adminstrs. in Higher Edn., Stamford Cath. H.S. Alumni Assn. (bd. dirs. 1989-91). Avocations: skiing, tennis, golf, bicycling, guitar. E-mail: dalems@optonline.net.

SWEENEY, DANIEL THOMAS, cable television company executive; b. N.Y.C., Sept. 25, 1929; s. Daniel Thomas and Rose Marie (Delorenzo) S.; m. Anita Geraldine Madeo, Feb. 14, 1953; children: John, William, Robert, Ellen, Daniel, David. BS, N.Y. State Maritime Coll., 1952; LLB, Fordham U., 1957; LLM, NYU, 1962. Bar: N.Y. Assoc. Kirlin, Campbell and Keating, N.Y.C., 1957-62; dep. county atty. Nassau County, Garden City, N.Y., 1962-65, undersheriff, 1965-66, dep. county exec., 1966-69; chmn., chief exec. officer Mitchel Field Devel. Corp., 1969-71; pres. Sweeney/Edman Enterprises Inc., Hempstead, N.Y., 1971-72; exec. v.p., chief oper. officer HBO, N.Y.C., 1972-73; dir. Cablevision Systems Corp., Woodbury, N.Y., 1973-94; pres. Channel 21, Sta. WLIW-TV, Garden City, 1970-74. Chmn. L.I. State Pk. and Recreation Com., Babylon, N.Y., 1976-83, Jones Beach State Pkwy. Authority, Babylon, N.Y., 1976-79; mem. L.I. Power Auth., 1996-97, chmn. Found. for Long Island State Parks, 1999-. Lt. comdr. USN, 1952-54, Korea. Democrat. Roman Catholic. Home: 94 Glenlawn Ave Sea Cliff NY 11579-2038 Office: Cablevision Systems Corp 1111 Stewart Ave Bethpage NY 11714-3581

SWEENEY, DAVID BRIAN, lawyer; b. Seattle, June 23, 1941; s. Hubert Lee and Ann Louise (Harmon) S.; m. Janice Kay Goins, June 18, 1983; children: Stuart, Jennifer, Ann, Katharine. BA Magna cum laude, Yale U., 1963; LLB, Harvard U., 1967. Bar: Wash. 1968, U.S. Dist. Ct. (we. dist.) Wash. 1968, U.S. Ct. Appeals (9th cir.) 1968. Assoc. Roberts, Shefelman, Lawrence, Gay and Moch, Seattle, 1968-75; ptnr. Roberts, Shefelman, Lawrence, Gay & Moch (then Robert & Shefelman, then Foster, Pepper & Shefelman), 1976—2002; of counsel Smith & Zuccarini, P.S., Bellevue, Wash., 2002—. Mem. Seattle-King County Bar Assn., Wash. State Bar Assn., ABA, Estate Planning Council of Seattle. Clubs: College, Harbor. Republican. Presbyterian. Home: 17506 SE 46th St Bellevue WA 98006-6527 Office: Smith & Zuccarini PS Rainier Plz Ste 2250 777 108th Ave NE Bellevue WA 98004 Office Fax: 425-453-4454. E-mail: david@smithzuccarini.com.

SWEENEY, DEIDRE ANN, lawyer; b. Hackensack, N.J., Mar. 17, 1953; d. Thomas Joseph and Robin (Thwaites) S. AB cum laude, Mt. Holyoke Coll., 1975; JD, Fordham U., 1978. Assoc. Curtis, Mallet-Prevost, Colt & Mosle, N.Y.C., 1978—84, Eaton & Van Winkle, N.Y.C., 1984—86; ptnr. Jacobs, Persinger & Parker, 1986—2002; of counsel McCanliss and Early, 2002—. Adj. instr. Adelphi U., N.Y.C., 1982-86. Class agt. Mt. Holyoke Coll. Alumni Fund, South Hadley, Mass., 1975-80; chmn. nominating com. Mt. Holyoke Class of 1975, 1990-94; mem. Archdiocese N.Y. Bequests and Planned Gifts Com., 1988-97; mem. Hi-Five Scholarship com. CUNY, 2000—. Mem. Assn. of Bar of City of N.Y. (uniform state laws com. 1982-85).

SWEENEY, DENNIS JOSEPH, judge; b. New London, Conn., Sept. 25, 1946; m. Judy K. Winchel, July 27, 1968; 1 child, Shawna Marie. BBA, Gonzaga U., 1968, JD, 1972; LLM, U. Va., 1995. Bar: Wash., U.S. Dist. Ct. (ea. dist.) Wash., U.S. Ct. Appeals (9th cir.), U.S. Tax Ct., U.S. Supreme Ct.; CPA, Wash. Acct. Roger Fruci & Assocs. CPAs, Spokane, Wash., 1969-71; public defender Spokane County Public Defenders Office, 1971-72; ptnr. Leavy, Schultz & Sweeney P.S., Pasco, Wash., 1972-91; elected judge divsn. III Wash. State Ct. Appeals, Spokane, 1991, chief judge divsn. III, 1996-98, presiding chief judge, 1998-99. Presenter seminars, lectr. in Continuing Legal Edn. Program, Wash., 1990—, lectr. at Wash. State Judicial Coll. Contbr. articles to law revs. and ednl. legal jours. Bd. dirs. Heritage Coll., Toppenish, Wash., Benton Franklin Legal Aid, 1972—; mem. jurisprudence com. Access to Justice Bd.; vol. Richland Repertory Theater, benefit sausagefest for Christ the King ch.; Lt. U.S. Army, 1972. Named Appellate Judge of Yr., Wash. State Trial Lawyers Assn. Fellow Am. Coll. Trial Lawyers; mem. AICPA, Wash. Soc. CPAs, Am. Bd. Trial Advocates. (office), (home). Office: Ct Appeals State of Wash PO Box 2159 Spokane WA 99210-2159 E-mail: Dennis.Sweeney@courts.wa.gov., Dsween2150@aol.com.

SWEENEY, EILEEN PATRICIA, lawyer; b. Evanston, Ill., Nov. 6, 1951; d. Howard J. and Kathleen P. Sweeney; m. Lawrence Andrew Johnston, Sept. 1, 1979; children: Edward, Matthew, Kathleen. BA, Northwestern U., Evanston, 1973; JD, Northwestern U., Chgo., 1976. Bar: Ill. 1976, D.C. 1980. Staff atty. Legal Assistance Found. Chgo., 1976-79, Nat. Sr. Citizens Law Ctr., Washington, 1980-91; dir. gov. affairs Children's Def. Fund, 1991-98; dir. state low income initiatives project Ctr. on Budget and Policy Priorities, 1998—. Mem. SSI modernization panel Soc. Security Administn., Balt., 1990-92; mem. tech. com. Earnings Sharing, Washington, 1985-88. Contbr. articles to profl. jours. Bd. dirs. Nat. Ctr. on Poverty Law, 1993—; mem. commn. legal problems of elderly ABA, Washington, 1990-91; mem. expert panel rethinking disability policy, 1993-96. Recipient Reginald Heber Smith award Nat. Legal Aid and Def. Assn., Washington, 1985, Alumna Yr. Regina Dominican H.S., Wilmette, Ill., 1985. Mem. Nat. Acad. Soc. Ins. Roman Catholic. Office: Ctr Budget and Policy Priorities 820 1st St NE Ste 510 Washington DC 20002-8035

SWEENEY, EMILY MARGARET, prosecutor; b. Cleve., May 2, 1948; d. Mark Elliot and Neydra (Ginsburg) Mirsky; m. Patrick Anthony Sweeney, Dec. 30, 1983; 1 child, Margaret Anne. BA, Case Western Res. U., 1970; JD, Cleve. Marshall Coll. Law, 1981. Bar: Ohio 1981. Tchr. English Cleve. Pub. Schs., 1970; plant mgr. Union Gospel Press Pub. Co., Cleve., 1971-73; publ. specialist Cleve. State U., 1973-82; asst. U.S. atty. Dept. Justice, Cleve., 1982—; now U.S. atty., 1993—. Precinct committeeman, Woodmere, Ohio, 1978; mem. Atty. Gen.'s Adv. Com. U.S. Attys., 1993—96, 1998—99, chmn. office mgmt. and budget subcom., 1993—2001, mem. asset forfeiture, civil issues, controlled substances and drug demand reduction, LECC/victim witness subcoms., 1993—2001; chmn. law enforcement coord. com. No. Dist. Ohio, 1993—. Recipient Eddy award for graphic design, 1977, Spl Achievement award U.S. Dept. Justice, 1985. Mem.: Fed. Bar Assn. Democrat. Office: US Atty's Office 1800 Bank One Ctr 600 Superior Ave E Ste 1800 Cleveland OH 44114-2600

SWEENEY, EUGENE WILLIAM, dermatologist; b. Bklyn., May 25, 1934; s. John Edward and Marion Elizabeth (Leonard) S.; m. Dianne Card, Oct. 24, 1964; children: Edward L., E. Sean. BS, Manhattan Coll., 1956; MD, NYU, 1960. Diplomate Am. Bd. Dermatology. Intern The Bklyn. Hosp., 1960-61; resident, fellow Columbia Physicians and Surgeons Med. Ctr./St. Luke's Hosp., N.Y.C., 1963-66; pvt. practice Teaneck, N.J., 1966—. Office: 773 Teaneck Rd Teaneck NJ 07666-4846

SWEENEY, FRANCIS E. state supreme court justice; b. Jan. 26, 1934; married; 4 children. BSBA, Xavier U., 1956; JD, Cleve.-Marshall Law Sch., 1963. Profl. football player Ottawa Rough Riders, Ont., Can., 1956-58; mem. legal dept. Allstate Ins. Co., Cleve., 1958-63; asst. prosecuting atty. Cuyahoga County, 1963-70; judge Cuyahoga County Ct. of Common Pleas, 1970-88; judge (8th cir.) U.S. Ct. Appeals, 1988-92; justice Ohio Supreme Ct., Columbus, 1992—. With U.S. Army, 1957-58. Recipient Legion of Honor award Xavier U., 1956, Outstanding Jud. Svc. award Ohio Supreme Ct., 1972-85, Alumnus of Yr. award Xavier U., 1977. Office: Ohio Supreme Ct 30 E Broad St Fl 3 Columbus OH 43215-0001*

SWEENEY, GEORGE BERNARD, petrochemical industry executive, investor, broadcast executive, travel agency executive; b. Cleve., May 9, 1933; s. George Bernard and Ethel E. (Wise) S.; m. Molly Jane O'Neill, July 13, 1963; children: Brian, Kelly, Mark, Kevin, Kim. BSBA, John Carroll U., 1955; MBA, U. Pa., 1957; DHL (hon.), John Carroll U., 2000. With Exxon Corp., 1956-78; chmn., pres. Esso Pakistan Fertilizer Co., Karachi, 1969-74; v.p. Exxon Corp. and Exxon Chem. U.S.A., Houston, 1974-78; dir., prin., exec. v.p. Chagrin Valley Co. Ltd., Cleve., 1977-83; dir. Nevamar Corp., Odenton, Md. Pres., prin. Questers, Inc., Houston, 1979-86; pres., prin. Stas. KMUV/KPHD/KSSO, Conroe, Tex., 1984-89, Sweeney Broadcasting Co., 1984-89, Travel Network, Sweeney Travel Quest, Inc., 1987-93. Bd. dirs., v.p., bd. advs. Houston Symphony, 1976—; trustee John Carroll U., Cleve., 1977—, Strake Jesuit Coll. Prep., Houston, 1979—85; trustee, chmn. bd. Trinity Coll., Washington, 1974—80; exec bd. Wharton Grad. Sch., U. Pa., 1980—85; trustee, bd. dirs., exec. com. U. St. Thomas, Houston, 1982—88; mem. parents com. U. Va., Charlottesville, 1984—91; bd. dirs. Tex. Hunter-Jumper Assn., 1981—87; dir., v.p. Houston Hunter Jumper Charity Horse Show, 1983—88; founding trustee, bd. dirs. Franciscan Mission Svc., Silver Spring, Md., 1987—91, mem. audit com.; mem. nat. bd. dirs. U.S. Equestrian Team, Gladstone, NJ, 1989—94; bd. dirs. Ctr. for Family Studies U. of Miami, 1999—. Served to 1st lt. Transp. Corps. U.S. Army, 1958. Recipient in Pakistan U.S. State Dept. citation of appreciation, 1974, John Carroll U. Centennial medal, 1986, Sullivan award John Carroll U., 1980, 85, 90, 95, 2000, Alumni Svc. award, 1995, Bus. Sch. 50 Finest award, 1995. Mem. Houston Club, Palm Beach Polo and Country Club, Houston Oaks Golf Club, Ancient Order of Hibernians. Home: 24112 Macedonia Rd Hockley TX 77447-6010 also: 12563 Mallet Cir Wellington FL 33414-8408

SWEENEY, JACK, publishing executive; BA in English, King's Coll. With adv. dept. Washington Post, 1968; adv. dir. Trenton Times, 1974, Boston Herald, 1978, Houston Chronicle, 1980, dir. sales and mktg., 1983, v.p. sales and mktg., 1986, v.p., gen. mgr., 1991, assoc. pub., 1998, pres., 1998—, pub., 2000—. Leader United Way Tex. Gulf Coast, Greater Hosuton Partnership, Houston Image Group, Chidren's Assessment Ctr. Found., Houston Symphony, Houston Internat. Festival, BBB. Mem.: Tex. Daily Newspaper Assn. (Pat Taggart Newspaper Exec. of Yr.), Newspaper Assn. Am. (mem. bd. dirs., mem. exec. com.). Office: Houston Chronicle 801 Texas Ave Houston TX 77002 Office Fax: 713-220-6677.*

SWEENEY, JAMES RAYMOND, lawyer; b. Chgo., Feb. 19, 1928; s. John Francis and Mae J. (McDonald) S.; m. Rhoda W. Davis, May 15, 1987; children from previous marriage: Margaret Elizabeth, John Francis, Thomas Edward. BS, U. Notre Dame, 1950; JD, Northwestern U., 1956. Bar: Ill. 1956. With firm Schroeder, Hofgren, Brady & Wegner, Chgo., 1956-61; ptnr. Hofgren, Wegner, Allen, Stellman & McCord, 1962-71, Coffee, Wetzel, Sweeney, Chgo., 1971-72, Coffee & Sweeney, 1972-76, Mason, Kolehmainen, Rathburn & Wyss, Chgo., 1976-82, McWilliams, Mann, Zummer & Sweeney, 1983-86, Mann, McWilliams, Zummer, & Sweeney, 1986-89, Lee, Mann, Smith, McWilliams & Sweeney, 1989-91, Lee, Mann, Smith, McWilliams, Sweeney & Ohlson, 1991—; dir. ctr. intellectual property law John Marshall Law Sch., 1998—. Commr. for disbarment matters Ill. Supreme Ct., 1963-73; mem. hearing div. Atty. Registration and Discipline Commn., 1974-77, chmn. commn. 1983-90; chmn. Ctr. for Intellectual Property Law adv. bd. John Marshall Law Sch., 1997-99. Bd. dirs., sec. Highland Park (Ill.) Hosp., 1972-79. Served as lt. (j.g.) USN, 1950-53; lt. comdr. Res. ret. Mem. ABA (coun. patent, trademark and copyright sect., sec. 1978-82), Ill. State Bar (assembly 1990-96), Chgo. Bar Assn. (sec. 1977-79), Bar Assn. 7th Cir., Intellectual Property Law Assn. Chgo., Patent Law Assn. Chgo. (pres. 1974), The Lawyers Club, Skokie (Ill.) Country Club, Union League Club. Home: 505 N Lake Shore Dr Chicago IL 60611-3427 Office: Lee Mann Smith McWilliams Sweeney & Ohlson 209 S La Salle St Ste 410 Chicago IL 60604-1203 also: John Marshall Law Sch 315 S Plymouth Ct Chicago IL 60604-3969 E-mail: 7Sweeney@jmls.edu.

SWEENEY, JOHN ADRIAN, psychologist; b. Cin., May 2, 1952; PhD, Syracuse U., 1974—80. Psychologist Cornell U. Med. Ctr., N.Y.C., NY, 1979—90, University of Pitts., Pa., 1990—2001; ctr. dir. U. Ill. Chgo., Ill., 2001—. Office: Neuropsychiatric Inst 912 South Wood St Ste 235 Chicago IL 60612 Business E-Mail: jsweeney@psych.uic.edu.

SWEENEY, JOHN E. congressman; b. Troy, N.Y. children: Kelly, John, Mary. AAS, Hudson Valley C.C.; BS in Polit. Sci., Criminal Justice, Russell Sage Coll.; JD, Western New Eng. Coll., 1990. Bar: N.Y. 1990. Dir. Rensselaer County Stop-DWI program, Troy; ptnr. Sweeney, Cholakis & Wollowitz; commr. of labor State of N.Y., Albany, 1995-97, dep. sec. to Gov. George Pataki, 1997-99; mem. U.S. Congress from 22d N.Y. dist., 1999—; mem. appropriations com. Serves on Banking and Fin. Svcs., Small Bus., Transp. and Infrastructure coms.; vice chmn. Aviation subcom.; mem. ground transp., capital mkts. and housing subcoms. Chmn. N.Y. Rep. Party, 1992-95. Elected to U.S. Ho. Reps. in 1998 to succeed retiring 10-term Rep. Gerald Solomon. Republican. Office: 416 Cannon Ho Office Bldg Washington DC 20515*

SWEENEY, JOHN J(OSEPH), lawyer; b. N.Y.C., Dec. 28, 1924; s. John J. and Rose H. (Galligan) S.; m. Rita V. Colleran, Aug. 27, 1955; children: Jean Maria, John J., Peter F., Thomas P., Michael J., Roseanne. LLB, St. John's U., 1951, BA, 1952. Bar: N.Y., 1951. Vol. lawyer Felony Ct. Legal Aid Soc., N.Y.C., 1951-52; asst. gen. counsel U.S. Trucking Corp., 1952-55; pvt. practice, 1955-83; editor. N.Y. State Tax Monitor, 1983-84; mortgage real estate loan officer, 1985-90; tchr. DeWitt Clinton H.S., 1990-92; pvt. practice Scarsdale, 1992—. Spl. master Supreme Ct., N.Y. County; pre-trial master Civil Ct., N.Y. County; commr., referee, receiver and guardian ad litem Supreme and Surrogate's Ct.; arbitrator Am. Arbitration Assn., Civil Ct., N.Y. County, Better Bus. Bur.; arbitrator, mediator N.Y. State Mediation Bd.; litigator local, state, and fed. cts. Pres. Arthur Manor Assn., Scarsdale, 1970-73, Cath. Big Bros., N.Y.C., 1971-73; mem. nominating com. Village Trustee, Scarsdale, 1970-76, mem. nominating com. sch. bd., 1973-76; mem. Scarsdale Hist. Soc., 1980—. With U.S. Army, 1943-46. Decorated Silver star, two Bronze stars, two Purple Hearts and three Battle stars, Combat Infantry Badge. Mem. Guild Cath. Lawyers (pres. 1969-71), Scarsdale Antiques Running Club (pres. 1984-86). Democrat. Avocations: marathon running, tennis, platform tennis, softball, writing. Home and Office: 223 Boulevard Scarsdale NY 10583-5832

SWEENEY, KEVIN MICHAEL, lawyer; b. Westfield, Mass., May 28, 1965; s. Lawrence Arthur and Maureen Theresa (Cavanaugh) S.; m. Karen Elizabeth Marsian, May 15, 1993. BA, U. Mass., 1987; D Law, U. Wis., 1990. Bar: Mass., Wis.; U.S. Dist. Ct. (we. dist.) Wis., U.S. Dist. Ct. Mass. 2d v.p., assoc. gen. counsel Office Gen. Counsel Mass. Mut. Life Ins. Co., Springfield, Mass., 1993—2002; 2d v.p. law, asst. sec. and chief compliance officer Mass Mutual Internat., Inc., 1996—2002, Luxembourg, 1996—2002, also bd. dirs., 1999—2002; chief compliance officer Mass Mutual Internat. Bermuda, Ltd., Hamilton, 1996—2001; counsel, asst. sec. MML Reinsurance Bermuda, 1996-97; corp. sec. Mass Mutual Found. for Hartford, Inc., Hartford, Conn., 1996—2002, also bd. dirs., 2000—; asst. sec. Mass Mutual Holding Co., 1998-2000, C. M. Life Ins. Co., 1998-2000, MML Bay State Life Ins. Co., 1998-2000, Mass. Mutual Benefits Mgmt., Inc., 1998-2000; asst. clk. Mass Mutual Holding MSC, Inc., 1999-2000; corp. sec. MassMutual Trust Co., 2000—01; v.p. recruiting and opers., corp. human resources MassMutual Fin. Group, 2002—. Assoc. Bulkley, Richardson and Gelinas, Springfield, 1990-93; rsch. asst. U. Wis., Madison, 1988-90; law clk. Wis. Dept. Justice, Madison, 1989; project asst. and law clk. Legal Assistance to Institutionalized Persons, Madison, 1988-89, adj. prof. of law, We. New Eng. Coll. Sch. of Law, 2002—. Author: (paper) Restructuring Insurance Companies Through Mergers, Acquisitions and Other Affiliations, ABA Ann. Meeting, 1999; rsch. asst.: (book) Tournament of Lawyers, 1991. Legal counsel, bd. dirs., dir. fin. Mass. Hugh O'Brian Youth Leadership Found., Inc., Boston, 1991-93; atty. advisor Mass. Bar Assn. H.S. Mock Ct. Competition, Springfield, 1990-91; mem. Dem. Town Com., West Springfield, 1990-91. Tech. sgt. ANG, 1983-91. Mem. ABA (young lawyers divsn. in-house counsel com., planning bd. mem. 1994-96), State Bar Wis., Phi Kappa Phi. Democrat. Roman Catholic. Avocations: travel, reading, listening to music. Office: Mass Mut Financial Group 1295 State St Springfield MA 01111-0001

SWEENEY, LAWRENCE EARL, JR. computer company executive; b. Charleston, W.Va., Mar. 27, 1942; s. Lawrence Earl and Isabel Lenore Sweeney; m. Mary Elizabeth Davis, Sept. 13, 1969; children: Daniel, Blake. BSEE, Stanford U., 1960, MSEE, PhD, Stanford U. V.p. SRI Internat., Menlo Park, Calif., 1970—90; sr. v.p. Mirage Sys., Sunnyvale, 1990—91; v.p., gen. mgr. bus. devel. Tele Atlas N.Am., Menlo Park, 1991—. Mem.: SAE, IEEE, Calif. Alliance for Advanced Transp. Sys. (bd. dirs. 1995, award of excellence, CAATS Civic Entrepreneur). Office: Tele Atlas NAm 1605 Adams Dr Menlo Park CA 94025

SWEENEY, MARK OWEN, publisher; b. Cherryvale, Kans., Dec. 27, 1942; s. Paul Eldon and Clelia Eugenia (Bosette) S.; m. Janet Lynn Turner, July 24, 1964; children— Douglas, Jonathan. Grad., Moody Bible Inst., 1963; BA, Pacific Coll., 1965; MA, Wheaton Coll., Ill., 1967. Instr. history Cascade Coll., Portland, Oreg., 1967-70; editor Moody Bible Inst., Chgo., 1970-72; exec. producer Moody Corr. Sch., Moody Bible Inst. (Radio div.), 1972-74; dir. public relations Moody Bible Inst. (dir. Moody Lit. Ministries), 1974-77, mgr. publ. div., 1977-81; dir. Victor Books, Scripture Press Publs., 1981-83, v.p., 1983-90, pubr., COO Ill., 1990-94; corp. v.p., pub. Scripture Press Publs., Inc. and Victor Books, 1994-95; COO Killion McCabe and Assocs., Dallas, 1995-97; exec. dir., COO Leadership Network, 1997-98; sr. v.p., assoc. pub. W Pub Group, Thomas Nelson, Inc., Nashville, 1998—2001, sr. v.p., pub., 2001—. Mem. Christian Booksellers Assn., Evang. Christian Pubs. Assn. (past chmn. bd.). Home: 229 Waterbury Cir Franklin TN 37067-6204 Office: W Pub Group PO Box 141000 545 Marriott Dr Ste 750 Nashville TN 37214-5082 E-mail: msweeney@wpublishinggroup.com.

SWEENEY, MICHAEL ANDREW, newspaper editor; b. York, Pa., Nov. 27, 1948; s. Felix William and Deuris C. (Ehehalt) S.; m. Linda Carol Gillam, Nov. 20, 1976; children: Barbara Catherine, Matthew Allan. BA in Communication Art, Seton Hall U., 1972; MA in Polit. Sci., Rutgers U., 1981. Reporter The Courier-News, Bridgwater, N.J., 1972-75, asst. night editor, 1975-77, night editor, 1977-78, nat. editor, 1978-79, asst. news editor, 1980-81; news editor The Advocate Southern Conn. Newspapers Inc., Stamford, Conn., 1981-83, exec. news editor, 1983-85, asst. mng. editor, 1985-88; editorial page editor Greenwich Time/So. Conn. Newspapers, Inc., 1988—, columnist, 1991—. Contbr. articles to profl. jours. Roman Catholic. Avocations: gardening, computers, Mercedes-Benz automobiles. Office: Greenwich Time 20 E Elm St Greenwich CT 06830-6573

SWEENEY, MIKE, professional baseball player; b. Orange, Calif., July 22, 1973; Baseball player Kansas City (Mo.) Royals, 1995—. Office: Kansas City Royals PO Box 419969 Kansas City MO 64141-6969*

SWEENEY, NEAL JAMES, lawyer; b. Paterson, N.J., Nov. 1, 1957; s. Bernard Thomas and Mary Agnes (Keneally) S.; m. Mary Elizabeth Finocchiaro, Oct. 27, 1984; children: Daniel Fulton, Clare Kenneally, Moira Ann. BA in History and Polit Sci., Rutgers U., 1979; JD, George Washington U., 1982. Bar: Ga. 1982, U.S. Dist. Ct. (no. dist.) Ga. 1982, U.S. Dist. Ct. (no. dist.) Tex. 1982, U.S. Claims Ct. 1984, U.S. Ct. Appeals (5th cir.) 1987. Assoc. Smith, Currie & Hancock, Atlanta, 1982-87, ptnr., 1988-98; ptnr. Kilpatrick Stockton LLP, 1998—; chair dept. epidemiology, 2001—. Co-author: Construction Business Handbook, 1985, Holding Subcontractors to Their Bids, 1986, Subcontractor Default, 1987, The New AIA Design and Construction Documents, 1988, Proving and Pricing Claims, 1995, Fifty State Construction Lien and Bond Law, 2000, Who Pays For Defective Design?, 1997; editor: Construction Subcontracting, 1991, Common Sense Construction Law, 1997; editor Construction Law Update, 1992—; notes editor G.W.U.J. Internat. Law and Econs., 1981-82. Mem. ABA (pub. contract law sect., forum com. on constrn. industry), Atlanta Bar Assn., Am. Arbitration Assn. (panel of arbitrators), Water Environment Fedn. (editl. adv. bd. 1994-97), Design Build Inst. of Am. (exec. bd. s.e. chpt. 2002—). Roman Catholic. Home: 120 Forrest Lake Dr NW Atlanta GA 30327 Office: Kilpatrick Stockton LLP 1100 Peachtree St NE Ste 2800 Atlanta GA 30309-4530 E-mail: nsweeney@kilpatrickstock.com.

SWEENEY, PHILLIP PETER, poet; b. Towanda, Pa., Apr. 3, 1949; s. Robert Gerard and Theresa Alva Sweeney; children: Adam, Seth. BA, SUNY-Binghamton, 1973, MS in Edn., 1993. Cert. tchr., N.Y. Lang. arts instr. St. Michael's Sch., Memphis, 1983-84; tchr. poetry/creative writing alternative lit. programs State of N.Y., 1984-92; arts-in-edn. programs tchr. So. Tier Inst. for the Arts in Edn., 1984-92; tchr. poetry in the schs. program Imagination Celebration, Broome County, N.Y., 1984-92; instr. English and composition Afton (N.Y.) Ctrl. H.S., 1996—. Performance poet/writer Poets & Writers, Inc., 1984—. Author: Dark Shadows for a Thousand Points of Light, 1998; lead singer/songwriter: Truman's Cabin, 1984—. Bd. dirs., sec. So. Tier Ind. Living Ctr., Binghamton, 1995-96; drama dir. Afton Ctrl. H.S., 1997-98; SADD advisor, Afton, 1997—; founder, dir. SADD Care Cmty. Coffeehouse, 1997—; lectr. in field. Recipient Profl. Writing Residency, Blue Mtn. Ctr., 1984; Broome County Arts Coun. Career Enhancement grantee, 1990, United Cultural Fund grantee, 1996. Roman Catholic. Avocations: chess, music and guitar. Home: 137 Shamrock Pl #2 Harpursville NY 13787

SWEENEY, RANDALL W. aerospace transportation executive; BS in Edn., Ohio State U., 1972, MA in Pub. Adminstrn and Orgnl. Develop., 1977. Spl. asst. to regional adminstr. region V U.S. Small Bus. Adminstrn., 1980—81; pres. Def. and Aerospace Internat., Inc., Arlington, Va. Mem. Army Sci. Bd., Va.; dir., co-founder Nat. Ctr. Govt. Contracting, 1982—83; v.p. mktg. and contract adminstrn. Ferrotherm Co., Inc., 1985—. Mem. Ohio Elections Commn., Columbus, 1979—80; chmn. Ohio Bd. Tax Appeals , 1984—99. Mem.: Nat. Small Bus. Govt. Contractors Assn. (v.p. 1984—86, chmn. govt. affairs com. 1984—86). Office: SAAL-ASB Ste 11500 2511 Jefferson Davis Hwy Arlington VA 22202-3911*

SWEENEY, RICHARD JAMES, economics educator; b. San Diego, Jan. 13, 1944; s. John Joseph and Catherine Scott (Spahr) S.; m. Joan Long, June 19, 1965; children: Robin Scott, Erin Michaela. BA, UCLA, 1965; PhD, Princeton U., 1972. Acting asst. prof. econs. UCLA, 1968-71; asst. prof. Tex. A&M U., College Station, 1971-73; dep. dir. office of internat. monetary research U.S. Dept. Treasury, Washington, 1973-77; Charles M. Stone prof. econs. and fin. Claremont (Calif.) McKenna Coll., 1977-89, chmn. dept. econs., 1987-89; Bolton Sullivan & Thomas A. Dean chair internat. fin. Georgetown U., Washington, 1989—. Vis. assoc. prof. econs. U. Va., Charlottesville, 1975; vis. prof. bus. adminstrn. Dartmouth Coll., Hanover, N.H., 1979; vis. prof. fin. Gothenburg (Sweden) Sch. Econs., 1991—. Author: A Macro Theory with Micro Foundations, 1974, Principles of Microeconomics, Macroeconomics, 1980, Wealth Effects and Monetary Theory, 1988, Profit-Making Speculation in Foreign Exchange Markets, 1992; author, editor: Capital Control in Emerging Market Economies, 1997, Exchange-Rate Policies for Emerging Market Economies, 1999; contbr. articles to profl. jours. Fellow NSF 1966-68, Woodrow Wilson Found. 1965; grantee Gen. Electric Found., 1980, Mid.-Am. Found., 1987, Earhart Found., 1988. Mem. Western Econ. Assn. (editor Econ. Inquiry jour. 1984-96), Am. Econ. Assn., Am. Fin. Assn., Western Fin. Assn., Phi Beta Kappa. Democrat. Avocations: writing, weightlifting, walking, aerobics. Office: McDonough Sch Bus Georgetown U Washington DC 20057-0001 E-mail: sweeneyr@georgetown.edu.

SWEENEY, ROBERT DAVID, communications engineer; b. Nashville, Aug. 28, 1921; s. John Henry and A. Letty (Bateman) S.; m. Mildred Kathleen Rose, July 14, 1941 (dec. Aug. 1973); children: Robert, Mary, Barbara; m. Marie Ruby Simmons, Dec. 14, 1974; children: Robert Jr., Rick, Mary, Alan, Barbara, Robbie. Comm. Engr., Capitol Radio Engring. Inst., Washington, 1942; Elec. Engr., U.S. Mil. Acad., West Point, N.Y., 1950. Commd. U.S. Army, 1951, advanced through grades to col., 1969; comm. and electronic instr. Norwich U., Norfield, Vt., 1948-50; asst. instr. U.S. Army Mil. Acad., West Point, 1950-51; bn. comdr., asst. divsn. signal officer 1st Armored Divsn., Ft. Hood, Tex., 1951-52; commdg. officer 59th Signal Support Co., 1952-53; radio engr. Japan Signal Bn., 1953-56; signal officer 61st Anti Aircraft Artillery Groups, Milw., 1956-60; officer in charge Down Island Comm. Systems, U.S. Comm. Detachment, Taiwan, 1960-61; comm.-electronics officer 28th N.Am. Air Defense Command, Hamilton AFB, Calif., 1961-64; chief Pacific field office U.S. Army Strategic Comm. Command, Okinawa, 1964-67; post signal officer The Infantry Ctr., Ft. Benning, Ga., 1967-68; dep. dir. Comm. Systems Engring. Mgmt. Agy., 1st Signal Brigade, Vietnam, 1968-69; dept. dir. comm.-electronics dept. U.S. Army Infantry Sch., Ft. Benning, 1969-73; congl. aide-dist. rep. Congressman 3rd Dist. Ga., Washington, 1974-83. Counselor Boy Scouts Am., Ft. Riley, Kans., 1950—. Decorated Legion of Merit with oak leaf cross, Bronze Star with 3 oak leaf crosses, Air Medal, Purple Heart. Mem. Assn. Elec. Engrs., Armed Forces Comm.-Elec. Assn. (charter pres. 1968, merit award), Fraternal Order Eagles, Odd Fellows. Democrat. Baptist. Avocations: amateur radio, chess, football, baseball, tennis. Home: 4828 Allegheny Dr Columbus GA 31907-1734 E-mail: sweeneyrd@hotmail.com.

SWEENEY, THOMAS FREDERICK, lawyer; b. Detroit, Feb. 10, 1943; s. Harold Eugene and Marion Genevieve (Lunz) S.; m. Susan Carol Horn, Dec. 27, 1968; children: Sarah Elizabeth, Neal Thomas. AB, U. Mich., 1965, JD, 1968. Bar: Mich. 1968, U.S. Dist. Ct. (ea. dist.) Mich, 1968, U.S. Tax Ct. 1979, U.S. Supreme Ct. 1985. Assoc. Fischer, Franklin, Ford, Simon & Hogg, Detroit, 1969—73, ptnr., 1974—85, Houghton, Potter, Sweeney & Brenner, Detroit, 1986—95; mem. Clark Hill, Birmingham, 1995—2002, mem. exec. com., 1999—. Spkr. Inst. CLE. Contbr. articles to legal jours. Mem. Birmingham (Mich.) Charter Rev. Commn., 1977; bd. dirs. Cmty. House Assn., 1990—98, pres., 1993—95; trustee Baldwin Pub. Libr., Birmingham, 1981—, pres., 2002—. Mem. ABA, Oakland County Bar Assn. (chmn. taxation com. 1988-89), Forest Hills Swim Club (pres. 1985-87). Roman Catholic. Home: 1493 Buckingham Ave Birmingham MI 48009-5866 Office: Clark Hill 255 S Old Woodward Ave Ste 301 Birmingham MI 48009-6182 E-mail: tsweeney@clarkhill.com.

SWEENEY, THOMAS JOSEPH, JR. lawyer; b. N.Y.C., Oct. 29, 1923; s. Thomas Joseph and Johanna M. (Flynn) S.; m. Robin Virginia Thwaites, May 30, 1947; children: Thomas Joseph, III, Deidre Ann. BA, N.Y. U., 1947; JD, Columbia U., 1949. Bar: N.Y. 1949. Assoc. in law Columbia U. Law Sch., 1949-50; assoc. Cravath, Swaine & Moore, N.Y.C., 1950-62; with Morgan Guaranty Trust Co. N.Y., 1962-89, v.p., 1965-76, sr. v.p., sr. trust officer, 1976-89, chmn. instl. trust and investment com., 1989-99; ptnr. Decker, Hubbard, Welden & Sweeney, N.Y.C. Bd. dirs. W.R. Kenan Fund. Trustee Pinkerton Found., Jean and Louis Dreyfus Found. 2d lt. USAAF, 1943-45. Mem. N.Y. State Bar Assn. Democrat. Roman Catholic. Home: 525 Teaneck Rd Ridgefield Park NJ 07660-1100 Office: Decker Hubbard 420 Lexington Ave New York NY 10170

SWEENY, ARTHUR, III, realtor; b. N.Y.C., Nov. 11, 1933; BA, Hobart Coll., 1956. V.p. Braisin, Porter & Wheelock, N.Y.C., 1958-82; v.p., dir. William J. Dwyer & Co., 1982-87, Cross & Brown Co., N.Y.C., 1987-92. Home: 83 Landing Ave Colchester VT 05446-6955

SWEENY, DONNA BOZZELLA, writer, editor; b. Bklyn., Apr. 11, 1945; d. Joseph and Kaarin (Pajula) Bozzella; m. H.W. Allen Sweeny, Jan. 2, 1981; stepchildren: Peter, Christine, Catherine, David. BA, St. John's U., 1966; MBA, Fordham U., 1982; postgrad., CUNY, 1982-84. Employment interviewer, divsn. employment N.Y. State Dept. Labor, Bklyn., 1967-72; travel coord. Am. Jewish Com., 1974-75; adminstrv. asst. to pres. Bell & Howell Edn. Group, Evanston, Ill., 1976-78; legal coord. Internat. Std. Brands (later Nabisco Brands), N.Y.C., 1978-80; dir. tng. and adminstrn. Arthur Andersen, Tokyo, 1984-86; freelance writer and editor 1986—. Cooking columnist Tokyo Weekender, 1986-90; staff writer Coconut Grove Times, 1997—, Brickell Post, 1997—, South Miami Times, 1999—; publicity writer Streets of Mayfair Mall, 1997-99; editor Voice of the Grove, 1994-97; editor: Coconut Grove Mag., 1998—. Pres. Coconut Grove (Fla.) Federated Rep. Women's Club, 1992-93; mem. exec. com. Ambs. of Mercy Hosp., Miami, Fla., 1993—; bd. dirs. Mercy Found., 2001-02; trustee Miami Mus. Sci., 1994, mem. adv. bd., 1995; mem. adv. coun. La Salle H.S., Miami, 1996-98; committeewoman dist. 20 Dade County Rep. Exec. Com., 1997-98; mem. spl. events com. Coconut Grove Playhouse, 1998-99; bd. dirs. Coconut Arts Festival, 1999—, v.chmn. 2002. Mem. Coconut Grove C. of C. (bd. dirs. 1997-2000, Coconut Club award 1997). Roman Catholic. Avocations: photography, ikebana, collecting political memorabilia, cooking. Home: 2000 S Bayshore Dr Coconut Grove FL 33133-3256

SWEENY, KENNETH S. graphic design consultant; b. Trenton, N.J., Aug. 8, 1948; s. Russell Lawrence and Elva Marion (Sibbitt) S.; m. Geraldine Ann Condemi, May 25, 1969 (div. Oct. 28, 1980). AA, Sch. Visual Arts, N.Y.C., 1970. Graphic artist Lasky Advt., Bloomfield, N.J., 1970-71; assoc. art dir. Ziff-Davis, N.Y.C., 1971-72, Warner Communications, N.Y.C., 1972-75; graphic designer NBC Network Mktg. Sales, 1976-78; owner, creative dir. Sweeny Ink, Belleville, N.J., 1975-78; art dir. Al Paul Lefton Advt., N.Y.C., 1978-80, Corporations & Advt. Agencies, N.Y.C., Conn., N.J, 1978-80; graphic design cons. staff Loral Electronic Systems, Yonkers, N.Y., 1980-90. Cons. in field; practitioner of letterforms through use of alphabets and typography; part-time substitute tchr. elem.-h.s., 1987—; part-time adult edn. instr. Designer INEWS Electronic Shield, 1985, N.J. Bankers Assn., 1972, Logo Designs and Trends, 1990, Graphics Jour. Com. chairperson Forum Employees Assn., Yonkers, 1983-84. Recipient DESI award Graphics: USA, 1978, 82, 84, 85, 88, 90, Bestsellers gold award Pub. Designers Assn., 1983, silver, gold and merit awards N.J. Art Dirs. Club, 1982, 84, 85, 88, 90. Mem. Nat. Computer Graphics Assn., Inter-Soc. Color Coun., Art Dirs. Club (merit award 1983), Type Dirs. Club, Advt. Club Westchester (silver, gold, copper awards 1984, 85, 86, 88), Advt. Club Fairfield (silver award 1986, 87, 88), Art Dirs. Club N.J., Am. Irish Genealogists, Nat. Mgmt. Assn. (Achievement award 1982), Am. Mgmt. Assn., Airforce Aviation Assn. (Achievement award 1984). Republican. Roman Catholic. Home and Office: PO Box 1532 New Canaan CT 06840-1532

SWEENY, STEPHEN JUDE, academic administrator; b. N.Y.C., Sept. 15, 1943; s. Herbert Vincent and Isabel Mary (Dolan) S.; m. Barbara Mary Stasz, Aug. 7, 1976. BA in Spanish, Cath. U., 1966; MA in Theology, Manhattan Coll., 1971, MA in Counseling Psychology, 1976; PhD, NYU, 1991. Prin. Incarnation Elem. and Jr. High Sch., N.Y.C., 1969-73; dir. campus ministry Manhattan Coll., 1973-76; asst. to provost Coll. of New Rochelle, N.Y., 1976-78, mem. edn. dept., 1976—, exec. asst. to pres., 1978-80, v.p. for planning, 1980-81, sr. v.p., 1981-97, pres., 1997—. Bd. trustees exec. com., com. on fin. and adminstrn. Commn. Ind. Colls. and Univs.; bd. trustees, chmn. acad. affairs com., chmn., student affairs com. Coll. St. Elizabeth; bd. trustees strategic planning com., mem. com. LaSalle Acad., Network of Sacred Heart Schs.; membership com. Network of Sacred Heart Schs.; bd. dirs. Neylan Commn. Colls. and Univs., Cardinal McCloskey Svcs., Women's Coll. Coalition. Mem.: Soc. Friendly Sons St. Patrick (N.Y.C.), Soc. Friendly Sons of St. Patrick (Westchester), Sovereign Mil. Order of Malta (med. com.), Knights of the Holy Sepulchre. Roman Catholic. Office: The College of New Rochelle 29 Castle Pl New Rochelle NY 10805-2338

SWEENY, WENDY PRESS, lawyer; b. Coral Gables, Fla., June 24, 1960; d. Samuel and Carol Sue Press; m. Kermit P. Sweeny Jr., Sept. 3, 1989; 1 child, Briana Mikel. AA in Bus., Broward C.C., 1981; BA in Bus., U. South Fla., 1983; JD, Nova U., 1987. Fla. 1987, Wyo. 1988, U.S. Dist. Ct. Wyo. 1988. Assoc. Messenger & Jurovich, Thermopolis, Wyo., 1987-91; county prosecuting atty. Waskakie County, Worland, 1991-95; pvt. practice, 1995—. Mem. Girl Scouts USA. Mem. Bus. and Profl. Women's Assn. (pres. 1998). Avocation: rock climbing. Office: 1116 Robertson Ave Worland WY 82401-2826 E-mail: wsweeny@trib.com.

SWEET, BRUCE, writer, educator; b. N.Y.C., Dec. 24, 1935; s. Charles Mason and Ella S.; m. Madeleine Riordan, Aug. 8, 1988; children: Antonia, Gabriela, Aaron, Jonathan, Donna, Alexandra, Melinda. BS, SUNY, Geneseo, 1960; MA, U. Iowa, 1962; PhD, NYU, 1981. Dir. theatre, instr. U. Iowa H.S., 1960-62; chmn. speech and drama prof. St. Mary's Coll., Notre Dame, Ind., 1962-64; dir. theatre, instr. Patrick Henry H.S., Mpls., 1964-66; dir. lab. theatre prof. SUNY, Cortland, 1966-69; dir. theatre, instr. James Sperry H.S., Henrietta, N.Y., 1969-71; artistic dir., tchr., supr. Arts Coun. of Tulsa, Okla., 1971-72; program head, dir., instr. Rolsyn (N.Y.) H.S., 1972-78; artistic dir. Strasberg Inst., N.Y.C., 1981; prof. artist in residence Towson (Md.) State U., 1981-82; prof., directing supr. St. Cloud U., 1982-84; writer, performing, dir., educator N.Y.C., 1985-96; writer-in-residence, prof. St. John Fisher Coll., Rochester, 1996-99. Writer-in-residence St. John Fisher Coll. Adirondack Lake Ctr. for the Arts, Pathfinder Village, United Cerebral Palsy Ctr. of Rochester, Writers and Books of Rochester, Aesthetic Edn. Inst. of Rochester, U. Rochester, SUNY Brockport, N.Y., Geva Theatre Rochester, Jewish Cmty. Ctr. of Rochester, Young Audiences of Rochester, Blue Mountain Ctr., N.Y.; adj. prof. English Saint John Fisher Coll., Pittsford, N.Y., 1996—. Contbr. articles to profl. jours. With U.S. Army, 1954-56. Mem. APR, Poets and Writers, Writers and Books, Meml. Art Gallery. Avocations: music, sports, animals, travel, cooking. Home: 34 Hannahs Terr Rochester NY 14612

SWEET, CHARLES WHEELER, retired executive recruiter; b. Chgo., June 11, 1943; s. Charles Wheeler and Alice Naomi (Grush) Sweet; m. Joy Ann Weidernmiller, Mar. 23, 1968; children: Charles III, Kimberly Ann, Rebecca Townsend. AB, Hamilton Coll., Clinton, N.Y., 1965; MBA, U. Chgo., 1968. Salesman Procter & Gamble, Chgo., 1965-67; with pers. Ford, Dearborn, Mich., 1968-69, R.R. Donnelley, Chgo., 1969-72; exec. recruiter A.T. Kearney Inc. Exec. Search, 1972—87, pres., 1987-99, chmn., 2000—01; ret., 2001. Bd. dirs. Gt. Bank Algonquin. Chmn. bd. dirs., exec. advisor No. Ill. U., 1979—88; bd. dirs. Rehab. Inst. Chgo., 1987—. Mem.: Assn. Exec. Search Cons., Barrington Hills Country Club (bd. dirs. 1993—96). Avocations: tennis, bridge. Home: 92 Meadow Hill Rd Barrington IL 60010-9601

SWEET, CYNTHIA KAY, business administrator; b. Highland, Kans., Feb. 21, 1949; d. Jack Wendull and Ruthanna (Dittemore) Hedrick; m. Roger Keith Alexander, 1968; children: Karen Joyce, Melinda Ruth Anne; m. Erich Christian Sweet, Oct. 31, 1990. Student, U. Kans., 1968, North Peralta Coll., 1973-74, U. Colo., 1976-79; BS in Bus. Tech., Empire State Coll., 1984. Computer operator Computer Ctr. U. Colo., Boulder, 1977-79; subscription coord. Inst. Arctic & Alpine Rsch., 1979; computer operator Computer Ctr. Rensselaer Poly. Inst., Troy, N.Y., 1979-80, dir. devel. info. svcs., 1982-85; rsch. analyst N.Y. State Mus., Albany, 1979-80, project mgr., 1980-82; product mgr. Info. Assocs., Rochester, N.Y., 1985-89, sr. program mgr., 1990-92; applications mgr. Claris Corp., Santa Clara, Calif., 1989-90; custom programming mgr. Datatel, Fairfax, Va., 1992-94; exec. dir. advancement solutions TRG, Phoenix, 1994-96; dir. profl. svcs. USA Group Info. Solutions, 1996-97; v.p. InfoSolutions.edu, 1997-99; higher edn./pub. sector practice mgr. The Hunter Group, San Francisco, 1999-2001; realtor RE/MAX Excalibur, Scottsdale, 2001—. Freelance fundraising cons., Albany and Rochester, 1984-89. Contbr. articles to profl. jours. Activity coord. Info. Assocs./United Way, Rochester, 1985—89, 1991—92; mem. festival staff Meml. Art Gallery, 1987—89; mem., vol. Desert Bot. Garden, Phoenix, 2001—; bd. dirs. Draper Dance Theatre, Rochester, 1988—92. Mem. Am. Mgmt. Assn., Nat. Assn. Realtors, Scottsdale Assn. Realtors. Avocations: camping, hiking, gardening, gourmet cooking, reading. Office: RE/MAX Excalibur 15160 N Hayden Rd Scottsdale AZ 85260 E-mail: c.sweet@remax.com.

SWEET, CYNTHIA RAE, small business owner; b. Oelwein, Iowa, Apr. 4, 1958; d. Garth Wayne and Shirley Jean (Bond) Huffman; m. Stanton Logan Sweet, May 30, 1981; children: Ashley Anne, Devin Logan, Tyler Bond. BA with honors, U. No. Iowa, 1979. Office mgr. Midway Devel. Corp., Cedar Falls, Iowa, 1979-84; adminstrv. asst. D.T.S., Inc., 1984—, Montessori Sys. Sch., Cedar Falls, 1995—2002; owner Sweet Press, 2002—. Author: Nuts and Bolts - How to Build a Bell Program, 1986, The Rottink Family of the Netherlands, 1986, Silver Celebration: A History of the Sturgis Falls Celebration, 2000; co-author: The Descendants of John Bond, 1992, David Elliott, Loyalist, and his Descendants, 1995, The Life and Family of Rev. Joshua Sweet, 2001; editor annual Sturgis Falls Celebration Program Book, 1996—. Adminstrv. asst. Sturgis Falls Celebration, Inc., Cedar Falls, 1987—; music dir. handbell program First United Meth. Ch., Cedar Falls, 1979-95. Home and Office: 1116 Washington St Cedar Falls IA 50613-3070

SWEET, HARVEY, theatrical set designer, lighting designer; b. Detroit, Oct. 27, 1943; s. Sam and Rose Sweet; m. Susan Perrett, Mar. 16, 1964 (div. Mar. 1975); children: Deborah Anne, Rebecca Lynn, Jason Aaron; m. Patricia Ravn, Sept. 9, 1978 (div. July 1987). BS, Ea. Mich. U., 1965; MS, U. Wis., 1967, PhD, 1974. Instr. U. N.D., Grand Forks, 1967-69; asst. prof. Boise (Idaho) State Coll., 1972-73; instr. U. Wis., Madison, 1973-74; prof. of theater arts U. No. Iowa, Cedar Falls, 1974-89; dir. lighting Landmark Entertainment Group, L.A. and Tokyo, 1989-91; cons. Advanced Tech., Tokyo, 1991; tech. writer Walt Disney Imagineering, Glendale, Calif., 1992; project mgr., sr. designer, sr. estimator, tech. writer Tru Roll, Inc., 1993-99; project mgr. estimator tech. sales LVH Entertainment Sys., Oxnard, 1999—2001, divsn. head, cons., 2001—. Owner, operator Sweet Studios Theatrical Equipment, Cedar Falls, 1981-89; dir. theater tech. and design U. No. Iowa, 1974-87. Author: Graphics for the Performing Arts, 1982, Handbook of Scenery, Properties and Lighting I and II, 1988, 2nd edit., 1995, The Complete Book of Drawing for the Theatre, 1995; scenic designer Summer Repertory Theatre, 1988, Timberlake Playhouse, 1988-89; lighting designer, scenic designer, tech. dir. various coll. theatrical prodns., 1964-89; themed lighting designer Sanrio Puroland, Tokyo, 1989, exec. dir. lighting, 1990. Mem. U.S. Inst. for Theatre Tech. (vice commr. 1979-81, commr. 1981-87, mem. graphic stds. bd. 1979-86, evaluation commn. 1983-88, mem. publs. com. 1986-89, bd. dirs. 1989). Avocations: travel, cooking. Office: LVH Entertainment Sys 300 Irving Dr Oxnard CA 93030 E-mail: cre8tivguy@aol.com.

SWEET, JAMES BROOKS, oral and maxillofacial surgeon; b. Darlington, Pa., Mar. 28, 1934; s. Lufay Anderson and Margaret Jean (Brooks) S.; m. N. Gayle Laird, Oct. 11, 1958; children: James Brooks II, Laird Anderson, Bradley Stephen. BA, Lafayette Coll., 1956; DDS, U. Pitts., 1964, DMD, 1974; MS in Dentistry, NYU, 1975. Aviation flight officer USNR, 1957; advanced through grades to dir. USPHS; rotating intern USPHS Hosp., Staten Island, N.Y., 1964-65, resident oral and maxillofacial surgery, 1970-73; chief dept. dentistry Fed. Correctional Inst. Hosp., Ashland, Ky., 1965-67, Terminal Island, Calif., 1967-70; chief oral and maxillofacial surgery Clin. Ctr. NIH, Bethesda, Md., 1973-80; chief dept. dentistry and oral and maxillofacial surgery USPHS Hosp., Nassau Bay, Tex., 1980-81; ret. USPHS, 1981; assoc. prof. dept. oral and maxillofacial surgery Health Sci. Ctr. U. Tex., Houston, 1981-84; prof., 1984—95; prof. emeritus, 2002—. Asst. clin. prof. med. br. U. Tex., Galveston, 1980-; assoc. attending physicianBen Taub Gen. Hosp., Houston, 1984-; cons. oral and maxillofacial surgery self study guides, Stoma Press, Seattle, 1983-; cons. VA Hosp., Houston, 1986-. Contbr. articles to profl. jours.; editorial reviewer: Annals of Internal Medicine, 1977-. Coach basketball Olney (Md.) Boys Club, 1975-80; mem. aim rev. Tex. area USCG, 1981-82. Lt. USNR, 1957-64. Fellow Am. Assn. Oral and Maxillofacial Surgeons; mem. Tex. Soc. Oral and Maxillofacial Surgeons, Houston Soc. Oral and Maxillofacial Surgeons, Am. Assn. Dental Schs., USPHS Profl. Assn., NIH Sailing Club, Omicron Kappa Upslion (pres. Mu Mu chpt. 1993-94). Presbyterian. Avocations: sailing, swimming, real estate, travelling. Home: 2013 Sweet St Navarre FL 32566-3042 Office: U Tex Health Sci Ctr 6516 John Freeman St Houston TX 77030-3402 E-mail: jbsweet16@aol.com.

SWEET, LOWELL ELWIN, lawyer, writer; b. Flint, Mich., Aug. 10, 1931; s. Leslie E. and Donna Mabel (Latta) S.; m. Mary Ellen Ebben, Aug. 29, 1953; children: Lawrence Edward, Diane Marie, Sara Anne. BA in Psychology, Wayne State U., 1953; LLB, U. Wis., 1955. Bar: Wis. 1955, U.S. Dist. Ct. (ea. dist.) Wis. 1955, U.S. Dist. Ct. (no. dist.) Ill. 1958. Ptnr. Morrissy, Morrisy, Sweet & Race and predecessor firms, Elkhorn, Wis., 1957—70; ptnr., pres. Law Office Lowell E. Sweet SC, 1970—2001. Instr. gen. practice sect. U. Wis. Law Sch., 1978, 79, 86, 90; lectr. real estate law Wis. Bar, Gateway Tech., Carthage Coll. Inst., 1974—. Author: Phased Condominiums for Matthew Bender, 1992; co-editor: Condominiuim Law Handbook, 1981, 93; mem. editl. bd. Workbook for Wis. Estate Planners, 1990. Mem. Walworth County Rep. com.; sect. Wis. Jt. Survey Commn. on Debt Mgmt. With CIC, U.S. Army, 1955-57. Named Outstanding Young Man of Am., Elkhorn Jaycees, 1966; recipient citation for svc. in drafting Wis. Condominium Law, Wis. Legislature, 1978. Fellow ABA, Wis. Law Found.; mem. Wis. Bar Assn. (gov. 1972-75, 91-93, 99-01), Walworth County Bar Assn., Am. Judicature Soc., The Best Lawyers in Am., Am. Coll. Real Estate Lawyers, Kiwanis, Lions, Moose, KC. Home: 3530 Westshire Cir Delavan WI 53115 Office: Law Office of Lowell E Sweet SC 114 N Church St Elkhorn WI 53121-1202

SWEET, MARC STEVEN, financial executive; b. Bklyn., Aug. 15, 1945; s. Edward I. and Bess G. (Freiman) S.; m. Naomi Charna Fishbein, Aug. 22, 1971; children: Erica Rebekah, Miriam Shoshana, Benjamin Lewis. BBA, Pace Coll., 1967; postgrad., Columbia U., 1967-68. CPA, N.Y. Sr. staff auditor Arthur Young & Co., 1969-71; asst. corp. contr. Liberty Fabrics N.Y., Inc., 1971-72; dir. acctg. Tetley, Inc., N.Y.C., 1972-75, dir. fin., 1975-81; corp. contr., asst. sec. Jetro Holdings, Inc. and subs., 1981-84; corp. contr. Elmhurst Milk & Cream Co., Inc. and subs. and assoc. corps., Queens, N.Y., 1984-86; CFO Modell Group, N.Y.C., 1986-99; corp. contr. Sci. Components, Inc. and assoc. entities, 1999—. Asst. scoutmaster Boy Scouts Am., 1963-66, mem. Flatbush dist. com., 1965-67; vice chmn. ann. fund com. Pace U., 1992-93, chmn., 1993-95, mem. alumni campaign adv. com., 1994-96, dir. Lubin Sch. Bus. Alumni Assn., 1995—, campaign adv. com. Lubin Sch., 1996-2000, sec. Alumni Fedn., 1999-2001, vice chmn. Alumni Fedn., 2001—. Trustees scholar Pace Coll., 1967, N.Y. Texaco Co. scholar. Mem. AICPA, Am. Philatelic Soc., N.Y. State Soc. CPAs, Scottish Deerhound Club Am. Home: 1282 E 29th St Brooklyn NY 11210-4631

SWEET, PHILIP W. K., JR. former banker; b. Mt. Vernon, N.Y., Dec. 31, 1927; s. Philip W.K. and Katherine (Buhl) S.; m. Nancy Frederick, July 23, 1950; children— Sandra H., Philip W.K. III, David A.F. AB, Harvard U., 1950; MBA, U. Chgo., 1957. Pres., dir. The No. Trust Co., Chgo., 1975-81; chmn., chief exec. officer No. Trust Corp., 1981-84. Alderman City of Lake Forest, Ill., 1972-74; vis. com. U. Chgo. Grad. Sch. Bus.; trustee Chgo. Zool. Soc., past chmn. 1988-93; life trustee Rush-Presbyn.-St. Luke's Med. Ctr.; vestryman Episc. Ch., 1971-74, 86-89. Mem. Soc. Colonial Wars (gov. Ill. chpt. 1978-80), Chgo. Sunday Evening Club (trustee, chmn. 1997-2000), Econ. Club, Comml. Club, Chgo. Club, Commonwealth Club (past pres.), Old Elm Club (Highwood, Ill.), Onwentsia Club (gov.), Shoreacres Club (past pres. Lake Bluff).

SWEET, PORTIA ANN, retired human resources specialist; b. Charleston, W.Va., Jan. 14, 1939; BA, U. Houston, 1973. Sr. profl. in human resources. Adminstrv. mgr. Great Am. Ins. Co., Houston, Cin., Denver, 1973-81; cons., owner Sweet Encounters, Greeley, Colo., 1982-89; risk mgmt. splst. Hi/LO Auto Supply, Houston, 1991-94; human resources mgr. Chevron Products/MKTG, 1994-2000; ret., 2000. Vol. dir. Greeley Conv. Bur., 1986; bd. dirs. Women's Resource Ctr., Durango, Colo., 1988-89; vol. Houston Area Women's Ctr., 1990-91. Recipient Cert. Appreciation A Woman's Place, 1981. Mem. NAFE, NOW, Human Resources Mgmt. Assn. (bd. sec. 1995-96), Soc. Human Resources Mgmt., Houston Human Resources Mgmt. Assn., Risk and Ins. Mgmt. Soc., Ind. Ins. Agents (Big I). Episcopalian. Avocations: needlework, flower gardening, classical music. Home: 5800 Lumberdale Rd Apt 80 Houston TX 77092-1512 Office: Chevron Products Co 5959 Corporate Dr Houston TX 77036-2302

SWEET, ROBERT BURDETTE, adult education educator; b. Chgo., Feb. 21, 1930; s. Arthur B. and Helen (Rippe) Sweet. BA, Cornell Coll., 1951; MA, Middlebury Coll., 1960; PhD, U. Denver, 1970. Tchr. New Trier H.S., Winnetka, Ill., 1952—60; instr. Wright Jr. Coll., Chgo., 1961—63, Kendall Coll., Evanston, 1964—68, San Jose State U., Calif., 1970—93. Avocation: Avocations: painting, sculpting, composing. Home: 1761 Edgewood Rd Redwood City CA 94062-3219

SWEET, ROBERT WORKMAN, federal judge; b. Yonkers, N.Y., Oct. 15, 1922; s. James Allen and Delia (Workman) S.; m. Adele Hall, May 12, 1973; children by previous marriage— Robert, Deborah, Ames, Eliza. BA, Yale U., 1944, LL.B., 1948. Bar: N.Y. 1949. Asso. firm Simpson, Thacher & Bartlett, 1948-53; asst. U.S. atty. So. Dist. N.Y., 1953-55; asso. firm Casey, Lane & Mittendorf, 1955-65, partner, 1957-65; counsel Interdepartmental Task Force on Youth and Juvenile Delinquency, 1958-78; dep. mayor City of N.Y., 1966-69; partner firm Skadden, Arps, Slate, Meagher & Flom, N.Y.C., 1970-77; mem. hearing office N.Y.C. Transit Authority, 1975-77; U.S. dist. judge So. Dist. N.Y., N.Y.C., 1978—. Participant USIA Rule of Law Program in Albania, 1991; observer Albanian elections, 1992. Pres. Community Service Soc., 1961-78; trustee Sch. Mgmt. Urban Policy, 1970— , Taft Sch.; vestryman St. Georges Epis. Ch., 1958-63. Served to lt. (j.g.) USNR, 1943-46. Recipient Alumni citation of merit Taft Sch., 1985, various other awards, citations for service as dept mayor N.Y.C. Mem. ABA, Assn. of Bar of City of N.Y., N.Y. Law Inst., N.Y. County Lawyers Assn., State Bar Assn., Am. Legion (comdr. Willard Straight Post) Clubs: Quaker Hill Country, Century Assn., Merchants, Indian Harbor Yacht, Mid City Rep.

SWEET, WILLIAM, educator, author, administrator; b. Edmonton, Alberta, Can., Apr. 22, 1955; s. William Donald and Joyce Leila (Taylor) S. DEA, U. Sorbonne, Paris, 1987; PhD, U. Ottawa, Can., 1994; DPh, St. Paul U., Can., 1996. Lectr. U. Saskatchewan, Saskatoon, Can., 1980-83, Coll. de l'Outaouais, Hull, Que., Can., 1983-85, U. Ottawa, 1983-85, 87-88, Carleton U., Ottawa, 1989-90; asst. prof. to prof. St. Francis Xavier U., Antigonish, Nova Scotia, 1990—. Sec.-gen. World Union of Cath. Philos. Socs., Washington, 1998—. Author: (book) Idealism and Rights, 1997, Antifoundationalism, Faith, and Community, 2001; editor: Collected Works of Bernard Bosanquet, 1999, Idealism, Metaphysics, and Community, 2001, The Bases of Ethics, 2000, God and Argument, 1999. Chair of senate. St. Francis Xavier U., Antigonish, 1995-96, chair of faculty of arts, 1998-2000, chair univ. faculty, 2001-02; mem. St. Martha's Regional Hosp. Mission Assurance Adv. Coun., 1999—; mem. ethics com. Ea. Regional Health Bd., Nova Scotia, 1999-2000. Rsch. grantee Social Scis. and Humanities Rsch. Coun. of Can., 2000—; Nimishakkavi K. Subbaiah Naidu Endowment lectr. U. Madras, India, 1999, Royal Inst. of Philosophy lectr. U. Wales, Cardiff, 1999; Dharma Endowment lectr., Bangalore, India, 2001. Mem. Can. Jacques Maritain Assn. (pres. 1999—), Can. Soc. for Study of Religion (mem. exec. and mem. sec. 1999-2001), Can. Philos. Assn. (bd. dirs. 1997-99), Can. Soc. Christian Philosophers (v.p. 1996-99, pres. 2000-02), Istituto Internazionale Jacques Maritain (v.p. 2002--). Avocations: travel, rock climbing, literature. Office: St Francis Xavier Univ Antigonish PO Box 5000 Nova Scotia NS Canada B2G 2W5 E-mail: wsweet@stfx.ca.

SWEETEN, EDWARD DREW, administrator; b. Tucson, Feb. 26, 1950; s. Edward Drew and Lilly (Denham) S.; m. Sharon Marie Kamp, May 27, 1972; children: Michael, Jennifer. BS in Zoology, U. Nev., 1972, AS in Radiology Tech., 1973, AA, 1987; MD, Spartan Health Scis. U., 1985. RN, Nev. Radiology tech. Sunrise Hosp., Las Vegas; adminstr., owner Patable X-Ray Nev.; case mgr. Sierra Health Svc.; sr. assoc. Med./Legal Cons. Mem. Am. Soc. Radiology Tech., Am. Radiology Nurses Assn., Am. Coll. Health Care Adminstrs. Republican. Baptist. Avocations: flying, water sports. Home: 6521 Elton Ave Las Vegas NV 89107-2413

SWEETING, CHARLES HARVARD, columnist, film director; b. Derby, Eng. s. Treleaven William and Josephine Harvard (Taylor) S. MA, Dublin U., Ireland, 1959. Writer Associated British/Warner Bros., Elstree, Hertfordshire, Eng., 1954-55; film coord. theatre arts dept. Pa. State U., 1969-70; columnist Union Jack monthly, San Diego, 1984—; founder Brit. & Commonwealth Inst. N.Y., N.Y.C., 1979—. Author: A Film Course Manual, 1971; asst. film dir. Reach for the Sky, Anastasia, St. Joan, 6 TV series including Robin Hood, The Invisible Man; 1st asst. dir. Freedom's Finest Hour (narrated by Ronald Reagan). Served with RAF. Recipient George Washington Honor Gold medal Freedoms Found., 1965, Golden Eagle award Coun. on Internat. Nontheatrical Events, 1965. Mem. The Broadcasting, Entertainment, Cinematograph and Theatre Union (London), Australian Soc. N.Y., Can. Soc. N.Y. (life), St. David's Soc. N.Y. (life), St. George's Soc. N.Y. (assoc. life), Dublin U. Grad. Assn. (life), Dublin U. Players (hon.), Dublin U. Philos. Soc. (hon.), Episcopal Actors' Guild (N.Y.), Savage Club (life, London), Trinity Coll. Dublin Dining Club London (life), London Press Club, Overseas Press Club Am., Britannia Lodge (N.Y.C.), Victory Club (London), Brit. War Vets. Am., Oxford Alumni. Office: Brit & Commonwealth Inst St George's Soc NY 175 9th Ave New York NY 10011-4924

SWEETLAND, LORAINE FERN, librarian, educator; b. Morristown Corners, Vt., Aug. 13, 1933; d. William Eric and Sylbil Bedina (Bailey) Bloomfield; m. Ronald David Sweetland, July 1, 1950; children: Kathy L. (dec.), Dale J. Bettis. BS in Elem. Edn., Columbia Union Coll., 1968; MS in LS, Syracuse U., 1973. Tchr. 1st and 2d grade Beltsville (Md.) Seventh-day Adventist Sch., 1960-67; asst. libr., cataloger Vt. Tech. Coll., Randolph Ctr., 1968-69; middle sch. libr. Barre (Vt.) City Schs., 1970-74; tchg. prin. Cen. Vt. Seventh-day Adventist Sch., Barre, 1974-76, Brooklawn Seventh-day Adventist Sch., Bridgeport, Conn., 1976-81; med. libr. Washington Adventist Hosp., Takoma Park, Md., 1981-85; dir. libr. svcs. Seventh-day Adventists World Hdqs., Silver Spring, 1985-95. Med. libr. cons., Balt., 1983-95; pres. Oasis, 1993-94; tchr. Home Study Internat., Silver Spring, Md., 1995-98, IPS-Info. Problem Solvers, Crossville, Tenn., 1998—. Book reviewer Libr. Jour., 1990-98. Trustee Randolph (Vt.) Pub. Library, 1970-71; sec. Nat. Area Hosp. Council, Washington, 1985; treas. Plateau Food Buying Club, 1999—. Mem. Assn. Seventh-day Adventist Librs., Laurel Rotary Club (bull. editor 1990-94). Republican. Avocations: gardening, computers, Internet. E-mail: lauriefern@charter.net.

SWEETSER, GENE GILLMAN, quality assurance professional, state legislator; b. Burlington, Vt., Apr. 24, 1948; s. Archelaus William and Stella Ruth (Brink) S.; m. Elizabeth Ann Hannett, Apr., 1967 (div. May 1972); 1 child, Analei; m. Susan Williams, Aug. 27, 1978 (div. Feb. 1995); 1 child, Virginia Lucretia. BA Polit. Sci. and Environ. Sci., Johnson State Coll., Vt., 1978; MS in Adminstrn., St. Michael's Coll., Vt., 1993. Maintenance machinist Avdel Internat., Inc., Parsippany, N.J., 1982-84; machine shop supr. Mitec Systems, Inc., Williston, Vt., 1984-84; maintenance supr. Fonda, Inc., Albans, 1985-88; asst. quality control mgr. Chatham Precision, Hinesburg, 1988-91; state representative Vt. State Ho. of Reps., 1990—; prodn. control IBM, Essex, Vt., 1992—. Mem. Bd. Civil Authority, Essex, Vt., 1988—, Justice of the Peace, 1988—; mem. com. ways and means Vt. State Ho. of Reps., 1991—. Founder, bd. dirs. paper recycling program Worcester Vol. Fire Dept., 1978-82; founder, bd. dirs. Worcester Film Soc., 1978-82, Worcester Views Newsletter, 1978-82; vice chmn. Ctrl. Ct. Regional Planning Commn., 1980-82; vol. The Holiday Project, 1987-89; coach Essex Youth Soccer, 1988, 89; player agt. for minor league Essex Little League Assn., 1990; v.p. Survivors of Crime, Inc. With USMC, 1969-72, Vt. Army nat. Guard, 1978—. Address: 28 Foster Rd Essex Junction VT 05452-3316

SWEETSER, MARIE-ODILE GAUNY, retired foreign language educator; b. Verdun, Meuse, France, Dec. 28, 1925; came to U.S., 1949; d. Eugene Auguste and Madeleine (Schwab) Gauny; m. Franklin Pratt, Dec. 17, 1955; 1 child, Caroline Gauny Sweetser. Grad., U. Nancy, France, 1945; MA, Bryn Mawr Coll., 1950; PhD, U. Pa., 1956. Instr. Mills Coll., Oakland, Calif., 1957-60; from asst. prof. to assoc. prof. French CUNY, 1960-69; from assoc. prof. to prof. French U. Ill., Chgo., 1969-97, ret., 1997. Mem. adv. bd. Papers on French Seventeenth Century Lit., Paris, Seattle, Tübingen, Germany. Author: Les Conceptions dramatiques de Corneille d'après ses écrits théoriques, 1962, La Dramaturgie de Corneille, 1977, La Fontaine, 1987; editor, contbr. articles to profl. jours. Marcelle Parde scholar, 1949-50, Newberry Libr. Found. fellow, 1980. Mem. Mouvement Corneille (bd. dirs. 1980—), Soc. des Amis de la Fontaine (v.p. 1996—), Ctr. Internat. Rencontres sur le 17th Siecle (bd. dirs. 1991—). Avocations: music, theater. Home: 311 Hirst Ct Lake Bluff IL 60044-2754

SWEEZY, JOHN WILLIAM, political party official; b. Indpls., Nov. 14, 1932; s. William Charles and Zuma Frances (McNew) S.; BS in Mech. Engring., Purdue U., 1956; MBA, Ind. U., 1958; student Butler U., 1953-54, U. Ga., 1954-55, Ind. Cen. Coll., 1959; m. Carole Suzanne Harman, July 14, 1956; children: John William, Bradley E. Design, test engr. Allison div. GM, Indpls., 1953-57; power sales engr. Indpls. Power & Light Co., 1958-69; dir. pub. works City of Indpls., 1970-72; chmn. Marion County Rep. Cen. Com., 1972—; bd. dirs. Lorco Engring., Indpls., Indpls. Industrial Products, Acme Screw & Mfg., Inc., Telnet, Inc., Landmarks Ltd., Innovative Investment Co. Bd. dirs. Indpls. Humane Soc.; chmn. 11th Dist. Rep. Com., 1970, 73—; chmn. Nat. Assn. Urban Rep. County Chmn.; alt. del. Rep. Nat. Conv., 1968, del., 1972, 76, 80, 84, 88, 92, 96, del., mem. credentials com., 1984, 88; mem. credentials com., 1980, spkr. presenter, 1996; mem. Rep. Nat. Com., 1984—, exec. com., 1984— ; mem. Warren Schs. Citizens Screening Com., 1958-72; bd. dirs. Warren Devel. Com. With AUS, 1953-55. Mem. AMA, Mensa, Sigma Iota Epsilon. Home: 2089 S German Church Rd Indianapolis IN 46239-9620 Office: 12 N Delaware St Indianapolis IN 46204-3205

SWEIG, MICHAEL TERRY, building services company executive, consultant; b. N.Y.C., May 31, 1946; s. Morton and Charlotte (Phillips) S. BS, NYU, 1968, MBA, 1969. V.p. sales Nat. Cleaning Group, N.Y.C., 1969-77, sr. v.p. sales, 1977-81, exec. v.p., 1981-85, pres., CEO, 1985-90; chmn., CEO, Lakeside Bldg. Co., Chgo., 1991—. Bd. dirs., owner Amonk (N.Y.) Tennis Club, 1986—. Contbr. articles to profl. jours. Named Man of Yr., AFL-CIO, N.Y., 1986. Mem. Chgo. Soc. Clubs, Sports Club L.A. Republican. Avocations: skiing, flying, tennis, racquetball, golf. also: 2112 Century Park Ln Los Angeles CA 90067-3300

SWEITZER, MICHAEL COOK, healthcare product executive; b. Cin., July 29, 1961; s. Charles Samuel and Louise (Cook) S. BS in Biomedical Engring., Rensselaer Poly. Inst., 1983, M in Engring., 1985. Product specialist Siemens Med. Sys., Iselin, N.J., 1985-89, tech. mgr, 1989-90, nat. sales mgr., 1993-94, product mgr., 1994-96, cons., 1996-98, product specialist San Francisco, 1990-92; product mgr. Toshiba Am. Med. Sys., S. San Francisco, 1992-93. Contbr. chpt. to MRI Guide for Technologists, 1994. Mem. Am. Healthcare Radiology Adminstrs., Inst. for Indsl. Engrs. Office: Varian Med Sys Inc MS E 263 3100 Hansen Way Palo Alto CA 94304-1129

SWELL, LILA, education educator; b. N.Y.C., Sept. 7, 1936; d. Isidore and Bessie (Abramson) S. BA in Psychology, NYU, 1956; MSW, U. Mich., 1958; EdD, Columbia U., 1964. Lectr. U. Mich. Sch. of Social Work, Ann Arbor, 1964-65; asst. prof. U. Chgo. Sch. Social Svcs. Adminstrn., 1965-68; vis. asst. prof. U. Ill., Chgo., 1969-70; assoc. prof. Queens Coll. CUNY, 1970—. Author: Success You Can Make It Happen, 1977, Self Esteem in the Classroom, Techniques for Teachers, 1991, Educating for Success: Theory Manual, Workbook and Leaders Guide, 1990, My Journal of Success (K-12) Teacher's Guide, 1992, Lets Work it Out: A Problem Solving Journal (5-12) Teacher's Guide, 1994; contbr. monographs, jour. articles, creative publs., audio and video tapes, films and revs.; TV appearances U.S., Australia; radio appearances U.S., Australia, New Zealand. Mem. Kappa Delta Pi, Pi Lambda Theta. Home: 130 E 67th St New York NY 10021-6136 Office: CUNY Queens Coll Dept Elem Early Child Edn 65-30 Kissena Blvd Flushing NY 11367-1575 E-mail: LilaSwell@aol.com.

SWENKA, ARTHUR JOHN, retired food products executive; b. Lone Tree, Iowa, Oct. 21, 1937; s. Samuel Joseph and Verdis Mary (Weed) S.; m. Elizabeth Simms, July 1956 (div. 1976); children: Lee Arthur, Timothy John; m. Dixie Jo Meade, Feb. 1982. Gen. equivalency diploma, U.S. Army, 1957. Truck driver U.S. Mail, Oelwein, Iowa, 1958-59, Stiles Supermarket, Oelwein, 1959-60; salesman Hoxie Inst. Wholesale Co., Waterloo, Iowa, 1960-68, slaes mgr., 1968-69, br. mgr., 1969-70, Waterloo and Mason City, 1970-72, Nobel Inc., Albuquerque, 1972-81; pres. Nobel/Sysco Food Svcs. Co., 1981-84, Denver, 1985-95; sr. v.p. ops. Sysco Corp., Houston, 1995—2000. Mem. Dirs. Coun., Houston, 1985—2000. Treas., bd. dirs. Albuquerque Conv. and Visitors Bur., 1975-80; v.p., bd. dirs. Albuquerque Internat. Balloon Festival, 1975-82; bd. dirs. New Day Home for Runaway Children, Albuquerque, 1980-89, Found. St. Joseph's Hosp.; pres. Kodak Internat. Balloon Fiesta, Albuquerque, 2001—, Manzano Morning Assn., Inc., 2001—. Republican. Roman Catholic. Avocation: hot air ballooning. Home: 30 Twin Peaks Dr Estancia NM 87016-9732

SWENSEN, CLIFFORD HENRIK, JR. psychologist, educator; b. Welch, W.Va., Nov. 25, 1926; s. Clifford Henrik and Cora Edith (Clovis) S.; m. Doris Ann Gaines, June 6, 1948; children— Betsy, Susan, Lisa, Timothy, Barbara BS, U. Pitts., 1949, MS, 1950, PhD, 1952. Diplomate Am. Bd. Profl. Psychology. Instr. U. Pitts., 1951-52; clin. psychologist VA, 1952-54; from asst. prof. to assoc. prof. U. Tenn., Knoxville, 1954-62; assoc. prof. psychology Purdue U., West Lafayette, Ind., 1962-65, prof., 1965—, dir. clin. tng., 1975-85; vice chair U. Senate, 1994-95. Vis. prof. U. Fla., 1968-69, U. Bergen, Norway, 1976-77, 83-84; cons. VA, 1981 White House Conf. on Aging, others; Am. Psychol. Assn.-NSF Disting. Sci. lectr., 1968-69; Fulbright-Hays lectr., Norway, 1976-77 Author: An Approach to Case Conceptualization, 1968; Introduction to Interpersonal Relations, 1973; contbr. chpts. to books, articles to profl. jours. Mem. Ind. Gov.'s Task Force Alzheimer's Disease and Related Senile Dementia, 1998—. Served with USN, 1944-46 Recipient Gordon A. Barrows Meml. award for disting. contributions to psychology, 1990; named to Hall of Fame, Brentwood Pa. H.S., 2001. Fellow APA (pres divsn. cons. psychology 1976-77, Presdl. citation 1999, Cert. achievement 2000), Am. Psychol. Soc., Soc. Personality Assessment, Am. Assn. Applied and Preventive Psychology, Acad. of Clin. Psychology; mem. Midwestern Psychol. Assn., Southeastern Psychol. Assn., Ind. Psychol. Assn., Gerontol. Soc., Sigma Xi, Psi Chi. Republican. Mem. Ch. of Christ Home: 611 Hillcrest Rd West Lafayette IN 47906-2349 Office: Purdue U Dept Psychol Scis West Lafayette IN 47907 E-mail: cswensen@psych.purdue.edu.

SWENSEN, JOHN SCOTT, investment manager; b. Somerville, N.J., June 16, 1952; s. John Henry and Jacqueline Ann (Tingaud) S.; m. Linda Kathryn Daley Conaty, Aug. 11, 1973 (div. June 1984); children: Rebecca Lynn, Caroline Marie, Jeffery Scott; m. Cynthia Sharrah, May 14, 1988. B of Engring. with high honors, Stevens Inst. Tech., 1974; MBA, NYU, 1979. V.p. Chase Manhattan Bank, N.Y.C., 1973-84; mng. dir. Banque Paribas, 1984-93; lead investment mgr., mng. dir. Scudder Kemper Investments, 1993—. Bd. dirs. Aguaytia Energy, Lima, Peru, ELCOSA, Puerto Cortes, Honduras, Jamaica Energy Ptnrs., Kingston, Termotasajero, Bogata, Colombia; treas. bd. dirs. 200 W. 86th Corp. Mem. The Univ. Club, Lake Naomi (Pa.) Club (bd. govs. 1997, trustee, CFO 2000), Tau Beta Pi. Republican. Lutheran. Avocations: squash, tennis, skiing, hunting, golf. Home: 200 W 86th St Apt 18G New York NY 10024-3379 Office: 345 Park Ave New York NY 10154-0004

SWENSEN, MARY JEAN HAMILTON, graphic artist; b. Laurens, S.C., June 25, 1910; d. Elvin A. and Della (Brown) Hamilton; m. Oliver Severn Swensen, Mar. 3, 1943 (dec.). BS, Columbia U., 1956, MA, 1960; Cert. Notable, U. Madrid, Spain; postgrad., Ariz. State U., 1974-80. Mem. 1st USSA sr. internat. cross-country skiing team. One person shows at Colo. Fed. Savs. and Loan Assn., Denver, 1978, Panoras Gallery, N.Y.C., 1963; exhibited in group shows at Soc. Western Artist, M.H. de Young Mus., San Francisco, 1964, Nat. Art Roundup, Las Vegas, 1965, Fine Arts Bldg., Colo. State Fair, Pueblo, 1965, Duncan Gallery, Paris, 1974, Colo. Fed. Savs. & Loan Assn., Denver, 1978; graphics arts in pub. collections at Met. Mus. Art, N.Y.C., Nat. Graphic Arts Collection, Smithsonian Inst., Laurens (S.C.) Pub. Libr., N.Y.C. Pub. Libr. Assoc. Libr. of Congress, Archael. Inst. Am., Smithsonian Instn., Johns Hopkins. Recipient Duncan Gallery Prix de Paris, 1974, Notable award M.H. de Young Mus., 1964, YWCA of U.S.A. Gold Medal as most admired athlete of yr., 1977, USSA Nat. Vets. X-Country Racing Team Gold, Silver and Bronze medals for downhill, giant slalom, slalom, and cross-country sr. citizen and vet. races, 1963-79. Mem. Internat. Platform Assn., Am. Mensa, Columbia Club N.Y., Delta Phi Delta.

SWENSEN, SWEN RUSSEL, surgeon; b. Provo, Utah; s. Russel Brown and Buelah (Strickler) S.; m. Gretel Ann Foxley, Sept. 4, 1970; children: James, Gretel, Kirsten, Cathrine, Matthew. BA, Brigham Young U., 1963; MS, George Washington U., 1968, MD, 1969. Intern Latter Day Saints Hosp., Salt Lake City, 1969-70, staff mem., 1974-99, co-dir. surg. edn. students & residents, 1976-93; surg. resident U. Utah, 1970-74, clin. instr. surgery, 1974-78, asst. clin. prof. surgery, 1978-84, clin. prof., 1984-2001. Bishop Ch. Jesus Christ Latter Day Saints, Salt Lake City, 1982—87, mission pres. Vienna, 1993—96; venue med. officer Winter Olympis, Salt Lake City, 2002. Fellow ACS, South West Surg. Congress; mem. Salt Lake Surg., Soc. Surgery Alimentry Tract. Avocations: mountain climbing, basketball, travel, hiking, swimming. Home: 2954 Benchmark Dr Salt Lake City UT 84109-1465 Office: Bryner Clinic 745 E 300 S Salt Lake City UT 84102-2299

SWENSON, ANN-MARIE, education educator; b. Ogden, Iowa, Dec. 30, 1921; d. Algot Valentine and Ruth Polly (Jacobson) Christofferson; m. John Hilbert Swenson, July 4, 1942; children: John H. Jr., Frederick Lawrence, Sonja Christine. Student, Bethany Coll., Lindsborg, Kans., 1939-40, Augustina Coll., Rock Island, Ill., 1942; BA in Elem. Edn., U. Denver, 1960, MA in Spl. Edn., 1975; postgrad., U. Lund, Sweden, 1972. Tchr. Sapinero Rural Sch., Gunnison County, Colo., 1949-50, Brighton-Whittier Sch., 1954-55, Westlake Sch. Adams Dist., Thornton, Colo., 1961, Pocatello Idaho Elem., 1961-62, Boulder (Colo.) Valley Schs., 1962-74; resource tchr. Walden (Colo.) Jr. Sr. H.S., 1974-83; tchr. Tempe (Ariz.) Elem. Sch., 1983-86, Tempe (Ariz.) Union H.S. Dist., 1986-90. Pres. North Parks Schs. Edn. Assn., 1982-83; parent and child advocacy, Ariz. Edn. Dept., Phoenix, 1987-89. Mem. State Commn. Profl. Rights and Responsibilities, Boulder, Colo., 1966-68. Recipient Tuition scholarship Climax Molibdenum Co., Leadville County, Colo., 1975. Mem. NEA, Colo. Edn. Assn., Boulder Valley Edn. Assn., Ariz. Edn. Assn. Democrat. Avocations: reading, hiking, walking, sewing, volunteering. Home: 1055 Adams Cir Apt 502 Boulder CO 80303-1848

SWENSON, CHRISTINE ERICA, microbiologist; b. N.Y., Apr. 27, 1953; d. Oscar Adolf and Marjorie Claire Swenson; m. James Yasinski, Sept. 6, 1980; children: Jeffrey, Emma. BA, Middlebury Coll., 1975; PhD, Cornell U., 1980. Postdoctoral fellow Rockefeller U., N.Y., 1980-82, U. Calif., San Francisco, 1982-84; scientist The Liposome Co., Inc., Princeton, N.J., 1984-88, dir. preclin. devel., 1988—. Office: Elan Pharms Inc One Research Way Princeton NJ 08540

SWENSON, CONSTANCE N. artist; b. Mpls., Aug. 7, 1920; d. Marion Edward and Myrtle Evelyn Norman; widowed June, 1994; children: Norman, David Erik, Stephen Scott. Student, Mpls. Sch. Art, Gustavus Adolphus Coll. Home: 1722 Lakeview Dr SW Rochester MN 55902-4228

SWENSON, DIANE KAY, lawyer; b. Sioux Falls, S.D., June 16, 1952; d. Clarence Donald and Mildred Ann (Meyer) S. BA magna cum laude, Augustana Coll., 1974; JD, Hamline U., 1981. Bar: Minn. 1981. Tchr. Malvern (Iowa) Pub. Schs., 1974-76, Rosemount Pub. Schs., Apple Valley, Minn., 1976-78; legis. asst. to Senator Larry Pressler, U.S. Senate, Washington, 1981-86; exec. v.p. Am. Tort Reform Assn., 1986-99, Nat. Assn. Fed. Credit Unions, Washington, 1999—. V.p. Emmanual Luth. Ch., Bethesda, Md., 1997. Mem. ABA. Republican. Lutheran. Avocation: skiing. Home: 6140 Stonehenge Place Rockville MD 20852-5807 Office: Nat Assn Fed Credit Unions 3138 10th St N Arlington VA 22201-2149 E-mail: dswenson@nafcunet.org., dks@erols.com.

SWENSON, GEORGE WARNER, JR. electronics engineer, radio astronomer, educator; b. Mpls., Sept. 22, 1922; s. George Warner and Vernie (Larson) S.; m. Virginia Laura Savard, June 26, 1943 (div. 1970); children: George Warner III, Vernie Laura, Julie Loretta, Donna Joan; m. Joy Janice Locke, July 2, 1971. BS, Mich. Coll. Mining and Tech., 1944, E.E., 1950; MS, MIT, 1948; PhD, U. Wis., 1951. Asso. prof. elec. engring. Washington U., St. Louis, 1952-53; prof. U. Alaska, 1953-54; asso. prof. Mich. State U., 1954-56; faculty U. Ill., Urbana, 1956—, prof. elec. engring. and astronomy, 1958-88, prof. emeritus, 1988—, acting head dept. astronomy, 1970-72, head dept. elec. and computer engring., 1979-85. Dir. Vermilion River Obs., 1968-81; vis. scientist Nat. Radio Astronomy Obs., 1964-68; cons. to govt. agys. and other sci. bodies; sr. rsch. assoc. U.S. Army Constrn. Engring. Rsch. Lab., 1988--; adj. prof. elec. engring. Mich. Technol. U., 1996—. Author: Principles of Modern Acoustics, 1953, An Amateur Radio Telescope, 1980; co-author: Interferometry and Synthesis in Radio Astronomy, 1986, 2d edit., 2001; contbr. articles to profl. jours. 1st lt. signal corps U.S. Army, WWII. Recipient citation for disting. service to engring. U. Wis., 1984; Guggenheim fellow, 1984-85 Fellow IEEE, AAAS; mem. NAE, Am. Astron. Soc., Internat. Sci. Radio Union (U.S. nat. com. 1965-67, 80-82), Internat. Astron. Union, Inst. Noise Control Engring. (cert.), Sigma Xi, Eta Kappa Nu, Tau Beta Pi, Phi Kappa Phi. Achievements include chairing conceptual design group which produced the concept/proposal for the Very Large Array of National Radio Astronomy Observatory; designed and built two large innovative radio telescopes for the University of Illinois. Home: 1107 Kenwood Rd Champaign IL 61821-4718 Office: U Ill 328 CSL 1308 W Main St Urbana IL 61801-2307

SWENSON, KATHLEEN SUSAN, music and art educator; b. Reno, Oct. 23, 1938; d. Harold Ruthaford McNeil and Hollyce Margaret (Scruggs) McNeil Biggs; m. James Michael Phalan, 1956 (div. 1974); children: David Michael, Jeanine Louise Phalan Lawrence, Gregory Sean; m. Gerald Allen Swensen, Nov. 1976 (div. 1987); stepchildren: Craig Allen, Sarah Ann, Eric Sander. Student, U. Nev., Reno, 1956-58, Foothill Coll., 1966-68; AA, West Valley Coll.; BA, U. Calif., Santa Cruz, 1983. Concert pianist, Nev.,Calif, 1950-64; pvt. piano instr. various locations, 1963—; pvt. art instr., 1970—; pvt. astrology instr., 1973—; founder, pres. AAM Triple Arts, Aptos, Calif., 1974—; founder, owner Aptos (Calif.) Acad. Music, 1991—. Producer, instr. art instrn. videos, music instrn. films, books. Mem. Soc Western Artists, Calif. Piano Tchrs. Assn., Los Gatos Art Assn. (pres. 1985-86), Saratoga Contemporary Artists (v.p. 1984-85), Nat. League Am. Pen Women (honorarian 1985), Soroptomists, Phi Beta Kappa. Republican. Episcopalian. Home and Office: Aptos Acad Music 3000 Wisteria Way Aptos CA 95003-3318 E-mail: Aamtriplearts@aol.com., aptsacademymusic@aol.com.

SWENSON, L. ANNE, publisher; b. Blue Island, Ill., Mar. 27, 1936; d. Eugene Martin and Golda Merle (Standard) S.; m. Douglas Hieber, Feb. 15, 1957 (div. May 1959); m. Warren Tunis Wognum, Nov. 25, 1965 (div. May 1997); children: Nicholas Evan Wognum, Sandra Anne Wognum. Student, Cornell Coll., Mt. Vernon, Iowa, 1954-56, U. Minn., 1964, Roosevelt U., 1964-65. Book buyer Maeyama's, Park Forest, Ill., 1960-63; pub./owner Milestones, Inc., Ely, Minn., 1977—. Chmn. Donald G. Gardner Humanities Trust, Ely, 1995-00, design rev. com., City of Ely, 1993-94; chmn. Ely Greenstone Pub. Arts, 1998—. Editor: (book) Ely, Since 1888, 1988; pub. (weekly newspaper) The Ely Echo, 1977—; columnist/writer, 1976—. Com. chmn. Ely C. of C., 1994-96; bd. dirs. No. Lakes Arts Assn., Ely, 1995-2000, Voyageur Winter Festival, Ely/Winton Bicentennial Com., Ely, 1975-76; troop leader Girl Scouts, Rome, 1956-57. Mem. St. Louis Co. Hist. Soc., Ely/Winton Hist. Soc. Home: 2647 Van Vac Rd Ely MN 55731-8426 Office: Milestones Inc/Ely Echo 2 E Sheridan St Ely MN 55731-1257 E-mail: thepub@elyecho.com.

SWENSON, MARK GREGORY, architect; b. Mpls., Nov. 29, 1949; s. Stanley S. and Linnea Marie (Anderson) S.; m. Marcy Gayle Stevenson, Apr. 6, 1974; 1 child, Gregory Peter. B in Environ. Design, U. Minn., 1971, MArch, 1973. Registered architect, Minn., Colo., Ariz., Wis., Mich., Ohio, Fla., Ill., Iowa, La., Nev., Penn., Tex., N.J., Ga. N.H. Project planner Ellerbe, Inc., Bloomington, Minn., 1972-78; prin., pres. BRW Architects, Inc., Mpls., 1978-96, also bd. dirs.; prin., pres. Elness Swenson Graham Architects Inc., 1996—. Lectr. architecture U. Minn., Mpls., 1974-82. Bd. edn. Minnehaha Acad., Mpls., 2000—. Evans scholar Western Golf Assn., 1967-71. Mem. AIA (lectr. profl. devel. 1983-87, pres. Mpls. chpt. 2002). Home: 5501 Dever Dr Edina MN 55424-1641 Office: Elness Swenson Graham Architects Inc Thresher Sq 700 S 3rd St Minneapolis MN 55415-1130 E-mail: markswenson@esgarch.com.

SWENSON, SUE, foundation administrator, former health and education administrator; married; 3 children. BA, MA, U. Chgo.; MBA, U. Minn. Mktg. mgr. Barr Engring., Minn. Heart and Lund Inst., U. Minn.; commr. Adminstrn. on Developmental Disabilities, 1998—2001; exec. dir. Joseph P. Kennedy Jr. Foundation, Washington, 2001—. Cons. subcom. on disability policy U.S. Senate, Washington. Fellow Joseph P. Kennedy Jr. Found., 1996. Office: Joseph P. Kennedy Jr. Foundation 1325 G Street NW Ste 500 Washington DC 20005*

SWENSON, SUSAN ANN, engineering recruiting company executive; b. Lansing, Mich., July 30, 1948; d. Milton Cecil and Dorothy Frances (Manuel) Taylor; m. John William Deutschmann, Apr. 17, 1982 (div. Oct. 1995); 1 child, Danielle Cecile. BA in Sociology, U. Wis., 1971; MSW, Mich. State U., 1974. Cert. social worker. Vocat. rehab. counselor, Portland, Oreg., 1982-88; recruiter rschr. Corp. Builders, 1989; engring. recruiter Fran Low, Ltd., 1989-91; owner Swenson & Assocs., Scottsdale, Ariz., 1991—. Social and rehab. svcs. trainee U.S. Govt. Mich. State U., East Lansing, 1972-73, 73-74. Asst. coach Arcadia Scottsdale United Soccer Club, 1995; soccer player N.W. United Women's Soccer, 1980-93, DiHearts Soccer Team, 1996—; soccer player, mgr. Misfits Soccer Team, 1993-95. Mem. AAUW, Nationwide Interchange Svc., Inc., Ariz. Assn. Pers. Svcs. Democrat. Avocations: soccer, country line dancing, creative writing, reading. Home and Office: Swenson & Assocs 8502 E Cholla St Scottsdale AZ 85260-6612

SWENSON, TAMI CHARLOTTE, technical advisor, research analyst; b. St. Croix Falls, Wis., Dec. 30, 1969; d. Stuart and Charlotte S. BS, Carroll Coll., 1992; MA, Tex. A&M U., 1996. Rsch. assoc. Ctr. Demographic and Socioecon. Rsch. and Edn., College Station, 1998—2002; rsch. fellow Sch. Pub. Health, U. Minn., Mpls., 2002—. Rsch. paper panelist Midwest Polit. Sci. Annual Meeting, 1995, So. Rural Sociology Annual Meetings, 2001; presenter in field. Author: monographs; editl. asst. Jour. Politics, 1993; contbr. numerous articles to profl. jours. Mem. Our Saviour's Luth. Ch., Bryan, Tex., 1992-2001. Younger scholar rsch. grantee NEH, 1990, Food Assistance Rsch. grantee So. Rural Devel. Ctr. USDA, 1999, travel grantee joint internat. activities Brit. Acad., 1999. Mem. Am. Polit. Sci. Assn. (rsch. paper panelist annual meetings 1999-2000), Am. Sociol. Assn. (rsch. paper panelist annual meetings 1997-2000), Internat. Soc. Advancement of Socioecons. (rsch. paper panelist 1998-99). Avocations: gardening, politics, needlework. Office: University of Minnesota School of Public Health Minneapolis MN 55455-0381

SWENSON, TREE, poet; MPA in Nonprofit Mgmt., Harvard U., 1996. Co-founder, exec. dir., pub. Copper Canyon Press, Port Townsend, Wash., 1972—92; dir. programs Mass. Cultural Coun., 1992—2002; exec. dir. Acad. Am. Poets, N.Y.C., 2002—. Art dir. Graywolf Press, 1984—93; lectr. Emerson Coll., 1993—97; cons. PEN New Eng., 1993—97; book designer W.W. Norton, 1993—97, Graywolf Press, 1993—97, Ecco Press, 1993—97, Sarabande Books, 1993—97, New Directions, 1993—97; corrd. pub. module grad. writing seminars Bennington Coll., 1993—; grant fellowship panel Nat. Endowment for Arts, N.Y. State Coun. on Arts, Wash. State Arts Commn., Ill. Arts Coun.; mem. leadership devel. com. Nat. Assembly of State Arts Agy., 1999—. Grantee grantee, Nat. Endowment for Arts, Lila Wallace-Reader's Digest Fund, Andrew W. Mellon Found. Office: The American Academy of Poets 588 Broadway Ste 1203 New York NY 10012-3210*

SWENSSON, EARL SIMCOX, architect; b. Nashville, July 28, 1930; s. Earl Ebenezer and Viola Lazelle (Simcox) Swensson; m. Suzanne Dickenson, June 6, 1953; children: Krista, Lin, Kurt. BS in Bldg. Design, Va. Poly. Inst. and State U., 1952, MSArch, 1953. Registered 28 states. Founder, prin. Earl Swensson Assocs., Inc., Nashville, 1961—. Adj. prof. Va. Poly. Inst. and State U., Blacksburg, 1971—72, Auburn U., 1976—83; lectr. in field; apptd. chairholder Jennings and Rebecca Jones Chair of Excellence in Urban and Regional Planning, Mid. Tenn. State U., 1999. Contbr. articles; author (with Richard L. Miller): (books) New Directions in Hospital and Healthcare Facility Design, 1995. Mem. arch. program adv. coun. Auburn U., 1990—94; bd. dirs. Metro Arts Commn., 1979—86; Middle Tenn. Health Systems, 1973—78; Leadership Nashville Alumni Groups, 1984—; bd. advisors U. Tenn. Sch. Arch., 1982, chmn., 1985—88. Named Outstanding Nashvillian of Yr., Downtown Kiwanis Club, 1992, One of Top 100 Alumni of Greatest Distinction Throughout 128-yr. History, Va. Poly. Inst. and State U., 2001; recipient Jefferson award, Am. Inst. Pub. Svc. (Nashville chpt.), 1985. Fellow: AIA. Presbyterian. Achievements include patents for on systamodule for pharmacies. Office: Earl Swensson Assocs 2100 W End Ave Ste 1200 Nashville TN 37203-5239

SWENSSON, EVELYN DICKENSON, conductor, composer, librettist; b. Woodstock, Va., Sept. 18, 1928; d. Glenn Gilmer and Evelyn Christine (Ring) Dickenson; m. Sigurd Simcox Swensson, June 9, 1949; children: Lisë, Karen, Erik, Jon. Cert. in piano, Ward-Belmont Coll., 1946; BA in Piano and Voice, Hollins Coll., 1949; MusM, Westchester U., 1972. Condr. Aldersgate Meth. Ch., Wilmington, Del., 1969—2002, Brandywiners Ltd., Kennett Sq., Pa., 1973-86, Opera Del., Wilmington, 1974—, Bi-Centennial Chorus, Wilmington, 1976; guest condr. Del. Symphony Orch., 1977; condr. Ardensingers, 1978-80; condr. 200th Anniversary Meth. Ch. Am., Balt., 1984. V.p. Opera for Youth Inc.; dir. family opera theater Opera Del., Wilmington, 1974—. Condr.: inaugural concert for Gov. P.S. duPont IV, 1977, condr.: Sleeping Beauty (Respighi), 1977, condr.: The Zoo (Sullivan and Rowe), 1980, condr.: The Lion, the Witch and the Wardrobe (John McCabe), 1980, condr.: celebration of Swedes Landing, 1988, condr.: The Boy Who Grew Too Fast (Menotti), 1982, condr.: Charlotte's Web (Strouse), 1989, condr.: A Wrinkle in Time (Larsen), 1992, composer, condr.: The Enormous Egg, 1993, composer, condr.: The Adventure of Beatrix Potter, 1994, composer, condr.: The Jungle Book, 1995, composer, condr.: Anne of Green Gables, 1996, composer, condr.: The Homecoming, 1997, composer, condr.: The Legend of Redwall Abbey, 1998, composer, condr.: All Through the Night, 1999, composer, condr.: The Trumpet of the Swan, 2000, composer, condr.: The Mixed-Up Files of Mrs. Basil E. Frankweiler, 2002. Recipient W. W. Laird Music award, Opera Del., Wilmington, 1987, Internat. Reading Coun. Literacy award, 1989, Disting. Alumna award, West Chester U., 1989, 5 competition awards, Nat. League Am. Pen Women, 2000. Mem.: Am. Guild Organists (choir master). Home: 58A Heyburn Rd Chadds Ford PA 19317

SWERDLOFF, ILEEN POLLOCK, lawyer; b. Bronx, N.Y., July 15, 1945; d. Seymour Pollock and Selma (Goldin) Feinstein; m. Mark Harris Swerdloff, Dec. 24, 1967; 1 child, Jonathan Edward. BA, SUNY, 1967; JD, Western New Eng. Sch. of Law, 1978. Bar: Conn. 1979, U.S. Dist. Ct. Conn. 1981, U.S. Supreme Ct. 1985. Mng. ptnr. Swerdloff & Swerdloff, West Hartford, Conn., 1980—. Sec. Chrysalis Ctr., Hartford, Conn., 1988-91, pres., 1991-92. Mem. Am. Bar Assn., Conn. Bar Assn., Hartford County Bar Assn., Hartford Assn. Women Attys. Jewish. Avocations: knitting, aerobics. Home: 9 Beacon Heath Farmington CT 06032-1524 Office: Swerdloff & Swerdloff 61 S Main St West Hartford CT 06107-2486

SWERDLOFF, MARK HARRIS, lawyer; b. Buffalo, Sept. 7, 1945; s. John and Joan (Harris) S.; m. Ileen Pollock, Dec. 24, 1967; 1 child, Jonathan Edward. BA, SUNY, Buffalo, 1967; JD, U. Conn., 1975. Bar: Conn. 1975, U.S. Dist. Ct. Conn. 1975, U.S. Ct. Appeals (2d cir.) 1983, U.S. Supreme Ct. 1985, Fla. 1977. Assoc. Wilson, Asbel & Channin, Hartford, Conn., 1975-78; ptnr. Swerdloff & Swerdloff, West Hartford, 1978—. Pres. Arpus Enterprises, Old Saybrook Conn., 1993—; trial fact finder Superior Ct., Hartford, 1990—; arbitrator Dispute Resolution Inst., Hartford, 1990—. Mem. ABA, Conn. Bar Assn., Conn. Trial Lawyers Assn. Democrat. Jewish. Avocations: photography, travel, cooking. Home: 9 Beacon Heath Farmington CT 06032-1524 Office: Swerdloff & Swerdloff 61 S Main St West Hartford CT 06107-2486 E-mail: mhsips@mindspring.com.

SWERDLOFF, RONALD S. medical educator, researcher; b. Pomona, Calif., Feb. 18, 1938; s. Julius Lewis and Eva (Kelman) S.; m. Christina Wang; children: Jonathan Nicolai, Peter Loren, Paul Im, Michael Im. BS, U. Calif., 1959, MD, 1962. Diplomate Am. Bd. Internal Medicine, Am. Bd. Endocrinology. Intern U. Wash., Seattle, 1962-63, resident, 1963-64; rsch. assoc. NIH, Bethesda, Md., 1964-66; resident UCLA Sch. Medicine, 1966-67; rsch. fellow Harbor-UCLA Med. Ctr., Torrance, Calif., 1967-69, asst. prof., 1969-72, assoc. prof. divsn. Endocrinology, 1972-78, chief divsn. Endocrinology, 1973—, prof., 1978—, assoc. chair dept. medicine, 1997—; dir. UCLA Population Rsch. Ctr., 1986-92, Mellon Found. Ctr. in Reproductive Medicine, 1997—. Dir. WHO Collaborating Ctr. Reprodn., Torrance; cons. WHO Geneva, 1982-90, NIH, Bethesda, 1982—, UN Fertility Planning Assn., Geneva, 1983—, Am. Bd. Internal Medicine, Phila., 1989—; inaugural lectr. Australian Soc. Reproductive Biology, Perth, 1990; mem. tech. adv. com. Contraceptive R&D Agy. (CONRAD, AID), 1992—. Editor 3 books; contbr. 100 chpts. to books, 250 articles to profl. jours. Bd. dirs., vice chair Harbor-UCLA Rsch. and Edn. Inst. Fellow: ACP; mem.: We. Soc. Clin. Rsch. (pres. 1983—84, UCLA Sherman Mellinkoff award, Mayo Soley award 2000), Endocrinology Soc., Pacific Coast Fertility (pres. 1984, Squibb award, Outstanding Rsch. award 1976, 1984, Wyeth award 1984), Am. Soc. Clin. Rsch. (pres. we. sect. 1972—73), Am. Assn. Physicians, Am. Soc. Andrology (pres. 1992—93, Serono award 1986). Office: Harbor UCLA Med Ctr Divsn Endocrinology 1000 W Carson St Torrance CA 90502-2004 E-mail: swerdloff@gcrc.rei.edu.

SWERDLOW, AMY, historian, educator, writer; b. N.Y.C., Jan. 20, 1923; d. Joseph and Esther (Rodner) Galstuck; m. Stanley H. Swerdlow, Nov. 27, 1949 (dec. Sept. 1991); children: Joan Swerdlow-Brandt, Ezra, Lisa, Thomas. BA, NYU, 1963; MA, Sarah Lawrence Coll., 1973; PhD, Rutgers U., 1984. Prof. emerita Sarah Lawrence Coll., Bronxville, N.Y., 1981-95, dir. grad. studies in women's history, 1983-95, dir. women's studies program, 1983-95. Mem. adv. bd. Feminist Press, 1973—. Editor: Memo, Women Strike for Peace, 1969—73; editor, co-author Families in Flux, 1980, (reprint), 1989; author: Women Strike for Peace, Traditional Motherhood and Radical Politics in the 1960s , 1993; editor: Feminist Perspective on Homework and Childcare , 1978; co-editor: Class, Race, and Sex: The Dynamics of Control, 1983, Rethinking Women's Peace Studies , 1995; contbr. Sights on the Sixties, Reflections on a Critical Time, Women and Militarism: Essays in History, Politics and Social Theory, Give Peace a Chance; (books) The Abolitionist Sisterhood: Women's Political Culture in Antebellum America, 1994; contbr. American History as Women's History, Red Diapers, Growing Up Red, Dissent, Women's America. Peace History Soc. non-govtl. rep. to UN, 1994—2002. Rutgers U. fellow, 1977-81, Woodrow Wilson Dissertation fellow, 1980. Mem. Orgn. Am. Historians, Berkshire Conf. in Women's History. Home: 33 Wheelock Walk East Hampton NY 11937-3937 E-mail: amnerm@aol.com.

SWERDLOW, MARTIN ABRAHAM, physician, pathologist, educator; b. Chgo., July 7, 1923; s. Sol Hyman and Rose (Lasky) Swerdlow; m. Marion Levin, May 19, 1945; children: Steven Howard, Gary Bruce. Student, Herzl Jr. Coll., 1941-42; BS, U. Ill., 1945; MD, U. Ill., Chgo., 1947. Diplomate Am Bd Pathology. Intern Michael Reese Hosp. and Med. Center, Chgo., 1947-48, resident, 1948-50, 51-52, mem. staff, 1974—, chmn. dept. pathology, v.p. acad. affairs, 1974-90; pathologist Menorah Med Ctr, Kansas City, Mo., 1954—57. Asst prof, pathologist Univ Ill Col Med , Chicago, 1957—59, assoc prof, 1959—60, clin prof, 1960—64, prof, pathologist, 1966—72, assoc dean, prof pathology, 1970—72; prof pathology, chmn Univ Mo, Kansas City, 1972—74; prof pathology Univ Chicago, 1975—89, Geever prof, head pathology emeritus, 1993—; mem comt standards Chicago Health Sys Agency, 1976—. With MC U.S. Army, 1944—45. Recipient Alumnus of the Yr Award, Univ Ill Col Med, 1973, Instructorship Award, Univ Ill, 1960, 1965, 1968, 1971, 1972. Mem.: AMA, Inst Med, Am Soc Dermatopathology, Am Acad Dermatology, Int Acad Pathology, Col Am Pathologists, Am Soc Clin Pathologists, Chicago Pathology Soc (pres 1980—). Jewish. Office: U Ill Coll Medicine Dept Pathology 1819 W Polk St Chicago IL 60612-7331 E-mail: maswerdl@uic.edu. *My credo these years has been to care about patients, students, colleagues, employees, my institution and the many publics I serve. Honesty and thoroughness has been a basic life style, irrespective of the cost. With all, competence is a necessity and ongoing. Continuous responsibility for my education and learning is my way of living.*

SWERDLOW, STEVEN HOWARD, hematopathologist; b. Chgo., Sept. 1, 1950; m. Jennifer Margaret Goodman, May 18, 1975; children: Deborah, Naomi. AB in Biology summa cum laude, Brandeis U., 1971; MD, Harvard U., 1975. Diplomate Am. Bd. Pathology. From asst. to assoc. prof. pathology and lab. medicine U. Cin., 1983-92; dir. divsn. hematopathology, assoc. prof. to prof. pathology U. Pitts., 1992—. Author: Biopsy Interpretation of Lymph Nodes, 1992; mem. editl. bd. jour. Human Pathology, Am. Jour. Surg. Pathology; contbr. articles to Am. Jour. Pathology, Human Pathology, Blood, Leukemia, others. Mem. Am. Soc. Hematology, Am. Soc. Investigative Pathology, U.S. Can. Acad. Pathology (coun. 2001—), Soc. Hematopathology (v.p. 2002—), Europe Assn. Haematopath (exec. com. 2002—), Phi Beta Kappa. Achievements include research in defining centrocytic/mantle cell lymphoma as a distinct clinicopathologic entity. Office: UPMC-Presbyterian Divsn Hematopath PUH C606 200 Lothrop St Pittsburgh PA 15213-2546

SWERLING, JACK BRUCE, lawyer; b. N.Y.C., May 30, 1946; s. Benjamin Fidel and Jeanette (Fidler) S.; m. Erika Andrea Helfer, Jan. 17, 1970; children: Bryan, Stephanie. BA, Clemson U., 1968; JD, U. S.C., 1973. Bar: S.C. 1973, U.S. Dist. Ct. S.C. 1973, U.S. Ct. Appeals (4th cir.) 1974, U.S. Supreme Ct. 1978. Ptnr. Law Firm of Isadore Lourie, Columbia, S.C., 1973-83, Swerling,

Harpootlian & McCulloch, Columbia, 1983-92; pvt. practice, 1992—. Mem. Pre-Trial Intervention Adv. Com., 1980-82; mem. adv. com. Child Victim Ct. Notebook divsn. Pub. Safety Programs, 1987; mem. S.C. Bd. Law Examiners, 1987-92, S.C. Bd. Grievances and Discipline, 1994-97; adj. prof. U. S.C. Sch. Law, Columbia, 1986—; clin. prof. dept. Neuropsychiatry Sch. Medicine, 1988—; mem. S.C. Supreme Ct. com. on model criminal jury instructions, chmn. bule ribbon task force criminal docketing com. Author: South Carolina Criminal Trial Notebook, 1991; co-author: Criminal Trial Advocacy, 1998; contbr. articles to profl. jours. Co-pres. Jewish Cmty. Ctr., Columbia, 1977. Fellow Am. Coll. Trial Lawyers, Am. Acad. Appellate Lawyers, Am. Bd. Criminal Lawyers, S.C. Bar Found.; mem. ABA, ATLA, Am. Judicature Soc., Nat. Assn. Criminal Def. Lawyers, S.C. Trial Lawyers Assn. (chmn. criminal law sect. 1979-82), S.C. Bar Assn. (chmn. criminal law sect. 1985-86), Richland County Bar Assn. (chmn. criminal law sect. 1988-89). Democrat. Jewish. Avocation: shooting sporting clays. Office: 1720 Main St Ste 301 Columbia SC 29201-2850

SWETLIK, WILLIAM PHILIP, orthodontist; b. Manitowoc, Wis., Jan. 31, 1950; s. Leonard Alvin and Lillian Julia (Knipp) S.; m. Cheryl Jean Klein, June 30, 1973 (div.); children: Alison Elizabeth, Lindsey Ann, Adam William; m. Joyce M. Caris, Mar. 10, 1995. Student, Luther Coll., Decorah, Iowa, 1968-70; DDS, Marquette U., 1974; MS in Dentistry, St. Louis U., 1977. Diplomate Am. Bd. Orthodontics. Resident in gen. dentistry USPHS, Norfolk, Va., 1974-75; practice dentistry specializing in orthodontics Green Bay, Wis., 1977—. Instr. oral pathology NE Wis. Tech. Coll., Green Bay, 1979-86. Author: (with others) Orthodontic Headgear, 1977. Mem. Prevention Walking Club, Family Crisis Ctr. of Green Bay. Served as lt. USPHS, 1974-75. Fellow Coll. Diplomates Am. Bd. Orthodontics; mem. ADA, Am. Assn. Orthodontists, Wis. Dental Assn. (Continuing Edn. award 1986), Wis. Soc. Orthodontists, Orthodontic Edn. and Research Found., Brown Door Kewaunee Dental Soc. (program chmn. 1985-86, sec., treas. 1986-87, v.p. 1987-88, pres. 1988-89), St. Louis U. Orthodontic Alumni Assn. (pres. 1988-89), Acad. Gen. Dentistry, Violet Club of Am. Roman Catholic. Avocations: racquetball, skiing, jogging, raising violets, recording equipment. Home: 2160 Greenleaf Rd De Pere WI 54115-8621 Office: 115 Alpine Ct Shawano WI 54166-2041 E-mail: jayecars@aol.com.

SWETMAN, GLENN ROBERT, English language educator, poet; b. May 20, 1936; s. Glenn Lyle and June (Read) S.; m. Margarita Ortiz, Feb. 8, 1964 (div. 1979); children: Margarita June, Glenn Lyle Maximilian, Glenda Louise. BS, U. So. Miss., 1957, MA, 1959; PhD, Tulane U., 1966. Instr. U. So. Miss., 1957-58, asst. prof., 1964-66; instr. Ark. State U., 1958-59, McNeese U., 1959-61; instr. English Univ. Coll. Tulane U., 1961-64, spl. asst. dept. elec. engring., 1961-64; assoc. prof. La. Inst. Tech., 1966-67; prof., head dept. langs. Nicholls State Coll., Thibodaux, La., 1967-69, head dept. English, 1969-71, prof., 1971-91; prof. emeritus William Carey Coll., Gulfport, Miss., 1991—. Writer in residence, prof. English William Carey Coll., Gulfport, 1991—; ptnr. Breeland Pl., Biloxi, 1960—; stringer, corr. Shreveport (La.) Times, 1966—; ptnr. Ormuba, Inc., 1975—; cons. tech. writing Union Carbide Corp., Am. Fedn. Tchrs. State v.p. Nat. Com. to Resist Attacks on Tenure, 1974—. Book reviewer Jackson (Miss.) State Times, 1961; contbr. poetry to various publs. including Poet, Prairie Schooner, Trace, Ball State U. Forum, Film Quar., Poetry Australia, numerous others worldwide; author: (books of poems) Tunel de Amor, 1973, Deka #1, 1973, Deka #2, 1979, Shards, 1979, Concerning Carpenters, 1980, Son of Igor, 1982, Poems of the Fantastic, 1990; contbr. numerous articles to encys.; cons. editor (poetry) Paon Press, 1974—, Scott-Foresman, 1975; mem. editl. bd. Scholar and Educator, 1980—. Subdivsn. coord. Rep. Party, Hattiesburg, Miss., 1964. With AUS, 1957. Recipient Poetry awards KQUE Haiku contest, 1964, Coll. Arts contest, L.A., 1966, Black Ship Festival, Yoqosuka, Japan, 1967, Green World Brief Forms award Green World Poetry Editors, 1965. Mem. MLA, S. Cen. MLA, So. Literary Festival Assn. (v.p. 1975-76, 82-83, pres. 1984-85), Coll. Writers Soc. La. (pres. 1971-72, exec. dir. 1983—), IEEE, Am. Assn. Engring. Edn., La. Poetry Soc. (pres. 1971-74, 86—), Internat. Boswellian Inst., Nat. Fedn. State Poetry Socs. (2d v.p., nat. membership chmn. 1972-74, pres. 1976-77), Nat. Soc. Scholars and Educators (bd. dirs. 1982—, sec. exec. bd. 1986—, sec. bd. dirs. 1968—, sec. soc. 1989—), Am. Fedn. Tchrs. (chpt. pres. 1973-78), Nat. Fedn. State Poetry Socs. (1st v.p. 1975-76, exec. bd. 1972—), Phi Eta Sigma, Omicron Delta Kappa. Home: PO Box 146 Biloxi MS 39533-0146 Office: William Carey Coll 1856 Beach Dr Gulfport MS 39507-1508

SWETNAM, DANIEL RICHARD, lawyer; b. Columbus, Ohio, Dec. 22, 1957; s. Joseph Neri and Audrey Marguerite (Mason) S.; m. Jeannette Deanna Dean, June 7, 1980; children: Jeremiah Daniel, Laura Janelle, Andrew Michael. BA, Ohio State U., 1979; JD, U. Cin., 1982. Bar: Ohio 1982, U.S. Dist. Ct. (so. dist.) Ohio 1982, U.S. Ct. Appeals (6th cir.) 1986, U.S. Supreme Ct. 1986. Assoc. Schwartz, Warren & Ramirez, Columbus, 1982-88, ptnr., 1989-96; prin. Schottenstein, Zox & Dunn, 1997—. Deacon Grace Brethren Ch., Worthington, Ohio, 1989—; mem. Grace Brethren Christian Schs. Commn., 1993-98. Mem. ABA, Ohio State Bar Assn., Columbus Bar Assn., Comml. Law League Am., Order of Coif. Republican. Avocations: golf, tennis. Home: 2178 Stowmont Ct Dublin OH 43016-9563 Office: Schottenstein Zox & Dunn 41 S High St Columbus OH 43215-6101

SWETNAM, MONTE NEWTON, petroleum exploration executive; b. Alexandria, La., Oct. 9, 1936; s. Montreville Morris and Margaret Elizabeth (Cullison) S.; m. Elaine Adelia Taylor, Dec. 21, 1957; children: Scott David, Robert Troy. Student, Johns Hopkins, 1955-58; BS in Geology, U. Wyo., 1960, MS in Geology, 1961; MBA in Bus. Adminstrn, Pepperdine U., 1978. Registered geologist, Calif. Exploration geologist Amerada Petroleum Corp., Durango, Colo., 1961-63; exploration geologist Tenneco Oil Co., 1963-65, dist. project geologist Bakersfield, Calif., 1965-69, div. staff geologist, 1969; partner Argonaut Oil & Gas Cons., Denver, 1969-71; internat. exploration mgr. Tesoro Petroleum Corp., San Antonio, 1971-73, v.p. internat. exploration, 1973-74, sr. v.p. exploration, 1974-82; pres. Tesoro-Bolivia Petroleum Co., 1975-82, Tesoro-Algeria Petroleum Co., 1975-82; sr. v.p. exploration Natural Resource Mgmt. Corp./NRM, Dallas, 1983-86; sr. v.p. exploration and prodn. Harken Energy Corp., 1987-89, exec. v.p., 1991-93; pres. Harken Exploration Co., 1988-91, Harken Bahrain Oil Co., 1989-93; exec. v.p., chief oper. officer Giant Exploration and Prodn. Co., Farmington, N.Mex., 1994-96; v.p. refining ops. Giant Industries, Inc., Scottsdale, Ariz., 1996-97, v.p. corp. affairs, 1997-98, exec. v.p. adminstrn. and corp. affairs, 1998-2000. Contbr. articles to profl. jours. Mem. Am. Assn. Petroleum Geologists, Geol. Soc. Am., Sigma Xi. Clubs: Alamo Yacht, Lake Canyon Yacht. Republican. Home: 420 Marina Dr Port Aransas TX 78373-4907 Office: 420 Marina Dr Port Aransas TX 78373-4907 Fax: 361-749-3093. E-mail: emenes@the-i.net.

SWETNAM, RUTH E. DANGLADE, curriculum director; b. Marion, Ind., Jan. 27, 1940; d. Harold Davis and Elizabeth (Lake) Neel; m. James K. Danglade, Sept. 2, 1961 (div. Nov. 1979); children: Annette, John, Douglas, Adam, Matthew; m. Gary L. Swetnam, June 19, 1993. BS, Ball State U., 1961, MA, 1964. Cert. elem., secondary bus., spl. edn. and speech pathology tchr., sch. adminstrn., Ind. Tchr. orthopedically handicapped Muncie (Ind.) Community Schs., 1961-67, tchr. of multiply handicapped, 1969-74, tchr. learning disabled, 1976-79; spl. edn. instr. Ball State U., Muncie, 1974-79; asst. dir. spl. edn. Delaware County Spl. Edn. Coop., 1979-91; dir. curriculum Muncie Community Schs., 1991-98; dir. Inst. Cmty. Edn. Devel. and Sch. Improvement Ball State U., Muncie, 1998—; profl. devel. cons., 1998—. Sci. curriculum cons. NSF, Muncie, 1976-78; learning disabilities instr. Ball State U., 1974-80. Bd. dirs. Delaware County Easter Seal Soc., Minnetrista Cultural Found., Inc.; chairperson adv. coun. Ball State U. Coll. Bus., 1985-90; mem. adminstrv. bd. High St. United Meth. Ch., Muncie, 1984-88, youth coord., 1985-88; mem. adv. bd. Delaware County 4-H, 1991-98; chair allocations panel United Way of Delaware County, chmn. budget panel; mem. Muncie StarPress Ptnrs. for Literacy Adv. Bd. Mem. ASCD, Ind. ASCD, Assn. for Children with Learning Disabilities, Coun. Exceptional Children (pres. Delaware County chpt. 1977-78), Nat. Staff Devel. Coun., Ind. Staff Devel. Count., Muncie-Delaware County C. of C. (bus. edn. partnership), Phi Delta Kappa, Pi Beta Phi. Methodist. Avocations: music, reading, traveling, walking, hiking. Office: Ball State U Teachers College 1003 Muncie IN 47306-0001 E-mail: rswetnam@bsu.edu.

SWETS, JOHN ARTHUR, psychologist, researcher; b. Grand Rapids, Mich., June 19, 1928; s. John A. and Sara Henrietta (Heyns) Swets; m. Maxine Ruth Crawford, July 16, 1949; children: Stephen Arthur, Joel Brian. BA, U. Mich., 1950, MA, 1953, PhD, 1954. Instr. psychology U. Mich., Ann Arbor, 1954—56; asst. prof. psychology MIT, Cambridge, 1956—60, assoc. prof. psychology, 1960—63; v.p. Bolt Beranek & Newman Inc., 1964—69, sr. v.p., 1969—74, gen. mgr. rsch., devel. and cons., dir., 1971—74; chief scientist BBN Labs., 1975—98, chief scientist emeritus, 1998—; sr. rsch. assoc. dept. radiology Brigham and Women's Hosp., 1997—. Lectr. dept. clin. epidemiology Harvard Med. Sch., 1985—88, dept. health care policy, 1988—; mem. corp. Edn. Devel. Ctr., Newton, Mass., 1971—75; Regent's prof. U. Calif., 1969; advisor vision com., com. on hearing and bioacoustics NAS-NRC, 1960—96; mem. Commn. on Behavioral Social Scis. and Edn., NRC, 1988—92, vice chair, 1992—93, chmn., 1993—96; ex-officio mem. governing bd. NRC, 1994—96, mem. various coms., 1960—. Author: Signal Detection Theory and ROC Analysis in Psychology and Diagnostics, 1996; co-author (with D.M. Green): Signal Detection Theory and Psychophysics, 1966; co-author: (with R.M. Pickett) Evaluation of Diagnostic Systems: Methods From Signal Detection Theory, 1982; editor: Signal Detection and Recognition by Human Observers, 1964; editor: (with L.L. Elliott) Psychology and the Handicapped Child, 1974; editor: (with D. Druckman) Enhancing Human Performance, 1988; mem. editl. bd.: Med. Decision Making, 1980—85, mem. editl. bd.: Psychol. Sci., 1989—94, mem. editl. bd.: , 1999—, mem. editl. bd.: Psychol. Rev., 1995—97, mem. editl. bd.: Jour. Exptl. Psychology: Applied, 1995—97, mem. editl. bd.: Human Factors, 1997—2001; contbr. articles to profl. jours. Mem. bd. dirs. German-Am. Rsch. Coun. Found., 1999—2001; mem. corp. Winchester Hosp., Mass., 1981—84. Fellow vis. rsch. fellow, Philips Labs., The Netherlands, 1958. Fellow: APA (Disting. Sci. Contbn. award 1990), AAAS (coun. 1986—89), Am. Psychol. Soc., Soc. Exptl. Psychologists (chmn. 1986, exec. com. 1986—89, Howard Crosby Warren medal 1985), Am. Acad. Arts and Scis., Acoustical Soc. Am. (exec. coun. 1968—71); mem.: NAS (chmn., Troland award com. 1991, chair psychology sect. 1998—2001, nominating com. 2001), Soc. Math. Psychology, Psychometric Soc., Psychonomic Soc., Tequesta Country Club, Sigma Alpha Epsilon, Sigma Xi. Congregationalist (Moderator). Home: 10411 SE Terrapin Pl 103-C Tequesta FL 33469-1827 E-mail: swets@bbn.com.

SWETT, ALBERT HERSEY, retired lawyer, business executive, consultant; b. Medina, N.Y., Feb. 18, 1923; s. Raymond Fuller and Marion (Hersey) S.; m. Mary Stewart, Oct. 10, 1944; children: Marion Hersey Swett Robinson, Margaret Stewart Swett Haskell, Albert Louis. Grad., The Hill Sch., 1941; B.Engring., Yale U., 1944; LL.B., Harvard U., 1949. Bar: N.Y. 1949. Assoc. Harris, Beach & Wilcox, Rochester, N.Y., 1949-56, ptnr., 1957-66; v.p., gen. counsel Xerox Corp., Stamford, Conn., 1966-75, Coca-Cola Co., Atlanta, 1975-78, v.p., counsel to chmn., 1978-80; ind. cons., 1980—. Trustee Practising Law Inst., 1977-83. Served with USNR, 1942-46. Mem. Assn. Gen. Counsel (emeritus), Tau Beta Pi. Lodges: Masons. Republican. Methodist. Home: Apt 615 1570 East Ave Rochester NY 14610-1640 E-mail: ahs30319@aol.com.

SWETT, RICHARD NELSON (DICK SWETT), diplomat, former congressman; b. Bryn Mawr, Pa., May 1, 1957; s. Philip Eugene Sr. and Ann (Parkhurst) S.; m. Yvonne Katrina Lantos, Aug. 29, 1980; children: Chelsea, Sebastian, Keaton, Chanteclaire, Kismet, Atticus, Sunday. BA in Architecture, Yale U., 1979. Lic. contractor, Calif.; lic. architect, Calif., N.H. Arch. Skidmore Owings & Merrill, San Francisco, 1979-82; pres. Bastion Group, Inc., San Mateo, 1982-87; project mgr. Grosvenor Properties, San Francisco, 1986-87; pres. Veritas Group Inc., Gilford, N.H., 1987-90; mem. 101st-102d Congresses from 2nd dist. N.H., Washington, 1990-95; mem. pub. works and transp. com. U.S. Ho. of Reps., 1991-95, mem. sci., space, and tech. com., 1991-95, mem. select com. on aging, 1991-95; amb. to Denmark, Am. Embassy, Copenhagen, 1998-2001. Founding mem. adv. bd. European Ctr. of Calif., 2001—; mem. bd. Sunrise Capital Ptnrs., 2001—; mem. U.S. Govt. Gen. Svcs. Adminstrn. Peer Rev. Bd. Del. N.H. Dem. Conv., Henniker, 1988; bd. advisors, Hans Christian Andersen Found., Denmark; state chmn., U.S. Olympic Com., 1992-98, 2001—. Presented 1st Comdr. Order of Danabrog, Queen Margrethe II of Denmark, 2001; named as one of Top Ten Outstanding Young Ams., U.S. Jr. C. of C., 1993. Fellow AIA; mem. Nat. Hist. Preseervation Soc., Ind. Power Producers N.H. Assn., Yale Club N.H., Sierra Club, Winnipesaukee Yacht Club. Avocations: athletics, piano, art, sailing. E-mail: rswett@attbi.com.

SWETT, STEPHEN FREDERICK, JR. artist, educator; b. Englewood, N.J., Sept. 14, 1935; s. Stephen Frederick and Frances (Gulotta) S.; m. Annette Palazzolo, Nov. 18, 1961; children: Susan, Kimberly Ann, Stephen Laurence. BA, Montclair State Coll., 1959, MA, 1965; EdD in Ednl. Adminstrn., Rutgers U., 1976; grad., North Light Art Sch., 1995. Tchr. Long Branch (N.J.) H.S., 1961-62, Roselle Park (N.J.) H.S., 1962-73; rsch. asst. Rutgers U., New Brunswick, N.J., 1973-74; instrnl. supr. Elmwood Park (N.J.) Schs., 1974-76, Morris Hills Regional Schs., Denville, N.J., 1976-77; asst. prin. Lawrence H.S., Lawrenceville, 1977-79; prin. Stafford Intermediate Sch., Manahawkin, 1979-94; recreation and art cons., 1994—. Participant NSF Inst. in physics, chemistry and math. Seton Hall U., 1964, Newark Coll. Engring., 1965, Stevens Inst. Tech., summers 1966-68; rschr. sch. fin. Exhibited in group shows at Sheldon Meml. Art Gallery, 1998, Period Gallery, Omaha, 1998, 99, Montserrat Gallery, N.Y.C., 2000, The Looking Glass Art Gallery, Hawley, Pa., 2000. With AUS, 1959-61. Mem. Roselle Park Edn. Assn. (pres. 1971-73), Nat. Soc. Study Edn., Am. Assn. Physics Tchrs., Am. Inst. Physics, Am. Assn. Sch. Adminstrs., N.J. Assn. Sch. Adminstrs., Nat. Assn. Elem. and Mid. Sch. Adminstrs., N.J. Assn. Elem. and Mid. Sch. Adminstrs., Nat. Assn. Secondary Sch. Prins., Phi Delta Kappa (sec. Rutgers chpt. 1977-80, v.p. 1980-82, pres. 1983-84). Home: 306 Tenth Ave Belmar NJ 07719-2313

SWETT-BRASEFIELD, SUSAN, chemical engineer; b. Newark, Sept. 25, 1962; d. Stephen F. and Annette (Palazzolo) Swett. BSChE, Stevens Inst. Tech., Hoboken, N.J., 1984. Registered profl. engr., N.J. Sr. staff engr. environ. div. T&M Assocs., Middletown, N.J., 1984-93; project engr. Killam Assocs., Freehold, 1993-97; project mgr. Bay Pointe Engring. Assocs., Point Pleasant, 1997-2001; sr. project mgr. Maser Cons. P.A., Matawan, 2001—. Mem. AIChE, ASCE, Soc. Women Engrs., N.J. Profl. Engrs. Soc. Home: 33 Hialeah Ct Howell NJ 07731-2437 Office: Maser Cons PA 30 Freneau Ave Rte 79 Matawan NJ 07747 E-mail: S.Brasefield@maserconsulting.com.

SWETTE, BRIAN T. online computer executive; BA in Econ., Az. State U. Mgr. Procter & Gamble; exec. v.p./chief mktg. officer Pepsi-Cola, 1981-01. Office: EBay Inc 2145 Hamilton Ave San Jose CA 95125

SWEZEY, CHRISTOPHER STEPHEN, geologist; b. Lexington, Va., Dec. 5, 1964; s. Charles Mason and Mary Evelyn (Knight) S. Student, U. Paris, 1985-86; BS, Duke U., Durham, N.C., 1987; MA, U. Texas, Austin, 1991, PhD, 1997. Sound and lighting tech. Duke Tech. Svcs., Durham, N.C., 1983-87; mus. tech. U.S. Geol. Survey, Menlo Park, Calif., 1987-88; teaching asst. U. Tex., Austin, 1988-92, rsch. asst., 1993-94; fulbright scholar U. Louis Pasteur, Strasbourg, France, 1992-93; rsch. asst. U. Tex. at Austin, 1993-94; Chateaubriand scholar CNRS, Strasbourg, France, 1995; rsch. asst. Bur. Econ. Geology, Austin, Tex., 1996-97; geologist BP Exploration, Inc., Houston, 1997-98, BP Amoco Exploration, Houston, 1999-2000, U.S. Geol. Survey, Reston, Va., 2000—. Author: Geology of Montreat, 1992; contbr. over 10 articles to profl. jours. Mem. AAAS, Internat. Assn. of Sedimentologists, Geol. Soc. Am., Soc. for Sedimentary Geology, nat. Speleological Soc. Avocations: guitar, dulcimer, photography, hiking. E-mail: cswezey@usgs.gov.

SWIATEK, MARY ANN, psychologist; b. South Plainfield, N.J., Dec. 27, 1965; married. BA in Psychology with honors, Oberlin Coll., 1988; PhD, Iowa State U., 1993. Lic. psychologist, Pa. Asst. prof. psychology SUNY, Fredonia, 1993-96, Lafayette Coll., Easton, Pa., 1996-2000, adj. asst. prof. psychology, 2000—; rsch. specialist Carnegie Mellon Inst. for Talented Elem. Students, Pitts., 2000—. Rsch. cons. Lafayette Coll. Counseling Ctr., Easton, 2000—; psychologist Kids Peace Nat. Hosp., 2002—. Contbr. articles to profl. jours. Recipient award for excellence in rsch. Am. Mensa Edn. and Rsch. Found., 1992 Mem. APA, Am. Psychol. Soc., Nat. Assn. Gifted Children, World Coun. Gifted and Talented Children, Pa. Assn. Gifted Edn.

SWIBEL, STEVEN WARREN, lawyer; b. Chgo., July 18, 1946; s. Morris Howard and Gloria Swibel; m. Leslie S. Swibel; children: Deborah, Laura. BS, MIT, 1968; JD, Harvard U., 1971. Bar: Ill. 1971, U.S. Dist. Ct. (no. dist.) Ill. 1971, U.S. Tax Ct. 1973, U.S. Ct. Appeals (7th cir.) 1981. Assoc. Sonnenschein Carlin Nath & Rosenthal, Chgo., 1971-78, ptnr., 1978-84, Rudnick & Wolfe, 1984-93, Schwartz, Cooper, Greenberger, Krauss Chartered, Chgo., 1993—. Adj. prof. taxation Ill. Inst. Tech. Kent Coll. Law, Chgo., 1989-2001; lectr. in field; contbr. articles to profl. jours. Ednl. counselor MIT, 1979—; bd. dirs. MIT Alumni Fund, 1992-95, Ragdale Found., 1987-00, treas, 1987-92; bd. dirs. Kids In Danger, 1998—. Recipient Lobdell Disting. Svc. award MIT Alumni Assn., 1989. Mem. ABA (com. partnerships sect. taxation), Ill. Bar Assn., Chgo. Bar Assn. (fed. taxation com., exec. subcom. 1984—, chmn. subcom. on real estate and partnerships 1986-87, vice-chmn. 1988-89, chmn. 1990), Met. Club, MIT Club (dir. Chgo. chpt. 1980-91, 96—, sec. 1980-87, pres. 1987-89), Sigma Xi, Tau Beta Pi, Eta Kappa Nu. Office: Schwartz Cooper Greenberger & Krauss Chartered 180 N La Salle St Ste 2700 Chicago IL 60601-2757 E-mail: swibel@alum.mit.edu.

SWICK, HERBERT MORRIS, medical educator, neurologist; b. Baton Rouge, Nov. 22, 1941; s. Edgar Haight and Mary Ellen (Morris) S.; m. Mary Lynne McCluggage, June 29, 1963; children: Kristin Ann, Elizabeth May, Diane Marie. BA with honors, Johns Hopkins U., 1963, MD, 1966. Cert. Am. Bd. Psychiatry and Neurology, Am. Bd. Pediatrics. Resident in pediat. Johns Hopkins U., Balt., 1966-69; resident in neurology U. Ky., Lexington, 1971-74, asst. prof. neurology and pediat., 1974-75; from asst. to prof. neurology and pediat. Med. Coll. Wis., Milw., 1975-94, asst. dean med. edn., interim chmn. dept. neurology, 1987-88, from assoc. to sr. assoc. dean acad. affairs, 1988-93, sr. assoc. dean for acad. programs, 1993-94; prof. neurology U. Kans. Sch. Medicine, Kansas City, 1994-99, sr. assoc. dean acad. affairs, 1994-98; acting chmn. dept. history and philosophy of medicine Sch. Medicine U. Kans., 1995; interim exec. dean U. Kans. Sch. Medicine, 1995-97; scholar-in-residence Assn. Am. Med. Colls., 1998-2000; exec. dir. Inst. Medicine and Humanities, Missoula, Mont., 2000—; prof. U. Mont., 2000—; clin. assoc. prof. medicine U. Wash. Sch. Medicine, 2001—. Chief dept. neurology Children's Hosp. Wis., Milw., 1981-87; vis. prof. neurol. edn. Mayo Clinic and Found., Rochester, Minn., 1985; bd. dirs. Inst. Medicine and Humanities. Contbr. numerous articles to profl. jours. Bd. dirs. Milw. Chamber Music Soc., 1982-88, pres. 1986-88; bd. dirs. Missoula Cultural Coun., 2001—, Mont. Natural History Ctr., 2001—. Served to lt. commdr., USN, 1969-71. Fulbright sr. scholar, 1978. Fellow Am. Acad. Neurology (edn. com., undergrad. edn. subcom. 1985-89); mem. Am. Assn. History Medicine, Child Neurology Soc. (archives and history com. 1981-88, exec. com. 1982-86, sci. selection com. 1983, 84), Columbia History of Medicine Club, Internat. Child Neurology Assn., Milw. Acad. Medicine (coun. 1993-94), Profs. of Child Neurology, Wis. Neurol. Soc. (sec.-treas. 1981-82, pres.-elect 1982-84, pres. 1984-85), Assn. Univ. Profs. in Neurology (undergrad. edn. com. 1979-86), Assn. Am. Med. Colls. (coun. deans 1995-97, group on ednl. affairs 1986-98, group on student affairs 1986-94, faculty affairs profl. devel. conf. planning com. 1997-98). Office: Inst Medicine & Humanities PO Box 4587 Missoula MT 59806-4587

SWICK, JANE MULLER, artist; b. Detroit, Nov. 7, 1932; d. Arthur Herman and Elma Lee Muller; m. Howard James Swick, Oct. 3, 1952; children: Kathryn, John, Susan, Patti. Student, Calif. Coll. Arts and Crafts, Oakland, 1995—. Exhibited in galleries at Lakeside and Bandon, Oreg., also Kauai, Hawaii; solo shows at Walnut Creek Art Festival, Kingren Found., Walnut Creek, Evergreen Ct. Exhbn., Coos Bay; group shows at Willowbrook Art Show, Napa, ullerton Cmty. Park, Coquille Art Ctr. Gallery, Coos Bay Art Mus. Gallery, Coos Bay Pub. Libr., others; represented in pvt. collections. Recipient 1st and 2d place awards at various county fairs and art exhbns. Mem. Bay Area Artist's Assn., Coquille Valley Artist's Assn., Art Mus. of Coos Bay. Avocation: model trains. Home: 67308 Fern Rd North Bend OR 97459 E-mail: janemswick@charter.com.

SWID, STEPHEN CLAAR, business executive; b. N.Y.C., Oct. 26, 1940; s. David and Selma (Claar) S.; m. Nan Goldman, Mar. 1, 1963; children: Robin, Scott, Jill. BS, Ohio State U., 1962. Mgmt. trainee Alside Aluminum Co., Akron, Ohio, 1962-63; securities analyst Dreyfus Fund, N.Y.C., 1963-66; sr. investment officer Oppenheimer Fund, 1966-67; gen. ptnr. City Assocs., 1967-69, Swid Investors, N.Y.C., 1970-78; co-chmn. bd. Gen. Felt Industries Inc., Saddle Brook, N.J., 1974-86, Knoll Internat., 1977-86; chmn. bd., CEO SBK Entertainment World, Inc., N.Y.C., 1986-89; chmn., CEO SCS Comm., 1989—, SESAC, 1992—. Trustee Solomon Guggenheim Mus.; mem. vis. com. 20th century art Met. Mus. Art; past trustee Horace Mann Sch., N.Y.C.; former exec. vp. bd. dirs. Lenox Sch. N.Y.; dir. Mcpl. Art Soc. Mem.: Coun. Fgn. Rels. Office: SCS Communications 152 W 57th St New York NY 10019-3310

ŚWIECICKI, MARCIN, politician, economist; b. Warsaw, Poland, Apr. 17, 1947; s. Andrzej and Jadwiga (Wierusz-Kowalska) S.; m. Joanna Maria Szyr, June 24, 1969; children: Tomasz, Jaroslaw, Ignacy, Konstancja. BSc in Sociology, Warsaw U., 1970, M in Econ. Sci., 1971; student, George Washington U., 1975-76; D in Econ. Sci., Inst. of Planning, Warsaw, 1981; vis. scholar, Harvard U., 1984-85. From councillor to chief specialist Planning Com. Warsaw, 1972-82; dir. for study and analysis Cons. Econ. Coun. Warsaw, 1982-87, gen. sec., 1987-89; sec. PZPR Cen. Com., Warsaw, 1989; minister fgn. econ. coop. Warsaw, 1989-91; ind. advisor Warsaw, 1991—94, 2001—02; mayor City of Warsaw, 1994-99; undersec. of state and mem. negotiating team Min. of Econs. responsible for relations with EU, 1999—2000; coord. econ. and environ. activities Orgn. for Security and Devel. in Europe, 2002—. Scientific worker Polish Acad. of Sics., Warsaw, 1991-94; participant Round Table Debates, Warsaw, 1989; adv. to Lithuanian Govt., Warsaw, 1993, the Pres. of Lithuania, 2000-2001; dep. chmn. Parliamentary Commn. for Fgn. Rels., Warsaw, 1993. Co-author: The Economy of Ukraine, 1993; contbr. articles to profl. jours. Active Polish United Workers Party, Warsaw, 1974-90, Freedom Union, Warsaw, 1993—; nat. coun. mem. Dem. Union, Warsaw, 1994—; dep. Polish Parliament, Warsaw, 1989-91, 93-96; co-founder, pres. Polish Com. Supporting Establishment of Mus. of History of Polish Jews, 1997—. Fullbright fellow 1975-76, 84-85. Mem. Polish Assn. for Club of Rome (treas. 1987), Polish Fullbright Alumni Assn. (founder, v.p. 1993), Bus. Ctr. Club. Roman Catholic. Avocations: mountain hiking, jogging, volleyball, political books, memoirs. Home: Wegrzyna 29 00 769 Warsaw Poland Office: OSCE Kärtner Ring 5-7 A-1010 Vienna Austria E-mail: m.swiecicki@melog.com.pl.

SWIFF, KELLY, food products executive, civic volunteer, writer; Student, Cordon Bleu Cookery Sch., London, LaVarenne Cookery Sch., Paris, Burgundy, France. Model The Dialing for Dollars, Good Morning Houston; pres. 1773 Am. Tea Co. Instr. self-esteem courses, modeling courses, culinary courses, gala fund-raising. Author: Music Theory with F, A & C, Harp Theory with F, A & C, Take A Look Inside Yourself, Gala Fund Raising Fundamentals, Tea—The New American Revolution; contbr. articles to profl. publs. Founder, chair Woodlands Literary Gala for South Montgomery County; founder, pres. South Montgomery County Libr. Guild; founder Savoir-Faire Etiquette Program, Houston Fire Mus. Gala; past pres., Argonauta Women's Group; founder Neartown Bicycle Tour benefitting Houston Police Dept. Recipient Women of Distinction award; named Top 94 Citizen, People Scene mag. Achievements include invention of of porcelain tea bag steeper. Avocations: cooking, floral design, painting, sewing.

SWIFT, CALVIN THOMAS, electrical and computer engineering educator; b. Quantico, Va., Feb. 6, 1937; s. Thomas and Elsie (Hill) S.; m. Joanne Taylor, Sept. 5, 1959; children: Pamela, Janet. BS, MIT, 1959; MS, Va. Poly. Inst., 1965; PhD, William and Mary Coll., 1969. Research engr. N. Am. Aviation Co., Downey, Calif., 1959-62; aerospace technologist NASA, Hampton, Va., 1962-81; prof. elec. and computer engring. U. Mass., Amherst, 1981—2001, prof. emeritus, 2001—. Cons. engring., Amherst, 1981— Editor: Transactions on Geoscience and Remote Sensing, 1980-84; assoc. editor: Jour. Oceanic Engring., 1980-84. F.L. Thompson fellow NASA, 1977; faculty fellow U. Mass., 1997. Fellow IEEE (life); mem. Internat. Union Radio Sci. (chmn. Commn. F 1988-91), Antennas and Propagation Soc. (adminstrv. com. 1974-77, 80-85), Geosci. and Remote Sensing Soc. (adminstrv. com. 1978-86, pres. 1985, Disting. Achievement award 1994). Office: U Mass Dept Elec & Computer Engring Amherst MA 01003

SWIFT, EDWARD FOSTER, III, investment banker; b. Chgo., Nov. 1, 1923; s. Theodore Philip I and Elizabeth (Hoyt) S.; m. Joan McKelvy, July 2, 1947; children: Theodore Philip II, Edward McKelvy, Lockhart McKelvy, Elizabeth Hoyt; m. Carol Coffey Whipple, June 21, 1968. Grad., Hotchkiss Sch., 1941; BA, Yale U., 1945. With Esmark, Inc. (formerly Swift & Co.), 1947-75, asst. to v.p. charge meat packing plants, 1958, asst. v.p., 1958-59, v.p. for provisions, fgn., casings and storage, 1959-64, exec. v.p., 1964-75; vice-chmn. Chgo. Corp., 1975-79; vice chmn. Bacon, Whipple & Co., Chgo., 1980-84; mng. dir. A.G. Becker Paribas Inc., 1984-85; with E.F. Hutton and Co., 1985-87; mng. dir. Shearson Lehman Hutton Inc. 1987-92. Bd. dirs. Santa Fe Pacific Pipelines, Inc. Chmn. So. Ind. chpt. United Negro Coll. Fund, 1956; trustee Northwestern U., Evanston, Ill.; bd. dirs. Northwestern Meml. Hosp., Chgo. Served to capt. U.S. Army, 1942-46. Mem. Chgo. Assn. Commerce and Industry (bd. dirs.), Scroll and Key, Chgo. Club, Racquet Club, Econ. Club, Valley Club, Comml. Club, Onwentsia Club, Old Elm ClubBirnam Wood Golf Club, Aurelian Honor Soc. Home: 1500 N Astor St Chicago IL 60610-1635 Office: 70 W Madison St Ste 1400 Chicago IL 60602-4267

SWIFT, FRANK MEADOR, lawyer; b. N.Y.C., Dec. 27, 1911; s. Frank Meador and Alberta (Rankin) S.; m. Harriet Elizabeth Simpson, May 30, 1944; children: Frank Meador (dec.), Thomas Lamar. Student, Emory U., 1930-32; LL.B., U. Ga., 1935. Bar: Ga. 1935. Partner Swift, Currie, McGhee & Hiers, Atlanta, 1965-82, of counsel, 1982—. Served to comdr. USNR, 1942-46. Mem. Am., Ga. bar assns., Lawyers Club Atlanta, Clubs: Piedmont Driving. Republican. Presbyterian. Home: 201 Neptune Rd Apt 455 Saint Simons GA 31522-4246 Office: Swift Currie McGhee & Hiers 1355 Peachtree St NE Ste 300 Atlanta GA 30309-3238

SWIFT, JANE MARIA, governor; b. North Adams, Mass., Feb. 24, 1965; d. John Maynard and Jean Mary (Kent) S.; m. Charles T. Hunt III, Feb. 19, 1994. BA in Am. Studies, Trinity Coll., Hartford, Conn., 1987. Exec. mgmt. trainee G. Fox. & Co., Hartford, 1987-88; adminstrv. aide Sen. Peter C. Webber, Boston, 1988-90; mem. Mass. State Senate, 1991-96, 3d asst. minority leader, 1993-96; coord. strategic devel. of regional airports Mass. Port Authority, 1997; dir. consumer affairs and bus. regulation Commonwealth of Mass., lt. gov., 1999-2001, gov., 2001—. 3d asst. minority leader, 1993-96. Republican. Roman Catholic. Office: State House Rm 360 Boston MA 02133

SWIFT, JILL ANNE, industrial engineer, educator; b. Memphis, Nov. 12, 1959; d. Gary Green and Sharon (Willoughby) Brown; m. Fredrick Wallace Swift, June 12, 1987; children: Andrew, Samantha. BS, Memphis State U., 1981, MS, 1982; PhD, Okla. State U., 1987. Registered profl. engr., Fla.; cert. quality mgr., quality engr. Design engr. DuPont Co., Glasgow, Del., 1982-83; head dept. physics Coll. Boca Raton, Fla., 1983-87; asst. prof. indsl. engring. U. Miami, Coral Gables, 1987-96; quality cons., 1996—; dir. quality assurance Cubic Transp. Systems, Tullahoma, Tenn., 1997—. Vis. scholar Air Force Inst. Tech., Wright-Patterson AFB, Ohio, 1988; cons. A.T. Kearney, Amman, Jordan, 1990; quality liaison U. Miami Inst. Study of Quality in Mfg. and Svc., 1988—; cons., spkr. in field. Author: Introduction to Modern Statistical Quality Control and Management, 1995, Principles of Total Quality Control, 1996; co-author: Principles of Total Quality, 1997; contbr. articles to profl. publs. Mem. IIE (chpt. dir. 1988-90, Christmas toy dr. coord. 1989, 90), Am. Soc. Engring. Edn., Am. Soc. Quality Control, Phi Kappa Phi, Alpha Pi Mu (faculty adviser 1988-96), Tau Beta Pi. Republican. Avocations: cross-stitch, reading. E-mail: jill.swift@cubic.com.

SWIFT, JOHN FRANCIS, health care advertising company executive; b. N.Y.C., June 15, 1935; s. John F. and Mary Veronica (Kehoe) S.; m. Eleanor H. Cunniff, Oct. 10, 1964; children— John Francis, Sharon Ann. BS in Bus. Adminstrn, Seton Hall U., 1960, postgrad., 1960-61. Mktg. research mgr. Lederle Labs. div. Cyanamid Internat., 1960-63; account exec. Robert A. Becker Advt. Agy., N.Y.C., 1963-66; mgr. new products Chesebrough Ponds Co., 1966-68; v.p. Frohlich Intercon Co., 1968-72; pres., CEO, Lavey/Wolff/Swift, Inc., 1972-91, chmn., CEO, 1991-94; pres., CEO, BBDO Health & Med. Comms. Inc., 1977-91; chmn., CEO, Health & Med. Comm. Inc., 1991-95, chmn. emeritus, 1995—; vice-chmn. Lyons Lavey Nickel Swift, Inc., 1995—. Bd. govs. Cathedral Healthcare Systems, 1991—; chmn. Cathedral Healthcare Found., 1994—. Served with USN, 1955-57. Mem. Pharm. Advt. Coun. (pres. 1979), Bio-Med. Mktg. Assn., Canoe Brook CC (Summit, N.J.), Manasquan River Golf Club, Skytop Club (Pa.), Royal Palm Yacht and Country Club, Boca Raton Resort and Club, N.Y. Athletic Club. Home: 32 Peppermill Rd Chatham NJ 07928-1312 also: 600 S Ocean Blvd Boca Raton FL 33432-6265 also: 76 Bay Point Harbour Point Pleasant NJ 08742-5509 Office: Health & Med Comm Inc 220 E 42d St New York NY 10017

SWIFT, JOHN GOULDING, lawyer; b. Lake Charles, La., Nov. 12, 1955; s. Goulding William Jr. and Betty Jane (Richardson) S.; m. Jan Lynette Whitehead. BS, La. State U., 1977, JD, 1980. Bar: La. 1980, U.S. Dist. Ct. (we. dist.) La. 1982, U.S. Ct. Appeals (5th cir.) 1983, U.S. Dist. Ct. (mid. dist.) La. 1985, U.S. Dist. Ct. (ea. dist.) Tex. 1986, U.S. Dist. Ct. (ea. dist.) La. 1986, U.S. Ct. Appeals (4th cir.) 1992, U.S. Supreme Ct. 1997. Law clk. to presiding justice U.S. Dist. Ct. (we. dist.) La., Lake Charles, 1980-81; assoc., ptnr. Davidson, Meaux, Sonnier, McElligott & Swift, Lafayette, La., 1981—2001; ptnr. Swift & Rhoades L.L.P., 2001—. Mem. Gulf Coast Conservation Assn.; bd. dirs. Hidden Hills Cmty., Inc., 1987-93, pres., 1989-93; bd. dirs. Lafayette Parish unit Am. Cancer Soc., 1992-99, pres., 1996-97, bd. dirs. La. divsn., 1995-96; youth dir., mem. adminstrv. bd. Meth. Ch., 1992-93, chair staff-parish rels. com., 1996, mem. adminstrv. bd., 1996, 98, 99, trustee, 1996-98, chair, 1998. Mem.: ABA, La. Def. Counsel, La. Bar Found. (bd. dirs. 1997—, sec.-treas. 2000—02), Acadiana Inns of Ct., 15th Jud. Dist. Bar Assn. (pres. 1993—94), Lafayette Parish Bar Assn. (bd. dirs. 1988—95, pres. 1993—94), La. Bar Assn. (com. to study permanent disarmament, ho. of dels. 1996—), La. State U. Alumni Fedn., Ducks Unltd., Kiwanis. Republican. Avocations: running, fishing, hunting. Home: 105 Oakwater Dr Lafayette LA 70503-2227 Office: Swift & Rhoades LLP PO Box 53107 Lafayette LA 70505 E-mail: jswift@swiftrhoades.com.

SWIFT, JONATHAN, educator, television host, tenor; b. Glasgow, Scotland, Apr. 26, 1932; came to U.S., 1948, naturalized, 1954; s. John Francis and Catherline Little (McGowan) S. MA, Wayne State U., 1957; postgrad., Ecole Normale Superieure, Paris, 1954-55; studied with Georges Jouatte, 1954-56; cert., Conservatoire Nat. de Musique, France, 1955; postgrad., U. Mich., 1959, Cambridge U., 1981; PhD, Mich. State U., 1983. On-camera tchr. French Sta. WTVS, Detroit, 1955-56, tchr. Am. lit., 1960-62; instr. French Wayne State U., 1955-60; tchr. English, French and social studies Detroit Pub. Schs., 1957-64; tchr. English and history Glasgow Corp. Schs., 1967; tchr. English and French Livonia (Mich.) Pub. Schs., 1967; chmn. English dept. Stevenson H.S., Livonia, 1970-78, dir. Sch. Global Edn., 1978-98; dir. Ctr. Internat. Studies Madonna U., Mich., 1998—. Sr. lectr. Mich. State U. Debut in opera as Alfredo in La Traviata, 1961; host PBS TV and cmty. TV series Global Connections, Time Out for Opera, Dining Out With Jonathan Swift; leading tenor with Detroit Piccolo Opera Co., 1981-86, Detroit Grand Opera Assn., 1965, Mich. Opera Co., 1961-64; concert soloist with major symphonies in U.S., Can., Europe, Australia, 1961-81; appeared as tenor soloist in various radio and TV programs, 1961-81; rec. artist with Scotia and Andis, U.K.; contbr. articles and poems to profl. and lit. jours. Recipient French Govt medal, 1954, tribute Mich. State Legislature, 1984, NEA Applegate-Dorros award, 1987, MEA Siddall Internat. award, 1987, Philo Farnsworth award Alliance Cmty. Media, 1990, 94, 95, 98, 99, 2000, 2002, Hometown award Nat. Fedn. Local Cable Programmers, 1994, 99, 2001, Nat. TV award Nat. Assn. Telecomm. Officers and Advs., 1995, Human Rels. award, Livonia, 1999, Multi-Cultural award, Birmingham, Mich., 2000; Fulbright scholar, 1954-55; named to Hall of Fame, Mich. Model UN, 1999. Mem.: Chevalier de la Confrerie de la Chaine des Rotisseurs, Descs. Knights of Garter, Soc. Friends of St. George. Roman Catholic. also: 4200 Telegraph Rd # 489 Bloomfield Hills MI 48302-2038 E-mail: jswift@madonna.edu., jonswift@earthlink.net.

SWIFT, PAUL, editor; b. Spokane, Wash., June 29, 1942; s. Paul Lawrence and Kathleen (O'Reilly) S.; m. Mary McCall Nettles, May 18, 1976; children: Zachary Benner, Nicole Elizabeth. BA, Gonzaga U., 1968; MA, Boston Coll., 1973. Program officer, editor John D. Rockefeller 3rd, N.Y.C., 1970-72; ind. writer various orgns., 1973-80; assoc. dir. Bard Coll. Ctr., Annandale-on-Hudson, N.Y., 1978-82; editor Pub. Rel. Quar., Rhinebeck, 1982-98. Editor: Edward Bernays' The Later Years, 1987, Publishing Newsletters, 1992, 98, Justus von Lengerke, 1996, Restaurant Newsletters that Pay Off, 1997; editor Newsletter on Newsletters, N.Y., 1982-2001, publ., editor, 2001— (APEX grand award for publication excellence 2000); contbg. editor Pub. Rels. Strategist, 1999—. Recipient APEX Grand award Excellence Pub., 2000, Comm. Concepts, Inc. Mem. Chamber Music Soc. (bd. dirs. 1984-85), Dollars For Scholars (bd. dirs. 1986-90), Newsletter and Elec. Pubs. Assn. Roman Catholic. Home: 20 W Chestnut St Rhinebeck NY 12572-1314 Office: Newsletter on Newsletters 20 W Chestnut St Rhinebeck NY 12572-1314 E-mail: pswift123@aol.com.

SWIFT, RICHARD G(ENE), composer, educator; b. Middlepoint, Ohio, Sept. 24, 1927; s. Lisle Russell and Josephine (Ladd) S.; m. Dorothy Zackrisson, Feb. 10, 1951; children: Jeremy, John, Joel. MA, U. Chgo., 1956. Assoc. prof. music U. Calif., Davis, 1956-67, prof., 1967-91, prof. emeritus, 1991—, chmn. dept., 1963-71. Vis. prof. Princeton U., 1977; faculty research lectr. U. Calif., 1983-84. Composer: A Coronal, 1954, String Quartet I, 1956, II, 1958, III, 1964, Sonata for Clarinet and Piano, 1957, Sonata for Solo Violin, 1958, Eve, 1959, Stravaganza III for Clarinet, Violin and Piano, 1960, Concerto for Piano and Chamber Ensemble, 1961, Extravaganza for Orchestra, 1962, Domains, I, II, III, 1963, Bucolics, 1964, Concerto for Violin and Chamber Ensemble, 1967, Music for A While, 1969, Thanatopsis, 1971, Prime, 1973, Quartet IV, 1973, Specimen Days, 1976, Mein blaues Klavier, 1979, Concerto II for piano and chamber ensemble, 1980, Quartet V, 1982, Things of August, 1985, Roses Only, 1991, In Arcadia, 1994, Stravaganza XI, 1995, Getting Back In, 1997, Stravaganza XII, 1998, Stravaganza XIII, 1999, Stravaganza XIV, 2001, Stanzas, 2001; cons. editor 19th Century Music. Served with AUS, 1950-52. Recipient award Rockefeller Found., 1956, 68; award Fromm Found.; Composers String Quartet award, 1973; award Nat. Endowment for Arts, 1976; Inst. award Am. Acad. and Inst. Arts and Letters, 1978; Disting. Teaching award U. Calif., 1980 Fellow Inst. Creative Arts; mem. Am. Music Ctr., ASCAP, Am. Musicological Soc., Soc. for Music Theory, The Soc. of Composers. Home: 568 S Campus Way Davis CA 95616-3523

SWIFT, ROBERT FREDERIC, music educator; b. Ilion, N.Y., July 7, 1940; s. Frederic Fay and Ruth Eleanor (Ainslie) S.; m. Margot Sue Werme, Nov. 24, 1962; children: Jeffrey Robert, Jennifer Sue. BS, Hartwick Coll., 1962, MA, 1968; PhD, Eastman Sch. Music, Rochester, N.Y., 1970. Music instr. West Winfield (N.Y.) Cen. Sch., 1962-67, N.Y. State Music Camp, Oneonta, 1962—, Brighton High Sch., Rochester, 1970-71; asst. prof. music Eastman Sch. Music, 1971-76; assoc. prof. music Memphis State U., 1976-79; prof. music, dept. chmn. Plymouth State Coll. of U. N.H., Plymouth, 1979—. Choral conductor USA, United Kingdom, Australia, New Zealand, South America, Can. Author: Music from the Mountains: The New York State Music Camp, 1947-96; compuser numerous musical compositions. Ch. musician Christian Sci., Presbyn., Bapt. chs. NDEATitle IV fellow U. Rochester, 1967-70; recipient Disting. Tchg. award Memphis State U., 1979, Disting. Tchg. award Coll. for Lifelong Learning of U. System of N.H., 1987, Disting. Tchg. award Plymouth State U., 1998. Mem. N.H. Music Edn. Assn. (Music Educator of Yr. award 1998), Music Educators Nat. Conf., Am. Choral Dirs. Assn., Coll. Music Soc., Royal Sch. Ch. Music., Phi Mu Alpha Sinfonia, Kappa Delta Pi. Republican. Mem. Christian Science Ch. Home: PO Box 125 Plymouth NH 03264-0125 Office: Plymouth State Coll Dept Music And Theatre Plymouth NH 03264 E-mail: rswift@mail.plymouth.edu.

SWIFT, STEPHEN CHRISTOPHER, lawyer; b. N.Y.C., Jan. 7, 1954; s. James Stephen and Rhoda Emma Jean (Howd) S. AA, Lansing C.C., 1980; BA, Mich. State U., 1983; JD, Wayne State U., 1988. Bar: Mich. 1988, Hawaii 1989, D.C. 1991, Va. 1995, Md. 1998, U.S. Dist. Ct. D.C. 1997, U.S. Dist. Ct. Md. 1998, U.S. Dist. Ct. (ea. and we. dists.) Va. 1995, U.S. Dist. Ct. Hawaii 1989, U.S. Dist. Ct. (ea. dist.) Mich. 2002, U.S. Ct. Fed. Claims 1990, U.S. Ct. Internat. Trade 2000, U.S. Bankruptcy Ct. (ea. and we. dists.) Va. 1995, U.S. Tax Ct. 1997, U.S. Ct. Appeals (fed., D.C., 9th cirs.) 1990, U.S. Ct. Appeals (4th cir.) 1995, U.S. Supreme Ct. 1992; registered patent atty. 1994. Pvt. practice, Honolulu, Hawaii, 1989-94, Arlington, Va., 1995—. Mem. ABA, Fed. Bar Assn., Fed. Cir. Bar Assn., Am. Intellectual Property Law Assn. Office: Swift Law Office 2231 Crystal Dr Ste 500 Arlington VA 22202-3736 Fax: 703-418-1895. E-mail: steve@swift-law.com.

SWIFT, STEPHEN JENSEN, federal judge; b. Salt Lake City, Sept. 7, 1943; s. Edward A. and Maurine (Jensen) S.; m. Lorraine Burnell Facer, Aug. 4, 1972; children: Carter, Stephanie, Spencer, Meredith, Hunter. BS, Brigham Young U., 1967; JD, George Washington U., 1970. Trial atty. U.S. Dept. Justice, Washington, 1970-74; asst. U.S. atty. U.S. Atty.'s Office, San Francisco, 1974-77; v.p., sr. tax counsel Bank Am. N.T. & S.A., 1977-83; judge U.S. Tax Ct., Washington, 1983—. Adj. prof. Golden Gate U., San Francisco, 1976-83, U. Balt., 1987—. Mem. ABA, Calif. Bar Assn., D.C. Bar Assn. Office: US Tax Ct 400 2nd St NW Washington DC 20217-0002

SWIGART, JOAN B. artist, art consultant; b. Peoria, Ill., Jan. 30, 1930; d. Claude S. and Elvera V. (Seeber) Bradley; m. Lynn S. Swigart, Mar. 30, 1952; children: Christopher, Paul Tag, Ann, Leigh. Student, Bradley U., 1948-50, 79-81, Ill. State U., Normal, 1981-84. Dir. multimedia arts inst. Bradley U., Peoria, 1973, 74, program dir. Econs. Fair, 1976, 77; artist-in-residence for several Ill. sch. dists. Ill. Arts Coun., Chgo., 1983, 84, 85. Vice pres. bd. dirs., chair cultural outreach Peoria Arts and Sci. Coun., 1986—88; chair pub. art com. Peoria City Beautiful Commn., 1986—88; bd. dirs. Peoria Art Guild, 1969—88; chaiir resident artist coun. Westport (Conn.) Art Ctr., 1990—92; bd. dirs. Gloucester (Mass.) Cultural Coun., chmn., 2002—. Exhibited in numerous solo, 2-person and group exhbns., 1980—. Dir. Sch. of Art, Peoria Art Guild, 1972-76; bd. dirs. Peoria Arts Festival, 1987-88, Urban League, Peoria, 1970-76, Planned Parenthood, Peoria, 1981-86; mem. edn. com. Lakeview Mus., 1985-88. Grantee Ill. Arts Coun., 1983, 84, 85. Democrat. Home: 13 Marble Rd Gloucester MA 01930-4324 Office: Swigart Studios 119 Main St Gloucester MA 01930-4324

SWIGER, L. A. agricultural studies educator, educator; BS in Animal Husbandry, Ohio State U., 1954; MS, Iowa State U., 1957, PhD, 1960. Geneticist USDA, Lincoln, Neb., assoc. prof. animal sci., experiment sta. statistician Nebr., 1959—65; grad. chmn. Ohio State U.; prof. animal sci. Va. Tech, Blacksburg, 1965—80, head dept. animal sci., 1980-86, assoc. dean rsch. Coll. Agrl. and Life Scis., 1986-92, interim dean, 1992-93, dean, 1993—. Recipient Rockefeller Prentice Meml. award Am. Soc. Animal Sci., 1984. Office: Va Tech Coll Agrl and Life Sci Blacksburg VA 24061-0402 E-mail: swiger@vt.edu.

SWIGERT, JAMES MACK, lawyer; b. Carthage, Ill., Sept. 25, 1907; s. James Ross and Pearl (Mack) S.; m. Alice Francis Titcomb Harrower, July 7, 1931 (dec. 1990); children: Oliver, David Ladd, Sally Harper (Mrs. Hamilton). Student, Grinnell Coll., 1925-27; SB, Harvard U., 1930, LLB, 1935. Bar: Ill. 1935, Ohio 1937. With Campbell, Clithero & Fischer, Chgo., 1935-36, Taft, Stettinius & Hollister, Cin., 1936—, ptnr., 1948-79, sr. ptnr. and chmn. exec. com., 1979-85, of counsel, 1985—. Dir., mem. exec. com. Union Cen. Life Ins. Co., 1963-79; dir., chmn. audit com. Philips Industries, 1975-82. Author articles on labor rels. and labor law. Bd. dirs. Cin. Symphony Orch., 1976-78; trustee, chmn. exec. com. Am. Music Scholarship Assn., 1987-92. Mem.: Queen City (past dir.), Cincinnati Country (past v.p., dir.), Queen City Optimists (past pres.), Tennis (past pres.), Recess (past pres.), Harvard Law (past pres.) (Cin.). Republican. Presbyterian. Home: 2121 Alpine Pl Cincinnati OH 45206-2690 Office: 1800 Star Bank Ctr Cincinnati OH 45202 E-mail: swigert@taftlaw.com.

SWIGGART, CAROLYN CLAY, lawyer; b. Bloomington, Ill., Sept. 19, 1958; AB, Wellesley Coll., 1980; JD, U. Conn., 1983. Bar: Mass. 1983, Conn. 1985, U.S. Dist. Ct. Mass. 1985, U.S. Dist. Ct. Conn. 1986, U.S. Supreme Ct. 1989. Sole practice; of counsel Pierson Law Firm, Darien, Conn. Author: Shades of Gray: The Clay and McAllister Families of Bryan County, Georgia during the Plantation Years. Dist. rep. Representative Town Meeting, Darien, Conn., 1990-94. Mem. ABA, Conn. Bar Assn. (co-chmn. Basic Practice Manual 1991-94, editor Basic Practice Manual 1986-91, exec. com. family law sect. 2001-), Stamford Regional Bar Assn., Indian Harbor Yacht Club. Avocation: sailing. Office: Pierson Law Firm 777 Post Rd Darien CT 06820 Address: PO Box 941 Darien CT 06820-0941

SWIGGER, KATHLEEN MARY, computer science educator; b. South Bend, Ind., July 2, 1947; d. Harry Francis and Helen Francis (Kranitz) Gallagher; divorced; Jessica, Nathaniel. BA, U. Iowa, 1969, MA, 1972, PhD, 1977. Dir. acad. computing East Tex. State U., Commerce, 1977-78, asst. prof., 1978-80; asst. prof. computer sci. U. North Tex., Denton, 1980-84, assoc. prof., 1985-91, prof., 1991—. Cons. Ernst & Young, Denton, 1990—, UCLA, 1990—, Hughes Air Craft, Arlington, Tex., 1990—, Trinsic Corp., 1993. Editor: IEEE Computer; contbr. articles to sci. jours., chpts. to books. Grantee TWA, 1986, USAF Office Sci. Rsch., 1986-87, E-Systems, 1986-87, Ernst & Young Found., 1988-90, 92-93, NSF, 1991-94, 2000—, Tex. Instruments, 1993, Fund for Improvement in Post Secondary Edn., 1996, NSF, 1999—. Mem. Assn. for Artificial Intelligence (sec. North Tex. chpt. 1987-89), Assn. for Computing Machinery, Human Factors Soc., IEEE Computer Soc. (bd. govs. 2000—). Democrat. Avocations: antiques, jogging, music. Office: U North Tex PO Box 13886 Denton TX 76203-6886 E-mail: kathy@cs.unt.edu.

SWIGGER, KEITH, dean; b. Hutchinson, Kans., Feb. 3, 1943; s. Paul Clarke and Loneta (Miller) S.; children: Jessica, Nathaniel; m. Cindy Johnson Potter, Nov. 29, 1997. BA, U. Chgo., 1965, MA, 1975, Ind. U., 1967; PhD, U. Iowa, 1973. Sketchwriter Marquis Who's Who, Chgo., 1963-67; teaching asst. Ind. U., Bloomington, 1967, U. Iowa, Iowa City, 1968-73, lectr., 1973-74, libr., 1976-77; asst. prof. East Tex. State U., Commerce, 1977-81; asst. prof. libr. scis. Tex. Woman's U., Denton, 1981-85, assoc. prof., 1985-89, prof., 1989—, interim dean Sch. Libr. Sci., 1991-92, dean Sch. Libr. and Info. Studies, 1992-2000, dir. Ctr. for Consulting and Planning, 1997—, dean Coll. Profl. Edn., 2000—. Co-editor Jour. of Youth Svcs., 1997-2000; contbr. numerous articles to profl. jours. Bd. dirs. ACLU, Denton, 1990-92, Emily Fowler Pub. Libr., Denton, 1995-97, vice chair, 1997; mem. Tex. Edn. Tech. Coord. Coun., 2000-. Rsch. grantee OCLC, Inc., 1990-91, Career Tng. grantee U.S. Office Edn., 1990-98; postdoctoral fellow Coun. on Libr. Resources U. Chgo., 1974-75; recipient Svc. award Nat. Storytelling Assn., 1998. Mem. ALA, Tex. Libr. Assn., Libr. and Info. Tech. Assn., Tex. Faculty Assn., Assn. Libr. Info. Sci. Edn. Office: Tex Womans Univ Coll Profl Edn PO Box 425769 Denton TX 76204-5769 E-mail: kswigger@twu.edu.

SWIGGETT, HAROLD E. (HAL SWIGGETT), writer, photographer; b. Moline, Kans., July 22, 1921; s. Otho Benjamin and Mildred (Spray) S.; m. Wilma Caroline Turner, Mar. 1, 1942; children: Gerald, Vernon. Grad. h.s. Ordained minister So. Bapt. Ch. Staff photographer San Antonio Express-News, 1947-67, head dept., 1955-67; free-lance writer/photographer San Antonio, 1947—; full-time, 1967—. Contbg. author books on game gunting, gun-oriented paperbacks; author: Hal Swiggett on North American Deer, 1980; sr. editor Harris Publs., Guns/Hunting; editor: Handguns 95; contbg. editor N.Am. Hunter. Minister So. Bapt. Ch. With USAAC, World War II. Recipient 10th ann. Outstanding Am. Handgunner award, 1982, Lifetime Cicero award, 1991, St. Gabriel Possenti medal, 1991; named to Am. Handgunner Hall of Fame, 1987, Anschutz/PSI Gun Writer of Yr., 1990, Handgun Hunter Hall of Fame, 1991. Mem. NRA (life), Wildlife Unltd. (pres. chpt. 1955-58), Outdoor Writers Assn. Am. (dir. 1969-72), Tex. Outdoor Writers Assn. (pres. 1967-68), Ducks Unltd., Tex. Rifle Assn. (life), Internat. Handgun Metallic Silhouette Assn. (life), Game Conservation Internat. Home: 539 Roslyn San Antonio TX 78204-2456

SWIHART, H. GREGG, real estate company executive; b. San Francisco, Sept. 25, 1938; s. Lawson Benjamin and Violet Mary (Watters) S.; m. Ilse Paula Rambacher, Dec. 24, 1958; children: Tatjana Etta, Brett Marc, Natascha Theda. BA, U. Ariz., 1958; postgrad., Heidelberg (Germany) U., 1961-65, Harvard U., 1959-60; MA, Boston U., 1961; postgrad., Freiburg (Germany) U., 1961-65. Cert. property mgr. Stockbroker Walston & Co., Tucson, 1966-71; with Solot Co., 1971-74; pres. Cienega Properties, Inc., property mgmt. and investment, 1975-77, GT Realty Assocs., Ltd., Tucson, 1977—. Me.m Tucson Com. Fgn. Rels., 1973—; pres. Forum for Greater Outdoors, 1977-79; bd. dirs. Tucson Mus. Art, 1968-74, pres., 1969-70; pres. and trustee, Canelo Hills Sch., 1977-79. Mem. Tucson Bd. Realtors, Inst. Real Estate Mgmt. (pres. Tucson-So. Ariz. chpt. 1982, mem. nat. governing coun. 1985-87), Inst. Real Estate Mgmt. (governing coun. 1985-87, Property Mgr. of Yr. award So. Ariz. chpt. 1988), Realtors Nat. Mktg. Inst., Harvard Club (pres. 1973-74), Active 20-30 Club (pres. 1969-70), Downtown Tucson Club. Home: Tunnel Springs Ranch PO Box 555 Sonoita AZ 85637-0555 Office: 5643 E Broadway Blvd Tucson AZ 85711

SWIHART, STEVEN TAYLOR, judge; b. Alexandria, Va., Sept. 7, 1942; s. Albert Taylor and Marian Dorothy (Lille) S.; 1 child, Sarah Ann Swihart. BA, Univ. Nebr., 1966, JD, 1972. Bar: Nebr. 1972. Staff atty. Panhandle Legal Svcs., Scottsbluff, Nebr., 1972-73, Lincoln (Nebr.) Legal Aid Soc., 1974; atty., advisor Health/Human Svcs., Social Security Adminstrn. Office Hearing Appeals, Omaha, 1975-77; ptnr. Christian, Krieg & Swihart, 1978-88; adminstrv. law judge SSA, Office Hearing Appeals, Denver, 1989—. 1st lt. U.S. Army, 1966-69, Vietnam. Mem. Nebr. State Bar Assn. Democrat. Avocations: music, reading, chess. Office: Office Hearings Appeals 1244 Speer Blvd Denver CO 80204-3518 E-mail: sswi185037@aol.com.

SWILDENS, KARIN JOHANNA, sculptor; b. Amsterdam, The Netherlands, June 22, 1942; arrived in U.S., 1979; d. Petrus Bernardus Swildens and Ceclia Thecla Maria Vernimmen; m. Gilles Roger Basset, Mar. 25, 1963 (div. Jan. 1968); children: Eric Gilles Basset, Laurent Patrice Basset; m. Claude Maurice Gaignaire, June 28, 1972; 1 child Gazelle Gaignaire. Diploma in art, L'Ecole des Arts Decoratifs, Paris, 1963. Exhibitions include Artscape, Long Beach, Calif., Speak Easy Gallery, L.A., Art Home, Sag Habor, N.Y., Waldo Collection, West Hollywood, Calif., Trios Gallery, Solana Beach, Calif., Tops, Malibu, Calif., Hamilton Gallery, Santa Monica, Calif., Bric a Brac Gallery, Haarlem, The Netherlands, Glass Garage Gallery, West Hollywood, Calif. Vol. instr. Brentwood Unified Sci. Magnet Sch., 1979—82. Recipient Daumier Sculpture award, 1993. Home and Office: 1872 Midvale Ave Apt 303 Los Angeles CA 90025-6349

SWILLER, RANDOLPH JACOB, internist; b. N.Y.C., Jan. 21, 1946; s. Abraham Irving and Helen (Emmer) S.; m. Florence Tena Davis, Sept. 3, 1967; children: Jeremy Adam, Rebecca Susan, Steven Eric. BA in Biology cum laude, Hofstra U., 1968; MD, Chgo. Med. Sch., 1972. Diplomate Am. Bd. Psychiatry and Neurology, Am. Bd. Med. Examiners. Intern Long Island Jewish-Hillside Med. Ctr., New Hyde Park, N.Y., 1972-73; psychiatric resident SUNY Downstate Med. Ctr., Bklyn., 1973-76; asst. attending psychiatrist Maimonides Med. Ctr., 1976-78; medical resident, mem. med. ethics com. Jewish Hosp. Med. Ctr. of Bklyn., 1978-80; fellow in hematology North Shore U. Hosp., Manhasset, N.Y., 1980-81; attending physician in internal medicine Fla. Med. Ctr., Lauderdale Lakes, 1982—, mem. med. utilization rev. com., 1986—, mem. credentials and qualifications com., 1990—; attending physician in internal medicine Coral Springs (Fla.) Med. Ctr., 1987—, mem. med. utilization rev. com., 1987-89; asst. attending physician in internal medicine North Ridge Med. Ctr., Ft. Lauderdale, Fla., 1997—. Mem. ACP, AMA, Am. Soc. Internal Medicine, Fla. Med. Assn., Broward County Med. Assn., Am. Psychiat. Assn., Fla. Psychiat. Soc. Democrat. Jewish. Achievements include research in disseminated intravascular coagulation in obstetrical practice, angioimmunoblatic lymphadenopathy syndrome. Avocation: piano. Office: 1881 N University Dr Ste 200 Coral Springs FL 33071-6094

SWINBURN, CHARLES, lawyer; b. Bowness on Windermere, Cumbria, Eng., Apr. 11, 1942; came to U.S., 1949; s. Joseph and Myra (Sullivan) S.; m. Carol Ann Ditzler, Dec. 16, 1972; children: Ann Elizabeth, Catherine Knowles. BA in Psychology, Princeton U., 1963; MBA, Harvard U., 1971; JD, U. Pa., 1993. Industry analyst U.S. Dept. Transp., Washington, 1971-73, chief Industry Analysis Div., 1973-76, dep. asst. sec., 1979-83; assoc. adminstr. fed. assistance Fed. R.R. Adminstrn., 1976-79; v.p. FS Rollins Environ. Svcs. Inc., Wilmington, Del., 1983-90; atty. Morgan, Lewis & Bockius, Washington, 1993—. Mem., bd. dirs. RailAmerica, Inc. Capt. USMC, 1963-69; major USMCR, 1970-75. Decorated DFC (2), Air medal (35); recipient Presdl. Disting. Exec. award, 1980, Dept. Transp. Meritorious Achievement award, 1976, 78, 81 Home: 1713 Maple Hill Pl Alexandria VA 22302-3927 E-mail: chaarles@aol.com.

SWINDELL, ARCHIE CALHOUN, JR. research biochemist, statistician; b. Sept. 26, 1936; s. Archie Calhoun and Louise Evelyn (Ellis) S.; m. Dolores Dyer Holland, Dec. 28, 1962; children: Randy Zidick, Matthew Earle. BS in Chemistry, So. Meth. U., 1958; M in Nutritional Sci., Cornell U., 1965, PhD in Biochemistry, 1968. NIH postdoctoral fellow Duke U. Med. Ctr., Durham, N.C., 1968-70; rsch. sci. positions in biochemistry, pharmacology, statis. Pfizer, Inc., Groton, Conn., 1970-95; statis. cons., 1995—. Contbr. articles on cholesterol metabolism, hormone action, cell culture, actions of drugs, data analysis, stats. to profl. jours., 1968-2001; patentee several anti-atherosclerosis agts. Mem. Town Coun., Groton, 1991-95, Bd. of Edn., 1997—. With U.S. Army, 1958-61. Mem. AAAS, Am. Statis. Assn., Am. Heart Assn., Am. Assn. Artificial Intelligence, Sigma Xi. Avocations: astronomy, nataure photography. Home and Office: 192 Monument St Groton CT 06340-3915 E-mail: swindell.ct@snet.net.

SWINDLE, MARVIN MICHAEL, veterinarian, researcher, consultant; b. Dallas, Aug. 19, 1946; s. Marvin Mayo and Dolorose Claire Swindle; m. Paula Ann Swindle, Mar. 18, 1972; children: Katelyn, Ashley. BS, Tex. A&M U., 1968, DVM, 1969. Diplomate Am. Coll. Lab. Animal Medicine. Owner Aberdeen (Md.) Vet. Clinic, 1972-79; lab. animal vet. Med. Sch. Johns Hopkins U., Balt., 1979-85; prof., chmn. dept. comparative medicine Med. U. S.C., Charleston, 1985—. Contbr. chpts. to books, articles to profl. jours. Mem. leadership coun. Am. Heart Assn., bd. dirs. 1987-00. Capt. U.S. Army, 1969-72, Vietnam. Recipient Smith award for rsch. Am. Heart Assn., 1996. Fellow: Acad. Surg. Rsch. (pres. 1988—89, 1991—93, Von Recum award 1996); mem.: ECLAM (diplomate), AVMA, ACLAM (diplomate), Am. Soc. Lab. Animal Practitioners (bd. dirs. 2000—), Am. Assn. Lab. Animal Sci. (bd. trustees 1990—94), KC, Rotary Internat. Republican. Roman Catholic. Avocation: certified wine judge. Office: Med U SC PO Box 250777 114 Doughty St Rm 648 Charleston SC 29425

SWING, MARCE, producer, publisher; b. Wichita, Kans., Dec. 3, 1943; d. Eldon Derry and Ruth (Biddle) S. Bus. mgr. Old Westport Med. Assn., Kansas City, Mo., 1972-73; dept. chmn., instr. Ft. Bragg (N.C.) Nursery and Kindergarten, 1965-66, Luth. Schs., Tex. Dist., Irving, 1966-68, Kansas City (Kans.) Sch. Dist. 500, 1973-78, Extension Dept. U. Calif., Northridge, 1979-82, Pima Coll., Tucson, 1983-84, Kinder Care, Lake Buena Vista, Fla., 1989-90; TV/motion picture exec. producer, dir., writer Swing Prodns., Orlando, 1989—; owner, pres. Swing Enterprises/Swing Prodns., 1978—, Living for Edn., Inc., Orlando, 1994—; owner Edn. in the New Millennium, Inc., 2002; founder, pres. Digital Media Arts Incubator Lab, Inst. Ind. Filmmakers, Orlando, Fla.; projects prodr. read24-7.com. Exec. mgmt., acctg. andmktg. cons. to major internat. corps.; lectr., seminar instr., guest speaker, anchorperson, moderator, panelist. Exec. producer, dir., writer, featured talent on-air live and taped programming for networks, network affiliates and cable, feature motion pictures, on air internationally and web sites, interactive TV episodes, with msde, 34 children's books and CD ROMS, puppets and collectables, V series, mini series, 30 celebrity profiles, 36 documentaries, 14 televents, 45 pub. svc. spots, 30 minute infomat, 12-hour entertinment Christmas Eve project; developer entertainment informational, ednl. and indsl. TV programs and videos; contbr. articles to profl. jours. Corp. adminstr., TV exec. producer, dir., fundraiser nat. hdqrs. March of Dimes, White Plains, N.Y., 1984-86, Arthritis Found., Atlanta, 1985; ofcl. hostess Seattle World's Fair; mem. Nat. Task Force for Child Care, Nat. Task Force for Youth Suicide, Nat. Task Force for Child Abuse; mem. Ariz. Commn. on Arts. Recipient local, regional and nat. art and craft awards. Mem. NEA, NAFE, AAUW, Am. Mgmt. Assn., Nat. Assn. Women Artists, Profl. Assn. Producers and Dirs., Nat. Printmaker's Assn., Nat. Thespian Soc., Thousand Oaks Art Assn., Internat. Digital Media Arts Alliance (founding mem.), Orange County, Fla. Govt. Arts and Cultural Affairs, Coun. Art Edn. and Resources, Show of Hands Gallery, Nat. Youth Camps. Lutheran. Avocations: reading, writing, photography, cooking, mural painting.

SWING, WILLIAM LACY, ambassador; b. Lexington, N.C., Sept. 11, 1934; s. Baxter Dermot and Mary Frances (Barbee) S.; m. Yuen Fong Cheong; children: Brian Curtis, Gabrielle. AB, Catawba Coll., 1956, LLD (hon.), 1980; BD, Yale U., 1960; postgrad., Oxford (Eng.) U., U. Tuebingen, Germany, 1961, Hofstra U., LLD (hon.), 1994. Vice consul Am. Consulate, Port Elizabeth, Republic of South Africa, 1963-66; internat. economist Bur. Econ. Affairs Dept. State, 1966-68; consul, chief consular sect. Am. Consulate Gen., Hamburg, Germany, 1968-72; internat. rels. officer, desk officer Fed. Republic Germany Dept. State, Washington, 1972-74; dep. chief of mission, counselor Am. Embassy, Bangui, Ctrl. African Republic, 1974-76; fellow Ctr. for Internat. Affairs Harvard U., 1977-79; amb. to People's Republic of Congo, 1979-81; amb. to Republic of Liberia Monrovia, 1981-85; amb. to South Africa, 1989-92; amb. to Fed. Republic of Nigeria, 1992-93; amb. to Haiti, 1993-98; amb. to Dem. Republic of the Congo (formerly Zaire), Am. Embassy, Kinshasha, 1998—2001; spl. rep. of UN Sec.-Gen. for Western Sahara, 2001—. Dir. Fgn. Svc. Career Devel. and Assignments, 1985-87; sr. dep. asst. sec. state for pers., 1987-89. Co-editor: Education for Decision, 1963, U.S. African Policy and the Case of South Africe: Dilemas and Priorities, 1977, Haiti: In Physical Contact with History, 1995. Recipient Meritorious Honor award USIA, 1971, Superior Honor award Dept. State, 1985, Presdl. Disting. Svc. award, 1985, Presdl. Meritorious Svc. award, 1987, 90, 94, Equal Employment Opportunity award Dept. State, 1988, Disting. Honor award, 1994, Valor award, 1995, Disting. Svc. award, 1996, Disting. Pub. Svc. award USCG, 1998, U.S. Presdl. Cert. of Commendation, 1998. Mem. Army and Navy Club. Yale Club (Washington and N.Y.C.), Harvard Club, Internat. Club, Lions. Mem. United Ch. of Christ. Office: MINURSO-HQ Laayoune PO Box 5846 Grand Central Sta New York NY 10163-5846 Home: 6002 Paradise Point Dr Miami FL 33157 E-mail: Swing@UN.Org.

SWINNEY, CAROL JOYCE, secondary education educator; Langs. tchr. Hugoton (Kans.) High Sch., 1972-98; dir. distance learning S.W. Plains Regional Svcs. Ctr., Kans., 1998—. Named Kans. Tchr. of Yr., Disney for Lang. Tchr. of Yr., 1993, Milken Nat. Educator, 1992. Office: PO Drawer 1010 Sublette KS 67877-1010

SWINNEY, HARRY LEONARD, physics educator; b. Opelousas, La., Apr. 10, 1939; s. Leonard Robert and Ethel Ruth (Bertheaud) S.; m. Gloria Luyas, Oct. 21, 1967 (dec. Oct. 1997); 1 child, Brent Luyas (dec.); m. Lizabeth Kelley, Aug. 12, 2000. BS in Physics, Rhodes Coll., 1961; PhD in Physics, Johns Hopkins U., 1968. Vis. asst. prof. Johns Hopkins U., 1970-71; asst. prof. physics NYU, 1971-73; assoc. prof. CCNY, 1973-77, prof., 1978; prof. physics U. Tex., Austin, 1978—, Trull Centennial prof., 1984-90, Sid Richardson Found. regents chair, 1990—, dir. Ctr. Nonlinear Dynamics, 1985—. Morris Loeb lectr. Harvard U., 1982. Editor: Hydrodynamic Instabilities and the Transition to Turbulence, 1985; contbr. articles to profl. jours. Regents chair Sid Richardson Found., 1990—. Grantee NSF, Dept. Energy, NASA, Office Naval Rsch., Welch, others; Guggenheim fellow, 1982-83. Fellow AAAS, Am. Phys. Soc. (exec. bd. 1992-94, Fluid Dynamics prize 1996); mem. NAS, Am. Acad. Arts and Scis., Am. Assn. Physics Tchrs. Democrat. Methodist. Office: U Tex Dept Physics Ctr Nonlinear Dynamics Austin TX 78712 E-mail: Swinney@physics.utexas.edu.

SWINSON, BETTY WHITE, composer; b. New Castle, Ind., Aug. 20, 1934; d. Odie Paul and Ella Mildred (Dragon) White; m. Owen Isaac Swinson, Sept. 21, 1963; children: Jo Ann Swinson King, Lea Etta Swinson Walker. Grad. high sch., Mt. Summit, Ind. Author: (song book) A Song to Sing-A Story to Tell, vol. 1, 1983, vol. 2, 1988, vol. 3, 1996. Mem. Broadcast Music Inc., Traditional Country Gospel Music Assn. Avocations: traveling, crocheting, bird watching. E-mail: musicman@hrtc.net.

SWINTON, JOHN RALPH, retired language educator, writer; b. Plainfield, N.J., June 5, 1939; s. John Swinton and Helen Ada Robbins; m. Cordelia Westervelt, June 29, 1963; children: John Robbins, Rebecca Welser, Margaret Jennings. BA in English, Ursinus Coll., 1962; MA in English, Pa. State U., 1970. Freelance folk singer, 1959—62; tech. writer Gannett Fleming Engrs., Harrisburg, Pa., 1963—65; mem. faculty Pa. State U., University Park, 1968—96. Author: Bufflehead & Other Poems, 2000; editor: Blindness Research, 1969, Educating for Careers, 1976. Founder, pres. State College Meals on Wheels, Pa., 1971. Mem.: Outdoors Writers Assn. Am., Pa. Outdoors Writers Assn. (parliamentarian). Avocations: fishing, birdwatching, camping, swimming. Home and Office: 915 W Beaver Ave State College PA 16801

SWINTON, SONYA DEVONNE, government agency administrator; b. Muskogee, Okla., Dec. 3, 1957; d. Billy Clarence Swinton and Edna Lonetta Atkinson (Eggleston) Swinton. BS, U. Ark., 1980; MEd, Pa State U., 1982. Mgmt. divsn. Corp. For Cmty. and Nat. Svc., Washington, 1994—; cable tv coord. Cablevision, Inc.- Govt. Channel, New Carrollton, Md., 1987—94; edn. adminstr. USMC, Quanitico, Japan, 1982—86. Dir. Children's Cable TV Workshop-Entertainment Divsn., New Carrollton, 1987—90; exec. dir. Cmty. TV USA Network, Washington, DC, 1990—; v.p. advt. & mktg. Swinton Internat. Enterprises, Washington, 2000—. Author: (book) STAR POWER: Internet Celebrity, 2002, ROYAL DESTINY: USA, 2003. Chief executor Royal Swinton Soc., Washington, 2002. Sgt. USMC, 1982—86, Okinawa,Japan and Quanitco, VA. Named disting. alumna award, Nat. Assn. for Equal Opportunity in Higher Edn., 1998; recipient Cmty. Svc. Award, Taste of DC Festival Commn., 2001. Mem.: Soc. of Motion Picture & TV Engineers, Royal TV Soc. of N.Am., Nat. Acad. of TV Arts & Sciences (awards com. 1998), Am. Women In Radio TV (photographer 1998), Nat. Acad. of Rec. Arts & Sciences (assoc.; musicare bd. 1999), Royal Photographic Soc. of Gt. Britain. Baptist. Avocation: photography, sports and writing. Office: Community TV USA Network L'EnFant Plaza PO 23722 Suite 400 Washington DC 20026 Business E-Mail: SonyaS@ctvnusa.com.

SWIONTKOWSKI, MARC FRANCIS, orthopedist; b. Elizabeth, N.J., Sept. 15, 1951; s. William Robert and Agnes Eileen (Baker) S.; m. Beth Ellen, Sept. 2, 1972. BA, Calif. State U., 1973; MD, U. So. Calif., 1979. Gen. surgeon Univ. Wash., Seattle, 1979-80, orthopaedic residence, 1980-84; orthopedic cons. KIlimanjoro Christian Med. Ctr., Moshi, Tanzania, 1984; research assoc. Lab. for Experiment, Davos, Swit.; asst. prof. Vanderbilt Univ. Surgery, Nashville, 1985-86; assoc prof. Vanderbilt Univ., 1986-88; assoc. prof. Univ. Wash., Seattle, 1988-91, prof., 1991-97; prof., chair dept. orthop. surgery U. Minn., Mpls., 1997—. Fellow Am. Acad. Orthopaedic Surgery, Soc. Internat. Chgo., Chirurgie Orthopaedic Traumatology, Am. Coll. Surgery, Am. Bd. Orthopaedic Surgery (bd. dirs. 1999—). Democrat. Avocations: bicycle riding, carpentry. Office: U Minn Dept Ortho Surgery 420 Delaware St SE # Minneapolis MN 55455-0374

SWIRE, EDITH WYPLER, music educator, musician, violist, violinist; b. Boston, Feb. 16, 1943; d. Alfred R. Wypler Jr. and Frances (Glenn) Emery Wypler; m. James Bennett Swire, June 11, 1965; 1 child, Elizabeth Swire Falker. BA, Wellesley (Mass.) Coll., 1965; MFA, Sarah Lawrence Coll., Bronxville, N.Y., 1983; postgrad., Coll. of New Rochelle, 1984-85. Tchr. instrumental music, viola, violin The Windsor Sch., Boston, 1965-66; tchr., dir. The Lenox Sch., N.Y.C., 1967-76; music curriculum devel. The Nightingale-Bamford Sch., 1968-69; head of fine arts dept. The Lenox Sch., 1976-78, head of instrumental music, 1978-80; founder, dir., tchr. of string sch. Serpentine String Sch., Larchmont, N.Y., 1981—. Mem. founding com. Inter Sch. Orch., N.Y.C., 1972, trustee, 1976—; panelist Nat. Assn. Ind. Sch. Conf., N.Y.C., 1977. Mem. music and worship com., Larchmont Ave. Ch., 1978-82, 88. Mem. Westchester Musicians Guild, N.Y. State Music Tchrs. Assn., Music Tchrs. Nat. Assn., Music Tchrs. Coun. Westchester (program com.), Violin Soc. Am., Wellesley in Westchester, Am. String Tchrs. Assn., The Viola Soc. of N.Y. Avocations: study of Alexander technique, chamber music, encouraging music in schools. Home and Office: 11 Serpentine Trail Larchmont NY 10538-2618

SWIRE, JAMES BENNETT, lawyer; b. Bklyn., July 10, 1942; AB, Princeton U., 1963; LLB, Harvard U., 1966. Bar: N.Y. 1967, D.C. 1976. Assoc. Rogers Hoge & Hills, N.Y.C., 1966-73; ptnr. Townley & Updike, 1982-95, chmn. mgmt. com., 1990-95; ptnr. Dorsey & Whitney, LLP, 1995—, office head, 1998—, mem. mgmt. com., 1999—2001. Guest lectr. food and drug law Seton Hall Law Sch., 1977. Trustee Cancer Care, Inc., 1978—, v.p., 1982-86, chmn. exec. com., 1986-90, pres. 1990-95; chmn. cmty. bd. Beth Israel-St. Luke's Roosevelt Cancer Ctr., N.Y.C., 1999—. Mem. Assn. Bar City N.Y. (chmn. com. medicine and law 1977-80, sec. com. on trademarks and unfair competition 1985-88), N.Y. State Bar Assn., Internat. Trademark Assn. (assoc.). E-mial. Office: 250 Park Ave New York NY 10177-0001 E-mail: swire.james@dorseylaw.com.

SWIRSKY, JUDITH PERLMAN, arts administrator, consultant; b. Bklyn., Oct. 31, 1928; d. Samuel and Rose (Klein) Perlman; m. Leo Jerome Swirsky, June 26, 1949; 1 child, Marjorie Ann Swirsky Zelner. BA, NYU, 1947; postgrad., Columbia U., 1947-48. Rsch. asst. The Bklyn. Mus., 1947-49, vol. coord., 1983-89; exec. dir. Grand Cen. Art Galleries Edn. Assn., N.Y.C., 1988-90; freelance curator Genest Gallery, Lambertville, N.J., 1990; dir. vol. resources Snug Harbor Cultural Ctr., S.I., 1992-95, dir. spl. events, 1994-95. Dir. art sales and rental Gallery The Bklyn. Mus., 1974-77; del. Vol. Com. of Art Mus., Balt., 1973, panelist, 1979; mem., co-founder Vol. Program Adminstrs., N.Y.C., Cultural Inst., 1984—; ind. curator travelling exhbn. Four Objects, Four Artists, Relatively Speaking: Mothers and Daus. in Art, 1994—, Memory and Desire, Paintings and Watercolors by Harriet Shorr, Charles Parness: A Different View of Life and the World. Co-author: On Exhibit, 1993-98. Pres. Community Com. for the Bklyn. Mus., 1969-70; bd. dirs. Greater N.Y. Girl Scouts U.S., 1965-71; founder Children's Sch. Time Program and Women's League, Bklyn. Acad. Music, 1961-64; chmn. Bklyn. Guild for Opera, 1966-77; bd. dirs. Arthritis Found. Greater N.Y., 1969-79; trustee Bklyn. Home for Children, 1961-70, Julia Bernstein League of the Free Nurses Inst., 1952-60. Mem. Am. Assn. Mus., Assn. Vol. Adminstrn. (cert., editor region II newsletter), Am. Assn. Mus. Vols., Civitas. Avocations: travel, cooking. Home and Office: 57 Montague St Brooklyn NY 11201-3374

SWISHER HARNETTY, STACEY ELAINE, mechanical engineer; b. Columbus, Ohio, Nov. 12, 1966; d. George Monroe and Linda Sue Swisher; m. Patrick M. Harnetty. BSME, Tenn. Tech. U., 1989; MSME, Va. Poly. Inst. and State U., 1991. Engr. in tng., Tenn. Process engring. mech. engr. Eastman Chem. Co., Kingsport, Tenn., 1991-94, devel. mech. engr., 1994-97, plant mech. engr., 1997-98, maintenance gen. supr., 1998—. Contbr. articles to sci. jours.; patentee in field. Supporter United Way, Kingsport, 1991—, Safehouse, Kingsport, 1991—; free engring. svcs. Kingsport Ctr. for Opportunity, 1993. Mem.: NSPE (Young Engr. of Yr. 2002), ASME (v.p. bd. pub. info. 2001—, chair exec. com. on plant engring. and maintenance 2000—01, panel mem. Young Engrs. Forum with PBS 1998—99, Young Engr. of Yr. 1997), Sigma Xi. E-mail: swishers@asme.org.

SWISLOCKI, JAMES PAUL, music educator, soccer coach; b. Middleburg Heights, Ohio, Nov. 7, 1977; s. Paul Darwin and Maryanne Teresa Swislocki; m. Michelle Marie Jonas, Dec. 29, 2001. MusB in Edn., Baldwin-Wallace Coll., 2000. Cert. Tchr. State of Ohio Dept. Edn., 2000. Asst. marching band dir. Westlake City Sch., Westlake, Ohio, 1999—2000; instrumental music tchr. Painesville Twp. Local Sch., Painesville, 2000—. Jazz band dir. Painesville Twp. Local Sch., 2000—, jr. high coed soccer coach, 2001—, mid. sch. girls soccer intramurals, 2000—; summer band tchr. Westlake City Sch., 1999—2001; mid. sch. pit dir. LaMuth Mid. Sch. Drama Club, Painesville, 2001—. Recipient Crystal Apple award, The Plain Dealer, 2002. Mem.: Ohio Music Edn. Assn., Music Educators Nat. Conf. (Future Tchr. of Am. Honor Band award 2000), Kappa Delta Pi. Roman Catholic. Avocations: saxophone, basketball, tennis, baseball card collecting, baseball.

SWIST, MARIAN IRENE, emergency nurse; b. Pottsville, Pa., Oct. 26, 1941; d. Thomas Francis and Marian C. (Munster) Moran; m. John J. Swist, Aug. 3, 1963 (dec.); children: Christine M. Swist Mullen, Robert J. Diploma in nursing, Reading (Pa.) Hosp., 1962. RN, Pa.; CEN; cert. emergency nursing pediatric course. Staff nurse Reading Hosp. Med. Ctr., 1962-65; staff nurse emergency dept. Pottstown Meml. Med. Ctr., 1971—. Mem. Emergency Nurses Assn., Alumni Assn. Reading Hosp. Sch. Nursing.

SWISTAK, PIOTR TOMASZ, mathematician, sociologist; b. Warsaw, Dec. 22, 1954; s. Stefan and Lucyna Swistak; m. Karyna Ditta Witoszka, Apr. 16, 1979. MS in Math., U. Warsaw, 1978, MA in Sociology, 1979; MA in Stats., U. Chgo., 1985, PhD in Sociology, 1987. Lectr. U. Warsaw, 1979-83; Searle fellow U. Chgo., 1983-86; asst. prof. SUNY, Stony Brook, 1987-88; assoc. prof. U. Md., College Park, 1988—. Contbr. numerous articles to profl. jours. Founding mem. Solidarity, Warsaw, 1980-82. Recipient U. Warsaw Pres.'s award for rsch. achievements, 1981, The Susan Colver Rosenberg prize U. Chgo., 1987, Excellence in Tchg. award U. Md., 1997, Vis. Scholar award Russell Sage Found., 1998-99; Harvard U. fellow, 1983, Calif. Inst. Tech. fellow, 1983, U. Chgo. fellow, 1983. Mem. Am. Polit. Sci. Assn. (Heinz Eulau award 1997, 98). Office: Univ of Maryland Dept Govt and Politics College Park MD 20742 E-mail: pswistak@gvpt.umd.edu.

SWITALSKI, MICHAEL MATHEW, secondary educator, lawyer; b. Milw., Nov. 25, 1963; s. Robert R. and Vera P. S. BA in History, Marquette U., 1985; JD, U. Wis., 1988; postgrad. tchg. cert., U. Wis., Milw., 1992. Dir. campus ministry, tchr. Newman H.S., Wausau, Wis., 1992—. Varisty soccer coach Newman H.S., 1992—; referee U.S. Soccer Fedn., 1992—. Bd. dirs. Wausau Soccer Club, 1994—; mem. St. Michael Parish Liturgy Commn., Wausau, 1992—. Lt. comdr. USN, 1988-91. Mem. Soc. for Historian of Am. Fgn. Rels., Wis. Soccer Coaches Assn., Nat. Soccer Coaches Assn., Wis. Bar Assn., Phi Alpha Theta. Roman Catholic. Avocations: raquetball, soccer, basketball, hiking, reading. Office: Newman HS 1130 W Bridge St Wausau WI 54401

SWITHERS, DAVID JOHNATHAN, computer engineer; b. Beverly, Mass., Dec. 28, 1954; s. David George and Patricia Ann (Harris) S.; m. Marel Waterman Hyland, Aug. 26, 1978; children: Kristen Sue, Melissa Elizabeth, Amy Katherine. BS in Math., U. Tex., 1979; MSCS, Old Dominion U., 1988. Commd. ensign USN, 1974, advanced through grades to lt., 1981, ret., 1984; engr. Tektronix, Newport News, Va., 1984-86, EDO Corp., Chesapeake, 1986-88, Gen. Instrument, Westwood, Mass., 1988-89, Whistler Corp., Westford, 1989-91; engring. mgr. Computer Identics, Canton, 1991-98; pres. Advanced Electronic Design, Taunton, 1998—. Mem. IEEE. E-mail. Home: 22 Connie Ln North Attleboro MA 02763-4056 Office: 300 Myles Standish Blvd Taunton MA 02780 E-mail: dswithers@ieee.org.

SWITLO, JANICE GEORGINA ALICE E. barrister, solicitor, mediator, negotiator, legal and business consultant; b. Vancouver, B.C., Can., Jan. 10, 1959; d. Alexander Donald and Mary (Shutka) Switlo; married; 1 child. LLB, Osgoode Hall, Toronto, 1986; B.Commerce, U. B.C., 1981. Mgmt. cons. Control Data Can. Ltd., Vancouver, 1981-83; barrister, solicitor Aydin & Co., 1987-88; legal counsel Dept. Justice of Can., 1989-93; gen. counsel Westbank Indian Band, Westbank, B.C., 1993-94; barrister, solicitor, cons. Switlo & Co., Peachland, 1993-97; candidate fed. election Okanagan-Coquihaila, 1997; legal advisor Ministry Aboriginal Affairs, Govt. N.W.T., 1999-2000. Mem. adv. coun. on multiculturalism, adv. coun. to Minister of Multiculturalism, B.C., 1996-98; presenter in field. Author: (book/screenplay) Sookinchute, 2001, (treatise) Trick or Treaty?, 1995, Apple Cede: First Nations Land Management Regime, 1999, In a perfect world...Modern day colonialism in Canada, 2001, The River Forks Here: Canada's attempt to execute the 1969 White Paper and Indigenous Peoples, 2002, (book) Gustafsen Lake: Under Seige, 1997. Dir. B.C. Parents in Crisis Soc., Vancouver, 1991—93, Orpheum Kids Club Soc., Vancouver, 1991, Vancouver Youth Theatre, 2001. Recipient various univ. scholarships. Mem. Internat. Bar Assn., Internat. Commn. Jurists (Can. sect.), Can. Counsel on Internat. Law, York U. Alumni Assn., U. B.C. Commerce Alumni Assn., Phi Delta Phi. Office: Switlo & Co 10654 Whyte Ave Ste 170 Edmonton AB Canada T6E 2A7 E-mail: switlo@hotmail.com, janice@switlo.com.

SWITZER, BRIAN CARL, strategic systems designer; b. Cleve., Sept. 13, 1938; s. Robert Charles and Patricia Davison S.; m. Nicole S., Dec. 31, 1964; children: Michelle, Stephanie. BA, Ohio Wesleyan U., 1960; MBA, Ohio State U., 1964. Founder, pres. M.C.O. Solutions, Inc., Shaker Heights, Ohio, 1962—; founder Strategic Alliance Team, 1997—. Bd. dirs. Cons. Assocs. Internat., Inc., Pepper Pike, Ohio, 1998—. Author: How to Sell Overseas, 1966. Mem. Rotary. Republican. Episcopal. Avocation: photography. Home: 11615 Pleasant Ridge Pl Cleveland OH 44136-4523 Office: MCO Solutions 23400 Stanford Rd Shaker Heights OH 44122

SWITZER, CAROLYN JOAN, artist, educator; b. Petoskey, Mich., Apr. 20, 1931; d. Eugene Constant and Burnis Hazel (Lower) S. Student, Wayne State U., 1954-55, St. John's Coll., Santa Fe, N.Mex., 1993; BA, Mich. State U., 1953, MA, 1964. Cert. tchr., Mich. Art tchr. Ferndale Bd. of Edn., 1953-56, Birmingham Bd. of Edn., Mich., 1956-96. Exhbns. include local shows, galleries and pvt. collections. Cons. Girl Scouts U.S., Birmingham, Petoskey, Mich.; mem. Crooked Tree Arts Coun., Petoskey AAUW scholar, Mich. State, 1962; recipient recognition award for svc. to community, Birmingham Edn. Assn. Coun., 1967, Outstanding Senior Woman Lantern Night MSU, 1953. Mem. AAUW, Nat. Art Edn. Assn., Mich. Art Edn. Assn., Mich. Edn. Assn., Detroit Inst. Art, Nat. Mus. for Women in Arts, Mich. Coun. for Arts. Avocations: music/singing, reading, exercise class, walking, photography. Home: 805 Lindell Ave Petoskey MI 49770-3159

SWITZER, FREDERICK MICHAEL, III, lawyer, arbitrator, mediator; b. St. Louis, Sept. 7, 1933; s. Frederick Michael Jr. and Viola Marie (Bardenheier) S.; m. Suzanne Elizabeth Reichardt, Aug. 28, 1970. BA cum laude, U. Notre Dame, 1956; JD, Washington U., 1959, LLM, 1972. Bar: Mo. 1959, U.S. Ct. Mil. Appeals 1960, U.S. Supreme Ct. 1962, U.S. Dist. Ct. (ea. dist.) Mo. 1993, U.S. Tax Ct. 1974, U.S. Ct. Appeals (8th cir.) 1978, U.S. Dist. Ct. (we. dist.) Mo. 1992, U.S. Ct. Appeals (4th cir.) 1994. Assoc. Switzer, Barnes & Toney, St. Louis, 1963-65, ptnr., 1965-75, Fordyce & Mayne, St. Louis, 1975-87, Coburn Croft, St. Louis, 1987-92, Danna, McKitrick, P.C., St. Louis, 1992—. Dir. Bardenheier Wine Co., St. Louis, 1983-85; instr. St. Louis Univ., 1971-72. Pres., dir. St. Louis Industry Adv. Group, 1971-90; dir. St. Louis Abbey Sch. Soc., 1975—; mem. employee benefits adv. com. City of Ladue (Mo.), 1980—, St. Louis Indsl. Rsch. Assn., 1991—; secr., dir. Citizens for Mo.'s Children, St. Louis, 1986-91; adv. bd. Am. Youth Found., St. Louis, 1989—, pres. Friends of Am. Youth Found., 2000—. Capt. USNR, 1959-63. Recipient Mitchell award for playwriting, Univ. Notre Dame, 1959. Mem. ABA (labor employment section, equal employment opportunity law com., immigration law com., litig. section, gen. practice section), ATLA, Assn. Atty. Mediators, Mo. Bar Assn. (labor law com., chmn. mil. law com. 1969-71, bar jour. com.), St. Louis Bar Assn. (labor law com., anti-trust com.), Strathalbyn Farms Club (past dir., past asst. secr.), Phi Delta Phi. Republican. Roman Catholic. Avocations: sailing, hiking, equestrian activities, tennis. Office: Danna McKitrick PC 150 N Meramec Ave Fl 4 Saint Louis MO 63105-3779 E-mail: fswitzer@dmfirm.com.

SWITZER, JO ELLEN YOUNG, academic administrator, dean; b. Huntington, Ind., Mar. 4, 1948; d. John Frederick and Miriam Lucile (Kindy) Young; children: Sarah Kate Keller, John Christian Keller. BA, Manchester Coll., 1969; MA, U. Kans., 1977, PhD, 1980; postdoctoral, Ind. U., 1983, Harvard U., 1995. English tchr., Dearborn Heights, Mich., 1969-70, Fenton High Sch., Bensenville, Ill., 1970-73; asst. instr. U. Kans., Lawrence, 1977-79; asst. prof. Ind. U.-Purdue, Ft. Wayne, Ind., 1979-82; assoc. prof. Manchester Coll., North Manchester, 1982-87, Ind. U.-Purdue, Ft. Wayne, 1987-93; v.p., dean for acad. affairs and prof. comm. studies Manchester Coll., 1993—. Recipient E. C. Buehler award U. Kans., 1978; grantee NEH, 1983. Mem. Central States Comm. Assn. (Outstanding Young Educator award 1982), Nat. Comm. Assn. Home: 3069 E 1200 N Roanoke IN 46783 Office: Manchester Coll Office Acad Affairs 604 E College Ave North Manchester IN 46962-1276 Fax: 260-982-5042. E-mail: jyswitzer@manchester.edu.

SWITZER, JON REX, architect; b. Shelbyville, Ill., Aug. 22, 1937; s. John Woodrow and Ida Marie (Vadalabene) S.; m. Judith Ann Heinlein, July 7, 1962; 1 child, Jeffrey Eric. Student, U. Ill., 1955-58; BS, Millikin U., 1972; MA, U. Ill., Springfield, 1981. Registered architect Ill., Mo., Ohio, Colo.; registered interior designer, Ill. Architect Warren & Van Praag, Inc., Decatur, Ill., 1970-72; prin., 1972-81, Bloomington, Ill., 1981-83; architect Hilfinger, Asbury, Cufaude, Abels, 1983-84; ptnr. Riddle/Switzer, Ltd., 1984-86; with bldg., design and constrn. div. State Farm Ins. Cos., 1986-89; architect The Riddle Group, 1989-91; prin. J. Rex Switzer, Architect, 1991—. Elder Presbyn. Ch., 1996. With U.S. Army, 1958-61. Mem. AIA (pres. Bloomington chpt. 1983, Decatur chpt. 1976, v.p. Ill. chpt. 1986-87, sec. 1985, treas. 1984), Am. Archtl. Found., Chgo. Architecture Found., Nat. Trust Hist. Preservation, Frank Lloyd Found., Decatur C. of C. (merit citation 1974, merit award 1979), Am. Legion, Masons (32d degree). Republican. Presbyterian. Avocations: swimming, hunting, fishing, reading, drawing, travel. Home: 9 Mary Ellen Way Bloomington IL 61701-2014 Office: 2412 E Washington St Ste 6A Bloomington IL 61704-1613

SWITZER, MAURICE HAROLD, journalist; b. Toronto, Ont., Can., Mar. 28, 1945; s. Harold Switzer and Ruby (Marsden) Hicks; m. Mary Helene Pavlik; children: Andrea Zimperi, Adin, Lisa Doracka. Student, Trent U., Peterborough, Ont., 1964-65. Journalist Belleville (Ont.) Intelligencer, 1965-67, sports editor, 1967-72, mng. editor, 1972-79, Oshawa (Ont.) Times, 1979-81; pub. Timmins (Ont.) Daily Press, 1981-86, Sudbury (Ont.) Star, 1986-92, Winnipeg (Man.) Free Press, 1992-94; owner Media Help Svcs.,

1994—. Faculty Aboriginal Media First Nations Tech. Inst., 1996—97; dir. comm. Assembly of First Nations, Ottawa, 1997—2000, Union Ont. Indians, North Bay, 2000—; adj. prof. comms. Huntington U., Sudbury, Ont., Canada. Author: Bruno Cavallo a Conversation, 1991. Mem. elders coun. Mississaugas of Alderville First Nation. E-mail: swimau@anishinabek.ca.

SWITZER, ROBERT LEE, biochemistry educator; b. Clinton, Iowa, Aug. 26, 1940; s. Stephen and Elva Delila (Allison) S.; m. Bonnie George, June 13, 1965; children: Brian, Stephanie. BS, U. Ill., 1961; PhD, U. Calif., Berkeley, 1966. Research fellow Lab. Biochemistry, Nat. Heart Inst., Bethesda, Md., 1966-68; asst. prof. biochemistry U. Ill., Urbana, 1968—73, assoc. prof., 1973—78, prof. biochemistry and basic med. scis., 1978—2002, prof. emeritus, 2002—, dept. head, 1988—93. Mem. biochemistry study sect. NIH, 1985-89, chmn., 1987-89; guest prof. U. Copenhagen, 1995; mem. microbial physiology and genetics study sect., NIH, 1998-2000. Author: (with Liam F. Garrity) Experimental Biochemistry, 3rd rev. edit., 1999; mem. bd. editors Jour. Bacteriology, 1977-82, 85— , Archives Biochemistry and Biophysics, 1977-98, Jour. Biol. Chemistry, 1980-85; contbr. articles to profl. jours. NSF predoctoral fellow, 1961-66; NIH postdoctoral fellow, 1966-68; Guggenheim fellow, 1975 Mem. Am. Soc. for Biochemistry and Molecular Biology, Am. Soc. Microbiology, Am. Chem. Soc., AAAS, Sigma Xi. Home: 404 W Michigan Ave Urbana IL 61801-4948 Office: U Ill Dept Biochemistry 600 S Mathews Ave Urbana IL 61801-3602 E-mail: rswitzer.@uiuc.edu.

SWITZER, SAMUEL THOMAS, non-profit administrator; b. Cowgill, Mo., Feb. 5, 1951; s. William Thomas and Lova Nadine (Hayden) S. (dec.); m. Carolyn Beth Stephens, Aug. 7, 1971; children: Samuel Andrew, Jennifer Elaine. BSBA summa cum laude, William Jewell Coll., 1973; cert. mgmt. program, Rockhurst Coll., 1978. CPA, Mo. Asst. bank examiner Fed. Res. Bank St. Louis, 1973-74; cashier, asst. contr. Kansas City (Mo.) Life Ins. Co., 1974-77; contr., asst. treas. Belsaw Machinery Co., Kansas City, Mo., 1977-80; coord. spl. projects Kansas City Power and Light Co., 1980-81; dir., sec.-treas. Scudder Communications Assocs., Inc., Gladstone, Mo., 1982-87; treas. Midwestern Sem. Housing Corp., Kansas City, 1981-93; v.p. Midwestern Bapt. Theol. Sem., 1981-93; sr. v.p. United Cerebral Palsy of Greater Kansas City, 1993—; prin., owner Switzer Homeplace Farms of Kearney, Kidder, Cowgill, Mo., 1988—, Switzer No. Lights Ranch, Minitonas and Swan River, Canada, 2001—. Chmn. So. Bapt. Sems. Bus. Officers Coun., 1986, 91; notary pub., State of Mo., 1982-94. Bd. dirs. Kearney (Mo.) Devel. Corp., 1977-80; deacon 1st Bapt. Ch., Kearney, 1977—, chmn. fin. com., pers. com., tchr. Sunday sch.; league treas., dir. of ofcls., coach Kearney Holt Youth Soccer Club, 1982-93; mem. businessmen's group study exch. tour Rotary Club Internat., West Germany and Berlin, 1987; league coord., coach Kearney Holt Recreation Assn., 1985-91; mem. religious life com. William Jewell Coll., Liberty, Mo., 1989-98, chmn. 1989-92, chmn. alumni athletic commn., 1998—, pub. address announcer Nat. Assn. Intercollegiate Athletics soccer team, 1995—; bd. dirs. Kearney R-1 Sch. Bd., 1991-94, liaison mem. strategic planning com., 1992; mem. Sr. Link Adv. Bd., 1994—; pres. William Jewell Coll. Soccer Booster Club, 1995-99; bd. dirs. William Jewell Coll. Cardinal Athletics Booster Club, 1998—; stadium announcer semi-pro football team Mo. Wolfpack, 1999-2000; pianist Tryst Falls (Mo.) Bapt. Ch., 1996-98; gold crown mem. Clay County Devel. Commn.; stadium announcer Clay County River Bandits Collegiate Mo.-Iowa-Nebr.-Kans. League Baseball Team, 1997—. Named one of Outstanding Young Men Am., 1984, 86, 89, 90. Mem. NRA, Kansas City C. of C., William Jewell Coll. Alumni Assn. (bd. govs. 1998—, exec. adv. com. 1999-2000), Cmty. Assn. Not-for-Profit Bus. Execs. (founder 1998, bd. dirs.), N.Am. Hunting Club (life), Mo. Mchts. and Mfg. Assn. (bd. dirs., mem. exec. adv. com. 2001). Republican. Avocations: hunting, skiing, boating, farm management, conservation. Home: 17009 NE 134th Ter Kearney MO 64060-8910 Office: United Cerebral Palsy of Greater Kansas City 1044 Main Ste 600 Kansas City MO 64105 E-mail: sswitzer@ucpkc.org.

SWITZER, STEPHEN STUART, school superintendent; b. Defiance, Ohio, Oct. 1, 1949; s. Alfred Lyle and Lora M. (Snyder) S.; m. Laura Marie Prochaska, Aug. 7, 1976; children: Matthew Stephen, Andrew Peter. BA in English, U. Findlay, 1971; MEd in Counseling, Bowling Green State U., 1973, PhD in Edn. Adminstrn., 1987. Cert. English tchr., sch. counselor, sch. supt., h.s. prin., Ohio. Secondary sch. educator Defiance City Schs., 1970-71, Arlington (Ohio) local schs., 1971-73; counselor Paulding (Ohio) Exempted Village Sch., 1973-74; h.s. prin. Holgate (Ohio) local schs., 1974-82; supt. Pettisville (Ohio) local schs., 1982—. Exec. dir. Pettisville Sch. Found., 1986—; adj. assoc. prof. edn1. adminstrn. Bowling Green State U., 1997—. Recipient Exemplary Ednl. Leadership award Buckeye Assn. Sch. Adminstrs., 1994. Home: PO Box 92 Pettisville OH 43553-0092 Office: PO Box 1 Pettisville OH 43553-0001

SWITZER, TOCCOA, artist; b. Clinton, S.C., Dec. 14, 1930; d. Hercules Milledge and Mercer Bailey (Vance) Wise; m. James Layton Switzer, Feb. 20, 1954 (dec.); children: James Layton Jr., Toccoa Bailey, Paul Kent III; m. Paul Kent Switzer, Jr., Oct. 12, 1990. AA, Stephens Coll., Columbia, Mo., 1951; BFA, Ohio State U., Columbus, 1953. Chmn. Switzer/Wise Investment LP, Union, S.C., 1989—. Bd. dirs. M.S. Bailey and Son, Bankers, Clinton, Clinton Investment Co.; mem. adv. bd. Anchor Fin. Corp., Myrtle Beach, S.C. Den mother Cub Scouts Am., Union, 1962-65; vol. ARC, Union, 1968—; Sunday Sch. tchr. Grace United Meth. Ch., Union, 1954-95, chmn. bldg. com., 1976-77, bd. trustees 1985—; bd. dirs. Great Town Program, Union, 1976-82; bd. dirs. Union Main St. Program, 1983-84; mem. bldg. com. Union Carnegie Libr., 1983-85; bd. mem. Union County Health Care Found., Union, 1993—; bd. trustees Wofford Coll., Spartanburg, S.C., 1990—; bd. dir. Bailey Found., Clinton, 1989—; bd. mem. U. S.C.-Union Partnership Bd., 1989—. Recipient Founder Day award U.S.C., Union, 1999. Mem. Friends of the Libr., Union Cotillion Club (pres.), Book and Garden Club (pres. 1989-90), Union County C. of C. (pres. 1981-82). Methodist. Avocations: painting, gardening, reading.

SWOAP, DAVID BRUCE, government affairs consultant; b. Kalamazoo, Aug. 12, 1937; s. Orlo Frederick and Aileen Esther (Hempy) S. BA in Govt. with honors, Denison U., 1959; MA in Govt, Claremont Grad. Sch., 1961; DSc (hon.), U. Osteo. Medicine and Health Scis., Des Moines, 1981. Asst. sec. Calif. State Pers. Bd., Sacramento, 1972-73; chief dep. dir., acting dir. Calif. State Dept. Social Welfare, 1973, dir., 1973-74, Calif. State Dept. Benefit Payments, 1974-75; sr. rsch. asso. Rep. Study Com., U.S. Ho. of Reps., Washington, 1975-76; profl. staff mem. U.S. Senate Com. on Fin., 1976-79; legis. dir. U.S. Senator William L. Armstrong, 1979-81; dep. sec. HHS, 1981-83; sec. health and welfare State of Calif., Sacramento, 1983-85; ptnr. Franchetti & Swoap, San Francisco, 1985-90; vice chmn. Sacramento Advs., 1991-98; chmn. bd. dirs. Hope Unltd. Internat., San Diego, 1991-96, chmn. bd. internat. advisors, 1996—; owner The David Bruce Gallery, Carlsbad, Calif., 1995-97. Owner Mana Olana Farms, Hakalau, Hawaii, 1989-97. Elder Presbyn. Ch.; bd. dirs. Friends of SOS Children's Villages, 1989-91; mem. bd. regents John F. Kennedy U., 1990-93. Rotary Club Found. fellow, 1961-62 Mem. Wycliffe Assocs., Phi Beta Kappa, Delta Upsilon. Republican.

SWOFFORD, DONALD ANTHONY, architect; b. Houston, Apr. 14, 1947; s. Harry and Henrian (Engbrock) S.; 1 child, James McShea. BArch, Tex. A&M U., 1969; MArch, U. Va., 1976. Registered arch., Va., Tex., D.C., Nat. Coun. Archtl. Registration Bds.; lic. instrument pilot. Arch., urban designer City of Dallas, 1970-72, Office Milton L. Grigg, FAIA, Archs., 1972-78; prin., owner DASA, PLC, Charlottesville, Va., 1978—. Pres. Traditional Am. Concepts, Ltd., 1983—. Author Dallas Hist. Landmark Program, 1972; prin. works include Joseph Jarvis residence, 1978, Shrinemont Conf. Ctr., Episcopal Diocese of Va., Orkney Springs, 1981, United Coal/Martha Washington Inn, Bristol, Va., 1985, office and studio WVIR TV, 1985, restoration Farley, Culpeper, Va., 1987, restoration St. Francis Assisi Cath. Ch., Stanton, Va., 1988, restoration and additions Goochland County (Va.) Courthouse, 1989, Montpelier, home of James Madison, 1986, George M. McMath residence, Locustville, Va., 1991, restoration of Higlands, home of James Monro, Charlottesville, 1991, Holy Name of Mary, Bedford, Va., 1994, restoration of Clover Hill Tavern, Appomattox, Va., 1994, hist. rehab. of Danville Rail Passenger Sta., restoration of Gen. George C. Marshall Home, Leesburg, Va., 1994, Danville City Courthouse, Danville, Va., 1995, Danville Cts. and Jails Bldg., 1999, Charlotte County Clks. Office, Va., 1999, Congl. Cemetary, Washington, 1999, Ct. Sq. F&M Bank, Winchester, Va. (Nat. Honor award Nat. Trust for Hist. Preservation). Cub master Pack 119, Stonewall Jackson Coun., 1994-98. Recipient Tex.-AIA Design award, 1969-70, Loudoun County award for Jarvis Residence, 1985; Jefferson fellow, 1972-73. Fellow: AIA (James River chpt. Design award for Danville Rail Passenger Sta. 1995); mem.: Assn. Preservation Tech., Soc. Archtl. Historians, Nat. Trust Historic Preservation, Albemarle County Hist. Soc., Va. Soc. Archs. Office: DASA 812 E High St Charlottesville VA 22902-5126 Fax: 434-293-8534. E-mail: das@dasaonline.com.

SWOFFORD, ROBERT LEE, newspaper editor, journalist; b. Berryville, Ark., Aug. 22, 1949; s. Andrew Madison and Verna Mae (England) S.; m. Karen King, Jan. 24, 1969 (div. 1977); children: Teri, Toby; m. Sandra Dunn, 1978 (div. 1979); m. B. Joanna Rongren, Feb. 14, 1981; 1 child, Tyler. AA, Coll. of the Sequoias, 1969; student, Calif. State U., 1969-71. Photographer, reporter, news editor The Advance-Register, Tulare, Calif., 1965-78; city editor The Record Searchlight, Redding, 1978-81; suburban editor, Neighbors editor The Sacramento Bee, 1981-86; assoc. metro. editor, cmty. editor The Orange County Register, Santa Ana, Calif., 1986-89; exec. news editor The Press Democrat, Santa Rosa, 1989-90, mng. editor, 1990—. Mem. Am. Soc. Newspaper Editors, Assoc. Press Mng. Editors, Calif. Soc. of Newspaper Editors (bd. dirs.). Office: The Press Democrat 427 Mendocino Ave Santa Rosa CA 95401-6385

SWOGER, JAMES WESLEY, magician; b. Wilkinsburg, Pa., Jan. 26, 1918; s. George Edmond and Iva Edna (Heacox) S.; m. Willie Williams, Jan. 8, 1944 (div. 1967); children: Melinda, James Michael, Andrina; m. Violet Elizabeth Pettit, Oct. 29, 1968. Owner House of Enchantment, Oceanside, Calif., 1937—. Owner, magician Museum of Magic, 1937, Magic Follies of Tomorrow, 1938-41; active numerous war bond drive shows, camp shows, ship entertainment and concert tours in Australia, New Guinea and the Philippines, 1943-46; starred in Magic on Showboat Rhododenron Season, 1965—, Mr. Roger's Neighborhood, Army Hour, 1943; lectr. Magic Castle, 1995; magician Pitts. Children's Theatre, 1941-43, Bascom Prodns., 1941-43, Austin Prodns., 1941-43; bd. dirs. Awesome Balloons, Inc. Magician for more than 79 yrs. Named Magician of Yr. 1960, 50 Yrs Svc. Magic, Internat. Magicians Ring 13 IBM, 1973, Faithful Yr. Svc. Magic, 42d Annual Magicfest, 1973, 60 Yr. Svc. Magic, 1983; named to Order of Arrow Boy Scouts Am. Mem. Soc. Am. Magicians (pres.), Internat. Brotherhood Magicians (pres., Order of Merlin Excalibur 1995), Craftsmen Printers Guild, Mystic 52 (pres.), Acad. Magical Arts Scis., Fellowship Christian Magicians, San Diego Ring 76 IBM, Awesome Balloons (bd. mem. 2000). Republican. Avocations: inventing stage effects, model illusions. Home: 3542 Mira Pacific Dr Oceanside CA 92056-3932

SWOOPES, SHERYL DENISE, professional basketball player; b. Brownfield, Tex., Mar. 25, 1971; d. Louis Swoopes; m. Eric Jackson; 1 child, Jordan. Student, South Plains Jr. Coll., Tex.; BA, Tex. Tech. U., 1993. Basketball player USA Women's Nat. Team, 1995-96, Houston Comets (named MVP and Defensive Player of the Year, 2000), 1997—. Mem. 1995 Pan Am. Games Womens Basketball Team. Recipient bronze medal as mem. 1994 World Championship Team, gold medal as mem. 1994 Women's Goodwill Games Team; named 1993 Nat. Player of the Yr., MVP 1993 NCAA Final Four, 1992 and 1992 SWC Player of Yr., 1992 SWC Newcomer of the Yr.; mem. WNBA champion Houston Comets, 1997, 98, 99, ESPY Award for Women's Pro-Basketball Player of the Year, 2001. Achievements include having a Nike basketball shoe named in her honor. Office: Houston Comets Two Greenway Plz Ste 400 Houston TX 77046 Address: 908 E Felt St Apt 111 Brownfield TX 79316-3703*

SWOPE, ALAN JOSEPH, psychologist, educator; b. Cleve., Apr. 24, 1942; s. Floyd Keene and Leone Louise Swope; m. Bonnie Lee Swope, June 1976 (div. Oct. 1997); children: Alison, Laura. BA, Hiram Coll., 1964; PhD, Columbia U., 1969. Lic. psychologist, Calif. Psychologist City of Berkeley, Calif., 1970-81; pvt. practice as psychotherapist Berkeley, 1971—; prof. Wright Inst., 1978—, Calif. Sch. Profl. Psychology, Alameda, 1982—. Hon. life bd. mem. Calif. Psychology Internship Coun., Berkeley, 1992—. Contbr. articles to profl. jours. Fellow: Am. Bd. Profl. Psychology (diplomate); mem.: APA, No. Calif. Soc. for Psycoanalytic Psychology. Avocations: writing, reading, tennis, piano. Office: 3155 College Ave Berkeley CA 94705-2755

SWOPE, CHARLES EVANS, bank president, lawyer; b. West Chester, Pa., June 16, 1930; s. Charles S. and Edna (McAllister) S.; m. Stephanie Swope; 1 child, Charles E. BS, Bucknell U., 1953; JD, Washington and Lee U., 1959; MS, Ind. Coll., 1966; attended Naval War Coll., Judge Adv. Gen. Sch., 1957; attended, Command and Staff Coll., 1969; D in Pub. Svc. (hon.), West Chester U., 1994. Assoc. Gawthorp & Greenwood, Attys., West Chester, Pa., 1960; pres., chmn. bd., sr. trust officer 1st Nat. Bank, Chester County, 1965—, also chmn. bd. dirs. Pres. Eachus Dairy Co., 1970-84; pres., bd. dirs. West Chester Corp.; bd. dirs. Madison Co., Penjerdel, Penn Mut. Ins. Co., dir. 1st Nat. Bank Chester County; pres. Automobile Assn. Chester County; lectr. corp. law. Pres. West Chester Civic Assn., 1964; co-chmn. Chester County Heart Assn. Dr., West Chester Cmty. Ctr. Bldg. Dr., 1970-90, 175th Anniversary West Chester, 200th Anniversary West Chester, co-chmn.; mem. Nat. Football Found. and Hall of Fame; dir. Chester County coun. Boy Scouts Am., 1961-97; bd. dirs. Chester County Svc.; pres. Swope Found. Trust; bd. dirs., pres. West Chester U. Found.; mem. Marine Corps Scholarship Fund; chmn. Bus. and Indsl. Coun. Chester County, pres., 1981; chmn. Easter Seal Soc. Chester County; mem. Com. to Restore Tun Tavern; trustee West Chester U., 1962-72, pres. bd. trustees, 1966-72; trustee Chester County Devel. Fund, Dr. Charles S. Swope Scholarshpi Fund, Hatfield Home; YMCA trustee Chester County Hosp. Corp. Maj. USMC, 1952-58, col. Res. Decorated Legion of Merit, Nat. Def. medal, Navy Commendation medal, Meritorious Svc. medal; recipient Coll. Football Centennial award, 1970; Congl. Medal of Merit, 1981; Disting. Eagle Scout award Boy Scouts Am., 1983; Legion of Hon. Gold medallion Chapel of Four Chaplains, 1998; named to Hall of Fame, West Chester U., 1997, West Chester H.S., 1999; recipient CEO of Yr. Chester County C. of C., 2000. Mem. ABA (life), VFW (life), Am. Bankers Assn., Pa. Bankers Assn. (chmn. legis. com. 1965, 70), U.S. Naval Inst., Assn. Univ. Trustees Pa., Am. Soc. Internat. Law, Chester County Bar Found. (v.p.), Greater West Chester C. of C. (pres. 1963), Marine Corps League Chester County (vice comdr. 1960-72), Freedoms Found., Am. Legion (life), Chester County Hist. Soc. (Founder's award), Mil. Order of the World Wars, Marine Corps Res. Officer Assn. (nat. pres. 1982-83, vice chmn. bd. dirs.), Marine Corps League, Pa. C. of C., Navy League U.S., Washington and Lee Law Sch. Assn., Bucknell Alumni Assn., West Chester U. Alumni Assn., Pa. Economy League, Brandywind Valley Assn., Maxwell Football Club, West Chester Club, Golf and Country Club, Union League Club (Phila), Applebrook Country club, Italian Social Club, Sky Top Club, Great Oaks Yacht and Country Club, Masons, Rotary (pres. West Chester, Pa. club 1968-69, Paul Harris fellow), Elks, Phi Alpha Delta, Phi Kappa Psi. Republican. Methodist (ofcl. bd.). Home: 200 W Ashbridge St West Chester PA 19380-2371 Office: First Nat Bank 9 N High St West Chester PA 19380-3015

SWOPE, DONALD DOWNEY, retired banker; b. Martinsville, Ill., Feb. 26, 1926; s. Roy V. and Dorothy Irene (Downey) S.; m. Earla Long Markert, Aug. 16, 1960. BS, Ind. State U., 1950. With Ill. Savs. and Loan Commn., Springfield, Ill., 1950-77, chief dept. commr., 1971-77; exec. v.p. Bank for Savs. & Loan Assn., Chgo., 1977-81, pres., 1981-90, dir. Dir., treas. Country Fair White Elephant, Green Valley, Ariz. With USNR, 1944-63. Mem. VFW (life), Nat. Assn. State Savs. and Loan Suprs. (pres. 1972-73), Am. Legion (life), C. C. Green Valley, Kiwanis (pres. Crete, Ill. 1977-78, treas. Green Valley, Ariz. 1994, 95), Elks (treas.).

SWOPE, FRANCES ALDERSON, retired librarian; b. Richmond, Va., Dec. 5, 1911; d. Joseph Newman and Frances (Richardson) Alderson; m. Kenneth Dabney Swope, Dec. 27, 1958; stepchildren: Jeanne Weikel, Lee Smith. BA, U. Ky., Lexington, 1933; BS in Libr. Sci., U. Ill., 1939; postgrad., U. Va., U. Mich., U. London. Tchr. Alderson (W.Va.) H.S., 1933-39; ext. libr. Circleville (Ohio) Pub. Libr., 1939-41, Kanawha County Pub. Libr., Charleston, W.Va., 1941-43; alt. custodian hqrs. Commandants Confidential & Secret Files, 3rd Naval Dist., N.Y.C., 1943-45; cataloguer Yale U. Libr., New Haven, 1946-47; chief ext. libr. Kanawha County Pub. Libr., 1947-67; archivist Greenbrier Hist. Soc., Lewisburg, W.Va., 1969-97. Named W.Va. History Hero, 1997. Mem. Nat. Trust Historic Preservation, Nat. Soc. Colonial Dames in Am., W.Va. Libr. Assn. Lt. USNR, 1943-45. Democrat. Presbyterian. Avocation: walking. Home: 1130 Highland Pl Apt 303 Harrisonburg VA 22801

SWOPE, JEFFREY PEYTON, lawyer; b. Evanston, Ill., June 11, 1945; s. Oliver P. and Elspeth E. (Cahill) S.; m. Linda Lee, Aug. 26, 1967; children: Matthew, Gregory, Timothy. AB, Harvard U., 1967, JD, 1970. Bar: Mass. 1970, U.S. Dist. Ct. Mass. 1971, U.S. Ct. Appeals (1st cir.) 1973, U.S. Ct. Claims 1974, U.S. Supreme Ct. 1979. Assoc. Palmer & Dodge, Boston, 1970-76, ptnr., 1977—. Treas. Social Law Libr., Boston, 1984—. Treas. Ella Lyman Cabot Trust, Holliston, Mass., 1979—. Mem. Mass. Audubon Soc. (bd. dirs. 1985—2002). Home: 54 Hyde St Newton MA 02461-1206 Office: Palmer & Dodge LLP 111 Huntington Ave Boston MA 02199-7613

SWOPE, RICHARD MCALLISTER, retired lawyer; b. West Chester, Pa., Apr. 19, 1940; s. Charles Seigel and Edna McPherson (McAllister) S.; m. Karen Diane Glass, Aug. 24, 1963 (div. 1972). BS in Edn., Bucknell U., 1962; LLB cum laude, Washington and Lee U., 1968. Bar: Va. 1968. Ret., 1998. Instr. Nat. Inst. Trial Advocacy, 1982-86. Mem. Virginia Beach Beautification Commn.; bd. dirs. Virginia Beach Orchestral Assn., 1982-88; v.p., bd. dirs. Swope Found., West Chester, Pa., 1961—; v.p. Swope Scholarship Found. Capt. USMC, 1962-65. Mem. Va. Assn. Def. Attys. (bd. dirs. 1975-78, 88-90), Va. State Bar Assn., Norfolk/Portsmouth Bar Assn., Virginia Beach Bar Assn., Virginia Beach C. of C., Rotary (pres. 1982, Paul Harris fellow). Avocation: golf. Home: 936 Poquoson Cir Virginia Beach VA 23452-4646 Office: 936 Poquoson Cir Virginia Beach VA 23452-4646

SWOPE, SCOTT PAUL, lawyer; b. Trenton, Mich., Nov. 9, 1968; AA, St. Petersburg Jr. Coll., 1990; BS, U. South Fla., 1994; JD, U. Fla., 1997. Bar: Fla. 1997, U.S. Dist. Ct. (mid. dist.) Fla. 1997. Deputy sheriff Pinellas County Sheriff's Office, Largo, Fla., 1988-94; atty. Tew, Zinober, Barnes, Zimmet & Unice, Clearwater, 1997-98, Gassman & Gulecas, P.A., Clearwater, 1998-2001, Swope & Assocs., P.A., Clearwater, 2001—. U. Fla. Coll. Law scholar, Gainesville, 1994-97. Mem. Pinellas County Estate Planning Coun., Clearwater Bar Assn. (civil traffic infraction hearing officer 2000-). Office: Swope & Assocs PA 2555 Enterprise Rd Ste 15 Clearwater FL 33763 Fax: 727-726-9500. E-mail: sswope@swopelegal.com.

SWOPE, WILLIAM RICHARDS, retail executive; b. Washington, Oct. 17, 1920; s. King and Mary Margaret (Richards) S.; m. Bobbie Wylie Stringfellow, June 17, 1944 (div. Sept. 1993); children: Robert Cromwell, William Richards Jr.; m. Dorothy S. Taylor, Feb. 3, 1994. AB, U. Ky., 1941; LLB, Harvard U., 1947. Bar: Ky. 1947. V.p., sales mgr. Stringfellow Lumber Co., Inc., Birmingham, Ala., 1951—58; pres., owner Swope Co., Inc., 1958—98. Bd. deacons Ind. Presbyn. Ch., Birmingham, 1953—56, 1961—64, 1971—74. Maj. U.S. Army, 1942—45. Mem.: Lincoln's Inn Soc., Nat. Fedn. Ind. Bus., N.Am. Wholesale Lubmer Assn., ABA, Idle Hour Country Club (Lexington), Lions (pres. 1957—58), The Club, Birmingham Country Club, Ph Delta Theta, SAR, First Families Va., Ams. Royal Descent, Order of the Crown. Republican. Presbyterian. Died Aug. 25, 1998.

SWYDEN, ROBERT GENE, family practice physician; b. Tipton, Okla., Nov. 5, 1931; s. Namon S. and Blanche (Andrews) S.; m. Sara Lou Swinney, Jan. 8, 1955; children: Robert G., Lisa Ann. BS, U. Okla., 1953, MD, 1956. Physician USAMC, Korea, 1957-59, Ft. Sill, Okla., 1959; pvt. practice Bell, Calif., 1959-92, Downey, 1992—. Fellow: Am. Acad. Family Physicians; mem. AMA, Calif. Med. Assn., Calif. Assn. Family Practice, L.A. County Med. Assn. Republican. Avocations: bicycling, cooking, coin collecting, reading, sports. Home: 9920 Casanes Ave Downey CA 90240-3501 Office: 8535 Florence Ave Downey CA 90240-4014

SWYERS, DONALD G. information scientist; b. Syracuse, N.Y., Mar. 30, 1958; s. William A. Swyers and Corinne Prall Neville; m. Nancy C. Bargesser, Jan. 2, 1993; 1 child. BS in Mgmt. Sci., SUNY, Geneseo, 1980; MBA in Corp. Investment, U. Hartford, 1991. Cert. computer profl. Inst. Cert. Computing. Database analyst Xerox, Webster, N.Y., 1980-87; computer automated sys. engring. tool cons. Aetna, Hartford, Conn., 1987-94; cons., 1994-99; information engr. Citigroup-Travelers Life & Annuity, 1999—. Home: 575 Bridge Rd Unit 10-6 Florence MA 01062-1089 Office: Citigroup Travelers Life and Annuity 1 Tower Sq # 9ms Hartford CT 06183-0001

SWYGERT, HAYWOOD PATRICK, university president, law educator; b. Phila., Mar. 17, 1943; s. LeRoy and Gustina (Rogers) Huzzy; m. Sonja Branson, Aug. 22, 1969; children: Haywood Patrick, Michael Branson. AB in History, Howard U., 1965, JD cum laude, 1968. Bar: D.C. 1968, Pa. 1970, N.Y. 1970. Law clk. to chief judge U.S. Ct. Appeals (3d cir.), Phila., 1968—69; assoc. Debevoise, Plimpton, Lyons & Gates, N.Y.C., 1969—70; adminstrv. asst. to Congressman Charles B. Rangel NY, 1971—72; spl. asst. dist. atty. Phila., 1973; from asst. prof. to prof. law Temple U., 1972—90, v.p. adminstrn., 1982—88, exec. v.p., 1988—90; pres. SUNY, Albany, 1990—95, Howard U., Washington, 1995—. Bd. dirs. Fannie Mae, 1999. Gov.'s rep. Southeastern Pa. Transp. Authority, 1987—90; bd. trustees Inst. Pub. Adminstrn., 1992—; mem. exec. com. Pub. Law Ctr., Phila., 1980—88, N.Y. State Coun. on Humanities, 1991—; chmn. N.Y. State Spl. Commn. on ednl. structure, policies and practices, 1993—; co-chair joint task force grad. edn. Nat. Assn. State Univs. and Land Grant Colls., Am. Assn. State Coll. and Univs., 1993—; Bd. dirs. New Community Devel. Corp., HUD, 1980—82; bd. dirs. Nat. Pub. Radio, 1995—. Mem.: The Victory Funds (trustee), Middle States Assn. Colls. and Schs. (commn. on higher edn. 1992—95), Amnivs. Coun. Edn. Commn. Women in Higher Edn., ABA. Home: 3119 Arizona Ave NW Washington DC 20016-3420 Office: Howard U Office of Pres 2400 6th St NW Ste 402 Washington DC 20059-0002*

SWYSTUN-RIVES, BOHDANA ALEXANDRA, dentist; b. Kopychynci, Ukraine, Jan. 31, 1925; came to U.S., 1951; d. Peter and Maria (Ottawa) Swystun; m. John Rives, June 20, 1952 (div. 1960); 1 child, Peter A. DMD, Ludwig Maximillians Universitat, Munich, 1951; DDS, NYU, 1960. Dentist Dr. Joseph Matriss, East Rutherford, N.J., 1960-61; gen. practice dentistry Clifton, 1961-99. Vol. dentist Felician Sisters Orphanage, Lodi, N.J., 1982—; mem. Presdl. Task Force, Washington. Mem. ADA (award for commitment to professionalism and health), Ukrainian Med. Assn., Ukrainian Nat. Assn., Ukrainian Inst. Am., Clifton-Pasaic (N.J.) C. of C. Republican. Ukrainian Catholic. Avocations: reading, fgn. langs., walking, gold jewelry. Home: 149 Village Circle Glasgow KY 42141-7038

SYAT, SCOTT MITCHELL, lawyer; b. Boston, Aug. 16, 1968; s. Stephen Richard and Deborah S.; m. Shari Lynn Kaye, Oct. 4, 1998. BA, U. Mass., 1990; JD, New Eng. Sch. of Law, 1993. Bar: Mass. 1993, U.S. Dist. Ct. Mass. 1994. Mem. ABA, ATLA, Mass. Bar Assn., Mass. Acad. of Trial Attys., Mass. Criminal Defense Lawyers Assn. Office: 21 McGrath Hwy Ste 505 Quincy MA 02169

SYBINSKY, ESTRELLA BESINGA, political science educator; b. Cuindulman, Philippines, Dec. 5, 1947; d. Cornelio Rana Besinga and Josefa Olano Felisan; m. Peter Andrew Sybinsky, Jyly 29, 1972; children: Cristina Felice, Andrea Catherine. BA cun laude, U. San Carlos, Cebu City, Philippines, 1968; MA in Polit. Sci., U. Hawaii, 1971, postgrad., 1981—. Lectr. U. Hawaii, Honolulu, 1973-75, instr. Kaneohe, 1975-86, Windward C.C., Kanoehe, 1987-88; acting asst. dean, instr. U. Hawaii, 1986-87, prof. polit. sci., 1988-95; owner Felice Catherines Antiques, San Anselmo, Calif., 1996-98; asst. prof. polit. sci. Sonoma State U., Rohnert Park, 1998-99; assoc. faculty Ind. U., Columbus, 2000—; faculty polit. sci. dept. Butler U., Indpls., 2001. Spkr. in field. Author of poems. Mem.: NEA, AAUW, Tenn. Tchrs. Assn., World Affairs Coun. No. Calif., Nat. Acad. Polit. Sci., Marin Poetry Ctr., Writers Ctr. Indpls. Democrat. Roman Catholic. Avocation: writing. Home: 185 St Andrews Dr Franklin TN 37069

SYCHOV, ALYAKSANDR, diplomat; b. Homel, Belarus, Sept. 19, 1951; married; 2 children. Ministry Fgn. Affairs, Belarus, 1979-84; with Belarus permanent mission to UN office, Geneva, 1984-90; head internat. econ. rels. dept. Ministry Fgn. Affairs, Belarus, 1991-92, dep. fgn. min. Belarus, 1992-94; permanent rep. of Belarus UN, N.Y., 1994-2000, dep. fgn. min., 2000—. Mem. bur., chmn. of session com. Econ. Commn. for Europe, 1988-90; chmn. com. on internat. security and disarmament matters 51st Session UN Gen. Assembly, 1996-97, chmn. 1st com. 19th spl. session UN Gen. Assembly, 1997, vice-chmn. ECOSOC, 1998-99. Office: Ministry Fgn Affairs Belarus 19 Lenin Str Minsk Belarus

SYCKS, DAVID BRENT, music educator, musician; b. Coshocton, Ohio, Jan. 3, 1964; s. Richard Allen and Martha Virginia Sycks; m. Linda Margaret Braden, Dec. 21, 1965; children: Jane, Emily, Megan. MusB, Capital U., 1986; MusM, Ind. U., 1989. Cert. tchr. Wright State U. Band dir. Bluffton (Ohio) H.S., 1994—; applied trumpet Bluffton Coll., 2001—. Big band jazz musician. Mem.: Orgn. of Am. Kodaly Educators, Kodaly Educators of N.W. Ohio (v.p. 1999—2002), Internat. Assn. of Jazz Educators, Ohio Music Educators Assn., Internat. Trumpet Guild. Office: Bluffton H S 106 West College Bluffton OH 45817 Personal E-mail: sycksd@bf.noacsc.org.

SYDNEY, DORIS S. sports touring company executive, interior designer; b. N.Y.C., Feb. 18, 1934; d. Morris and Frances (Terrace) Steinman; m. Herbert P. Sydney, Oct. 20, 1957; children: Madeleine Jane, Peter Samuel. Student, Vassar Coll., 1950-52; BS, Columbia U., 1952-55; postgrad., NYU, 1956-57, N.Y. Sch. Interior Design, 1974. Cert. documentor Equitable Life Ins. Co., N.Y.C, 1955-57; rschr. Fairchild Publs., N.Y.C., 1957-58; furniture sales Steinman's Inc., 1958-60; interior designer, prin. Doris S. Sydney Interiors, Armonk, N.Y., 1975; exec. asst. Tennis Europe Inc., Conn., 1984—. Pres. Coman Hill Sch. PTA, 1971-72, Byram Hills H.S. PTA, 1977-79, also chair; pres. Byram Hills Scholarship Fund, 1980-82, Non-partisan Nominating Com., 1982-84; coun. del. Vassar Coll. Alumni Assn., Poughkeepsie, N.Y., 1973-77; chair Fred Caruolo Meml. Fund, 1979-81; pres. bd. trustees North Castle Pub. Libr., 1981-90; v.p. Friends North Castle Pub. Libr., 1993—; treas., pres. Armonk Hadassah, 1980—. Republican. Jewish. Home: 65 Windmill Rd Armonk NY 10504-2833 E-mail: dorissyd@aol.com.

SYDNOR, EDGAR STARKE, lawyer; b. Lynchburg, Va., Nov. 30, 1943; s. Charles Raine and Louise Allen (Starke) S.; m. Rita Frances Johnson, Dec. 28, 1965; children: Edgar Starke Jr., Elizabeth Sydnor Norris, Carlton Allen. BA in English, Washington and Lee U., 1966, JD, 1973. Bar: Va. 1973. Assoc. Edmunds, Williams, Robertson, Sackett, Baldwin & Graves, Lynchburg, 1973-75, ptnr., 1975-81; atty. Vulcan Materials Co., Birmingham, Ala., 1981-84, gen. atty., 1984-88, asst. gen. counsel, dir. pub. affairs, 1988-95, elected officer of co., 1992-2000, asst. gen. counsel chem. and environ., 1995-2000; ret., 2000. Capt. USAF, 1966-71. Presbyterian.

SYDNOR, WILLIAM ANDREW, special education educator, writer; b. Wilmington, Del., July 8, 1957; s. Margaret Elizabeth Brault and Walter Andrew Sydnor (d.1978); life ptnr. William K. Goodman. BS in Liberal Arts, Barry U., 1986; MS in Edn., Nova Southeastern U., 1996. Cert. learning disabilities/emotional handicaps Fla. Dolphin trainer, marine mammal handler Ocean World, Inc., Fort Lauderdale, Fla., 1974—81; buyer Bahia Mar Marine Store, 1981—93; spl. edn. tchr. Dade County Schools, Miami, 1988—91; curriculum specialist Broward County Sch., Fort Lauderdale, 1994—. Adj. prof. coll. of edn. Nova Southeastern U., Davie, Fla., 2000—. Author, illustrator Mitchell's Magical Day With Frank and Ivy Stranahan, 2000, Mitchell's Magical Day on the New River, 2002, illustrator (poster) Nat. Minority AIDS Coun.; contbr. Vol. grant & program writer Stranahan Ho., Inc., Fort Lauderdale, 1994—. Grantee Ednl. grant, Fla. Dept. of State, Bur. of Hist. Preservation, 2000, Tolerance/Diversity grant, CitiBank Broward Edn. Found., 2001, Gov.'s Reading Initiative grant, Fla. Dept. of Edn., 2001, Safe and Drug Free Schools Enhancement grant Broward County Schools, State of Fla. Dept. of Edn., 2002, Ednl. grant, Fla. Dept. of State, Bur. of Hist. Preservation, 2002. Mem.: NEA. Avocations: boating, bicycling, painting. Office: Broward County Schools 600 Southeast Third Avenue Fort Lauderdale FL 33301 Personal E-mail: sydnor@hotmail.com. Business E-Mail: sydnor@hotmail.com.

SYDOW, MICHAEL DAVID, lawyer; b. Dec. 12, 1950; m. Kelli McDonald; children: Kristen, David, Wyatt. BA, Southwestern U., 1973; JD with honors, U. Tex., 1976. Bar: Tex. 1976, U.S. Ct. Claims 1977, U.S. Ct. Appeals (5th cir.) 1977, U.S. Dist. Ct. (so. dist.) Tex. 1977, U.S. Dist. Ct. (ea. dist.) Tex. 1979, U.S. Supreme Ct. 1980, U.S. Dist. Ct. (no. dist.) Tex. 1985, U.S. Dist. Ct. (we. dist.) Tex. 1986; cert. in civil trial law Tex. Bd. Legal Specialization. Trial atty. Office Gen. Counsel USN, Arlington, Va., 1976-77; mem. firm Eastham, Watson, Dale & Forney, Houston, 1977-84, Hagans & Sydow, LLP, Houston, 1985-90, Reynolds & Sydow, LLP, Houston, 1993-94; pvt. practice, 1990-93; with Sydow & McDonald, LLP, 1995-97; shareholder Verner, Liipfert, Bernhard, McPherson & Hand, Houston, 1997—. Fellow Tex. Bar Found., Houston Bar Found.; mem. Houston Bar Assn. (chmn. jud. liaison com. 1988-90, Pres.'s award 1990), Maritime Law Assn. U.S. (mem. com. on gen. average 1977-88, practice and procedures com. 1988—), State Bar Tex., Phi Delta Phi. Address: Verner Liipfert Bernhard McPherson & Hand Chartered 1111 Bagby St Ste 4650 Houston TX 77002-2543

SYED, ELIZABETH CHANCE, medical/surgical nurse; b. Clermont, Fla., Oct. 18, 1958; d. Brooker Lawson and Beulah Catharine (Lord) Chance; m. Mohsin M. Syed, Dec. 30, 1993; children: Adam, Jibran. B in Gen. Studies, Howard Payne U., 1981; MA in Comm. without thesis, SW Bapt. Theol. Sem., 1985; ADN, Ea. N.Mex. U., 1988. Cert. CCRN, program nurse sr. options, med. office mgr. Critical care nurse Meml. Hosp. & Med. Ctr., Midland, Tex., 1990—, Angelo Cmty. Med. Ctr., San Angelo, 1992; staff nurse ICU Med. Ctr. Hosp., Odessa, 1998; mental health nurse Glenwood Hosp., Midland, 1998—; office mgr. Family Care Clinic, 1998—. Instr. ACLS. Mem. Cmty. Chorale, Farmington, N.Mex., 1981, Roswell, N.Mex., 1989-90. Mem. AACN (rsch. assoc. Thunder Project 1991-92). Baptist. Avocation: music. Office: Family Care Clinic 4506 Briarwood Ave Midland TX 79707-2642

SYED, IBRAHIM BIJLI, medical educator and physicist, writer, philosopher, theologist, public speaker, writer; b. Bellary, India, Mar. 16, 1939; came to U.S., 1969, naturalized, 1975; s. Ahmed Bijli and Mumtaz Begum (Maniyar) S.; m. Sajida Shariff, Nov. 29, 1964; children: Mubin, Zafrin. BS with honors, Veerasaiva Coll., Bellary U., Mysore, 1960; MS with honors and distinction, Bangalore U., Mysore, 1962; diploma, U. Bombay, 1964; DSc, Johns Hopkins U., 1972; PhD (hon.), Malta, 1985. Cert. hazard control officer, 1980, internat. health care safety profl., 1980; diplomate Am. Bd. Radiology, Am. Bd. Health Physics. Lectr. physics Veerasaiva Coll., Bellary U., Mysore, 1962-63; med. physicist, radiation safety officer Victoria Hosp., India, 1964-67, Bowring and Lady Curz on Hosp. & Postgrad. Med. Rsch. Inst., Bangalore, India, 1964-67; cons. med. physicist, radiation safety officer Ministry of Health, Govt. of Karnataka, India, 1964-67, Bangalore Nursing Home, India, 1964-67; med. physicist, radiation safety officer Baystate Med. Ctr., Springfield, Mass., 1973-79; assoc. prof. Springfield Tech. C.C.; also adj. prof. radiology Holyoke (Mass.) C.C., 1973-79; asst. clin. prof. nuclear medicine U. Conn. Sch. Medicine, Farmington, 1975-79; cons. med. physicist Mercy Hosp., Springfield, 1973-79, Wing Meml. Hosp., Palmer, Mass., 1973-79; med. physicist, radiation safety officer VAMC, Louisville, 1979—, exec. officer radiation safety com., 1979—; prof. medicine U. Louisville Sch. Medicine, 1979—, dir. nuclear med. scis., 1980—; mem. Instl. Review Bd. Veterans Admin. Medical Ctr., Louisville, 2000—. Guest lectr. religious studies program U. Louisville, 1979—; vis. prof. Bangalore U., 1987—88, Gulbarga U., India, 1987—88; vis. scientist Bhabha Atomic Rsch. Ctr., Bombay; invited spkr. Veerasaiva Coll., Bellary, India, 1996, Vijayanagar Coll., Hospet, 1996, Vajayanagar Inst. Med. Scis., Bellary, 1996, Deccan Coll. Med. Scis., Hyderabad, India, Bhabha Atomic Rsch. Ctr., Bombay, 1997, 15th Ann. Islamic Conf. New Eng., Islamic Coun. New Eng., 1999, Coun. for a Parliament of the World's Religions, Cape Town, South Africa, 1999, Garden City Coll. Bangalore, 2000, Veerasaiva Coll., Bellary, 2000, Islamic Rsch. Found., Mumbai, India, 2001, Islamic Assn. of Essex, England, 2001, Assn. Muslim Social Scientists, Detroit, 2001; PhD thesis examiner Allahabad U., 1996—; course dir. licensing for nuclear cardiologists U. Louisville, 1980—, mem. admissions com. nuclear medicine program, 1980—; guest relief examiner Am. Bd. Radiology, 1991; examiner in radiol physics, 95, 97, 98, 2000; mem. panel of examiners Am. Bd. Health Physics ; PhD thesis examiner U. Delhi, Internat. Inst. for Advanced Study, Clayton, Mo., 1985—, Allahabad (India) U., 1996—; faculty mem. Med. Physicists of India Ann. Meeting, 1987; IAEA tchr. expert in nuclear medicine on mission to People's Republic of Bangladesh, 86; to Guatemala, 94; founder, pres. Islamic Rsch. Found. for Advancement of Knowledge, Louisville, 1988—; convener Internat. Conf. on Islamic Renaissance: Action Plan for the 21st Century, Chgo., 1995; cons. Coun. Sci. and Indsl. Rsch., Govt. India, 0809—, Am. Coun. Sci. and Health, 1980—; cons. gastroenterology and urology divsn. FDA, HHS, 1988—, cons. radiopharm. divsn., 1989—; cons. Govt. India in nuclear medicine, diagnostic radiol. physics, therapeutic radiol. physics and radiation safety, 1992; cons. radiol. and med. nuc. physics Govt. India, Un Devel. Program, 1992; convenor Internat. Conf. on Islamic Renaissance, Chgo., 1995; guest spkr. Muslim Cmty. Ctr., Chgo., 1988; invited spkr. objective studies and Islamic voice, Bangalore, 96, Parliament of World Religions, Chgo., 1993, Cape Town, South Africa, 99. Author: Radiation Safety for Allied Health Professionals, Radiation Safety Manual, 1979; contbg. editor Jour. of Islamic Food and Nutrition Coun. of Am., 1986—, health and sci. column Muslim Jour., 1989—; freelance writer Minaret Biweekly, N.Y.C., 1975—, Islamic Voice, India, 1988—, Al-Balaagh, Lenasia, South Africa, 1989—, AL'FURQAN Internat., Norcross, Ga., 1990, Message Internat., Jamaica, N.Y., 1990, Minaret Monthly Mag., L.A., 1995—, The Message, London, 1998—, The Minaret, Botswana, 1998—; editor: Science and Technology for the Developing World, 1988; mem. editl. bd. Jour. Islamic Med. Assn., 1981—; regular contbr. Pres.'s Page; manuscript reviewer for sci. and med. jours., 1973; assoc. editor AAlim, 1998—; contbr. more than 100 articles to sci. jours.; pub. internat. more than 110 articles on various topics of Islam in jours. and mags. Moderator fgn. policy workshop U.S. Dept. State, Louisville, 2000; spkr. Dayton (Ohio) Islamic Ctr., 2000, Muslim Student Assn. U. Cin., 2000; spkr.. Muslim Cmty. Ctr., Chgo., 2001; invited spkr. Muslim Assn. of Cleveland East, Cleve., 2002. Recipient Disting. Cmty. Svc. award India Cmty. Found., 1982, Hind Rattan Jewel of India Title award Govt. India, 1994; WHO fellow, Govt. India scholar Bhabha Atomic Rsch. Ctr., Bombay, 1963-64; USPHS fellow Johns Hopkins U., 1969-72. Fellow Inst. Physics (U.K.), Am. Inst. Chemists, Royal Soc. Health, Am. Coll. Radiology, Internat. Acad. Med. Physics; mem. Am. Assn. Physicists in Medicine, Am. Coll. Nuclear Medicine, Health Physics Soc., Am. Acad. Health Physics, Soc. Nuclear Medicine (faculty mem. ann. meeting 1987, convenor internat. conf. 1995), Nat. Assn. Ams. of Asian Indian Descent (chmn. state pub. rels. com. 1982—), Islamic Med. Assn. N.Am. (life, faculty 1994, 96, 98), Internat. Inst. Islamic Medicine (faculty Orlando, Fla. 1996, 97, Birmingham, U.K. 1998), Islamic Soc. N.Am. (faculty Chgo. 1998), Islamic Soc. Balt. (founding mem.), Islamic Cultural Ctr., Louisville, Islamic Assn. Maritime Provinces Can., Halifax, N.S. (asst. sec. 1967-69), Health Physics Soc. (chmn. med. health physics com. 1989—, affirmative action com. 1984—), Am. Assn. Physicists in Medicine (biol. effects com.), Assn. Muslim Scientists and Engrs. N.Am. (program chmn. ann. conf. 1987, treas. 1987-88, sec. 1988—), AAUP, Soc. Nuclear Medicine India (life, faculty mem. ann. meeting 1987, invited spkr. and faculty ann. meeting 1996), Assn. Med. Physicists India (life, invited spkr. and faculty ann. meeting Madras 1996), Med. and Biol. Physics (divsn. Can.) Assn. Physicists, Hosp. Physicists Assn., N.Y. Acad. Scis., Islamic Assn. Maritime Provinces of Can., Ky. Med. Assn., Jefferson County Med. Soc. (assoc.), Sigma Xi. Islamic. Home: 7102 W Shefford Ln Louisville KY 40242-6462 Office: 800 Zorn Ave Louisville KY 40206-1433 E-mail: irfi@iname.com.

SYED, YASSER FOUAD KHADERI, electrical engineer; b. Halifax, Nova Scotia, Can., Sept. 9, 1968; s. Asif Syed, Amtul Syed; m. Romana Yasser Shahdad; children: Arva Hanan. BS cum laude, Rensselaer Polytechnic Inst., 1990; MS Elec. Engring., U. So. Calif., L.A., 1992; DPhil Elec. Engring., U. Tex., 1999. Sr. systems engri. SpectraPoint Wireless, Richardson, Colo., 1996—2000; project mgr. emerging digital video techs. CableLabs, Louisville, 2000—. Assoc. mem. INCITS, Washington, 2000—. Named Dean's List, Rensselaer Polytechnic Inst., 1986—90; grantee, Tex. Instruments, 1998; scholar, Hewlett-Packard, 1990. Mem.: IEEE (3d pl. Grad. Paper Contest 1998), Greater Dallas Indo- Am. C. of C. (bd. dirs. 1999—2000), Alpha Phi Omega, Eta Kappa Nu, Tau Beta Pi. Office: Cable Television Laboratories Inc 400 Centennial Pkwy Louisville CO 80027 Personal E-mail: yasser_syed@ieee.org.

SYEED, SAYYID MUHAMMED, religious organization administrator; , naturalized, U.S. PhD in Sociolinguistics, Ind. U., 1984; LittD (hon.) , Grad. Theol. Found., Donaldson, Ind., 2001. Sec. gen. Internat. Islamic Fedn. Student Orgns., 1984—88; dir. acad. outreach Internat. Inst. Islamic Thought, Washington, 1984—94; sec. gen. Islamic Soc. N.Am. Mem. bd. advisors Coun. Am.-Islamic Rels. Founder Am. Jour. Islamic Social Scis., editor-in-chief, 1984—94, mem. bd. adv. editors Mid. East Affairs Jour., chmn. editl. bd. Islamic Horizons, 1982—84. Bd. trustees Coun. for Parliament of World's Religions. Recipient Lifetime Achievement award, Cath. Heritage Found., 2001. Office: Islamic Soc NAm PO Box 38 Plainfield IN 46168-0038

SYGNECKI, CHRISTINA, sales executive; b. Forest Hills, N.Y., Aug. 30, 1954; d. Rene Julien and Marie Helene (Popovic) S.; m. Mark Spencer Conroy, May 22, 1977 (div. Dec. 1988). BA, U. Miami, 1974. Outside sales mgr. Cream of the Valley, Sacramento, 1983-84; dept. mgr. Oakville Grocery, San Francisco, 1984-85; store mgr. La Ferme Beaujolaise, 1985-86; chef, owner Nina Rent-A-Chef, 1986-88; mdse. coord. Carnival Cruise Lines, Miami, 1988-93; sales mgr. duty free Greyhound Leisure Svcs., 1993-95; sales mgr. cruise ships Weitnauer Am. Trading, 1995-96; mgr. Pertex Textile Products, Bloomfield Hills, Mich., 1996-97; metro mgr. Artisans and Estates of Kendall Jackson Winery, Santa Rosa, Calif., 1997—2002; territory mgr. Corterra Wines of Kendall Jackson Winery, 2002—. Mem. Seigneurs de Corbieres, France. Mem. Chaine des Rotisseurs (vice echanson, Merit award 1996), Sommelier Guild (v.p. 1993—), Ordre des Canardiers. Republican. Roman Catholic. Avocations: yoga, travel, wine collecting, literature, music. Home and Office: 6559 Harvey Ave Pennsauken NJ 08109-2459

SYKES, ALAN O'NEIL, lawyer, educator; b. Bethesda, Md., Oct. 10, 1954; s. Alan O'Neil and Emily (Adams) S.; m. Maureen J. Gorman, June 29, 1980; children: Madeleine, Sophie. BA, Coll. William and Mary, 1976; JD, Yale U., 1982, PhD in Econs., 1987. Bar: Mass., D.C. Atty. Office of Arnold & Porter, Washington, 1982-86; asst. prof. law U. Chgo., 1986-90, prof. law, 1990—, Frank and Bernice Greenberg prof., 2002—. Ind. law cons., Chgo., 1990—; vis. prof. law Harvard U., Cambridge, Mass., 1991, NYU, 1996. Author: Product Standards for International and Integrated Goods Markets, 1995, Legal Problems of International Economic Relations, 2002. NSF fellow, 1976-79. Mem. ABA, Am. Econ. Assn., Am. Law and Econs. Assn. (bd. dirs. 1999—). Office: U Chgo Sch of Law 1111 E 60th St Chicago IL 60637 E-mail: alan_sykes@law.uchicago.edu.

SYKES, DIANE S. state supreme court justice; b. Milw. children: Jay, Alexander. B, Northwestern U., 1980; JD, Marquette U., 1984. Reporter Milw. Jour.; law clk. to Hon. Terence T. Evans; assoc. Whyte & Hirschboeck S.C.; judge Milw. County Ct., 1992, Wis. Supreme Ct., Madison, 1999—. Office: Wis Supreme Ct PO Box 1688 Madison WI 53702*

SYKES, GRESHAM M'CREADY, sociologist, educator, artist; b. Plainfield, N.J., May 26, 1922; s. M'Cready and Beatrice (Evans) S.; m. Carla Adelt, July 13, 1946. AB summa cum laude, Princeton U., 1950; PhD (Woodrow Wilson fellow 1950-51, Univ. fellow 1951-52), Northwestern U., 1953; MA (hon.), Dartmouth Coll., 1961. Instr. sociology Princeton U., 1952-54, asst. prof., bicentennial preceptor, 1954-58; assoc. prof. Northwestern U., Evanston, Ill., 1958-60; prof. sociology Dartmouth Coll., Hanover, N.H., 1960-63, chmn. dept., 1961-63; exec. officer Am. Sociol. Assn., 1963-65; research prof. law and sociology, dir. adminstrn. of justice program U. Denver, 1965-72; chmn. dept. sociology U. Houston, 1973; prof. sociology U. Va., Charlottesville, 1974-88, chmn. dept., 1978-81, emeritus prof., 1988—. Chmn. Salzburg (Austria) Seminar in Am. Studies, summer 1965; working as artist, with frequent group and one-man exhbns., 1988—. Author: Crime and Society, rev. edit., 1967, The Society of Captives, 1958, Law and the Lawless, 1969, Social Problems in America, 1971, Criminology, 1978, rev. edit., 1992, The Future of Crime, 1980; criminology editor Jour. Criminal Law, Criminology and Police Sci., 1959-64; assoc. editor Rev. Am. Sociol. Assn., 1960-62, Contemporary Sociology, 1977-80, Criminology, 1980-84; contbr. articles and revs. to Ency. Britannica, profl. jours. Served to capt., C.E. AUS, 1942-46, ETO. Recipient Edwin H. Sutherland award Am. Soc. Criminology, 1980. Home: 311 2nd St NW # B Charlottesville VA 22902-5011 E-mail: gms6m@virginia.edu.

SYKES, MELVIN JULIUS, lawyer; b. Balt., Jan. 9, 1924; s. Philip Louis and Sara (Klein) S.; m. Judith Janet Konowitz, Sept.24, 1950; children: David K., Rachel A. (dec.), Daniel E., Israel J. Grad., Balt. City Coll., 1940, Balt. Hebrew Coll., 1941; AB with honors, Johns Hopkins U., 1943; LLB magna cum laude, Harvard U., 1948. Bar: Md. 1949, U.S. Ct. Appeals (4th cir.) 1949, U.S. Dist. Ct. Md. 1950, U.S. Supreme Ct. 1955. Law clk. to Judge Morris A. Soper U.S. Ct. Appeals (4th cir.), 1948-49; pvt. practice Balt., 1949—. Draftsman Md. Dept. Legislative Reference, 1949—50; rsch. cons. Md. Commn. Adminstrv. Orgn., 1951—52; reporter Md. Commns. to Study Judiciary, 1953, Md. commns. to revise law relating to pub. svc. commn. , 1953—55; mem. standing com. on rules of practice, procedure Md. Ct. Appeals, 1954—72, 1978—; mem. legis. coun. Commsn. on Revision Condemnation Laws, 1961—63; mem. Balt. Charter Revision Com., 1962—63; pres. Bar Libr. Balt., 1962—63; mem. Md. Constl. Conv. Commn., 1966—67; cons. Gov. Md. Commn. to Revise Testamentary Laws, 1967—69; mem. Gov. Md. Commns. tostudy state aid to nonpub. edn., 1969—71, Md. Code Revision Commn., 1970—78. Co-author: West's Maryland Procedural Forms, 1964, Jewish Law (Mishpat Ivri), Cases and Materials, 1999; co-translator Elon, Jewish Law--History, Principles, Sources, 1994. Bd. dirs. Balt. Neighborhoods; mem. governing coun. Am. Assn. Jewish Edn., 1968—81; Balt. Jewish Coun., 1970—72; bd. dirs. Balt. chpt. Am. Jewish Com.; former mem. and chmn. bd. trustees Balt. Hebrew U. With USAF, 1943—45. Fellow Am. Coll. Trial Lawyers, Am. Coll. Trust and Estate Counsel, Am. Bar Found., Md. Bar Found. (chmn. 1981-83); mem. ABA, Am. Law Inst., Md. Bar Assn., Balt. City Bar Assn. (lectr. continuing edn. programs), Am. Jewish Congress, Balt. Zionist Dist., B'nai B'rith, Phi Beta Kappa Fellows. Democrat. Home: 3811 Fords Ln Baltimore MD 21215-2804 Office: Ste 1701 120 E Baltimore St Baltimore MD 21202-6701

SYKES, PAULA MARIE, school counselor; b. Somers Point, N.J., July 6, 1954; d. Richard Issac and Eleanor Marie (Landry) Cressey; m. Joseph William Sykes Jr., July 10, 1981; children: Kristina Marie, Teighan Marie. BA in Elem. Edn., Glassboro State Coll., 1978, MA in Student Pers. Svcs., 1981. Cert. tchr., N.J.; cert. sch. counselor, N.J. 3d grade tchr. Egg Harbor Twp. (N.J.) Bd. Edn., 1978-81, sch. counselor, 1981—, mem. pupil assessment com., 1994, chairperson pupil intervention com., 1989—99, coord. presdl. acad. fitness award com., 1987—, coord. Children are People com., 1990—, coord. peer leadership tng., 1994-98, peer mediation coord., instr., 1995—, pupil assistance com., 1999—, intervention and referral svc. team, 2000—, 504 com., 1995—. Mem. Absecon PTO, past assembly com., past tchr.-of-yr. com.; vol. Atlantic City Med. Ctr., 1986-87; bd. dirs. Egg Harbor Twp. Cmty. Ctr., 1995-98. Mem. Alpha Delta Kappa (altruistic chairperson 1990). Republican. Roman Catholic. Home: 605 Chelsea Rd Absecon NJ 08201-1618 Office: Egg Harbor Twp Bd Edn EHT Intermediate Sch 25 Alder Ave Egg Harbor Township NJ 08234-5315

SYKORA, BARBARA ZWACH, state legislator; b. Tracy, Minn., Mar. 5, 1941; d. John M. and Agnes (Schueller) Zwach; m. Robert G. Sykora, 1965; children: Mona, John, Kara, Mary. BA, St. Catherine Coll., 1963. Tchr. Springfield (Mass.) Sch., 1963-64, Roseville (Minn.) Sch., 1964-66; mem. Minn. Ho. of Reps., St. Paul, 1994—. Bd. dirs. Beacon Bank. Vice chmn. 2d Congl. Dist. Rep. Com., Minn., 1978-82; chmn. 6th Congl. Dist. Rep. Com., 1982-86, 2d congl. dist. Senator Durenberger Campaign, 1980-82, Senator Pillsbury Campaign, Wayzata, Minn., 1980; chair Ind. Rep. State Com., Minn., 1987-93; dist. dir. Office Congressman Rod Grams, 1993-94; bd. dirs. Animal Humane Soc. Hennepin County, Minn. Acad. Excellence Found.; chair Family and Early Childhood Edn. Com., 1999-2002; chair Legis. Commn. on lEcon. Status of Women, 2001—. Mem. Excelsior C. of C., Hopkins/Minnetonka Rotary. E-mial. E-mail: bsykora@uswestmail.net.

SYKORA, HAROLD JAMES, military officer; b. Tripp, S.D., Mar. 10, 1939; s. James J. and Mary (Tucek) S.; m. Patricia Ann Friedrich, Dec. 26, 1962; children: Montgomery James, Gina Marie. BS, U. S.D., 1961, MA in Math., 1965; postgrad., U. Wis., 1971-72, Indsl. Coll. Armed Forces, Ft. McNair, Washington, 1987-88. Math. tchr. Mitchell (S.D.) Sr. H.S., 1961-64, 65-71, 72-74; commd. U.S. Army; advanced through grades to maj. gen.; with U.S. Army Command and Gen. Staff Coll., Ft. Leavenworth, Kans., 1974-75; exec. officer hdqs. 147th F.A. S.D. N.G., Pierre, 1975-80; tng. officer hdqrs. S.D. N.G., Rapid City, 1980-83, chief of staff, 1983-87, adj. gen., 1988-98; pvt. practice def. industry cons., 1998—. Bd. dirs. Am. Sys. Corp., Inc., Am. Sys. Internat. Alumni Achievement award U. S.D., 1996. Mem. N.G. Assn. S.D. (pres. 1979-80), N.G. Assn. U.S. (chmn. fire support task force 1998—), Am. Legion, Assn. U.S. Army, Adjutant's Gen. Assn. U.S. (sec. 1991-97, Army res. forces policy com. 1992-97, chmn. Army res. forces policy com. 1995-97), Rapid City Area C. of C. Republican. Roman Catholic. Home and Office: 5204 Pinedale Hts Rapid City SD 57702-2079 E-mail: sykorajh@aol.com.

SYKORA, PETR, professional hockey player; b. Plzen, Czechoslovakia, Nov. 19, 1976; Center Cleve. Lumberjacks, 1993-94, Detroit Vipers, 1994-95, AHL, Albany; center, left wing, right wing N.J. Devils, 1995—2002, Anaheim Mighty Ducks, 2002—. Named to NHL All-Rookie Team, 1995-96. Office: Anaheim Mighty Ducks Arrowhead Pond of Anaheim 2695 East Katella Ave. Anaheim CA 92806*

SYLER, ELEANOR GRACE, psychology educator, writer; b. Rockcastle County, Ky., Dec. 6, 1933; d. Casper Martin and Elsie Mae (Hale) Owens; m. Clair Wade Syler, Aug. 20, 1953; children: Dana Lee, Christopher Wayne. BS, Evangel U., 1977; MS, S.W. Mo. State U., 1978; EdD, Nova Southeastern U., 1990. Asst. to dean of students Evangel U., Springfield, Mo., 1978-82, dir. Ctr. for Effective Learning, 1982-98, asst. prof. behavioral scis., 1982—2000, assoc. prof. behavioral scis., 1996—2000, prof. emeritus, 2000—. Field reader Dept. Edn., Office Postsecondary Edn., Washington, 1990-2000. Author: Successful Study Skills for Serious Students, 1986; contbr. articles to profl. jours. Lic. min. Assemblies of God, Springfield, Mo.; dir. Christian edn. First Assembly of God, Strafford, Mo., 1992—. Recipient Cert. Appreciation Nat. Assn. Devel. Edn., 1996, Gov.'s award for excellence in tchg., Mo., 1998, Disting. Svc. award Evangel U. Alumni Assn., 2001. Mem. M.W. Regional Assn. Devel. Edn. (pres.-elect 1991-92, pres. 1992-93, Outstanding Educator award 1997), Mo. Writer's Guild, Ozarks Writers League, Christian Writer's Club. Republican. Assemblies of God. Avocations: writing Christmas plays and performances, emboidery. Home: PO Box 251 Strafford MO 65757 E-mail: sylere@aol.com.

SYLK, LEONARD ALLEN, housing company executive, real estate developer; b. Phila., Feb. 25, 1941; s. Harry S. and Gertrude (Bardy) S.; m. Barbara Ann Lovenduski, Dec. 1, 1975; children: Tristan, Tyler, Galen. BS in Econs., U. Pa., 1963; MBA, Columbia U., 1965. Cert. comml. property builder. Founder, chmn. bd., CEO Shelter Systems Corp., Hainesport, N.J., 1965-99; ret.; prin., CEO Property Mgmt. Svcs., Hainesport, N.J. Bd. dirs. Home Owners Warranty Corp., N.J., v.p., 1988-95; bd. dirs. Internat. Housing Com., Nat. Comml. Builders Coun., 1986-97; vice chmn. USA Bancshares, Inc., 1998-2000; chmn., bd. govs. Mid. East Forum; trustee Nat. Bldg. Sys. Coun., 1986—; presdl. advisor on housing trade with Soviet Union, 1990; bldg. industry advisor U.S. Dept. Commerce, 1997-99. Contbr. articles to industry publs. Chmn. ann. awards dinner Jewish Nat. Fund, Phila., 1987, v.p., bd. dirs.; bd. dirs. Phila. Orch. Assn., 1990-98; bd. dirs. Pa. Ballet, 1994-99, exec. com., 1996-99, vice-chmn., pres., 1998; bd. dirs. Resources for Childrens' Health, 1993-96, Acad. Music, Phila., 1990-96, Rock Sch. of Pa. Ballet, 1995-98, Young Scholars Charter Sch., 2000—, Merion Civic Assn., 2000—; bd. dirs. Jewish Nat. Fund, 1987—, v.p., 2000—; N.J. chmn. Builders for Bush, 1988; trustee Hahnemann U. and Hosp., 1991-96; vice chmn., trustee St. Christopher's Hosp. for Children, Phila., 1994—, chmn. St. Christophers Found. for Children, 1999, v.p., bd. dirs., 1999—; chmn. 1999 , bd. dirs., vice chmn. St. Peter's Sch, Phila., 1995—; trustee Allegheny U. Hosps., 1998; bd. govs. Young Scholars Charter Sch. Phila., 1999—. Named Man. of Yr., 1988, Man of Yr., N.J. C. of C., 2002; recipient Tree of Life award presented by R. Hon. Margaret Thatcher, 1995. Mem. Nat. Assn. Homebuilders (com. chmn., nat. bd. dirs. 1984—, mem. exec. com. 1990, 97, fundraising chmn. 1991, Man of Yr. in Industrialized Housing 1990), Wood Truss Coun. Am. (bd. dirs. 1983—, pres. 1987, named to Hall of Fame 1990), Builders League South Jersey (v.p., bd. dirs. 1984-94), N.J. Builders Assn. (bd. dirs., com. chmn., exec. com. 1990-96), Merion Civic Assn. (bd. dirs. 1999—), Le Club (N.Y.C.), Atlantic City Country Club, Vesper Club, Union League, Capitol Club (Washington), Masons. Republican. Home: 350 N Highland Ave Merion Station PA 19066-1708 Office: Property Mgmt Svcs PO Box 9 Hainesport NJ 08036-0009

SYLLA, RICHARD EUGENE, economics educator; b. Harvey, Ill., Jan. 16, 1940; s. Benedict Andrew and Mary Gladys (Curran) S.; m. Edith Anne Dudley, June 22, 1963; children: Anne Curran, Margaret Dudley. BA, Harvard U., 1962, MA, 1965, PhD, 1969. Prof. econs. and bus. N.C. State U., Raleigh,

1968-90; Henry Kaufman prof. history fin. insts. and markets NYU, N.Y.C., 1990—, prof. econs., 1990—. Cons. Citibank NA, N.Y.C., 1979-82, Chase Manhattan Bank, N.Y.C., 1983-85; vis. prof. U. Pa., Phila., 1983, U. N.C., Chapel Hill, 1988; rsch. assoc. Nat. Bur. of Econ. Rsch., 1983—; trustee Mus. Am. Fin. History, 2002-. Author: The American Capital Market, 1975; co-author: Evolution of the American Economy, 1980, 2d edit., 1993, A History of Interest Rates, 1991, rev. edit., 1996; co-editor: Patterns of European Industrialization, 1991, Anglo-American Financial Systems, 1995, The State, The Financial System, and Economic Modernization, 1999; editor Jour. Econ. History, 1978-84. Trustee Mus. Am. Fin. History, 2002—. Study fellow NEH, 1975-76; Rsch. grantee NSF, 1985-94, 98-02, Sloan Found., 1995-97. Mem. Am. Econs. Assn., Econ. History Assn. (v.p. 1987-88, trustee 1977-88, Arthur H. Cole prize 1970, pres. 2000-2001), Bus. History Conf. (trustee 1991-94, 2002—), So. Econ. Assn. (v.p. 1981-82), Cliometrics Soc. (trustee 1997-2000, trustee chair 1998-2000). Avocations: golf, hiking, stamp collecting, arts. Home: 110 Bleecker St Apt 23D New York NY 10012-2106 Office: NYU 44 W 4th St New York NY 10012-1106 E-mail: rsylla@stern.nyu.edu.

SYLVESTER, GEORGE HOWARD, retired air force officer; b. Riverside, N.J., Aug. 10, 1927; s. Ralph Davis and Dorothy Clarisse (Mealley) S.; m. Elaine Ruth Winderling, June 7, 1949; children— Wendy, Susan, David. BS, U.S. Mil. Acad., 1949; MA, Georgetown U., 1956. llama farmer, 1999—. Commd. 2d lt. USAF, 1949, advanced through grades to lt. gen., 1976; pilot, 1949-54; asst. prof. social scis. U.S. Mil. Acad., 1956-60; long-range planner Hdqrs. U.S. Air Force, 1961-64; mil. asst. to sec. def., 1964-66; squadron comdr. F-4 squadron Vietnam, 1966; comdr. Danang Air Base, Vietnam, 1967; dir. test Eglin AFB, Fla., 1968-70; asst. dir. tactical systems test and evaluation Office Sec. Def., 1970-73; dep. for systems ASD, Wright-Patterson AFB, Ohio, 1973-74, vice comdr., 1974-76, comdr., 1976-79; vice comdr. AF Systems Command, Andrews AFB, Md., 1979-81; ret., 1981; ind. aerospace cons., 1981—. Chmn. Shenandoah County Water Resources Com. Decorated D.S.M. with 1 oak leaf cluster, Legion of Merit with 2 oak leaf clusters, D.F.C., Air medal with 7 oak leaf clusters. Lutheran. Home: 4839 Conicville Rd Mount Jackson VA 22842-2800

SYLVESTER, JOHN EDWARD, social worker; b. N.Y.C., Apr. 13, 1949; s. John and Esther (Larkin) S.; m. Dolores Alcantara, July 2, 1974. BA in Psychology, CUNY, 1975; cert. in social work, Fordham U., 1977. Program coord. Mid. Bronx (N.Y.) Sr. Citizen's Coun., 1980-82; assoc. editor N.Y.C. Self-Help Clearing House, 1978-80; case worker Cath. Guardian Soc., N.Y.C., 1982-83, Assn. for Advancement of the Blind, Queens, N.Y., 1984-86; probation officer N.Y.C. Dept. of Probation, Bronx, 1987-88; parole officer N.Y. State Div. of Parole, N.Y.C., 1988-92; program dir. Ehrlich Supported Housing Program for Homeless Univ. Consultation and Treatment Ctr. for Mental Hygiene, Bronx, 1992-95; tenant organizer N.W. Bronx Cmty. and Clergy Coalition, 1998-2000; intensive case mgr. Steinway Child and Family Svc., Queens, 2000—. Mem. Am. Servicemen's Union, N.Y.C., 1968; vol. ARC, N.Y.C., 1973; hot line vol. The Samaritans of N.Y., N.Y.C., 1998—. With USMC, 1967-70, Vietnam. Named one of Outstanding Young Men in Am., U.S. Jaycees, 1982. Mem. Assn. Black Social Workers, Amnesty Internat. Home: 637 Willow Brook Rd Clinton Corners NY 12514-2539 Fax: 718-391-9665. E-mail: talktous@steinway.org.

SYLVESTER, KATHRYN ROSE, lawyer; b. Camden, N.J., Jan. 20, 1968; d. Frank Albert and Bergetta Anne Sylvester; m. William S. Palmieri; 1 child McKinley Kathryn Palmieri. BA, Rosemont (Pa.) Coll., 1990; MS in Environ. Law, Vt. Law Sch., South Royalton, 1991, JD, 1994. Bar: Conn., U.S. Dist. Ct. Conn.; mem. Gaming Disputes Ct., Mohegan Tribe. Temp. asst. clk. Milford (Conn.) Superior Ct., 1994-97; assoc. Waller, Smith & Palmer, P.C., New London, Conn., 1997-98, Hunt, Leibert Chester & Jacobson, Hartford, 1998—. Mem. ABA, New Haven County Bar Assn. Avocations: blues music, travel, antiquarian books, antiques, cooking. Home: 270 Wooding Hill Bethany CT 06524-3407 Office: Hunt Leibert Chester & Jacobson 94 Hungerford St Hartford CT 06106-4638

SYLVESTER, RICHARD RUSSELL, economist, management executive; b. Jan. 10, 1938; s. Leslie Gardner and Effie (Williams) S.; m. Irene Elizabeth Lehman, Apr. 17, 1976; children: Bonnie Ann, Vicky Ellis, Juliesta Elaine. BA, UCLA, 1959; MBA, U. So. Calif., 1962; PhD, UCLA, 1970, postgrad., 1971-74; JD, Loyola U., 1981. Designer corp. offices GM Corp., Warren, Mich., 1958; sr. analyst Lockheed Aircraft Corp., Burbank, Calif., 1962-66; sr. planner corp. offices Hughes Aircraft Co., Culver City, 1966-68; sr. staff economist, staff mgr. TRW, Inc., Redondo Beach, 1969-70; pres. Def. Rsch. Co., 1970-81, Sylvester Consulting Group, 1970—, PhD Pub. Co., 1970—, Sylvester Appraisal Co., 1970—, U.S. Electropower Controls Corp., 1970-71. Asst. prof. Calif. State U., 1970-73; mgr. corp. planning Brunswick Def./Celesco, Costa Mesa, Calif., 1973-75; staff specialist strategic planning Gen. Dynamics Corp., 1981-83; strategic analysis specialist Northrop Corp., 1983-89; cons. econs., engring. and fin., L.A., 1970—; lectr. Northrop U., U. Calif., U. So. Calif., Loyola U., La Verne U., 1961-81; asst. prof. Calif. State U., 1970-73, lectr., 1989—; assoc. prof. Pepperdine U., 1975-76, lectr., 1994—; lectr. U. Redlands, 1997—, UCLA, 1999—; co-founder Theta Cable TV, L.A., 1966-67. Author: Management Decisions and Actions, 3d edit., 1988, Investment Strategy, 1982, Tax Planning, 4th edit., 1980, Strategic Planning, 6th edit., 1990, Investment Planning and Tax Planning Software, 1983-93, Strategic Financial Planning, 1993, Future Challenge, Financial Strategy and Tax Planning, 1993, International Transfer Pricing, 1994, Quantitative Methods, 1997, Calculus for Executive Decisions, 1999, 2d edit, 2002, Mathematical Methods for Economics and Law, 1999; contbr. tech. reports to profl. lit. Fellow UCLA, 1970; postdoctoral scholar in engring., UCLA, 1971-74; GM scholar, 1953-57; Ford Found. grantee, 1965, U.S. Fed. Govt. rsch. grantee, 1967-70. Mem. Westwood Hills Christian Ch. (bd. dirs. 1978-81, 91-93), Beta Gamma Sigma, Alpha Kappa Psi. Home: 4253 Beethoven St Los Angeles CA 90066-5705

SYLVESTER, ROBERT J. academic administrator; b. Jessup, Pa., May 26, 1936; s. Frank J. and Ellen N. Sylvester; m. Joan J. Luciani, Oct. 4, 1958; children: Beth E. Sylvester Jennings, Robert J. Jr., Leah M. Sylvester Timlin. BS, U. Scranton; MA, Cert. Advanced Studies in Adminstrn., Fairfield U. Instr. Am. history and constnl. history Fairfield (Conn.) U. Coll. Prep. Sch., 1959—72, chmn. dept. social studies, 1962-72, dir. admissions, sr. housemaster, 1972-74, assoc. prin. for admissions and pub. rels., 1974—79, dir. devel. and alumni rels., 1979-83; v.p. instnl. advancement U. Scranton, Pa., 1983—, emeritus, 2001—; pres. RJS Assocs. Consulting, 2001. Cons. in field. Pres. Jesuit Advancement Adminstrs. Conf., 1988-91; bd. dirs. Un. Scranton Alumni Coun.; past pres. Milford (Conn.) Babe Ruth League; bd. dirs. Diocesan Sch. Bd., 1995—, Scranton Cultural Ctr., 1998-2001, Scranton/Lackawanna Human Devel. Agy., 1985-2000, Friendship House, 1998-2000, Downtown Scranton Bus. Assn., Easter Seal Soc., 1984-96, Scranton Prep. Sch. Trustees, 1990-96, Boys and Girls Clubs of Scranton, 1992-98, Northeastern Pa. Philharm., 1987-99, Forest Lakes coun. Boy Scouts Am.; exec. com. UNICO Nat. Svc. Orgn., 1998—; pres. bd. dirs. Serving Seniors, 1985-90. Recipient J. Barry McGannon, S.J. award Jesuit Advancement Adminstrs., 1997. Mem. Nat. Soc. Fundraising Execs. (Fundraiser of Yr. award 1994), N.E. Pa. Devel. Coun., Coun. for Advancement and Support of Edn. (Retirement award for svc. to profession 2001), Glen Oak Country Club (mem. strategic planning com.), Scranton Club, Alpha Sigma Nu. Avocations: golf, outdoor activities. Address: 1009 Woodland Way Clarks Summit PA 18411

SYLVESTRE, JEAN GUY, former national librarian; b. Sorel, Que., Can., May 17, 1918; s. Maxime Arthur and Yvonne Marie (Lapierre) S.; m. Francoise Poitevin, Feb. 27, 1943; children: Marie, Jean, Paul. BA, U. Ottawa, 1939, B.Ph., 1940, MA, 1942, D.L.S. (hon.), 1969, D.Litt. (hon.), 1970, LL.D. (hon.), 1974, 75, 82. Translator Dept. Can. Sec. of State, 1942-44; editor Wartime Info. Bd., 1944-45; asst. pvt. sec. to minister of justice, 1945-47; pvt. sec. to sec. of state for external affairs, 1947-48; pvt. sec. to prime minister, 1948-50; adminstrv. officer Dept. Resources and Devel., 1950-53; asst. librarian Library of Parliament, Ottawa, Ont., 1953-56, asso. parliamentary librarian, 1956-68, nat. librarian, 1968-83; pres., chmn. bd. Can. Inst. for Hist. Microprodns., 1983-86; chmn. Ottawa Valley Book Festival, 1988-92; hon. chmn., 1993—. Author: Louis Francoeur, journaliste, 1941, Situation de la poésie canadienne, 1941, Anthologie de la poésie canadienne-française, 1943, 58, 64, 66, 68, 74, Poétes catholiques de la France contemporaine, 1944, Sondages, 1945, Impressions de théâtre, 1950, Amours, délices et orgues, 1953, Panorama des lettres canadiennes-francaises, 1964, Canadian Writers, 1964, Literature in French Canada, 1967, A Century of Canadian Literature, 1967, The Future of the National Library of Canada, 1980, Guidelines for National Libraries, 1987 French, Spanish and Arabic edits., 1988; also articles in profl. jours., encys.; editor: A Canadian Errant (J.P. Manion), 1960; editor: Canadian Universities Today, 1961, Structures sociales du Canada francais, 1967. Chmn. Gov. Gen.'s Lit. Awards, 1960-62; organizer, chmn. World Poetry Conf., Expo 1967; chmn. Can. Council Com. on Aid-to-Publs., 1960-68; lectr. U. Ottawa Library Sch., 1954-71; v.p. Can. Library Week Council, 1965-67; Bd. dirs. Can. Writers Found., pres., 1960-61. Decorated comdr. Ordre International du Bien Public, officer Order of Can.; comdr. Order of Merit of Poland; recipient Centennial medal., Outstanding Pub. Service award, Internat. Fedn. Libr. Assn. medal. Fellow Royal Soc. Can. (hon. sec. 1959-62, pres. sect. I 1963-64, hon. libr. 1969-91, pres. 1973-74); mem. Soc. Ecrivains Canadiens, Can. Libr. Assn. (life), Ont. Libr. Assn. (hon. life), Can. Assn. Info. Sci. (pres. 1971-72), Assn. Scis. et Techniques (life). Home: 2286 Bowman Rd Ottawa ON Canada K1H 6V6

SYLVIS, ROBIN, dental hygiene educator; b. Bklyn., June 10, 1954; d. Seymour and Isabel Bassman; m. Frank Llewellyn Sylvis, Aug. 21, 1977; children: Mariel Elizabeth, Brandon Michael. BS, West Liberty State Coll., W.Va., 1975; MS, Pa. State U., 1980. Registered dental hygienist, Pa. Dental hygienist, Pa., 1975—; dental hygiene instr. Pa. Tech. Coll., Williamsport, 1978-80; assoc. prof. Middlesex C.C., Bedford, Mass., 1980-90; clin. faculty U. Pa. Sch. of Dental Medicine, Phila., 1991; clin. dir., assoc. prof., sci. dept. coord. Harcum Coll., Bryn Mawr, Pa., 1990—. Rpfol. cons. Probex Dental Edn. Cons., Harrisburg, Pa., 1999—, Biotrol Internat., Louisville, 1997-99; clin. cons. Middlesex County C.C., 1996. Contbg. cons. Clinical Practice of the Dental Hygienist, 1994; contbr. Stedman's Concise Med. Dictionary for Health Professionals, 1997; contbr. articles to profl. publs. including Am. Dental Assn. Edn. Jour. Mem. PTA, Bryn Mawr, 1990—. Mem. Am. Dental Edn. Assn., Am. Dental Hygienists Assn., Main Line Dental Hygiene Study Club, Sigma Phi Alpha (past co-chair 1992-93), Eta Sigma Gamma. Avocations: jazzercise, swimming, reading. Office: Harcum Coll 750 Montgomery Ave Bryn Mawr PA 19010

SYMCHOWICZ, SAMSON, retired biochemist; b. Krakow, Poland, Mar. 20, 1923; came to U.S., 1954; s. Chiel and Esther M. S.; m. Sarah R. Nussbaum, May 24, 1953; children: Esther, Beatrice, Caren. Chem. engr., Poly. Inst. Prague, Czechoslovakia, 1950; MS in Chemistry, Bklyn. Poly. Inst., 1956; PhD in Biochemistry, Rutgers U., 1960. Asst. biochemist McGill U., Montreal, Que., Can., 1951-54, SUNY, 1954-56; biochemist Schering-Plough Corp., Bloomfield, N.J., 1956-73, assoc. dir. biol. rsch., 1973-80, dir. drug metabolism, 1980-92; ret. Editorial bd. Drug Metabolism and Disposition; contbr. over 90 sci. papers to profl. publs. Mem. Internat. Soc. Study of Xenobiotics, Am. Chem. Soc., N.Y. Acad. Sci., Soc. Pharmacology and Exptl. Therapeutics.

SYME, DANIEL BAILEY, rabbi, institution executive; b. Sharon, Pa., Feb. 6, 1946; s. Monte Robert and Sonia (Hendin) S.; m. Jill Susan Young; 1 child, Joshua. BA, U. Mich., Ann Arbor, 1967; BHL, MAHL, Hebrew Union Coll.-Jewish Inst. Religion, Cin., 1972; MEd, Columbia U., 1977, EdD, 1980. Ordained rabbi, 1972. Asst. dir. Nat. Fedn. Temple Youth, 1972-73; rabbi Stamford (Conn.) Fellowship for Jewish Learning, 1973-77; asst. nat. dir. edn. Union of Am. Hebrew Congregations, N.Y.C., 1973-77, dir., 1977—; asst. dir. Commn. Jewish Edn. for Reform Movement, 1973-77, dir., 1977—, Union of Am. Hebrew Congregations TV Inst., N.Y.C., 1982-83, exec. asst. to pres., 1983-85, v.p., 1985-91, sr. v.p., 1991-96; sr. rabbi Temble Beth El, Bloomfield Hills, Mich., 1996—. Chmn. coalition for Alternatives in Jewish Edn., N.Y.C., 1978-80; mem. Nat. Assn. Temple Educators, 1972-91, Commn. on Teaching of Israel and Zionism, World Zionist Orgn., 1980-84; dir.-at-large Jewish Nat. Fund, Jewish Fedn. Met. Detroit, 2000—, internat. bd. Meml. Found. for Jewish Culture; nat. cabinet mem. Am. Zionist Movement, v.p. Am. Zionist Youth Movement; bd. dirs. United Israel Appeal, Ecumenical Inst. Author: 100 Essential Books for Jewish Readers, Finding God, My Body is Something Special, Prayer Is Reaching, I'm Growing, I Learn About God, Books Are Treasures, Jewish Home, What Happens After I Die?, Why I Am a Reform Jew, Drugs, Sex and Integrity, The Jewish Wedding Book, The Book of the Jewish Life; exec. prodr. T.V. programs A Conversation with Menachem Begin, 1981, Choosing Judaism, 1981, To See the World Through Jewish Eyes, 1983, A Conversation with Yitzchak Navon, 1983, You Can Go Home Again, Jewish Youth and Cults, 1984; contbr. articles to religious publs. Mem. Rabbinic Adv. Coun., United Jewish Appeal, Nat. Religious Edn. Assn. (exec. bd.), Nat Coun. Jewish Edn. (exec. bd.), Econ. Club Detroit (bd. dirs.). Office: 7400 Telegraph Rd Bloomfield Hills MI 48301-3876

SYMENS, MAXINE BRINKERT TANNER, marketing professional; b. Primghar, Iowa, June 12, 1930; d. George Herman and Irene Marie (Dahnke) Brinkert; m. Jack Frederiksen Tanner, Dec. 28, 1950 (dec. Oct. 1976); m. Delbert Glenn Symens, Sept. 26, 1981. BS magna cum laude, Westmar Coll., 1970. Cert. tchr., Iowa. Elem. tchr. Rural Sch. O'Brien Co., Primghar, 1949-54, Gaza (Iowa) Com. Sch., 1954-60; secondary tchr. Primghar Com. Sch., 1960-81; fitness salon owner Slim 'N' Trim, George, Rock Rapids, Iowa, 1982-87; restaurant owner George Cafe, 1985-90, Pizza Ranch, 1988-96; with network mktg. divsn. Espial, 1997-99; dir. Coastal Vacations, 2000—. Advt. sales cons. Internet advt., 1997-99, Antique & Gift Shop, 1998-2000. Pres. Primghar Edn. Assn., 1970-71. Mem. George C. of C., George Kiwanis Club (sec. 1991-95), Coast Club (bd. dirs. 1999—), Delta Kappa Gamma. Lutheran. Home: 307 Dell St NE George IA 51237-1030

SYMENS, RONALD EDWIN, electrical engineer, consultant; b. Britton, S.D., Jan. 16, 1951; s. Edwin Donald and Dora Marie (Larson) S.; children: Amy Marie, Chad Ronald. BSEE, S.D. Sch. Mines and Tech., 1973. Jr. engr. Firestone Tire Co., Akron, Ohio, 1973-74, engr., 1974-76, sr. engr., 1977-78; systems engr. Hewlett Packard, Cleve., 1977-79; pres. Comml. Timesharing Inc., Akron, 1980—. Inventor defect marker. Deacon Manchester Trinity Chapel, Akron, 1984-88, chmn. deacon bd., 1987-88; mem. Akron Regional Bd. Republican. Avocation: family camping, church, hunting, golfing. Office: Comml Timesharing Inc 2650 S Arlington Rd Akron OH 44319-2010

SYMES, LAWRENCE RICHARD, computer science educator, university dean; b. Ottawa, Ont., Can., Aug. 3, 1942; s. Oliver Lawrence and Maybell Melita Blanche (Gilliard) S.; m. Evelyn Jean Hewett, Apr. 3, 1964; children: Calvin Richard, Michelle Louise, Erin Kathleen. BA, U. Sask., Saskatoon, Can., 1963, postgrad. in math., 1964; MS, Purdue U., 1966, Phd, 1969. Asst. prof. Purdue U., West Lafayette, Ind., 1969-70; assoc. prof. computer sci. U. Regina, Sask., Can., 1970-74, prof. Can., 1974—, dir. computer ctr. Can., 1970-75, head dept. computer sci. Can., 1972-81, dean of sci. Can., 1982-92, dean grad. studies, assoc. rsch. v.p. Can., 1997-99, dir. info. svcs. Can., 1999—. Dir. tng. Software Tech. Ctr., 1993-94; exec. dir. postsecondary svcs. br. Saskatchewan Edn. Tng. and Employment Govt. of Saskatchewan, 1994-95, exec. dir. multimedia learning, 1995-96; invited lectr. Xian Jiaotong U., 1983, Shandong Acad. Sci., People's Republic of China, 1987 Contbr. articles to profl. jours. Bd. dirs. Hosp. System Study Group, Saskatoon, 1978-94, chmn. bd., 1980-83; dir. SSTA Computer Svcs., Regina, 1972-89; mem. adv. coun. Can./Sask. Advanced Tech. Agreement, 1985-87; mem. Sask. Agrl. Rsch. Found. Bd., 1987-88; mem. steering com. IBM/Sask. Agreement, 1990-92. Can. Fed. Govt. grantee, 1977-84. Mem. Assn. Computing Machinery, Can. Info. Processing (pres. 1979-80, accreditation com. 1988-94), IEEE Computer Soc., Sask. ADA Assn. (bd. dirs. 1990-93), Sask. Tech. Ctr. (bd. dirs. 1993-98), Sask. Comm. Network (bd. dirs. 1996—, chmn. 1998—, Provl. Action Com. on the Economy 1998-2000). Office: U Regina Info Svcs 3737 Wasaona Pkwy Regina SK Canada S4S 0A2

SYMES, PETER DAVID, engineer; b. Chester, U.K., Apr. 30, 1946; naturalized U.S. citizen, 1999; s. Geoffrey Leonard and Dorothy S.; m. Stephanie Kean, June 14, 1969; children: Helen, Neil. BSEE with hons., U. Coll. of North Wales, Bangor, 1967. Engr., planning and installation Brit. Broadcasting Corp., London, 1967-73; product mgr. Pye Tvt, Ltd., Cambridge, Eng., 1973-76, Cen. Dynamics, Ltd., Montreal, Can., 1976-83, Grass Valley Group, Nevada City, Calif., 1983-86, staff engr., 1986-94, mgr. advanced technology, 1994—. Short program lectr. U. of Calif., L.A., 1996—. Patentee: Digital Video Processing Architecture, 1989; author: (book) Video Compression, 1998, Video Compression Demystified, 2001. Fellow: Soc. Motion Picture and TV Engrs. (various offices, v.p. engring. 2002—, various awards); mem.: IEEE (sr.). Avocations: bird watching, photography. Office: Grass Valley Group 400 Providence Mine Rd Nevada City CA 95959-2953 E-mail: p.d.symes@ieee.org.

SYMLAR, JESSE LEE, executive; b. Cleve., Aug. 4, 1951; s. Jesse Lee and Willa Leeann S. BA in Pub. Adminstrn., Christopher Newport U., 1982; MBA. MS in Tech. Mgmt., U. Md., 2001. Project mgr. VYCOR Corp., Washington, 1986-90; multimedia tng. Multimedia Tng. Inst., 1987-88; program analyst Det. Vets. Affairs, 1990; program mgmt. U.S. Dept. Agrl., 1990-93; program analyst Dept. Vets. Affairs, 1993-99; bus. process engr. Multimedia, Upper Marlboro, Md., 1998-2000; CEO Kyi Internat., 2000—. Author of poems. Mentor Each-One-Teach-One, Upper Marlboro, 1997-99. Sgt. USAF, 1975-79. Mem. Amherst Soc., Internat. Soc. Poets (disting.). Avocations: art, poetry, music, chess, sports, computers. Home: 4746 King John Way Upper Marlboro MD 20772

SYMMES, DANIEL LESLIE, technology executive, producer, director; b. Los Angeles, June 26, 1949; s. Louis Leslie and Mary (Warkentine) S. Student, Columbia Coll., Hollywood, Calif., 1970-71. Co-founder Stereovision Internat., Inc., North Hollywood, Calif., 1971; cons. Dimension 3e, Beverly Hills, 1975-87; pres., chmn. Spatial Techs. Inc., 3D Video Corp., Hollywood, 1987-95; pres., CEO Dimension 3, Beverly Hills, 1995—. Responsible for comml. 3D TV in U.S. and abroad; known worldwide as Mr. 3D. Author: Amazing 3-D; contbr. numerous articles to profl. jours.; dir. photography local 659 IATSE; patentee 3-D TV; inventor 1st reflex widescreen 3D filming system. Mem. SMPTE. Avocations: photography, expert scuba photography.

SYMMONDS, RICHARD EARL, gynecologist; b. Greensburg, Mo., Mar. 19, 1922; s. Emmett E. S. AB, Central Coll., Fayette, Mo., 1943; MD, Duke U., 1946; MS in Ob-Gyn, U. Minn., 1953. Intern Los Angeles County Hosp., 1946, resident in Ob-Gyn, 1950-53, resident in gen. surgery, 1954-56; practice medicine specializing in gen. surgery Rochester, Minn., 1958—; mem. faculty Mayo Clinic, 1953—, prof. gynecologic surgery, 1960—, chmn. dept., 1970-84, chmn. emeritus, 1984—. Contbr. articles to profl. jours. Served with USN, 1947-49. Fellow A.C.S.; mem. Am. Gynecol. Soc., Am. Assn. Obstetricians and Gynecologists, Soc. Pelvic Surgeons, Soc. Gynecologic Oncologists, Am. Coll. Obstetricians and Gynecologists. Office: 200 1st St SW Rochester MN 55905-0001

SYMONDS, PAUL SOUTHWORTH, mechanical engineering educator, researcher; b. Manila, Aug. 20, 1916; came to U.S., 1917; s. George R.B. and Claire Louise (Southworth) S.; m. Ilese Powell, Jan. 23, 1943; children: Alan Powell, Robin Peter. BS, Rensselaer Poly. Inst., 1938; MS, Cornell U., 1941, PhD, 1943; Docteur en Sciences Appliquées (hon.), Faculté Polytechnique de Mons, Belgium, 1988. Instr. mechanics Cornell U., Ithaca, N.Y., 1941-43; physicist Naval Research Lab., Washington, 1943-47; asst. prof. engring. Brown U., Providence, 1947-51, assoc. prof., 1951-54, prof., 1954-83, prof. engring. rsch. emeritus, 1983—, chmn. div. engring., 1959-62. Mem. editl. bd. Quar. Applied Math., 1965—; mem. editl. adv. bd. Internat. Jour. Impact Engring., 1983—; also numerous papers in tech. jours. Recipient Fulbright award 1949-50, 57-58; fellow Imperial Chem. Industries, Cambridge, U.K., 1950-51; Guggenheim fellow Swansea, Wales, 1957-58; NSF sr. postdoctoral fellow Oxford, Eng., 1964-65. Fellow ASME, ASCE, Am. Acad. Mechanics; mem. Internat. Assn. Bridge and Structural Engring. Home: 229 Medway St Apt 110 Providence RI 02906-5300 Office: Brown U Divsn Enging Providence RI 02912-0001 E-mail: paul_symonds@brown.edu.

SYMONS, DOROTHY ANNA, accountant; b. Sudbury, Ont., Can., June 9, 1925; came to U.S., 1961; d. Thomas Summers and Marion Georgina (Souter) Wilson; m. John Jeffrey Symons; children: Judith, Thomas, Joanne. BA, B in Commerce, Queens U., 1947. Rsch. asst. Bank of Can., Ottawa, Ont., 1947-49; asst. contr. Henry Morgan and Co., Montreal, Que., Can., 1950-57; contr. Milton Kreis Enterprises, Beverly Hills, Calif., 1968-71, Edison Bros.-Jeans West, L.A., 1972-75, Edison Bros.-United Sporting Goods, L.A., 1975-78; dir. fin. svcs. UCLA, 1978-84; mgmt. cons. Jane Fonda Workout, Beverly Hills, 1985-87, Siemens-Tel Plus, Van Nuys, Calif., 1988. Cons. Tax Counseling for Elderly, Hemet, Calif., 1990—; bd. dirs. Valley Restart Homeless Shelter, Hemet, treas. 1992-95; bd. dirs. La Vista Drug and Rehab. Ctr., Hemet, treas. 1995-97. Mem. AAUW (treas. 1996—, named gift honoree 1997). Republican. Episcopalian. Avocations: bridge, travel.

SYMONS, EDWARD LEONARD, JR. lawyer, educator, investment advisor; b. Pitts., Dec. 21, 1941; s. Edward Leonard and Lillian Mae (Daniel) S.; m. Louise Quinn, July 18, 1970; children: Amy, Colin. BA, Cornell U., 1963; JD summa cum laude, U. Pitts., 1969. Assoc., ptnr. Reding, Blackstone, Rea & Sell, Pitts., 1969-72; asst. atty. gen., chief counsel Pa. Dept. Banking, Harrisburg, 1972-74; prof. law U. Pitts. Sch. Law, 1974-98; CEO, Symons Capital Mgmt., Inc., 1983—. Tax cons., Wash., 1987, Del., 95; exec. v.p. investments Smithfield Trust Co., 1996—2000; mem. adv. coun. Conflict Resolution Ctr. Internat., 1994—; mem. bd. internat. scholars Ctr. for Comml. Law Studies, Queen Mary and Westfield Coll., U. London, 1993—. Co-author: Pennsylvania Professional Corporations, 1974, Banking Law Teaching Materials, 1984, 3d edit., 1991, Regulation of Financial Institutions, 1998; contbr. articles to profl. jours. Commr., Mt. Lebanon, Pa., 1976—80; chmn. St. Clair Hosp. Found., Pitts., 1996—; bd. dirs. Performing Arts for Children, 1980—84, Mt. Lebanon Hosp. Authority, 1993—, St. Clair Hosp., 1995—. 1st. lt. arty., AUS, 1964—66. Mem. ABA (banking law com., consumer fin. svcs. com., devel. in investment svcs. com.), Order of Coif. Office: Symons Capital Mgmt Inc 250 Mount Lebanon Blvd Ste 301 Pittsburgh PA 15234-1248

SYMONS, ROBERT SPENCER, electronic engineer; b. San Francisco, July 3, 1925; s. Spencer W. and Avesia (Atkins) S.; m. Alice Faye Smith, Dec. 21, 1960; children: Julia Ann, Robert Spencer Jr. BS, Stanford U., 1946, MS, 1948. Engr. Eitel-McCullough, Inc., San Bruno, Calif., 1947, Heinz & Kaufman, South San Francisco, 1948, Pacific Electronics Co., Los Gatos, Calif., 1949; sr. engring. mgr. Varian Assocs., Palo Alto, 1950-83; tech. dir. CTO Litton Sys., Inc., San Carlos, 1983—. Patentee in field. 1st lt. AUS, 1950-53. Recipient Charles B. Thornton award for Advanced Tech. Achievement, 1991, 99. Fellow IEEE (assoc. editor Transactions on Electron Devices jour. 1980-83); mem. Commonwealth of Calif. Club, Phi Beta Kappa, Tau Beta Pi. Home: 290 Surrey Pl Los Altos CA 94022-2180 Office: Litton Industries 960 Industrial Rd San Carlos CA 94070-4194

SYMOSEK, PETER FRANK, research scientist; b. Lawrence, Mass., Sept. 22, 1953; s. Frank John and Theresa Alice (McTiernan) S. BS, Merrimack Coll., North Andover, Mass., 1978; ScM, Brown U., 1980, PhD, 1985. Sr. prin. rsch. scientist Honeywell, Inc., Mpls., 1985—. Condr. workshops on computer vision. Contbr. articles to IEEE Jour., Computer Graphics Image Processing, Pattern Recognition; patentee in field. Mem. IEEE (tech. program.), Soc. Photo-optical Instrumentation Engrs., Toastmasters. Avocations: golfing, scuba diving, swimming, bicycling, reading. Office: Honeywell Labs MN65-2500 3660 Technology Dr Minneapolis MN 55418-1096 E-mail: peter.symosek@honeywell.com.

SYMS, HELEN MAKSYM, educational administrator; b. Wilkes Barre, Pa., Nov. 12, 1918; d. Walter and Anna (Kowalewski) Maksym; m. Louis Harold Syms, Aug. 16, 1947; children: Harold Edward, Robert Louis. BA, Hunter Coll., 1941; MS, Columbia U., 1947; teaching credentials, Calif. State U., Northridge, 1964. Statis. clk. McGraw Hill Pub. Co., N.Y.C., 1941-42; acct. Flexpansion Corp., 1943-47, Oliver Wellington & Co., N.Y.C., 1947-48, Broadcast Measurement Bur., N.Y.C., 1948-51; tchr. Calif. State U., Northridge, 1964, Burbank (Calif.) Unified Sch. Dist., 1964-79; chmn. bus. edn. dept. Burbank H.S., 1974-79; docent, acct. arts coun. Calif. State U., Northridge, 1979—; tchr. MEND-Meet Each Need with Dignity Learning Ctr., Pacoima, Calif., 1987-89; assoc. dir. M.E.N.D. (Meet Each Need with Dignity) Learning Ctr., 1989-96. Mem. Phi Beta Kappa, Delta Kappa Gamma (pres. 1972-74, treas. Xi chpt. 1982-90, 92—, treas. area IX 1975-78). Home: 9219 Whitaker Ave Northridge CA 91343-3538

SYNAN, HAROLD VINSON, minister, university dean; b. Hopewell, Va., Dec. 1, 1934; s. Joseph and Minnis Evelyn (Perdue) S.; m. Carol Lee Fuqua, Aug. 13, 1960; children: Mary Carol, Virginia Lee, Vinson Jr., Joseph. BA, U.

Richmond, 1958; MA, U. Ga., 1964, PhD, 1967. Ordained to ministry Pentecostal Holiness Ch., 1957. Pastor Pentecostal Holiness Ch., Va., Ga., 1958-75; tchr. Emmanuel Coll., Ga., 1960-75; gen. sec. Pentecostal Holiness Ch., Oklahoma City, 1973-77, asst. gen. supt., 1977-85; chmn. N.Am. Renewal Svc. Com., 1984-2001; tchr. Oral Roberts U., 1991-94; dean Sch. Div., Regent U., Virginia Beach, Va., 1994—. Author: Holiness-Pentecostal Movement, 1971, Emmanuel College: The First Fifty Years, 1968, Old Time Power, 1973, Charismatic Bridges, 1974, Azusa Street, 1976, In the Latter Days, 1984, Twentieth-Century Pentecostal Explosion, 1987, Launching the Decade, 1990; editor: Aspects of Pentecostal-Charismatic Origins, 1975, Century of the Holy Spirit, 2001; contbr. articles to profl. jours. Mem. Soc. Pentecostal Studies (pres. 1974). Republican. Home and Office: 939 Copper Stone Cir Chesapeake VA 23320-8285 Office: Regent Univ 1000 Regent University Dr Virginia Beach VA 23464 E-mail: vinssyn@regent.edu. *I have but one goal in life; to see the power of the Holy Spirit so released in the Church and the world that every person on earth can have an opportunity to know Jesus Christ as personal Savior and Lord.*

SYNEK, MIROSLAV, physicist, chemist, world affairs independent consultant, researcher; b. Prague, Czechoslovakia, Sept. 18, 1930; came to U.S., 1958, naturalized, 1963; s. Frantisek and Anna (Kokrment) S.; children: Mary Rose, Thomas Robert. Student, Indsl. Chemistry Tech. Sch., Prague, 1946-50; cert. in liberal arts, Prague, 1951; MS in Physics with distinction, Charles U., Prague, 1956; PhD in Physics, U. Chgo., 1963. Analytical chemist Indsl. Medicine Inst., Prague, 1950-51; rsch. physicist Acad. Scis., 1956-58; from asst. to assoc. prof. De Paul U., Chgo., 1962-67; prof. Tex. Christian U., Ft. Worth, 1967-71; lectr., rschr. U. Tex., Austin, 1971-75, tenured faculty San Antonio, 1975-95. Sci. advisor Tex. Edn. Agy., Austin, 1971-73, U. Tex., 1971-73; advisor Student Physics Soc., active numerous univ. coms. Contbr. numerous articles to sci. jours., abstracts to presentations. Campaigner United Way, San Antonio, 1975-95; judge Alamo Sci. Fairs and Tex. Acad. of Sci. Fairs, annually; grand award judge Internat. Sci. and Engring. Fairs, 1998, 99. Rsch. grantee Robert A. Welch Found., 1968-71, 76-83, 93-95. Fellow AAAS, Am. Phys. Soc. (life), Tex. Acad. Sci., Am. Inst. Chemists; mem. NEA, Tex. State Tchrs. Assn., AAUP, DAV Comdrs. Club, Am. Assn. Physics Tchrs., Am. Mus. Natural History, Libr. Congress, Smithsonian Instn., Nat. Trust Hist. Preservation, N.Y. Acad. Scis., Am. Chem. Soc. (San Antonio edn. com. chmn.), Czechoslovak Nat. Coun. Am. (dist. sec. Chgo. 1961-63, chmn. 1967), Czechoslovak Soc. Arts and Scis. Am., Internat. Soc. Poets (disting. mem.), Sheriffs' Assn. Tex. (assoc.), San Antonio Astronomical Assn., World Affairs Coun. San Antonio (diplomat mem.), Bexar County Czech Heritage Soc. of Tex., Sigma Xi (life), Sigma Pi Sigma (sustaining). Roman Catholic. Achievements include research in atomic structure calculations of laser-active lanthanides, analytical relativistic self-consistent field theory, approximate estimate of the extra-terrestrial intelligence probability, nuclear age requiring free elections. Home and Office: Independent Consultant PO Box 5937 San Antonio TX 78201-0937 E-mail: m.synek@juno.com.

SYNNESTVEDT, KIRSTIN, musician, educator; b. Bryn Athyn, Pa., Jan. 8, 1940; d. Raymond Harvey and Katherine Riefstahl Synnestvedt. Student, Tanglewood Berkshire Mus. Ctr., Lenox, Mass., 1956-59; BS, Juilliard Sch., 1963; MusM, Syracuse U., 1966; D of Musical Arts, U. Iowa, 1979. Coll. organist, instr. music Doane Coll., Crete, Nebr., 1966-69; ch. organist, choir dir., solo recitalist Chgo., 1973—. Organ concert broadcasts Sta. WNIB, Chgo., Sta. WDCB, Glen Ellyn, Ill., Sta. WMWA, Glenview, Ill.; adjudicator organ contests, Lincoln, Nebr., Des Moines, Iowa, Chgo. Creator, performer one-woman show of hats. Mem. Fire Buffs of Ill., Chgo., Ill. Fire Safety Alliance, Mt. Prospect, Ill.. Hon. scholar Juilliard Sch., 1961-63. Mem. Nat. Assn. Tchrs. Singing, Music Tchrs. Nat. Assn., Am. Guild Organists, Soc. for Preservation and Appreciation of Antique Motorized Fire Apparatus, 5-11 Club, Chgo. Club Women Organists (pres. 1980-82, 87-90), Pi Kappa Lambda (hon. mem.). Avocations: creative writing, cooking, gardening, modern dance, fast walking.

SYNNOTT, MARCIA GRAHAM, history educator; b. Camden, N.J., July 4, 1939; d. Thomas Whitney and Beatrice Adelaide (Colby) S.; m. William Edwin Sharp, June 16, 1979; children: Willard William Sharp, Laurel Beth Sharp. AB, Radcliffe Coll., 1961; MA, Brown U., 1964; PhD, U. Mass., 1974. History tchr. MacDuffie Sch., Springfield, Mass., 1963-68; instr. U. S.C., Columbia, 1972-74, asst. prof., 1974-79, assoc. prof. history, 1979-97, dir. grad. studies history dept., 1990-92, prof. history, 1997—. Author: The Half-Opened Door, 1979; contbr. essays to books. Active university-wide cmty. svc. projects. Fulbright scholar, 1988; Am. Coun. Learned Socs. grantee, 1981. Mem. Am. Hist. Assn., So. Hist. Assn., Orgn. Am. Historians (membership com. 1990-93), S.C. Hist. Assn. (pres. 1994-95), History of Edn. Soc. (mem. editl. bd. 1996, 97, 98, bd. dirs. 2000—). Avocations: historic sites and museums, snow skiing, walking. Office: U SC Dept History Columbia SC 29208-0001

SYNNOTT, WILLIAM RAYMOND, retired management consultant; b. Fall River, Mass., Dec. 29, 1929; s. William Joseph and Marie Aurore (Labrie) S.; m. Suzanne Pauline Moseley, Oct. 21, 1967; children— Dianne, Mark, Amy Grad. cert., Rutgers U. Stonier Grad. Sch. Banking, 1958; BS summa cum laude, Boston U., 1973; grad. advanced mgmt. program, Harvard Bus. Sch., 1973. Sr. v.p. Bank of Boston, 1967-87; sr. dir. The Yankee Group, Boston, 1987-88; dir. Nolan Norton & Co., Lexington, Mass., 1988-91; pres. W.R. Synnott Assocs., Wellesley Hills, 1990-94. Lectr., seminar leader on info. technology worldwide. Author: The Information Weapon, 1987; co-author: Information Resource Management, 1981. Served as sgt. U.S. Army, 1951-53, Korea. Avocations: skiing, tennis, golf. Home: Green Hill Rd Jackson NH 03846 also: 1630 Winding Oaks Way #101 Naples FL 34109 E-mail: wilsyn@aol.com.

SYNODINOS, JOHN ANTHONY, academic administrator; b. Balt., Sept. 6, 1934; s. Anthony John and Jean (Asimakes) S.; m. Glenda J. Davis, Sept. 5, 1959; children: Jean Louise, Victoria Lynn Gertenbach. BS, Loyola Coll., Balt., 1959; EdM, Temple U., 1977; DHL, Lebanon Valley Coll., 1996, Loyola Coll., 1997. Control buyer Montgomery Ward, Balt., 1959-60; asst. dir. admissions Johns Hopkins U., 1960-63, dir. spl. events, 1963-65, assoc. dir. pub. rels., 1965-67, asst. dir. Ctr. for Study Social Orgn. Schs., 1960-68; assoc. dir. devel. Franklin & Marshall Coll., Lancaster, Pa., 1968-70, asst. to pres., 1970-71, v.p. advancement, 1971-84; pntr. John A. Synodinos & Assocs., 1984-88; pres. Lebanon Valley Coll., Annville, Pa., 1988-96, pres. emeritus, 1996—; of counsel Franklin Cons. Group, 2002. Trustee, pres. Children and Family Svcs. Found., 1996-2002; trustee Lebanon Valley Coll., 1997—; bd. dirs. WITF FM/TV Pub. Broadcasting Bd., 1996-2002, Greater Harrisburg Found., 1999-2002. With U.S. Army, 1952-55. Named Disting Citizen of Yr., Pa. Dutch Coun. Boy Scouts Am., 2002. Mem. Fortnightly Club (Lancaster, pres. 1980). Greek Orthodox. Home: 25 Cart Way Lebanon PA 17042-9469

SYPHERS, JAMES EDGAR, social work educator; b. Exeter, N.H., Feb. 21, 1933; s. Albion Lionel and Mary Pinkham (Collins) S.; m. Joyce Caswell, June 22, 1952 (div. Mar. 1969); m. Barbara Walters, Dec. 31, 1974; children: Gail N., Dale A., Paul N., Neal A., Dennis L., Marcia W. Syphers Turner. BA in Psychology, U. N.H., 1955; MSW, U. Pitts., 1965; BD, Oberlin Coll., 1968; PhD in Higher Edn., Walden U., 1978. Acting. coord., dir. cmty. affairs Hill House Assn., Pitts., 1965-69; instr., acting dir. human svcs. Lincoln U., Pa., 1969-75; asst. prof., dir. social work and human svcs. Widener U., Chester, 1975-76; assoc. prof., asst. dir. human svcs. program Lincoln U., 1977-79; assoc. prof., chair, field coord. dept. social work Saginaw Valley State U., University Center, Mich., 1980-87; asst. prof., field coord. dept. social work Western Carolina U., Cullouhee, N.C., 1987-91; dir. social svc. Downingtown (Pa.) Indsl. and Agrl. Sch., 1991-92; asst. prof., acting chair dept. social work and gerontology California U. Pa., 1992—. Evaluator gang control programs City of Phila. and Youth Svc. Inc., 1973-75; cons., evaluator Dauphin Commn. on Drugs and Alcohol, Harrisburg, Pa., 1978; sec. Saginaw County Mental Health/Mental Retardation Adv. Bd., 1982-86; cons. social work program Curlow Coll., Pitts., 1994-99 Author, co-editor: Community Action for Social Change, 1972; contbr. (booklet) The Community is Our Client, 1966. Mem. gen. com., devel. com. Friends Com. on Nat. Legislation, Washington, 1973-79. Recipient grad. fellowship NIMH, 1963-65, rsch. fellowship NIH, 1964, Human Svc. Program grant SRS of HEW, 1970-76. Mem. NASW (western north ctrl. unit sec. 1980—), NAACP (student chpt. v.p. 1953-2001), AAUP, Coun. on Social Work Edn. (del. 1980—), Mich. Assn. Baccalaureate Social Work Programs (pres. 1980-87), Pa. Assn. Undergrad. Social Work Edn. (pres. 1974-76, 92-2001), Phi Alpha. Democrat. Mem. Soc. Of Friends. Avocations: hiking, construction, travel, social justice activities, counseling. Office: Calif Univ Pa Social Work and Gerontology Box 90 California PA 15419 E-mail: syphers@CUP.edu.

SYPOLT, DIANE GILBERT, federal judge; b. Rochester, N.Y., June 14, 1947; d. Myron Birne and Doris Isabelle (Robie) Gilbert; m. Dwight Douglas Sypolt; children: Andrew, David. BA, Smith Coll., Northampton, Mass., 1969; postgrad., Stanford U., 1977-78, Georgetown U., 1978; JD, Boston U., 1979. Bar: D.C. 1979, Mass. 1979. Law clk. to judge D.C. Ct. Appeals, Washington, 1979-80; assoc. Peabody, Lambert & Meyers, 1980-83; asst. gen. counsel Office of Mgmt. and Budget, 1983-86; dep. gen. counsel U.S. Dept. Edn., 1986-88, acting gen. counsel, 1988-89; legal counselor to V.P. of U.S., White House; counsel Pres.'s Competitiveness Coun., Washington, 1989-90; judge U.S. Ct. Fed. Claims, 1990—. Bd. dirs. Democracy Devel. Inst. Recipient Young Lawyer's award Boston U. Law Sch., 1989. Mem. Fed. Am. Inn of Ct. (Master), Federalist Soc. Office: US Ct Fed Claims 717 Madison Pl NW Washington DC 20439-0002

SYRON, RICHARD FRANCIS, financial executive, economist; b. Boston, Oct. 25, 1943; s. Dominick Richard and Elizabeth (McQuire) S.; m. Margaret Mary Garatoni, Oct. 21, 1972; children: Erin Elizabeth, Brendan Paul BS in Econs.-Acctg. with high honors, Boston Coll., 1966; MA in Econs., Tufts U., 1969, PhD in Econs., 1971. Dep. dir. budget Commonwealth of Mass., 1973-74; v.p., economist Fed. Res. Bank of Boston, 1974-82, sr. v.p., econ. advisor, 1982-85; exec. asst. to sec. U.S. Treasury, Washington, 1979-80, dep. sec. for econ. policy, 1980-81; asst. to Chmn. Volcker Fed. Res. Bd., Washington, 1981-82; pres., CEO Fed. Home Loan Bank of Boston, 1986-88; pres., chief exec. officer Fed. Res. Bank of Boston, 1989-94; chmn. Am. Stock Exch., N.Y.C., 1994-99; chmn., CEO Thermo Electron, Waltham, Mass., 1999—. Past chmn. Boston Coll.; past chmn. Boston Pvt. Industry Coun.; bd. dirs. John Hancock Mut. Life Ins. Co., Boston, Dreyfus Corp., Am. Stock Exch. Author: Urban Fire Insurance, 1972; contbr. articles to profl. jours. Teaching fellow Tufts U., 1966-69. Mem.: Comml. Club Boston, Boston Econ. Club, Wianno Yacht Club, Clover Club Boston. Office: 81 Wyman St Waltham MA 02451-1223

SYROPOULOS, MIKE, retired school system director; b. Kato Hora, Navpactos, Greece, Jan. 18, 1934; came to U.S., 1951; s. Polykarpos Dimitri and Constantoula P. (Konstantinopoulos) S.; m. Sandra Francis Flick, Jan. 3, 1942; children: Pericles, Connie, Tina. BS, Wayne State U., 1960, MEd, 1965, EdD, 1971. Cert. secondary tchr., Mich. Tchr. Detroit Pub. Schs., 1960-66, dept. head, 1966-67, acting supr., 1967-69, rsch. asst., 1969-74, program assoc., 1976-97; asst. dir. Wayne (Mich.) County Intermediate Dist., 1974-76; pres. Rsch. & Evaluation Specialists Inc., Clinton Twp., Mich., 1997—. Pres. Rsch. & Evaluation Specialists, Inc., Clinton Twp., Mich., 1997—. Contbr. articles to reports. V.p. St. John Greek Orthodox Ch., Sterling Heights, Mich., 1987, pres., 1988; bd. dirs. U. Mich. Modern Greek Studies, 2000—; external v.p. Hellenic Soc. Paedeia Mich., 2001—. With U.S. Army, 1956-58. Mem.: Mich. Edn. Rsch. Assn., Mich. Assn. Supervision Curriculum (bd. dirs. 1994—), Am. Hellenic Edn. Progressive Assn. (athletic dir. 1992, treas. 1994, sec. 1995, lt. gov. 1996, gov. 1997, supreme gov. 1998—2000, bd. dirs. Nat. Edn. Found.), ASCD. Greek Orthodox. Avocation: golfing. Home: 46602 Red River Dr Macomb MI 48044-5442 Office: Rsch & Evaluation Specialists Inc PO Box 380102 Clinton Township MI 48038-0060 E-mail: msyropou@aol.com.

SYTEK, DONNA P. former state legislator; b. Haverhill, Mass., Dec. 14, 1944; m. John Sytek; 1 child. AB, Regis Coll., 1966, MA. Chmn. rules com. N.H. Ho. of Reps., Concord; mem. N.H. Ho. of Reps. (dist. 26); chmn. Jud. Conduct Commn. , Bow, NH, 2001—. Chmn. N.H. Rep. Com., 1982-84; pres. Nat. Rep. Legislators Assn., 1992-93; del. to Rep. Nat. Conv., 1980, 84, 88, 84 Const. Conv., Assembly on the Legislature, chmn., 1991-92; mem. exec. com. NCSL, 1990-94, 97-98, Coun. State Govt., 1989—. Mem. Dist. Nursing Assn. (bd. dirs. 1989—), Boys and Girls Club (bd. dirs. 1989-97). Roman Catholic. Avocation: travel. Office: Jud Conduct Commn 501 South St Bow NH 03304-3413*

SYTSMA, FREDRIC A. lawyer; b. Grand Rapids, Mich., Jan. 12, 1944; BA, Mich. State U., 1964; JD, U. Mich., 1968. Bar: Mich. 1968. Mem. Varnum, Riddering, Schmidt & Howlett, Grand Rapids. Fellow Am. Coll. Trust and Estate Counsel; mem. ABA, State Bar Mich. (mem. coun. probate and estate planning sect. 1977—, chmn. 1986-87), Grand Rapids Bar Assn. Office: Varnum Riddering Schmidt & Howlett PO Box 352 333 Bridge St NW Grand Rapids MI 49501-0352 E-mail: fasytsma@varnumlaw.com.

SYVERTSON, CLARENCE ALFRED, engineering and research management consultant; b. Mpls., Jan. 12, 1926; s. Alfred and Esther Louise (Goertemiller) S.; m. Helen Hammond Gonnella, May 4, 1953 (dec. May 1981); 1 child, Marguerite Louise.; m. JoAnn Mary Caruso, May 8, 1982. B. Aero. Engring., U. Minn., 1946, MS, 1948; postgrad., Stanford U., 1950-57; grad., Advanced Mgmt. Program, Harvard U., 1977. Research scientist Ames Aero. Lab., NACA, Moffett Field, Calif., 1948-58; exec. dir. Joint Dept. Transp./NASA Civil Aviation Research and Devel. Policy Study, 1970-71; with Ames Research Center, NASA, Moffett Field, 1958-84, dep. dir., 1969-78, dir., 1978-84. Mem. adv. bd. Coll. Engring., U. Calif., Berkeley, 1980-85; cons. prof. Stanford U., 1985-88; hon. prof. Northwestern Poly. U., Xian, China, 1998. Served with U.S. Army, 1946-47. Recipient invention and contbn. award NASA, 1964, Exceptional Service medal, 1971, Disting. Service medal, 1984, Outstanding Achievement award U. Minn., 1982, Commanders award for civilian service U.S. Army, 1984 Fellow AIAA (Lawrence Sperry award 1957), Am. Astronautical Soc., Calif. Coun. Sci. and Tech.; mem. Nat. Acad. Engring. Home: 14666 Springer Ave Saratoga CA 95070-5748

SZABAN, MARILYN C. small business owner; b. Palmer, Mass., Dec. 24, 1942; d. Joseph J. and Sophie V. (Duda) Martowski; m. Richard J. Szaban, June 9, 1962 (dec. 1993); children: Gregory John, Deborah Ann, Michael John. BFA summa cum laude, U. So. Maine, 1986; student, Notre Dame Coll., 1983. Owner, pres. Automotive Parts and Supply Co., Inc., Ramsdell & Van Dyke, Worcester, Mass., 1977—; co-owner, pres. Plymouth (N.H.) Auto Supply, Inc., 1980-96; owner, pres. Transfigurations, Worcester, 1996—. Bd. dirs. APSCO, Worcester, PASCO, Plymouth; art tchr. Jewish Comm. Ctr., Worcester, 1991, 92. Designer for Transfigurations, 1996; artist Portland Rev. of the Arts, 1986. Bd. dirs., art tchr. gallery com., Art Guild of Farmington, Conn., 1988-90. Recipient hon. mention Manchester Inst. Arts & Scis., 1981, 82, recognition award, 1983, Nat. Competition Juried Art Shows, Northeast and Mid-Atlantic States, 1981—. Mem. Plymouth C. of C. Avocations: fine arts, competition in juried art shows. Address: 116 Village Blvd Ste 200 Princeton NJ 08540-5700

SZABLYA, HELEN MARY, writer, language professional, lecturer; b. Budapest, Hungary, Sept. 6, 1934; came to U.S., 1963; d. Louis and Helen (Bartha) Kovacs; m. John Francis Szablya, June 12, 1951; children: Helen, Janos, Louis, Stephen, Alexandra, Rita, Dominique-Mary. Diploma in Sales, Mktg., U.B.C., 1962; BA in Fgn. Lang., Lit., Wash. State U., 1976. Freelance writer, translator, 1967—; columnist Cath. News, Trinidad, W.I., 1980-91; adult educator TELOS Bellevue (Wash.) C.C., 1987-89; adult educator Pullman-Spokane (Wash.) C.C., 1976-80; faculty Christian Writers' Conf., Seattle, 1983-88, Pacific N.W. Writers' Conf., Seattle, Tacoma, 1987—; hon. consul for Wash., Oreg., Idaho Republic of Hungary, 1993—. Lectr. Washington Commn. for Humanities, 1987-89. Author: (with others) Hungary Remembered, 1986 (Guardian of Liberty award, 1986, George Washington Honor medal, Freedoms Found. award 1988), 56-os Cserkészcsapat, 1986, (with others) The Fall of the Red Star, 1996 (Hungarian translation 1999, 1st prize Wash. Press Assn., 1st prize Nat. Fedn. Press Women); pub., editor Hungary Internat. newsletter, 1990-93; columnist Hungarian Bus. Weekly, 1994-95; translator: Emlékezünk, 1986, Mind Twisters, 1987. Recipient Nat. 1st place editl. Nat. Fedn. Press Women, 1987, Senator Tom Martin Meml. award Pacific N.W. Writers Conf., 1979; grantee Hungarian Am. Assn. Wash., 1986, Wash. Com. for Humanities, 1986; named Cmty. Woman of Yr., Am. Bus. Women Assn., 1990. Mem. AAUW, Wash. Press Assn. (pres. 1987-88, 1st and 2nd place awards, several editorial and profile awards 1983, 87, 89, 90, 91, 92, 96, Communicator of Achievement award 1987), Nat. Fedn. Press Women (Affiliate Pres.' award 1988, bd. dirs. edn. fund N.W. quadrant, mem. 21st century planning com.), Authors Guild, Am. Translators Assn., Arpad Acad. (Gold medal 1987), Nat. Writers Club, Internat. P.E.N. Club, Sigma Delta Chi (editl. award 1989). Avocations: children, reading, dancing, swimming, traveling. Home and Office: PO Box 578 Kirkland WA 98083-0578

SZABLYA, JOHN FRANCIS, electrical engineer, consultant; b. Budapest, Hungary, June 25, 1924; came to U.S., 1963, naturalized, 1979; s. John and Alexandra (Huszar) S.; m. Helen Bartha-Kovacs, June 12, 1951; children: Helen A., Janos L., Louis J., Stephen J.P., Alexandra H.R., Anita H.C., Dominique-Mary H. Diploma engring., Jozsef Nador U., Budapest, 1947, diploma edn., D in Econs., Jozsef Nador U., Budapest, 1948. Registered profl. engr., Wash., Mont., Alaska, Wyo., Oreg., Colo., Idaho, B.C. and Ont., Can. Design engr. Ganz Elec. Works, Budapest, 1947-56; assoc. prof. Tech. U. Budapest, 1951-56, U. B.C., Vancouver, Can., 1957-63; prof. elec. engring. Wash. State U., Pullman, 1963-82, now prof. emeritus; mgr. elec., instrumentation and control engring. EBASCO Svcs., Inc., Bellevue, Wash., 1981-90; ret., 1990; cons. engr., v.p. Szablya Cons., Inc., Kirkland, Wash., 1990—. Vis. prof. Technische Universitat Braunschweig, 1973-74, U. W.I., St. Augustine, Trinidad and Tobago, 1983—, U. Wash., Seattle, 1985—, Seattle U., 1987. Contbr. numerous articles to profl. jours. Recipient Zipernowszky medal Hungarian Inst. Elec. Engrs., 1954, diploma of recognition, 1998, Arpad Academia Gold medal, 1990. Fellow IEEE, Instn. Elec. Engrs. (London); mem. Osterreichischer Verband der Elekrotechnik, Hungarian Acad. Scis., European Register Higher Tech. Professions, Sigma Xi. Roman Catholic. Home: PO Box 578 Kirkland WA 98083-0578

SZABO, ALBERT, architect, educator; b. N.Y.C., Nov. 7, 1925; s. Benjamin and Jane (Margolies) S.; m. Brenda Dyer, Dec. 26, 1951; children: Ellen Bryna Szabo, Stephen, Rebecca Szabo Salvadori, Jeannette. Student, Bklyn. Coll., 1942-47, Inst. Design, Chgo., 1947-48; MArch, Harvard U., 1952. Apprentice Marcel Breuer Architect, 1947-48; instr. Inst. Design, Chgo., 1951-53; prof. architecture Grad. Sch. Design Harvard U., Cambridge, Mass., 1954-96; prof. emeritus, 1996—; chmn. dept. archtl. scis. Harvard U., Cambridge, Mass., 1964-68, assoc. chmn., head tutor dept. visual and environ. studies, 1968-70, prof. visual and environ. studies, chmn. dept. visual and environ. studies, 1970-72, sec. faculty design, 1964-74, prof. visual and environ. studies, 1970-91; archtl. design practice with Brenda Dyer Szabo, Chgo. and Cambridge, 1953—; ptnr. Soltan/Szabo Assocs., Inc., Cambridge, 1967-71. Vis. prof. Rensselaer Poly. Inst., 1967-68; Fulbright cons. to municipality of Tehran, Iran; Fulbright Hayes lectr. in architecture, Tehran, 1972, Kabul U. Afghanistan, 1974-76; cons. U.S. AID, Afghanistan, 1974-76, Govt. Afghanistan, 1974-76; acting curator Loeb Fellowship in Advanced Environ. Studies, 1974, cons. King Faisal U. Coll. Architecture and Planning, 1983; mem. edn. com. Boston Archtl. Ctr. Sch. Architecture, 1981-90; Osgood Hooker prof. visual art Faculty of Arts and Scis., 1991-96, prof. emeritus, 1996—. Author: (with others) The Shape of Our Cities, 1957; editor: (with others) Housing generated by User Needs, 1972, (with B.D. Szabo) Preliminary Notes on Indigenous Architecture of Afghanistan, 1978, (with T.J. Barfield) Afghanistan: An Atlas of Indigenous Domestic Architecture, 1991 (Outstanding Acad. Book award ALA 1992). Served with USAAF, 1944-45. Recipient Alpha Rho Chi medal Harvard U., 1952; Wheelwright travelling fellow Harvard U., 1963, Nat. Endowment for Arts fellow, 1980; Tozier Fund rsch. grantee Harvard U., 1963, Milton Fund rsch. grantee, 1966, 72, 77, 84, 87, Faculty rsch. grantee, 1978, The Aga Khan Program Islamic Architecture grantee, 1988, Faculty of Arts and Scis. Clark Fund Rsch. grantee, 1997; 1st One Man Show, Carpenter Center for the Visual Arts, 2001. Mem. Assn. Collegiate Schs. Architecture (N.E. regional dir. 1969-70). Office: Harvard U Carpenter Ctr 19 Prescott St Cambridge MA 02138-3902 E-mail: szabo@fas.harvard.edu.

SZABO, ANDRAS, internist; b. Sopron, Hungary, Nov. 9, 1967; m. Edit Szabo. MD summa cum laude, Debrecen U., 1993. Diplomate Am. Bd. Internal Medicine. Ward physician Hollos Istvan Psychiatry Clinic, Doba, Hungary, 1993-95; resident Meridia Huron Hosp./Cleve. Clin. Health Sys., 1995-98; internist Wagner (S.D.) Cmty. Meml. Hosp. and Clinic, 1998—. Mem. ACP, AMA, Am. Soc. of Internal Medicine, S.D. State Med. Assn., Am. Diabetes Assn. (profl. sect.), Am. Acad. Pain Mgmt. Roman Catholic. Avocations: classical music, history, wildlife. Office: Wagner Cmty Clinic 3d and Walnut Sts Wagner SD 57380 E-mail: aszabo@charles-mix.com.

SZABO, AUGUST JOHN, consulting engineering firm executive; b. Baton Rouge, Sept. 27, 1921; s. August J. and Maggie (Farr) S.; m. Ruth Goss, Aug. 5, 1945; children: Robert G., John F., Rebecca R. BS in Civil Engring., La. State U., 1943; MS in Sanitary Engring., Harvard U., 1950. Pub. health engr. La. State Dept. Health, Monroe and Lafayette, 1946-55; assoc. prof. civil engring. U. Southwestern La., Lafayette, 1955-63; prin. Domingue, Szabo & Assocs., 1957—. Bd. dirs. Coun. for a Better La., Baton Rouge, 1986—; trustee La. Coll., Pineville, 1978-83. 1st lt. U.S. Army, 1943-46, PTO. Recipient Arthur Sidney Bedell award La. Water Pollution Control Assn./Water Environ. Fedn., 1968. Fellow Am. Consultin Engrs. Coun.; mem. ASCE (life), NSPE (dir. 1973-77), Am. Water Works Assn. (life, George Warren Fuller award 1985), Am. Acad. Environ. Engrs. (life, diplomate), La. Conf. on Water Supply, Sewerage and Indsl. Wastes (pres. 1969-71, S.L. Perry award 1987), La. Engr. Found. (bd. dirs., pres. 1984-95), Consulting Engrs. Coun. La., Profl. Engrs. in Pvt. Practice, Water Environ. Fedn. (life), La. Engring. Soc. (pres. 1970-71, Leo M. Odom award 1976), Rotary Club of Lafayette (pres. 1969-70), Greater Lafayette C. of C. (dir. 1971-74, 84-86, v.p. 1986), Chi Epsilon. Home: 1117 Kim Dr Lafayette LA 70503-4127 Office: Domingue Szabo & Assocs Inc Ste 1100 PO Box 52115 400 E Kaliste Saloon Rd Lafayette LA 70505-2115

SZABO, BARNA ALADAR, mechanical engineering educator, mining engineer; b. Martonvasar, Hungary, Sept. 21, 1935; came to U.S., 1967, naturalized, 1974; s. Jozsef and Gizella (Ivanyi) S.; m. Magdalin Gerstmayer, July 23, 1960; children: Mark, Nicholas. BASc., U. Toronto, Ont., Can., 1962; MS, SUNY, Buffalo, 1966, PhD, 1968; D. honoris causa, U. of Miskolc, Hungary, 1998. Registered profl. engr., Mo. Mining engr. Internat. Nickel Co. Can., 1960-62; engr. Acres Cons. Services Ltd., Niagara Falls, Can., 1962-66; instr. SUNY, Buffalo, 1966-68; mem. faculty Washington U., St. Louis, 1968—, prof. mech. engring., 1974—, Albert P. and Blanche Y. Greensfelder prof., 1975—. dir. Ctr. Computational Mechanics, 1977-92; chmn. engring. software Rsch. and Devel., Inc., 1989—. Author: (with Ivo Babuska) Finite Element Analysis, 1991; contbr. articles to profl. jours. Fellow U.S. Assn. Computational Mechanics (founding mem.); mem. ASME, Hungarian Acad. Sci., Soc. Engring. Sci. Home: 48 Crestwood Dr Clayton MO 63105-3033 Office: PO Box 1129 Saint Louis MO 63188-1129 E-mail: szabo@me.wustl.edu.

SZABO, DANIEL, government official; b. Budapest, Hungary, Mar. 23, 1933; came to U.S., 1950, naturalized, 1954; s. Alexander and Maria (Berger) S.; m. Corinne Holiber, July 3, 1955; children— Nancy Beth, Peter Stuart. BA, CCNY, 1957; MA, Johns Hopkins U., 1959. Internat. economist U.S. Tariff Commn., 1959-60; desk officer for Vietnam, Cambodia and Laos U.S. Dept. Commerce, 1960-63; spl. asst. to U.S. Senator Jacob K. Javits, 1963-69; dep. asst. sec. state for Inter-Am. Affairs, Washington, 1969-74; sr. adviser Inter-Am. Devel. Bank, 1974-95; cons Rockville, Md., 1995—. Mem. nat. adv. coun. Am. Jewish Com. Bd. dirs. Washington area chpt. Am. Jewish Com.; v.p. Md. Interfaith Legis. Com., 1999—. With U.S. Army, 1954-56. Home: 11600 Danville Dr Rockville MD 20852-3716 E-mail: dans3693@erols.com. *In approaching life I want my work to represent a service to our society. I am attracted to new ideas and new ways of solving old problems.*

SZABO, DENIS, criminologist, educator; b. Budapest, Hungary, June 4, 1929; s. Jenö and Catherine (Zsiga) S.; m. Sylvie Grotard; children— Catherine, Marianne. Doctorate in Social and Polit. Scis., U. Louvain, Belgium, 1956; diploma in criminology, Sorbonne U., Paris, 1958; hon. doctorate, U. Sienna, Italy, 1984, U. Budapest, Hungary, 1985, U. Aix-Marseille, 1992, Panteios U., 1996. Asst. in sociology U. Louvain, 1951-56; lectr. sociology Cath. Univs., Paris, Lyon, 1956-58; mem. research group Centre Nat. de la Recherche Scientifique, Paris, 1954-58; asst. prof. sociology U. Montreal, 1958, assoc. prof., 1959-66, founder, dir. dept. criminology, 1960-70, prof., 1966—; founder, dir. Internat. Center for Comparative Criminology, 1969-84; prof. emeritus, 1995—. Emeritus prof. law U. Ecuador,

Quito, 1984 Author (editor): Canadian Criminal Justice System, 1977, Criminologie et Politique Criminelle, 1978, La Criminologie Empirique au Quebec, 1985, Science et Crime, 1986, De L'Anthropologie a la criminologie comparee, 1993, La Criminologie: Ses Fondements ul sa Fondation, 1998; co-author (with Marc LeBlanc): Le Traite di criminologie Empirique, 1993, The Criminal Justice System, 2001. Decorated officer Order Can.; recipient Beccaria award German Society Criminology, 1970; named prof. emeritus Law Faculty, Central U. Ecuador, Quito, 1984; named Comdr. Nat. Order Merite Hungarian Republic, 1996, Chevalier Des Arts et des Lettres, France, 1996. Fellow Royal Soc. Can., Am. Sociol. Soc., Am. Soc. Criminology (exec. coun., Sutherland award 1968); mem. Internat. Soc. Criminology (pres. 1978-85, hon. pres.), Can. Soc. Criminology (v.p. 1962-64), Soc. de Criminology (v.p. 1962-64), Soc. de Criminologie du Que. (sec.-gen. 1960-70), Ordre Nat. du Québec (officer 1998—), Internat. Assn. Sociology, Nat. Order of Merit (comdr. Ivory coast 1987), Hungarian Acad. Scis. (elected). Roman Catholic. Home: 66 Carré Copp Georgeville QC Canada J0B 1T0 Office: U Montreal Internat Ctr Com Crim CP 6128 succursale Centre-ville Montreal QC Canada H3C 3J7

SZABO, ELIZABETH MARYANN, lawyer; b. Passaic, N.J. d. William Guy and Stasia (Siejwa) S. BA cum laude, Wilson Coll., 1976; JD, N.Y.U., 1986. Bar: N.J. 1988, U.S. Dist. Ct. N.J. 1988, Pa. 1988, N.Y. 1991, U.S. Dist. Ct. (ea. dist.) N.Y. 1991, U.S. Dist. Ct. (so. dist.) N.Y. 1991, U.S. Supreme Ct. 1994. Asst. dir. Multistate Legal Studies, N.Y.C., 1986-90; pvt. practice, 1991—. Arbitrator Small Claims Ct., Civil Ct. City of N.Y., 1997—; columnist Immigration Law, Asenta Newspaper, 1997—, Weekly Bengalee, 1994-96, India Horizons, 1995. Fundraiser Campaign for Coun. Woman Jenny Lim, N.Y.C., 1997; vol. Housing Ct. Lawyers Project, N.Y.C., 2002—. Mem. Nat. Lawyers Guild (exec. com. 1996-98, sec. N.Y. chpt. 1996-99, lectr. immigration law), N.Y. County Lawyers Assn. (consumer bankruptcy com. 1994-98, immigration com. 1994-98, Pro Bono award 1994, 95), N.Y. State Bar Assn. (public interest com. 1995-97), Small Claims Arbitrators Assn., Fed. Bar Assn. Democrat. Episcopalian. Avocations: photography, poetry, painting, acting. Office: 401 Broadway Ste 605 New York NY 10013-3005

SZABO, JOSEPH LASZLO, management consultant; b. Darby, Pa. s. Laszlo and Judith S.; m. Stacey Allen, May 31, 1986; children: Brandon, Bradley, Tyler, McKenzie. BSCE, S.D. Sch. Mines Tech., 1986; Exec. MBA, U. Pa., 2000. Owner PC Board Svcs., Ardmore, Pa.; mng. dir. info. tech. Avanta Credit Card, Horsham, Fleet Credit Card, Horsham; chief info. officer Internet Capital Group, King of Prussia, Pa.; CEO, mng. dir. Szabo Cons. Internat., LLC. Capt. USAF, 1980-85. Mem. Presdl. Round Table. Republican. Baptist. Avocations: golf, scuba diving, skiing, boating. Home: 43 Washington Ln Coatsville PA 19320 Office: Szabo Consulting Internat LLC 900 E 8th Ave King Of Prussia PA 19406 E-mail: jszabo@szaboconsulting.com.

SZABO, PETER JOHN, investment company executive, financial planner, mining engineer, lawyer; b. Bklyn., Nov. 22, 1946; s. Paul Simon and Marita Ellen (Coughlin) S.; m. Dorothy Anne Steward, Nov. 14, 1970; children: Peter, David, John Paul Steward. BS in Mining Engring., Columbia U., 1968; LLB, LaSalle Law Sch., 1975; MS in Fin. Planning, Coll. Fin. PLanning, 1994. registered profl. engr., CFP. Mining engr. Halecrest Co., Mt. Hope, N.J., 1973-74; mgr. solid fuels & minerals Ford, Bacon & Davis, N.Y.C., 1974-75; asst. v.p. Mfrs. Hanover Trust Co., 1975-77, Irving Trust Co., N.Y.C., 1977; v.p. Republic Nat. Bank of Dallas, 1977-80; mgr. bus. devel. AMOCO Minerals, Denver, 1980-84; investment broker B.J. Leonard, 1984-85; investment exec. Wedbush Nobel Cook, 1985; regional sr. v.p. Alliance Fund Distbrs., N.Y.C., 1985-92, sr. v.p., 1992—. Mining engr. U.S. Bur. Mines, Dallas, 1971-72, IRS, Washington, 1972-73. Treas. Columbia Sch. Engring., 1968—. Lt. USMC, 1969-71, Vietnam, capt. Res. Mem. VFW (post sr. vice comdr. 1993-94, post comdr. 1994-95, all state team post comdrs. 1995, 16th dist. jr. vice comdr. 1995—, 16th dist. sr. vice comdr. 1996—, nat. aide-de-camp 1995-96), Mil. Order of the Cootie (sr. vice comdr. 1994-95). Republican. Roman Catholic. Avocations: sailing, golf, tennis, jogging, scripophily. Home and Office: Alliance Fund Distbrs 810 Oxford Way Benicia CA 94510-3646

SZABO, PETER STUART, management consultant; b. Washington, Nov. 1, 1963; s. Daniel T. and Corinne (Holiber) S.; m. Norah L. McVeigh. BA magna cum laude, U. Rochester, 1985; MA, MPPM, Yale U., 1990. Cons. IBRD, Washington, 1990-91; exec. asst. to commr. Conn. Dept. Transp., Newington, 1991-93, dep. commr. bur. policy & planning, 1993-95; engagement mgr. N.Y. Consulting Ptnrs., N.Y.C., 1995—. Mem. Phi Beta Kappa. Democrat. Jewish. Avocations: writing, hiking, photography.

SZABO, VALERIE, lawyer; b. Greenville, Mich., Mar. 6, 1956; d. Bernard and Shirley (Fine) S.; m. Glenn Goldenhorn, Sept. 27, 1987. BA, U. S.C., 1977; JD, George Mason U., 1980. Assoc. Ilona Ely Freedman, Alexandria, Va., 1981-83; pvt. practice Arlington, 1984-96; ptnr. Szabo & Angus, PLLC, 1996-99, Valerie Szabo, PLLC, 2000—. Mem. ABA, ATLA, Va. Bar Assn., Va. Trial Lawyers Assn., Fairfax County Bar Assn., Arlington County Bar Assn., Delta Theta Phi. Democrat. Office: Ste 203 1313 Dolley Madison Blvd Mc Lean VA 22101-3926 Fax: 703-841-5404.

SZABO, YURIKA LIN, marketing executive, advertising executive; b. Long Beach, Calif., Mar. 1, 1967; d. Sandor Alex and Taeko (Tsujimura) S. Student, Calif. State U., Long Beach, 1985-90. Dir. mktg. Adolphs Food Svc., Lakewood, Calif., 1991—; publicist, cons. L.A. Access Video, 1996—; graphic designer Peepod Prodns., Los Alamitos, Calif., 1996—. Reporter Studio 12, Lakewood, 1997, camera operator, 1997; cons. L.A. Access Video, 1996—. Author of poems. Recipient Editor's Choice award Nat. Libr. Poetry, 1996; Calif. Scholar Fedn. Svc. scholar, 1981-85. Mem. Internat. Soc. Poets (disting.). Avocations: writing, computer graphics, body sculpting, acting, skating.

SZAKSZTYLO, KATHEE, training specialist; b. Chgo., Nov. 19, 1969; d. Casimir and Lillian Marie Szaksztylo. Film studies internship, Moscow U., 1992; BA in cinema, photography, So. Ill. Univ., 1993; MFA in tng., edn., Roosevelt U., Schaumburg, Ill., 1998. Program dir. Vill. of Hawthorn Woods (Ill.), 1988—94; sales support mgr. Corporate Computing, Bannockburn, Ill., 1994—96; tng. coord. W.W. Grainger, Inc., Lincolnshire, 1996—98, tng. specialist Lake Forest, 1998—2001, tech. tng. specialist, 2002—. Mem. Chgo. Data Processing Edn. Coun. Roman Catholic. Avocations: painting, writing, environmental, landscaping. Home: 3407 Peacock Ln Rolling Meadows IL 60008-2525 Office: WW Grainger Inc 100 Grainger Pkwy Lake Forest IL 60045-5201

SZALAPSKI, ROBERT FRANCIS, theoretical physicist; b. St. Paul, Dec. 21, 1964; s. Edward William and Judith Mary (Raines) S.; m. Jeanne Therese Lanson, Sept. 17, 1985; children: Jacob Daniel, Maxwell Martin, Damien Alexander. BS in Physics, U. Minn., 1988; PhD in Physics, U. Wis., 1994. Rsch. assoc. Nat. Lab. for High Energy Physics, Tsukuba, Japan, 1994-96, rsch. fellow Japan, 1996-98; mem. physics faculty U. Rochester, N.Y., 1998-99. Adj. physics faculty SUNY Brockport, 2000. Contbr. articles to profl. jours. Fellowship NSF, 1996-97, postdoctoral fellowship Japan Soc. for the Promotion of Sci., 1996-97, grad. fellowship Dept. of Edn., 1989-93 Avocations: tennis, running, skiing. Home: 43 Smallwood Dr Pittsford NY 14534-3433 Office: Avant! Sys Divsn 117 Victor Heights Pkwy Victor NY 14564-8938 E-mail: robs@avanticorp.com.

SZALKOWSKI, CHARLES CONRAD, lawyer; b. Amarillo, Tex., Apr. 14, 1948; s. Chester Casimer and Virginia Lee Szalkowski; m. Jane Howe, Dec. 28, 1971; children: Jennifer Lee, Stephen Claude. BA, BS in Acctg., Rice U., 1971; MBA, JD, Harvard U., 1975. Bar: Tex. 1975. Assoc. Baker Botts L.L.P., Houston, 1975-82, ptnr., 1983—. Speaker in field. Chmn. ann. fund campaign Rice U., Houston, 1991-93, chmn. Fund Coun., 1995-96; chmn. adminstrv. bd. St. Luke's United Meth. Ch., Houston, 1994, chmn. bd. trustees, 1997; chmn. DePelchin Children's Ctr., Houston, 2002-; bd. dirs. Meth. Children's Home, Waco, MIT Enterprise Forum of Tex., Houston. Mem.: ABA (fed. regulation of securities com.), Assn. Corp. Growth (bd. dirs. Houston chpt.), Tex. Bus. Law Found. (bd. dirs., mem. exec. com. 1988—, chmn. 1998—2000), Harvard Law Sch. Assn. Tex. (pres. 1983—84), Houston Bar Assn. (chmn., corp. counsel sect. 1989—90), State Bar Tex. (chmn. bus. alw sect. 1991—92), Am. Law Inst., Assn. Rice U. Alumni (bd. dirs. 1999—2002). Office: Baker Botts LLP 1 Shell Plz 910 Louisiana St Ste 3000 Houston TX 77002-4991

SZALLER, JAMES FRANCIS, lawyer; b. Cleve., Jan. 22, 1945; s. Frank Paul and Ellen Grace (O'Malley) S.; m. Roberta Mae Curtin, Oct. 23, 1967 (div. Aug. 1975); m. Charlene Nancy Smith, Apr. 28, 1984. AA, Cuyahoga Community Coll., 1967; BA, Cleve. State U., 1970, JD cum laude, 1975. Bar: Ohio 1975, U.S. Dist. Ct. (no. dist.) Ohio 1975, U.S. Supreme Ct. 1982, U.S. Ct. Appeals (6th cir.) 1983, U.S. Ct. Appeals (4th cir.) 1986. Assoc. Metzenbaum, Gaines & Stern, Cleve., 1975-79; sr. ptnr. Brown & Szaller Co., L.P.A., 1979—. Lectr. law Cleve. State U., 1977-81. Mem. editorial bd. Cleve. State U. Law Rev., 1973-75.; contbr. articles to profl. jours. Mem. Ohio State Bar Assn., Greater Cleve. Bar Assn., Cleve. Acad. Trial Lawyers, Ohio Acad. Trial Lawyers (Disting. Svc. award 1996), Assn. Trial Lawyers Am., Nat. Coll. Advocacy (advocate). Democrat. Roman Catholic. Avocations: gourmet cooking, automobile racing. Office: Brown & Szaller Co LPA 14222 Madison Ave Cleveland OH 44107-4510 E-mail: szaller@lawandhelp.com.

SZANTAI, LINDA MARIE, speech and language therapist; b. Phila., Dec. 21, 1957; d. Richard George Reckeweg and Eileen Theresa (Wrenn) Renders; m. Paul Matthew Vidunas, July 22, 1978 (div. Dec. 1987); m. Stephen Michael Szantai, Sept. 16, 1989. BS, Coll. N.J., 1986. Cert. in speech correction, N.J. Speech/lang. therapist Dept. Corrections, State of N.J., Skillman, 1986-89, Ventnor (N.J.) Sch. Dist., 1989—2001, Port Republic (N.J.) Sch., 1989-92, Estell Manor (N.J.) Sch. Dist., 1995-97, Brigantine Sch. Dist., NJ, 2001—, Mainland Regional High Sch., 2001—. Mem. Kappa Delta Pi (pres. Greater Trenton chpt. 1985-86, recognition award 1986), Phi Kappa Phi (Outstanding Freshman Achievement award 1983).

SZANYI, KEVIN ANDREW, lawyer; b. Buffalo, Jan. 7, 1960; s. Andrew John and Alice M. (Degenhart) Szanyi; m. Lyn Barnes Szanyi, Dec. 28, 1996; children: Colin Joseph, Lauren Elizabeth. BA, U. Dayton, 1982; JD, SUNY, Buffalo, 1985. Bar: N.Y. 1985. Assoc. Hodgson Russ Andrews Woods & Goodyear, Buffalo, 1985-92, ptnr., 1993-95, Harris Beach & Wilcox, Buffalo, 1995-99; mng. ptnr. Webster Szanyi LLP, 1999—. Mem. Def. Rsch. Inst., Nat. Assn. R.R. Trial Counsel. Office: Webster Szanyi LLP 1400 Liberty Bldg Buffalo NY 14202 E-mail: kszanyi@websterszanyi.com.

SZAPIRO, TOMASZ JERZY, economist, researcher; b. Warsaw, Poland, Dec. 23, 1950; s. Jerzy and Maria Danuta (Ksiazkiewicz) S.; m. Ewa Maria Podedworna, Jan. 17, 1981; children: Katarzyna, Hanna, Michal. MSc in Physics, U. Warsaw, 1973; PhD in Math., Polish Acad. Scis., 1981; habilitation in economy, Warsaw Sch. Econs., 1992. Rsch. asst. Warsaw Sch. Econs., 1973-78, sr. rsch. asst., 1978-81, asst. prof., 1981-93, assoc. prof., 1992-96, dean grad. sch., 1992-96. Adj. prof. studies in internat. bus. U. Minn., 2000—; vice dir. Sch. Reflective Practitioners, Warsaw, 1994-97. Author: Pondering Decisions, 1993; co-author: Calculus, 1996; guest co-editor Annals of Ops. Rsch., 2001; contbr. articles to profl. jours. Mem. Internat. Soc. for MCDM, Polish Math. Soc., INFORMS (exec. bd. Polish chpt. 1995-97). Avocations: music, reading, walking. Office: Warsaw Sch Econs Al Niepodleglosci 162 02-554 Warsaw Poland

SZÁRA, STEPHEN ISTVÁN, pharmacologist, consultant; b. Budapest, Hungary, Mar. 21, 1923; arrived in U.S., 1957; s. János Szára and Mária Katona; m. Madeleine Gadányi, Sept. 5, 1959 (div. June 1980); 1 child Christopher. D of Natural Scis., Petrus Pázmány U., Budapest, 1950; MD, Med. U. Budapest, 1951. Asst. prof. Dept. Biochemistry Med. U. Budapest, 1950—53; chief biochemistry lab. State Inst. for Nervous Disorders, Budapest, 1953—56; vis. scientist Clin. Sci. Lab. NIMH, Bethesda, Md., 1957—61, sect. chief Washington, 1961—71; br. chief NIDA NIH, Rockville, Md., 1971—90; sci. cons. Kensington, 1990—. Assoc., clin. prof. psychiatry George Washington U., Washington, 1966—75; mem. adv. bd. Heffter Rsch. Inst., Santa Fe, 1993—. Co-author (with H. Weil-Malherb): Biochemistry of Functional and Experimental Psychoses, 1971; co-editor (with M. Braude): The Pharmacology of Marihuana, 1976; editor: Neurobiology of Behavioral Control of Drug Abuse, 1986; contbr. Recipient Meritorious Achievement award, ADAMHA/PHS/DHHS, 1984. Fellow: Coll. Internat. Neuro-Psychopharmacology, Am. coll. Neuro-Psychopharmacology; mem.: Am. Soc. Pharmacol. Exptl. Therapy. Achievements include discovery of hallucinogenic effects of NN-Dimethyltryptamine in man. Avocation: Avocations: sailing, computer programming. Home: 10901 Jolly Way Kensington MD 20895-1111

SZAREK, GENE, religious studies educator; b. Chgo., Jan. 3, 1941; BS in Math., Licentiate in Philosophy, St. Louis U., 1963, MA in Math., 1965; MA in Theology, U. San Francisco, 1971; PhD, Marquette U., 1975. Chair math. dept. Gordon Tech H.S., Chgo., 1967—71; asst. prof. Mundelein Coll., 1975—76; pastor St. Stanislaus B. & M. Church, 1976—81; prin. Archbishop Weber H.S., 1981—90; asst. prof. Loyola U., 1990—. Sec. bd. dirs. Gordon Tech H.S., Chgo., 1994—2002; provincial councilor Congregation of the Resurrection, 1996—; corp. mem. Resurrection Ctr., Woodstock, 1999—. Editor: Oaxaca Newsletter: Partners in Mission, 1990. Chaplain, advisor Alpha Delta Gamma Fraternity, Chgo., 1995—2002; spkr. many religious and civic groups Chgo., N.Y.C., St. Louis. Named Polish-Am. Citizen of Yr., Cook County Bd. Commrs., 2001. Home: 2226 North Hoyne Ave Chicago IL 60647 Office: Loyola Univ 6525 North Sheridan Rd Chicago IL 60626 Personal E-mail: genocarl@hotmail.com.

SZAREK, STANISLAW JERZY, mathematics educator; b. Ladek Zdroj, Poland, Nov. 13, 1953; came to U.S., 1980, naturalized, 1994; s. Mieczyslaw and Bronislawa (Brzezinska) S.; m. Malgorzata Chwascinska, June 22, 1980 (div. 1996); children: Martina, Natalia; 1 stepchild, Olga. M in Math., Warsaw (Poland) U., 1976; PhD in Math. Scis., Polish Acad. Scis., Warsaw, 1979. Rsch. asst. Math. Inst. Polish Acad. Scis., Warsaw, 1976-79, rsch. fellow, 1979-83; asst. prof. Case Western Res. U., Cleve., 1983-87, prof., 1987—, chair math. dept., 1994-96; prof. U. Paris, 1996—. Vis. positions U. Ill., Urbana, 1980, Ohio State U., Columbus, 1981, U. Tex., Austin, 1981-83, Inst. des Hautes Etudes Scientifiques, Bures-Sur-Yvette, France, 1986-89, U. Paris, 1990, 92, 95, Math. Scis. Rsch. Inst., Berkeley, Calif., 1996. Contbr. articles to profl. jours. Recipient Prize of Sci. Sec., Polish Acad. Scis., 1979; rsch. grantee NSF, 1983—, U.S.-Israel Binat. Sci. Found., 1993-97; Sloan fellow Alfred P. Sloan Found., 1986-88. Mem. Am. Math. Soc. Avocations: skiing, sailing, diving, bridge, travel. Office: Case Western Res U Dept of Math Cleveland OH 44106 E-mail: szarek@cwru.edu.

SZAREK, WALTER ANTHONY, chemist, educator; b. St. Catharines, Ont., Can., Apr. 19, 1938; s. Anthony and Sophia (Kania) S. BSc, McMaster U., 1960, MSc, 1962; PhD, Queen's U., 1964. Postdoctoral fellow in chemistry Ohio State U., Columbus, 1964-65; asst. prof. biochemistry Rutgers U., New Brunswick, N.J., 1965-67; asst. prof. chemistry Queen's U., Kingston, Ont., 1967-71, assoc. prof., 1971-76, prof., 1976—, dir. Carbohydrate Research Inst., 1976-85; founding mem., prin. investigator Neurochem, Inc., 1993—. Cons. to govt. and industry; mem. Premier's Coun. Tech. Fund. Mem. editl. adv. bd. Carbohydrate Rsch. jour., 1973-97, Jour. of Carbohydrate Chemistry, 1994-2001; contbr. articles on chemistry of carbohydrates to profl. jours. Recipient Tchg. Excellence award Queen's U. Arts and Sci. Undergrad. Soc., 1988-89, Tchg. Excellence in Chemistry award, 1993, 2000, 2002. Fellow Chem. Inst. Can.; mem. AAAS, Am. Chem. Soc. (chmn. divsn. carbohydrate chemistry 1982-83, Claude S. Hudson award in carbohydrate chemistry 1989, Melville L. Wolfrom award 1992), Inst. Theol. encounter with Sci. and Tech., Royal Soc. Chemistry, N.Y. Acad. Scis., Soc. Glycobiology. Roman Catholic. Office: Dept Chemistry Queens Univ Kingston ON Canada K7L 3N6 Fax: 613-533-6532. E-mail: szarekw@chem.queensu.ca.

SZARLETA, ELLEN JEAN, economics educator; b. Bellefonte, Pa., June 28, 1959; d. Norbert Edward and Jean (Donatelli) S. BA, SUNY, Fredonia, 1981; PhD in Agrl. Econs., U. Wis., 1987; JD, U. Iowa, 1995. Agrl. economist U. W.I., U.S. AID, Burkina Faso, West Africa, 1984-85; rsch. assoc. Oak Ridge (Tenn.) Nat. Lab., 1987-89; asst. prof. econs. Wright State U., Dayton, Ohio, 1989-90, Canisius Coll., Buffalo, 1990-92; asst. prof. econ. Ind. U.–N.W., 1997—; prosecutor Lake County, Ind., 1995-96; atty. Willie Harris & Assoc., 1996-97; magistrate Lake Superior Ct., 2000—. Speaker Dayton Coun. on World Affairs, 1990. Mem. ABA, Am. Econ. Assn., Ind. State Bar Assn., Omicron Delta Epsilon, Sigma Delta Pi. Avocations: jogging, reading, cross-country skiing, biking. Office: Ind U NW SPEA 3400 Broadway Gary IN 46408-1101 E-mail: eszarlet@iun.edu.

SZASZ, SUZY, librarian, writer; b. Bethesda, Md., July 3, 1955; d. Thomas Stephen and Rosine (Loshkajian) S.; m. Larry Isaac Palmer, May 7, 1995. AB summa cum laude, Syracuse U., 1976, MLS, 1978; postgrad., U. Va., 1978-79. Ref. libr. Cornell U., Ithaca, N.Y., 1979-82, libr., 1982—. Author: Lupus: Living With It, 1991, 95; editor-in-chief: Microform Rev., 1991-93, mem. editl. bd., 1993—. Ch. historian 1st Congregational Ch., Ithaca, 1997—. Winner N.Y. State essay contest Philip Morris Co., 1987. Mem. Phi Beta Kappa. Avocations: knitting, cooking, reading. Home: 45 Whitetail Dr Ithaca NY 14850-9458

SZASZ, THOMAS STEPHEN, psychiatrist, educator, writer; b. Budapest, Hungary, Apr. 15, 1920; came to U.S., 1938, naturalized, 1944; s. Julius and Lily (Wellisch) S.; m. Rosine Loshkajian, Oct. 19, 1951 (div. 1970); children: Margot Szasz Peters, Susan Marie Szasz Palmer. AB, U. Cin., 1941, MD, 1944; DSc (hon.), Allegheny Coll., 1975, U. Francisco Marroquin, Guatemala, 1979; LHD (hon.), Towson U., 1999; D Sc(hon.), SUNY, 2001. Diplomate: Nat. Bd. Med. Examiners, Am. Bd. Psychiatry and Neurology. Intern 4th Med. Service Harvard, Boston City Hosp., 1944-45; asst. resident medicine Cin. Gen. Hosp., 1945-46, asst. clinician internal medicine div. out-patient dispensary, 1946; asst. resident psychiatry U. Chgo. Clinics, 1946-47; tng. research fellow Inst. Psychoanalysis, Chgo., 1947-48, rsch. asst., 1949-50, staff mem., 1951-56; practice medicine, specializing in psychiatry, psychoanalysis Chgo., 1949-54, Bethesda, Md., 1954-56, Syracuse, N.Y., 1956—; prof. psychiatry SUNY Health Sci. Ctr., 1956-90, prof. psychiatry emeritus, 1990—. Vis. prof. dept. psychiatry U. Wis., Madison, 1962, Marquette U. Sch. Medicine, Milw., 1968, U. N.Mex., 1981; holder numerous lectureships, including C.P. Snow lectr. Ithaca Coll., 1970; E.S. Meyer Meml. lectr. U. Queensland Med. Sch.; Lambie-Dew orator Sydney U., 1977; Mem. nat. adv. com. bd. Tort and Med. Yearbook; cons. com. mental hygiene N.Y. State Bar Assn.; mem. research adv. panel Inst. Study Drug Addiction; adv. bd. Corp. Econ. Edn., 1977— Author: Pain and Pleasure, 1957, The Myth of Mental Illness, 1961, Law, Liberty and Psychiatry, 1963, Psychiatric Justice, 1965, The Ethics of Psychoanalysis, 1965, Ideology and Insanity, 1970, The Manufacture of Madness, 1970, The Second Sin, 1973, Ceremonial Chemistry, 1974, Heresies, 1976, Karl Kraus and the Soul-Doctors, 1976, Schizophrenia: The Sacred Symbol of Psychiatry, 1976, Psychiatric Slavery, 1977, The Theology of Medicine, 1977, The Myth of Psychotherapy, 1978, Sex by Prescription, 1980, The Therapeutic State, 1984, Insanity: The Idea and its Consequences, 1987, The Untamed Tongue: A Dissenting Dictionary, 1990, Our Right to Drugs: The Case for a Free Market, 1992, A Lexicon of Lunacy, 1993, Cruel Compassion, 1994, The Meaning of Mind, 1996, Fatal Freedom, 1999, Pharmacracy: Medicine and Politics in America, 2001, Liberation By Opperession: A Comparative Study of Slavery and Psychiatry, 2002; editor: The Age of Madness, 1973; cons. editor of psychiatry and psychology: Stedman's Medical Dictionary, 22d edit, 1973; contbg. editor: Reason, 1974—, Libertarian Rev., 1986—; mem. editorial bd. Psychoanalytic Rev, 1965—, Jour. Contemporary Psychotherapy, 1968—, Law and Human Behavior, 1977—, Jour. Libertarian Studies, 1977—, Children and Youth Services Rev, 1978—, Am. Jour. Forensic Psychiatry, 1980—, Free Inquiry, 1980—. Comdr. M.C., USNR, 1954-56. Recipient Stella Feiss Hofheimer award U. Cin., 1944, Holmes-Munsterberg award Internat. Acad. Forensic Psychology, 1969; Wisdom award honor, 1970; Acad. prize Institutum atque Academia Auctorum Internationalis, Andorra, 1972; Distinguished Service award Am. Inst. Pub. Service, 1974; Martin Buber award Midway Counseling Center, 1974, Thomas S. Szasz award Ctr. Ind. Thought , 1990, Alfred R. Lindesmith award for achievement in field of scholarship and writing Drug Policy Found., 1991, Rollo May award APA, 1998; others; named Humanist of Year Am. Humanist Assn., 1973; Hon. fellow Postgrad. Center for Mental Health, 1961, Mencken award, 1981, Humanist Laureate, 1984, Statue of Liberty-Ellis Island Found. Archives Roster, 1986. Fellow Am. Psychiat. Assn. (life), Am. Psychoanalytic Assn., Internat. Psychoanalytic Soc., Western N.Y. Psychoanalytic Soc. Home: 4739 Limberlost Ln Manlius NY 13104-1405 Office: 750 E Adams St Syracuse NY 13210-2306 E-mail: tszasz@aol.com.

SZCZECHOWICZ, GRETCHEN, medical/surgical nurse; b. Middletown, Conn., Apr. 13, 1939; d. Norman and Ellen G. (Green) Wilson; m. Fred Szczechowicz, Oct. 3, 1968; 1 child, Christopher. Diploma, Salem Hosp. Sch. Nursing, 1959; student, Boston U., Emmanuel Coll., St. Joseph's Coll. Cert. coll. health nurse, ANCC. Staff nurse Salem Hosp., Mass., supr., med. surg.; health svc. coord. Salem State Coll. Recipient Mass. Commonwealth Citation for Outstanding Performance, Merit awards. Mem. APHA, Am. Coll. Health Assocs., New Eng. Coll. Health Assn.

SZCZEPANIAK, JANE CAMILLE, childbirth educator; b. Phila., Apr. 13, 1947; d. John and Jane (Feltowicz) S.; m. James Patrick Gillece, Apr. 24, 1971 (div. 1998); children: Jessica, Jocelyn, Jillian, James, Juliette, John Szczepaniak-Gillece. BA, Rosemont Coll., 1968. Cert. childbirth educator. Pvt. practice childbirth edn., Balt., 1978-95; childbirth educator Becoming a Family, N.J., 1996—. Dir.-at-large Cesarean Prevention Movement, Syracuse, N.Y., 1984-86; exec. com. C/SEC, Framingham, Mass., 1981—. Mem. Internat. Childbirth Edn. Assn. (cesarean ops. com. 1981-92), ASPO, C/SEC. Democrat. Roman Catholic. Avocations: sewing, beachwalking, biking, volunteer religious education, pastoral care. Home: 629 Wesley Ave Ocean City NJ 08226-3855

SZCZEPANSKI, SLAWOMIR ZBIGNIEW STEVEN, lawyer; b. Lodz, Poland, Mar. 9, 1948; s. Wladyslaw and Janina Szczepanski; m. Cynthia Ellen Weagley, Sept. 30, 1972; children: Christine, Diana. BS in Chem. Engring., Rensselaer Poly. Inst., 1971; MS in Chem. Engring., Rensselaer Poly. Inst., 1972; JD, Union U., Albany, N.Y., 1975. Bar: N.Y. 1976, D.C. 1976, Ill. 1977, U.S. Dist. Ct. (no. dist.) Ill. 1977, U.S. Ct. Appeals (fed. cir.) 1988. Atty. Philips Petroleum Co., Washington, 1975-77; from assoc. to ptnr. Willian, Brinks, Hofer, Gilson & Lione, Chgo., 1977-95; of counsel Arnold White and Durkee, 1996-99; shareholder Jenkens & Gilchrist, 2000—. Author: Licensing in Foreign and Domestic Operations, 1985-98; editor (legal periodical) Licensing Law and Business Report, 1986-98; contbr. articles to profl. jours. Mem. ABA, ATLA, Am. Intellectual Property Law Assn., Internat. Assn. Protection Indsl. Property, Nat. Advocates Soc., Licensing Execs. Soc. Intellectual Property Law Assn. Chgo., Univ. Club. Avocations: tennis, sailing. Home: 641 W Willow St Apt 107 Chicago IL 60614-5176 Office: Jenkens & Gilchrist Ste 2600 225 W Washington St Chicago IL 60606-3416 Fax: (312) 425-3909. E-mail: sszczepanski@jenkens.com.

SZCZERBA, VICTOR BOGDAN, electrical engineer, sales engineer; b. Chgo., Oct. 21, 1966; s. Bogdan and Zosia (Mika) S. BSEE, Marquette U., 1989; MBA, U. Calif., Berkeley, 1999. Sales engr. New Vision Computers, Milw., 1988-89; mktg. engr. Cypress Semicondr., San Jose, Calif., 1989-91; regional sales mgr. AMD/NEXGEN, Milpitas, 1991-96; sr. acct. mgr. Sun Micro Sys., Mountain View, 1996-99; cons. McKinsey & Co., Warsaw, 1999-2001; v.p. sales and mktg. Utopy Inc. , San Francisco, 2001—. Sales engr. Trinity Tech., Mountainview, Calif., 1991-92; cons. S3, Santa Clara, 1991-92; tutor Project Read. Mem. Knights of St. Patrick (pres. 1988-89), Sigma Phi Delta (v.p. 1987-88). Republican. Roman Catholic. Avocations: skiing, investing. Home: 235 Middlefield Rd Palo Alto CA 94301-1343 Office: Utopy Inc 330 Fell St San Francisco CA 94102 also: 330 Fell St San Francisco CA 94102 E-mail: victor@szczerba.com.

SZCZESNIAK, RAYMOND ALBIN, systems analyst, researcher; b. Buffalo, Nov. 28, 1940; s. Vincent John Szczesniak, Irene Genevieve Szczesniak; m. JoAnne Edmundine Maleskis (dec. Apr. 26, 1985); children: Peter, David, Philip, Carl. PhD Medicinal Chemistry, U. Mich., 1967. Sr. rsch. scientist E. R. Squibb & Sons, Inc., New Brunswick, NJ, 1968—73; database adminstr. Comerica Bank, Dallas, 1994—. Cons. Cardinal Capital Corp., Dallas, 1982—84. Author: Thru The Mist, 1985. Faithful capt. KC-4th Degree, Dallas, 1978—79. Recipient, Merck & Co., 1963. Mem.: Mensa (life; sec., treas 1978—80). Achievements include patents for radioimmunoassay, 1974. Avocation: chess. Home: 4042 Mendenhall Dr Dallas TX 75244 Personal E-mail: rayszc@msn.com.

SZCZUREK, THOMAS EUGENE, business executive; b. Chgo., Aug. 29, 1957; s. Eugene and Anne (Potaniec) S.; m. Vickie Lynn Dodds, Oct. 20, 1984. AAS, Morton Coll., 1977; BBA with highest honors, Western Ill. U., 1979; MBA, U. Cin., 1981. Assoc. account mgr. Burroughs Corp., Chgo., 1979-80; sr. mktg. analyst NCR Corp., Dayton, Ohio, 1982-84; mktg. and bus. mgr.

Monarch Marking Systems, 1984-86; mktg. mgr. Reynolds & Reynolds, 1986-87, dir. mktg., 1987-90, dir. product mgmt., dir. nat. accounts mktg., 1990-91; v.p. mktg. Evenflo Juvenile Products Co., Piqua, Ohio, 1991-96; v.p. corp. mktg. Monarch Marking Sys., Dayton, 1996-97; v.p. sales and mktg. Century Products Co., Cleve., 1997-2000; pres. Cosco Home and Office Products, Columbus, Ind., 2001—. Chmn. Cicero Young Adults Assn., 1979-80; mem. Republican Senatorial Inner Cir., v.p. Woodview Estates Homeowners Assn., 1988-90, pres., 1990-93. Named one of Outstanding Young Men of Am. U.S. Jaycees, 1986; recipient Republican Senatorial Medal of Freedom award, 1999. Mem. Am. Mktg. Assn. (chmn. promotion com. 1978-79), Worldwide Mktg. Leadership Panel, Phi Beta Lambda, Phi Kappa Phi, Beta Gamma Sigma, Alpha Mu Alpha. Avocations: golf, investing. Home: 9851 Fitzwater Rd Brecksville OH 44141-1307 Office: 2525 State St Columbus IN 47201-7494

SZE, DANIEL YUNG-HO, medical educator; b. Pitts., June 5, 1961; s. Tsung Wei and Frances Tung Sze; m. Cynthia Ruth Harris, Aug. 14, 1993; children: Katherine Lily, Michael Jason. BA, Harvard U., 1983; PhD, MD, Stanford U., 1991. Asst. prof. Stanford U., 1997—. Office: Divsn Cardiovascular and Interventional Radiology Stanford U Stanford CA 94305

SZE, GORDON, neuroradiologist; b. N.Y.C., Mar. 6, 1955; s. Kenneth and Denise Sze. BA summa cum laude, Harvard U., 1976, MD, 1981; MA (hon.), Yale U., 1997. Intern, resident, fellow U. Calif., San Francisco, 1981-86; asst. prof. Cornell Med. Sch., N.Y.C., 1986-89; chief neuroradiology Yale Med. Sch., New Haven, 1989—, assoc. prof., 1989-97, prof., 1997—. Mem. editl. bd. Am. Soc. Neuroradiology, 1992—; editl. bd., assoc. editor Radiol. Soc. N.Am., 1999—. Mem. Phi Beta Kappa. Office: Yale Univ Sch of Medicine Dept Radiology 20 York St New Haven CT 06512

SZE, MICHAEL MING-CHIH, actuary, consultant; b. Shanghai, China, June 1, 1940; came to U.S., 1968; m. Elsie Sim-Yee Chin, Aug. 19, 1972; children: Benjamin, Samuel, Timothy. BS, U. Hong Kong, 1964; MS, Calif. State U., Hayward, 1969; PhD in Math., Ohio State U., 1975. Pension cons., ptnr. Hewitt Assocs, Lincolnshire, Ill., 1975-96; pres., fin. planner Sze Assocs., Toronto, Can., 1996—. Adj. prof. U. Mich., Ann Arbor, 1998—99; mem. tech. panel adv. bd. Social Security Adminstrn., Washington, 1994—96, Washington, 1999; cons. Nat. Social Security Inst. Bulgaria, Sofia, 1997, Sofia, 99; cons. on actuarial profession Kazakhstan Govt., Almaty, 1999—2002; cons. on social security Bhutan Govt., 2000—02. Mem. editl. bd. Jour. Actuarial Practice, 1996—; acting assoc. editor N.Am. Actuarial Jour., 1998—; co-author: Carswell's Benefits Manual, 1999—. Fellow Soc. Actuaries (bd. govs. 1994-97), Can. Inst. Actuaries (com. on investment practice 1994-96); mem. Acad. Social Scis., N.Y. Acad. Scis. Roman Catholic. Avocations: bridge, YMCA sports. Office: Sze Assocs 45 Francine Dr Willowdale ON Canada M2H 2G5

SZEFLER, STANLEY JAMES, pediatrics and pharmacology educator; b. Buffalo, Aug. 24, 1948; s. Stanley and Bernice Laura (Platt) Szefler; m. Christine M. Drezek, Dec. 26, 1970; children: David, Paul. BS, SUNY, Buffalo, 1971, MD, 1975. Resident pediat. Children's Hosp. Buffalo, 1975—77; postdoctoral fellow in clin. pharmacology and allergy immunology SUNY, Buffalo, 1977—79, asst. prof. pediat. and pharmacology, 1979—82; assoc. prof. pediat. and pharmacology U. Colo., Denver, 1982—90, prof. pediat., pharmacology, 1990—. Dir. clin. pharmacology Children's Hosp., Buffalo, 1979—82, Nat. Jewish Ctr. for Immunology and Respiratory Medicine, Denver, 1982—. Contbr. articles to profl. jours. Mem. steering com., Asthma Camp for Children Am. Lung Assn., Denver, 1987—96. Maj. USAR, 1979—88. Grantee NIH, 1980—84, 1990—, FDA, Denver, 1988—91. Fellow: Am. Acad. Pediat. (liaison mem. com. drugs), Am. Acad. Allergy, Asthma and Immunology (chmn. asthma, rhinitis and respiratory disease interest sect. 1995—97). Avocations: baseball, soccer. Office: Nat Jewish Med & Rsch Ctr Dept Pediat 1400 Jackson St Denver CO 80206-2761

SZEGO, CLARA MARIAN, cell biologist, educator; b. Budapest, Hungary, Mar. 23, 1916; came to U.S., 1921, naturalized, 1927; d. Paul S. and Helen (Elek) S.; m. Sidney Roberts, Sept. 14, 1943. AB, Hunter Coll., 1937; MS (Garvan fellow), U. Minn., 1939, PhD, 1942. Instr. physiology U. Minn., 1942-43; Minn. Cancer Research Inst. fellow, 1943-44; rsch. assoc. OSRD, Nat. Bur. Standards, 1944-45, Worcester Found. Exptl. Biology, 1945-47; rsch. instr. physiol. chemistry Yale U. Sch. Medicine, 1947-48; mem. faculty UCLA, 1948—, prof. biology, 1960—. Guggenheim fellow, 1956; named Woman of Year in Sci. Los Angeles Times, 1957-58; named to Hunter Coll. Hall of Fame, 1987. Fellow AAAS; mem. Am. Physiol. Soc., Am. Soc. Cell Biology, Endocrine Soc. (CIBA award 1953), Soc. for Endocrinology (Gt. Britain), Biochem. Soc. (Gt. Britain), Internat. Soc. Rsch. Reprodn., Phi Beta Kappa (pres. UCLA chpt. 1973-74), Sigma Xi (pres. UCLA chpt. 1976-77). Achievements include rsch. and numerous publs. on steroid protein interactions, mechanisms of hormone action and lysosome participation in normal cell function. Home: 1371 Marinette Rd Pacific Palisades CA 90272-2627 Office: U Calif Dept Molecular Cell & Devel Biology Los Angeles CA 90095-1606 E-mail: cmszego@ucla.edu.

SZENBERG, MICHAEL, economics educator, editor, consultant; b. Sosnowiec, Poland, Apr. 8, 1934; came to U.S., 1961, naturalized, 1966; s. Henry and Sara (Rosensaft) S.; m. Miriam Silverstein, Sept. 2, 1962; children: Naomi, Avi. Student, Bar Ilan U., Israel, 1959-61; BA summa cum laude, L.I. U., 1963; PhD, CUNY, 1970. Faculty L.I. U., Bklyn. Center, 1965—, prof. econs., 1974-83; disting. prof. econs. Lubin Grad. Sch. Bus. Pace U., 1983—; chmn. fin. and econ., 2000—; dir. Ctr. Applied Rsch., 1994—. Adj. prof. Hunter Coll., 1970-76, Pace U., 1975-83; founder, dir. Lecture Bur. Econs., 1973; chmn. 1st Met. Grad. Conf. Econs., 1973; assoc. mem. Ctr. Tech. Assessment, Newark Coll. Engring., 1973; vis. prof. econs. NYU, summers 1977, 78, 79; cons. in field. Author: Economics of the Israeli Diamond Industry, 1973, The Welfare Effects of Trade Restrictions: A Case Study of the United States Footwear Industry, 1977, The Economics of the American Footwear Industry, 2d edit., 1984; editor: Essays in Economics, The John Commons Memorial Lectures, 1986, Eminent Economists: Their Life Philosophies, 1992, Passion and Craft, Economists at Work, 1999; assoc. editor: Am. Economist, 1973-75, editor-in-chief, 1975—; econs. co-editor: Cambridge Univ. Press Encyclopedia; contbr. articles to profl. jours. and chpts. to books. Served with Israeli Air Force, 1956-59. Recipient Dean Hudson award L.I. U., 1962, Am. Coll. Abroad award, 1962, Dean Abelson award CUNY, 1963; fellow econs. CUNY, 1963; grantee Israel Diamond Inst., 1970; recipient Irving Fisher Monograph award, 1971; fellow Internat. Honor Soc. in Econs., 1972; grantee Dept. Labor, 1975; recipient Kenan award for teaching excellence Pace U., 1983, Schalkenbach Found. Research award, 1987, First Prize Recognition award for scholarly productivity, 1989, Tchr. of the Year Pace U., 1992, Teaching Excellence award Acad. Bus. Admin., 1993, Achievement award CUNY, 1993, Outstanding Publication award Pace U., 1993, 94, 95, Outstanding Svc. award Pace U., 1996, scholarly rsch. awards for basic and applied rsch. Pace U., 1996. Mem. Atlantic Econ. Soc., Internat. Trade and Fin. Assn., Internat. Fedn. Sci. Editors, Ea. Econ. Assn., Am. Econ. Assn., Assn. Cultural Econs., Internat. Honor Soc. Econs. (exec. bd. 1975—, regional dir. 1971-74), Optimates Soc. (pres. 1972-80). Home: 1442 E 9th St Brooklyn NY 11230-6405 E-mail: mszenberg@pace.edu.

SZENDE, BÉLA, pathologist; b. Budapest, Hungary, July 29, 1936; s. Béla and Júlia (Mesterházy) S.; m. Béláné Gabriella Kiss; children: Katalin, Gabriella. BA, Vörösmarty Grammar, Budapest, 1954; MA, Budapest U., 1960. Resident Budapest U., 1960-63, asst., 1963-71, sr. lectr., 1971-75, reader, 1975-82, prof., 1982—. Contbr. articles to profl. jours. Recipient J. Balo award Hungarian Soc. Pathologists, Budapest, 1995. Mem. Coll. Hungarian Pathologists (pres. 1995-2000), Pathol. Soc. Gt. Britain, Internat. Acad. Pathologists. Home: Üllöi ut 55 1091 Budapest Hungary Office: Semmelweis U Üllöi ut 26 Budapest Hungary E-mail: bszende@korb1.sote.hu.

SZEP, PAUL MICHAEL, editorial cartoonist; b. Hamilton, Ont., Can., July 29, 1941; came to U.S., 1966; s. Paul Joseph and Helen (Langhorne) S.; m. Angela Diane Garton, Feb. 27, 1965 (div. 1976); children: Amy, Jason. A.O.C.A., Ont. Coll. Art, 1964; A.O.C.A. hon. degree, 1975, Framingham State Coll., 1975, Worcester State Coll., 1980, William Penn Coll., 1981. Sports cartoonist Hamilton Spectator, 1958-61; graphics designer Financial Post, Toronto, Ont., 1965-66; editorial cartoonist Boston Globe, 1966—. Vis. fellow Harvard U., 1981; lectr. various univs. Author: In Search of Sacred Cows, 1967, Keep Your Left Hand High, 1969, At This Point in Time, 1973, The Hader They Fall, 1975, Unvote for a New America, 1976, Them Demaned Pictures, 1977, Warts and All, 1979, To a Different Drummer, 1983, The Gang of Eight, 1985, The Next Szep Book, 1985, Often in Error, Never in Doubt, 1987, And Then Jack Said to Arnie, 1991, And Then Arnie Told Chi Chi and Then Chi Chi Said to Fuzzy, 1993, And Then Fuzzy Told Seve, 1996, Not Just Another Szep Book, 1997, And Then Seve Told Freddy, 1997, Then Freddy Told Tiger, 1998, And Then Tiger Told the Shark, 1999, Talking on Tour, 2001, And Then the Shark Told Justin, 2002; editl. cartoonist: Sta. WNEV-TV, creator comic strip: Mr. Zeep, 1999; contbr. . Served with F.A. Royal Canadian Army, 1957-58. Recipient Pulitzer prize, 1974, 77, award Sigma Delta Chi, 1974, 77, Toyl award Boston Jaycees, 1976, Headliners award, 1977, Reuben award for best editl. cartoonist Nat. Cartoonist Soc., 1979, Thomas Nast award; Internat. Cartoonist award, Best Sports Cartoonist award Nat. Cartoonists Soc., 1988. Mem. Soc. Illustrators, Kittansett Club, Harvard Club, Weston Golf Club. Home: 7 Stetson St Brookline MA 02446-7106 E-mail: paulszep@peoplepc.com., paulszep@attbi.com.

SZEPESHAZI, KAROLY ISTVAN, pathologist; b. Budapest, Hungary, July 19, 1938; came to U.S., 1989; s. Istvan and Marta (Borszeky) S.; m. Eszter Maria Faluhelyi, Aug. 1, 1984; children: Zsolt, Kinga. MD, U. Med. Sch., Budapest, Hungary, 1963, PhD, 1977. Resident Inst. Traumatology, Budapest, Hungary, 1963-66, asst. prof. dept. pathology Hungary, 1966-68; sr. lectr., chief lectr. 1st Inst. Pathology, Cancer Rsch. U. Sch. Medicine, Hungary, 1968-80; head dept. pathology Jahn Hosp., Hungary, 1980-89; rsch. prof. dept. medicine Tulane U., New Orleans, 1989—. Contbr. articles to profl. jours., chpts. to books. Mem. New Orleans Mus. Art, Smithsonian Inst., 1996-97. Mem. AAAS, N.Y. Acad. Scis. Avocations: travel, hiking, tennis. Office: Tulane U Dep Medicine 1601 Perdido St New Orleans LA 70112-1207 E-mail: karoly@tulane.edu.

SZEREMETA-BROWAR, TAISA LYDIA, endodontist; b. Geneva, Mar. 21, 1957; d. Swiatoslaw Bohdan and Stefania (Melnyk) Szeremeta; m. Andrew Wolodymyr Browar, Sept. 19, 1981. BS in Dentistry, Case Western Res. U., 1978, DDS, 1980; cert. specialty endodontics magna cum laude, U. Ill., Chgo., 1982. Pvt. practice Hinsdale (Ill.) Periodontics and Endodontics, 1982—; asst. clin. prof. Northwestern U. Dental Sch., Chgo., 1986-97, clin. prof., 1997—. Counselor, mem. Plast-Ukrainian Scouting, 1963—; presenting team Worldwide Marriage Encounter, Chgo., 1985-94; mem. parish coun. Sts. Volodymyr and Olha, Chgo., 1985-94. E. Wach rsch. grantee U. Ill., Chgo., 1980. Mem. ADA, Am. Assn. Endodontists, Am. Coll. Stomatologic Surgeons, Ukrainian Med. Assn. (chair membership 1983-88), Ill. Assn. Endodontists (pres. 1990-91), Ill. State Dental Soc., Chgo. Dental Soc. (sec. table clinic 1990, vice chair 1991, chair 1992), Hinsdale C. of C. Ukrainian Catholic. Avocations: embroidery, marriage enrichment, marriage preparation, theology. Office: Hinsdale Periodontics & Endodontics 40 S Clay St Ste 111W Hinsdale IL 60521-3280

SZERI, ANDRAS Z. engineering educator; b. Nagyvarad, Hungary, June 6, 1934; came to U.S., 1967; s. Andras F. and Julie (Farkas) S.; m. Mary J. Parkinson, Apr. 25, 1962; children: Andrew J., Elizabeth C., Maria J. BS with honors, U. Leeds, Eng., 1959, PhD, 1962. Research engr. English Electric Co., Stafford, Eng., 1962-64; prof. Universidad Santa Maria, Valparaiso, Chile, 1964-66; asst. prof. U. Pitts., 1967-70, assoc. prof., 1970-76, prof. math., 1977-93, prof. mech. engring., 1977-94, chmn. dept. mech. engring., 1984-87, William Kepler Whiteford prof. engring., 1990-94; Robert Lyle Spencer prof. mech. engring., chmn. U. Del., Newark, 1994, interim dean Coll. Engring., 1998-2000. Cons. Westinghouse Electric Co., Pitts., 1967-82; external examiner U. W.I., 1989-95. Editor: Tribology: Friction, Lubrication, and Wear, 1980, Fluid Film Bearings, Theory, and Design, 1998. Fellow ASME (assoc. editor Jour. Tribology 1978-87, tech. editor 1987-93); mem. Am. Acad. Mechanics, The Soc. Rheology, Soc. Engring. Sci., Soc. Natural Philosophy. Office: U Del Dept Mech Engring Newark DE 19716 E-mail: szeri@me.udel.edu.

SZETELA, REBECCA E. COOMBE, engineer; b. Detroit, Nov. 07; d. Robert C. and Phyllis M. Coombe; m. Michael D. Szetela, Oct. 17, 1951. AS, Oakland C.C., Royal Oak, Mich., 1979; student, Oakland U., Macomb C.C., Warren, Mich., 1984. Detailer, designer Network Comms., Romulus, Mich., 1979-81; design coord. Beta Tech, Inc., Roseville, 1981-88; die design engr. Piecemaker, Troy, 1988-90; die designer Lamina, Oak Park, 1990-93; CAD designer Saturn, Rochester Hills, 1993-95; assoc. engr. TRICO, 1996—. Mem. N.Am. ACAD Users Group. Avocations: golfing, swimming, waterskiing, snow skiing, running. Office: TRICO Products Corp 3255 W Hamlin Rd Rochester Hills MI 48309-3231

SZETO, HUNG, publisher; b. Hoyping, Canton, People's Republic of China, Sept. 8, 1936; s. Cheong Yee and Sau King(Kwan) S.; m. Sau Hing Chow, Jan. 27, 1962; children: Roland, Lisa, Nancy. B in adminstrn., Tsing Hua Coll., Hong Kong, 1969. Mgr. Far East Trade Ctr., Seattle, 1975-81; editor Seattle Chinese Post, 1982; pres. APC Group, Seattle, 1986—; pub. Chinese Bus. Jour., 1989—; pres. Sino-Am. Econ. Devel. Assn., 2002—. Mem. Asian Am. Journalists Assn., Chinese-Lang. Press. Inst., Northwest Minority Pubs. Assn., Sino-Am. Econ. Devel. Assn. (pres. 2000--). Avocations: writing, consulting. Office: APC Group 659 S Weller St Seattle WA 98104-2944 *Personal philosophy: Serving the community by providing information.*

SZETO, PAUL (CHEUK-CHING SZETO), religious mission executive; b. Canton, China, July 28, 1940; came to U.S., 1962; s. Fai and Oi-wain (Wong) S.; m. Dorcas Chow, July 8, 1967; children: Tedd, Christine, Melissa. BA, Seattle Pacific U., 1966, MA, 1968; MDiv, Yale U., 1970; D of Missiology, Fuller Theol. Sem., Pasadena, Calif., 1980. Sr. minister Chinese Bapt. Ch., Seattle, 1971-78; dir. ch. planting ABC Pacific N.W., 1978-80; gen. dir. Evangelize China Fellowship, Inc., Monterey Park, Calif., 1980—. Founding dir. N.Am. of Chinese Evangelicals, 1972; participant Internat. Conf. for Itinerant Evangelists 1983, 86; bd. dirs. Chinese Coordination Ctr. of West Hong Kong, 1976-80; Lausanne II, Manila, 1989. Author: Seven Directions of Modern Theology, 1978, Suffering and Hope, 1982, Higher Ground, 1997, My Mentor: J. Edwin Orr, 2002; translator: Amazing Grace, 1966, Evangelical Awakening in Eastern Asia, 1981; compiler: The Abundant Life, 1987, Committed to Serve, 1985, The Boundless Power of Prayer, 1987. Mem. Greater Seattle Asian Am. Coun., 1972; mem. Royal Brougham Found., Seattle, 1974; mem. Campaign for Yale, L.A., 1977; trustee Azusa (Calif.) Pacific U., 2000. Resident scholar Oxford U., 1991. Mem. Greater L.A. Chinese Ministers Assn., U.S. Chaplains Assn., 1998, Edn. & Culture Found., (pres. 1998). Office: Evangelize China Fellowship 437 S Garfield Ave Monterey Park CA 91754-3328 Fax: 626 288-6727.

SZEWCZYK, SAMUEL HIDEYO, financial economist, educator; b. Phila., Nov. 7, 1952; s. Vincent and Miyuki (Morinaga) S.; m. Anne Hsu, Aug. 8, 1981. BS, Pa. State U., 1974, MBA, 1981, PhD, 1987. Assoc. prof. fin. Drexel U., Phila., 1987—. Contbr. articles to profl. jours. Lt. USN, 1975-78. Mem. Am. Fin. Assn. Fin. Mgmt. Assn., Eastern Fin. Assn., Southern Fin. Assn., Beta Gamma Sigma. Republican. Roman Catholic. Home: 732 Parker Ln Springfield PA 19064-1305 Office: Drexel U Fin Dept Philadelphia PA 19104

SZGALSKY, HELEN A. pediatric nurse practitioner, school nurse; LPN, Hartford (Conn.) Hosp., 1976; BSN summa cum laude, U. Bridgeport Coll. Nursing, Conn., 1982; MSN, U. Pa., 1983. Cert. Pediatric Nurse Practitioner, U. Pa. Sch. Nursing, 1983; cert. RN, Pediatric Nurse Practitioner, Am. Nurse's Assn., 1983, recertified 1988, 1993. Coronary intensive care unit nurse, team leader Hartford Hosp., 1976-82; staff nurse Staff Builders, Bala Cynwyd, Pa., 1982-83; pediatric nurse practitioner intern Penn-Urban HMO, Jefferson Child and Youth Clinic, Phila., 1982-83; pediatric nurse practitioner Gloucester County Health Ctr., Woodbury, N.J., 1983-89; part-time faculty Gloucester County Coll., Sewell, 1984-85; adj. clin. prof. U. Pa., Phila., 1984-89, Rutgers U., Camden, N.J., 1984-89; pediatric nurse practitioner Woodbury Pediat., Woodbury Heights, 1985-87; part-time faculty Cumberland County Coll., Vineland, 1986; pediatric nurse practitioner, case mgr., cons. Emmanuel Cancer Found., Bloomfield, 1987-89; pediatric nurse practitioner Thomas Jefferson U. Outpatient Pediat. Children's Health Ctr. Phila., 1989-93, Thomas Jefferson U. Enuresis Clinic at A.I. DuPont Inst., Wilmington, Del., 1992-93, Del. County Pediat., Drexel Hill, Pa., 1993-94, Salem County Dept. Health, Salem, N.J., 1995—. Co-preceptor for med. students from The Jefferson Med. Coll. of Thomas Jefferson U. and residents of the Underwood-Meml. Hosp. Family Practice Residency Program, Woodbury, N.J., 1983-89; clin. preceptor and instr. for jr. and sr. med. students from Thomas Jefferson Med. Coll., 1989-93; faculty mem. Salem C.C., 1999—; adj. faculty Salem (N.J.) C.C. Mem. Am. Acad. Nurse Practitioners, Nat. Assn. Pediatric Nurse Assoc. Practitioners, Sigma Theta Tau, Phi Kappa Phi. Office: 17 W Red Bank Ave Ste 201 Woodbury NJ 08096-1630

SZIGETI, MICHELLE MARIE, critical care nurse; b. South Bend, Ind., Mar. 21, 1954; d. Eugene Peter and Patricia Joyce (May) S. RN, Meml. Hosp., South Bend, 1976; BS, St. Francis Coll., Joliet, Ill., 1990. Cert. critical care nurse. Charge nurse cardiac intermediate care Meml. Hosp., South Bend, 1976-83, charge nurse cardio vascular intensive care, 1983—; tchr. cardiovasular intensive care Meml. Hosp. of South Bend, 1991—. Mem. AACN. Home: 112 S Mccombs St South Bend IN 46637-3330

SZILAGYI, GEORGE, microbiologist, physician; b. Carei, Romania, Dec. 30, 1916; s. Adolph Szilagyi and Lotte Kepecs; m. Magdalena Virag, Aug. 11, 1945; children: Edith, Andrew. MD, Franz Joseph U., 1942. Lab. physician, microbiologist Lab. Hygiene, Oradea, Romania, 1942-49; chief dept. of labs. Anti-Epidemic Ctr., Satu-Mare, Romania, 1949-62; rsch. assoc. Montefiore Hosp., Bronx, N.Y., 1963-69; dir. microbiology Albert Einstein Hosp., 1969-96, asst. prof. microbiology and immunology, 1971-79, assoc. prof. microbiology, immunology and lab. medicine, 1979-93, assoc. prof. microbiology, immunology and pathology, 1993-96; assoc. prof. emeritus Albert Einstein Coll. Medicine, 1996—. Contbr. articles to sci. and profl. jours. Fellow Am. Acad. Microbiology. Avocations: photography, hiking, travel. Home: 67-71 Yellowstone Blvd Forest Hills NY 11375 Office: Jack D Weiler Hosp 1825 Eastchester Rd Bronx NY 10461-2301

SZILAGYI, MIKLOS NICHOLAS, electrical and computer engineering educator; b. Budapest, Hungary, Feb. 4, 1936; came to U.S., 1981; s. Karoly and Ilona (Abraham) S.; m. Larissa Dorner, Feb. 23, 1957 (div. July 1970); 1 child, Gabor; m. Julia Levai, May 31, 1975; 1 child, Zoltan Charles. MS in Engring., Physics with honors, Tech. U. Leningrad, USSR, 1960; PhD, Electrotech. U. Leningrad, 1965; D Tech., Tech. U. Budapest, 1965; DSc with exceptional distinction, Hungarian Acad. Scis., 1979. Research asst. phys. electronics Tech. U. Leningrad, 1958-60; research assoc., Inst. Tech. Physics Hungarian Acad. Scis., 1960-66; head electron optics lab. Tech. U. Budapest, 1966-71; prof., head dept. phys. scis. K. Kando Coll. of Elec. Engring., Budapest, 1971-79, pres., 1971-74; cons. Deutsches Elektronen-Synchrotron DESY, Hamburg, Federal Republic of Germany, 1980-81; vis. sr. research assoc., applied and engring. physics Cornell U., 1981-82; prof. elec. and computer engring. U. Ariz., 1982—. Sci. adv. Nat. Inst. Neurosurgery, Budapest, 1966-70; vis. prof. Enrico Fermi Inst., U. Chgo., Lawrence Berkeley Lab, U. Calif., Stanford Linear Accelerator Ctr., Stanford U., 1976-77, Inst. Physics, U. Aarhus, Denmark, 1979-81, 88, 89, 90, Delft U. Tech., The Netherlands, 1988-89, U. Heidelberg, Fed. Republic of Germany, Max Planck Inst. Nuclear Physics, Heidelberg, 1984, pres. The Tucson Inst., 1993—. Author eleven books, including Introduction to the Theory of Space-Charge Optics, 1974, Fachlexikon Physik, 1979, Electron and Ion Optics, 1988, How To Save Our Country, 1993; contbr. over 95 articles to profl. jours., also contbr. to internat. confs; editor The New Common Sense. UN Indsl. Devel. Orgn. fellow, 1976. Mem. IEEE (sr.), Am. Phys. Soc., Internat. Soc. Hybrid Microelectronics, European Soc. Stereotactic and Functional Neurosurgery, L. Eotvos Phys. Soc. (Brody prize 1964), J. Neumann Soc. for Computer Sci., Danish Phys. Soc., Danish Engring. Soc. Contbr. to devel. of various particle beam devices, provided solution to problem of electron optical synthesis. Avocations: swimming, music, literature and fine arts, social philosophy. Office: U Ariz Dept Elec And Computer Engri Tucson AZ 85721-0001

SZILAGYI, SHERRY ANN, psychotherapist, lawyer; b. Cheverly, Md. d. John Alex and Mary Ann Szilagyi. BA in Edn.-Social Work-Psychology magna cum laude, U. Md., Catonsville, 1989; MSW summa cum laude, U. Md., Balt., 1990, JD cum laude, 1995. Bar: N.Mex. 1996, D.C. 1997, U.S. Supreme Ct. 2000; lic. cert. social worker, clin.; supr. cert. health ins. analyst; lic. child and civil rights advocate, tchr., Md. Dir. Teen and Community Ctr., Crofton, Md., 1987-89; social worker Dept. Social Svcs. and Child Protection, Hyattsville, 1988-89; clin. therapist Mental Health Ctr., Annapolis, 1989-90; pvt. practice, Columbia, 1990—; clin. therapist Sexual Assault Crisis Ctr., Annapolis, Md., 1990—. Tutor, rschr. U. Md., College Park, 1989—; cmty. chair Balt. Domestic Violence Advocacy Project, 1994—; pro bono atty. for pub. interest and animal rights. State of Md. scholar, 1988. Acad. Law scholar, 1995. Mem. ABA, APA, AACD, NASW, NOW, Women's Bar Assn., Psi Chi, Phi Kappa Phi. Avocations: skiing, computers, research, massage, travel. Office: ACPC 6535 Huntshire Dr Ste B Elkridge MD 21075-6165

SZILASSY, SANDOR, retired lawyer, library director, educator; b. Magyarbarnag, Hungary, Apr. 9, 1921; came to U.S., 1957; s. Sandor Sr. and Jolan (Fenyves) S.; m. Clara Ida Varkonyi, July 21, 1951; children: Peter S., Thomas S., Paul A.D. LLD, U. Budapest, Hungary, 1944, Lawyer-Judge Dipl., 1949; MA, Ind. U., 1959. Practicing atty., pres. law firm, Veszprém, Hungary, 1944-56; asst. libr. Anderson (Ind.) Coll. Libr., 1959-61; head div. sci. and tech. Auburn (Ala.) U. Libr., 1961-68; head libr., assoc. prof. Ind. State U., Evansville, 1968-69; dir. libr., prof. U. Tampa, Fla., 1969-72; dir. librs. Rowan U. of N.J., 1972-94. V.p. Ala. Acad. Sci., 1963-68; pres. Coun. N.J. Coll. and Univ. Librs., 1978-79, 89-90, Librs. Unltd., N.J., 1981-82, 88-89; cons. numerous orgns; radio commentator, Sta. WTEL, Phila., 1987-91. Author: Revolutionary Hungary, 1971 (Arpad Acad. Gold medal 1972), Ein Amerikanischer Diplomat uber Ungarn, 1974, Hungary's Road to Trianon, 1988, Hungary at the Brink of the Cliff, 1997, From Barnag to Miami, 1999, numerous others; author book chpts.; mem. editorial bd. Ency. Hungarica, 1989—; contbr. essays, studies, articles to profl. jours., newspapers, mags.; editor Egyesült Amerikai Magyarság. Bd. elders Presbyn. Ch., Lakeland, Fla., 1970-72; 1st Hungarian United Ch. of Christ, Miami, 1996—. Recipient Legion of Honor award Chapel of Three Chaplains, 1981. Mem. N.J. Acad. Libr. Network (exec. bd. 1988—), Tri-State Coll. Libr. Coop. (pres. 1975-76, 88-89, Johanniter Order Knights (Germany), Arpad Acad. (sect. pres. 1979—), Miami Kossuth Club (pres.), Phi Alpha Theta. Mem. Reformed Ch. Avocations: research, writing, reading, swimming, hiking. Home: 133 N Pompano Beach Blvd Pompano Beach FL 33062-5720 E-mail: aracsi@webtv.net.

SZOKA, EDMUND CASIMIR CARDINAL, archbishop; b. Grand Rapids, Mich., Sept. 14, 1927; s. Casimir and Mary (Wolgat) S. BA, Sacred Heart Sem., 1950; J.C.B., Pontifical Lateran U., 1958, J.C.L., 1959. Ordained priest Roman Catholic Ch., 1954; asst. pastor St. Francis Parish, Manistique, Mich., 1954-55; sec. to bishop Marquette, 1955-57, 59-62; chaplain St. Mary's Hosp., 1955-57; tribunal, notary, defender of bond, 1960-71; asst. chancellor Diocese of Marquette, 1962-69, chancellor, 1970-71; pastor St. Pius X Ch., Ishpeming, Mich., 1962-63, St. Christopher Ch., Marquette, 1963-71; bishop Diocese of Gaylord, Mich., 1971-81; archbishop of Detroit, 1981-90; elevated to cardinal, 1988; pres. Pontifical Commn for Vatican City State, Vatican. Sec.-treas. Mich. Cath. Conf., Lansing, 1972-77; chmn. region VI Nat. Conf. Cath. Bishops, 1972-77; treas., mem. adminstrv. bd. and adminstrv. com., budget and fin. com. Nat. Conf. Cath. Bishops/U.S. Cath. Conf., 1981-84; trustee, mem. exec. com., chmn. com. for univ. relations Cath. U. Am., 1981-90; trustee Nat. Shrine of the Immaculate Conception, Washington, 1981-90; chmn. bd. trustees Cath. Telecommunications Network Am., 1984-90; pres. Prefecture for Econ. Affairs of the Holy See, 1990-97, pres. Pontifical Commn. For Vatican City State, 1997, pres. Governatorato; mem. Secretariat of State, 2d sect. Coun. for Rels. with States. Mem. Congregation for Insts. Consecrated Life and Socs. Apostolic Life, Congregation for Causes of Saints, Congregation for Bishops, Congregation for Evangelization of Peoples, Congregation for Clergy. Address: Governatorato 00120 Vatican City Italy

SZOKE, JOSEPH LOUIS, psychologist, mental health facility administrator; b. Rahway, N.J., May 6, 1947; s. Louis Joseph Sr. and Julia Dorothy (Jasa) S.; m. Carolyn Kay Orr, Jan. 13, 1971; children: Elizabeth, Amy. BS, U. Dayton, 1969, MA, 1973. Cert. clin. psychologist, mental health adminstr. Psychologist Dayton (Ohio) Mental Health Ctr., 1969-71; dir. psychol. and social services Dayton Bur. Drug Abuse, 1971-73; assoc. dir. Montgomery County Bd. Mental Health, Dayton, 1973-74; exec. dir. Tri-County Bd. Mental Health, Troy, Ohio, 1974-90; exec. dir. alcohol and drug addiction Mental

Health Svcs. Bd. for Montgomery County, Dayton, 1990—. Adj. prof. U. Dayton, Ohio, 1975—, Sinclair Coll., Dayton, 1973—78; cons. Applications Rsch. Corp., Dayton, 1973—74. Pres. Metro Behavioral Health Care Network, 1998—2001; treas. Hospice of Miami County, Troy, Ohio, 1986—, Epilepsy Assn. Miami County, Troy, 1986—90. Capt. U.S. Army, 1969—72. Fellow: Assn. Behavioral Healthcare Mgmt. (pres. 1988, Adminstr. of Year award 1991); mem.: Ohio Assn. County Behavioral Health Authorities (pres. 2001), Ohio Assn. Cmty. Mental Health Bds. (treas. 1987—89), Nat. Assn. Rural Mental Health, Am. Evaluation Assn., Kiwanis (pres. Troy club 1983), Kiwanis (pres. Troy club 1983). Roman Catholic. Avocations: running, softball, stamp collecting, woodworking. Home: 1675 Old School House Rd Troy OH 45373-4435 E-mail: jszoke@adamhs.co.montgomery.oh.us.

SZOLNOKI, JOHN FRANK, special education educator, administrator; b. N.Y.C., Apr. 16, 1956; s. Jacob and Anna (Reinwald) S.; m. Judy Lynn Gitterman, June 7, 1981; children: Melissa Beth, David Jacob. BS, Manhattan Coll., 1978; MS, Coll New Rochelle, 1981; MEd, Columbia U., 1983, EdD, 1988. Cert. tchr. spl. edn., sch. adminstr., supr., dist. adminstr., N.Y. Therapy aide Office Mental Health, N.Y. State Bronx Psychiat. Ctr., 1978; tchr. sci. 6th-8th grades Sts. Philip and James Sch., Archdiocese of N.Y., 1978-79; program supr. occpf. edn. classes St. Mary's Habibilitation Inst. Inst. Applied Human Dynamics, Bronx, N.Y., 1979-83; sch. supr. Assn. for Help of Retarded Children Bronx Habilitation Ctr., N.Y.C., 1983-87; spl. educator Mt. Pleasant-Blythedale Union Free Sch. Dist., Valhalla, N.Y., 1987-88; spl. edn. educator Bd. Coop. Ednl. Svcs. So. Westchester, White Plains, 1988-98, Dobbs Ferry (N.Y.) H.S., 1995-96, Harrison (N.Y.) H.S., 1996-97. Adj. prof. Western Conn. State U., Danbury, 1988-89, St. Thomas Aquinas Coll., Sparkill, N.Y., 1990, 91, Coll. New Rochelle, N.Y., 1994, CUNY Hunter, 1994—; team leader Bd. Coop. Ednl. Svcs., So. Westchester, 1989-93, site coord. extended sch. yr. program Rye Lake campus, 1991-95; presenter in field; Ctr. Spl. Edn. and Tng. Resource Ctr., workshop presenter supts. day, 1995. Vol. firefighter, sec. hook & ladder Harrison (N.Y.) Fire Dept., 1993-95, lt., 1996, 97, capt., 1998 (Firefighter of Yr. 1990); mem. com. Very Spl. Arts,White Plains, N.Y., 1990; parent rep. exec. bd. Harrison Children's Ctr., 1991-93, 95—; lector, tchr. catechism St. Gregory the Gt. Roman Cath. Ch., 1994-95; EMT vol. Harrison Ambulance Corps, 1993-94; aux. police officer N.Y.C. Police Dept., 1975-77; mem. Ctrl. Westchester Vicariate Coun., Archdiocese of N.Y., 1998—; mem. parish coun. St. Gregory the Great, 1998—; panel mem. surrogate decision making com. N.Y. State Commn. on Quality Care for the Mentally Disabled, 1999—. Grantee: Readers Digest Found., Westchester Edn. Coalition, 1990, Innovation Network, Westchester, Rockland Impact II, Adaptor award, 1991, 92, 93, 94, 95, 97, 98. Mem. Am. Assn. on Mental Retardation (rsch. project norming examiner adaptive behavior scale 1991), Coun. for Exceptional Children (pres. Hunter Coll. chpt. 1997—, regional rep. to bd. dirs. N.Y. State Fedn. 1990-93, treas. 1993-96, exec. bd. dirs. 1993-96, del. Nat. conv. 1998, co-chair N.Y. state conv. 1997), Kappa Delta Pi, Phi Delta Kappa. Avocation: marathon runner (finisher N.Y.C. 1989, 92, 93). Home: 127 Webster Ave Harrison NY 10528-2913 Office: Bd Coop Ednl Svcs So Westchester 1606 Old Orchard St White Plains NY 10604-1049

SZONNTAGH, EUGENE L. chemical engineer, chemistry educator, archaeometrist, musicologist, organist, historian; b. Budapest, Hungary, July 31, 1924; s. Jenö Szonntag and Anna Vaisz; m. Nora Jenser, July 27, 1950; children: Desi, Thomas. Diploma in Chem. Engring., Tech. U. Budapest, 1948, DTech, 1975, PhD, 1999. Registered profl. engr., Pa.; profl. indsl. hygienist. Asst. to assoc. prof. Veszprem (Hungary) U., 1950-56; from scientist to sr. scientist Leeds and Northrup Co., North Wales, Pa., 1957-72; prin. engr. Honeywell, Inc., Ft. Washington, Clearwater, Fla., 1972-86; assoc. prof. U. South Fla., Tampa, 1987-91, prof., 1991—. Contbr. over 100 articles to profl. jours., including 20 on Roman organ of Aquincum, 8 chpts. to books; author 38 patents in field. Dir. music, organist, St. Alfred's Ch., Palm Harbor, Fla., 1983—93, Faith Luth. Ch., 1994—95, Holy Spirit Episcopal Ch., Safety Harbor, Fla., 1995—. Recipient Indsl. Rsch. 100 award Chromatography, 1964, Star Inventor award Honeywell, 1982. Mem. Am. Inst. Archaeology, Am. Musicological Soc., Am. Mus. Instrument Soc., Organ Hist. Soc., N.Y. Acad. Scis., Am. Chem. Soc. (emeritus), Am. Indsl. Hygiene Assn., Instrument Soc. Am. (historian 1978-82), Am. Guild Organists (acad. mem.; cert. choir master, chpt. dean 1970-72, 84-86). Avocations: collecting musical instruments, travel, archaeology, photography. Home: 1161 Cane Mill Ln Bradenton FL 34212 Office: U South Fla MDC-56 13201 Bruce B Downs Blvd Tampa FL 33612 E-mail: eszonntagh@aol.com.

SZOVERFFY, JOSEPH, educator, medieval scholar; b. Clausenbourgh, Transylvania, June 19, 1920. MA, State Coll. H.S. Tchrs., Budapest, 1944; PhD, Budapest U., 1943; PhD, U. Fribourg, 1950. Prof. fgn. lang. Glenstall Coll. (Ireland), 1950-52; archivist Irish Folklore Commn., Dublin, 1952-57; spl. prof. classics and medieval Latin U. Ottawa, 1957-58, asst. prof., 1958-59; from asst. prof. to assoc. prof. German philology U. Alta., 1959-62; assoc. prof. mediaeval German lit. Yale U., 1962-65; prof. German, medieval lit. Boston Coll., 1965-70, acting chmn. German studies, dir. grad. studies, 1968-70; prof. comparative lit. SUNY-Albany, 1970-77, chmn. dept., 1972-75; vis. prof. Byzantine studies Dumbarton Oaks Ctr. Byzantine Studies, Washington, 1977-78; prof. medieval lit. Sch. Hist. Studies, Inst. Advanced Study, 1978-79; Richard Merton vis. prof. Inst. Medieval Studies Freie U., Berlin (W.Ger.), 1980— ; hon. rsch. assoc. Harvard Ukrainian Research Inst., Harvard U., 1975—; with Inst. Advanced Studies, Berlin, 1983-84; vis. prof. Medieval Studies U. Vienna, Austria, 1984-85, 87-88. Author: Der hl Christophorus und sein Kult, 1942; Irisches Erzahlgut im Abendland, 1957; Annalen der lateinischen Hymnendichtung I-II, 1964-65; Weltliche Dichtungen des lateinischen Mittelalters, 1970; Peter Abelard's Hymnarius Paraclitensis Vol I-II, 1975; Germanistische Abhandlugen, 1977; A Guide to Byzantine Hymnography, Vol I-II, 1979-80; Repertorium Novum Hymnorum Medii Aevi, Vol I-IV, 1982, Religious Lyrics of the Middle Ages, 1983, A Concise History of the Medieval Latin Hymnody, 1985, Typology of Latin Hymns, 1988, Turnhout Across the Centuries...Harvard Lectures, 1988, Secular Latin Lyrics, Vol. I-IV, 1992-95, Memoirs, 1996. Recipient Chgo. Folklore prize U. Chgo., 1954; fellow Guggenheim Found. 1961, 69-70, Am. Philos. Soc., 1965, 72, Ctr. Medieval and Early Renaissance Studies, SUNY, 1973—, NEH, 1978-79; grantee Guggenheim Found. 1963, 71, 75. Mem. Mediaeval Acad. Am., MLA, Am. Comparative Lit. Assn., Conn. Acad., West Berlin Acad. Deceased.

SZTANDERA, LES MARK, computer science educator; b. Zabrze, Poland, Dec. 19, 1961; came to U.S., 1989; s. Felix and Regina (Sowa) S.; m. Wanda Monica Wietrzycka, Apr. 5, 1986; 1 child, Claudia Sabrina. Diploma, Cambridge (Eng.) U., 1989; MS, U. Mo., 1990; PhD, U. Toledo, Ohio, 1993. Rsch., tchg. asst. U. Mo., Columbia, 1989-90, U. Toledo, 1991-93; asst. prof. Phila. U., 1993-98, assoc. prof., 1998—, head computer sci. dept., 1997—. Reviewer coll. textbooks Prentice Hall Co., Englewood Cliffs, N.J., 1993—, McGraw-Hill Co., N.Y.C., 1993—, profl. jours. in field; organizer, mem. coms., chmn. various internat. confs. Contbr. numerous articles to profl. jours. Rsch. grantee Am. Heart Assn., Washington, 1991, Cray-Pitts. Supercomputing Ctr., 1992, 94, 96, NSF, Washington, 1996, Nat. Textile Ctr., Wilmington, 1998-2002, Dept. Commerce, Washington, 1998-2002. Mem. Assn. for Computing Machinery, N. Am. Fuzzy Info. Processing Soc., Can. Soc. for Fuzzy Info. and Neural Systems. Achievements include development of fuzzy neural trees, contributions to fuzzy set theory. Avocations: travel, literature. Office: Phila Univ Computer Info Sys Philadelphia PA 19144 E-mail: sztanderal@philau.edu.

SZTEINBAUM, EDWARD, psychiatrist; b. San Francisco, Dec. 1, 1955; s. Victor and Betty (Braverman) Szteinbaum; m. Marian Meyer, Nov. 1989; children: Jesse, Sabrina. MD, Javeriana, Bogota, 1979. Diplomate Am. Bd. Psychiatry. Outpatient psychiatrist Maimonides Med. Ctr., Bklyn., 1988-90; adult and addiction outpatient, day program psychiatrist St. Vincent's Med. Ctr., S.I., 1990-97; outpatient adult and addiction psychiat. profl. U. Medicine and Dentistry, Edison, N.J., 1997-99; med. dir. Princeton House Outpatient Divsn. Princeton (N.J.) U., 1999—. Chmn. morbidity com./psychiatry dept. St. Vincent's Med. Ctr., S.I., 1992-97; mem. faculty practice com. U. Medicine and Dentistry, Piscataway - New Brunswick, N.J., 1997-99. Mem. APA, N.J. Psychiat. Assn., Hispanic Rsch. Group, North Richmond Rsch. Group. Office: Princeton House Outpatient 253 Witherspoon St Princeton NJ 08540-3211

SZUCH, CLYDE ANDREW, lawyer; b. Bluefield, W.Va., Nov. 22, 1930; s. Nicholas and Aranka (Rubin) S.; m. Rosalie Hirschman Wulfson, Sept. 5, 1954; children: Peter Alan, Richard Coleman. BA, Rutgers, 1952; LLB, Harvard U., 1955. Bar: N.J. 1955, U.S. Dist. Ct. N.J. 1955, U.S. Ct. Appeals (3rd cir.) 1958, U.S. Supreme Ct. 1962. Law clk. to assoc. justice William J. Brennan Jr. U.S. Supreme Ct., Washington, 1956-57; asst. U.S. atty. U.S. Attys. Office, Newark, 1957-58; assoc. Pitney, Hardin & Kipp, 1958-62; ptnr. Pitney, Hardin, Kipp & Szuch, Morristown, N.J., 1962-2000, of counsel, 2001—. Mem. panel Ctr. for Pub. Resources, N.J.; bd. dirs. Vt. Rlwy. Inc., Clarendon & Pittsford R.R. Co., Burlington, Vt., Brennan Ctr. for Justice; panelist AAA Large Complex Cases. Gov. N.J. region Nat. Conf. for Cmty. and Justice. Fellow Am. Bar Found.; mem. ABA, Am. Law Inst., N.J. State Bar Assn., Morris County Bar Assn., Essex County Bar Assn., Fed. Bar Assn. (N.J. chpt.), N.J. C. of C. (bd. dirs.), Nat. Legal Aid Defender Assn., Hist. Soc. U.S. Ct. Appeals for 3d Cir. Office: Pitney Hardin Kipp & Szuch PO Box 1945 Morristown NJ 07962-1945

SZUCS, ANDREW ERIC, program manager; b. Cleve., Apr. 25, 1946; s. Andrew Elmer and Katherine (Krizsak) S.; m. Laura Jean Nyhan, June 4, 1971; children: Andrew Edward, Eric Stephen. BA, U. Dayton, 1968; Diploma, Cleve. Inst. Electronics, 1972; MBA, Wright State U., 1984. Pub. affairs specialist USAF, Laughlin AFB, Tex., 1968-70; exhibit rschr., writer USAF Orientation Group, Wright-Patterson AFB, Ohio, 1970-73; cmty. rels. dir., 1973-77; publ. mgr. Air Force Logistics Command, 1977-85, chief pub. officer, 1985-90; civilian command tng. mgr./adminstrn. Air Force Materiel Command, 1990-2001; program mgr. Materiel Sys. Group Supply Logistics Wright-Patterson AFB, 2001—. Contbr. articles to profl. jours. (AWA Jour. award 1986). Staff sgt. USAF, 1968—73. Named Disting. Alumnus, St. Ignatius High Sch., Cleve., 1994. Mem. Soc. Aerospace Communicators, Nat. Press Club, Am. Radio Relay League, Amateur Satellite Corp., U.S. Soccer Fedn. (referee), Ohio High Sch. Athletic Assn. (referee), Wright State U. Bus. Alumni Assn. (rec. sec. 1985-89), Nat. Assn. Sports Ofcls. Roman Catholic. Avocations: ham radio operator, creative writing, trainer for pvt. soccer team. Home: 1135 Mint Springs Dr Fairborn OH 45324-5728 Office: Material Sys Group/SLR Wright Patterson AFB OH 45433

SZUCS, LORETTO DENNIS, internet publishing executive, editor; b. Bklyn., Apr. 14, 1941; d. Joseph Raymond and Muriel Dennis; m. Robert John Szucs, May 27, 1961; children: Juliana Smith, Diana Sullivan, Patricia Stitz, Laura Pfeiffer. BA in History, St. Joseph's Coll., Rensselaer, Ind., 1990. Archives specialist Nat. Archives & Records Adminstrn., Great Lakes Region, Chgo., 1990-92; acquisitions editor Ancestry Pub., Salt Lake City, 1992-97; v.p. Ancestry.com, Provo, 1997—. Author: They Became Americans, 1998, Chicago & Cook County Sources, 1996; co-editor: The Source: A Guidebook of American Genealogy, 1997, The Archives: A Guide to National Archives, 1988 (ALA Choice 1988). Mem. history adv. com., Statue of Liberty-Ellis Island Found., 1991. Recipient award of merit, Nat. Geneal. Soc., 1997, award of excellence in geneal. methods and sources, 1991. Mem. ALA (genealogy com.), Fedn. Geneal. Socs. (v.p., David S. Vogels Jr. award 1990). Roman Catholic. Office: Ancestry.Com 360 W 4800 Provo UT 84604

SZWALBENEST, BENEDYKT JAN, lawyer; b. Poland, June 13, 1955; s. Sidney and Janina (Bleishtif) S.; m. Shelley Joy Leibel, Nov. 8, 1981. BBA, Temple U., 1978, JD, 1981. Law clk. Fed. Deposit Ins. Corp., Washington, 1980; law clk. to presiding justice U.S. Dist. Ct. (ea. dist.) Pa., Phila., 1980-81; staff atty., regulatory specialist Fidelcor, Inc. and Fidelity Bank, 1981-86; regulations specialist sr. regulatory staff Fed. Res. Bank of N.Y., N.Y.C., 1986-89; s.v.p. regulatory compliance, sec. Custodial Trust Co. subs. Bear Stearns, Princeton, 1990—2001, pres., CEO, 2001—; mng. dir. Bear Stearns & Co., Inc., 1998—. Author: Federal Bank Regulation, 1980. Mem. Commonwealth of Pa. Post-secondary Edn. Planning Commn., Harrisburg, 1977-79; trustee Pop Warners Little Scholars, Phila., 1981-86. Recipient E. Gerald Corrigan Pres.'s Award for Excellence, 1988. Mem.: ABA (nat. sec., treas. law student divsn. 1980—81, Silver Key award 1980, Gold Key award 1981), N.J. Bankers Assn. (legis. and compliance com. 1992—), Securities Industry Assn. (anti-money laundering com. 2001—), Temple U. Sch. Bus. Alumni Assn. (sec. 1982—84, v.p. 1984—86, pres. 1986—88, bd. dirs. gen. alumni assn. 1986—88), Am. Bankers Assn. (cert. compliance specialist, lectr. 1984—), Am. Judicature Soc., Omicron Delta Epsilon. Avocations: baseball, tennis, skiing. Home: 1504 Brookfield Rd Yardley PA 19067-3930 Office: Custodial Trust Co 101 Carnegie Ctr Princeton NJ 08540-6231

SZYBALSKI, WACLAW, molecular geneticist, educator; b. Lwów, Poland, Sept. 9, 1921; came to U.S., 1950, naturalized, 1957; s. Stefan and Michalina (Rakowska) S.; m. Elizabeth Hunter, Feb. 5, 1955; children: Barbara A. Szybalski Sandor, Stefan H. BSChemE, Politechnika Lwów, 1944; MSChemE, Politechnika Slaska, Gliwice, Poland, 1945; DSc, Inst. Tech., Gdańsk, Poland, 1949; PhD (hon.), U. Marie Curie, Lublin, Poland, 1980, U. Gdańsk (Poland), 1989, Inst. of Tech., Gdańsk, 2001, Med. U. Gdansk, Poland, 2000, Inst. Tech., Gdansk, 2001. Asst. prof. Inst. Tech., Gdańsk, 1945—50; staff Cold Spring Harbor (N.Y.) Biol. Labs., 1951—55; asst. prof. Inst. Microbiology, Rutgers U., New Brunswick, N.J., 1955-60; prof. oncology McArdle Lab., U. Wis.-Madison, 1960—. Mem. recombinant DNA adv. com. (RAC) NIH, 1974-78; Wendel H. Griffith meml. lectr. St. Louis U., 1975; Raine vis. prof. U. Western Australia, Perth, 1997. Author numerous papers, revs., abstracts and books in field; editor-in-chief: Gene, 1976-96, hon. and founding editor-in-chief, 1996—; mem. editorial bd. other jours. Recipient Karl A. Forster lecture award U. Mainz, 1970, A. Jurzykowski Found. award in biology, 1988, Hilldale award in biology U. Wis., 1994, Gold G.J. Mendel Hon. medal for merit in biol. scis. Acad. Scis. of Czech Republic, 1995; Cogene lectr. Internat. Union Biochem., Nairobi, 1987, Cairo, 1988, Harare, Zimbabwe, 1989. Mem. AAAS, Am. Soc. Biochemists, Genetic Soc. Am., Am. Soc. Microbiologists (chmn. virology divsn. 1972-74, chmn. divsn. IV 1974-75), European Molecular Biology Orgns. (lectr. 1971, 76), Polish Soc. Microbiologists (hon.), Italian Soc. Exptl. Biology (hon.), Polish Med. Alliance (hon.), Polish Acad. Scis. (fgn. mem.). Home: 1124 Merrill Springs Rd Madison WI 53705-1317 Office: U Wis McArdle Lab Madison WI 53706 E-mail: szybalski@oncology.wisc.edu. *The profession should also be the hobby and a constant source of enjoyment and satisfaction.*

SZYBICKI, EDMUND, executive; b. Bulkowo, Poland, June 7, 1927; s. Jan and Ewa (Turbacz) S.; m. Margareta Anna Persson, Nov. 7, 1957. B Engring., Stockholms Tekniska Inst., 1948; BS in Math., U. Stockholm, 1954. Head group Ericsson L.M., Stockholm, 1958-70, ITT-Teleco. Labs., Madrid, Spain, 1970-74, coord. Paris, 1974-77; mgr. Bell No. Rsch., Montreal, Can., 1977-80, Soc. Gen. Industry, Geneva, 1980-82; cons. Internat., 1982-86; tech. dir. IST Systems, 1986—. Cons. in field; invited prof. U. Cauca, Popayan, Colombia, 1986, 89. Inventor in field; contbr. articles to profl. jours. Mem. N.Y. Acad. Scis. Avocation: tennis. Fax: +41-22-782 22 36.

SZYDLOWSKI, RALPH, retired die maker, formability consultant; b. Alpena, Mich., Nov. 14, 1942; s. Chester and Bridget (Romel) Sedloske; m. Geraldine Bryson, Oct. 8, 1971; children: Denise E., George S., Ruth A., Regina M. Assoc. in Indsl. Tech. summa cum laude, Baker Coll., Flint, Mich., 1991, B of Indsl. Mgmt. summa cum laude, 1994. With Flint Metal Ctr., Draw Die Tryout, 1972-96; die maker Flint Metal Ctr., 1996—2001, formability cons., 1995—2001. Served with U.S. Army, 1962-69. Decorated Silver Star, Purple Heart. Mem. VFW, DAV, Am. Legion, Mil. Order of the Purple Heart, 26th Inf. Regt. Assn., Soc. 1st Inf. Divsn., Eagles. Roman Catholic. Avocations: woodworking, travel, books. E-mail: rsgs42@aol.com.

SZYGENDA, STEPHEN A. electrical and computer engineering educator, researcher; b. McKeesport, Pa., Oct. 5, 1938; s. Stephen A. Sr. and Elizabeth B. (Zolczer) S.; m. Marie A. Deli, Apr. 2, 1960; children: Stepahnie Burden, Diana Easton, Mark. BS, Fairleigh Dickinson U., 1965; MS, Northwestern U., 1967, PhD, 1968. Registered profl. engr., Tex. Engr. Comprehensive Design, N.J., 1959-62; mem. tech. staff Bell Telephone Labs., N.J., Ill., 1962-68; assoc. prof. elec. engring. and computer engring. U. Mo., Rolla, 1968-70; prof. elec. engring. and computer engring. So. Meth. U., Dallas, 1970-73, U. Tex., Austin, 1973-86, dir. Ctr. for Tech. Tran., 1986-89, Clint Murchison Sr. Chair of Free Enterprise prof., 1986-96, chmn. elec. and computer engring. dept., 1993-96; dean sch. engring. U. Ala., Birmingham, 1996-2000; dean Sch. Engring. So. Meth. U., Dallas, 2000—. Pres. CCSS, Austin, 1972-81, Comsat Gen. Int. Sys., Austin, 1981-83, SBI, Inc., Austin, 1985—; pres., CEO Rubicon Group, Austin. 1983-85; active Tex. Gov. Coun. for Sci. and Tech., 1984-87. Contbr. articles to profl. jours. Dir. Laguna Gloria Mus., Austin, 1981-83; pres. bd. Austin Ballet, 1983. With USN, 1956-59. Fellow IEEE (bd. dirs. 1973-75 Svc. awards 197, 79, 83, 87, 96), Soc. for Design and Process Sci.; mem. Assn. Computing Machinery (Svc. award 1975, 79, 87, 88, Disting. lectr. 1991-95). Roman Catholic. Achievements include pioneering in CAD, simulation, fault tolerant computing, telecommunications, entrepreneurship, and software engineering. Home: 5227 Beckington Ln Dallas TX 75287 Office: Southern Methodist Univ Sch of Engring Dallas TX 75275

SZYMANSKI, BOLESLAW KAROL, computer scientist, educator, entrepreneur; b. Paslek, Poland, Apr. 22, 1950; came to U.S., 1982; s. Kazimierz and Aniela Marta (Langer) S.; m. Emilia Haraf, Dec. 15, 1973; children: Peter Rafal, Witold Andrew. M in Engring. Electronics, Warsaw Poly. Inst., Poland, 1973; PhD in Computer Sci., Nat. Acad. of Scis., Warsaw, 1976. Asst. prof. Warsaw Polytech., 1973-75; rschr. Inst. Sci. Technol. and Econ. Info., Warsaw, 1975-78; divsn. head Inst. STEI, 1979-82; postdoctoral fellow Aberdeen U., U.K., 1978; vis. asst. prof. U. Pa., Phila., 1982-85, assoc. prof. computer sci., 1985-89; prof. computer sci. CSCI, 1990—, acting chmn., 1993-94; assoc. dean info. tech. Rensselaer Polytech. Inst., Troy, N.Y., 1997—; founder/chmn. bd. dirs. Premonitia, Inc., Boston, 2000. Cons. IBM, Poughkeepsie, N.Y., 1992-96, GE Rsch. and Devel. Ctr., Schenectady, N.Y., 1987-90; expert UN Indsl. Devel. Office, Vienna, Austria, 1990-96; chief sci. officer CCCC, Phila., 1984-87; editor-in-chief Scientific Computing IOS Press, Amsterdam, 2000—. Author: Parallel Functional Languages and Compilers, 1993; editor: Languages, Compilers & RT Systems, 1996; developer Tempest parallel system for ecol. simulations, EPL parallel computer language. Expert witness U.S. Congress, Washington, 1987. Rsch. grantee IBM, Lucent, DARPA, ARO, NSF, ONR, 1986—; recipient Tech. Innovation award NASA, 1998, SuPaCup '98 German Computer Soc., Mannheim, 1993. Fellow IEEE; mem. Assn. for Computing Machinery (nat. lectr. 1987-88). Avocations: tennis, history. Home: 6 Hollow Rd Newtonville NY 12110-5100 Office: Rensselaer Polytech Inst 110 8th St Troy NY 12180-3590 E-mail: bkszym@yahoo.com., szymab@rpi.edu.

SZYMANSKI, CHRISTOPHER JOHN, consulting company executive; b. Providence; s. Frank Joseph and Janet Fairbanks Mitchel Szymanski; m. Virginia Jean Artley, Apr. 14, 1984 (dec. Jan. 1998); m. Virginia Ann Weil, Sept. 12, 1999; children: Jennifer Bushman, Tauna, Nicholas Langman, Todd, Andrea Langman. BA in History and Internat. Rels., U. N.H., 1970; MA in Polit. Sci., Brown U., 1972, PhD in Polit. Sci., 1975. Fgn. svc. officer Dept. of State, Washington, 1974-87; dep. amb. U.S. Embassy, Rangoon, Burma, 1987-90, min.-counselor for econ. affairs Beijing, 1993-95; sr. advisor to under-sec. of state for econ. affairs Dept. of State, Washington, 1995, sr. fgn. svc. officer, 1987-97, sr. coord. for bus. affairs, 1997; pres. The Artley Group, Ltd., 1998—. Columnist China Online.com., 2001—; contbr. articles and papers to profl. jours. Chmn. bd. Internat. Sch., Rangoon, 1989-90; sr. advisor Ctr. for Democracy, Washington, 1999—. Mem. Phi Beta Kappa. Office: The Artley Group Ltd 1101 15th St NW Ste 505 Washington DC 20005-5002 E-mail: president@artleygroup.com.

SZYMANSKI, EDNA MORA, dean; b. Caracas, Venezuela, Mar. 19, 1952; came to U.S., 1952; d. José Angel and Helen Adele (McHugh) Mora; m. Michael Bernard, Mar. 30, 1973. BS, Rensselaer Poly. Inst., 1972; MS, U. Scranton, 1974; PhD, U. Tex., 1988. Cert. rehab. counselor. Vocat. evaluator Mohawk Valley Workshop, Utica, N.Y., 1974-75; vocat. rehab. counselor N.Y. State Office Vocat. Rehab., 1975-80, sr. vocat. rehab. counselor, 1980-87; rsch. assoc. U. Tex., Austin, 1988-89; asst. prof. U. Wis., Madison, 1989-91, assoc. prof., 1991-93, assoc. dean sch. edn., 1993-97, dir. rehab. rsch. and tng. ctr., 1993-96, prof. rehab. psychology and spl. edn., 1993-99, chair dept. rehab. psychology and spl. edn., 1997-99, fellow tchg. acad., 1997; dean Coll. Edn. U. Md., College Park, 1999—. Cons. Rsch. Assocs. Syracuse, N.Y., 1988-90. Co-author various book chpts.; co-editor: Rehabilitation Counseling Basics and Beyond, 1992, 98; co-editor Work and Disability, 1996—, Rehabilitation Counseling Bull., 1994-2000; contbr. articles to profl. jours. Mem. Pres.'s Com. on Employment of People with Disabilities, Washington, 1987-97. Recipient Rsch. award Am. Assn. Counselor Edn. and Supr., 1991. Mem. ACA (chair rsch. com. 1992-94, Rsch. awards 1990, 93, 95), Am. Rehab. Counseling Assn. (pres. 1985-86, rsch. award 1989, 94, Disting. Profl. award 1997, James F. Garrett award for disting. career in rehab. rsch. 1999), Coun. Rehab. Edn. (chair rsch. com. 1990-95, v.p. 1993-95, 97), Nat. Coun. Rehab. Edn. (chair rsch. com. 1992-99, Rehab. Edn. Rschr. of Yr. 1993, New Career in Rehab. Edn. award 1990). Office: U Md Coll Edn 3119 Benjamin Bldg College Park MD 20742-1100 E-mail: ednas@deans.umd.edu.

SZYMANSKI, JOHN MATTHEW, investment officer; b. N.J., July 18, 1958; s. Edward and Mary F., m. Helen Louise Sisler, April 20th, 1985; 3 children. BS, Columbia U., N.Y.C, 1980. cert. Certified Fin. Planner. Cons. Arthur Anderson, N.Y.C, 1980-82, Bankers Trust, N.Y.C., 1982-83; fin. adv., Smith Barney, Paramus, N.J., 1983-86; fin. adv. Shearson Lehman Hutton, 1986-90; assoc. v.p. Prudential Securities, 1990-96; sr. v.p. First Union Securities, 1996—. Author: Five Secrets to Successful Investing, 1996. Avocations: swimming, golf, travel, politics. Office: First Union Securities 45 Eisenhower Dr Paramus NJ 07652

SZYMCZAK, EDWARD JOSEPH, mechanical engineer; b. Anderson, Tex., Sept. 28, 1938; s. Harold and Verna (Walkoviak) S.; m. Lorena Jane Sharp, Sept. 26, 1964; children: Denise, Lisa, Brian. Student, U. St. Thomas, 1958; BSME, Tex. A&M, 1961; MBA, U. Houston, 1970. Registered profl. engr., Tex. Engr. trainee to engring. mgr. Cameron Iron Works, Houston, 1961-90; dir. engring. ea. hemisphere Cooper Oil Tool Div./Cooper Industries, London, 1990-91; dir. engring. Houston, 1991-95, Cameron div. Cooper Cameron Corp., Houston, 1995-97; mgr. design process tech. ABB Vetco Gray, 1998—. Mem., past chmn. indsl. adv. bd. U. La., Lafayette (formerly U. Southwestern La.), 1991—; trustee Tex. A&M U. Rsch. Found., College Station, 1994—; mem. mech. engring. adv. bd. U. Tenn., Knoxville, 1996-2000. Patentee (8) on oil tool equipment. Mem. ASME, Tex. A&M Former Students Assn., Tex. A&M 12th Man Found., Tex. A&M Mech. Engring. Acad. Disting. Grads., Soc. Petroleum Engrs., Nat. Assn. Corrosion Engrs., Tau Beta Pi. Republican. Roman Catholic. Avocations: ranching, farming, mechanic, investing, technical and personnel recruiting. Home: 4002 Cypress Hill Dr Spring TX 77388-5717

SZYMKOWIAK, MARY L. non-profit organization administrator; b. Buffalo, Oct. 31, 1961; d. Edward and Patrica Marie (Kobielski) S.. BA, Cornell U., 1984. Asst. treas. Union BAnk of Switzerland, N.Y.C., 1985—88; asst. v.p. 1st Am. Bank N.Y., 1989—90; mgr. Union Sq. Cafe, 1993—94; controller Gramercy Tavern, 1994—96; mgr. Kaufman-Dahl, Inc., 1996—98; nat. coord. The Human Adventure Corp., 1998—, CFO, 1998—, also bd. dirs. Bd. dirs. Resources, Inc., Bklyn., sec., 1998—. Roman Catholic. Office: The Human Adventure Corp 420 Lexington Ave # 2754-55 New York NY 10170

SZYMONIAK, ELAINE EISFELDER, retired state senator; b. Boscobel, Wis., May 24, 1920; d. Hugo Adolph and Pauline (Vig) Eisfelder; Casimir Donald Szymoniak, Dec. 7, 1943; children: Kathryn, Peter, John, Mary, Thomas. BS, U. Wis., 1941; MS, Iowa State U., 1977. Speech clinician Waukesha (Wis.) Pub. Sch., 1941-43, Rochester (N.Y.) Pub. Sch., 1943-44; rehab. aide U.S. Army, Chickasha, Okla., 1944-46; audiologist U. Wis., Madison, 1946-48; speech clinician Buffalo Pub. Sch., 1948-49, Sch. for Handicapped, Salina, Kans., 1951-52; speech pathologist, audiologist, counselor, resource mgr. Vocat. Rehab. State Iowa, Des Moines, 1956-85; mem. Iowa Senate, 1989—2000; ret., 2000. Bd. dir. On With Life, Terrace Hill Found. Adv. bd. Iowa State Inst. for Social and Behavioral Health; mem. Child Care Resource and Referral Cmty. Empowerment Bd., Greater Des Moines Coun. for Internat. Understanding, United Way, 1987—88, Urban Dreams, Iowa Maternal and Child Health com.; pres. Chrysalis Found., 1997; mem. City-County Study Commn.; bd. dirs. On with Life; Mem. Des Moines City coun., 1978—88; bd. dirs. Nat. League Cities, Washington, 1982—84, Civic Ctr., House of Mercy, Westminster House, Iowa Leadership Consortium, Iowa Comprehensive Health Assn. Named Woman of Achievement, YWCA, 1982, Visionary Woman, 1993, Young Women's Resource Ctr., 1989; named to Iowa Women's Hall of Fame, 1999; named Des Moines Woman of Influence, Bus. Record, 2000. Mem. Am. Speech Lang. and Hearing Assn., Iowa Speech Lang. and Hearing Assn. (pres. 1977-78), Nat. Coun. State Legislators (fed.

state com. on health, adv. com. on child protection), Women's Polit. Caucus, Nexus (pres. 1981-82, mem. Supreme Ct. Select Com.), Wellmark Found. (adv. bd.). Avocations: reading, traveling, swimming, whitewater rafting. Home: 2116 44th St Des Moines IA 50310-3011 E-mail: ElaineSzy@aol.com.

SZYMONIK, PETER TED, information scientist, consultant, systems analyst; b. Boleslawiec, Jelena, Poland, Nov. 13, 1963; came to U.S., 1964; s. Jan and Genowefa (Bielak) S.; m. Stephanie Christine Sans, Feb. 14, 1991. BA in History and Polit. Sci., U. Conn., 1988. Sys. adminstr. Cummings & Lockwood, Hartford, 1989-94, tech. mgr., 1994-95; law office technology practice mgr. Advanced Computing Techniques, Glastonbury, Conn., 1996-97; technology practice mgr. Source Svcs. Corp., Manchester, 1997-98; tech. practice mgr. Romac Emerging Technologies, 1998-99; dir. e-commerce RCG Info. Technologies, 1999-2000; prin. Price Waterhouse Coopers LLP, 2000-01; dir. client svcs. Integrated Delivery Solutions, Inc., 2001—02; CEO, founder Tech. Adv. Group, LLC, Manchester, 2002—; dir. client svcs. Tymetrix , Hartford, 2002—. Sys. operator GE Info. Network, Rockville, Md., 1986-95; asst. sys. operator The Microsoft Network, 1995-98; cons. Sacred Hoop of Am. Resource Exch., Greenwich, 1988-89. Editor and pub. mags. Simulations Online, 1991, Genie Games RT NewsLetter, 1991, Source Legal Tech. Newsletter, 1998-99; editor Ebay Wargame Collectors Jour.; contbg. editor Strategy Plus mag., 1991-95. Avocations: conflict simulations, hist. analysis, internat. relations. Home and Office: 209 Jenny Clfs Manchester CT 06040-6862 E-mail: xorg@cox.net., szymonik@cox.net.

SZYSZKA, ROSWITA EVELYN, artist; b. Chgo., Apr. 5, 1955; d. John and Regina (Rizinger) Schilli; m. Michael C. Szyszka, Jan. 29, 1977; children: David M., Eric S. AA, Am. Acad. Art, 1976. Author: The World Healing Book; artist: Looking Out, Looking In; (Top 100 artists of the 20th Century). Mem. Woodstock Artist Assn., The Woodstock Guild. Office: PO Box 637 Bearsville NY 12409-0637 E-mail: RoswitaSzyszka@hotmail.com.

TA, TAI VAN, lawyer, researcher; b. Ninh Binh, Vietnam, Apr. 16, 1938; came to U.S., 1975; s. Duong Van and Loan thi (Pham) T.; m. Lien-Nhu Tran, Oct. 26, 1967; children: Becky, John, Khuong Virginia, Dora. LLB, U. Saigon, Vietnam, 1960; MA, U. Va., 1964, PhD, 1965; LLM, Harvard U., 1985. Bar: Mass. 1986, U.S. Dist. Ct. Mass. 1987. Prof. U. Saigon Law Sch., 1965-75, Nat. Sch. Adminstrn., 1965-75; ptnr. Tang thi Thanh Trai & Ta Van Tai, 1968-75; legal rschr. Reed Smith Shaw & McClay, Pitts., 1975; rsch. assoc. Harvard U. Law Sch., Cambridge, Mass., 1975—, adj. lectr., 1998—; pvt. practice, Brookline, 1986—; rsch. scholar NYU Law Sch., N.Y.C., 1990-94. Cons. Milbank Tweed Hadley & McCloy, N.Y.C., 1979, Shearman & Sterling, N.Y.C., 1979, Paul Weiss Rifkind Wharton and Garrison, N.Y.C., 1989, 90. Co-author: The Laws of Southeast Asia, 1986, The Le Code: Law in Traditional Vietnam, 1987, Investment Law in Vietnam, 1990; author: Vietnamese Tradition of Human Rights, 1988; contbr. articles to profl. jours. Commr. Mass. Govs. Asian-Am. Coun., 1992—. Fulbright scholar 1960-62; grantee Asia Found., 1972, Ford Found., 1975-76, Aspen Inst. 1993. Avocations: piano, swimming, foreign languages. Home: 145 Naples Rd Brookline MA 02446-5748 Office: Harvard U Law Sch Pound 423 1563 Massachusetts Ave Cambridge MA 02138-2903

TAAM, RONALD EVERETT, physics and astronomy educator; b. N.Y.C., Apr. 24, 1948; s. Lawrence and Julia (Louie) T.; m. Rosa Wen Mei Yang, Oct. 19, 1974; children: Jonathan, Alexander. BS, Poly. Inst., N.Y.C., 1969; MA, Columbia U., 1971, PhD, 1973. Postdoctoral fellow U. Calif., Santa Cruz, 1973-76, vis. faculty Berkeley, 1976-78; asst. prof. Northwestern U., Evanston, Ill., 1978-83, assoc. prof., 1984-86, prof. physics and astronomy, 1986—, chmn. physics and astronomy, 1995-98. Fellow Am. Phys. Soc.; mem. Am. Astron. Soc., Royal Astron. Soc., Internat. Astron. Union. Office: Dept Physics and Astronomy Northwestern U 2145 Sheridan Rd Evanston IL 60208-0834 E-mail: r-taam@northwestern.edu.

TABACHNICK, MICHAEL NEIL, physicist, educator; b. N.Y.C., Apr. 7, 1944; s. Isadore David Tabachnick and Yadvega (Rabinowitz) Yellen; m. Roslyn Shapelow, Aug. 1969 (div. Sept. 1987); children: Robert, Susan; m. Naomi Rosalie Berlin, Nov. 29, 1987; children: Lawrence Weisberg, Michael Weisberg, Susan Juliano. AB in Physics, Temple U., 1965; MA in Physics, Columbia U., 1967. Grad. tchg. asst. Rutgers U., New Brunswick, N.J., 1967-68; assoc. prof. physics Delaware Valley Coll., Doylestown, Pa., 1968—. Adj. faculty Trenton (N.J.) State Coll., 1980-85. Mem. AAUP, Pa. Assn. Univ. Profs., Sigma Pi Sigma, Alpha Phi Omega. Avocations: concert pianist, photography, boat building, sailing. Office: Delaware Valley Coll 700 E Butler Ave Doylestown PA 18901-2607 E-mail: tabachnM@devalcol.edu.

TABACHNICK, NORMAN DONALD, psychiatrist, educator; b. Toronto, Ont., Can., Feb. 21, 1927; BS, U. Ill., 1947, MD, 1949; PhD in Psychoanalysis, So. Calif. Psychoanalytic Inst., 1977. Diplomate Am. Bd. Med. Examiners, Am. Bd. Psychiatry and Neurology. Intern Michael Reese Hosp., 1949-50; resident in psychiatry U.S. VA Hosp., Bedford, Mass., 1950-51, U.S. AFB, Biloxi, Miss., 1951-52, L.A. County Gen. Hosp., 1953-54; staff psychiatrist Sepulveda VA Hosp., 1976-78; pvt. practice L.A.; mem. staff Resthaven Sanitarium, U. So. Calif. Med. Ctr., L.A. County, Westwood Hosp., Edgemont Hosp., Cedars-Sinai Med. Ctr.; mem. staff Neuropsychiatric Inst. UCLA; clin. prof. psychiatry U. So. Calif., L.A., 1970-75, UCLA, 1975—. Hon. mem. med. staf. Resthaven Cmty. Med. Health Ctr., 1973; guest lectr. Cedars-Sinai Med. Ctr., 1985; mem. adv. bd. divsn. psychoanalysis Nassau County Med. Ctr.; mem. faculty Calif. Sch. Profl. Psychology, L.A. Ctr. Group Psychotherapy, Grad. Ctr. Child Devel. and Psychotherapy; cons. L.A. County Coroner's Office, 1963-70, Bur. Vocat. Rehab., Jewish Family Svc., profl. adv. bd. Resthaven Sanitarium, Marianne Frostig Sch. Ednl. Therapy, W. Valley Ctr. Edl. Therapy. Author: Accident or Suicide?, 1973; mem. edtl. bd. Jour. Acad. Psychoanalysis, book rev. editor, 1978; mem. edtl. bd. Internat. Jour. Psycho-analytic Psychotherapy, 1979-83; reviewer Am. Jour. Psychiatry, 1983—, Jour. Neuropsychiatry and Clin. Neuro Scis., 1988-90; contbr. articles to profl. jours.; cons. (film) Suicide Prevention: The Physician's Role, 1967, Highlights of the 1964 American Psychiatric Association; cons., participant The Thin Edge--Guilt., 1975. Assoc. chief psychiatrist L.A. Suicide Prevention Ctr., 1968-76, prin. investigator; adv. com. Walter Briehl Human Rights Found., 1984; v.p., bd. dirs. Suicide Prevention Ctr., Inc.; bd. dirs. Inst. Suicide Prevention, L.A., 1996, chmn. funding a crisis line com., 1997; bd. dirs. We. divsn. Am. Found. Suicide Prevention, 1998—. Rsch. grantee Founds. Fund Rsch. Psychiatry, 1963, NIMH, 1970. Fellow Am. Psychiatric Assn. (life), Am. Acad. Psychoanalysis (pres. 1974, chmn. nominating com. 1975, trustee, chmn. com. on rsch., mem. editl. bd. The Acad., presdl. citation 1975); mem. Internat. Psychoanalytic Assn., Internat. Assn. Suicide Prevention, Am. Psychoanalytic Assn. (cert., mem. com. liason with AAAS 1977-80), Am. Assn. Suicidology, (founder, mem. editl. bd. Life-Threatening Behavior, cert. recognition 1996) Inst. Contemporary Psychoanalysis (founding mem., trustee 1990-93), So. Calif. Psychoanalytic Inst. (pres., tng. and supervising analyst, selection rsch. clin. assocs. com., dir. rsch. divsn. 1970-81, chief investigator 1976-88, chmn. com. rsch. award stds. 1979, pres.-elect 1980, 86, pres. 1981, 87-90), Am. Coll. Psychiatrists, Med. Rsch. Assn. So. Calif., So. Calif. Psychiat. Soc. (consultation and violence panel), L.A. County Med. Assn., Am. Coll. Psychiatry. Office: 505 N Bonhill Rd Los Angeles CA 90049-2325

TABACKMAN, STEVEN CARL, lawyer; b. Balt., Apr. 2, 1950; s. Nathan and Evelyn (Caplan) T.; m. Leslie Adele Stout, Dec. 27, 1986; children: Alexa, Robert, Julia, Lia. BA with distinction, U. Va., 1971, JD, 1976. Bar: Va. Supreme Ct. 1976, D.C. Ct. Appeals 1977, U.S. Dist. Ct. D.C. 1978, U.S. Dist. Ct. Md. 1990, U.S. Dist. Ct. (ea. dist.) Va. 1992, U.S. Ct. Appeals (D.C. cir.) 1978. Law clk. to Hon. Leonard Braman D.C. Superior Ct., Washington, 1976-77; law clk. to Hon. Theodore R. Newman, Jr. D.C. Ct. Appeals, 1977-78; asst. U.S. atty. U.S. Atty.'s Office D.C., 1978-88; assoc., ptnr. Perkins Coie, 1988-94; ptnr. Tighe, Patton, Tabackman & Babbin, 1994-99, Oblon Spivak McClelland Maier & Neustadt, Arlington, Va., 1999—2002, Tighe Patton Armstrong Teasdale, Washington, 2002—. Mem. editorial bd. Money Laundering Law Reporter, 1990-2000; contbr. articles to profl. jours. Gen. counsel Duke Ellington Fund, Washington, 1988—. Fellow Am. Bd. Criminal Lawyers; mem. ABA, Nat. Assn. Criminal Def. Lawyers. Home: 1458 Highwood Dr Mc Lean VA 22101-2517 Office: Tighe Patton Armstrong Teasdale 1747 Pennsylvania Ave NW Washington DC 20006

TABAK, LAWRENCE, federal agency administrator; b. Bklyn. BS, City Coll. of City U. of N.Y.; DDS, Columbia U.; PhD, SUNY at Buffalo. Certificate of Proficiency in Endodontics SUNY at Buffalo. Sr. assoc. dean for rsch., Sch. Medicine and Dentistry U. Rochester, prof., dentistry, biochemistry and biophysics, dir., Ctr. Oral Biology, AAB Inst. Biomedical Scis.; dir. Nat. Inst. Dental and Craniofacial Rsch., 2000—. Vis. scientist Nat. Inst. Dentistry and Craniofacial Rsch., prin. investigator for tng. grants, co-chair planning com. for workshop on saliva and other fluid-based diagnostics, ad hoc reviewer, intramural rsch. program. Fellow: AAAS; mem.: Soc. Glycobiology, Am. Assn. for Dental Rsch., Internat. Assn. for Dental Rsch. Office: 45 Center Dr Bethesda MD 20892*

TABAK, STEVEN WILLIAM, cardiologist; b. L.A., May 7, 1952; MD, Johns Hopkins U., 1977. Intern Cedars-Sinai Med. Ctr., L.A., 1977-78, resident in internal medicine, 1978-81, fellow in cardiovascular disease, 1981-83; assoc. clin. prof. medicine UCLA; clin. chief of cardiology Sinai Med. Ctr., 1996-98. Pvt. practice. Fellow Am. Coll. Cardiology; mem. AMA, ACP. Office: 414 N Camden Dr Ste 1100 Beverly Hills CA 90210-4532

TABANDERA, KATHLYNN ROSEMARY, secondary education educator; b. Honolulu, Aug. 6, 1960; d. William Fernandez and Sakae Sandra (Shibata) Rosa; m. Russell Takao Tabandera, Dec. 24, 1979 (div. 2000); children: Tiffany Nohelani, Christine Lei, Angela Nani, Nicole Ku'ulei, Ricky William Kanaina. BA in Psychology, BA in Econs., BBA in Bus. Adminstrn., Tchr. Edn. Program, U. Hawaii, Hilo, 1988, Profl. Edn. Program, 1989, Natural Sci. Certificate Program, 1994; MEd, Almeda Coll. and U., 2002. Profl. cert. secondary educator, Hawaii; cert. paralegal. Adminstr. Tabandera Fishing Co., Hilo, Hawaii, 1980-85; realtor assoc. Ala Kai Realty Inc., 1985—; owner Tracks Enterprises, 1985—; tchr. Kohala High Sch. Alternative Learning Ctr., 1989-91; social studies tchr. Honoka'a High Sch., 1991-92; real estate appraiser Hilo, 1992. Tchr. Hilo H.S. Alt. Learning Ctr., 1992-94, Waiakea H.S., 1994-2001, social studies tcht. Teoau H.S., 2001–; mentor, tutor Kamehameha Schs. Talent Search, 1993-94; commr. on mayor's com. on people with disabilities, 1993-96; sales dir. Amerivox, 1995-97; adminstrv. asst. Newmans Nursery, 1995-97. Named to Dean's List, U. Hawaii, 1985-88. Mem. AAUW, NEA, NAFE, ASCD, Am. Soc. Profl. Appraisers, Hawaii Island Bd. Realtors, Hawaii Assn. Realtors, Nat. Assn. Realtors, Hawaii State Tchrs. Assn., Adminstrn. of Justice. Avocations: animal breeding and raising, ornamental horticulture, reading.

TABATZNIK, BERNARD, retired physician, educator; b. Mir, Poland, Jan. 8, 1927; came to U.S., 1959, naturalized, 1966; s. Max and Fay (Ginsberg) T.; m. Marjorie Turner, Jan. 8, 1956; children: Darron Mark, Keith Donald, Ilana Wendy; m. Charline Edwards Harmon, Aug. 7, 1992. BSc, U. Witwatersrand, South Africa, 1945, MB, BChir, 1949. Intern Baragwanath Hosp., Johannesburg, South Africa, 1950-51, Hillingdon Hosp., Ashford Hosp., also research unit Canadian Red Cross Meml. Hosp., Taplow, Eng., 1951-54; med. registrar Ashford Hosp., 1954-56, Johannesburg Gen. Hosp., 1956-58; physician Baragwanath Hosp., 1958-59; fellow in medicine Sch. Medicine Johns Hopkins U., Balt., 1959-60, fellow in cardiology, 1960-61, asst. prof. medicine, 1966-97, ret., 1997; head cardiopulmonary divsn. Sinai Hosp., 1961-72, assoc. chief medicine, 1964-72; chief cardiology dept. North Charles Gen. Hosp., Balt., 1972; also dir. med. edn., dir. Postgrad. Inst., coord. ambulatory svcs.; med. dir. Nurse Practitioner-Physician Asst. Program, Ch. Hosp., Balt., 1987-90. Contbr. articles to profl. jours. Recipient Save-A-Heart Humanitarian award, 1977, Maimonides award, 1983, Shaarei Zion Humanitarian award, 1987. Fellow Royal Coll. Physicians (London); mem. South African Cardiac Soc., Am. Heart Assn., Md. Heart Assn. (chmn. health careers 1964-66), Laennec Cardiovasc. Sound Group. Home: HC 3 Box 180 Monterey VA 24465-9313 E-mail: btabatznik@aol.com.

TABER, DAVID O. urological surgeon; b. Panama City, Panama, June 30, 1938; s. Alden Pugh and Virginia (Kresler) Taber; m. Rebecca M.; children: Sharon Taber Silverman, Jeffrey, Andrew, Richard; m. Rebecca M. Taber, Dec. 20, 1987. BA, Syracuse U., 1959; MD, George Washington U., 1963. Diplomate Am. Bd. Urology. Urologic surgeon in pvt. practice, El Paso, Tex., 1972—. Chief med. staff Columbia West Hosp., El Paso, 1975-76, chief of urology, 1998-99; chief of surgery Sierra Med. Ctr., El Paso, 1977-78, chief of urology, 1995-97; prof. urology Tex. Tech Sch. Medicine, El Paso, 1998-99. Mem. state com. on prostate cancer Am. Cancer Soc., Austin, 1998-99; bd. dirs. El Paso unit Am. Cancer Soc., 1999; mem. Tex. Rangers Found., Waco, 1998-99. Served to lt. U.S. Army, 1963-72. Fellow ACS; mem. AMA, Tex. Urol. Soc., Am. Urol. Assn., Tex. Med. Assn., Am. Fertility Soc., Am. Lithotripsy Soc., Alpha Epsilon Delta, Pi Sigma. Episcopalian. Avocation: photography. Office: 125 W Hague Rd Ste 170 El Paso TX 79902-5811

TABER, FRANCES KATHRYN, geriatrics nurse, administrator; b. Chattanooga, Dec. 8, 1923; d. Buren M. and Evelyn V. (Keyes) Farr; m. John W. Taber, Dec. 18, 1945; children: Shelley, Jay. Diploma, St. Joseph's Sch. Nursing, Mt. Clemens, Mich., 1945; BSPA, St. Joseph's Coll., Windham, Maine, 1966; Cert. Nursing Home Adminstr., Wayne State U., 1972. RN, Mich.; cert. social worker, Mich. Instr. student nurses St. Joseph's Retreat, Dearborn, Mich., 1946-47; staff nurse Wayne State U., Detroit, 1947-54; dir. nursing Bortz Health Care Facilities, West Bloomfield, Mich., 1966-72, adminstr., v.p., 1972-85; adminstr. Oak Manor, Troy, 1985—. Legal expert for nursing homes Am. Coll. Nursing Home Adminstrs., 1992. With U.S. Navy, 1945. Mem. Oakland County Nursing Home Assn. (past v.p. and pres.). Home: 2536 Robindale Ln Bloomfield Hills MI 48302-0761 Office: 2316 John R Rd Troy MI 48083-2590

TABER, MARGARET RUTH, electrical engineering technology educator, electrical engineer; b. St. Louis, Apr. 29, 1935; d. Wynn Orr and Margaret Ruth (Feldman) Gould Stevens; m. William James Taber, Sept. 6, 1958 B of Engring. Sci., BEE, Cleve. State U., 1958; MS in Engring., U. Akron, 1967; EdD, Nova Southeastern U., 1976; postgrad., Western Res. U., 1959-64. Registered profl. engr., Ohio; cert. engring. technologist. From engring. trainee to tng. dir. Ohio Crankshaft Co., Cleve., 1954-64; from instr. elec.-electronic engring. tech. to prof. Cuyahoga C.C., 1964-79, chmn. engring. tech., 1977-79; assoc. prof. elec. engring. tech. Purdue U., West Lafayette, Ind., 1979-83, prof., 1983-2000, prof. emeritus, 2000—. Lectr. Cleve. State U., 1963-64; mem. acad. adv. bd. Cleve. Inst. Electronics, 1981—; cons. in field. Author: (with Frank P. Tedeschi) Solid State Electronics, 1976; (with Eugene M. Silgalis) Electric Circuit Analysis, 1980; (with Jerry L. Casebeer) Registers, 1980; (with Kenneth Rosenow) Arithmetic Logic Units, 1980, Timing and Control, 1980, Memory Units, 1980; 6809 Architecture and Operation, 1984, Programming I: Straight Line, 1984; contbr. articles to profl. jours. Bd. dirs. West Blvd. Christian Ch., deaconess, 1974-77, elder, 1977-79; deacon Federated Ch., 1981-84, 86-89, Stephen Leader, 1988—; mem. Cancer Support Group; vol. Lafayette Reading Acad., 1992—; ednl. resource vol., vol. tchr. Sunburst Farm Rainbow Acres, Inc., Ariz., 1988—. Recipient Helen B. Schleman Gold Medallion award Purdue U., 1991, The Greater Lafayette Cmty. Survivorship award, 1994, Outstanding Alumni award U. Akron Coll. Engring., 1994, Disting. Alumni award, Cleve. State U., 2002; Margaret R. Taber Microcomputer Lab. named in her honor Purdue U., 1991; NSF grant, 1970-73, 78; Rainbow Acres Computer Lab named The Marge Taber Computer Lab., 2002. Fellow Soc. Women Engrs. (counselor Purdue chpt. 1983-94, Disting. Engring. Educator award 1987); mem. IEEE (life sr.), Am. Cancer Soc. (co-chair svc. and rehab com. 1992-94, vol. coord. CanSurmount 1993-98, chair Cmty. Connections, mem. Resource, Info. and Guidance CoreTeam, 1994-98, v.p. Tippecanoe bd. dirs. 1996-98, relay for life hon. chair 1999), Am. Bus. Women's Assn. (ednl. chmn. 1964-66), Am. Soc. Engring. Edn., Am. Tech. Edn. Assn., Tau Beta Pi (hon.), Phi Kappa Phi. Avocations: robotics; camping; housekeeping. Home: 3036 State Rd 26 W West Lafayette IN 47906-4743 Office: Purdue U Elec Engring Tech Dept Knoy Hall Tech West Lafayette IN 47907

TABER, PATRICK E. computer programmer; b. Lawrence, Kans., June 4, 1972; s. Patrick E. and Shirley M. (Pruske) T. BS, Trinity U., San Antnonio, Tex., 1994. Tech. support/programmer Southwest Software, Austin, 1995-98; cons. Integration Svcs., Inc., 1998—. Home: 511 S Elm St Georgetown TX 78626-5651

TABERNILLA, ARMANDO ALEJANDRO, lawyer; b. Palm Beach, Fla., Nov. 24, 1959; s. Francisco H. and Hilda M. (Molina) T.; m. Holly B. Susac, May 11, 1991; children: Christian A., Sofia F. BSE, Duke U., 1981; JD, U. Va., 1984. Assoc. Steel, Hector & Davis, Miami, 1984-90, ptnr., 1990-92; assoc. gen. counsel IVAX Corp., 1992-94, v.p., gen. counsel, 1994-96, sr. v.p., gen. counsel, 1996-98; v.p., gen. counsel Fla. Crystals Corp., Palm Beach, 1998—. Mem. ABA, Phi Beta Kappa. Avocations: woodworking, golf, reading, art. Office: Fla Crystals Corp One North Clematis #200 West Palm Beach FL 33401

TABIBI, S. ESMAIL, pharmaceutical researcher, educator; b. Khoy, Iran, May 26, 1945; came to U.S., 1978; s. S. Ebrahim and Sharifeh Tabibi; m. Shahnaz Rahaie, Mar. 28, 1975; children: Shahrzad, Shirazeh, Shabnam. PharmD, U. Tabriz, Iran, 1969; PhD, U. Md., Balt., 1982. Lab. scientist I biochemistry dept. U. Md., 1979-82; vis. fellow Nat. Cancer Inst., Bethesda, Md., 1982-83; rsch. assoc. Roxane Labs., Inc., Columbus, Ohio, 1983-86; dir. pharm. R & D, H.G. Pars Pharm. Lab., Inc., Cambridge, Mass., 1986; dir. pharm. R & D MediControl Corp., Newton, 1986-89, v.p. R & D, 1989-90; v.p. R & D, mem. sci. adv. bd. Micro Vesicular Systems, Inc., Nashua, N.H., 1990-92; assoc. prof. pharms. dept. U. R.I., Kingston, 1992-93; project officer PRB, NCI, NIH, 1993—2001; founder, v.p. R & D Avicenna Pharms., Rockville, Md., 2001—. Adj. assoc. prof. Mass. Coll. Pharmacy, Boston, 1989-93; mem. sci. adv. bd. Cell Rsch. Corp., Newton, 1989-93; mem. equal employment opportunity adv. group Nat. Cancer Inst., 1996-99; founder, first prin. The Islamic Sch. of Potomac, Md., 1996-99; founder, dir., sec., bd. dirs. Ibn Sina Health Found. N.Am., Md., 1997—. Contbr. articles to sci. jours., chpt. to book. Vice chmn. PTO, Chelmsford, Mass., 1991; founding mem. Ahlul Bayt Assembly N.Am., 1997—. Mem. Am. Pharm. Assn., Am. Assn. Pharm. Scientists (chmn. publ./newsletter com., biotech. sect. 1995-98), Controlled Release Soc., Rho Chi. Achievements include patents on oral cavity and dental microemulsion products, hexamethylmelamine containing parenteral emulsions, wax emulsion as liquid control releas drug delivery, lipid-vesicles having an alkyd wall forming material; heat-dehydrated emulsion composition; patents pending on liposomal gel products; heat-dehydrated liposomal compositions, water-insoluble drug delivery system. Office: NIH - Nat Cancer Inst Pharm Resources Br 6130 Executive Blvd Rockville MD 20852-4910 E-mail: setabibi@hotmail.com., tabibie@dtpepn.nci.nih.gov.

TABIN, JULIUS, patent lawyer, physicist; b. Chgo., Nov. 8, 1919; s. Sol and Lillian (Klingman) T.; m. Johanna Krout, Sept. 7, 1952; children: Clifford James, Geoffrey Craig. BS, U. Chgo., 1940, PhD in Physics, 1946; LL.B., Harvard U., 1949. Bar: Calif., D.C. 1949, Ill. 1950. Jr. physicist metall. lab. U. Chgo., 1943-44; physicist Los Alamos Sci. Lab. (U. Calif.), N.Mex., 1944-45, Argonne Nat. Lab., AEC, Chgo., 1946; staff mem., group supr. Inst. Nuclear Studies, Mass. Inst. Tech., 1946-49; patent examiner U.S. Patent Office, Washington, 1949-50; asso. firm Fitch, Even, Tabin & Flannery, Chgo., 1950-52; mem. firm Fich, Even, Tabin & Flannery, 1952—. Lectr. U. Chgo., 1959 Mem. Am., D.C., Calif., Ill., Chgo. bar assns., Sigma Xi. Home: 162 Park Ave Glencoe IL 60022-1352 Office: 120 S La Salle St Chicago IL 60603-3403

TABLER, NORMAN GARDNER, JR. lawyer; b. Louisville, Oct. 15, 1944; s. Norman Gardner and Marie (Grant) T.; m. Dawn Carla Martin, May 6, 1989; 1 child, Rachel Ann Ayres-Tabler. BA, Princeton U., 1966; MA, Yale U., 1968; JD, Columbia U., 1971. Bar: Ind. 1971, U.S. Dist. Ct. (so. dist.) Ind. 1971. Assoc. Baker & Daniels, Indpls., 1971-77, ptnr., 1978-96; sr. v.p. corp. affairs, gen. counsel, chief compliance officer, sec. Clarian Health Ptnrs., Inc., 1996—. Adj. prof. Ind. U. Law Sch., Indpls., 1984-88; mem. adv. com. Ctr. for Law and Health, Ind. U., Indpls., 1987-91; mem. antitrust task force Ind. Dept. Health, 1993-94; lectr. Ind. U. Law Sch., 1992-96. Bd. dirs. Ind. Repertory Theatre, Inc., Indpls., 1984-97, Indpls. Art Ctr., 1988-93, chmn., 1989-92; bd. dirs. Indpls. 500 Festival, 1992-98, Brickyard 400 Festival, 1993-98, Found. of Indy Festivals, 1995-98, Indy Festivals, 1995-98; bd. dirs. Indpls. Pub. Broadcasting, 1992—, chmn., 1997-2001; mem. Ind. Sec. of State's Com. on Revision of Ind. Nonprofit Corp. Act, 1989-92, Ind. Ednl. Fin. Authority, 1989-93; mem. Ind. Recreational Devel. Commn., 1993—, vice chmn., 2002; mem. Medicaid Task Force Ind. Commn. Health Policy, 1990-92, Ind. Commn. on CLE, 1999—; mem. nat. bd. lay reps. PBS, 1997—. Mem. ABA (health care com. sect. antitrust law, health law sect.), Ind. Bar Assn. (health law sect.), Indpls. Bar Assn. (health law sect.), Am. Health Lawyers Assn. (com. on antitrust, com. on fraud and abuse, self-referrals and false claims, in-house counsel com. and tchg. hosps., acad. med. ctrs. com.), Ind. Health and Hosp. Assn. (com. on hosp. governance 1999—), Ind. U. Parents Assn., Ind. U. Parents Ann. Fund (nat. chmn. 1995-98), U.S. Squash Racquets Assn., Princeton Alumni Assn. Ind. (pres. 1988-97), Indpls. Athletic Club (bd. dirs. 1994-2000), Skyline Club (bd. govs. 1992—), Princeton Club N.Y., Lawyers Club (Indpls.), Five Seasons Country Club (Indpls.). Methodist. Avocations: reading biographies, squash. Address: General Counsel & Senior VP Legal Dept Clarian Health Partners Inc PO Box 1367 Indianapolis IN 46206-1367

TABLER, SHIRLEY MAY, retired librarian, artist; b. Washington, Mar. 18, 1936; d. Howard Leon and Ella May (Miles) Bosley; m. Edward Charles Sepelak, July 30, 1954 (div. 1965); children: David Edward, Linda May, William Bryan; m. Carlton Byard Tabler, June 27, 1968 (dec. May 1993); stepchildren: Roger Byard, Charlotte Virginia. BS in Art Edn., U. Md., 1977, BA in Libr. Sci., 1978, MA in Art Edn., 1981, MLS, 1990. Sec. Nat. Capital Housing Authority, Washington, 1954-55; clk. Vitro Corp., Silver Spring, Md., 1956-57; hostess, cashier Hot Shoppes, Wheaton, 1960-63; new accounts sec. State Nat. Bank, Bethesda, 1966-68; media aide, art tchr. Montgomery County Pub. Schs., Rockville, 1968-86, libr., cataloguer, computer tech., 1986-93. Exhibited in group shows at Arts Club, Washington, 1990, 91, 92, 93, 94, 95, 96, 97, Rockville Mcpl. Gallery, 1992, 93, 94, 95, 97, 98, 99, 2000, 2001, 2002, Sugar & Fricht Gallery 1994, 95, Ten Oaks Gallery-Clarksville, 1994, 95, 97, 98, 99, 2000, Town Ctr. Gallery, 1994, Kensington Gallery, 1994, 95, 96, 97, 98, 99, 2000, 2001, 2002, Strathmore Hall, 1998, 99, 2000, 2001, 2002, World-Wide Internat. Miniature Art Show, Eng., 1995, Hobart, Tasmania, 2000, Sandy Spring Mus. Art Gallery, 2000, Rockville Unitarian Gallery, 2001, Washington Area Printmakers Calendar, 1997, 98, 99, 2000, 2001, 2002; one-person shows include Rockville Mcpl. Gallery 1989, Landon Gallery, Bethesda, Md., 1990, Washington Printmakers Gallery, 1994, 97, 2000, 2002, Galleries at Savage Mill, 1996, 97, Cafe Monet Gallery, 1997, 98, 99, 2000, 2002. Leader, advisor Girl Scouts U.S., Rockville, 1964-82. Mem. ALA, Soc. Librs. Internat., Am. Art League, Nat. League Am. Pen Women (past pres. Chevy Chase, pes. 2000-02), Md. Printmakers, Miniature Painters, Sculptors and Gravers Soc., D.C., Cider Painters Am., Art Gallery of Fells Point, Miniature Art Soc. Fla., Olney Art Assn. (newsletter editor 1984-91, show chmn. 1993, 98, libr. show chmn. 1992-94, program chmn. 1995, 96, 97, 98, joint show chair 1998), Rockville Art League, Phi Kappa Phi. Democrat. Methodist. Avocations: camping, leather tooling, painting, quilting, ceramics. Home: 123 Charles St Rockville MD 20850-1510 Office: Genevieve Roberts Studio 17521 Shenandoah Ct Ashton MD 20861-9774 E-mail: ladybugtab@juno.com.

TABOADA, JAVIER GUSTAVO, neurologist; b. Trujillo, Peru, Feb. 20, 1940; came to U.S., 1966; s. Manuel and Esperanza (Vives) T.; m. Martha Rivas-Plata, June 25, 1966; children: Lucia, Martha, Suzanne, Tina. BS, Nat. U. Trujillo, Peru, 1960, MD, 1966. Diplomate Am. Bd. Psychiatry, Am. Bd. Neurology. Neurology residency Georgetown U., Washington, 1968-72; capt. U.S. Army, 1969, advanced through grades to col., 2000; psychiatry residency N.Y. Hosp.-Cornell, White Plains, N.Y., 1972-75, chief geriatric unit; chief neurology svc. USPHS Hosp., S.I., 1975-78; pvt. practice Assoc. Neurologists of N.J., PA, Trenton, 1978—, pres., 1990—; clin. asst. prof. SUNY Downstate, Bklyn., 1975-78; clin. asst. prof. neurology Hahneman U., Phila., 1980—; chief neurology svc. H. Fuld Med. Ctr., Trenton, N.J., 1994—. Fellow ACP, Am. Acad. Neurology, Royal Med. Soc.; mem. Mercer County Med. Soc. (exec. coun. 1990—, v.p. 1995-96, pres. 1997-98), KC. Roman Catholic. Avocation: soccer. Office: Assoc Neurologists of NJ PA 1245 Whitehorse Ave Trenton NJ 08619 E-mail: kapoed24@aol.com.

TABONE, WILLIAM L. financial planner; s. Peter J. and Jeanne E. Tabone; m. Carol Ann Serino, July 15, 1967; children: Justin, Gavin. BS in Chemistry, U. Scranton, 1966; MBA, Fairleigh Dickenson U., 1969. Cert. Ohio Agent's Life, Accident and Health, and Variable Products Ins. 2002; gen. securities rep. Series 7 NYSE/NASD, 2002, registered investment advisor rep. Series 66 2002, cert. managed futures rep. Series 31 2002. Gen. mgr. Europe Inmont Corp., Watford, England, 1977—81; mng. dir. United Techs., Barcelona, 1981—82; gen. mgr., mktg. dir. USA, L.Am., Asia BASF Corp., Cin.,

1982—94; mng. dir., gen. mgr. Europe Michelman Internat. and Co. SNC, Aubange, Belgium, 1994—99; mng. dir., gen. mgr. Europe and Asia Fusion Automation Inc., Harlow, England, 2000—01; fin. advisor Morgan Stanley, Cin., 2001—. Mng. dir., gen. mgr. Europe and Asia Fusion Gmbh, Niederwuerzbach, Germany, 2000—01. Mem.: Kikuoka Country Club, Luxembourg (pres. 1995—99), Ivy Hills Country Club (bd. mem. mga 2002). Avocations: languages, golf, tennis, travel. Home: 2346 Bedford Ave Cincinnati OH 45208 Office: Morgan Stanley Atrium II 221 E Fourth St 22nd Fl Cincinnati OH 45202 Office Fax: 513-651-1136. Personal E-mail: billtabone@aol.com. E-mail: william.tabone@morganstanley.com.

TABOR, ANNA MARIE, writer; b. Feb. 28, 1972; BA, St. Mary's Coll., Notre Dame, Ind., 1994; postgrad., U. Notre Dame, 1995-97. English tchr. Orden Bunka Ctr., Tsu City, Japan, 1994-95; ESL tchr. Nishikawa, Bremen, Ind., 1996; Japan program adminstr., asst. and tour guide coord. St. Mary's Coll., Notre Dame, 1996; writer Indpls., 1997—; tchr. English as a 2d lang. South Bend English Inst., 2000—. Author: The Wager, 1997, Geohisousamadeshita, 2001.

TABOR, BEVERLY ANN, retired elementary school educator; b. Dallas, Feb. 12, 1943; m. Charles W. Tabor, Aug. 22, 1964; children: Shawn, Josh. BS in Edn., U. N. Tex., 1964, MEd in Guidance, Counseling, 1970. Cert. tchr. elem. art, guidance and counseling, supr., Tex. Elem. tchr. Ft. Davis (Tex.) Ind. Sch. Dist., 1964-65, Mesquite (Tex.) Ind. Sch. Dist., 1965-69, 71-97; counselor Amarillo (Tex.) Ind. Sch. Dist., 1970-71; ret. Mem. ins. adv. com. Tchr. Retirement Sys. of Tex., Austin, 1986-97; chmn. site based mgmt. com. Tosch Elem. Sch., Mesquite, 1992-94, mentor for new tchrs., student tchrs., H.S. students considering the tchg. profession. Life mem. Tosch Elem. PTA, 1985—. Named to Apple Corps, 1995. Mem. Tex. State Tchrs. Assn. (life), Mesquite Edn. Assn., Alpha Delta Kappa (past pres. Mesquite). Avocations: arts and crafts. Home: 271 County Road 2504 Mineola TX 75773-3143

TABOR, CURTIS HAROLD, JR. librarian, minister; b. Atlanta, July 3, 1936; s. Curtis Harold and Gerturde Olive (Casey) Tabor; m. Dorothy May Corbin, June 30, 1957 (dec. June 1996); m. Paulene C Pennington, July 12, 1997; children: Timothy M, John M. AA, Fla. Coll., Temple Terrace, 1957; BA, Harding Coll., 1960; MA, Butler U., 1967; MDiv, Bapt. Missionary Assn. Theol. Sem., Jacksonville, Tex., 1974; MLS, Tex. Woman's U., 1977. Min. Ch. of Christ, Bowling Green, Ky., 1960-61, Hamilton, Ont., Can., 1961-64, Indpls., 1964-67, Nacogdoches, Tex., 1967-75, Dallas, 1976-77, Columbus, Miss., 1977-79, Tampa, Fla., 1993-97, Maryville, Tenn., 1997—; reference libr. Blount County Pub. Libr., 1998—. Teacher Great Lakes Christian Col, Beamville, Ont, Canada, 1961—64; bible chair dir Stephen F Austin State Univ, Nacogdoches, 1967—75; participated archeological excavations, Tell Gezer, Israel, 1969, Tell Lachish, Israel, 80; profl libr sci Fla Col, Temple Terrace, 1979—85, libr dir, 1985—97. Author (with others): (book) Resurrection, 1973, The Lord of Glory, 1980, Making A Difference: Florida College, the First Fifty Years, 1996. Cub master Boy Scouts Am, Nacogdoches, 1970—75; pres Nacogdoches Baseball Asn, 1974—75; vol driving instr 55 Alive AARP, 1998—. Recipient Scouters Key, Cub Scouts Ams, 1975. Mem.: SAR, Tampa Bay Library Consortium (treas 1986—89), Nat Geneological Soc, Beta Phi Mu, Eta Beta Rho. Republican. Mem Ch Of Christ. Avocations: amateur radio (KC4XS), locksmithing. Home: 1906 Raulston View Dr Maryville TN 37803-2868 E-mail: haltabor@yahoo.com.

TABOR, EDWARD, physician, researcher; b. Washington, Apr. 30, 1947; BA, Harvard U., 1969; MD, Columbia U., 1973. Intern and resident Columbia-Presbyn. Med. Ctr., N.Y.C., 1973-75; rsch. investigator Bur. Biologics, Bethesda, Md., 1975-83; dir. divsn. anti-infective drug products FDA, Rockville, 1983-88; assoc. dir. for biol. carcinogenesis Nat. Cancer Inst./NIH, Bethesda, 1988-95; dir. divsn. transfusion transmitted diseases FDA, Bethesda and Rockville, Md., 1995-99; assoc. dir. med. affairs Office Blood Rsch. and Rev., FDA, Rockville, 1999—. Author: Infectious Complications of Blood Transfusion, 1982; editor: (with others) Etiology, Pathology, and Treatment of Hepatocellular Carcinoma in North America, 1991, Hepatitis C Virus and its Involvement in the Development of Hepatocellular Carcinoma, 1995, Liver Cancer, 1997; contbr. more than 250 articles to profl. jours. Capt. USPHS, 1975—. Achievements include research in hepatitis viruses, hepatocellular carcinoma. Office: FDA/CBER HFM-300 1401 Rockville Pike Rockville MD 20852-1448

TABOR, HERBERT, biochemist; b. N.Y.C., Nov. 28, 1918; s. Edward and Henrietta (Tally) T.; m. Celia White, Apr. 8, 1946; children: Edward, Marilyn, Richard, Stanley. AB, Harvard U., 1937, MD, 1941. Intern Yale U. and New Haven Hosp., 1942; with Lab. Biochem. Pharmacology Nat. Inst. Diabetes, Digestive and Kidney Disease, Bethesda, Md., 1943. Editor in chief Jour. Biol. Chemistry; contbr. articles to profl. jours. Mem. NAS, Am. Soc. Pharm. and Exptl. Therapeutics, Am. Chem. Soc., Am. Soc. for Biochemistry and Molecular Biology, Am. Acad. Arts and Scis. Office: NIH 8 Center Dr Bldg 8 Rm 223 Bethesda MD 20892-0830 E-mail: tabor@helix.nih.gov.

TABOR, LINDA J. educator; b. Bridgeport, Conn., May 10, 1965; d. James Atwood Tabor and Ruth Paula Sykes. BFA magna cum laude, U. Bridgeport, 1999. Tchr. drama and dance Music and Arts Ctr. for the Handicapped, Bridgeport, 1987-2000, co-coord. new visions dance project, 1989-91; tchr. drama and dance Charles D. Smith Jr. Found., 1993-94. Tutor Literacy Vols. of Am., Bridgeport, 1995-96. Mem. Phi Kappa Phi. Avocations: music, reading, T'ai Chi, writing children's books.

TABOR, MARY LEEBA, b. Balt., Mar. 3, 1946; d. Gerson and Freda (Roseman) T.; m. Ardell Louis Persinger, Sept. 16, 1984; children: Benjamin George Hammerschlag, Sarah Esther Hammerschlag. BA with high honors, U. Md., 1966; MA in Teaching, Oberlin Coll., 1967; postgrad., U. Chgo., 1968; MFA in Creative Writing, Ohio State U., 1999. Tchr. Towson (Md.) High Sch., 1967-70; employment profl. Ctr. for Naval Analyses, Alexandria, Va., 1970-71; tchr. adult edn. Montgomery County (Md.) Bd. Edn., 1975-80; editor pub. affairs Am. Petroleum Inst., Washington, 1980-83, writer, editor-in-chief, 1983-86, mgr. environ., health and pub. affairs, 1986-89, dir. pub. affairs writing, 1989-96; assoc. fiction editor The Jour., lit. mag. Ohio State U., Columbus, 1996-99, contbg. editor, 1999—. Adj. prof. creative writing and Am. lit. George Washington U., 1999—; advisor on high sch. sci. curriculum reform NSTA, Washington, 1991-96; lectr. Smithsonian Instn. Campus-on-the-Mall, 2001—. Debate judge Nat. Cath. Forensic High Sch. League, Bethesda (Md.)-Chevy Chase High Sch., 1991-93; bd. dirs. Bethesda Jewish Congregation, 1993-96. Mem. Phi Beta Kappa, Phi Kappa Phi, Alpha Lambda Delta. Office: George Washington U Dept English 801 22D St NW Rm 760 Washington DC 20052-0001

TABORN, KAREN FAYE, ethnomusicologist; b. Cleve., Dec. 29, 1956; d. Albert Lorenzo and Jeannette Ann Taborn. MA, N.Y.U., 1988. Prof. New Sch. Social Rsch., N.Y.C., 1993—. Cons. Harlem C. of C., N.Y.C., 1992—95. Author: What Made Harlem Famous, 1992. Recipient Art Commn. award, City of N.Y., 1991—92; grantee Faculty Devel. grant, New Sch. Social Rsch., 2001.

TABRIZI, MEHDI FAKHER, obstetrician/gynecologist; b. Tabriz, Iran, Jan. 6, 1931; MD, Faculty Medicine, 1957. Diplomate Am. Bd. Ob-Gyn. Intern St. Francis Hosp., Bronx, N.Y., 1959-60; resident Sibley Meml. Hosp., Washington, 1960-64; ob-gyn Fairfax Hosp., Va.; tchg. staff George Washington Med. Sch.; pvt. practice Arlington, Va., 1967—. Fellow ACOG; mem. Fairfax County Med. Soc. Office: 9204 A Old Court House Rd Vienna VA 22182

TABUSSI, STEPHEN JOHN, banker; b. Bklyn., July 21, 1949; s. Angelo G. and Eileen (Pryce) T. BA, Bklyn. Coll., 1971; MA, U. So. Calif., 1978. Mgr. media ops. Mfrs. Hanover Trust, N.Y.C., 1973-75; supr. ops. Union Bank, Los Angeles, 1975-77; media specialist Los Angeles Community Coll. Cist., 1977-78; asst. v.p. communications Western Bancorp, Los Angeles, 1978-81; v.p., advt. mgr. First Interstate Bancorp, 1981—. With U.S. Army, 1971-73.

TACAL, JOSE VEGA, JR. retired public health official, veterinarian; b. Ilocos Sur, Philippines, Sept. 5, 1933; came to U.S., 1969; s. Jose Sr. and Cristina (Vega) T.; m. Lilia Caccam, 1959; children: Joyce, Jasmin, Jose III. DVM, U. Philippines, Quezon City, 1956; diploma, U. Toronto, 1964. Diplomate Am. Coll. Vet. Preventive Medicine; lic. vet., Calif. Provincial veterinarian Philippine Bur. Animal Industry, Manila, 1956-57; instr. vet. medicine U. Philippines, Quezon City, 1957-64, asst. prof., chmn. dept. vet. microbiology, pathology and pub. health, 1965-69; pub. health veterinarian San Bernardino (Calif.) County Dept. Pub. Health, 1970-83, sr. pub. health veterinarian, program mgr., sect. chief, 1984-2000. Zoonotic diseases lectr. Calif. State U., San Bernardino, spring 1984; lectr. U. Calif. Extension, Riverside, spring, 1985; vis. prof. vet. pub. health U. Philippines at Los Banos, Laguna, 1988; participant 1st Internat. Conf. on Emerging Zoonoses, Jerusalem, 1996; program presenter 4th Internat. Symposium on Ectoparasites of Pets, U. Calif., Riverside, 1997; poster presenter 8th Ann. Rabies in the Ams. Conf., Kingston, Ont., Can., 1997; mem. rabies and ferret adv. group Calif. Dept. Health Svcs., 1998; program presenter 48th Western Poultry Disease Conf., Vancouver, B.C., Can., 1999, 10th Ann. Rabies in Ams. Meeting, San Diego, 1999. Columnist L.A. Free Press, 1991, Pilipinas Times, 1993, Mabuhay Times, 1994-95; contbr. more than 50 articles to profl. jours. Pres. Filipino Assn. of San Bernardino County, Highland, Calif., 1979; charter mem. Greater Inland Empire Filipino Assn., Highland, 1986-99; del. First Filipino Media Conf. N.Am., L.A., 1993; mem. San Bernardino County Africanized Honey Bee Task Force, 1993-2000; participant 1st Internat. Conf. on Emerging Zoonoses, Jerusalem, 1996. Recipient Donald T. Fraser Meml. medal U. Toronto, 1964, Cert. of Merit, Hon. fellow, Philippine Coll. Vet. Pub. Health, 2002, Philippine Vet. Med. Assn., 1965, Cert. of Appreciation Calif. State Bd. Examiners in Vet. Medicine, 1979, 84, Cert. of Recognition, Congressman George E. Brown Jr., 42d Congl. Dist. Calif., 1994, Assemblyman Joe Baca, 62d Assembly Dist., Calif. State Legis., 1994, Vet. Medicine/Journalism award Greater Inland Empire Filipino Assn., 1999; Colombo Plan Study fellow Can./Philippine Govts., 1963-64; hon. fellow Philippine Coll. Vet. Pub. Health, 2002. Mem.: ACLU, AVMA, AAAS, Highland Area Hist. Soc., San Bernardino City Libr. Found, Rare Fruit Growers (Inland Empire chpt.), Soc. for Advancement of Rsch., Western Poultry Disease Conf., Am. Vet. Med. History Soc., Phi Sigma, Phi Kappa Phi. Office: PO Box 1023 Highland CA 92346-1023

TACHA, ATHENA, sculptor, educator; b. Larissa, Greece, Apr. 23, 1936; came to U.S., 1963; MA, Nat. Acad. Fine Arts, Athens, Greece, 1959; MA in Art History, Oberlin Coll., 1961; PHD, U. Paris, 1963. Curator modern art Allen Art Mus., Oberlin, Ohio, 1963-73; prof. art Oberlin Coll., 1973-2000; adj. prof. art U. Md., College Park, 1999—. One-woman shows include Zabriskie Gallery, N.Y., 1979, 81, Max Hutchinson Gallery, N.Y., 1984, High Mus. Art, Atlanta, 1989, Franklin Furnace, N.Y., 1994, Beck Ctr., Cleve., 1998-99, Found. for Hellenic Culture, N.Y., 2001, also numerous other exhibits throughout the world, 1966—; prin. pub. commns. include sculptures at Am. Airlines Ctr., Dallas., City of Phila., Dept. Environ. Protection, Trenton, N.J., Case-Western Res. U., Cleve., Low Water Dam Riverfront Pk., Tulsa, Dept. of Transp., Hartford, Conn., City of Sarasota, Fla., Ecology Dept. U. Minn., St. Paul; collections include Hirshhorn Mus., Washington, Albright-Knox Art Gallery, Buffalo, Mus. Fine Arts, Houston, Nat. Coll. Fine Arts, Washington, Cleve. Mus. Art, Munson-Williams-Proctor Inst., Uttica, Nelson-Atkins Mus. Art, Kansas City, Allen Art Mus., Oberlin, Speed Art Mus., Louisville; author: (as A. T. Spear) Rodin Sculpture in the Cleveland Museum of Art, 1967, Brancusi's Birds, 1969; contbr. articles to profl. jours.; subject of book Cosmic Rhythms: Athena Tacha's Public Sculpture (E. McClelland), 1998, Dancing in the Landscape: The Sculpture of Athena Tache, 2000. Recipient 1st prize May Show, Cleve. Mus. Art, 1968, 71, 79; NEA grantee, 1975. Home: 3721 Huntington St NW Washington DC 20015-1817 E-mail: at89@umail.umd.edu.

TACHA, DEANELL REECE, federal judge; b. Jan. 26, 1946; BA, U. Kans., 1968; JD, U. Mich., 1971. Spl. asst. to U.S. Sec. of Labor, Washington, 1971—72; assoc. Hogan & Hartson, 1973, Thomas J. Pitner, Concordia, Kans., 1973—74; dir. Douglas County Legal Aid Clinic, Lawrence, 1974—77; assoc. prof. law U. Kans., 1974—77, prof., 1977—85, assoc. dean, 1977—79, assoc. vice chancellor, 1979—81, vice chancellor, 1981—85; judge U.S. Ct. Appeals (10th cir.), Denver, 1985—; U.S. sentencing commr., 1994—98; chief judge U.S. Ct. Appeals (10th cir.), Denver, 2001—. Office: US Ct Appeals 10th Cir 643 Massachusetts St Ste301 Lawrence KS 66044-2292

TACHAU, HERMAN, structural engineer; b. Braunschweig, Germany, Nov. 12, 1920; came to U.S., 1936; s. Paul and Ilse Lea (Sternthal) T.; m. Heidi Elisabeth Mazur, Jan. 18, 1948; children: Judith Ilse, Robert David, Paul Alfred. BSCE, Ill. Inst. Tech., 1942; MSCE, Harvard U., 1946. Registered prof. engr. N.Mex., Ariz. Asst. prof. civil engring. U. Iowa, Iowa City, 1949-53; bridge designer N.Mex. State Hwy. Dept., Santa Fe, 1953-63, bridge design engr., 1963-68, asst. bridge engr., 1968-73, bridge engr., 1973-82; structural engr. H.W. Lochner Inc., Santa Fe, 1983-87; bridge engr. Scanlon & Assocs., 1987-93. Mem. subcom. bridges and structures Am. Assn. State Hwy. Ofcls., Washington, 1973-82; chmn. tech. com. concrete masonry design, 1978-82, mem. nat. coop. hwy. rsch. project, 1975-82. Contbr. tech. papers. Recipient 1st award Welding Contest, J.F. Lincoln Arc Welding Found., 1956. Mem. ASCE (v.p. N.Mex. sect. 1975-76), NSPE, Am. Concrete Inst. (bridge com. 1981-94).

TACHAUER, ALLAN DINU, internist; b. Timisoara, Romania, Mar. 26, 1960; came to U.S., 1987; s. Ernest and Ecaterina T.; m. Alessandra, June 9, 1986; 1 child, Allana. MD, Carol Davila Inst. Medicine, Bucharest, 1985. Diplomate Am. Bd. Internal Medicine. Resident Ravenswood Hosp., Chgo., 1989-92; fellow in med. ethics U. Chgo., 1992-93; assoc. program dir. Ravenswood Hosp., 1997-99; pvt. practice Chgo., 1993—; clin. asst. prof. U. Ill., 1997—. Fellow ACP; mem. Am. Soc. Bioethics & Humanities, AAAS. Avocations: violin, foreign languages, computers. Office: RMPG 4211 N Cicero Ave Chicago IL 60641-1604 E-mail: atachauer@rhmc.com.

TACHE, YVETTE FRANCE, neurogastroenterologist; b. Feb. 1, 1945; d. Lucien Joseph Laurant and Jeanne Marthe Fouillat; m. Jean Arthur Tache, June 20, 1970 (dec. Apr. 1979); children: Stephanie, Veronique. Master's degree, U. Claude Bernard, Lyon, France, 1968, DEA, 1969; PhD, U. Montreal, Can., 1974; Dr. Honoris Causa, U. Pecs, Hungary, 1994. Asst. rschr. U. Montreal, 1977-78; vis. scientist Salk Inst., La Jolla, Calif., 1978-80; from asst. rsch. prof. to assoc. rsch. prof. U. Montreal, 1980-82; assoc. prof. in rsch. UCLA, 1982-85, prof. medicine, 1985—. External referee Specialized Sci. Jour., 1977—, Med. Rsch. Coun., Que., Can., 1981—; mem. selection com. Med. Rsch. Coun., Que., 1982. Contbr. articles to profl. jours. Recipient Sr. Scientist award NIMH, 1988-98, Merit award NIH, 1996—, Janssen award in gastroenterology, 1998. Mem. Am. Physiol. Soc., Am. Gastroenterol. Soc., Soc. Neurosci., Hans Selye Found. (v.p. 1984—). Democrat. Roman Catholic. Avocations: tennis, travel, skiing. Office: CURE: DDRC West La VA Med Ctr 11301 Wilshire Blvd Los Angeles CA 90073-1003 E-mail: ytache@ucla.edu.

TACHI, DOUGLAS PAUL, architect, interior designer; b. Chgo., Mar. 1, 1945; s. Sadayoshi and Ruth Nobuko (Shikami) T.; m. Fleta Ross Collins, Dec. 27, 1987; children: Erin Paige, Brett Spencer. BS in Arch., Wash. U., St. Louis, 1968, MArch, 1974. Apprentice in arch. Mies van der Rohe, Chgo., 1961-63; designer Anselevicius & Rupe, St. Louis, 1974-76; project designer Harry Weese & Assocs., Washington, 1976-77, chief designer, v.p. in charge of design Miami, Fla., 1977-83; ptnr., v.p. Tilden, Tachi and Pales, 1983-87; ptnr., pres. Loggia Arch., Orlando, Fla., 1987—. Master plan cons. Rollins Coll., Winter Park, Fla., 1996-97; chief designer Miami Metrorail, 1977-83; project mgr. stas. L.A. Rapid Transit Dist., 1981. Exec. prodr. documentary: Bruyeres: The Courage of Our Fathers, 2000. Mem. master plan com./architect Miami Downtown Govt. Ctr., 1979-84; architect Art in Transit Screening Com., Miami, 1979-82. With U.S. Army, 1969-71. Recipient Master Plan award U. Miami, 1985, Architecture award Downtown Devel. Assn., Orlando, 1989. Mem. AIA (assoc., Henry Adams Cert. for Excellence in Arch. 1972). Avocations: Biblical archaeology, fly fishing, yacht design.

TACK, THERESA ROSE, women's health nurse; b. Lunenburg, Vt., Nov. 10, 1940; d. Gustave L. and Blanche Rose Fournier; m. Dennis M. Tack, Sept. 2, 1961; children: Lynelle Scullard, Karyn Terry, LeAnn Gomez. Diploma, Cen. Maine Gen. Hosp., 1961. Cert. ACLS, neonatal resuscitation Am. Heart Assn. Staff nurse neurosurgery unit Hillcrest Med. Ctr., Tulsa, 1961-62; staff nurse cardiovascular unit Meth. Hosp., Houston, 1962-65; staff nurse St. John's Hosp., Red Wing, Minn., 1979-85, Wasatch County Hosp., Heber City, Utah, 1985-97. Columnist, Nurses Notes in Wasatch Wave, Heber City, Utah, 1990-97.

TACKE, ELEANOR, photographic archivist; b. Highland Park, Mich., Feb. 13, 1939; d. Harold Starr and Margaret Eleanor (Gillett) Atherton; m. Carl Ewald Tacke, Nov. 24, 1961; children: Lisa Kathleen, Paul Christopher. B Gen. Studies, Wayne State U., 1991, M of Libr. Info. Sci., 1998. Sec. Gen. Motors Corp., Warren, Mich., 1961-65, exec. sec., 1979-95; tng. archivist Wayne State U., Detroit, 1996-97, grad. rsch. asst., 1997-98; photog. archivist Schroeder Info. Sys., Inc., 1998—2000. Pres., Warren Coop. Nursery, 1971-72, Friends of Interlochen Pub. Libr. Mem. AAUW, LWV of Grosse Pointe (v.p. 1995-2000), Mich. Archival Assn., Soc. Am. Archivists. Avocations: swimming, reading, travel, going to concerts and plays. Home: 5713 Bush Rd Interlochen MI 49643-9592

TACKER, WILLIS ARNOLD, JR. medical educator, researcher; b. Tyler, Tex., May 24, 1942; s. Willis Arnold and Willie Mae (Massey) T.; m. Martha J. McClelland, Mar. 18, 1967; children: Sarah Mae, Betsy Jane, Katherine Ann. BS, Baylor U., 1964, MD, PhD, 1970. Lic. physician, Ind., Alaska, Tex. Intern Mayo Grad. Sch. Medicine Mayo Clinic, Rochester, Minn., 1970-71; pvt. practice Prudhoe Bay, Alaska, 1971; instr. dept. physiology Baylor Coll. Medicine, Houston, 1971-73, asst. prof. dept. physiology, 1973-74; clin. prof. family medicine Ind. U. Sch. Medicine, West Lafayette, Ind., 1981—; vis. asst. prof. Biomed. Engring. Ctr., Purdue U., 1974-76, assoc. prof. Sch. Vet. Medicine, 1976-79; assoc. dir. William A. Hillenbrand Biomed. Engring. Ctr., Purdue U., 1980-93, prof. Sch. Vet. Medicine, 1979—, acting dir., 1991-93; exec. dir. Hillenbrand Biomed. Engring. Ctr., 1993-95. Vis. rsch. fellow Sch. Aerospace Medicine, Brooks AFB, San Antonio, 1982; with Corp. Sci. and Tech., State of Ind., 1985-88; presenter, cons. in field. Author: Some Advice on Getting Grants, 1991; co-author: Electrical Defibrillation, 1980; author: (with others) Handbook of Engineering and Medicine and Biology, 1980, Implantable Sensors for Closed-Loop Prosthetic Systems, 1985, Encyclopedia of Medical Devices and Instrumentation, 1988, (with others) Defibrillation of the Heart, 1994; contbr. numerous articles to profl. jours. Chmn. bd. dirs. Assn. Advancemnt Med. Instrumentation Found., Arlington, Va., 1987-95. Mem. Am. Heart Assn. (bd. dirs. Ind. affiliate 1975-81, med. edn. com. 1975-81, pub. health edn. com. 1975-81, chmn. ad hoc com. CPR tng. for physicians 1976-77, rsch. review com. 1988-90), Am. Physiol. Soc., Ind. State Med. Assn., Tippecanoe County Med. Soc., Assn. Advancement Med. Instrumentation (chmn. various coms., bd. dirs. 1981-84, pres. 1985-86), Am. Men and Women Sci., Alpha Epsilon Delta, Beta Beta Beta, Soc. Sigma Xi. Achievements include research in biomedical engineering, cardiovascular physiology, medical education, emergency cardiovascular care, motor evoked potentials, skeletal muscle ventricle; patents for an apparatus and method for measurement and control of blood pressure, electrode system and method for implantable defibrillators, pressure mapping system with capacitive measuring pad. Office: Purdue U Lynn Hall West Lafayette IN 47907 E-mail: tacker@vet.purdue.edu.

TACKET, HALL SANFORD, retired internist; b. Dyer, Tenn., Apr. 12, 1921; s. John Otis and Lucile (Sanford) T.; m. Jeanne Snedecor, Apr. 17, 1925; children: Lynn, Carol, Hall Sanford Jr. BS, U. Tenn., 1943, MD, 1944. Diplomate Am. Bd. Internal Medicine, 1952. Instr. to assoc. prof. medicine U. Tenn. Coll. Medicine, Memphis, 1950-64, clin. prof., 1964-87, prof., 1987-96, emeritus prof., 1996—; internist pvt. practice, 1950-86. Chief gen. internal med. Baptist Meml. Hosp., Memphis, 1979-91, dir. med. edn., 1979-91. Contbr. articles to profl. jours. Cpt. U.S. Army, 1945-47. Master ACP (gov. Tenn.); fellow Am. Coll. Cardiology. Home: 8100 Connecticut Ave Apt 1609 Chevy Chase MD 20815-2821 E-mail: halltacket@pol.net.

TACKETT, CHERYL L. reporter, writer; b. Washington, Sept. 19, 1948; d. Kenneth A. and Mary Ellen Charley; m. Les Horst, June 25, 1969 (div. Aug. 1989); children: Melynda, Sheri, Michael; m. James Franklin Tackett, June 3, 1995. AA, Vincennes (Ind.) U., 1987—89; MA , Ind. State U., Terre Haute, 1995; student, John G. Lake Ministry Coun., 2001. Adult svcs. libr. Starke County Libr., Knox, Ind., 1995—98; prof. asst. summer sch. Ind. State U., Terre Haute, 1994—99; news dir. WKVI News Dept., Knox, Ind., 1999; reporter and writer The Leader Review, 2001. Author: (short stories) Word Aflame Prisons of the Past, 1994 (1st place Writer's Contest, 1994). Publicist, writing Coalition Against Domestic Abuse, Starke County, 2001, Phoenix House, Starke County, 2001. Named Pfennig Scholar Ind. State U., 1989—90, 1990—92; recipient William C. Ball award, Ind. State U., 1992, 1st place Best Ongoing News Coverage, Hoosier State Press Assn., 2001. Mem.: Friends of the Library, Eta Sigma Pi, Phi Delta Kappa, Sigma Tau Delta. Pentecostal. Avocations: cooking, reading. Office: The Leader 4 S Main St Box 38 46534 E-mail: tackett@nitline.net.

TACKETT, STEPHEN DOUGLAS, education services specialist; b. Waverly, Ohio, Apr. 27, 1939; s. James Elbert and Zelma Iola (Manahan) T.; m. Magdalena Schneider, Jan. 4, 1958; children: Doris, Janice, Jerry, Suzanne. AA, El Paso C.C., 1974; BS, SUNY, Albany, 1976; MA, Ball State U., 1979. Nat. cert. counselor; lic. profl. clin. counselor. Enlisted U.S. Army, 1955, advanced through grades to Command Sgt. Maj., 1973, retired, 1982; instr. Mt. Wachusett C.C., Gardner, Mass., 1979-81; asst. dir. Evaluation U.S. Army Sgts. Maj. Acad., Ft. Bliss, Tex., 1981-82; dir. substance abuse treatment Sun Valley Hosp., El Paso, 1982-84; from guidance counselor to ednl. svcs. officer U.S. Army, Germany, 1984-86, 88-90; edn. advisor U.S. Army Sgts. Maj. Acad., Fort Bliss, 1990-92; edn. svcs. specialist Mil. Entrance Processing Sta., El Paso, 1992—. Mem. adv. bd. for Counselor Edn. U. Tex., El Paso, 1983. Cubmaster Boy Scouts Am., Ft. Leonard Wood, Mo., 1970-71, com. mem., Frankfurt, Germany, 1972-73, asst. scoutmaster, Kaiserslautern, Germany, 1976-79. Mem. ACA, Assn. for Career and Tech. Edn., Nat. Assn. Secondary Sch. Prins., Tex. Assn. Secondary Sch. Prins., Tex. Counseling Assn. Office: Mil Entrance Processing Sta Ste E 6380 Morgan Ave El Paso TX 79906-4610

TACKITT, SYLVAN WRIGHT, lawyer; b. Banta, Ind., June 12, 1909; s. Mitchell Albert Ward and Carrie Blanche (Stewart) T.; m. Elizabeth Estelle Stephenson, Sept. 6, 1934 (dec. Nov. 1970); children: Stephen Wright (dec.), Martha Anne Distler; m. Harriet Martin Cartmel, May 13, 1972 (dec. Dec. 1, 1995); m. Edith Boyer Schuman, May 14, 1997. BS in Bus., Ind. U., 1931, LLB, 1933. Bar: Ind. 1931. Pvt. practice, Bloomington, 1933—; prosecuting atty. Monroe County, Ind., 1942-46, county atty., 1964-65. Mem. 1st Christian Ch., Bloomington, 1934—; pres. YMCA, Bloomington, 1951-52; bd. dirs. Monroe County Pub. Libr., Monroe County Pub. Libr. Found.; govt. appeal agt. 1948-68. Recipient Sagamore of Wabash award Gov. of Ind., 1982. Mem. ABA, Ind. State Bar Assn. (bd. mgrs. 1970-72), Monroe County Bar Assn. (pres. 1960-61), Bloomington Country Club, Columbia Club (Indpls.), Masons, Lions (Melvin Jones fellow, pres. Bloomington chpt. 1947-48), Sigma Alpha Epsilon. Republican. Avocations: golf, bridge, cryptograms, collecting marbles and orientalia. Home: 1304 E 2d St Bloomington IN 47401-5104 Office: 103 N College Ave Ste 203 Bloomington IN 47404-3977

TACKMAN, ARTHUR LESTER, newspaper publisher, management consultant; b. Chgo., July 28, 1916; s. Arthur Lester and Lucy Louise (Gutekunst) T.; m. Mary Lillian Connor, Mar. 31, 1939; children: Arthur Lester III, Laurence Connor, Alan Rhead. BA, Ohio State U., 1938, MPA, 1939. With various depts. U.S. Govt., Washington, 1938-49; staff asst., mem. pers. policy bd. Dept. Def., 1949; asst. mgr. Savannah river plant AEC, Aiken, S.C., 1950-55, asst. dir. inspection Washington, 1955-59, dir. pers., 1959-65, HUD, Washington, 1965-70; mgmt. cons. Glenwood, N.Mex., 1970-78; owner, operator Deep Creek Ranch, Inc., 1972—; publisher Catron Co. Pub. Co., Inc., Reserve, N.Mex., 1986-91. Pres. Gila Nat. Forest Permittees, Reserve, 1978-86; mem., treas. N.Mex. Pub. Lands Coun., Albuquerque, 1967-87; coun. mem. Boy Scouts Am., S.C., Washington, 1950-65. Lt. USN, 1943-46. Recipient Man Yr. Award Aiken County C. of C., 1953, Citation for Meritorious Svc. United Def. Fund, 1957. Mem. N.Mex. Press Assn. Democrat. Unitarian Universalist. Home: 9504 San Rafael Albuquerque NM 87109

TACKWELL, ELIZABETH MILLER, social worker; b. Caney, Kans., Mar. 14, 1923; d. Jesse Winfield and Mattie (Shuler) Miller; m. Joseph J. Tackwell, Dec. 13, 1946 (dec. Mar. 1988); children: Steven, Tiana Tackwell David, Christy Tackwell. BA cum laude, U. Okla., 1953, MSW, 1962. Bd. cert. diplomate Am. Bd. Examiners in Clin. Social Work; lic. social worker, Okla. Social worker Dept. Pub. Welfare, Tulsa/Cleve./Okla. County, Okla., 1958-59, med. social analyst, 1960-61; assoc. John Massey M.D. Clinic, Oklahoma City, 1964-69; clin. asst. prof. Okla. U. Sch. Social Work, 1964—; asst. prof., clin. instr. dept. psychiatry/behavioral scis. Okla. U. Health Scis. Ctr., 1963—;

psychiat. social worker VA Med. Ctr., 1961-97, chief mental health sect., 1976-97, adminstrv. dir. day treatment ctr., 1993-97; pvt. practice, 1971—. Psychiat. surveyor Health Care Fin. Adminstrn., Dept. Human Svcs., Washington, 1985—. Recipient Svc. Commendation award DAV, 1980, Awards Am. Ex-Prisoners of War, 1994, 95, 96. Mem. NASW (diplomate in clin. social work, pres. Okla. chpt. 1971-73, Social Worker of the Yr. Western Okla. chpt. 1975, Lifetime Achievement award Okla. chpt. 1997), Am. Psychotherapy Assn. (cert. diplomate), Acad. Cert. Social Workers, Okla. Health and Welfare Assn. (conf. chmn. 1975—), Pi Gamma Mu. Home and Office: 1328 Tarman Cir Norman OK 73071-4846

TADDEI, LOIS ANNETTE MAGOWAN, artist, decorator; b. Phila., Sept. 17, 1935; d. Frank Rue Magowan and Grace Gloria (Valentino) Weinstein; m. Robert Matthew Taddei, May 21, 1960; 1 child, Robyn Grace. Degree, Pierce Coll. Represented by Phila. Mus. of Art. Watercolor botanicals shown at Phila. Mus. Art; one-woman shows include Pa. Hort. Soc., Phila, La Grande Gallery, Moorestown, N.J., Camden County Libr.; group shows include Art at Armory, Phila, Great Galleries, New Hope, Pa., Hardcastle Gallery, Wilmington, Del., Hockessin, Del., Gallery I, Chadds Ford, Pa., Rhoads Gallery, Gwynedd Valley, Pa., Festival Arts, Cape May, N.J., Ocean City (N.J.) Arts Festival; designer Vassar Designers Showcase House, 1991-92, Haddonfield Design Showcase House, 1992, Barry Decorators Haddonfield & Cherry Hill, Interiors by Marilouise, West Chester, Pa., Rocco Marianni & Assoc. Interior Design, Haddonfield. Mem. Graphic Artist Guild, United Visual Artists, Burlington Country Art Guild. Avocations: gardening, needlepoint, ballet, museums.

TADDEO, DOMINIC J. transportation executive; b. Montreal, Que., Can., Mar. 21, 1939; s. Donat and Loretta (DiGiovanni) T.; m. Angela Nucci; children: Anthony, Mark. B.Commerce, Loyola Coll., 1959. Internal auditor Thorne, Riddell & Co.; sr. internal auditor, chief acct. Pratt & Whitney Aircraft of Can. Ltd.; asst. treas., controller McLean Kennedy, Inc.; dir. fin. Montreal Port Auth., dir. fin. and adminstrn., dir. ops., pres., CEO, 1984—. Bd. dirs. Laurentian Bank, 1998. Chmn. bd. Electronic Data Interchange for Commerce, Montreal, 1990; co-chmn. fund raising campaign Montreal Symphony Orch., 1996-97; v.p. corp. campaign Heart and Stroke Found. of Que.; 1996-97; former dir. St. Mary's Hosp. Found., chmn. ball, 1991; co-chmn. ann. collection Ch. of Montreal, 1992, 93; past mem. bd. dirs. Cedars Cancer Fund of Royal Victoria Hosp.; past v.p. La Commission Scolaire Baldwin-Cartier. Recipient Golden Lion award Order of Sons of Italy, 1985; named Transport Personality of the Yr., Province of Que., 1989; recipient Award of Distinction Faculty of Commerce and Adminstrn. of Concordia U., 1989; Dimensions 1995 award Order of Charterd Adminstrs. of Que., 1995. Mem.: Internat. Assn. Ports and Harbors (exec. com. 1986—, pres. 2000—01), Am. Assn. Port Authorities (chmn. 1989—90), Assn Can. Ports and Harbours (pres. 1982—83). Office: Montreal Port Authority Wing #1 Cite du Havre Port Montreal Bldg Montreal QC Canada H3C 3R5

TADDESSE, SAMUEL, economist, consultant; b. Addis Ababa, Shoa, Ethiopia, Oct. 16, 1944; came to U.S., 1968; s. Altaye and Askale (Yitabarek) T.; m. Sarah Louise Samuel; children: Tsehay, Samson, David. BSc, Haile Selassie 1st U., 1968; MBA, Fairleigh Dickinson U., 1970; PhD in Fin. and Applied Econs., U. Pa., 1975. Asst. prof. fin. and econs. Bernard Baruch Coll. CUNY, N.Y.C., 1973-77; sr. economist Fed. Res. Bank of N.Y., 1977-80; dist. mgr. AT&T, Morristown, N.J., 1980-87; v.p. Debo Enterprises, Inc., Washington, 1987—. Sr. cons. Mgmt. Systems Internat., Washington, 1992—. Founder World Class Schs., Inc. Mem. Am. Bus. Assn. of Kenya, Internat. Soc. for African Devel., Soc. for Internat. Devel., Am. Econ. Assn. Republican. Jewish. Avocation: camping. Home: Apt 701 5300 Columbia Pike Arlington VA 22204-5816 Office: Apt 701 5300 Columbia Pike Arlington VA 22204-5816

TADEO, ELVIA, artist; b. Ensenada, B.C., Mex., Nov. 21, 1970; d. Austreberto and Consuelo (Tadeo) T. Student art, Rafael Contreras, Ensenada, 1986-89, Lorraine M. Rowley, San Diego, 1990-96, Silvia Moonier, 1997-98, Edward Mores, 1998-99. Represented by The Gallery on Broadway, San Diego. Juror La Jolla Art Assn., 1999-2001, Del Mar Fair, Calif., 2001—. Contbg. artist pastel painting: Baja 4 You, 1999; poetry pub. in Art Venues Mag., Newsletter of Pastel Soc. San Diego, Pastel Soc. West Coast; exhibited at LaJolla (Calif.) Art Assn. Gallery, 1997-2001, Galerias Internacionales of Hotel Hyatt Regency, Guadalajara, Mex., 1996-98, Gallery of Pastel Soc. of West Coast, Camino, Calif., 1997, Ceudonium de la Mujer, Ensenada, 1999-2001, Galeria de la Ciudad de Ensenada, B.C., Mex., 2000, Giorgio Santini's Gallery of Fine Arts, Rosarito, Mex., 2000-2001, El Centro Cultural San Angel, Mexico City, 2000, Centro Cultural Riviera, Ensenada, 2000, Centro Cultural Siglo 21, Mexico City, 2001, Hosp. Tembre, Mexico, 2001, Teatro la Cjuda-deia, Mexico, 2001, Hosp. of Pemex City, 2002, House of Reps., Mexico City, 2002, The Gallery on Broadway, San Diego; rep. Gallery on Broadway, San Diego, Gallery Giorgio Santini, Rosarito, San Diego Mus. of Art, Artist Guild, 2002-03. Art cons. Cultural Ctr. of Ensenada, 2000—; nat dir. Mexican Rep. in the Art Miles project, United Nations U.S.A. rep., 2002-03. Recipient 1st place Del Mar Fair, 1996, Spl. award, 1996. Mem. LaJolla Art Assn. (publicity chair 1999-2001), Pastel Soc. of West Coast, Degas Pastel Soc., Pastel Soc. San Diego, Carlsbad and Oceanside Art League, Internat. Assn. Pastels, Directorio Enciclopedico de las Artes Plasticas, Directorio of Artistas Plasticos de la Cordinacion Nacional de Artes Plasticas de Bellas Artes. Roman Catholic. Avocations: horseback riding, hiking. Office: PO Box 2229 Vista CA 92085 E-mail: elviatadeo@aol.com.

TADEUSIEWICZ, RYSZARD, scientist, biomedical engineer, educator; b. Sroda Slaska, Wroclaw, Poland, May 5, 1947; s. Stanislaw and Jozefa (Kubiak) T.; m. Malgorzata Anna Jaworowska, Sept. 15, 1968; 1 child, Joanna. MSc, AGH Tech. U. Cracow, 1971, PhD, 1975, habilitation, 1981. Asst., assoc. prof. AGH Tech. Univ., Cracow, Poland, 1971-86, prof., 1986—. Cons. Bank BPH, Cracow, 1994—. Author: Neural Networks, 1993, Problems of Biocybernetics, 1991; contbr. numerous articles to profl. jours. Mem. IEEE (sr.), Internat. Fedn. Automatic Control, Internat. Neural Network Soc., Polish Cybernetic Soc. (hon.), Sci. Rsch. Com. Home: Opolska 13/17 31-276 Cracow Poland Office: AGH Tech Univ Al Mickiewicza 30 30-059 Cracow Poland E-mail: rtad@biocyb.ia.agh.edu.pl.

TADIAN, LUANNE F. B. financial analyst, consultant, researcher; b. Colorado Springs, Colo., Mar. 29, 1965; d. Carlos Solomon and Josie Dolores (Vigil) C'DeBaca; m. Nishan Thaddeus Tadian, Dec. 30, 1985; children: Joshua Abel, Zachary Solomon. BS in Psychology and Biology, U.N.Mex., 1988; MBA, Calif. State U., L.A., 199. Lic. in real estate law, series 6 and 63, Nat. Assn. Securities Dealers. Jr. v.p. prodn. Sentry Mortgage, Albuquerque, 1988-89; rsch. cons., L.A., 1991-93; account mgr. Beverly Hills Group Fin. Mgmt. Specialists, 1993-96; mgr. customer support Daylight Transport/DayWest Express, 1996—. Bd. dirs., chmn. vol. recognition, mem. pub. rels. and resource devel. coms. Calif. Litracy, San Gabriel, 1993—; del. Rep. Planning Com. Mem. NAFE, Nat. Assn. Women Bus. Owners, Nat. Assn. Life Underwriters, Beta Gamma Sigma. Republican. Roman Catholic. Home: House C 269 S Walnut Grove Ave San Gabriel CA 91776-1711

TADIKAMALLA, PANDU R. computer scientist, educator; s. Satyanarayana and Saraswati Tadikamalla; m. Rama D. Chimakurty, June 10, 1955; children: Raghu, Sara. PhD, U. of Iowa, 1975. Prof. U. of Pitts., Pitts., 1992—. Chmn. of the bd. of dir. S.V. Temple, Pitts., 1995—96. Office: University of Pittsburgh 25h Mervis hall Pittsburgh PA 15260 Home Fax: 412-648-1693; Office Fax: 412-648-1693. Personal E-mail: pandu@katz.pitt.edu. E-mail: pandu@katz.pitt.edu.

TADLOCK, ANDREW BRIAN, music educator; b. Sioux City, Iowa, Mar. 28, 1960; s. Melvin Eugene and Mary Viola Tadlock; m. Pamela Joan Keister, July 25, 1997; children: Randal Hensel, Brian Hensel, Jaclyn, Jason Hensel. MusB, U. Iowa, 1982, MA, 1995. Lic. Bd. Ednl. Examiners. Music specialist St. Lukes Regional Med. Ctr., Sioux City, 1982—85; dir. vocal music Winnebago (Nebr.) Cmty. Schs., 1985—86; vocal music specialist Sioux City Cmty. Sch. Dist., 1986—87; dir. vocal music Camanche (Iowa) Cmty. Sch., 1987—2001, Davenport (Iowa) Cmty. Sch. Dist., 2001—. Dir. music ministry Jesus Christ, Prince of Peace Parish, Clinton, 1991—. Mem.: KC, NEA, Nat. Pastoral Musicians Assn., Am. Choral Dirs. Assn. Roman Catholic. Avocations: technology, theater , golf.

TADLOCK, ANITA CONNER, volunteer; b. New Orleans, Sept. 11, 1944; d. Marion and Lorena (Dobyns) Conner; m. Norman Edward Tadlock, June 25, 1966; children: Edward Scott, Stephanie Lee, Elizabeth Conner, Stephen Dobyns. BMusic, Queens Coll., Charlotte, N.C., 1966; student, U. Vienna, 1964, Colegio de Espana, Salamanca, Spain, 1993. Social worker Bur. Children's Svcs., Morristown, N.J., 1966-67, 69-70; pvt. piano tchr., 1966-82. Donations chair Am. Women's Assn. Singapore, 1992, chair cmty. svcs. com., 1993, 1st v.p., 1994, pres., 1994-95; bd. dirs. Am. Assn. of Singapore, 1994-95; chair in charge of food George Washington Ball com., 1996-97; bd. dirs. Am. Club of Singapore, 1994-96, membership chair, 1996-97; docent Singapore Nat. History Mus., 1995-97; mem. fin. com. Trinity United Meth. Ch., Hackettstown, N.J., 1998-2000; active Jr. League of London, 1984-91, non-resident sustainer, 1991—; active Boy Scouts Am., Girl Scouts U.S.; pres. PTA, 1982-84. Recipient Outstanding Vol. award Am. Assn., Singapore, 1996, Am. Women's Assn., Singapore, 1996. Mem. DAR, Jr. League of London, Delta Omicron, Kappa Delta. Methodist. Avocations: travel, reading, antiquing.

TAESCH, RICHARD EDMUND, music educator; b. San Diego, Dec. 17, 1942; s. Edmund Thomas Taesch and Ann Marcella Simeone; m. Sandra Aiken, June 15, 1968 (div. Jan. 0, 1980). Literary Braill Libr. of Congress, 1988, Music Braille Libr. of Congress, 1992. Tchr. Adler Music Acad., Van Nuys, Calif., 1961—71, Van Nuys Music (pvt. studio), Van Nuys, 1971—94, LA City Coll., Los Angeles, 1983—90; tchr., chair (dept of guitar) So Calif Conservatory of Music, Sun Valley, 1976—, tchr., founder (braille music div) La Canada, 1992—. Br. pres. Music Teachers Assn. Calif, San Fernando East Valley, Calif., 1971—79; music specialist Calif Transcribers and Educators of Visually Handicapped, Los Angeles, Calif., 1996—; bd. mem. So Calif Cons of Music, Sun Valley, Calif., 2000—. Author: (book) An Introduction to Music for the Blind Student Parts I & II; contbr. articles to profl. jours. Founder Music Edn. Network for the Visually Impaired, Sun Valley, Calif., 1996. Recipient Ptnr. Sch. Award, Blend School-LAUSD, 1999. Mem.: Nat. Assn. of Schools of Music, Nat. Braille Assn. Roman Catholic. Achievements include development of founder of 1st functional Cal Transcribers and Educators of the Visually Handicapped music committee; developed curriculum for teaching of braille music. Avocations: hiking, ham radio, pilot. Office: SCCM Braille Music Div 245 Berkshire Ave La Canada CA 91011 Office Fax: 818-790-5903.

TAFAZOLI, MANSOUR MANNY, radiologist; b. Tehran, Iran, Feb. 17, 1939; came to U.S., 1988; s. Hassan Tafazoli and Fatemeh Ghoddousi; m. Soraya Nowbar Berry, 1969; children: Sara, Maryam. MD, Tehran Med. Sch., 1964. Diplomate Am. Bd. Radiology. Assoc. prof. radiology Tehran Med. Sch., 1979-88; radiologist Kingman (Ariz.) Regional Med. Ctr., 1998—. Mem. Radiologic Soc. N.Am. Office: Kingman Regional Med Ctr 3269 Stockton Hill Rd Kingman AZ 86401-3619

TAFEL, EDGAR, architect; b. N.Y.C., Mar. 4, 1912; s. Samuel and Rose (Chary) T. Student, NYU, 1930-32; DFA (hon.), SUNY, Geneseo, 2001. Sr. fellow Frank Lloyd Wright's Taliesin Fellowship, Spring Green, Wis., 1932-41; practice architecture N.Y.C., 1946—. Lectr. USIS, Eng., Israel, India, Netherlands, 1972-73, New Sch. for Social Rsch., N.Y.C., 1974; faculty Smithsonian Instn., 1978; co-producer, actor (video) The Frank Lloyd Wright Way. Author: Years with Frank Lloyd Wright, 1993, Frank Lloyd Wright, 1993; contbr. articles to profl. jours.; Prin. works include: Protestant Chapel at Kennedy Airport, 1964, First Presbyn. Ch. Addition, 1959, De Witt Ch., all N.Y.C., Fine Arts Bldg., State U. N.Y. at Geneseo, 1967, Fulton-Montgomery Community Coll, Johnstown, N.Y., 1969, Grace Ch, White Plains, 1970, Allentown (Pa.) Art Mus. addition, 1975, Columbia-Greene Community Coll, Hudson, N.Y., 1974, Salvation Army Corps Community Centers; master plans for: State Coll. at Geneseo, York Coll., N.Y.C., Cadet Corps Hdqrs., Bronx, N.Y.; designed over 100 residences. Bd. dirs. N.Y.C. Mission Soc. Served with AUS, World War II, CBI. Recipient award of merit for Presbyn. Ch. Fifth Ave. Assn., N.Y.C., service citation State U. N.Y. Coll. at Geneseo, 1970 Fellow AIA; mem. Nat. Acad. Arts (assoc.), Taliesin Fellowship (coun.), Fallingwater (adv. com.). Home and Office: 14 E 11th St New York NY 10003-4402

TAFERO, ARTHUR H. computer company executive; b. Jersey City, May 7, 1947; s. Arthur H. Tafero and Mary Guida Tafero; m. Maryanne A. Bannon, Mar. 25, 1951; 1 child Geoffrey Gee 1 child Thomas ;1 child Elise. MA, Columbia U., 1976. Dir. EasternStudiesDatabase.com, Hollis, NY, 1997—; faculty instr. BarnesandNobleUniversity.com, NY, 2002—. Editor: (book) The Encyclopedia of China, 1995; author: (AOL world history sect.) Chinese History and Philosophy, 1996, (Internet course) Understanding Mao, 2002, Taoism, 1996, Confucianism, 1996, Indian History and Philosophy, 1997, Japanese History and Philosophy, 1997, Understanding Vietnam, 2002, Korean History and Philosophy, 2002, The Way of Chuang Tzu, 1996, TaoTeChing, Asian Economics, 2001, Mythology, 1998, Christianity, 2001, Judaism, 2001, The Bible, 2000, Islam, 1999, The Qur'an, 1999, Hinduism, 1999, Buddhism, 1998, Terrorism, 2001. American Taoist. Avocations: fantasy baseball, tennis, films. Home: Ste B73 87-30 204th St Jamaica NY 11423 Office: EasternStudiesDatabase.com Ste B73 87-30 204th St Jamaica NY 11423 Home Fax: 718-776-2153; Office Fax: 718-776-2153. Personal E-mail: easternstudies@aol.com. Business E-Mail: easternstudies@aol.com.

TAFFE, WILLIAM JOHN, computer science educator; b. Albany, N.Y., Feb. 3, 1943; s. William Berchmans and Ellen Ann (Upton) T.; m. Betty Jo Miller, Dec. 27, 1965; children— Daniel David, Michael Andrew. B.S., Le Moyne Coll., 1964; M.S., U. Chgo., 1967, Ph.D., 1968. Research physicist Air Force Cambridge Research Lab, Bedford, Mass., 1968-69; asst. prof. physics Colby Coll., Waterville, Maine, 1969-71; assoc. prof. physics Plymouth State Coll., N.H., 1971-81, prof. physics, 1981-82, prof., chmn. computer sci., 1982— ; vis. prof. U. N.H., Durham, 1980; mem. accrediting team N.H. post secondary edn. commn., Concord, 1982-89. Contbr. articles to profl. jours. on atmospheric physics and computer sci. edn.; monograph N.H. phys. environ. Chmn. Planning Bd. Rumney, N.H., 1983-90. N.Y. State Bd. Regents scholar, 1960-64; NSF grantee, 1972, 74, 76, 79, Spaulding Potter Charitable Found., 1975, Rotary grantee, 1994—. Mem. Assn. for Computing Machinery, Spl. Interest Group on Computer Graphics, Nat. Intercollegiate Soccer Officials Assn., N.H. Soccer Ofcls. Assn., New Eng. Lacrosse Ofcls. Assn. Roman Catholic.

TAFLOVE, ALLEN, electrical engineer, educator, researcher, consultant; b. Chgo., June 14, 1949; s. Harry and Leah T.; m. Sylvia Hinda Friedman, Nov. 6, 1977; children: Michael Lee, Nathan Brent. BS with highest distinction, Northwestern U., 1971, MS, 1972, PhD, 1975. Assoc. engr. IIT Rsch. Inst., Chgo., 1975-78, rsch. engr., 1978-81, sr. engr., 1981-84; assoc. prof. Northwestern U., Evanston, 1984-88, prof., 1988—, Charles Deering McCormick prof., 2000—; master Lindgren/Slivka Residential Coll. Sci. & Engring., 2000—. Author: Computational Electrodynamics: The Finite-Difference Time-Domain Method, 1995; co-author: Computational Electromagnetics: Integral Equation Approach, 1993, Computational Electrodynamics: The Finite-Difference Time-Domain Method, 2d edit., 2000; editor: Advances in Computational Electrodynamics: The Finite-Difference Time-Domain Method, 1998; contbr. 12 book chpts. , 80 articles to profl. jours.; patentee in field. Fellow: IEEE. Achievements include pioneer of finite-difference time-domain method in computational electromagnetics. Office: Northwestern U Dept Elec and Comp Engring 2145 Sheridan Rd Evanston IL 60208-0834 E-mail: taflove@ece.northwestern.edu.

TAFT, BOB, governor; b. Jan. 8, 1942; m. Hope Taft; 1 child, Anna. BA, Yale U., 1963; MA, Princeton U., 1967; JD, U. Cin., 1976. Pvt. practice; mem. Ohio Ho. of Reps., Columbus, 1976-80; commr. Hamilton County, Ohio, 1981-90; sec. of state State of Ohio, Columbus, 1991-99, gov., 1999—. Office: 30th Fl 77 S High St Fl 30 Columbus OH 43215-6117*

TAFT, DAVID DAKIN, chemical executive; b. Cleve., Mar. 27, 1938; s. Kingsley A. and Louise D. T.; m. Sararose Leonard, July 8, 1961; children: Amy Rose, Kingsley Leonard, Elisabeth. AB, Kenyon Coll., 1960; PhD in Chemistry, Mich. State U., 1963. Sr. rsch. chemist Archer-Daniels Midland, 1964-67; mgr. polymer rsch. Ashland Chem., 1967-72; dir. comml. devel. Gen. Mills Chems., 1972-74; v.p., dir. R&D, Henkel Corp., 1973-78, group v.p. consumer and splty. products, 1978-81, exec. v.p. chem. products div., dir., 1981-82; gen. mgr. materials div. Raychem Corp., Menlo Park, Calif., 1983-84; gen. mgr. Telecom group, 1983-86; v.p. Raychem Corp., 1984-93, v.p. manufacuturing, 1986-93; COO Landec Corp., Menlo Park, Calif., 1993—. Author: Fundamentals of Powder Coatings; bd. editors: Rsch. Mgmt. Jour.; patentee in field. Trustee Mpls. Soc. Fine Arts, 1981-83, Kenyon Coll., 1990—; vice chmn. Mem. Comml. Devel. Assn., Indsl. Research Inst., Am. Chem. Soc., Kenyon Alumni Assn. (pres. 1978), Circus Club. Republican. Office: Landec Corp 3603 Haven Ave Menlo Park CA 94025-1010 E-mail: dtaft@landec.com.

TAFT, EARL JAY, mathematics educator; b. N.Y.C., Aug. 27, 1931; s. David and Terry (Gordon) T.; m. Hessy Levinsons, Jan. 18, 1959; children: Nina, Alexander. BA, Amherst Coll., 1952; MA, Yale U., 1953, PhD, 1956. Instr. Columbia U., N.Y.C., 1956-59; asst. prof. Rutgers U., New Brunswick, N.J., 1959-62, assoc. prof., 1962-66, prof. math., 1966—. Exec. editor: Communications in Algebra, 1974-99, math. series Marcel Dekker Inc., 1974—; contbr. numerous articles to profl. jours. NSF grantee. Mem. Am. Math. Soc., Math. Assn. Am., Phi Beta Kappa, Sigma Xi. Home: 65 Central Park W Apt 8A New York NY 10023-6009 Office: Rutgers U Dept Math New Brunswick NJ 08854-8019

TAFT, JOHN THOMAS, television producer, writer; b. Dublin, Ireland, July 7, 1950; came to U.S., 1957; s. William Howard and Barbara (Bradfield) T.; m. Christine Rinehart Jordan, June 28, 1990; children: Stephen Alexander Rinehart. BA, Yale U., 1972, U. Oxford, Eng., 1974, MA, 1979, Johns Hopkins U., 1981. Stringer New Republic mag., Washington, 1977-79; pres. Taft Assocs./TV Prodn., 1984—; Washington editor Harper's mag., N.Y.C., 1987-89. Cons. Panoptic Prodns., London, 1984-89. Contbr. articles to profl. jours.; author: Mayday at Yale, 1976, American Power, 1989; producer TV documentary: After the War, 1987, America's Century, 1989; mem. adv. bd. Jour. Popular Film and TV, 1991—. Mem. Author's League of Am., Manuscript Soc. (trustee 1979-85, 92—), Elizabethan Club (bd. govs. 1970-72), Cosmos Club. Avocations: skiing, skating, golf. Home: 3013 44th Pl NW Washington DC 20016-3556 Office: Taft Assocs TV Prodn 1015 33rd St NW Apt 501 Washington DC 20007-3531

TAFT, NATHANIEL BELMONT, lawyer; b. Tarrytown, N.Y., Aug. 12, 1919; s. Louis Eugene and Etta Minnie (Spivak) Topp; m. Norma Rosalind Pike, May 22, 1943 (dec. Dec. 1997); children: Charles Eliot, Stephen Pike. BS in Econs., Fordham U., 1940; JD, Harvard U., 1948. Bar: N.Y. 1949. Asst. to gen. counsel N.Y. State Ins. Dept., Albany, 1948-50; law dept. N.Y. Life Ins. Co., N.Y.C., 1951-65, group dept., 1965-84, ret. as group v.p., 1984; sole practice law White Plains, N.Y., 1985—. Lectr., author on healthcare reform, 1992—. Contbr. articles to profl. jours.; author monographs on group ins. regulation. Bd. dirs. Westchester Philharmonic, 1991-2002, pres., 2001-02. Mem. ABA, N.Y. State Bar Assn., Nat. Assn. Physicians (sec.-treas. 1991—). Republican. Jewish. Avocations: golf, writing. Home and Office: 16 Sparrow Cir White Plains NY 10605-4624 E-mail: nat@nattaftlaw.com.

TAFT, NELLIE LEAMAN, artist; b. Cin., May 22, 1937; d. Hulbert and Elizabeth (Brady) Sutphin; m. A.M. Gammell, Dec. 1, 1973 (div. Apr. 1981). AB, Briarcliff Jr. Coll., 1957; BA, Columbia U., 1968; MA, Tchrs. Coll., 1970. Counselor Oreg. State Sch. for Deaf, Salem, 1960; asst. tchr. art Brearley Sch., N.Y.C., 1961; tchr. pottery Greenwich House Pottery, 1965-66; tchr. Lexington Children's Ctr., 1965-66; intern New World Sch., Hackensack, N.J., 1969-70; tchr. The Caedmon Sch., N.Y.C., 1970-73; founder, prin. The Learning Ctr., East Greenwich, R.I., 1978-81. Cons. in field. One-woman shows include Carnegie Art Ctr., Ky., 1984, Closson's Gallery, Cin., 1986, 1989, 1995, Wooden Tent Gallery, Mass., 1990, Gallery 68, Belfast, Maine, 1992, Between the Muse Gallery, Rockland, Maine, 1996, St. Botolph Club Odyssey's, Boston, 2002, exhibited in group shows at John S. Ames Gallery, Belfast, Ireland, 1994, Contemporary Art Ctr., Cin., 1994, Nielsen Gallery, Boston, 1998, 1999, 2001, Muse Gallery, 1998, 1999, Maine Coast Artist Gallery, 1999, Represented in permanent collections Cin. Art Mus., Cin. Bell Tel. Bd. dirs. Cambridge Art Assn.; nat. com. mem. Whitney Mus. Fellow, Va. Ctr. for Creative Arts, 2002; scholar Clarissa Bartlett Traveling scholar, 1991, Albert H. Whitin Traveling scholar, 1991. Mem. St. Botolph Club (art com.), Camargo Club. Avocations: tennis, golf, kayaking, flying, dancing.

TAFT, S. TUCKER, computer scientist; b. Cleve., Mar. 4, 1953; s. Seth C. and Frances P. (Prindle) T.; m. Phyllis Robin Yale, June 27, 1982; children: Rebecca Yale, Maia Yale. AB summa cum laude, Harvard Coll., 1975. Programmer U. Hosps., Cleve., 1970-71, Digital Equipment Corp., Maynard, Mass., 1972; sys. programmer Harvard U., Cambridge, 1975-79; computer scientist AverStar, Inc. (formerly Intermetrics, Inc.), 1980-87, chief scientist, 1988-2000; chief tech. officer AverCom Corp., Burlington, Mass., 2000—02; pres. SofCheck, Inc., Lexington, 2002—. Author: (programming language) Ada 95, 1995; contbr. articles to profl. jours. Bd. dirs. Lexington (Mass.) Montessori Sch., Lexington; mem. Jackson Lab., Bar Harbor, Maine, 1987—. Mem. Assn. for Computing Machinery, IEEE Computer Society. (assoc.). Democrat. Avocations: tennis, skiing, biking, roller blading. Home: 14 Moon Hill Rd Lexington MA 02421-6113

TAFT, SETH CHASE, retired lawyer; b. Cin., Dec. 31, 1922; s. Charles Phelps and Eleanor K. (Chase) T.; m. Frances Prindle, June 19, 1943; children: Frederick, Thomas, Cynthia, Tucker. BA, Yale U., 1943, LL.B., 1948. Bar: Ohio 1948. Assoc. Jones, Day, Reavis & Pogue, Cleve., 1948-59, ptnr., 1959-88. Mem. Cuyahoga County (Ohio) Bd. Commrs., 1971—78, pres., 1977—78; mem. Cuyahoga County Charter Commn., 1958—59; pres. Fedn. for Cmty. Planning, Cleve., 1986—89, Cleve. Internat. Program, 1990—94; chmn. Substance Abuse Initiative Greater Cleve., 1989—, Coun. Internat. Programs USA, 1999—2002, Cleve. Coun. World Affairs, 2000—02; Rep. candidate for mayor of Cleve., 1967; for gov. of Ohio, 1982. With USNR, 1943—46. Home: 6 Pepper Ridge Rd Cleveland OH 44124-4904 Office: Jones Day Reavis & Pogue 901 Lakeside Ave E Cleveland OH 44114-1190 E-mail: sethtaft@aol.com.

TAFT, SHELDON ASHLEY, lawyer; b. Cleve., Mar. 2, 1937; s. Kingsley Arter and Louise Parsons (Dakin) T.; m. Rebecca Sue Rinehart, Dec. 26, 1962; children: Mariner R., Ashley A., Curtis N. BA, Amherst Coll., 1959; LLB, Harvard U., 1962. Bar: Ohio 1962. Assoc. Vorys, Sater, Seymour & Pease, Columbus, Ohio, 1965-69, 71-73, ptnr., 1974—2001, of counsel, 2002—; chief legal counsel Pub. Utilities Commn. Ohio, 1969-71. Ohio bd. advisors Chgo. Title Ins. Co., 1967-98. Rep. candidate for justice Ohio Supreme Ct., 1974; trustee Opera Columbus, 1989—, pres., 1991-93, life trustee, 1995—. 1st lt. USAF, 1963-65. Mem. ABA (pub. utilities sect.), Ohio State Bar Assn. (pres. pub. utilities com. 1984-87), Columbus Bar Assn. (pub. utilities com.), Ohio Camera Collectors Soc. (pres. 1985-87), Rocky Fork Hunt and Country Club, Capital Club, 41 Club. Congregationalist. Avocation: camera collecting. Home: 27 Sessions Dr Columbus OH 43209-1440 Office: Vorys Sater Seymour & Pease PO Box 1008 52 E Gay St Columbus OH 43216-1008

TAFT, WILLIAM HOWARD, IV, federal agency administrator; b. Washington, Sept. 13, 1945; s. William Howard and Barbara Hoult (Bradfield) T.; m. Julia Vadala, May 4, 1974; Maria Consetta, William Howard V, Julia Harris. BA, Yale U., 1966; JD, Harvard U., 1969. Bar: D.C. 1969. Assoc. Winthrop, Stimson, Putnam & Roberts, N.Y.C., 1969-70; atty.-advisor to chmn. FTC, Washington, 1970; prin. asst. to dep. dir. Office of Mgmt. and Budget, 1970-72, exec. asst. to dir., 1972-73; exec. asst. to sec. HEW, 1973-76, gen. counsel, 1976-77; ptnr. Leva, Hawes, Symington, Martin & Oppenheimer, 1977-81; gen. counsel The Pentagon, 1981-84; dep. sec. def. Dept. Def., 1984—; perm. rep. U.S. Mission to NATO, 1989—92; ptnr. Fried Franks, Washington, 1992—2001; legal adviser U.S. Dept. State , 2001—. Recipient Disting. Service award HEW, 1975 Mem. D.C. Bar Assn., Lit. Soc. (Washington) Clubs: Cosmos (Washington), Leo (Washington). Republican. Office: US Dept State Legal Adviser 2201 C St NW Washington DC 20520*

TAFURI, WILLIAM, sculptor; Student, SUNY, Farmingdale, 1966-67; student in Jewelry Design, Fashion Inst. Tech., N.Y., 1978, Mechanics Inst., 1978; student in Interior Design, N.Y. Inst. Tech., 1982. Instr. in design and technique Acad. Goldsmiths and Jewellers, N.Y., 1988-97; tchr. applied arts Herricks Union Free Sch. Dist., New Hyde Park, 1993-95. Artist-in-residence Art Camp, New Milford, Conn., 1994; lectr. in field. One-man exhbns. include Russell Salon, Oyster Bay, N.Y., 1994, Baffa Art Gallery, Sayville, N.Y., 1996; group exhbns. include Forum Gallery, Jamestown, N.Y., 1992, Stamford (Conn.) Art Assn., 1992, Downey (Calif.) Mus. Art, 1992, Corp. Art Works, Ltd., Schaumburg, Ill., 1992, Outrlimits Art Gallery, N.Y.C., 1992, 93,

Macy's, L.I., N.Y., 1992, Islip (N.Y.) Art Mus., 1993, 94, Art 54 Gallery, Soho, N.Y., 1993, Shelter Rock Art Gallery, Manhasset, N.Y., 1994, Sea Cliff (N.Y.) Gallery, 1994, Chelsea Ctr., Muttontown, N.Y., 1995, Design Gallery, Davis, Calif., 1995, George and Gertrude Wisser Meml. Libr., Old Westbury, N.Y., 1995, 1-800-Flowers, Massapequa Park, N.Y., 1995, Gallery Authentique, Roslyn, N.Y., 1995, Broom St. Gallery, Soho, N.Y., 1996, AHRC Mansion, Brookville, N.Y., 1996, Paterson (N.J.) Mus., 1997, Poly. U. Libr., Farmindale, N.Y., 1997, Arizona Iced Tea, Lake Success, N.Y., 1997, Chesterwood Mus., Stockbridge, Mass., 1998, Multevend, Inc., Bay Shore, N.Y., 1998, Mather Meml. Hosp., Pt. Jefferson, N.Y., 1999; contbr. articles to profl. jours. Mem. Internat. Sculpture Ctr., Profl. Sculptors Guild, N.Y. Artists Network, Nassau County Mus. Art. Studio: 266 Middle Island Rd Unit 6 Medford NY 11763-1525

TAGATZ, GEORGE ELMO, retired obstetrician, gynecologist, educator; b. Milw., Sept. 21, 1935; s. George Herman and Beth Elinore (Blain) T.; m. Susan Trunnell, Oct. 28, 1967; children: Jennifer Lynn, Kirsten Susan, Kathryn Elizabeth. AB, Oberlin Coll., 1957; MD, U. Chgo., 1961. Diplomate Am. Bd. Obstetricians and Gynecologists, Am. Bd. Reproductive Endocrinology (examiner, bd. reproductive endocrinology 1976-79). Rotating intern Univ. Hosps. of Cleve., 1961-62, resident in internal medicine, 1962-63; resident in ob-gyn U. Iowa, 1965-68; sr. research fellow in endocrinology U. Wash. dept. obstetrics and gynecology, 1968-70; asst. prof. ob-gyn U. Minn. Med. Sch., 1970-73, assoc. prof., 1973-76, prof., 1976-2000, ret., 2000, asst. prof. internal medicine, 1970-73, dir. div. reproductive endocrinology, 1974-92. Mem. fertility and maternal health adv. com. FDA, USPHS, HHS, 1982-86; cons. in field, 1986-87. Ad hoc editor: Am. Jour. Ob-Gyn, Fertility and Sterility; contbr. articles to profl. publs. Served with M.C. U.S. Army, 1963-65. Mem. AMA, Minn., Hennepin County med. socs., Minn. Obstet. and Gynecol. Soc., Am. Coll. Ob-Gyn (subcom. on reproductive endocrinology 1979-82), Endocrine Soc., Am. Fertility Soc., Central Assn. Obstetricians and Gynecologists, U. Iowa Ob-Gyn Alumni Soc. Home: 5828 Long Brake Trl Edina MN 55439-2622

TAGER, LOUISE ARLENE, supreme court advocate; b. Johannesburg, South Africa, Nov. 4, 1935; d. Abe Harold and Fanny (Stein) Cohen; m. Harris Hirsch Joseph Tager, July 5, 1955; children: Erle, Beverley, Saul. BA, U. Witwatersrand, 1965, LLB, 1970, diploma in Tax Law, 1975; ML, Harvard Law Sch., 1978. cert. advocate supreme ct. South Africa. Tutor Sch. Law U. Witwatersrand, 1969, sr. bursar Sch. Law, 1970, lectr. Sch. Law, 1971-74, sr. lectr. Sch. Law, 1975-78, prof. Sch. Law, 1978-89, hon. prof. Sch. Law, 1990-94; exec. dir. The Law Review Project, 1985-96, dean faculty of law, 1980-85; prof. extraordinarius, dept. mercantile law U. South Africa, 1995-96; resigned, 1997; prof. extraordinary dept. mercantile law U. Orange Free State, 1999-2001. Dir. Zakhelizwe, 1988-97, Progress Through Employment, 1989-97, Alexandra TREK Recration Edn. Ctr., 1990-97; bd. dirs. TRANSNET Ltd., 1990—, chmn. 1996—; chmn. U.S. S. Africa Leadership Devel. Exchg. Program USSALEP, 1990-96, Rural and Urban Devel. Corp., 1991—, ORT Science and Tech. Edn. Project, 1992, The Law Review Project, 1985-96, Barloworld Ltd., 1992—, Legal Assist Ltd., 1993-96, Women's Devel. Bus., 1993—, Wooltru Ltd., 1993—, Theta Securities Ltd, 1996, Ind. Bus. Enrichment Ctr., 1993-98, Ind. Bus. Finance Ctr., 1993-98, Truworths Internat. Ltd., 1998—, South African Inst. Bus. Ethics Ltd., 1991—, Nt. Industrial Chamber, 1991—, Coun. Free Market Found., 1992—; trustee Internat. Assn. Students Interested in Economic & the Mgmt. Process (AIESEC), 1995—. Author: Negotiable Instruments Lawsa Student Texts, 1984; contbr. chpts. to books. Chmn. VATWATCH, South Africa, 1990-91, Bus. Practices Com., 1988-99; mem. standing com. Sml. Claims Ct. Johannesberg, 1985—, Coord. Consumer Coun. of South Africa, 1988-95; mem. deregulation com. Competition Bd. of South Africa, 1987-94; mem. Land Affairs Adv. Com., 1989-92; mem. Nat. Manpower Commn., 1993-94, Nat. Health Legislation Rev. Com., 1995-96, mem. standing adv. commn. on company law, 1996-99. Recipient Paul Harris award Rotary Internat. Mem. Soc. Advs. South Africa. Jewish. Avocations: aerobics, gardening. Home: 48 8th Ave Lower Houghton Johannesburg 2198 South Africa

TAGGART, G. BRUCE, government program executive; b. Phila., Apr. 8, 1942; s. Robert Henry Taggart and Rachael Elizabeth Burtt. BS in Physics, Coll. William and Mary, 1964; postgrad. in engineering mechanics, U. Pa., 1964-65; PhD in Physics, Temple U., 1971. Instr. dept. physics Drexel U., Phila., 1970; asst. prof. dept. physics Va. Commonwealth U., Richmond, 1971-77, assoc. prof., 1977-82, prof., 1982-83; from mgr. materials sci. tech. to prin. staff mem., phys. scis. tech. divsn. BDM Internat., McLean, Va., 1983-90; program dir. materials theory, divsn. materials rsch. NSF, Washington, 1990—. Vis. asst. prof. dept. physics Temple U., Phila., 1970-71; rsch. assoc. with theory group Oak Ridge (Tenn.) Nat. Lab., 1974; vis. prof. dept. theoretical physics Oxford (Eng.) U., 1978, Fed. U. Pernambuco, Recife, Brazil, 1980; vis. assoc. prof. dept. physics U. Ill., Urbana, 1978-79; guest worker with statis. physics group thermophysics divsn. Nat. Inst. Standards and Tech., Gaithersburg, Md., 1978-88; lectr. dept. physics and astronomy U. Md., College Park, 1989-90; vis. scientist divsn. materials rsch. on leave from BDM Internat., NSF, 1989-90; presenter in field. Referee (jours.) Phys. rev., Physics Letters, Jour. of the Physics and Chemistry of Solids, Acad. Press, Dept. Energy, Def. Advanced Rsch. Projects Agy., NSF, AAAS; numerous profl. jours. Scholar Coll. William and Mary, 1964; Ford fellow U. Pa., 1964-65; NSF summer fellow and Univ. fellow Temple U., 1971. Mem. AAAS, Am. Phys. Soc. (condensed matter physics divsn., materials physics divsn., polymer physics divsn.), Materials Rsch. Soc., Sigma Pi Sigma. Achievements include research in condensed matter physics, materials science and statistical mechanics. Office: Nat Sci Found Divsn Materials Rsch 4201 Wilson Blvd Arlington VA 22230-0002

TAGGART, GANSON POWERS, management consultant; b. Albany, N.Y., Aug. 16, 1918; s. Ralph Cone and Ruth Harriett (Townsend) T.; m. Paulett Long, June 30, 1945; children: H.Tee, Paulett Long, Cornelia V.C. BSChemE, U. Mich., 1940, MSChemE, 1941; postgrad., Northea. Sch. Advanced Mgmt., 1964. Registered engr., Mass. Mng. dir. Badger N.V., The Hague, The Netherlands, 1965-70; v.p. world sales Badger Co., Cambridge, Mass., 1970-71; sr. v.p., dir. Badger Co. Inc., 1978-82; mgmt. cons. Devel. Scis. Inc., Sandwich, Mass., 1972-77; chmn. bd. Serapis Energy Inc., Boston, 1982-85, dir.; pres. Mgmt. Sys. Inc., 1984—. Chmn. bd. dirs. William K. Stout Pub. Co., 1995—; bd. dirs. E.F. Schumacher Soc. Contbr. articles to mags. Oil mem. Energy Facilities Siting Coun. Mass., Boston, 1979-82; mem. Winchester (Mass.) Planning Bd., 1971-77, Winchester Town Meeting, 1960-64; mem. exec. com. Internat. Sch. The Hague, 1965-70; trustee Ledges Condominium Assn., 1992-98, chmn., 1998; trustee USS Constn. Mus., 1989-95, treas. 1991-92; moderator Winchester Unitarian Soc., 1983-93; active Mus. Sci., Boston, Found. Global Cmty. Lt. (j.g.) USNR, 1944-48. Mem. AIChE (chmn. Boston sect. 1955, Order of Xiphias), Soc. Chem. Industry (London), Conservation Law Found., Am. Chem. Soc., World Bus. Acad., Inst. Noetic Scis., Chemists Club (N.Y.C.), Annisquam Yacht Club (Gloucester, Mass.), Downtown Club (Boston). Office: PO Box 516 7 Church St Winchester MA 01890-1862 *Hard work and flexibility in doing and thinking pays big dividends, as long as you are honest with yourself and others. I have always tried to see things from the other person's point of view, to give them the benefit of the doubt. I strive always to do the best I can and I do not spend a lot of time analyzing or criticizing what is wrong with others. And most important is a wonderful wife who accepts constructively life as it is dealt to you.*

TAGGART, HELEN M. adult education educator, nurse; b. Savannah, Ga., Dec. 6, 1946; d. Thomas Anthony and Ruth Elizabeth (Sisson) McKenzie; m. Thomas Robert Taggart, Mar. 9, 1968; children: Kathleen Taggart Swanner, Thomas Robert Jr. BSN, Armstrong State Coll., 1978; MSN, Ga. So. U., 1992; postgrad., U. Ala., Birmingham, 1995—. Staff nurse St. Joseph's Hosp., Savannah, 1967-68, 77-89, head nurse Ga., 1971-74, St. Mary's Hosp., Athens, 1968-71; instr. Armstrong State Coll., Savannah, 1989-92; asst. prof. Armstrong Atlantic State U., 1992—. Profl. adv. com. Nat. Multiple Sclerosis Soc., Atlanta, 1992-96; bd. mem. Ga. Bd. Nursing, Atlanta, 1994—; mem. Clin. Simulation Task Force Nat. Coun. State Bds. Nursing, Chgo., 1996-99. Editor, contbr.: Adult Nursing in Acute Community, 1998; contbr. articles to profl. jours. and chpts. to books. Counselor Multiple Sclerosis Support Group, Savannah, 1989-97. Nat. Assn. Orthop. Nurses rsch. grantee, 1996, U. Ala. (Birmingham) traineeship grantee, 1997, Armstrong Atlantic State U. rsch. grantee, 1997-98. Mem. Nat. League Nurses (exec. bd. 1996-98), Assn. Bus. Women Am. (exec. bd. 1994-96), Nat. Assn. Orthop. Nurses (rsch. com. 1995-99), Ga. Nurses Assn. (exec. bd. 1992-96). Avocations: gardening, swimming, snow skiing. Home: 6 Mulberry Bluff Dr Savannah GA 31406-3226 Office: Armstrong Atlantic State University 11935 Abercorn St Savannah GA 31419-1989

TAGGART, JOHN K. operations executive; b. Teaneck, N.J., Feb. 6, 1953; s. John Frances and Lillian (McGlew) T.; m. Janet Taggart, Oct. 6, 1984; children: Jenna, Michael. BS in Indsl. Engring., Newark Coll. of Engring., 1975. Cert. Practitioner Inventory Mgmt., Integrated Resource Mgmt. MFG planner Ohaus Scale Corp., Florham Park, N.J., 1975-77; MRP co-ordinator inventory sys. mgr. Singer Sewing Corp., Elizabeth, 1978-80; mfr. cons. Sperry Univac, Parsippany, 1981-86, UNISYS, Berkley Heights, 1986-92; v.p. ops. Dragoco, Totowa, 1992—. Mem. U.S. Del. on Materials Mgmt. to Soviet Union, 1991. Mem. Am. Prdn. & Inventory Ctrl. Soc. Roman Catholic. Avocations: karate, auto club. Home: 14 Rillo Dr Wayne NJ 07470-3419 Office: Dragoco 10 Gordon Dr Paterson NJ 07512-2204

TAGGART, LINDA DIANE, women's health nurse; b. Balt., June 14, 1940; d. Louis and Annie Helena (Heertje) Glick; divorced; 1 child, Keri Anne. AS in Nursing, Pensacola Jr. Coll., 1967; BA, U. West Fla., 1970; postgrad., St. Joseph's Coll., 1976-78. RN, Fla., Ala. Staff nurse Bapt. Hosp., Pensacola, Fla., 1967-70, head nurse, 1970-72; dir. in-svc. edn. Baycrest, Inc. Extended Care Facility, 1973, DON, 1973-74, Medica Media, Pensacola, 1974; clinic adminstr. Cmty. Healthcare Ctr. (formerly Medica Media), 1974—. Dir. sex and health edn. Cmty. Healthcare Ctr., Pensacola, 1974—; regional dir. Medica Media, ea. U.S., 1990; testified before Jud. com. U.S. Ho. of Reps., 1994. Contbr. project, articles; appeared on (documentaries) Dateline NBC, 48 Hours, Nightline, Turning Point, ABC, CNN, (HBO documentaries) Soldiers in the Army of God, 2000, Keeping It Real, Program of RCRC, South Africa, 2002. Bd. dirs. Rape Crisis Ctr., Pensacola, 1976-91, chair, 1980, 84, 89 (Addie Brooks award 1984); mem. exec. com. Lakeview Community Mental Health Ctr., Pensacola, 1989 (Expression of Appreciation award 1980-91). Recipient Pioneer/Heroe award Fla. Abortion Coun., 1989, Woman of Yr. award NOW, 1995, Women's Equity Day award 1986. Mem. ACLU, Am. Assn. Sex Educators, Counselors and Therapists (cert. sex educator), Feminist Majority Found., Religious Coalition for Reproductive Choice (bd. dirs. 2000—), People for Am. Way, So. Poverty Law Ctr., Internat. Platform Assn., Planned Parenthood Fedn. Am. Democrat. Presbyterian. Avocations: skiing, jewelry design, cross-stitch, reading, ballroom dancing. Office: Cmty Healthcare Ctr 6770 N 9th Ave Pensacola FL 32504-7346

TAGGART, THOMAS MICHAEL, lawyer; b. Sioux City, Iowa, Feb. 22, 1937; s. Palmer Robert and Lois Allette (Sedgwick) T.; m. Dolores Cecilia Baroway Renfro, Jan. 4, 1963; children: Thomas Michael Jr., Theodore Christopher; m. Mary Ann Gribben, Feb. 7, 1976. BA, Dartmouth Coll., 1959; JD, Harvard U., 1965. Bar: Ohio 1965, U.S. Dist. Ct. (so. dist.) Ohio 1967, U.S. Dist. Ct. (no. dist.) Ohio 1981, U.S. Supreme Ct. 1997. Ptnr. Vorys, Sater, Seymour & Pease, Columbus, Ohio, 1965—. Lectr. Ohio Legal Ctr. Inst., Ohio Mfrs. Assn., Capital U. Ctr. for Spl. and Continuing Legal Edn. Capt. USMC, 1959-63. Mem. ABA, Ohio Bar Assn. (bd. govs. 1991-99, liability ins. com. 1996-97, 99-00, pres. 1997-98, trustee Found. 1996-98, 2000—, chair commn. on jud. evaluations 2000, Ohio Bar medal 1999), Columbus Bar Assn. (bd. govs., pres. 1989-90), Ohio Assn. Civil Trial Attys., Am. Arbitration Assn., Columbus Area C. of C. Methodist. Home: 145 Stanbery Ave Columbus OH 43209-1465 Office: Vorys Sater Seymour & Pease 52 E Gay St Columbus OH 43215-3161

TAGGE, ANNE, writer, not-for-profit organization administrator; b. Waltham, Mass., Oct. 20, 1954; d. Raymond and Anne (Weller) T. BA, Wellesley Coll., 1977. Pres., founder Susan Lee Campbell Inst., Wellesley, Mass., 1986—. Spkr. in field. Contbr. to newspapers, mags., jours., books. Recipient U.S./UNEP Achievement award, honoree Rolex awards for Enterprise; Town of Wellesley scholarship, Fulbright scholar; Salzburg Seminar fellow; French Ministry Fgn. Affairs grantee. Mem. Explorers Club. Home: Moshup Trail Aquinnah Marthas Vineyard MA 02535 Office: 37 Avon Rd Wellesley MA 02482-4618

TAGGETTE, DEBORAH JEAN, special education educator; b. Dover Foxcroft, Maine, Sept. 24, 1952; d. Ernest Lyford and Arlene Elizabeth (Dority) Fairbrother; m. Berton Louis Taggette, July 19, 1975; children: Angela Beth, Chad Berton. BS in Edn., U. Maine, Fort Kent, 1975. Asst. tchr. spl. edn. Community High Sch., Fort Kent, 1978-79, substitute tchr. spl. edn., 1980, tchr. severly handicapped, 1984-92, resource rm. tchr., 1992-94, self contained tchr., 1994—. Transistion team of disabled students Community High Sch., 1993. Tchr. religious edn. St. Charles Parish; foster parent. Mem. DAV (life mem.), Order of Ea. Star (Miriam 140), Order of Rainbow for Girls (worthy advisor chpt. 17 1970-71), Grand Assembly (Grand Cross of Colors 1970), Vet. Meml. Fund of St. Francis. Avocations: reading, sewing, snowmobiling, boating, camping. Home: 1033 Main St Saint Francis ME 04774-9701 Office: SAD 27 Community High Sch Pleasant St Fort Kent ME 04743-1240

TAGIURI, CONSUELO KELLER, child psychiatrist, educator; b. San Francisco; d. Cornelius H. and Adela (Rios) Keller; m. Renato Tagiuri; children: Robert, Peter, John. BA, U. Calif.-Berkeley; MD, U. Calif.-San Francisco. Diplomate Am. Bd. Psychiatry and Neurology. Resident psychiatry Mass. Gen. Hosp., Boston; staff psychiatrist Children's Hosp., 1951-59; med. dir. Gifford Sch., Weston, Mass., 1965-85; chief psychiatrist Cambridge (Mass.) Guidance Ctr., 1961-84; mem. faculty dept. psychiatry Harvard Med. Sch., 1965—; cons. early childhood program Children's Hosp., 1985—. Contbr. articles in field to books. Fellow Am. Orth. Psychiat. Assn., Mass. Med. Soc., New Eng. Coun. Child Psychiatry.

TAGLIAFERRI, LEE GENE, investment banker; b. Mahanoy City, Pa., Aug. 14, 1931; s. Charles and Adele (Cirilli) T.; B.S., U. Pa., 1957; M.B.A., U. Chgo., 1958; m. Maryellen Stanton, Apr. 29, 1962; children— Mark, John, Maryann. Div. comptroller Campbell Soup Co., Camden, N.J., 1958-60; securities analyst Merrill, Lynch, Pierce, Fenner & Smith, Inc., N.Y.C., 1960-62; asst. v.p. U.S. Trust Co. of N.Y., 1962-71; v.p. corporate finance div. Laidlaw & Co., Inc., N.Y.C., 1972-73; pres. Everest Corp., N.Y.C., 1973— ; dir. Fairfield Communities Inc., UEC, Inc., LRA, Inc., Industrialized Bldg. Systems, Inc. Past pres. West Windsor Community Assn. Trustee Schuyler Hall, Columbia, Madison Sq. Boys Club. Served with AUS, 1953-55. K.C. Clubs: University of Pa., Princeton (N.Y.C.). Home: 77 Lillie St Princeton Junction NJ 08550-1307 Office: 1 Penn Plz New York NY 10119-0002

TAGLIATTINI, MAURIZIO, construction executive, research historian, writer; b. Messina, Italy, June 2, 1933; came to U.S., 1959, naturalized, 1970; s. Giovanni and Vittoria (Federighi) T.; m. Marsha Croce, Nov. 4, 1973 (div. 1979). Diploma of Geometra, Inst. Tech. per Geometri, Modena, Italy. Founder, past pres. Tagliattini Marble Co., N.Y.C. Author: The Discovery of North America by European Navigators (with a critical study on the origin of Christopher Columbus), 1992. With NATO Air Force, 1957-58. Roman Catholic.

TAGLIENTE, JOSEPHINE MARLENE, artist; b. Chisholm, Minn., Nov. 23, 1939; d. Joseph and Carmela (DeLuca) T.; m. Wayne W. Brown, May 28, 1960 (div. 1972); children: Michael Anthony, Troy Tagliente, Roben Tagliente, Angela Monique, Ninon Terese, Anina Maria (dec.). Student, Mpls. Coll. Art and Design, 1957-59, Mankato State Coll., 1966, Kansas City Art Inst., 1972; MFA, U. Guanajuato, Mex., 1974. Artist-in-residence Jewish Cmty. Ctr., Wilmington, 1969; illustration chairperson, mem. faculty Ray Coll. of Design, Chgo., 1980-87; adj. faculty Paradise Valley C.C., Phoenix; spkr. in field. One-woman exhbn. Natalini Gallery, Chgo., 1986; group exhbns. include Windbell Gallery, Wilmington, Del., Newark (Del.) Gallery, Galeria San Miguel, Mex., Galeria Osman, Mex., Galeria Condor, Mex., Torres Gallery, Albuquerque, Dartmouth Gallery, Albuquerque, Edith Lampert Gallery, Santa Fe, La Luna Nueva, Santa Fe, Herberger Theatre, Phoenix Little Theatre, Artesimo Gallery, Scottsdale, Ariz., Del. Art Mus., Wilmington, Sky Harbor Airport, 1994, Westaff, UK-Ariz., Canticles: Sight and Sound, 2002, others; represented in corp. collections Collins, Miller & Hutchins, Chgo., Mt. Sinai Hosp., N.Y.C.; also pvt. and pub. permanent collections; represented by Artisimo Gallery, Scottsdale; illustrations published in books; poetry published in anthologies; inventor garden products, office implements. Vol. art educator St. Anne's Intercity, Wilmington, 1967-68, Recreation Intercity, Chgo., 1978-79; cultural advocate for homeless Cultural Labor Party, Chgo., 1980-87, cultural advocate for minority concerns, 1985-88. Recipient Fine Art award Artist's Guild of Chgo., 1977, Print Drawing award, 1978, Educator/Svcs. award Sauk Area Career Ctr., 1984. Mem. Nat. Mus. Women in Arts, The Drawing Soc., Soc. Children's Book Writers and Illustrators, Statue of Liberty-Ellis Island Found. Social Democrat. Avocations: writing, digital painting, raising turtles and studying their habitat. E-mail: joyfulsunrise@qwest.net.

TAGUE, CHARLES FRANCIS, retired engineering, construction and real estate development company executive; b. N.Y.C., Aug. 16, 1924; s. Charles and Isabelle (Carey) T.; m. Alicia Patricia Murtha, Aug. 6, 1949; children: Patrick, Charles, Thomas, Mary Alicia Haberman, James, Beth Anne Giuliano BS, Fordham U., 1952. Auditor Scovell, Wellington & Co., N.Y.C., 1951-57; comptroller Chem. Constrn. Corp., 1957-75; contr. Burns and Roe, Inc., Oradell, N.J., 1975-81; fin. dir. Alfred Sanzari Enterprises, Hasbrouck Heights, 1981-84; v.p. fin. Alexander Summer Co., 1984-93; ret., 1993. Mem. Colts Neck (N.J.) Sports Found.; active Boy scouts Am.; mem. Lacawac Sanctuary Steering Com.; pres. parish coun. Ch. of Presentation; mem. pastoral coun. St. Thomas More Cath. Ch. With USNR, 1943-46, PTO, ETO, NATOUSA. Mem. Controllers Inst., Nat. Contract Mgmt. Assn., Assn. Govt. Accts., Scranton Club. Democrat. Roman Catholic. Address: Seabrook Village 506 North Shore Neptune NJ 07753

TAHA, ASSAD M. surgeon; b. Nabatieh, Lebanon, Dec. 12, 1955; came to U.S. 1980; s. Muhyddin S. and Hind (Jaber) T. BS, Am. U. Beirut, 1976, MD, 1980; PhD, Med. Coll. Ohio, Toledo, 1992. Diplomate Am. Bd. Surgery, Am. Bd. Surg. Critical Care. Surgery resident Good Samaritan Hosp., Cin., 1980-82, Med. Coll. Ohio, Toledo, 1982-85, attending surgeon, 1985-94, Am. U. of Beirut, Lebanon, 1994—, assoc. prof. surgery and physiology Lebanon, 1994—. Dir. hyperbaric medicine Med. Coll. Hosp., Toledo, 1987—94, dir. surg. intensive care, 1988—94, assoc. prof. surgery; vis. surgeon surg. critical care Brigham & Women's Hosp., Harvard Med. Sch., Boston, 2000—01; vis. assoc. prof. Harvard U., 2000—01. Mem. editl. bd. European Jour. Emergency Surgery and Intensive Care; contbr. articles to profl. jours. Recipient AMA Physician Recognition award, 1987, 1991, 1997, 2000; grantee, Ohio Lions, 1987—92, Am. U.- Beirut U. Rsch. Bd., 1993—2000. Fellow ACS, Am. Physiologic Soc., Am. Soc. Gastrointestinal Endoscopy, European Assn. Trauma and Emergency Surgery, Royal Coll. Surgeons Can., Soc. Critical Care Medicine, Undersea and Hyperbaric Med. Soc., Am. Soc. Laser Medicine and Surgery, Am. Coll. Nutrition, Internat. Coll. Surgeons, Assn. Acad. Surgery, Shock Soc., European Soc. Intensive Care Medicine, World Assn. Disaster and Emergency Medicine; mem. AAUP, numerous others. Avocations: chess, bridge. Office: Am U of Beirut 850 3d Ave 18th Fl New York NY 10022-6222 Fax: 212-583-7650, 961-135-4305. E-mail: at03@aub.edu.lb.

TAHIR, MARY ELIZABETH, retail marketing and management consultant; b. Greenwood, Miss., Dec. 14, 1933; d. Mahmoud Ibrahim and Mary Constance Tahir. Student, U. Miss., 1951-53. Cert. Profl. Cons., Acad, Profl. Cons. and Advisors. Mgmt. trainee Neiman-Marcus Co., Dallas, 1954-56; asst. buyer D.H. Holmes Co. Ltd., New Orleans, 1956-58, buyer, 1958-65, assoc. divisional mdse. mgr., 1965-67, divisional v.p., 1969-79, corp. v.p., gen. mdse. mgr., 1979-89; pres. Liz Tahir & Assocs., 1990—. Bd. dirs. World Trade Ctr. *Liz Tahir was one of the first women nationally to be named a corporate vice president of a major retail organization, the 142 year old D.H. Holmes Company, Ltd. in New Orleans. She has expanded her career to international marketing, as an entrepreneur founding Liz Tahir & Associates Consulting. She writes for various business magazines and newsletters, and has been interviewed and quoted in such publications as The Wall Street Journal, Inc. Magazine, Advertising Age. In her international professional speaking, she presents seminars and lectures on such topics as Branding/Positioning, Negotiation Skills, Merchandising, and Leadership across the U.S. as well as Brazil, Mexico, Australia, New Zealand, and Japan.* Author: Mexico's Cosmetic and Fragrance Market: Past, Present and Future Opportunities, 1991, The Changing World of Mexican Retail Opportunities, 1991, Mexico: Window of Opportunity, 1991, Art of Negotiating, 1993, Negotiating More Profitable with Your Suppliers, Customers and Employees, 1994, Sizzling Customer Service, 1998. Bd. dirs. Vieux Carre Property Owners Assn., New Orleans, 1990, YWCA, 1996—. Recipient Role Model award YWCA, 1990, Woman Bus. Owner of the Yr. award, 1996. Mem. Women's Profl. Coun. (pres. 1998, chmn. New Choices 1989), Fashion Group Internat. (Alpha award 1987-88, Lifetime Achievement award 1993), Nat. Spkrs. Assn., Am. Mktg. Assn. (bd. dirs. 1996—, pres. 1997), Am. Assn. Profl. Cons., Am. Mgmt. Assn., Fgn. Rels. Assn. (bd. dirs. 1992—, pres. bd. dirs. 1994-96), Nat. Retail Fedn. Avocations: art collecting, textiles collecting. Home: 817 Esplanade Ave New Orleans LA 70116-1940 Office: Liz Tahir & Assocs 201 Saint Charles Ave Ste 2500 New Orleans LA 70170-2500 E-mail: liz@liztahir.com.

TAI, CHEN-TO, electrical engineering educator; b. Soochow, China, Dec. 30, 1915; came to U.S., 1943; m. Chia Ming Shen, Apr. 28, 1941; children: Arthur, Bing, Julie, David, James. BSc, Tsing Hua U., Beijing, 1937; DSc, Harvard U., 1947. Rsch. fellow Harvard U., Cambridge, Mass., 1947-49; sr. rsch. scientist Stanford Rsch. Inst., Palo Alto, Calif., 1949-54; assoc. prof. Ohio State U., Columbus, 1954-56, prof., 1960-64, Tech. Inst. Electronics, Brazil, 1956-60, U. Mich., Ann Arbor, 1964-86, prof. emeritus, 1986—. Author: Dyadic Green's Functions, 1971, 2d edit., 1994, Generalized Vector and Dyadic Analysis, 1991, 2d edit., 1997; contbr. numerous articles to profl. jours. Fellow IEEE (life, Centennial award 1985, Heinrich Hertz medal 1998); mem. U.S. Nat. Acad. Engring. Home: 1155 Arlington Blvd Ann Arbor MI 48104-4023 Office: Univ of Mich Dept EECS Ann Arbor MI 48109 E-mail: ctnming@aol.com., tai@eecs.umich.com.

TAI, CHONG-SOO STEPHEN, political scientist, educator; b. Seoul, Oct. 15, 1940; came to U.S., 1969, naturalized, 1983; s. Hyung-Kyoon and Ock-Hee (Park) T.; m. Susan Gillja Kang, Aug. 28, 1965; children: Audrey, Elizabeth, Michael. BA, Yonsei U., Seoul, 1963; MA, Ill. State U., 1972, Northwestern U., 1972, PhD, 1974. Lectr. Northwestern U., Evanston, Ill., 1974-75; asst. prof. U. Ark., Pine Bluff, 1976-80, assoc. prof. polit. sci., 1980-86, prof. polit. sci., 1986—, dir. polit. sci. program, 1980—. Fulbright program adviser, 1986—; great decisions coordinator Fgn. Policy Assn., Pine Bluff, 1977-84; cons. S.E. Ark. Planning Commn., Pine Bluff, 1979-80; active Southwestern Internat. Studies Consortium, Mex., 1986; pres. Internat. Faculty Club, U. Ark., Pine Bluff, 1986-91; vis. prof. polit. sci., Kyung Hee U., Korea, 1992-93. Contbr. articles to profl. jours. Bd. dirs. Korean Cmty. Assn. Little Rock, 1996—. Served with Korean AF, 1963-67. Grantee KOTN radio sta., 1978, Ark. Endowment for Humanities, 1979-80, NEH, 1980; Fulbright-Hays scholar, China, 1985. Fellow Internat. Ctr. for Asian Studies; mem. Am. Polit. Sci. Assn., Ark. Polit. Sci. Assn., Assn. for Asian Studies, Assn. Korean Polit. Studies N.Am. Roman Catholic. Avocation: golf, swimming, collecting jazz albums, Samurai films, and Chinese and Japanese paintings and calligraphy. Home: 11324 Hickory Hill Rd Little Rock AR 72211-4368 Office: U Ark Pine Bluff 1200 University Dr Pine Bluff AR 71601-2799 E-mail: tai_c@vx4500.uapb.edu.

TAI, ELIZABETH SHI-JUE LEE, library director; b. Si-Ann, China, Aug. 12, 1942; came to the U.S., 1965; d. Jun-Yee Lee and Fang-Yee Liu; m. Hsiang Tai, Dec. 29, 1969; children: Alan C., Victoria C., Brian C. BA in English Lang. and Lit., Nat. Cheng Kung U., Taiwan, 1965; M in Libr. and Info. Sci., Tex. Woman's U., 1967. Sr. libr. Queens (N.Y.) Borough Pub. Libr., 1967-73; asst. regional libr. Cin. Pub. Libr., Libr. for Blind and Physically Handicapped, 1973-75; libr. Ga. State Libr., Atlanta, 1975-78; dir. Poquoson (Va.) Pub. Libr., 1979—. Vol. Va. chpt. ARC-York County, 1980—; vice-chair Peninsula Ret. Sr. Vol. Program Coun., Newport News, Va., 1994—99, chair, 2000; mem. York County (Va.) Sch. Sys. Extend Program Coun., 1997; mem. Va. social svcs. bd. York County/City of Poquoson, 2002—; bd. dirs. Peninsula Ret. Sr. Vol. Program Coun. , Newport News, Va., 2001—. Named City Employee of Yr., City of Poquoson, 1989; recipient Letter of Commendation, Va. Gov. James Gilmore III, 2001. Mem. ALA, Va. Libr. Assn., Va. Pub. Libr. Dirs. Assn. (Outstanding Pub. Rels. award 1998, Outstanding Facility award 1998, Outstanding Young Adult Program award 1999, Outstanding Children's Program award 1999, Outstanding Pub. Rels. Project award 2001, Outstanding

Pub. Rels. Project award 2002), Tidewater Area Libr. Dirs. Coun. Avocations: reading, gardening, swimming, tennis. Home: 129 Loblolly Dr Yorktown VA 23692-4254 Office: 500 City Hall Ave Poquoson VA 23662-1996 E-mail: etai@ci.poquoson.va.us.

TAI, EMILY SOHMER, history educator, writer; b. N.Y.C., Feb. 24, 1959; d. Bernard and Margot (Rosette) Sohmer; m. Paul Maurice Tai, June 7, 1986; children: Ariella Victoria, Cordelia Elizabeth. BA summa cum laude, Queens Coll., 1982; PhD, AM, Harvard U., 1996. Tchg. fellow dept. history Harvard U., Cambridge, Mass., 1985-86, sect. leader core curriculum, fall 1985; assoc. prof. history Queensborough C.C., Bayside, NY, 1997—; rsch. fellow CUNY, 2001—02. Adj. asst. prof. history Queensborough C.C., N.Y.C., 1996-97; scholars' rep. scholars' svcs. com. N.Y. Pub. Libr., N.Y.C., 1995; C.C. Humanities Assn. fellow, Ford Found. seminar Library of Congress, 1999; presenter papers in field. Contbr.: (ency.) Medieval Trade, Travel, and Exploration, 2000, (jour.) Reconstruction, 1994. N.Y. Regents scholar, Jewish Found. for Edn. of Women scholar, 1982-85; Harvard U. History Dept. traveling fellow, 1988, Fulbright-Hays rsch. fellow, 1989-90, rsch. fellow, Libr. Congress, 1999; PSC-CUNY Rsch. grantee, 2001-2002. Mem.: Am. Soc. LEgal History, Coord. Coun. of Women in Hist. Profession, Medieval Club of N.Y. (treas.), Mediterranean Studies Assn., World History Assn., Medieval Acad. Am., Am. Hist. Assn. (contbr. monthly mag. 1996), CUNY/PSC Union, Phi Beta Kappa, Phi Alpha Theta. Jewish. Office: Queensborough C C Dept History Med Arts 408 22205 56th Ave Flushing NY 11364-1432

TAIGANIDES, E. PAUL, agricultural and environmental engineer, consultant; b. Polymylos, Macedonia, Greece, Oct. 6, 1934; s. Pavlos Theodorou and Sophia ((Elezidou) T.; m. Maro Taiganides, Dec. 25, 1961; children: Paul Anthony, Tasos E., Katerina. BS in Agri. Engring., U. Maine, 1957; MS in Soil and Water Engring., Iowa State U., 1961, D of Environ. Engring., 1963. Cert. engr., Iowa, Colo. Rsch. assoc., asst. prof. Iowa State U., Ames, 1957-65; prof. Ohio State U., Columbus, 1965-75; mgr., chief tech. adviser UN, FAO, Singapore, Singapore, 1975-84, mgr., chief engr. Singapore, 1984-85, mgr., chief tech. adviser Kuala Lumpur, Malaysia, 1985-87; mgr., owner EPT Cons., Columbus, 1987—. Cons. EPD/Hong Kong, 1988-92, WHO, UN, Denmark, Poland, Czechoslovakia, 1972-75, Internat. Devel. Rsch. Ctr., Can., China, Asian, 1984-89, NAE, Thailand, 1990, FAO, Malaysia, Foxley & Co., Nu-Tek Foods; environ. advisor to Bertam Devel. Corp., Kuala Lampur, Malaysia, 1992—; waste cons. to U.S. Feed Grains Coun., Taiwan, Malaysia, 1992, Venezuela, 1993; pres. Fan Engring., (US) Inc., 1991—, Red Hill Farms, Ohio, 1992—. Author: (video) Waste Resources Recycle, 1985, Pig Waste Treatment and Recycle, 1992; editor: Animal Wastes, 1977; co-editor Agricultural Wastes/ Biological Wastes, 1979; contbr. articles to profl. jours. Bd. govs., v.p. Singapore Am. Sch., Singapore, 1978-83; clergy-leity congress Greek Orthodox Ch., Houston, 1974. Recipient rsch. awards EPA, 1971-75, Water Resources Inst., 1968-73; rsch. grantee UNDP, FAO, IDRC, GTZ, Asean, 1975-88. Fellow Am. Soc. Agrl. Engrs. (chmn. dept., A.W. Farral award 1974), Am. Assn. Environ. Engrs. (diplomate); mem. Am. Soc. Engring. Edn. (div. chmn.), Singapore Lawn Tennis Assn. (v.p. 1980-84), Am. Club (mgmt. com. 1980-85), Sigma Xi. Greek Orthodox. Avocations: tennis, classical music, folk dancing. Home and Office: 1800 Willow Forge Dr Columbus OH 43220-4414

TAILLON, JAMES HOWARD, orthotist; b. Watertown, N.Y., May 21, 1946; s. Howard James and Pauline (Henderson) T.; m. Carolyn Ann Davidson, Sept. 1, 1970 (div. Oct. 1981); children: Michelle Nicole, Andrew James, Karen Elizabeth; m. Diane Marie Schomers, May 5, 1984; children: Stafford James, Elliot James. BSET, Memphis Naval Air Tech. Tng. Unit, 1967; postgrad., NYU, 1973. Cert. orthotist. Staff orthotist Frees & Tyo, Syracuse, N.Y., 1973-76; chief othotist U. Mich. Med. Ctr., Ann Arbor, Mich., 1976-78; dir. othotics and prosthetics D.T. Watson Hosp. for Children, Sewickley, Pa., 1978-80; dir. rsch. Camp Internat., Jackson, Mich., 1980-84; ptnr. The Brace Ctrs. Ltd., Green Bay, Wis., 1984-98; pres. The Elford Group, Ltd., 1998-2000; CEO Argent Corp., 2000—02; investment advisor William R. Hough & Co., Naples, Fla., 2002—. Inventor multicentric knee joint, pelvic stabilization device, Rolz scar massage device. With USN, 1965-69. Fellow Am. Back Soc.; mem. Am. Acad. Orthotists/Prosthetists, Am. Orthotic/Prosthetic Assn., Internat. Soc. Prosthetics and Orthotics, Rehab. Engring. Soc. of N.Am. Avocations: sport aviation, hiking, travel. Home: 5633 Turtle Bay Dr # 27 Naples FL 34108 Office: Wm R Hough & Co 500 S 5th Ave Ste 509 Naples FL 34102 E-mail: jtaillon@hough.com.

TAIMUTY, SAMUEL ISAAC, physicist; b. West Newton, Pa., Dec. 20, 1917; s. Elias and Samia (Hawatt) T.; BS, Carnegie Inst. Tech., 1940; PhD, U. So. Calif., 1951; m. Betty Jo Travis, Sept. 12, 1953 (dec.); children: Matthew, Martha; m. Rosalie Richards, Apr. 3, 1976; stepchildren: Charles Scott Holman, Martha Ruth Holman, Elizaeth Ann Holman. Physicist, U.S. Naval Shipyard, Phila. and Long Beach, Calif., 1942-46; rsch. asst. U. So. Calif., 1947-51; sr. physicist U.S. Naval Radiol. Def. Lab., 1950-52, SRI Internat., Menlo Park, Calif., 1952-72; sr. staff engr. Lockheed Missiles & Space Co., Sunnyvale, Calif., 1972-89; cons. Sci. Applications Internat. Corp., 1990—; cons. physicist, 1971—. Mem. Am. Phys. Soc., Sigma Xi. Episcopalian. Contbr. articles to sci. pubs. Patentee in field. Home: 3346 Kenneth Dr Palo Alto CA 94303-4217 E-mail: staimnty@sigmaxi.org.

TAINTER, JOSEPH ANTHONY, archaeologist; b. San Francisco, Dec. 8, 1949; s. George Washington and Elizabeth Anne (O'Reilly) T.; m. Bonnie Catherine Bagley, Nov. 4, 1977; 1 child, Emmet Bagley. BA, U. Calif., 1972; MA, Northwestern U., 1973, PhD, 1975. Asst. prof. U. N.Mex., Albuquerque, 1975-78; rsch. asst. prof. Eastern N.Mex. U., Portales, 1978-80; archaeologist USDA Forest Svc., Albuquerque, 1980-94; project leader Rocky Mountain Rsch. Sta., 1994—. Pres. N.Mex. Archaeol. Coun., Albuquerque, 1979-80; cons. U.S. Nat. Com. of Scientific Com. on Problems of the Environ., UN, 1995, Monts Mandingues Classified Forest, Bamako, Mali, 1992-93, Nat. Directorate of Arts and Culture, Mali, 1998, 99; dirs. lectr. Getty Rsch. Ctr., 1994; plenary address Internat. Soc. Ecological Econs., 1994. Author: The Collapse of Complex Societies, 1988, 10th printing, 1999, Korean edit., 1999; co-editor: Evolving Complexity and Environmental Risk in the Prehistoric Southwest, 1996; co-editor: The Way the Wind Blows: Climate, History and Human Action, 2000. Grantee NSF, 1974-75. Mem. AAAS, Am. Anthropol. Assn., Soc. for Am. Archaeology. Achievements include developed and tested new theory explaining why societies and civilizations collapse; developed and tested new theory that relates economic sustainability to sociopolitical complexity; developed first archaeological research program in USDA Forest Service Research. Home: PO Box 145 Corrales NM 87048-0145 Office: Rocky Mountain Rsch Sta 333 Broadway SE Ste 115 Albuquerque NM 87102-3497

TAISHOFF, LAWRENCE BRUCE, publishing company executive; b. Washington, Aug. 30, 1933; s. Sol Joseph and Betty (Task) T.; m. Nancy Lee Stuckey, Sept. 17, 1962 (div. 1979); children: Robert Paul, Randall Lawrence, Jonathan Bradford. AB, Duke U., 1955. Asst. dir. Sta. WTOP-TV, Washington, 1955-56; with Broadcasting Publs., Inc., 1958—, pres., pub., 1971-91, chmn., 1991—, also dir.; adviser Cahners Consumer/Entertainment Pub. divsn. Cahners Pub. Co., 1991—; v.p. Jolar Corp., 1952-72, dir., 1958-72. Gen. ptnr. Jolar Assocs., Washington, 1972—; chmn. bd., pres. Graphictype, Inc., 1976-86, also dir.; chmn., pres. Solar Corp., 1982-86; chmn. Broadcasting-Taishoff Found., 1982-2001; chmn., CEO Chuckie Broadcasting, Ardmore, Okla., 1993—, Trustco, Washington, 1988—; CEO Solar Investments, Naples, Fla. Co-author radio and TV segment Britannica Book of the Yr., 1983—. Trustee Washington Journalism Ctr., 1982-93, Nat. Press Found., 1993—, mem. adv. bd., 1993—; bd. dirs. Nat. Press Found., 1982—, mem. exec. com., 1990-94; mem. journalism and comms. exec. com. Capital Campaign for Arts and Scis., Duke U., 1984—, mem. athletic adv. bd., 1999—; bd. advisors Am. Journalism Ctr., Budapest, 1991-95; mem. White House Press Corps, 1983—; mem. Met. Washington Bd. Trade, 1970—; team capt. pubs. divsn. United Givers Fund drive, 1965; mem. admissiosn adv. com. Duke Alumni Assn., 1968-70; mem. U.S. Senate and Ho. of Reps. Periodical Press Gallery, 1958—; trustee Broadcast Pioneers Ednl. Fund Inc., 1985; judge VFW Voice of Democracy contest, 1978—; mem. bd. judges Peabody awards, 1985-91; mem. Am. U. Sch. Comms. Disting. Adv. Commn., 1985—; mem. Founders Soc. Duke U., 1985—, Duke Athletic Adv. Bd., The Mus. of TV and Radio Roundtable, 1988-89; bd. dirs. Ardissone, Naples, Fla., 1994-99; chmn., trustee Taishoff Family Found. With AUS, 1956-58. Mem. IEEE (sr.), Internat. Radio & TV Soc., Broadcast Pioneers (life, bd. dirs., exec. com. Broadcast Pioneers Libr.), Am. Sportscasters Assn. (exec. com. 1990—), White House Corrs. Assn., Nat. Press Club, Woodmont Country Club (Rockville, Md.), Cosmos Club (Washington), Sigma Delta Chi, Zeta Beta Tau. Jewish. Office: 4420 Mercantile Ave Naples FL 34104-3348

TAIT, C(OLUMBUS) DOWNING, JR. physician, medical educator; b. Valdosta, Ga., Sept. 3, 1923; s. C. Downing Sr. and Mary Lucretia (Jacobs) T.; m. Nancy Reep, Aug. 25, 1956; children: Carl, Jennifer. BA in Philosophy, U. Va., 1943, MD, 1947; cert. in psychoanalytic medicine, Columbia U., 1957. Diplomate Am. Bd. Psychiatry and Neurology; cert. in adult psychoanalysis. Intern Bellevue Hosp., N.Y.C., 1947-48; resident in psychiatry Compton (Calif.) Sanitarium, 1948-49, N.Y. State Hosp., Orangeburg, 1950-51; psychoanalytic trainee Columbia U., N.Y.C., 1950-51, 53-57; pvt. practice, 1953-64; assoc. prof. Emory U. Sch. of Medicine, Atlanta, 1964-67, prof. psychiatry, 1967-81; pvt. practice N.Y.C., 1953-64, Atlanta, 1977—. Geographical tng. and supervising psychoanalyst Emory Columbia U. Psychoanalytic Tng., Atlanta, 1966-78; dir. rsch. Ga. Mental Health Inst. Emory U. and State, Atlanta, 1965-71. Co-author: Delinquents, Their Families, and the Community, 1962; contbr. articles to profl. jours. Cons. to juvenile ct. judges Atlanta, 1966-71; Lt. USNR, 1951-53. Rsch. fellowship Atomic Energy Commn., Duke U., 1949, Yale U., 1950. Fellow Ga. Psychiat. Assn., Am. Psychiat. Assn.; mem. AMA, Atlanta Med. Assn., Ga. Med. Assn., Internat. Psychoanalytic Assn., Am. Psychoanalytic Assn., Atlanta Psychoanalytic Assn. (pres. 1979-81). Avocations: travel, music. Home and Office: 3895 Chaucer Wood NE Atlanta GA 30319-1687

TAIT, JOHN REID, lawyer; b. Toledo, Apr. 7, 1946; s. Paul Reid and Lucy Richardson (Rudderow) T.; m. Christina Ruth Bjornstad, Mar. 12, 1972; children: Gretchen, Mary. BA, Columbia U., 1968; JD, Vanderbilt U., 1974. Bar: Idaho 1974, U.S. Dist. Ct. Idaho 1974, U.S. Ct. Appeals (9th cir.) U.S. Supreme Ct., Nez Perce Tribal Ct. Assoc. Keeton & Tait, Lewiston, Idaho, 1974-76, ptnr., 1976-86, 89—, Keeton, Tait & Petrie, Lewiston, 1986-88; nominated. Chmn. bd. No. Rockies Action Group, Helena, Mont., 1985-86, bd. dirs., 1981-88; mem. Lewiston Hist. Preservation Commn., 1975-94, chmn., 1988-94; bd. dirs. Idaho Legal Aid Svcs., Boise, 1975-99, Idaho Housing Agy., Boise, 1984-91, St. Joseph Regional Med. Ctr. Found., Inc., 1989-94, Lewiston Ind. Found. for Edn., Inc., 1996—; Dem. precinct committeeman, 1976-86, state committeeman, 1977-94, 2000—; del. Dem. Nat. Conv., 1980, 84; regional coord. Idaho State Dem. Party, 1996-99; treas. Larry LaRocco for Congress, 1990, 92. With U.S. Army, 1968-71. Recipient Pro Bono Svc. award Idaho State Bar, 1988, Cmty. Recognition award Lewiston Intergovtl. Coun., 1992, Spl. Recognition award Idaho Legal Aid Svcs., 1993. Mem. ABA, ATLA, Idaho Trial Lawyers Assn. (regional dir. 1976-77, 86-88, 97—), Idaho State Bar (bd. dirs. worker's compensation sect. 2002-), Clearwater Bar Assn. (sec. 1974-76, pres. 1984-86), Consumer Attys. Calif., Workplace Injury Litigation Group (bd. dirs. 2002-). Office: Keeton & Tait PO Drawer E 312 Miller St Lewiston ID 83501-1944 Fax: 208-746-0962. E-mail: lewlawus@lewiston.com.

TAIT, ROBERT E. lawyer; b. Lima, Ohio, Sept. 3, 1946; s. Robert and Helen (Smith) T.; m. Donna G. Dome, June 22, 1968; children: Heather, Jennifer, Robert. BA, Kenyon Coll., 1968; JD, U. Mich., 1973. Bar: Ohio 1973, U.S. Dist. Ct. (so. dist.) Ohio. 1976, U.S. Dist. Ct. (no. dist.) Ohio 1976, U.S. Dist. Ct. Md. 1980, U.S. Ct. Appeals (6th cir.) 1981, U.S. Supreme Ct. 1982. Ptnr. Vorys, Sater, Seymour & Pease, LLP, Columbus, Ohio, 1973—. Staff counsel Govs. Select Com. on Prevention Indsl. Accidents, Columbus, 1977-78. Served with U.S. Army, 1969-70. Fellow Columbus Bar Found.; mem. ABA (litigation sect., products liability com.), Ohio Bar Assn. (worker's compensation com.), Columbus Bar Assn. (workers compensation and professionalism coms.), Def. Rsch. Inst. (workers compensation com.), Columbus Def. Assn., Assn. Def. Trial Attys. (exec. com. 1991-94, treas., 2002-), Fedn. Def. and Corp. Counsel. Home: 2045 Wickford Rd Columbus OH 43221-4223 Office: Vorys Sater Seymour & Pease PO Box 1008 52 E Gay St Columbus OH 43215-3161

TAITT, EARL PAUL, psychiatrist, army officer; b. L.A., Nov. 6, 1956; s. Earl and Mary (Freitas) T.; m. Puruca Estepa, May 11, 1985; children: Anamaria, Earl. AA, East L.A. Coll., 1976; BS, U. Calif., Irvine, 1978; MD, Northwestern U., Chgo., 1984. Commd. capt. U.S. Army, 1984, advanced through grades to maj., 1991; intern in psychiatry Tripler Army Med. Ctr., Honolulu, 1984-85; resident in psychiatry Eisenhower Army Med. Ctr., Ft. Gordon, Ga., 1985-88; staff psychiatrist Community Mental Health Ctr., 1988; div. psychiatrist, chief mental health 10th Mountain Div., Ft. Drum, N.Y., 1988-90; staff psychiatrist Community Mental Health Ctr., Ft. Meade, Md., 1990—; chief resident in psychiatry U.S. Army Hosp., Ft. Gordon, Ga., 1988. Cons. Army Drug and Alcohol Program, Ft. Drum, 1988-90, Installation Detention Facility, Ft. Meade, 1990—. Mem. San Gabriel (Calif.) Mission Parish Coun., 1975-76; pres. Medicai Soc., L.A., 1976. Mem. Assn. U.S. Army, Order of Green Key. Republican. Roman Catholic. Home: 14403 Altamaha Ct Orlando FL 32837-5425

TAK, TAHIR, cardiologist, researcher; b. Lahore, Punjab, Pakistan, July 18, 1951; arrived in U.S., 1985; s. E. Tak and E. Nathaniel. BS, Govt. Coll., Lahore, 1971; MD, U. Nijmegen, Holland, 1980; PhD, U. Maastricht, Holland, 1989. Diplomate in internal medicine and in cardiovasc. diseases Am. Bd. Internal Medicine. Asst. prof. medicine U. So. Calif., L.A., 1989—96; assoc. prof. medicine U. Nev., Las Vegas, 1996—98; cardiologist Scott and White Clinic, Temple, Tex., 1998—2001; assoc. prof. Tex. A&M U. HSC, 1998—2001; cardiologist Marshfield (Wis.) Clinic, 2001—; clin. prof. U. Madison Sch. Medicine, 2002—. Fellow: ACP, Am. Coll. Cardiology, Am. Coll. Chest Physicians, Am. Heart Assn., European Soc. Cardiology. Home: 1213 W State St Marshfield WI 54449 Office: Marshfield Clinic 1000 N Oak St Marshfield WI 54449

TAKABE, KAZUAKI, gastroenterology surgeon, research scientist; b. Nishinomiya City, Hyougo, Japan, Aug. 12, 1966; s. Tokuji and Ayako T. MD, Niigata U., 1992; PhD, Yokohama City U., 1999. Rsch. trainee dept. legal medicine Niigata (Japan) U. Sch. of Medicine, 1992-93; surg. resident Niigata U. Hosp., 1993-94, Akita (Japan) Red Cross Hosp., 1994-95; surg. fellow Yokohama (Japan) U. Hosp., 1995-97; rsch. assoc. The Salk Inst., PBL, La Jolla, Calif., 1997—. Prof., chmn. gene diagnosis and therapy Internet Med. Coll., 2000—; com. mem. Soc. of Rsch. Fellows The Salk Inst., 1999—. Contbr. articles to profl. jours. Yoshida scholarship found. fellowship, 1997-2000. Mem. The Endocrine Soc., Internat. Liver Transplantation Soc., Internat. Assn. of Surgeons and Gastroenterologists, Japan Surg. Soc., Japanese Soc. of Gastroenterology, Japan Hepatology Soc. Office: The Salk Inst PBL 10010 N Torrey Pines Rd La Jolla CA 92037 Fax: 858-552-1546; Office Fax: 858-657-0925. E-mail: ktakabe@aim.salk.edu.

TAKACH, PATRICK BERNARD, small business owner; b. Columbia, S.C., Aug. 8, 1950; s. John Joseph and Eleanor (Hollis) T. BS, U. S.C., 1972, MA in Health and Phys. Edn., 1975. Beverage mgr. Steak and Ale, Columbia, 1973, Columbia Country Club, 1973-74, Tivoli Gardens, Columbia, 1974-75; mgr. Overlook Restaurant, Hilton Head Island, S.C., 1975-76; electrician Columbia, 1976-78; mgr. Scandinavian Health Spas, Akron, Ohio, 1978-80, European Health Spas, West Palm Beach, Fla., 1980-81; pres., chief exec. officer Southeastern Health Svcs., Inc. (Physicians Weight Loss Ctrs.), Columbia, 1981—. Founder Acad. Success, Columbia, 1984. Republican. Home: 140 Walnut Ln Columbia SC 29212-8609 Office: Southeastern Health Svcs Inc Physicians Weight Loss Ctrs 12A Clusters Ct Columbia SC 29210-4832

TAKACS, MICHAEL JOSEPH, educator; b. N.Y.C., July 28, 1940; s. Michael and Elizabeth Agnes (Scharschmidt) T. AB in Sociology, Fordham U., 1964; MA in Sociology, St. John's U., 1968. Tchr. Bklyn. Prep. Sch., 1964-67, Turtle Hook Sch., Uniondale, N.Y., 1968-73, 74-95, Nairobi U., 1971, Colegio San Ignacio, Rio Piedras, P.R., 1973-74. Vis. scholar Robert Black Coll., Hong Kong U., 1975, Ramkamhang U., Bangkok, 1975. Vol. cmty. outreach program Our Holy Redeemer Ch., Freeport, N.Y., L.I. Assn. for AIDS Care, L.I. People with AIDS Coalition, Advocacy Counseling Entitlements Svcs. of Ret. and Sr. Vol. Program, Safe Horizon 9/11 Disaster Assistance Program; advisor Nat. Jr. Honor Soc.; mem. Sr. Action in Gay Environment., L.I. bears. Mem. Nat. Coun. for Social Studies, Mid. States Coun. for Social Studies, L.I. Coun. for Social Studies, N.Y. State Coun. for Social Studies. Episcopalian. Home: 13915 83rd Ave Briarwood NY 11435-1561

TAKACS, WENDY EMERY, economics educator; b. Wayne, N.J., Aug. 3, 1947; d. Wendell Sherwin and Louise Marie (Shay) Emery. BA, Douglass Coll., 1969; MA in Internat. Rels., John Hopkins U., 1971, MA in Econs., 1973, PhD in Econs., 1976. Rsch. asst. Pres.' Commn. on Internat. Trade and Investment Policy, Washington, 1970-71; economist Internat. Fin. Div. Bd. Govs. Fed. Res. System, 1975-76; asst. then assoc. prof. U. Md., Balt., 1976—; profl. lectr. John Hopkins SAIS, Washington, 1976—. Rsch. fellow The Brookings Instn., Washington, 1973-74; vis. fellow dept. econs. U. Bristol, Eng., 1984-87, Inst. for Internat. Econs., Washington, 1986-87, Inst. for Internat. Econ. Studies, Stockholm, Sweden, 1987; cons. The World Bank, Washington, 1988—; co-dir. UNDP/World Bank Trade Expansion program, 1993—. Co-author Auction Quotas and U.S. Trade Policy, 1987; contbr. articles to profl. jours. Mem. Am. Econ. Assn., Can. Econ. Assn., Internat. Trade and Fin. Assn. (bd. dirs. 1991-93), Western Econ. Assn., Md. Combined Tng. Assn. (sec. 1980-82). Avocations: dressage and combined training, long distance walking. Office: U Md Dept Econs Baltimore MD 21228 Home: 1900 Long Corner Rd Mount Airy MD 21771-3738

TAKADA, FUJIO, jewelry store owner; b. Osaka, Japan, Dec. 20, 1955; s. Fujikazu Takada and Misako Kusunoki; m. Ryoko Shimaoka, June 3, 1986; children: Yuka, Yoshikuni. LLB, Kwansei Gakuin U., Nishinomiya, 1978; diploma in gemology, Gemological Inst. Am., Santa Monica, Calif., 1979. Pres., owner Takada Jewelry & Co., Ltd., Naniwaku, Japan. Gemological Inst. Great Britain fellow, 1980. Mem. Internat. Colored Stone Assn., Chibjo, Ono Grand Country Club, Tokyo Diamond Exch. Club. Avocation: golf. Office: Takada Jewelry & Co Ltd 1-13-8 Nambanaka 7th Fl Gombi-Nissei Bldg Naniwaku Osaka 556-0011 Japan

TAKAHASHI, JOSEPH S. neuroscientist, educator; b. Tokyo, Dec. 16, 1951; s. Shigeharu and Hiroko (Hara) T.; m. Barbara Pillsbury Snook, June 28, 1985; children: Erika S., Matthew N. BA, Swarthmore (Pa.) Coll., 1974; PhD, U. Oreg., 1981. Pharmacology rsch. assoc. NIMH, NIGMS, Bethesda, Md., 1981-83; asst. prof. Northwestern U., Evanston, Ill., 1983-87, assoc. chmn. neurobiology and physiology, 1988-96, assoc. prof. neurobiology and physiology, 1987-91, prof. neurobiology and physiology, 1991-96, Walter and Mary Elizabeth Glass prof. life scis., 1996—, acting assoc. dir. Inst. for Neurosci., 1988-95; investigator Northwestern U. Howard Hughes Med. Inst., 1997—. Psychobiology and behavior rev. com. NIMH, 1988-92; mem. Nat. Mental Health Adv. Coun., 1997—; neurosci. adv. com. Klingenstein Fund, 1999—. Assoc. editor Neuron; mem. adv. bd. Jour. Biol. Rhythms, 1984—; contbr. over 120 articles to profl. jours. Grantee Bristol-Myers Squibb, 1995—; recipient Alfred P. Sloan award A.P. Sloan Found., 1983-85, Searl Scholars award Chgo. Cmty. Trust, 1985-88, Merit award NIMH, 1987, Honma prize in biol. rhythms Honma Found., 1986, Presdl. Young Investigator award NSF, 1985-90, 6th C.U. Ariens Kappers award Netherlands Soc. for Advancement Nat. Scis., Medicine and Surgery, 1995, W. Alden Spencer award Columbia U., 2001. Fellow Am. Acad. Arts and Sci.; mem. Am. Soc. Human Genetics, Genetics Soc. Am., Soc. Neurosci., Soc. for Rsch. on Biol. Rhythms (adv. bd. 1986—), Mammalian Genome Soc. Achievements include discovery of the expression of circadian oscillations in cells from vertebrates; and identification of first circadian clock gene in mice. Office: Northwestern U Howard Hughes Med Inst 2153 N Campus Dr Evanston IL 60208-0877

TAKAHASHI, STEVEN SHIGERU, lawyer; b. Seattle, Sept. 12, 1962; s. George Etsu and Toshiko Takahashi. BA in Society and Justice, U. Wash., 1985; JD, U. Oreg., 1989. Bar: Wash. 1989. Staff atty. Assoc. Counsel for the Accused, Seattle, 1989—2001, Allstate Staff Counsel, Seattle, 2001—. Avocations: bodybuilding, travel, cooking, investing, fine dining. Office: 900 4th Ave Ste 1470 Seattle WA 98164 Home: Apt 202 120 1st Ave W Seattle WA 98119-4249

TAKAMURA, JEANETTE CHIYOKO, dean; b. Honolulu, Aug. 1, 1947; d. Jiro and Jane Chiseko (Ishida) Chikamoto; m. Carl Takeshi Takamura, May 17, 1974; 1 child, Mari Leigh. BA, U. Hawaii, 1969, MSW, 1972; PhD, Brandeis U., 1985. Program dir. Moiliili Community Ctr., Honolulu, 1972-74; instr. sch. medicine and social work U. Hawaii, 1975-78, asst. prof., 1982-86; dir. exec. office on aging Office of Gov., 1987-94; dep. dir. State Dept. of Health, 1995-97; asst. sec. for aging U.S. Dept. HHS, Washington, 1997—2002; endowed chair in applied gerontology and pub. svc. Calif. State U., L.A., 2001—02; dean, Sch. Social Work Columbia U., N.Y.C., 2002—. Ptnr. Browne/Takamura, Honolulu, 1985-86. Contbr. articles to profl. jours. and chpts. to books; editorial bd.: Aging Today, 1991—. V.p. Moiliili Community Ctr., 1977; adv. com. long term care Milbank Meml. Fund; adv. com. on aging issues World Econ. Forum. Grantee NIMH, 1982-84, U.S. Dept. HHS, 1985, 86, 89-90, 91. Mem. Nat. Assn. Statute Units on Aging (2d v.p. 1991-92), Am. Soc. on Aging (program planning com. 1992-93, exec. com. 1996—, nat. adv. bd. White House Conf. on Aging, 1995), Gerontology Soc. Am., Futurist Soc. Congregationalist. Avocations: travel, reading, walking. Office: Columbia U Sch Social Work McVickar Hall Rm 204 622 W 113th St New York NY 10025*

TAKANISHI, RUBY N. foundation administrator, researcher; b. Waimea Kaua'i, Hawaii, July 9, 1946; d. Kazuo and Misae (Tokushige) T.; m. Louis L. Knowles, Aug. 23, 1969; 1 child, Marika T. Knowles. AB in psychology with great distinction and honors, Stanford U., 1968; AM, U. Mich., 1969; PhD, Stanford U., 1973; postgrad., U. Chgo., 1969-70, Harvard U., 1978-79. Teaching asst. Bing Nursery Sch. Stanford U., 1968, teaching asst. Sch. Edn., 1972, 73; asst. prof. dept. edn. Grad. Sch. Edn. UCLA, 1973-80, acting head early childhood devel. specialization, 1974, faculty Bush Tng. Program in Child Devel. and Social Policy, 1978-80, assoc. prof., 1980-86; exec. dir. Carnegie Coun on Adolescent Devel Carnegie Corp., N.Y., 1986—. Vis. asst. prof. dept. psychology Yale U., 1980; adj. assoc. prof. Tchrs. Coll., Columbia U., 1981-82; exec. dir. Fedn. Behavioral, Psychol. and Cognitive Scis., Washington, 1982; co-investigator Asian-Am. Edn. Project, 1973-76; bd. dirs. Grantmakers for Children, Coun. Founds.; rsch. assoc. Stanford Ctr. for Rsch. and Devel. in Teaching, Stanford U., 1973; adv. bd. Ms. Found. for Women, 1992, divsn. biobehavioral scis. and mental disorders Inst. Medicine, 1992; U.S. rep. UNESCO Mexico Conf., 1972; Harvard-Henry A Murray Ctr., Cambrige, Mass., 1997, Agy. Health Care Rsch. and Quality/U.S. Dept. Health and Human Svcs., Washington, 1997—; cons. to numerous insts. Assoc. editor: Am. Psychologist; consulting editor: Rehab. Psychology, Young Children; mem. editorial bd. Early Childhood Rsch. Quar.; mem. bd. reviewing editors: Ednl. Researcher; reviewer Am. Ednl. Rsch. Journ., Child Devel., Health Psychology, Psychology of Women Quar., Rev. Ednl. Rsch.; contbr. articles to profl. jours., chpts. to books; co-author: Preparing Adolescents for the 21st Century, 1997. Bd. trustees St. Augustine-by-the-Sea Sch., Santa Monica, Calif., 1976-77; mem. child care com. Calif. LWV, 1975-77; legis. asst. Office of Senator Daniel K. Inouye, Washington, 1980-81. Named one of Outstanding Young Women of Am., 1978. Mem. AAAS, APA (fellow, dir. office sci. affairs 1984-86, adminstrv. officer for children, youth and family policy office of nat. policy studies 1982-83, pub. interest, ethnic minority), APHA, Am. Ednl. Rsch. Assn. (program chair learning and devel. 1978, program chair spl. interest group in early edn. 1980), Nat. Assn. Edn. Young Children (chair com. orgnl. history and archives 1976-78), Soc. Rsch. in Child Devel. (program com. 1985-89, governing coun. 1989-95), Soc. Rsch. in Adolescence, Phi Beta Kappa. Avocation: volunteering for community service. E-mail: ffcd-ruby@worldnet.att.net.

TAKASHIMA, KOICHI, technical specialist; b. Saitama City, Saitama, Japan, June 30, 1965; MBA(hon.) , U. Central Oklahoma, Edmond, OK, 1994—97. Telephone Charges Dept. NTT (Nippon Telegraph & Telephone Corporations, Kawagoe City, Japan, 1984—91; Technical Specialist Goldman Sachs, New York, NY, 1998—2002.

TAKASHIMA, SHIRO, biophysics educator; b. Tokyo, May 12, 1923; s. Atsuharu and Yoshie (Miyoshi) T.; m. Yuki Morita, June 26, 1953; children: Nozomi L., Makoto D. BS, U. Tokyo, 1947, PhD, 1955. Assoc. prof. Osaka U., Japan, 1959-63; rsch. scientist Walter Reed Med. Ctr., Washington, 1963-64; asst. prof. U. Pa., Phila., 1964-70, assoc. prof., 1970-76, prof. bioengring., 1976-92; prof. emeritus, 1993—. Mem. editorial bd. J. Biol. Physics., The Netherlands, 1977-97. Author: Electrical Properties of Biopolymers and

Membrane, 1989; (book chpt.) Principles and Technics of Protein Chemistry, 1968; contbr. articles to profl. jours.; organizer internat. confs. Bd. dirs. Japanese Assn. of Greater Phila., 1983-90. Recipient Vis. Prof. grants Ministry of Edn., Italy, 1984, Japan Soc. of Sci., 1977, Yamada Found., 1990, Disting. Svc. award overseas Japanese Edn., Kensho-Kai, Japan, 1997; decorated for disting. achievements in sci. and edn., Japanese Govt., 1997. Mem. IEEE, Biophysical Soc., N.Y. Acad. Scis. Democrat. Methodist. Achievements include rsch. into dielectric relaxation of biopolymers, electrical properties of excitable mempranes from nerves and muscles. Home: 659 Niblick Ln Wallingford PA 19086-6675 Office: U Pa Dept Bioengring Philadelphia PA 19104-6392 E-mail: Stakashima@earthlink.net., Takashim@eniac.seas.upenn.edu.

TAKASUGI, NAO, state official, business developer; b. Oxnard, Calif., Apr. 5, 1922; s. Shingoro and Yasuye (Hayashi) T.; m. Judith Shigeko Mayeda, Mar. 23, 1952; children— Scott, Russell, Ronald, Tricia, Lea. BS, Temple U., 1945; MBA, U. Pa. Wharton Sch., 1946. Mem. city council City of Oxnard, Calif., 1976-82, mayor, 1982-92; mem. Calif. State Assembly, 1992-98, chmn. revenue and taxation com. Bus. developer, cons.; commr. Oxnard Harbor Dist., 2000—. Profiled in Tom Brokaw's The Greatest Generation, 1999. Mem. Oxnard Planning Commn., 1974-76; pres. World Trade Ctr. Assn., Oxnard; apptd. (by Calif. gov.) chmn. UN Anniversary; assemblyman Calif. State Assembly 37th Dist.; bd. govs. Japanese Am. Nat. Mus. Decorated Order of Sacred Treasure with Gold Rayette medal Japanese Gov., 1992. Mem. Ventura County Japanese Am. Citizens League, World Trade Ctr. Assn. (pres. Oxnard chpt.), U.S. Conf. Mayors (mem. nat. adv. bd.), Nat. League of Cities (nat. bd. dirs.), Ventura County Transp. Com., League Calif. Cities (bd. dirs.), South Coast Area Bd. Dirs. (chmn. transp. com.), Assn. Ventura County Cities, Oxnard Housing Authoritry (chmn.), Oxnard Redevel. Agy. (chmn.), Optimists Club (Oxnard). Republican. Methodist. Home: 1221 El Portal Way Oxnard CA 93035-2511

TAKASUGI, ROBERT MITSUHIRO, federal judge; b. Tacoma, Sept. 12, 1930; s. Hidesaburo and Kayo (Otsuki) T.; m. Dorothy O. Takasugi; children: Jon Robert, Lesli Mari. BS, UCLA, 1953; LLB, JD, U. So. Calif., 1959. Bar: Calif. bar 1960. Practiced law, Los Angeles, 1960-73; judge East Los Angeles Municipal Ct., 1973-75, adminstrv. judge, 1974, presiding judge, 1975; judge Superior Ct., County of Los Angeles, 1975-76; U.S. dist. judge U.S. Dist. Ct. (cen. dist.) Calif., 1976—. Nat. legal counsel Japanese Am. Citizens League; guest lectr. law seminars Harvard U. Law Sch. Careers Symposium; commencement spkr.; mem. Legion Lex U. So. Calif. Law Ctr.; mem. Civil Justice Reform Act and Alt. Dispute Resolution Com., mem. Adv. Com. on Codes of Conduct of the Jud. Conf. of the U.S., 1987-92, Code of Conduct of Judges. Mem. editorial bd. U. So. Calif. Law Rev., 1959; contbr. articles to profl. jours. Calif. adv. com. Western Regional Office, U.S. Commn. on Civil Rights, 1983-85; chmn. blue ribbon com. for selection of chancellor L.A. C.C. With U.S. Army, 1953-55. Harry J. Bauer scholar, 1959; recipient U.S. Mil. Man of Yr. award for Far East Theater U.S. Army, 1954, Jud. Excellence award Criminal Cts. Bar Assn., cert. of merit Japanese-Am. Bar Assn., Lifetime Achievement award, 2000, Disting. Svc. award Asian Pacific Ctr. and Pacific Clinics, 1994, Freedom award Sertoma, 1995, Pub. Svc. award Asian Pacific Am. Legal Ctr. So. Calif., 1995, Trailblazer award So. Calif. region NAPABA, 1995, Spl. award Mex.-Am. Bar Assn., 1996, Spirit of Excellence award ABA, 1998, Pub. Svc. award Japanese Am. Citizens League, 1999; named Judge of Yr. Century City Bar Assn., 1995. Mem. U. So. Calif. Law Alumni Assn. (dir.). Office: US Dist Ct 312 N Spring St Los Angeles CA 90012-4701

TAKEDA, YASUNIKO, pathologist; b. Iiyama, Nagano, Japan, Mar. 16, 1927; arrived in U.S., 1953; s. Hideyoshi and Hanna Takeda; m. Tamako Kawai Takeda, May 5, 1958; children: James, Mary, Clara, Basil. MD, Chiba Sch. Medicine, Japan, 1952. Diplomate Am. Bd. Pathology, lic. physician Colo., 1969. Intern Bethesda Hosp., Cin., 1953—54; resident Sacred Heart Hosp., Spokane, Wash., 1954—56; resident in clin. pathology U. Colo. Hosp., Denver, 1956—58; instr. dept. medicine U. Colo., 1963—64, asst. prof., 1965—69, assoc. prof., 1969—78, prof., 1978—88, prof. emeritus medicine, 1988—, dir. immunoassay lab., 1972—86, dir. hematology lab., 1986—88, dir. Medicine 501 course, 1970—82. Reviewer manuscripts. Contbr. Recipient Career Devel. award, NIH, 1967—72; fellow Rsch. fellow, Am. Heart Assn., 1964—66; grantee Rsch. grantee, NIH, 1969—78. Fellow: Am. Soc. Clin. Pathologists, Coll. Am. Pathologists; mem.: Am. Physiol. Soc. Avocations: Go, gardening, ballroom dancing, fishing. Home: 635 Dexter St Denver CO 80220-5037 Office: University of Colorado Sch of Medicine 4200 E 9th Ave Denver CO 80262

TAKEI, GEORGE HOSATO, actor; b. L.A., Apr. 20, 1937; s. Takekuma Norman and Fumiko Emily (Nakamura) T. BA, UCLA, 1960, MA, 1964. Dir., chmn. Golden Security Bancorp, Alhambra, Calif., 1981--. Appeared in films, including Green Beret, 1967, Star Trek I-VI, 1979-91, Return from the River Kwai, 1989, Blood Oath, 1990, Prisoners of the Sun, 1990, Live by the Fist, 1993, Oblivion, 1994, Chongbal, 1994, Oblivion 2: Backlash, 1996, Trekkies, 1997, Bug Buster, 1998, Mulan, 1998, Who Gets the House, 1999; plays include The Wash, 1990, Undertow, 1988, Year of the Dragon, 1974, Macbeth, 1972; TV shows include, Star Trek, 1966-69, Playhouse '90, 1959, Hercules, 1998; (TV movie) Kissinger and Nixon, 1995, The Best Bad Thing, 1997. Trustee, Japanese Am. Nat. Mus., L.A. Theatre Ctr., 1984—; dir., v.p. So. Calif. Rapid Transit Dist., L.A., 1973-84. Mem. Nat. Japanese-Am. Citizens League (cultural affairs chmn. 1970-73), SAG, Assn. of Asian Pacific Am. Artists, Am. Pub. Transit Assn. (v.p. 1978-80). Democrat. Buddhist. Avocations: running, architecture, historic preservation. Mailing: 419 N Larchmont Blvd # 41 Los Angeles CA 90004-3013

TAKESHITA, TORU, computer software research scientist; b. Nishinomiya, Hyogo, Japan, Dec. 16, 1931; s. Hajime and Chiho (Kubota) T.; m. Yumiko Taniguchi, Oct. 20, 1962; children: Chikako, Jun. BA in Sci., U. Kyoto, Japan, 1957; PhD in Computer Sci., U. Beverly Hills, 1983. With IBM Japan Ltd., Tokyo, 1957-91; cons. software tech. IBM Hdqrs., Riji, Japan, 1983-87; mgr. Software Tech. Computer Sci. Inst. Tokyo Rsch. Lab., 1988-90, mgr. Computer Sci. Inst., 1990-91; sr. tech. staff mem. IBM, 1984-91, Tech. Coun. IBM Acad. Tech., 1989-91; prof. info. sci. Chubu U., 1991—; dir. Information Systems Ctr., 1993-97; dep. dir. Rsch. Inst. Information Sci., 1993-96; dir. Rsch. Inst. Info. Sci., 1997—. Author 30 books related to computer programming; contbr. numerous articles to profl. jours. Mem. IEEE, Assn. Computing Machinery, Info. Processing Soc. Japan, Japan Soc. Software Sci. and Tech., Japan Soc. Artificial Intelligence. Avocations: reading, photography, travel. Home: 3 11 1 410 Soshigaya Setagaya-ku Tokyo 157-0072 Japan Office: Chuba U Coll Bus Adm/Inf Sc 1200 Matsumoto-cho Kasugai-shi 487-8501 Japan

TAKETOMI, SUSAMU, physicist, researcher; b. Chiba City, Japan, Sept. 25, 1950; s. Manjiro and Kimie (Kida) T. B of Engring., U. Tokyo, 1975; DSc, Keio U., Yokohama, Japan, 1989. Rschr. Ctrl. Rsch. Lab. Fuji Elec. Co. Ltd., Yokosuka City, Japan, 1975-85; rschr. Matsumotoyushi Seiyaku Co. Ltd., Yao City, Japan, 1985—; vis. rschr. Keio U., Yokohama, Japan, 1985-89, Seikei U., Tokyo, 1990-95, U. Ctrl. Fla., 1995-96, U. Wash., Seattle, 1996-98, Kans. State U., Manhattan, 1998-2000, Nat. Inst. Stds. and Tech., Gaithersburg, Md., 2001—. Lectr. in field. Author: (book) Magnetic Fluids: Principle and Application, 1988, Magnetic Fluid Handbook, 1995. Mem. Am. Phys. Soc., Japan Phys. Soc., Japan Applied Phys. Soc. Avocation: playing violin. Home: 311 W Side Dr #304 Gaithersburg MD 20878 Office: Magnetic Materials Grp Bldg 223 Nat Inst Stds and Tech Gaithersburg MD 20899-8552

TAKEUCHI, HIROSHI, investment company executive, consultant; b. Okayama, Japan, Apr. 23, 1938; s. Buichi and Shigeko (Ueda) T.; m. Nobuko Hayashi, May 10, 1967; 1 child, Tsuruichi. degree in lit., degree in lang., Osaka U., 1962. Chief exports Mitsui Engr. & Shipbuilding Co., Tokyo, 1965-69, mgr. off-shore bus. devel., 1973-81; spl. rep. Mitsui Engring. & Shipbuilding Co., London, 1969-73; gen. mgr., exec. v.p. Mitsui Zosen (U.S.A.), Inc., Houston, 1981-90; exec. v.p., dir. Global Tech. Inc., 1990-93, Arlington, Va., 1993—. Mktg. cons. Iben, Albuquerque, N.M., 1993—, Takt Internat., N.J., 1993—. Avocations: writing, swimming, tennis, reading, diving. Office: Global Tech Inc 9576 Basket Ring Rd Columbia MD 21045-3420

TAKSAR, MICHAEL I. mathematician, educator, mathematician, researcher; b. Moscow, Sept. 9, 1949; s. Joshua M. Taksar, Tamara V. Vitold; m. Tanya S. Kuznetsova, Oct. 1, 1994; children: Maxime, Serge. PhD, Cornell U., 1979. Asst. prof. Stanford U., Palo Alto, Calif., 1979—84; assoc. prof. Fla. State U., Tallahassee, 1984—87; prof. SUNY, Stony Brook, 1987—. Mem.: IEEE (sr.), Inst. for Ops. Rsch. and Mgmt. Scis. Office: U Mo Columbia Dept Maths Columbia MO 65211 Home Fax: 573-882-1869. Personal E-mail: taksar@math.missouri.edu.

TAKUMI, ROY MITSUO, state legislator; b. Honolulu, Oct. 13, 1952; m. Wanda A. Kutaka; children: Aisha, Jaron. BA, Friends World Coll., 1991; MPA, U. Hawaii, 1993. Cmty. organizer, Osaka, Japan, 1977-83; program dir. Am. Friends Svc. Com., Honolulu, 1984-90; polit. dir. Hawaii State AFL-CIO, 1990-92, comms. dir., 1992—. Rep. Ho. of Reps., Honolulu, 1992—. Office: State Ho Reps State Capitol Honolulu HI 96813 E-mail: reptakumi@capitol.hawaii.gov.

TAL, JACOB, electronics executive; b. Tiberias, Israel, Nov. 29, 1940; s. Refael and Seniora Tboul; 1 child, Tomer; m. Rivka Barlev. BS, Technion, Haifa, Israel, 1966; MS, U. Minn., 1968, PhD, 1970. Research fellow U. Minn., Mpls., 1970-71; elec. engring. prof. U. Utah, Salt Lake City, 1971-78; research engr. Hewlett Packard, Palo Alto, Calif., 1978-81; founder, owner Motion Control Seminar, Mountain View, 1981—; founder, pres. Galil Motion Control, 1983—. Cons. Control Data, Mpls., 1970-75, Electro Craft, Mpls., 1970-78, Ford Motor Corp., Detroit, 1976-78, Burroughs Corp., Westlake, Calif., 1981-82. Author: Motion Control by Microprocessors, 1984, (with others) Incremental Motion Control, 1978, Motion Control Applications, 1989; contbr. articles to profl. jours. Mem. IEEE, Electronic Motion Control Assn. Avocations: folk dancing, hiking, windsurfing. Office: Galil Motion Control 3750 Atherton Rd Rocklin CA 95765 E-mail: jacobt@galilmc.com.

TALACHIAN, REZA, filmmaker; b. Isfahan, Iran, Dec. 1, 1944; arrived in U.S., 1972; s. Ramezan Talachian and Taybeh Ajalouiean. BS in Motion Picture Prodn., So. Ill. U., 1977, MA in Pub. Visual Communication, 1981. Bank mgr. Bank Saderat, Shaikh-Bahiee, 1969—72; sales mgr. Southwestern Co., Franklin, Tenn., 1975—76; instr. Sch. Cinema and TV, Tehran, Iran, 1977—79; creative arts project coord. Sta. WSIU-TV, Carbondale, Ill., 1979—81; owner, prodr., editor Megatrend Visual Prodns., Hollywood, Calif., 1981—82. (screenwriter): (films) Darraab, 1977; Ashura, 1979; (animator, editor): Graphic and Edn. Tech., 1978; (co-prodr., writer): (films) How to count from 1 to 5, 1978; (prodr., dir., editor) Bazzar, 1979; author: (book) Brief Critical History and Survey Catalogue of Iranian Films from 1896 to 1975, 1981, Discover Your Mind, 1987, The Hidden Path, 1997. Home: 400 Broadway # 503 Seattle WA 98122-5380

TALAFOUS, JOSEPH JOHN, SR. lawyer; b. N.Y.C., Sept. 6, 1929; s. Karol J. and Anna (Sulik) T.; m. Louise Lukac, June 18, 1955; children: Mary Lou, Joseph J. Jr., Caroline, Theresa. AB, Rutgers U., 1954; JD, Seton Hall U., 1959. Bar: N.J. 1959, U.S. Dist. Ct. N.J. 1959, U.S. Dist. Ct. (so. dist.) N.Y. 1959, U.S. Dist. Ct. (ea. dist.) N.Y. 1965, U.S. Supreme Ct. 1965, U.S. Ct. Internat. Trade 1982, N.Y. 1984. Practice (now Talafous & Talafous), Jersey City, 1959—. Asst. prosecutor Hudson County, N.J., 1962-63; asst. corp. csl. City of Jersey City, 1965-72; judge Mcpl. Ct., Jersey City, 1974-77; commr. N.J. Gov.'s Commn. Internat. Trade. Pres., Slovak Am. Heritage Found., Inc., 1976—; v.p. Slovak League Am.; Slovak mem. Gov.'s Ethnic Coun. Served with U.S. Army, 1951-53, Korea. Mem. ABA, N.J. Bar Assn., N.Y. State Bar Assn., Assn. of Bar of City of N.Y., Hudson County Bar Assn., Hague Acad. Internat. Law. Office: 61 Sip Ave Jersey City NJ 07306-3106

TALAL, MARILYNN GLICK, poet; b. N.Y.C. d. Philip Howard and Dorothy (Barchoff) Glick; m. Norman Talal, June 21, 1959; children: Andrew, Melissa. BA in English, Sarah Lawrence Coll., 1959; MA in British Lit., Columbia U., 1963; PhD in Creative Writing, U. Houston, 1993. Tchr. adult edn. U. Va. Ext., Arlington, 1965-66; poet, tchr. Bel Aire Sch., Tiburon, Calif., 1974-78, Calif. Poets in Schs., 1978-82, Marin county coord., 1979-82; tchr. assoc. U. Tex., San Antonio, 1982-85; writing cons. Jonathan Netanyahu Acad., 1986-87. Presenter writing workshops, 1993—. Contbr. poetry to lit. jours. and articles to profl. jours. Nat. Endowment for Arts Creative Writing fellow, 1991, Stella Erhart Meml. fellow U. Houston, 1987-88, Writers' League of Tex. poetry fellow, 2001, Writer's League of Tex., 2001; recipient 1st place award Napa Valley Poetry Conf., 1981. Mem. Acad. Am. Poets, PEN West.

TALALAY, PAUL, pharmacologist, physician; b. Berlin, Mar. 31, 1923; arrived in U.S., 1940, naturalized, 1946; s. Joseph Anton and Sophie (Brosterman) Talalay; m. Pamela Judith Samuels, Jan. 11, 1953; children: Antony, Susan, Rachel, Sarah. SB, Mass. Inst. Tech., 1944; student, U. Chgo. Sch. Medicine, 1944—46; MD, Yale U., 1948; DSc (hon.) , Acadia U., 1974. House officer, asst. resident surg. services Mass. Gen. Hosp., Boston, 1948—50; asst. prof. surgery U. Chgo., 1950—51, asst. prof. biochemistry, 1955—57, assoc. prof., then prof., 1957—63; asst. prof. Ben May Lab. Cancer Research, 1951—57, assoc. prof., then prof., 1957—63; John Jacob Abel prof., dir. dept., pharmacology and exptl. therapeutics Johns Hopkins Sch. Medicine, 1963—75, John Jacob Abel Distinguished Service prof., 1975—. Am. Cancer Soc. prof., 1958—63, 1977—. Sr. asst. surgeon USPHS, 1951—53; vis. prof. Guy's Hosp. Med. Sch., London, 1970, London, 1974—76; nat. adv. cancer coun. USPHS, 1967—71; vis. com. dept. biology MIT, 1964—67; bd. sci. advisers Jane Coffin Childs Meml. Fund for Cancer Rsch., 1971—80; bd. sci. consultants Sloan-Kettering Inst. Cancer Rsch., 1971—81. Hon. editl. adv. bd. Biochem. Pharmacology, 1963—68, editl. bd. Jour. Biol. Chemistry, 1961—66, Molecular Pharmacology, 1965—68, 1971—80, editor-in-chief, 1968—71. Recipient Premio Internationale la Madonnina Milan, 1978, Med. Alumni Disting. Svc. award, U. Chgo., 1978; fellow Guggenheim Meml., 1973—74; scholar Am. Cancer Soc., 1954—58. Fellow: Am. Acad. Arts and Scis.; mem.: NAS, AAAS (Theobald Smith award med. scis. 1957), Am. Soc. Pharm. and Exptl. Therpeutics, Am. Chem. Soc., Biochem. Soc., Am. Soc. Clin. Investigation, Am. Soc. Biochem. Molecular Biology, Am. Philos. Soc., Alpha Omega Alpha, Sigma Xi, Phi Beta Kappa. Home: 5512 Boxhill Ln Baltimore MD 21210-2039 Office: Johns Hopkins U Sch Medicine 725 N Wolfe St Baltimore MD 21205 Fax: 410-502-6818. E-mail: ptalalay@jhmi.edu.

TALAMANTES, ROBERTO, developmental pediatrician; b. Juarez, Chihuahua, Mex., June 19, 1952; came to U.S., 1955; s. Cruz and Viviana (Monarez) T.; m. Blanca Yolanda Chavez, Aug. 19, 1972; children: Christian, Steven. BS in Biology, U. Colo., 1972; MD, U. Autonoma Ciudad Juarez, 1979. Rotating intern Baylor Coll. Medicine, Houston, 1980-81, pediat. resident, 1981-84, devel. pediat. fellow, 1984-86; pvt. practice Gen. Devel. Pediatrics, Las Cruces, N.Mex., 1986—. Pres. IPA N.Mex., 1993-98; chmn. bd. dirs. Cimarron HMO, 1997—; pres. elect med. staff Meml. Med. Ctr., Las Cruces, 1993-94, pres., 1994-95, sec., 1992-94. With U.S. Army, 1972-74. With U.S. Army, 1972—74. Fellow Am. Acad. of Pediatrics, Soc. of Devel. Pediatrics; mem. N.Mex. Pediatric Soc., N.Mex. Med. Soc. Republican. Avocations: chess, guitar. Office: Hillside Circle Las Cruces NM 88011

TALAPATRA, DIPAK CHANDRA, aerospace engineer; b. Laur, Bangladesh, Jan. 20, 1942; s. Upendra Chandra and Jalada Sundari Talapatra; m. Brigitte Hildegard Fischer; children: Indrani, Anika. B with honors, Indian Inst. Tech., Kharagpur, 1963; M in Engring., McGill U., 1968; PhD, U. BC, Vancouver, Can., 1972. Sr. scientist ENSCO Inc., Springfield, Va., 1972—77; sr. rsch. engr. Gen. Tire, Akron, Ohio, 1977—80; mech. engr. Naval Ordinance Sta., Indian Head, Md., 1980; aerospace engr. NASA, Goddard Space Flight Ctr., Greenbelt, 1982—83, mgr. flight support sys., 1983—85, structural dynamics mgr., 1985—87; mgr. Can. programs NASA, Space Sta. Program Office, Reston, Va., 1987—92; mgr. NASA liaison in Can. Internat. Space Sta. Program, Montreal, 1992—. Patentee light weight arch type structures for large reflective mirrors for space and ground based telescopes (U.S. Patent #406634, 1977); contbr. articles. Presenter HS-Space Awareness Presentation, Montreal, 2000, Internat. Tng. Environ. Leadership Group, Brazil Environ. Observations from Space, Montreal, 1995—. Recipient NRC of Can. Rsch. Assistantship, McGill U., 1966—68, U. BC, 1968—72. Mem.: ASME. Avocations: tennis, swimming, badminton, reading, art. Office: NASA International Space Station Program 2101 NASA Road 1 Houston TX 77058-3963 Office Fax: 450-926-4948. Business E-mail: dipak.talapatra@space.gc.ca.

TALARICO, MARIA THERESA, tax accountant; b. Chgo., July 11, 1960; d. Alfredo and Maria Rose (Altomari) Talarico. BS in Commerce, DePaul U., Chgo., 1982, MS in Taxation, 1988. CPA, Ill. Jr. tax acct. Harris Trust and Savs. Bank, Chgo., 1982-86, tax acct., 1986-87, sr. tax acct., 1988-89; tax supr. Aon Corp., 1989-91; sr. tax. cons. Arthur Andersen & Co., 1991-92, experienced sr. tax cons., 1992-94, asst. tax mgr., 1994-97, tax mgr., 1997—2001, Deloitte & Touche, 2001—. Mem. AICPA, Ill. Soc. CPAs.

TALARICO, RUDOLPH DOMINIC, retired urologist; b. Newark, May 7, 1934; s. Gaetan and Frances (Corbo) T.; m. Pamela Nelson, July 30, 1966; children: Patricia Jane Kelly, Christine Frances. BA, Seton Hall U., 1956; MD, N.J. Coll. Medicine, 1960; MA, Monmouth U., 1993. Diplomate Am. Bd. Urology. Intern Jersey City Med. Ctr., 1960-61; resident in surgery Georgetown U. Hosp., Washington, 1961-62; resident in urology St. Luke's Hosp., N.Y.C., 1964-68; pvt. practice, Neptune and Brick, N.J., 1968-97; ret., 1997. Capt. U.S. Army, 1962-64, Korea. Recipient cmty. svc. citation State of N.J., 1995. Fellow ACS; mem. N.Y. Acad. Medicine, Am. Urol. Assn., Phi Alpha Theta. Roman Catholic. Avocations: hunting, medical missionary work. Home: 114 Washington Ave Spring Lake NJ 07762-1428

TALAVERA, FRANCISCO, pharmacist, writer; b. Lorain, Ohio, Mar. 12, 1957; s. Francisco Talavera and Alida Rodriguez; m. Wei Tong; 1 child Iesele. BS, U. P.R., 1980; MS, N.D. State U., 1983; PhD, Wash. State U., 1987; PharmD , Creighton U., 1999. Registered pharmacist Nebr., 1999. Fellow U. Mich., Ann Arbor, 1989—95; pharmacy editor eMedicine.com Inc., Omaha, 1999—. Pharmacist PharMerica, Omaha, 2001—. Author: (book) Pharmacy Review, 2001; contbr. articles. Recipient Nat. Rsch. Svc. award, Nat. Cancer Inst., 1989—92; scholar, Hoffman-La Roche, 1995—99. Mem.: Am. Soc. Hosp. Pharmacists, Am. Pharm. Assn. Avocation: martial arts. Office Fax: 402-891-2368. Business E-Mail: ftalaver@cox.net.

TALBERT, CHARLES HAROLD, religion educator; b. Jackson, Miss., Mar. 19, 1934; s. Carl E. and Audrey (Hale) T.; m. Betty O'Neal Weaver, June 30, 1961; children: Caroline O'Neil, Charles Richard. BA, Samford U., 1956, LittD (hon.), 1990; BD, So. Bapt. Theol. Sem., Louisville, 1959; PhD, Vanderbilt U., 1963. Asst. prof. Wake Forest U., Winston-Salem, N.C., 1963-68, assoc. prof., 1968-74, prof., 1974-89, Wake Forest prof., 1989-96; disting. prof. religion Baylor U., Waco, Tex., 1996—. Author: Reading Luke, 1982, Reading Corinthians, 1987, Learning Through Suffering, 1991, Reading John, 1992, The Apocalypse, 1994, Reading Acts, 1997, Romans , 2002. Postdoctoral fellow U. N.C., 1968-69, Soc. for Values in Higher Edn., 1971-72. Mem. Soc. Bibl. Lit. (editor SBL Dissertation Series, N.T. 1984-86, 87-89, editorial bd. jour. 1984-89), Cath. Bibl. Assn. (assoc. editor Cath. Bibl. Quar. 1991-98, pres. 1999-00), Nat. Assn. Bapt. Profs. Religion (pres. 1985), Studiorum Novi Testamenti Societas. Democrat. Baptist. Home: 9602 Old Farm Rd Waco TX 76712-6402 Office: Baylor Univ Dept Religion PO Box 97284 Waco TX 76798-7284 E-mail: Charles_Talbert@baylor.edu.

TALBERT, DOROTHY GEORGIE BURKETT, social worker; b. Rison, Ark.; d. Booker T. and Dorothy (Ragan) Burkett; m. Ernest Talbert, May 14, 1949; children— Ernest George, Dorothy Ernette. A.B., Ark. State A. M. and N. Coll., 1946; M.S.W., Atlanta U., 1948; postgrad. U. Pa., 1962, Tulane U., 1965. Caseworker child welfare services Miss. Dept. Pub. Welfare, 1948-49, Ill. Pub. Aid Commn., Chgo., 1951-53; probation counselor Family Ct. Del., 1956-58; with Del. State Dept. Pub. Welfare, Dover, 1958-71, unit supr., 1962-64, supr. licensing and day care services, 1964-67, chief program devel. Child Welfare Services, 1967-68, chief services to families and children, 1968-71; asst. dir. family services, div. social services Del. Dept. Health and Social Services, 1971-78, dep. dir. adult and spl. services, 1978-82, adult crisis intervention coordinator, Newark, 1982— , staff tng./resource developer, 1985— ; instr. continuing edn. program U. Del., part time 1968—, ret. 1989—; mem. social services adv. com. Del. Adolescent Program, 1969-75, bd. dirs., 1969-75; mem. State Adv. Council on Alcoholism, 1972-76; mem. Del. Devel. Disabilities Planning Council, Del. Adv. Council for Coordination of Services to Handicapped; social work edn. adv. com. Del. State Coll., 1978— . Bd. dirs. United Way of Del., 1979. Mem. Nat. Assn. Social Workers, Am. Pub. Welfare Assn., Nat. Council Pub. Welfare Adminstrs., Black Profl. Forum (sec. 1979), Nat. Caucus Black Aged, NAACP, Delta Sigma Theta. Home: 3007 W 3rd St Wilmington DE 19805-1703 Office: Div State Service Ctrs 501 Ogletown Rd Newark DE 19711-5403

TALBERT, GEAL FUKUMOTO, investment representative; b. Honolulu, Aug. 22, 1961; d. Alvin J. and Geraldine S. Fukumoto BBA, U. Hawaii, 1983. CLU, ChFC. Sales agt. Prudential, Long Beach, Calif., 1986-94; investment rep. Edward Jones, Kaneohe, Hawaii, 1994—. Mem. Kaneohe Bus. Group, 1994—, v.p., 1996, pres., 1998; mem. Edward Jones Grass Roots Task Force, 1997-2001, Edward Jones hiring team, 2000-2002. Vol. Jr. Achievement, 1994-98; bd. dirs. Nat. Fedn. Ind. Bus., 1997-99; mem. Hawaii Estate Planning Coun., 1996—. Mem. Am. Soc. CLUs (bd. dirs. Harbor chpt. 1992-94, chmn. continuing edn. 1992-93), Am. Bus. Womens Assn. (Ulupono charter chpt. 1994-98), Securities Industry Assn. of Hawaii (dir., govt. affairs chair 1999-2000, pres. 2002-), Small Bus. Hawaii (bd. dirs. 1999—), Rotary (Kaneohe chpt., chmn. youth svcs. 1996, sec. 1997-98, pres. 2000-2001), Investment Soc. Hawaii (bd. dirs. 1997-2000). Avocations: travel, reading. Office: Edward Jones 45-1144 Kamehameha Hwy Ste 403 Kaneohe HI 96744-3226

TALBERT, ROY, JR. history educator; b. Cheraw, S.C., Aug. 1, 1943; s. Roy and Betty Jean (Harper) T.; BA (Furman Scholar), Furman U., 1965; MA (NDEA fellow), Vanderbilt U., 1967, PhD, 1971; grad. Inst. Ednl. Mgmt., Harvard U., 1981; grad. Computer Literacy Inst., Pepperdine U., 1983; Jane Boyd Holbert, Oct. 24, 1986; children: Matthew, Rebecca Anne, Drew, Elizabeth. Sr. teaching fellow Vanderbilt U., Nashville, 1967-70; asst. prof. history Ferrum (Va.) Coll., 1974-76, dir. curriculum and programs, 1976-79; vice chancellor for acad. affairs Coastal Carolina U., Conway, 1979-84, assoc. prof. history, 1979-89, prof., 1989—, chmn. 1991—; producer, host The Public Eye, TV show, 1978-79; host Waccamaw Mag., TV show, 1983; project dir. numerous film, TV and pub. programming projects for community and civic groups, 1975-79. Served to capt. U.S. Army, 1970-72. Mem. So. Hist. Assn., Orgn. Am. Historians. Methodist. Author: FDR's Utopian: Arthur Morgan of the TVA, 1987, Negative Intelligence: The Army and the American Left, 1917-41, 1991, No Greater Legacy: The Centennial History of Willcox, McLeod, Buyck and Williams, 1995. Home: 106 Wofford Ln Conway SC 29526-8823 Office: Coastal Carolina Univ History Dept Conway SC 29526

TALBOT, DONALD ROY, consulting services executive; b. Bridgeport, Conn., Jan. 23, 1931; s. Grant Edward and Elvera (Gilbert) T.; m. Beverly Rinebold, Aug. 15, 1953; children: Donna, Randall, Theodore, Timothy, Thomas. B in Marine Engring., N.Y. State Maritime Coll. Project engr. atomic power equipment div. GE, San Jose, Calif., 1952-58; mgr. nuclear labs., nuclear div. Martin Marietta Corp., Balt., 1958-62, project dir. nuclear div., 1962-67, dir. spl. studies Friendship, Md., 1967-71, project dir. environ. programs Balt., 1971-74, dir. environ. tech. ctr. Relay, Md., 1974-83, gen. mgr. environ. systems div. Columbia, 1984-87; corp. v.p. Versar, Inc., Springfield, Va., 1987-89; pres. R.E. Mgmt. Svc., Inc., Towson, Md., 1989—. Recipient Antarctica Svc. medal Civil Engrs. Corps USN, 1965, Cert. of Appreciation Sec. Dept. Commerce, 1975 Avocation: outdoor activities. Home: 712 Hickory Lot Rd Baltimore MD 21286-1427 Office: R E Mgmt Svcs Inc PO Box 10614 Baltimore MD 21285-0614 E-mail: remsdrt@comcast.net.

TALBOT, EMILE JOSEPH, French language educator; b. Brunswick, Maine, Apr. 12, 1941; s. Joseph Emile and Flora Talbot; m. Elizabeth Mullen, Aug. 6, 1966; children: Marc, Paul. BA, St. Francis Coll., Biddeford, Maine, 1963; MA, Brown U., 1965, PhD, 1968. Instr. French U. Ill., Urbana, 1967-68, asst. prof., 1968-73, assoc. prof., 1973-86, prof., 1986—, head dept. French, 1988-94. Author: (book) Stendhal and Romantic Esthetics, 1985, Stendhal Revisited, 1993, Reading Nelligan, 2002; editor: La Critique Stndhalienne, 1979; assoc. editor: Quebec Studies, 1993—96, rev. editor: The French Rev., 1979—82, rev. editor: Quebec Studies, 1988—93, mem. editl. bd.: Nineteenth-Century French Studies, 1986—, mem. editl. bd.: La Revue Francophone, 1990—96, mem. editl. bd.: Etudes Francophones, 1996—. Decorated chevalier Ordre des Palmes Académiques (France); fellow, Ctr. Advanced Study U. Ill., 1973, Assoc., 1988, NEH, 1973—74, Camargo Found., France, 1976. Mem.: MLA, Am. Coun. Quebec Studies (v.p.

1995—97, pres. 1997—99), Assn. Can. Studies in U.S., Am. Assn. Tchrs. French. Roman Catholic. Office: U Illinois Dept French 707 S Mathews Ave Urbana IL 61801-3625 E-mail: ejtalbot@uiuc.edu.

TALBOT, LEE MERRIAM, ecologist, educator, association executive; b. New Bedford, Mass., Aug. 2, 1930; s. Murrell Williams and Zenaida (Merriam) T.; m. Martha Walcott Hayne, May 16, 1959; children: Lawrence Hayne, Russell Merriam. BA, U. Calif., Berkeley, 1953, MA, PhD, U. Calif., Berkeley, 1963. Biologist Arctic Research Lab., Point Barrow, Alaska, 1951; staff ecologist Internat. Union for Conservation, Brussels, 1954-56; ecologist, dir. East African ecol. research project Nat. Acad. Scis., Govts. of Kenya and Tanzania, 1959-63; wildlife advisor UN Spl. Fund, Africa, 1963-64; dir. S.E. Asia project Internat. Union for Conservation, 1964-65; resident ecologist, field rep. for internat. affairs Smithsonian Instn., Washington, 1966-70; sr. scientist, dir. internat. activities Pres.'s Council on Environ. Quality, 1970-78; sr. sci. advisor Internat. Council Sci. Unions, Paris, 1978-83; dir. conservation, spl. sci. advisor World Wildlife Fund Internat., Switzerland, 1978-80; dir. gen. Internat. Union for Conservation of Nature and Natural Resources, Gland, Switzerland, 1980-83; research fellow Environ. and Policy Inst., East West Ctr., 1983-87; vis. fellow World Resources Inst., Washington, 1984-89; sr. environ. advisor World Bank, 1984—; pres. Lee Talbot Assocs. Internat., 1991—; sr. prof. environ. scis., internat. affairs and pub. policy George Mason U., Va., 1994—. Cons. UNESCO, World Bank, Asian Devel. Bank, Nat. Geog. Soc., Inter-Am. Devel. Bank, The Nature Conservancy, U.S. Govt., U. Calif., UN Spl. Fund, WHO, UN Environment Program, UN Univ., UN Devel. Programme Govts. Laos, People's Republic China, Bhutan; conservation coord. Internat. Biol. Program, 1965-70; bd. dirs., chmn. bd. Ecologically Sustainable Devel., Inc., Inst. Ecosys. Studies, World Found. for Environ. and Devel.; mem. corp. N.Y. Bot. Gardens. Author 17 books and monographs; contbr. articles to profl. jours. Active Boy Scouts Am., Geneva, 1980-82, Washington, 1987-95. With USMC, 1953-54. Decorated officer Order of Lion (Senegal); recipient Fgn. Field Rsch. award Nat. Acad. Scis., 1959, CINE Golden Eagle award, 1969, Albert Schweitzer medal, 1975, Regents Lectureship award U. Calif.-Santa Barbara, 1986, Pierre Chaleur prize for lit. French Acad. Scis., 1993; finalist Univ.-Wide Tchg. Excellence award George Mason U., 1997. Fellow Royal Geog. Soc., Royal Soc. Arts, AAAS, N.Y. Zool. Soc.; mem. Am. Inst. Biol. Scis. (Disting. Svc. award 1979), Acad. Medicine, World Conservation Union (hon.), Am. Assn. for Club of Rome, Am. Soc. Mammalogists, Ecol. Soc., Wildlife Soc. (Outstanding Publ. award 1963), Soc. for Conservation Biology, Internat. Soc. for Ecol. Econs., Boone and Crockett Club (N.Y.C.), Explorers Club (N.Y.C.), Cosmos Club (Washington), Sigma Xi, Phi Kappa Sigma. Achievements include incorporation of ecological principles in international development; development of new principles for management of wild resources; biodiversity conservation; definition of ecosystem dynamics of tropical savannahs including role of fire, feeding habits and migrations of wild herbivores; development and negotiation of international agreements for environmental protection. Home: 6656 Chilton Ct Mc Lean VA 22101-4422 *My career is based on two premises: first, that our most important challenges are environmental issues which determine the earth's carrying capacity for human life and, equally important, the quality of that life; and second, that it is important to obtain direct experience in as much of the world as possible (over 127 countries so far) to understand the human ecological setting as a basis for action to improve it.*

TALBOT, MARTHA HAYNE, conservationist, biologist; b. San Francisco, Aug. 3, 1932; d. Francis Bourn and Anna (Walcott) Hayne; m. Lee Merriam Talbot, May 16, 1959; children: Lawrence Hayne, Russell Merriam. BA, Vassar Coll., 1954. Co-founder, asst. dir. student conservation program U.S. Nat. Parks, 1955-59; co-dir. East African Ecol. Rsch. Project, Kenya and Tanzania, 1959-63; asst. dir. S.E. Asia Project, Internat. Union for Conservation of Nature/Natural Resources, 1964-65; asst. coord. Internat. Biol. Programme, London, 1966; rsch. assoc. Smithsonian Instn., Washington, 1966-75; mem., treas. Fairfax County Park Authority, Fairfax, Va., 1973-77; sec.-treas. Talbot Racing Assocs., McLean, 1983—; owner, dir. Talbot Hayne Vineyard, St. Helena, Calif., 1988—; sec.-treas. Lee Talbot Assocs. Internat., McLean, 1991—. Bd. dirs. Student Conservation Assn., 1966-78, 83-87, hon. dir., 1987— (Svc. Honor award), Defenders of Wildlife, 1974-77, Audubon Naturalist Soc., 1975-78, Rachel Carson Coun., 1975-94, treas., 1994-98, v.p., 1998—. Co-author: Introduction to the Landscape, East Africa, 1961, (monograph) The Wildebeest in Western Masailand East Africa, 1963, Renewable Natural Resources in the Philippines, 1964, Conservation of the Hong Kong Countryside, 1966; co-editor: Conservation in Tropical South East Asia, 1968; contbr. numerous articles to sci. jours. Cub Scout troop leader Boy Scouts Am., Geneva, 1978-83, transp. coord., McLean, 1989-95. Recipient Outstanding Pub. award The Wildlife Soc., 1963, Cinema Golden Eagle award Documentary Film, 1968, Disting. Alumna award Katharine Branson Sch., 1981, Conservation Svc. award U.S. Dept. Interior, 1986, Bd. Tribute to co-founder, Student Conservation Assn., 1984, Resolution of Honor, 1999; N.Y. Zool. Soc. grantee, 1961. Mem. Soc. Women Geographers (bd. dirs. 1972-75, treas. 1984-89, treas. Washington group 1990-96), Napa Valley Grape Growers Assn. Avocations: hiking, backpacking, bicycling, skiing, travel. Home: 6656 Chilton Ct Mc Lean VA 22101-4422

TALBOT, MARY LEE, minister; b. Cleve., Apr. 18, 1953; d. Richard William and Mary Helen (Jacobs) T. BA, Coll. Wooster, 1975; MDiv, Andover-Newton Theol. Sch., 1979; MPhil, Tchrs. Coll. Columbia U., 1990; PhD, Columbia U., 1997. Ordained to ministry Presbyterian Ch. (U.S.A.), 1981. Asst. in ministry Grace Congl. Ch., Framingham, Mass., 1975-78; resources coord. Women's Theol. Coalition, Boston, 1977-79; assoc. editor Youth Mag., Phila., 1979-80; co-dir. youth and young adult program Presbyn. Ch. U.S.A., N.Y.C., 1981-88; cons. in religious edn., 1988-90; dir. continuing edn. Pitts. Theol. Sem., Pitts., 1990—2001; interim pastor Clinton, 2002—. Bd. dirs. Christian Assn., U. Pa., 1979-81; mem. religion com. Chautauqua Inst., 1988-91. Author, editor: (program resource) Suicide and Youth, 1981, (newsletter) Trackings, 1986-88; editor: Racism and Anti-Racism, 1982, One Fantastic Book, 1982, My Identity: A Gift from God, 1987, A Guidebook for Presbyterian Youth Ministry, 1988, God's Gift of Sexuality, 1989, Celebrate Bible Study, 1990; contbr. articles to Youth Mag., Alert, Chautauquan Daily, others. Bd. dirs. Christian Assn., U. Pa., 1979-81. Recipient English award Bus. and Profl. Women, 1971. Mem. Assn. Presbyn. Ch. Educators, Assn. Presbyn. Clergywomen, Religious Edn. Assn. (bd. dirs. 1986-91), History of Edn. Soc., Kappa Delta Pi. Democrat. Office: 1767 Rte 30 Clinton PA 15026

TALBOT, PAMELA, public relations executive; b. Chgo., Aug. 10, 1946; BA in English, Vassar Coll., 1968. Reporter Worcester, Mass. Telegram and Gazette, 1970-72; account exec. Daniel J. Edelman, Inc., Chgo., 1972-74, account supr., 1974-76, v.p., 1976-78, sr. v.p., 1978-84, exec. v.p., gen. mgr., 1984-90; pres. Edelman West, 1990-95; pres., COO Edelman U.S., 1995—. Office: Edelman Pub Rels 200 E Randolph Dr Ste 6300 Chicago IL 60601-6436 E-mail: pam.talbot@edelman.com.

TALBOT, PETER JENNINGS, financial services executive; b. Norwalk, Conn., June 11, 1961; s. Edward Richmond Talbot and Ellen Jennings Grevatt; m. Kathryn Lynn Nichols, Aug. 18, 1984; children: Kaitlyn Elizabeth, Peter Jennings II. BBA, U. North Fla., 1987. Republican. Episcopalian. Dealer svcs. rep. Chrysler First Comml. Corp., Atlanta, 1987-88, acct. mgr. Bloomington, Minn., 1988-89, sr. acct. mgr. St. Louis, 1989-91, dist. sales mgr. Irving, Tex., 1991-92; credit and collections mgr. PHH-NTS, Ft. Worth, 1992-93; region mgr. Transamerica Comml. Fin. Corp., Schaumburg, Ill., 1993-97; ops. mgr. GE Capital Vendor Fin. Svcs., Danbury, Conn., 1997-98; internat. ops. mgr. GE Capital Telecom Fin. Svcs., 1998—2001; client integration and support mgr. GE Capital Trade Payables Svcs., 2000—; v.p. quality GE Distbn. Fin., Jacksonville, Fla., 2001—. Corp. sec. Cmty. Christmas, Inc., Cary, Ill., 1993-97. Mem. Water's Edge Country Club, Rudder Bluc, St. Johns Country Club, Sigma Nu. Avocations: sailing, genealogy, golf, gardening. Home: 4020 Grande Vista Blvd #308 Saint Augustine FL 32084 Office: GE Distbn Fin 4899 Belfort Rd Jacksonville FL 32256 E-mail: pequot61@aol.com.

TALBOT, PHILLIPS, Asian affairs specialist; b. Pitts., June 7, 1915; s. Kenneth Hammet and Gertrude (Phillips) T.; m. Mildred Aleen Fisher, Aug. 18, 1943; children: Susan Talbot Jacox, Nancy, Bruce Kenneth. BA, BS in Journalism, U. Ill., 1936; student, London Sch. Oriental Studies, 1938-39, Aligarh Muslim U., India, 1939-40; PhD, U. Chgo., 1954; LL.D. (hon.), Mills Coll., 1963. Reporter, Chgo. Daily News, 1936-38, corr. India and Pakistan, 1946-48, 49-50; assoc. Inst. Current World Affairs, 1938-41, 46-51; instr. U. Chgo., 1948-50, Columbia U., N.Y.C., 1951; exec. dir. Am. Univs. Field Staff, 1951-61; asst. sec. Near Eastern and S. Asian affairs Dept. State, 1961-65; U.S. ambassador to Greece, 1965-69; pres. Asia Soc., N.Y.C., 1970-81, emeritus, 1981—. Phi Beta Kappa vis. scholar, 1973-74 Author: (with S.L. Poplai) India and America, 1958, India in the 1980s, 1983; editor: South Asia in the World Today, 1950. Trustee emeritus Aspen Inst., U.S.-Japan Found.; counselor United Bd. for Christian Higher Edn. in Asia; elder Presbyn. Ch. 2d lt. cav. Officers Res. Corps, 1936; 1st lt. N.G., 1937-38; lt. comdr. USNR, 1941-46. Recipient Padma Shri honors, India, 2002. Mem. Am. Acad. Diplomacy, Coun. Am. Ambs., Coun. Fgn. Rels., Century Assn., Cosmos Club. Address: 200 E 66th St New York NY 10021-9175 E-mail: talbotp@pipeline.com.

TALBOT, PIERRE JOSEPH, microbiologist, researcher; b. Quebec City, Que., Can., July 11, 1956; s. Arthur and Suzanne (Hudon) T.; m. France Ouellet, July 29, 1977; children: Natalie, Benoit, Dominic. BSc in Biochemistry, Laval U., Ste-Foy, Que., 1977; PhD in Biochemistry, U. B.C., Vancouver, 1981. Rsch. assoc. Scripps Clinic and Rsch. Found., La Jolla, Calif., 1981-84; asst. prof. Inst. Armand-Frappier U. Que., Laval, 1984-89; assoc. prof. Inst. Armand-Frappier, Que., 1989-92, prof., 1992—, dir. Human Health Rsch. Ctr., 1998—. Com. reviewer Med. Rsch. Coun., Ottawa, Ont., Can., 1989-96, 98-2000, Multiple Sclerosis Soc., Toronto, Ont., 1993-96, Nat. Sci. Engring. Res. Coun., Ottawa, 1999-2002. Mem. editl. bd. Viral Immunology, San Antonio, 1990-99; contbr. articles to Virology, Jour. Virology, Annals Neurology, Jour. Immunology. Fonds de la Recherche en Santé du Que. scholar of exceptional merit, 1992-97. Mem. AAAS, Am. Soc. Virology, Am. Soc. Microbiology, Can. Soc. Microbiologists (Fisher Sci. award 1987), Can. Soc. Immunology, Assn. Can.-Francaise Pour L'Avancement des Scis., Internat. Soc. Neuroimmunology, Internat. Soc. Neurovirology. Achievements include research in immuno- and molecular biology of neurotropic coronaviruses and possible involvement in multiple sclerosis. Home: 38 59th Ave Laval QC Canada H7V 2A9 Office: INRS Inst Armand-Frappier 531 Boul Des Prairies Laval QC Canada H7V 1B7 E-mail: pierre.talbot@inrs-iaf.uquebec.ca.

TALBOT, STEPHEN HENDERSON, television producer, writer; b. Hollywood, Calif., Feb. 28, 1949; s. Lyle and Margaret (Epple) T.; m. Pippa Gordon; children: Dashiell, Caitlin. BA, Wesleyan U., 1970. Asst. to pres., lectr. Am. studies SUNY, Old Westbury, 1970-73; reporter Internews, Berkeley, Calif., 1973-79; producer, reporter KQED-TV, San Francisco, 1980-89; producer, writer Frontline (PBS), 1992—; series editor Frontline World, 2002—. Appeared in Leave It To Beaver as Gilbert, 1958-63, also Twilight Zone, Perry Mason, Lassie, others; prodr., co-writer for Frontline: The Best Campaign Money Can Buy (Columbia U. Dupont award), 1992, Rush Limbaugh's America, 1995, The Long March of Newt Gingrich, 1996, Justice for Sale, 1999 (Gold medal Houston Internat. Film Festival 2000); writer, co-prodr.: (PBS-TV) Beryl Markham, 1986, Ken Kesey, 1987, Carlos Fuentes, 1989, Maxine Hong Kingston, 1990, John Dos Passos, 1994, Frontline: Spying on Saddam, 1999; prodr., writer: (documentary) The Case of Dashiell Hammett, 1982 (Peabody award, Edgar Allan Poe award), 1968: The Year That Shaped a Generation, 1998, Frontline: The Battle Over School Choice, 2000 (First prize Edn. Writers Assn.); co-prodr., reporter: (documentary) Broken Arrow, 1980 (George Peabody & George Polk award), others; contbr. articles to mags. including Salon and Washington Post Mag. Recipient Thomas Storke Internat. Journalism award World Affairs Coun. No. Calif., San Francisco, 1983, 86, Golden Gate award San Francisco Film Festival, 1986, 89, Emmy award NATAS, 1980-83, 87-88, 90-91. Mem. Writer's Guild Am. West, Am. Fedn. TV and Radio Artists. Office: Frontline World care KQED-TV 2601 Mariposa San Francisco CA 94110-1400 E-mail: stalbot@KQED.org.

TALBOTT, BEN JOHNSON, JR. lawyer; b. Louisville, May 2, 1940; s. Ben Johnson and Elizabeth (Farnsley) T.; m. Sandra Riehl, Oct. 19, 1963; children: Elizabeth, Betty, John, Ben, Sandra. AB magna cum laude, Xavier U., Cin., 1961; LLB, Harvard U., 1964. Bar: Ky. 1965, U.S. Ct. Appeals (6th cir.) 1967. Law clk. to presiding justice U.S. Dist. Ct. Ky., Louisville, 1964-65; assoc. Middleton, Reutlinger & Baird, 1965-68, ptnr., 1968-80, Westfall, Talbott & Woods, Louisville, 1980-2000, Talbott & Talbott, PLLC, Louisville, 2000—. Atty. Stitzel-Weller Distillery, 1970—72, Louisville Gen. Hosp., 1974—83, Louisville and Jefferson County Bd. Health, 1974—80, U. Louisville, 1980—95; bd. dirs. Strategia Corp. Mem. adv. bd. Louisville 15, Sta. WKPC-TV, bd. dirs., 1972-74, pres. 1974; past bd. dirs. U. Louisville Found., U. Louisville Med. Sch. Fund Orgn.; bd. dirs. Louisville Theatrical Assn., 1971—, pres., 1975-76, chmn., 1977-78; bd. dirs. Def. Enterprise Fund, 1994—; bd. dirs. Macauley Theatre, 1975, TARC Adv. Com., 1971, Jefferson County Capital Constrn. Com., 1971, Louisville Orch., 1976-86, pres., 1979-81; bd. trustees, trustee U. Louisville, 1970-79, sec., 1974, vice chmn., 1975, chmn. fin. com., 1976; bd. dirs. Ky. Ctr. for the Arts, 1983—, Louisville Lung Assn., 1974-75, treas., 1975; bd. dirs. Historic Homes Found., 1972-78, 95-97, 2000-01, v.p. 1978, advisor, atty. 1978-98; bd. regents Whitehall, 1993-2001. Named Outstanding Young Man of Louisville, Louisville Jaycees, 1976. Mem.: SAR, ABA, Louisville Bar Assn. (past mem. exec. com.), The Def. Rsch. and Trial Lawyers Assn., Ky. Bar Assn. (chmn. 1989, Gen. Practice Session of CLE), Big Sand Lake Club, Louisville Country Club, Filson Club, Mayflower Soc., Harvard Law Sch. Assn. Ky. (sec. 1965, pres. 1989—), Soc. Colonial Wars, Pendennis Club, Louisville Boat Club, U. Louisville Club, Phi Kappa Phi (bd. dirs., treas. Louisville chpt. 1990—). Avocations: golf, tennis, skiing. Home: 566 Blankenbaker Ln Louisville KY 40207-1167 Office: Talbott & Talbott 501 S 2nd St Louisville KY 40202-1864 E-mail: ben@talbottandtalbottlaw.com.

TALBOTT, EUNICE TILLMAN, club organizer; b. Springfield, Mo., Jan. 25, 1911; d. Sidney Ellis and Nancy Elizabeth (Denney) Tillman; B.S. (Ed.), U. Tampa, 1947; postgrad. U. Fla., 1959-61; m. William W. Talbott, June 23, 1933; 1 dau., Sharon Lynn Webb. Tchr., Hillsborough County, Fla., 1947-68; lectr. table settings; port. Recipient awards flower shows, 1968— . Mem. NEA, Fla. Edn. Assn., English Council (program chmn. Hillsborough County 1963-65), DAR (regent 1970-72), Colonial Dames (pres. 1977-79), Magna Charta Dames, Tampa and Fla. Fedn. Garden Clubs, Plantagnet Soc., Tri Sigma. Democrat. Methodist. Clubs: Sundial Garden (pres. 1970-72), State Jr. Garden (chmn. 1945-47), Tampa Woman's (librarian 1979-80), Jasmine Garden Circle, Order of Crown. Home: 2810 W Parkland Blvd Tampa FL 33609-5318

TALBOTT, FRANK, III, lawyer; b. Danville, Va., Mar. 26, 1929; s. Frank and Margaret (Jordan) T.; m. Mary Beverley Chewning, July 11, 1952; children: Beverley, Frank IV. BA, U. Va., 1951, LLB, 1953. Bar: Va. 1952. With firm Meade, Talbott & Tate, Danville, 1956—59, Talbott, Wheatley & Talbott, Danville, 1959—66; with Dan River Inc., 1966-76, v.p., gen. counsel, 1968-76; ptnr. firm Clement, Wheatley, Winston, Talbott & Majors, Danville, 1977-78; individual practice law, 1979-92; gen. counsel Va. Mfrs. Assn. Inc., 1983-92; of counsel Woods, Rogers & Hazlegrove, Danville, Va., 1992—. Chmn. adv. bd. NationsBank, Danville, 1984-94. Vice-chmn. Danville Sch. Bd., 1964-70; trustee Va. Student Aid Found., 1963-68; bd. dirs. United Fund Danville, 1959-63, Meml. Hosp., Danville, 1977-90. Served with AUS, 1953-56. Decorated Commendation medal. Fellow Am. Bar Found. (life); mem. Va. Bar Assn. (v.p. 1965-66, exec. com. 1967-70), Danville Bar Assn. (pres. 1965-66), Am. Judicature Soc., Newcomen Soc., U. Va. Alumni Assn. (bd. mgrs.), Danville Golf Club, Farmington Country Club, Country Club Va., Country Club of North Carolina, Delta Psi, Phi Alpha Delta. Methodist. Home: 221 Salisbury Cir Danville VA 24541-3532 Office: PO Box 560 Danville VA 24543-0560

TALBOTT, GEORGE ROBERT, physicist, mathematician, educator; b. San Diego, Oct. 1, 1925; s. George Fletcher and Mary (Lanz) T. BA with honors, UCLA, 1960; DSc, Ind. No. U., 1973. Physicist, tech. staff Rockwell Internat. Co., Anaheim, Calif., 1960-85; lectr. computer sci. Calif. State U., Fullerton, 1979—. Cons. physics, computer sci.; disting. guest lectr. Brunel U., London, 1974, 76; spl. guest Forschungsbibliothek, Hannover, W. Ger., 1979; assoc. editor KRONOS jour., Glassboro (N.J.) U., 1978—; chief computer scientist and ednl. videotape dir. Specialized Software, Wilmot, Wis., 1982—; phys. scientist and rsch. assoc. San Diego Mus. Man, 1993—. Author: Electronic Thermodynamics, 1973, Philosophy and Unified Science, 1977, Computer Applications, 1989, Sir Arthur and Gravity, 1990, Fermat's Last Theorem, 1991, The Signal Processing Library, 1995, Etwas Von Niohts, 2000, A Twelfth Dynasty Egyptian Mathematical Papyrus, 2001, Finding Molecular Weight By Light Scatter, 2001, Mostowski's Theorem In Digital Signal Processing, 2001, Lecomte Du Nouy and The Beauty of Precision, 2001, A New Equation for Orbital Velocities, 2001, Derivatives in Cardinal Arithmetic, 2002; mem editl. bd.: KRONOS jour., 1978—; co-inventor burner, —. With M.C., U.S. Army, 1956. Recipient Vis. Scholars award Western Mich. U., 1979; named to Herbert Hoover H.S. Hall of Fame, San Diego, 1998. Mem. Am. Soc. Med. Technologists, Am. Math. Soc., Math. Assn. Am., Am. Soc. clin. Pathologists (lic. med. lab. technologist), Sigma Xi. Buddhist. Home: 4031 E Charter Oak Dr Orange CA 92869-2611 E-mail: ptahseti@aol.com.

TALBOTT, JOHN, mayor; m. Claudia Field; 2 children. BA in Soc. Sci., Coll. Great Falls, 1976; MA in Polit. Sci., Ctrl. Mich. U., 1978. Enlisted USAF, advanced through grades to col., ret., 1982, served in various assignments including Joint Svc. Commands, past comdr. commn. squadron Mont.; with Jet Propulsion Lab, to 1989; former mayor City of Spokane. Active cmty. devel. and politics, Spokane, 1989—.*

TALCOTT, JAMES AUSTIN, internist, oncologist, educator; b. Gt. Falls, Mont., Aug. 27, 1951; s. James Grant and Doris Duane (Austin) T.; m. Joan Barbara Mannick, Apr. 25, 1987; children: Wesley John, Nicholas James, William Austin. BS, Stanford U., 1973; BA, Oxford U., 1976; MD, Yale U., 1980; SM in Epidemiology, Harvard U. Diplomate Am. Bd. Internal Medicine, Am. Bd. Med. Oncology. Intern and resident in internal medicine U. Wash. Affiliated Hosps., Seattle, 1980-83; chief resident Harborview Med. Ctr., 1983-84; fellow in med. oncology Dana-Farber Cancer Inst.-Harvard U. Med. Sch., Boston, 1984-87, instr., 1987-92, asst. prof., 1992—; dir. Ctr. for Outcomes Rsch. Mass. Gen. Hosp. Cancer Ctr., 1997—. Contbr. articles to med. jours. HEW Presdl. scholar, 1969, Rhodes scholar, 1974. Democrat. Methodist. Avocations: outdoor activities, microcomputing. Home: 27 Carroll Cir Weston MA 02493-2029 Office: Mass Gen Hosp B75 230 55 Fruit St Boston MA 02114 E-mail: jtalcott@partners.org.

TALENT, JAMES M. former congressman, lawyer; b. Des Peres, Mo., Oct. 18, 1956; m. Brenda Lyons, 1984; children: Michael, Kathleen Marie, Christine. BA in Polit. Sci., Washington U., 1978; JD, U. Chgo. Law Sch., 1981. Law clk. 7th Ct. Appeals, 1981-82; adj. prof. law, 1982-84; mem. Mo. State Ho. Reps., 1984-93; minority leader, 1989-93; mem. 103rd-106th Congresses from 2nd Mo. Dist., 1993—2001, mem. edn. and the workforce com., armed svcs. com., chmn. small bus. com. Legislative Achievement award Mo. Hosp. Assn., 1989. Mem. Mo. Bar Assn. (Award for significant contbns. to adminstrv. justice 1989), Mo. C. of C. (Spirit of Enterprise award 1990), Order of the Coif. Republican. Office: 9433 Olive Blvd Saint Louis MO 63132*

TALER, GEORGE ABRAHAM, medical educator; b. Marburg, Lahn, Germany, Aug. 18, 1949; came to the U.S., 1950; s. Joseph and Bronislawa (Frenkiel) T.; m. Cyndy Renoff, May 14, 1977; children: David Joachim, Jordan Houghton. BS, Johns Hopkins U., 1971; MD, U. Md., 1975. Cert. family medicine and geriatric medicine. Asst. prof. U. Md., Balt., 1980-97, assoc. prof., 1997—. Pres. Md. Gerontol. Assn., Balt., 1990, Md. Geriatrics Soc., Balt., 1995-96. Recipient Svc. award Md. Gerontol. Assn., Balt., 1996. Mem. Am. Acad. Home Care Physicians (pres. 1998-2000, bd. dirs.), Am. Acad. Family Physicians, Am. Geriatrics Soc., Am. Med. Dirs. Assn. Office: Washington Hosp Ctr 110 Irving St NW Washington DC 20010-2975 E-mail: george.taler@medstar.net.

TALERMAN, ALEKSANDER, pathologist, educator; b. Warsaw, Poland, Jan. 8, 1932; came to U.S., 1979; s. Nattali and Stanislawa (Naiman) T.; m. Karin Margaretha Barkland, Feb. 28, 1962; children: Robert Alexander, Edward Mark Olof. MB, BChir, U. Sheffield, Eng., 1957, MD, 1968. Lectr. pathology U. London, 1965-70; sr. lectr. pathology, head dept. pathology Rotterdam (The Netherlands) Cancer Inst., 1970-79; prof. pathology and ob-gyn. U. Chgo., 1979—90; Peter A. Herbut prof. pathology and cell biology Thomas Jefferson U., Phila., 1990—. Co-author: Atlas of Germ Cell Tumors, 1989; editor: Pathology of the Testis and its Adnexa, 1985; contbr. articles to profl. jours. With Royal Air Force, 1960-63. Recipient Silver medal German Cancer Soc., 1979. Fellow Royal Coll. Pathologists; mem. Internat. Soc. Gynecol. Pathologists (exec. coun. 1976-82, sec. 1982-86, pres. 1990-92), Internat. Acad. Pathology, European Soc. Pathology, Path. Soc. Great Britain and Ireland. Home: 243 S 4th St Philadelphia PA 19106-3803 Office: Thomas Jefferson Univ Dept Pathology Main Bldg 11th & Walnut Sts Rm 285Q Philadelphia PA 19107-5244 Fax: 215-923-1969.

TALESE, GAY, writer; b. Ocean City, N.J., Feb. 7, 1932; s. Joseph Francis and Catherine (DiPaola) T.; m. Nan Ahearn, June 10, 1959; children—Pamela, Catherine. BA in Journalism, U. Ala., 1953. Staff writer N.Y. Times, N.Y.C., 1955-65; writer Esquire mag., 1960. Author: New York - A Serendipiter's Journey, 1961, The Bridge, 1964, The Overreachers, 1965, The Kingdom and the Power, 1969, Fame and Obscurity, 1970, Honor Thy Father, 1971, Thy Neighbor's Wife, 1980, Unto the Sons, 1992; co-author: (with Barbara Lounsberry) The Literature of Reality, 1995; contbr. articles to Esquire mag., others. Served to 1st lt. AUS, 1954-56. Mem. P.E.N. (v.p. 1984-87, bd. dirs. 1980—), Phi Sigma Kappa. Home: 109 E 61st St New York NY 10021-8101 also: 154 E Atlantic Blvd Ocean City NJ 08226-4511

TALESNICK, STANLEY, lawyer; b. Indpls., June 4, 1927; s. Louis and Rose (Galerman) T.; m. Joan Goldstone, Mar. 16, 1952 (div. Feb. 1967); children: Jill Wilkins, Jane Talesnick, Kay Gilmore; m. Claudia Jean Ferrell, Nov. 28, 1969 (dec.). AB, Ind. U., 1948, LLB, 1950, JD, 1967. Bar: Ind. 1950, U.S. Dist. Ct. (no. and so. dists.) Ind. 1950, U.S. Dist. Ct. (ea. dist.) Wis. 1991, U.S. Ct. Appeals (7th cir.) 1961, U.S. Supreme Ct. 1980; cert. bus. bankruptcy law Am. Bd. Cert. Ptnr. Dulberger, Talesnick, Claycombe & Bagal, Indpls., 1952-57, Bagal & Talesnick, Indpls., 1957-67, Talesnick & Kleiman, Indpls., 1967-74, Dann Pecar Newman Talesnick & Kleiman, Indpls., 1974-94; bankruptcy and creditor's rights counsel Leagre, Chandler & Millard, 1995-1999; of counsel Ancel & Dunlap, LLP, 2000—01, Sommer & Barnard PC (merger), 2002—. Asst. city atty. City of Indpls., 1959-67; instr. bus. law Butler U., Indpls., 1981-82. Chmn. Ind. bd. NCCJ, 1974-76; v.p. Jewish Fedn. Greater Indpls., 1985-89, pres. 1989-91; bd. dirs. Coun. Jewish Fedns. (now United Jewish Cmtys.), 1986-90; treas. Indpls. Hebrew Congregation, 1967-70; v.p. Indpls. Hebrew Congregation Found., 1992-96. With USN, 1945-46, USNR. Disting. fellow Ind. Bar Assn.; recipient Liebert I. Mossler Cmty. Svc. award outstanding & enduring vol. svcs. Jewish Fedn. Greater Indpls. Inc., 1997. Fellow Comml. Law Found., Intenrat. Bar Found.; mem. Ind. State Bar Assn. (ho. of dels. 1985—), Indpls. Bar Assn. (v.p. 1989-90, chmn. comml. and bankruptcy sect. 1985, bd. mgrs. 1994-96), Lawyers Assn. Indpls., Comml. Law League Am., Am. Bankruptcy Inst., B'nai Brith (local pres. 1957-58). Democrat. Jewish. Home: 140 Olde Mill Cir S Dr Indianapolis IN 46260-2373 E-mail: stalesnick@sommerbarnard.net.

TALHELM, DANIEL RODERICK, economics consulting firm executive, educator; b. Evart, Mich., May 31, 1941; s. Calvin B. and Marjory (Kirk) T.; m. Susan E. Devries, Apr. 21, 1964 (div. Dec. 1980); children: Jennifer, Charles; m. Lynne Louise Croxford, Feb. 14, 1981; children: Alan, Thomas. BS, U. Mich., 1964, M of Forestry, 1965; PhD, N.C. State U., 1972. Rsch. forester USDA Forest Svc., Asheville, N.C., 1965-67; rsch. fellow N.C. State U., Raleigh, 1967-70; rsch. assoc. U. Ill., Urbana, 1971; resource economist State of Mich., Lansing, 1971-75; asst. prof. Mich. State U., East Lansing, 1975-84, vis. assoc. prof., 1984-94; vis. prof., 1994—; pres., chief exec. officer Resource Econometrics, East Lansing, 1984—. Bd. tech. experts Great Lake Fishery Commn., Ann Arbor, 1980-85; sci. adv. bd. societal com. Internat. Joint Commn., Windsor, Ont., Can., 1987-91. Spl. editor Trans. Am. Fishery Soc., 1987; contbr. articles to profl. jours. Mem. Gov.'s Great Lakes Fishery Adv. Commn., Lansing, 1979-85. Recipient Meritorious Svc. award Great Lakes Fishery Commn., 1988, Conservation award Fedn. of Ont. Naturalists, 1981. Mem. Am. Agrl. Econ. Assn., Assn. Environ. and Resource Economists, Cen. States Travel and Tourism Rsch. Assn., Am. Econ. Assn., Am. Fisheries Soc. (pres. socio-econs. sect. 1986-87), Am. Soc. Pub. Adminstrn. (bd. dirs. environ. and natural resources sct. 1987-90), Soc. Am. Foresters, Xi Sigma Pi. Unitarian Universalist. Avocations: running, hunting, fishing. Office: Mich State U Natural Resources Bldg East Lansing MI 48824

TALIAFERRO, HENRY BEAUFORD, JR. lawyer; b. Shawnee, Okla., Jan. 12, 1932; s. Henry Beauford Sr. and Laudys L. (Anthony) T.; m. Janet Stewart Myers, Nov. 23, 1955 (div. Feb. 1985); children: Sarah Stewart T. deLeon, Henry B. III, William N.; m. Patricia Ann Calloway, May 16, 1987. BA, U. Okla., 1954, JD, 1956. Bar: Okla. 1956, U.S. Supreme Ct. 1966, D.C. 1969, U.S. Claims Ct. 1970. Assoc. Monnet, Hayes & Bullis, Oklahoma CIty, 1956-59, ptnr., 1959-66; exec. dir. O.E.O. legal svcs. program Oklahoma County, 1966-67; dir. congl. rels., acting exec. dir. Pres.'s Nat. Adv. Commn. on Civil Disorders, Washington, 1967-68; assoc. solicitor for Indian Affairs Dept. of the Interior, 1968-69; pvt. practice, 1969-70; ptnr. Casey, Lane & Mittendorf, 1970-80; exec. v.p., gen. counsel The GHK Cos., Oklahoma City, 1980-83; of counsel Kerr, Irvine & Rhodes, 1987—. Cons. Gas Pipeline Acquisitions & Mgmt., Oklahoma City, 1983-87; mem. Interstate Oil and Gas Compact Commn., 1980—, Okla. Commn. on Nat. Gas Policy, 1991-99, Okla. Energy Resources Bd., 1994—, vice-chair, 1996-97, chair, 1997-99. Author: (with others) Report of Presidents National Advisory Commission on Civil Disorders, 1968; contbr. articles to profl. jours. Candidate 5th dist. U.S. Ho. of Reps., Okla., 1966; mem. planning commn. Fairfax County, Va., 1973, platform com. Dem. Nat. Conv., San Francisco, 1984. Mem. ABA, Okla. Bar Assn., D.C. Bar Assn., Met. Club (Washington), Oklahoma City Golf and Country Club. Democrat. Episcopalian. Avocations: fishing, golf. Office: Kerr Irvine Rhodes & Ables 201 Robert S Kerr Ave Ste 600 Oklahoma City OK 73102-4267

TALIAFERRO, JAMES HUBERT, JR. communications educator; b. Chattanooga, Feb. 21, 1924; s. James Hubert and Ida Estelle (Gilbert) T. Student, Davidson Coll., 1942-43; BS, U. Denver, 1948; MS, Columbia U., 1949; PhD, NYU, 1976. Advt. exec. McCann-Erickson Inc., N.Y.C., 1951-53, Grey Advt. Agy., N.Y.C., 1953-55, Kenyon & Eckhardt, Inc., N.Y.C., 1955-61, Sullivan Stauffer Colwell & Bayles, N.Y.C., 1961-68; instr. speech Bklyn. Coll., CUNY, 1968-75, asst. prof., 1975-82, dep. chmn. dept. speech, 1980-82; prof. dept. communications Rutgers U., New Brunswick, N.J., 1982—; ptnr. Lifestory, Inc., 1985-94. Vis. prof. Fashion Inst. Tech., N.Y.C., 1987-90; ptrn. Taliaferro/Grau & Assocs., Ltd.; cons. in field; assoc. producer New Am. Playwright Series, 1970; assoc. dir. Reading for Blind, Bklyn. Coll., 1976-80; drama critic Housatonic Valley Pub. Co. newspapers, 1973-85. Author plays: Inside Out, 1963; Tour de Force, 1963; also articles, papers. Chmn. Foun. for Mus. of Am. Theatre, 1974-80; trustee Rahway Landmarks Assn. (N.J.), 1983-85; bd. dirs. 320 E 57th St. Corp., 1982-86; bd. dirs., dir. pub. rels. Health House, Chattanooga; bd. dirs. Chattanooga Cares; mem. vestry Christ Ch., Chattanooga. With U.S. Army, 1943-45. Mem. Am. Soc. Theatre Rsch., Internat. Communication Assn., Speech Communication Assn., Eastern Communication Assn., Huguenot Soc. Am., SAR Democrat. Episcopalian. Home: 249 Sunset Dr Rising Fawn GA 30738-4120 Office: Rutgers U Dept Comm Sch Comm Info Libr Sci New Brunswick NJ 08903

TALIAFERRO, ROBERT See BROOKE, TAL

TALIAFERRO, YVON ROCHELLE, accountant, consultant; b. Washington, May 1, 1957; d. Kenneth Wayne and Shirley Yvonne (Dixon) Smith. BS in Acctg., Loma Linda U., 1981. Mgr., personnel cons., acct. K&W Security Patrol, Valiejo, Calif., 1981-85; account exec. Alamo Assocs., Concord, 1986-88; credit mgr. BTS Group, Oakland, 1988-91; owner, pres. AAA Notary Svc., Danville, 1990—; adminstrv. asst. Strategic Fin. Svcs., Walnut Creek, 1992—; customer svc. rep. Bank of Am., Concord, 1993—. Contracting cons. VIP Bus. Svcs., Danville, Calif., 1990-91; entrepreneur, investor, Walnut Creek, 1991—. Mem. NAFE, Nat. Notary Assn. (notary pub.). Avocations: musician, recording artist, racing cars, tennis, horseback riding.

TALL, FRANKLIN DAVID, mathematics educator; b. N.Y.C., Apr. 21, 1944; s. Martin and Faye Tall; m. Tomoko Ueda, 2000. AB, Harvard U., 1964; PhD, U. Wis., 1969. Asst. prof U. Toronto, Ont., Can., 1969-74, assoc. prof. Can., 1974-80, prof. math. Can., 1980—, assoc. chair Can., 1998-2000. Author: (monograph) Set Theoretic Consistency Results and Topological Theorems Concerning the Normal Moore Space Conjecture and Related Problems, 1977, The Work of Mary Ellen Rudin, 1993. Nat. Scis. and Engring. Rsch. Coun. Can. grantee, 1973—. Mem. Am. Math. Soc., Can. Math. Soc., Assn. Symbolic Logic, Canada-Japan Soc. of Toronto, Can. Assn. Neurolinguistic Programming. Office: U. Toronto Dept Math Toronto ON Canada M5S 3G3 E-mail: tall@math.utoronto.ca.

TALL, LAMBERT, engineering educator, consultant; b. Sydney, Australia, Jan. 25, 1933; came to U.S., 1955; s. Jack and Leontine E. (Eisman) T.; m. Rita Augusta Csallner, Dec. 26, 1959. B.E. in Civil Engring., U. Sydney, 1954; M.S. in Civil Engring., Lehigh U., 1957, Ph.D. in Civil Engring., 1961. Bridge design engr. New South Wales (Australia) Dept. Main Roads, 1954-55; grad. asst., instr. Lehigh U., Bethlehem, Pa., 1955-61, asst. prof., 1961-64, assoc. prof., 1964-69, prof., 1969-79, dir., 1966-78; vis. fellow U. New South Wales (Australia), 1964; liaison scientist U.S. Office Naval Research, London, 1971-72; dir. U.S.A./Egypt Coop. Program on Low-Cost Housing, 1976-79; dean Coll. Tech., Fla. Internat. U., Miami, 1979-83, prof. civil engring., 1983— . Mem. Fla. Task Force on Sci., Engring., and Tech. Service to Industry, 1980-81. Served with Royal Australian Art., 1955. John Simon Guggenheim Found. fellow, 1964. Fellow ASCE, Instn. Engrs. Australia (Chapman medal 1964); mem. Am. Welding Soc. (Davis silver medal 1963, 71), Internat. Inst. Welding, Internat. Assn. Bridge and Structural Engring., AAAS, ASTM, Am. Soc. Engring. Edn., Assn. Profl. Engrs. Australia, Structural Stability Research Council, Soc. for History of Tech., Am. Mgmt. Soc., Sigma Xi. Editor, chief author: Structural Steel Design, 1st edit., 1964, 2d edit., 1974; mem. editorial adv. bd. Welding Design and Fabrication; contbr. articles to profl. jours. Office: Sch Engring Fla Internat U Miami FL 33199-0001

TALLEDO, OSCAR EDUARDO, medical educator; b. Sullana, Piura, Peru, Aug. 1, 1929; s. Jorge Antonio and Flora Natividad (Cordova) T.; m. Jeanette McCarley, June 8, 1959; children: Roy Anthony, Paul Frederick, Linda Jeanette. BS, San Marcos U., 1948, MD, 1955. Diplomate Am. Bd. Ob-Gyn., Am. Bd. Laser Surgery. Intern Crawford W. Long Hosp., Atlanta, 1956-57, resident, 1957-58, Med. Coll. Ga., Augusta, 1958-60, fellow in gynecology, 1960-61, chief gynecologic oncology, 1961—, prof. ob-gyn, 1970—, instr., 1961-63, asst. prof., 1963-68, assoc. prof., 1968-71, prof., 1971—, acting chmn., 1981-82. Nat. Heart Inst. grantee, 1965 Fellow Am. Coll. Ob-Gyn, ACS, Gynecologic Oncology Soc.; mem. Soc. Gynecologic Investigation, AMA, Am. Fertility Soc., Richmond County Med. Soc., Ga. Ob-Gyn Soc., So. Med. Assn., S. Atlantic Assn. Ob-Gyn, Gyn-Urology Soc., Ga. Med. Assn. Clubs: Augusta Country. Lodges: Rotary (chmn. world community service com., Augusta 1983). Presbyterian. Home: 817 Aumond Pl W Augusta GA 30909-3106 Office: Med Coll Ga Dept Gyn Oncology Dept Ob Gyn Augusta GA 30912

TALLENT, ROBERT GLENN, chemical and environmental engineer, entrepreneur; b. Nashville, July 4, 1954; s. Glenn Oliver and Virginia Jo (Bell) T.; m. Sandra Marie McKenzie, Aug. 2, 1986; 1 child, Emily Suzanne (dec.). BE, Vanderbilt U., 1976; MS, George Washington U., 1996. Cert. Scuba diving instr. trainer, emergency med. technician. Dir. tng. Am. Watersports Co., Oxon Hill, Md., 1980—83; chem. engr. Naval Sea Systems Command, Washington, 1980—87; pres. Caribbean Ventures, Alexandria, Va., 1984—88; dist. course dir. Profl. Assn. Diving Instrs., Va., Md., Del., Washington, 1984—; staff Am. Systems Corp., Chantilly, Va., 1988-89; account exec. Data Link Info. Solutions, Inc., Falls Church, 1989—90; pres. Internat. Diving Inst., 1988—91, Nut'N But Nuts, Stafford, Va., 1990—91, Earthworks Internat., Stafford, 1991—96; engr. Info. Spectrum, Inc., 1994—96, SEMCOR, 1996—97; pres. The Triton Found., 1997—; project mgr. MACI, 1998—. Author: Caribbean Ventures Dive Travel Notebook, 1986. Commr. Boy Scouts Am., Stafford, Va., 1988—2001. Lt. (j.g.) USN, 1976—80. Recipient Wood badge, Boy Scouts Am., 1994, Silver Beaver award, 2000, Outstanding Achievement award, PADI, 2001, Cmty. Svc. award, PADI Internat., 1993, 1997. Mem. Nat. Eagle Scout Assn. (life mem.), Luv-N-Laffs Clowns, Undersea Med. Soc., Clowns of Am. Internat. Republican. Methodist. Avocations: squash, boxing, music, clowning, scuba diving. Home: 30 Larkwood Ct Stafford VA 22554-1585

TALLENT, STEPHEN EDISON, lawyer; b. Columbus, Nebr., Aug. 10, 1937; s. William E. and Helen Tallent; m. Martha Sutcliffe, Apr. 6, 1971; 1 child, Jennifer Diane. BA, Stanford U.; JD, U. Chgo.; LLD (hon.), Lincoln U. Bar: Calif. 1963, U.S. Dist. Ct. (so. and cen. dists.) Calif. 1965, U.S. Dist. Ct. (so. and ea. dists.) N.Y. 1989, U.S. Ct. Appeals (D.C. cir. 1981), U.S. Ct. Appeals (2d cir.) 1987, U.S. Ct. Appeals (3d. cir.) 1980, U.S. Ct. Appeals (4th cir.) 1982, U.S. Ct. Appeals (9th cir.) 1968, U.S. Ct. Mil. Appeals 1965, U.S. Supreme Ct. 1973. Ptnr. Gibson, Dunn & Crutcher, L.A., 1962-96; pvt. practice Washington, 1997—. Former adj. prof. Loyola Law Sch., L.A.; mem. vis. com. U. Chgo. Law Sch.; former mem. Calif. Atty. Gen.'s adv. com. for Evaluation of Anti-Organized Crime Programs; mem. L.A. Town Hall, L.A. World Affairs Council; mem. bd. visitors Stanford Law Sch.; founding dir. Am. Employment Law Coun., 1993—. Fellow Coll. Labor and Employment Lawyers (founding, pres. and gov. 1995—); mem. ABA (chair labor and employment law sect. 1998-99), Indsl. Rels. Rsch. Assn. Home: PO Box 512 Reedville VA 22539-0512 Office: 1050 Connecticut Ave NW Ste 900 Washington DC 20036-5320

TALLENT, WILLIAM HUGH, chemist, research administrator; b. Akron, Ohio, May 28, 1928; s. Charles Othar and Agnes Annette (Johnson) T.; m. Joy Anne Redfield, Aug.23, 1952; children: Elizabeth Ann, Cinda Marie, Raymond Charles. BS, U. Tenn., 1949, MS, 1950; PhD, U. Ill., 1953. Chemist Nat. Heart Inst., Bethesda, Md., 1953-57, G.D. Searle & Co., Skokie, Ill., 1957-64; head new crops evaluation investigations Agr. Rsch. Svc., USDA, Peoria, 1964-69, chief indsl. crops lab., 1969-74, asst. dir., 1974-75, ctr. dir. No. Regional Rsch. Ctr., 1975-83, regional adminstr. N.E. region, 1983-84, asst. adminstr. Washington, 1984-94, tech. transfer advisor Beltsville, Md., 1994—. Editor Jour. Am. Oil Chemists Soc., 1998-2001. Recipient Merit award Gamma Sigma Delta, 1979, Presdl. Rank award for Sr. Execs., 1988, NASA Tech. 2002 award for lifetime achievement in tech. transfer, 1992. Mem. AAAS, Am. Oil Chemists' Soc., Am. Chem. Soc., Soc. Econ. Botany. Home and Office: 831 West Side Dr Iowa City IA 52246-4309 Fax: 319-354-4059.

TALLERICO, DELMA DOLORES, museum educator; b. Pricedale, Pa., May 2, 1952; d. Thomas Delmar Hepple and Elizabeth Theresa (Katchmark) Ambler; m. Samuel Joseph Tallerico, Aug. 9, 1975; children: Robert Peter, Michael James, Patrick Joseph. BA, Seton Hill Coll., 1974; MA in Tchg., U. Pitts., 1975; diploma, Inst. Children's Lit., 1994. Lic. real estate broker, Pa. Counselor Youth Corps, Greensburg, Pa., 1972-74; intern Greensburg (Pa.)-Salem, 1974-75; tchr. St. James Elem., Pitts., 1975-80; real estate agt. Metro Realty, 1989-92; mus. tchr. Frick Art and Hist. Ctr., 1993—. Minority machine inspection clk. City of Pitts., Shadyside, Pitts., 1993-97; mem. St. Paul Cathedral Choir. Republican. Roman Catholic. Avocation: piano.

TALLETT, ELIZABETH EDITH, biopharmaceutical company executive; b. London, Apr. 2, 1949; d. Edward and Edith May (Vickers) Symons; m. James Edward Wavle Jr.; children: James Edward Tallett, Alexander Martin Tallett, Christopher Andrew Wavle. BS with honors, U. Nottingham (Eng.), 1970. Ops. rsch. analyst So. Gas Bd., 1970-73; mgmt. svcs. mgr. Warner-Lamber (UK), Eastleigh, Eng., 1973-77, strategic planning mgr., 1977-81; internat. dir. strategic planning Warner-Lambert, Morris Plains, N.J., 1981-82, corp. dir. strategic planning, 1982-84; dir. mktg. ops. Parke-Davis, 1984-87; exec. v.p. therapeutic products Centocor, Malvern, Pa., 1987-89, pres. pharms. div., 1989-92; pres., CEO Transcell Techs., Inc., Monmouth Junction, N.J., 1992-96, Dioscor, Inc., Stockton, 1996—. Bd. dirs. Prin. Fin. Group, Varian, Inc., Coventry Health Care, Inc., IntegraMed Am. Inc., Immunicon Inc., Varian Semi Conductor, Equipment Assoc. Inc.; dir. Biotech. Coun. N.J. Contbr. articles to profl. jours. Mem. Ch. Of Eng. Avocations: acting, badminton, travel, skiing.

TALLEY, BEVERLY M. music educator; b. Mobile, Ala., June 17, 1940; d. Lowell Manning and Edna Blake Estes; m. Clarence Daniel Talley; stepchildren: Joseph, Lisa, Dan, Barbara Ann, Jessie. Student, U. South Ala., 1994—. Pvt. practice piano educator, Houston, 1975-93, Mobile, 1994—. Various positions Cypress Creek Music Tchrs. Assn., Houston, 1980-93; music chmn., v.p. Mobile Piano Ensemble, 1994-96, piano concerto soloist, 1995, piano duo artist, 1997. Mem. Nat. Music Tchrs. Assn., Ala. State Music Tchrs. Assn., Mobile Music Tchrs. Assn. (Sonata contest v.p. 1994-96. pres. 2000-02), Suzuki Assn. of the Ams., U.S. Achievement Acad. (scholastic all Am.), Alpha Theta Chi. Democrat. Baptist. Home: 6424 Lubarrett Way Mobile AL 36695-3823

TALLEY, CAROL LEE, newspaper editor; b. Bklyn., Sept. 10, 1937; d. George Joseph and Viola (Kovash) T.; children— Sherry, Jill, Scott. Student, U. Ky., 1955-57, Ohio U., 1957-58. Reporter Easton (Pa.) Daily Express, 1958-60; reporter N.J. Herald, 1962-64, edn. editor, 1964-66; reporter Daily Advance, Dover, N.J., 1966-68, polit. editor, investigative reporter, from 1969, mng. editor, 1974-81; editor Evening Sentinel, Carlisle, Pa., 1982—. Mem. A.P. Task Force N.J., 1970, Pa. Associated Press Mng. Editor's Bd. Dirs. Past bd. dirs. Helen Stevens Cmty. Mental Health Ctr. (chair), Carlisle; past pres. bd. dirs. Stevens Mental Health Ctr., Carlisle. Recipient pub. service awards Nat. Headliners, 1971, Sigma Delta Chi, 1971, George Polk Meml. award for local reporting, 1974, Dew Meml. award Pa. Newspaper Pub.'s Assn., 1985. Mem. Pa. Newspaper Editors Soc., Kiwanis Club. Office: 457 E North St Carlisle PA 17013-2655

TALLEY, CHARLES RICHMOND, commercial banking executive; b. Richmond, Va., Dec. 23, 1925; s. Charles Edward and Marie (Thorckmorton) Talley; m. Anne Marie Smith, June 4, 1948; children: Laurie Anne, Charles Richmond Jr. BA in Econs, U. Richmond, 1949; postgrad., Sch. Banking Rutgers U., 1959-61, Sch. Fin. Pub. Relations, Northwestern U., 1954-55; grad. exec. program, U. Va., 1974. Asst. cashier 1st & Mchts. Nat. Bank, Richmond, 1955-57, asst. v.p., 1957-63, v.p., 1963-69, sr. v.p., 1969-73, exec. v.p., 1973-84; corp. exec. officer Sovran Bank N.A., 1984-86, ret., 1986, 1986. Bd dirs Security Atlantic Life Ins Co; vpres, bd dirs Security Atlantic Ins Agency; bd dirs Sovran Properties Inc; vice chmn bd dirs Va Educ Loan Authority, 1983—87, chmn, 1988—91; vpres, mem exec comt Richmond Eye and Ear Hosp, pres, 1988—91. Pres Richmond Jr Cof C, 1960—61; treas Richmond chpt Nat Found, 1956—; pres Baptist Extension Bd Va, 1973—75; bd dirs Commonwealth Eye and Ear, 1986—89, Richmond Symphony Orchestra, Richmond Better Bus Bur. With USNR, 1944—46. Mem.: Richmond Clearing House Asn (pres 1977), Richmond Metropolitan CofC (bd dirs 1979—89), Tides Lodge Golf and Country Club (Irvington, Va), Bull and Bear Club, Willow Oaks Country Club Richmond (pres 1971), Rotary (bd dirs Richmond 1981—83). Home: 4301 Stratford Rd Richmond VA 23225-1060 also: Bldg 2 Unit 2 The Green At Tides Lodge Irvington VA 22480

TALLEY, DANIEL ALFRED, economics educator; BS in Econs., U. Puget Sound, 1990; PhD in Econs., U. Oreg., 1996. Prof. econs. Dakota State U., Madison, S.D., 1996—. Trustees scholar U. Puget Sound, 1986-90, Kleinsorge Rsch. scholar, 1993. Mem. Am. Econ. Assn., Midwest Econ. Assn., Omicron Delta Epsilon. Avocations: racquetball, strategy gaming. Office: Dakota State U 820 N Washington Ave Madison SD 57042-1735

TALLEY, HAYWARD LEROY, communications executive; b. Nov. 3, 1923; s. Roy and Reta (Hayward) T.; m. Emma Mae Chandler, Sept. 2, 1950; children: Brian, Kevin. BS, U. Ill., 1948. Chief engr. Sta. WOKZ-AM-FM, Alton, Ill., 1948-50; pres., gen. mgr. Talley Broadcasting Corp. (sta. WSMI AM and FM), Litchfield, 1950—; pres. Talley Broadcasting Co. (sta. KBKB AM and FM), Ft. Madison, Iowa, 1960-99, North Cen. Iowa Broadcasting Co. (stas. KLSS, KSMN), Mason City, 1963-83, Talley Broadcasting Corp. (sta. WAOX), Staunton, Ill., 1999—. Chmn. ofcl. bd. Meth. Ch., 1961-63, 65-66; adv. bd. Lewis & Clark Coll., 1978—. With Signal Corps, U.S. Army. Mem.: Ill. Broadcasters Assn. (Broadcaster or Yr. 2002), Nat. Assn. Broadcasters, Am. Legion, Masons, Rotary (pres. Litchfield Club 1989—90). Home: 1414 N Harrison St Litchfield IL 62056-1209 Office: Sta WSMI PO Box 10 Litchfield IL 62056-0010

TALLEY, JIM ALLEN, minister, counselor; b. Swink, Okla., Dec. 20, 1942; s. Herbert Lee and Dora Murdice (Robirds) T.; m. C. Joyce Burr, Dec. 22, 1961; children: Renee Talley Ridgeway, Paul, Kent. AA, Bakersfield (Calif.) Jr. Coll., 1962; BA, Calif. State U., Turlock, 1971; MA, Mennonite Sem., Fresno, Calif., 1978; PhD, Columbia Pacific U., San Rafael, Calif., 1991. Ordained to ministry Bapt. Ch., 1971. Elder Ch. in the Pk., Modesto, Calif., 1970-76; min. single adults 1st Bapt. Ch., 1976-91; pvt. practice counseling Oklahoma City, 1991—. Dir. west coast Nat. Cmty. Marriage Policy, Modesto, 1988-91. Author: Relationship Instruction, 1984, Reconciliation Instruction, 1988; co-author: Too Close Too Soon, 1981, Reconcilable Differences, 1985, True Colors, 1991, Life After Divorce, 1991. Republican. E-mail: drtalley@drtalley.com. *Integrity is the ability to ware a helmet around all day that prints out our thought life on a screen for everyone to read.*

TALLEY, JOSEPH EUGENE, psychologist; b. Springfield, Mass., May 27, 1949; s. Joseph Addison and Miriam Louise (Ayers) T.; m. Vibeke Absalon, Jan. 3, 1981; children: Kirsten, David, Jonathan. BA, U. Richmond, 1971; MA, Radford Coll., 1973; PhD, U. Va., 1978. Diplomate Am. Bd. Profl. Psychology; lic. psychologist, N.C.; cert. health svc. provider, N.C. Assoc. clin. prof. dept. psychiatry and behavioral scis. Duke U. Med. Ctr., Durham, N.C., 1977—, coord. rsch., program evaluation and testing svcs., 1979—; gen. practice psychotherapy, 1980—. Author: Study Skills, 1981, Performance Prediciton of Law Enforcement Personnel, 1990, The Predictors of Successful Very Brief Psychotherapy, 1992; author, editor: Counseling and Psychotherapy Services, 1985, Counseling and Psychotherapy with College Students: A Guide to Treatment, 1986, Multicultural Needs Assessment with College and University Populations, 1995, Seeking Something Sacred: Managing Our Frustrations, Losses and Fears, 2001; contbr. articles to profl. jours. Bd. deacons Hillsborough Presbyn. Ch., N.C., 1983-85, chmn., 1985, bd. elders, 1987-94, v.p. bd. trustees, 1992-94; bd. dirs. Orange County Mental Health Assn., Chapel Hill, N.C., 1982-83, mem. legis. com., 1983, site visitor for accreditation. Mem. APA, Acad. Counseling Psychology (pres. 1995-97, Disting. Svc. award 2002), Am. Bd. Profl. Psychology (sect./treas. coun. of pres.'s psychology splty. acads. 1997-98, chmn./CEO 2000—), N.C. Psychol. Assn., Nat. Soc. Clin. Hypnosis (cert. and approved cons., supr. and practitioner, ethics com. 1995-97), Phi Kappa Phi, Omicron Delta Kappa, Psi Chi, Phi Kappa Sigma. Democrat. Presbyterian. Home: 134 E Tryon St Hillsborough NC 27278-2550 Office: Duke U Counseling & Psychol Svcs PO Box 90955 214 Page Bldg Durham NC 27708-0955 E-mail: jtalley@acpub.duke.edu.

TALLEY, LINDA JEAN, food scientist, dietitian; b. Hearne, Tex., July 15, 1948; d. Roy Wesley and Dorothy Louise (Allen) Dugger; m. Thomas James Talley, May 15, 1970; children: John Paul, Jo Ann. BS in Food Tech., Tex. A&M U., 1969, MS in Food Sci. and Tech., 1979, PhD in Food Sci. and Tech., 1981. Registered dietitian Am. Dietetic Assn.; registered sanitarian; lic. dietitian, Tex. Technician I soil and crop scis. dept. Tex. A & M U., College Station, 1969-72; technician I in horticulture scis. Tex. A&M U., 1977-78, grad. asst., 1978-81; quality assurance mgr. food products divsn. Southland Corp., Ft. Worth, 1972-73; pub. health inspector Ft. Worth Pub. Health Dept., 1973-74; dir. quality assurance plant sanitation and product devel. Kimbell Foods, Inc., Mfg. Divsn., Ft. Worth, 1974-75; profl. cons., 1975-76; v.p., cons. TALCO, Dallas, 1981-91; sr. food scientist Enersyst Devel. Ctr., Inc., 1990-98; v.p. Med. Arts Software, Inc., 1998—2002; prof. human sci. dept. Tarleton State Univ., Stepenville, Tex., 2001—. Presenter in field. Contbr. articles to profl. jours. Mem. Inst. Food Techs., Sigma Xi, Phi Tau Sigma. Avocations: gardening, reading, needlework. Home: 2225 W Overhill Dr Stephenville TX 76401-2067 Office: 2225 W Overhill Dr Stephenville TX 76401-2067

TALLEY, RICHARD BATES, lawyer; b. Oklahoma City, Mar. 19, 1947; s. Olin Jack and Betty Lee (Bates) T.; m. Joan Walker, Sept. 15, 1992; children from a previous marriage: Richard Bates Jr., Samuel Logan, Bradley Dale, Rachel Alexandra. BBA, Okla. U., 1969, JD, 1972. Bar: Okla. 1972, U.S. Dist. Ct. (we. dist.) Okla. 1972, U.S. Ct. Appeals (10th cir.) 1973, U.S. Dist. Ct. (no. dist.) Tex. 1987, U.S. Tax Ct. 1987.; CPA, Okla. Atty. Talley, Crowder & Gallagher, Norman, Okla., 1995. Bd. dirs. Bacchus Enterprises, Inc., Norman, The Top of the Center, Inc. Pres. Cleveland Co. YMCA. Mem. ABA, Okla. Bar Found., Okla. Bar Assn., Okla. Trial Lawyers Assn., Okla. Soc. CPAs, Cleve. County Bar Assn., Soc. CPAs. Democrat. Methodist. Avocations: clock collecting, motorcycling, golf, boating. Home: 1819 Joe Taylor Cir Norman OK 73072-6650 Office: Talley Crowder & Gallagher 219 E Main St Norman OK 73069-1304 E-mail: rtalley@mmcable.com.

TALLEY, RICHARD WOODROW, accountant; b. Birmingham, Ala., Sept. 10, 1941; s. Alton Woodrow and Alta O. (Tittle) T.; m. Anita Marcell Moses, Jan. 14, 1966; children: Richard Woodrow Jr., Leah Michelle. BS in Commerce and Bus. Adminstrn., U. Ala., 1964. CPA Ala. Pres. Smither, Talley & Mauldin, P.C., Decatur, Ala., 1964—. Officer Boy Scouts Am., Decatur, Austin Band Boosters, Decatur, PTA, Decatur; mgr., coach Dixie Youth Baseball, Decatur; deacon Ch. of Christ. Served as sgt. USAR, 1964-70. Named Boss of Yr. Decatur Jaycees, 1980. Mem. AICPA, Tenn. Soc. CPAs, Ala. Soc. CPAs, Commerce Execs. Soc. U. Ala., Lions (sec. 1982-83, treas. 1985-86, sec.-treas. 1994-95). Avocations: genealogy, photography. Home: 1266 Brandywine Ln SE Decatur AL 35601-4582 Office: Smither Talley & Mauldin PC PO Box 2067 Decatur AL 35602-2067

TALLEY, ROBERT COCHRAN, medical school dean and administrator, cardiologist; b. May 26, 1936; m. Katherine Ann Plocar; children: Andrew, Katherine, David. BS, U. Mich., 1958; MD, U. Chgo., 1962. Diplomate Nat. Bd. Med. Examiners (mem. medicine com. 1984-88, com. chair 1988-93), Am. Bd. Internal Medicine, subsplty. cardiovascular diseases. Asst. prof., dept. physiology and medicine U. Tex. Med. Sch., San Antonio, 1969-71, head, sect. cardiovascular diseases, 1971-75, assoc. prof., dept. medicine, 1971-75; acting chief medicine VA Hosp., 1974, chief cardiology service, 1973-75; chmn. dept. internal medicine U. S.D. Sch. Medicine, Sioux Falls, 1975-87, Freeman prof. medicine, 1984-87, interim v.p., dean, 1986-87, v.p., dean, 1987—. Mem. Liaison Com. on Med. Edn., 1998—; mem. adminstrn. bd., coun. of deans Assn. Am. Med. Colls., 1999-2000. Contbr. 33 articles to med. jours. Served to surgeon USPHS, 1966-68. Tchg. scholar Am. Heart Assn. U. Chgo., 1972-75; Outstanding Tchr. and Clinician award U. Tex., San Antonio, 1969-70, Ann. Tchg. award for Best Clin. Instr., U. Tex., San Antonio, 1971-72, Anton Hyden Disting. Prof. award. U. S.D. Sch. Medicine, 1979, Faculty Recognition award U. S.D. Sch. Medicine, 1981. Fellow ACP, Am. Coll. Cardiology; mem. AMA, Am. Heart Assn. (bd. dirs. Dakota affiliate), Am. Fedn. Clin. Rsch. Home: 1305 Cedar Ln Sioux Falls SD 57103-4512 Office: U SD Sch Medicine 1400 W 22nd St Sioux Falls SD 57105-1505*

TALLEY, ROBERT MORRELL, aerospace company executive; b. Erwin, Tenn., Mar. 13, 1924; s. Robert Taylor and Anna Laura (Morrell) T.; m. Mary Sue Williams, June 5, 1948; children: David, Carol. Student, East Tenn. State Coll., 1942-43, U. Va., 1943-44; BS U. S.C., 1945; MS, U. Tenn., 1948, PhD, 1950. Chief infrared br., chief solid state div. U.S. Naval Ordnance Lab., White Oak, Md., 1951-58; mgr. lab. Santa Barbara Rsch. Ctr. subs. Hughes Aircraft, Calif., 1958-69, v.p., 1969-76, pres., 1976-89, ret. Contbr. articles to profl. jours.; patentee in field. Trustee U. Calif.-Santa Barbara Found.; bd. dirs. Industry Edn. Coun., Santa Barbara. With USN, 1943-46. Fellow Am. Phys. Soc.; mem. Optical Soc. Am., LaCumbre Club, Sigma Xi

TALLEY, TRUMAN MACDONALD, publisher; b. N.Y.C., Feb. 3, 1925; s. Truman Hughes and Helen Nicholson (Macdonald) T.; m. Madelon DeVoe, Oct. 17, 1953 (dec. 1997); children: Melanie, Macdonald, Marina. Student, Buckley Sch., Deerfield Acad., Sorbonne, 1945-46; grad. cum laude, Princeton U., 1949. Assoc. editor New Am. Libr. of World Lit., N.Y.C., 1949-59, editorial v.p., 1959-64; pres., editl. dir. Weybright & Talley, N.Y.C., 1966-78; pub. Truman Talley Books with Times Books, 1978-82; with E.P. Dutton, 1983-98, St. Martin's Press, N.Y.C., 1998—. Mem. grad. bd. Princeton Tiger, 1950—. Trustee Clinton Hall Assn. Merc. Libr., N.Y.C. With AUS, 1943-46, ETO. Decorated Purple Heart. Mem. P.E.N. Clubs: Anglers, Brook, Maidstone, Southampton Beach. Office: Truman Talley Books St Martin's Press 175 5th Ave New York NY 10010-7703

TALLEY, WILLIAM GILES, JR. manufacturing company executive; b. Adel, Ga., Sept. 25, 1939; s. William Giles and Mary (McGlamry) T.; m. Jacqueline Vickery, Apr. 14, 1962; children: William Giles, John Lindsey, Bronwyn Ashley. BSBA, U. S.C., 1961. Mgmt. trainee Talley Veneer & Crate Co., Inc., Adel, 1961-62; with Talley's Box Co., Leesburg, Fla., 1962-69, plant mgr., ptnr., 1967-69; gen. mgr. Growers Container Coop., Inc., 1969-96; pres. Talley Acres, Inc., 1979—, Talley Ent., Inc., 1997—. Bd. dirs. Sun Trust Bank Ctr. Fla., N.A., Orlando. Past chmn., bd. dirs. Leesburg Hosp. Assn.; bd. dirs. Hospice of Lake Sumter, Inc., 1997—, pres., 1999; bd. dirs., treas., mem. exec. com. Ctrl. Fla. Healthcare Devel. Found., Inc.; bd. trustees Bethune-Cookman Coll., Daytona Beach, Fla., 1999—. Mem. Leesburg C. of C., Sigma Alpha Epsilon. Republican. Methodist. Home: 2206 Talley Court Rd Leesburg FL 34748-3177 Office: Po Box 49817 Leesburg FL 34749-0817

TALLIO, KEVIN VERNE, engineering supervisor; b. Detroit, June 13, 1960; s. Verne Samuel Jr. and Patricia Anne (Perry) Tallio; m. Eileen Patricia Dooner, June 30, 1981 (1991); m. Nancy Lee Strand, Sept. 2, 1995; children: Clarissa, Jacob, Kyle. AA, Atlantic C.C., Mays Landing, N.J., 1982; BS in Mech. Engring., Drexel U., 1985, MS in Mech. Engring., 1987, PhD, 1998. Rsch. engr. Sci. Rsch. Lab. Ford Motor Co., Dearborn, Mich., 1989-98, tech. specialist Sci. Rsch. Lab., 1998-99, supr. V-engine engring., 1999—. Frederic O. Hess rsch. fellow Drexel U., 1987. Mem. Soc. Automotive Engrs., Sigma Xi. Achievements include patent for engine performance improvement. Office phone. Home: 6407 Bedview Dr Saline MI 48176 Office: 21500 Oakwood Blvd # Md53poee Dearborn MI 48124-4080 E-mail: ktallio@ford.com.

TALLMAN, RICHARD C. federal judge, lawyer; b. Oakland, Calif., Mar. 3, 1953; s. Kenneth A. and Jean M. Tallman; m. Cynthia Ostolaza, Nov. 14, 1981. BSC, U. Santa Clara, 1975; JD, Northwestern U., 1978. Bar: Calif. 1978, Wash. 1979, U.S. Dist. Ct. (no. dist.) Calif. 1979, U.S. Dist. Ct. (we. dist.) Wash. 1979, U.S. Ct. Appeals (9th cir.) 1979, U.S. Dist. Ct. Hawaii 1986, U.S. Supreme Ct. 1997, U.S. Dist. Ct. (ea. dist.) Wash. 1998. Law clk. to Hon. Morrell E. Sharp U.S. Dist. Ct. (we. dist.) Wash., Seattle, 1978—79; trial atty. U.S. Dept. Justice, Washington, 1979—80; asst. U.S. atty. (we. dist.) Wash., Seattle, 1980—83; ptnr. Schweppe, Krug & Tausend, PS, 1983—89; mem. Bogle & Gates, PLLC, 1990—99; ptnr. Tallman & Severin, LLP, 1999—2000; apptd. U.S. cir. judge U.S. Ct. Appeals (9th cir.), 2000—. Chmn. western dist. Wash. Lawyer Reps. to Ninth Cir. Jud. Conf., 1996—97. Instr. Nat. Pk. Svc. Seasonal Ranger Acad., Everett and Mt. Vernon, Wash., 1983—93; chmn. Edmonds C.C. Found., Lynnwood, 1990—92; gen. counsel Seattle-King County Crime Stoppers, 1987—99; mem. exec. bd. Chief Seattle coun. Boy Scouts Am., 1997—. Mem.: FBA (we. dist. trustee 1992—93, v.p. 1994, pres. 1995), ABA, Seattle-King County Bar Assn., Wash. Athletic Club, Rainier Club. Avocations: hunting, hiking, fishing. Office: Park Place Bldg 1200 Sixth Avenue 21st FL Seattle WA 98101-3123

TALLMAN, ROBERT HALL, investment company executive; b. Creston, Iowa, Aug. 10, 1915; s. Ralph H. and Hazel Verne (Hall) T.; m. Elizabeth Childs, Sept. 19, 1938; children: Susan, Mary, Timothy. BS, U. Nebr., 1937. Trainee to dist. mgr. Firestone Tire & Rubber Co., Akron, Ohio, 1937-50; pres. Tallman Oil Co., Fargo, N.D., 1950-80; chmn. bd. State Bank of Hawley, Minn., 1966-70, 1st Nat. Bank of Barnesville, 1965-88; pres. Tallman Investment Ent., Fargo, 1980—; pres., dir. Dak Tech. Inc. Dir. Bell Farms. Past pres. Fargo Bd. Edn., N.D. Petroleum Coun.; past pres. St. Lukes Hosp. Assn.; past chmn. trustees 1st Congl. Ch. of Fargo; trustee U. Nebr. Found., 1987—. Mem. Fargo C. of C. (past pres.), Am. Assn. Ret. Persons, Nat. Rifle Assn., N.D. State U. Teammakers Club (past pres.), Fargo Country Club, Kiwanis (past pres.), Masons, Shriners, Elks. Republican. Congregationalist. Avocations: golf, hunting, fishing, travel, photography. Home: 3201 16th Ave S Fargo ND 58103-4517 Office: Box 9886 2108 S University Dr Fargo ND 58103-5342

TALLMAN, SUSAN PORRI, library director; b. Oneida, N.Y., Oct. 24, 1948; d. Charles Stuart and Mary Jane Porri Blackton; m. Owen Harold Tallman, July 23, 1977; 1 child, Alexander Charles. BA in History, U. Rochester, 1971. Co-owner Carnivorous Garden, Hamilton, N.Y., 1977-83; sci. libr. asst. Colgate U., 1982-84; asst. dir. Ritter Meml. Libr., Lunenburg, Mass., 1988-92, dir., 1992—. Mem. state adv. coun. librs. Mass. Bd. Libr. Commrs., Boston, 1995-98. Mem. steering com. Lunenburg Sch. Linked Svcs., 1996—. Named Citizen of the Yr. Lunenburg Grange, 1996. Mem. Mass. Libr. Aid Assn. (bd. dirs. 1996—). Democrat. Home: 852 Massachusetts Ave Lunenburg MA 01462-1328 Office: Ritter Meml Libr 960 Massachusetts Ave Lunenburg MA 01462-1300 E-mail: stallman@cwmars.org.

TALLMER, MARGOT SALLOP, psychologist, psychoanalyst, gerontologist; b. N.Y.C., Sept. 8, 1925; d. Harry and Mildred (Schifrin) Sallop; m. Jonathan Tallmer, Apr. 12, 1949 (dec.); children— Mary, Megan, Jill, Andrew. MS, NYU, 1948; MA, Yeshiva U., 1962, PhD, 1967; postgrad., NYU, 1976. Faculty dept. psychol. founds. Hunter Coll., N.Y.C., 1969-76, assoc. prof., 1976-79, prof., 1979—94, prof. emeritus; staff psychologist Mt. Sinai Hosp., 1967-68; postgrad. Center for Mental Health, 1968-69; pvt. practice N.Y.C., 1967—2002; faculty, trustee, bd. dirs. Nat. Psychol. Assn. for Psychoanalysis; faculty N.Y. Ctr. for Psychoanalytic Tng. Author: Sex in Later Life, 1996; editor: Sex and Life Threatening Illness, HIV Testing Positive, The Child and Death, Sexuality and the Older Adult; co-author: Suicide in the Elderly; mem. editl. bd. Current Issues in Psychoanalysis, Psychoanalytic Rev.; contbr. chpts. to textbooks, articles to profl jours. Mem. APA, Boston Soc. Gerontologic Psychiatry, N.Y. State Psychol. Assn. (pres. divsn. adult devel. and aging). Address: 515 E 85th St New York NY 10028-0246 E-mail: mamadoc4@aol.com.

TALLO, DIANE, endocrinologist; b. Sharon, Pa., May 31, 1947; d. Edward Paul and Helen T.; m. Youell Spencer, July 1, 1993. BS, Youngstown State U., 1969, MS, 1971; MD, Ohio State U., 1974. Diplomate Am. Bd. Internal Medicine, Am. Bd. Endocrinology and Metabolism. Intern then resident Ohio State U., Columbus, 1974-77, fellow in endocrinology, 1977-79, asst. prof. internal medicine, 1979-85, clin. prof. medicine, 1985—; staff Riverside Meth. Hosp., 1985—. Contbr. articles to profl. jours. Mem. Endocrinology and Metabolism Soc. Avocations: tennis, gardening, cooking.

TALLY, LURA SELF, state legislator; b. Statesville, N.C., Dec. 9, 1921; d. Robert Ottis and Sara (Cowles) Self; A.B., Duke U., 1942; M.A., N.C. State U., Raleigh, 1970; m. J.O. Tally, Jr., Jan. 30, 1943 (div. 1970); children: Robert Taylor, John Cowles. Tchr., former guidance counselor Fayetteville (N.C.) city schs.; mem. N.C. Ho. of Reps. from 20th Dist., 1971-83, chmn. com. higher edn., from 1975, also 1980-83, vice chmn. com. appropriations for edn., 1973-86; state senator from 12th Dist. N.C., 1983-95; chmn. N.C. Senate Com. of Natural Resources, Community Devel. and Wildlife, 1987, Environment and Natural Resources, 1989-94. Past pres. Cumberland County Mental Health Assn., N.C. Historic Preservation Soc.; trustee Fayetteville Tech. Inst., 1981-94; mem. Legis. Research com. Mem. Am. Personnel and Guidance Assn., Fayetteville Bus. and Profl. Women's Club, Kappa Delta, Delta Kappa Gamma. Methodist. Club: Fayetteville Woman's (past pres.). Office: W Jones St Raleigh NC 27601

TALMADGE, PHILIP ALBERT, former state supreme court justice, former state senator; b. Seattle, Apr. 23, 1952; s. Judson H., Jr. and Jeanne C. Talmadge; m. Darlene L. Nelson, Sept. 6, 1970; children: Adam, Matthew, Jessica, Jonathan, Annemarie. BA magna cum laude, Yale U., 1973; JD, U. Wash., 1976. Bar: Wash. 1976. Assoc. Karr Tuttle Campbell, 1976—89; pres. Talmadge & Cutler, P.S., 1989—95; senator State of Wash., 1979—94; justice Supreme Ct. Wash., 1995—2001; ptnr. Talmadge & Stockmeyer PLLC, 2001—. Author: The Nixon Doctrine and the Reaction of Three Asian Nations, 1973; editor: Law Rev., 1975—76; contbr. articles to profl. jours. Chair Senate Judiciary Com., 1981, 1983—87, Senate Health and Human Svcs. Com., 1992—95, Wash. Senate, 1978—94, ways and means com., children and family svcs. com., edn. com. Fellow: Am. Assn. Appellate Lawyers; mem.: King County Bar Assn., Wash. State Bar Assn. Office: 18010 Southcenter Pkwy Tukwila WA 98188*

TALMAGE, DAVID WILSON, microbiology and medical educator, physician, former university administrator; b. Kwangju, Korea, Sept. 15, 1919; s. John Van and Eliza (Emerson) Talmage; m. LaVeryn Marie Hunicke, June 23, 1944; children: Janet, Marilyn, David, Mark, Carol. Student, Maryville (Tenn.) Coll., 1937—38; BS, Davidson (N.C.) Coll., 1941; MD, Washington U., St. Louis, 1944. Intern Ga. Baptist Hosp., 1944—45; resident medicine Barnes Hosp., St. Louis, 1948—50, fellow medicine, 1950—51; asst. prof. pathology U. Pitts., 1951—52; asst. prof., then assoc. prof. medicine U. Chgo., 1952—59; prof. medicine U. Colo., 1959—, prof. microbiology, 1960—86, disting. prof., 1986—, chmn. dept., 1963—65, assoc. dean, 1966—68, dean, 1969—71; dir. Webb-Waring Lung Inst., 1973—83, assoc. dean for research, 1983—86. Mem. nat. council Nat. Inst. Allergy and Infectious Diseases, NIH, 1963—66, 1973—77. Author (with John Cann): Chemistry of Immunity in Health and Disease; editor: Jour. Allergy, 1963—67; editor: (with M. Samter) Immunological Diseases. Served with M.C. AUS, 1945—48. Scholar Markle, 1955—60. Mem.: Am. Assn. Immunologists, Am. Acad. Allergy, Inst. Medicine, NAS, Alpha Omega Alpha, Phi Beta Kappa. Fax: 303-388-6955. E-mail: davidtal@juno.com.

TALMAGE, EDWARD ARTHUR, anesthesiologist; b. East Orange, N.J., 1927; AA, Princeton U., 1948; MD, N.Y. Med. Coll., 1952. Diplomate Am. Bd. Anesthesiology, Am. Bd. Pain Medicine. Intern St. Luke's Hosp., Bethlehem, Pa., 1952-53; pvt. practice Newton, N.J., 1953-56; resident in anesthesiology Robert Packer Hosp., Sayre, Pa., 1956-57, Jackson Meml. Hosp., Miami, Fla., 1957-58; instr. anesthesiology U. Miami (Fla.) Med. Sch., 1958-60; chief anesthesiologist No. Miami Gen. Hosp., 1960-63, Robert Packer Hosp., Sayre, Pa., 1963-65; with Meml. Bapt. Hosp., Houston, 1965-70; chief anesthesiology Guthrie Clinic, Robert Packer Hosp., Sayre, 1970-78; with S.W. Meml. Hosp., Houston, 1978-85; physician in interventional pain medicine West Houston Med. Ctr., 1985—. Assoc. clin. prof. Tex. U. Med. Sch. Fellow Am. Coll. Pain Medicine, Am. Coll. Chest Physicians; mem. AMA, Internat. Soc. Study Pain, World Soc. Pain Clinicians, So. Med. Assn., Am. Soc. Regional Anesthesiologists, Soc. Critical Care Medicine, Am. Acad. Pain Medicine, Am. Pain Soc., Tex. Pain Soc., Am. Neuromodulation Soc., Internat. Spine Injection Soc. Office: West Houston Doctors Ctr 12121 Richmond Ave Ste 403 Houston TX 77082-2439

TALMAGE, KENNETH KELLOGG, business executive; b. Morristown, N.J., Jan. 16, 1946; s. Edward Taylor Hunt Jr. and Dorothy Rogers Talmage. BA, Claremont Men's Coll., 1968; MBA, Boston U., Brussels, 1976. Aide to U.S. ambassador to Austria, Vienna, 1969-72; asst. to chmn. Fin. Com. to Re-elect Pres. Nixon, 1972-73; assoc. Hon. Leonard K. Firestone, L.A., 1973-74; attaché Am. Embassy, Brussels, 1974-77; mgmt. cons. strategic planning and fin. Arthur D. Little, Inc., Cambridge, Mass., 1977-80; sr. v.p. Boston Safe Deposit & Trust Co., 1980-87; pres. Lloyd's, Inc., Denver, 1987-92. Bd. dirs. Monterey Water Co., 1992—, pres., 1995-97, chmn., CEO, 1997—; bd. dirs. Pure West Industries, Inc., vice-chmn., 1993-95. Mem. exec. com. Outward Bound, U.S.A., 1980—85; dir. Vols. for Outdoor Colo., 1988—94, Breckenridge Outdoor Edn. Ctr., 1989—92; advisor Hurricane Island Outward Bound Sch., Maine, 1987—, bd. trustee, 1979—87, chmn. bd. trustees, 1980—83; bd. trustee Colo. Outward Bound Sch., 1990—96, vice chmn., 1995—96, bd. govs., 1996—. With USNR, 1968—69. Mem. The Country Club (Mass.), Denver Country Club, The Spanish Bay Club (Pebble Beach). Home: PO Box 1526 Carmel CA 93921-1526 Office: Monterey Water Co 1158 S Main St Manteca CA 95337-9505 E-mail: kktalm@aol.com.

TALMAGE, LANCE ALLEN, obstetrician/gynecologist, career military officer; b. Vandergrift, Pa., Feb. 23, 1938; s. Guy Wesley and Martha Lois (Bradstock) T.; m. Diana Elizabeth Heywood, June 23, 1962; children: Tamara, Lance Jr., Tenley. BS in Chem. Engring., U. Toledo, 1960; MD, U. Mich., 1964. Flight surgeon 24th Infantry Divsn. U.S. Army, Europe, 1966-69; resident U. Mich. Med. Ctr., Ann Arbor, 1969-73; clin. prof. Med. Coll. Ohio, Toledo, 1987—2000; med. dir. Ctr. for Women's Health, 1987—. Brigadier gen. 112th Med. Brigage Ohio Army Nat. Guard, Columbus, 1995-97; pres. med. staff Toledo Hosp., 1989-91, chair dept. Ob-gyn., 1979-86; pres. Toledo Lucas County Acad. Medicine, 1994-95; mem. Toledo Hosp. Found. Bd., 2000—; mem. adv. com. Promedia Bd. of Trustees; bd. trustees Accreditation Assn. Ambulatory Health Care, 2000—. Cabinet mem. United Way, Toledo, 1994-96; hon. chmn. March of Dimes Mothers-March, Toledo, 1989; pres. Ottawa Hills (Ohio) Athletic Boosters, 1986-88, team physician, 1981—. Named to, Ohio Vets. Hall Fame, 2001; recipient Garde Nationale Trophy, Ohio Army Nat. Guard, 1998, Outstanding Team Physician, 2002, Blue T award, U. Toledo, 2002. Fellow Am. Coll. Surgeons, Am. Coll. Obstetricians & Gynecologists (dist. chair 1996-99, v.p. 2000—); mem. AMA (mem. ho. of dels.), Ohio State Med. Assn. (pres. 1998-99), Kiwanis, Pi Kappa Phi Alumni Assn., U. Toledo Alumni Assn. (bd. trustees 1996—, pres. 2000-01), Lucas County Domestic Violence Task Force. Republican. Lutheran. Office: The Toledo Hosp 2142 N Cove Blvd Toledo OH 43606 E-mail: latalmage@voyager.net.

TALMERS, WILLIAM NICHOLAS, economist, educator; b. Manchester, N.H., Dec. 29, 1919; B.S. with highest distinction, Babson Inst., Wellesley, Mass., 1951; Ph.D. in Econs., M.I.T., 1954; m. Danae Apostolides, Mar. 24, 1950; 1 dau., Lydia Evangeline. Teaching fellow M.I.T., 1953-54; asst. prof. econs. Bucknell U., Lewisburg, Pa., 1954-56; economist, v.p. European-Am. Econ. Corp., N.Y.C., 1956-67; propr. W.N. Talmers Co., N.Y.C., 1967-78; asso. prof. econs. Molloy Coll., Rockville Centre, N.Y., 1979— . Served with USAAF, World War II. Mem. Am. Econ. Assn., Fin. Analysts Fedn., N.Y. Soc. Security Analysts. Died, July 9, 1992. Address: 150 Greenway Ter Forest Hills NY 11375-5267

TALMI, YOAV, conductor, composer; b. Kibbutz Merhavia, Israel, Apr. 28, 1943; m. Erella Gottesmann; 2 children. Diploma, Rubin Acad. Music, Tel Aviv; postgrad., Julliard Sch. Music; D (hon.), Laval U., 2001. Artistic dir., condr. Gelders Symphony Orch., Arnhem, 1974-80; prin. guest condr. Munich Philham. Orch., 1979-80; artistic dir. Israel Chamber Orch., 1984-88; music dir. New Israeli Opera, 1985-89, San Diego Symphony Orch., 1990-96, Waterloo Festival, N.J., 1994-95, Que. Symphony, Can., 1999—, Hamburg (Germany) Symphony, 2000—. Guest condr. Berlin Philharm., Munich Philharm., London Philharm., Philharmonia, Royal Philharm., Concertgebouw, Paris Orch. Nat., Israel Philharm., Tokyo Symphony, New Japan Philharm., Vienna Symphony, St. Petersburg Philharm., Pitts. Symphony, Detroit Symphony, St. Louis Symphony, Houston Symphony, Dallas Symphony, Montreal Symphony, N.Y. Chamber Symphony, L.A. Chamber Orch., Oslo Philharm., Tonhalle Orch., Zurich, others. Composer: Dreams for choir a capella, Music for Flute and Strings; Overture on Mexican Themes (recorded), 3 Monologues for Flute Solo (pub.), Inauguration Fanfare, Elegy for Strings, Timpani, and Accordion, 1997; recs. include: Bruckner 9th Symphony (Oslo Philharm.), Tchaikovsky 1st Symphony (Quebec Symphony), Gliere 3d Symphony, Brahms Sextet/4 Serious Songs, Rachmaninov's Isle of the Dead, Berlioz:Symphonie Fantastique, Overtures, Harold in Italy, Romeo and Juliette, (San Diego Symphony), Tchaikowsky/Schoenberg, Bloch/Barber/Grieg/Puccini (Israel Chamber Orch.); (with Erella Talmi) works for flute and piano. Recipient Boskovitch prize for composition, Israel, 1965, Koussevitzky Meml. Conducting prize, Tanglewood, 1969, Ruppert Found. Condr. competition award, London, 1973, Ahad Ha'am award L.A. Ctr. Jewish Culture and the Am.-Israel Cultural Found., 1997. Home: PO Box 1384 Kfar Sava 44113 Israel Office: ICM Artists 40 W 57th St Fl 16 New York NY 10019-4098 Fax: 972-9-765-6553. E-mail: talmi@netvision.net.il.

TALPOS, GARY B. surgeon; b. 1948; MD, U. Mich., 1974. Diplomate Am. Bd. Surgery. Intern, then resident U. Hosp.-U. Mich. Med. Ctr.; fellow vascular lab. rsch. Kings Coll., London, 1977-78; staff surgeon Henry Ford Hosp., Detroit; pvt. practice managed care HMO. Mem. ACS, Assn. Acad. Surgery, Am. Assn. of Endocrine Surgeons, Internat. Assn. of Endocrine Surgeons, Soc. Internat. De Chirurgie, Western Surg. Assn., Am. Assn. of Clin. Endocrinologists, Am. Coll. of Endocrinology, Ctrl. Surg. Assn. Office: Henry Ford Hosp Dept Surgery 2799 W Grand Blvd Detroit MI 48202-2689

TALSANIA, BHARAT HIMATLAL, sales and marketing executive; b. Bombay, Mar. 24, 1948; s. Himatlal Jagjivan and Vasant Himatlal (Mehta) T.; m. Shalini Bharat Surati, May 25, 1978. BS, St. Xavier's Coll., 1968; MBA, Wharton Sch. Fin., 1971. Asst. to assoc. controller U. Pa., Phila., 1971-73; supr. cost dept. Sterling Drug (Can.) Ltd., Toronto, 1973-74; corp. acctg. mgr. Ortho Pharm. (Can.) Ltd., 1974-83, mgr. spl. projects, 1976-79, mgr. mktg. fin. services, 1979-81, mgr. sales mktg. adminstrn., 1981-83; mgr. sales info. svcs. Janssen Pharm. (U.S.A.) Inc., Piscataway, N.J., 1983-86; dir. sales adminstrn. Adria Lab., Columbus, Ohio, 1986-90; dir. worldwide customer affairs Centocor Inc., Malvern, Pa., 1990-92; prin. CSC Ptnrs. Cons., Inc., Wayne, 1993-95; ptnr. Talsania Assocs., L.A., Phila., Calif., 1995-2000, pres., 2001—; v.p. market intelligence Ligand Pharms., San Diego, 2000-2001. Mem. Gujarati Mandal Cen. Ohio, 1987-88. Mem. Nat. Wholesalers' Drug Assn., Drug Distbn. Data Systems, Assn. MBA Execs., Postal Commemorative Soc., Am. Mgmt. Assn., Asian Am. Bus. Group Cen. Ohio. Hindu. Avocations: travel, tennis, swimming, squash, sailing. Home: 800 Fairview Ave Apt 12 Arcadia CA 91007-6645 Office: Talsania Assocs 800 Fairview Ave Ste 12 Arcadia CA 91007 E-mail: btusa@yahoo.com.

TALT, ALAN R. lawyer; b. Stockton, Calif., June 17, 1929; s. Daniel Henry and Josephine (LeSaffre) T.; m. Marjorie Schutte, Sept. 12, 1953; children: Bradley Alan, Stephen Scott, Mark Kevin, Karen Talt Beardsley. BA, U. Calif., Berkeley, 1951, JD, 1954. Bar: Calif. 1955, U.S. Dist. Ct. (no. and so. dists.) Calif. 1955, U.S. Ct. Appeal (9th cir.) 1955. Law clk. to the chief judge U.S. Ct. Appeal (9th cir.), San Francisco, 1954-55; pvt. practice, L.A. and Pasadena, Calif., 1955—. Gen. counsel Kirkhill Rubber Co., Brea, Calif., 1988—2000; gen. counsel, bd. dirs. KAPCO, Brea, 1985—; gen. counsel Caine, Farber & Gordon, Pasadena, Calif., 1986—. Asst. editor: Williston Casebook Contract Law, 1953. Pres. San Gabriel Valley Learning Soc., Pasadena, 1976-77; nat. v.p. Newman Clubs Am., 1949-50. Samuel Bell-McKee fellow, 1948; U. Calif. Berkeley Alumni scholar, 1947. Mem. Calif. State Bar, Jonathan Club, Valley Club (pres.), Ironwood Country Club. Avocations: fly fishing, philately. Home: 1375 St Albans Rd San Marino CA 91108-1860 Office: 790 E Colorado Blvd Ste 710 Pasadena CA 91101-2190 E-mail: artaltlaw@aol.com.

TALTY, LORRAINE CAGUIOA, accountant; b. Makati, Manila, The Philippines, July 3, 1957; came to the U.S., 1973, naturalized, 1983; d. Leon Perez and Asuncion (Rodriguez) Caguioa; m. Kevin Michael Talty, Jan. 23, 1982; 1 child, Leah Marie. BBA in Acctg. magna cum laude, Chaminade U., 1979. Office mgr., comptr. Caro of Honolulu, 1976-82; acct. David Schenkein, CPA, Latham, N.Y., 1984-86; sales rep. Caromat Corp., Torrance, Calif., 1985-86; owner Kevlor Internat., Fairport, N.Y., 1985—; acct. Cortland L. Brovitz & Co., CPA's, Rochester, 1986-87; pvt. practice acctg. Fairport, 1986—. Comptr. Tal-Tee Assocs., Inc., Webster, N.Y., 1995—. Newsletter editor Country Knolls West Civic Assn., Clifton Park, 1984-85, civic com. rep., 1985-86. Bd. dirs., vol. coord. Rochester Children's Theatre, 1994-96; treas. adv. com. St. Joseph's Sch., Penfield, N.Y., 1995-99, chair, 1999-2000; treas. Fil-Am Assn., Rochester, 1998-99; class of 2006 parents' bd. rep. Our Lady of Mercy H.S., 2000—, sec. parent's assn, 2001—. Home: 8 Silver Fox Dr Fairport NY 14450-8665 E-mail: ktalty1@rochester.rr.com.

TALUCCI, SAMUEL JAMES, retired chemical company executive; b. Newark, Feb. 13, 1929; s. Anthony and Josephine (Valocchi) T.; m. Charlotte Sisofo, Sept. 22, 1951 (dec. Oct. 1985); children: Samuel J., Charlene, Anthony, Catherine, Christina, Louisa; m. Louise Coulter, Oct. 1987. BS, U. Del., 1951. Resident mgr. Italian Subs. Rohm & Haas Co., Milan, 1956-58, gen. mgr. Italian Subs., 1958-66, mng. dir. Brit. Subs., 1966-68, dir. European ops. Phila., 1968, asst. gen. mgr. Internat. div., 1971, v.p. gen. mgr. Plastics div., 1974, v.p. corporate bus., group dir. agrl. and indsl. chems. Plastics div., 1975-83, regional dir. N.Am. region, 1983-89, ret., 1989. Bd. dirs. Rosemont Coll. Mem. Nat. Agrl. Chems. Assn. (bd. dirs.), Pa. Chamber Bus. & Industry (bd dirs.), Middle States Assn. Colls. and Secondary Schs. (mem. commn. on secondary schs.) Address: 9 Thatcher Ct 251 Montgomery Ave Haverford PA 19041

TALWANI, MANIK, geophysicist, educator; b. Patiala, India, Aug. 22, 1933; came to U.S., 1954; s. Bir Sain and Saraswati (Khosla) T.; m. Anni Fittler, Apr. 3, 1958; children: Rajeev Manik, Indira, Sanjay. BSc with honors, Delhi U., India, 1951, MSc, 1953; PhD, Columbia U., 1959; PhD (hon.), Oslo U., 1981. From rsch. scientist to assoc. prof. Lamont-Doherty Geol. Obs., Columbia U., N.Y.C., 1959-70, dir. obs., 1972-81; prof. Columbia U., 1970-82; dir. Ctr. for Crustal Studies Gulf R & D Co., Pitts., 1981-83, chief scientist exploration div. Houston, 1983-85; Schlumberger prof. geophysics Rice U., 1985—. Cons. Govt. of Iceland, 1982-92, Lockheed Martin, 1998-2000; dir. Geotech. Rsch. Inst., Houston Advanced Rsch. Ctr., Woodlands, 1985-98; Sackler disting. lectr. U. Tel Aviv, 1987; prin. investigator Apollo 17 first gravity measurements on moon. Co-author: Geophysical Atlas of the Norwegian Sea; editor 12 books on earth sci., Maurice Ewing Meml. Symposium; co-editor: Geophysical Atlases of Indian, Atlantic and Pacific Oceans; contbr. over 150 papers to profl. jours. Recipient Krishnan award Indian Geophys. Union, 1964, Exceptional Sci. Achievement award NASA, 1973, Guggenheim award, 1974, Alfred Wegener medal European Union Geoscis., 1993; Fulbright-Hays fellow, 1974. Fellow AAAS, Am. Geophys. Union (James B. Macelwane award 1964, Maurice Ewing award 1981), Geol. Soc. Am. (George P. Woollard award 1984); mem. Soc. Exptl. Geophysicists, Am. Assn. Petroleum Geologists, Norwegian Acad. Scis., Petroleum Club, Acad. Nat. Scis. Russian Fedn., Houston Geophys. Soc. (hon. mem. 1993), Houston Philos. Soc, Sigma Xi. Home: 1111 Hermann Dr Apt 10 D Houston TX 77004-6929 Office: Rice U PO Box 1892 Houston TX 77251-1892 E-mail: manik@rice.edu.

TALWAR, PANKAJ, physician; b. New Delhi, Oct. 30, 1957; came to U.S., 1984; s. Surinder Nath and Urmil (Anand) T.; m. Vandana, Jan. 14, 1984; children: Neel Sagar, Ashima, Nikhil Sagar. MB BS, Maulana Azad Med. Coll., New Delhi, 1980; DVD, U. Delhi, New Delhi, 1984. Intern Good Samaritan Hosp., Balt., 1986-87; resident Good Samaritan Hosp. & John Hopkins Hosp., 1987-89; physician pvt. practice, Rockville, Md., 1989—. Office: 50 W Edmonston Dr Ste 401 Rockville MD 20852-1244

TAM, FRANCIS MAN KEI, physics educator; b. Macao, Asia, Dec. 7, 1938; came to U.S., 1960; naturalized, 1974; s. Anthony Wai Chiu and Agatha (Yeung) Tam; m. Margaret McGann, Oct. 28, 1978; children: Mary Christina, Peter Anthony, Matthew Philip. Gen. cert. edn., U. London, 1959; cert. of matriculation, U. Hong Kong, 1959; BA, U. Calif., Berkeley, 1963; MS, U. Minn., 1967. Reader U. Calif., Berkeley, 1962-63; teaching asst. U. Minn., Mpls., 1963-65, rsch. asst., 1965-67; asst. prof. physics Frostburg (Md.) State U., 1967-95, assoc. prof. physics, 1995. Cons. sci. fair projects Regional Edn. Svc. of Appalachia, Cumberland, Md., 1989-96. Author: Thunderstorm Electrification, 1972; reviewer textbooks in field; contbr. articles to profl. publs. Pastoral leader Mary, Servant of the Lord Prayer Community, St. Peter and Paul's Cath. Ch., Cumberland, 1977-80; advisor Dem. Club, Frostburg State Coll., 1969-70. Westinghouse Corp. grantee, 1990; recipient Outstanding Alumnus award Yuet Wah Coll., 1970. Mem. Am. Phys. Soc., Am. Geophys. Union, Am. Meteorol. Soc., Am. Assn. Physics Tchrs. (Disting. Svc. award Appalachian sect. 1991, sect. rep. 1991—, sec.-treas. 1981-91, pres. 1978-79, chmn. com. on minorities in physics edn. 1989-91, mem. com. on profl. concerns 1991-94, membership and benefits com., 1994, nominating com. 1997, com. on history and philosophy 1999—). Roman Catholic. Avocations: collecting Chinese antiques, table tennis, tai chi. Home: 33 Teaberry Ln Frostburg MD 21532-2301 Office: Frostburg State U Physics Dept Frostburg MD 21532 E-mail: ftam@frostburg.edu.

TAM, PATRICK, information technology executive; b. Canton, China, June 7, 1948; m. Angelika Huttner, Sept. 14, 1976. SB, MIT, 1971, SM, 1972; PhD, U. Calif., Berkeley, 1979. CEO The Software Revolution, Inc., Bothell, Wash., 1999—2001, also bd. dirs.; pres. Arrae Internat., Inc., Kenmore, 2001—; exec. dir. Spokane Intercollegiate Rsch. and Tech. Inst., 2002—. Mem.: MIT Alumni Club of Puget Sound (pres. 2002). Home: 6150 NE 192d St Seattle WA 98028 Personal E-mail: tam@alum.mit.edu.

TAM, PATRICK SAI-WAH, research engineer; b. Hong Kong, Apr. 16, 1955; came to U.S., 1974; s. Jim and Tai (Kong) T. BS in Chem. Engring., U. Wis., 1977; MS in Chem. Engring., U. Mass., 1981, PhD in Chem. Engring., 1986. Research engr. KSE Inc., Amherst, Mass., 1983-86; research assoc. Tex. A&M U., College Station, 1987, Morgantown (W.Va.) Energy Tech. Ctr., 1988—. Patentee process purifying hydrocarbonaceous oils. Mem. Am. Inst. Chem. Engrs., Am. Chem. Soc., Sigma Xi. Office: Morgantown Energy Tech Ctr PO Box 880 Mail-stop N05 Morgantown WV 26507

TAMADA, JANET AYAKO, biomedical engineer; b. Seattle, Sept. 15, 1962; d. Henry Shiyoso and Katsuko T. BSChemE, Caltech., 1984; PhD in Chem. Engring., U. Calif., Berkeley, 1989. Fellow MIT, Cambridge, Mass., 1989-91; rsch. scientist, sr. scientist, sr. mgr., exec. dir. Cygnus Inc., Redwood City, Calif., 1991—. Contbr. articles to profl. jours. Grad. fellow NSF, U. Calif., Berkeley, 1984. Mem. AIChE, Am. Chem. Soc., Controlled Release Soc. Democrat. Achievements include patents for electrotransport and glucose monitoring.

TAMARELLI, ALAN WAYNE, chemical company executive; b. Wilkinsburg, Pa., Aug. 13, 1941; s. John Adam Tammarelli and Florence Eleanor (Heacock) T.; m. Carol Ann Crawford, Aug. 3, 1963; children: Robin Carol, Alan Wayne. BS, Carnegie Mellon U., 1963, MS, 1965, PhD, 1966; MBA, NYU, 1972. Engr. Exxon Corp., Linden, N.J., 1966, project leader, 1968-70; corp. planner Engelhard Minerals & Chem. Corp., Newark, 1970-71, asst. to exec. v.p., 1971-74, gen. mgr., 1974-77, v.p., 1977-79, group v.p., 1979-81; sr. v.p. Engelhard Corp., Iselin, N.J., 1981-83; chmn., chief exec. officer Dock Resins Corp, Linden, NJ, 1983—. Mem. exec. com. nat. adv. coun. for environ. policy and tech. U.S. Dept. Environment Protection, Gov's. Econ. Task Force, N.J.; mem. exec. com. Alliance for Union County. Capt. U.S.

Army, 1966-68. NSF fellow, 1963-66 Mem. Synthetic Organic Chems. Mfrs. Assn. (chmn., vice chmn., bd. govs.), Am. Chem. Soc., N.Y. Paint and Coatings Assn. (chmn., pres., v.p., sec., treas., bd. dirs.), Chem. Industry Coun. (chmn., bd. dirs., exec. com.), N.J. Energy Rsch. Inst. (founding trustee), Am. Mgmt. Assn., N.Y. Acad. Scis., Scabbard and Blade, Rotary (pres., v.p., sec. Linden Club), Linden Indsl. Assn. (pres.), Sigma Xi, Tau Beta Pi, Phi Kappa Phi, Omicron Delta Kappa. Home: 49 Wexford Way Basking Ridge NJ 07920-2432 Office: Dock Resins Corp 1512 W Elizabeth Ave Linden NJ 07036-6385

TAMAREN, MICHELE CAROL, special education educator, personal coach; b. Hartford, Conn., Aug. 2, 1947; d. Herman Harold and Betty (Leavitt) Liss; m. David Stephen Tamaren, June 8, 1968; 1 child, Scott. BS in Elem. Edn., U. Conn., 1969; MA in Spl. Edn., St. Joseph Coll., West Hartford, Conn., 1976. Cert. elem. and spl. edn. tchr., Conn., Mass. Tchr. N.Y. Inst. for Spl. Edn., Bronx, 1971-74; ednl. cons. Renbrook Sch., West Hartford, 1975-78; grad. instr. St. Joseph Coll., 1978; elem. tchr. Acton (Mass.) Pub. Schs., 1969-70, tchr. spl. edn., 1978-94; learning specialist and writer Educators Pub. Svc., Cambridge, Mass., 1994-96; inclusion and behavioral specialist Acton (Mass.) Pub. Schs., 1996-2000. Ednl. cons. to schs., parents, orgns., pubs., 1980-00; internat. and nat. lectr. on bldg. self-esteem in classroom, 1988-00. Author: I Make a Difference!, 1992; also articles. Bd. dirs. United Way, Acton-Boxborough, 1996—99. Horace Mann grantee Mass. Dept. Edn., 1987, 88, Mass. Gov.'s Alliance Against Drugs, 1992. Mem. Phi Kappa Phi, Kappa Delta Pi. Avocations: travel, writing, reading, distance walking. Home and Office: 34 Constitution Way Apt D Marblehead MA 01945-4652 E-mail: mtamaren@aol.com.

TAMARGO, MAURICIO J. federal agency administrator; b. Cuba; m. Tara Tamargo; children: Greg, Erin. BA in History, U. Miami; JD, Samford U. Bar: Fla., D.C., U.S. Supreme Ct. Adminstrv. asst. Fla. State Rep. Ileana Ros-Lehtinen; legis. dir. Congresswoman Ileana Ros-Lehtinen; staff dir., counsel subcom. on internat. econ. policy and trade House Internat. Rels. Com., staff dir., counsel subcom. on Africa, staff dir. internat. ops. and human rights subcom.; chief of staff, legal counsel Congresswoman Ileana Ros-Lehtinen; chmn. Fgn. Claims Settlement Commn. U.S. Dept. Justice, Washington, 2002—. Office: US Dept Justice Fgn Claims Settlement Commn 600 E St NW Washington DC 20579*

TAMARGO, RAFAEL J. neurological surgeon, educator; b. Havana, Cuba, Mar. 22, 1958; AB magna cum laude, Princeton U., 1980; MD, Columbia U., 1984. Diplomate Am. Bd. Neurol. Surgery. Intern Columbia Coll. Physicians and Surgeons, N.Y.C., 1984-85; resident in neurosurgery Johns Hopkins Hosp., Balt., 1985-92, active staff, 1992—, asst. prof. neurosurgery, 1992-98, assoc. prof. otolaryngology-head and neck surgery, 1998—. Fellow ACS; mem. Am. Assn. Neurol. Surgeons, Am. Heart Assn. Office: Johns Hopkins Hosp 600 N Wolfe St Meyer 8-181 Baltimore MD 21287-0001 E-mail: rtamarg@jhmi.edu.

TAMARO, GEORGE JOHN, consulting engineer; b. Weehawken, N.J., Mar. 16, 1937; s. Giorgio Angelo and Giacomina T.; m. Rosemary Ann Volta, June 24, 1961; children: Peter Louis, Jean Marie, Paul Anthony, Mark Joseph. B of Civil Engring., Manhattan Coll., 1959; M of Civil Engring., Lehigh U., 1961; M of Archtl. Tech., Columbia U., 1969. Profl. engr., N.Y., N.J., D.C., Md., Pa., Calif., Ill., Tex., La., Wis., Wash., R.I., Ark., Mo., Miss., Idaho; structural engr., Ill., Mass.; geotech. engr., Calif.; chartered engr., U.K.; registered European engr. Staff engr. Port Authority of N.Y. & N.J., N.Y.C., 1961-71; v.p., chief engr. ICOS Corp. Am., 1971-80; sr. ptnr. Mueser Rutledge Cons. Engrs., 1980—. Patentee in field; author tech. papers. Chmn. Bergen County Planning Bd., N.J., 1978-82; vice-chair Leonia (N.J.) Planning Bd., 1971-89; mem. Bd. Adjustment, Leonia, 1974-76; councilman Borough Governing Body, Leonia, 1972. Fellow ASCE (Martin S. Kapp Found. Engr. award 1987, Homer Gage Balcom award 2002), Instn. Civil Engrs. U.K., Instn. Structural Engrs. U.K.; mem. Nat. Acad. Engring., Internat. Soc. Soil Mechs. and Found. Engrs., Post-Tensioning Inst. (com. on rock and soil anchors), Deep Found. Inst. (Disting. Svc. award), The Moles (past pres.), Coun. on Tall Bldgs. and Urban Habitat, Chi Epsilon (hon. mem. award 1990), Tau Beta Pi. Avocations: sailing, photography. E-mai. Office: Mueser Rutledge Cons Engrs 225 W 34th St New York NY 10122-0002 E-mail: gtamaro@mrce.com.

TAMBARO, MARIE GRACE, health specialist, nursing educator; b. N.Y.C., June 28, 1946; d. Louis Vincent and Jeanette (Motto) Nunziato; m. Arthur Michael Tambaro, Sept. 20, 1964; children: Celeste, Joseph, Arthur Michael Jr., Louis Derek. BSN with honors, CUNY, 1981; postgrad., Seton Hall U., 1985. CCRN, ACLS. Critical care staff nurse Richmond Meml. Hosp., S.I., N.Y., 1980-83; nursing insgr. Brookdale C.C., Lincroft, N.J., 1983—; health specialist Holmdel (N.J.) Bd. Edn., 1990—. Apptd. to Holmdel Twp. Bd. of Health, 1989—, Holmdel Bd. of Edn. Dist. Instrnl. Coun., 1994; chair Holmdel Drug and Alcohol Commn., 1986-88; rep. to N.J. State Drug and Alcohol Commn., 1987. Mem. AAUW. Republican. Roman Catholic. Avocations: reading, gourmet cooking, fitness. Home: 15 Seven Oaks Dr Holmdel NJ 07733-1924 Office: Holmdel Twp Bd Edn 4 Crawfords Corner Rd Holmdel NJ 07733-1908

TAMBERRINO, FRANK MICHAEL, professional association executive; b. Wilmington, Del., May 3, 1955; s. Frank and Mary Pauline (Wilson) T.; m. Charlotte Jane Yates, June 4, 1982; children: F. Michael, Cara J. BA in Urban Affairs, Va. Poly. Inst. and State U., 1977, M in Urban Regional Planning, 1979. Grad. teaching asst. Va. Poly. Inst. and State U., Blacksburg, 1979; rsch. asst. R. Yearwood Enterprises, 1979; sr. planner Pinellas County Planning Commn., Clearwater, Fla., 1979-83; exec. dir. com. of 100 Citrus County, Inverness, 1983-86; exec. dir. Citrus County Indsl. Devel. Authority, Crystal River, 1986-89; sr. v.p. econ. devel. Pensacola (Fla.) Area C. of C., 1990-97; exec. dir. Sarasota (Fla.) Com. Econ. Devel., 1997-99; pres. Maury Alliance, Columbia, Tenn., 1999—. Mem. practitioners adv. com. Fla. Dept. Commerce, 1988, 91-96, chmn., 1994-96; mem. adv. coun. Enterprise Fla. Practitioners, 1996-99. Contbr. articles to profl. jours. Mem. Citrus County Extension Svc. Adv. Com., Inverness, 1987-89, Pvt. Industry Coun. Escambia County, 1995-96; bd. dirs. Crystal River chpt. Jr. Achivement, 1987, Com. of 100 Citrus County, 1987-88, USO Greater Pensacola, 1995-97, Sarasota-Manatee Wages Coalition, 1997-99, Tenn. Econ. Partnership, 2002-; mem. devel. bd. Escarosa Regional Workforce, 1996-97; mem. adv. coun. Sarasota-Bradenton Internat. Airport, 1997-99; mem. adv. bd. Keiser Coll., 1999; mem. Tenn. Indsl. Devel. Coun., 2000—, bd. dirs., 2001—. Recipient So. Practitioners award So. Bus. and Devel., 1995. Mem. Fla. Econ. Devel. Coun. (bd. dirs. 1988-92, v.p. 1989, pres.-elect 1990, pres. 1991, Profl. or Yr. award 1994), So. Indsl. Devel. Coun. (state bd. dirs. 1989-90, 97—), Ducks Unltd. (chmn. Crystal River chpt. 1987-89), Rotary (pres. Inverness 1987-88, mem. Five Flags 1990-97, Sarasota Bay 1997-99, bd. dirs. 1998-99, Columbia chpt. 2000—). Roman Catholic. Office: Maury Alliance PO Box 1076 Columbia TN 38402-1076 E-mail: frank@mauryalliance.com.

TAMBOLI, AKBAR RASUL, consulting engineer; b. Babhulgon, India, July 20, 1942; s. Rasul M. and Chandbi T.; m. Rounkbi A. Tamboli, May 21, 1969; children: Tahira, Ajim, Alamgir. BS, U. Poona, India, 1965; MS, Stanford U., 1967. Sr. engr. Miller Assocs., Pottsville, Pa., 1967-69; assoc. Edwards & Hjorth, N.Y.C., 1970-76; sr. project engr. Engrs. Inc., East Orange, N.J., 1977-80; v.p. Office of Irwin G. Cantor PC, N.Y.C., 1981-91; cons. engr. CUH2A Inc., Princeton, N.J., 1992-98; sr. v.p. Thornton-Tomasetti Group, N.Y.C., 1999—. Editor: Steel Design LFRD Method Handbook, 1996, Handbook of Structural Steel Connection Design and Details. Vol. Cancer Fund Drive, N.J., 1986. Fellow ASCE; mem. Am. Steel Constrn., Am. Soc. Welding. Avocations: golf, boating. Home: 10 Davenport Dr Princeton Junction NJ 08550-3001 Office: Thornton-Tomasetti Group 641 Ave of the Americas New York NY 10011-2014

TAMBOLI, PRABHAKAR, agriculturist, educator; b. Gwalior, India, Dec. 19, 1929; s. Mahadeo and Gangu T.; m. Sunila Muley, Feb. 6, 1953; children: Ashlesha, Satish. BS, Victoria Coll., Gwalior, 1950; PhD, Iowa State U., 1962. Cert. agrl. scientist. Assoc. dean Jawahar Lal Agr. U., Jabalpur, 1952-67; expert FAO, Rome, 1967-73; sr. agriculturist World Bank, Washington, 1974-92; adj. prof. U. Md., College Park, 1992—, exec. dir., sr. advisor, 1998—, dir., 1998-99. Cons. World Bank, Washington, 1992-99. Avocations: music, travel, tennis. Home: 6409 Greentree Rd Bethesda MD 20817-3370 Office: U Md Jh Patterson Hl College Park MD 20742-0001 Fax: 301-469-8445. E-mail: ptamboli@deans.umd.edu.

TAMBORLANE, WILLIAM V., JR. physician, biomedical researcher, pediatrics educator; b. N.Y.C., Aug. 25, 1946; s. William and Eleanor (Bernabo) T.; m. Kathleen Mary Blinn, Dec. 27, 1969; children: Melissa, Amy, James. BS, Georgetown U., 1968, MD, 1972. Diplomate Am. Bd. Pediatrics, Am. Bd. Pediatric Endocrinology. Attending physician Yale New Haven Hosp., 1977—. Asst. prof. pediatrics Yale U., New Haven, 1977-81, dir. Children's Diabetes Ctr., 1977—; assoc. prof. pediatrics Sch. Medicine, New Haven, 1982-83; chief pediatric endocrinology and diabetes Yale Sch. Medicine, 1985—, prof. prdiatrics, 1986—; program dir. Yale Children's Clin. Rsch. Ctr., N.H., Conn., 1986—; chmn. Lawson Wilkens Diabetes Com., 1988-89; dir. Yale Pediatric Pharmacology Rsch. Unit, 1999—. Editor: Yale Guide to Children's Nutrition, 1997. Recipient Jonathan May award, Charles Best award Am. Diabetes Assn., 1979, Clin. Investigator award NIH, 1979-82. Mem. Am. Fedn. Clin. Rsch., Am. Soc. Clin. Investigation, Endocrine Soc., Soc. Pediatric Rsch., Phi Beta Kappa. Office: Yale U Sch Med Children's Clin Rsch Ctr 333 Cedar St New Haven CT 06510-3289

TAMBS, LEWIS ARTHUR, diplomat, historian, educator; b. San Diego, July 7, 1927; s. Fred B. and Marguerite Johanna (Tambs) Jones; m. Phyllis Ann Greer, 1982. BS, U. Calif.-Berkeley, Berkeley, 1953; MA, U. Calif.-Santa Barbara, 1962, PhD, 1967. Plant engr. Standard Brands, San Francisco, 1953-54; pipeline engr. Creole Petroleum Co., Caracas, Maracaibo, Venezuela, 1954-57; gen. mgr. Cacyp, Maracaibo, 1957-59; instr. Creighton U., 1965-67, asst. prof., 1967-69; prof. history Ariz. State U., Tempe, 1969—82, 1987—2002, dir. Center Latin Am. Studies, 1972-76; cons. Nat. Security Council, 1982-83; U.S. ambassador to Colombia, 1983-85; U.S. ambassador to Costa Rica, 1985-87. Author: East European and Soviet Economic Affairs, 1975, Historiography, Method and History Teaching, 1975, (Geopolitics of the Pacific, (english trans.), 2002, with others) Hitler's Spanish Legion, 1979; editor: United States Policy Toward Latin America, 1976, Inter-American Policy for the 80's; co-editor: Santa Fe IV, 2000, English translation of Karl Haushofer's Geopolitics of the Pacific, 2002; co-author periodical guides; contbr. articles to profl. jours. Bd. dirs. Ariz.-Mex. Commn., 1974-82, Coun. Inter-Am. Security, 1979-90. With U.S. Army, 1945-47, 50-51. Faculty grantee Ariz. State U., 1970, 71, 74, 78, 79. Roman Catholic.

TAMBURRO, GIOVANNA M. artist; b. Corona, N.Y., Nov. 06; d. Carlo and Grace (Emanuela) Parente; m. Americo M. Tamburro; children: Luana, Robert, Lisa. Assoc. in Fine Arts, Nassau C.C., 1977; postgrad., N.Y. Tech. Inst., 1982-83. Chiropractic asst. Office of Dr. Robert Tamburro, Hicksville, N.Y., 1985—. Art tchr. to deaf children, Westbury and Hicksville, N.Y., 1974; health and wellbeing contbr. low fat diet Nassau County Med. Ctr., N.Y. State Coll. Human Ecology, Cornell U., Ithaca, N.Y. Exhibited in shows at Firehouse Gallery, 1973 (1st prize in graphics), Stix-Port Washington Libr., Stix-L.I. Black Artist Assn., 1977, N.Y. Tech. Inst., 1982-83, Huntington Art League (award 1990), East Islip Art League, 1990 (award), Jean Paris/Blossom Show (award), Graphic Eye Gallery, Port Washington, 1992, L.I. Librs., Lynn Kottler Galleries; contbr. poems to Nat. Libr. Poetry, The Poet Band Co. Va., Kent Publs., Nat. Soc. Poets. Recipient award Internat. Soc. Poets, 1994. Mem. Trustees of Nat. Mus. of Women in Arts (assoc.).

TAMBURRO, PETER JAMES, JR. secondary school educator; b. Hoboken, N.J., Jan. 20, 1947; s. Peter James and Rose Catherine (Verta) Tamburro; m. Andrea Everitt Huber, Aug. 21, 1976 (div. 1998); children: Peter James III, Christopher Harding, Matthew Everitt. BA in Polit. Sci, Dickinson Coll., 1969; MAT in Social Studies, Trenton State Coll., 1973. Cert. secondary sch. tchr., social studies N.J. Tchr. Morris Sch. Dist., Morristown, N.J., 1973-76, Hanover Park Regional H.S. Dist., East Hanover, NJ, 1976—. Cross country coach Hanover Park H.S., East Hanover, 1983—, volleyball coach, 1990—98, asst. basketball coach, 1994—2001; judge Bicentennial Com., NJ; asst. basketball coach Caldwell (N.J.) Coll., 1989—93; cons. Hist. Commn., East Hanover, 1989—92; cons. for developing AP history programs, reader AP exams ETS; mem. hist. com. Washington Twp., 1994—97, curriculum adv. com., 1996—97; adj. prof. William Paterson U., NJ, 1999—; spkr. in field. Author: (book) Gateway to Morris, 1993, Learn Chess from the Greats, 2000; editor (with Dale Brandreth): The Chess Diary of Rudolph Spielmann; editor: Atlantic Chess News, 1973—76, 2000—; contbr. articles to chess mags.; nationally syndicated columnist: U.S. Chess Fedn., 1994—. Mem. Hist. Commn., Washington Twp., NJ, 1994—96; scoutmaster Boy Scouts Am., 1994—97; team capt. Rep. Nat. Conv., 2000; Rep. County Committeeman Hanover Twp., NJ, 1984—88; legis. aide Assemblyman Robert Martin, Trenton, 1985—89. Named N.J.'s Outstanding Tchr. History, DAR, 1990, Cross Country State Section Champions, 1987, 2000, 2001, Morris County Coach of the Yr., Cross Country, 2000; fellow Taft Inst. Two Party Govt., Fairleigh Dickinson U., 1984, Woodrow Wilson Found., 1991, Nat., Coun. Basic Edn., Washington, 1993; grantee, NSF, 1978, Dodge Found., Madison, N.J., 1987. Mem.: Chess Journalists Am. (v.p. 1990—99, pres. 1999—, awards 1995, 1996, 1997), U.S. Chess Fedn. (nat. chmn. hist. com. 1994—99), N.J. Edn. Assn., Hanover Park Regional Ednl. Assn. (v.p. 1994—95, pres. 1995—2001), Morris County Hist. Soc., Nat. Coun. Social Studies. Avocations: rare books, chess. Home: 22 Budd St Morristown NJ 07960-5304 Office: Hanover Park High Sch 63 Mount Pleasant Ave East Hanover NJ 07936-2601

TAMBWEKAR, UNMESH AJAY, management consultant; b. Bombay, Nov. 4, 1971; s. Ajay B. and Ujwala Tambwekar. BS, St. Peter's Coll., Jersey City, 1992; M in Engring. Mgmt., Stevens Inst. Tech., 1996; Exec. M in Tech. Mgmt., U. Pa., 1999. Fin. analyst PaineWebber Group, Weehawken, N.J., 1990-92; sys. analyst Toys R Us, Somerset, 1992-94; mgr. Baker & Taylor, Bridgewater, 1994-96, Noblestar Sys., Parsippany, 1996-97; founding ptnr., chief info. officer Brownstone Techs., Hoboken, 1995-97; sr. mgr. Ernst & Young, Lyndhurst, 1998-2000; mgr. Answerthink Cons. Group, N.Y.C., 2000—. Contbr. articles to profl. jours. Mem. Internat. Soc. Strategic Mgmt., N.Y. New Media Assn. Avocations: reading, triathalons, skiing, travel. Home: 1109 Green Hollow Dr Iselin NJ 08830-2942 Office: Answerthink Cons Group # 17 500 7th Ave New York NY 10018-4502 Fax: 212-629-4818. E-mail: utam@home.com.

TAMELING, GARY WILLIAM, sales executive; b. Islip, N.Y., Dec. 15, 1969; s. Hermann Heinrich and Rosina Marie T. BS in Bus. Adminstrn. and Mgmt. Sci., SUNY, Oswego, 1993. Acct. exec. Sears, Roebuck and Co., Bay Shore, N.Y., 1994-97; quality control warehouse person Cablevision Sys. Corp., Hauppauge, 1994-97, sales and mktg. analyst Riverhead, NY, 1997—2001, sr. sales coord. Riverhead and Port Jefferson, 2001—. Mem. Co. H. 119th N.Y. Vols. Hist. Assn. (Willis Co.). Avocations: Civil War living history, weightlifting, racquetball, tennis, soccer. Home: 7 Tex Ct Islip NY 11751-2620 Office: Cablevision Sys Corp Industrial Rd Port Jefferson Station NY

TAMEN, HARRIET, lawyer; b. Yonkers, N.Y., May 17, 1947; d. Saul and Lily (Balglau) T. AB, Bryn Mawr Coll., 1969; JD, George Washington U., Washington, 1973. Bar: N.Y. 1974, U.S. Dist. Ct. (so. dist.) N.Y. 1975. Atty. W.T. Grant, N.Y.C., 1974-76, City of N.Y. Office Econ. Devel., divsn. Real Property, N.Y.C., 1977-81, Credit Lyonnais Bank, N.Y.C., 1981-86, Chase Manhattan Bank, 1986-89; v.p., counsel internat. corp. fin. Citibank, 1989-92; ptnr. Claugus Tamen & Orenstein, 1992-93; pvt. practice N.Y.C., 1994—. Bd. dirs. Dromenon Theatre, N.Y., 1980-86, Nat. Dance Inst., N.Y., 1982, chmn. bd. dirs., 1984-87; chmn. bd. dirs. Theatre & Dance Alliance, 1989-90; del. exch. program Women in Law, South Am., 1987—; mem. campaign staff Ed Koch for Mayor, N.Y.C., 1977; mem. steering com. Soviet Am. Banking Law Working Group, 1991—; guest lectr. Moscow Conf. on Banking, 1992, Ulaan Baatar, Mongolia, 1993-94, 96, Harriman Inst. of Columbia U., 1994; co-chair N.Y. Lawyers Com. for Clinton-Gore; mem. adv. coun. U.S. Export Import Bank, 2000. Mem. ABA, Assn. of Bar of City of N.Y.

TAMEZ, LORRAINE DIANE, writer, nurse; b. Pueblo, Colo., Nov. 26, 1950; d. Daniel and Mary Ann (Abeyta) Tamez; children: David, Christopher, Lauren. cert. in nursing, student, Trinidad State Jr. Coll., Colo. Poetry editor Purgatoire Mag. Author: Prairie Woman, 1989; contbr. poetry (as L.D. Thames) various mags. With U.S. Army, 1969-71. Mem. PEN, Poets and Writers. Democrat. Roman Catholic. Avocations: photography, photojournalism, writing poetry. Home and Office: PO Box 181 Trinidad CO 81082-0181

TAMIOLAKIS, EMMANUEL, economist; b. Serres, Greece, Apr. 6, 1957; came to U.S., 1981; s. Thomas and Maria (Fragiadaki) T.; m. Danuta Kloczko, Apr. 22, 1982. BA in Econs. and Bus., Athens Grad. Sch. Econs. & Bus. Sci., Athens, Greece, 1980; MA, New Sch. for Social Rsch., N.Y.C., 1984. Asst. treas. Maritime Realty Corp., N.Y.C., 1985—. Mem. Am. Econ. Assn., Am. Hellenic Ednl. and Progressive Assn. Democrat. Home: 15124 19th Ave # 2 Flushing NY 11357-3104

TAMIR, THEODOR, electrophysics researcher, educator; b. Bucharest, Romania, Sept. 17, 1927; came to U.S., 1958, naturalized, 1968; s. Martin and Helena (Hart) Berman; m. Hadassah Cohen, Oct. 5, 1949; children: Jonathan, Yael. BS Technion, Israel Inst. Tech., 1953, Dipl. Ingenieur, 1954, MS, 1958; PhD, Poly. Inst. Bklyn., 1962. Instr. Technion Israel Inst. Tech., Haifa, 1956-58; mem. rsch. staff Poly. Inst., Bklyn., 1958-62; mem. faculty Poly. Univ., 1962—; prof. electrophysics Poly. Inst. N.Y., 1969-92, Univ. prof., 1992—, head dept. elec. engring., 1974-79. Sci. and engring. cons. to indsl. and govtl. labs. Editor, author: Integrated Optics, 1975 (transl. into Russian and Chinese), Guided Wave Optoelectronics, 1988 (transl. into Russian); co-editor: Springer Series in Optical Sciences, 1979-96; contbr. chpts. to books, articles to profl. jours. Served with Israeli Army, 1947-49. Awarded Instn. Premium, 1964, Electronics Premium, 1967, Instn. Elec. Engrs., London; citation for disting. research Polytechnic chpt. Sigma Xi, 1978 Fellow IEEE, Instn. Elec. Engrs. (London), Optical Soc. Am.; mem. Internat. Union Radio Sci., Sigma Xi. Home: 981 E Lawn Dr Teaneck NJ 07666-6604 Office: Polytechnic Univ Elec & Comp Engring Dept 5 MetroTech Ctr Brooklyn NY 11201 E-mail: ttamir@duke.poly.edu.

TAMKIN, CURTIS SLOANE, real estate development company executive; b. Boston , Sept. 21, 1936; s. Hayward and Etta (Goldfarb) T.; m. Priscilla Martin, Oct. 18, 1975; 1 child, Curtis Sloane. BA in Econs., Stanford U., 1958. V.p., treas., dir. Hayward Tamkin & Co., Inc., mortgage bankers, L.A., 1963-70; mng. ptnr. Property Devel. Co., 1970-82; pres. The Tamkin Co., 1982—2000; chmn. Tamkin Capital Group L.L.C., 1999—. Mem. bd. govs. Music Ctr. L.A., 1974—98; pres. L.A. Master Chorale Assn., 1974—78; mem. vis. com. Stanford U. Librs., 1982—86; bd. dirs., mem. exec. com. L.A. Philharm. Assn., 1985—, chmn. bd. overseers, 2001—. Lt. (j.g.) USNR, 1960—63. Mem.: Pacific County Internat. Policy, L.A. Jr. C. of C. (dir. 1968—69), Founders League L.A. Music Ctr. (pres. 1988—98, chmn. emeritus 1998—), Hillcrest Country Club, Burlingame Country Club. Home: 1230 Stone Canyon Rd Los Angeles CA 90077-2920 Office: 9460 Wilshire Blvd Beverly Hills CA 90212-2732

TAMKIN, S. JEROME, business executive, consultant; b. L.A., Apr. 19, 1926; s. William W. and Thelma (Brandel) T.; m. Judith Deborah, Mar. 23, 1963; children: Windy Lynn, Gary William, Sherry Dawn. BS, U. So. Calif., 1950; MA, Fremont Coll., 1951, PhD, 1952; LL.D., St. Andrews U., London, 1954. Mem. rsch. staff chemistry dept. U. Calif. at Los Angeles, 1943; rsch. chemist, analyst supr. synthetic rubber div. U.S. Rubber Co., 1943-44; pres., gen. mgr. Majicolor, Inc., Los Angeles, 1947-49; rsch. engr. Coll. Engring., U. So. Calif., 1946-48; gen. mgr. Pan Pacific Oil Co., Long Beach, Calif., 1948-55; plant mgr. indsl. sales and mfg., 1953-55; v.p., sales mgr. Wilco Co., Los Angeles, 1948-55, v.p. charge indsl. sales and mfg., 1953-55; v.p., sales mgr. Unit Chem. Corp., Los Angeles, 1955-56; pres. Phillips Mfg. Co. (merger Instl. Food Equipment Corp.), 1957-62, Waste King Corp. (subs. Instl. Food Equipment Corp.), 1962-67; also dir.; v.p., dir. Dyna Mfg. Co., Los Angeles, 1962-68; pres., dir. Profl. Rsch. Inc., 1965-73; exec. v.p. Am. Med. Internat., Inc., Beverly Hills, Calif., 1966-71, dir., 1966-89; sec., dir. Rodger Young, Inc., L.A., 1971-77; pres., chmn. bd. TGT Petroleum Corp., Wichita, 1972—; pres., dir. Tamkin Cons. Corp., 1978—; owner, operator Tamkin Securities Co., 1979-86; vice chair bd., dir. Integrated Voice Solutions Inc., Chattanooga, 1991-96; bd. dirs. CAPP Care Inc., Newport Beach, Calif., 1991-99. Tech. cons. Daylin Inc., Beverly Hills, 1973-75; bd. dirs. Healthcare Decisions, Inc., Newport Beach, Calif., 1996-99. Contbr. articles to profl. jours.; patentee electronic gas detector, circuits for automatic control hazardous vapors. Cmty. warden W. Adams-Baldwin Hills Cmty. CD, 1950—52; bd. govs. West Los Angeles County coun. Boy Scouts Am., Technion-Israel Inst. of Tech., 2001—; dep. sheriff L.A. County, 1949; bd. dir. Sunair Home Asthmatic Children; city commr. L.A. Bd. Environ. Quality, 1972—73; bd. dir. Recovery Found., Fund for Higher Edn.; mem. exec. com. adv. coun. crime prevention L.A. Police, 1985—; trustee, bd. visitors U. Calif.-Irvine Coll. Medicine, 1989—; bd.. visitors UCLA Sch. Medicine, 1990—; trustee Scripps Found. for Medicine and Sci., 1996—; bd. dir. U. of Judaism, 1999—, UCLA Brain Mapping Found., 1999—; trustee Morehouse Sch. Medicine, 1995—. Officer USNR, 1944—46. Mem. AIM, Am. Mgmt. Assn., Inst. Aero. Scis., Am. Soc. Naval Engrs., Soc. Am. Mil. Engrs., Am. Chem. Soc., IEEE, Soc. Motion Picture and TV Engrs., Am. Inst. Chem. Engrs., Soc. Advancement Mgmt., U.S. Naval Inst., Calif. Scholarship Fedn. (life), Nat. Eagle Scout Assn., Sunrise Country Club, The Springs Country Club, Malibu Riding and Tennis Club, Alpha Eta Rho. Office: 2100 Sawtelle Blvd Ste 201 Los Angeles CA 90025-6264

TAMM, ELEANOR RUTH, retired accountant; b. Hansell, Iowa, July 20, 1921; d. Horace Gerald and Sibyl (Armstrong) Wells; m. Roy C. Tamm, Oct. 18, 1941 (dec. Jan. 1980); children: Larry LeRoy, Marilyn Ruth Tamm-Schmitt. Grad., Am. Soc. Travel Agts., Inc., 1970; student, Iowa Cen. C.C., 1983, 85; grad., Inst. Children's Lit., 1994. Tchr. Howard County Rural Sch., Riceville, 1939-41; bookkeeper, cashier Cen. States Power and Light Co., Elma, Iowa, 1941-42; office supr. J.C. Penney Co., Goldsboro, N.C., 1942-44, bookkeeper West Palm Beach, Fla., 1945; head teller Iowa State Bank, Clarksville, Iowa, 1955-69; office and group mgr. Allen Travel Agy., Charles City, 1969-81, tour conductor, tour organizer and planner, 1971-81; office mgr. Arora Clinics, P.C., Fonda, Iowa, 1986-90; freelance collaborator on children's books Clarksville, 1989—. Author: Flight to the Everlands, 1993, Firm Foundations, 1996, Adventure Down Under, 2001. Leader Girl Scouts U.S.A., Clarksville, 1946-47; tchr. St. John Luth. Ch., Clarksville, 1946-66, ch. sec., 1954-66, sec.-treas. Altar Guild, 1993-94; United Fund sec.-treas. Clarksville Cmty. Fund, 1956-66; sec.-treas. Clarksville Band Boosters, 1964-66. Lutheran. Avocations: reading, music, writing, decorating, designing and sewing fashions. Home: 408 E 3rd St Fonda IA 50540-0425

TAMM, MARY ANNE DECAMP, social services administrator; BA, George Washington U., 1971; MA, U. Okla., 1974; postgrad., Temple U., 1975-77; MSW, Rutgers U., 1980. Instr. U.S. Army Edn. Ctr., Ft. Kobbe, Canal Zone, 1971-72, guidance counselor Canal Zone, 1972-73; social worker Norfolk (Va.) Social Svc. Bur., 1973-75; spl. asst. to regional commr. Office Edn., HEW, Phila., 1975-77; from social worker to supr. divsn. youth and family svcs. State of N.J., Camden, 1977-82, asst. dist. office mgr. divsn. youth and family svcs., 1982-85, dist. office mgr. divsn. youth and family svcs., 1985-98, county svc. specialist, 1998—. Councilwoman Twp. of Cherry HIll, N.J., 1983-88; coun. liaison Local Assistance Bd., Youth Adv. Bd., Social Svc. Bd., Sr. Citizen Adv. Bd., Health Adv. Bd., Alcohol and Drug Abuse Adv. Bd., 1983-88; mem. County Inter-Agy. Coordinating Coun.; mem. Commn. on Missing/Abused Children; mem. Youth Svcs. Commn., mem. human svcs. adv. coun.; advisor YMCA; trustee Trinity Presbyn. Ch. Mem. NASW.

TAMMELLEO, A. DAVID, lawyer, editor, publisher; b. Providence, Aug. 9, 1935; s. Anthony and Kathleen (Gilleran) T.; m. Marylouise Kenney, Aug. 8, 1964; children: David A., Kathy. BA cum laude, Providence Coll., 1957; JD cum laude, Boston Coll., 1961. Bar: R.I. 1962, U.S. Dist. Ct. R.I., U.S. Ct. Appeals (1st cir.), U.S. Supreme Ct. Spl. investigative legal counsel State of R.I., Providence, 1961-69; sr. ptnr. A. David Tammelleo & Assocs., 1962—; chief trial counsel Monti & Monti, 1969-78; chief legal counsel Dept. Employment Security State of R.I., 1978-82; pres., pub. and CEO Medica Press Inc., Med. -Legal Pub. Co.; pub. Medica Press Inc., 1984—, editor-in-chief, 1984—. Lectr. on hosp., med. and nursing law through U.S., 1984—; legal cons. Med. Econs. mag., 1984—. Editor: Nursing Law's Regan Report, 1984—; Hospital Law's Regan Report, 1984—, Medal Law's Regan Report, 1984—; mem. editl. bd. RN mag., 1984-94; contbg. editor RN Jour., 1984—; columnist Legally Speaking, Advice of Counsel, 1984—; contbr. articles to legal jours. Atty., mem. biomed. ethics commn. Diocese of Providence,

1984—. Fellow R.I. Bar Found. (editl. bd. R.I. Bar jour. 1975-90, R.I. Bar Assn. (med.-legal com., joint com. with R.I. Med. Soc.); mem. ABA, Am. Judicature Assn., Am. Acad. Hosp. Attys., Nat. Health Lawyers Assn., R.I. Bar Assn., Cath. Health Assn., New Eng. Conf. Cath. Health Assn., Boston Coll. Law Sch. Deans Coun., Boston Coll. Law Sch. Alumni Assn. Avocations: sailing, tennis, jogging, astronomy, aeronautics. Office: Crossroads Office Pk Ste 212 75 Sockanossett Cross Rd Cranston RI 02920-5558 E-mail: Adtlaw@aol.com.

TAMMEN, RONALD, international politics educator; b. Portland, Oreg., Nov. 30, 1943; s. Clement William and Wanda Wave (Hamner) T.; m. Susan Smith, May 20, 1970. BA in Polit. Sci., Pacific U., 1965; cert., Reed Coll., 1966; MA in Polit. Sci., U. Mich., 1966, PhD in Polit. Sci., 1975. Def. analyst CIA, 1966-69; staff cons. Arms Control and Fgn. Policy Caucus, 1969-72; legis. asst. to Senator William Proxmire, 1972-82, chief of staff to, 1982-89; pres. The Tammen Group, Washington, 1989-91; mng. ptnr. Potomac Ptnrs., 1989-91; prof. nat. strategy Nat. War Coll., 1991-94, assoc. dean of faculty, 1994-98, dept. chair, 1998-2000; dir. Mark O. Hatfield Sch. Govt., Portland State U., 2000—. Editor: The Economics of Defense Spending, 1971; author: MIRV and the Arms Race, 1973; co-author: Power Transitions, 2000; contbr. articles to profl. publs. Home: 15855 Oswego Shore Ct Lake Oswego OR 97034-3601 E-mail: tammen@pdx.edu.

TAMMEUS, WILLIAM DAVID, journalist, columnist; b. Woodstock, Ill., Jan. 18, 1945; s. W. H. and Bertha H. (Helander) T.; m. Marcia Bibens, Nov. 29, 1996; children: Lisen, Kate; stepchildren: Christopher L. Johnston, Daniel Bednarczyk, Kathryn Bednarczyk, David Bednarczyk. BJ, U. Mo., Columbia, 1967; postgrad., U. Rochester, 1967-69. Reporter Rochester (N.Y.) Times-Union, 1967-70; reporter Kansas City (Mo.) Star, 1970-77, Starbeams columnist, 1977—; syndicated columnist N.Y. Times News Svc., 1989-99, Knight Ridder/Tribune Info. Svcs., 2000—. Author: A Gift of Meaning, 2001; editor-at-large Presbyn. Outlook, 1993; contbg. editor Mo. Life mag., 1980-81; commentator Sta. KCPT-TV, 1979-90. Co-recipient Pulitzer prize for gen. local reporting of Hyatt Regency Hotel disaster, 1982, recipient 1st pl. opinion-editl. divsn. Heart of Am. award Kansas City Press Club, 1991, 93, 1st pl. column divsn., 1994, 1st pl. award for best column/humor divsn. Mo. Press Assn., 1997, Best In-Depth Reporting on Religion award Am. Acad. Religion, 2001. Mem. Nat. Soc. Newspaper Columnists (v.p. 1990-92, pres. 1992-94, 1st pl. items divsn. Writing award 1992, 3d place humor writing, 1999, 2000), Soc. Profl. Journalists. Presbyterian. Office: 1729 Grand Blvd Kansas City MO 64108-1413 E-mail: tammeus@kcstar.com.

TAMPAS, JOHN P. radiologist; children: Jessica, Peter, Andrea, Christiana. BS, U. Vt., 1951, MD, 1954. Diplomate Am. Bd. Radiology. Radiology resident U. Vt., Burlington, 1957—60; teaching fellow pediat. radiology L.A. Children's Hosp., 1960—61; NIH Nat. Heart Inst. resident fellow cardiovascular radiology U. Ind., Indpls., 1961—62; attending radiology Med. Ctr. Hosp. Vt., Burlington, 1962—; asst. prof. radiology Coll. Medicine U. Vt., 1962—70; prof. & chmn. dept. radiology Med. Ctr. Hosp. Vt., Burlington, 1970—96. Contbr. articles to profl. jours. Recipient Karl Jefferson Thompson Meml. Excellence in Tchg. award, 1969, 1975; scholar, James Picker Found./NRC, 1962—65. Fellow: Am. Coll. Radiology (pres. 1987—88, bd. chancellors, emergency radiology com., accreditation com., chmn. mem. ins. com., adminstrv. affairs commn., radiologic practice commn., Gold medal 1996); mem.: AMA, Vt. Med. Soc., Vt. Radiol. Soc., Assn. Univ. Radiologists, Soc. Chmn. Acad. Radiology Depts., New Eng. Roentgen Ray Soc., Radiol. Soc. N.Am., Am. Roentgen-Ray Soc. (pres. 1982—83), Soc. Pediat. Radiology, Alpha Omega Alpha. Office: Fletcher Allen Health Ctr 111 Colchester Ave Burlington VT 05401-1416 also: Hosp Vt Med Ctr Dept Radiology Burlington VT 05401

TAMSEN, CHRISTI MARIE, secondary school educator, coach; b. Port Washington, Wis., Mar. 27, 1956; d. Leland John and Peggy Jean (Paegelow) Wagner; m. Michael Dean Tamsen, Aug. 11, 1979; children: Michelle, Tricia. BS, U. Wis., Oshkosh, 1979. Coach basketball, jr. varsity and freshman track and field Cedarburg (Wis.) H.S., 1980—85, coach volleyball, varsity, jr. varsity and freshmen, 1981—2002, tchr. phys. edn. and health edn., 1986—. Mem.: Wis. Alliance Phys. Edn. Health and Recreation. Home: 6776 Larkspur Ln Saukville WI 53080 Office: Cedarburg H S W68 N611 Evergreen Cedarburg WI 53012

TAMULONIS, FRANK LOUIS, JR. lawyer; b. Pottsville, Pa., Sept. 26, 1946; s. Frank Louis Sr. and Cecelia Florence (Hoffman) T.; m. Jane Alice Troutman, June 26, 1976; children: Kathryn Lydia, Frank Louis III. AB, Cornell U., 1968; JD, Villanova Law Sch., 1971. Bar: Pa. 1971, U.S. Supreme Ct. 1975, U.S. Ct. Appeals (3d cir.) 1981. Law clk. to dist. judge U.S. Dist. Ct. (ea. dist.), Phila., 1971-74; assoc. Kassab, Cherry & Archbold, Media, Pa., 1974-76, Zimmerman, Lieberman & Derenzo, Pottsville, 1976—. Contbr. articles to profl. jours. Mem. Am. Trial Lawyers Assn., Def. Research Inst., Pa. Def. Inst., Inst. Pa. Trial Lawyers Assn., Pa. Bar Assn., Schuylkill County Bar Assn. Republican. Roman Catholic. Office: Zimmerman Lieberman Tamulonis & Crossen PO Box 238 111 E Market St Pottsville PA 17901-2914

TAMURA, CARY KAORU, consultant; b. Honolulu, Jan. 9, 1944; s. Akira and Harue T.; m. Denise Jeanne Mitts, Oct. 17, 1987; children: Jennifer Joy, Matthew D. Student, U. Hawaii, 1961-63; BA in Philosophy, Nyack Coll., 1966; MA in Theology, Fuller Sem., 1986. Cert. fund-raising exec. Dir. svc. tng. ops. Fin. Adv. Clinic of Hawaii, Honolulu, 1972-76; dir. planned giving The Salvation Army, 1976-78, Portland, Oreg., 1981—85; planned giving cons. InterVarsity Christian Fellowship, 1978-80; account exec. Am. Income Life, 1980-81; dir. devel., planned giving U. So. Calif., 1985-90; dir. gift planning UniHealth America, Burbank, Calif., 1990-94; pvt. practice Brea, 1995—. Bd. dirs. Nat. Com. on Planned Giving, Indpls., 1991-93, sec. exec. com., 1993; mem. adv. com., adj. faculty UCLA Extension; lectr. in field. Bd. dirs. Japanese Evang. Missionary Soc., 1990-95, v.p., 1993; bd. deacons Evang. Free Ch., 1992-95. With U.S. Army, 1969-72. Mem. Planned Giving Round Table So. Calif. (pres. 1989-91, Pres.'s award 1992), Nat. Soc. Fund Raising Execs., (bd. dirs. Greater L.A. chpt. 1990-97, v.p. 1993, 95, treas. 1996-97, Profl. Fund Raiser of Yr. award 1995), So. Calif. Assn. Hosp. Developers. Republican. Avocations: photography, golf, travel. Home and Office: 1413 Robert Ct Brea CA 92821-2165 E-mail: visionkeeper1@netzero.net.

TAMZARIAN, ARMIN PETROVICH, physician; b. Kiev, Ukraine, Soviet Union, Feb. 29, 1936; Came to U.S., 1982; s. Piotyr Danielovich Tamzarian and Rivka Moisovna Gershovitz; m. Anya Ivanovna Rubinstein, Apr. 15, 1965; children: Marta, Aaron, Avram, Katya. BS in Biochemistry, Moscow U., 1955; MD, U. Riga, Riga Latvia, 1959; PhD, U. Heidelberg, 1963; PhD Litterae Humanorae, U. Berlin, 1970. Cert. medicine. Med. intern State Mental Hosp., Heidelberg, 1960-62, asst. processor, 1962-64; chmn. med. wing Comintern, Leningrad, 1964-75; chmn. Franco-Soviet Med. Alliance, Paris, 1975-82; pvt. physician Amity Clinic, N.Y.C., 1982-89; staff physician Fairview Clinics, Edina, Minn., 1989—. Author: Health in the Imperial Russian Court, 1964, The Use and Abuse of Laudanum in History, Literature, and the Lively Arts, 1975, Health in the Shtetl: The Diaspora's Silver Lining, 1979, Power Trip: Addictive Personalities and the Quest for Political Dominance, 2001. 1st lt. Red Guard, 1951-53. Jewish. Office: Tovarich Outreach 3406 E 24th St Minneapolis MN 55406-1472 Fax: 612-922-5221. E-mail: killbubba@usa.net.

TAN, ALEXANDER CO, political science educator; b. Manila, Philippines, July 5, 1964; s. Serafin Haw Tan and Anita Co; m. Chungwei Jessie Chu, Oct. 21, 1961. PhD, Tex. A&M U., 1996. Tower postdoct. fellow So. Meth. U., Dallas, 1996-98; asst. prof. poli. sci. U. North Tex., Denton, 1998—. Mem. editl. bd. Polit. Rsch. Quarterly, 2000, Electoral Studies, 1999, Electoral Studies, 1999; contbr. articles to profl. jours. Mem. Dallas Com. Fgn. Rels., Dallas, 2001. John G. Tower fellow John Goodwin Tower Ctr. Polit. Studies, 1996-98. Roman Catholic. Office: U North Tex PO Box 305340 Denton TX 76203-5340

TAN, AMY RUTH, writer; b. Oakland, Calif., Feb. 19, 1952; d. John Yueh-han and Daisy Ching (Tu) T.; m. Louis M. DeMattei, Apr. 6, 1974. BA in Linguistics and English, San Jose (Calif.) State U., 1973, MA in Linguistics, 1974; LHD (hon.), Dominican Coll. San Rafael, 1991. Specialist lang. devel. Alameda County Assn. for Mentally Retarded, Oakland, 1976-80; project dir. M.O.R.E. Project, San Francisco, 1980-81; free-lance writer, 1981-88. Author: The Joy Luck Club, 1989 (Nat. Book Critics Circle award for best novel nomination 1989, L.A. Times Book award nomination 1989, Gold award for fiction Commonwealth Club 1990, Bay Area Book Reviewers award for best fiction 1990), The Kitchen God's Wife, 1991, The Moon Lady, 1992, The Chinese Siamese Cat, 1994, The Hundred Secret Senses, 1995, The Bonesetter's Daughter, 2001; also numerous short stories and essays; screenwriter, prodr.: (film) The Joy Luck Club, 1993. Recipient Best Am. Essays award, 1991. Office: care Ballantine Publ Publicity 201 E 50th St New York NY 10022-7703

TAN, BOEN HIE, analytical biochemist, biomedical scientist; b. Padangan, Java, Indonesia, Dec. 14, 1926; s. King Hoo and Bwan Nio (Oei) T. BS, U. Leyden, Holland, 1952, MS, 1955, ScD, 1962. Profl. nuclear medicine specialist. Fellow, asst. prof. U. Leyden, Holland, 1953-55, 62-64; fellow, rsch. assoc. Max Planck Inst., Gottingen, Germany, 1961-62, U. Minn., Mpls., 1955-61, 64-68, 1972-73; rsch. assoc. N.Y. Hosp., Cornell Med. Ctr., N.Y.C., 1968-72; rsch. assoc., prof. U. Groningen, Maastricht, Holland, 1973-81; rsch. assoc. U. South Ala., Mobile, 1982-92; analytical biochemist Ala. Dept. Environ. Mgmt., Montgomery, 1992—. Contbr. over 55 articles to profl. jours. Treas. "Aesculapius" Leyden U. Pharm. Student Assn., 1952-53. Mem. Nederlandse Vereniging voor Nucleaire Geneeskunde, Am. Assn. for Clin. Chemistry, FASEB, AAAS, Am. Chem. Soc. Achievements include research on sulfhydryl, disulfide groups in denatured, renatured proteins; purification, analysis, pharmacokinetic, pharmacological activities of new drugs; alpha-1-antitrypsin, plasma proteins, enzymes, inhibitors, fibrin formation lysis; vanadate-sulfhydryl complexes and PDE activities, DNA damage and repair; diabetes and the heart. Home: PO Box 230451 Montgomery AL 36123-0451 Office: Ala Dept Environ Mgmt 1890 Dickinson Dr # A Montgomery AL 36109-2604

TAN, ENG MENG, immunologist, biomedical scientist; b. Seremban, Malaysia, Aug. 26, 1926; came to U.S., 1950; s. Ming Kee and Chooi Eng (Ang) T.; m. Liselotte Filippi, June 30, 1962; children: Philip, Peter. BA, Johns Hopkins U., 1952, MD, 1956. Intern Duke U., Durham, N.C., 1956-57; resident, fellow Case-We. Res. U., Cleve., 1957-62; rsch. assoc. Rockefeller U., N.Y.C., Calif., 1962-65; asst. prof. Washington U. Sch. Medicine, St. Louis, 1965-67; assoc. mem. Scipps Rsch. Inst., LaJolla, 1967-77; prof. U. Colo. Sch. Medicine, Denver, 1977-82; dir. Autoimmune Disease Ctr., LaJolla, Md., 1982—. Chmn. allergy & immunology rsch. com. NIH, Bethesda, Md., 1982-84; mem. nat. arthritis adv. bd. HHS, Washington, 1981-85. Contbr. chpts. in books, articles to profl. jours. Named an hon. prof., Shanghai 2d Med. U.; named to Nat. Lupus Hall Fame, 1984; recipient US Sr. Scientist award, Humbolt Found., Germany, 1986, Ciba-Giegy-Internat. League against Rheumatism, 1989, Carol Nachman award, Wiesbaden, Germany, 1989, Lee Howley Sr. award, Arthritis Found., 1989, Paul Klemperer award and medal, NY Acad. Medicine, 1993, City Medicine award, Durham, NC, 1996, Disting. Med. Alumnus award, Duke U., 2000, Mayo Soley award, Western Soc. Clin. Investigation, 2002. Fellow AAAS; mem. Am. Coll. Rheumatology (pres. 1984-85, chmn. Blue Ribbon com. Future Acad. Rheumatology 1997-98, Disting. Investigator award 1991, Gold medal award 1998), Assn. Am. Physicians, Am. Soc. Clin. Investigation, Western Assn. Physicians (v.p. 1980-81), Am. Assn. Immunologists, Brazilian Soc. Rheumatology (hon.), Australian Ryeumatism Assn. (hon.), Brit. Soc. Rheumatology (hon.), Mex. Nat. Acad. Medicine (hon.). Achievements include research on antibodies and antigens in cancer and in autoimmune diseases, systemic lupus erythematosus, scleroderma, Sjogren's syndrome, myositis and mixed connective tissue disease; relationship of autoantibodies to pathogenesis; recipient Mayo Soley award, Western Soc. Clin. Investigation, 2002. Home: 8303 Sugarman Dr La Jolla CA 92037-2224 Office: Scripps Rsch Inst 10550 N Torrey Pines Rd La Jolla CA 92037-1000 E-mail: emtan@scripps.edu.

TAN, HUI QIAN, computer science and civil engineering educator; b. Tsingtao, China, June 12, 1948; s. Dumen Tan and Ruifan Rao; m. Ren Zhong, June 16, 1994; children: William W., Danny D. BA, Oberlin Coll., 1982; MS, Kent State U., 1984, PhD, 1986. Asst. prof. computer sci. and civil enginng. U. Akron, Ohio, 1986-89, assoc., 1990—; rsch. prof. Kent (Ohio) State U., 1987. Contbr. articles to profl. jours. Grantee NASA, 1987—, 91—, NSF, 1988-92. Mem. IEEE Computer Soc., Assn. for Computing Machinery, SIGSAM Assn. for Computing Machinery, Phi Beta Kappa. Avocations: classical music, history, literature, swimming, cycling.

TAN, JAMES, internist, educator; b. Aug. 3, 1938; married. AA, U. Philippines, 1960, MD, 1965. Diplomate in internal medicine and infectious disease Am. Bd. Internal Medicine; cert. physician, Ohio. Intern Philippine Gen. Hosp., Manila, 1964-65, resident in internal medicine, 1965-67; tng. Bangkok, 1967-68; fellow in infectious diseases U. Cin. Coll. Medicine, 1968-71; mem. staff U. Cinn. Med. Ctr., other Cin. hosps., 1971-74; active staff Summa Health System, 1975—; prof. medicine Northeastern Ohio Univs. Coll. Medicine, Rootstown, 1979—, vice chmn. dept. internal medicine, 1993—, chmn. infectious disease sect., 1977—; chmn. dept. of programs Summa Health Sys., Akron, Ohio, 1992—. Contbr. articles to profl. jours.; reviewer for jours. Fellow Am. Coll. Chest Physicians, Infectious Disease Soc. Am. (sec. Ohio 1994—), ACP-Am. Soc. Internal Medicine (master, gov. Ohio chpt. 1995-99); mem. Am. Soc. for Microbiology, Ohio Med. Soc., Soc. for Hosp. Epidemiologists, Assn. Program Dirs. in Internal Medicine, Alpha Omega Alpha. Office: Summa Health Sys 75 Arch St Ste 303 Akron OH 44304-1432 E-mail: tanj@summa-health.org.

TAN, LI-SU LIN, accountant, insurance executive, investment consultant; b. Keelung, Taiwan, Republic of China, Mar. 7, 1956; came to U.S. 1985; d. I-Chang and Sung-Mei (Chen) Lin; m. Bert T. Tan, Aug. 19, 1985; children: Patricia Tan, Peter Puwen Tan, Lotus Tan. BBA, Nat. Taiwan U., 1978; MBA, Ill. Inst. Tech., 1991. CPA, Ill., Taiwan; lic. ins. agt., Ill.; registered investment advisor. Asst. mgr. T.N. Soong & Co. (mem. firm of Arthur Anderson & Co., SC), Taipei, 1978-85; practitioner Li-Su Lin, CPA, 1981-85, Li-Su Lin Tan, CPA, Naperville, Ill., 1988-90; pres. Lisu L. Tan & Co., Ltd., CPAs, 1990—; agt. Mut. of Omaha Co., Lombard, 1991-94, Met. Life and Affiliated Cos., Bloomingdale, 1993-98, GE Fin. Assurance, Oak Brook, 1999—. Chair family Naperville Chinese Assn., 1990. Mem.: AICPA (tax divsn., quality control program), Ill. Soc. CPAs, Buddha's Light Internat. Assn. (pres. 2002—, bd. dirs. 2002—), Chinese Am. Culture Found. (bd. dirs. 2000—, pres. 2001—), Nat. Taiwan U. Alumni Assn. Greater Chgo. (bd. dirs. 1999—), World Taiwanese C. of C. (dep. treas. 1998—99), Taiwanese C. of C. N.Am. (treas. 1998—99, bd. dirs. 2002—), Greater Chgo. Area Taiwanese Am. C. of C. (bd. dirs. 1995—), Taipei First Girls High Alumni Assn. (treas. 1990—94). Buddhist. Avocations: travel, art collecting, photography. Office: Lisu L Tan & Co Ltd CPAs 6S235 Steeple Run Dr #200 Naperville IL 60540-3754 E-mail: main@lisutancpas.com.

TAN, LI-ZHE, engineering educator, researcher; b. Huainan, Anhui, China, Apr. 30, 1963; came to U.S., 1985; s. Zhi-neng and Wan-shun (Yu) T.; m. Jean Qian Jiang, June 29, 1989; children: Ava, Alexander, Amber. BS, Southeast U., Nanjing, China, 1984; MS in Structural Engring., U. N.Mex., 1987, MS in Elec. Engring., 1989, PhD in Elec. Engring., 1992. Tchg. and rsch. asst. U. N.Mex., Albuquerque, 1986-91, rsch. assoc., 1992-93; sr. software/rsch. engr. Am. Laser Games Inc., 1993-94; prin. scientist Iterated Systems Inc., Atlanta, 1994-97; prof. DeVry U., Decatur, 1997—. Patentee in field. Mem. IEEE (sr.; advisor Atlanta sect.), IEEE Circuits and Systems Soc., IEEE Signal Processing Soc., IEEE Comm. Soc. Avocations: music, travel. Home: 375 Victorian Ln Duluth GA 30097-5769 Office: DeVry U 250 N Arcadia Ave Decatur GA 30030-2198 E-mail: ltan@faculty.atl.devry.edu.

TAN, LUCAS G. anesthesiologist; b. Maasin, Leyte, Philippines, Oct. 18, 1932; s. Yu Chin and Nga sio (Go) Tan; m. Victoria A. Ong, Oct. 18, 1967; children: Lowell, Vivian, Verna, Violeta. MD, U. Santo Tomas, 1960. Diplomate Am. Bd. Anesthesiology. Intern Pitts. Mercy Hosp., 1962-63; resident in surgery Lebanon Hosp., Bronx, N.Y. 1963-67; resident in anesthesiology U. Toronto, 1969-70; fellow in anesthesiology St. Luke's Hosp., Cleve., 1971-72; chmn. dept. anesthesiology Alexian Bros. Hosp., San Jose, Calif., 1978-83, vice-chmn. dept. anesthesiology, 1984-85, chmn. dept. anesthesiology, 1991-1992. Com. mem. surg. care Alexian Bros. Hosp., 1979-80, respiratory care, 1984-85, continuing edn. and libr., 1990-91, continuing med. evaluation, 1992-93. Fellow Am. Coll. Anesthesiology; mem. Am. Soc. Anesthesiologists, Calif. Soc. Anesthesiologists. Office: 10165 Dougherty Ave Morgan Hill CA 95037-9212 E-mail: lucvic@aol.com.

TAN, SENG C. research scientist, materials research executive; b. Kluang, Johore, Malaysia, June 4, 1955; came to U.S., 1980; s. Kim L. and Chen (Lee) T.; m. Ming Yung Chen, Aug. 3, 1985; children: Anthony Wenwei, Max Bowen, James Seemin. BS in Mech. Engring., Nat. Taiwan U., 1978; PhD, U. Utah, 1983. Teaching asst. Nat. Taiwan U., Taipei, 1978-79; rsch. asst. U. Utah, Salt Lake City, 1980-83; rsch. assoc. NRC, Washington, 1984-86; sr. rsch. scientist AdTech Sys. Rsch. Inc., Dayton, Ohio, 1986-90; rsch. fellow, rsch. assoc. prof. Northwestern U., Evanston, Ill., 1991-92; pres., CEO Wright Materials Rsch. Co., Beavercreek, Ohio, 1990—. Author: Stress Concentration in Laminated Composites, 1994; contbr. more than 50 articles to profl. jours.; patentee in field. Recipient fellowships, contracts, and grants. Mem. ASME, SPIE, Am. Soc. for Composites (founder-mem.), SAMPE, Soc. Mfg. Engrs. Avocations: jogging, ballroom dancing, music, badminton. Home: 3591 Apple Grove Dr Beavercreek OH 45430-1480 Office: Lab 1187 Richfield Ctr Beavercreek OH 45430-1165

TAN, TJIAUW-LING, psychiatrist, educator; b. Pemalang, Java, Indonesia, June 2, 1935; came to U.S., 1967; naturalized, 1972; s. Ping-Hoey and Liep-Nio (Liem) T.; m. Esther Joyce Kho, June 2, 1961; children: Paul Budiman, Robert Yuling, Alice Ayling. BS, U. Indonesia Faculty Medicine, 1957, MD, 1961; postgrad., U. Indonesia, Jakarta, 1961-65, UCLA, 1967-71, Pa. State U., 1971-72. Diplomate Am. Bd. Psychiatry and Neurology, Am. Bd. Gen. Psychiatry, Am. Bd. Geriat. Psychiatry. Lectr. psychiatry U. Indonesia, Jakarta, 1965-67; psychiat. cons. Ctrl. Gen. Hosp., 1965-67; postdoctoral fellow UCLA Brain Rsch. Inst., 1967-69; asst. rsch. psychiatrist, dept. psychiatry Neuropsychiat. Inst., UCLA, 1969-70; asst. prof. psychiatry Pa. State U., 1972-87, assoc. prof. psychiatry, 1987-99, prof. psychiatry, 1999—. Chief inpatient psychiatry Univ. Hosp. Milton S. Hershey Med. Ctr., 1972—, dir. Behavioral Medicine Clinic, co-dir. Biofeedback Lab., 1975—; cons. psychiatry Family and Children's Svc. Lebanon County, Lebanon, Pa., 1971-79. Contbr. articles to profl. jours. Bd. dirs. Retarded Children's Assn. Dauphin County, Inc., 1971-73. Fellow Am. Psychiat. Assn. (life); mem. Pa. Psychiat. Soc., Ctrl. Pa. Psychiat. Soc., Assn. Advancement Behavior Therapy, Assn. Applied Psychophysiology and Biofeedback, Soc. Behavioral Medicine, Assn. Psychophysiol. Study of Sleep, Am. Acad. Sleep Disorder Medicine, Am. Assn. for Geriat. Psychiatry, Am. Geriat. Soc. Home: 1478 Bradley Ave Hummelstown PA 17036-9143 Office: Pa State U Coll Medicine Dept Psychiatry 500 University Dr Hershey PA 17033-2390 E-mail: lingtan@psu.edu., lingtan@aol.com.

TAN, WILLIAM LEW, lawyer; b. West Hollywood, Calif., July 25, 1949; s. James Tan Lew and Choon Guey Louie; m. Shelly Mieko Ushio. BA, U. Pa., 1971; JD, U. Calif. Hastings Coll. Law, San Francisco, 1974. Bar: Calif. 1975, U.S. Dist. Ct. (cen. dist.) Calif. 1975, U.S. Ct. Appeals (9th cir.) 1975, U.S. Supreme Ct. 1979. Assoc. Hiram W. Kwan, Los Angeles, 1974-79; ptnr. Mock & Tan, 1979-80; sole practice, 1980-81; ptnr. Tan & Sakiyama, L.A., 1981-86, 88—, Tan & Sakiyama, P.C., L.A., 1986-88. Bd. dirs. Am. Bus. Network, L.A.; pres. bd. dirs. Asian Rsch. Cons., L.A., 1983—85; mem. adv. bd. Cathay Bank, 1990—91; bd. dirs. Asian Pacific Am. Legal Ctr.; mem. Calif. State Bd. Psychology, 2002—. Co-founder Asian Pacific Am. Roundtable, L.A., 1981; chmn. bd. dirs. Leadership Edn. for Asian-Pacifics, L.A., 1984-87; alt. del. Dem. Nat. Conv., San Francisco, 1984; mem. Calif. State Bd. Pharmacy, Sacramento, 1984-92, v.p., 1988-91, pres., 1991-92; mem. L.A. City and County Crime Crisis Task Force, 1981, L.A. Asian Pacific Heritage Week Com., 1980-85, Asian Pacific Women's Network, L.A., 1981, L.A. City Atty.'s Blue Ribbon Com. of Advisors, 1981, cmty. adv. bd. to Mayor of L.A., 1984, allocations vol. liaison team health and therapy divsn. United Way, L.A., 1986, mem. nominating com. bd. dirs. 1994-99; bd. dirs. Chinatown Svc. Ctr., L.A., 1983; conf. advisor U.S.-Asia, L.A., 1981-83; mem. L.A. city atty. Housing Adv. Com.; mem. Pacific Bell Consumer Product Adv. Panel, 1986-90; vice chair cmty. adv. bd. Sta. KCET-TV, PBA, 1993-94; mem. adv. commn. State of Calif. Com. on State Procurement Practices, 1989-90; mem. L.A. City Attys. Citizens' Task Force on Pvt. Club Discrimination, 1989-90; mem. Calif. Med. Summit, 1993; mem. Mayor's Commn. Children, Youth and Families, 1993-96; mem. pub. access subcom. Mayor's Spl. adv. Com. on Tech. Implementation, 1994-96; bd. dirs. Asian Pacific Am. Legal Ctr., 1993—, vice chair, 1999—. Named one of Outstanding Young Men of Am., 1979. Mem.: Japanese Am. Bar Assn., Nat. Asian Pacific Am. Bar, Asian Pacific Bar of Calif., Minority Bar Assn. (chmn. 1981—82, sec. 1980—81, chmn. adv. bd. 1982—83), So. Calif. Chinese Lawyers Assn. (pres. 1980—81, chmn. 1987—88, mem. various other coms.), L.A. County Bar Assn. (trustee 1984—86, vice chair human rights com. 1980—82, mem. numerous other coms.), Calif. State Bar Assn. (vice chmn. com. ethnic minority rels. 1983—85, chmn. pub. affairs com. 1981—82, mem. other coms.), Soc. Intercultural Edn. (conf. coord., advisor panelist tng. and rsch. com. 1983), Bench and Bar Media Coun. Avocations: gourmet cooking, bicycling, swimming, tennis, water color painting. Office: 201 S Figueroa St Ste 390 Los Angeles CA 90012-2543 E-mail: wltlaw@aol.com.

TANAHASHI, KAZUAKI, artist, writer; b. Kokora, Fukuoka, Japan, Oct. 4, 1933; came to the U.S., 1977; s. Shigeo and Suzuko T.; m. Linda Beth Hess, Nov. 2, 1980; children: Karuna Izumai, Ko Hanshan. Scholar in residence, San Francisco Zen Ctr., 1977-84. One-man shows include Everson Mus. Art, 1993, Calif. Mus. Art, 1994, Erlangen Mus. Art, Germany, 1997; author: Enku: Sculptor of a Hundred Thousand Buddhas, 1982, Penetrating Laughter: Hakuin's Zen and Art, 1984, Brush Mind, 1990; editor: Moon in a Dewdrop: Writing of Zen Master Dogen, 1985, Elightenment Unfolds: The Essential Teachings of Zen Master Dogen, 1999; co-editor: Essential Zen, 1994. Project coord. Plutonium Free Future, Berkeley, Calif., 1991—; coord. Ten Millennium Future, Berkeley, 1997—. Fellow World Acad. Art and Sci. Home: 1520 Blake St Berkeley CA 94703-1806 E-mail: tanahashi@aol.com.

TANAKA, J(EANNIE) E. lawyer; b. L.A., Jan. 21, 1942; d. Togo William and Jean M. Tanaka. BA, Internat. Christian U., Tokyo, 1966; MSW, UCLA, 1968; JD, Washington Coll., 1984. Bar: Calif. 1984, U.S. Dist. Ct. (cen., no. dists.) Calif. 1985, U.S. Ct. Appeals (9th cir.) 1985, D.C. 1987. Instr. Aoyama Gakuin, Meiji Gakuin, Sophia U., Tokyo, 1968-75; with program devel. Encyclopedia Britannica Inst., 1976-78; instr. Honda, Mitsubishi, Ricoh Corps., 1975-80; with editorial dept. Simul Internat.; assoc. Seki and Jarvis, L.A., 1984-86, Jones, Day, Reavis & Pogue, L.A., 1986-87, Fulbright, Jaworsky and Reavis, McGrath, L.A., 1987-89; asst. counsel Unocal, 1989-91; pvt. practice, 1991—; counsel Calif. Dept. Corps., 1993—. Active Japan-Am. Soc., L.A., 1984-95, Japanese-Am. Citizens League, L.A., 1981, 92—, Japanese Am. Cultural and Cmty. Ctr., 1986-89; vol. Asian Pacific Am. Legal Ctr. So. Calif., 1985-86. Mem. Japanese-Am. Bar Assn., Mensa. Democrat. Mem. Foursquare Meth. Ch. Avocations: Japanese language, Chinese language, U.S.-Far East relations, martial arts. Address: 5203 Summertime Ln Culver City CA 90230

TANAKA, KOUICHI ROBERT, hematologist, educator; b. Fresno, Calif., Dec. 15, 1926; s. Kenjiro and Teru (Arai) T.; m. Grace Mutsuko Sakaguchi, Oct. 23, 1965; children— Anne M., Nancy K., David K. BS, Wayne State U., 1949, MD, 1952. Intern Los Angeles County Gen. Hosp., 1952-53; resident, fellow Detroit Receiving Hosp., 1953-57; instr. Sch. Medicine, UCLA, 1957-59, asst. prof. medicine, 1959-61, assoc. prof. medicine, 1961-68, prof., 1968-97, prof. emeritus, 1998—; chief divsn. hematology Harbor-UCLA Med. Ctr., Torrance, 1961-97, chief hematology 1998-2000. Served with AUS, 1946-48. Master ACP (gov. So. Calif. region I 1993-97); mem. Am. Fedn. Med. Rsch., Western Soc. Clin. Investigation, L.A. Soc. Internal Medicine (pres. 1971), Am. Soc. Hematology, Internat. Soc. Hematology, Western Assn. Physicians, Am. Soc. Clin. Investigation, Assn. Am. Physicians, Sigma Xi, Alpha Omega Alpha. Achievements include research on red cell metabolism. Home: 4 Cayuse Ln Palos Verdes Estates CA 90275-5172 Office: Harbor-UCLA Rsch and Edn Inst Bldg C-1 Rm 12 1124 W Carson St Torrance CA 90502

TANAKA, PATRICE AIKO, public relations executive; BA, U. Hawaii, 1974. Editor Hawaii Press Newspapers, 1974-77; dir. pub. rels. Hotel Inter-Continental Maui, 1977-79; from acct. exec. to sr. v.p. and creative dir. Jessica Dee Comm., N.Y.C., 1979-87, exec. v.p., gen. mgr., 1987-90; CEO, creative dir. PT&Co., 1990—. Featured in books: Dive Right in The Sharks Won't Bite The Entrepreneurial Woman's Guide to Success, 1995, featured in books: American Dreamers, Visionaries and Entrepreneurs, 1995. Bd. dirs. Girl Scout Coun. Greater N.Y., 1996—. Named one of nation's 500 Most Influential Asian Ams., Avenue mag., 1996; recipient Mothering That Works award, Working Mother mag., 1994, Women Mean Bus. award, Bus. and Profl. Women, 1999. Mem.: Coun. Pub. Rels. Firms (bd. dirs.), Women Execs. in Pub. Rels., N.Y. Women in Comm. (pres.-elect 2001—02, Matrix award for pub. rels. 1996), Asian Pacific Am. Women's Leadership Inst. (founding bd. dirs.), U. Hawaii Alumni Assn. (bd. dirs. N.Y. chpt.), U.S. Fund for UNICEF (bd. dirs.). Home: One River Pl #2610 New York NY 10036 Office: Patrice Tanaka & Co Inc 320 W 13th St Fl 7 New York NY 10014-1200

TANAKA, RICHARD I. computer products company executive; b. Sacramento, Dec. 17, 1928; s. G. and Kei Tanaka; m. Edith M. Arita, Aug. 18, 1951; children: Steven Richard, Jean Elizabeth, John Richard, Anne Mariko. BS with highest honors, U. Calif., Berkeley, 1950, MS, 1951; PhD, Calif. Inst. Tech., 1958. Sr. rsch. engr. N.Am. Aviation, Inc., 1951-54; mem. tech. staff Hughes Aircraft Co., 1954-57; dept. mgr., sr. mem. comuter rsch. Lockheed Missiles & Space Co., Palo Alto, Calif., 1957-65; sr. v.p. Cal Comp (Calif. Computer Products, Inc.), Anaheim, 1966-77; pres. Internat. Tech. Resources Co., Tustin, Calif., 1977-80; pres., CEO Systonetics, Inc., Fullerton, 1980-86; pres. Lundy Electronics & Sys., Inc., Glen Head, N.Y., 1986-89; chmn., CEO, pres. Scan-Optics, Inc., Manchester, Conn., 1989-97; chmn., CEO V-Sys., Inc., San Juan Capistrano, Calif., 1999-2000. Vis. prof. U. Calif., Berkeley, 1962 Author: Residue Arithmetic and Its Applications to Computer Technology, 1967. Hughes fellow Calif. Inst. Tech., 1955-57 Fellow IEEE (pres. computer soc. 1965-66, centennial medal, Golden Core award 1996); mem. Internat. Fedn. Info. Processing (pres. 1974-77, hon. life mem., U.S. del.), Am. Fedn. Info. Processing Socs. (pres. 1969-71, disting. service award 1983), Phi Beta Kappa, Tau Beta Pi, Eta Kappa Nu. Home: 10321 Shadyridge Dr Santa Ana CA 92705-1568

TANAKA, RICHARD KOICHI, JR. architect, planner; b. San Jose, Calif., Oct. 16, 1931; s. Richard Inoru and Mae Yoshiko (Koga) T.; m. Barbara Hisako Kumagai, Oct. 7, 1961; children: Craig, Todd, Sandra, Trent. BArch, U. Mich., 1954; M in Urban Planning, Calif. State U., San Jose, 1978. Exec. v.p. Steinberg Group, San Jose, L.A., 1954—. Chair, bd. dirs. Happi House Restaurants, Inc., 1972—. Author: American on Trial, 1988. Dir. Human Rels. Com., San Jose, 1969-73; dir., pres. Bicentennial Com., San Jose, 1974-77; bd. dirs. Santa Clara County Sch. Bd. Assn., 1980—; pres. Internment of Local Japanese Ams., San Jose, 1984—; past pres., trustee East Side H.S. Dist., San Jose, 1971-92, Japanese Am. Citizens League, San Jose; mem. bd. govs. Boy Scouts Am., San Jose, 1978—, NCCJ, San Jose, 1976—; past pres. Tapestry and Talent, 1976-80; trustee San Jose/Evergreen C.C., 1992—, pres., 1993-94, 97-98; bd. dirs. Calif. C.C. Trustees, 1993-2002, pres., 1997-98. Mem. AIA, Am. Planning Inst., Constrn. Specification Inst., Rotary. Avocations: golf, painting. Home: 14811 Whipple Ct San Jose CA 95127-2570 Office: 60 Pierce Ave San Jose CA 95110-2819 E-mail: rktanaka@msn.com.

TANCIN, CHARLOTTE ANN, librarian; b. Hazleton, Pa., Sept. 3, 1950; d. Steven Tancin and Charlotte Elizabeth (DeVries) Tancin Bacenko. BA in Philosophy, Mount St. Mary's Coll., 1973; MLS, U. Pitts., 1983. Cataloger and circulation desk staff Albany County Public Libr., Laramie, Wyo., 1980-81, reference and circulation desk staff, 1982; reference staff Carnegie Libr. of Pitts., 1984; asst. libr. Hunt Inst. for Bot. Documentation, Carnegie Mellon U., Pitts., 1984-87, libr., sr. rsch. scholar, 1987—. Bd. dirs. Pa. Preservation Consortium, Pitts.; Bookkeeper product evaluation team mem. Libr. of Congress, Pitts., 1993-94; bd. trustees Pitts. Regional Libr. Ctr., 1994-95, chair preservation adv. com., 1991-94. Mem. ALA, Coun. on Bot. and Horticultural Librs. (pres. 1996-97, sec. 1999—), Pa. Libr. Assn. (chair preservation roundtable 1992), Spl. Librs. Assn., Soc. for the History of Natural History, Pitts. Bibliophiles (chair 1998—). Democrat. Avocations: quiltmaking, genealogy, backpacking, gardening, recreational gardening. Office: Hunt Inst for Bot Documentation Carnegie Mellon Univ Pittsburgh PA 15213

TANCOUS, JEAN JACOBS, chemist; b. Cin., Jan. 20, 1926; d. George Joe and Nellie Ruth (McGee) Jacobs; m. Ernest Tancous, Dec. 2, 1950; children: John, Judy Tancous Thompson. BA, U. Cin., 1946, MS, 1949. Rsch. assoc. Leather Industries Am. Lab. U. Cin., 1949-86; dir. U.S. Hide, Skin and Leather Assn. Lab., Cin., 1988—. Author: Skin, Hide, and Leather Defects, 1959, rev. edit., 1986; contbr. more than 40 articles to profl. jours. Recipient Hall of Fame award U.S. Hide, Skin, and Leather Assn., 1997. Mem. Am. Leather Chemists Assn. (Alsop award 1962, Prize Paper award 1965, Fred O'Flaherty Svc. award 1996, Wilson Meml. Lectr. award 1975). Achievements include research in tannery problems, cattlehide fiber orientation defect and chrome recovery. Home: 3369 Fiddlers Green Rd Cincinnati OH 45248-2807

TANCREDI, JAMES J. lawyer; b. Hartford, Conn., Apr. 1, 1954; s. Joseph I. and Angelina C. (Lanza) T.; children: Lauren, Jamie, Brian. BA in Urban Studies and Polit. Sci., Coll. Holy Cross, 1976; JD, U. Conn., 1979. Bar: Conn. 1979, U.S. Dist. Ct. Conn. 1979, U.S. Ct. Appeals (2d cir.) 1982, U.S. Dist. (so. dist.) N.Y. 1988, U.S. Supreme Ct., 1991. From assoc. to chmn. bankruptcy dept. Day, Berry & Howard, Hartford, Conn., 1979—2001, chmn. bankruptcy dept., 2001—02. Editor: CT Bankruptcy Desk Book. Bd. dirs. Conn. Mental Health Assn., Hartford, 1986-89, 2001—. Mem. ABA (bus. sect.), Am. Bankruptcy Inst., Conn. Bar Assn. (exec. com. mem. bankruptcy section), Hartford County Bar Assn. (dir., chair cmty. comml. law 1997—). Congregationalist. Office: Day Berry & Howard LLP CityPlace I Hartford CT 06103 E-mail: jjtancredi@dbh.com.

TANCREDI, LAURENCE RICHARD, law and psychiatry educator, physician; b. Hershey, Pa., Oct. 15, 1940; s. Samuel N. and Alvesta (Pera) T. AB in English, Franklin and Marshall Coll., 1962; MD, U. Pa., 1996; JD, Yale U., 1972. Diplomate Am. Bd. Neurology and Psychiatry; Bar: N.Y. 1982. Sr. profl. assoc. Inst. Medicine, NAS, Washington, 1972-74; fellow in psychiatry Columbia U. Coll. Physicians and Surgeons, N.Y.C., 1974-75; postdoctoral fellow in psychiatry Yale U. Med. Sch., New Haven, 1975-77, assoc. prof. psychiatry, 1977-84; Kraft Eidman prof. medicine and law U. Tex. Health Sci. Ctr., Houston, 1984-92, dir. health law program, 1983-92; clin. prof. psychiatry NYU, 1992—; clin. prof. health care scis. U. Calif., San Diego, 1993—; mem. staff Brookhaven nat. Labs. Clin. Ctr., 1994-96; pvt. practice N.Y.C., 1994—. V.p. Internat. Acad. Law and Mental Health, 1987-95; bd. dirs. Internat. Acad. Law and Mental Health, 2002—; mem. tech. bd. dirs. Milbank Meml. Fund, N.Y.C., 1981-84; mem. adv. com. on transplantations Health Care Fin. Adminstrn., Dept. Health and Human Svcs., 1981-84; nat. adv. bd. NIMH Ctr. for the Study of Pub. Mental Health N.Y. State Office Mental Health, 1994—; mem. cmty. svcs. bd. Dept. Mental Health, Mental Retardation and Alcohol Svcs., City of N.Y., 1995-2001; mem. sci. adv. com. Am. Suicide Found., 1995--; cons. Commn. on Med. Profl. Liability, co-prin. investigator study ABA, 1978-80; cons. in field. Fellow: N.Y. Acad. Med. Office: 129B E 71st St New York NY 10021-4201

TANCREDO, THOMAS G. congressman; b. North Denver, Colo., Dec. 20, 1945; m. Jackie Tancredo; 2 children. BA, U. No. Colo., 1968. Mem. Colo. State Ho. Reps., 1977-81; regional rep. U.S. Dept. Edn., 1981-93; mem. U.S. Congress from 6th Colo. dist., 1999—; mem. edn. and workforce, internat. rels., and resources coms. Office: US Ho Reps 418 Cannon Ho Office Bldgce Bldg Washington DC 20515-2701 also: Ste 100 5901 S Middlefield Rd Littleton CO 80123-2891*

TANCS, LINDA ANN, lawyer; b. Elizabeth, N.J., Sept. 27, 1963; d. Tibor Louis and Rose Tancs. Student, U. Warwick, Coventry, Eng., 1984; BA, Rutgers Coll., 1985; JD cum laude, Seton Hall U. Sch. Law, 1993. Bar: N.J. 1993, N.Y., 1994, U.S. Dist. Ct. (N.J.) 1993, U.S. Ct. Appeals (fed. cir.) 2001. Paralegal Fox and Fox, Counsellors at Law, Newark, 1985-88, Vol. Lawyers for Arts, N.Y.C., 1988; corp. paralegal Wilentz, Goldman & Spitzer, Woodbridge, N.J., 1988-90, assoc., 1993-96; staff atty. Muze, Inc., N.Y.C., 1996-97; mem. legal dept. IMS Internat., Inc., Totowa, NJ, 1997—99; sr. assoc. Norris, McLaughlin & Marcus, Somerville, 2000—. V.p. Pro Agents, Inc., 1995-96; adj. prof. acctg. and legal studies dept. Middlesex County Coll., Edison, N.J., 1998—; adj. prof. paralegal studies Fairleigh Dickenson U., 1999. Assoc. editor Seton Hall Law Rev. Mem. ABA, N.J. Bar Assn., N.Y. State Bar Assn. (chair young entertainment lawyers com. 1994-96), Phi Beta Kappa, Phi Sigma Iota, Delta Phi Alpha. Home: 411 Roosevelt St Roselle Park NJ 07204-1509

TANDE, TERESA LYN, secondary educator; b. Scobey, Mont., May 8, 1954; d. Lyder Christian and Isabelle Louise (Eklund) Tande; m. Doug Darling; 1 stepchild, DJ. BS in English, Minot State U., 1976; MS in Edn., U. N.D., 1995. English tchr. Towner (N.D.) Schs., 1977-80; English 8-12, libr. K-12 Starkweather (N.D.) Schs., 1980-90; English 8, prodn. Ctrl. Middle Sch., Devils Lake, N.D., 1990—; speech and edn. tchr. Lake Region State Coll., 1988—; English tchr. Mayville (N.D.) State, summer 1997. Workshop presenter, 1988—; state accreditation mem. DPI State Accreditation, Bismarck, N.D., 1994-2001; co-dir. No. Plains Writing Project, Minot, 1992-2001; co-dir. speech camp Devils Lake Pub. Schs., Devils Lake, 1996-98, Respect and Protect chair; mem. N.D. Lang. Arts State Test Writing Team. Mem. N.D. Dem. Party, 1976—, nat. del. 1980; tchr., drama dir., mem. coun. Our Saviors Luth. Ch., Devils Lake, 1984—, coun. pres., 199--2000; sec. Ft. Totten Trail Riders, Devil Lake, 1982-85, mem., 1982-95. Named State Educator of Yr. State Farm Bur., 1994, Devils Lake Tchr. of Yr., 1995. Mem. NEA, N.D. Edn. Assn. (state chair), Nat. Coun. Tchrs. English (Outstanding English Tchr. 2000), N.D. Coun. Tchrs. English (bd. dirs. 1994—), Nat. Middle Level N.D. Edn. Democrat. Lutheran. Avocations: reading, singing, writing lyrics, walking. Home: 2213 Hwy 20 Devils Lake ND 58301 Office: Ctrl Middle Sch 325 7th St Devils Lake ND 58301-2488

TANDLER, BERNARD, cell biology educator; b. Bklyn., Feb. 18, 1933; s. Arthur and Pauline (Solomon) T.; m. Helen Weisman, Dec. 25, 1955 (dec. Aug. 14, 1986); children: Janice Dena, Evan Charles. BS, Bklyn. Coll., 1955; AM, Columbia U., 1957; PhD, Cornell U., 1961; DMD (hon.), U. Cagliari, 1997. Instr. anatomy NYU, N.Y.C., 1962-63; assoc. Sloan Kettering Inst., 1963-67; asst. prof. cell biology Cornell U., N.Y.C., 1965-67; assoc. prof. Case Western Res. U., Cleve., 1967-72, prof. oral biology, 1972-91, acting chmn. dept. oral biology, 1987-89. Affiliate prof. oral biology U. Wash., Seattle, 1993—; vis. prof. U. Copenhagen, 1973, U. Cagliari, 1983, Kyushu Dental Coll., 1994-98; sr. rsch. scientist Tex. Tech U., Lubbock, 1999-01; cons. NIH, NSF, VA. Author: (with C.L. Hoppel) Mitochondria, 1972; assoc. editor: Anatomical Record, 1974-98; guest editor: Microscopy Rsch. and Technique, 1993-94, European Jour. Morphology, 1995-2000, 02—; contbr. chpts. to books, articles to profl. jours. Recipient Disting. Alumnus award Bklyn. Coll., 1981, Robert E. Kennedy award for Acad. Freedom, Ohio chpt. AAUP, 1992, Disting. Scientist award Am. Assn. Dental Rsch., 1999; USPHS fellow, 1957-62. Mem. Am. Assn. Anatomists, Am. Soc. Cell Biology, Electron Microscopy Soc. Am., Japanese Soc. Oral Biology, Japanese Assn. Anatomists, Internat. Assn. Dental Rsch. (Disting. Scientist award 1999) Am. Soc. Mammalogists, Italian Soc. Anatomy (hon.), Sigma Xi.

TANDON, RAJIV, psychiatrist, educator; b. Kanpur, India, Aug. 3, 1956; came to U.S., 1984; s. Bhagwan Sarup and Usha (Mehrotra) T.; m. Chanchal Nammi Vohra; children: Neeraj, Anisha, Gitanjali. Student, St. Xavier's Coll., Bombay, India, 1974; BS, All India Inst., New Delhi, 1980; MD, Nat. Inst. of MH, India, 1983. Sr. resident Mental Health and Neuro-Scis., India, 1983-84; resident U. Mich. Hosps., Ann Arbor, 1984-87, attending psychiatrist, 1987-2000. Dir. schizophrenia program, dir. hosp. svcs. divsn. U. Mich., Ann Arbor, 1987—2000, assoc. prof., 1993—99, prof., 1999—; cons. Lenawee County Cmty. Mental Health, Adrian, Mich., 1985—99. Author: Biochemical Parameters of Mixed Affective States; Negative Schizophrenic Symptoms: Pathophysiology and Clinical Implications; contbr. more than 120 articles to profl. jours. Recipient Young Scientist's award Biennial Winter workshop on Schizophrenia, 1990, 92, Travel award Am. Coll. Neuropsychopharmacology/Mead, 1990, Rsch. Excellence award Am. Assn. Psychiatrists from India, 1993, Sci. award, Best Drs. in Am. award, 1994-98, Gerald Klerman award for outstanding rsch. by a Nat. Alliance for Rsch. in Schizophrenia and Depression young investigator, 1995, FuturPsych award CINP, 1997. Mem. Am. Psychiat. Assn. (Wisniewski Young Psychiatrist Rschr. award 1993), World Fedn. Mental Health, Soc. for Neurosci., N.Y. Acad. Scis., Soc. Biol. Psychiatry, Mich. Psychiat. Soc. Democrat. Hindu. Office: U Mich Med Ctr Dept Psychiatry Box 0120 1500 E Medical Center Dr # 9C Ann Arbor MI 48109-0005

TANDON, RAJIV, training company executive; b. Allahabad, India, May 9, 1944; came to U.S., 1969; s. Jagdish Bihari and Vimla Devi (Mehrotra) T.; m. Priti Khanna, Sept. 1969; children: Ribhu Dev, Veeti. BTech with honors, Indian Inst. of Tech., 1966, MS in Ops. Rsch., 1972; MBA, U. Minn., 1972, PhD, 1987. Trainee Kumardhubi (India) Engring. Works, 1966-67, prodn. control officer, 1967-69; ops. rsch. analyst Nat. Car Rental, Mpls., 1971-72, mgr. ops. rsch., 1972-75, dir. fin. analysis, 1975-77, corp. v.p., MIS, 1977-81, corp. v.p., gen. mgr. car rental, 1981-86; dir. venture mgmt. U. St. Thomas, 1988-93, dir. corp. venturing, 1993-95; pres., CEO Learning Byte Internat. (formerly Inst. for Advanced Tech.), 1995—2001, Adayana, Inc., Mpls., 2001—. Mgmt. cons., 1986-95 Exec. editor New Venture Rev., 1985-90; contbr. articles to profl. jours. Pres. Planners League, 1978. Mem. Am. Mgmt. Assn., Inst. of Noetic Sci., Inst. of Mgmt. Scis. (sec. upper Midwest chpt. 1975-76, v.p. 1976-77, pres. 1977-78). Avocations: reading, news. Home: 8109 Rhode Island Ave S Bloomington MN 55438-1146 Office: 4444 W 76th St Minneapolis MN 55435 E-mail: rtandon@adayana.com.

TANDY, JEAN CONKEY, art educator; b. Reese, Mich., May 17, 1931; d. Samuel Hall and Christine Margaret (Walker) Conkey; m. Norman Edward Tandy, Jan. 25, 1952; children: Michelle Tandy Ryan, Kristen, Peter Spence. BA, Mich. State U., 1962, MA in Fine Arts, 1965. Instr. French Bath (Mich.) Cmty. Schs., 1961-62, designer program art curriculum, instr., 1962-67; instr. art Mahar Regional Schs., Orange, Mass., 1966-67, Athol (Mass.)-Royalston Regional Schs., 1967-68; invited designer, developer art curriculum Mt. Wachusett C.C., Gardner, Mass., 1968, chair art dept., 1968-97, prof. art, 1968-97, prof. emeritus, 1997—. Watercolors and clay exhibited on regular basis, 1950—. Mt. Wachusett C.C. grantee, 1970-96, Fed. Govt. grantee, 1968; chosen for subject of Mount Wachusett C.C. Most Valuable Faculty Series film. Mem. Women's Caucus for Art, Mass. C.C. Coun., Women in Arts, Teaching Faculty Assn. (v.p. 1979-80, pres. 1980-81, grievance officer 1981-82); honored with a cast bronze for contbn. to fine arts ctr. coll. Independent. Avocations: gardening, writing poetry and children's stories, reading, travel. Home: 539 Whipple Hill Rd PO Box 2 Winchester NH 03470-0002

TANE, SUSAN JAFFE, retired manufacturing company executive; b. N.Y.C. d. Irving and Beatrice (Albert) J.; m. Irwin R. Tane; children by previous marriage: Robert Wayne, Stephen Mark. BS, Boston U., 1964; postgrad., Hofstra U., C.W. Post U. Elem. sch. tchr., Long Beach, N.Y., 1964-67; pres. Fashions by Appointment, Glen Cove, 1967-71; adminstrv. asst. Peerless Sales Corp., Elmont, 1967-71; from sales mgr. to mktg. dir. United Utensils Co., Inc., Port Washington, 1973-78; v.p. ops. and control United Molded Products divsn. United Utensils Co., Inc., 1978-80; v.p. mktg. Utensco, 1980-88. Bd. dirs. Peerless Aerospace Corp. Co-inventor plastic container and handling assembly. Life mem. Ronald McDonald House; mem. Friends of the Arts-L.I. U.; friend N.Y. Pub. Libr.; pres. Susan Jaffe Tane Found.; fellow Morgan Libr.; trustee, sr. v.p. Am. Jewish Congress; life mem. Hadassah; chair Commn. for Women's Equality/Am. Jewish Congress; bd. dirs. Poe Found. Mem. Boston U. Alumni Assn., Lotos Club (mem. libr. com.). Home: 12 Sands Light Rd Sands Point NY 11050-1228

TANENBAUM, BASIL SAMUEL, engineering educator; b. Providence, Dec. 1, 1934; s. Harry Milton and Rena Ada (Herr) T.; m. Carol Binder, Aug. 26, 1956; children: Laurie, Stephen, David. BS summa cum laude, Brown U., 1956; MS, Yale U., 1957, PhD in Physics, 1960. Staff physicist Raytheon Co., Waltham, Mass., 1960-63; prof. engring. Case Western Res. U., Cleve., 1963-75; dean of faculty Harvey Mudd Coll., Claremont, Calif., 1975-93, prof. engring., 1975—, Norman F. Sprague, Jr. prof. of life scis., 1996—. Vis. scientist Cornell U., Arecibo (P.R.) Obs., 1968-69; vis. assoc. prof. Northwestern U., Evanston, Ill., 1970; vis. scholar U. Calif. Irvine Beckman Laser Inst., 1993-94, 98, 2000—; mem. sci. adv. com. Nat. Astronomy and Ionosphere Ctr., 1972-77, Calif. Poly. Inst., Pomona, 1976-87; mem. engring. and sci. adv. com. Calif. State U., Fullerton, 1976-87; mem. nat. adv. com. Rowan Coll., Glassboro, N.J., 1993-2000, chmn. curriculum subcom.; mem. Eisenhower adv. com. Calif. Postsecondary Edn. Com., 1993-97; dir. Minority Engrs. Indsl. Opportunity Program, 1973-75; dir. summer sci. program Thacher Sch., Ojai, Calif., 1977-82; vice chmn. pres.'s adv. coun. Olin Coll. Engring., Needham, Mass., 2001—; mem. biomed. engring. adv. com. U. Calif., Irvine, 2000--; cons. various corps., univ. labs., govt. agys. Author: Plasma Physics, 1967. Trustee Western U. Health Scis., Pomona, Calif., 1997—. Woods Hole Oceanog. Inst. fellow, 1959; NSF fellow Yale U., 1956-60; sr. Sterling fellow Yale U., 1959; recipient Case Western Res. U. Wittke tchg. award, 1974, Henry T. Mudd prize Harvey Mudd Coll., 1996. Mem. AAAS, Am. Phys. Soc., Am. Soc. for Engring. Edn., IEEE, AAUP, Sigma Xi (rsch. award 1969) Home: 611 W Delaware Dr Claremont CA 91711-3458 Office: Harvey Mudd Coll 301 E 12th St Claremont CA 91711-5901 E-mail: sam_tanenbaum@hmc.edu.

TANENBAUM, BERNARD JEROME, JR. corporate executive; b. Little Rock, Nov. 26, 1934; s. Bernard Jerome and Naomi (Dante) T.; m. Patricia Wise, June 9, 1955; children: Bernard Jerome III, Albert Wise. BBA, Tulane U., 1956; D.Pub. Service, Ark. Bapt. Coll., 1974. Salesman Dantan Co., Dumas, Ark., 1955; buyer Dantes Stores, 1956-61; exec. v.p. Dante and Tanenbaum, 1961; pres. UDS Inc. (formerly United Dollar Stores, Inc.), 1967—. Pres. Pudata Inc.; chmn. JAT II, Inc., vice chmn. Ark. Tax Revision Commn. County chmn. ARC, 1957-60; v.p., dir. Desota coun. Boy Scouts Am.; pres. Henry S. Jacobs Camp, S.W. region Union Am. Hebrew Congregations, also vice chmn. bd. trustees, mem. exec. com., mem. nat. com. camps and instns., rep. S.W. region to long-range planning com.; past chmn. N.Am. bd. World Union Progressive Judiasm, 1995, mem. exec. governing body, 1989; pres., dir. Camp Assn. So. Temples; mem. bd. govs. Hebrew Union Coll.-Jewish Inst. of Religion; trustee adv. bd. Tulane U.; trustee Leo N. Levi Hosp., 1994, treas., 1998; bd. dirs. Dante & Tanenbaum Found., Ark. dept. NCCJ, Ark. chpt. Arthritis Found., Hot Springs Music Festival, 1995, "50 for the Future", Hot Springs, 1995; bd. dirs., chmn. Hot Spring Documentary Film Inst., 1996—; founding chmn. Arza/World Union-N.Am.; sr. v.p. World Union for Progressive Judaism, 2001—. Recipient Ark. Ten Outstanding Young Men award, 1971, Outstanding Service award Sickle Cell Anemia Found., 1973, Distinguished Arkansan award, 1974, Internat. Humanitarian award World Union for Progressive Judaisms, 2000. Mem. Ark. Retail Mchts. Assn. (dir.), Dumas Mchts. Assn. (past chmn.), Dumas Jr. C. of C. (past pres.), Ark. Jr. C. of C. (past internat. dir.), Dumas C. of C., Zeta Beta Tau.; mem. B'nai B'rith (past dir.) Jewish religion (past pres., trustee temple). Club: Mason (32). Home: 130 S Lakeland Pt Hot Springs National Park AR 71913-7608 Office: 130 S Lakeland Pt Hot Springs National Park AR 71913

TANENBAUM, JAY HARVEY, lawyer; b. N.Y.C., Nov. 17, 1933; s. Leo Aaron and Regina (Stein) T.; m. Linda Goldman, May 28, 1961; children: Susan Hillary, Steven Eric. BA, Hobart and William Smith Colls., 1954; LLB, Union U., 1957, JD, 1961. Bar: N.Y. 1957, U.S. Dist. Ct. (so. dist.) N.Y. 1961, U.S. Supreme Ct. 1967. Internat. trader Associated Metals and Minerals Corp., N.Y.C., 1960-64; pvt. practice, 1964—. Corp. counsel Internat. Gate Corp., Gen. Gate Corp. Mem. N.Y. State Bar Assn., N.Y. Trial Lawyers Assn., Bronx County Bar Assn. Clubs: St. James (London), Le Club (N.Y.). Jewish.

TANENBAUM, JILL NANCY, graphic designer; b. Glen Cove, N.Y., Dec. 18, 1954; d. Joseph and Barbara Sally (Kosberg) W.; m. Alan Lloyd T. BA in Studio Arts, SUCO, Oneonta, 1976; MA in Publ. Design, U. Balt., 1981. Asst. art dir. John Wine Design, Washington, 1981-82; pres. art dir. Jill Tanenbaum Graphic Design and Advt., Inc., Bethesda, Md., 1982—. Judge Graphic Design USA. Works included in: S.D. Warren Idea Exchange and Promotional Services Library, Logobook, The Best of Business Card Design, 1994, works included in: The Best of Brochure Design II, 1995, works included in: The Best of Business Card Design III, 1996, works included in: The Best of Brochure Design 3, 1996, works included in: Letterhead Logo Design 4, 1996, works included in: Creativity 26, 1997, works included in: The Best of Brochure Design 4, 1998, works included in: Creative Low Budget Publication Design, 1998, works included in: American Corporate Identity 16, 2000, works included in: The Big Book of Design Ideas, 2000, works included in: Creativity 30, 2001, works included in: Graphic Design USA, 2001. Recipient Cert. Excellence Strathmore Graphics Gallery, Westfield, Mass., 1984, Excellence award Hopper Paper Co., 1994, Beckett Paper Co., 1994, 2 design awards Graphic Design U.S.A., 1995, Design award Graphic Design USA, 1998, 99, Gold award Calendar Mktg. Assn., 2000. Mem. Am. Inst. Graphic Arts (bd. dirs. 1992-94), Women of Washington, Art Dirs. Club Washington. Office: 4701 Sangamore Rd Bethesda MD 20816-2508

TANENBAUM, KENNETH, construction executive; B.Econs., U. Pa. V.p. bus. devel. LaFarge Can. Inc., Toronto, Canada. Office: LaFarge Canada 4 Union St Toronto ON Canada M6N 3M9*

TANENBAUM, SETH R. cardiologist; b. Queens, N.Y., May 20, 1954; s. Joseph and Bernice T.; m. Deborah, Mar. 30, 1980; children: Molly, Jessica. BA, Swarthmore Coll., 1976; MD, U. Chgo., 1980. Diplomate Am. Bd. Internal Medicine and Cardiovascular Disease, Am. Bd. Critical Care Medicine. Office: 2800 N Sheridan Rd Ste 400 Chicago IL 60657-6156 E-mail: s-tanenbaum@nwu.edu.

TANEV, KALOYAN STEFANOV, psychiatrist; b. Sofia, Bulgaria, Aug. 4, 1964; s. Stefan Ginev and Violeta Grivishka Tanev; m. Gayle Marie Elisabeth Spence-Tanev, Oct. 23, 1999. MD, Med. Acad. Sofia, 1990. Diplomate Am. Bd. Psychiatry & Neurology. Nursing asst. 2d Surgery Clin., Sofia, 1985-86; med. asst. Emergency 1st Aid Brigade, 1986-89; nursing companion Caring Nurse's Agy., Boynton Beach, Fla., 1991-93; lab. tech. WPB Lab., Lantana, 1992-93; resident in psychiatry Brown U., Providence, 1994-98; psychiatrist Tri-County Mental Health Ctr., Bennettsville, 1998—2002; fellow in neuropsychiatry, 2002—. Mem. Am. Psychiat. Assn., S.C. Psychiat. Assn., Am. Neuropsychiat. Assn. Avocations: bicycling, skiing, tennis, traveling, music. Home: Apt 2 51 W Main St Warner NH 03278-4213 Office: DHMC 1 Med Ctr Dr Lebanon NH 03756

TANG, C. MARK, investment advisor, venture capitalist; b. Jiangyin, China, June 21, 1964; s. Jinghua Tang and Ruifen Kong; m. Shaomei Sharon Guo, Jan. 20, 1994; children: Alexander, Gloria. BS in Biochemistry, Nanjing (China) U., 1985; PhD in Biochemistry and Molecular Biol., U. Calif., 1993; MBA in Fin., NYU, 2000. Postdoctoral rsch. assoc. Rockefeller U., N.Y.C., 1993-96; assoc. v.p. merchant banking and venture capital DH Blair Investment Banking Corp., 1996-98; co-founder, CFO, vice chmn. Aegisoft Corp. unit RealNetwork Inc., Rockville, Md., 1998-2000; investment advisor UBS PaineWebber, Inc., N.Y.C., 1998-2000, Morgan Stanley, Jersey City, 2001—. *A book entittled" The Eisential Biotech Investor" is expected to be published in the U.S & Asia late 2002.* Founding editor, biotech. analyst: Bio/Med. Tech. Stock Newsletter, 1994-98; contbr. articles to profl. jours., chpts. to books. Mem. Orgn. Chinese Am. Avocations: tennis, golf, volleyball, reading, writing. Home: 30-806 Newport Pky Jersey City NJ 07310 Office: Morgan Stanley Harborside Fin Ctr 149 Plz 3 Jersey City NJ 07311 Office Fax: 201-395-4013. E-mail: cmtang21@aol.com., c.mark.tang@morganstanley.com.

TANG, CHAO, physicist; b. Nanchang, China, Oct. 2, 1958; came to U.S., 1981; s. Danlin Tang and Yansheng Cheng; m. Laurel Q. Peng, Apr. 10, 1994; children: Daniel, Olivia. BS, U. Sci. Tech. China, 1981; PhD, U. Chgo., 1986. Rsch. assoc. Brookhaven Nat. Lab., Upton, N.Y., 1986-88, Inst. Theoretical Physics, Santa Barbara, Calif., 1988-91; rsch. scientist NEC Rsch. Inst., Princeton, N.J., 1991-97, sr. rsch. scientist, 1998—. Contbr. articles to profl. jours.; referee Phys. Rev. and Phys. Rev. Letters, 1987—, Europhysics Letters, Jou. de Physique, 1992—, Jour. Statis. Physics, 1992—, Sci., 1996—, Chem. Phys. Letters, 1996—. Recipient Telegdi prize, U. Chgo., 1982. Fellow Am. Phys. Soc. Achievements include discovery of self-organized criticality and contributions in areas of statistical physics, nonlinear dynamical systems, condensed matter physics, and protein folding. Home: 4 Dannys Way West Windsor NJ 08550-2943 Office: NEC Rsch Inst 4 Independence Way Princeton NJ 08540-6685 E-mail: tang@research.nj.nec.com.

TANG, ESTHER DON, development consultant, retired social worker; b. Tucson, Mar. 5, 1917; d. Don Wah and Yut (Gnan) Fok; m. David W. Tang, June 14, 1942; children: Patricia Karen Tang Crowley, Diana Cheryl Tang Simoes, David. Jr., Elizabeth Carol. Student, Draughn's Bus. Sch., San Antonio, 1936, U. Ariz., 1938-41, DHL (hon.), LHD (hon.), U. Ariz., 1992.

Owner, operator supermarket, Tucson, 1940-66; exec. dir. Pio Decimo Ctr., Cath. Diocese, 1966-85; cons., ptnr., vice chmn. bd. Netwest Devel. Corp., 1985—. Mem. Tucson Airport Authority, 1975—, Pima County Crime and Pub. Safety Coun., 1999; chmn. Tucson-Taichung Sister Cities, 1979-91; chmn. Tucson Sister Cities Steering Com., 1984—, Sister Cities Assn. Tucson, 1990, Ariz. Pers. Bd.; chmn. bd. dirs. Pima Community Coll., 1975-85; pres. bd. dirs. Pima Coun. on Aging, 1986-90; coord. U.S. Bicentennial, Tucson; mem. adv. bd. Ariz. Dept. Econ. Security; master of ceremonies to welcome Pres. Clinton, City of Tuscon, 1999. Named Woman of Yr., City of Tucson, 1955, Woman of Yr. in Adminstrn., 1968, Lady Comdr. the Holy Seplucher Jerusalem; recipient Disting. Friend of the Humanities award Nat. Adv. Bd., 1989, Jefferson award Ariz. Daily Star, 1987, Svc. award Pima Coun. on Aging, 1987-89, Disting. Svc. award U. Pima C.C. Found., 1988, Roots and Wings Comty. award, 1988, Rosie award So. Ariz. Ctr. Against Sexual Assault, 1990, Lifetime Achievement award YWCA, 1992, 93, La Doña de los Descendientes del Precido de Tucson, 1997-98, centennial alumni award U. Ariz., 1998, Pan-Asian Cmty. Leadership award, 1999, Arthritis Humanitarian award, 1999, Altrusa Women in Svc. award, 2000, Asia Am. Times Devel. Mgmt. Excellence award, 2000, Voices into the Millennium award Ariz. Border Patrol, Dynamic Duo—Pointing Lives in New Directions award Compass Health Care, Congl. Recognition, 2002, Lulac Nat. Presdl. citation, 2002, award Agave Ariz. Hist. Tape TV, 2002, Lifetime award U. Ariz. Coll. Agr. and Life Sci., 2002; Learning Svc. Bldg. and Gallery named in her honor, U. Ariz., 2001 Mem. Soroptimist (hon., Women Who Helped Build Tucson award), Rotary Club Tucson (4 way test award 1998). Roman Catholic. Avocations: travel, cooking, golf. Home: 701 E Camino De Los Padres Tucson AZ 85718-1921 Office: Netwest Devel Corp 2221 E Broadway Blvd Ste 211 Tucson AZ 85719-6032

TANG, GEORGE CHICKCHEE, investment company executive; b. Hong Kong, Nov. 8, 1964; came to U.S., 1984; s. George and Margaret Tang. BS, Case Western Res. U., 1987; MS, Northwestern U., 1989. Registered securities rep., commodity rep., ins. agt., Ill.; CFA, CFP, cert. investment mgr. cons., portfolio mgr. With AT&T Bell Labs., Naperville, Ill., 1989-92; fin. cons. Salomon Smith Barney, Oakbrook, 1992—, 2d v.p. for investments, 1998-2000, v.p. for investments, 2000-01, 1st v.p. investments, 2001—. Spkr., lectr. in field. Contbr. fin. columns to Chgo. Chinese Daily News, 1993—, Chinese Am. News, 1993—, China Jour., 1994-97. Writer ARC, Cleve., 1985-86; spkr. on environ. protection City Coun. Hong Kong, 1982. Recipient Champion of Wildlife Conservation award Hong Kong Std., 1982. Mem. Inst. CFA's (chartered), Assn. for Investment and Rsch., Inst. for Investment Mgmt. Cons. (cert.), Orgn. Chinese Ams. (internal v.p. Chgo. chpt. 1994-95, pres. 1995-97). Avocations: tennis, swimming, bridge, golf, art. Office: Salomon Smith Barney 1 Tower Ln Ste 2200 Villa Park IL 60181-4636

TANG, HANSONG, computational fluid dynamics researcher; b. Hunan, China, Aug. 13, 1961; came to U.S., 1998; s. Zemin Tang and Degui Zeng; m. Yan Qin, Sept. 30, 1989; 1 child, Da. BS, Wuhan (China) U. Electric-Hydraulic Engring., 1983, MEng, 1986; DSc, Peking U., Beijing, 1993; PhD, Ga. Inst. Tech., 2001. Lectr. Changhsa Comm. Inst., China, 1986-90; rsch. fellow Beijing U. Aeronautics and Astronautics, 1993-95, assoc. prof., 1995-98; rsch. scientist Stevens Inst. Tech., Hoboken, NJ, 2001—. Cons. Dictionary Chinese Educationalists, Hong Kong, 1998; mem. Sci. Com. on China Aerospace Corp., China Ocean Press, 1997. Editor: Jour. Hydrodynamics, 1999—, China Ocean Press, 1999—, Comm. on Nonlinear Scis. and Numerical Simulations, Elsevier, 1999—; contbr. articles to sci. jours., including Jour. Computational Physics, Math. Numerical Sinica, SIAM Jour. on Numerical Analysis. Grantee Natural Sci. Found. China, 1996, Aeronautics Sci. Found. China, 1996; 1995-97 Excellent Paper award Zhou Peiyuan Sci. Found., 1999. Avocations: table tennis, swimming. Office: HfMI Stevens Inst Tech Hoboken NJ 07030 E-mail: HansongTang@hotmail.com.

TANG, IRVING CHE-HONG, mathematician, educator; b. Macau, China, Dec. 29, 1931; came to U.S., 1948; s. Man-yan and Susie Wei-chun (Chung) T. BS, U. Calif., Berkeley, 1952; MS, U. Ill., 1953; DS, Washington U., St. Louis, 1965. Chartered engr., Brit. Engring. Coun. Design engr. Friden Calculators, San Leandro, Calif., 1955-56; staff engr. IBM Corp., San Jose, 1956-66; postdoctoral fellow U. Oslo, 1966-68; head math. dept. NSW Inst. Tech., Sydney, Australia, 1969-76, Hong Kong Poly., 1977-89; prof. math. Phillips U., Enid, Okla., 1989-91, Oklahoma City C.C., Rose State Coll., 1991-94, Okla. State U., Oklahoma City, 1994-97, 99—, Ednl. Testing Svc., Princeton, N.J., 1997-99. Contbr. articles to profl. jours. Fellow Brit. Computer Soc.; mem. Math. Assn. Am., Hong Kong Math. Soc. (pres. 1977-81), Sigma Xi, Tau Beta Pi, Eta Kappa Nu. Office: Okla State U Math Dept Oklahoma City OK 73107 E-mail: ictang@osuokc.edu., tangic@AltaVista.net.

TANG, JUN, research scientist, educator; b. Shanghai, China, Aug. 6, 1935; came to U.S., 1987; m. Dong Zheng, Feb. 3, 1962; children: Minjia, Peijia. Diploma in English Advanced Studies, Beijing Fgn. Lang. U., 1986; diploma in civil structural engring., Shanghai Urban Constn. Coll., China, 1953; PhD in Engring. Mechanics, Peking U., Beijing, 1964. Asst. structural engr. Shanghai Metallurgy Industry Design Inst., 1954-56; structural and software engr. Shanghai Chem. Industry Design Inst., 1964-81; ctr. dir., prin. engr. Shanghai Pharm. Industry Design Inst., 1982-87; vis. rsch. scientist Inst. of Stds. and Tech., Gaithersburg, Md., 1987-90; sr. rsch. scientist U. Iowa, Iowa City, 1991—. Adj. prof. Tong-Ji U., Shanghai, 1984-87, Shanghai Jiao-Tong U., 1985-87, U. Iowa, 1993—. Mem. ASME (pressure vessel and piping divsn.), Soc. Automotive Engrs., Chinese Applied Mechanics Soc. (vice-chmn. popular edn. com.), Shanghai Soc. Mechanics (divsn. chair, standing com.), Shanghai Soc. of Civil Engring. (standing com.) Avocations: software development, classical music, bridge, dancing. Home: 1714 12th Ave Coralville IA 52241-1006 Office: U Iowa 226 ERF Iowa City IA 52242

TANG, KAI, software specialist, researcher; b. Nanjing, Jiangsu, China, Apr. 14, 1959; came to U.S., 1984; s. Hong Tang and Li Yun Deng; m. Yan Hong, Oct. 22, 1962; children: Jonathan, Caroline. BS in Engring., Nanjing Inst. Tech., 1982; PhD in Computer Sci., U. Mich., 1990. Software specialist Unigraphics Solutions, Ann Arbor, Mich., 1991—. Chief engr. Allvox, Ann Arbor, 1999—. Editor: Detroit Times, 2000—. Prin. Annhua Chinese Sch., Ann Arbor, 1999—. Home: 3133 Fawn Meadow Ct Ann Arbor MI 48105 Office: 4251 Plymouth Rd Ste 3200 Ann Arbor MI 48105-3649 E-mail: kai-tang@yahoo.com.

TANG, MAN-CHUNG, engineer, administrator; b. Xiao Qing, China, Feb. 22, 1938; came to U.S., 1968; s. Yu-Fung and Jing Tse Tang; m. Yee-Yun Fung, Aug. 26, 1966; children: Chin-Chung, Chin-Ning. BSc, Chu-Hai Coll., Hong Kong, 1959; MS, Tech. U. Darmstadt, Germany, 1964, PhD, 1965; DLitt (hon.) , Chu-Hai U., Hong Kong, 1997. Registered profl. engr., N.Y., Mass., Fla., Ill., Wash., others. Bridge engr. GHH, Germany, 1965-68; sr. engr. Severud & Assocs., N.Y.C., 1968-70; v.p., chief engr. Dyckerhoff & Widmann, 1970-78; pres. DRC Cons. Inc., 1978—; chmn. bd. T.Y. Lin Internat., San Francisco, 1995—. Contbr. more than 100 articles to profl. jours. Recipient Leadership award Am. Segmental Bridge Inst., 1991, Roebling Life Achievement award Internat. Bridge Conf., 1998. Mem. ASCE (hon., named N.Y. Civil Engr. of Yr. 1989, Roebling award 1999), Nat. Acad. Engring. (life), Chinese Acad. Engring. (life mem.). Achievements include pioneer work in design and construction of cable-stayed and segmental bridges. Office: TY Lin Internat 825 Battery St San Francisco CA 94111-1528 E-mail: mtang@tylin.com.

TANG, NG BING, librarian; b. Singapore, Apr. 10, 1950; d. Lim Koh and Wan Tik; m. Ng Theng Kioh, Mar. 4, 1978; children: Huang Lihui, Huang Lijie, Huang Lijing. BA with honors, Nanyang U., Singapore, 1973. Asst. libr. Nat. Libr., Singapore, 1973-80; head resource ctr. Ministry of Trade and Industry, from 1981. Cons. Singapore Tourist Promotion Bd., 1993. Recipient Efficiency Medal for 1988 Nat. Day awards Govt. Singapore. Mem. Libr. Assn. Singapore. Christian. Avocations: reading, cooking, gardening, travel, flower arrangement. Home: 24 King's Rd Singapore 1026 Singapore

TANG, PAUL CHI LUNG, philosophy educator; b. Vancouver, B.C., Can., Jan. 23, 1944; came to U.S., 1971; s. Pei-sung and Violet (Wong) T. BSc with high distinction, U. B.C., 1966; MA in Edn., Simon Fraser U., Vancouver, 1971; MA, Washington U., St. Louis, 1975, PhD, 1982; cert. in bioethics, Kennedy Inst. Ethics, 1983; diploma in piano, Royal Conservatory Music, Toronto, 1962. Teaching asst. philosophy of edn. Simon Fraser U., 1969-71; instr. philosophy St. Louis C.C. at Meramec, Kirkwood, Mo., 1975-82; instr., lectr. philosophy Washington U., 1972-76; adj. asst. prof. Harris-Stowe State Coll., St. Louis, 1980-82; asst. prof. philosophy Grinnell (Iowa) Coll., 1982-85; asst. prof. to assoc. prof. to prof. dept. philosophy Calif. State U., Long Beach, 1985—, chmn. dept. philosophy, 1988-94, acting chmn., 1998. Vis. lectr. philosophy So. Ill. U., Edwardsville, 1978-79. Editor: Philosophy of Sci. Assn. Newsletter, 1985—90; asst. editor: Philosophy of Sci. acad. jour., 1972—75, dep. editor: The Social Sci. Jour., 1999—; contbr. articles to profl. publs., revs. to profl. publs. Senator Internat. Parliament for Safety and Peace, Palermo, Italy. Decorated knight Templar Order of Jerusalem, knight Order Holy Cross of Jerusalem, knight comdr. Lofsenic Ursinius Order, chevalier Grand Croix de Milice du St. Sepulcre; recipient cert. of merit Student Philosophy Assn., 1988-90, 93-94, spl. award, 1992, Calif. State Senate Recognition award for commitment to edn., 1997; named faculty advisor of yr. Assoc. Students, 1987, 90, 91, 95, Highland Lord of Camster, Scotland, 1995; Paul Tang prize in philosophy named in his honor, 1996-99; fellow Washington U., 1971, summer rsch. fellow Calif. State U., 1988, 96, NEH fellow Harvard U., 1988, NEH Summer Seminar fellow, 1988; internat. scholar Phi Beta Delta, interdisciplinary scholar Phi Kappa Phi, 1993, Phi Beta Kappa, 2000; grantee vis. philosophers program Coun. for Philos. Studies, 1987, 91, 92; Disting. Vis. Scholars and Artists Fund, Calif. State U., 1988, 89, rsch. grantee, 1995, 97, 99. Fellow: World Lit. Acad.; mem.: Maison Internat. des Intellectuels de l'Acad. Francaise, Soc. Philosophy and Psychology, Brit. Soc. Philosophy of Sci., Iowa Philos. Soc. (pres. 1985—86), Hastings Ctr., Kennedy Inst. Ethics, History of Sci. Soc., Philosophy of Sci. Assn., Am. Philos. Assn. (Excellence in Tchg. award 1995, 1997), numerous others, Order Internat. Fellowship (Eng.), Companion of Honour (Eng.), Golden Key Internat. Hon. Soc. (Internat. Man of Yr. 1995—96), Internat. Order Merit (Eng.). Avocations: hiking, tennis, chess, music, travel. Home: 5050 E Garford St Apt 228 Long Beach CA 90815-2859 Office: Calif State U Dept Philosophy 1250 N Bellflower Blvd Long Beach CA 90840-0006 E-mail: pcltang@csulb.edu.

TANG, SHENGMING, sociology educator; b. Shanghai, China, Sept. 5, 1951; s. Wenching Tang and Yunyu Wu; m. Qilin Gu, Aug. 30, 1981; 1 child, Shawn Tang. BA, East China Normal U., Shanghai, 1982, MA, 1985; PhD, U. Nebr., 1992. Lectr. East China Normal U., Shanghai, 1985—88; asst. prof. Kenyon Coll., Gambier, Ohio, 1992—93, Western Ill. U., Macomb, 1993—97, assoc. prof., 1997—2002, prof., 2002—, dir. sociology grad. program, 1998—2000. Authro: Practical Approaches to Social Research, 1998; contbr. articles to profl. jours. Advisor Chinese Student Orgn., Western Ill. U., 1997—. Summer Rsch. grantee Western Ill. U., Macomb, 1999. Mem. Am. Sociol. Assn., Ea. Sociol. Soc., Western Sociol. Soc. Avocations: reading, classical music, playing piano, table tennis. Home: 310 Jamestown Rd Macomb IL 61455-9328 Office: Western Ill Univ 1 University Cir Macomb IL 61455-1390 E-mail: mfst@wiu.edu.

TANG, SHUANG, computer programmer, researcher; b. Beijing, Dec. 24, 1957; s. Yijie and Diayun (Yue) T.; m. Joy Z. Zhang, June 12, 1983; 1 child, Brady. BS, U. Sci. and Tech. China, Hefei, 1982; PhD, SUNY, Stony Brook, 1988. Rsch. assoc. U. Md., College Park, 1988-92, Oreg. State U., Corrallis, 1992-95; sr. program developer Veson Computer Inc., N.Y.C., 1995—. Contbr. articles to profl. jours. Avocations: bridge. Home: 171 E 84th St Apt 23A New York NY 10028-2082 Office: Veson Computer Inc 29 Broadway Rm 1002 New York NY 10006-3101 E-mail: shuangtang@yahoo.com.

TANG, XIANMIN, physicist, researcher; b. China; PhD, Coll. of William and Mary. Asst. prof. Wuhan (China) U., 1994—95; rschr. Coll. of William and Mary, Williamsburg, Va., 1996—2000; rsch. scientist Applied Materials, Inc., Santa Clara, Calif., 2000—. Contbr. articles to profl. jours. Mem.: AAAS, Am. Phys. Soc., Am. Vacuum Soc. (Merit Rsch. award 1999). Office: Applied Materials Inc MS 1158 3320 Scott Blvd Santa Clara CA 95054

TANG, YI, radiologist, researcher; b. Yichang, Hubei, China, Dec. 20, 1963; s. Zhongni and deying (Liu) T.; m. Xuling Huang, Oct. 2, 1988; 1 child, Chicao. MD, Sun Yat-Sen U. of Med. Scis., Guangzhou, China, 1987; PhDd., Kumamoto (Japan) U., 2000. Resident Guangdong Provincial People's Hosp., Guangzhou, 1987-93, attending physician, 1993-95; guest rschr. Kumamoto U., 1995-96; postdoctoral fellow MD Anderson Cancer Ctr., 2000-2001; rsch. fellow Mass. Gen. Hosp., 2001—. Reviewer Jour. of Magnetic resonance Imaging, 1999; contbr. articles to profl. jours. Higo Yiyoku Seshikai scholar, 1998, Konan Asia Internat. Found. scholar, 1999. Mem. Radiol. Soc. N.Am., Japanese Soc. of Magnetic Resonance Imaging. Avocations: table tennis, swimming, driving. Office: Mass Gen Hosp CMIR/Radiology 13th St # 5420 Bldg 149 Boston MA 02129 E-mail: tangyiradiology@hotmail.com.

TANG, YIN SHENG, physicist; b. Zongyang, Anhui, China, Oct. 23, 1962; s. Song Wu and Zhen Zhu (Gao) T.; m. Hua Chun Shi, Jan. 12, 1987; children: Astera, Sherwin. BSc, Hefei Poly. U., China, 1983; MSc, Xi'dian U., Si'an, China, 1985; DSc, U. Sci. and Tech. of China, 1988. Rsch. scientist Inst. Semiconductors, C.A.S., China, 1986-88; vis. fellow Surrey (Eng.) U., 1988-90; faculty rsch. fellow Glasgow (Scotland) U., 1990-96, UCLA, 1996-99; sr. photonic rsch. engr. R&D Lab., Culver City, Calif., 1999—. Patentee in field. Mem.: Materials Rsch. Soc. Avocations: badminton, hill walking, driving, photography, computers. Office: R&D Lab 5800 Uplander Way Culver City CA 90230-6608 E-mail: ystang@usa.com.

TANGORA, MARTIN CHARLES, mathematician, educator; b. N.Y.C., June 21, 1936; s. Albert and Virginia T.; m. Linda Perry, June 17, 1973; children: Charles, Elizabeth. BS, Calif. Inst. Tech., 1957; MS, Northwestern U., 1958, PhD, 1966. Instr. Northwestern U., Evanston, 1966-67, U. Chgo., 1967-69; asst. prof. U. Ill., Chgo., 1970-72, assoc. prof., 1972—. Temp. lectr. U. Manchester, Eng., 1969-70; sr. vis. fellow U. Oxford, Eng., 1973-74. Author: Computing the Homology of the Lambda Algebra, 1985; co-author: Cohomology Operations and Applications in Homotopy Theory, 1968; editor: Computers in Algebra, 1988, Computers in Geometry and Topology, 1989, Algebraic Topology Oaxtepec 1991 (conf. proc.), 1993. Bd. dirs. Landmarks Preservation Coun. Ill., Chgo., 1971—, pres., 1976, v.p. 1997—. Mem. Math. Assn. Am., Am. Math. Soc. Office: U Ill Chgo Math M/C 249 851 S Morgan St Chicago IL 60607-7042

TANGRETTI, THOMAS ALAN, state legislator; b. Pitts., Sept. 20, 1946; m. Sandra Shearer Leshock; stepchildren: Leigh Ann Leshock, Christopher Leshock; children: Leigh Ann, Thomas Jon. BA in Econs. and Polit. Sci., Indiana U. Pa., 1968; MPA, U. Pitts., 1974. Legis. asst. U.S. Rep. John H. Dent, Washington and Greensburg, Pa., 1969-72; dist. office adminstrv. asst. Greensburg, 1973-78; dir. adminstrn. Mark Lines Inc., 1978-83; county contr. Westmoreland County, Pa., 1983-88; mem. Pa. Ho. of Reps., Harrisburg, 1988—. Mem. appropriations com., chmn. subcom. on counties of local govt. com., mem. policy com., ins. com.; chmn. S.W. Dem. Caucus. Recipient cert. of excellence Govt. Fin. Officers Assn., 1987. Address: 327 S Main St Greensburg PA 15601-3111 Office: Pa Ho of Reps 328 South Office Bldg PO Box 202020 Harrisburg PA 17120-2020

TANHAM, GEORGE KILPATRICK, retired research company executive; b. Englewood, N.J., Feb. 23, 1922; s. Francis Thomas and Irene (Kilpatrick) T.; m. Mary Finch, 1958 (div. 1962); m. Barbara Hunt, May 27, 1966 (div. 1989); children: George K., Gerald Francis, Helen Tanham Woods, Barbara Tanham Stampora, Maedi Carney, Ruth Tanham Marshall, Ramsey; m. Kathleen Van Wyck, Oct. 27, 1989. BA, Princeton U., 1943; MA, Stanford U., 1947, PhD, 1951. Assoc. prof., master student houses Calif. Inst. Tech., Pasadena, 1947-55; research staff Rand Corp., Santa Monica, Calif., 1955-58, dep. to v.p. Washington, 1958-64, 65-68, v.p., trustee, 1971-82, sr. researcher, 1982-87, cons., 1987—; assoc. dir. AID, Saigon, Vietnam, 1964-65; minister counsellor U.S. Embassy, Bangkok, Thailand, 1968-70. Cons. SAIC, McLean, Va.; lectr. in field. Author: Communist Revolutionary Warfare: The Vietminh in Indochina, 1961, 67, 85, War Without Guns: American Civilians in Rural Vietnam, 1966, Contribution a l'Histoire de la Resistance Belge, 1971, Trial in Thailand, 1974; co-author: (with Douglas S. Blaufarb) Who Will Win a Key: An Answer to the Puzzle of Revolutionary War, 1989, (with Marcy Agmon) The Indian Air Force: Trends and Prospects, 1996, (with K. Bhapal and A. Mattoo) Securing India, (with Ralph Salmi and Cesar Majul) Conflict Resolution in Islam, 1997. Bd. visitors Patterson Sch. of Diplomacy and Internat. Commerce, U. Ky., 1985-95 , U. Pitts., 1982-92; bd. dirs. Ethics and Pub. Policy Ctr., 1988-98; adv. trustee Rand Corp., 1988—. Served with U.S. Army, World War II Decorated Purple Heart, Silver Star with oak leaf cluster, Air medal; Croix de Guerre avec etoile d'argent (Republic of France); Most Exalted Order of White Elephant (Thailand); Belgian-Am. Edn. Found. grantee, 1950; Ford Found. fellow, 1952-53; Social Scis. Research Council grantee, 1955-57; grantee U.S. Inst. Peace and Rockefeller Found., 1989-91, Alton Jones Found. 1996-98; Rajiv Gandhi Found. vis. fellow, New Delhi, 1995. Mem. Coun. Fgn. Rels., Cosmos Club, Spl. Forces Club (London), India Internat. Ctr. (New Delhi). Avocations: music, travel, gardening, sports. Home: PO Box 373 Strasburg VA 22657-0373 Office: Rand 1333 H St NW Washington DC 20005-4707

TANI, DANIEL M. astronaut; b. Ridley Park, Pa., Feb. 1, 1961; m. Jane Egan. BS in Mech. Engring., MIT, 1984, MS in Mech. Engring., 1988. Design engr. Hughes Aircraft Corp., El Segundo, Calif.; dept. exptl. psychology Bolt Beranek and Newman, Cambridge, Mass.; sr. structures engr. Orbital Scis. Corp., Dulles, Va., mission ops. mgr., launch ops. mgr.; astronaut NASA, Redmond, Wash., 1996, with Astronaut Office Computer Support Br. Recipient Outstanding Tech. Achievement award, Orbital Scis. Corp., 1993. Mem.: Aircraft Owners and Pilots Assn., Japanese Am. Citizens League, Alpha Delta Phi. Achievements include logged over 11 days in space; mission specialist STS-108 Endeavour (2001). Avocations: golf, flying, running, tennis, music. Office: Astronaut Office/CB NASA Johnson Space Ctr Houston TX 77058*

TANICK, MARSHALL HOWARD, lawyer, law educator; b. Mpls., May 9, 1947; s. Jack and Esther (Kohn) T.; m. Cathy E. Gorlin, Feb. 20, 1982; children: Lauren, Ross. BA, U. Minn., 1969; JD, Stanford U., 1973. Bar: Calif. 1973, Minn. 1974. Law clk. to presiding justice U.S. Dist. Ct., Mpls., 1973-74; assoc. Robins, Davis & Lyons, 1974-76; ptnr. Tanick & Heins, P.A., 1976-89, Mansfield & Tanick, Mpls., 1989—. Prof. constrn., real estate and media law U. Minn., Mpls., 1983—, Hamline U., St. Paul, 1982—; prof. constl. law William Mitchell Coll. Law, 1994. Editor: Hennepin Lawyer, Bench, Bar and Litigation mag.; contbr. articles to mags. Avocation: writing. Home: 1230 Angelo Dr Minneapolis MN 55422-4710 Office: Mansfield & Tanick 900 2nd Ave S Ste 1560 Minneapolis MN 55402-3383

TANIERE, ROMAIN ANDRE, pharmaceutical company scientist; b. Dijon, France, July 1, 1972; came to U.S., 1998; s. Pierre Jean Taniere and Evelyne Ida Morize. Ingenieur chimiste, ENSCM, Montpellier, France, 1996; MS, U. Kent. at Canterbury, Eng., 1996. Cooperant du service nat. en entreprise Merck-Lipha, Hitchin, England, 1996-98; scientist Dey, L.P., Napa, Calif., 1998-2001, Inhale Therapeutic Systems Inc., San Carlos, 2001—. Mem. Am. Chem. Soc., Royal Soc. of Chemistry, Am. Assn. of Pharm. Scientists. Avocations: oenology, skiing, cinema. Office: Inhale Therapeutic Systems Inc 150 Industrial Rd San Carlos CA 94070 Home: 7 Clarence Ct East Palo Alto CA 94303-1115 E-mail: rtaniere@inhale.com.

TANIS, JAMES ROBERT, library director, history educator, clergyman; b. Phillipsburg, N.J., June 26, 1928; s. John Christian and Bertha Marie (Tobiasson) T.; m. Florence Borgmann, June 26, 1963; children— Marjorie Martha, James Tobiasson. BA, Yale, 1951; B.D., Union Theol. Sem., N.Y.C., 1954; Dr. Theol., U. Utrecht, Netherlands, 1967; LittD (hon.), Dickinson Coll., Carlisle, Pa., 1994. Ordained to ministry Presbyn. Ch., 1954. Co-pastor Greystone Presbyn. Ch., Elizabeth, N.J., 1954-55; librarian, mem. faculty Harvard Div. Sch., 1956-65; univ. librarian Yale U., 1965-68; mem. faculty Yale Div. Sch., 1968-69; dir. libraries, prof. history Bryn Mawr (Pa.) Coll., 1969-97; guest curator Phila. Mus. Art, 1997—2002; parish assoc. Valley Forge Presbyn. Ch., King of Prussia, Pa., 1973—. Author: Calvinistic Pietism in the Middle Colonies, 1967; co-author: Bookbinding in America, 1983, Images of Discord/De Tweedracht Verbeeld, 1993, Fantasy and Fashion, 1996, Leaves of Gold: Manuscript Illumination from Philadelphia Collections, 2001. Decorated officer Order Orange-Nassau. Home: 105 Burnside Rd Villanova PA 19085-1315 E-mail: james.tanis@verizon.net.

TANK, GERHARD WILLI, obstetrician and gynecologist; b. Jan. 26, 1926; s. Frederick Karl and Martha Marie (Lade) T. BSc in Med. Sci., U. Wis., 1951, MD, 1953. Diplomate Am. Bd. Ob-Gyn. Rsch. asst. dept. physiology U. Wis. Med. Sch., Madison, 1949-51; intern Swedish Hosp., Seattle, 1953—54, resident in ob-gyn., 1954—56, Calif. Hosp./Orange County Hosp., 1956-57; practice medicine specializing in ob-gyn. Grants Pass, Oreg., 1957-90; ptnr. Grants Pass Clin., 1957-90, ptnr. emeritus, 1990; med. staff Josephine Gen. Hosp., 1957—90, chief of staff, 1968, bd. dirs., 1984-94; ret., 1990. Pres. Rogue Valley Physicians Svc., Medford, Oreg., 1972; bd. dirs. Our Valley Clinic, So. Oreg. Regional Area Health Edn. Ctr., Siskiyou Cmty. Health Ctr. Contbr. articles to profl. jours. Vol. Project Hope, 1967, 72. Fellow Am. Coll. Ob-Gyn.; mem. Pacific N.W. Soc. Ob-Gyn. (emeritus), Oreg. Med. Assn. (past trustee). E-mail: gwtank@atiinternet.com.

TANK, ROD GAILLARD, orthopaedic physical therapist; b. Harlan, Iowa, Jan. 12, 1947; s. Gaillard B. and Irene B. (Thraen) T.; m. M. Sue Howard, Dec. 15, 1972; children: Karynn S., Brad S. BS, U. Nebr., 1970; grad. in phys. therapy, Mayo Clinic, Rochester, Minn., 1972; MPA, Tex. Tech U., 1979. Dir. phys. therapy VA Hosp., Big Spring, Tex., 1974-76, Tex. Tech U. Sch. Medicine, Lubbock, 1976-78; exec. dir. ambulatory clinics Tex. Tech U. Health Sci. Ctr., 1980-82; asst. hosp. adminstr. Rosewood Hosp., Houston, 1982-83; COO AMI Heights Hosp., 1983-90, Winona Meml. Hosp., Indpls., 1990-92; sr. phys. therapist Physiotherapy Assocs., 1992-97; clin. dir. Replay Physical Therapy, Noblesville, Ind., 1997—. Parish coun. Our Lady of Mt. Carmel Cath. Ch., Carmel, Ind., 1993-95. Maj.. USAR, 1976-86. Mem. Am. Phys. Therapy Assn. (cert. orthopaedic clin. specialist), Am. Coll. Healthcare Execs. (diplomate), Am. Acad. Orthop. Manual Phys. Therapists. Republican. Avocations: running, reading, church lector. Home: 13772 Laredo Dr Carmel IN 46032-5257 Office: Replay Physical Therapy 641 Westfield Rd Noblesville IN 46060-1323

TANKERSLEY, REBECCA ELIZABETH GULDI, lawyer; b. Boston, Nov. 26, 1969; d. Richard L. and Sara S. (Pearce) G. BA with distinction, U. Mich., 1992, JD, 1995. Bar: Tex. 1995. Assoc. Locke Liddell & Sapp LLP, Dallas, 1995-99; asst. gen. counsel Software Spectrum, Inc., Garland, Tex., 1999—. Dir. Dallas Legal Hospice, 1996-1999. Mem. Dallas Assn. Young Lawyers (co-chair AIDS Legal Assistance com. 1996-98, mock trial com. 1998—), Dallas Bar Assn. Office: Software Spectrum Inc 2140 Merritt Dr Garland TX 75041

TANKOOS, SANDRA MAXINE, court reporting services executive; b. Bklyn., Nov. 12, 1936; d. Samuel J. and Ethel (Seltzer) Rich; m. Kenneth Robert Tankoos, Mar. 17, 1957; children: Robert Ian, Gary Russell, Jenine Sheryl. AA, Stenotype Inst., 1957; BA, Queens Coll., 1969; MA, C.W. Post Coll., 1973. Cert. stenotype reporter, 1959. Ct. reporter free lance, N.Y.C., 1957-70; tchr. Spanish various high schs., L.I., 1970-76; pres. Tankoos Reporting, N.Y.C., 1976—, Ar-Ti Recording, Mineola, N.Y., 1977—. Contbr. articles to profl. jours. Past pres., bd. dirs. Temple Sinai, Roslyn Hts., N.Y., 1989-91, Am. Jewish Acad., West Hempstead, 1984-94, LWV, Roslyn, 1969-75, NOW, Nassau County, 1975-77, bd. dirs. Religious Action Ctr., Washington, 1995—, ARZA, 1997—. Mem.: N.Y. State Shorthand Reporters Assn. (bd. dirs. 1998—2002). Avocations: writing, piano. Home: 77 Shepherd Ln Roslyn Heights NY 11577-2508 Office: Ar-Ti Recording Inc 142 Willis Ave Mineola NY 11501-2613 also: Tankoos Reporting Co 305 Madison Ave New York NY 10165 E-mail: sandra@tankoos.com.

TANNEBAUM, SAMUEL HUGO, accountant; b. Aug. 15, 1933; s. Simon L. and Eva (Kapp) T.; m. Nita Mae Levy, June 12, 1955; children: Joel L., Marilyn J. BBA with spl. distinction, U. Okla., 1955. CPA. Tex., Okla. Staff acct. Alford, Meroney & Co., Dallas, 1955-61; pvt. practice acctg., 1961-63; ptnr. Tannebaum & Bindler CPAs, 1963-67; mng. ptnr. Tannebaum, Bindler & Lewis, 1967-80, Tannebaum Bindler & Co. CPAs, Dallas, 1980-84; pres. Tannebaum Bindler & Co., PC, 1984-94; sr. exec. ptnr. Weaver & Tidwell LLP, 1995-99; cons., 1999—; mng. dir. Weaver and Tidwell Fin. Advisors, 2000—. Mem. adv. coun. Cmtys. Found. Tex., 1987—; bd. dirs. Dallas Home for Jewish Aged, 1973-76, Mental Health Assn. Greater Dallas, treas. 1998-2000; trustee Temple Emanu-El, Dallas, 1976-83, treas., 1980-82, v.p., 1982-83; trustee Found. Jewish Fedn. Greater Dallas, 1987-96. Mem. AICPA (coun. 1979-82, 95-97, personal fin. specialist), Tex. Soc. CPAs (dir., past v.p., past chpt. pres., CPA of Yr. Dallas chpt. 1976), Nat. Assn. Estate Planners (accredited estate planner), Nat. Assn. Estate Planning Couns. (dir. 1978-82, treas. 1982-83, v.p. 1983-84, pres. 1984-85), Dallas Estate Planning Coun. (past pres.), Brookhaven Country Club. Home: 5820 Meletio Ln Dallas TX 75230-2108 Office: Ste 1300 12221 Merit Dr Dallas TX 75251-2280 E-mail: shtannebaum@weaveranatidwell.com.

TANNEHILL, DARCY ANITA BARTINS, academic administrator; b. Pitts., May 14, 1958; d. Joseph Paul Bartins and Ileane Anita (Roy) Bartins Yerman; m. Gary Edward Mack, Oct. 28, 1979 (div. Apr. 1989); 1 child, Courtney Anita; m. Norman Bruce Tannehill Jr., Feb. 14, 1991; stepchildren: Andrea, Bruce. BA, Duquesne U., 1978, MSEd, 1986; postgrad., U. Pitts., 1993—. Rsch. asst. U. Pitts., 1979-81; adult edn. tchr. Allegheny Intermediate Unit, Pitts., 1985-86, counselor, statistician, 1986-90; coord. evening programs Robert Morris U., Moon Twp., 1990—92, asst. dir. academic svcs., 1992—93, assoc. dir. academic svcs., 1993—94, assoc. dean admissions, 1994—96, assoc. dean of enrollment mgmt. adult and cont. edn., 1996—97, assoc. dean student affairs and enrollment mgmt., 1997—99, dean Pitts. Ctr., 1999—2002, dean Sch. Adult and Continuing Edn., 2002—. Mem. AAHE, Nat. Assn. Women in Edn., Pa. Am. Coun. on Edn., Nat. Identification Program, Nat. Assn. Coll. Admissions Counselors, Continuing Edn. Assn., Am. Coun. on Adult and Experiential Learning, Exec. Women Internat. Republican. Presbyterian. Avocations: reading, music. Home: 4482 Battleridge Rd Mc Donald PA 15057-2587 Office: Robert Morris U 881 Narrows Run Rd Moon Township PA 15108 E-mail: tannehil@rmu.edu.

TANNEHILL, NORMAN BRUCE, JR. consultant, educator; b. Pitts., Aug. 22, 1950; s. Norman B. and Maxine (Hart) T.; m. Marianne Witt, Sept. 22, 1979 (div. July 1990); children: Andrea, Norman Bruce III; m. Darcy Anita Bartins, Feb. 14, 1991; 1 child, Courtney. BSBA, Robert Morris Coll., Coraopolis, Pa., 1975, MS, 1989. Owner, CEO Tannehill Info. Sys. Ltd., Coraopolis, 1989—. Mem. adj. faculty Robert Morris Coll., 1989-97, C.C. of Allegheny County, Pitts., 1991—, C.C. of Beaver County, Monaca, Pa., 1994—, Waynesburg Coll., 1998—. Mem. IEEE Computer Soc., Assn. for Computing Machinery, Assn. for Ednl. Comms. Tech., Mensa. Home: 4482 Battleridge Rd Mc Donald PA 15057-2587

TANNEHILL, NORMAN BRUCE, retired radiologist; b. Girard, Pa., Apr. 24, 1917; s. Joseph and Ona Ethlyn (Frazier) T.; m. Maxine Hart; children: R. Fred, Norman. BS, U. Pitts., 1941, MD, 1942. Intern Allegheny Gen. Hosp., Pitts., 1942-43; resident diagnostic radiology Aspinwall VA Hosp., 1947-48, resident radiology, 1949-50; resident radiology, radiation therapy Western Pa. Hosp., Pitts., 1949; mem. staff Ohio Valley Gen., McKees Rocks, Pa., 1950-91; pvt. practice Coraopolis. Fellow Am. Coll. Radiology; mem. AMA, Radiol. Soc. N.Am. Office: 1506 Beaver Grade Rd Coraopolis PA 15108-2907

TANNENBAUM, BARBARA LEE, curator, art historian; b. Chgo., Aug. 15, 1952; m. Mark Soppeland. BA, Reed Coll., 1975; MA, U. Mich., 1977, PhD, 1993. Dir. Ox-Bow Summer Sch. of Art, Saugatuck, Mich., 1980-81; curator Seymour Rosofsky Meml. Found., Chgo., 1981-85; instr. Oberlin (Ohio) Coll., 1985-97; chief curator Akron (Ohio) Art Mus., 1985-97, chief curator, head pub. programs, 1997—. Instr. human values in medicine program N.E. Ohio Univs. Colls. of Medicine, 1986-96; nat. adv. bd. Photo Americas, Portland, 2000—. Editor, contbr: Akron Art Museum: Art Since 1850, An Introduction to the Collection, 2001, Ralph Eugene Meatyard: Am American Visionary, 1991. Com. mem. Campus Fine Art and Design com., U. Akron, 1988—; organizer Women at the Summit Festival, 1997, A Festival of Women Photographers, N.Y.C., 1996-97. Recipient Achievement award No. Ohio Live mag., 1998; Luce Found grant U. Mich., 1988-89; postbaccalaureate fellowship Danforth Found., 1979. Mem. Art Table, Oracle, Phi Beta Kappa. Office: Akron Art Mus 70 E Market St Akron OH 44308 E-mail: btannenbaum@akronartmuseum.org.

TANNENBAUM, BERNICE SALPETER, national religious organization executive; b. N.Y.C. d. Isidore and May Franklin; 1 child, Richard Salpeter. BA, Bklyn. coll. Chmn. Commn. on the Status of Women of the World Jewish Congress; mem. exec. bd. Am. sect. World Jewish Congress; chmn. internat. affairs com.; mem. Zionist Gen. Coun.; active Exec. World Zionist Orgn. Bd. dirs., mem. gen. assembly Jewish Agy.; bd. dirs., v.p. United Israel Appeal; mem. exec. com. Am. Zionist Movement; former chair Hadassah mag.; nat. pres. Hadassah, 1976-80; nat. chmn. Hadassah Internat., 1984-95; sec. Jewish Telegraphic Agy.; bd. govs. Hebrew U. Office: Hadassah 50 W 58th St New York NY 10019-2590

TANNENBAUM, HARVEY, defense technology consultant; b. N.Y.C., June 26, 1923; s. Alfred and Ida (Kolbe) T.; m. Mildred Cohen, July 4, 1946; children: David Bruce, Mark Scott, Lynne Ellen. BS, NYU, 1946; postgrad., George Washington U., 1963-64. Chemist U.S. Army Chem. R & D Ctr., Aberdeen Proving Ground, Md., 1949-62, chief remote sensing, 1962-79; prin. staff engr. Honeywell, Inc., Clearwater, Fla., 1979-84; cons. Reistertown, Md., 1984-86; sr. program dir. SRI, Internat., 1986-88. Cons. EPA, CIA, Arms Control and Disarmament Agy., USAF, 1962-79; group chmn. NATO panel of experts on laser monitoring of atmosphere, Norway, 1976. Contbr. articles to profl. jours.; patentee in field. Served to cpl. USAF, 1942-45, ETO. Mem. Optical Soc. Am., Internat. Soc. Optical Engring., Infrared Symposia, Sigma Xi. Jewish. Avocations: bridge, photography. Home and Office: 12611 Mt Laurel Ct Reisterstown MD 21136-1801

TANNENBAUM, MICHAEL J(AY), physicist; b. N.Y.C., Mar. 10, 1939; s. Morris and Ann Tannenbaum; m. Barbara C. Moshinsky, July 15, 1973; children: Nina Fay, Lisa Marie. AB magna cum laude, Columbia U., 1959, MA, 1960, PhD, 1965. Vis. scientist CERN, Geneva, 1965-66, 91, attache scientifique, 1973-84; from asst. prof. to assoc. prof. Harvard U., Cambridge, Mass., 1966-71; assoc. prof. Rockefeller U., N.Y.C., 1971-80; physicist Brookhaven Nat. Lab., Upton, NY, 1980-87, sr. physicist, 1987—, group leader, 2001—. Contbr. articles to profl. jours. Ernest Kempton Adams fellow, 1965, NSF fellow, 1959-63, 66, Alfred P. Sloan Found. fellow, 1967-69. Fellow: AAAS, Am. Phys. Soc.; mem.: NY Acad. Scis., Sigma Xi, Phi Beta Kappa. Home: 245 E 93rd St Apt 10F New York NY 10128-3965 Office: Physics Dept Brookhaven Nat Lab Bldg # 510C Upton NY 11973-5000 E-mail: mjt@bnl.gov.

TANNENBAUM, STEVEN ROBERT, toxicologist, chemist; b. N.Y.C., Feb. 23, 1937; m. Carol Eigen, Sept. 6, 1959; children: Lisa, Mark. BS in Food Tech, MIT, 1958, PhD in Food Sci. and Tech, 1962. Asst. prof. MIT, Cambridge, 1964-69, assoc. prof., 1969-74, prof. chemistry and toxicology divsn. toxicology, registration and admissions officer, 1981-95, dir. divsn., 1996-98, co-dir. divsn. bioengring. and environ. health, 1998—2002, co-dir. biol. engring. divsn., 2002—. Vis. prof. Hebrew U. of Jerusalem, 1973-74; BASF vis. prof. U. Kaiserslautern, 1994; mem. adv. com. on biochemistry and chem. carcinogenesis Am. Cancer Soc., 1977-81, Inst. Medicine, Nat. Acad. Sci., 1996; bd. sci. advisors divsn. cancer etiology, NCI, 1994-95, Frederick Cancer Sch. Facility, 1995—, Nat. Cancer Inst., 1989-93; mem. cancer spl. program adv. com., 1979-82; mem. peer rev. com. Nat. Toxicology Program, 1983-85; founder, bd. dirs. Vicam, Ltd., Partnership. Editor: (with R.I. Mateles) Single-Cell Protein, 1968, (with D.I.C. Wang) Single-Cell Protein II, 1975, (with others) The Economics, Marketing and Technology of Fish Protein Concentrate, 1974, (with J.R. Whitaker) Food Proteins, 1977, Nutritional Safety Aspects of Food Processing, 1979, (with others) Gastrointestinal Cancer: Endogenous Factors, 1981, (with R.A. Scanlan) N-Nitroso Compounds, 1981; mem. editl. bd. Japanese Jour. Cancer Rsch., 1986—, Chem. Rsch. Toxicology, 1988-91, 95—, Cancer Epidemiology, Prevention and Biomarkers, 1990—, Cancer Rsch., 1993—; contbr. over 350 articles to profl. jours. Mem. AAAS, Nat. Acad. Scis., Inst. Medicine, Am. Chem. Soc., Inst. Food Technologists (sect. councillor N.E. chpt. 1966-69, Samuel Cate Prescott Rsch. award 1970, Babcock Hart award 1980), editorial bd. sci. jour. 1970-73, Am. Inst. Nutrition, Inst. of Medicine, Nat. Acad. of Sci., Am. Assn. Cancer Rsch., Soc. Toxicology, Oxygen Soc., Sigma Xi. Achievements include 9 U.S. patents. E-mail: srtcmit.edu. Office: MIT Div Bioengring Environ Hlth 77 Mass Ave Rm 56-731A Cambridge MA 02139-4307 *Motto: Crisis equals danger plus opportunity.*

TANNENBERG, DIETER E. A. retired manufacturing company executive; b. Chevy Chase, Md., Nov. 24, 1932; s. E.A. Wilhelm and Margarete Elizabeth (Mundhenk) T.; m. Ruth Hansen, Feb. 6, 1956; 1 child, Diana Sylvia Tannenberg. BSME, Northwestern U., 1959. Registered profl. engr., N.Y., Ohio, Ill., Ind., Wis., N.J. Supervising engr. Flexonics div. Calumet & Hecla, Inc., Chgo., 1959-61, chief engr., 1961-63, program mgr. advanced space systems, 1963-65, dir. mfg. services, 1965-67; dir. mfg. engring. SCM Corp., Cortland, N.Y., 1967-69; tech. dir. internat. Singer Co., N.Y.C., 1969-71; v.p. ops. internat. div. Addressograph-Multigraph Corp., Cleve., 1971-74; mng. dir. Addressograph Multigraph GmbH, Frankfurt/Main, W. Ger., 1974-78; v.p., gen. mgr. Europe, Middle East, Africa AM Internat. Inc., Chgo., 1978-79; pres. AM Bruning div., 1979-82, AM Multigraphics Div., Mt. Prospect, Ill., 1982-86; corp. v.p. AM Internat., Inc., 1981-83, corp. sr. v.p., 1983-86; chmn. bd. dirs., pres., chief exec. officer Sargent-Welch Sci. Co., Skokie, Ill., 1986-89; pres., CEO ExhibitGroup, Inc., Elk Grove Village, 1990-91, Bell & Howell Document Mgmt. Products Co., Chgo., 1991-94, Bell & Howell Postal Sys. Inc., Chgo., 1994-97; corp. v.p. Bell & Howell Co., Skokie, Ill., 1991-97. Chmn. AM Internat. GmbH, Frankfurt, 1977-86; bd. dirs. Gerard Daniel Worldwide INc. Contbr. chpts. to handbooks, articles to tech., trade mags.; patentee in machinery field. Served with M.I., U.S. Army, 1953-56. Named Man of Yr. Quick Print Mag., 1985. Mem. NSPE, ASME, Assn. Reprodn. Materials Mfrs. (bd. dirs. 1979-82, v.p. 1980-82), Nat. Assn. Quick Printers (bd. dirs. 1982-84), Nat. Printing Equipment and Supplies Mfg. Assn. (bd. dirs. 1983-86, chmn. govt. affairs com. 1985-86), Computer and Bus. Equipment Mfg. Assn. (bd. dirs. 1983-86, 91-93), Soc. Am. Value Engrs. (hon. v.p. 1985—), Value Found. (trustee 1985—), Barrington Hills Country Club, Pi Tau Sigma.

TANNENWALD, LESLIE KEITER, rabbi, justice of peace, educational administrator, chaplain; b. Boston, May 5, 1949; d. Irving Jules and Barbara June (Caplan) Keiter; m. Robert Tannenwald. BA, Brandeis U., 1971, MA, 1976; MA in Edn. and Counseling, Simmons Coll., Boston, 1972. Cert. social worker, tchr., Mass.; justice of the peace. Sr. assoc. Combined Jewish Philanthropies of Greater Boston, 1977-84; ednl. cons. Bur. Jewish Edn., Boston, 1985-87; ednl. dir. Congregation Shalom Emeth, Burlington, 1987-92; religious sch. dir. Falmouth (Mass.) Jewish Congregation, 1993-99; pres. Jewish Life Svcs., Newton, Mass., 1993—; rabbi Temple Emmanuel , Chelsea, 2001—. Cons. Selected Ednl. Orgns., Boston, 1972; chaplain, rabbi to local nursing home facilities. Author: Curriculum, Male and Female, 1979 (Honors award 1971), Understanding the Holocaust, 1990, Awakening: Alternative Creative Learning Techniques, 1995. Officer, bd. dirs. Combined Jewish Philantropies of Greater Boston , 1972—; mem. Am. Jewish Congress, Boston, 1976—; rabbi, religious leader Sherborn Congregation, 1995—97, Congregation Agudath Achim (Medway), 1999—2001; title of damsel Imperial Order St. John Ecumenical Found. Recipient Leadership award Inst. Leadership Devel. and Fund Raising Mem. Nat. Alliance Profl. & Exec. Women, Alumni Assn. Benjamin S. Hornstein Program of Jewish Communal Svc., Assn. Jewish Community Personnel. Democrat. Avocations: swimming, watercolor painting, music. Home: 6 Clifton Rd Newton MA 02459-3147 E-mail: rabbiles18@aol.com.

TANNENWALD, PETER, lawyer; b. Washington, Apr. 8, 1943; s. Judge Theodore and Selma (Peterfreund) T.; m. Carol B. Baum, May 25, 1969; 1 child, Jonathan Mark. AB, Brown U., 1964; LLB, Harvard U., 1967. Bar: U.S. Dist. Ct. D.C. 1968, U.S. Ct. Appeals (D.C. cir.) 1968, U.S. Supreme Ct. 1972. Assoc. Arent, Fox, Kintner, Plotkin & Kahn, Washington, 1967-74, ptnr., 1975-94; v.p. Irwin, Campbell & Tannenwald, P.C., 1995—. Columnist The LPTV Report, 1988-92. Mem. cmty. coun. Sta. WAMU-FM, Washington, 1986-93, 94-97; dir. Brown Broadcasting Svc., Inc., Providence, 1970—; chmn. maj. law firms divsn. Nat. Capital Area affiliate United Way, 1977-79. Mem. Harvard Law Sch. Assn. D.C. (pres. 1979-80), Harvard Law Sch. Assn. (sec. 1982-84). Avocations: electronics, photography. Office: Irwin Campbell Tannenwald PC 1730 Rhode Island Ave NW Washington DC 20036-3101

TANNER, ALTHEA CLAIRE, artist; b. New Orleans, Aug. 3, 1918; d. Tabor Orme and Rose Janette (McTogue) Dodson; m. Warren Tanner, Mar. 1948 (div. 1955). Student, Augustine Bus. Sch., New Orleans, 1939. Sales person Sears, Roebuck & Co., New Orleans, 1939-41; layout Metairie (La.) Herald; furniture artist, lettering Barnett's, New Orleans, 1954-62; layout Metairie (La.) Herald, 1963; lettering artist Motion Picture Advt., New Orleans, 1964-72; typing, filing, lettering art T. Smith & Son Stevedoring Co., 1972-82. One-woman show Aerial Gallery, N.Y.C., 1992; exhibited in group shows at Winners Circle Gallery, Van Nuys, Calif., 1984, Arts Council of New Orleans, 1992; represented in permanent collection Old State Capitol, Baton Rouge, 1992. Contbr. donated art works WYES, channel 12, 1980-95, Arts for Aids, 1986-97, Contemporary Arts Ctr., 1992, Pops Found. 1995-96; active seminars Arts Coun. of New Orleans, 1992. Mem. Nat. Mus. of Women in the Arts, La. Women's Caucus for Art, La. Watercolor Soc., New Orleans Mus. Art, Contemporary Art Ctr. of New Orleans. Republican. Roman Catholic. Avocations: art work, crafts, poetry. Home: 513 Arlington Dr Metairie LA 70001-5515

TANNER, BARBARA ANN, pediatrics nurse; b. Paia, Maui, Hawaii, Apr. 26, 1938; d. Samuel S.F. and Aileen L.Y. (Mau) Hew; m. Edwin Paul Tanner, Jan. 22, 1960; children: Rhonda, Bonnie, Eugene. BSN, U. Colo., 1960; cert. PNP, U. Hawaii, 1982; MS, U. Hawaii at Manoa, 1990. Cert. pediatric nurse practitioner, cmty. health nurse, advanced practice nurse. Evening charge nurse Maui Meml. Hosp., Wailuku; pub. health nursing supr. Hale Makua Home Health Svc.; pub. health nurse State. Dept. Health, pediatric nurse practitioner, project mgr. perinatal support svcs., 1990-95; clin. asst. prof. U. Hawaii, Manoa, 1997—. Commr. Maui County Commn. on Children and Youth, 1998-2000. Chair Keiki Booster Coalition, 1997. Recipient Educenter for Nursing Leadership award, 1990, Innovation in Improving Health Care Quality Mgmt. award Am. Coll. Physician Execs., 1992, March of Dimes Maui Divsn. Leadership award, 1992, State award for excellence Am. Acad. of Nurse Practitioners,, Healthy Mothers, Healthy Babies Nat. Achievement award, 1993, Sustained Superior Performance award Hawaii Dept. Health, 1994, March of Dimes chpt. of the Pacific, Maui County Excellence in Maternal and Child Health Care award, 1996; Ann L. Clark Nursing Rsch. Fund grantee, 1990. Mem. Nat. Assn. Pediatric Nurse Assocs. and Nurse Practitioners, Hawaii Nurses Assn. (bd. dirs., Excellence in Nursing Practice award 1991), Maui Nurses Assn. (pres., sec., bd. dirs.), Sigma Theta Tau (Gamma Psi chpt. 1991). Home: 175 Ehilani St Makawao HI 96768-8315 E-mail: atanner@maui.net.

TANNER, CANDACE JOANN, retired pre-school educator; b. Houston, Oct. 20, 1949; d. Joe Thomas and Deline Ivy Bahr; m. David Charles Tanner, Dec. 24, 1986; children: JoLynn, RaeAnn, Aaron, Jason. Cert. in Child Devel., Renton Tech. Coll., 1999. Pre-sch. tchr. Olympic View Christian, Wash., Childtime Learning Ctr.; program dir. Kid's Country Learning; child care giver Home Day Care Ctr., Anchorage; realtor ERA Bowden Co. Avocations: camping, fishing, reading, walking, travel. Home: 107 Natoma St Folsom CA 95630

TANNER, CRAIG RICHARD, fire and explosion engineer; b. Buffalo, July 24; s. Chester William and Gloria Ann (Steffan) T. Student, SUNY, Buffalo, 1971-75, St. Petersburg Jr. Coll., Clearwater, Fla., 1986—, U. Md., 1991—. Plant supr./cons. Indsl. Motors, Inc., North Tonawanda, N.Y., 1968—; pres. Metal Reclaiming Plant, 1975-77; mgr., pres. Seneca Electric, Buffalo, 1976-81; pres. TRC Industries/Tanner Imports, Clearwater, 1985—, Tanner Agy., Clearwater, 1985—; fire investigator, pub. adjuster Nat. Fire Adjusters, Inc., 1986-90, Nat. Casualty and Fire Adjusters, Inc., Clearwater, 1990—. Recipient Letter of Commendation, U.S. Dept. Justice. Mem. Elec. Apparatus Svcs. Assn., Nat. Assn. Investigative Specialists, Nat. Assn. Fire Investigators, Internat. Assn. Arson Investigators. Republican. Roman Catholic. E-mail: CraigFire@scientist.com.

TANNER, DANIEL, curriculum theory educator; b. N.Y.C., Sept. 22, 1926; s. Jack and Lillian (Jupiter) T.; m. Laurel Nan Jacobson, July 11, 1948 (div. 1988). BS with honors, Mich. State U., 1949, MS, 1952; PhD, Ohio State U., 1955. Asst. prof. edn. San Francisco State Coll., 1955-60; assoc. prof. edn., coord. Midwest program on airborne TV instrn. Purdue U., 1960-62; assoc. prof. edn., assoc. dir. internat. program for edn. leaders Northwestern U., 1962-64; assoc. prof. rsch. divsn. tchr. edn. CUNY, 1964-66; prof. edn., dir. Ctr. for Urban Edn., U. Wis.-Milw. Sch. Edn., 1966-67; prof. edn., dir. grad. programs in curriculum theory and devel. Grad. Sch. Edn., Rutgers U., New Brunswick, N.J., 1967—, chmn. dept. curriculum and instrn., 1969-72, faculty rsch. fellow, 1974-75, 88-89. Vis. lectr. U. Kansas City, summer 1956, Tchrs. Coll. Columbia, summer 1966; vis. prof. Emory U., summer 1968, SUNY, Binghamton, winter 1968, U. London, 1975, King Abdulaziz U., Saudi Arabia, winter 1992, U. Iowa, summer 1996; disting. lectr. ASCD, 1985, 86, Dewey Meml. lectr., 1984, Raths Meml. lectr., SUNY, 1984; Leadership Inst. lectr. U. Del., summer 1990; disting. lectr. Rider U., 1996; vis. scholar U. London Inst. Edn., 1974-75; mem. rev. bd. coll. work-study program U.S. Office Edn., 1965; mem. symposium on comparative curriculum history Inst. Sci. Edn. Kiel U., Fed. Republic Germany, 1989; del. leader Citizen Amb. Program, People-to-People Internat., Republic of South Africa, 1996, China, 1997, Dem. Citizenship Project Czech Republic, USIA, 1996-98; cons. U. Tex. Med. Ctr., 1961-62, Chgo. Sch. Survey, 1964-65, ctr. Urban Edn., N.Y.C., 1964-65, West Chgo. Sch. Survey, 1963-64, Nat. Ednl. TV Ctr., N.Y.C., 1963, Campbell County (Va.) Sch. Survey, 1970, Memphis Schs., 1977-78, Perth Amboy (NJ) Schs., 1996-97; ASCD Commn. on Gen. Edn., 1980-81, West Orange, N.J., Curriculum Study, 1984, ASCD Commn. on Secondary Sch. Practices, 1985, ASCD Ednl. Policy Task Force, 1985, NASSP Curriculum Coun., 1985-95; SUNY Buffalo External Evaluation, 1988; dir. Nat. Curriculum Inst., 1987; delivered Founder's Day address Delaware Valley Coll., 1985, Keynote address Nat. Conf. Citizen Edn., Palacky U., Czech Rep., 1998. Author: Schools for Youth: Change and Challenge in Secondary Education, 1965, Secondary Curriculum: Theory and Development, 1971, Secondary Education: Perspectives and Prospects, 1972, Using Behavioral Objectives in the Classroom, 1972, Curriculum Development: Theory into Practice, 3rd edit., 1995, Supervision in Education, 1987, History of the School Curriculum, 1991, Crusade for Democracy: Progressive Education at the Crossroads, 1991, 2002; founding editor, contbg. author: Rsch. Rev. for Sch. Leaders, 1996, 98, 00, Philosophy of Edn. Ency., 1996, Curriculum Issues, 87th Yearbook NSSE, 1988, 98th Yearbook, 1999, Ency. of Ednl. Rsch., 5th edit., 1982, Readings in Education Psychology, 1965, Yearbook of the Association for Student Teaching, 1962, The Great Debate, Our Schools in Crisis, 1959, Educational Issues in a Changing Society, 1964, Programs, Teachers and Machines, 1964, Views on American Schooling, 1964, The Training of America's Teachers, 1975, Curriculum and Instruction, 1981; co-author: Teen Talk: Curriculum Materials in Communications, 1971; co-editor: Improving the School Curriculum, 1988, Restructuring for an Interdisciplinary Curriculum, 1992, Curriculum Issues and the New Century, 1995; contbg. editor: Ednl. Leadership, 1969-74; mem. editl. bd. Tex. Tech. Jour. Edn., 1984-89, Tchg. Edn., 1986-90, Jour. Curriculum Supervision; editorial cons.: Ency. of Ednl. Rsch., 5th edit., Jour. Ednl. Psychology; founding editor Rev. of Rsch. for Sch. Leaders; contbr. Atlantic Monthly, Bull. of Atomic Scientists and other nat. mags., ednl. jours. Trustee Delaware Valley Coll., Doylestown, Pa., 1981-95; bd. dirs. Ohio State Alumni Assn. N.J., 1990-96. Recipient Excellence award Edn. Press Am., 1989, Distinguished Educator award Rider U., 1996; Univ. scholar Ohio State U., 1955. Fellow AAAS, John Dewey Soc. (bd. dirs. 1985-88, archivist 1989—, chmn. lectrs. commn. 1999—, pres. 2001—); mem. AAUP, Am. Ednl. Rsch. Assn., N.Y. Acad. Scis., Am. Polit. Sci. Assn., Am. Ednl. Studies Assn., Nat. Soc. Study Edn., Phi Kappa Phi, Phi Delta Kappa (Svc. award 1957). Home: Highwood Rd Somerset NJ 08873 Office: Grad Sch Edn Rutgers U New Brunswick NJ 08901-1183 Fax: 732-732-6803. *The essential quality of education and life is growth. Hence problems must be seen as opportunities and not as limitations if solutions are to be found and progress is to be made.*

TANNER, DAVID HAROLD, professional roof consultant; b. Union City, Pa., Nov. 20, 1945; s. Harold Oliver and Doris Louise (Wright) T.; m. Janet Patterson, Aug. 24, 1968; children: Jonathan David, Daniel James. BS in Edn., California U. of Pa., 1967; MS in Edn., SUNY, Oswego, 1968; grad., USAF Air Command & Staff Coll., 1995. Cert. U.S. Naval aviator, 1969, USAF sr. pilot, 1979; FAA cert. comml. pilot; cert. tchr., Pa., N.Y. Structural steel layout Erie (Pa.) City Iron Works, 1968; navy P-3 pilot USN Atlantic Fleet, Jacksonville, Fla., 1968-72; indsl. edn. tchr. Carlisle (Pa.) Area Sch. Dist., 1972, So. Middleton Sch. Dist., Boiling Springs, Pa., 1972-73, Cumberland Valley Sch. Dist., New Cumberland, 1973-74; mgr. engring. svcs. Carlisle Syntec, Inc., 1974-79; v.p. Carroll-Tanner Assocs., Corning, N.Y., 1980-81; tech. dir. C.F. Evans Roofing & Sheet Metal, Elmira, 1982-86; roofing dir. HCFF Architects, 1986-96; pres. Tanner Roof Cons., Horseheads, N.Y. and Dauphin, Pa., 1996—. Asbestos bldg. inspector N.Y. State Dept. Health, Albany, N.Y., 1989—; dir. intelligence 914 Airlift Wing, Air Force Res., Niagara Falls, N.Y., 1988-97, ret., 1997. Author: Owner's Manual of Roof Inspection, Maintenance and Repair, 1992. Sunday sch. tchr. Maranatha Christian & Missionary Alliance Ch., Horseheads, N.Y., 1981-2002. Lt. USN, 1968-72, Atlantic and Europe; vet. Operation Desert Shield/Storm, 1990-91, Persian Gulf, Asst. Wing Intelligence Officer, Maj. USAF. Recipient Full Grad. Sch. fellowship Title V, U.S. Dept. Edn., SUNY, Oswego, 1967; named Disting. Naval grad., 1969, Disting. grad. USAF Intelligence Command, 1989. Mem. Constrn. Specifications Inst., Res. Officer Assn., Classic Chevy Club, Am. Legion, Nat. Warplane Mus., Nat. Trust for Hist. Preservation, Epsilon Pi Tau, Phi Sigma Pi, Phi Delta Kappa. Mem. Christian and Missionary Alliance Church. Avocations: hunting, historical restoration, cabinetmaking, antique autos, motorcycling. Home and Office: 711 Sam Hill Ln Dauphin PA 17018 E-mail: tannerroofconsul@comcast.net.

TANNER, DEE BOSHARD, retired lawyer; b. Provo, Utah, Jan. 16, 1913; s. Myron Clark and Marie (Boshard) T.; m. Jane Barwick, Dec. 26, 1936 (div. Aug. 1962); children: Barry, Diane McDowell; m. Reeta Walker, Dec. 6, 1981. BA, U. Utah, 1935; LLB, Pacific Coast U., 1940; postgrad., Harvard U., 1936, Loyola U., L.A., 1937. Bar: Calif. 1943, U.S. Dist. Ct. (so. dist.) Calif. 1944, U.S. Ct. Appeals (9th cir.) 1947, ICC 1964, U.S. Dist. Ct. (ea. dist.) Calif. 1969, U.S. Supreme Ct. 1971. Assoc. Spray, Davis & Gould, L.A., 1943-44; pvt. practice, 1944; assoc. Tanner and Sievers, 1944-47, Tanner and Thornton, L.A., 1947-54, Tanner, Hanson, Meyers, L.A., 1954-64; ptnr. Tanner and Van Dyke, 1964-65, Gallagher and Tanner, L.A., 1965-70; pvt. practice Pasadena, Calif., 1970-95; retired, 1995. Mem. L.A. Bar Assn., World Affairs Assn., Harvard Law Sch. Assn., Lawyers' Club L.A. Home and Office: 1720 Lombardy Rd Pasadena CA 91106-4127 E-mail: rpltd@aol.com.

TANNER, DOUGLAS ALAN, lawyer; b. Palo Alto, Calif., Aug. 30, 1953; s. Bernard R. and Caroline (Orris) T.; m. Carol Scilacci, May 28, 1977; children: Lauren Elizabeth, Wynn Ann, Leigh Caroline. AB in History, Stanford U., 1974, MBA, JD, Stanford U., 1978. Bar: Calif. 1978, U.S. Dist. Ct. (no. dist.) Calif. 1978, U.S. Ct. Appeals (9th cir.) 1979, N.Y. 1987. Law clk. to judge U.S. Ct. Appeals (9th cir.), San Francisco, 1978-79; assoc. Orrick, Herrington & Sutcliffe, 1979-83, ptnr. San Jose, Calif., 1984-86, N.Y.C., 1986-89, Milbank, Tweed, Hadley & McCloy, L.A., 1989-92, Hong Kong, 1992-2001, Palo Alto, Calif., 2001—. Mem. San Francisco Barristers (chmn. corps. com. 1981-82), Order of Coif, Phi Beta Kappa. Republican. Episcopalian. Office: 630 Hansen Way Fl 2 Palo Alto CA 94304-1022 E-mail: dtanner@milbank.com.

TANNER, EDWARD CLEIN, orthopedist, medical educator; b. Amsterdam, N.Y., May 17, 1949; m. Elizabeth Treiber. BSChE, U. Rochester, N.Y., 1972; MD, U. Rochester, 1976. Clin. asst. prof. U. Rochester, 1981—; assoc. chief orthopedics Rochester Gen. Hosp., 1991-96, chief orthopedics, 1996—. Mem. AMA (del.), Am. Acad. Orthopedic Surgeons (bd. councilors 1998--), Med. Soc. State of N.Y. (del., treas. 1991-93, 2d vice chair 1993-95, vice chair publs. com. 1999—), Monroe County Med. Soc. (treas. 1984-87, pres. 1989-90), Rochester Orthop. Soc. (pres. 1994—). Office: Rochester Gen Hosp 1425 Portland Ave Rochester NY 14621-3095

TANNER, ERIC BENSON, lawyer; b. St. Louis, Aug. 27, 1949; s. Robert H. and Delores (Benson) T.; m. Rosalind Grace Tanner, June 23, 1978; children: Jacob, Adam. BA, U. Mo., Columbia, 1971; JD, U. Mo., Kansas City, 1975; cert., Coll. Fin. Planning, Denver, 1988. Bar: Mo. 1975. Instr. paralegal program Avila Coll., Kansas City, 1982-84; staff atty. Legal Aid Western Mo., 1975-83; pvt. practice, 1983-86; asst. v.p. trust dept. United Mo. Bank, NA, 1986-90; staff atty. Shook, Hardy & Bacon, 1990-93; v.p., trust counsel Commerce Bank, N.A., 1993—. CLE lectr. on estate planning topics to various bar assns. and univs., 1975—. Contbr. articles to law jours. Mem. planned giving com. Nat. Kidney Found., Kans. and Kansas City met. area, 1995-97; vol. Habitat for Humanity, 1997, 99, 2002; bd. dirs. Prime Health, 1980-86. Mem. ABA, Mo. Bar Assn., Kansas City Met. Bar Assn., Lawyers Assn. Kansas City, Kansas City Corp. Fiduciaries Assn. (pres. 1997), Estate Planning Soc. Kansas City. Office: Commerce Bank NA 1000 Walnut St Ste 800 Kansas City MO 64106-2160

TANNER, HAROLD, investment banker; b. N.Y.C., May 7, 1932; s. Irving and Pauline (Steinlauf) T.; m. Estelle Newman, July 6, 1957; children: David, James, Karen. BS, Cornell U., 1952; MBA, Harvard U., 1956. V.p., dir. Blyth & Co. Inc., N.Y.C., 1956-69; exec. v.p. New Court Securities Corp., 1969-76, Blyth Eastman Dillon & Co., Inc., N.Y.C., 1977-80; ptnr. Salomon Bros. Inc., 1980-81, mng. dir., 1981-87; pres. Tanner & Co., Inc., N.Y.C., 1987—. Co-founder Vol. Urban Cons. Group. Pres. Am. Jewish Com.; chmn. bd. trustees Cornell U., Russell Sage Found., Revson Found., Classroom Inc. Lt. (j.g.) USNR, 1952—54. Mem. Coun. on Fgn. Rels., Century Country Club, Harmonie Club. Home: 2 Morris Ln Scarsdale NY 10583-6053 Office: Tanner & Co 650 Madison Ave New York NY 10022-1029

TANNER, HELEN HORNBECK, historian, consultant; b. Northfield, Minn., July 5, 1916; d. John Wesley and Frances Cornelia (Wolfe) Hornbeck; m. Wilson P. Tanner, Jr., Nov. 22, 1940 (dec. 1977); children: Frances, Margaret Tanner Tewson, Wilson P., Robert (dec. 1983) AB with honors, Swarthmore Coll., 1937; MA, U. Fla., 1949; PhD, U. Mich., 1961. Asst. to dir. pub. rels. Kalamazoo Pub. Schs., 1937-39; with sales dept. Am. Airlines Inc., N.Y.C., 1940-43; teaching fellow, then teaching asst. U. Mich., Ann Arbor, 1949-53, 57-60, lectr. extension svc., 1961-74, asst. dir. Ctr. Continuing Edn. for Women, 1964-68; project dir. Newberry Libr., Chgo., 1976-81, rsch. assoc., 1981-95, sr. rsch. fellow, 1995—. Expert witness in Indian treaty litigation, 1963—; dir. D'Arcy McNickle Ctr. for Indian History, 1984-85; cons., expert witness Indian treaties; mem. Mich. Commn. Indian Affairs, 1966-70 Author: Zespedes in East Florida 1784-1790, 1963, 89, General Green Visits St. Augustine, 1964, The Greeneville Treaty, 1974, The Territory of the Caddo Tribe of Oklahoma, 1974, The Ojibwas, 1992; editor: Atlas of Great Lakes Indian History, 1987, The Settling of North America: An Atlas, 1995. NEH grantee, 1976, fellow, 1989; ACLS grantee, 1990. Mem. Am. Soc. Ethnohistory (pres. 1982-83), Am. Hist. Assn., Conf. L.Am. History, Soc. History Discoveries, Chgo. Map Soc., Fla. Hist. Soc., Hist. Soc. Mich. Home: 5178 Crystal Dr Beulah MI 49617-9618 Office: The Newberry Libr 60 W Walton St Chicago IL 60610-3380 E-mail: hhtanner@aol.com.

TANNER, JANE, mathematics educator; b. Syracuse, N.Y., Aug. 20, 1956; d. Francis Duane and Barbara Ann (Zimmerman) Tanner; m. David Allen Covillion, Apr. 18, 1980 (dec. Sept. 1996); m. Andrew Rowe, June 30, 2001. AB, Cornell U., 1978; MS, SUNY, Oswego, 1982; postgrad., SUNY, Syracuse, 1983-86. Cert. elem. and math. tchr., N.Y. Math. tchr. 7th grade Ray Jr. High Sch., Baldwinsville, N.Y., 1978-79; math. tchr. 6th/7th grades Zogg Mid. Sch., Liverpool, 1979-81; tchr. math. Liverpool High Sch., 1981-82; prof. Onondaga C.C., Syracuse, 1982—; tchr. math. Lafayette (N.Y.) H.S., 1986. Text reviewer in field. Co-author: Mathematics Teacher, 1978; contbr. articles to profl. jours. Mem. planning com. Syracuse Sci. Fair, 1982-96. N.Y. State Regents scholar, 1974, James L. Sears Found. scholar, 1974. Mem. AAUW, Nat. Coun. Tchrs. Math., Assn. Math. Tchrs. N.Y. State, Math. Assn. Am., Assn. for Women in Math., N.Y. State United Tchrs., Am. Fedn. Tchrs., Onondaga County Math. Tchrs., N.Y. State Assn. Two-Yr. Colls., N.Y. State Math. Assn. Two-Yr. Colls. (pres., state scholarship chair), Am. Math. Assn. Two-Yr. Colls (prodn. mgr. AMATYC Rev.), Onondaga C.C. Fedn. Tchrs. (sec. 1987-2001, del.-at-large 2001—), Embroiderers Guild Am., Am. Needlepoint Guild (v.p.), Delta Kappa Gamma (rec. sec., pres. Beta Kappa chpt., state exec. sec., state pres.), Alpha Phi (house corp. bd. Delta chpt., sec., pres. Fingerlakes alumnae chpt.). Republican. Avocations: traveling, crossword puzzles, reading, crafts. Home: 231 Searles Rd Parish NY 13131 Office: Onondaga Community Coll Math Dept Syracuse NY 13215 E-mail: tannerj@aurora.sunyocc.edu.

TANNER, JIMMIE EUGENE, college dean; b. Hartford, Ark., Sept. 27, 1933; s. Alford C. and Hazel Ame (Anthony) T.; m. Carole Joy Yant, Aug. 28, 1958; children— Leslie Allison, Kevin Don. BA, Okla. Baptist U., 1955; MA, U. Okla., 1957, PhD, 1964. Assoc. prof. English, Franklin Coll., Ind., 1964-65; prof. English, Okla. Bapt. U., Shawnee, 1958-64, 65-72; v.p. acad. affairs Hardin-Simmons U., Abilene, Tex., 1972-78, La. Coll., Pineville, 1978-80; dean William Jewell Coll., Liberty, Mo., 1980-97, prof. English, 1997—, interim pres., 1993-94. Contbr.: The Annotated Bibliography of D.H. Lawrence, Vol. 1, 1982, Vol. 2, 1985. Mem. Shawnee Sch. Bd., 1966-72; mem. edn. commn. So. Bapt. Conv., 1967-72. So. Fellowships Fund fellow, 1960-61; Danforth fellow, 1962-63. Democrat. Baptist. Avocations: tennis; photography. E-mail: tanner@william.jewell.edu Home: 609 Lancelot Dr Liberty MO 64068-1023 Office: William Jewell Coll Liberty MO 64068 *As I reflect on my life, the thought that presses on me is my incredible luck at having been born in America in the 20th century, my good fortune in having the opportunity for education, for a satisfying career, for supportive family, friends, mentors at every stage of my life. I must recognize any accomplishment as communal as well as individual.*

TANNER, JOHN DOUGLAS, JR. history educator, writer; b. Quantico, Va., Oct. 2, 1943; s. John Douglas and Dorothy Lucille (Walker) T.; m. Jo Ann Boyd, Jan. 1964 (div. Aug. 1966); 1 child, Lorena Desiree; m. Laurel Jean Selfridge, Dec. 19, 1967 (div. Oct. 1987); children: John DouglasIII, Stephen Douglas, Elizabeth Jane; m. Karen H. Olson, Apr. 16, 1988. BA, Pomona Coll., 1966; MA, Claremont Grad. U., 1968; postgrad., U. Calif., Riverside, 1976, 84-86, U. Calif., San Diego, 1984-87, U. Pacific, 1993. Cert. tchr. Calif. Asst. swimming, water polo coach Pomona Coll., 1966-69; rsch. asst. history dept. Claremont Grad. U., 1967-69; prof. history Palomar Coll., San Marcos, Calif., 1969—, pres. faculty, 1970-71, v.p. faculty senate, 1971-72. Author: Olaf Swenson and his Siberian Imports jour., 1978 (Dog Writers Assn. Am. Best Series award 1979), Campaign for Los Angeles, 1846-47, 69; co-author: Last of the Old-Time Outlaws: The George West Musgrave Story, 2002; co-editor: Don Juan Forster, 1970, Alaskan Trails, Siberian Dogs, 1998; contbr. articles to profl. jours. Citizens com. Fallbrook (Calif.) San. Dist., 1980; merit badge counselor Boy Scouts Am., 1975-85; Martin County Hist. Soc., Morgan County Hist. Soc., Fallbrook Hist. Soc., San Diego Opera Guild, San Diego Classical Music Soc., Opera Pacific Guild. Chautauqua fellow NSF, 1979. Mem. Nat. Assn. for Outlaw and Lawman History, Inc., Western Outlaw-Lawman History Assn. (adv. bd.), Custer Battlefield Hist. and Mus. Assn. (life), Western Writers Am., Old Trail Drivers Assn. Tex., The Westerners, So. Calif. Siberian Husky Assn. (pres. 1972-79), U.S. Shooting Team (Inner Circle), Sons of the Rep. of Tex., Western History Assn., Ariz. Hist. Soc., N.Mex. Hist. Soc., Siberian Husky Club Am. (bd. dirs. 1974-78, 1st v.p. 1978-79). Republican. Episcopalian. Avocations: collecting S.W. Indian art, backpacking, wine making, writing, opera. Home: 2308 Willow Glen Rd Fallbrook CA 92028-8605 Office: Palomar Coll 1140 W Mission Rd San Marcos CA 92069-1415

TANNER, JOHN D. real estate developer, contractor; b. Calgary, Alta., Can., Feb. 2, 1939; came to U.S., 1956; s. Earl Pingree and Betty (Bridge) T.; m. Barbara Steed, Dec. 27, 1965; children: Jeffrey, Scott, Daniel, David, William, Joanna, Trisha. BS, Brigham Young U., 1965. Constrn. engr. Tide Water Oil Co., Sacramento, 1965-67; regional constrn. engr. Phillips Petroleum Co., Inc., San Francisco, 1967-69; mgr., v.p. Staiger Constrn. Co., Inc., Sacramento, 1969-71, owner, pres., 1971-76, Tanner Industries, Inc., Roseville, Calif., 1972—, Western Single Ply. Nev., Inc., Las Vegas, 1987—, Western Single Ply. Calif. Inc., Loomis, 1981—. Pres. sch. bd. dirs. Eureka Sch. Dist., Granite Bay, Calif., 1987—. Mem. Granite Bay Golf Club (founding mem.). Republican. Mem. Lds Ch. Home: 7150 J Bar B Dr Granite Bay CA 95746-9453

TANNER, JOHN S. congressman, lawyer; b. Dyersburg, Tenn., Sept. 22, 1944; s. E.B. and Edith (Summers) T.; m. Betty Ann Portis, Sept. 2, 1967; children: Elizabeth Tanner Atkins, John Portis. BS, U. Tenn., 1966, JD, 1968. Bar: Tenn. 1968. Mem. Tenn. Ho. of Reps., 1976-88, 101st-107th Congresses from 8th Tenn. dist., Washington, 1988—. Mem. Ways and Means, Cong. Sportsmen's Caucus (founding mem. The Blue Dog Coalition). Active Obion County Cancer Soc.; former mem. bd. visitors USAF Acad.; bd. visitors U.S. Naval Acad.' former mem. bd. visitors U.S. Mil. Acad. Lt. USN, 1968-72; col. Tenn. Army N.G., 1974- 2000. Mem. Obion County C. of C., Obion County Bar Assn., Rotary. Democrat. Mem. Christian Ch. (Disciples Of Christ). Avocations: golf, hunting. Office: US House of Reps 1226 Longworth Hob Washington DC 20515-0001

TANNER, JOSEPH R. astronaut; b. Ill., 1950; married; 2 children. BSc in Mech. Engring., BS, U. Ill., 1973. Commd. 2d lt. USN, 1973, pilot, 1975—84; astronaut NASA, Houston, 1992—. Astronaut Space Shuttle Atlantis, 1994, svc. to Hubble Space Telescope, 1997, aboard Endeavour, 2000. Recipient Outstanding Alumnus award, U. Ill. Avocations: swimming, camping, mountaineering, time with family. Office: Astronaut Office CB NASA Johnson Space Ctr Houston TX 77058*

TANNER, LAUREL NAN, education educator; b. Detroit, Feb. 16, 1929; d. Howard Nicholas and Celia (Solvich) Jacobson; m. Daniel Tanner, July 11, 1948; m. Kenneth J. Rehage, Nov. 25, 1989. BS in Social Sci, Mich. State U., 1949, MA in Edn., 1953; EdD, Columbia U., 1967. Pub. sch. tchr., 1950-64; instr. tchr. edn. Hunter Coll., 1964-66, asst. prof., 1967-69; supr. Milw. Pub. Schs., 1966-67; mem. faculty Temple U., Phila., 1969—, prof. edn., 1974-89, prof. emerita, 1993—; prof. edn. U. Houston, 1989-96. Vis. professorial scholar U. London Inst. Edn., 1974-75; vis. scholar Stanford U., 1984-85, U. Chgo., 1988-89; curriculum cons., 1969—; disting. vis. prof. San Francisco State U., 1987. Author: Classroom Discipline for Effective Teaching and Learning, 1978, La Disciplina en la enseñanza y el Aprendizaje, 1980, Dewey's Laboratory School: Lessons for Today, 1997 ; co-author: Classroom Teaching and Learning, 1971, Curriculum Development: Theory into Practice, 1975, 3d edit., 1995, Supervision in Education: Problems and Practices, 1987, (with Daniel Tanner) History of the School Curriculum, 1990; editor Nat. Soc. Study Edn. Critical Issues in Curriculum, 87th yearbook, part 1, 1988. Faculty rsch. fellow Temple U., 1970, 80, 81; recipient John Dewey Rsch. award, 1981-82, Rsch. Excellence award U. Houston, 1992, Outstanding Writing award Am. Assn. Colls. Tchr. Edn., 1998; Spencer Found. rsch. grantee, 1992. Mem. ASCD (dir. 1982-84), Soc. Study Curriculum History (founder, 1st pres. 1978-79), Am. Edn. Rsch. Assn. (com. on role and status of women in ednl. R & D 1994-97), Profs. Curriculum Assn. (Factotum 1983-84, chair membership com. 1994-95), Am. Ednl. Studies Assn., John Dewey Soc. (bd. dirs. 1989-91, pres. 2000-01), Alumni Coun. Tchrs. Coll. Columbia U. *In my view, America has progressed over the years, and the best days are still to come. We have the single necessary resource to solve our most urgent problems and achieve our deepest moral values — human intelligence.*

TANNER, LYNN, actress; b. N.Y.C., Mar. 22, 1953; d. Harry J. and Barbara Sylvia (Hirschman) Maurer; m. Allen Barry Witz, Aug. 31, 1975. BS, NYU, 1975; JD, DePaul U., 1980. Bar: Ill. 1980. Actress, various, 1980—. Appeared (films) Human Error, 1987, Another Time, Another Place, 1988, Twisted, 1995, actress (pilot TV series) Hollywood Flat , Pack of Lies, Back at the Blue Dolphin Saloon, Toyer; actor: Burying Rose; actress Dolores and Her Loved Ones, Final Placement, Facing the Dragon, The Workroom, Sign in Sidney Brusteins Window , Summer and Smoke, The Maids, Under Milkwood, Dark at the Top of the Stairs , Rosa; co-author: (film scripts) Wrong Turn , Tessa Deare, Reasons. Mem. SAG, AFTRA, Actors Equity Assn., Women in Film, Women in Theatre, Ill. Bar Assn. E-mail: lynnjettstar@adelphia.net.

TANNER, MARTIN ABBA, statistics and human oncology educator; b. Highland Park, Ill., Oct. 19, 1957; s. Meir and Esther Rose (Bauer) T.; m. Anat Talitman, Aug. 14, 1984; 1 child, Noam Ben. BA, U. Chgo., 1978, PhD, 1982. Asst. prof. stats. and human oncology U. Wis., Madison, 1982-87, assoc. prof., 1987-90; dir. lab., prof. and dept. chair biostatistics U. Rochester, 1990-94; prof. dept. statistics Northwestern U., 1994—. Cons. Kirkland & Ellis, 1980-82; mem. Nat. Inst. Allergy and Infectious diseases study sect., 1994-98; reviewer NIH, NSF, VA. Assoc. editor Jour. Am. Stat. Assn., 1987-99; editor Jour. of Am. Statis. Assn., 1999—; contbr. articles to profl. jours. Recipient New Investigator Rsch. award NIH, 1984, Mortimer Spiegelman award Am. Pub. Health Assn., 1993; NSF grantee, 1983, 95, NIH grantee, 1986—. Fellow Royal Statis. Soc., Am. Statis. Assn. (Continuing Edn. Excellence award); mem. AAAS, Mensa, Sigma Xi. Avocations: classical guitar, medieval poetry. Office: Northwestern U 2006 Sheridan Rd Evanston IL 60208-0852 E-mail: mat132@nwu.edu.

TANNER, MICHAEL CARL, mental health services professional; b. Bklyn., June 7, 1962; s. Carl F. and Mary J. Tanner; m. Pattie M. Albanese, Dec. 31, 1989 (div. 1998); 1 child, Gabrielle Kirsten. Mental health therapy aide Pilgrim Psychiat. Ctr., Brentwood, N.Y., 1988-96; devel. aide L.I. Devel. Ctr., Ridge, 1996—; cashier Suffolk County Regional Off-Track Betting Corp., Hauppauge, 1997—. Congl. liaison Assn. State, County and Mcpl. Employees, Washington, 1988—. Coord. Neighborhood Watch, 1995; v.p. Bay Area Civic Assn., Shirley, N.Y., 1999; mem. Legis. Adv. Com., Shirley, 1997—. With N.Y. Army Nat. Guard, 1990-93. Mem.: AARP, KC (2nd degree 1998—), Law Enforcement Alliance Am., Govt. Employees' Assn., Acad. Polit. Sci., Internat. Assn. Women Police, Am. Police Hall of Fame (guardian angel), Nat. Assn. Chiefs Police, Hispanic Nat. Law Enfocement Assn. N.Y. (hon.), Mastic Park (N.Y.) Civic Assn., Medford (N.Y.) Civic Assn., Cath. War Vets., Internat. Brotherhood Teamster Hauppauge, Moriches Bay (N.Y.) Civic Assn., Am. Legion (adjutant 1998). Roman Catholic. Home: PO Box 389 Rocky Point NY 11778-0389 Office: LI Devel Ctr 64 Ridge Rd Ridge NY 11961-1008

TANNER, PEGGY, retired nurse; b. N.Y.C., N.Y., Sept. 9, 1929; d. Denis Michael Hegarty and Minnie Daly; m. Henry V. Tanner, Sept. 5, 1959; children: Denise Fontenelli, James. Student, Iona Coll., 1974. RN N.Y. Staff nurse Queen Mary's Hosp., Sidcup, England, 1950—53, Jewish Meml. Hosp., New York, NY, 1955—59; med. asst. Dr. Arthur Antenucci, N.Y.C., 1960—62; claimes examiner Am. Prog. Ins., Mount Vernon, 1962—65; interviewer N.Y. State Unemployment Office, New Rochelle, 1973—76; staff nurse New Rochelle Hosp., 1977—92, ret., 1992. Author: Tales of Two Countries, 1997, The Joy of the Journey, 1999. Adv. com. Parks & Recreation, New Rochelle, 1971—75; oral history recorder Bicentennial Com., 1975—76; dist. leader Rep. Party, 1970—74. Mem.: Jersey Shore Writers Guild, Irish History Roundtable. Personal E-mail: pegoty4@aol.com.

TANNER, R. MARSHALL, lawyer; b. Santa Monica, Calif., Dec. 4, 1946; s. Stanley Robert and Kathryn (Lau) Tanner; m. Colleen Bonner, Sept. 3, 1969; children: David, Brent, Julie, Glenn, Scott, Holly. BA, Brigham Young U., 1970; JD, UCLA, 1977. Ptnr. Lawler, Felix & Hall, L.A., 1977-86, Pettit & Martin, Newport Beach, Calif., 1986-95, Sheppard, Mullin, Richter & Hampton, 1995—. Lt. USNR, 1970-74. Mem. Calif. State Bar Assn., Orange County Bar Assn. Mem. Lds Ch. Office: Sheppard Mullin Richter & Hampton 650 Town Center Dr Fl 4 Costa Mesa CA 92626-1993 E-mail: mtanner@smrh.com.

TANNER, ROBERT DENNIS, chemical engineering educator; b. Detroit, Jan. 17, 1939; s. Albert and Shary (Roth) T.; m. Ruth Taissa Kellman, Jan. 27, 1963; children: David S., Benjamin J. BSE in Math., U. Mich., 1961, BSChemE, 1962, MSChemE, 1963; PhD, Case Western Res. U., 1967. Pilot plant engr. Diamond Shamrock Rsch. Labs., Concord Township, Ohio, 1963; engring. assoc. R & D Merck & Co., Rahway, N.J., 1967-72; prof. Vanderbilt U., Nashville, 1972—. Cons. Smith Kline & French Labs., Phila., 1981-87; vis. prof. Swiss Fed. Inst. Tech., Zurich, Switzerland, 1981-82. Contbr. numerous articles to profl. jours. Mem. Am. Chem. Soc. (chmn. div. microbial and biochem. tech. 1979-80). Office: Vanderbilt U Chem Engring Dept Nashville TN 37235

TANNER, ROBERT HUGH, engineer, consultant; b. London, July 22, 1915; s. George John and Evelyn (Stratton) T.; m. Joan Margaret Garnham, July 6, 1940; children: Christopher John, Rosemary June, Peter Pinckney, David Stephen. BS in Engring., U. London, 1936, MS in Engring., 1962; LLD, Concordia U., 1989. From TV to rsch. engr. BBC, London, 1936-47; from engr. to dir. info. No. Electric Co., Ltd., Ottawa, Can., Ont., 1947-70; dir. info. Bell-No. Rsch., Ont., 1970-72; pres. IEEE, N.Y.C., 1972; dir. indsl. rsch. Can. Dept. Comm., Ottawa, 1973-75; pvt. practice cons. engr. Naples, Fla., 1975—. Cons. in field. Inventor various patents. Maj. Brit. Army, 1939-45, ETO. Fellow IEEE (pres. 1972, McNaughton Gold medal 1974, Pratt award 1981, Award for Engring Professionalism, 1993), Acoustical Soc. Am., Engring. Inst. Can., Instn. of Elec. Engrs.; mem. Nat. Coun. Acoustical Cons. (bd. dirs. 1982-88). Episcopalian. Office: PO Box 655 Naples FL 34106-0655 Fax: 239-254-1186. E-mail: nfn20071@naples.net.

TANNER, W(ALTER) RHETT, lawyer; b. Athens, Ga., May 16, 1938; s. Johnnie Bryson and Walterette (Arwood) T.; m. Carolyn Laverne Watson, Nov. 11, 1967; 1 child, Walter Rhett (dec. 1989). AB cum laude, U. Ga., 1960, JD cum laude, 1962. Bar: Ga. 1961; cert. neutral Ga. Office of Dispute Resolution. Assoc. Hansell, Post, Bandon & Dorsey, Atlanta, 1963-66, ptnr., 1966-89, Jones, Day, Reavis & Pogue, Atlanta, 1989-95, of counsel, 1995-99, retired, 1999; mediator Resolution Resources, 1999—. Panelist Am. Arbitration Assn., 1995—. Bd. dirs. Atlanta Symphony Orch., 1975—95, mem. exec. com., 1977—86, v.p., 1978, chmn. maj. gifts campaign, 1980, bd. counsellors, 1996—; mem. Leadership Atlanta, 1980, Leadership Ga., 1982; mem. bd. visitors Grady Meml. Hosp., 1983—92; trustee Ga. Legal History Found., 1986—, pres., 1996—; hon. chmn. Atlanta Decorators Show House, 2002; trustee, vice chmn. Sr. Citizens Svc. Met. Atlanta, Inc., 2000—. Lt. comdr. USNR, 1964—72. Mem. Atlanta Bar Assn. (bd. dirs. 1982-87, exec. com. 1983-87), State Bar Ga. (vice chmn. bar and media com. 1979-82), Atlanta Bar Found. (trustee 1985-91), U. Ga. Alumni (pres. chpt. 1973-74, chmn. Atlanta/Met. coun. 1975, mem. state bd. mgrs., v.p. 1976-78), Rotary Club, Gridiron, Capital City Club, Phi Beta Kappa, Omicron Delta Kappa, Phi Kappa Phi, Phi Delta Phi, Delta Tau Delta. Home: 2097 Bohler Rd NW Atlanta GA 30318-1515 Office: Jones Day Reavis & Pogue 3500 Suntrust Plz 303 Peachtree St NE Ste 3500 Atlanta GA 30308-3263 E-mail: wtanner516@aol.com.

TANNIAN, FRANCIS XAVIER, economist, educator; b. Boston, Dec. 5, 1933; s. John Joseph and Marie (Killian) T.; m. Beatrix Laube, May 19, 1962; children— Monica, Margaret Joyce, Mark, Michele BA, Boston Coll., 1955, MA, 1959; PhD, U. Va., 1965. Bus trainee Gen. Electric Co., Schenectady, 1955-56; asst. prof. econs. Duquesne U., Pitts., 1962-66; assoc. prof. econs. U. Del., Newark, 1967-72, prof. urban econs., 1972—, assoc. dean, 1978-79. Vis. prof. U. Stuttgart, Fed. Republic Germany, 1972-73, U. Karlsruhe, Fed. Republic Germany, 1982, San Diego State U., 1989, U. Nitra, Czechoslovakia, 1990; cons. Fed. Water Pollution and Control Adminstrn., 1965-68, Deutsche Gesellschaft, Frankfurt, Fed. Republic Germany, 1982-83; lectr. urban studies U.S. Dept. State, Budapest, Bucharest, Belgrade, 1975; guest lectr. Czechoslovakian Acad. Scis., 1975 Editor: Externalities, 1972; contbr. articles to profl. jours. Mem. Del. Gov.'s Econ. Adv. Council, 1969-72; bd. dirs. Del. OIC, Wilmington, 1970-78; bd. dirs. Parity Econ. Devel. Corp., Wilmington, 1978-84; mem. Wilmington Mayor's Econ. Devel. Com., 1976-82. Served with U.S. Army, 1957-58 Mem. Am. Econ. Assn., So. Econs. Assn., Am. Real Estate and Urban Econs. Assn. Democrat. Roman Catholic. Home: 910 Baylor Dr Newark DE 19711-3128 Office: U Del Coll Urban Affairs Newark DE 19711

TANNOUS, ROBERT JOSEPH, lawyer; b. Amman, Jordan, June 4, 1962; came to U.S., 1968; s. Jerry J. and Nadia Tannous; m. Marlo B. Tannous, Apr. 22, 1989; children: Mallory E., Alexander B. BSBA, Ohio State U., 1984, JD, 1987. Bar: Ohio 1987, U.S. Dist. Ct. (so. dist.) Ohio 1987. Ptnr. Porter, Wright, Morris & Arthur LLP, Columbus, Ohio, 1987—. Trustee Children First Inc., Columbus, 1996-00, Ohio Hist. Found., Columbus, 1999-02, Ohio Historical Soc. Devel. counsel; fundraiser, com. various charitable orgns., Columbus, 1987—; team walk coord. March of Dimes, 1988-90; mem. Columbus Mus. of Art, Columbus Zoo. Recipient Forty Under 40 award Bus. First, 1997; named one of Ten Outstanding Young Citizens U.S. Jr. C. of C., 1997. Mem. ABA (bus. law sect.), Ohio Sate Bar Assn., Columbus Bar Assn. (corps. law com., sports and entertainment law com., securities law com.), Capital Club, Columbus Investment Interest Group, Columbus Coun. on World Affairs, Columbus Area C. of C. (capt. club 1991-92), Alpha Lambda Delta, Phi Eta Sigma, Phi Alpha Kappa, Beta Gamma Sigma (past pres.). Republican. Episcopalian. Avocations: golf, travel, reading, Ohio State Buckeyes. Office: Porter Wright Morris & Arthur LLP 41 S High St Ste 2800 Columbus OH 43215-6194 E-mail: rtannous@porterwright.com.

TANOUS, HELENE MARY, radiologist, educator; b. Zanesville, Ohio, Oct. 22, 1939; d. Joseph and Rose Marie (Mokarzel) T.; m. John Camp, 1986 (dec. 1990). BA, Marymount Coll., 1961; MD, U. Tex., 1967. Diplomate Am. Bd. Radiology. Intern County Hosp., L.A., 1967-68; resident in radiology Cedars-Sinai Med. Ctr., 1968-69, U. So. Calif. Hosp., L.A., 1969-71; pvt. practice medicine specializing in radiology, 1972-73; instr. radiology U. So. Calif. Med. Sch., 1971-72; asst. prof. diagnostic radiology Baylor Med. Sch., Houston, 1973-75; dir. med. student elective in diagnostic radiology Ben Taub Hosp., 1973-75; pvt. practice diagnostic radiology Largo, Fla., 1975—. Chief Radiology Diagnostic Clinic, Largo, Fla.; asst. prof. diagnostic radiology U. South Fla. Med. Sch., 1980—; asst. prof., dir. med. student edn. in diagnostic radiology U. Tex., Galveston, 1988-91. Pres., founder Children's Advs., Inc., 1977-85; bd. dirs. Fla. Endowment for Humanities, 1979-83. Decorated Chevalier des Palmes Academiques Govt. of France, 1988. Mem. AMA, So. Med. Assn., L'Alliance Francaise of Tampa (bd. dirs. 1984—, pres. 1985-87), Fedn. Alliances Francaises U.S.A. (bd. dirs. 1987-89), Houston Com. Fgn. Rels. E-mail: helenetanousmd@aol.com.

TANOUS, PETER JOSEPH, banker; b. N.Y.C., May 21, 1938; s. Joseph Carrington and Rose Marie (Mokarzel) T.; m. Barbara Ann MacConnell, Aug. 18, 1962; children: Christopher, Helene, William. BA in Econs., Georgetown U., 1960. With Smith Barney & Co., Inc. (now Salomon Smith Barney, Inc.), N.Y.C., 1963-78, 2d v.p., mgr. Paris office, 1967, v.p., 1968-78; resident European sales mgr. in Paris Smith Barney & Co., Inc. (now Salom0n Smith Barney, Inc.), 1969-71; internat. sales mgr. Smith Barney & Co., Inc. (now Salomon Smith Barney, Inc.), 1971-78, 1st v.p., 1975-78; chmn. bd. Petra Capital Corp., 1978-81; pres. Lynx Investment Advisory Inc., Washington, 1992—. Exec. v.p. Bank Audi (USA), N.Y.C., 1984-92; del. U.S.-Saudi Arabian Joint Econ. Commn. Bus. Dialogue; trustee Browning Sch., N.Y.C., 1987-93; bd. dirs. Cedars Bank, L.A., Interstate Resources, Inc., Rosslyn, Va., MPS Group, Inc. (formerly Modis Profl. Svcs., Inc.), Jacksonville, Fla., Kistler Aerospace Corp., Seattle. Author: Investment Gurus, 1997, The Wealth Equation, 1999. Recipient Nat. Order of Cedar, Govt. of Lebanon, 2002. Office: 1100 Connecticut Ave NW Washington DC 20036-4101

TANOWITZ, HERBERT BERNARD, internist, parasitologist and medicine educator; b. Bklyn., Sept. 6, 1941; s. Joseph and Esther Tanowitz; children: Pamela, Meredith, Jill. BS, Bklyn. Coll., 1963; MD, Yeshiva U., Bronx, N.Y., 1967. Diplomate Am. Bd. Internal Medicine, Am. Bd. Infectious Diseases. Intern Bellevue Hosp., N.Y.C., 1967-68; resident Lincoln Hosp., Bronx, 1968-71; fellow in infectious diseases Albert Einstein Coll., 1971-73; USN physician Naval Hosp., Quantico, Va., 1973-75; asst. prof. pathology and medicine Albert Einstein Coll. Medicine, 1975-80, assoc. prof. pathology and medicine, 1980-86, prof. pathology and medicine, 1986—. Capt., USNR, 1973—. Office: Albert Einstein Coll Medicine 1300 Morris Park Ave Bronx NY 10461-1926 E-mail: tanowitz@aecom.yu.edu.

TANPHAICHITR, KONGSAK, rheumatologist, allergist, immunologist, internist; b. Bangkok, Feb. 22, 1946; came to U.S., 1971; s. Boonchoo and Hong (Nayakovit) T.; m. Sirirat Tareesung, June 17, 1973; children: Saksiri Marc, Marisa. Student, Mahidol U., Bangkok, Thailand, 1964-66, MD cum laude, 1970. Diplomate Am. Bd. Internal Medicine, Am. Bd. Rheumatology, Am. Bd. Allergy and Immunology; cert. Rheumatologist Royal Coll. Physicians Can. Straight med. intern Detroit Gen. Hosp.-Wayne State U., 1971-72; resident Barnes Hosp.-Washington U., St. Louis, 1972-74, fellow in rheumatology and immunology, 1974-76; instr. in medicine Washington U., 1976-77, asst. prof. medicine, 1977-97, assoc. prof. medicine, 1997—; attending physician Barnes Hosp., 1976—, Jewish Hosp. of St. Louis, 1981—. Dir. Allergy, Rheumatology & Immunology Specialists, St. Louis; cons. rheumatology Washington U., St. Louis, 1976—. Author: Amyloid Fibrils in Joint Fluid, 1976, Studies of Tolerance in NZB/NZW Mice, 1977, Vasculitis and Multiple Sclerosis, 1980, Buddhism and Science, 1987, Buddhism: Answers to Common Questions, 1990, Buddhism Answers Life, 1995, Mindfulness: The Key to Perfect One's Life, 1997, Mind and Universe, Mindfulness and Stress Management, 1998, Awakened Life for the New Millennium, 2000, Ethics and Morality, 2000, Parenting, 2000, Buddhism Beyond Non-Violence, 2001, Mom, 2001, The Best, the Worst and the Horrible of 9/11 , 2001, Miracle of the Buddha's Wisdom, 2002. Dharma tchr., bd. dirs., sec. Wat Phrasriratanaram Buddhist Temple, St. Louis, 1983—; co-dir. Buddhist Coun., St. Louis, 1985-90; chmn. Buddhist Coun. Greater St. Louis, 1999—. Fellow: ACP, Royal Coll. Physicians Can., Am. Coll. Rheumatology, Am. Acad. Allergy, Asthma, and Immunology; mem.: Thai-Am. Physicians Found. (treas., bd. dirs. 2000—), Thai Physicians Assn. Am. (treas. Midwest chpt. 1994, sec. Midwest chpt. 1997, nat. treas. 1998, nat. bd. dirs. 1999—2001, nat. treas. 2000), Thai Assn. Greater St. Louis (pres.), Thai Temple Karate Shorinryu Club (Black Belt). Avocations: karate, karaoke, insight meditation. Home: 12413 Ladue Rd Saint Louis MO 63141-8100 Office: Allergy Rheum & Immun Specs 11115 New Halls Ferry Rd Florissant MO 63033-7613

TANSELLE, GEORGE THOMAS, English language educator, foundation executive; b. Lebanon, Ind., Jan. 29, 1934; s. K. Edwin and Madge R. (Miller) T. BA magna cum laude, Yale U., 1955; MA, Northwestern U., 1956, PhD, 1959. Instr. Chgo. City Jr. Coll., 1958-60, U. Wis., Madison, 1960-61, asst. prof., 1961-63, assoc. prof., 1963-68, prof. English, 1968-78; v.p. John Simon Guggenheim Meml. Found., 1978—; adj. prof. English and comparative lit. Columbia U., 1980—. Mem. Planning Inst. Commn. on English, 1961; mem. exec. com. Ctr. for Edits. Am. Authors, 1970-73; mem. adv. com. for drama for bicentennial Kennedy Ctr., 1974-76; mem. Soviet-Am. symposium on editing Ind. U., 1976; mem. adv. com. Howells Meml., Kittery Point, 1976-78; exec. com. Ctr. for Scholarly Edits., 1976-81; mem. nat. adv. bd. Ctr. for Book, Libr. of Congress, 1978—; mem. adv. bd. Burton's Anatomy of Melancholy, 1978—, Pub. and Printing History, A Guide to Manuscript Resources in the U.S., 1980—; bd. dirs. Lit. Classics of U.S., Inc., 1979—, chmn. editl. standards com., 1979—, corp. sec., 1989—; mem. adv. com. N.Am. imprints program, 1980-92; Hanes lectr. U. N.C., 1981; mem. adv. coun. Rosenbach Mus. and Libr., 1980—; mem. adv. coun. Ind. U. Inst. Adv. Study, 1983—; mem. faculty Summer Rare Book Sch., Columbia U., 1984-87; mem. adv. bd. Ctr. for Am. Culture Studies, Columbia U., 1985-94; mem. adv. coun. Am. Trust for the Brit. Libr., 1987—; Rosenbach lectr. U. Pa., 1987; mem. adv. coun. Am. Literary Manuscripts project, 1988—; bd. dirs. 18th Century Short-Title Catalogue/N.Am., Inc., 1988—, chmn., 1994—, Mark Twain Edition Project, 1991—; mem. vis. com. Lilly Libr., 1988-92; mem. adv. bd. Ctr. for Renaissance and Baroque Studies, U. Md., 1990—; mem. adv. com. Writings of J.F. Cooper, 1990—; Sandars lectr. Cambridge U., 1997; mem. adv. bd. Blake Archive, 1998—; bd. dirs. Am. Newspaper Repository, 1999—; mem. faculty Beineke Libr. Master Classes, 1999—. Author: Royall Tyler, 1967, Guide to the Study of United States Imprints, 1971, A Checklist of Editions of Moby-Dick, 1976, Selected Studies in Bibliography, 1979, The History of Books as a Field of Study, 1981, Textual Criticism since Greg, 1987, A Rationale of Textual Criticism, 1989, Parkman Dexter Howe Library, Hawthorne and Melville, 1989, Textual Criticism and Scholarly Editing, 1990, Libraries, Museums, and Reading, 1991, A Description of Descriptive Bibliography, 1992, The Life and Work of Fredson Bowers, 1993, Literature and Artifacts, 1998; co-editor: The Writings of Herman Melville, 1968—, Samuel Johnson's Translation of Sallust, 1993; editor: Library of Am. Melville, 1982-83, Books as a Way of Life: Essays by Gordon N. Ray, 1988; mem. editorial bd. Contemporary Literature, 1962-91, Abstracts of English Studies, 1964-78, Papers of Bibliog. Soc. Am, 1968-80, Resources for American Literary Study, 1971—, Analytical and Enumerative Bibliography, 1977—, Review, 1978—, Am. Literature, 1979-82, Literary Research, 1986-90, Common Knowledge, 1991—, Book History, 1996—, Leviathan, 1998—; contbr. articles to books and profl. jours. Mem. coun. Friends of Columbia U. Librs., 1990-94; bd. dirs. Friends of Lilly Libr., 1990-92. Recipient Kiekhofer Teaching award U. Wis., 1963, Jenkins award for bibliography, 1973; Guggenheim fellow, 1969-70; Am. Council Learned Socs. fellow, 1973-74; Nat. Endowment for the Humanities fellow, 1977-78, Laureate award Am. Printing History Assn., 1987. Mem. MLA (mem. exec. com. bibliog. evidence group 1974-75, methods of lit. rsch. div. 1979-83, chmn. 1982, mem. Hubbell award Com. Am. lit. sect. 1978-82, chmn. 1982, mem. com. on prize for ind. scholars 1983-87, chmn. 1985-87, chmn. ad hoc com. on future of print record 1993-95), Modern Humanities Rsch. Assn., Bibliog. Soc. London (pres. Am. Friends 1992—), Bibliog. Soc. Australia, Bibliog. Soc. Am. (mem. council 1970-94, vice chmn. publs. com. 1974-76, chmn. 1981-84, sec. 1976-78, chmn. com. on regional groups, 1978-80, 2d v.p. 1978-80, 1st v.p. 1980-82, pres. 1984-88), Bibliog. Soc. U. Va. (pres. 1992—), Oxford, Cambridge, Edinburgh, Birmingham, No. Ill., Can. bibliog. socs. (mem. coun. 1996—), Soc. for Bibliography of Natural History, Printing Hist. Soc. (Am. corr. 1970-84), Am. Printing Hist. Assn. (trustee N.Y. chpt. 1979-85), Pvt. Librs. Assn., Ind. Research Libraries Assn. (com. on standards for rare book cataloging in machine-readable form 1978-79), Fellows Morgan Libr., Manuscript Soc. (bd. dirs. 1974-79), Am. Pub. Libr. Film Project (bd. advisors 1993—), Am. Antiquarian Soc. (mem. publs. com. 1972-81, chmn. com. 1978-81, mem. council 1974-92, hon. councillor, 1992—, del. to Am. Coun. Learned Socs. 1978-93, exec. com. dels., 1987-89, chmn. exec. com. program on book in Am. culture 1983-89, com. on edn., 1982-85, chmn., 1983-85, chmn. com. on libr. 1988-91), Soc. Textual Scholarship (adv. bd. 1979—, pres. 1981-83), The Johnsonians (chmn. 1993), Melville Soc. (pres. 1982, Electronic Melville Com. 1997—), Book Club Calif., Typophiles, Guild Book Workers, Wis. Acad. Scis., Arts and Letters, Renaissance Soc. Am., Am. Soc. 18th-Century Studies, Renaissance English Text Soc., Assn. Documentary Editing (chmn. Julian Boyd award com. 1986, Boydston award com. 1995), Soc. Scholarly Pub., Assn. internationale de bibliophilie, Soc. History of Authorship, Reading and Publishing (bd. dirs. 1993—), Phi Beta Kappa. Clubs: Century, Yale, Caxton, Grolier (publs. com. 1979-82, 83-87, 97—, council 1980—, small exhbns. com. 1979-87, chmn. 1980-82, sec. 1982-86, chmn. library com. 1985-86, pres. 1986-90), Odd Volumes. Office: John Simon Guggenheim Meml Found 90 Park Ave Fl 33 New York NY 10016-1301

TANSEY, LISA REBECCA, database administrator, dancer, masseuse, musician; b. Palo Alto, Calif., Sept. 25, 1959; d. David Arthur and Beverly Joy Tansey. BS, U. Victoria, B.C., Can., 1983. Rsch. assoc. Syntro Corp., San Diego, 1983-87; programmer analyst Electronic Online Systems, Inc., Carlsbad, 1988-98; engring. ops. mgr. Litton PRC, La Mesa, 1998-2000; engring. ops. site mgr. Northrop Grumman, 2000—. Prin. Virtually There, San Marcos, Calif., 1992—. Pres. Moreton Bay Fig Morris, San Diego, 1986, 2000, 01; leader San Dieguito Drum Cir., Solana Beach, Calif., 1997—. Avocations: dancer, musician. Home: 2364 Greenwing Dr San Diego CA 92123 Office: 7777 Alvarado Rd Ste 520 La Mesa CA E-mail: Tansey_Lisa@prc.com., LisaWare@aol.com.

TANSILL, FREDERICK JOSEPH, lawyer; b. Washington, Feb. 27, 1948; s. Frederick Riker and Mary Eileen (Loftus) T.; m. Joan Louise Trefsgar, July 10, 1971; children: Brendan Frederick, Brooke Charlotte, Charlotte Trefsgar. BA with honors, Brown U., 1970; JD, Georgetown U., 1974, LLM in Taxation, 1982. Bar: D.C. 1974, U.S. Tax Ct. 1976, Va. 1983. Assoc. Cross, Murphy & Smith, Washington, 1974-77; ptnr. Bird & Tansill, 1977-79; assoc. Ober, Grimes & Shriver, 1979-81; ptnr. Lewis, Mitchell & Moore, Vienna, 1981-86; counsel Boothe, Prichard & Dudley, McLean, 1986-87; ptnr. McGuire, Woods, Battle & Boothe, 1987-90; shareholder Verner, Liipfert, Bernhard, McPherson & Hand, Chartered, 1990-97; owner-mgr. Frederick J. Tansill & Assocs., LLC, 1997—. Gen. counsel No. Va. Cmty. Found., 1995-98, 1st v.p., 1998-99, pres., 1999-2000. Fellow Am. Coll. Trust and Estate Counsel; mem. ABA, Va. Bar Assn. (exec. coun. taxation sect. 1989-92, coun. and legis. com. wills sect. 1993-99—, trusts and estate sect. 1983-99, bd. govs. 1988-96, chmn. bd. govs. 1991-92, co-chmn. spl. task force lawyers as fiduciaries 1993-95), D.C. Bar Assn. (steering com. estates, trusts and probate law sects. 1995-97, co-chair 1997-99), Fairfax County Bar Assn. (will sect. 1986, chmn. tax sect. 1987-88, CLE com. 1988-89), No. Va. Estate Planning Coun. (exec. com. 1987-92, pres. 1990-91), Tower Club (bd. dirs. 1988—). Office: Frederick J Tansill & Assocs 1749 Old Meadow Rd Ste 301 Mc Lean VA 22102-4310 Fax: (703) 847-1357. E-mail: Fjtansill@aol.com.

TANSKI, JAMES MICHAEL, lawyer; b. Bristol, Conn., Feb. 11, 1946; s. John William and Stephanie J. (Kasek) T.; m. Janet E. Burlingame, Sept. 5, 1975; children: John Matthew, Susan Burlingame. BS, U.S. Mil. Acad., 1968; JD, U. Conn., 1976. Bar: Conn. 1976, U.S. Dist. Ct. Conn. 1977, U.S. Ct. Appeals (2d cir.) 1977. Commd. 2d lt. U.S. Army, 1968, advanced through ranks to capt., 1970, resigned, 1973; assoc. Law Offices of F. Timothy McNamara, Hartford, Conn., 1976-77, Adinolfi, O'Brien & Hayes, P.C., Hartford, 1977-80; ptnr. O'Brien, Tanski & Young, 1980—. Decorated Purple Heart with oak leaf cluster, Bronze Star, Air medal with 4 oak leaf clusters and 3 silver leaf clusters, Army Commendation medal with oak leaf cluster. Mem. Conn. Bar Assn. (profl. ethics com. 1982-83), Conn. Def. Lawyers Assn., Hartford County Bar Assn. (co-chair legal-med. com. 1999-2002), Def. Rsch. Inst., Conn. Med. Def. Lawyers Assn. Roman Catholic. Office: O'Brien Tanski & Young Cityplace II 185 Asylum St Hartford CT 06103-3402

TANSOR, ROBERT HENRY, investor; b. Chgo., Apr. 1, 1935; s. John S. and Leora Caroline (Buhmann) T.; m. Stephanie Trainor, Sept. 10, 1977; children: John Frederick, Adam Robert. BS, Northwestern U., 1957. CPA, Ill., N.J. Sr. acct. Arthur Young & Co., Chgo., 1961-65; mem. corp. staff Litton Industries, 1965-67; v.p. fin., controller Royal Typewriter Co., Conn., 1968-72, Sweda Internat. div. Litton Industries, Pinebrook, N.J., 1973-75; v.p. fin., adminstrn. Paramount Pictures Corp., N.Y.C., 1975-77, Otis Elevator Corp., Farmington, Conn., 1977-83; v.p. fin., chief fin. officer Gulton Industries Inc., Princeton, N.J., 1983-86; sr. v.p., treas., chief fin. officer The Polymer Corp., Reading, Pa., 1986-89; pvt. investor, 1989—. Served to lt. (j.g.) USN, 1957-61; ret. comdr. USNR, 1980. Mem. Fin. Execs. Inst. Republican. Roman Catholic. Avocations: golf, swimming, theater, music.

TANSY, MICHAEL, psychologist; b. Indpls., Nov. 28, 1954; s. Paul Myron and Peggy Jo Tansy; m. Susan McGuirl, Jan. 3, 1981 (div. Feb. 1992); children: Kathleen Megan, Sean Michael; m. Anne Moody. BA, Ariz. State U., 1976, Master Counseling, 1979, PhD, 1996. Cert. profl. counselor. Counselor St. Luke's Hosp., Phoenix, 1979-80; dir. Maricopa Med. Ctr., 1980-82, Phoenix Camelback Hosp., 1982-84; adminstr. Scottsdale (Ariz.) Camelback Hosp., 1984-87; pvt. practice Mesa, Ariz., 1984—; adminstr. Charter Hosp. E. Valley, Chandler, 1987-88; lead psychologist Gilbert (Ariz.) Unified Sch. Dist., 1995—. Chair allied health profls. Scottsdale Camelback Hosp., 1990-92. Mem. editl. bd. Current Issues Edn., 1978—; contbr. articles to profl. jours. Chair Sch. Psychology Grad. Sch. Assn., Ariz. State U., Tempe, 1990-94. Mem. APA, Am. Counseling Assn., Nat. Assn. Sch. Psychologists, Ariz. Assn. Sch. Psychologists. Democrat. Episcopalian. Home: 217 E Riviera Dr Tempe AZ 85282 Office: 1731 W baseline Rd 101 Mesa AZ 85202 E-mail: mtansy@aol.com.

TANTRA, MULJADI, corporate marketing professional; b. Selatpanjang, Riau, Indonesia, July 1, 1971; came to U.S., 1988; s. Pingardi and Lesmina Tantra; m. Vivi Effendy, Nov. 24, 1996; children: Vincent, Grace. BS, Iowa State U., 1992; MBA, San Diego State U., 1996. Ops. rsch. engr. Cymer, Inc., San Diego, 1996-98, mktg. analysis mgr., 1998-2000; dir. corp. mktg. Lam Rsch., Fremont, Calif., 2000—. Inventor, patentee in field. Mem. AAAS, Sigma Xi (rsch. grantee 1995), Beta Gamma Sigma, Phi Beta Delta. Buddhist. Avocations: music, tennis, scuba diving, travel. Home: 2667 Torrey Ct Pleasanton CA 94588 Office: Lam Rsch 4650 Cushing Pky Fremont CA 94538 E-mail: muljadi.tantra@lamrc.com.

TANTUM, JAMES KENT, educational facilitator, publisher; b. Miami, Fla., Dec. 7, 1964; s. James Kent Tantum and Penelope Elaine Davis. BA, Temple U., 1990. Facilitator, presenter World Game Inst., Phila., 1994—2001; owner Tantum Mfg., 1998—. Author: Teleological Expressionism, 1998; co-author: Sex Notes, 1998; author of short stories; photographer A Year in the Life of Rittenhouse Square Show, 1995; artist (calendar) Jim Calendar, 1997, 98, 99, 2000, 2001; designer Pogany flatware, 1996, Wrax cd rack, 1995; creator, M.C., Jim's Ann. All-Invitational Road Rally, 1995—. Avocation: travel. Home: PO Box 42733 Philadelphia PA 19101 Office: Tantum Mfg PO Box 42733 Philadelphia PA 19101 E-mail: TanTummfg@aol.com.

TANUR, JUDITH MARK, sociologist, educator; b. Jersey City, Aug. 12, 1935; d. Edward Mark and Libbie (Berman) Mark; m. Michael Isaac Tanur, June 2, 1957; children: Rachel Dorothy, Marcia Valerie. BS, Columbia U., 1957, MA, 1963; PhD, SUNY, Stony Brook, 1972. Analyst Biometrics Rsch., N.Y.C., 1955-67; lectr. SUNY, Stony Brook, 1967-71, from asst. prof. to prof. sociology, 1971-94, disting. teaching prof., 1994—. Cons. NBC, N.Y.C., 1976—89, Lang. of Data Project, Los Altos, Calif., 1980—89, Inst. for Rsch. on Learning, 1994—95; mem. com. on nat. stats. NAS, 1980—87, com. on applied and theoretical stats., 1997—2000; trustee NORC, U. Chgo., 1987—; bd. dris. Social Sci. Rsch. Coun. Author: The Subjectivity of Scientists and The Bayesian Approach, 2001; editor: Statistics: A Guide to the Unknown, 1972, Internat. Encyclopedia of Statistics, 1978, Cognitive Aspects of Survey Methodology, 1984, Questions About Questions, 1991, Cognition and Survey Research, 1999, The Subjectivity of Scientists and the Baynesian Approach, 2001, (Jour.) Internat. Ency. of Social Scis., 1963—67; contbr. articles to sci., stats., and social sci. jours. Bd. dirs. Vis. Nurse Svc., Great Neck, N.Y., 1970-2000; bd. govs. Gen. Soc. Survey, Chgo., 1989-92. Sr. rsch. fellow, Am. Statis. Assn./NSF/Bur. Labor Statistics, 1988-89. Fellow, AAAS, Am. Statis. Assn. (Founders award 1997); mem. Internat. Statis. Inst., Phi Beta Kappa. Home: 17 Longview Pl Great Neck NY 11021-2508 Office: SUNY Dept Sociology Stony Brook NY 11794-0001

TANZER, JED SAMUEL, lawyer, financial consultant; b. Arverne, N.Y., Nov. 16, 1947; s. David and Mildred (Bondy) T.; m. Sally Jane Ketcham, July 10, 1971. BS with honors in Social Sci., SUNY, Oneonta, 1970; JD cum laude, MBA, Syracuse U., 1978. Bar: N.Y. 1979, Fed. Dist. Ct. 1979, U.S. Tax. Ct. 1979; permanent tchg. cert. N.Y. State. Tchr., union grievance chmn. Ctrl. Sch. Dist., Windsor, N.Y., 1970-75; rsch. asst. Sch. Mgmt. Syracuse (N.Y.) U., 1977-78; sr. atty. Ayco/Am. Express Corp., Albany, N.Y., 1978-82, assoc. regional mgr., 1982-85, v.p., regional mgr., 1986-92, regional v.p., 1988-91, v.p. counseling, 1992-93, fin. cons., 1978-93; v.p. Sanford Bernstein Co., Palm Beach, Fla., 1993-99; dir. Newberger & Berman, LLC, 1999, regional v.p., 1999—. Bd. dirs. Cobb Youth Chorus, 1988-93, treas. 1988-93; bd. dirs. Martin County Coun. for Arts, 1998-2000, Neuberger Berman Trust Co. of Fla., 2001. Mem. ABA (com. state and local taxation 1981-82), N.Y. State Bar Assn., Justinian Law Soc., Beta Gamma Sigma, Kappa Delta Pi. Home: 1116 Abbeys Way Tampa FL 33602-5957 E-mail: jtanzer@tampabay.rr.com.

TANZI, DAVID E. military officer; BS in Edn., SUNY, Cortland, 1965; MEd, Ohio State U., 1967; postgrad., Squadron Officer Sch., Air Command and Staff Coll. Commd. 2d lt. USAF, 1969, advanced through grades to maj. gen., 2000; F-100 fighter pilot 166th Tactical Fighter Squadron, Lockbourne AFB, Ohio, 1970—72; F-105 pilot 465th Tactical Fighter Squadron, Tinker AFB, Okla., 1972—73; F-100 instr. pilot, flighter exainer 128th Tactical Fighter Squadron, Dobbins AFB, Ga., 1973—77; F-104 and F-4 flight examiner 457th Tactical Fighter Squadron, Carswell AFB, Tex., 1977—81; comdr. 89th Tactical Fighter Squadron, Wright-Patterson AFB, Ohio, 1981—85; dep. comdr. ops. 906th Tactical Fighter Group, 1985; dep. comdr. ops., comdr. 917th Tactical Fighter Group, Barksdale AFB, La., 1985—87; comdr. 906th Fighter Group, Wright-Patterson AFB, Ohio, 1987—93, 419th Fighter Wing, Hill AFB, Utah, 1993—99; dir. plans and programs Hdqrs. AF Res. Command, Robins AFB, Ga., 1999—2002; comdr. 10th Air Force Naval Air Sta. Joint Res. Base, Ft. Worth, 2002—. Decorated Legion of Merit with oak leaf cluster, Air medal. Mem.: Air Force Assn., Res. Officer Assn., Order of Sword, Order of Daedalians. Office: Naval Air Sta Joint Res Base Carswell Field Fort Worth TX 76127-6200

TANZMAN, EDWARD ALAN, lawyer; b. Chgo. s. Jack and Mary (Grodman) T.; m. Ellen Louise Partridge. BA in Polit. Sci. with honors, U. Chgo., 1973; JD, Georgetown U., 1976. Bar: Ill. 1976, D.C. 1979. Legis. asst. U.S. Senator John A. Durkin, Washington, 1976-79; various rsch. and adminstrv. staff positions Argonne (Ill.) Nat. Lab., 1979—, group leader social scis. and law, 2000—; legis. counsel Palau Nat. Congress, Koror, Palau, 1980-81. Adv. bd. Lawyers Alliance for World Security, Washington; adv. bd. DePaul U. Internat. Human Rights Law Inst., Chgo., 1998—. Co-author: Manual for National Implementation of the Chemical Weapons Convention, 1998; contbr. articles to internat. law jours. Chairperson bd. dirs. Health Rsch. Inst., Inc., Naperville, 1996—; cmty. rep. Nettelhorst Locl Sch. Coun., Chgo., 1989-2000; pres. Friends of Nettelhorst Sch., Chgo., 1992—. Fellowship Leadership Greater Chgo., 1993-94; recipient Award of Merit Health Rsch. Inst., Inc., 1989. Office: Argonne Nat Lab 9700 Cass Ave Argonne IL 60439-4832 Fax: 630-252-5327. E-mail: tanzman@anl.gov.

TANZMAN-BOCK, MAXINE M. psychotherapist, consultant; b. New Brunswick, N.J., Mar. 30, 1957; BA is Sociology, Rutgers U., 1980; MSW, Fordham U., 1984. Lic. clin. social worker. Therapist Van Ost Inst. for Family Living, Englewood, N.J.; pvt. practice Wayne, 1986—. Cons. Union City Schs., N.J., Physicians Weight Loss Ctr., Wayne; psychotherapist Cath. Cmty. Svcs., Paramus, N.J.; with Family Svcs. Bergen County, N.J.; vol. probation counselor, residence counselor Svc. Ctrs., N.J.; social worker St. Lawrence Rehab. Ctr., N.J.; designer and presenter workshops. Featured cable TV 1990; host weekly call in therapy show on radio, 1991-92. Mem. NASW, Acad. Cert. Social Workers, Am. Assn. Behavioral Therapists. Office: 25 Packanack Lake Rd Wayne NJ 07470-5809

TAO, CHIA-LIN PAO, humanities educator; b. Soochow, Kiangsu, China, July 7, 1939; came to U.S., 1961; d. Tsung-han and Hoi-chin Pao; m. Jing-shen Tao, Aug. 22, 1964; children: Rosalind, Jeanne, Sandy. BA, Nat. Taiwan U., Taipei, 1961; MA, Ind. U., 1963, PhD, 1971. Assoc. prof. Nat. Taiwan U., Taipei, 1969-76, 78-79; vis. assoc. prof. dept. East ASian studies U. Ariz., Tucson, 1976-78, 79-85, assoc. prof., 1989-2000, prof., 2000—. V.p. Hist. Soc. for 20th Century China in N.Am., 1992-93, pres., 1993-94. Editor, author: Studies in Chinese Women's History, 5 vols., 1979—2001. Mem. Tucson-Taichung Sister-City Com., Tucson, 1984—; sec. Ariz. Asian Am. Assn., 1989, dir., 1989-93. Rsch. grantee Nat. Sci. Coun., Taipei, 1971-72, 73-74, Harvard-Yenching Inst., Cambridge, Mass., 1972-74, Pacific Cultural Found., Taipei, 1984-85. Mem. Assn. for Asian Studies (pres. Western conf. 1994), Tucson Chinese Am. Profl. Soc. (pres. 1996), Tucson Chinese Assn. (bd. dirs. 1996-98). Democrat. Office: U Ariz Dept E Asian Studies Tucson AZ 85721-0001 E-mail: cpaotao@email.arizona.edu.

TAO, FU-MING, chemist; b. Suzhou, Jiangsu, China, June 26, 1960; s. Yungen and Heimei (Shen) Tao; m. Fuzhen Shi, May 1, 1985; children: Li, Jim, Emily. BS in Chemistry, U. Sci. and Tech. of China, Hefei, 1982; MS in Chemistry, Suzhou (China) U., 1985; PhD in Chemistry, Boston Coll., 1991. Asst. prof. dept. chemistry Suzhou U., 1985-86; rsch. asst. Cellular and Molecular Rsch. Lab. Mass. Gen. Hosp., Boston, summer 1987; teaching asst. dept. chemistry Boston Coll., Chestnut Hill, Mass., 1986-91; postdoctoral rsch. assoc. Brown U., Providence, 1991-92; postdoctoral fellow dept. chemistry Harvard U., Cambridge, Mass., 1992-95; asst. prof. dept. chemistry Calif. State U., Fullerton, 1995—. Contbr. articles to profl. jours. Mem. Am. Chem. Soc. Home: 2540 Country Hills Rd Apt 142 Brea CA 92821-4627

TAORMINA, CHARLES ANTHONY, writer, editor, artist; b. Johnstown, Pa., Apr. 2, 1948; s. Anthony James and Shirley Ruth (Wagner) T.; m. Brenda Gail Gilbert, Aug. 8, 1970 (div. 1981); 1 child, Angela Loraine. BA in Liberal Arts, Indiana U. of Pa., 1970. Contbg. editor/reporter Times of Charlottesville, Va., 1976-78; editor Blue Ridge Rev., Charlottesville, 1978-79, VIRTU, Uniontown, Pa., 1993—; writer, editor, mgr. The Renaissance Workshop, 1990—. Spkr. World Future Soc., Bethesda, Md., 1989, 93; mem., actor Actors & Artists of Fayette County, Scottdale, Pa., 1993; contbg. author/mem. writing workshop project-Projects, Inc. Author: (novels) Abbas & Merdan, Endgames, Karma Bums, Gratuity, Legacy, The Entropy Wars, (novella) Of Rifles & Butterflies, (drama) Freedom One, Tauromenium, Rally!, Catalyst, (nonfiction) Along the Journalistic Path, Infinity, Vision, Ardour, Keystone, Quintessence, Autobiography (story collections), Early Tales, Moments, Shared Lives, (poetry) Rain Folio, also monographs,(audio cassette) Renaissance: An Introduction; editor: Commercial Book and Story Editing; contbr. fiction to Blue Ridge Rev., Samisdat, Gargoyle, Fool's Jour., William and Mary Rev.; contbr. nonfiction to Daily Progress, The Sun, Harper's Weekly, others; contbr. photography to Washington Post, Gargoyle, others; contbr. on-line arts newsletter PRIVY, Write Advice, poetry to Am. Poetry Ann.; dramas staged Gemini Theater, Pitts., 1998. Freedom writer Amnesty Internat., N.Y.C., 1989—; mem. regeneration project Rodale Press, Emmaus, Pa., 1989; workshop leader VISTA Literacy Project, Ravenna, Ohio, 1988; pub. rels. worker Nat. Road Heritage Park Project, Uniontown, 1993. Recipient Honorable Mention award Soc. for Am. Cuisine, 1987. Mem. Dramatists Guild (assoc.), Am. Christian Writers Assn., Renaissance Soc. Am., Union of Concerned Scientists. Roman Catholic. Avocations: sketching, cosmology, travel, music listening, hiking. Office: The Renaissance Workshop 860 Chalker St Fl 1 Akron OH 44310-2116 also: 103 Camden Ave Johnstown PA 15904-2302 E-mail: CATAORMINA@prodigy.net.

TAPE, GERALD FREDERICK, former association executive; b. Ann Arbor, Mich., May 29, 1915; s. Henry A. and Flora (Simmons) T.; m. Josephine Waffen, June 18, 1939; children: Walter Richard, James William, Thomas Gerald. AB, Eastern Mich. U., 1935, Sc.D. (hon.), 1964; MS, U. Mich., 1936, PhD, 1940. Asst. physics Eastern Mich. U., 1933-35, U. Mich., 1936-39; instr. physics Cornell U., 1939-42; staff mem. radiation lab. Mass. Inst. Tech., 1942-46; asst., then assoc. prof. physics U. Ill., 1946-50; asst. to dir., then dep. dir. Brookhaven Nat. Lab., 1950-62; v.p., then pres. Associated Univs., Inc., 1962-63, pres., 1969-80, spl. asst. to pres., 1980-82; commr. AEC, 1963-69; U.S. rep. to IAEA with rank of amb., 1973-77; former pres., cons. Associated Univs., Inc. Dir. Sci. Svc. Inc., 1971—2002 , Atomic Indsl. Forum, 1970-73; mem. Pres.'s Sci. Adv. Com., 1969-73, Def. Sci. Bd., 1970-73, chmn., 1970-72; mem. sci. adv. com. IAEA, 1972-73; mem. gen. adv. com. ERDA, 1975-77; mem. adv. council Electric Power Rsch. Inst., 1978-85; mem. U. Chgo. bd. govs. for Argonne Nat. Lab., 1982-85; cons. Def. Nuclear Facilities Safety Bd., 1991-2000. Author: (with L.J. Haworth) Relay Radar Chapter of MIT Radiation Laboratory Technical Series, 1947; also papers, reports. Recipient Army-Navy Certificate of Appreciation, 1947, Meritorious Civilian Service medal Sec. Def., 1969, Dept. State Tribute Appreciation, 1969, Dept. Def. medal for pub. service, 1973; Henry DeWolf Smyth Nuclear Statesman award Atomic Indsl. Forum/Am. Nuclear Soc., 1978; Disting. Pub. Service award NSF, 1980; Disting. Assoc. award Dept. Energy, 1980; Enrico Fermi award U.S. Energy Dept., 1987; decorated comdr. Order Leopold II, Belgium. Fellow Am. Phys. Soc., Am. Nuclear Soc., AAAS; mem. Nat. Acad. Engring., Am. Astron. Soc., Phi Beta Kappa, Sigma Xi, Phi Kappa Phi, Kappa Delta Pi. Home: 9707 Old Georgetown Rd 2518 Bethesda MD 20814

TAPE, JAMES WILLIAM, physicist, researcher; b. Urbana, Ill., Apr. 6, 1946; s. Gerald Frederick Tape, Josephine Waffen Tape; m. Virginia Elizabeth Slusser; children: Sean, Christopher. PhD, Rutgers U., 1972; BA, Johns Hopkins U., 1967. Post doctoral rschr. U. of Wash., Seattle, 1972—74, Bell Lab. Rutgers U., Murray Hill, NJ, 1974—75; technical staff mem. Los Alamos Nat. Lab., Los Alamos, N.Mex., 1975—79, mgr., 1979—98, sr. policy adv. office of assoc. dir. for threat reduction, 1998—. Explorer adv. Explorer Post 20 BSA, Los Alamos, 1986—96. Fellow: Inst. of Nuclear Materials Mgmt. (pres. 1995—96); mem.: Am..Phys. Soc. Home: 90 Camino Espejo Santa Fe NM 87507 Office: Los Alamos National Laboratory PO Box 1663 Los Alamos NM 87545

TAPHORN, JOSEPH BERNARD, lawyer; b. Beckemeyer, Ill., Oct. 9, 1921; s. Herman Henry and Marie (Gasser) T.; m. Anna Marie Klinge, June 25, 1944 (dec. Dec. 1991); children: Robert J., Joanne M., John F.; m. Joan Campen Klemmer, July 13, 1996. BS in Agr., U. Ill., 1943; BS in Engring., George Washington U., 1949, LLB, 1950. Bar: N.Y. 1952, D.C. 1952, U.S. Dist. Ct. (so. and ea. dists.) N.Y. 1952, U.S. Dist. Ct. (no. dist.) N.Y. 1991, U.S. Dist. Ct. D.C., 1952, U.S. Ct. Appeals (D.C. cir.) 1961, U.S. Ct. Appeals (fed. cir.) 1996, U.S. Supreme Ct. 1961. Patent examiner U.S. Patent Office, Washington, 1946-49, patent classifier, 1949-50; patent agt. Pollard and Jonston, N.Y.C., 1950-52; patent atty. IBM Corp., 1952-59, patent mgr., counsel various locations, 1959-70, copyright counsel Armonk, N.Y., 1970-78, copyright and trademark counsel, 1978-88; pvt. practice Poughkeepsie, 1989—. Chmn. bd. U.S. Dynamics, Yonkers, N.Y. 1975-77. Contbr. articles to profl. jours. Pres. Huntley Civic Assn., Eastchester, N.Y., 1958-59; trustee Copyright Soc. USA, N.Y.C., 1985-88. Capt. U.S. Army, 1943-46, ETO. Mem. ABA (com. chmn. 1983-87), N.Y. State Bar Assn., Dutchess County Bar Assn., Am. Intellectual Property Law Assn., N.Y. Intellectual Property Law Assn. (com. chmn. 1987-89), Ea. N.Y. Intellectual Property Law Assn., Dutchess Golf and Country Club, Americana Tennis Club. Republican. Roman Catholic. Avocations: golf, hunting, fishing, tennis, skiing. Home and Office: 8 Scenic Dr Poughkeepsie NY 12603-5521 E-mail: jbtaphorn@prodigy.net.

TAPIA, JOANN, educational association administrator, rancher; b. San Francisco, Jan. 22, 1943; d. Jose Matias Tapia and Anna Maria Lopez; m. Robert F. Voltura, Sept. 1, 1961 (div.); children: Anna Maria Voltura, Marc Voltura; m. John P. Eastham (div.); children: John P. Eastham(dec.) , Marina Eastham. BA in Edn., Coll. Santa Fe, 1971; MA in Edn. Foundations, U. N.Mex., 1972; EdD, Harvard U., 1980, MPA, 1981. Cert. social studies tchr. K-12 N.Mex., bilingual-ESL tchr. N.Mex., in spl. edn. N.Mex. Owner La Esquelita Daycare Ctr., Santa Fe, 1961—70; tchr. Southwestern Coop. Ednl. Lab., Albuquerque, 1970—71; spl. asst. Exec. Office of Pres., Washington, 1982—83; program dir. U.S. Dept. Transp., 1983—84; asst. sec. pub. and Indian housing HUD, 1983—84; ESL specialist, coord. Govt. of D.C., 1986—89; bilingual edn. specialist Boston Pub. Schs., 1989—92; dir. curriculum and instrn. Dulce Ind. Sch. Dist., Dulce, N.Mex., 1992—93; legis. analyst to Rep. Ron Gentry Santa Fe, 1993—96; founder, dir. La Escuelita, 2001—. Pres. bd. dirs. Edn. Found., Santa Fe, 2001—; head tchr. Cochiti Pueblo Tribal Schs., N.Mex., 1968—70; headstart tchr. Pueblo of San Juan Tribal Ter., San Juan Pueblo, N.Mex., 1965—68; univ. faculty mem. (summers) Pedagogical

Inst. Yaroslav, U. Kazan, Russia, 1990—93; sr. cons. Diversified Mgmt. Assocs., Washington, 1983. Author: Characteristics of Primary Level Students, 1970; news reporter, writer: Sta. KOAT-TV. Founder Annie Tapia Found.; county chair Rep. Party N.Mex., 1997—99; precinct chair Rep. Party Santa Fe, 2000—. Recipient award, Women's Club of Am.; fellow Littaur fellow, Harvard U., 1980. Mem.: various edn. and religious orgns. Roman Catholic. Avocations: golf, skiing, travel. Office: Edn Found PO Box 22382 Santa Fe NM 87502 E-mail: ilovekidsalot@qwest.net.

TAPIA, JUAN CARLOS, entrepreneur, producer; b. Panama City, Panama, Feb. 5, 1942; s. Raul Santiag Tapia and Rosa Maria Rodriguez de Tapia; m. Ligia Velarde, Aug. 15, 1963 (div. July 1973); children: Juan Carlos, Lia Malena; m. Carmen Amalia Rosas, Jan. 31, 1976; children: Juan Carlos, Carmen Lorena, Ana Cristina. Student, Inst. Nat. H.S., Panama City, Panama, 1959; BS, Univ. de Panama Economy, 1960—64. Salesman Agencias Santiago Tapia, Panama City, Panama, 1960-62; gen. mgr., salesman Ency. Britanica, 1962—65; sales supr. mutual funds Investors Overseas Svc., 1965—67; gen. mgr. mutual funds Gramco Internat., 1969-70; regional mgr. Gramco Internat. Iberia, Spain, 1967—69; v.p. sales The Circle Club, Panama City, 1970-72; pres. Descuento S.A., 1972-74; prodr., dir., host Lo Mejor del Boxeo, 1975—; sales rep. Lat. Am., Asia Top Rank, Inc., 1979—2001, Don King Prodns., Panama City, 1986-95. Dealer Casinos Nacioles, Panama City, 1962-65; sales rep. Latin Am. and Asia for Main Events, 1990-2000, Latin Am. and Asia for Cedric Kushner Promotions, 1992-2000, Latin Am., ESPN Internat., 1989—, Latin Am. Hallmark Channel, 1995—. Pres. Fundacion Bel Canto, 2001—. Listed in Guinness Book of World Records (1st time 4 World Champion Fights were transmitted live in the world), 1978; named Best Sports Events Prodr. El Morro de Am., 1983, Best TV Prodr. Circulo de Espectaculos de Periodistas Mex., 1983, 86, 88, Golden Eagle award Channel 9, Argentina, 1983, Best TV Prodr. World Boxing Assn., 1993. Mem. World Assn. Sports Journalists, Lions. Avocation: wine collection. Office: PROTESA PO Box 201 Panama 9A Panama

TAPIA, MARIO EDUARDO, cultural organization administrator; b. San Felipe, Chile, Sept. 11, 1947; came to U.S., 1973; s. Viterbo Topia and Maria Ernstina Guerrero; m. Cecilia C., July 11, 1970 (div. Oct. 1985); 1 child, Susana C. MA in Edn., Cath. U., Valparaiso, Chile, 1971. Pres., CEO Centro Gerontologio Latino, N.Y.C., 1991—. Pres. Chilean Civic Ctr., N.Y.C., 1995—. Recipient Illustrious Son award Mcpl. of San Reude, Chile, 1994. Office: Centro Gerontologico Latino 120 Wall St 23rd Flr New York NY 10005

TAPLETT, LLOYD MELVIN, human resources management consultant; b. Tyndall, S.D., July 25, 1924; s. Herman Leopold and Emiley (Nedvidek) T.; m. Patricia Ann Sweeney, Aug. 21, 1958; children: Virginia Ann, Sharon Lorraine, Carla Jo, Carolyn Patricia,m Catherne Marie, Colleen Elizabeth. BA, Augustana Coll., 1949; MA, U. Nebr., 1958; postgrad., S.D. State U., U. S.D., U. Iowa, Colo. State U. Accredited personnel dir.; prof. human resources; cert. tchr. & counselor. Tchr. Sioux Falls (S.D.) pub. schs., 1952-69; with All-Am. Transport co., Sioux Falls, 1969-78, Am. Freight System, Inc., Overland Park, Kans., 1978-79; dir. human resources & pub. rels., corp. affirmative action Chippewa Motor Freight, Inc., Sioux Falls, 1979-80; human resources & mgmt. cons., 1980-81; mgr. Sioux Falls Job Svcs., 1981-85, Pioneer Enterprises, Inc., 1985-86; ops. mgr. ATE Environ., Inc., 1986-88; cons. Royal River Casino, 1988-90; acad. dean Huron U., Sioux Falls, 1990-97; instr. econs. Coll. Bus., 1992—. Chmn. Chippewa Credit Union; mem. adv. bd. dirs. Nelson Labs., Sioux Dalls, 1981-82; evening mgmt. instr. Nat. Coll., Sioux Falls, 1981-90, chmn. adv. com., 1984—, Huron U., 1990-97, S.F. Washington High Sch. Sports Heritage, 1989-98. Contbr. articles to nat. mags. Past bd. dirs. Jr. Achievement, United Way, Sioux Vocat. Sch. Handicapped; past mem. Gov.'s Adv. Bd. Cmty. Adult Manpower Planning; chmn. bus. edn. adv. com. Sioux Falls Pub. Schs., 1982-85; chmn. adv. com. South East Area Vocat. Sch., 1982-85; mem. alumnae bd. Augustana Coll., 1985-88; commencement spkr. Capt. USMC, 1943-46, 50-52, WWII, Korea. Recipient VFW Commendation award, 1990, Liberty Bell award S.D. Bar Assn., 1967, Sch. Bd. award NEA/Thom McAn Shoe Corp., 1966, S.D. Unsung Heroes Edn. Recognition award Sta. KSFV-TV, 1998; named Boss of Yr., Sioux Falls, 1977. Mem. NEA (life, Pacemaker award), Am. Soc. Personnel Adminstrn. (accredited personnel mgr., life, S.D. dist. dir. 1980-84), Am. Trucking Assn. (mem. pub. rels. coun.), S.D. Edn. Assn. (life), Sioux Falls Personnel Assn. (past pres.), Sales & Mktg. Club Sioux Falls, Sioux Falls Traffic Club, VFW (life, Nat. Polit. Action Recognition award 1990), Am. Legion, Toastmasters (past gov. dist. 41, Disting. Toastmaster award, Outstanding Toastmaster award dist. 41, Hall of Fame 1977), Elks. Republican. Roman Catholic.

TAPLEY, JAMES LEROY, retired lawyer, railway corporation executive; b. Greenville, Miss., July 10, 1923; s. Lester Leroy and Lillian (Clark) T.; m. Priscilla Moore, Sept. 9, 1950. AB, U. N.C., 1947, JD with honors, 1950. Bar: N.C. 1951, D.C. 1962. With So. Ry. Co., Washington, 1953-83, gen. solicitor, 1967-74, asst. v.p. law, 1974-75, v.p. law, 1975-83; v.p. Washington counsel Norfolk So. Corp., Washington, 1983-87; ret., 1987. Mem. Phi Beta Kappa, Kappa Sigma. Clubs: Chevy Chase.

TAPLEY, PHILIP ALLEN, English language and literature educator; b. Blackwell, Okla., June 11, 1938; s. Robert G. Sr. and Valena M. (Simmons) T.; m. Mary Stringer, Aug. 10, 1974; children: Mary Margaret, Laura Katherine. BA, U. North Tex., 1960, MA, 1962; PhD, La. State U., 1974; Cert. in Victorian Lit., U. London, 1966. Cert. secondary tchr., Tex. Tchg. asst. U. North Tex., Denton, 1960-61, La. State U., Baton Rouge, 1961-65, 68-69, instr., 1965-68; from asst. prof. to assoc. prof. La. Coll., Pineville, 1969-80, acting chmn. dept. English, journalism and langs., 1980, prof. dept. English, journalism and langs., 1980—. Tchr. Karamay U. Liberal Arts and Scis., China, summer, 1998, 2001, condr. study tour from La. Coll. to Ireland, spring, 1999; maj. scholar, presenter La. Endowment for the Humanities, Alexandria, 1977—; vis. cons. Ctrl. La. Electric Co., Pineville, 1989-95; mem. faculty coun. La. Coll., 1998-2000, vice chmn. faculty, 1999-2000. Author: A History of First United Methodist, 1976, 2d edit., 1989, (with others) Proceedings of the Red River Symposium, 1987, 2d edit., 1991; contbr. Issues and Indentities in Literature, 1997, Survey of Long Fiction, 2d revised edit., 2001, Critical Survey of Short Fiction, 2nd revised edit., 2000; also contbr. articles to profl. jours. Pres., Friends of Rapides Libr., Alexandria, 1985-86, 97, bd. dirs., 1996-99; adv. bd. Arna Bontemps Mus., 1995—; lay eucharistic minister Epis. Ch., 1997—; aux. del. to annual conv. of western La., Diocese of Episcopal Ch., 2000, 01, 02; dir. Inst. Adult Edn., St. James Episcopal Parish, 2002. Recipient 30-yr. Svc. award La. Coll., 1999; Mellon Found. fellow, 1982, 88, Ford Found. fellow, 1989. Mem. MLA, AAUP, South Ctrl. MLA (program chair so. lit. 1979), La. Folklore Soc. (vice pres., 1977-78, pres. 1978-79), Hist. Assn. Ctrl. La. (pres. 1978-80, bd. dirs. 1978-98), Phi Kappa Phi, Alpha Chi, Sigma Tau Delta (nat. scholarships and awards com. 2001, 02, 25 Yr. award as local chpt. faculty sponsor), Omicron Delta Kappa, Sigma Delta Chi. Democrat. Episcopalian. Avocations: reading, music, historic preservation, folklore collecting. Home: 1721 Polk St Alexandria LA 71301-6334 Office: La Coll English Dept 1140 College Dr Pineville LA 71360-5122

TAPLIN, FRANK E., JR. trustee education and arts institutions and associations; b. Cleve., June 22, 1915; s. Frank Elijah and Edith R. (Smith) T.; m. Ngaio I. Thornton, Sept. 3, 1943 (div. Mar. 1951); children: Caroline I. Taplin Ruschell, Jennifer Taplin Jerome, David F.; m. Margaret A. Eaton, Apr. 27, 1953; stepchildren: Jennifer A. Sichel Dickerman, Martha D. Sichel Kelly, Susan Sichel Panella. BA in History, Princeton U., 1937; MA in Jurisprudence (Rhodes scholar), Oxford U., 1939; JD, Yale U., 1941; MusD (hon.), Cleve. Inst. Music, 1981; DHL (hon.), Fordham U., 1984; Dr. Mus. Arts (hon.), Manhattan Sch. Music, 1984; LLD (hon.), Rider Coll., 1988. Bar: Ohio 1946. With firm Jones, Day Cockley & Reavis, Cleve., 1946-50; dir. NACCO Industries, Inc., 1946—97, trustee Environ. Def. Fund., 1990-2001; asst. to Sen. Taft in Ohio senatorial campaign, 1950; pvt. bus. investments Cleve., 1951-57; asst. to pres. Princeton U., 1957-59; chmn. bd. Scurry-Rainbow Oil, Ltd., 1954-74; trustee Inst. for Advanced Study, 1972-88; pres. Cleve. Inst. Music, 1952-56; trustee Cleve. Orch., 1946-57, pres., 1955-57, Nat. Council Met. Opera, 1961-64; dir. Met. Opera Assn., 1961-91, pres., chief exec. officer, 1977-84; hon. trustee Bradford (Mass.) Coll.; trustee Princeton (N.J.) Day Sch., 1966-72, Princeton Area United Community Fund, 1963-76; mem. Princeton U. Music Dept. Adv. Council, 1960-85, chmn., 1965-71; trustee Sarah Lawrence Coll., 1969-77, chmn., 1973-77, hon. trustee, 1977—; trustee Lincoln Center for Performing Arts, 1972-88, vice chmn., 1981-84; trustee, founding pres. Lincoln Center Chamber Music Soc., 1969-73; fellow Morgan Library; mem. council Friends Princeton Library; chmn. bd. Marlboro Sch. Music, 1964-70; trustee Woodrow Wilson Nat. Fellowship Found., 1972—93, Am. Schs. Oriental Rsch., 1970—75, Western Res. Hist. Soc., Cleve.; internat. bd. dirs. United World Colls., London, 1973-76; also chmn. United World Colls. (U.S. com.), 1973-75; bd. dirs. Am. Friends of Covent Garden and Royal Ballet, Friends of Aldeburgh Festival.; mem. vestry Trinity Ch., Princeton, 1984-87. Chmn. adv. coun. Princeton U. Environ. Inst., 1998—. Vice chmn. council of fellows Morgan Library, 1987-90. Served from ensign to lt. comdr. USNR, 1941-46. Decorated hon. mem. (mil. div.) Order Brit. Empire.; recipient Gold Medal award Nat. Inst. Social Scis., 1983, Disting. Service award Third St. Music Sch. Settlement, 1983 Mem. ABA, Assn. Am. Rhodes Scholars, Am. Philos. Soc., Am.-Scandinavian Found. (exec. trustee), Univ. Club (N.Y.C.), Century Assn. (N.Y.C., bd.mgmt. 1981-84), Springdale Golf Club, Nassau Club (Princeton), Pretty Brook Club (Princeton), Tavern Club (Cleve.).

TAPLIN, WINN LOWELL, historian, retired senior intelligence operations officer; b. Saint Albans, Vt., Oct. 3, 1925; s. Winn Lowell and Elinor (Cunningham) T.; m. Ellajean Allard, July 16, 1949; children: Leslie Taplin Baumann, Mark Allard. BSCE, U. Mich., 1946, AB, 1948, AM, 1950, PhD, 1956. Oper. officer CIA, Washington, Saigon, Bucharest, Geneva, Bangkok, 1955-81; cons. Stowe, Vt., 1981-94, Sarasota, Fla., 1994—. Author: Secret New England: Spies of the American Revolution, 1991, We Vermonters, 1992. Mem. U.S. del. to UN Commn. on Human Rights, 1969; pres. Vt. Hist. Soc., 1989-93, trustee, 1983-96; mem. Sarasota Geneal. Soc., v.p., 1999-2001, pres., 2001—; pres. Mansfield View Water Corp., Stowe, 1989-92. 1st lt. USMC, 1943-46, 50-52, Korea. Decorated Bronze Star, Intelligence Medal of Merit. Mem. Central Intelligence Retirees Assn., Assn. Former Intelligence Officers, First Day Cover Soc., Am. Philatelic Assn., Am. Legion, DAV, U. Mich. Club Sarasota (dir. 1994—), Sigma Chi. Avocations: historical research, genealogy, classical music, stamp collecting. Home: 7618 Sandalwood Way Sarasota FL 34231-5334

TAPP, MAMIE PEARL, educational association administration; b. Aiken, S.C., July 20, 1955; d. Willie Lee and Nancy (Madison) Garrett; m. Anthony Karl Tapp, Aug. 13, 1983; children: Anthony K. II, Barry Garrett, Myles Jarvis. BA, CUNY, 1977; MA, New Sch. for Social Rsch., 1984; postgrad., Nova Southeastern U., 1994—. Flight attendant Capitol Airlines, Jamaica, N.Y., 1976-81; pers. assoc. Cmty. Svc. Soc., N.Y.C., 1982-83; pers. specialist Marriott Hotel, Tampa, Fla., 1983-84; dir. placement Tampa Coll., 1984-86, facility coord., 1986-87, compliance officer, 1987-88; career counselor Alpha House, Tampa, 1988-91; career specialist U. Tampa, 1991-96, adj. prof., 1992-93; career specialist Jr. Achievement Greater Tampa, Inc., Tampa, 1996—, tchr. asst. program adv. com. mem., 1996-98. Tchr. asst. program adv. com. Hillsborough H.S., 1996-97; sr. edn. svc. mgr. Jr. Achievement, 1997—. Author: (novels) Resumes, 1992, Cover Letters, 1991, Thank You Letters, 1992, (poetry) Inner Peace, 1999; co-editor: I Cried, 2001, Life, 2002. Bd. dirs. Children's Mus. Tampa, 1992-94; com. mem. United Way, Tampa, 1994-95; mem. bd. St. Peter Claver Cath. Sch., Tampa, 1995-99, exec. com. Glee Club, 1995; vol. Scout troop leader, 1997-98. Recipient Outstanding Bus. Woman award Am. Bus. Women's Assn., Tampa, 1987, Cmty. Svc. award Tampa Connections, 1993, Editor's Choice award Internat. Libr. of Poetry, 1999. Mem. AAUW, Am. Vocat. Assn., Fla. Assn. Women in Edn. Roman Catholic. Avocations: reading, sewing. Office: Jr Achievement Central Maryland Inc 10711 Red Run Blvd Ste 110 Owings Mills MD 21117 E-mail: tapptbjpt@earthlink.net.

TAPPAN, JANICE RUTH VOGEL, animal behavior researcher; b. Pasadena, Mar. 13, 1948; d. Robert Samuel and Etta (Berry) Vogel; m. David Stanton Tappan IV, Dec. 20, 1970 (div. Mar. 20, 2001); children: Stacey, Christina, Danny. BA in Anthropology, U. Calif., Berkeley, 1970. Rsch. asst. L.A. Zoo, 1982—; owner Fiddlers Crossing, Pasadena, 1989—. Calif. Arts Coun. folklore grantee, 1989-90. Mem. Scottish Fiddling Revival (v.p. 1986—, judge fiddling 1989—), Scottish Fiddlers of Calif. (v.p. 1986—), Calif. Traditional Music Soc. (devel. dir. 1990-94, v.p. 1994—), Scottish Fiddlers of L.A. (music dir. 1990—), Phi Beta Kappa. Democrat. Mem. Soc. Of Friends. Avocations: music. Home: 1938 Rose Villa St Pasadena CA 91107-5046

TAPPÉ, ALBERT ANTHONY, architect; b. Pitts., Aug. 12, 1928; s. Albert Anthony and Martha Ann (McKee) T.; m. Jean Bates, June 27, 1963; children: Eliza Bruce, Albert Anthony III. Student, William and Mary Coll., 1947-48, Fontainebleau Fine Art and Music Sch., 1951; BS, U. Va., 1952; M.Arch., MIT, 1958, M.City Planning. Designer, McLeod & Ferrara (Architects), Washington, 1954-55; planner Boston City Planning Bd., 1957-58; architect and planner Architects Collaborative, Cambridge, Mass., 1958-61; partner Huygens & Tappé, Inc. (architects and planners), Boston, 1962-80; pres. A. Anthony Tappé & Assocs., Inc., 1980—. Instr. dept. city planning MIT, 1959-60; instr. in office of exec. edn. Harvard U., 1989—; cons. architect Mass. Bur. Library Extension, 1965-76; chmn. bldg. commn., Brookline, Mass., 1977, mem. bd. examiners, Brookline; v.p. Guild Religious Architecture; mem. Back Bay Archtl. Commn.; bd. dirs. Boston Archtl. Center, 1980, bd. overseers, 2001—; vis. architect Am. Acad. in Rome, 1997. Author: Guide to Planning a Library Building, 1967; important works include: Longy Concert Hall, Cambridge, Mass., Campus N.H. Coll., Franklin Park Zoo, Boston, Lynn Inst. for Savs., Interfaith Religious Ctr., Columbia, Md., student housing W.Va. Wesleyan Coll., Hotel, Costa Smeralda, Sardinia, Newton Pub. Libr., Beverly Pub. Libr., Am. Coll., Athens, Greece, Morse Inst. Library, Natick ,Mass., Newton Public Library, Mass., Ctrl. Sch., Longmeadow, MA.; also residences in U.S., France, Switzerland, housing projects in New Eng. Served with AUS, 1946-47, 52-54. Recipient Progressive Architecture Design award, 1966, 1st place single family category Plywood Design Awards Program, 1973, award of Merit, 1974 Fellow AIA (mem. nat. urban planning and design com. 1975, citation, hon. mentions 1969, 1st honor award 1970, honor award New Eng. Regional Council 1976); mem. Mass. Assn. Architects (exec. com.), Boston Soc. Architects (dir., v.p. 1981-82, pres. 1982-83, award 1998), Am. Inst. Planners, Am. Planning Assn., Am. Inst. Cons. Planners, Harvard Travelers Club. Clubs: Union Boat (Boston), Eastern Point Yacht (Gloucester, Mass.), Harvard Club (Boston), Bass Rocks Golf Club (Gloucester, Mass.). Home: 58 Euston St Brookline MA 02446-4045 Office: Tappe Assocs Inc 6 Edgerly Pl Boston MA 02116-5327

TAPPER, DAVID, pediatric surgeon; b. Balt., Aug. 26, 1945; s. Herman A. and Sylvia Phyllis (Golomb) T.; m. Susan Irene Wagner, June 25, 1968; children: JoEllen, Erica, Jacalyn, Aaron. BS, U. Md., College Park, 1966; MD, U. Md., Balt., 1970. Intern and resident in surgery U. Calif. San Francisco Med. Ctr., 1970-73; pediatric surg. rsch. fellow Boston Children's Hosp., 1973-75; sr. and chief surg. resident U. Calif., San Francisco, 1975-77; sr. and chief pediatric surg. fellow Children's Hosp., Boston, 1977-79; asst. prof. surgery Harvard Med. Sch., 1979-83; surgeon-in-chief Children's Hosp. Med. Ctr., Seattle, 1983—; prof. surgery and pediatrics U. Wash., 1983—, vice-chmn. dept. surgery, 1986—. Exec. com. Am. Bd. Surgery, Phila., 1996-98, chmn. surg. forum, 1998-2000. Maj. USAR, 1971-82. Fellow ACS; mem. Am. Surg Assn., Am. Pediatric Surgery Assn. (bd. govs. 1993-96, pres. 2001), Soc. Univ. Surgeons, Pacific Coast Surg. Soc. (councilor N.W. region 1999—), Halsted Surg. Soc., Seattle Surg. Soc. (pres. 1999). Jewish. Office: Childrens Hosp Med Ctr 4800 Sand Point Way NE Seattle WA 98105-3901 E-mail: dtappe@chmc.org.

TAPPER, MICHAEL LEITNER, physician; b. N.Y., Mar. 9, 1945; s. Albert Michael and Jean (Leitner) T. BA cum laude, Columbia, 1965, MA, 1966, MD, 1970. Diplomate Am. Bd. Internal Medicine, Am. Bd. Infectious Diseases, Nat. Bd. Medical Examiners. Internship Harlem Hosp. Ctr., 1970-71, residency, 1971-73; fellow dept. medicine Meml. Sloan-Kettering Cancer Ctr., 1973-75; chief of infectious diseases Lenox Hill. Hosp., N.Y., 1977—, hosp. epidemiologist, 1977—; medical dir. AIDS program Lenor Hill. Hosp., 1989—. Asst. prof. clinical medicine Columbia Univ., 1975-77, clinical asst. prof. medicine Cornell Univ., 1978—; clinical prof. medicine, NYU Sch. Medicine, 1994—; asst attending physician dept. medicine Harlem Hosp. Ctr., 1973-80, Roosevelt Hosp., 1975-77; adj. physician infectious disease svc. Meml. Hosp., 1975-91, Lenox Hill Hosp., 1976-77; assoc. physician chief section of infectious disease, Lenox Hill Hosp., 1977-81; com. mem. for numerous confs. Co-editor: Clinical Treatment Section AIDS, 1992-93; editorial bd. Infection Control and Hospital Epidemiology; contbr. numerous articles to profl. jours. AIDS adv. coun. N.Y. State AIDS Coun., adv. com. N.Y. State Health Dept., chmn. 1995-98; chmn. AIDS com. Soc. Hosp. Epidemiology of Am., 1991-92, chmn. AIDS/TB Com., 1992—. Fellow: ACP, N.Y. Acad. Medicine, Infectious Disease Soc. Am.; mem.: APHA, N.Y. Soc. Infectious Diseases (v.p. 1993—94, pres.-elect 1994—95, pres. 1995—96), Soc. Healthcare Epidemiology Am., Royal Soc. Medicine, Med. Soc. State N.Y., Med. Soc. County of N.Y., Internat. Soc. Infections in Immunocompromised Hosp, Internat. AIDS Soc., Hosp. Infection Soc., Brit. Infection Soc., Brit. Soc. Antimicrobial Chemotherapy, Assn. Practitioners in Infection Control, Am. Soc. Microbiology. Office: Lenox Hill Hosp 100 E 77th St New York NY 10021-1850 Office Fax: 212-434-2574. E-mail: mtapper@lenoxhill.net.

TAPSCOTT, CHRISTOPHER PETER, sociologist; b. Edgeware, Middlesex, U.K., Sept. 5, 1952; s. Peter Gordon and Elizabeth Catherine (Smyth) T.; m. Gretta Eve Melck, July 29, 1985; children: Kimberley, Claire. BS with honors, U. Cape Town, S. Africa, 1974, M Pub Adminstrn, 1977; MSc, U. Birmingham, 1978; PhD, London Sch. Econs., 1992. Urban studies officer Cape Town City Coun., S. Africa, 1975-77, prin. urban studies officer S. Africa, 1979-81; dir. Inst. for Mgmt. and Devel. Studies/U. Transkei, Umtata, S. Africa, 1981-86, Namibian Inst. for Social/Econ. Rsch., Windhoek/Nambia, 1990-93; head Social Scis. Divsn. U. Nambia, 1993-94; dir. Sch. Govt. U. Western Cape, Cape Town, S. Africa, 1994—. Task team mem. Presdl. Rev. comm. on Pub. Sector Reform, S. Africa, 1997-98; coord. tech. drafting team white paper on Transformation of Pub. Svc., S. Africa, 1995; mem. core adv. group on Inter-Govtl. Rels., Pretoria, S. Africa, 1998—; mem. Inter-Agy. World Congress on Agrl. Reform and Rural Devel., Rev. Mission to Nambia, 1994; trustee Joint Univs. Pub. Mgmt. Edn. Trust, chmn. 1997-99; mem. Internat. Panel of Experts on Fishing Incentives, Rome, FAO, 2000. Contbr.: (books) Power of Development, 1995, The Two-Edged Sword, 1996, The Worldwide Diffusion of The European Model of the State, 1999; co-editor: Intervoernmental Relations in South Africa, 2001; contbr. articles to profl. jours. Mem. exec. com. Cmty. Peace Found., Cape Town, 1995-98; mem. So. Democracy Ctr. Coun., Cape Town, 1997-98; trustee Local Govt. Learning Network Trust, 1997—, We. Cape Pub. Adminstrn. and Mgmt. Forum, 1995—. Grantee Soc. for Protection of Sci. and Learning, London, 1987, Canon Collins Trust, London, 1988, Africa Edn. Trust, London, 1988. Mem. Internat. Inst. Adminstrv. Scis. Avocations: scuba diving, tennis. Office: Sch Govt/Univ Western Cape Pvt Bag X17 Bellville 7535 South Africa E-mail: ctapscott@unc.ac.za.

TAQUEY, ANTONY, accountant; b. Albert, Somme, France, Aug. 13, 1953; arrived in U.S., 1955; s. Charles Henri and Ruth McVitty Taquey; m. Karen Elizabeth Anderson, June 17, 2001. BA in Econs., New Eng. Coll., 1976; MS in Acctg. and Fin., Johns Hopkins U., 1997. Editor(pub.): War is Personal, 2001. Republican. Episcopalian. Home: PO Box 1751 Clemmons NC 27012

TAR, LASZLO, artist; b. Szabolc, Hungary, June 9, 1922; arrived in U.S., 1956; s. Laszlo Tar; m. Olga Vida; children: Julia LaScalere, Leslie, Julius. BA, Royal Acad. Fine Arts, Budapest, 1948; apprentice, Italiam master Giorgio Morandi, 1946; postgrad., New Sch., N.Y.C.; student, Art Students League, N.Y., 1971—77. Artist, 1927—; with WestPoint Pepperell, F. Schumacher & Co. Exhibitions include Washington Sq. Park Outdoor Art Show, exhibitions include Budapest Galeria, 1989, one-man shows include various locations throughout Hungary, exhibitions include N.Y. Consulate of Republic of Hungary, 2000, Huntington Arts Counzel Art in the Atrium, 2001, Represented in permanent collections Budapest Mus. of Fine Art, Mcpl. Mus., Rome. Home: 3 Cliftwood Dr Huntington NY 11743 Personal E-mail: ltar@tarart.com.

TARAN, LEONARDO, classicist, educator; b. Galarza, Argentina, Feb. 22, 1933; came to U.S., 1958, naturalized, 1976; s. Miguel and Liuba Taran; m. Judit Sofia Lida, Dec. 10, 1971; 1 child, Gabriel Andrew. Legal degree, U. Buenos Aires, 1958; PhD in Classics, Princeton U., 1962. Jr. fellow Inst. Research in Humanities, U. Wis., 1962-63, Center Hellenic Studies, Washington, 1963-64; asst. prof. classics U. Calif., Los Angeles, 1964-67; mem. faculty Columbia U., 1967—, prof. Greek and Latin, 1971—, Jay prof. Greek and Latin, 1987—, chmn. dept., 1976-79. Mem. Inst. Advanced Study, Princeton, N.J., 1966-67, 78-79; trustee Assn. Mems. Inst. Advanced Study, 1974-79; mem. mng. com. Am. Sch. Classical Studies, 1976— Author: Parmenides, 1965, Asclepius of Tralles, Commentary to Nicomachus' Introduction to Arithmetic, 1969, Plato, Philip of Opus and the Pseudo-Platonic Epinomis, 1975, Anonymous Commentary on Aristotle's De Interpretatione, 1978, Speusippus of Athens, 1981, Collected Papers (1962-1999), 2001; co-author: Eraclito: Testimonianze e imitazioni, 1972; Editorial bd.: Columbia Studies in the Classical Tradition, 1976-80. Am. Coun. Learned Socs. fellow, 1966-67, 71-72, Guggenheim Found. fellow, 1975, NEH fellow, 1986-87; grantee Am. Philos. Soc., 1963, 71, 75, Am. Coun. Learned Socs., 1968, 72, NEH, 1985-87, 88-89. Mem. Am. Philol. Assn., Classical Assn. Atlantic States, Soc. Ancient Greek Philosophy, Assn. Guillaume Bude. Home: 39 Claremont Ave New York NY 10027-6802 Office: Columbia U 615 Hamilton Hall New York NY 10027 E-mail: lt1@columbia.edu.

TARANIK, JAMES VLADIMIR, geologist, educator; b. Los Angeles, Apr. 23, 1940; s. Vladimir James and Jeanette Downing (Smith) T.; m. Colleen Sue Glessner, Dec. 4, 1971; children: Debra Lynn, Danny Lee. BSc in Geology, Stanford U., 1964; PhD, Colo. Sch. Mines, 1974. Chief remote sensing Iowa Geol. Survey, Iowa City, 1971-74; prin. remote sensing scientist Earth Resources Observation Systems Data Ctr., U.S. Geol. Survey, Sioux Falls, S.D., 1975-79; chief non-renewable resources br., resource observation div. Office of Space and Terrestrial Applications, NASA Hdqrs., Washington, 1979-82; dean mines Mackay Sch. Mines U. Nev., Reno, 1982-87, prof. of geology and geophysics, 1982—, Arthur Brant chair of geophysics, 1996—; pres. Desert Research Inst., Univ. and C.C. Sys. Nev., 1987-98, Regent's prof. and pres. emeritus, 1998—; adj. prof. geology U. Iowa, 1971-79; vis. prof. civil engrng. Iowa State U., 1972-74; adj. prof. earth sci. U. S.D., 1976-79; program scientist for space shuttle large format camera expt. for heat capacity mapping mission, liaison Geol. Scis. Bd., Nat. Acad. Scis., 1981-82; dir. NOAA Coop. Inst. Aerospace Sci. & Terrestrial Applications, 1986-94; program dir. NASA Space Grant consortium Univ. and Community Coll. System Nev., Reno, 1991-2000, dir. NASA EPSCOR program, 1998—; dir. Great Basin Ctr. Geothermal Energy, 2000—. Team mem. Shuttle Imaging Radar-B Sci. Team NASA, 1983-88, mem. space applications adv. com., 1986-88; chmn. remote sensing subcom. SAAC, 1986-88; chmn. working group on civil space commercialization Dept. Commerce, 1982-84, mem. civil operational remote sensing satellite com., 1983-84; bd. dirs. Earth Satellite Corp., Newmont Mining Corp.; mem. adv. com. NASA Space Sci. and Applications Com., 1988-90, Nat. Def. Exec. Res., 1986-94, AF studies bd., com. on strategic relocatable targets, 1989-91; mem. pre-launch rev. bd., NASA, Space Radar Lab., 1993-94; mem. fed. lab. rev. task force, NASA, 1994-96; prin. investigator Japanese Earth Resources Satellite, 1991-94; mem. environ. task force MEDEA, Mitre Corp., McLean, Va., 1993-98; mem. mapping scis. com. Nat. Rsch. Coun., 2001—; cons. Jet Propulsion Lab., Calif., Hughes Aircraft Corp., Lockheed-Marietta Corp., Mitre Corp., TRW; developer remote sensing program and remote sensing lab. for State of Iowa, ednl. program in remote sensing for Iowa univs. and U. Nev., Reno; program scientist for 2d space shuttle flight Office Space and Terrestrial Applications Program; mem. terrestrial geol. applications program NASA, 1981-82; co-investigator Can. Radarsat Program, 1995—; program dir. NASA Space Grant and NASA EPSCOR, Nev., 1998—; mem. mapping scis. com. Nat. Rsch. Coun., 2001—. Contbr. to profl. jours. Served with C.E. U.S. Army, 1965-67; mil. intelligence officer Res. Decorated Bronze Star medal; recipient Spl. Achievement award U.S. Geol. Survey, 1978, Exceptional Sci. Achievement medal NASA, 1982, NASA Group Achievement award Shuttle imaging radar, 1990, NASA Johnson Space Ctr. Group Achievement award for large format camera, 1985; NASA prin. investigator, 1973, 83-88, prin. investigator French Spot-1 Program to Evaluate Spot 1986-88; NDEA fellow, 1968-71. Fellow: AAAS, Am. Soc. Photogrammetry Remote Sensing, Explorers Club, Geol. Soc. Am.; mem.: AIAA (sr.), IEEE (sr.), Soc. Econ. Geologists, Am. Geol. Inst. Found. (trustee 1999—), Am. Inst. Metall. Engrs., Am. Astron. Soc. (sr.), Soc. Mining Engrs. Am., Am. Assn. Petroleum Geologists (chmn. rsch. com. 2000—), Am. Geophys. Union, Soc. Exploration Geophysicists, Internat.

Acad. Astronautics, Bohemian Club San Francisco. Home: PO Box 7175 Reno NV 89510-7175 E-mail: jtaranik@mines.unr.edu. *I have always been in awe of the universe in which we live and the little time we have on earth to perceive and understand it.*

TARANOW, GERDA, English language educator, researcher, author; b. N.Y.C. d. Samuel and Sabina (Ostro) Taranow. BA, NYU, 1952, MA, 1955; PhD, Yale U., 1961, postgrad., 1962-63. Instr. English, U. Ky., Lexington, 1963-65, asst. prof., 1965-66, U. Syracuse, N.Y., 1966-67; asst. prof. English, Conn. Coll., New London, 1967-70, assoc. prof., 1970-76, prof., 1976—. Referee NEH, Washington, 1972—. Author: (book) Sarah Bernhardt: The Art Within the Legend, 1972, The Bernhardt Hamlet: Culture and Context, 1997. Fellow, Yale Univ, 1962—63, NEH, 1980—81. Mem.: MLA, Soc Histoire Théâtre (France), Int Fedn Theatre Research, Soc Theatre Research (Eng), Am Soc Theatre Research. Avocations: opera, theatre, ballet. Office: Conn Coll PO Box 5567 New London CT 06320 Fax: 860-447-0128. E-mail: gtarhamlet@earthlink.net.

TARANTINO, DOMINIC A. retired professional services firm executive; b. San Francisco, Aug. 1, 1932; m. Leona Lazzareschi, July 24, 1954; children: John Robert, Stephen, Leanne. BS, U. San Francisco, 1954. With Price Waterhouse, 1957-98, mem. policy bd. and mgmt. com., 1979-93, vice chmn. tax svcs., 1982-88, co-chmn. bd., mng. ptnr., 1988-93; chmn. Price Waterhouse World Firm, 1995-98. Mem. IRS Commr.'s Adv. Group, 1978. Chair bd. trustees U. San Francisco, 1999—; treas., bd. dirs. Bus. Opportunities for Leadership Diversity, 1988--. Recipient Delta Sigma Pi Career Achievement award, 1997. Mem. AICPA (bd. dirs. 1988-95, vice chair 1992-3, chmn. 1993-94, Dixon Meml. award 1990, Gold medal for disting. svc. 2000). Address: Mead Point Nipowin Ln Greenwich CT 06830 E-mail: dominic.tarantino@us.pwcglobal.com.

TARANTINO, LOUIS GERALD, business executive, consultant, lawyer; b. Bridgeport, Conn., Sept. 7, 1934; s. Louis Gerald and Mary Louise (Boyle) T. BA, U. Pa., 1955, LLB, 1958. Bar: Conn. 1958, N.Y. 1960. Assoc. Beekman & Bogue, 1959-67, ptnr., 1968-76; pres., bd. dirs. Berkeley Mgmt. Assocs., Inc., Boston, 1984—. Mem. enterprise adv. bd. Photonics Ctr., Boston U.; ptnr. Berkeley Investment Ptnrs., N.Y.C., Wintzen Pharms, L.P., The Netherlands, Startup Ptnrs., Boston; bd. dirs. SiteLab Corp., Portsmouth, N.H., EachNet-.com.Ltd.,Cayman Islands, Shanghai and Hong Kong, Anyparty.com.inc., Boston, Comml. Exch. Co. Inc., Boston; bd. dirs. The Inst. for New Medicine, Washington. Mem. Bar Assn. City N.Y., N.Y. Bar Assn., Conn. Bar Assn., SAR, Huguenot Soc. Pa., St. Anthony Hall, Knickerbocker Club, India House (N.Y.C.), St. Anthony Club (Phila.). Home: One Devonshire Pl Apt 3409 Boston MA 02109

TARANTO, MARIA ANTOINETTE, psychology researcher and educator; b. Framingham, Mass., Dec. 28, 1941; d. Gaetano (Tom) Peter and Rose Marie (Busceme) T.; m. John Curtis Mahon, June 5, 1988. BA in Psychology, Bennington Coll., 1965; MA in Psychology, George Peabody Coll., 1968; M Philosophy in Psychology, Columbia U., 1981, PhD, 1985. Tchr. Head Start Pub Sch. System, Pitts., 1966-67; rsch. assoc. Hofstra U., Hempstead, N.Y., 1968-69, instr., 1969-72; co-dir. Inst. for Piagetian Studies, 1972-76; instr. Nassau C.C., Garden City, N.Y., 1976-78, asst. prof., 1978-85, assoc. prof. psychology, 1985-95, prof. emeritus, 1996—. Jour. reviewer Baywood Pub. Co., Long Island, N.Y., 1989, Karger, Basel, Switzerland, 1989. Co-author: (monographs) A Study of Number..., 1972, Liquid Conservation, 1976; contbr. articles to profl. jours and govt. pubs. Mem. Union of Concerned Scientists, 1981—, Amnesty Internat., 1987—; sponsor Pearl S. Buck Found., 1984—. Recipient Mellon fellowship CUNY, N.Y.C., 1987. Mem. Am. Psychol. Assn., Jean Piaget Soc., Gerontol. Soc., New Eng. Psychol. Assn., Filicudi Assn. Avocations: hiking, gardening, picniking.

TARAR, AFZAL MUHAMMAD, management consultant; b. Gujranwala, Punjab, Pakistan, Apr. 1, 1962; came to the U.S., 1989; s. Abdul Wahid and Ghulam Sugra Tarar. BE in Computer Engring., Tsinghua U., 1988; MS in Computer Sci., Case Western Res. U., 1991. Systems specialist EG&G, Inc., Beijing, 1986-89; cons. Cap Gemini Am., Cleve., 1990-91; officer, project mgr. KeyCorp./Key Svcs. Corp., 1991-95; mgr. Deloitte & Touche Consulting Group, N.Y.C., 1995-98; sr. prin. Am. Mgmt. Sys., Inc., 1998-2000; prin. ZEFER, 2000-01, IBM Global Svcs., N.Y.C., 2001—. Mem. Am. Mgmt. Assn., Internat. Assn. Knowledge Engrs., Soc. for Mgmt. Applied Intelligent and Relevant Techs. in Fin. Svcs., Japan Soc. Cleve. (trustee 1992-94), Strategic Leadership Forum.

TARAS, PAUL, physicist, educator; b. Tunis, Tunisia, May 12, 1941; emigrated to Can., 1957, naturalized, 1962; s. Wladimir and Benita (Koort) T.; m. Marja-Leena Malinen, Aug. 3, 1963; children— Lisa Helene, Michele Anne. BASc., U. Toronto, 1962, MA, 1963, PhD, 1965. Asst. prof. physics U. Montreal, Que., Can., 1965-70, assoc. prof., 1970-76, prof., 1976—. Spokesman U. Montreal in rsch. projects. Helios, SDC, Babar. Rsch. on nuclear and particle physics; co-managed conception and constrn. of 8pi Spectrometer, Chalk River Nuclear Labs, 1984-86; contbr. articles to profl. jours.; presenter papers to profl. confs. U. Toronto, Province of Ont., U.K. Atomic Energy Authority fellowships; France-Que., NRC, Natural Scis. and Engring. Research Council Can. grantee. Mem. Am. Phys. Soc., Can. Assn. Physicists, Soc. Galilée (mem. exec. bd.), Babar Collaboration (bd. dirs.). Home: 1639 Norway Rd Montreal QC Canada H4P 1Y3 Office: Univ de Montreal Lab Physique Nucleaire Montreal QC Canada H3C 3J7 E-mail: taras@lps.umontreal.ca.

TARASCIO, LINDA SCOTT, management executive; b. Ft. Smith, Ark., Sept. 20, 1942; d. Thomas Nelson and Mary Altha (Tankersley) Scott; m. Vincent Joseph Tarascio, Mar. 30, 1964; children: Linda, Mark, Eugene, Anthony. BA, Rice U., 1964. Pres. Publ. Mgmt. Svcs., Inc., Chapel Hill, N.C., 1977—. Prodn. and editl. mgr. So. Econ. Jour., Chapel Hill, 1977-97; cons., prodn. mgr. Econ. Inquiry, Long Beach, Calif., 1985-86. Editor: Economic Inquiry Cumulative Index, 1987, Journal of Marketing Cumulative Index, 1989 ; co-editor: Journal of Finance Cumulative Index, 1985, Southern Economic Journal Cumulative Index, 1985. Office: Pub Mgmt Svcs Inc PO Box 2213 Chapel Hill NC 27515-2213

TARASCIO, VINCENT JOSEPH, economist, educator; b. Hartford, Conn., Feb. 5, 1930; s. Mario and Sarina (Cartelli) T.; m. Linda Scott Tarascio, Mar. 30, 1964; children: Linda A., Mark, Eugene, Anthony. AS, U. Hartford, 1951; BA, San Jose (Calif.) State U., 1961; PhD, Rice U., 1966. With U. N.C., Chapel Hill, 1964—, assoc. prof., 1969-72, prof., 1972—2001, prof. emeritus, 2001—. Cons. Ford Found., N.Y.C., 1975; cons. bd. regents U. Fla., 1981. Author: Pareto's Methodological Approach to Economics, 1968, Wage and Employment Theory, 1971, Fiscal Aspects of Human Resource Development, 1971; cons. editor: JAI Press, 1983-92; mng. editor: So. Econ. Jour., 1969—. Mem. Am. Econ. Assn. (nominating com. 1976), Atlantic Econ. Soc. (exec. com. 1993-95), Western Econ. Assn., So. Econ. Assn. (exec. com. 1969-97), History Econs. Soc. (pres. 1974-75). Office: Univ NC CB # 3305 Gardner Hall Chapel Hill NC 27599

TARASI, LOUIS MICHAEL, JR. lawyer; b. Cheswick, Pa., Sept. 9, 1931; s. Louis Michael and Ruth Elizabeth (Records) T.; m. Patricia Ruth Finley, June 19, 1954; children: Susan, Louis Michael III, Elizabeth, Brian, Patricia, Matthew. BA, Miami U., Ohio, 1954; JD, U. Pa., 1959. Bar: Pa. 1960, U.S. Dist. Ct. (we. dist.) Pa. 1960, U.S. Ct. Appeals (3d cir.) 1964, U.S. Supreme Ct. 1969, U.S. Dist. Ct. (we. dist.) Tex. 1988, U.S. Ct. Appeals (5th cir.) 1989, U.S. Ct. Appeals (4th cir.) 1994, U.S. Ct. Fed. Claims 1987, U.S. Dist. Ct. Colo. 1998; cert. civil trial adv. Nat. Bd. Trial Advocacy. Assoc., owner Burgwin, Ruffin, Perry & Pohl, Pitts., 1960-68; ptnr. Conte, Courtney & Tarasi, Beaver County, Pa., 1968-78, Tarasi & Tighe, Pitts., 1978-82, Tarasi & Johnson, P.C., Pitts., 1982-95, Tarasi & Assocs., P.C., Pitts., 1995-99, The Tarasi Lawfirm, P.C., Pitts., 1997-2001, Tarasi, Tarasi & Fishman, P.C., Pitts., 2001—. Mem. parish coun. St. James Ch., Sewickley, Pa.; mem. Sewickley Borough Allegheny Coun., 1978-1982. With U.S. Army, 1954-56. Fellow: Internat. Soc. Barristers; mem.: Am. Coll. Barristers (sr. counsel), Am. Bd. Trial Advs., Melvin Belli Soc., St. Thomas More Soc. (award 1991), West Pa. Trial Lawyers Assn. (pres. 1975), Pa. Bar Assn., Allegheny County Bar Assn., Acad. Trial Lawyers Allegheny County, Pa. Trial Lawyers Assn. (pres. 1979—80), Assn. Trial Lawyers Am. (gov., rep.). Democrat. Roman Catholic. Avocations: reading, golf, lecturing. Home: 1 Way Hollow Rd Sewickley PA 15143-1192 Office: Tarasi Tarasi & Fishman 510 3d Ave Pittsburgh PA 15219-2107

TARASKO, ALEXANDRA, nursing educator; b. Austria, Jan. 15, 1949; came to U.S., 1955; d. Peter Stephen and Alexandra (Narizna) Bazylewsky; m. Basil Paul Tarasko, Aug. 15, 1970; children: Andrei, Michael. BSN, Hunter Coll., 1973; MA in Nursing Edn., NYU, 1980; mental health/psychiat. nursing cert., Adelphi U., 1996. Psychiat. nurse Roosevelt Hosp., N.Y.C., 1974-76, head nurse, 1976-78; prof. Queensborough C.C., Bayside, N.Y., 1981—. Adj. lectr. NYU, N.Y.C., 1980; coord. Older Adults: Health Care '90's, Bayside, 1990, AIDS Conf., Bayside, 1991, Role of Spirituality in Health Conf., 2002; participant TV and radio appearances, 1989, 91. Apptd. mem. Health Careers Task Force, N.Y.C., 1991, CUNY Health Professions Task Force, Psychosocial Svcs., 1994-95; leader Health Explorer post Boy Scouts Am., Queensborough C.C., 1988-90. New Visions for Edn. grantee CUNY, 1998, 2000. Mem. Nurse Healers-Profl. Assn., Am. Holistic Nurses' Assn. Avocations: antiques, auctions. Home: 36-46 212th St Bayside NY 11361-2049 Office: Queensborough CC Springfield Blvd And Fifth Ave Flushing NY 11364

TARASZKIEWICZ, WALDEMAR, physician; b. Wilno, Poland, July 6, 1936; came to U.S., 1979; s. Michal Taraszkiewicz and Nina (Lutomska) Dylla; m. Teresa Barbara Szwarc, Oct. 15, 1966. MD, Med. Acad., Gdansk, Poland, 1961, internal medicine specialty, 1967, internal medicine specialty II, 1972. Diplomate Am. Bd. Family Practice. Family physician Out Patient Clinic, Sopot, Poland, 1962—64; resident doctor U. Hosp., Gdansk, 1965—71; allergist Clinic of Allergy, 1965—75; physician Cardiology Dept., 1971—75, Hôpital Civil, Telagh, Algeria, 1975—79; surg. asst. Hinsdale (Ill.) Hosp., 1979—82; resident physician St. Mary of Nazareth Hosp., Chgo., 1982—85, emergency room physician, 1984—85; family practice medicine Brookfield, 1985—88, Westmont, 1988—89, Chgo., 1987—; med. dir. Winston Manor Nursing Home, 1989—90; clin. asst. prof. U. Ill. Med. Coll., 1994—. Sr. asst. dept. cardiology Univ. Hosp., Gdansk, 1971-75; mem. adminstrv. com., pres. med. staff Hôpital Civil, Telagh, 1976-79. Contbr. articles to profl. jours. Recipient Bronze medal Polski Zwiazek Wedkarski, 1970, cert. 3d place, 1971. Fellow Am. Acad. Family Practice; mem. AMA (continuing edn. award), Ill. Med. Soc., Chgo. Med. Soc. (practice mgmt. com.), World Med. Assn., Am. Acad. Allergy and Immunology, Am. Coll. Allergy and Immunology, Polish Med. Alliance, N.Y. Acad. Scis. Avocations: art collecting, fishing. Office: 5946 N Milwaukee Ave Chicago IL 60646 E-mail: waldemar_taraszkiewicz@yahoo.com.

TARAVELLA, CHRISTOPHER ANTHONY, lawyer; b. Pueblo, Colo., Sept. 19, 1951; s. Frank Louis and Ann Jean T.; m. Kathleen; children: Nicholas M., John L. BS in Engring. Mechanics, USAF Acad., 1973; JD, U. Colo., 1976; postgrad., Harvard U., 1996. Bar: Iowa 1976, Colo. 1976, U.S. Ct. Mil. Appeals 1976, U.S. Dist. Ct. Colo. 1976, Fla. 1977, U.S. Supreme Ct. 1982, U.S. Ct. Appeals (fed. cir.) 1983, D.C. 1984, U.S. Claims Ct. 1984, Mich. 1985. Commd. 2nd lt. USAF, 1973, legal intern Staff Judge Adv. Denver, 1973-76, advanced through grades to lt. col. Hurlburt Field, Fla., 1976-78, asst. staff judge adv. Zaragoza, Spain, 1978-81, chief cir. trial counsel Washington, 1981-83; chief Constitutional Torts Br. Civil Litigation, 1983-85; resigned USAF, 1985; asst. gen. counsel Chrysler Motors Corp., Highland Park, Mich., 1985-90; asst. gen. counsel comml. affairs, chief patent counsel Chrysler Corp., Auburn Hills, 1990-96; v.p., gen. counsel Daimler Chrysler Svcs. N.Am. LLC, Southfield, 1997—. Mem. governing com. Conf. on Consumer Fin. Law. Staff Judge Adv. USAFR, 927 Air Refueling Group, Selfridge Air NG Base, Mich., 1985-94. Mem. Am. Fin. Svcs. Assn. (bd. dirs.). Office: Daimler Chrysler Svcs N Am LLC CIMS 465-25-02 27777 Franklin Rd Southfield MI 48034-2337 Business E-Mail: cat8@daimlerchrysler.com.

TARAVELLA, ROSIE, actress, writer; b. Mt. Morris, N.Y., July 8, 1962; d. Charles James and Carrie (Sardinia) T.; m. Michael Anthony Valerio, May 27, 1994. BA in Dramatic Arts, San Diego State U., 1985. Entertainment dir., staff trainer Johnny Rockets, Inc., L.A., 1986-98; staff writer, voice talent The Rick Dees Weekly Top 40, 1990-93; freelance writer, voice talent The Premiere Comedy Radio Network, 1992-98; actress, 1992—; writer L.A. Times Calendar Live! Website, 1999—. Theatrical prodr., cons. The Tamarind Theater, L.A., 1993-94. Author (plays) Rose's Bowl-O-Rama, 1992, The Wives, 1994, Pa's Funeral, 1995; (with Diane Kelber) Blue Grass, 1999; screenwriter: Carlo's Wake, 1997; actress (commls.) AT&T, Dial, Radio Shack and others, 1992—, (TV) Who's the Boss, Ellen, Full House, Married with Children, The Client, Almost Perfect, Brooklyn South, Sinatra, Norma Jean and Marilyn, George and Leo, Roswell; actress, co-writer (film) Carlo's Wake, 1999. Pres. Boards and Boards Prodns., North Hollywood, Calif., 1994-98. Recipient Am.'s Best Sitcom Writing Competition award, 1999. Mem. Mus. TV and Radio, KCRW-Nat. Pub. Radio, Am. Soc. Prevention Cruelty Animals, Nat. Geog. Soc. Democrat. Roman Catholic. Avocations: cooking, genealogy, Internet, film and TV history. Office: Broads and Boards 12828 Victory Blvd Ste 334 North Hollywood CA 91606-3013

TARBI, WILLIAM RHEINLANDER, secondary education educator, curriculum consultant, educational technology researcher; b. San Bernardino, Calif., Feb. 23, 1949; s. William Metro and Sue (Rheinlander) T.; m. Jenny Workman, Apr. 10, 1980 (div. 1985); m. Michele Hastings, July 4, 1990; children: Amy, Melissa. AA, Santa Barbara City Coll., 1969; BA in History, U. Calif., Santa Barbara, 1976; MA, U. Redlands, 1992. Cert. secondary edn. social studies tchr., Calif. Reporter AP, Santa Barbara, Calif., 1976-80, UPI, Seattle, 1980-85, Golden West Radio Network, Seattle, 1980-85; tchr. Redlands (Calif.) Unified Sch. Dist., 1988—. Cons. IMCOM, Redlands, 1985—. Mrm. E Clampus Vitus, Phi Delta Kappa. Avocations: painting, photography, writing, gardening, fencing.

TARBOX, GURDON LUCIUS, JR. retired museum executive; b. Plainfield, N.J., Dec. 25, 1927; s. Gurdon Ludius and Lillie (Hodgson) T.; m. Milver Ann Johnson, Sept. 25, 1952; children: Janet Ellen LeGrand, Joyce Elaine Schumacher, Paul Edward, Lucia Ann Raatma. BS, Mich. State U., 1952; MS, Purdue U., 1954; D Pub. Svc., U. S.C., 1993. Asst. dir. Brookgreen Gardens, Murrells Inlet, S.C., 1954-59, trustee, 1959-94, dir., 1963-94, pres., 1990-94. Bd. dirs. Bartlett Tree Expert Co. Chmn. Georgetown County Mental Health Commn., 1964-66; mem. exec. coun. Confedn. S.C. Local Hist. Socs., 1976-80; trustee S.C. Hall Fame, 1976, S.C. Heritage Trust, 1981-86, S.C. Mansion Commn., 1986-99. Served with AUS, 1946-48. Recipient Order of Palmetto, State of S.C., 1999, Francis K. Hutchinson medal for svc. to conservation The Garden Club of Am., 1995. Mem. Soc. Am. Foresters, Am. Assn. Bot. Gardens and Arboreta (dir. 1971-74, sec.-treas. 1982, v.p. 1983, pres. 1985-86), Georgetown County Hist. Soc. (pres. 197-74), Am. Hort. Soc., Royal Hort. Soc., Am. Assn. Mus. (coun. 1983), Southeastern Mus. Conf. (dir. 1977-80), S.C. Fedn. Museums (pres. 1974-76), Am. Assn. State and Local History, S.C. Confedn. Local Hist. Socs., Rotary (pres. 1979-80). Episcopalian. Home: 641 Crooked Oak Dr Pawleys Island SC 29585-8104

TARBUTTON, LLOYD TILGHMAN, franchise consultant; b. Easton, Md., Jan. 3, 1932; s. William Lloyd and Ethel Ford T.; m. Virginia Rachael Johnson, Nov. 1, 1952 (div. 1977); children: Gregory Alan, Kenton Lyle.; m. Layne E. Johnson, Apr. 15, 1981; 1 stepchild, C. Todd Woolston. Dr Comml. Sci. in Mktg., Pacific Western U. Grad. Realtors Inst.; cert. franchise exec., La. State U., cert. hotel adminstr. Divsn. sales mgr. Reuben H. Donnelley Corp. (advt. agy.), Norfolk, Va., 1953-58; chmn. bd., dir. Tarbutton Assocs., Inc., 1962—; founder, dir., pres., chmn. bd. Econo Lodges of Am., 1967-83; chmn. bd. emeritus Econo Lodges of Am. (formerly Econ-Travel Motor Hotel Corp.), 1983—. Co-founder, chief judge Franchising Hall of Fame, Washington, 1979-82; co-founder, chmn. Coun. Franchise Suppliers, Washington, 1986-88. Author: Franchising--The How To Book, 1986. Trustee Edn. Found. Old Dominion U., 1979-86, chmn. bd. trustees Ctr. Econ. Edn., Old Dominion U., 1983-84. Recipient Hon. Tchr. award Maury High Sch., Norfolk, 1959. Mem. Internat. Franchise Assn. (hon. life, chmn. bd. dirs., chmn. 1st Asian Symposium on Franchising, Tokyo 1978, 1st European Symposium on Franchising, Amsterdam 1978, 1st Indonesian Symposium on Franchising, Jakarta 1991), 1st Ea. Europe Franchise Symposiums (Varna, Bulgaria, 2000, inducted into Franchise Hall of Fame 2000), Internat. Councl Hotel/Motel Mgmt., Realtor's Inst. Norfolk (chmn. 1965), Internat. Sales Execs. Club (Distinguished Sales award 1957), Internat. Platform Assn., Airplane Owners and Pilots Assn., Cavalier Golf and Yacht Club, Town Point Club, Registry Resort Tennis Club, The Club at Pelican Bay. Presbyterian. Home: 7911 Grand Bay Dr Naples FL 34108-7556 Office: 700 Oriole Dr Ste 116A Virginia Beach VA 23451-4960 E-mail: ltarbutton@aol.com. *I believe the greatest assist to my progress in business and personal life came when I became more aware of the "value of self" and thus others.*

TARCA, MIHAI, economist, educator; b. Pascani, Romania, Aug. 4, 1941; s. Vasile and Ecaterina (Popoaia) T.; m. Ana Lazar, June 19, 1970; children: Viorel, Mihaela. Degree, Acad. Econ. Studies, Bucharest, 1965; Phd in Econs., Acad. of Econ. Studies, 1972. Asst. Al I Cuza U., Iasi, Romania, 1965-69, lectr. Romania, 1969-74, assoc. prof. Romania, 1974-90, prof. Romania, 1990—, chief dept. econs. Romania, 1974-91, dean faculty of econs. Romania, 1991-95. .vis. prof. U. Wis., Madison, 1975-76, U. N.C., Chapel Hill, 1976, Univ. Paris XI, 1994; fellow U. Nebr. Omaha, 1993; dir. Inst. of Enterprise Adminstrn., Iasi, 1994—, pres., 1998—. Author, editor: Statistics, 1970, Privatization and the Market Economy, 1993; author: An Introduction to Demographic Prognosis, 1974, Statistics, 1979, Statistics, 1980, The Romanian Population: Past, Present and Future Trends, 1993, Regression and Correlation, 1994, Demography, 1997, Treatise of Applied Statistics, 1998; editor-in-chief University Annales, 1976-94; contbr. articles to profl. jours. Mem. Assn. of Romanian Statisticians, Gen. Assn. of Economists, World Population Soc., Internat. Union for the Sci. Study of Population, European Assn. for Population Studies, Romanian Acad. Sci. (v.p. Iasi br. 1992-98, pres. 1998—). Home: Aleea Rozelor #9 6600 Iasi Romania Office: Univ Al I Cuza IEAI Bd Copou nr 11 6600 Iasi Romania E-mail: tarca@dragon.uaic.ro.

TARDIO, THOMAS A. public relations executive; V.p. strategic planning and other positions Columbia Pictures Industries, 1979-88; CFO, v.p. adminstrn. Rogers & Cowan, Inc., L.A., 1988-89, exec. v.p. entertainment sect., 1989-91, pres., CEO, 1991-95, co-chmn., mng. dir., 1996—2000; mng. dir. Shandwick Convergence, 1997—2000; pres. Shandwick, United States, 1998—2000; pres., COO, Weber Shandwick, Western Region , 2001—. Mem. IBM mobile computing mktg. adv. bd. Mem. bd. visitors adv. bd. Loyola Law Sch. Mem. Pub. Rels. Soc. Am., Nat. Acad. Recording Arts and Scis., Pub. Communicators L.A., Contry Music Assn. Office: Rogers & Cowan 1888 Century Park E Ste 500 Los Angeles CA 90067-1709

TARDOS, ANNE, artist, writer, composer; b. Cannes, France, Dec. 1, 1943; d. Tibor and Berthe (Steinmetz) T.; m. Oded Halahmy, Nov. 6, 1976 (div. Dec. 1979); m. Jackson Mac Low, Jan. 20, 1990; step-children: Mordecai-Mark Mac Low, Clarinda Mac Low. Attended, Akademie für Musik und Darstellende Kunst, Vienna, Austria, 1961-63, Art Students League of N.Y., 1963-69. Guest tchr. Sch. Visual Arts, N.Y.C., 1974, 87, SUNY, Albany, 1986, U. Calif., San Diego, 1990, Schule für Dichtung in Wien, Vienna, Austria, 1992—. Author: Cat Licked the Garlic, 1992, Mayg-shem Fish, 1995, Uxudo, 1999; composer: (CD) The Dik-dik's Solitude: New and Selected Works, 2002, Chance Operation: Tribute to John Cage, 1993, Open Secrets, 1993, Museum Inside the Telephone Network, 1991, (cassette) Gatherings, 1980, Songs and Simultaneities, 1985;exhibitions include Jack Tilton Gallery, N.Y.C., 1989, Mus. of Modern Art, Bolzano, Italy, 1989, Venice Biennale, 1990, Galerie 1900-2000, Paris, 1990, Mus. Modern Art, N.Y.C., 1993; author: (radio plays) Stimmen, 1986, Phoneme Dance for John Cage, 1986, Among Men, 1996. E-mail: annetardos@worldnet.att.net.

TARDUNO, JOHN ANTHONY, geophysicist, department chairman; m. Beth Tarduno. BS, Lehigh U., 1983; MS, PhD, Stanford U., 1987. Prof. geophysics Rochester (N.Y.) U., 2000—, chair, dept. earth & environ. sci., 1998—. Fellow: Geol. Soc. Am.; mem.: Phi Beta Kappa. Office: U Rochester Dept Earth and Environ Sciences Rochester NY 14627

TAREN, JAMES ARTHUR, neurosurgeon, educator; b. Toledo, Nov. 10, 1924; s. Joseph Clarence and Mary Frances (Walker) T. BS, U. Toledo, 1948; MD, U. Mich., 1952. Diplomate Am. Bd. Neurosurgery. Intern U. Mich. Hosp., Ann Arbor, 1952-53, resident in surgery, 1953-54, resident neurosurgery, 1955-57; clin. instr. U. Mich. Med. Sch., 1955-57, instr. neurosurgery, 1957-58, asst. prof., 1958-63, assoc. prof., 1963-67, prof. neurosurgery, 1967—, dir. neurobehavioral sci. program, 1975-78, assoc. dean acad. programs, 1978-87, dir. Brain Tumor Lab., 1985-88; dir. Integrated Acad. Info. Mgmt., 1988-89; dir. neuromodulation program U. Mich. Med. Sch., Ann Arbor, 1994-97. Neurosurgeon Wayne County Gen. Hosp., Eloise, Mich., 1957-71, VA Hosp., Ann Arbor, 1957-73, U.S.S. Hope (Project Hope), Peru, 1962, Ecuador, 1963, Guinea, 1965; vis. prof. Hosp. Foch, Paris, 1966-67, St. Anne Hosp., Paris, 1981, Karolinski Inst., Stockholm, 1981, Haukland Sykehus, Bergen, Norway, 1984, Gumma U., Japan, 1989, Nihon U. Sch. Medicine, Tokyo, 1990. Author, co-editor: Correlative Neurosurgery, 1969, 3rd edit., 1982; contbr. articles to profl. jours. Dep. med. examiner Washtenaw County Dept. Health, Ann Arbor, 1962-90; pres. Hawaii Youth New Leadership Forum, 2000. Active U.S. Armed Forces, 1943-46, PTO. Fellow NIH, 1953; rsch. fellow in neurosurgery Boston Children's Hosp., Peter Bent Brigham Hosp., Boston, 1955. Fellow ACS; mem. AMA, Congress of Neuro. Surgeons, Am. Assn. Neuro. Surgery, Am. Assn. Med. Colls., Am. Soc. for Stereotactic and Functional Neurosurgery, Am. Neuromodulation Soc. (treas. 1994-98, v.p. 1998-99), Royal Soc. Medicine (affiliate), Brit. Med. Soc., Internat. Assn. Study of Pain, Ferrari Club Am. E-mail: jtaren@ilhawaii.met.

TARGOVNIK, SELMA E. KAPLAN, physician; b. N.Y.C., Apr. 22, 1936; d. Harry A. and Helen (Goodstein) Kaplan; m. Jerome H. Targovnik, Dec. 2, 1961; children: Nina Rebecca, Labe Eric (dec.), Diane Michelle. BA, NYU, 1957; MD, Albert Einstein Col. Medicine, 1961. Diplomate Am. Bd. Dermatology. Intern Kaiser Found. Hosp., San Francisco, 1961-62; resident in internal medicine Bellevue Hosp., NYU Med. Ctr., 1962-63, U. Colo. Med. Ctr., Denver, 1963-64; rsch. fellow, resident in dermatology Boston U. Med. Ctr., 1964-66, mem. staff, 1968-69, NYU Med. Ctr., 1966-68; practice medicine specializing in dermatology Phoenix, 1969-98; ret. Part-time staff Carl Hayden VA Hosp., Phoenix, 1998—; mem. staff St. Joseph's Hosp., Phoenix, St. Luke's Hosp., Phoenix, Columbia Hosp., Phoenix; mem. staff Good Samaritan Hosp., Phoenix, chief divsn. dermatology, 1985-90; adj. assoc. prof. Midwestern U. Coll. Medicine, Glendale, Ariz., 1998—. Bd. dirs. ACLU, Ariz., 1973-78, 83-94, Congregation Beth El, Phoenix, 1971-75, Flagstaff Festival of the Arts, 1984-86; active Jewish Nat. Fund. Fellow Am. Acad. Dermatology, Assocs. for the Weizmann Inst. Sci., Assocs. for the Technion Inst.; mem. Am. Technion Soc. (bd. dirs. 1988—, pres. Ariz. divsn. 1990-92), Dermatology Found., Sonoran Dermatologic Soc., Southwestern Dermatologic Soc., Pacific Dermatologic Soc., Noah Worcester Dermatologic Soc., Phi Beta Kappa, Mu Chi Sigma, Pi Delta Phi, Beta Lambda Sigma. Democrat. Jewish. Home: 3706 E Rancho Dr Paradise Valley AZ 85253 E-mail: selmaderm@cox.net.

TARGOWSKI, ANDREW STANISLAW, computer information educator, consultant; b. Warsaw, Poland, Oct. 9, 1937; came to U.S., 1980; s. Stanislaw Adam and Halina (Krzyzanska) T.; m. Alicja Kowalczyk, Jan. 22, 1966 (div. 1977); 1 child, Stanislaw; m. Irmina Dura, Mar. 11, 1978; children: Agnieszka, Kubas, John. MS in Indsl. Engring., M in Indsl., Warsaw Poly., 1961, PhD in Computer Sci., 1968. Head dept. systems design Inst. Orgn. and Machinery Industry, Warsaw, 1961-64; pres. Warsaw Computer Svc. Ctr., 1965-71; sr. v.p. Bur. for Info. Tech., 1971-74; assoc. prof. Hamilton Coll., Clinton, N.Y., 1974-75; cons. Machinery Industry Ministry, Warsaw, 1976-79; prof. computer info. systems Western Mich. U., Kalamazoo, 1980-82, 85—; prof. Hofstra U., Hempstead, N.Y., 1982-84, Ea. Ky. U., Richmond, 1984-85; chmn., chief exec. officer Semantex, Systems Architects, Inc., 1988—. Chmn. Greater Kalamazoo Telecity USA Project. Author: Organization of Computer Centers, 1971, Organization of Data processing Process, 1975, Informatics, Models of Systems and Development, 1980, Red Fascism, 1982, The Architecture and Planning of Enterprise-wide Information Management Systems, 1990, The Momentary End of History, 1991, In the Pursuit of Time, 1993, Defense of Poland, 1993, Vision of Poland, 1995, Global Information Infrastructure, 1996, Enterprise Information Infrastructure, 2000, Fate of Poland and World, 2000, Informatics Without Illusion-Memoirs, 2001. Pres. Polish Tennis Assn., Warsaw, 1971-72; chair planning com. Polish Study Ctr.; chmn. steering com. Kalamazoo Telecity; bd. dirs. Polish Am. Congress, 2001; pres. World Rsch. Coun. of Poles Living Abroad, 2001;pres. Colleagues Internat., 2000-01. Mem. Assn. Info. Resources Mgmt. (v.p.), Polish Inst. Arts and Scis., U.S. Tennis Assn., YMCA. Roman Catholic. Avocations: tennis, sailing, skiing, reading. Home: 5485 Saddle Club Dr Kalamazoo MI 49009-9774 Office: Western Mich U Dept Bus Info Systems Kalamazoo MI 49008

TARIM, TUNA BEGUM, electrical design engineer, researcher; b. Izmir, Turkey; s. Muazzez and Aydin T. PhD, Istanbul Tech. U., 1999. Vis. scholar Analog VLSI Lab. Ohio State U., Columbus, 1997-1999; elec. design engr. Tex. Instruments, Inc., Dallas, 1999—. Contbr. numerous articles to profl. jours., chpts. to books. Recipient 3rd Place Best Paper award Midwest Symposium on Circuits and Systems, 1999. Avocations: singing, drawing, tennis. Office: Tex Instruments Inc 12500 TI Blvd MS 8729 Dallas TX 75243 E-mail: tarim@ee.eng.ohio-stae.edu.

TARINO, GARY EDWARD, lawyer; b. Jersey City, Oct. 3, 1951; s. Edward G. and Veronica Tarino; m. Maureen Fitzpatrick, May 9, 1987. BA summa cum laude, Rutgers U., 1973, JD, 1976. Bar: N.J. 1976, U.S. Dist. Ct. N.J. 1976, D.C. Ct. Appeals 1978, U.S. Supreme Ct. 1980, N.Y. 1982, U.S. Dist. Ct. (so. dist.) N.Y. 1988, U.S. Dist. Ct. (ea. dist.) N.Y. 1990. Assoc. Winne, Banta, Rizzi & Harrington, Hackensack, N.J., 1976-79; asst. pros. Bergen County Pros. Office, 1979-83, chief organized crime squad, 1981-83; atty. Automatic Data Processing, Inc., Roseland, N.J., 1983—, assoc. gen. counsel, staff v.p., 1994—. Pub. defender Borough of Maywood, N.J., 1978; bd. dirs. N.J. Coun. Econ. Edn., 1990—; master Sidney Reitman Employment Law Am. Inn Ct., 1995-2000. Bd. dirs. Am. Heart Assn., N.J., 1976-81, Middlesex County (N.J.) chpt., 1973-81; trustee Integrity, Inc., 1991-97; grad. Leadership N.J., 1989; cubmaster pack III Boy Scouts Am., 2000—. Recipient cert. of appreciation U.S. Treasury Dept., 1983, letter of commondation PBA, 1983, Alumni Vol. Leadership award 1st Ann. Leadership N.J., 1991. Office: Automatic Data Processing 1 A D P Blvd Roseland NJ 07068-1786

TARIO, TERRY C(HARLES), broadcasting executive; b. L.A., Aug. 28, 1950; s. Clifford Alexander and Marion Charlene (Olive) T.; 1 child; Brian Paul. Grad. high sch., Hermosa Beach, Calif., 1968. Gen. mgr. South Bay Power Tools, Hermosa Beach, 1973-76; v.p., gen. mgr. Sta. KEZJ-FM and KLIX AM-FM, Twin Falls, Idaho, 1976—; pres. Money Music, music and record pub. co., 1995—. Dir. mktg. Pet Complex, Boise and Salt Lake City, 1985-90; v.p. Admagination. Creator commls. John Lennon Meml. (Best of Yr. award 1982), Pets Unltd., 1983 (Best of Yr. award 1983), Depot Grill, 1984 (Best of Yr. award 1984), Eyecenter (Best of Yr. award 1986). Mem. adv bd. Cactus Pete's Resort Casino. Served with USN, 1968-72. Recipient Best of Yr. Pub. Svc. award, 1990. Mem. BMI, Idaho Broadcasters Assn. (Best Pub. Svc. award 1990), Advt. and Mktg.Cons. (pres.). Avocations: skiing, running, writing. Office: Stas KEZJ FM and KLIX-AM-FM 415 Park Ave Twin Falls ID 83301-7752 E-mail: terrytario@clearchannel.com.

TARIQ, MASOOD, communications executive; married; 2 children. BSEE, M in Computing Sci.; postgrad., U. N.C. Pres. Unified Product Solutions and Internat. Optical Networks; with Nortel Networks, Brampton, Canada, 1978, pres. Asia Pacific Canada. Office: Nortel Asia Pacific 8200 Dixie Rd Ste 100 Brampton L6T 5P6 Canada

TARITAS, KAREN JOYCE, customer service administrator; b. Ft. Wayne, Ind., June 5, 1957; d. George and Patricia Louise (Smith) T. BS, Purdue U., 1988; AAS, Ind. U., 1980. Cert. managed healthcare profl. Billing rep., experience analyst Lincoln Nat. Life Ins. Co., Ft. Wayne, 1974-82; customer svc. rep., underwriting asst. K&K Ins. Co., 1984-86; telemarketing mgr. Stanley Steemer Carpet Cleaner, 1990-98; svc. cons. AETNA U.S. Healthcare, 1998—2002; managed health profl. Ins. & Risk Mgmt., 2002, customer svc. rep., 2002—. Mem. Nat. Geographic Soc., Am. Mus. Nat. History, Smithsonian Instn., Nat. Womens History Mus., Purdue U. Alumni Club, Ind. U. Alumni Club, Delta Sigma Pi. Avocations: collecting music boxes, cross stitch/needlepoint. Home: 4414 Hanna St Fort Wayne IN 46806-4744

TARJAN, ROBERT WEGG, retired information services executive, part-time math teacher; b. Evanston, Ill., July 28, 1943; s. Robert David and Constance Rita (Wegg) T.; m. Elizabeth Lindner; children: Robert J., Anne Marie, Katie, Michael, Eileen. BS in Math., Loyola U., Chgo., 1965. Programmer Kemper Nat. Ins. Cos., Long Grove, Ill., 1965-67, supr., 1967-79, teleprocessing mgr., 1969-78, tech. systems mgr., 1978-81, ops. and system support mgr., 1981-85, asst. mgr. info. svcs., 1985-96, v.p. info. svcs., 1986-97. Bd. dirs. Acord, Pearl River, N.Y.; math. tchr. Loyola Acad., Wilmette, Ill., 1998-2001. Roman Catholic. Avocations: golf, travel, bridge.

TARKINGTON, STEVEN EDWARD, health services director; b. Elizabeth City, N.C., May 30, 1958; s. William Edward and Jean (Aydlett) T.; m. Lynn Gotschalk, May 9, 1981. RN, Norfolk (Va.) Gen. Hosp., 1980; BBA, Averett Coll., 1994, MBA, 1996. Staff nurse ICU Henrico Drs. Hosp., Richmond, 1980-81, asst. dir. clin. nursing, 1981-82, dir. critical care nursing, 1982-86, head nurse cardiac surgery, ICU, 1986-90; dir. Heart Transplant Svcs., 1990-92; chief nurse exec., 1992-96; clin. dir. heart transplant Henrico Drs. Hosp., Richmond, Va., 1996-97; v.p. patient care svcs., chief nursing officer Ctrl. Fla. Regional Hosp., Sanford, 1997-99, COO/chief nursing officer, 1999-2000; clin. resource mgr. Osceola Reg. Med. Ctr., Kissimmee, Fla., 2000-2001, critical care, cardiovasc. svcs. dir., 2001—02; adminstrv. dir. critical care/cardiovascular svcs. Henrico Doctors Hosp., Richmond, Va., 2002—. Nurse cons. on "Shock" video for Creative Specialist, Inc.; adv. bd. J. Sargent Reynolds C.C. Sch. Nursing, John Tyler C.C. Sch. Nursing, 1992-96, Seminole C.C. Sch. Nursing, 1997-2000, U. Ctrl. Fla. Sch. Nursing, 1999-2000; chmn. Ctrl. Va. Organ Donation Com.-Lifenet Transplant Svcs. Recipient Estelle Rankin award Med. Staff, Norfolk Gen. Hosp., 1980, Nursing Leadership award Nursing Div., Henrico Doctors' Hosp., 1989, God and County award Boy Scouts Am., 1970. Mem. ARC. Home: 12133 Ormond Dr Richmond VA 23233

TARKOWSKI, LARRY MICHAEL, town official; b. Flint, Mich., May 15, 1952; s. Lavern Joseph and Barbara Ann (Wade) T.; children: Jonathon, Logan. B in Gen. Studies, U. Mich., Ann Arbor, 1974. Supt. Warren Smith Contracting, Flagstaff, Ariz., 1979-89; dir. pub. works Town of Prescott Valley, 1989—. Chmn. No. Ariz. Coun. Govt. Transp. Bd., Flagstaff, 1990-97; mem. Ariz. Town Hall, 1997; gov. appointee State Groundwater Users Adv. Coun.; co-chair Yavapai County Water Adv. Coun.; cert. referee, soccer coach; mem. Ariz. Gov.'s Water Tech. Adv. Com., Ariz. Gov.'s Water Mgmt. Commn. Named Profl. Man of Yr., Prescott Valley Rotary Club, 1993, Man of Yr., Ctrl. Ariz. Sr. Assn., 2001. Mem. Am. Water Works Assn., Am. Pub. Works Assn. (pres. No. Ariz. br. 1995), Solid Waste Assn. N.Am., Ctrl. Yavapai Transp. Planning Orgn., Ctrl. Yavapai Assn. Govts. (chmn. tech. adv. coun.), Prescott Valley Hist. Soc., Prescott Valley C. of C., Lions (pres. 1994), Yavapai Soccer Club (coord. 1992—, bd. dirs. 1997—), Prescott Valley C. of C. (roastee), Ariz. Youth Soccer Assn. (bd. dirs.). Avocations: soccer, softball, skiing, hiking. E-mail: ltarkowski@pvaz.net.

TARLETON, LARRY WILSON, newspaper editor; b. Wadesboro, N.C., July 19, 1943; s. Harold Wilson and Martha (Roberson) T.; m. Judith Elaine Huntley, Sept. 8, 1963; children: Laurie Leigh, Larry Huntley. BA in Journalism, U. N.C., 1965. Reporter The Charlotte (N.C.) Observer, 1965-73; sports writer The Miami (Fla.) Herald, 1973-74; sports editor The Charlotte Observer, 1974-76; exec. sports editor, mng. editor, exec. editor The Dallas Times Herald, 1976-88; asst. pub. The Post and Courier, Charleston, SC, 1988—2000, pub., 2000—. Mem. Am. Soc. Newspaper Editors, S.C. Press Assn., Dallas Press Club (pres. 1988). AP Mng. editors, AP Sports Editors. Avocations: golf, travel. Home: 27 New St Charleston SC 29401-2405 Office: The Post and Courier 134 Columbus St Charleston SC 29403-4800*

TARLOV, ALVIN RICHARD, former philanthropic foundation administrator, physician, educator, researcher; b. Norwalk, Conn., July 11, 1929; s. Charles and Mae (Shelinsky) T.; m. Joan Hylton, June 12, 1956 (div. 1976); children: Richard, Elizabeth, Jane, Suzanne, David. BA, Dartmouth Coll., 1951; MD, U. Chgo., 1956. Intern Phila. Gen. Hosp., 1956-57; resident in medicine U. Chgo. Hosps., 1957-58, 62-63, research assoc., 1958-61; asst. prof. medicine U. Chgo., 1963-68, assoc. prof., 1968-70, prof., 1970-84, chmn. dept. medicine, 1969-81; chmn. grad. med. edn. nat. adv. com. HHS, Washington, 1980; pres. Henry J. Kaiser Family Found., Menlo Park, Calif., 1984-90; sr. scientist New Eng. Med. Ctr., Boston, 1990-99, exec. dir. The Health Inst., 1995-99; prof. of Pub. Health Harvard U., 1990-99; prof. of medicine Tufts U., 1990-99; dir. Tex. Inst. for Soc. and Health Rice U., Tex., 1999—. Dir. Tex. Inst. for Soc. and Health, James Baker III Inst. for Pub. Policy, Rice U. Pres. Med. Outcomes Trust, Inc., 1993—; chmn. bd., pres. Mass. Health Data Consortium, 1994-98. Served to capt. U.S. Army, 1958-61. Recipient Research Career Devel. award NIH, 1962-67; John and Mary Markle Found. scholar, 1966-71. Mem. ACP (master), Inst. Medicine of Nat. Acad. Scis. Office: Tex Program Soc & Health Rice U Baker Inst Pub Policy 6100 Main St Houston TX 77005 E-mail: atarlov@rice.edu.

TARN, NATHANIEL, poet, translator, educator; b. Paris, June 30, 1928; s. Marcel and Yvonne (Suchar) T.; children : Andrea, Marc. BA with honors, Cambridge (Eng.) U., 1948, MA, 1952; postgrad., U. Sorbonne, U. Paris, 1949-51; MA, U. Chgo., 1952, PhD, 1957; postgrad., London Sch. Econs., 1953-58. Anthropologist, Guatemala, Burma, Alaska, and other locations, 1952—; prof. comparative lit. Rutgers U., 1970-85, prof. emeritus modern poetry, comparative lit, anthropology, 1985. Vis. prof. SUNY, Buffalo and Princeton, 1969-70. Author: Old Savage/Young City, 1964, Where Babylon Ends, 1968, The Beautiful Contradictions, 1969, October, 1969, A Nowhere for Vallejo, 1971, Lyrics for the Bride of God: Section: The Artemision, 1972, The Persephones, 1974, Lyrics for the Bride of God, 1975, The House of Leaves, 1976, Birdscapes, with Seaside, 1978, The Desert Mothers, 1985, At the Western Gates, 1985, Palenque, 1986, Seeing America First, 1989, Flying the Body, 1993, Multitude of One, 1995, Views from the Weaving Mountain: Selected Essays in Poetics and Anthropology, 1991, Scandals in the House of Birds: Shamans & Priests on Lake Atitlan, 1997, The Architextures, 2000, Three Letters From The City: The St. Petersburg Poems 1968-1998, 2000, Selected Poems 1950-2000, 2002; co-author: (with Janet Rodney) The Forest, 1978, Atitlan/Alashka, 1979, The Ground of Our Great Admiration of Nature, 1978; contbg. author: Penguin Modern Poets No. Seven: Richard Murphy, Jon Silkin, Nathaniel Tarn, 1965, A.P.E.N. Anthology of Contemporary Poetry, 1966, The Penguin Book of Modern Verse Translation, 1966, Poems Addressed to Hugh MacDiarmid, 1967, Music and Sweet Poetry: A Verse Anthology, 1968, Frontier of Going: Anthology of Space Poetry, 1969, Shaking the Pumpkin, 1972, America: A Prophecy, 1973, Open Poetry, 1973, Active Anthology, 1974, Symposium of the Whole, 1983, Random House Book of Twentieth Century French Poetry, 1983, Beneath a Single Moon: Buddhism in American Poetry, 1991, American Poetry since 1950: Innovators and Outsiders, 1993; translator: The Heights of Macchu Picchu (Pablo Neruda), 1966, Stelae (Victor Segalen), 1969, Zapotec Struggles, 1993; editor, co-translator: Con Cuba: An Anthology of Cuban Poetry of the Last Sixty Years, 1969, Selected Poems (Pablo Neruda), 1970; editor Cape Edits. and founder-dir. Cape Goliard Press, J. Cape Ltd., 1967-69. Recipient Guinness prize for poetry, 1963. Office: PO Box 8187 Santa Fe NM 87504-8187

TARNEY, KAREN, organization executive; b. Milw., Apr. 18, 1940; d. Nathan and Myn (Apter) Paschen; children: Charles Green, Roberta Green Young; m. Richard Tarney, Oct. 6, 1985. BS with honors, U. Wis., Milw., 1978, MS in Nursing with honors, 1982. Tchg. asst. U. Wis., Milw., 1982, lectr., 1984; instr. Med. Coll. Wis., 1984-87; co-founder Citizens Against Drug-Impaired Drivers (CANDID). Guest spkr., workshop creater-presentor in grief and loss, wellness, prevention and community. Book reviewer; contbr. articles to profl. jours. Mem. exec. com. Nat. Safety Coun., Milw. Address: PO Box 170970 Milwaukee WI 53217-8086 E-mail: candid@candid.org.

TARNOFF, EILEEN FELDMAN, social worker; b. N.Y.C., Sept. 11, 1947; d. Murray M. and Mildred (Milstein) Feldman; m. Michael B. Tarnoff, June 14, 1970; 1 child, Adam M. BA, Nat.-Louis U., Evanston, Ill., 1969; MA in Social Work, Univ. Chgo., 1971. Lic. clin. social worker; diplomate Am. Bd. Clin. Social Workers. Dept. chmn. Nat. Louis U., Evanston, 1983-87; faculty Nat.-Louis U., 1980—; pvt. practice Highland Park, Ill., 1980—. Cons. Youth Orgn. Umbrella, Evanston, 1987-92, Glencoe (Ill.) Children's Ctr., 1982-90, others; clin. dir. SHALVA, 1996-2001; divorce mediator, 1997; lectr., cons., trainer in field. Mem. Acad. Cert. Social Workers (diplomate). Home: 861 Barberry Rd Highland Park IL 60035-3821 Office: Nat Louis Univ 2840 Sheridan Rd Evanston IL 60201-1796 E-mail: ethomemail@aol.com.

TARNOFF, JEROME, lawyer; b. June 22, 1931; s. Meyer and Anne (Soshnick) T.; children: Marcy Jane, Margery Lynne; m. Nancy Radin, 1990. AB, Syracuse U., 1952; JD, Columbia U., 1957. Bar: N.Y. 1957, U.S. Dist. Ct. (so. and ea. dists.) N.Y. 1960, U.S. Ct. Appeals (2d cir.) 1961. Ptnr. Sheldon and Tarnoff, N.Y.C., 1957-78, Feldesman, D'Atri, Tarnoff & Lubitz, N.Y.C., 1978, Baskin and Sears, P.C., N.Y.C., 1979-84, Baskin & Steingut P.C., 1984-85, Berger & Steingut, 1986-92, Morrison, Cohen, Singer & Weinstein, LLP, 1993—. Contbr. article to legal jour. Chmn. policy com. N.Y. Dem. Party, 1975-78, vice chmn. N.Y. County, 1978—, mem. nat. com., 1980-88; mem. Cmty. Planning Bd. #8, 1966-75; bd. dirs. Grand St. Settlement, 1973—, Assoc. Y's of N.Y., 1972-88. With U.S. Army, 1952-54. Recipient Disting. Svc. award NAACP, 1975, Cert. Achievement, El Diario-La Prensa, 1977. Mem. ABA, N.Y. State Bar Assn., Assn. of Bar of City of N.Y., N.T. County Lawyers, Am. Arbitration Assn. (nat. panel arbitrators), Phi Alpha Delta, Sunningdale Country Club (Scarsdale, N.Y.), Harmonie Club (N.Y.C.), Audubon, Masons. Jewish. Office: Morrison Cohen Singer & Weinstein 750 Lexington Ave New York NY 10022-1200 E-mail: jtarnoff@mcsw.com.

TARNOFF, PETER, former federal agency administrator, business consultant; b. N.Y.C., Apr. 19, 1937; s. Norman Tarnoff and Henrietta (Goldfarb) Laing; m. Daniele Oudinot, Jan. 13, 1962 (div. Oct. 1981); children: Nicholas, Alexander; m. Mathea Falco, Dec. 24, 1981; 1 child, Benjamin. Student, U. Paris, 1956-57, postgrad., 60-61; BA, Colgate U., 1958; postgrad., U. Chgo., 1958-60. Joined Fgn. Svc., Dept. State, 1961; spl. asst. to amb. Am. Embassy, Bonn, Fed. Republic Germany, 1969; trainee Nat. Sch. Adminstrn., Paris, 1970; prin. officer Am. Consulate Gen., Lyon, France, 1971-73; dep. chief of mission Am. Embassy, Luxembourg, 1973-75; dir. Office Rsch. and Analysis for Western Europe Dept. State, Washington, 1975-76, exec. sec. Dept. State, 1977-81, fgn. affairs fellow San Francisco, 1981-82; exec. dir. World Affairs Coun. No. Calif., 1983-86; pres., dir. Coun. on Fgn. Rels., N.Y.C., 1986-93; under sec. state for polit. affairs Dept. State, Washington, 1993-97; pres. Internat. Adv. Corp., San Francisco, 1997—. Office: Internat Adv Corp 2028 Green St San Francisco CA 94123-4813 E-mail: iacmail@aol.com.

TARNOPOL, MICHAEL LAZAR, bank executive; b. 1936; s. Irving and Charlotte (Weber) T.; m. Lynne Lichtenstein, June 29, 1958; children: Lisa Silverman, Lori Moore. Gen. ptnr., sr. mng. dir., also bd. dirs. Lehman Bros. Inc., 1959-75; with Bear Stearns & Co. Inc., 1975—, vice-chmn., bd. dirs.; chmn. investment banking divsn., bd. dirs. Bear Stearns Internat. Mem. pres.'s coun. Solomon R. Guggenheim Found.; vice chmn. bd. trustees U. Pa., bd. overseers Wharton Sch.; bd. overseers Meml. Sloan Kettering Cancer Ctr.; Bd. dirs. Cap Cure Found., U.S. Polo Tng. Found., Robert Steel Found., Inc. Mem. Palm Beach Country Club, Harmonie Club, East Hampton Tennis Club, Atlantic Golf Club, Quaker Ridge Golf Club, Trump Internat. Golf Club. Office: 245 Park Ave New York NY 10167-0002

TARNOVE, LORRAINE, medical association executive; b. Atlantic City, July 26, 1947; d. Leonard Robert Tarnove and Jeanne Tarnove Yudkin; m. Steven B. Friedman, June 1, 1969; children: K. Brooke, Ari-Benjamin. BA, U. Md., 1969. Pres. Lorraine Tarnove Consulting, Columbia, Md., 1985-93; exec. dir. Am. Med. Dirs. Assn. Contbr. chpt. to book. Office: AMDA 10840 Little Patuxent #760 Columbia MO 21044*

TARNOW, FREDRIC HERMAN, science educator; b. Chgo., Jan. 6, 1933; s. Harold B. and Maria (Kropp) T.; m. Beverly L. Weber, Dec. 5, 1953; children: Lillian Marie, Fredric H., LaVerne A. Kind. BS in Secondary Edn., Biology, Northeastern Ill. U., 1972; MA in Ednl. Adminstrn., Northern Ill. u., 1974. Tchr. Sch. Dist. # 54, Schaumburg, Ill., 1972-78, 85-87, chmn. sci., 1978-85; ednl. cons. North Cook Ednl. Svc. Ctr., Glenview, Ill., 1987-93; instr. Govs. State U., University Ctr., 1980—, Aurora (Ill.) U., 1990—. Adj. prof., Nat. Coll., Evanston, Ill., 1986—, vis. lectr., instructor Northeastern U., Chgo., 1989—. Contbr. articles to profl. jours. With U.S. Army, 1954-56, res., 1956-89. Recipient Presdl. award State of Ill., 1986, 87. Mem. Nat. Biology Tchrs. Assn. (elem. chmn. 1985-88), Nat. Sci. Tchrs. Assn., Nat. Coun. Tchrs. Math., Nat. Sci. Supr. Assn., Ill. Sci. Tchrs. Assn. (regional dir. 1985-87), Assn. Supervision Curriculum Devel., Assn. Sch. Sci. Math. Home: 3657 N St Louis Ave Chicago IL 60618-4225 Office: Hands-On Minds-On Learning 3657 N Saint Louis Ave Chicago IL 60618-4225

TARNOW, MALVA MAY WESCOE, post-anesthesia care nurse; b. Allentown, Pa., July 27, 1942; d. Frederick H. and Malva M. (Tharp) Wescoe; m. Donald F. Tarnow, Aug. 5, 1967; children: Dean, Elizabeth. Diploma, Bellevue Sch. Nursing, N.Y.C., 1963; BS in Hosp. Mgmt., Pacific Christian Coll., 1978. Cert. peri anesthesia nurse. Staff nurse recovery rm. Bellevue Hosp., N.Y.C., 1963-66; charge nurse recovery rm. Los Angles County Gen. Hosp., L.A., 1966-68; staff nurse post anesthesia care unit Los Robles Regional Med. Ctr., Thousand Oaks, Calif., 1968-70, 73-93; staff nurse ICU and CCU Ventura County Gen. Hosp., Ventura, 1970; charge nurse peri anesthesia care unit Granada Hills (Calif.) Community Hosp., 1989—. Mem. Am. Soc. Peri Anesthesia Nurses (Calif. alt. dir. 1990-93), Peri Anesthesia Nurses Assn. Calif. (dist. bd. dirs. 1980-84, 89-90, treas. 1984-86, v.p. 1986-87, pres. 1987-88).

TARONJI, JAIME, JR. lawyer; b. N.Y.C., Nov. 20, 1944; s. Jaime and Ruth T.; m. Mary Taronji, May 16, 1970; children: Ian A., Mark N., Nicole V. BA, George Washington U., 1972; JD, Georgetown U., 1976. Bar: Va. 1977, DC 1978, Ohio 1996. Asst. to dep. staff dir. U.S. Commn. on Civil Rights, Washington, 1972-76; trial atty. FTC, 1976-79; antitrust counsel Westinghouse Electric Corp., Pitts., 1979-81; group legal counsel Dana Corp., Toledo, 1982-88; v.p., gen. counsel Packaging Corp. Am. subs. Tenneco, Evanston, Ill., 1988-95; law v.p. NCR Corp., Dayton, 1996-99; v.p., gen. counsel, sec. Dayton Superior Corp., 1999—. Adv. bd. mem. Corp. Counsel Inst., Georgetown U. Law Ctr. Author: The 1970 Census Undercount of Spanish Speaking Persons, 1974; editor: Puerto Ricans in the U.S., 1976. Capt. M.I., U.S. Army, 1965-70, Vietnam. Mem. ABA (antitrust sect.), Am. Corp. Counsel Assn., Minority Corp. Counsel Assn., Hispanic Nat. Bar Assn. Democrat. Roman Catholic. Home: 5 Grandon Rd Dayton OH 45419-2548 Office: Ste 130 7777 Washington Village Dr Dayton OH 45459-3976 E-mail: jimtaronji@daytonsuperior.com.

TARPEH-DOE, LINDA DIANE, controller; b. Laramie, Wyo., Mar. 19, 1957; d. Leland Dean and Marilyn Lee (McClurg) Wheeler; m. Nyenpan Tarpeh-Doe, Jan. 16, 1982 (div. Nov. 1985); 1 child, Nyenpan Tarpeh-Doe II. BS in Acctg., U. Colo., 1979. CPA, Cert. Govt. Fin. Mgr. Asst. auditor First Bank Holding Co., Lakewood, Colo., 1979-80; internat. devel. intern USAID, Monrovia, Liberia, 1981-82, sys. acct. Washington, 1982-84, fin. analyst Kingston, Jamaica, 1984-88, macs coord. Washington, 1988-93, contr. Colombo, Sri Lanka, 1993-97, REDSO, Nairobi, Kenya, 1997-2000, USAID/Ethiopia, Addis Ababa, 2000—02, USAID, Indonesia, 2002—. Mem. AICPA, Assn. Govt. Accts. Democrat. Methodist. Avocations: music, reading. Home: 3851 Paseo Del Prado Boulder CO 80301-1527 Office: Am Embassy Jakarta Unit 8135 USAID FPO AP 96520-8135 E-mail: ltarpeh-doe@usaid.gov.

TARPENNING, EMILY, music educator; b. Portsmouth, N.H., Dec. 9, 1942; d. Alvie Earl and Alta Bernice (Crenshaw) Ryan; m. Bobby Gene Tarpenning, Sept. 1, 1961 (div. Apr. 1983); children: Virginia Lynn Richards, Michael Darrin. BA, Tex. Wesleyan U., 1993; MMus, U. North Tex., 1997. Tchr. piano, music theory, Bethany, Okla., 1969-72, Keller, Tex., 1972-86; tchr. piano Ft. Worth, 1986—, Tarrant County Coll., Hurst, 1993—2000, Fossil Ridge High Sch., Ft. Worth, 1998. Adj. prof. Am. Coll. Musicians, 1994—. Author: Fanny Mendelssohn Hensel: A Bridge Between, 1997; composer many piano and choral compositions. Music dir., pianist Haslet (Tex.) United Meth. Ch., 1997—, chmn. worship com., 1999; choir dir., pianist Light World Lutheran Ch., Ft. Worth, Tex., 2000-; charter mem. mental health task force First United Meth. Ch., Ft. Worth, 1993-97; state theory test designer, Tex. Music Tchrs. Assn., 2001—. Mem. Am. Coll. Musicians, Nat. Guild Piano Tchrs., Music Tchrs. Nat. Assn., Tex. Music Tchrs. Assn., Mid-Cities Music Tchrs. Assn., Ft. Worth Music Tchrs. Assn. (cert. chmn. 1997-98). Democrat. Avocations: cross-stitch, knitting, reading, crafts, painting. Home: 9048 Magnolia Blossom Trail Fort Worth TX 76131-4126

TARPGAARD, PETER THORVALD, naval architect; b. Knoxville, Tenn., Sept. 25, 1937; s. Peter Thorvald and Edith Margurite (Mees) T.; m. Judith Ann Burgess; 1 child, Andrew Christian. BS, U.S. Naval Acad.; SM mech. engr., naval engr., MIT, 1968, PhD, 1970. Spl. project asst. Office of the Chief of Naval Devel., Washington, 1970-73; profl. staff U.S. Arms Control & Disarmament Agy., 1973-76; design supr. Portsmouth Naval Shipyard, Portsmouth, N.H., 1976-79; prin. analyst Congressional Budget Office, Washington, 1979-85; mgr. submarine programs Draper Lab., Cambridge, Mass., 1985-92; prof. U.S. Naval War Coll., Newport, R.I., 1992-97; mgr. Noesis Inc., 1997—. Cons. Congressional Office of Tech. Assessment, Washington, 1991-92. Contbr. articles to profl. jours. With U.S. Navy, 1959-79. Mem. Soc. Naval Architects & Marine Engrs., Assn. for Public Policy Analysis & Mgmts., U.S. Naval Inst. Episcopalian. Home: 5 Longmeadow Ave Middletown RI 02842-5225 Office: Noesis Inc 83 Dr Marcus F Wheatland Bd Newport RI 02840 E-mail: ptarpgaard@alum.mit.edu.

TARPLEY, JAMES DOUGLAS, journalism educator, magazine editor; b. Los Angeles, May 2, 1946; Cert. tchr., Mo. BS in Edn., S.W. Mo. U., 1968, MA in English, 1972; MA in Mass Comm., Ctrl. Mo. U., 1976; PhD in Journalism, So. Ill. U., 1983. Prof. journalism Evangel Coll., Springfield, Mo., 1976-87; chmn. Sch. of Journalism Regent U. (formerly Christian Broadcasting Network U.), Virginia Beach, Va., 1987—; dir. The Wash. Grad. Journalism Ctr. Guest lectr. Cen. Mo. U., S.W. Mo. U., So. Ill. U., U. Ohio summer journalism workshops, 1976—. Youth page editor Eldon Advertiser, 1972-76, mng. editor Home Free, 1988-90, High Adventure, 1983-87, Criminal Justice Management, 1978-81, editor Ranger News, 1979-81, design and layout editor Vision Mag., 1984-87; free-lance writer, contbr. biog. entries to profl. publs.; free-lance photographer; graphic artist, copywriter Disco-Fair advt. dept., 1964-68. Exec. com. Eldon PTA, 1971-74; youth dir. Eldon Assembly of God, 1968-75; Sunday sch. supt. Cen. Assembly of God, Springfield, Mo., 1978-82; mem. Sch. Effectiveness Evaluation Team Springfield Pub. Schs., 1985-86, 86-87. Recipient Mo. Journalism Tchr. Yr. award, 1976, Cert. of Merit Columbia U., 1984, Gold Medal of Merit Columbia U. Scholastic Press Assn., 1984, Ruritan Gov.'s award, 1997, Ruritan of Yr. award Great Bridge Ruritans, 1998, 99; named Outstanding Grad., Dept. Mass Communication Cen. Mo. U. 1976; fellow U. Pa. and Freedom Found. project on press freedom, 1984, Nat. Newspaper Fund Fellow Dow Jones and U. Mo., 1975; named fellow of Scripps-Howard CCCU Washington D.C. Capstone proj., 1995, 2002, Am. Press Inst. fellow. Mem. Assn. Christian Collegiate Media (nat. exec. dir. 1995—), Coll. Media Advisers (bd. dirs., chmn. various coms., pres. citation 1981, 84-89), Soc. Coll. Journalists (pres. 1992—, exec. dir. 1983-92, pres. citation 1981, 85, 87, 90), Assn. Christian Collegiate Media (exec. dir. 1995—), Assn. Edn. in Journalism and Mass Comm., Nat. Conf. Editl. Writers (com. scholarly rsch. 1985), Soc. Newspaper Design (edn. com. 1986-88), Broadcast Edn. Assn. (intern. com. 1984), Assn. Journalism Historials, Inst. Cert. Photographers, Mo. Tchrs. Assn., Evang. Press Assn., Ruritan Outstanding Club Pres. award Holland dist. 1999), Pi Delta Kappa. Republican. Avocations: writing, photography, painting. E-mail: Doc44685@aol.com., dougtar@regent.edu.

TARPLIN, RICHARD J. federal agency administrator; b. Tarrytown, N.Y., Dec. 23, 1959; m. Linda Eisheid, Oct. 6. 1990; 2 children. BA with honors, Skidmore Coll., 1981. Legis. asst. to Rep. Leon E. Panetta State of Calif., 1982-85, mem. profl. staff senate labor and resources com., 1985-88; staff dir. subcom. children, family, drugs alcoholism U.S. Senate, 1988-93; prin. dep. asst. sec. legis. HHS, Washington, 1993-96, asst. sec. legis., 1997—2001; v.p. Timmons and Co. , 2001—. Office: Timmons & Co 1850 K St NW, Ste 850 Washington DC 20006-2213*

TARPY, ELEANOR KATHLEEN, social worker; b. Pawtucket, R.I. d. Stephen and Mary F. (Nolan) T. AB, Brown U., 1937; MS in Social Work, Boston U., 1947. Lic. social worker, Mass. Social worker R.I. Child Welfare, Providence, 1937-47, supr., 1947-49, VA Regional Office, Providence, 1949-54, VA Med. Ctr., Brockton, Mass., 1954-90; ret., 1990. Contbg. author: Current Psychiatric Therapies, vol. 4, 1964. Mem. Nat. Assn. Social Work, (past com. chair). Home: 929 Armistice Blvd Pawtucket RI 02861-3321

TARPY, THOMAS MICHAEL, lawyer; b. Columbus, Ohio, Jan. 4, 1945; s. Thomas Michael and Catherine G. (Sharshal) T.; m. Mary Patricia Canna, Sept. 9, 1967; children: Joshua Michael, Megan Patricia, Thomas Canna, John Patrick. AB, John Carroll U., 1966; JD, Ohio State U., 1969. Bar: Ohio 1969, U.S. Dist. Ct. (so. dist.) Ohio 1972, U.S. Dist. Ct. (no. dist.) Ohio 1974, U.S.

Ct. Appeals (6th cir.) 1982, U.S. Supreme Ct. 1997. Assoc. Vorys, Sater, Seymour & Pease LLP, Columbus, 1969-76, ptnr., 1977-85, 87—; v.p. Liebert Corp., 1985-87. Chmn. Columbus Graphics Commn., 1980; mem. Columbus Area Leadership Program, 1975. With U.S. Army, 1969-75. Fellow Coll. Labor and Employment Lawyers; mem. ABA, Ohio Bar Assn., Columbus Bar Assn. Office: Vorys Sater Seymour & Pease LLP PO Box 1008 52 E Gay St Columbus OH 43215-3161

TARR, CURTIS W. business executive; b. Stockton, Calif., Sept. 18, 1924; s. F.W. and Esther (Reed) T.; m. Elizabeth May Myers, 1955 (div. 1978); children: Pamela Elizabeth, Cynthia Leigh; m. Marilyn Van Stralen, 1979 (div. 1991); m. Mary Katherine Stegmiller, 1992. BA, Stanford U., 1948, PhD, 1962; MBA, Harvard U., 1950; L.H.D., Ripon Coll., 1965, Grinnell Coll., 1969, Lincoln Coll., 1980; LL.D., Lawrence U., 1974, Ill. Wesleyan U., 1980. Rsch. asst., instr. Harvard U., 1950-52; v.p. Sierra Tractor & Equipment Co., Chico, Calif., 1952-58; staff mem. 2d Hoover Commn., 1954-55; asst. dir. summer session Stanford U., 1961-62, dir., 1962-63, asst. dean humanities and scis., 1962-63, lectr. bus. sch., 1962-63; pres. Lawrence U., Appleton, Wis., 1963-69; asst. sec. for manpower and res. affairs Air Force, 1969-70; dir. SSS, Washington, 1970-72; under sec. state for security assistance, 1972-73; acting dep. under sec. state for mgmt., 1973; v.p. overseas devel. Deere & Co., Moline, Ill., 1973, v.p. parts distbn. and materials mgmt., 1973-81, v.p. mgmt. devel., 1981-83; dean and prof. Johnson Sch. Mgmt., Cornell U., 1984-89, prof. mgmt., 1989-90, dean emeritus, 1990—; vice chmn. Intermet Corp., 1992-95. Bd. dirs. Phyton Corp., Ithaca, N.Y., 1985-2002, State Farm Ins. Companies, 1985-98, Banta Corp, 1976-95, Intermet Corp., 1984-98; mem. Internat. Rsch. Coun. Ctr. for Strategic and Internat. Studies, Washington, 1989-92; adj. prof. mgmt. Emory U., 1991-93. Author: Private Soldier, 1976, By the Numbers, 1981, Youth, 1994. Trustee Inst. Paper Chemistry, 1963-69, Morehouse Sch. Medicine, Atlanta, 1994—; chmn. Task Force on Govt. Orgn., Fin. and Tax Distbn. for State Wis., 1967-69; chmn. Def. Manpower Commn., 1974-76, Ill. State Scholarship Commn., 1978-79, Quad Cities Grad. Study Ctr., 1982-84, Rep. candidate for Congress 2d Dist., Calif., 1958; trustee Am. Coll., Bryn Mawr, Pa., 1989-92; dir. Bethesda Home, Savannah, Ga., The Mighty 8th Air Force Mus., Savannah. With AUS, 1943-46, ETO. Recipient Exceptional Civilian Service medal Air Force Dept., 1970; Distinguished Service award SSS, 1975 Mem. Univ. Club (Chgo.), Cosmos Club (Washington). Methodist.

TARR, JOEL ARTHUR, history and public policy educator; b. Jersey City, May 8, 1934; s. Max Alfred and Florence (Levin) Tartalsky; m. Arlene Green, Sept. 2, 1956 (dec. June 1969); children: Michael Jay, Joanna Sue; m. Tova Brafman, Aug. 11, 1978; children: Maya Leah, Ilana Ariel. BS, Rutgers U., 1956, MA, 1957; PhD, Northwestern U., 1963. Asst. prof. Calif. State U., Long Beach, 1961-66; vis. prof. U. Calif., Santa Barbara, 1966-67; asst. prof. Carnegie Mellon U., Pitts., 1967-70, assoc. prof., 1969-72, prof. history and pub. policy, 1973-90, Richard S. Caliguiri prof. urban and environ. history and policy, 1990—, dir. program in tech. and soc., 1975-87, co-dir. program in applied history and social sci., 1978-86, acting dean Sch. Urban and Pub. Affairs, 1986, assoc. dean Coll. Humanities and Social Sci., 1988-91, acting dean Coll. Humanities and Social Sci., 1991-92, acting head dept. history, 1992-93. Author: A Study in Boss Politics, 1971; editor: Patterns of City Growth, 1974, Retrospective Technology Assessment, 1977, Transportation Innovation and Spatial Change in Pittsburgh, 1850-1934, 1978, Pittsburgh-Sheffield: Sister Cities, 1986, Technology and the Rise of the Networked City in Europe and America, 1988, The Search for the Ultimate Sink: Urban Pollution in Historic Perspective, 1996. Bd. dirs. Action Housing, Pitts., 1983; trustee Hist. Soc. Western Pa., 1993—. NEH fellow, 1969-70; grantee NSF, 1975-79, 78-80, 83-85, 95-98, NOAA, 1982-84; recipient Robert Doherty Prize for contbns. to excellence in edn., 1992, Choice Outstanding Acad. Book award, 1997. Mem. AAAS, Pub. Works Hist. Soc. (pres. 1982-83, Abel Wolman prize 1989), Orgn. Am. Historians, Pub. History Assn., Am. Soc. Environ. History, Soc. for the History of Tech., Urban History Assn. (pres. 1999). Democrat. Jewish. Home: 5418 Normlee Pl Pittsburgh PA 15217-1116 Office: Carnegie-Mellon U Schenley Pk Pittsburgh PA 15213 E-mail: jt03@andrew.cmu.edu.

TARR, RALPH WILLIAM, lawyer, former federal government official; b. Bakersfield, Calif., Sept. 29, 1948; BA, Dartmouth Coll., 1970; MPA, Calif. State U., 1973; JD, U. Calif., Hastings, 1976. Extern to assoc. justice Calif. Supreme Ct., 1976; rsch. atty. to presiding justice Ct. Appeal (5th dist.) Calif., 1976-77; assoc. Baker, Manock & Jensen, Fresno, Calif., 1977-81, dir., mem. exec. com., 1981-82; mem. adminstrv. com. Fed. Register, Washington, 1982-85; dep. asst. atty. gen. U.S. Dept. Justice, 1982-84, acting asst. atty. gen., 1984-85; solicitor U.S. Dept. Interior, 1985-89, counselor, 1989-90; pvt. practice L.A., 1990—. Home: 24011 Alder Pl Calabasas CA 91302-2394 Office: Andrews & Kurth LLP 601 S Figueroa St Ste 1725 Los Angeles CA 90017-5747

TARR, ROBERT JOSEPH, JR. publishing executive, retail executive; b. Freeport, N.Y., Dec. 7, 1943; s. Robert Joseph and Janet Christman (Laughton) T.; m. Molly Worthington Upton, Feb. 28, 1970; children: William Upton, Robert Joseph, III, David Worthington. BS, U.S. Naval Acad., 1966; MBA, Harvard U., 1973; MA, Fletcher Sch. Law & Diplomacy, 1976. Asst. v.p. corp. fin. Paine Webber Jackson Curtis, Boston, 1973-75; dir. corp. planning, then v.p., treas. Gen. Cinema Corp., Chestnut Hill, Mass., 1976-78, sr. v.p., 1978-83, exec. v.p., COO, 1983-85, pres., COO, 1985-91; pres., CEO, COO Harcourt Gen., Inc. (Gen. Cinema Corp., 1993), 1991-97. Pres., CEO, COO The Neiman Marcus Group, Inc., 1987—91, pres., bd. dirs., CEO, COO, 1991—97; bd. dirs. John Hancock Mutual Life Ins. Co., Barneys, NY, WESCO Distbn. Co., Inc.; chmn., pres., CEO HomeRuns.com, Inc., 1999—2001. Lt. USN, 1966-71. Mem. Comml. Club Boston, Brae Burn Country Club, Kiawah Island Club., Wianno Yacht Club, The Oyster Harbors Club. Home: 3 Commonweealth Ave Unit 2 Boston MA 02116-

TARRANCE, VERNON LANCE, JR. public opinion research executive; b. Harlingen, Tex., Dec. 4, 1940; s. Vernon Lance Sr. and Mary Gilmore (Rea) T.; m. Eugenia Aline McCuistion, July 2, 1966; children: Vernon Lance III, Haloway McCuistion, Kyle Rea. BA, Washington & Lee U., 1962; postgrad., U. Mich., 1971; MA, Am. U., 1973; postgrad., Harvard U., 1973-74. Dir. rsch. Tex. Rep. Com., Austin, 1964-67, Rep. Nat. Com., Washington, 1969-70; spl. asst. to dir. U.S. Census Bur., 1970-73; v.p. Decision Making Info. Inc., Santa Ana, Calif., 1974-77; pres., founder Tarrance, Hill, Newport & Ryan, Houston, 1977-92; pres., mng. dir. Gallup China Ltd., Beijing, 1993-95; vis. prof. polit. sci. Tex. A&M U., College Station, 1995-96; scholar in residence Washington and Lee U., Va., 1996; mng. dir. Burson-Marsteller, Washington, 1997-99. Bd. dirs. Gallup Orgn., 1987-92; cons. Gallup Internat. Rsch. Ctr., Lincoln, Nebr.; co-chmn. adv. adjustment panel U.S. Census. Co-author: The Ticket Splitter, 1990, Checked and Balanced, 1998; editor: Texas Precinct Votes '66, '68, '70. Fellow John F. Kennedy Inst. Politics Harvard U., 1973-74; named one of 150 People Who Influence Fed. Govt. Nat. Jour. Mag., 1986. Mem. Am. Polit. Sci. Assn., Kappa Sigma. Avocations: mountain trekking, golf, aviculture, travel.

TARRANT, R(ICHARD) J(OHN), classicist, educator; b. Bklyn., Apr. 4, 1945; s. John Joseph and Bertha (Slaney) T.; m. Jacqueline Brown, Sept. 14, 1968. BA, Fordham U., 1966; DPhil, Oxford U., 1972; AM (hon.), Harvard U., 1982. P.S. Allen jr. research fellow Corpus Christi Coll., Oxford, Eng., 1968-70; lectr. Univ. Coll., Toronto, Ont., Can., 1970-71, asst. prof. Can., 1971-74, assoc. prof. Can., 1974-79; prof. U. Toronto, 1979-82; prof. Greek and Latin Harvard U., Cambridge, Mass., 1982-87, Carl A. Pescosolido prof. Roman civilization, 1987-93, Pope prof. Latin language and Literature, 1993—, Harvard Coll. prof., 1999—, chmn. dept., 1988-94, acting dean Grad. Sch. Arts and Scis., 1995-96. Vis. Mellon prof. Inst. for Advanced Study, Princeton, 1991-92; vis. fellow Corpus Christi Coll. U. Oxford, 1992. Author: Greek and Latin Lyric Poetry in Translation: A Bibliographical Survey, 1972, Seneca, Agamemnon, 1976, (with others) Texts and Transmission: A Survey of the Latin Classics, 1983, Seneca's Thyestes, 1985; editor Phoenix: Jour. Classical Assn. Can., 1978-82, Harvard Studies in Classical Philology, 1985-88, 93-94; editorial bd. Toronto Medieval Latin Texts, 1977—, Cambridge Classical Texts and Commentaries, 1992—; advisory bd. Text: Transactions of the Soc. for Textual Scholarship, 1994—, Materiali e discussioni comitato scientifico, 2002–; contbr. articles to profl. jours. Cabot fellow, 1993-94; Marshall scholar, 1966-69. Mem. Am. Philol. Assn. (bd. dirs. 1987-89, v.p. publs. 1992-95), Cambridge Philol. Assn., Classical Assn. Can., Classical Assn. New Eng., Phi Beta Kappa. Office: Harvard U Dept Classics Boylston Hall Cambridge MA 02138 E-mail: tarrant@fas.harvard.edu.

TARRANTS, WILLIAM EUGENE, government official; b. Liberty, Mo., Dec. 9, 1927; s. Joseph Eugene and Mildred Jane (Wright) T.; m. Mary Jo Edman, Jan. 19, 1952 (div. 1981); children: James Timothy, Jennifer Lynn; m. Lorna D. Lundberg, Sept. 24, 1988; stepchildren: David Murphy, Christine Walls, Janelle McCrea. B in Indsl. Engring., Ohio State U., 1951; MS in Indsl. Engring., 1959; PhD, NYU, 1963. Registered profl. engr., Calif., Ohio, N.Mex. Instr. indsl. engring. Ohio State U., Columbus, 1958-59; asst. prof., research asso. N.Y. U., 1959-64; chief accident research div. Bur. Labor Stats., Dept. Labor, Washington, 1964-67; dir. manpower devel. div. Nat. Hwy. Traffic Safety Adminstrn., Dept. Transp., 1967-80; chief scientist Office of Program and Demonstration Evaluation, 1980-84; program analyst Office of Occupant Protection, 1984-87, program analyst evaluation staff, 1987-90, also chmn. sci. and tech. info. adv. bd., 1984-91. Instr. Johns Hopkins U., 1984-91, U. Md., 1991-92; planning and adminstrn. transp. safety mem. Transp. Rsch. Bd., NAS; cons. on safety program evaluation Indsl. Commn. Ohio, 1959; exec. com. Related Accreditation Commn., 1994—; accreditation bd. Engring. and Tech., Inc., 1994—. Contbr.: chpt. to Selected Readings in Safety, 1973, Readings in Industrial Accident Prevention, 1980; Author: chpt. to A Selected Bibliography of Reference Materials in Safety Engineering and Related Fields, 1967, Dictionary of Terms Used in the Safety Profession, 1971, Measurement of Safety Performance, 1980, Handbook of Occupational Safety and Health, 1987, also manuals and articles in field; mem. editorial bd.: Jour. Safety Research, Accident Analysis and Prevention, An Internat. Jour.; editor-in-chief: Traffic Safety Evaluation Research Rev. Trustee, ch. chmn. Evang. Covent Ch., 1976-80, 84-88, region 8 rep. to bd. trustees East Coast Conf., 1986-92. Capt. USAF, 1951-57. Recipient Founder's Day award NYU, 1963, 1st pl. Nat. Tech. Paper awards, 1961, 63, 67, cert. for outstanding performance Nat. Hwy. Traffic Safety Adminstrn., 1973, 86, Disting. Svc. to Safety award Nat. Safety Coun., 1989, Disting. Career Svc. award U.S. Dept. Transp., 1990; inducted into Safety and Health Hall of Fame Internat., 1990. Fellow Am. Soc. Safety Engrs. (dir., v.p. rsch. and tech. devel., pres. 1977-78, chmn. acad. accreditation coun. 1978-97, chmn. profl. and ednl. stds. com. 1997—, fellow rev. bd. 1980-88, Pres.'s award 1996); mem. AAAS, Am. Soc. Safety Rsch. (trustee), Am. Inst. Indsl. Engrs., Human Factors Soc., System Safety Soc., Evaluation Rsch. Soc., Vets. of Safety, Am. Nat. Stds. Inst. (stds. com.), Soc. for Risk Analysis, Nat. Safety Coun. (chmn. rsch. projects com. 1973-78, exec. com. indsl. conf. 1977-78, Disting. Svc. award 1989), Alpha Pi Mu, Kappa Delta Pi. Mem. Evangelical Covent Ch. (trustee, ch. chmn. 1976-80, 84-88). Home: 606 Woodsmans Way Crownsville MD 21032-2317 Office: 400 7th St SW Washington DC 20590-0001 *We often look with awe at the successful person, much as we admire a well designed structure or a beautiful painting. Behind the finished product usually lies exhaustive effort, frustration, disappointment, and even failure which is obscured by the glow of accomplishment. Success is achieved by some ability, lots of hard work, perserverance, courage of convictions, help and support from others, a desire to reach a goal, self-discipline, and considerable personal sacrifice as we make choices concerning the use of our limited resources. The ability to bounce back from adversity is crucial. Most important of all is the strength and insight gained through prayer and the willingness to permit your life to be guided by Christian faith.*

TARRO, GIULIO, virologist; b. Messina, Italy, July 9, 1938; s. Emanuele and Emanuela (Iannello) T. MD, U. Naples, 1962, postgrad. in Nervous Diseases, 1968, PhD in Virology, 1971; postgrad. in Med. and Biol. Scis., Roman Acad., 1979; hon. degree in Medicine, U. Pro Deo, Albany, N.Y., 1989; hon. degree in immunology, St. Theodora Acad., N.Y., 1991; hon. degree in bioethics, Constantinian U., Cranston, R.I., 1996. Asst. in med. pathology Naples U., Italy, 1964-66; rsch. assoc. divsn. virology and cancer rsch. Children's Hosp., Cin., 1965-68; asst. prof. rsch. pediat. U. Cin. Coll. Medicine, 1968-69; rsch. fellow Nat. Rsch. Coun., Naples, 1966-74, rsch. chief, 1974; prof. oncologic virology Coll. Medicine U. Naples, 1971-85, prof. microbiology and immunology Sch. Specialization, 1972—; chief divsn. virology D. Cotugno Hosp. for Infectious Diseases, Naples, 1973—, head dept. diagnostic labs A.O., 2002—, head dept. diagnostic labs, 2002—; dean faculty natural and phys. scis. Nobile Accademia di Santa Teodora Imperatrice, Capua, Italy, 1993—; head dept. medicine Naples People U., 2000—. Sr. scientist Nat. Cancer Inst. Frederick (Md.) Ctr., 1973; project dir. Nat. cancer Inst., Bethesda, Md., 1971-75; edn. min. rep. Zool. Sta., Naples, 1975-79; cons. Italian Pharmacotherapic Inst., Rome, 1980-98; pres. De Beaumont Bonelli Found. for Cancer Rsch., Naples, 1978—, nat. com. on bioethics, 1995-98; sci. coord. extracorporeal hyperthermia in HCV patients First Circle Med., Mpls., 2000—. Author: Virologia Oncologica, 1979, Patologia dell'AIDS, 1991, Con il Cancro si PuÓ Vivere, 1992, AIDS Cosa Possiamo Fare Cosa Dobbiamo Sapere, 1994, Pocket File Research Collection, 1997, Pocket File Research Collection, 5th edit., 2002, To Prevent Is To Win, 1998, Bioethics and Culture of Prevention, 2001; editor-in-chief: Internat. Jour. Clin. Investigation, 2000—; contbr. over 350 articles to profl. jours. Pres. Sci. Cultural Com., Torre Annunziata, Italy, 1984, Tumor Prevention Assn., Rome, 1984; mem. acad. senate Constantinian U., Providence, 1990, U. Pro Deo, N.Y., 1994; hon. acad. U. Sancti Cyrilli, Valletta, Malta, 2001; mem. UNESCO-Hebrew U. Jerusalem Internat. Sch. of Molecular Biology and Microbiology. Maj. Italian Navy, 1982-84, lt. col., 1993-95. Decorated comdr. Nat. Order of Merit, Star of Europe, knight grand cross Sovereign Constantinian Order St. George, gt. officer Italian Republic; recipient Internat. Lenghi award Lincei Acad., 1969, Gold Microscope award Italian Health Min., 1973, Knights of Humanity award Internat. Register of Chivalry, Malta, 1978, gold medal of Culture, Pres. of Italian Republic, 1975, Culture award, 1985, 1st prize in Biomed. Rsch., Italian Acad. Arts and Scis., 1987, Castello di Pietrarossa award, Italy, 1991, gold Cesare award Padova, 1991, 20th Century award in Medicine, 1994, Gold Little Horse, Transnat. European Fedn., Rome 1996, Man of Yr. award Am. Biog. Inst., 1998, 2000, King Manfredi award Manfredonia, 1999, Equestris Ordinis S. Sepulcri of Jerusalem, Rome, 1999, Gold medal of Health Pres. of Italian Republic, 1999. Fellow: AAAS; mem.: UNESCO, European Soc. Clin. Virology, Internat. Sch. for Molecular Biology and Microbiology, N.Y. Acad. Scis., Nat. Order Journalists, AIDS Soc. Asia and the Pacific, Assn. Res. Prevention of Cancer (sci. com. 1995), Italian Assn. Viral Study and Rsch. (pres. 1995—), Italian Soc. Immuno-Oncology (v.p. 1975—, pres. 1990—), Internat. League Drs. for Abolition of Vivisection (pres. 1992—), Internat. Assn. Leukemias, Am. Assn. Cancer Rsch., Am. Soc. Microbiology, Rotary, Lions (pres. Pompei chpt. 1987—89, vice gov. dist. 1991—92, pres. com. fight cancer 1992—94, pres. com. sci. and life 1994—95, pres. com. fight drug addiction and AIDS 1995—97, pres. com. transplant and donations 1998—99, pres. com. oncology 2000—, Melvin Jones fellow 1993). Roman Catholic. Achievements include patents in field; discovery of RSV virus in infant deaths in Naples and of tumor liberated protein as a tumor associated antigen, 100 kilodalton protein overexpressed in lung tumors and other epithelial adenocarcinomas. Home: 286 Posillipo 80123 Naples Italy Office: A O D Cotugno Hosp 54 Quagliariello 80131 Naples Italy E-mail: gitarro@tin.it.

TART, CHARLES THEODORE, psychologist, educator; b. Morrisville, Pa., Apr. 29, 1937; s. Charles Samuel Tart and Alma Mathilda Pfleger; m. Judith Ann Bamberger, Feb. 11, 1958; children: Catherine Lucinda Tart Walker, David Theodore. Student, MIT, 1955-57; BA in Psychology, U. N.C., 1960, MA in Psychology, 1962, PhD in Psychology, 1963. Diplomate in exptl. hypnosis Am. Bd. Examiners Psychol. Hypnosis. Radio engr. various comml. broadcasting stas., 1955-59; rsch. asst. Round Table Found., Glen Cove, Maine, 1957; rsch. asst. psychophysiology lab. Duke U., 1958-60; tchg. asst. U. N.C., 1960-61, rsch. asst., 1961; lectr. in psychology Stanford U., 1964-65; instr. in psychiatry Sch. Medicine U. Va., 1965-66; prof. psychology U. Calif., Davis, 1966-94, prof. emeritus, 1994—; sr. rsch. fellow Inst. Noetic Scis., Sausalito, Calif., 1987—; prof. psychology Inst. Transpersonal Psychology, Palo Alto, 1994—. Cons. SRI Internat., 1977-78; vis. prof. East-West psychology Calif. Inst. Integral Studies, San Francisco, 1994-95; disting. vis. prof., Bigelow chair consciousness studies U. Nev., Las Vegas, 1997-98. Author: Altered States of Consciousness, 1969, On Being Stoned: A Psychological Study of Marijuana Intoxication, 1971, Transpersonal Psychologies, 1975, States of Consciousness, 1975, (with P. Lee, R. Ornstein, D. Galin and A. Deikman) Symposium on Conciousness, 1975, Learning to Use Extrasensory Perception, 1976, Psi: Scientific Studies of the Psychic Realm, 1977, (with H. Puthoff and R. Targ) Mind at Large: Institute of Electrical and Electronic Engineers Symposia on the Nature of Extrasensory Perception, 1979, Waking Up: Overcoming the Obstacles to Human Potential, 1986, Open Mind, Discriminating Mind: Reflections on Human Possibilities, 1989, Living the Mindful Life, 1994, Body Mind Spirit: Exploring the parapsychology of Spirituality, 1997, Mind Science: Meditation Training for Practical People, 2000; editor: Archives of Scientists' Transcendent Experiences. Bd. advisors Albert Hoffman Found., Ctr. for Study of Personality and Spirituality; mem. adv. bd. Forge Inst. for Spirituality and Social Change, Internat. Transpersonal Ctr. USPHS rsch. fellow U. N.C., 1961-63, Stanford U., 1963-65; recipient Elmer and Alyce Green award Internat. Soc. for Study of Subtle Energies and Energy Medicine, 1994, Disting. Sci. Contbns. award APA, 2000. Mem. Acad. Religion and Psychical Rsch. (adv. coun.), Am. Soc. Psychical Rsch., Internat. Assn. for Near-Death Studies, Multidisciplinary Assn. for Psychedelic Studies, Parapsychol. Assn. (Outstanding Career award 1999), Soc. for Sci. Exploration. Avocations: hiking, camping, meditation. Office: Inst Transpersonal Psychology 744 San Antonio Rd Palo Alto CA 94303-4632 E-mail: cttart@ucdavis.edu.

TARTAGLIA, RICHARD V. priest; b. White Plains, N.Y., Nov. 6, 1946; s. Valentine Tartaglia and Louise M. DiPopolo. BA, St. Mary's Coll., St. Mary, Ky., 1968; MDiv, Mt. St. Mary's Seminary, Emmitsburg, Md., 1972. Ordained priest St. John the Bapt. Cathedral, 1972. Deacon St. Clement Ch., Dover, NJ, 1971—72; assoc. pastor St. Andrew Ch., Clifton, 1972—73, Holy Family Ch., Forham Park, 1973—74, St. Mary Ch., Denville, 1974—. Advisor Juvenile Conf. Com., Denville, 1977—87. Mem.: KC (chaplain 1975—). Roman Catholic. Avocations: photography, tennis, baseball, electronics, military history. Home: 15 Myers Ave Denville NJ 07834 Office: St Marys Ch 15 Myers Ave Denville NJ 07834

TARTAGLIONE, CHRISTINE MARGARET, state legislator; b. Phila., Sept. 21, 1960; AS, Pierce Jr. Coll. From legal asst. to sr. exec. asst., Phila.; mem. Dist. 2 Pa. Senate, Harrisburg, 1994—; bus. rep. United Food and Comml. Workers Union, Phila. Chair., Democratic Party of Pennsylvania. Mem. Assn. of State Dem. Chairs. Office: State Legislature Rm 458 Main Capitol Bldg Harrisburg PA 17120 also: 1061 Bridge St Philadelphia PA 19124-1824*

TARTELL, ROBERT MORRIS, retired dentist; b. Bronx, N.Y., June 22, 1926; s. Julius and Ida (Saunders) Tartell; m. Lottie Haid Schachter, June 12, 1948; children: Ross Howard, Marc Sorrel, Adam Ethan(dec.). BA, N.Y.U., 1945, DDS, 1948. Lic. dentist N.Y. V.p., dir. Medden, Inc., Valley Stream, N.Y., 1957-71; mng. ptnr. Profl. Investors, N.Y.C., 1957-91; pres., dir. Roberts Adv. Svc., Inc., 1957-91; dir. postgrad. edn. Am. Soc. Study of Orthodontics, 1971-72; mng. ptnr. RBT Co., Elmsford, N.Y., 1987-91; v.p., bd. dirs. Sport World of Am. Inc., West Chester, 1992-94;, 1995. Prodr.: Gilbert and Sullivan Yiddish Light Opera Co., 1980—, (cassette and CD recs.): Der Yiddisher Pinafore, 1994—, Der Yiddisher Mikado, 1995—. Pres. West Hempstead Sch. Commn. League, 1968—69; dir., founder West Hempstead Scholarship Fund, 1970—71. 1st lt. U.S. Army, 1952—54, Panama. Mem.: ACLU, N.Y. Acad. Scis., 1st Dist. Dental Assn., ADA, League for Yiddish, Gen. Semantics Inst., Common Cause, Gallatin, Mason, Mensa. Jewish. Home: 690 Hawthorne St West Hempstead NY 11552-3112 E-mail: gnsyiddish@aol.com.

TARTER, CURTIS BRUCE, physicist, science administrator; b. Louisville, Sept. 26, 1939; s. Curtis B. and Marian Turner (Cundiff) T.; m. Jill Cornell, June 6, 1964 (div. 1975); 1 child, Shana Lee; m. Marcia Cyrog Linn, Sept. 6, 1987. BS, MIT, 1961; PhD, Cornell U., 1967. Tchg. asst. Cornell U., Ithaca, N.Y., 1961-63, rsch. asst., 1964-67; physicist Lawrence Radiation Lab., Livermore, Calif., summers 1962, 63; staff mem. theoretical physics divsn. U. Calif., Lawrence Livermore Nat. Lab., 1967-69, group leader macroscopic properties of matter, 1969-71, assoc. divsn. leader, 1971-74, group leader opacities, 1972-78, divsn. leader, 1974-84; dep. assoc. dir. for physics Lawrence Livermore Nat. Lab., 1984-88, assoc. dir. for physics, 1988-94, dep. dir., 1994; dir., 1994—. Sr. scientist Applied Rsch. Labs. Aeronutronic divsn. Philco-Ford Corp.; cons. Hertz Found., 1970—, field com. study on astronomy in the 80's, NRC, 1980; mem. Army Sci. Bd., Washington, 1989-96; adj. prof. dept. applied sci., U. Calif., Davis, 1999; mem. Calif. Coun. on Sci. and Tech., 1996—, Pacific Coun. on Internat. Policy, 1998, lab. opers. bd. DOE, 1998—, Nuclear Energy Rsch. Adv. Bd., 1999—, Coun. Fgn. Rels., 1999—. Contbr. numerous articles to profl. jours. Recipient Roosevelts Gold Medal award for sci. Fellow Am. Phys. Soc.; mem. AAAS, Am. Astron. Soc., Internat. Astron. Union. Republican. Avocations: golf, squash, bridge. Home: 676 Old Jonas Hill Rd Lafayette CA 94549-5214 Office: Lawrence Livermore Nat Lab PO Box 808 Livermore CA 94551-0808 E-mail: tarter1@llnl.gov.

TARTER, FRED BARRY, advertising executive; b. Bklyn., Aug. 16, 1943; s. Irving and Edna (Kupferberg) T.; m. Lois; children: Scott Andrew, Heather Michelle, Megan Elizabeth. BS, CCNY, 1966. Pres. Jamie Publs. Hootenanny Enterprises, Inc., 1962-65; mdse. dir. Longines Symphonette Soc., 1965-67; with Universal Communications, Inc., N.Y.C., 1967—, pres., CEO, 1969-74; exec. v.p. Deerfield Communications, Inc., 1974-87, pres., CEO, 1977-88; pres. Deerfield Books, Inc., 1988-89; pub. S.E.W. mag., 1977-88; pres. The Rainbow Group Ltd., 1988—; chmn. Stagebill Mag., 1997-2001; pres., CEO The Lakeside Group of Cos., 2001—; chmn. The Telephone Co. LLC , 2001—. Bd. dirs. Caribbean Internat. News Corp., Lakeside Group, Inc., Boardwalk Entertainment, Ltd.; chmn. Stagebill Enterprises, LLC, 1997—2001; vice chmn. Affinity Comm., Inc., 1997—2001; pres., CEO The Telephone Co. LLC; exec. prodr. Joanne Carson's VIP's Miss Am. Teenager Pageant, 1972—73; pres. The Programme Exch., U.K. Ltd.; prodr. Spenser Judas Goat, 1995, Ceremony, 1996, Wounded Heart, 1996, Lover's Leap, 1996, Hearts Adrift, 1995, Marriage Counselor, 1994, Spenser: Pale Kings & Princes, 1995, Spenser: A Savage Place, 1995, Reasons of the Heart, 1996. Mem. Friars Club, The Reform Club (London), Met. Club (N.Y.). Home: 578 Westport Tpke Fairfield CT 06430-1670 Office: The Lakeside Group Ltd 210 E 39th St New York NY 10016-2754 E-mail: ftarter@lakesideglobal.com. *An integral part of success is the capacity for failure. Persistence, combined with responsibility, has proven to be the winning combination time and again.*

TARTER, JAMES GORDON, chemistry educator; b. San Angelo, Tex., Dec. 21, 1954; s. Delbert Gordon and Margaret Watkins Tarter; m. Victorija Dalia Laucius, July 17, 1982; children: James, Nathan, Aaron, Kara. PhD, Ariz. State U., 1981. Cert. profl. chemist. Asst. prof. chemistry U. North Tex., Denton; dir. lab. svcs. TALEM, Inc., Ft. Worth, 1989-94; assoc. prof., chair phys. sci. dept. Coll. So. Idaho, Twin Falls, 1995—. Vis. assoc. prof. chemistry Tex. Wesleyan U., Ft. Worth, 1994-95. Editor: Ion Chromatography, 1987. Asst. scoutmaster troop 200 Boy Scouts Am., Twin Falls, 1999-2001; mentor Twin Falls Sch. Dist., 1996-2001. Recipient Outstanding Acad. Faculty award Coll. So. Idaho Found. and 1st Security Bank of Idaho, 1999-2000. Fellow Am. Inst. Chemists. Office: U So Idaho PO Box 1238 Twin Falls ID 83303-1238 Office Fax: (208) 736-2136. E-mail: jimtarter@yahoo.com., jtarter@csi.edu.

TARTER, MICHAEL ERNEST, biostatistician, educator; b. Bronx, N.Y., Dec. 20, 1938; s. William Tarter and Frieda Browdy; m. Orna Benzenburg, Aug. 30, 1975; children: Douglas, Robin. BA in Math., UCLA, 1959, MA in Math., 1961, PhD in Biostats., 1963. Asst. prof. U. Mich., Ann Arbor, 1964-66, assoc. prof., 1967, U. Calif., Irvine, 1968-70, Berkeley, 1970-76, prof., 1977—. Author books and articles; editor: Jour. Am. Statis. Assn. (screening editor for applications 1971-80). Fellow Am. Statis. Assn. (chmn. com. resources biometrics sect. 1981—, editorial bds. computational stats. and data analysis 1983-86, biometrics 1976-84, stats. 1977-97). Office: U Calif Sch Pub Health Dept Biomed Environ Health Scis 140 Warren Hall Berkeley CA 94720-7360 E-mail: Tarter@uclink@Berkeley.edu.

TARTER, RONALD LEWIS, urban planner, educator; b. Somerset, Ky., Dec. 19, 1947; s. Oral Lee and Alta Marie Tarter; m. Em Thi Tarter, Dec. 14, 1971; children: Kim A.T., David Michael, Linda Marie. BA in Regional Planning, Ea. Ky. U., 1974, MA in Geography, 1977, postgrad. Transp. planner Ky. Dept. Transp., Frankfort, 1975, Lake Cumberland Area Devel. Dist., Russell Springs, 1976—82, regional planner, 1983—91, planning dir., 1991—. Transp. advisor Appalachian Devel. Coun., Berea, Ky., 1977—80. Author: The God Theory, 2001. With USN, 1968—72. Mem.: Am. Inst. Cert. Planners,

Am. Planning Assn., Masons. Avocations: gardening, fishing, guitar, jogging, Karate. Home: 918 Winding Ridge Dr Somerset KY 42503 Office: Lake Cumberland Area Devel Dist 2384 Lakeway Dr Russell Springs KY 42642

TARTTER, PAUL IAN, breast surgeon, educator; b. Edinburgh, Scotland, Aug. 21, 1951; came to U.S., 1956; s. Jean Royal and Jean (Walker) T.; m. Vivien Carol Rothman, Oct. 13, 1972; children: Eric Walter, Alexander Charles. BS in Biology, Brown U., 1973, MD, 1977. Resident in surgery Mt. Sinai Med. Ctr., N.Y.C., 1977-82, instr. in surgery, 1982-84, asst. prof. surgery, 1984-87, assoc. prof. surgery, 1987—. Chief breast svc. Mt. Sinai Med. Ctr., 1989-98. Author: Immunologic Aspects of Blood Transfusion, 1992; co-author: Non-Palpable Breast Cancer, 1992; contbr. articles to profl. jours. Mem. AAAS, Assn. Acad. Surgery, Collegium Internat. Chirugiae Digestive, Internat. Soc. Preventive Concology, N.Y. Cancer Soc., N.Y. Met. Breast Group, N.Y. Surg. Soc., Soc. Italiana di Chirurgia et Immunobiologia, Soc. for Surg. of Alimentary Tract, Soc. Surg. Oncology, Surg. Infection Soc. Avocations: sailing, skiing. Office: 425 W 59th St Ste 7A New York NY 10019-1104 E-mail: paul_tartter@slrhc.org.

TARTZ, ROBERT SCOTT, engineering executive; b. Cin., Nov. 6, 1964; s. Ralph Kurt and Virginia Ann Tartz; m. Juliana Tirtasari, Dec. 4, 1999. BSEE, Ohio No. U., 1987; MA in Psychology, Alliant Internat. U., 1995, PhD in Clin. Psychology, 2002. Design engr. Sundstrand Aerospace Corp., Rockford, Ill., 1987—89; project engr. Geetronics, Cin., 1989—93; clin. intern Union Pan Asian Communities, San Diego, 1994—96; software/usability cons. Bizint Solutions/Naval Health Rsch. Ctr., 1994—2000; clin. intern North County Interfaith Coun. - Annex Counseling Ctr., Escondio, 1996—97, Cath. Charities Ctr. Counseling, San Diego, 1997—98; sr. software/usability engr. V2Commerce Corp, La Jolla, 1999—2000; sr. software/human factors engr. eAnywhere Tech, Inc., San Diego, 2000—01; cons. Wireless Custom Solutions, Inc., 2001—. Rsch. cons. Saybrook Inst., San Francisco, 1994—, MythSeeker Inst., L.A., 1998—; presenter in field. Contbg. author: book A Rainbow that Trancends Forever, 2002; contbr. articles to profl. jours. Mem.: ACM - Computer-Human Interaction (SIGCHI), Applied Exptl. and Engring. Psychology, wUsability Professionals' Assn., Assn. Computing Machinery, APA. Avocations: lapidary, drums, silversmithing, goldsmithing, rockhounding. Home: 4218 Iowa St San Diego CA 92104 Personal E-mail: rtartz@aol.com.

TARULLI, DONNA MARIE, healthcare industry consultant; b. N.Y.C., May 9, 1951; d. Dominick and Rosalie Meo T. BSN, Point Loma Coll., 1975; MSN, UCLA, 1979, postgrad., 1981. RN, MN. Clin. nurse II, med. div./med.-surgical oncology UCLA Hosps. and Clinics, 1975-77; coord./nurse oncologist, Dept. Nursing, Ob-Gyn Cedars-Sinai Med. Ctr., L.A., 1977-78, nursing supr., 1978-79; clin. nurse specialist, Dept. Nursing/Surgical Div. UCLA Hosps. and Clinics, 1979-81; cons., lectr. Nat. Ctr. Continuing Edn., Roseville, Calif., 1979-81; assoc. dir., Dept. Risk Mgmt. Cedars-Sinai Med. Ctr., L.A., 1981-87; founding ptnr., exec. dir. MedLaw, Inc., 1981—; cons., lectr. Profl. Ednl. Systems, Inc., Eau Claire, Wis., 1988-93; cons. O'Mara and Assocs., L.A., 1988-91; adminstrv. dir. The Paris Group, Marina Del Rey, Calif., 1996—. Presenter seminars in field; mem. Risk Mgmt. Adv. Panel to Joint Commn., 1986. Mem. Am. Soc. Healthcare Risk Mgmt., So. Calif. Assn. Health Care Risk Mgmt.(pres. 1985-86, bd. dirs. 1986-87, 87-88), Sigma Theta Tau.

TARUN, ROBERT WALTER, lawyer; b. Lake Forest, Ill., Sept. 1, 1949; s. Donald Walter and Bonnie Jean (Cruickshank) T.; m. Helen J. McSweeney, May 1, 1987; children: Abigail Esch, Tyler Vincent, Parker Donald, Aimée Dakota. AB, Stanford U., 1971; JD, DePaul U., 1974; MBA, U. Chgo., 1982. Bar: Ill. 1974, Calif. 1975, U.S. Dist. Ct. (no. dist.) Ill. 1974, U.S. Dist. Ct. (we. dist.) Ark. 1986, U.S. Dist. Ct. (so. dist.) Ind. 1995, U.S. Dist. Ct. (no. dist.) Calif. 1995, U.S. Dist. Ct. (ea. dist.) Mich. 1996, U.S. Dist. Ct. (ea. dist.) Wis. 2000, U.S. Dist. Ct. (ctrl. dist.) Ill. 2001, U.S. Ct. Appeals (7th cir.) 1975, U.S. Ct. Appeals (5th cir.) 1992, U.S. Ct. Appeals (3d cir.) 1993, U.S. Ct. Appeals (Fed. cir.) 1995, U.S. Ct. Appeals (9th and 11th cirs.) 1996, U.S. Supreme Ct. 1978. Asst. atty. gen. State of Ill., Chgo., 1974-76; asst. U.S. atty. U.S. Dept. Justice, 1976-79, dep. chief criminal div., 1979-82, exec. asst. U.S. atty. no. dist. Ill., 1982-85; ptnr. Reuben & Proctor, 1985-86, Isham, Lincoln & Beale, Chgo., 1986-88, Winston & Strawn, Chgo., 1988—. Lectr. in law U. Chgo., 2001—; adj. prof. Northwestern U. Sch. Law, 1999—2001, lectr. criminal law parctice, 2000—01; instr. Atty. Gen.'s Advocacy Inst., Washington, 1980—85, Nat. Inst. Trial Advs., 1990. Author (with Dan K. Webb): Corporate Internal Investigations, 1993—2002. Bd. dirs. Chgo. Ctrl. Area Com., 1994—. Fellow Am. Coll. Trial Lawyers (mem. fed. criminal procedure com. 1993—, admission to fellowship com. 1997-2000); mem. ABA (white collar crime inst. 1997—, planning com.), Bar Assn. San Francisco, Chgo. Bar Assn., Nat. Assn. Criminal Def. Lawyers, U. Chgo. Grad. Sch. Bus. Alumni Assn. (bd. dirs. 1986), Racquet Club, Wong Sun Soc. (San Francisco), Kenilworth Club, H.O.G. (Black Hills chpt.), Chgo. Stanford Assn. Presbyterian. Avocations: architecture, screenplays, forensic science. Office: Winston & Strawn 35 W Wacker Dr Ste 4700 Chicago IL 60601-1614 Home: 219 Leicester Rd Kenilworth IL 60043-1244

TARUTIS, WILLIAM JOHN, JR. ecology educator, wetlands scientist; b. Wilkes-Barre, Pa., Nov. 16, 1963; s. William John and Ardith (Jones) T.; m. Mary Ann Jean Trudnak, Aug. 28, 1993. BS, Wilkes Coll., 1986; MS, Pa. State U., 1989, PhD, 1993. Rsch. asst. Pa. State U., Univ. Pk., Pa., 1986-93; asst. prof. Wilkes U., Wilkes-Barre, 1993-97; assoc. prof. Lackawanna Coll., Scranton, 1998—, chair math./computer info. sys./sci. divsn., 2000—. Contbr. articles to profl. jours. Active Pa. Interscholastic Athletic Assn. official basketball and football. Mem. Soc. Wetland Scientists (cert. profl. wetland scientist), Ecol. Soc. Am. (cert. ecologist), Soil Sci. Soc. Am., Pa. Acad. Sci., Ind. Order Odd Fellows (past grand), Sigma Xi. Office: Lackawanna Coll Math/Comp Info Sys/Sci Div Scranton PA 18509 E-mail: tarutisw@ljc.edu.

TARVER, MARGARET LEGGETT, lawyer, forensic scientist; b. Birmingham, Ala., Mar. 7, 1942; d. Booker Thomas and Ernestine Williametta (Rutland) Leggett; divorced; children: James, Derrick. BS, Talladega (Ala.) Coll., 1962; MS, Howard U., 1966; JD, Seton Hall U., 1982. Bar: Pa., 1982, N.J., 1982, U.S. Dist. Ct. (ea. dist.) Pa., 1983, U.S. Dist. Ct. N.J., 1982, U.S. Supreme Ct. 2000. Rsch. asst.med. sch. Howard U., Washington, 1962-64; sci. cons. Bd. Edn., 1966-68; instr. Tech. Tng. Project, Newark, 1970-71; sr. learning ptnr. SUNY, Albany, 1972-74; tech. dir. N.J. State Police Lab., Hammonton, 1976—. Cons., emergency med. technician U. Medicine and Dentistry N.J., 1975. Vol. atty. Phila. Lawyers Vol. Indigent Program, 1983-2001; bd. dirs. YWCA, Paterson, N.J., 1976-81, Women's Haven Battered Women's Program, Paterson, 1976-81. Mem. ABA, N.J. State Bar Assn. (bd. dirs. minorities in the profession sect. 1990-96, jud. adminstrn. com. 1999—, by-laws com. 1999—, editor-in-chief minorities in the profession sect. newsletter 1990-95), Pa. Bar Assn., Burlington County Bar Assn., Phila. Bar Assn., Northeastern Assn. Forensic Scientists, Am. Acad. Forensic Scis. (jurisprudence sect. 1997, program co-chair ann. meeting 2000), Mid-Atlantic Assn. Forensic Scientists, N.J. Assn. Forensic Scientists (bd. dirs. 1998—), Assn. Black Women Lawyers-South Jersey (mem.-at-large 1999-2001, pres. 2001—), Talladega Coll. Alumni Assn. (pres. Phila. chpt. 1983-85). Avocations: pianist, organist, oil painting, tennis, bicycling. Home: 42 Garland Ln Willingboro NJ 08046-3012 Office: NJ State Police South Regional Lab 1101 S White Horse Pike Hammonton NJ 08037-0271 E-mail: mltarveresq@worldnet.att.net.

TARVESTAD, ANTHONY M. psychiatrist; BA magna cum laude, Winona State U., 1973; JD, William Mitchell Coll. of Law, 1977. Exec. dir. Am. Bd. Physical Medicine and Rehab. Named Super Lawyer Minn. Jour. Law and Politics, 1994. Mem. Am. Coll. Healthcare Execs., Am. Health Laywers Assn., ABA, Am. Arbitration Assn. (arbitrator), Minn. State Bar. Assn. Office: Am Bd PM&R 21 1st St SW Ste 674 Rochester MN 55902-3007*

TARZIAN, ANITA JEANNE, nurse, researcher, ethicist; b. Chgo., Apr. 10, 1962; d. George Martin and Myra Ann Tarzian; m. Janes Allen Fill, Mar. 21, 1998. BA, Knox Coll., 1984; BSN, Rush U., 1986; MSN, U. Md., Balt., 1995, PhD in Nursing, 1998. RN, Ill. Nurse Rush-Presbyn.-St. Luke's Med. Ctr., Chgo., 1986-90, 92-93; vol. U.S. Peace Corps, La Descubierta, Dominican Republic, 1990-92; rsch. asst. U. Md. Sch. Nursing, 1993-98; rsch. assoc. law and health program U. Md. Sch. Law, 1999—. Hospice nurse Vis. Nurses Assn. Md., Balt., 1994—; rsch. and ethics cons., Balt., 1998—. Elizabeth Collins Lee scholar U. Md. Sch. Nursing, 1996. Mem. ANA (sdv. bd. Ctr. for Ethics and Human Rights 2000—), Am. Soc. for Bioethics and Humanities, Hospice and Palliative Nurses Assn., Md. Nurses Assn. (co-chmn. Ctr. for Ethics and Human Rights 2000—), Md. Healthcare Ethics Com. Network (chmn. edn. com. 2000—), Sigma Theta Tau. Democrat. Avocations: travel, hiking, reading. Fax: 410-706-4045. E-mail: atarzian@juno.com.

TAS, GURAY, physicist; b. Erzincan, Turkey, Feb. 1, 1965; s. Hulusi and Naciye Tas; m. Clara Esther Castro-Ponce, July 19, 1997. PhD, Brown U., 1996. Postdoctoral rsch. assoc. U. Ill., Urbana, 1995-97, Brown U., Providence, 1997-98; mgr. advance applications Rudolph Techs., Inc., Flanders, N.J., 1998—. NATO sci. scholar Sci. and Tech. Coun. Turkey, 1989-92. Mem. AAAS, Am. Phys. Soc., Sigma Xi. Office: Rudolph Techs Inc 1 Rudolph Rd Flanders NJ 07836 Office Fax: 973-691-5480. E-mail: gtas@rudolphtech.com.

TASA, KENDALL SHERWOOD, college dean; b. Greenville, Tex., Apr. 29, 1947; s. Kenneth A. and Juanita (Holley) T.; m. Patricia Ann Langford, Mar. 28, 1969; children: Laura Ann, Heather Denise. BS, East Tex. State U., 1967, MS, 1969, EdD, 1973. Tchr. Lone Oak (Tex.) High Sch., 1969-72; prof. chemistry Brazosport Coll., Lake Jackson, Tex., 1973-97, pres. faculty assembly, 1990-91, chmn. div. Math. and Sci., 1991-97, dean ednl. programs and svcs., 1998—. Contbr. articles to sci. jours. Chmn. adminstrv. bd. 1st United Meth. Ch., Angleton, Tex., 1991-93. Mem. Nat. Coun. Instrnl. Adminstrs., Rotary. Republican. Avocations: golf, upland bird hunting, astronomy. Office: Brazosport Coll 500 College Dr Lake Jackson TX 77566-3136

TASCHNER, DANA BRADLEY, lawyer; Pvt. practice, L.A.; U.S. jud. settlement officer. Named Calif. Lawyer of Yr., 1998; recipient Congl. Svc. award, 1998. Mem.: FBA (past nat. co-chair trial and appellate practice com.), ABA (gen. practice sect., Sole Practitioner of Yr. 1998), Sons Am. Legion (Freedom in Law award 1998), Sigma Alpha Epsilon (Nat. Alumni T.H.E. award 1999). Fax: 310-552-4885. E-mail: dbtaschner@aol.com.

TASDIZEN, TOLGA, electrical engineer; b. Istanbul, Turkey, Aug. 1, 1973; s. Akin and Serap T. PhD, Brown U., 2001. Rsch. asst. Brown U., Providence, 1995-2000, postdoctoral rsch. fellow, 2000-2001, U. Utah, Salt Lake City, 2001—. Mem. IEEE. Home: Unit 1 1312 Logan Ave Salt Lake City UT 84105 Office: U Utah Rm 3169 Central Campus Dr Salt Lake City UT 84112-9205 Fax: 401-863-1157. E-mail: tolgatasdizen@hotmail.com.

TASH, MARTIN ELIAS, publishing company executive; b. N.Y.C., Jan. 24, 1941; s. David and Esther (Milch) T.; m. Arlene Sue Klein, June 23, 1962; children: Nathan, Faye, Jill. BBA, Baruch Sch. City Coll. N.Y., 1962. C.P.A. Staff accountant S.D. Leidesdorf & Co. (C.P.A.'s), N.Y.C., 1962-66; v.p. fin., dir. LMC Data Inc., 1966-71; with Plenum Pub. Corp., 1971-98, chmn. bd., pres., 1977-98; chmn. bd., pres., CEO Gradco Systems, Inc., 1990—. Office: Gradco Systems Inc 3753 Howard Hughes Pkwy Ste 200 Las Vegas NV 89109-0952

TASH, PAUL CLIFFORD, editor, publishing executive; b. South Bend, Ind., July 17, 1954; s. Robert N. and Barbara R. (Eller) T.; m. Karyn E. Krayer, Aug. 19, 1983; children: Kaley Marie, Kendyl Barbara. BA, Ind. U., 1976; LLB, Edinburgh (Scotland) U., 1978. Reporter St. Petersburg Times, 1978-83, city editor, 1983-86, metro editor, 1986-89, editor, pub. Fla. Trend Mag., 1990-91, Washington bur. chief, 1991-92, exec. editor, dep. chmn., 1992-2000, pres., editor, dep. chmn., 2000—. Bd. dirs. Times Pub. Co., Com. to Protect Journalists, Mich. Journalism Fellows, Fla. Trend Mag., Congressional Quar., Poynter Inst. Media Studies. Chmn. Fla. First Amendment Found.; mem. adv. bd. Ind. U. Sch. Journalism. Marshall Aid Commemoration Commn. scholar, 1976-78. Mem.: Tampa Bay Area Com. on Fgn. Rels., Fla. C. of C. (bd. govs.), Am. Soc. Newspaper Editors. Home: 111 Bay Point Dr NE Saint Petersburg FL 33704-3805 Office: St Petersburg Times 490 1st Ave S Saint Petersburg FL 33701-4204 also: PO Box 1121 Saint Petersburg FL 33731-1121

TASHIMA, ATSUSHI WALLACE, federal judge; b. Santa Maria, Calif., June 24, 1934; s. Yasutaro and Aya (Sasaki) Tashima; m. Nora Kiyo Inadomi, Jan. 27, 1957; children: Catherine Y., Christopher I., Jonathan I. AB in Polit. Sci., UCLA, 1958; LLB, Harvard U., 1961. Bar: Calif. 1962. Dep. atty. gen. State of Calif., 1961—67; atty. Spreckels Sugar divsn. Amstar Corp., 1968—72, v.p., gen. atty. Spreckels Sugar divsn., 1972—77; ptnr. Morrison & Foerster, L.A., 1977—80; judge U.S. Dist. Ct. (ctrl. dist.), Calif., 1980—96, U.S. Ct. Appeals (9th cir.), Pasadena, 1996—. Mem. Calif. Com. Bar Examiners, 1978—80. With USMC, 1953—56. Mem.: ABA, L.A. County Bar Assn. Democrat. Office: Richard A Chambers US Ct Appeals PO Box 91510 125 S Grand Ave Pasadena CA 91109-1510*

TASHIMA, CHRIS, actor, theatre artist; b. Cambridge, Mass., Mar. 24, 1960; s. A. Wallace and Kiyo I. Tashima. Student, U. Calif., Santa Cruz, 1978-80, UCLA, 1980-82. Dir. Cedar Grove Prodn. Co., L.A., 1996—. Actor: (play) East West Players, L.A., 1986, Berkeley Repertory Theatre, Berkeley, Calif., 1991, Celebration Theatre, L.A., 1994, Ind. TV Svc., (film) Open City Films, and Ghost Pictures, Chgo., 1997, Chrome Dragon Films, Shanghai, China, Hilo, Hawaii, 1998; set designer: (musical theatre prodn.) Into the Woods, 1992 (DramaLogue award 1992), Sweeney Todd, 1994 (Ovation award 1995); actor, dir., co-writer: (short film) Visas and Virtue, 1997 (Acad. award 1997); dir., prodr., writer, editor: (short film) Chisai Samurai, 1986. Mem. short film award selection com. L.A. Asian Pacific Film and Video Festival, 1999; film festival jurist Chilean Internat. Short Film Festival, Santiago, Chile, 1998. Recipient Theatre award L.A. Weekly Theater, 1994, Humanitarian award The 1939 Club, 1997, Cmty. award Japanese Am. Svc. Com., 1998, Asian Am. Leadership award Bridge Builder, A. Mag., 1998. Mem. SAG, AFTRA, Acad. Motion Picture Arts and Scis. (acad. awards short films awards rev. and nominating com. 1998-2000), Actors Equity Assn., Coalition Asian Pacifics in Entertainment, Visual Comms. (hon. bd. dirs. film fest 2000). Democrat. Office: Cedar Grove Prodns PO Box 29772 Los Angeles CA 90029-0772 E-mail: cedarmail@aol.com.

TASINI, MIRIAM FINDER, medical educator, psychiatrist, psychoanalyst; b. Apr. 4, 1936; MD, Albert Einstein Coll. Medicine, 1971. Instr. Harvard Med. Sch., Boston, 1975-77; prof. UCLA Med. Sch., L.A., 1977-85, assoc. prof., 1985-97, prof., 1997—. Mem.: Am. Psychoanalytic Assn. Office: 1081 Moraga Dr Los Angeles CA 90049-1620

TASKER, JOHN BAKER, veterinary medical educator, college dean; b. Concord, N.H., Aug. 28, 1933; s. John Baker and Catherine Mabel (Baker) T.; m. Grace Ellen Elliott, June 17, 1961; children: Sybil Alice, Sarah Catherine, Sophia Ethel DVM, Cornell U., 1957, PhD, 1963. Instr. Cornell U., Ithaca, N.Y., 1960-61, from assoc. prof. to prof., 1967-78; from asst. prof. to assoc. prof. Colo. State U., Fort Collins, 1963-67; prof. vet. clin. pathology, assoc. dean La. State U., 1978-84; dean Coll. Vet. Medicine Mich. State U., East Lansing, 1984-94; prof. vet. pathology Coll. Vet. Medicine/Mich. State U., 1984-95; dean, prof. emeritus Mich. State U., 1995. Cons. Ralston-Purina Co., St. Louis, 1978, Universidad Nacional P. Urena, Dominican Republic, 1980, U. Nebr., Lincoln, 1982-83 Editor: Veterinary Clinics of North America, 1976 Served to 1st lt. U.S. Army, 1958-60 Recipient Outstanding Instr. award Colo. State U. Vet. Coll., 1967; Norden Teaching award Cornell U. Vet. Coll., 1977 Mem. AVMA, Am. Coll. Vet. Pathologists (diplomate; examiner 1972-74), Am. Soc. Vet. Clin. Pathology (pres. 1971-72), Assn. Am. Vet. Med. Colls. (exec. com. 1986-91, pres. 1989-90). Avocations: reading, travel. Home: 501 Emory Ct # 303 Salisbury MD 21804 E-mail: jbt2@prodigy.net.

TASKER, MOLLY JEAN, lawyer; b. Cumberland, Md., Feb. 13, 1945; d. Samuel Paul Tasker and Peggy Evelyn Purinton; m. Richard Mark Curtis, June 7, 1985. AA, Santa Fe Jr. Coll., 1968; BA, Fla. Atlantic U., 1970; JD, Fla. State U., 1973. Bar: Fla. 1973, U.S. Supreme Ct. 1992, U.S. Dist. Ct. (mid. dist.) Fla. 1997. Atty., advisor CIA, Washington, 1974-82, asst. gen. counsel, 1983-95, chair publs. rev. bd., 1993-95; ptnr. Tasker & Stephens, PA, Indian Harbour Beach, Fla., 1996—. Bd. dirs. Brevard County Emergency Med. Svc. Found., Melbourne, Fla., Cmty. Housing Initiative, Melbourne; guest lectr. Fla. So. Coll., Lakeland, 1997-01. Exec. sec. Brevard County (Fla.) Juvenile Justice Coun., 1997—; vice-chair Brevard County Dem. Exec. Com., 1997-98; chair govtl. affairs com. C. of C., Melbourne, 1998-99. Recipient Spl. Recognition award Brevard County Legal Aid, Inc., Fla., 1997, 2000; Fulbright Travel grant Fla. State U. Ctr. for Slavic and East European Studies, 1972. Mem. AAUW, LWV, Phi Alpha Delta, Phi Gamma Nu. Lutheran. Avocations: photography, reading, tennis, boating. Home: 4050 Carolwood Dr Melbourne FL 32934-7179 Office: 244 E Eau Gallie Blvd Indian Harbour Beach FL 32937-4874

TASMAN, ALLAN, psychiatry educator; b. Louisville, Feb. 8, 1947; s. Goodman and Zelda Tasman; m. Cathy Faye Goldstein, May 24, 1970. BA in Chemistry, Franklin and Marshall Coll., 1969; MD, U. Ky., 1973. Diplomate Am. Bd. Psychiatry and Neurology. Resident in psychiatry U. Ky. Med. Sch., Lexington, 1973-74, U. Cin. Med. Ctr., 1974-76; asst. prof. psychiatry U. Conn. Med. Sch., Farmington, 1976-82, assoc. prof. psychiatry, 1982-88, prof. psychiatry, 1988-91; prof. psychiatry and behavioral scis., tenure and chmn. U. Louisville Sch. Medicine, 1991—. Editor: Annual Review of Psychiatry, Vol. ll, 1992, Clinical Challenges in Psychiatry, 1993, Less Time to Do More, 1993, Textbook of Psychiatry, 1996 (sr. editor); dep. editor Jour. of Psychotherapy Practice and Rsch. Fellow Am. Psychiat. Assn. (v.p. 1996-98, pres.-elect 1998-99, pres. 1999-00, Nancy Roeske award for excellence in med. student edn. 1991); mem. Am. Assn. Dirs. of Psychiat. Residency Tng. (pres. 1993-94), Assn. Acad. Psychiatry (pres. 1993-94, Educator of Yr. award 2000), Am. Assn. of Chmn. of Depts. of Psychiatry (pres. 1996-97, 97-98). Office: U Louisville Sch Medicine Dept Psychiatry & Behavioral Louisville KY 40292-0001

TASSÉ, ROGER, lawyer, former Canadian government official; b. Montreal, Que., Can., 1931; BA, Coll. St. Marie, Montreal, 1952; Lic. in Law, U. Montreal, 1955; diploma d'Etudes Superieures, U. Ottawa, Ont., Can., 1957. Bar: Que. 1956, Ont. 1986; called to Queens Counsel 1971. Joined Dept. Justice, 1956, civil law counsel for Can. govt., from 1957, supt. bankruptcy, 1965-68, asst. dep. min. consumer and corp. affairs, 1968-72; dep. min. Dept. of Solicitor Gen., 1972-77; dep. min. of justice, atty. gen. of Can., 1977-85; ptnr. Land Michener Lash Johnston, Toronto and Ottawa, Noel Décary Aubry & Assocs., Hull, Que., 1985-88; exec. v.p. legal and environ. affairs Bell Can., 1988-91; of counsel Fraser & Beatty, Toronto, 1992-95, Gowling, Lafleur & Henderson, Ottawa, 1995—. Prin. constl. advisor to Spl. Joint Com. of the Senate and the House of Commons on a Renewed Can., 1991-92. Mem. Citizens' Forum on Canada's Future, 1990; co-chair task force Can. Mags., 1993; mem. DTH Panel, 1995. Decorated officer Order of Can. Avocations: skiing, tennis. Office: Gowling Lafleur Henderson LLP 160 Elgin St Ste 2600 Ottawa ON Canada K1P 1C3 Fax: (613) 563-9869. E-mail: roger.tasse@gowlings.com.

TASSINARI, MELISSA SHERMAN, toxicologist; b. Lawrence, Mass., Sept. 26, 1953; m. R. Peter Tassinari (dec.); children: Michael, Emily, Sara. AB, Mt. Holyoke Coll., 1975; postgrad., U. St. Andrews, Scotland, 1973-74; PhD, Med. Coll. Wis., 1979. Diplomate Am. Bd. Toxicology. Rsch. asst. in orthopedic surgery., Lab. Human Biochemistry Children's Hosp. Med. Ctr., Boston, 1981-83; rsch. affiliate in toxicology Toxicology Dept. Forsyth Dental Ctr., 1983-86, staff assoc., 1986-89; asst. prof. cell biology U. Mass. Med. Ctr., Worcester, 1989-91; mgr. reproductive and developmental toxicology Pfizer Global R&D., Groton, Conn., 1991-97, asst. dir., 1997-99, group dir. toxicol. scis., 2001—. Rsch. fellow oral biology Harvard Sch. Dental Medicine, Boston, 1978-81, instr. oral biology and pathophysiology, 1981-83; asst. prof. biol. scis. Wellesley Coll., Mass., 1985-91, biology Simmons Coll., Boston, 1986-87. Contbr. abstracts, articles to profl. jours. Mem. Teratology Soc. (coun. 2000—), Neurobehavioral Teratology Soc., Mid. Atlantic Reproduction and Teratology Assn. (steering com. 1994), Midwest Teratology Assn., Soc. Toxicology. Office: Pfizer Global R&D Eastern Point Rd Groton CT 06340

TASSONE, BRUCE ANTHONY, chemical company executive; b. Phila., Sept. 8, 1960; s. Bruno Anthony and Julia A. (D'Alonzo) T. BSME, Univ. Pa., Phila., 1982; MBA with distinction, Univ. Pa., 1986. Asst. sales mgr. Gen. Electric, Schenectady, N.Y., 1982-84; dir., gen. mgr. Teleflex, King of Prussia, Pa., 1986-96; pres. Mendit Chemical, Bridgeport, 1996—. Bd. dirs. Friends Assn. for Children. Nominee, Entrepreneur of Year, Del. Valley, Phila., 1989. Mem. Soc. of Mech. Engrs., Beta Gamma. Republican. Roman Catholic. Avocations: fin. mgmt, reading, sports activities. Home: 1722 Ridgeway Rd Havertown PA 19083-1614

TASSOS, ALICE CROWLEY, writer, linguist; b. Dallas, June 19, 1925; d. Thomas Francis and Geneiva Edna (Lee) Crowley; m. John Tassos, Mar. 4, 1950 (div. June 1960); 1 child, Penelope Geneiva Tassos Grima. BA in English, French, BS in Journalism, So. Meth. U., 1945, BA in Psychology, 1960; MA in French, Columbia U., 1947. Solo pilot cert. Sec. to fashion editor Vogue Mag., N.Y.C., 1945-46; airline stewardess Trans-Caribbean Airline, 1946; embassy libr. U.S. Info. Svc. Fgn. Svc. Dept. State, Athens, Greece, 1947-49; jr. exec. J. Walter Thompson Co., N.Y.C., 1950-51; city side reporter Miami Daily News, 1952; pub. rels. exec. Boca Raton (Fla.) Hotel & Club, 1953; pvt. practice writer, linguist Dallas, 1960—. Author poems. Canvasser Am. Heart Assn., New Canaan, Conn., 1959; office sec. Easter Seals, Dallas, 1960-61; vol. recreational therapy asst. Timberlawn Psychiat. Hosp., Dallas, 1961-64; vol. March of Dimes, Dallas, 1997. Sr. scholar So. Meth. U., Dallas Woman's Club, 1944-45; consumer price index pub. svc. commendation Dept. Commerce, Dallas, 1999. Mem. AAUW, NAFE, Cmty. of the Holy Spirit (assoc.), Daus. of the King, Alpha Theta Phi, Theta Sigma Phi, Psi Chi. Episcopalian. Avocations: skin diving, swimming, cycling, walking.

TAST, MARCI, consultant; b. Syracuse, Nebr., Oct. 15, 1963; d. Donald Ervin and Carol Ann (Pike) Wachter; m. Alan H. Tast, Sept. 11, 1993. AAS in Bus. Adminstrn., S.E. C.C., Lincoln, Nebr., 1991; BS (summa cum laude) in Computer Info. Sys., Bellevue U., 1997. Cert. in prodn. and inventory mgmt., 1995. Word processing specialist Nebr. Dept. Revenue, Lincoln, 1981-84, word processing technician, 1984-89, info. svcs. supr., 1989-92; tech. svcs. mgr. Lozier Corp., Omaha, 1993-97; sr. electronic commerce analyst Koch Industries, Inc., Wichita, Kans., 1997-99; specialist Data Systems Internat., Overland Park, 1999—. Exec. sec. Vintage Thunderbird Club Internat., Wichita, 1997—2001; webmaster Kans. Cornhusker Club, Wichita, 1998—2002. Named competent Toastmaster, Toastmasters Internat., 1996. Mem.: Project Mgmt. Inst., Am. Prodn. and Inventory Control Soc. Avocations: reading, research on the Internet, traveling. Home: 17547 W 158th Pl Olathe KS 66062 Office: Data Systems Internat 7801 W 110th St Overland Park KS 66210-2305

TATA, GIOVANNI, publishing executive; b. Taranto, Italy, Apr. 26, 1954; came to U.S., 1974, naturalized, 1982; s. Vito and Angela (Colucci) T.; m. Brenda Susan Smith, Feb. 14, 1978; children: Elizabeth Ariana, Katherine Allison, Margaret Anne, Michael Anthony, Hanna Amelia. BS cum laude, Brigham Young U., 1977, MA, 1980; grad. cert. area studies, U. Utah, 1980, PhD, 1986; postgrad., U. Turin, Italy, 1980-81. Archaeologist Utah State Hist. Soc., Salt Lake City, 1979; instr. dept. langs. U. Utah, 1983-85; Mediterranean specialist Soc. Early Hist. Archaeology, Provo, Utah, 1978-91; rsch. fellow Direzione Gen. Cooperazione Sci. Culturale e Technica, Rome, 1980-81; mus. curator Pioneer Trail State Park, Salt Lake City, 1982-83; instr. dept. art Brigham Young U., Provo, 1982-84, dir. creative works, 1996—; rsch. curator Utah Mus. Fine Arts, Salt Lake City, 1985-87; pres. Mus. Info. Sys., 1987-93, Transoft Internat., Inc., 1988—. Chmn. 35th Ann. Symposium on the Archaeology of the Scriptures, 1986, Taras Devel. Corp., 1994—97, Muse-Media, Inc., 1995—2000. Patentee method and system for computerized learning, response, and evaluation. Brigham Young U. scholar. Mem.: Intellectual Property Owners Assn., Assn. Univ. Tech. Mgrs., Nat. Coun. Museums, Am. Assn. Museums. Republican. Mem. Ch. Jesus Christ of Latter-day Saints. Home: PO Box 2194 Provo UT 84603-2194 Office: Transoft Internat 3325 N University Ave Ste 300 Provo UT 84604-7412 E-mail: tata@lexinet.com.

TATA, ROBERT JOSEPH, retired geographer, educator; b. New Britain, Conn., Mar. 3, 1935; s. Rosario and Anna Marie Tata; m. Maryann Hanson; children: Virginia Tata-Phillips, Amy Tata-Winslow, Steven. AB in Geography, Syracuse U., 1957, MA in Geography, 1961, PhD in Geography, 1968; MA in Econ., Fla. Atlanta U., 1975. Asst. prof. Fla. Atlantic U., Boca Raton, 1964—67, assoc. prof., 1968—80, chair geography, 1970—76, prof., 1980—99, prof. emeritus, 1999—. Cons. faculty U.S. Army Command & Gen. Staff, Ft. Leavenworth, Kans., 1967—80; cons. Pan Am Inst. Geography & History, 1974—75; reviewer NSF, Washington, 1982—98. Author: (book) Structural Changes in Puerto Rico's Economy, 1980, Haiti: Land of Poverty, 1982; editl. bd.: The Southeastern Geographer, 1968—72; contbr. articles. Col. U.S. Army, 1957—86. Grantee Rsch. grant, U.S. Army Engr. Rsch. Inst.

Mem.: Assn. Am. Geographers, Fla. Soc. Geographers (past. v.p., past pres. 1977—79, Profl. Cartography award 1966), Ret. Officers' Assn., Sigma Xi. Avocations: reading, travel, fishing, baseball. Home: 2637 SW Cranbrook Ct Boynton Beach FL 33436 Office: Fla Atlantic Univ 500 NW 20th St Boca Raton FL Home Fax: 561-738-7519. Personal E-mail: b33bacchus@earthlink.net.

TATAR, ARNOLD MARSHALL, internal medicine physician, educator; b. Chgo., June 26, 1933; s. Louis and Rose Goldberg Tatar; m. Marina Deull-Wirszup, Aug. 30, 1959; children: Carolyn Beth, Audrey Michelle, Lauren D. W. BA in Chemistry, U. Ill., 1954; BS in Medicine, U. Ill., Chgo., 1955, MD cum laude, 1957. Lic. physician, Ill.; cert., recert. Am. Bd. Internal Medicine. Resident in internal medicine Michael Reese Hosp. and Med. Ctr., Chgo., 1957-60, chief med. resident, 1960-61, attending physician, 1961—; pres. Drs. Tatar, Tatar, Buchanan and Hunt, 1961—; attending physician Northwestern Meml. Hosp., 1991—. Assoc. prof. internal medicine U. Chgo., 1973-91; asst. prof. internal medicine Northwestern U., Evanston/Chgo., 1991—; dir. med. intensive care Michael Reese Hosp., Chgo., 1969-76, dir. investigative hypertension clinic, 1964-76, pres. med. staff, 1988-90, hosp. trustee, 1982-91. Contbr. rsch. articles to profl. jours. Pres. Parent-Tchr. Orgn., John F. Kennedy Sch., Highland Park, Ill., 1970-72. Lt. col. U.S. Army, 1967-69. Named one of Chgo.'s Top Drs., Chgo. Mag., 1997, 2001, Outstanding Primary Care Physicians in U.S., Town and Country Mag., 1999. Fellow Am. Coll. Chest Physicians, Am. Coll. Angiology, Am. Heart Assn. (coun. on hypertension, coun. on clin. cardiology), Am. Soc. Internal Medicine. Avocations: music, theater, dance, bicycling, skiing. Home: Apt 5-East 189 E Lakeshore Dr Chicago IL 60611 Office: Drs Tatar Tatar Buchanan and Hunt Ste 1919 111 N Wabash Chicago IL 60602

TATARIAN, MARY LINDA, retailer, real estate broker; b. Montclair, N.J., Mar. 18, 1947; d. Vincent Lawrence and Marietta Buongiorno Franciosi; m. Jerry Tatarian, Aug. 29, 1970. BA, Syracuse U., 1969. Lic. real estate broker, Fla., cert. tchr., N.J. Pres. Island Amusements, Inc., Fort Myers Beach, Fla., 1986—; real estate broker Beach Realty Inc., 1996—. Contbr. various articles on video to local newspapers, 1988—. Sponsor Ft. Myers Beach Youth Basketball League, 1995—. Mem. Video Software Dealers' Assn. (incorporating bd. mem. for chpt. regional leaders tng., 1994-95, 98-99, S.W. Fla. chpt., sec. 1993-94, treas., 1994-95, pres., 1995-97, 98-99, 99—, nat. scholarship com. 1998, 99, Svc. awards 1993, 94, 95, 96), Greater Ft. Myers Beach C. of C. Avocations: writing, travel, swimming. Office: Island Amusements Inc 8357 Lagoon Rd Fort Myers Beach FL 33931-5211

TATARINOV, KIRILL, computer software industry expert; b. Moscow, Sept. 17, 1964; came to U.S., 1994; s. Lev Gorinshteyn and Inna Tatarinova; m. Osksana Grekina Tatarinov, Jan. 18m 1986; children: Katherine, Konstantin. MS in Elec. Engring., Moscow U. Railroad Engring., 1986; MBA, Houston Bapt. U., 1997. Tech. lead Fibronics Ltd., Haifa, Israel, 1990-91; dir. R&D Patrol Software Pty. Ltd., Sydney, Australia, 1991-94; v.p. R&D BMC Software, Inc., Houston, 1994-98, v.p. strategic planning, 1998-2000, sr. v.p., chief tech. officer, 2000—02; chmn. Kontora, LLC, 2002—. Inventor: System for monitoring and managing computer resources, 1997, 99. Office: PO Box 550412 Houston TX 77255 Address: 110 Carnarvon Dr Houston TX 77024 E-mail: kirill@tatarinov.com.

TATARSKII, VALERIAN IL'ICH, physics researcher; b. Kharkov, USSR, Oct. 13, 1929; s. Il'ya A. and Elizabeth A. (Lapis) T.; m. Maia S. Granovskaia, Dec. 22, 1955; 1 child, Viatcheslav V. MS, Moscow State U., 1952; PhD, Acoustical Inst. Acad. Scis., 1957; DSc, Gorky State U., 1962. Scientific rschr. Geophys. Inst. Acad. Sci. USSR, Moscow, 1953-56, Inst. Atmospheric Physics, Acad. Sci. USSR, Moscow, 1956-59, sr. scientific rschr., 1959-78, head lab., 1978-90; head dept. Lebedev. Phys. Inst. Acad. Sci., 1990-91; sr. rsch. assoc. U. Colo. Coop. Inst. for Rsch. in Environ. Sci., Boulder, 1991—2001; sr. rsch. assoc. environ. tech. lab. Zel Technologies NOAA/ERL, 2001—. Author: Wave Propagation in a Turbulent Medium, 1961, 67, The Effect of the Turbulent Atmosphere on Wave Propagation, 1971, Principles of Statistical Radiophysics, 1989; contbr. articles to profl. jours. Recipient of Max Born award, 1994, Optical Soc. of Am., USSR State prize, 1990. Fellow Optical Soc. Am. (Max Born award 1994), Inst. of Physics; mem. Russian Acad. Sci., U.S.A. Nat. Acad. Engring., N.Y. Acad. Sci. Avocations: classical music, kayaking. Office: NOAA ERL ETL 325 Broadway St Boulder CO 80305-3337 E-mail: vtatarskii@hotmail.com.

TATE, CURTIS E., JR. management educator; b. Trezvant, Tenn., July 5, 1920; s. Curtis E. and Mary Kathryn (Haskins) T.; m. Evelyn Ruth Mann, Apr. 12, 1945 (div. May, 1969); m. Mary Jim Combs, Aug. 28, 1977; children: Curtis Emory, Milton Oglesby. Student, N. Ga. Coll., 1943-44, U. Ga., 1945-46; AB, Bethel Coll., 1946; MS, U. Tenn., 1952. Clk. Family Gen. Grocery, Trezevant, Tenn., 1938-42; clk. purchasing dept. P&G Defense Corp., Milan, 1942; plant mgr. Keathley Pie Co., Memphis, 1946-50; instr. Furman U., Greenville, S.C., 1952-53; bus. mgr. Lander Coll., Greenwood, 1953-56; from asst. to assoc. prof. Coll. of Bus. Adminstrn. U. Ga., Athens, 1956-92; prof. emeritus Terry Coll. of Bus. U. Ga., 1991—. Bd. dirs. Flexible Products, Inc., Marietta, Ga., 1968-76; asst. dean fund raising, 1991—. Co-author: Successful Small Business Management, 1975, latest rev. edit., 1985, Complete Guide to Your Own Business, 1977, Dow-Jones-Irwin Business Papers, 1977, Bus. Policy: Administrative, Strategic and Constitigency Issues, 1983, 92, Managing for Profits, 1984, Small Business Management and Entrepreneurship, 1992. With U.S. Army, 1942-45, ETO. Fellow N. Am. Case Rsch. Assn. (sec., v.p., bd. dirs., pres. so. casewriters, Outstandinc Case Contbr. 1992), Acad. Mgmt., NACRA (past pres. adv. coun. 1998), Kiwanis, Sigma Iota Epsilon, Beta Gamma Sigma. Home and Office: 1640 Broadlands Dr Watkinsville GA 30677-2288

TATE, FRAN M. small business owner; b. Auburn, Wash., Oct. 5, 1929; d. Frank Joseph and Theresa Mary (Bingesar) Pfulg; m. Rory Tate, Sept. 30, 1970 (div.); children: Michael C., Joseph M.; m. Juan Ramon Ramirez, Sept. 6, 1981 (div. May 1986). Student, U. Wash. Gen. mgr. Sorensen Heating Co., Auburn, 1952-70; cons. Success Motivation Inst., Bellevue, Wash., 1970-72; field engr., draftsman J. Dalton and Assocs., Point Barrow, Alaska, 1973-75; pres., owner Inupiat Water Delivery Co., 1977—, Elephant Pot Sewage Haulers, Point Barrow, 1977—; pres., owner, operator Pepe's North of the Border Restaurant, 1978—; pres., owner Tate Enterprises, Inc., Burger Barn, 1984—. Disc jockey, Sta. KBRW, Barrow. Guest of Johnny Carson Show, 1984; featured on Carson Comedy Classics and Stephen Cox book Here's Johnny. Mem. Barrow Zoning Commn.; mem. citizens adv. bd. Barrow Mus. and Cultural Ctr., 1989-91; regional coord. Gov.'s Conf. for Small Bus., 1989-90. Recipient Boss of Yr. award Credit Women Internat., 1969, Outstanding Svc. award Barrow PTA; named Alaska's Outstanding Women, State Commn. for Status of Women, 1984, Outstanding Radio Vol. of Yr., State of Alaska, 1991; Paul Harris fellow for cmty. svc. Rotary Found. Rotary Internat. Mem. NAFE, Barrow C. of C. (pres. 1989—, bd. dirs.), Blues Alley Music Soc., Nat. Geog. Soc., Smithsonian Instn., Jazz Heritage Found., Arctic Slope Scholarship Found., Las Vegas Jazz Club. Roman Catholic.

TATE, GENA WELLS, piano educator; b. Phila., Oct. 1, 1960; d. Gerald Charles Wells and Marilyn Zane (Wood) Wells Black; m. Brian Thomas Tate, Mar. 5, 1994; 1 child, Breanna Frances. AA in Acctg., Hinds C.C., Raymond, Miss., 1980; B Piano Music Edn. summa cum laude, Miss. State U., 1983. Tchr. choral music Forest (Miss.) Mcpl. Sch. Dist., 1983-85; pvt. tchr. piano, Forest, 1983-85, Morton, Miss., 1985-94, Columbus, 1994-96, Columbia, Tenn., 1997—. Pianist Morton 1st Bapt. Ch., 1984-94; organist early worship svc. Fairview Bapt. Ch., Columbus, 1995-96; keyboardist, substitute pianist First Bapt. Ch., Columbia, Tenn., 1998—. Annie Laurie Lyle piano scholar Miss. State U., 1983. Mem.: Nat. Guild Piano Tchrs., Nashville Area Music Tchrs. Assn., Tenn. Music Tchrs. Assn. (cert.), Music Tchrs. Nat. Assn. (cert.). Baptist. Avocations: writing and playing music, travel, movies, dining out.

TATE, HAROLD SIMMONS, JR. lawyer; b. Taylors, S.C., Sept. 19, 1930; s. Harold Simmons and Cleone (Clayton) T.; m. Elizabeth Anne Coker, Dec. 22, 1952; children— Mary Elizabeth Anne, Martha Coker, Virginia Clayton. Grad. cum laude, Harvard U., 1951, JD, 1956, postgrad., 1954. Bar: S.C. 1956. Ptnr. Haynsworth Sinkler Boyd, PA, Columbia, S.C., 1962—. Chmn. U.S. Dist. Ct. (S.C.) Adv. Com., 1984—; lectr. Am. Law Inst.-ABA seminars; adv. com. on rules and procedures U.S. Ct. Appeals (4th cir.), 1990-95 Co-author: South Carolina Appellate Practice, 1985; bd. editors Federal Litigation Guide Reporter, 1985—; co-draftsman S.C. Rules of Evidence, 1995; contbr. articles and book revs. to profl. jours. Chmn. Richland County Mental Health Ctr., 1965-66; co-chmn. Columbia Hearing and Speech Ctr., 1962-64; mem. admission and scholarship com. Harvard U., 1961—; chmn. subcom. on legislation, legislation and fin. study commn. Gov.'s Adv. Group on Mental Health Planning, 1963-65; chmn. Columbia Bd. Supervisory of Registration, 1961-70; pres. Columbia Philharm. Orch., 1966-67, Town Theatre, 1967-70; bd. trustee Richland County Pub. Libr., 1973-78, Hist. Columbia Found., 1971-75, Caroliniana Soc., 1978—, Bostick Charitable Trust, 1968—, Archaeol. Rsch. Trust, 2000—; bd. mgrs. S.C. Hist. Soc., 1993-99, 2002—; commr. S.C. Commn. of Archives and History, 1995—. Capt. U.S. Army, 1951-53. Recipient DuRant award Disting Pub. Svc., 2001. Fellow Am. Coll. Trial Lawyers; mem. ABA, Am. Law Inst., Am. Judicature Soc., S.C. Bar Assn., Assn. Bar City N.Y., Richland County Bar Assn., Harvard Law Sch. Assn. S.C. (sec.-treas. 1968-70, pres. 1988—), Forest Lake Country Club, Columbia Drama Club (pres. 1963-64), Palmetto Club (sec. 1963-70, pres. 1973-76), The Forum Club, Harvard Club (N.Y.C.), Harvard Club S.C., Carolina Yacht Club. Episcopalian. Home: 15 Gibbes Ct Columbia SC 29201-3923 Office: Haynsworth Sinkler Boyd PA 1426 Main St Ste 1200 Columbia SC 29201-2843 Business E-Mail: state@sinklerboyd.com.

TATE, LORETTA CLARA, health educator; b. Elberton, Ga., Mar. 6, 1948; d. Huit and Roberta (Edmond) T.; m. James Lucien Crump Jr., Oct. 16, 1980; chidlren: James Lucien III, Brendan Patrick. BS, St. Louis U., 1973; MS, SUNY, Buffalo, 1978; postgrad., Temple U., 1981, NYU, 1983. Staff radiographer Providence Hosp., Washington, 1968-69, Yonkers (N.Y.) Gen. Hosp., 1969, Mercy Hosp., Buffalo, 1970-73, Alexian Bros. Hosp., St. Louis, 1972-73; clin. instr. Thomas Jefferson U., Phila., 1974-76, instr., 1978-79, asst. prof., 1979-81, chmn. dept. radiation tech., 1981-85; dir. program and spl. projects Greater Phila. Health Action, Inc., 1985-87; health educator Educare, Phila., 1990—. Cons. radiologic tech. texts F.A. Davis Pubs., Phila., 1982-83. Inventor health education game. Corr. sec. Ivy Leaf Parents Coun., Phila., 1990-94; mem. environ. edn. com. Awbury Arboretum Assn., Phila., 1990-92; asst. leader Boy Scouts Am., Cub Scout Pack 358, Phila., 1989-90. Recipient Mallinckrodt award Johns Hopkins Hosp., 1968. Mem. Phila. Soc. Radiologic Technologists (bd. chairperson, pres. elect., pres. 1980-84, cons. bd. dirs., 1990-92). Democrat. Baptist. Avocations: cake decorating, baking, cycling. Home: 1031 E Haines St Philadelphia PA 19138-1533

TATE, LYNNE ALLEN, interior designer; b. Columbus, Ga., Oct. 11, 1951; d. Anthony Joseph and Betty Sue (Thompson) Allen; m. John Robert Mendenhall II, Apr. 20, 1974 (div. Sept. 1978); m. Kevin Michael Tate, Feb. 16, 1985; 1 child, Martha Grayson. BS in Interior Furnishings, Auburn U., 1973. Interior designer Carriage House Columbus (Ga.), Inc., 1973-78; mgr., designer Crabapple, Columbus, 1978-81; owner, designer Lynne Allen Interiors, 1981—. Mem. Am. Soc. Interior Designers, Auburn Alumni Assn., The Luncheon Club, Quadrille. Lodges: Soroptimist Internat. (2d v.p. Columbus 1986—, YCA chair So. region 1986-88—). Roman Catholic. Avocations: needlework, reading, entertaining. Office: Lynne Allen Interiors 1151 Brown Ave Columbus GA 31906-2404

TATE, ROBERT HALE, academic administrator; b. Radford, Va., Sept. 24, 1958; s. Robert Dewitt and Phyllis Hale T. BA, Va. Tech., 1980, MA, 1983; PhD, Fla. State U., 1997. Instr. Fla. So. Coll., Lakeland, 1982-85, asst. prof., 1986-97, assoc. prof., 1997—, sr. devel. officer, 1998-99, exec. dir. devel., 1999, v.p. for advancement, 2000—. Cons. Cohen & Assocs., Tampa, 1986-98. Mem. Rotary, Omicron Delta Kappa (Tchr. of Yr. award/Fla. So. Coll. 1986, faculty sec. 1992-2000, province vice-dir. 1998-2000), Phi Eta Sigma (Lover of Wisdom award 1987), Phi Kappa Phi, Sigma Tau Delta. Methodist. Office: Fla So Coll 111 Lake Hollingsworth Dr Lakeland FL 33801-5607 E-mail: rtate@flsouthern.edu.

TATE, SHEILA BURKE, public relations executive; b. Washington, Mar. 3, 1942; d. Eugene L. and Mary J. (Doherty) Burke; m. William J. Tate, May 2, 1981 (dec. Aug. 1998); children: Hager Burke Patton, Courtney Paige Patton Manzel. BA in Journalism, Duquesne U., 1964; postgrad. in mass communications, U. Denver, 1975-76. Rsch. asst. Westinghouse Air Brake Co.; asst. account exec. Falhgren and Assos.; copywriter Ketchum, MacLeod and Grove, 1964-66; account exec. Burson-Marsteller Assocs., Pitts., 1967, sr. v.p. Washington, 1985-87; public rels. mgr. Colo. Nat. Bank, Denver, 1967-70; account exec. Hill and Knowlton, Inc., Houston, 1977-78, v.p. Washington, 1978-81; dep. to the chmn. Hill and Knowlton Inc., 1987-88; press sec. to First Lady White House, 1981-85; press sec. George Bush for Pres. Campaign, 1988; press sec. to Pres.-elect George Bush, 1988-89; vice chmn. Cassidy and Assocs. Pub. Affairs, Washington, 1989-91; pres. Powell Tate, 1991-99, vice-chmn., 1999—. Bd. dirs. Corp. for Pub. Broadcasting (former mem.), vice chmn., 1990-92, chmn., 1992-94; bd. dirs. Ethics Resource Ctr., Washington. Chmn. civilian pub. affairs adv. bd. U.S. Mil. Acad.; mem. adv. bd. Ronald Reagan Inst. Emergency Medicine, George Washington U. Hosp., Washington; mem. nat. adv. bd. The Salvation Army; bd. dirs. First Tee of Greater Washington. Mem. Nat. Press Club, Duquesne U. Century Club, Washington Golf and Country Club, Farmington Country Club, Belfair Club. Office: Powell Tate 700 13th St NW Ste 1000 Washington DC 20005-5926 E-mail: state@webershandwick.com.

TATE, STANLEY G. diversified business executive, expert witness; b. N.Y., Apr. 25, 1928; s. Jack A. and Anna B. Tatelman; m. Joanne Marilyn Greenwood, Sept. 10, 1949; children: J. Kenneth, James David, Linda Sue Tate Best. BA, U. Fla., 1946, BS, 1948, postgrad., 1949, Columbia U., NYU. Nat. cert. appraiser; lic. gen. contractor, Fla.; cert. in forensic documentaton Am. Bd. Forensic Examiners. Founder Stanley Tate Builders, Inc., North Miami, Fla., 1954—, Investment Diversified Ltd., North Miami, 1964—, High Point of Delray Builders, Inc., North Miami, 1969—, Tate Enterprises, North Miami, 1986—. Chmn. bd. Envirocivil Engring. Corp.; receiver for real estate devels. and other bus. entitites throughout U.S.; expert witness in fed. and state cts. on real estate matters in litigation, before U.S. Ho. of Reps. and Senate coms. on fed. legis. in housing and banking areas; pres., COO, King Internat. Corp., 1985-86, CEO Assoc. Mortgage Investors, 1971-81; past dir., chmn. region I adv. bd. Nat. Bd. Resolution Trust Corp.; mem. adv. bd. BlueStone Capital Ptnrs., N.Y.C., BlueStone Capital Online, Inc.; bd. dirs. KFx, Inc.; charter mem. adv. coun. U. Fla. Sch. Bldg. Constrn.; hon. mem. adv. staff Apt. and Constrn. News; guest lectr. U.Miami Bus. Sch.; guest spkr., lectr., participant numerous industry-related seminars and programs; dir. Team Fla./Free Trade Ams. Contbr. numerous articles on gen. real estate and condominium develing, mktg. and Property devel. to profl. publs. Past bd. dirs. Miami Heart Inst., Fla. League Cities; past trustee pub. health trust Met. Dade County, Fla., also past mem. exec. com.; past mem. Performing Arts Ctr. Trust, Inc., Dade County; past mem. and vice chmn. bd. Fla. Endowment Fund for Higher Edn.; past pres. Temple Israel, Miami Fla., now trustee; past bd. dirs. and mem. exec. com. Miami City Ballet; past chmn. Metro Dade County Housing Oversight Com.; past bd. dirs. and vice chmn. Magnet Ednl. Choice Assn., Inc.; past chmn. Dade County Housing and Urban Devel. Adv. Bd.; past mem. adv. exec. com. YWCA Miami; mem. campaign cabinet United Way Dade County; trustee Fla. Taxwatch, Inc., James E. Scott Cmty. Assn., Mt. Sinai Med. Ctr.; bd. dirs. Miami Jewish Home and Hosp. for Aged, Keep Dade Beautiful, Dade County unit Am. Cancer Soc., Miami-Dade C.C. Found., Fla. Coun. of 100, Fla. Coun. on Econ. Edn., Easter Seals Dade County; mem. bd. trustees St. Thomas U., Kids Voting U.S.A.; mem. United Way Dade County Trustees; mem. family counseling svcs. adv. bd. Family Svc. Found., Inc.; mem., chmn. Fla. Prepaid Postsecondary Edn. Expense Bd., 1st chmn., 1987-; mem., chmn. Fla. Prepaid Coll. Found.; mem. cmty. adv. bd. Jr. League Miami; mem. exec. com. Fla. Guardian Ad Litem Program for 11th Jud. Cir.; hon. trustee Miami Children's Mus.; mem. program coordinating com. Dade County Family Self Sufficiency Program; mem. adv. coun. Voices for Children; past asst. mayor and mayor. City pf Bay Harbor Islands, Fla.; endowed tchg. chair Miami-Dade C.C. Med. Campus; pres. bd. dirs. Elephant Forum; mem. Ptnrs. in Productivity Task Force; mem. Fannie Mae's Nat. Housing Impact Adv. Coun., Miami-Dade Adv. Bd. Gulf Coast Jewish Family Svcs. (non-custodial parent employment program), Assn. of Governing Bd. of Univ.'s, Am. Nurses Credentialing Ctr., Fla. Bd. of Edn. adv. council, Council of 100 Edn. Governanace Task Force. Recipient Shalom award State of Israel, 1971, Ben Gurion award, spl. honoree Israel Bonds Campaign and Greater Miami Jewish Fedn., Cmty. Star award Family Counslng Svcs. Greater Miami, 1991, award for devoted outstanding cmty. svc. B'nai B'rith, 1992, Dorothy Shula award United Way, 1996, Unsung Hero award Youth Law Ctr., 1996, Most Valuable Protector Vol. award Voices for Children, 1999, Disting. Svc. award Coll. Savs. Plan-USA Network, 1999, Eagle award for Outstanding Cmty. Svc., Miami-Dade County Rep. Party, 2001; recipient Outstanding Citizen award and named hon. Dade County Mayor, 1998; named Bus. Assoc. of Yr., Hurricane chpt. Am. Bus. Women's Assn., 1988, hon. treas. State of Ala., 1989. Fellow Am. Coll. Forensic Examiners; mem. Nat. Assn. Home Builders, Nat. Assn. Real Estate Appraisers (cert.), Nat. Assn. Rev. Appraisers and Mortgage Underwriters (cert.), Internat. Real Estate Inst., Latin Builders Assn., Hispanic-Am. Builders Assn. (dir. dirs.), Home Builders Assn. South Fla. (past dir., named to Hall of Fame 1994), Am. Israel Pub. Affairs (nat. exec. com.), Jewish Nat. Fund (investment com.), U.S. Senatorial Trust, Westview Country Club (past 1st v.p. and dir.), Bankers Club, Hound Ears Lodge and Club, Jockey Club. Republican. Jewish. Avocations: golf, tennis. Office: Tate Enterprises 1175 NE 125th St Ste 102 North Miami FL 33161 E-mail: stanley@Tateenterprises.com.

TATE, STONEWALL SHEPHERD, lawyer; b. Memphis, Dec. 19, 1917; m. Janet Graf; children: Adele Shepherd, Shepherd Davis, Janet Reid Walker. BA, Southwestern at Memphis (now Rhodes Coll.), 1939; JD, U. Va., 1942; LLD (hon.), Samford U., 1979, Suffolk U., 1982, Capital U., 1989, Rhodes Coll., 1993. Bar: Va. 1941, Tenn. 1942. Chmn. bd. Martin, Tate, Morrow & Marston, P.C. (and predecessor firms), Memphis, 1947—. Chmn. pres.'s coun. Rhodes Coll., 1995-96, sec. bd. trustees, 1967-77, 80-84. Pres. Episcopal Churchmen of Tenn., 1961-62; sec. standing com. Episcopal Diocese of Tenn., 1969-71; pres. Chickasaw Coun. Boy Scouts Am., 1967-78. With USNR, 1942-46; comdr. USNR; ret. Decorated Order of Cloud Banner (China); recipient Silver Beaver award Boy Scouts Am., 1963, Disting. Eagle Scout award, 1980, Disting. Svc. medal Rhodes Coll., 1978, Disting. Alumni award, 1991, Lawyers' Lawyer award Memphis Bar Assn., 1990; Memphis Rotary Club Civic Recognition award, 1983; Paul Harris fellow, 1985. Fellow Am. Bar Found., Am. Coll. Trust and Estate Counsel, Internat. Acad. Estate and Trust Law, Coll. Law Practice Mgmt. (hon.), Tenn. Bar Found., Memphis and Shelby County Bar Found.; mem. ABA (chmn. standing com. on profl. discipline 1973-76, chmn. standing com. on scope and correlation of work 1977, chmn. task force on lawyer advt. 1977, pres. ABA 1978-79, chmn. standing com. on lawyer competence 1986-92, mem. coun. sr. lawyers divsn. 1997-2001), Am. Judicature Soc. (past bd. dirs.), Am. Law Inst., Lawyer-Pilots Bar Assn., Tenn. Bar Assn. (pres. 1963-64), Memphis and Shelby County Bar Assn. (pres. 1959-60), Nat. Conf. Bar Pres. (pres. 1972-73, Alumnus of Yr. 1996), U.S. 6th Cir. Jud. Conf. (life), U. Va. Law Sch. Alumni Assn. (mem. exec. coun. 1974-77), Rhodes Coll. Alumni Assn. (pres. 1951-53), Rotary (pres. 1982-83, bd. dirs. 1974, 80-84, 89-90), Raven Soc., Order of Coif, Phi Beta Kappa, Omicron Delta Kappa, Phi Delta Phi, Sigma Alpha Epsilon (highest effort award N.Y.C. Alumni Assn. 1979). Office: Martin Tate Morrow & Marston PC Falls Bldg 22 N Front St Ste 1100 Memphis TN 38103-1182 E-mail: sstate@martintate.com.

TATE, THADDEUS W(ILBUR), JR. (THAD TATE), history educator, historical institute executive, historian; b. Winston-Salem, N.C., May 27, 1924; s. Thaddeus Wilbur and Elizabeth Kent (Llewellyn) T. AB, U. N.C., 1947, MA, 1948; PhD, Brown U., 1960. Historian U.S. Nat. Park Service, 1948-54; research assoc. Colonial Williamsburg Found., (Va.), 1954-57, asst. dir. research, 1957-61; book rev. editor William and Mary Quar., Williamsburg, 1961-66, editor, 1966-72; asst. prof. history Coll. William and Mary, 1961-64, assoc. prof., 1964-69, prof. 1969-90, Murden prof. humanities, 1990-92, emeritus, 1992—; dir. Inst. Early Am. History and Culture, Williamsburg, 1972-89, Commonwealth Ctr. for Study of Am. Culture, Williamsburg, 1988-92. Author: Negro in Eighteenth-Century Williamsburg, 1966; co-author: Colonial Virginia: A History, 1986, The College of William and Mary: A History, 1993; co-editor, contbg. author: Chesapeake in the Seventeenth Century, 1979; co-editor: Saints and Revolutionaries, 1984, An Uncivil War: The Southern Backcountry in the American Revolution, 1985; mem. adv. bd.: Environ. Rev., 1976-85; chair editorial adv. bd.: Papers of John Marshall. Mem. Williamsburg Wetlands Bd., 1980-93; chair bd. dirs. Va. Found. for Humanities and Pub. Policy, 1989-95; mem. tercentary commn. Coll. William and Mary, 1988-93. With USNR, 1943-46. Recipient Grad. Alumni citation Brown U., 1985; Thomas Jefferson award Coll. William and Mary, 1986; Brown U. fellow, 1949-51; NEH fellow, 1982-83; fellow Am. Council Learned Socs., 1970-71 Mem. Orgn. Am. Historians, Am. Hist. Assn., So. Hist. Assn., Va. Hist. Soc. (hon.), Am Soc. Legal History, Mass. Hist. Soc., Am. Soc. Environ. History, Assocs. John Carter Brown Library, Am. Antiquarian Soc., Hist. Soc. Episcopal Ch. (1st v.p. 1996-99, pres. 1999—), Phi Beta Kappa, Phi Alpha Theta. Democrat. Episcopalian. Home: 313 Half Burns Lane Williamsburg VA 23185-3908

TATEL, DAVID STEPHEN, federal judge; b. Washington, Mar. 16, 1942; s. Howard Edwin and Molly (Abramowitz) Tatel; m. Edith Sara Bassichis, Aug. 29, 1965; children: Rebecca, Stephanie, Joshua, Emily. BA, U. Mich., 1963; JD, U. Chgo., 1966. Bar: Ill. 1966. Instr. U. Mich., Ann Arbor, 1966—67; assoc. Sidley & Austin, Chgo. and Washington, 1967—69, 1970—72; dir. Chgo. Lawyer's Com., 1969—70, Nat. Lawyers Commn. for Civil Rights Under Law, Washington, 1972—74; dir. Office for Civil Rights HEW, 1977—79; assoc., ptnr. Hogan & Hartson, 1974—77, ptnr., 1979—94; cir. judge U.S. Ct. Appeals (D.C. cir.), 1994—. Lectr. Stanford U. Law Sch., 1991—92; co-chmn. Nat. Lawyers Com. for Civil Rights Under Law, Washington, 1989—91; chmn., bd. dirs. Spencer Found., Chgo., 1990—97. Bd. dirs. Carnegie Found. for Advancement in Tchg., Stanford, Calif., 1997—. Office: US Ct Appeals 333 Constitution Ave NW US Courthouse Washington DC 20001-2866*

TATEOKA, REID, lawyer; b. Salt Lake City, Jan. 11, 1954; s. Matt M. and Ida S. (Shimizu) T.; m. Shauna Reid, June 3, 1977; children: Jacob Reid, Elizabeth Ann, John Robinson. BA, U. Utah, 1978; JD, Brigham Young U., 1981. Bar: Utah 1981, U.S. Dist. Ct. (cen. dist.) Utah 1981, U.S. Ct. Appeals (10th cir.) 1986. Assoc. McKay, Burton, Thurman & Condie, Salt Lake City, 1981-85; ptnr., shareholder, dir. McKay, Burton & Thurman, 1985-89, pres., 1989—. Lectr. on problem collections in Utah, 1988, 90. Treas. Japanese Am. Citizens League, Salt Lake City, 1983, 88-90, pres., 1991-96, bd. dirs., 1997—; active Salt Lake coun. Boy Scouts Am. Mem. Am. Inns of Cts., Phi Delta Phi (provincial pres. 1984—). Mem. Lds Ch. Avocations: skiing, golf, fishing. Office: McKay Burton & Thurman Gateway Tower East Ste 600 Salt Lake City UT 84133 E-mail: reid@mbt-law.com.

TATERA, JAMES FRANK, chemist, process analysis specialist; b. Milw., June 27, 1946; s. Harry Frank and Agnes Rose (Szymanowski) T.; m. Kaaren Marie Piekarski, Sept. 9, 1972; children: Patrick, Monica, David. BS in Chemistry, Math., U. Wis., Oshkosh, 1968; postgrad., U. Minn., 1968, 71-73; MBA, Cen. Mich. U., 1982. Cert. specialist in analytical tech. Tchg. rsch. assoc. chemistry dept. U. Minn., Mpls., 1968, 71-73; analytical chemist Dow Corning Corp., Midland, Mich., 1973-76, scale up engr. new products commercialization, 1976-78, prodn. bldg. supt. prodn. dept., 1978-80; analytical systems specialist project and plant engring. Dow Corning Ltd., Barry, Wales, 1981-84; analytical systems supr. plant engring. & maintenance Dow Corning Corp., Carrollton, Ky., 1984-85, analytical systems specialist plant engring. and maintenance, 1985-87, sr. analytical and control specialist project engring., 1988-90, sr. analytical systems specialist strategic change program, 1991-98, sr. analytical sys. specialist Process Analysis Expertise Ctr., 1998-2000; ret., 2000; sr. process analysis cons. Tatera & Assocs. Inc., Madison, Ind., 2001—. Session developer, panelist, course instr., presenter in field; U.S. nat. com. Internat. Electrotech. Commn., Paris, 1993, Milan, 1994, Montreal, 1996, Houston, 1998, Beijing, 2002, U.S. nat. com. tech. advisor subcom. 65D, 1993—. Editl. adv. bd. InTech mag., 1998—; contbr. articles to profl. jours., chpts. to books. 1st lt. U.S. Army, 1969-71. Decorated Bronze Star, Bronze Star with oak leaf cluster. Fellow Instrumentation Sys. and Automation Soc. (formerly Instrument Soc. Am.) (dir.-elect, sec.-treas. analysis divsn. 1994-96, dir. 1996-98, chmn. SP 76 stds. com. 1991-96, pres. N.E. Mich. sect. 1979-80, various sect. offices 1976-79, Louisville sect. del. 1995—, com. mem. 1998—, various divsn. and dept. positions 1998—); mem. Am. Chem. Soc. (Louisville sect. chair 1999-2001, rep. vol. in pub. outreach program Louisville sect. chmn.-elect 1998-99, sect. careers program and nat. chemistry week com. 1992-99), Air and Waste Mgmt. Assn. (optical sensing divsn. indsl. issues and applications com. on enhanced monitoring 1993-99), Elks, Am.

Legion, VFW, KC, Delta Sigma Phi, Phi Lambda Upsilon, Sigma Iota Epsilon. Roman Catholic. Home and Office: 2038 Ridgewood Dr Madison IN 47250-2729 E-mail: jtatera@seidata.com.

TATGENHORST, ROBERT (CHARLES TATGENHORST), lawyer, educator; b. Cin., Apr. 21, 1918; s. Charles and Clara (Strebel) T.; m. Louise Thompson, Sept. 6, 1951; children: David, John, James, Richard. AB, Dartmouth Coll., 1940; LL.B., U. Cin., 1947. Bar: Ohio 1947. Asst. atty. gen., State of Ohio, 1947-49; asso. firm Taft, Stettinius & Hollister, Cin., 1951-58; ptnr. firm Tatgenhorst & Tatgenhorst, 1958-61; prin. firm Robert Tatgenhorst & Assos., 1961-85; ptnr. Tatgenhorst & Bruestle, 1986—, 1986-95. Adj. prof. law Chase Coll. Law, No. Ky. U., 1962-86. Pres. Westwood Civic Assn., Cin., 1959, Meth. Union, 1960; chmn. dist. Boy Scouts Am., 1970; trustee Twin Towers Retirement Ctr., 1968-93, Westwood United Meth. Ch., bd. trustees 1985-88, pres., 1990-92, trustee, 1992. With CIC U.S. Army, 1942-46. Mem. Ohio State Bar Assn., Cin. Bar Assn. (sec. 1973-75), Ryland Lakes Country Club, Optimists (pres. Cin. club 1962), Dartmouth of Cin. Club (pres. 1965), Masons (33 deg.), Sigma Alpha Epsilon, Phi Alpha Delta (pres. 1946). Republican.

TATHAM, DAVID FREDERIC, art historian, educator; b. Wellesley, Mass., Nov. 29, 1932; s. Richard Merton and Florence Elizabeth (Mallette) T.; m. Cleota Reed, Dec. 12, 1979. AB, U. Mass., 1954; MA, Syracuse U., 1960, PhD, 1970. Dean students Syracuse (N.Y.) U., 1966-71, assoc. prof. fine arts, 1972-78, prof., 1978—, chmn. dept. fine arts, 1980-86. Author: The Lure of the Striped Pig, 1973, Prints and Printmakers of New York State, 1986, Winslow Homer and the Art of the Book, 1990, Winslow Homer and the Illustrated Book, 1992, Fishing in the North Woods, 1995, Winslow Homer in the Adirondacks, 1996, Winslow Homer and the Pictorial Press, 2002, (exhbn. catalogs) Winslow Homer Drawings, 1979, Art, Artists and Museums, 1980, Bolton Brown, 1981, Abraham Tuthill, 1983; contbr. articles to profl. jours. Served with U.S. Army, 1956. Daniels research fellow, 1974; Am. Philos. Soc. grantee, 1980, 86, 98; Am. Art Jour. award for outstanding scholarship, 1984; NEH grantee, 1987-88. Fellow Athenaeum of Phila.; mem. Am. Antiquarian Soc. (rec. sec. 1988-93), Coll. Art Assn. Home: 329 Westcott St Syracuse NY 13210-2107 Office: Syracuse U Dept Fine Arts Bowne Hall Syracuse NY 13244-1200 E-mail: dftatham@syr.edu.

TATHAM, ROBERT HAINES, geophysicist, educator; b. Merced, Calif., Dec. 10, 1943; s. Robert and Dorothy (Fitzgerald) T.; m. Henna E. Solomin, Aug. 29, 1970; children: Sarah, Rachel, Benjamin. BS in Physics, Calif. State U., Northridge, 1967; MS in Applied Geophysics, U. Houston, 1970; PhD in Geophysics, Columbia U., 1975. Geophysicist Texaco Inc., Houston, 1967-71, spl. projects geophysicist, 1975-81; rsch. geophysicist Geosource, 1981-86; mgr. geophys.rsch. Texaco Inc., 1986-99; prof., Shell Centennial chair U. Tex., Austin, 1999—. Adj. prof. U. Houston, 1988-99. Co-author: Multicomponent Seismology in Petroleum Exploration; contbr. articles to tech. jours. and books. Mem. IEEE, Soc. Exploration Geophysicists (Disting. Lectr. 2001), European Assn. Exploration Geophysicists, Am. Assn. Petroleum Geologists, Am. Geophys. Union, Seismol. Soc. Am., Geophys. Soc. Houston (pres. 1998-99). Democrat. Jewish. Avocation: gardening. Home: 3807 Laurel Ledge Ln Austin TX 78731-4051 E-mail: tatham@mail.utexas.edu.

TATIBOUET, ANDRE STEPHAN, condominium and resort management firm executive; b. Honolulu, Mar. 10, 1941; s. Joseph J. F. and Annalie (Knaack) T.; m. Jane Inez Barrows, Apr. 19, 1968; children: Cartier, Cecily. BA in Russian and Am. History, U. Hawaii, 1964. Cert. Hotel Adminstr. Owner, developer Pacific Beach Hotel, Honolulu, 1968-69; founder, pres. Aston Hotels & Resorts (formerly Hotel Corp. of Pacific), 1969—; chmn., CEO Aston Hotels & Resorts; bd. dirs. ResortQuest Internat. Inc., 1998-2000, AFM Hospitality Corp., 2000—. Life mem. founders circle Punahou Sch., 1981—; mem. Hebrew U., 1982—; emeritus mem. U. Hawaii Pres. Club, 1983—; state chmn. U.S. Commn. on Civil Rights, 1985-95; 2d v.p. Waikiki Improvement Assn., 1985-90; mem. travel industry mgmt. adv. com. U. Hawaii, 1986—; mem. Honolulu Symphony Soc., 1986—, vice chmn. bd. dirs., 1988-89; mem. travel industry mgmt. adv. coun. Hawaii Pacific Coll., 1988—; mem. Hawaii Coun. Econ. Edn., 1988—; trustee Honolulu Chamber Music Soc., 1975-85, Jewish Fedn. Hawaii, 1982-86; bd. dirs. Hawaii Performing Arts Co., 1982-87, Hawaii Visitors and Convention Buraeu, 1987—, Filipino Cmty. Ctr., 1996—; regent Chaminade U., 1986-90; mem. Ctrl. Union Congregational Ch., 1968—, deacon, 1996-99, investment com., 1998-2000. Recipient Gov.'s award for svc. as mem. of Commn. on Yr. 2000, 1978, Man of Yr. award Temple Emanu-El, 1986, Beautification award Hawaii Outdoor Circle, 1987, Judah L. Magnes Gold Medal award Am. Friends Hebrew U., 1988, Exec. of Yr. award Hawaii chpt. Profl. Secs. Internat., 1988, Disting. Alumni Outstanding Svc. award U. Hawaii, 1990, Hope Award Nat. Multiple Sclerosis Soc., 1997, Enterpreneur of Yr. in Hawaii-Hospitality Ernst & Young, 1997, Junior Achievement Hawaii award Bus. Hall of Fame, 1998. Mem. Hawaii Execs. Coun., Hawaii Hotel Assn. (pres. 1987-88, treas. polit. action com. 1985-90), Am. Hotel and Motel Assn. (nat. bd. dirs. 1985-87, Lawson A. Odde award 1997), Waikiki Beach Operators Assn. (founding charter mem., exec. dir. 1984—), Soc. of Family Hoteliers of Am. Hotel and Motel Assn., Hawaii ParkConv. Coun. (founding dir., sustaining mem.), Young Pres.' Orgn., Skal Club Hawaii, Plaza Club, Beverly Hills Country Club, Honolulu Club, Oahu Country Club, Outrigger Canoe Club, Lambda Alpha Internat. Congregationalist. Avocations: tennis, music, history, literature. Office: Aston Hotels & Resorts 3075 La Pietra Cir Honolulu HI 96815-4514

TATNALL, ANN WESLAGER, reading educator; b. Uniontown, Pa., June 1, 1935; d. Clinton Alfred and Ruth Georgia (Hurst) Weslager; m. George Gress Tatnall, Oct. 8, 1954; children: Peggy Ann, George Richardson. BS in Edn., U. Del., 1967; MA in Edn., Glassboro State Coll., 1978. Cert. reading specialist, cert. supr., cert. elem. tchr., N.J. Tchr. reading Oldmans Twp. Bd. of Edn., Pedricktown, N.J., 1972-78, reading specialist, 1978-95, reading supr., 1981-95. Mem. N.J. Dept. of Edn. Minimum Basic Skills Test Devel. Com., Trenton, N.J., 1981-82; mem. Quad-Dist. Reading Coordination Com., Salem County, N.J., 1987-95; chairperson Adminstrv. Com. of Oldmans Twp. Schs., Pedricktown, N.J., 1993-95. Chair Woodstown (N.J.) Candlelight House Tour, 1983-99, homes chair, 2000—; pres. Pilesgrove-Woodstown Hist. Soc., 1994-99, 2002-, v.p., 1999-2001, pres. 2002—; v.p. Pilesgrove Libr. Assn., 1994—; sec. Hist. Preservation Commn., Woodstown, 1989—; mem. Jr. Bd. of Wilmington (Del.) Med. Ctr., 1969—, treas. Thrift Shop, 1970-75; bd. trustees United Way of Salem County, 1997-99; mem. Salem County Cultural and Heritage Commn., 1997—. Recipient Gov.'s Tchr. Recognition Program award Gov. of N.J., 1988; selected Hands Across the Water, Russian/USA Tchr. Exchange, 1990-91; named Salem County Woman of Achievement, 1998. Mem. AAUW, Internat. Reading Assn., N.J. Reading Assn., Woman's Club of Woodstown. Avocations: travel, reading, Univ. of Del. football, restoration of historic houses, granddaughters. Home: 209 N Main St Woodstown NJ 08098-1227

TATNALL, GEORGE JACOB, aeronautical engineer; b. Cin., Aug. 9, 1923; s. George Henry and Ida Mae (Hazelbaker) T.; m. G. Virginia Morgan, Feb. 5, 1949; children: Robert, William, Jeffrey, Thomas, Jane. BSME in Aeronautics, U. Pitts., 1949. Devel. engr. Naval Air Devel. Ctr., Warminster, Pa., 1949-57, supr. electro-mech. design br., supr. radome antenna sect., 1957-62, 63-78; engrng. group leader Corning (N.Y.) Glass Works, 1962-63; cons. Semcor, Inc., Warminster, 1979-81; cons. pvt. practice, 1982-84; cons. Rome Rsch. Corp., New Hartford, N.Y., 1993-95. Tech. advisor Seventh Fleet USN, S.E. Asia, during Vietnam War, 1971. Contbr. to sci. papers presented at confs. (many also pub. in proceedings); author: (with others) chpt. in book Environmental Simulation and Test Data; author: manuals and documentation aircraft equipment. With US Army AF, 1943-45, China. Mem. AIAA (pres. U. Pitts. chpt. 1948), VFW, Flying Tiger U.S. 14th Air Force Assn. Achievements include patents for Speed Brake Retarding Mechanism for an Air Dropped Store, Air Dropped Minature Sonobuoy, Rotatable and Tiltable Radome with ind. scan and tilt antenna; developed low noise coupling through laminar boundary layer for acoustic homing missile, test facilities for supersonic rain erosion of aircraft materials. Home: 551 Walter Rd Warminster PA 18974-5553

TATNALL, PETER COOLIDGE, civil engineer; b. Worcester, Mass., Sept. 20, 1938; s. Rodman R. and Amy (Taylor) T.; m. Mary Lou Olen, Sept. 16, 1988; children: Lori Tucker, Lynn Ralph, Leah Dennis. BCE, Rensselaer Polytech. Inst., 1962. Ops. mgr. Lehigh Portland Cement Co., Allentown, Pa., 1965-76; dir. concrete aggregates Genex/London (Ky.) Inc., 1976-77; plant mgr. Blue Grass Art Cast, Winchester, Ky., 1977-79; tech. mgr. Redi Mix Assocs., Aurora, Ill., 1979-81; product mgr. Bekaert Corp., Marietta, Ga., 1981-98; dir. underground constrn. Novocon Internat., Inc. (now S.I. Concrete Sys.), 1998—. Editor: (pubs.) Measurement of Properties, 1988. Bd. dirs. City Zoning Appeals Bd., Geneva, Ill., 1980-84. 1st lt. U.S. Army, 1963-65. Fellow Am. Concrete Inst. (chmn. 1996-2002); mem. Mem. ASCE, ASTM (chmn. subcom. 1990—), Am. Shotcrete Assn. (treas. 1998, pres. 2000), Transp. Rsch. Bd. Home: 3800 Bays Ferry Trl Marietta GA 30062-5287 Office: SI Concrete Sys 3800 Bays Ferry Trl Marietta GA 30062-5287

TATONE, KATHY, lawyer; b. Ft. Dodge, Iowa, Apr. 27, 1957; d. Peter and Maria Terranova; m. Marc Tatone, Aug. 29, 1978; children: Michael, Matthew. BA, U. Minn., 1981; JD cum laude, William Mitchell Coll. of Law, 1985. Bar: Minn. 1985, U.S. Ct. Appeals (8th cir.) 1985. Assoc. Karon Jepsen & Daly, St. Paul, 1985-90; ptnr. Rath Thue & Tatone, Mpls., 1990-92; pvt. practice, 1992—. Author, editor, columnist Minn. Trial Lawyers Mag., 1985—; mem. editl. bd. Barrister Mag., 1993-94; contbr. articles to profl. pubs. Mem. Minn. Trial Lawyers (exec. com., bd. govs. 1990-94), Minn. Women Lawyers, Minn. State Bar Assn., Minn. Million Dollar Round Table. Office: 3036 Kyle Ave N Minneapolis MN 55422

TATRO, NORBERT, journalist, educator; b. Milw., Jan. 24, 1943; s. Norbert J. Tatro and Della Leonore Jones; m. Elaine Feldman, Feb. 24, 1996. BA with honors, U. Iowa, 1965; MS in Journalism, Northwe. U., 1965; postgrad., Columbia U., 1969-70. News prodr.-writer CBS Sta. WBBM-TV, Chgo., 1966-70; news prodr. Sta. WTMJ-TV, Milw., 1971-74; news prodr.-writer NBC Network and Sta. WMAQ-TV, Chgo., 1975-97; asst. prof. comm. Truman State U., Kirksville, Mo., 1998-2000; asst. prof. journalism Roosevelt U., Chgo., 2001—. Recipient Chgo. Emmy, Spot News Nat. Acad. TV Arts and Scis., 1976-77, 88-89, Peter Lisagor award Bus. Journalism Soc. Profl. Journalists, 1994; CBS News fellow Columbia U., 1969-70. Mem. Broadcast Edn. Assn. Avocation: running Boston marathons. Office: Roosevelt U 430 S Michigan Ave Chicago IL 60605 Fax: 312-281-3231. E-mail: ntatro@roosevelt.edu.

TATUM, ARTHUR, III, educator, lexicographer, pianist; b. Sumpter, S.C., July 7, 1935; s. Art Tatum and Lillie Bell. Cert. tchr. Prin. Youth in Action, N.Y.C., 1964-67; prin., tutor Cmty. Action, 1968-72; performer Jazz Hall of Fame, L.A., 1975-79; music tutor Morgan Coll., Balt., 1980-83, Coppin State Coll., Balt., 1985-90, lang. tutor, 1995-96. Author: (Ebonese dictionary) Afro American Language, 1994, (gospel in ebonese) Gospel According to St. Matthew, 1996, Solar-Harmonic Systems (original method for reading and writing music). Lang. tutor Neighborhood Youth Corp., Charles Villa Balt., 1995-97. Avocations: sand-lot baseball, golf, table-tennis. Office: Tatum Publs 2330 Guilford Ave Baltimore MD 21218-5206 E-mail: arthurtatum@webtv.net.

TATUM, BETTY JOYCE, secondary school educator; b. Oklahoma City, Dec. 19, 1949; d. Howard and Elaine (Easley) Lisby; m. Frank Dennis Tatum, Dec. 27, 1980. BA, Okla. State U., 1972, MS, 1984. Cert. secondary tchr., Okla. 9th grade English tchr. Ponca City (Okla.) Pub. Schs., 1972-80, 7th grade English tchr., 1985-87, H.S. English tchr., 1988—; tchr. learning disabilities students Calcasieu Sch. Sys., Lake Charles, La., 1981-83. Mem profl. devel. task force com. Ponca City Schs., 2000-01. Recipient Citation of Tchr. Appreciation, Okla. Sch. Sci. and Math., 1997. Mem. NEA, Okla. Edn. Assn., Nat. Coun. Tchrs. English, Ponca City Panhellenic, Alpha Delta Pi, Okla. State U. Alumni Assn. (bd. dirs. 1993-96), Delta Kappa Gamma. Avocations: bridge, reading, travel, crafts, writing. Home: 621 Greenbriar Rd Ponca City OK 74601-1622 Office: Ponca High HS 927 N 5th St Ponca City OK 74601-3302

TATUM, LAURICE M. security firm executive; b. Birmingham, Ala. s. Darcey Thornton Tatum and Elizabeth Younger Burnham; m. Janet Welsted Strorier, Feb. 4, 1984; 1 child Louise "Libby" Elizabeth. AAS in Police Adminstrn., No. Va. C.C., Alexandria, 1976; BS in Adminstrn. Justice, Am. U., 1978, MPA in Internat. Affairs, 1980; MS in Criminal Justice, U. Ala., Birmingham, 1981. Statis. analyst FBI, Washington, 1974—79; res. dep. sheriff Jefferson County Sheriff's Dept., Birmingham, Ala., 1980—81; police officer Irondale Police Dept., 1981—83; investigator, pres., owner Tatum Agy. Investigations, Birmingham, 1983—84, 1988—; elected constable Constable Dist. 46, Montgomery, 1984—88. Program's officer Civil Air Patrol/Potomac Squadron, Washington, 1976—80, Civil Air Patrol/Bessemer Squadron, Birmingham, 1980—82; committeeman Jefferson County Rep. Exec. Com., 1989—. Recipient Freedom Found. award, Freedom Found., 1973. Mem.: Assn. Cert. Fraud Examiners (pres. Ala. chpt. 2001—02). Avocation: woodenship modeling. Office: Tatum Agy Investiation Southeastern Legal Bldg 1920 Huntington Rd Birmingham AL 35209

TATUM, STEPHEN LYLE, lawyer; b. New Orleans, Apr. 3, 1954; s. Gail Douglas and Barbara (Lyle) T.; m. Nenetta Carter, July 5, 1977; children: Carter Ann, Stephen Lyle Jr. BS in Anthropology, So. Meth. U., 1976; JD, U. Tex., 1979. Bar: Tex. 1979, U.S. Dist. Ct. (no. dist.) Tex. 1980, U.S. Dist. Ct. (ea. dist.) Tex. 1986, U.S. Dist. Ct. (we. dist.) Tex. 1991, U.S. Ct. Appeals (5th and 11th cirs.) 1981, U.S. Ct. Appeals (10th cir.) 1986, U.S. Supreme Ct. 1993; cert. in civil appellate law Tex. Bd. Legal Specialization. Law clk. Judge David O. Belew Jr. U.S. Dist. Ct., Ft. Worth, 1979-80; assoc. Cantey & Hanger, 1980-85, ptnr., 1985-90; sr. ptnr. Thompson & Knight, P.C., 1990-93; ptnr. Brown, Herman, Dean, Wiseman, Liser & Hart LLP, 1993—. Bd. dirs. Tex. Dept. Health, Austin, 1992-95, Trinity River Authority, Arlington, Tex., 1990-92; trustee Southwestern U., Georgetown, Tex., 1997—, Ft. Worth Country Day Sch., 1993—; chair bd. trustees YMCA of Tarrant County, Ft. Worth, 1987-91. Named Outstanding Young Leader of Tarrant County, Tarrant County Jaycees, Ft. Worth, 1988. Mem. Fedn. Ins. and Corp. Counsel, Internat. Assn. Def. Counsel, State Bar of Tex. (adminstrn. of justice com. 1987-91). Methodist. Avocations: soccer, golf, reading, drumming. Office: Brown Herman Dean Wiseman Liser & Hart LLP 306 W 7th St Ste 200 Fort Worth TX 76102-4905

TATUM, THOMAS DESKINS, film and television producer, director; b. Pineville, Ky., Feb. 16, 1946; s. Clinton Turner and Gaynelle (Deskins) T.; m. Laura Ann Smith, Aug. 15, 1968 (div. 1974); m. Suzanne Pettit, Sept. 29, 1983 (dec. 1998); children: Rhett Cowden, Walker Edwin; m. Kathryn Vinson, Nov. 28, 1998. BA, Vanderbilt U., 1968; JD, Emory U., 1974. Bar: Ga. 1974, D.C. 1980. Spl. asst. City of Atlanta, 1974-76; dep. dir. fed. relations Fed. Relations Nat. League of Cities, Washington, 1977-78; dir. communications Office of Conservation and Solar Energy, 1979-80; chmn. exec. producer Tatum Communications., Inc., Hollywood, Calif., 1981—; chmn., pres. Western Film & Video, Inc., Telluride, Colo., 1987—; pres., COO Planet Central TV, 1995-96. Prodr. feature film Winners Take All, 1987; prodr., dir. documentaries Double High, 1982 (award), Maui Windsurf, 1983, home videos Greenpeace in Action, Girls of Winter/Skiing mag., US Pro Ski tour, 1983-90, Action Sports of the 80's ESPN, 1984-88, Am. Ultra Sports with Prime Network, 1989-94, various TV, cable and home video sports and health programs, 1982—, series Eco Sports, 1995—, Body, Mind, and Spirit, 1996-97, Beyond Extreme—Sports, 1999, Ouray Ice Festival, Oln, 2000—, Super Crashes, Splashes and Wipeouts Series, 2001—. Dep. campaign mgr. Maynard Jackson, 1973, Jimmy Carter primary campaign, 1976, staff conf. Dem. Mayors, 1974-75, media cons. Greepeace, 1988; bd. dirs. Atlanta Ballet, v.p., 1975; nat. urban affairs coord. Carter Mondale campaign 1976, mem. Carter Mondale transition team 1976-77; mem. adv. bd. Solar Electric Light Fund, Washington, 1990-98, Green Peace. Mem. Ga. Bar Assn., Hollywood Film and TV Soc., L.A. Tennis Club. Presbyterian. Avocations: skiing, sailing, Yoga, tennis, travel. Home: PO Box 944 Telluride CO 81435-0944 Address: PO Box 253 Costilla NM 87524 E-mail: utemtn@aol.com.

TATYREK, ALFRED FRANK, consultant, materials and environmental engineer, analytical and research chemist; b. Hillside, N.J., Jan. 23, 1930; s. Frank Peter and Frances (Luxa) T. BS, Seton Hall U., 1954; postgrad., Rutgers U., 1956-57. Rsch. chemist Bakelite div. Union Carbide, Bloomfield, N.J., 1953-58, U.S. Radium Corp., Morristown, 1959-62; analytical chemist insp. Chem. Procurement Dist. U.S. Army, N.Y.C., 1962-64, rsch. chemist Picatinny Arsenal Dover, N.J., 1964-73; chem. materials engr. U.S. Army Armament Rsch., Devel. and Engrng. Ctr., 1973-95. Cons. polymer materials, environ. chemistry. Patentee pyrotechnic compositions, chemiluminescent compounds and processes, crank case oil vacuum purification sys. for internal combustion engines, method for the removal of thermoset potting compound from the electronics package of a munitions item; lectr., contbr. articles on mountaineering expdns. and adventures in the great mountain ranges of N.Am., S.Am., Europe and Africa to mags.; contbr. more than 50 sci. and tech. reports. 1st aid instr. ARC, Essex County, N.J., 1969-82; chief 1st aid Maplewood (N.J.) CD, 1971-91; patrol dir. Nat. Ski Patrol, Phoenicia, N.Y., 1978-84, sr. status, 1979-, lifetime Nat. Ski patroller So. N.Y. region, 1993-. Staff sgt. N.J. Air N.G., 1948-57. Recipient comdr.'s award for pub. svc. Dept. of Army, 1996. Mem. Nat. Soc. Inventors, Nat. Assn. Underwater Instrs. (cert. advanced diver and underwater photographer 1971—, cert. for Nitrox diving), Magician's Roundtable (life), Internat. Magician's Soc., Alpine Club of Can. (life mem., hiking leader), Appalachian Mountain Club, Sierra Club, Sigma Xi, The Scientific Rsch. Soc. (pres. Picatinny chpt. 1974-75, 79-80, 85-86). Roman Catholic. Achievements include 6 patents in field. Also climbed 15,771 feet Mt. Blanc, highest mountain peak in Europe; climbed to highest summit on Point Uruhu on 19,730 feet on Mt. Kilimanjaro, highest mountain peak in Africa, 1972; leader of climb on Matterhorn and Monte Rosa, Switzerland's highest peak; participant in numerous mountain expdns. in U.S. and Can., including 3 first ascents in No. Cascades of Wash. (S.E. ridge of Mt. Goode, Aug. 1963, Peak 7732 via the Snow Chute, Aug. 1964, East ridge of Bear Mountain Aug. 1964); numerous undersea photography trips to Caribbean and South Pacific coral reefs. Home: 27 Orchard Rd Maplewood NJ 07040-1919 E-mail: atatyrek@worldnet.att.net. *"God has given us a world rich in physical and intellectual beauty as well as intriguing scientific discovery. To earn these rewards we must seek out and meet the challanges of life, not as distasteful burdens, but as true opportunities upon which to build where others have failed or left off, using all the infinite resources that God has given to all of us".*

TAUB, AARON MYRON, healthcare administrator, consultant; b. Jersey City, Dec. 21, 1935; s. Isadore and Beatrice (Grotsky) T.; m. Rosemary Elizabeth Dessel, July 24, 1967; children: Michael David, Deborah Anne. BS, Wagner Coll., 1960; PhD, SUNY, Buffalo, 1965. Mgr. med. svcs. Fisons Can., Toronto, 1969-72; mgr., dir. quality control Fisons Corp., Bedford, Mass., 1972-82, dir. regulatory affairs, 1982-84, sr. scientist, 1984, dir. project mgmt., 1985-88, dir. new product coord. Rochester, N.Y., 1988-96. Mem., chmn. Bd. of Health, Stow, Mass., 1977-82. With USNR, 1953-55. Predoctoral fellow NIH, SUNY, 1962-64. Mem. Sigma Xi. Avocation: reading. Home: 5 Glen Cannon Trl Pittsford NY 14534-2346

TAUB, AMY F. dermatologist; b. Chgo. d. Max and Martha Forman; m. Jeff M. Taub, Sept. 6, 1992; 1 child, Zachary. MD, Northwestern U., 1985. Diplomate Am. Bd. Dermatology. Med. dir. div. dermatology Northwestern Meml. Physicians Group, Chgo., 1998—; founder, CEO Skinfo, LLC, Buffalo Grove, Ill., 1999—. Founder skin care website Skinfo.com, 2000. Fellow Am. Acad. Dermatology, Am. Soc. Dermatologic Soc., Am. Soc. Laser Medicine and Surgery, Chgo. Dermatol. Soc., Ill. State Dermatol. Soc. (chair laser subcom. 2000-01). Jewish. Office: Ctr Adv Dermatology and Laser Surgery 1535 Lake Cook Rd Ste 406 Northbrook IL 60062 Office Fax: 847-753-9356. E-mail: drtaub@skinfo.com., ataub@nmh.org.

TAUB, EDWARD, psychology researcher; b. Bklyn., Oct. 22, 1931; s. Samuel Hart and Ida Pearl (Kimmel) T.; m. Mildred Allen Taub, Aug. 13, 1959. BA, Bklyn. Coll., 1953; MA, Columbia U., 1959; PhD, NYU, 1969. Rsch. asst. Columbia U., N.Y.C., 1956, Dept. Exptl. Neurology, Jewish Chronic Disease Hosp., N.Y.C., 1957-60, rsch. assoc., 1960-68; dir. Behavioral Biology Ctr., Inst. for Behavioral Rsch., 1968-83; assoc. dir. Inst. for Behavioral Rsch., 1978-83; univ. prof. psychology U. Ala., Birmingham, 1986—, sr. scientist ctr. for aging, univ. prof., 2000—; standing guest prof. U. Konstanz, Germany, 1995—; guest prof. U. Jena, Germany, 1996—. Asst. prof. dept. psychiatry Johns Hopkins U., Balt., 1972-82; vis. prof. grad. prog. dept. psychology CUNY, 1984-85; vis. prof. U. Tuebingen, U. Trier, U. Muenster, Humboldt U., Germany, 1993—. Contbr. articles to profl. jours.; co-inventor technique of thermal biofeedback, 1970-71. Recipient Pioneering Rsch. Contbn. award, 1989, Disting. Scientist of 1998 award Assn. of Applied Psychophysiol. and Biofeedback, Ireland Prize for Scholarly Distinction U. Ala., Birmingham, 1997, Humboldt Rsch. award, 2000; Guggenheim Found. fellow, 1983-84. Fellow AAAS, APA (exec. com. div. 6), Soc. for Behavioral Medicine, Am. Psychol. Soc. (charter, William James Fellow award 1997); mem. Soc. for Neurosci., Biofeedback Soc. Am. (pres. 1978-79, Outstanding Rsch. Contbn. award 1988), Am. Physiol. Soc. (exec. com. neurosci. sect. 1988-91). Office: U Ala at Birmingham 712 CPM 1530 3d Ave S Birmingham AL 35294-0018 E-mail: etaub@uab.edu.

TAUB, ELI IRWIN, arbitrator, lawyer; b. N.Y.C., July 6, 1938; s. Max and Belle (Slutsky) T.; m. Nancy Denise Bell, May 15, 1983; 1 child, Jennifer. BA, Bklyn. Coll., 1960; JD, NYU, 1963. Bar: N.Y. 1964, U.S. Dist. Ct. (no. dist.) N.Y. 1979. Ptnr. Silverman, Silverman & Taub, Schenectady, N.Y., 1971-77; pres. Eli I. Taub, P.C., 1978-2001; judge Schenectady County (N.Y.) Family Ct., 2001; staff Fed. Mediation & Conciliation Svc., 2001—. Arbitrator Am. Arbitration Assn., N.Y. State Pub. Employment Rels. Bd., 1966-; N.Y. State Pub. Employers Rels. Bd.; hearing officer, paralegal adv. com. Schenectady County C.C. Chmn. trustees Joseph Egan Supreme Ct. Library, Schenectady, 1980, 81, 84; pres. Schenectady County Republican Club, 1985-86; v.p. Jewish Fedn. Schenectady, 1983-86; mem. surrogate decision making com. N.Y. State Commn. on Quality of Care for the Mentally Disabled; bd. dirs. Jewish Cmty. Ctr., Jewish Family Svcs. N.Y. Adolescent Pregnancy Prevention Svcs.; advocate Nat. Coll. of Advocacy; vice-chmn. Schenectady Co. Indsl. Devel. Agy. Recipient Vol. of Yr. award Jewish Family Svcs., 1998, Humanitarian of Yr. award Alcohol and Substance Abuse Coun., 2001. Mem.: ATLA, Indsl. Rels. Rsch. Assn., Nat. Orgn. Social Security Claimant Reps., Schenectady County Bar Assn., N.Y. State Trial Lawyers Assn., N.Y. State Bar Assn., N.Y. State Family Ct. Judges Assn., Am. Judges Assn., Am. Arbitration Assn., B'nai B'rith (pres. 1976—77, Youth Svcs. award 1985). Home: 105 N Ferry St Schenectady NY 12305-1610 Office: 105 N Ferry St Schenectady NY 12305 Fax: 518-393-0719.

TAUB, ETHAN, neurosurgeon; b. Boston, June 15, 1964; s. Arthur and Sheila Taub. AB magna cum laude, Harvard U., 1984, MD, 1988. Intern in surgery Mass. Gen. Hosp., Boston, 1988-89; instr. Harvard/MIT Divan. Health Sci. and Tech., 1989-90; resident, chief resident N.Y. Hosp./Cornell Med. Ctr., N.Y.C., 1990-95; E. M. Botterall fellow in functional neursurgery U. Toronto, Ont., Can., 1995-96; Moreley travelling fellow harvard Med. Sch., 1996-97; neurosurgeon U. Zurich, Switzerland, 1997-99; head functional neurosurgery U. Bern, Switzerland, 1999—. Contbr. numerous articles to profl. jours.; translator (from French) the Neurosurgical Treatment of Parkinson's Disease, 1997; translator chpts.: (from German) Contemporary Psychiatry, 2001. Mem. Am. Assn. Neurol. Surgeons, Phi Beta Kappa. Achievements include research on surgical treatment of movement disorders, pain and epilepsy. Home: Bellariastrasse 61 8038 Zurich Switzerland Office: Dept Neurosurgery Inselspital 3010 Bern Switzerland Fax: (+41) 31-382-2414. E-mail: ethan.taub.md@swissonline.ch., ethan.taub@insel.ch.

TAUB, JESSE J. electrical engineering researcher; b. N.Y.C., Apr. 27, 1927; s. Julius and Ida (Orlansky) T.; m. Eva Pollack, Dec. 24, 1955 (dec. Nov. 1973); children: Richard Lawrence, Jocelyn Cara, Suzanne Mara; m. Naomi Etta Trachtenberg, June 30, 1974. BEE, CCNY, 1948; MEE, Poly. U., 1949. Group leader microwave electronics, Material Lab. USN, Bklyn., 1949-55; engr. Airborne Instruments Lab., Mineola, N.Y., 1955-58, sect. leader, 1958-61, engrng. cons., 1961-75; chief scientist AIL Systems Inc., Melville, 1975-93; cons., 1993—. Mem. engring. adv. bd. N.Y. Tech., Hofstra U. Author: (with others) Microwave Measurements, 1963; contbr. numerous papers to profl. publs.; patentee microwave techniques With USN, 1945-46. Fellow IEEE (Centennial medal 1984, 3rd Millenium medal 2000, C.A. Fowler award 1993, Region 1 William Terry award 2001, adminstrv. com. 1972-74, program chmn. microwave symposium, steering com., chmn. L.I. sect. awards, USAB Divsn. award 2002); mem. Archaeology Inst. Am. Democrat. Jewish. Avocations: classical musician, contract bridge, archaeology. Home and Office: 115 Northgate Cir Melville NY 11747-3045 E-mail: jjtaub@aol.com.

TAUB, NADINE, law educator; b. Jan. 21, 1943; BA with distinction, Swarthmore Coll., 1964; LLB, Yale U., 1968; diploma with distinction, Stockholm U., 1973. Bar: N.Y., N.J., U.S. Ct. Appeals (2d and 3d cirs.), U.S. Supreme Ct. Asst. prof., assoc. prof. Rutgers Sch. Law, 1973-82, prof., 1982—, dir. Women's Rights Litigation Clinic, 1973—, prof. law II, 1988—. Project dir. Cmty. Legal Action Workshop ACLU, Newark, 1969-72, part-time lectr. Stockholm U. Sch. Social Work, 1972-73, 98; rschr. and presenter in field. Co-editor: Reproductive Laws for the 1990s: A Briefing Handbook, 1988, Reproductive Laws for the 1990s, 1989; co-author: Adult Domestic Violence: Statutory, Constitutional and Equitable Issues, 1981, The Law of Sex Discrimination, 1988, 2d edit., 1993, Sex Discrimination and the Law: History, Theory and Practice, 1984, 2d rev. edit., 1996; contbr. articles to profl. jours., chpts. to books. Reginald Heber Smith fellow Morrisania Legal Svcs., Bronx, 1968-69; S.I. Newhouse scholar, 1991—. Mem. Soc. Am. Law Tchs. (bd. trustees), N.J. Bar Assn., Assn. Bar City N.Y. Office: Rutgers Sch Law 123 Washington St Newark NJ 07102-3026 E-mail: taub@andromeda.rutgers.edu.

TAUB, RICHARD PAUL, social sciences educator; b. Bklyn., Apr. 16, 1937; s. Martin Glynn and Frances (Israel) T.; m. Doris Susan Leventhal, Aug. 14, 1961 (dec. Feb. 1996); children: Neela Robin, Zachariah Jacob; m. Betty G. Farrell, June 21, 2000. BA, U. Mich., 1959; MA, Harvard U., 1962, PhD in Social Relations, 1966. Asst. prof. sociology Brown U., Providence, 1965-69; from asst. prof. to Paul Klapper prof. of social scis. U. Chgo., 1969—, assoc. dean Coll. of Univ., 1982-86, chmn. com. on human devel., 2000—. Adv. bd. Neighborhood Preservation Initiative, 1993-2000; chair adv. bd. Nat. Cmty. Devel. Initiative, 1991-95; dir. South Ark. Rural Devel. Study, 1988—; Disting. visitor Mac Arthur Found., 1998. Author: Community Capitalism, Bureaucrats Under Stress, (with D. Garth Taylor and Jan Dunham) Paths of Neighborhood Change, (with Doris L. Taub) Entrepreneurship in India's Small Scale Industries; editor: (with Doris L. Taub) American Society in Tocqueville's Time and Today; co-editor Studies of Urban Soc., 1978—; contbr. articles to profl. jours. Chmn. bd. St. Thomas the Apostle Sch., Chgo., 1983-86; bd. dirs. Hyde Park Kenwood Cmty. Conf., Chgo., 1972-75; bd. seminary Coop Bookstore, Chgo., 1994—; chair com. on human devel., U. Chgo., 2000—. Angell scholar U. Mich., 1956; Woodrow Wilson fellow Harvard U., 1959-60, W.E.B. DuBois Inst. fellow, 1997-98; grantee Am. Inst. Indian Studies, Ford Found., MacArthur Found., NSF, Wieboldt Found., Nat. Inst. Justice. Mem. Am. Sociol. Assn., Midwest Sociol. Soc., Assn. for Asian Studies. Avocations: bicycling, music. Office: Univ Chgo 5730 S Woodlawn Ave Chicago IL 60637 E-mail: rpt2@uchicago.edu.

TAUB, ROBERT ALLAN, lawyer; b. Denver, Nov. 25, 1923; s. Clarence Arthur and Mary Frances (Jones) T.; m. Doris Irene Schroeder, Dec. 22, 1945; children: Amanda, Jonathan, Barbara. BA, U. Chgo., 1944, JD, 1947. Bar: Ill. 1947. Legal staff Marshall Field & Co., Chgo., 1947-50; mgr. exec. compensation Ford Motor Co., Dearborn, Mich., 1950-63, asst. sect., 1963-74, dir. corp. affairs planning, 1974-98. Pres. Dearborn Community Arts Council, 1971-72; trustee Internat. Mus. Photography, George Eastman House, Rochester, N.Y., 1976—, chmn., 1979-82; mem. adv. bd. U. Mich. Dearborn, 1980—, Met. Mus. Art, N.Y.C., 1987—; trustee Henry Ford Hosp., Detroit, 1983—; chmn. Dearborn Pub. Libr., 1986—; bd. dirs., mem. exec. com., chmn. fin. com., Health Alliance Plan, 1992—. Mem. ABA, Ill. Bar Assn, Art Inst. Chicago, 1998—. Presbyterian. Home: 1824 Hawthorne St Dearborn MI 48128-1448 E-mail: rataub@mediaone.net.

TAUB, STEPHEN RICHARD, lawyer; b. N.Y.C., Oct. 5, 1944; s. Irving Robert and Sylvia T.; m. Alyson Zoe Winter, Dec. 23, 1968. BA, Queens Coll., 1965; JD, NYU, 1968. Bar: N.Y. 1969, U.S. Dist. Ct. (ea. and so. dists.) N.Y. 1970, U.S. Ct. Appeals (2nd cir.) 1971, U.S. Supreme Ct. 1972. Asst. dist. atty., bur. chief Kings County Dist. Attys. Office, Bklyn., 1970—77; pvt. practice Garden City, 1977—96; ptnr. Ostrow and Taub, LLP, 1996—2000, Schlissel, Ostrow, Karabatos, Poepplein & Taub, PLLC, Mineola, NY, 2000—02; pvt. practice, 2002—. Matrimonial case neutral evaluator Nassau County Supreme Ct., Mineola, 1997—. Village Justice Village Kensington, Great Neck, N.Y., 1986-98; Acting Village Justice Village Old Brookville, N.Y., 1998—. Fellow Am. Acad. Matrimonial Lawyers; mem. ABA, N.Y. Family Law Am. Inn of Ct. (master), N.Y. State Bar Assn., N.Y. State Magistrates Assn., Nassau County Bar Assn., Nassau County Magistrates Assn. (pres. 1993-94). Avocation: tennis. Office: 190 Willis Ave Mineola NY 11501

TAUB, THEODORE CALVIN, lawyer; b. Springfield, Mass., Jan. 1, 1935; s. Samuel and Sara Lee (Daum) T.; m. Roberta Mae Ginsburg, Aug. 23, 1959; children: Tracy, Andrew, Adam. AB, Duke U., 1956; JD, U. Fla., 1960. Bar: Fla., 1960, U.S. Supreme Ct. Atty. Shumaker, Loop & Kendrick, LLP, Tampa. Asst. city atty. City of Tampa, 1963-67; city atty. City of Temple Terrace, Fla., 1974—; panelist in field. Contbr. articles to profl. jours. Chmn. Tampa-Hillsborough (Fla.) County Expy. Authority, 1974-84; mem. Hillsborough County Charter Commn., 1966-69, Local Govt. Mgmt. Efficiency Com., 1979, State of Fla. Environ. Efficiency Study Commn., 1986-88; founder Tampa Bay Performing Arts Ctr. Fellow: Am. Bar Found; mem. ABA (chmn. real property litigation com. 1981-86, chmn. com. on housing and urban environ. 1989-91), Am. Coll. Real Estate Lawyers (bd. govs.), Am. Land Title Assn. (lenders' counsel group), Fla. Bar Assn. (bd. cert. real estate lawyer), Fla. Jaycees (pres.), Tau Epsilon Phi. Democrat. Jewish. Home: 4937 Lyford Cay Rd Tampa FL 33629-4828 Office: Bank of Am 101 E Kennedy Blvd Ste 2800 Tampa FL 33602-5869 E-mail: ttaub@slk-law.com.

TAUBE, HENRY, chemistry educator; b. Sask., Can., Nov. 30, 1915; arrived in U.S., 1937, naturalized, 1942; s. Samuel and Albertina (Tiledetski) Taube; m. Mary Alice Wesche, Nov. 27, 1952; children: Linda, Marianna, Heinrich, Karl. BS, U. Sask., 1935, MS, 1937, LLD, 1973; PhD, U. Calif., 1940; PhD (hon.) , Hebrew U. of Jerusalem, 1979; DSc (hon.) , U. Chgo., 1983, Poly. Inst., N.Y., 1984, SUNY, 1985, U. Guelph, 1987, Seton Hall U., 1988, Lajos Kossuth U. Debrecen, Hungary, 1988; DSc, Northwestern U., 1990, U. Athens, 1993. Instr. U. Calif., 1940—41; instr., asst. prof. Cornell U., 1941—46; faculty U. Chgo., 1946—62, prof., 1952—62, chmn. dept. chemistry, 1955—59; prof. chemistry Stanford U., 1962—90; prof. emeritus Stanford U, 1990—; Marguerite Blake Wilbur prof. Stanford U., 1976, chmn. dept., 1971—74. Baker lectr. Cornell U., 1965. Recipient Harrison Howe award, 1961, Chandler medal, Columbia U., 1964, F. P. Dwyer medal, U. NSW, 1973, Nat. medal of sci., 1976—77, Excellence in Grad. Tchg. and Innovative Sci. award, Allied Chem., 1979, Nobel prize in chemistry, 1983, Bailar medal, U. Ill., 1983, award in chemistry, Robert A. Welch Found., 1983, Disting. Achievement award, Internat. Precious Metals Inst., 1986, Merit award, Brazilian Order of Sci., 1994; fellow, Guggenheim, 1949, 1955. Fellow: Royal Soc. Can. (hon.), Indian Chem. Soc. (hon.), Royal Soc. Chemistry (hon.); mem.: NAS (award in chem. scis. 1983), Royal Soc., Royal Danish Acad. Scis. and Letters, Finnish Acad. Sci. and Letters, Am. Philos. Soc., Royal Physiographical Soc. of Lund, Am. Chem. Soc. (award for nuclear applications in chemistry 1955, Kirkwood award 1965, Disting. Svc. in Advancement Inorganic Chemistry award 1967, Nichols medal 1971, Willard Gibbs medal 1971, T.W. Richards medal 1980—81, Monsanto Co. award in inorganic chemistry 1981, Linus Pauling award 1981, Priestley medal 1985, Oesper award 1986, G.M. Kosolapoff award 1990), Engrng. Acad. Japan (assoc.), Am. Acad. Arts and Scis., Australian Acad. Scis. (corr.), Brazilian Acad. Scis. (corr.), Chem. Soc. Japan (hon.), Hungarian Acad. Scis. (hon.), Can. Soc. Chemistry (hon.), Coll. Chemists of Catalonia and Beleares (hon.), Sigma Xi, Phi Beta Kappa, Phi Lambda Upsilon (hon.). Office: Stanford U Dept Chemistry Stanford CA 94305-5080 E-mail: cdpiercy@stanford.edu.*

TAUBENFELD, HARRY SAMUEL, lawyer; b. Bklyn., June 27, 1929; s. Marcus Isaac and Anna (Engelhard) T.; m. Florence Spatz, June 17, 1956; children: Anne Gail Weisbrod, Stephen Marshall. BA, Bklyn. Coll., 1951; JD, Columbia U., 1954. Bar: N.Y. 1955, U.S. Supreme Ct. 1965, U.S. Dist. Ct. (so. and ea. dists.) N.Y. 1976. Assoc. Benjamin H. Schor, Bklyn., 1955-58; ptnr. Zuckerbrod & Taubenfeld, Cedarhurst (N.Y.), N.Y.C., 1958—; bd. dirs. Cornerstone Real Estate Income Trust, 1993—, Next Generation Mktg., Inc., 1996-99. Village atty. Village of Cedarhurst, 1977-88, trustee, 1989-2001; mem. bd. Downtown Cedarhurst Bus. Improvement Dist., 1993; legis. chmn., counsel Nassau County Village Ofcls., 1979-86, v.p., 1991-93, pres., 1993-94, mem. exec. com., 1989-99, chmn. intergovtl. liaison com., 1991-93; mem. legis. com. N.Y. State Conf. Mayors, 1979-87, 92-93; mem. exec. bd. Tri-County Village Ofcls., 1991-95, pres., 1993-94; arbitrator Am. Arbitration Assn. Dist. Ct. Nassau County, 1980—, Assessment Rev. Panel, Supreme Ct., Nassau County, 1981—; mem. Constl. Bicentennial Com., 1987-89; hon. trustee Cong. Beth Shalom, Lawrence, N.Y., 1990-2001; nat. bd. dirs. Zionist Orgn. Am. Assoc. chmn. Am. Zionist Fedn., 1985-87; pres. Herut Zionists Am., 1977-79; v.p. Hartman YMHA, 1983-87; del. World Zionist Congress, 1977, 82, 87; mem. Zionist Gen. Coun., 1977-83; bd. govs. Jewish Agy., 1983-92; mem. exec. com. World Zionist Orgn., 1983-92; trustee United Jewish Appeal, 1986-91; bd. dirs. United Israel Appeal, 1986-91; hon. vice chmn., bd. dirs. Jewish Nat. Fund, 1987-89; nat. bd. dirs. Am. for a Safe Israel; hon. pres. World Coun. Herut Hatzoa, Jerusalem, Internat. Bd. Youthtown of Israel. Recipient Centenial award Jabotinsky Found. 1981, Betar Youth award World Betar 1982, award Internat. League for Repatriation of Russian Jews 1977, Youth Towns of Israel Leadership award 1973, Israel Bonds Leadership award 1976, Life Time Achievement award Israel Bonds 1991, Defender of Jerusalem award 1991, Israel Bonds Menachem Begin Leadership award, 1999. Mem.: Internat. Assn. Jewish Lawyers and Jurists, Beth El (New Rochelle, N.Y.), Zionist Orgn. of Am., Jewish War Vets., B'nai B'righ, Nordau Circle Club. Home: 21 N Chatsworth Ave Larchmont NY 10538 Office: PO Box 488 575 Chestnut St Cedarhurst NY 11516-2223

TAUBER, JEAN A. healthcare management executive; b. Erie, Pa., Nov. 1, 1954; d. William Lester and June Ann Maurer; m. Robert Joseph Tauber, July 23, 1983; 1 child, William Joseph. BS in Edn., Edinboro U., 1976; MS in Info. and Libr. Sci., SUNY, Buffalo, 1979. Corp. libr. Hammermill Paper Co., Erie, Pa., 1979-82; dir. edn./libr. Hamot Health Found., 1982-92; program leader St. Vincent Health Ctr., 1992-96; mgr. outreach svcs. Erie Pub. Libr. Sys., 1996-97; dir. performance improvement Shriners Hosps. Children, 1997—. Exec. bd., pres. N.W. Pa. Interlibrary Coop., Erie, 1982-91, ASTD, Erie, 1989-94; exec. bd., examiner Quality Awards Bd., Erie, 1990-99; bd. dirs. Family Svcs. N.W. Pa., Erie. Trustee exec. bd. First Presbyn. Ch. Covenant, 1994-2000. Mem. Am. Coll. Healthcare Execs. Avocations: cooking, gardening. Office: Shriners Hosps for Children 1645 W 8th St Erie PA 16505-5007 E-mail: jtauber@shrinenet.org.

TAUBER, MARK J. lawyer; b. Detroit, Mar. 25, 1949; s. Max M. and Beatrice R. (Roth) T.; m. Anita L. Tilben, June 23, 1970; children: Melissa A., Benjamin M., Allison B. BA, U. Mich., 1970; JD, George Washington U., 1973. Bar: D.C. 1973, Md. 1974, U.S. Supreme Ct. 1980. Assoc. Pierson, Ball & Dowd, Washington, 1973-79, ptnr., 1980-82, Piper & Marbury, Washington, 1982-99, Piper, Marbury, Rudnick & Wolfe, Washington, 1999—2002, Piper Rudnick LLP, 2002—. Home: 11515 Big Piney Way Potomac MD 20854-1365 Office: Piper Rudnick LLP 1200 19th St NW Washington DC 20036-2430

TAUBER, SONYA LYNN, nurse; b. Harford County, Md., Apr. 22, 1963; d. Daniel Raymond and Helen Tauber. AA, Harford Community Coll., 1987; student, Frostburg State Coll., 1981-83; BSN, Notre Dame Nursing Coll., 1997. Cert. geriatric aide, intravenous therapy. Nurse Bel Air (Md.) Convalescent Ctr.; staff nurse orthopedic fl., developer policies and procedure Greater Balt. Med. Ctr., 1987-95; hospice home care Stella Maris Hospice Home Care, Balt., 1995-97; nurse Blakehurst Retirement Cmty. Health Care Ctr., 1997-98; program dir./nurse adult med. day program United Cerebral palsy of Ctrl. Md., Essex, 1998—.

TÄUBER, UWE CLAUS, physicist; b. Rehau, Germany, Sept. 12, 1963; s. Adolf and Gertraud (Dietrich) T.; m. Karin Ziegler, July 19, 1990; children: Lilian Alexandra, Judith Melanie. Physics Diploma, Tech. U. Munich, Germany, 1988, DrRerNat, 1992; DrRerNatHabil, Tech. U. Munich, 1999. Rsch. staff Tech. U. Munich, 1988-93; postdoctoral fellow Harvard U., Cambridge, Mass., 1993-95; rsch. assoc. Oxford (Eng.) U., 1995-97; habilitation fellow Tech. U. Munich, 1997-98; asst. prof. physics Va. Tech., 1998—. Contbr. articles to Phys. Rev. B/E, Phys. Rev. Letters, Ency. of Applied Physics, others. Recipient various scholarships; DFG postdoctoral rsch. fellow, 1993, Marie Curie fellow, 1996, DFG habilitation fellow, 1997; NSF rsch. grantee, 2000. Mem. German Phys. Soc., Am. Phys. Soc., European Phys. Soc., Franco-Bavaria. Lutheran. Avocations: golf, piano. Home: 6104 Albemarle Ln Blacksburg VA 24060-8116 Office: Va Polytechnic Inst and U Physics Dept Blacksburg VA 24061-0435 E-mail: tauber@vt.edu.

TAUBMAN, MARTIN ARNOLD, immunologist, educator; b. N.Y.C., July 10, 1940; s. Herman and Betty (Berger) T.; m. Joan Petra Mikelbank, May 30, 1965; children: Benjamin Abby, Joel David. BS, Bklyn. Coll., 1961; DDS, Columbia U., 1965; PhD, SUNY, Buffalo, 1970; MA (hon.), Harvard U., 1997. Asst. mem. staff Forsyth Dental Center, Boston, 1970—, head immunology dept., 1972—, assoc. mem. staff, 1974-80; sr. staff mem. The Forsyth Inst., 1980—; asst. clin. prof. oral biology and pathophysiology Harvard U. Sch. Dental Medicine, 1976-79, assoc. clin. prof., 1979-97, prof. oral biology, 1997—. Mem. oral biology and medicine study sect. NIH, 1980-84 Editor: (with J. Slots) Contemporary Microbiology and Immunology; contbr. articles to profl. jours., chpts. to books. Recipient Rsch. Career Devel. award, 1971-76, Fred Birnberg Alumni award for disting. dental rsch. Columbia U. Assn. Dental Alumni, Disting. Faculty award Harvard Sch. Dental Medicine, 1990, MERIT award NIH, 1991-2000; USPHS fellow, 1962-63; postdoctoral fellow, 1966-70. Mem. Am. Soc. Microbiology, Soc. Mucosal Immunology, Internat. Assn. Dental Research (Oral Biology award 1991), Am. Assn. Immunologists, Am. Assn. Dental Research (v.p. 1987—, pres. elect 1988, pres. 1989). Office: The Forsyth Inst 140 Fenway Boston MA 02115-3799

TAUBMAN, WILLIAM CHASE, political science educator; b. N.Y.C., Nov. 13, 1941; s. Howard and Nora (Stern) T.; m. Jane Dea Andelman, May 18, 1969; children— Alexander, Phoebe. AB, Harvard U., 1962; MA, cert. of Russian Inst., Columbia U., 1965, PhD, 1969; MA (hon.), Amherst Coll., 1978. Instr. Amherst Coll., Mass., 1967-69, asst. prof., 1969-73, assoc. prof., 1973-78, prof. dept. polit. sci., 1978-83, Bertrand Snell prof., 1983—. Mem. planning staff U.S. Dept. State, Washington, 1970-71; mem. bd. Internat. Rsch. and Exch. Bd., N.Y.C., 1971-74, mem. selection com., 1984-85; vis. assoc. prof. Yale U., New Haven, spring 1975; chmn. adv. com. Cold War Internat. History Project, Woodrow Wilson Ctr., Washington, 1993—; mem. Internat. Acad. Adv. Group, Russian Fgn. Ministry Archives, 1992-97; assoc. Davis Ctr. for Russian Studies, Harvard. Author: The View from Lenin Hills, 1967; Governing Soviet Cities, 1973; Stalin's American Policy, 1982; co-author: (with Jane Taubman) Moscow Spring, 1989; editor, translator: Khrushchev on Khrushchev (Sergei N. Khrushchev), 1990; editor: Globalism and Its Critics, 1973; co-editor: Nikita Khrushchev, 2000. Woodrow Wilson Nat. Found. fellow, 1962; Ford Found. fellow, 1963-67; Council Fgn. Relations fellow, 1970-71; Rockefeller Found. fellow, 1983; Columbia U. Harriman Inst. sr. fellow, 1987; grantee Nat. Council Soviet and East European Research, 1984; Fulbright-Hays Faculty Rsch. fellow, 1988, NEH fellow, 1992, Woodrow Wilson Internat. Ctr. for Scholars fellow, 1999-2000. Mem. Council Fgn. Relations, Authors Guild. Home: 43 Hitchcock Rd Amherst MA 01002-2500 Office: Amherst Coll Dept Polit Sci Amherst MA 01004-2259 E-mail: wctaubman@amherst.edu.

TAUC, JAN, physics educator; b. Pardubice, Czechoslovakia, Apr. 15, 1922; came to U.S., 1969, naturalized, 1978; s. Jan and Josefa (Semonska) T.; m. Vera Koubelova, Oct. 18, 1947; children: Elena (Mrs. Milan Kokta), Jan. Ing.Dr. in Elec. Engrng., Tech. U. Prague, 1949; RNDr., Charles U., 1956; Dr.Sc. in Physics, Czechoslovak Acad. Scis., 1956. Scientist microwave research Sci. and Tech. Research Inst., Tanvald and Prague, 1949-52; head semiconductor dept. Inst. Solid State Physics, Czechoslovak Acad. Scis., 1953-69; prof. exptl. physics Charles U., 1964-69, dir. Inst. Physics, 1968-69; mem. tech. staff Bell Telephone Labs., Murray Hill, N.J., 1969-70; prof. engrng. and physics Brown U., 1970-83, L. Herbert Ballou prof. engrng. and physics, 1983-92, L. Herbert Ballou prof. emeritus, 1992—, dir. material research lab., 1983-88. Dir. E. Fermi Summer Sch., Varenna, Italy, 1965; vis. prof. U. Paris, 1969, Stanford U., 1977, Max Planck Inst. Solid State Research, Stuttgart, Germany, 1982; UNESCO fellow, Harvard, 1961-62 Author: Photo and Thermoelectric Effects in Semiconductors, 1962, also numerous articles; editor: The Optical Properties of Solids, 1966, Amorphous and Liquid Semiconductors, 1974; co-editor: Solid State Communications, 1963-92. Recipient Nat. prize Czechoslovak Govt., 1955, 69; Sr. U.S. Scientist award Humboldt Found., 1981, Silver medal Union of Czechoslovak Mathematicians and Physicists, 1992. Fellow AAAS, Am. Phys. Soc. (Frank Isakson prize 1982, David Adler award 1988); mem. NAS, European Phys. Soc. (founding), Czechoslovak Acad. Scis. (corr. 1963-71, 90-91, fgn. 1991-92, Hlavka medal 1992), Czech Learned Soc. (hon.). Office: Brown U Divsn Engring Providence RI 02912-0001

TAUCHERT, THEODORE RICHMOND, mechanical engineer, educator; s. Elwyn Harding and Eleanor (Richmond) T.; m. Ann Dudley Bradlee, May 10, 1958; children: Amy T. Tauchert, Sarah T. Rushing, Rebecca T. McGowan, Charles W., Macy G. Casperson. BSE., Princeton U., 1957; M.Eng., Yale U., 1960, D.Eng., 1964. Structural engr. Sikorsky Aircraft, Stratford, Conn., 1957-61; research asoc., lectr. Princeton U., N.J., 1964-65, asst. prof., 1965-70; assoc. prof. U. Ky., Lexington, 1970-76, prof. engrng. mechanics, 1976—, chmn. dept., 1980-84, 88-94. Editorial bd.: Acta Mechanica, 1976—, Jour. Thermal Stresses, 1981— ; author: Energy Principles in Structural Mechanics, 1974; contbr. articles to profl. jours. Served to 2d lt. U.S. Army, 1957-58. Mem. ASCE, ASME, Am. Soc. Engrng. Edn., Soc. Engrng. Sci., Sigma Xi Home: 1620 Richmond Rd Lexington KY 40502-1620 Office: U Ky Dept Mech Engring Lexington KY 40506-0001

TAUDIEN, EDWARD PAUL, retired construction executive; b. N.Y.C., Jan. 25, 1932; s. Edward Peter Paul and Lucia Sylvia (Linder) T.; m. Patricia A. Dean, June 14, 1958; children: Mark, Glenn, Evan. BS in Engring., Cooper Union Sch. Engrng., N.Y.C., 1959. Registered profl. engr., N.Y., N.J., Fla. V.p. Skinner & Cook, Inc., Roselle Pk., N.J., 1954-81; mgr. ops. So. Bldg. Divsn. Perini Corp., West Palm Beach, Fla., 1981-86; v.p., gen. mgr. Proctor Constrn. Co., Vero Beach, 1987; area ops. mgr. Dawson Constrn. Co., Fla., N.C., 1988-93. Mayor Branchburg (N.J.) Twp., 1980; committeeman, 1975, 77-81; mem. Branchburg Planning Bd., 1977-81, Zoning Bd. Appeals, Palm Beach Gardens, Fla., 1984-87. Trustee Plainfield (N.J.) Masons Welfare & Pension Funds, 1974-77. Cpl. U.S. Army, 1952-54. Decorated Occupation Medal Germany, 1952, Nat. Def. Svc. Medal, 1953. Republican. Presbyterian. Avocations: world travel, history. Home: 4992 SE Mariner Village Ln Stuart FL 34997-2151

TAUER, PAUL E. mayor, educator; b. 1935; m. Katherine Eldredge, Sept. 1, 1956; children: Paul E. Jr., Edward, Roch, Eugene, Kathryn, Tammie, Andrew, Timothy. BA in Historyand Edn., Regis Coll., 1961; MA in Edn. Adminstrn., U. No. Colo., 1964. Tchr. Denver Pub. Schs., 1961-92; ret., 1992. Mayor City of Aurora, Colo., 1987—, mem. Aurora City Coun., 1979-1987; mem. Adams County Coordinating Com., Gov.'s Met. Transp. Roundtable; active Aurora airport coms. Mem. N.O.I.S.E. Office: Office of Mayor 1470 S Havana St Aurora CO 80012-4014 E-mail: ptauer@ci.aurora.co.us.*

TAULBEE, THOMAS LESTER, psychotherapist, educator; b. Normal, Ill., June 12, 1947; s. Marion L. and Marjorie S. T. BS, Ill. State U., 1970; MS, Tex. A&M U., 1971, EdD, 1973. Cert. marriage and family therapist; cert. sports counselor. Psychotherapist Human Resource Devel. Ctr., Dallas, 1974-76; prof. psychology Richland Coll., 1976—, prof. history, 1994—. North Tex. regl. dir. Nat. Inst. Sports, 2000—; bd. advisors Revival Fires Ministries, Branson West, Mo., 1997-99, bd.dirs. Sports Sys. Internat., 2001—, N. Tex. Regl. Dir. of Nat. Inst. of Sports, 2000—. Co-author: Psychology from a Personal Perspective, 1992, rev. edit., 1997; editor, co -author: Personal Applications of Psychology, 1997. Dir. Superior Student Roundtable, Parker, Tex., 1993, 1996—. Ctr. for Behavioral Studies U. North Tex., Denton, 1973-74; named Basketball All-Am., Ill. State U., 1969; named to Ill. State U. Athletic Hall of Fame. Mem. Tex. Jr. Coll. Teachers Assn., Nat. Assn. Scholars, Assn. Behavior Analysis. Avocations: world travel, scuba diving, cooking. Office: Richland Coll 12800 Abrams Rd Dallas TX 75243-2173 E-mail: taulbee@flash.net.

TAUNTON, KATHRYN JAYNE, accountant; b. Thomaston, Ga., Nov. 3, 1953; d. Mack Doudal and Martha Jayne (Goolsby) T. AA, Cypress Coll., 1973; BA in Accounting, Calif. State U., 1977. Circulation clk. Buena Park Library Dist., Buena Park, Calif., 1973-76; account supr. ORCO State Employees Credit Union, Santa Ana, 1977-78, Santa Ana City Credit Union, 1978-79; self employed Reliable Credit Union Service, Buena Park, 1979-95. Avocations: music, travel, theater, cooking.

TAUNTON, ROMA LEE, nurse educator and researcher; Diploma, Ida V. Moffett Sch. Nursing, 1959; BS In Nursing, U. Ala., 1963; M in Nursing, Emory U., 1965; PhD in Ednl. Psychology, U. Kans., 1983. Chief nurse children & youth project U. Ala. Med. Ctr., Birmingham, Ala., 1967-68; coord. children & youth project U. Ark. Med. Ctr., Little Rock, 1968-69; coord. pediatric nursing Grady Meml. Hosp., Atlanta, 1970-74; dir. pediatric nurse practitioner project Am. Nurses Assn., 1974-76, dir. nursing practice dept. Mo., 1976-79; assoc. prof. Sch. Nursing U. Kans. Med. Ctr., 1983-92, prof., 1992—; co-investigator Nat. Database Nursing Quality Indicators. Cons. in field. Contbr. numerous articles to profl. jours. Recipient Cert. Outstanding Svc. in Nursing and Health Programs Met. chpt ARC, 1973, Mable Korsell award, 1975, Outstanding Young Women Am. award, 1974, Investigator Recognition award U. Kans. Med. Ctr., 1989, Dean's Rsch. award U. Kans. Sch. Nursing, 1989, Am. Jour. Nursing Books of the Yr. award, 1986, 88, 89, Chancellor's award for Outstanding Teaching, 1992, Kemper fellow, 1997; rsch. grantee Am. Nurses Found., NIH, Sigma Theta Tau Pinnacle Mentor award, 2002. Fellow Am. Acad. Nursing; mem. ANA, Midwest Nursing Rsch. Soc., Acad. for Health Svcs. Rsch., Sigma Theta Tau (rsch. grantee, Pinnacle Mentor award 2002). Home: 4417 Wyoming St Kansas City MO 64111-4370 Office: U Kans Med Ctr Sch Nursing 39th Rainbow Blvd Kansas City KS 66160-0001

TAUNTON-RIGBY, ALISON, pharmaceutical executive; b. Barnsley, Eng., Apr. 23, 1944; came to U.S., 1968; d. Charles Francis and Joan (Willis) Forster; m. Roger Taunton-Rigby, 1966 (div. Nov. 1985); children: Jonathan Forster, Rolf Kristian, Jason Erik, Liv Kathryn. BSc, Bristol (Eng.) U., 1965, PhD, 1968; AMP, Harvard U., 1985. V.p. R & D Genome Therapeutics, Waltham, Mass., 1969-83; v.p. bus. devel. Biogen, Cambridge, 1983-84; v.p., gen. mgr. Vivotech, Newton, 1984-86; sr. cons. ADL, Cambridge, 1986-87; sr. v.p. biotherapeutics Genzyme Corp., 1987-93; pres., CEO Mitotix, Inc., 1993-94, Cambridge Biotech Corp., 1995-96, Aquita Biopharm., Worcester, Mass., 1996—. Bd. dirs. CML Group, Synaptic Pharm., Aquita Biopharm.; pres. Mass. Biotech Coun., 1994-96, bd. dirs.; chmn. ECS Biotech. Industry Orgn., 1994—. Author chpts. in books; contbr. articles to profl. jours. Mem. New Eng. Brit. Bus. Assn. (bd. dirs. 1986-90), Assn. Biotech. Cos. (bd. dirs. 1984-87), Centaur (bd. dirs. 1984-87), Boston Club (bd. dirs. 1991-95), The Initiative (bd. dirs. 1991-93). Achievements include 5 patents.

TAUR, YUAN, physicist, researcher; b. Nanchang, Jiangxi, China, Sept. 27, 1946; came to U.S., 1968; s. Tang and Ping-Chung Seh Taur; m. Betty Chu, Apr. 20, 1974; children: Ying, Hsuan. BS in Physics, Nat. Taiwan U., 1967; PhD in Physics, U. Calif., Berkeley, 1974. Postdoctor U. Calif., Berkeley, 1974-75; rsch. assoc. Goddard Inst. Space Studies NASA, N.Y.C., 1975-79; mem. tech. staff Rockwell Internat. Sci. Ctr., Thousand Oaks, Calif., 1979-81; rsch. staff mem., mgr. T. J. Watson Rsch. Ctr. IBM, Yorktown Heights, NY, 1981—2001; prof. U. Calif., San Diego, 2001—. Co-author: Fundamentals of Modern VLSI Devices, 1998; contbr. articles to profl. jours. Fellow IEEE (subject editor Electron Device Letters 1996-99, editor-in-chief 1999—). Achievements include 12 patents. Avocations: tennis, skiing, bridge, mahjong. Office: U Calif San Diego Dept Elec and Computer Engring La Jolla CA 92093

TAUREL, SIDNEY, pharmaceutical executive; b. Casablanca, Morocco, Feb. 9, 1949; came to U.S., 1986; s. Jose and Marjorie (Afriat) T.; m. Kathryn H. Fleischmann, Mar. 22, 1977; children: Alexis, Patrick, Olivia. BSBA, Ecole des Hautes Etudes Commerciales, Paris, 1969; MBA, Columbia U., 1971. Mktg. assoc. Eli Lilly Internat. Corp., Indpls., 1971-72; mktg. planning mgr. Eli Lilly Do Brasil Limitada, Sao Paulo, Brazil, 1972-75, gen. mgr. Brazil, 1982-83; mgr. pharm. ops. Eastern Europe Eli Lilly and Elanco Gesmbh, Vienna, 1976; sales mgr. pharm. Eli Lilly France SA, Paris, 1977-79, mktg. dir. pharm., 1980-81; v.p. Europe Lilly European ops., London, 1984-85; exec. v.p. Eli Lilly Internat. Corp., Indpls., 1986, pres., 1986-91, exec. v.p. pharm. divsn., 1991-93; exec. v.p. Eli Lilly and Co., 1993—, pres. pharm. divsn., 1993—, bd. dirs., 1991—; pres., COO Eli Lilly & Co., 1996-98, CEO, 1998—. Chmn. Eli Lilly & Co., 1999—; bd. dirs. McGraw-Hill, Cies, IBM, ITT Industries; bd. overseers Columbia Bus. Sch. Bd. dirs. RCA Tennis Championships. Recipient Ellis Island medal of honor, 2000; named to Order

Knight of the French Legion of Honor, 2000. Mem. Pharm. Rsch. and Mfrs. Assn. Avocations: tennis, music. Office: Eli Lilly and Co Lilly Corporate Ctr Indianapolis IN 46285 E-mail: staurel@lilly.com.*

TAURO, JOSEPH LOUIS, federal judge; b. Winchester, Mass., Sept. 26, 1931; s. G. Joseph and Helen Maria (Petrossi) T.; m. Elizabeth Mary Quinlan, Feb. 7, 1959 (dec. 1978); children— Joseph L., Elizabeth H., Christopher M.; m. Ann Lefavour Jones, July 12, 1980. AB, Brown U., 1953; LLB, Cornell U., 1956; JD (hon.), U. Mass., 1985, Suffolk U., 1986, Northeastern U., 1990, New Eng. Sch. Law, 1992, Boston U., 1997, Brown U., 1998. Bar: Mass. 1956, D.C. 1960. Assoc. Tauro & Tauro, Lynn, Mass., 1958-59; asst. U.S. atty. Dept. Justice, Boston, 1959-60; ptnr. Jaffee & Tauro, Boston and Lynn, Mass., 1960-71; chief legal counsel Gov. of Mass., Boston, 1965-68; U.S. atty. Dept. Justice, 1972; judge U.S. Dist. Ct., 1972—; chief judge U.S. Dist. Ct., Mass., 1992-99. Mem. exec. com. Cornell Law Assn., Ithaca, N.Y., 1968-71; mem. adv. coun. Cornell Law Sch., Ithaca, 1975-80; vis. prof. law Boston U. Law Sch., 1977—; mem. Jud. Conf. U.S., 1994-97, mem. com. on operation of jury sys., 1979-86, mem. adv. com. on codes of conduct, 1988-94. Trustee Brown U., 1978—, Mass. Gen. Hosp., Boston, 1968-72, Children's Hosp. Med. Ctr., Boston, 1979-94. 1st lt. U.S. Army, 1956-58. Recipient Disting. Alumnus award Cornell U. Law Sch., 1992, Brown Bear award Brown U., 1993; named one of 10 Outstanding Young Men, Greater Boston Jaycees, 1966. Fellow Am. Bar Found.; mem. Mass. Bar Assn., Boston Bar Assn. (coun. 1968-71), D.C. Bar Assn., Boston Yacht Club (Marblehead, Mass.). Republican. Roman Catholic. Avocations: sports; reading; music; films; theater. Office: 1 Courthouse Way Ste 7110 Boston MA 02210-3009

TAUSCH, JOHANNES, mathematician, educator; b. Schwandorf, Bavaria, Germany, Aug. 13, 1963; married. Diplom math., Julius Maxmilians U., Wurzburg, Germany, 1989; PhD, Colo. State U., 1995. Postdoctoral assoc. MIT, Cambridge, 1995—98; asst. prof. So. Meth. U., Dallas, 1998—. Office: So Meth Univ Dept Math Dallas TX 75275-0156

TAUSCHER, ELLEN O. congresswoman; b. Newark, 1951; m. William Y. Tauscher; 1 child, Katherine. BS in early Childhood Edn., Seton Hall U., 1974. With Bache Securities, N.Y.C., N.Y. Stock Exchange; dir. Tauscher Found.; mem. U.S. Congress from 10th Calif. dist., 1997—; mem. house armed svcs. com., house transp. com. U.S. Ho. Reps. Founder The ChildCare Registry; bd. regents Seton Hall U.; co-chair Delaine Eastin's State Supt. Pub. Instrn. Campaign, 1994; transp. and infrastructure com., surface transp. and water resources and environ. Author: The ChildCare Sourcebook, 1996. Active The Coalition, New Dem. Coalition, Bipartisan Freshman Campaign Fin. Reform Task Force, House Cancer Awareness Working Group, Congl. Caucus on the Arts; vice-chair Calif. Dem. Del.*

TAUSCHER, JOHN WALTER, retired pediatrician, emeritus educator; b. LaSalle, Ill., Feb. 3, 1929; s. John Robert and Ella (Danz) Tauscher; m. Mary Claire Cline, June 19, 1954 (dec. 1989); children: Michael, John, Claire, Mark, Matthew; m. Delphine Bonanni, Oct. 26, 1991. BS, U. Ill., 1952, MD, 1954. Diplomate Am. Bd. Pediatrics. Intern Cook County Hosp., Chgo., 1954-55; resident in pediatrics Hurley Med. Ctr., Flint, Mich., 1958-60; practice medicine specializing in pediatrics, 1960-75; assoc. prof. human devel. Coll. Human Medicine, Mich. State U., East Lansing, 1975-80, prof. pediatrics and human devel., 1980-94, prof. emeritus, 1994; ret., 1994. V.p. After Hours Pediatric Care, P.C., Flint, 1972-87; chmn. pediatrics Hurley Med. Ctr., 1980-90, dir. pediatric edn., dir. primary care pediatrics, 1991-94; dir. clin. svcs. Mott Children's Health Ctr., 1981-85, v.p. health affairs, 1985-91. Served with USAF, 1955-58 Decorated Air Force Commendation medal; recipient Outstanding Tchg. award Coll. Human Medicine, Mich. State U., 1977, 84, 85, Clin. Instr. of Yr. award St. Joseph Hosp., 1977, Disting. Cmty. Faculty award Mich. State U., 1989. Mem. AMA, Genesee County Med. Soc. (pres. 1990), Mich. State Med. Soc., Northeastern Mich. Pediatric Soc., Am. Acad. Pediatrics Roman Catholic. Home: 1069 Rayna Dr Davison MI 48423-2845 also: 1010 Ibis Ct Bradenton FL 34209-7323

TAUZIN, W. J. BILLY, II (WILBERT J. TAUZIN), congressman; b. Chackbay, La., June 14, 1943; s. Wilbert Joseph and Enola (Martinez) T.; m. Cecile Bergeron, May 29, 1993; children: Kristie René, Wilbert J. III, John Ashton, Thomas Nicholas, Michael James. BA, Nicholls State U., 1964; JD, La. State U., 1967. Bar: La. 1967. Practice, Houma and Thibodaux, La., 1967-80; mem. firm Marcel Fanguy & Tauzin, 1967-72, Tauzin-Sonnier, 1972-80; mem. La. Ho. of Reps., 1971-80, house floor leader, 1974-79, chmn. Teche Clearinghouse Rev. Bd., 1975-78, chmn. house natural resources com., 1975-80; mem. U.S. Congress from 3d La. Dist., 1980—; mem. commerce com., mem. resources com.; chmn. energy and commerce com.; dep. whip Ho. of Reps., 1995—. Mem. Thibodaux Playhouse, 1967-75; mem. Criminal Justice Inst. Recipient Thibodaux Outstanding Young Man award, 1971 Mem. ABA, La. State Bar Assn., Lafourche Parish Bar Assn. (past pres.), Chackbay-Choupic Jr. C. of C. (past pres.), Nicholls Alumni Council (v.p.) Lodges: Kiwanis; K.C. Home: Rienzi B-5 PO Box 1407 Thibodaux LA 70302-1407 Office: US House of Reps 2183 Rayburn House Office Bldg Washington DC 20515-1803

TAVAKOLI, AMIR, civil engineer, educator; b. Tehran, Iran, Sept. 19, 1957; came to U.S., 1975; s. Abbas and Roghieh (Shanizadeh-Asli) T.; 1 child, Omid. BCE, U. Wash., 1978; MCE, Ga. Tech., 1979, MS in Indsl. Mgmt., 1982, PhD in Civil Engring., 1983. Registered profl. engr., Ohio; cert. cost engr. Engr. civil design Planners and Engrs. Collaborative, Atlanta, 1981-83; asst. prof. constrn. So. Ill. U., Edwardsville, 1983-85; head, Constrn. Engring. and Mgmt. Program Case Western Res. U., Cleve., 1985-92; gen. mgr. Tavakoli & Assocs., Inc., Cleve., Atlanta, 1988—. Cons. in field. Contbr. articles to profl. jours. Mem. ASCE, Am. Assn. Cost Engrs. (pres. N.C. Ohio sect. 1988-89, dir. 1989—), Am. Soc. Engring. Edn. Avocations: swimming, soccer, travel, outdoor activities. Office: PO Box 241033 Cleveland OH 44124-8933

TAVALLALI, MORAD, plastic and reconstructive surgeon; b. Tehran, Iran, Feb. 10, 1959; came to U.S., 1976; s. Djamchid and Nini (Chaicar) T.; m. Pascale Helene Dubois, Mar. 4, 1962; children: Caspian, Calista. BS, Georgetown U., 1980, MS, 1981, MD, 1985. Diplomate Am. Bd. Plastic Surgery, Nat. Bd. Med. Examiners. Intern, then resident in surgery Lenox Hill Hosp., N.Y.C., 1985-90; fellow in plastic surgery Baylor U. Coll. Medicine, Houston, 1990-92, U. Brussels, 1992-93; pvt. practice, Chevy Chase, Md., 1993—. Mem. staff Fairfax Hosp., Sibley Hosp., Suburban Hosp. Contbr. chpt. to book, articles to sci. publs. Bhussvy Meml. scholar Georgetown U., Washington, 1983; recipient Sandoz award Sandoz Pharm. Co., 1984. Mem.: ACS, Nat. Capital Soc. Plastic Surgeons, Am. Soc. for Aesthetic Plastic Surgery, Am. Soc. Plastic Reconstructive Surgeons, Alpha Omega. Avocations: contemporary art, travel, music. Office: Ste 310 3299 Woodburn Rd Annandale VA 22003-7356

TAVARES, TONY, professional hockey and baseball leagues executive; b. Fall River, Mass., Oct. 17, 1949; m. Elizabeth Tavares; children: Sheila, Kristen, Mark. BS in Acctg., Roger Williams Coll. Comptroller, acting dir. Providence Civic Ctr.; with Centrum, Worcester, Mass., New Haven Vets. Meml. Coliseum, Nassau Vets. Meml. Coliseum, Uniondale, N.Y., Spectacor Mgmt. Group, pres., CEO; cons. Walt Disney Co.; pres. Anaheim Sports Inc., Anaheim, Calif., 1992—2002; chmn., gov. Mighty Ducks of Anaheim, 1993—2002; pres. Anaheim Angels, 1996—2002, Montreal Expos , 2002—. Mem. Internat. Assn. Auditorium Mgrs. Office: Montreal Expos Olympic Stadium 4549 Pierre-de-Coubertin Ave Montreal QC H1V 3N7 Canada*

TAVASSOLI, FATTANEH ABBAS-ZADEH, pathologist, consultant; b. Teheran, Iran, Mar. 30, 1949; came to U.S., 1963; d. Hossein Abbas-zadeh and Homa (Rassadi) T.; m. Bahman Jabbari, Dec. 30, 1975. BS in Chemistry, S.W. Mo. State Coll., 1968; MD, St. Louis U., 1972. Diplomate Am. Bd. Pathology. Intern, resident in pathology Barnes Hosp., St. Louis, 1972-75; fellow in gynecol. pathology St. John's Mercy Med. Ctr., 1975-76; from staff pathologist to vice chmn. Armed Forces Inst. Pathology, Washington, 1976-92; dir. gynecology and breast pathology, dir. rsch. Fairfax Hosp., Falls Church, Va., 1992-94, chmn. dept. gynecology and breast pathology, Armed Forces Inst. Pathology, 1994. Adj. prof. pathology Uniformed Svcs. Sch. Health Scis., Bethesda, Md., 1987-92; cons. NIH, Bethesda, 1991—; clin. prof.. pathology George Washington U. Author: Pathology of the Breast, 1992, Expert Computer System: Breast Pathology, 1990; contbr. over 70 articles to profl. jours., chpts. to books. Mem. Am. Soc. Clin. Pathologists (coun. in anatomic pathology 1991-96, course dir.), Internat. Acad. Pathology, U.S.-Can. Acad. Pathology (former mem. abstract rev. com., moderator gynecol. subsplty., panel 1993-95), Internat. Soc. Gynecol. Pathologists (at-large), Arthur Purdy Scout Soc. Surg. Pathologists (bd. editors Modern Pathology, Human Pathology, Internat. Jour. Gynecol. Pathology, The Breast Jour.). Avocations: gold-gilding and marbelizing furniture, interior design, writing peotry. Office: Dept Gynecologic & Breast Pathology Armed Forces Institute Of Pa Washington DC 20306-0001

TAVEGGIA, THOMAS CHARLES, business educator; b. Oak Lawn, Ill., June 15, 1943; s. Thomas Angelo and Eunice Louise (Harris) T.; m. Brigitte I. Adams, Jan. 23, 1965; children: Michaela, Francesca. BS, Ill. Inst. Technology, 1965; MA, U. Oreg., 1968, PhD, 1971. Prof. U. Oreg., Eugene, 1970, U. B.C., Vancouver, Can., 1970-73, U. Calif., Irvine, 1973-74, Ill. Inst. Technology, Chgo., 1974-77; mgmt. cons. Towers, Perrin, Forster, & Crosby, 1977-80; ptnr. Manplan Cons., 1980-81, Coopers & Lybrand, San Francisco, 1981-86, Touche Ross, San Francisco, 1986-88; prof. Calif. Sch. Profl. Psychology, Berkeley, 1988-98, U. Ariz., Tucson, 2000—. Author: (with Dubin and Arends) From Family and School to Work, 1967; (with Dubin) The Teaching-Learning Paradox: A Comparative Analysis of College Teaching Methods, 1968; (with Dubin and Hedley) The Medium May Be Related to the Message: College Instruction by TV, 1969; contbr. articles to profl. jours. NDEA Title IV fellow, 1967-71; U. B.C. faculty rsch. grantee, 1970, 71, 73; grantee Calif. Sch. Profl. Psychology, 1993-98. Mem. Acad. Mgmt., Nat. Bur. Cert. Cons. Home: 1506 W Canada Hills Dr Tucson AZ 85737-9052

TAVEL, MARK KIVEY, money management company executive, economist; b. Cambridge, Mass., May 9, 1945; s. Bernard Benjamin and Elizabeth (Rogers) T.; m. Susana Sara Doño, Dec. 14, 1980; children: Sarah Emily, Rachel Florence, Amanda Victoria, Nathaniel Benjamin, Roberto Aaron Doño. BA cum laude, Harvard U., 1967; MBA, Columbia U., 1968. Sr. mng. dir. Rothschild Asset Mgmt., Inc., N.Y.C.; bd. dirs. N. M. Rothschild Internat. Asset Mgmt., London. Bd. dirs. Rothschild Asset Mgmt., Inc. Trustee, treas. Trevor Day Sch., N.Y.C. Mem. Harvard Club (N.Y.C.). Home: 110 Riverside Dr New York NY 10024-3715 Office: Rothschild Inc 44th Fl 1251 Ave of the Americas New York NY 10020-1193

TAVENAS, FRANÇOIS, civil engineer, educator; b. Bourg de Péage , Drôme, France, Sept. 12, 1942; arrived in Can., 1966; s. Adrien and Marie Thérèse (Bazin) T.; m. Gundula Schlichting, Apr. 27, 1963; children: Anne Catherine, Philippe, Sophie. BCE, Inst. Nat. Scis. Appliquées, Lyon, France, 1963; PhD, U. Grenoble, France, 1965. Registered profl. engr., Que. Engr. Piette & Assocs., Que., Can., 1966-70; asst. prof. civil engring. Laval U., 1970-73, assoc. prof., 1973-79, prof., 1979-85, 97—, dean, 1985-89; vice-prin. planning and resources McGill U., Montreal, Que., 1988-97; rector Laval U., Can., 1997—. Cons. Golder & Assocs., Toronto, 1973-75, Terratech, Montreal, 1975-85, Soc. d'Energie de la Baie James, Montreal, 1980-84; mem. coun. Natural Scis. and Engring. Rsch. Coun. Can., 1989-95; bd. dirs. Groupe Pour l'avancement Technique et Indsl., Que.; pres. RISQ (Que. Internet), 1998—; v.p. Conf. Rectors and Prins. of Univs. in Que., 1997-99, pres., 1999-2001; chmn. bd. Québec Metro Hi Tech Park; bd. dirs. Assn. Univs. and Colls. of Can., 1998—; mem. Adv. Com. for On-Line Learning, Industry Can., 2000-2001. Author: (with others) Embankments On Soft Soils, 1985; contbr. articles to profl. jours. Recipient Chevalier of the French Legion of Honor, 1999. Mem. Can. Geotech. Soc. (v.p. 1982-85, pres.-elect 1990, pres. 1991-92), Internat. Soc. Soil Mechanics and Found. Engring., Assn. Can. Francaise pour L'Avancement des Scis. (pres. 1997-98). Avocations: tennis, travel, sailing. Office: Univ Laval Quebec QC Canada G1K 7P4 E-mail: francois.tavenas@rec.ulaval.ca.

TAVERAS, JUAN MANUEL, physician, educator; b. Dominican Republic, Sept. 27, 1919; came to U.S., 1944, naturalized, 1950; s. Marcos M. and Ana L. (Rodriguez) T.; m. Bernice Helen McGonigle, June 12, 1947 (dec. 1990); children: Angela Forbes Summers, Louisa Helen Taveras Koranda, Jeffrey Lawrence; m. Mariana Margarita Bucher, Mar. 18, 1991. BS, Normal Sch. Santiago, Dominican Republic, 1937; MD, U. Santo Domingo, Dominican Republic, 1943, U. Pa., 1949; MS honoris causa, Harvard Med. Sch., 1971; Dr. honoris causa, Univ. Nacional Pedro Henriquez Ureña, Dominican Republic, 1987; Doctor Honoris Causa, U. Catolica Madre Y Maestra, Santiago, Dominican Republic, 1992. Diplomate: Am. Bd. Radiology. Instr. anatomy U. Santo Domingo, 1943-44; fellow radiology Grad. Hosp. U. Pa., 1945-48; rotating intern Misericordia Hosp., Phila., 1949-50; asst. radiologist Presbyn. Hosp., N.Y.C., 1950-52, asst. attending radiologist, 1953-56, assoc. attending radiologist, 1956-60, attending radiologist, 1960-65; dir. radiology Neurol. Inst., N.Y.C., 1952-65; cons. USPHS Hosp., S.I., N.Y., 1952-65, Morristown (N.J.) Meml. Hosp., 1957-65, St. Barnabas Hosp., N.Y.C., 1959-65, VA Hosp., Bronx, N.Y., 1960-65; asst. instr. radiology U. Pa. Sch. Medicine, 1947-48; faculty Columbia Coll. Phys. and Surg., 1950-65, prof. radiology, 1959-65; prof. radiology, chmn. dept., dir. Mallinckrodt Inst. Radiology, Washington U. Sch. Medicine, St. Louis, 1965-71; radiologist-in-chief Barnes and Allied Hosps., 1965-71; cons. neuroradiology service Unit 1 St. Louis City Hosp., 1966-71; cons. radiology Jewish Hosp., St. Louis, 1966-71; prof. radiology Harvard Med. Sch., 1971-89, prof. radiology emeritus, 1989—; radiologist-in-chief Mass. Gen. Hosp., Boston, 1971-88. Pres. VII Symposium Neuroradiologieum, 1964; hon. prof. U. Chile, 1978, Peruvian U. Cayetano Heredia, 1994; founder, cons. Diagnosis and Advanced Medicine Ctr. in Juan M. Taveras Health Plaza, Santo Domingo, Dominican Republic, 1997—. Author: Neuroradiology, 1996; (with Ross Golden) Roentgenology of the Abdomen, 1961, (with Ernest H. Wood) Diagnostic Neuroradiology, 1964, 2d edit., 1976, (with Norman Leeds) Dynamic Factors in Diagnosis of Supratentorial Brain Tumors by Cerebral Angiography, 1969, (with F. Morello) Normal Neuroradiology, 1979, (with James Provenzale) Clinical Cases in Neuroradiology, 1994, (with Laszlo Szlavy) Noncoronary Angioplasty, 1994; editor: (with others) Recent Advances in the Study of Cerebral Circulation, 1970, Cysticercosis of the Central Nervous System, 1983, Radiology: Diagnosis, Imaging, Intervention, 1986, Radiologia e Imagen, Diagnostica y Terapeutica, 1998, 99; chief editor: Am. Jour. Neuroradiology, 1980-89; contbr. numerous articles to profl. jours. Bd. dirs. Edward Mallinckrodt, Jr. Found., 1980-96. Decorated knight Order of Duarte Sanchez y Mella (Dominican Republic) 1972; Juan M. Taveras professorship established in his honor Harvard Med. Sch., 1988. Fellow: Am. Coll. Radiology (gold medal 1985); mem.: AMA, Japan Radiol. Soc., Hungarian Radiologic Soc., Radiol. Assn. Ctrl. Am. an dPanama, Tex. Radiol. Soc., Rocky Mountain Radiol. Soc., Radiol. Soc. Venezuela, Iberrian Latin Am. Soc. Neuroradiology (pres. 1988—91, pres. IC congress 1992), New Eng. Roentgen Ray Soc., Brazilian Radiol. Soc., Colombia Neurol. Soc., Costa Rica Soc. Radiology, Mass. Radiol. Soc., Assn. U. Radiologists (gold mdeal 1985), Nat. Acads. Practice, N.Y. Acad. Scis., Am. Soc. Neuroradiology (pres. 1962—64, gold medal 1995), World Fedn. Neurology, Am. Assn. Neurol. Surgeons (assoc.), Phila. Roentgen Ray Soc. (hon.), European Soc. Neuroradiology (hon.), Mexican Neuroradiology Soc. (hon. prize of merit award), Inter-Am. Coll. Radiology, Mass. Med. Soc., Radiol. Soc. N.Am. (gold medal 1981), Am. Roentgen Ray Soc. (gold medal 1988), Am. Neurol. Assn., Alpha Omega Alpha. Republican. Home: 85 E India Row Apt 40F Boston MA 02110-3394 Office: Mass Gen Hosp 55 Fruit St Boston MA 02114-2696

TAVERNA, RODNEY ELWARD, financial services company executive; b. Springfield, Ill., Aug. 8, 1947; s. Jerome Thomas and Virginia (Holcomb) T.; m. Cheryl Ann Walters, Sept. 4, 1968 (div. 1983); children: Lara Lyn, Melinda Marie, Ryan Thomas; m. Caroline Whiffen, Apr. 1985. BA, U. Mo., 1969; MBA in Fin., Nat. U., 1988. Commd. 2d lt., supply officer USMC, 1969, advanced through grades to maj., 1979; supply officer Central Svcs. Agy., Danang, Vietnam, 1970-71, Marine Air Control Squadron, Futenma, Okinawa, 1977-78; logistics officer Hdqrs. Marine Corps Recruit Depot, Paris Island, S.C., 1972-75; support officer Marine Barracks, Treasure Island, San Francisco, 1975-77; regimental supply officer 1st Marine Divsn., Camp Pendleton, Calif., 1978-79, asst divsn. supply officer, 1985-88; brigade supply officer 1st Marine Brigade, Kaneohe Bay, Hawaii, 1980-82; exec. officer 1st Maintenance Bn., Camp Pendleton, 1982-85; asst div. supply officer 1st Marine Div., 1985-88; pres. Freedom Fin. Group, 1991—; br. mgr. WMA Securities, Inc., 1994-97; sr. field dir. Premier Fin. Am., 1997-2000. Owner, mgr. Opportunities Unltd., Oceanside, Calif., 1985-91; cons. Incentive Leasing Corp., San Diego, 1985-86, The Profit Ctr., Santa Ana, Calif., 1991; founding mgr. Meditrend Internat., San Diego, 1987-88; founding dir. Am. 3-D Corp., Henderson, Nev., 1990-91. Republican. Avocations: computers, snow skiing, racquetball, scuba diving. Home and Office: 1632 Avenida Andante Oceanside CA 92056-6905 E-mail: FreedomFinancial@cox.net.

TAVLIN, MICHAEL JOHN, manufacturing executive; b. Lincoln, Nebr., Dec. 16, 1946; BEd, Oklahoma City U., 1970; JD, U. Nebr., 1973; LLM in Taxation, Washington U., St. Louis, 1977. Bar: Nebr. 1973, Mo. 1974. Ptnr. Nelson & Harding, Lincoln, 1973-77; sr. tax. mgr. Deloitte & Touche, Lincoln and Tulsa, 1979-84, PriceWaterhouseCoopers, Tulsa, 1984-86; v.p., treas., sec. Aliant Comm. Inc. and subs., Lincoln, 1986-99; sr. v.p., CFO, treas., sec. Interactive Intelligence, Inc. and subs., Indpls., 1999—2001; CFO, gen. counsel Speedway Motors, Inc., Lincoln, 2001—. Bd. dirs., treas. Cmty. Health Endowment, Lincoln, 1998, Woods Charitable Fund, Lincoln, 2000. Named Disting. Alumnus Oklahoma City U., 1995. Office: Speedway Motors Inc PO Box 81906 Lincoln NE 68501

TAVORMINA, JOHN WILLIAM, lawyer; b. Elizabeth, N.J., Dec. 14, 1953; s. Joseph B. and Anne F. (Arace) T.; m. Leslie Rohrer, July 5, 1988; children: Jena Leigh, Taylor Lynn, Tori Anne. BA, Tulane U., 1975, JD, 1978. Bar: La. 1978, N.Y. 1980, Tex. 1983; cert. in personal injury, trial law, Tex. Bd. of Legal Specialization. Atty. Exxon Corp. various offices, N.Y.C., Houston, & La., 1978-87; assoc. Helm, Pletcher, Bowen & Saunders, Houston, 1987-89, ptnr., 1989—. Contbr. articles to Tulane Law Rev., 1977-78; speaker at legal seminars, 1990—. Mem. Am. Bd. Trial Advocates, Tex. Bar Found., Coll. of State Bar Tex., Million Dollar Advocates Furum. Office: Helm Pletcher Bowen & Saunders 2929 Allen Pkwy Ste 2700 Houston TX 77019-7102

TAVROW, RICHARD LAWRENCE, lawyer, corporate executive; b. Syracuse, N.Y., Feb. 3, 1935; s. Harry and Ida Mary (Hodess) T.; m. Barbara J. Silver, Mar. 22, 1972; children— Joshua Michael, Sara Hallie. AB magna cum laude, Harvard U., 1957, LL.B., 1960, LL.M., 1961; postgrad., U. Copenhagen, 1961-62, U. Luxembourg, 1962. Bar: N.Y. bar 1961, U.S. Supreme Ct. bar 1969, Calif. bar 1978. Atty. W.R. Grace & Co., N.Y.C., 1962-66; asst. chief counsel Gen. Dynamics Corp., 1966-68; chief counsel office of fgn. direct investments U.S. Dept. Commerce, Washington, 1969-71; ptnr. Schaeffer, Dale, Vogel & Tavrow, N.Y.C., 1971-75; v.p., sec., gen. counsel Prudential Lines, Inc., 1975-78, also bd. dirs.; v.p., sec., gen. counsel Am. Pres. Lines, Ltd., Oakland, Calif., 1978-80, sr. v.p., sec., gen. counsel, 1980-91, also bd. dirs.; sr. v.p., sec., gen. counsel Am. Pres. Cos., Ltd., 1983-91, also bd. dirs. Calif.; sr. ptnr. Law Offices of R.L. Tavrow, 1991—; chmn., pres., CEO Diabetes Healthcare & Life Enhancement Ltd., 2000—. Instr. Harvard Coll., 1959-61; lectr. Am. Mgmt. Assn., Practising Law Inst., other assns. Recipient Silver Medal award Dept. Commerce, 1970; Fulbright scholar, 1961-62 Mem. ABA, State Bar Calif., Internat. Bar Assn., Am. Soc. Internat. Law, Am. Corp. Counsel Assn., Am. Soc. Corp. Secs. Inc., Harvard Law Sch. Assn., Navy League, Harvard Club (N.Y.C.).

TAW, DUDLEY JOSEPH, sales executive, director; b. Cleve., Mar. 11, 1916; s. William C. and Ella (Gedeon) T.; m. Louise E. Forshey, Sept. 10, 1938; children: Judith (Mrs. William W. Beck, Jr.), Dudley Joseph. Student, Hiram Coll., 1938. With McKesson & Robbins, Inc. (pharm. co.), after 1937, sales mgr., 1947, v.p. sales N.Y.C., 1953-60; v.p. Revlon, Inc., 1960-64; v.p. mktg. East Ohio Gas Co., Cleve., 1964-74, pres., 1975-81, chmn., 1981-82, Middtaw, Ltd., Inc., 1982. Bd. dirs. No. New England Gas Corp., First Union Mgmt. Co., Biskind Devel. Co., Vt. Gas Systems Inc. Mem. Better Bus. Bur., Cleve., chmn., 1973; trustee Lakewood Hosp.; treas. Salvation Army, Cleve. With USNR, 1946-47. Named Sales Exec. of Year Sales and Mktg. Execs. Cleve., 1966, Man of Year, 1977 Mem. Sales and Mktg. Execs. Cleve. (pres. 1969-70), Westwood Country Club, Union Club, Pepper Pike Club, Rotary (pres. Cleve. 1972-73). Methodist. Home: 20975 Avalon Dr Cleveland OH 44116-1303

TAWA, WAKO, foreign language educator; b. Japan, Sept. 22, 1948; naturalized U.S. citizen, 1981; children: John, Christina, Liam. BA, SUNY, Buffalo, 1971; MA, Internat. Christian U., Tokyo, 1975; PhD, Pa. State U., 1986. Lectr. Internat. Christian U., Tokyo, 1972-75, U. Hawaii, Honolulu, 1976-80; instr. Pa. State U., University Park, 1983-86; asst. prof. Conn. Coll., New London, 1986-88, Amherst (Mass.) Coll., 1988-94, assoc. prof., 1994-00, prof., 2000—. Dir. summer program Pa. State U., University Park, 1984-86; vis. asst. prof. Harvard Summer Sch., Cambridge, 1986, 91, 93. Co-editor: Issues on Empty Categories, 1987; contbr. articles to profl. jours. Dana Faculty fellow Conn. Coll., 1986, Trustees' Faculty fellow Amherst Coll., 1991-92; grantee Culpeper Found., 1998-2000. Mem. Internat. Cognitive Linguistics Assn., Internat. Linguistic Assn., Assn. Asian Studies, Assn. Tchrs. Japanese, Am. Coun. on the Teaching Fgn. Langs., Linguistic Soc. Am. Office: Amherst Coll PO Box 5000 Amherst MA 01002-5000 E-mail: wtawa@amherst.edu.

TAWEH, ZIAD MICHAEL, internist; b. Zahle, Lebanon, Feb. 15, 1968; came to U.S., 1986; s. Michael Elias Taweh and Nadia Tahtouh; m. Jocelyne S. Taweh, June 20, 1998. BA, Cen. Conn. State U., 1992; MD, St. George's U., 1996. Instr. ARC, New Britain, Conn., 1988-92; med. resident in internal medicine and primary care Maimonides Med. Ctr., Bklyn., 1997—2000; med. dir. Harborside at Glen Hill, Danbury, Conn., 2002—; staff physician Danbury Hosp., 2000—. Bd. dirs. sci. adv. bd. Nutrition Superstores, West Palm Beach, Fla. Mem. ACP (1st prize 1999), ARC, Nat. Assn. Interns and Residents, Am. Soc. Internal Medicine, Alpha Phi Omega. Avocations: traveling, languages, reading. Office: 20 Germantown Rd Danbury CT 06810 E-mail: ztaweh@aol.com.

TAWSHUNSKY, ALAN NEAL, lawyer; b. N.Y.C., Oct. 14, 1954; s. Ben and Myrtle (Fink) T. BA, Queens Coll., 1976; JD, Georgetown U., 1984. Bar: N.Y. 1985, D.C. 1986. Mathematician U.S. Energy Info. Adminstrn., Washington, 1977-84; law clk. U.S. Dist. Ct., Wilmington, Del., 1984-85; atty. Covington & Burling, Washington, 1985-90, Cadwalader, Wickersham & Taft, Washington, 1990-93, Akin, Gump, Strauss, Hauer & Feld, Washington, 1993—. Mem. ABA, D.C. Bar Assn., N.Y. State Bar Assn.

TAXY, JEROME B. pathologist; b. Chgo., Sept. 13, 1945; s. Morton and Dorothy (Epstein) T.; m. Gail Sokol, July 6, 1969; children: Benjamin, Cara. BA, U. Ill., 1967; MD, U. Ill., Chgo., 1971. Diplomate Am. Bd. Pathology (Anatomic and Clin.). Intern in pediatrics U. Mich., Ann Arbor, 1972; resident in pathology Northwestern U., Chgo., 1976; rsch. pathologist U.S. Army, Frederick, Md., 1976-77; staff pathologist US Army Walter Reed Hosp., Washington, 1977-78; asst. prof. pathology Johns Hopkins Med.Sch., Balt., 1978-82; staff pathologist Luth. Gen. Hosp., Park Ridge, Ill., 1982—; clin. assoc. prof. pathology Northwestern U. Med. Sch., Chgo., 1983-99, clin. prof. pathology, 1999—. Mem. editl. bd. Am. Jour. Clin. Pathology, 1990—, Am. Jour. Surg. Pathology, 1999. Mem. editl. bd. Am. Jour. Surg. Pathology, 1999—; contbr. 71 articles to peer reviewed jours., 9 book chpts., 15 abstracts, 2 revs. Major U.S. Army, 1976-78. Named one of 4 best Chgo. pathologists, Chgo. Mag., 1992. Mem. A.P. Stout Soc. Surgical Pathologists, U.S.-Can. Acad. Pathology, Chgo. Pathology Soc., Am. Soc. Clin. Pathologists, Am. Soc. Hematologists. Avocations: violin, running, tennis, bridge. Office: Luth Gen Hosp 1775 Dempster St Park Ridge IL 60068-1143

TAYLER, IRENE, English literature educator; b. Abilene, Tex., July 13, 1934; d. B. Brown Smith and Madeline (Bowron); m. Edward W. Tayler, June 3, 1961 (div. 1971); children: Edward Jr., Jesse; m. Saul Touster, Jan. 14, 1978. BA in Philosophy, Stanford U., 1956, MA in Am. Lit., 1961, PhD in English Lit., 1968. Tchr. Breadloaf Sch. of Eng., Middlebury, Vt., 1970, 71, 75, 76; teaching asst. Stanford U., Calif., 1958-60; lectr. Columbia U., N.Y., 1961-71; asst. prof. CUNY, 1971-73, assoc. prof., 1973-76, MIT, Cambridge, 1976-82, prof., 1982-96, sec. of the faculty, 1993-95, retired, 1996. Chair gov. com. The English Inst., 1981. Author: (book) Blake's Illustrations to the Poems of Gray, 1971, Holy Ghosts: The Male Muses of Emily and Charlotte Bronte, 1990; contbr. numerous articles to profl. jours. Internat. Inst. Edn. fellow U. Munich, 1957-58; Wilson fellow Stanford U., 1961-62; ACLS study grantee, 1968-69; Faculty Rsch. Found. grantee CUNY, 1972-73; NEH sr. scholar fellow, 1980; Mac Vicar faculty fellow MIT, 1993—. Mem.: Cosmopolitan Club (N.Y.C.), St. Botolph Club (Boston) (pres. 2000—). E-mail: itayler@mit.edu.

TAYLOR, A. JEFFRY, lawyer; b. L.A., Nov. 29, 1943; s. Henry Allen and Jane Clara (Bosco) T.; m. Kate Colemen Hanrahan, Apr. 10, 1965; children: Jennifer, Stefanie, Bryce, Zachary. BA, UCLA, 1965; JD, Loyola U., L.A.,

1969. Bar: Calif. 1970, Vt. 1972, U.S. Supreme Ct. 1976, U.S. Tax Ct. 1985, U.S. Claims Ct. 1988, U.S. Ct. Appeals (1st cir.) 1990, U.S. Dist. Ct. (ctrl. dist.) Calif. 1970, U.S. Dist. Ct. Vt. 1972. Law clk. U.S. Dist. Judge 9th Cir. Ct. Appeals, L.A., 1969-70; trial atty. U.S. Dept. Justice Antitrust Divsn., 1970-72; corp. counsel Vt. Elec. Power Co., Rutland, 1972-79; hearing officer Vt. Dept. Edn., Montpelier, 1979-88; bar counsel Vt. Profl. Conduct Bd., 1979-88; adj. prof. law Vt. Law Sch., Royalton, 1978-88, 95-96; pvt. practice Rutland, 1979—. Contbr. articles Vt. Law Rev., 1997—. Vt. state counsel Clinton/Gore '92 and '96; Vt. rep. Nat. Lawyers Coun./Dem. Nat. Com., State Counsel, Gore 2000; Vt. bd. mem. UN Assn. U.S.; presdl. elector for State of Vt., 2000. Mem. Am. Soc. Internat. Law. Democrat. Unitarian Universalist. Avocations: opera, trout fishing. Home: 1415 East St North Clarendon VT 05759-9765 Office: One Justice Sq Rutland VT 05701 E-mail: jeffreyT905@aol.com.

TAYLOR, ALAN CHARLES, chaplain, counselor, researcher, consultant; b. Saratoga Springs, N.Y., Dec. 30, 1958; s. Alfred Tobias and Mary Catherine (Gunn) T.; m. Susan Laurence McCall, Sept. 20, 1997. BA cum laude in Art, SUNY, Plattsburgh, 1980; MS in Ednl. Psychology and Stats., SUNY, Albany, 1988, MS in Rehab. Counseling, 1992; postgrad., Russell Sage Coll., Albany, 1990-91; MA in Ministry with honors, Bibl. Theol. Sem., Hatfield, Pa., 2000; postgrad., Bibl. Theol. Sem., 2000—. Cert. rehab. counselor; credentialed alcoholism and substance abuse counselor; lic. min. Grad. asst., evaluator intern Evaluation Consortium SUNY, Albany, 1988-89, grad. asst. dept. ednl. psychology and stats., 1989-90; rsch. asst. Regents Coll., 1990-91, vocat. rehab., alcohol and drug counselor, 1993-97; residence dir. Bibl. Theol. Sem., 1999—. Cons. tchg. asst. Sch. Edn. Computing Facility U. Albany, 1987—88, summers, 1989, 90; adj. faculty Coll. St. Rose, spring, 1991; pastoral counseling and tng. Albany Area Bibl. Counseling, 1995—98; chaplain asst. Frederick Mennonite Cmty., 1999—2000; residence dir. Bibl. Theol. Sem., 2000; chaplain Ruidoso (N.Mex.) Downs Race Track, 2001; pray ministry, devel. Messianic Jewish Alliance Am., 2001—. Editor software Inst. for Internat. Rsch., Washington, 1989; contbg. editor: Commitment e-jour., 1999; contbr. presentations to profl. mtgs.; co-editor: (tng. manual) Improving the Efficiency of Educational Systems, Volume 1: DOS, Enable, SPSS/PC, Lotus, Introduction to Statistics, Volume 2: Manpower Education and Planning Model, Volume 3: Manpower Education and Planning Model, 1989; photographs exhibited in various shows. Mem.: AACD, Internat. Ministerial Fellowship, Soc. Biblical Lit., Race Track Chaplaincy Am. (bd. dirs.), Evang. Theol. Soc., Grad. Network Edn. (co-founder 1987, pres. 1990—92), New Eng. Ednl. Rsch. Orgn. (program com. ann. mtg. 1991), Am. Assn. Christian Counselors, Ea. Ednl. Rsch. Assn. (assoc. Disting. Paper award 1988), Mensa. Avocations: reading, travel, photography, writing. Address: Apt 104 2748 Cowpath Rd Hatfield PA 19440-2601

TAYLOR, ALEX, painter, sculptor, exhibit designer; b. Wichita, Kans., Aug. 13, 1952; s. Lewis W. and Jane (Barclay) T.; m. Vickie Halverson, July 1, 1978; 1 child: Charles Ethan. BFA in Painting, Ariz. State U., 1976. Exhibit and graphic designer Phoenix Zoo, 1972-76; exhibit designer Minn. Zoo, Apple Valley, 1976-78; imagineer Walt Disney Co., Glendale, Calif., 1979-83; owner Emerge Design, Alhambra, 1983-90; painter, sculptor La Cañada, 1990—. Patentee press fit sign framing sys. Mem. L.A. Art Assn., Huntington Westerners. Democrat. Mem. Soc. Of Friends. Avocations: collecting books, studying American history.

TAYLOR, ALFRED RALEIGH, geologist, director; b. Eure, Gates County, N.C., July 7, 1928; s. Raleigh Jackson and Annie B. Taylor; m. Eugenia Dare Eure, Nov. 9, 1946; children: Patricia Dare, Teri Ann. BS in Geology, U. N.C., 1955. Cert. geologist Va. Geologist U.S. Geol. Survey, Worldwide, 1955-81, Minerals Mgmt. Svc., Reston, 1981-82, Bur. Land Mgmt., 1982-83; geol. cons. Somerset, Ky., 1984-87; sr. geologist Va. Divsn. of Mineral Resources, Cedar Bluff, Va., 1988-89; geol. cons., 1989; geologist supr. Va. Divsn. Min. Resources, Dept. Mines, Minerals & Energy, Abingdon, Va., 1990-2000, scientist mgr., geologist mgr., 2000—. Adj. faculty in geology and geography Somerset C.C. of U. Ky., Somerset, 1968-77, 86-88. Contbr. over 55 articles and chpts. to books and profl. jours. S/sgt. USMC, PTO, ATO; lt. USNR. Recipient Antarctic Svc. medal, commendation U.S. Dept. Interior, 1961, citations U.S. Geol. Survey; Taylor Outlier Mountain in Antarctica named for him; named Ky. Col. Mem. DAV (life), Am. Assn. Petroleum Geologists, Am. Inst. Profl. Geologists (cert. prof. geologist), Ky. Soc. Profl. Geologists, Fleet Res. Assn., VFW (life), Am. Legion (life), Naval Res. Assn., Marine Corps League (life), Sigma Gamma Epsilon. Office: Va Divsn Mineral Resources PO Box 144 Abingdon VA 24212-0144

TAYLOR, ALLAN BERT, lawyer; b. Cin., June 28, 1948; s. H Ralph and Henrietta Irene (Medalia) Taylor; m. Sally Ann Silverstein, June 6, 1971; children: Rachel Elizabeth, Karen Ruth. AB, Harvard U., 1970, M in Pub. Policy, JD, Harvard U., 1975. Bar: Conn 1975, US Ct Appeals (DC cir) 1977, US Dist Ct (so dist) NY 1979, US Ct Appeals (2d cir) 1979, US Supreme Ct 1979, US Ct Appeals (1st and 10th cirs) 1991. Law clk. to J. Skelly Wright D.C. Cir., Washington, 1975-76; law clk. to Thurgood Marshall U.S. Supreme Ct., 1976-77; assoc. Day, Berry & Howard, Hartford, Conn., 1977-83, ptnr., 1983—. Overseer Bushnell Meml Hall Corp, Hartford, 1992—. Bd dirs Hartford Infant Action Project, 1990—, pres, 1999; elected mem Hartford City Coun, 1981—87; mem. Hartford Bd. Edn., 1989—93, v.p., 1991—93; mem. Conn .State Bd. Edn., Hartford, 1994—; chmn. charter revision comns. City of Hartford, 1999—2002; bd dirs Conn Asn Bds Educ, Hartford, 1989—93, Hartford Stage Co, 1993—2001. Mem.: ABA, Hartford Bar Asn, Conn Bar Asn, Phi Beta Kappa. Democrat. Jewish. Avocations: astronomy, reading. Home: 238 Whitney St Hartford CT 06105-2270 Office: Day Berry & Howard City Place Hartford CT 06103 E-mail: abtaylor@dbh.com.

TAYLOR, ALLAN RICHARD, retired banker; b. Prince Albert, Sask., Can., Sept. 14, 1932; s. Norman and Anna Lydia (Norbeck) T.; m. Shirley Irene Ruston, Oct. 5, 1957; children: Rodney Allan, Leslie Ann. LLD (hon), U. Regina, Sask., 1987, Concordia U., Montreal, Can., 1988; DBA (hon.), Laval U., Quebec City, Can., 1990; LLD (hon.), Queen's U., Kingston, Ont., 1991; Doctorate of Univ. (hon.), U. Ottawa, 1992. With Royal Bank of Can., Toronto, Ont., Can., 1949-95, pres., COO, dir., 1983-86, chmn., CEO, dir., 1986-94, chmn., 1994-95, ret., 1995. Bd. dirs. Fairmont Hotels & Resorts, Inc., Toronto, GM Can. Ltd., Oshawa, Ont., Canada, Max Bell Found., Calgary, The Can. Ditchley Found., Toronto, Can. Inst. for Advanced Rsch., NeuroScience Can. Found, Montreal; mem. adv. coun. Can. Exec. Svc. Overseas; former chmn. Can. Bankers Assn.; past pres. Internat. Monetary Conf.; bd. dirs. Fairmont Hotels and Resorts, Toronto. Former chmn. corp. program IMAGINE; mem. adv. bd. Can. Found. AIDS Rsch.; chmn. hon. adv. bd. Can. Assn. for Cmty. Living. Decorated officer Order of Can. Address: 200 Bay St 18th Fl North Tower Toronto ON Canada M5J 2J5

TAYLOR, ALLAN ROSS, linguist, educator; b. Palisade, Colo., Dec. 24, 1931; s. Athel Ross and Marjorie Verle (Walters) T.; m. Mary Callas, Sept. 8, 1958; children: Artemisia, Anthony, Peter, Anna, Yoana. AB, U. Colo., Boulder, 1953; PhD (Woodrow Wilson fellow, Fulbright fellow, NDEA fellow), U. Calif., Berkeley, 1969. Teaching asst., lectr. U. Calif., Berkeley, 1958-63; instr. U. Colo., 1964-65, asst. prof., 1965-70, assoc. prof., 1970-77, prof., 1977-93, prof. emeritus, 1993—, also past chmn. dept. linguistics, dept. French and Italian. Cons. bilingual edn. for Native Ams. Active Dem. Party and in environ. issues. With U.S. Army, 1954-57. NEH grantee, 1972-76, 80-82, 87-90, 89-93. Mem. Linguistic Soc. Am., Am. Anthrop. Assn. Home: 787 17th St Boulder CO 80302-7601 Office: U Colo Dept Linguistics PO Box 295 Boulder CO 80309-0295 E-mail: allan.taylor@colorado.edu. *Reading in physical anthropology and genetics, and many years of an advocacy role in environmental issues, have convinced me that man's highest calling is custodial: to protect, preserve, and pass on inviolate the world and all of its inhabitants, even when it may appear to be against our own short-term interest to do this. For the grand plan, if there is any, is to allow diversity to make the choices which prove ultimately to be the only viable ones.*

TAYLOR, ANDREW T. medical association administrator; b. Jackson, Tenn., Jan. 14, 1942; MD, Duke U., 1968. Cert. nuclear medicine Splty. Bd. 1, internal medicine Splty. Bd. 2. Prof. radiology Emory U. Sch. Med., co-dir. nuc. medicine; resident U. Hosp.-U.C.S.D., San Diego, 1970, 1972—74, intern, 1969. Office: Am Bd Nuclear Medicine 900 Veteran Ave Rm 13-152 Los Angeles CA 90024-2703 Office Fax: 310-794-4821.*

TAYLOR, ANN, human resources specialist, educator; b. Gordonville, Pa., Feb. 28, 1940; d. Gideon S. and Elizabeth L. Stoltzfus; m. James R. Taylor III, Feb. 18, 1983 (dec. Sept. 1995). BA, Ea. Mennonite U., 1966; MEd, Millersville (Pa.) U., 1979; EdD, Temple U., 1995. Caseworker Lancaster (Pa.) Welfare Dept., 1969-72, Lancaster County Probation Parole Dept., 1967-69; parole agent Pa. Bd. Probation, Parole, Harrisburg, 1972-85; human resource cons., trainer Taylor Assocs., Lancaster, 1985—. Adj. prof. bus. mgmt. Pa. State U., Lancaster, 1979-2000; spkr. in field; free lance trainer Hamilton Bank, Lancaster, 1985-91, Armstrong World Industries, Lancaster, 1987, 91; adv. com. staff trainer Vantage Drug and Alcohol Facility, Lancaster, 1983-85. Co-author: Fire Up Your Brilliance; co-author articles to profl. jours. Vol. Lancaster County Mental Health Ctr., 1983-94; seminar leader Fulton County (Pa.) C. of C., 1985-86, York County (Pa.) C. of C., 1985-86, Lancaster County C. of C., 1985-88. Mem. Internat. Coaching Fedn. Democrat. Episcopalian. Avocations: travel, reading, gardening, hiking. Office: 214 E King St Lancaster PA 17602 E-mail: brilliance@comcast.com.

TAYLOR, ANNA DIGGS, judge; b. Washington, Dec. 9, 1932; d. Virginius Douglass and Hazel (Bramlette) Johnston; m. S. Martin Taylor, May 22, 1976; children: Douglass Johnston Diggs, Carla Cecile Diggs. BA, Barnard Coll., 1954; LLB, Yale U., 1957. Bar: D.C. 1957, Mich. 1961. Atty. Office Solicitor, Dept. Labor, W, 1957-60; asst. prosecutor Wayne County, Mich., 1961-62; asst. U.S. atty. Eastern Dist. of Mich., 1966; ptnr. Zwerdling, Maurer, Diggs & Papp, Detroit, 1970-75; asst. corp. counsel City of Detroit, 1975-79; U.S. dist. judge Eastern Dist. Mich. Detroit, 1979—. Hon. chair, trustee United Way Cmty. Found., S.E. Mich., Detroit Inst. Arts; co-chair, vol. Leadership Coun.; trustee Henry Ford Health Sys., Cmty. Found. for S.E. Mich. Mem. Fed. Bar Assn., State Bar Mich., Wolverine Bar Assn. (v.p.), Yale Law Assn. Episcopalian. Office: US Dist Ct 740 US Courthouse 231 W Lafayette Blvd Detroit MI 48226-2700

TAYLOR, ANTHONY BALDWIN, civil engineer; b. Nassau, Bahamas, Nov. 25, 1971; came to U.S., 1990; s. Anthony Baldwin Sr. and Ruth Inez (McKenzie) T.; m. Kaaryn Wilaine Rogers, July 2, 1994; children: Anthony Baldwin III, Andrew Benjamin. BSCE, N.C. State U., 1994; PhD, Columbia State U., 1997. Owner/engr. TNT Constn., Nassau, 1992-94; constrn. engr. Greenman Pedersen Inc., Durham, N.C., 1994-96; resident engr. Parsons, Butner, 1996—2000, dir. of engring. Newport, 2000—. Mem. Am. Soc. Civil Engr., Assn. for the advancement of Cost Engring. Avocations: reading, writing, basketball, sport shooting, fishing. Home: 4885 E Wolf Tree Ave Terre Haute IN 47805-9414

TAYLOR, AUBREY ELMO, physiologist, educator; b. El Paso, Tex., June 4, 1933; s. Virgil T. and Mildred (Maher) Taylor; m. Mary Jane Davis, Apr. 4, 1953; children: Audrey Jane Hildebrand, Lenda Sue Taylor Brown, Mary Ann. BA in Math. and Psychology, Tex. Christian U., 1960; PhD in Physiology, U. Miss., 1964. Fellow biophysics lab. Harvard U. Med. Sch., Boston, 1965-67; from asst. prof. to prof. dept. physiology U. Miss. Coll. Medicine, Jackson, 1967-77; prof., chmn. dept. physiology U. South Ala. Coll. Medicine, Mobile, 1977—2002, disting. prof. emeritus, 2002—. Pulmonary score com. mem. Nat. Heart, Lung and Blood Inst., 1976; with Surgery and Anesthesiology, 1979—82, Manpower Com., 1985—95; chmn. RAP, 1983. Mem. editl. bd.: Jour. Applied Physiology, 1994—, mem. editl. bd.: Critical Care Medicine, 1991—97, mem. editl. bd.: Circulation Rsch., mem. editl. bd.: Am. Jour. Physiology, mem. editl. bd.: Internat. Pathophysiology, mem. editl. bd.: Microcirculatory and Lymphatic Rsch., mem. editl. bd.: Chinese Jour. Physiology, mem. editl. bd.: Microcirculation, mem. editl. bd.: Jour. Biomed. Sci., mem. editl. bd.: Am. Rev. Resp. and Critical Care Jour., mem. editl. bd.: Internat. Soc. Pathology, author 9 books: ; contbr. chapters to books, over 730 articles to profl. jours.; N.Am. editor: Clin. Scis., 1998—. With U.S. Army, 1953—55. Named Disting. Physiologist Am. Coll. Chest Physicians, 1994; recipient Lederle Faculty award, 1967—70, Philip Dow award, U. Ga., 1984, NIH Merit award, 1987—97, Lucian award, McGill U., 1988, John Whitney award, U. Ark., 1990, Gelen award, Intestinal Shock Soc., 1991, Arthur C. Guyton award, U. Miss Coll. Medicine, 1993, Disting. Alumnus award, Tex. Christian U., 1998, Disting Svc. award, USA med. Alumni Assn., 2000, Myerson-De Luzio Lectr., Tulane Sch. Medicine, 1997, Disting. Lectr., La State U., Shreveport, 1997, Abreu Meml. Keynote Spkr., U. Tex. Sch. Medicine, Galveston, 1998, Med. Student Rsch. Conf., 1998, Wu-Ho-Su Meml. Symposium Spl. Lectr., Louise Lenoir Locke eminent scholar chair, USA Coll. Medicine, chmn. med. student rsch. award com., Am. Heart Assn., 1992—94, Wiggers award, Am. Physiol. Soc., 1987, Eugene Landis Rsch. award, Micro Circulatory Soc., 1985, State Rsch. award, Acad. Scis, 1988, Cecil Drinker Rsch award, N.Y. Acad. Scis., 1988; grantee NIH, 1964—. Fellow: Royal Soc. Medicine (dir. R.S.M. Found.), Am. Heart Assn. (So. regional rev. com. 1977—81, cardiopulmonary, critical care coun. 1977—, chmn. 1979—81, EIA Rev. Com. 1986—95, pulmonary and devel. rev. com. 1987—95, nat. rsch. com. 1990—95, del. assembly 1990—99, chmn. 1993—98, chmn. grant/rev.com 1994—95, coun. affairs com. 1994—98, nominating com. 1998—99, basic sci. com. 1998—, circulation coun., chmn. elect. , AALAC bd. trustees rep., Bronze award Miss. AHA 1976, Dickinson W. Richards award 1988, Outstanding Ala. AHA program 1993, Sci. Coun. Achievement award 1995, Disting. Svc. award 1995, Rsch. Achievement award 1997, So. Ala. Dist. Achievement award 2000, Gala honoree 2000, Hall of Fame Spring Hill Hosp. Heart Assn. 2001), AAAS; mem.: European Respiratory Soc. (sec. lung injury group), Am. Thoracic Soc., Fedn. Am. Socs. for Exptl. Biology (bd. dirs. 1988—90, reorganizing com.), Biophys. Soc., N.Y. Acad. Scis., Internat. Pathophysiology Soc. (v.p. 1991—99), N. Am. Soc. Lymphology (pres. 1988—90, Cecil Drinker Rsch. award 1988), Internat. Lymphology Soc., Ala. Acad. Scis. (Ann. State Rsch. award 1988), Micro Circulatory Soc. (coun. 1977—81, pres. 1981—83, Eugene Landis Rsch. award 1985), Assn. Dept. Chairs of Physiology (exec. com. 1996—, sec. treas. 1998—2002), Am. Physiol. Soc. (coun. 1984—87, chmn. mem. com. 1985—87, pres. 1987—90, hon. com., chmn. 1993—96, chmn. Perkins fellow com. 1996—98, Cannon lectr. 1999, Wiggers award 1987, Achievement award 2002), NAS (com. for Internat. Union Physiol. Sci.), Sigma Xi, Alpha Omega Alpha. Democrat. Presbyterian. Achievements include research in in cardio-pulmonary physiology, fluid balance, edema, microcirculation and capillary exchange of solute and water and inflammatory processes in the lung. Home: 11 Audubon Pl Mobile AL 36606-1907

TAYLOR, BARBARA ALDEN, public relations executive; b. Dallas, Aug. 21, 1943; d. Harold Earl and Sally Alden (Howard) T. BA, Smith Coll., 1965; MA, Antioch Coll., 1971. Vol. Peace Corps., India, 1966-68; tchr. Upper Merion Sch. Dist., King of Prussia, Pa., 1969-70, Cheltenham Sch. Dist., Elkins Park, 1970-74; pub. rels. dir. Princess Hotels Internat., N.Y.C., 1974-75; chmn. Taylor & Hammond Ltd., 1975-84; pres. Doremus/Marketshare, 1984-86; exec. v.p. Porter/Novelli, N.Y.C., 1986-90; sr. v.p. Hill and Knowlton, Inc., 1990-93; sr. v.p. corp. comm. Lancaster Group Worldwide, 1993-95; sr. v.p. Coty Inc. and Benckiser Group, 1995-97; exec. v.p. Edelman Pub. Rels. Worldwide, N.Y.C., 1997—. Bd. dirs. Madison Square Boys' and Girls' Club N.Y., 1978—, also mem. women's bd. Boys' Club N.Y. Named to Acad. of Women Achievers YWCA, 1985; bd. dirs. Up With People, Tucson, 1990—; trustee Smith Coll., 1999—. Mem. Women in Comms., Pub. Rels. Soc. Am. (counselors acad.), Internat. Women's Forum, Advt. Women N.Y., Cosmetic Exec. Women, Fashio Group, Doubles Internat., Smith Coll. Alumnae Assn. (bd. dirs. 1993-96), Club N.Y., Lyford Cay Club, Jr. League City N.Y. Avocations: tennis, walking. Office: Edelman Pub Rels Worldwide 1500 Broadway Ste 504 New York NY 10036-4048

TAYLOR, BARBARA ANN OLIN, writer, educational consultant; b. St. Louis, Feb. 8, 1933; d. Spencer Truman and Ann Amelia (Whitney) Olin; m. F. Morgan Taylor Jr., Apr. 5, 1954; children: Frederick M. III, Spencer O., James W., John F. AB, Smith Coll., 1954; M in Mgmt., Northwestern U., 1978, PhD, 1984; LHD, U. New Haven, 1995. Mem. faculty Hamden (Conn.) Hall Country Day Sch., 1972-74; cons. Booz, Allen & Hamilton, Inc., Chgo., 1979; program assoc. Northwestern U., Evanston, 1982; co-founder, exec. dir. Nat. Ctr. Effective Schs. R&D, Okemos, Mich., 1986-89, rsch. assoc., 1987; cons. on effective schs. rsch. and reform Nat. Ctr. Effective Schs. R&D U. Wis., Madison, 1990-96; pres. Excelsior! Found., Chgo., 1994—. Mem. exec. com. Hudson Inst., New Am. Schs. Devel. Corp. Design Team, 1990-94; Danforth Disting. lectr. U. Nebr., Omaha, 1993. Co-author: Making School Reform Happen, 1993, Keepers of the Dream, 1994, The Revolution Revisited: Effective Schools and Systemic Reform, 1995; editor: Case Studies in Effective Schools Research, 1990; contbr. articles to profl. jours. Pres. Jr. League of New Haven, 1967-69; pres. NCCJ, New Haven, 1971-73; co-chair Coalition Housing and Human Resources, Hartford-New Haven, 1970-73; co-chair steering com. Day Care Conn., Hartford, 1971-73; trustee U. New Haven, 1961-71, Smith Coll., Northampton, Mass., 1984-90, Choate Rosemary Hall Sch., 1973-78, Lake Forest Coll., 1996—, Hudson Inst., 1989-97, Northwestern U., 1998—. Recipient Humanitarian award Mt. Calvary Bapt. Ch., 1988, Outstanding Alumna award John Burroughs Sch., 1994, Pres.'s award U. New Haven. Mem. ASCD, Nat. Commn. Citizens Edn. (bd. dirs. 1980-86), Nat. Staff Devel. Coun., Phi Delta Kappa (Internat. award for Outstanding Svc. 2000). Episcopalian. Office: Nat Ctr Effective Schs Rsch & Devel 222 E Wisconsin Ave Ste 301 Lake Forest IL 60045-1723

TAYLOR, BARBARA JO ANNE HARRIS, government official, civic and political worker; b. Providence, Sept. 09; d. Ross Cameron and Anita (Coia) Harris; m. Richard Powell Taylor, Dec. 19, 1959; 1 child, Douglas Howard. Student, Georgetown U., 1956-59, 62-63, BS cum laude, 1963. Adminstrv. asst. profl. devel. and welfare NEA, Washington, 1956-59; asst. to dir. Georgetown U., 1956-59; exec. asst. All Am. Conf. to Combat Communism, 1960; spl. legis. asst. mil. affairs to chmn. mil. R & D subcom. U.S. Senate Armed Svcs. Com., 1971-72; U.S. nat. commr. UNESCO, 1982—, mem. exec. com. U.S. nat. commn., 1983—, sr. advisor 22d gen. conf., 1983. Speaker in field. Contbr. articles to profl. jours. Del. numerous internat. confs.; U.S. commr. Nat. Commn. Librs. and Info. Sci., 1985-96, mem. various coms.; gen. chmn. George Bush for Pres. Md. State Steering Com., 1987-88; co-chmn. Md. del. Rep. Nat. Conv., 1988, 92; dep. chmn. Md. Victory '88, Bush-Quayle Campaign; mem. Nat. Fin. Com. Reagan for Pres., 1980, Reagan-Bush, 1984; state fin. chmn. Md. Rep. Party, 1980; mem. Nat. Rep. Club; mem. exec. bd. Salvation Army Aux., Washington, 1967-75, chmn. membership com., 1969-70, chmn. fund-raising com., 1968-69, mem. exec. com. of exec. bd., 1970-75, treas., mem. fin. com., 1970-71, v.p., 1971-72, historian, 1972-73, editor newsletter, 1968-69, chmn. nominating com., 1974-75, spl. awards. for exceptional vol. svc., 1969, 72; mem. exec. bd. Welcome to Washington Internat., 1969-74, bd. advisers, 1969-74, dir. workshop, 1969-74; exec. bd. Am. Opera Sch. Soc., Washington, 1970-85, v.p., 1974-85; mem. Episc. Ch. Home for Aged Women's Aux., 1970-75, Episc. Ctr. for Emotionally Disturbed Children Women's Aux., 1970-75; exec. bd. St. David's Episc. Ch. Aux., 1970-72, 73-74; bd. dirs., treas. Spanish-Portuguese Study Group, 1970-72; mem. exec. bd. League Rep. Women D.C., 1964-67, 75-77, treas., 1964-67; mem. nat. coun. Women's Nat. Rep. Club, N.Y.C., 1969—, chmn. Washington-Md.-Va. legis. com., 1970-75; mem. Nat. Fedn. Rep. Women, 1964—; mem. nat. fin. com. Reagan for Pres., 1979-80; mem. governing bd. Capital Speakers Club, 1973-75, chmn. by-laws com., 1973-74; mem. exec. bd. Nat. Vols. in Action, 1975-77; mem. adv. com. Rock Creek Found. Mental Health, 1982-87; mem. 50th anniversary com. Save the Children; mem. fund-raising com. Washington Choral Arts Soc., 1982-84; state fin. chmn. Reagan-Bush campaign Md. Rep. Com., 1980; Md. coord. Nat. Inaugural Com., 1981, 85; trustee Crossnore Sch., Inc., N.C., 1983—, vice chmn. bd; trustee Kate Duncan Smith DAR Sch., Grant, Ala., 1983-86, Tamassee (S.C.) DAR Sch., 1983-86; adviser Bacone Am. Indian Coll., Inc., Muscogee, Okla., 1983-88. Mem. ALA, Spl. Librs. Assn., Coun. on Libr. Resources (commn. on preservation and access), Am. Libr. Trustees Assn., Libr. Adminstrn. and Mgmt. Assn., Assn. Coll. and Rsch. Librs., Am. Antiquarian Soc., Internat. Platform Assn., Spanish-Portuguese Study Group, Nat. Lawyers' Wives, Nat. Capital Law League, Nat. Soc. DAR (chmn. nat. resolutions com. 1980-83, chmn. nat. Nat. Soc. DAR sch. com. 1983-86; state historian 1978-80, mem. state bd. mgmt. 1973—, Nat. Soc. DAR libr. gen., mem. exec. com. and nat. corp. bd. mgmt. 1986-89, chmn. nat. commemorative events com. 1992-95, 98-2001, Nat. Soc. DAR libr. centennial com. 1995-98), Nat. Soc. Children Am. Revolution (sr. nat. asst. registrar 1978-80, mem. sr. nat. bd. mgmt. 1978-80, sr. nat. exec. com. 1978-80), Nat. Assn. Parliamentarians, World Affairs Coun., League of Rep. Women, Md. Fedn. Rep. Women, Women's Nat. Republican Club, Nat. Fed. Rep. Women, Commn. on Preservation and Access, Lit. Vols. Am. (Washington Met. area affiliate), Exec. Women in Govt., Gen. Soc. Mayflower Descendants, Am. News Women's Club, Internat. Club, Capitol Hill Club, Univ. Club Washington, Washington Club, Congl. Country Club (Potomac, Md.).

TAYLOR, BARRY NORMAN, physicist; b. Phila., Mar. 27, 1936; s. Morris and Sarah (Weiss) T.; m. Sheila Anne Cohen, Dec. 28, 1958; children: Deborah Susan, David Joel, Denise Beth. AB, Temple U., Phila., 1957; MS, U. Pa., 1960, PhD, 1963. Instr., then asst. prof. physics U. Pa., 1963-66; mem. tech. staff RCA Rsch. Labs., 1966-70; chief absolute elec. measurements sect. Nat. Bur. Standards (name changed to Nat. Inst. of Standards and Tech. 1988), Gaithersburg, Md., 1970-74, adminstr. NIST Precision Measurement Grants Program, 1974-2000, chief electricity divsn., 1974-89; mgr. Fundamental Cons. Data Ctr., 1989-2001, scientist emeritus, 2001—. Instr. Rider Coll., Trenton, N.J., 1969-70; mem., chairperson nat. and internat. tech. coms. Co-author: Fundamental Constants and Quantum Electrodynamics, 1969; co-editor: Precision Measurement and Fundamental Constants, 1971; Co-editor: Precision Measurement and Fundamental Constants II, 1984; contbr. articles to sci. jours. Recipient Silver medal U.S. Dept. Commerce, 1975, Gold medal, 1989, John Price Wetherill medal Franklin Inst., 1975, Codata prize, 2000, Disting. Exec. award Sr. Exec. Svc. of USA U.S. Pres., 2000. Fellow IEEE, Am. Phys. Soc. (chair topical group on fundamental constants and precise tests of phys. laws 1990-92); mem. Sigma Xi. Office: Nat Inst of Stds and Tech 100 Bureau Dr Stop 8401 Gaithersburg MD 20899-8401 E-mail: barry.taylor@nist.gov.

TAYLOR, BERNARD J., II, banker; b. Phila., Nov. 10, 1925; s. Bernard and Marie (Pearce) T.; m. Barbara Silverstein; children: Dorothy Taylor Tomlinson, Lawrence Dean, David Stewart. BS, U. Pa., 1949. Asst. mgr. McCrory Stores Corp., Phila., 1949-51; fin. analyst Fidelity Bank, 1951-57, asst. to v.p. investments, 1957-59, asst. to pres., 1959-60, corp. sec., 1960-63, v.p., sec., 1963-66, sr. v.p. in charge adminstrn. dept., 1966-72, exec. v.p., 1972-74; v.p. Fidelcor, Inc. (parent co. Fidelity Bank), 1969-72, exec. v.p., 1973-76; sr. exec. v.p., 1976-79; pres., dir. Fidelity Bldg. Corp., 1970-79; pres., CEO Wilmington (Del.) Trust Co., Del., 1979-92, dir., 1979-98, chmn., 1980-92. Ptnr. Golf Ptnrs. (Hartefield Nat. Golf Course), 1993-99. Pres. Savoy Opera Co., Phila., 1961-63, prodn. mgr., dir., 1970-75; pres., bd. dirs. Pa. Opera Theatre, 1975-80, treas., bd. dirs., 1980-93; mem. adv. bd. mgrs. Inglis House Phila., 1967-70; mem. Del. Round Table, 1980-92; bd. dirs. Greater Wilmington Devel. Coun., 1980-84, Sta. WHYY, PBS-TV, Phila., 1980-92; bd. dirs., 1986-91; bd. dirs. Del. Theatre Co., 1987-91. With AUS, 1944-46, PTO. Inducted to State of Del. Bus. Leaders Hall of Fame, 1999. Mem.: Orpheus (Phila); Wilmington Country; Jonathan's Landing Golf. Home: 8 Oak Tree Hollow Rd West Chester PA 19382-8341

TAYLOR, BEVERLY LACY, stringed instrument restorer, classical guitarist; b. Denver, Mar. 1, 1928; d. Frederick Thurlow and Ruth (Rogers) Lacy; m. Arthur D. Taylor, Mar. 18, 1967. BA, Wheaton Coll., Norton, Mass., 1949; postgrad., U. Denver, 1951-53, U. Colo., 1953. Scene designer, tech. dir. Piper Players, Idaho Springs, Colo., 1949-51; art instr. Denver Art Mus., 1952; craft and speech instr. Wallace Sch., Denver, 1953; illustrator dept. native art Denver Art Mus., 1954-56; designer, owner The Art Studio, Santa Fe, 1956-58; instr., owner Classic Guitar Studio, 1959—; instr. classical guitar Santa Fe Conservatory of Music, 1966-67, Coll. Santa Fe, 1971-72; stringed instrument restorer Lacy Taylor Studio, Santa Fe, 1967—. One-woman shows of mosaic panels include Mus. N.Mex., Santa Fe, 1959; exhibited in group shows at Mus. New Mex., 1962, 63; executed mosaic panels Denver Art Mus. Bd. mem. Renesan, Elderhostel Inst. Network. Recipient Miriam Carpenter Art prize Wheaton Coll., 1949, prize N.Mex. State Fair, 1959, 61. Mem. Guild Am. Luthiers, Assn. String Instrument Artisans. Avocations: drawing, gardening, dog training, horse therapy programs for handicapped adults and children. Home: 1210 Canyon Rd Santa Fe NM 87501-6128

TAYLOR, BLANCHE MURRAY, organist; b. Phila., Aug. 23, 1927; d. James Andrew and Anna Delores (Best) Murray; widowed; 1 child, Renee Phillips. Student, Settlement Music Sch., Phila., 1945-48, Zechwer Hahn's Conservatory, 1948-51. Cert. med. adminstr. Organist Reunion Choir of Phila., 1989—; ch. organist, dir. Oak Grove Bapt. Ch., Phila., 1990-95; ch. organist Trinity AME Ch., 1995—. Composer, arranger Spiritual Medley, 1996; singer Tomlin Accapella Choir, Phila., Famous Ward Singers, Phila., Willettes, Phila.,

1945-49. Recipient citation City Coun. Phila., Presdl. acknowledgment for 50 yrs. as ch. organist, 1993. Mem. Nat. Assn. Negro Musicians. Mem. AME Ch. Avocation: window shopping. Home: Apt 305 6300 Old York Rd Philadelphia PA 19141-2013

TAYLOR, BRETT DAVIS, music educator; b. Silver Spring, Md., Aug. 8, 1975; s. Bette Ann Taylor; m. Jennifer Leigh Harrill, July 20, 2002. BS, Towson U., Towson, MD, 1993—97; Maser of Music, U. of Md., College Park, MD, 2000—02. Teaching Certificate Md. State Dept. of Edn., 1998. Instrumental music tchr. Good Counsel H.S., Wheaton, Md., 2002—; grad. asst. U. of Md. Bands, College Park, 2000—02; instrumental music tchr. Montgomery County Pub. Schools, Rockville, 1998—2000. Scholar C. James Velie Meml. Scholarship, Towson U., 1997. Mem.: Music Educators Nat. Conf., Tau Beta Sigma Nat. Hon. Band Svc. Sorority (hon.), Kappa Kappa Psi Nat. Hon. Band Svc. Frat. (hon.). Personal E-mail: brett8@comcast.net.

TAYLOR, BRUCE STEVENSON, architect, planner; b. N.Y.C., Sept. 3, 1946; s. James Stevenson and Linnea Sarrah (Hendrickson) T.; m. Sandra Dee Butzman, Oct. 9, 1970; 1 child, Eric Stevenson. BArch, Miami U., Oxford, Ohio, 1969. Registered architect, Mass., Conn., N.H., Vt., Maine, N.Y. Design draftsman Architects Collaborative, Cambridge, Mass., 1969-73; project architect W.M. Design Group, Nahant, 1973-76; pvt. practice architecture West Newbury, 1976-78; corp. dir. Claude Miquelle Assocs., Inc., Melrose, 1978-85; architect, planner Bruce S. Taylor, Architect, West Newbury, 1985—. Vis. critic Boston Archtl. Ctr., 1976-77; student counselor Students from Boston Archtl. Ctr., 1980-85. Archtl. projects featured in mags. Bd. dirs. Bd. Health, West Newbury, 1981-83, chmn., 1984-85. Recipient Merit award Builder Mag., 1984, 1st Honor award Soc. Am. Registered Architects, 1984, Grand award Nat. Assn. Home Builders and Better Homes and Gardens, 1984. Mem. Nat. Council Archtl. Registration Bds., AIA, Boston Soc. Architects. Lutheran. Avocations: skiing, fishing, model railroading, historical architecture. Home and Office: 248 Main St West Newbury MA 01985-1414

TAYLOR, CARL ERNEST, physician, educator; b. Landour, Mussoorie, India, July 26, 1916; s. John C. and Elizabeth (Siehl) Taylor; m. Mary Daniels, Feb. 14, 1943; children: Daniel, Elizabeth, Henry. BS, Muskingum Coll., 1937, DSc, 1962; MD, Harvard, 1941, MPH, 1951, DPH, 1953; LHD (hon.) , Towson U., 1974. Diplomate Am. Bd. Preventive Medicine. Intern, resident pathology, surg. staff, tropical disease rsch. Gorgas Hosp., Panama, 1941—44; charge med. service Marine Hosp., Pitts., 1944—46; supt. Meml. Hosp., Fategarh, India, 1947—50; rsch. assoc. Harvard Sch. Pub. Health, Boston, 1950—52, asst. prof. epidemiology, 1957—59, assoc. prof., 1959-61; prof. preventive and social medicine Christian Med. Coll., Ludhiana, India, 1953—56; prof. internat. health, chmn. dept. internat. health Johns Hopkins Sch. Hygiene and Pub. Health, Balt., 1961—83, prof. emeritus, 1984—. Cons. AID, 1959—; UNICEF country rep. in China, 1984—87; expert com. WHO, 1963, 1966—67, 1970—73, 1975; mem. Nat. Adv. Commn. Health Manpower; chmn. Nat. Council for Internat. Health. Contbr. articles to profl. jours. Fellow: Am. Pub. Health Assn., Royal Soc. Tropical Medicine and Hygiene, Royal Coll. Physicians; mem.: Nat. Acad. Medicine, Inst. Medicine, Indian Assn. for Advancement Med. Edn., Am. Soc. Tropical Medicine and Hygiene, Assn. Tchrs. Preventive Medicine. Achievements include research in rural health, population dynamics, nutrition, epidemiology of leprosy. Home: Bittersweet Acres 1201 Hollins Ln Baltimore MD 21209-2209 Office: Johns Hopkins Sch Hygiene and Pub Health 615 N Wolfe St Baltimore MD 21205-2103 *The growing complexity of human relationships around this increasingly crowded world presents new challenges to concerned scientists. Solutions to our problems must come from new collaborative styles of work bridging the usual boundaries between people, since the problems we face are mutual.*

TAYLOR, CARL G. foundation administrator; b. Miami Beach, Fla., Jan. 18, 1956; s. Jack Samuel and Elly Taylor; m. Susan M. Moore, June 5, 1993. B degree, Goddard Coll., 1982, M degree, 1986. Case worker State of Vt. Social Rehab. Svcs. NEKCA Youth Svcs., Newport, 1985-86; social worker B Social Rehab. Svcs., 1986-89; pres. Newport Adolescent Programs, 1989—. Founder Mt. Sinai Hosp., Miami Beach, 1993. Bd. dirs. NEKCA Drug and Alcohol Programs, Newport, 1989-92; panelist Diversion Bd., Newport, 1991-93; ednl. surrogate parent Vt. Dept. Edn., Montpelier, 1989-93. Mem. Am. Counseling Assn., Vt. Counseling Assn., Am. Hort. Therapy Assn., Nat. Alcohol Drug Abuse Counselors Assn., Nat. Alcohol Drug Abuse Counselors Assn. Jewish. Avocations: canoeing, gardening, fishing, traveling, reading. Address: PO Box 785 Newport VT 05855-0785 Office: PO Box 785 Newport VT 05855-0785

TAYLOR, CARMEN KAYE, apparel company executive; b. Greensburg, Pa., Oct. 15, 1952; d. Bruce Lowell and Mildred Louise (Montgomery) Taylor; m. John Douglas Kellum, Aug. 2, 1975 (div. May 1987). Student, MacMurray Coll., 1971-72, Elgin Community Coll.; AA, Coll. DuPage, 1975; BA with honors, Nat. Louis U., 1978. Cert. tchr. Aide occupational therapy Mercy Ctr., Aurora, Ill., 1972-76; tchr. behavior disorders Lake Park High Sch., Roselle, 1978-80, Salk Pioneer Sch., Roselle, 1980-81; mgr. So-Fro Fabrics Stores, Lombard, Joliet & Chgo., Ill., 1981-84; offshore coord. Florsheim Shoe Co., Chgo., 1984-90; mgr. Linens N Things, Rolling Meadows, Ill., 1990-91, House of Fabrics, Aurora, 1992-94, Glen Ellyn, 1994; store mgr. T.J. Maxx, Naperville and W. Dundee, 1994-97, W. Dundee, 1996-97; mgr. Toys R Us, Schaumburg, 1997-98, Kmart, Villa Park, Ill., 1998-99, Kohl's, Downers Grove, 1999—. Mem. Internat. Dyslexia Assn., Nat. Assn. Female Exec., Kappa Delta Pi. Lutheran. Avocations: dance, swimming, sewing, needlepoint, choir. Home: 30 W 156 Wood Ct and Hwy 59 PO Box 8137 Bartlett IL 60103-8137 Office: Kohl's 2920 Finley Rd Downers Grove IL 60515-1042

TAYLOR, CAROL,¨rehabilitation nurse; b. York, Pa., June 26, 1949; d. James Vincent and Arlene Catherine (Rosenzweig) Kavanagh; m. David Eugene Taylor, June 9, 1983; children: Shannon Kathleen Kaye, Kevin Christopher, David Jason, E. J. Meyer. RN diploma, E.J. Meyer Meml. Hosp. Sch. Nursing, Buffalo, 1970; student, SUNY, Buffalo, 1967-68, 72-73, U. South Miss., Gulfport, 1984; BSN, U. South Ala., Mobile, 1989; MS in Health Sci., Tex. Wesleyan U., 1991; student nurse anesthesia, U.S. Army-Weslyan U., 1990-92. Cert. registered nurse anesthetist. Nurse operating rm. Biloxi (Miss.) Regional Med. Ctr.; nurse operating rm./recovery rm. Meml. Hosp., Gulfport, Miss.; charge nurse operating rm. Sacred Heart Hosp., Pensacola, Fla., 1987-88; staff nurse rehab. HCA West Fla. Regional Med Ctr. Rehab. Inst., 1989-90; nurse anesthetist Fitzsimons Army Med. Ctr., Aurora, Colo., 1993-95, Lyster Army Hosp., Ft. Rucker, Ala., 1995-97, The Anesthesia Group of Sarasota, Fla., 1997, James A. Haley VA Hosp., Tampa, 1997—. Maj. U.S. Army, 1990-2000. Mem. AANA. Home: 906 133rd St E Bradenton FL 34212-9209

TAYLOR, CARROLL STRIBLING, lawyer; b. Port Chester, N.Y., Jan. 14, 1944; s. William H. Jr. and Anna P. (Stribling) T.; m. Nancy S. Tyson, Apr. 7, 1968; children: Heather, Kimberly, Tori, Tiffany, Tacy. AB, Yale U., 1965; JD, U. Calif., Berkeley, 1968. Bar: Hawaii 1969, Calif. 1969, U.S. Dist. Ct. Hawaii 1969, U.S. Dist. Ct. (cen. dist.) Calif. 1975, U.S. Ct. Appeals (9th cir.) 1975. Rschr. Legis. Reference Bur., Honolulu, 1968-70; reporter Jud. Coun. Probate Code Revision Project, 1970-71; assoc. Chun, Kerr & Dodd, 1971-75; ptnr. Hamilton & Taylor, 1975-80; officer, dir. Char, Hamilton, Taylor & Thom, 1980-82, Carroll S. Taylor Atty. at Law, A Law Corp., Honolulu, 1982-86; ptnr. Taylor & Leong, 1986-91, Taylor, Leong & Chee, Honolulu, 1991—. Adj. prof. Richardson Sch. Law U. Hawaii, Honolulu, 1981-86, 88-90, 97; mem. Disciplinary bd. of Supreme Ct. of Hawaii, 1994—, vice chair, 1997-99, chair, 2000—; dir. Am. Nat. Lawyers Ins. Reciprocal, 1997-2000; mem., bd. dirs. Hanahauoli Sch., 1992-97. Fellow Am. Coll. Trust and Estate Counsel; mem. ABA, Calif. Bar Assn., Hawaii State Bar Assn., Hawaii Inst. Continuing Legal Edn. (pres. 1986-88), Pla. Club (Honolulu). Episcopalian. Home: 46-429 Hololio St Kaneohe HI 96744-4225 Office: 737 Bishop St Ste 2060 Honolulu HI 96813-3214 E-mail: ctaylor@hawaii.rr.com.

TAYLOR, CARSON WILLIAM, electrical engineer; b. Superior, Wis., May 24, 1942; s. William Stanley and Elizabeth Marie (Christophersen) T.; m. Gudrun Renate Leistner, Dec. 28, 1966; 1 child, Natasha Marie. BSEE, U. Wis., 1965; M in Engring., Rensselaer Poly. Inst., 1969. Elec. engr. U.S. Bur. Reclamation, Billings, Mont., 1967-68, Bonneville Power Adminstrn., Portland, Oreg., 1969-89, prin. engr., 1989—. Prin. Carson Taylor Seminars, Portland, 1986—. Author: Power System Voltage Stability, 1994; contbr. papers to profl. publs.; patentee in field. Lt. U.S. Army, 1965-67. Lt. U.S. Army, 1965-67. Fellow IEEE (chmn. subcom. 1982—); mem. Conférence Internationale des Grands Réseaux Électriques a Haute Tension (CIGRE, disting. mem.), Eta Kappa Nu. Lutheran. Avocations: fishing, hunting, woodworking, reading, computers. Office: Bonneville Power Adminstrn PO Box 491 Vancouver WA 98666-0491

TAYLOR, CARTER W. aviation educator; b. St. Louis, Oct. 10, 1937; s. George Wellford and Carola Whitman T.; children by a previous marriage: Carter W. Jr., Patricia L.; m. Judy Hall Taylor, Nov. 16, 1991; children: G. Scott Moore, Tamara Moore Polson. BS, N.Mex. State U., 1961. Cert. flight instr. FAA; cert. airline transport pilot FAA. Tchr. El Paso Pub. Sch., 1962-63; air traffic controller FAA, Jacksonville, Fla., 1963-64; pilot Eastern Airlines, Inc., Miami-N.Y.C., 1964, Am. Airlines, Inc., N.Y.C.-Dallas, 1964-67, capt., 1967-97, flight instr. Dallas, 1983-95, sr. flight instr., 1995-97. Recipient World Speed Record Dallas to London Fedn. Aeronautique Internat., 1997, World Speed Record London to Dallas Fedn. Aeronautique Internat., 1997, Nat. Speed Record Chgo. to Dallas Nat. Aeronautic Assn., 1997. Mem. Antique Automobile Club Am. (nat. dir. 1991-92), Antique Automobile Libr. and Rsch. Ctr. (bd. dirs. 1985-86). Avocations: antique automobiles, antique aircraft, photography. Home: 1228 Old Spartanburg Rd Greer SC 29650-3266 Fax: 864-244-9511. E-mail: captcwt@aol.com.

TAYLOR, CASPER R., JR. state legislator; b. Cumberland, Md., Dec. 19, 1934; married. BA, U. Notre Dame, 1956. State del. Dist. 2A Md. State Delegation, 1975-94, state del. Dist. 1C, 1995—, vice chmn. econ. matters com., 1978-86, chmn. econ. matters com., 1987-94, co-chmn. spl. house com. on econ. devel. strategy, mem. legis. policy, rules and exec. nominations com., 1987—94; spkr. of ho., 1994—. Co-chair, Legis. Policy Com., 1994-(mem., 1987-), Special Joint Com. on Econ. Devel. Strategy, 1988-91; chair, Western Md. Del., 1982-86, Allegany Co. Del., 1987-94. Mem. Gov.'s Task Force to Study Pub. Svc. Commn. Law, Spl. Joint Com. on Transp., Joint Com. on Energy and Joint Com. on Md. Port; pres. Allegany County Liquor Dealers; adv. bd. Sacred Heart Hosp.; mem. Cumberland Bus. and Civic Assn. Mem., Savings and Loan Oversight Com., 1986, Spl. Joint Com. on Energy Pricing, 1990-91, Tort and Ins. Reform Oversight Com., 1991-93, Spending Affordability Com., 1994-2000; bd. dirs. Nat. Spkrs. Conf., State Legis. Leaders Found., 2000-; Citizens Adv. Bd., Gov.'s Commn. on Md. Military Monuments, 1989-, State House Trust, 1994-, Md. Environ. Trust, 1995-, Gov.'s Redistricting Adv. Com., 2001-; Del. Dem. Nat. Conv., 2000; Mem. Md. Wildlife Fedn., Acad. Polit. Sci. (chpt. pres.), Elks, Alhambra, Eagles, C. of C., K.C. Served in U.S. Air Force R.O.T.C., 1952-54. Address: 72 Pershing St Cumberland MD 21502-3013 Office: 101 State House Annapolis MD 21401-1991*

TAYLOR, CELIANNA ISLEY, information systems specialist; b. Youngstown, Ohio; d. Paul Thornton and Florence (Jacobs) Isley; divorced; children: Polly, Jerry, Jim. BA in Philosophy, Denison U., 1939; MLS, Western Res. U., 1942. Worked in several pub. librs. and univ. librs., 1939-50; head Libr. Cataloging Dept. Battelle Mem. Inst., Columbus, Ohio, 1951-53; head pers. office, assoc. prof. libr. adminstrn. Ohio State U. Librs., 1954-65; coord. info. svcs., assoc. prof. libr. adminstrn. Nat. Ctr. for Rsch. in Vocat. Edn., Ohio State U., 1966-70; sr. rsch. assoc., adminstrv. assoc., assoc. prof. libr. adminstrn. dept. computer and info. sci. Ohio State U., 1970-86, assoc. prof. emeritus Univ. Librs., 1986—. Mem. Task Force on a Spl. Collections Database, Ohio State U. Librs., Columbus, 1988-89, comm. systems and recs. coord. Ohio State U. Retirees Assn., Columbus, 1992-93, info. specialist, MacForum, Ohio State U., Columbus, 2001—; cons. for several profl. orgns. including Ernst & Ernst CPA's and Oreg. State Sys. of Higher Edn., 1961-82. Author: (with J. Magisos) Guide for State Voc-Tech Edn. Dissemination Systems 1971, (with A.E. Petrarca, and R.S. Kohn) Info. Interaction 1982; editor Highlights-Coun. for Ethics in Econs., 1997—; contbr. several articles to profl. jours.; designer info. sys.: CALL Sys., 1977-82, Channel 2000 Proj. Home Info. Svc., 1980-81, Continuing Education Info. Ctr., 1989-90, Human Resources (HUR) Sys., 1976-77,1979-82, DECOS, 1975-86, Computer-asst. libr. Sys., Optical Scan Sys., 1972-73, ERIC Clearinghouse for vocat. edn., 1966-70. Bd. dirs. Columbus Reg. Info. Svc., 1974-78, Cmty. Info. Referral Svc., Inc. 1975-81; chmn. subcom. on design, info. and ref. com. Columbus United Cmty. Coun., 1972-73; dir. Computer Utility for Pub. Info. Columbus, 1975-81; acct. coord. Greater Columbus Free-net, 1994-98; info. specialist, coord. LWV Met. Columbus Webside Com., 2001-02. Mem. ALA, Assn. Computing Machinery (Ctrl. Ohio chpt.), Am. Soc. Info. Sci.,Assn. Faculty and Profl. Women Ohio State U., Columbus Metro Club, Coun. for Ethics in Econs., Olympic Indoor Tennis Club. Avocations: bicycling, bird watching, gourmet cooking, tennis, water aerobics. Home and Office: 3471 Greenbank Ct Columbus OH 43221-4724

TAYLOR, CHARLES ELLETT, biologist, educator; b. Chgo., Sept. 9, 1945; s. Stewart Ferguson and Barbara (Ellett) T.; m. Minna Glushien, June 22, 1969. AB, U. Calif., 1968; PhD, SUNY, Stony Brook, 1973. Prof. U. Calif., Riverside, 1974-80, UCLA, 1980—. Cons. artificial life and population genetics; dir. UCLA Cognitive Sci. Rsch. Program, 1990-99; mem. adv. bd. Computer Mus. Fishtank. Co-author: Artifical Life II, 1992, Artifical Life VI, 1998; editor: Artificial Life, 1997—2002; assoc. editor: IEEE Transactions on Evolutionary Computing, 1997—99; contbr. articles to profl. publs. Mem. Santa Fe Inst. Office: Dept Organismic Biology Ecology and Evolution UCLA Box 951606 Los Angeles CA 90095-1606 E-mail: ctaylor@ucla.edu.

TAYLOR, CHARLES H. congressman; b. Brevard, N.C., Jan. 3, 1941; m. Elizabeth Owen; 3 children. BA, Wake Forest U., 1963, JD, 1966. Tree farmer, N.C.; mem. N.C. Ho. of Reps., Raleigh, 1967-73, minority leader, 1969-73; mem. N.C. Senate, 1973-75, minority leader, 1973-75; mem. U.S. Congress from 11th N.C. dist., Washington, 1991—; mem. appropriations com., commerce, justice, state jud. subcom., subcom. on interior. chmn. subcom. on legis. branch. Republican. Baptist. Office: US Ho of Reps 231 Cannon Ho Office Bldg Washington DC 20515-3311 also: 22 S Pack Sq Ste 330 Asheville NC 28801-3503*

TAYLOR, CHARLES HENRY, psychoanalyst, educator; b. Boston, Oct. 2, 1928; s. Charles Henry and Rosamond (Stewardson) T.; m. Diana Burgess, 1950; children: Stephen, Diana Beth, Charles S., Eleanor; m. Patricia Finley, 1988. BA, Yale U., 1950, MA, 1952, PhD, 1955; postgrad., Cambridge (Eng.) U., 1950-51. From instr. to asst. prof. English Ind. U., 1955-61; from asst. dean to assoc. dean, also assoc. prof. English Yale U., 1961-63, acting provost, 1963-64, provost, prof. English, 1964-72, pres. rep., 1972-76; grad. C.G. Jung Inst., N.Y., 1979; pvt. practice, 1976—. Bd. dirs. Meridian Audio, Ltd. Author: The Early Collected Editions of Shelley's Poems, 1958, (with Patricia Finley) Images of the Journey in Dante's Divine Comedy, 1997; editor: Essays on the Odyssey, 1963; contbr. articles to profl. jours. Mem. com. on libr. Yale U. Coun., 1990-95; trustee Hampshire Coll., 1988-93, 99—, chair, 2000—. Mem. Internat. Assn. Analytical Psychology, Archive for Rsch. in Archetypal Symbolism (pres. 1987-93, treas. 1993—), N.Y. Assn. Analytical Psychology, Nat. Assn. for Advancement Psychoanalysis, Phi Beta Kappa. Home: 40 Rogers Ave Milford CT 06460-6435

TAYLOR, CHARLES LEWIS, political scientist; b. Ware Shoals, S.C., Nov. 8, 1935; s. Humphrus Lee and Sue (Brissey) Taylor; m. Mary Frances Taylor, June 1, 1958; children: Susan, James. BA, Carson-Newman Coll., Jefferson City, Tenn., 1957; MA, Yale U., 1959, PhD, 1963. Asst. prof. Coll. William & Mary, Williamsburg, Va., 1962-66; rsch. assoc. Yale U., New Haven, 1966-70; prof. Va. Tech., Blacksburg, Va., 1970—. John Marshall profl Budapest (Hungary) U. Econ. Scis., 1991-92; recurring vis. rsch. prof. Berlin Sci. Ctr., 1993—. Author: World Handbook of Political and Social Indicators, 1972, 83. Pastor Roanoke Valley Presbyn. Ch., Blacksburg, 1985—. Democrat. Avocations: hiking, travel. Office: Va Tech Mailcode 0130 Blacksburg VA 24061

TAYLOR, CHRIS, journalist, writer; b. Toronto, Ont., Can., May 24, 1972; arrived in U.S., 2000; s. Bryce and Carole Taylor. BA in English Lit. and Religious Studies, McGill U., 1994; M in Journalism, Carleton U., 1997. Reporting intern Montreal Gazette, 1997; rschr. TV Ont., Ottawa, 1997—98; asst. editor B.C. Bus. Mag., Vancouver, 1998—2000; staff writer Smart Money Mag., N.Y.C., 2000—. V.p. bd. dirs. Western Mag. Awards Found., Vancouver, 1999—2000, judge, 2001, 02, Nat. Journalism Awards, 2002. Vol. Make-A-Wish Found., 2002. Mem.: Can. Assn. Journalists, Soc. Profl. Journalists, Can. Soc. of N.Y. Avocations: travel, theater , guitar. Office: Smart Money Mag 1755 Broadway 2d Fl New York NY 10019 E-mail: ctaylor@hearst.com.

TAYLOR, CLIFFORD OTIS, retired principal; b. Ft. Pierce, Fla., Jan. 4, 1926; s. Thomas Archie and Margaret Emeline (Tyler) T.; m. Dorothy Ann Pearce, Dec. 27, 1952. BA, Fla. State U., 1950; MEd, U. Ill., Urbana, 1954; postgrad., U. Miami, Appalachian State U. Cert. tchr., prin. Tchr. Fairlawn Sch., St. Lucie County, Ft. Pierce, North Grade Sch., Palm Beach County Bd. Edn., West Palm Beach, Fla.; prin. South Grade Sch., Palm Beach County Bd. Edn., Kirklane Elem. Sch., Palm Beach County Bd. Edn., West Palm Beach, ret., 1991. Hon. mem. state and nat. PTA. With USN, 1944-46. Kirklane Elem. Sch. renamed Clifford O. Taylor/ Kirklane Elem. Sch. in his honor. Mem. ASCD, NAESP, Palm Beach County Prins. Assn., So. Assn. Schs. and Colls., Fla. Assn. Sch. Adminstrs., Retired Educators Assn., Lions, Phi Delta Kappa. Episcopalian. Home: 1811 N J Ter Lake Worth FL 33460-6523

TAYLOR, CLIFFORD WOODWORTH, state supreme court justice; b. Delaware, Ohio, Nov. 9, 1942; s. Alexander E. and Carolyn (Clifford) T.; m. Lucille Taylor; 2 children. BA, U. Mich., 1964; JD, George Washington U., 1967. Asst. prosecuting atty. Ingham County, 1971-72; ptnr. Denfield, Timmer & Taylor, 1972-92; judge Mich. Ct. of Appeals, 1992-97, Supreme Ct. Justice, 1997—. Mem. standing com. on professionalism Mich. State Bar, 1992. Bd. dirs. Mich. Dyslexia Inst., 1991—, Friends of the Gov.'s Residence, 1991—; mem. St. Thomas Aquinas Ch. With USN, 1967-71. Fellow Mich. State Bar Found.; mem. Mich. Supreme Ct. Hist. Soc., Federalist Soc., Cath. Lawyers Guild, State Bar. Home: 9760 Sunny Point Dr Laingsburg MI 48848 Office: Mich Supreme Ct PO Box 300052 Lansing MI 48909*

TAYLOR, CONCIERE MARLANA, writer; b. N.Y.C., Oct. 30, 1950; d. George Allen and Celestine Winifred Taylor. AA, Queensborough C.C., Bayside, N.Y., 1971; BFA, honors program cert., L.I. U., 1974, postgrad., 1976-80. Editor Source mag. Queens Coun. on Arts, Jamaica, N.Y., 1976-79, literary arts coord., 1979-82; pvt. practice, 1982—. Author (with others): Shock Treatment, 1988; writer, editor Tips & Tour Rock mag., 1979-81; contbr. poems Mensa Soc. Lit. mag., various anthologies, others. Mem.: Internat. Women's Writing Guild, Poets and Writers. Avocations: collecting limited edition books and popular culture items, reading, anglophilia. Home: 67-08 Parsons Blvd #6B Flushing NY 11365

TAYLOR, CORA HODGE, social worker; b. Fayetteville, N.C., Nov. 25, 1942; d. John Marlin and Cora Louise (Mitchell) Hodge; m. Charles L. Taylor, June 26, 1965; children: Charles L., John M. BS, N.C. Coll., Durham, 1963; MSW, U. N.C., Chapel Hill, 1965. Clin. social worker VA Hosp., Bedford, Mass., 1965-68, 73-79; chief social worker Regional Health Center, Wilmington, 1978-79; clin. social worker VA Hosp., Bedford, 1979-91, supervisory social worker geriatrics and long term care, 1991—, coord. contract programs, 1993—. Field instr. Boston U. Sch. Social Work, 1979-87, Smith Coll. Sch. of Social Work, 1986-89; instr., cons. primary care residents Tufts U. Med. Sch., Regional Health Center, Wilmington, Mass., 1978-79. Mem. Town Meeting, Billerica, Mass., 1981—; precinct clk., 1981, 82, 89, precinct chmn., 1984, 85, 86; deacon first Congl. Ch., 1986—; women vets. coord. VA Bedford; Social Work Leadership Tng. program, 1998. Mem. LWC (dir. 1970-73), Acad. Cert. Social Workers, Nat. Assn. Social Workers. Home: 35 Wildbrook Rd Billerica MA 01821-5647 Office: 200 Springs Rd Bedford MA 01730-1114

TAYLOR, CRAIG BARR, psychiatrist; b. Salt Lake City, June 8, 1945; s. Lee Neff and June (Bitner) T.; m. Suesan Westwood, May 30, 1968; 1 child, Megan. AB, Columbia Coll., N.Y.C., 1966; MD, U. Utah, 1970. Resident in psychiatry U. Utah, Salt Lake City, 1970-71, asst. prof., 1975-77; resident in psychiatry Stanford (Calif.) Med. Ctr., 1973-75, asst. prof., 1977-84, assoc. prof., 1984-91, prof. psychiatry, 1991—; dir. behavioral sci. Stanford Ctr. for Rsch. in Disease Prevention, 1984-90; co-dir. Stanford Cardiac Rehab. Program, 1984—; dir. adult psychiatry residency tng. prgm. Stanford, 1995—, dir. Lab. for Study of Behavioral Medicine, 2000—; med. dir. Kinetics Found., 2000—. Author: (with Bruce Arnow) Nature and Treatment of Anxiety Disorders, 1988, Shadow of the Salmon, 1994, (with Nancy Houston Miller) Lifestyle Management in Patients with Coronary Heart Disease, 1995; contbr. articles to profl. jours. Grantee NHLBI, NICHD, NIMH, 1978—. Mem. Soc. Behavioral Medicine (pres. 1995-96). Achievements include research in field of eating disorders, anxiety disorders, computer-assisted therapy and development of methods for cardiovascular risk reduction and cardiac rehabilitation; helped establish field of behavioral medicine. Avocations: fly fishing, watercolor painting. Office: Stanford Med Sch Dept Psychiatry Stanford CA 94305-5722 E-mail: btaylor@stanford.edu.

TAYLOR, DARLA JEAN, nurse; b. L.A., Feb. 21, 1959; d. Samuel and Darlene Taylor. AS, Compton C.C., 1983; student, U. Phoenix, 2000. Pediatric nurse Harbor UCLA Med. Ctr., Torrance, Calif., 1983-86, U. So. Calif., L.A., 1986-89, recovery rm. nurse, 1989-91, health facilities evaluator I, 1991—. Author, editor: (video) Living With Illness as a Teenager, 1985. author: (manuel) Medications Policy and Procedures, 1986. Mem. ANA, Black Nurses Assn., Devel. Disabilities Nurses Assn., Calif. Nurses Assn. Avocations: reading, bicycling, walking. Office: 5555 Ferguson Dr Ste 320 Los Angeles CA 90022-5152

TAYLOR, DAVID BROOKE, lawyer, banker; b. Salt Lake City, Oct. 14, 1942; s. Lee Neff and June Taylor; m. Carolyn Kaufholz, May 29, 1965; children: Stewart, Allison. BA, U. Utah, 1964; JD, Columbia U., 1967. Bar: N.Y. 1967, N.C. 1995. Ptnr. Wickes, Riddell, Bloomer, Jacobi & McGuire, N.Y.C., 1967-79, Morgan, Lewis & Bockius, N.Y.C., 1979-89; banker, lawyer Chase Manhattan Bank, N.A., 1989-92; pres. Geoenertec Corp., 1992-93; ptnr. Fennebresque, Clark, Swindall & Hay, Charlotte, N.C., 1994-98, McGuire & Woods, LLP, Charlotte, 1999—. Mem. ABA, N.Y. State Bar Assn., N.C. Bar Assn. Home: 3815 Beresford Rd Charlotte NC 28211-3713 Office: McGuire & Woods LLP 100 N Tryon St Ste 2900 Charlotte NC 28202-4022

TAYLOR, DAVID GEORGE, retired banker; b. Charlevoix, Mich., July 29, 1929; s. Frank Flagg and Bessie (Strayer) T.; m. Robyne T. McCarthy, July 28, 1990; children from previous marriage: David, Amy, Jeanine. BS, Denison U., 1951; MBA, Northwestern U., 1953. With Continental Ill. Nat. Bank and Trust Co. Chicago, 1958-86, asst. cashier, 1961-64, 2d v.p., 1964-66, v.p., 1966-72, sr. v.p., 1972-74, exec. v.p., 1974-80, exec. v.p., treas., 1980-83, vice chmn., 1983-84, chmn., chief exec. officer, 1984; vice chmn. Irving Trust Co., N.Y.C., 1986-89; group exec. Chem. Bank, N.Y.C., 1989-94, ret., 1994. Mem. Dealer Bank Assn. Com. on Glass-Steagall Reform, 1985-86. Bd. dirs. Evanston Hosp., Glenbrook Hosp.; trustee Art Inst. Chgo., 1981-86; advisor J.L. Kellogg Grad. Sch. Mgmt., Northwestern U., 1984—; bd. dirs. CNA Income Shares. Served to lt. USN, 1953-56. Mem. Pub. Securities Assn. (bd. dirs. 1977-78, chmn. 1977, treas. 1978), Govt. and Fed. Agys. Securities Com. (chmn. bd. dirs. 1982-83), Assn. Res. City Bankers (asset/liability com/govt. relations com. 1983—). Republican. Presbyterian.

TAYLOR, DAVID KERR, international business educator, consultant; b. Oxford, N.C., Oct. 11, 1928; s. David Kerr and Myrtle Norman (Shamburger) T.; m. Isabel de Sousa Botelho de Albuquerque, Apr. 23, 1960; children: Anne de Albuquerque Taylor Grave, Katherine Rowena Taylor. BA, Duke U., 1947, JD, 1949. Bar: N.Y., N.C. Atty. Ins. Co. N.Am., N.Y.C., 1949-51, Milbank, Tweed, Hadley & McCloy, N.Y.C., 1954-55; internat. exec. Mobil Corp., N.Y.C., Washington, Can., Portugal, Nigeria, France, others, 1955-86; adj. prof. internat. affairs, sr. fellow intrnat. bus. Georgetown U. Sch. Fgn. Svc., Washington, 1987-2000. Pres. Luso-Am. Bus. Coun., 1987-89; bd. visitors Duke U. Law Sch. 1st lt. U.S. Army, 1951-54, Germany. Mem. Am. Portuguese Soc. (bd. dirs., pres. 1968-70, 76-80), Washington Export Coun., Washington Inst. Fgn. Affairs, Dacor Bacon House, Cosmos Club, Phi Beta Kappa. Avocation: singing. Home: 2737 Devonshire Pl NW Washington DC 20008-3479

TAYLOR, DAVID SPENCER, engineer; b. Salt Lake City, May 27, 1944; s. Spencer Campbell and Estella Richards Taylor; m. Kathleen Maughan, Aug. 20, 1969; children: Christopher, Joel, April, Jesse. BSChemE, U. Utah, 1969; MBA, Utah State U., 1973. Process engr. Shell Chem. Co., Torrance, Calif., 1969-71; human resource cons., evaluation specialist Manpower Devel. Svc., Logan, Utah, 1973-75; retail bus. owner The Music Taylor, 1975-78; mfg.

engr. Thiokol Corp., Corinne, Utah, 1979-83, 94-95, project mgr., 1983-85, chief propellant engr., 1985-86, 90-94, sr. engr., scientist, 1996-99, program mgr., tech. contracts, 1999—. Author: Christmas Songs for 5-String Banjo, 1977. Advisor Jr. Achievement, Torrance, 1970-71; dist. chmn. Rep. Party, Smithfield, Utah, 1976-78; scoutmaster, varsity scout coach, commr. Boy Scouts Am, Smithfield, 1983-97. Recipient Silver Beaver award Boy Scouts Am., 1995, Silver Snoopy award NASA, 2000. Mem. AIAA, Phi Kappa Phi. Mem. Lds Ch. Avocations: hiking, mountain climbing, folk singing, carpentry, sports.

TAYLOR, DAVID WYATT AIKEN, retired clergyman; b. Tsingkiangpu, Kiangsu, China, Dec. 13, 1925; s. Hugh Kerr and Fanny Bland (Graham) T.; m. Lillian Ross McCulloch, Aug. 25, 1951; children: Frances Bland, David Wyatt. BA, Vanderbilt U., 1949; B.D. cum laude, Union Theol. Sem. Va., 1952; Th.M., Princeton Theol. Sem., 1953; D.D. (hon.), King Coll., Bristol, Tenn., 1959. Ordained to ministry Presbyn. Ch. U.S., 1952. Pastor chs., Elkton, Va., 1953-55, Bristol, 1955-62; ednl. sec. bd. world missions Presbyn. Ch. U.S., 1962-68, program div. dir., 1968-73, ecumenical officer gen. assembly mission bd., 1973-82; pastor Orange Park Presbyn. Ch., Orange Park, Fla., 1982-86; gen. sec. for strategy and interpretation Consultation on Ch. Union, Princeton, N.J., 1986-88, gen. sec., 1988-93; ret., 1993. Instr. Bible Presbyn. Jr. Coll., Maxton, N.C., 1951; mem. program bd., div. Christian edn. Nat. Council Chs., 1965-69, bd. mgrs., dept. edn. for mission, 1962-68, mem. program bd., div. overseas ministries, 1968-78, mem. governing bd., 1976-80, chmn. governing bd. credentials com., 1978; chmn. Church World Service, Inc., 1973-75; mem. adminstrn. and fin. com. Nat. Council Chs., 1973-75, mem. commn. on faith and order, 1978-93; mem. commn. on interchurch aid World Council Chs., 1973-75; mem. 5th Assembly, 1975; rep. Presbyn. Ch. U.S. to World Alliance Ref. Chs., 1976-82; bd. dirs. Presbyn. Survey mag., 1963-68; mem. Consultation on Ch. Union, 1974-93; chmn. Nat. Ecumenical Officers Assn., 1978-81 Bd. dirs. Abingdon Presbytery's Children's Home, Wytheville, Va., 1958-62. Served with AUS, 1944-46, PTO. Mem. Sigma Chi. Home: 3113 Glenhope Ct Cary NC 27511

TAYLOR, DEAN ALAN, physicist; b. Pitts., Oct. 30, 1953; s. George Benjamin and Jeanne Lenore (Garner) T.; m. Diana Lynn Swiecki, July 4, 1976; children: Logan Alan, Lauren Alexandra. BS in Biol. Scis., Fla. Inst. Tech., 1976; MS in Radiol. Scis., U. Wash., 1991. Commd. ensign USN, 1976, advanced through grades to lt. comdr., retired, 1995; diagnostic physicist, radiation safety officer Union Hosp., Terre Haute, Ind., 1995—. Cons. in field. Bd. dirs. Vigo County Youth Soccer Assn., 2000—. Decorated Meritorious Svc. medal, Navy Commendation medal, Navy Achievement medals (2). Mem. Am. Assn. Physicists in Medicine, Health Physics Soc., Am. Coll. Med. Physics, Ret. Officers Assn. (life). Avocations: scuba diving, photography. Home: 5696 S Ernest St Terre Haute IN 47802-9499 Office: Union Hosp 1606 N 7th St Terre Haute IN 47804-2780 E-mail: hxdat@uhhg.org.

TAYLOR, DEBORAH ANN, court visitor, retired paralegal; b. Columbia, S.C. Asst. long term care ombudsman State of Alaska Sr. Svcs., Anchorage, 1989-95, ins. counseling and asst. coord., 1993-98, info. and referral officer, 1996-98; ret., 1998; ct. visitor, 1999—. Chair N.W. Alliance Info. & Referral Sys., 1997-98. Bd. dirs. Coll. Rd. Svc. Dist., Fairbanks, Alaska, 1985-87, North Star Borough Planning and Zoning Com., Fairbanks, pres. Village Green Homeowners Assn. 1983-85, Fairbanks, Grand Larry Condominium Assn., Anchorage, 1987-96. Mem. Alaska State Employees Assn. (sec. treas. 1993-95, pres. Anchorage chpt., 1991-95, sec. 1988-91), Alaska Bar Assn. (elder law sect.), Ret. Pub. Employees of Alaska (treas. Anchorage chpt. 1999-2000). E-mial. E-mail: data@alaskalife.net.

TAYLOR, DONALD, retired manufacturing company executive; b. Worcester, Mass., June 2, 1927; s. John A. B. and Alice M. (Weaver) T.; m. Ruth L. Partridge, June 24, 1950; children: Linda Taylor Robertson, Donald, Mark, John. BSME, Worcester Poly. Inst., 1949; grad., Northeastern U. Mgmt. Devel. Program, 1962, Harvard Bus. Sch. Advanced Mgmt. Program, 1979. Registered profl. engr., Mass. With George J. Meyer Mfg. Co., Milw., 1954-69; pres. mfg. div. A-T-O, Inc., 1969; exec. v.p. Nordberg div. Rex Chainbelt, Inc., Milw., 1969-73; v.p. ops. Rexnord Inc., Brookfield, Wis., pres., chief operating officer, 1978-85, chief exec. officer, from 1985, chmn., 1985-88; pres. Nordberg Machinery Group, Milw., 1973-78. Dir. Harnischfeger Corp., Banta Corp. Bd. dirs. Blood Ctr. Southeastern Wis., Greater Milw. Com., Met. Milw. YMCA; bd. dirs. Milw. Symphony Orch. Served with USNR, 1951-54. Mem. ASME. Clubs: Milw. Country, Milw. Town, Univ., Masons. Office: 1 Runnymede Dr North Hampton NH 03862-2328

TAYLOR, DONALD ARTHUR, marketing educator; b. Windsor, Ont., Can., Sept. 27, 1923; came to U.S., 1947, naturalized, 1955; s. David Cameron and Eva (Perry) T.; m. Shirley Marion Jenner, 1949; children: John Cameron, Stephen Bruce, Michael James. BA, U. Western Ont., 1947; MBA, U. Mich., 1949, PhD (Horace H. Rackham fellow), 1955. Asst. prof. marketing Mich. State U. at, East Lansing, 1955-58, asso. prof., 1958-62, prof., 1962—, chmn. dept. marketing and transportation adminstrn., 1969-81, prof., 1981-84, chmn. dept. mktg. and transp. adminstrn., 1984-86, chmn., prof. emeritus, 1986—. Adviser, chief of party to mission at various univs., Brazil, 1956-58, 62-64; dir. Latin Am. Studies Center, 1968-69; also co-dir. Latin-Am. Market Planning Center, sr. cons. food distbn. studies, N.E. Brazil, Colombia; cons. Geigy Agrl. Chems., Johnson & Johnson Domestic Operating Co., Ford Motor Co., Westinghouse Electric Corp., Whirlpool Corp., Burroughs Corp.; dir. Clark-Graveley Corp., 1972-77 Author: (with D.J. Luck, D.A. Taylor, H. Wales, R. Rubin) Marketing Research, 6th edit, 1982, (with T.A. Staudt, D.A. Taylor and D.J. Bowersox) A Managerial Introduction to Marketing, 3d edit, 1976, (with D.A. Taylor) Institution Building in Business Administration: The Brazilian Experience, 1968, (with Bowersox, Cooper, Lambert and Taylor) Management in Marketing Channels, 1980. Mem. bd. edn. Holt Sch. Dist., 1960-62. Recipient Homenagen Especial award 1st graduating class Escola de Administracao de Empresas, Sao Paulo, Brazil, 1958; named hon. prof., 1964 Mem. Am. Marketing Assn. (bd. dirs. 1969) Home: 3724 Harolds Rd Traverse City MI 49686-9435

TAYLOR, DONNA BUESCHER, marriage and family therapist; b. Andalusia, Ala., Sept. 16, 1953; d. Robert C. and Mary Kate (Vickers) Bush; m. Davis H. Buescher, Nov. 22, 1973 (div. Feb. 1992); children: Tracy Marie, Robert Davis, Kyle Moore; m. Thomas W. Taylor, Apr. 30, 1994. BA, Samford U., 1975; MA in Psychology, Austin Peay State U., 1989; postgrad., Tex. Woman's U., 1989-90. Tchr. Liberty Hall Acad., Williston, Fla., 1977, Bunnell Elem. Sch., Williston, 1978; tchr. geography Flagler-Palmcoast (Fla.) H.S., 1979; tchr. St. Joseph's Sch., Lakeland, 1980, St. Alban's Sch., Waco, Tex., 1981-83; sch. psychologist Dallas Ind. Sch. Dist., 1989-94, Plano (Tex.) Ind. Sch. Dist., 1994-96; marriage and family therapist Plano, 1994-98; pvr. practice Cleveland, Miss., 1998—. Parent educator Practical Parent Edn., Plano, 1996-98; adj. instr. Delta State U., Cleveland, 1999—; program dir. Early Learning Mentoring Program. Tchr. Sunday sch. So. Bapt. Orgn., 1973—; mem. nominating com. 1st Presbyn. Ch., Cleveland. Fellow Christian Athletes; mem. NASP, Tex. Assn. Sch. Psychologists, Collin County Psychol. Assn., Delta State Faculty Wives, Garden Club. Republican. Home: 1010 College St Cleveland MS 38732-3111

TAYLOR, DORIS DENICE, physician, entrepreneur, oncology consultant; b. Indpls., Sept. 19, 1955; d. Eugene and Mary Catherine (Ryder) T. BA, U. Minn., 1976, cert. behavior analyst, 1977, MD, 1983; BS, Purdue U., 1979. Diplomate Nat. Bd. Med. Examiners. Pvt. practice Locumtenens, 1989—; mng. dir. Sebree-Watkins-Ovbokhan Meml. Cancer Fund, Indpls. Pres., CEO Taylors of Indy Corp., Indpls.; oncologic svcs. cons. and developer; del. People to People Amb. Programs, 2002; CEO One Bed One Chair Charitable Found., Indpls. Lange scholar, U. Minn., 1980, Joseph Collins Found. scholar, 1980-81, Nat. Med. Fellowship scholar, 1980-81. Mem. AMA, Nat. Med. Assn., Am. Soc. for Therapeutic Radiology and Oncology, Am. Soc. Clin. Oncologists, People to People Amb. Programs (del. 2002). Office: PO Box 11278 Fargo ND 58106-1278 E-mail: locumradonc@aol.com., ticorpindy@aol.com.

TAYLOR, DOUGLAS HOWARD, translator; b. Washington, Apr. 4, 1961; s. Richard Powell and Barbara Jo Anne (Harris) T. BA, Amherst Coll., 1984; MA, Am. U., 1990, cert. translator. Freelance Russian and French translator, Germantown, Md., 1988—; v.p. Taylor Enterprises, 1996—. Editor-in-chief Landon News, 1979-80; editor mag. Nat. Soc. for Children of Am. Revolution, 1979-80; contbr. articles to profl. jours. Mem. fin. com. Md. Reagan/Bush Campaign, Potomac, 1984; asst. to chmn. Md. Bush/Quayne Campaign, Bethesda, 1988. Mem. Phi Beta Kappa. Republican. Episcopalian. Avocations: numismatics, bowling, tennis, running, reading. Home and Office: 14914 Spring Meadows Dr Germantown MD 20874-3444

TAYLOR, DUNCAN PAUL, research neuropharmacologist; b. Bremerton, Wash., Feb. 4, 1949; s. Alan Earl and Barbara Eleanor (Thiel) T.; m. Jeanne Louise Damgaard, Apr. 8, 1972; 1 child, Aubrey Elizabeth. BS in Chemistry, Calif. Inst. Tech., 1971; PhD in Biochemistry, Oreg. State U., 1977. Technician analytical svcs. Carnation Co. Rsch. Labs., Van Nuys, Calif., 1967-70; Peace Corps vol. Princess Margaret Secondary Sch., St. Johns, Antigua and Barbuda, 1971-73; grad. teaching and rsch. asst. biochemistry and biophysics Oreg. State U., Corvallis, 1973-77; rsch. assoc. sect. biochemistry and pharmacology NIMH, Bethesda, Md., 1977-79; scientist, neuropharmacologist, rsch. assoc. Pharm. div. Mead Johnson & Co., Evansville, Ind., 1979-80, sr. scientist, group leader, 1980-82; sr. scientist, group leader, neuropharmacologist Pharm. R & D div. Bristol-Myers Co., 1982-83, sr. rsch. scientist, mgr., 1983-85, rsch. fellow preclin. cen. nervous system rsch., 1985-89; sr. rsch. fellow preclin. cen. nervous system rsch. Pharm. Rsch. Inst. Bristol-Myers Squibb Co., Wallingford, Conn., 1989-94; dir. pharmacology Symphony Pharms., Malvern, Pa., 1994-95; cons., 1995-96; analyst bus. devel. Pharmacia & Upjohn, Kalamazoo, 1996-98, dir. Strat. Rsch. Assessment, 1998—. Mem. external adv. bd. dept. chemistry U. So. Miss.; grant reviewer NSF, 1981, 2, Med. Rsch. Coun. Can., 1987, 88; frequent presenter to profl. confs. Contbr. numerous articles and abstracts to profl. jours. Bd. dirs. Posey County chpt. Am. Cancer Soc., 1983—85; mem... Tri-State Cursillo Community; mentor Horizons Leadership Acad., Evansville-Venderburgh Sch. Corp., 1985; cons. Project Bus. Jr. Achievement, 1988; mem. chancel choir 1st United Meth. Ch., Mt. Vernon, Ind., 1976—86; mem. adult choir South Congl. Ch., Middletown, Conn., 1986—96, deacon, 1987—90, 1995—96, co-chmn., 1989—90, 1996, mem. coun., 1989—90, mem. task force on long-range planning, 1989—90; mem. adult choir 2d Reformed Ch., Kalamazoo, 1997—, mem. handbell choir, 1997—, mem. worship coun., 1997—2000, elder, 1998—2001, consistory mem., 1998—2001, ch. outreach coun., 2000—01. Scholar Carnation Co., 1967-70, Calif. State scholar, 1967-68, 70; rsch. fellow NSF, 1970, Cold Spring Harbor Labs., 1974. Fellow: Am. Inst. Chemists; mem.: AAAS, Soc. Competitive Intelligence Profls., Internat. Brain Rsch. Orgn.-World Fedn. Neuroscientists, Fedn. Am. Socs. for Exptl. Biology, European Brain and Behavior Soc., Brit. Brain Rsch. Assn, Soc. for Neurosci. (v.p. Conn. chpt. 1989—93), Am. Soc. for Pharmacology and Exptl. Therapeutics, Am. Chem. Soc., Phi Lambda Upsilon, Sigma Xi. Democrat. Achievements include patent for method and treatment of ischemia in the brain; made significant efforts in identification and development of new antipsychotics and antidepressants; identification of potential mechanism of action of the antipsychotic BMY14802; research in receptors, in etiology, expression and pharmacotherapy of psychiatric disorders. Home: 8722 W F Ave Kalamazoo MI 49009-8895

TAYLOR, EDNA JANE, retired employment program counselor; b. Flint, Mich., May 16, 1934; d. Leonard Lee and Wynona Ruth (Davis) Harvey; children: Wynona Jane MacDonald, Cynthia Lee Zellmer. BS, No. Ariz. U., 1963; MEd, U. Ariz., 1967. Tchr. high sch. Sunnyside Sch. Dist., Tucson, 1963-68; employment program counselor employment devel. State of Calif., Canoga Park, 1968-98, ret., 1998. Mem. adv. coun. Van Nuys Cmty. Adult Sch., Calif., 1983-96, steering com., 1989-91, leadership coun., 1991-92; mem. adv. coun. Pierce C.C., Woodland Hills, Calif., 1979-81; first aid instr., recreational leader ARC. Mem. NAFE, Internat. Assn. of Pers. in Employment Security, Calif. Employment Counselors Assn. (state treas. 1978-79, state sec. 1980), Delta Psi Kappa (life). Avocations: writing, tennis, health and fitness, gardening. E-mail: baunitoo@hotmail.com.

TAYLOR, EDWARD STEWART, physician, educator; b. Hecla, S.D., Aug. 20, 1911; s. Robert Stewart and Sylvia Frances (Dewey) T.; m. Ruth Fatherson, June 15, 1940; children: Edward Stewart, Elizabeth Dewey Taylor Bryant, Catherine Wells Taylor. BA, U. Iowa, 1933, MD, 1936. Diplomate Am. Bd. Ob-Gyn (dir. 1962-69). Intern, Hurley Hosp., Flint, Mich., 1936-37; splty. tng. ob-gyn L.I. Coll. Hosp., 1937-41; prof. ob-gyn, chmn. dept. Sch. Medicine, U. Colo., 1947-76, clin. prof., 1976-81, prof., chmn. emeritus, 1981—. Nat. cons. ob-gyn to surg. gen. USAF, 1958-62. Author: Manual of Gynecology, 1952, Essentials of Gynecology, 4th edit.; editor: Beck's Obstetrical Practice, 10th edit.; editor-in-chief for obstetrics: Obstetrical and Gynecol. Survey, 1967-92. Trustee Denver Symphony Orch., 1979-85. Served to lt. col. AUS, 1942-45. Endowed ob-gyn. chair U. Colo., 1999. Fellow ACS, Am. Coll. Obstetricians and Gynecologists (Disting. Svc. award 1984); mem. AMA, Am. Gynecol. Soc. (v.p. 1974-75), Am. Assn. Obstetricians and Gynecologists (pres. 1970-71), Ctrl. Assn. Obstetricians and Gynecologists, S.W. Obstet. and Gynecol. Soc. (hon.), Am. Gynecol. and Obstet. Soc., Assn. Profs. Ob-Gyn (pres. 1974-75), Western Surg. Soc., Finnish Gynecol. Soc. (hon.), University Club (Denver), Alpha Omega Alpha. Clubs: University (Denver). Congregationalist. Home: 80 S Dexter St Denver CO 80246-1051

TAYLOR, ELDON, psychological researcher; b. Anchorage, Jan. 27, 1945; s. Blaine Eldon and Helen Gertrude (George) T.; children: Roy, William, Angela, Eric, Cassandra, Hillarie, Preston. Student, Weber State Coll., Ogden, Utah, 1971-74; BS, MS, DD, U. Metaphysics, L.A., PhD in Pastoral Psychology, 1986; PhD in Clin. Psychology, St. John's U., Springfield, La., 1990; HHD (hon.), Sem. Coll., 1987; PhD in Pastoral Psychology (hon.), World U. Roundtable, Benson, Ariz., 1988. Diplomate Am. Psychotherapy Assn. Dir. Bulwark, Salt Lake City, 1977-84; pres., dir. Progressive Awareness Rsch., Spokane, Wash., 1984—. Bd. dirs. World U. Roundtable, Benson, Ariz.; mem. adj. faculty St. John's U., 1989—. Author: Thinking Without Thinking, 1995, Subliminal Communication, 1986, Subliminal Learning, 1988, Simple Things and Simple Thoughts, 1989, Wellness: Just a State of Mind, 1993, Just Be: A Little Cowboy Philosophy, 1997, Subliminal Technology, 1998, Self Empowerment, 1999, others; contbr. numerous articles and poetry to various pubs.; author numerous audiocassettes on self-improvement; patentee whole brain info. audio processor. Spiritual advisor Intermountain Hospice Ctr., Salt Lake City, 1987-88; counselor Utah State Prison, Draper, 1986-88; sports motivation trainer U.S. Judo Team, Colorado Springs, Colo., 1989—. Named Ky. Col., State of Ky., 1984; recipient Golden Poet award Am. Poetry Soc., 1985-87. Fellow Nat. Assn. Clergy Hypnotherapists; mem. Am. Psychol. Practitioners Assn., Am. Law Enforcement Officers Assn., Internat. Assn. for Forensic Hypnosis, Am. Counselors Soc., Internat. Soc. Stress Analysts, Am. Assn. Religious Counselors. Avocations: physics, horses. Home: PO Box 13249 Spokane WA 99213-3249 Office: Progressive Awareness Rsch 21203 W Beechwood Rd Medical Lake WA 99022-8630 E-mail: etaylor@iea.com., dretaylor@inntertalk.com.

TAYLOR, ELDON DONIVAN, government official; b. Holdenville, Okla., July 29, 1929; s. Rome B. and Alma (Collins) T.; m. Hypatia Ethel Roberts, Feb. 7, 1953; 1 child, Teresa Lynn. Student, Murry State A. and M. Coll., 1948-49, George Washington U., 1949-50; BS cum laude, Am. U., 1959, MA, 1966, postgrad., 1966-68. Research budget analyst, budgetary adminstrn. Office Naval Research, Navy Dept., Washington, 1949-51, 55-56; chief research and devel. budget sect., research and devel. planning adminstrn. Bur. Ordnance, 1956-60; dir. program rev. and resources, mgmt. div. research, devel. planning and adminstrn. Office Space Scis., NASA, Washington, 1960-70; dep. asst. adminstr. for resources mgmt. EPA, 1970-73; asst. dir. adminstrn. NSF, 1973-79; insp. gen. NASA, 1979-80; dir. adminstrn. Va. Ctr. Innovative Tech., 1984-85; v.p. Assn. Univs. for Research in Astronomy, 1985-86; pres. Taylor Mgmt. Assistance Inc., 1987—. Served with USAF, 1951-55. Recipient Commendation award for outstanding performance Dept. Navy, 1958; William A. Jump Meritorious award for achievement in pub. adminstrn., 1964; Exceptional Service award NASA, 1969; Disting. Service award NSF, 1978 Mem. Pi Sigma Alpha, Phi Theta Kappa. Home and Office: 7931 Wolf Run Hills Rd Fairfax Station VA 22039-2101

TAYLOR, ELISABETH COLER, retired secondary school educator; b. N.Y.C., Jan. 24, 1942; d. Gerhard Helmut and Judith Coler; m. Billie Wesley Taylor II, Jan. 27, 1960; children: Letitia Rose, Billie Albert. Student, Wilmington Coll., 1959-60; BS, Wayne State U., Detroit, 1969; MS, The Ohio State U., 1980; postgrad., Wright State U., Dayton, Ohio, 1989—. Cert. home economist. H.s. tchr. home econs., computer sci., lang. arts Dayton (Ohio) City Schs., 1972-99. Bd. mem. Camp Fire Girls, 1970-71, vol. Detroit Mus. of Art, 1970-71, group leader Camp Fire Girls, Boy Scouts, Detroit, 1968-74. Mem. AAUW (life), Am. Mensa Ltd. (life). Avocations: birding, travelling, needlework. Home: 131 Snow Hill Ave Dayton OH 45429-1705

TAYLOR, ELIZABETH JANE, investment consultant, real estate and international marketing executive; b. Tiffin, Ohio, Oct. 27, 1941; d. Albert Joseph Lucas and Mary Jane Siebenaller-Swander; m. Gaylen Lloyd Taylor, July 11, 1977. Student, Heidelberg Coll., 1961, Austin (Tex.) C.C., 1983-84; grad., Real Estate Edn. Ctr., 1984, Inst. Real Estate, 1988, Real Estate Inst., 1989; Tex. Realtors Inst., 1989; student, Rockhurst Coll., 1991-92. Dir. regional mktg. Sibrow, Inc., Ottawa, Can., 1981-83; realtor assoc. Alliance Sales, Austin, 1985-88; assoc. Broadway Comml. Investments, 1988-91; prin. Taylor & Assocs. Internat. Mktg. & Bus. Devel., 1980-98. Cons., Hypnosis Conn., Ohio, Tex. and Ariz., 1967—; tchr. mktg. and bus. develop., 1980-96. Author: (poetry) Letters from Home, 1986, Best New Poets of 1986, American Poetry Anthology, vol. VI., #3, 1986, Unfinished Business and the Tapestry, 2001, (novel) Unfinished Business, 2002; columnist Austin Women Mag., 1984-86. V.p. Am. Congress on Real Estate, 1982-83; arbitrator Better Bus. Bur., 1984-89, sr. arbitrator, Austin, 1989-95; spkrs. bur. Austin Womans Ctr., 1985-88; v.p. Austin World Affairs Coun., 1984-94; adv. panel Austin Woman Mag., 1984-86. Nominee to Tex. Womens Hall of Fame, 1984. Mem. NAFE (network dir. 1980-88), Am. Biog. Inst. Rsch. (hon., bd. advisors 1988). Avocations: writing, behavior research. Home: 3926 E Cherokee St Phoenix AZ 85044-3827

TAYLOR, FANNIE TURNBULL, social education and arts administration educator; b. Kansas City, Mo., Sept. 11, 1913; d. Henry King and Fannie Elizabeth (Sills) Turnbull; m. Robert Taylor, Dec. 2, 1938 (div. 1974); children: Kathleen Muir Taylor Isaacs, Anne Kingston Taylor Wadsack. BA, U. Wis., 1938; LHD (hon.), Buena Vista Coll., Storm Lake, Iowa, 1975. Mem. faculty U. Wis., Madison, 1941—, prof. social edn., 1949—, emerita, 1979—. Dir. Wis. Union Theater, 1946-66, coord. univ. systems arts coun., 1967-70, assoc. dir. Ctr. Arts Adminstrn., 1970-72, coord. Consortium for Arts, 1976-84; cons. in field. Author: The Arts at a New Frontier: The National Endowment for the Arts, Wisconsin Union Theater: Fifty Golden Years (Book award of Merit, State Hist. Soc. Wis. 1990); contbr. articles to profl. jours. Program dir. music Nat. Endowment Arts, 1966-67, program info. dir., 1972-76; bd. dirs. Wis. Arts Coun., 1964-72, Wis. Found. Arts, 1976-91, Madison Civic Music Assn., 1976-84, Madison Children's Mus., 1983-96, Elvehjem Mus. Art Coun., 1976—, chair 1983-86; Madison Civic Ctr. Found., 1981-94; hon. chair Wis. Union Theater Program Endowment Fund, 1985—; bd. dirs. Wis. chpt. Nature Conservancy, 1963-84, chmn. 1976-77; bd. dirs. Shorewood Hills Found., 1976—, pres., 1976-81. Recipient Oak Leaf award Nature Conservancy, 1981, Wis. Gov.'s award in Support of the Arts, 1992, Leadership award Madison Cmty. Found., 2002; named Woman of Distinction, Madison YWCA, 1994. Fellow Wis. Acad. Scis., Arts and Letters; mem. Assn. Performing Arts Presenters (founder, exec. dir. 1957-72, 1st recipient Fannie Taylor award 1972), Am. Assn. Dance Cos. (bd. dirs. 1967-72), Nat. Assn. Regional Ballet (bd. dirs. 1975-77), Nat. Guild Cmty. Music Schs. Arts (bd. dirs. 1977-80), Women in Comm. (Writers' Cup 1980), U. Wis. Found., U. Wis. Alumni Assn. (Disting. Svc. award 1979, Madison Civics Club (pres. 1969-70), Univ. Club (pres. 1982-85), Blackhawk Club. Home: 8301 Old Sauk Rd Apt 220 Middleton WI 53562-4393 E-mail: ftaylor@facstaff.wisc.edu.

TAYLOR, FOSTER JAY, retired university president; b. Gibsland, La., Aug. 9, 1923; s. Lawrence Foster and Marcia Aline (Jay) T.; m. Lou Kavanaugh; 1 son, Terry Jay. Student, La. Poly. Inst., 1940-42; BA, U. Calif., Santa Barbara, 1948; MA, Claremont (Calif.) Grad. Sch., 1949; PhD, Tulane U., 1952. Assoc. prof. history, dean men. La. Coll., Pineville, 1952-56, prof., 1956-62, dean coll., 1960-62; pres. La. Tech. U., Ruston, 1962-87, pres. emeritus, 1987—. Past chmn. La. Labor Mediation Bd.; arbitrator Am. Arbitration Assn., Fed. Mediation and Counciliation Svc.; former mem. La. Adv. Coun. on Vocat.-Tecy. Edn.; bd. dirs. First Guaranty Bank, Pizza Inn, Inc. Author: The United States and the Spanish Civil War, 1936-39, 1956, Reluctant Rebel, The Secret Diary of Robert Patrick, 1861-1865, 1959. Served to lt. comdr., aviator USNR, 1942-46. Mem. Am. Hist. Assn., Miss. Valley Hist. Assn., So. Hist. Assn., Nat. Acad. Arbitrators., Phi Alpha Theta. Clubs: Rotary. Home: 2502 Tanglewood Dr Ruston LA 71270-2244

TAYLOR, FRANCIS MICHAEL, auditor, municipal official; b. Munich, Germany, 1960; came to the U.S., 1961; BS, Va. Tech., 1982. CPA Va., cert. internal auditor. Pub. acct., Roanoke, Va., 1982-84; controller ARC Roanoke, Inc., 1984-87; audit supr. City of Roanoke, 1987-94; city auditor City of Stockton (Calif.), 1994—. Mem. AICPAs, Nat. Assn. Local Govt. Auditors (pres.), Calif. Soc. CPAs, Inst. Internal Auditors, Govt. Fin. Officers Assn., Info. Sys. Audit and Control Assn. Office: 425 N El Dorado St Stockton CA 95202-1951

TAYLOR, FRED, professional football player; b. June 27, 1976; , U. Fla. Running back Jacksonville Jaguars, Fla., 1998—. Ranks fourth on U. Fla. all-time rushing list; played in 3 college bowl games; team was 14-0 in games in which he had over 100 yds. rushing. Office: Jacksonville Jaguars 1 Alltel Stadium Pl Jacksonville FL 32202-1917*

TAYLOR, FREDERICK WILLIAM, JR. (FRITZ TAYLOR), lawyer; b. Cleve., Oct. 21, 1933; s. Frederick William Sr. and Marguerite Elizabeth (Kistler) T.; m. Mary Phyllis Osborne, June 1, 1985. BA in History, U. Fla., 1957; MA in Near East Studies, U. Mich., 1959; JD cum laude, NYU, 1967. Bar: N.Y. 1968, Calif. 1969, U.S. Dist. Ct. (cen. dist.) Calif. 1969. Govt. rels. rep. Arabian Am. Oil Co., Dhahran, Saudi Arabia, 1959-63, oil supply coord. N.Y.C., 1963-68, sr. counsel Dhahran, 1969-71, gen. mgr. govt. rels. orgn., 1971-74, v.p. indsl. rels., 1974-78; assoc. O'Melveny & Myers, L.A., 1968-69; ptnr. Burt & Taylor, Marblehead, Mass., 1978-80; pres., chief exec. officer Nat. Med. Enterprises Internat. Group, L.A., 1980-82; counsel Chadbourne, Parke & Afridi, United Arab Emirates, 1982-84; ptnr. Sidley & Austin, Cairo, 1984-87, Singapore, 1987-93; spl. counsel Heller Ehrman White & McAuliffe, L.A. and Singapore, 1993-95; legal advisor, corp. counsel law divsn. Lucent Techs. Internat. Inc., Riyadh, Saudi Arabia, 1995—. Contbr. articles to profl. jours. Mem. ABA, Calif. Bar Assn., Order of Coif, Singapore Cricket Club, Tanglin Club, Changi Sailing Club, Singapore Am. Club, Dirab Golf Club. Home: 9875 E Shadowlake Ct Claremore OK 74017-1444 Office: Lucent Techs Int Inc PO Box 4945 Khurais Rd Riyadh 11412 Saudi Arabia

TAYLOR, G. DON, industrial engineering educator; b. Anchorage, Mar. 25, 1960; s. Gaylon Don and Rita M. (Eudy) T.; m. Jo Ellen Gibson, June 6, 1987; children: Daniel Alexander, Caroline Frances. BS in Indsl. Engring., U. Tex., Arlington, 1983, MS in Indsl. Engring., 1985; PhD, U. Mass., 1990. Registered profl. engr., Ark. Mfg. engr., supr. Tex. Instruments Inc., Lewisville, 1983-86; process engr. Digital Equipment Corp., Enfield, Conn., 1987-89; asst. prof. U. Ark., Fayetteville, 1990-94, assoc. prof. indsl. engring., 1994-98; prof., dir. The Logistics Inst., 1998—99; Mary Lee and George P. Guthie Chair in Engring. Logistics U. Louisville, 2000—. Dir. Ctr. for Engring Logistics and Distbn, U. Louisville, Ky., 2001—. Contbr. articles to profl. jours. Mem. Am. Soc. Engring. Edn., Inst. Indsl. Engrs. (sr. mem., faculty advisor 1992-93), Sigma Xi, Tau Beta Pi. Achievements include principal investigator on research grants totaling more than $4 million. Home: 2909 Pin Oak Dr La Grange KY 40031-9490 Office: Univ Ark 4207 Bell Engineering Ctr Fayetteville AR 72701

TAYLOR, GAIL RICHARDSON, freelance writer, civic worker, lawyer, former university official; b. Cleve., July 16, 1949; d. Allen Barnd and Margaret Christine (Thomas) Ricardson; m. William David Taylor, May 16, 1987; 1 child, William Robert. BA, Wellesley Coll., 1971; MS in Journalism, Northwestern U., 1978; JD magna cum laude, Case Western Reserve U., 1993. Bar: Ohio, 1993. Co-editor Time Sharing Today, Phila., 1972-73; reporter Today's Spirit (Montgomery Pub. Co.), Hatboro, Pa., 1973-76, The Argus Leader (Gannett Co.), Sioux Falls, S.D., 1978-82; writer, editor Case Western Res. U., Cleve., 1982-83, sr. writer, editor, 1983-84, dir. news svcs., 1984-87, coord. govt. rels., 1987-90, dir. govt. rels., 1990-97; freelance writer, 1999—. Contbr. articles to newspapers and mags. Chmn. bd. trustees United Protestant Campus Ministries in Cleve., 1996-97; trustee Hot Meals, Oberlin, Ohio;

mem. Oberlin Bd. Edn., 1998-99, Christ Episcopal Ch.; oblate Benedictine Sisters of Erie, Pa. Independent. Avocations: gardening, golf, ice skating, school volunteering. Home: 317 Elm St Oberlin OH 44074-1404 E-mail: gailt317@aol.com.

TAYLOR, GARRY LANCE, music educator; b. Cullman, Ala., Sept. 9, 1954; s. Henry Leslie and Helen Lavern Taylor; m. Sheila Jan Rucks, June 25, 1976; children: Erin Lee, Hanna Beth. BS, Auburn U., Auburn, AL, 1976; MA, U. North Ala., Florence, AL, 1979. Band dir. Brooks H.S., Killen, Ala., 1976—83, Hanceville H.S., Hanceville, 1983—84, Cullman H.S., Cullman, 1984—. Camp coord. Southeastern Summer Music Camp, Cullman, Ala., 1990—. Mem.: Internat. Assn. Jazz Educators (pres., ala. chpt. 1997—99), Ala. Bandmasters Assn. (rec. sec. 1999—2001), Ala. Bandmasters Assn. (vice-president 2001—02). Office: Cullman High School Band 510 13th Street NE Cullman AL 35055

TAYLOR, GARY JAY, fire services professional; b. Altadena, Calif., Feb. 10, 1948; s. Howard and Virginia Taylor; m. Julie Elizabeth Pruett, Dec. 19, 1970; children: Yvette, Dawna. AS, Victor Valley Coll., Victorville, Calif., 1974. Firefighter Heperia (Calif.) Fire Dept., 1975-80, paramedic, 1977-83, fire capt., 1980-93, divsn. chief, 1993—. Author Emergency Ops. Manual, City of Hesperia Emergency Ops. Plan, 1999. Chmn. Emergency Resource Group, Victorville, 1999—. Sgt. U.S. Army, 1968-70, Vicenzia, Italy. Mem. Emergency Resource Group (chmn. 1999-2001). Republican. Presbyterian. Avocations: flying, horseback riding, fishing, golf, bicycling. Home: PO Box 214 Victorville CA 92393 Office: Hesperia Fire Dept 17288 Olive St Hesperia CA 92345 Fax: 760-244-9174. E-mail: gtaylor@ci.hesperia.ca.us.

TAYLOR, GENE, congressman; b. New Orleans, Sept. 17, 1953; m. Margaret Gordon; children: Sarah, Emily, Gary. BA, Tulane U., 1974; grad., U. So. Miss. Sales rep. Stone Container Corp.; city councilman Bay St. Louis, 1981—83; dist. 46 sen. Miss. State Sen., 1984-89; mem. U.S. Congress from 5th Miss. dist., 1989—; ranking mem. house armed svcs. com., mem. transp. and infrastructure com. With USCGR, 1971-1984. Mem. Lions, Rotary, Kappa Sigma. Roman Catholic. Office: US House of Reps 2311 Rayburn Hob Washington DC 20515-2405*

TAYLOR, GEORGE ALLEN, advertising agency executive; b. Lake City, Iowa, Oct. 26, 1906; s. Bertrand Franklin and Mabel (Minard) T.; m. Regina Helen Wickland, July 3, 1938 (div. 1956). PhB in Fine Arts, Northwestern U., 1947, MEd, 1951, postgrad., 1951-54; art edn. diploma, U. No. Iowa, 1926. Art supr. pub. schs., Indianola, Iowa, 1926-29; instr. art Simpson Coll., 1926-29; designer Modern Art Studios, Chgo., 1929-30; display designer W.J. Rankin Corp., 1930-35; creative dir. Arthur Meyerhoff Assocs., Inc., Milw., 1935-38, br. mgr. L.A., 1938-42, account exec. Chgo., 1942-59, account supr., 1959-61, v.p. adminstrn., 1961-65, vice chmn., 1965-80. Pres. GATA Ltd.; lectr. semantics Ill. Inst. Tech., Chgo., 1947-50, Northwestern U. Sch. Commerce, 1948. Lyricist popular songs. Reader Recs. for Blind, Inc., 1956-94, CRIS Radio, 1981-85. Recipient 1st place awards in copy and layout L.A. Advt. Club, 1940. Life mem. Emeritus, Life mem. Art. Inst. Chgo. also: Unit 1910 8515 Costa Verde Blvd San Diego CA 92122-1150

TAYLOR, GEORGE FREDERICK, newspaper publisher, editor; b. Portland, Oreg., Feb. 28, 1928; s. George Noble and Ida Louise (Dixon) T.; m. Georga Bray, Oct. 6, 1951; children— Amelia Ruth, Ross Noble. BS, U. Oreg., 1950. Reporter Astoria (Oreg.) Budget, 1950-52, Portland Oregonian, 1952-54; copy reader Wall St. Jour., 1955-57, reporter, 1957-59, Detroit Bur. chief, 1959-64, Washington corr., 1964-68, asst. mng. editor, 1968-69, mng. editor N.Y.C., 1970-77, exec. editor, 1977-86; pub. North Bend (Oreg.) News, 1981-86, Prime Time, 1987—, Coquille Valley Sentinel, 1989-2000. Lt. USAF, 1955-57. Mem. Oregon Newspaper Publishers Assn. (bd. dirs. 1997-2000). E-mail: Ftaylor@harborside.com.

TAYLOR, GEORGE KIMBROUGH, JR. lawyer; b. Atlanta, Aug. 28, 1939; s. George Kimbrough and Helen Whiteside (Shepard) T.; m. Carol Ann McKinney, July 1, 1961 (div. 1976); children: George Kimbrough III, Thomas Haynes; m. Triska Ashley Drake, Oct. 2, 1981. BA, Emory U., 1961; LLB, U. Va., 1964. Bar: Ga. 1964, U.S. Dist. Ct. (no. dist.) Ga. 1964, U.S. Ct. Appeals (11th cir.) 1964. Assoc. Kilpatrick & Cody, Atlanta, 1964-70, ptnr., 1970-96, Kilpatrick Stockton LLP (formerly Kilpatrick & Cody), 1997—. Bd. dirs. Ont. Reins. Co. Ltd., Atlanta; pres., bd. dirs. Norcros U.S.A., Inc., Atlanta, U.S. Properties, Inc., Atlanta, 1983-92. Chmn. bd. dirs. Spl. Audiences, Inc., Atlanta, 1985-87; bd. dirs. Atlanta Symphony Orch., 1986—, treas., 1995-97; trustee Woodruff Arts Ctr., Atlanta, 1997—; bd. dirs. Atlanta Opera, 1995—, Ga. Humanities Coun., Atlanta, 1986-93, Ga. Conservancy, 1979-85; bd. dirs. Ga. Coun. Internat. Visitors, Atlanta, 1987-94, pres., 1993; bd. dirs. Brit.-Am. Bus. Group, 1989-95, pres., 1994; bd. visitors Emory U., Atlanta, 1993-96, Brit.-Am. Bus. Coun., 1997—, chmn. 1997-98; mem. alumni coun. U. Va. Law Sch.; active Leadership Atlanta. Woodrow Wilson fellow, 1961. Mem. ABA, Internat. Bar Assn., Atlanta Bar Assn., Order of Coif, Soc. Internat. Bus. Fellows, Capital City Club, Phi Beta Kappa, Omicron Delta Kappa. Democrat. Avocations: sailing, skiing. Office: Kilpatrick Stockton LLP 1100 Peachtree St NE Ste 2800 Atlanta GA 30309-4530 E-mail: ktaylor@kilstock.com.

TAYLOR, GINGER GAY OHLENBUSCH, interior designer; b. Lubbock, Tex., Apr. 21, 1947; d. Albert Bernhardt and Wilma (Limmer) Ohlenbusch; m. Howard Edward Taylor, Dec. 18, 1971 (div. June 1980); children— Julie Elizabeth, Leslie Ann. B.F.A., U. Denver, 1969. Cert. tchr., Colo. Tchr. elem. art Jefferson County Pub. Schs., Lakewood, Colo., 1971-74; owner, interior designer Taylor'd Designs, Denver, 1974-80, 84— ; interior designer Spectrum III, Inc., Littleton, Colo., 1980-81; exec. adminstr. Overthrust Resources, Ltd., Denver, 1981-82; interior designer Davis & Shaw, Denver, 1982-84; instr. interior design Denver YWCA Programs, 1977-79. Mem. Interior Design Soc. (assoc.), Am. Soc. Interior Design (assoc.). Republican. Lutheran. Avocations: skiing; tennis; floral designing. Home: 3655 S Verbena St Apt F302 Denver CO 80237-3509 Office: Taylor'd Designs PO Box 73043 Las Vegas NV 89170-3043

TAYLOR, GLEN, printing and graphics company executive, professional sports team executive; State senator Minnesota Senate, 1980-90; chmn. Taylor Corp., Mankato, Minn.; owner Minnesota Timberwolves, Minneapolis, 1994—. Office: Taylor Corp 1725 Roe Crest Dr Mankato MN 56003-1807 also: Minnesota Timberwolves Target Ctr 600 1st Ave N Minneapolis MN 55403-1416

TAYLOR, HAROLD ALLEN, JR. industrial mineral-speciality metals marketing consultant; b. San Jose, Calif., June 27, 1936; s. Harold Allen and Marie Anna (Briody) T.; m. Theresa Josephine Kustritz, Aug. 29, 1963; children: Harold Allen III, Ruth F. Cook, Jonathan L.E. BA, Brown U., 1958; MA, U. Minn., 1968. Project leader Office Mineral Supply, U.S. Bur. Mines, Phila., 1968-70, commodity specialist divsn. ferrous metals Washington, 1970-74; commodity analyst U.S. internat. Trade Commn., 1974-80; sr. commodity specialist br. indsl. minerals U.S. Bur. Mines, 1980-95; pres. Basics Mines, Summit Point, W.Va., 1995—. Pub., editor Dimension Stone Advocate News, Graphite Advocate News, Bismuth Advocate News, Indium Advocate News, 2000—; contbr. articles to profl. jours. and encys. Pres. Arlington (Va.) Interfaith Coun., 1994, 95. Mem. AIME (sec 1983-84, 1st vice chmn. 1984-85, chmn. 1985-86, mem. exec. adv. bd. mineral econs. subsect. 1981-83, 87-91), ASTM (chmn. subcom. nomenclature of com. on dimension stone 1987—, sec. of com. 1990-95), Soc. Govt. Economists (chmn. materials policy panels, 1979-84), Capitol Metals Forum (steering com. 1979-85), Toastmasters (pres. 1978, 81, 87, 91, asst. area gov. 1978-79, area gov. 1979-80, dep. divsn. lt. gov. 1989-90), Sigma Gamma Epsilon. Address: PO Box 185 Summit Point WV 25446-0185

TAYLOR, HARRIS C. consultant endocrinologist, diabetologist; b. Bklyn., Apr. 30, 1940; s. William and Florence Ruth T.; m. Diana Kahn, Sept. 3, 1962; children: Brian David, Rebecca Lynn. BS, Queens Coll., 1961; MD, U. Chgo., 1965. Diplomate Am. Bd. Internal Medicine, Am. Bd. Endocrinology and Metabolism. Cons. endocrinologist Kaiser Found., Cleve., 1972-86; chief divsn. endocrinology Luth. Med. Ctr., 1977-96, dir. endocrinology & radioimmunoassay lab., 1978-96, dir. internal medicine residency, 1985-94, dir. rsch., internal medicine residency program Fairview Health Sys., 1996—. Sr. clin. instr. Case Western Reserve U. Sch. Medicine, Cleve., 1977-81, clin. asst. prof., 1981-88, clin. assoc. prof. medicine (endocrinology), 1988—. Contbr. articles to profl. jours. Chmn. program com. Diabetes Assn. Cleve., 1976-81, exec. com. mem., 1978-85, pres.-elect, 1981-82, pres., 1982-84. Sr. asst. surgeon USPHS, 1966-68. Named One of Best Drs. in Cleve., Cleve. Mag., 1998, 2002. Fellow: ACP (reviewer Annals of Internal Medicine 1986—, Master Tchr. award 2001), Am. Coll. Endocrinology (editl. bd. Endocrine Practice 1997—); mem.: Endocrine Soc., Am. Thyroid Assn., Am. Assn. Clin. Endocrinologists, Phi Beta Kappa. Jewish. Avocations: philately, classical music. Office: Luth Hosp Cleve Clinic Health Sys 1730 W 25th St Cleveland OH 44113-3170

TAYLOR, HELEN SHIELDS, civic worker; b. Bloomington, Ind., Nov. 27, 1922; d. Lester Howard Shields and Mary Margaret (Galyan) Shields-Fleener; m. Richard R. Hurst, July 29, 1945 (div. Feb. 1959); children: Pamela Hurst Hayes, Richard S.; m. Clyde Leon Taylor, Dec. 2, 1961; 1 child, John P. AA, Coll. Sequoias, 1975; BA, Calif. State U., Fresno, 1979. Active Bd. Edn. Pipeline Program; bd. dirs. Taylor Machinery, Inc., Visalia, Calif. Author: Japanese Invasion of the Philippines, 1977, Russia Today, 1979. Active in registration of legal immigrants with County; bd. dirs. Town Hall, Inc., Fresno, 1990-96; past pres. Tulare County Symphony, Visalia, Meth. Women, Visalia, 1952-96; mem. Ice House Theatre, Visalia, 1980-96; mem. justice and edn. Tulare County Grand Jury, 2000-01. Mem. AAUW (grantee 1979), U.S. Fgn. Policy Assn. (co-chair 1986-96), Alpha Gamma Sigma. Democrat. Avocations: investing, travel, book reviewing, public speaking. Home: 1545 S Chinowth St Visalia CA 93277-3909 Office: Taylor Machinery Inc 6988 Avenue 304 Visalia CA 93291-9510

TAYLOR, HELEN VIRGINIA, minister; b. Oakland, Ill., Apr. 4, 1920; d. Peter Beightel, Nancy Elizabeth McQueen; m. Jackson Taylor (dec. 1975); children: Ronald, Roy, Pete, Rowena, Rachel, John, David. Ordained minister 1971. Pastor, Hugo, Ill., 1978—84; founder House of Refuge Christian Outreach, Brocton, 1993—. Hourse mother Living Hope Renewal Mission, Orlando, Fla. Home: 405 N County Rd 2560E Brocton IL 61917

TAYLOR, HENRY SPLAWN, literature educator, poet, writer; b. Loudoun County, Va., June 21, 1942; s. Thomas Edward and Mary Marshall (Splawn) T. BA, U. Va., 1965; MA, Hollins (Va.) Coll., 1966. Instr. English Roanoke (Va.) Coll., 1966-68; asst. prof. U. Utah, 1968-71; faculty Am. U., Washington, 1971—, prof. lit., 1976—, co-dir. MFA program in creative writing, 1982—, dir. Am. studies program, 1983-84. Dir. U. Utah Writers' Conf., 1970-72; writer-in-residence Hollins Coll., 1978; poet-in-residence Wichita State U., 1994, Randolph-Macon Woman's Coll., 1997; prof. poetry U. Cin., 2002. Author: (poems) The Horse Show at Midnight, 1966, Breakings, 1971, An Afternoon of Pocket Billiards, 1975, Desperado, 1979, The Flying Change, 1985 (Pulitzer prize 1986), (essays) Compulsory Figures: Essays on Recent American Poets, 1992, (textbooks) Poetry: Points of Departure, 1974, The Water of Light: A Miscellany in Honor of Brewster Ghiselin, 1976, (cassette album) Landscape with Tractor, 1985; co-translator: The Children of Herakles, 1981, (poems) Understanding Fiction: Poems 1986-96, 1996, Brief Candles: 101 Clerihews, 2000; contbg. editor: Hollins Critic, 1971-78, 97—; editl. cons. Magill's Literary Ann., 1972-90; adv. editor Bellingham (Wash.) Rev., New Va. Rev., 2000—; cons. editor Poet Lore, 1977-84; translator: Plautus' The Weevil, 1995, Sophocles' Electra, 1998. Recipient Michael Braude award for Light Verse, Am. Acad. Arts & Letters, 2002; fellow, Nat. Endowment Arts, 1978, 1986; grantee, NEH, 1980—81. Mem. PEN, Am. Lit. Translators Assn. Democrat. Mem. Soc. Of Friends. Home: 6930 Selkirk Dr Bethesda MD 20817 Office: Am U Dept Lit Washington DC 20016-8047 E-mail: htaylor@american.edu.

TAYLOR, HENRY AUGUSTUS, psychologist; b. Bryn Mawr, Pa., Apr. 23, 1941; s. James and Elizabeth (L'Engle) T.; m. Mary Hearn, June 17, 1962 (div. 1980); children: Henry, Katharine. AB, Princeton U., 1962; PhD, Stanford U., 1966. Lic. psychologist, N.J. Asst. prof. psychology Douglass Coll., New Brunswick, N.J., 1966-70; rsch. assoc. Rutgers U., 1970-73; br. chief psychologist Union County Psychiat. Clinic, Elizabeth, N.J., 1974-78; chief psychologist, dir. tng. Elizabeth Gen. Med. Ctr., 1978-86; clin. dir. Ctr. for Brief Therapy and Hypnosis, Metuchen, N.J., 1986-98, Meadowlands Ctr. for Counseling and Psychotherapy, Secaucus, 1988-97. Mem. APA, Ea. Psychol. Assn., N.J. Psychol. Assn., Am. Soc. Clin. Hypnosis, Internat. Soc. Hypnosis, Internat. Soc. for Study of Dissociation. Office: 111 Quimby St Ste 6 Westfield NJ 07090-2185 E-mail: hataylor@alumni.princeton.edu.

TAYLOR, HERMAN IVAN, JR. production and distribution executive; BS in Civil Engring. Tech., Fla. A&M U., 1981; MBA, Amber U., Garland, Tex., 1991; MS in Internat. Mgmt., U. Tex., Dallas, 1995. Cert. plant engr., cert. facilities mgr. Mfg. engr. supr. Tex. Instruments, Inc., Dallas, 1985-88, facilities team leader, 1988-91, facilities maintenance mgr., 1991-94, infrastructure project mgr., 1994-96; def. mgr. Raytheon Sys. Co., 1996-99; v.p. prodn. and distbn. Am. Heart Assn., 1999—. Pres. Ivan's Engring., Inc., Garland, 1990—; mem. Planning and Zoning Commn., Sachse, Tex., 1993; mem. HVAC adv. bd. Cedar Valley C.C., Dallas, 1992. Capt. C.E., U.S. Army, 1981-85; maj. USAR. Mem. Internat. Facilities Mgmt. Assn., Assn. for Facilities Engring., Inst. for Supply Mgmt., Fla. A&M U. Alumni Assn. Baptist. Avocations: golf, sports, chess, travel.

TAYLOR, HUMPHREY JOHN FAUSITT, information services executive; b. Meshed, Iran, Sept. 6, 1934; came to U.S., 1976; s. Geoffrey Fausitt and Frances Margaret (Kenyon) T.; m. Penelope Helen Taylor, Dec. 19, 1970; children: Zanthe, Helena. BA with honors, Cambridge (Eng.) U., 1958. Dist. officer Govt. of Tanganyika, 1959-62; mktg. and opinion researcher Nat. Opinion Poll, Eng., 1963-66; mng. dir. Opinion Rsch. Ctr., Eng., 1966-76; with Louis Harris and Assocs., N.Y.C., 1976-81; pres. Harris Interactive Inc., 1981-98, CEO, 1992-98; chmn. The Harris Poll, 1997—. Trustee U.S. com. UNICEF, N.Y.C., 1981—87; trustee Overseas Devel. Coun., Washington, 1987—2001; trustee, chmn. Am. Health Found., 1988—91; trustee Royal Soc. Medicine Found., 1992—; mem. Coun. on Grad. Med. Edn., 2000—. 2d lt. Brit. Army, 1953—55. Fellow: Am. Acad. Ophthalmology (hon.; trustee); mem.: Nat. Coun. Pub. Polls (chmn.). Avocations: history, biographies, skiing, tennis, travel. Address: Louis Harris & Assoc 111 5th Ave Fl 8 New York NY 10003-1005

TAYLOR, IAN LOGAN, dean; b. Eng. MD, PhD, Liverpool Med. Sch. Fellow in gastrointestinal rsch. UCLA, mem. Wadsworth V.A. Tng. Program, various positions, prof. medicine; chief of gastroenterology Duke U., 1986—89, dir. Sarah W. Stedman Ctr. for Nutritional Studies, 1989—90, prof. physiology, dept. cell biology, 1990—93; prof. and chmn. dept. medicine Med. U. S.C., 1993—2001, pres. U. Med. Assocs., 1999—2001; dean Sch. Medicine Tulane U., 2001—. Office: Tulane Health Scis Ctr 1430 Tulane Ave New Orleans LA 70112*

TAYLOR, JAMES, JR. lawyer; b. Florence, S.C., Dec. 6, 1942; s. James and Thelma (Baker) T.; m. Jayne S.C. Bridge, May 19, 1974; children: James Robson, Ashley Baker. BA cum laude, U. of the South, 1965; JD, Georgetown U., 1973. Bar: D.C. 1973, U.S. Ct. Internat. Trade 1977, U.S. Ct. Appeals (fed. cir.) 1982, U.S. Supreme Ct. 1978. Assoc. Busby Rivkin Sherman Levy and Rehm, Washington, 1973-76, Busby and Rehm, Washington, 1977-78; ptnr. Busby Rehm and Leonard, 1979-87, Dorsey & Whitney, Washington, 1988-92, Stroock & Stroock & Lavan, Washington, 1992-95, Ablondi, Foster, Sobin & Davidow, P.C., Washington, 1996—2001, Adduci, Mastriani & Schaumberg LLP, Washington, 2001—. Lt. USN, 1967-70; Vietnam. Mem. ABA, D.C. Bar Assn., Club Interallié (Paris). Episcopalian. Avocations: sailing, fishing, languages. Home: PO Box 101 4153 School Rd Broomes Island MD 20615 Office: Adduci Mastriani & Schaumberg LLP 1200 17th St NW Washington DC 20036

TAYLOR, J(AMES) BENNETT, management consultant; b. Sarasota, Fla., June 15, 1943; s. Thurman Ralph and Lucille (Bennett) Taylor; 1 child Kelly Christine. BS in Advt., U. Fla., 1965. Dist. mgr. Coca-Cola Co., Shreveport, La., 1966-68, allied product splst. Dallas, 1968-70, dist. mgr. Cin. and Indpls., 1970-75; v.p. Ott R&D, Miami, Fla., 1975-78; pres., CEO Exec Group, Inc., Tampa, 1978-98, Think Track Inc., Miami, 1998—. Fellow Career Mgmt. Internat. Bd. Career Mgmt. Cert., 1996. Home: 1700 SW 1st Ave Miami FL 33129-1158 Office: 2000 S Dixie Hwy Ste 104 Coconut Grove FL 33133-2441 E-mail: jbtaylor@thinktrack.com.

TAYLOR, JAMES DANIEL, consulting engineer; b. Tifton, Ga., June 30, 1941; s. Albert Lee and Josephine (Smith) T.; m. Rachel Zilber, Dec. 31, 1966 (dec. May 1994). BSEE, Va. Mil. Inst., 1963; MSEE, Air Force Inst. Tech., 1977. Registered profl. engr., Fla. Commd. 2d lt. AUS, 1963, advanced through grades to capt., 1968; commd. capt. USAF, 1968, advanced through grades to lt. col., 1978; engring. officer Hollowman AFB, N. Mex.; engring. officer Avionics Lab. USAF, Wright-Patterson AFB, Ohio, 1977-81, staff engr. electronic systems div. Hanscom AFB, Mass., 1981-91, retired, 1991. Editor: Introduction to Ultrawideband Radar Systems, 1995, Ultrawideband Radar Technology, 2000; patentee elec. pulse generator, variable gemoetry airship; author tech. papers, reports. Mem. IEEE, AIAA, SPIE, Assn. Unmanned Vehicle Systems (Outstanding Contbr. award 1988), Assn. Old Crows. Avocations: photography, computers, writing. Home and Office: 2620 SW 14th Dr Gainesville FL 32608-2045

TAYLOR, JAMES FRANCIS, marketing professional; b. Detroit, Sept. 5, 1951; s. Harold James and Mary Frances (Law) T.; m. Janet Elizabeth Joss, May 21, 1977; children: Jonathan Harold, Jessica Frances, Jenna Leigh, Jeanette Mary. BA in Polit. Sci., Mich. State U., 1976; postgrad., Thomas Cooley Law Sch., 1979. Product mgr. Gen. Aluminum Products, Charlotte, Mich., 1975-77; sales mgr. Empire Metal Products, Columbus, Ohio, 1978; bus. mgr. Law Offices of Paul Martin, Lansing, Mich., 1978-79; dir. mktg. and sales Feather-Lite Mfg. Co., Troy, 1979-81; v.p. mktg. and sales Innovative Products Corp., Madison Heights, 1981-82; pres. J.F. Taylor Assocs., Inc., Durham, N.C., 1982—, Meadowcrest Group, Inc., 1989—; pres., bd. dirs. The Taylor-Grant-Joss Found., Durham, N.C.; COO C.J. Woodmaster, Inc., 1998—. Corp. sec., bd. dirs., CFO of All Corps. Unifinished Furniture Express, Inc., 1997—, Durham, N.C., C.J. Woodmaster of Charlotte Inc., C.J. Woodmaster of Raleigh, Inc.; CFO C.J. Woodmaster of Cary, Inc., 1999—; CFO, corp. sec. C.J. Woodmaster Devel., Inc., Durham, N.C. Mem. Univ. Club Mich. State U., Hope Valley Country Club, Rotary, Carolina Club. Republican. Roman Catholic. Home: 4 Roswell Ct Durham NC 27707-5070 Office: 2327 Englert Dr Ste 201 Durham NC 27713-4448 E-mail: cjwoodmaster@aol.com.

TAYLOR, JAMES JOHN, academic administrator; b. Mpls., July 26, 1940; s. James John and Mary Elizabeth (Mason) T.; m. Margaret Claire Zacha, Dec. 28, 1976; children: Jerry William, John Allen. BA, Oblate Coll. of S.W., 1966; MEd, St. Louis U., 1969, MBA in Fin., 1972; cert. of advanced studies, Harvard U., 1977; PhD in Adminstrn., Curriculum and Instrn, U. Nebr., 2002. Dept. head, tchr. Althoff High Sch., Belleville, Ill., 1966-71; asst. to controller U. of South Fla., Tampa, 1972-79; project mgr. W.Va. Bd. of Regents, Morgantown, 1979-83; prin., project dir. Am. Mgmt. Systems, Arlington, Va., 1983-90; mng. cons. Taylor Mgmt. Group, 1990-91; v.p. bus. and finance Guam Community Coll., 1991—. Founder, treas. Guam Ednl. Radio Found., KPRG-FM, 1992-99; organizer Chief Bus. Officers of the Pacific, 1997, 98, 99. Member adv. com. on spl. edn. Arlington Sch. Bd., 1981-83; founder, producer St. Louis High Sch. Film Makers Festival, 1968-72; contbr. articles to profl. jours. Founding mem. Harvard Club at Nat. Press Club; mem. Rotary. Avocations: photography, duplicate bridge, scuba diving. Home: 29 Cruz Hts Talofofo GU 96930-4736

TAYLOR, JAMES L. naval officer; Grad., U.S. Naval Acad., 1965; M in Computer Systems, Naval Post Grad. Sch., Monterey, Calif., 1977, M in Mech. Engring., 1979. Commd. ensign USN, 1965, advanced through grades to rear adm., 1996; various assignments to dep. dir. for shipyard mgmt. Naval Sea Systems Command Hdqtrs., 1989-90; dir. Supportability, Maintenance and Modernization Divsn. Chief of Naval Opers., 1994-96; fleet maintenance officer, dep. chief of staff U.S. Pacific Fleet, 1996-99; sr. v.p., group mgr. SAIC AMSEC LLC, 1999—. Decorated Legion of Merit, Meritorious Svc. medal, Disting. Svc. medal. E-mail: james_taylor@amsec.com.

TAYLOR, JAMES MARION, II, automotive wholesale executive; b. Andalusia, Ala., Jan. 20, 1926; s. Marion Doby and Catherine (Hill) T.; m. Abbie Chapman Henderson, Mar. 22, 1947; children: Cathy, James III, Merrily, Abbie, John. Student, U.S. Merchant Marine Acad., 1944-46, Auburn U., 1946-47. Salesman Taylor Parts, Inc., Andalusia, 1947-49, salesman, dir., 1950, v.p., sales mgr., 1950-61, v.p., gen. mgr., 1961-62, pres., 1962-88, chmn., chief exec. officer, 1988-92. Bd. dirs. Covington County Bank, Andalusia; chmn. Southern Nat., Andalusia, 1986—; mem. adv. bd. Shatter-proof Glass Co., Detroit, 1968, AC-Delco, Detroit, 1966-67, Walker (Tenneco), Racine, Wis., 1985. Bd. dirs. Ala. Wildlife Fedn., Montgomery, 1974-77, pres., 1977-78; bd. dirs. Lurleen B. Wallace Jr. Coll. Found., Andalusia, 1986-89, Covington County Bd. Edn., Andalusia, 1960-74, City of Andalusia Downtown Devel. Authority, 1989-96, City of Andalusia Indsl. Devel. Bd., 1969-71. Mem. Nat. Assn. Wholesalers (bd. dirs. and 1st vice chmn. 1988-90, chmn.-elect 1991, chmn. 1992, treas. 1993-94), Automotive Hall of Fame (Midland, Mich. bd. dirs. 1986-94), Automotive Info. Coun. (bd. dirs. 1987-92), Andalusia C. of C. (bd. dirs. 1960-62, 89-92), Auburn Alumni Assn. (life), Kiwanis (pres. Andalusia club 1969-70), Am. Legion. Republican. Baptist. Avocations: hunting, fishing, gun collecting. Home: 104 S Ridge Rd Andalusia AL 36420-4214 Office: Taylor Parts Inc GPI PO Box 1068 Andalusia AL 36420-1068

TAYLOR, JAMES SHEPPARD, communications educator; b. Montgomery, Ala., Dec. 15, 1943; s. Elbert Ruppert and Mary Pinckard (Bryan) T.; m. Mary Ann Luck, Mar. 30, 1972; children: John Brinson Overstreet, Laura Luck Biering. BA in Speech, Auburn U., 1965, MA in Speech, 1966; PhD in Rhetoric and Pub. Address, Fla. State U., 1968. Grad. asst. Auburn (Ala.) U., 1965-66, asst. prof. speech, 1969-73; grad. asst. Fla. State U., Tallahassee, 1966-68; asst. prof. speech N.C. State U., Raleigh, 1968-69; assoc. prof., chair comms. Houston Bapt. U., 1973-94, prof., chair comms., assoc. dean arts and humanities, 1994-98, dean arts and humanities, 1998—. Editl. assoc. So. Speech Jour., 1967-68; mem. editl. bd. N.C. Jour. Speech, 1966-69; news and notions editor So. Speech Comm. Jour., 1972-75. Recipient Tchg. Excellence and Campus Leadership award Sears-Roebuck Found., 1989-90. Mem. Tex. Speech Comm. Assn., So. States Comm. Assn., Speech Comm. Assn. (ERIC evaluator 1973-76), Phi Kappa Phi, Phi Delta Kappa, Kappa Delta Pi, Omicron Delta Kappa. Democrat. Methodist. Avocations: golf, running, tennis, hiking, reading. Office: Houston Bapt U 7502 Fondren Rd Houston TX 77074-3298 E-mail: jtaylor@hbu.edu., jsheppardtaylor@msn.com.

TAYLOR, JAMES WALTER, business and management educator; b. St. Cloud, Minn., Feb. 15, 1933; s. James T. and Nina C. Taylor; m. Joanne Syktte, Feb. 3, 1956; children: Theodore James, Samuel Bennett, Christopher John. BBA, U. Minn., 1957; MBA, NYU, 1960; DBA, U. So. Calif., 1975. Mgr. research div. Atlantic Refining, Phila., 1960-65; dir. new product devel. Hunt-Wesson Foods, Fullerton, Calif., 1965-72; prof. mktg. Calif. State U., 1972-95; mng. dir. Innovative Mgmt. Devel. Co., Laguna Beach, Calif., 1975—. Cons. Smithkline Beecham Corp., Tokyo, Govt. of Portugal, Lisbon, Austrade, Govt. of Australia, Hagenfeldt-Affarerna AB, Stockholm. Author: Profitable New Product Strategies, 1984, How to Create a Winning Business Plan, 1986, Competitive Marketing Strategies, 1986, The 101 Best Performing Companies in America, 1987, The Complete Manual for Developing Winning Strategic Plans, 1988, Every Manager's Survival Guide, 1989, Developing Winning Strategic Plans, 1990, How to Develop Successful Advertising Plans, 1993, Marketing Planning: A Step by Step Guide, 1997, The Marketing Strategy and Planning Workbook, 2000. Fulbright scholar Ministry of Industry, Lisbon, Portugal, 1986-87, U. We. Sydney, Australia, 1989-90; recipient Merit award Calif. State U., 1986-90. Mem. The Planning Forum, Am. Mktg. Assn., Strategic Mgmt. Assn., Assn. for Consumer Rsch., Acad. Mktg. Sci. Home: 3190 Mountain View Dr Laguna Beach CA 92651-2056

TAYLOR, JANET DROKE, legal secretary; b. Bristol, Tenn., Feb. 26, 1961; d. Jimmie D. and Nancy Bell (Sluder) Droke; children: Leslie Ann, Laurie Elizabeth; m. Terry E. Taylor. AA, East Tenn. State U., 1980; student, Milligan Coll., Johnson City, Tenn., 1988-89. With Sullivan County Election Commn., Blountville, Tenn., 1978; legal sec. Boarman & Vaughn, Johnson City, 1980-84; legal asst. Bob McD. Green and Assocs., 1985-89; fed. judicial sec. to U.S. cir. judge U.S. Ct. Appeals, 4th Cir., Abingdon, Va., 1989—. Adv. bd. legal asst. program Milligan Coll., Johnson City, 1988-89. Mem. Tenn. Paralegal Assn. (treas. 1989, pub. rels. dir. 1990), Appalachian Paralegal

Assn., Fed. Judicial Secs. Assn. (4th cir. rep. 1998-2000). Republican. Avocations: reading, piano, travel. Home: PO Box 727 Bluff City TN 37618-0727 Office: US Court of Appeals 4th Cir PO Box 868 Abingdon VA 24212-0868

TAYLOR, JANIE, ballerina; b. Houston; Student, Giacobbe Acad. Dance, New Orleans, Sch. Am. Ballet, 1994—95. Apprentice N.Y.C. Ballet, 1998, mem. corps de ballet, 1998—2001, soloist, 2001—. Dancer (films) Center Stage, (ballets) Divertimento No. 15, A Midsummer Night's Dream, The Nutcracker, Scotch Symphony, Western Symphony, Swan Lake, The Four Seasons, Harmonielehre, Burleske, Them Twos, Viva Verdi, many others. Office: NYC Ballet NY State Theatre 20 Lincoln Ctr Plz New York NY 10023-6913*

TAYLOR, JAY GORDON, lawyer; b. Paducah, Ky., Nov. 18, 1940; s. William Edward Taylor and Ruah Loraze Suer; m. Barbara M. McCrea; children: Julia, Sarah, Brian. BSME, U. Cin., 1964; JD, Ind. U., 1967. Bar: Ind. 1967, Ill. 1967, U.S. Dist. Ct. (no. dist.) Ill., 1970, U.S. Patent Office 1970, U.S. Ct. Appeals (7th cir.) 1975, U.S. Ct. Appeals (2d cir.) 1980, U.S. Ct. Appeals (fed. cir.) 1982, U.S. Dist. Ct. (so. and no. dists.) Ind. 1990. Ptnr. Kirkland & Ellis, Chgo., 1967-77, Haight & Hofeldt, Chgo., 1977-90, Ice Miller Donadio & Ryan, Indpls., 1990—. Capt. U.S. Army, 1967-69. Mem. ABA, Fed. Cir. Bar Assn., Am. Intellectual Property Law Assn., Intellectual Property Law Assn. Chgo., Order of Coif, Pi Tau Sigma. Office: Ice Miller Donadio & Ryan Box 82001 One American Sq Indianapolis IN 46282 Office Fax: 317-592-4779. E-mail: taylor@icemiller.com.

TAYLOR, JEAN ELLEN, mathematics researcher and educator; b. San Mateo, Calif., Sept. 17, 1944; d. Richard Lachlan and Donna Taylor; m. John Mark Guckenheimer, Apr. 18, 1969 (div.); m. Frederick J. Almgren, Oct. 6, 1973 (dec. 1997); 1 child Karen Taylor Almgren stepchildren: Ann Almgren, Robert Almgren; m. William T. Golden, July 8, 2001. AB summa cum laude, Mt. Holyoke Coll., 1966, DSc (hon.), 2001; MS in Chemistry, U. Calif., Berkeley, 1968; MS in Math., U. Warwick, Coventry, Eng., 1971; PhD, Princeton U., 1973. Instr. MIT, Cambridge, Mass., 1972-73; asst. prof. Rutgers U., New Brunswick, N.J., 1973-77, assoc. prof., 1977-82, prof., 1982-87, prof. II, 1987—. Mem. Inst. for Advanced Study, Princeton, N.J., 1974-75, 77-78, 85, 95-96; Miller vis. prof. U. Calif., Berkeley, 1999; vis. scholar Stanford (Calif.) U., 1989; visitor Princeton U., 1980-81; mem. Geometry Computing Group (permanent faculty of the Nat. Sci. and Tech. Ctr. for Computational and Visualization of Geometric Structures); cons. Nat. Bur. Standards, Gaithersburg, Md.; guest expert 3-2-1 Contact program Children's TV Workshop, 1978; mem. exec. com. Conf. Bd. of the Math. Scis., 2000-2002; lectr. in field. Contbr. articles in math., physics and materials sci. to profl. jours. Recipient Presdl. Pub. Svc. award Rutgers Coll. Class of 1962, 1999; Sloan Found. fellow, 1976-78; NSF grad. fellow, 1966-72, hon. fellow Woodrow Wilson Found.; rsch. grantee NSF, 1973—, Air Force Office Sci. Rsch., 1987—. Fellow: AAAS (bd. dirs. 1995—99), Assn. for Women in Sci., Am. Acad. Arts and Scis.; mem.: Soc. for Indsl. and Applied Math., Materials, Mining and Metall. Soc., Assn. for Women in Math. (pres. 1999—2001), Math Assn. Am., Materials Rsch. Soc., Am. Math. Soc. (v.p. 1994—97, exec. com. 1985—88, coun. 1984—89, nominating com. 1977—78), Assn. Princeton Grad. Alumni (governing bd. 1999—), Phi Beta Kappa. Democrat. Achievements include proof that, in the context of Geometric Measure Theory, the singular set in a mathematical model for soap bubble clusters and soap films on wire frames is what is physcally observed, thereby solving a 100 year old problem; development of mathematical models for treating shapes of surfaces and interfaces for crystalline materials and use of them to model crystal growth. Avocations: backpacking, gardening, reading, jogging, skiing. Office: Rutgers U Math Dept New Brunswick NJ 08903 E-mail: taylor@math.rutgers.edu.

TAYLOR, JEFFREY LEE, political science educator, author; b. Spencer, Iowa, Jan. 30, 1961; s. James Lee and Judith Lane Taylor; m. Shirley Jean Bentz, Dec. 29, 1990; 1 child, William Taylor (dec.). BA magna cum laude, Northwestern Coll., 1983; MA, U. Iowa, 1985; PhD, U. Mo., 1997. Libr., instr. No. State U., Aberdeen, S.D., 1985-90; libr. Lincoln U., Jefferson City, Mo., 1994-95, Univ. Ctr. Rochester, Minn., 1997—; instr. polit. sci. Rochester Cmty. and Tech. Coll., 1999—. Instr. S.D. Pub. Library Tng. Inst., Pierre, 1987, Southea. Libraries Coop., Rochester, 1997-98. Author: From Radical to Respectable, 1997. Clair Boone County Green Party, Columbia, Mo., 1994-96, Mo. Green Party, 1996; chair Olmsted County Green Party, Rochester, 2001-02. State of Iowa scholar, 1979. Mem. Am. Polit. Sci. Assn., Acad. Polit. Sci., Minn. Library Assn. Mem. Soc. of Friends. Office: Univ Ctr Rochester 851 30th Ave SE Rochester MN 55904

TAYLOR, JILL OLSEN, lawyer, artist; b. Logan, Utah, June 1, 1955; d. Keith Conrad and Norma Elveda (Correll) Olsen; m. Bruce T. Taylor, July 3, 1979; children: Jenny, Benjamin, Christina. BA summa cum laude, Brigham Young U., 1977, JD, 1980. Bar: Utah 1980. Dep. county atty. Emery County, Utah, 1980-81; corp. atty. Physicians Emergency Svc., Price, 1981-88; pvt. practice Provo, 1986—. Bd. dirs., pres. Covered Bridge Canyon Homeowners Assn., 1983-89; mem. Utah County Planning Commn., 1993—, chair planning commn., 1993-2000. Mem.: ABA, Order of Barristers (headmaster Meridian Sch. 2001—), Utah State Bar Assn., Am. Immigration Lawyers Assn. (chair Utah chpt. 1996, bd. govs.), Phi Kappa Phi. Republican. Mem. Lds Ch.

TAYLOR, JOB, III, lawyer; b. N.Y.C., Feb. 18, 1942; s. Job II and Anne Harrison (Flinchbaugh) T.; m. Mary C. August, Oct. 24, 1964 (div. 1978); children: Whitney August, Job IV; m. Sally Lawson, May 31, 1980; 1 child, Alexandra Anne. BA, Washington & Jefferson Coll., 1964; JD, Coll. William and Mary, 1971. Bar: N.Y. 1972, U.S. Dist. Ct. (no., so. ea. and we. dists.) N.Y. 1973, U.S. Ct. Appeals (2d cir.) 1973, U.S. Ct. Claims 1974, U.S. Tax Ct. 1974, U.S. Supreme Ct. 1975, U.S. Ct. Appeals (9th cir.) 1976, U.S. Ct. Mil. Appeals 1977, U.S. Ct. Appeals (D.C. and 10th cirs.) 1977, D.C. 1981, U.S. Ct. Internat. Trade 1981, U.S. Ct. Appeals (fed. cir.) 1982, U.S. Dist. Ct. (no. dist.) Calif. 1983, U.S. Ct. Appeals (6th cir.) U.S. Dist. Ct., 1987, U.S. Ct. Appeals (3d cir.) 1990, U.S. Dist. Ct. Conn. 1996. Ptnr. Olwine, Connelly, Chase, O'Donnell & Weyher, N.Y.C., 1971-85, Latham & Watkins, N.Y.C., 1985—. Served to lt. USN, 1964-68. Mem. ABA, Assn. Bar City N.Y., La Confrerie des Chevaliers du Tastevin, Racquet and Tennis Club, Wee Burn Country Club (Darien, Conn.), New Canaan Country Club.. Republican. Episcopalian. Avocations: squash, tennis, golf, reading. Office: Latham & Watkins 885 3rd Ave Fl 9 New York NY 10022-4834

TAYLOR, J(OCELYN) MARY, museum administrator, zoologist, educator; b. Portland, Oreg., May 30, 1931; d. Arnold Llewellyn and Kathleen Mary (Yorke) T.; m. Joseph William Kamp, Mar. 18, 1972 (dec.); m. Wesley Kingston Whitten, Mar. 20, 2001. BA, Smith Coll., 1952; MA, U. Calif., Berkeley, 1953, PhD, 1959. Instr. zoology Wellesley Coll., 1959-61, asst. prof. zoology, 1961-65; assoc. prof. zoology U. B.C., 1965-74; dir. Cowan Vertebrate Mus., 1965-82, prof. dept. zoology, 1974-82; collaborative scientist Oreg. Regional Primate Research Ctr., 1983-87; prof. (courtesy) dept. fisheries and wildlife Oreg. State U., 1984-95; dir. Cleve. Mus. Nat. History, 1987-96, dir. emerita, 1996—. Adj. prof. dept. biology Case Western Res. U., 1987-96. Assoc. editor Jour. Mammalogy, 1981-82. Contbr. numerous articles to sci. jours. Trustee Benjamin Rose Inst., 1988-93, Western Res. Acad., 1989-94, U. Circle, Inc., 1987-96, The Cleve. Aquarium, 1990-93, Cleve. Access to the Arts, 1992-96; corp. bd. Holden Arboretum, 1988-98, The Cleve. Mus. Natural History, 1996—, The Catlin Gabel Sch., 1998-2000, The Inst. for the Northwest, 1999—2001. Recipient Lake County Environ. award, Lake county metro parks.; Fulbright scholar, 1954-55; Lalor Found. grantee, 1962-63; NSF grantee, 1963-71; NRC Can. grantee, 1966-84; Killam Sr. Rsch. fellow, 1978-79 Mem. Soc. Women Geographers, Am. Soc. Mammalogists (1st v.p. 1978-82, pres. 1982-84, Hartley T. Jackson award 1993, hon. mem. 2001), Australian Mammal Soc., Cooper Ornithol., Assn. Sci. Mus. Dirs. (v.p. 1990-93), Rodent Specialist Group of Species Survival Commn. (chmn. 1989-93), Sigma Xi. Home: 2718 SW Old Orchard Rd Portland OR 97201-1637 E-mail: taylorjm@teleport.com.

TAYLOR, JOE, JR. writer, consultant; b. Haverford, Pa., Jan. 24, 1973; s. Joseph M. and Catherine M. Taylor; m. Lori Ann Johns. BS Commn., Ithaca Coll., 1994. Prin. Spincycle Media, Inc., Miami, 1994—; prodr. WXPN/World Cafe, Phila., 1994—2001. Author: (book) Grow Your Band's Audience, 2002; prodr.: (live at the world cafe) CD Series, 1995, (radio series) Live at the Writers House, 1997. Adv. bd. mem. Writers Ho., Philadelphia, PA., 1996—2002. Mem.: NARAS. Democrat. Roman Catholic. Avocation: travel, music, art. Office: Spincycle Media Inc 8345 NW 66th St #3261 Miami FL 33166 Business E-Mail: info@spinme.com.

TAYLOR, JOE CLINTON, judge; b. Durant, Okla., Mar. 28, 1942; s. Luther Clinton and Virena (Parker) T.; m. Margaret Pearl Byers, June 8, 1963; children: Marna Joanne, Leah Alison, Jocelyn Camille. Student, Southeastern State Coll., 1960-62; BA, Okla. State U., 1965; JD, U. Okla., 1968. Bar: Okla. 1968. Pvt. practice, Norman, Okla., 1968-69; apptd. spl. dist. judge Durant, 1969-72; assoc. dist. judge Bryan County, Okla., 1972-76; dist. judge, chief judge 19th Dist. Ct., 1976-93; presiding judge Southeastern Okla. Jud. Adminstrv. Dist., 1984-92, Choctaw Tribal Ct., 1979-83; pres. Okla. Jud. Conf., 1987-88; chmn. Assembly Presiding Judges, 1989-90; presiding judge trial div. Okla. Ct. on the Judiciary, 1991-93; Okla. Ct. of Tax Rev., 1992—; judge Okla. Ct. of Civil Appeals, Tulsa, 1993—. Chmn. bd. dirs. Durant Youth Svcs., 1976-93; bd. dirs. Bryan County Youth Svcs., Inc., 1971-93. Lt. Col. USAR. Lt. col. USAR, ret. Mem. Lions, Phi Sigma Epsilon, Delta Theta Phi. Mem. Ch. of Christ. Home: PO Box 329 Durant OK 74702-0329 Office: Ct Civil Appeals 601 State Bldg 440 S Houston Ave Tulsa OK 74127-8922 E-mail: joe.taylor@oscn.net.

TAYLOR, JOE WILLIAM, publishing executive, writer; b. Cin., Jan. 27, 1949; s. William Louis Taylor and Mary Louise Cox; m. Patricia Lou Willey, Dec. 12, 1982. BA in Philosophy, U. Ky., 1975; MA, Fla. State U., 1981, PhD, 1985. Pub. Swallow's Tale Press, Tallahassee, 1984—; dir. Livingston Press, U. West Ala., Livingston, 1992—. Prof. U. West Ala., 1990—. Author: Oldcat & Ms. Puss: A Book of Days, 1996. Mem. MLA, Associated Writing Program, Pubs. of the South Assn. Home: RR 2 Box 90-d Coatopa AL 35470-9642 E-mail: jwt@uwa.edu.

TAYLOR, JOEL SANFORD, retired lawyer; b. Hazleton, Pa., Oct. 8, 1942; s. Robert Joseph and Alice Josephine (Sanford) T.; m. Donna Rae Caron, Mar. 26, 1967; children: Jason, Adam, Jeremy. BA, Swarthmore Coll., 1965; LLB, Columbia U., 1968. Bar: N.Y. 1969, U.S. Ct. Appeals (2d cir.) 1970, U.S. Dist. Ct. (no. dist.) Ohio 1974, U.S. Supreme Ct. 1974, U.S. Dist. Ct. (so. dist.) Ohio 1975, U.S. Ct. Appeals (6th cir.) 1975, U.S. Dist. Ct. (ea. dist.) Ky. 1979. Law clk. hon. Constance B. Motley U.S. Dist. Ct., N.Y.C., 1968-69; assoc. Paul, Weiss, Rifkind, Wharton & Garrison, 1969-72; exec. asst. Ohio Office of Budget & Mgmt., Columbus, Ohio, 1972-74; asst. atty. gen. Ohio Atty. Gen., 1974-83, chief counsel, 1983-91; ptnr. Dinsmore & Shohl, 1991-2000; fin. dir. City of Columbus, 2000—. Pres. Ohio Sundry Claims Bd., Columbus, 1972-74, Ohio State Controlling Bd., Columbus, 1973-74; mem., bd. trustees Ohio State Tchrs. Retirement Sys., Columbus, 1986-91, Solid Waste Authority Ctrl. Ohio, 2001—. Mem. Govt. Fin. Officers Assn., Columbia Law Alumni Assn., Ohio Sierra Club, Nat. Wildlife Fedn., Nature Conservany. Office: City Hall 90 W Broad St Columbus OH 43215-9000 E-mail: jstaylor@cmhmetro.net.

TAYLOR, JOHN CALVIN, missionary, dentist; b. Cin., July 22, 1914; s. John Calvin Taylor V and Magdala Elizabeth Siehl; m. Adah Packard Boggs, Mar. 7, 1941; children: Sarah, Margaret, Virginia, John, Frederick, Alison, Carla. BSc, Muskingum Coll., 1937; BD, Cedarville Sem., 1939; DDS, U. Pitts., 1949; cert. excellence in Hindi and Urdu, Lang. Sch., Landour, India, 1940, 41. Diploma Acad. Gen. Dentistry. Missionary Reformed Presbyn. Synod, Roorkee, India, 1939-46; moderator, pastor Reformed Presbyn., Pitts., Fairview, Pa., 1946-47; nat. missions missionary Presbyn. Bd. Home Missions, Pitts., Tyre, 1947-52; missionary dentist United Presbyn., Pitts., Seattle, 1953-59; dir. Meth. Mission Hosp. Dental Clinic, Bariely, India, 1954—55; founder Dental Clinic Landour Cmty. Hosp., Mussoorie, India, 1955-59; pres. Rotary Club Internat., Mount Union, Pa., 1964-65; pastor 3 chs. Mt. Union, Johnsonburg and St. Mary areas, 1964-68; founder Shanta Bhawan Hosp. Dental Clinic, Katmandu, Nepal, 1968; dental missionary Missionary Dentist, Inc.-E.L.W.A. Hosp., Liberia, 1977, Pakistan, 1980—81, Shell, Ecuador, 1983; free dentist Dental Care, India, 1984—; founder Oral Clinic Ctr., Dera Dun, India, 1981—. Tchr. emergency dentistry Vellore (India) Med. Coll., 1958; dentist Youth With a Mission, Mercy Ship, Hawaii, 1985. Author: Wildlife in India's Tiger Kingdom, 1980, Face the Devil's Roar, 1995. Co-founder, life mem. Wildlife Preservation Soc., Dehra-Dun, India, 1954—, organizer, founder Rajpur Wildlife Park, 1954—. Recipient Cert. of Honor for 50 Yrs. of Dedicated Svc. to Dentistry, ADA, 1999. Mem. Herminie Lions Club (fgn. chmn. 1988—, Lions Hat award 1993), N.Am. Hunting Club, NRA. Republican. Presbyterian. Avocations: zoology, hunting, taxidermy, photography, music. Home: 110 Highland Ave Herminie PA 15637-1310 E-mail: tgrtlr@juno.com.

TAYLOR, JOHN BRIAN, federal agency administrator, economist, educator; b. Yonkers, N.Y., Dec. 8, 1946; s. John Joseph and Lorraine (Crowley) T.; m. Raye Allyn Price, Dec. 30, 1972; children: Jennifer Lynn, John Andrew. AB in Econs. summa cum laude, Princeton U., 1968; PhD, Stanford U., 1973. Asst. prof. econs. Columbia U., N.Y.C., 1973-77, assoc. prof., 1977-79, prof., 1979-80; prof. econs. and pub. affairs Princeton U., 1980-84; prof. econs. Stanford U., 1984—, dir. Ctr. for Econ. Policy Rsch., 1994-97, dir. Introductory Econs. Ctr., 1997-2001; under sec. treasury for internat. affairs U.S. Treasury, Washington, 2001—. Vis. prof. econs. Yale U., 1980; sr. staff economist Pres.'s Coun. Econ. Advisers, 1976—77, mem., 1989—91; econometric cons. Townsend-Greenspan and Co., NY, 1978—81; rsch. advisor Fed. Res. Bank, Phila., 1981—84; rsch. assoc. Nat. Bur. Econ. Rsch., 1980—2001; rsch. economist Bank of Japan, Tokyo, 1987, hon. adviser, 1994—2001; panel of econ. advisers Congl. Budget Office, 1995—2001. Author: (non-fiction) Macroeconomics, 1986, Macroeconomic Policy in the World Economy, 1993, Economics, 1995, Unemployment, Inflation, and Monetary Policy, 1998, Monetary Policy Rules, 1999, Handbook of Macroeconomics, 2000; co-editor: Am. Econ. Rev., 1985—89; editor (assoc.): Econometrica, 1981—85, (jour.) Jour. Econ. Dynamics and Control, 1978—85, Jour. Monetary Econs., 1978—83, Jour. Econ. Perspectives, 1997—2001; contbr. articles to profl. jours. NSF grantee, 1979-81, 81-83, 83-86, 86-89, 92-95; Guggenheim Found. fellow, 1983-84; sr. fellow Hoover Instn., 1996—. Fellow Econometric Soc., Am. Acad. of Arts and Sci.; mem. Am. Econ. Assn. (exec. com. 1991-94, v.p. 2000-01). Office: US Dept Treasury 1500 Pennsylvania Ave NW Washington DC 20220*

TAYLOR, JOHN DARRYL, computer scientist; b. Tuscaloosa, Ala., Apr. 24, 1963; s. John DePriest and Mattie Beatrice (Terry) T.; m. Patricia Anne Smith, June 10, 1995; children: Joseph Smith, James Smith, Chrystal Smith. BS, Stillman Coll., Tuscaloosa, 1985. Night watchman Fitts Industries, Tuscaloosa, 1983; cartographer Def. Mapping Agy., Louisville, 1985-89; computer specialist Nat. Imagery & Mapping Agy., Bethesda, Md., 1989—; sr. database adminstr. Raytheon Corp., Springfield, Va., 2000. Author: (book of poetry) Complete Works of John Taylor, 1996. Stillman Coll. Presdl. scholar, 1985. Mem. Internat. Exec. Guild. Democrat. Christian Ch. Avocations: pocket billiards, table tennis, Star Trek books and video, movie collecting. Home: 18828 Mcfarlin Dr Germantown MD 20874-1439 Office: National Imagery and Mapping Agency 4600 Sangamore Rd Bethesda MD 20816-5003 E-mail: IAMBORGHUE@aol.com.

TAYLOR, JOHN DAVID, retired humanities educator; b. Colorado Springs, Colo., Jan. 19, 1938; s. John Albert Wojtacha, Jimmie Royce Taylor (Stepfather), Margaret Virginia Bordenelli; m. Marilyn Moncure, May 3, 1967 (div. Sept. 1995). BA in History, Md. U., 1963; MEd, U. Va., 1969; MA in History, Georgetown U., 1972. Tchr. 8th grade Social Studies, English Fairfax County Schs., Fairfax, Va., 1963—68, tchr., history, govt., polit. sci., Russian history, 1969—95; ret., 1995. Editor newsletter The Ark Va. Fedn. Humane Societies, 1978—. Sp=4 U.S. Army, 1956—59, Germany. Recipient Humanitarian award, Va. Fedn. Humane Societies, 1978; fellow, Nat. Endowment for Humanities, 1989. Democrat. Avocations: weightlifting, martial arts, reading, travel. Home: 6614 S Wakefield Dr Alexandria VA 22307

TAYLOR, JOHN JACKSON (JAY TAYLOR), writer, documentalist, retired foreign service officer; b. Little Rock, Dec. 4, 1931; s. Alfred Wesley and Annie Laurie (Cain) T.; m. Elizabeth Rose, July 9, 1954; children: John Jr., Laurie, Amy, Cynthia. BA, Vanderbilt U., 1952; MA, U. Mich., 1968. 3d sec. U.S. Fgn. Service, Accra, Ghana, 1957-59, 2d sec. Taichung and Taipei, Republic of China, 1960-65; Chinese affairs analyst Dept. State, Washington, 1966-67; staff assoc. Ctr. for Chinese Studies, U. Mich., Ann Arbor, 1967-68; U.S. consul Kuching, Malaysia, 1968-70; chief external affairs reporting U.S. Consulate Gen., Hong Kong, 1970-74; officer-in-charge Chinese affairs Dept. State, Washington, 1974-75; staff mem. E. Asian affairs Nat. Security Council, 1975-77; polit. counselor U.S. Embassy, Pretoria/Capetown, 1977-80, polit. cons. Peking, 1980-82; rsch. fellow Fairbanks Ctr. for East Asian Studies Harvard U., Cambridge, Mass., 1982-83; dir. East Asian analysis Dept. State, Washington, 1983-85; dep. asst. sec. state Bur. Intelligence and Research, Dept. State, 1986-87; chief of mission U.S. Interests Sect., Havana, Cuba, 1987-90; diplomat in residence Carter Presdl. Ctr., Emory U., 1990-92; sr. mem. State Task Force 2000, 1992-93; sr. assoc. Global Bus. Access; assoc. in rsch. Fairbank Ctr. for East Asian Studies, Harvard U.; prodr., writer, dir. ?Why Prodns. Guest faculty Emory U. and Spelman Coll. Author: China and Southeast Asia, 1974, 1976, The Dragon and the Wild Goose, 1987, 1990, The Rise and Fall of Totalitarianism, 1993, The Generalissimo's Son, 2000, (documentaries) Ubuntu, African and Afrikaner, 2000; contbr. , columns in newspapers. Served as Naval Aviator with USMC, 1953-57. Mem.: Wash. Inst. Fgn. Affairs, Asian Soc., Fgn. Svc. Assn. E-mail: jaytaylor888@sprintmail.com.

TAYLOR, JOHN JOSEPH, nuclear engineer, researcher; b. Hackensack, N.J., Feb. 27, 1922; s. John J.D. and Johanna F. (Thibideau) T.; m. Lorraine Crowley, Feb. 5, 1943; children: John B., Nancy M., Susan M. BA, St. John's U., Jamaica, NY, 1942, St. John's U., Jamaica, N.Y., 1942; DSc (hon.), 1975; MS, U. Notre Dame, 1947. Mathematician Bendix Aviation Corp., Teterburo, N.J., 1946-47; engr. Kellex Corp., N.Y.C., 1947-50; v.p. water reactor div. Westinghouse Electric Corp., Pitts., 1950-81; v.p. nuclear power Electric Power Rsch. Inst., Palo Alto, Calif., 1981-95; energy cons., 1995—. Mem. adv. com. Oak Ridge (Tenn.) Nat. Lab., 1973-83, Brookhaven Nat. Lab., Upton, N.Y., 1986-92, Inst. for Nuclear Power Ops., 1988-95; mem. adv. com. Argonne (Ill.), Nat. Lab., 1980-86, bd. dirs.; cons. Office Tech. Assessment, Washington, 1975-93; mem. internat. adv. group IAEA, Vienna, Austria, 1992-95; mem. nuclear rsch. rev. com. NRC, 1995-97; mem. U.S.-Russian Commn. on Weapons Plutonium Disposition, 1996-2001, Nat. Acad. Bd. Radioactive Waste Mgmt., 1998-2001, DOE Nuclear Energy Rsch. Adv. Bd., 1998—. Co-author: Reactor Shielding Manual, 1953, Naval Reactor Physics Manual, 1956, Nuclear Power, Policy and Prospects, 1987, Management and Disposition of Excess Weapons Plutonium; contbr. articles to profl. jours. Bd. regents St. Mary's Coll., Moraga, Calif. Lt. (j.g.) USN, 1942-45. Recipient Order of Merit, Westinghouse Electric Corp., 1957, George Westinghouse Gold medal ASME, 1990. Fellow AAAS, Am. Phys. Soc., Am. Nuclear Soc. (bd. dirs. Walter Zinn award 1993); mem. NAE, Nat. Acad. Engring., Cosmos Club (Washington). Republican. Roman Catholic. Home: 15 Oliver Ct Menlo Park CA 94025-6685 Office: Electric Power Rsch Inst PO Box 10412 3412 Hillview Ave Palo Alto CA 94304-1344

TAYLOR, JOHN LOCKHART, former city official; b. N.Y.C., Nov. 4, 1927; s. Floyd and Marian (Lockhart) T.; m. Barbara Becker, July 19, 1952; children: Catherine Fair, Robert, William, Susan. AB, Middlebury Coll., 1952; M.Govtl. Adminstrn., U. Pa., 1956. Reporter Providence Jour.-Bull., 1952-54; adminstrv. intern City of Xenia, Ohio, 1955-56; mcpl. mgr. Borough of Narberth, Pa., 1956-60, Twp. of Lakewood, N.J., 1960-64; asst. city mgr. Fresno, Calif., 1964-65; city mgr., 1965-68, Kansas City, Mo., 1968-74, Berkeley, Calif., 1974-76; lectr. U. Pa., 1957-58, Golden Gate U., 1977; sr. urban mgmt. specialist Stanford Research Inst., 1977-80; dir. Internat. Devel. Center, 1980-82; clk. of bd. suprs. City of San Francisco, 1982-98, spl. asst., 1998—. Pres. Calif. Clks. Bd. Suprs. Assn., 1988-89. Served with USN, 1945-48. Mem. Internat. City Mgrs. Assn., Am. Soc. Pub. Adminstrn., Mcpl. Execs. Assn. (pres. 1991-93, 98). Address: 1005 Creston Rd Berkeley CA 94708-1503 E-mail: misterclerk@email.msn.com.

TAYLOR, JOHN MCKOWEN, lawyer; b. Baton Rouge, Jan. 20, 1924; s. Benjamin Brown and May (McKowen) T.; 1 child, John McKowen. BA, La. State U., 1948, JD, 1950. Bar: La. 1950, U.S. Supreme Ct. 1960. Assoc. Taylor, Porter, Brooks, Fuller & Phillips, Baton Rouge, 1950-55, Huckaby, Seale, Kelton & Hayes, Baton Rouge, 1955-58; ptnr. Kelton & Taylor, 1958-61; pvt. practice, 1961—. With AUS, 1943-46; maj. USAR, 1946—, ATO, ETO, PTO. Mem. ABA, AAAS, La. State Bar Assn., Baton Rouge Bar Assn., Mil. Order of World Wars, Am. Radio Relay League, Baton Rouge Country Club, City Club of Baton Rouge, Baton Rouge Amateur Radio Club, Camelot Club, SAR, Sigma Chi, Pi Gamma Mu, Phi Delta Phi. Republican. Presbyterian. Home and Office: 2150 Kleinert Ave Baton Rouge LA 70806-6712 E-mail: jmcktaylor@cox.net.

TAYLOR, JOHN MICHAEL, research director; b. Birmingham, Eng., Feb. 15, 1943; s. Eric John and Dorothy Irene T.; m. Judith Moyle, 1965; children: Michael James, Miranda Elizabeth, David Charles, Lydia Jane. MA, U. Cambridge, U.K., 1965, PhD, 1969. Rsch. engr. Gen. Electric Co., London, 1965-66; sr. sci. officer Signals R & D Establishment, Christchurch, U.K., 1969-77; head divsn. Royal Signals and Radar Establishment, Malvern, U.K., 1978-80, Admiralty Surface Weapons Establishment, Portsmouth, U.K., 1980-81, head dept. U.K., 1982-84; lab. dir. Hewlett Packard Labs., Bristol, U.K., 1984-86, dir. U.K., 1986-98; exec. dir. Hewlett Packard Ltd., U.K., 1992-98; dir. gen. rsch. couns. Office of Sci. and Tech., U.K. DTI, 1999—. Vis. prof. Bristol U., 1986—, Imperial Coll., London U., 1990—. Contbr. articles to profl. jours.; patentee in field. Fellow Royal Soc., U.K. Instn. Elec. Engrs. (pres. 1998-99), Brit. Computer Soc., Royal Soc. Arts, Royal Acad. Engring. Avocations: family, sailing, photography, theatre. Office: OST, Albany House 94-98 Petty France London SW1 9ST England

TAYLOR, JOHN READ, JR. financial management company executive; b. N.Y.C., July 16, 1943; s. John Read and Patricia (Green) T.; m. Sandra Shackelford Brown, June 28, 1969 (div. 1988); 1 child, Louise Tiffany; m. Joyce Manis, Jan. 28, 1989; 1 child, John Read III. AB, Princeton U., 1965; postgrad. in polit. sci., U. N.C., 1966-69. Asst. mgr. Chem. Bank, N.Y.C., 1969-73; asst. v.p. First Nat. Bank Chgo., 1973-74; v.p. Citibank, N.Y.C., 1974-78, Gesellschaft fur Trendanalysen, N.Y.C., 1978-79; pres. EMCOR Mgmt., 1979-81; chmn. FX Concepts, Inc., 1981—. Chmn. J3 Biologics, Inc., N.Y.C., 1992-98, U.S. Transgenics, Inc., 1999-2002, Am. Integrated Biologics, Inc., 2002—. Bd. dirs. Franklin Coll. Switzerland, Lugano, 1975—, chmn., 1980-90, vice chmn. 1995—; bd. dirs. Hemophilia Assn. N.Y., 1990—; chmn. Coalition for Hemophilia B, N.Y., 1990—. Home: 45 E 89th St New York NY 10128-1251 Office: FX Concepts Inc 225 W 34th St Ste 710 New York NY 10122-0710

TAYLOR, JOSEPH B. former state legislator; b. Forest Hills, N.Y., Apr. 21, 1927; s. William Dee and Gladys H. (Bacon) T.; m. Emily Warren, 1956; children: Prudence H.T. (Mrs. David W. Wicks), Theodore W. BS, U. Maine, 1950; MS, MIT, 1956. Mem. from dist. 42 Maine Ho. of Reps., 1995-98. Mem. Sigma Psi, Delta Tau Delta. Address: 14 Lawn Ave Cumberland Center ME 04021-9506

TAYLOR, JOSEPH HENRY, lawyer; b. Chgo., Mar. 2, 1934; s. Joseph Henry and Blanche (Murnane) T.; m. Marie Theresa Dietz, Feb. 20, 1960 (div. Dec. 21 1975); children: Lisa Marie Moose, Joseph John, Matthew Edward, Nicole; m. Joyce Louise Eriks, Jan. 1, 1977; children: Sean Philip, Ryan Joseph, Colin, Michael, Zachary. BS in Philosophy, Loyola U., Chgo., 1960, JD, 1965. Bar: Ill. 1965, U.S. Dist. Ct. (no. and so. dists.) Ill. 1965. Assoc. Pentis & Tourek, Chgo., 1965-66; pvt. practice Chgo. and Palos Heights, Ill., 1966—. Prosecutor City of Palos Heights, 1976—. Alderman City of Palos Heights, 1974-76. Cpl. USMC, 1951-54. Mem. ATLA, Ill. Trial Lawyers Assn., Ill. State Bar Assn., Chgo. Bar Assn., S.W. Suburban Bar Assn. (pres. 1970), DuPage County Bar Assn., Criminal Def. Lawyer. Avocations: pilot, motorcycles, marathon runner. Office: 7330 W College Dr Palos Heights IL 60463-1157

TAYLOR, JOSEPH HOOTON, JR. radio astronomer; b. Phila., Mar. 29, 1941; s. Joseph Hooton and Sylvia Hathaway (Evans) T.; m. Marietta Bisson, Jan. 3, 1976. BA in Physics, Haverford Coll., 1963; PhD in Astronomy, Harvard U., 1968; DSc (hon., U. Chgo., 1985, U. Mass., 1994. Research fellow, lectr. Harvard U., 1968-69; asst. prof. astronomy U. Mass., Amherst, 1969-72, assoc. prof., 1973-77, prof., 1977-81; prof. physics Princeton U., 1980—, James McDonnell Disting. prof. physics, 1986—, dean of faculty, 1997—. Author: Pulsars, 1977. Recipient Dannie Heineman prize in astrophysics, Am. Inst. Physics/Am. Astron. Soc., 1980, prize in gravitation and cosmology, Tomalla Found., 1985, Magellanic Premium award, Am. Philos.

Soc., 1990, Einstein prize laureate, Albert Einstein Found., 1993, Wolf Prize in Physics, Wolf Found., 1992, Nobel Prize in Physics, Nobel Found., 1993; fellow MacArthur fellow, 1981. Fellow: Am. Phys. Soc., Am. Acad. Arts and Scis.; mem.: Internat. Astron. Union, Internat. Sci. Radio Union, Am. Astron. Soc., Am. Philos. Soc., NAS. Mem. Soc. Of Friends. Home: 272 Hartley Ave Princeton NJ 08540-5656 Office: Princeton U Dept Physics 215 Jadwin Hall PO Box 708 Princeton NJ 08544-0001*

TAYLOR, JUDITH ANN, marketing and sales executive; b. Sheridan, Wyo., July 9, 1944; d. Milo G. and Eleanor M. (Wood) Rinker; m. George I. Taylor, Sept. 15, 1962; children: Monte G., Bret A. Fashion dept. mgr. Montgomery Ward, Sheridan, 1968-73; pers. mgr., asst. mgr. Dan's Ranchwear, 1973-80; sales/prodn. coord. KWYO Radio, 1981-83; sales mgr., promotions coord. KROE Radio, 1984-96; mng. editor BOUNTY Publ., 1993-96; dir. sales and marketing Best Western Sheridan Ctr., 1996—. Notary pub. State of Wyo., 1985—; lectr., instr. BSA Merit U.; lectr. acad. achievement LVA Adv. Bd., 1993—, instr. Tongue River Middle Sch. Academic Enrichmen t Program, 1994-95; S.C. Ambs., 1980—, pres., 1995-96. Mng. editor BOUNTY Publ., 1993-96. Sec.-treas. Sheridan County Centennial Com., 1986-89; local sec.-treas. Wyo. Cenntennial Com., Sheridan, 1986-90; exec. dir. Sheridan-Wyo. Rodeo bd., 1983—; bd. dirs. Sheridan County Fair Bd., 1991-96, treas., 1995—; bd. dirs. "Christmas in April" Sheridan County, 1992—, Cowboy Mus. of the West, 1998—; mem. WJTP Coun., Cheyenne, 1990-92; mem. adv. coun. Tutor-Literacy Vols. of Am., 1993—; Sheridan High Sch. Key Club sponsor, 1994—; Sheridan Jr. High Sch. Builders Club sponsor, 1996—; mem. City of Sheridan CVB Bd., 1996—, treas., 1998-2000, v.p., 2000—; ; Mrs. Santa Claus for local groups; vol. coord. AIDS Quilt; local chmn. March of Dimes Walkamerica, 1997—; mem. steering com. Ronald McDonald House; mem. adv. bd. Sheridan Coll. Hospitality Program, 2000—. Named Person of Week, Sheridan County Cmty., 1998. Mem. Wyo. Assn. Broadcasters, S.C. C. of C. (dir. 1988—, pres. 1989-91, 97-98), UMWA Aux. (pres. 1982-89), Kiwanis (v.p. 1992—, pres. 1994), S.C. Ambassadors (pres. 1995-96), Ft. Phil Kearney/Bozeman Trail (bd. dirs. 1995—). Republican. Christian Ch. Office: Best We Sheridan Ctr PO Box 4008 Sheridan WY 82801-1208 E-mail: judyt@fiberpipe.net.

TAYLOR, JUDITH CAROLINE, entrepreneur; b. Quincy, Ill., June 23, 1948; d. Earl George and Caroline Clara (Knuffman) Schenk; m. Richard Odell Taylor, Nov. 28, 1970; children: Alexander James and Nicholas James (twins). BA, Quincy (Ill.) U., 1985; grad., Unity Sch. Religious Studies, 1997. Ordained Unity minister, 1997. Resident mgr. Landing Heights Apts., Brighton, N.Y., 1973-75; facilitator adult student program Quincy U., 1983-85; dist. mgr. Creative Expressions, 1981-85; mgr. mem. svcs. Quincy Conv. and Visitors Bur., 1985; sales dir. Motor Inn Hotel, Quincy, 1986; entrepreneur Taylor Enterprises, 1985—; exec. dir. The Kensington, 1987-90; sales mgr., co-owner Taylor's Fine Furniture & Gifts, 1990-95; pastor, minister Unity Ch. Quincy, 1997-99; minister Christ Ch. Unity, 1999—. Cons., freelance designer. Designed, marketed series I and II Quincy Postcards, 1987, 90; photo show John Wood C.C., 1993. House tour chairperson Quincy Perserves Bd., 1989; pres. Quincy Newcomers Club, 1980; pres. Great Rivers Mothers of Twins, Quincy, 1979; student min. Unity Ch., Quincy, 1996, 97; vol. chaplain Blessing Hosp., Quincy, 1998—; br. mgr. Quincy Alzheimer's Assn., 1999—. Recipient Americanism award VFW, Quincy, 1966. Mem. AAUW, Older Womens League (pres. 1988), Altrusa Club, League of Women Voters, Quincy Area Ministerial Assn. (v.p. 1999—). Avocations: photography, poetry writing. Home: 1461 Maine St Quincy IL 62301-4260

TAYLOR, KAREN ANNETTE, mental health nurse; b. Kinston, N.C., Oct. 7, 1952; d. Emmett Green and Polly Ann (Taylor) Tyndall; m. Paul Othell Taylor Jr, June 24, 1979 (div. 1996); 1 child Clarissa Anne. AA, Lenoir C.C., Kinston, 1972; Diploma, Lenoir Meml. Hosp. Sch. of, Nursing, 1984; student, St. Joseph's Coll., Windham, Maine, 1993-94. RN NC. Staff nurse Lenoir Meml. Hosp., 1984-86; staff nurse, relief patient care dir. Brynn Marr Hosp., Jacksonville, N.C., 1987-90; staff nurse, quality assurance Naval Hosp., Camp Lejeune, 1990-92. Recipient Meritorious Unit Commendation, Am Fedn Govt Employees, 1992. Baptist. Avocations: reading, crocheting. E-mail: karent@ncfreedom.net.

TAYLOR, KATHLEEN (CHRISTINE TAYLOR), physical chemist, researcher; b. Cambridge, Mass., Mar. 16, 1942; d. John F. and Anna M. (Maloney) T. BA in Chemistry, Douglass Coll., New Brunswick, N.J., 1964; PhD in Phys. Chemistry, Northwestern U., 1968. Postdoctoral fellow U. Edinburgh, Scotland, 1968-70; assoc. sr. rsch. chemist Gen. Motors Rsch. Labs., Warren, Mich., 1970-74, sr. rsch. chemist, 1974-75, asst. phys. chemistry dept. head, 1975-83, environ. sci. dept. head, 1983-85, phys. chemistry dept. head, 1985-96; physics and phys. chemistry dept. head Gen. Motors Global Rsch. & Devel. Operations, 1995-98, materials and protesses dir., 1998—2002. Recipient Mich. Sci. Trailblazer award Detroit Sci. Ctr., 1986. Fellow AAAS, mem. NAE, Am. Chem. Soc. (Garvan medal 1989), Materials Rsch. Soc. (treas. 1984, 2d v.p. 1985, 1st v.p. 1986, pres. 1987), Soc. Automotive Engrs., The Catalysis Soc., Sigma Xi.

TAYLOR, KATHY DEANNE, marketing executive; b. Peoria, Ill., Sept. 20, 1951; d. Chas S. and Carol A. (McDonough) Guynn; m. Harold N. Taylor Jr. (dec. Nov. 1982); 1 child, Shawn. AA in Bus., Ill. Cen. Coll., Peoria; student in mktg. mgmt., Sangamon State, Springfield. Mgr. sales Credit Bur. Accounts, Inc., Peoria, 1986-87; sales exec. Rsch. Inst. Am., N.Y.C., 1987-93, mem. adv. coun., 1989, pres. bd., 1990-91; sales exec. Paramount Comm., Waterford, Conn., 1993-95; govt. sales cons. West Group Thompson Legal Pub., 1995—2001; pres. bd. Million Dollar Club, 1998, 2 Million Dollar Club, 2000; owner A Sweet Arrangement, 1999—; sales exec. Lexis-Nexis , 2001; propr. A Sweet Arrangement, 2000—. Dir. cardiac ctr. Proctor Community Hosp., 1972-81, risk mgmt. coord., 1981-83; pres. Cen. Ill. Risk Mgmt., Inc., 1983-86. Chmn. bd. Tri-County Heart Assn., Peoria, 1987-88, pres., 1986-87; div. and regional mgr. Am. Heart Assn., Ill. affiliate, Springfield, 1985-89, mem. speakers bur., risk factor com., 1972-81; bd. dirs. Dept. Rehab. Svcs., 1989-91; active ARC hospice tng. Meth. Med. Ctr. Vol. Svcs.; asst. CE dir. Springfield Rd. Bapt. Ch., 2001-02. Mem. NAFE, Am. Inst. Banking, Peoria Jaycee Women (v.p. 1984), Ill. Jaycee Women (state chaplain, mgr. family life program 1984-85), Morton Jayceettes (pres. 1980). Republican. Home and Office: No Oaks Estates 2 Locust Grove Ct Groveland IL 61535-9764

TAYLOR, KENDRICK JAY, microbiologist; b. Manhattan, Mont., Mar. 17, 1914; s. William Henry and Rose (Carney) T.; m. Hazel Marguerite Griffith, July 28, 1945; children: Stanley, Paul (dec.), Richard. BS, Mont. State U., 1938; postgrad. (fellow), U. Wash., 1938-41, U. Calif., Berkeley, 1952, Drama Studio of London, 1985. Rsch. microbiologist Cutter Labs., Berkeley, Calif., 1945-74; microbiologist Berkeley Biologicals, 1975-86. Committeeman Mount Diablo coun. Boy Scouts Am., 1955, dist. vice-chmn., 1960-61, dist. chmn., 1962-65, cubmaster, 1957, scoutmaster, 1966; active Contact Ministries, 1977-80; bd. dirs. Santa Clara Cmty. Players, 1980-84; vol. instr. ESL, 1979-80; vol. ARC Blood Ctr., 1985-96, VA Hosp., 1986-96, San Jose; life mem. PTA; census taker, 1980; mem. Berkely Jr. C. of C., 1946-49. With AUS, 1941-46, lt. col. Res., ret. Recipient Scout's Wood badge Boy Scouts Am., 1962, Golden Diploma Mont. State U., 1988, Silver Diploma, 1998. Mem. Am. Soc. Microbiology (chmn. local com. 1953, v.p. No. Calif. br. 1963-65, pres. 1965-67), Sons and Daus. Mont. Pioneers, Mont. State U. Alumni Assn., Mont. Hist. Soc., Gallatin County Hist. Soc., Headwaters-Heritage Hist. Soc., Am. Legion (post 89), PTA Calif. (life). Presbyterian (trustee 1951-53, elder 1954—). Home: 550 S 13th St San Jose CA 95112-2361

TAYLOR, KENNETH DOUGLAS, stockbroker, finance and computer consultant, educator; b. Topeka, Nov. 21, 1942; s. Olin Orlando and Lola Louise (Conley) T.; AB, George Washington U., 1964, MS in Stats., 1966; MS in Computer Sci. SUNY, 1990, PhD in Math. Eurotech, 1992, (univ. fellow); student of Peter Hilton; postgrad., McGill U., 1974, Bowdoin Coll., U. Montreal; m. Joy Ellen Rice, May 25, 1973 (div. Nov. 1981); m. Elizabeth Flanagan Brunner, May 6, 1995. Registered rep./stockbroker, options principal. Sr. programmer C-E-I-R, Inc., 1963, 69; instr. Army Map Svc., 1964-65; student instr. McGill U., 1966-71; rsch. assoc. U. Va. Med. Sch., 1972; fin. and computer cons., Plymouth, N.Y., 1973-87; computer scientist USAF, 1989-90; broker Russell Hawkes Assoc./Linsco/Pvt. Ledger, 1993-94, LESKO Fin Svcs, 1994—; sec. Richmond (Va.) Computer Club, 1977. Contbr. articles to profl. jours. Summer grantee NSF, Can. Research Council. Mem. ASTM, Am. Math. Soc. Home: PO Box 288 Montrose PA 18801-0288 Office: LESKO Fin Svcs Centre Plz 53 Chenango St Binghamton NY 13901-2820

TAYLOR, KENNETH GRANT, chemistry educator; b. Paterson, N.J., May 12, 1936; s. Ulysses Grant and Susan (De Haan) T.; m. Carla May Rydell, June 17, 1961; children: Koren Lynn, Kevin Grant, Kaylyn Jo. BA, Calvin Coll., 1957; PhD, Wayne State U., 1963. Rsch. assoc. MIT, Cambridge, 1963-64; sr. rsch. assoc. Wayne State U., Detroit, 1964-66; from asst. to assoc. prof. chemistry U. Louisville, 1966-73, prof., 1974—, acting chmn., 1973-74, vice chmn., 1976-78, chmn., 1978-87, assoc. dean. Rsch., Arts and Scis., 1991-97. Prof. associé Univ. de Nancy I, France, 1974-75, 82-83; vis. prof. U. Lund, Sweden, 1991, Ecole Nationale de Chimie-Montpellier, France, 1997. Contbr. numerous articles to profl. jours.; co-author, presentor numerous papers at sci. meetings. Rsch. and teaching grantee NIH, NSF, Am. Cancer Soc., Am. Chem. Soc., Dept. Interior, U. Louisville, 1966—. Fellow AAAS; mem. Am. Chem. Soc., Ky. Acad. Sci. Democrat. Presbyterian. Home: 1838 Yale Dr Louisville KY 40205-2031 Office: U Louisville Dept Chemistry Louisville KY 40292-0001

TAYLOR, KENNETH J. diagnostic sonologist; b. Rochford, Essex, Eng., Mar. 8, 1939; s. William Albert and Florence (Soulsby) T.; m. Anne Bowen Simpkins, Apr. 8, 1964 (div. Nov. 1968); 1 child, Sally-Anne; m. Caroline Rix, May 17, 1975; children: Andrew, Ian. BSc, London U., 1961; MBBS, London U./Guys Hosp., Eng., 1964, PhD, 1972; MD, U. London, 1975; MA, FACP, Yale U., 1979. House surgeon Royal Surrey Hosp., Guildford, Eng., 1964-66; sr. house surgeon Guys Maudsley Hosp., London, 1966-67; jr. lectr. Guys Hosp. Med. Sch., 1967-70, lectr., 1970-72; sr. fellow Royal Marsden Hosp., Sutton, Surrey, Eng., 1973-75; assoc. prof. radiology Yale U., New Haven, 1975-77, assoc. prof., 1977-79, prof., 1979—, prof. vascular surgery and ob-gyn., 2000—; assoc. Yale-New Haven Hosp., 1975—; med. dir. Yale New Haven Sch. for Ultrasonography, 1975—. Co-dir. Yale Ctr. for Ultrasonics and Sonics, New Haven, 1991—; dir. Yale Vascular Lab., 1992—; ad hoc adv. bd. NIH, Washington. Chmn. editl. bd. Clinics in Diagnostic Ultrasound, 1978-2000; co-editor: Doppler in Clinic Diagnosis, 1988, 2d edit., 1995; assoc. editor Radiology Jour., 1992-97; author: Atlas of Ultrasound, 1978-2001, 2d edit., 1984; cons. to editor Radiology Jour., 1997-2000; mem. editl. bd. Ultrasound Med. Biology, 1975--, Jour. Ultrasound Medicine, 1980-2001, 02--, Clin. Ultrasound, Jour. Clin. Ultrasound. Bd. dirs. Friends of Hospice, New Haven, 1980. Lt. Royal Navy Res., 1962-65. Rsch. grantee Am. Cancer Soc., N.Y., 1976, 82, NIH Cancer Inst., Washington, 1988-89, 88-91. Fellow ACP, Am. Inst. Ultrasound Med. (bd. gov. 1978-82); mem. Radiol. Soc. N.Am. Achievements include pioneering applications for grey scale ultrasound, applications of Doppler ultrasound; ultrasonic contrast agents diagnosis and therapy of liver tumors. Avocations: travel, classical music, swimming, cycling, Italian culture. Home: 1611 Great Hill Rd Guilford CT 06437-3647 Office: 333 Cedar St New Haven CT 06510-3206 E-mail: kenneth.taylor@yale.edu.

TAYLOR, KENNETH NATHANIEL, publishing executive, writer; b. Portland, Oreg., May 8, 1917; s. George Nathaniel and Charlotte Bodwell (Huff) T.; m. Margaret Louise West, Sept. 13, 1940; children: Becky, John, Martha, Peter, Janet, Mark, Cynthia, Gretchen, Mary Lee, Alison. BA, Wheaton Coll., 1938, DLitt (hon.), 1965; student, Dallas Theol. Sem., 1940-43; ThM, No. Bapt. Theol. Sem., 1944; DLitt (hon.), Trinity Evang. Div. Sch., 1972; LHD (hon.), Huntington Coll., 1974, Taylor U., 1989. With Moody Press (pub. protestant religious lit.), Chgo., 1947-63, dir., 1948-62, Moody Lit. Mission (prodn. and distbn. lit.), 1948-62; pres. Tyndale House Publishers, 1963-84, chmn. bd., 1984—, Coverdale House Pubs., London, Eng., 1969-79. Pres. Tyndale House Found., 1964-79, bd. dirs., 1964—; dir. Inter-Varsity Christian Fellowship, 1956-59, Evang. Lit. Overseas, 1951-70, Short Terms Abroad, 1963-77; pres. Living Bibles Internat., Wheaton, Ill., 1968-77, internat. pres., 1977-90, internat. chmn. emeritus, 1990-92; chmn. Unilit., Inc., Portland, 1972-73 Author: Is Christianity Credible, 1946, Living Letters: The Paraphrased Epistles, 1962; juveniles Stories for the Children's Hour, 1953, Devotions for the Children's Hour, 1954, I See, 1958 (reprinted as Small Talks About God, 1995), Bible in Pictures for Little Eyes, 1956, Lost on the Trail, 1959, Romans for the Children's Hour, 1959; Living Prophecies - The Minor Prophets Paraphrased, 1965, Living Gospels, 1966, Living Psalms and Proverbs With the Major Prophets Paraphrased, 1967, The Living New Testament, 1967, Almost 12, 1968, revised, 1995, Living Lessons of Life and Love, 1968, Living Books of Moses, 1969, Living History of Israel, 1970, The Living Bible, 1971, Taylor's Bible Story Book, 1970, The Lord Is My Strength, 1975; juveniles What High School Students Should Know About Creation, 1983, What High School Students Should Know About Evolution, 1983, Big Thoughts for Little People, 1983, Giant Steps for Little People, 1985, Wise Words for Little People, 1987, Next Steps for New Christians (originally How To Grow), 1989, My First Bible in Pictures, 1989 (ann. Angel award 1990, Platinum Book award 1990), The Good Samaritan, 1989, Jesus Feeds A Crowd, 1989, The Lost Sheep, 1989, The Prodigal Son, 1989; Good News for Little People, 1991 (ann. Angel award 1992), My Life, A Guided Tour, 1991, Daniel and the Lions' Den, 1992, Noah's Ark, 1992, Family-Time Bible in Pictures, 1992, A Boy Helps Jesus, 1994, The Good Neighbor, 1994, Noah Builds a Boat, 1994, A Very Special Baby, 1994, The Story of Noah's Ark, 1994, Small Talks About God, 1995, Everything a Child Should Know About God, 1996; co-editor: The Bible for Children, 1990 (ann. Angel award 1991); pub. The Christian Reader, 1964-92, Have a Good Day, 68—; co-author: My First Bible Words: A Kid's Devotional, 1998, Right Choices, 1999, Family Devotions With Children, 1999, A Child's First Bible, 2000. Bd. dirs. Christian Libr. Svc., 1972-75, InterSkrift forlage Aktiebolag, Sweden, Internat. Bible Soc., 1992-94; trustee Living Bible Found., Fuller Theol. Sem.; mem. adv. bd. Internat. Bible Reading Assn. Recipient citation Layman's Nat. Bible Com., 1971; award Religious Heritage Am., 1972; disting. svc. citation Internat. Soc. Christian Endeavor, 1973; Nelson Bible award, 1973; Better World award VFW Aux., 1974; disting. pub. svc. award 1974; Recognition award Urban Ministries, Inc., 1977; Svc. award Wheaton Coll. Alumni Assn., 1977; Crusader award Wheaton Coll., 1979; Gutenberg award Chgo. Bible Soc., 1981; Internat. Christian Edn. Assn. award, 1983, Disting. Svc. to Family award Wheaton Coll. Alumni Assn.; Inducted into DuPage County Heritage Gallery, 1983; named Man of Yr. Com. Internat. Goodwill, 1983; recipient 1st Ann. Lit. award Evang. Lit. Overseas, 1983; Svc. award YFC/USA, 1984; Gold Medallion Achievement award Evang. Pubs. Assn., 1984; named to Christian Booksellers Hall of Fame, 1989; recipient Ann. James DeForest Murch award Nat. Assn. Evangelicals, 1995, Annual Golden Word award Internat. Bible Soc., 1996. Evangelical Christian Publ. Assn. awd. for leadership, example, integrity, creativity, and passion for communicating the Word of God, 1997. Mem. Wheaton Coll. Scholastic Honor Soc., Wheaton Coll. Alumni Assn. (Disting. Svc. to Family award 2000). Home: 1515 E Forest Ave Wheaton IL 60187-4469 Office: 351 Executive Dr Carol Stream IL 60188-2420 *Who but God could make an unending universe, sized by billions of light years? And who could dream of knowing such a God personally? I am one who believes this, and have based my life on the Bible as God's message to mankind, and to you and me. But how to manage Bible reading when it is in such an ancient language? How to crack the shell of the coconut and find the milk and meat? That is why I spent 16 years translating the Bible into living English, with 40 million copies now in print.*

TAYLOR, KENT (PAUL TAYLOR), poet, medical researcher; b. New Castle, Pa., Nov. 8, 1940; s. Paul Douthitt and Goldie Lucille (McKee) T.; m. Joan Czaban; 1 child, Mark; m. Helen Gladys Chapman (dec.); stepchildren: Sylvia Hughes, Robert Hughes. BA, Ohio Wesleyan U., 1962. Rsch. technician Case Western Res. U., Cleve., 1963-65, St. Vincent's Charity Hosp., Cleve., 1965-67; rsch. asst. Cleve. Met. Gen. Hosp., 1967-68, Mt. Sinai Hosp., Cleve., 1968-70; staff rsch. assoc. U. Calif., San Francisco, 1970-84. Author: Torn Birds, 1969, Cleveland Dreams, 1971, Driving Like the Sun, 1976, Aleatory Letters, 1964, Late Stations, 1966, Night Physics, 2002, also 11 other books; contbr. numerous poems to periodicals and anthologies. Avocations: sprinting, football, reading. Home: 1450 10th Ave San Francisco CA 94122-3603

TAYLOR, LANCE JEROME, economics educator; b. Montpelier, Idaho, May 25, 1940; s. Walter Jerome and Ruth (Robinson) T.; m. Yvonne S.M. Johnsson, May 31, 1963; children: Ian Lance, Signe Marguerite. BS with honors, Calif. Inst. Tech., 1962; PhD, Harvard U., 1968. Instr. econs. Harvard U., Cambridge, Mass., 1967-68, asst. prof., assoc. prof., 1970-74; research assoc. MIT, Cambridge, 1968-70, prof. econs., 1974-93, New Sch. for Social Rsch., N.Y.C., 1993—. Vis. prof. U. Brasilia, 1974, Pontifical Cath. U. Rio de Janeiro, 1981, U. Delhi, 1987-88, Stockholm Sch. Econs., 1990; Marshall lectr. Cambridge U., 1986-87; cons. World Bank, UN, various fgn. govts. Author: Macro Models for Developing Countries, 1979, Models of Growth and Distribution for Brazil, 1980, Structuralist Macroeconomics, 1983, Varieties of Stabilization Experience, 1988, Income Distribution, Inflation, and Growth, 1991, The Market Meets its Match: Restructuring the Economies of Eastern Europe, 1994, Global Finance at Risk, 2000, Restructuring Macroeconomics: Structuralist Proposals and Critiques of the Mainstream, 2003. Fulbright fellow, 1962-63 Mem. Am. Econ. Assn., Royal Econ. Soc. Home: PO Box 378 Washington ME 04574-0378 Office: New School for Social Rsch Grad Faculty 65 5th Ave New York NY 10003-3089 E-mail: lance@midcoast.com.

TAYLOR, LAWRENCE DOW, geologist, educator; b. Boston, Oct. 6, 1932; s. Theodore and Dorothea Mae (Dow) T.; m. Jean Ann Ryland, Sept. 24, 1955; children: Charles, Keith. AB, Dartmouth Coll., 1954, MA, 1958; PhD, Ohio State U., 1962. Geologist geophysics br. U.S. Geol. Survey, Boston, and Greenland, 1954-55, geologist fuels br. Denver, 1958; rsch. assoc. Dartmouth Coll., Hanover, N.H., and Greenland, 1957-58, Ohio State U. Inst. Polar Studies, Columbus, Ohio, and Antarctica, 1962-63, Glacier Bay, Alaska, 1959-60; asst. prof. Coll. of Wooster, Ohio, 1963-64, Albion (Mich.) Coll., 1964-68, assoc. prof., 1968-77, prof., 1977-98, prof. emeritus, 1998—, chair dept. geol. scis., 1968-85. Chief glaciologist Trans-Antarctic Traverse, NSF, U.S. Antarctic Rsch. Program, 1962-63. Contbr. articles to profl. jours. With U.S. Army, 1955-57. Grantee NSF, 1960, 62-63, 65, 69, Hewlett Melon Found., 1981, Pew Sci. Program, 1991, Albion Coll., 1992-97; recipient Exemplary Tchr. award United Meth. Ch., 1997, Mich. Campus Compact Cmty. Svc. award, 1998, Antarctic Svc. Congl. medal; Taylor Hills, Antarctica, named in his honor. Fellow Geol. Soc. Am., Am. Quaternary Assn., Am. Geophys. Union, Nat. Assn. Geology Tchrs. (pres. East Ctrl. sect. 1984-85), Explorers Club, Rotary, Sigma Xi. Avocations: mountain climbing, backpacking, cross country skiing, tennis. Office: Albion Coll Dept Geol Scis Albion MI 49224

TAYLOR, LEE, organization development practitioner; b. Knoxville, Tenn., 1950; d. Albert B. and Mary E. (Rhyne) Cleveland; divorced; 1 child, Mark Alyn. Diploma, St. Mary's Sch. Nursing, Knoxville, 1979; BA in Mgmt., Maryville Coll., 1990; MBA, Bristol U., 1992. Cert. psychiat./mental health nurse. Nurse adminstr. PRNS, Morristown, 1983-85; dir. nursing, adminstr. Meth. Med. Ctr. Home Health, Oak Ridge, Tenn., 1985-89; dir. quality assurance Superior Home Health Care Oak Ridge, 1989-91, asst. adminstr., 1991-93, adminstr., 1993-96; surveyor. J.C.A.H.O. Home Care Accreditation Svcs., 1992—; chief fin. officer, rsch. dir. Diagnostic Mgmt., Inc., 1995—; CFO, sr. cons., orgn. devel. practitioner Lazarus Consulting Group, 1995—. Nursing adv. com. Roane State Coll.; cons. home health agys.; rschr. in field. Recipient Sister Celeste Leadership award, 1978-79. Mem. Alpha Sigma Lambda. Home: Box 30244 Knoxville TN 37930-0244

TAYLOR, LEIGH HERBERT, college dean; b. Chgo., Oct. 23, 1941; s. Herbert and Leona Taylor; m. Nancy E. Young; children: Jennifer, Jeremiah. BA, U. Tulsa, 1964, JD, 1966; LLM, NYU, 1969. Bar: Okla. 1966, Ill. 1976. Trial atty. Civil Rights div. Dept. Justice, Washington, 1966-68; prof. DePaul U. Coll. Law, Chgo., 1969-77, asst. dean, 1972-73, assoc. dean, 1973-77; dean Coll. Law, Ohio No. U., Ada, 1977-78, Sch. Law Southwestern U., L.A., 1978—. Mem. adv. bd. 1st Woman's Bank of L.A., 1981-85; dir. Law Sch. Admissions Svcs., Inc., 1982-86; chmn. audit com. Law Sch. Admissions Coun., 1989-91, trustee, 1991-98, chair-elect, 1994-95, chair, 1995-97; mem. bd. trustees Coun. on Legal Edn. Opportunity, 1993-96, NALP Found., 1999-2003. Editor-in-chief Tulsa Law Jour., 1966; author: Strategies for Law-Focused Education, 1977; (with others) Law in a New Land, 1972; mem. editorial bd. Family Law Quarterly, 1977-78. Bd. dirs. Criminal Def. Consortium Cook County (Ill.), Inc., 1975-77, L.A. Press Club Found., NALP Found., 1999—. With AUS, 1959. Fellow Am. Bar Found.; mem. ABA (accreditation com. 1991-95), Law in Am. Soc. Found., Ill. Bar Assn., Chgo. Bar Assn. (rec. sec.), L.A. County Bar Assn., Okla. Bar Assn. Office: Southwestern U Sch Law Office of Dean 675 S Westmoreland Ave Los Angeles CA 90005-3905 E-mail: ltaylor@swlaw.edu.

TAYLOR, LEONARD STUART, engineering educator, consultant; b. N.Y.C., Dec. 28, 1928; m. Lillian Rachel Schlang, Apr. 12, 1954; children: Robin Jolie, Allyn Lise. AB, Harvard Coll., 1951; MSc, N.Mex. State U., 1955, PhD, 1960. Microwave engr. Raytheon Mfg. Co., Bedford, Mass., 1950-55; research physicist Gen. Electric Co., Phila., 1960-63; assoc. prof. Case Western Res. U., Cleve., 1964-67; prof. U. Md., College Park, Md., 1967-96, prof. emeritus, 1996—. Cons. USN, Silver Spring, Md., 1967-96. Contbr. articles to profl. jours; inventor Microwave Scalpel, Implantable Microwave Hyperthermia Applicator and numerous others. Recipient Disting. Alumni award, N.Mex. State U., 1975. Fellow IEEE (life), Am. Soc. for Laser Medicine and Surgery; mem. Am. Phys. Soc., Optical Soc. of Am., Bioelectromagnetics Soc. Avocations: tennis, music. Office: U Md Dept Ee College Park MD 20742-0001

TAYLOR, LESLI ANN, pediatric surgery educator; b. N.Y.C., Mar. 2, 1953; d. Charles Vincent Taylor and Valene Patricia (Blake) Garfield. BFA, Boston U., 1975; MD, Johns Hopkins U., 1981. Diplomate Am. Bd. Surgery. Surg. resident Beth Israel Hosp., Boston, 1981-88; rsch. fellow Pediatric Rsch. Lab. Mass. Gen. Hosp., 1984-86; fellow pediatric surgery Children's Hosp. of Phila., Phila., 1988-90; asst. prof. pediatric surgery U. N.C., Chapel Hill, 1990-97, assoc. prof. pediat. surgery, 1997—. Author: (booklet) Think Twice: The Medical Effects of Physical Punishment, 1985. Recipient Nat. Rsch. Svc. award NIH, 1984-86. Fellow Am. Coll. Surgeons; mem. AMA, Am. Acad. Pediatrics, Am. Pediat. Surg. Assn. Achievements include research on organ preservation for pediatric liver transplantation and short bowel syndrome. E-mail: lataylor@med.unc.edu.

TAYLOR, LESLIE GEORGE, mining and financial company executive; b. London, Oct. 8, 1922; came to U.S., 1925; s. Charles Henry and Florence Louisa (Renouf) T.; m. Monique S. Schuster, May, 1964 (div. 1974); children: Leslie G. Anthony II, Sandra J. Mira, Linda S. Marshall (dec. Feb. 17, 2002); m. Wendy Ann Ward, July 4, 1979. BBA, U. Buffalo, 1952. Asst. to pres. Kelsey Co., 1952-60; pres. Aluminum Industries and Glen Alden Co., Cin. and N.Y.C., 1960-63; pres., chmn. bd. dirs. DC Internat. (and European subs.), Denver, 1963-68; prin. Taylor Energy Enterprises, 1968—, Taylor Mining Enterprises, Denver, 1968—, Leslie G. Taylor and Co., Denver, 1968—. Del. Internat. Astronautical Soc., Stockholm, 1968, London, 69, Speditur Conv., 1976; bd. dir. Merendon Mining Internat., Calgary, Alta, Agri Health Internat., Agaro Internat., Inc.; sr. adv. Voice Mobility, Inc., Richmond, BC, Canada. Mem. USCG Aux. Mem. Soc. Automotive Engrs., Shriners, Masons, Scottish Rites. Republican. Episcopalian.

TAYLOR, LESTER DEAN, economics educator, consultant; b. Toledo, Mar. 8, 1938; s. Samuel George and Willa Emma (Brown) T.; m. Carol Austin, Aug. 13, 1966 (div. May 1980); children: James, Rebecca. BA, U. Iowa, 1960; PhD, Harvard U., 1963. Instr. Harvard U., Cambridge, Mass., 1963, asst. prof. econs., 1964-68; staff economist Coun. Econ. Advisers, Washington, 1964-65; adviser Harvard Inst. Internat. Devel., Bogotá, Colombia, 1967-68; assoc. prof. econs. U. Mich., Ann Arbor, 1969-74; prof. U. Ariz., Tucson, 1974—. Author: (with H.S. Houthakker) Consumer Demand in the U.S., 1966, 2d. rev. edit., 1970, Telecommunications Demand in Theory and Practice, 1980, 2d edit., 1994, Capital, Accumulation and Money, 2000. Woodrow Wilson fellow Harvard U., 1960-62. Mem. Am. Econ. Assn., Econometric Soc., Royal Econ. Soc., Phi Beta Kappa. Avocations: art, golf, numismatics. Office: U Ariz Dept Econs Tucson AZ 85721-0001

TAYLOR, LEWIS JEROME, JR. priest; b. Norfolk, Va., Feb. 22, 1923; s. Lewis Jerome and Roberta Page (Newton) T.; m. Pauline Rector Green, Nov. 24, 1945; children: Lewis J. III, Michael R., John B., Mary F., Joan E. BS in Engring., U.S. Naval Acad., 1944; MDiv, Seabury-Western Theol. Sem., Evanston, Ill., 1961; PhD in Religion, Duke U., 1972. Ordained priest Episcopal Ch., 1962. With George R. Green, Inc., White Post, Va., 1949-52, Travelers Ins. Co., Norfolk, 1956-58; chaplain Coll. William and Mary, Williamsburg, Va., 1961-63; rector St. Aidan's Episc. Ch., Virginia Beach,

1963-68; prof. theology St. Andrews Sem., Manila, The Philippines, 1971-76; rector Ch. of the Messiah, Chester, N.J., 1978-86; interim rector of various parishes Diocese of Southern Va., 1986-93; instnl. chaplain Indian Creek Correctional Ctr., Chesapeake, Va., 1993-98. Mem. Dept. Missions Diocese of Newark, 1965-68, Commn. on Ministry, Newark, 1979-82; dean Lay Sch. of Christian Studies, Newark, 1977-82; chmn. Commn. on Racism, Southern Va., 1992-95. Author: In Search of Self: Life, Death, and Walker Percy, 1985; contbr. articles to profl. jours. Bd. dirs. Samaritan House, Virginia Beach, 1995—. Comdr. USN, 1944-49, 52-56; PTO. Trinity Inst. grantee, 1986. Mem. Rotary (pres. 1980-86). Democrat. Avocations: tennis, camping, reading, writing.

TAYLOR, LINDA P. director, corporate financial executive; b. Maywood, Calif., June 30, 1950; d. Wm. Kenneth and Beverly Duncan Palmer; m. Sterling H. Taylor; 1 child Mark. BS in Engring., U. Calif., Irvine, 1972, MS in Engring., 1973; MBA, Pepperdine U., 1977. Cert. life and health Calif. Dept. Ins.; lic. NASD series 6, 63 & 65, cert. coll. funding advisor. Rsch. engr. Chevron Oil Field Rsch. Co., La Habra, Calif., 1973—77; oil and gas engr. Chevron USA, San Francisco, 1977—80, chief engr. Goleta, 1980—88; prin. engr., ops. mgr. Harding Lawson Assocs., Thousand Oaks, 1988—91; v.p. ops. Taylor Motorsports Mktg., Oxnard, 1991—96; prin. adviser, CEO Coll. Funding Assocs., Inc., Agoura Hills, 2002. Charter mem. Coll. Fin. Referral Network (R), Agoura Hills, 1999—. Author: (book) Motorsports Advantage Program Workbook, 1992, Sending Your Child to College Without Going Broke, 2000, Christian Family's Guide to Sending Your Child to College WIthout Going Broke, 2002. Mem.: Conejo Valley LeTip, Camarillo Pride Lions Club. Avocation: motorcycling. Office: Coll Funding Assocs Inc Ste 101 30401 Agoura Rd Agoura Hills CA 91301 Office Fax: 818-597-9780. Business E-Mail: lindaptaylor@hotmail.com.

TAYLOR, LINDA RATHBUN, investment manager; b. Rochester, N.Y., May 25, 1946; d. Lewis Standish and Elizabeth (Florence (Hunt) Rathbun; m. Donald Gordon Taylor, Mar. 1, 1975; children: Alexander Standish, Abigail Elizabeth, Elizabeth Downing. BA, Vassar Coll., 1968; MBA, Harvard U., 1973. Chartered fin. analyst. Assoc. corp. fin. Donaldson, Lufkin & Jenrette, N.Y.C., 1973-75; cons. IBRD, Washington, 1975; fin. analyst U.S. Treas. Dept., 1976-78; chief investment officer United Mine Workers Fund, 1978-85; investment mgr. Cen. Pension Fund Internat. Union Oper. Engrs., Washington, 1985-86; investment banker Saranow Co., 1986-89; pvt. investor, 1990—; mng. ptnr. Sakonnet Mgmt., LLC, 1998-2000. Pres. Boundary Farm Inc.; CEO CMAC, LLC, 2001—; bd. dirs. J.P. Morgan Venture Capital Investors, J.P. Morgan Corp. Fin. Investors. Contbr. articles to profl. jours. Trustee Montgomery County (Md.) Employees' Retirement Sys., 1987-93; bd. dirs. Washington Internat. Horse Show, 1995—; com. mem. Vassar Coll. Endowment Fund, 1992—; elder Bradley Hills Presbyn. Ch., 1992-95; bd. pensions Presbyn. Ch. U.S.A., 1996-99; dir. Va. Horse Shows Assn. Found., 1998—. Recipient Disting. Alumni award Carolina Day Sch., 1996. Mem. Jr. League Washington, Washington Soc. Investment Analysts (bd. dirs. 1984-85), Fin. Analyst Fedn. Republican. E-mail: ponyprod@aol.com.

TAYLOR, LINDSAY DAVID, JR. health care executive; b. Balt., Dec. 15, 1945; s. Lindsay David Sr. and Lillian Helen (Wagner) T.; children: Sarah Ruth, John David, Margaret Katherine. B in Mech. Engring., Rensselaer Poly. Inst., 1967; MBA, Dartmouth Coll., 1969. Bus. assoc. U.S. Steel Corp., Pitts., 1968-70; spl. asst. to asst. sec. for health HEW, Washington, 1970-71, mgr. operational planning, 1971-74, dep. asst. sec. mgmt., 1977-79; programming officer World Bank, 1974-76; dir. exams. and supervision Fed. Home Loan Bank Bd., 1979-81; exec. v.p. Perpetual Bank, Alexandria, Va., 1981-89; pres., CEO Columbia (Md.)-FreeState Health Sys., 1989-91, Preferred Health Network, 1992-96; CEO Alpha Health Plan, 1997-99; COO NPD, LLC, Bethesda, Md., 1999—, Nat. Assn. Cmty. Health Ctrs., Washington, 2001—. Cons. Nat. Acad. Pub. Adminstrn., Washington, 1985—86, Ctr. for Advancement of Health, Washington, 1988—89, Diabetex Corp., Balt., 1996—2001; trustee Md. Sci. Ctr., 1996—2000; co-chair Greater Balt. Health Care Coun., 1996—2001, Leadership Md., 1996; bd. adv. Found. for Island Health, 2001—02. Recipient Mgmt. Improvement award Pres. U.S., 1973, 77. Mem. Ctr. for Excellence in Govt. (prin. 1986-2002), Washington Coun. Govts. (devel. policy com. 1986-89), Tau Beta Pi, Pi Tau Sigma, Edward Tuck Scholar. Avocations: photography, folk music instruments, travel, wilderness, basketball. Office: 4800 Montgomery Ln Ste 1000 Bethesda MD 20814-3472 also: Ste 210 7200 Wisconsin Ave Bethesda MD 20814 E-mail: L_DavidTaylor@yahoo.com.

TAYLOR, LISA CANTER, poet, writer; b. Hartford, Conn., June 16, 1954; s. Daniel and Helen Joy Canter; m. Russell W. Taylor, Jr., Aug. 8, 1981; children: Justin, Kira. BA, U. Conn., 1979, MA, 1981. Psychotherapist EASTCONN., Columbia, 1997—99; staff devel. specialist, writer-in-residence EASTCONN, Hampton, 2000—. Author: Falling Open, 1993, Safe Love and Other Political Arts, 1995, poetry in anthologies, 1995, 1996; contbr. Recipient Nat. Scholastic Writing award 1st prize Poetry award, 1972. Mem. Poetry Soc. Am., Still River Writers. Avocations: walking, reading, bicycling. Home: PO Box 484 Mansfield Center CT 06250 E-mail: dreamingchange@hotmail.com.

TAYLOR, LIVINGSTON VERNON, retired newspaper reporter; b. Charleston, Ill., July 25, 1930; s. Edson Homer and Beryl Inglis Taylor; m. Lynn Putney, June 12, 1954 (div. Nov. 1961); children: Laurie Taylor Mitchell, Matthew E., Robin Pintar; m. Elizabeth Ann Hall, Nov. 24, 1967 (div. Mar. 1982); m. Sarah Kaighn Tignor, Nov. 26, 1983. BSJ, Northwestern U., 1952. Aviation cadet, navigation instr. USAF, Waco and Houston, 1952-56; reporter Muncie (Ind.) Star, 1956-60; reporter So. Ind. news bur. Louisville Courier-Jour., New Albany, Ind., 1961-63, reporter State Capital news bur. Frankfort, Ky., 1964-66; reporter Louisville Times, 1966-67; freelance reporter Frankfort, 1967-68; news bur. mgr. UPI, 1968-69; reporter State Capital news bur. Louisville Courier Jour., 1969-87. Mem. delegation to observe civil war and peace efforts Witness for Peace, Nicaragua, 1987; chmn. Spl. Commn. on Election Reform, Frankfort, 1988; chmn. Ky. Exec. Br. Ethics Commn., Frankfort, 1992-95; Bible study leader Franklin County Jail, Frankfort, 1988—; staff mem. Pulitzer Prize for Pub. Svc., 1966. Recipient award for Outstanding Reporting of Pub. Affairs, Am. Polit. Sci. Assn., 1958; Gerald Loeb award for disting. bus. and fin. journalism UCLA, 1976; named to Ky. Journalism Hall of Fame, 1991, Nat. Pub. Pks. Tennis champion, 65 and over singles, 1995, 70 and over doubles, 2001. Mem. Soc. Profl. Journalists. Presbyterian. Avocations: tennis, gardening. Home: 1196 Nineveh Rd Frankfort KY 40601-8433

TAYLOR, LYN ANN, principal; b. N.Y.C., Dec. 27, 1942; d. Edward H. and Ann G. McGuire; m. Turner Worthington Taylor, Feb. 1, 1975; children: Christopher Edward, Adam Worthington. BS in Elem. Edn., St. John's U., Jamaica, N.Y., 1964; MA in Edn. Adminstrn., LaSalle U., 2000. Tchr. grade 2 St. Mary's Sch., Manhasset, N.Y., 1964-65; tchr. grades 2, 4, 5 and 6 Wantagh (N.Y.) Sch. Sys., 1965-69; tchr.-prin. grades K, 1, 2 and 4 Dept. Def. Overseas Sch., Japan, Philippines, Cuba, 1969-74; substitute tchr. Health, Edn. and Welfare, P.R., 1975-77, various schs., R.I., 1980-89; pres. sch. bd. St. Lucy's Sch., Middletown, R.Il., 1982-86; prin. St. Joseph's Sch., Beverly, N.J., 1995—. Team leader Dept. Def., Japan, Philippines, Bahamas, Cuba, 1969-74; pres. sch. bd. St. Lucy's Sch., Middletown, R.I., 1982-84. Mem. ASCD, NAFE, Nat. Cath. Educators Assn. (chairperson conv. New Orleans 1999), Pvt. Sch. Mgmt. Roman Catholic. Avocations: oil painting, dancing, traveling, raising Great Danes. Home: 24 Merion Rd Marlton NJ 08053 Office: St Josephs Sch 805 Warren St Beverly NJ 08010

TAYLOR, MARGARET TURNER, clothing designer, architectural designer, economist, writer, planner; b. Wilmington, N.C., May 7, 1944. A.B. in Econs., Smith Coll., 1966; M.A. in Econ. History, U. Pa., 1970, now Ph.D. candidate in City and Regional Planning. Tchr. Jefferson Jr. High Sch., New Orleans, 1966-69; instr. econs. U. Tex.-El Paso, 1974-75; adj. prof. econs., Salisbury State U., Md., 1976-78; prin. mgr., designer Margaret Norriss, women's clothing, Salisbury, Md., 1980-95; owner Functional Design Ideas, Inc., 1995—; planner at Wharton Ctr. Applied Research, Phila., 1985-86; planning cons., writer.

TAYLOR, MARGARET UHRICH, educational administrator; b. Lebanon, Pa., Nov. 27, 1952; d. William Murray and Anne (Schultz) Uhrich; m. Timothy Norman Taylor, Sept. 29, 1979; 1 child, Walter Marshall. BA, Shippensburg U., 1974. Adminstrv. asst. Patriot-News Co., Harrisburg, Pa., 1974; reporter Pub. Opinion sect., Chambersburg, 1975-78; assoc. editor, Miami bur. chief OAG, Inc., N.Y.C., 1978-79; dir. mktg., pub. affairs Wilson Coll., Chambersburg, 1980-90, co-founder women in transition program, 1985; pres. Margaret Taylor's Mktg. Comms., 1989; sr. rschr. Brizius & Foster, McConnellsburg, Pa., 1990, pvt. practice cons., 1990—; exec. dir. Fulton County Econ. Devel. Corp., 1993-96, Fulton Indsl. Devel. Assn., McConnellsburg, 1997-2000; comm. chair Pa. Econ. Devel. Assn., 1997-2000; owner McConnellsburg Inn, 1992-2000; dir. instnl. advancement Pa. State U. Mt. Alto Campus, 2000—. Adj. faculty Shippensburg U., Pa., 1981-90; lectr. comms. Wilson Coll. Founding mem. Commonwealth Assn. Students, 1972; charter mem. Friends of Fulton County Libr., McConnellsburg, 1975; founder Unforgettable Charity Ball, Chambersburg, 1983-86; active Gotemba Sister-City Com., Borough of Chambersburg, 1981-90; pub. rels. counsel Greater Chambersburg Area United Way, 1985-90; cons. dir. Straight Love Franklin County, Chambersburg, 1982-83; founder Women's Network Franklin County, 1982-90; bd. dirs. Fulton County Med. Ctr. Corp., 1987-93, sec. 1989-90, vice-chmn. 1990-91, chmn. 1992-93; bd. dirs. Pa. Downtown Ctr. Assn., 1998-2000, Fulton County Tourist Promotion Agy., 1995-2000, Pa. Rural Devel. Coun., 1999-2001. Mem. Soc. Profl. Journalists (treas. Central Pa. chpt. 1981-82, v.p. 1982-83, pres. 1983-84, chmn. freedom of info. com. 1980-81, chpt. del. nat. conv. 1977). Rotary (bd. dirs. 2000—). Home: 121 W Market St Mc Connellsburg PA 17233-1007

TAYLOR, MARGARET WISCHMEYER, retired language educator; b. Terre Haute, Ind., Aug. 5, 1920; d. Carl and Grace (Riehle) Wischmeyer; m. John Edward Taylor, Sept. 5, 1942 (dec. 1988); children: Deborah Ann, Tobin Edward, Mary Leesa. BA magna cum laude, Duke U., Durham, 1941; MA, John Carroll U., Cleve., 1973. Feature writer Dayton (Ohio) Daily News, 1945-53; freelance writer Cleve., 1953—; asst. to Dr. Joseph B. Rhine Duke U. Parapsychology Lab., Durham, NC, 1941; asst. prof. English and journalism Ea. Campus, Cuyahoga CC, Cleve., 1973-92, prof. emeritus, 1992—, advisor campus newspaper, 1973-84, dir. Writers Conf., 1975-90. Writing cons., editor various cos. and pubs., Cleve., 1973—; founder, operator Grammar Hot Line, 1987-92. Author: Crystal Lake Reflections, 1985, English 101 Can Be Fun, 1991, The Basic English Handbook, 1995. Recipient top state honors Ohio Newspaper Women's Assn., 1947, award for best ednl., best overall stories Am. Heart Assn., 1970, Besse award for tchg. excellence, 1980, Profl. Excellence award, 1985, Provost's Pride award, 1987, Nat. Tchg. Excellence award Coun. for Advancement and Support of Edn., 1989; named Ohio Outstanding Citizen, Ohio Ho. Reps., 1987, 89, Innovator of Yr., League for Innovations in C.C.s, 1988, Pres.'s award Cuyahoga C.C., 1992. Mem. Mensa, Phi Beta Kappa, Pi Beta Phi. Presbyterian. Avocations: tennis, reading, writing. Home: 27900 Fairmount Blvd Cleveland OH 44124-4616 E-mail: taylorstock@ameritech.net.

TAYLOR, MARILYN L. finance educator, consultant; b. Hamilton, Ontario, Can., Apr. 27, 1942; arrived in U.S.A., 1956; d. Dwight S. and Reta (Finch) Levere; m. Robert E. Taylor, Apr. 1963; children: Theresa, Christopher. BA, U. So. Fla., 1967; MBA, Harvard U., 1974, DBA, 1979. Program dir. U. So. Fla., Tampa, Fla., 1967—72; from asst. prof. to prof. U. Kans., Lawrence, Kans., 1977—87, prof., 1987—94; from chair strategic mgmt. to dir. exec. MBA program U. Mo., Kans. City, Mo., 1994—2000, dir. exec. MBA program, 2000—. Bd. dir. European Case Clearing House Babson Coll., Wellsley, Mass., The Workman Found., Leavenworth, Kans.; cons. in field, 1975—. Mem. editl. bd.: Case Rsch. Jour., 1988—; contbr. articles to profl. jours.; co-author: The ICIC Program - an Executive MBA Business School Service-Learning Program Model, 2000—; co-author: (with Greg Dess & Thomas Lumpkin) Cases for Strategic Management, 2002—. Adv. bd. Initiative for Competitive Inner City-Kans. City, Kans. City, 1995—; local adv. bd. Local Initiative Support Corp., 1999—. Recipient Faculty Pioneer award, Aspen Inst. & World Resources Inst., 2001; scholar, The Ewing Marion Kauffman Found., 2001—. Fellow: No. Am. Case Rsch. Assn. (v.p. membership 1986—88, v.p. programs 1989—90, pres. 1991—92); mem.: Mid West Acad. Mgmt. (founding track chmn. 1998—2000, case rsch. com. 1998—2000), Nat. Bus. Sch. Network (steering com. 1998—2001, C.R. Christensen award 2000, Nat. finalist field studies project 2001, Nat. winner field studies project 2000, Outstanding Leadership award 2001), Acad. Mgmt. Avocations: piano, walking, reading, swimming, travel. Office: Bloch School Bus & Pub Administration Univ Mo 5110 Cherry Kansas City MO 64110

TAYLOR, MARK, lt gov; b. Atlanta, May 7, 1957; Degree in polit. sci., Emory U.; degree in law, U. Ga. Exec. Fred Taylor Co., Albany; mem. Ga. Senate, Atlanta, 1987—; asst. adminstrn. floor leader then adminstrn. floor leader Gov. Zell Miller; sec. transp. com.; mem. appropriations, ethics, ins. and labor, rules coms.; also reapportionment com.; lt. gov. State of Ga., Atlanta, 1999—. Mem. bd. dirs. March of Dimes, Albany/Dougherty 2000 Partnership, Thronateeska Heritage Found. Mem. Ga. Bar Assn., Dougherty County Bar Assn., Leadership Albany (charter), Artesian City Sertoma Club (past pres.), Rotary. Democrat. Office: Rm 240 State Capitol Atlanta GA 30334 E-mail: mtaylorx@legis.state.ga.us.*

TAYLOR, MARK ALAN, academic administrator; b. Mt. Vernon, Ill., Apr. 10, 1959; s. Roy Jr. and Lora Kathleen (Ashby) T.; m. Kimberly June Weldon, June 15, 1996. BS, Ariz. State U., 1981; PhD, Purdue U., 1986. Rsch. scientist Purdue U., West Lafayette, Ind., 1986-87; faculty assoc. Ariz. State U. West, Tempe, 1987-90; asst. prof. Grand Canyon U., Phoenix, 1987-92, assoc. prof., 1992-94, asst. v.p., 1990-92, prof., 1994—, v.p. program devel., 1992—. Lectr. Agrl. Coll., Urumchi, China, summer 1988; adj. assoc. prof., coord. med. edn. Kirksville (Mo.) Coll. Osteo. Medicine/S.W. Ctr., 1990-94, assoc. dean for adminstrv. affairs, 1994-95, asst. to pres., 1995—; acad. liaison and design cons. Alcyone Group Inc., 1995—; mem. Ariz. Advanced Placement Bd., Phoenix, 1987—, Ariz. Biology Conf., Phoenix, 1988—, Ariz. Alliance Sci. and Tech. Edn., Phoenix, 1987—. Author: Biochemistry of the Cell, 1989, Genetics: A Human and Molecular Approach, 1990, Microbiology: A Medical Frontier, 1989, Biology: Cell Structure and Function, 1989, 2d edit., 1991, Developmental Biology, 1991, Cell Biology, 1992, 96, 98, Careers in Health Care and Medicine, 1992, 94, 98; contbr. numerous articles to profl. jours. Mem. adv. coun. Salvation Army, Phoenix, 1990-93. Recipient James S. Mountain Meml. award, Founder's award Woods Hole Oceanographic Inst., 1984. Mem. AAAS, Soc. Devel. Biology, Am. Soc. Cell Biology, Am. Inst. Biol. Scis., N.Y. Acad. Sci., Ariz.-Nev. Acad. Sci., Sigma Xi, Phi Beta Kappa, Phi Kappa Phi. Republican. Methodist. Achievements include research in the regulation of translation and meiotic maturation in Xenopus laevis; development of health care education programs and consortiums. Avocations: basketball, fishing, international travel. Office: Grand Canyon Univ 3300 W Camelback Rd Phoenix AZ 85017-1097

TAYLOR, MARK DOUGLAS, publishing executive; b. Geneva, Jan. 16, 1951; s. Kenneth Nathaniel and Margaret Louise (West) T.; m. Carol E. Rogers, May 28, 1973; children: Jeremy Peter, Kristen Elizabeth, Margaret Louise, Rebecca Cynthia, Stephen Rogers. BA, Duke U., 1973. Exec. dir. Tyndale House Found., Wheaton, Ill., 1973-78; v.p. Tyndale House Pubs., 1978-84, pres., chief exec. officer, 1984—. Dir. Living Bibles Internat. U.S., Naperville, Ill., 1972-92; bd. trustees Taylor U., 1998—. Author The Complete Book of Bible Literacy, 1992. Mem. Wheaton Liquor Control Commn., 1986—, chmn., 1994—; chmn. bd. dirs. Outreach Cmty. Ctr., 1986-93. Mem. Internat. Bible Soc. (bd. dirs. 1992-96). Office: Tyndale House Publishers Inc PO Box 80 Wheaton IL 60189-0080 *What we accomplish in life is soon forgotten. Our best legacy is to pass on to our children and grandchildren our positive values.*

TAYLOR, MARTHA ELIZABETH (BETSY TAYLOR), investment company executive; b. Phila., Dec. 30, 1950; d. Harry Colvin and Jeannette M. (Hartwell) Taylor; 1 child, Jeannette E. Student, Phila. Coll. of Textiles & Science, Phila., 1990—. Telecommunications mgr. Miller Anderson & Sherrerd, West Conshohocken, Pa., 1985-89; asst. treas./sec., mgr. gen. affairs LTCB-MAS Investment Mgmt., Inc., 1989—. Office: LTCB-MAS Investment Mgmt Inc 1 Tower Brg Ste 1000 West Conshohocken PA 19428

TAYLOR, MARVA JEAN SHIPMAN FOULKS, social worker; b. Toledo, July 22, 1952; d. Marvin Morgan and Virginia Caroline (Wyse) Shipman. BA in Social Welfare and Psychology, Olivet U., 1973; MSW, U. Ill., Chgo., 1987. Lic. clin. social worker, Ill.; cert. sch. social worker. Social worker Ill. Dept. Mental Health, Manteno, 1973-84; social worker, child protective investigator Ill. Dept. Children and Family Svcs., Kankakee, 1984-99; social worker Tinley Park (Ill.) Mental Health Ctr., 1999—. Clarinetist Kankakee Mcpl. Band, 1989—. Mem. Nat. Assn. Social Workers, Acad. Cert. Social Workers. Mem. Nazarene Ch. Avocations: music, water sports, reading. Office: Tinley Park Mental Health Ctr 7400 W 183d St Tinley Park IL 60477

TAYLOR, MARVIN EDWARD, JR. lawyer; b. Smithfield, N.C., Oct. 15, 1937; s. Marvin Edward and Ellen Borden Broadhurst T.; m. Karin Gunilla Guggenheim, Nov. 29, 1969; 1 child, Karin Elizabeth Guggenheim. AB, U. N.C., 1960, JD with honors, 1965. Bar: N.Y. 1966, N.C. 1968, U.S. Dist. Ct. (ea. dist.) N.C. 1973, U.S. Ct. Appeals (4th cir.) 1974, Calif. 1976. Assoc. Nixon Mudge Rose Guthrie Alexander & Mitchell, N.Y.C., 1965-67, Sanford Cannon Adams & McCullough, Raleigh, N.C., 1967-71; atty. pvt. practice, 1972-75, 1984—; corp. counsel Memorex Corp., Santa Clara, Calif., 1975-80; atty. pvt. practice, Hickory, N.C., 1983. Dept. counsel GE Co., Hickory, NC, 1980—82; mem. staff N.C. Law Rev., 1964, rsch. editor, 65. Dir. Parents' Assn. N.C. State U., Raleigh, 1989-93, Coun. Entrepreneurial Devel, Research Triangle Park, N.C., 1985-88, chmn. pub. com., 1985-88; participant N.C. Ctr. Nonprofits Pro Bono Program, Raleigh, 1994—. With USAF, 1960-62. Mem.: Swedish-Am. C. of C. WSA (sec. 1999—2000), N.C. Bar Assn. (com. comml. banking and bus. law 1970—75, subcom. securities regulation 1972—75, bus. law sect. coun. 1982—90, internat. law com. 1990—92, internat. law and practice sect. coun. 1992—95, pub. info. com. 1995—2000, lawyers in the schs. com. 1999—, comm. com. 2000—), Swedish-Am. C. of C. of N.C. (co-founder, dir., sec.-treas. 1998—), Order of Coif. Democrat. Episcopalian. Avocations: skiing, photography, reading. Office: 119 SW Maynard Rd Cary NC 27511-4472

TAYLOR, MARY CURTIS SMITH, musician; b. Shepherdsville, Ky., Jan. 9, 1937; d. Curtis Waldo and Hazel Dell (Trunnell) Smith; m. John G. Taylor, Aug. 16, 1958; children: John Gordon Jr., Tiffany May, Whitney Adams. Student, U. Louisville, 1954-55, postgrad., 1966; MusB, Murray State U., 1958, MEd, 1960, Cert. in Sch. Libr. Media, Sch. Adminstrn. and Supervision, 1981; postgrad., U. So. Calif., 1976; MLS, Vanderbilt U., 1985. Pvt. tchr. music, 1954-91; tchr. music and phys. edn. Benton City Schs., Ky., 1958-60; tchr. music Jefferson County Sch. Dist., Louisville, 1960-64; with Nashville Symphony Orch., 1969-92; asst. prof., supr., student tchr. Murray (Ky.) State U., 1974-76; libr. technician Ky. Dept. for Librs. and Archives Field Svcs., 1981-89; dir. Calloway County Pub. Libr., Murray, 1989-90, West Wyandotte Libr., Kansas City, Kans., 1993—; string specialist USD500, 1993, Conroe Independent Sch. Dist. (ISD), Conroe, TX, 1993—. Music tchr. upward bound project Alice Lloyd Coll., Pippa Passes, Ky., 1967; music instr. string class Bethel Coll., McKenzie, Tenn., 1980; coord. KENCILIP/Inter-Libr. Loan, Murray, 1980. Touring Broadway musicals: Sound of Music, Hello, Dolly!, A Funny Thing Happened on the Way to the Forum, West Side Story, Carnival, Nutcracker Suite (concertmaster), Fiddler on the Roof. First violinist Nashville Symphony Orch., 1963-92; concertmaster Jackson Symphony Orch., 1974-88; first violin sect. Paducah (Ky.) Symphony Orch., 1981-91, The Des Moines Metro Summer Festival of Opera, Indianola, Iowa, 1978, Murfreesboro Symphony Orch. Middle Tenn. State U., 1973-91, Nashville Baroque Orch., 1974-76, Jackson Symphony Orch., 1969-91, Louisville Symphony Orch., 1969-76, Owensboro (Ky.) Symphony; concertmaster Louisville Youth Orch., 1955, Louisville Civic Orch., 1954-55, St. Joseph Symphony, Mo., 1991-92, Brazos Valley Symphony, 1993—, Tex. Acadiana Symphony, Lafayette, La., 1993—, Symphony S.E. Tex., Beaumont, 1993—, The Kingwood (Tex.) Pops Orch., 1996—; founder Conroe Symphony Orch., 1997—. Mem. ALA, AAUW, Am. String Tchrs. Assn., Am. Fedn. Musicians, Colonial Dames 17th Century, Sigma Alpha Iota. Avocations: collecting books, needlework, home decorating, travel, reading. Bus. Home: 8 Kensington Dr Conroe TX 77304-2707 E-mail: mataylor@conroe.isd.tenet.edu.

TAYLOR, MARY KAY, medical, surgical nurse; b. Knoxville, Iowa, Jan. 26, 1954; d. Wendell Shawver and Margery Ethel (Beebe) Kubli; m. Gregory Taylor, Sept. 4, 1993. ADN, Indian Hills Community Coll., 1979; BSN, Teikyo Marycrest U., 1993. RN, Iowa. Staff nurse Mercy Hosp., Des Moines, 1979-81, Knoxville Area Community Hosp., 1981-83, VA Med. Ctr., Knoxville, 1983-98, Iowa Meth. Med. Ctr., Des Moines, 1998—. Home: PO Box 646 Knoxville IA 50138-0646 E-mail: mtaylor@lisco.com.

TAYLOR, MARY LEE, retired college administrator; b. Amarillo, Tex., Nov. 13, 1931; d. David Kelly and Bessie F. (Peck) McGehee; m. Lindsey Taylor, Sept. 13, 1950 (dec. Aug. 1985); children: Gary, Kent, Ronald. BS, W. Tex. State U., 1959; MEd, Tex. Tech U., 1975. Tchr. Mesquite (Tex.) Pub. Schs., 1961-63; resource tchr. Amarillo Pub. Schs., 1971-79, supr., 1979-80; reading instr. Amarillo Coll., 1981-88, asst. prof. reading, 1988-93, assoc. prof., 1994-95; instr. GED Ctr. for Neighborhood Ministries, Phoenix, 2002—. Project dir. Tex. Edn. Agy., Austin, 1984-85, 85-86, Amarillo Coll., 1988-89. Mem. Tex. Assn. for Children with Learning Disabilities (meritorious svc. award 1985), Coll. Reading and Learning Assn. (spl. interest group leader 1987-89, cert. 1988, editor newsletter 1987-89), Am. Assn. Cmty. and Jr. Colls., North Plains Assn. for Learning Disabilities (pres. 1987-88, coord. accessibility svcs. 1993—), Tex. Assn. Developmental Educators (membership chmn. 1992-93), Assn. of Higher Edn. and Disabled Students. Avocations: camping, hiking. Office: GED Ctr for Neighborhood Ministries 1918 W Van Buren Phoenix AZ 85009 E-mail: mlltaylor@aol.com.

TAYLOR, MERYL CHRISTINE, protective services official; b. Tacoma; d. Tisdale Merlin Eugene and Lisa Valerie (Smith) Kuto; m. Stanley Johnson, Sept. 6, 1975 (dec. Aug. 1981); children: Brittainy Johnson, Zachary Johnson; m. Richard L. Jaylor Jr., Feb. 2, 1985; children: Ashley Fay, Nicholas Koai. BS in Psychology, Kent State U., 1977, A in Law Enforcement, 1979; cert. in bus. adminstrn., J.H. Thompson Acad., Erie, Pa., 1987; cert. peace officer, Sheriff's Acad., Jefferson, Ohio, 1991. Store detective Hills Dept. Store, Ashtahwa, Ohio, 1979-80, Fisher's Big Wheel, Conneaut, 1980-83, J.A. Conley 10, Kingsville, 1985-86, Nichols Dept. Store, Saybrook, N.Y., 1986-87, K-Mart, Ashtahwa, 1995-97; corrections officer Conneaut Police Dept., 1998—. Author: Earthbound, 1987, Scraps, 1988. Recipient Golden Poet award World Poetry, 1985, 87, Silver Poet award, 1988; Named Poet of Yr. Ash. Co. Writers Guild, 1995. Democrat. Lutheran. Avocations: writing, reading. Home: 416 Bank St Conneaut OH 44030-2804 Office: Conneaut Police Dept 294 Main St Conneaut OH 44030-2650

TAYLOR, MICHAEL ALAN, psychiatrist; b. N.Y.C., Mar. 6, 1940; s. Edward D. and Clara D. T.; m. Ellen Schoenfield, June 28, 1963; children—Christopher, Andrew. BA, Cornell U., 1961; MD, N.Y. Med. Coll., 1965. Intern Lenox Hill Hosp., N.Y.C., 1965-66; resident N.Y. Med. Coll., 1966-69, asst. prof. psychiatry, 1971-73; asso. prof. SUNY Med. Sch., Stony Brook, 1973-76; prof. psychiatry Univ. Health Scis., Chgo. Med. Sch., 1976—, dept., 1976-94. Author: The Neuropsychiatric Mental Status Examination, 1981; sr. author: General Hospital Psychiatry, 1985, The Neuropsychiatric Guide to Modern Everyday Psychiatry, 1993, The Fundamentals of Neuropsychiatry, 1999; editor-in-chief Neuropsychiat., Neuropsychology and Behavioral Neurology Jour.; also numerous articles. Served to lt. comdr. M.C. USNR, 1969-71. Grantee NIMH, 1971-73; Grantee Ill. Dept. Mental Health, 1976-81; VA grantee, 1985-93. Mem. Am. Psychopath. Assn. Office: FUHS Chgo Med Sch 3333 Green Bay Rd North Chicago IL 60064-3037

TAYLOR, MICHAEL BROOKS, economist, educator; b. Ann Arbor, Mich., Mar. 18, 1944; s. William Brooks and Roma G. (Sims) T.; m. Cynthia Wiebol dt, Sept. 26, 1972 (div.); children: William B., Catherine Hallie. BA, Carleton Coll., 1966; PhD, Harvard U., 1976; MBA, Ohio U., 1984. Asst. prof. Occidental Coll., L.A., 1974-76, Berea (Ky.) Coll., 1976-77, Marietta (Ohio) Coll., 1977-86, assoc. prof., 1986-94, prof., 1994—. Vis. assoc. prof. mgmt. Southwestern U. of Finance & Econ., China, 1986-87; vis. prof. Fgn. Affairs Coll., China, 1996. Co-author: Pictorial Guide to America Spinning Wheels, 1975; author (book chpt.): Ready for the Real World, 1994. Recipient McCoy Disting. Professorship, Marietta Coll., 1994-99. Mem. Soc. Values of Higher Edn., Am. Mktg. Assn. (Mid-Ohio Valley chpt. pres. 1992-93). Avocations: spinning wheel historian, golf, tennis. Office: Marietta College 102 Thomas Hall Marietta OH 45750

TAYLOR, MICHAEL GEORGE, lawyer; b. Harvey, Ill., Aug. 28, 1955; s. Howard George Taylor; m. Diann Marie Taylor, Aug. 11, 1984; children: Christopher, Sarah, Nathan, Daniel, Jacob. BA in Philosophy, U. Wis., 1977;

MA in Philosophy, U. Mich., 1979, JD, 1984. Bar: Minn. 1984. Shareholder Leonard, Street and Deinard, Mpls., 1991—. Mem. Phi Beta Kappa. Office: Leonard Street and Deinard 150 S 5th St Ste 2300 Minneapolis MN 55402-4238

TAYLOR, MICHAEL LESLIE, lawyer; b. Boonville, Mo., Nov. 2, 1954; s. Paul Howard and Nora Lee T.; m. Janet S. Finke, June 23, 1990. AA, Kansas City Communtiy Coll., 1977; BGS, U. Kans., 1979, JD, 1982. Bar: Mo. 1982, U.S. Dist. Ct. Mo. 1982, U.S. Ct. Appeals (10th cir.) 1986, U.S. Ct. Appeals (8th cir.) 1987, U.S. Supreme Ct. 1999. Assoc. atty. Watkins, Boulware, Lucas & Miner, St. Joseph, Mo., 1982-85, ptnr., 1986-87, Watkins, Boulware, Lucas, Miner, Murphy & Taylor, St. Joseph, 1987—. Instr. Mo. Western State Coll., St. Joseph, 1985-94. Bd. mem. Midland Empire Diabetes Assn., St. Joseph, 1984; mem. United Way Allocations Com., St. Joseph, 1985-86; pres. East Hills Homes Assn., St. Joseph, 1987-89; co-chair Leadership Tomorrow, St. Joseph, 1985-88; pres. Center Court Homes Assn., St. Joseph, 2002--. Recipient Outstanding Vol. Svc. to the City Vol. award City St. Joseph, 1985, Lon O. Hocker Meml. Trial LAwyer award Mo. Bar Found., 1989. Fellow Am. Acad. Matrimonial Lawyers; mem. ABA, Mo. Bar Assn., St. Joseph Bar Assn., Million Dollar Advocates Forum. Avocations: reading, tennis, weightlifting. Office: Watkins Boulware Lucas Miner Murphy & Taylor 3101 Frederick Ave Saint Joseph MO 64506-2911 E-mail: mike.taylor@wblmmt.com.

TAYLOR, MILDRED LOIS, nursing home administrator; b. Conroe, Tex., July 23, 1927; d. George Carl and Bertha Elizabeth (Swift) Ferguson; student Hunter Coll., 1944, U.S. Navy Hosp. Corps Sch., Bethesda, Md., 1944, corr course Am. Sch., Chgo., 1971, Central Tex. Coll., 1971, U. Tex., Austin, 1975; m. Thomas Nielsen Taylor, Dec. 1, 1945; children— Linda Sue, Thomas Grant, Charles Nielsen. Nurse aide St. David's Hosp., Austin, Tex., 1965-67; adminstr.-in-tng. North Lamar Nursing Home, Austin, 1971-72, adminstr., 1973-75; adminstr. Austin Nursing & Convalescent Center, 1976— , sec., treas., 1976— . Pres. Episcopal Women of the Ch., Austin, 1966; mem. Tex. Nursing Home Adminstrs. Polit. Action Com., 1976— . Served with WAVE, USNR, 1944-45. Lic. nursing home adminstr., Tex. Mem. Tex. Nursing Home Assn., Am. Health Care Assn., Austin C. of C., U.S. C. of C. Clubs: Lost Creek Country, Order Eastern Star, St. David's Hosp. Women's Aux. (Austin). Office: 110 E Live Oak St Austin TX 78704-4355 Home: 301 Nicole Way Bastrop TX 78602-6629

TAYLOR, MINNA, lawyer; b. Washington, Jan. 25, 1947; d. Morris P. and Anne (Williams) Glushien; m. Charles Ellett Taylor, June 22, 1969; 1 child, Amy Caroline. BA, SUNY, Stony Brook, 1969; MA, SUNY, 1973; JD, U. So. Calif., 1977. Bar: Calif. 1977, U.S. Dist. Ct. (cen. dist.) Calif. 1978. Extern to presiding justice Calif. Supreme Ct., 1977; field atty. NLRB, L.A., 1977-82; dir. employee rels., legal svcs. Paramount Pictures Corp., 1982-85, v.p. employee rels. legal svcs., 1985-89; dir. bus. and legal affairs Wilshire Ct. Prodns., 1989-91; sr. counsel Fox Broadcasting Co., 1991-92, v.p. legal affairs, 1992-97, sr. v.p. legal affairs, 1997—. Webmaster www.ifcome.com, 2001—. Editor notes and articles: U. So. Calif. Law Rev., 1976-77. Mentor MOSTE, L.A., 1986-87, 88-89; pres. Beverly Hills chpt. ACLU, L.A., 1985. Fellow ABA, Calif. State Bar (mem. copyright subcom. 1994-95), L.A. County Bar Assn.; mem. Beverly Hills Bar Assn., L.A. Bead Soc. (membership sec. 1992-94, mem. bd. dirs. 1994-95), Order of Coif. Office: Fox Broadcasting Co 10201 W Pico Blvd Los Angeles CA 90064-2606

TAYLOR, MURRY ALLAN, retired forester; b. Fresno, Calif., Mar. 1, 1941; s. Hubert Murry and Patricia Ann (Rooney) Taylor; 1 child Eric Murry. BS in Forest Mgmt., Humboldt State U., Arcata, Calif., 1965. Smokejumper U.S. Forest Svc., Redding, Calif., 1965, forester Ft. James, 1966—72, Idyllwild, 1969—73; smokejumper Alaska Fire Svc., Fairbanks, 1973—80; horse logger Greenview, Calif., 1980; smokejumper Bur. Land Mgmt., Boise, Idaho, 1987, Alaska Fire Svc., Fairbanks, 1988—2001; ret., 2001. Tchr. San Jacinto C.C., Calif., 1973; lectr. in field. Author: (book) Jumping Fire: A Smokejumper's Memoir, 2000 (named to L.A. Times List of Best Books of 2000). Mem. Scott Valley II Land Planning Group, Ft. James, 1975—78. Mem.: Nat. Smokejumpers Assn. (life; bd. dirs. 1999—2002), Jane Goodall Inst. Green Party. Avocations: solar power, racing dirt track cars.

TAYLOR, NATHALEE BRITTON, nutritionist; b. Lubbock, Tex., June 8, 1941; d. Nathaniel E. and Dessie Pauline (Moss) Britton; children by previous marriage: Clay H., Bret N. Courtney. BS in Home Econs., Tex. Tech U., 1963. Home economist Pioneer Gas, Lubbock, Tex., 1963-65; dietitian Tex. Tech U., 1966-71; home economist South Plains Electric Co-op., 1986; mgr. quality control Rip Griffins Enterprises, Tex., 1987; sales rep. Time Chem., 1987—; with Sentry; mktg. rep. Dodson Group Ins., Farmers Ins., Lubbock, Southwestern Bell Wireless. Co-author: (cookbook) From Our House to Yours, 1975; columnist: Lubbock Lights mag.; presenter TV show Southwestern Cooking Sta. KTXT. Bd. dirs. Am. Heart Assn., Lubbock, 1985-87; mem. Home Economist in Bus. (pres. Lubbock chpt., 1985); culinary co-chmn. Lubbock C. of C. Arts Festival, 1982, 83, 84. Named Lincoln County Fair Queen. Mem. Tech. Home Econs. Alums (sec./treas.), Am. Home Econs. Assn. (v.p., sec./treas.), Bd.-Cove, Soroptomist (v.p. Lubbock club). Democrat. Avocations: gardening, writing, cooking, horseback riding.

TAYLOR, NELL COCHRANE, non-profit association executive; b. Bklyn., Dec. 25, 1929; d. Zeddie Marshall and Eunice Hamilton C.; m. Timothy M. Taylor, Sr., June 11, 1955 (div. June 1988); children: Timothy, Stuart, Blair, Scott, Marshall. AB cum laude, Smith Coll., Northampton, Mass., 1951; MA, Yale U., 1952; postgrad., Hunter Coll., 1952-56, The New Sch., N.Y. U., 1952-56. English tchr., guidance counselor Hunter Coll. H.S. of CUNY, N.Y.C., 1953-59; instr. lang. arts Coll. at Purchase/SUNY, N.Y., 1978-79; program adminstr. for tng. County of Westchester, White Plains, 1979-80; mgr. cmty. coll. rels., asst. to v.p. human resources The Continental Group, Stamford, Conn., 1980-84; mgr. rsch. comms. Cyrus J. Lawrence, Inc., N.Y.C., 1985-86; dir. adminstrv. svcs. Sheltering Arms Chldrn.'s Svc., 1988-90; exec. dir. The White Plains Child Day Care Assn., Inc., 1990-97; ednl. cons. Scarborough, N.Y., 1998—. Devel. cons. County of Westchester, Dept. Cmty. Mental Health, White Plains, 1987-88; mem. Not-for-Profit Mgmt. Ctr. Adv. Bd., White Plains, 1995-97; v.p. Child Care Coun. of Westchester, White Plains, 1994-95, bd. dirs. 1992-98; exec. steering com. Ctr. for Pub. Rsch., N.Y.C., 1981-84; mem. Nat. Urban League's Commerce and Industry Coun., N.Y.C., 1981-84. Contbg. author: Social Aspects of Education, 1962. Bd. dirs. Scarborough Manor Owners Corp., 1999-2002; elder Mt. Kisco Presbyn. Ch., N.Y., 1999-2001; v.p. Yale Alumni Assn. of Westchester, White Plains, 1990-91, bd. dirs. 1990-93; bd. dirs. Planned Parenthood of Westchester/Rockland, White Plains, 1989-93; trustee No. Westchester Hosp. Ctr., Mt. Kisco, 1987-99, Smith Coll., Northampton, 1979-89; councilwoman Town of New Castle, Chappaqua, N.Y., 1976-79; mem. Westchester County Women's Adv. Bd., 2000—. Named Black Achiever in Industry, Harlem YMCA, 1982; recipient John M. Greene award Smith Coll., 1994, Jan Silverman award White Plains Child Day Care Assn., 1998. Mem. Rotary Club (Paul Harris fellow Westchester Club 1994, bd. dirs. 1995-98). Democrat. Avocations: reading, writing, piano. Home: Scarborough Manor 3H-1 PO Box 307 Scarborough NY 10510-0807

TAYLOR, NELLIE RUBY, artist, poet; b. Lundale, W.Va., Apr. 18, 1946; d. John Otis and Blanche L. (Wright) Taylor; m. Ivan Lee Hurt, July 31, 1965 (div. Nov. 1982); children: Ivan Lee Hurt Jr., Bradley Allen Hurt. MA, Masters Art, Usa, 1995—95. Adminstr. Cleve. Sch., Cleveland, Ohio, 1987—; nursing Mary Farmes Nurses, Cleveland Heights, 2002—02; agent A.L. Williams Ins., Athens, 1984—87; tchr. Manor-Care, Mayfield Heights, 2002—. Author: (book) Mental Education; inventor Hopter-Copter; prodr.: (television) In Time Like These; founder & pres. (corporation) The Mean Corporation. Recipient Award of Excellence, Ohio Sch. Bd. Assn, 1985—87, Lifetime Congl. award, U.S. Congress 11th Dist., 1998. Mem.: Am. Fedration of Teachers. Avocations: writing, traveling, traveling, drama. Home: 2826 E 130th Unit # 102 Shaker Heights Cleveland OH 44120

TAYLOR, NICHOLAS C. state agency administrator, energy executive; b. Washington, Sept. 18, 1937; s. James Spear Taylor and Helen Livingston MacGregor Strauss; m. Catherine Blaffer, Jan. 1, 1999; children: Nicholas Van Kempen, Katherine C., Christie. AB, Harvard U., 1959; JD, Georgetown U., 1963. Assoc. Wilson, Woods & Villalon, Washington, 1964-65, Shearman & Sterling, N.Y.C., 1965-70, Locke, Liddell, Sapp, Dallas, 1970-74; shareholder Stubbeman, McRae, Sealy, Laughlin & Browder, Inc., Midland, Tex., 1974-93; atty., 1993—; pres. Mexco Energy Corp.; chmn. State Securities Bd. of Tex. Mem. Tex. Jud. Coun., 1990. Recipient Am. Jurisprudence prizes for constnl. law, oil, and gas taxation So. Meth. U. Law Sch. Mem. Natural Gas Prodrs. Assn., Permian Basin Petroleum Assn., Midland Downtown Lions Club. Episcopalian. Office: Mexco Energy Corp PO Box 10502 Midland TX 79702-7502 E-mail: mexco@msn.com.

TAYLOR, NICK, writer; Pres. Author's Guild, N.Y.C., 2002—. Lectr. Sandhills writer's conf. Augusta Coll., Ga.; lectr. annual writer's conf. Marymount Manhattan Coll., NY. Contbr. articles, ; author: Laser: The Inventor, the Nobel Laureate, and the Thirty-Year Patent War, 2000, 7 additional books. Office: The Authors Guild 31 East 28th St 10th Floor New York NY 10016*

TAYLOR, PAMELA ANN, social worker; b. Paterson, N.J., Aug. 25, 1940; d. John William and Alberta M. (Henderson) T. BA, Colby Coll., 1962; MSW, U. Hawaii, 1970. Diplomate in clin. social work; cet. ACSW, LCSW, BCD. Social worker Welfare Dept. Aid To Families with Dependent Children, Cambridge, Mass., 1963-65; supr. Welfare Dept. AFDC, 1965-68; social worker Child and Family Svcs. of N.H., Laconia, 1970-72, regional dir. Lakes Regional Office, 1972-75; chief clinic social worker N.H. Program Alcohol and Drug Abuse, Concord, N.H., 1975-78; mental health supr. Pleasant Point Health Ctr., Perry, Maine, 1978-80; dir. of social work Mid-Maine Med. Ctr., Waterville, 1980-84, Maine Med. Ctr., Portland, 1984-91. Specialist geriatric mental health Cmty. Health and Counseling Svcs., Bangor, 1991—. Bd. dirs. Mt. St. Joseph Nursing, Home, Waterville, 1982-84, Alliance for Mentally Ill, Portland, 1986-89; mem. ancillary advisor com. to Maine Health Care Fin. Commn. Profl. Adv. Com., 1984-85; mem. Aging Adv. Com. of Maine Hosp. Assn., 1988-91. Recipient Cert. of Achievement Maine Hosp. Assn., 1990. Mem. Nat. Assn. Social Workers (sec. N.H. chpt. 1975-77, pres. elect 1977-78, COI chairperson Maine chpt. 1981-84, clin. practice task force, 1987-89, nat. com. on inquiry, 1982-87), Soc. for Hosp. Social Work Dirs. (pres. 1983-84, 87-88, named hosp. social work dir. of yr. Maine chpt. 1989).

TAYLOR, PAUL FRANKLIN, college dean; b. Portsmouth, Ohio, Oct. 28, 1946; s. Frank Claude and Geneva Ruth (Jones) T.; children: Victoria Carol, Matthew Winston, Kate Franklin. BA, U. Ky., 1970; MA, Gerogetown (Ky.) Coll., 1972. Sports writer Lexigton (Ky.) Herald-Leader, 1970-71; dir. admissions and fin. aid Shawnee State U., Portsmouth, Ohio, 1971-73; guidance counselor Cen. Ky. State Vocat. Tech. Sch., Lexington, 1973-74; dir. training Bluegrass Employment and Training Program, 1974-76; career counselor Lexington Tech. Inst., 1976-77; asst. dir. student svcs. Lexington C.C., 1977-86, dean enrollment and student affairs, 1986—. Mem. Am. Assn. Collegiate Registrars and Admissions Officers (bd. dirs., v.p. admissions and enrollment mgmt. 1999-2002, pres.-elect 2002--), So. Assn. Collegiate Admissions Ofcrs. and Registrars (exec. com. 1990-91, v.p. for profl. devel. 1992-94, v.p. for membership states and regionals 1994-96, pres. 1997), Ky. Assn. Collegiate Admissions Ofcrs. and Registrars (v.p. admissions 1984-86, pres. 1987-88), Ky. Assn. for Promotion Coll. Admissions (pres. 1983-84), Ky. Assn. Collegiate Admissions Counselors. Democrat. Avocations: snow skiing, golf, volleyball, softball, running. Office: Lexington Community College Cooper Dr Lexington KY 40506-0235 E-mail: pault@uky.edu.

TAYLOR, PAUL PEAK, pediatric dentist, educator; b. Childress, Tex., May 11, 1921; s. Noah Peak and Lois C. (Vinson) T.; m. LaVerne Countryman, Aug. 11, 1945; chi dren: Scott, Peri Ann. Student, W. Tex. State Coll., 1938-40; DDS, Baylor U., 1944; MS, U. Mich., 1951. Diplomate Am. Bd. Pediatric Dentistry (examining mem. 1977-84, chair 1983). Prof. Baylor U. Coll. Dentistry, Dallas, 1958-86, chmn. grad. pediatric dentistry, 1960-69, chmn. dept. pediatric dentistry, 1969-86, prof. emeritus, 1986—; dir. dental svcs. Children's Med. Ctr., 1965-86, dir. emeritus dental svcs., 1986—; dir. dental svcs. Tex. Scottish Rite Hosp. for Children, 1965-86, dir. emeritus dental svcs., 1986—. Contbr. articles to Jour. of Dentistry for Children, 1960-82; author (with others) Pediatric Dentistry, 1986, Current Therapy in Pediatric Infectious Disease, 1989; mem. edtl. and publs. com. Jour. Dentistry for Children. Capt. U.S. Army, 1951-53. Named to Baylor Coll. Dentistry Hall of Fame, 1999; Mott Found. fellow, 1949-51. Fellow Am. Coll. of Dentists (life); mem. ADA (life), Tex. Dental Assn., Dallas County Dental Assn. (Dentist of Yr. 1999, Lifetime Achievement award 2002), Masons (life, 32d degree), Shriners. Episcopalian. Avocation: golf. Home: 2615 Briarcove Dr Plano TX 75074-4905

TAYLOR, PEYTON TROY, JR. gynecologic oncologist, educator; b. Tuscaloosa, Ala., July 21, 1941; s. Peyton Troy Sr. and Frances (Sutter) T.; m. Helena Ström, Sept. 23, 1967; children: Annika, Karin, Sarah. BS, U. Ala., 1963; MD, Med. Coll. Ala., 1968. Intern U. Va. Hosp., Charlottesville, 1968-69, resident, 1969-70, 72-75; asst. prof. ob-gyn U. Va., 1976-79, assoc. prof., dir. divsn. ob-gyn., 1981-87, Richard N. and Louise R. Crockett prof., 1987—; prof. ob-gyn., dir. divsn. ob-gyn. U. Va. Health Scis. Ctr., 1981-97; med. dir. Cancer Ctr. U. Va., 1996—; clin. assoc. surgery Nat. Cancer Inst., Bethesda, Md., 1970-72. Assoc. prof. U. Ala., Birmingham, 1979-81. Contbr. articles to profl. jours. Served with USPHS, 1970-72. Fellow ACS, Am. Coll. Obstetricians and Gynecologists; mem. Assn. Acad. Surgeons, Soc. Gynecol. Oncologists, Soc. Surg. Oncology, Am. Soc. of Clin. Oncology, Am. Assn. for Cancer Rsch., Internat. Gynecol. Cancer Soc., So. Surg. Assn. Episcopalian. Office: U Va PO Box 10016 Charlottesville VA 22906-0016

TAYLOR, PHILIP HARLEY, JR. software engineer; b. Pensacola, Fla., Mar. 27, 1959; s. Philip Harley Sr. and Sheila Ann (McNamee) T. BS, U. Md., 1984. Programmer Gee & Jenson, West Palm Beach, Fla., 1982; programmer Goddard Space Flight Ctr. NASA, Greenbelt, Md., 1983-84; programmer Intran, Rosslyn, Va., 1984-85, SAIC, Tysons Corner, 1985; sr. programmer TRW, Alexandria, 1985-87, Claritas, Alexandria, 1987-88; cons. Boeing, IBM, Microsoft, Chase Manhattan, A.C. Neilson, Vienna, 1988-90; mgr. spl projects Softview, Oxnard, Calif., 1990-91; sr. software engr. Borland, Scotts Valley, 1991-92; staff engr. Kaleida Labs., Mountain View, 1993—. Author: 3D Graphics Programming in Windows; contbr. book revs., instrnl. courseware. Mem. restructuring bus. com. North Monterey County (Calif.) H.S., 1991-92. Mem. IEEE, Assn. Computer Machinery. Home: 15932 Manion Way NE Duvall WA 98019-8528

TAYLOR, PRISCILLA SHEPPARD, editor; b. Pottstown, Pa., Sept. 15, 1931; d. George B. and Priscilla S. Sheppard; m. John Maxwell Taylor, July 6, 1957; children: Alice Spaulding Taylor McVeigh, Katharine Maxwell Taylor Shaibani, James Sheppard Taylor. BA summa cum laude, Agnes Scott Coll., 1953; MA with distinction, London Sch. Econ., 1955. Editor/analyst CIA, 1955-59; tchr. English, history Internat. Sch. Bangkok, 1962-63; lectr. history U. Va., 1964-65; sr. editor Editorial Experts, Inc. (now EEI Comms.), Alexandria, Va., 1976—. Editor: The Editorial Eye, 1982-83, columnist, 1992—; editor: The Key Reporter, Washington, 1984-2001; Disting. Centennial lectr. Agnes Scott Coll., 1989. Editor: Manuscripts: The First Twenty Years, 1984, The Great Grammar Challenge, 1999. Fulbright scholar, 1953-55. Mem. Mortar Bd., Phi Beta Kappa. Avocation: tennis. Home: 1939 Lorraine Ave Mc Lean VA 22101-5331 E-mail: priscillataylor@erols.com.

TAYLOR, R. ERVIN, JR. archaeologist; b. Los Angeles, Jan. 15, 1938; s. Royal Ervin and Francys Ellen (McMurtry) T.; m. Marilynn Julia Lampley, Aug. 30, 1959; children: Gregory Michael, Karen Louane. BA, Pacific Union Coll., 1960; MA, UCLA, 1965, PhD, 1969. Asst. prof. Calif. State U., Northridge, 1967-70; from assoc. prof. to prof. anthropology U. Calif., Riverside, 1970—, chmn. dept. anthropology, 1994-2000. Author: Radiocarbon Dating, 1987; editor: Chronologies in New World Archaeology, 1978, Advances in Obsidian Glass Studies, 1980; co-editor: Radiocarbon After Four Decades, 1992, Chronometric Dating in Archaeology, 1997. Grantee NSF, 1978—. Fellow AAAS, Am. Anthropol. Assn.; mem. Southwestern Anthropol. Assn. (pres. 1975-76), Soc. Archaeol. Scis. (pres. 1982, gen. sec. 1982—). Home: 25155 Crestview Dr Loma Linda CA 92354-3508 Office: U Calif Radiocarbon Lab Riverside CA 92521-0001 E-mail: retaylor@citrus.ucr.edu.

TAYLOR, RALPH ARTHUR, JR. lawyer; b. Washington, Jan. 19, 1948; s. Ralph Arthur Sr. and Mary Florence Taylor; m. Joanna Lamb Moorhead, Jan. 30, 1988; children: Alison M., John Duncan. BS in Engring. with honors, Princeton, 1970; JD, U. Va., 1975. Bar: Va. 1975, D.C. 1976, Md. 1989, U.S. Dist. Ct. D.C. 1977, U.S. Dist. Cts. (ea. and we. dists.) Va. 1986, U.S. Dist. Ct. Md. 1988, U.S. Dist. Ct. Colo. 1998, U.S. Ct. Appeals (4th cir.) 1991, U.S. Ct. Appeals (D.C. cir.) 1977, U.S. Ct. Appeals (6th cir.) 1991, U.S. Ct. Claims 1985, U.S. Supreme Ct. 1980. Program advisor U.S. EPA, Boston, 1970-72; assoc. Steptoe & Johnson, Washington, 1975-84, Shaw, Pittman, Potts, & Trowbridge, Washington, 1984-86, ptnr., 1986-2001, leader tech. and intellectual property litigation group, co-leader Yr. 2000 practice group; ptnr., co-chair intellectual property litigation group Dorsey & Whitney, LLP, 2000—. Assoc. editor Litigation News, 1985-99, exec. editor, 1999—; notes editor Va. Law Rev., 1974-75; contbg. author: International Technology Transfers, 1995. Pres. Cloisters West Homeowners Assn., Washington, 1989, 90; pres. 1625 Q St. Condominium Assn., Washington, 1982-86; mem. grad. bd trustees Princeton Quadrangle Club. Lt. USPHS, 1970-72. Mem. Order of the Coif, Met. Club (Washington), Kenwood Golf and Country Club, Barristers, Princeton Club (Washington). Protestant. Avocations: sailing, skiing, tennis, squash, amateur radio. Office: Dorsey & Whitney LLP Ste 400 South 1001 Pennsylvania Ave NW Washington DC 20004

TAYLOR, RALPH ORIEN, JR. real estate developer, investor; b. Kansas City, Mo., Jan. 6, 1919; s. Ralph Orien Sr. and Genevieve (Sturgeon) T.; m. Betty Boswell, Dec. 7, 1940 (dec. Oct. 1959); children: Ralph Bradley, Nancy Virginia Stevens; m. Deborah Rosemary Berger, Oct. 10, 1982. BS in Bus. and Pub. Adminstrn., U. Mo., 1940. Ptnr. Sturgeon & Taylor, Kansas City, Mo., 1940-42; chmn., pres. Sturgeon & Taylor, Inc., Kansas City, Prairie Village (Kans.), 1946, Sturgeon & Taylor Devel. Co., Inc., Prarie Village, Kans., 1949—, Sturgeon & Taylor, Co., Prarie Village, 1955-90, Roth & Taylor Devel. Co., Inc., Prarie Village, 1989—; ptnr., co-founder ScripTpro LLC, Pharmacy Robotics & Automation, Mission, 1994. Mem. Johnson County (Kans.) Real Estate Bd., Kansas City Real Estate Bd. Lt. comdr. USNR, 1942-46, PTO, ETO. Decorated Bronze Star with combat V; recipient Alumnus of Yr. award, Phi Delta Theta Fraternity, 2000, Ralph and Debbie Taylor Phi Delta Theta Baseball Stadium dedicated in his honor, U. Mo., 2000. Charter mem. Nat. Assn. Home Builders (life bd. dirs.), Home Builders Assn. Greater Kansas City (pres. 1951-52, life bd. dirs., Builder of Yr. award 1979); mem. , Indian Hills Country Club (Mission Hills, Kans.), Ft. Lauderdale Country Clu b, Lauderdale Yacht Club, Phi Delta Theta (Raymond L. Gardner Alumnus of Yr. award 2000). Republican. Mem. Christian Ch. Avocations: golfing, boating. Home: 411 W 46th Ter Apt 903 Kansas City MO 64112-1437 Office: 1050 Seminole Dr PHB Fort Lauderdale FL 33304-3225 also: Sturgeon & Taylor Devel Co Inc PO Box 3328 Olathe KS 66063 E-mail: RalphoTaylor@aol.com.

TAYLOR, RANDALL WILLIAM, quality assurance administrator; b. Paulding, Ohio, Mar. 10, 1948; s. Virgil Myron and Deloris Elizabeth (Myers) T.; m. Patricia Helen Rager, Apr. 29, 1972. AAS in Supervision, Purdue U., Ft. Wayne, 1979, student, 1986-88; BSM, Ind. Wesleyan U., 1989. Broadcaster Radio Sta. WTVB-WANG, Coldwater, Mich., 1969; quality control inspector tire div. B.F. Goodrich, Woodburn, Ind., 1969-74; quality engr. Uniroyal Goodrich Tire Co., 1987-90; Michelin Americas Small Tires corp. sr. quality engr., 1990-94; gen. mgr. Universal Metalcraft, Inc., Decatur, Ind., 1994-96; client mgr. Brit. Stds. Ams., Inc., 1996-2000, sr. client mgr., 2000—. V.p. Big Bros./Big Sisters, Ft. Wayne, 1982-86. Mem. Ind. State Trapshooting Assn. (bd. dirs. 1984-90). Lodges: Masons. Avocations: trapshooting, golf, fishing, travel. Fax: 330-874-8013.

TAYLOR, RAY, state senator; b. Steamboat Rock, Iowa, June 4, 1923; s. Leonard Allen and Mary Delilah (Huffman) T.; m. Mary Allen, Aug. 29, 1924; chidlren: Gordon, Laura Rae Taylor Hansmann, Karol Ann Taylor Rogers, Jean Lorraine Taylor Mahl. Student, U. No. Iowa, 1940-41, Baylor U., 1948-49. Farmer, Steamboat Rock, Iowa, 1943—; mem. Iowa Senate, 1973-95. Bd. dirs., sec. Am. Legis. Exch. Coun., 1979-94; sec. Hardin County Farm Bur., 1970-72; mem. Iowa divsn. bds. Am. Cancer Soc.; chmn. Am. Revolution Bicentennial com.; mem. Steamboat Rock Cmty. Sch. Bd., 1955-70; coord. Rep. youth, 1968-72; chmn. bd. Faith Bapt. Bible Coll., past chmn. acad. com.; pres. Eldora Area Chamber and Devel. Coun., 1998—2001; mem. Eldora Indsl. Corp., 1998—; pres. Am. Coun. Christian Chs.; chmn. Iowans for Responsible Govt.; bd. dirs. Iowans for Tax Relief, 1995—; chmn. Steamboat Rock Schoolhouse Com., 2000—. Named Guardian of Small Bus. NFIB/Iowa, 1989-90, for outstanding support for good govt. and accessible, affordable health care in Iowa, Iowa Physician Asst. Soc., 1991; Ind. Bapt. fellow of the Midwest, Christian Patriots, 1994, Hon. alumnus Faith Bapt. Bible Coll. & Theol. Sem., 1995; recipient Contenders award Am. Coun. Christian Chs., 1991, Legislator of Yr. award Iowa Soc. of Friends, 1991-92. Mem. Wildlife Club, Eldora Rotary (v.p. 2001). Baptist. Home: 31363 185th St Steamboat Rock IA 50672-8107 E-mail: raymaryt@netins.net.

TAYLOR, RICHARD BERTROM, accountant; b. Cuthbert, Ga., Nov. 1, 1951; s. Wilburn Bertrom and Marjorie (Hixon) T.; m. Sherrie L. Lieber; children: Kenneth, Douglas, Andrew. AS cum laude, Andrew Coll., 1971; BBA, U. Ga., 1973. CPA, Ga., Fla. Staff acct. Lester Witte & Co., Atlanta, 1973-79; mgr. HLB Gross Collins, PC, 1979-84, ptnr., 1984—, also v.p., bd. dirs. Mem. adv. bd. acctg. dept. Kennesaw State U., 1989—; exec. com. HLB-USA, Inc., 1997—. Bd. dirs. North Cobb Christian Sch., 1989-90. Mem. AICPAs, Ga. Soc. CPAs, Pinetree Country Club (bd. dirs. 1983-87, 91-93, treas. 1984-85, 91, v.p. 1986, pres. 2001—), Optimists (sec. 1982-84), French-Am. C. of C. (dir. Atlanta chpt. 2000—, treas. 2000—), Phi Kappa Phi, Beta Alpha Psi, Phi Theta Kappa. Methodist. Avocations: gardening, football, travel, golf, dance. Office: HLB Gross Collins PC 2625 Cumberland Pkwy SE Ste 400 Atlanta GA 30339-3911 E-mail: artrbt@bellsouth.net., rtaylor@bellsouth.net.

TAYLOR, RICHARD CHARLES, lawyer; b. Crookston, Minn., June 1, 1942; s. Robert E. and Frances (Freegrad) T.; m. Mary Jane Collins, Oct. 11, 1969; children: David Robert, Allison Jane, Kevin James. BS in Indsl. Engring., U. N.D., 1965, JD, 1967; postgrad., U. Calif., San Francisco, 1981; cert. of completion, Lawyers Post Grad. Clinic, 1975-76. Bar: Minn. 1967, N.D. 1967, Colo. 1971, U.S. Dist. Ct. Minn. 1979, U.S. Dist. Ct. N.D. 1982. Ptnr. Dickel, Johannson, Taylor & Rust, P.A., Crookston, 1971-98; judge U.S. Dist. Ct. 9th Jud. Dist., 1998—. Mem. Minn. Lawyers' Bd. Profl. Responsibilty, St. Paul, 1983-91, Minn. Supreme Ct. Adv. Commn. on Lawyer Discipline, 1992-93. Mem. editorial bd. U. N.D. Law Rev., 1966-67. Bd. dirs., v.p. riverview Hosp. Assn., Crookston, 1979-88, Diocese of Crookston, 1984-98, Maple Lake Improvement Dist., 1989-93, Phoenix Industries, 1992-99, L&R Industries, 1988-98. Decorated Bronze Star, D.S.M. Mem. ATLA, Am. Bd. Trial Advocates, Minn. State Bar Assn. (bd. govs. 1991-98, cert. civil trial specialist 1991—), Minn Leading Attys., 14th Dist. Bar Assn. (pres. 1987-88), Minn. Trial Lawyers Assn., Minn. Def. Lawyers Assn., Minn. Diocesan atty's Assn., Am. Arbitration Assn. (panel of arbitrators), Arbitration Forum (panel of arbitrators), Am. Legion, Minakwa Country Club, Elks. Roman Catholic. Avocations: hunting, fishing, skiing. Home: RR 2 Box 95A Erskine MN 56535-9368

TAYLOR, RICHARD HENRY, minister; b. Paterson, N.J., Oct. 6, 1943; s. John Henry and Dorothy (Hutton) T. BA, Marietta Coll., 1965; MDiv, Andover-Newton Theol. Sch., 1969. Ordained to ministry United Ch. of Christ, 1969. Pastor St. Luke's United Ch. of Christ, Kittanning, Pa., 1968-72, 1st Congl. Ch., Hinsdale, Mass., 1972-80, Congl. Ch., Middlefield, 1972-80, 1st Congl. Ch., Andover, Conn., 1980-87, 1st Congl. Ch. Benton Harbor, Mich., 1987-99, Beneficent Congl. Ch., Providence, 1999—. V.p. Congl. Christian Hist. Soc., Boston, 1981—; hist. cons. Census Project, United Ch. Bd. for Homeland Ministries, N.Y.C., 1983; convenor Task Force on Small Chs., United Ch. of Christ, Framingham, Mass., 1978-80; sec. Hist. Commn., United Ch. of Christ, N.Y.C., 1974-75; mem. Hist. Coun. United Ch. of Christ, 1991—. Author: Historical Directory of the Berkshire Association, 1979, The Churches of Christ of the Congregational Way in New England, 1989, The Congregational Churches of the West, 1992, Southern Congregational Churches, 1994, Congregations of the German Evangelical Synod of North America and Related Groups, 1998; co-author: Religious Congregations and Membership in the United States, 2000, 2d edit., 2002; contbr. articles to profl. jours. Pres. Hop River Homes for Elderly, Andover, 1981-87; chmn. Hist. Commn., Hinsdale, 1977-80; founder Armstrong County Hist. Mus., Kittanning, 1971-72; bd. dirs. Beneficent Ho., Providence, 1999—, Black Heritage Soc. R.I., Providence, 2000—; mem. United Ch. of Christ Coalition for Lesbian, Gay, Bisexual and Transgender Concerns, 1983—. Mem. Assn.

Statisticians Am. Religious Bodies (1st v.p. 1996-97, pres. 1997-2000), Am. Congl. Assn. (bd. dirs. 1986-87, 2000—), Omicron Delta Kappa. Address: 70 Oak St Apt B Providence RI 02909-1932

TAYLOR, RICHARD JAMES, lawyer; b. Merrill, Wis., Jan. 19, 1939; s. M.N. and Billie (Mead) T.; m. Nancy Hildebrand, Nov. 25, 1966. BA, U. Wis., 1962; DEF, U. Orleans, France, 1963; JD, U. Mich., 1966; postgrad., U. Paris II, 1971-72. Bar: N.Y. 1968. Assoc. Langner Parry Card & Langer, N.Y.C., 1966—68, Conboy Hewitt O'Brien & Boardman, N.Y.C., 1968—71; asst. prof. U. Paris I Law Sch., 1973—78; trademark and copyright counsel Colgate-Palmolive Co., N.Y.C., 1978—2001. Seminar leader Am. Law and Lang., N.Y.C., 1987—; pro bono counsel Hearts and Voices, N.Y.C., 1992—95; mem. com. of experts World Intellectual Property Orgn. Trademark Law Treaty, Geneva, 1993—94; lectr. intellectual property symposia. Co-author: Doing Business in France, 1973, Worldwide Trademark Transfers, 1992; contbr. chpt. to book, articles to Nat. Law Jour., Trademark Reporter, Jour. Japan Trademark Assn., Bus. Latin Am., others. Mem. ABA (chair com. on internat. trademark treaties and laws 1990-91, del. to World Trademark Symposium 1992), Internat. Trademark Assn. (chair internat. com. 1987-89, mem. internat. task force 1989-90, bd. dirs. 1992-95, mem. task force on trademark law treaty 1991-95, publ. bd. 1995—).

TAYLOR, RICHARD POWELL, lawyer; b. Phila., Sept. 13, 1928; s. Earl Howard and Helen Moore (Martin) T.; m. Barbara Jo Anne Harris, Dec. 19, 1959; 1 child, Douglas Howard. BA, U. Va., 1950, JD, 1952. Bar: Va. 1952, D.C. 1956. Law clk. U.S. Ct. Appeals for 4th Circuit, 1951-52; assoc. Steptoe & Johnson LLP, Washington, 1956-61, ptnr., 1962—, chmn. transp. dept., 1978—; sec., corp. counsel Slick Corp., 1963-69, asst. sec., 1969-72, also bd. dirs., 1965-68; sec., corp. counsel Slick Indsl. Co., 1963-72; sec., bd. dirs. Slick Indsl. Co. Can. Ltd, 1966-72. Bd. dirs. Intercontinental Forwarders, Inc., 1969-72. Mem. Save the Children 50th Anniversary Com., 1982; gen. counsel Am. Opera Scholarship Soc., 1974—; mem. lawyer's com. Washington Performing Arts Soc., 1982—; mem. adv. com. Rock Creek Found. Mental Health, 1982—; mem. nat. adv. bd. DAR, 1980-83, chmn., 1983—; mem. men's com. Project Hope Ball, 1980—; nat. vice chmn. for fin. Reagan for Pres., 1979-80; mem. exec. fin. com. 1981 Presdl. Inauguration; mem. President's Adv. Com. for Arts, 1982—, Rep. Nat. Com., 1983—; Md. fin. chmn. Reagan-Bush '84, Bush-Quayle '88. Served to lt (j.g.), Air Intelligence USNR, 1952-56. Mem. ABA (co-chmn. aviation com. 1964-76, chmn. 1976-77), Fed. Bar Assn., D.C. Bar Assn., Va. Bar Assn., Fed. Energy Bar Assn., Am. Judicature Soc., Assn. Transp. Practitioners, Internat. Platform Assn., Raven Soc., Order of Coif, Univ. Club, Capital Hill Club, Nat. Aviation Club, Aero Club, Congl. Country Club (Washington), Potomac (Md.) Polo Club. Episcopalian. Home: 14914 Spring Meadows Dr Germantown MD 20874-3444 Office: 1330 Connecticut Ave NW Washington DC 20036-1704 E-mail: rtaylor@steptoe.com. *Everyone should devote a portion of his or her life to efforts which help ensure that our country remains free and strong and that its concept of government under law is maintained and expanded throughout the world.*

TAYLOR, RICHARD TRELORE, retired lawyer; b. Kewanee, Ill., Aug. 5, 1917; s. Earl G. and Lucile (Cully) T.; m. Maureen Hoey, Feb. 9, 1946. BS, U. Ill., 1939, JD, 1946; LL.M., Columbia U., 1947; LHD (hon.), Marlboro Coll., 2001. Bar: Ill. 1946, N.Y. 1947. Assoc. Cadwalader, Wickersham & Taft, N.Y.C., 1947-57, ptnr., 1957-87, presiding ptnr., 1977-87, of counsel, 1988-89. Trustee Marlboro Coll., Vt. Served with U.S. Army, 1941-45. Decorated Bronze Star Mem. ABA, Univ. Club (N.Y.C.). Home: 870 United Nations Plz New York NY 10017-1807

TAYLOR, RICHARD WIRTH, political science educator; b. Cleve., Jan. 15, 1923; s. Robert and Irmgard (Wirth) T.; m. Sadie White, Sept. 19, 1946; children: Peter, Karla, Mark, Stephen. BA, U. Ill., 1947, MA, 1948, PhD, 1950. Instr. polit. sci. U. Minn., Mpls., 1950-52; asst. prof. polit. sci. Lehigh U., Bethlehem, Pa., 1952-55, Wis. State U., Stevens Point, 1955-56; vis. asst. prof. Northwestern U., Evanston, Ill., 1956-57; assoc. prof. Coe Coll., Cedar Rapids, Iowa, 1957-60, chmn., prof., 1960-67; prof. polit. sci. Kent State U., Ohio, 1967-92, prof. emeritus, 1992—, chmn., 1974-82. Vis. prof. Karl-Marx-Universität, Leipzig, Fed. Republic Germany, 1990. Co-exec. editor Peace and Change, 1986-87. Mem. policy com. Am. Friends Com. Nat. Legis., Washington, 1964-85, exec. com., 1986-87; mem. acad. adv. com., ombudsman com. Internat. Bar Assn., Edmonton Alta., Can., 1980—; mem. Friends World Com. on Consultation, 1991-98, Friends Svc. Com., 2000—, clerk Lake Erie/CAP Yearly Meeting, 1977-79. Home: 115 Kendal Dr Oberlin OH 44074-1905

TAYLOR, ROBERT BROWN, medical educator; b. Elmira, N.Y., May 31, 1936; s. Olaf C. Taylor and Elizabeth (Place) Brown; m. Anita Dopico; children: Diana Taylor Root, Sharon Taylor Oliverio. Student, Bucknell U., 1954-57; MD, Temple U., 1961. Diplomate Am. Bd. Family Practice. Gen. practice medicine, New Paltz, N.Y., 1964-78; faculty physician Sch. Medicine Wake Forest U., Winston-Salem, N.C., 1978-84; prof. dept. family medicine Oreg. Health Scis. U. Sch. Medicine, Portland, 1984—, chmn., 1984-98. Mem. comprehensive part II com. Nat. Bd. Med. Examiners, Phila., 1986-91. Author: Common Problems in Office Practice, 1972, The Practical Art of Medicine, 1974; editor: Family Medicine: Principles and Practice, 1978, 5th edit., 1998, Health Promotion: Principles and Clinical Applications, 1982, Difficult Diagnosis, 1985, Difficult Medical Management, 1991, Difficult Diagnosis II, 1992, Fundamentals of Family Medicine, 1996, Fundamentals of Family Medicine, 1998, Manual of Family Practice, 1997, 2d edit., 2002, Taylor's Review of Family Medicine, 1998, Manual of Ten-Minute Diagnosis, 2000; contbg. editor Physicians Mgmt. Mag., 1972-99; editl. bd. The Family Practice Rsch. Jour., 1980-90, The Female Patient, 1984—, Am. Family Physician, 1990-98, Jour. of Family Practice, 1990-93, Med. Tribune, 1993-99. Served as surgeon USPHS, 1961-64. Fellow Am. Acad. Family Physicians (sci. program com., Thomas Johnson award, bd. curators found. archives), Am. Coll. Preventive Medicine; mem. Soc. Tchrs. Family Medicine (bd. dirs., cert. of excellence), Assn. Am. Med. Colls., Am. Assn. for Study Headache, World Orgn. Family Physicians (chmn. sci. program com.), Portland City Club, Multnomah Athletic Club, Phi Beta Kappa, Alpha Omega Alpha.. Home: 1414 SW 3rd Ave Apt 2904 Portland OR 97201-6629 Office: Oreg Health Scis U Sch Medicine Mail Code FP 3181 SW Sam Jackson Park Rd Portland OR 97201-3011

TAYLOR, ROBERT EDWARD, foreign language educator; b. Portland, Oreg., Nov. 22, 1919; s. Dolph J. and Lula May (Nicholas) T.; m. Naomi Ellen Klatt, Feb. 13, 1943 (div. 1962); 1 child, Thomas Robert; m. Olga Zazuliak, May 19, 1962; 1 child, Anne-Marie. BA, Reed Coll., 1943; MA, Columiba U., 1947, PhD, 1951. Instr. french Columbia Univ., N.Y.C., 1947-50; instr. to prof. french NYU, 1950-62, prof. french, 1962-63; prof. French U. Mass., Amherst, 1963-90, dept. head, 1963-70, prof. emeritus, 1990—. Seminar assoc. Columbia Univ., 1959-80; chair Nat. Fulbright Com. for France, N.Y.C., 1963-65; dir. programs in France, Univ. Mass., 1971, 1990-91, 1997-98. Cons. editor Merriam-Webster's 3rd Internat. Dictionary, 1961; contbg. editor: Bibliographie Internat. de l'Humanisme et de la Renaissance; contbr. articles to Renaissance Soc. of Am., Modern Lang. Assn. 1st lt. USAAF, 1942-46. Decorated Chevalier dans l'Ordre des Palmes Académiques. Mem. Modern Lang. Assn. (asst. ed. 1950-55), Am. Assn. Tchrs. French, Assn. des Prof. de Lang. Modernes. Avocations: music, theatre. Home: 154 Lincoln Ave Amherst MA 01002-2011

TAYLOR, ROBERT HOMER, quality assurance professional, pilot; b. Rochester, N.Y., Mar. 18, 1922; s. C. Gilbert and Josephine Mary (Woodward) T.; m. Mignon Jane Beight, Aug. 1945; children: Robert Jr., Douglas Beight, Scott Woodward, Sondra Lee. BSME, Case Western Res. U., 1947. Commd. 2d lt. USAF, 1944, advanced through grades to lt. col., 1975; v.p., gen. mgr. Taylor Corp., 1947-53; mgr. quality assurance Spectra Physics Laserplane, Dayton, Ohio, 1976-89; pres., gen. mgr. CON-AV Corp., Tipp City, 1989—, pres., sec., 1990—. Chief quality assurance staff on NASA Mercury Booster for USAF, Cape Canaveral, Fla., 1961-63; mgr. nuc. tng. weapons devel. USAF Weapons Lab., 1964-67; CAT I test mgr. F-111, 1967-68; instr. pilot C-7, tng. officer, Vietnam, 1969; project element monitor T-43, attache, A-37, C-130 aircraft, Pentagon, 1970-74; br. chief WPAFB, 1974-75. Advisor Aero Scis. Alternatives, Tipp City, 1990—. Lt. col. CAP, Vietnam. Decorated Air medal with three oak leaf clusters, DFC; named to Aviation Hall of Fame, 1986. Mem. VFW, Exptl. Aircraft Assn., Flying Angels, Inc. (pres. 1991), Vets. Am., Masons, Beta Theta Pi (Case chpt. pres. 1942), Theta Tau, Early Birds. Episcopalian. Avocations: boating, flying, fishing, refurbishing antique aircraft. Home: 5855 Us Route 40 Tipp City OH 45371-9419 Office: CON-AV Corp 5855 Us Route 40 Tipp City OH 45371-9419

TAYLOR, ROBERT LARRY, author, freelance writer; b. Abilene, Tex., July 22, 1940; s. Larry Thornton and Virginia (Kerby) T.; life ptnr. Theodore Thomas Nowick, June 22, 1975. BA in Journalism, Tex. Tech U., 1962. Editor NHSC Newsletter, Nat. Home Study Coun., Washington, 1968-72; asst. editor Music Educators Jour., Music Educators Nat. Conf., 1972-76; editor Transp. USA mag. U.S. Dept. Transp., 1976-80; dep. text editor Am. Illustrated mag. USIA, 1980-86; freelance writer and author, Blue Hill, Maine, 1986—. Author: (novels) The Innocent, 1997, All We Have Is Now, 2002, (short stories) Revelation and Other Stories, 2002; contbg. author: Gay Pride: Photographs from Stonewall to Today, 1994; contbr. short stories to publs. Trustee Pierre Monteux Meml. Found., treas., 1994—97; mem. nat. coun. America Speaks Out, 2001—; exec. com. Pierre Monteux Meml. Found., 1997—2002, v.p., 2002—. Decorated Bronze Star; recipient Blue Pencil award as 1st place for best mag. Nat. Assn. Govt. Communicators, 1980, Outstanding Alumnus award Tex. Tech U. Sch. Mass Comm., 1986. Democrat. Avocations: singing, making handmade books. Home: Morgan Bay Rd Blue Hill ME 04614 E-mail: kailuum@downeast.net.

TAYLOR, ROBERT LEE, lawyer, former judge; b. North Wildwood, N.J., Sept. 6, 1947; s. Louis Edward and Elizabeth (Zuccato) T.; m. Julie Ann Adams, Apr. 28, 1979; children: Tracy, Jennifer, Kathryn, Robyn. BS, James Madison U., 1969; JD, Washington and Lee U., 1974. Bar: N.J. 1974, U.S. Dist. Ct. N.J. 1974, U.S. Ct. Appeals (3d cir.) 1982, U.S. Supreme Ct. 1991. Assoc. George M. James, Wildwood, 1974-78; ptnr. Way, Way, Goodkin & Taylor, 1978-81, Way, Way, & Taylor, Wildwood, 1981-82; pvt. practice law Stone Harbor, N.J., 1982—; judge Mid. Twp. Mcpl. Ct., 1984-89. Organizer, dir. First so. State Bank, Avalon, N.J.; mem. dist. 1 ethics com. N.J. Supreme Ct., 1994-96; solicitor Lower Twp., N.J., 1994-96; diplomate N.J. Mcpl. Law. Advisor Law Explorers Boy Scouts Am., 1981, exec. bd. so. N.J. coun., 1995-2000; chmn. Cape May County Dem. Com., 1996-98. With U.S. Army, 1969-71. Mem. ABA, N.J. Bar Assn. (gen. coun. 1978-82), Cape May County Bar Assn. (pres. 1980-81), Cape May County Mcpl. Judges Assn. (treas. 1987-89), N.J. Jud. Conf. (del. 1978-82), Am. Legion, DAV (life), Delta Theta Phi. Democrat. Roman Catholic. Avocations: skiing, tennis, golf. Office: 9712 3rd Ave # 4 Stone Harbor NJ 08247-1931 E-mail: rltaylor@pro-usa.net.

TAYLOR, ROBERT LEWIS, management educator; b. Pitts., Dec. 10, 1939; s. Robert William and Elinor (Miller) T.; m. Linda Taylor Shapiro, Oct. 28, 1988; 1 child, Kara; children by previous marriage: Rob, Mike. AB in Am. Studies, cum laude, Allegheny Coll., 1961; MBA, Ohio State U., 1966; D in Bus. Adminstrn., Mgmt., Ind. U., 1972. Asst. prof., dir. rsch. USAF Acad., Colorado Springs, Colo., 1971-77, assoc. prof., dir. instrn. dept. econ., geography, mgmt., 1977-79, prof. mgmt., head dept. econs., geography, mgmt., 1980-81; assoc. dean Coll. Letters and Sci., head div. Bus. and Econs., Carl N. Jacobs Prof. of Bus. U. Wis., Stevens Point, 1981-84; dean Coll. Bus. Pub. Adminstrn. U. Louisville, 1984—. Chmn. bd. dirs. Ky. Wood Floors, Louisville, 1988-98; bd. dirs. Banc One Ky. Corp., Louisville, 1988-2000, The Rawlings Co., Louisville, Logan Aluminum, AACSB: Internat., St. Louis, chmn. 1999-2000; cons., advisor Kellogg Nat. Fellowship program Kellogg Found., Battle Creek Mich., 1985-89. Co-author, editor: Contemporary Issues in Leadership, 1984, 5th edit., 2001, Leadership Challenges for Today's Manager, 1988, Military Leadership: In Pursuit of Excellence, 4th edit., 2000; contbr. articles to profl. jours. Chmn. Mayor's Strategic Planning Group, Louisville, 1986—; mem. Gov.'s Econ. Devel. Com., Frankfort, Ky., 1987-89, exec. com. Bus. Advs., 1988-92, task force on econ. devel. Ky. Legis. Rsch. Coun., 1991, Leadership Louisville, 1986, Leadership Ky., 1987; bd. trustees Jewish Hosp. Healthcare Svcs., Louisville, 2000—. Mem. Acad. Mgmt. (proceedings editor 1976-77, newsletter editor 1983-86), Louisville C. of C. (bd. dirs., exec. com 1990-94), Sigma Xi, Beta Gamma Sigma, Pi Gamma Mu. Mem. Eastern Orthodox Ch. Avocations: travel, walking, stamp collecting, reading. Home: 1516 Sylvan Way Louisville KY 40205-2408 Office: U Louisville Coll Bus & Pub Adminstrn Louisville KY 40292-0001 E-mail: Robert.L.Taylor@louisville.edu.

TAYLOR, ROBERT M. minister; b. Englewood, N.J., Mar. 5, 1932; s. Robert M. and Irene Maude T.; m. Anna Elizabeth Taylor, Dec. 27, 1953 (dec. Sept. 1970); m. Beverly Ann Taylor, Nov. 7, 1971; children: Robert M., William Harrison, Joanne Elizabeth, Susan Ruth. BA cum laude, Lafayette Coll., 1953; MDiv, Princeton Seminary, 1956. Ordained to ministry Presbyn. Ch., 1956. Pastor Mahoning Presbyn. Ch., Danville, Pa., 1956-59; asst. pastor Harundale Presbyn. Ch., Glen Burnie, Md., 1959-62; pastor Cen. Presbyn. Ch., Downingtown, Pa., 1962-69; sr. pastor The Presbyn. Ch., New Brunswick, N.J., 1969-75, Rosedale Gardens Presbyn. Ch., Livonia, Mich., 1975-79, Immanuel Presbyn. Ch., Albuquerque, 1979-85; interim pastor Community Presbyn. Ch., Mountainside, N.J., 1985-86; interim sr. pastor First Presbyn. Ch., Matawan, 1986-88; pastor Christ Ch. on Quaker Hill, Pawling, N.Y., 1988-94, Hope Presbyn. Ch., Lakewood, N.J., 1994-97; retired, 1997. Commr. Gen. Assembly/Presbyn. Ch., Mpls., 1968; supr. Princeton Sem. Tchg. Ch., New Brunswick, N.J., 1969-75; v.p. Inter-Ch. Coalition on Mission in Southwest, Phoenix, 1984; mem. Monmouth Presbytery, 1994—; mem. ethics com. Harlem Valley Psychiat. Ctr.; mem. Interfaith Clergy Coun.; bd. dirs., v.p. Cmty. Resource Ctr. Pawling, 1988-94. Mem. United Fund Bd. Govs., Downingtown, 1969, Citizen's Adv. Com., 1969, Mayor's Youth Adv. Com., East Brunswick, 1973; sec. Coll. Scholarship Found., 1975. Fellow in Pastoral Leadership Devel., Princeton Theol. Seminary, 1973. Mem. Rotary, Alpha Chi Rho (pres. 1952-53). Home: 2201 Monroe Village Jamesburg NJ 08831 *Life is a marvelous journey of caring and sharing with continual opportunities for growth. The challenge is to remain open to God's leading, even when the necessary hurdles are many.*

TAYLOR, ROBERT MORGAN, electronics executive; b. Orange, N.J., May 13, 1941; s. Morgan H. M. Taylor and Grace Anna (Bonynge) Loding; m. Sandra Ruth Cox, Sept. 11, 1965; children; Scott Joseph, Karen Lynne. BA in Chemistry, Williams Coll., 1963; PhD in Chemistry, Pa. State U., 1968; MBA, Drexel U., 1973. Scientist Leeds & Northrup Co., North Wales, Pa., 1968-70, sr. scientist, 1970-72, prin. scientist, 1972-84, corp. scientist, 1984-85, dir. R&D, 1985-92, dir. analytical mktg., 1990-93; v.p. The Capital Controls Group, Colmar, 1993-99; pres. RMT Cons., Lansdale, 1999—. Contbr. articles to profl. jours.; 3 patents in dissolved oxygen sensing. Chmn. indsl. com. Montgomery County (Pa.) Sci. Rsch. Competition, 1987-99. Mem. IEEE, Electrochem. Soc. (fin. com. 1971-73, controlling mems. com. 1977), Am. Chem. Soc., Instrument Soc. Am. (sr.), Indsl. Rsch. Inst. (rep.). Republican. Presbyterian. E-mail: rmtaylor@viocenet.com.

TAYLOR, ROBERT P. lawyer; b. Douglas, Ariz., May 6, 1939; s. Paul Burton and Mary Ruth (Hart) T.; m. Sybil Ann Cappelletti, May 30, 1963 (div. Apr. 1974); children: David Scott, Nicole; m. Anne Dale Kaiser, Sept. 21, 1991. BSEE, U. Ariz., 1961; JD, Georgetown U., 1969. Bar: U.S. Ct. Appeals (9th circ.) 1969, U.S. Ct. Appeals (1st, 2d, 3d, 6th, and Fed. circs.), U.S. Supreme Ct., 1975. Elec. engr. Motorola Corp., Phoenix, 1961, Bell & Howell, Pasadena, Calif., 1964-65; examiner U.S. Patent Office, Washington, 1966-69; atty. Pillsbury Madison & Sutro, San Francisco, 1969-96, Howrey, Simon, Arnold & White, LLP, Menlo Park, Calif., 1996—. Mem. adv. commn. Patent Law Reform, Washington, 1990-92; mem. adv. bd. Litigation Risk Analysis, Palo Alto, Calif., 1985—. Contbr. articles to profl. jours. Dir. Ind. Colls. of No. Calif., San Francisco, 1982-96, officer, 1988-96. Fellow Am. Coll. Trial Lawyers; mem. ABA (chair sect. antitrust 1991-92), Am. Law Inst. Avocations: bicycling, cooking, hiking. Office: Howrey Simon Arnold & White LLP 301 Ravenswood Ave Menlo Park CA 94025-3434

TAYLOR, ROBERT ROWE, communications executive, consultant; b. Wellsville, N.Y., June 12, 1953; s. Robert Eugene and Dortha Louise (Gordon) T.; m. Marion Helga Gross, Nov. 28, 1975; children: Jacqueline Alvis, Justin Rowe, Robert Brewster. BS in Comm., Boston U., 1975. Asst. dir. annual giving Boston U., 1975-78; dir. annual fund Kalamazoo Coll., 1978-79; dir. direct mktg. ABA, Chgo., 1979-81; dir. devel. Ill. Inst. Tech., 1981-89; pres. Evang. Health Sys. Found., Oak Brook, Ill., 1989-95; v.p. devel. Nat. Easter Seal Soc., Chgo., 1995; pres. The Marlin Group, Glen Ellyn, Ill., 1996—. Bd. dirs. Am. Cancer Soc., Pk. Forest, Ill., 1981-93, Cmty. Supportive Living Sys. Inc., Chgo., 1992-94, Lifelink Charities, Bensenville, Ill., 1996—, Chgo. AIDSWalk. Author: (with others) Transitional Development Repositioning for Planned and Major Gifts, 1997, Four Hundred Years: A History of the Taylor Family, 1999. Pres. Boston Univ. Alumni Club, Chgo., 1979-84; precinct committeeman Ill. Rep. Party, Will County, 1985-90. Recipient Most Improved Ann. Fund award Coun. for Advancement and Support of Edn., Washington, 1976, 78, 82, Silver Echo award Direct Mktg. Assn., N.Y.C., 1980, William Arbruster award Ill. Jaycees, Park Forest, 1985. Mem. Nat. Soc. Fund Raising Execs., Union League Club. Republican. Mem. United Ch. of Christ. Avocations: music, golf, coin collecting, history, writing. Office: The Marlin Group 568 Raintree Dr Glen Ellyn IL 60137-6715 E-mail: marlinrob@aol.com.

TAYLOR, ROBERT WILLIAM, professional society administrator; b. Brownsville, Tenn., July 28, 1929; s. Charles William and Annie Laura (Taliaferro) T.; m. Jeanette Henshaw, Jan. 4, 1953; children: Robert William, Teresa, Mark Thomas. BS in Chemistry, Murray (Ky.) State U., 1949; MS in Journalism, Ohio U., 1950. Asst. editor Jour. Petroleum Tech., 1953, editor, 1954-63; exec. dir., sec. AIME, 1963-68; exec. v.p., gen. mgr. Soc. Mfg. Engrs., 1968-81; publishing dir. Mfg. Engring., 1968-81; pres. Am. Soc. Assn. Execs., Washington, 1981-98, ASAE Found., Washington, 1981-98, ASAE Service Corps., Washington, 1981-98, ASAE Ins. Co., 1993—, IMM Global Mgmt. Group, 1998—. Assoc. editor: Petroleum Prodn. Handbook, 1961. Past bd. dirs. One to One Found., Mfg. Engring. Edn. Found.; hon. co-chmn. Clinton/Gore Inaugural; chmn. Nat. Ctr. for Nonprofit Enterprise, 1999—. Served to 2d lt. USAF, 1951-53. Fellow Soc. Mfg. Engrs., Jr. Engring. Tech. Soc. (past dir.), Am. Soc. Engring. Edn. (past dir.), Council Engring. and Sci. Soc. Execs. (past pres.), Am. Assn. Engring. Socs. (past dir.) Home: 1401 N Oak St Apt 605 Arlington VA 22209-3685 Office: Pres GMG Solutions & Assn Mgmt Solutions 1110 N Glebe Rd Ste 580 Arlington VA 22201-4795

TAYLOR, ROGER DALE, lawyer; b. Booneville, Ark., Apr. 6, 1950; s. Carl Edward and Amanda (Wilkins) T.; m. Elizabeth Payne, Feb. 20, 1988; children: Zachary, Grace, Greta, Wilkins. BSEE, U. Ark., 1972; JD with honors, George Washington U., 1980. Bar: D.C. 1980, Tex., 1981, Ga., 1996. Assoc. Vinson & Elkins, Houston, 1981-83, Busby, Rehm & Leonard, Washington, 1983-85, Finnegan, Henderson, Washington, 1985-90, ptnr. Tokyo, 1990-92, Washington, 1992-96, Atlanta, 1997—, Alston & Bird, Atlanta, 1996-97. Adj. prof. Law Sch. Cath. U. Am., Washington, 1992-95. Mem. Am. Intellectual Property Assn., Atlanta Soc. Clubs, Licensing Execs. Soc. (chmn. Japan com. 1994—), World Trade Ctr. Atlanta, Order of the Coif, Tau Beta Phi, Etta Kappa Nu. Office: Finnegan Henderson 3200 Suntrust Plz 303 Peachtree St NE Atlanta GA 30308-3201

TAYLOR, ROGER LEE, lawyer, academic administrator; b. Canton, Ill., Apr. 6, 1941; s. Ivan and Pauline Helen (Mahr) T.; m. E. Anne Zweifel, June 13, 1964. BA, Knox Coll., 1963; JD cum laude, Northwestern U., 1971. Bar: Ill. 1971, U.S. Dist. Ct. (no. dist.) Ill. 1971, U.S. Dist. Ct. (no. dist.) Tex. 1975, U.S. Ct. Appeals (7th cir.) 1972, U.S. Ct. Appeals (5th and 11th cirs.) 1981, U.S. Supreme Ct. 1975. Assoc. Kirkland & Ellis, Chgo., 1971-78, ptnr., 1978—; pres. Knox Coll., Galesburg, 2002—. Trustee Knox Coll., interim pres. 2002. Mem. ABA, Chgo. Coun. Lawyers, Friends of the Parks (bd. dirs.), Order of Coif, Univ. Club, Mid-Am. Club Chgo., Soangetaha Country Club (Galesburg, Ill.). Office: Knox College Galesburg IL 61401

TAYLOR, RONALD LEE, academic administrator; b. Urbana, Ill., Nov. 11, 1943; s. Lee R. and Katherine L. (Becker) Taylor; m. Patricia D. Fitzimmons, Mar. 10, 1973; children: Jamie, Lara, Meredith, Dana. AB, Harvard U., 1966; MBA, Stanford U., 1971. Asst. contr. Bell & Howell, Chgo., 1971-73; pres. DeVry Inc./Keller Grad. Sch., 1973—. Bd. dirs. La Petite Acad., Inc.; mem. Commn. Ednl. Credit and Credentials, 1997—2000, Commn. Govt. and Pub. Affairs, 2001—. Pres. Hinsdale (Ill.) Sch. Bd., 1983—91; com. chmn. Ill. Bd. Higher Edn., Springfield, 1985—; mem. mgmt. bd. Stanford U. Sch. Bus. Mem.: Am. Coun. Edn., Ill. C. of C. (edn. com. 1987—, bd. dirs.). Office: DeVry Inc 1 Tower Ln Ste 1000 Hinsdale IL 60181-4663 E-mail: rtaylor@devry.com.

TAYLOR, RONALD FULFORD, physician; b. Bethesda, Md., Mar. 23, 1956; s. Harold Bernard and Evelyn (Stansbury) T.; m. Sharon Delyn Stevenson, Mar. 7, 1987. BS, Frostburg (Md.) State Coll., 1978; MD, Med. Coll. Va., 1982. Intern Vanderbilt U., Nashville, 1982-83, resident, 1983-85, fellow in pulmonary and critical care medicine, 1985-87; practice pulmonary and critical care medicine, sleep medicine Jackson (Tenn.) Clinic, 1987—. Contbr. articles to profl. jours. Bd. dirs. Am. Lung Assn. of Tenn., Nashville, 1987-95. Mem. Am. Coll. Chest Physicians. Office: Jackson Clinic 616 W Forest Ave Jackson TN 38301-3966

TAYLOR, ROSE PERRIN, social worker; b. Lander, Wyo., Feb. 11, 1916; d. Wilbur Rexford Perrin and Agatha Catherine (Hartman) Perrin DeMars; m. Louis Kempf Kugland, Sept. 1942 (div. 1951); children: Mary Louise, Carolyn Kugland McElhany; m. Wilfred Taylor, Oct. 13, 1962 (dec. 1991). AB, U. Mich., 1937; MSW, U. Denver, 1956; student, Columbia U., 1936, Santa Rosa Jr. Coll., 1974-93, Coll. of Marin, 1995-98. Group worker Dodge Community House, Detroit, 1937-38; case worker Detroit Welfare Dept., 1938-40; child welfare worker Fremont County Welfare Dept., Lander, Wyo., 1940-42; worker children's svcs. Laramie County Welfare Dept., Cheyenne, 1951-57, dir., 1957-58; supr. San Mateo (Calif.) County Health & Welfare, 1958-74; dir. Fed. Day Care Project, San Mateo, 1964—. Tchr. Sch. Pub. Health Nursing, U. Wyo., 1951-55; tchr. Sch. Social Work, U. Calif., San Jose, 1962-63; workshop leader NIMH, Prescott, Ariz., 1961, Ariz. State U., Phoenix, 1962, Oreg. State Welfare Dept., Otter Crest, 1973; cons. day care workshops. Contbr. articles to profl. jours. Adminstrv. vol. Buck Ctr. for Rsch. in Aging, Marin County, 1994-95, vol. epidemiol. rschr. nutrition validation study for people in their 80's and 90's, 1995; bd. dirs. Friends of Redwoods, 2000—, Cmty. Ch. of Mill Valley, United Ch. of Christ, 2002—. Recipient Resolution of Commendation, Calif. State Senate, 1974; Annual Rose Taylor award San Mateo Child Care Coordinating Coun., 1982, Founder's Recognition award, 1997. Mem. NASW. Democrat. Mem. United Ch. of Christ. Avocations; artist, writer children's fiction, poetry. Home: The Redwoods # 10105 40 Camino Alto Mill Valley CA 94941-2943 E-mail: rosept@aol.com.

TAYLOR, ROSEMARY, artist; b. Joseph, Oreg. d. Theodore and Sarah A. (Lambright) Resch; m. Robert Hull Taylor; children: Barbara Taylor Ryalls, Robert H. Student, Cleve. Inst. Art, 1937-40, NYU, 1947. Tchr. pottery Rahway (N.J.) Art Ctr., 1950-55. Pottery cons. McCalls Mag., 1962-72. One woman shows include Paterson (N.J.) Coll., 1964, Westchester (Pa.) Coll., 1970, Gallery 100, Princeton, N.J., 1967, George Jensen's, N.Y.C., 1972, Artisan Gallery, Princeton, 1974, Am. Crafts (Ohio), 1979-99, Guild Gallery, 1986-91, Little Art Gallery, N.C., 1985-99, Olde Queens Gallery (N.J.), 1987, N.J. Designer Craftsmen, 1990, 97, 98, 99 (bd. dirs. 1986-87, std. chmn. 1994), Creative Hands, 1995, 97, 98, 99, Princeton, 1994; group shows include Mus. Natural History, N.Y.C., Newark Mus., Trenton (N.J.) Mus., Montclair (N.J.) Mus., Phila. Art Alliance , Pa. Horticulture Soc., 1988, Nat. Design Center, N.Y.C., Michener Mus., Pa., 1996; represented in permanent collection Westchester Coll. Bd. dirs. Solebury Cmty. Sch.; mem. Fulbright award com., 1982, 83. Mem. LWV (pres. Plainfield, N.J. chpt.), Am. Craft Coun., N.J. Designer-Craftsmen, Phila. Craft Group, Bucks County (Pa.) C. of C., Visual Artists and Galleries Assn., Nat. Assn. Am. Penwoman, Michener Mus., Doylestown, Pa., Women in the Arts (charter). Democrat. Unitarian Universalist. E-mial. Home: 10 Ingham Way New Hope PA 18938 Office: PO Box 282 Stockton NJ 08559-0282 E-mail: romy282@nni.com.

TAYLOR, ROSLYN DONNY, family physician; b. Columbia, S.C., Feb. 14, 1941; d. Otto G. and Roslyn Elizabeth (Alfriend) Donny; divorced; children: Cynthia Gambill Taylor Veal, Kevin Emory. BA, Emory U., 1963, MD, 1967. Diplomate Am. Bd. Family Practice. Rotating intern Jacksonville (Fla). Naval Regional Med. Ctr., 1967-68; pvt. practice, Green Cove Springs, Fla., 1968-70; resident in family practice Spartanburg (S.C.) Regional Med. Ctr., 1974-76; pvt. practice, Imman, S.C., 1976-78; staff physician student health svc. U. S.C., Columbia, 1978-82, mem. faculty dept. family medicine, 1979-87, med. dir. Woodrow Intermediate Care Facility, 1983-86; attending physician Pain Therapy Ctr., Richland Meml. Hosp., 1986—87; vis. prof. dept. family and preventive medicine U. Utah, Salt Lake City, 1987-88, dir. family practice residency, 1988-94; assoc. dir. family practice residency Meml. Med.

Ctr., Savannah, Ga., 1994—2001; interim program dir., chair dept. family medicine Mercer U. Sch. Medicine, 2002. Contbg. author: Saunders Manual of Medical Practicd, 1996, 98, The Primary Care Patient's Teaching Guide, 1998; mem. editl. bd. Family Practice News, 1990—; also articles. Vol. physician Homeless Shelter Clinic, Salt Lake City, 1990-94; chmn. rural physician loan assistance program com. State of Utah, 1990-94; mem. Chatham County Bd. Health, Savannah, 1998—. Lt. comdr. M.C., USNR, 1967-73. Named Physician of Yr., Columbia Mayor's Com. on Employment Handicapped, 1984, Outstanding Clin. Faculty in Family Medicine, Mercer U. Sch. Medicine, 1998. Fellow Am. Acad. Family Physicians (editl. bd. Home Study and Self Assessment program 1994-96); mem. AMA, Soc. Tchrs. Family Medicine, Ga. Med. Soc., Ga. Acad. Family Physicians, Med. Assn. Ga., Phi Beta Kappa, Alpha Omega Alpha. Presbyterian. Avocations: photography, reading, beach combing. Office: Meml Med Ctr Family Practice 1107 E 66th St Savannah GA 31404-5701

TAYLOR, ROWAN SHAW, music educator, composer, conductor; b. Ogden, Utah, June 1, 1927; s. Hugh Taylor and Lucille (Olsen) Gaenger; m. Dorothy Foulger, June 26, 1946 (div. 1953); children: Kathleen, Scott; m. Priscilla Pulliam, Aug. 29, 1957; children: Mark, Dianne, Paul, John (dec.), Eric, Brent, Charlotte. BA, Brigham Young U., 1952, MA, 1957. Tchr. San Juan Sch. Dist., Blanding, Utah, 1948-50; with C.F. Braun Engring. Firm, 1950-58; tchr. L.A. Unified Dist., 1958-64; from instr. to prof. L.A. C.C., Woodland Hills, Calif., 1964—. Condr., composer numerous symphonies and mus. works. With U.S. Army, 1955-56, Korea. Republican. Mem. Ch. Jesus Christ of LDS. Avocation: collecting cologne bottles. Home: 22544 Tiara St Woodland Hills CA 91367-3335

TAYLOR, ROY LEWIS, botanist, educator; b. Olds, Alta., Can., Apr. 12, 1932; s. Martin Gilbert and Crystal (Thomas) T. B.Sc., Sir George Williams U., Montreal, Que., Can., 1957; PhD, U. Calif. at Berkeley, 1962; DSc (hon.), U. B.C., Vancouver, Can., 1997. Pub. sch. tchr. Olds Sch. Div., 1949-52; jr. high sch. tchr. Calgary Sch. Bd., Alta., 1953-55; chief taxonomy sect., research br. Can. Agrl. Dept., Ottawa, Ont., 1962-68; dir. Bot. Garden, prof. botany, prof. plant scis. U. B.C., Vancouver, 1968-85; pres., CEO Chgo. Hort. Soc., 1985-94; dir. Chgo. Bot. Garden, Glencoe, Ill., 1985-94; exec. dir. Rancho Santa Ana Bot. Garden, Claremont, Calif., 1994-99; prof. botany, chmn. botany program Claremont Grad. U., 1994-99, dir. emeritus, 1999. Pres. Western Bot. Svcs. Ltd. Author: The Evolution of Canada's Flora, 1966, Flora of the Queen Charlotte Islands, Vols. I and II, 1968, Vascular Plants of British Columbia: A Descriptive Resource Inventory, 1977; The Rare Plants of British Columbia, 1985; assoc. editor Pacific Horticulture, 2001—. Mem. State of Ill. Bd. Natural Resources and Conservation, 1987-94; trustee Nature Ill. Found., 1990-94, Elisabeth C. Miller Bot. Garden Trust, Seattle, 1994—, Elisabeth C. Miller Bot. Garden Endowment, 2001—, The Arbor Fund, Seattle, 1997—, chmn., 2002—; bd. dirs. Milner Gardens and Woodland Soc., Qualicum Beach, B.C., Can., 2000—, vice-chmn., 2000—. Fellow Linnean Soc. London (hon.); mem. Can. Bot. Assn. (pres. 1967-68), Biol. Coun. Can. (pres. 1973-74), Am. Assn. Mus. (accreditation com. 1980-85, chmn. 1985-91, chmn. ethics commn. 1991-93), Am. Assn. Bot. Gardens and Arboreta (hon. life; pres. 1976, 77, award of merit 1987), Am. Soc. Bot. Artists (bd. dirs. 1997—), Claremont C. of C. (bd. dirs. 1995-98), Ottawa Valley Curling Assn. (pres. 1968-69), B.C. Soc. Landscape Archs. (hon.), U. B.C. Bot. Garden (hon.), Chgo. Hort Soc. (life, medal 1994), Gov. Gen.'s Curling Club Can. (life). E-mail: taylor.rl@shaw.ca.

TAYLOR, RUSSELL BENTON, mining executive; b. Eskridge, Kans., May 16, 1925; s. Bayard Charles and Eva May (Russell) T.; m. Arlene Marie Krehbiel, Aug. 14, 1959; 1 child, Bruce Charles. BSBA, U. Kans., 1949; JD, U. Kans, 1951. Asst. cashier Eskridge (Kans.) State Bank, 1951-57, cashier, 1957, pres., 1958-69, chmn., 1969-78; v.p., dir South Standard Mining Co., Salt Lake City, 1978-96. Mayor City of Eskridge, Kans., 1959. Decorated Purple Heart. Mem. Kans. Bar Assn., Kiwanis, Masonic, Arab Shrine. Republican. Methodist. Avocations: traveling, ranching. Home and Office: 6th & Locust Eskridge KS 66423 E-mail: rbt@kansas.net.

TAYLOR, RUTH ARLEEN LESHER, marketing educator; b. Riverton, Iowa, Mar. 7, 1941; d. Clyde Almond and Bernice Emogene (Graves) Lesher; m. Leslie (Milburn) Taylor, Aug. 10, 1963; children: Treg Anthony, John Leslie II. BS in Home Econs. Edn. magna cum laude, U. Houston, 1975; MEd, Tex. Christian U., 1977; PhD, U. N. Tex., 1981. Prof. mktg. Tarrant County C.C., Ft. Worth, 1977-78, North Tex. State U., Denton, 1978-81, Southwestern U., Georgetown, Tex., 1982-87, S.W. Tex. State U., San Marcos, 1981-82, 87—. Dir. travel to China, Japan, Hong Kong, Costa Rica, Morocco, Europe, Eng. and Mex.; faculty intern Tex. Dept. Econ. Devel. and Tex. Sec. of State Office. Author: Text Maps Study Guides, 1994—; contbg. author: The Psychology of Fashion, 1985, Ethics in Accounting, 1994; contbr. articles to profl. jours. Mem. Lost Creek Garden Club, Austin, Tex., 1985—, v.p.; vol. Bob Bullock State Hist. Mus. Grantee Merrick Found., 1991. Mem.: DAR, Am. Soc. for Competitiveness, Winthrop Soc., French Huguenot Soc., Colonial Dames, Internat. Hospitality Coun. (bd. dirs.), Mayflower Soc., Mktg. Mgmt. Assn., Western Mktg. Educators Assn., Am. Mktg. Assn., Alpha Mu Alpha, Alpha Kappa Psi, Phi Delta Kappa, Phi Epsilon Omicron, Beta Gamma Sigma. Avocations: travel, gardening, reading, entertaining. Office: SW Tex State Univ 601 University Dr San Marcos TX 78666-4685

TAYLOR, SAMUEL STUART, pharmaceutical executive, writer; b. Richmond, Va., Jan. 15, 1958; BS, Old Dominion U., 1981; MBA, Va. Commonwealth U., 1999. Specialist in student devel. U. Tex., Austin, Tex., 1981—86; trainer Merck & Co. Inc., Glen Allen, Va., 1987—. Author: Why Do African Americans Call Themselves the N...Word?, 2000. Recipient Brotherhood award, Nat. Conf. Christians & Jews, 1976. Mem.: Alpha Phi Alpha, Omicron Delta Kappa. Avocation: scuba diving. Office: Jameir Productions PO Box 2081 Glen Allen VA 23058-2081 Fax: 804-364-5279. E-mail: jameir@msn.com.

TAYLOR, SCOTT ALLEN, music educator secondary schools; b. Dayton, Ohio, May 7, 1963; s. Donald F. Taylor and Grace Jane (Childers) Stewart; m. Kelly Kay Knepshield, July 23, 1988; children: Kelsey Rae, Kyle Scott. B of Music Edn., Morehead State U., 1985; MA in Edn., No. Ky. U., 1990. Cert. music tchr. grades kindergarten-12, Ky., Ohio. Jr. high, asst. h.s. band dir. Carlisle (Ohio) Schs., 1986-87, h.s. band dir., 1987-88; h.s. band and choral dir. Newport (Ky.) Ind. Schs., 1988—. Judge marching bands Ky. Music Educators Assn., Calvert City, Ky., 1987—. Nominee Tchr. Merit award Ashland (Ky.) Oil, 1990, Golden Apple award Ky. Post, Covington, 1993. Mem. Ky. Edn. Assn. (assembly del. 1991-93, pres. 1994), Newport Tchrs. Assn. (pres. 1994—), Ky. Music Edn. Assn., No. Ky. Band Dirs. Assn. (chmn. select band 1988—, 92, 93). Republican. Mem. Ch. of Christ. Avocations: golf, fishing, gardening, reading. Home: 7 Jillian Ct Highland Heights KY 41076-1626 Office: Newport HS 900 E 6th St Newport KY 41071-2018

TAYLOR, SCOTT MAXFIELD, sales and marketing executive; b. Evanston, Ill., Aug. 13, 1953; s. Brett Maxfield and Gretchen Pauline (Porter) T. Jr. BA, Coe Coll., 1975; M in Mgmt., Northwestern U., 1977; MSc, New Sem., 1985; EdD, U. St. Thomas, 2002. Sales mgr. Daytons, Mpls., 1977-78, asst. buyer, 1978-79; store mgr. Brett's Dept. Store, Mankato, Minn., 1979-80, buyer jr. dept., 1981-83, v.p., 1981-87, divsn. mdse. mgr., 1984-85, gen. mdse. mgr., 1985-89, pres., 1988-92, also bd. dirs.; v.p. sales and mktg. Phenix Biocomposites, Inc., 1993-95; founder Expanded Awareness Inst., 1985-. Adj. faculty Minn. State U., Mankato, 1996-98; bd. dirs. New Music Network; prof. small bus. mgmt. South Ctrl. Tech. Coll., 1999—. Bd. dirs. Blue Earth County Hist. Soc., Mankato, 1984-87, Mankato Area Conv. and Vis. Bur., 1986-89, chmn., 1987-88; Presbyn. deacon, 1986-88, moderator, 1987-88. George F. Baker scholar, 1975. Mem. Omicron Delta Epsilon, Kiwanis (bd. dirs. 1984-90, pres. 1988-89, named Disting. Club Pres. 1988-89), Nat. Retail Fedn. (bd. dirs. 1991-92), Rotary. Avocation: curling. Home: 38342 Timber Trail Saint Peter MN 56082-9757 also: S Ctrl Tech Coll PO Box 608 New Ulm MN 56073 E-mail: scottt@sctc.mnscu.edu.

TAYLOR, SHAREN RAE (SHAREN MCCALL), special education educator; b. Springfield, Ill., Feb. 26, 1946; d. Robert Jr. and Marie Elizabeth (Motley) McCall; m. Robert Lawrence Taylor, Aug. 13, 1966; children: Rhett Alan, Ryan Andrew, Raegan Alyssa. BS in Elem. Edn., Ill. State U., 1968; MA in Spl. Edn., Northeastern Ill. U., 1990. Cert. trainable mentally handicapped, children and adolescent tchr., Ill. Tchr. 1st grade Argenta (Ill.) Oreanna Schs., 1968; tchr. 3d grade Auburn (Ill.) Pub. Schs., 1968-69, substitute tchr., 1970-73; substitute tutor Virden (Ill.) Pub. Schs., 1970-73, Warrensburg (Ill.) Pub. Schs., 1974-75; tchr. kindergarten Peppermint Stick Pre-Sch., Grayslake, Ill., 1981-84; tchr.'s asst. Laremont Sch., Gages Lake, 1984-86, job coach, 1986-87; tchr. trainable mentally handicapped Laremont Satellite Class, Mundelein, 1987-91, Oak Grove Sch, Libertyville, 1991-95, O'Plaine Sch., Gurnee, 1995-98, Viking Sch., Gurnee, 1998—. Fin. sec. Faith Bapt. Ch., Grayslake, 1985-88, deaconess, 1989-91. Mem. Coun. for Exceptional Children. Republican. Avocations: reading, music, movies, theatre. Home: 18750 W Deerpath Rd Grayslake IL 60030-2912

TAYLOR, SHERRIL WIGHTMAN, broadcasting company executive; b. Salt Lake City, Jan. 4, 1924; s. Kenneth E. and Florence May (Wightman) T.; m. Josephine Vermillion, May 2, 1970; 1 child by previous marriage, Sarah. Student, U. Utah, 1943-46; BJ, U. Mo., 1947; postgrad., Yale U. Promotion mgr. KSL Radio, Salt Lake City, 1947-51; sales promotion mgr. CBS, Hollywood, Calif., 1951-53, CBS radio sales N.Y.C., 1953-56; dir. sales promotion and advt. CBS Radio; also v.p. Radio Advt. Bur., 1956-58; sr. group head J. Walter Thompson, Chgo., 1958-61; ind. TV producer Kukla, Fran, and Ollie Show, N.Y.C., 1961-64; v.p. Nat. Assn. Broadcasters, Washington, 1964-67, dir., 1969-78; v.p. affiliate relations CBS, 1967-79. Cons. Bonneville Internat. Corp., 1979-85; pres. Taylor Co., 1985-91; vice chmn. Coltrin & Assoc., 1991—; pvt. sector coordinator USIA, Washington, 1982, cons., 1982—; chmn. adv. com. Voice of Am., Washington, 1989—; vis. lectr. Brigham Young U., Provo, Utah, 1980— , Emerson Coll., Boston, Mich. Central U., Southern Vt. Coll.; adv. faculty-industry seminar, 1980, 81; bd. dirs. Am. Communications Inc., Utica-Rome TV Svcs. Inc., 1988—. Author: Radio Programming in Action, 1967. Mem. Carnegie Hall com. for Utah Symphony, Park Avenue Preservation Com.; past trustee The Helene Toolen Inst. Med. Rsch., Bennington, Vt., 1985—; mem. futures com. Bennington Mus., 1985—; bd. dirs. Nautical Ventures Inc., N.Y.C., 1987—; chmn. bd. Cmty. Action Network-N.Y., 2000-01. Recipient Nat. Assn. Broadcasters Ann. Conv. Am. Broadcast Pioneer award, 1998. Mem. So. Calif. Broadcasters Assn. (dir.), Internat. Radio and TV Soc. (v.p., bd. dirs., pres., chmn., bd. dirs. found.), Broadcasters' Found. (dir.), Food and Wine Soc. (N.Y. chpt.), Belleair (Fla.) Country Club, Yale Club of N.Y., Sigma Chi (Significant Sig award 2000). Episcopalian. Home: 430 E 86th St New York NY 10028-6441

TAYLOR, SONYA KAYE, legal assistant, writer; b. Gainesville, Ga., Mar. 6, 1952; d. Mark Otwey Taylor, Anita Louise Taylor. Student, U. Ga., 1971—75, Atlanta Law Sch., 1977—79, New Sch. N.Y., 2001. Paralegal Appalachian Cmty. Devel. Com., Bethlehem, Ga., 1990—2001. Mem.: ACLU, Order Ea. Star. Avocation: Avocations: writing plays, screenwriter, writing mysteries.

TAYLOR, STEPHEN CRAIG, philosophy educator, researcher, lecturer; b. Salisbury, Md., May 12, 1954; s. Billy Brown and Bernetta Ann (Anderson) T. Student, Salisbury State Coll., 1973-75; BA, U. Md., 1977, MA, 1979; student in Philosophy, Bryn Mawr Coll., 1991—. Philosophy instr. Del. State Coll., Dover, 1981-85; philosophy asst. prof. Del. State U., 1985—. Dir. Del. State Coll. Lecture Series, 1984-86; vis. scholar, mem. speakers bur. Del. Humanities Forum, 1986—; resident ethicist instnl. animal care and use com. Del. State U.; resident ethicist hospice svcs. adv. com. Del. Hospice, Inc.; ethicist Newborn Screening and Genetics adv. com. State of Del.; lectr. ethical issues numerous orgns. and colls. Contbr. numerous articles on ethics to profl. jours. Mem. Am. Philol. Assn., AAUP, Del. Humanities Forum (affiliate Nat. Endowment for the Humanities). Office: Del State U Philosophy Dept 1200 N Dupont Hwy Dover DE 19901-2202

TAYLOR, STEPHEN H. state commissioner; m. Gretchen Taylor; 3 children. Grad., U. N.H. Reporter and editor daily newspaper; owner, operator dairy and maple, Meriden Village, N.H.; commr. N.H. Dept. Agr., Markets and Food. Active numerous charitable and civic orgns. Served with U.S. Army. Office: NH Dept Agr Markets and Food PO Box 2042 Concord NH 03302-2042 E-mail: staylor@agr.state.nh.us.

TAYLOR, STEPHEN LLOYD, food toxicologist, educator, food scientist; b. Portland, Oreg., July 19, 1946; s. Lloyd Emerson and Frances Hattie (Hanson) T.; m. Susan Annette Kerns, June 23, 1973; children: Amanda, Andrew. BS in Food Sci. Tech., Oreg. State U., 1968, MS in Food Sci. Tech., 1969; PhD in Biochemistry, U. Calif., Davis, 1973. Research assoc. U. Calif., Davis, 1973-74, research fellow, 1974-75; chief food toxicology Letterman Army Inst., San Francisco, 1975-78; asst. prof. food toxicology U. Wis., Madison, 1978-83, assoc. prof., 1983-87; head dept. food sci. technology, dir. Food Processing Ctr. U. Nebr., Lincoln, 1987—. Cons. in field, 1978—. Contbr. articles to profl. jours. Fellow: Inst. Food Technologists (divsn. chmn. 1981—82, sect. chmn. 1984—85, exec. com. 1988—91), Nat. Acad. Scis. (bd. food and nutrition), Nat. Inst. Environ. Health Scs.; mem.: Soc. Toxicology, Am. Chem. Soc., Am. Acad. Allergy, Asthma and Immunology. Democrat. Presbyterian. Home: 941 Evergreen Dr Lincoln NE 68510-4131 Office: U Nebr Dept Food Sci Tech Lincoln NE 68583-0919 E-mail: staylor@unl.edu.

TAYLOR, STEPHEN MICHAEL, music educator; b. Columbus, Ohio, Jan. 29, 1967; s. Ralph Edward Taylor Jr. and Dorothy Ann Taylor; m. Mary Nicole Suter, Nov. 20, 1999. Bachelors of Music in Edn., Carson-Newman Coll., Jefferson City , TN, 1984—88. Department of Education The State of Tenn., 1993. Knox county schools Farragut H.S., Knoxville, Tenn., 1993—, Farragut Mid. Sch., Knoxville, 1992—98, Rule H.S., Knoxville, 1989—91. Mem.: Tenn. Bandmasters Assn. (assoc.), Music Educators Nat. Conv. (assoc.), Tenn. Music Educators Assn. (assoc.), Nat. Band Assn. (assoc.), East Tenn. Sch. Band &Orch. Assn. (assoc.). R-Consevative. Avocations: travel, history, music.

TAYLOR, STEVE HENRY, zoologist; b. Inglewood, Calif., Mar. 18, 1947; s. Raymond Marten and Ardath (Metz) T.; 1 child, Michael Travis; m. Sarah Margaret Young, May 14, 1993. BA in Biology, U. Calif.-Irvine, 1969. Animal keeper Los Angeles Zoo, 1972-75, assoc. curator, 1975-76; children's zoo mgr. San Francisco Zoo, 1976-81; zoo dir. Sacramento Zoo, 1981-88; dir. Cleve. Met. Zoo, 1989—. Bd. dirs. Sacramento Soc. Prevention Cruelty to Animals, 1983-87, Sacramento Red Cross, 1988-89, Conv. and Visitor Bur. of Greater Cleve., 1995—, Leadership Cleveland Class 1997; mem. admissions com. United Way, 1999. Recipient Robert P. Bergman Impact award Convention & Visitors Bur. Greater Cleve., 2000. Fellow Am. Assn. Zool. Parks and Aquariums (infant care diet advisor 1979, 85, bd. dirs. 1987-93, pres. 1991-92, chmn. pub. edn. com. 1987-89, bd. regents, mgmt. sch., chmn. accreditation com. 1998, 99, Outstanding Svc. award 1979, 85, 88, 89, 91, 95, 98, 99, 2001); mem. Conservation Breeding Specialist Group, World Assn. Zoos and Aquariums, The Wilds (bd. dirs. Ohio club), Sierra Club, Audubon Soc. Democrat. Home: 1265 Elmwood Rd Rocky River OH 44116-2236 Office: Cleveland Metroparks Zoo 3900 Wildlife Way Cleveland OH 44109-3132 E-mail: sht@clevelandmetroparks.com.

TAYLOR, STRATTON, state legislator, lawyer; b. Sallisaw, Okla., Jan. 25, 1956; s. Owen and Velma T. AA, Claremore (Okla.) Jr. Coll., 1976; BSE with hons., U. Tulsa, 1978, JD, 1983. Bar: Okla. 1983. State rep. State of Okla., 1978-82, state senator, 1982—; ptnr. Taylor, Burrage, Foster & Singhal, Claremore, 1985—; commr. Uniform Commrs. on State Laws, 1985—; pres. of Okla.Sen., 1995—. Chmn. Okla. Senate Jud. com., 1985-88, appropriations chmn., 1988-94; bd. dirs. State Legis. Found., Oklahoma City, 1988—, Acypl Tour of Japan. Mem. Okla. Bar Assn. Democrat. Baptist. Home: PO Box 309 Claremore OK 74018-0309 Office: Oklahoma State Senate 422 State Capital Bldg Oklahoma City OK 73105*

TAYLOR, STUART ROSS, geochemist, author; b. Ashburton, New Zealand, Nov. 26, 1925; s. Thomas Stuart and Anne Grace (Lloyd) T.; m. Noel Elvie White, May 21, 1958; children: Susanna, Judith, Helen. BSc, U. New Zealand, 1948, MSc, 1951; PhD, Ind. U., 1954; DSc, Oxford U., 1978. Lectr. U. Oxford, Eng., 1954-58; sr. lectr. U. Cape Town, South Africa, 1958-60; professorial fellow Australian Nat. U., Canberra, 1961-90, vis. fellow, 1990-99, prof. emeritus, 1997; prof. U. Vienna, 1992, 96. Vis. scientist Lunar and Planetary Inst., Houston, 1969-90. Author: Lunar Science: Post-Apollo View, 1975, Planetary Science, 1982, Solar System Evolution, 1992, (with others) Continental Crust, 1985, Destiny or Chance: Our Solar System and Its Place in the Cosmos, 1998, Solar System Evolution, 2d edit., 2001; contbr. more than 220 articles to profl. jours. Recipient Goldschmidt medal Geochem. Soc., 1993, Gilbert award Geol. Soc. Am., 1994, Bucher medal Am. Geophys. Union, 2002; Asteroid 5670 named Rosstaylor, 1997. Fellow Royal Soc. New Zealand (hon.), Australian Acad. Sci., Geol. Soc. London (hon.), Geol. Soc. India (hon.); mem. NAS (fgn. assoc.), Meteoritical Soc. (pres. 1989-90, Leonard medal 1998). Office: Australian Nat U Dept Geology Canberra 0200 Australia E-mail: ross.taylor@anu.edu.au.

TAYLOR, SUSAN C. dermatologist; b. Phila., Oct. 7, 1957; d. Charles and Ethel T.; m. Keld Dawkins; children: Morgan Elizabeth, Madison Lauren. BS, U. Pa., 1979; MD, Harvard, 1983. Diplomate Am. Bd. Dermatology, Am. Bd. Internal Medicine. Dermatologist Soc. Hill Dermatology, Phila., 1989—; staff dermatologist/dir. St. Lukes-Roosevelt Hosp. Ctr., New York, 1999—, dir. skin of color ctr. Mem. Am. Acad. Dermatology, Pa. Med. Soc., Phila. Co. Med. Soc., Nat. Med. Assn. Office: Societ Hill Dermatology 932 Pine St Philadelphia PA 19107-6128 also: 1090 Amsterdam Ave New York NY 10025-1737

TAYLOR, SUSAN CHANDLER, state judge; b. Albemarle, N.C., Nov. 20, 1952; d. Aubrey M. and Vivian S. Chandler; m. Michael W. Taylor, Aug. 14, 1977; children: William C.B., Samuel M.G., John C.E. BA, U. N.C., Greensboro, 1975; JD, U. N.C., Chapel Hill, 1978. Cert. juvenile ct. judge, N.C. Asst. dist. atty. 14th dist. State of N.C., Durham, 1978-81, 20th dist. State of N.C., Albemarle, 1981-90, dist. ct. judge, 1990—2002, superior ct. judge, 2002—. Mem. N.C. Assn. Dist. Ct. Judges. Democrat. Baptist. Home: PO Box 65 Albemarle NC 28002-0065 Office: Dist Ct Judges Offices PO Box 1607 Albemarle NC 28002-1607

TAYLOR, SUSAN MERRIL See HORGAN, SUSAN BEDSOW

TAYLOR, SUSAN S. communications executive; b. Minneapolis, Oct. 17, 1945; d. Lucius O. and Mary Elizabeth (McNaughton) T. BS in Edn., U. Minn., 1967; MS in Ednl. Rsch. & Testing, Fla. State U., Tallahassee, 1971, PhD in Instl. Sys., 1974. Cert. tchr., Minn., Mo. Tchr. Minnetonka Pub. Schs., Kansas City, Mo., 1968-70; tchr./author CAI lab.-K.C. Pub. Schs., 1968-70; grad. asst. Fla. State U., Tallhassee, 1970-74; cons./mgr. Control Data Corp., 1974-88; tech. dir. WICAT Sys., Orem, Ut., 1989-90; owner/cons. SST Enterprises, Bloomington, Minn., 1990—. Presenter in field. Author: (chap. book) Create: A Computer-Based Authorizing Curriculum, 1979. Sec. Minn. Episcopal Cursillo Coun., Minn., 1998—2001. Mem. Internat. Soc. Performance Improvement (co-chair independent cons., past pres., treas. Minn. chpt.), Am. Soc. Tng. & Devel. Avocations: gardening, genealogy, reading, walking, crafts. Office: SST Enterprises 7430 Autumn Chace Dr Ste 203 Bloomington MN 55438-1115 E-mail: sstenterprises@aol.net.

TAYLOR, SUZANNE S. educational association administrator, educator; b. Meriden, Conn. d. Clifford I. and Gladys Saunders; children: Patricia Ann, Scott Seth; m. George Brown, 2001. PhD, U. Conn., 1971. Coord. rsch. Conn. Higher Edn., Hartford, 1970-72; rsch. coord. univ. svc. rep. Conn. Edn. Assn., 1972-92; exec. dir. AAUP, Kingston, RI, 1992—2001. Commr. Conn. Commn. on Status of Women, Hartford, 1976-79, U.S. Civil Rights Commn., Hartford, 1980-86; adj. prof. Labor Rels., U. R.I., Kingston, 1988—; chair Old Saybrook (Conn.) Pension Bd., 1990—. Author: Public Employee Retirement Systems, 1988, Negotiating Health Insurance, 1992, Coming of Age in Academia, 1999. Mem. Rep. Town Com., Mansfield, 1976-80, Old Saybrook, 1984-90. Mem.: Am. Assn. Individual Investors, Assn. Fin. Counseling and Planning Edn., Indsl. Rels. Rsch. Assn., Phi Delta Kappa. Avocation: gardening. Home: PO Box 408 Old Saybrook CT 06475-0408 Office: Labor Rsch Ctr URI Kingston RI 02881

TAYLOR, SUZONNE BERRY STEWART, real estate broker; b. Memphis, Sept. 27, 1926; d. Sue Hodge (Berry) Stewart; m. Robert Allen Taylor, Sr., June 15, 1946; children: Robert A. Jr., Suzonne Stewart Taylor Davids. Student, Rhodes Coll., 1944-45, U. S.C., 1969. Cert. residential specialist CRS Coun., 1996; grad. Realtors Inst.; cert. real estate broker; accredited buyer's rep. Am. Bd. Realtors. Sales agt. E. Roy Stone Realtors, Greenville, S.C., 1967-69; realestate broker Aven Assoc. Realtors, Dover, Del., 1970-80, Emerson & Co. Realtors, Dover, 1980—. Active Cresent Music Club, Greenville, 1955, Wildwood Garden Club, Greenville, 1960; mem., costume chmn. Greenville Little Theater, Jr. League Greenville, 1956-66, sustaining mem., 1966—, Jr. League Wilmington, Del., 1999—, dir., 1999. Mem. Nat. Bd. Realtors, Del. Bd. Realtors, Kent County Bd. Realtors, Del. Hist. Soc., Biggs Mus., Alpha Omicron Pi. Republican. Episcopalian. Home: 517 Greenhill Rd Dover DE 19901-3766 Office: Emerson ERA Harrington 1404 Forest Ave Dover DE 19904 E-mail: suetaylor@doverhouses.com.

TAYLOR, TERESA MARIE, realtor; b. San Antonio, Nov. 21, 1949; d. Willie G. and Theresa (Page) Murillo; m. Ralph W. Taylor, June 30, 1972 (div. 1979); children: Lisa, Phillip; m. Michael Brock Toon, Nov. 29, 1997. Grad., Exec. Sectl. Sch., 1969; student, Richland Coll., 1989, Brookhaven Coll., 1990. Lic. real estate agt., Tex. Sec. to controller Steak and Ale Restaurants, 1969-73; sec. Henry S. Miller Co., 1974-75; exec. sec. to sr. v.p. of fin. Jet Fleet Corp., 1976-78; exec. sec. to exec. v.p. and sr. v.p. J.L. Williams & Co., Inc., 1978-80; exec. sec. U.S. Lend Lease Inc., 1980-82; exec. sec. to gen. mgr. Melrose Hotel, 1982-83; exec. sec. to dir. North Tex. sales MCI Telecommunications, 1986-91; leasing agt. Lou Smith Realtors, Dallas, 1988; sales assoc. Christensen Realtors, 1988-97; adminstrv. asst. to info. tech. group, pntr. Kenneth Leventhal & Co., 1991-95; adminstrv. asst. to regional v.p. Bristol Hotel Co., 1995-98; sales assoc. Henry S. Miller Realtors, 1997—2001, Coldwell Banker, 2001—. Active Profl. Members League, Dallas Mus. Art, 1993-95; bd. dirs., v.p. fund raising Am. Kidney Fund, 1989-93, chmn. for ann. fund raiser; bd. dirs. Restart Orgn., 1990-93; fundraiser Nat. Marrow Donor Program, 1995-97; vol. KERP Channel 13, 1994—. Named Multi-Million Dollar Prodr. Mem.: Greater Dallas Assn. Realtors (Paint the Town participant 1989—92, Leadership alumni 2000—), Tex. Assn. Realtors, Nat. Assn. Realtors, Am. Bus. Women's Assn. (bull. editor 1987—88, publicity editor 1988—90, program chmn. 1989—90, hostess chmn. Dallas area coun. 1988—90, chn. pub. rels. com. 1990—92, Woman of the Yr. 1990). Republican. Roman Catholic. Avocations: tennis, snow skiing, cooking, needlepoint. Home: 4149 Republic Dr Frisco TX 75034-6327

TAYLOR, TERRY R. editor, educator; b. Valley Forge, Pa., Oct. 4, 1952; d. Thomas R. and Anna P. (Bystrek) T. BA in Journalism, Temple U., 1974. Reporter gen. assignments, sch. news Charlotte (N.C.) News, 1974-77; supr., writer AP, Phila., 1977-81, supr., writer sports desk N.Y.C., 1981-85, asst. editor sports, 1985-87, dep. editor sports, 1987-91, asst. chief bur., 1991-92, editor sports, 1992—; asst. editor sports N.Y. Times, 1991. Assoc. in journalism Columbia U., N.Y.C., 1991-95; adv. bd. Honda Awards, 1996—. Recipient John A. Domino Meml. award St. Bonaventure U., 1996, Founder's award Temple U., 1999; inductee Delaware County Sports Hall of Fame, 1998. Roman Catholic. Office: AP Sports 50 Rockefeller Plz New York NY 10020-1605

TAYLOR, THEODORE LANGHANS, author; b. Statesville, N.C., June 23, 1921; s. Edward Riley and Elnora Alma (Langhans) T.; m. Gweneth Ann Goodwin, Oct. 25, 1946; children: Mark, Wendy, Michael; m. Flora Gray Schoenleber, Apr. 18, 1981. Student, Fork Union Mil. Acad., 1939-40, U.S. Mcht. Marine Acad., 1942-44. Reporter Portsmouth (Va.) Star, 1941-42, Bluefield (W.Va.) News, 1946-47; sportswriter NBC-Radio, N.Y.C., 1942; asst. dir. pub. relations N.Y. U., 1947-48; dir. pub. relations YMCA Schs. and Colls., N.Y.C., 1948-50; publicist Paramount Pictures, Hollywood, Calif., 1955-56; assoc. producer Perlberg-Seaton Prodns., 1956-61. Free lance writer 1961—; author: The Magnificent Mitscher, 1954, Fire on the Beaches, 1957, People Who Make Movies, 1968, The Cay, 1969 (Jane Addam's Children's Book award 1970), The Children's War, 1971, Air Raid: Pearl Harbor, 1971, The Maldonado Miracle, 1973, Rebellion Town, 1973, Showdown, 1973, Teetoncey, 1974, Teetoncey and Ben O'Neal, 1975, Battle in the Arctic Seas, 1976, The Odyssey of Ben O'Neal, 1977, A Shepherd Watches, A Shepherd Sings, 1977, Jule, 1979, Battle of Midway Island, 1981, The Trouble with Tuck, 1981, Sweet Friday Island, 1981, HMS Hood vs Bismarck, 1982, Battle in the English Channel, 1983, The Cats of Shambala, Rocket Island, 1985, Walking Up a Rainbow, 1986, The Stalker, 1987, The Hostage, 1988, Monocolo, 1989, Sniper, 1989, Tuck Triumphant, 1991, The Wierdo, 1991, Maria, 1992, To Kill the Leopard, 1993, Timothy of the Cay, 1993, The Bomb, 1995, Rogue Wave, 1996, The Flight of Jesse Leroy Brown, 1998, A Sailor Returns, 2000, The Boy Who Could Fly Without A Motor, 2002, Lord of The Kill, 2002. Served with USNR, 1945-46, 50-55. Recipient Lewis Carroll Shelf award, 1970, Silver medal Commonwealth Club, 1970, Best Book award So. Calif. Coun. on Children's Lit., 1970, Best Book award U. Calif. at Irvine, 1970, 74, Best Non-Fiction award Western Writers Am., 1977, Young Reader's Medal Calif. Reading Assn., 1984, 92, Edgar Allan Poe award, 1992, Utah Young Adult Book award, 1993, Md. Children's Book award, 1994, Scott O'Dell Best Hist. Fiction award, 1995, The Kerlan Body of Work award, 1997. Mem. Calif. Writers Guild, Acad. Motion Picture Arts and Scis., Screen Writers Guild. Republican. Lutheran. Address: 1856 Catalina Laguna Beach CA 92651-3340

TAYLOR, THOMAS WILLIAM, lawyer; b. Columbus, Ind., Feb. 11, 1943; s. Virgil W. and Margaret Emma (Voiles) T.; m. Linda Kay Followell, Jan. 1, 1964; children: Pamela Kay, William Lansing. AB with honors, Ind. U., 1965; LLB cum laude, Harvard U., 1968. Bar: Mass. 1968, U.S. Dist. Ct. Mass. 1969. Assoc. Ropes & Gray, Boston, 1968-78, ptnr., 1978-98, of counsel, 1999—. Lectr. Pres.'s urban policy program seminars U.S. Coun. of Mayors, 1982; chmn. tax panel nat. workshop Coun. of Infrastructure Financing Authorities, 1993; vol. astronomer Chaco Obs., Chaco Culture Nat. Hist. Park, 2000, prin. astronomer, 2001; Wilderness First Responder, 2002—. Mem. Nat. Assn. Bond Lawyers (opinions com., chmn. securities law panel Washington workshop 1992, lectr. atty.'s workshop Chgo. 1983-97), Am. Coll. Bond Counsel (founding fellow), Appalachian Mountain Club Stewardship Soc. Avocations: rock climbing, snowboarding, orienteering, trumpet playing. Office: Ropes & Gray 1 International Pl Fl 4 Boston MA 02110-2624

TAYLOR, THOMAS FULLER, religious society administrator; b. Evanston, Ill., May 7, 1937; s. Lewis Archer and Margaret Fox (Nicholson) T.; m. Nancy Louise Emmons, June 16, 1963; children: Jennifer Louise, Clarke Bentley. BA in Physics, Earlham Coll., 1959; MusM, Northwestern U., 1962, PhD in Musicology, 1967. Instr. Oakwood Sch., Poughkeepsie, N.Y., 1959-61, Earlham Coll., Richmond, Ind., 1962-64; lectr. Northwestern U., Evanston, 1964-66, Ind. U., Bloomington, 1966-67; assoc. prof. musicology U. Mich., Ann Arbor, 1967-87; assoc. sec. Friends World Com. Consultation (Quakers), London, 1986-91, gen. sec., 1992-98. Author: The Catalog of Works of Jeremiah Clarke, 1973, Cheerfully over the World, a Handbook for Isolated Friends, 2000; editor Soc. of Friends publs. Clk., chmn. Ann Arbor Friends Meeting, 1974-78; mem. policy com. Friends Com. on Nat. Legislation, 2000—. Avocations: walking, music, travel.

TAYLOR, T(HOMAS) ROGER, educational consultant, educator; b. Urbana, Ill., May 31, 1945; s. Thomas and Ora Wilma Taylor; m. Beverly Milam, Dec. 19, 1981; 1 child, Whitney Brinson. BS, U. Ill., 1967; MA, So. Ill. U., 1972, PhD, 1980. Tchr. Mt. Vernon (Ill.) Schs., 1967-71; cons. Ill. Dept. State, 1971-74; dir. Area Svc. Ctr. for Gifted Children, South Cook County, Ill., 1975-79; prof. urban edn. Govs. State U., 1975-79; cons. Ednl. Cons. Assocs., Denver, 1977-82, also dir. Pres. Curriculum Design for Excellence, Oak Brook, Ill.; former sr. ptnr. T & H Investments, Hinsdale, Ill. V.p. Mt. Vernon C.C. Orch. Named Ky. Col., 1979, Outstanding Young Men of Am., YMCA, 1980, Best of the Best, IDEA Fellows Program, 1992, 93. Mem. NRA, NEA, Ill. Edn. Assn. (bd. dirs.), Nat. Assn. Gifted Children, World Coun. for Gifted, Assn. Childhood Edn. Internat., U. Ill. Alumni Assn. (dir. 1967-71), Profl. Assn. Diving Instrs., Demolay Club, Phi Delta Kappa. Home: 1907 Midwest Club Pkwy Oak Brook IL 60523-2525 Office: PO Box 4505 Hinsdale IL 60522-4505

TAYLOR, TIMOTHY LEON, college dean; b. Danville, Ill., May 7, 1963; s. Howard L. and A. Jane (Pate) T.; m. Melisa Sue Swenny, May 25, 1991. AAS in Electronics Tech., Danville Area C.C., 1985, AAS in Indsl. Maintenance, 1986; BS in Electronics Mgmt., So. Ill. U., 1989, MS Ed. in Vocat. Edn., 1991. Store mgr. Marty K Restaurant, Danville, 1979-86; owner, operator Tayco Sys., Pekin, Ill., 1986-87; mgr. Gatsby's Bar & Billiards, Carbondale, 1988-91; machine operator Ambrosia Chocolate Co., Milw., 1991-92; dir. electronics MBTI Bus. Tng. Inst., 1992-94; assoc. dean indsl. occupations, agr. and apprenticeship Blackhawk Tech. Coll., Janesville, Wis., 1994—. Cons., owner Taylor Info. Mgmt. Sys., Stoughton, Wis., 1991—. Recipient Curriculum Devel. award Accrediting Coun. Indpendent Colls. and Schs., 1993. Mem. ASCD. Baptist. Avocations: music performance, basketball, baseball, football. Office: Blackhawk Tech Coll 6004 Prairie Ave Janesville WI 53547

TAYLOR, VELANDE PINGEL, author, publisher; b. N.Y.C., Sept. 10, 1923; d. Regnar Sophus Albert Pingel and Ella Charlotte Pries; m. Bert Raymond Taylor Jr., Oct. 28, 1961. BA, CUNY, 1944; MA, Columbia U., 1945, PhD, 1947. Instr. Paul Smith's (N.Y.) Coll., 1946-47; asst. prof. East Carolina Coll/U., Greenville, 1947-58; prof., head humanities divsn. Colo. Woman's Coll., Denver, 1958-66; vis. prof. St. Mary's U., San Antonio, 1966-69; prof. Mid. Ga. Coll., Cochran, Ga., 1969-72; lectr., cons. Wing Kwong Coll., Kowloon, Hong Kong, 1974-75; lectr., writer-in-residence Hong Kong Bapt. Coll., 1975-84; cons., founder WordCraft By Lan, Seattle, 1990—; editor, pub. WordCraft Books, 1995—. Cons. in field; appearances on radio programs RTHK, Hong Kong, 1984, WWWS-FM, N.C., 1956-58, KOA, Co., 1961-63, TV programs WNCT, N.C., 1954-58; editor Hong Kong Bapt. Coll. Acad. Jour., 1977-84. Author: (fiction) Fragments of A Broken Mirror, 1983, Tales from the Archetypal World, 1998, Between the Lines, 1999, (non-fiction) An American Utilitarian: Richard Hildreth As A Philosopher, 1948, Icologs in Communication, 1962, Icolog Concept Training Cards, 1965, Mode and Muse in a New Generation, 1978, Homilies in the Marketplace, 1996, rev. edit., 1998, Flowing Water, Singing Sand: The Metaphysics of Change, 1999, Gallery, 2001, (poems: Catalyst, 1951, Copper Flowers, 1996, rev. edit. 1999, Immortal Dancer, 1968, Mood Montage, 1968, Walking Songs, 1997, rev. edit., 1998, Zbyx: Tokens, 1997, The Zodiac Affair, 2000, Gallery, 2001, (syntonic research) Gypsy: A Cymagonic Ode, 1968, Hemisphere Happenings: San Antonio Commemorative Suite, 1968; contbr. essays, stories, poems and articles to profl. publs.; designer games Journeys, Word-Worlds, Options, Vision Quest. Hon. trustee Am. Indian Relief Coun., S.D., 1994—; pro bono cons. Joint Adv. Commn. on Edn., Seattle, 1992-95; vol. spl. svcs. ARC, N.Y.C., 1943-48; svc. vol. Cabrini Pastoral Care Ministry, Seattle, 1994—. Recipient Cert. of Merit, Internat. Mark Twain Soc., 1947, Gold medal order of the Dannebrog, 1951, Bronze medal Freedoms Found., 1952, Gold medal Freedoms Found., 1953, Disting. Svc. Bronze plaque Hong Kong Bapt. Coll., 1982, Cert. of Appreciation, Am. Indian Relief Coun., 1998, 99, 2000, 01, 02. Mem. Am. Philos. Assn., Acad. Am. Poets, Poets and Writers, Nat. Authors Registry, Grünewald Guild. Avocations: art, music, reading, games design, walking.

TAYLOR, VESTA FISK, real estate broker, educator; b. Ottawa County, Okla., July 15, 1917; d. Ira Sylvester and Judie Maude (Garman) Fisk; m. George E. Taylor, Aug. 17, 1957 (dec. Oct. 1963); stepchildren: Joyce, Jean, Luther. AA, Northea. Okla. A&M, 1936; BA, N.E. State U., Tahlequah, Okla., 1937; MA, Okla. State U., 1942. Life cert. Spanish, English, history, elem. Tchr. rural sch. grades 1-4, Ottawa County, Okla., 1931-33; tchr. rural sch. grades 1-8, 1933-38; tchr. H.S. Spanish, English Wyandotte, Okla., 1938-42; tchr. H.S. Spanish, English, math. Miami, 1942-57; tchr. H.S. Spanish Jacksonville, Ill., 1960-65; tchr. H.S. Spanish, English Miami, 1965-79; owner, broker First Lady Realty, 1979—; tchr. real estate for licensing N.E. Okla. Vocat.-Tech., Afton, 1980-94. Radio spellmaster weekly-county groups Coleman Theater Stage, 1954-57; radio program weekly 4-H, Miami, 1953-57; weekly radio program telling story of Pilot Club Internat., Jacksonville, Ill., 1960-61. Author: (poem) The Country School, 1994. Vol. sec. Ottawa County Seniors' Ctr., 1993—; mem. restoration com. Friends of Theater, 1993—; mem. Friends of the Libr., 1994—. Named Outstanding Coach Ottawa County 4-H Clubs, Miami, 1955, 67, Outstanding Alumnus All Yrs. H.S. Reunion, Wyandotte, Okla., 1992, Champion Speller N.E. Okla. Retirees, Oklahoma City, 1991. Mem. AAUW (pres. 1978-80, treas. 1994-98), Ottawa County Ret. Educators (treas. 1990-95, corr. sec. 1995—), Miami Classroom Tchr. (v.p. 1973-77), Tri-state Travel Club (purser 1989-95), Kappa Kappa Iota (pres. 1988-92, treas. 1986-88). Democrat. Baptist. Avocations: gardening, reading, travel, volunteering. Home: 821 Jefferson Blvd Miami OK 74354-4910 Office: First Lady Realty 821 Jefferson St Miami OK 74354-4910

TAYLOR, VICKY ANN, telephone company executive; b. Fairfield, Ala., July 31, 1958; d. Eddie Richardson and Ruth Hans Bogar. BS, Miles Coll., Fairfield, Ala., 1981. Info. case analyst FBI, Washington, 1981-89; adminstrv. sec. D.C. Pub. Schs., 1991-95; maint. adminstr. Bell Atlantic, Greenbelt, Md., 1995—. Sub. tchr. Prince George's County Pub. Schs., Md., 1996—. Poet/writer Nat. Libr. of Poetry, Owing Mills, Md., 1996—. Alto Mass Choir Glendale Bapt. Ch., Landover, Md., 1998, mem. newsletter ministry, 1998—, asst. ch. clk., 1999—. Avocations: bowling, baseball, volleyball, cooking, singing. Home and Office: 2002A Fort Davis St SE Washington DC 20020-1306 Office: PO Box 1056 Forestville MD 20753

TAYLOR, WALTER WALLACE, retired lawyer; b. Newton, Iowa, Sept. 18, 1925; s. Carrol W. and Eva (Greenly) T.; m. Mavis A. Harvey, Oct. 9, 1948; children: Joshua Michael (dec. 1980), Kevin Eileen, Kristin Lisa, Jeremy Walter, Margaret Jane, Melissa E., Amy M. AA, Yuba Coll., 1948, AB, 1950; MA, U. Calif., 1955; JD, McGeorge Coll. Law, 1962. Adminstrv. analyst USAF, Sacramento, 1951-53; personnel, research analyst Calif. Personnel Bd., 1954-56; civil svc., personnel analyst, chief counsel, gen. mgr. Calif. Employees Assn., 1956-75; staff counsel, chief profl. standards Calif. Commn. Tchr. Credentialing, 1975-88, ret., 1988. Staff counsel State Office Real Estate appraiser Licensing and Certification, 1992-94, ret.; tchr. discipline civil service, personnel cons. Author: Know Your Rights, 1963-64. Served USCGR, 1943-46. Mem. Calif. State Bar, Am., Sacramento County Bar Assns. Democrat. Home e-mail: walt. Home: 4572 Fair Oaks Blvd Sacramento CA 95864-5336 E-mail: walt_taylor@quiknet.com.

TAYLOR, WATSON ROBBINS, JR. investment banker; b. Montgomery, Ala., Mar. 16, 1956; s. Watson Robbins and Ernestine (Jenkins) T.; m. Davis Anne Denson, July 12, 1980; children: Watson Robbins III, Caroline Davis, Davis Denson. BS, Auburn U., 1979, MBA, 1982. Ranch foreman Johnston & Sons, Letohatchee, Ala., 1975-76; estimator Standard Roofing Co., Montgomery, 1976-78, v.p., 1978-84; pres. Standard Roofing USA, Inc., 1984-93, Standard-Taylor Industries, 1990-93; ptnr. First Commerce Capital, Inc., Montgomery, 1993-98; mgr. agribus. and middle market fin. group Morgan Keegan, 1998-99; pres. W.R. Taylor & Co., LLC, 1999—. Bd. dirs. Auburn U. Sch. Bus., Montgomery, Montgomery Acad. Fin. chmn. Ala. Rep. Com., Birmingham, 1989; trustee YMCA Endowment Found., Montgomery, 1989; bd. dirs. ARC, 1989, Montgomery coun. Boy Scouts Am., 1989. Mem. Montgomery Area C. of C. (bd. dirs. 1989-92), Ala. Alliance Bus. and Industry (bd. dirs. 1989-92), Rotary (past dir.), Young Pres.'s Assn. (Rebel chpt.), Montgomery Country Club, Ocean Reef Club. Methodist. Avocations: tennis, hunting, fishing, travel. Home: 3809 Colline Dr Montgomery AL 36106-3357 E-mail: rtaylor@wrtayco.com.

TAYLOR, WATSON ROBBINS, construction company executive; b. Wetumpka, Ala., Sept. 7, 1925; s. Henry Watson and Helen Robbins Taylor; m. Ernestine Jenkins, Sept. 10, 1949; children: Jane Albright, W. Robbins Jr., George Lewis. BS, U. Ala., 1948; DSc (hon.), Auburn (Ala.) U., 1986. Estimator Std. Roofing Co., Montgomery, Ala., 1948-52, v.p., 1952-66, pres., CEO, 1966-97, CEO, chmn. bd., 1997—; chmn., pres. Std.-Taylor Industries Inc., 1979—. Chmn. bd. Union Bank and Trust Co., Montgomery, 1980-94. Chmn. bd., founding chmn. Auburn U., Montgomery, 1967-80; dir. Ala. Shakespeare Festival, 1995—, Ala. State Docks, Mobile, 1992—. Lt. j.g. USN, 1943-45. Named Contractor of Yr. RSI mag., 1999; named univ. ctr. in his honor Watson Robbins Taylor Ctr. Auburn U., 1999. Republican. Episcopalian. Avocations: golf, hunting. Home: PO Box 1 Letohatchee AL 36047-0001 Office: Std Roofing Co 516 N Mcdonough St Montgomery AL 36104-2645

TAYLOR, WESLEY ALAN, accountant, consultant; b. Johnson City, Tenn., Oct. 27, 1958; s. Wesley Wentworth and Charlotte Marie (Holly) T.; m. Robin Ann Whitehead, Aug. 3, 1996. BS in Acctg., U. Tenn., 1980. CPA, Tenn., Va.; registered rep. Nat. Assn. Securities Dealers; cert. pvt. pilot FAA. Staff acct. Wesley W. Taylor CPA, P.C., 1980-85; sr. acct. Blackburn, Childers & Stegall, CPAs, Elizabethton, Tenn., 1985-88; acct., mgr. BCS & Co., CPAs, Bristol, 1988-89; pvt. practice, Elizabethton, 1989; tax sr. Brown, Edwards & Co., CPAs, Abingdon and Bristol, Va., 1989-91; pvt. practice Elizabethton, Tenn., 1991—. Auditor for various local Miss Am. preliminary pageants, 1985-97, local state fair pageant judge, 1992, 98, local parade judge, 1994-95, local chief judge festival pageant. Mem. AICPA, Johnson City Jaycees (pres., v.p., treas., Keyman of Yr., Jaycee of Yr., Presdl. award of excellence, others), Tenn. Jaycees (state sec.-treas.), Aircraft Owners and Pilots Assn. (pvt. pilot 1996—), Nat. Aeronautic Assn., Exptl. Aircraft Assn., Profl. Assn. Diving Instrs. (open water diver 1988), Am. Motorcyclist Assn., Diving Soc. of Profl. Assn Diving Instrs. Republican. Christian. Avocations: water- and snowskiing, motorcycling, boating, aviation, scuba diving. Home: 140 Andi Brandon Ln Johnson City TN 37601 Office: 308 E F St Elizabethton TN 37643-3270 E-mail: watcpa@mounet.com.

TAYLOR, WESLEY BAYARD, JR. retired army officer; b. Covington, Ky., June 5, 1944; s. Wesley B. Sr. and Varina Martha (Morgan) T.; m. Linda L. Taylor, June 2, 1967; children: Kathleen C., Clint C. BS, U.S. Mil. Acad., 1965; MA in Internat. Rels., U. Calif., Santa Barbara, 1973; student, U.S. Army War Coll., 1985-86. Commd. 2d lt. U.S. Army, 1965, advanced through grades to brig. gen., 1990; asst. bn. advisor, sr. bn. advisor Airborne Divsn. Adv. Detachment, U.S. Mil. Assitance Command, Vietnam, 1967-68; staff officer Dept. of Army, Washington, 1980-81; bn. comdr. 3rd Bn., 5th Inf. U.S. Army, Republic of Panama, 1981-83; bn. comdr. 1st Ranger Bn. Hunter Army Airfield, Ga., 1983-85; strategic fellow U.S. Army War Coll., Carlisle Barracks, Pa., 1986-87; regimental comdr. 75th Ranger Regiment, Ft. Benning, Ga., 1987-89; asst. divsn. comdr. 1st Armored Divsn., Germany, 1989-91; dep. dir. ops, readiness and mobilization Dept. of Army, Washington, 1991-92; dep. asst. sec. of def. for policy and missions Office Sec. of Def., 1992-94; pres., CEO Cal Farley's Boys Ranch & Affiliates, U.S.A., Amarillo, Tex., 1995-99. Dist. commr. Boy Scouts Am., Germany, 1989-91. Decorated DSM, Def. Superior Svc. medal, Silver Star, Legion of Merit, Def. Meritorious Svc. medal, Bronze Star medal with oak leaf cluster, Air medals. Mem. Assn. U.S. Army, U.S. Army Ranger Assn., 75th Ranger Regiment Assn., Soc. Vietnamese Airborne Advisors, Soc. 173rd Airborne Brigade. Methodist. Avocations: fishing, hunting.

TAYLOR, WILLIAM AL, church administrator; b. Danville, Va., Sept. 26, 1938; s. Preston Floyd and Helen Elizabeth (Doss) T.; m. Brenda Flo Owen, June 4, 1961 (dec. 1996); children: Fawnia Rae Ricks, Albert Todd, Athena Dawn Jarman; m. Norma S. Pierce, June 28, 1997. AA, Lee Coll., 1957; postgrad., U. Calif., Santa Barbara, 1980. Br. mgr. Ency. Britannica, Greensboro, N.C., 1960-62, divsn. trainer Mpls., 1963, dist. mgr. Omaha, 1964-72; adminstrv. asst. Forward in Faith Internat. Broadcast, Cleveland, Tenn., 1972-80; gen. mgr. Sta. WQNE-FM, 1980—; dir. stewardship Ch. of God Internat. Offices, 1980—. Pres. Pathway Credit Union, Cleveland, 1985—, Vision Found., Cleveland, 1985—, exec. dir., 1979-80; chmn. Internat. Commn. on Prayer, Cleveland, 1986—. Author: Proving God, 1991, Days of Heaven on Earth, 1993, Stewardship Masterplanning, 1993. Pres. Clean Water Soc., Gastonia, N.C., 1974-75; speaker Citizens Against Legalized Liquor, Bradley County, Tenn., 1973, 75; advisor Mothers on March, Cleveland, 1976; active Nat. Conf. on Drug Abuse, Washington, 1978; master of ceremonies Nat. Religious Leaders Conf. on Alcohol and Drug Abuse, Indpls., 1979; pres. Ch. of God Found., 2002. Recipient Mass Communications award Ch. of God Media Ministries, 1980, Stephen award Ch. of God Lay Ministries, 1990. Mem. Nat. Assn. Evangelicals (bd. adminstrs. 1985-98, chmn. stewardship commn. 1985-89), Christian Stewardship Assn. (bd. dirs. 1990-96, nat. prayer com. 1999—, Outstanding Stewardship Profl. award 2000). Avocations: flying, travel, racquetball. Office: Ch of God Dept Stewardship 2490 Keith St NW Cleveland TN 37311-1309 E-mail: stewardcog@mindspring.com. *We are all spending the precious gift of life, and we have been given the privilege to decide upon what we shall spend it. I have found the most worthy and fulfilling investment of life is God's stated purpose, "that we be conformed to the image of His son Jesus Christ".*

TAYLOR, WILLIAM BROCKENBROUGH NEWTON, engineer, consultant, management consultant; b. Norfolk, Va., Mar. 11, 1925; s. Lewis Jerome and Roberta Page (Newton) T.; m. Nancy Dare Aitcheson, June 12, 1945; children: William B. N. Jr., Anne P. Taylor Cregger, Paul K., Katharine C.Taylor Nace, David A. BS, U.S. Mil. Acad., West Point, N.Y., 1945; MS in Engring., Johns Hopkins U., 1951. Profl. engr., D.C., Va. Commd. 2d lt. U.S. Army Corps of Engrs., 1945, advanced through grades to maj., 1953, retired, 1954; gen. engr. Army AEC Nuclear Power Program, Washington, Ft. Belvoir, Va., 1955-60; engring. mgr. Army Mapping R&D, Ft. Belvoir, 1960-62; aerospace engr. NASA, Washington, 1962-67; R&D mgr. staff Army Hdqrs., 1967-69; tech. dir. Army R&D Lab., Ft. Belvoir, 1969-73; chief R & D U.S. Army Corps of Engrs., Washington, 1973-77; prin. engr. Planning Rsch. Corp., McLean, Va., 1978-80; consulting engr. and mgmt. cons. Alexandria, 1980—. Mem. study com. Nat. Rsch. Coun., Washington, 1983; mem. constrn. mgmt. task force Grace Commn. on Cost. Control, Washington, 1982. Contbr. articles to The Mil. Engr. jour., Wash. Acad. Scis. jour., others. Participant various civic activities. Fellow Soc. Am. Mil. Engrs. (pres. Fort Belvoir chpt. 1972); mem. AIAA, SAR, SCV, Order of Founders and Patriots Am., Washington Acad. Scis., Sigma Xi. Republican. Episcopalian. Achievements include program definition of NASA's Apollo applications program; designs for geothermal energy power plant for Dominica; 5 military nuclear power plants; international technology transfer among U.S., U.K., Germany, Sweden, and Russia involving governmental and industrial clients. Home and Office: 4001 Belle Rive Ter Alexandria VA 22309-3004

TAYLOR, WILLIAM JAMES (ZAK TAYLOR), lawyer; b. Milw., Jan. 26, 1948; s. William Elmer and Elizabeth Emily (Lupinski) T.; m. Marlou Belyea, Sept. 20, 1975; children: Danielle Belyea, James Zachary Belyea. BA in Econs., Yale U., 1970; JD, Harvard U., 1976. Bar: Calif. 1976, U.S. Dist. Ct. (cen. dist.) Calif. 1976, U.S. Dist. Ct. (no. dist.) Calif. 1977, U.S. Ct. Appeals (9th cir.) 1977, U.S. Dist. Ct. (ea. dist.) Calif. 1980, U.S. Supreme Ct. 1980, U.S. Tax Ct. 1988. Law clk. to hon. Shirley M. Hufstedler U.S. Ct. Appeals (9th cir.), L.A., 1976-77; assoc. Broebeck, Phleger & Harrison, San Francisco, 1977-83; ptnr. Broebeck, Phleger and Harrison, 1983-95; shareholder Taylor & Jenkins, P.C., Oakland, Calif., 1995-96, Chilvers & Taylor, P.C., Oakland, 1996-99; of counsel Brobeck, Phleger & Harrison, LLP, San Francisco, 2000—. Bd. dirs. Berkeley (Calif.) Law Found., 1988-91, Legal Svcs. for Children (recipient Jean Waldman Child Advocacy award, San Francisco 1988), 1983-89; co-chmn. Attys. Task Force for Children, San Francisco, 1983-89. Editor-in-chief Harvard Civil Rights, Civil Liberties Law Rev., 1976; bd. editors No. Dist. Calif. Digest, 1978-83; co-author: California Antitrust Law, 1991; contbg. editor: Calif. Bus. Law Reporter, 1995-96, Antitrust Law Developments, 1997, 2d edit., 2002. With U.S. Army, 1970-73. Mem. ABA, Bar Assn. San Francisco (bd. dirs. 1986-87, chair antitrust sect. 1987, chair fed. cts. sect. 1995-97), Am. Bus. Trial Lawyers Assn., Nat. Health Lawyers Assn., Calif. Soc. Healthcare Attorneys, Barristers of San Francisco (bd. dirs. 1980-82, v.p. 1982-83). Democrat. Office: Brobeck Phleger & Harrison LLP 1 Market Spear Tower San Francisco CA 94105-1420 E-mail: wtaylor@brobeck.com., wta9786011@cs.com.

TAYLOR, WILLIAM JESSE, JR. international studies educator, research corporation president; b. Florence, S.C., Dec. 28, 1933; s. William J. and Dorothy (Byrd) T.; m. Louise Inger Haegerstrom, Apr. 9, 1977; 1 child, Nicolaus; children by previous marriage: Juliana C., William J. III, L. Scott, Christopher B., Helen B. BS, U. Md., 1962; MA, Am. U., 1964, PhD, 1967. Enlisted U.S. Army, commd. 2d lt., 1955, advanced through grades to col., 1976; prof. U.S. Mil. Acad., West Point, N.Y., 1970-81; vis. prof. U.S. Nat. War Coll., 1975-76; ret. col. U.S. Army, 1981; dir. polit. mil. studies Ctr. for Strategic and Internat. Studies Georgetown U., Washington, 1980-83; exec. dir., chief operating officer Ctr. for Strategic and Internat. Studies, 1983-87, v.p. internat. security programs, 1987-92; sr. v.p. Internat. Security Affairs, 1992-99, sr. advisor, 1999-2000; pres. Taylor Assocs. Inc., 1984—. Internat. lectr., debater, T.V. mil. analyst, 1970—. Author: Future of Conflict: U.S. Interests, 1982, Future of Conflict into the 21st Century, 1987; co-author: American National Security: Policy and Process, 1981, 83, 89, 93, 99; co-editor: Defense Manpower Planning, 1980, The Future of Conflict in the 1980's, 1982, Strategic Requirements for the Army to the Year 2000, 1983, Strategic Responses to Conflict in the 1980's, 1984, Nordic Defense: Comparative Decisionmaking, 1985, Strategic Dimensions of Military Manpower, 1987, The Future of U.S.-Republic of Korea Security Ties, 1989, The Korean Peninsula: Prospects for Arms Control, 1990, Korea 1991: The Road to Peace, 1991, Elvis in The Army, 1995, 97. Mem. Presiding Bishop's Nat. Episc. Roundtable, 1983-86. Decorated Bronze Star with oak leaf cluster, Legion of Merit (2), Air Medal (3), Air medal for valor, Vietnam Cross of Gallantry, Combat Infantry Badge; recipient Pitman Potter Medal Am. U., 1964; named to Infantry Officer Hall of Fame, 1976; named Disting. Alumnus, Episcopal Acad., 1995. Mem. St. Anthony Club. Republican. Episcopalian. Home: 6010 Maiden Ln Bethesda MD 20817-6261 E-mail: wjtaylor44@aol.com., wtaylor@csis.org.

TAYLOR, WILLIAM OSGOOD, newspaper executive; b. Boston, July 19, 1932; s. William Davis and Mary (Hammond) T.; m. Sally Coxe, June 20, 1959; children: William Davis II, Edmund C., Augustus R. BA, Harvard U., 1954. With Globe Newspaper Co., Boston, 1956—, treas., 1963, bus. mgr., 1965-69, gen. mgr., 1969—; chmn. emeritus The Boston Globe, 1998—; chmn. Fed. Res. Bank of Boston. Trustee Boston Pub. Libr., Boston Pub. Libr. Found.; chmn. emeritus The Freedom Trail Found.; dir. Internat. Crisis Group; chmn. founder's com. Boston Mus. Project. With U.S. Army, 1954-56. Address: Globe Newspaper Co Three School St Boston MA 02108-4317

TAYLOR, WILLIAM WOODRUFF, III, lawyer; b. Richmond, Va., July 30, 1944; s. William Woodruff Jr. and Ida (Winstead) T.; m. Susan Broadhurst, Sept. 29, 1984; children: Katherine Lowell, Matthew Gordon. AB, U. N.C., 1966; LLB, Yale U., 1969. Bar: N.C. 1969, D.C. 1970, U.S. Ct. Appeals (2nd, 4th, 5th and 11th cirs.), U.S. Supreme Ct. Law clk. to judge U.S. Dist. Ct. Del., Wilmington, 1969-70; staff atty. Pub. Defender Service, Washington, 1970-75; assoc. Ginsburg, Feldman and Bress, 1975-78; ptnr. Zuckerman, Spaeder L.L.P., 1978—. Instr. dept. forensic sci. George Washington U., Washington, 1973-74; adj. prof. Columbus Sch. Law, Cath. U. Am., Washington, 1973-76; mem. D.C. Commn. on Jud. Disabilities and Tenure, 1978-83, chmn., 1979-83; vis. prof. U. N.C. Law Sch., fall 1991. Fellow Am. Coll. Trial Lawyers; mem. ABA (criminal justice sect., vice chmn. for govtl. affairs 1989-92, chair criminal justice sect. 1996-97), Nat. Inst. for Trial Advocacy (faculty 1978—, chmn. pub. defender svc. assn. 1984-89). Episcopalian. Avocations: fly fishing, tennis. Office: Zuckerman Spaeder LLP Taylor & Kolker LLP 1201 Connecticut Ave NW Washington DC 20036-2638

TAYLOR, WILSON H. retired diversified financial company executive; Grad., Trinity Coll., 1964. With Conn. Gen., 1964—82; v.p. Aetna Ins. Co., 1975; exec. v.p., CFO Cigna Corp., Phila., 1982-88, pres. property casualty group, 1983-88, COO, 1988, pres., chief exec. officer, 1988—2000; ret., 2000. Phi Beta Kappa.*

TAYLOR-BROWN, CAMERON ANN, artist, educator, consultant; b. L.A., Oct. 2, 1953; d. James Hutton and Ann Rossner (Hinsdale) Taylor; m. Charles Albert Brown, July 8, 1978; children: Julia, Peter. Student, Vassar Coll., 1970-71; BA, U. Calif., Berkeley, 1975; BS, Phila. Coll. Textiles, 1977. Fabric stylist Cheney Bros., N.Y.C., 1977-79; design instr. Phila. Coll. Textiles, 1979-83; rsch. assoc., curator Goldie Paley Design Ctr., Phila., 1980-83; arist, educator Phila. and L.A., 1979—; regional rep. fibers L.A., 1983—; ednl. cons. ACCESS Cmty. Arts and Edn., 1997—. Mem. com. Getty Edn. Inst./Fairfax Family Sch., L.A., 1997; lectr., workshop presenter Bobbinwinders, Creative Weavers Guild, the Shepherdess, South Coast Spinners and Weavers, So. Calif. Guild Handweavers. Artist, contbr. Fiberarts mag., 1985, 87, Fiberarts Design Book 4, 1991, Design Book 5, 1995, Design Book 6, 1999 Shuttle, Spindle & Dyepot, 1997; exhbns. include Artspace Gallery, Woodland Hills, Calif., 1992, Del Mano Gallery, 1994, Downey Mus. Arts, 1995, Riverside Mus. Art, 1997, Wignall Gallery, 1999 Mem. program devel. com., fundraiser, cmty. outreach com., grant writer Friends of Third St. Sch., L.A., 1989-99, co-pres., 1997-99—. Recipient Woman of Larchmont Cmty. Svc. award Larchmont Chronicle, 1997. Mem. Textile Group L.A. (bd. dirs. 1984-90), Designing Weavers (Bd. dirs. 1992-95, 97—), Calif. Fibers (regional liaison 1993—). Avocations: reading, gardening, travel, skiing.

TAYLOR DYE, JUDY ANGIE, engineer, consultant; b. Cantho, Vietnam, Mar. 15, 1970; came to U.S., 1975; d. Carl Eugene and Phyllis Lynn (Le) T. BS in Engring., Fla. Atlantic U., 1994. Engr., intern Wescon Cons., Deerfield Beach, Fla., 1994, project engr., 1994-95, project mgr., 1995-96, project mgr., gen. mgr., 1996-97; owner, pres. C.E.M. Cons., West Palm Beach, Fla., 1997-2001; project engr., team leader LBFH Inc., Palm City, 2001—. Democrat. Office: LBFH Inc 3550 SW Corporate Pkwy Palm City FL 34990

TAYLOR-LOVELL, SARAH, biologist; b. Plattsburgh, N.Y., Jan. 31, 1970; d. Howard Wayne and Mary Beth Taylor; m. Jeffrey James Lovell, June 11, 1994; children: Morgan Beth Lovell, Evan James Lovell. BS, U. Ill., 1992, MS, 1995, PhD, 2000. Rsch. biologist Zeneca Agrl. Products, Champaign, Ill., 1995-97; grad. rsch. asst. U. Ill., 1997-2000; field devel. biologist Dow AgroScis., Indpls., 2000—. Instr. Ill. Agrl. Pesticide Conf., Champaign, 2000. Contbr. articles to profl. jours. Recipient Lang Aldrich award Ill. Fertilizer and Chem. Assn., 1993; Frerichs grad. fellow, U. Ill., 1992-94, Slife grad. fellow, 1999. Mem. Weed Sci. Soc. Am., Agronomy Soc. Am., North Ctrl. Weed Sci. Soc., Phi Eta Sigma. Methodist. Home: 3000 Mallard Ave Lorimor IA 50149 E-mail: staylor-lovell@dow.com.

TAYLOR SWISHER, DEBORA DIANNE, home health nurse; b. Canton, Ill., Apr. 5, 1959; d. Richard Jean and Barbara Elaine (Bump) T.; m. Duane E. Swisher, Aug. 8, 1998. AAS, Carl Sandburg Coll., 1980; BSN, U. Ill., Chgo., 1990. Cert. provider BLS, Am. Heart Assn. Staff nurse pediatrics St. Mary Med. Ctr., Galesburg, Ill., 1980-94, staff nurse home health, 1994—, operational support nurse, 1998—2000, performance improvement/edn. coord./home health aide supr., 2000—. Clin. instr. LPN program Carl Sandburg Coll., Galesburg, 1990-92; home health nurse UpJohn Healthcare Svcs., Rock Island, Ill., 1990-92; chmn. recruitment and retention com. St. Mary Med. Ctr., 1991-92; mem. nominating com. 5th dist. I.N.A., Moline, Ill., 1990-91; cons. in devel. of parenting programs, 1990; CPR instr. Am. Heart Assn.; CPR and first aid instr. ARC. Guest speaker childcare class Galesburg High Sch, 1989; mem. Knox County Cardiovascular Task Force; active Young Reps., Galesburg, 1990; supt. Sunday sch. Henderson (Ill.) United Meth. Ch., 1986—92. Mem. ANA, U. Ill. Nursing Alumni Assn. (bd. dirs., award 1990), Sigma Theta Tau. Avocations: reading, walking, cross-stitching, singing. Home: 1713 N Seminary St Galesburg IL 61401-1921 Office: St Mary Med Ctr 3333 N Seminary St Galesburg IL 61401-1251

TAYLOR-WHITE-GRIGSBY, QUEEN DELORES, minister, consultant; b. Oklahoma City, Aug. 21, 1948; d. Barnett C., Sr. and Bedell Boles Dewitt Taylor; m. Walter Thomas White II, Nov. 26, 1966 (div. June 1976); children: Walter Thomas III, Robin Orlando; m. James O. Grigsby, Sept. 19, 1976 (dec. Dec. 1976); 1 child, James Jumaané. BS, Howard U., 1970. Ordained to ministry Ray Deliverance Found., 1989. Assoc. cons. Trust Inc., Richmond, Va., 1973-80, Orgnl. Devel. Cons., Richmond, 1974—; founder, cons., pres. Taylor & Co., Phoenix, Richmond, Va., Atlanta, Okla. City, Possum Hollow, Ark., 1973—; founder, min. Man Child Ministries, Phoenix, 1988—. Cons. MARTA Atlanta, 1978-79, Frederick County, Md., 1974, Richmond Pub. Sch. System, 1977, Black Police Officers, Tulsa, 1986. Author, poetess. Advocate child welfare Dept. of Corrections, Phoenix, 1990, advocate tchr. rights, 1991; active tchr. rights Phoenix Pub. Sch. System, 1992; supr. elections County Election Bd., Maricopa County, Ariz., 1987; cons., coord. YMCA, Maricopa County, 1991-92, trainer, developer internat. analysis model for residential housing for abused women and their families YWCA; coord. asst. swim program YWCA, Glendale Recreation Dept.; active food programs and ministry Internat. Healing Cathedral/Hall of Deliverance and Dessert Moon Found., 1982—; active children and youth program Phoenix Women's League, 1991-92 Lucille McMahn scholar, 1965, Nellie Green scholar, 1965; recipient Danforth Leadership award, 1965, Philip Morris Scholarship, 1983, Golden Poet award, 1991. Mem. Soc. Tng. and Devel. (cert. housing specialist), Housing Specialist Inst. Independent Republican. Avocations: reading, swimming, hunting, fishing, camping. Office: Taylor & Co 1138 N Bath Ave Oklahoma City OK 73117-2602

TAYMOR, JULIE, theater, film and opera director and designer; b. Newton, Mass., 1952; d. Melvin L. and Betty Taymor. BA, Oberlin Coll., 1974. Founder Teatr Loh. Dir. Way of Snow, The Transposed Heads, 1984, The Tempest, 1986, Liberty's Taken, 1985, Juan Darién, 1988, Fool's Fire, 1992, Titus Andronicus, 1994, Oedipus Rex, 1992, The Magic Flute, Salomé, The Flying Dutchman, The Lion King, 1997, (Tony awards for best director and costume design 1998), operas, classical plays and exptl. theater projects; prodr. Shakespeare plays and operas; designer puppets, masks, imaginative costumes and other visual elements. MacArthur grantee, Watson fellow, 1974-79, Obie awards, 1988. Office: Internat Creative Mgmt 40 W 57th St New York NY 10019-4001*

TAYSON, RICHARD ALLAN, office management director, writer, educator; b. San Bernardino, Calif., Jan. 24, 1962; came to U.S., 1962; s. Virgil Dean Tayson and Kathryn Marie (Beresford) Drake. BA, Colo. State U., 1988; MA, NYU, 1992. Tchg. asst. NYU, N.Y.C., 1991, program coord. Goldwater Hosp. Writing, 1993-94; adj. faculty New Sch. Social Rsch., 1995—; dir. office mgmt. Philip Johnson/Alan Ritchie Architects. Author: Look Up For Yes, 1997, The Apprentice of Fever, 1998. Recipient Beatrice Slote award Prairie Schooner Rev., Lincoln, Nebr., 1995, Pushcart prize Pushcart Press, 1996, Wick Poetry prize Kent (Ohio) State U., 1997. Avocations: movie history, contemporary American poetry, disability and gay activism. Home: 8675 Midland Pkwy Apt 4N Jamaica NY 11432-3034 Office: Philip Johnson/Alan Ritchie Architects 375 Park Ave New York NY 10152-0002

TAZEAU, YVETTE NICOLE, psychologist; b. Mar. 25; BA, U. Calif., Davis, 1988; MS, Pacific Grad. Sch. Psychology, Palo Alto, Calif., 1993, PhD, 1995. Clin. asst. Stanford (Calif.) Med. Ctr., 1990-91, The Children's Health Coun., Palo Alto, 1991-96; intern VA Med. Ctr., 1993-94; dist. mgr., psychologist San Andreas Regional Ctr., Campbell, Calif., 1997-99; pvt. practice San Jose, 1998—. Mem. APA, Calif. Psychol. Assn., Hispanic Neuropsychol. Soc., Soc. Indsl. & Orgnl. Psychology, Nat. Soc. Hispanic MBAs.

TCHIVZHEL, EDVARD, music director; b. Leningrad, Russia, Jan. 29, 1944; Music dir. Fort Wayne Philharm Orch., Ft. Wayne, Tex., 1993-98, Greenville Symphony Orch., Greenville, S.C., 1999—. Office: Greenville Symphony Orch 200 S Main St Greenville SC 29601-2832*

TCHOBANOGLOUS, GEORGE, civil engineering educator; b. Patterson, Calif., May 24, 1935; s. Christo and Penelope (Megdani) T.; m. Rosemary Ash, June 16, 1957; children— Kathryn, Lynn, Julianne. B.C.E., U. Pacific, 1958; M.C.E., U. Calif., Berkely, 1960; PhD, Stanford U., 1969. Registered profl. engr., Calif. Research engr. U. Calif.-Berkeley, 1960-62; cons. Metcalf & Eddy Engrs., Palo Alto, Calif., 1963-81, Nolte & Assocs., Sacramento, 1981—, Calif. Water Resources Control Bd., 1972-80; assoc. prof. U. Calif.-Davis, 1970-76, prof. engring., 1976—. Prin. author: Wastewater Engineering: Collection, Treatment, Disposal, 1972; author: (with R. Smith and R. Crites) Wastewater Management: A Guide to Information Sources, 1976, (with H. Theisen and R. Eliassen) Solid Wastes: Engineering Principles and Management Issues, 1977, (with Schroeder) Water Quality: Characteristics, Modeling, Modification, 1985, (with Peavy and Rowe) Environmental Engineering, 1985, (with H. Theisen, S.A. Vigil) Integrated Solid Waste Management: Engineering Principles and Management Issues, 1993. (with R. Crites) Small and Decentralized Wastewater Management Systems, 1998; co-author: Wastewater Engineering: Treatment, Disposal, Reuse, 1991; author, editor: Wastewater Engineering: Collection and Pumping of Wastewater, 1981; co-editor: Pumping Station Design, 1989; contbr. numerous articles to profl. jours. Mem. bd. Calif. Integrated Waste Mgmt.; lectr. T.R. Camp, 1990. Mem. AAAS, ASCE, Assn. Environ. Engring. Profs. (bd. dirs., past pres.), Am. Acad. Environ. Engrs., Water Environ. Fedn. (Gordon Masken Fair medal 1985), Am. Water Works Assn. (Thomas R. Camp lectr. 1991), World Mariculture Soc., Sigma Xi. Home: 662 Diego Pl Davis CA 95616-0123

TCHOSHANOV, MOURAT ASHIROVICH, education educator; b. Dashoguz, Turkmenistan, July 11, 1959; arrived in U.S., 1998; s. Ashir Tchoshanov and Amangul Tchoshanova; m. Natalia Ivanovna Tchoshanova, Mar. 17, 1989; 1 child Aina Mouratovna Tchoshanova. Specialist degree, Turkmen State Inst., Chardjou, Turkmenistan, 1980; Candidate of Sci., Kazan (Russia) State Inst., 1987; DSc, postgrad., Kazan State U., 1996. Prof. math. Tatar-Am. Inst., Kazan, 1992—97, Kostroma State Tech. U., Russia, 1997—98; prof. tchr. edn. U. Tex., El Paso, 2000—. Vis. scholar Case Western Res. U., Cleve., 1994—95; vis. prof. Ohio State U., Columbus, 1998—2000; adv. bd. mem. Supporting and Strengthening Stds.-based Math. Tchr. Preparation NSF, Austin, Tex., 2001—. Author: Flexible Technology of Problem-based Modular Instruction, 1996, Visual Mathematics, 1997, America Learns to Count, 2001. Recipient Fulbright award, U.S. Info. Agy., Washington, 1994. Fellow: Fulbright Assn.; mem.: N.Y. Acad. Sci., Internat. Group on Psychology Math. Edn. Office: U Tex El Paso 500 W University Ave El Paso TX 79968

TCHOUNWOU, PAUL BERNARD, environmental health specialist, toxicologist, educator; b. Bangou, Cameroon, Aug. 14, 1960; came to U.S., 1985; s. Maurice and Christine (Kouanang) Seumo; m. Martha Namondo Mondoa, Aug. 3, 1990; children: Christine K., Hervey M., Solange S. BSc, U. Yaounde, Cameroon, 1983, MSc, 1984; MS in Pub. Health, Tulane U., 1986, ScD, 1990. Cert. toxicologist Nat. Environ. Health Assn.; registered sanitarian La. State Bd. Examiners for Sanitarians. Tchg. asst. Tulane Sch. Pub. Health, New Orleans, 1988-90; med. rschr. Inst. Med. Rsch., Yaounde, 1991-94; asst. prof. Faculty Medicine, 1992-94; rsch. assoc. Xavier & Tulane Univs., New Orleans, 1994-96; assoc. prof., dir. environ. sci. PhD program Jackson State U., Jackson, 1996—; adj. assoc. prof. sch. pub. health Tulane U., 1999—; prof., dir. environ. sci. doctoral program Jackson State U., 2001—. Adj. assoc. prof. Tulane U. Sch. Pub. Health, 1999—; environ. health cons. Orstom & UNICEF, Yaounde, 1992-93, U.S. AID, Kaele, 1991-93; rsch. supr. Tulane Sch. Pub. Health, New Orleans, 1994—; tng. and rsch. fellow U.S. AID, Washington, 1985-90; adj. assoc. prof. environ. health scis. Tulane U. Sch. Pub. Health and Tropical Medicine, 1999—. Editl. bd. Internat. Jour. Environ. Toxicology and Water Quality, 1994—; guest editor Internat. Jour. Molecular Scis., 2002; regional editor USA-Environ. Toxicology, 2002--; mem. overseas editl. bd. Jour. Environ. Biology, 2002--; contbr. articles to profl. jours. Grantee, Internat. Devel. Rsch. Ctr., 1992—93, Nat. Aeronautics and Space Adminstrn., 1977—99, NIH, 1998—, Nat. Oceanic and Atmospheric Adminstrn., 2001—. Mem. APHA, AAUP, AAAS, Am. Assn. Cancer Rsch., Water Environ. Fedn., Cameroon Bioscis. Soc., Cameroon Assn. Epidemiology, Nat. Environ. Health Assn., N.Y. Acad. Scis., Soc. Environ. Toxicology and Chemistry, Soc. Toxicology, Delta Omega. Roman Catholic. Avocations: travel, playing tennis, watching TV sport programs. Home: 230 Clark Farms Rd Madison MS 39110-8112 Office: Jackson State U Sch Sci & Tech PO Box 18540 Jackson MS 39217

TEACHOUT, TERRY, writer, critic; b. Cape Girardeau, Mo., Feb. 6, 1956; s. H.H. and Evelyn (Crosno) Teachout. BS, William Jewell Coll., 1979. Sr. editor Harper's Mag., N.Y.C., 1985-87; editl. writer Daily News, 1987-93, classical music and dance critic, 1993-2000; music critic Commentary Mag., 1995—; contbr. Time Mag., 1998—; arts columnist Washington Post, 1999—. Author: City Limits, 1991; editor: Ghosts on the Roof: Selected Journalism of Whittaker Chambers, 1989, Beyond the Boom, 1990, A Second Mencken Chrestomathy, 1995, The Skeptic: A Life of H.L. Mencken, 2002. Home and Office: 205 W 84th St Apt B New York NY 10024-4660 E-mail: terryteachout@earthlink.net.

TEAGAN, JOHN GERARD, newspaper executive; b. Detroit, Sept. 23, 1947; s. Stanley John and Margaret Suzanne (Sullivan) T.; m. Carla Kay Eurich, Sept. 13, 1975; 1 child, Elizabeth Margaret. BBA, U. Notre Dame, 1969. C.P.A., Mich. Audit supr. Ernst & Whinney (C.P.A.s), Detroit, 1969-73; acctg. mgr. Detroit Free Press, 1973-77, treas., controller, 1977-83, v.p. fin., treas., 1983-89, v.p., bus. mgr., 1989—. Adv. bd. Providence Hosp., Southfield, Mich., 1984-93, sec., 1989, vice chmn. 1990, chmn., 1991; trustee Grosse Pointe (Mich.) Acad., 1990-96, Children's Home Detroit, Grosse Pointe, 1997—; bd. dirs., treas. Free Press Charities, Inc.; bd. dirs. Providence Hosp. and Med. Ctrs., Southfield, 1998—; Metro Detroit bd. dirs. Am. Heart Assn., 1999—; bd. dirs. Boysville of Mich., Inc., 2001—' cmty. adv. bd. Knight Found., 2002—. Mem. AICPA, Internat. Newspaper Fin. Execs., Mich. Assn. CPAs, Grosse Pointe Yacht Club. Roman Catholic. Office: Detroit Free Press Inc 600 W Fort St Detroit MI 48226-2706 E-mail: teagan@freepress.com.

TEAGLE, DAVID BRYAN, manufacturing executive; b. Abilene, Tex., Nov. 18, 1956; s. Ollie Bryan Teagle and Carolyn Ann Dorr; m. Colinda Jean Torrez, Sept. 17, 1999; 1 child from previous marriage Kezia Anne. BBA, Abilene Christian U., 1979, MBA, 1980. Freelance photographer; with energy sys. divsn. NCR Corp., 1980—81; with ARCO Exploration/ARCO Oil, 1981—84, Burroughs Sys., 1985—86, Continental Airlines, 1986—92; freelance press photographer, 1992—2002; actor, 1992—2002; pres. Am. Ventilation Equipment Co., 2002—. Author: Fallen Angels of Sans Espair, 1997. Recipient Ernest Hemingway 1st Book award. Mem.: Nat. Press Photographer Assn. Achievements include patents for Enviroblower. Home: 403 W Cherry St Kaufman TX 75142

TEAGUE, BERNICE RITA, accountant; b. Lowell, Mass., Nov. 1, 1957; d. Francis Joseph and Agnes Lena (Laferriere) T. Grad. h.s., Lowell, Mass. Student aide Hanscom AFB, Bedford, Mass., 1974; sec. asst. Family Svcs. of Greater Lowell, 1975—, asst. bookkeeper, 1976-86, bookkeeper, 1986, asst. bus. mgr., 1987-88, prin. acct., 1988-89; bus. mgr., 1989-99; acctg. clk., billing rep. Med Life Pharmacy, N. Billerica, Mass., 2000—01. Mem. NAFE, Smithsonian Instn., Planetary Soc., Nat. Trust for Hist. Preservation, Am. Inst. Profl. Bookkeepers, Internat. Platform Assn. Democrat. Roman Catholic. Avocations: embroidery, crafts, reading, fishing, gardening. Home: 163 A St Lowell MA 01851-4117

TEAGUE, BRUCE WILLIAMS, chiropractor; b. Dayton, Ohio, Sept. 6, 1947; s. Bige Barnett and Lena Teague; m. Germaine Lee Mullican, Oct. 15, 1977; children: Deanna, Katrina, Bret, Travis, Krystal. BBA, Ea. Ky. U., 1970; D.Chiropractic, Palmer Coll. Chiropractic, 1977. Chiropractor, pres., dir. Teague Chiropractic Ctr., Anchorage, 1980—. Mem. L.A. Coll. Chiropractic Orthopedics, 1988—. Mem. Am. Chiropractic Assn. (mem. nutrition coun., coun. on sports injuries and phys. fitness), Coun. Diagnostic Imaging, Am. Coll. Chiropractic Edn. and Rsch., Alaska Chiropractic Soc., Internat. Chiropractors Assn., Palmer Coll. Alumni Assn., Moose, Rotary. Office: Teague Chiropractic Ctr 11435 Old Seward Hwy Anchorage AK 99515-3041

TEAGUE, FRANCES NICOL, English language educator; b. Toronto, Ont., Can., Jan. 16, 1949; d. William Kennedy and Phyllis Christine (Bowie) Nicol; m. Ben Teague, May 25, 1968. BA, Rice U., 1970; PhD, U. Tex., 1975. Asst. prof. English, U. Ga., Athens, 1977-84, assoc. prof., 1984-91; prof., 1991—. Author: The Curious History of "Bartholomew Fair," 1985, Shakespeare's Speaking Properties, 1991, Bathsua Makin, Woman of Learning, 1998; editor: (with John Velz) One Touch of Shakespeare, 1986, Acting Funny, 1993, The Early Modern Englishwoman, series II, vol. 5: Educational and Vocational Books, 2001. Summer grantee Am. Coun. Learned Socs., London, 1981; fellow Folger Shakespeare Summer Inst., 1982. Mem. MLA, Shakespeare Assn. Am., Southeastern Renaissance Conf. (v.p. 1989-90, pres. 1990-91), South Atlantic MLA.

TEAGUE, LAVETTE COX, JR. systems educator, consultant; b. Birmingham, Ala., Oct. 8, 1934; s. Lavette Cox and Caroline Green (Stokes) T. Student, Auburn U., 1951-54; BArch, MIT, 1957, MSCE, 1965, PhD, 1968; MDiv with distinction, Ch. Div. Sch. Pacific, 1979. Cert. computer profl. Inst. Cert. Computer Profls. Archtl. designer Carroll C. Harmon, Birmingham, 1957, Fred Renneker, Jr., Birmingham, 1958-59; architect Rust Engring. Co., 1959-62, Synergetics, Inc., Raleigh, N.C., 1962-64, Rust Engring. Co., Birmingham, 1964-68; rsch. asst., instr., rsch. assoc. MIT, Cambridge, 1964-68; dir. computer svcs. Skidmore Owings & Merrill, San Francisco, Chgo., 1968-74; postdoctoral fellow UCLA, 1972; adj. assoc. prof. arch. and civil engring. Carnegie-Mellon U., Pitts., 1973-74; archtl. systems cons. Chgo., 1974-75, Berkeley, Calif., 1975-80, Pasadena, 1980-82, Altadena, Calif., 1982—. Lectr. info. systems Calif. State Poly. U., Pomona, 1980-81, prof., 1981-98, prof. emeritus, 1998—, asst. chair, 1990-91, chair, 1991-93, 96-98; Fulbright lectr., Uruguay, 1985. Author: Event-Based Analysis and Design: An Introduction to Structured Methods, 2000; co-author: Structured Analysis Methods for Computer Information Systems, 1985. Mem. adv. bd. Ch. Div. Sch. of the Pacific. Recipient Tucker-Voss award MIT, 1967; Fulbright scholar, 1985. Mem. AIA (Arnold W. Brunner scholar 1966), Assn. Computing Machinery, Sigma Xi, Phi Eta Sigma, Scarab, Scabbard and Blade, Tau Beta Pi, Chi Epsilon, Beta Gamma Sigma. Episcopalian. Home: 1696 N Altadena Dr Altadena CA 91001-3623 Office: 3801 W Temple Ave Pomona CA 91768-2557 E-mail: lcteague@csupomona.edu.

TEAGUE, MARY ELIZABETH, small business owner; b. Mt. Vernon, Tex., Aug. 18, 1928; d. Jodie Felter and Martha Willie (Crafts) T. AAS, C.C. of Air Force, 1987. Advanced through grades to chief master sgt. USAF, 1950, retired, 1988. Editor, publ.: (cmty. newsletter) Waterwood News, 1990—. Lutheran. Avocations: travel, handicrafts, writing. Home: 4027 Waterwood Pass Dr Elmendorf TX 78112-6024

TEAGUE, PETER WESLEY, superintendent, academic administrator; b. Gary, Ind., Jan. 15, 1952; s. Robert Wesley and Gladys Eve (Dunlop) T.; m. Paulette Joan Neymeyer, June 23, 1973; children: Robert, Angela, Jessica, Nicole. BS in Bus. Adminstrn./Psychology, Sterling Coll., 1973; MA in Christian Edn., Luther Rice Sem., 1987; EdD in Ednl. Aminstrn., Nova Southeastern U., 1995. Mgmt. trainee Skaggs Drug Co., Denver, 1973-74; spl. asst. to dir. Grace & Truth Evangelistic Assn., York, Pa., 1974-75; dir. devel. Christian Sch. of York, 1975-79, supt., 1979; dean undergrad. edn. Lancaster Bible Coll., 1998—99, pres., 1999—. Elder York (Pa.) Gospel Ctr., 1977-86, 89-90, chmn. bd., 1984-86, 89-90, adult s.s. tchr., 1977—, mem. Christian edn. com., 1977-86; workshop presenter for various convs. Contbg. author: Handbook for Christian Living, 1991; co-editor: Manual for Christian Sch. Adminstrs., 1988. Mem. Corp. Bd. Lancaster (Pa.) Bible Coll., 1989—. Mem. Assn. Christian Schs. Internat. (regional coun. 1983-91), Mid-Atlantic Christian Schs. Assn. (conv. dir.), Nat. Assn. Secondary Prins. Home: 4 Crestlyn Dr York PA 17402 *I am amazed how important encouragement is to a person. A word fitly spoken can change the outlook of a person for the day.*

TEAGUE, RANDAL CORNELL, SR. lawyer; b. Durham, N.C., May 19, 1944; s. Roy M. Sr. and Lottie (Rhew) T.; children: R. Cornell, R. Townsend, Mary Robb Durham, James K.B. BA, Am. U., 1967; JD, George Washington U., 1971, LLM with highest honors, 1972; LLD (hon.), Allen U., 1973. Bar: Fla. 1972, D.C. 1972, U.S. Dist. Ct. D.C. 1972, U.S. Tax Ct. 1972, U.S. Ct. Mil. Appeals 1972, U.S. Ct. Appeals (D.C. and fed. cirs.) 1972, U.S. Ct. Appeals (5th cir.) 1973, U.S. Supreme Ct. 1975, Mass. 1979, U.S. Ct. Appeals (1st cir.) 1979, U.S. Dist. Ct. Mass. 1979, U.S. Ct. Internat. Trade. Coordinator policy devel. OEO, Washington, 1971-73; adminstrv. asst., legis. counsel to Rep. Jack F. Kemp Ho. of Reps., 1973-79; div. counsel Cabot Corp., 1979-81; counsel Vorys, Sater, Seymour & Pease LLP, Washington, 1981-83, ptnr., 1984—. Pres. Internat. Exch. Coun., 1984—; trustee Fund Am. Studies, Washington, 1976—, chmn., 1998—; trustee, dir. Air Force Acad. Found., Colorado Springs, Colo., 1983—; chmn. adv. com. voluntary aid U.S. AID, 1987-91; trustee Earth U., Costa Rica, 1987—; councillor Atlantic Coun. of U.S., 1990—; co-founder Am. Inst. on Polit. and Econ. Sys., Charles U., Prague, 1993—; founder Internat. Inst. Polit. and Econ. Studies, Athens, Greece, 1996—; dir. Salzburg Seminar, 1997—. Named one of Outstanding Young Men Am., 1973; recipient George Washington medal Freedoms Found., 1978. Mem. ABA, FBA, Fla. Bar Assn. Clubs: University (Washington). Republican. Episcopalian. Office: Vorys Sater Seymour & Pease LLP 1828 L St NW Fl 11 Washington DC 20036-5109 E-mail: rcteague@vssp.com.

TEAHON, JEAN ANN, county official; b. Dunning, Nebr., June 19, 1936; d. Norman Arthur and Margaret Elsa (Terwilliger) Linder; m. Charles Gerald Teahon, Aug. 31, 1958; children: Geri Ann, Peggy Lynn, Tedd Norman. AA, Kearney State Coll., 1958. Cert. assessor Nebr. Elementary tchr. Compton Sch., Valentine, Nebr., 1956, Calamus Valley Sch., Ainsworth, 1956-57, Willow Lake Sch., Elsmere, 1957-59, German Valley Sch., Brewster, 1968-72; dep. county clk. Blaine County, 1980-90, county clk./assessor, 1995—; office mgr. Ctrl. Sandhills Area Ext., Thedford, Nebr., 1992-94. Author: Blaine County History, 1988. Active Dunning United Ch. of Christ, 1949—, memorial chair, 1992—. Mem. Nat. Assn. County Ofcls., Nebr. Assn. County Ofcls. Democrat. Office: Blaine County # 1 Lincoln Ave Brewster NE 68821 E-mail: jteahon@yahoo.com.

TEAL, ELISABETH JANE, business educator, researcher; b. Carrollton, Ga., Mar. 10, 1958; d. Dewey E. and Ramona T. BS cum laude, Brenau U., 1980; MBA, U. Ga., 1991, PhD, 1998. V.p. Sun Trust Bank, Gainesville, Ga., 1980-88; grad. tchg. asst. U. Ga., Athens, 1992-97; asst. prof. Hankamer Sch. Bus. Baylor U., Waco, Tex., 1997—. Contbr. articles to profl. jours. Recipient Carland award Acad. Entrepreneurship, 1999. Mem. U.S. Assn. Small Bus. and Entrepreneurship (program chair small bus. divsn. 2000, v.p. elect 2001, v.p. 2002), Acad. Mgmt. (Am. Assembly Collegiate Schs. Bus., com. entrepreneurship divsn. 1999—, Heizer cert. 1999), Internat. Coun. Small Bus., S.W. Acad. Mgmt. Baptist. Avocations: travel, tennis, music. Office: Baylor U Hankamer Sch Bus PO Box 98006 Waco TX 76798-8006

TEAL, MONIKA JOSEPHA, artist; b. Bennettsville, S.C., May 25, 1950; arrived in Switzerland, 1992; d. William Benny and Anita Josepha (Geigenmueller) T.; children: Natalie Teal McAllister. BS, U. Minn., 1974; postgrad., Sch. Visual Concepts, Seattle, 1981-84; MA, Western Carolina U., 1988. Lectr. in field; mem. grants rev. com. N.C. Arts Coun.; adj. faculty mem. Western Carolina U., 1991, U. N.C., Asheville, 1991; lectr. Inst. for English and Lit., U. Bern, Switzerland, 1994; art restoration and conservation apprentice, 1999. One-woman shows include Asheville Art Mus., 1987, Kinston Arts Coun., N.C., 1991, Western N.C. Arts Coun., 1991, Forum, ETC, Bern, 1992, Frauenzentrum, Bern, 1993, Galerie Boulangerie, Switzerland, 1994, Chelsea Gallery, Western Carolina U., 1995, Saülenhalle des Landhaus. Solothurn, Switzerland, 1996, Fulton-Burt Gallery, Sarasota, Fla., 1998, U. N.C., Pembroke, 1999, Gallery Leontine, Fla., 1999; exhibited in group shows at Women's Cultural Ctr., Seattle, 1986, Fremont Gallery, Seattle, 1986, Marianne Partlow Gallery, Olympia, Wash., 1986, 87, Chelsea Gallery, Western Carolina U., 1987, 90, Wilson (N.C.) Art Ctr., 1989, Henley S.E. Spectrum, Winston-Salem, N.C., 1989 (Best in Show award), Upstairs Gallery, Tryon, N.C., 1990, Woman's Caucus for Art, Miami, Fla., 1990, Weizenblatt Gallery, 1990, Knight Gallery, Charlotte, N.C., 1991, Asheville (N.C.) Art Mus., 1991, Solothurn Kunstmuseum, 1991, Trade St. Gallery, N.C., 1992, GSMBK Galerie, Bern, Switzerland, 1993, Winthrop (S.C.) U. Gallery, 1996, others; also in pub. and pvt. collections. N.C. Visual Arts fellow, 1990.

TEALDI, JAVIER HERNAN, computer/network support specialist; b. Buenos Aires, Dec. 26, 1971; came to U.S., 1979; s. Alberto Maria and Susanne Isabel Tealdi. AS in Mech. Engring. magna cum laude, Norwalk (Conn.) Tech. Coll., 1994; BA in Environ. Engring. cum laude, N.Y. Inst. Tech., 1996. Cert. Microsoft systems engr. Environ. engr. Green Tech. Group, Pawling, N.Y., 1996-98; computer specialist Ascom Hasler, Shelton, Conn., 1998-2000; computer/network support specialist Alliance Capital/Bernstein, White Plains, N.Y., 2000—. Mem. Delta Sigma Phi. Avocations: travel, camping, hiking, computers. Office: 1 N Lexington Ave White Plains NY 10601-1712 E-mail: vajt@excite.com.

TEARE, SCOTT WILLIAM, physicist; b. London, Can., Nov. 7, 1961; s. Chester William Albert and Nancy Hellen (Scott) T.; m. Janice Christina McQuay, Sept. 30, 1989. BSc, U. Guelph, Ont., Can., 1986, MSc, 1987, PhD, 1991. Cons. Lexus Corp., London, Can., 1987-88; scientist Ont. Hydro, Toronto, Can., 1990—. Contbr. articles to profl. jours. Mem. IEEE. Office: Ontario Hydro 595 Bay St Toronto ON Canada M5G 1X6

TEARPOCK, DANIEL J. geologist; b. Mocanaqua, Pa. s. John G. and Laura (Tiberi) T.; m. Silvia Cantu; children: Nicole, Danielle. BS, Bloomsburg Univ., 1970; MA, Temple Univ., 1977. Cert. petroleum geologist. Mgr. tech. svcs. Cert. Ctr., King of Prussia, Pa., 1970-72; pres., ptnr. Atlantic Computer Svcs., Pennsauken, N.J., 1972-74; geothermal devel. specialist Sperry Rand, Jackson, Miss., 1977-79; petroleum cons. Atwater Cons., New Orleans, 1979-85; proj. geologic engr. Tenneco, Lafayette, 1985-87, sr. geologic engr., 1987-88; CEO/pres. Subsurface Cons. & Assocs., 1988—. CEO, pres. SPX Oil & Gas Co., 1996—; tech. adv. PDVSA Venezuela, 1996—; geology instr. Montgomery Coll., Blue Bell, Pa., 1974-75, instr. Hinds Jr. Coll., Jackson, Miss., 1979-80, adj. asst. prof. Tulane U., 1984-85; guest lectr. U. S.W. La., 1993-95. Author: Applied Subsurface Geological Mapping, 1990, Quick Look Techniques for Prospect Evaluation, 1994; contbr. numerous articles to profl. jours. Mem. Rep. Nat. Com. Recipient Best Paper award New Orleans Geological Soc., 1990, 91. Mem. Am. Assn. Petroleum Geologists, Gulf Coast Am. Geol. Soc., Lafayette Geol. Soc., Geol. Soc. Am., Indonesian Petroleum Soc., Houston Geol. Soc., New Orleans Geol. Soc. Office: Subsurface Cons & Assocs LLC 400 E Kaliste Saloom Rd Lafayette LA 70508-8508

TEAS, CHARLES BRYANT, physical education educator; b. Bellaire, Tex., July 18, 1938; s. Fred Augustus and Blanche (Bryant) T.; m. Karen Sue Keith, Oct. 20, 1962; children: Timothy Bryant, Tamara Annette. BS, Tex. A&M U., 1962; MEd, Sam Houston State U., 1968. Cert. health and phys. edn. tchr., Tex. Assoc. phys. dir. Longview (Tex.) YMCA, 1962-64; gymnastic specialist San Angelo (Tex.) Ind. Sch. Dist., 1964-67; fellow Sam Houston State U., Huntsville, 1967-68; prof. phys. edn. Del Mar Coll., Corpus Christi, Tex., 1968-92. Recipient numerous awards for swimming and diving, including 1st Place Clown Diving award U.S. Masters Diving, 1974, 2d Place 1 Meter Diving award U.S. Masters Diving, 1974, 2d Place 3 Meter Diving award U.S. Masters Diving, 1974, 3d Place 3 Meter Diving award Masters Games, Toronto, Ont., Can., 1985. Mem. Tex. Assn. Health, Phys. Edn., Recreation and Dance (aquatics chmn. 1973, gymnastics chmn. 1975, 78), Am. Alliance Health, Phys. Edn. Recreation and Dance, Tex. Jr. Colls. of Tex., U.S. Gymnastics Fedn., Gymnastics Assn. Tex. (life). Home: 4421 Gaines St # 14 Corpus Christi TX 78412-2585

TEAS, JOHN FREDERICK, small business owner; b. Bellaire, Tex., Oct. 10, 1934; s. Fred A. and Blanche (Bryant) T.; m. Patsy Tutt, 1967. Degree in horticulture, Tex. A&M U., 1957. Cert. nurseryman, Tex. With Teas Nursery Co., Inc., Bellaire, 1957—, v.p., since 1974. Assoc. bd. dirs. Weslayan Bank, Houston; tchr. plant identification Houston C.C. and U. Houston, 1991—. Mem. AAN (gov. region 2 1991), Am. Soc. Agriculture Cons., Tex. Soc. Landscape Architects (pres. 1975-77), Houston Landscape Nurserymen's Assn. (pres. 1974-75), Tex. Assn. Nurserymen (pres. region II 1978), SCV, Garden Ctrs. Am. (pres. 1986). Recipient Faith in God award Houston Jaycees, 1968. Mem. Am. Soc. Agriculture Cons., Tex. Soc. Landscape Architects (pres. 1975-77), Houston Landscape Nurserymen's Assn. (pres. 1974-75), Am. Assn. Nurserymen, Tex. Assn. Nurserymen (pres. region II 1978), SCV, Garden Ctrs. Am. (pres. 1986). Lodges: Rotary (bd. dirs. Houston chpt.). Avocation: geneology. Home: 16 Town Oaks Pl Bellaire TX 77401-4237 Office: Teas Nursery Co Inc 4400 Bellaire Blvd Bellaire TX 77401-4398

TEAS, RICHARD HARPER, lawyer; b. Streator, Ill., Sept. 24, 1930; s. Bert H. and Audrey C. Teas; m. Janice K. Eikenmeyer, July 29, 1960 (dec.); children: Catherine L. Teas-Rogers, Amelia H. AB, U. Ill., 1957, LLB, 1960. Bar: Ill. 1960, U.S. Dist. Ct. (so. dist.) Ill. 1960. Probate adminstr. Continental Nat. Bank and Trust Co. of Chgo., 1960-66; ptnr. Tracy, Johnson, & Wilson Law Offices, Joliet, Ill., 1966—. Comdr. USNR, 1952-69. Mem. Ill. State Bar Assn. (trust and estates sect. coun., standing com. on legislation, task force on unauthorized practice of law), Will County Bar Assn. (probate com.), Am. Coll. of Trust and Estate Counsel, Estate Planning Coun. of Greater Joliet (pres. 1976). Avocations: tennis, golf. Home: 20853 Rock Run Dr Joliet IL 60431-9323 Office: Tracy Johnson & Wilson 116 N Chicago St Ste 600 Joliet IL 60432-4224 E-mail: rhteas@ameritech.net.

TEASDALE, KENNETH FULBRIGHT, lawyer; b. St. Louis, Nov. 8, 1934; s. Kenneth and Ann (Fulbright) T.; m. Elizabeth Driscol Langdon, June 13, 1964; children: Caroline, Doug, Cindy. AB, Amherst Coll., 1956; LLB, Washington U., St. Louis, 1961. Bar: Mo. 1961. Atty. antitrust div. U.S. Dept. Justice, Washington, 1961-62; asst. counsel Dem. Policy Com. U.S. Senate, 1962-63, gen. counsel Dem. Policy Com., asst. to majority leader, 1963-64; assoc. Armstrong, Teasdale, Kramer & Vaughan, St. Louis, 1964-67, ptnr., 1967-86; mng. ptnr. Armstrong, Teasdale, Schlafly & Davis, 1986-93, chmn. of firm, 1993—. Trustee United Way Greater St. Louis, Sci. Ctr. St. Louis, St. Louis Art Mus. ; trustee, chmn. bd. regents St. Louis U.; mem. nat. coun. Washington U. Law Sch., 1988—. Mem. ABA, Bar Assn. Mo., Bar Assn. St. Louis, Racquet Club, Noonday Club, Old Warson Country Club. Episcopalian. Office: Armstrong Teasdale Schlafly & Davis Metropolitan Sq Saint Louis MO 63102-2733

TEASE, JAMES EDWARD, judge; b. Sheffield, Ala., Dec. 28, 1939; s. James Albert and Hattie Wayne (Counts) T.; m. Anne Elizabeth Gilley, Sept. 2, 1972. BS, Florence State U., 1961; LL.B., U. Ala., 1964; grad., Nat. Coll. State Judiciary, 1971. Bar: Ala. 1964. Gen. practice law, Florence, 1965-67; city prosecutor, 1966-67; dep. dist. atty. Lauderdale County, Ala., 1967-71; circuit judge 11th Jud. Cir. Ala., Florence, 1971-89; extra judge Ala. Ct. Civil Appeals, 1989; U.S. adminstrv. law judge Social Security Adminstrn., Office Hearings & Appeals, Florence, Ala., 1989—. Mem. Ala. Constl. Commn.; chmn. Ala. Citizens Adv. Com. on Election Reform; judge Ala. Ct. of Judiciary, 1981-89. Bd. dirs. Regional Library System. Served with AUS, 1964-65. Named Florence Outstanding Young Man Jaycees, 1974, Alumnus of Year U. N. Ala., 1975 Mem. Am. Judicature Soc., Nat. Conf. State Trial Judges, Ala. Assn. Circuit Judges (pres. 1986), Lauderdale County Bar Assn. (pres.), Am. Legion, Sigma Delta Kappa. Baptist. Home: 1926 Monticello Rd Florence AL 35630-2740 Office: Walnut St Exec Ctr 205 S Walnut St Ste D Florence AL 35630-5721

TEASLEY, ELLA LORAINE, educational association administrator; b. Memphis, Oct. 6, 1951; d. Pete Turner and Ruth Roberta Teasley. Student, Wayne State U., 1969, Madonna Coll., Livonia, Mich., 1993, Marygrove Coll., Detroit, 1970—; B of Mgmt., Detroit Inst. Tech., 1973. Tchr. Semi-Quois Cmty. Ctr., Detroit, 1983; pres., CEO Mich. Latchkey Assn., Inc., 1984—; v.p. Detroit Sch. Age Inc., 1991—. Bd. dirs. Wayne County Child Care Coordinating Coun., Detroit, 1998—. Co-author: How to Start a Latchkey Program, 1990; presenter workshops. Mem. Wayne County Sch. Age Coalition, 1985—; mem. Detroit Pub. Sch. Latchkey Task Force, 1988; mem. Mich. Dept. Edn. Office of Spl. Edn. Svcs., 1997. Mem. Ch. of Christ. Avocations: travel, reading, movies. Home: 3352 Kendall St Detroit MI 48238-3817 Office: Mich Latchkey Assn Inc PO Box 27132 Detroit MI 48227-0132

TEAT, HERBERT LEROY, retired music educator; b. El Paso, Tex., May 14, 1923; s. Herbert Leroy Teat and Martha Motee Shannon; m. Angelien Francis, Aug. 4, 1951 (div. Jan. 1975); children: Herbert L. III, James Stephen, Adonna Mary; m. Sue Ellen French, Dec. 17, 1976 (div.); 1 child, Timothy Shannon. MusB, North Tex. State Tchrs. Coll., 1948; MusM, Westminster Choir Coll., 1954. Cert. music tchr., Tex., Ala. Band dir., music dir. Rusk (Tex.) Sch. Dist., 1948-52; choral dir., music dir. Longview (Tex.) Sch. Dist., 1954-69, Tarleton State U., Stephenville, Tex., 1969-83, U. North Ala., Florence, 1984-86; ret. Cons. choral music edn. Contbr. articles to profl. jours.; mem. editl. bd. Southwestern Musician mag., 1958-62; author workbook: EEV Music Reader, 1968. Chmn. campaign March of Dimes, Cherokee County, Tex., 1950; charter mem., v.p. Tex. Choral Dirs. Assn., 1955; state v.p. Music Educators Assn., 1958-60, state pres., 1960-62, mem. state pres. assembly nat. conf., Washington, 1962. Mem. San Gabriel Writers League, Tex. Music Educators (hon. life mem.), Congress of Parent-Tchrs. (hon. life mem.). Methodist. Home: 1105 Church Georgetown TX 78626 E-mail: herble@thegateway.net.

TEATER, DOROTHY SEATH, retired county official; b. Manhattan, Kans., Feb. 11, 1931; d. Dwight Moody and Martha (Stahnke) Seath; m. Robert Woodson Teater, May 24, 1952; children: David Dwight, James Stanley, Donald Robert, Andrew Scott. BS, U. Ky., 1951; MS, Ohio State U., 1954. Home econs. tchr. Georgetown (Ky.) City Schs., 1951-53; extension specialist Ohio Coop. Extension, Columbus, 1967-73; consumer affairs adminstr. City of Columbus, 1974-79, Bank One Columbus NA, 1980-85; councilmember Columbus City Coun., 1980-85; commr. Franklin County, Columbus, Ohio, 1985-2000; ret. Mem. Columbus Met. Area Cmty. Action Orgn.; mem. adv. bd. Ohio Housing Trust; chairwoman Franklin County Children's Cabinet. Bd. dirs. BBB; mem. hon. adv. bd. Girl Scouts. Recipient Outstanding Alumnus award U. Ky., 1989, Women of Achievement award YWCA, 1995, Disting. Svc. award Ohio State U., 1997; named Disting. Alumni, Ohio State U., 1977. Mem. County Commrs. Assn. Ohio (pres. 1994), Columbus Met. Club, Greater Columbus C. of C. (Columbus award 1997). Republican. Methodist. Avocations: gardening, sewing.

TEATES, CHARLES DAVID, radiologist, educator; b. Luray, Va., July 1, 1936; s. Gilbert Grove and Mae Frankie (Pierce) T.; m. Mary Bruce Bucher, June 6, 1958; children— Elizabeth Susan, David Bruce, Mary Catherine BS, Lebanon Valley Coll., Annville, Pa., 1958; MS, MD, U. Va., Charlottesville, 1963. Diplomate Am. Bd. Radiology, Am. Bd. Nuclear Medicine. Intern U. Kans. Med. Ctr., 1963-64; resident in radiology U. Va. Med. Ctr., 1964-67; Asst. prof. radiology U. Va., Charlottesville, 1969-73, assoc. prof., 1973-79, prof., 1979-2000, emeritus prof., 2000—. Contbg. author books on radiology and nuclear medicine Served to maj. M.C., U.S. Army, 1967-69, Vietnam Mem. Am. Coll. Radiology (pres. Va. chpt. 1984-85), Soc. Nuclear Medicine (pres. Mid-Eastern chpt. 1984-86), AMA, Alpha Omega Alpha Home: 4635 Watts Passage Charlottesville VA 22911-5932 Office: U Va Med Ctr PO Box 170 Charlottesville VA 22908-0001

TEBBEN, SHARON LEE, education educator; b. Fairfield, Iowa, Oct. 15, 1943; d. Richard Paul and Arline Marie (Sires) Brandt; m. E. Marvin Tebben, Sept. 7, 1963; children: Laurel Ann, Leslie Kay, Paul Marvin. BS, Mankato State U., 1965; MS, U. Wyo., 1973; EdD, U. St. Thomas, 1992. Tchr. chemistry San Diego City Schs., 1965-68, Alhambra City Schs., Calif., 1968-70; tchg. asst. U. Wyo., Laramie, 1970-73; mem. faculty Presentation Coll., Aberdeen, S.D., 1974-92, chmn. dept. chemistry, 1975-92; asst. prof. edn. Northern State U., 1992-95, assoc. prof., 1995—, assoc. dean sch. of edn., dir. grad. studies, 1995, dean of edn., 1999—; NCA cons./evaluator, 1990—. NDEA fellow, 1971-73. Mem. AAUW, ASCD, North Ctrl. Assn. (cons., evaluator, mem. accreditation review coun.), Phi Kappa Phi, Alpha Lambda Delta, Phi Delta Kappa. Office: Northern State U 1200 S Jay St Aberdeen SD 57401-7155 E-mail: tebbens@northern.edu.

TEBLUM, GARY IRA, lawyer; b. Phila., Apr. 25, 1955; s. Milton and Marlene Ann (Rosenberg) T.; m. Lisa Ida Goldsmith, May 13, 1979; children: Corey Harris, Jeremy Brett. BS, U. Del., 1976; JD cum laude, U. Pa., 1979. Assoc. Trenam, Simmons, Kemker, Scharf, Barkin, Frye & O'Neill, Tampa, Fla., 1979-84; ptnr. Trenam, Kemker, Scharf, Barkin, Frye, O'Neill & Mullis, 1984—. Editor U. Pa. Law Rev., 1978-79. Mem. ABA, Fla. Bar Assn., Hillsborough County Bar Assn. Jewish. Home: 14039 Shady Shores Dr Tampa FL 33613-1934 Office: Trenam Kemker Scharf et al 2700 Bank of America Plz Tampa FL 33602

TECCO, ROMUALD GILBERT LOUIS JOSEPH, violinist, concertmaster; b. Toulon, Var, France, May 1, 1941; came to U.S., 1960; s. Raymond Charles and Angele (Cornille) T. Student, Paris Conservatoire, 1954-60; diploma, postgrad. diploma, Juilliard Sch. Music, 1967-68. Mem. N.Y. String Quartet, 1969-72; concertmaster Juilliard Ensemble, N.Y.C., 1969-72, St. Paul Chamber Orch., 1972-98; soloist Chgo. Symphony, Bavarian Radio Orch., Orch. of Mex., Orchestre Colonne, Paris, Rotterdam Philharm.; performer numerous festivals, Sweden, Finland, France, Italy, U.S. Recs. with Aaron Copland and Lou Harrison Chamber Music. Served with French Navy, 1964-65, NATO hdqrs. Recipient first prize in violin Conservatoire Paris; recipient first prize chamber music Conservatoire Paris Mem. St. Paul Univ. Club.

TECK, KATHERINE, musician, writer; b. Mineola, N.Y., Dec. 31, 1939; d. Walter Henry and Helen Elliot (Bennett) Weintz.; m. Alan Teck, June 15, 1963; children: Rachel, Daniel. BA, Vassar Coll., 1960; student, Mannes Coll. Music, 1961; MA in Composition, Columbia U., 1964; cert. arts mgmt., Purchase Coll., 1995. Mem. concert music dept. Broadcast Music Inc., N.Y.C., 1964-66; founder, pres. Modern Listener's Record Club, 1966-67; staff Dover Publs. Inc., 1967-69; freelance horn player Westchester County, 1971-90; studio musician for dance SUNY, Purchase, 1978-83; events coord. Borders Books & Music, 1996-98; dir. mktg. Musicians Showcase Recs., 1999-2000; coord. sch. programs Emelin Theatre, Mamaroneck, NY, 2002—. Author: (books) Bears Beat Bowls in the Bathtub, 1996, Ear Training for the Body, 1994, Movement to Music, 1990, Music for the Dance, 1989; contbr. articles to profl. jours. Seidl fellow Columbia U., 1962. Mem. Internat. Guild Musicians in Dance (founding). Home: 44 Havilands Ln White Plains NY 10605-3009

TECLAFF, LUDWIK ANDRZEJ, law educator, consultant, author, lawyer; b. Czestochowa, Poland, Nov. 14, 1918; came to U.S., 1952, naturalized, 1958; s. Emil and Helena (Tarnowska) T.; m. Eileen Johnson, May 30, 1952. Mag Iuris, Oxford (Eng.) U., 1944; MS, Columbia U., 1955; LLM, NYU, 1961, JSD, 1965. Attaché Polish Fgn. Ministry, London, 1943-46; consul in Ireland, Polish Govt. in London, 1946-52; student libr. Columbia U. Sch. Libr. Sci., 1953-54; libr. Bklyn. Pub. Libr., 1954-59; rsch. librar. Fordham U. Sch. Law, 1959-62, asst. prof. law, 1962-65, assoc. prof. law, 1965-68, prof. 1968-89, prof. emeritus, 1989—, dir. law libr., 1962-86; cons. in field. With Polish Army, 1940-43, France, Eng. Recipient Clyde Eagleton award in internat. law NYU, 1965. Mem. Am. Soc. Internat. Law, Internat. Law Assn., Am. Law Librs. Assn., Internat. Coun. Environ. Law, Internat. Water Law Assn. Roman Catholic. Author: The River Basin in History and Law, 1967; Abstraction and Use of Water, 1972; Legal and Institutional Responses to Growing Water Demand, 1978; Economic Roots of Oppression, 1984, Water Law in Historical Perspective, 1985; editor: (with Albert E Utton) International Environmental Law, 1974, Water in a Developing World, 1978, International Groundwater Law, 1981, Transboundary Resources Law, 1987; contbr. articles on water law, law of the sea and environ. law to law jours. Office: Fordham U Sch Law 140 W 62nd St New York NY 10023-7407

TEDD, MONIQUE MICHELINE, artist; b. Sotteville-les-Rouen, France, Jan. 25, 1943; came to U.S., 1968; d. Maurice Joseph and Dolly Jeanne (Carpentier) T.; m. Asiat A. Ali, Dec. 23, 1967; 1 child, Asiat Allum Ali. MFA in Painting, Beaux-Arts Sch. of Rouen, Seine Rouen Maritime, France, 1967. Art tchr. Vernon, France, 1967-68; advt. Hahn J. Shoes, Washington, 1968-69, Magrams, Burlington, Vt., 1974—. Set decorator Lyric Theater, Burlington, Vt., 1975. One-woman shows include St. Michael's Coll., Winooski, Vt., 1972, 91, Peel's Gallery, Danby, Vt., 1978-79, Gov.'s Corridor, State Capital, Montpelier, Vt., 1980, The Living and Learning Ctr., U. Vt., Burlington, 1982, Passepartout Gallery, Winooski, 1983, Gallery Two, Woodstock, 1984; exhibited in group shows at The Gallery, Washington, 1969, N.Y. First Internat. Art Show, 1970, Galerie des Trois Arts, Burlington, Vt., 1970-71, Fleming Mus., Burlington, 1972, Frog Hollow, Middlebury, 1973, The Four Winds Gallery, North Ferrisburg, Vt., 1975, Norwich U. Armory Show, Hanover, N.H., 1976, Old Bergen Art Guild Touring Exhibit, 1978-80, Stratton Art Festival, Stratton, Vt., 1979, Women's Ednl. Ctr., Essex Junction, Vt., 1981-82, Pocketbook Wood Gallery, Montpelier, 1981-82, Window, a Women's View, Burlington, 1981-82, Passepartout Gallery, 1985, Smith Coll., 1985, Wood Art Gallery, Montpelier, 1985, 86, 87, Helen Day Ctr., Stowe, Vt., 1986-87, Gallery Two, 1991, Shelburne Mus., 1996, Beaux Arts Studio, Essex Junction, Vt., 1998—; selected for exhibit and calendars Paysage de France, a 12-city exhibit, 1965. Recipient 1st prize Rouen C. of C., 1964, 3rd prize Grand Prix Internat. of Deauville, 1987, open studio 7th Vt. Craft Coun., 2000. Home: 9 Seneca Ave Essex Junction VT 05452-3521

TEDDER, THOMAS FLETCHER, immunology educator, researcher; b. Chateauroux, France, May 14, 1956; came to U.S. 1959; s. Raymond Percy and Barbara (Hagemann) T. AA, Okaloosa-Walton Community Coll, Niceville, Fla., 1976; BS with honors, U. Fla., 1978, MS, 1980; PhD, U. Ala., Birmingham, 1984. Rsch. fellow in pathology Harvard Med. Sch., Boston, 1984-85, instr. pathology, 1986-88, asst. prof. pathology, 1988-93; assoc. prof. pathology Harvard U. Med. Sch., 1993; prof. immunology Duke U. Med. Ctr., Durham, N.C., 1993—, chmn. dept. immunology, 1993—. Alter Geller prof. rsch. in immunology Duke U. Med. Ctr., 1997—. Assoc. editor Jour. Immunology, 1989-93, sect. editor, 1993-98; contbr. numerous articles to med. jours., including Jour. Immunology, Nature, Lancet, Immunity. Recipient LeRoy Collins Disting. Alumnus award Fla. Assn. C.C.'s; named 25th Anniversary Disting. Alumnus, Okaloosa-Walton C.C., 1989; Damon Runyon-Walter Winchell rsch. fellow, 1985-87; scholar Leukemia Soc. Am., 1991-96, Stohlman scholar, 1995-96. Mem. Am. Soc. for Microbiology (Pres. Fellow 1982), Am. Assn. Immunologists, Sigma Xi, Phi Kappa Phi. Achievements include identification and determination of structure and function of many human B lymphocyte cell-surface molecules. Office: Duke U Med Ctr Dept Immunology PO Box 3010 Durham NC 27710-0001 E-mail: thomas.tedder@duke.edu.

TEDESCHI, GORDON J. music educator; s. Gabriel Tedeschi and Dolores Tedeschu; m. Carleen E. Cunningham, June 16, 1984; children: Jennifer. B of Music, No. Ill. U., 1977. Orch. dir. East Brunswick H.S., NJ, 1977—. Part-time lectr. Rutgers U., New Brunswick, NJ, 1996—. Mem.: CJMEA, NJMEA, MENC. Office: East Brunswick HS 380 Cranbury Rd East Brunswick NJ 08816

TEDESCHI, JOHN ALFRED, historian, librarian; b. Modena, Italy, July 17, 1931; came to U.S., 1939, naturalized, 1944; s. Caesar George and Piera (Forti) T.; m. Anne Wood Christian, Sept. 8, 1956; children: Martha, Philip, Sara. BA, Harvard U., 1954, MA, 1960, PhD, 1966. Bibliographer European history and lit. Newberry Library, Chgo., 1965-84, curator rare books and manuscripts, head dept. spl. collections, 1970-82, dir. Ctr. Renaissance Studies, 1979-84; curator rare books and spl. collections Meml. Library U. Wis.-Madison, 1984-96. Lectr. history U. Chgo., 1969-71; vis. prof. U. Ill.-Chgo., 1972-73, adj. prof., 1979-84 Co-editor: (series) Corpus Reformatorum Italicorum, 1968-96; editor-in-chief: Bibliographie Internat. de L'Humanisme et de la Renaissance, 1977-82; editor: Italian Reformation Studies in Honor of Laelius Socinus, 1965, (with Anthony Molho) Renaissance Studies in Honor of Hans Baron, 1971, (with Gustav Henningsen) The Inquisition in Early Modern Europe: Studies on Sources and Methods, 1986, The Prosecution of Heresy: Collected Studies on the Inquisition in Early Modern Italy, 1991 (transl. into Italian 1997), Tomasso Sassetti, Il Massacro di San Bartolomeo, 1995, The Italian Reformation of the Sixteenth Century and the Diffusion of Renaissance Culture: A Bibliography of the Secondary Literature (c. 1750-1997), 2000, The correspondence of Roland H. Bainton and Delio Cantimori, 1932-66, 2002; translator: (with Anne Tedeschi) The Cheese and the Worms. The Cosmos of a Sixteenth-Century Miller (Carlo Ginzburg), 1980 (named an Outstanding Acad. Book by Choice mag.), The Night Battles. Witchcraft and Agrarian Cults in the Sixteenth and Seventeenth Centuries (Carlo Ginzburg), 1983, Clues, Myths, and the Historical Method (Carlo Ginzburg), 1989, Hans Urs von Balthasar: A Theological Style (Angelo Scola), 1995, Domenico Scandella Known as Menocchio: His Trials Before the Inquisition (1583-1599) (Andrea Del Col), 1996, The Protestant Reformation in Sixteenth-Century Italy (Salvatore Caponetto), 1999, Books of the Body: Anatomical Ritual and Renaissance Learning (Andrea Carlino), 1999; mem. editl. com.: Index des Livres Interdits (Sherbrooke), Collected Works of Erasmus (Toronto); mem. editl. bd.: Studi e Testi per la Storia Religiosa Italiana del '500 (Florence), The Peter Martyr Libr. (Kirksville, Mo.); contbr. articles to profl. jours. Served with U.S. Army, 1954-56. Grantee Am. Philos. Soc., 1961; grantee NEH, 1967; Old Dominion fellow Harvard U. Ctr. Renaissance Studies, Florence, Italy, 1967-68; fellow Inst. Research in Humanities, U. Wis.-Madison, 1976-77; Huntington Library fellow, 1984. Mem. Am. Soc. Reformation Research (pres. 1972), Renaissance Soc. Am. (exec. bd. 1971-96), 16th Century Studies Conf. (pres. 1987), Am. Hist. Assn., Am. Cath. Hist. Assn. Home: 57211 Rush Creek Rd Ferryville WI 54628 E-mail: tede@frontiernet.net.

TEDESCO, ANNE CAVOLO, music educator, concert pianist; b. Valley Stream, N.Y., Oct. 5, 1951; d. Andrew and Elizabeth (St. Thomas) Cavolo; m. Carmine Tedesco, Aug. 15, 1976; children: Gregory, Louis. MusB cum laude, SUNY, Potsdam, 1973; MusM, Manhattan Sch. of Music, 1975. Adj. assoc. prof. music St. John's U., Jamaica, N.Y., 1982—. Lectr. on music history for various arts groups and univs., Met. N.Y. area. Piano debut Carnegie Recital Hall, 1981; concert painist N.Y. Metro area. Manhattan Sch. of Music scholar, 1973-75. Mem. AAUP, Am. Keyboard Artists, N.Y. Music Tchrs. Assn., Friday-Woodmere Music Club, Nassau Music Educators Assn. Avocations: concerts, opera. Home: 394 Cornwell Ave Malverne NY 11565-1532 Office: St Johns U Dept Fine Arts Music Divsn Jamaica NY 11439-0001

TEDESCO, FRANCIS JOSEPH, university administrator; b. Derby, Conn., Mar. 8, 1944; s. Lena (Tufano) Tedesco; m. Luann Lee Ekern, Aug. 1, 1970; 1 child, Jennifer Nicole. BS cum laude, Fairfield U., 1965; MD cum laude, St. Louis U., 1969. Asst. instr. Hosp. of U. Pa., Phila., 1971-72; asst. prof. Washington U. Sch. Medicine, St. Louis, 1974-75, U. Miami (Fla.) Sch. Medicine, 1975-77, co-dir. clin. research, 1976-78, assoc. prof., 1977-78, Med. Coll. Ga., Augusta, 1978-81, chief of gastroenterology dept., 1978-88, prof., 1981—, acting v.p. clin. activities, 1984, v.p. for clin. activities, 1984-88, Interim dean Sch. of Medicine, 1986-88, pres., 1988—2001, pres. emeritus, 2001—. Cons. Med.-Letter/AMA divsn. drugs, Dwight D. Eisenhower Army Med. Ctr., Ft. Gordon, Ga., VA Med. Ctr., Augusta, Walter Reed Army Med. Ctr., Washington; mem. gastroenterology spl. study sect. NIH, Washington, 1982—, mem. nat. digestive disease adv. bd., 1985-88, vice chmn., 1986-87, chmn., 1987-88; mem. Ty Cobb Found. Scholarship Bd., 1998—. Contbr. numerous articles to profl. jours. Bd. dirs. Augusta Country Day Sch., 1981-83, Am. Cancer Soc., Augusta, 1985—, v.p., 1986—; bd. dirs., exec. com. Ga. Coalition for Health, 1995-2002; chmn. Gov.'s Health Strategies Coun., 1992-2002; bd. visitors CDC, 1998—; nat. adv. bd. Ga. Acad. Sci., Math. and Engring., 1998—; mem. Ty Cobb Fedn. Bd., 1998—. Recipient Eddie Palmer award for gastrointestinal endoscopy, 1983, cert. of appreciation Am. Cancer Soc., 1986, Outstanding Faculty award Med. Coll. Ga. Sch. Medicine, 1988, Profl. Achievement award Fairfield U., 1993, alumni merit award St. Louis U. Sch. Medicine, 1996; Avalon Found. scholar St. Louis U., 1968-69, Paul Harris fellow Rotary, 1990, Spirit of Ga. award Ga. Econ. Devel. Assn., 1998. Fellow ACP, Am. Fedn. Clin. Investigation, Am. Gastroent. Assn., Am. Soc. Gastrointestinal Endoscopy (treas. 1981-84, pres.-elect 1984-85, pres. 1985-86, Rudolph Schindler award 1993); mem. Am. Coll. Gastroenterology, So. Soc. Clin. Investigation, Richmond County Med. Soc., Med. Assn. Ga. Roman Catholic. Avocations: reading, swimming. Home: 2810 Peachtree Pl Augusta GA 30909 Office: Med Coll Ga Office Pres 1120 15th St Augusta GA 30912-0006

TEDESCO, FRANK MARIO, management consultant; b. N.Y.C., May 6, 1945; s. Anthony George and Nina Emily (Sorrentino) T.; m. Annetta Conrad, Dec. 22, 1990; children: Michael, Daniel, Robert, Laura, Doug. AS in Chem. Tech., B of Tech., U. Dayton, 1967; MBA in Gen. Mgmt., Fairleigh Dickenson U., 1977. Dir. quality ITT Rayonier, Inc., Stamford, Conn., 1967-83; mgr. quality Union Carbide Corp., Chgo., 1983-84; sr. exec. cons., v.p. Juran Inst., Wilton, Conn., 1985—. Speaker, presenter papers to numerous orgns. Co-author: (course texts) Management of Quality - Manufacturing, 1990, Total Service Quality, 1990. With U.S. Army, 1969-71. Mem. AAAS, ASTD, Am. Chem. Soc., Tech. Assn. of the Pulp and Paper Industry, Am. Soc. for Quality Control. Office: Juran Inst Inc 11 River Rd # 811 Wilton CT 06897-4025

TEDESCO, PAUL HERBERT, humanities educator; b. Nashua, N.H., Dec. 28, 1928; s. Steven R. and Ruth (Weaver) T.; m. Eleanor Martha Hollis, Jan. 24, 1953; children: Steven Anthony, Sara Adams Tagget, James Beattie. AB in History, Harvard Coll., 1952; AM in History, Boston U., 1955, PhD in History, 1970; CAGS in Adminstrn., Northeastern U., Boston, 1974. Instr. humanities Mich. State U., East Lansing, 1955-60; tchr. history Great Neck (N.Y.) North H.S., 1960-62; chmn. dept. social studies Canton (Mass.) H.S., 1962-65; prof., chmn. edn. Northeastern U., Boston, 1965-87; Fulbright prof. history Peking U., Beijing, China, 1988-89; historian-in-residence City of Haverhill, Mass., 1989-90; lectr. bus., history, govt. edn. Asian divsn. U. Md., Korea, Japan, Guam, 1990-94; team leader, lectr. Joint Siberian-Am. Faculty, Irkutsk State U., Siberia, 1994-95; edn. coord. Asian divsn. U. Md., 1995-97; lectr. U. Md. European divsn., 1997—. Nat. dir. BHelp (Bus., History and Econ. Life Program), Boston, 1968—; cons. in field. Author: Teaching with Case Studies, 1978, A New England City: Haverhill Massachusetts, 1987, Attleboro, Massachusetts: The Hub of the Jewelry Industry, 1979, Protection, Patriotism and Prosperity: James M. Swank, the AISA, and the Tariff, 1872-1913, 1985; author, editor: The Creative Social Science Teacher, 1970, The Thunder of the Mills, 1981, Dover, Mass., 2000. Mem. Town Fin. Com., Canton, Mass., 1966-68. With U.S. Army, 1952-54. Recipient FEI Nat. collegiate award, 1985, Freedoms Found. George Washington medal for econ. edn., 1984. Mem. New Eng. History Tchrs. Assn. (past pres., Kidger award 1975), Dover Hist. Soc. (pres.).

TEDESCO, RICHARD ALBERT, minister; b. Phila., Sept. 14, 1942; s. Vito and Esther (Iannelli) T.; m. Joyce Lea Morando, Aug. 1, 1964; children: Lisa Renee, Stephanie Ruth. Grad., N.E. Bible Inst., 1964; BS in Bible, Valley Forge Christian Coll., 1976; M of Bible in Theology, Internat. Bible Inst. & Sem., Orlando, Fla., 1985; PhD in Theology, Honolulu U., 1988; DD (hon.), Clarksville Sch. Theology, 1985. Ordained to ministry Christian Ch. N.Am., 1967, Covenant Ministries Internat. Inc., 1988; lic. clin. pastoral counselor. Pastor Christian Assembly Ch., Uhrichsville, Ohio, 1967-69, Follansbee, W.Va., 1969-73; bus. mgr., sec./treas. dept. missions Gen. Coun. Christian Ch. N.Am., 1973-80, gen. sec.-treas. Gen. Coun., 1975-82, exec. dir. dept. home and fgn. missions, 1981-85, asst. gen. overseer for fgn. concerns, 1981-85; staff min., dir. dept. missions and world outreach Faith Fellowship Ministries World Outreach Ctr., Sayreville, N.J., 1988—; founding trustee, exec. adminstrv. sec. Covenant Ministries Internat., 1988—. Recipient cert. of honor Pentecostal Christian Ch. Argentina, 1984, Outstanding Achievement award Christian Ch. of N.Am., 1984, 87, Merit award Nat. Assn. Evangelicals, 1990.

Fellow Internat. Acad. Edn.; mem. Nat. Christian Counselors Assn. (profl. assoc. mem.). Office: Covenant Ministries Internat 2707 Main St Sayreville NJ 08872-1457 E-mail: rtedesco@ffmwdc.org. *Let me quote the song writer: "If I've gained any praise, let it go to Calvary," for I am what I am and do what I do by the strength and enablement of our Lord, Jesus Christ.*

TEDFORD, CHARLES FRANKLIN, biophysicist; b. Lawton, Okla., June 26, 1928; s. Charles E. and Loula B. (Waters) T.; m. Julie Reme Sauret, Sept. 15, 1951; children: Gary Franklin, Mark Charles, Philip John. BS with distinction in Chemistry, S.W. Tex. State U., 1950, MS, 1954; postgrad. in radiobiology Reed Coll., 1957, in biophysics U. Calif., Berkeley, 1961-63. Enlisted USN, 1945-47, commd. ensign, 1950, advanced through grades to capt., 1968; biochemist U.S. Naval Hosp., San Diego, 1953-54, U.S. Naval Biol. Lab., Oakland, Calif., 1954-56; sr. instr., radiation safety officer Nuclear, Biol. and Chem. Warfare Def. Sch., Treasure Island, Calif., 1956-61; asst. chief nuclear medicine div. Navy Med. Sch., Bethesda, Md., 1963-66; adminstrv. program mgr. radiation safety br. Bur. Medicine and Surgery, Washington, 1966-72; dir. radiation safety and health physics program Navy Regional Med. Center, San Diego, 1972-74; mgr. Navy Regional Med. Clinic, Seattle, 1974-78, ret., 1978; dir. radiation health unit Ga. Dept. Human Resources, Atlanta, 1978-79; dir. Ariz. Radiation Regulatory Agy., Tempe, 1979-91; chief, Radiological Health Prog., Juneau, Alaska, 1991-93, ret. 1993; cons. 1993—. elected chmn. Conf. Radiation Program Dirs., 1987; named Ariz. Southwestern Low Level Radioactive Waste Compact Commr., 1990. Recipient Ariz. Adminstr. of Yr. award Ariz. Adminstrs. Assn., 1988; decorated Legion of Merit, Meritorious Service medal. Mem. Health Physics Soc., Am. Nuclear Soc. Contbr. articles on radiation safety to profl. publs.

TEDFORD, JACK NOWLAN, III, construction executive, small business owner; b. Reno, Jan. 1, 1943; s. Jack Nowlan Jr. and Elizabeth (Kolhoss) T.; m. Nancy Joanne Stiles, Feb. 27, 1971; children: Jack Nowlan IV, James Nathan. BS, U. Nev., 1966, MBA, 1969. Bus. mgr. Los Angeles Bapt. Coll., Newhall, Calif., 1969-71; v.p. Jack N. Tedford, Inc., Fallon, Nev., 1971-98; owner/broker Tedford Realty, 1974-94; owner/mgr. Tedford Bus. Systems, 1978-94; pres. JNT, Inc., 1994—. Pres., Jack N. Tedford, Inc., 1998—. Author numerous computer programs. Mem. Selective Svc. Local Bd., Fallon, 1971-76; chmn. City of Fallon Bd. Adjustment, 1972-95, chmn. Churchill Co. Reps., Fallon, 1976-80; mem. ctrl. com. Nev. Reps., 1976-2002; del. Nat. Conv., Detroit, 1980, Dallas, 1984; former coun. ofcls. Western Nev. Devel. Dist.; former treas. Lahontan Valley Environ. Alliance; mem. Fellowship of Cos. for Christ Internat. Mem. Assn. Gen. Contractors (past pres., former v.p., treas. Nev. chpt., dir.), Nat. Bd. Realtors, State Bd. Realtors, Sierra Nevada Assn. Realtors, CEDA Bus. Coun. (bd. dirs. 1991-97), Nat. Asphalt Pavement Assn. (state dir., nat. dir. 2000-2001), Rotary (bd. dirs. 1980-81), Master's Coll. (bd. dirs. 1971-95), Slavic Gospel Assn. (bd. dirs.), Nat. Assn. Gen. Contractors (bd. dirs. open shop com., closely held bus. com.), Fellowship of Cos. for Christ Internat. Republican. Baptist. Avocations: computers, family activities, golf. Home and Office: PO Box 7937 Incline Village NV 89452 E-mail: jack@jntinc.com.

TEDLOCK, BARBARA HELEN, anthropologist, educator, academic administrator; b. Battle Creek, Mich., Sept. 9, 1942; d. Byron Taylor and Mona Gerteresse (O'Connor) McGrath; m. Dennis E. Tedlock, July 19, 1968. BA in Rhetoric, U. Calif., Berkeley, 1967; MA in Anthropology, Wesleyan U., 1973; PhD in Anthropology, SUNY, Albany, 1978. Lectr. in music Tufts U., Medford, Mass., 1977-78, asst. prof. anthropology, 1978-82, assoc. prof., 1982-87; assoc. prof. anthropology SUNY, Buffalo, 1987-89, prof. anthropology, 1989—, chair dept. anthropology, 1998—2000, 2002—, assoc. dean undergrad. edn., 2000—01. Vis. mem. Inst. for Advanced Study, Princeton, 1986. Author: Time and the Highland Maya, 1982, The Beautiful and the Dangerous Encounters with Zuni Indians, 1992, The Woman in the Shaman's Body: Reclaiming the Feminine in Religion and Medicine, 2002; editor: Dreaming: Anthropological and Psychological Interpretations, 1987; co-editor: Teaching From the American Earth, 1975; assoc. editor Jour. of Anthropol. Rsch., 1987-93; sr. editor Dreaming, 1990-95; assoc. editor Latin Am. Rsch. Rev., 1992—; mem. editl. adv. bd. Encyc. Cultural Anthropology, 1993-95, Handbook of Qualitative Research, 1998—. Adv. bd. Mus. of Indian Arts, Santa Fe, 1991-95; mem. Roycrofters-at-large East Aurura, N.Y., 1989—; mem. Cultural Survival, 1980—; mem. humanities panel WGBH, Boston, 1983-84; judge pottery Southwestern Assn. on Indian Affairs, Santa Fe, 1981-83. Fellowships NEH, 1986, 93, sr. fellowship Am. Coun. of Learned Socs., 1994, Weatherhead fellowship Sch. of Am. Rsch., 1980, sr. fellowship Ctr. for the Study of World Religions/Harvard U., 1998; recipient Charles Bordon, Geoffrey Bushnell Juan Cosmos prize in linguistics Internat. Congress of Americanists, 1979. Fellow Am. Anthropol. Assn. (bd. dirs. 1991-93, editor-in-chief Am. Anthropologist 1994-98, Pres.'s award for leadership 1997), Soc. for Cultural Anthropology, Am. Philosophical Soc.; mem. AAUW, PEN (elected), Soc. for Humanistic Anthropology (pres. 1991-93, Writing prize 1986), Soc. for Psychol. Anthropology (bd. dirs. 1993-96), Assn. for Study of Dreams (bd. dirs. 1990-95), Soc. for Ethnohistory (exec. bd. 1980-82), Am. Studies Assn. (exec. bd. 1983-85), Assn. on Am. Indian Affairs. Avocations: skiing, running, swimming, dancing, videoing. E-mial. Office: SUNY Buffalo Dept Anthropology Buffalo NY 14261-0001 E-mail: tedlockb@acsu.buffalo.edu.

TEDOLDI, ROBERT LOUIS, JR. financial planner, consultant; b. Meriden, Conn., Jan. 4, 1967; s. Robert Louis and Carol (Amesbury) T. BA in Journalism, U. S.C., 1989. Assoc. Coordinated Fin. Planning, Farmington, Conn., 1990-92; jr. ptnr. Benefit Plans Design & Adminstrn., Inc., Vernon, 1992-96; pres., CEO Tedoldi Fin., South Windsor, 1996—; pres., ptnr. DiSanto Bertoline Fin. Svcs. LLC, Glastonbury, 1999—. Team capt. March of Dimes, Hartford, Conn., 1992, 93; bd. dirs. Plum Ridge Condo Assn., South Windsor, Conn., 1994—, pres., 1997—; mem. Greater Hartford Jaycees, 1991—. Recipient Conn. Ofcl. citation Gov. of Conn./House and Senate, 1992-93. Mem. Internat. Assn. Fin. Planning, Nat. Assn. Life Underwriters (voting del. 1990), U.S. Golf Assn., Conn. State Assn. Life Underwriters, Hartford Life Underwriters Assn. (bd. dirs. 1991—, cmty. svc. chmn. 1991, 92, Pres.'s award 1993, 96, golf com. chmn. 1996-97, Pres.'s award 1996), Tolland County C. of C. (bd. dirs., mem. golf com. 1995—), Ellington Ridge Country Club (green com. 1990—), Pi Kappa Phi. Republican. Roman Catholic. Avocations: golf, hockey, boating, water and snow skiing, mountain hiking.

TEDROW, JOHN CHARLES FREMONT, soils educator; b. Rockwood, Pa., Apr. 21, 1917; s. John Wesley and Emma Grace (Younkin) T.; m. Mary Jane Lough, Mar. 20, 1943 (dec. Mar. 1991); children: John Charles Fremont, Thomas Lough (dec.). BS, Pa. State U., 1939; MS, Mich. State U., 1940; PhD, Rutgers U., 1950. Jr. soil technologist Dept. Agr., 1941-42, soil scientist, 1946-47; instr. Rutgers U., New Brunswick, N.J., 1947-50, asst. prof., 1950-53, assoc. prof., 1953-57, prof. soils, 1957-84, prof. emeritus, 1984—. Cons. N.S. Research Found., 1949— ; sr. pedologist Boston U., 1953— ; prin. investigator Arctic Inst. N.Am., Washington, 1955-68, NSF, 1961-62, Atomic Energy Commn., Washington, 1961-63; cons. to govt. and industry. Author: (with R.C. Murray) Forensic Geology: Earth Sciences and Criminal Investigation, 1974, Soils of the Polar Landscapes, 1977, (with K.A. Linell) Soil and Permafrost Surveys in the Arctic, 1981, Soils of New Jersey, 1986, (with R.C. Murray) Forensic Geology, 1991; editor in chief Soil Science, 1968-79; editor: Antarctic Soils and Soil Forming Processes, 1966. Served to lt. USNR, 1942-46. Recipient Lindback Research award Rutgers U., 1978, Antarctic Service medal. Fellow Am. Soc. Agronomy, Soil Sci. Soc. Am., Arctic Inst. N.Am.; mem. Internat. Soc. Soil Sci., Am. Geophys. Union, Am. Arbitration Assn., Sigma Xi, Alpha Zeta (hon.), Phi Mu Delta. Achievements include investigation of polar soils in Alaska, Can., Greenland, Scandinavia, Siberia and Antarctica. Home: 5 Bluebird Ct Edison NJ 08820-3677 Office: Rutgers U Ecology Evolution and Natural Resources PO Box 231 New Brunswick NJ 08903-0231

TEEGARDEN, KENNETH LEROY, clergyman; b. Cushing, Okla., Dec. 22, 1921; s. Roy Albert and Eva B. (Swiggart) T.; m. Wanda Jean Strong, May 28, 1944; children: David Kent, Marshall Kirk. Student, Okla. State U., 1938-40; AB, Phillips U., 1942, MA, 1945, D.D., 1963; B.D., Tex. Christian U., 1949, D.D., 1976, Bethany Coll., 1974; LL.D., Lynchburg Coll., 1975; L.H.D., Culver-Stockton Coll., 1975. Ordained to ministry Christian Ch. (Disciples of Christ), 1940; pastor in Kaw City, Okla., 1941-43, Chandler, 1944-47, Texas City, Tex., 1947-48, Healdton, Okla., 1948-49, Vernon, Tex., 1949-55, Fort Smith, Ark., 1955-58; exec. minister Christian Ch. in, 1958-65; asst. to pres. Christian Ch. in U.S. and Can., Indpls., 1965-69; exec. minister Christian Ch. in Tex., 1969-73; gen. minister, pres. Christian Ch. in U.S. and Can., 1973-85; faculty Brite Div. Sch., Tex. Christian U., 1985-89. Mem. governing bd. Nat. Council Chs., 1973-85; del. 5th Assembly of World Council Chs., Nairobi, Kenya, 1975, 6th Assembly, Vancouver, B.C., Can, 1983; rep. Nat. Council Chs. in Exchange of Ch. Leadership with Soviet Union, 1974 Author: We Call Ourselves Disciples, 1975. Named Disting. Alumnus Tex. Christian U., 1973, Phillips U., 1975; Outstanding Citizen Vernon, Tex., 1954 Home: 7013 Serrano Dr Fort Worth TX 76126-2317 E-mail: kltfwt@msn.com.

TEEGUARDEN, DENNIS EARL, forest economist, educator; b. Gary, Ind., Aug. 21, 1931; s. Gary Leon and Mary Dessa (Purciful) T.; m. Sally Annette Gleason, Dec. 23, 1954; children— Jason Earl, Julie Annette, Justin Gary. BS in Forestry with honors, Mich. Tech. U., Houghton, 1953; M.Forestry, U. Calif., Berkeley, 1958, PhD in Agrl. Econs. (Bidwell research fellow 1962-63), 1964. Rsch. aid U.S. Forest Service, 1957; asst. rsch. specialist U. Calif., Berkeley, 1958-63, mem. faculty, 1963-91, prof. forestry econs. Sch. Forestry, 1963-91, S.J. Hall prof. forest econs., 1989-91, prof. emeritus, 1991—, chmn. dept. forestry and resource mgmt., 1978-86, acting dir. forest products lab., 1987-88, assoc. dean for acad. affairs, 1990-92, assoc. dean rsch. and extension, 1992-93. Mem. Calif. Commn. on Agr. and Higher Edn., 1993-95, com. scientists Dept. Agr., 1977-80; cons. in field; mem. adv. bd. U. Calif. Forest Products Lab., 1994-98; mem. adv. coun. Alberta Heritage Found. for Sci. and Engring. Rsch., 2001—. Co-author: Forest Resource Management: Decision-Making Principles and Cases, 1979; contbr. articles to profl. jours. Trustee Mich. Tech. Fund, Mich. Tech. U., Houghton, 1994—. Lt. USNR, 1953-57, Korea. Recipient Outstanding Alumnus award Mich. Tech. U., 1993, Berkeley citation U. Calif., Berkeley, 1994; grantee U.S. Forest Svc., Bur. Land Mgmt.; named to Honor Acad. Sch. Forestry and Wood Products, Mich. Tech. U., 1995. Fellow Soc. Am. Foresters; mem. Western Forest Economists, Calif. Water Fowl Assn. Home: 4732 Westwood Ct Richmond CA 94803-2441 Office: U Calif Coll Natural Resources Berkeley CA 94720-0001

TEEM, JOHN MCCORKLE, retired association executive; b. Springfield, Mo., July 23, 1925; s. Lon Vester and Judith (McCorkle) T.; m. Sylvia Victoria Konvicka; children— Judith Majka Teem Donald, Paul Norman AB, Harvard U., 1949, MA, 1951, PhD, 1954. Sr. research fellow Calif. Inst. Tech., Pasadena, 1954-60; v.p., chief scientist Electro Optical Systems, 1960-67; dir. tech. staff, research and devel. Xerox Corp., Stamford, Conn., 1967-72; asst. gen. mgr., dir. phys. research AEC, Washington, 1973-75; asst. adminstr. ERDA, 1975-76; pres. Assn. Univs. for Research in Astronomy, 1977-86. Served with U.S. Army, 1943-46 Recipient Disting. Service medal AEC, 1975; named Fairchild Disting. scholar Calif. Inst. Tech., 1976-77 Fellow AAAS; mem. Am. Astron. Soc. Democrat. Roman Catholic. Home: 3800 Fairfax Dr Apt 1710 Arlington VA 22203-1723 E-mail: jmandsteem@earthlink.net.

TEEM, PAUL LLOYD, JR. bank executive; b. Gastonia, N.C., Mar. 10, 1948; s. Paul Lloyd Sr. and Ruth Elaine (Bennett) T. BA, U. N.C., 1970; Cert., Inst. Fin. Edn., Chgo., 1984, Diploma, 1985, Degree of Distinction, 1989. Cert. tchr. N.C., cert. consumer credit exec.; lic. real estate broker. Exec. v.p., sec. Citizens South Bank, Gastonia, NC, 1983—; exec. v.p., sec., bd. dirs. Citizens South Fin. Svcs. Inc., 1988—; exec. v.p., sec. Citizens South Holdings, Mut. Holding Co., 1998—, Citizens South Banking Corp., Inc., 1998—. Bd. dirs. Gastonia Mchts. Assn., Inc., 1981-83; lay reader Episcopal Ch. Decorated Order Purple Cross, Legion of Honor; named Ky. Col., 1995. Fellow Soc. Cert. Credit Execs.; mem. Nat. Soc. Sons and Daus. of Pilgrims, SAR, Sons of Confederate Vets., Mil. Order of Stars and Bars, Masons (32d degree, bd. dirs. 1981—, Disting. Svc. award 1987, Gold Honor award 1988, Active Legion of Honor 1989, Order of the Purple Cross of York 1990), Shriners, KT, Royal Order of Scotland, Hon. Order Ky. Cols., Phi Alpha Theta. Democrat. Avocation: genealogy. Home: 1208 Poston Cir Gastonia NC 28054-4634 Office: Citizens South Bank PO Box 2249 Gastonia NC 28053-2249 E-mail: paul.teem@citizenssouth.com.

TEEPEN, THOMAS HENRY, newspaper editor, journalist; b. Nashville, Jan. 19, 1935; s. Albert George and Elizabeth Blanche (Winfree) T.; m. Nancy Irene Roux, Feb. 2, 1957 (div. 1974); children— Kristina Lynn, Jeremy Roux; m. Sandra Jean Richards, May 14, 1975; 1 stepchild, Jennifer Koerlin BS in Journalism, Ohio U., 1957. Reporter Urbana (Ohio) Daily Citizen, 1957-58; asst. editor Kettering-Oakwood Times, Dayton, Ohio, 1958-59; from reporter to editorial writer Dayton Daily News, 1959-68, editorial page editor, 1968-82, Atlanta Constitution, 1982-92; nat. corr. Cox Newspapers, Atlanta, 1992-2000, columnist, 2000—. Contbg. columnist Liberal Opinion Week. Former pres. Joel Chandler Harris Assn., Atlanta; mem. Atlanta Opera, 1985—, Joint Internat. Observer Group, Ethiopian Elections, 1992; mem. internat. adv. com. The African-Am. Inst., N.Y.C., 1985-97; bd. dirs. Capital Area Mosaic, Genesis Shelter. Profl. journalism fellow Stanford Univ., 1967 Home and Office: 900 Charles Allen Dr NE Atlanta GA 30308-1722 E-mail: tteepen@earthlink.net., teepencolumn@coxnews.com.

TEEPLE, FIONA DIANE, librarian, lawyer; b. St. Thomas, Ont., Can., Jan. 9, 1943; d. William Lloyd and Grace (Hathaway) T. BA, U. Western Ont., London, 1964; BLS, U. B.C., Vancouver, 1965; MLS, U. Toronto, Ont., 1976; LLB, York U., Toronto, 1980. Bar: Ont., 1985. Asst. law librarian U. Western Ont., London, 1965-70; reference librarian York U. Law Library, Toronto, 1971-77; adminstrv. asst. Ont. Legis. Library, 1980, exec. asst., 1981-83; chief librarian Supreme Ct. of Can., Ottawa, 1983-90, dir. libr., 1990—. Editor: Practitioner's Desk Book, 1976-80; mng. editor CALL Newsletter, 1973-75; contbr. articles, revs., book chpts. in field. Mem. Can. Assn. Law Librs., Law Soc. Upper Can. Mem. United Ch. Can.

TEERLINK, J(OSEPH) LELAND, real estate developer; b. Salt Lake City, July 16, 1935; s. Nicholas John and Mary Luella (Love) T.; m. Leslie Dowdle, Nov. 5, 1975; children: Steven, David, Andrew, Suzanne, Benjamin. Student, U. Utah, 1953-55. Sales rep. Eastman Kodak Co., Salt Lake City, 1960-69; founder Graphic Systems, Inc., 1969-82, pres., 1969-79, chmn. bd., 1979-82; founder Graphic Ink Co., 1973, pres., 1975-79, chmn. bd., 1979-82; founder G.S.I. Leasing Co., 1975, pres., 1975-82; chmn. bd. Graphic Sys. Holding Co., Inc., 1978-82; dir. leasing and acquisitions Terra Industries, Inc., real estate developers, 1982-86, ptnr., 1986—. Bd. dirs. ARC, Salt Lake City, 1979-82; co-founder, dir. Hope Living Ctr. Found. for Mothers and Children, 1993-99; vice consulate of the Netherlands for Utah, 1977-92; mem. active corps of execs., SBA, 1979-83; mem. adv. bd. House of Hope Mothers and Children Utah Alcoholism Found., 1992-94. Recipient Masters award Salt Lake Bd. Realtors, 1993; named Small Businessman of the Yr. for Utah, SBA, 1978. Mem. Graphic Arts Equipment and Supply Dealers of Am. (dir. 1978-82), Printing Industry of Am., Nat. Assn. Indsl. and Office Parks (pres. Utah chpt. 1986-87), Nat. Fedn. Ind. Businessman, Million Dollar Club (life). Republican. Mem. Lds Ch. Home: 2984 Thackeray Pl Salt Lake City UT 84108-2517 Office: 6925 Union Park Ctr Midvale UT 84047-4135 E-mail: receptionist@terrautah.com.

TEES, RICHARD CHISHOLM, psychology educator, researcher; b. Montreal, Que., Can., Oct. 31, 1940; s. Ralph Charles and Helen Winnifred (Chisholm) T.; m. Kathleen F. Coleman, Sept. 1, 1962; children: Susan M., Carolyn V. BA, McGill U., 1961; PhD, U. Chgo., 1965. Asst. prof. U. B.C., Vancouver, 1965-67, assoc. prof., 1969-75, prof. psychology, 1975—, head dept. psychology, 1984-94, 99—. Rsch. prof. U. Sussex, Brighton, Eng., 1972-73, 77-78; chmn. grant selection panel Nat. Scis. and Engring. Rsch. Coun. Can., Ottawa, 1993-96, B.C. Health Care Rsch. Found., Vancouver, 1984-87; chmn. studentship com. Med. Rsch. Coun., Ottawa, 1985-92; chmn. Can. Coun. Dept. Psyc., 1987-93. Author: (with Kolb) Cerebral Cortex of the Rat, 1990; mem. editorial bd. Can. Jour. Exptl. Psychology, 1975-84, 87—; contbr. articles to profl. jours., chpts. to books. Research fellow Killam Found., 1972-73, 77-78; research fellow Can. Council, 1972-73 Fellow APA, Am. Psychol. Soc., Can. Psychol. Assn.; mem. Soc. for Neurosci., Psychonomic Soc., Can. Soc. Brain, Behaviour, and Cognitive Sci. (pres. 1997-98), U. B.C. Senate, Nat. Ctr. Excellence Can. Stroke Network. Home: 1856 Acadia Rd Vancouver BC Canada V6T 1R3 Office: U BC Dept Psychology Vancouver BC Canada V6T 1Z4 E-mail: rtees@cortex.psych.ubc.ca.

TEESDALE, RANDALL LEE, consumer products company executive; BS in Indsl. Tech., Ea. Ill. U., 1976; MBA, Govs. State U., 1981. Various distbn. logistics and supply chain mgmt. positions Boise Cascade Office Products, Itasca, Ill., 1984—93; v.p. distbn. ops. Corp. Express, Inc., Broomfield, Colo., 1993—2000; v.p. distbn. svcs. World Kitchen, Inc., Elmira, NY, 2000—. Mem.: Warehousing Edn. Rsch. Coun., Coun. Logistics Mgmt. Office: World Kitchen Inc One Pyrex Place Elmira NY 14902

TEETER, DWIGHT LELAND, JR. journalism educator; b. L.A., Jan. 6, 1935; s. Dwight Leland and Ruth Elizabeth (Sauer) T.; m. Letitia Ruth Thoreson, July 7, 1956; children: Susan Letitia Hall, John Thoreson, William Weston. AB in Journalism, U. Calif.-Berkeley, 1956, M.J., 1959; PhD in Mass Communications, U. Wis., 1966. Reporter Waterloo Daily Courier, Iowa, 1957-60; asst. prof. Iowa State U., Ames, 1964-66; asst. to assoc. prof. U. Wis., Madison, 1966-72; assoc.prof. to prof. U. Ky., Lexington, 1972-77, dir. journalism dept., 1975-77; prof. journalism, chmn. dept. journalism U. Tex., Austin, 1977-84, William P. Hobby Centennial prof. communication, 1983-87; prof., dept. mass communications U. Wis., Milw., 1987-91; dean, prof. Coll. Communications U. Tenn., Knoxville, 1991—. Vis. assoc. prof. U. Wash., Seattle, 1969-70; treas. Journalism Council, Inc., N.Y.C., 1972-81 Author: (with Bill Loving) Law of Mass Communications, 10th edit., 2001, (with Jean L. Folkerts) Voices of a Nation: A History of Media in the United States, 4th edit., 2002, (with Ratner) Fanatics and Fire-Eaters: Newspaper Publications Leading to Civil War, 2002; contbr. articles to legal, hist., comm. jours. Chair Headliners Club of Tex. Media Contest, 1979-83; judge Tex. Bar Assn. Media Contest, 1981-85; mem. pub. affairs com. Tex. State Bar, 1985-87. Recipient Tex. Excellence in Teaching award Tex. Ex-Students' Assn., 1983, Harold L. Nelson award U. Wis., 1985. Mem. Assn. for Edn. in Journalism and Mass Comm. (chmn. prof. freedom and responsibility com. 1971-73, pres. 1985-86), Soc. Profl. Journalists (Disting. Tchr. award 1991), Phi Kappa Phi, Kappa Tau Alpha. Office: U Tenn 330 Communication Knoxville TN 37996-0330 E-mail: dwight-teeter@utk.edu.

TEETERS, BRUCE A. lawyer; b. Jackson Center, Ohio, Dec. 29, 1965; s. Richard Leon and Janet Elaine Teeters; m. Julie Ann Thiel, June 17, 1995; children: Madison Anna, Noah Richard, Elaine Lindsay. BS in Polit. Sci./Acctg., Ohio No. U., 1988; JD, U. Cin., 1991. Bar: Ohio 1991, U.S. Dist. Ct. (so. dist.) Ohio 1992. Atty. Chernesky, Heyman & Kress, Dayton, Ohio, 1991—. Bd. dirs. Bus. Adv. Com., Oakwood, Ohio, 1996—, Jackson Center Edn. Found. Mem. ABA (bus. law divsn.), Ohio State Bar Assn. (bus. law divsn.), Dayton Bar Assn. Office: Chernesky Heyman & Kress Ten Courthouse Plz SW Dayton OH 45402

TEETERS, JOSEPH LEE, mathematician, consultant; b. Caney, Kans., Dec. 10, 1934; s. Jesse L. and Marie (Tapper) Teeters; m. Janet L. Hamm, June 18, 1984; children: Jeffrey, Susan, Christopher. Student, Colo. Sch. Mines, 1956, U. Kans., 1957; MA in Math., U. No. Colo., 1960, EdD in Math., 1968. Cert. secondary sch. tchr., Colo., Ill., hazard waste profl., OSHA. Exploration geologist Ohio Oil Co., Rawlings, Wyo., 1956-57; instr. Stout State U., Menomonie, Wis., 1960-62; asst. prof. Baker U., Baldwin City, Kans., 1962-65; temp. instr. U. No. Colo., Greeley, 1965-68; asst. prof. Western State Coll., Gunnison, Colo., 1968-69; prof. U. Wis., Eau Claire, 1969-88; cons. assoc. Delphi Data, Corona, Calif., 1989-98; ind. mathematician and cons., Lake Zurich, Ill., 1998—. Land surveying cons. Donaldson Engring., Menomonie, 1960-62; land boundary cons. ACLU, Eau Claire, 1974; lectr., spkr., cons. in field. Author: Creating Escher-Type Drawings, 1977; designer tessellation art; contbr. cover designs for profl. publs. Active Forest Lake (Ill.) Cmty. Assn., 1990—; sr. citizen trainer Marathon Challenge, St. Louis, 1994; mem. Golden Colo. Civic Orch., 1956; unicyclist Kans. State Sunflower State Games. Grantee NSF, 1965, U. New Orleans, 1987. Mem. Internat. Assn. for Math. Geology, Internat. Platform Assn., Stanton County Kans. Hist. Assn., No Man's Land Hist. Soc., Santa Fe Trail Assn., Kans. Trails Assn., Am. Volkssport Assn. (triathlete), Colo. Sch. of Mines Assn., Tiblow Trailblazers (sports cons. 1994—), Sherman County Kans. Hist. Soc., Kappa Kappa Psi, Sigma Gamma Epsilon, Phi Delta Kappa. Achievements include creation of magnetic fishing tool for small sand screen well openings, designing and development of motion activated vortiginous reflector system(s) for bicycles, creation of a multi-function recursive algorithm which yields (with each use) a unique random lottery number ball quick-pick selection result, and two successful completions of the Boston Marathon as well as six other 26.2 mile running events. Avocations: raising St. Bernards, designing birdhouses, planning and building full size windmills. Home and Office: 21635 W Ravine Rd Lake Zurich IL 60047-8890

TEETERS, NANCY HAYS, economist, director; b. Marion, Ind., July 29, 1930; d. S. Edgar and Mabel (Drake) Hays; m. Robert Duane Teeters, June 7, 1952; children: Ann, James, John. AB in Econs., Oberlin Coll., 1952, LLD, 1979; MA in Econs., U. Mich., 1954, postgrad., 1956-57, LLD, 1983, Bates Coll., 1981, Mt. Holyoke Coll., 1983. Tchg. fellow U. Mich., 1954-55, instr., 1956-57, U. Md. Overseas, Germany, 1955-56; staff economist govt. fin. sect. Bd. Govs. of FRS, Washington, 1957-66, mem. bd., 1978-84; economist (on loan) Coun. Econ. Advs., 1962-63; economist Bur. Budget, 1966-70; sr. fellow Brookings Instn., 1970-73; sr. specialist Congl. Rsch. Svc., Library of Congress, Washington, 1973-74; asst. dir., chief economist Ho. of Reps. Com. on the Budget, 1974-78; v.p., chief economist IBM, Armonk, N.Y., 1984-90. Bd. dirs., trustee Prudential Mut. Funds, 1985—. Author: (with others) Setting National Priorities: The 1972 Budget, 1971, Setting National Priorities: The 1973 Budget, 1972, Setting National Priorities: The 1974 Budget, 1973; contbr. articles to profl. publs. Recipient Comfort Starr award in econs. Oberlin Coll., 1952; Disting. Alumnus award U. Mich., 1980 Mem. Nat. Economists Club (v.p. 1973-74, pres. 1974-75, chmn. bd. 1975-76, gov. 1976-79), Am. Econ. Assn. (com. on status of women 1975-78), Am. Fin. Assn. (dir. 1969-71) Democrat. Home: 243 Willowbrook Ave Stamford CT 06902-7020

TEETS, CHARLES EDWARD, international business consultant, lawyer; b. Terra Alta, W.Va., Feb. 11, 1947; s. Chester Carlton and Wilye Katherine (Martin) T.; m. Judith Marlene Kildow, Dec. 19, 1970; children: Melissa Catherine, Brant Randolph. BS, Salisbury State Coll., 1973; MBA, So. Ill. U., 1980; JD, U Wis., 1994. Bar: Wis. 1994, Fla. 1997. Sr. cost acct. Perdue, Inc., Salisbury, Md., 1973-74; sect. chief acctg. terminal sys. divsn. NCR, Millsboro, Del., 1974-76; contr. SPS Techs., Anasco, P.R., 1976-79; mgr. mfg. acctg. instrumentation divsn. Baxter Travenol Labs., Savage, Md., 1979-81; contr. Coated Abrasives N.Am. divsn. Std. Oil Co., Niagara Falls, N.Y., 1981-83; v.p., sec., treas. Carborundum Abrasives Co., 1983-86; v.p., CFO LeRoy (N.Y.) Industries, Inc., 1986-91; ind. cons., 1991—; mng. ptnr. Teets Kildow Internat., Dunedin, Fla., 1994-99; ptnr. Tatum CFO Ptnrs., Atlanta, 1999—. Adj. prof. Schiller Internat. U., 1995—, Hillsborough Coll., 1995—, Keller Graduate Sch. Mgmt., 1998—, Nova Southeastern U., 1997—; lectr. Cash Mgmt. Inst., Holliston, Mass., 1983—; bus. guest, Beijing, 1986-87; mem. Korean trade mission Dept. Commerce, Washington, 1987; del. U.S./China Joint Session on Industry, Trade and Econ. Devel., Beijing, 1988; econ. and legal advisor Vietnam C. of C. and Industry, Hanoi, 1994, Ministry of Sci. and Tech., Govt. of Brazil, 1998—; lectr. U. Tampa Vis. Bus. Leaders Program Bulgarian Ministry of Industry seminar, 1997, The Stetson U., U.S.-Brazil Internat. Negotiations seminar, 1996, U. South Fla. Ctr. for Small Bus. Devel., 1997; spkr. profl. series seminar Global Alliance USA, Brazil, 1998, 2000; spkr. in field. Sgt. U.S. Army, 1967-70, Vietnam. Recipient Wall St. Jour. award Dow Jones Co., 1973; Asia Found. grantee 1994. Mem. ABA, State Bar of Wis., State Bar Fla., Nat. Assn. Accts., Am. C. of C. (Hong Kong chpt.), St. Petersburg Fla. C. of C., Beta Gamma Sigma. Republican. Methodist. Avocations: boating, traveling, golf. Home: 550 Neel Reid Dr Roswell GA 30075 Office: 550 Neel Reid Dr Roswell GA 30075 E-mail: charles.teets@tatumcfo.com.

TEETS, PETER B. federal agency administrator; b. 1942; BS, U. Colo., MS, 1978. V.p. Denver Aerospace subs. Martin Marietta Corp., Colo., 1980-85, corp. v.p., pres., 1985-87, sr. v.p., 1987—; pres., COO, Info. & Tech. Svcs. Sector Lockheed Martin Corp., Bethesda, M.D.; under secy. of air force U.S. Dept. Defense, Washington, 2001—. Sr. v.p., group pres., Martin Marietta Corp. Office: US Dept Defense Under Secy Air Force 1670 Air Force Pentagon Washington DC 20330-1670 Office Fax: 703-693-4303.*

TEETS, WALTER RALPH, accounting educator; b. Boulder, Colo., Oct. 1, 1950; s. Otis E. and Elsie (Purchase) T.; m. Mary Anne Clougherty; stepchildren: Katherine Wierman, Elizabeth Wierman. B in Music Edn., U. Colo., 1973; MMus, U. Wis., Madison, 1976; MS in Edn., U. Wis., Whitewater, 1981, MS in Acctg., 1985; PhD, U. Chgo., 1989. CPA. Asst. prof. Wash. U., St. Louis, 1986-89, U. Ill., Urbana-Champaign, Ill., 1989-94, Gonzaga U., Spokane, Wash., 1994-99, assoc. prof., 1999—. Continuing profl. edn. spkr. Gonzaga U., 1996—2002, Wash. Soc. CPAs, numerous others; vis. assoc. prof. U. Notre Dame, 2000. Editor Fin. Reporting Jour., 1998—; spl. guest editor Issues in Acctg. Edn., 2001-02; contbr. articles to profl. jours. Recipient Outstanding Acctg. Educator award Wash. Soc. CPAs, 1998-99; Acad. acctg. fellow Office of Chief Acct., U.S. SEC, 1997-98. Mem. Am. Acctg. Assn. (editor Fin. Reporting Jour. newsletter Fin. Acctg. and Reporting sect. 1998—), K.C. (fin. sec. 1990-93, 99—). Avocations: music, cross-country skiing, four-wheeling. Office: Gonzaga Univ 502 E Boone Ave Spokane WA 99258-0001 Fax: 509-323-5811. E-mail: teets@gem.gonzaga.edu.

TEETSELL, JANICE MARIE NEWMAN, business owner, lawyer; b. N.Y.C., Aug. 11, 1951; d. Robert and Clara (White) Swindler; m. Roger Kevin Newman, Jan. 20, 1972 (div. 1980); 1 child, Germaine M. Swindler-Newman (dec.); m. Robert Charles Teetsell, Dec. 29, 1998. BA, Smith Coll., 1973; JD, Rutgers U., 1980. Bar: N.J. 1983, U.S. Supreme Ct. 1987. Adminstrv. asst. Corp. Ann. Reports, N.Y.C., 1972-73; pub. rels. asst. Lippincott & Margulies, 1973; journalist Essex Forum Newspaper, East Orange, N.J., 1973; pub. info. officer City of Newark, 1974-82; producer, host Newark and Reality TV show, Newark, 1974-85; asst. communications dir. Mayor's Office, 1982-86; legis. liaison, publ. info. officer N.J. Div. on Women, Trenton, 1988-90, acting dir., 1990, women svcs. coord., 1990-91; environ. issues specialist N.J. Dept. Environ. Protection and Energy, 1991-92; comm. specialist Dept. Environ. Protection, Lawrenceville, N.J., 1992-95; pvt. practice South Orange, 1994—; host, prodr. New Jersey Issues TV Show, 1995-98. Mem. working group N.J. Supreme Ct. Domestic Violence, 1994-96; pres. JM Newman & Assocs.; chair Interest on Lawyers Trust Accounts, 1995-96, mem., 1986-96; dir. Legal Consultation Svc. Resource Ctr. Women, 1997-99. Mem. editl. bd. N.J. Lawyer mag., 1987-96, The Voice, Episcopal Diocese of Newark, 1999—; design editor: The Voice, 1993-94; contbr. articles to mags. Bd. dirs. Instrns. Exposures Experiences, 1983-87, Greater Newark Conservancy; 2d v.p. Women's Polit. Caucus, N.J., 1991-92, 1st v.p., 1992-93; appt. to N.J. Supreme Ct. Com. on Women in the Cts., 1990-94, Com. on Character, 1992—, N.J. Women Vets. Adv. Com., 1993-94; lay reader, Episc. Diocese of Newark, 1980—, eucharistic lay min., 1993—, parliamentarian, 1992-94; sr. warden, House of Prayer Espisc. Ch., Newark, 1992; vestry clk. St. Andrew Holy Communion Episcopal Ch., 1997-99, warden, 2002—. Recipient Pub. Svc. award N.J. Voice Newspaper, 1977, Achievement award Minority Contractors and Craftsmen Trade Assn., 1982, award Nat. Council Negro Bus. and Profl. Women Legal Achievement, 1987, award N.J. Unit Nat. Assn. Negro Bus. and Profl. Women's Clubs, 1987; named to Outstanding Young Women Am. U.S. Jaycees, 1984. Mem. Nat. Assn. Media Women (rec. sec. 1985-87, Media Woman of Yr. award 1985, pres. N.J. chpt. 1986-88), N.J. Bar Assn. (pub. rels. com. 1987—, 2d vice chmn. women's rights sect., 1990-92, 1st vice chmn. women's rights sect., 1992-93, chmn., 1993-95, trustee minorities in the profession sect., Cmty. Svc. award young lawyers divsn. 1989), N.J. State Bar Found. (trustee 1994-95), N.J. Women Lawyers Assn. (pres. 1986-88, trustee pub. rels. com., entertainment and arts com., Essex County Bar Assn., Nat. Coun. Negro Women, Garden State Bar Assn., Essex County Women Lawyers (trustee 1991-94, v.p. 1997-99), Rotary (pres. South Orange 1999-2000, Paul Harris fellow 2000, dist. 7470 youth exchange program comms. chair 2000-01, asst. gov. 2001—). Democrat. Episcopalian. Home: 40 Woodland Ave East Orange NJ 07017 also: 76 S Orange Ave Ste 308 South Orange NJ 07079-1923 E-mail: Jteetsell@aol.com.

TEEVAN, RICHARD COLLIER, psychology educator; b. Shelton, Conn., June 12, 1919; s. Daniel Joseph and Elizabeth (Halliwell) T.; m. Virginia Agnes Stehle, July 28, 1945; children— Jan Elizabeth, Kim Ellen, Clay Collier, Allison Tracy. BA, Wesleyan U., Middletown, Conn., 1951; MA, U. Mich., 1952, PhD, 1955. Rubber buffer Sponge Rubber Product Co., Derby, Conn., 1939-41; with U. Mich., 1951-57, teaching fellow, 1951-53, instr., 1953-57; asst. prof. Smith Coll., 1957-60; assoc. prof. Bucknell U., 1960-64, prof., 1964-69; chmn. psychology, prof. SUNY-Albany, 1969—; pres. Teevan Assocs., Cons., 1991—. Cons. on coll. teaching, 1989—. Author: Reinforcement, 1961, Instinct, 1961, Color Vision, 1961, Measuring Human Motivation, 1962, Theories of Motivation in Learning, 1964, Theories of Motivation in Personality and Social Psychology, 1964, Motivation, 1967, Fear of Failure, 1969, Readings in Elementary Psychology, 1973; contbr. articles to sci. jours. Served to capt. AUS, 1941-47; prisoner of war 1943-45, Ger. Office Naval Research grantee, 1958-72; recipient Lindbach award Bucknell U., 1966 Mem. AAAS, AAUP, Am. Psychol. Assn. (Disting. visitor 1981-85), Eastern Psychol. Assn., Phi Beta Kappa, Sigma Xi. Home: 45 Pine St Delmar NY 12054-3413 Office: SUNY Dept Psychology 1400 Washington Ave Albany NY 12222-0100

TEGEDER, VINCENT GEORGE, historian, educator, archivist; b. La-Crosse, Wisconsin, Oct. 1, 1910; s. William John and Hilda Catherine (Ruegg) Tegeder. BA in History, St. John's U., 1933; MA in History, U. Wis., 1942, PhD of History, 1949. Ordained priest 1937. Instr. history St. John's Prep Sch., Collegeville, Minn., 1934—42; prof. history St. John's U., 1946—79, prof. emeritus history, 1979—. Archivist St. John's U., Collegeville, 1975—94, St. John's Abbey, Collegeville, 1978—96, archivist emeritus, 1996—, St. John's U., Collegeville, 1994—; vis. prof. history Sacramento State Coll., 1965—67, Sophia U., Tokyo, 1973—74, U. San Francisco, 1966. Contbr. articles to profl. jours. Grantee, Louis and Maud Hill Found., 1961, U.S. Office Edn., 1970. Mem.: Minn. Hist. Soc., Cath. Hist. Soc. Roman Catholic. Avocations: fishing, travel, history. Home: Saint Johns Abbey PO Box 2015 Collegeville MN 56321-2015

TEGENU, MESFIN, health services administrator, consultant; b. Addis Ababa, Ethiopia, Mar. 24, 1956; s. Tegenu Tekil-Agaist and Adanch Habtemariam; m. Nina Minale, Feb. 22, 1996; children: Sephanit, Mahalet. BPharm, Addis Ababa U., 1980; MS, St. John's U., 1988. Registered pharmacist. Coord. injectable and ctrl. supplies program HIP of N.Y., N.Y.C., 1991-94, mgr. corp. pharmacy programs, 1994-96, mgr. pharm. contracting/materials mgmt., 1996-98; assoc. v.p. pharmacy svcs. Keystone Mercy Health Plan, Phila., 1998-2001, v.p. pharmacy affairs, 2001—. Mem. Am. Managed Care Pharmacy. Home: 15 N Koewing Pl West Orange NJ 07052-4014 Office: Keystone Mercy Health Plan 200 Stevens Dr Philadelphia PA 19113-1522 E-mail: MTegenu@aol.com.

TEGGE, FRANK ALLEN, stock brokerage company executive; b. Dearborn, Mich., Oct. 29, 1942; s. Frank Alfred and Marjorie Mildred (Allen) T.; 1 child from previous marriage, Kurt Eric; m. Sophia Branoff. BA, Albion Coll., 1964; postgrad., Garrett Theol. Sem., Evanston, Ill., 1965-66, Loyola U., Chgo., 1966-67, Wayne State U., 1967-68; cert. investment mgmt. analyst, U. Pa., 1992. Registered investment advisor. Stock broker Manley, Bennett, McDonald & Co., Lansing, Mich., 1970-73, ltd. ptnr., 1973-75, ptnr., 1975-82, sr. v.p., 1982-84; v.p. Thomson McKinnon Securities, Inc., 1984-89; 1st v.p. McDonald and Co. Securities, Inc., East Lansing, Mich., 1989-94, sr. v.p., 1994—. Bd. dirs. Manley, Bennett, McDonald, Detroit. Bd. trustees Cen. United Meth. Ch., Lansing, 1985-88, Woldumar Nature Ctr., Lansing, 1986-92, R.E. Olds Mus., Lansing, 1984-86, Chief Okemos Coun., Boy Scouts Am.Trust Fund, Lansing, 1988—, coun. exec. com., 1989—, dist. com., asst. scoutmaster, Wharton Ctr. for Arts, Mich. State U., 1993—; mem. investment com. YMCA, Lansing, 1987-93; bd. dirs. Mid-Mich. chpt. ARC, 1993—; mem. long range planning com. Capital area United Way, 1994—; mem. deans com. coun. Coll. Arts and Letters Mich. State U., 1995—. Decorated Bronze star, Purple Heart, Army Commendation medal with oak leaf cluster; named One of 100 Best New-Style Brokers of 1994, Fin. Planning on Wall St. mag., 1994. Mem. Internat. Assn. Fin. Planners, Investment Mgmt. Cons. Assn., Comdrs. Club of Mich. (pres. 1984), Rotary (bd. dirs. 1989-92, pres. 1992-93). Republican. Avocations: fishing, hunting, camping. Office: McDonald and Co Securities 4660 S Hagadorn Rd Ste 190 East Lansing MI 48823-6804 Home: 310 W Spring Meadows Ln Dewitt MI 48820-8700

TEGTMEIER, RONALD EUGENE, physician, surgeon; b. Omaha, Jan. 16, 1943; s. Harvey and Edna T.; children: Anne, Amy; m. Victoria Susan, June 28, 1985; children: Justina Becerra, Gregory Galvan, Mark Tegtmeier. AB, Dartmouth Coll., 1965; BMS, Dartmouth Med. Sch., 1966; MD, Harvard Med. Sch., 1968. Diplomate Am. Bd. Plastic Surgery. Internship in surgery U. Colo. Med. Ctr., Denver, 1968-69, residency in gen. surgery, 1969-70; plastic surgery preceptorship Kingston-upon-Hull, England, 1973; residency in plastic surgery U. Mexico, Albuquerque, 1974-76, fellowship, 1976; plastic surgeon pvt. practice Arvada, Colo., 1977—, Artistic Ctr. for Cosmetic Surgery, Golden, 1988—. Pres. Clear Creek Valley Med. Soc., Lakewood, Colo., 1983-84; speaker of ho. Colo. Med. Soc., denver, 1985-87. Author: Aesthetica Tapes, 1988—; contbr. numerous papers and publs. to profl. jours. Named Outstanding Bus. Person, Arvada Jaycees, 1978; recipient Arvada Image award, 1981, Denver Post Gallery of Fame award, 1979. Mem. Am. Soc. Plastic and Reconstructive Surgeons, Am. Soc. for Aesthetic Plastic Surgery, Am. Soc. Laser Medicine and Surgery, Am. Acad. of Anti-Aging Medicine. Avocations: scuba, music, skiing, tennis, model trains, flying, aquariums. Office: Artistic Ctr Cosmetic Surgery 14062 Denver West Pkwy Bldg 52 Golden CO 80401-3187 E-mail: www.beautyac@aol.com.

TEHIE, JANICE BEVERIDGE, education educator; b. May 20, 1965; BA in Psychology cum laude, Fairleigh Dickinson U., 1987; MEd in Counselor Edn., Pa. State U., 1988, PhD in Ednl. Founds., 1996. Adj. Centenary Coll., Hackettstown, N.J., 1990-91; tchg. asst. dept. edn. founds. Pa. State U., University Park, 1993-95; asst. prof. edn. St. Peter's Coll., Jersey City, 1996-99, U. Pitts., Bradford, 1999—. Home: 440 Congress St Apt 7B Bradford PA 16701 Office: U Pitts Edn Dept Bradford 231 Hanley Libr 300 Campus Dr Bradford PA 16701-2812 E-mail: janteh@aol.com.

TEHRANI, FLEUR TAHER, electrical engineer, educator, researcher; b. Tehran, Iran, Feb. 16, 1956; came to U.S., 1984; d. Hassan and Pourandokht (Monfared) T.; m. Akbar E. Torbat, June 16, 1997. BS in Elec. Engring., Arya-Mehr U. of Tech., Tehran, 1975; DIC in Comm. Engring., Imperial Coll. Sci. and Tech., London, 1977; MSc in Comm. Engring., U. London, 1977, PhD in Elec. Engring., 1981. Registered profl. engr., Calif. Comm. engr. Planning Orgn. of Iran, Tehran, 1977-78; lectr. A elec. engring. Robert Gordon's Inst. Tech., Aberdeen, U.K., 1982-83; lectr. II elec. engring. South Bank U., London, England, 1983—84; asst. prof. elec. engring. Calif. State U., Fullerton, 1985-91, assoc. prof. elec. engring., 1991-94, prof. elec. engring., 1994—, dir. pharm. engring. program, 1999-2001. Vis. assoc. prof. elec. engring. Drexel U., Phila., 1987-88; sys. cons. Telebit Corp., Cupertino. Calif., 1985; engring. cons. PRD, Inc., Dresher, Pa., 1989-92; mem. NASA/Am. Soc. Engring. Edn. summer faculty Jet Propulsion Lab., Calif. Inst. Tech., Pasadena, 1995, 96. Contbr. articles to profl. jours.; patentee in field. Recipient Best Rsch. Manuscript award Assn. for the Advancement of Med. Instrumentation, 1993, NASA/Am. Soc. Engring. Edn. Recognition award for rsch. contbns., 1995, 96. Fellow Inst. for Advancement of Engring.; mem. IEEE, Women in Sci. and Engring. (chair Calif. State U. chpt. 1990-91), Assn. Profs. and Scholars of Iranian Heritage (pres. 1991-92), Sigma Delta Epsilon. Avocations: music, literature, poetry, stamp collecting. Office: Calif State U Coll Engring & Computer Sci 800 N State College Blvd Fullerton CA 92831-3547 E-mail: ftehrani@fullerton.edu.

TEHRANIAN, MAJID, political economy and communications educator; b. Iran, Mar. 22, 1937; m. Katharine Kia; children: Terrence, Yalda, John, Maryam. BA in Govt., Dartmouth Coll., 1959; MA in Middle Eastern Studies, Harvard U., 1961, PhD in Polit. Economy and Govt., 1969. Asst. prof. econs. Lesley Coll., 1964-69; assoc. prof. polit. sci. New Coll. U. South Fla., 1969-71; dir. social planning Plan Orgn. of Iran, 1971-72; sr. analyst, dir. rsch. Indsl. Mgmt. Inst., 1972-74; dir. prospective planning project Nat. Iranian Radio & TV, 1974-75; prof., founding dir. Iran Communications & Devel. Inst., 1976-78; program specialist communication planning and studies Div. Devel. of Communication Systems UNESCO, Paris, 1979-80; fellow Communication Inst., East West Ctr., 1981-82; chair dept. communication U. Hawaii, Manoa, 1986-88, prof. dept. communication, 1981—, dir. Matsunaga Inst. Peace, 1990-92, dir. Toda Inst. Global Peace Policy Rsch., 1996—. Vis. scholar Inst. for Communication Rsch., Stanford U., 1977; vis. fellow St. Anthony's Coll., Oxford U., 1978-79; vis. scholar Ctr. for Internat. Affairs MIT, 1980-81, Can., U.S. and USSR universities, 1988; rsch. affiliate Ctr. for Middle Eastern Studies, Harvard U., 1980-81; vis. prof. dept. govt. Harvard Summer Sch., 1989-90; dir.-elect and dir. Inst. for Peace, U. Hawaii, coun. and exec. com., 1986—; rsch. fellow Social Sci. Rsch. Inst., U. Hawaii, Manoa, 1982-83, 84-86; lectr. in field. Author: Towards a Systematic Theory of National Development, 1974, Socio-Economic and Communications Indicators in Development Planning, 1981, Technologies of Power, 1990; co-author: The Middle East: Its Government and Politics, 1972, The Global Context of the Formation of Domestic Communications Policies, 1975, Policy Towards Social Sciences in Asia and Oceania, 1978, Worlds Apart: Human Securityand Global Goverance, 1999, Asia Peace: Security and Goverance in the Asia Pacific Region, 1999, Global Communication and World Politics, 1999, Choose Dialogue, 1999; editor: Communications Policy for Development, 1977, Letters from Jerusalem, 1990, Deconstructing Paradise: Dependency, Development and Discourse in Hawaii, 1990, Peace and Policy; co-editor: Restructuring for World Peace: On the Threshold of the 21st Century, 1992, Toward Democratic Governance 2000, Choose Dialogue, 2000 (in Japanese); contbr. articles to profl. jours.; reviewer in field. Scholar Dartmouth Coll., 1955-59, Fujio Matsuda scholar, 1990-91; Jane Addams Peace Found. fellow, 1961, Ford Found. fellow Harvard U., 1959-61, fellow St. Anthony's Coll., Oxford, 1978-79, fellow East West Ctr. Communication Isnt., 1977, 81, 82; rsch. grantee Social Sci. Rsch. Inst., U. Hawaii, Manoa, 1982-85, UNESCO rsch. grantee, 1983-84, Can. Studies Faculty Enrichment grantee, 1988, Hawaii Interactive TV System Curriculum Devel. grantee, 1989; recipient Dartmouth Colby & Grimez Prizes, 1959, Excellence in Teaching award 1989, Soka U. award of highest honor, Disting. Svc. award Assn. Edn. in Journalism and Mass Communication, 1998. Fellow World Acad. Art & Sci.; mem. Internat. Inst. Comm. (bd. trustees 1979-81), Internat. Comm. Assn. (conf. theme chair for Asia 1989), Pacific Telecomm. Coun., Middle East Studies Assn. N.Am., Middle East Econs. Assn. (nat. adv. bd.), Soc. for Iranian Studies (founding exec. sec. 1967-71), Worldview Internat. Found. Avocations: swimming, tennis, chess, poetry. Home: 2627 Manoa Rd Honolulu HI 96822-1767 Office: U Hawaii Sch of Communication Honolulu HI 96822 also: Toda Inst 1600 Kapiolani Blvd Ste 1111 Honolulu HI 96814-3806 Fax: 808 955-6476.

TEI, TAKURI, accountant; b. Korea, Feb. 25, 1924; s. Gangen and Isun (Song) T.; came to U.S., 1952, naturalized, 1972; diploma Concordia Theol. Sem., 1959; B.D., Eden Theol. Sem., 1965; M.Ed., U. Mo., 1972; m. Maria M. Ottwaska, Dec. 1, 1969; 1 dau., Sun Kyung Lee. Partner, Madeleine Ottwaska & Assos., St. Louis, 1968— ; pres. TMS Tei Enterprises Inc., Webster Groves, Mo., 1969— ; instr. Forest Park Community Coll. Mem. Am. Coll. Enrolled Agts. (pres. 1976—), Am. Accounting Assn., Am. Taxation Assn., Assn. Asian Studies, NAACP. Republican. Lutheran. Home and Office: 7529 Big Bend Blvd Saint Louis MO 63119-2103

TEICH, ALAN HARVEY, psychology educator, clinical psychologist; b. East Meadow, N.Y., May 29, 1955; s. Robert and Sonia (Kahan) T.; m. Diane Lees; children: Sarah, Daniel. BS, SUNY, Brockport, 1977; MA, SUNY, Geneseo, 1979; PhD, U. Miami, 1987. Lic. psychologist, Pa. Asst. lab. instr. U. Pitts., Johnstown, Pa., 1979-82; tchg./rsch. asst. U. Miami, Coral Gables, Fla., 1982-87; asst. prof. U. Pitts., Johnstown, 1987-94, assoc. prof., 1995—, interim chairperson natural scis. divsn., 1997-98, chairperson natural scis. divsn., 1998—. Presenter in field. Contbr. articles to profl. jours. Bd. dirs. Victim Svcs., Johnstown, 1992—, Johnstown Concert Ballet, 1995—. Mem. APA, Soc. Behavioral Medicine, Pa. Soc. Behavioral Medicine, Laurel Mountain Psych. Assn. (exec. bd. dirs., pres. 1993-95). Home: 2240 Spear Ave Johnstown PA 15905-1646 Office: U Pitts Johnstown 116 Engring and Sci Bldg Johnstown PA 15904

TEICH, ALBERT HARRIS, professional society administrator; b. Chgo., Dec. 17, 1942; s. Maurice and Ina (Szuldiner) T.; m. Carolyn R. Richmond, June 3, 1965 (div. 1987); children: Mitchell Craig, Kenneth David; m. Jill H. Pace, Jan. 29, 1989; 1 child, Samantha Lynne. BS, MIT, 1964, PhD, 1969. Rsch. fellow Syracuse (N.Y.) U. Rsch. Corp., 1969-71, dir., sci. and tech. studies, 1971-73; coord. rsch. SUNY, Binghamton, 1973-74; dir. rsch. SUNY Inst. for Pub. Policy Alternatives, Albany, 1974-76; assoc. prof. pub. affairs and dep. dir., grad. program sci. tech. and pub. policy George Washington U., 1976-79; mgr., sci. policy studies AAAS, Washington, 1980-84, head, office of pub. sector programs, 1984-89, dir. sci. and policy programs, 1989—. Cons. Nat. Acad. Scis., Office of Tech. Assessment, Washington, 1976-95, Orgn. for Econ. Cooperation and Devel., Paris, 1994—; chmn. SRS adv. com. NSF, Washington, 1988-90; pres. Technosci. Assocs., Inc., Silver Spring, Md., 1977-82; chair Ga. Inst. Tech., Sch. Pub. Adv. Bd., 2001-; mem. bd. govs. US-Israel Binational Sci Found., 2001—. Editor: Science and Technology in the U.S.A., 1986, Technology and the Future, 8th edit., 2000; editor, author: Scientists and Public Affairs, 1974; mem. editl. bd. Science Communication, 1991—, Science, Technology and Human Values, 1994—, Prometheus, 1999—. Fellow AAAS (chmn. sect. X 1988); mem. Tech. Transfer Soc. (v.p. 1985-91), Am. Soc. for Pub. Adminstrn. (mem. editl. bd. 1985-89), Soc. for Social Studies of Scis., Sigma Xi. Avocations: swimming, photography, travel writing. Office: AAAS 1200 New York Ave NW Washington DC 20005-3941 E-mail: ateich@aaas.org.

TEICH, HOWARD BERNARD, lawyer, activist, public affairs specialist; b. Huntington, N.Y., Nov. 1, 1946; s. Samuel and Beatrice Ann (Kay) T. AB, U. Pa., 1967; JD, Boston U., 1970. Bar: N.Y., 1971, U.S. Dist. Ct. (so. dist.) N.Y. 1984. Counsel N.Y. State Senator Emanuel Gold, N.Y.C., 1971-72; law sec. N.Y. State Supreme Ct. Justin Martin Evans, 1972-75; assoc. pub. Firehouse mag., 1975-79; pub. Midtown South Bus., 1985-87; prin. Law Offices Howard B. Teich, 1980—; sr. cons. The Kamber Group, Washington, 1995—; sr. counsel McLaughlin & Stein, P.C., N.Y.C., 1997—. Founder, chair New Dem. Dimensions, N.Y.C., 1981-91, Nat. Task Force on Life Safety for Handicapped, Washington, 1979-81; bd. dirs. Boys Choir of Harlem, N.Y.C., 1983-85, Assn. on Am. Indian Affairs, 1990-97, adv. bd., 1997—; chmn. New Leadership of Israel Bonds, N.Y.C., 1977-79; pres. Am. Jewish Congress Met. Region N.Y.C., 1992—, past nat. v.p.; bd. dirs. Jewish Comty. Rels. Coun., N.Y., 1995—, past v.p., 1995-98; co-chair Jewish Heritage, N.Y.C., 1997—;dep. dir. N.Y. state citizens com. McGovern for Pres., 1972, Samuels for Gov., 1974, Carey for Gov., 1974; dep. dir. N.Y. state primary campaign Carter for Pres., 1980; co-chair N.Y. state citizens com. Glenn for Pres., 1984, Mondale/Ferraro '84, 1984; bd. dirs. Manhattan Playhouse. Recipient Robert Briscoe award Emerald Isle Immigration Soc., 1996, Israel Leadership award Israel Bonds, 1979, Martin Luther King Jr. Living-the-Dream award, Gov. George Pataki, N.Y., 1999. Mem. AJ Congress Met Region (pres. 1992—), U. Pa. Club, Assn. on Am. Indian Affairs (bd. dirs., nat. adv. bd.). Democrat. Jewish. Avocations: N.Y.C. marathon, softball, tennis, reading, theatre, dance. Home: 185 E 85th St New York NY 10028-2140 Office: 260 Madison Ave New York NY 10016-2401

TEICH, JEFFREY ERNEST, business educator, entrepreneur; b. Rush City, Minn., June 11, 1960; s. Ernest Albert and Evelyn Ann Teich; m. Gabriele Teich, Feb. 26, 1999; 1 child, Lara Margareta. BS, Ariz. State U., 1982, MS, 1984; PhD, SUNY, Buffalo, 1991. Faculty assoc. Ariz. State U., Tempe, 1984-86; grad. asst. SUNY, Buffalo, 1986-90; from asst. to assoc. prof. N.Mex. State U., Las Cruces, 1990—. Vis. prof. Helsinki Sch. Econs., 1998, vis. scholar, 89; vis. prof. electronic commerce Rotterdam Sch. Mgmt., 2002—. Contbr. articles to profl. jours. including Electronic Markets, Decision Support Sys. Mgmt. Sci.; inventor (software) NegotiAuction, 2000. Mem. Internat. Soc. Multiple Criteria Decision Making, Decision Scis. Inst., INFORMS, Alpha Iota Delta, Beta Gamma Sigma. Avocations: computers, tennis, beach paddle ball, backgammon, travel. Office: NMex State U Dept Mgmt Las Cruces NM 88003

TEICH, MALVIN CARL, electrical engineering educator; b. N.Y.C., May 4, 1939; s. Sidney R. and Loretta K. Teich SB in Physics, MIT, 1961; MSEE, Stanford U., 1962; PhD in Quantum Electronics, Cornell U., 1966. Research scientist MIT Lincoln Lab., Lexington, Mass., 1966-67; prof. engring. sci. Columbia U., N.Y.C., 1967-96, prof. emeritus, 1996—, chmn. dept. elec. engring., 1978-80, mem. Columbia Radiation Lab., faculty applied physics dept.; prof. elec. computer engring., biomed. engring., physics Boston U., 1995—. Mem. Photonics Ctr., Boston U., also Ctr. Adaptive Sys., Hearing Rsch. Ctr.; mem. sci. bd. Inst. Physics, Czech Acad. Scis., Prague. Author: (with B.E.A. Saleh) Fundamentals of Photonics, 1991; dep. editor Quantum Optics, 1988-92; bd. editors Jour. Visual Comm. and Image Representation, 1989-92, Jemná Mechanika a Optika, 1994—; contbr. articles to profl. jours.; patentee in field. Recipient Citation Classic award Inst. for Sci. Info., 1981; Meml. Gold medal of Palacky U., Czech Republic, 1992; Guggenheim Meml. Found. fellow, 1973. Fellow AAAS, IEEE (Browder J. Thompson Meml. prize 1969, Morris E. Leeds award 1997), Optical Soc. Am. (editl. adv. panel Optics Letters 1977-79), Am. Phys. Soc., Acoustical Soc. Am.; mem. Sigma Xi, Tau Beta Pi. Office: Boston U Dept Elec and Computer Engr 8 Saint Mary's St Boston MA 02215-2421 E-mail: teich@bu.edu.

TEICH, STEPHEN S. forensic psychiatrist; b. Huntington, N.Y., June 5, 1941; s. Samuel and Beatrice Ann T. BA, Princeton U., 1962; MD, SUNY, Bklyn., 1967. Diplomate in psychiatry and forensic psychiatry Am. Bd. Psychiatry and Neurology. Dir. mental health Manhattan Ho. Detention for Men, N.Y.C., 1972-73; staff psychiatrist Ryan Health Ctr., 1974-75; cons. Richmond Fellowship, 1974-75; forensic psychiatrist, 1971—. Served to major U.S. Army, 1971-72. Mem. Am. Acad. Psychiatry & the Law, Internat. Acad. Law & Mental Health, Internat. Soc. Traumatic Stress Studies, Am. Psychiat. Assn., Physicians for Human Rights, Physicians for Social Responsibility. Office: 40 W 24th St New York NY 10010-3215 E-mail: ssteichmd@aol.com.

TEICHER, HENRY EARL, retired education educator; b. Jersey City, July 9, 1922; s. Leo and Anna Binn Teicher; m. Anne Severin, Aug. 14, 1962; 1 child Rikke Jordahn. BA, State U. Iowa, 1946; MA, Columbia U., 1947, PhD, 1950. From asst. prof. to prof. Purdue U., West Lafayette, Ind., 1951—67; asst. prof. Stanford U., Palo Alto , Calif., 1955—56; assoc. prof. NYU, N.Y.C., 1960—62; prof. Columbia U., 1967—68, Rutgers U., New Brunswick, NJ, 1968—93; ret., 1993. Cons. Radio Corp. Am., Indpls., 1967. Author: Probability Theory: Independence, 1977, Interchangeability, 1987, Martingales, 1997; contbr. articles to profl. jours. With U.S. Army, 1943—46. Fellow: Inst. Math. Statis.; mem.: Phi Beta Kappa. Avocations: reading, music. Home: 15 Elberon Ave Allenhurst NJ 07711

TEICHER, MARTIN, lawyer; b. N.Y.C., Nov. 16, 1945; s. Aaron and Gertrude (Mark) T.; m. Barbara Langner, Sept. 13, 1970; children: Nina Rebecca, Ira Kenneth. BA, CUNY, Flushing, 1967; JD, NYU, 1970. Bar: N.Y. 1971, U.S. Dist. Ct. (so. and ea. dists.) N.Y. 1972, U.S. Ct. Appeals (2d cir.) 1975, U.S. Supreme Ct. 1976. Assoc. Kronish, Lieb, Shainswit, Weiner & Hellman, N.Y.C., 1970-79; atty. spl. litigation dept. Am. Cyanamid Co., Wayne, N.J., 1980-88; asst. gen. counsel, chief litigation counsel CIBA-GEIGY Corp., Ardsley, N.Y., 1988-97; sr. corp. counsel Pfizer, Inc., 1997—. Speaker drug liability, environ. ins. coverage claims, food & drug law. Mem., bd. of trustees Ahavath Torah Congregation, Englewood, N.J., 1983—, treas., 1986-88, pres., 1988-91; participant Keystone Ctr. AIDS Vaccine Liabity project, 1988-90. Mem. N.Y. State Bar Assn., Assn. of Bar of City of N.Y. (product liability com., 1981-86, tort litigation com. 1986-89, medicine and law com., 1989-91), Nat. Acad. Scis. (adv. com. on liability issues associated with AIDS vaccines 1987). Home: 453 Cape May St Englewood NJ 07631-4720 Office: Pfizer Inc 201 Tabor Rd Morris Plains NJ 07950 E-mail: martin.teicher@pfizer.com.

TEICHER, OREN JONATHAN, trade association executive; b. Toronto, Aug. 7, 1949; came to U.S., 1956; s. Morton Irving and Mildred (Adler) T.; m. Alison Eden Greene, June 20, 1976; children: Carrie Lee, Jessica Anne, Zachary Saul. BA in Pub. Affairs, George Washington U., 1972. Adminstrv. asst. to rep. U.S. Ho. of Reps., Washington, 1974-80; dir. corp. comms. March of Dimes Birth Defects Found., White Plains, N.Y., 1980-84; exec. dir. Ams. for Constitutional Freedom, N.Y.C., 1987-90; assoc. exec. dir. Am. Booksellers Assn., 1990-95, dir. govt. affairs, 1995-97, COO. N.Y., 1997—. Pres. Am. Booksellers Found. for Free Expression, Tarrytown and N.Y.C., 1990-98; chmn. Media Coalition, N.Y.C., 1992-94. Trustee White Plains Libr., 1995-2000; del. Dem. Nat. Conv., 1992, 96. Jewish. Home: 10 Richbell Rd White Plains NY 10605-4111 Office: Am Booksellers Assn 828 S Broadway Tarrytown NY 10591-6602

TEIG, MARLOWE GILMAN, investment banker; b. Fargo, N.D., Sept. 13, 1938; s. Julius Berner Teig and Inez (Hedlund) Teig-Erickson; m. Carole Lynne Werner, Nov. 25, 1961; children: Jennifer Lynne, Alan Gilman. BA, U. Mich., 1961; postgrad., CCNY, 1962-64. With Harcourt Brace Jovanovich, 1964-80, Houghton Mifflin Co., 1980-87, Macmillan, Inc., 1987-88; mng. dir. Berkery, Noyes & Co., Newton, Mass., 1990—. Home: 40 Kirkstall Rd Newton MA 02460-2218

TEILLON, L. PIERRE, JR. lawyer; b. N.Y.C., Nov. 15, 1943; AB, Yale U., 1965; LLB, Columbia U., 1968. Bar: Pa. 1968. Mem. Heckscher, Teillon, Terrill & Sager, P.C., West Conshohocken, Pa. Mem. Am. Coll. Trust and Estate Counsel, Pa. Bar Assn. (real property, probate and trust sects.), Phila. Bar Assn. (past chmn. probate sect.). Office: Heckscher Teillon Terrill & Sager 100 Four Falls Corp Ctr Ste 300 West Conshohocken PA 19428 Fax: 610 940-6042. E-mail: perry@htts.com.

TEIMAN, RICHARD B. lawyer; b. Bklyn., May 19, 1938; AB, Princeton U., 1959; LLB, Harvard U., 1962. Bar: N.Y. 1963. Ptnr. Winston & Strawn and predecessor Cole & Deitz, N.Y.C., 1968—. Trustee Citizens Budget Commn., 1993—. Mem. Assn. Bar City N.Y. (com. Admiralty 1975-78, 87, chair 1988-91), Maritime Law Assn. (com. Maritime Financing 1980—, chmn. subcom. Recodification U.S. Ship Mortgage Act 1986-91, chmn. subcom. U.S. Coastguard, Citizenship and Related Matters 1988-94), Phi Beta Kappa. Home: 5 Pryer Ln Larchmont NY 10538-4012 Office: Winston & Strawn 200 Park Ave Rm 4100 New York NY 10166-0005 E-mail: rteiman@winston.com.

TEIRSTEIN, PAUL SHEPHERD, physician, health facility administrator; b. N.Y.C., July 5, 1955; s. Alvin Stanley and Alice Teirstein. BA in Biology, Vassar Coll., 1976; MD, CUNY, 1980. Diplomate Am. Bd. Internal Medicine and Cardiovascular Diseases. With Lab. of Vision Rsch. NIH, Bethesda, Md., 1977-79; intern and resident Brigham & Women's Hosp., Boston, 1980-83; fellow in cardiology Stanford (Calif.) U., 1983-86; fellow in advanced coronary angioplasty Mid-Am. Heart Inst., Kansas City, Mo., 1986-87; fellow in stents, artherectomy and lasers NIH, Bethesda, 1987; dir. interventional cardiology Scripps Clinic and Rsch. Found., La Jolla, Calif., 1987—. Presenter at Am. Coll. Cardiology, 1987-94, Am. Heart Assn., 1990-93, The French Hosp., San Luis Obispo, Calif., 1989, St. Luke's Med. Ctr., Phoenix, 1989, Cardiology for the Cons., Rancho Santa Fe, 1989, U. Calif., Irvine, 1989, ACP, Scottsdale, Ariz., 1989, Presbyn. Hosp., Whittier, Calif, 1989, St. Jude Med. Ctr., Fullerton, Calif., 1990, Oscala Med. Ctr., Osaka, Japan, 1992, Cedars-Sinai Med. Ctr., L.A., 1993, European Congress of Cardiology, Nice, France, 1993, Tokyo U., 1993, Lenox Hill Hosp., N.Y., 1993, Japanese Soc. Internat. Cardiology, 1994, Nat. Hindu Hosp., Bombay, 1994, G.B. Pant Hosp., Delhi, India, 1994, Escort's Hosp., 1994, B.M. Birla Hosp., Calcutta, 1994, Shaare Zedek Med. Ctr., Jerusalem, 1994, XV Gongresso da Sociedad de Cardiology de Sao Paulo, Ribeirao Preto, Brazil, 1994, and others. Grantee NSF, 1975 Fellow Am. Coll. Cardiology, Assn. for Rsch. in Vision and Ophthalmology, Beta Beta Beta, Alpha Omega Alpha. Office: Scripps Clinic & Rsch Found 10666 N Torrey Pines Rd La Jolla CA 92037-1092

TEISON, HERBERT J. editor, publisher; b. N.Y.C., Nov. 22, 1927; s. Irving and Celia (Wolkowisky) Teitelbaum. BS, CCNY, 1949. Writer Mexico City News, 1950-51; announcer, prodr. Sta. XELA, Mexico City, 1950-51; pub. rels. dir. Schwerin Rsch., N.Y.C., 1952-53; asst. rsch. dir. Dumont TV Network, 1954-55; advt. mgr. St. Regis Publs., 1956-59; assoc. pub. programs Saturday Rev., 1960-73; adj. prof. New Sch. Social Rsch., 1961-75; editor, pub., pres. Comms. House/Travel Smart, Dobbs Ferry, N.Y., 1973—. Co-author: Travel Smarts, 1996; author: Daniel, Molly & Me, 1997. Mem. Soc. Am. Travel Writers, Music Therapy Soc. (v.p. 1965—). Avocations: gardening, collecting, language tutoring.

TEISSONNIERE, GERARDO, musician, educator; b. Ponce, PR; MMus, Cleve. Inst. Music, 1989. Mem. piano faculty Cleve. Inst. Music, 1989—. Recipient Arthur Loesser Meml. award Cleve. Inst. Music, 1985. Mem. Music Tchrs. Nat. Assn. Office: Cleve Inst Music 11021 East Blvd Cleveland OH 44106-1705

TEITEL, SIMON, economist, educator; b. Buenos Aires, Dec. 5, 1928; came to U.S., 1961; s. Gregorio and Regina (Tarnorudzka) T.; m. Raquel Schenkolewski, June 20, 1954; children: Rut Gabriela, Ariel Dan. BS in Indsl. Engring., U. Buenos Aires, 1956, MS in Indsl. Engring., 1963; PhD in Econs., Columbia U., 1969. Econ. affairs officer Ctr. for Indsl. Devel., UN, N.Y.C., 1963-67; sr. indsl. devel. officer policies and programming div. UN Indsl. Devel. Orgn., Vienna, 1967-68; sr. cons. Office Program Advisor to Pres., Inter-Am. Devel. Bank, Washington, 1968-76, sr. econ. advisor econ. and social devel. dept., 1976-89; sr. rsch. adv., 1989-92; rsch. cons. World Bank, Washington, 1992-94; econ. cons. UN, 1994—2002; rsch. fellow ICER , Turin, Italy. Adj. assoc. prof. econs. Cath. U. Am., Washington, 1971-77, adj. prof., 1977-81, prof., 1981-88; adj. prof. Am. U., 1992; professorial lectr. Georgetown U., Washington, 1996-98; vis. lectr. internat. econs. Yale U., New Haven, 1977-78; lectr. to numberous profl. assns. and univs.; occasional referee Econ. Devel. and Cultural Change, Jour. Devel. Econs., World Devel., L.Am. Rsch. Rev.; mem. spl. internat. panel on appropriate techs. for developing countries Bd. on Sci. and Tech. for Internat. Devel., NAS-NAE, 1974-77. Author: Politica Economica en Centro y Periferia, 1976, Integracion Economica, 1977, Trade, Stability, Technology and Equity in Latin America, 1982, Symposium on Technological Change and Industrial Development, 1984, Growth, Reform and Adjustment: Latin America's Trade and Macroeconomic Policies in the 1970s and 1980s, 1986, Handbook of Latin American Studies, Library of Congress, Economics: Argentina, 1989, Towards a New Development Strategy for Latin America, 1992, Industrial and Technological Development, 1993, Technology and Enterprise Development, 1994, Resources, Industrialization and Exports in Latin America, 1998, Technology and Skills in Zimbabwe's Manufacturing. From Autarky to Competition, 2000, Technology Policy and Innovation Systems in Semi-Industrialized Countries, 2002; contbr. articles to profl. jours. Fellow: Internat. Ctr. for Environ. Rsch.; mem.: Am. Econ. Assn. Jewish. Home: 5610 Wisconsin Ave Apt 606 Chevy Chase MD 20815-4432 E-mail: steitel@starpower.net.

TEITELBAUM, HARRY, English educator; b. Leipzig, Germany, Sept. 23, 1930; came to U.S., 1939; s. Simon and Rencia (Spindel) T.; m. Marilyn L. Nober, Nov. 7, 1953; children: Mark, David, Deborah. BA, Bkyn. Coll., 1952, MA, 1953; ABD, NYU, 1968. Cert. tchr. English, math., supr. secondary edn., N.Y.; cmty. coll. instr. liberal arts, Calif. Teaching fellow Bklyn. Coll., 1953; instr. U.S. Armed Forces Inst., Germany, 1954-55; substitute tchr. N.Y.C. High Schs., Bklyn., 1955; tchr. English Elmont (N.Y.) Meml. High Sch., 1955-60; tutor SAT Plainview, N.Y., 1963-68; English tchr. Plainview-Old Bethpage Sch. Dist., 1960-85; dept. chmn. John F. Kennedy High Sch., Plainview, 1966-70; adj. prof. Hofstra U., Hempstead, N.Y., 1958-74, Suffolk County C.C., Selden, 1974-87, Saddleback Coll., Mission Viejo, Calif., 1988—2001. Judge various writing and speaking contests, L.I., N.Y., 1964-85; scholar-lectr. Orange County Calif. Librs., 1989. Author: How to Write a Thesis, 1964, 75, 94, 98, How to Write Book Reports, 1975, 89, 95, 98; co-author: How to Write Themes and Essays, rev. edit., 1994; contbr. articles to profl. jours. and newspapers. Cpl. U.S. Army, 1953-55. Recipient Disting. Tchr. award Alpha Sigma Lambda Hofstra U., 1969, John F. Kennedy High Sch., 1979. Avocations: skiing, tennis, woodworking, jogging. Home: 29562 Avante Laguna Niguel CA 92677-7949 Office: Saddleback C C 28000 Marguerite Pky Mission Viejo CA 92692-3635

TEITELBAUM, HOWARD S. academic administrator; BA in mathematics, Calif. State Polytech. Coll., Pomona; MA in curriculum devel., PhD in philosophy and statistics, MD, Mich. State U.; MPH, Harvard Sch. Pub. Health. Cert. preventive medicine, diplomate Nat. Bd. Examiners for Osteo. Physicians and Surgeons. Intern Mount Clemens (Mich.) Gen. Hosp.; chief resident in preventive medicine Yale U. Sch. Medicine, Dept. Epidemiology and Pub. Health; prof. Coll. Osteo. Medicine, Mich. State U.; dean Coll. Osteo. Medicine and Surgery, Des Moines U., 2000—. Pres. Am. Osteo. Coll. Occupl. and Preventive Medicine, 1996—98. Named Prof. of Yr., Yale Sch. Medicine, 1988; recipient Spl. Golden Apple award for Tchg., 1992, Outstanding Golden Apple award for Tchg., 1996. Fellow: Am. Osteo. Coll. Preventive Medicine. Office: Coll Osteo Medicine and Surgery 3200 Grand Ave Des Moines IA 50312*

TEITELBAUM, LEONARD H. state legislator; b. Bklyn., Feb. 27, 1931; married; 1 child. BME, Rensselaer Poly. Inst., 1953. Pres. Terminal Data Corp., Rockville, Md.; mem. dist. 19 Md. Ho. of Dels., Annapolis, 1987-95; environ. matters com.; vice-chmn. com. on bi-county agencies; mem. dist. 19 Md. Senate, Annapolis, 1995—, mem. fin. com., 1997—. Sen. fin. com., health sub-com., jt. com. on health care delivery and fin., sen. chmn., jt. adv. com. on legis. data sys., joint com. on children, youth and families, task force to conquer cancer, task force on quality of care in nursing homes. Bd. dirs. Montgomery County unit Am. Cancer Soc.; mem. Md. Dem. Ctrl. Com., Montgomery County, 1978-81; mem. Washington Suburban Sanitary Commn., 1981-87, vice chmn., 1982-83, 86-87, chmn., 1983-84. Recipient Outstanding Svc. award Jewish Cmty. Coun. of Greater Washington, 1985. Mem. B'nai B'rith. Address: 454 Miller Senate Office Bldg Annapolis MD 21401

TEITELBAUM, MARILYN LEAH, special education educator; b. Bklyn., June 12, 1930; d. Abraham and Fay (Ingis) Nober; m. Harry Teitelbaum, Nov. 7, 1953; children: Mark, David, Deborah. BA, Bklyn. Coll., 1953; MS, Queens Coll., 1968, L.I. U., 1982. Cert. tchr., N.Y. Elem. and spl. edn. tchr., Franklin Square, N.Y., 1955-57; elem. tchr. Manetto Hill Sch., Plainview, 1968-70, Northport (N.Y.) Sch. Dist., 1970-78, spl. edn. tchr., 1978-87; pvt. spl. edn. tchr. Laguana Niguel, Calif., 1988—. Author: Teachers as Consumers-What They Should Know About the Hearing Impaired Child, 1981. V.p. Friends of Libr., Laguna Niguel Pub. Libr., 1988—. Recipient outstanding tchr. award Northport PTA, 1987. Mem. NEA, Coun. Exceptional Children, United Tchrs. Northport, Orange County Dyslexic Soc. Avocations: reading, travel, painting, piano. Home: 29562 Avante Laguna Niguel CA 92677-7949

TEITELBAUM, PHILIP, psychologist; b. Bklyn., Oct. 9, 1928; s. Bernard and Betty (Schechter) T.; m. Osnat Boné; children: Benjamin, Daniel, David, Jonathan, Gideon. BS, CCNY, 1950; MA, Johns Hopkins U., 1952, PhD, 1954. Instr., asst. prof. physiol. psychology Harvard U., 1954-59; assoc. prof. psychology U. Pa., Phila., 1959-63, prof., 1963-73; prof. psychology U. Ill.-Urbana-Champaign, 1973-85, emeritus prof., 1985—, Disting. prof. Ctr. Advanced Studies, 1980-85; grad. research prof. U. Fla., Gainesville, 1984—. Author: Fundamental Principles of Physiological Psychology, 1967; editor: (with E. Satinoff) Motivation: Handbook Behavioral Neurobiology, 1983. Contbr. chpts. to books, articles to profl. jours. Fellow Ctr. for Advanced Study in Behavorial Scis., Stanford U., 1975-76, Fulbright fellow Tel Aviv U., 1978-79, Guggenheim fellow, 1984-85, Carnegie Found. fellow Inst. Neurol. Scis., U. Pa. Med. Sch., 1958-59. Fellow APA (pres. div. physiol. psychology, disting. sci. contbn. award 1978), Am. Psychol. Soc. (William James fellow); mem. NAS, AAAS, Am. Physiol. Soc., Soc. for Neurosci., Soc. Exptl. Psychology. Home: 2239 NW 17th Ave Gainesville FL 32605-3909 Office: U Fla Dept Psychology Gainesville FL 32611

TEITELBAUM, STEVEN LAZARUS, pathology educator; b. Bklyn., June 29, 1938; s. Hyman and Rose Leah (Harnick) T.; m. Marilyn Ruth Schaffner; children: Caren Beth, Aaron Michael, Rebecca Lee. BA, Columbia U., 1960; MD, Washington U., St. Louis, 1964. Intern Washington U. Sch. Medicine, St. Louis, 1964-65, 3d. yr. asst. resident, ACS clin. fellow, 1967-68; intern NYU, 1965-66, 2d yr. resident, 1966-67; assoc. pathologist Jewish Hosp. at Washington U. Med. Ctr., St. Louis, 1969-89, pathologist-in-chief, 1987-96; assoc. pathologist Barnes-Jewish Hosp., 1986—; pathologist St. Louis Shriners Hosp. for Crippled Children, 1986—; Wilma and Roswell Messing prof. pathology Washington U. Sch. Medicine, St. Louis, 1987—. Mem. Othopedics and Musculoskeletal Study Sect. NIH, 1983-87. Contbr. numerous sci. articles to med. jours., 1965—, 12 chpts. to med. books and texts, 1976—; mem. editorial bd. Calcified Tissue Internat., 1980-85, 89-91, Human Pathology; mem. bd. assoc. editors Jour. Orthopaedic Rsch., Jour. Cellular Biochemistry. Mem. Am. Soc. Clin. Investigation, Assn. Am. Physicians, Am. Acad. Orthopaedic Surgeons (Ann Doner Vaughan Kappa Delta award 1988), Paget's Disease Found. (adv. panel), Am. Soc. for Bone and Mineral Rsch. (pres. 1993, William F. Neuman award 1998), Fed. Am. Soc. Expl. Biology (bd. dirs. 1997—, pres. 2002–). Office: Washington U Sch Medicine 216 S Kingshighway Blvd Saint Louis MO 63110-1026 E-mail: teitelbs@medicine.wustl.edu.

TEITELL, CONRAD LAURENCE, lawyer, author; b. N.Y.C., Nov. 8, 1932; s. Benson and Belle (Altman) T.; m. Adele Mary Crummins, May 26, 1957; children: Beth Mary, Mark Lewis. AB, U. Mich., 1954; LL.B., Columbia U., 1957; LL.M., N.Y. U., 1968. Bar: N.Y. 1958, D.C., 1968. Mem. Prerau & Teitell, White Plains, N.Y., 1964-96, Cummings & Lockwood, Stamford, Conn., 1996—. Dir. Philanthropy Tax Inst., Old Greenwich, Conn., 1964—. Author: Philanthropy and Taxation, 5 vols., 1993-2002; editor, pub. Taxwise Giving, 1964—; contbr. articles to legal jours. Served with U.S. Army, 1957. Recipient Disting. Svc. to Higher Edn. award Am. Coll. Pub. Relations Assn., 1970, Disting. Svc. award Nat. Com. on Planned Giving, 1990, Harrison Tweed Spl. Merit award Am. Law Inst./ABA, 1992. Fellow Am. Coll. Trust and Estate Counsel; mem. ABA (former co-chmn. com. charitable giving, trusts, founds.), Assn. of Bar of City of N.Y. Home: 16 Marlow Ct Riverside CT 06878-2614 Office: Cummings & Lockwood 4 Stamford Plz Stamford CT 06902-3834 also: PO Box 299 Old Greenwich CT 06870-0299 E-mail: cteitell@cl-law.com.

TEITELMAN, RICHARD BERTRAM, judge; b. Phila., Sept. 25, 1947; s. Nathan and May B. (Schreibman) T. BA in Math., U. Pa., 1969; JD, Washington U., St. Louis, 1973. Bar: Mo. 1974. Pvt. practice, St. Louis, 1974-75; staff atty. Legal Svcs. Ea. Mo., 1975-76, mng. atty., 1976-80, exec. dir., gen. counsel, 1980—; judge Mo. Ct. Appeals (ea. dist.), 1997—2000, Supreme Ct., 2002—. Bd. dirs., Citizens for Mo.'s Children, St. Louis, 1988—. Recipient Durward K. McDaniel award, Am. Coun. of Blind, 1986. Mem. ABA, Mo. Bar, Bar Assn. Met. St. Louis (pres. 1989-90; award of merit, young lawyers sect., 1985), Mound City Bar Assn., Lawyers Assn., St. Louis, Women Lawyers' Assn. Greater St. Louis, St. Louis County Bar Assn., Am. Blind Lawyers Assn., St. Louis Bar Found., Am. Judicature Soc. (bd. dirs. 1986—), Leadership St. Louis. Office: Legal Svcs Ea Mo 625 N Euclid Ave Saint Louis MO 63108-1660*

TEIXEIRA, ARTHUR ALVES, food engineer, educator, consultant; b. Fall River, Mass., Jan. 30, 1944; s. Arthur Araujo and Emelia (Alves) T.; m. Jean E. Lamb, Dec. 26, 1966 (dec. Dec. 1983); children: A. Allan, Scott C.; m. Marjorie St. John, June 28, 1986; 1 stepchild, Craig St. John. PhD, U. Mass., 1971. Registered profl. engr., Fla., Mass. Rsch. engr. Ross Labs., Columbus, Ohio, 1971-73, R&D group leader, 1973-77; sr. cons. Arthur D. Little, Inc., Cambridge, Mass., 1977-82; assoc. prof. U. Fla., Gainesville, 1982-89, prof., 1989—. Sci. advisor Escola Superior de Biotecnologia, Porto, Portugal, 1991-96, FMC Corp., Santa Clara, Calif., 1989-92; internat. cons., Brazil, Chile, Cuba, Hungary, Kenya, Poland, Portugal, Peru, Romania, and Bulgaria; reviewer USDA, Washington, 1991—. Author: Computerized Food Processing Operations, 1989; contbr. 8 chpts. to books, 50 articles to profl. jours. Judge Internat. Sci. Fair, Orlando, Fla., 1991. Recipient Golden Retort Award of Merit (IFTPS), 1994, Fulbright scholar award, Portugal, 1990—91, Sr. Faculty award, U. Fla. chpt. Gamma Sigma Delta, 1996, Fulbright scholar award, Peru, 2000, Disting. Food Engr. award, IAFIS/FPEI/ASAE, 2001; fellow, NATO, 1988—89. Fellow Am. Soc. Agrl. Engrs. (dir. 1988-90, Paper awards 1988-89, 2001, assoc. editor Transactions of ASAE 1985—); mem. AIChE, ASAE, Inst. Food Technologists (mem. editl. bd. 1980-83), Am. Soc. Engring. Edn., Inst. Thermal Process Specialists, Coun. on Agrl. Sci. and Tech., R & D Assocs., Gamma Sigma Delta (chpt. pres. U. Fla. 1999-2000). Roman Catholic. Achievements include design of on-line process control system to assure safety of sterilized canned foods; tech. and econ. feasiblity for radiation sterilization of disposable feeding devices; research in computer optimization and control of food sterilization processes and mathematical modelling of bacterial spore population dynamics in processed foods. Office: U Fla Rogers Hall Gainesville FL 32611-0570 E-mail: atex@agen.ufl.edu.

TEIXEIRA DE OLIVEIRA, CARLOS ALBERTO, financial company executive; b. B.Horizonte, Brazil, Aug. 7, 1951; s. João Evangelista and Geraldina (Teixeira) O.; m. Maria Auxiliadora G.T. Oliveira, July 8, 1976; children: Michelle G. Teixeira, Carlos Frederick G., Danielle G. B.Econs. and Bus. Adminstrn., PUC - MG, Brazil, 1977. V.p., CEO Safra Nat. Bank of N.Y., N.Y.C., 1982-85; dir., CEO Banco Rural S.A., Belo Horizonte, Brazil, 1986; pres., chmn. bd. Banco de Crédito Real de Minas Gerais S.A., Brazil, 1987; chmn. bd. Indi, Ceag and João Pinheiro Found., 1988-90; pres., chmn. bd. BDMG - Banco de Desenvolvimento de Minas Gerais S.A., 1988-90; sec. State Planning, Industry and Commerce, Mining and Energy, 1990; pres. Consultrade Ltd., 1987—; dir. Tenenge S.A., São Paulo, 1991—; pres. MinasPart/Meracado Comum, Belo Horizonte, Minas, Brazil, 1993—. Gen. dir. Faculdade Estácia de Sá de Belo Horizonte; dir. Comercial Assn. of State of Minas Gerais. Author: Minas Gerais 1989 Economy, 1989, Além de Pero Vaz: Carta Brasileira ao Seculo XX1; Contbr. articles to profl. jours. Mem. Clube dos Diretores Lojistas, Belo Horizonte, 1988—, Forum do Pensamento Economico Minas Gerais, Belo Horizonte, 1990—. Recipient Santos Dumont medal MG Govt., Santos Dumont, 1990, MG Congress medal, 1988; named Mgr. of Yr. Minas Gerais Conselho Regional de Administração, 2000. Mem. Internat. Brazilian C. of C. (v.p. 1989-91, dir.), Brazilian Assn. of Devel. Banks (pres. 1988-90), Inst. Brasileiro Executivos Financeiros (Fin. Exec. of the Yr. 1988), Brazilian Accountancy Acad. Home: Rua California 729/1201 30315-500 Belle Horizonte MG Brazil Office: MinasPart Desenv Econ Mercado Comum Av do contorno 4 667-Serra 30090110 Belo Horizonte MG Brazil

TEJA, AMYN SADRUDIN, chemical engineering educator, consultant; b. Zanzibar, Tanzania, May 11, 1946; came to U.S., 1980; s. Sadrudin N. and Amina (Dharsi) T.; m. Carole Rosina Thurlow, July 3, 1971; children: Kerima Amy, Adam Riaz. BSc in Engring., U. London, London, 1968; PhD, U. London, 1972. Intern Warren Springs Lab., Stevenage, Eng., summer 1966, Brit. Gas Corp., London, summer 1968; rsch. fellow in chem. engring. Loughborough (U.K.) U. Tech., 1971-74; chem. engring. lectr. Loughborough (Eng.) U. Tech., 1974-80; assoc. prof. chem. engring. Ga. Inst. Tech., Atlanta, 1980-83, prof., 1984-90, regents prof. Woodruff Sch. Mech. Engring., 1991—2001, regents prof. Sch. Chem. Engring., 1990—, dir. Fluid Properties Rsch. Inst., 1985—, co-dir. Specialty Separations Ctr., 1992—, assoc. chair grad. studies, 1994—. Vis. assoc. prof. chem. engring. U. Del., Newark, 1978—78, Ohio State U., 1980; cons. Laporte Chems., England, 1971, Mobil Rsch. and Devel. Co., NJ, 1979, Conoco Ltd., Humberside Refinery, England, 1980, Milliken Chem. Co., Spartanburg, SC, 1981—83, Hoechst Celanese Corp., Corpus Christi, Tex., 1984, Charlotte, 92, Philip Morris U.S.A., Richmond, Va., 1984—87, DuPont Co., 1988, Union Carbide Corp., South Charleston, W.Va., 1989—96, Shell Oil Co., 1989—93; presenter in field, reviewer various jours. Editor: Chemical Engineering and the Environment, 1981; mem. editl. bd. Reports on the Progress of Applied Chemistry, 1972-76, Critical Reports on Applied Chemistry, 1976-80, Jour. Chem. and Engring. Data, 1991-96, Chem. Engring. Rsch. Compendium, 1990—, Jour. Supercritical Fluids, 1990—; assoc. editor The Chem. Engring. Jour., 1973—; contbr. more than 200 articles to profl. jours. Recipient Hinchley medal Instn. Chem. Engrs., 1968, IBM Rsch. scholarship, 1968-71, Gas Coun. Rsch. scholarship, 1968-71, Brit. Coun. Younger Rsch. Workers award, 1977, Outstanding Tchr. award Omega Chi Epsilon, 1990. Mem. AIChE (pub. com. 1992—, jour. rev.), Am. Soc. Engring. Edn., Am. Chem. Soc., Sigma Xi (v.p. Ga. Tech. chpt. 1991-92, pres. 1992-93, Supr. Outstanding MS Thesis in Engring. 1984, 90, Supr. Outstanding PhD Thesis 1993, 96, Sustained Rsch. award 1987). Avocations: tennis, science fiction. Home: 6282 Indian Field Norcross GA 30092-1372 Office: Ga Inst Tech Sch Chem Engring Atlanta GA 30332-0100 E-mail: amyn.teja@che.gatech.edu.

TEJADA, AUDREY DOLAR, artist, writer; b. Manapla, Philippines, Dec. 29, 1957; came to U.S., 1961; d. Peter Infante and Mary Placentero (Dolar) T.; m. Joseph Yu, June 14,1986. BA in English, Cornell U., 1982; MS in Broadcast Journalism, Boston U., 1996. Intern Fgn. Svc. Diplomatic Corps, Washington, 1980, Bur. Pub. Affairs U.S. Dept. State, Washington, summers '80, 81; intern World News Tonight with Peter Jennings ABC News, N.Y.C., 1995; witn CNN Internat., Atlanta, 1996-97; Hearst fellow in broadcast news WCVB, Boston, 1997-98; v.p. cmty. devel. and media rels. Save Ourselves PC Prodns. and Cons., 1999—. Prodr., writer, dir.: (film) Rage, 1981; author; Strange Tango, 1992; work reviewed by Pentangle Films, 1981; writer, prodr. (CD ROM) Balikbayan, 1995; exec. prodr., rschr. Cyberspace@COM, 1995-96; contbr. articles to internet mag.; book reviewer Gustavus Myers nat. book award. Bd. trustees Cornell U., Ithaca, N.Y.; officer Harvard U., Cambridge, Mass.; mem. Mass. Commn. on Asian Ams., 1999. Recipient Chase Manhattan Found. fellowship, 1982. Mem. Quill and Dagger Soc., Asian Am. Journalists Assn. (nat. bd. dirs.), Unity Journalists of Color. E-mail: adtejada@hotmail.com.

TEJADA, FRANCISCO, physician, educator; b. Moyobamba, San Martin, Peru, July 25, 1942; s. Francisco Tejada and Semiramis Reatequi; m. Barbara Ann Kotowski, Feb. 1, 1970; children: Anamaria, Semiramis, Barbara Lee, Francisco, James. BS, U. Nacional Mayor de San Marcos, Lima, Peru, 1961; MD, U. Peruana Cayetano Heredia, Lima, 1967. Diplomate Am. Bd. Internal Medicine, Am. Bd. Oncology. Resident in medicine Johns Hopkins U., Balt., 1969-72; sr. cancer researcher Nat. Cancer Inst., NIH, Bethesda, Md., 1972-75; asst. clin. dir. Comprehensive Cancer Ctr. Fla., Miami, Fla., 1975-80; asst. prof. U. Miami, 1975-79, assoc. prof., 1979-85, prof., 1985—; vis. prof. U. Peruana Cayetano Heredia, Lima, 1994—; sr. ptnr. Oncology Assocs., Miami, 1980-85; chief cancer control Papanicolaou Cancer Ctr., 1984-86; assoc. dir. AMC Cancer Rsch. Ctr., Denver, 1986-87; pres. Am. Oncology Ctrs., Miami, 1985—; prof. U. San Agustin, Arequipa, Peru, 1992—, U. Peruana Cayetano Heredia, Lima, Peru, 1994—; clin. rsch. scientist UM/Sylvester Comprehensive Cancer Ctr., 2001—. Oncology expert Pan Am. Health Orgn., Washington, 1975-85, Nat. Cancer Inst., Bethesda, Md., 1984-86; dir. Miami Cancer Inst., 1980—; dir. Peruvian-Am. Endowment Inc., 1993-99, v.p., 1995-97; bd. dirs. Integrated Med. Svcs. Fla. Keys, Key West, 1997-2000; dir. oncology dept. Clinica Ricardo Palma, Lima, Peru, 1991-99; med. dir. Fla. Comprehensive Cancer Control Initiative, 2000—; dir. CureMe-Doctor Inc., 2002—. Editor Miami Health Letter, 1986—; inventor cancer risk assessment. Mem. Beacon Coun., Miami, 1984, Latin Am. Cancer Info., Washington, 1976, Hispanic Cancer Rsch. Network, Washington, 1990; chpt. pres. Peruvian Am. Med. Soc., Miami, 1986; trustee Pub. Health Trust Miami-Dade County, 2002. Lt. Peruvian Army, 1966-67. Decorated comendador Orden Sociedad (Peru); comendador Peruvian U. Cayetano Heredia; recipient Gold Medal Merit award Ministry of Edn., Lima, 1959, Hipolito Unanue award Hipolito Unanue Inst., Lima, 1968. Fellow ACP, Johns Hopkins U., Nat. Cancer Inst.; mem. Colegio Medico del Perú, Am. Assn. Cancer Rsch., Am. Soc. Clin. Oncology, Am. Soc. Hematology, Bolivian Cancer Soc. (hon. mem.), Peruvian Cancer Soc. (hon. mem.), Chilean Soc. Cancer (hon. mem.), Argentinian Soc. Head and Neck Pathology (hon. mem.). Roman Catholic. Avocations: hiking, photography, reading. Office: 1801 NW 9th Ave Rm 200F Miami FL 33136

TEJEDA, MANUEL J. business school educator; b. Camagüey, Cuba, Oct. 19, 1964; s. Manuel Jacinto Tejeda, Aida Josefina Moreno-Tejeda; life ptnr.. AB, U.Miami, 1985; MSEd, U. Miami, 1990; PhD, U.Miami, 1994. Cert. Teacher 1985. Rsch. asst. prof. U. Miami, Miami, Fla., 1994—98; asst. prof. Gettysburg Coll., Gettysburg, Pa., 1998—2000, Barry U. Andreas Sch.of Bus., Miami Shores, Fla., 2000—. Contbr. articles to profl. jours. Avocations: travel, gardening, bassett hounds. Office: Barry University 11300 Northeast Second Ave Miami Shores FL 33161-6695 Business E-Mail: mtejeda@mail.barry.edu.

TE KANAWA, KIRI, opera and concert singer; b. Gisborne, N.Z., Mar. 6, 1944; d. Thomas and Eleanor Te Kanawa; m. Desmond Park, Aug. 30, 1967 (div. 1997); children— Antonia Aroha, Thomas Desmond. Student, St. Mary's Coll., Auckland, N.Z., 1957-60, London Opera Centre, 1966-69; DMus (hon.), Oxford U., Dundee U., 1983, Warwick U., Auckland U., Waikato U., Nottingham U., Chgo. U., Durham U., Cambridge U. Joined Royal Opera House, London, 1971; appeared in role of Countess in Le Nozze di Figaro, 1971; U.S. debut in Santa Fe Festival, 1971; Met. Opera debut as Desdemona in Otello, 1974; appearances with all major European and Am. opera houses, including Australian opera cos., Royal Opera House, Covent Garden, London, Paris Opera, Munich Opera, La Scala, others; opera appearences include Boris Gudonov, Carmen, Don Giovanni, the Magic Flute, Eugene Onegin, La Boheme, Manon Lescaut, many others; appeared in film Don Giovanni as Elvira, 1979; recs. include Blue Skies, 1986, Kiri Sings Gershwin, 1987, Kiri Te Kanawa: Italian Opera Arias, 1991, Kiri Her Greatest Hits, Ave Maria, Kiri on Broadway, The Kiri Selection, Kiri Side Tracks, My Fair Lady, Maori Songs; PBS appearance: Great Performances: West Side Story, 1985; author: Land of the Long White Cloud, 1989, Opera for Lovers, 1996. Decorated comdr. Order Brit. Empire, 1973, Dame Comdr. Brit. Empire, 1983, Order of Australia, 1990, Order of New Zealand, 1995. Address: care Nick Grace Mgmt Ltd 2 Union Ct Sheen Rd Richmond TW9 1AA England

TEKINER, DENIZ HALIL, sociologist, writer; b. New Rochelle, N.Y., July 20, 1952; s. Sami and Roselle Tekiner. PhD, New Sch. for Social Rsch., N.Y., 1992. Adj. prof. Hunter Coll., N.Y.C., 1989; instr. adult divsn. New Sch., N.Y.C., 1993—95. Author: Modern Art and the Romantic Vision, 2000; contbr. articles to profl. jours.. Democrat. Home: 355 E 86th St New York NY 10028 E-mail: d.tekiner@worldnet.att.net.

TEKIPPE, RUDY JOSEPH, civil engineer; b. Decorah, Iowa, Dec. 2, 1943; s. Roman R. and Florence (Gesing) T.; m. Sheryl Ellen Bresnahan; children: Cynthia, Timothy, Michele, Ted. BSCE, Iowa State U., 1965, MSCE, 1966; PhD, U. Wis., 1969; Advanced Mgmt. Program, Harvard U., 1992. Registered profl. engr., Calif., La., Utah. Cons. engr. L.P. Erdman, Decorah, 1963-65; engr., sr. engr., supr. J.M. Montgomery, Cons. Engr., Pasadena, Calif., 1969-74, v.p., 1974-83, sr. v.p., 1984—, dir. technology, 1992—. Assoc. prof. Iowa State U., Ames, 1983-84. Co-author 3 tech. text and reference books; contbr. tech. papers to profl. publs. Recipient Disting. Svc. award U. Wis., Madison, 1992. Mem. Tau Beta Pi, Chi Epsilon, Phi Beta Phi, Sigma Nu. Achievements include design of water pollution control facilities including municipal and industrial wastewater management and treatment plants. Home: 2222 Kinneloa Ranch Rd Pasadena CA 91107-1100 Office: Montgomery Watson Americas 300 N Lake Ave Ste 1200 Pasadena CA 91101-4184

TELANG, NITIN T. cancer biologist, educator; b. Bombay, India, July 3, 1943; came to U.S., 1976; s. Trimbak Pandharinath and Madhumalati (Kanitkar) T. BSc, U. Poona, India, 1963, MSc, 1966, PhD, 1974. Assoc. rsch. scientist Tata Meml. Hosp. Cancer Rsch., Bombay, 1974-76; rsch. assoc. U. Nebr., Lincoln, 1976-78; staff fellow Am. Health Found., Valhalla, N.Y., 1978-81; rsch. assoc. Sloan-Kettering Inst., N.Y.C., 1981-85; asst. attending biochemist Meml. Sloan-Ketering Cancer Ctr., 1985-91; assoc. prof. Cornell U. Med. Coll., 1991—; dir. divsn. carcinogenesis & prevention Strang-Cornell Cancer Rsch. Lab., 1991-95, dir. carcinogenesis and nutrition core lab., 1991—; dir. divsn. carcinogenesis and prevention Strang Cancer Rsch. Lab., The Rockefeller U., 1995—, sr. scientist, head Julian H. Robertson Jr. Chemoprevention Rsch. Lab., Strang Cancer Prevention Ctr., 1998—. Vis. investigator The Rockefeller U., N.Y.C., 1985-89. Contbr. numerous articles to profl. jours. Mem. Am. Assn. Cancer Rsch., Am. Soc. Cell Biology, Am. Inst. Nutrition, European Assn. Cancer Rsch. Office: Strang Cancer Rsch Lab Rockefeller Univ 1230 York Ave New York NY 10021-6307 E-mail: telangn@rockvax.rockefeller.edu.

TELEGDI, ANDREW, member of parliament; b. Budapest, Hungary, May 28, 1946; arrived in Can., 1957; s. Alexander Sandor and Elenora Maria (Friedrich) T.; m. Nancy Curtin; 1 child, Erin. , U. Waterloo. Mem. Waterloo City Coun., 1985-93, Waterloo Regional Coun., 1988-93; M.P. for Waterloo Ho.of Commons., 1993-97, vice chair standing com. on human rights and disabled, 1994-95, vice chair pub. accounts standing com., 1995-96; mem. justice com. Ho. of Commons, 1997-98, mem. caucus com. on postsecondary edn., 1996—, vice chair, regional licensing com.; assoc. mem. fin., environ., and industry coms. Ho. of Commons; M.P. for Kitchener-Waterloo Ho. of Commons. Exec. dir. Youth in Conflict with the Law, 1976-93; coord. Justice Week, Waterloo, 1979—; pres. Fedn. of Students, U. Waterloo, 1973-75; councillor City of Waterloo, 1985-93; advisor to Prime Min., Budapest Conf. on Security and Coop. in Europe, 1994; mem. standing com. on citizenship and immigration, Ho. of Commons, Ottawa, 1998-2000; parliamentary sec. to Minister of Citizenship and Immigration, 1998-2000. Bd. dirs. The Working Centre and St. John's Soup Kitchen, 1986—, Kitchener House, 1979—; pres. K.W. Multicultural Centre, 1987-89; chair Conestoga Coll. Basic Job Readiness Tng. Adv. Group, 1980-84; mem. clin. adv. com. Cath. Family Counselling Centre, 1986-87, family violence com.; chair People, Working and Learning Inc., 1984-86. Mem. Waterloo Uptown Bus. Assn., Kitchener-Waterloo C. of C. (bus. edn. com.). Office: House of Commons 285 Confederation Bldg Ottawa ON Canada K1A 0A6 E-mail: telega@parl.gc.ca.

TELENCIO, GLORIA JEAN, elementary education educator; b. Trenton, N.J., Sept. 3, 1955; d. John and Anne (Tymoch) T. BA cum laude, Georgian Ct. Coll., 1977. Cert. elem. edn. Math and sci. tchr. grade 8 St. Anthony's Grammar Sch., Trenton, 1977-78; elem. tchr. grade 7 St. Mary's Assumption Sch., 1978-79; elem. tchr. grade 2 Hamilton Twp. Bd. Edn., 1979-85, elem. tchr. grade 1, 1985—. Sch. coord. Regional Curriculum Svc. Unit, Learning Resource Ctr.-Ctrl., 1990-95. Tech. rep., exec. bd. PTA, 1981-91, 1994-97. Recipient State of N.J. Gov.'s Tchr. Recognition award State of N.J., 1991, Resolution of Commendation, Town Coun. of the Twp. of Hamilton, 1991; named Tchr. of Yr., Hamilton Twp. Dist., 1999-00; mini-grantee Bd. Edn., 1987-88, McDonald's Classroom grantee, 1999. Mem. NEA, N.J. Edn. Assn., Hamilton Edn. Assn., Sunnybrae PTA (tchr. rep. exec. bd. 1981-91, co-chair PTA 25th Anniversary com. 1990-91), Kappa Delta Pi, Sigma Tau Delta, Pi Delta Phi, Delta Tau Kappa. Republican. Byzantine Catholic. Avocations: reading, theatre, music. Home: 31 Newkirk Ave Trenton NJ 08629-1429 Office: Sunnybrae Elem Sch 166 Elton Ave Trenton NJ 08620-1622

TELEPAS, GEORGE PETER, retired lawyer; b. Kingston, N.Y., Nov. 20, 1935; s. Peter G. and Grace Telepas; m. Regina Tisiker, Sept. 6, 1969 (div.); m. Patricia Kilstofte, Apr. 30, 1995. BS, U. Fla., 1960; JD, U. Miami, 1965. Bar: Fla. 1965, Colo. 1986. Assoc. Preddy, Haddad, Kutner & Hardy, 1966-67, Williams & Jabara, 1967-68; pvt. practice Miami, Fla., 1968-98. Mem. citizens bd. U. Miami. With USMC, 1954-56. Mem. ATLA, ABA, Fla. Bar Assn., Colo. Bar Assn., Dade County Bar Assn., Fla. Trial Lawyers Assn., Dade County Trial Lawyers Assn., Delta Theta Phi, Sigma Nu. Address: 13320 Marsh Landing Palm Beach Gardens FL 33418

TELESETSKY, WALTER, government official; b. Boston, Jan. 22, 1938; s. Keril and Nellie (Krelka) T.; m. Sharron-Dawn Lamp, July 15, 1961; children: Stephanie Ann, Anastasia Marie. BS in Mech. Engring., Northeastern U., 1960; MBA, U. Chgo., 1961; postgrad., Harvard U., 1977. Engr. trainee Chrysler Corp., Detroit, 1956-59; rsch. asst. Microtech Rsch. Co., Cambridge, Mass., 1959-60; engr. Allis Chalmers Mfg. Co., Milw., 1960-61; mem. tech. staff The Mitre Corp., Bedford, Mass., 1962-68; sr. mem. tech. staff Data Dynamics, Inc., Washington, 1969; phys. scientist NOAA, Rockville, Md., 1970-71, U.S. Gate Project coord., 1972-74, dir. U.S. Global Weather Experiment Project Office, 1974, dir. Program Integration Office, 1975-77, dir. Programs and Tech. Devel. Office, 1977-79, dir. Programs and Internat. Activities Office, 1979-81; dep. assoc. dir. for tech. svcs., chief AFOS ops. div. Nat. Weather Svc., Silver Spring, 1981-86, dir. Office of Systems Ops., 1986-2000, dir. Office Operational Sys., 2000—. Liaison to NAS coms. on atmospheric scis., geophysics studies and internat. environ. programs, 1975-81; U.S. coord. U.S./Japan Coop. Program in Natural Resources, 1980-88; chmn. U.S.-Japan Marine Resources and Engring. Coordination Com., 1980-88; U.S. del. governing coun. UN Environ. Program and World Meteorol. Orgn.; mem. commn. for Basic Systems World Meteorol. Orgn., 1988—; speaker in field. Contbr. articles to profl. publs. Recipient Silver medal Dept. Commerce, 1975, Gold medal Dept. Commerce, 1998. Mem. AAAS, Am. Geophys. Union, Am. Meteorol. Soc., Am. Soc. Mech. Engrs., Marine Tech. Soc. Home: 16 Eton Overlook Rockville MD 20850-3003 Office: 1325 E West Hwy Silver Spring MD 20910-3280

TELFER, MARGARET CLARE, internist, hematologist, oncologist; b. Manila, The Philippines, Apr. 9, 1939; came to U.S., 1941; d. James Gavin and Margaret Adele (Baldwin) T. BA, Stanford U., 1961; MD, Washington U., St. Louis, 1965. Diplomate Am. Bd. Internal Medicine, Am. Bd. Hematology, Am. Bd. Oncology; lic. Ill., Mo. Resident in medicine Michael Reese Hosp., Chgo., 1968, fellow in hematology and oncology, 1970, assoc. attending physician, 1970-72, dir. Hemophilia Ctr., 1971—, interim dir. div. hematology and oncology, 1971-74, 81-84, 89—, attending physician, 1972—, Rush-Presbyn. St. Luke's Hosp., 1999—, Olympia Fields (Ill.) Hosp., 1999—, Cook County Hosp., Chgo., 2000—; asst. prof. medicine U. Chgo., 1975-80, assoc. prof. medicine, 1980-85, assoc. prof. clin. medicine, 1985-89; assoc. prof. medicine U. Ill., Chgo., 1990-2001, Rush U., Chgo., 2001—. Mem. med. adv. bd. Hemophilia Found. Ill., 1971, chmn., 1972—83, lectr. annual symposium, 1978—84; mem. med. adv. bd. State of Ill. Hemophilia Program; dir. hematology-oncology fellowship program Michael Reese Hosp., 1971—75, 1981—84, 1989—2000, lectr. and mem. numerous coms.; lectr. Cook County Grad. Sch. Medicine, 1980—85, U. Chgo., ARC. Contbr. articles to profl. jours. Fellow ACP; mem. Am. Soc. Clin. Oncology, Am. Assn. Med. Colls., Am. Soc. Hematology, World Fedn. Hemophilia, Blood Club (Chgo.), Thrombosis Club (Chgo.). Office: Florsheim Bldg 29th & Ellis Chicago IL 60616

TELFORD, GORDON LAING, surgeon, educator; b. Warrington, Eng., Dec. 3, 1944; came to U.S., 1946; s. Wayne M. and Helen Telford. BA, Drake U., Des Moines, 1967; MD, U. Chgo., 1971. Intern U. Fla., 1971-72; resident in surgery U. Iowa, 1972-74, U. Md., 1976-80; rsch. fellow in GI physiology Mayo Clinic, 1980-82; prof. surgery Med. Coll. Wis., Milw., 1982—, chmn. GI and minimally invasive surgery, 1998—. Mem. adv. commn. med. ethics Archdiocese Milw., 1987-92; bd. dirs. Ranch Cmty. Svcs., Menomonee Falls, Wis., 1994-98. Mem. ACS, Am. Surg. Assn. Ctrl. Surg. Assn., Phi Beta Kappa. Avocations: hiking, fishing, canoeing, biking, history. Office: Med Coll Wis 9200 W Wisconsin Ave Milwaukee WI 53226-3522

TELFORD, KENNETH ALDERMAN, philosopher, educator, humanities educator; b. Springfield, Mass., Apr. 13, 1922; s. Harold George Telford Sr. and Edna Clara Alderman; m. Nancy Jo Taylor, 1948 (div. 1968); children: Clinton, Cassie, Laurie. BA, Denison U., 1948; MA, U. Chgo., 1954, PhD, 1961. From instr. to full prof. and chmn. humanities divsn. Chgo. City Coll., 1953—78; prof. New Sch. for Social Rsch., N.Y.C., 1968—69. Author: Aristotle's Poetics, Translation and Analysis, 1961, The Origins of the Modern Morgan, 1988, The Lippitt Register, 1990, Selected Poems, by Kenneth A. Telford, 1992, Collected Writings on Equine Topics, 1993, What Ever Happened to the Pacer?, 1995, Aristotle's Nicomachean Ethics, Translation, 1997, Aristotle's Nicomachean Ethics, Commentary, 1997, Aristotle's Organon, Vol. I, Categories and On Interpretation, with Commentaries, 1998, Aristotle's Organon, Vol. II, Prior Analytics, with Commentary, 1998, Aristotle's Organon, Vol. III, Posterior Analytics, with Commentary, 1998, Aristotle's Organon, Vol. IV, On Topics and On Sophistical Refutations, with Commentary, 1999, Aristotle's Physics, Translation, 1999, Aristotle's Physics, Commentary, 1999, Aristotle's On the Heaven, with Commentary, 2000, Aristotle's On Genesis and Destruction, with Commentary, 2000, Aristotle's On the Soul, with Commentary, 2000, Aristotle's Metaphysics, Translation, 2000, Aristotle's Metaphysics, Commentary, 2000, Aristotle's Politics, Translation, 2001, Aristotle's Politics, Commentary, 2001, Aristotle's Poetics, with Commentary, 2001, Plato's Republic, Book I, with Commentary, 2001, Plato's Phaedo, with Commentary, 2001. Sgt. maj. U.S. Army, 1942—47, ETO. Home: 4877 Vt Route 12 Randolph VT 05060

TELGENHOF, ALLEN RAY, lawyer; b. Flint, Mich., Jan. 31, 1964; s. Gerald H. and Bernice Kay Telgenhof; m. Judy Michele Campbell, Sept. 5, 1986; children: Tyler, Allyson, Will, Luke. BA, Mich. State U., 1987; JD cum laude, Thomas M. Cooley Law Sch., 1989. Bar: Mich. 1989, U.S. Dist. Ct. (ea. dist.) Mich. 1992, U.S. Ct. Appeals (6th cir.) 1992, U.S. Dist. Ct. (we. dist.) Mich. 1997. Legis. analyst Mich. Ho. of Reps., Lansing, 1989; assoc. Hicks & Schmidlin, P.C., Flint, 1990-93; pvt. practice law Clio, Mich., 1993-94; ptnr. Pointner, Joseph, Corcoran & Telgenhof, P.C., Charlevoix, 1994-98, Joseph, Corcoran & Telgenhof, P.C., Charlevoix, 1998-2000, Joseph, Corcoran, Telgenhof & Snyder, P.C., Charlevoix, 2000—. Advisor Clio H.S. Law Club, 1992-94; founder, pres. Clio Area Edn. Found., 1992-94; presenter in field. Trustee Clio Bd. Edn., 1992-94, Charlevoix Bd. Edn., 1995—, pres., 1997—; commr. City of Charlevoix Planning Commn., 1995-96. Named Alumnus of Yr. Clio H.S., 1999. Mem. ABA, Charlevoix-Emmet Bar Assn. Avocations: sports, sailing, family activities. Office: Joseph Corcoran Et Al PO Box 490 203 Mason St Charlevoix MI 49720-1337 Fax: 231-547-3014. E-mail: atelgenhof@chartermi.net.

TELICZAN, CASIMIR JOSEPH, secondary school educator; b. Grand Rapids, Mich., Sept. 12, 1953; s. Edmund Raphael Teliczan (dec.) and Marjorie Ann VanTuinen; m. Michelle Marie Teliczan, Jan. 29, 1983; children: Sean (dec.), Cheri, Gregory. AA in Mgmt., L.A. C.C., 1979; AAS in Interpreting and Translating, C.C. of AF, 1985, AAS in tech. instructing, 1986; BS in Liberal Studies, Excelcior Coll., Albany, 1989; MEd in Secondary and Adult Edn., Grand Valley State U., 1999; PhD of Alternative Edn., Concordia U., 2001. Cert. tchr., Mich. Enlisted USAF, 1973, advanced through grades to sr. master sgt., linguist Thailand and The Philippines, 1973-78, counselor Calif., 1979-82, chief collection mgr. Hahn AB, Germany, 1983-86, chief European tng. Goodfellow AFB, Tex., 1987-91, supt., 1991-92, exec. officer, 1992-93, ret., 1993; sci. tchr., head dept. River Valley Acad., Rockford, Mich., 1994—, tech. liaison, 2000—, summer sch. dir., 2000—. Rugby coach Hahn AB, 1983-86, Goodfellow AFB, 1987-93, Cedar Springs, Rockford, 1997-98; rugby officiator, 1983—; treas. NCO Acad. Grads. Assn., 1991. Edn. grantee Rockford Edn. Found., 1998-2001. Mem. Air Force Assn. (life), Mich. Alternative Edn. Orgn., Rockford Edn. Assn. Avocations: fishing, rugby, hunting, karate. Office: River Valley Acad 350 N Main St Rockford MI 49341-1020 E-mail: cteliczan@rockford.k12.mi.us.

TELITCHEV, IGOR YEVGENIEVICH, aerospace engineering educator, researcher; b. Dzerzhinsk, Gor'ki, Russia, Mar. 20, 1964; s. Yevgeni Nikolayevich and Nina Timopheyevna T.; m. Elena Arturovna Lushnikova, Apr. 15, 1964; children: Kirill, Ivan. MS in Aerospace Engring., Samara State Aerospace U., Russia, 1987, PhD, 1996. Rsch. scientist Samara State Aerospace U., 1987-96, asst. prof., 1996-99, assoc. prof., 2000—. Guest scientist Fraunhofer Ernst-Mach-Inst., Freiburg, Germany, 1997; vis. prof. Rein-Westphalia Tech. U., Aachen, Germany, 2000-01; rsch. fellow U. Calgary, Alta., Can. Contbr. articles to profl. jours. and confs. Grantee European Space Agy., 1997, German Rsch. Assn., 1997, Ernst-Mach-Inst., Germany, 1998, Internat. Union Applied and Theoretical Mechanics, 2000, German Sci. Exch. Svcs., 2000; recipient Soros award in physics George Soros Found., 2000. Mem. Hypervelocity Impact Soc. (grantee 1996). Office: U Calgary MEB 2500 Univ Dr NW Calgary AB Canada T2N 1N4 also: 320 Jackson Pl NW Calgary AB Canada T3B 2V3 Fax: 403-282-8406. E-mail: telitchev@mail.ru.

TELL, WILLIAM KIRN, JR. oil company executive, lawyer, retired; b. Evanston, Ill., Feb. 27, 1934; s. William Kirn and Virginia (Snook) T.; m. Karen Nelson, July 16, 1960; children— Catherine, Caroline, William F. BA in Govt., Dartmouth Coll., 1956; JD, U. Mich., 1959. Bar: Ohio, 1960, D.C., 1979. Sr. v.p. Texaco Inc., Washington and N.Y.C., 1979-97; pres. corp. comm. divsn. Texaco Corp., 1989-97, ret., 1998. Adj. fellow Am. Enterprise Inst., 1997—. Mem. adv. bd. dirs. Met. Opera, N.Y.C., 1983-98; trustee Am. Coun. Trustees and Alumni, 1992—. Mem.: Inst. for Am. Values (mem. bd. 2001—), Am. Hwy. Users Assn. (chmn. 1991, 1995, 1996, chmn. emeritus 1997—), Fgn. Policy Assn. (bd. govs. 1991—), Manhattan Inst. (trustee 1997—), Everglades Club, Met. Club, Congressional Club, Greenwich Country Club. Home: 633 Steamboat Rd Greenwich CT 06830-7145 Office: 660 Steamboat Rd Greenwich CT 06830-7150

TELLE, LEWIS DONALD, surgeon; b. Chgo., Nov. 22, 1920; s. Samuel Kenneth and Goldie (Krueger) T.; m. Nancy Carolyn Bearden, Dec. 7, 1946; children: Lindaly, L. Donald II. AA, Herzl Jr. Coll., Chgo.; BS, Ctrl. Y Coll., Chgo.; MD, U. Ill., Chgo. Diplomate Am. Bd. Surgery. Intern Cook County Hosp., Chgo.; resident surgery and family practice Charlotte (N.C.) Meml. Hosp.; family practice physician Martin Meml. Hosp., Mt. Airy, N.C.; resident gen. surgery Cleve. (Ohio) VA Hosp., Case Western Res. U.; chief surgery U.S. Army Hosps., Ft. Chaffe, Ark., Ft. McClellan, Ala.; pvt. practice gen. surgery various hosps., Pomeroy, Marietta, Ohio; pvt. practice family practice and surgery Family Practice and Surgery Ctr., Jay (Fla.) Hosp., Family Practice Med. Ctr., Pensacola, Fla. Lt. col. U.S. Army Med. Corps, 1955-59. Fellow ACS, South-Ea. Surg. Soc.; mem. AMA, Fla. Med. Assn. Republican. Methodist. Home: 106 Cypress Pt E Pensacola FL 32514-7934 Office: Med Care Ctrs North Fla 3799 N Davis Hwy Pensacola FL 32503-3023 Fax: 850-432-9685.

TELLEEN, JUDY, counselor; b. Chgo., Dec. 13, 1942; d. Kurt Theodore and Gertrude Lillian Lockwood Johnson; m. David Roger Telleen; June 15, 1964; children: Karin, Kirstin, Erik. BA, Lawrence U., 1964; MA, U. Mich., 1967, PhD, 1970. Program dir. counseling svcs. Asian Human Svcs., Chgo., 1994-95, coord. of counseling svcs., 1995-96, coord. of case mgmt., 1997-98; adj. prof. Governor's State Univ., University Park, Ill., 1995-99; counselor Arlington Heights, 1999—. Adv. com. mem. Bd. Suprs. and Sch. Bd., Va., 1993; mem. Pub. Policy and Legis. com. Ill. Counseling Assn., 1994, mem. governing coun., 2000—. Author: (book) A Predictive Model of the Cumulative Academic Achievement of Indian Students , 1970, Guidance Factors Influencing Indian Students to Attend the University of Michigan , 1971; mem. editl. bd. (periodical) Ill. Counseling Assn. Quarterly, 1995—98. Youth advocate Bridge Youth & Family Svcs., Palatine, Ill., 1994—96; chairperson learning com. All Saints Lutheran Ch., 1993—2001. Mem. Am. Counselor's Assn., Ill. Counselor's Assn., Ill. Assn. of Couples & Family Couns. (pres.), Ill. Assn. for Multicultural Counseling, Ill. Assn. of Mental Health Counselors, Assn. for Multicultural Counseling Develop., Internat. Assn. of Marriage & Family Counselors, Internat. Assn. of Addictions & Offender Counselors, Pi Lambda Theta, Phi Kappa Phi. Lutheran. Office: Ste 102 1040 S Arlington Heights Rd Arlington Heights IL 60005-3162

TELLEM, SUSAN MARY, public relations executive; b. N.Y.C, May 23, 1945; d. John F. and Rita C. (Lietz) Cain; m. Marshall R.B.. Thompson; children: Tori, John, Daniel. BS, Mt. St. Mary's Coll., L.A., 1967. Cert. pub. health nurse; RN. Pres. Tellem Pub. Rels. Agy., Marina del Rey, Calif., 1977-80, Rowland Grody Tellem, L.A., 1980-90; chmn. The Rowland Co., 1990—; pres., CEO Tellem, Inc., 1992-93. Instr. UCLA Extension, 1983-97; adj. prof. Pepperdine U., 1999—; speaker numerous seminars and confs. on pub. rels. Editor: Sports Medicine for the '80's, Sports Medicine Digest, 1982-84. Bd. dirs. Marymount High Sch., 1984-87, pres., 1984-86; bd. dirs. L.A. Police Dept. Booster Assn., 1984-87; mem. Cath. Press Coun.; mem. pres.'s coun. Mus. Sci. and Industry. Mem. Am. Soc. Hosp. Mktg. and Pub. Rels., Healthcare Mktg. and Pub. Rels. Assn., Pub. Rels. Soc. Am. (bd. dirs. 1994—), L.A. Counselors, PETA, Am. Lung Assn. (chair comm. com. L.A. chpt.) Soc. for Prevention of Cruelty to Animals (chair PetSet), Sports Club (L.A.). Roman Catholic. Avocations: reading, tennis, aerobic dance. Office: 23852 Pacific Coast Hwy # 928 Malibu CA 90265-4879 Fax: 310-589-6101.

TELLER, PAULINE IVANCOVICH, artist; b. Ross, Calif., May 3, 1914; d. Baldo Aloysius and Marien Barron Ivancovich; m. Frederic de Peyster Teller II, Aug. 29, 1941; children: Joan Teller Coda, Peter Ivancovich, Anne Teller Wallace, Frederic de Peyster III. BFA, Dominican Coll., 1936. One-woman shows include San Francisco Mus. Modern Art, 1940, Dominican Coll. Libr., 1975, Ross Valley Clinic, 1976, Marin Civic Ctr. Adminstrn. Bldg Gallery, 1981, Mus. Mission San Juan Capistrano, 1987, Hobar Gallery, Santa Barbara, Calif., 1989; exhibites include San Francisco Art Assn., 1939, Fine Arts Bldg GGIE, 1940, San Francisco Women Artists, 1945, Marin Soc. Artists, 1936-85, Terra Linda Art Assn., 1936-85, Soc. Western Artists, 1936-85, Marin Art Guild, 1970-85, Calif. State Fair, Sacramento, 1970-85, Gilbert Gallery, San Francisco, 1970-85, Shorebirds Gallery, Tiburon, 1970-85, L.A. Design Ctr., 1987, Village Artistry, Carmel, Calif., 1988-89, Linda Vida Gallery, Ruidoso, N.Mex., 1988-89, Hobar Gallery, Santa Barbara, Calif., 1989-90, Vigil Gallery, Sonoma, Calif., 1990, Nevada City, Calif., 1990, Linda Lundeen Gallery, Las Cruces, N.Mex., 1991, Projects Gallery, San Rafael, Calif., 1991, Arlene Siegel Gallery, N.Mex.; represented in permanent collections at Mrs. J.H. Dollar, Hr., Kentfield, Dr. Gary Boero, San Rafael, Domonican Coll., Leafy Mayhew, Sacramento, Stanford (Calif.) U., San Domenico Sch. San Anselmo, Calif., Stanford U. Hosp., Saiter Packard Children's Hosp., Stanford, Calif., others. Mem. Nat. Mus. Women in Arts (charter). Home: 290 Harvard Dr Larkspur CA 94939-1112

TELLES, MARELYN V. TAYLOR, psychiatric clinical nurse specialist; b. N.Y.C., July 30; d. Edward J. and Mary J. (Byrnes) Taylor. Diploma, St. Mary's Hosp., Waterbury, Conn., 1963; AA in Psychology, San Diego Mesa Coll., 1980; BSN magna cum laude, U. San Diego, 1982, MSN, 1984. ARNP, N.H.; cert. adult psychiat. and mental health clin. nurse specialist ANCC. Psychiat. clin. nurse specialist VA Med. Ctr., San Diego, 1985-86, Manchester, N.H., 1986—. Clin. adj. faculty Rivier Coll., Nashua, N.H., 1994—. Grantee NIMH, 1982-83; recipient award for disting. govt. svc. N.H. Fed. Execs. Assn., 1990. Mem. ANA, N.H. Nurses Assn. (editl. adv. bd. Nursing News 1986—. bd. dirs. 1986-91), Sigma Theta Tau. Home: 752 Mammoth Rd Manchester NH 03104-4526 Office: 718 Smyth Rd Manchester NH 03104-7004

TELLIER, HENRI, retired Canadian military officer; b. Montreal, Que., Can., Sept. 1, 1918; s. Henry Joseph and Jeanne (St. Cyr) T.; m. Virginia Wright, July 23, 1945; children: Pierre, Michele, Suzanne, John, Nicole. Student, U. Montreal, 1935-40, U. Ottawa, 1946-47, Canadian Army Staff Coll., 1942-43, Imperial Def. Coll., London, Eng., 1966, Dept. Def. Computer Inst., Washington, 1968; PhD in mil. sci., H.C. With Robert Howard & Co. (ins. brokers), Montreal, 1937-40; commd. 2d lt. Canadian Army, 1940, advanced through grades to lt. gen., 1973; asst. sec. to minister (Nat. Def.), 1945-48; comdg. officer (Royal 22d Regt.), 1948-51; instr. (Canadian Army Staff Coll.), 1951-54; army mem. (Joint Intelligence Staff), 1954-57; mil. adviser Vietnam, 1957-58; chief of staff (Que. Mil. Dist.), 1958-60; mil attache Rome, 1960- 63; dir. mil. ops. and plans Army, 1963-64, dir. internat. plans, 1964-65; comdr. (Canadian Contingent), Cyprus, 1965-66; dir. gen. plans (Forces Hdqrs.), Ottawa, Ont., 1967-70, chief plans, 1970-71; Canadian mil. rep. to mil. com. (NATO Hdqrs.), Brussels, 1971-73; ret., 1973. Assoc. nat. commr. Canadian Red Cross Soc., Toronto, Ont., 1973-75, nat. commr., 1975, sec.-gen., 1981-83, hon. v.p.; pvt. mem. Refugee Bd., 1984-89; chmn. Canadian sect. Mil. Coop. Com. Can.-U.S., Joint Permanent Bd. Def. Can.-U.S.; commr. Commn. for Strategic and Internat. Studies; mem. adv. council Can. Exec. Services Orgn. Decorated Mem. Order of Canada; Disting. Service Order (Canada); Queens medal Netherlands; comdr. Order of Merit (Italy), officer Order of Red Cross. Mem. Canadian Inst. Internat. Affairs., Can. Exec. Svc. Orgn., Inst. Assn. Execs., The Empire Club of Can., Royal 22 Regiment Assn., UN Assn. Office: 19 Bay Hill Ridge Stittsville ON Canada K2S 1B9

TELLIER, PAUL M. railroad transportation executive; b. Joliette, Que., Can., May 8, 1939; s. Maurice J. and Eva M. (Bouvier) T.; m. Andree Poirier, June 6, 1959; children: Claude, Marc. BA, U. Ottawa, 1959, LLL, 1962; BLitt, Oxford U., 1966; LLD (hon.) , U. Alta., Can., 1996, U. Ottawa, 2000; DCommerce (hon.) , St. Mary's U., 2001. Bar: Que. bar 1963. Sr. gov. official, Can., 1967-92; dep. minister Indian affairs and no. devel., 1979-82; dep. minister energy, mines and resources, 1982-85; chmn. governing bd. Internat. Energy Agy., 1985-92; clk. of Privy Council and sec. to Cabinet Govt. of Can., Ottawa, 1985-92; dir. Petro Can., 1985-92; pres., CEO Canadian Nat. Railway Co., 1992—. Bd. dirs. Alcan Aluminum Ltd., Montreal, Can., BCE/Bell Can., Montreal, McCain Foods Ltd., Florenceville, Can., Bombardier, Montreal, Can. Coun. of Chief Execs., Conf. Bd., Grand Truck, Assoc. Am. R.R., Rlwy. Assoc., Can. Decorated companion Order of Can.; recipient Pub. Policy Forum Outstanding Achievement award, 1988, Gov. Gen.'s Outstanding Achievement award, 1990, Right Hand Man award Greenbrier, 1996, B'nai Brith Can. award of merit, 2000, Partnership award Am. Short Line and Regional R.R. Assn., 2001, Partnership award Am. ShortLine & Regional R.R. Assn., 2001, McCullough Logistics Exec. of Yr. award, 2001; named to Queen's Privy Coun., Her Majesty Queen Elizabeth, 1992; Queen's counsel, 1981; named Transp. Person of Yr., 1997, Railroader of Yr., 1997, Grand Montréalais, 1998, CEO of Yr., 1998, Personality of Yr., Les Affaires jour., McCullough Logistics Exec. of Yr., 2001. Mem. Que. Bar, Railway Assn. Can. (dir.), Assn. Am. Railroads (dir.). Roman Catholic. Office: Can Nat Railway Co 935 De La Gauchetiere St West Montreal QC Canada H3B 2M9 also: PO Box 8100 Montreal QC Canada H3C 3N4

TELLIER, RICHARD DAVIS, management educator; b. Darby, Pa., Feb. 18, 1942; s. Joseph Campbell and Jane Grace (Davis) T.; m. Susan Gammon, June 10, 1974; children: John-Jo and Tiekka (twins). BSEE, Drexel U., 1967; MBA, Fla. State U., 1971, DBA, 1973. Elec. engr. Philco-Ford Corp., Phila., 1960-67; aerospace sys. engr. GE, Cape Canaveral, Fla., 1967-70; lectr. Fla. State U., Tallahassee, 1970-73; prof. mgmt. Calif. State U., Fresno, 1973-2000, chmn. dept. mgmt. and mktg., 1979-84, assoc. dean Sch. Bus., 1984-85, asst. dean, 1990-92, assoc. provost acad. resources, 1995-99, prof. emeritus, 2000—. Cons. ops. mgmt., market rsch. orgnl. behavior. Author: Operations Management: Fundamental Concepts and Methods, 1978, Production and Operations Management Test Bank, 1990 ; contbr. articles to profl. jours. Grantee 1975; recipient Meritorious Performance award, 1987, 88, 90. Mem. Ops. Research Soc. Am., Phi Kappa Phi. Home: 8294 N Academy Ave Clovis CA 93611-9454 Office: Calif State U Shaw and Maple Ave Fresno CA 93740-0001 E-mail: rickt@csufresno.edu.

TELLIS, GERARD J. business educator; b. Bombay, India, Mar. 27, 1950; came to U.S., 1979; s. Aloysius Louis and Lucy Tellis; m. Cheryl Anne Evelyn, Mar. 5, 1980; children: Neil, Viren, Kethan, Sonia. BS, U. Bombay, 1975; PGDBM, Xavier Inst. Mgmt., Jamshedpur, India, 1977; PhD, U. Mich., 1983. Sales devel. mgr. Johnson & Johnson, Bombay, 1977-79; assoc. prof. mktg. U. Iowa, Iowa City, 1983-88; prof. mktg. U. So. Calif., L.A., 1989-95, Neely chair in Am. Enterprise LA, 1996—. Author: Advertising and Sales Promotion Strategy, 1998, Will & Vision, 2001. Dir. coaches Am. Youth Soccer Assn., Hacienda Heights, Calif., 1996-2002, tournament dir., 1998-2002. Recipient Frank M. Bass award Mktg. Sci., 1998, William F. Odell award Jour. Mktg. Rsch., 1998, Harold D. Maynard award, Jour. Mktg., 2001. Mem. Am. Mktg. Assn., Inst. Ops. Rsch. and Mgmt. Sci., Assn. Consumer Rsch. Avocations: soccer, hiking, gardening. Office: U So Calif Dept Bus Los Angeles CA 90089-0001

TELLIS, VIVIAN ANTHONY, transplant surgeon, administrator; b. Calcutta, India, Jan. 2, 1939; s. Vivian Joseph and Monica (Mascarenhas) T.; m. Patricia Joan Gioscio, Apr. 20, 1968; children: Audrey, Eileen. MBBS, All-India Inst. Med. Scis., New Delhi, 1960. Diplomate Am. Bd. Surgery; lic. physician, N.Y. Intern Jersey City Med. Ctr., 1963-64; resident Harlem Hosp., 1965-66, Montefior Med. Ctr., 1966-68, fellow in transplantation, 1968-70; attending surgeon Montefiore Med. Ctr., Bronx, N.Y., 1970—. Asst. prof. surgery Albert Einstein Coll. Medicine, Bronx, 1972-78, assoc. prof. surgery, 1978-87, prof. surgery, 1987—; transplant cons., med. rev. bd., end stage renal disease, N.Y., 1998—. mem. med. adv. bd. Transplant Recipients Internat. Orgn. (Triangle award 1996). Contbr. over 100 articles to profl. jours. Pub. spkr. for increased organ donor awareness, various support and ch. groups, 1980—; mem. bd. trustees Nat. Kidney Found., 1993— (Lester Hoenig award 1994). Mem. ACS, Am. Soc. Nephrology, Transplantation Soc., Internat. Pediat. Transplant Soc., Am. Soc. of Transplantation, Am. Soc. Transplant Surgeons, N.Y. Transplantation Soc. (pres. 1985-86), N.Y. Regional Transplant Program (pres. 1989-90). Democrat. Roman Catholic. Avocations: skiing, origami, music. Office: Montefiore Med Ctr 111 E 210th St Bronx NY 10467-2401 E-mail: vtellis@montefiore.org.

TELLO, RICHARD J. radiologist, researcher; b. Mexico City, Dec. 24, 1960; s. Mona Joan Lener; m. Jeanette M. Pratt, Dec. 27, 1983; 1 child, Rebecca. BS in Math., BSE in Mech. Engring., MIT, 1982, MSME, 1983, postgrad., 1984—; MD, Stanford U., 1989; MPH, Harvard U., 1998. Diplomate Am. Bd. Med. Examiners, Am. Coll. Radiology; certificate Diagnostic Radiology 1994, Special Competence Nuclear Medicine 1995. Rsch. asst. The Kidney Ctr., Boston, 1979, Beth Israel Hosp., Boston, 1980-81; rsch. engr. Extracorporeal Med. Specialties, King of Prussia, Pa., 1980; engr. IBM, Boulder, Colo., 1981-82, researcher, engr. Palo Alto, Calif., 1982-83; internal med. intern St. Mary's Hosp., San Francisco, 1989-90; radiology resident New England Deaconess Hosp., Boston, 1990-94; fellow nuclear medicine Harvard U., 1993-94; fellow MRI Brigham & Women's Hosp., 1994-95; dir. clin. MRI rsch. U. Melbourne, Australia, 1995-96; assoc. radiologist Alfred Hosp., Melbourne, Australia, 1996; assoc. prof. radiology Boston U., 1996—, assoc. prof. of epidemiology and biostats., 1999—, dir. cardiac MRI, radiology rsch., 2000—, prof., dir. MRI, 2001—, prof. radiology, epidemiology and biostats., 2001—. Adv. bd. Magnetic Resonance Imaging & Single Photon Emission Computed Tomography St. Mary's Hosp., 1990, Digital Radiology New England Deacness Hosp., 1991, Internet Tech. and Care, Boston U.; admissions panel Stanford Med. Sch., 1983; tchr., lectr. and presenter in field. Editor-in-chief: Internat. Jour. Radiology; author: tech. reports and conf. proceedings; contbr. articles to profl. jours. Nat. Hispanic Scholarship Fund scholar, 1979-88, Leopold Schepp Found. scholar, 1979-84, 1987-89, Nat. Med. Found. scholar 1983-84, Paul W. Mayer scholar Alliance for Engring. in Med. and Biology, 1986; Recipient Clapp and Poliak Eng. and Design award, 1980, Luis de Flores award MIT, 1982, special projects award and Rolex award for Innovation, 1993; MIT rsch. fellow 1983, MIT-Harvard HST/Whitaker Found. fellow 1984-87; grantee Sigma Xi, 1981, Hearst Found., 1985-87. Mem. ASME, Internat. Soc. Magnetic Resonance in Medicine, Radiological Soc. of No. Am. (rsch. resident award 1992), N.Y. Acad. Sci. (Otto P. Bergdorf honor 1978), Am. Roentgen Ray Soc. (New England chpt., pres. award 1994, Exec. Coun. award 2001), Internat. Soc. of Magnetic Resonance in Medicine, Pi Tau Sigma, Sigma Xi. Achievements include patents in field of biomedical extracorporeal blood perfusion and filtration with additional work on continuous monitoring of blood pressure via development of new instrumentation; notable work in image analysis with emphasis on three dimensional anatomic reconstruction, on biomedical flow analysis with emphasis on cardiac and kidney function. Office: Boston Univ/Boston Med Ctr Dept Radiology 88 E Newton St Boston MA 02118-2308 Fax: 617-638-6616. E-mail: tello@alum.mit.edu.

TELMER, FREDERICK HAROLD, steel products manufacturing executive; b. Edmonton, Alta., Can., Dec. 28, 1937; Ingar and Gertrude Bernice (Floen) T.; m. Margaret Goddard Hutchings, Oct. 30, 1959; children: Christopher, Kevin, Colin. BA in Econs., U. Alberta, 1961, MA in Econs., 1964. With Stelco, Inc., Hamilton, Ont., Can., 1963—, gen. mgr. corp. affairs and strategic planning Can., 1984-85, v.p. corp. affairs and strategic planning Can., 1985-87, pres. Stelco Steel Can., 1988-90, dir. Can., 1989, chmn., chief exec. officer Can., 1991-97, chmn. Can., 1997—. Founding dir. Japan Soc. Mem. Toronto Club, Burlington Golf and Country Club, Hamilton Golf and Country Club, Delta Kappa Epsilon. Avocations: golf, woodworking, tennis, skiing, piano. Office: Stelco Inc 100 King St W PO Box 2030 Hamilton ON Canada L8N 3T1 E-mail: ftelmer1@cogeco.ca.

TELNACK, METHODIUS RICHARD, priest, monk, craftsman; b. Detroit, May 9, 1928; s. John Joseph Telnack, Anna Catherine Capitan. BA, Sem. of the Holy Ghost, Conyers, Georgia, 1957; PhLic, Pontifical U. of St. Thomas, Rome, Italy, 1962. Ordination to priesthood 1957. Cantor Monastery of the Holy Ghost, Conyers, Ga., 1962—83; procurator Monastery of the Holy Ghost,Inc, 1991—. Prof. philosophy/ theology Monastery of the Holy Ghost, 1962—94. Represented in permanent collections Our Lady of Lourdes Ch., Daytona Beach, Fla., St. Andrew Cath. Ch., St. Brendan Cath..Ch., Clearwater, Fla., St. Mary Cath. Ch., Johnson City, Tenn. Corp. USMC, 1946—48, China/Guam. Mem.: South Rockdale Civic Assn., Conyers/Rockdale C. of C. Roman Catholic. Avocation: music composition. Home and Office: Monastary of the Holy Spirit 2625 Hwy 212 SW Conyers GA 30094

TELSER, LESTER GREENSPAN, educator, economist; b. Chgo., Jan. 3, 1931; s. Asher and Edith (Greenspan) T.; m. Sylvia R. Trossman, June 24, 1956; children— Joshua, Tamar. AB, Roosevelt U., 1951; student, Harvard, 1951-52; A.M., U. Chgo., 1953, PhD in Econs, 1956. Asst. prof. econs. Iowa State U., 1956; mem. faculty Grad. Sch. Bus., U. Chgo., 1958-64; prof. econs. U. Chgo., 1965—. Cons. to industry, 1964— Author: Competition, Collusion and Game Theory, 1972, Functional Analysis in Mathematical Economics, 1972, Economic Theory and the Core, 1978, A Theory of Efficient Cooperation and Competition, 1987, Theories of Competition, 1988. Served with AUS, 1956-58. Fellow Am. Statis. Assn. (asso. editor jour. 1966-69), Econometric Soc.; mem. Am. Econs. Assn. Home: 1456 E 56th St Chicago IL 60637-1866

TELSER, SYLVIA RUTH, retired family life educator, social worker; b. Montreal, Que., Can., Mar. 7, 1930; d. Isaak Isidore and Katherine (Dubiner) Trossman; m. Lester Greenspan Telser, June 24, 1956; children: Joshua, Tamar. BA, McGill U., 1951, MSW, 1953. Psychiat. social worker Jewish Gen. Hosp., Montreal, 1953-55; family caseworker Jewish Family and Community Svc., Chgo., 1955-56; pvt. practice Monterey, Calif., 1957-58; social worker, supr., therapist Children's Home and Aid Soc., Chgo., 1971-86; family life educator Jewish Family and Cmty. Svc., 1986-95. Mem. Hadassah (local program chair 1984-88, pres. 1988—, met. chair Jewish family edn. 1995—). Republican. Jewish. Avocations: gardening, tennis, cross-country skiing. Home: 1456 E 56th St Chicago IL 60637-1866

TEMA-LYN, LAURIE, management consultant; b. Bklyn., Mar. 25, 1951; d. Morton and Jeanne (Lite) Carlin. BA, Bklyn. Coll., 1972. Mgmt. supr. Rapp & Collins, Inc., N.Y.C., 1972-78, v.p., 1978-80; assoc. Synectics, Cambridge, Mass., 1980-83; founder, gen. ptnr. IdeaScope Assocs., 1983-95; prin. Practical Imagination Enterprises, Carlisle, Mass., 1995—. Presenter European Conf. on Innovation and Creativity, 1987, 94. Contbr. articles to bus. publs. Bd. dirs. Arica Inst., N.Y.C., 1979-80; pres. bd. dirs. Savoyand Light Opera Co. Mem. Creative Problem Solving Inst. (presenter, leader), Am. Mktg. Assn., Direct Mktg. Assn. (presenter), Product Devel. Mgmt. Assn., Creative Edn. Found., New Eng. Bus. Assn. for Social Responsibility, Qualitative Rsch. Cons. Assn., Boston Womens Network, Mgmt. Roundtable, Sharing a New Song. Office: Practical Imagination Enterprises 18 Losey Rd Ringoes NJ 08551-1206 E-mail: laurie@practical-imagination.com.

TEMARES, LEE BARNETT, rare book dealer, book appraiser; b. N.Y.C., July 21, 1939; d. Morris Mosses and Estelle (Klugsberg) Barnett; m. Myron Alvin Temares; children: Mark, Matthew, Kari. BA, N.Y.U., 1960. Rare book dealer Manhasset (N.Y.) Art and Antiques Ctr., 1963—. Contbr. articles to profl. jours. Treas. Manhasset Jewish Cmty. Coun., Manhasset, N.Y. 1988—; v.p. Temple Beth Sholom, Flushing, N.Y., 1987—; pres. Friends of Manhasset Pub. Libr. Mem. L.I. Antiquarian Book Dealers Assn. (pres. 1986-90, fair chair 1978—), L.I. Profl. Antiques Dealers Assn., L.I. Book Collectors, N.Y./N.J. Bookdealers Assn., Barbara Johnson Democratic Club. Democrat. Jewish. Avocations: travel, community service, bargain hunting. Home: 50 Heights Rd Plandome NY 11030-1413 Office: Manhasset Art and Antique Ctr 9 George St Manhasset NY 11030-2313 E-mail: tembooks@aol.com.

TEMARES, M. LEWIS, university dean, academic administrator; b. N.Y.C., Feb. 5, 1941; s. Nathan and Gertrude (Weiss) T.; m. Eleanor Liebman, Dec. 8, 1962 (div. Mar. 1975); m. Louise Cortinovis Delphus, Jan. 1, 1989; chidlren: Scott, Stacy, Christy, Jennifer. BBA, MBA; MS, Columbia U.; PhD. V.p. and dean of engring. U. Miami, Fla. Office: Univ of Miami Info Tech Miami FL 33146

TEMERLIN, LIENER, advertising agency executive; b. Ardmore, Okla., Mar. 27, 1928; s. Pincus and Julie (Kahn) T.; m. Karla Samuelsohn, July 23, 1950; children: Dana Temerlin Crawford, Lisa Temerlin Gottesman, Hayden Crawford, Sandy Gottesman. BFA, U. Okla., 1950. Assoc. editor Sponsor Mag., N.Y.C., 1950-51; copywriter Glenn Advt. Inc., Dallas, 1952-54, creative dir., 1954-70, chief oper. officer, 1970-74; pres. Glenn, Bozell & Jacobs, Inc., 1974-79; chmn. bd. dirs. Bozell & Jacobs Inc., 1979-86, Bozell, Jacobs, Kenyon & Eckhardt, Dallas, 1986-89; chmn. Bozell, 1989-92, Temerlin McClain, 1992—. Bd. dirs. East/West Inst. Chmn. Winston Churchill Found. award dinner, 1986; chmn. Dallas Symphony Assn., 1986-88, pres., 1984-86, mem. bd. govs., 1982-84, pres. coun., 1989—; mem. Blair House Restoration Com., 1987-88; vice chmn. Am. Film Inst., 1992-93, bd. trustees, 1992—; bd. dirs. United Way of Met. Dallas Exec. Com., 1986-89, Dallas Bus. Com. for Arts, 1989, Dallas Citizen's Coun., 1984-86, 92; trustee Southwestern Med. Found., 1988—, bd. trustees, 1992—, So. Meth. U., trustee com. Univ. devel., 1988, exec. bd., 1990-91; trustee and chmn. of devel. com. Dallas Mus. Art, 1993-96; mem. steering com. Susan G. Komen Found., 1989-91, art acquisition com. Meyerson Symphony Ctr., 1989-92, exec. coun. Daytop/Dallas, 1989—; chmn. grand opening fortnight Morton H. Meyerson Symphony Ctr., 1989; mem. Madison Coun. Libr. Congress, Washington, 1991—; hon. chair 2d ann. rsch. dinner Am. Lung Assn. Tex., 1996; corp. chmn. Sr. Citizens Greater Dallas for Spirit of Generations Award to Stanley Marcus, 1997; fundraising campaign chmn. Lieberman Rsch. Bldg., Baylor Med. Ctr., 1997; hon. chmn. ann. dinner Make A Wish Found., 1998; mem. exec. bd. Meadows Sch. Arts, So. Meth. U., 2001; co-chair ann. fundraising event Vogel Alcove Child Care Ctr. for the Homeless, 2001; mem. fund devel. adv. com. Jr. League of Dallas, 2001—. Recipient Bill D. Kerss award Dallas Advt. League, 1983, Brotherhood award NCCJ, 1984, Susan G. Komen Found. for Breast Cancer Rsch. Community award, 1989, Neiman Marcus (formerly James K. Wilson) Silver Cup award, 1990, Linz award 1990, Silver Medal award Dallas Advt. League, 1991, Vol. Fundraiser of Yr. award Nat. Soc. Fundraising Execs., 1991, Best Man in Advt. award McCall's Mag., 1992; named Dallas Father of Yr., 1991, So. Meth. U. Sch. of Advertising named Temerlin Advertising Inst. for Edn. and Rsch., 2001.

TEMES, GABOR CHARLES, electrical engineering educator; b. Budapest, Hungary, Oct. 14, 1929; s. Erno and Rozsa (Angyal) Wohl-Temes; m. Ibi Kutasi-Temes, Feb. 6, 1954; children: Roy Thomas, Carla Andrea. Dipl.Ing., Tech. U. Budapest, 1952, DSc (hon.), 1991; Dipl. Phys., Eotvos U., Budapest, 1954; PhD, U. Ottawa, Ont., Can., 1961. Asst. prof. Tech. U. Budapest, 1952-56; project engr. Measurement Engring. Ltd., 1956-59; dept. head No. Electric Co. Ltd., 1959-64; group leader Stanford Linear Accelerator Center, 1964-66; corp. cons. Ampex Corp., 1966-69; prof. elec. engring. UCLA, 1969-90, chmn. dept., 1975-80; dept. head Oreg. State U., Corvallis, 1990—. Cons. Xerox Corp., ANT GmbH Author: (with others) Introduction to Circuit Synthesis and Design, 1977, Analog MOS Integrated Circuits for Signal Processing, 1986; assoc. editor: (with others) Jour. Franklin Inst, 1971-82; co-editor, contbg. author: (with others) Modern Filter Theory and Design, 1973, Oversampling Delta-Sigma Data Converters, 1991. Recipient Western Electric Fund award Am. Soc. Engring. Edn., 1982, Humboldt Sr. Rsch. award, 1991; NSF grantee, 1970— Fellow IEEE (life, editor Transactions on Circuit Theory 1969-71 Best Paper award 1969, 81, 85, Centennial medal 1984, Edn. award 1987, Tech. Achievement award 1989, Grad. Tchg. award 1998, Millenium medal 2000, CAS Golden Jubilee medal 2000). Home: 7100 NW Grandview Dr Corvallis OR 97330-2708 Office: Oreg State U Dept Elec Engring Corvallis OR 97331 E-mail: temes@ece.orst.edu.

TEMIN, DAVIA B. marketing executive; b. Cleve., June 5, 1952; d. J.T. and Sylvia (Black) T.; m. Walter T. Kicinski, Aug. 10, 1991. BA, Swarthmore Pa./Coll., 1974; MA, Columbia U., 1976. Cmty. svcs. specialist Commonwealth Mass., Boston, 1975; editor-in-chief, founder Hermes mag. Columbia U. Bus. Sch., N.Y.C., 1976-79, dir. publ. affairs, 1979-83; v.p., dir. mktg. Citicorp Global Investment Bank, 1983-86; v.p., dir. corp. mktg. Scudder, Stevens & Clark, 1986-89; pres. The Temin Group, 1989-90; v.p., dir. mktg. Schroder Wertheim & Co., Inc., 1990-96; corp. v.p., head corp. mktg. GE Capital, 1996-98; pres. Temin and Co., Inc., 1998—. Exec. prodr. The Night & The Music Prodns., 1994—; bd. dirs. Soma Found.; chmn., bd. dirs. Mark Taylor Dance Co.; advisor to pres. Swarthmore Coll., 1994—, trustee, 1995—99, chair long range planning task force on ednl. leadership and visibility, devel. com., 1995—; bd. advisors Knight-Bagelot Fellowship Journalism Sch. Columbia U., 1995—; pres. bd. dirs., exec. com. Pub. Rels. Soc., N.Y.; bd. advisors Office.com, 2000—; bd. dirs. The Women's Leadership Fund, The White House Project, Women's E-News; adv. bd. Goldman Sachs Investment Mgmt. Fin. Resend Initiative. Chair Women's Counseling Project, 1978-81, Beth Cachet Dance Co., 1980-90; bd. trustees The Elaine Kaufman Cultural Ctr., 2000—. Recipient Meritorious Svc. award Commonwealth of Mass., 1976. Mem. Fgn. Policy Assn., Fin. Women's Assn., Women Pres.'s Orgn., Women Inc., Nat. Arts Club, Strategic Adv. Bd., Devel. Com., Comm. Com., Columbia Bus. Sch. Club, Swarthmore Club, Princeton Club. Home: 530 E 90th St Apt 5K New York NY 10128-7860 Office: Temin and Co Inc Ste 1700 136 E 57th St New York NY 10022-2707

TEMIN, MICHAEL LEHMAN, lawyer; b. Phila., July 18, 1933; s. Henry and Annette (Lehman) T.; children: Aaron Lehman, Seth Lehman; m. Anne L. Hearn, 2000. BA magna cum laude, Yale U., 1954; LL.B. cum laude, U. Pa., 1957. Bar: Pa. 1958, Del. 2000, U.S. Ct. Appeals (3d cir.) 1958, U.S. Supreme Ct. 1969, U.S. Ct. Appeals (2d cir.) 1986, U.S. Ct. Appeals (9th cir.) 1992, U.S. Ct. Appeals (11th cir.) 2002. Asst. U.S. atty. U.S. Atty.'s Office, Phila., 1958-59; assoc. Wolf, Block, Schorr and Solis-Cohen, 1959-66, ptnr., 1966—. Lectr. Law Sch., U. Pa., Phila., 1982-90, adj. prof., 1990-93, 94-95; Thomas A. O'Boyle vis. disting. practitioner, 1985, I. Grant Irey lectr., 1988. Editor U. Pa. Law Rev., 1955-57 Vice chmn. Ednl. Nominating Panel, Phila., 1981-83; bd. dirs. Citizens Com. in Pub. Edn., Phila., 1970-96, pres. 1980-82. Fellow Am. Coll. Bankruptcy (regent); mem. Phila. Bar Assn. (chmn. bankruptcy com., sect. corp., banking and bus. law 1979-86, chmn. profl. guidance com. 1985, sec. sect. corp. banking and bus. law 1985, treas. sect. corp. banking and bus. law 1986, vice chmn. sect. corp. banking and bus. law 1987, chmn. sect. corp. banking and bus. law 1988), Pa. Bar Assn. (ho. of dels. 1985-89, 90—), ABA (bus. bankruptcy com. of sect. corp. banking and bus. law chmn. rules subcom., 1985-92, vice chmn. chpt. 11 subcom. 1992-96, vice chmn. ea. dist. Pa. bankruptcy conf. 1994-95, chmn. ea. dist. Pa. bankruptcy conf., 1995-96), Order of Coif. Jewish. Office: Wolf Block Schorr & Solis-Cohen LLP 22d Flr. 1650 Arch St Philadelphia PA 19103-2029 E-mail: mtemin@wolfblock.com.

TEMIN, PETER, economist, educator; b. Phila., Dec. 17, 1937; s. Henry and Annette T.; m. Charlotte Brucar Fox, Aug. 21, 1966; children: Elizabeth Sara, Melanie Wynn. BA, Swarthmore Coll., 1959; PhD, MIT, 1964. Mem. faculty MIT, 1965—, prof. econs., 1970—. Author: Iron and Steel in Nineteenth Century America, 1964, The Jacksonian Economy, 1969, Casual Factors in American Economic Growth in the 19th Century, 1975, Did Monetary Forces Cause the Great Depression?, 1976, Taking Your Medicine: Drug Regulation in the United States, 1980, The Fall of the Bell System, 1987, Lessons from the Great Depression, 1989, Inside the Business Enterprise, 1991, (with C. Feinstein and G. Toniolo) The European Economy Between The Wars, 1997. Mem. Am. Econ. Assn., Econ. History Assn., Econ. History Soc., Phi Beta Kappa. Home: 15 Channing St Cambridge MA 02138-4713 Office: MIT Dept Econs Cambridge MA 02139

TEMKIN, HARVEY L. lawyer; b. Madison, Wis., Jan. 1, 1952; s. Joe L. and Sylvia (Libanoff) T.; m. Barbara Jean Myers, June 13, 1976; children: James, Daniel, Eli. BA, U. Wis., 1974; JD, U. Ill., 1978. Bar: Wis. 1978. Assoc. Foley & Lardner, Madison, 1978—83; prof. Tulane Law Sch., New Orleans, 1983-87; ptnr. Foley & Lardner, Madison, 1987—2002, Reinhart Boerner Van Deuren, s.c., Madison, 2002—. Lectr. U. Wis. Law Sch., 1990-93; mem. U.S. Senator Feingold's Bus. Adv. Group. 1st v.p. Hillel Found., Madison, 1982-83, bd. dirs., 1987-95; chmn. edn. com. Beth Israel Synagogue, Madison, 1980-82; chmn. Downtown Madison, Inc., 1989-91; chmn. Jewish edn. panel Madison Jewish Community Coun., 1993-98. Fellow Am. Coll. Real Estate Lawyers; mem. ABA (real property probate and trust sect., reporter significant legis. panel 1983-85, significant lit. panel 1985-87). Home: 2313 Sugar River Rd Verona WI 53593-8741 Office: Reinhart Boerner Van Deuren 22 East Mifflin St PO Box 2018 Madison WI 53701-2018 E-mail: htemkin@reinhartlaw.com.

TEMKIN, ROBERT HARVEY, accountant; b. Boston, Oct. 21, 1943; s. Max and Lillian (Giller) T.; m. Ellen Phyllis Band, Sept. 25, 1966; 1 child, Aron; m. Debra Gottlieb, Oct. 3, 1998; 1 child, Rachel; m. Douglas Moore, Feb. 29, 1999; 1 child, Joshua. BBA, U. Mass., 1964. CPA, Mass. With Ernst & Young LLP, 1964—72, 1973—2002, ptnr., 1976—2002, nat. dir. auditing standards, 1980-88; prin. in acctg. practice, 2002—. Assoc. prof. NYU, 1982. Bd. dirs. Jewish Home for Elderly of Fairfield County, 1979-94, pres., 1985-87; mem. Bd. Edn., Weston, Conn., 1983-87; dir. United Synagogue of Conservative Judaism, 1984-99; mem. bus. adv. coun. U. Mass., chmn. acctg. alumni advisory coun.; bd. dirs., vice chair Jewish Cmty. Ctrs. of Greater Boston, Combined Jewish Philanthropies of Greater Boston, exec. com., 1995-99, 2000—, bd. dirs. 1993—; treas. Synagogue Coun., Mass., 1988-93; dir. Hillel Found., U. Mass., 1992-99. Recipient Acctg. Alumni award U. Mass., 1978, Alumnus Award Sch. Mgmt. U. Mass., 1986. Mem. AICPA (staff dir. commn. on auditors responsibilities 1976-78, peer rev. com. 1982-84, auditing stds. bd. 1984-88, chmn. internat. auditing task force 1988-90), Mass. Soc. CPAs (Silver medal 1964), N.Y. State Soc. CPAs, Mass. Bd. Pub. Accountancy (sec. 1996, 2001, chmn. 1997, 2002). Home and Office: 1611 Commonwealth Ave Newton MA 02465-2800 E-mail: robert.temkin@ey.com.

TEMKO, ALLAN BERNARD, writer; b. N.Y.C., Feb. 4, 1924; s. Emanuel and Betty (Alderman) T.; m. Elizabeth Ostroff, July 1, 1950 (dec. Aug. 1996); children: Susannah, Alexander. AB, Columbia U., 1947; postgrad, U. Calif., Berkeley, 1949-51, Sorbonne, 1948-49, 51-52. Lectr. Sorbonne, 1953-54, Ecole des Arts et Metiers, Paris, 1954-55; asst. prof. journalism U. Calif., Berkeley, 1956-62, lectr. in city planning and social scis., 1966-70, lectr. Grad. Sch. Journalism, 1991; lectr. art Stanford U., 1981, 82; architecture critic San Francisco Chronicle, 1961-93, art editor, 1979-82. Archtl. planning cons.; chmn. Yosemite Falls Design Workshop, 1992; Pulitzer Prize juror, 1991-92; architecture advisor Roman Cath. Cathedral, Oakland, Calif., 2000—. Author: Notre Dame of Paris, 1955, Eero Saarinen, 1962, No Way To Build a Ballpark and Other Irreverent Essays on Architecture, 1993; contbr. articles to U.S. and fgn. mags. and newspapers; West Coast editor, Archtl. Forum, 1959-62. Served with USNR, 1943-46. Recipient Gold medal Commonwealth Club Calif., 1956, Silver medal, 1994, Journalism award AIA, 1961, Silver Spur award San Francisco Planning and Urban Renewal Assn., 1985, AIA Inst. Honor award, 1991, Nathaniel A. Owings award AIA Calif. Coun., 1995, 1st prize in archtl. criticism Mfrs. Hanover/Art World, 1986, Critic's award Mfrs. Hanover/Art World, 1987, Profl. Achievement award Soc. Profl. Journalists, 1988, Pulitzer Prize for criticism, 1990; grantee Rockefeller Found., 1962-63, 20th Century Fund, 1963-66, NEA, 1988, Graham Found., 1990; Guggenheim fellow, 1956-57. Home: 1015 Fresno Ave Berkeley CA 94707-2517 *My chief intellectual and professional goal has always been to create excellence in a democratic America and, where possible, in the world at large. This Jeffersonian aim, which came to me directly from Lewis Mumford, naturally includes architecture, environmental planning, the fine arts, and literature. Through education, in which history, criticism, and serious journalism play important roles, I think it is still possible to attain such excellence despite the complex problems of technological civilization.*

TEMKO, STANLEY LEONARD, lawyer; b. N.Y.C., Jan. 4, 1920; s. Emanuel and Betty (Alderman) T.; m. Francine Marie Salzman, Mar. 4, 1944 (dec. Dec. 1998); children: Richard J., Edward J., William D. AB, Columbia U., 1940, LLB, 1943. Bar: N.Y. 1943, D.C. 1951. Practice in, N.Y.C., 1943, 46-47; law clk. Mr. Justice Wiley Rutledge, U.S. Supreme Ct., Washington, 1947-48; legal counsel Econ. Coop. Adminstrn., 1948-49; assoc. Covington & Burling, Washington, 1949-55, ptnr., 1955-90, sr. counsel, 1990—. Editor-in-chief: Columbia Law Rev, 1942-43. Trustee Beauvoir Sch., 1963-69; trustee Columbia U., 1980-91, trustee emeritus, 1991—, mem. bd. visitors Sch. Law, 1961-98, mem. emeritus, 1999—; mem. bd. govs. St. Albans Sch., 1967-73, chmn., 1971-73. 2nd lt. U.S. Army, 1943-46. Decorated Bronze Star; recipient medal for conspicuous alumni svc. Columbia U., 1979. Fellow Am. Bar Found. (chmn. rsch. com. 1970-72); mem. ABA, Am. Law Inst., D.C. Bar Assn., Columbia U. Sch. Law Alumni Assn. (pres. 1982-84), Met. Club, Nat. Press Club, Phi Beta Kappa. Home: 4811 Dexter Ter NW Washington DC 20007-1020 Office: Covington & Burling 1201 Pennsylvania Ave NW Washington DC 20004-2401 E-mail: stemko@cov.com.

TEMME, MARCIA E. See HARDCASTLE, MARCIA E.

TEMMER, JAMES DONALD, museum director; BA, U. Wis., 1987; MA, Marquette U., 1991; postgrad., Pa. State U., 2002—. Dir. Stonefield, Wis., 1996—99, H.H. Bennett & History Ctr., Wisconsin Dells, 1999—2002, Charles Allis/Villa Terr. Art Mus., Milw., 2002—. Recipient Nancy Hanks award for Profl. Excellence, Am. Assn. Mus., 2001. Mem.: State Hist. Soc. Wis. Office: Charles Allis Art Museum 1801 N Prospect Ave Milwaukee WI 53202

TEMMERMAN, ROBERT EUGENE, JR. lawyer; b. Detroit, Dec. 5, 1952; s. Robert E. and Jeanne M. (Schultz) T.; m. Lisa Diane Harvey, Sept. 14, 1985; children: Diane, Alicia, Robert III. BA, Boston Coll., 1975; JD, Santa Clara U., 1980. Bar: Calif. 1980, U.S. Dist. Ct. (no. dist.) Calif. 1980, U.S. Ct. Appeals (9th cir.) 1989, U.S. Supreme Ct. 1997. Pvt. practice Robert E. Temmerman, Jr., Atty. at Law, Campbell, Calif., 1980-98; ptnr. Temmerman & Desmarais, LLP, 1998-99, Temmerman, Desmarais & Phillips, LLP, Campbell, 1999-2000, Temmerman & Desmarais LLP, Campbell, 2000, Temmerman & Cilley LLP, San Jose, 2000—. Co-author: Post Mortem Trust Administration, 1996. Mem. State Bar Calif. (chair exec. com. estate planning, trust and probate law sect. 1997-98). Avocations: wine making, river rafting, skiing. Office: Temmerman & Cilley LLP Ste 150 1960 The Alameda San Jose CA 95126-1441

TEMPEL, JEAN CURTIN, venture capitalist; b. Hartford, Conn., Mar. 23, 1943; d. John J. and Sally (Miller) Curtin Jr.; m. Louis J. Tempel, Nov. 23, 1968 (div. 1978); m. Peter A. Wilson, May 10, 1980. BA in Math., Conn. Coll., 1965; MS in Computer Sci., Rensselaer Poly. Inst., 1972; advanced mgmt. program cert., Harvard U., 1979. Various sr. mgmt. positions Conn. Bank and Trust Co., 1965-80; mgr. strategic planning and mktg. Bank New Eng., 1980-82; sr. v.p., mgr. of custody The Boston Co., 1983, pres. Boston Safe Clearing Corp., 1984-90, exec. v.p., chief ops., info. officer, 1985, exec. v.p., COO, 1988-90; prin. Tempel Ptnrs. Inc., Boston, 1991; pres., COO Safeguard Scientifics Inc., Wayne, 1992-93, bd. dirs.; gen. ptnr. TL Ventures LP, Boston, 1994-96, spl. ltd. ptnr., 1997-99; founder, mng. ptnr. First Light Capital Inc., 2000—. Bd. dirs. Cambridge (Mass.) Tech. Ptnrs., Cambridge, Mass., 1991-98, Centocor, Malvern, Pa., Sonesta Internat. Hotels, Inc., Boston; trustee Scudder Funds, Boston, Northeastern U., Conn. Coll. Trustee Northeastern U., Conn. Coll. Mem. Internat. Women's Forum (dir.). Avocations: skiing, bicycling, sailing. Office: First Light Capital Inc 60 State St Fl 5 Boston MA 02109

TEMPELIS, CONSTANTINE HARRY, immunologist, educator; b. Superior, Wis., Aug. 27, 1927; s. Harry and Thelma Marie (Hoff) T.; m. Nancy Louise Foster, Aug. 27, 1955; children: William H., Daniel S. BS, U. Wis.-Superior, 1950; MS, U. Wis.-Madison, 1953, PhD, 1955. Project assoc. immunology U. Wis., Madison, 1955-57; instr. immunology U. W.Va., Morgantown, 1957-58; asst. rsch. immunologist U. Calif., Berkeley, 1958-66, assoc. prof. immunology, 1966-72, prof., 1972-95, prof. emeritus, 1995—, prof. grad. sch., 1996—. Vis. scientist Wellcome Rsch. Labs., Beckenham, Kent, Eng., 1977-78, U. Innsbruck, Austria, 1985, 90, 91; cons. in field. Contbr. articles to profl. jours. Served with USNR, 1945-46. Recipient Rsch. Career Devel. award, 1965-70; Fogarty sr. internat. fellow NIH, 1977-78 Mem. AAAS, Am. Assn. Immunologists, Fedn. Am. Soc. Exptl. Biology, Sigma Xi. Office: U Calif Sch Pub Health Berkeley CA 94720-0001 E-mail: chtemp@uclink4.berkeley.edu.

TEMPEST, RICK, state representative; m. Donna Tempest; 2 children. Grad. U. Wyo. Mem. Wyo. Ho. of Reps., 1986—, former chmn. appropriations com., former majority floor leader, speaker, 2000—. Active Am. Legis. Exchange Coun.; mem. Energy Coun. Dir. Wyo. Cmty. Devel. Authority; founder Wyo. Bus. Coun.; bd. dirs. Casper Econ. Devel. Alliance. Republican. Avocations: golf, travel, the arts. Office: Speaker of the House 111 W Second # 508 Casper WY 82601 Office Fax: 307-234-2784.*

TEMPESTA, MICHAEL STEVEN, pharmaceuticals company executive, chemist; b. Mpls., Sept. 28, 1952; BA in Chemistry, U. Minn., 1978; MS in Organic Chemistry, U. Ariz., 1980, PhD in Organic Chemistry, 1981. Postdoctoral fellow Suntory Inst. for Bioorganic Rsch., Japan, 1982-83, Columbia U., 1983; asst. prof. organic chemistry U. Mo., Columbia, 1983-90; v.p. chemistry and discovery Shaman Pharms., Inc., San Carlos, Calif., 1990-92, 1993—94, chief tech. officer, 1994—95; chief sci. officer LaRex, Inc., Mpls., 1996—97; sr. v.p. R&D Pharmaprint, Irvine, Calif., 1997—98; pres. NatProd Consulting Svcs., El Granada, 1995—. Presenter confs. including 3d SUNBOR Symposium, Symposio Internacional de Productos Naturales, Post-IUPAC Symposium, AAAS Annual Meeting; rsch. presenter univs. including U. P.R., Nat. Cancer Inst.-Frederick Rsch. Cancer Facility, N.E. Mo. State U., U. Minn., U. Okla., Columbia U., Kans. State U., U. Ariz., U. Hawaii, So. Ill. U., U. Mo.-Columbia and N.W. Mo. State U. Author: (with others) Stereochemistry and Reactivity of Systems Containing Pi Electrons, 1983, Biological, Biochemical and Structural Information, 1990; assoc. editor Internat. Jour. Crude Drug Rsch.; article referee, reviewer jours. including Internat. Jour. Crude Drug Rsch., Jour. Natural Products, Jour. Organic Chemistry, Planta Medica, Sci., Tetrahedron, Tetrahedron Letters. Recipient George T. Walker Rsch. award, 1977, SUNBOR Rsch. award, 1984-86; grantee Am. Chem. Soc.-Petroleum Rsch. Fund, 1984-86, Suntory Found., 1984-87, Mo. Rsch. Assistance Act, 1987-88, Eli Lilly, 1988-89, 89-90, USDA/OIC/ICD, 1988, NSF, 1988, 89-94, Nat. Corn Growers Assn., 1988-89, 89, Formula Funds, 1989, Archer Daniels Midland, 1989-90, Food for 21st Century, 1989-90, MRAA, 1989-90, Shaman Pharms., 1990-91, SBIR-NIH-NDDKD, 1990-91. Mem. AAAS, Am. Chem. Soc. (treas. and sec. Mo. chpt. 1988-89), Am. Soc. Pharmacognosy (mem. awards and funds com. 1989-94), Internat. Union Pure and Applied Chemistry, Phytochem. Soc. Europe, Sigma Xi, Alpha Chi Sigma. Home: PO Box 2439 El Granada CA 94018-2439

TEMPLE, DONALD, retired allergist and dermatologist; b. Chgo., May 21, 1933; s. Samuel Leonard and Matilda Eve (Riff) T.; m. Sarah Rachel Katz, Sept. 29, 1957; children: Michael A., Matthew D., Madeline B. AB in Biology cum laude, Harvard U., 1954; MD, U. Chgo., 1958. Diplomate Am. Bd. Allergy and Immunology, Am. Bd. Dermatology, Nat. Bd. Med. Examiners; lic. Intern Michael Reese Hosp., Chgo., 1958-59; resident in dermatology U. Chgo. Hosps., 1959-62; clin. asst., dept. dermatology Boston U. Sch. Medicine, 1963-64; clin. instr. dermatology Stanford U. Sch. Medicine, 1965; preceptee in allergy Offices of Leon Unger, M.D., and Donald Unger, M.D., Chgo., 1965-69; pvt. practice Des Plaines, Ill., 1969-76; with allergy dept. Glen Ellyn (Ill.) Clinic, 1972-97; ret., 1997. Dermatology and allergy staff Louis A. Weiss Hosp., Chgo., 1965-73, allergy sect. Loyola U. Med. Ctr., Maywood, Ill., 1977-80, exec. and contract medicine coms. Glen Ellyn; clin. asst. prof. dermatology Abraham Lincoln Sch. Medicine, U. Ill., 1972-75; clin. asst. prof. medicine sect. allergy and dermatology, Loyola U., 1977-85; mem. staff Cen. DuPage Hosp., Winfield, Ill., 1973-97, Glen Oaks Med. Ctr., Glendale Heights, Ill., Glendale Heights Community Hosp., 1980-92. Contbr. articles to profl. jours. Bd. dirs. Am. Lung Assn., DuPage, McHenry counties, 1980-91; chmn. Contract Medicine, HMO Com., Glen Ellyn Clinic, 1985, mem. exec. com., 1988-92. Fellow Am. Coll. Chest Physicians, Am. Assn. Cert. Allergists, Am. Coll. Allergists, Am. Acad. Allergy, Ill. Soc. Allergy and Clin. Immunology, Chgo. Dermatol. Soc.; mem. AMA, Ill. State Med. Soc., DuPage County Med. Soc., Chgo. Med. Soc., Fla. Med. Assn. Collier County Med. Soc. Jewish. Avocations: sailing, investing. Home: 6595 Nicholas Blvd Ph 3 Naples FL 34108-7210 Also: 110 E Delaware Pl Apt 2004 Chicago IL 60611-4904 E-mail: chiples@aol.com.

TEMPLE, DONALD EDWARD, medical association executive; b. N.Y.C., Nov. 28, 1946; s. James Edward and Helen Louise (Gannon) T.; m. Lucy Chirinos de Lorentzen, Feb. 23, 1974 (div. 1989); 1 child, Gail Marie. BBA, St. Francis Coll., Bklyn., 1968. Vol. U.S. Peace Corps, Lima, Peru, 1968-72; asst. to pres., gen. mgr. Barrons Ednl. Series, Inc., Hauppauge, N.Y., 1973-78; dir. supply svc. Am. Lung Assn., N.Y.C., 1978-84; bus. mgr. Am. Jour. Respiratory and Critical Care Medicine, 1985—, Am. Jour. Respiratory Cell and Molecular Biology, N.Y.C., 1989—; dir. bus. affairs Am. Lung Assn., 1985-89, dep. mng. dir. bus. affairs, 1990-94; dir. bus. affairs Am. Thoracic Soc., 1994—. Mailers tech. adv. com. U.S. Postal Svc., Washington, 1987-93. Vol. L.I. Assn. AIDS Care, 1994-98. Recipient Merit award Soc. for Tech. Communication, 1990. Mem. Soc. Scholarly Pub., Alliance Non-Profit Mailers (bd. dirs., chmn. tech. com. 1986-94, v.p. 1990-94), Am. Soc. Assn. Execs., Healthcare Mktg. Comms. Coun., N.Y. Soc. Assn. Execs., Soc. Scholarly Pub. Home: 63 Vanderwater St Farmingdale NY 11735-5235 Office: Am Thoracic Soc 61 Broadway New York NY 10006-2747 E-mail: dtemple@thoracic.org.

TEMPLE, JACK DONALD, JR. physician, medical educator; b. Miami, July 30, 1952; s. Jack Donald and Helen (Underhill) T.; m. Regina Ann Kramer, Jan. 14, 1984; children: Laura, Kathleen, Elizabeth. AA, Miami-Dade C.C., 1972; BS in Chemistry, U. Miami, 1974, MD, 1978. Diplomate Nat. Bd. Med. Examiners. Med. intern Jackson Meml. Hosp., Miami, 1978-79, med. resident, 1978-81, clin. fellow, 1981-85, attending physician, 1985—, dir. hematology clinic, 1985-92; clin. instr. U. Miami, 1981-82, asst. prof., 1985-91, assoc. prof., 1991—. Chief med. svc. U. Miami Hosp., 1993—; dir. Harrington Lat. Am. Tng. Programs, Miami, 1992—. Contbr. chpt. to book, articles to med. jours. Named Dr. of Yr. S. Fla. Mag., 1991. Mem. AAAS, Leukemia Soc. Am. (bd. trustees S. Fla. 1992—), U. Miami Alumni Assn. (pres. medicine 1991-94). Achievements include development of new treatments for sickle cell anemia and lymphomatoid granulomatosis. Office: U Miami Sch Medicine Sylvester Cancer Ctr 1475 NW 12th Ave Miami FL 33136-1002

TEMPLE, JOHN R. publishing executive; Mng. editor, pub. & pres. Rocky Mountain News, Denver. Office: Rocky Mountain News 100 Gene Amole Way Denver CO 80204*

TEMPLE, JOSEPH GEORGE, JR. retired pharmaceutical executive, retired chemicals executive; b. Bklyn., Aug. 29, 1929; s. Joseph George and Helen Frances (Beney) T.; m. Ann Elizabeth McFerran, June 21, 1952; children: Linda Jo, James, John. BSChemE, Purdue U., 1951, DEng (hon.), 1988. With Dow Chem. Co., Midland, Mich., 1951-89, v.p. mktg., 1976-78, dir., 1979-94; pres. Dow Chem. Latin Am., Coral Gables, Fla., 1978-80; group v.p. human health Dow Chem. Co., Cin., 1980-83; chief exec. officer, pres. Merrell Dow Pharms. Inc., 1983-87; exec. v.p. Dow Chem. Co., 1983-89; chief exec. officer, chmn. bd. dirs. Merrell Dow Pharms. Inc., Cin., 1988-89; chmn., chief exec. officer Marion Merrell Dow, Inc., Kansas City, Mo., 1989-92, also bd. dirs., chmn., 1992-94, vice chmn., 1994-95; ret., 1995. Former trustee Com. for Economic Devel. Mem. pres.'s coun. Purdue U., 1978—; bd. fellows Saginaw Valley State U., 1987-89. Recipient Disting. Engr. Alumni award Purdue U., 1978, Outstanding Chem. Engr. award Purdue U., 1993. Mem. Am. Inst. Chem. Engrs., Soc. Plastics Industry (bd. dirs. 1980-82), Pharm. Mfrs. Assn. (bd. dirs. 1981-83), Mgmt. Assn. (Silver Knight award 1976, Gold Knight award 1982). Episcopalian.

TEMPLE, LARRY EUGENE, lawyer; b. Plainview, Tex., Dec. 26, 1935; s. Herman Edward and Grace Eileen (Ivey) T.; m. Laura Louann Atkins, Feb. 23, 1963; children: Laura Allison, John Lawrence. BBA, U. Tex., 1957, LLB with honors, 1959; LLD (hon.), Lamar U., 1985. Bar: Tex., U.S. Dist. Ct. (we. dist.) Tex., U.S. Ct. Appeals (5th cir.), U.S. Supreme Ct. Law clk. to justice Tom Clark U.S. Supreme Ct., Washington, 1959-60; assoc. Powell, Rauhut, McGinnis, Reavley & Lochridge, Austin, Tex., 1960-63; legal adminstrn. asst., exec. asst. Tex. Gov. John B. Connally, 1963-67; spl. counsel to pres. Lyndon Baines Johnson, Washington, 1967-69; pvt. practice Austin, 1969—. Bd. dirs. Temple-Inland, Inc., Guaranty Fed. Bank. Mem. U. Tex. Cancer Found., Houston, 1978-84, U. Tex. Devel. Bd., Austin, 1980-85, 90—, chmn., 1993-95; pres. U. Tex. Ex-Students Assn., 1997-98; mem. Tex. Higher Edn. Coordinating Bd., Austin, 1983-89, chmn., 1983-87; chmn. Select Com. for Higher Edn., Austin, 1985-87; bd. dirs. Lyndon B. Johnson Found., 1986—, vice chmn., 1989-2000, pres., 2000—; trustee U. Tex. Law Sch. Found., 1989—. Recipient Faculty award U. Tex. Law Sch., 1987, Humanitarian award Austin region NCCJ, 1988, Santa Rita award U. Tex. System, 1989, Disting. Alumnus award U. Tex., Austin, 1990, Outstanding Alumnus award U. Tex. Law Sch., 1999. Fellow Tex. Bar Found.; mem. ABA, Tex. Bar Assn. (chmn. legis. com. 1980, 83-86), Tex. Jr. Bar Assn. (chmn. bd. dirs. 1967), Austin Jr. Bar Assn. (pres. 1962-63). Democrat. Episcopalian. Home: 2606 Escondido Cv Austin TX 78703-1610 Office: 400 W 15th St Ste 1510 Austin TX 78701-1648

TEMPLE, LEE BRETT, architect, songwriter; b. Balt., June 7, 1956; BArch, Cornell U., 1979. Cert. Nat. Coun. Archtl. Registration Bds. Gen. ptnr. Temple Gebelein Partnership, Ithaca, N.Y., 1981-91; prin. and sole propr. Lee Temple Architect AIA, Ithaca and Crestone, Colo., 1985-98. Vis. critic dept. architecture Cornell U., Ithaca, 1981; vis. prof. architecture Hobart Coll., 1981-82, prof., 1992-93; asst. prof. architecture Syracuse (N.Y.) U., 1982-87. Prin. works include Athena Residence, Chapelle Frontenac; author: Medieval Town Study, 1981; songwriter (CDs) Thunderstormin', Reel Whirl, Last Eagle. Chmn. social justice com. Cornell Cath. Cmty., Ithaca, 1989-92, trustee parish coun., 1989-90; mem. founding bd. dirs. Eco Village at Ithaca, 1991-93; mem. steering com. Tibetan Resettlement Project at Ithaca, 1991-92; founder Sustainable Resource Ctr., Crestone, 1993; founder Temple Mountain Music, 1996. Recipient 1st prize Storey Com. Compact House Competition, 1983; Eidlitz fellow dept. arch. Cornell U., 1979, 81, Design Excellence award AIA, 1987, Residential Design award N.Y. chpt. AIA, 1985-86. Mem. ASCAP, Cousteau Soc. Home and Office: PO Box 220 Crestone CO 81131-0220

TEMPLE, ROBERT, physician, federal agency administrator; b. N.Y.C., July 18, 1941; s. Samuel A. and Judith (Coslow) T.; m. Bonnie Streifer, Oct. 27, 1963; 1 child, James. BA magna cum laude, Harvard U., 1963; MD, NYU, 1967. Diplomate Am. Bd. Internal Medicine, Am. Bd. Clin. Pharmacology. Intern Columbia-Presbyn. Med. Ctr., N.Y.C., 1967-68, resident, 1968-69; clin. assoc. Nat. Inst. Arthritis and Metabolic Disease, NIH, Bethesda, Md., 1969-72; med. officer FDA, Rockville, 1972-74, asst. to dir., bur. of drugs, 1974-76, dir. div. cardio-renal drug products, 1976-82, dir. office drug research and rev., 1982-84, dir. office of drug evaluation I, 1984—. Mem. coop. studies rev. com. VA, 1977-80. Contbr. articles to profl. jours. Served with USPHS, 1969-72. Recipient Disting. Alumni award NYU Sch. Medicine, N.Y. 1987; Pub. HealthSuperior Svc. award HHS, 1986, Disting. Svc. award, 1991. Fellow Am. Coll. Clin. Pharmacology (hon.); mem. Soc. Clin. Trials (bd. dirs. 1983, v.p. 1986, pres. 1987), Am. Soc. Clin. Phrmacology and Therapeutics (awards and com. memberships 1983, bd. dirs. 1987-90, 92—), Alpha Omega Alpha. Democrat. Jewish. Avocations: model trains, tennis, gardening, cooking. Home: 3325 Rowland Pl NW Washington DC 20008-3226 Office: FDA 5600 Fishers Ln Rockville MD 20852-1750

TEMPLE, ROBERT WINFIELD, chemical company executive; b. New Albany, Ind., Feb. 25, 1934; s. Edgar Winfield and Kathryn (Rady) T.; m. Katrina Voorhis, Jan. 4, 1954 (div. Oct. 1970); children: James V., Robert K., Jennifer Anne; m. Katharine Ann Stobbs, Apr. 29, 1977 (div. June 1985); children: Andrew, Philip; m. Angela J. Temple, Aug. 5, 1986; 1 child, Sarah Louise. BSChE, BS in Indsl. Mgmt., postgrad., MIT, 1955, NYU, 1955-58, Columbia U., 1966. Dist. sales mgr. ACF Industries, 1955-59; sr. staff cons. Arthur D. Little, Inc., 1959-64; dir. planning and devel. Am. Cryogenics, Inc., Atlanta, 1964-69; v.p. Williams Bros. Co., 1969; pres. Lang Engring., Coral Gables, Fla., 1970-74; CEO Western Process Co., Geneva and Houston, 1974—87; head agribus and biotechnology Brit.-Am. Tobacco Co., London, 1988—91; pres. TMR-Viterra Interant., Ltd., 1989-92; CEO Gulfcrest Internat., 1987—, Newco Internat., 1999—2001; sr. advisor Bacteria Bar Codes Inc., 1998—2001, Wynthecon, 1999—2001; CEO Surface BioSolutions Inc., 2001—; adv. dir. Telerad, 2002—. Dir. World Congress on Super Conductivity, Global Econ. Action Inst. Conf. on African Devel.; dir. MIT Enterprise Forum (former chmn.); spkr. on mgmt. and mktg. various seminars. Contbr. articles to profl. jours. Fellow Am. Inst. Chemists and Chem. Engrs.; mem. Am. Chem. Soc., Am. Mgmt. Assn., Chem. Mktg. Rsch. Assn., Internat. Food Technologists (chmn. seminars on food irradiation 1995, 99), MIT Alumni Assn. (past regional pres., mem. adv. bd.), Houston Fresh Fruit and Vegetable Assn. (dir., past pres.), Sigma Chi Alumni Assn. Presbyterian. Home: 14134 Bluebird Ln Houston TX 77079-6836 Office: Gulfcrest Internat PO Box 19435 Houston TX 77224-9435 E-mail: rwt@ev1.net.

TEMPLE, WAYNE CALHOUN, historian, writer; b. nr. Richwood, Ohio, Feb. 5, 1924; s. Howard M. and Ruby March (Calhoun) T.; m. Lois Marjorie Bridges, Sept. 22, 1956 (dec. Apr. 1978); m. Sunderine Wilson, Apr. 9, 1979; 2 stepsons, James C. Mohn, Randy E. Mohn. AB cum laude, U. Ill., 1949, AM, 1951, PhD, 1956. Rsch. asst. history U. Ill., 1949-53, tchg. asst., 1953-54; curator ethnohistory Ill. State Mus., 1954-58; editor-in-chief Lincoln Herald, Lincoln Meml. U., 1958-73, assoc. editor, 1973—, also dir. dept. Lincolniana, dir. univ. press, John Wingate Weeks prof. history, 1958-64; with Ill. State Archives, 1964—, now chief dep. dir. Lectr. U.S. Mil. Acad., 1975; sec.-treas. Nat. Lincoln-Civil War Council, 1958-64; mem. bibliography com. Lincoln Lore, 1958—; hon. mem. Lincoln Sesquicentennial Commn., 1959-60; advisory council U.S. Civil War Centennial Commn., 1960-66; maj. Civil War Press Corps, 1962—; pres. Midwest Conf. Masonic Edn., 1985. Author: Indian Villages of the Illinois Country: Historic Tribes, 1958, rev. edits., 1966, 77, 87, Lincoln the Railsplitter, 1961, Abraham Lincoln and Others at the St. Nicholas, 1968, Alexander Williamson-Tutor to the Lincoln Boys, 1971, (with others) First Steps to Victory: Grant's March to Naples, 1977, Lincoln and Grant: Illinois Militiamen, 1981, Stephen A. Douglas: Freemason, 1982, Lincoln as a Lecturer, 1982, By Square and Compasses: The Building of Lincoln's Home and Its Saga, 1984, Lincoln's Connections with the Illinois and Michigan Canal, 1986, Dr. Anson G. Henry: Personal Physician to the Lincolns, 1988, Abraham Lincoln: From Skeptic to Prophet, 1995, Thomas and Abraham Lincoln as Farmers, 1996, Alexander Williamson: Friend of the Lincolns, 1998, By Square and Compass: Saga of the Lincoln Home, 2002; co-author: Illinois's Fifth Capitol: The House that Lincoln Built, 1988; contbg. author: Capitol Centennial Papers, 1988; editor: Campaigning with Grant, 1961, 72, The Civil War Letters of Henry C. Bear, 1961; 71 radio scripts A. Lincoln 1809-1959, Indian Villages of the Illinois Country: Atlas Supplement, 1975; editorial advisory bd. Am. Biog. Inst., 1971— , Ency. Indians of Ams., 1973— ; contbr. articles to profl. jours., encys. Sponsor Abraham Lincoln Bay, Washington Nat. Cathedral; mem. adv. com. Abraham Lincoln Bicentennial Commn.; mem. Ill. State Flag Commn., 1969—; trustee, regent Lincoln Acad. Ill., 1970-82; bd. govs. St. Louis unit Shriners Hosps. for Crippled Children, 1975-81; mem. commissioning com., hon. crew mem. and plank owner USS Springfield submarine, 1990—; hon. crew mem. USS Abraham Lincoln aircraft carrier, 1989—. With U.S. Army, 1943-46, gen. Res. (ret.). Decorated Bronze Star Medal, Silver Citizenship medal SAR, 1993, Literary Merit Gold medal Ill. Lodge of Rsch., 1993; recipient Order of Arrow Boy Scouts Am., 1957, Scouters award, 1960, Scouter's Key, also medallion, 1967, Lincoln medallion Lincoln Sesquicentennial Commn., 1960, award of Achievement U.S. Civil War Centennial Commn., 1965, Algernon Sydney Sullivan medallion, 1969, Distinguished Service award Ill. State Hist. Library, 1969, 77, I.H. Duval Distinguished Service award, 1971, legion of honor Internat. Supreme Council, Order of De Molay, 1972, Disting. Service award Civil War Round Table of Chgo., 1983, 91, Cert. Excellence Ill. State Hist. Soc., 1985, Archbishop Richard Chenevix Trench award, 1999;Lincoln Diploma Honor, Lincoln Meml. U., Harrogate, Tenn., 1963, Lifetime Achievement award 2001; named Hon. Ky. Col., Marshal of Okla. Territory. Fellow Royal Soc. Arts (life); mem. Lincoln Group D.C. (hon.), U. Ill. Alumni Assn., Ill. State Hist. Soc., Board of Advisors, The Lincoln Forum, Ill. Profl. Land Surveyors Assn., Ill. State Dental Soc. (citation plague 1966), Res. Officers Assn., Lincoln Fellowship of Wis., NRA (endowment), Iron Brigade Assn. (hon. life), Mil. Order Loyal Legion U.S. (hon. companion), Mil. Order Fgn. Wars U.S., Masons (33 degree, Meritorious Svc. award, Red Cross of Constantine, grand rep. from Grand Lodge of Colo.), Shriners, K.T., Kappa Delta Pi, Phi Alpha, Phi Alpha Theta (Scholarship Key award), Chi Gamma Iota, Tau Kappa Alpha, Alpha Psi Omega, Sigma Pi Beta (Headmaster), Sigma Tau Delta (Gold Honor Key award for editorial writing), Zeta Psi. Presbyterian (elder). Home: 1121 S 4th Street Ct Springfield IL 62703-2200 Office: Ill State Archives Springfield IL 62756-0001 *Only in America could a poor farm boy from Ohio work his way through a great university, like the University of Illinois, and receive a doctor's degree. Life has been kind to me, and I have tried hard and worked hard. I am proud to be an American.*

TEMPLE, WICK, journalist; b. Little Rock, Oct. 24, 1937; s. Robert Wickliffe and Lorene (Bullard) T.; m. Margaret A. McCay, May 27, 1989; children: Wick III, Ellen Wallace, Carol Halter, Shawn Temple. AA, Texarkana Coll., 1957; postgrad., U. Tex., 1958-59. Reporter, sports editor Texarkana (Tex.) Gazette-News, 1954-58; reporter Austin (Tex.) American-Statesman, 1958-59; reporter, news editor AP, Little Rock, 1959-65, corr. St. Louis, 1965-66, bur. chief Helena, Mont., 1966-68, Seattle, 1968-73, sports editor N.Y.C., 1973-80, mng. editor, 1980-85, dir. human resources, 1985-88, v.p., 1988, dir. newspaper membership, 1988—. Home: 10 Berkeley Rd Millburn NJ 07041-2012 Office: AP 50 Rockefeller Plz New York NY 10020-1605

TEMPLER, DONALD IRVIN, psychologist, educator; b. Chgo., Aug. 26, 1938; s. Irvin Lennox and Berthe Elizabeth (Litwin) T. BA in Psychology, Ohio U., 1960; MA, Bowling Green U., 1961; PhD, U. Ky., 1967. Lic. psychologist, Ky., N.J., Calif. Dir. dept. psychology Western State Hosp., Hopkinsville, Ky., 1965-67; asst. prof. Western Ky. U., Bowling Green, 1967-68; chief psychologist Carrier Clinic, Belle Mead, N.J., 1969-73; dir. psychology Pleasant Grove Hosp., Louisville, 1973-74; chief psychologist Waterford Hosp., St. John's, Newfoundland, 1974-75; pvt. practice Louisville, 1975-78; faculty Calif. Sch. Profl. Psychology, Fresno, 1978—. Contbr. articles to Jour. Abnormal Psychology, Jour. Consulting and Clin. Psychology, Acta Neurologica Scandanavia, Archives Gen. Psychiatry, and Develop. Psychology, Am. Jour. Mental Deficiency, Perceptual and Motor Skills, Physiology and Behavior, Am. Psychologist, Jour. Clin. Psychology, British Jour. Psychiatry, Psychol. Documents, Internat. Jour. Addictions, Rsch. Communications in Chem. Pathology and Pharmacology, others; author 3 books; editorial bd. Omega; reviewer Addictive Behaviors, Internat. Jour. Aging and Human Devel., Jour. Abnormal Psychology, Jour. Rsch. in Personality, Perceptual and Motor Skills, others. Fellow Am. Psychol. Soc., Am. Psychol. Assn. Office: Calif Sch Profl Psychology 1350 M St Fresno CA 93721-1808

TEMPLETON, ALAN ROBERT, biology educator; b. Litchfield, Ill., Feb. 28, 1947; s. John Smith and Lois Arlene (McCormick) T.; m. Bonnie A. Altman, Dec. 20, 1969; children: Jeremy Alan, Jeffrey Alan. BA, Washington U., 1969; MS in Stats., PhD in Genetics, U. Mich., 1972. Jr. fellow Mich. Soc. Fellows, Ann Arbor, 1972-74; asst. prof. U. Tex., Austin, 1974-77; assoc. prof. Washington U., St. Louis, 1977-81, prof., 1981—, Charles Rebstock prof. biology, 2001—. Cons. St. Louis Zool. Park, 1979—; founding mem., dir. Soc. for Conservation Biology, 1985—. Editor: Theoretical Population Biology, 1981-91; mem. editorial bd. Molecular Phylogenetics & Evolution, 1991—, Brazilian Jour. of Genetics, 1991-97, Genetics and Molecular Biology, 1998—; assoc. editor Am. Naturalist, 2002-; contbr. numerous article to profl. jours. Grantee NSF, 1974-80, 90—, NIH, 1980—, Nixon Griffis Fund for Zool. Rsch., 1986-87, Burroughs Welcome Fund for Functional Genomics, 2000—. Fellow AAAS; mem. Soc. for Study Evolution (v.p. 1982, pres. 1996-97), Genetics Soc. Am., Soc. Conservation Biology (bd. dirs. 1985-88), Nature Conservancy (trustee Mo. chpt. 1988—, v.p. 1996-2000). Avocations: hiking, caving, music, ethnomusicology, scuba diving. Office: Washington U Dept Biology Saint Louis MO 63130-4899

TEMPLETON, ANN, artist, educator; b. Houston, July 2, 1936; d. Lawrence L. and Marie L. (Bergeron) St. Pe'; m. James D. Templeton, Nov. 19, 1955; children: Pamela A., Donna M., James D. II, Donald L. Student, Massey Bus. Coll. Sec. A.M. Lockett Inc., Houston; owner Studio I and Gallery II; self-employed artist, instr. Ann Templeton Arts Inc., Ruidoso Downs, N.Mex. Instr. workshops and seminars, 1983—; juror at numerous art shows; instr. Okla. Christian Coll., Norman, 1997, Grayson County Coll., Tex., 1986, Jackson Jr. Coll., Tenn., 1983, 86, Lufkin Jr. Coll., Tex., 1986, San Juan Coll., Farmington, N.Mex., 1988, 90, 92, Ea. N.Mex. U., Ruidoso, 1994; artist-in-residence Fairmont (W.Va.) State Coll., 1998; represented by Brazier Fine Arts, Richmond, Va., Mahon Fine Arts, Ruidoso, Hilton Head Isle, S.C., Total Arts Gallery, Taos, N.Mex., Riverbend Gallery, Marble Falls, Tex., Jayne Gallery, Kansas City, Mo., Rich Designs, Colorado Springs, Colo., Rice Gallery, Denver, Ann Hughes Ballery, Dallas. Exhibited in group shows at Colony Show, Ruidoso, 1990, 91, Tex. Arts Festival, Lubbock, 1990, 96, N.Mex. State Arts Fair, 1990, 91, Knickerbocker N.Y., 1990, Mus. of the Horse, Ruidoso, 1992-95, 97, Shasta County Western Invitational, 1993, Tres Amigoes, Ruidoso, 1993-97, N.Mex. State Capitol, 1994, Roby Mills Exhbn., Colorado Springs, Colo., 1995, Permian Basin Art Inst., Odessa, Tex., 1995-96, Lafayette Art Assn., 1996, N.Mex. Pastel Soc., 1996, N.W. Pastel Soc., Washington, 1996, Pratt Gallery, San Diego, 1996, 98, 99, Bardean Gallery, Albuquerque, 1997, 98, Allied Artists Am., 1997, Brazier Fine Arts, Richmond, Va., 1998, Carlsbad (N.Mex.) Mus., 1998, Fairmont State Coll., W.Va., 1998, Heart Inst., Magnolia, Ark., 1998, Quinlan Art Ctr., Gainsville, Ga., 1999; represented in permanent collections at San Juan C.C., Farmington, N.Mex., Brownsville (Tex.) Art Mus., Hill Country Arts Found., Ingram, Tex., Coupeville (Wash.) Arts Ctr., Ellen Noe'l Art inst. of Permian Basin, Odessa, Carlsbad Art Mus., also corp. and pvt. collections. Recipient Best and Brightest award Scottsdale Artists Sch., 1989, awards N.Mex. Art League, 1993, Franklin Sq., N.C., merit award J.R. Mooney Debut, 1994, Harbor County competition, 1995, Grumbacher Gold medal Lafayette Art Assn., 1996, 2d pl. award Mus. of the Horse, 1997, Slide Registry award Internat. Assn. Pastel Socs., 1998, 2d pl. award EuroFare Internat. Art Competition. others. Mem. N.Mex. Art Guild (life mem., hon. mem.), Gulf Coast Art Guild (pres.), Pasadena Gulf Coast Art Soc. (hon., past pres.), Women in Arts, N.Mex. State Arts Assn., N.Mex. Art League (hon., award 1993), Oil Painters Am. (assoc.), Allied Artists Am. (assoc.), Pastel Soc. Am. (assoc.), Knickerbocker Artists USA (signature), Kans. Soc. Oil Painters (signature, award 1987). Roman Catholic. Avocations: music, books. Home: PO Box 651 Ruidoso Downs NM 88346-0651

TEMPLETON, DAVID HENRY, JR. chemist, educator; b. Houston, 1920; s. David Henry Templeton and Miriam Clark; m. Lieselotte Kamm; children: Diana Killen, Alan. BS, La. Tech U., 1941; MA, U. Tex., 1944; PhD, U. Calif., Berkeley, 1947, U. Uppsala, 1977. Chemist Manhattan Project, Chgo., 1944—46; instr., asst. prof., assoc. prof. U. Calif., Berkeley, 1947—58, prof., 1958—90, prof. emeritus, 1990—. Dean coll. of chemistry U. Calif., Berkeley, Calif., 1970—75. Grantee John Simon Guggenheim Fellowship, Guggenheim Found., 1954—68. Fellow: AAAS; mem.: Am. Chem. Soc., Am. Crystallographic Assn. (pres. 1984, A.L.Patterson Award (with Lieselotte Templeton) 1987). Home: 1244 Brewster Dr El Cerrito CA 94530 Personal E-mail: dhtem@aol.com.

TEMPLETON, DENNIE, III, educational administrator, consultant; b. San Antonio, Dec. 12, 1948; s. Dennie E. and Helen (Gamble) T.; m. Debra Roberts, July 17, 1992. BA in Bus., U. Hawaii, 1987; BA in Vocat. Edn., So. Ill. U., 1991; M of Tech. Edn., U. Ga., 1995, EdD, 1998. Master chief petty officer/LTJG (lieutenant JG) U.S. Navy, 1971, served, 1971-92; retired USN, 1992; rsch., tng. U. Ga., Athens, 1993-97; dir. instrnl. devel. and distance edn. Patrick Henry C.C., Martinsville, Va., 1997-99; dir. distance edn. Radford Univ., 1999—. Cons. U. Ga., 1996. Rschr. in field. Mem. Internat. Tech. Edn. Assn., Tng. Devel. Assn., USS Nevada Assn. Avocations: music, golf, tennis. Office: Radford U PO Box 6719 Radford VA 24142-6719 Home: 189 Fairway Dr Radford VA 24141-3905

TEMPLETON, HILDA B. psychiatrist, educator; BA in Biology, Rutgers U., Newark, 1962, MS in Biol. Scis., 1965; MD, U. Medicine and Dentistry N.J., 1978. Diplomate Am. Bd. Psychiatry and Neurology. Tchg. asst. in physiology Rutgers U., 1963-65; field dir. state of La. Med. Com. for Human Rights, 1965; dir. health and welfare The Urban League of Essex County, N.J., 1965-67; rsch. asst. dept. anatomy U. Medicine and Dentistry N.J., 1970-71; tchr. Ctrl. Mid. Sch., Orange, N.J., 1971-74; intern N.J. Med. Sch., 1978-79; resident Rutgers Med. Sch., 1981, chief resident, 1981; sr. resident Princeton (N.J.) Med. Ctr., 1982; pvt. practice Livingston, N.J., 1982—; clin. asst. prof. psychiatry and behavioral medicine N.Y. Coll. Osteo. Medicine N.Y. Inst. Tech., 1998—. Attending physician dept. psychiatry, dept. ob-gyn. St. Barnabas Med. Ctr., Livingston, 1982—, chair dept. psychiatry, 1997-2000, clin. chief dept. psychiatry, 1986-90, 91-93, 95-97, assoc. clin. chief dept. psychiatry, 1985-86, acting chair dept. psychiatry, 1986-87, mem. various hosp. coms.; clin. instr. dept. psychiatry U. Medicine and Dentistry of N.J., 1987-97; cons. Kessler Inst. for Rehab., 1982-91, Cmty. Psychiat. Inst., 1982-85, Jewish Vocat. Svcs., 1982-88; med. dir. interim out-patient program East Orange (N.J.) Gen. Hosp., 1982-83; mem. assoc. med. staff Fair Oaks Hosp., Summit, N.J., 1980-82; lectr. in field. Chair Newark Arts and Scis. Devel. Coun., Rutgers U. Found., 1995—; mem. leadership com. Campaign for Cmty., Diversity and Ednl. Excellence, 1994—96; nat. bd. dirs. Down Syndrome Soc., 2001—; mem. med. adv. bd. No. N.J. chpt. Nat. Multiple Sclerosis Soc., 1982—86; mem. governing bd. The Cmty. Mental Health Ctr. of the Oranges, Maplewood and Millburn, 1983—84. Mem. AMA, Am. Soc. Psychosomatic Ob-Gyn., Am. Psychiat. Assn., Med. Women's Assn., Post Partum Internat., Depression After Delivery, N.J. Acad. Medicine, N.J. Psychiat. Assn., Tri-County Med. Soc., Essex County Med. Soc. (chmn. com. mental health 1998—). Office: 22 Old Short Hills Rd Ste 217 Livingston NJ 07039-5605 E-mail: hbtmdi@msn.com.

TEMPLETON, JOHN ALEXANDER, II, coal company executive; b. Chgo., Mar. 31, 1927; s. Philip Henry and Florence (Moore) T.; m. Norma Frazier, Aug. 10, 1949; children: Lori, Linda, Leslie, Sally. BS, Ind. U., 1950. Agt. Conn. Mut. Life Ins. Co., Terre Haute, Ind., 1949-51; ptnr. Miller, Templeton, Scott Ins. Agy., 1951-64, elected chmn., 1994, also bd. dirs.; pres. Sherwood Templeton Coal Co., Inc., Indpls., 1968—, also bd. dirs. Bd. dirs. Plumb Supply Co., Des Moines, Dicksons, Inc., Seymour, Ind., Mchts. Nat. Bank Terre Haute. Chmn. Vigo County Goldwater for Pres. Com., 1964; trustee Union Hosp., 1968—, v.p., 1975—, chmn. bd. dirs., 1986-91; bd. dirs. Ind. State U. Found., 1970—; trustee U. Evansville, 1974-77; v.p., trustee Ind. Asbury Towers, Greencastle, 1980-83. With U.S. Army, 1946-48. Mem. Ind. Assn. Ins. Agts. (pres. 1959-60), Ind. Coal Assn. (bd. dirs.), Lynch Coal Ops. Reciprocal Assn., Interstate Coal Conf., Ind. C. of C. (bd. dirs. 1981-95), Ind. U. Alumni Assn. (exec. coun. 1983-86), Masons, Elks. Republican. Methodist.

TEMPLETON, JOHN MARKS, JR. retired pediatric surgeon, foundation executive; b. N.Y.C., Feb. 19, 1940; s. John Marks and Judith Dudley (Folk) T.; m. Josephine J. Gargiulo, Aug. 2, 1970; children: Heather Erin, Jennifer Ann. BA, Yale Coll., 1962; MD, Harvard U., 1968; hon. degree, Beaver Coll., Buena Vista U., Va. Commonwealth U., Alvernia Coll. Intern Med. Coll. Va., Richmond, 1968-69, resident, 1969-73; prof. pediat. surgery U. Pa. and Children's Hosp. Phila., 1995, dir. trauma program, 1989-95. Chmn. bd. Templeton Growth Fund, Ltd. Assoc. editor: Textbook of Pediatric Emergencies, 1993; pub. 6000 Name Geneology, 1997, A Searcher's Life, 1999. Chmn. health and safety, exec. bd. Cradle of Liberty coun. Boy Scouts Am.; mem. exec. bd. Eastern U., Fgn. Policy Rsch. Inst., Nat. Recreation Found., Melmark Charitable Found.; nat. bd. dirs., pres. Pa. divsn. Am. Trauma Soc.; bd. dirs. Nat. Bible Assn., Nat. Liberty Mus., Phila.; elder Proclamation Presbyn. Ch.; pres. John Templeton Found. With M.C., USNR, 1975-77. Barclay fellow Templeton Coll., Oxford U., Eisenhower Exch. fellow, fellow George H. Gallup Internat. Inst.; mem. Order of Charlemagne. Mem. ACS, AMA, Am. Pediat. Surg. Assn., Am. Acad. Pediats., Am. Assn. Surgery Trauma, Ea. Assn. Surgery Trauma, Phila. Coll. Physicians, Union League, Lyford Cay Club, Merion Cricket Club, Athenaeum Club London, Rotary Internat., White's London, United Oxford and Cambridge U. Club (London). Republican. Evangelical. Office: 5 Radnor Corp Ctr Ste 100 Radnor PA 19087-4534 E-mail: mcgraw@templeton.org.

TEMPLETON, JOHN MARKS, investment counsel, financial analyst; b. Winchester, Tenn., Nov. 29, 1912; s. Harvey Maxwell and Vella (Handly) T.; m. Judith Dudley Folk, Apr. 7, 1937 (dec. Feb. 1951); children: John Marks, Anne Dudley, Christopher Winston; m. Irene Reynolds Butler, Dec. 31, 1958 (dec. Nov. 1993). AB, Yale U., 1934; MA (law) (Rhodes scholar), Balliol Coll., Oxford, Eng., 1936; LLD (hon.), Beaver Coll., 1965, Marquette U., 1980, Jamestown Coll., 1983, Maryville Coll., 1984, Babson Coll., 1992, Rhodes Coll, 1992, U. Rochester, 1992, La. Coll., 1993, Moravian Coll., 1994; D.Litt. (hon.), Wilson Coll., 1974; D.D. (hon.), Buena Vista Coll., 1979; D.C.L. (hon.), U. of South, 1984; DLitt (hon.), Manhattan Coll., 1990; LHD, U. Dubuque, 1992, Fla. Southern Coll., 1992; DLitt (hon.), Campbell U., 1993; LLD, Moravian Coll., 1994; DPhil (hon.), Stonehill Coll., 1995; LHD (hon.), Furman U., 1995; LLD (hon.), Notre Dame U., 1996, Methodist Coll., 1997; LHD (hon.), Brigham Young U., 1998, Queens Coll., 1999. CFA. Sec.-treas., v.p., dir. Nat. Geophys. Co., Dallas and N.Y.C., 1937-41; pres., dir. Templeton, Dobbrow & Vance, Inc., N.Y.C., 1941-65; chmn. Templeton Damroth Corp., 1959-62; v.p., dir. First Trust Bank Ltd., Bahamas, 1963—; pres., dir. Templeton Funds Inc., 1977-86, Templeton Global Funds Inc., 1981-86, Templeton Growth Fund Can., Ltd., Toronto, 1954-85; chmn Templeton Galbraith & Hansberger Ltd, 1986-92. Author: The Humble Approach, 1981; co-author: The Templeton Touch, 1985, The Templeton Plan, 1987, Global Investing, 1988, The God Who Would Be Known, 1989, Riches for the Mind and Spirit, 1990, Looking Forward, 1993, Discovering the Laws of Life, 1994, Is God the Only Reality?, 1994, Evidence of Purpose, 1994, Future Agenda, 1995; contbr. articles to fin. publs. Past pres. Lyford Cay (Bahamas) Property Owners Assn.; Chmn. YMCA Bergen County, 1952-54; dir., campaign chmn. Englewood Community Chest, 1953-54; trustee Englewood Hosp., 1953-56, Soc. for Promoting Christian Knowledge, 1984-87, Balliol Coll. Endowments (Oxford), Templeton Project Trust (Eng.); chmn. bd. trustees Princeton Theol. Sem., 1967-73, 79-85, trustee for restoration of Westminster Abbey, 1991—; trustee Wilson Coll., 1941-73, Buena Vista Coll., 1981—, Templeton Found. Inc., 1952—, John Templeton Found. Inc., 1987—, council on theol. sems. United Presbyn. Ch. U.S.A., 1946-83; mem. Ctr. Theol. Inquiry, 1979-92, Commn. on Ecumenical Mission, 1961-70; bd. corporators Presbyn. Ministers Fund, Inc., 1960-93; bd. visitors Harvard Div. Sch., 1981-88; adv. bd. Harvard Ctr. for the study of World Religions, 1975-89; bd. mgrs. Am. Bible Soc., 1972-92; mgmt. Council Templeton Coll. (Oxford); pres. Templeton Theol. Sem., Bahamas, 1984-88; hon. rector Dubuque U., 1982-92. Decorated knight Order of Brit. Empire, Knight of St. John; recipient Churchman of Yr. award Religious Heritage Am., 1979, Internat. Churchman of Yr. award, 1981, Ecumenical Patriarch's Hon. Order of Mt. Athos, Free Enterprise award Palm Beach Atlantic Coll., 1984, Centennial medal N.Y. Mayflower Soc., 1987, award USA Today, 1991, award for excellence in investment mgmt., 1991, Benjamin Franklin award Royal Soc. Arts, 1994, Lifetime Achievement award Laymans Nat. Bible Assn., 1995, Nat. Bus. Hall of Fame award Jr. Achievement Assn., 1996, Interfaith gold medallion Internat. Coun. Christians and Jews, 1997, Abraham Lincoln award, 1997, Ind. award Brown U., 1998, Alexis de Tocqueville award Ind. Inst., Calif., 1998, Faith and Freedom award Action Inst., 2000, Faith and Fredom award Action Inst., 2000; named to Wall Street Week Hall of Fame, 1990. Mem. Soc. Security Analysts, World Pres. Orgn., Chief Execs. Orgn. (pres. 1968-69), Bahamas C. of C. (bd. dirs. 1976-79), Internat. Acad. Religious Scis., Mt. Pelerin Soc., Elihu Club, Elizabethan Club (New Haven), Yale Club, University Club (N.Y.C.), Lyford Cay Club of Bahamas (dep. chmn. 1980-86), Lansdowne Club, Royal Overseas League, Athenaeum (Eng.), United Oxford and Cambridge Univs. Club (Eng.), White's Club (Eng.), Rotary (Bahamas), Phi Beta Kappa., Zeta Psi. Office: Box N7776 Nassau The Bahamas

TEMPLETON, ROBERT EARL, engineering and construction company executive; b. Pitts., June 21, 1931; s. Robert James and Alice Wilma (Scheppele) T.; m. Barbara Ann McDonald, June 9, 1956; children: Shirley Anne (dec.), Susan Elaine, Sally Irene. BSCE, Carnegie Mellon U., 1953, MSCE, 1954; MBA in Mgmt., NYU, 1960. Registered profl. engr., N.Y. With M.W. Kellogg Co., Houston, 1954-93, project engr., 1963-66, mgr. contract status, 1966-68, mgr. sales forecasting, 1968-72, mgr. market forecasting, 1972-73; mgr. Venture Analysis, 1973-74, mgr. analysis and methods divsn., 1974-76, mgr. Project Cost Services divsn., 1976-81, mgr. Cost Mgmt. Services divsn., 1981-85, project control mgr., 1985-93; pres. Templeton Enterprises Inc., 1993—; project mgmt. profl. cons. Steege Kingston & Assocs., Inc., 1993-96, Team Assocs. Inc., Houston, 1996—. Cons. project mgmt. profl., total cost mgmt., work process improvement, reengring., benchmarking, electronic data interchange Internat. Stds. Orgn., 9000 Quality Sys. Stds., Houston, 1993—. Mem. editl. bd. Engring. and Process Econs., 1976-85. Area chmn. United Campaign, Summit, N.J., 1969-70; v.p. Jefferson Sch. PTA, Summit, 1965-67, pres., 1967-69; security chmn. Fonn Villas Civic Assn., Houston, 1973, chmn. archtl. stds. com., 1974, v.p., 1975, pres., 1976; mem. exec. com., bd. dirs. Houston Advs. for Mentally Ill Children; active Can Care of Houston Inc., For-By-To Cancer Survivors (ch. ministry), Income Tax Assistance (VITA), Tax Counseling for the Elderly (TCE), AARP, Houston. J. Waldo Smith Hydraulic fellow ASCE, 1953-54 Fellow Am. Assn. Cost Engrs. (award of merit 1977, award of recognition 1980, cert. cost engr.; nat. pres. 1971-72, nat. adminstrv. v.p. 1970-71, nat. adv. staff 1973—, spl. projects chmn. 1974-75, cert. bd. chmn. 1976-79, chmn. assn. standards and recommended practices com. 1985-89, chmn. quality mgmt. com. 1988—, chmn. inter-orgnl. liaison com. 1995-98, co-chair enabling technologies com., 1998—); mem. N.Am. Soc. Corporate Planners (program dir. 1974, chmn. ad hoc cert. com. 1986—), Am. Assn. Engring. Socs., Project Mgmt. Inst. (cert. project mgmt. profl., v.p. certification Houston chpt. 1993-94, v.p. edn. 1985-86, 87-88, 91-92, pres. 1988-89, chmn. advisor 1989-90), Sigma XI (Sec. M.W. Kellogg br. 1973-74), Sigma Xi (2d v.p. 1976-77, 84-85, 1st v.p. 1985-86), Houston Comml. Bridge League (v.p. 1973-75), Houston C. of C. (life mem., dir. engring. and constrn. internat. bus. network exec. com.), Am. Mktg. Assn., Acad. for Health Services Mktg. (profl. mem.), Health Services Mktg. Soc. (bd. dirs.), Tau Beta Pi, Beta Theta Pi. Republican. Presbyterian (deacon 1956-59, elder 1980-82). Club: M.W. Kellogg Quarter Century (pres. 1986-87) Home and Office: 12718 Old Oaks Dr Houston TX 77024-4016 E-mail: 102501.36@compuserve.com.

TEMPLIN, CARL ROSS, college dean, educator; b. Salt Lake City, Jan. 8, 1951; s. Carl Alma and Darlene (Bunkall) T.; m. Shirley Oram, May 4, 1973; chldren: Carl Allen, David Brian, Aaron Michael, Angela Ruth, Joshua Ryan. BA in Humanities, Brigham Young U., 1975; MBA, U. Wyo., 1979; PhD in Bus., Ariz. State U., 1988. Missile launch officer 90th Strategic Missile Wing, Warren AFB, Wyo., 1975-79; contracting officer Ogden Air Logistics Ctr., Hill AFB, Utah, 1980-85; from asst. prof. to assoc. prof. contracting Air Force Inst. Tech., Wright-Patteson AFB, Ohio, 1988-94, dean, 1994-95; dean Sch. Bus. So. Utah U., Cedar City, 1997—, interim provost, 2001-02. Mem. acquisition adv. coun. Def. Logistics Agy., Washington, 1991-92. Mem. editl. adv. bd. Air Force Jour. Logistics, 1994-95; contbr. articles to profl. jours. Mem. Iron County Econ. Devel. Com., Cedar City, 1998—. Recipient Field award in contracting edn. Dayton chpt. Soc. Logistics Engrs., 1990. Mem. Nat. Assn. Purchasing Mgmt., Phi Kappa Phi, Beta Gamma Sigma, Sigma Iota Epsilon. Avocation: music. Home: 2170 W Cedar Hills Dr Cedar City UT 84720-8275 Office: So Utah U Coll Bus and Tech Cedar City UT 84720 E-mail: templin@suu.edu.

TEMPLIN, KENNETH ELWOOD, paper company executive; b. Mason City, Nebr., Jan. 26, 1927; s. Otto Rudolph and Marianna (Graf) T.; m. Harriet Elaine Ressel, Aug. 24, 1951; children: Steven, David, Daniel, Benjamin, Elizabeth. BS in Bus. Adminstrn, U. Nebr., 1950; MBA, Wayne State U., 1961. Fin. analyst Ford Motor Co., 1950-54; fin. analyst, corp. staff Chrysler Corp., 1955-60, div. controller marine engine div., 1961-63, gen. sales mgr., 1964-65; v.p. Marsh and Templin, N.Y.C., 1966-69; v.p., gen. mgr. operating group Saxon Industries, 1970-79, group v.p., 1979-82, sr. v.p., c.o.o., 1982-85; v.p.-converting Paper Corp. Am., Wayne, Pa., 1985-86; exec. v.p. Quality Park Products Inc., St. Paul, 1986-88, 1986-88, pres., 1988-96, ret., 1996. Mem. exec. com. Single Service Inst., 1971-79 Regional chmn. Minn. devel. com. Nat. Multiple Sclerosis Soc., 1970-71; co-pres. Home and Sch. Assn., Bernardsville, N.J., 1975-76; bd. dirs. West Hennepin Counseling Svcs., Inc., 1996-2000, Brain Injury Assn. Minn., 1997-2001; mem. Svc. Corps Ret. Execs. (SCORE), 1996—, chmn. Mpls. chpt., 1999-2000; bd. dirs. Hennepin History Mus., 2000—. With U.S. Army, 1945-47, 50-51. Mem. Envelope Mfrs. Assn. Am. (postal affairs com. 1989-96, fin. com. chmn. 1994-95, bd. dirs. 1990-91, 93-95). Presbyterian. E-mail: templink@aol.com.

TENBOSCH, GERALD JOHN, fundraising executive; b. Cin., Dec. 22, 1950; s. Karl Alfred and Gertrude (Lowenbeg) T.; m. Betsy Ann Tenbosch, Jan. 16, 1976; children: David, Gabe, Abby. AA, U. Cin., 1971, BS, 1973, MS, 1981. Youth supr., career mgr. Citizen's Com. on Youth, Cin., 1973-78; project mgr. Cin. Bd. Edn./Pub. Schs., 1978-81; project dir. Workshop for Retarded Citizens, 1981-82; asst. dir. regional office City of Hope Med. and Rsch. Ctr., 1982-84; resource devel. dir. Cin. Speech and Hearing Ctr., 1984-96; exec. dir. Invest in Neighborhoods Inc., Cin., 1996—. Mem. adv. bd. Ret. Sr. Vol. Program, Cin., 1983-89. Bd. dirs. Finneytown Elem. PTA, Cin., 1988-95. Mem. Nat. Soc. Fundraising Execs. (treas., officer 1984-90), Assn. Vol. Adminstrn., Finneytown Athletic Assn. Jewish. Avocations: sports, coaching, golf, family activities. Home: 1009 Pinehollow Ln Cincinnati OH 45231-5732 Office: Invest in Neighborhoods Inc 927 Mcpherson Ave Cincinnati OH 45205-1814

TENCA, ALEXANDRE FERREIRA, computer engineer, educator; b. President Prudente, São Paulo, Brazil, Apr. 23, 1958; s. Jabes Pinto and Dirce (Ferreira) Tenca; m. Williane Munhoz Ribeiro, May 29, 1965; children: Jean, Caio. BE in Elec. Engring., Sch. Polytech. U. São Paulo, Brazil, 1981; MS in Elec. Engring., Sch Polytech. U. São Paulo, Brazil, 1990; MS in Computer Sci., Sch. of Engring. and Applied Sci. UCLA, 1994; PhD in Computer Sci., Sch. of Engring. and Applied Sci.UCLA, 1998. Cert. Elec. Engr., CREA, Brazil, 1981. Prof. Sch. Polytech. U. São Paulo, Brazil, 1989—97; rschr. and project mgr. Fundação para o Desenvolvimento Tecnológico da Engenharia, Brazil, 1981—92; rsch. asst. UCLA, 1997—98, tchg. fellow, 1997, tchg. assoc., 1993—96; prof. Oreg. State U., ECE, Corvallis, Oreg., 1998—. Contbr. articles to profl. jours.sci. papers to confs., lectr. notes. Recipient CAREER Award, NSF, 2001-2005, Citation: Outstanding PhD, Sch. of Engineering and Applied Sci., Computer Sci. Dept., 1998, Scholarship, CNPq, 1992. Mem.: IEEE Computer Soc. (chair session on computer arithmetic 1999—), SPIE. Office: Oreg State Univ - ECE Dept 220 Owen Hall Corvallis OR 97331-3211 Office Fax: 541-737-1300. Business E-Mail: tenca@ece.orst.edu.

TENDLER, DAVID, international trade company executive; b. N.Y.C., Jan. 15, 1938; s. Philip and Pearl (Berman) T.; m. Beatrice Weisberg, Oct. 11, 1958; children: Pearl, Karen. BBA in Internat. Econs., CCNY, 1959. With Philipp Bros. Co., 1960—, mgr. Far Eastern ops., 1968-75, pres., 1975—; dir. parent corp. Engelhard Minerals & Chems. Corp. (name changed to Phibro Corp. 1981), 1975-85, vice chmn. bd., 1979-81, chmn. bd., chief exec. officer, 1981—; co-chmn., co-chief exec. officer Phibro-Salomon Inc., 1983-84; ptnr. Tendler Beretz, L.L.C. Ltd., 1985—. Chmn. subcom. trade U.S.-German Dem. Rep. Trade and Econ. Coun., 1978—84; bd. dirs., mem. exec. com. U.S./USSR Trade and Econ. Coun., 1979—85, U.S.-China Bus. Coun., 1983—94; chmn. exec. com., bd. dirs. V.I. Technologies, Inc., Watertown, Mass., 1994—. Mem. bd. overseers NYU Grad. Sch. Bus., 1981-85; trustee Lenox Hill Hosp., 1981-94; trustee, mem. exec. com. N.Y. Blood Ctr., 1987—; bd. dirs., mem. exec. com. Fgn. Policy Assn., 1983-96; bd. dirs. Ctr. for Gender Equality, N.Y.C., 1999—; mem. adv. coun. Weissman Ctr. for Internat. Bus., Baruch Coll., 2001. Recipient Torch of Liberty award metals and metal products div. Anti-Defamation League, 1976, Edith and Herbert Lehman award Henry St. Settlement, 1982; named Man of Yr., Fgn. Trade Soc., Baruch Coll., CUNY, 1985 Office: Tendler Beretz LLC 150 E 52nd St New York NY 10022-6017 E-mail: tenchan@aol.com.

TENENBAUM, BERNARD HIRSH, entrepreneur, educator; b. Long Beach, N.Y., Dec. 23, 1954; s. Abraham Benjamin and Helen Pearl (Wahrhaft) T. BA, Columbia Coll., 1976; postgrad., Stanford U., 1976-77; MBA, U. Pa., 1981. Mgr. Lido Beach (N.Y.) Hotel, 1976-77; gen. mgr. Sound Spectrum, Huntington, N.Y., 1977-78; dir. Small Bus. Ctr., Phila., 1980-84; asst. dir. Entre Ctr., 1984-85, assoc. dir., 1986-88; prof. entrepreneurial studies, dir. Fairleigh Dickinson U., Madison, N.J., 1988-93; v.p. corp. devel. Russ Berrie & Co., Inc., 1993-97; pres. Children's Leisure Products Group, The Jordan Co., N.Y.C., 1997—. Cons. Phila. Phillies, 1984-85; bd. dirs. WPI Group, Inc., Ogontz Ave. Redevel. Corp., West Phila. Ptnership; dir. Russ Berrie & Co. Del. Securities Exchange Commn. on Small Bus. Capital Formation, 1984-86; vice chmn. Small Bus. Devel. Ctr. adv. bd., Phila., 1983—; bd. dirs. Pvt. Industry Council, Phila., 1983-88; chmn. Small Bus. Fair, Phila., 1983-88. Mem. Phila. C. of C. (vice chmn. small bus. coun. 1982-86, chmn. 1986-88), Venture Assn. N.J. (v.p.). Democrat. Jewish. Avocations: swimming, sports cars, music, literature, film. Office: The Jordan Co 767 5th Ave New York NY 10153-0023 E-mail: bernie@btenenbaum.com.

TENENBAUM, J. SAMUEL, lawyer; b. Frankfurt, Germany, Mar. 5, 1949; s. Josef and Chana Tenenbaum; m. Susan Kay Nabedrick, Nov. 11, 1973; 1 child, Benjamin. BA, Ohio State U., 1970; JD cum laude, Northwestern U., 1973. Bar: Ill. 1973, U.S. Dist. Ct. (no. dist.) Ill. 1974, U.S. Ct. Appeals (7th cir.) 1974, U.S. Ct. Appeals (10th cir.) 1975, U.S. Ct. Appeals (9th cir.) 1976, U.S. Supreme Ct. 1977. Law clk. to judge U.S. Dist. Ct. (no. dist.) Ill., Chgo., 1973-75; ptnr. Tenenbaum & Senerowitz and prior firms, 1975-91, Schwartz, Cooper, Greenberger & Krauss, Chgo., 1991-95, Sachnoff & Weaver, Ltd., Chgo., 1995—. Instr., adj. prof. clin. trial advocacy Northwestern U. Sch. Law, Chgo., 1985—. Contbr. articles to profl. jours. Pres. Beth Hillel Congregation, 1992-94; nat. chmn. Northwestern U. Law Sch. Fund, 1990-92; golf coach Jewish Cmty. Ctr. MACABBI. Avocations: golf, rafting, travel, reading. Office: Sachnoff & Weaver Ltd 30 S Wacker Dr Fl 29 Chicago IL 60606-7429 E-mail: stenenbaum@sachnoff.com.

TENENBAUM, JEFFREY MARK, academic librarian; b. Phila., Apr. 10, 1945; s. Paul and Hansi (Barber) T. BA, Pa. State U., 1966; MLS, McGill U., 1968. Documents librarian, then reference librarian U. Toronto (Ont., Can.) Library, 1968-72; reference librarian U. Mass. Library, Amherst, 1973—. Vis. ref. libr. McGill U., Montreal, 1984, Nat. Libr. Can., Ottawa, Ont., 1999; mem. Info. Access Co. Acad. Libr. Product Adv. Bd., Foster City, Calif., 1992-94. Mem. Amherst Pub. Art Commn., 1994-2000. Mem. ALA, Assn. Can. Studies in U.S., Am. Coun. Que. Studies, Mid-Atlantic and New Eng. Conf. for Can. Studies (sec. 1992-96), Pioneer Valley Assn. Acad. Librs. (pres. 1989-90), Assn. Coll. and Rsch. Librs., Beta Phi Mu, Phi Alpha Theta, Pi Gamma Mu. Jewish. Home: 27 Montague Rd Apt 48 Amherst MA 01002-1043 Office: U Mass U Libr 154 Hicks Way Amherst MA 01003-9275 E-mail: jmt@library.umass.edu.

TENENHAUS, MAYER, plastic surgeon; b. Montreal, Feb. 7, 1960; s. Moshe and Malka (Danhi) T. BS, SUNY, Stony Brook, 1981; MD, Sackler Sch. Med. Tel Aviv U., 1987. Diplomate Am. Bd. Gen. Surgery, Am. Bd. Plastic and Reconstructive Surgery. Intern Albany (N.Y.) Med. Coll., 1987-88; resident in gen. surgery Case Western Res. U., Cleve., 1989-93; fellow in burn and critical care U. Calif., San Diego, 1993-95; fellow in plastic surgery Nassau County Med. Ctr., Long Island, N.Y., 1995-97; clin. instr. plastic surgery U. Calif., San Diego, 1997-98, asst. clin. prof. plastic and reconstructive surgery, 1998—; chief divsn. plastic and reconstructive surgery VA Med. Ctr., 1998—. Specialist in cosmetic and burn reconstructive surgery. Fellow Am. Coll. Surgeons; mem. AMA, Am. Burn Assn., San Diego Plastic Surg. Soc. Avocations: photography, sailing, motorsports, sculpting.

TENER, CAROL JOAN, retired secondary education educator; b. Cleve., Feb. 10, 1935; d. Peter Paul and Mamie Christine (Dombrowski) Manusack; m. Dale Keith Tener, Feb. 13, 1958 (div. Aug. 1991); children: Dean Robert, Susan Dawn Tener Belair. Student, Cleve. Mus. Art, 1948-53, Cleve. Art Inst., 1953-54; BS in Edn. cum laude, Kent State U., 1957; MS in Supervision, Akron U., 1974; postgrad., Kent State U., 1964, 81, 88-90, Akron U., 1975, 79, John Carroll U., 1982, 83, 85-86, Ohio U., 1987, Baldwin Wallace Coll., 1989. Cert. permanent K-12 tchr., Ohio. Stenographer Equitable Life Iowa, Cleve., 1953-54; tchr. elem. art Cuyahoga Falls (Ohio) Bd. Edn., 1957-58, 62-63, 65-68, tchr. jr. high sch., 1968-69; tchr. high sch. Brecksville (Ohio)-Broadview Heights Sch. Dist., 1969-94; chmn. dept. art Brecksville-Broadview Heights (Ohio) H.S., 1979-94, chmn. curriculum devel., 1982, 89; ret., 1994. Instr. for children Kent State U., 1956; advisor, prodr. cmty. svc. in art Brecksville Broadview Heights Bd. of Edn., 1969-94; former tchr. recreation and adult art edn. 1967-68, City of Cuyahoga Falls, 1967-68; com. mem. North Ctrl. Evaluation Com., Nordonia City, Ohio, 1978, Solon City, Ohio, 1989; chmn. north ctrl. evaluation com. Garfield Heights H.S., 1991; chair pilot program curriculum devel. com. in art/econs. Brecksville-Broadview Heights H.S., 1985-86, 86-87. Contbr. articles to newspapers, brochures, mags.; commd. artist for mural Brecksville City's Kids Quarters, 1994, Christopher Columbus/John Glen portraits in relief commemorating Columbus Day, 1961, Wooster (Ohio) Products Co.; editor Greater Cleve. chpt. Ohio Ret. Tchrs. Assn., 1998-2002. Chmn. Artmart Invitational Exhibit PTA, 1982-94; active Meals on Wheels program in Brecksville and Broadview Hts., 1995-98, Heart Disease collection, 1995, Stow-Glen Assisted Living Visitations, 1994-95, NCR Assisted Living transp. provision to hosps. and dr. in neighboring county; trustee, sec. Gettysburg Devel. Block Group Parma, 1995-96, Kids Quarters, 1994; Med Save fraud vol. Cuyahoga County Dept. Sr. and Adult Svcs., 2000-2002, spkrs. bur.; sr. health ins. info. program vol. Ohio Dept. Ins., 2001—. Recipient Ohio Coun. on Econ. Edn. award, 1985-86, award for significant svc. to cmty. Ret. and Sr. Vol. Program of USA, 1996, GCC/ORTA Svc. award, 1998, ORTA Pub. Rels. award, 1999-2001, Outstanding Svc. award Sr. Medicare Patrol Projects, Cert. of Appreciation, U.S. Dept. Health and Human Svcs. Adminstrn. on Aging, 2002; Pres.'s scholar Kent State U., 1954-57. Mem.: NAFE, ASCD, NEA (life), AAUW, S.W. Area Ret. Educators (co-chair 1996—98, program chair 1996—98, program coord. 1999—2000), Nat. Mus. Women in Arts, Cleve. Mus. Art, Acad. Econ. Edn., Brecksville Edn. Assn., Internat. Platform Assn., Nat. Art Edn. Assn., Ohio Ret. Tchrs. Assn. (life; registration chair 1997—98, pres.-elect Cleve. chpt. 1998, program chair 1998, interim editor 1998, circulation mgr. 1998—2002, chpt. pres. 1999, editor 1999—2002, trustee 2000, nominating chair 2000—01, bylaw chair 2000—01, editor/circulation mgr. 2000—, by-law chair 2000—01), Phi Delta Kappa Pi. Roman Catholic. Avocations: European and American museum tours, photography, collecting books on architecture, painting. Home: 7301 Sagamore Rd Parma OH 44134-5732

TENER, GEORGE E. investor; b. Edgeworth, Pa., May 5, 1917; s. Alexander Campbell and Marion (Clement) T.; m. Patricia Ann Buehner Talcott, Apr. 13, 1945 (div. June 1964); children: Roberta T. Kerkam, Jenifer E.; m. Anne Powell Potts Faber, Oct. 11, 1966. BA, Yale U., 1940. Fgn. svc. officer Dept. State, Italy, Philippines, 1948-54; fin. analyst J&W Seligman & Co., N.Y.C., 1957-64; bd. dirs. Inst. Philos. Rsch., Chgo., 1967-93. Dir. Nat. Assn. for the So. Poor, 1965—. Lt. Am. Field Svc., 1942-44. Decorated Brit. Empire medal, 1945. Mem. Univ. Club (N.Y.), Met. Club, City Tavern Club. Democrat. Episcopalian. Avocations: writing, travel, photography. Home: 3202 Scott Pl NW Washington DC 20007-2946

TENET, GEORGE JOHN, government agency official; b. N.Y. m. A. Stephanie Glakas; 1 child. BS in Fgn. Svc., Georgetown U., 1976; MIA, Columbia U., 1978. Legis. asst. to Sen. H. John Heinz III Senate Select Com. on Intelligence, Washington, 1985-86, designee to vice chair Sen. Patrick J. Leahy, 1986-89, dir. oversight of arms control negotiations Soviet Union/US, 1989-93, staff dir., 1993; mem. presdl. transition team Nat. Security Coun., 1993-95, spl. asst. to pres., sr. dir. intelligence programs, 1995-97; dep. dir. CIA, 1995-96, acting dir., 1996-97, dir., 1997—. Author: The Ability of U.S. Intelligence to Monitor the Intermediate Nuclear Force Treaty. Office: CIA Off of Dir Washington DC 20505-0001 Office Fax: 703-482-1739.*

TENG, LEE CHANG-LI, researcher in accelerator physics; b. Peiping, China, Sept. 5, 1926; came to U.S., 1947, naturalized, 1962; s. Tsuei Ying and Chien Min (Ho) T.; m. Nancy Lai-Shen Huang, Sept. 21, 1961; 1 child, Michael Nan-Hao. B.S., FuJen U., Peiping, 1946; M.S., U. Chgo., 1948, Ph.D., 1951. Asst. prof. U. Minn., Mpls., 1951-53; assoc. prof. Wichita State U., Kans., 1953-55; leader accelerator theory group Argonne Nat. Lab., Argonne, Ill., 1955-62, dir. particle accelerator div., 1962-67; professorial lectr. U. Chgo., 1964-67; dept. chmn. accelerator theory dept. Fermi Nat. Accelerator Lab., Batavia, Ill., 1967-72, head advanced projects, 1974-79, assoc. head accelerator div., 1972-81, head accelerator physics dept., 1986-87, head dept. spl. projects, 1987-89; head accelerator physics, advanced photon source project, Argonne (Ill.) Nat. Lab., 1989—; bd. dirs. Synchrotron Radiation Research Ctr., Taiwan, China; adj. prof. physics U. Wis., Madison, 1991—94; hon. prof. Beijing Normal U.; chmn. numerous confs., workshops, schs., and coms.; cons. various univs., labs., and cos. Contbr. articles to profl.

jours. Recipient Gold medal of Achievement Chinese Ministry of Edn., 1956; Disting. Service award Immigrants Service League, 1963. Fellow Am. Phys. Soc. (exec. com. 1980-82); mem. Academia Sinica (academician), AAUP, Inst. High Energy Physics, Chinese Acad. Sci. (hon. adv.), Chinese Student and Alumni Svcs. (pres. 1973), FuJen Alumni Assn. (hon. chmn.), Chinese C. of C. and Professions (chmn. bd. 1988-91), Phi Tau Phi (pres. 1963-66), Sigma Xi (pres. Wichita chpt. 1954). Republican. Avocations: violin, tennis, skiing. Home: 400 E 8th St Hinsdale IL 60521-4506 Office: Argonne Nat Lab 9700 Cass Ave Argonne IL 60439-4803

TENG, SHUYE, research scientist; b. Huaihua, Hunan, China; B in Engring., Hunan U., 1993; M in Engring., Tsinghua U., Beijing, China, 1996; PhD, Tex. A&M U., 2000. Rsch. asst. Tsinghua U., Beijing, 1993-96, U. Houston, 1996, Tex. A&M U., 1997-99; rsch. sci. Heat Transfer Rsch. Inc., College Sta., Tex., 2000—. Contbr. articles to profl. jours. Recipient Jiangchumin award, 1989, Panlison award, 1990, 91, Dupont award, 1992, Outstanding Grad. Student award Min. of Machinery and Elec. Industry, China, 1993, artificial environ. engring. award Tsinghua Artificial Environ. Co., 1993. Mem. ASME. Fax: 979-690-3250. E-mail: shirley_teng@yahoo.com.

TENGBOM, LUVERNE CHARLES, retired religion educator; b. Poskin, Wis., May 30, 1919; s. Carl John and Ida Carolina (Carlson) T.; m. Mildred Helena Hasselquist, May 23, 1953; children: Daniel, Judith, Janet, David. BA, Gustavus Adolphus Coll., 1943; MDiv, Augustana Sem., 1946; ThM, Luther Sem., St. Paul, 1962; PhD, Hartford Sem. Found., 1977. Ordained to ministry Luth. Ch. in Am., 1946. Pastor 1st Luth. Ch., Calgary, Alta., Can., 1946-56; missionary, mem. bd. world missions Augustana Luth. Ch., Tanzania, 1956-67; prof. Luth. Bible Inst., Anaheim, Calif., 1967-85, acad. dean, 1976-85, prof., 1987-91, prof. emeritus, 1994—. Sec. Can. Conf., Augustana Luth. Ch., 1950-56; mem. commn. on world mission Pacific S.W. Synod, Luth. Ch. in Am., 1981-85, bd. world missions, 1985-87; prof. Trinity Theol. Coll., Singapore, Singapore Bible Coll., 1985-87. Author: Fill My Cup, Lord, 1978, Bible Readings for Families, 1981. Sec. Luth. Bible Inst., Camrose, Alta, 1946-56; dean Luth. Bible Sch., Moshi, Tanzania, 1960-61. Home: 789 N Cambridge Ave Claremont CA 91711-4258 E-mail: ltengbom@aol.com. *My purpose and prayer in life has been to have a greater commitment to the Lord Jesus, to proclaim the good news with greater conviction, and to have a greater concern for others.*

TENGS, TAMMY ORA, educator; b. Roseburg, Oreg., Sept. 2, 1959; d. Allan Leighton and Muriel Maxine Tengs. BS in Psychology, U. Oreg., 1983; MS in Indsl. Engring., U. Mass., 1987; DS in Health Policy and Mgmt., Harvard U., 1994. Dir. Lifesaving Priorities Project, Harvard Ctr. Risk Analysis, Boston, 1992-94; asst. rsch. prof. Duke U. Ctr. Health Policy Rsch. and Edn., Durham, NC, 1994-96. Mem. Am. Pub. Health Assn., Assn. Pharmacoecons. and Outcomes Rsch., Assn. Pub. Policy Analysis and Mgmt., Soc. Med. Decision Making (trustee 1998-2000). Office: U Calif Sch Social Ecology Irvine CA 92697-7076 Fax: 949-824-8286. E-mail: tengs@uci.edu.

TEN HAKEN, RICHARD ERVIN, retired educational administrator; b. Clymer, N.Y., Apr. 28, 1934; s. James Henry and Irma Clarabelle (Legters) Ten H.; m. Marilyn Kay Gallup, July 1, 1954; children: Valorie, Vivian. BA, Hope Coll., Holland, Mich., 1956; MS, Syracuse U., 1963, EdD, 1967. Acct., mgmt. trainee GE, Syracuse, N.Y., 1955-56; sales rep. Corry-Jamestown, Chgo. and Corry, Pa., 1956-58; tchr. Carthage (N.Y.) Cen. Sch. Dist., 1958-59; asst. supt. schs. Watertown (N.Y.) City Sch. Dist., 1959-63, Byram Hills Cen. Sch. Dist., Armonk, N.Y., 1963-64; supt. schs. Ticonderoga (N.Y.) Cen. Sch. Dist., 1964-68, Rush-Henrietta (N.Y.) Cen. Sch. Dist., 1968-70; chief exec. officer, dist. supt. schs. Monroe 2-Orleans Bd. Coop. Ednl. Svcs., Spencerport, N.Y., 1970-93; ret., 1993. Trustee, chmn., pres. N.Y. State Tchrs.' Retirement Bd., Albany, 1972-94; bd. dirs., pres. J.P. Morgan Funds, N.Y.C. Trustee, chmn. audit com., 2001; Chase Vista Mut. Funds Group, N.Y.C., 1987-2001, Pinnacle Govt. Fund, Inc., Rochester, 1985-90, Trinity Assets Trust, Rochester, 1989-92; participant Seminar on Internat. Investing-Global Understandings, Japan, 1988; prof., adj. vis. prof. Syracuse, U., U. Buffalo, SUNY Genesco; pres., CEO Ten Haken & Assoc., Inc., 1992—. Author: (monographs) Guide for Successful Bonding 1968, School Administrator Personnel Planning, 1989. Charter mem. bd. dirs. Finger Lakes Regional Edn. Ctr. for Econ. Devel., 1983-93; mem. exec. com. Nat. Coun. on Tchrs. Retirement, Austin, Tex., 1986-91; trustee Asbury United Meth. Ch., 1993-99, chmn. Asbury Investment com., 1993—, Rochester Area Cmty. TV Assn.; investment com. Rochester Area Cmty. Found., 1990—; dir. United Meth. Found., 1998—. Recipient award for rsch. in sch. fin. NEA, 1968, James M. Manwaring award Syracuse U., 1985. Mem. Am. Assn. Ednl. Svc. Agys. (bd. dirs. 1984-87, pres. 1986-87 Nat. Disting. Svc. award 1993), Am. Assn. Sch. Adminstrs (legis. com.), Am. Mgmt. Assn. (President's Assn.), N.Y. State Coun. Sch. Supts. (chmn. membership). Methodist. Avocations: flying, sailing, fishing, golf. Home: 4 Barnfield Rd Pittsford NY 14534-2544

TENHOEVE, THOMAS, academic administrator; b. Bklyn., Oct. 1, 1935; s. Thomas and Adeline Ruth (Vander Hill) T.; m. Suzanne Underwood, June 7, 1957; children: Thomas III, Carol, Timothy. AB, Hope Coll., 1956; MA, U. Mich., 1957; PhD, U. Toledo, 1965; postgrad., U. Western Mich. Biology tchr. South Haven. Mich. Pub. Schs., 1957-58; biology instr. Northwestern Coll., Orange City, Iowa, 1958-63; supr. biology students U. Toledo, Ohio, 1963-65; acad. dean, acting pres. Northwestern Coll., Orange City, 1965-70; pres. Butler (Pa.) County Community Coll., 1970-84, Oakton Community Coll., Des Plaines, Ill., 1984-95. Bd. dirs. Sister Cities Internat., 1986-95, 98—, nat. v.p., treas., 2001-; trustee Northwestern Coll., 1988-95; mem. Ill. C.C. State Found. Bd., 1993-95, Ill. Math. and Sci. Acad. Selection Bd., 1986, 87, Cook County Sheriff's Scholarship Panel; exec. com. Golden Corridor, 1986-92. Recipient Pacesetter award Nat. Coun. for Community Rels., 1986, Orchard Village award. Mem. Am. Coun. on Internat. Intercultural Edn. (chmn. 1992-95), Coun. North Ctrl. Two-Yr. Colls. (state rep. 1988-92, exec. bd. 1989-95, 2d v.p. 1990-91, 1st v.p. 1991-92, pres. 1992-93).

TENICELA, RUBEN ANTIALON, anesthesiologist; b. Peru, 1929; MD, U. Nat San Marcos, Lima, 1957. Diplomate Am. Bd. Anesthesiology. Intern. St. Joseph's Hosp., 1960; resident Balt. City Hosp., 1961-62, Pitts. U. Health Ctr., 196-64; from instr. to prof. Pain Control Ctr. U. Pitts., 1965-95. Mem. AMA. Am. Soc. Anesthesiologists, Internat. Assn. for Study of Pain. Home: 4 Wynnecliffe Dr Carnegie PA 15106-3835 E-mail: Rtenicela3@att-bi.com.

TENISON, GARY V. sales executive; b. Akron, Ohio, Jan. 20, 1967; s. David and Mary Tenison; m. Elizabeth Tenison, July 20, 1985; 4 children. BS in Aero. Engring., Ohio State U., 1985; MBA in Mktg., U. Minn., 1993. Project engr. BF Goodrich, Uniontown, Ohio, 1985—90; project mgr. Fluidyne Corp., Mpls., 1990—92, sr. program mgr. aero. systems engring., 1992—94, mktg. and sales mgr., 1994—96; pres., CEO Tenison Engring., Akron, 1996—98; nat. sales mgr. Eaton Aeroquip, Jackson, Mich., 1998—. Avocations: skiing, golf, literature. E-mail: gtenis@compuserve.com.

TENKOTTE, PAUL ALLEN, history and international studies educator; b. Covington, Ky., June 30, 1960; s. Harry Vincent and Mary Margaret (Meier) T. BA in History, Thomas More Coll., 1982; MA in History, U. Cin., 1983, PhD in History, 1989. Charles P. Taft fellow U. Cin., 1982, 84, 85, grad. asst. Carl Blegen Libr., 1983, Lenore McGrane fellow, 1986-87; prof. history Thomas More Coll., Crestview Hills, Ky., 1987—, dir. internat. studies, 1991-2001. Regional coord. 3 U.S. Congl. dists for Nat. Bicentennial Competition on the Constn. and Bill of Rights, Ctr. for Civic Edn., 1987-89. Author: A Heritage of Art and Faith; contbr. articles to profl. jours. and encyclopedias. Active Miami Purchase Assn. Historic Preservation, Cin., 1985-92; coord. historic restoration Mother of God Ch., Covington, 1986-94, v.p. governing bd., 1987-89; trustee Internat. Visitors Coun. Greater Cin., 2000-2001; mem. Ky. Underground Railroad Adv. Com., 1997—. Groesbeck scholar for historic preservation Nat. Soc. Colonial Dames Am. in Ohio, 1986; Cultural Exch. grantee Japan Travel Bur., 1991; recipient Thomas More Coll. Alumni Assn., 1999 Mem. Dinsmore Homestead Found. (adv. coun. 1989-92), Kenton County Hist. Soc. (v.p. 1981-82, pres. 1982), Phi Alpha Theta (Dr. A.F. Zimmerman scholar 1982, Dr. John Pine scholar 1985). Avocations: photography, architecture, bicycling, travel. Office: Thomas More Coll 333 Thomas More Pky Covington KY 41017-3428

TENN, JOSEPH SIMON, physics and astronomy educator; b. L.A., May 11, 1940; s. Sol and Edith I. Tenn; m. Eileen Michelle Levitin, Dec. 23, 1967; children: Shoshanna, Steven. BS, Stanford (Calif.) U., 1962; MS, U. Wash., 1966, PhD, 1970. Asst. prof. Sonoma State U., Rohnert Park, Calif., 1970-74, assoc. prof., 1974-80, prof., 1980—, chair, 2001—. Contbr. articles to Mercury and Griffith Observer. Grantee Sonoma State U., 1989, Am. Inst. Physics, 1994. Mem. Astron. Soc. of the Pacific (mem. history com. 1986-2002, chair 1993-99), Am. Phys. Soc., Am. Assn. Physics Tchrs., Am. Astron. Soc. Home: 1625 Hillview Ter Santa Rosa CA 95405-7521 Office: Dept Physics and Astronomy Sonoma State U Rohnert Park CA 94928

TENNANT, JOHN RANDALL, management advisory company executive; b. North Bend, Wash., Aug. 23, 1940; s. Maurice Andrew and Jane Downing (Vinnedge) T.; m. Nikki Mae Priem, July 17, 1965 (div.); children: Ann Elizabeth, Randall Warren; m. Deborah Ann Francis, Oct. 25, 1986 (div.); 1 child, Alyssa Jane. BS in Indsl. Engring., Stanford U., 1962; MBA, U. Wash., 1966. Registered profl. engr., Wash. Sr. rsch. engr. Boeing Co., Seattle, 1962-68; mgr. Price Waterhouse, 1968-73, ptnr. Tokyo, 1973-79, Los Angeles, 1979-89; founder, CEO, Manex, Inc., Newport Beach, Calif., 1989—; dir. subs. Price Waterhouse Assocs., Pacific region, 1975-79. Mem. John Tracy Clinic Men's Com., Santa Catalina Island Conservancy, pres., 1985-87; capt. Long Beach Mounted Police. Mem. NSPE, Japan Computer Assn. (founder, pres. 1976-77), Japan Modapts Assn. (founder), Japan Am. Soc., Inst. Mgmt. Cons., Am. Inst. Indsl. Engrs. (pres. Seattle chpt. 1970-71), Data Processing Mgmt. Assn., Tokyo Lawn and Tennis Club, L.A. Country Club, Jonathan Club, Empty Saddle Club, Los Rancheros Visitadores Club, Los Caballeros Club. Home: 13 Village Park Way Santa Monica CA 90405 E-mail: tennant_john@smc.edu.

TENNANT, ROY, librarian; b. Greencastle, Ind., July 19, 1957; BA in Geography, Humboldt State U., 1985; M of Libr. and Info. Studies, U. Calif., Berkeley, 1986. Reference and collection devel. libr. The Libr. U. Calif., Berkeley, 1987-89, coord. for automated circulation The Libr., 1988-89, pub. svc. automated sys. coord. The Libr., 1989-92, head info. sys. instr. and support The Libr., 1993-95, digital libr. project mgr. The Libr., 1995-2000; mgr. eScholarship Web & svcs. design Calif. Digital Libr., Oakland, 2000—. Cons. in field, Sonoma, Calif., 1993—. Author: Crossing the Internet Threshold: An Instructional Handbook, 1993, Practical HTML: A Self-Paced Tutorial, 1996; editor: XML in Libraries, 2002.. Recipient Network Citizen award Libr. Apple Computer Inc., 1992. Mem. ALA. Avocation: whitewater rafting. Office: Calif Digital Libr 4th Fl 415 20th St Oakland CA 94612 Office Fax: 510-893-1212. E-mail: roy.tennant@ucop.edu.

TENNE, DONALD PAUL, financial planner; b. Bronx, N.Y., Nov. 28, 1954; s. Gerard Lawrence and Rita Rose (Delli Bovi) T.; m. Marybeth Rose Taylor, Oct. 12, 1985; children: Melissa Rose, Daniel Benjamin. Grad., Adirondack C.C., 1973-75. Acct. rep. Met. Ins. Co., Glens Falls, N.Y., 1982-87; fin. planner MetLife Securities, Inc., 1987—; instr. SUNY, Canton, 1998-99, Jefferson C.C., Watertown, N.Y., 1998-99. Fin. editor Sta. WCKM Radio, Lake George, N.Y., 1994—; instr. Skidmore Coll., Saratoga, N.Y., 1989—, Boces, Hudson Falls, N.Y., 1989—; Metlife Leaders Conf. qualifier, 1994-96, 1999; Metlife Pres. Conf. qualifier, 1996-98, 2000; mem. Metlife Income and Investment adv. coun., 1998-2000, Metlife Securities Fin. Planning Adv. Coun., 1999-2001, MSI Fin. Planning Mktg. Adv. Coun., 2000-2001, Metlife mature markets specialist, 1999. Guest columnist Glens Falls Bus. Jour., 1990. Fund raising com. Literacy Vols. of Glens Falls, 1990-93. Mem. Masons (past master), Fin. Planning Assn. Avocations: racketball, golf, reading. Office: MetLife Securities Inc PO Box 788 Glens Falls NY 12801-0788 E-mail: dtenne@metlife.com.

TENNEN, KEN, lawyer; b. Belmont Shore, Calif., June 30, 1947; s. Morris and Clair (Rose) T.; m. Diane Janet Sussman, Dec. 25, 1982; children: Sterling M, Skyler Alexander. Cert. counseling, UCLA, 1973; lic., U. Los Ams., Cholula Puebla, Mex., 1975; MA, Georgetown U., 1977; JD, LaVerne Coll. Law, 1996. Bar: Calif. 1996. Cons. Booz Allen & Hamilton, Washington, 1974-77; with Multinat. Corp., L.A., 1977-92; sole practitioner West Hills, Calif., 1996—. Bd. dirs., chief exec. officer Suntree Townhomes, Tarzana, Calif. Chmn. Happy Valley Sch. Bd., Ojai, Calif., 1991-2000; chmn. Happy Valley Found., 1990—, pres., 2000—; bd. dirs. Rec. for the Blind, 1999—. Mem. Calif. State Bar (com. on legal profls. with disabilities 1999—), Calif. Conf. Dels. Avocations: gardening, photography, scuba. Office: 24372 Vanowen St Ste 202 West Hills CA 91307-2800 E-mail: ken@kentennen.com.

TENNENBAUM, MICHAEL ERNEST, private investor; b. St. Petersburg, Fla., Sept. 17, 1935; s. Reubin and Frieda (Miller) T.; m. Suzanne Stockfisch; children by previous marriage— Mark Stephen, Andrew Richard. BS, Ga. Inst. Tech., 1958; MBA with honors, Harvard U., 1962. Assoc. Burnham & Co., N.Y.C., 1962-64, Bear, Stearns & Co., N.Y.C., 1964-69, sr. mng. dir., 1969-96, vice chmn. investment banking div., 1988-93; chmn. bd. dirs. Tech. Park, Atlanta, 1978-81; mng. mem. Tennenbaum & Co., LLC, L.A., 1996—. Bd. dirs. TelePacific Corp., Pemco Aviation Group (chmn.), Party City Corp; bd. visitors UCLA Sch. Medicine, 2000—; bd. dirs. L.A. World Affairs Coun., 1997—. Bd. govs., nat. bd. trustees Boys and Girls Clubs Am.; mem. nat. adv. bd. Ga. Inst. Tech., 1971-77; mem. vis. com. Harvard U. Sch. Bus., Cambridge, Mass., 1986-92, bd. assocs., 1992—; bd. trustees Ga. Inst. Tech. Found., Inc., Atlanta, 1988-96; bd. dirs. Joffrey Ballet, 1990-92, chmn. exec. com., 1991-92; bd. dirs. Music Ctr. L.A. County Unified Fund Cabinet, 1990-91; chmn. L.A. Mayor's Spl. Adv. Com. on Fiscal Adminstrn., 1993-94; commr. Calif. Intercity HighSpeed Ground Transp. Commn.; chmn. Calif. High Speed Rail Authority, 1998-2001. Mem. L.A. World Affairs Coun. (dir. 1997—). Home: 118 Malibu Colony Rd Malibu CA 90265-4642 Office: Tennenbaum & Co LLC 11100 Santa Monica Blvd Ste 210 Los Angeles CA 90025-3335 Fax: 310-566-1010. *The older I get, the luckier I feel.*

TENNENT, VALENTINE LESLIE, accountant; b. Apia, Western Samoa, Apr. 5, 1919; came to U.S., 1922; s. Hugh Cowper and Madge Grace (Cook) T.; m. Jeanne Marie Elder, Dec. 10, 1941; children: Madeline Jeanne Walls, Hugh Cowper II, Michael Waller, Val Leslie, Paul Anthony. Student, U. Calif., Berkeley, 1938-40. CPA, Hawaii, La. Mgr. Tennent & Greaney, CPAs, Hilo, Hawaii, 1945-50; ptnr. Cameron, Tennent & Dunn, CPAs, Honolulu, 1950-56, KPMG LLP, Honolulu, 1956-79, cons., 1979-84. Ind. rschr. pub. fin. and banking, polit. economy, moral philosophy, San Diego, 1984-2000. Founding trustee, pres., treas. Tennent Art Found., Honolulu, 1955-77; trustee, treas. Watumull Found., Honolulu, 1963-90; bd. dirs. Iolani Sch., Inst. for Human Svcs., Honolulu, Lyman Mus., Hilo. Capt. USAF, 1941-45. Recipient Bishop's Cross for disting. svc. Protestant Episcopal Ch., Dist. Hawaii, 1965, G.J. Watumull award for disting. achievement Watumull Found., Honolulu, 1982. Mem. AICPA (governing coun. 1961-64), Hawaii Soc. CPAs (pres. 1960). Episcopalian. Avocations: swimming, fine arts, music, literature. Home and Office: Unit 1411 8515 Costa Verde Blvd San Diego CA 92122-1146 *Joy in life comes from knowing the things you want to accomplish within God's overall purpose, pursuing them to the end regardless of difficulties, and accepting full responsibility for inevitable failures.*

TENNEY, FRANK PUTNAM, marketing executive; b. Orono, Maine, Oct. 6, 1937; s. Carl Bither and Velma May (Williamson) T.; m. Margaret Anne Seymour, Apr. 23, 1960; children: Jane Dossiere, Carl B., Janet M., Alan F., Janice M. Lovell. Cert. notary public, Maine. Nat. sales mgr. Shaw & Tenney Oar & Paddle Co., Orono, 1958-68; sales mgr. George D. Wetherill, Phila., 1968-69; with R.M. Flagg, Veazie, Maine, 1968-69; salesman DuBois Chem., Cin., 1969-76; Maine sales mgr. Rochester (N.Y.) Midland Co., 1976-82; with H.A. Manning Co., BellowsFalls, Vt., 1982-86; dist. sales mgr. U.S. West Mktg. Resources, Loveland, Colo., 1986-90; sales mgr. City Directory, Inc., Belmond, Iowa, 1990—92; with RAK Industries, 1993; v.p. Maine Mktg. Resources, Brewer, Maine, 1994—. Assoc. Prepaid Legal. Adv. bd. Salvation Army. Tech. sgt. Maine ANG, 1955-87, ret. Mem.: KC (past grand knight Pine Cone coun., 4th degree, past faithful navigator Pine Cone assembly), VFW, Greater Bangor C. of C., Golden Cir. (Averill plaque), 40/8, Profl. Sales Club Bangor, Am. Legion (Americanism officer 1997, post comdr. 1999—2000, adjutant 2001—03, past vice comdr. II). Republican. Roman Catholic. E-mail: mten@midmaine.com.

TENNEY, LISA CHRISTINE GRAY, healthcare administrator; b. Pitts., Feb. 5, 1952; d. Elmer Burtt and Elizabeth (Scharding) Gray; m. Robert Howard Tenney, Mar. 8, 1972; children: Brian, David, Michael. BSN, W.Va. U., 1974. Cert. emergency nurse; cert. ACLS instr., CPR instr./trainer. Staff nurse Suburban Hosp., Bethesda, Md., 1979-80, Holy Cross Hosp., Silver Spring, 1980—; pvt. practice nursing Gaithersburg, 1982—88; co-founder, assoc. dir. Md. Profl. Staffing Svcs., Bethesda, 1987—94; asst. nurse mgr. emergency dept. Holy Cross Hosp., Silver Spring, Md., 1995—99, project mgr. acute care svcs. adminstrn. Silver Sping, 1999—, clin. ops. trainer, BLS-AHA cmty. tng. ctr. mgr., 1999, dir. nursing resources, 2001—. Speaker in field. Contbr. articles to profl. jours. Mem. Emergency Nurses Assn., Sigma Theta Tau. Home: 9226 Bluebird Ter Gaithersburg MD 20879-1739

TENNEY, NOEL W. humanities educator; b. Tallmansville, W.Va., Oct. 11, 1944; s. Lloyd William and Macie Mills Tenney. BS Edn., Concord Coll., 1969; MAT, W.Va. Wesleyan Coll., 1979; postgrad., Pa. State U., 1981—82. Cert. tchg. cert. W.Va. Tchr. Upshur County Bd. Edn., Backhannon, W.Va., 1969—81, Pa. State U., State College, 1981—82; instr., mus. specialist Salem (W.Va.) Coll., 1983—89; instr., cultural specialist Fairmont (W.Va.) State Coll., 1992—. Ednl. cons., storyteller Hill Lorists, Tallmansville, W.Va., 1989—; adj. instr. W.Va. Wesleyan Coll., Buckhannon, 1989—; cultural specialist W.Va. Folklife Ctr., Fairmont State Coll., Fairmont, W.Va., 1999—. Author: (nonfiction) This Mountain Place, 1990, All About Upshur County, 1993; co-editor: (jours.) Traditions and Hillchild, 1993—. Bd. dirs. Staunton/Parkersburg Turnpike Alliance, Beverly, W.Va., 2001—. Recipient award of merit, Am. Assn. State and Local History, 1995, Southeastern Region Ednl. award, Nat. Storytelling Assn., 1998, Citizen of Yr. award, Record Delta, 2001; fellow Paul Harris fellow, Rotary Found. Internat., 1997. Mem.: Upshur County Hist. Soc. (dir. spl. projects 1982—). Home: PO Box 8 Tallmansville WV 26237 Office: Fairmont State Coll WV Folklife Ctr Locust Ave Fairmont WV 26554 Personal E-mail: noeltenney@aol.com.

TENNEY, SARAH G. music educator; b. N.Y.C., Apr. 30, 1948; d. John Wool Griswold and Margaret Brett Tenney. BA, Bennington Coll., 1971; MusM, New Eng. Conservatory, 1976. Founder Spectrum Young Audiences Trio, Boston, 1976-80; marimba, percussion tchr. Rivers Music Sch., Weston, Mass., 1976-80, 85—, St. Ann's Sch., Bklyn., 1980-85; founder, dir. Marimba Magic, Weston, 1987—; tchr. improvisation Northeastern U., Boston, 1991-95. Percussionist on 6 Revel records; percussionist/timpanist in Christmas Revels, 1980—; presenter in field. Composer: (composition/musical) Gamelon Dream, 1989, Mysterious Waltz, 1991, Whole Tone Dream, 1996, Adventures, 1999, Machines, 2000, Jaja Mani Dreams, 2001, (composition/musical) Drum Circle, 2002. Concert performer Concerts for Children, 1976-80, Cambridge World's Fair, 1997, 98. Mem. Music Tchrs. Nat. Assn. (conf. presenter 1991), Musicians Union, Music Educators Nat. Conf. (presenter ea. conf. 1992, 96), Percussive Arts Soc. (presenter internat. conv. 1989, 97), Orff Schulwerk Assn. (presenter nat. conf. 1996) presenter European Piano Tchrs. Assn., Internat. Conf., Budapest, 2000, Internat. Marimba Conf., Belgium, 1992. Office: The Rivers Music Sch 337 Winter St Weston MA 02493-1072

TENNEY, TOM FRED, bishop; b. DeRidder, La., Dec. 6, 1933; s. Fred and Jenny Veve (Nichols) T.; m. Thetus Pearl Caughron, Dec. 27, 1952; children: Tom Gregory, Teri Denise Tenney Spears. Student, Apostolic Bible Inst., St. Paul, 1952; DD (hon.), 1992. Ordained to ministry United Pentecostal Ch., 1954. Pastor United Pentecostal Ch., Monroe, La., 1953-56, DeRidder, 1976-78, youth pres. La. dist., 1953-60, dist. supt. for La., 1978—; youth pres. United Pentecostal Ch., Internat., St. Louis, 1960-69, dir. fgn. missions, mem. exec. bd., 1969-76, mem. gen. bd., 1978—. Internat. radio speaker Harvestime, St. Louis, 1976-78. Author: Pentecost: What's That?, 1975, The Flame Still Burns, 1989, The Main Thing, 1993, Advice to Pastors and Other Saints, 1995, Beyond Sunrise, 1996, Some Things I've Learned, 1998, Secret Sources of Power, 2000. Trustee Tupelo (Miss.) Children's Mansion, Spirit of Freedom, Metairie, La., Lighthouse Ranch for Boys, Hammond, La. Democrat. Home and Office: PO Box 248 Tioga LA 71477-0248

TENNEY, WILLIAM FRANK, pediatrician; b. Shreveport, La., June 5, 1946; s. William Bonds and Pat (Patton) T.; m. Elizabeth Carter Steadman, Oct. 4, 1973; children: Amy Karen, William Allen. BA, Vanderbilt U., 1968; MD, La. State U., New Orleans, 1972. Diplomate Am. Bd. Pediatrics, sub-Bd. Pediatric Nephrology. Intern Grady Meml. Hosp., Atlanta, 1972-73; resident in pediatrics Emory U. Affiliated Hosps., 1973-74, fellow in pediatric nephrology and inorganic metabolism, 1974-76; practice medicine specializing in pediatric nephrology St. Helens, Oreg., 1976-79, Shreveport, 1979-85, 97—, Seattle, 1985-97; mem. staff Children's Orthopedic Hosp. and Med. Ctr.; chief dept. pediatrics Swedish Hosp. Med. Ctr., 1987-90, 95-97; assoc. prof. pediatrics La. State U. Sch. Medicine, 1997-2001; dir. La. Children's Kidney Ctr., 2000-01; chief, divsn. pediat. nephrology La. State U. Sch. Medicine, 2000-01; chief pediat. nephrology, dir. S.C. Children's Kidney Ctr., Greenville (S.C.) Hosp. Sys., 2001. Clin. asst. prof. pediatrics La. State U. Sch. Medicine, 1979-85, U. Wash. Sch. Medicine, Seattle, 1985-97; chmn. Renal com. Schumpert Med. Ctr., Shreveport, 1982, co-chmn. 1979-81, mem. 1983-84, co-dir. Renal Dialysis Unit, 1979-84, mem. renal transplantation com., 1984; cons. pediatric nephrology Shriner's Hosp. Crippled Children, Shreveport, 1979-84, Shreveport Regional Dialysis Ctr., 1979-84, Bossier Dialysis Ctr., Bossier City, La., 1983-84, Natchitoches (La.) Dialysis Facility, 1984; co-dir. La. Children's Kidney Ctr., 1998—; co-dir. La. Children's Kidney Ctr., 1999—. Author: (with others) Pediatric Case Studies, 1985; contbr. articles to profl. jours. Mem. Union Concerned Scientists, Cambridge, Mass., 1986-95, Internat. Physicians for Prevention of Nuclear War, Boston, 1986-95. Fellow Am. Acad. Pediatrics; mem. Am. Soc. Pediatric Nephrology, North Pacific Pediatric Soc., AMA, Wash. State Med. Assn., Internat. Soc. Peritoneal Dialysis, Empirical Soc. Emory U., King County Med. Soc., Northwest Renal Soc., Southwest Pediatric Nephrology (mem. study group 1981-84). Avocations: oil painting, rockhounding, camping, jogging. Home: 103 Fillery Dr Greenville SC 29615 Office: Pediat Nephrology 205 Enterprise Dr Ste 200 Greenville SC 29615

TENNIES, ROBERT HUNTER, headmaster; b. Bogotá, Colombia, Aug. 19, 1952; s. Leo C. and Ruth (Winston) T.; m. Ruth Ellen Fischer, June 14, 1975; children: Debbie, Julie. BS, Wheaton (Ill.) Coll., 1973; MA, U. South Fla., 1975; EdS, Fla. Atlantic U., 1978, EdD, 1982. Sci. tchr. Cypress Lake Middle Sch., Ft. Myers, Fla., 1973-77, Boca Raton (Fla.) Christian Sch., 1977-78, asst. adminstr., 1978-84, headmaster, 1984—, min. of children, 1984-90; interim. min. of edn., 1991-93. Spkr. Internat. Conf. Religious Edn., Petrozavodsk, Russia; mem. Nat. Rev. Panel Blue Ribbon Schs., 1999. Recipient Excellence in Edn. award Nat. Assn. Elem. Prins., 1990, 97. Mem. Nat. Sci. Tchrs. Assn., Assn. of Christian Schs. Internat. (accreditation commn.), Nat. Assn. Elem. Sch. Prins. Avocation: camping. Home: 2415 NW 30th Rd Boca Raton FL 33431-6214 Office: Boca Raton Christian Sch 315 NW 4th St Boca Raton FL 33432-3739 E-mail: Tennies_r@popmail.firn.edu., bocachristian@bocachristian.org.

TENNOV, DOROTHY, psychologist; b. Montgomery, Ala., Aug. 29, 1928; d. Daniel Edgar Tennow and Lois Estelle (Moore) Miller; children: Randall, Russell, Daniel. BA, CUNY, 1950; MA, U. Conn., 1954, PhD, 1964. Prof. U. Bridgeport, Conn., 1964-86; pvt. cons. in self-mgmt. and personal decision-making Millsboro, Del., 1986—. Pvt. practice cons., Westport, Conn., 1970-74, Stratford, Conn., 1975-80. Author: Psychotherapy: The Hazardous Cure, 1975, Super Self, 1976, Love and Limerence, 1979, reissue, 1999 (2d Press Women award 1980), Mem. AAAS, APA, Am. Psychol. Soc., Authors Guild, Assn. Politics and the Life Scis., Internat. Soc. Human Ethology, Human Behavior and Evolution Soc. Home and Office: RR 9 Box 251 Millsboro DE 19966-9545 E-mail: tennov1@mchs1.com.

TENNYSON, EDSON LEIGH, transportation engineer; b. Orange, N.J., July 6, 1922; s. William Edwin and Jane Virginia (Leigh) T.; m. Shirley Louise Forward, July 15, 1944; children: Marilyn Elizabeth, Constance Virginia, Marjorie Leigh. BS in Mgmt. Engring., BEngring. in Mgmt., Carnegie Inst. Tech., 1947. Registered profl. indsl. engr., Ohio, Pa. Rsch. analyst Pitts. Railways Co., 1947-49; v.p. Kenosha Motor Coach Inc., Milw., 1949-51; traction commr. Youngstown (Ohio) City, 1951-56; dep. commr. Dept. Pub. Property, Phila., 1956-71; dep. sec. Dept. Transp., Harrisburg, Pa., 1972-79; planning coord. Pub. Works, Arlington County, Va., 1983-92; transp. cons. San Diego, N.J., 1980-82, 93-94. Cons. to Nat. Capital Transit Agy., Washington, 1962-63. Mem. Citizens Adv. Com. No. Va., 1997—, transp. rsch. bd. Nat. Rsch. Coun., 1972—, mem. emeritus; cons. rail electrification study Pa. Corridor, 2001; mem. budget com. Nat. Capital Presbytery, Washington,

1993-96; chmn. tech. adv. com. Del. Valley Regional Planning Commn., 1970-76; asst. scoutmaster Boy Scouts Am., Mt. Lebanon, Pa., 1947-49; chmn. planning commn. Middletown, Pa., 1980-83; elder, Presbyn. Ch., Chestnut Hill, Phila., 1962-68; trustee Vienna Presbyn. Ch., Va., 1998-2000. 1st lt. U.S. Army, 1946. Westinghouse Meml. scholar, Pitts., 1940-45; recipient Disting. Svc. award U.S. Dept. Transp., Washington, 1978; named Arlington's Most Valuable Employee, 1987. Mem. Westwood Country Club, Tau Beta Pi, Omicron Deltea Kappa, Delta Upsilon. Avocations: tennis, swimming, travel, transit research. Home and Office: 2233 Abbotsford Dr Vienna VA 22181-3220

TENNYSON, JOSEPH ALAN, engineering executive; b. St. Paul, May 28, 1958; s. Walter Arnold and Carol Jean (Hauenstein) T.; m. Patricia Ann Jordan, Aug. 29, 1981; children: Alexa Jordan, Ryley Joseph. BSBA, AA in Lib. Arts, U. Minn., 1981. Fin. planner K.A. Richard & Assocs., St. Paul, 1981-83; reporting analyst Control Data Corp., Mpls., 1983-84, systems analyst, 1984-85, fin. analyst, 1985-86; dir. ops. Michaud, Cooley, Erickson, 1986-89, corp. sec., 1986—, v.p. fin. and adminstrn., 1989-93, prin., 1993—. Bd. dirs. Compas. Mem. Leadership Mpls., 1988-89; bd. dirs. United Arts Partnership Fund, 1996-98, Wolf Ridge Environ. Learning Ctr., 1999-2000; mem. assembly com. on intercollegiate athletics U. Minn., 1994-97; trustee Minnatonka Found. for Excellence, 2000—. Mem. Mpls. Club, U. Minn. Alumni Assn. (nat. bd. dirs. 1995-97), Sigma Chi (Grand Consul citation 1983, L.G. Balfour award 1981), Omicron Delta Kappa, Order of Omega. Avocations: computers, fly fishing, golf. Office: Michaud Cooley Erickson 333 S 7th St Ste 1200 Minneapolis MN 55402-2422 Home: 20260 Excelsior Blvd Excelsior MN 55331-8731

TENNYSON, PETER JOSEPH, lawyer; b. Winona, Minn., Mar. 18, 1946; s. Richard Harvey and Sylvia Josephine (Jadrich) T.; m. Mary Eileen Fay, Jan. 3, 1970; children: Mark Christian, Rachel Christine, Matthew Patrick, Erica Ruth/ BA, Purdue U., 1968; JD, U. Va., 1975. Bar: Calif. Assoc. atty. O'Melveny & Myers, L.A., 1975-82; v.p., gen. counsel Cannon Mills Co., Kannapolis, N.C., 1982-84; ptnr. Stradling, Yocca, Newport Beach, Calif., 1984-89, Jones, Day, Reavis & Pogue, Irvine, 1990-95, Paul, Hastings, Janofsky & Walker, Costa Mesa, 1995—. Mem. Calif. Commn. on Future of Legal Profession and State Bar, 1994; lectr. in field. Mem. adv. com. St. Joseph Hosp., Orange, Calif., 1987-93; bd. dirs. Lincoln Club Orange County, 1991-93, South Coast Symphony, 1989-92; mem. found. bd. Orange County H.S. Arts. Capt. U.S. Army, 1968—72. Mem. Orange County Bar Assn., Performing Arts Bus. Alliance South Coast Repertory Silver Circle. Roman Catholic. Avocations: downhill skiing, swimming. Home: 2621 Circle Dr Newport Beach CA 92663-5616 Office: Paul Hastings Janofsky & Walker LLP 695 Town Center Dr Fl 17 Costa Mesa CA 92626-1924 E-mail: petertennyson@paulhastings.com.

TENORIO, MANOEL FERNANDO DA MOTA, computer engineering educator; b. Maceio, Alagoas, Brazil, Oct. 24, 1957; came to U.S., 1981; s. Igor Souza and Maria Luiza (Maia) T.; m. Anne Elizabeth Grant, July 4, 1987; children: Joshua Emanuel, Jonathan Daniel, Katherine Anna. BSEE, Nat. Inst. Telecomm., Brazil, 1979; MSEE, Colo. State U., 1984; PhD, U. So. Calif., 1987. Teaching asst., instr. Nat. Inst. Telecomm., 1977-79; dir. R&D C.S. Systems and Components Ltda, Itajuba, MG, Brazil, 1979-80; rsch. asst. Colo. State U., Ft. Collins, 1981-82, U. So. Calif., L.A., 1982-85; lectr. elec. engring. UCLA, 1985-86, U. So. Calif., L.A., 1985-86; rsch. scientist Varian Rsch. Ctr., Palo Alto, Calif., 1986-87; asst. prof. elec. engring. Purdue U., West Lafayette, Ind., 1987—, coord. parallel distributed processing structures lab., 1988—. Vis. researcher Ctr. for Computer Tech., Campinas, Sao Paulo, Brazil, 1982-85; lectr., panelist, presenter workshops, cons. in field; assoc. researcher Inst. Logic, Theory and Philosophy of Sci., ILTC, Rio de Janeiro, 1990—. Mem. editorial bd. sci. computing and automation Elsevier, 1989-90; contbr. articles, tech. reports to profl. publs., chpts. to books. Conselho Nacional de Pesquisa scholar, 1981-85, Coordenadoria de Aperfeicoamento de Pessoal de Ensino Superior scholar, 1979-80; grantee Davis Ross, 1988, 87-89, Knowles Electronics, 1987, Battelle, 1990, Army Rsch. Office, 1989-92, Dept. HHS, 1988—, GE Found., 1991-92. Mem. IEEE (neural network coun. com. 1991—), Assn. for Computing Machinery, Am. Assn. Artificial Intelligence, Internat. Neural Network Soc. Achievements include patents for parallel knowledge processing method for integrated circuit implementation, randomlike information decoding system, dynamical system circuit for dense memory storage, communication system employing chaotic signals. Office: Purdue U Sch Elec Engring West Lafayette IN 47907

TENT, JAMES FOSTER, historian; b. Ridgewood, N.J., Jan. 15, 1944; s. James Robert and Virginia June (Foster) T.;m. Margaret Bunting Wyman, Aug. 17, 1968; children: John Fleming, Virginia Foster. AB, Dartmouth Coll., 1966; MA, U. Wis., 1969, PhD, 1973. Vis. asst. prof. Cornell Coll., Mt. Vernon, Iowa, 1973-74; from asst. prof. to dept. chmn. U. Ala., Birmingham, 1974—2002, dept. chmn., 2002—. Guest prof. U. Hanover, Germany, 1982-83, Free Univ. Berlin, 1985-88. Author: Mission on the Rhine: Denazification & Reeducation in Germany, 1982, The Free University of Berlin: A Political History, 1988, E-Boat Alert: Defending the Normandy Invasion Fleet, 1996; author, editor: Academic Proconsul: E.Y. Hartshorne and Reopening German Universities, 1998. Ford Found. grantee, 1969-72. Mem. Am. Hist. Assn., German Studies Assn., So. Hist. Assn., Birmingham Soc. Piping, Phi Kappa Phi. Avocations: reading, hiking, gardening, model aircraft building, flying. Office: U Ala Dept History 1212 University Blvd Birmingham AL 35294-0001 E-mail: jtent@uab.edu.

TENTSER, ALEXANDER, music educator, conductor; b. Kiev, Ukraine, Nov. 23, 1965; arrived in U.S., 1990; s. Mikhael and Dina Tentser; m. Anna Gendler, Jan. 19, 1985; 1 child Misha. M in Piano Performance, Russian Music Acad., Moscow, 1989; D in Musical Arts, U. Ariz., 1996. Cert. coll. tchr. Ariz. Tchr. piano and music theory Pima C.C., Tucson, 1997—; music dir. Pima C.C. Orch., 2001—. Founder, music dir. Cochise Coll. Chamber Orch., Sierra Vista, Ariz., 1999—2001; tchr. piano Cochise Coll., Sierra Vista, Ariz., 1997—2001; founder, artistic dir. Adirondack Piano Inst., Saranac Lake, NY, 2001—; lectr. Extended U. Ariz., Tucson, 1996—. Grantee profl. devel. grantee, Ariz. Commn. on Arts, Phoenix, 1994. Mem.: Music Tchrs. Nat. Assn. Avocation: travel. Office: Pima CC 2202 W Anklam Rd Tucson AZ 85709

TENTZERIS, EMMANOUIL M. engineering educator, researcher; b. Athens, Greece, Mar. 20, 1970; came to U.S., 1992; s. Markos E. Tentzeris and Irene M. Tentzeri. Diploma summa cum laude, Nat. Tech. U. Athens, 1992; MSc, U. Mich., 1993, PhD, 1998. Asst. prof. Ga. Inst. Tech., Atlanta, 1998—. Invited profl. Tech. U. Munich, 2002; RF thrust leader NSF-GT-Packaging Rsch. Ctr., 1998; broadband tech. hardware, subthrust leader Yamacraw Rsch. Initiative of State of Ga., 2000; tech. program co-chair Automatic Radio Frequency Techniques Group, Atlanta, 1999; vice-chair IEEE-Components Packaging and Mfg. Tech. Tech. Com. 16 Radio Frequency/Wireless. Author: (with others) Advances Computational FM, 1998, Electronic Packaging, 2000, The RF and Microwave Handbook, 2001; reviewer in field. Recipient Best Paper award, Internat. Microelectronics and Packaging Soc. Symposium, 1997, Applied Computational Electromagnetics Soc. Symposium, 2001, Career award NSF, 2000, Ga. Tech.-ECE Outstanding Jr. Faculty award 2002; Greek Acad. Excellence fellow Greek Dept. Edn., 1988-92; Papastavridios Greek Math Excellence fellow Greek Govt., 1989. Mem. IEEE (MTT-AP Atlanta chpt., bd. com. mem., tech. session chair 1996, 2000, 2001, 2002, chair steering com. mem. 1998), Ga. Tech. Wireless Inst., Tech. Chamber of Greece. Avocations: sports, history books, travel. Home: 5121 Lenox Park Cir Atlanta GA 30319 Office: Ga Inst Tech Sch ECE 777 Atlantic Dr Atlanta GA 30332-0250

TENUTA, LUIGIA, lawyer; b. Madison, Wis., June 4, 1954; d. Eugene P. and Nancy (Gardner) T. AB in Internat. Studies with honors, Miami U., Oxford, Ohio, 1976; JD, Capital U., 1981; postgrad., Pontifical Coll. Josephinum, 1987-88. Bar: Ohio 1981. With internat. mktg. dept. Dresser Industries, Columbus, Ohio, 1976-80, analyst strategic planning, 1980, mgr. internat bus. planning Stratford, Conn., 1981; pvt. practice law Columbus, 1981—. Former mem. devel. com. Miami U. Mem. Ohio Bar Assn., Columbus Bar Assn. Roman Catholic. Office: 6400 Riverside Dr Dublin OH 43017-5197

TEPE, JUDITH MILDRED, vocal music teacher, choral director; b. Merrill, Wis. d. Herbert August and Mildred Lorna (Utech) Zamzow; m. Roger Charles Tepe, Aug. 7, 1976; children: Elizabeth, Jonathan, Rachel. BA in Music Edn., Concordia Coll., Moorhead, Minn., 1972; ME in Curriculum and Instrn., Lesley Coll., Cambridge, Mass., 1993. Choral and gen. music tchr. Shawano (Wis.) Sch. Dist., 1972-74, Howard-Suamico Schs., Green Bay, Wis., 1974-77; dir. music Pilgrim Luth. Ch., 1975-80; choral and band tchr. NEW Luth. H.S., 1977-78; dir. music Faith Luth. ch., 1982-91; artistic dir. Green Bay Boy Choir, DePere, Wis., 1990—; vocal music specialist Green Bay Pub. Schs., 1991—. Recipient Golden Apple Tchr. of Distinction award Green Bay C. of C., 1997. Mem. Am. Choral Dirs. Assn., Music Educators Nat. Conf., Voice Care Network. Democrat. Avocations: reading, golf, cooking, travel, the outdoors. Home: 1187 Robin St De Pere WI 54115-3132 Office: Green Bay Boy Choir 1016 N Broadway De Pere WI 54115-2610

TEPHLY, THOMAS ROBERT, pharmacologist, toxicologist, educator; b. Norwich, Conn., Feb. 1, 1936; m. Joan Bernice Clifcorn, Dec. 17, 1960; children: Susan Lynn, Linda Ann, Annette Michele. BS, U. Conn., 1957; PhD, U. Wis., 1962; MD, U. Minn., 1965. Research asst. U. Wis., Madison, 1957-62, instr., 1962; asst. prof. U. Mich., Ann Arbor, 1965-69, assoc. prof., 1969-71; prof. pharmacology U. Iowa, Iowa City, 1971—. Contbr. articles to profl. jours. Rsch. scholar Am. Cancer Soc., 1962-65; recipient John Jacob Abel award, 1971, Kenneth P. Dubois award, 1992; Fogarty sr. internat. fellow NIH, 1978; rsch. grantee NIH, 1966—. Mem. Am. Soc. Pharmacology and Exptl. Therapeutics, Soc. Toxicology, AAAS, Am. Soc. Biochem. Molecular Biologists. Home: 6 Lakeview Dr NE Iowa City IA 52240-9142 Office: U Iowa Dept Pharmacology 2-452 BSB Iowa City IA 52242

TEPLEN, PHILIP H. lawyer; b. N.Y.C., Apr. 26, 1957; s. Martin Joseph and Pearl Faye Teplen; m. Patti Anne Teplen, Sept. 22, 1984; children: William, Amanda. BSBA in Fin., Georgetown U., 1979, Oxford U., 1979; JD, Bklyn. Law Sch., 1982. Prin. Teplen & Assocs. PLLC, N.Y.C., 1984—; founder, pres. Tepco Fin., 1986-88; gen. counsel, v.p. Baron Devel., 1988-91; founder, pres. Intelligent Solutions, 1994-96; exec. v.p. Rupert Techs. Group Inc., 2002—. Guest lectr. Fla. Internat. U. Miami, 1999. Avocations: boating, tennis, golf. Office: 350 Fifth Ave New York NY 10118 E-mail: pteplen@phtlawyers.com.

TEPLITZ, ROBERT FORMAN, lawyer; b. Miami, Fla., Dec. 20, 1970; s. Alan Forman and Judith (Roberts) T. BA magna cum laude, Franklin & Marshall Coll., 1992; JD cum laude, Cornell U., 1995. Bar: Pa. 1995, U.S. Dist. Ct. (mid. dist.) Pa. 1997. Litigation assoc. McNees, Wallace & Nurick, Harrisburg, Pa., 1995-98; policy dir. Casey for Gov. campaign, 2001—02; dep. chief counsel Dept. Auditor Gen., Harrisburg, 1998—2001, spl. asst. to chief of staff, 2002—. Bd. dirs. Am. Cancer Soc., Harrisburg, 1996—, Harrisburg Jewish Cmty. Ctr., 2000—. Mem. Phi Beta Kappa. Office: Casey for Gov 300 N 2nd St Harrisburg PA 17101 E-mail: robteplitz@aol.com.

TEPLITZKY, PHILIP HERMAN, information technology executive; b. Bklyn., Apr. 12, 1949; s. Moe and Blanch (Lewis) T.; m. Harriet Grossman, Aug. 8, 1982; 1 child, Ben. BA, Harpur Coll., Binghamton, N.Y., 1970; MS, Sch. Advanced Tech., Binghamton, 1977. Ptnr. Plagman Group, N.Y.C., 1981-85; sr. mgr. Price Waterhouse, 1985-86; dir. Coopers & Lybrand, 1988-92; mng. dir. tech. SystemHouse, 1992—99; chief tech. officer The Vitamin Shoppe, 2001—; chief info. officer Harry Fox Agy., 2001—. Mem. industry adv. panel NYU, N.Y.C., 1991—. Mem. editorial adv. bd. Auerbach Data Security Jour., 1991. Treas. Jewish Family Svc., Rockland County, 1992—. Mem. IEEE, Assn. Computing Machinery. Home: 2 Southerly Pl New City NY 10956-6622

TEPLOW, THEODORE HERZL, retired valve company executive; b. Brockton, Mass., Apr. 14, 1928; s. Edward Abraham and Evelyn (Stone) T.; m. Charlotte Leah Savitz, June 14, 1953; children: Rachel P., David I., Deborah R., Evan S., Jonathan P. BS, U.S. Mcht. Marine Acd., 1950; MBA, Harvard U., 1953; DHL honoris causa, Hebrew Coll., 1999. Mgmt. trainee to pres. Crosby Valve Inc. a Tyco Internat. Ltd. Co., Wrentham, Mass., 1953-82, cons., 1982-99; dir. Emerson Investment Mgmt., Inc., Boston, 1985—. Cons. Firesafe Products Corp., N.Y.C., 1982-96. Trustee Am. Mcht. Marine Mus. Found., Kings Point, N.Y., 1988-98, Rofeh Internat., Boston, 1990—, Hebrew Coll., Brookline, Mass., 1971—, chmn., 1992-99; chmn. Hebrew Coll. Bd. Mgrs. of Trust Property, 1999—; trustee Kings Point Challenge, 1997—; v.p., bd. dirs. Internat. Catacomb Soc., Boston, 1982-99; bd. dirs. Cong. Beth El-Atereth Israel, Newton Center, Mass., 1975-85, Beth El Cmty. Hebrew Sch., Newton Center, 1965-85, USMMA Found., Kings Point, 1988—; asst. treas., dir. Am. Com. for Weizmann Inst. Sci., N.Y., 1987—; gov. Weizmann Inst. Sci., Rehovoth, Israel, 1991—; bd. dirs. Wilstein Inst. Jewish Policy Studies, L.A., Boston, 1993—, Stone Charitable Found., 1982-99; dir. Archives for Hist. Documentation, Boston, 1994—. Comdr. USNR, ret. Recipient Outstanding Profl. Achievement award U.S. Mcht. Marine Acad. Alumni Assn., 1970, Meritorious Alumni Svc. award, 1990, Disting. Svc. award, 1995. Democrat.

TEPPER, CLIFFORD, allergist, immunologist, educator; b. Schenectady, N.Y., Oct. 26, 1922; s. Solomon B. and Annette (Lifset) T.; m. Cynthia S. Tepper; children: Stewart, Nancy, Henry, Audrey. Chief allergy dept. Ellis Hosp., Schenectady, 1990—; allergist allergy asthma immunology ctr. Albany Med. Coll., Albany, N.Y., 1992—. Prof. pediatrics Albany (N.Y.) Med. Coll., 1973—; cons. in field. Trustee Schenectady Mus., 1987-99, Schenectady Pub. Libr., 1985—. Mem. Coll. Allergy and Immunology, Am. Acad. Pediatrics, Am. Acad. Allergy and Immunology, New Eng. Soc. Allergy (pres. 1990-92), N.Y. State Allergy Soc. (treas. 1993-95), Physicians for Social Responsibility. Avocations: bird watching, art history. Home: 2216 Stoneridge Rd Niskayuna NY 12309-5524 Office: Allergy Asthma Immunology Ctr Albany Med Coll 1201 Washihngton Ave Ext Albany NY 12205 Fax: 518 452 2683. E-mail: CTEPPER804@aol.com.

TEPPER, GARY, engineering educator; b. Latrobe, Pa., Sept. 8, 1965; s. William and Clara Tepper; m. Pooran Tepper; children: Ryan, Roya. PhD in Engring. Physics, U. Calif., San Diego, 1993. Asst. prof. engring. physics W.Va. Wesleyan Coll., Buckhannon, 1996—97; assoc. prof. chem. engring. Va. Commonwealth U., Richmond, 1997—. Pres. Sentor Techs. Inc., Glen Allen, Va., 1998—. Contbr. articles to profl. jours. Recipient Ralph E. Powe Outstanding Jr. Faculty award, Oak Ridge Associated Univs., 1998. Mem.: Va. Acad. Sci. (sect. chair 2001—), Internat. Soc. Optical Engring. Office: Va Commonwealth U 601 West Main St Richmond VA 23284 Office Fax: 804-828-3846. Business E-Mail: gctepper@saturn.vcu.edu.

TEPPER, HOWARD, partner; b. Jan. 31, 1963; BA in Acctg. and Info. Sys., CUNY, 1984, MBA in Healthcare Adminstrn., 1988. Adminstr. Mt. Sinai Med. Ctr., N.Y.C., 1984-87, Beth Israel Med. Ctr., N.Y.C., 1989-91; adminstrv. dir. St. Vincent's Hosp. and Med. Ctr., 1991-93; dir. adminstrn. Univ. Medicine and Dentistry, Newark, 1993—2002; ptnr. Grassi Healthcare Consulting, 2002—. Contbr. chpts. to books.

TEPPER, LLOYD BARTON, physician; b. L.A., Dec. 21, 1931; m. Lamonte Leverage; children: Jeffrey Hamilton, Evan Clothier. AB, Dartmouth Coll., 1954; MD, Harvard U., 1957, MIH, 1960, ScD in Hygiene, 1962. Diplomate in occupational medicine Am. Bd. Preventive Medicine. Rsch. fellow Harvard Med. Sch., Boston, 1958-59; clin. fellow Mass. Gen. Hosp., 1958-60; rsch. assoc. MIT, Cambridge, 1959-61; physician U.S. AEC, Washington, 1962-65; prof. environ. health U. Cin., 1965-72; assoc. dir. Kettering Lab., Cin., 1965-72; assoc. commr. U.S. FDA, Washington, 1972-76; corp. med. dir. Air Products and Chems., Inc., Allentown, Pa., 1976-97; adj. prof. medicine Jefferson Med. Coll., 1998—2001. Dir. Chem. Industry Inst. Toxicology, Research Triangle Park, N.C., 1982-89; trustee Am. Bd. Preventive Medicine, vice chair, 1986-94; adj. prof. emergency medicine U. Pa., 2000—. Editor Jour. Occupational Medicine, 1979-91. Fellow Am. Coll. Occupational and Environ. Medicine, Am. Acad. Occupational Medicine (pres. 1980-81). E-mail: lbtepper@icdc.com.

TEPPER, LYNN MARSHA, gerontology educator; b. N.Y.C., Mar. 16, 1946; m. William Chester Tepper, Aug. 27, 1967; children: Sharon Joy, Michelle Dawn. BS, SUNY, Buffalo, 1967; MA, Wayne State U., 1971; MS, Columbia U., 1977, EdM, 1978, EdD, 1980. Instr. John F. Kennedy Sch., Berlin, 1967-68, ednl. counselor, 1968-69; ednl. coordinator Army Edn. Ctr., 1969-71; psychologist U.S. Dept. Def., 1971-73; prof. Gerontology L.I. U., 1979-99, Columbia U., N.Y.C., 1982—. Cons. NATO, Naples, Italy, 1969-71, SHAPE, Brussels, 1969-71, also numerous nursing homes, N.Y., 1978—, Found. for Long Term Care, 1992—; prof. gerontology Mercy Coll., Dobbs Ferry, 1979—; dir. Gerontology Resource Ctr., Ctr. for Geriatrics and Gerontology, Columbia U., N.Y.C., 1980-85, dir. Behavioral Sci. Program, 1982—; del. White House Conf. on Aging, 1980. Author: (textbooks) Long Term Care, 1993, Respite Care, 1993; contbr. articles to profl. jours., chpts. to books. Advisor Office on Aging, State of N.Y., Albany, 1980-90; dir. Mercy Coll., Inst. Gerontology, 1990—; trustee, St. Cabrini Nursing Home, 1988-98, Morningside Nursing Home, 1998—; bd. dirs. Found. Long Term Care. Brookdale Inst. on Aging fellow, 1983; rsch. grantee NIH, Nat. Inst. on Aging, U.S. Dept. Edn., U.S. Bur. Health Professions, interdisciplinary geriat. tng. U.S. Dept. Health Resources Svcs. Adminstrn. Fellow Gerontol. Soc. Am.; mem. Northeastern Gerontol. Soc., Am. Psychol. Assn. Avocations: physical fitness, hiking. Home: Burnside Dr Yonkers NY 10706-3013 Office: Columbia U Med Campus Box 20 630 W 168th St New York NY 10032-3702

TEPPER, RICHARD EDWARD, infectious disease physician; b. Phila., Sept. 5, 1955; s. Milton and Bernice (Hurwitz) T.; m. Ellen Robin Licht, Aug. 20, 1983; children: David, Daniel. BS, Muhlenberg Coll., 1977; MD, Pa. State U., 1981. Diplomate Am. Bd. Internal Medicine, Am. Bd. Infectious Diseases. Intern Med. Coll. of Pa., Phila., 1981-82, resident in internal medicine, 1981-84, chief resident in internal medicine, 1984-85; coord. internal medicine residency program Frankford Hosp., 1984-85; infectious disease fellow SUNY, Bklyn., 1985-87; infectious disease physician Jeanes Hosp., Phila., 1987—, co-chmn. med. rev. com., 1993-98, med. dir. transitional care unit, 1996-99, chmn. med. rev. com., 1998—. Mem. ACP, AMA, Am. Soc. Microbiology, Pa. State Med. Soc., Phila. County Med. Soc., Infectious Disease Soc. Am., Phi Beta Kappa. Avocations: computers, tennis. Office: PO Box 187 Southampton PA 18966-0157

TEPPER, ROBERT ERIC, physician; b. Bklyn., Sept. 8, 1963; s. Stanley and Sandra (Lippan) T.; m. Linda Ellen Kanarvogel, Nov. 20, 1993. BA in Premed. Sci. summa cum laude, Lehigh U., 1985; MD, Med. Coll. Pa., 1987. Diplomate Nat. Bd. Med. Examiners, Am. Bd. Internal Medicine, Am. Bd. Gastroenterology. Intern in medicine NYU Med. Ctr., N.Y.C., 1987-88, resident in medicine, 1988-90, chief resident, 1990-91; fellow in gastroenterology Montefiore Med. Ctr., Bronx, N.Y., 1991-93; physician gastroenterology Nassau Gastroenterology Assocs., P.C., Great Neck, 1993—. Teaching asst. in medicine NYU Sch. Medicine, 1989—; sr. asst. attending physician North Shore Univ. Hosp., Manhasset, N.Y., 1993—, L.I. Jewish Med. Ctr., New Hyde Park, N.Y., 1994—, St. Francis Hosp., Roslyn, N.Y., 1994—. Contbr. articles to profl. jours. Fellow Am. Coll. Gastroenterology, ACP; mem. AMA, Am. Gastroent. Assn., Med. Soc. State of N.Y., Crohn's and Colitis Found. Am. (co-chmn. med. adv. com. L.I. chpt.), Nassau County Med. Soc., Phi Beta Kappa, Alpha Omega Alpha. Republican. Jewish. Avocations: popular music, sports, U.S. coin collecting. Office: Nassau Gastroenterology Assocs PC 1000 Northern Blvd Great Neck NY 11021-5312

TEPPERMAN, BARBARA-DAWN A. clinical psychologist, marriage/family therapist; b. N.Y.C., June 17, 1947; d. David and Sarah Tepperman; m. Dr. John H. Yoepp. BA, Hunter Coll., 1972; MA, New Sch. for Social Rsch., 1975; PhD, Fla. Inst. Tech., 1982; grad., Landmark Forum. Clin. psychologist Lincoln Ctr. the Whole Person, Melbourne, 1989—. Cons. Wellsprings Health Ranch, Melbourne, 1984—87, Child Care Assoc., Cocoa, Fla., Devereux Hosp. and Children's Ctr., Melbourne, Alpha Med. Ctr., Melbourne; group movement/dance therapist Humanist Growth Ctr., Melbourne; psychology instr. Brevard C.C., Barry U., Rollins Coll.; psycho remedial therapist Madeline Borg Child Guidance Ctr., N.Y.C., Homes Regional Med. Ctr.; mem. continuing med. edn. com. Women's Healthcare Adv. Coun. ; assoc. med. staff Cirs. of Care. Columnist: Heartlines, 1992; (personality): radio and TV talk shows; (presenter in field): ; contbr. art and articles to media. Hunter Coll. Alumni grantee, 1971. Mem.: BMAS, Fla. Native Plant Soc., Nat. Coalition of Art Therapy Assns. (presenter Healing the Healer 1991), Brevard Assn. Human Svcs., Fla. Art Therapy Assn., South Brevard Profl. Women's Network (steering com. 1990—2000), Fla. Psychol. Assn (chpt. edn. chair 1996—98, pres. 1998—2000, chpt. edn. chair 2002—), Strawbridge Art League, Bonsai Soc. Avocations: art, music, dance, nature, health. Office: Lincoln Ctr for the Whole Person 701 E Lincoln Ave Melbourne FL 32901-4646 E-mail: Dr.Tepperman@cs.com.

TER-ABRAMYANTS, LALA ABRAMOVNA, artist, educator; b. Myaundzha, Kclyma, USSR, Aug. 4, 1956; d. Abram Moiseevitch and Valentina Vasilevna (Shestakova) T.-A.; m. Vitaliy Alexandrovich Osminin, July 8, 1980 (div. Sept. 1988); 1 child, Veronika Osminina; m. Alex Korsunsky, Jan. 5, 1991; 1 child, Abram Korsunsky. Student, Art Inst. Moscow, 1990. Photo retoucher Armavir (Russia) Photo Studio, 1974-75; artist designer Rwy. Sta. Dept., Moscow, 1975-80; archivist Art Inst. Moscow, 1983-86; graphic artist Newspaper Pub. House, Moscow, 1986-87; visual artist Factory of Art Prodn., 1987-90, silk painter, 1990-92; pvt. tchr. drawing and painting Bronx, N.Y., 1994—; instr. painting on silk Riverdale YM-YWHA, N.Y.C., 1995. Batic textile artist OUS Co. Inc., 1993—. Exhibited in group shows at Moscow Textile Fabrics, Oslo, Norway, 1991, Ctrl. House of Painters, Moscow, 1992, Princeton, N.Y., 1992, Madison Sq., N.Y.C., 1992, NYANA, N.Y.C., 1993, L.I., N.Y., 1994, Lincoln Sq., N.Y.C., 1996. Avocations: theater, cinema, music, reading, cooking. Home: 3871 Sedgwick Ave Apt 6J Bronx NY 10463-4467

TERAMURA, ALAN HIROSHI, science educator; b. L.A., Dec. 26, 1948; s. Kuniyoshi and Mineko (Nakamura) T.; m. Karen Lee McKnight, Sept. 10, 1974; 2 children. BA, Calif. State U., 1971, MA, 1973; PhD, Duke U., 1978. Asst. prof. botany U. Md., College Park, 1979-82, assoc. prof. botany, 1982-88, prof. botany, 1988-93; dean Coll. Natural Scis. U. Hawaii, Honolulu, 1994—, sr. v.p. for rsch., dean grad. divsin., 1997—. Guest prof. Botanishes Inst., Karlsruhe, Germany, 1982-83; chmn. sci. adv. bd. Ctr. Global Change, College Park, 1989-93; cons. USDA, EPA, Nat. Acad. Sci., Washington, 1982—. Contbr. chpts. to 12 books and 80 articles to profl. jours. Grantee NSF, 1977, 1996, U.S. EPA, 1980-90, USDA, 1989-93. Mem. Am. Soc. Plant Physiologists, Botanical Soc. Am., Ecol. Soc. Am., Sigma Xi. Achievements include advanced research on effects of global climate change. Office: U Hawaii Office Dean Coll Natural Scis 102 Bilger Honolulu HI 96822

TERANES, PAUL S. county judge, mediator; b. Milw., June 25, 1935; s. Stephen Raymond and Anne Teresa Teranes; m. Barbara J. Teranes, Dec. 28, 1966; children: Richard, Jane, Daniel, Amy. AB, Coll. Holy Cross, Worcester, Mass., 1958; JD, U. Mich., 1961. Bar: Mich. 1961. Asst. prosecuting atty. Wayne County, Detroit, 1962-82; cir. ct. judge Wayne County Circuit Ct., 1982—. Trustee Upshaw Inst. for Blind, Detroit, 1982-2001, pres., 1995; trustee Great Lakes Ctr. Ind. Living, Detroit, 1988-94; chmn. disabilities com., Mich. Open Justice Commn., 1998—; bd. trustees Leader Dog Sch. for Blind, Rochester, Mich., 1998—, sec., 2000—. Voted in top 5 most respected Mich. judges, Lawyers Weekly newspaper poll, 1991; named Outstanding Profl. Alumnus, U. Detroit H.S., 1985. Mem. Cath. Lawyers Assn. (bd. trustees), Mich. Judges Assn., Mich. Bar Assn., Detroit Met. Bar Assn., Witenagamode Soc. Avocation: bicycling. Office: Wayne County Circuit Ct 2 Woodward Ave CYMB Detroit MI 48226

TERAUDS, JURIS, science educator; b. Jelgava, Latvia, Oct. 15, 1936; s. Janis Hermanis and Tatjana Terauds; m. Shirley Jean Henry, Jan. 4, 1961 (div. Oct. 15, 1986); children: Jeffry Juris, Dana Kelly, Kimberly Kirsten. BS, Univ. Dubuque, Dubuque, IA, 1961; MS, Biomechanics, LA State Univ., Lost Angeles, CA, 1965; PhD (hon.) , Univ. Md., College Park, MD, 1972. Instr. Univ. Md., College Park, Md., 1968—72; assoc. prof. Univ. Tex., Odessa, 1972—75; prof. Univ. Alta., Edmonton, Canada, 1975—80; adj. prof. San Diego State Univ., San Diego, 1981—86; prof./dept. head Colo. State Univ., Fort Collins, 1986—90, prof. emeritus, 1991—. Pres. Internat. Soc. of Biomechanics Sports, San Diego, 1978—85, Rsch. Ctr. for Sports, Fort Collins, Colo., 1978—; ceo X-Iser Industries, Fort Collins, Colo., 1991—. Author: (several books on) Biomechanics, over 80 articles. Editor IAF Internat. Olympic Com., London, England, 1978—90, IAAF Internat. Olympic Cmte., London, England, 1978—90; rsch. dir. Olympics of Montreal, Montreal, Canada, 1976; chmn. SPIE Photooptical Instruments, 1982; chmn. photooptical instruments SPIE, 1982. Recipient Superior Contbn., Internat. Olympic Cmte., 1976, Profl. Achievement, Univ. Dubuque, IA, 1999; fellow, Internat. Soc. of Biomechanics in Sports, 1998. Fellow: Internat. Soc. of Biomechanics in Sports (dir. 1978—2002); mem.: Internat. High Speed Cinematography & Videography (chmn. 1982—88). Achievements include invention of Stepping Exercise Machine, 1977-2002. Avocations: reading, digital motion analysis, digital motion analysis, videography. Home: 3319 Lone Jack Road Encinitas CA 92024-7014 Office: X-Iser Industries RCS 1501 West Lake Fort Collins CO 80521 Office Fax: 858-756-2478.

TERBORG-PENN, ROSALYN MARIAN, historian, educator; b. Bklyn., Oct. 22, 1941; d. Jacques Arnold Sr. and Jeanne (Van Horn) Terborg; 1 dau., Jeanna Carolyn Terborg Penn. BA in History, Queens Coll. CUNY, 1963; MA in History, George Washington U., 1967; PhD in Afro-Am. History, Howard U., 1978. Daycare tchr. Friendship House Assn., Washington, 1964-66; program dir. Southwest House Assn., 1966-69; adj. prof. U. Md.-Balt. County, Catonsville, 1977-78, Howard C.C., Columbia, Md., 1970-74; prof. history Morgan State U., Balt., 1969—, project dir. oral history project, 1978-79, coord. grad. programs in history, 1986—. Project dir. Assn. Black Women Hist. Rsch. Conf., Washington, 1982-83. Author: (with Thomas Holt and Cassandra Smith-Parker) A Special Mission: the Story of Freedman's Hospital, 1862-1962, 1975, African American Women in the Struggle for the Vote, 1850-1920, 1998; editor: (with Sharon Harley) The Afro-American Woman: Struggles and Images, 1978, 81, 97, (with Darlene Clark Hine and Elsa Barkley Brown) Black Women in America: An Historical Encyclopedia, 1993, 94, (with Sharon Harley and Andrea Benton Rushing) Women in Africa, 1987, (with Andrea Benton Rushing) Women in Africa and the African Diaspora: A Reader, 1996, (with Janice Sumler-Edmond) Black Women's History at the Intersection of Knowledge and Power, 2000; history editor Feminist Studies, 1984-89; mem. editl. bd. Md. Hist. Mag., 1988-94. Founding mem. Howard County Commn. for Women. Ford Found. fellow, 1980-81, Smithsonian Instn. fellow, 1982, 94-95; Howard U. grad. fellow in history, 1973-74, recipient Rayford W. Logan Grad. Essay award Howard U., 1973, Letitia Woods Brown Meml. prize for best article, 1988, Anna Julia Cooper award for disting. scholarship Sage Women's Ednl. Press, 1993, Letitia Woods Brown Meml. Book prize, 1998. Mem. Assn. Black Women Historians (co-founder, 1st nat. dir. 1980-82, nat. treas. 1982-84, cert. outstanding achievement 1981, Lorraine A. Williams Leadership award 1998), Am. Hist. Assn. (mem. com. on women historians 1978-81, Joan Kelly Prize com. 1984-86, chair com. on women historians 1991-94), Orgn. Am. Historians (mem. black women's history project adv. com. 1980-81), Alpha Kappa Alpha (mem. Internat. Archives and Heritage com. 1994-96). Office: Morgan State U 1700 E Cold Spring Ln Baltimore MD 21251-0002

TERCHEK, RONALD JOHN, political science educator; b. Cleve., July 29, 1936; s. John Allen Terchek and Ann Marie (Race) Eckart; m. Mary Ellen Joseph, Mar. 23, 1968; children: Kristin, Daniel. BA, U. Chgo., 1958, MA, 1960; PhD, U. Md., 1965. From asst. prof. to prof. govt. and politics U. Md., College Park, 1963—. Lectr. numerous colls. in U.S., Can., Europe, and India; chmn. Founds. of Polit. Theory, 1990-93, bd. dirs.; chmn. Spitz Award Com. Conf. for the Study of Polit. Thought, 1986-89, 94. Author: Making of the Test Ban Treaty, 1970, Republican Paradoxes and Liberal Anxieties, 1997, Gandhi: Struggling for Autonomy, 1998; editor: Foreign Policy as Public Policy, 1982, Democratic Theory: A Reader, 2001; editl. adv. bd. Gandhian Studies; contbr. articles to profl. jours. Grantee Lilly Found., 1993-94, U. Md. Mem. Am. Polit Sci. Assn. (coms., program organizer, Profl. award 1989), So. Polit. Sci. Assn., Southwestern Polit. Sci. Assn., Northeastern Polit Sci. Assn., Soc. for the Philos. Study of Polit. and Legal Thought. Democrat. Roman Catholic. Avocations: music, reading, gardening, hiking. Home: 919 Sligo Creek Pky Takoma Park MD 20912-5810 Office: U Md Dept Govt And Politics College Park MD 20742-0001 Fax: 301-314-9690. E-mail: rterchek@gupt.umd.edu.

TERENZIO, MARION ANN, college program executive; b. Stamford, Conn., Aug. 8, 1954; d. Emanuele and Josephine Terenzio. AB in Music, Vassar U., 1976; MA in Music Therapy, Tex. Woman's U., 1979; MA in Cmty. Psychology, Sage Grad. Sch., Troy, N.Y., 1989; PhD in Cmty. Psychology, Mich. State U., 1991. Prof. psychology and arts The Sage Colls., Troy, 1999—, v.p. campus life, 1999—. Cons. music therapy various allied health agencies, 1985-98, Albany (N.Y.) Med. Ctr., 1993-96, colls. and univs., 1998—. Founding editor N.Am. Assn. Masters in Psychology newsletter, 1994-97; contbg. editor jour. Psychology and Mgmt., 2001. Bd. dirs. Troy Area United Ministries, 1994-98, Troy Savs. Bank Music Hall, 1996—, Rensselear County C. of C., Troy, 1999; mem. program com. Regional Art Ctr., Troy, 1994-98. Recipient Rubin Found. grant, 1998, Faculty Study award Pew Charitable Trust, 1998, grant Very Spl. Arts Washington, 1999, Disting. Svc. award Hudson McHawk Assn., 1999, Alumnae award Friend of Russell Sage Coll., 2000, Nat. Fellowship Program award for higher edn. adminstr. Am. Coun. on Edn. Mem. APA, Soc. Rsch. (chair com. on women 1995), N.Am. Assn. for Masters in Psychology, Nat. Music Therapy Assn., Nat. Assn. for Student Pers. Adminstrs. Avocation: karate (black belt). Office: The Sage Colls 45 Ferry St Troy NY 12180-4115 E-mail: terenm@sage.edu.

TERESI, JOSEPH, publishing executive; b. Mpls., Mar. 13, 1941; s. Cliff I.A. and Helen Ione (Leslie) (dec.); 1 child, Nicholas (dec.). CEO Jammer Cycle Products Inc., Burbank, Calif., 1968—80, Paisano Pubs. LLC , Agoura Hills, 1970—; chmn. bd., CEO V-Twin Expo, 1998—. Promoter motorcycle events; prodr. Easyriders Video mag.; owner Teresi Dyno Drags. Pub. (mags.) Easyriders, 1971—, In the Wind, 1974—, Biker, 1986—, Tattoo, 1986—, Am. Rodder, 1987-2001, Womens Enterprise, 1987-89, V-Twin News, 1989—, V-Twin, 1989, Tattoo Flash, 1993—, Tattoo Savage, 1993—, VQ, 1994—, Early-Riders, 1994-96, Quick Throttle, 1995-99, Roadware, 1995—, Tailgate, 2000, Tattoo Industry, 2000, Highbeams, 2003. Achievements include holding the world speed record for motorcycles set at 322 miles per hour, 1990. Avocations: motorcycles, race cars, boats, marlin fishing, skiing. Office: Paisano Pubs LLC PO Box 3000 Agoura Hills CA 91376-3000

TEREZIS, NICK LOUIS, surgeon; b. Wheeling, W.Va., Jan. 14, 1932; MD, U. Pitts., 1956. Diplomate Am. Bd. Surgery. Intern Ohio State U. Hosp., 1956-57; resident surgery Pitts. Med. Ctr. Hosp., 1957-58, 60-62; fellow surgery Pitts.-Presbyn. Hosp., 1957-63; mem. staff Ohio Valley Hosp., Steubenville; pvt. practice, 1963—. Fellow ACS, Am. Coll. Chest Physicians; mem. AMA.

TER HORST, JERALD FRANKLIN, public affairs counsel; b. Grand Rapids, Mich., July 11, 1922; s. John Henry and Maude (Van Strien) ter H.; m. Louise Jeffers Roth, Jan. 20, 1945; children: Karen Bayens Morris, Margaret Fulton Brosnan, Peter Roth, Martha Morgan Lubin. Student, Mich. State U., 1941-42; AB, U. Mich., 1947. Reporter Grand Rapids Press, 1946-51; mem. staff Detroit News, 1953-74, city and state polit. writer, 1953-57, Washington corr., 1958-60; chief Detroit News (Washington bur.), 1961-74; White House press sec. to Pres., 1974; columnist Detroit News/Universal Press Syndicate, 1974-81; nat. dir. public affairs Ford Motor Co., 1981-91; fgn. assignments include Berlin crisis Geneva Fgn. Ministers Conf., Yugoslavia, 1959, 70, Israel, 1960, Eng., Ireland, Germany, Italy and France, 1963, 69, Vietnam, India and Pakistan, 1966, 70, China, 1972, Moscow, 1974, Africa, 1978. Writer N.Am. Newspaper Alliance, 1958-74 Author: Gerald Ford and Future of the Presidency, 1974, The Flying White House: The Story of Air Force One, 1979; contbr. to mags. and TV documentaries. Bd. dirs. Nat. Press Found., 1982-98, Gridiron Found., WETA-TV (Channel 26), 1988-99, Grad. Sch. Polit. Mgmt., George Washington U., 1985-96, Washington, Brady Campaign to Prevent Gun Violence, 1992-2002. Officer USMCR, 1943-46, 51-52. Mem. Pub. Rels. Soc. Am., Soc. Profl. Journalists, Psi Upsilon. Presbyterian (elder). Clubs: Gridiron, Nat. Press. Overseas Writers.

TERILLI, JOSEPH ANTHONY, secondary education educator; b. Winthrop, Mass., June 14, 1948; s. Joseph Anthony and Mary Grace (Colontuoni) T.; m. Carol Ann Saccardo, Oct. 8, 1971; 1 child, Joseph Anthony III. BS, Boston Coll., 1970, MEd, 1973. Tchr., adminstr. Boston Pub. Schs., 1972-77; tchr. Coolidge Jr. H.S., Reading, Mass., 1977-84, Reading Meml. H.S., 1984—, mentor tchr., 1988—. Pres., CEO Terilli Enterprises Devel. Corp., Aruba, 1986—; mem. Profl. Devel. Com., Reading, 1988-92. Author: Blood on the Chalkboard, How Children Succeed, also newspaper articles, booklets, monographs and mock trial; pub. (newsletter) Political Action Network (PAN). Mem. exec. bd., Mass. state chair Dem. Party (New Dems.). Mem. C. of C., Kiwanis (past sec.). Roman Catholic. Avocations: politics, travel, writing, collecting comic books. Home: 27 Lawndale Rd Stoneham MA 02180-1014 Office: Reading Meml HS 62 Oakland Rd Reading MA 01867-1613

TERJUNG, BIRGIT, internist, researcher; b. Bonn, Germany, Feb. 17, 1966; came to U.S., 1998; d. Sigurd and Brigitta (Goerbing) T.; m. Stephan Repges. Grad. in Arch., U. Bonn, 1985-88, 89-91, MD, 1996; student, U. Vienna, Austria, 1988-89; lic. physician, U. Munich, 1993. Resident dept. internal medicine U. Munich, 1991-93; fellow dept. internal medicine U. Bonn, 1993-97, 2000—; postdoctoral rsch. fellow dept. medicine Columbia U., N.Y., 1998-2000. Contbr. chpt. to Autoimmune Liver Disease, 1998, articles to profl. jours. Postdoctoral fellow Deutscher Akademischer Austauschdienst, Bonn, 1998-2000, Lise-Meitner award, 2000—. Mem. Am. Gastroenterol. Assn., German Assn. for Internal Medicine, German Assn. for the Study of the Liver. Home: Gut Capellen 4 53913 Swisttal Germany E-mail: bterjung@uni-bonn.de.

TERK, GLENN THOMAS, lawyer; b. Feb. 27, 1949; s. Raymond Arthur and Marguerite Ida (Nichols) T.; m. Mary Ann Michaud, Sept. 25, 1982. BSME, Clarkson Coll. Tech., 1971; JD, U. Conn., 1976. Bar: Conn. 1976, U.S. Dist. Ct. Conn. 1976. Engr. Combustion Engrng. Co., Windsor, Conn., 1971-76; assoc. Francis, Kroopnick & O'Neil, Hartford, 1976-78; ptnr. Brignole & Terk, 1993-95; pvt. practice, 1995—. Mem. Dem. Town Com., Windsor, 1978-79, Windsor Inland Wetlands Commn., 1978-79, Rep. Town com., Wethersfield, 1997—; chmn. Trinity United Meth. Ch. adminstrv. bd., Windsor, 1982-83, finance chmn. 1997—. Mem. Conn. Bar Assn. (lawyers and cmty. subcom. 1981-85, real property exec. com. 1994—, comml. law com. 1994—). Home: 445 Old Reservoir Rd Wethersfield CT 06109-3956 Office: 81 Wolcott Hill Rd Wethersfield CT 06109-1242 E-mail: Gterk@cs.com.

TERKELSEN, KENNETH G. psychiatrist, hospital administrator; b. Boston, Dec. 13, 1943; s. George Conrad and Joan Marie Terkelsen; m. Kathleen Felz, Aug. 9, 1967; children: David, Erin. BA, Georgetown U., 1965; MD, Jefferson Med. Coll., 1969. Diplomate Am. Bd. Psychiatry and Neurology. Dir. day treatment N.Y. Presbyn. Hosp., White Plains, 1987-95, dir. core care divsn., 1995-98, dir. residency edn., 1998—99; med. dir. inpatient svcs. Mass. DMH at Cape Cod Islands, 1999—. Manuscript reviewer Psychiat. Svcs., Washington, Cmty. Mental Health Jour.; lectr., presenter in field; affiliate faculty Ctr. for Study of Issues in Pub. Mental Health, Nathan Kline Inst. for Psychiat. Rsch., 1993-99. Contbr. articles to profl. jours. Bd. dirs. Search for Change, Inc., 1985-91. Mem. Am. Psychiat. Assn. (mem. com. on rehab. 1990-91, chair com. on psychiat. disability and rehab. 1991-95), Nat. Alliance for Mentally Ill (Exemplary Psychiatrist award 1992), Alpha Omega Alpha. Avocations: hiking, sailing, woodworking, dogs. Office: Cape Cod & Islands CMHC 830 County Rd Pocasset MA 02559-2110 E-mail: Kenneth.Terkelson@dmh.state.ma.us.

TERKLA, DAVID GABRIEL, economics educator; b. Portland, Oreg., May 12, 1953; s. Louis Gabriel and Phyllis Jean (Cohn) T.; m. Dawn Rose Geronimo, Aug. 30, 1975; children: Michael, Heather. BA, Williams Coll., 1975; MA, U. Calif., Berkeley, 1977, PhD, 1979. Asst. prof. Boston U., 1979-87; assoc. prof. U. Mass., Boston, 1987—. Mem. tech. adv. group for mgmt. of Boston Harbor/Mass. Bay Exec. Office Environ. Affairs Commonwealth of Mass., Boston, 1986—, mem. tech. adv. com. for Boston Harbor/Mass. Bay, 1988—. Author: Invisible Facotrs in Local Economic Development, 1987, New England Fishing Economy, 1986; former mem. editorial bd. Estuaries; assoc editor Marine Resource Economics, 1990—. Grantee Jessie B. Cox Found., 1986-90. Mem. Am. Econ. Assn. Democrat. Unitarian Universalist. Avocations: fishing, hiking, camping, gardening. Office: U Mass Dept Econs Harbor Campus Boston MA 02125-3393

TERMAN, C. RICHARD, science educator; b. Mansfield, Ohio, Sept. 8, 1929; s. William J. and Virginia Ferne (Bowen) T.; m. Phyllis L. McAdam, June 15, 1951; children: Gregory William, Krista Karyl, Jonathan Richard. AA, Spring Arbor Jr. Coll., 1950; BA, Albion Coll., 1952; MS, Mich. State U., 1954, PhD, 1959. NIH postdoctoral fellow Johns Hopkins U., Balt., Penrose Rsch. Lab., Phila.; assoc. prof. Taylor U., Upland, Ind., 1961-63; from assoc. to full prof. Coll. of William and Mary, Williamsburg, Va., 1963-96, rsch. prof. biology emeritus, 1996—. Exch. scientist U.S. and Polish Nat. Acad. Scis., 1974. Contbr. articles to sci. rsch. jours. Recipient Horsely Rsch. award Va. Acad. Sci., Career Rsch. Devel. award NIH, 1970-74, Phi Beta Kappa award, 1970; fellow Animal Behavior Soc. and AAAS, 1983, NATO sr. sci. fellow Oxford U., 1974. Mem. Animal Behavior Soc. (program officer 1971-73, treas. 1976-78). Avocations: camping, fly fishing. Home: 109 Oak Rd Williamsburg VA 23185 Office: Coll of William and Mary Biology Dept Williamsburg VA 23185 E-mail: DickPhyl@aol.com.

TERMAN, LEWIS MADISON, electrical engineer, researcher; b. San Francisco, Aug. 26, 1935; s. Frederick Emmons and Sibyl (Walcott) T.; m. Barbara Chertok, Aug. 28, 1958. BS in Physics, Stanford U., 1956, MSEE, 1958, PhD, 1961. Mem. rsch. staff T.J. Watson Rsch. Ctr., IBM, Yorktown Heights, N.Y., 1961-89, sr. mgr., 1989-91, sr. mem. tech. planning staff, 1991-93; mgr. VLSI processor design IBM, NY, 1993-94; program mgr., 1994—2001. Co-chmn. Symposium on Very Large Scale Integrated Technology, Systems and Application, Taiwan, 1989, 91, 93, 95, 97, 99, 01, tech. program co-chmn., 1985, 87; tech. program chmn. Internat. Solid State Cirs. Conf., N.Y.C., 1983; chmn. Symposium on Very Large-Scale Integrated Tech., Kobe, Japan, 1985, San Diego, 1986, Symposium on Very Large-Scale Integrated Cirs., Karuizawa, Japan, 1988, Kyoto, Japan, 1989, Symposium on Low Power Electronics, San Diego, 1994. Contbr. articles to profl. jours.; holder 24 patents. Pres. Twin Lakes Water Works Corp., S. Salem, N.Y., 1980—. Recipient IEEE Solid-State Cirs. Tech. Field award, 1995. Fellow: AAAS; mem.: IEEE (chmn. tech. mtgs. coun. 1993—94, treas. 1995—98, chair strategic planning and rev. com. 1999—2000, v.p. elect 2000, v.p. 2001, tech. activities bd.), Nat. Acad. Engrng., Circuits and Sys. Soc. of IEEE (adminstrv. com. 1981—83), IEEE Solid-State Circuits Soc. (editor jour. 1974—77, v.p. 1996—97, pres. 1998—99, treas. 1988-89), Electron Devices Soc. of IEEE (v.p. 1988-89, pres. 1990-91, Disting. Svc. award 1995), IBM Acad. Tech. (co-chair tech. program com. 1996, chair components and processes com., tech. coun. 1996—98, pres. 2001—). Avocations: music, theatre, opera, hiking. Home: 61 Twin Lakes Rd South Salem NY 10590-1012 Office: IBM TJ Watson Rsch Ctr PO Box 218 Yorktown Heights NY 10598-0218

TERMEER, HENRICUS ADRIANUS, biotechnology company executive; b. Tilburg, Holland, Feb. 28, 1946; came to U.S., 1971, naturalized, 1999; s. Jacques and Mary (Van Gorp) T. Student, Economisch Hogeschool, Rotterdam, The Netherlands, 1969; MBA, U. Va., 1973. Mgr. mgmt. svcs. Norvic Co., Norwich, England, 1969-71; mgr. internat. product planning Baxter Travenol, Inc., Deerfield, Ill., 1973-74, internat. mktg. mgr., 1975-76; gen. mgr. Travenol GMBH, Munich, 1976-79; v.p. Hyland Therapeutics divsn. Baxter Travenol, Glendale, Calif., 1979-81, exec. v.p., 1981-83; pres. Genzyme Corp., Inc., Boston, 1983—, COO, 1983-85, CEO, 1986—, chmn., 1988—. Dir. Autoimmune Corp. Abiomed, Mass. Cystic Fibrosis Found., Diacrin Corp., Biotech. Industry Orgn., PHRMA, Mass. High Tech., H&Q Lifescis. Fund. Trustee Hambrecht & Quist Healthcare Investors Fund, Mus. Sci., Boston, Darden Bus. Sch. U. Virginia. Served to 1st lt. Netherlands Royal Air Force, 1966-67. Fellow AAAS. Office: Genzyme Corp 1 Kendall Sq Cambridge MA 02139-1562

TERMES, A. DICK, artist; b. Spearfish, S.D., Nov. 7, 1941; s. Joe and Nonie (Christensen) T.; m. Markie Scholz; children: Lang, Kabe. BS in Edn., Black Hills State U., 1960-64; MA, U. Wyo., 1969; MFA, Otis Art Inst., 1971. Art instr. Henley Jr. High and H.S., Klamath, 1964-66, Sheridan (S.D.) H.S. and Elem. Sch., 1966-68, Black Hill State U., 1971-72; artist in schs. S.D. Arts Coun., 1973—2002. One-man shows include Visual Arts Ctr., Sioux Falls, S.D., 1999, Bantlesville Cmty. Ctr., Okla., 1998, Termesphere Gallery, Spearfish, S.D., 1993-2002, Arts on Grand, Spencer, Iowa, 1996, U. Ill. Sch. of Architecture, 1993, Mont. Moon Gallery, Chgo., 1989, Iowa State U., 1986, Charleston Hgts. Art Ctr. Las Vegas, 1986, U. Ky., 1983, Ariz. State U., 1982, Bergdorf Goodman, N.Y.C., 1981, Calif. State Poly., U. Pomona, 1979, Gallery '72, Omaha, 1978, U. of the Pacific, 1977, U. N.D., 1973, The Grace Mus., Abilene, Tex., 2001, U. So. Ala., Mobile, 2002, Eastern Shore Art Ctr., Fairhope, Ala., 2002, Evansville (Ind.) Mus., 2002, Calif. State U., Bakersfield, 2002, U. South Ala., Mobile, 2002, Evansville (Ind.) Mus., 2002; exhibited in group shows Extrasensory Mus. Travel Show, Japan, 1998-2000, M.C. Escher Centennial Congress, U. Rome, 1998, Sphere Mus., Tokyo, 1991-99, Fuller Mus., Brockton, Mass., 1990, U. Ariz., Tucson, 1989, Gallery on the Green, Lexington, Mass., 1989-93, Mont. Moon Gallery, Chgo., 1988-89, Moravian Coll., Bethlemen, Pa., 1987, Del. Art Must., Nat. Acad. Fantastic Art, 1987, Smithsonian-Air and Space Mus., Washington, 1986, Otis Art Inst., L.A., 1985, Indigenous Image Gallery, Palm Desert, Calif, 1984, Mus. of Fun, Japan, 1984, Chgo. Design Fest, Chgo., 1983, The Pillsbury's American Art, St. Paul, 1981, U. Rome, 1998, Extrasensory Mus., Japan, 1999-2000, Burbank Creative Art Ctr., 2000, U. Wis., O'Claire, 2001. Recipient scholarship Otis Art Inst., 1969-71, Four S.D. Arts Coun. fellow, 1976-80, 84, 94, S.D. Mus. of Art Artistic Achievement citation, 1986, Gov.'s award for creative achievement in S.D., 1999. Home and Office: 1920 Christensen Dr Spearfish SD 57783-8037

TER-MIKIRTYCHEV, VALERII VARTANOVICH, physicist, researcher; b. Krasnodar, Russia, Sept. 26, 1966; s. Vartan Petrovich and Vera Ervatovna (Nazaretian) T.-M.; m. Ekaterina L'vovna Arestova, Apr. 9, 1994; 1 child, Vladimir Valer'evich. MS, Moscow Physics/Engrng. Inst., 1990, PhD, 1994. Physical diplomate. Staff rsch. scientist Gen. Physics Inst. Russian Acad. Scis., Moscow, 1994-98; rsch. scientist Kyoto (Japan) Sangyo U., 1994-98; vis. fellow, rsch. scientist Dept. Physics U. Otago, Dunedin, New Zealand, 1996; staff mem. Sci. and Engrng. Svcs. Inc., Burtonsville, Md., 1999-2000. Sr. laser engr. advanced R & D OEM Bus. Unit Spectra-Physics Lasers Inc., Mountain View, Calif., 2001-2002; mem. Optical Sci. Group, 1995—, Laser Sci. Group, 1995—, Optical Soc. Am., Washington, 1993—. Inventor in field; contbr. more than 60 publs. and 60 conf. papers to profl. jours. Mem. Optical Soc. Am. Achievements include inventor of room-temperature stable color center lasers, ultrabroadband lasers and diode-pumped solid-state lasers which have no analogs in the world due to their unique characteristics. E-mail: valeriit@hotmail.com.

TERMINI, ROSEANN BRIDGET, lawyer, educator; b. Phila., Feb. 2, 1953; d. Vincent James and Bridget (Marano) T. BS magna cum laude, Drexel U., 1975; MEd, Temple U., 1979, JD, 1985, grad. in food and pharmacy law, 1998. Bar: Pa. 1985, U.S. Dist. Ct. (ea. dist.) Pa. 1985, D.C. 1986. Jud. clk. Superior Ct. of Pa., Allentown, 1985-86; atty. Pa. Power & Light Co., 1986-87; corp. counsel food and drug law Lemmon Co., Sellersville, Pa., 1987-88; sr. dep. atty. bur. consumer protection plain lang. law Office of Atty. Gen., Harrisburg, 1988-96; prof. Villanova U. Sch. Law, 1996-2000; prof. food and drug law Temple U. Sch. Pharmacy, 1998—2000, St. Joseph U., 2000—. Spkr. continuing legal edn.-plain lang. laws, environ. conf.; adj. prof. Widener U. Sch. Law, 1993—, Dickinson Sch. Law; specialized food, drug, cosmetic and med. device law course dir. Immaculata Coll., 2002; mem. on-line distance learning legal issues pharmacy promotion St. Joseph U., 2002. Author: Food, Drug and Medical Device Law: Topics and Cases, 2001; contbr. articles to profl. jours, law revs. Active in Sr. Citizens Project Outreach, Hospice, 1986—; mem. St. Thomas More Law Bd.; mem. pres.' coun. Immaculata Coll., 2002. Mem. ABA (various coms.), Bar Assn. D.C., Pa. Bar Assn. (ethics, exceptional children and environ. sects., Plain English award 1999), Temple U. Law Alumni Assn., Drexel U. Alumni Assn., Omicron Nu, Phi Alpha Delta. Avocations: tap dancing, hiking, cross-country skiing. E-mail: rtermini@attorney.com. *Notable cases include: Waste Conversion case, 1990, violation of Pa. Solid Waste Mgmt. Act.*

TERNBERG, JESSIE LAMOIN, pediatric surgeon; b. Corning, Calif., May 28, 1924; d. Eric G. and Alta M. (Jones) T. AB, Grinnell Coll., 1946, Sc.D. (hon.), 1972; PhD, U. Tex., 1950; MD, Washington U., St. Louis, 1953; Sc.D. (hon.), U. Mo., St. Louis, 1981. Diplomate: Am. Bd. Surgery. Intern Boston City Hosp., 1953-54; asst. resident in surgery Barnes Hosp., St. Louis, 1954-57, resident in surgery, 1958-59; research fellow Washington U. (Sch. Medicine), 1957-58; practice medicine specializing in pediatric surgery St. Louis, 1966—; instr., trainee in surgery Washington U., 1959-62, asst. prof. surgery, 1962-65, assoc. prof., 1965-71, prof. surgery in pediatrics, 1975-96, prof. surgery, 1971-96, chief div. pediatric surgery, 1972-90, prof. emeritus, 1996—; mem. staff Barnes Hosp., 1974-90, pediatric surgeon in chief, 1974-90, mem. operating room com., 1971-90, mem. med. adv. com., 1975-90. Mem. staff Children's Hosp., dir. pediatric surgery, 1972-90. Contbr. numerous articles on pediatric surgery to profl. jours. Trustee Grinnell Coll., 1984—. Recipient Alumni award Grinnell Coll., 1966, Faculty/Alumni award Washington U. Sch. Medicine, 1991, 1st Aphrodite Jannopaulo Hofsommer award, 1993. Fellow ACS, AAAS; mem. SIOP, Am. Pediatric Surg. Assn., We. Surg. Assn. (2d v.p. 1984-85), St. Louis Med. Soc., Soc. Surgery of the Alimentary Tract, Am. Acad. Pediatrics, Soc. Pelvic Surgeons (v.p. 1991-92), Brit. Assn. Paediatric Surgeons, Assn. Women Surgeons (disting. mem. 1995), Mo. State Surg. Soc., St. Louis Surg. Soc. (pres. 1980-81), St. Louis Pediatric Soc., Soc. Surg. Oncology, Pediatric Oncology Group (chmn. surg. discipline 1983-96), St. Louis Childrens Hosp. Soc. (pres. 1979-80), Acad. Sci. St. Louis (Trustees award 2002), St. Louis Met. Med. Soc. (hon., councilor, trustee), Barnes Hosp. Soc., Phi Beta Kappa, Sigma Xi, Iota Sigma Pi, Alpha Omega Alpha. Office: St Louis Childrens Hosp 1 Childrens Pl Saint Louis MO 63110-1002 E-mail: ternbergj@msnotes.wustl.edu.

TERNER, RON M. artist, photographer; b. N.Y.C., May 27, 1949; s. Hugo and Alice Terner; m. Susan Rios; 1 child, Rajeev Terner. Artist, dir. Focal Point Gallery, Bronx, N.Y., 1974—, pres., 1984—. Author: Nudes 1975-85, 1985, Nudes 1986-91, 1991. Bd. dirs. City Island (N.Y.) Cmty. Ctr., 1998—. Office: Focal Point Gallery 321 City Island Ave Bronx NY 10464 E-mail: RonTerner@aol.com.

TERNUS, JEAN ANN, nursing educator; b. Columbus, Nebr., Feb. 29, 1944; d. Maurice Henry and Marcella (Huntemer) T. BS in Nursing, Mt. Marty Coll., 1966; MS, Kans. State U., 1977. RN Kans., Mo., Nebr. Staff nurse Brian Meml. Hosp., Lincoln, Nebr., 1966-67, VA Hosp., Milw., 1967-69, Kansas City, Mo., 1969-72; nursing instr. Kansas City (Kans.) Community Coll., 1973—; cardiovascular nurse specialist Meth. Hosp., Houston, 1973. Mem. AAUW, NEA, AACN, Kans. State Nurses Assn. (pres. dist. II 1980-82, chair dist. newsletter 1980-2000, editor newsletter 1980-98, Dist. 2 bd. dirs. 2001—, 2d v.p. 1986-90, 1st v.p. 1990-92, sec. dist. II 1993—, v.p. 1993-95), NLN, Gerontol. Nurses Assn., Kans. Nurses Found. (bd. dirs. 1990-91, sec. 1992—, pres.-elect 1995—, pres. 1997—), Sigma Theta Tau, Delta Kappa Gamma. Democrat. Roman Catholic. Home: 5342 Juniper Dr Shawnee Mission KS 66205-2225 Office: Kansas City CC 7250 State Ave Kansas City KS 66112-3003 E-mail: jternus@toto.net. *Personal philosophy: "Treat people as if they were what they ought to be and you help them become what they are capable of being" (Goethe).*

TERNUS, MARSHA K. state supreme court justice; b. Vinton, Iowa, May 30, 1951; BA, U. Iowa, 1972; JD, Drake U., 1977. Bar: Iowa 1977, Ariz. 1984. With Bradshaw, Fowler, Proctor & Fairgrave, Des Moines, 1977—93; justice Iowa Supreme Ct., 1993—. Editor-in-chief: Drake Law Rev., 1976—77. Mem.: Polk County Bar Assn. (pres. 1984—85), Order of Coif, Phi Beta Kappa. Office: Iowa Supreme Ct State Capital Bldg Des Moines IA 50319-0001*

TERNUS, MONA PEARL, critical care nurse, flight nurse, educator; b. Levittown, N.J., Nov. 3, 1961; d. William Joseph and Sarah (Tanne) Tillis; married, July 1998; 1 child, Kattey; stepchildren: Dale, Brian, Megan, Duncan. BA, NYU, 1982; MSN, Pace U., 1986. Cert. critical care nurse, trauma nurse, staff devel. nurse; instr. ACLS and critical care. Nursery nurse No. Westchester Hosp. Ctr., Mt. Kisco, NY, 1987—88; ICU nurse Meth. Hosp., Houston, 1988—89; dir. nursing Golden Age and Winslow Nursing Homes, 1989; hospice case mgr. Vis. Nurse Assn., 1989—91; critical care charge nurse Woodlands (Tex.) Meml. Hosp., 1990—92; commd. 1st lt. USAF, 1992, charge nurse surg. ICU 59th Med. Wing Tex., 1992—94, critical care educator, 1994—95; flight nurse 23d Aeromed. Evacuation Squadron, Pope AFB, NC, 1996—97; 2nd in command Mobile Aeromed. Staging Facility NATO Implementation Force, Tuzla AB, Bosnia-Herzegovina, 1996—97; res. officer 433d Aeromed. Evacuation Squadron, Kelley AFB, Tex., 1997—98; edn. specialist U. Tex., MD Anderson Cancer Ctr., Houston, 1997—98; prof. Auburn U., Montgomery, Ala., 1998—2002; res. officer 908th Aeromed. Evacuation Squadron, Maxwell AFB, 1998—2002; advanced through grades to maj. USAF, 2000; res. officer USAF HQ Surgeon Gen.'s Tactical Action Team, 2002—; prof. Old Dominion U., Norfolk, Va., 2002—; USAF surgeon gen.'s tactical action team IMA, 2002—. Mem. Air Force Surgeon Gen. Tactical Action Team. Mem. AACN, ANA, Ala. Nurses State Assn., Air Force Assn., Officers Club, Assn. Mil. Surgeons U.S., Res. Officers

Assn., Ret. Officers Assn., Aerospace Med. Assn., Pi Alpha Alpha, Pi Sigma Alpha, Sigma Theta Tau (v.p. Kappa Omega chpt.). Jewish. Avocations: travel, reading, holistic healing. Home: 804 Beckley Ln Chesapeake VA 23322

TERP, DOUGLAS C. academic administrator; b. Arlington, Mass., Feb. 22, 1962; s. Charles Jensen and Lorna May (Cook) Terp; m. Wanda Lee Terp, Aug. 17, 1986; 1 child Charles Jensen. BA, Colby Coll., 1984; MBA, Thomas Coll., 1995. Exec dir. Vt. Rep. Party, Montpelier, 1986—87; computer sales cons. McAuliffe Inc., Burlington, 1987; asst. dir. pers. Colby Coll., Waterville, Maine, 1987—90, dir. pers., 1990—2001, assoc. v.p. adminstrn., 2001—. Dir., treas. Health Reach Network, Waterville, 1997—2001; dir. Good Will Hinckley (Maine) Sch., Hinckley, 1998—. Bd. dirs. United Way Mid-Maine, Waterville, 1993—97, chmn., 1994—95. Methodist. Avocation: running. Office: Colby Coll 4585 Mayflower Hill Waterville ME 04901-8845

TERP, THOMAS THOMSEN, lawyer; b. Fountain Hill, Pa., Aug. 12, 1947; s. Norman T. and Josephine (Uhran) T.; m. Pamela Robinson; children: Stephanie, Brian, Adam; step-children: Taylor Mefford, Grace Mefford. BA, Albion (Mich.) Coll., 1969; JD, Coll. of William and Mary, 1973. Bar: Ohio 1973, U.S. Dist. Ct. (so. dist.) Ohio 1973, U.S. Ct. Appeals (6th cir.) 1973, U.S. Supreme Ct. 1979. Assoc. Taft, Stettinius & Hollister, Cin., 1973-80, ptnr., 1981—. Bd. dirs. Starflo Corp., Orangeburg, S.C., Attorneys' Liability Assurance Soc., Ltd., Hamilton, Bermuda, ALAS, Inc., Chgo. Editor-in-chief William & Mary Law Rev., 1972-73; mem. bd. editors Jour. of Environ. Hazards, 1988—, Environ. Law Jour. of Ohio, 1989—. Mem. Cin. Athletic Club, Coldstream Country Club, Epworth Assembly (Ludington, Mich.), Lincoln Hills Golf Club (Ludington), Queen City Club. Avocations: tennis, golf, travel. Office: 1800 Firstar Tower 425 Walnut St Cincinnati OH 45202 E-mail: terp@taftlaw.com.

TERPENING, DONALD LESTER, science educator, medical technologist; b. Poughkeepsie, N.Y., Nov. 13, 1949; s. Kenneth B. and Marion A. T.; m. Barbara Hale, Nov. 23, 1974; children: Ethan Kenneth, Nathaniel Albert. BA in Biology, Marist Coll., 1973; MS in Med. Biology, C.W. Post Col. Long Island U., 1975. Lab tech. Vassar Bros. Hosp., Poughkeepsie, N.Y., 1969-71, med. tech., 1971-73, supervisor hematology dept., 1973-74; prog. dir. med. lab. tech. prog. Ulster County C.C., Stone Ridge, 1976-81, biology prof., 1975—. Dir. tchg. ctr. Ulster County C.C., Stone Ridge, N.Y., 1997-2000. Pres. Ulster Adv. Council, Kingston, N.Y., 1978-83; chmn. Recreation Com., Town of Olive, West Shoken, N.Y., 1992-99. Mem. Am. Soc. Clinical Pathologists, Empire State Assn. Two Year Coll. Biologists (treas. 2000—). Avocations: muzzle-loading sports, archery, woodworking, Revolutionary War reenactor. Office: Ulster County CC Cottekill Rd Stone Ridge NY 12484 E-mail: terpenid@sunyulster.edu.

TERPENING, VIRGINIA ANN, artist; b. Lewistown, Mo., July 17, 1917; d. Floyd Raymond and Bertha Edda (Rodifer) Shoup; m. Charles W. Terpening, July 5, 1951; 1 child by previous marriage, V'Ann Baltzelle Deatrick. Student, William Woods Coll., Fulton, Mo., 1936-37, Washington U. Sch. Fine Arts, St. Louis, 1937-40. Lectr. on art; jurist for selection of art for exhibits Labelle (Mo.) Centennial, 1972; chmn. Centennial Art Show, Lewistown, 1971, Bicentennial, 1976; dir. exhibit high sch. student for N.E. Mo. State U., 1974; supt. ann. art show Lewis County (Mo.) Fair, 1975-90. One-woman shows include Culver-Stockton Coll., Canton, Mo., 1956, Creative Gallery, N.Y.C., 1968, The Breakers, Palm Beach, Fla., 1976, others; group shows include Mo. Ann. Show, City Art Mus., St. Louis, 1956, 65, Madison Gallery, N.Y.C., 1960, Ligoa Duncan Gallery, N.Y.C., 1964, 78, Two Flags Festival of Art, Douglas, Ariz., 1975, 78-79, Internat. Art Exhibit, El Centro, Calif., 1977, 78, Salon des Nations, Paris, 1985, UN World Conf. of Women, Narobi, Kenya, 1985, William Woods Coll., Fulton, Mo., 1992-95, La Junta Coll. Art League Internat., 1992, 94, Coffret Musée, Paris, 1995; represented in permanent collection Nat. Mus. of Women in Art, 1990; executed Mississippi RiverBoat oil painting presented to Pres. Carter by Lewis County Dem. Com., Canton, 1979. Mem. Lewistown Bicentennial Hist. Soc.; charter mem. Canton Area Arts Coun. of N.E. Mo. Recipient Cert. of Merit Latham Found., 1960-63, Mo. Women's Festival of Art, 1974, Bertrand Russell Peace Found., 1973, Gold Medallion award Two flags Festival of Art, 1975, Safeco purchase award El Centro (Calif.) Internat. Art Exhibit, 1977, 1st Pl. award LaJunta (Colo.) Fine Arts League, 1981, diploma Univ. Delle Arti, Parma, Italy, 1981, Purchase award Two Flags Art Festival, 1981, award Assn. Conservation and Mo. Dept. Conservation Art Exhibit, 1982, Purchase award Canton Area Arts Coun., 1988, Colorado Springs Art Festival, 1989; paintings selected for Competition '84 Guide by Nat. Art Appreciation Soc., 1984, 1st Pl. award New Orleans Internat. Art Exhibit, 1984, Two Flags Festival of Art, 1986, Sunflower Judges award Harlin Mus., West Plains, Mo., 1994, Key to City, Lifetime award, 1998; named artist laureate, Nepenthe Mondi Soc., 1984. Mem. Artist Equity Assn., Internat. Soc. Artists, Internat. Platform Assn., Nat. Mus. Women in Art (charter), Animal Protection Inst. Mem. Christian Ch. (Disciples Of Christ). Address: 105 S Vine St PO Box 117 Lewistown MO 63452-0117

TERR, ABBA ISRAEL, allergist, immunologist; b. Cleve., 1930; MD, Case Western Res. U., 1956. Diplomate Am. Bd. Allergy and Immunology. Intern U. Wis. Hosps., Madison, 1956-57; resident in internal medicine U. Mich. Med. Ctr., Ann Arbor, 1957-60, fellow in allergy, 1960-62; physician Stanford (Calif.) U. Med. Ctr. and U. Calif. SF Med. Ctr.; clin. prof. medicine U. Calif. Med. Ctr., San Francisco. Fellow ACP, Am. Acad. Allergy, Asthma, and Immunology; mem. Am. Thoracic Soc. Address: 450 Sutter St Rm 2534 San Francisco CA 94108-4204 E-mail: abbaterrmed@attglobal.net.

TERR, LENORE CAGEN, psychiatrist, writer; b. N.Y.C., Mar. 27, 1936; d. Samuel Lawrence and Esther (Hirsch) Cagen; m. Abba I. Terr; children: David, Julia. AB magna cum laude, Case Western Res.,U., 1957; MD with honors, U. Mich., 1961. Diplomate Am. Bd. Psychiatry and Neurology, Subspecialty Bd. Child and Adolescent Psychiatry. Intern U. Mich. Med. Ctr., Ann Arbor, 1961-62; resident Neuropsychiat. Inst. U. Mich., 1962-64, fellow Children's Psychiat. Hosp., 1964-66; from instr. to asst. prof. Case Western Res. U. Med. Sch., Cleve., 1966-71; pvt. practice Terr Med. Corp., San Francisco, 1971—; from asst. clin. prof. to clin. prof. psychiatry Sch. Medicine U. Calif., 1971—. Lectr. law, psychiatry U. Calif., Berkeley, 1971—90, Davis, 1974—88; dir. Am. Bd. Psychiatry and Neurology, 1988—96, chair psychiatry coun., 1996. Author: Too Scared to Cry, 1990, Unchained Memories, 1994, Beyond Love and Work, 1999; contbr. articles to profl. jours.; exhibited works in art show at Canessa Gallery, San Francisco, 2002. Recipient Career Tchr. award, NIMH, 1967—69, Child Advocacy award, APA, 1994; grantee project grant, Rosenberg Found., 1977, William T. Grant Found., 1986—87, Leon Lowenstein Found., 2002; scholar scholar-in-residence, Rockefeller Found., Italy, 1981, 1988. Fellow: Am. Acad. Child and Adolescent Psychiatry (coun. 1984—87), Am. Coll. Psychiatrists (program chair 1991—92, Bowis award 1993), Am. Psychiat. Assn. (Child Psychiatry Rsch. award 1984, Clin. Rsch. award 1987, Marmor Sci. award 2002); mem.: Phi Bet Kappa, Alpha Omega Alpha. Avocations: piano, walking, travel, gardening, needlepoint. Office: Terr Med Corp 450 Sutter St Rm 2534 San Francisco CA 94108-4204

TERRACINA, ROY DAVID, private investor; b. Chgo., Aug. 24, 1946; s. Angelo R. and Josephine T.; m. Dana Wheeler, July 6, 1984; children: Joseph, Vincent, Angela, Peter, Paul. BS in Fin., Marquette U., 1968, MBA, 1972. Officer First Wis. Nat. Bank, Milw., 1968-71; account exec. Robert W. Baird Co., 1971-74; v.p. mktg. Midwest Retail Group, 1974-76; mgmt. cons. Anderson-Roethle, 1976-77; v.p., treas. Farm House Foods Corp., 1977-84; pres. Sterling Foods, Inc., San Antonio, 1984-93, pvt. investor, 1994—. Instr. personal fin. Marquette U.; instr. fin. Trinity U.; bd. dir. US Global Investors, Norwood Promotional Products Inc., JP Morgan Chase , San Antonio. Roman Catholic. Office: 7900 Callaghan Rd San Antonio TX 78229-2327

TERRAGNO, PAUL JAMES, information industry executive; b. Ogden, Utah, May 17, 1938; s. Charles L. and Florence E. (Gabardi) T.; m. Nancy Robinson, Aug. 26, 1961; children— Thomas C., Paul A., Teresa A. BA, U. Utah, 1960; MS, U. Wyo., 1962. Vice pres. Westat, Inc., Rockville, Md., 1962-70; vice pres. Remac Information, Gaithersburg, 1970-76; dir. U.S. Patent Office, Washington, 1976-80; v.p. Pergamon Internat., McLean, Va., 1980-84; pres. Pergamon InfoLine, 1984-87, Pergamon ORBIT InfoLine, McLean, 1987-89, Maxwell Online, Inc., 1989-92. Pres. Pergamon Orbit InfoLine, Ltd., London, 1984-89, Pergabase, Inc., Gainesville, Fla., 1985-92, pres. Topate Info. Svcs. Inc., 1992-97; dir. Eagle Design and Mgmt., Inc., Bethesda, Md. Contbr. articles to various publs. Mem. Am. Soc. Info. Sci. Roman Catholic. Home: 10607 Vantage Ct Rockville MD 20854-4244 Office: 7830 Old Georgetown Rd Bethesda MD 20814-2432 E-mail: terragno@erols.com.

TERRAS, AUDREY ANNE, mathematics educator; b. Washington, Sept. 10, 1942; d. Stephen Decatur and Maude Mae (Murphy) Bowdoin. BS with high honors in Math., U. Md., 1964; MA, Yale U., 1966, PhD, 1970. Instr. U. Ill., Urbana, 1968-70; asst. prof. U. P.R., Mayaguez, 1970-71, Bklyn. Coll., CUNY, 1971-72; asst. prof. math. U. Calif.-San Diego, La Jolla, 1972-76, assoc. prof., 1976-83, prof., 1983—. Prin. investigator NSF, 1974-88; vis. positions U. Aachen, Germany, 1998, Tsuda Coll., Tokyo, 1999, MIT, fall 1977, 83, U. Bonn (W.Ger.), spring 1977, Inst. Mittag-Leffler, Stockholm, winter, 1978, Inst. Advanced Study, spring 1984, Math. Scis. Rsch. Inst., Berkeley, Calif., winter 1992, spring 1995, CRM, U. Montreal, 1999, others; dir. West Coast Number Theory Conf., U. Calif.-San Diego, 1976, AMS joint summer rsch. conf., 1984; lectr. in field. Author: Harmonic Analysis on Symmetric Spaces and Applications, Vol. 1, 1985, Vol. II, 1988, Fourier Analysis on Finite Groups and Applications, 1999; editor: The Selberg Trace Formula and Related Topics, 1986; contbr. chapters to books, articles to profl. jours. Woodrow Wilson fellow, 1964, NSF fellow, 1964-68; NSF grantee Summer Inst. in Number Theory, Ann Arbor, Mich., 1973. Fellow: AAAS (nominating com. math. sect. project 2061); mem.: Assn. for Women in Sci., Assn. for Women in Math. (travel grants com. 1996), Soc. Indsl. and Applied Math., Math. Assn. Am. (program com. for nat. meeting 1988—90, chair joint program com. Am. Math. Soc. and Math. Assn. Am. 1991), Am. Math. Soc. (com. employment and ednl. policy com. on coms., coun., trans. editor, com. for the yr. 2000, western sect. program com., assoc. editor book revs. Bull., assoc. editor Notices). Achievements include research in harmonic analysis on symmetric spaces and number theory. Office: U Calif San Diego Dept Math La Jolla CA 92093-0112

TERRAS, VICTOR, Slavic languages and comparative literature educator; b. Poltsamaa, Estonia, Jan. 21, 1921; came to U.S., 1952, naturalized, 1956; s. Evald and Elena (Rosenberger) T.; m. Rita Schubert, 1951; 1 child, Alexander Mag. Phil., U. Tartu, Estonia, 1942; PhD, U. Chgo., 1963. Lectr. U. Tartu, 1943-44; instr. to assoc. prof. U. Ill., Urbana, 1959-64, prof. Slavic langs., 1965-66; prof. U. Wis., Madison, 1966-70; prof. Slavic langs. and comparative lit. Brown U., Providence, 1970-88, prof. emeritus, 1988—. Author: The Young Dostoevsky: A Critical Study, 1969, Belinskij and Russian Literary Criticism, 1974, A Karamazov Companion, 1981, Vladimir Mayakovsky, 1983; editor: Handbook of Russian Literature, 1984, The Idiot: An Interpretation, 1990, A History of Russian Literature, 1991, Russian Poetry of the Silver Age, 1998, Reading Dostoevsky, 1998. Mem. Am. Assn. Advancement Slavic and East European Studies, Am. Assn. Tchrs. Slavic and East European Langs. (pres. 1981-82), Internat. Dostoevsky Soc. (v.p. 1983—). Home: 70470 Tamarisk Ln Rancho Mirage CA 92270-2445 Office: Brown U Box E Providence RI 02912

TERREAULT, CHARLES, engineer, management educator, researcher; b. Montreal, Que., Can., Mar. 21, 1935; s. Charles Terreault and Antonia Clark; m. Marie Rolland, Sept. 10, 1960; children: Genevieve, François, Patrick, Olivier-Hugues. BA, Coll. Stanislas, Montreal, 1954; BA in Sci., Ecole Poly., Montreal, 1959; hon. doctorate, U. Que., 1986. Engr. Bell Can., Montreal, 1959-65, staff engr., 1967-69, chief engr., 1971-73, asst. v.p. rsch., 1978-91; researcher Bell Telephone Labs., Holmdel, N.J., 1965-67; dir. planning Bell No. Rsch., Ottawa, Ont., Can., 1969-71, v.p. systems engring. Montreal, 1973-78; Jvr Cyr prof. mgmt. tech. Ecole Poly., 1991-96. Bd. dirs. Natural Scis. and Engring. Rsch. Coun. Can., Ottawa; chmn. Imatex Comm. Inc., SILONEX, Inc., Simpler Networks, Inc.; chmn. Can. Inst. Telecomm. Rsch. Contbr. articles to profl. jours. Fellow IEEE (Armstrong award 1984), Canadian Acad. Engring., Ordre Ingénieurs de Que., Que. Assn. Indsl. Rsch. (Annual award 1992). Avocations: computers, classical music, skiing. Home and Office: 1665 Victoria Ave # 804 Saint Lambert QC Canada J4R 2T6 E-mail: cterreault@sympatico.ca.

TERREL, RONALD LEE, civil engineer, business executive, educator; b. Klamath Falls, Oreg., Sept. 2, 1936; s. Theodore Thomas and Ruth Margaret (Fausset) T.; m. Susan Laura Harrower, Feb. 28, 1959 (div. July 1981); children: Douglas Scott, Nancy Dawn, Janet Lynn; m. 2d Alice Marie Blanchard, July 23, 1981. BSC.E., Purdue U., 1960, MS, 1961; PhD, U. Calif.-Berkeley, 1967. Estimator J.H. Pomeroy & Co., San Francisco, 1955; lab. asst. Purdue U., 1956-60; asst. field geologist Bear Creek Mining Co., Mpls., 1957-58; materials engr. U.S. Bur. Reclamation, Denver, 1960-64; project engr. J.H. Pomeroy & Co., Antigua, B.W.I. and, Calif., 1964-65; research asst. U. Calif.-Berkeley, 1965-67; asst. prof. civil engr. U. Wash., Seattle, 1967-70, assoc. prof., 1970-75, prof., 1975-85, prof. emeritus, 1985—, head Transp. Constrn. and Geometronics divsn., 1976-79; prof., sr. researcher Oreg. State U., 1989-94; pres. Pavement Systems Inc., 1970-82; exec. v.p. Seattle Engring. Internat., Inc., 1979-81; pres. Terrel Assocs., Inc., 1981-85; owner Terrel Research LLC, 1986—; v.p. Pavement Technologies Inc., 1985-86; chmn., CEO RL Techs. Ltd., 1996—. Bd. dirs., v.p. Hydrogenesis, Inc.; cons. in field. Patentee in field. Co-founder, dir. Wash. State Transp. Ctr., 1981-84. Nominated Constrn. Man of Yr. Engring. News-Record, 1972; Purdue Alumni scholar, 1959-60; Ford fellow, 1965-67 Mem. ASTM, ASCE, Tranps. Rsch. Bd., Assn. Asphalt Paving Technologists (bd. dirs. 1979-83, Emmons award 1983, 95, award of merit 1990), Triaxial Inst. (chmn. 1971-73), Can. Tech. Asphalt Assn., Internat. Soc. for Asphalt Pavements (founding mem. 1987), Sigma Xi, Tau Beta Pi, Chi Epsilon, Sigma Gamma Epsilon. Office: 9703 241st Pl SW Edmonds WA 98020-6512 E-mail: rterrel@u.washington.edu.

TERRELL, A. JOHN, retired university telecommunications director; b. Pasadena, Calif., Dec. 27, 1927; s. Harry Evans and Elizabeth (Eaton) T.; m. Elizabeth Schalk, June 6, 1949; children: Patricia Elyse, Marilee Diane, John Scott. Student, Chaffey Coll., 1947-48; BBA, U. N.Mex., 1952. Communications cons. Mountain States Tel. & Tel., Albuquerque, 1951-56; mgr. office and communications services A.C.F. Industries, Inc., 1956-62; mgr. communications and services Norton Simon Industries, Inc., Fullerton, Calif., 1962-68; v.p. gen. mgr. Wells Fargo Security Guard Service div. Baker Industries, 1968-71; adminstrv. mgr., budget adminstr. Hyland div. Baxter-Travenol Labs. Inc., Costa Mesa, Calif., 1971-77; exec. v.p. Am. Tel. Mgmt. Inst. Inc., Newport Beach, 1977-78; telecommunications dir. UCLA, 1978-89; ret., 1989. Contbr. articles to profl. jours. Rep. candidate for state rep., Albuquerque, 1960; precinct chmn. and mem. Barnalillo County Rep. Central Com., 1961-62; Rep. candidate for N.Mex. State Bd. Edn., 2d Jud. Dist., 1962; colonial aide-de-camp Gov. N.Mex., Santa Fe, 1968. Served with U.S. Mct. Marine, 1944-45, U.S. Army, 1946-47, USAR, 1947-50. Mem. Nat. Assn. Accts. (dir. 1967-77, Most Valuable Mem. 1974-75), Telecommunications Assn., Am. Legion, VFW. Lodges: Greater Irvine Lions (charter pres. 1975-76), Albuquerque Jaycees (v.p., treas. 1956-62). Episcopalian. Home: 2727 Island View Ln Corona Del Mar CA 92625-1309 E-mail: ajterrell@fea.net.

TERRELL, G. IRVIN, lawyer; b. Houston, Sept. 28, 1946; s. George I. and Adella (Weichert) T.; m. Karen Steenberg, Jan. 8, 1984; 1 child, Katharine. BA, U. Tex., 1968, JD, 1972. Bar: Tex., U.S. Supreme Ct., U.S. Ct. Appeals (3d and 5th cirs.), U.S. Dist. Ct. (so., no. and ea. dists.) Tex., U.S. Dist. Ct. (we. dist.) Pa. Assoc. Baker & Botts, Houston, 1972-79, ptnr., 1980—. Mem. ABA, Houston Bar Assn., Internat. Soc. Barristers. E-mail: irv.terrell@bakerbotts.com.

TERRELL, HOWARD BRUCE, psychiatrist; b. Feb. 19, 1952; BS magna cum laude, Calif. State U., Hayward, 1974; MD, U. Calif., San Diego, 1980. Diplomate in psychiatry and in forensic psychiatry Am. Bd. Psychiatry and Neurology. Intern. Kaiser Found. Hosp., Oakland, Calif., 1980-81; resident in psychiatry U. Calif., San Francisco/Fresno, 1982-85; staff psychiatrist Kings View Corp., Reedley, Calif., 1985-87, sr. staff psychiatrist, 1987-88, dir. outpatient psychiatry, 1988-89; dir. dual diagnosis and affective disorders programs Sierra Gateway Hosp., Clovis, 1989-91. Asst. clin. prof. psychiatry U. Calif. Sch. Medicine, San Francisco; lectr. in field. Contbr. articles to profl. jours. Fellow Am. Coll. Forensic Psychiatry, Am. Psychiat. Assn.; mem. Am. Acad. Psychiatry and the Law, Ctrl. Calif. Psychiat. Soc. (pres. Sierra chpt. 1996-98). Avocations: golf, computers, photography, enology, music. Office: 3100 Willow Ave Ste 102 Clovis CA 93612-4741

TERRELL, J. ANTHONY, lawyer; b. N.Y.C., Sept. 20, 1943; s. Claude M. and Kathleen L. (Prevost) T.; m. Karen E. Terrell, Aug. 8, 1969; 1 child, Elizabeth S. BA, NYU, 1965, LLM in Taxation, 1975; JD, Villanova U., 1968. Bar: N.Y. With Frueauff, Farrell, Sullivan & Bryan, N.Y.C., 1970-74, ptnr., 1974; assoc. Thelen Reid & Priest LLP, N.Y.C., 1974-76, ptnr., 1977—. Mem. ABA (sect. bus. law, sect. pub. utility, comm. and transp. law, vice chmn. corp. finance com.), Internat. Bar Assn. (bus. law sect.), Nat. Assn. Bond Lawyers, Belle Haven Club, Met. Club, Coral Beach and Tennis Club. Home: Indian Harbor Greenwich CT 06830 Office: Thelen Reid & Priest LLP 40 W 57th St New York NY 10019-4097

TERRELL, JAMES (NELSON JAMES TERRELL), physicist; b. Houston, Aug. 15, 1923; s. Nelson James Sr. and Gladys Delphine (Stevens) T.; m. Elizabeth Anne Pearson, June 9, 1945; children— Anne (dec.), Barbara, Jean BA, Rice U., 1944, MA, 1947, PhD, 1950. Research asst. Rice U., Houston, 1950; asst. prof. physics Western Res. U., Cleve., 1950-51; mem. staff Los Alamos Nat. Lab., U. Calif., 1951-89, assoc., 1989-94; affiliate, 1994—. Producer (computer generated movie) The X-Ray Sky, 1969-76; contbr. articles to profl. jours. and encys. Served to 1st lt. AUS, 1944-46 Graham Baker scholar Rice U., 1943-44; fellow Rice U., 1946-48, AEC, 1948-50 Fellow Am. Phys. Soc., AAAS; mem. Am. Astron. Soc., Internat. Astron. Union, Phi Beta Kappa, Sigma Xi Achievements include research in relativity, quasars, x-ray and gamma ray astronomy, nuclear physics, lasers. Home: 85 Obsidian Loop Los Alamos NM 87544-2528 Office: Los Alamos Nat Lab Mail Stop D436 Los Alamos NM 87545-0001

TERRELL, JAMES DANIEL, lawyer; b. Kansas City, Oct. 22, 1956; s. D. Ronald and Bobbie L. (Graham) T.; m. Lori J. McAlister, May 31, 1980; children: Justin Daniel, Christopher James, Alexander Graham. BS, Ctrl. Mo. State U., 1979; JD, U. Mo., 1982. Bar: Mo. 1982, U.S. Dist. Ct. (we. dist.) 1982, U.S. Dist. Ct. (ea. dist.) Mo. 1984. Assoc. Wasinger, Parham & Morthland, Hannibal, Mo., 1982-87; ptnr. Wasinger, Parham, Morthland Terrell & Wasinger, 1987—. Bd. dirs. Marion County Svcs. for the Developmentally Disabled, Hannibal, 1989—. Mem.: 10th Jud. Cir. Bar Assn. (pres. 2001—), Mo. Bar Assn. (family law sect.), U. Mo. Alumni Assn. (life), Phi Delta Phi. Office: Wasinger Parham Morthland Terrell & Wasinger 2801 Saint Marys Ave Hannibal MO 63401-3775

TERRELL, JEFFREY E. otolaryngologist, researcher, educator; b. Takoma Park, Md., Jan. 14, 1962; s. Robert Louis and Joan Estelle Terrell; m. Linda Bjork, June 27, 1992; 2 children. Student, Marshall U., 1984; BA in Biology, U. Chgo., 1984; MD, Harvard U., 1988. Diplomate Am. Bd. Otolaryngology. Assoc. prof. otolaryngology U. Mich. Med. Sch., Ann Arbor, 1993—; dir. Mich. Sinus Ctr., Livonia, 1999—. Contbr. numerous articles to profl. jours. Fellow: Am. Rhinologic Soc., Am. Acad. Otolaryngology; mem.: Phi Beta Kappa. Office: U Mich Health Sys TC 1904D 1500 E Medical Center Dr Ann Arbor MI 48109-0312 Fax: (734) 936-9625. E-mail: terrelj@umich.edu.

TERRELL, PAMELA SUE, pharmacist; b. Richmond, Ind., Feb. 1, 1965; d. Kenneth Duane and Phyllis J. (Preston) T. BS in Pharmacy with honors, PharmD, Purdue U., 1991. Registered pharmacist, Ind.; bd. cert. pharmacotherapy specialist. Pharmacist Reid Hosp. and Health Care Svcs., Richmond, 1992-94, Owl Drugs, Muncie, Ind., 1994-95, Cardinal Health Sys., Inc., Muncie, 1996—; resident in pharmacy practice Meth. Hosp. Ind., Indpls., 1995-96; adj. instr. pharmacy practice Butler U. Sch. Pharmacy and Health Scis., 1995-96. Cons. pharmacist H&R Healthcare Cons., Muncie, 1994-95. Mem. Am. Coll. Clin. Pharmacy, Fellowship of Christian Pharmacists Internat., Ind. Coll. Clin. Pharmacy, Rho Chi, Phi Kappa Phi. Avocations: needlework, travel, cooking. Home: 2917 W Applewood Ct Muncie IN 47304-7502 Office: Cardinal Health System 2401 W University Ave Muncie IN 47303-3428 E-mail: psterrell@comcast.net.

TERRELL, W(ILLIAM) GLENN, university president emeritus; b. Tallahassee, May 24, 1920; s. William Glenn and Esther (Collins) T.; m. Gail Strandberg Terrell; children by previous marriage: Francine Elizabeth, William Glenn III. BA, Davidson Coll., 1942, LLD (hon.), 1969; MS, Fla. State U., 1948; PhD, State U. Iowa, 1952; LLD (hon.), Gonzaga U., 1984, Seattle U., 1985. Instr., then asst. prof. Fla. State U., Tallahassee, 1948-55; asst. prof., then assoc. prof., chmn. dept. psychology U. Colo., Boulder, 1955-59, acting dean Coll Arts and Scis., 1963-65; prof. psychology, dean Coll. Liberal Arts and Scis., U. Ill. at Chgo. Circle, 1963-65, dean faculties, 1965-67; pres. Wash. State U., Pullman, 1967-85, pres. emeritus, 1985—. Pres. Nat. Assn. State Univs. and Land-Grant Colls., 1977-78; cons. The Pacific Inst., Seattle, 1987—. Contbr. articles to profl. jours. Served to capt. inf. U.S. Army, 1942-46, ETO. Recipient Disting. Alumnus award U. Iowa, 1985; Disting. Grad. Dept. Psychology, U. Iowa, 1996. Fellow APA, Soc. Rsch. in Child Devel.; mem. AAAS, Sigma Xi, Phi Kappa Phi. Avocations: golf, reading, travel. Home: 2438 36th Ave W Seattle WA 98199-3704 Office: The Pacific Inst 1709 Harbor Ave SW Seattle WA 98126-2073 E-mail: gterrell@pacinst.com.

TERRELL-MCDANIEL, ROBIN F. nursing administrator; b. Charlton Heights, W.Va., May 9, 1961; d. Clarence E. Sr. and Dorothy Mae (Smith) T.; m. Charles Kevin McDaniel, Aug. 4, 1990. ADN, W.Va. Inst. Tech., 1982; BSN, W.Va. U., 1987. Emergency room charge nurse Montgomery (W.Va.) Gen. Hosp., 1982-87, nursing supr., 1987-88; coord. utilization rev. MedCert, Charleston, W.Va., 1988-89; vis. asst. prof. nursing W.Va. Inst. Tech., Montgomery, 1989-90; critical care nurse W.Va. Gen. Hosp., 1990-97, cardiac rehab. nurse, 1995-97, dir. acute care nursing, cardiac rehab. intensive care, 1997-2000, chief nursing officer, 2000—. Mem. Am. Assn. Cardiovascular and Pulmonary Rehab. Home: PO Box 345 Pratt WV 25162-0345

TERRILL, KAREN STAPLETON, retired medical planning consultant; b. Milw., Mar. 21, 1939; d. Thomas John and Olive Patrea (Thorbjornsen) Stapleton; m. Max Kurt Winkler, Dec. 18, 1965 (dec. June 1976); m. Richard Terrill, Jan. 23, 1991 (dec. May 1991). BS in Nursing, U. Mich., 1961; MBA, U. Nev., 1974. RN, Calif. Project nurse Langley Porter N.P.I., San Francisco, 1962-64; asst. dir. nursing Milw. County Mental Health Ctr., 1964-66; instr. Fond du Lac (Wis.) Sch. Dist., 1966-67; sch. nurse Inglewood (Calif.) Sch. Dist., 1968-69; instr. nursing U. Nev., Reno, 1969-74; health planner manpower State of Nev. Comp B. Agy., Carson City, 1974-75; planning analyst St. Mary's Hosp., Reno, 1974-76; sr. system analyst U. Calif., San Francisco, 1976-79; med. planning cons. Stone Marraccini & Patterson, 1979-93. Mem. citizen's adv. group City of Richmond, Calif., 1987-88; founding dir. of B.O.A.T. non-profit corp. to promote ferry transit on San Francisco Bay. Mountain State Regional Planning Commn. grantee, 1973-74. Home: 1308 Mallard Dr Richmond CA 94801-4113 E-mail: ktturkish@aol.com.

TERRILL, RICHARD LESLIE, investment management consultant; b. Dallas, Sept. 9, 1965; s. Richard A. Terrill and Linda Joyce (Jones) Knox; m. Monica Lynn Hesley, Mar. 30, 1991; 1 child, Olivia Caroline. BBA, Stephen F. Austin State U., 1988. V.p. investments AG Edwards & Sons, Inc., Dallas, 1991—. Mem. Dallas Estate Planning Coun., 1994—; instr. Richland Coll., Dallas, 1995—. Mem. Internat. Assn. Fin. Planners, Inst. Cert. Fin. Planners. Avocation: cycling. Office: AG Edwards & Sons Inc 2305 Cedar Springs Rd Ste 300 Dallas TX 75201-7807

TERRILL, ROBERT CARL, hospital administrator; b. Oklahoma City, Dec. 10, 1927; s. D. Willard and Velma (Mitchell) T.; m. Jessica Doe, Dec. 14, 1957; children— Thane Bennett, Sarah Haven. BA, U. Okla., 1948, MA in History, 1961; MA in Hosp. Adminstrn., State U. Iowa, 1954; EdD in Ednl. Adminstrn., Ind. U., 1978. Adminstrv. resident Mary Fletcher Hosp., Burlington, Vt., 1953-55, asst. adminstr., pers. dir., 1955-57, assoc. adminstr., 1957-65; adminstr. Hosps. of U. Okla., Oklahoma City, 1965-72; dir. Ind. Univ. Hosps., Indpls., 1972-77; assoc. prof. Coll. Mgmt. U. Mass., Boston, 1977-87; preceptor in hosp. adminstrn. Washington U., St. Louis, Trinity U., San Antonio; asst. prof. U. Okla. Health Scis. Center. Pub. edn. planning svcs. corp., 1987—. Fellow Am. Coll. Hosp. Adminstrs.; mem. Mass. Hosp. Assn., Am. Hosp. Assn., Assn. Programs in Hosp. Adminstrn., Pub. Health Assn., New Eng. Hosp. Assembly, Nat. League for Nursing, State U. Iowa. Alumni

Assn., Ind. U. Alumni Assn. Clubs: Rotarian. Home: 30 N Sandyside Ln Yarmouth Port MA 02675-1749 Office: 923 Old Kings Hwy Yarmouth Port MA 02675 E-mail: materrill@capcod.net.

TERRILL, ROSS GLADWIN, author, educator; b. Melbourne, Australia; came to U.S., 1965, naturalized, 1979; s. Frank and Miriel (Lloyd) T. BA with honors, U. Melbourne; PhD, Harvard U., 1970. Tutor in polit. sci. U. Melbourne, 1962-63; staff sec. Australian Student Christian Movement, 1964-65; teaching fellow Harvard, 1968-70, lectr. govt., 1970-73, asso. prof., 1974-78, research fellow East Asian studies, 1970—; dir. student programs Harvard (Center Internat. Affairs), 1974-78; contbg. editor Atlantic Monthly, 1970-84; research fellow Asia Soc., 1977-79. Vis. prof. U. Tex., Austin, 1999—. Author: China Profile, 1969, China and Ourselves, 1971, 800,000,000: The Real China, 1972, R.H. Tawney and His Times, 1973, Flowers on an Iron Tree, 1975, The Future of China, 1978, The China Difference, 1979, Mao: A Biography, 1980, revised 1993, 2000, White-Boned Demon, 1984, The Australians, 1987, Madam Mao, 1992, revised, 1993, 99, China in Our Time, 1992, The Australians: How We Live Now, 2000; contbr. numerous articles to profl. jours. Recipient Nat. Mag. award, 1972; George Polk Meml. award outstanding mag. reporting, 1972; Sumner prize, 1970. Mem. Authors Guild, PEN. Clubs: Harvard of N.Y.C. Home: 87 Gainsborough St Boston MA 02115-4911 E-mail: terr@compuserve.com.

TERRILL, W(ALLACE) ANDREW, political scientist; b. Pasadena, Calif., Aug. 15, 1954; s. Wallace and Gloria (Acheson) T. BA in Polit. Sci., Calif. State Poly. U., 1975; MA in Polit. Sci., U. Calif., Riverside, 1976; PhD in Internat. Rels., The Claremont Grad. Sch., 1983. Rsch. asst. Analytical Assessments Corp., L.A., 1978-80, rsch. assoc., 1980-87; part-time instr. Calif. State Poly. U., Pomona, 1987-89; asst. prof. polit. sci. Old Dominion U., Norfolk, Va., 1989-93; sr. internat. security analyst Lawrence Livermore Nat. Lab., Livermore, Calif., 1993—2001; rsch. prof. Strategic Studies Inst., U.S. Army War Coll., Carlisle, Pa., 2001—. Vis. prof. U.S. Air War Coll., Maxwell AFB, Ala., 1998-99; cons. Sys. Rsch. and Devel. Corp., L.A., 1987-89; adj. asst. prof. Occidental Coll., L.A., 1988-89; adj. prof. Los Positas Coll., 2001; workshop leader; interviewed on TV, radio and in print media on Mid. Eastern and nonproliferation issues. Contbr. numerous book revs. and articles to acad. jours. Served with USAR, 1976—, lt. col., 1997. Decorated Meritorious Svc. medal, 1991; recipient Haynes Found. dissertation fellowship, 2 Claremont Grad. Sch. full-tuition fellowships. Office: US Army War Coll Strategic Studies Inst Carlisle Barracks PA 17013

TERRIQUEZ-KASEY, LAURA MARIE, emergency nurse; b. Bronx, N.Y., May 12, 1950; d. Gilbert Manuel and Elizabeth (Arevena) Terriquez; m. William Kasey, July 23, 1988 (dec. May 1995). AAS, SUNY, Morrisville, 1971; BSN, Long Island U., 1980; MSN, CUNY, 1985. RN, N.Y., Tex. Commd. 2d lt. AUS, 1974, advanced through grades to maj., 1993; staff nurse emergency svc. Bellevue Hosp. Ctr., N.Y.C., 1971-73, head nurse emergency svc., 1973-81, nursing supr., 1981-84; clin. nurse coord. South Nassau Cmty. Hosp., Oceanside, N.Y., 1984-85; staff nurse Brooke Army Med.Ctr., San Antonio, 1985-86; head nurse vascular surg. ward Brooke Army Med. Ctr., 1987-89, charge nurse, EMT, head nurse PACU, 1987-89; staff nurse med. ICU William Beaumont Army Med. Ctr., Ft. Bliss/El Paso, Tex., 1985-90, staff nurse trauma unit, 1990-91, head nurse trauma unit, 1991-92, asst. chief nurse, 1992-93; nurse mgr. emergency/trauma svcs. Bassett Health Care Sys., Cooperstown, N.Y., 1993-2000, adminstr. emergency and svc. tng. program, 1997-98, co-chair network adv. group, nurse advisor emergency svcs.; clin. instr. SUNY Sch Nursing, Binghamton, 2000—. Instr. U. El Paso, Tex., 1991-92; mem. com. nursing adv. Southwest Organbank, El Paso, 1992—; adj. instr. U. Tex. Dept. Nursing, El Paso, 1992; Advanced Emergency Med. Technic Critical Care, N.Y. State Dept. Health sponsor for EMS programs, 2000-02. With disaster med. assistance team Team Houston, Tex., 2001; with disaster med. assistance team team response Anthrax Postal Response, N.Y.C., 2001. Decorated Army Commendation medal with 3 oak leaf clusters, Army Achievement award; recipient Meritorious Svc. award San Antonio Police Dept., 1988, Svc. award ARC, 1980, Cert. Appreciation N.Y. Emergency Med. Svcs., 1984. Mem.: Disaster Med. Assistance Team (NY), Emergency Nurses Assn., Am. Legion, Sigma Theta Tau. Avocations: swimming, biking. Home: 125 Park Dr Angel Heights Oneonta NY 13820 Office: Decker Sch Nursing Box 6600 SUNY Binghamton Binghamton NY 13902 E-mail: laurakasey@catskill.net.

TERRIS, ALBERT, metal sculptor; b. N.Y.C., Nov. 10, 1916; s. Aaron and Fania (Rosenthal) Teraspulsky; children: Susan, Abby, David, Enoch. BSS, CCNY, 1939; postgrad., NYU Inst. Fine Arts, 1939-42. Lectr. Met. Mus. Art, 1941-42; tchr. fine arts N.Y.C. High Sch. System, 1947-54; prof. emeritus Bklyn. Coll., 1947-86. Steel sculptures include Non-Fixed Relationship, 1948, Homely Cosmology, 1948, Anti-Gravity, 1950, Giraffes, 1953, Short Art, 1953, Pro-Gravity Chains, 1956, Tools, 1956, Crushed Sculpture, 1956, Words, 1957, Discursive-Illegible-Boustrophedon, 1975, Plates of Charlemagne, 1975, Fireharps, 1975, Cycle of Life, 1977, Wipes, 1996, Quantum Photography, 1995, Meals, 1998, Visitors, 1998, Twigs Door Music, 2001; one-man shows: Saidenberg, 1955, Duveen-Graham, 1958, Carnegie Internats., 1958, 62, Bklyn. L.I. Artists Bklyn. Mus. (awarded first prize), 1960, Allan Stone, 1962, Critics Choice, 1972, Artists Space, 1975, Gloria Cortella, 1977, (retrospective) The Artist in the Civil Service Bklyn. Coll. Gallery, 1985; exhibited in group shows at Tanager Gallery, 1952-61, Stable Anns., 1952-60, Mus. Modern Art, N.Y.C., 1962, others; represented in permanent collections: Stephen Paine, Boston, Arnold Maremont, Evanston, G. David Thompson Estate, NBC-TV, others. Served with 1st Allied Airborne, 1942-45. Home and Office: 280 S Ocean Ave Freeport NY 11520-4939

TERRIS, LILLIAN DICK, psychologist, association executive; b. Blooomfield, N.J., May 5, 1914; d. Alexander Blaikie and Herminia (Doscher) Dick; m. Louis Long, Apr. 22, 1935 (dec. Sept. 1968); 1 son, Alexander Blaikie Long; m. Milton Terris, Feb. 6, 1971. BA, Barnard Coll., 1935; PhD, Columbia U., 1941. Diplomate Am. Bd. Examiners in Profl. Psychology. Instr. psychology Sarah Lawrence Coll., Bronxville, N.Y., 1937-40; jr. pers. tech. SSA, Washington, 1941; sr. pers. clk. OWI, N.Y.C., 1941-43; dir. profl. examination svc. Am. Pub. Health assn., 1943-70; pres., 1970-79; pres. emeritus, 1979—. Assoc. editor: Jour. Pub. Health Policy, 1979—; contbr. articles to profl. jours. Recipient Nat. Environ. Health assn. award, 1976, Cert. Svc. award Bd. Preventive Medicine, 1979. Fellow Am. Psychol. Assn., Am. Coll. Hosp. Adminstrs. (hon.); mem. Am. Pub. Health Assn., N.Y. State Psychol. Assn., Phi Beta Kappa, Sigma Xi. Home: 208 Meadowood Dr South Burlington VT 05403-7401 Office: 475 Riverside Dr New York NY 10115-0122 E-mail: jphpterris@aol.com.

TERRIS, SUSAN, physician, cardiologist; b. Morristown, N.J., Sept. 5, 1944; d. Albert and Virginia Terris. BA in History, U. Chgo., 1967, PhD in Biochemistry, 1975, MD, 1976. Diplomate in internal medicine, endocrinology and metabolism, cardiovasc. disease Am. Bd. Internal Medicine. Resident in internal medicine Washington U., Barnes Hosp., St. Louis, 1976-78; fellow in endocrinology and metabolism U. Chgo., 1978-80, fellow cardiology, 1980-83, U. Mich., Ann Arbor, 1983-85, instr. cardiology, 1985-86; head cardiac catheterization lab., head cardiology Westland (Mich.) Med. Ctr., 1985. Contbr. articles to Jour. Biol. Chemistry, Am. Jour. Physiology, Am. Jour. Cardiology, Jour. Clin. Investigation, other profl. publs. Grantee Juvenile Diabetes Found., 1978-80, NIH, 1978-79. Mem. AAAS, Am. Heart Assn., N.Y. Acad. Sci. Achievements include rsch. demonstrating dependence of intracellular degradation of insulin upon its prior receptor-mediated uptake by liver; studies on the electrophysiologic effect of cathecholamimes on sheep Parkinje fibers and on the hemodynamic effects of various drugs on the human circulatory system.

TERRIS, SUSAN DUBINSKY, writer, educator; b. St. Louis, May 6, 1937; d. Harold William and Myra Friedman Dubinsky; m. David Warren Terris, Aug. 31, 1958; children: Dan, Michael, Amy Terris Orgish. BA, Wellesley Coll., 1959; MA, San Francisco State U., 1965. Author: (books) The Upstairs Witch and the Downstairs Witch, 1970, The Backwards Boots, 1971, On Fire, 1972, The Drowning Boy, 1972, Plague of Frogs, 1973, Pickle, 1973, Whirling Rainbows, 1974, The Pencil Families, 1975, Amanda, the Panda, and the Redhead, 1975, The Chicken Pox Papers, 1976, No Boys Allowed, 1976, Two P's in a Pod, 1977, Tucker and the Horse Thief, 1979, Stage Brat, 1980, No Scarlet Ribbons, 1981, Wings and Roots, 1982, Octopus Pie, 1983, Baby-Snatcher, 1984, The Latchkey Kids, 1986, Author! Author!, 1990, Nell's Quilt, 1996; (poems) Killing in the Comfort Zone, 1995, Curved Space, 1998, Angels of Bataan, 1999, Eye of the Holocaust, 1999, Minnesota Fishing Report, 2000, Susan Terris: Greatest Hits, 2000, Fire is Favorable to the Dreamer, 2002; contbr. articles to profl. jours. Mem. PEN Internat., Authors Guild, Poetry Soc. Am. Democrat. Jewish. Avocations: hiking, canoeing, baking. Home and Office: 11 Jordan Ave San Francisco CA 94118

TERRITO, MARY C. health facility administrator, oncologist; BS in Biology, Wayne State U., 1965, MD, 1968. Intern/resident in internal medicine Parkland Hosp., Dallas, 1971-73; fellow in hematology/oncology Harbor-U. Calif., L.A., 1973-74, UCLA, 1974-75; rsch. assoc. Wadsworth VA Hosp., L.A., 1975-81; asst. prof. dept. medicine UCLA, 1975-81, assoc. prof., 1981-96, prof., 1996—, dir. bone marrow transplant program Ctr. Health Scis., 1981—. Contbr. articles to profl. jours. Office: UCLA Bone Marrow Transplantation Program Ctr 42-121 CHS 10833 Le Conte Ave Los Angeles CA 90095-3075

TERRY, B. BRENT, laywer; b. Louisville, Dec. 7, 1968; s. Bobby Swede and Eleanor (Foster) T.; m. Lee Ann, May 22, 1993. BA in History, William Jewell Coll., 1991; JD, Emory U., 1994. Bar: Ga. 1994. Sr. assoc. Attys. at Law Smith, Atlanta, 1994-99, Misner, Scott, and Grate, Atlanta, 1999—. Risk mgmt. com. Briarlake Bapt. Ch., Decatur, Ga., 1996-98. Mem. ABA, ATLA, Ga. Trial Lawyers Assn., Christian Legal Soc., Atlanta Bar Assn. Avocations: choral music, reading, politics, church activities, sports. Office: Ste 1010 1050 Crown Pointe Pkwy Atlanta GA 30338

TERRY, CLIFFORD LEWIS, journalist; b. Highland Park, Ill., Jan. 19, 1937; s. Clifford Lewis and Isabelle (Marlow) T.; m. Patricia West Dickelman, Sept. 1, 1966; children: Christopher West, Scott Marlow. Student, Carleton Coll., Northfield, Minn., 1954-55; BA, Trinity Coll., Hartford, Conn., 1958; postgrad., Columbia U., 1962-63. Tchr., English and history Mt. Hermon (Mass.) Sch., 1958-59; police reporter City News Bur. Chgo., 1959-60; mem. staff Chgo. Tribune, 1960-94, movie critic, 1965-70; assoc. editor Chgo. Tribune (Sunday mag.), 1970-82, feature writer, 1982-85, TV critic, 1985-89, arts feature writer, 1989-94; ind. writer, 1994—. Author: Chicago: Off the Beaten Path, 2001. Served with AUS, 1960. Nieman fellow Harvard U., 1969-70 Mem. Phi Beta Kappa.

TERRY, DAVID WILLIAM, lawyer; b. Temple, Tex., May 21, 1958; s. Victor Lewis and Jon Gayle (Kirschner) T.; m. Katherine Ellen Noll, Dec. 5, 1987; children: Nicholas William, John Benjamin. BA, Colo. Coll., 1981; JD, South Tex. Coll. Law, 1985. Bar: Tex. 1986, U.S. Dist. Ct. (no. and ea. dists.) Tex. Briefing atty. U.S. Ct. Appeals (4th cir.), San Antonio, 1986-87; pvt. practice Dallas, 1987—. Exec. editor South Tex. Law Rev., 1985. Pres. East Dallas Cppr. Parish, 1992. Mem. Tex. Trial Lawyers Assn. (bd. dirs. 1992—), Am. Assn. Portrait Artists, Dallas Trial Lawyers Assn. (bd. dirs. 1994—), ATLA, Coll. State Bar Tex. (pro bono coll.). Democrat. Methodist. Avocations: oil painting, portraits and landscapes. Office: 12221 Merit Dr Ste 1650 Dallas TX 75251-3102 E-mail: davidterry@davidterry.com.

TERRY, ELIZABETH HAYS, calligrapher, needlepoint designer; b. Bryn Mawr, Pa., July 29, 1935; d. James Franklin and Mary Ellen (Carmichael) Hays; m. Charles L. Terry, III, Feb. 8, 1958; children: Elizabeth Harllee Carmichael Terry Moran, Charles L. IV. AB, Smith Coll., 1957. Asst. to profs. Harvard U., Cambridge, Mass., 1957-58; art tchr. Exeter (N.H.) Day Sch., 1968-72; asst. editor Phillips Exeter Acad. Alumni Quarterly, 1972-75, dir. alumni records, 1975-85; owner Elizabeth Terry, Needlepoint Design, Exeter, N.H., 1980—. Tchr. needlepoint Guild of Strawbery Banke, Portsmouth, N.H. Dir. for Town of Exeter-Save Our Shores, 1972. Mem. Smith Coll. Class of 1957 (class fund agt. 1972-77, alumnae fund com. 1977-80, class bequest chair 1982—, com. on deferred giving 1990—), N.H. Colonial Dames (pres. 1989-92, nat. historian 1992-94, nat. v.p. 1994-2000). Episcopalian. Avocations: tennis, needlepoint, historic preservation. Home and Office: 77 Brookside Dr Stratham NH 03885-2128 E-mail: ceterry@rcn.com.

TERRY, FREDERICK ARTHUR, JR. lawyer; b. Buffalo, May 24, 1932; s. Frederick Arthur and Agnes Elizabeth (Tranter) T.; m. Barbara Anderson. BA, Williams Coll., 1953; LLB, Columbia U., 1956. Bar: N.Y. 1957, U.S. Dist. Ct. (so., no. and ea. dists.) : N.Y., U.S. Tax Ct.:, U.S. Supreme Ct.:. Law clk. to Hon. Sterry R. Waterman, U.S. Ct. Appeals (2d cir.), 1956—57; assoc. Sullivan & Cromwell, N.Y.C., 1957-65, ptnr., 1965-99, sr. counsel, 2000—. Bd. dirs. Eisenhower Fellowships, Natural Resources Def. Coun., McIntosh Found., Weinman Found., Rockefeller U.; trustee Harold K. Hochschild Found.; chmn. Flagler Found. Mem. ABA, N.Y. State Bar Assn., Assn. of Bar of City of N.Y., Century Assn., River Club, Union Club, India House, Doubles, Maidstone Club (East Hampton, N.Y.), The Bathing Corp. (Southampton, NY), Lyford Cay Club (Bahamas). Office: Sullivan & Cromwell 125 Broad St Fl 25 New York NY 10004-2400

TERRY, GARY A. lawyer, former trade association executive; b. Ogden, Utah, Apr. 2, 1935; s. Hyrum Aceal and Viola (Sorenson) T.; m. Carole Ann Eitel, June 23, 1962; children— Stephanie Ann, Brendan Gary BA in Polit. Sci., UCLA, 1964; JD, George Washington U., 1968. Bars: Va. 1969 D.C. 1969. Mem. staff U.S. Ho. of Reps., Washington, 1964-65; Washington staff Bethlehem Steel Corp., 1965-69; atty. HUD, Washington, 1969; exec. v.p. Am. Land Devel. Assn. (now Am. Resort Devel. Assn.), 1969-82, pres., 1982-91, also dir.; with Jones, Waldo, Holbrook & McDonough, Washington, 1991-95, St. George, 1995-97. Dir. Internat. Found. for Timesharing, Washington, 1981-91, mem. consultative council Nat. Inst. Bldg. Scis., Washington, 1982-85; U.S. rep. land use and town planning com. Internat. Real Estate Fedn., Brussels, 1984-91; mem. Found. for Internat. Meetings, Washington, 1984-92; del. Lincoln Inst. Land Policy, Harvard U., 1984, 85 Contbr. articles to profl. jours. Asst. to exec. dir. Presdl. Inaugural Com., 1969-70; mem. adv. bd. NOAA, Washington, 1972; bd. dirs. Zacchaeus Free Med. and Legal Clinics, Washington, 1991-95, co-chair lawyers com., 1992-95; bd. dirs. Celebrity Concert Series, St. George, 1999—; chmn. Pioneer Ctr. for the Arts Found., St. George, 2000-02, bd. trustees, 1998—. Seved with USN, 1953-56. Decorated Am. Spirit of Honor medal. Mem. Va. Bar Assn., D.C. Bar Assn. Mem. Lds Ch. Avocations: music; literature; architectural design; art; travel. Home: 952 Lizzie Ln Saint George UT 84790-2255

TERRY, JOHN ALFRED, state supreme court judge; b. Utica, N.Y., May 6, 1933; s. Robert Samuel and Julia Berenice (Collins) T. BA magna cum laude, Yale U., 1954; JD, Georgetown U., 1960. Bar: D.C. 1960. Asst. U.S. atty. for D.C., 1962-67; staff atty. Nat. Commn. Reform of Fed. Criminal Laws, Washington, 1967-68; pvt. practice law, 1968-69; chief appellate div. U.S. Atty.'s Office for D.C., 1969-82; judge D.C. Ct. Appeals, 1982—. Mem. D.C. Bar (bd. govs. 1977-82), ABA, Phi Beta Kappa Office: DC Ct Appeals 500 Indiana Ave NW Washington DC 20001-2138

TERRY, JOHN JOSEPH, transportation investor; b. Chgo., July 29, 1937; s. Michael Parnell and Honore (Ryan) T.; m. Terese Rose Mulkern, Dec. 31, 1960; children: Michael P., Gregory, Deirdre BS, Loyola U., Chgo., 1959; postgrad., U. So. Fla., 1967. C.P.A., Ill. With Touche, Ross & Co., 1959-65; v.p. Nat. City Lines, Denver, 1965-71; v.p. fin. Pepsico Transp., Inc., Tulsa, 1971-74; v.p. U.S. Rwy. Assn., Washington, 1974-76; chmn. P.I.E. Transport Europe, 1976-79; exec. v.p. IU Internat. Corp., Wilmington, Del., 1976-85; pres. Transp. Mgmt. Investment Group, Inc., Phila., 1985—. V.p.-at-large Am. Trucking Assn., Washington, 1984-85, chmn., internat. competitiveness task force, 1991, tax policy com., 1987—; bd. dirs. Caldwell Freight Lines, Lenoir, N.C., Basin Western, Inc., Roosevelt; cons. freight transp. World Bank and European Bank for Reconstrn. and Devel., 1986—. Served with U.S. Army, 1960-63 Recipient Best Motor Carrier Rsch. award Transp. Rsch. Forum, 1991. Office: Transp Mgmt Investment Group Inc 210 Locust St Apt 11B Philadelphia PA 19106-3923

TERRY, JOSEPH RAY, JR. lawyer; b. Vicksburg, Miss., Aug. 10, 1938; s. Joseph Ray Sr. and Alma Blanche (Smith) T.; m. Louise Caroline Beland, July 17, 1965; children: Kathleen A., Marie L., Bernard R. JD, Loyola U., 1965. Bar: D.C. 1966, Miss. 1968, U.S. Ct. Appeals (5th cir.) 1971, Ga. 1973, U.S. Dist. Ct. (no. and so. dists.) Ga. 1973, U.S. Ct. Appeals (D.C. cir.) 1973, U.S. Supreme Ct. 1973, U.S. Ct. Appeals (8th cir.) 1974, U.S. Dist. Ct. (we. dist.) Tenn. 1983, U.S. Ct. Appeals (6th cir.) 1989; cert. mediator. Trial atty. civil rights div. U.S. Dept. Justice, Washington, 1966-69; assoc. regional counsel U.S. Dept. HUD, Atlanta, 1969-70; ptnr. Crosland, Myer, Rindskopf & Terry, 1974-76; regional counsel EEOC, 1970-73, supr. trial atty. Litigation Cen., 1976-79, regional atty. Memphis, 1979-96, dep. gen. counsel Washington, 1996-99, cons., lectr., mediator, 1999—. Part-time asst. atty. City of Atlanta, 1975-76; cons. NLRB, Memphis, 1981-82; adj. prof. law Emory U., 1971-75; vis. prof. law St. Louis U., 1973-74, William C. Wefel disting. vis. prof. law, 1998—; acting program dir. EEOC, Washington, 1983, acting dist. dir., Memphis, 1984-85; bd. dirs. Fed. Credit Union, 1984-91; mem. adv. com. to U.S. Dist. Ct. for western dist. Tenn., 1990-93, chmn. case mgmt. subcom., 1991-98; mem. faculty Southwestern Legal Found., Dallas, spring 1998; cons. equal employment, 1999—; cert. gen. civil mediator Supreme Ct. Tenn., 2000. Author: (jour.) Eliminating the Plaintiff's Attorney in Equal Employment Litigation: A Shakespearean Tragedy, Labor Lawyer, 1989, Memphis and Race, The Commercial Appeal, 1987. Cons. Alaska Human Rights Commn., Anchorage, 1981; bd. dirs. Nat. Kidney Found. of West Tenn., Memphis, pres., 1984-85; bd. dirs. United Meth. Neighborhood Ctr., 1985-88; bd. dirs. St. Patrick's Parish Coun., Memphis, pres., 1986-88; mem. Leadership Memphis, 1988-99; bd. dirs. Place of Grace Ministries, Carlisle, Pa., 1997—. Named Honor Law Graduate U.S. Atty. Gen., 1965. Mem. ABA (EEOC liaison com. 1987-89), Fed. Bar Assn. (bd. dirs. 1988-89, v.p. West Tenn. chpt. 1991-92, pres. 1993-94, nat. com. 1996-99, named Younger Fed. Lawyer of Yr. 1973), Supreme Ct. Hist. Soc., St. Thomas More Lawyers Guild, Salvation Army (bd. dirs. 1995-96, 2001-02). Roman Catholic. Avocations: tennis, golf, skiing, hiking, reading. Home: 1560 Harbert Ave Memphis TN 38104-5033

TERRY, KAY ADELL, marketing executive; b. Portland, Oreg., July 11, 1939; d. Langdon Alcott and Emma Francis (Meyer) Howard; m. Frank F. Terry, Aug. 31, 1963 (div. Mar. 1988); 1 child, Kimberly Sue. CPC, CIPC. Office mgr. Merck Sharp & Dohme, Portland, 1959-63; asst. dir. admissions Seattle Pacific U., Seattle, 1963-66; owner United Personnel Svc., 1966-86; pres., CEO Ram Force Cos., 1986-91; pres. N.W. region Robert Half Internat., 1991-93; pres., CEO Terry & Assocs., 1993—; CEO Key Staff, LLC, 1996—, also bd. dirs. Bd. dirs. Ram Force Cos., Seattle Acctg. Force, Inc., Seattle, Office Force, Inc., Seattle, Data Force, Inc., Seattle. Contbr. articles to profl. jours. Vol. Spl. Olympics, Seattle. Named 16th Fastest Growing Co. in Wash. State, 1999, 2000; recipient Best Co. to Work for award, Wash. CEO mag., 1996—2000; fellow, Seattle Pacific U., 1989. Mem. Women Bus. Owners, Nat. Assn. Accts. (bd. dirs. 1985-87, Mem. Achievement award 1987, Disting. Svc. award 1987), Nat. Staffing Pers. Svcs. Assn. (vice-chmn. 1993), Wash. Athletic Club, Washington Software Assn., Nat. Tech. Svcs. Assn., Desert Falls Country Club, Columbia Tower Club. Republican. Avocations: travel, tennis, swimming, golf. E-mail: KTerry1010@aol.com., Kay@Keystaff.com.

TERRY, LEE R. congressman, lawyer; b. Omaha, Jan. 29, 1962; s. Leland R. Terry; m. Robyn L. Terry, Feb. 14, 1992; children: Nolan E., Ryan, Jack. BS, U. Nebr., 1984; JD, Creighton U., Omaha, 1987. Bar: Nebr. 1987, U.S. Dist. Ct. Nebr. 1987. Staff atty. Schrempp & Salerno, Omaha, 1987-92; ptnr. Schrempp, Salerno & Terry, 1992-93, Terry & Kratville, Omaha, 1993-98; mem. U.S. Congress from 2d Nebr. dist., 1999—; former mem. banking and fin. svcs. com.; former mem. govt. reform and oversight com.; former mem. transport and infrastructure com.; mem. Energy & Commerce Com., Omaha City Coun., 1991—98. Co-author: Trying the Soft Tissue Case in Nebraska, 1995. Mem. Omaha City Coun., 1991—, pres., 1995-97; chair elect Am. Diabetes Assn., Great Plains, 1996-97, chair Nebr. area, 1997-99. Named One of Ten Outstanding Young Omahans, Omaha Jaycees-C. of C., 1994. Mem. Nebr. Assn. Trial Attys. (dir. 1995—), Suburban Rotary. Republican. Methodist. Avocations: travel, playing, spending time with family. Office: Ho Reps 1513 Longworth House Office Bldg Washington DC 20515-0001 Home: 35 Spyglass Pt Valley NE 68064-9325 Office: Dist Office 11640 Arbor St Omaha NE 68144*

TERRY, LEON CASS, neurologist, educator; b. Dec. 22, 1940; s. Leon Herbert and Zella Irene (Boyd) T.; m. Suzanne Martinson, June 27, 1964; children: Kristin, Sean. Pharm. D., U. Mich., 1964; MD, Marquette U., 1969; PhD, McGill U., 1982; MBA, U.D. Fla., 1994. Diplomate Am. Bd. Psychiatry and Neurology, Am. Bd. Med. Mgmt. Intern U. Rochester, N.Y., 1969-70; staff assoc. NIH, 1970-72; resident in neurology McGill U., Montreal, Que., Can., 1972-75; MRC fellow, 1975-78; assoc. prof. U. Tenn., Memphis, 1978-81; prof. neurology U. Mich., Ann Arbor, 1981-89; assoc. prof. physiology, 1982-89; asst. chief neurology VA Med. Ctr., Ann Arbor, 1982-89; prof. neurology and physiology, chmn. dept. neurology Med. Coll. of Wis., Milw., 1989-2000. Dir. clin neurosci. ctr. and multiple sclerosis clinic, Med. Coll. Wis.; assoc. dean for amb. care, 1996-98; vice chief of staff Froedtert Hosp., 1994-97; chief of staff, 1997-98; chief med. officer cenegenics, 1997-98. Contbr. articles to profl. jours, chpts. to books. Served to lt. comdr. USPHS, 1970-72. NIH grantee, 1981-92; VA grantee, 1980-92; VA Clin. Investigator award, 1980-81. Mem. AMA, Am. Soc. Clin. Investigation, Cen. Soc. Clin. Investigation, Am. Neurol. Assn., Am. Coll. Physician Execs. (vice chmn. academic health ctr. soc. 1994-95, chair, 1995-98, leader forum health care delivery 1995-98), Am. Coll. Healthcare Execs., Endocrine Soc., Am. Acad. Neurology, Internat. Soc. Neuroendocrinilogy, Internat. Soc. Psychoeuroendocrinilogy, Soc. Neurosci., Soc. Rsch. Biol. Rhythms, Milw. Acad. Physicians, Wis. Neurol. Assn., Wis. State Med. Soc. (del.-elect 1995-96), Med. Soc. Milw. County, Milw. Neuropsychiatric Soc. (pres.-elect.). Avocations: pilot, skiing, scuba diving, computers. Office: Med Coll Wis Dept Neurology Froedtert Hosp 9200 W Watertown Plank Rd Milwaukee WI 53226-3557 E-mail: cass@ross-terry.com., cass@megapathdsl.com.

TERRY, MARSHALL NORTHWAY, JR. English language educator, author; b. Cleve., Feb. 7, 1931; s. Marshall Northway and Margaret Louise (Carpenter) T.; m. Antoinette Barksdale, Sept. 5, 1953; children: Antoinette Terry Bryant, Mary Marshall Terry Benton. Student, Amherst Coll., 1949-50, Kenyon Coll., 1950-51; BA, So. Meth. U., 1953, MA, 1954. Teaching fellow English So. Meth. U., Dallas, 1954, dir. pub. relations, lectr. English, 1957-64, instr. English, 1956, 65-67, asst. dir., 1968, assoc. prof., 1969-71, prof. English, 1972—, chmn. dept., 1971-75, 79-82, dir. creative writing program. Book critic Dallas News, 1970-75; pres. faculty senate So. Meth. U., 1993-94, assoc. provost, 1994-98, E.A. Lilly prof. Eng., 1998—. Author: Old Liberty, 1961, Tom Northway, 1968, Dallas Stories, 1986, Ringer, 1987, My Father's Hands, 1993, Land of Hope and Glory, 1996, Angels Prostate Fall, 2000; contbr. short stories to various jours. and mags.; editor Prize Stories, 1986. Past trustee Incarnate Word Coll., San Antonio; sec. bd. trustees Fort Burgwin Research Ctr., Ranchos de Taos, N.Mex. Recipient Jesse H. Jones fiction award Tex. Inst. Letters, 1968, Best Short Story award S.W. Rev., 1973, S.W. Writer of Yr. award, 1988, Willis M. Tate award So. Meth. U., 1990, 94, Lon Tinkle award for continuing excellence in Letters, Tex. Inst. Letters, 1991. Mem. AAUP (chpt. pres. 1971), Coll. Conf. Tchrs. English, South Central MLA, Tex. Inst. Letters (pres. 1977-79, councilor 1980—) Democrat. Methodist. Home: 2717 Lovers Ln Dallas TX 75225-7905 Office: So Meth Univ Dept English Dallas TX 75275-0001 E-mail: mterry@mail.smu.edu.

TERRY, MARTIN MICHAEL, visual artist, art therapist; b. Poughkeepsie, N.Y., Dec. 17, 1952; s. Gustave Paul Thury and Philomena (Casale) Terry; m. Loretta Mary Bunten, Oct. 6, 1990. AS, Dutchess C.C., 1972; attended, SUNY, New Paltz, 1973-90, U. N.Mex., 1991-96. Engraver's asst. Dell Pub. Co., Poughkeepsie, 1972-75; therapy aide Hudson River Psychiatry Ctr., 1975-80; art therapist N.Y. State Dept. Corrections, Stormville, 1980-85; program dir. Dutchess Horizons, Poughkeepsie, 1980-91. Artist-in-residence Albuquerque Pub. Schs., 1991-96. Mem. Cmty. Cultural Planning Com., Albuquerque, 1991-93. Mem. N.Mex. Art League (bd. pres. 1993-95, exhibit com. 1991-93, Best in Show award 1995), Albuquerque United Artists. Home: 503 Highmore Dr Duncanville TX 75116-2924

TERRY, MICHAEL JOSEPH, legal process supervisor, court trainer; b. Mount Ayr, Iowa, Aug. 26, 1957; s. John Stanley and Kathryn Marie (Williams) T. BS in Psychology, Santa Clara U., 1979, paralegal cert., 1987. Dep. ct. clk. Santa Clara County Mcpl. Ct., San Jose, Calif., 1980-86; ct. attendant Santa Clara County Superior Ct., 1986-87, courtroom clk., 1987—94, lead courtroom clk., 1994—2001, supr., 2001—. Mem. faculty Ct. Clk. Tng. Inst. Editor: Crimson Warrior Pub., 1992—. Mem. Coalition of Trial Ct. Clks. Assn., Superior Ct. Clks,. Assn. Calif. (pres.), Phi Delta Phi. Democrat. Avocations: literature, travel, theatre. Office: Superior Ct 191 N 1st St San Jose CA 95113

TERRY, MYRA, administration administrator; b. Newark , Feb. 16, 1944; d. Jules and Amalia Wallach (Goldberg) T.; div. 1981; children: Cynthia Anne Terry-Meisner, Julie Lynn Terry-Meisner; m. Milton Kaplan, June 12, 1988. Cert. in merchandising, Lab. Inst. of Merchandising, 1963; cert. in design, N.Y. Sch. of Interior Design, 1973. Pres. NJ Design Cons., Inc., Mountainside, 1973-92; exec. dir. Ctr. for Women in Crisis, Maplewood, N.J., 1977-81; dir. Divorce Support Ctr., Mountainside, N.J., 1981-92; chair Choice NJ, 1992-93; pres. NOW-NJ, Trenton, 1992-95; exec. dir. Women's Fund of N.J., Union, 1996—. Chair NOW-NJ Found., NJ Advisory Coun. Status of Women, 1994-96, Transition Team Gov. Christine Todd Whitman, 1993. Columnist: Decorators Notebook, 1986-88. Coordinator, Religious Coalition for Abortion Rights, 1982-92. Mem. Allied Bd. Trade, NOW (pres. Essex County chpt. 1981-83), Nat. Council of Jewish Women (v.p. 1971), NOW-N.J. (coordinator Homemakers Rights Task Force 1980-83, coord. divorce reform task force 1988-92). Democrat. Avocation: biking. Home: 588 Longview Rd South Orange NJ 07079-1325 E-mail: myranow@aol.com.

TERRY, PAMELA MAYS, psychology educator; b. Macon, Ga., Oct. 20, 1949; d. Thomas Littleton and Nancy Valune Smith M.; m. Stephen Wesley Terry, Feb. 4, 1984; 1 child, Valyne Kathryne. AB, U. Ga., 1971, MS, 1974, PhD, 1975. Rsch. psychologist U.S. Army Rsch. Inst., Fort Benning, Ga., 1976-92; asst. prof. psychology Gordon Coll., Barnesville, 1999—. Tech. cons. U.S. Army Infantry Sch., Ft. Benning, 1986-92, U.S. Army Basic Tng. Task Force, Ft. Benning, 1983-85; spl. equal employment opportunity officer Fort Benning, 1985. Mem. Forsyth Womens Club, 1996-98. Fellowship NSF, U. Ga., 1972-75. Mem. Am. Psychol. Soc., Ga. Sociol. Assn., Phi Beta Kappa, Sigma Xi, Phi Kappa Phi. Southern Baptist. Avocations: playing piano, genealogy. Home: 22 Brooklyn Ave Forsyth GA 31029 Office: Gordon Coll Divsn Bus and Social Sci 419 College Dr Barnesville GA 30204

TERRY, PAUL WILLIS, physicist; b. Salt Lake City, Apr. 2, 1952; s. Evan Ray and Joan Eliza Terry; m. Gloria Benita Gutierrez, Dec. 30, 1975; children: Paul Willis Terry Jr., Laura Joan, Stephen Michael. PhD, U. of Tex. at Austin, Austin, Texas, 1976—81. Prof. of physics U. of Wisconsin-Madison, Madison, Wis., 1994—. assoc. prof. of physics, 1991—94, asst. prof. of physics, 1988—91; rsch. scientist Inst. for Fusion Studies, U. of Tex. at Austin, Austin, Tex., 1987—88, rsch. assoc., 1983—87, rsch. fellow, 1981—83; vis. scientist Culham Lab., UK Atomic Energy Agy., Culham, United Kingdom, 1989—89, Free U. of Brussels, Brussels, Belgium, 1980—80; rsch. asst. U. of Tex. at Austin, Austin, Tex., 1976—81, MIT, Cambridge, Mass., 1974—76. Chmn. U.S. Transport Task Force, 2002—; mem. Exec. Com., Internat. Sherwood Fusion Theory Conf., 2001—, Exec. Com., U. Fusion Associates, 1996—98; assoc. editor The Physics of Fluids B, New York, NY, 1990—92; mem. Joint Inst. for Fusion Theory Adv. Com., 1992—; pvt. cons. to Bolt, Beranek, and Newman, Cambridge, Mass., 1974—75. Author: (papers) Physics of Fluids, Physics of Fluids B, Physics of Plasmas, (paper) Physics of Fluids A, (papers) Physical Review Letters, Nuclear Fusion, Plasma Physics and Controlled Fusion, Physics Letters A, Comments on Plasma Physics, (review article) Reviews of Modern Physics, (paper) Astrophysical Journal, Celestial Mechanics, Journal of Mathematical Physics, Journal of Applied Physics, Physica D. Recipient Vilas Assoc. Faculty Award, U. of Wisconsin-Madison, 1998; fellow Fellow, Am. Phys. Soc., 1993; scholar Richard Ln. Scholarship in Classical Physics, U. of Tex. at Austin, 1978. Fellow: Am. Phys. Soc.; mem.: Phi Beta Kappa. Achievements include discovery of Suppression of turbulence and turbulent transport by stable flow shear in fusion plasmas and fluids. Office: University of Wisconsin-Madison 1150 University Avenue Madison WI 53706 Office Fax: 608-262-7205. E-mail: pwterry@wisc.edu.

TERRY, RICHARD FRANK, data transcriber; b. Ogden, Utah, July 19, 1949; s. Frank Nebeker and Gertrude Angeline (Berghout) T. BA, Weber State Coll., 1979. Data transcriber IRS, Marriott, Utah, 1976—. Recipient Hon. Alumnus award, Oglala Lakota Coll., 2001. Mem. Ch. of Jesus Christ of Latter Day Saints. Avocation: reading the Spanish Bible.

TERRY, ROBERT BROOKS, lawyer; b. Kansas City, Mo., July 7, 1956; s. Frank R. and Susan S. (Smart) T.; m. Penny Susan Kanterman, July 2, 1987; children: Ryan, Kevin, Erin. Student, Vanderbilt U., 1974-75; BS in Acctg., U. Mo., 1978, JD, 1981. Bar: Mo. 1981, U.S. Dist. ct. (we. dist.) Mo. 1981, U.S. ct. Appeals (8th and 10th cirs.) 1983. Assoc. Spencer, Fane, Britt & Browne, Kansas City, Mo., 1981—89; v.p., gen. counsel Farmland Industries, Inc., 1993—, pres., CEO, 2002—. Mem. ABA, Kansas City Mo. Bar Assn., Lawyers' Assn. Kansas City, Order of Coif. Avocation: baseball. Home: 4952 W 132nd Ter Leawood KS 66209-3460 Office: Farmland Industries Inc PO Box 7305 3315 N Oak Trfy Kansas City MO 64116-2798*

TERRY, ROBERT DAVIS, neuropathologist, educator; b. Hartford, Conn., Jan. 13, 1924; m. Patricia Ann Blech, June 27, 1952; 1 son, Nicolas Saul. AB, Williams Coll., 1946, DSc (hon.), 1991; MD, Albany (N.Y.) Med. Coll., 1950. Diplomate: Am. Bd. Pathology, Am. Bd. Neuropathology. Postdoctoral tng. St. Francis Hosp., Hartford, 1950, Bellevue Hosp., N.Y.C., 1951, Montefiore Hosp., N.Y.C., 1952-53, 54-55, Inst. Recherches sur le Cancer, Paris, France, 1953-54, sr. postdoctoral fellow, 1965-66; asst. pathologist Montefiore Hosp., 1955-59; assoc. prof. dept. pathology Einstein Coll. Medicine, Bronx, N.Y., 1959-64, prof., 1964-84, acting chmn. dept. pathology, 1969-70, chmn., 1970-84; prof. depts. neuroscis. and pathology U. Calif.-San Diego, 1984-94, prof. emeritus, 1994—. Mem. study sect. pathology NIH, 1964-68; study sects. Nat. Multiple Sclerosis Soc., 1964-72, 74-78; mem. bd. sci. counselors Nat. Inst. Neurol. and Communicative Disorders and Stroke, NIH, 1976-80, chmn., 1977-80; mem. nat. sci. coun. Huntington's Disease Assn., 1978-81; mem. med. and sci. adv. bd. Alzheimer Assn., 1978-88; mem. sci. adv. bd. Max Planck Inst., Martinsried, 1990-96. Mem. editorial adv. bd. Jour. Neuropathology and Exptl. Neurology, 1963-83, 85-88, Lab. Investigation, 1967-77, Revue Neurologique, 1977-87, Annals of Neurology, 1978-82, Ultrastructural Pathology, 1978-86, Am. Jour. Pathology, 1985-89. Served with AUS, 1943-46, ETO. Recipient Potamkin prize for Alzheimer Rsch., 1988, Met. Life Found. award, 1991. Fellow AAAS, Am. Acad. Arts and Sci.; mem. Am. Assn. Neuropathologists (pres. 1969-70, Meritorious Contbn. award 1989), N.Y. Path. Soc. (v.p. 1969-70, pres. 1971-73), Am. Assn. Pathologists, Am. Neurol. Assn., Am. Acad. Neurology. Achievements include research and publications on Alzheimer's disease and Tay Sachs disease. Office: U Calif San Diego Dept Neurosci La Jolla CA 92093

TERRY, ROBERT MEREDITH, foreign language educator; b. Danville, Va., Dec. 16, 1939; s. Willard Terry and Martha Willeford; m. Anne Reynolds Beggarly, Jan. 30, 1965; children: Michael Reynolds, Christopher Robert, Meredith Anne. BA in French, Randolph-Macon Coll., Ashland, Va., 1962; PhD in Romance Langs., Duke U., Durham. N.C., 1966. Asst. prof. French U. Fla., Gainesville, Fla., 1966-68; assoc. prof. U. Richmond, Richmond, Va., 1968-83, prof., 1983—. Pres. Am. Coun. on Tchg. Fgn. Langs., 1994, mem. exec. coun., 1983-85, 2000—. Co-author: Accent: Conversational French I, 1980, Vous Y Etes!, 1990, Intersections, 1991; editor Dimension, So. Conf. on Lang. Tchg., 1991-97; assoc. editor ACTFL Foreign Language Education Series, 1994, 96, 98, 99, 2000; editor N.E. Conf. Report, 2000; articles editor NECTFL Rev.; contbr. articles to profl. jours. Recipient Stephen A. Freeman award N.E. Conf. on Teaching Fgn. Lang., 1990, Robert J. Ludwig Nat. Fgn. Lang. Leadership award, 1995. Mem. Am. Coun. on Tchg. Fgn. Langs., Fgn. Lang. Assn. Va., Am. Assn. Tchrs. French, So. Conf. on Lang. Tchg. Home: 1504 Cloister Dr Richmond VA 23233-4035 Office: Univ Richmond PO Box 25 28 Westhampton Way University Of Richmond VA 23173-0025 E-mail: rterry@richmond.edu.

TERRY, ROGER, pathologist, consultant; b. Waterville, N.Y., May 8, 1917; s. Orrin and Mary Isabelle (Kennedy) T.; m. Eleanor Virginia Wallace, Dec. 13, 1942; children: Robin, Orrin. AB magna cum laude, Colgate U., 1939; MD, U. Rochester, 1944. Cert. anatomic pathologist. Intern then resident Strong Meml. Hosp., Rochester, N.Y., 1944-51; asst. prof. U. Rochester Sch. Medicine, 1951-56, assoc. prof., 1956-61, prof. pathology, 1961-69, U. So. Calif. Sch. Medicine, Los Angeles, 1969-82; pathologist San Gabriel (Calif.) Valley Med. Ctr., 1982—. Exec. dir. Calif. Tumor Tissue Registry, Los Angeles, 1969-84. Contbr. articles to profl. jours. Served to capt. USAF, 1954-56. Fellow Am. Soc. Clin. Pathologists, Coll. Am. Pathologists; mem. AMA, Internat. Acad. Pathology (councilor 1973-76), Am. Soc. Investigative Pathology, L.A. Soc. Pathologists, Am. Soc. Cytopathology, Internat. Soc. Dermatopathology, Phi Beta Kappa, Sigma Xi, Alpha Omega Alpha. Republican. Episcopalian. Avocations: ballroom dancing, snorkeling, tandem bike riding. Home: 2841 Shakespeare Dr San Marino CA 91108-2230 Office: San Gabriel Valley Med Ctr 438 W Las Tunas Dr San Gabriel CA 91776-1216 Fax: 626-457-3201.

TERRY, ROGER HAROLD, minister, musician, composer, author, editor; b. Salisbury, N.C., Feb. 3, 1925; s. Roger Harold and Marie (Kneeburg) T.; m. Martha Frye, June 30, 1948 (div. July 1973); children: Barbara (dec.), Ruth, Julia, Glenn; m. Kathryn Wagoner, Nov. 22, 1973. AB, Lenoir-Rhyne Coll., Hickory, N.C., 1945, D Sacred Music (hon.), 1973; BD, Lutheran Theological Southern Seminary, Columbia, S.C., 1948; MS in Theology, Union Theological Seminary, 1955. Asst. pastor St. John Luth. Ch., Salisbury, N.C., 1948-50; pastor Emanuel Luth. Ch., Ridgefield Park, N.J., 1950-53, St. Mark Luth. Ch., China Grove, N.C., 1953-59; worship/music editor Bd. Parish Edn. United Luth. Ch. in Am., 1959-62; worship/music editor div. for parish services Luth. Ch. in Am., Phila., 1963-77; pastor Peace Luth. Ch., Gibsonville, N.C., 1977-83, Macedonia Luth. Ch., Burlington, 1983-84, Nazareth Luth. Ch., Rural Hall, 1985-87; interim pastor Friedens Luth. Ch., Gibsonville, 1991—. Program dir. Lutheridge Sch. Music, Arden, N.C., 1956-72; pres. Council of Chs., Ridgefield Park, N.J., 1952-53; chaplain Internat. Order of St. Luke Physician, 1978—; interim pastor Messiah Luth. Ch., Burlington, N.C., 1997—; pastor emeritus Macedonia Luth. Ch., Burlington, 1997—. Author: Church School Hymnal for Children, 1964, Young Children Sing, 1967, Music Resource Book, 1967, Music in Christian Education, 1969, Sing! Hymnal for Youth and Adults, 1970, Children Sing, Books 1-3, 1972-77, Celebrate, 1974-77, (with others) Hymnal Companion to the Lutheran Book of Worship, 1981; editor: (quar. jour.) Soli Deo Gloria, 1992—; editor, author of numerous Luth. curriculum resources; contbr. articles to religious publs. Sec., bd. trustees Lowman Home for Aged, White Rock, S.C., 1957-59; vol. relief worker, fund raiser Hurricane Hugo victims, 1989-90; interim pastor Friedens Luth. Ch., Gibsonville, N.C., 1991-92. Mem. Forsyth Luth. Council. (pres. 1986-87), Am. Guild Organists (exec. com. 1985-86), Hymn Soc. Am. (pres. Phila. chpt. 1970-72). Clubs: Rotary. Republican. Avocations: organic gardening, small scale tree farming. Home and Office: 402 Trinity Oaks Dr Salisbury NC 28144-5761 *The love of power, the addiction of dictators, dehumanizes and destroys. The power of love, which Jesus revealed, creates willing hands and servant hearts to heal brokenness and bring good out of evil. Our destiny depends upon how we choose.*

TERRY, STEPHEN, gynecologist, obstetrician; b. N.Y.C., Jan. 3, 1936; s. James Hendrick and Theodosia Ruggles Hatch T.; m. Barbara Anne Brown, Sept. 3, 1960; children: Stephen Wilson, Andrew Brock, Sarah Elizabeth. BA in Chemistry cum laude, BA in Zoology cum laude, U. Ariz., 1957; MD, Columbia U., 1961. Diplomate Am. Bd. Ob/Gyn. Intern in medicine, surgery Bellevue Hosp., N.Y.C., 1961-62; resident in ob-gyn N.Y. Lying-In Hosp., 1962-65; ob-gyn U.S. Army Med. Corps, Nuremberg, Germany, 1965-68, Okla. City Clinic, 1968-69; fellow in gynecol. oncology M.D. Anderson Hosp., Houston, 1969-70; pvt. practice ob-gyn Tucson, 1970-95. Clin. asst. Cornell Med. Sch., N.Y.C., 1963-65, U. Okla. Med. Sch., Oklahoma City, 1968-69; co-chief ob-gyn Pima County Hosp., Tucson, 1970; bd. dirs. Gaslight Enterprises, Tuscon; lect. U. Ariz. Med. Sch., Tuscon, 1992—; rsch. cons., investigator Argus Rsch., Tucson, 1993-95, mem. investigational rev. bd., 1997—. Maj. USAR. Recipient commendation medal U.S. Army, 1968, certificate of achievement, 1967. Fellow Am. Coll. Ob-Gyn., Am. Fertility Soc., Am. Urogynecol. Soc.; mem. S.W. Obstet.-Gynecol. Soc. (coun. 1989, pres. 1994), Med. Soc. U.S. and Mex., Am. Soc. Colposcopy, Am. Assn. Gynecol. Laparascopists, Am. Gynecol. Laser Soc., Tucson Obstet. and Gynecol. Soc. (pres. 1982), Social Register Assn., Knights of the Vine, Phi Beta Kappa, Delta Sigma Phi (social chmn., scholarship chmn.), Phi Lambda Upsilon, Beta Beta Beta. Avocations: genealogy, philately, oenology. Home: 6121 E San Marino Tucson AZ 85715-3017 Office: 5295 E Knight Dr Tucson AZ 85712-2147

TERRY, WAYNE GILBERT, healthcare executive, hospital administrator, consultant and mediator in health services management; b. Plymouth, Mass., Oct. 2, 1932; s. Lawrence Arthur Terry and Betty Frances (Boutemain) McClellan; m. Barbara Bromwell, Sept. 20, 1980; children: Karleton Wayne, Dale Duane, Kendrick Shane, Kristen Alayne, Tammye Van Clief, Wade Bromwell Delk. AA, Allan Hancock Coll., Santa Maria, Calif., 1960; BBA, U. Hawaii, 1966; M. Hosp. Adminstrn., Med. Coll. Va., 1973; PhD in Health Svcs. Mgmt., LaSalle U., 1999. Commd. 2d lt. USAF Med. Svc. Corps, 1967, advanced through grades to maj., 1976; asst. adminstr. for registrar activities USAF Hosp., Orlando AFB, Fla., 1966-67; assoc. adminstr. aeromed. evacuation activities USAF, Hickam AFB, Hawaii, 1967-71; adminstrv. resident USAF Regional Hosp., Langley AFB, Va., 1972-73; CEO USAF Hosp., Columbus AFB, Miss., 1973-75; nat. health edn. and tng. program advisor Office of Surgeon Gen., Dept. of Air Force, Washington, 1975-78; dir. health professions pers. planning and policy divsn. Office of Asst. Sec. Def. for Health Affairs, The Pentagon, 1978-80; dep. project mgr./adminstrv. dir. King Faisal U. Teaching Hosp., Al-Khobar, Saudi Arabia, 1980-82; dep. project mgr., hosp. dir. North Yemen Healthcare Project, As-Salem Hosp., Sadah, Yemen Arab Republic, 1982-83; hosp. dir., CEO western area Armed Forces Hosps., Khamis Mushayt, Saudi Arabia, 1983-84; chief adminstr./commissioning team chief Orbit Summit Health, Ltd., Riyadh, Saudi Arabia, 1984-85; hosp. dir., adminstrv. dir. Truk State Dept. Health Svcs., Moen, Federated States of Micronesia, 1985-87; assoc. adminstr. support svcs. King Fahad Hosp., Saudi Arabian N.G., Riyadh, 1987-90; project mgr., CEO N.W. Armed Forces Hosps. Program, Tabuk, Saudi Arabia, 1990-98, cons. in health svcs. mgmt. Saudi Arabia, 1998-99; cons., mediator in health svcs. mgmt. Crozet, Va., 1999-2000; exec. dir. Southside Area Health Edn. Ctr. Longwood U., Farmville, 2000—. Apptd. cons. in healthcare planning Air Force Surgeon Gen., 1979; apptd. preceptor program in health care adminstrn. to U. Mich. for adminstrv. residents at N.W. Armed Forces Hosps. Programs, Tabuk, Saudi Arabia, 1993; lectr. in field; cons. in field; mem. supervisory bd. Royal Coll. Surgeons in Ireland, Dublin, Ireland, 1990-98; active various symposium organizing coms.; sr. grant specialist, grants reviewer. Author books and monographs in field; contbr. articles to profl. jours. Warden to Am. Cmty. N.W. Region of Yemen Arab Republic to Am. Embassy in Sanaa, 1982-83, warden to Am. Cmty. N.W. Region of Saudi Arabia to Am. Embassy in Riyadh, 1990-99; mem. Internat. Sch. Sys. Coord. Com., Tabuk, 1990-99; bd. dirs. Taif Sch. Dist. Sys., Saudi Arabia, 1981-82, Ctrl. Va. Health Planning Agy., Richmond, Va., 2001—, Va. Tobacco Settlement Found., Richmond, Va., regional adv. bd., 2001-, Regional Southside Area Health Edn. Ctr., Longwood U., Farmville, Va., 2001—. Decorated Def. Meritorious Svc. medal, Air Force Meritorious Svc. medal with 3 oak leaf clusters, Air medal with 2 oak leaf clusters, Air Force Commendation medal with 2 oak leaf clusters, Republic of Vietnam Gallantry Cross with palm, Sec. of Def. Svc. medal/badge, Air Force Chief Med. Svc. Corps badge; recipient Citation of Appreciation Nat. Coun. Social Welfare, Seoul, Republic of Korea, 1963, Suchan Province Gov., Choong Nam, Republic of Korea, 1963, award of merit Pacific Air Forces Command, Hickam AFB, Hawaii, 1965, Outstanding Rsch. award Med. Coll. Va., 1973, Men of Achievement award, Cambridge, Eng., 1982, Citation of Appreciation Gov. Truk State, Federated States of Micronesia, 1987, Citation of Merit Internat. Red Cross Commn., 1991, N.W. Armed Forces Hosps., Ministry of Def. and Aviation, Tabuk, Saudi Arabia, 1991, Citation of Appreciation Presidency of Gen. Staff Hdqs., 1992, 93, 95, 96, 97, 98, 99, Disting. Alumni award Allan Hancock Coll., Santa Maria, Calif., 2000, Personality of the South award, 1975. Fellow Am. Coll. Healthcare Execs., Royal Soc. Health; mem. Am. Hosp. Assn., Am. Mgmt. Assn., Air Force Med. Svc. Corps Assn., Air Force Assn., Assn. Mil. Surgeons of U.S., Nat. Area Health Edn. Ctrs. Assn. Republican. Baptist. Avocations: tennis, numismatics, hiking. Office: Southside Area Health Edn Ctr Longwood Univ 201 High St Farmville VA 23909

TERRY, WILLIAM FERRELL, pediatrician; b. Nashville, Nov. 16, 1949; s. J.T., Jr. and Ferrell Locke T.; m. Jo Willoughby, June 2, 1979; children: Laura, Elizabeth, Julia. BA, Vanderbilt U., Nashville, 1970; MD, Columbia U., 1974. Diplomate Am. Bd. Pediatrics, Am. Bd. Pediatric Hematology-Oncology. Resident in pediat. Duke U., Durham, N.C., 1974-77, fellow in pediat. hematology and oncology, 1977-79; pvt. practice, Knoxville, Tenn., 1979—. Chief staff East Tenn. Children's Hosp., Knoxville, 1985-86, dir. Pediat. Hematology-Oncology Clinic, 1979-92. Pres. Ronald McDonald House, Knoxville. Mem. AMA, Am. Acad. Pediatrics, Tenn. Med. Assn., Knoxville Acad. Medicine. Methodist. Avocations: reading, jogging, music, hiking. Home: 1428 Kensington Dr Knoxville TN 37922-6038 Office: Knoxville Pediat Assocs 2201 W Clinch Ave Knoxville TN 37916-2203

TERRY, WILLIAM HUTCHINSON, insurance executive; b. New Orleans, July 4, 1951; s. Arthur Hutchinson III and Betty (Brown) T.; m. Victoria Lyn Rosich, July 30, 1984; children: Tonya, Amanda, Arthur Hutchinson IV. BA, Tulane U., 1978. Underwriter Marine Office of Am., Inc. (Continental Ins. Co.), 1978-79, Ins. Co. of N.Am. (Tex.), 1979-82; account exec. Corroon & Black of New Orleans, Inc., 1982; v.p. Muller-Young & Assocs., Inc., 1982-87; pres. Griffon Internat. Underwriters & Mgrs., Ltd., 1987-88, Cygnus Ins. Svcs., Ltd., 1989—. Mem. Presdl. Round Table. With USN, 1972-75. Mem. World Trade Club, Caribbean Shippers Assn., Surplus Lines Assn., U.S. C. of C. Republican. Episcopalian. Avocations: tennis, yachting, painting, gardening. Office: Cygnus Ins Svcs Ltd 106 Park Pl Ste 301 Covington LA 70433-5018

TERSCHAN, FRANK ROBERT, lawyer; b. Dec. 25, 1949; s. Frank Joseph and Margaret Anna (Heidt) T.; m. Barbara Elizabeth Keily, Dec. 28, 1974; 1 child, Frank Martin. BA, Syracuse U., 1972; JD, U. Wis., 1975. Bar: Wis. 1976, U.S. Dist. Ct. (ea. and we. dists.) Wis. 1976, U.S. Ct. Appeals (7th cir.) 1979, U.S. Ct. Appeals (10th cir.) 1989, U.S. Supreme Ct. 1992. From assoc. to ptnr. Frisch, Dudek & Slattery Ltd., Milw., 1975-88; ptnr. Slattery and Hausman Ltd., 1988-94, Terschan & Steinle Ltd., Milw., 1994-96, Terschan, Steinle & Ness, Milw., 1996—. Mem. Wis. Jud. Conduct Adv. Com., 2002—. Treas., sec. Ville du Park Homeowners Assn., Mequon, Wis., 1985-86; cub scout packmaster pack 3844 Boy Scouts Am., 1989-90, asst. scoutmaster Troop 865, 1991-93. Mem. ABA, Am. Bd. Trial Advocates, Wis. Bar Assn., Milw. Bar Assn., Assn. Trial Lawyers Am., Wis. Acad. of Trial Lawyers (bd. dirs. 1996—), 7th Cir. Bar Assn. (judicial conduct adv. com. 2002—), Order of Coif. Republican. Lutheran. Avocations: swimming, coin collecting, reading, outdoor activities. Home: 10143 N Lake Shore Dr Mequon WI 53092-6109 Office: 2600 N Mayfair Rd Ste 700 Milwaukee WI 53226-1314 E-mail: frt@tsn-law.com.

TERUYA, JUN, hematologist, clinical pathologist; b. Tokyo, Feb. 8, 1954; s. Kunimitsu and Yukiko Teruya; m. Naoko Taniguchi, Apr. 23, 1979; children: Ami, Miho. MD, Hokkaido U. Sch. Medicine, Sapporo, Japan, 1979; DSc, Teikyo U., Tokyo, 1988. Cert. Bd. Internal Medicine Japan, Bd. Hematology Japan, Bd. Transfusion Medicine Japan, diplomate Clin. Pathology and Blood Bank/Transfusion Medicine Am. Bd. Pathology, Internat. Bd. Acad. Clin. and Applied Thrombosis/Hemostatis, lic. physician Mass., Pa., Ill. Resident dept. cardiovascular surgery Tokyo Women's Med. Coll., 1979-80, resident dept. medicine, 1980-82; instr. divsn. hematology dept. internal medicine Teikyo U. Sch. Medicine, Tokyo, 1983-86, asst. prof. divsn. hematology, 1986-89; rsch. fellow pathology Harvard Med. Sch., Boston, 1989-91; asst. prof. divsn. hematology Teikyo U. Sch. Medicine, Tokyo, 1991-92; clin. fellow pathology Harvard Med. Sch., Boston, 1992-95; assoc. prof. dept. transfusion medicine Juntendo U. Sch. Medicine, Tokyo, 1995-97; asst. med. dir., assoc. med. dir. blood transfusion svc. Teikyo U. Sch. Medicine, Chiba, Japan, 1986-89, 91-92; resident, chief resident clin. pathology Mass. Gen. Hosp., Boston, 1992-94, acting asst. dir. blood transfusion svc., 1993-94, asst. dir. blood transfusion svc., 1994-95; assoc. med. dir. blood transfusion svc. Juntendo U. Hosp., Tokyo, 1995-97; med. dir. transfusion medicine and coagulation MCP Hahnemann U. Health Scis., Hahnemann Hosp., Phila., 1997-99; dir. hemostasis and blood bank Northwestern Meml. Hosp., 1999—2001; assoc. med. dir. Clin. Lab., 2000; asst. prof. pathology and lab. medicine MCP Hahnemann U. Health Scis., Phila., 1997-99; chief clin. coagulation svcs. Allegheny U. Health Scis., 1998-99; asst. prof. pathology Northwestern Univ., 1999—2001; dir. hemostasis lab and blood bank Northwestern Meml. Hosp., 1999—2001; dir. coagulation and blood bank Tex. Children's Hosp. and Meth. Hosp., 2001—; asst. prof. pathology Baylor Coll. Medicine, 2001—. Lectr. Teikyo U. Sch. Medicine, Tokyo, 1986—89, Mass. Gen. Hosp., Boston, 1993—95. Contbr. Mem.: AMA, Japan Soc. Blood Transfusion, Japan Hematol. Soc., Am. Soc. Apheresis, Japanese Soc. Internal Medicine, Mass. Med. Soc., Coll. Am. Pathologists, Am. Soc. Clin. Pathologists, Am. Assn. Blood Banks, Internat. Soc. Blood Transfusion, Internat. Soc. Thrombosis and Hemostatis. Avocations: tennis, music, piano, flute. Office: Tex Children's Hosp Dept Pathology MC2-2261 6621 Fannin St Houston TX 77030-2399 E-mail: jxteruya@texaschildrenshospital.org.

TERWILLEGAR, JANE CUSACK, librarian, educator; b. Warsaw, Nov. 7, 1935; d. James Scott and Estella B. (Ackerman) Cusack; m. Gordon H. Terwillegar, July 26, 1958 (div. Mar. 1989); children: Sarah Ann Terwillegar Smedley, Arne Matthew. BA, Elmira (N.Y.) Coll., 1957; MLS, SUNY, Geneseo, 1960; EdS, U. Ga., 1977. Cert. tchr., Fla. Instr. U. Ga., Athens, 1975-81; libr. Palm beach County Libr., West Palm Beach, Fla., 1981-83, Palm Beach County Schs., Royal Palm Beach, 1983-94, dist. libr. media svcs. mgr. West Palm Beach, 1994—2000; dir. Lake Park Public Libr., 2000—. Lectr. Sch. Libr. and Info. Sci., U. South Fla., Tampa, 1987—, Nova U., Ft. Lauderdale, Fla., 1995—; task force mem. SUNLINK project Fla. Dept. Edn., 1995-2000; mem. adv. coun. Fla. Libr. Svcs. and Tech. Act., 1999—. Co-author: Commonsense Cataloging, 3d edit. 1983, 4th edit. 1990; reviewer Sch. Libr. Jour., 1986—; contbr. articles to profl. jours. Pres. Staff Assn. Palm Beach Sch. Dist., 1997-99. Mem. ALA, AAUW (pres. No. Palm Beach br. 2001-), Am. Assn. Sch. Librs. (exec. bd. 1990-94), Assn. for Libr. Svc. to Children (Newbery com. 1988-89), Fla. Assn. Media in Edn. (sec. 1988-89, bd. dirs. 1997—, pres. 1999-2001), Ednl. Media Assn. Fla. (pres. 1988), Kiwanis Club of Lake Park, Delta Kappa Gamma, Phi Beta Kappa, Delta Kappa Phi, Phi Delta Kappa. Avocations: scuba diving, sports cars. Home: 911 Oak Harbour Dr Juno Beach FL 33408-2173 Office: Lake Park Public Libr 529 Park Ave West Palm Beach FL 33403-

TERZIAN, GRACE PAINE, publisher; b. Boston, Oct. 19, 1952; d. Thomas Fite and Grace Hillman (Benedict) Paine; m. Philip Henry Terzian, Oct. 20, 1979; children: William Thomas Hillman, Grace Benedict Paine. BA in Art History, Williams Coll., 1974. Art dir. The New Republic, Washington, 1976-78; asst. editor The Chronicle of Higher Edn., 1978-79; rsch. editor Archtl. Digest, L.A., 1982-85; pub. The Women's Quar., Arlington, Va., 1994—. Editor Ex Femina, 1996—; sr. v.p. Ind. Women's Forum. Mem. Soc. Colonial Dames in Am., Phi Beta Kappa. Episcopalian. Home: 10505 Adel Rd Oakton VA 22124-1605 Office: The Women's Quarterly PO Box 3058 Arlington VA 22203-0058 E-mail: gterzian@radix.net.

TERZIAN, KARNIG YERVANT, civil engineer; b. July 4, 1928; came to U.S. s. Yeznig and Marie Terzian; m. Helen S., Dec. 21, 1958. BCE, Am. U. Beirut, Lebanon, 1949; MCE, U. Pa., 1954. Assoc. L. T. Beck & Assocs., 1956-60; prin. Urban Engrs., Inc., Phila., 1960-93, sr. v.p., sec.-treas., 1960-93, co-founder, ptnr., 1993-99. Cons. major transp. projects in Pa., N.Y., N.J., Nigeria, Zaire; cons., exec. Urban Engrs., 1993—. Bd. dirs. Armenian Sisters Acad., 1970-74. Mem. ASCE (Life Membership award 1993), ASTM, Prestressed Concrete Inst. Armenian Apostolic. Office: Urban Engrs Inc 530 Walnut St Fl 14 Philadelphia PA 19106-3621

TERZIAN, PHILIP HENRY, journalist; b. Kensington, Md., July 5, 1950; s. L.A. and Louise (Anderson) T.; m. Grace Barrett Paine, Oct. 20, 1979; children: William Thomas Hillman, Grace Benedict Paine. BA, Villanova U., 1973; DTS, Episcopal Theol. Sem., Va., 1995; postgrad., Oxford (Eng.) U., 1976. Desk editor Reuters, Washington, 1973, U.S. News & World Report, Washington, 1973-74; asst. editor The New Republic, 1974-78; mem. policy planning staff Dept. State, 1978-79; asst. editor Anniston (Ala.) Star, 1979-80; assoc. editor Lexington (Ky.) Herald, 1980-82; asst. editor of editorial pages L.A. Times, 1982-86; editor of editorial pages Providence Jour., 1986-92; assoc. editor, syndicated columnist Providence Jour. (Knight-Ridder/Tribune News Svc.), 1992—. Panelist Washington Week in Review, C-SPAN, Fox News, etc. Contbr. articles to newspapers and jours. Pres. Providence Com. Fgn. Rels., 1989-92. Recipient Edn. Writers award Edn. Writers Assn., 1981, Ida Lee Willis Svc. to Preservation award Ida Lee Willis Found., 1982; named finalist Pulitzer prize Disting. Commentary, 1991, Pulitzer Prize juror, 1994-95; media fellow Hoover Instn., Stanford U., 2002. Fellow Am. Journalism Found.; mem. Am. Coun. on Germany, Va. Hist. Soc., St. Andrew's Soc. Washington, Soc. King Charles the Martyr, Sons of Union Vets. of Civil War, Wolver Beagles (hon. whip), Nat. Press Club, Order Hosp.

St. John of Jerusalem, Nat. Beagle Club. Republican. Episcopalian. Home: 10505 Adel Rd Oakton VA 22124-1605 Office: Providence Jour 1325 G St NW Ste 250 Washington DC 20005-3124 E-mail: pterzian@belo-dc.com.

TERZIAN, SHOHIG GARINE SHERRY, mental health facility administrator; d. Ebraxé Momjian and Ardashes Garabed T. AB in Eng. Literature cum laude, Radcliffe Coll., 1937; MS in Libr. and Info. Sci., Columbia Univ., 1942, student, UCLA, Univ. Wis., New Sch. for Social Rsch., 1940-65. First libr. neurol. inst. Columbia Presbyn. Med. Ctr., N.Y.C., 1940-41; referee asst. Vassar Coll. Libr., Poughkeepsie, N.Y., 1942-43; picture editor, rsch. asst. U.S. Office War Info., N.Y.C., 1943-46; rsch. libr. Time, Inc., 1947-48; libr. Prudential Ins. Co. Western Home Office, L.A., 1948-61; mem. faculty dept. psychiatry & biobehavioral scis. UCLA Med. Sch., 1961-86; dir. mental health info. svc. UCLA Neuropsychiatric Inst., 1961-86; rsch. cons., 1987—. Picture editor, rsch. asst. U.S. War Dept. Civil Defense, U.S. Dept. of State, Office Internat. Info. and Cultural Affairs, N.Y.C., 1943-46. Bibliographer; contbr. Bertrand Russell Soc. Quarterly, Santayana Soc. Bulletin, Ararat Quarterly, LA Times. Mem. Armenian Gen. Benevolent Union, UCLA Emeriti, UCLA Faculty Ctr., Spl. Libr. Assn. Washington, Saroyan Soc. Calif., Santayana Soc., Calif. Libr. Soc., Statue of Liberty Ellis Island Found. Armenian Orthodox. Avocations: reading, writing. Home: 11740 Wilshire Blvd # A1602 Los Angeles CA 90025-6536

TERZIAN, YERVANT, astronomy and astrophysics educator; b. Alexandria, Egypt, Feb. 9, 1939; came to the U.S., 1960, naturalized, 1971; s. Bedros and Maria (Kiriakaki) T.; children: Sevan, Tamar. BS, Am. U., Cairo, 1960; MS, Ind. U., 1963, PhD, 1965, DSc (hon.), 1989, Yerevan State U., 1994, Aristotle U. Thessaloniki, Greece, 1997, Union Coll., N.Y., 1999. Rsch. assoc. Arecibo Obs., P.R., 1965-67; asst. prof. astronomy and astrophysics Cornell U., Ithaca, N.Y., 1967-72, assoc. prof., 1972-77, prof., 1977—, chmn. dept. astronomy, 1979-99, dir. Pew Program in Sci. Edn., 1988-99, James A. Weeks prof. in phys. scis., 1990-99, David C. Duncan prof. in phys. scis., 1999—. Editor: Interstellar Ionized Hydrogen, 1968, Planetary Nebulae, 1978; co-editor: Cosmology and Astrophysics, 1982, Carl Sagan's Universe, 1997; sci. editor The Astrophys. Jour., 1989-99; contbr. over 200 articles to tech. jours. Recipient Clark Disting. Tchg. award Cornell U., 1984. Fellow AAAS; mem. Internat. Astron. Union, Internat. Sci. Radio Union, Am. Astron. Soc., Armenian Acad. Sci. Office: Cornell U Astronomy Dept Space Scis Bldg Ithaca NY 14853 E-mail: yt28@cornell.edu.

TESAR, PATRICIA MARIE, academic coordinator; b. Cleve., Oct. 7, 1955; d. John Joseph and Florence Louise Tesar. BA in Interpersonal Com., Cleve. State U., 1982; MA in Rehab. Counseling, Gallaudet Coll., 1986; PhD in Spl. Edn. Adminstrn., Gallaudet U., 2002. Ind. living counselor ind. living program Health Hill Hosp., Cleve., 1982-83; practicum rehab. counselor for the deaf Va. Dept. Rehabilitative Svcs., Springfield, 1985; career counselor student spl. svcs./career ctr. Gallaudet U., Washington, 1984-90, coord. spl. svcs. Office for Students with Disabilities, 1990—. Co-chair subcom. adult employment Developmental Disabilities State Planning Coun. D.C., 1997—. Recipient Mima Bravo Counseling award, 1986, U.S. Congl. award of achievement, 1986, 92, Nat. Disting. Svc. Registry Counseling award, 1990; Quota Internat. fellow, 1986; Mary Pickford scholar, 1985; Gallaudet U. Pres.'s scholar, various yrs. Mem. ASCD, Am. Deafness and Rehab. Assn. (sec. met. Washington chpt. 1986-88, pres. 1988-90, 90-92), Am. Assn. Counseling and Devel., Nat. Rehab. Assn., Nat. Assn. for Deaf, Am. Assn. for Deaf-Blind, Md. Career Devel. Assn., Md. Rehab. Counseling Assn., Washington Consortium of Univs. Career Devel. Group, Washington Consortium of Univs. Student Support Svcs. Coalition (regional conf. coord.), Met. Washington Assn. Deaf-Blind, Coll. Placement Coun., Registry of Interpreters for the Deaf, Assn. on Higher Edn., Coun. for Exceptional Children, Kappa Delta Pi. Baptist. Avocations: reading, sign language interpreting. Home: 6500 Alexis Dr Bowie MD 20720-4755 E-mail: Patricia.Tesar@gallaudet.edu.

TESAREK, DENNIS GEORGE, retired business consultant, writer, educator; b. Chgo., Jan. 2, 1935; s. George Joseph and Mary (Basl) T.; m. Caroline Arrena Myers, Jan. 1956 (div. Oct. 1968); children: William Paul, Dianne, Peter Bond; m. Kathleen Leigh Holm, Nov. 26, 1969; children: Philip Shawn, Leigh-Anne. BA in Math., U. Mo., 1956; postgrad., Systems Rsch. Inst., 1966, UCLA, 1984, Harvard U., 1985, MIT, 1986. Saleman Conn. Mut. Life Ins. Co., Dallas, 1959-61; systems engr. IBM, Phoenix, 1961-66, instr. L.A., 1966-68, mgr. Houston, 1968-74, industry mgr. White Plains, N.Y., 1974-76, project mgr. L.A., 1976-78, planning cons. Houston, 1978-84, cons. in bus. transformation, planning and gen. mgmt., 1984-97; owner Tesarek Enterprises (Consulting and Investments), 1997—. Adj. prof. Ariz. State U., 1963-65; guest lectr. U. Houston, 1980, 81, 83, 87. Author: Distributed Information Systems Planning Methodology, 1982, Information Systems Management Effectiveness Assessment, 1983, Business Systems Planning for Competitive Advantage Methodology, 1986, Executive Strategy Session Methodology, 1987, Management Planning Session Methodology, 1987, Steps in Strategic Investment Methodology, 1989. Tutor Vols. in Pub. Schs., Houston Ind. Sch. Dist., 1972-74, 80-82. 1st lt. USMC, 1956-59. Republican. Mem. Christian Sci. Ch. Avocations: color photography and printing, wood working, reading, jogging. E-mail: dtesarek@earthlink.net.

TESAREK, WILLIAM PAUL, business consultant, writer, financial executive; b. Albuquerque, May 6, 1958; s. Dennis George and Caroline Arrena (Myers) T.; m. Nancy Anne Pence, May 12, 1984 (div. Feb. 1991); children: Michelle Marie, Allison Elaine. BS in Econs., U. Houston, 1986, MA in Econs., 1988, MBA in Fin., 1993, PhD, 1994. Instr. econs. U. Houston, 1987-88; sr. sales tax analyst Tex. State Comptroller, Austin, 1988-89; adj. prof. fin. U. Houston, 1989-93; sr. economist Asset Analysis & Mgmt., Houston, 1993; sr. fin. economist Asset Dynamics, 1993-94; owner The Tesarek Group, 1994—. Cons. in strategic planning and process reengring. mgmt. Author: Housing Price and Regional Real Estate Cycles: Market Adjustments in Houston, 1991; Beyond Counting the Beans: How Chief Financial Executives Use Knowledge to Advance the Corporation, 1995. With USN, 1976-80. Econ. Honors. Soc. Achievement award, 1986. Mem. Am. Econs. Assn., Am. Fin. Assn., Western Econ. Assn., Tex. Econ. & Demographic Assn., Allied Soc. Sci. Assn., Houston Bus. Process Reengring. Share Group. Republican. Mem. Ch. of Christ. Avocations: wood working, photography. Home and Office: The Tesarek Grp 16011 Silver Valley Dr Houston TX 77084-2960

TESCHNER, DOUGLASS PAUL, social welfare administrator, state legislator; b. Cambridge, Mass., Oct. 29, 1949; s. Douglass P. Teschner and Mary Elizabeth (Bernt) Teschner Zeller; m. Martha Weaver, Sept. 26, 1981. BS in Forestry, U. Mass., 1971, EdD in Adminstrn., 1985; MS in Botany, U. Vt., 1978. Land surveyor Lincoln Engring. and Burnell Land Surveying, 1974, 78; tchr. White Mountain Sch., 1976; dir. Inst. Exptl. Studies, various locations, 1984-87; fin. officer Becket Acad., East Haddam, Conn., 1984-85; devel. dir. Riverbend Cmty. Mental Health, Concord, 1987—2002; state rep. N.H. Ho. Reps., 2000—02; project dir. Rwanda Nat. Assembly Support Project. Co-editor: Wilderness Challenge: Outdoor Education Alternatives for Youth in Need, 1984; contbr. articles to profl. jours. Mem. Haverhill Hist. Soc.; vol. Peace Corps, 1971-73; vice moderator Haverhill Congl. Ch. Mem. Appalachian Mountain Club. Avocations: mountaineering, hiking, rock and ice climbing, skiing. Home: 2100 Brushwood Rd Pike NH 03780-9706 Office: Riverbend Cmty Mental Hlth PO Box 2032 Concord NH 03302-2032

TESELLE, JOHN, federal judge; Chief bankruptcy judge U.S. Bankruptcy Ct. (we. dist.) Okla., Oklahoma City, 1987—. Office: 228 Old Post Office Bldg 215 Dean A McGee Ave Oklahoma City OK 73102-3440

TESK, JOHN ALOYSIUS, materials scientist; b. Chgo., Oct. 19, 1934; s. John August and Theresa Mary (Mattea) T.; m. Regina Sophia Budzyn, Dec. 10, 1966; 1 child, John A.W. BS in Engring. Sci., Northwestern U., 1957, MS in Metallurgy, 1960, PhD in Materials Sci., 1963. Asst. prof. U. Ill., Chgo., 1964-67; cons. Argonne (Ill.) Nat. Lab., 1964-67, asst. metallurgist, 1967-70; dir. rsch. Dental, Howmedica Inc., Chgo., 1970-77; dir. edn. svcs. Inst. Gas. Tech., 1977-78; gen. phys. scientist, group leader, materials coord. polymers divsn., sr. tech. advisor, indsl. liaison dir.'s office Nat. Inst. Stds. & Tech., Gaithersburg, Md., 1978—. Cons. Dentsply Internat., York, Pa., 1977-78; mem. review bd. Dental Sch. Case Western Res. U., Cleve., 1987-88, Biomaterials Program, Clemson U., 1972-74, Dental Sch., Tokushima U., Japan, 1997; mem. orthopaedic adv. bd. Clemson U., 1999-2001; chmn. dental stds. ADA, Chgo., 1980-86; leader U.S. Del. Internat. Stds. Orgn., 1980-86; organizer confs. Holder 8 patents; editl. bd. Jour. Dental Materials, 1988-91, Jour. Oral Implantology, 1984-2000, Biomaterials Forum, 1996—, Applied Biomaterials, 1998—; mem. editl. rev. bd. Nat. Inst. Stds. and Tech., 1996-2001; contbr. chpts. to books and articles to profl. jours. Mem. bldg. com. Divine Savior Parish, Downers Grove, Ill., 1971-72; chmn. troop 737 Cub Scouts, Highland, Md., 1980; adult supr. youth group Saint Louis Parish, Highland, 1982-83. Fellow Acad. Dental Materials (exec. com. 1987-94); mem. Am. Phys. Soc., Am. Soc. Metals (exec. com. Chgo. chpt. 1964-67, 78), Biomaterials Soc. (charter, nominating com. 1987, 96, editl. bd. Forum 1996—, Applied Biomaterials 1998—, stds. com. 1995—, contbg. editor Biomaterials Forum, co-chair stds. com. coun. 1996—, liaison com. 1996-98, program com. 1999), Am. Soc. Testing and Materials, 1995— (exec. com. 2000—), Internat. Assn. Dental Rsch. (treas. dental materials group 1987-94), Tech. Materials Soc. (exec. com. Chgo chpt. 1965), Japanese Soc. for Dental Materials (hon.). Roman Catholic. Avocations: gardening, boating, travel, walking. Home: 6759 Cortina Dr Highland MD 20777-9501 Office: Nat Inst Stds & Tech Rm A143 Bldg 224 Gaithersburg MD 20899-0001

TESKE, STEVEN CECIL, lawyer; b. Tucson, Mar. 4, 1960; s. Ronald Dean and Barbara Elizabeth T.; m. Deborah Ann Appling, Mar. 12, 1983; children: DeAnna Marie, Jacquelyn Suzanne, Joshua Stephen. AA, Clayton State Coll. & U., 1981; B of Indisciplinary Studies, Ga. State U., 1983, MA in Polit. Sci., 1988, JD, 1991. Bar: Ga. 1992, U.S. Dist. Ct. (no. dist.) Ga. 1995, U.S. Ct. Appeals (11th cir.) 1997, U.s. Supreme Ct. 1997. Paralegal Ga. Dept. Labor, Atlanta, 1981—84; parole officer Ga. Bd. Pardons & Parole, 1984—90, deputy chief, 1990—92, chief parole officer, 1992—94, asst. dir., 1994—95; assoc. Stephen E. Boswell, 1995—97; ptnr. Boswell & Teske, Jonesboro, 1997—99; judge Juvenile Ct. of Dlayton County, 1999—. Mem.: ABA, Am. Probation and Parole Assn., Nat. Coun. of Juvenile and Family Ct. Judges, Coun. of Juvenile Ct. Judges Ga., Clayton County Bar Assn., Am. Correctional Assn. (del. assembly 1993—95). Democrat. Methodist. Avocations: stamp collecting, swimming. Home: 1752 Brenda Dr Jonesboro GA 30236-3361 Office: clayton County Courthouse Annex 3 121 S McDonough St Jonesboro GA 30236

TESLER, DIANE ELAINE, artist; b. Ft. Wayne, Ind., Apr. 5, 1944; d. Howard Irving Becker and Helen Elizabeth Berg; m. Roy Tesler, Aug. 20, 1967 (div.); children: Theodore, Pearl; m. Patrick S. Stanaski, Dec. 29, 1986. BA, Antioch Coll., 1966. Instr. painting Art League Sch., Alexandria, Va., 1978—. Asst. dir. Torpedo Factory Art Ctr., Alexandria, 1979-80. Represented in permanent collections at MCI, Am. Gen. Fin., Sterling Winthrop, USAF, Washington Cathedral, Louisville Gas & Elec., others. Active Nat. Trust Historic Preservation, Washington, 1990—, Ind. Historic Landmarks Found., Indpls., 1998—. Recipient Butler Inst. Am. Art award Merit, Youngstown, Ohio, 1980; Va. Mus. Fine Arts fellow, Richmond, 1982. Mem. Art League (pres. 1990-91). Avocation: piano. Home: 2512 Dewitt Ave Alexandria VA 22301-1104 Office: Torpedo Factory Art Ctr 105 N Union St Alexandria VA 22314-3217 E-mail: d.e.tesler@erols.com.

TESLER, LAWRENCE GORDON, technology company executive; b. N.Y.C. , Apr. 24, 1945; s. Isidore and Muriel (Krechmer) T.; m. Shelagh Elisabeth Leuterio, Oct 4, 1964 (div. 1970); 1 child, Lisa Traci; m. Colleen Ann Barton, Feb. 17, 1987. BS in Math., Stanford U., 1965. Pres. Info. Processing Corp., Palo Alto, Calif., 1963—68; rsch. asst. Stanford U. Artificial Intelligence Lab., 1968—73; mem. rsch. staff Xerox Corp., Palo Alto, 1973—80; sect. mgr. Lisa divsn. Apple Computer, Inc., Cupertino, Calif., 1980—82, cons. engr., 1983—86, v.p. advanced tech., 1986—90, v.p. advanced products, 1990—92, v.p. engring., 1992—93, chief scientist, 1993—97, v.p. AppleNet divsn., 1996—97; pres. Stagecast Software, Inc., Redwood City, 1997—2001; v.p. engring. Amazon.com, 2001—. Bd. dirs. ARM Holdings, PLC; mem. Computer Sci. and Telecom. Bd., 1991-94. Contbr. articles to profl. jours., various computer software. Bd. dirs. Peninsula Sch., Menlo Park, Calif., 1974-78, Gorilla Found., Menlo Park, 2000—. Mem. Assn. Computing Machinery (conf. co-chmn. 1987-88). Office: Amazon dot com PO Box 81226 Seattle WA 98108 E-mail: tesler@pobox.com.

TESON, FERNANDO ROBERTO, law educator, consultant; b. Buenos Aires, Aug. 3, 1950; s. Roberto Julio and Marta (Grun) T.; m. Maria Teresa Martinez, Nov. 11, 1976 (div. Feb. 1992); children: Fernando, Marcelo; m. Bettina C. Rauleder, Oct. 11, 1996; 1 child, Carolina. Grad., U. Buenos Aires, 1975; lic. internat. law, U. Libre de Bruxelles, Brussels, 1982; SJD, Northwestern U., 1987. Assoc. prof. law Ariz. State U., Tempe, 1984-88, prof. law, 1988—2002; chmn., prof. Fla. State U. Sch. Law, Tallahassee, 2002—. Vis. prof. San Diego Summer Program, Mex., 1987, Dublin, Ireland, 1988, Paris, 1990, 93, Hastings Law Sch., San Francisco, Spring 1990, Cardozo Law Sch., N.Y.C., Fall 1992, Ind. U., Bloomington, Spring 1993, Cornell U., Ithaca, N.Y., 1994-95; permanent vis. prof. Di Tella U., Buenos Aires, 1996—; career diplomate Argentina Govt., Buenos Aires, 1977-81; prof. George Washington/Oxford U. Internat. Human Rights Program, New College, Oxford, 1999, 2001. Author: A Philosophy of International Law, Humanitarian Intervention: An Inquiry into Law and Morality, 2d edit.; contbr. articles to profl. jours. James N. Raymond fellow Northwestern U., 1982-83; Tobias Simon Eminent scholar Fla. State U. Sch. Law, 2002. Mem. Am. Soc. Internat. Law, Am. Soc. Social and Polit. Philosophy. Avocations: music, bridge, food. Home: 2609 Lotus Dr Tallahassee FL 32312 Office: Fla State U Coll of Law Tallahassee FL 32306-1601

TESONE, DANA V. information technology executive; b. Dover, Del., May 10, 1954; s. Leah M Tesone, William N Tesone. MS, MBA, Nova Southeastern U., PhD, 1995. Cert. mgr. 1986. V.p. human resouces Ocean Reef Club, Key Largo, Fla., 1992—94; asst. prof. U. Ctrl. Fla., Orlando, 2001—. Prof. trainer, cons. hospitality orgns., 1986—2002. Contbr. articles to profl. jours. Recipient Mgr. of Yr., Pier 66 Resort and Marina, 1986, Outstanding Teaching award, U. Hawaii, 2001. Personal E-mail: dtesone@mail.ucf.edu. Business E-Mail: dtesone@mail.ucf.edu.

TESORIERO, PHILIP JAMES, human resource consultant; b. Bklyn., Dec. 6, 1942; s. Vincent James and Marie Vivian (Agresti) T.; m. Michele Iannello; children: Maria, Sandra. B.S., Adelphi U., 1967; postgrad. N.Y.U., 1970; postgrad. in psychology New Sch. Social Research, 1972-74. Adminstrv. counselor OEO, Bklyn., 1964-69; personnel adminstr. Chase Manhattan Bank, N.Y.C., 1969-72; dir. tng. devel. Prentice Hall Co., N.Y.C., 1972-74; personnel dir. Am. Savs. Bank, N.Y.C., 1974-78; dir. personnel, adminstrn. Simplicity Pattern Co., N.Y.C., 1978-82; v.p. indsl. relations Boorum & Pease Co., Elizabeth, N.J., 1982-85; v.p. human resources cons. svcs. Soloway Assocs., N.Y.C., 1986-98; tng. coord. ISS Internat. Svc. System, Inc., N.Y.C., 1990-97; lectr. in field. Author: No Nonsense Basic Budgets, 1977; (mgmt. bus. game) Supervisor In-Basket, 1974; (tng. program) Facilitating Employment of Handicaps, 1980, (tng. program) Super Productivity, 1987; contbr. paper to profl. jour. Active Jr. Achievement. Mem. Am. Soc. Tng. and Devel., Internat. Found. Employee Benefits, Am. Mgmt. Assn., Am. Inst. Bankers, Human Resource Devel. Soc. Office: Philip James Inc 25 Trenton Ave Unit 10 Lavallette NJ 08735-2732 also: 350 5th Ave Ste 5404 New York NY 10118-5404

TESS, ALICE CHARLENE, writer, retired secondary school educator; b. El Paso, Tex., Nov. 9, 1943; d. Kenneth Richard and Alice (Adams) Bourland; m. Gerald William Tess, Feb. 14, 1986; children: Leigh A. Bramer, Lisa L. Black, Ana Tess. BS in Sec. Edn., U. Tex., El Paso, 1968. Lic. tchr., Tex. Tchr. Ysleta Ind. Sch. Dist., El Paso, 1964-69, 70-98, Gadsden Ind. Sch. Dist., Anthony, N.Mex., 1969-70; ret., 1998; ednl. cons. in English grammar and writing Pathway Press, Garland, Tex., 1996—. Cons. for Pathway Press doing tchr. inservice. Author: Simple Steps to Sentence Sense, 1996, The Cowboy's Treasure (1st pl. S.W. Writers Contest 1994), The Van Winkle Bride, 2001. Recipient Tchr. of Yr. award Ysleta Ind. Sch. Dist., 1998. Avocations: walking, swimming, reading. Office: Wordsworth Lit Svcs 2441 Anise Dr El Paso TX 79936-3503 E-mail: wwlitsrvcs@aol.com.

TESSA, MARIAN LORRAINE, talk show host, writer, producer, educator; b. N.Y.C., Sept. 23, 1950; d. Sylvester Joseph and Emma Carol (Chimento) T. BA in English, SUNY, Cortland, 1972; postgrad., N.Y. Sch. Broadcasting, 1972-73; MEd, Coll. Staten Island, 1996. Writer CBS, N.Y.C., 1972-75; show host, producer, writer Manhattan Cable, 1975—, S.I. Cable, 1988—. Educator, 1991—. Spokesperson Miss Universe/Miss U.S.A. Beauty Pageants, 1976, promotion benefits; guest appearances include David Susskind Show, 1978, ABC Wide World Spl., 1978, The Joe Franklin Show, 1980, The You Show, 1979, Natural Living Program, 1981; talk show host Kaleidoscope, 1983-85; voice over cable TV, 1975—; performer Off-Broadway, 1969; photographic model Penzo Spagnoli Gallery, Florence, Italy, 1984, San Francisco, N.Y.C. and London, 1988. Recipient Forensic award. Mem.: NAFE, NATAS, S.I. Svc. Tchrs. Assn., Am. Com. on Italian Migration, Nat. Fedn. Bus. and Profl. Women's Clubs Inc., United Fedn. Tchrs. Office: Tessa Prodns 10 Wagner St Staten Island NY 10305-2957

TESSEM, STEVEN E. energy executive; b. San Tome, Venezuela, Apr. 23, 1956; s. Earl V. and Majill A. Tessem; m. Joanne Clark, Oct. 19, 1960; children: Brynne, Nolan. BSME, Tex. A&M U., 1978; MBA, Rice U., 1990. Profl. engr., Tex. V.p. project devel. Asia Pacific Enserch Internat. Ltd., Florham Park, N.J., 1994-99; mng. dir. bus. devel. GPU Internat., Inc., Parsippany, 1997-99; dir. project devel. Consol. Edison Devel., Inc., N.Y.C., 1999—. Avocations: golf, motorcycling. Home: 103 Tallwood Ln Lincroft NJ 07738

TESSENEER-STREET, SUSAN, photographer, artist; b. Murray, Ky., Dec. 14, 1939; d. Ralph Athen and Susan Geneva (Kirkland) Tesseneer; m. Robert Beni Street Sr., Jan. 16, 1939; children: Robert Beni II, Ralph Calvin Sr. BA, S.E. Mo. U., 1974; student, Harvard U., 2002. Tchr., 1974-79; bus. owner, 1977-85; writer, 1984-86; photographer, 1990—; artist, 1998—. Author: (book) Gift in Celebration of Women. Mem. Sikeston Art League, 1980—, pres., 1990-94; sec., treas., organizer Cmty. Concert, Sikeston, 1989. Mem. Assoc. of Am. U. Women (charter), Profl. Photographers Am., Am. Soc. Portrait Artists, Hemingway Soc., Nat. Writers Club, Women in the Arts (charter), Am. Soc. Portrait Painters, Impressionist Soc. Office: Susan Tesseneer-Street Studio Gallery 1003 Allen Blvd Sikeston MO 63801-4711

TESSER, ABRAHAM, social psychologist; b. N.Y.C., May 24, 1941; s. Louis and Ruth (Buchholz) T.; m. Marsha Richman Rosenthal, June 4, 1967 (div. Feb. 22, 1983); children: Louis J., Rachel A.; m. Carmen Chaves, Dec. 15, 1990. BA, L.I. U., 1962; MS, Purdue U., 1965, PhD, 1967. Rsch. assoc. Inst. for Behavioral Rsch., U. Ga., 1971-78, assoc. dir., 1978-84, acting dir. Ctr. for Rsch. on Deviance, 1984-86, dir., 1984-94; from asst. prof. to assoc. prof. social psychology U. Ga., 1967-74, prof., 1974-89, rsch. prof. psychology, 1989-99, prof. emeritus, 2000—, sr. affiliate Inst. for Behavioral Rsch., 2001—. Vis. fellow Yale U., 1976-77, Princeton U., spring 1983; fellow Ctr. for Advanced Studies in the Behavioral Scis., Stanford, Calif., 1992-93, Ohio State U., 1999-2000. Editor Jour. Personality and Social Psychology, 1991-94; contbr. numerous articles to profl. jours. Mem. AAUP, APA, Am. Psychol. Soc., Soc. for Personality and Social Psychology (pres. 2000), Soc. Exptl. Social Psychology, So. Soc. for Social Psychology. Office: Inst Behavioral Rsch Barrow Hall U Ga Athens GA 30602

TESSER, DOROTHY, artist; b. Bklyn., Mar. 11, 1926; d. Max and Ethel Weber; m. Jack Tesser, Oct. 12, 1947; children: Clifford Charles(dec.) , Jean Karasic, Barbara Campbell. Degree in graphic art, Pratt Inst.; cert. art therapist, New Sch. U., 1983. Artist Famous Studios, N.Y.C.; owner, artist and prodr. D&J Films Animation; freelance artist All Animation Studios; art dir. D&R Animation, Storyboard, N.Y.C. One-woman shows include N.J. Ctr. Healing Arts, Red Bank, N.J., Freehold Area Hosp. Pediat. Ward. Mailing: 525 Ocean Blvd Apt 307 Long Branch NJ 07740-8910

TESSIER, DENNIS MEDWARD, paralegal, lecturer, legal advisor, consultant, cartoonist; b. Royal Oak, Mich., Sept. 20, 1956; s. Medward James and Marilyn (Pitsos) T.; m. Michelle Terri Zeichick, July 28, 1990; 1 child, Brian Jae. Cert. paralegal, U. West L.A., 1987, cert. atty. practice, 1990; cert. in epidemiology, U.S. CDC, 1991. Reprodn. analyst Burroughs Corp., Detroit, 1975-76; mixologist Holiday Inn, Inc., Belair, Calif., 1977-83; spl. asst. office of the gen. counsel U.S. Jud. Intelligence Agy., Pacific Sta., L.A., 1981—; mixologist R.W. Grace Inc., Marina Del Rey, Calif., 1984-86; paralegal O'Melveny & Myers, L.A., 1986, Haight, Brown & Bonesteel, Santa Monica, Calif., 1987-93, Helsell & Fetterman, Seattle, 1993-94, Nintendo of Am. Inc., Redmond, Wash., 1994-96, Tousley Brain PLLC, Seattle, 1996-98, Preston Gates & Ellis, Seattle, 1998—. Family law cons. Helping Svcs., L.A., 1990-93, L.A. Clinic, 1990; rschr. Tessier & Assocs. Rsch., Topanga Canyon, Calif., 1983—; with Starlight Found., Redmond, Wash., 1993—. Author: Beauty in Motion, 1983, Champerty and Barratry, 1998. Creek Rat Esquire, 1999, Federal Civil Trial Manual, 2001, Big Daddy Hotrod Cartoons; contbr. articles to profl. jours. Mem. ABA (sci. and tech. law, jud. adminstrn. sects.), ATLA, Soc. Epidemiology Rsch., Assn. Investigative Scis., Judges Advs. (JAG) Assn., King County Bar Assn., U.S. Nat. Acad. Scis. Academe Industry Program (spkr. CLE), Am. Legion. Democrat. Lutheran. Avocations: music, arts. Home: 21100 Pioneer Way Edmonds WA 98026-6947 Office: Preston Gates & Ellis 701 Fifth Ave Ste 5000 Seattle WA 98104 E-mail: dtessier@justice.com., dennist@prestongates.com.

TESSING, LOUISE SCIRE, graphic designer; b. Chgo., May 13, 1946; d. Rocco Roy and Ruth Louise (Knueppel) Scire; m. Arvid Victor Tessing, Jan. 18, 1975. BS in Visual Design, Ill. Inst. Tech., Chgo., 1968; MBA in Mktg., Loyola U., Chgo., 1986. Jr. designer Field Mus. of Natural History, Chgo., 1968-69, Charles MacMurray & Assocs., Chgo., 1969-74; designer, art dir. Grant-Jacoby Inc., 1974-76, Playboy Enterprises Inc., Chgo., 1976-78, Stevens Biondi Decicco Inc., Chgo., 1978-80; prin., owner Tessing Design Inc., 1980—. Lobby treas. Ill. Women's Agenda, Chgo., 1990-92. Mem.: Soc. Typographic Arts (v.p. 2000—), Internat. Assn. Bus. Communicators (v.p. comm. and design 1998—), Nat. Assn. Women Bus. Owners, Chgo. Women in Publ., Am. Ctr. for Design (bd. dirs. 1971—77, pres. 1976—77), Women in Design Chgo. (founder 1977, pres. 1977—78, 1991—93, Friend award 1990, Founder award 1997). Home and Office: Tessing Design Inc 3822 N Seeley Ave Chicago IL 60618-3912

TESSLER, ALEXANDER, aerospace engineer; b. Kiev, Ukraine, Apr. 5, 1950; came to U.S., 1973; s. Leonid Tessler and Ida Ryabinskaya; m. Barbara Sue Feldsher, June 27, 1982; children: Lee, Veronica, Michael. BS in Structural Engring., Inst. Civil Engring., Kiev, 1972; MS in Structural Mechs., UCLA, 1976, degree in engring., 1978, PhD in Structural Mechs., 1979. Sr. engr. Northrop Corp., Hawthorne, Calif., 1980-83; mech. engr. U.S. Army Materials Tech. Lab., Watertown, Mass., 1983-91; aerospace engr. NASA Langley Rsch. Ctr., Hampton, Va., 1991—. Adj. prof. mech. engring. Northeastern U., Boston, 1986-91, George Washington U., Washington, 1992—, Old Dominion U., Norfolk, Va., 1993—; cons. Internat. Space Sta., NASA, Huntsville, Ala., 1996; structures expert NASA/Russian Joint Working Group on Aeronautics, Hampton, 1995—; spkr. in field. Contbr. articles to profl. publs., chpt. to book. Recipient Spl. Act award U.S. Army, 1985, 89, Tech. Excellence Dual Career Ladder award NASA, 1992, Superior Accomplishment award NASA, 1993, 95. Mem. AIAA (structures tech. com.), U.S. Assn. Computational Mechs., Internat. Cmty. for Composites Engring. Achievements include pioneering of anisoparametric interpolation approach for penalty-type finite elements; development of innovative higher-order thick-composite beam, plate and shell theories applicable for computational mechanics. Avocations: running, photography. Home: 137 Chinquapin Orch Yorktown VA 23693-2322 Office: Langley Rsch Ctr Mail Stop 240 Hampton VA 23681-0001

TESSLER, ROBERT LOUIS, lawyer; b. Newark, Apr. 6, 1938; s. Max and Charlotte (Paskow) T.; m. Linda Gottlieb, 1991; 1 child, David Alan. BA, Hamilton Coll., 1959; JD, Columbia U., 1963. Bar: N.J. 1963, U.S. Dist. Ct. N.J. 1963, N.Y. 1983. Ptnr. Yankowitz & Tessler, Newark, 1963-78; assoc. Julien & Schlesinger, N.Y.C., 1978-84; ptnr. Toberoff, Tessler & Schochet, 1984—. Atty. Zoning Bd. of West Orange (N.J.), 1980-85. Chmn. Essex County chpt. ACLU, Newark, 1973-76; county committeeman N.J. Democratic Party, 1973-78; chmn. bd. Nat. Music Theater Network, 1989—. Mem. ATLA, N.Y. Trial Lawyers Assn., Am. Inns of Ct. Jewish. Avocation: musical theater organization devoted to developing new works in opera and musicals. Office: Toberoff Tessler & Schochet 350 5th Ave Ste 5314 New York NY 10118-5314

TEST, STACY MARIE, network engineer; b. Niskayuna, N.Y., Dec. 3, 1971; d. Ronald Allen and Lillian Mary Kane; m. Christopher Loren Test, Mar. 9, 1996. BSEE, Trenton State Coll., 1994; MSEE, Monmouth U., 2000. From cons. to sr. cons. Booz-Allen & Hamilton, Eatontown, NJ, 1994—2001; sr.

mem. tech. staff Tyco Electronics, 2001—. Mem. IEEE, Soc. Women Engrs. Roman Catholic. Avocations: softball, volleyball, music, sewing. Home: 353 Hilltop Rd Toms River NJ 08753-4221

TESTA, MICHAEL HAROLD, lawyer; b. N.Y.C., 1939; m. Carol Waldenberg, 1962; 2 children. BS summa cum laude, NYU, 1958, LLB cum laude, 1961, LLM in Taxation, 1967. Bar: N.Y. 1961. Assoc. White & Case, N.Y.C., 1962-71, Skadden, Arps, Slate, Meagher & Flom, N.Y.C., 1971-72, ptnr., 1972-91; conservation lawyer, 1992—. Advisor U.S. del. to UN Conf. on Straddling Fish Stocks and Highly Migratory Fish Stocks, 1994-95, U.S. del. to Kyoto Internat. Conf. on Sustainable Contribution of Fisheries to Food Security, 1995, to N.W. Atlantic Fisheries Orgn., 1996, 98, to 22d Session of FAO Com. on Fisheries, 1997, to Western and Ctrl. Pacific Fisheries Conf., 1998-2001; adj. assoc. prof. law NYU Law Sch., 1986; mem. consultative com. to secs. state and commerce N.W. Atlantic Fisheries Conv., 1996—. Assoc. editor, contbr.: NYU Law Rev., 1960-61; contbr. articles to legal jours. Mem. planning bd. Town of Tuxedo (N.Y.), 1971-76. Served to capt. USAFR, 1961-72. Root-Tilden-Snow scholar, 1958-61. Mem. ABA, Order of Coif. Home: 860 UN Plz New York NY 10017-1816 Office: Ste 28-424 4 Times Square New York NY 10036-6522

TESTA, STEPHEN MICHAEL, geologist, consultant; b. Fitchburg, Mass., July 17, 1951; s. Guiseppe Alfredo and Angelina Mary (Pettito) T.; m. Lydia Mae Payne, July 26, 1986; 1 child, Brant Ethan Gage. AA, Los Angeles Valley Jr. Coll., Van Nuys, 1971; BS in Geology, Calif. State U., Northridge, 1976, MS in Geology, 1978. Registered geologist, Calif., Oreg., Wyo.; cert. profl. geol. scientist., Idaho, Alaska; cert. engring. geologist, Calif.; cert. European geologist; registered environ. assessor, Calif. Engring. geologist R.T. Frankian & Assocs., Burbank, Calif., 1976-78, Bechtel, Norwalk, 1978-80, Converse Cons., Seattle, 1980-82; sr. hydrogeologist Ecology Environment, 1982-83; sr. geologist Dames & Moore, 1983-86; v.p. Engring. Enterprises, Long Beach, Calif., 1986-89; CEO Applied Environ. Svcs., San Juan Capistrano, 1990-94; pres. Testa Environ. Corp., 1994—; mine. insp. Calif. State Mining and Geology Bd., 2000—. Author: Restoration of Petroleum Contaminated Aquifers, 1990, Principles of Technical Consulting and Project Management, 1991, Geological Aspects of Hazardous Waste Management, 1994, The Reuse and Recycling of Contaminated Soil, 1997, Petroleum in the Environment, 2001, Restoration of Contaminated Aquifers: Petroleum Hydrocarbons and Organic Compounds, 2d edit., 2000; editor: Geologic Field Guide to the Salton Basin, 1988, Environmental Concerns in the Petroleum Industry, 1989, Environmental Geology, 1999, Petroleum Geology, 1999, Mining Geology, 1999, Engineering Geology, 1999, Hydrogeology, 1999; contbr. over 125 articles and abstracts to profl. jours.; author: In Situ Restoration of Metals Contaminated Sites, 2002; editor-in-chief Jour. Environ. Geoscis., 1998—, assoc. editor Jour. Oil Industry History, 2001—. Mem.: AAAS, Calif. Water Pollution Control Assn., Hazardous Materials Rsch. Inst., Mineral. Soc. Can., Environ. Assessment Assn., Assn. Mil. Engrs., Assn. Engring. Geologists, Assn. Ground Water Scientists and Engrs., Nat. Assn. State Bds. Geology (coun. examiners 1998—), South Coast Geol. Soc., Am. Geol. Inst. (found. trustee 1998—), Am. Mineral. Soc., Am. Assn. Petroleum Geologists (Pacific sect. environ. com., co-chmn. 1993—, chmn. liaison com. divsn. environ. geoscis. 1997, geoenviron. forum 1998, editor-in-chief Jour. Environ. Geoscis. 1998—2001, best environ. practices com. 2000—, divsn. environ. gas scis. best environ. practices com. 2000—, assoc. editor Oil Industry History Jour. 2001—, cert. of merit 1997, rsch. award 2000), Geol. Soc. Am., Am. Geol. Inst. (found. trustee), Geol. Soc. Am. (found. trustee 1998—, , Roy J. Shlemon mentor program honorarium 1998), L.A. Basin Geol. Soc. (pres. 1991—92), Am. Inst. Profl. Geologists (profl. devel. com. 1986, continuing edn. com. program chmn. 1988—, nat. screening bd. 1992—94, exec. bd. del. 1993, nat. v.p. 1994, chmn. 1995—, found. trustee 1995—, honors and awards com. 1996—97, nominating com. 1997, found. trustee 1997—, internat. affairs com. 1998, nat. pres. 1998, nominating com. 2000, chmn. coll. curriculum accreditation ad hoc com. 2000, honors and awards com. 2000—, nominating com. 2001—, presdl. Cert. of Merit 1987, Martin Van Couvering award 1999), Cosmos Club, Sigma Xi. Roman Catholic. Achievements include research igneous and metamorphic petrology, asphalt chemistry; development of methods for subsurface hydrogeologic characterization and remediation, proprietary processes for incorporation of contaminated soil and other materials considered toxic and hazardous via recycling into a variety of cold-mix asphaltic products; history of geology in the Far West. Home and Office: 19814 Jesus Maria Rd Mokelumne Hill CA 95245-9559 E-mail: stesta@goldrush.com.

TESTAIUTI, MARK A. neurosurgeon; b. Oct. 9, 1963; BS, SUNY, Stonybrook, 1985; MD, Hahnemann U. Sch. Med., Pa., 1989. Diplomate Am. Bd. Neurosurgery. Resident neurosurgery Albert Einstein/Montefiore Med. Ctr., New York, 1990-94, chief resident neurosurgery, 1994-95; asst. prof. neurosurgery UMDNJ/Robert Wood Johnson Med. Sch., Camden, N.J., 1995-99; acting chief divsn. neurosurgery Cooper Hosp./UMNDNJ, 1998-99, chief divsn. neurosurgery, 2001—02. Contbr. articles in profl. jours. Mem. Am. Assn. Neurol. Surgeons, N.J. Med. Soc. Office: Orthopedic and Neurosurg Specialists LLC 807 Haddon Ave Haddonfield NJ 08033 E-mail: m.testaiuti@aol.com.

TESTAVERDE, VINCENT FRANK (VINNY TESTAVERDE), professional football player; b. Bklyn., Nov. 13, 1963; Student, U. Miami, Fla. Quarterback Tampa Bay (Fla.) Buccaneers, 1987-92, Cleve. Browns, 1993-95, Balt. Ravens, 1996-98, N.Y. Jets, Hempstead, N.Y., 1998—; AFC East conf. champions, 1998-99; played in Pro Bowl, 1996. Recipient Heisman Trophy, 1986, Maxwell award, 1986, Davey O'Brien award, 1986; named quarterback The Sporting News coll. All-Am. 2d team, 1985, Coll. Football Player of Year, The Sporting News, 1986. Achievements include being a holder of the regular-season record as starting NFL quarterback, postseason record as starting NFL quarterback, Tampa Bay Buccaneers all-time records for most yards passing, also most touchdown passes, Balt. Ravens all-time records for most yards passing, also most touchdown passes. Office: c/o New York Jets 1000 Fulton Ave Hempstead NY 11550-1030*

TESTER, LEONARD WAYNE, psychology educator; b. Nampa, Idaho, Aug. 21, 1933; s. Walter Vernon and Dora Dorothy (Peters) T. BTh, Kansas City Coll., Overland, Kansas, 1957; MA, Abilene Christian Coll. (now Abilene Christian U.), 1961; STB, Harvard U., 1969; EdM, Columbia U., 1971, EdD, 1976, MPhil, 1979, PhD, 1981. Lic. psychologist, N.Y. Pers. mgr. Boston Safe Deposit & Trust Co., 1966-69; adj. instr. clin. counseling N.Y. Inst. Tech., Westbury, 1971-80, adj. asst. prof., 1980-84, sr. counselor, 1980-92, assoc. prof., 1984-92, dir., 1992-95, sr. counselor, 1980-92, prof., 1992—, prof., chmn., 1992-93, prof., dir., 1993-95. Cons., grad. asst. Bus. Sch. and Tchrs. Coll. Columbia U., 1977-81. Contbr. articles to profl. jours.; presenter workshops in field. Exec. dir. Ho. of the Carpenter, Boston, 1967-68; bd. dirs. Pierre (S.D.) Coun. of Arts, Counseling Ctr. Episcopal Ch., Great Neck, N.Y., Tech. Sch. in N.Y.C. William Wayne Jackson honors scholar Harvard Div. Sch. Fellow Am. Orthopsychiat. Assn.; mem. APA, N.Y. Soc. Clin. Psychologists, N.Y. Soc. Hypnosis and Psychotherapy, others. Home: PO Box 20107 New York NY 10023-1477 Office: NY Inst of Tech 1855 Broadway New York NY 10023-7692

TETA, TODD NICHOLAS, technology consultant, real estate developer; b. San Diego, Dec. 22, 1973; s. Amato Nicholas and Mary Ann Teta. BS, U. So. Calif., 1996. Cons. Andersen Cons., El Segundo, Calif., 1996-98; founder, ptnr. VisionCore Cons., Irvine, 1998—; founder, pres. Mission Street Devels., Inc., San Diego, 2000—. Vol. Habitat for Humanity, Long Beach, Calif., 1998—; assoc. mem. amb. bd. U. So. Calif. Mem. IEEE, Mensa. Office: VisionCore Cons Ste 1005-330 4790 Irvine Blvd Irvine CA 92620 E-mail: tteta@visioncore.com., todd.teta@usa.net.

TETEF, MERRY LYNN, internist, oncologist; b. Burbank, Calif., May 9, 1961; MD, Harvard U., 1987. Diplomate Am. Bd. Internal Medicine, Am. Bd. Oncology. Resident in internal medicine UCLA Med. Ctr., L.A., 1987-90; fellow in hematology, oncology City of Home Med. Ctr., Duarte, Calif., 1990-93, mem. staff dept. med. oncology and therpeutic rsch., 1993-99; oncologist South Orange County Hematology Oncology Assocs., Laguna Hills, Calif., 1999—2001, Oncology Ctr. of Orange County, Irvine, 2001—. Mem ACP, Am. Soc. Clin. Oncology. Office: Ste 300 33 Creek Rd Irvine CA 92604-7705 also: Oncology Ctr Orange County 33 Creek Rd Ste 300 Irvine CA 92604

TETELBAUM, SOLOMON DAVID, research engineer; b. Odessa, Ukraine, June 10, 1936; came to U.S., 1989; s. David Mossey and Dvoyra Peysach Tetelbaum; m. Shushana Barer, Dec. 29, 1962; children: Dina, Vladimir. MS in Mech. Engring. with honors, Polytechnic Inst., Odessa, 1958; PhD in Mech. Engring., Tech. Inst., Odessa, 1968. Cert. sr. scientist, USSR. Chief sci. rsch. dept., assoc. prof. Polytechnic Inst., Odessa, 1971-88; cons. Electric Power Rsch. Inst., Palo Alto, Calif., 1991-93; prin. engr. GE Co., San Jose, 1992-93; dir. engring. Ideation Internat., Santa Monica, 1995; rsch. engr. environ. svcs. dept. City of San Jose, 1995—. Bd. dirs. Sci. Tech. Soc. USSR. Author: (with others) Gases as Working Fluids of the Power Nuclear Installations, 1978, Thermodynamic Cycles and Schematics of High Temperature Gas Cooled Reactors, 1983, Simulation and Substance—Field Analysis of the Inventive Problems, 1984; contbr. numerous articles to profl. jours.; inventor in field. Recipient award Rsch. Achievement award of Calif. Water Environment Assn, 1998, All-Union Sci. Tech. Soc., 1981, prize Ship board Com., 1975.

TETELMAN, ALICE FRAN, small business owner; b. N.Y.C., Apr. 15, 1941; d. Harry and Leah (Markovitz) T.; m. Martin A. Wenick, Dec. 7, 1980. BA, Mt. Holyoke Coll., South Hadley, Mass., 1962. Rsch. and info. asst. Edn. and World Affairs, N.Y.C., 1963-67; legis. asst. U.S. Sen. Charles Goodell, Washington, 1968-70; land use and energy specialist Citizens Adv. Com. on Environ. Quality, 1973-74; sr. assoc. prog. mgr. Linton & Co., 1971-73, 75-76; pub policy cons., 1977-78; adminstrv. asst. U.S. Congressman Bill Green (N.Y.), 1978-81; cons. The Precious Legacy Project, Prague, Czechoslovakia, 1982-83; Rep. staff dir. Select Com. on Hunger, U.S. Ho. of Reps., Washington, 1984-85; dir. State of N.J. Washington Office, 1986-90; exec. dir. Coun. of Gov.'s Policy Advisors, Washington, 1991-94; dir. Washington Office, The City of N.Y., 1994-98. Pres. Italian Vacation Villas, Washington. Bd. dirs. Republican Women's Task Force, Nat. Women's Polit. Caucus, 1976-80, Women in Senate and House (WISH) List, 1998-2001. European Community grantee, 1975. Mem. Ripon Soc. (nat. exec. com. 1971-73). Office: Italian Vacation Villas PO Box 9586 Washington DC 20016-9586

TETENYI, PAL GABOR, research scientist, former national agency official; b. Budapest, Hungary, Oct. 3, 1929; s. Imre and Irén Meitin Tetenyi; m. Mária Halász, July 29, 1955; 1 child, Pal. B of Chemistry, State U., Moscow, 1954; PhD, Budapest U., 1960; D of Chem. Scis., Hungarian Acad. Scis., 1966. Dir. Inst. Isotopes, Budapest, 1959-70, 75-77; dep. gen. sec. Hungarian Acad. Scis., 1970-75; sec. Sci. Policy Com. Hungary, 1977-83; head Sci., Culture and Edn. Cen. Com. Hungarian Socialist Workers Party, 1983-85; pres. State Office for Tech. Devel., 1985-89, Hungarian Nat. Atomic Energy Commn., 1985-90; rsch. prof. Inst. of Isotopes, Budapest, 1989—. Mem. sci. adv. com. Hungarian Nat. Atomic Energy Com. Contbr. numerous articles to profl. jours. Recipient Golden Order of Labour Hungarian Presdl. Coun., 1962, 75, 81, State award, 1983, Order of Flag of the Republic, 1989. Mem. Hungarian Acad. Scis., Royal Acad. Scis. Eng. (fgn. mem. Sweden), Acad. Engring. Hungary, Internat. Catalysis Assn. Comm. Avocation: history. Home: 5-C Tátra Utca 1136 Budapest Hungary Office: Inst of Isotopes PO Box 77 H-1525 Budapest Hungary E-mail: tetenyi@alpha0.iki.kfki.hu.

TETER, JOSEPH GORDON, surgeon; b. St. Paul, Aug. 19, 1925; s. Howard Wallace and Gladys Lorraine (Evans) T.; m. Mary Kane Cushing, June 21, 1952; children: Douglas, John, Scott, Sarah (twins). MD, Harvard Med. Sch., 1948. Diplomate Am. Bd. Surgery. Intern Boston City Hosp., 1948-49, resident, 1949-50; resident in pathology W. Roxbury VA Hosp., Boston, 1950-51; res. Boston VA Hosp., 1953-56; pvt. practice surgery Menlo Park, Calif., 1957—. Hosp. appts: Stanford (Calif.) U. Hosp., Sequoia Hosp., Redwood City, Calif.; provisional staff Mills-Peninsula Hosp., Burlingame, Calif.; clin. prof. gen. surgery emeritus Stanford U. Med. Sch., 1995—; chair surgical sect. Sequoia Hosp., Redwood City, Calif. Pres. Citizens for Sensible Planning, Menlo Park, 1987—, Accountable Mgmt., Inc. Menlo Park, 1995. 1st. Lt. U.S. Army Med. Corps, 1951-53. Mem.: San Mateo County Med. Assn., Calif. Med. Assn., Rotary Club Menlo Park, Masons. Congregationalist. Office: 888 Oak Grove Ave Ste 14 Menlo Park CA 94025-4428

TETERIS, NICHOLAS JOHN, obstetrics educator; b. Martins Ferry, Ohio, Jan. 14, 1929; s. John Nicholas and Georgia D. (Begis) T.; children: John Nicholas, Georgia Yingling. Student, U. Cin., 1948; BA with honors, Washington & Jefferson Coll., 1950; MD, Ohio State U., 1954, M in Med. Sci., 1961. Diplomate Am. Bd. Ob-Gyn. (examiner). Intern Jefferson Med. Coll. Hosp., Phila., 1954-55; resident ob-gyn Ohio State U. Hosps., Columbus, 1958-61, chief resident ob-gyn, 1961-62, attending staff, 1962; instr. Dept. Ob-Gyn Ohio State U., 1960-65, asst. prof., 1965, assoc. prof., 1967, prof., 1970—; asst. to dir. Univ. Hosps., Columbus, 1962-66, asst. dir., 1966-70; asst. dean post MD edn. Ohio State U., 1967-69; assoc. med. dir. Univ. Hosps., Columbus, 1990—, dir. oper. rms., 1990—; asst. dean for research and post MD edn. Ohio State U., 1969-70, med. dir. oper. rm., 1990—, med. dir. ambulatory surgery unit 1990. Consulting staff Mt. Carmel Hosp., Columbus, 1962; cons. USAF Hosp. Wright-Patterson AFB, Ohio, 1962, Lockbourne AFB, Ohio, 1964; attending staff Gynecologic Cancer Clinic, Columbus, 1962-69; pres., bd. chmn. Med. R&D Found. Inc. Ohio State U. Hosps., 1986—. Contbr. articles to profl. jours., chpts. to books. Mem. utilization rev. com. Sun Ridge Nursing Home, program for Acad. Medicine Columbus and Franklin County; mem. Met. Health Com. United Community Council; pres. Greek Orthodox Cathedral. Served to capt. USAF, 1954-58, to maj. USAFR, resigned. Recipient Cert. of award Ohio State Med. Assn. Original Investigation, 1965. Mem. ACS, Am. Coll. Obstetricians and Gynecologists (hon. mention exhibit 1963), Am. Cancer Soc., Am. Soc. Study Sterility, AMA, Ohio State Med. Assn., Columbus Acad. Medicine, Columbus Obstetric and Gynecologic Soc. (1st award 1960), Soc. for Study Breast Disease, Cen. Assn. Obstetricians and Gynecologists. Clubs: Capital, Faculty (Columbus). Office: Ohio State Univ Room 519 Means Hall 1654 Upham Dr Rm 547 Columbus OH 43210-1250

TETHER, ANTHONY J. government agency administrator; BEE, Rensselaer Poly. Inst., 1964; MS, Stanford U., 1965, PhD in Elec. Engring., 1969. Exec. v.p. Systems Control Inc., 1969—78; dir. nat. intelligence office Office of the Sec. of Def., 1978—82; dir. strategic tech. office Dept. Def., 1982—86; v.p. tech. and advanced devel. Ford Aerospace Corp., 1986—92; v.p. advanced tech. sector, then v.p., gen. mgr. range systems Sci. Applications Internat. Corp., 1992—99; CEO Dynamics Tech., Inc.; CEO, pres., founder The Sequoia Group, 1996—2001; dir. Def. Advanced Rsch. Projects Agy., Washington, 2001—. Mem. Army Sci. Bd., Def. Sci. Bd.; mem. control policy R&D com. Office of Nat. Drug Control. Recipient Nat. Intelligence Medal, Civilian Meritorious Svc. medal, Dept. of Def. Mem.: IEEE. Office: DARPA 1400 Defense Pentagon Rm 34 750 Washington DC 20301-1400*

TETHER, ANTHONY JOHN, aerospace executive; b. Middletown, N.Y., Nov. 28, 1941; s. John Arthur and Antoinette Rose (Gesualdo) T.; m. Nancy Engle Pierson, Dec. 27, 1963 (div. July 1971); 1 child, Jennifer; m. Carol Suzanne Dunbar, Mar. 3, 1973; 1 child, Michael. AAS, Orange County C.C., N.Y., 1961; BS, Rensselaer Poly Inst., 1963; MSEE, Stanford (Calif.) U., 1965, PhD, 1969. V.p., gen. mgr. Sys. Control Inc., Palo Alto, Calif., 1968-78; dir. nat. intelligence Office Sec. of Def., Washington, 1978-82; dir. strategic tech. DARPA, 1982-86; corp. v.p. Ford Aerospace, Newport Beach, Calif., 1986-90, LORAL, Newport Beach, 1990-92; corp. v.p., gen. mgr. Sci. Application Internat., Inc., San Diego, 1992-94; CEO Dynamics Tech. Inc., Torrance, 1994-96; CEO, pres. Sequoia Group, Newport Beach, 1996-2001; dir. def. advanced rsch. project agy. Office of Sec. of Def., Washington, 2001—. Bd. dirs. Condyne Tech., Inc., Orlando, Fla., 1990—92, chmn., 1990—92; dir. Orincon, La Jolla, Calif., 1996—99, Evans & Sutherland, Salt Lake City, 2001; mem. def. sci. bd. Army Sci. Bd. Task Forces, 1998—2002; cons. Army Sci. Bd., Def. Sci. Bd. Contbr. articles to profl. jours. Recipient Nat. Intelligence medal DCI, 1986, Civilian Meritorious medal U.S. Sec. Def., 1986. Mem. IEEE, Cosmos Club, Sigma Xi, Eta Kappa Nu, Tau Beta Pi. Avocations: ham radio, skiing, golf. Home: 6400 Lyric Ln Falls Church VA 22044 E-mail: ttether@aol.com.

TETHERLY, JONATHAN COLLIESON, chaplain, educator; b. Boston, Nov. 12, 1944; s. Edgar Osborne and Margaret Rena (Collieson) T.; m. Katsuyo Handa, Nov. 4, 1972; children: Christine Yuriko, Naomi Collieson. BS cum laude, U. N.H., 1966; MS, U. Minn., 1971; MDiv, Andover Newton Theol. Sch., 1974. Ordained min. United Ch. of Christ. Instr. biology Assumption Coll., Richardton, N.D., 1968-71; min. Congl. United Ch. of Christ and United Ch. Christ, Willsboro and Wadhams, N.Y., 1974-79, Federated Ch., Chicopee, Mass., 1979-90; comty. min. Coun. of Chs. of Greater Springfield, 1990; chaplain Hampden County Sheriff's Dept. and Correctional Ctr., Ludlow, 1988—. Substitute tchr. Springfield, West Springfield, South Hadley, Holyoke, and Ludlow pub. schs., 1990—; mem. Coun. for Mission Outreach and Social Responsibility, Mass. Conf. of United Ch. of Christ, Framingham, Mass., 1983-87, founder, chair Criminal Justice Task Force, Mass. Conf. United Ch. of Christ, 1987-90; chair, mem. Hampden Assn. United Ch. of Christ missions, Hampden County, Mass., 1981-87, 89-96; bd. dirs. Mass. Citizens Against the Death Penalty, 1982—. Pres. Champlain Valley Housing Assn., Pt. Henry, N.Y., 1975-79; mem.-at-large Chicopee Sch. Com., 1986-91; rep. Ward 5 Chicopee Sch. com., 2000—; mem. Title XX Adv. Bd., Elizabethtown, N.Y., 1976-79; mem. legis. com. Mass. Assn. Sch. Coms., Boston, 1990-91, 2001—; bd. dirs. Union Cmty. Fund Pioneer Valley. Recipient Comty. Svc. award Valley Opportunity Coun., 1982, Haystack cert. of recognition Mass. Conf. of United Ch. Christ, 1995, recognition award Mass. Citizens Against Death Penalty, 1991. Mem. Mass. Assn. Profl. Substitute Tchrs. (pres.), Chicopee Clergy Assn., Greater Springfield Harriers. Democrat. Avocations: track, distance running, making maple syrup. Home: 29 Arlington St Chicopee MA 01020-2503 Office: Hampden County Correct Ctr 627 Randall Rd Ludlow MA 01056-1085

TETIRICK, JACK E. retired surgeon; b. Marysville, Ohio, Sept. 14, 1926; s. Harry Walker and Gladys Lew (Twitchell) T.; m. Helen Hartman, Dec. 20, 1947; children: Daniel, Ruth, James. BS, Ohio State U., 1948; MD, Harvard U., 1951. Diplomate Am. Bd. Surgery. Resident in surgery Mass. Gen. Hosp., Boston, 1951-56; from clin. instr. to assoc. clin. prof. Ohio State U., Columbus, 1956-90; ret., 1990. Dir. med. affairs Grant Hosp., Columbus, 1977-90; chmn. bd. dirs. Health Mgmt. Svcs., Columbus, 1985-89; med. dir. Health Svcs. Found., Columbus, 1985-88; adv. bd. Ohio Health Choice Plan, Columbus, 1984-88. Fellow Am. Coll. Surgeons; mem. Ohio State Med. Assn. (del. 1973-76). Republican. Avocations: farming, writing children's literature. Home: 6848 County Road 2 Zanesfield OH 43360-9742 E-mail: jacktet@bright.net.

TETLEY, GLEN, choreographer; b. Cleve., Feb. 3, 1926; s. Glenford and Eleanor (Byrne) T. Student, Franklin and Marshall Coll., 1944-46, DFA (hon.) , 2001; BS, NYU, 1948; student contemporary dance with, Hanya Holm, Martha Graham, 1946; student classical ballet with, Margaret Craske, Anthony Tudor at Met. Opera Ballet Sch., 1949; Doctor of Fine Arts (hon.) , Franklin and Marshall Coll., 2001. Choreographer Major Ballet Co., 1948—. Guest instr. Yale Dramatic Workshop, 1947-48, Colo. Coll., 1946-49, Hanya Holm Sch. Contemporary Dance, 1946-52, Ballet Rambert, 1966-68, Netherlands Dance Theatre, 1962-65, B. De Rothschild Found., Israel, 1965-67 Featured dancer in Broadway musical Kiss Me Kate, 1949, Out of This World, 1950, Juno, 1958; premiered in Broadway musical Menotti's Amahl and the Night Visitors, NBC Opera, 1951; soloist with Broadway musical, N.Y.C. Opera, 1951-54, John Butler's Am. Dance Theatre, 1951-55, Robert Joffrey Ballet, 1955-56, Martha Graham Dance Co., 1957-59, Am. Ballet Theatre, 1959-61, Jerome Robbins: Ballets USA, 1961-62, Netherlands Dance Theater, 1962-65, own co., 1962-69; made govt.-sponsored tour of Europe, 1969, appearances at Spoleto Festival, all maj. Am. dance festivals; guest choreographer, Netherlands Dance Theatre; artistic dir.: Netherlands Dance Theatre, 1969; guest choreographer, Am. Ballet Theatre, Ballet Rambert, Batsheva Co. Israel, Robert Joffrey Ballet, Alvin Alley Co., U. Utah Repertory Dance Theatre, Vancouver Festival, Royal Danish Ballet, 1969, Royal Ballet Covent Garden, Royal Swedish Ballet, Den Norske Opera, Hamburg State Opera, Stuttgart Ballet; former artistic dir., Stuttgart Ballet Co.; artistic assoc., Nat. Ballet of Canada, Toronto, 1987-89; ballets include Pierrot Lunaire, 1962, Birds of Sorrow, 1962, The Anatomy Lesson, 1964, Sargasso, 1964, Field Mass, 1965, Mythical Hunters, 1965, Ricercare, 1966, Chronochromie, 1966, Tehilim, 1966, Freefall, 1967, The Seven Deadly Sins, 1967, Dithyramb, 1967, Ziggurat, 1967, Circles, 1968, Embrace Tiger and Return to Mountain, 1968, Arena, 1968, Imaginary Film, 1970, Mutations, 1970, Field Figures, 1971, Rag Dances, 1971, Small Parades, 1972, Threshold, 1972, Laborintus, 1972, Strophe-Antistrophe, 1972, The Moveable Garden, 1973, Gemini, 1973, Voluntaries, 1973, Sacre du Printemps, 1974, Tristan, 1974, Strender, 1974, Daphnis and Chloe, 1975, Greening, 1975, Alegrias, 1975, Poeme Nocturne, 1977, Sphinx, 1978, Praeludium, 1979, The Tempest, 1979, Contredances, 1979, Summer's End, 1980, Dances of Albion-Dark Night: Glad Day, 1980, Firebird, 1981, Murderer Hope of Women, 1983, Revelation and Fall, 1984, Pulcinella, 1984, Dream Walk of the Shaman, 1985, Alice, 1986, Orpheus, 1987, La Ronde, 1987, Tagore, 1989, Dialogues, 1991, Oracle, 1994, Amores, 1997, Lux in Tenebris, 1999; off-Broadway choreographer-dir. ballets including Fortuna, 1961, Ballet Ballads, 1961. Patron Benesh Inst. Choreology; bd. dirs. Tag Found., N.Y.C. Served with USNR, 1944-46. Recipient German critics award for Die Feder; Queen Elizabeth II Coronation award Royal Acad. Dancing, 1981; recipient Prix Italia Rai prize, 1982, Tennant Caledonia award Edinburgh Festival, 1983, Ohioana Career Medal, 1986, achievement award N.Y.U., 1988; named knight Order Merit, 1997.

TETLIE, HAROLD, priest; b. Madison, Minn., Aug. 24, 1926; s. H. Ben and Anna (Mauland) T. BA cum laude, St. Olaf Coll., Northfield, Minn., 1951; MBA, U. Denver, 1956; postgrad., Cornell U., 1959-60; MDiv, Luther Sem., St. Paul, 1965. Ordained to ministry Am. Luth. Ch., 1965. Pastor Christ the King Chs. (Evang. Cath. Ch.), Alice, Tex., 1965—, congregation supr., 1969—. Cir. parish priest, Nuevo Leon, Tamaulipas, Hidalgo, San Luis Potosi, Mex. Author numerous poems. Coord. Joint Action in Cmty. Svc., Inc., Alice, 1970—. Sgt. U.S. Army, 1945-46, PTO. Recipient Svc. to Mankind award Sertoma Club, Corpus Christi, Regional Vol. of Yr. award Joint Action in Cmty. Svc., 1991, Michael Madhusudan award for poem, Calcutta, 1996; Ky. Col., 1992. Mem. NEA (life), VFW (life), Am. Legion (life), 40 et 8 (life), Family Motor Coach Assn., Sons of Norway, Order of Ky. Col., Internat. Platform Assn., Thousand Trails, WWII Tank Destroyer Soc. (chaplain). Home and Office: Christ the King Chs PO Box 1607 Alice TX 78333-1607 *It is by the Power of Jesus Christ: He tells us in John 13:34: "Love one another, even as I loved you.".*

TETLOW, ELISABETH MEIER, writer, researcher, scholar, lawyer; b. Cin., Mar. 26, 1942; d. Carl L. and Margaret (Hersey) Meier; m. L. Mulry Tetlow, July 5, 1970; children: Tania C., Maria A., Sonia M., Sarah A. BA, Columbia U., 1964; MA, Fordham U., 1967, MA, 1970, Columbia U., 1973; STM, Woodstock Coll., 1974; MDiv, Jesuit Sch. Theology, Berkeley, 1979; JD, Loyola U., New Orleans, 1984. Bar: La. 1984. Instr. Coll. of Mt. St. Vincent, Riverdale, N.Y., 1968-69, Fordham U., 1970, Loyola U., New Orleans, 1979-82; law clk. to Atty. Gen. of La., Dept. Justice, 1983; law clk. La. Supreme Ct., New Orleans, 1984-85; staff atty. U.S. Ct. Appeals (5th cir.), 1985-87; rsch. atty. Kierr, Gainsburgh, Benjamin, 1988; law clk. La. Ct. Appeals (4th cir.), 1989-91. Author: Women and Ministry in the New Testament, 1980, 2d edit., 1984, Partners in Service, 1983, The Spiritual Exercises of St. Ignatius Loyola, 1987, 2d edit., 1996; contbr. articles to profl. jours. Active Amnesty Internat., Bread for the World, Pax Christi, Oxfam, Epilepsy Coun., Spl. Olympics, Sierra Club, Audubon Soc., Women's Ordination Conf.; bd. dirs. New Orleans region Dystonia Med. Rsch. Found.; v.p., bd. dirs. Greater New Orleans region Nat. Assn. Riding for the Handicapped, 1995-97; bd. dirs. Symphony Chorus of New Orleans, 1996--. Recipient Disting. Svc. award Alliance for Affordable Energy, 1992, U.S. Gold Medal, USA Karate Fedn., 1989. Mem. ABA, Cath. Bibl. Assn. Am., Cath. Theology Soc. Am., Am. Acad. Religion, Soc. Bibl. Lit., Coll. Theology Soc., La. Bar Assn., La. Karate Assn., Internat. Shotokan Karate Fedn., Symphony Chorus New Orleans (bd. dirs.), Met. Opera Regional Auditions. Democrat. Roman Catholic. Avocations: shotokan karate, swimming, piano, choral music, hiking. Home and Office: 16 Fontainebleau Dr New Orleans LA 70125-3452

TETOR, DAVID R. agriculturist, consultant; b. Montour Falls, N.Y., Dec. 16, 1943; s. Donald Booth and Margaret Eva (Howell) Tetor; m. Louise Anne Weeks, Apr. 23, 1966; children: Brian David, Michael James, Eric John. BS, Cornell U., 1965. Cert. pesticide applicator/trainer N.Y. Dept. Environ.

Conservation. Student trainee USDA Soil Conservation Svc., summers, 1962—64, soil scientist Rochester, NY, 1965; systems analyst Cornell Coop. Ext., Ithaca, 1970; agr. program leader Herkimer (N.Y.) County Cornell Coop. Ext., 1970—72, Dutchess County Cornell Coop. Ext., Millbrook, NY, 1972—2000. Agr. cons.; pres. N.Y. State Assn. County Agrl. Agts., NY, 1972—, Cornell Coll. Agr. Alumni, Ithaca, NY, 1990—2000; co-chair Dutchess County Tourism Bd., Poughkeepsie, NY, 1998—2000. Treas. adv. bd. Pine Plains Future Farmers Am. , 1976—; supr. Town of Stanford, NY, 1992—95; pres. Pine Plains (N.Y.) Sch. Bd., 1982—87; bd. dirs. Dutchess County Indsl. Devel. Agy., Poughkeepsie, 1990—, Stanford Town Bd., 2002—; mem. coun. Cornell U., 2002—. Capt. U.S. Army, 1965—69. Named Outstanding Young Agt., Nat. Assn. County Agrl. Agts., 1979; named to Alumni Honor Roll, SUNY, 2000; recipient Disting. Svc. award, Nat. Assn. County Agrl. Agts., 1984, Outstanding Alumni award, Coll. of Agr. and Life Scis., Cornell U., 2002. Mem.: Dutchess County Farm Bur. (bd. dirs. 1990—), Dutchess County Agrl. Soc., N.Y. State Agrl. Soc. (bd. dirs. 2002—), Grange. Republican. Avocations: attending NASCAR races, coin collecting, stamp collecting, camping. Home: 5626 Rt 82 Clinton Corners NY 12514 Office: Dave Tetor Agr Cons PO Box 46 Stanfordville NY 12581

TETREAULT, DONALD RICHARD, education educator; b. Pawtucket, R.I., Mar. 16, 1955; s. Richard Earl and Theresa Elizabeth (Coleman) T.; married, Aug. 23, 1986; children: Jesse Martin, Jeremy Richard. BS magna cum laude, Springfield (Mass.) Coll., 1977; MA in Tchg., N.Mex. State U., 1978; PhD, U. So. Calif., 1997. Mgr. Nautilus Pacifica, Long Beach, Calif., 1979-81; program dir. Calif. Primary Physicians, L.A., 1981-84; H.S. tchr. L.A. Unified Sch. Dist., 1985-93; asst. prof. sch. fin. and edn. policy analysis U. S.C., Columbia, 1996—. Cons. in field. Author: (monographs) State of the States: School Finance, 1999; contbr. chpt. to book. Recipient awards for outstanding dissertation. Mem. Am. Edn. Rsch. Assn. (chair spl. interest group 2000—), Am. Edn. Fin. Assn. (bd. dirs. 2002--), Assn. Sch. Bus. Ofcls, (chair fin. com. 2002—), Phi Delta Kappa. Avocation: jazz guitar. Office: U SC 313 A Wardlaw Columbia SC 29208-0001 E-mail: dtetreault@sc.rr.com.

TETTLEBAUM, HARVEY M. lawyer; m. Ann Safier; children: Marianne, Benjamin. AB, Dartmouth Coll., 1964; JD, AM in History, Washington U. Sch. Law, 1968. Asst. dean Washington U. Sch. Law, 1969-77; asst. atty. gne., chief counsel Consumer Protection and Anti-Trust Div., 1970-77; pvt. practice Jefferson City, Mo., 1977-90; mem., chmn. health law practice group Husch & Eppenberger, LLC, 1990—. Contbr. articles to profl. jours. Treas. Mo. Rep. State Com., 1976—; v.p. Moniteau County R-1 Sch. Dist. Bd., 1991-95, pres., 1995-96; mem. Calif. R-1 Sch. Bd., 1990-96, v.p., 1993-95, pres., 1995-96. [e]m. Am. Health Lawyers Assn. (bd. dirs. 1993-99, co-chair long-term care and the law program 1993-2001, chair 2001—, chair long-term care and law program 2001—, chair long term care substantive law com. 1997-2001), Mo. Bar Assn. (health and hosp. law com., chmn. adminstrv. law com., vice chair delivery of legal svc. com., Mo. statewide legal svc. com.), Am. Health Care Assn. (legal subcom. 1994—). Home: 56295 Little Moniteau Rd California MO 65018-3069 Office: Husch & Eppenberger LLC Monroe House Ste 300 235 E High St PO Box 1251 Jefferson City MO 65102-1251

TETZLAFF, CHARLES ROBERT, prosecutor; b. Oct. 15, 1938; s. Donald H. and Harriet (Ranney) T.; m. Joan Seugling, July 1, 1962; children: Julie Lynn Mulrow, Carl Lawrence. BA, U. Vt., 1960; LLB, Boston U., 1963; LLM, NYU, 1964. Bar: Vt. 1964, U.S. Supreme Ct. 1970. Judge advocate USAF, 1965-68; dep. state's atty. Chittenden County, Vt., 1968-70; ptnr. Latham, Eastman, Schweyer and Tetzlaff, 1969-93; U.S. atty. dist. Vt. Office U.S. Atty., Burlington, 1993—; gen. counsel U.S. Sentencing Commn., Washington, 2002—. Trustee Vt. Legal Aid, 1976-78; chair Dist. 4 Environ. Commn., 1979-83, Gov. Sentencing Study Commn., 1985-86; active Vt. Bd. Bar Examiners, 1980-84, State Police Adv. Commn., 1985-86, Gov. Bail Amendment Task Force. Capt. USAF, 1965-68. Mem. ABA, Vt. Bar Assn., Chittenden County Bar Assn. Office: US Sentencing Commn One Columbus Circle NE Washington DC 20002-8002

TETZLAFF, THEODORE R. lawyer; b. Saukville, Wis., Feb. 27, 1944; AB magna cum laude, Princeton U., 1966; LLB, Yale U., 1969. Bar: Ind. 1969, D.C. 1969, Ill. 1974. Legis. asst. to Congressman John Brademas, 1970; exec. dir. Nat. Conf. Police Community Rels., 1970-71; acting dir. U.S. Office Legal Svcs., Office Econ. Opportunity, Washington, 1972-73; counsel, Com. Judiciary U.S. Ho. of Reps., 1974; v.p., legal and external affairs Cummins Engine Co., 1980-82; gen. coun. Tenneco, Inc., Greenwich, Conn., 1992-99; ptnr. Jenner & Block, Chgo., 1976—80, 1982—2001; mng. ptnr. McGuireWoods LLP, 2002—. Bd. dirs. Continental Materials Corp., Chgo. Pres. Chgo. area Found. Legal Svcs., 1983—; commr. Pub. Bldg. Commn. Chgo., 1990—. Reginald Heber Smith fellow, 1969-70. Mem. ABA (chair sect. litigation 1991-92), Ill. State Bar Assn., Ind. State Bar Assn., D.C. Bar. Office: McGuireWoods LLP Suite 4400 77 West Wacker Dr Chicago IL 60601

TEUBNER, FERDINAND CARY, JR. retired publishing company executive; b. Phila., Sept. 22, 1921; s. Ferdinand Cary Teubner and Esther Roslyn (Test) Alperstein; m. Ruth May Hazen, Nov. 1, 1953; 1 child, Janell Caron Teubner Crispyn. Student, U. Pa., 1940-41; grad., Charles Morris Price Sch. Advt. and Journalism, 1949. Rep. W.H. Hoedt Studios, Inc., Phila., 1945-52; account exec. Patterson Prodns., Inc., 1955-56, v.p., 1956-57; staff exec. Am. Assn. Advt. Agys., N.Y.C., 1957-59; rep. W.H. Martin & Co., Inc., 1959-62; advt. salesman Editor & Pub. Co., Inc., 1962-65, advt. mgr., 1965-76, gen. mgr., treas., 1976-78, treas., pub., 1978-95, dir., 1969-95; sec.-treas., dir. E & P Research, Inc., 1985-95, ret., 1995. Served with USAAF, 1942-45, ETO; served with U.S. Army, 1952-55, Korea, ret. maj. AUS, 1981. Decorated Purple Heart; recipient Silver Shovel award Internat. Newspaper Mktg. Assn., 1993. Mem. Sales Execs. Club N.Y.C., Res. Officer Assn. Clubs: Union League, Lake Valhalla Country. Episcopalian. Home: 18 Lenape Dr Montville NJ 07045-9795

TEUFEL, WILLIAM LOCKWOOD, emergency physician; b. Cleve., Mar. 21, 1941; s. William John and Dorothy Margaret (Lockwood) T.; m. Margaret Ong, June 28, 1969 (div. Sept. 1980); 1 child, Drew William; m. Zoe Ann Zimmerman (dec. Oct. 1999); children: Thea Anna, Kallie Abra. BS in Chemistry, Denison U., 1963; MD, U. Cin., 1967. Resident in gen. surgery Highland Hosp., Oakland, Calif., 1968-69; resident in emergency medicine U. Cin., 1971-73; from asst. dir. to dir. emergency svc. Highland Gen. Hosp., Oakland, 1973-76, San Francisco Gen. Hosp., 1976-80; sr. ptnr. Calif. Emergency Physicians Med. Group, Oakland, 1982-91; med. dir. emergency svc Marin Gen. Hosp., Greenbrae, Calif., 1986-99; med. dir. Coastal Valleys Emergency, Santa Rosa, 1999—. Oral examiner Am. Bd. Emergency Medicine, Lansing, Mich., 1981—; health coun. County of Marin, San Rafael, Calif., 1997-2002. Lt. comdr. USNR. Fellow Am. Acad. Emergency Medicine (bd. dirs. Calif. chpt. 1998—). Avocations: motorcycling, native plant gardening. Office: Calif Emergency Physicians 2101 Webster St Ste 1770 Oakland CA 94612-9700 Home: PO Box 471 437 Meadow Way San Geronimo CA 94963-0471 E-mail: wlteufel@aol.com.

TEUSCHLER, MICHAEL ALEXANDER, computer consultant; b. Chgo., Nov. 30, 1953; s. Edward Michael and Josephine Anastasia (Bien) T. Assoc. editor Peacock N.W. News, Chgo., 1972-74; polit. activist Citizen's Action Program, 1974; stockman Cotter & Co., 1974-77; asst. mgr. Cloona Health Ctr., Westport, Ireland, 1977-78; computer programmer Sears Roebuck & Co., Chgo., 1978-90; sr. computer cons. Cap Gemini Am., Milw., 1991-2000; sr. cons. Keane, Inc., 2000—. Pres. Old Town Renaissance Consort, Chgo., 1985-89, 2100 N. Albany Block Club, Chgo., 1988-89; vice chmn. fin. com. St. Philomena Parish, Chgo., 1976. Mem. ASPCA, Wis. Assn. Sys. Mgrs., Morning Star Fellowship of Isis (founding mem.), Internat. Platform Assn., Humane Soc. of U.S., Nat. Arbor Day Soc., World Wildlife Fund, Nat. Audubon Soc., Nat. Wildlife Fedn. Leaders Club, Defenders of Wildlife, Am. Diabetes Assn., Doris Day Animal League, Sierra Club, Wilderness Soc., Internat. Fund for Animal Welfare, Animal Legal Def. Fund. Avocations: renaissance dance, ancient religions. Home: 7625 W Wind Lake Rd Wind Lake WI 53185-2253 Office: 11270 W Park Pl Milwaukee WI 53224-3623 E-mail: mteuschler@bigfoot.com.

TEUTSCH, MONICA, health services administrator; b. N.Y.C., Mar. 7, 1955; d. Edward and Annemarie (Jung) T. BS, Guilford Coll., 1975; MPH, U. Ill. Sch. Pub. Health, 1980. Dir. Hot Springs (N.C.) Health Program; dir. divsn. human resources Mtn. Resource Ctr., Cullowhee, N.C.; dir. children's dental program Mission St. Joseph's, Asheville. Cons. in field. Office: GCHC Children's Dental 509 Biltmore Ave Asheville NC 28801-4601 E-mail: monica.teutsch@msj.org.

TEVRIZIAN, DICKRAN M., JR. federal judge; b. Los Angeles, Aug. 4, 1940; s. Dickran and Rose Tevrizian; m. Geraldine Tevrizian, Aug. 22, 1964; children: Allyson Tracy, Leslie Sara. BS, U. So. Calif., 1962, JD, 1965. Tax acct. Arthur Andersen and Co., Los Angeles, 1965-66; atty., ptnr. Kirtland and Packard, 1966-72; judge Los Angeles Mcpl. Ct., 1972-78, State of Calif. Superior Ct., Los Angeles, 1978-82; ptnr. Manatt, Phelps, Rothenberg & Tunney, 1982-85, Lewis, D'Amato, Brisbois & Bisgaard, Los Angeles, 1985-86; judge U.S. Dist. Ct., 1986—. Adv. dir. sch. pub. policy U. Calif., L.A. Adv. dir. UCLA Sch. Pub. Policy. Named Trial Judge of the Yr., Calif. Trial Lawyers Assn., 1987, L.A. County Bar Assn., 1994-95; recipient Peter the Great Gold Medal of Honor Russian Acad. Natural Scis., 1998, Ellis Island Medal of Honor award, 1999. Mem. Calif. Trial Lawyer's Assn. (trial judge of yr. 1987), L.A. County Bar Assn. (trial judge of yr. 1994-95), Malibu Bar Assn. (fed. ct. trial judge of yr. 1998). Office: US Dist Ct Royal Federal Bldg 255 E Temple St Los Angeles CA 90012-3332

TEW, E. JAMES, JR. management services company executive; b. Dallas, July 7, 1933; s. Elmer James and Bessie Fay (Bennett) T.; children: Teresa Annette, Linda Diane, Brian James. Student, Arlington State Jr. Coll., 1955-57; BBA in Indsl. Mgmt., So. Meth. U., 1969; MS in Quality Systems, U. Dallas, 1972, MBA in Mgmt., 1975; EdD in Adult Edn., Nova U., 1986. Registered profl. engr., Calif. Mgr. quality assurance ops. Tex. Instruments Inc., Dallas, 1957-98; chmn. corp. metric implementation com. Texins Credit Union, co-chmn. credit com. Adj. faculty Richland Coll. Mountain View Coll., LeTourneau U.; precinct chmn., election judge, del. several county and state convs.; bus. computer info. systems adv. bd. U. North Tex., bd. dirs. ctr. for quality and productivity U. North Tex.; bd. examiners Malcolm Baldridge Nat. Quality award, U.S. Dept. Commerce, Nat. Inst. Standard and Tech., 1988, 89, 90, 91, 95, 96; chmn. panel judges, fellow Tex. Quality Award, 1993-2001; cons. nat. quality award Govt. Singapore, 1994; spkr. in field; bd. examiners Presdl. Quality Award, 1994-96, judge 1997-2000; quality examiner U.S. Army, 1996—; sr. quality examiner USAF, 1995-98, postdoctoral edn. in mediation and arbitration edn., 1998, 99; vol. mediator for dispute mediation svc., 1998—. Spkr. in field. Contbr. articles to profl jours. Decorated Army Commendation medal with oak leaf cluster, Meritorious Svc. medal, Legion of Merit. Fellow Am. Soc. Quality Control (cert. quality auditor, cert. quality mgr., cert. as quality and reliability engr., chmn. Dallas-Ft. Worth sect. 1974-75). Fellow U.S. Metric Assn. (cert., chmn. cert. bd. 1986-87); mem. U.S. Res. Officers Assn., Dallas C. of C. (chmn. world mfg. com. 1974-77, chmn. spl. tasl force career edn. adv. bd. 1973-74), Mensa (mem. air force blue ribbon commn. on assesments and evaluations 1996-98), Sigma Iota Epsilon, Phi Delta Kappa. Baptist. Clubs: Texins Rod and Gun (pres. 1969-70), Texins Flying, Masons (32 degree). Fax: 214-349-3686. E-mail: ejtew@swbell.net.

TEWARSON, REGINALD PRABHAKAR, retired mathematics educator, consultant; b. Pauri, Garhwal, India, Nov. 17, 1939; came to U.S., 1957; s. Seth Narottam and Chand (Mani) T.; m. Hedi Thomann, July 1, 1960 (div. Nov. 1990); children: Anita Jasmine, Monique Shanti. MA, Agra (Ind.) U., 1952; PhD, Boston U., 1961. Lectr. Lucknow (Ind.) U., 1951-57; sr. mathematicisn Honeywell EDP, Wellesley Hills, Mass., 1960-64; leading prof. applied math. and stats. SUNY, Stony Brook, 1964-2000, leading prof. physiology and biophysics dept., 1964-2000, leading prof. emeritus, 2001—. Cons. NIH, Washington, 1971-74. Author: Sparse Matrices, 1973; mem. editorial bd. Applied Math. Letters, 1986—, Math. Computer Modeling, 1991—, Pan. Am. Math. Jour., 1991—; contbr. articles to profl. jours. Centenary scholar Govt. of India, 1946-50, Crusade scholar U.S. Coun. Chs., 1957-59; rsch. grantee NIH, 1973-97, Air Force Office Sch. Rsch. Math. and Info. Scis., 1983-85, NSF, 1993-95. Mem. Am. Math. Soc., Soc. Indsl. and Applied Math., Soc. for Math. Biology. Democrat. Achievements include pioneering research on sparse matrices based largely on own research; co-development of mathematical model of kidney concentrating mechanism, of computer model of neuronal function. Avocations: carpentry, cooking, biking, gardening. Home: 22 Night Heron Dr Stony Brook NY 11790-1108 Office: SUNY Dept Applied Math And Stats Stony Brook NY 11794-0001 E-mail: tewarson@ams.sunysb.edu.

TEWELL, JOSEPH ROBERT, JR. electrical engineer; b. Albany, N.Y., May 19, 1934; s. Joseph Robert and Florence Edna Tewell; m. Barbara Ann Johnson, Nov. 20, 1960; children— Patricia Ann, Donna Lynn, Joseph Robert, III. B.E.E., Rensselaer Poly. Inst., 1955, M.E.E., 1958. Rsch. engr. N.Am. Aviation, Inc., Downey, Calif., 1955; assoc. rsch. engr. Lockheed Aircraft Corp., Burbank, 1956; instr. Rensselaer Poly. Inst., 1957-64; sr. rsch. scientist Martin Marietta Corp., Denver, 1964-79, mgr. advanced programs Michoud, La., 1979-87, mgr. shuttle-C project, 1988-90, mgr. computer-aided productivity, 1991-93, mgr. sys. engring., 1994-96; ret., 1996; pvt. cons., 1996—. Founding sponsor Challenger Ctr.; cons. Redford Corp., Scotia, N.Y., 1961. Contbr. articles to profl. jours.; inventor dual action single drive actuator, spacecraft docking and retrieval mechanism Founding sponsor Challenger Ctr. Served with Army Security Agy., 1957. Recipient NASA Manned Awareness citation, 1970, NASA Skylab Achievement award, 1974, NASA New Tech. award, 1976, Tech. Achievement award Martin Marietta Corp., 1977, Sustained Performance award Martin Marietta Corp., 1981, NASA cert. of recognition, 1977, Author of Yr. award, 1986, also 38 publ. awards, 1965— Fellow Explorers Club; mem. AIAA, Smithsonian Assocs., Air and Space Mus., Unmanned Vehicle Sys., Nat. Audubon Soc., Sigma Xi, Eta Kappa Nu, Tau Beta Pi, Theta Chi. Home and Office: 619 Legendre Dr Slidell LA 70460-3427

TEXAS, SAM FAYAD, small business owner, political activist; b. Monrovia, Liberia, Oct. 20, 1958; came to U.S., 1979; naturalized; s. Moufid and Elizabeth (Mowad) Fayad. Student, U. Houston, 1977-80. Handler pub. complaints against govt. agencies, 1980-90; owner, mgr. Texas Sam Import/Export, Houston, 1990—. Contbr. articles to jours. and newspapers. Vol. Bib Brothers, Houston, 1990—, Human Rights Watch, Houston, 1990—, Amnesty Internat., Houston, 1990—, Habitat for Humanity, Houston, 1990—, ARC; precinct judge, Houston, 1990, 91; del. to state and nat. Rep. and Dem. convs., 1992; mgr. local polit. campaigns, 1990; investigator genicide in Bosnia, 1996; Dem. nominee for Tex. Ho. of Reps., 1992. Named Outstanding Citizen, Mayor of Tex. and Gov. of Tex., 1988, 90, 92, 93; recipient outstanding vol. award Amnesty Internat., 1994. Republican. Roman Catholic. Avocations: prison ministry, councillor for needy, teaching Sunday school, counseling youth. Home: PO Box 55707 Houston TX 77255-5707 Office: Texas Sam Import/Export 6510 Sivley St Houston TX 77055-5362 E-mail: samtexas@samtexas.simplenet.com.

TEXEL, TIMOTHY J. state agency director; b. Lincoln, Nebr., 1964; s. Keith W. and Barbara J. T.; m. Joan C. Texel, 1998. BA in English, BA in Polit. Sci., U. Nebr., 1988, JD, 1991. Bar: Nebr. Judge advocate U.S. Army, Schofield Barracks, Hawaii, 1991-94; asst. atty. gen. Nebr. Dept. Justice, Lincoln, 1995-98; exec. dir. and gen. counsel Nebr. Power Rev. Bd., 1998—. Capt. U.S. Army, 1991-94. Presbyterian. Office: Nebr Power Rev Bd PO Box 94713 Lincoln NE 68509-4713 E-mail: tjtexel@linux3.nrc.state.ne.us.

TEXON, MEYER, cardiologist, internist, pathologist, researcher; b. N.Y.C., Apr. 23, 1909; s. Morris David and Eva (Kaizer) T.; m. Ami Atheda Gold, Oct. 23, 1941; children: Stephen, Sylvia. BA, Harvard Coll., 1930; MD, NYU, 1934. Diplomate Am. Bd. Internal Medicine, Am. Bd. Cardiovascular Diseases. Sr. clin. asst. in medicine Mt. Sinai Hosp., N.Y.C., 1938-96; asst. med. examiner City of New York, 1957-61; assoc. prof. forensic medicine NYU Med. Ctr., 1955—; attending physician Beth Israel Hosp. North, N.Y.C., 1960-96. Author: (books) Heart Disease and Industry, 1954, Can the Cardiac Stand Trial?, 1987, Hemodynamic Basis of Atherosclerosis, 1980, Hemodynamic Basis of Atherosclerosis with Critique of the Cholesterol-Heart Disease Hypothesis, 2d. edit., 1996. Fellow ACP, Am. Heart Assn. (mem. coun. atherosclerosis, clin. cardiology), N.Y. Acad. Medicine; mem. AMA (Hektoem silver medal 1958), N.Y. County Med. Soc. (pres. 1982-83). Home: 365 West End Ave New York NY 10024-6511 E-mail: mtexon@aol.com.

TEXTOR, ROBERT BAYARD, cultural anthropology writer, consultant, educator; b. Cloquet, Minn., Mar. 13, 1923; s. Clinton Kenney and Lillian (Nickles) T.; divorced; children: Alexander Robertson, Marisa Elizabeth. Student, Lafayette Coll., 1940-41, Antioch Coll., 1941-43; BA in Asian Studies, U. Mich., 1945; PhD in Cultural Anthropology, Cornell U., 1960. Civil info. and edn. officer Mil. Govt., Kyoto-Wakayama, Japan, 1946-48; rsch. fellow anthropology and S.E. Asia studies Yale U., 1959-60, assoc., 1960-61; rsch. fellow in stats. Harvard U., 1962-64; assoc. prof. edn. and anthropology Stanford U., 1964-68, prof. edn. and anthropology, 1968-86, prof. anthropology, 1986-90, prof. anthropology emeritus, 1990—; courtesy prof. internat. studies U. Oreg., 1991—. Vis. prof. U. Saar, Saarbrücken, Germany, 1984-85; cons. Motorola, Inc., 1991—, Ministry of Planning, Kuwait, 1999; mem. S.E. Asia Coun., 1974-77; cons. cultural anthropology to govt. agys., 1957-58, 61-62. Author: Roster of the Gods: An Ethnography of The Supernatural in a Thai Village, 6 vols., 1973, Austria 2005: Projected Sociocultural Effects of the Microelectronic Revolution, 1983, Anticipatory Anthropology, 1985, (with Sippanondha Ketudat) The Middle Path for the Future of Thailand, 1990, (with others) Uncompromising Integrity: Motorola's Global Challenge, 1998; assoc. editor Jour. Conflict Resolution, 1965-70; mem. editorial bd. Human Orgn., 1966-71, Jour. Cultural Futures, 1979-87; adv. editor Behavior Sci. Rsch., 1974-86. Bd. dirs. Vols. in Asia, Stanford, Calif., 1968-73; mem. Metro Portland Future Vision Commn., 1993-95; mem. Portland, Oreg., Organizing Com. for Lewis and Clark Bicentennial, 1996-97. Served with U.S. Army, 1943-46. Fellow Rockefeller Found., 1951-52, fgn. area tng. fellow Ford Found., Thailand 1955-58, Carnegie fellow, 1958-59, Fulbright West Europe rsch. fellow, 1984-85, East-West Ctr. fellow, 1988-90; NSF grantee, Thailand, U.S., 1969-73, Volkswagen Found. grantee, Thailand and Germany, 1984. Fellow Am. Anthrop. Assn. (life), Soc. Applied Anthropology; mem. Siam Soc. (life), Assn. Asian Studies (life), Council on Anthropology and Edn. (pres. 1974-75), AAUP (pres. Stanford chpt. 1975-76), Phi Kappa Phi. E-mail: robertbtextor@attbi.com.

TEZAK, EDWARD GEORGE, mechanics educator; b. Steelton, Pa., Oct. 16, 1940; s. John Frank and Mary Cecilia (Shiprak) T.; m. Martha Katherine Leyko, Sept. 10, 1966; children: Christine Louise, Edward Scott. BS, U.S. Mil. Acad., 1963; MS in Astrodynamics, UCLA, 1967; PhD in Engring. Mechanics, Va. Poly. Inst. and State U., 1979. Commd. 2d lt. U.S. Army, 1963, advanced through grades to col., 1985; co. comdr., XO B Co. 13th Engr. Battalion, Camp Casey, Korea, 1964-65; engr. battalion advisor 6th ARVN Engr. Group, QuiNhon and DaNang, Vietnam, 1967-68; instr., then asst. prof. dept. mechanics U.S. Mil. Acad., West Point, N.Y., 1969-72; plans officer U.S. Army Engr. Group, Saigon, Vietnam, 1972-73; USMA fellow Army War Coll., Carlisle, Pa., 1982-83; group dir. dept. mechanics U.S. Mil. Acad., 1976-88, dep. head dept. mechanics, 1988, assoc. dean, 1989-93; ret. U.S. Army, 1993; dean Sch. Info. Sys. and Engring. Tech. SUNY, Utica, 1993-97, dean Coll. Tech. Alfred State, 1998-99; assoc. prof. Alfred State Coll., 1999-2000, prof. mechanics, 2000—; sec., treas. Coun. for Engring. Tech. N.Y. State (CET-NYS), 2000—. Mem. adv. bd. dept. math. U.S. Mil. Acad., 1993-97. Mem. Cmty. Counsel, Utica, 1994-97. Decorated Legion of Merit. Mem. ASME, Am. Soc. Engring. Edn. (bd. dirs., chair PIC III 1993-95, exec. com. mech. divsn., program chair, divsn. chair 1989-93, vice program chair engring. tech. divsn. 2001—, Outstanding Campus Liaison Rep. award Mid. Atlantic sect. 1991, Outstanding Tchr./Educator of Yr award St. Lawrence sect. 2001),), Phi Kappa Phi. Roman Catholic. Avocations: bowling, golf, skiing. Home: 450 N Main St Wellsville NY 14895-1042

TEZDUYAR, TAYFUN ERSIN, engineering educator; b. Elazig, Turkey, Aug. 6, 1954; s. Kamil and Esma Tezduyar; m. Tomoko Sasaki, Oct. 15, 1988. MS in Mech. Engring., Calif. Inst. Tech., 1978, PhD in Mech. Engring., 1982; Hon. Doctorate, Slovak Republic, 2001. Postdoctoral rsch. engr. in mech. engring. Stanford U., Palo Alto, Calif., 1982-83; asst. prof. in mech. engring. U. Houston, 1983-87; assoc. prof. in aerospace engring. and mechanics U. Minn., Mnpls., 1987-91, prof. in aerospace engring. and mechanics, 1991-97, disting. McKnight Univ. prof., 1997-98; James F. Barbour prof. engring. Rice U., Houston, 1998—, chmn. dept. mech. engring. and materials sci., 1999—. Dir. Army High Performance Computing Rsch. Ctr., Mpls., 1994-98. Authored over 100 jour. papers, 30 book chpts., 120 conf. papers; editor 10 jour. vols. various internat. jours. Recipient Presdl. Young Investigator award NSF, 1986, Comdr.'s Ednl. award for excellence U.S. Army Soldier Sys. Command, Natick, Mass., 1996, Computational Mechanics award Japan Soc. Mech. Engrs., Tokyo, 1997. Fellow ASME, U.S. Assn. Computational Mechanics (Computational Fluid Dynamics award 1997); mem. Internat. Assn. Computational Mechanics (Computational Mechanics award 1998). Avocations: coin collecting, biking. Office: Rice Univ Mech Engr & Mat Scis 6100 Main St Houston TX 77005-1892 E-mail: tezduyar@rice.edu.

TEZLA, ALBERT, English educator; b. S. Bend, Ind., Dec. 13, 1915; s. Mihály and Lucza (Szénási) Tezla; m. Olive Anna Fox, July 26, 1941; children: Michael William, Kathy Elaine. BA, U. Chgo., 1941, MA, 1947, PhD, 1952. Instr. Ind. U. Ext., S. Bend, 1946-48; from instr. to assoc. prof. U. Minn., Duluth, 1949-61, prof., 1961-82, prof. emeritus, 1982—. Vis. prof. Hungarian lit. Columbia U., N.Y.C., 1966, cons., 1967-71, 77-81, vis. scholar, 1975; cons. U. Minn., Mpls., 1968-83; project reviewer NEH, Washington, 1979-82; vis. prof. Hungarian lit. U. Minn., Duluth, 1998. Author: An Introductory Bibliography to the Study of Hungarian Literature, 1964, Hungarian Authors: A Bibliographical Handbook, 1970, The Hazardous Quest: Hungarian Immigrants in the United States, 1895-1920, 1993; co-author: Academic American Encyclopedia, 1980, World Authors, 1975-80, 1985, Benét's Readers Encyclopedia, 1987, World Authors, 1980-85, 1991; editor, contbg. translator: Ocean at the Window: Hungarian Prose and Poetry since 1945, 1980, Three Contemporary Hungarian Plays, 1992; contbg. translator: Hungarian Short Stories, 1983, The Kiss: 20th Century Hungarian Short Stories, 1993; translator: God in the Wagon: Ten Short Stories (Ferenc Sánta), 1985 (Hungarian Pubs. award 1985), The Fifth Seal (Ferenc Sánta), 1986 (Hungarian Pubs. award 1986), Somewhere in a Distant Fabled Land: American Hungarians, 1895-1920, 1987, On the Balcony: Selected Short Stories (Iván Mándy), 1988 (Hungarian Pubs. award 1988), Hungary: A Brief History (István Lázár), 1990, An Illustrated History of Hungary (István Lázár), 1992, Memoir of Hungary, 1944-48 (Sándor Márai), 1996, Once There Was a Central Europe: Selected Short Stories and Other Writings (Miklós Mészöly), 1997, A Wartime Memoir, Hungary, 1944-45 (Alaine Polcz), 1998; editl. cons. Holmes and Meier Pubs., 1998. Lt. (s.g.) USN, 1942-46, PTO. Recipient Diplome d'honeur, Inst. Cultural Rels., Hungary, 1970, Commemorative medal, 1970, Endre Ady Medallion, Presidium Hungarian PEN Ctr., 1986, Pro Cultura Hungarica award, Rep. Hungary, 1996, Abraham Lincoln award, Am. Hungarian Found., 1998; fellow Fulbright Rsch. fellow, Associated Bd. Rsch. Coun., 1959—60, Rsch. fellow, Internat. Co. Traveling Grants, 1963—64, Internat. Rsch. and Exchs. Bd., 1978; grantee Rsch. grantee, Am. Coun. Learned Socs., 1961, 1968, NEH, 1978—82. Mem. Internat. Assn. Hungarian Studies (mem. exec. com. 1978-83, John Lotz Meml. award 1986), Am. Hungarian Educators' Assn., Fulbright Assn. Democrat. Avocations: gardening, physical fitness, reading, classical films. Home: 5412 London Rd Duluth MN 55804-2511

THACHER, BARBARA AUCHINCLOSS, history educator; b. Oyster Bay, N.Y., July 27, 1918; d. Hugh and Frances Coverdale (Newlands) Auchincloss; m. Thomas Thacher, Aug. 4, 1942; children: Barbara Burrall Thacher Plimpton, Elizabeth Coverdale Thacher Hawn, Thomas Day II, Hugh Auchincloss, Peter Anthony, Andrew. BA cum laude, Bryn Mawr Coll., 1940; MA in History, Columbia U., 1965. Editl. rschr. Newsweek, N.Y.C., 1940-41, 44; writer N.Y. Times Sunday Mag., News of Week Rev., 1941-43; co-editor Christmas Booklist for Children Harper's Mag., 1957-59; asst. history dept. Barnard Coll., 1964-65; rsch. asst. Ctr. Urban Edn., 1966. Bd. dirs. Bryn Mawr Coll., 1966-88, chair bd. trustees, 1980-87, emeritus, 1988—, City Univ. of N.Y., trustee, 1970-73, WNET-TV-Channel 13, trustee, 1978-88; active Sheltering Arms Children's Svc., Istanbul Women's Coll., Leake & Watts Children's Home Svcs., Yonkers and N.Y.C., 1961-83, emeritus, 1983—, N.Y.C. Park Assn., Riverdale Girls Sch.; trustee Tchrs. Coll. Columbia U. Mem. Cosmopolitan Club (gov.), North Haven Casino. Democrat. Presbyterian. Home: Apt 311 88 Notch Hill Rd North Branford CT 06471-1852

THACKER, JERRY LYNN, school administrator; b. Mishawaka, Ind., July 7, 1950; s. Burl Willis and Azzie Dell (Davidson) T.; m. Donna Lee, Aug. 11, 1973. BA, Bethel Coll., Mishawaka, Ind., 1972; MS, Ind. U., S. Bend, 1975;

EdD, Andrews U., Berrien Springs, Mich., 1987. Tchr., individually guided edn. team leader Penn-Harris Madison Sch. Corp., Osceola, Ind., 1972-85; elem. prin. Twin lakes Sch. Corp., Monticello, 1985-89; dir. curriculum Saginaw (Mich.) Ind. Sch. Dist., 1989-90; dir. elem. edn. MSD Lawrence Twp., Indpl., 1990-96, asst. supt. for Human Resources, 1996-98; supt. of schs. Logansport (Ind.) Cmty. Sch. Corp., 1998—. Presenter in field; contbr. numerous articles to profl. publs. Recipient various grants; recipient Award for Svc. to Profession, Ind. Assn. Curriculum Devel., others. Mem. ASCD, Nat. Assn. Elem. Prins., IAEMSP (pres.), AASA, Internat Reading Assn., Pi Lambda Theta, Phi Delta Kappa. Home: 831 Meadowview Dr Logansport IN 46947-1333

THACKER, STEPHEN BRADY, medical association administrator, epidemiologist; b. Independence, Mo., Dec. 30, 1947; m. 1976; 2 children. AB, Princeton U., 1969; MD, Mt. Sinai Sch. Medicine, 1973; MSc, London Sch. Hygiene and Tropical Medicine, 1984. Chief consolidated surveillance and cmty. activity epidemiol. program office Ctrs. Disease Control and Prevention, Atlanta, 1978-83, dir. surveillance and epidemiol. studies, 1983-86; asst. dir. sci. Ctrs. Environ. Health and Injury Control, 1986-89; dir. epidemiol. program office Ctrs. Disease Control and Prevention, 1989—, acting dep. dir., 1998, acting dir. Nat. Ctr. Injury Prevention and Control, 1999-2000, acting dir. Nat. Ctr. Environ. Health, 1993-95. Mem. steering com. Assn. Behavioral Sci. Med. Edn., 1971-74; assoc. Dept. Cmty. Medicine, Med. Ctr. Duke U., Durham, N.C., 1975-76; lectr. Cmty. Ctr. Mt. Sinai Sch. Medicine, N.Y.C., 1978—, Sch. Medicine Emory U., Atlanta, 1985-86; cons. epidemiology Arab Republic Egypt, 1979-91; clin. asst. prof. cmty. health Sch. Medicine Emory U., 1986-91; adj. prof. Emory U. Sch. Pub. Health, 1992—. Editor: Epidemiologic Revs., 1990—. Clin. scholar Robert Wood Johnson Found., 1974-75; recipient Mosby Book award for excellence, 1973, Pub. Health Svc. Outstanding Svc. medal, 1987, Pub. Health Svc. Meritorious Svc. medal, 1988, Saul Horowitz Jr. Meml. award, 1990, Supervisory award for contbr. advantage of women, 1991, Pub. Health Svc. Commendation medal, 1991, Pub. Health Svc. Disting. Svc. medal, 1993, Pub. Health Svc. Surgeon Gen.'s Exemplary Svc. medal, 1993, Pub. Health Svc. Disting. Svc. medal, 1997, Medal of Excellence William C. Watson, Jr. Achievements include rsch. public health surveillance, infectious disease, environ. health, injury prevention, alcohol abuse, health care delivery, meta-analysis, technology assessment. Office: Ctrs for Disease Control and Prevention MS C08 1600 Clifton Rd NE Atlanta GA 30329-4018 Business E-Mail: sbt1@cec.gov.

THACKER, STROM CRONAN, educator; b. Marysville, Calif., June 23, 1966; s. Roger Dean Thacker and Terry Kristen Strom; m. Isabelle Paine, Aug. 10, 1991; children: Matthew, Caroline. BA, Pomona Coll., 1988; PhD, U. N.C., 1996. Legal asst. Hancock Rothert and Bunshoft, San Francisco, 1988-89; asst. prof. Inst. Tech., Mexico City, 1995-96, Boston U., 1996—. Author: Big Business, the State and Free Trade: Constructing Coalitions in Mexico, 2000. Tinker Found. rsch. grantee, U. N.C., 1990; Summer fellow Inst. L.Am. Studies, U. N.C., 1992, Fulbright fellow, 1993-94. Mem. Am. Polit. Sci. Assn., L.Am. Studies Assn. Office: Boston U Dept IR 152 Bay State Rd Boston MA 02215

THACKER, VASANT MUKUND, obstetrician, gynecologist; b. 1945; MD, Calcutta Nat. Med. Inst. Diplomate Am. Bd. Ob-Gyn. Intern Waltham-Weston Hosp., Waltham, Mass., 1973-74; resident St. Elizabeth Hosp., Brighton, 1974-77; active staff Winchester (Mass.) Hosp.; mem. staff Mt. Auburn Hosp., Cambridge, Mass. Office: 101 Main St Ste 210 Medford MA 02155-4530

THACKERAY, JONATHAN E. lawyer; b. Athens, Ohio, July 30, 1936; s. Joseph Eugene and Betty Rutherford (Boright) T.; m. Sandra Ann McMahon; children: Jennifer, Sara, Amy, Jonathan. AB cum laude, Harvard U., 1958, JD, 1961. Bar: Ohio 1961, U.S. Dist. Ct. (no. dist.) Ohio 1961, U.S. Supreme Ct. 1972, U.S. Ct. Appeals (6th cir.) 1973, U.S. Ct. Appeals (9th cir.) 1982, N.Y. 1993. Assoc. Vorys, Sater, Seymour & Pease, Columbus, Ohio, 1961, Baker & Hostetler, Cleve., 1965-72, ptnr., 1973-93; v.p., gen. counsel The Hearst Corp., N.Y.C., 1993—. Served to lt. USNR, 1961-65. Mem. ABA, Ohio Bar Assn., Cleve. Bar Assn., Am. Law Inst. Office: The Hearst Corp 959 8th Ave New York NY 10019-3795 *Notable cases include: administrative proceedings leading to approval of joint newspaper operating agreements in Cincinnati, Seattle and Las Vegas; litigation of newspaper antitrust cases in Memphis, Trenton and Dallas.*

THACKRAY, ARNOLD WILFRID, historian, foundation executive; b. Eng., July 30, 1939; came to U.S., 1967, naturalized, 1982; s. Wilfrid Cecil and Mary (Clarke) T.; m. Barbara Hughes, 1964 (div. 1990); children: Helen Mary, Gillian Winifrid, Timothy Arnold; m. Diana Schueller, 1994; 1 stepchild, Gregory Jordan. B.Sc., Bristol (Eng.) U., 1960; MA, Cambridge (Eng.) U., 1965, PhD, 1966. Research chemist Robert Dempster and Co., Yorkshire, Eng., 1960-61; research fellow Churchill Coll., Cambridge U., 1965-68; prof. history and sociology of sci. U. Pa., Phila., 1968-96, Joseph Priestley prof. emeritus history/sociology of sci., 1996—, chmn. dept., 1970-77, dir. Beckman Ctr. for History of Chemistry, 1982-96; prof. history, prof. chemistry, dean grad. studies and research U. Md., 1985-86. Exec. dir., libr. Chem. Heritage Found., 1987-96, pres., 1996—; vis. lectr. Harvard U., 1967-68; vis. fellow All Souls Coll., Oxford, Eng., 1977-78; mem. Inst. Advanced Study, 1980. Editor: Isis, an Internat. Rev. of History of Science and its Cultural Influences, 1978-85, Osiris, 1985-94, Science After '40, 1992, Constructing Knowledge in the History of Science, 1995, Private Science, 1998, (with others) Science and Values, 1974, Toward a Metric of Science, 1978; author: Atoms and Powers, 1970, John Dalton, 1972, (with others) Gentlemen of Science, 1981-82, Chemistry in America, 1985, (with others) Arnold O. Beckman, 2000; contbr. articles to profl. jours. Recipient Gladstone Essay prize, also pub. speaking prize Churchill Coll., Cambridge U.; Guggenheim fellow, 1971-72, 85-86; Ctr. for Advanced Study in Behavioral Scis. fellow, 1973-74, 83-84 Fellow AAAS, Am. Acad. Arts and Scis., Royal Hist. Soc., Royal Chem. Soc.; mem. Am. Chem. Soc. (Dexter award 1983), Am. Hist. Assn., Manchester Llt. and Philos. Soc. (corr.), History of Sci. Soc., Am. Coun. Learned Socs. (bd. dirs., treas. 1985-96), Soc. for Social Studies of Sci. (pres. 1981-83), Am. Coun. on Edn. (bd. dirs. 1987), Société Chimie (bd. dirs. 1997—), Cosmos Club (Washington). Episcopalian. E-mail: athackray@chemheritage.org.

THACKSTON, EDWARD LEE, engineer, educator; b. Nashville, Apr. 29, 1937; s. Guy Carleton and Sydney Virginia (Adams) T.; m. Betty Tucker, Mar. 19, 1961; children: Carol Elizabeth Thackston Nixon, Leah Virginia Thackston Hawkins. BE summa cum laude, Vanderbilt U., 1961; MS, U. Ill., 1963; PhD, Vanderbilt U., 1966. Registered profl. engr., Tenn. City engr. City of Lebanon, Tenn., 1959; design engr. City of Nashville, 1961-62; instr. Vanderbilt U., Nashville, 1965-66, asst. prof., 1966-69, assoc. prof., 1969-75, prof. engring., 1975-2000, chmn. dept. civil and environ. engring., 1980-99. Asst. to gov. for environ. affairs, State of Tenn., 1972-74; cons. in field. Author book, tech. reports; contbr. to profl. publs. Bd. dirs. Tenn. Environ. Coun., Nashville, 1971-76; bd. dirs. Tenn. Conservation League, Nashville, 1974—, v.p., 1977, pres., 1978-80; trustee Cumberland Mus., Nashville, 1986-92; trustee Cumberland U., Lebanon, 1996—, mem. exec. com., 1996—2002, sec.-treas., 2000—2002. Recipient Tenn. Lifetime Environ./Conservation Stewardship award State Tenn. 1996, Engr. of Yr. Mid. Tenn. Tenn. Soc. Prof. Engring., 2001, Landmark Paper award Assn. Environ. Engring. and Sci. Profs., 2001; named Tenn. Conservationist of Yr., 1974. Fellow ASCE; mem. Am. Water Works Assn. (life), Water Environ. Fedn. (life), Assn. Environ. Engring. Profs. (Landmark Paper award 2001), Mid. Tenn. Soc. Profl. Engrs. (Engr. of Yr. 2001), Tenn. Hist. Soc., Tau Beta Pi, Chi Epsilon. Republican. Episcopalian. Avocations: genealogy, history, photography. Office: Vanderbilt U PO Box 1831 Nashville TN 37235

THADANI, UDHO, physician, cardiologist; b. Hyderabad, India, Apr. 1, 1941; came to U.S., 1980; s. Vensimal Mulchand and Gopi Thadani; m. Dorothy Ann Thadani, 1974; 1 child, Emma Sarala. MBBS, All India Inst. Med. Scis., New Delhi, 1964. Lic. physician, Okla., Ont., Can., Eng., India; cert. internal medicine, U.K., Can.; cert. cardiology, Can.; diplomate in internal medicine and cardiovasc. diseases Am. Bd. Internal Medicine. Intern All India Inst. Med. Scis., New Delhi, 1964-65, house physician, surgeon, 1965-66; house physician in medicine Joyce Green Hosp., Dartford, Kent, Eng., 1966-67; sr. house physician in medicine Kingston Gen. Hosp., Hull, Eng., 1967-69, registrar, rsch. fellow in medicine and cardiology Eng., 1969-71, U. Leeds (Eng.), The Gen. Infirmary at Leeds, 1971-75; sr. rsch. fellow, clin. asst. medicine Queen's U., Kingston Gen. Hosp., Ont., Can., 1975-78; asst. prof. medicine Queen's U., Kingston, 1978-80; staff physician Kingston Gen. Hosp., 1978-80; assoc. prof. medicine U. Okla. Health Scis. Ctr., Oklahoma City, 1980-83; prof. medicine Okla. U. Health Scis. Ctr., 1983—2001, prof. emeritus medicine, 2001, mem. cardiology fellowship com., 1980-82; dir. clin. cardiology Okla. U. Health Scis. Ctr. and VA Med. Ctr., 1980-87, vice chief cardiovascular sect., 1981-99, dir. clin. rsch., 1987-99. Vice chmn. rsch. and devel. com. VA Med. Ctr., Oklahoma City, 1989-92, chmn. physiology-pharmacology categorical rev. com., 1989-94, chmn. rsch. and devel. com., 1992-94; sr. rsch. fellow Ont. Heart Found., 1978-80, rsch. fellow, 1976-78; rsch. fellow dept. medicine Queen's U., Kingston, Ont., 1975-76; rsch. fellow U. Leeds, Pub. Health and Ciba Found., dept. medicine and cardiovascular sect. Leeds Gen. Infirmary, 1971-75. Editor: Medical Therapy of Ischemic Heart Disease, 1992, Nitrates Updated, 1996; contbr. over 100 articles to profl. jours., chpts. to books; mem. editl. bd. panel Cardiology Drug Facts and Comparison, 1989; contbg. rev. panel Drug Facts and Comparisons, 1989—; mem. editl. bd. Internat. Jour. Cardiology, 1987-93, Cardiovascular Drugs and Therapy, 1987—, Heart Diseases, 1999-, Am. Jour. Pharmacology, 2000-; reviewer Circulation, Jour. Am. Coll. Cardiology, Am. Jour. Cardiology, Brit. Heart Jour., Internat. Jour. Cardiology, Can. Jour. Cardiology, European Heart Jour., Annals of Internal Medicine, New Eng. Jour. Medicine, Archives of Internal Medicine, Cardiovascular Drugs and Therapy, Drugs, European Jour. Pharmacology, Clin. Pharmacology and Therapeutics. Fellow: Royal Coll. Physicians and Surgeons Can., Coun. Clin. Cardiology Am. Heart Assn. (coun. rep. Okla. 1989—2000), Am. Coll. Cardiology (mem. cardiovasc. drug com. 1990—94), Royal Soc. Medicine London, Royal Coll. Physicians Can.; mem.: Can. Cardiovasc. Soc., Royal Coll. Phycisians U.K., Phi Kappa Phi (mem. FDA cardiovasc. and renal drugs adv. com. 1995—99). Avocations: gardening, tennis, travel. Office: Okla U Health Sci Ctr Cardiology Sect 920 SL Young WP 3120 Oklahoma City OK 73104 E-mail: udho-thadani@ouhsc.edu.

THADDEUS, MICHAEL, mathematician, educator; b. N.Y.C., Jan. 12, 1967; s. Patrick and Janice (Farrar) T. AB, Harvard Coll., 1988; PhD, U. Oxford, Eng., 1991. Jr. rsch. fellow St. John's Coll., Oxford, 1991—. Rhodes scholar St. John's Coll., Oxford, 1988, Garside Sr. scholar Corpus Christi Coll., Oxford, 1990. Home: St Johns College Oxford OX1 3JP England Office: Mathematical Inst 24-29 St Giles Oxford OX1 3LB England

THADDEUS, PATRICK, physicist, educator; b. Wilmington, Del., June 6, 1932; s. Victor and Elizabeth (Ross) T.; m. Janice Petherbridge Farrar, Apr. 6, 1963; children: Eva, Michael. B.Sc., U. Del., 1953; MA, Oxford (Eng.) U., 1955; PhD, Columbia U., 1960. Research assoc. Columbia Radiation Lab., 1960-61; research assoc. Goddard Inst. Space Studies, N.Y.C., 1961-63, mem. sci. staff, 1963-86; mem. faculty Columbia U., 1965-86, adj. prof. physics, 1971-86; prof. astronomy and applied physics Harvard U., 1986-2000, Robert Wheeler Willson prof. applied astronomy, 2000—; mem. sci. staff Smithsonian Astrophys. Obs., 1986—. Vis. com. Nat. Radio Astronomy Obs., 1973-76, 91-94; mem. Astronomy Survey Com., 1978-80, 89-90; chair task group on Space Astronomy and Astrophysics, 1996-97; Fairchild Disting. Scholar Calif. Inst. Tech., 1994; Russell Marker lectr. Pa. State U., 1989; vis. fellow Inst. Astronomy, Cambridge, Eng., 1983. Author papers on microwave spectroscopy, optical and radio astronomy. Recipient Exceptional Sci. Achievement medal NASA, 1970, 85; John C. Lindsay Meml. award Goddard Space Flight Center, 1976; Alexander von Humboldt award, 1983; Herschel medal Royal Astron. Soc., 2001; Fulbright fellow, 1953-55. Fellow Am. Phys. Soc.; mem. Am. Astron. Soc., Am. Acad. Arts and Scis., Nat. Acad. Scis., Internat. Astronomical Union, Saturday Club, Sigma Xi. Address: 58 Garfield St Cambridge MA 02138-1802

THADEN, EDWARD CARL, history educator; b. Seattle, Apr. 24, 1922; s. Edward Carl and Astrid (Engvik) T.; m. Marianna Theresia Forster, Aug. 7, 1952. BA, U. Wash., 1944; student, U. Zurich, Switzerland, 1948; PhD, U. Paris, 1950. Instr. Russian history Pa. State U., 1952-55, asst. prof., 1955-58, assoc. prof., 1958-64, prof., 1964-68, prof. emeritus, 1992—. Vis. prof. Ind. U., 1957, U. Marburg, 1965, U. Ill., Urbana, 1980, U. Halle, Germany, 1988, U. Helsinki, Finland, 1990; prof. U. Ill., Chgo., 1968—, chmn. dept. history, 1971—73; editl. cons. Can. Rev. Studies in Nationalism, 1973—78; vis. rsch. scholar USSR Acad. Scis., 1975, 88, 90; project prin. rschr. Ford Found., 1975—78; U.S. rep. Internat. Congress of Hist. Scis., 1980; project dir. NEH grant, 1980—82. Author: Conservative Nationalism in Nineteenth-Century Russia, 1964, Russia and the Balken Alliance of 1912, 1965, Russia Since 1801: The Making of a New Society, 1971, Russia's Western Borderlands, 1710-1870, 1984, Interpreting History: collected Essays on Russia's Relations with Europe, 1990, Essays in Russian and East European History: Festschrift in Honor of Edward C. Thaden, 1995, The Rise of Historicism in Russia, 1999; co-author, editor: Russification in the Baltic Provinces and Finland, 1955-1914, 1981; co-author, co-editor: Finland and the Baltic Provinces in the Russian Empire, 1984; mem. editorial bd. Jour Baltic Studies, 1984-93, assoc. editor, 1987-93, East European Quarterly, 1998—. Served to lt. (j.g.) USNR, 1943-46. Carnegie Inter-Univ. Com. travel grantee to USSR, 1956; Fulbright rsch. grantee Finland, 1957-58, Germany, 1965, Poland and Finland, 1968; Soc. Sci. Rsch. Coun. grantee, 1957; Am. Coun. Learned Socs. grantee, 1963, 65-66; fellow Woodrow Wilson Internat. Ctr. for Scholars, 1980 Mem. Am. Assn. for Advancement Slavic Studies (pres. Midwest br. 1975-76, exec. sec. 1980-82), Chgo. Consortium for Slavic and Ea. European Studies (pres. 1982-84), Baltische Historische Kommission, Göttingen (corr. mem. 1985—), Commn. Internat. des Etudes Historiques Slaves (v.p. 1985-95, pres. 1995-2000, pres.d'honneur 2000—). Office: U Ill Dept History 913 UH (M/C 198) 601 S Morgan St Chicago IL 60607-7100

THAKER, AMISH A. engineer; b. New Delhi, Apr. 28, 1968; came to U.S., 1989; parents Arvind R. and Shashikala A. Thaker BTech, Indian Inst. Tech. Kanpur, India, 1989; MS, U. Va., 1992, PhD, 1997. Rsch. assoc. U. Va., Charlottesville, 1989-97, rsch. scientist, 1998-99; tech. support engr. Fluent Inc., Lebanon, N.H., 1999—. Contbr. papers to profl. jours. Mem. AIAA, Sigma Xi (assoc.). Avocations: R.C. gliders, motorcycles, sports. Office: Fluent Inc 10 Cavendish Ct Lebanon NH 03766-1442 E-mail: aat@fluent.com.

THAKOR, NITISH VYOMESH, biomedical engineering educator; b. Nagpur, India, Feb. 9, 1952; came to U.S., 1976; s. Vyomesh H. and Jayshree V. Thakor; m. Ruchira N. Thakor, Dec. 17, 1983; children: Mitali N., Milan N., Jai N., Vir N. B of Tech., Indian Inst. Tech., Bombay, 1974; PhD, U. Wis., 1981. Engr. Philips India Ltd., Bombay, 1974-76; rsch. asst. U. Wis., Madison, 1977-81; asst. prof. Northwestern U., Evanston, Ill., 1981-83, Johns Hopkins U., Balt., 1984-87, assoc. prof., 1987-94, prof., 1994—. Cons. Biomed. Instrumentation, 1984—. Assoc. editor Jour. Ambulatory Monitoring, Med. Design and Material, 1978—, IEEE Jour. Transactions on Biomed. Engring., IEEE Transactions Info. Tech. Biomedicine, 1988-92, Jour. Biol. Sys., 1993-97; contbr. 120 articles to profl. jours.; patentee in field. Recipient Presdl. Young Investigator award 1985, NIH Rsch. Career Devel. award Centennial medal U. Wis. Sch. Engring.; Fulbright scholar 1987; grantee NSF, NIH, Dept. Edn. Fellow IEEE, Am. Inst. Med. and Biol. Engring.; mem. Sigma Xi. Achievements include devel. of micro-computer-based ambulatory ECG monitor; techniques for arryhythmia detection in implantable pacemakers and defibrillators, neurological signal processing and monitoring instrumentation, medical microsystems and MEMS. Home: 12010 Misty Rise Ct Clarksville MD 21029-1256 Office: Johns Hopkins U Med Sch Biomed Engring Dept 720 Rutland Ave Baltimore MD 21205-2109 E-mail: nthakor@bme.jhu.edu.

THAL, HERBERT LUDWIG, JR. electrical engineer, engineering consultant; b. Mt. Vernon, N.Y., Feb. 15, 1932; s. Herbert Ludwig and Mildred (Martinson) T.; m. Joan Madeline Ragsdale, Jan. 30, 1954; children: Herbert Ludwig III, Wayne, Carolyn, David, Eric. BEE, Rensselaer Poly. Inst., 1953, MEE, 1955, PhDEE, 1962. Rsch. assoc. Rensselaer Poly. Inst., Troy, N.Y., 1953-56; project engr. GE, Schenectady, 1956-67, staff engr. King of Prussia, Pa., 1967-77, mgr. electromagnetics, 1977-89; v.p. Microlab/FXR, Livingston, N.J., 1989-92. Adj. prof. Drexel U., Phila., 1983-90; adj. assoc. prof. U. Pa., Phila., 1986-87. 2d lt. U.S. Army, 1957. Fellow IEEE, Sigma Xi, Tau Beta Pi, Eta Kappa Nu. Presbyterian. E-mail: thal@ieee.org.

THALACKER, ARBIE ROBERT, lawyer, director; b. Marquette, Mich., Apr. 17, 1935; s. Arbie Otto and Jeanne (Emmett) T.; m. Rita Annette Skaaren, Sept. 11, 1956 (div. July 1992); children: Marc Emmett, Christopher Paul, Robert Skaaren; m. Deborah B. Garrett, Jan. 10, 1998. AB, Princeton U., 1957; JD, U. Mich., 1960. Bar: N.Y. 1961, U.S. Ct. Appeals (2d cir.) 1962. Assoc. Shearman & Sterling, N.Y.C., 1960-68, ptnr., 1968—. Dir. Detrex Corp., Detroit, 1981—, chmn. bd., 1993-96. Leader Rep. Dist. Com., 1966-68; v.p., trustee Greenwich Village Soc. for Hist. Preservation; trustee Naropa Univ.; bd. dirs. Meredith Monk House Found., Shambhala Internat. Mem. ABA, N.Y. Bar Assn., Assn. Bar City N.Y. (securities regulatory commn. 1975-78), Wine and Food Soc. (bd. dirs. 1976-78, 85-93, 94—), Chevaliers du Tastevin, Commanderie de Bordeaux, Siwanoy Country Club (bd. govs. 1976-79), Derby Club, Links Club, Verbank Hunting and Fishing Club. Home: 17 Commerce St New York NY 10014-3763 Office: Shearman & Sterling 599 Lexington Ave Fl C2 New York NY 10022-6069

THALDEN, BARRY R. architect; b. Chgo., July 5, 1942; s. Joseph and Sibyl (Goodwin) Hechtenthal; m. Irene L. Mittleman, June 23, 1966 (div. 1989); 1 child, Stacey; m. Kathyn McKnight, Sept. 1996. BArch, U. Ill., 1965; M in Land Architecture, U. Mich., 1969. Landscape architect Hellmuth, Obata, Kassebaum, St. Louis, 1969-70; dir. landscape architecture PGAV Architects, 1970-71; pres. Thalden Corp. Architects, 1971—; ptnr. Thalden-Boyd Architects. Prin. works include Rock Hill Park, 1975 (AIA award, 1977), Wilson Residence, 1983 (AIA award), Nat. Bowling Hall of Fame, 1983 (St. Louis RCGA award, 1984), Village Bogey Hills (Home Builders award, 1985, St. Louis ASLA award, 1994), St. Louis U. Campus Mall (St. Louis ASLA award, 1989), Horizon Casino Resort, Lake Tahoe, Nev., St. Louis Airport's Radisson Hotel, Lady Luck, Treasure Bay, Palace Casinos, Biloxi, Miss., Boomtown Casino, New Orleans, Pres. Casino on the Admiral, St. Louis, Plaza of Champions, Busch Stadium, Ho Chunk Casino, Wisconsin Dells (ABC award Best Bldg. in Wis., 2000), Potowatomi Casino, Milw., Terrible's Casino, Las Vegas. Bd. dirs. St. Louis Open Space Coun., 1973—83, St. Louis Art., Ednl. Coun.; bd. trustees Las Vegas Art Mus.; apptd. Mo. Lands Architect Coun., 1990—94. Named Architect of Yr. Builder Architect mag., 1986. Fellow Am. Soc. Landscape Architects (nat. v.p. 1979-81, pres. St. Louis chpt. 1975, trustee 1976-79, nat. conv. chair 1991); mem. AIA, World Future Soc. (pres. St. Louis chpt. 1984-94, keynote conf. spkr. 1995). Avocations: painting, gardening, tennis, guitar. Home: 2204 Chatsworth Ct Henderson NV 89074-5307 Office: Thalden Corp 7777 Bonhomme Ave Ste 2200 Saint Louis MO 63105-1911

THALER, CRAIG H. lawyer; b. Queens, N.Y., Sept. 13, 1965; s. Michael S. and Karen A. T.; m. Diane P. Heller, Nov. 17, 1991; children: Justin, Eli. BA cum laude, Brandeis U., 1987; JD, Hofstra U., 1990. Bar: N.J. 1990, U.S. Dist. Ct. N.J. 1990, N.Y. 1991. Assoc. Milbank, Tweed, Hadley & McCloy, N.Y.C., 1990-95, Luskin, Stern & Eisler, LLP, N.Y.C., 1995-96; v.p., sr. counsel and asst. sec. IBJ Whitehall Bank & Trust Co., 1996-99, dir. legal svcs., 1999—; sr. v.p., chief legal officer, sec. IBJ Whitehall Bus. Credit Corp., 1999—. Avocations: marathon running, hiking, biking. Office: IBJ Whitehall Bus Credit Corp One State St New York NY 10004 E-mail: cthaler@ibjwhitehall.com.

THALER, RICHARD WINSTON, JR. investment banker; b. Boston, Apr. 9, 1951; s. Richard Winston and Victoria Louise (Sears) T.; m. Mary Alice Gast, June 28, 1980; children: Julia Davis, Sarah Sears, Hannah Warren. BA in Am. Polit. History cum laude, Princeton U., 1973; MBA, Harvard U., 1978. Salesman Media Networks, N.Y.C., 1973-74; banker Bank of Boston, Rio de Janeiro, 1975-77, Boston, 1978-80; mng. dir. investment banking Lehman Bros., N.Y.C., 1980-96, Deutsche Banc Securities, N.Y.C., 1996—. Spl. gifts solicitor Princeton U. Ann. Giving, N.Y.C., 1987-88, 97-98, class agt., 1988-93; del. Dem. Nat. Conv., 1996; trustee Daily Princetonian, 1989—, Episc. Divinity Sch., Cambridge, Mass., 1995—; mem. vestry Chapel of St. James the Fisherman, Wellfleet, Mass.; trustee at large Plimouth Plantation, Plymouth, Mass., 1995—; active Dem. Leadership Coun. Mem. Mass. Soc. Mayflower Descendants, Harvard Club, Siwanoy Country Club, University Cottage Club. Democrat. Episcopalian. Avocations: gardening, sailing, Am. polit. hist., exotic travel.

THALHOFER, PAUL TERRANCE, lawyer; b. Eugene, Oreg., Oct. 27, 1954; s. Paul Albert and Elizabeth Ann (Wathen) T.; m. Cindy Ann Whitney, Aug. 7, 1977; 1 child, Brian Allen. BA, U. Colo., 1977; JD, U. Oreg., 1986. Disbursing fin. officer USMC, Okinawa, Japan, 1978-79, El Toro, Calif., 1979-80, Tustin, 1980-83; with law program dept. U. Oreg. USMC, Eugene, 1983-86; prosecuting atty. USMC, Camp Pendleton, Calif., 1986-87, def. atty., 1987, adminstrv. law atty., 1988-90, operational law atty., 1989-90, sr. legal advisor Marine Air Contingency Force Honduras, 1988; trial team leader Legal Team Delta/USMC, Camp Pendleton, Calif., 1990; legal advisor to commanding gen. USMC Forces/Operation Desert Shield, Saudi Arabia, 1990; legal advisor to comdg. gen. 3d marine aircraft ops. Desert Shield/Storm Wing, Bahrain, Saudi Arabia, 1990-91; trial team leader Legal Team Delta, Camp Pendleton, Calif., 1991-92; civil litigation atty. Bullivant, Houser, Bailey, Pendergrass & Hoffman, Portland, Oreg., 1992-93; assoc. Reif & Reif, Canby, 1993-95; ptnr. Reif, Reif & Thalhofer, 1996—. Adv. I Marine Expeditionary Force Augmentation Command Element, Camp Pendleton, Calif., 1996—. Lt. col. USMCR. Mem. Oreg. State Bar Assn., Clackamas County Bar Assn., Computer Law Assn., Vaquero Riding Club (pres. 1983), Phi Delta Phi (v.p. chpt. 1985-86). Avocations: skiing, golf, fishing. Home: 335 SE 7th Way Canby OR 97013-8763 Office: Reif Reif & Thalhofer 273 N Grant St Canby OR 97013-3697

THALL, BURNETT MURRAY, retired newspaper executive; b. Toronto, Ont., Can., Sept. 27, 1922; s. Henry and Selina (Harris) Rosenthal; m. Eleanor Langbord, Sept. 23, 1945; children: Nelson Spencer, Martin Evan. BASc., U. Toronto, 1945, MASc., 1947, PhD, 1949. Registered profl. engr., Ont. Spl. lectr. applied sci. and engring. U. Toronto, 1947; cons. engr., then prodn. engr. Toronto Star, 1947-50, v.p., 1958-68, sr. v.p., 1968-96, also dir. Chmn. Toronto Star Newspapers Ltd., elected chmn. bd., 1996-99. Trustee Atkinson Charitable Found.; hon. trustee Women's Coll. Hosp. Urgent Care Ctr.; founding trustee Princess Margaret Hosp. Urgent Care Centre named in his honour Women's Coll. Hosp., 1989. Mem. Assn. Profl. Engrs. Ont. (Citizenship medal 1991). Home: 15 Rosemary Ln Toronto ON Canada M5P 3E7 Office: The Toronto Star 1 Yonge ST Toronto ON Canada M5E 1E6

THALL, RICHARD VINCENT, school system administrator; b. San Francisco, Sept. 12, 1940; s. Albert Vincent and Alice Stella (O'Brien) T.; m. Ellyn Marie Wisherop, June 15, 1963; children: Kristen Ellyn, Richard Vincent Jr. AA, City Coll. San Francisco, 1961; BA, San Francisco State Coll., 1964; MA, San Francisco State U., 1971. Cert. elem. tchr., Calif.; cert. secondary tchr., Calif.; cert. community coll. tchr., Calif. Tchr. biology San Francisco Unified Sch. Dist., 1965-66, Mt. Diablo Unified Sch. Dist., Concord, Calif., 1966-79, program dir. water environ. studies program, 1979—. Ranger/naturalist State of Calif., Brannan Island, 1973-78; naturalist Adventure Internat., Oakland, Calif., 1979-81; lectr. Princess Cruise Lines, 1982—, Sea Goddess, 1986—, Sun Lines, 1987, Sitmar Lines, 1989, Royal Caribbean Internat., 1989—; lectr. naturalist Posh Talks, Inc., 1982—; spkr. commencements U. Calif., Berkeley, 1989. Author: Ecological Sampling of the Sacramento-San Joaquin Delta, 1976; Water Environment Studies Program, 1986; co-author: Project MER Laboratory Manual, 1982. Mem. Contra Costa County (Calif.) Natural Resources Commn., 1975-78, vice-chmn., 1977-78; active Save Mt. Diablo, Concord, 1969-76, v.p., 1974-75; mem. citizens com. Assn. Bay Area Govt. Water Quality, 1979-82, vice-chmn., 1980-82; active John Marsh Home Restoration Com., Martinez, Calif., 1977-78; troop com. chmn. Boy Scouts Am., Concord, 1984-86, asst. scoutmaster, 1985-87. Recipient Recognition and Excellence cert. Assn. Calif. Sch. Adminstrs., 1984, Wood Badge award Boy Scouts Am., 1986; grantee State Calif., 1982, 84, San Francisco Estuary Project, 1992, EPA, 1992, Shell Oil Co., 1993. Mem. AAAS, Nat. Assn. Biology Tchrs., Nat. Audubon Soc., Am. Mus. Natural Hist., Nat. Geog. Soc., Smithsonian Instn. (assoc.). Republican. Roman Catholic. Avocations: skiing, jogging, reading, hiking, photography. Home: 1712 Lindenwood Dr Concord CA 94521-1109 Office: Mt Diablo Unified Sch Dist 1936 Carlotta Dr Concord CA 94519-1358 E-mail: rothall@aol.com.

THALL, ROBERT, photographer, educator; b. Chgo., Dec. 6, 1948; BA in Design, U. Ill., 1972, MFA in Photography, 1986. Prof. photography Columbia Coll., Chgo., 1976—, chmn. Photography Dept. Vis. artist U. Ill., Chgo., 1975; adj. asst. prof. art U. Ill., Chgo., 1980; lectr. in field. One-person shows include Evanston (Ill.) Art Ctr., 1980, Morning Art and Dance Ctr., Chgo., 1980, Edwynn Houk Gallery, Chgo., 1984, Art Inst. Chgo., 1994, Ehlers Caudill Gallery, Chgo., 1995, City of Chgo. Photography Gallery at Water Tower, 1999, Mus. Contemporary Photography, 1999; exhibited in group shows at Hodges Taylor Gallery, Charlotte, N.C., 1996, Mus. Contemporary Art, Chgo., 1996, Mus. Van Bommel-Van Dam, Venlo, The Netherlands, 1997, Milw. Art Mus., 1999, others; curated exhbns. include Truman Coll., 1980, Chgo. Ctr. Contemporary Photography, Columbia Coll., 1983; commns. include Historic Bldgs. Iowa, 1976, Ctrl. Mfg. Dist., 1983, Midway Airport Pub. Art Competition, 1999, others; represented in permanent collections Art Inst. Chgo., Calif. Mus. Photography, Riverside, Calif., Can. Ctr. Arch., Montreal, Chgo. Hist. Soc., Getty Ctr. History Art and Humanities, Santa Monica, Calif., Hallmark Collection, Kansas City, Mo., Milw. Art Mus., Mus. Fine Art, Houston, Mus. Folkwang, Essen, Germany, Mus. Modern Art, N.Y.C., Seagram Collection, N.Y.C., Victoria and Albert Mus., London, others; book and exhbn. reviewer Exposure and New Art Examiner, 1980-83; publs. include The Perfect City, 1994, The New American Village, 1999, City Spaces, 2002. Project Completion grantee Ill. Arts Coun., 1980; Graham Found. grantee, 1998; John Simon Guggenheim Meml. Found. fellow, 1998. Office: Columbia Coll Dept Photography 600 S Michigan Ave Chicago IL 60605-1900

THAM, HILARY, poet; b. Kelang, Malaysia, Aug. 20, 1946; d. Sun Hong Tham and Tuck Khoon Oo; m. Joseph Ray Goldberg, May 20, 1945; children: Ilana P., Shoshana M., Rebecca S. BA in English Lit., U. Malaysia, 1971. Poet-in-residence Howard County Poetry & Literacy Soc., Columbia, Md., 1993-94; artist-in-edn. Va. commn. Arts, Richmond, 1990—, The Kennedy Ctr. for Performing Arts, N.Y.C., 1999—; poet-in-residence Arlington-Fairfax (Va.) Jewish Congregation, 2000—; poetry editor Potomac Rev., Port Tobacco, Md., 1995—; editor-in-chief The Word Works, Inc., Washington, 1995—. Panel judge Va. Commn. Arts, 1994-98, Md. Arts Coun., Balt., 1986-97, N.J. Grants Mid-Atlantic Arts Found., Balt., 1997-98. Author of poems. Chair Coalition for Resettlement IndoChinese Refugees, Arlington, 1979-80; pres. sisterhood Arlington-Fairfax Jewish Congregation, 1988-89, pres., 1990-93, v.p., 1992-96. Artist-in-Edn. grantee Va. Commn. Arts, 1990-2001. Mem. Writer's Ctr. Avocations: painting, travel.

THAMES, SHELBY FRELAND, science educator; b. Miss., Aug. 10, 1936; m. Shirley D. Thames; children: Scott F., Dana G., Clay B. BS in Chemistry, U. So. Miss., 1959, MS in Chemistry, 1961; PhD in Organic Chemistry, U. Tenn., 1964. From asst. to full prof. polymer sci. U. So. Miss., 1964—, disting. univ. rsch. prof., 1986—, So. Soc. for Coatings Tech. disting. prof., 1992-96, founder, first chair polymer sci. dept., dean Coll. Sci. and Tech., v.p. adminstrn. and regional campuses, exec. v.p. Founder, exec. dir. Internat. Coatings and Formulations Inst.. Contbr. articles to profl. jours. Shelby Freland Thames Polymer Sci. Rsch. Ctr. named in his honor U. So. Miss., 1998. Mem. N.Am. Indsl. Hemp Coun., Inc (bd. mem. 1999-2000), Am. Oil Chemists Soc., Am. Chem. Soc., Fedn. Socs. for Coatings Tech., Soc. Plastics Engrs., So. Soc. for Coatings Tech., New Uses Coun. (past chair, Wheeler McMillan award 1998), Assn. for the Advancement Indsl. Crops (Anson Ellis Thompson Career Achievement award 1999) , Powder Coatings Inst. Achievements include patents for 8 in field. Home: 103 Darby Rd Hattiesburg MS 39402-2307 Office: Univ So Miss Box 10037 Hattiesburg MS 39406-0037 E-mail: Shelby.F.Thames@usm.edu.

THAMES, STEPHEN A. sales executive, writer, composer; b. Cortland, N.Y., June 25, 1955; s. Ray C. and Mary B. Thames; m. Kelly M. Thames, Aug. 15, 1980. BA in Bus., SUNY, 1978. Author: The State I'm In, 2001; composer: Wildly Alive with Music, 2001, Andrew James Instructional CD, 2001. Republican. Home: PO Box 884 Cortland NY 13045

THAMHAIN, HANS JURGEN, finance educator, researcher; b. Dresden, Saxony, Germany, Oct. 1, 1936; s. Hans Florenz Thamhain, Martha Thamhain; m. Ingrid Katharina Schwoch; children: Petra Lively, Thilo. BSEE, Ingenieurschule Koblenz, Germany, 1961; MSEE, U. Waterloo, Can., 1967; MBA, Syracuse U., 1972, PhD in Bus. Adminstrn., 1974. Elec. engr. Standard Electric Co.,ITT, Pforzheim, Germany, 1961—64, Westinghouse Corp., Hamilton, Canada, 1964—67; project mgr. Gen. Electric Co., Syracuse, NY, 1967—75; bus. mgr. GTE/Verizon, Needham, Mass., 1975—81; assoc. prof. mgmt. Worcester Polytech. Inst., Worchester, 1981—87; prof. mgmt. Bentley Coll., Waltham, 1987—, dir. project mgmt. programs, 1987—. Cons. tech. and project mgmt. with numerous worldwide cos., 1981—; vis. prof., guest lectr. numerous univs. and insts., 1981—. Author: Project Management for Small and Medium-Size Businesses, 1984, Engineering Program Management, 1985, Project Management Operating Guidelines, 1986 (Nat. Book award, AAP, 1993), Engineering Management, 1993; contbr. articles; seven patents, Germany, Can, and U.S. Scholar, Fulbright, 1998. Mem.: IEEE (life; Editorial Board 1985—date, Engrng. Mgr. of Year 2000), Project Mgmt. Inst. (Publications Advisory Board 1990—93, Dist. Contbn. award for Mgmt. Rsch. 1998, cert. project mgmt. profl. 1988), Am. Soc. Engrng. Mgmt. (Editorial Board 1987—date), Product Develop. Mgmt. Assn. (Publications Review Board 1990—date, cert. new product develop. profl. 2001), Phi Beta Delta. Avocations: ironman triathlete, marathons. Home: 25 Lanewood Ave Framingham MA 01701-3660 Office: Bentley Coll Forest St Waltham MA Home Fax: 781-891-2896; Office Fax: (781) 891-2896. Personal E-mail: hthamhain@bentley.edu. Business E-Mail: hthamhain@bentley.edu.

THAMPI, MOHAN VARGHESE, environmental health and civil engineer; b. Kuching, Sarawak, Malaysia, Mar. 25, 1960; s. Padmanabha Ramachandran and Sosamma (Varghese) T. Gen. Cert. Edn., Cambridge U., 1976; B in Tech. with honors, Indian Inst. Tech., Kharagpur, India, 1983; MS in Engrng., U. Tex., 1985; DSc (hon.), London Inst. Applied Rsch., 1992. Registered profl. engr., Tex., Fla., registered environ. mgr.; cert. safety tng. OSHA; cert. Nat. Coun. Examiners for Engrs. and Surveyors. Assoc. engr. Brown & Caldwell, Dallas, 1985-87, project mgr. Orlando, 1987-88, Stottler Stagg & Assocs., Cape Canaveral, Fla., 1988-91; sr. project engr. Chastain-Skillman, Inc., Lakeland, 1991-93; project mgr. Glace & Radcliffe, Inc., Winter Park, 1993-94; mgr. FDEP, West Palm Beach, 1995-96; project mgr. Office of Capital Projects Mgmt., Naples, 1996—. Author: Ultraviolet Disinfection Studies in a Teflon-Tube Reactor, 1985; contbr. articles to profl. jours. Active Rep. Pres.'s Citizens Adv. Comm., 1992. Recipient Cert. of Cont. Profl. Devel. award Fla. Engrng. Soc., 1992. Mem. NRA, NSPE, ASCE (assoc.), Project Mgmt. Inst., Internat. Assn. Water Pollution Rsch. and Control, Am. Mensa, Am. Water Works Assn., Water Pollution Control Fedn. (com. for preparing design practice manuals 1989—), Internat. Freelance Photographers Assn., Internat. Platform Assn., Internat. Assn. Air Travel Couriers, Am. Mgmt. Assn., Am. Smokers Alliance, Am. Gunsmithing Assn., Smithsonian Instn., Nat. Geog. Soc., Nat. Registry Environ. Professionals, U. Tex. Ex-Students Assn., Wine Soc. Am., Nat. Family Opinion, Internat. Deep Purple Appreciation Soc., Wilson Ctr. Assocs., I.I.T. Kharagpur Tech. Found., NASA Tech Briefs Reader Opinion Panel, Chemical Engring. Jour. Product Rsch. Panel, Nat. Rifle Assn., Plant Engrng. Editl. Quality Panel, Kharagpur Tech. Alumni Found., N.Am. Hunting Club, Knight Order of Templars (Jerusalem), PC Bug Computer Club. Mar Thoma Syrian Christian. Avocations: photography, music, travel, sports. Home: PO Box 11954 Naples FL 34101-2954 E-mail: thampimv@juno.com.

THANIKACHALAM, MOHAN, surgeon; b. Madras, Tamilnadu, India, Feb. 25, 1967; s. Sadagopan and Chandra Thanikachalam. B Medicine B Surgery, Kasturba Med. Coll., Manipal, India, 1991; MD, U.S. Med. Licensure Exam., 1992. Diplomate Am. Bd. Surgery, lic. physician. Transitional intern Carney Hosp./Boston U., 1993-94; surg. intern St. Elizabeth Med. Ctr./Tufts U., Boston, 1994-95, surg. resident, 1995-98, surg. chief resident, 1998-99, postdoctoral assoc., 1999—. Nat. rep. candidate assoc. soc. Am. Coll. Thoracic Sugery Coun. Contbr. articles to profl. jours. Rep. Student Coun. Mangalore U., Manipal, India, 1989. Recipient Thoracic Surgery Rsch. Fellowship award Thoracic Surgery Found. award, 2000—, Fellowship award Am. Heart Assn., 2000—. Fellow ACS (assoc., rep. candidate and associate soc. coun. reps.); mem. Internat. Soc. Heart and Lung Transplantation. Home: 300 Galen Dr Apt 302 Key Biscayne FL 33149-2149 Office: U Miami Dept Cardiothoracic Surgery ET 3072 1161 NW 12th Ave Miami FL 33136 E-mail: mthanika@med-miami.edu.

THANOS, DANIEL, retired obstetrician-gynecologist; b. 1919; BA, Syracuse U., 1941, MD, 1943. Intern Harper Hosp., Detroit, 1944, St. Joseph Hosp., Syracuse, N.Y., 1946-47; resident ob-gyn. U. Hosps., Cleve., 1947-49, chief resident obstetrics, 1949-50, chief resident gynecology, 1950-51; attending ob-gyn. U. Hosp. Cleve.-Lake County Hosp. Sys.; ret. Active Mil., 1944-46. Decorated Bronze star and commendation medal. Fellow Am. Coll. Ob-Gyn.; mem. AMA, Am. Bd. Ob-Gyn. (diplomate). Home: 38898 Andrews Pl Willoughby OH 44094-7829

THAPA, KHAGENDRA, survey engineering educator; b. Murtidhunga, Dhankuta, Nepal, Oct. 16, 1950; came to U.S., 1982; s. Ranadhoj and Krishna (Basnet) T.; m. Rajani Basnet, July 7, 1981; children: Samrat, Birat, Charisma. BSc, Tribhuran U., Kathmandu, Nepal, 1973, U. East London, 1978; MSCE, U. N.B., Fredericton, Can., 1980; MS, Ohio State U., 1985, PhD, 1987. Rsch. asst. U. N.B., Fredericton, 1978-80; researcher Geodetic Survey Can., Ottawa, 1980; lectr. Engrng. Inst. Tribhuvan U., Kathmandu, 1980-82; teaching/rsch. assoc. Ohio State U., Columbus, 1982-87; assoc. prof. Ferris State U., Big Rapids, Mich., 1987-91, prof., program coord. Coll. Tech., 1991—. Rschr. Ctr. for Mapping, Columbus, Ohio, 1990; cons. Techs., Archs. and Engrs. Consultancy, Kathmandu, 1980-82; chairperson Engrng. Topographic Mapping Com. Am. Soc. Photogrammetry and Remote Sensing, Washington, 1991—; evaluator accreditation bd. for engrng. and tech. Engrng. Accreditation Commn. Recipient Disting. Prof. award Mich. Assn. Governing Bd., 1996, Provost award for excellence; grantee NSF, Washington, 1989, 91. Mem. Royal Instn. Chartered Surveyors (rsch. grant 1988-89), Am. Congress on Surveying and Mapping, Am. Soc. Photogrammetry, Inst. Navigation, Geodetic Sci. Club (v.p. 1985-86). Achievements include devising a new technique to find inconsistent observations and constraints in horizontal networks, using linear programming in optimal design of leveling networks, devising a new method of line generalization in computer cartography and digital mapping; worked on critical points detection and data compression using zero-crossings; analysed the accuracy of spatial data used in geographic information system. Home: 20796 Edgewood Dr Big Rapids MI 49307-9024 Office: Ferris State U Coll Tech Surveying Engrng Program 915 Campus Dr Rm 312 Big Rapids MI 49307-2291

THARALDSON, GARY DEAN, hotel developer and owner; b. Valley City, N.D., Oct. 17, 1945; BA in Phys. Edn., Valley City State U.; postgrad., N.D. State U. Tchr., Leonard, N.D.; ins. agt., agy. owner, 1969-89; owner of 340 hotels, Valley City, 1982; pres. Tharaldson Enterprises, Fargo, N.D., 1982—. Office: Tharaldson Enterprises 1202 Westrac Dr Fargo ND 58103-2344

THARNEY, LAURA CHRISTINE, lawyer; b. New Brunswick, N.J., June 19, 1965; d. Thaddeus Raphael and Madeline Kay (Baumann) T. AA in Liberal Arts, Union County Coll., 1984; BA in History, Rutgers U., 1986, JD, 1991. Bar: N.J. 1991, U.S. Dist. Ct. N.J. 1991, N.Y. 1992. With Specialized Legal Svcs., N.Y. and N.J., 1991-96; dep. county counsel Office of Middlesex County Counsel, New Brunswick, 1992-94; assoc. Law Offices of Edward J. Buzak, Montville, N.J., 1994-95, Heine Assocs., P.A., Cherry Hill, 1995-96; pvt. practice Law Office of Laura C. Tharney, Milltown, 1996—. Mem. ABA, N.J. State Bar Assn. (mentor 1994—), N.Y. Bar Assn., Morris County Bar Assn. (mentor, mediator 1994—), Middlesex County Bar Assn., Phi Alpha Theta. Avocations: running, rock climbing, scuba diving. Office: 555 State Route 18 # 219 East Brunswick NJ 08816-3727

THARNEY, LEONARD JOHN, education educator, consultant; b. New Haven, Nov. 6, 1929; s. Lillian A. Batey; m. Denise A. Gauvin, June 20, 1981; children: Karen L., Linda L. BS, Trenton (N.J.) State Coll., 1954; MEd, Rutgers U., 1959; postgrad., Lehigh U., Bethlehem, Pa., 1963-70, Columbia U.; grad., Command & Gen. Staff Coll., Ft. Leavenworth, Kans., 1972. Cert. secondary math. and sci. tchr., elem. tchr. Tchr. (elem. demonstration) Trenton State Coll., 1954-60; tchr. (jr. high demonstration) Ewing Twp. (N.J.) Schs., 1960-63; cons., evaluator Am. Coun. on Edn., Washington, 1975-95, field coord., 1995—; cons., evaluator Mid. States Assn., Phila., 1987—; prof. Trenton State Coll., 1963-92, prof. emeritus, 1993—, dept. chmn., 1988-92. Cons. to internat. schs. for curriculum or sci. edn., Monrovia, Accra, Athens, Mogadishu, Cairo, Alexandria, Aleppo, Damascus, 1975—; tchr. grad. courses in curriculum and ednl. rsch. at overseas sites, Spain, Cyprus, Saudi Arabia, Syria, 1981—; exch. prof. Worcester Coll. Higher Edn., Eng., 1984-85; presenter sci. edn. workshops, AISA Internat. Conf., Nairobi, 1987; rep. from Coll. to Prins. Tng. Ctr., London, 1994; bd. dirs. Trenton, N.J. chpt. People to People Internat., 1995-98, chpt. pres., 1998—; N.J. del. Worldwide Conf. of People to People Internat., Chester, Eng., 1998, Hong Kong, 2000, Aalborg, Denmark, 2001, Kansas City, Mo., 2002, internat. trustee, 2000; 15th World Wide Conf. del., Kansas City, Mo., 2002, mem. Accrediting Commn. of the Distance Education and training Council, Wash., D.C., 2000—. Co-author 7 manuals for uniform constrn. codes. Col. AUS, 1947-81. Recipient ACE award for outstanding svc. in mil. evaluations, 1987, cert. of appreciation, presdl. citation, 1989, spl. plaque award, others, Outstanding Svc. and Support award 112th FA Assn., 1998; decorated meritorious svc. medal U.S. Army, 1981. Mem.: ASCD, Nat. Coun. Social Studies, Assn. for Edn. Tchrs. in Sci., Assn. Tchr. Educators, Am. Air Mus. in Britain (founding mem.), Torch Club Internat. (bd. dirs. 1998—2001, v.p. 2001—02, pres. Trenton club 2002—). Home: 20 Lawrenceville-Penning Rd Lawrenceville NJ 08648-1648

THARP, BENJAMIN CARROLL, JR. retired architect; b. Austin, Tex., Sept. 3, 1919; s. Benjamin Carroll Tharp and Norris (Ophelia) Wallis; m. Mae Sibley; children: Ronald Emery, Carolyn Jeanine Tharp Love. BArch, U. Tex., 1943. Registered architect, Tex. Draftsman Wurdeman & Beckett, L.A., 1944, Richard Neutra, L.A., 1945, Merrill Baird, L.A., 1946, Golemon & Rolfe, Houston, 1947, Milton Foy Martin, Houston, 1948; prin. Koetter & Tharp, 1949-64, Koetter, Tharp & Cowell, Houston, 1964-78; architect Koetter, Tharp, Cowell and Lockwood, Andrews, Newnam, 1978-81; ret. Lockwood, Andrews, Newnam, 1981. Bd. dirs. Harris County Soil and Water Conservation Dist., Houston, 1972-82; pres. Constrn. Industry Coun., Houston, 1970 Recipient 1st Restoration award Red Cedar Shingle and Handsplit Shake Bur./AIA, Seattle, 1975 Fellow AIA, Tex. Soc. Architects (chmn. hist. resources com. 1986); mem. Montgomery (Tex.) Hist. Soc., Optimist Club (pres. Houston chpt. 1970). Republican. Baptist. Home: 10410 Honea Egypt Rd Montgomery TX 77316-2489

THARP, CHRISTINE M. lawyer; 1 child Caseyann. JD, St. Mary's Sch. Law, 1980. Bar: Tex. 1980; cert. in family law Tex. Bd. Legal Specialization, 1988. Law clk. Mex. Am. Legal Def. and Edn. Fund, San Antonio, 1979; staff atty. Law Offices Charles Campion, 1979-86; of counsel Nicholas and Barrera, Inc., 1986-89; pvt. practice, 1989—. Bd. dirs. pro bono law project mem. Bexar County Legal Aid, 1988-89, adv. bd., 1988; vol. instr. for tng. Child Advocates fo San Antonio, 1990-91; mem. Bexar County Child Support Com., 1995; co-chair Bachelor Auction, March of Dimes. Named to Outstanding Young Women of Am., 1980; recipient Cert. of Appreciation, San Antonio Foster Parents. Mem. ABA (family law sect., entertainment law sect.), ATLA (Nat. Coll. Advocacy), Tex. Acad. Family Specialists, Bexar County Women's Bar Assn. (charter, bd. dirs. 1986-90, 92, bd. dirs. Women's Bar Found. 1989-90, 92, pub. rels. chair 1991-92), Am. Profl. Soc. on Abuse of Children, Nat. Assn. of Counsel for Children, San Antonio Family Lawyers Bar Assn. (bd. dirs. 1994—, treas. 1995-96, v.p. 1997-98, pres. 1998-99), San Antonio Bar Assn. (family law sect., fee dispute com. 1983—, chair 1987-88, 88-89), Tex. Trial Lawyers Assn. (author/lectr.), State Bar of Tex. (family law sect., lectr., mem. Coll. of the bar 1989—), Christian Legal Soc., Delta Theta Phi. Baptist. Office: 6217 Broadway St San Antonio TX 78209-4562

THARP, JAMES WILSON, lawyer; b. Hoisington, Kans., Nov. 22, 1942; s. James Alfred and Jeanette B. (Wilson) Tharp Adams; children: Jennifer, Juliana, Damien. AB, U. Kans., 1965, JD, 1968. Bar: Kans. 1968, U.S. Dist. Ct. Kans. 1968, Ohio 1969, U.S. Ct. Appeals (10th cir.) 1969, U.S. Dist. Ct. (so. dist.) 1970, U.S. Ct. Appeals (6th cir.) 1974, Hawaii 1977, U.S. Dist. Ct. Hawaii 1977, U.S. Ct. Appeals (9th cir.) 1977, U.S. Supreme Ct. 1978, No. Mariana Islands 1978, U.S. Dist. Ct. No. Mariana Islands 1978, U.N. Trust Territory Pacific Islands, 1978, Rep. of Marshall Island, 1983. Asst. atty. gen State of Ohio, 1969-70; gen. counsel Ohio Dept. Edn., 1970-72; pvt. practice Columbus, Ohio, 1972-74; counsel FHA, Columbus and L.A., 1974-76; area counsel HUD, 1976-79; pvt. practice law, Honolulu, 1979—; real estate broker Hawaii, 1980—. Adminstrv. hearing officer State of Hawaii, 1984—; arbitrator Hawaii Judiciary, 1987—; bd. dirs., chief academic advisor Pacific Western U. Dir., v.p. Hawaii Literacy, Inc., 1988-91; dir. Hawaii State Theatre Coun., 1988-93. Lever Brothers scholar, Scholarship Hall scholar, 1960-61. Mem. SAG, Hawaii Bar Assn. (rep. Gov.'s Coun. for Literacy 1987-91), Kansas Club Hawaii (gov. 1983-84), Masons. Avocations: reading, acting. Office: 1210 Auahi St Ste 104 Honolulu HI 96814-4922

THARP, KAREN ANN, insurance agent; b. Montpelier, Ohio, Sept. 24, 1944; d. Howard Wesley and Thelma (Myers) Skiles; children: Pamela Lyn Tharp Grasso, James Alan, Jennifer Ann Tharp McCue. Grad. high sch., Edon, Ohio. Sales agt. Equitable Life, Delray Beach, Fla., 1978-79; owner, pres. Fin. Profiles, Inc., Coral Springs, 1980—. Mem. Nat. Assn. Life Underwriters, Million Dollar Round Table. Republican. Avocations: sewing, art, spa. Home: 7306 NW 127th Way Parkland FL 33076-1980 Office: Fin Profiles Inc 10101A W Sample Rd Coral Springs FL 33065-3937 E-mail: INSpays@aol.com.

THARP, RICHARD, athletic director; b. Mar. 10, 1948; m. Melinda Siebert; children: Travis, Taylor, Tucker. BA, DePauw U., 1970; JD, U. Colo., 1973. Asst. univ. counsel Colo. U., 1973-76, v.p., univ. counsel, 1989-95; ptnr. Martin and Mehaffy, 1984-89. Former bd. dirs. Boulder Cmty. Hosp. Found., 1986-90, dir. Lifecare Internat., 1985—. Recipient British Blue, 1969. Mem. Colo. Bar Assn., Alumni C-Club (hon.). Office: Univ Colorado 368 UCB Boulder CO 80309-0368

THARP, ROLAND GEORGE, psychology, education educator; b. Galveston, Tex., June 6, 1930; s. Oswald Roland and Berma Lucille (Keefer) T.; m. Stephanie Dalton; children: Donald Martin, Thomas Roland, David Michael, Julie. Student, Middlebury Coll., 1956, 60; BA cum laude, U. Houston, 1957; MA, U. Mich., 1958, PhD, 1961. Cert. Am. Bd. Examiners in Profl. Psychology. Reporter Tex. City Sun, 1946-47; mgr. Tharp Lumber Co., LaMarque, Tex., 1949-54; intern VA Hosp., Menlo Park, Calif., 1960; asst. prof. U. Ariz., Tucson, 1961-65, assoc. prof., 1965-68; prof., dir. clin. studies, dir. multicultural ctr. for higher edn. U. Hawaii, Honolulu, 1968-87; provost and v.p. for acad. affairs U.S. Internat. U., San Diego, 1987-89; prof. edn., psychology U. Calif., Santa Cruz, 1990—; dir. Nat. Rsch. Ctr. for Diversity, 1995—. Dir. Ctr. for Rsch. on Edn., Diversity and Excellence, 1996—; prin. investigator Kamehameha Early Edn. Program, Honolulu, 1969-89; field selection officer Peace Corps, Washington, 1965-67. Author: (poetry) Highland Station, 1978; co-author: Behavior Modification in the Natural Environment, 1969, Self-Directed Behavior, 1980, Rousing Minds to Life, 1988, Teaching Transformed, 2000; writer, producer, dir. film Scenes from the Life, 1981 (Purchase prize The Contemporary Mus. 1981). Mem. Bd. Psychologist Examiners, Ariz., 1964-67; pres. Hawaii Literary Arts Coun., Honolulu, 1982. Robert Frost fellow Middlebury Coll., 1960; recipient Am. Film Mag. award for filmmaking Hawaii Internat. Film Festival, 1990, Grawemeyer award edn., 1993. Mem. Am. Ednl. Rsch. Assn., Am. Anthropol. Assn. Episcopalian. Avocations: tennis, painting. Office: U Calif CREDE 1156 High St Santa Cruz CA 95064-1077

THARP, TWYLA, dancer, choreographer; b. Portland, Ind., July 1, 1941; m. Peter Young (div.); m. Robert Huot (div.); 1 child, Jesse. Student, Pomona Coll.; BA in Art History, Barnard Coll., 1963; D of Performing Arts (hon.), Calif. Inst. Arts, 1978, Brown U., 1981, Bard Coll., 1981; LHD, Ind. U., 1987; DFA, Pomona Coll., 1987; studied with Richard Thomas, Merce Cunningham, Igor Schwezoff, Louis Mattox, Paul Taylor, Margaet Craske, Erick Hawkins. Dancer Paul Taylor Dance Co., 1963-65; freelance choreographer with own modern dance troupe and various other cos. including Joffrey Ballet and Am. Ballet Theatre, 1965-87; founder, choreographer Twyla Tharp Dance Found., N.Y.C., 1965-87; artistic assoc., resident choreographer Am. Ballet Theatre, 1987-91; teaching residencies various colls. and univs. including U. Mass., Oberlin Coll., Walker Art Ctr., Boston U. Choreographer White Oak Dance Project. Choreographer: Tank Dive, 1965, Re-Moves, 1966, One Two Three, 1966, Forevermore, 1967, Generation, 1968, Medley, 1969, After Suite, 1969, Dancing in the Streets of London and Paris, 1969, The One Hundreds, 1970, The Fugue, 1970, The Bix Pieces, 1971, Eight Jelly Rolls, 1971, The Raggedy Dances, 1972, Deuce Coupe, 1973, As Time Goes By, 1974, Sue's Leg, 1975, Ocean's Motion, 1975, Push Comes to Shove, 1976, Once More Frank, 1976, Mud, 1977, Baker's Dozen, 1979, When We Were Very Young, 1980, Nine Sinatra Songs, 1982, The Catherine Wheel, 1982, Bach Partita, 1984, The Little Ballet, 1984, (with Jerome Robbins) Brahms/Handel, 1984, At the Supermarket, 1984, In the Upper Room, 1987, Ballare, 1987, Stations of the Crossed, 1988, Everlast, 1989, Quartet, 1989, Bum's Rush, 1989, The Rules of the Game, 1990, Brief Fling, 1990, Grand Pas: Rhythm of the Saints, 1991, Deuce Coupe II, 1992, The Men's Piece, 1992, (with Mikhail Baryshnikov) Cutting Up, 1992-93, Demeter and Persephone, 1993, Waterbaby Bagatelles, 1994, Demeter and Persephone, 1994, Red, White & Blues, 1995, How Near Heaven, 1995, I Remember Clifford, 1995, Jump Start, 1995, Americans We, 1995; (film) Hair, 1979, Ragtime, 1981, Amadeus, 1984, White Nights, 1985, Valmont, 1989, I'll Do Anything, 1994; (video spls.) Making Television Dance, 1977, CBS Cable Confessions of a Corner Maker, 1980; (Broadway shows) Sorrow Floats, 1985, Singin' In The Rain, 1985; (TV) Baryshnikov by Tharp (Emmy award Outstanding Choreography 1985, Emmy award Outstanding Writing of Classical Music/Dance Programming 1985, Emmy award Outstanding Directing of Classical Music/Dance Programming 1985), The Catherine Wheel, 1982 (Emmy award nom. Outstanding Choreography 1982); author (autobiography): When Push Comes to Shove, 1992. MacArthur Found. Chgo. fellow, 1992; recipient Creative Arts award Brandeis U., 1972, Dance mag. award, 1981, Univ. Excellence medal Columbia U., 1987, Lions of the Performing Arts award N.Y. Pub. Libr., 1989, Samuel M. Scripps award Am. Dance Festival, 1990.

THARPE, FRAZIER EUGENE, journalist; b. Panama City, Fla., Jan. 10, 1941; s. Henry Clayton and Margaret Jane (Jenkins) T.; m. Barbara Ann Hembree, Oct. 30, 1971. BA in Polit. Sci. and History, Vanderbilt U., Nashville, 1963. Reporter Miami (Fla.) News, 1963; reporter U.P.I., Atlanta and Columbia, S.C., 1964; pub. relations exec. Atlanta, 1965-69; fin. editor Atlanta Constn., 1969-73. Editl. assoc., columnist, 1974-83, columnist Helpline, ConsumerWatch, 1983-98; editor Homefinder, 1999-2002.

THASE, GUNTER HERMANN, marketing executive; b. Bremen, Germany, Apr. 11, 1939; arrived in Can., 1963; s. Hermann and Elizabeth (Schroeder) T.; m. Ursula Widmer, Oct. 9, 1965; children: Philip, Monica. Mgr. internat. mktg. Brit. Metal Can., Toronto, 1973-78; gen. mgr. mktg. devel. Brit. Metal Can. & Amalgamet Can., 1978-82, sr. v.p., 1982-88; pres. Brit. Metal Can., Amalgamet Can. and Preussag Can., 1988—; dir. Premetalco Inc., 1988—. Former chmn. Christ the King Dietrich Bonnhoefer Luth. Ch. Lt. German Army, 1961. Mem. Nat. Club, Rotary, Cambridge Club. Office: Amalgamet Can 418-111 Richmond St W Toronto ON Canada M5H 2G4

THATCHER, ANNA MARIE, lawyer, law educator; b. Shenandoah, Iowa, Apr. 24, 1948; d. Gerald Eugene and Darlene Marie Teachout; m. Graham Thatcher, Apr. 4, 1970. BA, Dakota Wesleyan U., 1970; MA, U. S.D., 1972; JD, Hamline U., 1994. Bar: Minn. Theater dir., Rapid City, S.D., 1976-87; owner Anakota Arts, 1982-87; arts and non-profit cons. St. Paul, 1987-94; mng. producer Periaktos Prodns., Rapid City, 1994—. Co-columnist Arts and the Law, Minn. Lawyer, 1997-98 Mem. ABA, Minn. Bar Assn. Avocations: cooking, travel. Office: Periaktos Prodns 3213 W Main St # 272 Rapid City SD 57702-2314 E-mail: productions@periaktos.com.

THATCHER, GAYLE MARIE, community relations specialist; b. Arlington Heights, Ill., Dec. 29, 1969; d. Randall Hall and Mary Alice (Hartman) T. B in Liberal Studies, Bowling Green State U., 1992. Mktg. coord. R & M Imports, Waynesville, Ohio, 1992-93; advt. coord. Rocky Mountain Pub., Denver, 1993-94; found. adminstr. Keep the Lights Found., KCNC-TV, 1994-96; mgr. cmty. rels., spl. events Denver Mus. Natural History, 1996-97; freelance cons. mktg., pub. rels. and spl. events Denver, 1993—; nat. Internet sales mgr. USWEST dex.com Internet Yellowpages, 1997—. Mem. Assn. Women in Comm. Home: 2880 S Locust St Apt S705 Denver CO 80222-7165

THATCHER, GEORGE ROBERT, banker, columnist, author; b. Austin, Pa., Sept. 18, 1922; S. Walter Robert and Roberta Estelle (Bernard) T.; widowed; children: Georgia Anne Thatcher Faneca, Janie Estelle Thatcher

Holmes, Walter Wimberly. BA in English, U. Miss., 1948. Enlisted U.S. Army, 1942, advanced through grades to maj., 1948, stationed in Pacific, Korea, ret., 1952; ptnr. Rand-Thatcher Advt. Agy., Gulfport, Miss., 1948-81; pres. coast divsn. Magnolia Fed. Bank, 1981-92; councilman City of Gulfport, 1989; commissary Anglican Diocese of No. Malawi, 1995—; hon. canon St. Peter's Cathedral, Likoma Island, Malawi, 1997—; daily columnist The Sun Herald, Biloxi, Miss., 1998—. Bd. dirs. Union Planters Bank. Author: Misrepresentation in MS, 1954, Beach Walks, 1998, 2d edit., 1999, Beach Walks II, 2000. Mem. Miss. Arts Commn., 1991-2000; past chmn. United Way, Harrison County, Gulfport Carnegie Libr., Harrison County Libr.; past trustee Gulfport Meml. Hosp. Found.; past pres. Episcopal Laymen of Miss.; past sr. warden, layreader St. Peter's Episcopal Ch., Gulfport; mem., past dir. Miss. Hist. Assn. Decorated Bronze Star; named Outstanding Citizen Miss. Coast C. of C., 1998. Mem. Gulfport Rotary Club (pres. 1995-96, Citizen of Yr. 1993, Paul Harris fellow), Century Club (pres.), Gulfport Yacht Club, Bayou Bluff Tennis Club, Great So. Club, Miss. Gulf Coast C. of C. Republican. Avocations: tennis, chess, reading, classical music. Home: 1302 2nd St Gulfport MS 39501-2219 Office: Union Planters Bank 2200 14th St Gulfport MS 39501-2005 E-mail: grthatcher@aol.com.

THATCHER, JANET SOLVERSON, finance educator, educator; b. Sept. 24, 1946; m. John G. Thatcher, Mar. 20. 1976. BA, U. Wis., 1968, MBA, 1976, PhD, 1979. Svc. rep. Wis. Telephone Co., Beloit, 1968-71; trust dept. Baraboo (Wis.) Nat. Bank, 1971-73; pension, profit sharing trust dept. Firstar, Madison, 1973-74; asst. prof. fin. Va. Tech., Blacksburg, 1978-82, Clarkson U., Potsdam, N.Y., 1982-86; prof. U. Wis., Whitewater, 1986—2001. Contbr. articles to profl. jours. Home: 4546 Wavertree St San Luis Obispo CA 93401-7831

THATCHER, LAURA PATRICIA, social worker; b. Red Bank, N.J. 2 children. BA, Monmouth Coll., 1976; MSW, Rutgers U., 1987. Social worker family and adult svcs. Monmouth County, Freehold, N.J., 1980—. Office: Monmouth County Social Svcs PO Box 3000 Freehold NJ 07728-1250 Home: 2479 4th Pl Vero Beach FL 32962-1369

THATSNEYAKUL, YAOVARES, physician, consultant; b. Bangkok; m. Michael Pulaski, 1975. MD, Siriraj Med. Sch., Bangkok. Diplomate Am. Bd. Pediatrics. Cons. Dept. Human Svcs., State of N.J., 1985—. Office: Divsn Med Assistance and Health Svcs PO Box 712 Trenton NJ 08625-0712 E-mail: yaovares.thatsneyakul@dhs.state.nj.us.

THAU, WILLIAM ALBERT, JR. lawyer; b. St. Louis, June 22, 1940; s. William Albert and Irene Elizabeth (Mundy) T.; m. Jane Hancock, Sept. 7, 1961; children: William Albert, Caroline Jane, Jennifer Elizabeth. BS in Indsl. Mgmt., Ga. Inst. Tech., 1962; JD, U. Tex., 1965. Bar: Tex. 1965. Ptnr., head of real estate sect. Jenkens & Gilchrist, Dallas, 1965—. Chmn. real estate developer/builder symposium S.W. Legal Found, 1975-79; bd. dirs. Southwestern Film Archives, So. Meth. U.; lectr. Practicing Law Inst. Author: Negotiating the Purchase and Sale of Real Estate, 1975; editor Tex. State Bar Assn. Newsletter on Real Estate, Probate and Trust Law, 1978-81; contbr. articles to Real Estate Rev., 1983—. Bd. dirs. St. Philips Sch., Dallas, 1988, So. Meth. U.; trustee Dallas Can. Acad., 1987-88. Mem. ABA, Tex. State Bar Assn. (chmn. real estate, probate, trust law sect.), Am. Coll. Real Estate Lawyers. Republican. Office: Jenkens & Gilchrist 1445 Ross Ave Ste 3200 Dallas TX 75202-2799

THAUER, EDWIN WILLIAM, JR. financial services executive; b. Grand Rapids, Mich., May 24, 1953; s. Edwin William and Lucille Marie (Roy) T.; m. Karen Lee Alberts, Aug. 16, 1973; children: Susan Elizabeth, Angela Marie, Amanda Rose. Grad. high sch., Grand Rapids. Lic. life ins. counselor, Mich. Agt. The Bankers Life Co., Grand Rapids, 1977-80; pres., CEO Design Underwriting, Inc., 1980—. Mem. Am. Soc. CLU and Chartered Fin. Cons. (amb. polit. action com.), Nat. Assn. Life Underwriters, Life Ins. Leaders Mich. (life), Cascade Hills Country Club. Mem. Nazarene Ch. Home: 1875 Wilmont Dr SE Grand Rapids MI 49508-6591 Office: Design Underwriting Inc 985 Parchment Dr SE Grand Rapids MI 49546-3659 E-mail: ed.thauer@designunderwriting.com.

THAW, ARNOLD, clinical psychologist; b. N.Y.C., Apr. 21, 1931; s. Max and Rose Thaw. BA, NYU, 1952; MDiv, Starr King Sch. Ministry, Berkeley, Calif., 1956; PhD, Calif. Sch. Psychology, 1974. Lic. psychologist, Ariz. Chief psychologist Coconino Cmty. Guidance Ctr., Flagstaff, Ariz., 1974-77; mem. tng. faculty Gestalt Inst. of Phoenix, 1977-79, emeritus mem. tng. faculty, 1999—; pvt. practice clin. psychology Phoenix, 1977—. Minister Unitarian Universalist Ch. Office: Gestalt Inst of Phoenix 4302 N 32d St Phoenix AZ 85018-3904

THAW, MORT, writer; b. N.Y.C. s. Max and Sophie (Schwartz) T. Student, Bklyn. Coll. Writer over 150 produced teleplays and screenplays for The Untouchables, U.S. Steel Hour, NBC Matinee Theatre, Zane Grey, Robert Taylor's Detectives, Route 66, Ironside, Bonanza, The Waltons, Emergency, CHiPS, Paramount Pictures, Cinerama Releasing, Cameo Theatre, Day in Ct., others. Playwright: Together. T/sgt. USAAF. Mem. Writers Guild Am., West (chmn. plagiarism com. 1984-90, age discrimination com. 1982-93, tellers com. 1968—, human resources coordinating com. 1987-97, bd. nominating com. 1979-81, 83, 96, officers nominating com. 1997, election study com., 1991, others, bd. dirs. 1988-90, Svc. award 1987, Morgan Cox award 1996), Writers Guild Found. (bd. trustees 1986-97), Dramatists Guild. Democrat. Avocation: animal rights. Home and Office: 1263 N Flores St West Hollywood CA 90069-2973

THAWLEY, MICHAEL, diplomat; b. Eng., 1950; arrived in Australia, 1960; m. Deborah Wilkins; children: Samuel, Thomas, Cosimo. BA with honors, Australian Nat. U., 1971; postgrad. diploma in Russian, Surrey (Eng.) U., 1980. Joined Australian Fgn. Svc., 1972, first asst. sec. Prime Mins. Dept., 1993-96; nat. security advisor Prime Min. Australia, 1996; dep. sec. dept. fgn. affairs and trade; Australian amb. to the U.S. Washington, 2000—. Avocations: reading, music, gardening. Office: Embassy of Australia 1601 Massachusetts Ave NW Washington DC 20036-2273 Fax: 202-797-3209.

THAWORNWONG, SURAPHAN, candidate and graduate research assistant; b. Trang, Trang, Thailand, June 11, 1974; s. Suchart and Samphan Thawornwong. BEng., Mech. Engring., Prince of Songkla U., Thailand, 1995; MBA, U. Mo. Coll. Bus., Columbia, 1999; MS in Indsl. Engring., U. Mo., Columbia, 2000; postgrad. studies in Engring. Mgmt., U. Mo., Rolla, 2000—. Lic. profl. engr., Thailand, 1996. Grad. rsch. asst. Dept. Indusl. & Mfg. Systems Engring., U. Mo., Columbia, 1997—2000; grad. rsch. asst. Dept. Engring. Mgmt., U. Mo., Rolla, 2000—. Student asst. Ellis Libr., U. Mo., Columbia, 1999; presenter Computer Integrated Mfg. System Lab, Dept. Indusl.l & Mfg. Systems Engring. U. Mo., Columbia, 1999; MBA student cons. College of Bus., U. Mo., Columbia. Contbr. scientific papers to sci. confs. Recipient Student Assistance award, ASEAN Student Assistance Award Program, 1998-2000, Grant-In-Aid Scholarship, U. Mo. Curators Program, 1998-1999. Mem.: Internat. Assn. Fin. Engrs., Inst. Industrial Engrs., Inst. Ops. Rsch. and the Mgmt. Science. Office: Engring Mgmt Dept U Mo 1870 Miner Circle Rolla MO 65409

THAXTON, MARVIN DELL, lawyer; b. Electra, Tex., June 1, 1925; s. Montgomery Dell and Ida (Scheurer) T.; m. Carolyn Moore Alexander, Aug. 30, 1949; children: Rebecca Thaxton Henderson, Gail Thaxton Fogleman, Marvin D. Jr. JD, U. Ark., 1949. Bar: Ark. 1949, U.S. Dist. Ct. (ea. dist.) Ark. 1952, U.S. Dist. Ct. (we. dist.) Ark. 1978, U.S. Dist. Ct. (we. dist.) Okla., U.S. Supreme Ct. 1987. Prin. Thaxton Furniture Co., Newport, Ark., 1949-50; ptnr. Thaxton, Hout & Howard, Attys., 1950-97; retired, 1997. Spl. assoc. justice Ark. Supreme Ct., 1978, 84; examiner Ark. State Bd. Law Examiners, 1968-73, chmn. 1973. Pres. Newport Sch. Dist. Bd. Edn., 1964; past pres. Ea. Ark. Young Men's Clubs; adult leader Newport area Boy Scouts Am., 1949-94; bd. dirs. Newport Hosp. and Clinic Inc., 2000. Officer U.S. Mcht. Marine, 1945-46, PTO. Fellow Ark. Bar Found.; mem. ABA, Ark. Bar Assn. (honor cert. 1973), Newport C. of C. (pres. 1956, bd. dirs. 1997-2000), Newport Rotary Club (past pres., Paul Harris fellow 1990), Sigma Chi. Democrat. Methodist. Avocations: hunting, fishing, boating. Home: 12 Lakeside Ln Newport AR 72112-3914 E-mail: mdtjd@ipa.net.

THAXTON, MARY LYNWOOD, librarian, researcher; b. Detroit, Dec. 27, 1944; d. Osceola Alvin Jr. and Mary Phlegar (Penn) T. BA, Emory and Henry Coll., 1966; MLn, Emory U., 1967; AS, Ga. State U., 1978, MA, 1983, PhD, 1989. Reference libr. Coll. of William and Mary, Williamsburg, Va., 1967-71; reference libr., asst. prof. Ga. State U., Atlanta, 1971-77, social sci. bibliographer, assoc. prof., 1977-89; pvt. practice psychotherapy, gerontol cons., Tucker, Ga., 1989-91; gerontol. cons., psychotherapist in pvt. practice Marietta, 1991-95; Atlanta, 1996-99; behavioral sci. liaison, assoc. prof. Ga. State U., 1999—. Editor bibliography: Metropolitan Atlanta Rapid Transit Authority, 1982, Community Mental Health Services to the Elderly, 1984 (Libr. award 1984); contbr. articles to profl. jours. Office: Ga State U Pullen Libr University Plz Atlanta GA 30303 E-mail: lthaxton@gsu.edu.

THAYER, BRUCE ALLEN, automotive executive, artist; b. Eaton Rapids, Mich., Feb. 7, 1952; s. Alfred James and Beatrice Thayer; m. Ilene Alice Thayer, May 26, 1986. BS, Ctrl. Mich. U., 1974, BFA in Painting, 1975; MFA in Painting, Sch. Art Inst. Chgo., 1980. Sub. tchr. Lansing (Mich.) Schs., 1978-79; art instr. Kresge Art Mus. Mich. State U., East Lansing, 1998-2001; test driver GMC, Milford, Mich., 1988—. Vis. artist Aquinas Coll., Grand Rapids, Mich., 1998, G.M.I. Engring. Inst., Flitn, 1995; spkr., artist Aesthetic and Ideologies Conf., Mich. State U., East Lansing, 1999, Cranbrook Art Mus., Bloomfield Hills, Mich., 1995. Exhbns. include 15th Biennial Mich. Arts Exhbn., 1987 (Best of Show award 1987), Rutgers Nat. Works on Paper, 1986 (Purchase award 1986), 5th Ann. Mich. Fine Arts, 1983 (Best of Show award 1983), 20th Biennial Regional Arts Exhbn., 1999 (Purchase award 1999). Head juror San Jane Venable Scholarship, Lansing, 1993, 94; juror h.s. art Rep. U.S. Congress, East Lansing, 1998, 99. Fellow Art Matters, 1994; Visual Arts fellow Arts Midwest/NEA Regional, 1990; art grantee Mich. Coun. for the Arts, 1987. Mem. Soc. Am. Graphic Artists (Purchase award 1993), Cen. Mich. U. Art Alumni (adv. bd. dirs. 1999—). Avocations: horticulture, collecting arts and crafts, pottery. Home: 1515 Kelly Mason MI 48854 E-mail: brucellenethayer@aol.com.

THAYER, CARLYLE ALAN, educator; b. Nevada City, Calif., Nov. 5, 1945; arrived in Australia 1971; s. Alan Phillip and Roma Gertrude (Rogerson) T.; m. Zubeida Bibi Abdulla, July 1, 1969. AB, Brown U., 1967; MA, Yale U., 1971; PhD, Australian Nat. U., 1977. Tutor Australian Nat. U., Canberra, 1973, rsch. scholar, 1971-74; lectr. Bendigo Coll. Advanced Edn. (formerly Inst. Tech.), Bendigo, Victoria, 1975-78, RMC-Duntroon, Canberra, 1979-83; sr. lectr. Royal Mil. Coll./Duntroon, 1983-86, Australian Def. Force Acad., Canberra, 1986-89, assoc. prof., 1990—, head Sch. Politics, 1995—. Author: War By Other Means, 1989, The Vietnam Peoples's Army Under Doi Moi, 1994, Adelphi Paper 297, Beyond Indochina, 1995; co-author: Soviet Relations With India and Vietnam, 1992; review editor, Asian Studies Assn. of Australia, Canberra, 1980-87; co-editor: The Soviet Union as an Asian Pacific Power, 1987, Reshaping Regional Relations, 1993, Vietnam and the Rule of Law, 1993, Crisis of Expectations: UN Peacekeeping in the 1990's, 1995, Bringing Democracy to Cambodia, 1995. Nat. sec. Australian Soccer Referees Fedn., Canberra, 1989-95. With USN, 1963-64. Recipient PhD rsch. scholarship, Australian Nat. U., 1971-74, U.S. Nat. Def. Fgn. Language fellowship, Yale U. and Cornell U., 1969-71. Mem. Australasian Polit. Studies Assn. (nat. sec. 1996), Asian Studies Assn. of Australia, Australian Nat. Com., Coun. for Soc. Cooperation in the Asia Pacific, Australian Inst. Internat. Affairs, Am. Polit. Sci. Assn., Assn. Asian Studies, Nat. Press Club. Roman Catholic. Avocations: class 1 soccer referee, Nat. Soccer League, 1983-89. Home: 11 Ambara Pl Aranda ACT 2614 Australia Office: Australian Def Force Acad Sch Politics Canberra ACT 2600 Australia

THAYER, CHARLES J. investment banker; b. Abilene, Kans., Feb. 28, 1944; s. Bruce V. and Neoma (Obermeyer) T.; 1 child, Travis J. Grad., U. Kans., 1967. Exec. v.p., CFO Citizens Fidelity Bank, Louisville, 1977-87; exec. v.p. fin. PNC Bank Corp., Pitts., 1987-89; chmn., mng. dir. Chartwell Capital Ltd., Ft. Lauderdale, Fla., 1989—; interim chmn. Sunbeam-Oster, Providence, 1993. Adv. dir. Louisville Cmty. Devel. Bank, 1997—, Keefe Mgrs., Inc., N.Y.C., 1990-2002; bd. dirs. CogenAmerica, Mpls., Republic Bank, St. Petersburg, Fla. Trustee Cystic Fibrosis Found., Washington, 1980—; chmn. Cystic Fibrosis Svcs., Washington, 1994—. Avocation: sailing. Office: Chartwell Capital Ltd 420 Isle Of Capri Dr Fort Lauderdale FL 33301-2438 E-mail: CJT@chartwellCapital.com.

THAYER, DONALD WAYNE, food chemist, microbiologist; b. Kansas City, Mo., Jan. 15, 1937; s. Robert Page and Beatrice E. Thayer; m. Suzanne Cooper, Aug. 16, 1969. BS, Kans. State U., 1955—58, MS, 1963; PhD, Colo. State U., 1962—66. Resident rsch. assoc. chemist Naval Med. Rsch. Inst., Nat. Naval Med. Ctr., Bethesda, Md., 1966—67, rsch. chemist, 1967—69; asst. prof. biol. sciences Tex. Tech U., Lubbock, 1969—72, assoc. prof. biol. sciences, 1972—76, prof. biol. sciences, 1976—78; program mgr. applied biology NSF, Washington, 1978—81; chief food safety lab. USDA, Agrl. Rsch. Svc., Ea. Regional Rsch. Ctr., Wyndmoor, Pa., 1981—85, rsch. leader food safety mgmt. unit, 1985—2001, rsch. leader food safety intervention technologies rsch. unit, 2001—. Bd. of advisors Food Rsch. Inst., U. of Wisconsin-Madison, Madison, WIS., 1988—98; mem. u.s. del. who working group on health impact and control methods of irradiated foods WHO, Munich, 1986—86; mem. u.s. del. inter-american meeting harmonization of regulations on food irradiation in the americas Internat. Consultative Group on Food Irradiation, Food and Agrl. Orgn. of the UN (FAO), WHO (WHO), IAEA (IAEA), Orlando, FLA., 1989—89; mem. u.s. del. irradiation as a quarantine treatment of fresh fruits and vegetables Internat. Consultative Group on Food Irradiation, FAO, IAEA, WHO, Bethesda, MD., 1991—91; mem. u.s. del. irradiation as a pub. health intervention measure for food-borne diseases in l.am. and the caribbean Fao, Iaea, Who, Washington, 1992—92; u.s. del. and chair shelf-stable foods through irradiation processing Fao, Iaea, Vienna, 1993—93; usda rep. office of sci. and tech. policy (ostp) subcommitteee interagency radiation rsch. and policy coordination Nat. Sci. and Tech. Coun., Exec. Office of the Pres., Washington, 1994—98; co-chair cast com. radiation pasteurization of foods Coun. For Agrl. Sci. and Technolgy, Ames, IOWA, 1994—96; mem. u.s. del. internat. consultative group for food irradiation Fao, Iaea, Geneva, 2000—00. Editor: (book) Microbial Interaction with the Physical Environment, 1975, Actinomycete Taxonomy, 1980. E5 USNR, 1958—60, Bethesda, Maryland. Recipient Halpin Lectr., Poultry Sci. Dept., U. Wis. Madison, 1986, USDA-Unit Honor Award Superior Svc., U.S. Dept. Agr., 1988, Col. Rohland A. Isker Award, R & D Associates Mil. Food and Packaging Systems, Inc., 1992, Agrl. Rsch. Svc. Outstanding Scientist Yr., USDA, Agrl. Rsch. Svc., 1995, Julius Bauermann Lectureship Award, Philidelphia Affiliate Inst. Food Technologists, 1998, USDA Honor Award, US Dept. Agr., 2002. Fellow: Am. Acad. Microbiology; mem.: Am. Chem. Soc., Inst. Food Technolgists, Am. Soc. Microbiology, Internat. Assn. Food Protection (editl. bd. jour. food protection 1995), Soc. Sigma Xi (Regional Lectureship 1971). Avocation: genealogy. Office: Usda Ars, Errc 600 E Mermaid Ln Wyndmoor PA 19038-8598 Office Fax: 215-233-6406. Business E-Mail: dthayer@arserrc.gov.

THAYER, EDNA LOUISE, medical facility administrator, nurse; b. Madelia, Minn., May 21, 1936; d. Walter William Arthur and Hilda Engel Emily Ann (Geistfeld) Wilke; m. David LeRoy Thayer, Aug. 30, 1958; children: Scott, Tamara, Brenda. Diploma in nursing, Bethesda Luth., 1956; BS in Nursing Edn., U. Minn., 1960; MSN, Washington U., St. Louis, 1966; MS in Counseling, Mankato (Minn.) State U., 1972. Cert. nursing adminstr. advanced ANA. Nurse Bethesda Luth. Hosp., St. Paul, 1956-58, U. Minn. Hosp., Mpls., 1958; from nurse to asst. head nurse supr., edn. dir. Fairmont (Minn.) Community Hosp., 1959-63; instr. Alton (Ill.) Meml. Hosp., 1963-66; from nursing instr. to assoc. prof. and dean Sch. Nursing Mankato State U., 1966-77; asst. adminstr. Rice County Dist. One Hosp., Faribault, Minn., 1977-89; RN, adminstrv. supr. St. Peter (Minn.) Regional Treatment Ctr., 1990-96; spkr., 1996—. Nurse surveyor Minn. Dept. Tech. Edn., St. Paul, 1980-93; mem. adv. co. LPN and MA programs Tech. Inst., Faribault, 1977-2001. Mem. Rice County Ext. Bd., Faribault, 1986-91, adult leader 4-H Club, Rice County and St. Paul, 1971-97; advisor Med. Explorers, Faribault, 1977-89; mem. Rep. Rodosovich Health Com., Faribault, 1984-94; coun. mem. Our Savior's Luth. Ch., Faribault, 1984-87; mem. Rep. Boudreau Health Care Adv. Com., 1996-2001. Recipient alumni award Nat. 4-H Club, 1983, Disting. Friend of Nursing award Mankato State U., 1995. Mem. Minn. Orgn. Nurse Execs. (bd. dirs. 1987-89), Dist. F Nursing Svc. Adminstrs. (pres. 1980-82), Minn. Nurses Assn. (bd. dirs. 1982-87, Pres.'s award 1983, pres. 5th dist. 1974, 75, pres. 13th dist. 1984-86), AAUW, Sigma Theta Tau, Delta Kappa Gamma (pres. Pi chptr. 1982-84, Woman of Achievement award 1985), Hosp. Aux. Republican. Avocations: crafts, volunteer work, theater, plays. Home: 700 Roots Beach Ln Elysian MN 56028-9731

THAYER, EDWIN CABOT, musician; b. Weymouth, Mass., May 16, 1935; s. Elliot Pierce and Barbara (Senior) T.; m. Joan Peregoy, June 24, 1961; children: Bruce, Laura, Richard, William. MusB cum laude, U. Ill., 1957, MusM with performing honors, 1958. Instr. horn Brevard (N.C.) Music Center, summers 1957, 58, 62; grad. asst. U. Ill., 1957-58; prin. horn Washington Brass Choir, 1958-61, Richmond (Va.) Symphony, 1960-72, Norfolk (Va.) Symphony, 1961-65; assoc. prof. music Va. Commonwealth U. (formerly Richmond Profl. Inst.), Richmond, 1963-72; head piano dept. Va. Commonwealth U., 1965-69, music librarian, 1965-72, head brass and winds dept., 1969-72; prin. horn Washington Nat. Symphony, 1972-2000, 4th horn, prin. horn emeritus, 2000—; hornist Nat. Symphony Wind Soloists, 1978—, Euterpe Chamber Players, 1981-89, Chamber Soloists Washington, 1986—, Tanglewood (Mass.) Berkshire Music Festival Orch., summers 1955-56; hornist Brass Prins. and Woodwind Prins. Quintets Nat. Symphony Orch., 1988-2000; solo recitalist, chamber ensemble recitalist, horn soloist; guest artist Internat. Horn Workshops, Hartford, Ct., 1977, Potsdam, N.Y., 1981, Towson, Md., 1985; hornist 20th Century Consort, Washington, 1994—. Adj. faculty Cath. U. Am., 1973—, George Mason U., 1985—; mem. World Philharm. Orch., Rio de Janeiro, 1986, Highlands, N.C. Music Festival, 1995—. Served with AUS, 1958-61. Disting. tchr. White House Commn. on Presdl. Scholars, 1995. Mem. Internat. Horn Soc., Musicians Union, Pi Kappa Lambda, Phi Mu Alpha Sinfonia. Home: 11902 Triple Crown Rd Reston VA 20191-3016 Office: Kennedy Ctr for Performing Arts Nat Symphony Orch Washington DC 20566-0001 E-mail: cornu@juno.com.

THAYER, FREDERICK CLIFTON, public policy educator; b. Sept. 6, 1924; m. Carolyn Conn Easley, 1952; children: Jeffrey Lee, Sarah Diane. BS, U.S. Mil. Acad., 1945; MA, Ohio State U., 1954; PhD, U. Denver, 1963. Commd. 2d lt. USAF, 1945, advanced through grades to col., 1965, ret., 1969; assoc. prof. U. Pitts., 1969-83, prof., 1983-91; prof. European div. Troy State U., 1991-94, George Washington U., Washington, 1995-96; prof. public policy, dir. doctoral program So. U., Baton Rouge, 1997-99; vis. prof. U. of the Incarnate Word, San Antonio, 1999-2000, Ctrl. Mich. U., Mt. Pleasant, 2000—. Author: Air Transport Policy and National Security, 1965, An End to Hierarchy and Competition, 1973, 2d edit., 1981, Rebuilding America: The Case for Economic Regulation, 1984; contbr. articles to profl. jours. Office: Coll Extended Learning Ctrl Mich Univ Mount Pleasant MI 48859 E-mail: fthayer@yahoo.com.

THAYER, JANE See WOOLLEY, CATHERINE

THAYER, KEITH BAYARD, engineering company executive; b. Phoenix, Nov. 6, 1927; s. Ezra Weld and Claire (Pile) T.; m. Ruth O'Bryan, Oct. 6, 1951; children: Jane, John, Joe, Joan, Julie, Jill, Jim, Jacque. BSME with honors, Kans. State U., 1950. Registered engr. Tex., Okla., La., Kans., Miss. Machinist's helper MK&T Railroad, Parsons, Kans., 1943-45; assembler Douglas Aircraft, Santa Monica, Calif., 1946-47; engr. Phillips Petroleum Co., Bartlesville, Okla., 1950-51; piping design engr. Foster Wheeler, Houston, 1951-53; chmn. bd., pres. CDI Stubbs Overbeck, 1953-96; pres., CEO Garuda U.S., Inc., 1996—. Mem. industry adv. com. Tex. A&M U., Galveston, 1994-96; industry adv. coun. mech. and nuclear engring. dept. Kans. State U., Manhattan, 1999—; examiner Malcolm Baldridge Quality award, 2001—; pres. Sharpstown Save Our Park com., Houston, 1973-80; liturgy com. St. Francis de Sales Ch., Houston, 1978-81; mem. Silver Fox Advisors, 2001—. Recipient Frank L. Evans award Energy Sources Tech. Conf. & Exhbn., New Orleans, 1991. Fellow ASME Internat. (life; internat. pres. 1997-98, Andy Lewis award petroleum divsn. 1987, Thayer Best Mech. Achievement award 1996); mem. Soc. Piping Engrs. and Designers (dir. 1985-90), Tex. Assn. Mediators, Asia Soc., Sharpstown Civic Assn. (dir. 1997—), Greater Houston Partnership (CEO roundtable 1994—), River Bend Country Club, Silver Fox Advisers. Roman Catholic. Avocations: painting, woodworking, knifemaking, golf, hunting. Office: Garuda US Inc 6200 Savoy Dr Ste 733 Houston TX 77036-3324 E-mail: kbthayer@aol.com.

THAYER, MARTHA ANN, small business owner; b. Santa Fe, May 8, 1936; d. Duren Howard and Lena Odessa (Fox) Shields; m. Norman S. Thayer Jr., Jan. 30, 1960; children: Murray Norman, Tanya Noelle. BS, U. N.Mex., 1960. Child welfare worker State of N.Mex., Farmington and Santa Fe, 1961-64; owner Baskets by Thayer, Albuquerque, 1975-83, Noelle's, Albuquerque, 1985-89; ptnr., co-owner Indian Originals, 1989-94, Native Design, 1995-96; owner Martha A. Thayer, 1996-98; treas. DHS Properties, Inc., 1994—; agt. for Elizabeth Abeyta, Adrian Quintana, Alexandria Rohrscheib, Albuquerque, 1995—2001; owner Martha A. Thayer Enterprises L.L.P., 1998—2001; co-owner Shields Investments Enterprises L.L.P., 1998—2000. Crafts instr. Village Wool, Continuing Edn., Albuquerque, 1975-78; trustee Shields Trust, 1994—. Contbr. articles, revs. to craft publs.; juried show, Mus. of Internat. Folk Arts, 1975; baskets exhibited in group shows at N.Mex. State Fair, 1980 (1st place award), Women's Show, 1983 (1st place award). Campaign mgr. Dem. Candidate for State Supreme Ct., Bernalillo County, N.Mex., 1970; founding mem. Women's Polit. Caucus, Bernalillo County; chmn. Mother's March of Dimes, Bernalillo County, 1974. Mem. Hist. Preservation Soc., Petroleum Club, Genealogy Club of Albuquerque Pub. Libr., Mus. Albuquerque (assoc.). Avocations: genealogy, gardening, anthropology, politics, antiques, Native American art collector.

THAYER, RICHARD LEE, small business owner; b. Nelson, Nebr., Aug. 18, 1946; s. Lynn Earl and Patricia Ann (Doher) T.; m. MaryJo Ann Fager, Dec. 6, 1985. BA in Edn., U. Nebr., Kearney, 1969; M in Mgmt., Creighton U., 1993. Tchr. history Holdrege (Nebr.) H.S., 1969-73; salesman Cash-Wa Co., Kearney, 1973-75; from salesman to dist. mgr. Hanes Hosiery Inc., Omaha, 1975-89; owner, mgr. Exec. Mktg., 1989—, The Bakery/Deli, Omaha, 1993—. Founder, pres. Constl. Heritage Inst., Omaha, 1993-95. Republican. Baptist. Avocations: golf, political campaign advising.

THAYER, ROSEALYCE CULLEN, artist; b. Portland, Maine, July 1, 1928; d. Thomas Roswell and Helena (Murphy) Cullen; m. Edward P. Craig, II (dec.); children: Edward P., III, Thomas R., Peter A., Catherine C. (dec.); m. Charles V. Thayer, July 16, 1984; children: Charles W., David W. Diploma, Fryeburg Acad., Maine, 1946, Maine Coll. of Art, Portland, 1948, Westbrook Coll., 1948; BS, U. Maine, 1966; hon. degree, Maine Coll. Art, 2000. Dir. adult edn. S.D. Warren Co., Westbrook, Maine, 1961-73; art dir. SAD 55, Hiram, Maine, 1967-68; art tchr. North Yarmouth (Maine) Acad., 1961-64. Works collected in U.S., Can., Mexico. Trained victim advocate; instrumental in obtaining legis. for Immediate Search Law for Missing Children and Handicapped Persons, Vt. 1985 (adopted by Tex. 1997); active advocate stalking laws, Conn., Vt.; active Victims' Advocates, Victim Compensation and Victims' Rights, Nat. Victim Assistance Orgn., Washington, 1984—, Parents of Murdered Children, Cin., 1985; mem. Nat. Mus. Women Arts, Washington, 1997. Recipient life mem. award The Giraffe Project, Langley, Wash., 1993. Avocation: family. Home: 689 Breezy Hill Rd Springfield VT 05156-9467

THAYER, RUSSELL, III, airlines executive; b. Phila., Dec. 5, 1922; s. Russell and Shelby Wentworth (Johnson) T.; m. Elizabeth Wright Mifflin, June 12, 1947; children: Elizabeth, Dixon, Shelby, Samuel, David. Student, St. George's Sch., 1937-42; AB, Princeton U., 1949. Mgmt. trainee Eastern Air Lines, 1949-52; mgr. cargo sales and service Am. Airlines, Los Angeles, 1952-63; v.p. mktg. Seaboard World Airlines, N.Y.C., 1963-70; sr. v.p. Braniff Airways, Inc., Dallas, 1970-72, exec. v.p., 1972-77, pres., chief oper. officer, 1977-80, vice chmn., 1981-82; dir. (Braniff Airways, Inc.), 1971-82; v.p. Pan Am. World Airways, Inc., N.Y.C., 1982-84, sr. v.p., 1984-88, Airline Econs., Inc., Washington, 1988—, also bd. dirs., 1988—. Dir. Ft. Worth Nat. Bank, 1977-82; vice chmn. Airline Capital Assn; bd. dirs. Kiwi Internat. Airlines, Inc., World Aux. Power Corp. Mem. Trinity Ch. Ushers Guild, Princeton, N.J., 1968— ; Trustee Aviation Hall of Fame N.J. Served with USAAF, 1942-45, ETO. Decorated D.F.C., Air medal with 11 oak leaf clusters. Mem. Am. Aviation Hist. Assn., Air Force Assn., Exptl. Aircraft Assn., Nat. Aeros. Assn., Ivy Club (Princeton), Pretty Brook Tennis Club (Princeton), Bay Head (N.J.)

Yacht Club, Nassau Club (Princeton), Princeton Club (N.Y.C.), Phila. Club, Delta Psi. Home: Hulfish St Apt 17-I Princeton NJ 08542-3706 Office: Airline Capital Assocs Inc 535 5th Ave Rm 905 New York NY 10017-3610

THAYER, THOMAS MANOR, artist; b. Lansing, Mich., Apr. 8, 1958; BFA, U. Mich., 1981. Owner, lead artist Alexander Raymond Thomas Qaulity Fine Art, Camano Island, Wash., 1996—. One-man shows include Mountlake Terrace Civic Ctr. Gallery, Mountlake Terrace, Wash., 1999, Edmonds C.C., Edmonds, Wash., 1996, PACCAR Corp., Bellevue, Wash., 1995, Mountlake Terrace Libr., 1995, Cascade Estates Winery, Seattle, 1992, exhibited in group shows at The Artist's Mag. Competition, 2001, The Colored Pencil Soc. of Am. 9th Ann. Internat. Exhbn., San Francisco, 2001, Statements DC 207 Exhbn., Seattle, 2001, numerous others, including the Points of Color DC 207 Exhbn., Bothell, Wash., 2000; contbr. artwork. Mem.: Am. Soc. of Classical Realism, Colored Pencil Soc. of Am. Avocation: collecting and restoring classic cars of the 1960s and 1970s, snow skiing. Home: 1633 Hemlock Dr Camano Island WA 98282

THAYER, WALTER RAYMOND, internist; b. Providence, Apr. 16, 1929; s. Walter Raymond and Esther Veronica (Hulme) T.; children: Walter, Ida Marie, Peter; m. Meredith Marks, 1998. Intern R.I. Hosp., Providence, 1955-57; sr. asst. surgeon USPHS/NIH, Bethesda, Md., 1956-58; resident Georgetown U. Hosp., Washington, 1958-59; fellow in gastroenterology Yale U. Sch. Medicine, New Haven, 1959-61, rsch. fellow in internal medicine, 1961; from instr. to asst. prof. medicine Yale U., 1960-65; from assoc. prof. to prof. medicine Brown U. Sch. Medicine, Providence, 1965—. Nat. scientific adv. bd. Crohn's and Colitis Found., Inc., 1978-83, rsch. and tng. awards com., 1978-85, chmn., 1980-85, chmn. med. adv. bd. R.I. chpt., 1983; adv. bd. Nat. Coop. Crohn's Disease Study Group, 1981-83; mem. Cancer Control Bd. R.I., 1976-77. Editl. reviewer Gastroenterology, Digestive Disease and Scis.; contbr. articles to profl. jours. Sr. asst. surgeon USPHS, 1956-58. NSF fellow, 1972. Fellow Am. Coll. Physicians, Am. Coll. Gastroenterology (gov. for R.I. 1996-98); mem. Am. Gastroenterol. Assn. (Clinician of Yr. award 1999), Am. Fedn. Clin. Rsch., R.I. Med. Soc., R.I. Gastroenterology Soc., Providence Med. Soc. Avocations: cross country skiing, birdwatching, gardening. Home: 65 Bullocks Point Ave Riverside RI 02915-5318 Office: RIH Med Found 2 Dudley St Ste 370 Providence RI 02905-3248 E-mail: walter_thayer_jr@brown.edu.

THAYNE, DAREN, information technology executive; BME, MBA, Brigham Young U. Dir. devel. Novell, Inc., Corel USA Corp., Open Market, Inc.; chief tech. officer, v.p. devel. MyFamily.com, Inc., Provo, Utah. Office: Myfamily.com Inc 360 W 4800 N Provo UT 84604 Office Fax: 801-705-7001.*

THEALL, DONALD FRANCIS, retired university president; b. Mt. Vernon, N.Y., Oct. 13, 1928; s. Harold A. and Helen (Donaldson) T.; m. Joan Ada Benedict, June 14, 1950; children: Thomas, Margaret, John, Harold, Lawrence, Michael. BA with honors, Yale U., 1950; MA with 1st class honors, U. Toronto, 1951, PhD with 1st class honors, 1954. Teaching fellow U. Toronto, 1950-52, mem. faculty, 1952-65, prof. English, chmn. joint depts. English, 1964-65; dir. communication studies York U., also prof. English and communications, 1965-66; dir. English Atkinson Coll., 1965-66; mem. faculty McGill U., Montreal, Que., Can., 1966-79, prof. English, 1966-79, chmn. dept., 1966-74, Molson prof., 1972-79, dir. grad. program in communications, 1976-79, adj. prof. grad. comm. Que., Can., 1989-91; pres., vice chancellor, prof. English and cultural studies Trent U., Peterborough, Ont., 1980-87, univ. prof., 1987-94, univ. prof. emeritus, 1994—. Cultural exch. prof. Govt. of Can. and China, 1974; mem. adv. bd. Semiotic Inquiry, 1982—; cons. in field. Author: (with Robinson and Wevers) Let's Speak English, 4 vols., 1960-61, The Medium Is the Rear View Mirror: Understanding McLuhan, 1971, (with G.J. Robinson) Studies in Canadian Communications, 1975; Beyond the Word: Reconstructing Sense in the Joyce Era of Technology, Culture, and Communication, 1995 (short-listed Harold Adams Innis prize 1997), James Joyce's Techno-Poetics, 1997, The Virtual Marshall McLuhan, 2001; mem. editl. bd. Sci. Fiction Studies, 1976—, Can. Jour. Comm., 1979—, Jour. Can. Studies, 1980-87. Mem. Greater Peterborough Econ. Council, 1982-87; mem. fed. adv. council to minister employment and immigration for Peterborough area, 1986-87. Recipient awards Social Sci. and Humanities Rsch. Coun., 1991-94, 94-97, 97-2000, 2000—, Can. Fedn. Humanities-Aid to Scholarly Publs., 1994, 96, 2000; grantee Humanities Rsch. Coun. Can., 1954-56, 73-76, Ont. Dept. Edn., 1956-59, 91, Atkinson Found., 1960, CBC, 1961, Can. Coun., 1966-68, 73-76, Eastman Kodak Corp., Nat. Film Bd. Can., Can. Dept. Industry, Can. Dept. Trade and Commerce, Can. Ctrl. Mortgage and Housing, 1967-69, Que. Ministry Comm., 1977; sr. leave fellow Can. Coun., 1975. Corr. fellow Acad. Medicine (Toronto); mem. Internat. Communications Assn. (dir. 1978-81), Can. Communications Assn. (chmn. com. to investigate formation 1978, pres. 1979-80), MLA, Philol. Soc. Gt. Britain, Can. Assn. Chmn. English (founding chmn. 1971-74), Assn. Can. Univ. Tchrs. English, Internat. Inst. Communications, Soc. Arts Publs. (v.p. 1967-68), Sci. Fiction Research Assn., University Club of Toronto, Yale Club (Toronto), McGill Faculty Club, Elizabethan Club (Yale). Office: Trent Univ Grad Methodologies Program Peterborough ON Canada K9J 7B8 E-mail: dtheall@trentu.ca., dtheall@cogeco.ca.

THEBAUT, ANTHONY LENNON, surgeon; b. Atlanta, Dec. 24, 1938; s. Ben Robert Sr. and Arlouin (Lennon) T.; m. Joan Marie Sweet, May 1959 (div. June 1971); 1 child, Suzanne; m. Elizabeth Warwick, July 21, 1974; 1 child, Shannon. BS, Duke U., 1960; MD, Emory U., 1964. Diplomate Am. Bd. Surgery. Pvt. practice gen. surgeon, Palm Beach County, Fla., 1973—; staff Palm Beach Gardens (Fla.) Med. Ctr., 1976—, also bd. dirs.; staff Jupiter (Fla.) Hosp., 1979—. Chmn. dept. surgery Palm Beach Gardens Med. Ctr., 1984-86, chief of staff, 1986-87. Capt. U.S. Army, 1965-67, Vietnam. Recipient Bronze Star U.S. Army, 1967. Fellow ACS; mem. AMA, Fla. Med. Assn., Palm Beach County Med. Soc. Home: 12980 N Shore Dr Palm Beach Gardens FL 33410-1334 Office: 3355 Burns Rd Ste 305 Palm Beach Gardens FL 33410-4357 E-mail: athebaut@bellsouth.net.

THEEN, ROLF HEINZ-WILHELM, political science educator; b. Stadthagen, Germany, Feb. 20, 1937; came to U.S., 1956, naturalized, 1962; s. Walter and Gertrud (Tysper) T.; m. Norma Lee Plunkett, June 14, 1959; children: Tanya Sue, Terrell René. BA magna cum laude, Manchester Coll., 1959; MA, cert. with high distinction Russian and East European Inst., Ind. U., 1962, PhD, 1964. From asst. prof. to assoc. prof. Iowa State U., 1964-70; assoc. prof. polit. sci. Purdue U., West Lafayette, Ind., 1971-73, prof., 1974—. Dir. Purdue U.-Ind. U. study program U. Hamburg, 1980-81; translator, editor U.S. Joint Publs. Rsch. Svc. Author: Lenin: Genesis and Development of a Revolutionary, 1973, 74, 79; co-author: Comparative Politics: An Introduction to Seven Countries, 1992, 4th edit., 2000; editor, translator: The Early Years of Lenin (N. Valentinov), 1969; editor: The USSR First Congress of People's Deputies: Complete Documents and Records, 4 vols., 1991; contbr. articles to profl. jours., chpts. to books. Recipient Wilton Park award Iowa State U., 1971; Fgn. Area Tng. fellow Russian and East European Inst., 1962-64; grantee Am. Philos. Soc., Inter Univ. Com., Joint Com. Slavic Studies, Fulbright grantee, 1995; NEH sr. fellow, 1974-75, rsch. fellow Kennan Inst. Advanced Russian Studies, Woodrow Wilson Internat. Ctr. for Scholars, 1976, Ctr. Humanistic Studies fellow Purdue U., 1982, 88, 91. Mem. Am. Polit. Sci. Assn., Am. Assn. Advancement Slavic Studies, Am. Acad. Social and Polit. Sci. Mem. Ch. of the Brethren. Home: 717 Orchard Dr Lafayette IN 47905-4435 Office: Purdue U Dept Polit Sci Liberal Arts/Edn Bldg 2221 West Lafayette IN 47907-1363 Home (Winter): 6415 Midnight Pass Rd Unit 611 Sarasota FL 34242 E-mail: Theen@polscipurdue.edu.

THEERMAN, PAUL HAROLD, historian, archivist; b. Bartlesville, Okla., Oct. 12, 1952; s. Harold Bernard and Marie Anne (Rockenbach) Theerman; 1 child Virginia Marie. Student, Mich. State U., 1970-71; AB summa cum laude, Washington U., St. Louis, 1974; MA in History, U. Chgo., 1976, MS in Chemistry, PhD in History, 1980. Humanist-in-residence Mus. of Sci. & Industry, Chgo., 1980-81; asst. editor Joseph Henry Papers Smithsonian Instn., Washington, 1981-92, assoc. editor Joseph Henry Papers, 1992-93, assoc. archivist, 1993-98; head non-book collections history of medicine divsn. Nat. Libr. Medicine, Bethesda, Md., 1998—. Editor (books) Papers of Joseph Henry, vol. 5, 1985, vol. 6, 1992, vol. 7, 1996, Action and Reaction, 1993; author, editor: Experiencing Nature, 1997. Danforth Found. fellow, 1974, NSF fellow, 1974-78; recipient Morris Khorash award U. Chgo., 1974, Rsch. awards Smithsonian Instn., 1982. Mem. Soc. Am. Archivists, Am. Assn. for the History of Medicine, History of Sci. Soc. (chair meeting and programs 1997-98, program chair 1996, 2000), Am. Soc. Artificial Internal Organs (adv. bd. Project Bionics 2000—). Episcopalian. Avocations: hiking, camping, sailing, architecture. Home: 106 White Oak Ln Bluemont VA 20135 Office: History of Medicine Divsn Rm 1E-21 Nat Libr Medicine 8600 Rockville Pike Bethesda MD 20894 E-mail: paul_theerman@nlm.nih.gov.

THEIBERT, RICHARD WILDER, lawyer, educator; b. Akron, Ohio, June 20, 1951; s. Philip Richard and Ann (Conners) T.; m. Willis Anne Burton, July 25, 1981; children: Leslie, Elizabeth, Jillian. BS, Johns Hopkins U., 1974; JD, NYU, 1978. Bar: Md. 1979, Ala. 1991. Assoc. Weinberg & Green, Balt., 1979-80, Niles, Barton & Wilmer, Balt., 1980-85, Prem and Dumler, Balt., 1985-91, Najjar Denaburg, Birmingham, Ala., 1991—. Prof. U. Balt., 1987, Birmingham Sch. Law, 1991-2001. Pres. Birmingham Housing Devel. Corp., 1992-2000. Mem. ABA, Ala. Bar Assn., Ala. Real Estate Lawyers Assn. (pres.)., Birmingham Bar Assn. Episcopalian. Avocations: teaching, coaching. Home: 1000 31st St S Birmingham AL 35205-1108 Office: Najjar Denaburg 2125 Morris Ave Birmingham AL 35203-4274 E-mail: rtheibert@najjar.com.

THEIS, NANCY NICHOLS, community activist, mental retardation specialist; b. Seward, Alaska, Oct. 28, 1935; d. George Kenneth and Helen Edith Harriet (Fleig) Nichols; m. William Frederick Theis, Sept. 1, 1956 (dec.); children: David William (dec.), Susan Theis Ottenschot, Charles Howard. BS in Edn., SUNY, Brockport, 1958. Cert. tchr., N.Y. X-ray sheet film insp. Eastman Kodak Co., Rochester, 1954-55; switchboard operator Rochester (N.Y.) Tel. Corp., 1951-56; gen. office worker N.Y. Fire Ins. Rating Orgn., Rochester, 1957-58; substitute tchr. City of Rochester, 1959-63, 71-72, East Irondequoit Schs., Irondequoit, N.Y., 1972-74; village trustee Village of Webster, 1966-69; day habilitator United Cerebral Palsy Assn., Rochester, 1982-97, ret., 1997. Mem. informed consent com. United Cerebral Palsy Assn., 1990-97, United Way co-chair, 1988; liaison to planning bd. Village of Webster, 1966-69. Co-founder, registrar Webster Montessori Sch., 1966, 71-74; bd. dirs. Webster Mus. and Hist. Soc., 1979-83; mem. Monroe County Dem. Com., Rochester, 1985—; co-founder After Suicide Support Group, Rochester, 1987—. Mem. Women's Club of Webster (rec. sec. 1975-76, corr. sec. 1976-77, 1st v.p. 1977-79, pres. 1978-79, 2001-02). Baptist. Home: 72 Lapham Park Webster NY 14580-3236

THEIS, PAUL ANTHONY, publishing executive; b. Ft. Wayne, Ind., Feb. 14, 1923; s. Albert Peter and Josephine Mary (Kinn) T.; m. Nancy Ann Wilbur, Aug. 21, 1971; children: Mitchell A. BA in Journalism, U. Notre Dame, Ind., 1948; BS in Fgn. Svc., Georgetown U., 1949; postgrad., Am U., 1949-52. Reporter Army Times & Fairchild Pubs., Washington, 1950-53; corres. Newsweek Mag., 1953-54; adminstrv. asst. to U.S. Congressman, 1955-57; radio-TV dir. Nat. Rep. Congl. Com., 1957-60, dir. pub. rels., 1960-74; exec. editor to Pres. The White House, 1974-76; dep. undersec. Dept. Agr., Washington, 1976-77; staff cons. U.S. Ho. of Reps., 1977-81; pres. Headliner Editorial Svc., 1981—. Pub. rels. officer Pres. Eisenhower's Inaugural, Washington, 1957; vice chmn. publicity Pres. Nixon's Inaugural Com., 1969. Co-author: All About Politics, 1972; co-inventor game Hat in the Ring, 1965; co-editor Who's Who in Am. Politics, 1965-75. Alt. del. rep. Nat. Conv., Dallas, 1984, del., New Orleans, 1988, Houston, 1992; mem. D.C. Rep. Com., 1980-99. With U.S. Army Air Corps, 1943-46, ETO; maj. USAFR, Ret. Mem. Nat. Press Club, Capitol Hill Club, Cosmos Club. Roman Catholic. Home: 2903 Garfield St NW Washington DC 20008-3504

THEIS, PETER GEORGE, retired classics educator; b. Milw., Dec. 18, 1930; s. Peter Joseph and Laura Gertrude (Kornely) T.; m. Jane Elizabeth Grattan, Aug. 12, 1961; children: Peter Leo, Paul Joseph, Mary Ellen Brune, Thomas George. BA magna cum laude, Marquette U., 1952; AM, U. Chgo., 1957. Part-time instr. U. Wis., Milw., 1956; instr. Rockhurst U., Kansas City, Mo., 1960-61; instr., then asst. prof. classics Marquette U., Milw., 1961-90; ret., 1990. Mem. edn. bd. Holy Family Cath. Ch., Whitefish Bay, Wis., 1974-75; troop fundraising chmn. Boy Scouts Am., Whitefish Bay, 1976-77; pres. Post-Polio Resource Group of Southeastern Wis., Wauwatosa, 1987, Milw. Area Latin Tchrs. Assn., 1963-64, Fox River Valley Classical Assn., Milw., 1970-71, Wis. Latin Tchrs. Assn., Milw., 1976-78. Cpl. U.S. Army, 1953-55. NEH grantee, 1973. Mem. AAUP, DAV (life), Am. Classical League, Am. Philological Assn., Classical Assn. of the Mid. West and South, Wis. Assn. Fgn. Lang. Tchrs. (pres. 1980-82, Recognition award 1989), Marquette U. Retirees Assn. Avocations: reading, videotaping movies and documentaries. Home: 2328 W Apple Tree Rd Milwaukee WI 53209-3312

THEIS, STEVEN THOMAS, executive safety director; b. Trenton, N.J., June 16, 1959; s. Thomas Donald and Pauline (Ciko) T.; m. Mary L. Crane; children: Christopher William, Nicholas Thomas. BS, U. So. Calif., L.A., 1981; Cert. German Lang., Johann Wolfgang Goethe U., Frankfurt am Main, Germany, 1983; postgrad., Friedrich Alexander U., Erlangen, Germany, 1983-84; MS, U. Pa., 1999, MPhil, 2002. Cert. safety profl., cert. hazardous materials mgr., EMT, N.J. With Henkels & McCoy, Inc., various locations, 1978—, constrn. coord. Phoenix, 1982, project mgr. Burlington, N.J., 1985-87, safety dir. N.J. div., 1987-92; staff support coord. corp. office Henkels & McCoy, Blue Bell, Pa., 1992—, corp. dir. safety, 1992—; bd. dirs. Henkels & McCoy, Inc., 1996. Safety and health instr. ARC, Woodbury, N.J., 1984—, safety and health instr., trainer, 1990—; basic instr. OSHA constrn. ind. stds. U.S. Dept. Labor, Chgo., 1987—; chairperson safety and health com. Gloucester County ARC, Woodbury, 1991—. Patentee in field. 1st lt. West Deptford Emergency Squad, Thorofare, N.J., 1987-88, capt., 1989-90, hon. mem. 1991—; vice chmn. West Deptford Twp. Bd. Health, 1989-90, v.p. West Deptford Vol. Fire and Ambulance Assn., 1989-90; emergency med. spl. coord. West Deptford Office Emergency Mtmg., 1989-90. Named Mem. of the Yr., West Deptford Emergency Squad, 1988, Ditch Digger of Yr., Nat. Utility Contractors Assn., 2001; recipient Cameron award Nat. Safety Coun., 1992—93, 1993—94, Safety Dir. of Yr. award Distribution Contractors Assn., 2000. Mem.: APA, ASTM (membership sec. 1994, 1st vice-chmn. 2000—, rec. sec. 1998—99), Nat. Utility Contractors Assn., Nat. Electric Safety Code, Nat. Safety Coun., Am. Nat. Stds. Inst., Nat. Safety Coun., Am. Soc. Safety Engrs., Network of Employees for Traffic Safety, Common Ground Alliance. Republican. Roman Catholic. Avocations: antiques, classical music, model building, fishing. Office: Henkels & McCoy Inc 985 Jolly Rd Blue Bell PA 19422-1958

THEIS, WILLIAM HAROLD, lawyer, educator; b. Chgo., Nov. 8, 1945; s. Clarence M. and Marion K. (McLendon) T.; m. Maria Luisa Belfiore, Dec. 5, 1973; children: Catherine, Elizabeth. AB, Loyola U., Chgo., 1967; JD, Northwestern U., 1970; LLM, Columbia U., 1977, JSD, 1982. Bar: Ill. 1970, D.C. 1971, Wis. 1998, U.S. Ct. Appeals (7th cir.) 1971, U.S. Supreme Ct. 1974, Wis. 1998. Assoc. prof. La. State U. Law Ctr., 1972-78, Loyola U. Law Sch., Chgo., 1978-81; practiced in Chgo., 1981-99; pvt. practice Winnetka, Ill., 1999-2000; chief appellate atty. Fed. Defender Program, Chgo., 2000—. Part-time lectr. admiralty Northwestern Sch. Law, Chgo. Contbr. articles to legal jours. Lt. USNR, 1970-72. Mem. Am. Law Inst. Office: 55 E Monroe St Ste 2800 Chicago IL 60603

THEISEN, RUSSELL EUGENE, electrical engineer; b. Norfolk, Va., Aug. 3, 1937; s. Richard Roudolph and Pansie Mae (Garnette) T.; m. Mary Ann Asbury, May 30, 1963; children: Timothy Mark, Yvette Marie. BSEE, Old Dominion, 1962; MBA, Rollins Coll., 1973. Registered profl. engr., N.Y., Fla.; cert. project mgr.; Microsoft cert. systems engr. Windows 98 and NT. Svc. mgr. Mastercraft Elect., Norfolk, 1955-62; design engr. IBM Corp., Endicott, N.Y., 1962-64; plant mgr. Compton Industries, Vestal, 1964-66; sr. engr. Martin Marietta Aerospace, Orlando, Fla., 1966-74; sr. project engr. General Dynamics Corp., Longwood, 1974-76; sr. mem. profl. staff Martin Marietta Aerospace, Orlando, 1976-92; sr. sys. software analyst SCI Systems Inc., Huntsville, Ala., 1992-96; mgr. Worldwide Document Mgmt. and Control Systems, 1996-99, mgr. software quality control tech. divsn., 1999—2001; mgr. software quality for Sanmina-Sci EMS Divsn. Electronic Mfg. Svcs., 2001—. Nat. dir. Halbert Genealogy, Bath, Ohio, 1987-2002; pres. Theisen Enterprises Inc., 1994—; cert. mgr., 1996, Nat. Mgmt. Assn.; Ala. chmn. Profl. Devel., High Teck Valley Coun. Nat. Mgmt. Assn., 1996-98; dir. Nat. Computer Conf., 1983-85; POSIX Programming Language Standard IEEE 1986; 1094 Standard for Life Cycle Process 1989; dir. Am. Fedn. Info. Processing Socs., 1983-85; bd. dirs. Nat. Computer Conf., Software Processing Improvement Networks; dir. Tech. and Bus. Exhbn./Symposium, 1998-2001. Contbng. author: Reliability And Maintainibility, 1967; contbr. articles to profl. jours., Posix Prgmg. Language Standard IEEE, 1986; 1094 Standard for Life Cycle Process IEEE, 1989. Dir. Theisen Clan Theisen Genealogy Group, 1988-2002; dir. Fla. Libr. Adv. Bd., 1967-79; pres. Fla. chpt. Inst. Environ. Scis., 1967-69; pres. Theisen Enterprises Inc., 1994—, profl., Nat Soc. for Profl. Engrs., 1963-76, bd. dirs. Am. Fedn. Info. Processing Soc., 1983-85, Nat. Computer Confs., 1983-85, Internat. Svcs. Coun. Madison County, 1997—. With USMC, 1953-65. Mem. AIAA, IEEE (v.p. 1983-85, Fla. Coun. pres. 1987-89, aerospace policy com. 1989-2001, sr.), Inst. Environ. Scis., Assn. Software Quality, Huntsville Assn. Tech. Studies, Nat. Mgmt. Assn. (v.p. 1992-95, sr.), ACM (area chmn. 1987-89, sr.), Nat. Coun. Internat. Svcs. at Huntsville-Madison County (treas. 1997-2001, bd. dirs. 1997—), Huntsville New Tech. Users Group (bd. dirs. 1998—), Am. Soc. Quality, Huntsville Assn. Tech. Socs., Huntsville Area Visual Basic Users Group (sec. 2000-2001, bd. dirs. 2000-2001), Am. Legion, AARP. Achievements include development of data bus standard S-100, HPIB, IEEE-488; helped launch IEEE publications, including IEEE Computer Soc. Mag, Pattern Analysis and Machine Intelligence, IEEE Software, IEEE Micro, IEEE Design & Test; data metrics sys. for corp. info. sys., design and devel. Assets and Info. Mgmt. (AIM), EDM and PDM sys. for more than 95 worldwide facilities in 23 countries; instrumental in introducing e-mail to exec. office and congress 1978 and video conferencing and electronic voting in congress 1978. Office: Sanmina/SCI Tech Sys 215 Tech Divsn 8600 Memorial Pky SE Huntsville AL 35807-3001 E-mail: R.theisen@IEEE.org.

THEISEN, WILLIAM THOMAS, lawyer, freelance/self-employed columnist; b. Sandusky, Ohio, Apr. 30, 1975; s. Thomas William and Lori Anne Theisen; m. Errin Elaine Pocock, June 15, 2001; children: Richard Excalibur, Gordon Ceasar. JD, MBA, U. Toledo, 1999. Bar: Ohio 2000. Atty. Wilburn and Winthrop Law, Columbus, Ohio, 2001, sr. parnter, 2001—. Bd. dirs. Hamilton County Ethics Com., Columbus, Ohio. Author: (plays) The Seven, 2001 (Ohio Thespians Assn. Best New Playwright, 2002). Office vol. Green Party, Columbus, 2000—02; asst. scout master Troop 7 Boy Scouts Am., 1993—2002. Lt. col. N.G., 2000—02. Named Greenpeacekeeper of the Yr., Greenpeace U.S., 2001. Roman Catholic. Avocations: community acting, showdown trivia team. Home: 116 West Boalt St Sandusky OH 44870 Office: Wilburn and Winthrop Law 7892 High St Columbus OH 43689

THEISS, GENA LEE, genealogist, researcher; b. Caneyville, Ky., May 16, 1925; d. Clarence Harbon Johnson and Gracie Higdon; m. Robert Maple Hunt, Nov. 9, 1946 (div. May 1948); 1 child, Nancy Jane; m. George William Theiss, July 15, 1949; children: Patricia Sue, Donna Lee, Martha Rhea. Grad. h.s., Caneyville, Ky., 1943. Bookkeeper Lincoln Bank & Trust Co., Louisville, 1944-47, Citizens Nat. Bank, Louisville, 1948-56, First Nat. Bank, Louisville, 1957-84. Author, editor: Christian Weedman and his Descendants 1735-1986, 1986, revised edit., 1989, Descendants of John Higdon and Millicent, 1998, My Johnson Family in Butler County, Jentucky, 2002, Update on Christian Weedman and his Descendants, 2002, Possible Updare on John Higdon and Millicent, 2002. Active Hillview Cumberland Presbyn. Ch. Mem. Ky. Hist. Soc., DAR, Ea. Star Chpt. 154. Republican. Avocations: genealogy, quilting, photography, stamp collecting, traveling. Home: 8417 Burlingame Rd Louisville KY 40219-5205

THEISS, PATRICIA KELLEY, public health researcher, educator; b. Atlanta, Dec. 12, 1934; d. Charles Henry and Susie Carlota (Tate) Kelley; m. Erich Albert Theiss (div. Aug. 1996). BA, Wellesley Coll., 1956; MS, Howard U., 1958, Cert. in Secondary Edn., 1959. Rsch. asst. Armed Forces Inst. Pathology, Washington, 1959-61; heath edn. phone coord. Howard U. Cancer Ctr., 1977-81; program assoc. D.C. Lung Assn., 1981-85; co-project dir. Know Your Body Evaluation Project Georgetown U. Sch. Medicine, 1985-87; coord. minority health grant for cancer coalition Commn. Pub. Health, 1988-89, coord. data-based intervention rsch., 1989-93, protocol coord. immunization protocol NIH-DC initiative, 1994-97; pub. health advisor Dept. Health State Ctr. Health Stats. Inst. Minority Health Statistics Initiative, 1997—; coord. D.C. Healthy People 2010 Plan Initiative, 1998—; state contact U.S. Office Minority Health, Washington, 1999—. Mem. task force for substance abuse use Abuse Edn. for D.C. Pub. Schs., 1984-85; mem. Health Mothers/Health Babies Coalition, 1985-89. Contbr. articles to profl. jours. Chair health and welfare com. D.C. PTA, 1986-89; coord. AIDS awareness edn. State PTA, D.C., 1987-89. Recipient Cmty. Svc. award D.C. Assn. Health, Recreation and Dance, 1987. Mem. APHA, Met. Washington Pub. Health Assn. (pres. 1987-88). Democrat. Congregationalist. Avocations: oil painting, horseback riding. Home: 2501 Calvert St NW #902 Washington DC 20008 Office: DC Dept Health SCHS 825 N Capitol St NE Washington DC 20002-4210 E-mail: patricia.theiss@dc.gov.

THELEN, BRUCE CYRIL, lawyer; b. St. Johns, Mich., Nov. 24, 1951; BA, Mich. State U., 1973; JD, U. Mich., 1977. Bar: N.Y. 1978, Mich. 1980, Ill. 1992. Assoc. Dewey, Ballantine, Bushby, Palmer & Wood, N.Y.C., 1977-80; ptnr. Dickinson, Wright, Moon, Van Dusen & Freeman, Detroit, 1981-83, Dickinson Wright PLLC, Detroit, 1984—. Mem. U.S. Dept. Commerce-Mich. Dist. Export Coun., 1995—. Contbr. articles to profl. jours. Mem. allocation panel, mem. spkrs. bur., chmn. rsch. and info. svcs. com., mem. strategic planning com. and comty. leaders coun. United Way Cmty. Svcs., 1987—; mem. state of Mich. Task Force on Internat. Trade, Lansing, 1990; mem. Detroit Com. on Fgn. Rels., Greater Detroit-Windsor Japan Am. Soc. Decorated Order of Merit (Fed. Rep. Germany). Mem. N.Y. Bar Assn. (mem. internat. law sect.), State Bar Mich. (chmn. internat. law sect. 1990-91), Internat. Bar Assn., Am. Soc. Internat. Law, Ill. Bar Assn. (internat. law sect.), Internat. Inst. Detroit (bd. dirs. 1997-99, v.p. 1999-2000), French-Am. C. of C. of Detroit, German Am. C. of C. of Midwest (bd. dirs. 1992—, pres. Mich. chpt. 1994—), Mich. Israel C. of C. (bd. dirs. 1997-01), Greater Detroit C. of C. (chmn. European mission com. 1991-92, 95, export com. 1992-95, Leadership Detroit VIII program 1986-87), World Trade Club and Internat. Bus. Coun. (exec. com. 1992—), Internat. Bridge, Coun. Mentors, Wayne State U., Econ. Club Detroit, Detroit Athletic Club. Office: Dickinson Wright PLLC 500 Woodward Ave Ste 4000 Detroit MI 48226-3416

THELEN, EDMUND, research executive; b. Berkeley, Calif., May 8, 1913; s. Paul and Alice (Arnold) T.; m. Helen Naomi Betton, Oct. 30, 1965; children: Nancy Anne, Joan Arnold Thelen Hanson. BS, U. Calif., Berkeley, 1934. Asst. chemist Certain-Teed Products Corp., Richmond, Calif., 1934-35; chemist O. C. Field Gasoline Corp., Santa Maria, 1936-41; asst. mgr. Eclipse Pioneer divsn. Bendix Corp., Teterboro, N.J., 1946-47; sr. rsch. chemist Franklin Inst. Rsch. Labs., Phila., 1947-51, mgr. colloids and polymers br., 1951-74, v.p., dir. phys. and life scis. dept., 1974-76, Inst. fellow, sec. com. on sci. and the arts, 1976-82, mem., 1982-2001, emeritus, 2001—. Pres. Safety Surface Corp., 1983-88; mem. Coun. for Delivery of Dental Care, 1970-85; bd. govs. Franklin-Hahnemann Inst. Occupl. and Environ. Health, 1975-80, Mayor's Sci. and Tech. Adv. Com. on Environment, 1973-80; instr. dental medicine Hahnemann Med. Coll. and Hosp., 1964-74; v.p., dir. Pa. Environ. Coun., 1974-85; treas. Home Health Svcs. of Chester County and Vicinity, 1981-86. Co-author: (book) Porous Pavement for Runoff Control, 1978; editor Am. Assn. Ret. Persons, Eastern Chester County newsletter, 1994-97; contbr. papers to tech. publs. Bd. dirs. Neighborhood Vis. Nurse Assn., 1987-93. With USN, 1941-45; comdr. USNR, 1941-66. Recipient spl. recognition award Am. Soc. Landscape Archs., 1974. Mem. Franklin Inst., Sierra Club (ea. Pa. group chmn. 1968, Atlantic chpt. vice-chmn. 1971-73, founding chmn. Pa. chpt. 1974), Ret. Officers Assn. (treas. Valley Forge chpt. 1980-85, v.p. 1987, pres. 1988-89, sec. 1994-97), Toastmasters Internat. (dist. gov. 1960-61), Sunday Breakfast Spkrs. Club (pres. 1960-61), Sigma Xi. Home: 658 Davis Ln Wayne PA 19087-5418

THELEN, GIL, newspaper editor; b. Chgo., s. Gilbert Carl and Violet (Okonn) T.; m. Carol Abernathy, July 1966 (div. Apr. 1978); children: Deborah Brooke, Todd Foster; m. Cynthia Jane Struby, Sept. 2, 1979; children: Matthew David, Jonathan Whitfield. BA, Duke U., 1960. Reporter Milw. Jour., 1960-61, AP, Washington, 1965-72; writer Consumer Reports, Mt. Vernon, N.Y., 1972-77; reporter Chgo. Daily News, 1977-78; asst. met. editor Charlotte (N.C.) Observer, 1978-82, met. editor, 1982-83, asst. mng. editor, 1983-87; editor The Sun News, Myrtle Beach, S.C., 1987-90; exec. editor The State, 1990-97; cons. editor Knight-Ridder, Inc., Columbia, S.C., 1997-98; exec. editor The Tampa Tribune, 1998—. Adj. prof. U. S.C., Aiken, 1989-98.

Pres. Montgomery County Big Brothers, Bethesda, Md., 1967-69; co-founder Alpha Group, Myrtle Beach, S.C., 1989. Mem. Am. Soc. Newspaper Editors, Tampa Palms Rotary Club, Fla. Soc. Newspaper Editors, Leadership S.C., Leadership Columbia, Leadership Tampa, Phi Beta Kappa, Omicron Delta Kappa. Methodist. Avocations: golf, tennis, reading, classical music. Office: 200 S Parker St Tampa FL 33606-2308 also: The Tampa Tribune P.O. Box 191 Tampa FL 33601 E-mail: gtheien@tampatrib.com.

THELIN, JOHN ROBERT, academic administrator, education educator, historian; b. West Newton, Mass., Oct. 15, 1947; s. George Willard and Rozalija Katherine (Komarec) T.; m. Anna Sharon Blackburn, June 24, 1978. AB cum laude, Brown U., 1969; MA, U. Calif., Berkeley, 1972, PhD, 1973. Rsch. asst. Brown U., Providence, 1968-69; researcher, lectr. U. Calif., Berkeley, 1972-74; asst. prof. U. Ky., Lexington, 1974-77; asst. dean Pomona Coll., Claremont, Calif., 1977-79; from asst. dir. to rsch. dir. Assn. Ind. Calif. Colls. and Univs., Santa Ana, 1979-81; chancellor prof. Coll. William and Mary, Williamsburg, Va., 1981-93, pres. faculty assembly, 1990-91; prof. higher edn. & philanthropy Ind. U., Bloomington, 1993-96; prof. ednl. policy and history U. Ky., Lexington, 1996—, disting. univ. rsch. prof., 2001—. Vis. prof. grad. sch. Claremont U., 1978-81; vis. scholar U. Calif., Berkeley, 1995; curator Marquandia Soc., 1971-99; essay rev. editor Rev. of Higher Edn., 1979-91; rsch. cons. NSF, Washington, 1991; mem. faculty senate U. Ky., 1997—; guest faculty Coll. Bus. Mgmt. Inst., summer 1998, 99, 2000, 2001; mem., chair social sci. com. Grad. Coun., U.K., 1998-2001; keynote spkr. Sesquicentennial of Harvard Athletics Assn., Harvard U., 2002. Author: Higher Education and Its Useful Past, 1982, The Cultivation of Ivy, 1976, (with others) The Old College Try, 1989, Higher Education and Public Policy, 1991, Games Colleges Play, 1994; assoc. editor: (jour.) Higher Education: Theory and Research, 1983-91; guest columnist: Lenngton Herald-Leader, 2001. Pres., bd. dirs. United Way, Williamsburg, 1987-89; pres. Friends of Williamsburg Libr., 1989. Rsch. grantee Spencer Found., 1989-91, 99-2001; Regents fellow U. Calif., 1972; named to Order of Ky. Cols., 1998; recipient Outstanding Faculty Rsch. award Coll. of Edn., U. Ky., 2000. Mem. Assn. for Study of Higher Edn. (bd. dirs. 1988-90, keynote spkr. 1994, pres. 1999-2000), History of Edn. Soc. (editl. bd. 1988-91), Phi Beta Kappa (Faculty award for advancement of scholarship Alpha of Va. 1986, Alpha of R.I. 1969), Omicron Delta Kappa. Avocations: long-distance running, history of Los Angeles and California, sports history. Office: U Ky Edn Policy Studies Lexington KY 40503 Home: 1745 Richmond Rd Lexington KY 40502-0001 E-mail: JThelin@uky.edu.

THELIN, JOHN ROBERT, academic administrator, researcher; b. Evanston, Ill., Apr. 14, 1950; s. Harold John and Janet Flewell Thelin; life ptnr. Teresa Mary Warren. Student, Carleton Coll., 1968—70, Berklee Coll. of Music, 1970—71; BA magna cum laude in English, Colo. Coll., 1983; student, Colo. Tech. Coll., 1984, Colo. Mountain Coll., 1985; MFA in Writing, Vt. Coll., 1995. From rsch. asst. to devel. rsch. coord. Colo. Coll., Colorado Springs, Colo., 1985—97; adminstrv. mgr. Renaissance Acad., 1998—99; dir. of prospect rsch. Wash. and Lee U., Lexington, Va., 1999—. Instr. Word Waves, Colorado Springs, 1994—97; landscaper Avantgardens, Colorado Springs, 1997—99. Author numerous poems; actor: (TV commls.) , 2000—; poetry asst.: Shenandoah lit. jour., 2001—; editor: MUSE , 1995—98. Mem., lit. grant panel Colo. Coun. on the Arts, Denver, 1991—93; vol. coord. Colo. Springs Nuc. Freeze chpt., Colorado Springs, 1984—86; bd. dir. Poetry West, Colo. Springs, 1990—99. Mem.: Am. Acad. of Poets, Associated Writers' Program, Assn. Profl. Rschrs. for Advancement (treas. Va. chpt. 2002—), Women's Ednl. Soc. (life). Avocations: animals, music, films, dancing, hiking. Office: Washington and Lee University Development Building Lexington VA 24450-0303 Personal E-mail: poetvox@intelos.net. Business E-Mail: jthelin@wlu.edu.

THELIN, PETER CARL, economist, educator; b. Wellsley, Mass., June 26, 1945; s. George Willard and Rosalia (Komarec) T.; m. Gail Patricia Thelin, July 28, 1968 (div. Apr. 1985); children: Adam Carl Thelin, Dina Lyn Perkins. BS in Natural Resource Econs., U. Calif., Berkeley, 1968, MS in Natural Resource Econs., 1970, postgrad., 1974-80. Instr. in econs. West Valley Coll., Saratoga, Calif., 1970—. Author: A Road Less Traveled: An Alternative Path into the Realm of Introductory Economics, 2001; editor: A Commons Problem, 1993. Active Surfriders Found., Seabright Neighborhood Assn. Mem. Winter Moon, Acad. Martial Arts (student 1994—), Coll. Traditional Korean Healing Arts (student 1999-2001). Avocations: Tai Chi, bodysurfing, kayaking, reading, writing poetry. Home: 307 Mott Ave Santa Cruz CA 95062-3732 Office: West Valley Coll 14000 Fruitvale Ave Saratoga CA 95070-5640

THENELL, HEATHER JO, lawyer; b. Sturgeon Bay, Wis., Jan. 18, 1969; d. Roger H. and Faye A. Isaacson; m. Matthew J. Thenell, Jan. 19, 1996. BA cum laude, Carroll Coll., Waukesha, Wis., 1990; JD, U. Wis., Madison, 1993. Bar: Wis. 1993. Atty. Quincey, Becker & Schuessler, Mayville, Wis., 1993-95, Bachman Law Firm, Appleton, 1995-98; supervisory atty. Aid Assn. for Lutherans, 1998—. Sec., sr. officer AAL Bank and Trust, FSB, Appleton, 1998-2000; dir., officer Midwest Mortgage Corp., Appleton, 1998-00. Mentor Juvenile Diversion Program, Appleton, 1997-2002; mem. Outagamie County Estate Planning Coun. Mem. ABA, Outagamie County Bar Assn., Wis. Bar Assn. Home: 2539 W Sunnyview Cir Appleton WI 54914-1147 Office: AAL 4321 N Ballard Rd Appleton WI 54919-0001 E-mail: heather_thenell@aal.org.

THEOBALD, EDWARD ROBERT, lawyer; b. Chgo., Feb. 10, 1947; s. Edward Robert Theobald Jr. and Marie (Turner) Logan; m. Bonnie J. Singer, July 18, 1970; children: Debra Marie, Kimberly Ann. BA, So. Ill. U., 1969; JD, Ill. Inst. Tech., 1974. Bar: Ill. 1974, U.S. Dist. Ct. (no. dist.) Ill. 1974. Asst. state's atty. Cook County, Chgo., 1974-79, supr. felony trial divsn., 1980-81; assoc. Conklin, Leahy & Eisenberg, 1977; ptnr. Boharic & Theobald, 1981-83, owner, ptnr., 1983—. Legal adv. Sheriff of Cook County, Ill., 1986-89; spl. state's atty. U.S. Dist. Ct. no. dist. Ill., 1989-91; apptd. spl. corp. counsel City of Chgo., 1994. Mem. Parent adv. bd. Downers Grove (Ill.) South H.S., 1992-94. Named Number One Trial Atty. in Felony Trial Divsn. of Office of Cook County State's Atty., Felony Trial Divsn. Suprs., 1979. Mem. ABA (sect. on tort and ins. law, sect. on labor and employment law, chmn. com. on sentencing alternatives young lawyers sect. 1982-83, tort and ins. practice sect., labor and employment law sect.), ATLA, Chgo. Bar Assn. (mem. bd. mgrs. 1985-87, mem. labor and employment law com. 1983—, mem. com. on coms. 1990-94, mem. membership com. 1990-95, vice chair judicial evaluation com. 1999-2000), Ill. Bar Assn., Christian Legal Soc. (bd. dirs. Ill. chpt. 1993-2000). Roman Catholic. Home: 7104 Grand Ave Downers Grove IL 60516-3915 Office: 111 W Washington St Ste 759 Chicago IL 60602-2705

THEOBALD, SCOTT M. lawyer; b. Salt Lake City, Feb. 16, 1958; s. Bruce H. and Mary E. (Farnsworth) T.; m. Carol Jane Martin, Feb. 12, 1981; children: Jason S., Lindsay J., Zoe E., Sierra N. BA in Spanish, BSCE, U. Utah, 1983; MBA, JD, Columbia U., 1988. Bar: Ariz. 1988, U.S. Dist. Ct. Ariz. 1988. Assoc. Brown & Bain, Phoenix, 1988-94; ptnr. Brown & Bain, P.A., 1994-96, Meyer & Hendricks, Phoenix, 1996-99, Rogers & Theobald, LLP, Phoenix, 1999—. Vice gen. counsel Phoenix C. of C., 1995-96; bd. dirs. Social Venture Ptnrs. Ariz., Leadership Children's Found. Precinct committeeman Ariz. Rep. Party, Phoenix, 1988-96. Mem. Phoenix Country Club. Mem. Lds Ch. Avocations: hiking, travel, racquet sports, golf, films. Office: Rogers & Theobald LLP Ste 850 2425 E Camelback Rd Phoenix AZ 85016

THEOBALD, THOMAS CHARLES, banker; b. Cin., May 5, 1937; m. Gigi Mahon, Jan. 1987 AB in Econs., Coll. Holy Cross, 1958; MBA in Fin. with high distinction, Harvard U., 1960. With Citibank, N.A. div. Citicorp, 1960-87; vice-chmn. Citicorp, N.Y.C., 1982-87; CEO, chmn. Continental Bank Corp., Chgo., 1987-94; chmn. bd. dirs. Continental Bank N.A., 1987-94; ptnr. Blair Capital Ptnrs, LLC, 1994—. Bd. dir. Xerox Corp., Jones, Lang LaSalle US Realty Income & Growth Fund, Anixter Internat., Liberty Funds, Mac Arthur Found., MONY Group. Trustee Northwestern U. Office: William Blair Capital Partners 227 N Monroe Ste 3500 Chicago IL 60606-5307

THEODOLI-BRASCHI, GIOVANNI ANGELO (DUKE OF NEMI, GRANDEE OF SPAIN), investment banker; b. May 1, 1942; s. Marchese Pio and Marchesa Adriana Theodoli; m. Maria Milstein, Nov. 26, 1977; 2 children. JD, U. Bologna, 1966; MBA, Cornell U., 1972. Mktg. officer Texaco SpA, Italy, 1967-70; investment banker First Boston Corp., N.Y.C. and London, 1972-75; v.p. Europe Citicorp, Internat. Bank Ltd., London, 1975-82; dir. gen. Citibank España, Madrid, 1983-85; exec. dir. Citicorp Investment Bank, London, 1986-87; exec. dir. so. Europe County Natwest Ltd., 1987-92; dir. investment banking Natwest Markets, 1993-94, mng. dir. investment banking, 1995-98; CEO Redi Fin. Products Ltd., Dublin, Ireland, 1999—. Mem. Circolo della Caccia (Rome), Annabel's Club, Hurlingham Club, Puerta de Hierro Club (Madrid). Office: Redi & Ptnrs Ltd 12 Stanhope Gate London W1Y 5LB England

THEODORE, ARES NICHOLAS, research chemist; b. Kalamata, Greece, Oct. 28, 1933; came to U.S., 1954; s. Nicholas A. and Angeliki (Myseros) Theodoracopulos; m. Peggy Salvarakis, Sept. 3, 1961; children: Nicholas A., Angie A. BA cum laude, Westminster Coll., Salt Lake City, 1958; MS, U. Utah, 1961; postgrad., Case Western Res. U., 1967-68. Asst. prof. chemistry Westminster Coll., 1961-64; sr. rsch. chemist Diamond Shamrock Corp., Cleve., 1964-69; rsch. scientist Ford Motor Co., Detroit, 1969-73, sr. rsch. scientist, 1973-84, prin. rsch. scientist, 1984—. Contbr. articles to profl. jours.; patentee in field (59). Mem. ch. bd. Holy Cross Greek Orthodox Ch., Farmington Hills, Mich., 1986-88; campaigner Farmington Hills Dem. Com., 1986-88; mem. bus. coun. Boston Dem. Com., 1988—, Nat. Dem. Com., 1988—. U. Utah fellow, 1958-61, NSF fellow, 1964. Mem. Am. Chem. Soc. (treas. 1967), Ahepa (bd. govs. Dearborn, Mich. 1985-86). Avocations: swimming, golf, photography. Home: 34974 Valley Forge Dr Farmington Hills MI 48331-3210

THEODORE, CRYSTAL, artist, retired educator; b. Greenville, S.C., July 27, 1917; d. James Voutsas and Florence Gertrude (Bell) T. AB magna cum laude, Winthrop Coll., 1938; MA, Columbia U., 1942, EdD, 1953; postgrad., U. Ga., 1947. Instr. art Winthrop Coll., 1938-43; prof. art, head dept. Huntingdon (Ala.) Coll., 1946-52, E. Tenn. State U., 1953-57, Madison Coll., 1957-68; vis. prof. art World Campus Afloat Chapman Coll., Calif., 1967; prof. art James Madison U., Harrisonburg, Va., 1968-83, prof. emeritus. Contbr. articles to profl. jours.; paintings in regional and nat. art exhbns. Bd. dirs. Rockingham Fine Arts Assn., 1980—85, 1989, Citizens for the Downtown, 1989, Women's Coop. Coun. Harrisonburg and Rockingham County, 1976—79, Valley Coun. of the Arts, 1998—99, Shenandoah Coun. of the Arts, 1996—, pres., 1996—2002; founder OASIS Co-op Gallery, 2000. Served with USMC, 1944—46. Gen. Edn. Bd. of Rockefeller Found. fellow, 1952-53; recipient award Carnegie Found. Advancement of Tchg., 1947, 48, 49, 50; Ednl. Found. Program grantee AAUW, 1981-82; rsch. grantee Ednl. Radio and TV Ctr., 1956. Mem.: AAUW (cultural interests rep., nat. dir. 1980—82), Mensa, Va. Watercolor Soc., Pi Lambda Theta, Eta Sigma Phi, Kappa Pi. Democrat. Lutheran. Home: 150 Bear Wallow Ln Harrisonburg VA 22802-4822 E-mail: theodore@rica.net.

THEODORE, EUSTACE D. educational advancement consultant; b. Marietta, Ohio, Aug. 4, 1941; s. Demetrios E. and Nicoletta D. T.; m. Carol Nagy, June 13, 1964; children: Kyle James, Graham Clark. BA, Yale U., 1963; MA, Cornell U., 1965, PhD, 1967. Mem. faculty Hollins Coll., Roanoke, Va., 1967-71, Mt. Holyoke Coll., South Hadley, Mass., 1971-72; dean Calhoun Coll., Yale U., New Haven, 1972-81; exec. dir. Assn. Yale Alumni, 1981-97; pres. Coun. for Advancement and Support of Edn., Washington, 1997-2000; prin. eAdvancement.org, 2000—. Mgmt. and ednl. cons., 1965—. Contbr. articles to jours. Mem. Coun. Alumni Assn. Execs. (bd. dirs. 1991-97, pres. 1995-96), Coun. for Advancement and Support Edn. (trustee 1993-97, chair internat. task force 1994-97), CASE (Europe) (trustee 1995-2000), Commn. on Alumni Rels. (chair 1992-96). Office: eAdvancement.org 1301 21st St NW Washington DC 20036-1503

THEODORE, JOSE, hockey player; b. Sept. 13, 1976; Hockey player Montreal Canadiens, 1995—. Named Player of Week, Nat. Hockey League, 1999, Fredericton's Player of Yr., Am. Hockey League; named to World Hockey Championship 2nd All-Star team, 2000. Office: Molson Ctr 1260 d La Gauchetiere Street W Montreal QU 00012H3B 5E8 Canada Office Fax: 514-932-8736.*

THEODORESCU, RADU AMZA SERBAN, mathematician, educator; b. Bucharest, Romania, Apr. 12, 1933; emigrated to Can., 1968, naturalized, 1975; s. Dan and Ortensia Maria (Butoianu) T.; children: Dan, Paul, Anne. BSc, U. Bucharest, 1954, DSc, 1967; PhD, Acad. Romania, 1958. Asst. prof. Inst. Math. of Acad., 1954-57, sr. asst. prof., 1957-60, assoc. prof., sci. sec., 1960-64; prof., head dept. Center Math. Statistics, 1964-68; prof. U. Bucharest, 1968-69, Laval U., Quebec, Canada, 1969-2000, prof. emeritus Canada, 2000—; guest prof., lectr. univs. in Europe, N.Am. and Australia. Author: (with G. Ciucu) Processes with Complete Connections, 1960, (with S. Guiasu) Mathematical Information Theory, 1968, Uncertainty and Information, 1971, (with M. Iosifescu) Random Processes and Learning, 1969, (with W. Hengartner) Concentration Functions, 1973, 2d edit., 1980, Monte-Carlo Methods, 1978, (with E. Bertin and I. Cuculescu) Unimodality of Probability Measures, 1997; mem. editorial bd. Annales des Sciences Mathématiques du Québec, 1976-99, Optimization, 1970-2000, Statistics and Decisions; contbr. articles to profl. jours. Mem. bd. European Orgn. Quality Control, 1966-69. Recipient prize Acad. Romania, 1960 Fellow Inst. Math. Stats., Am. Soc. Quality; mem. Statis. Soc. Can. (hon.). Home: Apt 1603 9 Jardins Mérici Quebec QC Canada G1S 4S8 Office: Laval U Dept Math and Stats Quebec QC Canada G1K 7P4 E-mail: radutheo@mat.ulaval.ca.

THEODORIDIS, GEORGE CONSTANTIN, biomedical engineering educator, researcher; b. Braila, Romania, Dec. 3, 1935; came to U.S., 1959; s. Constantin George and Anastasia (Haritopoulos) T.; m. Lilly Kate Hyman, Sept. 20, 1975; 1 child, Alexander. BS in Mechanical and Elec. Engring., Nat. Tech. U. Athens, 1959; DSc, MIT, Cambridge, Mass., 1964. Rsch. assoc. MIT, Cambridge, Mass., 1964; sr. scientist Am. Sci. Engring., 1964-68; assoc. prof. in residence U. Calif., Berkeley, 1968-70; biomedical engring. U. Va., Charlottesville, 1970—; prof. elec. engring. U. Patras, Greece, 1976-83. Cons. Food and Drug Adminstrn., Washington, 1975-76, Applied Physics Lab, Columbia, Md., 1978-79. Author: Applied Math, 1983; contbr. articles to profl. jours. Den leader Boy Scouts Am., Charlottesville, Va., 1984-85. Fulbright fellow U.S. Govt., MIT, 1959-60; Nato fellow NATO, MIT, 1961-64; Spl. fellow NIH, U. Calif., 1968-70; recipient teaching award GE, MIT, 1963. Mem. Inst. Elec. and Electronics Engrs., Sigma Xi. Greek Orthodox. Avocations: history, travel. Home: 1817 Fendall Ave Charlottesville VA 22903-1613 Office: U Va Dept Biomed Engring PO Box 377 Charlottesville VA 22902-0377

THEODORU, STEFAN GHEORGHE, civil engineer, writer; b. Braila, Romania, June 11, 1921; came to U.S., 1965; s. Alexandru and Georgeta (Iovitz) T.; m. Nina Bogos, Jan. 31, 1945; children: Alexander, Radu. Degree in Civil Engring., Politech. Inst., Bucharest, Romania, 1947. Civil engr. Romanian Govt., Bucharest, 1947-64, Rella et Co., Vienna, Austria, 1964-65, Hydrotech. Corp., N.Y.C., 1965-66, Leon Selzer Assoc. P.E.C.P., N.Y.C., 1966-76; pvt. practice Long Island City, N.Y., 1976—. Author: Fata fara glas, 1993, Teatru , 1993, vol. V, 2002, Meeting in the Twilight, 1994, The Bag of Stars, 1995, Transylvania, 1995, (haiku) Centum, 1997, The Whispers of the Old Walnut Tree, 2001; author: ( ) Refugiatii, 2002; author, editor Vesuri vol. I, 1973, vol. II, La Lumina, 1993, A Wallachian Flag, 1977, Odiseea unui cuget, 1993, Un Milionar nebun, 1996, Genius, 1996, Nascuta in castelul lui Dracula, 1997, Marul din poveste, 1998, Adam si sotiile sale, 1998, Iac'asa, 1999, Drapelul de Margine, 1999, The Whispers of the Old Walnut Tree, 2001, Tati, 2002, author (anthologies) A Vision, a Verse, Vol. II, 1979; author: (anthologies) Dreams, 1963, 1980, Haiku World, 76, 1996, Numar Antologic 24, 1996, O Suta de Catarge, 92, 1997, Lumina Zorilor, 107-130, 1997, International Poetry and Art, 81, 88, 1997, Haiku Sans Frontiéres, 400, 1998, Light and Shadow, 36, 1998, Caligrafiile Clipei, 76-81, 1999, Culegatorii de Roua, 22, 1999, Almanah Origini, 75-84, 2000, Luna in Tandari, 58-59, 2000, Dimensiuni din Lumina Spiritului, 71-74, 2000, Poetii Romani de Haiku, 58, 2000, Crinkled Sunshine, 52, 2000, Haiku Printre Anotimpuri, 1, 3-7, 2000, Internet: Antologie de Haiku, 1997; contbr. work to profl. anthologies. Recipient numerous honors and awards including Daily Yomiuri, Tokyo, 1995, Panthon P.H. Semn, Romania, 1997, Romanian-Japanese Mag., 1997, Cultural Ctr. I. Perlea Orion, Romania, 1997, Internat. Ashya Haiku Festa, Hyogo, Japan, 2000, Tempus Found., Romania, 1998, V. Carlova award, Romania, 1995-98, Romanian Cinematography award 1952, Dacromanian Acad., 1999, Haiku award British H.S. J.W. Hackett Inst., 2000. Mem. Am. Romanian Relief Found., N.Y. Acad. Scis., Romanian Gen. Engring. Assn. (ct. tech. expert 1948, 64), Profl. Internat. Journalists Union Romania, Internat. Writers Assn. Ohio, Internat. Assn. Romanian Writers and Artists Ga., Am. Legion, Romanian Vexilologic Soc., Romanian Acad. Soc. Münich, Soc. Am. Inventors, Haiku Soc. Am., Haiku Soc. Romania, Constanta Haiku Soc. Romania. Achievements include co-inventor Pattern Recognition System. Home: 28-18 29th St Long Island City NY 11102

THEOFANOUS, THEO G. engineering educator, consultant; b. Athens, Greece, May 21, 1942; s. George T. and Smaro (Voudouris) T.; m. Danae P. Kembe, May 15, 1969; children: George, Lydia. BS in Chem. Engring., Nat. Tech. U., Athens, Greece, 1965; PhD in Chem. Engring., U. Minn., 1969; D in Laaperanta (hon.), U. Finland, 1999. Instr. in chem. engring. U. Minn., Mpls., 1968-69; asst. prof. chem. engring. Purdue U., West Lafayette, Ind., 1969-73, assoc. prof. chem. engring., 1973-74, assoc. prof. nuc. engring., 1974-76, prof. nuc. engring., 1976-85; prof. chem. and nuc. engring. U. Calif., Santa Barbara, 1985—, dir. Ctr. for Risk Studies and Safety, 1985—, prof. mech. and environ. engring., 1994—. V.p. Fauske, Grolmes, Henry & Theofanous, Ltd., Hinsdale, Ill., 1979-81; pres. Theofanous & Co., Inc., Santa Barbara, 1981—; cons. in field. Recipient Ernest Orlando Lawrence Meml. award U.S. Dept. of Energy, 1996. Fellow Am. Nuc. Soc.; mem. AIChE, AAAS, NAE. Achievements include finding the mechanism that caused the Sevesco accident; invented a methodology for risk assessment and mgmt. of high-consequence hazzards; contbr. in risk analyses of nuc. reactors and in mitigating the consequence of severe accidents. Office: U Calif Dept Chem Engring Santa Barbara CA 93106-5080 E-mail: theo@theo.ucsb.edu.

THEOHARIS, ATHAN GEORGE, history educator; b. Milw., Aug. 3, 1936; s. George A. and Adeline M. (Konop) T.; m. Nancy Artinian, Aug. 21, 1966; children: Jeanne, George, Elizabeth. AB, U. Chgo., 1956, AM, 1959, PhD, 1965. Instr. Tex. A&M U., College Station, 1962-64; asst. prof. Wayne State U., Detroit, 1964-68; assoc. prof. CUNY, S.I., 1968-69; assoc. prof. history Marquette U., Milw., 1969—76, prof., 1976—. Cons. select com. on intelligence activities U.S. Senate, Washington, 1975-76; cons. Nat. Archives FBI Records Task Force, Washington, 1980-81. Author: Seeds of Repression, 1972, Spying on Americans, 1978, The Boss, 1988, Chasing Spies, 2002, also author and/or author 13 other books. Mem. bd. dirs. ACLU-Wis., Mllw., 1975—. Recipient hon. mention Gavel award ABA, 1972, Outstanding Reference Source award database user sect. ALA, 1998, Haggerty award for rsch. excellence, 2002; 18 rsch. grants, Mem. Am. Hist. Assn. (nat. com. 1990-92), Orgn. Am. Historians (chmn. nat. com. 1980-82, Binkley-Stephenson award 1979), Am. Polit. Sci. Assn. Democrat. Greek Orthodox. Avocations: playing basketball, fan of professional and college sports. Home: 8527 N Manor Ln Fox Point WI 53217 Office: Marquette U PO Box 1881 Milwaukee WI 53201-1881

THEON, JOHN SPERIDON, meteorologist, researcher; b. Washington, Dec. 12, 1934; s. Lewis and Merope Theon; m. Joanne Edens, July 31, 1965; children— Christopher James, Catherine. BS in Aero. Engring. U. Md., 1957; BS in Meteorology, Pa. State U., 1959, MS, 1962; PhD in Engring. Sci. and Mechanics, U. Tenn., 1985. Aero. engr. Douglas Aircraft Co., Santa Monica, Calif., 1957-58; engr. U.S. Naval Ordnance Lab., White Oak, Md., 1962; rsch. meterologist, 1962-74; head meterology br. NASA Goddard Space Flight Center, Greenbelt, Md., 1974-77; asst. chief Lab. for Atmospheric Scis., 1977-78, Nimbus project scientist, 1972-78; mgr. global weather research program NASA Hdqrs., Washington, 1978-82, chief Atmospheric Dynamics and Radiation br., 1982-89, Spacelab 3 program scientist, 1979-86, chmn. space shuttle weather adv. panel, 1985-87; chief atmospheric, dynamics, radiation and hydrol. processes, 1989-93; chief phys. climate br., 1993-94; divsn. program scientist, 1994-95; exec. sec. task force on observations and data mgmt., 1994-95. Cons. Inst. for Global Environ. Strategies, 1995—, Orbital Scis. Corp., 1995-96, Cal Tech Jet Propulsion Lab., 1997-99. Contbr. articles to profl. jours. Served with USAF, 1958-60. Recipient Goddard Exceptional Performance award, 1978, NASA Exceptional Performance award, 1986, Radio Wave award Ministry of Posts & Telecomm. of Japan, 1995; name Disting. Alumnus U. Tenn., 1989. Fellow Am. Meteorol. Soc. Presbyterian. Home and Office: 6801 Lupine Ln Mc Lean VA 22101-1518

THEOPOLD, KLAUS HELLMUT, chemistry educator; b. Berlin, Apr. 18, 1954; came to U.S., 1978; s. Arnold and Gudula (Henjes) T.; children: Beatine Elise, Jessica Gudula, Nikolas McGeary, Karl Arnold. Vordiplom, U. Hamburg, Germany, 1977; PhD in Inorganic Chem., U. Calif.-Berkeley, 1982. Postdoctoral assoc. MIT, Cambridge, 1982-83; asst. prof. inorganic chem. Cornell U., Ithaca, N.Y., 1983-90; assoc. prof. inorganic chem. U. Del., 1990-95, prof. inorganic chem., 1995—, joint appointment in chem. engring., 1993. Vis. scientist inorganic chem., Oxford U., 1994; cons. Chevron Chem. Co., Kingwood, Tex., 1991-2001, Chevron Phillips Chem. Co., Bartlesville, Okla., 2001—. Contbr. articles to profl. jours. Served with German Army, 1974-75. Recipient Newly Appointed Young Faculty in Chemistry award Camille and Henry Dreyfus Fund, 1983, Presdl. Young Investigator award NSF, 1985; Alfred P. Sloan Rsch. fellow, 1992. Fellow AAAS; mem. Am. Chem. Soc., Gesellschaft Deutscher Chemiker, Sigma Xi. Office: U Del Dept Chemistry Biochem Newark DE 19716 E-mail: theopold@udel.edu.

THERING, HARLAN ROBERT, plastic surgeon, retired army officer; b. Plain, Wis., Oct. 17, 1934; s. Albert and Elizabeth (Lins) T.; m. Jane Edwards Sorenson, Dec. 27, 1956; children: Mary, Michael, Melissa, Mark. BS, Loras Coll., 1956; MD, Marquette U., 1960; postgrad. studies, Med. Field Svc. Sch., Fort Sam Houston, 1961-62. Diplomate Am. Bd. Surgery, Am. Bd. Plastic Surgery. Commd. officer M.C. U.S. Army, 1959, advanced through grades to col., ret., 1979; intern Brooke Army Med. Ctr., Ft. Sam Houston, Tex., 1960-61, resident gen. surgery, 1962-66; chief gen. surgery Bassett Army Hosp., Ft. Wainwright, Alaska, 1966-67, chief dept. surgery, 1967-68; resident plastic surgery Walter Reed Army Med. Ctr., Washington, 1968—70, asst. chief, 1970-72; chief plastic surgery svc. William Beaumont Med. Ctr., El Paso, Tex., 1972-79, cons. to plastic surgery svc., 1980—96; pvt. practice in plastic and reconstructive surgery, 1980—. Assoc. clin. prof. surgery Tex. Tech. U. Health Scis. Ctr., El Paso, 1974-89, assoc. clin. prof. surgery Tex. Tech. U. Med. Sch., 1980—; co-dir. burn unit Columbia Med. Ctr. West, El Paso, 1980-96; dir. Craniofacial Anomaly Clinic Border Children's Health Ctr., El Paso, 1989—; vice chmn. dept. surgery Providence Meml. Hosp., El Paso, 1994-95. Contbr. articles to profl. jours.; presenter at sci. symposia and seminars. Decorated Legion of Merit, Army Commendation medal. Mem. Am. Soc. Plastic Surgeons, Aesthetic Soc. Plastic Surgeons, Tex. Soc. Plastic Surgeons, Am. Coll. Surgeons, El Paso Soc. Plastic Surgeons (pres. 1999-2000), Cleft Palate Assn., Tex. Med. Assn., El Paso Med. Assn. Avocations: fishing, hiking, gardening, reading. Office: H Robert Thering MD, PA 125 W Hague Rd Ste 120 El Paso TX 79902-5803

THERNSTROM, STEPHAN, historian, educator; b. Port Huron, Mich., Nov. 5, 1934; s. Albert George and Bernadene (Robbins) T.; m. Abigail Mann, Jan. 3, 1959; children— Melanie Rachel, Samuel Altgeld. BS, Northwestern U., 1956; A.M., Harvard, 1958, PhD, 1962. Instr. history Harvard U., Cambridge, Mass., 1962-66, asst. prof., 1966-67, prof., 1973-81, Winthrop prof., 1981—, chmn. com. on higher degrees in history of Am. civilization, 1985-92; prof. Brandeis U., 1967-69, UCLA, 1969-73; Pitt. prof. Am. history and instns. Cambridge U., 1978-79; dir. Charles Warren Ctr. for Research in Am. History, 1980-83. Author: Poverty and Progress, 1964, Poverty, Planning and Politics in the New Boston, 1969, The Other Bostonians, 1973, History of the American People, 1984, 88; co-author: America in Black and White, 1997, Reflections on The Shape of the River, 1999; editor: Harvard Ency. Am. Ethnic Groups; co-editor: Harvard Studies in Urban History; Cambridge Interdisciplinary Perspectives on Modern History Series, Beyond the Color Line, 2001. Recipient Bancroft prize, R.R. Hawkins award, Faculty prize Harvard U. Press, Waldo G. Leland prize; Guggenheim fellow, John M. Olin fellow, ACLS fellow, sr. fellow Manhattan inst., 1998—. Office: Harvard U Robinson Hall Cambridge MA 02138

THERON, JOHANNES NICOLAAS, editor; b. Thabazimbi, Africa, Feb. 17, 1969; s. Diederik Johannes and Francina Petronella T.; m. Keri Lynne Crick, Oct. 9, 1999. B of Chem. Engring., U. Pretoria, South Africa, 1990; PhD, U. Cape Town, South Africa, 1990. Grad. trainee Gold Fields South Africa, Libanon, South Africa, 1991-92; dewatering mgr. Outokumpu Mintec,

Midrand, South Africa, 1996-98; sr. process engr. Outokumpu Am. Brass, Buffalo, 1998-2000; assoc. editor Chem. Engring. Mag., N.Y.C., 2000—. Mem. Am. Soc. Metals. E-mail: jantheron@hotmail.com.

THEROUX, DAVID JON, economist, educator, research executive; b. Lansing, Mich., May 25, 1949; s. Paul Richard and Marjorie Erma (Withrow) T.; m. Elaine Laconia Shipp, Mar. 20, 1976; children: Paul Jacques, Drake Emeri. A.B. in Applied Math., U. Calif.-Berkeley, 1973, B.S.M.E., 1973, M.S.M.E., 1974; M.B.A., U. Chgo., 1977. Rsch. asst. Richmond Field Sta., U. Calif.-Berkeley, 1974; project engr. Exxon Co. U.S.A., 1975-76; rsch. asst. U. Chgo., 1976, dir. vis. lecture program in econ. sci., 1977; v.p., dir. acad. affairs, dir. pub. policy studies Cato Inst., San Francisco, 1977-79; pres., dir. Pacific Inst. Pub. Policy Rsch., San Francisco, 1979-86; pres. The Ind. Inst., San Francisco, 1986—; pres., gen. ptnr. LTN Ptnrs., 1986—; pub., editor LibertyTree Network, 1986—; bd. dirs. Grocery Express, Ltd., 1986—; mem. Coun. for Monetary Reform, adv. bd. No. Calif. Econ. Seminars, 1981—. Mem. Mencken award book com. Free Press Assn., 1990—; trustee William Koch Found., 1978-79. With USAF, 1967-72. Recipient George Washington Honor medal for excellence Freedoms Found., 1983, Mencken award for Best Book Free Press Assn., 1988. Mem. Am. Econ. Assn., Royal Econ. Soc., Western Econ. Assn., So. Econ. Assn., Nat. Assn. Bus. Economists, Pub. Choice Soc., John Randolph Club, Pi Tau Sigma, Omicron Delta Epsilon. Sr. editor: Policy Report, 1978-79; editor: Cato Papers, 1978-79; The Energy Crisis: Government Policy and the Economy, 1978, (with P. Truluck) Private Rights and Public Lands, 1983, Politics and Tyranny: Lessons in Pursuit of Freedom, 1985. Home: 11990 Skyline Blvd Oakland CA 94619-2421 Office: 100 Swan Way Oakland CA 94621-1428

THEROUX, EUGENE, lawyer; b. Medford, Mass., Apr. 29, 1938; s. Albert and Anne (Dittami) T.; m. Phyllis Grissim, Feb. 13, 1963 (div. 1978); children: Christian, Elizabeth, Justin; m. Colleen Marie Pankratz, Feb. 27, 1982; children: Jean-Paul, Alexandra, Sebastien. Student, Harvard U., 1959, 60; BID, Pratt Inst., 1961, LittD, 1982; JD, Georgetown U., 1968. Bar: D.C. 1969, Mass. 1982, Va. 1985. Ptnr. Baker & McKenzie, Washington, 1969—, mem. policy com., 1992-94. Spl. counsel joint econ. com. U.S. Congress, Washington, 1972; adv. prof. Fudan U., Shanghai, People's Republic China, 1986—; adv. bd. Fletcher Sch. Law and Diplomacy, 1987—; trustee Monterey Inst. Internat. Studies. Author: (book) Joint Ventures In USSR, 1989, Business Guide To Moscow, 1990, Business Guide to Mongolia, 1996. Trustee Am. Leprosy Found., Washington, 1987—; v.p. U.S.-China Bus. Coun., Washington, 1973-75, dir., vice chair of bd., 1991-95. 1st lt. inf., U.S. Army, 1962-64, MAC/V So. Vietnam, 1968. Mem. ABA (chair Soviet law com. 1989-91), Metro. Club. Roman Catholic. Avocations: drawing, painting, running. Home: Short Hill Mountain Farm Lovettsville VA 20180 Office: Baker & McKenzie 815 Connecticut Ave NW Washington DC 20006-4004 E-mail: gene.theroux@bakernet.com.

THEROUX, PAUL EDWARD, author; b. Medford, Mass., Apr. 10, 1941; s. Albert Eugene and Anne (Dittami) T.; m. Anne Castle, Dec. 4, 1967 (div. 1993); children: Marcel, Louis; m. Sheila Donnelly, Nov. 18, 1995. BA, U. Mass., Amherst, DLitt, 1988, Trinity Coll., Washington, 1980, Tufts U., 1980. Lectr. U. Urbino, Italy, 1963, Soche Hill Coll., Malawi, 1963-65; faculty English dept. Makerere U., Uganda, 1965-68, U. Singapore, 1968-71; vis. lectr. U. Va., 1972-73. Author: (fiction) Waldo, 1967, Fong and the Indians, 1968, Girls at Play, 1969, Murder in Mt. Holly, 1969, Jungle Lovers, 1971, Sinning with Annie, 1972, Saint Jack, 1973, The Black House, 1974, The Family Arsenal, 1976, The Consul's File, 1977, Picture Palace, 1978 (Whitbread prize for fiction), A Christmas Card, 1978, London Snow, 1980, World's End, 1980, The Mosquito Coast, 1981, The London Embassy, 1982, Half Moon Street, 1984, O-Zone, 1986, My Secret History, 1988, Chicago Loop, 1990, Millroy and the Magician, 1993, My Other Life, 1996, Kowloon Tong, 1997, Collected Stories, 1997, Collected Short Novels, 1998, Hotel Honolulu, 2001; (nonfiction) V.S. Naipaul, 1973, The Great Railway Bazaar, 1975, The Old Patagonian Express, 1979, The Kingdom by the Sea, 1983, Sailing Through China, 1983, Sunrise with Sea Monsters, 1985, The White Man's Burden, 1987, Riding the Iron Rooster, 1988, The Happy Isles of Oceania, 1992, The Pillars of Hercules, 1995, Sir Vidia's Shadow, 1998, Fresh Air Fiend, 2000, Nurse Wolf and Dr. Sacks, 2001, Dark Star Safari, 2002; (film script) Saint Jack, 1979, Chinese Box, 1998. Recipient Editorial award Playboy mag., 1972, 76, 77, 79, Lit. award AAAL, 1977, James Tait Black award, 1982, Yorkshire Post Best Novel award, 1982, Thomas Cook Travel Book prize, 1989. Fellow Royal Soc. Lit., Royal Geog. Soc.; mem. AAAL.

THERRIEN, ANITA AURORE, elementary school educator; b. Lewiston, Maine, Apr. 1, 1937; d. Albert Leo and Florence (Clukey) T. Diploma, Ecole Pratique de Langue Francaise, Paris, 1957, diploma, 1963; BS in Edn., U. Maine, 1970, MEd, 1975. Cert. tchr., adminstr., Maine. Tchr. kindergarten St. Dominic Inst., Brookline, Mass., 1957-58; tchr. 1st and 3d grades St. Rita's Sch., Staten Island, N.Y., 1958-63; tchr. 1st and 4th grades Sabattus (Maine) Elem. Sch., 1967-92; ret., 1992. Scorer Maine Ednl. Assessment, Hinckley, 1988, mem. support team, 1988. Singer Holy Family Choir, Lewiston, 1984-88, Magic Pops Chorus, Lewiston, 1988-95. Honorable mention Alliance Francaise, 1958. Mem. Nat. Coun. Tchrs. of English, NEA (life), N.E. Coalition Ednl. Leaders, Sabattus Tchrs. Assn. (treas., chief negotiator 1967—), Maine Tchrs. Assn. Republican. Roman Catholic. Avocations: piano, singing, fishing, cross-country skiing, cycling.

THERRIEN, FRANCOIS XAVIER, JR. business and tax consultant; b. Amesbury, Mass. June 6, 1928; s. Francis Xavier and Doris Alma (Cote) T.; BS, U.S. Mil. Acad., 1950; MS, U. Ariz., 1962; Cert. tax profl., tax advisor, enrolled agt., environ. inspector, bd. cert. bus. appraiser; m. Yoshiko Kashima, July 22, 1969; children: Francois Xavier, Norman, Sakura, Izumi. Commd. 2d lt., U.S. Army, 1950, advanced through grades to lt. col., 1965, ret., 1970; dist. dir. R. J. Carroll Assoc., Inc., Atlanta, 1970-71; with Treasure Lake, Atlanta, 1971; pres. Identiseal of Fla., Orlando, 1972-74; owner Yoshiko Enterprises, Winter Park, Fla., 1974-87, bd. dirs., pres., 1988—; instr. Seminole Community Coll., 1974-79; regional rep. H.D. Vest Investment Securities, Inc., Irving, Tex., 1989—. Decorated Army Commendation medals (2), Air medal, Bronze Star medal, Silver Star, Croix DeGuerre with palm. Mem. Nat. Assn. Enrolled Agts. Roman Catholic. Office: 2265 Lee Rd Ste 223 Winter Park FL 32789-1858

THERRIEN, MICHEL, professional athletics coach; b. Nov. 4, 1963; m. Genevieve Therrien; children: Elizabeth, Charles. Coach Lvaal Titan, Granby Predateurs; 1st head coach Quebec Citadelles, 1999—2000; head coach Montreal Canadiens, 2000—. Office: Molson Ctr 1260 Gauchetiere St W Montreal QU H3B 5E8 Canada Office Fax: 514-932-8736.*

THESIER, LESLIE ANN EISEN, computer programmer, mathematician; b. Bklyn., June 29, 1964; d. Theodore and Elaine (Davies) E.; married; 2 children. BS in Computer Sci.-Math., SUNY, Binghamton, 1986, MA in Math., 1988. Cert. prin. Lotus cert. profl. Jr. programmer Chase Manhattan Bank, N.Y.C., 1986; asst. instr. SUNY, Binghamton, 1987-88, instr., 1988, cons., 1988-89; programmer/IT specialist IBM, Endicott, NY, 1989—. Home: 2709 Hamilton Dr Endwell NY 13760-2307

THESTRUP, PER, communications executive; b. Frederiksberg, Denmark, Nov. 6, 1935; s. Gudrun (Jensen) Thestrup; 1 child, Pia. Head news prodn. dept. Danmarks Radio, Soborg, Denmark, 1959—. Mem. town council Conservative, Herlev, Denmark, 1976-89; chmn. bd. Danish Com. Health Edn., Copenhagen, 1986—. With Danish Air Force, 1953-59. Office: Danish Broadcast Corp TV Ctr Indg 2 2860 Søborg Denmark Address: Porsevej 5 DK 4600 Kege Denmark

THEURER, BYRON W. aerospace engineer, business owner; b. Glendale, Calif., July 1, 1939; s. William Louis and Roberta Cecelia (Sturgiss) T.; m. Sue Ann McKay, Sept. 15, 1962 (div. 1980); children: Karen Marie, William Thomas, Alison Lee; m. Patricia Ann Pilcher, 2002. BS in Engring. Sci., USAF Acad., 1961; MS in Aero. Sci., U. Calif., Berkeley, 1965; MBA, U. Redlands, 1991. Commd. USAF, 1961, advanced through grades to lt. col., ret. 1978; project officer Space Shuttle Devel. Prog., Houston, 1971-76; chief of test F-15 Systems Prog. Office Wright Patterson AFB, Ohio, 1976-78; sr. engr. Veda, Inc., Dayton, 1979-81, Logicon Inc., Dayton, 1981-83; project mgr. Support Systems Assocs., Inc., 1983-84, CTA Inc., Ridgecrest, Calif., 1985-89; owner, operator The Princeton Rev. of Ctrl. Calif., 1989-92, San Luis Obispo, 1993—2002. Cons. in field. Decorated Silver Star, D.F.C., Air Medals (16); named Officer of the Yr., Air Force Flight Test Ctr., Edwards AFB, 1970. Mem. Air Force Assn., Assn. Old Crows, USAF Acad. Assn. Grads. (nat. bd. dirs. 1972-75, chpt. pres. 1981-83), Svc. Corps Ret. Execs. Republican. Episcopalian. Avocation: running. Home: PO Box 697 Cayucos CA 93430-0697

THEVENET, PATRICIA CONFREY, social studies educator; b. Norwich, Conn., Apr. 16, 1924; d. John George and Gertrude Pauline (Doolittle) Confrey; m. Rubén Thevenet, Dec. 15, 1945 (dec. Mar. 1983); chldren: Susanne, Gregory, Richard, R. James. BS, U. Conn., 1944; AM, U. Chgo., 1945; EdM, Columbia U., 1992, EdD, 1994. Cert. elem. tchr., N.J. Counselor testing and guidance U. Chgo., 1945; home economist Western Mass. Electric Co., Pittsfield, 1946; tchr. Unquowa Sch., Fairfield, Conn., 1950-53, Alpine (N.J.) Sch., 1968-86; program asst. soc. studies Tchrs. Coll. Columbia U., N.Y.C., 1987-93; ret., 1993. Historian Borough Northvale, N.J., 1987-94; participant summer seminar Smithsonian Instn., Washington, 1984. Del. 2d dist. rep. Town Mtg., Trumbull, Conn., 1954-56; pres., trustee Northvale Pub. Libr. Assn., 1957-63; trustee Northvale Bd. Edn., 1963-72, pres. Northvale Bd. Edn., 1969-70; exec. bd. dirs. Bergen County (N.J.) County Bds. Edn., 1965-72; mem. Evening Sch. Comm. No. Valley Regional Dist., Bergen County, 1976-83; trustee Voluntown Libr., 1997-2001. Mem. AAUW, Voluntown Hist. Soc., Friends of Slater Mus., DAR. Home: 88 N Shore Rd # B Voluntown CT 06384-1719

THEVUTHASAN, THEVA SUNTHARAMPILLAI, research scientist; b. Jaffna, Sri Lanka, June 15, 1957; came to U.S., 1986; s. Appiah and Parvathipillai (Sinnathamby) Suntharampillai; m. Rohini Nagalingam, Nov. 10, 1985; children: Sindhu, Senthuran, Sangeetha. BS in Physics with honors, U. Peradeniya, Kandy, Sri Lanka, 1981; MS, Asian Inst. of Tech., Bangkok, 1984; PhD, U. Maine, Orono, 1989. Rsch. asst. Asian Inst. Tech., Bangkok, 1984-86; postdoctoral rsch. assoc. U. Fla., Gainesville, 1989-90; postdoctoral fellow U. Hawaii, Honolulu, 1990-91; postgrad. rsch. assoc. U. Calif., Davis, 1991-93; rsch. scientist Pacific N.W. Nat. Lab., Richland, Wash., 1993-97, sr. rsch. scientist, 1998—. Contbr. articles to profl. jours. Scholar Can. Internat. Devel. Agy., Thailand, 1983. Mem. Am. Vacuum Soc. (bd. dirs. 1998—, short course exec. com. 1998—, sec. N.W. chpt., 1995—). Avocations: tennis, gardening, hiking. Office: EMSL Battelle MSIN K8-93 PO Box 999 Richland WA 99352-0999 E-mail: theva@pnl.gov.

THEYS, PHILIPPE PAUL, data quality professional; b. Lille, France, Feb. 20, 1949; came to U.S., 1994; s. Maurice and Paulette (Querleu) T.; m. Odile Marie-Paule Bechere, July 15, 1972; children: Sophie, Cedric, Alban, Alice. Diploma in Engring., Ecole Centrale De Paris, 1971; Lic., Scis. Econs., Assas, France, 1971; grad. in Plasma Physics, U. Paris-Orsay, France, 1972. Rsch. engr. French Atomic Commn., 1971-72; geophys. field engr. Schlumberger, France, Sweden, Germany, U.S., Australia, 1972-77, country mgr. Taiwan, 1978-79, interpretation devel. mgr. Ea. Hemisphere, 1980-81, mktg. mgr. United Arab Emirates, Indonesia, Norway, 1982-89, quality mgr. Worldwide, 1990-94, data quality mgr. Worldwide, 1994—. Vice chmn. Log Characterization Consortium, 1997-99. Author: Log Data Acquisition and Quality Control, 1999; editor (mag.) The Log Analyst, 1994-2000, Petrophysics, 2000—. Lt. French Army, 1971-72. Mem. Soc. Profl. Well Log Analysts (v.p. edn. 1997-98, v.p. tech. 1998-99, pres. 2000—), Am. Soc. for Quality, Soc. Petroleum Engrs. Roman Catholic. Avocations: skydiving, long distance running, photography. Office: Sugarland Product Ctr 110 Schlumberger Dr Sugar Land TX 77478 E-mail: theys5@slb.com.

THIAGARAJAN, SIVASAILAM, educational association administrator, educator; b. Madras, India, Mar. 21, 1938; came to U.S., 1967; s. Thiruvengadam and Valliammal (Nayagam) Sivasailam; m. Thayammal Subramaniam, May 27, 1965; 1 child, Raja Thiagarajan. BS, Loyola Coll., Madras, India, 1960; MS in Edn., Ind. U., 1970, PhD, 1971. High sch. tchr. T'Nagar High Sch., Madras, India, 1961-67; rsch. assoc. Ind. U., Bloomington, 1970-72; assoc. dir. Ind. U. Design Lab., 1972-75; chief instrn. designer U. Mid-Am., Lincoln, Nebr., 1975-76; prin. Workshops by Thiagi, Bloomington, Ind., 1976—. Chief of project, USAID Primary Edn. Project, Liberia, 1979-81. Author: (book) Giant Book of Team Techniques, 1980. Mem. Nat. Soc. for Performance & Instr. Avocations: magic, writing short stories. Home and Office: 4423 E Trailridge Rd Bloomington IN 47408-9633

THIBADEAU, EUGENE FRANCIS, education educator, consultant; b. N.Y.C., May 18, 1933; s. Eugene Servanis and Lillian (Archer) T.; 1 child, Christine. BA, NYU, 1959, MA, 1967, MA, 1968, PhD, 1973. Instr. NYU, N.Y.C., 1968; lectr. in philosophy Dowling Coll., Oakdale, N.Y., 1968-70; prof. edn. Indiana U. of Pa., Indiana, Pa., 1970—. Vis. assoc. prof. Adelphi U., Garden City, N.Y., 1974-75; vis. scholar NYU, N.Y.C., 1984-85; vis. prof. Hofstra U., Hempstead, N.Y., 1974, 75, 84, 86; cons. Central Bur. of Ednl. Visits, London, 1980-81, Commonwealth Speakers Bur., Harrisburg, Pa., 1983-85, U.S. Dept. Edn., Washington, 1983-85, Pa. Dept. Edn., Harrisburg, 1988—. Author: Opening Up Education-In Theory and Practice, 1976, Curriculum Theory, 1988, Existentialism in the Classroom, 1994; rev. editor: Focus on Learning, 1973-77, editor, 1977-84; contbg. editor: International Encyclopedia of Education, 2d edit., International Encyclopedia of Teaching and Teacher Education, 2nd edit., International Encyclopedia of Social and Behavioral Sciences; contbr. articles to profl. jours. Active in United Way, Indiana, Pa., 1980—, NAACP, Indiana, 1985—, Red Cross, Indiana, 1985—. Fulbright sr. lectr. Thames Polytechnic, London, 1978-79, Fulbright sr. scholar Janus Pannonius U., Peces, Hungary, 1990-91; foreign expert Shanghai (China) Tchrs. U., 1988; designated faculty rsch. assoc. Inst. for Applied Rsch. and Pub. Policy, Indiana U. of Pa., 1989; named Commonwealth Teaching fellow and Cert. Excellence in Teaching, Pa. State Colls. and Univ. Disting. Faculty Awards Com., 1976; recipient Founder's Day award, NYU, 1973, PSEA Outstanding Prof. Award, 1993. Fellow Am. Philosophy Edn. Soc.; mem. Am. Ednl. Studies Assn., AAUP, The S.W. Philosophy Edn. Soc., ASCD. Avocations: traveling, skiing, tennis, reading, chess. Home: 534 Chestnut Ridge Rd Penn Run PA 15765 Office: Indiana Univ Pa 131 Stouffer Hall Indiana PA 15705

THIBAUDEAU, MARY FRANCES, cultural organization administrator; b. Anaconda, Mont., Dec. 6, 1943; d. Frank Albert and Mary (May) T.; m. Alex W. Wells, Jr.; 1 child, Christopher. BA magna cum laude, U. Wash., Seattle, 1969. Therapist, counselor Thibaudeau and Assocs., Atlanta, 1976-88; chmn. Vietnam Reconciliation Bus. Group, 1988—. Cons. Ga. Vets. Leadership Program, Atlanta, 1994. Exec. prodr. (documentaries) Vietnam: POWs Return—The Final Healing, 2000, TET '68: Healing Wounds of War. . .30 Years After, 1998, TET Vietnam Reconciliation Documentary; co-author, editor (feature film screenplay) Perfume River, 2002. Exch. dir. Friendship Force Internat., Atlanta, 1993-94; co-founder, chmn. Tet Vietnam Reconciliation Found. for Internat. Healing/Friendship Ctr., 2002. Named Ga. Outstanding Citizen, Ga. Sec. State, 1994. Mem. Atlanta Vets. Assn. (hon.). Avocations: travel, reading, languages, hiking, photography. Home and Office: PO Box 767722 Roswell GA 30076-7722

THIBAUDEAU, MAY MURPHY, writer; b. Nasboro, Wis., May 8, 1908; d. Hugh Isadore and Laura (Brown) Murphy; m. Raymond Joseph Thibaudeau, June 16, 1941; children: Adele, Yvonne, Clairese, Camille, Valerie, Marguerete, Hugh. BS, U. Wis., Milw., 1973. Lic. tchr., Wis. Tchr. rural state graded, Fond du Lac County, Wis., 1927-34; tchr. city graded City of Peshtigo (Wis.), 1934-42; tchr. grade 3 St. Mary's Parish, South Milwaukee, Wis., 1956-75; writer, 1976—. Author: Life and Times of Frederick Layton, 1984, I Shall Not Die I Shall Live on in You, 1990 (State Assembly citation 1990), The Donkey Stayed in Ireland, 1980. Pres. Fond du Lac County Tchrs. Assn., 1933-34; mem. Wis. Edn. Assn., Madison, 1935-42, Nat. Cath. Edn. Assn., Washington, 1956-75, Common Cause, Washington, 1975—, LWV, Washington, 1985-90; leader Girl Scouts U.S., Milw., 1955-62. Mem. Wis. Regional Writers, Writers Ink, AAUW (Edn. Found. Name grantee 1990). Democrat. Roman Catholic. Avocations: perennial garden, ragtime organ music. Home: 1212 N Chicago Ave South Milwaukee WI 53172-1633

THIBAULT, J(OSEPH) LAURENT, service company executive; b. Sturgeon Falls, Ont., Can., Dec. 31, 1944; s. J. Rene and Leone (Doucet) T.; m. Paulette Patricia Lalonde, June 4, 1966; children—Alain, Andre BA in Econs., Laurentian U., Sudbury, 1966; MA in Econs., U. Toronto, Ont., 1968. Cons. Kates, Peat & Marwick Co., Toronto, 1968-72; dir. econs. and communications Can. Mfrs. Assn., 1972-76, v.p., 1976-81, sr. exec. v.p., 1981-84, pres., exec. dir., 1985-91; co-chair Can. Labour Force Devel. Bd., Ottawa, Ont., Can., 1991-95; fin. advisor Assante Capital Mgmt. Ltd., Mississauga, 1995—. V.p. World Skills; bd. dirs. William Osler Health Ctr. Found., Skills Can., Ontario. Mem. Can. Assn. Bus. Econs. (hon.). Home: 24 Cindebarke Terr Georgetown ON Canada L7G 4S5 Office: City Ctr Plz 1 City Centre Dr Ste 1520 Mississauga ON Canada L5B 1M2 E-mail: lthibault@assante.com.

THIBEAULT, GEORGE WALTER, lawyer; b. Cambridge, Mass., Sept. 21, 1941; s. George Walter and Josephine (Maraggia) T.; m. Antoinette Miller, June 30, 1963; children: Robin M., Holly Ann. BS, Northeastern U., 1964; MBA, Boston Coll., 1966, JD, 1969. Bar: Mass. 1969. Assoc. Gaston & Snow, Boston, 1969-73; ptnr. Testa, Hurwitz & Thibeault, 1973—. Mem. ABA, Mass. Bar Assn., Am. Arbitration Assn. Home: 181 Caterina Hts Concord MA 01742-4773 Office: Testa Hurwitz & Thibeault High St Tower 125 High St 22d Fl Boston MA 02110-2704 E-mail: thibeault@tht.com.

THIBEDEAU, RICHARD HERBERT, environmental planner, administrator; b. Needham, Mass., Apr. 2, 1942; m. Susan McAllister Richardson, Nov. 8, 1986; children: Susan, Richard, Catherine, Julie, Billy. BSFS, Georgetown U., 1964; M of Internat. Rels., U. Pa., 1967; M of Regional Planning, Harvard U., 1974. Field rep. CARE, Sri Lanka, 1967-70, asst. county dir. Korea, 1971-72; chief pvt. land planning Adirondack Park Agy., Ray Brook, N.Y., 1974-78; dep. dir. Mass. Coastal Zone Mgmt., Boston, 1978-80; chief planner Mass. Divsn. Water Resources, 1981-87, dir., 1987-90, Bur. Resource Protection Dept. Environ. Mgmt., Boston, 1990—. Reservist Fed. Emergency Mgmt. Agy., 1992-2000; chmn. Conn. River Flood Control Commn., Vt., N.H., Mass. and Conn., 1993-94. Treas. Christian Svc. Com. Old North Ch., Marblehead, 1998—. 1st lt. U.S. Army, 1964-66, Korea. Recipient Mass. Citation for Outstanding Performance, 1988, Mass. Cert. Performance, State Gov., 1990. Mem. Am. Planning Assn. (Disting. Leadership award N.E. chpt. 1989), Am. Inst. Cert. Planners (cert.), Am. Water Assn., Appalachian Mountain Club (com. chmn. 1986—). Avocations: hiking, skiing, kayaking. Home: 15 Village St Marblehead MA 01945-2212 Office: Mass Dept Environ Mgmt 251 Causeway St Ste 600 Boston MA 02114-2104

THIBERT, ROGER JOSEPH, clinical chemist, educator; b. Tecumseh, Ont., Can., Aug. 29, 1929; s. Charles and Violet (Hebert) T.; m. Audrey M. Wissler, July 10, 1954; children: Mark Roger, Robert Francis. BA, U. Western Ont., 1951; MS, U. Detroit, 1954; PhD, Wayne State U., 1958. Diplomate: Am. Bd. Clin. Chemistry, also past bd. dirs. Mem. faculty U. Windsor, Ont., Can., 1953—, prof. chemistry, 1967-94, dir. clin. chemistry, 1972-94, prof. emeritus, 1994—; prof. pathology Med. Sch. Wayne State U., Detroit, 1972-94; asso. div. head, clin. chemistry Detroit Receiving Hosp., Univ. Health Ctr., 1973-94; mem. med. staff Detroit Receiving Hosp.-Univ. Health Center, 1973-94. Cons. med. biochemistry Med. Labs. Windsor, Ont., Can., 1995-2000; scientific dir. Med. Labs., Windsor, Ont., Can., 2000—. Contbr. articles on chemistry, biochemistry, analytical chemistry, clin. chemistry to profl. jours. Recipient Smith Kline award Am. Assn. Clin. Chemistry, 1980, Alumni Teaching award U. Windsor, 1988, Alumni Award of Merit, 1994, Teaching award Ont. Confedn. U. Faculty Assns., 1990, Beckman Edn. Excellence award Canadian Soc. Clin. Chemists, 1992; Chem. Inst. Can. fellow, 1968—; Nat. Acad. Clin. Biochemistry fellow, 1978—; recipient grants Natural Scis. and Engring. Rsch. Coun., Can., award Union Carbide, Chem. Inst., Can., 1978. Fellow AAAS, Can. Acad. Clin. Biochemistry; mem. Am. Chem. Soc., Chem. Inst. Can., Assn. Chem. Profession Ont., Am. Assn. Clin. Chemistry, Nat. Acad. Clin. Biochemistry, Can. Soc. Clin. Chemists (Ames award 1988), Ont. Soc. Clin. Chemists, Am. Soc. for Biochemistry and Molecular Biology, Fedn. Am. Socs. Exptl. Biology, Can. Soc. Biochemistry and Molecular Biology, Can. Fedn. Biol. Scis., Can. Soc. for Chemistry, Sigma Xi. Roman Catholic. Home: 4612 Dali Ct Windsor ON Canada N9G 2M8 Office: U Windsor Dept Chemistry/Biochemistry Windsor ON Canada N9B 3P4

THIBIDEAU, REGINA, retail executive, social worker; b. Quincy, Mass., Sept. 18, 1943; d. Roy John Joseph Robicheau and Cora Drew Cross; m. Bruce Edward Maranda, Aug. 27, 1966 (div. June 1980); children: Hathaway Jakobsen, Kenseth Thibideau; m. Ronald William Joseph Thibideau, Sept. 24, 1984. BA, U. Vt., 1965; MEd, No. Ariz. U., 1998. Sec. clin. psychology office U. Mass., Amherst, 1966-67; social worker Mass. Dept. of Welfare, 1967-69, East Boston, 1969-70, Quincy, Mass., 1971-73; CPR coord. Am. Heart Assn., Hyannis, 1978-80; child advocate Office for Children, 1980; owner, retailer Maggie O'Shaughnessy's, Sun City West, Ariz., 1983—. Facilitator Mercy Otis Warren Women's Ctr., Hyannis, 1980-81. Contbg. writer T.J. Reid's Newsletter, Amite, La., 1999; writer Maggie's Newsletter, Sun City West, 1996—. Organizer Mother's Day Celebration, 1999, 2000; mem. Litchfield Park Libr. Assn., 1985-98. Named Top 10 Boutiques in Ariz., Ariz. Woman mag., 1999, 2000, 2001, One of Top Bus. in Ariz., 2000, 2001. Mem. AAUW, Sundome Merchants Assn. Avocations: travel, painting, computers, reading, walking. Home: 565 E Estero Ln Litchfield Park AZ 85340-4235 Office: 13521 W Camino Del Sol Sun City West AZ 85375-4416 E-mail: regina@maggie-o.com.

THIBODEAU, GARY A. academic administrator; b. Sioux City, Iowa, Sept. 26, 1938; m. Emogene J. McCarville, Aug. 1, 1964; children: Douglas James, Beth Ann. BS, Creighton U., 1962; MS, S.D. State U., 1967, MS, 1970, PhD, 1971. Profl. service rep. Baxter Lab., Inc., Deerfield, Ill., 1963-65; tchr., researcher dept. biology S.D. State U., Brookings, 1965-76, asst. to v.p. for acad. affairs, 1976-80, v.p. for adminstrn., 1980-85; chancellor U. Wis., River Falls, 1985-2000; sr. v.p. acad. affairs U. Wis. Sys., 2000—01. Mem. investment com. U. Wis., River Falls Found.; trustee W. Cen. Wis. Consortium U. Wis. System; bd. dirs. U. Wis. at River Falls Found.; mem. Phi Kappa Phi nat. budget rev. and adv. comm., Phi Kappa Phi Found. investment comm., comm. on Agrl. and Rural Devel., steering commn. Coun. of Rural Colls. and Univs., Joint Coun. on Food and Agrl. Scis., USDA. Author: Basic Concepts in Anatomy and Physiology, 1983, Athletic Injury Assessment, 1994, Structure and Function of the Body, 1996, The Human Body in Health and Disease, 1996, Textbook of Anatomy and Physiology, 1996. Mem. AAAS, Sigma Xi, Phi Kappa Phi, Gamma Sigma Delta, Gamma Alpha. Office: U Wis 116 N Hall River Falls WI 54022

THIBODEAU, ROBIN ANN, retired union official, mail carrier; b. Southington, Conn., Oct. 27, 1956; d. Robert Edward and Irene Josephine (Bendott) Dunbar; m. Roland Leo Thibodeau, Feb. 25, 1978 (div. Aug. 1983); children: Christina Ann Thibodeau, Desilyn Joanne Nelson. Grad. high sch., Southington; grad., Porter & Chesters Auto. Inst. Sec. Bd. of Edn., Southington, 1974-75; cashier, clk. Cumberland Farms, Plantsville, Conn., 1974; acctg. clk. to contr. Waterbury Farrel, Mfg., Cheshire, 1975-76; machinist Supreme Lake Mfg., Plantsville, 1976-77; auto transmission re-builder Transmission Works, Hartford, Conn., 1978-79; rural carrier substitute Southington Post Office, 1979-81, Terryville (Conn.) Post Office, 1980; regular rural carrier Plainville (Conn.) Post Office, 1981-84, Farmington (Conn.) Post Office, 1984—2000; ret., 2000. Local union steward Plainville Post Office, 1981-84; local/area steward Farmington Post Office, 1985-94. Republican. Avocations: computer bulletin board, RV travel, crafting, gardening. Home: 17 Spruce St Plainville CT 06062-2327 Office: Conn Rural Letter Carrier Assn 210 Main St Farmington CT 06032-9998

THIBODEAU, THOMAS RAYMOND, lawyer; b. St.Paul, Feb. 5, 1942; m. Mollie Nan Mylor, Sept. 24, 1966; 1 child, Matthew Raymond. BA in Polit. Sci. cum laude, U. St. Thomas, St. Paul, 1964; JD, U. Minn., 1967. Bar: Minn. 1967, U.S. Dist. Ct. Minn. 1967, U.S. Ct. Appeals (8th cir.) 1970, U.S. Supreme Ct. 1982, Wis. 1983, U.S. Dist. Ct. Wis. 1983, N.D. 2000, U.S. Dist. Ct. N.D., 2000; solicitor Supreme Ct. Eng. and Wales, 1996; cert. civil trial specialist Nat. Bd. Trial Advocacy. Ptnr. Johnson, Killen & Thibodeau, Duluth, Minn., 1967-2000, Thibodeau, Johnson & Feriancek PLLP, Duluth, 2000—. Pres. Legal Aid Service N.E. Minn., Inc., 1969-74; mem. civil justice reform act adv. com. U.S. Dist. Ct. Minn. Mem. revision Civil Jury Instruction Guide IV, 1997—. Chmn. Duluth City Charter Commn., 1976-78; vol. atty. St. Louis County Heritage and Arts Ctr., Duluth, 1980-87; pres. bd. trustees Marshall Sch., 1990-92. Recipient Disting. Alumni award U. St. Thomas, 1985. Fellow Internat. Soc. Barristers, Am. Coll. Trial Lawyers; mem. Am. Bd. Trial Advs. (advocate), Minn. Bar Assn. (chmn. specialization com. 1974-78, co-chmn. revision Civil Injury Instrn. Guide III com. 1982-85, 96-99), Minn. Def.

Lawyers Assn. (pres. 1988-89), Acad. Cert. Trial Lawyers of Minn. (pres. elect 1993, pres. 1994-95), Internat. Assn. Def. Counsel, Assn. Def. Trial Attys. Avocations: hunting, skiing, scuba diving and other water sports, reading. Office: Thibodeau Johnson & Feriancek PLLP 800 Lonsdale 302 W Superior St Duluth MN 55802-1802

THICKINS, GRAEME RICHARD, marketing professional, consultant; b. Perth, Australia, Apr. 4, 1946; came to U.S., 1952; s. Richard Percy and Lucie Joy (McDiarmid) T.; m. Jane Elizabeth Bantle, Nov. 6, 1969; children: Jeffrey, Christopher, Sarah. AA, Austin State Jr. Coll., 1967; postgrad., U. Minn., 1967-70. Editor Data 100 Corp., Edina, Minn., 1970-72; pub. rels. and promotion writer, editor MTS Sys. Corp., Eden Prairie, 1972-73; dir. pub. rels. svcs., writer, account exe. The Comm. Coalition, Inc., Edina, 1973-74; free-lance writer, cons. Mpls., 1974-75; mktg. comm. writer, asst. mgr. Medtronic, Inc., 1975-77; mktg. svcs. mgr., comm. mgr. Am. Med. Sys., Inc., 1977-78; account exec. D'Arcy-MacManus & Masius, Twin Cities, Minn., 1978; cons. editl. svcs., corp. comm. Controll Data Corp., Mpls., 1978-79, mgr. editl. svcs., 1979, mgr. promotion lit., 1980, mgr. creative svcs., 1981, mgr. advt. and promotion, sys. and svcs. co., 1982; cons. mktg., advt., direct mail, pub. rels., 1975-82; founder, pres. for emerging growth and tech. firms GT&A Strategic Mktg. Inc., 1982—. Spkr. in field. Co-chairperson mktg. and comm. Minn. Orch. Symphony Ball, 1986. Recipient numerous awards of excellence from various profl. assns. Mem. Assn. Online Profls., Am. Mktg. Assn., Coun. Growing Cos. (Minn. chpt. chair pub. rels. 1994-99), Minn. High-Tech Assn., Phi Gamma Delta. Avocations: photography, surfing, Hawaiiana, Internet communications. Home and Office: 8135 Kentucky Cir S Bloomington MN 55438-1230 E-mail: grt@gtamarketing.com.

THIE, GENEVIEVE ANN ROBINSON, retired secondary school educator; b. Aledo, Ill., Sept. 4, 1939; d. Leroy James and Wilma Elizabeth (Wood) Robinson; m. Irvin Emil Thie, Sept. 9, 1977; children: Vyona Ann, Daryl Irvin. BA, Iowa State Tchrs. Coll., Cedar Falls, 1961; MA, U. No. Iowa, Cedar Falls, 1969. Tchr. Cedar Rapids (Iowa) Sch. Bd., 1961-64, New Hartford (Iowa) Sch. Bd., 1965-68, Holmes Jr. High Sch., Cedar Falls, 1968-77; tchr. East Bay High Sch. Hillsborough County Sch. Bd., Tampa, Fla., 1979-84, tchr. Armwood High Sch., 1984-97, ret., 1997. Editor Iowa Coun. Tchrs. Math. Jour., 1975-78. Mem. NEA, Nat. Coun. Tchrs. Math., Math. Assn. Am., Fla. Coun. Tchrs. Math., Hillsborough County Tchrs. Math., Phi Delta Kappa. Episcopalian. Avocations: reading, golfing, traveling. Home: 265 Fairway Dr Spearfish SD 57783-3111

THIEBAUD, WAYNE, artist; b. Mesa, Ariz., Nov. 15, 1920; s. Morton J. and Alice Eugenia (LeBaron) T.; m. Betty Jean Carr, Dec. 11, 1959; children: Twinka, Mallary Ann, Paul LeBaron. BA, Sacramento State Coll., 1951, MA, 1952; MFA (hon.), Calif. Coll. Arts and Crafts, 1975. Art dir., N.Y.C.; also Hollywood, 1946-49; chmn. art dept. Sacramento City Coll., 1951; design cons. Calif. State Fair and Expn.; guest instr. San Francisco Art Inst., 1958; assoc. prof. art U. Calif. at Davis, now prof., Faculty Research lectr., from 1973. Vis. artist Cornell U., U. Hawaii, U. Wis., U. Utah, U. Ill., Yale, U. Va., Bradley U. One man shows include, Crocker Art Gallery, Sacramento, 1952, Artists Coop. Gallery, Sacramento, 1954, DeYoung Mus., San Francisco, 1962, Allan Stone Gallery, N.Y.C., 1962-70, Stanford, 1965, Galleria Schwarz, Milan, Italy, 1963, San Francisco Mus., 1967, Whitney Mus., 1972, Walker Art Ctr., Mpls., 1981, Ft. Worth Art Mus., 1981, Mus. Fine Arts, St. Petersburg, Fla., 1981, exhibited museums, U.S., Toronto, Can., Hague, Holland, Vienna, Berlin, Hong Kong, S.Am., traveling exhibit, Pasadena Mus. Art, 1967-68; one-man traveling exhibit Survey of Works, Oakland Mus., Phoenix Mus., U. So. Calif., Des Moines Mus., Boston Inst. Contemporary Art, 1976; U.S. rep. one-man traveling exhibit, Sao Paulo Biennale, 1966, Indocumenta, 1972; group exhbns. include, Santa Barbara Mus. Art, 1980, Bklyn. Mus., 1980, 81, Whitney Mus. Am. Art, 1981, San Antonio Mus. Art, 1981, Indpls. Mus. Art, 1981, Inst. Contemporary Art, U. Pa., 1981, Carnegie Inst., Pitts., 1981, Allan Stone Gallery, N.Y.C., 1982; represented permanent collections museums and galleries, Europe, U.S., including, Mus. Modern Art, Whitney Mus., Albright Knox Mus., Wadsworth Athenaeum, Library Congress, Woodward Found., Rose Art Mus., Brandeis U., Stanford, Sheldon Meml. Art Gallery U. Nebr., Fines Arts Mus. San Francisco, Utah Mus. Fine Arts U. Utah, Kemper Mus. Contemporary Art, Mo., U. Maine Mus. of Art, Spencer Mus. of Art U. Kans., Nat. Mus. Am. Art, Wash., Crown Point Press; also numerous pvt. collections, commd. fountain mobile sculpture, Calif. State Fair, 1952, Sacramento Municipal Utility Dist. Bldg., 1959; producer, dir. 12 ednl. motion pictures. (Recipient 1st prize Art Film Festival 1956, Golden Reel Film Festival award for Space, Calif. State Fair 1956, named Univ. Art Studio Tchr. of Yr., Coll. Art Assn. Am. 1981, Faculty Research medal U. Calif.-Davis, 1984, Award of Distinction, Nat. Art Schs. Assn., 1984, Spl. Citation, Nat. Assn. Schs. Art and Design, 1984); commd. to do paintings of Wimbledon Tennis Tournament, 1968, of Yosemite Ridge Line for Bicentennial Exhbn., 1976; sent to Kyoto, Japan to do woodblock prints by Crown Point Press, 1987; 42 works on paper at Arts Club Chgo., 1987. Author: etchings Delights, 1965, Prints, 1970-71, Seven Still Lifes and a Rabbit. Recipient Cyril Magnin award, San Francisco, 1987, Golden Plate award Am. Acad. Achievement, 1987, Nat. Medal of the Arts, 1994. Mem. Am. Acad. and Inst. Arts and Letters, Nat. Acad. Design (academician). "Wayne Thiebaud" exhbn. organized by San Francisco Mus. Modern Art for 50th anniversary, 1985, scheduled to travel to Newport Harbor, R.I., Milw., Columbus, Ohio and Kansas City. Office: Care Allan Stone Galle New York NY 10128

THIEBAUTH, BRUCE EDWARD, advertising executive, director; b. Bronxville, N.Y., Oct. 30, 1947; s. Bruce and Margaret Evelyn (Wiederhold) T.; m. Sherry Ann Proplesch, Aug. 31, 1968; 1 child, Bruce Revere. Student, Colby Coll., Waterville, Maine, 1965-66, Pace Coll., 1971; BA in Bus. Adminstrn. and Sociology magna cum laude, Bellevue Coll., 1972. Mgr. credit GE Credit Corp., Croton Falls, N.Y., 1971; mgr. ops. Bridal Publs., Inc., Omaha, 1972-73; regional mgr. Bridal Fair, Inc., 1973-74, sales mgr., 1974-76, chmn. bd., pres., 1976—. Bd. dirs. Collegiate Sports Adv. Network, LLC, dreamWeavers Media, Inc., Multi-Media Group, Inc., Bridal Fair mag.; pres. bd. dirs. Nat. Broadcasting Network, LLC, 1996—. With USAF, 1966-70. Recipient Nat. Def. Svc. medal, Somers (N.Y.) League Citizenship and Pub. Svc. award, 1965. Mem. Nat. Assn. Broadcasters, Airline Passengers Assn., Bellevue U. Alumni Assn., Paso Fino Horse Assn. Republican. Congregationalist. Office: 2242 S 156th Cir Omaha NE 68130-2505 E-mail: bethielbauth@csanhome.com., bridalfair@email.com.

THIEDE, RICHARD WESLEY, retired communications educator; b. Detroit, Mar. 30, 1936; s. Harold Victor and Blanche May (Gross) T. BS, Ea. Mich. U., 1961; MA, U. Ill., 1963; PhD, U. Mo., 1977. Tchg. asst. U. Ill., Urbana, 1961-62; tchr. Ctrl. H.S., Battle Creek, Mich., 1962-63, Shafer H.S., Southgate, 1963-64, Chadsey H.S., Detroit, 1964-68, Stevenson H.S., Livonia, 1968-71; part-time instr. Schoolcraft Coll., 1969-71; teaching/tech. asst. U. Mo., Columbia, 1971-74; instr. Ottumwa Hts. Coll., Iowa, 1975-76, Midland Luth. Coll., Fremont, Nebr., 1976-77; prof. comm. arts Defiance (Ohio) Coll., 1978-97, prof. emeritus, 1997—2002; ret., 1997. Tchr. summer sch. Southwestern H.S., Detroit, 1966, Cody H.S., Detroit, 1967, 68; tchr. evening sch. Chadsey H.S., 1965-67, Stevenson H.S., 1969-70; adj. instr. Northwest State C.C., Archbold, Ohio, fall 1997; part-time instr. Defiance (Ohio) Coll., spring, summer, fall, 1999. Mem. AARP, Eagles, Alpha Psi Omega, Kappa Delta Pi, Tau Kappa Epsilon (hon.). Democrat. Home: 615 W Sycamore St Columbus Grove OH 45830-1023

THIEL, DAVID BRIAN, physician assistant; b. Cin., July 2, 1956; s. Joseph Lee and Mary Jane (Otting) T. BA, Wabash Coll., Crawfordsville, Ind., 1978; AS with honors, Kettering Coll. Med. Arts, 1980. Cert. physician asst. Resident Los Angeles County-U. So. Calif. Med. Ctr., L.A., 1985-86; physician asst. in orthopedic surgery Ketchikan, Alaska, 1980-85; physician asst. in phys. medicine New Orleans, 1987—. In-svc. lectr. HealthSouth Rehab., Harahan, La., 1990—. Tannenbaum scholar, 1974-78. Fellow Sigma Xi. Republican. Avocations: swimming, skiing, sailing, orchid growing.

THIEL, PATRICIA ANN, chemistry educator; b. Adrian, Minn., Feb. 20, 1953; BA, Macalester Coll., 1975; PhD, Calif. Inst. Technology, 1981. Assoc. scientist Control Data Corp., Mpls., 1975-76; postdoctoral rsch. assoc. U. Munich, 1981, U. Calif., Berkeley, 1983; tech. staff mem. Sandia Nat. Lab., Livermore, Calif., 1981-83; tech. cons. Thermionics Labs. Inc., Hayward, 1983; asst. prof. chemistry Iowa State U., Ames, 1983-88, assoc. prof. chemistry, 1988-91, prof. chemistry, 1991—, chmn. dept., 1999—, program dir. Ames Lab., 1988—. Mem. adv. bd. Langmuir, 1989—; mem. adv. com. chem. divsn. NSF, 1992-93. Mem. editl. bd. Surface Sci., 1992-2000; contbr. articles to profl. jours. Recipient award for women in sci. and engring. NSF, 1991; Henry Dreyfus fellow, 1986-90, Alfred P. Sloan fellow, 1984-86, Alexander von Humboldt fellow, 1981, NSF Presdl. Young Investigator fellow, 1986-91. Fellow Am. Phys. Soc., Am. Vacuum Soc. (exec. com. 1989-92); mem. AAAS, Am. Chem. Soc., Materials Rsch. Soc. Office: Iowa State U Dept Chem 1605 Gilman Ames IA 50011-0001

THIEL, PHILIP, design educator; b. Bklyn., Dec. 20, 1920; s. Philip and Alma Theone (Meyer) T.; m. Midori Kono, 1955; children: Philip Kenji, Nancy Tamiko, Susan Akiko, Peter Akira (dec.). BSc, Webb Inst. Naval Architecture, 1943; MSc, U. Mich., 1948; BArch, MIT, 1952. Registered arch., Wash. Instr. naval architecture MIT, Cambridge, 1949-50; instr. U. Calif., Berkeley, 1954-56, asst. prof., 1956-60; assoc. prof. U. Wash., Seattle, 1961-66, prof. visual design and experiential notation, 1966-91; guest prof. Tokyo Inst. Tech., 1976-78; vis. prof. Sapporo (Japan) Sch. of Arts, 1992-98. Lectr., U.S., Can. Japan, Norway, Denmark, Sweden, Eng., Austria, Switzerland, Peru, Bolivia, Korea; cons. FAO, Rome, 1952; co-founder Environment and Behavior, 1969; founder Ctr. for Experiential Notation, Seattle, 1981. Author: Freehand Drawing, 1965, Visual Awareness and Design, 1981, People, Paths and Purposes, 1997; patentee in field. Soc. Naval Architects and Marine Engrs. scholar, 1947; Rehmann scholar AIA, 1960; NIMH grantee, 1967, Nat. Endowment for Arts, 1969, Graham Found., 1995. Mem. Soc. Naval Architects and Marine Engrs. (assoc.), Phi Beta Kappa, Sigma Xi.

THIEL, ROBERT JAMES, nutrition researcher; b. Detroit, Nov. 25, 1958; s. Robert F. Thiel and Judith F. (Schutz) Killian; m. Joyce Kay Mynders, Oct. 10, 1981; children: Michael J., Brian D., David P. BS in Acctg., U. LaVerne, Calif., 1980; MS in Systems Mgmt., U. So. Calif., 1982; PhD in Nutrition Sci., Union Inst., Cin., 1993; D Naturopathy, Internat. Coll. Naturopathy, 1999; D Naturopathy Medicine, First Nat. U. Naturopathy, 2001. Bd. cert. naturopathic physician. Internal auditor Martin Marietta Corp., Vandenberg AFB, Calif., 1980-81; asst. contr. Earth Technology Corp., Long Beach, 1981-84; div. contr. Indsl. Tectonics, Inc., Rancho Dominguez, 1984-87; v.p. Buckner, Inc., Fresno, 1987-93; nutrition rschr., health cons. Ctr. for Natural Health Rsch., Arroyo Grande, 1993—. Sci. editor Am. Naturopathic Med. Assn. Cons. Fresno Little Hoover Commn., 1991, Nutri-West, Medi-Foods, 1994. Named Rsch. Scientist of Yr., Am. Naturopathic Med. Assn., 1998, Physician of Yr., 1999, Disability Rschr. of Yr., 2001. Mem. Am. Coll. Nutrition, Calif. State Naturopathic Med. Assn. (pres.). Mem. Living Ch. of God. Office: Calif Health Group 1248 Grand Ave Ste C Arroyo Grande CA 93420-2429

THIEL, THOMAS JOSEPH, information scientist, consultant; b. Upper Sandusky, Ohio, Dec. 31, 1928; s. Otto Peter and Lillian Susan (Orians) T.; m. Alice Ellen Miller, June 18, 1955 (div. Dec. 1982); children: Susan Marie Schworer, Christine Ellen, Joseph Allen, John Andrew; m. Jean Karen Singer, Mar. 9, 1984. BS, Ohio State U., 1956, MS, 1959. Rsch. scientist USDA, Columbus, Ohio, 1957-63, rsch. adminstr. St. Paul, 1963-72, Peoria, Ill., 1972-84; div. mgr. Advanced Systems Devel., Alexandria, Va., 1984-91; pres. Info. and Image Mgmt. Techs., 1991—. Cons. Office of Sec. of Def., U.S. Army, USN, 1984-93, NATO, Mons, Belgium, 1988, Inst. De La Vie, Washington and Paris, 1991; dir. lab. U.S. Dept. Def. Author: CD-ROM Mastering for Information and Image Management, 1990, Automated Indexing of Document Image Management Systems, Ency. of Libr. and Info. Sci.; contbr. articles to Jour. Soil Sci. Soc. Am. Procs., 1960-62; contbr. articles to profl. jours. Sgt. U.S. Army, 1950-52, Korea, 1992-93. Fellow Soil and Water Conservation Soc. (life, bd. dirs. 1981-84, tech. transfer futures task force 1993—), Am. Soc. Agronomy (cert., emeritus), Soil Sci. Soc. Am. (emeritus), Assn. for Info. and Image Mgmt. (co-chair CD-ROM task force 1990--, chair electronic image mgmt. SIG 1991-92, chair emerging tech. adv. group 1992-93), Soc. for Applied Learning Tech. Achievements include research in the application of optical disk, compact disk read only memory and multimedia systems to office technical and scientific information management and dissemination, and in water movement in agricultural fields. Home: 19147 Park Place Blvd Eustis FL 32736-7262 Office: II-Tech 19147 Park Place Blvd Eustis FL 32736-7262

THIELE, HERBERT WILLIAM ALBERT, lawyer; b. Gananoque, Ont., Can., Apr. 14, 1953; s. Herbert and Bertha (Shields) T.; m. Kathi M. Brown, May 29, 1982; children: Herbert R. R., Eric W. R., Brian A. J., Kelly M. M., Kevin M. H., Karl S. H. BA, U. Notre Dame, 1975; JD, U. Fla., 1978. Bar: Fla. 1978, U.S. Dist. Ct. (so. dist. trial and gen. bars) Fla. 1979, U.S. Ct. Appeals (5th and 11th cirs.) 1981, U.S. Supreme Ct. 1982, U.S. Tax Ct. 1983, U.S. Dist. Ct. (no. dist.) Fla. 1991. Assoc. Law Offices of Roger G. Saberson, Delray Beach, Fla., 1979-81; asst. city atty. City of Delray Beach, 1979-81, city atty., 1981-90; county atty. Leon County, Tallahassee, 1990—. Bd. dirs. Delray Beach Mcpl. Employees Credit Union, 1985-88. Recipient award of recognition Stetson U. Law Rev., 1989, Ralph A. Marsicano award for Local Govt. Law, Fla. Bar, 1991. Mem. ABA (vice-chmn. urban, state and local govt. com. of gen. practice sect. 1991-95, mem. labor and employment law, litigation, govt. lawyers, gen. practice and trial practice com. sects.), ATLA, FBA, Fla. Bar (exec. coun. local govt. law sect. 1986-87, sec./treas. 1987-88, chmn.-elect 1988-89, chmn., 1989-90, immediate past chmn. 1990-91, ex-officio officer 1991—, trial, real property, gen. practice and labor and employment law sects., bar com. on individual rights and responsibilities 1986-90, long-range planning com. 1991-93, continuing legal edn. com. 1998-99, Paul S. Buchman award local govt. law sect. 2000), Tallahassee Bar Assn., Fla. Mcpl. Attys. Assn. (steering com. 1985-86, bd. dirs. 1980-89, sec./treas. 1989-90, Fla. Mcpl. Atty. of Yr. 1987), Fla. Assn. Police Attys., Nat. Inst. Mcpl. Law Officers (pers. and labor law com., trial practices and litigation com., legal advocacy com., 11th cir. rep. 1989-90), Am. Soc. for Pub. Adminstrn., Fla. Pub. Employer Labor Rels. Assn., Fla. Assn. County Attys. (chmn. coun. county attys. 1990-91, bd. dirs. 1991-93, treas. 1993, sec. 1993-94, v.p. 1994-95, pres. 1995-96, chmn. 1996-97, bd. dirs. 1997—, Recognition award 1994, Ethics in Govt. award 1998, 2001). Republican. Avocations: music, sports, philately. Home: 318 Milestone Dr Tallahassee FL 32312-3574 Office: Office of Leon County Atty Leon County Courthouse Tallahassee FL 32301

THIELE, HOWARD NELLIS, JR. lawyer; b. Dayton, Ohio, June 22, 1930; s. Howard Nellis and Irma Laura (Scheibe) T.; m. Alma Kuhn, Oct. 14, 1995; children: Leslie, Howard III, Craig. AB, Miami U., Oxford, Ohio, 1952; JD with distinction, U. Mich., 1955. Bar: Ohio 1955. Assoc., ptnr. Smith & Schnacke, LPA, Dayton, Ohio, 1957-89; ptnr. Thompson, Hine & Flory, 1989-95; ret., 1995. Pres. Dayton Art Inst., 1981-85; bd. dirs. Dayton Area chpt. ARC, 1983—, 1st vice chmn., 1990-91, chmn., 1992-94. Capt. USAF, 1955-57. Mem. Dayton Bar Assn., Order of the Coif, Engrs. Club, Phi Beta Kappa. Republican. Lutheran.

THIELE, LESLIE PAUL, political science educator; b. Moose Jaw, Sask., Can., Jan. 27, 1959; s. Jacob Zach and Wilfrida Maria Thiele; m. Susan Wapner, June 30, 1991; children: Jacob, Jonah. PhD, Princeton U., 1989. Asst. prof. Swarthmore (Pa.) Coll., 1989-91; asst. prof. polit. sci. U. Fla., Gainesville, 1991-95, assoc. prof., 1995-97, prof., 1998—, mem. affiliate faculty Coll. Natural Resources and Environ., 1996—. U. Fla. Rsch. Found. prof., 1997-99, chmn. dept., 1997—2002. Author: Friedrich Nietzsche and the Politics of the Soul, 1990, Timely Meditations: Martin Heidegger and Postmodern Politics, 1995, Thinking Politics, 1997, 2nd edit., 2002, Environmentalism for a New Millennium, 1999. Summer inst. grantee NEH, 1990; postdoctoral fellow Social Sci. and Humanities Rsch. Coun. Can., 1991-93; fellow Social Sci. Rsch. Coun.-MacArthur Found., 1994-96. Mem. Am. Polit. Sci. Assn. Democrat. Avocations: ultimate frisbee, hiking, canoeing. Office: U Fla Dept Polit Sci Anderson Hall Gainesville FL 32611-7325 Fax: 352-392-8127. E-mail: thiele@polisci.ufl.edu.

THIELEN, JEAN ROSE, artist; b. Racine, Wis., June 25, 1937; d. Floyd Adelbert Peck and Virginia Marjory Lutz; m. Daniel Peter Thielen, June 25, 1960; 1 child, Daniel Jerome. Student, U. Wis., Racine, 1957-59, Milw. Tech. Coll., 1977-79, U. Wis., Kenosha, 1978-80. Editl. artist Racine Jour. Times, 1981-87; dir. mktg. Porters of Racine, 1987-90; artist, art tchr. Racine, 1990—. Instr. U. Wis., Kenosha. Vol. art tchr. Olympia Brown Sch., Racine, 1998, Sacred Heart Sch., Racine, 1997-2001; fundraiser Arts Coun., S.E. Wis. AIDS Project, Channel 10, others. Recipient 1st pl. nat. Nat. Fedn. Press Women, 1985, 1st pl. Gold award Nat. Mag. Conf., 1990; named to St. Catherine's H.S. Hall of Fame, 1998, 100 of Am.'s Best Watercolor Painters, North Light Books, 2002. Mem. Midwest Watercolor Soc. (bd. dirs. 1998-99), Wis. Watercolor Soc. (bd. dirs., membership chair 1997—), League of Milw. Artists (bd. dirs. 1996-99, 2d pl. award 1997), Racine Art Guild (bd. dirs., v.p. 1996-97, Merit award 1996, 97, 99, 2000). Roman Catholic. Avocations: walking, bike riding. E-mail: jthielen@execpc.com.

THIELSCH, HELMUT JOHN, engineering company executive; b. Berlin, Nov. 16, 1922; came to U.S., 1939, naturalized, 1954; s. Kurt and Anna-Sibylle T.; m. Margaret E. McKenna, Aug. 16, 1952; children: Barbara Anne, Donald Kurt, Deborah Lee, Helmut John. BS, Auburn U., 1943; postgrad., U. Mich., 1943-45, Lehigh U., 1948. Registered profl. engr., R.I., Mass., Maine, N.J., Ga., Calif. Research engr. Allis Chalmers Co., Milw., 1945-46; metall. engr. Black, Sivalls & Bryson, Inc., Kansas City, Mo., 1946-47; research engr. Lukens Steel Co., Coatsville, Pa., 1948-49; engr. Welding Research Council, N.Y.C., 1949-52; dir. research Eutectic Welding Alloys Co., 1952-53; v.p., dir. research, devel. and engring. ITT Grinnell Corp., Providence, 1954-84; pres. Thielsch Engring., Inc., 1984—. Pres. HiTech Realty Assocs. Inc.; cons. on failure analysis to industry, public utilities, equipment builders, 1954—; lectr. at confs. on failures and failure prevention; mem. component tech. com. Argonne (Ill.) Nat. Lab.; bd. dirs. Ind. Energy, Inc. Author: Defects and Failures in Pressure Vessels and Piping, 1965; contbr. numerous articles to profl. publs.; patentee in field. Recipient Nat. Safety award, Nat. Bd. Boiler and Pressure Vessel Insps., 1990, John J. Tuohy Businessman of Yr. award, City of Cranston, 2000, Bus. Leadership award, Providence Bus. News Orgn., 2002. Fellow: ASME, Am. Bd. Forensic Examiners, Am. Welding Soc. (Adams Lecture award 1982), Am. Soc. Nondestructive Testing, Am. Soc. Metals; mem.: NSPE, TAPPI, ASTM, ACS, NSPE (Freeman award 1985), Nat. Fire Protection Assn., Tech. Assn. Pulp and Paper Industry, Am. Soc. for Metals, Am. Mgmt. Assn., Nat. Assn. Corrosion Engrs., Am. Nuclear Soc., Am. Soc. Quality Control, Am. Water Works Assn., Sigma Xi. Office: 195 Frances Ave Cranston RI 02910-2211 Fax: 401-467-2398. E-mail: hthielsch@theilsch.com.

THIEMANN, CHARLES LEE, banker; b. Louisville, Nov. 21, 1937; s. Paul and Helen (Kern) T.; m. Donna Timperman, June 18, 1960; children: Laura Gerette, Charles Lee, Rodney Gerard, Jeffrey Michael, Matthew Joseph. BA in Chemistry, Bellarmine Coll., 1959; MBA, Ind. U., 1961, DBA, 1963. Mem. rsch. dept. Fed. Res. Bank, St. Louis, 1963-64; with Fed. Home Loan Bank, Cin., 1964—, sr. v.p., then exec. v.p., 1974, pres., 1976—. Past chmn. bd. dirs. Office Fin.; trustee Fin. Instns. Retirement Fund; past mem. First Step Home. Bd. dirs. Habitat for Humanity Internat., Bellarmine U. Named Bellarmine Coll. Alumnus of Yr., 1999. Mem. Rotary Club, Queen City Club. Roman Catholic. Office: Fed Home Loan Bank 221 E 4th St Ste 1000 Cincinnati OH 45202-5139

THIEMANN, RONALD FRANK, dean, religion educator; b. St. Louis, Oct. 4, 1946; s. Frank Joseph and Marie Magdalene (Graeser) T.; m. Beth Arlene Barkow, June 15, 1968; children: Sarah Elizabeth, Laura Kristen. BA magna cum laude, Concordia Sr. Coll., Fort Wayne, Ind., 1968; MDiv, Concordia Sem., St. Louis, 1972; MA, Yale U., 1973, MPhil, 1974, PhD, 1976; postgrad., Eberhard-Karls Universitat, Tubingen, W.Ger., 1974-75. Asst. prof. dept. religion Haverford Coll., Pa., 1976-82, assoc. prof. dept. religion, 1982-85, prof. dept. religion, 1985-86, acting provost, 1985, acting pres., 1986; dean Div. Sch. Harvard U., Cambridge, Mass., 1986-98, John Lord O'Brian prof. divinity, 1986-98, prof. theology, religion & soc., 1998—, faculty fellow Hauser Ctr., JFK Sch. Govt. Vis. prof. honors program Villanova U., 1981; vis. asst. prof. Luth. Theol. Sem., Phila., 1977; mem. Ctr. Theol. Inquiry, Princeton, N.J., 1982-83; mem. consultation on Christianity and Marxism, U.S.A. nat. com. Luth. World Fedn., 1979-83, mem. consultation on civil religion, 1983-86, mem. consultation on problem of common good, 1985-88; bd. dirs. Trinity Press Internat.; mem. exec. com. Assn. Theol. Schs., 1994-2000; faculty mem. Hanser Ctr. JFK Sch. Govt. Harvard U., 1998—. Author: Revelation and Theology, 1985, Constructing a Public Theology: The Church in a Pluralistic Culture, 1991, Religion in Public Life: A Dilemma for Democracy, 1995, Who Will Provide? The Changing Role of Religion in American Social Welfare, 2001; editor: The Legacy of H. Richard Niebuhr, 1991, Why Are We Here? Everyday Questions and the Christian Life, 1998, Where Shall My Wandering Soul Begin: The Landscape of Evangelical Piety and Thought, 2000; mem. editl. bd.: Dialog, 1987—; contbr. numerous articles to profl. jours. Mem. bd. trustees Buckingham Browne & Nichols Schs., 1988-90; mem. task force on theol. education, Evang. Luth. Ch. in Am., 1989-91, task force on Luth.-Reformed Conversations, Evang. Luth. Ch. Am., 1988-92. Recipient Disting. Teaching award Lindback Found., 1982, Lilly Scholars award, 1998-99; Mellon Found. fellow, 1982-83; Deutscher Akademischer Austauschdienst fellow, 1974-75. Mem. Am. Acad. Religion, (chmn. narrative interpretation and theology group 1982-86), Soc. Christian Ethics, Am. Theol. Soc. Avocations: tennis; squash; piano. Home: 186 Shadyside Ave Concord MA 01742-2740 Office: Harvard Div Sch 45 Francis Ave Cambridge MA 02138-1911

THIEN-STASKO, VICKI LYNN, civil engineer technician; b. Scott Air Force Base, Ill., Apr. 22, 1953; d. Cordell Albert Knepper and Erna Rose (Studnicka) Knepper; m. Michael Lee Stasko, Nov. 19, 1988; stepchildren: Julie Stasko , Elliott Stasko ; m. William Frederick Thien, Mar. 12, 1971 (div.); 1 child Kyle Thien. Associates of Arch., Belleville Area Coll., 1982, Associates of Applied Sci., 1988; BSC cum laude, Greenville Coll., 1998. Civil engr. tech. St. Clair County Hwy. Dept., Belleville, Ill., 1982—2002; part-time real estate agent Better Homes & Gardens /Strano, 1993—94; part-time cosmetic cons. Christian Dior, 1995—97; part-time census enumerator U.S. Dept. Commerce-Census Dept., 2000—01. Co-chmn. "Operation Bag-It", Belleville, 1998—2002. Exhibitions include gingerbread creations/gingerbread scene Not a Creature was Stirring, 1996 (Best of Show, 1996), exhibitions include gingerbread creation/3'tall gingerbread Nutcracker Nuts Anyone?, 1997 (Merchant's award, 1997), exhibitions include gingerbread creation Frosty the Gingerbread Snowman, 1998 (Downtown Merchant's award, 1998), (Best of Show, 2000). Precinct committeewoman Dem. Party, Belleville, 1978—91; sec. Belleville Dem. Orgn., 1979—91; mayoral appointment/mem. Belleville Re-develop. Com., 1982—84; member St. Clair County Hist. Soc., 2000—02; ch. sch. bd. mem., tchr. Christ United Ch. of Christ, 1987—91. Recipient Ill. Gov.'s Hometown award, State of Ill., 1999. Protestant. Avocations: gardening, remodeling, travel. Office: St Clair County Hwy Dept 1415 N Belt W Belleville IL 62226 Office Fax: 618-233-0996.*

THIER, SAMUEL OSIAH, physician, educator; b. Bklyn., June 23, 1937; s. Sidney and May Henrietta (Kanner) Thier; m. Paula Dell Finkelstein, June 28, 1958; children: Audrey Lauren, Stephanie Ellen, Sara Leslie. Student, Cornell U., 1953—56; MD, SUNY, Syracuse, 1960, DSc (hon.) , 1987, Tufts U., 1988, George Washington U., 1988, Mt. Sinai Sch. Med., 1989, Hahnemann U., 1989; DSc (hon.) , U. Pa., 1994, Dartmouth Coll., 1996; LHD (hon.) , Rush U., 1988, Va. Commonwealth U., 1992, Med. Coll. Pa., 1992; LHD (hon.) , Brandeis U., 1994. Diplomate Am. Bd. Internal Medicine. Intern Mass. Gen. Hosp., Boston, 1960—61, asst. resident, 1961—62, sr. resident, 1964—65, clin. and research fellow, 1965, chief resident, 1966; clin. asso. Nat. Inst. Arthritis and Metabolic Diseases, 1962—64; from instr. to asst. prof. medicine Harvard U. Med. Sch., 1967—69; prof. medicine, health care policy Harvard Med. Sch., 1994—; asst. in medicine, chief renal unit Mass. Gen. Hosp., Boston, 1967—69; asso. prof., then prof. medicine U. Pa. Med. Sch., 1969—72, vice chmn. dept., 1971—74; assoc. dir. med. svcs. Hosp. U. Pa., 1969—71; David Paige Smith prof. medicine Yale U. Sch. Medicine, 1978—81, Sterling prof. medicine, 1981—85, chmn. dept., 1975—85; pres. Inst. Medicine NAS, Washington, 1985—91; pres., Univ. prof. Brandeis U., Waltham, Mass., 1991—94; pres. Mass. Gen. Hosp., Boston, 1994—97, Ptnrs. HealthCare Sys., Inc., Boston, 1994—96, 1997—, CEO, 1996—. Chief medicine Yale-New Haven Hosp., 1975—85, trustee, 1978—85; bd. dirs. Conn. Hospice, Inc., 1976—82; dir. Am. Bd. Internal Medicine, 1977—85, exec. com., 1981—85, chmn., 1984—85. Mem. editl. bd.: New Eng. Jour. Medicine, 1978—81; contbr. articles to med. jours. Mem. adv. com. to the dir. NIH, 1980—85. With USPHS, 1962—64. Recipient Christian R. and Mary F. Lindback Found. Disting. Tchg. award, 1971. Mem.: ACP (bd. regents 1982—85), Interurban Clin. Club, Assn. Am. Physicians, Assn. Profs. Medicine, Internat. Soc. Nephrology, Am. Physiol. Soc., Am. Soc. Nephrology, Am.

Fedn. Clin. Rsch. (pres. 1976—77), John Morgan Soc., Assn. Am. Med. Colls. (adminstrv. bd. coun. acad. socs.), Alpha Omega Alpha. Home: 99-20 Florence St Apt 4B Chestnut Hill MA 02467-1927

THIES, JULIE ANN, music educator; b. Janesville, Wis., Apr. 28, 1960; d. Allen Junior and Marion Luella (Hoeft) Pudleiner; m. Thomas Earl Thies, Aug. 28, 1982. MusB cum laude, U. Wis., 1982. Instr. piano Suzuki Music Acad. Chgo., 1983-84, Suzuki Piano Studio, Hazel Crest, Ill., 1985—. Mem. Music Tchrs. Nat. Assn. (nat. cert.), Suzuki Assn. of Ams., Ill. State Music Tchrs. Assn. (2nd v.p. membership 1995-99, rec. sec. 1993-95), South Suburban Music Tchrs. Assn. (pres. 1992-94, v.p. 1990-92, treas. 1988-90, Mem. of Yr. 1999). Avocations: bicycling, hiking, in-line skating. Home: 1825 Olive Rd Homewood IL 60430-2316 Office: Suzuki Piano Studio 3000 W 170th Pl Hazel Crest IL 60429-1174 E-mail: jtthies@earthlink.net.

THIES, MARGARET DIANE, nurse; b. Carroll, Iowa, Oct. 5, 1949; d. George Duane and Elizabeth Lee (Cram) Smith; children: Alicia Kay, Matthew John. Diploma in Nursing, Iowa Luth. Sch. Nursing, Des Moines, 1972; BSN, Creighton U., 1989; postgrad., Regis U., 1999—. RN, Nebr., Iowa, Colo. Staff nurse mental health unit Mary Greely Hosp., Ames, Iowa, 1972-73; staff nurse Kossuth County Hosp., Algona, 1973-74, 77-81; staff nurse med.-surg. unit U. Nebr. Hosp., Omaha, 1981-83, 87-89, charge nurse med.-surg. unit, 1983-87, quality assurance com. chairperson med.-surg. unit, 1984-88; quality assurance coord. Share Health Plan of Nebr., 1990-91; staff nurse med. Poudre Valley Hosp., Ft. Collins, Colo., 1992-95; quality resource specialist Poudre Valle Hosp., 1995—2001; quality improvement specialist Alegent Health Sys., Omaha, 2002—. Quality assessment and improvement com. chairperson, 1993-95, quality improvement spec., Alegent Health Sys., 2001—. Mem. City of Ft. Collins Parks and Rec. Commn., 1991-99, pres., 1995-97; mem. Family Support Coun., Foothills Gateway, 1995-96. Recipient Sec.'s Community Health Promotion award, 1990, Physician's award 1994. Home: 8722 Raven Oaks Dr Omaha NE 68152 Office: Alegent Health Sys Immanuel Med Ctr Omaha NE 68122-1799

THIES, RICHARD BRIAN, lawyer; b. Chgo., Dec. 14, 1943; s. Fred W. and Loraine C. (Mannix) T.; m. Anita Marie Rees, Aug. 5, 1972; children: Emily Marie, Richard Clarke. BA, Miami U., 1966; JD, Loyola U., 1974. Bar: (Ill. 1974), 1989 (U.S. Tax Ct.). Assoc. Wilson & McIlvaine, Chgo., 1974-78; assoc.-ptnr. Isham, Lincoln & Beale, 1978-88; ptnr. Wildman, Harrold, Allen & Dixon, 1988—, mem. exec. com., 1999—. Bd. govs. Chgo. Heart Assn., 1980-87, exec. com., 1982-87; bd. dirs. Juvenile Protective Assn., Chgo., 1984—; v.p. Samaritan Counseling Ctr., Evanston, 1989-94, pres., 1994. Mem. ABA, Chgo. Bar Assn., Chgo. Estate Planning Coun. Avocations: coaching children's sports, photography, music. Home: 305 Driftwood Ln Wilmette IL 60091-3441 Office: Wildman Harrold Allen & Dixon 225 W Wacker Dr Chicago IL 60606-1229

THIESENHUSEN, WILLIAM CHARLES, agricultural economist, educator; b. Waukesha, Wis., Feb. 12, 1936; s. Arthur Henry and Myrtle O. (Honeyager) T.; children— James Waring, Kathryn Hague, Gail Ann. BS, U. Wis., 1958, MS, 1960, PhD, 1965; M.P.A. (Danforth Found. fellow), Harvard U., 1962, postgrad., 1968-69. Instr. agrl. extension U. Wis., Madison, 1959-61; exec. asst. Land Tenure Center and Instituto de Economia Universidad de Chile research team in, Santiago, 1963-65, asst. prof. agrl. econs., 1965-68, asso. prof. agrl. econs., 1971-72, asso. prof. agrl. journalism, 1968-72, prof. agrl. journalism and agrl. econs., 1972—. Dir. Land Tenure Ctr., 1971-75, 94-98, prof. emeritus Agrl. Applied Econs., 1998—; asst. prof. econs. U. Wis., Milw., 1966-67; prof. agrl. econs. Escuela Nacional de Agricultura, Chapingo, Mex.; under AID contract, summer 1965; vis. prof. Universidad Autonoma de Madrid, Fulbright Program, 1977; cons., condr. seminars in field; Fulbright-Hays lectr., 1965, 72. Author: Chile's Experiments in Agrarian Reform, 1966, Reforma Agraria en Chile: Experimentos en Cuatro Fundos de la Iglesia, 1968, Broken Promises: Agrarian Reform and the Latin American Campesino, 1995; editor: Searching for Agrarian Reform in Latin America, 1989; mem. editl. bd. Latin Am. Rsch. Rev., Pakistan Devel. Rev.; contbr. articles to profl. jours. Served with USAR, 1960. Recipient award for best article Am. Jour. Agrl. Econs., 1969; Alpha Zeta nat. fellow, 1957; U. Wis. fellow, 1956; Harvard U. Adminstrn. fellow, 1962 Mem. Am. Agrl. Econs. Assn., Am. Econ. Assn., Latin Am. Studies Assn., Council Internat. Exchange Scholars (chmn. com. econs. selection 1979-80), Inter-Am. Found. (selection bd.), Wis. Acad. Scis., Arts and Letters, Phi Kappa Phi, Alpha Zeta, Sigma Delta Chi. Unitarian Universalist. Office: U Wis Land Tenure Ctr 1357 University Ave Madison WI 53715-1054 E-mail: wthiesen@facstaff.wisc.edu.

THIESSEN, DELBERT DUANE, psychologist; b. Julesberg, Colo., Aug. 13, 1932; s. David and Eva Peters (Wetherby) T.; children: Trevor, Theron, Kendell Courtney. BA in Psychology with distinction, San Jose (Calif.) State Coll., 1958; PhD, U. Calif., Berkeley, 1963. Extension instr. U. Calif., La Jolla, fall 1964; asst. sect. med. psychology, divsn. psychiatry and neurology Scripps Clinic and Research Found., 1962-65; faculty U. Tex., Austin, 1965-2000, prof. psychology, 1971-2000, prof. emeritus, 2000—. Rsch. cons. NIMH. Author: Gene Organization and Behavior, 1972, The Evolution and Biochemistry of Aggression, 1976, Bitter-Sweet Destiny: The Stormy Evolution of Human Behavior, 1996, Universal Desires and Fears: The Deep History of Sociobiology, 1997, Survival of the Fittest: The Darwinian Diet and Exercise Program, 1998; contbr. articles and chpts. to books. With AUS, 1952-54, Korea. Fellow USPHS, 1960-61; recipient Career Devel. award NIMH, 1967-72, grantee, 1967-78; grantee Russel Sage Found., NSF, U. Tex. Rsch. Inst. Fellow AAAS, APA; mem. Alumni Assn. Roscoe B. Jackson Meml. Lab., Am. Genetic Assn., Psychonomic Soc., Animal Behavior Soc., Southwestern Psychol. Assn., Behavior Genetics Assn., Sigma Xi, Phi Kappa Phi, Psi Chi. Home: 8760A Research Blvd Apt 241 Austin TX 78758-6420 E-mail: DelThiessen@msn.com.

THIGPEN, ALTON HILL, motor transportation company executive; b. Kinston, N.C., Feb. 3, 1927; s. Kirby Alton and Alice (Hill) T.; m. Rebecca Ann Braswell, May 16, 1953; children: David Alton, Jennifer Ann, Steven Roy. BS in Indsl. Engring, N.C. State U., 1950. With Asso. Transport, Inc., Burlington, N.C., 1950-71, engr., 1950-57, asst. terminal mgr., 1957-58, terminal mgr. Knoxville, Tenn., 1959, regional mgr. Valley region, 1960-62, South region, 1962-68, v.p.-dir. So. div., 1968-71; v.p. R.S. Braswell Co. Inc., Kannapolis, 1971-80, pres., 1980—, Hartford Motor Inn Inc., North Myrtle Beach, S.C., 1982—, A.T. Developers, Inc., North Myrtle Beach, 1983-97. Pres. Cherokee 2 Inc., Shelby, N.C., 1986-95, bd. dirs.; bd. dirs. First Union Nat. Bank, Earl Ownsby Studios Inc., Shelby. Bd. regents Berkshire Christian Coll., Lenox, Mass., 1975—; mem. adv. bd. Salvation Army, chmn. adv. bd., 1997-99. Served with USNR, 1945-46. Mem. Motor Carriers Va. (pres. 1967-68), N.C. Motor Carriers Assn. (dir. 1968—), Sigma Chi, Tau Beta Pi. Mem. Advent Christian Ch. Club: Mason (32 deg.), Lions. Home: 5395 Mooresville Rd Kannapolis NC 28081-8726 Office: PO Box 1197 Kannapolis NC 28082-1197

THIGPEN, JAMES TATE, physician, oncology educator; b. Columbia, Miss., June 6, 1944; m. Louisa Berdie Kessler, June 14, 1969; children: Monroe Tate, James Howard, Samuel Calvin, Richard Allen, David Albert. BS, U. Miss., 1964, MD, 1969. Intern Strong Meml. Hosp., U. Rochester, N.Y., 1969-70; resident U. Miss. Sch. Medicine, 1970-71, prof., dir. divsn. med. oncology dept. internal medicine, 1973—; also prof. ob-gyn. Nat. med. del. from Miss. Am. Cancer Soc., 1983-85, mem. nat. pub. issues com., 1983-85; mem. cancer clin. investigations rev. com. Nat. Cancer Inst., 1990-95, chmn., 1993-95. Nat. bd. govs. ARC, 1981-87. Fellow divsn. hematology/oncology dept. medicine, 1971-73. Fellow ACP; mem. AMA, Miss. Med. Assn., Ctrl. Med. Soc., Jackson Acad. Medicine, Miss. Acad. Scis., SW Oncology Group, Gynecologic Oncology Group (group vice chmn. sci. 1988—), Am. Fedn. Clin. Rsch., Am. Assn. Cancer Edn., Am. Soc. Clin. Oncology, Am. Assn. cancer Rsch., Am. Soc. Hematology, Soc. Gynecologic Oncologists, Soc. Assn. Oncology (pres. 1988-90), Am. Radium Soc., Optimists (internat. v.p. 1983-84, internat. pres. 1990-91). Baptist. (deacon 1978—, Sunday sch. tchr. 1979-85). Home: 3601 Kings Hwy Jackson MS 39216-3322 Office: Miss Oncology Assocs 2500 N State St Jackson MS 39216-4500 E-mail: jtthigpen@worldnet.att.net.

THIGPEN, LEWIS, engineering educator; b. Quincy, Fla., Aug. 29, 1938; s. Alonzo and Emma (Ray) T. BS magna cum laude in Mech. Engring., Howard U., 1964; MS, Ill. Inst. Tech., 1967, PhD, 1970. Profl. engr., Washington, D.C. Tech. staff mem. Sandia Nat. Labs., Albuquerque, 1969-73; asst. prof. Lowell (Mass.) Technol. Inst., 1973-75; from physicist to group leader Lawrence Livermore Lab., Livermore, Calif., 1975-88; chmn. mech. engring. Howard U., Washington, 1988—. Adv. com. mechanics NSF, Washington, 1990-91; program evaluator Mass. Higher Edn. Coord. Coun., Boston, 1991. Asst. leader Boy Scouts Am., Chgo., 1967-69; Served in U.S. Army, 1955-58, Germany. NASA fellow, 1964-67. Fellow ASME (region III com. chair 1996-98, accreditation bd. engring. and tech. evaluator 1991—, vice-chair nat. dept. heads com. 1999-2000, chair nat. dept. heads com. 2000-01); mem. AIAA, Am. Soc. Engring. Edn. (fellowship rev. panel 1990-94); Math. Throughout the Curriculum (adv. bd. 1996—), Ind. U., 1996—; Sigma Xi, N.Y. Acad. Scis. Achievements include patent in field and research in earth penetrating projectiles, constitutive modelling of geologic materials and theoretical seismology. Avocations: fishing, painting. Office: Howard U Dept Mech Engring 2300 6th St NW Washington DC 20001-2323 E-mail: thigpen@scs.howard.edu.

THIGPEN, MARY CECELIA, city official, consultant; b. L.A., Jan. 27, 1949; d. Tom Allen and Inell Theresa (Evans) Johnson; m. Willie Edward Thigpen, Apr. 30, 1971; children: Sonna Aminata, Monifa Ayodele. BA, Xavier U., New Orleans, 1971; MS in Urban Planning, U. New Orleans, 1979. Planner Urban Systems, Inc., New Orleans, 1977-79, Grimball/Garrandon/Savoy Engrs. and Architects, New Orleans, 1979-80; planner, cons. Mayor's Office, City of New Orleans, 1979; grants program evaluator Pinellas County Manpower Council, Clearwater, Fla., 1980-81; personnel mgmt. specialist Pinellas County Personnel Dept., 1981-83; adminstrv. analyst U. Calif., San Diego, 1983-85; sr. and personnel analyst City of Chula Vista, Calif., 1985—. Planning cons. Mayor's office, New Orleans, 1979; b.p. bd. dirs. Cajon Valley Ednl. Found., El Cajon, Calif., 1988—; v.p. personnel commn. City of El Cajon, 2000—. Writer poetry. Named Woman of Distinction, San Diego County Women, Inc., 1990; named Mother of Yr., Delta Sigma Theta of San Diego County, 1996. Mem. Nat. Med. Assn. Aux. (v.p. 1986—), Jack and Jill Am, Calif. Women in Govt., Internat. Pers. Mgmt. Assn., Altrusa Club of Chula Vista, Nat. Coalition of 100 Black Women, Inc. Roman Catholic. Avocations: fashion design, arts promotion, handcrafts, writing poetry and plays, photography. Home: 1551 Heron Ave El Cajon CA 92020-8810

THIGPEN, RICHARD ELTON, JR. lawyer; b. Washington, Dec. 29, 1930; s. Richard Elton and Dorothy (Dotger) T.; m. Nancy H. Shand, Dec. 15, 1951; children: Susan B., Richard M. AB, Duke U., 1951; LLB, U. N.C., 1956. Bar: N.C., 1956, U.S. Ct. Appeals (4th cir.) 1960, U.S. Ct. Appeals (5th cir.) 1960, U.S. Ct. Appeals (10th cir.) 1974, U.S. Tax Ct. 1958, U.S. Ct. Claims 1978. Lawyer FTC, Washington, 1956-58, Thigpen & Hines, Charlotte, N.C., 1958-84, Moore & Van Allen, Charlotte, 1984-88, Poyner & Spruill, Charlotte, 1988-93; gen. counsel Richardson Sports, 1994-98. Dir. Charlotte-Mecklenburg YMCA, 1964-88, Heineman Med. Rsch. Ctr., Charlotte, 1970—, Charlotte C. of C., 1982-85. Lt. USNR, 1951-53. Fellow Am. Bar Found., Am. Coll. Tax Counsel (regent 1989-95, vice chmn. 1992, chmn. 1993-94); mem. ABA, N.C. State Bar, N.C. Bar Assn. (pres. 1988-89, chmn. tax sect. 1976-80), Sports Lawyers Assn. (bd. dirs. 1995—, pres.-elect 2002). Avocation: golf, travel. Office: 1045 Providence Rd Ste 200 Charlotte NC 28207-2568

THILL, JOHN VAL, communications professional, writer, consultant; b. Milw., Dec. 27, 1953; s. Lewis Dominic and Carol Jean (Werner) T. BS, San Diego State U., 1977; MBA, U. San Diego, 1982. Mgr. Pacific Bell, San Diego, 1979-82; CEO Comm. Specialists of Am., Las Vegas, 1982—; pres. Bovee & Thill LLC, 1997—. Bd. dirs. Comm. Rsch. Inst., L.A. Author: Business in Action, 2000, Business Today, 2001, Excellence in Communication, 2001, Business Communication Today, 2002. Named Outstanding Bus. Communicator Am. Soc. Journalists, 1982, Nat. Cmty. Leadership award, 1997. Mem. Assn. Bus. Communication, 1985, Text and Acad. Authors Assn. Avocations: swimming, travel. Office: Bovee & Thill LLC 2950 E Flamingo Rd Ste B Las Vegas NV 89121-5208

THIMM, ALFRED LOUIS, management educator; b. Vienna, Austria, Dec. 10, 1923; came to U.S., 1939, naturalized, 1943; s. Hartwig H. and Olga F. (Felsner) T.; m. Patricia Mullen, Dec. 18, 1954; children: Alfred Louis, Peter H. BA, NYU, 1948, MA, 1949, PhD, 1959. Asst. prof. econs. St. Lawrence U., Canton, N.Y., 1953-55; research fellow NYU, 1955-56; assoc. prof. Clarkson Coll., Potsdam, N.Y., 1956-59; mem. faculty Union Coll., Schenectady, 1960-81, prof. econs. and indsl. adminstrn., 1968-81, dir. Inst. Adminstrn. and Mgmt., 1968-80, dir. Ph.D. program in adminstrn. and engring. systems, 1980-81; dean, dir. Sch. Bus. U. Vt., Burlington, 1981-85, prof. mgmt., 1981—. Mgmt. cons., 1973-81; cons. in field; vis. prof. Wirtschafts U., Vienna, 1980, 85-86, 89, 92, 93, 94, 95, Inst. Entscheidungs und Organisationsforschung, U. Munich, 1972, 74-75, 90, 91. Author: Economists and Society: From Aquinas to Keynes, 1973, 81, Business Ideologies in the Reform-Progressive: 1880-1914, 1976, Entscheidungstheorie, 1977, The False Promise of Codetermination, 1980, America's Stake in European Telecommuncation Policies, 1992, 94; contbr. articles to profl. jours., monographs. Grantee NSF, 1959, 61; grantee Ford Found., summers 1960, 62; Fulbright rsch. scholar Austria, 1967-68, 92. Mem. Am. Econs. Assn., Am. Statis. Assn., Inst. Mgmt. Sci. E-mail: thimm@bsadpo.emba.uvm.ebu., apthimm@together.net.

THIMOTHEOSE, KADAKAMPALLIL GEORGE, psychologist; b. Karipuza, India, Feb. 11, 1938; came to the U.S., 1976; s. K.G. and Mariamma Varghese; m. Mariamma Thimotheose, May 20, 1968 (div.); children: Geebee, Sonia. MA in Psychology, ME.D 1st class & rank, Kerala U., India, 1967, B in Edn., 1960, MA in Sociology, 1969; MA in History, PhD in Psychology, Kerala U., 1975; D Therapeutic Philosophy (hon.), World U., 1989. Lic. psychologist, marriage and family therapist, Mich.; diplomate Am. Bd. Med. Psychotherapists, Am. Bd. Psychotherapy, Am. Bd. Sexology, Am. Bd. Forensic Examiners, Am. Bd. Forensic Medicine, Am. Bd. Psychol. Specialities. Lectr., head dept. ednl. psychology S.N. Tchrs. Coll., Trivandrum, India; clin./adminstrv. dir. Alexandrine House, Inc., Detroit, 1976-81; chief exec. officer Cen. Therapeutic Svcs., Inc., Southfield, Mich., 1981—. Adv. bd. Trivandrum Med. Coll. Hosps., 1969-75; edn. faculty mem. U. Calicut, Kerala, India, 1969-75; v.p. forum ednl. rsch. and studies Kerala U., 1969-73. Author: Educational Psychology for B.Ed. Students, 1970; editor: Kerala University Journal of Education, 1969-73. Fellow Am. Bd. Med. Psychotherapists, Am. Acad. Clin. Sexologists. Am. Coll. Forensic Examiners, Am. Coll. Advanced Practice Psychologists; mem. APA, Am. Coll. Sexologists (sexologist), Am. Bd. Sexology (clin. supr.), World U. Round Table (hon. cultural doctorate in therapeutic philosophy), diplomate Am. Bd. Psychological Specialties. Republican. Avocations: photography, travel, reading, sightseeing. Home: 3048 Brewster West Bloomfield MI 48322-2471 Office: Cen Therapeutic Svcs Inc 17600 W 8 Mile Rd Ste 7 Southfield MI 48075-4316

THIRSK, ROBERT B. astronaut; b. New Westminister, Brit. Columbia, Aug. 17, 1953; m. Brenda Biasutti; 3 children. BSc in Mech. Engring., U. Calgary, 1976; MSc in Mech. Engring., MIT, 1978; MD, McGill U., 1982; MBA, MIT, 1998. Resident Queen Elizabeth Hosp., Montreal, Canada, 1982—83; astronaut Can. Astronaut Program, 1984—93; chief astronaut Can. Space Agy., 1993—94; sabbatical yr. Victoria, Canada, 1994—95; chief astronaut Can. Space Agy., 1996—98; astronaut NASA, Houston, 1998—. Dir. Can. Found. Internat. Space U.; crew comdr. CAPSULS mission, 1994; astronaut Space Shuttle mission STS-78, 1996. Recipient Disting. Alumni award, U. Calgary, 1985. Mem.: Coll. Physicians & Surgeons Ontario, Aerospace Med. Assn., Can. Aeronautics & Space Inst., Can. Coll. Family Physicians, Assn. Profl. Engrs. Ontario (Gold Medal award 1976). Avocations: flying, hockey, squash, playing the piano. Office: Astronaut Office CB NASA Johnson Space Center Houston TX 77058*

THIRTLE, MICHAEL ROBERT, community activist, consultant; b. Milw., Dec. 10, 1967; s. Robert Michael and Sandra Lee Thirtle; m. Denise Marie Domanico, June 10, 1990; children: Natalie Brooke, Jackson Ryan. BS, USAF Acad., 1990; MBA, Wright State U., 1993, MS, 1994; MPhil, Rand Grad. Sch., Santa Monica, Calif., 1997, PhD, 1999. Commd. 2d lt. USAF, Dayton, Ohio, 1990, advanced through grades to capt., 1994, ret., 1995; economist Rand Corp., Santa Monica, Calif., 1995-98; sr. cons. Pricewaterhouse Coopers, L.A., 1998-99; consulting dir. Nat. Data Corp., Chgo., 1999-2001; policy analyst, cons. RAND Corp., Santa Monica, Calif., 2001—. Adj. faculty fin. Cardean U., 2000—; adj. faculty econs. U. Phoenix, 2002--; content expert in econs. Jones INternat. U., 2002--. Author: The Predator ACTD, 1997, Seeing the Lighthouse, 1999; contbr. articles to profl. jours. Bd. dirs. Acad. Selection Com., Ill. 8th Dist., 1999; liaison officer USAF Acad., Dayton, 1992-95; v.p. Ch. Coun., L.A., 1997-99; sch. tutor Santa Monica (Calif.) H.S,. 1995-97. Maj. USAFR, 1995—. Mem. Air Force Acad. Assn. Grads., Am. Legion. Republican. Lutheran. Home: 1970 Marigold Ln Round Lake IL 60073-9540 Office: RAND Corp PO Box 2138 1700 Main St Santa Monica CA 90407-2138 E-mail: MThirtle@earthlink.net.

THIRUVATHUKAL, JOHN V. science educator, consultant; b. Cherthaca, Kerala, India, Aug. 4, 1939; s. Varkey K. and Rose Thiruvathukal; m. Teresa Kailath, Aug. 15, 1971; children: George J., Christina Stevenson. BS, St. Louis Univ., St. Louis, MO, 1961; MS, Mich. State Univ., East Lansing, MI, 1963; PhD, Oreg. State Univ., Corvallis, OR, 1968. Asst. prof. geology DePauw Univ., Green Castle, Ind., 1967—70; cons. NAS, Washington, 1968—87; prof. geoscience Montclair State Univ., Upper Montclair, 1970—. Author: (book) Elements of Oceanography. Chmn. MSU President's Commn. on Affirmative Action, Upper Montclair, NJ, 1987—89. Mem.: Soc. of Exploration Geophysicists, Am. Geophys. Union. Home: 56 Rabkin Drive Clifton NJ 07013 Office: Montclair State Univ 1 Normal Avenue Upper Montclair NJ 07043

THISSELL, JAMES DENNIS, physicist; b. Lincoln County, S.D., June 1, 1935; s. Oscar H. and Bernice G.J. (Olbertson) T. BA cum laude, Augustana Coll., 1957; MS, U. Iowa, 1963. Rsch. physicist U. Iowa, Iowa City, 1958-64; engr. McDonnell Douglas, St. Louis, 1965-66; scientist E.G. & G., Inc., Las Vegas, Nev., 1967-68; engr. Bendix Field Engring. Corp. Ames Rsch. Ctr., Moffett Field, Calif., 1970-77, Lockheed Missiles and Space Co., Sunnyvale, 1978—. Mem. AIAA, IEEE, Am. Phys. Soc., Am. Geophys. Soc., Sigma Xi. Republican. Lutheran. Home: 38475 Jacaranda Dr Newark CA 94560-4727 Office: LMTO 28-12 B158 FAC 1 PO Box 61687 Sunnyvale CA 94088-1687

THISTLETHWAITE, ALINE MCQUISTON, artist; b. Long Beach, Calif. d. John and Hazel McQuiston; children: Mark, Lote. BA, tchg. credential, UCLA, 1945; studied with, Barse Miller, Robert E. Wood, Mario Cooper, John Pike, Ed Whitney, Herb Olsen, Joan Irving, Rex Brandt. Tchr. drawing, painting and photography Santa Ana H.S. One-person shows include Laguna Beach (Calif.) Mus., Lido Island Yacht Club, Lido, Newport, Calif., Newport (Calif.) City Hall, Oxnard (Calif.) Plaza Gallery Fine Arts, Riverside (Calif.) Art Mus. Upstairs Gallery, Innpression Gallery, Rochioli Winery, Healdsburgh, Calif.; exhibited in group shows All. Calif. State Show, 1992, 94, Calif. Small Works, 1992, 93, 94, Newport City Open, Conejo Valley Ann., Hunt Libr., Fullerton, Calif., Sherman Gardens, Newport Beach, Calif., The Islander Gallery, Newport Beach, Armida Winery, 1996, Hopkilm Winery, Kendall Jackson Winery, 1998, 99, Cline Winery, 1998, 99, 2000, George Mason U. Art Gallery, Arlington, Va., 2000, Heritage Gallery, Lafayette, La., Nat. Acad. Design, N.Y., Watercolor U.S.A., Springfield, Mo., El Paso (Tex.) Mus., Oakland (Calif.) Mus., Wichita Centennial, St. Raymond's Ann., Whittier, Calif., Santa Paula Exhbn., Edward Dean Mus., Beaumont, Calif., Palm Springs Desert Mus., Brea (Calif.) Civic Ctr., Cerritos (Calif.) Coll., George Mason U., Arlington, Va.; featured in books: Southern California 100, Arts of Southern California XVII Watercolor. Recipient 1st prize Laguna Beach Mus., Jurors award San Bernardino Fine Arts Inst., Grumbacher Gold medal, 1994, 97, 2000, 2d prize for mixed media, 1992, 1st prize Long Beach Art Open, 1st prize Riverside Art Assn., Best in Show in watercolor, 1st in oil, 1st in watercolor Orange County Fair, 1st and 2d prize Torana Art Assn., 1st prize Santa Ana Ebell, 1st prize Kendall Jackson Tomatoe Festival, Best in Show, 1st prize Mixed Media, Sonoma Harvest Fair, others. Mem. Nat. Watercolor Soc., Watercolor West. Home: 401 Oak Brook Pl Santa Rosa CA 95409-6311

THISTLETHWAITE, DAVID RICHARD, architect; b. Burlington, Iowa, Aug. 24, 1947; s. Robert and Nona (Binder) T.; m. Carol Anne Armstrong, Aug. 22, 1970. BArch, Iowa State U., 1971. Registered arch., Calif., Minn.; registered Nat. Coun. Archtl. Registration Bds.; cert. Health Care arch., Am. Coll. Healthcare Archs., 2000. Designer Morrison Architects, St. Paul, 1971-73, Times Architects, Mpls., 1973-74; project architect Bentz/Thompson Assocs., 1974-77; project mgr. Setter Leach Lindstrom, 1977-78; project architect Wurster Bernardi Emmons, San Francisco, 1978-79, Strotz & Assocs., Tiburon, Calif., 1979-81, Hood Miller Assoc., San Francisco, 1981-84; prin., ptnr. R S T Architects, 1984-88; prin. Thistlethwaite Archtl. Group, 1988—. Contbr. articles to profl. jours. Mem. AIA (nat. profl. devel. com. 1983-86, treas. San Francisco chpt. 1985-86, chmn. Calif. coun. health facilities com. 1994-96, chmn. design com. Acad. Architecture for Health, 1994-96, mem. Calif. coun. ins. bd. trustees 1988-2000, mem. Calif. coun. legis. com. 1996-98), Am. Soc. Healthcare Engring., Design Profls. Safety Assn. (bd. dirs.). Office: 230 Powell St San Francisco CA 94102-2206 E-mail: dthistlethwaite@tagarchitects.com.

THIVIERGE, BETHANY, biomedical technical writer, editor; b. Lansing, Mich., Apr. 17, 1960; m. Randal J. Thivierge, May 8, 1982; children: Brianna, Kathelyn. BS in Biology, U. Mich., 1981; MPH in Health Promotion and Edn., Loma Linda U., 2001. Rsch. asst. U. Mich., Ann Arbor, 1981-84; clin. med. asst. Family Physicians, Camden, Maine, 1984-87; assoc. product mgr. FMC BioProducts, Rockland, 1987-91; owner, prin. Technicality Resources, 1991—. Editor: over 300 sci. and med. jour. articles; contbr. articles to profl. jours. Mem.: MENSA, Bd. Editors in Life Scis., Coun. of Sci. Editors (bd. editors Life Scis., cert. med. writer and editor), Am. Med. Writers Assn. (cert. editor of life scis.), Soc. for Tech. Comm. Avocations: theater, piano. Office: Technicality Resources PO Box 1132 Rockland ME 04841-1132 E-mail: bethiv@midcoast.com.

THIYAGARAJAH, AATHI R. physician; s. Kanapathipilla and Nagapooshani Thiyagarajah; m. Kalaivany Aathirayen, Mar. 15, 1996. MD, North Colombo Med. Ctr., Sri Lanka, 1993. Chief resident physician New Eng. Med. Ctr., Boston, 2000—01; clin. fellow in pain mgmt. Harvard Med. Sch., 2001—. Rschr. Spaulding Rehab. Hosp., Boston, 2001—02. Mem.: AMA (Physician Recognition award 2000), Assn. Acad. Physiatrists, Am. Acad. Phys. Medicine and Rehab. (vice chair membership com. 2000—01), Mass. Med. Soc. (mem. governing coun. resident physician sect., AMA del. 2000—02), Sri Lanka Med. Assn. (life). Hindu. Office: Spaulding Rehab Hosp 125 Nashua St Boston MA 02114 Business E-Mail: athiyaga@hms.harvard.edu.

THOM, JAMES ALEXANDER, novelist; b. Gosport, Ind., May 28, 1933; s. Jay Webb and Julia Elizabeth (Swain) T.; m. Dark Rain Thom, May 20, 1990; 2 stepchildren. AB, Butler U., Indpls., 1961, DHL, 1995. Reporter, columnist The Indpls. Star, 1961-67; mag. editor Rev. Pub. Co., Indpls., 1967-70; lectr. Sch. of Journalism Ind. U., Bloomington, 1977-80. Author 11 books incl.: Follow the River, 1981, Panther in the Sky, 1989 (Golden Spur from Western Writers of Am. 1990), The Red Heart, 1998, Sign-Talker, 2000; contbr. articles to profl. jours. Supporter, spokesman Hoosier Environ. Coun., Indpls., 1997—. Sgt. USMC, 1953-56; mem. Lewis & Clark Trail Heritage Found. Recipient Matrix award Women in Comm., 1995, Founders Cir. award Hoosier Environ. Coun., 1998, 99, 2000; named Sagamore of the Wabash, Gov. of Ind., 1978. Mem. The Authors Guild. Democrat. Avocations: woodcarving, sculptor, illustrator. Home and Office: 10061 W Stogsdill Rd Bloomington IN 47404

THOM, RICHARD DAVID, retired aerospace executive; b. St. Louis, Oct. 4, 1944; s. Reginald James and Vlasta (Koukl) T.; m. Linda Marie Hunt, Sept. 9, 1967; children: Elizabeth Marie, Robert James. BS in Physics, U. Mo., Rolla, 1967; MSEE, UCLA, 1971. Co-op engr. McDonnell Aircraft Corp., St. Louis, 1962-67; head advanced tech. group IR systems dept., aerospace group Hughes Aircraft Co., Culver City, Calif., 1967-72; mem. tech. staff Santa Barbara Rsch. Ctr., Hughes Aircraft Co., Goleta, 1972-76, asst. mgr. R&D Lab., 1976-80, mgr. advanced applications, 1980-83, chief engr., 1984-86, chief scientist, 1986-90, dir. tech., 1990-95; tech. program exec. Hughes Aircraft Co., 1995-98; asst. mgr. Raytheon Santa Barbara Rsch. Ctr., 1998-99; ret. Contbr. articles to profl. jours.; patentee in field. Recipient Hughes Group Patent award for pioneering contbns. in infrared detector tech., 1990. Mem. IEEE, Tau Beta Pi, Sigma Pi Sigma, Delta Sigma Phi. Republican. Avocations: freelance travel writing and photography, specializing in railway travel around the world. Home: 38 Fawn Run Pl PO Box 326 Coupeville WA 98239-0326 E-mail: Richthommail@aol.com.

THOMA, KURT MICHAEL, business owner; b. Boston, Aug. 9, 1946; s. Kurt Richard and Janet (Holdsworth) T.; divorced; children by previous marriage: Heather Anne, Heidi. Student, U. N.H., 1964-68. Clk., supr., asst. divsn. EDP coord., EDP coord. mutual funds divsn. 1st Nat. Bank, Boston, 1968-69; v.p. ctrl. N.H. bldg. corp. Barry Dashner, Inc., Sunapee, N.H., 1969-72; field rep. Acorn Structures, Inc., New London, N.H., Vt., 1972-75; v.p., treas. Design Structures Group, Inc., Quechee, Vt., 1975-76; pres. Withrow Assocs., Inc., New London, 1976-79; v.p. Confetti, Inc., Newport, R.I., 1978-89; pres., treas., propr. dessin batir, 1979-89; Christian Sci. practitioner Warner, N.H., 1990-93; ops. mgr. Arctic Dreams, New London, 1993—. With U.S. Army N.G., 1966-72. Avocations: writing, tennis, skiing, residential and furniture design, photography. Home and Office: PO Box 2064 New London NH 03257-2064 E-mail: kmthoma@tds.net. *"Prior" to the Knowledge or Science of Christ, I was an atheist. In King James Bible demonstrations, I Kings 17, II Kings 4, Daniel 3, Matthew, Mark, Luke, John, Acts 9, 14 and 20 all express the Christ Fact that there is no "death". In medical science "near death experience" is unfolding the same truth, which converges as One. "Death" is only in the "eye of the beholder". You will never see "death" for yourself.*

THOMA, RICHARD WILLIAM, chemical safety and waste management consultant; b. Milw., Dec. 7, 1921; s. Joseph Donath and Margaret Mary (Murphy) T.; m. Ida Mary Scharfschwerdt, Mar. 15, 1952; children: Adele, Richard W., Joseph O., John C. AA, U. Chgo., 1941; BS, U. Wis., Madison, 1947; MS in Biochemistry, U. Wis., 1949, PhD, 1951. R&D fermentation E.R. Squibb & Sons, Inc., New Brunswick, N.J., 1951-82; dir. process devel. New Brunswick Sci. Co., Inc., Edison, 1982-84, cons., 1984—; safety officer Harbor br. Oceanographic Instn., St. Lucie County, Fla., 1988-96. Editor Industrial Microbiology, 1977; contbr. articles to profl. jours.; patentee microbiol. transformation of steroids. Commr. Somerset County Bd. Elections, 1981-841 mem. Bridgewater Town Coun., 1975-81, Environ. Commn., 1974-75, Sewerage Authority, 1975-76, Police Commn., 1977-81; chmn. Bridgewater Dem. Mcpl. Com., 1980-87; alderman St. Lucie Village, 1996—. With AUS, 1942-46. Sr. rsch. fellow, 1980-82. Mem. VFW, Am. Chem. Soc., Am. Soc. Microbiology, Am. Acad. Microbiology (U.K.), Phi Beta Kappa, Sigma Xi, Phi Lambda Upsilon. Home and Office: 3772 Outrigger Ct Fort Pierce FL 34946-1911

THOMAE, MARY JOAN PANGBORN, special education educator; b. Sheboygan, Wis., July 19, 1958; d. Donald Rumsey and Joan Ruth (Thompson) Pangborn; m. Michael Jay Thomae, Oct. 27, 1990; 1 child, Zachary John. BA, Carthage Coll., Kenosha, Wis., 1981; MS in Edn., U. Wis., Whitewater, 1988. Cert. elem. tchr., learning disabled and emotionally disturbed edn., Wis. Tchr. learning disabled pub. schs., De Forest, Wis., 1981-85; tchr. asst. spl. edn. dept. U. Wis., Madison, 1985-86; tchr. learning disabled and emotionally disturbed pub. schs., Cambridge, Wis., 1985-86, Oak Creek, 1986—. Coord. designated vocat. instr. program Family and Consumer Edn. Dept., 1992—; active New Tchr. Mentor program, 2002. Mem. Coun. for Exceptional Children, Oak Creek Tchrs. Union (bldg. rep. 1987-89, 90-91, renaissance steering com. 1990—, chair new faculty recognition com. and fundraising com. 1994—). Avocations: aerobics, cooking, homemaking. Office: Oak Creek High Sch 340 E Puetz Rd Oak Creek WI 53154-3200

THOMAJAN, ROBERT, lawyer, management consultant; b. N.Y.C., May 4, 1941; s. Leon and Fay T. BS, NYU, 1962; JD, St. John's U., 1965. Bar: N.Y. 1965, Tex. 1987, U.S. Ct. Internat. Trade 1975, U.S. Supreme Ct. 1975, U.S. Ct. Appeals (9th cir.) 1976, U.S. Dist. Ct. (we. dist.) Tex. 1979. Atty. Nixon, Mudge, Rose, Guthrie, Alexander & Mitchell, N.Y.C., 1964-68; ptnr. Milgrim, Thomajan & Lee, 1968-90; pres. Eterna Investments, Austin, Tex., 1995—. Arbitrator Civil Ct., N.Y., 1981-86; mem. adv. bd. Ronald McDonald House, 1988-90; bd. dirs. Big Bros./Big Sisters, 1988-90; mem. World Econ. Forum, 1990-93. Mem. Am. Soc. Internat. Law, Internat. Law Assn.

THOMAN, CHARLES JAMES, chemistry educator; b. Wilkes-Barre, Pa., Nov. 4, 1928; s. Charles James Thoman and Anne Calistos Conway; m. Grace Ursula Garrett, May 28, 1983. BS in Chemistry, MA in Philosphy, Spring Hill Coll., 1953; MS in Chemistry, Fordham U., 1956; B of Sacred Theology, Woodstock Coll., 1959, M of Sacred Theology, 1960; PhD in Chemistry, U. Mass., 1966. Prof. U. Scranton, Pa., 1953-55, 66-82, 1984-87, Stephen F. Austin State U., Nacogdoches, Tex., 1987-89, U. Scis. Phila., Phila., 1989—. Rsch. assoc. La. State U. Sch. Medicine, Shreveport, 1982-83; vis. prof. U. Ala., Tuscaloosa, 1983-84. Pres. Pa. Regional Tissue & Transplant Bank, Scranton, 1978-82. Mem. Am. Chem. Soc. (chmn. Phila. sect. 1995). Roman Catholic. Avocations: basketball, history of the Mafia. Home: 402 Lark Dr Mount Laurel NJ 08054-4426 Office: U Scis Phila 600 S 43d St Philadelphia PA 19104

THOMAN, G. RICHARD, corporate and financial executive; b. Tuscaloosa, Ala., June 25, 1944; s. Richard S. and Evelyn (Zumwalt) Thoman; m. Wenke Helina Brier, Aug. 25, 1966 (div. Dec. 1987); children: Camille, Alexis; m. Lynn Susan Bendheim, Sept. 16, 1989; children: Kylie, Max, Amy, Eric. BA with honors, McGill U., 1966; MA, Grad. Inst. Internat. Studies, Geneva, 1968; MA in Internat. Econs., Tufts U., 1967, MA in Law and Diplomacy, 1969, PhD in Internat. Econs., 1971. Exec. trainee Citicorp, N.Y.C., 1968-69; sr. fin. analyst Exxon Corp., 1970-72; sr. assoc. McKinsey and Co., N.Y.C. and Paris, 1972-79; exec. v.p., CFO Am. Express Travel Related Svcs., N.Y.C., 1979-85, pres., Travel Related Svcs. Internat., 1985-89, chmn., CEO, 1989-92; pres., CEO Nabisco Internat. RJR Nabisco, Inc., 1992-94; sr. v.p., group exec. IBM Corp., Somers, N.Y., 1994-95, sr. v.p., CFO Armonk, 1995-97; pres., COO Xerox Corp., 1997-99, pres., CEO, 1999-2000, also bd. dirs.; pvt. investor; sr. advisor Evercore Ptnrs., N.Y.C., 2000—. Bd. dirs. Daimler-Chrysler AG, Union Bancaire Privee, Geneva; mem. U.S. adv. bd. INSEAD; mem. adv. bd. Deutsche Bank Capital Ptnrs. Author: Foreign Investment and Regional Development, 1972. Bd. dirs. Americas Soc., N.Y.C., 1990—, French-Am. Found.; bd. advisors Fletcher Sch. Law and Diplomacy, Tufts U., Medford, Mass., 1990—; mem. adv. bd. Sch. Mgmt. Yale U., Bus. Coun.; U.S. chair TransAtlantic Bus. Dialogue. Recipient Legion of Honors, Govt. of France, 1992. Mem.: Trilateral Commn., Coun. on Fgn. Rels. Avocations: tennis, reading, jogging, travel. Office: Evercore Ptnrs 65 E 55 St 33 Fl New York NY 10022

THOMAN, HENRY NIXON, lawyer; b. Cin., May 5, 1957; s. Richard B. and Barbara (Lutz) Thoman; m. Anne Davies, May 25, 2002; children: Victoria E., Nicholas B. BA, Duke U., 1979; JD, U. Chgo., 1982. Bar: Ohio 1982, U.S. Dist. Ct. (so. dist.) Ohio, 1982. With Taft, Stettinius & Hollister, Cin., 1982-88; sr. atty. John Morrell & Co., 1988-90; sr. counsel Chiquita Brands Internat. Inc., 1990-91, corp. planner, 1991-92; sr. dir. CTP ops. Chiquita Brands, Inc., 1993-94, chief adminstrv. officer Armuelles divsn., 1994-95; corp. counsel The Loewen Group, Covington, Ky., 1995-97; asst. chief counsel, asst. v.p. The Midland Co., Amelia, Ohio, 1997-99; v.p. orgnl. devel. Kendle Internat. Inc., 1999-2000, v.p. complementary ops., 2000—02; pvt. atty., 2002—. Mem. counselors com. U.S. Swimming, Colo., 1983-89; bd. dirs. Friends of Cin. Parks, 1990-93, 96-98, Starshine Children's Hospice, 1996-99, Cinci. Aquatic Club, 1997—, Kids Helping Kids, 2000-01, Mariemont Aquatic Club, v.p., 1992-93; pres. Club Atletico Y Socialde Chiriqui, 1994-95. Mem. ABA, Ohio State Bar, Cin. Bar Assn. E-mail: thoman.henry@fuse.net.

THOMAN, JOHN EVERETT, architect, mediator; b. Dixon, Ill., Aug. 6, 1925; s. George Dewey and Agnes Katherine (Fane) T.; m. Paula Ann Finnegan, Oct. 31, 1953; children: Shawn Michael, Brian Gerard, Kevin Charles, Trace Marie, Patricia Ann, Ronan Patrick, Caron Lynn. AA, UCLA, 1948; BArch cum laude, U. So. Calif., 1955. Registered architect, Calif. Project dir. A. Quincy Jones & Frederick E. Emmons, L.A., 1956-57, assoc., 1958, dir. constrn., 1958-73; dir. specifications A. Quincy Jones, FAIA & Assocs., 1973-77, Albert C. Martin, L.A., 1977-79; dir. constrn. and industry rels. Albert C. Martin and Assocs., 1979-95, assoc., 1979-90, sr. assoc., 1990—2002, dir. emeritus constrn. and industry rels., 1996—2002. Guest lectr. U. So. Calif. Lusk Sch. Real Estate, UCLA Grad. Sch., also various student, trade and tech. groups. Mem., vice chmn. Culver City (Calif.) Planning Commn., 1959; mem. Calif. Gov.'s Housing Commn., L.A., 1960, Community Redevel. Agy., Culver City, 1992-94. With U.S. Army, 1943-45, USAF, 1950-51. Mem. AIA (chmn. design awards com. L.A. 1960), Constrn. Specifications Inst. (bd. dirs. 1977-80, guest lectr.), Phi Eta Sigma, Tau Sigma Delta. Avocations: fishing, military history. Office: AC Martin Ptnrs 444 South Flower St Los Angeles CA 90071

THOMAN, MARK EDWARD, pediatrician; b. Chgo., Feb. 15, 1936; s. John Charles and Tasula Mark (Petrakis) T.; m. Theresa Thompson, 1984; children: Marlisa Rae, Susan Kay, Edward Kim, Nancy Lynn, Janet Lea, David Mark. AA, Graceland Coll., 1956; BA, U. Mo., 1958, MD, 1962. Diplomate Am. Bd. Pediat., Am. Coll. Toxicology (examiner). Intern U. Mo. at Columbia, 1962—63; resident in pediat. Blank Meml. Children's Hosp., Des Moines, 1963—65; cons. in toxicology USPHS, Washington, 1965—66; chief dept. pediat. Shiprock (N.Mex.) Navajo Indian Hosp., 1966—67; dir. N.D. Poison Info. Ctr.; also practice medicine specializing in pediat. Quain & Ramstad Clinic, Bismarck, ND, 1967—69; dir. Iowa Poison Info. Ctr., Des Moines, 1967—69; mem. pediat. exec. com. Broadlawns Med. Ctr., 1969—2000, pres. med. staff, 2000—01. Accident investigator FAA, 1976—, sr. aviation examiner, 1977—2000; sr. cons. in field; lectr. aviation seminars, 1977—; mem. faculty U. Osteo. Sci. & Health, 1969—2000, dir. cystic fibrosis clin., 1973—82; dir. Mid-Iowa Drug Abuse Program, 1972—76; mem. med. adv. bd. La Leche League Internat., 1965—; pres. Medic-Air Ltd., 1976—; chief med. officer Broadlawns Med. Ctr. , Des Moines, 2000—02. Editor-in-chief AACTION, 1975-90. Bd. dirs. Polk County Pub. Health Nurses Assn., 1969-77, Des Moines Speech and Hearing Ctr., 1974-79, Ecumenical Coun. Iowa, 1990-99; bd. govs. Mo. U. Sch. Medicine Alumni, 1988—, pres., 1997-99; elder mem. Cmty. of Christ Ch. With USMCR, 1954-59; lt. comdr. USPHS, 1965-66; capt. USNR, 1988-96, ret. 1996; dir. Dept. Health Svcs. USNR. Recipient N.D. Gov.'s award of merit, 1969, Cystic Fibrosis Rsch. Found. award, 1975, Am. Psychiat. Assn. Thesis award, 1962. Fellow Am. Coll. Med. Toxicology (diplomate 1996); mem. AMA (del. 1970-88), APHA, NRA (life), Assn. Am. Physicians & Surgeons (chief of staff, pres. Broadlawns Polk County Med. Ctr. 2000—), Polk County Med. Soc., Iowa State Med. Assn., Aerospace Med. Assn., Res. Officers Assn., Civil Aviation Med. Assn., Soc. Adolescent Medicine, Inst. Clin. Toxicology, Internat. Soc. Pediat., Am. Acad. Pediat. (chmn. accident prevention com. Iowa chpt. 1975-2000), Cystic Fibrosis Club, Am. Acad. Clin. Toxicology (trustee 1969-90, pres. 1982-84), Am. Assn. Poison Control Ctrs., Am. Coll. Physician Execs., U.S. Naval Inst., Flying Physicians Club, Aircraft Owners and Pilots Assn, Nat. Pilots Assn. (Safe Pilot award), Hyperion Field and Country Club. Republican. Home: 6896 NW Trail Ridge Dr Johnston IA 50131-1322 Office: PO Box 349 Johnston IA 50131-0349 E-mail: paro1795@aol.com., mthoman@broadlawns.org.

THOMAS, ADRIAN WESLEY, laboratory director; b. Edgefield, S.C., June 23, 1939; s. Hasting Adrian and Nancy Azalena (Bridges) T.; m. Martha Elizabeth McAllister, July 12, 1964; children: Wesley Adrian, Andrea Elizabeth. BS in Agrl. Engring., Clemson U., 1962, MS in Agrl. Engring., 1965; PhD, Colo. State U., 1972. Rsch. scientist USDA-Agrl. Rsch. Svc., Tifton, Ga., 1965-69, Fort Collins, Colo., 1969-72, rsch. leader Walkinsville, Ga., 1972-89, lab. dir. Tifton, 1989-98; retired. Mem. acad. faculty Colo. State U. Ft. Collins, 1969-72; acad. faculty U. Ga., Athens, 1973—, grad. faculty, 1988—. Contbr. agrl. rsch. articles to profl. jours. With U.S. Army, 1962-63. Mem. Am. Soc. Agrl. Engrs., Am. Soc. Agronomy, Soil and Water Conservation Soc. Am., Soil Sci. Soc. Am., Sigma Xi, Alpha Epsilon, Gamma Sigma Delta, Phi Kappa Phi. Lutheran. Avocations: reading, gardening, yard care, remodeling home, sports. E-mail: awthomas39@hotmail.com.

THOMAS, ALAN, candy company executive; b. Evansburg, Pa., Jan. 1, 1923; s. William Roberts and Letta (Garrett) T.; m. Marguerite Atria, July 1, 1972; children: Garrett Lee, Michael Alan, Randall Stephen, Brett Eliot. BS, Pa. State U., 1949; MS, U. Minn., 1950, PhD, 1954. Instr. Temple U., Phila., 1950-51, U. Minn., St. Paul, 1951-54; rsch. asst. Bowman Dairy Co., Chgo., 1954-56; rsch. project mgr. M&M Candies divsn. Mars, Inc., Hackettstown, N.J., 1956-60, product devel. mgr., 1961-64, chocolate rsch. dir., 1964; v.p. rsch. & devel. Mars Candies, Chgo., 1964-67, v.p. rsch. & devel. M&M/Mars divsn. Hackettstown, 1967-77, v.p. sci. affairs, 1977-78; gen. mgr. Ethel M, Las Vegas, 1978-83; cons., 1985; sr. cons. Knechtel Rsch. Scis., Inc., Skokie, Il., 1984; v.p. tech. Ferrara Pan Candy Co., Forest Park, Ill., 1986-92; cons., 1993—. Chmn. coun. industry liaison panel Food and Nutrition Bd., Nat. Acad. Scis./NRC, 1972-73; adv. U.S. del. Codex Alimentarius Com. on Cocoa and Chocolate Products, 1967-78. Served to 1st lt. inf. AUS, 1942-46. Recipient rsch. award Nat. Confectioners Assn. U.S., 1971. Mem. Grocery Mfrs. Am. (chmn. tech. com. 1975-76), Chocolate Mfrs. Assn. (chmn. FDA liaison com. 1975-77), Inst. Food Technologists, Am. Assn. Candy Technologists, Gamma Sigma Delta, Phi Kappa Phi. Home: 2005 Sedona Morning Dr Las Vegas NV 89128-8484 Office: Ferrara Pan Candy Co 7301 Harrison St Forest Park IL 60130-2016

THOMAS, ALBERT W, investment company executive, financial analyst; b. New York, Ny; s. Albert and Florence Thomas; m. Carolyn Meeth Thomas; children: Peter, Paulette. BS, Northwestern U., Chicago, IL, 1950; Naturopathic Dr., Bernadean U., Las Vegas, NV, 1972. Pres. Security Dynamics Investment Co., Chicago, Ill., 1966—68, Real Life Estate Inc., Chicago, 1969—70; fl. trader Mid Am. Cmty. Exch., 1964—81; pres. World Trading Group, Merritt Island, Fla., 1984—92, Williamsburg Investment Co., Merritt Island, 1988—. Cons. Various Companies. Author: (book) If it Doesn't Go Up, Don't Buy It; contbr. articles to profl. jours. Mem. adv. bd., pub. ofcl. Merritt Island Parks and Recreation Bd., Merritt Island, Fla., 2000—02. Pvt. US Army, 1944—46. Mem.: Space Coast Writers Guild, Mensa. Achievements include design of built and flew my own airplane, a Varieze. Avocations: fishing, travel. Home: 830 Waikiki Drive Merritt Island FL 32953-3276

THOMAS, ALLEN LLOYD, lawyer, private investor; b. Orange, N.J., Sept. 15, 1939; s. Richard Lloyd and Dorothy (Carr) Thomas; m. Virginia Dehnert, June 24, 1961 (div. 1974); children: Sarah Ann, Anne Marjorie; m. Barbara Singer, Mar. 12, 1978 (div. 2001); 1 child Allen Lloyd. BA, Wesleyan U., 1961; LLB, Yale U., 1964. Bar: N.Y. 1965, U.S. Ct. Appeals (D.C. cir.) 1981; solicitor, Eng. and Wales, 1996. Ptnr. Paul Weiss Rifkind Wharton & Garrison, N.Y.C., 1973—92; resident ptnr. Hong Kong, 1983-87; dir., gen. counsel Gerard Atkins & Co. Ltd., 1992-94; gen. counsel Gen. Atlantic Group Ltd, 1992-94. Chmn. Ockham Holdings PLC; bd. dirs. Penna Cons PLC, Eidos PLC, Moves Ltd., Blue Ocean PLC. Chmn. Urban Bus. Assis. Corp., N.Y.C., 1971-82; chmn. Hong Kong Ballet, 1985-87; co-chmn. Internat. Com., N.Y.C. Ballet, 1986-91; pres. Internat. Salzburg Assn. Am., 1987-92; dir., mem. exec. com., gen. counsel Child Care Action Campaign, 1990-92. Fellow Am. Coll. Investment Counsel, Hartford, Conn. Mem. River Club, N.Y. Boodle's Met. Club of Washington, Hong Kong Club, Hong Kong Jockey Club, Coral Beach and Tennis Club, Lenox Club, Buck's Club. Home: 3 Chester St London SW1X 7BB England E-mail: allenlloydthomas@hotmail.com.

THOMAS, ANDREW KYLE, lawyer; b. D.C., Apr. 8, 1966; s. Harold G. and Karen K. Thomas; m. Suzette Marie Thomas; children: Michelle Justine, Garrett Andrew. BA, James Mason U., 1988; JD, George Mason U., 1992. Assoc. Niles, Dulaney & Lauer, LLP, Culpeper, Va., 1996-99; ptnr. Dulaney, Parker, Lauer & Thomas, LLP, 1999—. Mem. ATLA, Va. Trial Lawyers Assn., Culpeper County Bar Assn., Fauquier County Bar Assn. Office: Dulaney Lauer & Thomas 209 N West St Culpeper VA 22701 Address: 98 Alexandria Pike Ste 11 Warrenton VA 20186

THOMAS, ANDREW PHILIP, physiologist; b. London, U.K., Oct. 22, 1955; s. William Robert and Christine Bessie (McSweeny) T.; m. Janette Alexander, Sept. 15, 1985; children: Samantha Jane, Jefferey McKinley. BS, U. Bristol, U.K., 1978; PhD, U. Bristol, 1981. Rsch. assoc. U. Bristol Med. Sch., 1983-85; asst. prof. Hahnemann U., Phila., 1985-86, Thomas Jefferson U., Phila., 1986-89, assoc. prof., 1989-94, prof., 1994-97, adj. prof., 1997—; prof./chmn. UMDNJ N.J. Med. Sch., Newark, 1997—. Mem. cell physiol. adv. panel, Nat. Sci. Found., Washington, 1988-92, initial rev. group, NIH, Bethesda, 1996—. Mem. Biochelmical Soc., Am. Soc. Biochemistry and Molecular Biology, Rsch. Soc. Alcoholism, Am. Assn. Advancement Sci. Office: UMDNJ Med Sch 185 S Orange Ave Newark NJ 07103-2757

THOMAS, ANDREW S.W. astronaut; b. Adelaide, S. Australia, Dec. 18, 1951; s. Adrian C. and Mary E. Thomas. B with hon. in Mech. Engring., U. Adelaide, 1973, PhD in Mech. Engring., 1978. From rsch. scientist to divsn. mgr. Lockheed Aero. Sys. Co., Marietta, Ga., 1977—87, mgr. flight sci. divsn., 1987—89; with Jet Propulsion Lab., Pasadena, Calif., 1989—92, NASA, Houston, 1992—93, astronaut, 1993—. Payload comdr. Endeavour Space Shuttle, 1996; bd. engr. 2 Russian Space Sta. Mir, 1998; with space flight STS-102, 2001; dep. chief astronaut office NASA. Mem.: Am. Inst. Aeronautics & Astronautics. Avocations: horseback riding, mountain biking, running, wind surfing, playing classical guitar. Office: Astronaut Office CB NASA Johnson Space Ctr Houston TX 77058*

THOMAS, ANN VAN WYNEN, law educator; b. The Netherlands, May 27, 1919; came to U.S., 1921, naturalized, 1926; d. Cornelius and Cora Jacoba (Daansen) Van Wynen; m. A.J. Thomas Jr., Sept. 10, 1948. AB with distinction, U. Rochester, 1940; JD, U. Tex., 1943; post doctoral degree, So. Meth. U., 1952. U.S. fgn. svc. officer, Johannesburg, South Africa, London, The Hague, The Netherlands, 1943-47; rsch. atty. Southwestern Legal Found., Sch. Law So. Meth. U., Dallas, 1952-67; asst. prof. polit. sci. So. Meth. U. Sch. Law, 1968-73, assoc. prof., 1973-76, prof., 1976-85, prof. emeritus, 1985—. Author: Communism versus International Law, 1953, (with A.J. Thomas Jr.) International Treaties, 1950, Non-Intervention—The Law and its Import in the Americas, 1956, OAS: The Organization of American States, 1962, International Legal Aspects of Civil War in Spain, 1936-1939, 1967, Legal Limitations on Chemical and Biological Weapons, 1970, The Concept of Aggression, 1972, Presidential War Making Power: Constitutional and International Law Aspects, 1981, An International Rule of Law—Problems and Prospects, 1974. Chmn. time capsule com. Grayson County Commn. on Tex. Sesquicentennial, 1986-88; co-chmn. Grayson County Commn. on Bicentennial U.S. Constn., 1988-93; co-chmn. com. Grayson County Sesquicentennial, 1994-97; co-chmn. Grayson County Commn. on the Millenium, 1997—. Recipient Am. medal Nat. DAR Soc., 1992. Mem. Tex. Bar Assn., Am. Soc. Internat. Law, Grayson County Bar Assn. Home: Spaniel Hall 374 Coffee Cir Pottsboro TX 75076-3164

THOMAS, ANNABEL CRAWFORD, writer; b. Columbus, Ohio, July 28, 1929; d. George Sheldon and Mary Ethel (Byers) Crawford; m. William Lawrence Thomas, Sept. 15, 1951; children: Stephen, Elizabeth Thomas Lantz, Katherine Thomas Reese, Michael. BA, Ohio State U., 1951. Author: The Phototropic Woman, 1981 (Iowa short fiction award 1981, citation Ernest Hemingway Found. 1982, New Writers award Great Lakes Colls Assn. 1982), Knucklebones, 1994 (Willa Cather award 1994); co-author: Human Atomy, 1993, Blood Feud, 1998, Stone Man Mountain, 2002. Home: PO Box 88 Ashley OH 43003-0088

THOMAS, ANNE MOREAU, former newspaper owner; b. Trenton, N.J., May 23, 1930; d. Daniel Howard and Lillis Dale (Simmonds) Moreau; m. Henry Seely Thomas, Jr., June 14, 1952 (dec. Aug. 1994); children: Catherine, John Martin II, Howard Moreau. BA, Middlebury Coll., 1951; DHL, Rutgers U., 1999; AA (hon.) , Raritan Valley C.C. Tchr. North Hunterdon H.S., Annandale, N.J., 1951-52, Hunterdon Adult Sch., Flemington, 1953-70; home and food editor Hunterdon County Democrat, 1954-99, owner, bd. sec., 1985-94, owner, chmn. bd., 1994—2001. Trustee Rutgers U., New Brunswick, N.J., 1985—, bd. govs., 1991—, chmn. bd. govs., 1995-98; mem. N.J. Commn. Higher Edn., Trenton, 1995-98. Recipient N.J. Food Communicator of Yr. award N.J. Dept. Agr., 1981, Golden award for cmty. svc. Hunterdon County C. of C., 1990, Eagle Leadership award Ctr./Urban cmty. Leadership, 1996, Hunterdon Disting. Citizen award Ctrl. N.J. Coun. Boy Scouts Am., 1999-2000; named Woman of Yr., Hunterdon County YMCA, 1997. Mem. N.J. Press Assn. (bd. dirs. 1977-85, pres. 1984, chmn. 1985), DAR, Copper Hill Country Club, N.J. Mus. Agr. (trustee), Hunterdon County Hist. Soc. (trustee). Republican. Presbyterian. Avocations: restoration of circa 1750 Cape Cod family homestead, gardening, cooking. Home: 38 Pennsylvania Ave Flemington NJ 08822-1222

THOMAS, ARCHIBALD JOHNS, III, lawyer; b. Jacksonville, Fla., Apr. 27, 1952; s. Archibald Johns and Jean (Snodgrass) T.; m. Martha Ann Marconi, Sept. 1, 1973. BA, U. So. Fla., 1973; JD, Stetson U., 1977. Bar: Fla. 1977, U.S. Dist. Ct. (mid. dist.) Fla. 1977, U.S. Ct. Appeals (11th cir.) 1981, U.S. Supreme Ct. 1981, U.S. Claims Ct. 1990; cert. labor and employment law, Fla. Law clk. to U.S. magistrate U.S. Dist. Ct., Tampa, Fla., 1977-78; 1st asst. fed. pub. defender U.S. dist. ct., Jacksonville, 1978-84; sr. ptnr. Thomas & Skinner, P.A., 1984-89; pvt. practice, 1990—. Mem. labor and employment law cert. com. Fla. Bar, 2002—. Mem.: NACDL, ATLA (employment rights sect.), Jacksonville Bar Assn., Fla. Nat. Employment Lawyers Assn. (pres. 2002), Nat. Employment Lawyers Assn. (co-chmn. Fla. chpt. 1992), Fed. Bar Assn., Fla. Bar Assn. (co-chmn. individual rights com. 2001). Democrat. Avocation: sailing. Home: 708 Mccollum Cir Neptune Beach FL 32266-3789 Office: Riverplace Tower Ste 1640 Jacksonville FL 32207 E-mail: archibald@job-rights.com.

THOMAS, BERTRAM DAVID, retired chemical engineer; b. Renton, Wash., May 5, 1903; s. David and Minnie Belle (Custer) T.; m. Dorothy Glorian Butler, Dec. 21, 1928 (dec. 1986); children: Preston David, Nancy Glorian, Lawrence Eldon. BS, U. Wash., 1929, PhD in Chemistry, 1933. Registered profl. engr., Ohio. Rsch. engr. Battelle Meml. Inst., Columbus, Ohio, 1934-40, asst. dir., 1940-56, pres., 1956-68; ret. Mem. adv. com. on environment, Santa Barbara, Calif., 1970-73. Patentee ore dressing and coal preparation methods; contbr. articles to sci. publs. Trustee Columbus Mus. Art, 1962-67, Ohio State U., Columbus, 1965-68, Santa Barbara Mus. Art, 1973—; trustee, pres. Santa Barbara Botanic Garden, 1974-82. Recipient Order Civil Merit 1st Class, Republic of Korea, 1965; DEng. (hon.), Mich. Coll. Mining and Tech., 1957; DSci (hon.) Ohio State U., 1963, Otterbein Coll., Westerville, Ohio, 1965, Cleve. State U., 1968. Fellow AAAS; mem. Chemists Club N.Y., Am. Che. Soc., Sigma Xi. Home: 300 Hot Springs Rd Apt 21 Santa Barbara CA 93108-2043

THOMAS, BESSIE, primary education educator; b. Shreveport, La., Nov. 30, 1943; d. Fleen and Tommie Lee (Anderson) Myles; m. Jesse Thomas, May 11, 1968 (dec. 1995). BS, Grambling Coll., 1966; MS, Grambling State U., 1976; postgrad., various colls. and univs., 1967-79. Cert. primary and elem. tchr., La. 1st grade tchr. Pine St. Sch., Hamburg, Ark., 1966-67, Pine Grove Elem. Sch., Shreveport, 1967-70, Mooringsport (La.) Sch., 1970-81; early childhood edn. tchr. Fairfield Elem. Sch., Shreveport, 1981-2000, Mooretown ECE Ctr., 2001—. Active Word of Faith Christian Ctr. Grantee Caddo Pub. Edn. Found., 1995—. Mem. NEA. Democrat. Avocations: inspirational reading, painting T-shirts, travel, interacting with children, viewing works of art. Home: 2831 Abbie St Shreveport LA 71103-2130 E-mail: blmt@bellsouth.net.

THOMAS, BETTY, director, actress; b. St. Louis, July 24, 1948; BFA, Ohio U. Former sch. tchr.; co-star Hill St. Blues, from 1981. Joined Second City Workshop, Chgo.; appeared on Second City TV, 1984; appeared in after sch. spl. The Gift of Love, 1985, Prison of Children, 1986. Appeared in The Fun Factory game show, 1976; (TV film) Outside Chance, 1978, Nashville Grab, 1981, When Your Lover Leaves, 1983, The Late Shift, 1996 (Drs. Guild Am. dramatic spl. award 1996); star TV series Hill Street Blues, 1981-87 (Emmy nominations 1981, 82, 83), (Emmy award, 1985); dir.: (TV) Dream On: "For Peter's Sake" (Emmy award, Outstanding Individual Achievement in Directing in a Comedy Series, 1993), 1993, Male Pattern Baldness, 1998; (films) Troop Beverly Hills, 1989, The Brady Bunch Movie, 1995, Private Parts, 1997, Doctor Dolittle, 1998, 28 Days, 1999; prodr.: Can't Hardly Wait, 1998. Recipient Women in Film Crystal award, 2001.*

THOMAS, BEVERLY IRENE, special education educator, educational diagnostician, substance abuse counselor; b. Del Rio, Tex., Nov. 12, 1939; d. Clyde Louis and Eve Naomi (Avant) Whistler; m. James Henry Thomas, Jan. 28, 1972; children: Kenneth (dec.), Wade, Robert, Darcy, Betty Kay, James III, Debra, Brenda, Michael. BM summa cum laude, Sul Ross State U., 1972, MEd, 1976, MEd in Counseling, 1992, MEd in Mid. Mgmt., 1996. Cert. music, elem. edn., music edn., learning disabilities, spl. edn. generic, ednl. diagnosis, ednl. counseling, spl. edn. counseling and mid. mgmt. Tchr. Pecos-Barstow-Toyah Ind. Sch. Dist., 1974—92, 1999—; edn. diagnostician West Tex. State Sch., Tex. Youth Commn., ret., 1999; tchr. spl. edn. and enhanced 5th grade Pecos-Barstow-Toyah Ind. Sch. Dist., 1999-2000; youth counselor Tex. Workforce Ctr., Pecos, 2000; substance abuse counselor Reeves County Detention Ctr., 2001—. Gifted-talented coordinator 5th grade, Pecos-Barstow-Toyah Ind. Sch. Dist., 1999-2000. Mem. AAUW, ASCD, NEA, MENSA, Assn. for Children with Learning Disabilities (local sec. 1974), Tex. State Tchrs. Assn. (treas. 1991-94), Tex. Ednl. Diagnosticians

Assn., Tex. Profl. Ednl. Diagnosticians, Reeves County Assn. of Children with Learning Disabilities, Nat. Coun. Tchrs. of Maths., Nat. Coun. Tchrs. English, Learning Disabilities Assn., Nat. Coun. for Geog. Edn., Learning Disabilities Assoc., Tex., Coun. for Exceptional Children, Tex. Counseling Assn., Am. Correctional Assn., Alpha Chi, Kappa Delta Pi, Chi Sigma Iota. Home: PO Box 128 Pecos TX 79772-0128

THOMAS, BROOKS, publishing company executive; b. Phila., Nov. 28, 1931; s. Walter Horstman and Ruth Sterling (Boomer) T.; m. Galen Pinckard Clark, Apr. 15, 1969 (div. 1973). BA, Yale U., 1953, LL.B., 1956; grad., Advanced Mgmt. Program, Harvard, 1973. Bar: Pa. 1957, N.Y. 1960. With law firm Winthrop, Stimson, Putnam & Roberts, N.Y.C., 1960-68; sec., gen. counsel Harper & Row, Pubs., Inc., 1968-69, v.p., gen. counsel, 1969-73, exec. v.p., 1973-79, chief operating officer, 1977-81, pres., 1979-87, chief exec. officer, 1981-87, chmn. bd., 1986-87. Chmn. bd. Harper & Row, Ltd., London, 1973-87; dir. Harper & Row, Pty. Ltd., Australia, Harla S.A. de C.V., Mex., Harper & Row Pubs. Asia, Pte. Ltd., Singapore. Pres., bd. dirs. Butterfield House, 1968-72, 90-93; trustee, dir. RADG, Inc., 1987-89; dir. Thompson Island Outward Bound Edn. Ctr., 1987-95, Colo. Outward Bound Sch., 1990-96, bd. govs., 1996—; bd. dirs. Young Audiences, Inc., 1977—, chmn., 1985—; trustee Outward Bound USA, 1980—, vice chmn., 1983-84, chmn., 1984-87; chmn. Nat. Book Awards, 1984-85, dir., 1985-87; mem. devel. bd. Yale U., 1985-89; adv. bd. Yale Sch. Orgn. and Mgmt., 1987-96; chmn. Vail Valley Inst., 1989—; dir. Outward Bound Internat., 1997—, dir. expeditionary learning, 2000-; trustee Episcopal Acad., 2000—. Lt. (j.g.) USNR, 1956-59. Mem. Am. Bar Assn., Assn. Bar City of N.Y., Assn. Am. Pubs. (bd. dirs. 1980-85, chmn. 1983-85), Council Fgn. Relations, Yale U. Alumni Assn. (law sch. rep. 1980-83) Clubs: Merion Cricket (Phila.); Century (N.Y.C.), Yale (N.Y.C.), University (N.Y.C.), N.Y. Yacht (N.Y.C.); Essex Yacht (Conn.). Home: 5 Tudor City Pl New York NY 10017-6853 also: 141 Saybrook Rd Essex CT 06426-1412 also: 63 Willow Pl Vail CO 81657-5304

THOMAS, CALVERT, lawyer; b. Balt., Nov. 1, 1916; s. William Douglas Nelson and Elizabeth Steuart (Calvert) T.; m. Margaret Somervell Berry, Sept. 1, 1943; children— Calvert Bowie, Carolyn Brooke Dold. Douglas Mackubin. BS, Washington and Lee U., 1938; LL.B., U. Md., 1940. Bar: Md. bar 1940, D.C. bar 1972, Mich. bar 1947, N.Y. State bar 1974, Conn. bar 1979. Asso. atty. Legal Aid Bur., Balt., 1940-41; atty. Lehmeyer & Moser, 1941-42, Solicitor's Office, Dept. Labor, Washington, 1942-43, Tax Ct. of U.S., Washington, 1943-44, Chief Counsel's Office, Bur. Internal Revenue, Washington, 1944-46; atty. legal staff Gen. Motors Corp., Detroit, 1946-72, asst. gen. counsel, 1972-78; sec., asst. gen. counsel in charge N.Y. legal staff, N.Y.C., 1973-78; chmn. Thomas Cadillac, Inc., 1978—. Councilman, Franklin Village, Mich., 1958-60, pres., 1960-64; Bd. dirs. Franklin Community Assn., 1956-58; vice chmn. Kingswood Sch., Cranbrook, 1968-69, chmn., 1969-71; trustee Cranbrook Schs., 1971-73, Washington and Lee U., 1975—; chmn. Old Guard West Hartford, 1992-93. Mem. Am., Fed., Detroit, Md., D.C., N.Y. bar assns., State Bar Mich. (chmn. tax sect. 1971-72), Am. Soc. Corp. Secs., So. Md. Soc., Soc. Colonial Wars, Lords of Md. Manors, Descendants of the Signers of the Declaration of Independence, Sons of the Am. Revolution, Soc. of the Ark and Dove, Soc. of Founders and Patriots of Am., Beta Theta Pi, Phi Delta Phi, Omicron Delta Kappa. Clubs: Hartford, Hartford Golf. Republican. Episcopalian. Home: 138 Stoner Dr West Hartford CT 06107-1306 Office: PO Box 1778 Hartford CT 06144-1778 E-mail: calt16@aol.com.

THOMAS, CARLTON EUGENE (SANDY THOMAS), electrical engineer, researcher; b. Cleve., Dec. 16, 1939; s. Clyde and Laura Bernice Thomas; m. Anne Edna Thomas, Jan. 28, 1961; children: Scott Carlton, Todd Clyde, Julie Anne, Penny Lynn. BSEE, U. Mich., 1961, MSEE, 1963, PhDEE, 1971. Rsch. scientist Conduction Corp., Ann Arbor, Mich., 1962-72; dir. laser and optics divsn. KMS Fusion, 1972-81; group leader Std. Oil Co., Cleve., 1981-86; sr. analyst Office Tech. Assessment U.S. Congress, Washington, 1986-87; fellow AAAS, 1987-88; legis. asst. Sen. Tom Harkin U.S. Senate, 1988-94; v.p. Directed Technologies, Inc., Arlington, Va., 1994—2001; pres. H2Gen Innovations, Alexandria, 2001—. Co-author: Five Minutes to Midnight, 1990; patentee in field; contbr. articles to profl. jours. Spkr. Nuclear Weapons Freeze Campaign, Cleve., 1981-84; bd. dirs. YMCA, Ann Arbor, Mich. Mem. AAAS (Sci., Arms Control and Nat. Security fellow 1987-88), IEEE, Soc. Automotive Engrs., Nat. Hydrogen Assn. (vice chmn. 1995-98), Eta Kappa Nu, Tau Beta Pi, Phi Kappa Phi. Avocations: gardening, wind-surfing, snorkeling, racquetball, tennis. E-mail: sandy_thomas@directed technologies.com. Office: H2Gen Innovations Inc 4740 Eisenhower Ave Alexandria VA 22304

THOMAS, CARMEN CHRISTINE, physician, consultant administrator; b. Germany, Apr. 15, 1908; came to U.S., 1921; d. Paul Ernest and Huberta (Mohr) T. AB, U. Del., 1929; MD, Woman's Med. Coll. Pa., 1932; DSc, U. Pa., 1940. Diplomate Am. Bd. Dermatology. Asst. chief resident Phila. Gen. Hosp., 1934-35; fellow in dermatology U. Pa., Phila., 1936-39, asst. prof. dermatology, 1940-67; prof. dermatology Woman's Med. Coll. Pa., 1941-68, dir. dept. oncology, 1952-66, emeritus prof. dermatology, 1968—; chief dermatologist Phila. Gen. Hosp., 1944-77; pvt. practice Phila., 1939-77. Cons. Vets. Hosp., Memor Hosp., Phila., 1950-77, Elwyn Inst., Devereux Sch., Delaware County, 1950-69. Contbr. articles to profl. jours. Fellow Phila. Coll. Physicians; mem. Am. Acad. Dermatology (life), Phila. Dermatol. Soc. (life, pres. 1942), Phila. County Med. Soc. (life), Phi Beta Kappa, Alpha Omega Alpha, Sigma Xi. Avocations: travel, photography, music archeology. Home: 600 E Cathedral Rd Apt G305 Philadelphia PA 19128-1929

THOMAS, CAROL LOUISE JOSEPH, community planning company executive; b. Poughkeepsie, N.Y., Aug. 29, 1923; d. Harold Kritzman and Charlotte Carolyn (Freiberg) Joseph; m. Charles Raymond Thomas, Mar. 21, 1943; children: Charles Joseph, Katharine Louise Thomas Noer. Student, Vassar Coll., 1941-43, Boston U., 1943, 49; AB cum laude, Syracuse U., 1948; MA, U. Conn., 1950; postgrad., MIT, 1950. Dir. Thomas Assocs. divsn. Universal Engring. Corp., Boston, 1969-78; pres. Thomas Planning Svcs., Inc., 1978—, TPS/China, Inc., 1995—. Mem. faculty U. R.I. Grad. Curriculum in Cmty. Planning and Area Devel., 1964— ; guest lectr. various colls., 1987-97, Harvard U., 1975-85; cons., author articles land use planning. Mem. parish com., 1958-60, mem. standing com. 1st and 2d ch. Unitarian Ch., 1958-60, 99—, chmn. 2001-2002. Named Hon. Citizen of Guangzhou, China. Fellow Am. Inst. Cert. Planners (chmn. 1984-86, pres. New Eng. chpt. 1965-67); mem. Am. Planning Assn. (pres. chpt. 1979-82, pres. pvt. practice divsn. 1988-92), Mass. Assn. Planning Dirs., Mass. Fedn. Planning Bds., Mass. Cons. Planners (vice chmn. 1984-88). Home: 151 Tremont St Apt 23P Boston MA 02111-1121 Office: 60 Temple Pl Boston MA 02111

THOMAS, CAROL MARIE, business manager, lawyer; b. Milw., June 28, 1954; d. Howard John and Elfriede Marie (Wachcic) Schuh; m. Gerald Bernard Thomas, July 1, 1978; children: Gerald, James, Michael, Kathryn. BA, Ariz. State U., 1976; MA, Mich. State U., 1978; JD, Thomas M. Cooley Law Sch., 1997; postgrad., Wayne State U., 1997—. Bar: Mich. 1997. Head resident advisor Mich. State U., Lansing, 1977; counselor, instr. Mort. C.C., Flint, Mich., 1978; admissions coord. Delta Coll., 1978-80; bus. mgr. Dr. G. Thomas, Saginaw, 1980-97. Pres. Saginaw Newcomers Club, 1986; v.p. North Saginaw Twp. Little League, 1993-95, Saginaw County Med. Aux., 1987. Mem. State Bar Mich. Republican. Roman Catholic. Avocation: piano. Home: 4691 Hamlet Dr S Saginaw MI 48603-1988 Office: 6420 Normandy Dr Saginaw MI 48603-4354

THOMAS, CHARLES ALLEN, JR. molecular biologist, educator; b. Dayton, Ohio, July 7, 1927; s. Charles Allen and Margaret Stoddard (Talbott) T.; m. Margaret M. Gay, July 7, 1951; children: Linda Carrick, Stephen Gay. AB, Princeton (N.J.) U., 1950; PhD, Harvard U., 1954. Rsch. scientist Eli Lilly Co., Indpls., 1954-55; NCR fellow U. Mich., Ann Arbor, 1955-57; prof. biophysics Johns Hopkins U., Balt., 1957-67; prof. biol. chemistry Med. Sch. Harvard U., Boston, 1967-78; chmn. dept. cellular biology Scripps Clinic & Rsch. Found., La Jolla, Calif., 1978-81; pres., dir. Helicon Found., San Diego, 1981—; founder, CEO The Syntro Corp., 1981-82; founder, CEO, now dir. of R&D Pantox Corp., 1989—. Mem. genetics study sect. NIH, 1968-72; mem. rsch. grants com. Am. Cancer Soc., 1972-76, 79-85. Mem. editorial bd. Virology, 1967-73, Jour. Molecular Biology, 1968-72, BioPhysics Jour., 1965-68, Chromosoma, 1969-79, Analytic Biochemistry, 1970-79, Biochim Biophys. ACTA, 1973-79, Plasmid, 1977—. With USNR, 1945-46. NRC fellow, 1965-66. Mem. AAAS, Am. Acad. Arts and Scis., Am. Fedn. Biol. Chemists, Genetics Soc. Am., Am. Chem. Soc. Achievements include rsch. in genetic and structural orgn. of chromosomes and devel. of a practical assessment of ind. antioxidant def. system by analytical biochemistry. Home: 1640 El Paso Real La Jolla CA 92037-6304 Office: Pantox Labs 4622 Santa Fe St San Diego CA 92109-1601 E-mail: cathomas@pantox.com.

THOMAS, CHARLES CARROLL, retired investment management executive; b. Feb. 15, 1930; s. Charles Carroll and Miriam (Smith) T.; m. Carolyn Rose Hirchert, June 16, 1951; children: Charles Carroll, Anne Hatheway, Megan Lloyd. Grad., Deerfield Acad., 1947; BA, Yale U., 1951. Divsn. retail programs mgr. Mobil Oil Corp., Boston, 1953-63; exec. v.p. Lionel D. Edie & Co., N.Y.C., 1963-72, Bank New Eng., Boston, 1972-76; v.p., dir. mktg. Loomis, Sayles & Co., 1976-85; pres. Concord Mgmt. Co., 1985-99; ret., 1999. Co-pub. Cons. Compendium Inc., 1985-95. Trustee Deerfield Acad., 1975-78, Babson Coll., 1976-82, 83-89, Cambridge Sch. of Weston, Mass., 1976-82, New Eng. Home for Little Wanderers, 1983-86, Maine Coll. of Art, 1993—, chair, 1999-2001. With USAF, 1951-53. Mem. Assn. of Investment Mgmt. Sales Execs. (pres. 1980-81, dir. 1980-84), Air Force Assn., Yale Club N.Y.C., Downtown Club Boston, Cumberland Club Portland. Republican. Home: 24 Hillside Ave Cumberland Center ME 04021-9333

THOMAS, CHARLES COLUMBUS, educator, artist; b. McAlester, Okla., Sept. 10, 1940; s. Claude Morris Thomas and Wilhelmina Rebecca Threat. BA in Music, Langston (Okla.) Coll., 1962; MFA in Speech, Theater, Bklyn. Coll., 1973; PhD in Equivalency, City U., 1980. Chmn. music Ben Franklin Jr. High, San Francisco, 1963-65; chmn. music and dance Lefferts Jr. High, Bklyn., 1965-70; asst. prof. Richmond Coll., S.I., N.Y., 1970-96, dir. african am. studies, 1972-73; assoc. prof., chmn. dance Coll. Staten Island, 1997—. Adj. asst. prof. N.Y. Tech. Coll., Bklyn., 1971—74; vis. prof. U. Ghana, 1972; cons. Sandy Ground Hist. Soc., S.I., NY, 1985—, Nuyorican Poets Cafe, N.Y.C., 1990—, N.Y. Housing Authority, S.I., 1999; vocalist-in-residence M. Eliot's Jazz Parlor, N.Y.C., 2001. Designer in field; actor: (Operas) Gethsemane Park, 2001. Adv. Richmond Historical Soc., S.I., 1994—; com. mem. Grammy Awards in the Schs., N.Y.C., 1995; lectr., performer Mayor's Counc. Youth & Physical Fitness, N.Y.C., 1969-73; mem. Urban League, S.I., 1998. Recipient Pres. citation, Nat. Assn. Equal Opportunity Higher Edn., Washington, 1995, Xi Phi Achievement award, Columbia U., 2000. Mem.: SAG, NATAS, NARAS, Omega Psi Phi (Man of Yr. 1982). Avocations: collecting African artifacts, dancing, memorabilia. Home: 1245 Park Ave New York NY 10128-1735 Office: College of Staten Island CUNY 2800 Victory Blvd Staten Island NY 10314-6600

THOMAS, CHARLES EDMUND, anesthesiologist, health facility administrator; b. Balt., Mar. 21, 1933; s. James Clayton and Emily Marie (Shimek) T.; m. Pamela Kay Daniel, May 10, 1986; children: James Philip, Lane Lynn Thomas, Cherylee Karin Bowman, Kevin Charles. DO, U. Health Scis. Coll. Osteo., Kansas City, Mo., 1959. Cert. Am. Osteo. Bd. Anesthesiology. Staff anesthesiologist Redford Receiving Hosp., Detroit, 1962-65, Bi-County Cmty. Hosp., Detroit, 1962-70, Detroit Osteo. Hosp., Detroit, 1962-70; chief dept. ansesthesiology Annie Warner Hosp., Gettysburg, Pa, 1970-72; staff anestheiologist Crippled Children's Hop., 1970-75; chmn. dept. anesthesiology, dir. ICU Hanover (Pa.) Gen. Hosp., 1975-97. Chmn. dept. anesthesiology Gettysburg Gen. Hosp., 1970-72. Mem. AMA, Am. Osteo. Assn., Internat. Anesthesia Rsch. Assn., Pa. Med. Assn., Pa. Osteo. Med. Assn., Pa. Cancer Pain Initiative. Republican. Methodist. Avocation: architecture. Office: 300 Baltimore St Hanover PA 17331-3239 E-mail: cethomas@netrax.net.

THOMAS, CHERRYL T. city buildings commissioner; Chief of staff Mayor Richard M. Daley City of Chgo., commr. Dept. Bldgs., 1994-98, chmn. U.S. Railroad Retirement Bd., 1998—. Office: City of Chgo Dept Bldgs 844 N Rush St Ste 804 Chicago IL 60611-1275*

THOMAS, CHERYL ANN, educational administrator; b. Elmhurst, Ill., Dec. 12, 1958; d. Donald Martin and Esther Irene St. John; m. David Stephen Thomas, Dec. 29, 1979; children: Joel, Seth. BS in Music Edn., King's Coll., 1980; MS in Music Edn. magna cum laude, Western Conn. State U., 1987; PhD in Ednl. Adminstrn., SUNY, Albany, 1998. Tchr. music Valhalla (N.Y.) Pub. Schs., 1980-83; tchr. various pvt. schs., N.Y., 1983-95; dean of students Webutuck Schs., Amenia, 1997-98; prin. Pawling (N.Y.) Mid. Sch., 1998—. Contbr. articles to profl. jours. Mem. ASCD, Mosaic Ministries (adv. bd. 1990-92). Republican. Baptist. Avocations: reading, writing, swimming, hiking, crafts. Home: One Blueberry Dr Wingdale NY 12594 Office: Pawling Ctrl Sch Dist 7 Haight St Pawling NY 12564-1114 E-mail: cheryl_thomas@aslan.com.

THOMAS, CHRISTOPHER YANCEY, III, surgeon, educator; b. Kansas City, Mo., Oct. 27, 1923; s. Christopher Yancey and Dorothea Louise (Engel) T.; m. Barbara Ann Barcroft, June 27, 1946; children— Christopher, Gregg, Jeffrey, Anne Student, U. Colo., 1942-44; MD, U. Kans., 1948. Diplomate Am. Bd. Surgery. Intern U. Utah Hosp., Salt Lake City, 1948-49; resident in surgery Cleve. Clinic Found., 1949-52; pvt. practice specializing in surgery Kansas City, Mo., 1954-89. Mem. staff St. Luke's Hosp., chief surgery, 1969-70; mem. staff Children's Mercy Hosp.; clin. prof. surgery U. Mo., Kansas City Med. Sch.; pres. St. Luke's Hosp. Edn. Found., 1977-83, Med. Plaza Corp., 1977-79; pres. Midwest Organ Bank, 1977-82. Editor IMTRAC investment adv. letter, 1978-2000. Served to capt. M.C., U.S. Army, 1952-54 Fellow ACS; mem. AMA, Southwestern Surg. Congress, Central Surg. Assn., Mo. State Med. Soc., Kansas City Surg. Soc. (pres. 1968), Jackson County Med. Soc. (pres. 1971) Clubs: Kansas City Country. Republican. Methodist. Home: 50 Coventry Ct Shawnee Mission KS 66208-5225 E-mail: barbtommy@aol.com.

THOMAS, CLARA MCCANDLESS, retired English language educator, biographer; b. Strathroy, Ont., Can., May 22, 1919; d. Basil and Mabel (Sullivan) McCandless; m. Morley Keith Thomas, May 23, 1942; children: Stephen, John. BA, U. Western Ont., London, 1941, MA, 1944; PhD, U. Toronto, 1962; DLitt (hon.), York U., 1986, Trent U., 1991; LLD (hon.), Brock U., 1992. Instr. English U. Western Ont., London, 1947-61, U. Toronto, 1958-61; asst. prof. English York U., Toronto, 1961-68, prof., 1969-84, prof. emeritus, Librs. Can. Studies Rsch. fellow, 1984—; acad. adv. panel Social Scis. and Humanities Research Council, 1981-84; mem. Killam Awards Selection Bd., 1978-81; rsch. fellow York U. Librs. Can. Studies, 1984—. Author biography of Anna Jameson, 1967, of Egerton Ryerson, 1969, of Margaret Laurence, 1969, 75, of William Arthur Deacon, 1982; Literary criticism (Can.), 1946, 72, 94, Memoir, 1999; mem. editl. bd. Literary History of Can., 1980—, Collected Works of Northrop Frye, 1993—. Recipient Internat. Coun. of Can. Studies prize No. Telecom, 1989; grantee Can. Coun., 1967, 73, Social Sci. and Humanities Rsch. Coun. Can., 1978-80 Fellow Royal Soc. Can.; mem. Assn. Can. Univs., Tchrs. English (pres. 1971-72), Assn. Can. and Que. Lit., Bus. and Profl. Women's Club, Assn. for Can. Studies. New Democratic. Office: York U 305 Scott Libr 4700 Keele St Downsview ON Canada M3J 1P3

THOMAS, CLARENCE, United States supreme court justice; b. Savannah, Ga., June 23, 1948; BA, Holy Cross Coll., 1971; JD, Yale U., 1974. Bar: Mo. Asst. atty. gen. State of Mo., Jefferson City, 1974—77; atty. Monsanto Co., St. Louis, 1977—79; legis. asst. to Sen. John C. Danforth, Washington, 1979—81; asst. sec. for civil rights Dept. Edn., 1981—82; chmn. U.S. EEOC, 1982—90; judge U.S. Ct. Appeals, 1990—91; assoc. justice U.S. Supreme Ct., 1991—. Office: US Supreme Court Supreme Ct Bldg 1 First St NE Washington DC 20543-0001*

THOMAS, CLAUDEWELL SIDNEY, psychiatry educator; b. N.Y.C., Oct. 5, 1932; s. Humphrey Sidney and Frances Elizabeth (Collins) T.; m. Carolyn Pauline Rozansky, Sept. 6, 1958; children: Jeffrey Evan, Julie-Anne Elizabeth, Jessica Edith. BA, Columbia U., 1952; MD, SUNY, Downstate Med. Ctr., 1956; MPH, Yale U., 1964. Diplomate Nat. Bd. Med. Examiners, Am. Bd. Psychiatry, Am. Bd. Forensic Medicine, Am. Bd. Psychological Splties. From instr. to assoc. prof. Yale U., New Haven, 1963-68, dir. Yale tng. program in social community psychiatry, 1967-70; dir. div. mental health service programs NIMH, Washington, 1970-73; chmn. dept. psychiatry U.M.D.N.J., Newark, 1973-83; prof. dept. psychiatry Drew Med. Sch., 1983—, chmn. dept. psychiatry, 1983-93; prof. dept. psychiatry UCLA, 1983-94, vice chmn. dept. psychiatry, 1983-93, prof. emeritus dept. psychiatry, 1994—; med. dir. Tokanui Hosp., TeAwamutu, N.Z., 1996. Cons. A.K. Rice Inst., Washington, 1978—80, SAMSA/PHS Cons., 1991—99; mem. LA County Superior Ct. Psychol. Panel, 1991—97; cons. psychiatrist L.A. County AB2034 Homeless Outreach Program (Skid Row Dual Diagnoses), 2001—. Author: (with B. Bergen) Issues and Problems in Social Psychiatry, 1966; editor (with R. Bryce LaPorte) Alienation in Contemporary Society, 1976, (with J. Lindenthal) Psychiatry and Mental Health Science Handbook; mem. editorial bd. Internat. Jour. Mental Health, Adminstrn. In Mental Health. Bd. dirs. Bay Area Found., 1987—. Served to capt. USAF, 1959-61. Fellow APHA, Am. Psychoanalytic Assn. (hon.), Am. Psychiat. Assn. (life), Royal Soc. Health, N.Y. Acad. Sci., N.Y. Acad. Medicine; mem. Am. Sociol. Assn., Am. Coll. Mental Health Adminstrs., Am. Coll. Forensic Examiners, Am. Coll. Psychiatrists, Sigma Xi. Avocations: tennis, racquetball, violin, piano. Office: 30676 Palos Verdes Dr E Palos Verdes Peninsula CA 90275-6354 also: 500 Pacific Coast Hwy Ste 208 Seal Beach CA 90740 E-mail: cysid32@ucla.edu. *Personal philosophy: Integrity sooner or later calls upon courage. If courage is not home integrity goes away.*

THOMAS, CRAIG, senator; b. Cody, Wyo., Feb. 17, 1933; s. Craig E. and Marge Oweta (Lynn) T.; m. Susan Roberts; children: Peter, Paul, Patrick, Alexis. BS, U. Wyo., 1955. V.p. Wyo. Farm Bur., Laramie, 1959-66; with Am. Farm Bur., 1966-75; gen. mgr. Wyo. Rural Elec. Assn., 1975-89; mem. Wyo. Ho. of Reps., 1984-89; rep. from Wyo. U.S. Ho. of Reps., Washington, 1989-94; senator from Wyo. U.S. Senate, 1995—. Mem. energy and natural resources com., environment and pub. works com., fgn. rels. com., Indian affairs com. Former chmn. Natrona County (Wyo.) Rep. Com.; state rep. Natrona County Dist.; del. Rep. Nat. Conv., 1980. Capt. USMC. Mem. Am. Soc. Trade Execs., Masons. Methodist. Office: US Senate 109 Hart Senate Office Bldg Washington DC 20510-0001*

THOMAS, DALE, film, video and live event producer; b. Pampa, Tex., July 6, 1951; s. Olan E. and Claudine Thomas. BA, Dallas Bapt. U., 1973; MEd, U. S.C., 1976. Coord. media svcs. U. S.C., Columbia, 1975-77; mgr. media svcs. Lexington Med. Ctr., 1977-85; exec. producer, mgr. LexCom Prodns., 1985-91; nat., internat. accounts mgr. Telemation, Denver, 1992-93; exec. v.p. Videosmith, Inc., Phila., 1993-94; mgr. creative svcs. Coors Brewing Co., Golden, Colo., 1994—. Prodr. mktg./sales/promotion, tng. and bus. theater programs. Bd. dirs. Palmetto Mastersingers, Columbia, 1988-91, performer, 1987-91. Named 1st Disting. Alumnus U. S.C. Media Arts, 1983; recipient 20 regional and nat. awards. Mem. Internat. TV Assn. (nat. bd. dirs. 1993-99, nat. v.p. 1990-91, nat. pres. 1992-93, chair festival adv. bd. 1989, chair internat. video festival 1988, regional v.p. 1985-87, chpt. pres. 1982-85, Chuck Web award 2000), S.C. Affiliate of Nat. Soc. to Prevent Blindness (chmn. bd. 1989-90, Robert Scott Meml. award 1984). E-mail: dale.thomas@coors.com.

THOMAS, DANIEL FOLEY, retired financial services company executive; b. Washington, Aug. 24, 1950; s. Richard Kenneth and Margaret (Foley) T.; m. Barbara Jane Clark, June 30, 1973; 1 child, Alison Clark. BS in Acctg., Mt. St. Mary's Coll., 1972. CPA, Va. Auditor Deloitte, Haskins and Sells, Washington, 1972-74; various fin. positions Communications Satellite Corp., 1974-78, asst. treas., 1984-85, treas., 1986-87, controller, 1987-89, Comsat Telesystems, Washington, 1978-79; mgr. acctg. and taxes Satellite Bus. Systems, McLean, Va., 1979-81, treas., 1981-84; v.p. fin. Comsat Tech. Products, Inc., Washington, 1985-86, Comsat Video Enterprises, Inc., Washington, 1989-90; exec. v.p. Leasetec Corp., Boulder, Colo., 1990—. Active cmty. svc. activities. Mem. AICPA, Va. Jaycees (life), Great Falls Jaycees (pres. 1978). Roman Catholic. Avocations: running, golf. Home: 1299 S Teal Ct Boulder CO 80303-1480 Office: Leasetec Corp 1000 S Mccaslin Blvd Superior CO 80027-9456 E-mail: dfthomas@aol.com.

THOMAS, DANIEL J. health services executive; BS, U. No. Iowa. Cert. public acct. Various positions Med. Care Internat., Inc.; exec. v.p. and COO OccuSystems, 1993—96, dir., pres. and COO, 1997, exec. v.p. and pres. practice mgmt. svcs., 1997—98; pres. and COO Concentra, 1998, CEO and dir., 1998—. Office: Concentra 3200 Highland Ave Downers Grove IL 60515*

THOMAS, DAVID ANSELL, retired university dean; b. Holliday, Tex., July 5, 1917; s. John Calvin Mitchell and Alice (Willet) T.; m. Mary Elizabeth Smith, May 18, 1946; 1 dau., Ann Elizabeth. BA, Tex. Tech. Coll., 1937; MBA, Tex. Christian U., 1948; PhD, U. Mich., 1956. C.P.A., Tex. Accountant Texaco, Inc., 1937-42; asso. prof. Tex. Christian U., 1946-49; lectr. U. Mich., 1949-53; prof. accounting Cornell U., Ithaca, N.Y., 1953-84; assoc. dean Cornell U. Grad. Sch. Mgmt., 1962-79; acting dean Cornell U. Grad. Sch. Bus. and Pub. Adminstrn., 1979-81; dean Samuel Curtis Johnson Grad. Sch. Mgmt. Cornell U., 1981-84. Author: Accelerated Amortization of Defense Facilities, 1958, Accounting for Home Builders, 1952; Contbr. numerous articles to publs.; Editor: Fed. Accountant, 1956-58. Pres. Exec. Investors, Inc.; exec. dir. Charles E. Merrill Family Found., 1954-57, Robert A. Magowan Found., 1957-60; adminstr. Charles E. Merrill Trust, 1957-81, Ithaca Growth Fund.; Bd. dirs. Ithaca Opera Assn., Cornell Student Agys. Served to capt. USAAF, 1942-46, PTO. Mem. Tex. Soc. C.P.A.'s, Nat. Assn. Accountants, Am. Accounting Assn., Phi Beta Kappa, Beta Alpha Psi. Clubs: Cornell of N.Y, University, Statler (pres., dir.). Home: Devenshire Park 1560 Jasper Ct Venice FL 34292-4336

THOMAS, DAVID LLEWELLYN, family practice physician; b. Clinton, Iowa, June 11, 1948; s. Marvin Llewellyn and Marjorie Emma (Mayer) T.; children: Tana, Paige, Drew, Aleksandr. BA in Zoology, U. Iowa, 1970, MD, 1974. Diplomate Am. Bd. Family Practice, Am. Bd. Geriatric Medicine. Resident in family medicine U. Ill., Rockford, 1977; pvt. practice pvt. practice, Marshalltown, Iowa, 1977-82; family physician Marshalltown Family Physicians, 1982-92, Ctr. for Family Medicine, Marshalltown, 1992-94, McFarland Clinic, PC, Marshalltown, 1994—, also bd. dirs., v.p., 1995-98, treas., 1999—. Clin. lectr. U. Iowa Coll. Medicine, Iowa City, 1981—. Bd. dirs. Iowa Found. for Med. Care, Des Moines, 1986—, Iowa Ctr. Agrl. Safety and Health, 1995-97; trustee Marshalltown Med. and Surg. Ctr., 1998—. Mem. Am. Health Quality Assn. (bd. dirs. 1995, v.p. 1997-2000, pres. 2000—). Republican. Episcopalian. Avocation: youth sports. Office: McFarland Clinic 303 Nicholas Dr Ste 1 Marshalltown IA 50158-4443 E-mail: dthomas@mcfarlandclinic.com.

THOMAS, DAVID LLOYD, accountant, consultant; b. Atlanta, May 10, 1942; s. Elbert and Evelyn Thomas; m. Mary Jo Ann Matney, June 25, 1966; children: Christine, Michael. BSBA, U. N.C., 1964. CPA, N.C. Auditor Price Waterhouse, N.Y.C., 1964, Atlanta, 1969-70; divsn. contr. Dart Industries, 1971; contr. Ithaca Industries, Inc., Wilkesboro, N.C., 1971-82, sec.-treas., 1982-91, CFO, bd. dirs., 1983-91; prin. David L. Thomas, CPA, 1991—. CFO Wilkes Regional Med. Ctr., 1993-2000, v.p., 1996-2000; sec. N.W. Health Care, 1994-95. Bd. dirs., mem. Wilkes Art Gallery, 1985-91; bd. dirs. Wilkes Edn. Found., 1988-91, N.C. Citizens for Bus. and Industry, 1989-92, John A. Walker Cmty. Ctr., 1996—, mem. exec. com., 1999—, v.p., 2000-01, pres., 2001-02—; mem. adv. bd. Wilkes C.C., 1989-97, vice chair, 1994-96, chmn., 1996-97, mem. vision 2010 cultural and quality of life com., 2001; mem. maj. firms calling com. Wilkes United Way, 1995—. Capt. MSC, U.S. Army, 1965-68. Fellow N.C. Assn. CPAs (sec. Catawba Valley chpt. 1982-83); mem. AICPA, Inst. Mgmt. Accts., Healthcare Fin. Mgrs. Assn., Wilkesboro C. of C. (bd. dirs. 1979-81, 90-92, v.p. 1982, 86, 91, trustee found. 1983-90). Republican. Methodist. Home and Office: 172 Walnut Pl Wilkesboro NC 28697-8775 E-mail: dlthomascpa@yahoo.com.

THOMAS, DEBI (DEBRA J. THOMAS), ice skater; b. Poughkeepsie, N.Y., Mar. 25, 1967; d. McKinley and Janice Thomas; m. Christopher Bequette, Nov. 1996; children: Christopher Jules II, Luc. BS, Stanford U.; MD, Northwestern U., 1997. Competitive figure skater, 1976-88. Winner U.S. Figure Skating Championship, 1986, 88, World Figure Skating Championship, 1986, World Profl. Figure Skating Championship, 1988, 89, 91. Recipient Am. Black Achievement Award, Ebony mag., named Women Athlete of Yr., 1986; winner Bronze medal Olympic Games, 1988; named to U.S. Figure Skating Hall of Fame, San Jose Sports Hall of Fame. Address: Mentor Mgmt 5610 Town Center Dr # 5 Granger IN 46530-

THOMAS, DENE, academic administrator, educator; 3 children. B Lit., S.W. State U., cert. in secondary edn., 1978; PhD English, U. Minn., 1984; course, Bryn Mawr's Women in Higher Edn. Adminstrn. program, 1990. Vice provost acad. affairs to tchr., dept. chmn., dean U. Idaho; pres. Lewis-Clark State Coll., 2001—. Office: Lewis-Clark State Coll 500 8th Ave Lewiston ID 83501*

THOMAS, DENNIS, paper company executive, former government official; b. Balt., Dec. 8, 1943; s. George Crosby and Justa Mae (Witherspoon) T.; m. Dawn Frances Haines, 1965; 1 son, William David. BS, Frostburg State Coll., 1965; MSW., U. Md., 1967. Asst. to Hon. J. Glenn Beall, Jr. U.S. Ho. of Reps., Washington, 1969-71, spl. asst., 1971-73, 1973-77, adminstrv. asst. to Hon. William V. Roth, Jr., 1977-81; asst. sec. legis. affairs Dept. Treasury, 1981-83; dep. asst. to Pres. for legis. affairs White House, 1983-85; ptnr. Touche Ross and Co., Inc., 1985; asst. to Pres., The White House, 1985-87; sr. v.p. pub. affairs and comm. Internat. Paper Co., Stamford, Conn., 1987—. Republican. Office: Internat Paper 400 Atlantic St Stamford CT 06921

THOMAS, DONALD A. astronaut; b. Cleve., May 6, 1955; s. Irene M. Thomas; m. Simone Lehmann Thomas; 1 child. BSc with hon. in Physics, Case We. Reserve U., 1977; MSc in Materials Sci., Cornell U., 1980, PhD in Materials Sci., 1982. Sr. mem. tech. staff AT&T Bell Lab., Princeton, NJ, 1982—87; with Lockheed Engring. & Sci. Co., Houston, 1987—88; materials engr. NASA, 1988—90, astronaut, 1990—. Astronaut Space Shuttle Columbia STS-65, 1994, Space Shuttle Discovery STS-70, 1995, Space Shuttle Columbia STS-83, 1997, Space Shuttle Columbia STS-94, 1997; adj. prof. in physics Trenton State Coll., Trenton, NJ. Mem.: Assn. Space Explorers, Tau Beta Pi. Avocations: swimming, bicycling, camping, flying. Office: Astronaut Office CB NASA Johnson Space Center Houston TX 77058*

THOMAS, DUKE WINSTON, lawyer; b. Scuddy, Ky., Jan. 25, 1937; s. William E. and Grace T.; m. Jill Staples, Oct. 24, 1964; children: Deborah L., William E. II, Judith A. BSBA, Ohio State U., 1959, JD, 1964. Bar: Ohio 1964, U.S. Dist. Ct. Ohio 1966, U.S. Ct. Appeals (3d cir.) 1971, U.S. Ct. Appeals (6th cir.) 1972, U.S. Supreme Ct. 1973, U.S. Ct. Appeals (7th cir.) 1979. Ptnr. Vorys, Sater, Seymour and Pease, LLP, Columbus, Ohio, 1964—. Bd. dirs. Ohio Bar Liability Ins. Co., Frontstep, Inc. Fellow Internat. Soc. Barristers, Am. Coll. Trial Lawyers (chmn. Ohio joint select com. on jud. compensation 1987), Am. Bar Found. (life), Ohio Bar Found., Columbus Bar Found.; mem. ABA (ho. of dels. 1985—, state del. 1989-95, bd. govs. 1995-98), Ohio Bar Assn. (pres. 1985), Columbus Bar Assn. (pres. 1978), Pres.'s Club Ohio State U., The Golf Club, Worthington Hills Country Club, Columbus Athletic Club. Home: 2090 Sheringham Rd Columbus OH 43220-4358 Office: Vorys Sater Seymour & Pease LLP PO Box 1008 52 E Gay St Columbus OH 43215-3161 E-mail: dwthomas@vssp.com.

THOMAS, DWIGHT REMBERT, writer; b. Savannah, Ga., Dec. 8, 1944; s. Huguenin and Alma (Sanders) Thomas. BA in English with honors, Emory U., 1967; PhD in Am. Lit., U. Pa., 1978. Fellow English dept. U. Pa., Phila., 1971-78; writer Savannah, 1979—. Cons. Film Odyssey, Washington, 1988—89. *Dr Thomas became a charter member of the Information Associates Program of the National Cancer Institute in 1994. He is now completing a large book dealing with new developments in American cancer medicine from 1970 to 2000.* Author: (book) The Poe Log: A Documentary Life of Edgar Allan Poe, 1987. Dir. Edgar Allan Poe Mus., Richmond, 1988—96. With U.S. Army, 1969—71. Mem.: MLA, Am. Med. Writers Assn., Mensa (treas. Savannah area 1985—88, local sec. 1989—90), Phi Beta Kappa. Roman Catholic. Avocations: German language, current cinema, bicycling. Home: 7 E Gordon St Savannah GA 31401-4925

THOMAS, EDWARD DONNALL, physician, researcher; b. Mart, Tex., Mar. 15, 1920; married; 3 children. BA, U. Tex., 1941, MA, 1943; MD, Harvard U., 1946; MD (hon.), U. Cagliari, Sardinia, 1981, U. Verona, Italy, 1991, U. Parma, 1992, U. Barcelona, Spain, 1994, U. Warsaw, Poland, 1996, U. Jagiellonski, Cracow, Poland, 1996. Lic. physician Mass., N.Y., Wash., diplomate Am. Bd. Internal Medicine. Intern in medicine Peter Bent Brigham Hosp., Boston, 1946—47, rsch. fellow hematology, 1947—48; NRC postdoctoral fellow in medicine dept. biology MIT, Cambridge, 1950—51; chief med. resident, sr. asst. resident Peter Bent Brigham Hosp., 1951—53, hematologist, 1953—55; instr. medicine Harvard Med. Sch., Boston, 1953—55; rsch. assoc. Cancer Rsch. Found. Children's Med. Ctr., 1953—55; physician-in-chief Mary Imogene Bassett Hosp., Cooperstown, NY, 1955—63; assoc. clin. prof. medicine Coll. Physicians and Surgeons Columbia U., N.Y.C., 1955—63; attending physician U. Wash. Hosp., Seattle, 1963—90; prof. medicine Sch. Medicine U. Wash., 1963—90, head divsn. oncology Sch. Medicine, 1963—85, prof. emeritus medicine Sch. Medicine, 1990—; dir. med. oncology Fred Hutchinson Cancer Rsch. Ctr., 1974—89, assoc. dir. clin. rsch. programs, 1982—89, mem., 1974—. Mem. hematology study sect. NIH, 1965—69; mem. bd. trustees and med. sci. adv. com. Leukemia Soc. Am., Inc., 1969—73; mem. clin. cancer investigation rev. com. NCI, 1970—74; 1st ann. Eugene C. Eppinger lectr. Peter Bent Brigham Hosp. and Harvard Med. Sch., 1974; Lilly lectr. RCP, London, 1977; Stratton lectr. Internat. Soc. Hematology, 1982; Paul Aggeler lectr. U. Calif., San Francisco, 1982; 65th Mellon lectr. U. Pitts. Sch. Medicine, 1984; Stanley Wright Meml. lectr. Western Soc. Pediat. Rsch., 1985; Adolfo Ferrata lectr. Italian Soc. Hematology, Verona, Italy, 1991. Mem. editl. bd. Blood, 1962—75, 1977—82, Transplantation, 1970—76, Proc. of Soc. for Exptl. Biology and Medicine, 1974—81, Leukemia Rsch., 1977—87, Hematological Oncology, 1982—87, Jour. Clin. Immunology, 1982—87, Am. Jour. Hematology, 1985—, Bone Marrow Transplantation, 1986—. With U.S. Army, 1948—50. Recipient A. Ross McIntyre award, U. Nebr. Med. Ctr., 1975, Philip Levine award, Am. Soc. Clin. Pathologists, 1979, Disting. Svc. in Basic Rsch. award, Am. Cancer Soc., 1980, Kettering prize, GM Cancer Rsch. Found., 1981, Spl. Keynote Address award, Am. Soc. Therapeutic Radiologists, 1981, Robert Roesler de Villiers award, Leukemia Soc. Am., 1983, Karl Landsteiner Meml. award, Am. Assn. Blood Banks, 1987, Terry Fox award, Can., 1990, Internat. award, Gairdner Found., 1990, Hong Kong prize, N.Am. Med. Assn., 1990, Nobel Prize in Medicine, 1990, Presdl. medal of sci., NSF, 1990. Mem.: NAS, Soc. Exptl. Biology and Medicine, Western Assn. Physicians, Swiss Soc. Hematology, Internat. Soc. Hematology, Internat. Soc. Exptl. Hematology, Am. Soc. Hematology (pres. 1987—88, Henry M. Stratton lectr. 1975), Am. Soc. Clin. Investigation, Am. Soc. Clin. Oncology (David A. Karnoksky Meml. lectr. 1983), Am. Fedn. Clin. Rsch., Assn. Am. Physicians (Kober medal 1992), Am. Assn. Cancer Rsch., Academie Royale de Medicine de Belgique (corr.), Nat. Acad. Medicine Mex. (hon.), Royal Coll. Physicians and Surgeons Can. (hon.), Swedish Soc. Hematology (hon.). Office: Fred Hutchinson Cancer Ctr 1100 Fairview Ave N D5-100 PO Box 19024 Seattle WA 98109-1024

THOMAS, EDWARD LABELLE, technical director; b. Milw., Dec. 13, 1951; s. Edward L. and Dorothy H. (Goggans) T.; m. Kay S. Olm, Aug. 8, 1972 (div. May 1986); 1 child, Johanna O.; m. Katharine E. Teeter, Oct. 4, 1986; children: Carlos, Marisol, Giancarlo. BA in Philosophy, Lakeland Coll., 1975; postgrad., Harvard Div. Sch., 1975; MBA, Bentley Grad. Sch. Bus., 2000. Radio engr. Sta. WBUR-FM, Boston, 1983-85; sr. audio engr. Bose Corp., Framingham, 1985-88; radio engr. Sta. WGHB-FM, Boston, 1988-90; tech. dir. Monitor Radio, 1988-97; tech. dir. religious prodn. Christian Sci. Pub. Soc., 1997—; dir. fin. and adminstrn. Peace Games, INc. Bd. dors. Boston Urban Gardeners, 1979-80, Boston Citizens Elderly Affairs, 1979-80; house facilitator Shared Living House, Boston, 1980-82. Fund For Theol. Edn. fellow, 1975-76. Home: 16 1/2 Woodbridge St Cambridge MA 02140-1220

THOMAS, ELIZABETH, lawyer; b. N.Y.C., Jan. 29, 1953; d. Howard E. and Edna Patrecia (McGuire) T.; m. Ronald L. Roseman, Aug. 14, 1986; 1 Child: Catherine Blake Roseman. BA, Wellesley Coll., 1975; JD cum laude, Harvard U., 1979. Bar: Mass., 1979, Wash., 1980. Law clk. to Hon. A. David Mazzone U.S. Dist. Ct. Mass., Boston, 1979-80; atty. Evergreen Legal Svcs., Seattle, 1980-87; assoc. Preston Gates & Ellis, 1987-89, ptnr., 1990—, chair environ. dept., 1997-98; chair energy & utilities practice group, 2001—. Contbr. articles to profl. jours. Chair Energy Facility Siting Process Rev. Com.; vice-chair rate adv. com. Seattle City Light Citizens; mem. conservation programs task force N.W. Power Coun.; mem. cost allocation adv. group energy com. Seattle City Coun.; tech. advisor Demand and Resource Evaluation Project Puget Sound Power & Light. Mem. ABA (mem. pub. utilities sect., mem. natural resources & enviroment sect.), N.W. Pub. Power Assn., Phi Beta Kappa. Office: Preston Gates & Ellis LLP 701 5th Ave Ste 5000 Seattle WA 98104-7078 E-mail: ethomas@prestongates.com.

THOMAS, ELIZABETH MARSHALL, writer; b. Boston, Sept. 13, 1931; d. Laurence K. and Lorna (McLean) Marshall; m. Stephen Thomas, 1956; children: Stephanie, Ramsay. Student, Smith Coll.; BA in English, Radliffe Coll., 1954. Writer, 1954—. Author: The Harmless People, 1959, Warrior Herdsmen, 1965, Reindeer Moon, 1987, The Animal Wife, 1990, The Hidden Life of Dogs, 1993, The Tribe of Tiger, 1994, Certain Poor Shepherds, 1998, The Social Lives of Dogs, 2000. Office: 80 E Mountain Rd Peterborough NH 03458-2318

THOMAS, ELLA COOPER, lawyer; b. Ft. Totten, N.Y. d. Avery John and Ona Caroline (Gibson) C.; m. Robert Edward Lee Thomas, Nov. 22, 1938 (dec. Jan. 1985); 1 child, Robert Edward Lee Jr. Student, Vassar Coll., 1932-34, U. Hawaii, 1934-35, George Washington U., 1935-36, JD, 1940. Bar: U.S. Dist. Ct. D.C. 1942, U.S. Ct. Appeals (D.C. cir.) 1943, U.S. Supreme Ct. 1947, U.S. Tax Ct. 1973. Secret maps custodian U.S. Dist. Engrs., Honolulu, 1941-42; contbg. editor Labor Rels. Reporter, Washington, 1942; assoc. Smith, Ristig & Smith, 1942-45; law libr. George Washington Law Sch., 1946-53; reporter of decisions U.S. Tax Ct., 1953-75. Computer vol. Mote Marine Lab., 1992—98. Author: Law of Libel and Slander, 1949. Mem. Inter-Am. Bar Assn. (coun. mem. 1973-99), D.C. Bar Assn. Avocations: physical fitness, crostics. Home: 1700 3rd Ave W Apt 118 Bradenton FL 34205

THOMAS, ELLEN LOUISE, private school administrator; b. Doylestown, Pa., Nov. 30, 1940; d. Edward Martin and Evelyn Graham (Axenroth) Happ; m. Eugene Greene Leffever, June 30, 1963 (dec. Nov. 1978); children: Eugene Greene II, Jeanette Ellen Dellaripa; m. William Dewey Thomas, Sept. 15, 1981; 1 child, Jeremiah David. BA in Edn., Immaculata (Pa.) Coll., 1962; postgrad., Pa. State U., 1962-67. Pvt. practice tutor, Doylestown, 1958-65; tchr. Cen. Bucks Sch. System, 1962-65; adminstr. The Curiosity Shoppe, 1965—, The Toddler Ctr., Doylestown, 1979—; exec. dir. Camp Curiosity, 1984—, Thomas Lea Equestrian Ctr., Doylestown, 1988—. Tchr. trainer Confortunity of Christian Doctrine, Doylestown, 1965-78; cons. early childhood Am. Sch. in Hong Kong, 1981-84; lectr. in early childhood Bucks County Community Ctr., Newtown, Pa., 1978-90; workshop facilitator Head Start, Phila., 1990; cons. day care Cen. Bucks C. of C., Doylestown, 1989-90; ednl. coord. Forest Grove Presbyn. Ch., 1984-90. Mem. U.S. C. of C., Washington, Bucks County C. of C., Doylestown, Nat. Fedn. of Ind. Bus., Washington; children's ministry coord. Jesus Focus Ministry, 1995—; trainer Pa. Child Care, 1995—; pres. Pa. Day Camp Assn., 1998-2000; Sunday sch. tchr. Hilton Bapt. Ch., 1995-2000; mem. Plumstead Christian Sch. Bd., 1995-2001; children's chmn. Central Bucks Village Fair, 2001-. Mem. ASCD, Assn. for Childhood Edn. Internat., United Pvt. Acad. Schs. Assn., Bucks County Assn. Edn. Young Children (pres. 1974-78). Office: The Curiosity Shoppe 4425 Landisville Rd Doylestown PA 18901-1134 E-mail: FaxThomdew@aol.com.

THOMAS, ESTHER MERLENE, elementary education educator; b. San Diego, Oct. 16, 1945; d. Merton Alfred and Nellie Lida (Von Pilz) T. AA with honors, Grossmont Coll., 1966; BA with honors, San Diego State U., 1969; MA, U. Redlands, 1977. Cert. elem. and adult edn. tchr. Tchr. Cajon Valley Union Sch. Dist., El Cajon, 1969—; sci. fair coord. Flying Hills Sch. Tchr. Hopi and Navajo Native Americans, Ariz., Utah, 1964-74, Goose and Gander Nursery Sch., Lakeside, Calif., 1964-66; dir., supt. Bible and Sunday schs. various chs., Lakeside, 1961-87; mem. sci. com., math. coun. Cajon Valley Union Sch. Dist., 1990-91, libr. com., 1997-98. Author: Individualized Curriculum in the Affective Domain; songwriter: for Hilltop Records, songwriter: songs Never Trouble Trouble, Old Glory, Jesus Is Our Lord, Daniel's Prayer, There Lay Jesus, God's Hands, 1996—97, songwriter: songs Washing Machine Charlie, Playmates, 1998, songwriter: songs The Kid in the Hall, 1999, songwriter: songs Spring Time on the Blue Ridge, Christ's DNA, 2000, songwriter: songs If You Need Me, 2001, songwriter: songs Chances, 2002, songwriter: songs Blame, 2002, songwriter: for Amerecord Records, songwriter: songs released Born to Win, 1996, songwriter: songs released Happy Birthday Dear Jesus, Christmas Lights, 2000, songwriter: songs released Walk the Line, 2000, songwriter: songs released You Don't Know What Repentance Is, 2001, songwriter: songs released I'm Asking You, 2001, songwriter: for Hollywood Artists Records, songwriter: songs released Clear the Path Lord, Aqua Forte, In the Volume of the Book, 1996, songwriter: songs released Home is Where the Heart Is, You Don't Even Know Who I Am, No Place to Cry, To Walk With God, Ixnay, If You Never Loved Me, 1997, songwriter: for Columbine Records Corp., songwriter: songs released Life of A Single Woman, 1997, songwriter: songs released Take This Pain Away, 1998, songwriter: songs released We Can Keep In Touch, 1999, songwriter: for Hollywood Stars Music Prodns., songwriter: The Star of Bethlehem, 2002, songwriter: Where the Eagle Flies, 2002; contbr. articles. Tem. U.S. Senatorial Club, Washington, 1984—, Conservative Caucus, Inc., Washington, 1988—, Ronald Reagan Presdl. Found., Ronald Reagan Rep. Ctr., 1988, Rep. Presdl. Citizen's Adv. Commn., 1989—, Rep. Platform Planning Com., Calif., 1992, at-large del. representing dist. #45, Lakeside, Calif., 1992, 1995—, Am. Security Coun., Washington, 1994, Congressman Hunter's Off Road Adv. Coun., El Cajon, Calif., 1994, Century Club, San Diego Rep. Century Club, 1995; mem. health articulation com. project AIDS, Cajon Valley Union Sch. Dist., 1988—, Concerned Women Am., Washington, Recruit Depot Hist. Mus., San Diego, 1989, Citizen's Drug Free Am., Calif., 1989—, The Heritage Found., 1988—; charter mem. Marine Corps Mus.; mem. Lakeside Centennial Com., 1985-86; hon. mem. Rep. Presdl. Task Force, Washington, 1986; del. Calif. Rep. Senatorial Mid-Term Conv., Washington, 1994; mus. curator Lakeside Hist. Soc., 1992-93. Recipient Outstanding Svc. award PTA, 1972-74; recognized for various contbns. Commdg. Post Gen., San Diego Bd. Edn., 1989. Mem. NRA, Tchrs. Assn., Calif. Tchrs. Assn., Cajon Valley Educators Assn. (faculty advisor, rep. 1980-82, 84-86, 87-88), Nat. Trust for Hist. Preservation, Christian Bus. and Profl. Women, Trust for Hist. Preservation, Ridgecrest Golden Terrace Park Assn. (pres. 1998-99), Nashville Songwriters Assn., Capitol Hill Women's Club, Am. Ctr. for Law and Justice, Internat. Christian Women's Club (Christian amb. to Taiwan, Korea, 1974). Republican. Avocations: world traveling, Christian teaching, vocal music, piano, guitar. Home: 13594 Hwy 8 # 3 Lakeside CA 92040-5235 Office: Flying Hills Elem Sch 1251 Finch St El Cajon CA 92020-1433

THOMAS, ETHEL COLVIN NICHOLS (MRS. LEWIS VICTOR THOMAS), counselor, educator; b. Cranston, R.I., Mar. 31, 1913; d. Charles Russell and Mabel Maria (Colvin) Nichols; Ph.B., Pembroke Coll. in Brown U., 1934; M.A., Brown U., 1938; Ed.D., Rutgers U., 1979; m. Lewis Victor Thomas, July 26, 1945 (dec. Oct. 1965); 1 child, Glenn Nichols. Tchr. English, Cranston High Sch., 1934-39; social dir. and adviser to freshmen, Fox Hall, Boston U., 1939-40; instr. to asst. prof. English Am. Coll. for Girls, Istanbul, Turkey, 1940-44; dean freshman, dir. admission Women's Coll. of Middlebury, Vt., 1944-45; tchr. English, Robert Coll., Istanbul, 1945-46; instr. English, Rider Coll., Trenton, N.J., 1950-51; tchr. English, Princeton (N.J.) High Sch., 1951-61, counselor, 1960-62, 72-83, coll. counselor, 1962-72, sr. peer counselor, 1986—. Mem. NEA, AAUW, Nat. Assn. Women Deans Adminstrs. and Counselors, Am. Assn. Counseling and Devel., Bus. and Profl. Women's Club (named Woman of Yr., Princeton chpt. 1977), Met. Mus. Art, Phi Delta Kappa, Kappa Delta Pi. Presbyn. Clubs: Brown University (N.Y.C.); Nassau.

THOMAS, FAYE EVELYN J. elementary and secondary school educator; b. Summerfield, La., Aug. 3, 1933; d. Reginald Felton and Atlee (Hunter) Johnson; m. Archie Taylor Thomas, Sept. 8, 1960; 1 child Dwayne Andre. *Faye Thomas' great great grandfather, Silas Thornton, was born in Macon County, Georgia in 1824. In 1848 Wiley Thornton took his family and his slaves, which included Silas Thornton and his mother, to Claiborne Parish in Louisiana. The Thornton family, white and black, has been educators and theologians. Silas was taught to read and write as a slave by the slave owner's son. He was the only black person in the community who knew how to read and write. He organized Fellowship Baptist Church and became the first minister and teacher in that community. His determination motivated following generations in education and theology.* BA, So. U., 1954; student, Tuskegee Inst., 1958, student, 1969, U. Detroit, 1961, student, 1962, student, 1963, Ctrl. Mich. U., 1965; MS, U. Ctrl. Ark., 1971, Cleve. State U., 1979. Tchr. Cullen (La.) Elem. Sch., 1957; tchr. English and social studies Charles Brown H.S., Springhill, 1957—70; tchr. English, Upward Bound Program, Grambling State U., 1968; tchr. English, Springhill H.S., 1970; elem. intermediate tchr. Riveredge Elem. Sch., Berea, Ohio, 1971—93; tchr. 7th grade English, Ford Mid. Sch., 1993—94. Tchr. asst. elem. coun. curriculum and instrn. Berea Sch. Dist., 1984—85. Author: When the Time Is Right, Move On. Dir. Non-Denominational Day Care Ctr., Cullen. Grantee, EDPA, 1970—71, Internat. Paper Found., 1958, 1960, NDEA, 1965; scholar Martha Holden Jennings scholar, 1984—85. Mem.: NEA, Assn. Supervision and Curriculum Devel., N.E. Ohio Tchrs. Assn., Berea Edn. Assn., Ohio Edn. Assn., Ohio Motorists Assn., Charles Brown Soc. Orgn. (trustee 1984—), Black Caucus NEA, People United to Save Humanity, Toastmasters, Order Eastern Star. Democrat. Baptist. Home: 19353 Bagley Rd Cleveland OH 44130-3319

THOMAS, FRANK EDWARD, professional baseball player; b. Columbus, Ga., May 27, 1968; Student, Auburn U. With Chgo. White Sox, 1990—. Named to Sporting News All-Star Coll. All Am. team, 1989; Sporting News All-Star team, 1991, 93-94; recipient Silver Slugger award, 1991, 93, 94; mem. Am. League All-Star Team, 1993-95; recipient Am. League MVP award, 1994; named Major League Player of Yr., Sporting News, 1993. Office: Chgo White Sox Comiskey Park 333 W 35th St Chicago IL 60616-3651*

THOMAS, FRANKLIN AUGUSTINE, lawyer, consultant; b. Bklyn., May 27, 1934; s. James and Viola (Atherley) T.; div.; children: Keith, Hillary, Kerrie, Kevin. BA, Columbia U., 1956, LL.B., 1963; LL.D. (hon.), Yale U., 1970, Fordham U., 1972, Pratt Inst., 1974, Pace U., 1977, Columbia U., 1979. Bar: N.Y. 1964. Atty. Fed. Housing and Home Finance Agy., N.Y.C., 1963-64; asst. U.S. atty. for So. Dist. N.Y., 1964-65; dep. police commr. charge legal matters N.Y.C., 1965-67; pres., chief exec. officer Bedford Stuyvesant Restoration Corp., Bklyn., 1967-77; pres. The Ford Found., 1979-96; atty., cons., 1996—. Bd. dirs. ALCOA, Avaya, Conoco, Inc., Citigroup, Cummins Engine Co., Lucent Techs., PepsiCo, Inc. Trustee Columbia U., 1969-75. Served with USAF, 1956-60. Recipient LBJ Found. award for contbn. to betterment of urban life, 1974, medal of excellence Columbia U., 1976, Alexander Hamilton award Columbia U., 1983

THOMAS, FRANKLIN RICHARD, American studies and language educator, writer; b. Evansville, Ind., Aug. 1, 1940; s. Franklin Albert and Lydia Elizabeth (Klausmeier) T.; m. Sharon Kay Myers, June 2, 1962; children: Severn Rhyl, Caerllion. AB, Purdue U., 1963, MA, 1964; PhD, Ind. U., 1970. Asst. prof. Purdue U., Hammond, Ind., 1969-71; asst. prof. Am. thought and lang. Mich. State U., East Lansing, 1971—, assoc. prof. Am. thought and lang., prof. Am. thought and lang. Editor, pub. Years Press, East Lansing, 1973—. Author: Literary Admirers of Alfred Stieglitz, 1983, Prism: The Journal of John Fish, 1992; editor: Americans in Denmark, 1990, The Landlocked Heart: Poems from Indiana, 1980; author 8 collections of poetry including Frog Praises Night, 1980, Death at Camp Pahoka, 2000. Fulbright grantee Country of Denmark, 1974-75, 85-86. Office: Mich State U Dept Am Thought Lang East Lansing MI 48824

THOMAS, FRANKLIN ROSBOROUGH, retired animator; b. Santa Monica, Calif., Sept. 5, 1912; s. Frank Waters and Ina Marcella (Gregg) T.; m. Jeanette Armentrout, Feb. 16, 1946; children: Ann Winfield, Gregg Franklin, Theodore William, Douglas Craig. Student, Fresno State Coll., 1929-31; AB magna cum laude, Stanford U., 1933; postgrad., Chouinard Art Sch., 1933-34, Walt Disney Studio, 1934. Directing animator Walt Disney Co., Burbank, Calif., 1934-78; ret., 1978. Lectr., spkr. in field; chmn. jury N.Y. Internat. Animated Film Festival, 1975. Animator for numerous films, including Show White and the Seven Dwarfs, 1937, Pinocchio, 1940, Bambi, 1942, The Three Caballeros, 1945, The Many Adventures of Winnie the Pooh, 1977; directing animator The Adventures of Ichabod and Mr. Toad, 1949, Cinderella, 1950, Alice in Wonderland, 1951, Peter Pan, 1953, Lady and the Tramp, 1955, Sleeping Beauty, 1959, 101 Dalmatians, 1961, Sword in the Stone, 1963, Mary Poppins, 1964, The Jungle Book, 1967, The Aristocats, 1970, Robin Hood, 1973, The Rescuers, 1977; supervising animator: The Fox and the Hound, 1981; also animator for numerous shorts; co-author: Disney Animation -- The Illusion of Life, 1981, Too Funny for Words, 1987, Bambi-The Story and the Film, 1990, Jungle Book Portfolio, 1993, Disney Villains, English edit., 1993, French edit., 1995; contbr. editor to sketch book series; Dixieland jazz pianist Firehouse Five Plus 2, 1949-68, appearing on radio and TV programs The Bing Crosby Show, The Milton Berle Show, Ed Wynn TV Shows, others; subject of documentary Frank and Ollie; exhibited drawings in Whitney Mus., N.Y.C., 1981. Guest spkr. Russian Govt. and Soyuzmultfilm and other East European countries, 1976, U.S. Info. Agy. Cultural Exch. Program, 1986. With USAF, 1942-45. Recipient numerous awards, including Annie award Internat. Animated Film Soc., 9 Old Men award Hon. Cinema Soc. Mem. Phi Beta Kappa. Address: 758 Flintridge Ave Flintridge CA 91011-4027

THOMAS, FREDDIE E. apparel designer, consultant; b. Cleve., Jan. 6, 1954; s. Charles Eugene Edwards and Ruth Elma Thomas; m. Angela Maria Elom, June 12, 1976; children: Sharron, Angela, Freddie Jr. Student, Cuyahoga C.C., 1975. Fashion show prodr. Cosmic Generation, Cleve., 1967—69, Plooki Fashions, Cleve., 1970—74, fashion designer, 1975—80, fashion commentator, 1980—84; fashion sales rep. Fashionfest Enterprises, 1985—87; promotion/pub. rels. dir. Duo Star Prodns., 1986—89; exec. dir. Cleve. Fashion Guild, 1988—. Guest designer Josephine Holmes Found., Cin., 1985; chief designer Liz Fashions, Atlanta, 1990; fashion cons. Plooki: The Enterprise, Cleve., 1996—; bus. cons. Servicemax & Assocs., East Cleveland, Ohio. Author: Theofashion: True Mode of Dress & Deportment, 2002; editor: (mag.) Plooki: The Magazine, 2002. Guest designer Bronner Bros. Show, Atlanta, 1990; sec. Black on Black 2000, East Cleveland, 2001. Mem.: Internat. Fashion Assn. (exec. dir., pres. 1994). Jehovah'S Witness. Avocations: cooking, music. Home: 13901 Crennell Ave Up Cleveland OH 44105

THOMAS, FREDERICK BRADLEY, lawyer; b. Evanston, Ill., Aug. 13, 1949; s. Frederick Bradley and Katherine Kidder (Bingham) T.; m. Elizabeth Maxwell, Oct. 25, 1975; children: Bradley Bingham, Stephens Maxwell, Rosa Macaulay. AB, Dartmouth Coll., 1971; JD, U. Chgo., 1974. Bar: Ill. 1974. Law clk. to hon. judge John C. Godbold U.S. Ct. Appeals (5th cir.), Montgomery, Ala., 1974-75; assoc. Mayer, Brown, Rowe & Maw, Chgo., 1975—80, ptnr., 1981—. Bd. dirs. St. Gregory Episcopal Sch., 1989—; bd. trustees La Rabida Children's Hosp., 1990—; bd. mgrs. YMCA Met. Chgo., 2002--. Mem. ABA, Chgo. Council Lawyers. Republican. Episcopalian. Office: Mayer Brown Rowe & Maw 190 S La Salle St Ste 3100 Chicago IL 60603-3441 E-mail: fthomas@mayerbrown.com.

THOMAS, GARNETT JETT, accountant; b. Farmington, Ky., July 27, 1920; s. Pinkney Madison and Ethel (Drinkard) T.; m. Katherine Gardner, Mary. 26, 1948 (dec. Sept. 1979); m. Nell Penton, May 23, 1981; stepchldren: Vernon Bice, Michael Bice, Gina Black. BS, Lambuth U., 1947; MS, Miss. State U., 1949. Clk., acct. Ill. Cen. R.R., Paducah, Ky., 1941-42; mgr. Coll. Bookstore Lambuth U., Jackson, Tenn., 1946-47; acct. Miss. Agrl. and Forestry Expt. Sta., Mississippi State, 1948-60, chief acct., 1960-75, administrv. officer and chief acct., 1975-85; administrv. officer emeritus, 1985—; pres. PBR Corp., Starksville, Miss., 1974-84. Fin. adminstr. seed tech., rsch. internat. programs Brazil, India, Guatemala, Columbia, Thailand, Kenya, 1958-85; pres. Govt. Employees Credit Union. Mem. adv. bd. Nat. Bank of Commerce of Miss., 1974—; fin. adminstr. seed tech, research internat. programs Brazil, India, Guatemala, Columbia, Thailand, Kenya, 1958-85; bd. dirs. Govt. Employees Credit Union, 1967-86, pres., 1969-73. With USN, 1942-46. Decorated Bronze Star with oak leaf cluster. Mem. Nat. Assn. Accts., Asn. Govt. Accts., Am. Assn Accts., Acad. Acctg. Historians, So. Assn. Agrl. Scientists, Rotary (pres., 1959-90, dist. 682 gov. 1977-78, adv. com. to pres. 1979-80, dist. chmn. Poloplus, 1987-90). Republican. Methodist. Home: 114 Grand Ridge Rd Starkville MS 39759-4112

THOMAS, GARY L. academic administrator; b. Willows, Calif., May 12, 1937; s. Leonel Richard and Myrtle Blanch (Moncur) T.; m. Margaret Anderson, Aug. 11, 1960 (div. 1975); children: Katelin, Elizabeth Ann, Derek Alan. AA, Modesto Jr. Coll., 1958; BS in Elec. Engring., U. Calif., Berkeley, 1960, MA in Physics, 1962, PhD in Elec. and Computer Engring., 1967. Acting asst. prof. U. Calif., Berkeley, 1967; asst. prof. elec. engring. SUNY, Stony Brook, 1967-70, assoc. prof. elec. engring., 1970-73, assoc. dean grad. sch., 1973-74, chairperson, prof. elec. engring., 1975-79; congl. fellow A.A.A.S., Washington, 1974-75; provost, v.p. acad. affairs N.J. Inst. Tech., Newark, 1980-98, prof. elec. & computer engring., 1980—; chancellor U. Missouri-Rolla, Rolla, Mo., 2000—. Student asst. bd. Dept. Higher Edn., N.J., 1980-97; chairperson rsch. adv. bd. PSE & G, Newark, 1986-90, Regional Transp. Rsch. Bd., N.Y. and N.J., 1987-90; bd. dirs. Kessler Inst. for Rehab., West Orange, N.J., 1988—; chair bd. dirs. Kessler Med. Rehab. Rsch. & Edn. Corp., 1997—. Author, editor: Fundamentals of Electrical and Computer

Engineering, 1983. State of Calif. scholar, 1960, Schumberger scholar, 1961; NSF grantee, 1973-79. Home: 506 W 11th St Rolla MO 65401-3959 Office: U. Missouri-Rolla 206 Parker Hall 1870 Miner Circle Rolla MO 65409-0910

THOMAS, GARY LYNN, financial executive; b. Port Vue, Pa., May 15, 1942; s. Willis L. and Luella M. (Rorabaugh) T.; m. Sharen A. Gibbons, May 13, 1967; children— Gregory Scott, Tara Elizabeth. BS in Bus. Adminstrn, Pa. State U., 1964; grad., Sch. Bank Adminstrn., U. Wis., 1973. CPA, Pa. Sr. auditor Arthur Andersen & Co., Los Angeles and Pitts., 1964-69; v.p. and dep. comptroller Pitts. Nat. Bank, 1969-77; v.p. and treas. Md. Nat. Corp., Balt., 1977-80; v.p., mgr. corp. fin. div. Md. Nat. Bank; exec. v.p. adminstrn. Peterson, Howell & Heather, Hunt Valley, Md., 1980-82; v.p. fin. Am. TeleServices, Inc, a Metromedia co., Balt., 1983-85; chief fin. officer First Cellular Group, Inc., 1985-88, Schelle, Warner, Murray & Thomas, Inc., Balt., 1988—. Mng. dir. Schelle Cellular Group, Inc., 1989—; pres. Ruxton Capital Group, Inc., 1989—; chief fin. officer Am. Personal Communications, Inc., Balt. and D.C., 1990—; adj. instr. Sch. Bank Adminstrn., U. Wis., 1975-80; speaker 14th ann. Bank Tax Inst., 1978. Mem. adv. bd., fin. com. St. Joseph Hosp., Balt.; bd. dirs. industry luncheon club Towson State U. Served with USAR, 1968. Inducted into McKeesport H.S. Hall of Fame, 1994. Mem. AICPA, Pa. Inst. CPAs, Md. Assn. CPAs (prior chmn. mems. in industry com.) Republican. Methodist. Home: 575 18th Ave S Naples FL 34102-7536

THOMAS, GARY WAYNE, actor; b. Oklahoma City, Dec. 28, 1953; s. Wayne Saxon and Thelma (Hitchcock) T. BBA, U. Okla., 1976. Actor films including Dark Before Dawn, 1988, Rain Man, 1988, Born on the Fourth of July, 1989, JFK, 1991, Robin Hood-Men in Tights, 1993, The Flintstones, 1994, Wild Bill, 1994, Mel Brooks Dracula, 1995, Pulp Fiction, 1995, Independence Day, 1996, L.A. Confidential, 1997, Outskirts, 1998, (TV shows) The Nearly Quiet Orb, 1990, Winchester, 1989, A House of Shadows and Lies, 1992, Melrose Place, 1992, 96, Long Shadows, 1994, Tracy Takes On..., 1995, (plays) Feiffer's People, 1988, Strip! Barely Legal, 1996. Mem. Actor's Fund Am. (life), Am. Film Inst., Screen Actors Guild. Democrat. Avocations: body building, movies, rappeling, dancing, piano. Home: 1208 SW 78th Ter Oklahoma City OK 73139-2420 E-mail: imgarythomas@worldnet.att.net.

THOMAS, HAROLD WILLIAM, avionics systems engineer, flight instructor; b. Cle Elum, Wash., Sept. 29, 1941; s. Albert John and Margaret Jenny (Micheletto) T.; children: Gregg Wallace, Lisa Michele. BS, U. Wash., 1964; M of Engring., U. Fla., 1968; Cert. Aviation Safety, U. So. Calif., 1994. Sci. programmer Aerojet Gen. Corp., Sacramento, 1964-65; systems analyst GE Co., Daytona Beach, Fla., 1965-69, systems engr. Phoenix, 1969-70; sr. software engr. Sperry Flight Systems, 1970-77; sr. systems engr. Honeywell, Inc., 1977-80; engr. section head Sperry Flight Systems, 1980-87; free lance flight instr., 1981—; tech. staff engr. Honeywell, Inc., Phoenix, 1987—. Designated engring. rep. Fed. Aviation Adminstrn., Long Beach, 1987—. Mem. AIAA, SAE Internat. Internat. Soc. Air Safety Investigators, Am. Mensa Ltd. Achievements include patent for rotating round dial aircraft engine instruments, patent for dynamic approach display format with plan and profile views. Home: 2514 W Pershing Ave Phoenix AZ 85029-1445 Office: Honeywell Inc 21111 N 19th Ave Phoenix AZ 85027-2700

THOMAS, HAYWARD, manufacturing company executive; b. Los Angeles, Aug. 9, 1921; s. Charles Sparks and Julia (Hayward) T.; m. Phyllis Mary Wilson, July 1, 1943; children: H. David, Steven T. BS, U. Calif., Berkeley, 1943. Registered profl. engr. Staff engr. Joshua Hendy Corp., Los Angeles, 1946-50; prodn. mgr. Byron Jackson Co., 1950-55; mgr. mfg. Frigidaire div. Gen. Motors Corp., Dayton, Ohio, 1955-70; group v.p. White Motor Corp., Cleve., 1971-73; sr. v.p. Broan Mfg. Co., Hartford, Wis., 1973-85; pres. Jensen Industries, Los Angeles, 1985-87; retired, 1987. Served to lt. USNR, 1943-46. Mem. Soc. Mfg. Engrs. (chmn. mfg. mgmt. council 1984-86). Republican. Episcopalian. Avocations: tennis, fishing. Home: 1320 Granvia Altamira Palos Verdes Peninsula CA 90274-2006

THOMAS, HAZEL BEATRICE, state official; b. Franklin, Tenn. d. William Henry Fuller and Mattie Betty (Covington) Fuller Young; m. Charles B. Thomas (dec. 1969); children; Charles Bradford Jr., Deborah Carlotta (dec.). BA, Fisk U., 1946; MA, Tenn. State U., 1972. Cert. elem. and secondary tchr., Tenn. Tchr. elem. Met.-Nashville Schs., 1954-87; rsch. assoc. Johns Hopkins U., Balt., 1978-79, Marquette U., Milw., 1979-86; exec. asst. to commr. edn. Tenn. Dept. Edn., Nashville, 1987—. Cons. Peer Mediated Learning System, Nashville, 1980-82; instr. Met. Schs. Tchr. Ctr., Nasvhville, 1985-87; mem. tech. assistance team for high schs. that work, So. Regional Edn. Bd., 1998-99. Author training modules Substitute Teaching, Tchr. Aides. Pres. Davidson County Dem. Women, Nashville, 1985-87; v.p. Tenn. Fedn. Dem. Women, 1989-91, pres., 2001—; pres. elect Nashville Women's Polit. Caucus, 1991—; pres. Tenn. Women's Polit. Caucus, 1994-95; mem. adminstrv. com. of bd. Nat. Women's Polit. Caucus, 1993-95, v.p., 1995—, v.p. edn. and tng., 2001—; mem. Tenn. Leadership, Inc., 1992—; spkr., polit. trainer U.S. Info. Agy., Nairobi, Kenya, 1997; mem. exec. bd. Citizen's Com. for Ann. Gov.'s Prayer Breakfast, 1992—; mem. exec. com. Tenn. Dem. Party, 2001—. Recipient Svc. to Edn. and Teaching Profession award Nat. Coun. Negro Women, 1988; Nat. Def. Edn. Act scholar, 1965, 67. Mem. Am. Bus. Womens Assn. (charter), Tenn. Edn. Assn. (pres. dept. classroom tchrs. 1974-75, state dept. affiliate, pres. 1988-90), Bellevue C. of C. (bd. govs. 1990-91), Assn. Classroom Tchrs. (pres. S.E. region 1975-76), Met. Nashville Edn. Assn. (exec. bd. 1971-77), Bellevue Sertoma Club (life, pres. 1990-91), Nat. Women's Polit. Caucus (v.p. 1995—). Democrat. Baptist. Avocations: reading, bridge. Office: Tenn Dept Edn Andrew Johnson Tower 710 James Robertson Pkwy Nashville TN 37243-1219 E-mail: hthomas@mail.state.tn.us.

THOMAS, HELEN A. (MRS. DOUGLAS B. CORNELL), newspaper bureau executive; b. Winchester, Ky., Aug. 4, 1920; d. George and Mary (Thomas) T.; m. Douglas B. Cornell. BA, Wayne U., 1942; LLD, Eastern Mich. State U., 1972, Ferris State Coll., 1978, Brown U., 1986; LHD, Wayne State U., 1974, U. Detroit, 1979; LLD, St. Bonaventure U., 1988, Franklin Marshall U., 1989, No. Michigan U., 1989, Skidmore Coll., 1992, Susquehanna U., 1993, Sage Coll., 1994, U. Mo., 1994; LLD, Northwestern U., 1995, Franklin Coll., 1995; Hon. degree, Mich. State U., 1996, Potsdam U., 1998, A Willenberg Univ., 1999; BA in law, Mount Vernon Coll., 1999. With UPI, 1943-2000, wire svc. reporter, 1943-74, White House bur. chief, 1974-2000; columnist Hearst Newspapers, 2000—. Author: Dateline White House. Recipient Woman of Yr. in Comm. award, Ladies Home Jour., 1975, 4th Estate award, Nat. Press Club, 1984, Journalism award, U. Mo., Al Newharth award, 1990, Ralph McGill award, 1995, Lifetime award, Internat. Media Found., Internat. Women's Press Found., 1996, White House Corr. Assn., 1998, Lowell Thomas award, Marist Coll., 2001. Mem. Women's Nat. Press Club (pres. 1959-60, William Allen White Journalism award), Am. Newspaper Women's Club (past v.p.), White House Corrs. Assn. (pres. 1976, Lifetime Achievement award 1998), Nat. Newspaper Assn. (Lifetime award 2002), Gridiron Club (pres. 1993), Sigma Delta Chi (fellow, Hall of Fame), Delta Sigma Phi (hon.). Home: 2501 Calvert St NW Washington DC 20008-2620

THOMAS, HELEN LEE, linguistics educator; b. Seymour, Ind., Feb. 4, 1951; d. Frank Walter and Virginia Ann (Kieffer) Voss; m. James Mitchell Thomas, Sept. 11, 1981 (div. 1989); children: Kyle, Kieffer. AB, Ind. U., 1973, MS, 1978, PhD in Linguistics, 1987. Dir. Intensive Edn. Lang. Ctr. U. Nev., Reno, 1982-88, dir. internat. programs, 1988-93, asst. prof., 1994-2000, assoc. prof., 2000—. Author: The English Language: An Owner's Manual, 1999; contbr. articles to profl. jours. including Modern Lang. Jour., English Jour. Fulbright Assn. scholar. Mem. Am. Assn. Applied Linguistics, Linguistic Soc. Am., Fulbright Assn., TESOL, Internat. Assn. World Englishes, Amnesty Internat. Avocations: skiing, hiking, sailing. Office: U Nev Reno English Dept 098 Reno NV 89509

THOMAS, HERMAN, state judge; b. Mobile, Ala., Jan. 6, 1961; s. Daniel Thomas and Bernice Young; m. Linda Grant, June 25, 1987; children: Brooke Alexis, Andrea Michelle. BS, U. S. Ala., 1983; JD, Fla. State U., 1985. Bar: Fla., Ala., U.S. Dist. Ct. (so. dist.) Ala., U.S. Dist. Ct. Appeals (11th cir.). Adminstrv. asst. Coll. Law Fla. State U., Tallahassee, 1985-86; asst. state atty. 4th Jud. Cir. Fla., Jacksonville, 1986, 1st Jud. Cir. Fla., Pensacola, 1986-87; asst. dist. atty. 13th Jud. Cir. Ala., Mobile, 1987-90, dist. ct. judge, 1990—. Adj. prof. U. S. Ala., Mobile, 1990-94, Spring Hill Coll., Mobile, 1994. Mem. sch. bd. McGill-Toolen H.S.; trustee U. S. Ala., Spring Hill Coll.; cmty. adv. Jr. League Mobile; bd. dirs. S. Ala. Med. Sci. Found., Family Exch. Ctr., Family Counseling Ctr., Parents as First Tchrs., Mobile Mental Health, Inc., Penelope Ho. Shelter, Mobile Sport Commn., Coalition Drug Free Mobile, Boys and Girls Club Greater Mobile, Inc., Am.'s Jr. Miss, Mobile Opera Bd., Ala. Civil Justice Found.; mem. A+ Coalition Better Edn.; cmty. chmn. Success by Six-United W ay; mem. adv. bd. Charter Hosp., Cath. Svc. Ctr., USA Comprehensive Sickle Cell Ctr., Autism Found. Ala.; mem. Challenge 2.0.0.0; mem. sch. bd. St. James, lector, Sunday sch. instr., youth club advisor; mem. Knights Peter Claver. 1st. lt. U.S. Army. Named Outstanding Young Man Am., 1986; recipient Disting. Citizen award. Mem. 100 Black Men Greater Mobile, Inc., U. S. Ala. Alumni (past pres., bd. dirs.), Mobile Sunrise Rotary, Mobile Inn Ct., Kappa Alpha Psi, Phi Kappa Phi. Democrat. Roman Catholic.

THOMAS, HILARY BRYN, telecommunications executive, interactivist, writer, speaker; b. Brignorth, Eng., Jan. 31, 1943; came to U.S., 1985; parents, Kenneth Bryn and Nancy Barbara Tench (Cullum) T. BSc with honors, U. Wales, 1965. Instr. U. Victoria, B.C., Can., 1967-73; rsch. asst. comm. studies group Univ. Coll., London, 1975-76; cons. Comm. Studies and Planning, Ltd., 1976-80; v.p. CSP Internat., Inc., London and N.Y.C., 1980-82, Aregon Internat., London and N.Y.C., 1982-85, Videodial, Inc., N.Y.C., 1985-88; pres. Minitel USA, Inc., 1988-92; pres., bd. dirs. Minitel Holdings, Inc., Del.; chmn. bd. dirs. Minitel Svcs. Co., 1988-92; pres. Interactive Telecom. Svcs. Inc., Denville, N.J., 1992—; pres., founder ISED Corp., Howell, 1992—; v.p. internat. bus. devel. eCHARGE Corp., Seattle, 1999-2001. Spkr. interactive svcs., electronic commerce, the Internet; cons. Contbr. articles to industry publs. Bd. dirs. Cor Cyry Gogledd Am., the N.Am. Welsh Choir, 1997-2001, Morris Conservatory Music, 1998-99. Mem. Internet Alliance (formerly Interactive Svcs. Assn., dir. emeritus 1997, bd. dirs. 1985-97, chmn. 1987-89, Disting. Svc. award 1989), World Inst. on Disability (bus. adv. coun. 1989-92), Internat. Inst. Interactivity (pres. 1997-2001). E-mail: hilary@interactivist.com.

THOMAS, HOWARD, business educator; b. Jan. 31, 1943; BSc, London U., 1964, MSc, 1965; MBA, U. Chgo., 1966; PhD, Edinburgh U., 1970. Prof. dept. bus. adminstrn. U. Ill., Urbana-Champaign, 1981-2000, dir. Office of Internat. Strategic Mgmt., 1990-2000, James F. Towey disting. prof. strategic mgmt., 1987-2000, acting dean Coll. Commerce and Bus. Adminstrn., 1991-92, dean Coll. Commerce and Bus. Adminstrn., 1992-2000, dean emeritus Commerce and Bus. Adminstrn., 2001—; dean Warwick Bus. Sch. U. Warwick, Coventry, U.K., 2000—. Vis. prof. MIT, 1986-87, Northwestern U., 1990. Office: Warwick Bus Sch U Warwick Coventry CV4 7AL England E-mail: deanht@wbs.warwick.ac.uk.

THOMAS, HOWARD LAMAR, chef, consultant, writer; b. Tucker, Ga., Jan. 30, 1956; s. William Lyle Thomas and Dorthea Mary (England) Whitelaw; (div. 1989). BA in Philosophy, West Ga. Coll., 1975; postgrad. in philosophy, U. Ga., 1989-91. Chef St. Orres, Gualala, Calif., 1980-83; owner, chef Olde Town Inn, Conyers, Ga., 1986-88; exec. chef GRO Enterprises: The Mansion, Atlanta, 1984-85, Windchimes, Point Arena, Calif., 1991-93, East-West Bistro, Athens, Ga., 1994—. Cons. Athens Coffee House, Cappi-Davis Corp., Athens, 1993; lectr. Rolling Pin Kitchens, Athens, 1996-2001; spkr. in field. Contbr. poetry to lit. jours. Parnassus, Nimrod, Wis. Rev., Poetry Motel, Am. Writing, hadden Oaks, Wanny Fanny, Clark St. Rev., other; , recipes to Atlanta Jour. Constn. Lectr. Athens-Clarke County Pub. Libr., 1996, 97, 98, 99, 2000; mem. Democratic Nat. Party, Ga., 1994—. Recipient 3d place award Circumference Lit. Jour., N.J. Coun. of Arts, 1994; finalist Pablo Neruda award 1999. Mem. ACLU, Am. Acad. Poets. Democrat. Baptist. Avocations: writing cookbooks, piano, modern literature, fly fishing, poetry. Office: East West Bistro 351 East Broad St Athens GA 30601

THOMAS, HOWARD PAUL, civil engineer, consultant; b. Cambridge, Mass., Aug. 20, 1942; s. Charles Calvin and Helen Elizabeth (Hook) T.; m. Ingrid Nybo, Jan. 4, 1969; children: Kent Michael, Lisa Karen, Karina Michelle. BS in Engring., U. Mich., 1965, MS in Engring., 1966. Registered profl. engr., Alaska, Calif. Engr. Ove Arup & Ptnrs., London, 1966-67; project engr. Woodward-Clyde Cons., San Francisco, 1967-73, assoc. Anchorage, 1975-89; spl. cons. Cowiconsult Cons., Copenhagen, 1973-75; prin. engr. Harding-Lawson Assocs., Anchorage, 1989-90; v.p., chief engr. EMCON Alaska, Inc., 1991-94; gen. mgr. Internat. Tech. Corp., 1994-96; assoc. GeoEngrs., Inc., 1996—2002; mem. Anchorage Mayor's Geotech. Adv. Commn., 1997—; prin. engr. CH2M Hill, Anchorage, 2001—. Chmn. Nat. Tech. Coun. Cold Regions Engring., 1988-89, chmn. com. program and publs., 1982-84; chmn. 4th Internat. Conf. Cold Regions Engring., Anchorage, 1986; liaison NAS/Nat. Rsch. Coun. Polar Rsch. Bd., 1989-99. Contbr. articles to profl. jours. Fellow ASCE (pres. Anchorage chpt. 1985-86, chair mgmt. group A. 1996-97, pres. Alaska sect. 1998-99, named Alaskan Engr. of Yr. 1986, Harold R. Peyton award 2001); mem. Soc. Am. Mil. Engrs., Cons. Engrs. Coun. Alaska (pres. 1989-90), Am. Cons. Engrs. Coun. (nat. dir. 1990-91), Project Mgmt. Inst. (v.p. Alaska chpt. 1991-95), Toastmasters (pres. Anchorage club 1984), Sons of Norway (pres. Anchorage lodge 2000-02). Lutheran. Avocations: playing French Horn in Anchorage Civic Orchestra, travel, skiing, sailing. Home: 2611 Brittany Dr Anchorage AK 99504-3332 E-mail: hthomas@ch2m.com.

THOMAS, IRV, journalist, publisher; b. San Francisco, Apr. 14, 1927; s. David Goldstein and Minnie Resnick; m. Vivian Laura Allen, Nov. 30, 1956; life ptnr.: Alice Joy. BA, U. Wash., 1990. Pub./editor Black Bart Brigade/Yin Times, Canyon, Calif., 1971-83; editor Earthstewards jour./newsletter, Bainbridge Island, Wash., 1985-89; pub./editor Ripening Seasons Jour., Seattle, 1995—. Tchr., workshop organizer Finding a Way Out, San Francisco, 1971-75; presenter World Futurist Conf., Toronto, Ont., 1980, Assn. for Humanistic Psychology Conv., Estes Park, Colo., 1976, Calif. Libr. Assn. Conv., Disneyland, 1972. Author, illustrator: Innocence Abroad, 1994, rev. edit., 2001; contbr. anthology: Alternative Papers, 1982; contbr. articles to profl. jours. Housing activist Seattle Sr. Housing Program Advocates, 1996-99; co-founder Afertlife.org, 2001. Avocation: hitchhiking. Home: 6545 Ravenna Ave NE #307 Seattle WA 98115 E-mail: irvthom1@attbi.com.

THOMAS, ISIAH LORD, III, former professional basketball player, basketball team executive, professional basketball coach; b. Chgo., Apr. 30, 1961; Grad. in Criminal Justice, Ind. U., 1987. With Detroit Pistons, 1981-94; v.p. Toronto Raptors, 1994-97, now v.p. basketball ops., owner, exec. v.p., 1996-97; sportscaster N.B.C. Sports, N.Y.C., 1997-00; head coach Indiana Pacers, Indianapolis, 2000—. Mem. U.S. Olympic Basketball Team, 1980, NBA Championship Teams, 1989-90. Named to All-Star team, 1982-93, All NBA First Team, 1984, 85, 86; recipient All-Star team MVP award, 1984, 86, NBA Playoff MVP award, 1990, NBA Finals MVP, 1990. Named to NBA All-Rookie team 1982. Address: Indiana Pacers 125 S Pennsylvania St Indianapolis IN 46204-3610*

THOMAS, J. EARL, retired physicist; b. Seattle, Sept. 7, 1918; s. Jacob Earl and Ursula May (Johnson) T.; m. Margaret Louise Johnston, June 15, 1977; children— Richard Bruce, Jacob Earl, John Calvin, James Hayden, Denise May, Stillman Jefferson. AB, Johns Hopkins U., 1939; PhD, Calif. Inst. Tech., 1943. Group leader rocket devel. Calif. Inst. Tech., Pasadena, 1942-45; group leader Manhattan Project, U. Calif., Los Alamos, 1945-46; asst. prof. elec. engring. M.I.T., Cambridge, 1946-51; mem. tech. staff Bell Telephone Labs., Murray Hill, N.J., 1951-52; group leader M.I.T. Lincoln Labs., Lexington, 1952-55; prof., chmn. dept. physics Wayne State U., Detroit, 1955-59; dir. research Sylvania Electric, Woburn, Mass., 1959-62; mgr. solid state devel. IBM, Poughkeepsie, N.Y., 1962-64; mgr. new product devel. Gen. Instrument Co., Newark, 1964-67; v.p. Carman Sapphire Co., Reseda, Calif., 1967-70; cons. Warnecke Electron Tubes, Des Plaines, Ill., 1970-71; dir. components research Victor Comptometer Co., 1971-75; mgr. advanced devel. NCR Corp., Ithaca, N.Y., 1975-84. Cons. pvt. cos. and govt. agys. Contbr. articles to sci. jours.; patentee in field. Active S.E. Asian refugee resettlement program. Recipient Service award U.S. Office Sci. Research and Devel., 1946 Fellow: IEEE (Millennium medal), Am. PHys. Soc.; mem.: Tau Beta Pi, Phi Beta Kappa, Sigma Xi. Democrat. Presbyterian. Home: 323 Savage Farm Dr Ithaca NY 14850-6503

THOMAS, J. MARK, minister, research fellow, sociology educator; b. Ft. Worth, Dec. 20, 1947; s. Jacob Gillespie and Eleanor Rose (Geivett) T.; m. Jacquelyn Higby, Sept. 2, 1978; children: Megan Lane, Drew Martin. BA, Tex. Christian U., 1971, MDiv, 1974; PhD, U. Chgo., 1983. Ordained to ministry United Ch. of Christ, 1974. Asst. prof. philosophy and religion, chaplain Drury Coll., Springfield, Mo., 1983-85; adj. asst. prof. religion, chaplain Ripon (Wis.) Coll., 1985-87; vis. asst. prof. philosophy and religion Beloit (Wis.) Coll., 1987-89; sr. rsch. fellow Au Sable Inst. Environ. Studies, Mancelona, Mich., 1989—. Sociology instr., lead tchr. social sci. dept. Madison Area Tech. Coll. Author: Ethics and Technoculture, 1987, (with others) Being and Doing, 1987, Philosophy and Technology, Vol. 10, 1990; editor: Paul Tillich, The Spiritual Situation in Our Technical Society, 1988, God and Capitalism, 1991. Chmn. planning com. Congress of Sci., Tech. and Religion for the Parliament of World Religion, 1993. Recipient Disting. Tchr. Yr., Madison Area Tech. Coll., 1999. Mem. Midwest Sociol. Soc., Communitarian Network. Democrat. Mem. United Ch. of Christ. Home: 816 Lincoln St Madison WI 53711-2163 Office: Madison Area Tech Coll Downtown Edn Ctr 211 N Carroll St Madison WI 53703-2211

THOMAS, JACQUELINE MARIE, lawyer; b. Rochester, N.Y., June 29, 1967; d. Robert J. and Frances P. (Pata) T.; m. Jeffrey W. Raetz, May 16, 1992. BA, St. John Fisher Coll., 1988; JD cum laude, Union U., 1991. Bar: N.Y. 1992. Assoc. Bouck, Holloway, Kiernan & Casey, Albany, NY 1991—94, Lacy, Katzen, Ryen & Mittleman, LLP, Rochester, 1994—2001, ptnr., 2001—. Mem. Trial Lawyers Assn. Am., N.Y. State Bar Assn., N.Y. State Trial Lawyers Assn., Monroe County Bar Assn. Office: Lacy Katzen Ryen and Mittleman 130 E Main St Ste 200 Rochester NY 14604-1620 E-mail: jthomas@lacykatzen.com.

THOMAS, JACQUELYN MAY, librarian; b. Mechanicsburg, Pa., Jan. 26, 1932; d. William John and Gladys Elizabeth (Warren) Harvey; m. David Edward Thomas, Aug. 28, 1954; children: Lesley J., Courtenay J., Hilary A. BA summa cum laude, Gettysburg Coll., 1954; student, U. N.C., 1969; MEd, U. N.H., 1971. Libr. Phillips Exeter Acad., Exeter, N.H., 1971-77, acad. libr., 1977—. Chair governing bd. Child Care Ctr., 1987-91; chair Com. to Enhance Status of Women, Exeter, 1981-84; chair Loewenstein Com., Exeter, 1982—; pres. Cum Laude Soc., Exeter, 1984-86; James H. Ottaway Jr. prof., 1990—; mem. bldg. com. Exeter Pub. Libr., 1986-88; chair No. New Eng., Coun. for Women in Ind. Schs., 1985-87; chmn. Lamont Poetry Program, Exeter, 1984-86. Editor: The Design of the Library: A Guide to Sources of Information, 1981, Rarities of Our Time: The Special Collections of the Phillips Exeter Academy Library. Libr. trustee, treas. Exeter Day Sch., 1965-69; bd. Exeter Hosp. Vols., 1954-59; mem. Exeter Hosp. Corp., 1978—; bd. dirs. Greater Portsmouth Cmty. Found., 1990—; active AAC&U, On Campus with Women, Wellesley Coll. Ctr. for Rsch. on Women; mem. People to People Amb. Program, sch. and youth svcs. libr. del. to People's Rep. China, 1998. Grantee N.H. Coun. for Humanties, 1981-82, NEH, 1982; recipient Lillian Radford trust award, 1989. Mem. ALA, Internat. Assn. Sch. Librs., New Eng. Libr. Assn., N.J., Ednl. Media Assn., New Eng. Assn. Ind. Sch. Librs., Am. Assn. Sch. Librs. (chmn. non-pub. sch. sect.), Phi Beta Kappa. Home: 17 Eagle Dr Newmarket NH 03857 Office: Acad Libr Phillips Exeter Acad 20 Main St Exeter NH 03833-2460 Fax: 603-777-4389. E-mail: jthomas@exeter.edu.

THOMAS, JAMES RAYMOND, accountant; b. Aberdeen, Wash., Jan. 22, 1947; s. Haywood and Ada Elnora (Gerhardt) T.; divorced; children: Ronald James, Wendy Gayle; m. Linda J. Jones, Mar. 23, 1991. AA, Wharton (Tex.) County Jr. Coll., 1967; BBA, U. Houston, 1970. CPA, Tex. Staff acct. Ernst & Young, Houston, 1970-71; acct. C&K Petroleum, Inc., 1972-73; contr. The Analysts, Inc., 1973; home builder Mountain Estates Constrn. Co., Cripple Creek, Colo., 1974-75; intermediate acct. Tenneco Realty, Inc., Houston, 1975-77; asst. contr. Weingarten Realty, Inc., 1977-78; pvt. practice Pearland, Tex., 1978-83; ptnr. Thomas Snyder MacAllister & Co., 1983-86; pvt. practice Friendswood, Tex., 1986—. Contbr. articles to newspapers. Bd. dirs., treas. Tri-County YMCA, Pearland, sustaining mem., 1986—; amb. Pearland-Hobby C. of C., 1984-85, Friendswood C. of C., 1986—; mem. founding bd. dirs. Pearland Multi-Svcs. Ctr., United Way. Mem. AICPA, Tex. Soc. CPA's, Friendswood C. of C., Rotary (bd. dirs. Pearland 1983-86, pres. 1986-87, mem. dist. 589 com. 1986—, mem. team to teach free enterprise principles to Poland and Hungary chpts. 1991, 92, 93, Paul Harris Fellow 1987). Republican. Methodist. Avocations: traveling, fishing. Home: 703 Woodview Friendswood TX 77546 Office: PO Box 2013 Friendswood TX 77549

THOMAS, JAMES ARTHUR, retired government official, electrical engineer; b. Meridian, Miss., Sept. 4, 1934; s. Walter James and Gladys Clarice (Harper) T.; m. Lily Juanita Purvis, Aug. 31, 1956; children: Karen Thomas Andrews, Chuck, Wendy Thomas Marks. BSEE, Miss. State U., 1962; MBA, Fla. State U., 1973. Sys. engr. NASA-Kennedy Space Ctr., Fla., 1962-74, Orbiter project engr., 1974-82, shuttle project engr., 1982-84, dir. launch and landing ops., 1985-86, dir. safety, reliability and quality assurance, 1987-90, dep. ctr. dir., 1990-97. Mem. Nat. Space Club, Rocket Pioneers Club. Baptist. Avocations: reading, writing, swimming. Home: 355 Pine Blvd Merritt Island FL 32952-5004

THOMAS, JAMES BERT, JR. government official; b. Tallahassee, Mar. 16, 1935; s. James Bert and Stella E. (Lewis) T.; m. Sharon Mae Kelly, June 16, 1962; children: James Bert III, Mary Elizabeth, John Christopher. BS, Fla. State U., 1957. C.P.A., Fla. Spl. auditor Office State Comptroller, Jacksonville, Fla., 1958; jr. auditor J.D.A. Holley & Co., C.P.A.'s, Tallahassee, 1959; sr. auditor Office of the State Auditor, 1959-60; trainee, audit dir. HUD audit div., Washington, 1960-71; asst. dir. Bur. Accounts ICC, 1972-75, dir. Bur. Accounts, 1977-80; inspector gen. U.S. Dept. HUD, 1975-77, U.S. Dept. Edn., Washington, 1980-95; dir. auditing Office of the Gov., State of Fla., Tallahassee, 1995—. Mem. Pres.'s Coun. Integrity and Efficiency, chmn. audit stds. subcom., 1984-95, chmn. audit com., 1989-90. Mem. AICPA (strategic planning com. 1987-90, chmn. govt. auditing standards adv. coun. 1991—), Inst. Internal Auditors (trustee Rsch. Found. 1991-92), Assn. Govt. Accts. (chmn. fin. mgmt. standards bd. 1985-86), Accts. Roundtable. Roman Catholic. Home: 4737 Tory Sound Ln Unit 601 Tallahassee FL 32309-2266 Office: Exec Office of Governor Rm 2107 The Capitol Tallahassee FL 32399-0001

THOMAS, JAMES EDWARD, accountant; b. Darlington, S.C., Oct. 18, 1944; s. Willie Thomas and Cleola (Sawyer) T.; m. Joan Yvette Grant, Mar. 15, 1945; 1 child, James E. II. BS in Acctg., Johnson C. Smith Coll., Charlotte, N.C., 1966; MA in Fin., C.W. Post Coll., Greenvale, N.Y., 1980; PhD in Edn., Fordham U., 1996; MBA, Pace U., 1976. Cert. paralegal. Asst. mgr. Mfrs. Hanover Trust, N.Y.C., 1970-78, Met. Savs. Bank, N.Y.C., 1978-81; auditor N.Y. State Dept. Social Svcs., 1981-83; acct. N.Y.C. Bd. Edn., 1983-86; acct., agt. IRS, N.Y.C., 1987-99; dir. fin. N.Y.C. Dept. Design and Constrn., Long Island City, 1999—. Instr. Katherine L. Gibbs, Inc., N.Y.C., 1987-89. Mem.: Internat. Platform Assn., Nat. Soc. Pub. Accts., Nat. Assn. Sch. Bus. Ofcls., Am. Mgmt. Assn., Assn. MBA Execs., Sigma Rho Sigma. Avocations: woodworking, basketball, basebell, track, reading. Home: 99-72 66th Rd# 3R Rego Park NY 11374

THOMAS, JAMES EDWARD, JR. brokerage house executive; b. Atlanta, Apr. 23, 1950; s. James Edward and Dortha Jean (White) Thomas; m. Leslie Ann Stagmaier, Sept. 6, 1975; children: Steele Stagmaier, Katherine Mills. BA magna cum laude, U. Ga., 1972, JD cum laude, 1975. Mgr. Genuine Parts Co., Atlanta, 1975-77; v.p. Robinson Humphrey Co., 1977-94; ptnr. J.C. Bradford and Co., 1994—; mng. dir. Wachovia Securities, 2000—. Bd. dirs. Enstar Comm. Corp., The Kinston Group, Inc., Atlanta, Tophat Soccer Club, Atlanta, Hall's Boathouse, Inc., Lakemont, Ga., Vista Environ. Info., Inc., San Diego. Pres. Castlewood Civic Orgn., Inc., Atlanta; mem. Lake Rabun Homeowners Assn., Lakemont, Ga.; mem. bd. advisors U. Ga., Habitat for Humanity. Mem. Internat. Platform Assn., Ga. Bar Assn., La Societe des Tetes Grandes, Capital City Club, U. Ga. LEADS Adv. Bd., Ga Tennis Found. (treas., trustee). Republican. Episcopalian. Avocations: boating, tennis, golf.

THOMAS, JAMES LEWIS, biomedical research scientist; b. Atlanta, May 18, 1949; s. Ruble Anderson and Mary Jo (Bass) T.; m. Kathleen Lee Hunter, Aug. 18, 1979; children: Jack, Mary Kate. BA, Emory U., 1971; PhD, U. Ala., Birmingham, 1981. Rsch. assoc. Washington U. Med. Sch., St. Louis, 1981-85, rsch. instr., 1985-91, rsch. asst. prof., 1991-2000; asst. prof. Mercer U. Sch. Medicine, Macon, 2000—. Contbr. articles to profl. jours. Mem. AAAS, Endocrine Soc., Soc. for Study of Reprodn., Pi Alpha, Delta Tau Delta. Achievements include research on structure/function relationships of enzyme catalytic amino acids; how changes in enzyme conformation participate in reaction mechanisms. Home: 4668 Savage Creek Dr Macon GA 31210 Office: Mercer U Sch Medicine Divsn Basic Med Scis 1550 College St Macon GA 31207 E-mail: Thomas_J@mercer.edu.

THOMAS, JAMES PATRICK, special education educator; b. Chgo., Sept. 24, 1946; s. Jacque Anthony and Dorothy Lucille (Brown) T.; m. Cathy E. Hanks, Sept. 29, 1979 (div. Aug. 1990); 1 child, Nicholas Jacque. BA in History and Polit. Sci., Drake U., 1973; MS in Pub. Adminstrn., Troy State U., 1983; MS in Spl. Edn., cert. advanced grad. studies, Johns Hopkins U., 1994. cert. spl. educator. Commd. 2nd lt. USAF, 1973, advanced through grades to maj., 1985; missile launch officer, instr., crew comdr., contr. 91st Strategic Missile Wing, Minot, N.D., 1974-78; exec. officer, asst. ops. officer, resource advisor 6916th Electronic Security Squadron, Hellenikon Air Base, Greece, 1978-81; chief programs br. 6940th Electronic Security Wing, Ft. Meade, Md., 1981-82; program mgr. USAF Ops. Security Hq USAF/XOEO Directorate of Electronic Combat, Washington, 1982-85; intelligence collection activities mgr./chief Hdqrs. U.S. European Command, Stuttgart, Germany, 1986-88; signals intelligence planning staff officer Nat. Security Agy., Ft. Meade, 1988-90; cons. spl. edn. Balt., 1991—. Adj. faculty mem. Catonsville (Md.) C.C., 1991—; spl. educator Howard County Sch. System, Columbia, 1992-94, Boonsborro (Md.) Middle Sch., 1994-96, Hiatt Mid. Sch., Des Moines, 1996-98, Johnston (Iowa) Mid. Sch., 1998-99, Johnston High Sch., 1999-2000, Variety Sch., Las Vegas, Nev., 2000—. Author: (pamphlet) Your Rights to Legal Advice, 1994; co-author: The Outcome of a Services Evaluation for Families of Vietnam Vets. with Children with Disabilities in the Balt. Met. Area, 1995. Pres. Cath. Men Parish Athens, Greece, 1979-81, Minot AFB, N.D., 1975-78; asst. den leader, dean leader Cub Scouts, Boy Scouts Am., Ellicott City, Md., 1987-90. With USN, 1964-73. Decorated Purple Heart, 2 Def. Meritorious Svc. medals, Meritorious Svc. medals, Air Force Commendation medal, Air medal, Air Force Achievement medal. Mem. VFW (life), Phoenix Soc., Mil. Order Purple Heart (life), Am. Legion China Post 1, Ret. Officers Assn. (life), Vets. Vietnam War (life), Soaring Assn. Am., Disabled Am. Vets. (life), Swiftboat Sailors Assn. Inc. (pres. 1995—), Phi Delta Gamma (v.p. Gamma chpt.). Roman Catholic. Avocations: pilot of sailplanes, sailing, snorkeling, golf, running, photography. Home: 1929 High Mesa Dr Henderson NV 89012-6182

THOMAS, JAMES RUSSELL, multimedia communications specialist; b. Palo Alto, Calif., Apr. 24, 1959; s. Samuel Harmon and Johy Dawn (Marler) T.; m. Sandy Holland, Feb. 17, 1994; children: Jason Andreau, Eric Hunter. AAS, Gadsen (Ala.) State U., 1983; BA, U. Md., 1987. Cert. legal video specialist. News and prodn. photographer Sta. KTXL, Sacramento, 1976-77; radio announcer Sta. KNDE Radio, 1976-77; sports anchor, news reporter Sta. WKAB, Montgomery, Ala., 1977-78; news anchor Sta. WAKA, 1977-80; news prodr., dir., assignment editor Sta. KTXL, Sacramento, 1980-82; radio announcer Sta. WHHY FM, Montgomery, 1978-80, Sta. KROY/KROI AM-FM, Sacramento, 1980-82; prodn. mgr., creative prodr. DBP Prodns., Montgomery, 1987-88; gen. mgr. LWT comms. LWT Advt., 1988; multimedia comms. specialist ALFA Ins. Group, 1989—. Author (mag. column) Comms. Climates, 1988—; contbg. editor ALFA Jour., 1988—; prodr., dir. tng. videos. Mem., bd. dirs. Op. Lifesaver, Montgomery, 1990—; bd. dirs. Carver Creative and Performing Arts Ctr., Montgomery, 1990—; gov. office hwy safety bd. Gov. of Ala., Montgomery, 1992—; mass comm. instr. Mont. City/County Pub. Schs., Montgomery, 1988—. Sgt. U.S. Army, 1983-87. Recipient Addy award Mont. Advt. Fedn., 1990, 91, 92, Gold award, 1993, 94, 95, Silver award 1996, Army Commendation medal, 2 awards for broadcasting excellence. Mem. Montgomery Advt. Fedn., Internat. TV Assn., Sigma Phi Epsilon. Republican. Baptist. Avocations: audiophile, film critic, music reviews, lecturing. Office: ALFA Ins Profl Devel Group 2108 E South Blvd Montgomery AL 36116-2015 Home: 2609 Royal Downing Ct Montgomery AL 36117-6813

THOMAS, JAMES WILLIAM, lawyer; b. N.Y.C., May 12, 1949; s. Howard and Alice (Brennan) T.; m. Cecilia Coleman Goad, July 7, 1973; children: James William, Brennan McKinney. BS, U. Dayton, 1971; JD, Ohio No. U., 1974. Bar: Ohio 1974, U.S. Dist. Ct. Ohio 1976. Ptnr. Earley & Thomas, Eaton, Ohio, 1974-89; pvt. rpactice, 1989—. Village solicitor Village of Lewisburg (Ohio), 1977-81, Village of Verona (Ohio), 1979-81; asst. pros. atty. Preble County (Ohio), 1980-81. Mem. Preble County Cmty. Corrections Planing Bd. Fellow Ohio State Bar Found.; mem. ABA, Ohio State Bar Assn., Ohio State Bar Coll., Ohio Acad. Trial Lawyers, Ohio Assn. Criminal Def. Lawyers, Preble county Bar Assn. (pres. 1982-84), Comm. Improvement Corp., Eaton Country Club, Rotary (dir. 1980-87, pres. 1987-88). Republican. Roman Catholic. Avocations: boating, tennis. Home: 761 Vinland Cv Eaton OH 45320-2536 Office: 112 N Barron St Eaton OH 45320-1702

THOMAS, JANET MARIE, economics educator; b. Providence; d. Lionel and Alice (Merrill) La Grandeur; m. David Joseph Thomas. BA in Econs., Framingham State Coll., 1981; MA in Econs., Boston Coll., Chestnut Hill, Mass., 1985, PhD in Econs., 1987. Fin. analyst, ops. mgr. Inleasing Corp., Providence, 1971-78; ops. mgr. residential mortgage Fleet Nat. Bank, 1978-79; vis. lectr. Framingham State Coll., Framingham, Mass., 1982; rsch./teaching asst. Boston Coll., Chestnut Hill, 1982-84, teaching fellow, 1984-87; asst. prof. econs. Bentley Coll., Waltham, Mass., 1987-93, assoc. prof. econs., 1993—. Mem. Am. Econ. Assn., Ea. Econ. Assn., So. Econ. Assn., Com. on the Status of Women in the Econs. Profession, Indsl. Orgn. Soc., Omicron Delta Epsilon. Roman Catholic. Office: Bentley Coll 175 Forest St Waltham MA 02452-4713

THOMAS, JEFFREY CONE, financial executive, consultant; b. New Orleans, Oct. 10, 1941; s. Eads Poitevent and Virginia Lee (King) T.; m. Brenda Gayle Ballard, June 7, 1969 (div. Mar. 1972). BA, La. State U., 1965. CLU; ChFC; CFP; CFS. Mgmt. trainee Am. Bank and Trust Co., Baton Rouge, 1965-68; supr. Travelers Ins. Co., 1968-71; dist. dir. Conn. Gen. Life Ins. Co., 1971-74; pres., CEO Pension & Profit Sharing Cons., 1974-77; pres. Fin. Advisor & Cons., 1977—. Adj. instr. adult eve. classes Coll. Fin. Planning, 1987-92; cons. Ethyl Corp., Baton Rouge, 1982, Dow Chem., Plaquemine, La., 1986. Contbr. article to Enterprise Mag., 1981. Vol. ARC, Baton Rouge, 1965-69; mem. adminstrv. bd. First Meth. Ch., Baton Rouge, 1987-89. Avocations: golf, tennis, fishing, gardening. Office: Fin Advisor & Cons PO Box 65238 Baton Rouge LA 70896-5238

THOMAS, JERRY ARTHUR, soil scientist; b. Logansport, Ind., Mar. 5, 1942; s. Purnal Kidd and Dorothy Helen (Smith) T.; m. Virginia Amy York, Oct. 17, 1964; 1 child, Charles Edward. BS in Agronomy, Purdue U., 1965; MS in Soil Fertility, Pa. State U., 1968. Libr. chemistry dept. Purdue Univ., West Lafayette, Ind., 1963, tech. aid USDA, ARS, agronomy dept., 1963-65; grad. teaching asst. agronomy dept. Pa. State U., University Park, 1965-67; soil scientist USDA Soil Conservation Svc., Indpls., 1967-85, Ind. State Bd. Health, Indpls., 1985—. Com. mem. Ind. State 4-H Rabbit com., West Lafayette, 1976—. Author publs. in field including Classification of the Sloping Soils of the West Baden Group in Monroe County, Ind., 1978, Soil Survey of Monroe County, Ind., 1981, Soil Survey of Lawrence County, Ind., 1985, Availability of Conservation Tillage Planting Systems for Northwestern Ind., 1985. Asst. scoutmaster Boy Scouts Am., Rensselaer, Ind., 1982-92. Recipient Innovative award Coun. State Govts., 1988; named Environ. Health Specialist of Yr., Environ. Health Assn., 1993. Mem. Am. Soc. Agronomy, Soil Sci. Soc. Am., Soil and Water Conservation Soc. Am., Ind. Acad. Sci., Ind. Assn. Profl. Soil Classifiers, Ind. Environtl. Health Assn., Masons, Eastern Star. Presbyterian. Home: 301 S Park Ave Rensselaer IN 47978-3037 Office: Ind State Bd Health Divsn Sanitary Engring 2 N Meridian St Indianapolis IN 46204-3003 E-mail: jthomas@isdh.state.in.us.

THOMAS, JIM GUS, music educator; b. El Paso, Tex., July 10, 1945; s. Gus Demetrios Thomopoulos and Antigone Mourgelas; m. Evi Deligianni Thomas, Aug. 15, 1970 (div. May 18, 1998); children: Gus James, Georgianna, Evi Deligianni. Bachelor Music Edn., Ariz. State U., Tempe, AZ, 1969, MA, 1975. Music educator Creighton Sch. Dist., Phoenix, 1970—; choral, gen. music educator Isaac Sch. Dist., 1972—76; founder, orchestral strings educator Paradise Valley Dist., 1976—79; music educator Cartwright Sch. Dist., 1979—. Dir., educator Summer Music Camp, Prescott, Ariz., 1993—; instr. Honors String Orch., 2002—, The Funky Fiddlers, 2002—; music curriculum coord. Cartwright Sch. Dist., Phoenix, 2002—, adminstrv. asst. to dist. music cons., 2002—. Composer: (greek folk dance for clarinet trio) Pentozalis. Mem.: Ariz. Music Educators Assn. (O.M. Hartsell Excellence Tchg. Music award 2002), Am. String Teachers Assn., Music Educators Nat. Conf. D-Liberal. Greek Orthodox. Achievements include two tours to Europe with music students. Avocations: biking, biking, biking, traveling, learning and performing multicultural music and instruments. Home: 4905 E Robin Lane Phoenix AZ 85054 Office: Peracta Elementary School 7125 West Encanto Phoenix AZ 85033

THOMAS, JIMMY LYNN, financial executive; b. Mayfield, Ky., Aug. 3, 1941; s. Alben Stanley and Emma Laura (Alexander) T.; m. Kristin H. Kent, Oct. 1986; children: James Nelson, Carter Danforth. BS, U. Ky., 1963; MBA, Columbia U., 1964. Fin. analyst Ford Motor Co., Detroit, 1964-66; asst. treas. Joel Dean Assocs., N.Y.C., 1966-67; asst. contr. Trans World Airlines, 1967-73; sr. v.p. fin. svcs., treas. Gannett Co., Inc., Arlington, Va., 1973-98. Bd. dirs. HSBC, Rochester, Tremont Ptnrs. Fundraiser United Negro Coll. Fund; bd. trustees, treas. Harley Sch., Rochester, N.Y.; bd. overseers Strong Meml. Hosp., Rochester; bd. govs. Genesee Hosp., Rochester; bd. dirs. Arlington Cmty. Found., Nat. Press Club Bldg., Washington. With U.S. Army, 1966-72. Ashland Oil Co. scholar, 1959-63, McKinsey scholar 1964; Samuel Bronfman fellow, 1963-64. Mem. Nat. Assn. Corp. Treas., U. Ky. Alumni Assn., Columbia U. Alumni Assn., Country Club of Rochester, Genessee Valley Club, Beta Gamma Sigma, Omicron Delta Kappa, Sigma Alpha Epsilon. Democrat. Mem. Christian Ch. (Disciples Of Christ). Home: 205 Fox Meadow Ln Orchard Park NY 14127-2883

THOMAS, JO, journalist; b. Long Beach, Calif., Dec. 7, 1943; d. Guy O'Neil DeYoung, Jr. and Josephine (Bradley) DeYoung; m. William L. Thomas III, June 12, 1965 (div. Sept. 1969); m. William F. Kelleher Jr., Dec. 19, 1985; children: Susan Elizabeth Kelleher, Kathleen DeYoung Kelleher. BA summa cum laude, Wake Forest U., 1965; MA, U. N.C., 1967. Reporter Cin. Post and Times-Star, 1966-70, Detroit Free Press, 1971-77; Washington corr. N.Y. Times, 1977-79, Miami bur. chief, 1979-81, asst. nat. editor, 1981-84, London corr., 1984-86, nat. corr., 1994-2001, writer, 2001—; assoc. prof. U. Ill., Urbana, 1987-94. Contbr. articles to newspapers and mags. Recipient Outstanding Reporting award Detroit Press Club, 1974-75, Robert F. Kennedy award, 1973; Nieman fellow Harvard U., 1970-71. Mem. Phi Beta Kappa, Kappa Tau Alpha. Office: NY Times-Nat 229 W 43d St New York NY 10036 E-mail: jothomas@nytimes.com.

THOMAS, JOAB LANGSTON, retired university president, biology educator; b. Holt, Ala., Feb. 14, 1933; s. Ralph Cage and Chamintney Elizabeth (Stovall) Thomas; m. Marly A. Dukes, Dec. 22, 1954; children: Catherine, David, Jennifer, Frances. AB, Harvard U., 1955, MA, 1957, PhD, 1959; DSc (hon.) , U. Ala., 1981; LLD (hon.) , Stillman Coll., 1987; LHD (hon.) , Tri-State U., 1994; LHD (hon.) , N.C. State U., 1998. Cytotaxonomist Arnold Aboretum, Harvard, 1959—61; prof. biology U. Ala., University, 1966—76, 1988—91, asst. dean Coll. Arts and Scis., 1964—65, 1969, dean for student devel., 1969—74, v.p., 1974—76, dir. Herbarium, 1961—76, dir. Arboretum, 1964—69, pres. Tuscaloosa, 1981—88; chancellor N.C. State U., Raleigh, 1976—81; pres. Pa. State U., University Park, 1990—95, pres. emeritus, 1995. Bd. dirs. Mellon Corp.; intern acad. adminstrn. Am. Coun. on Edn., 1971. Author: A Monographic Study of the Cyrillaceae, 1960, Wildflowers of Alabama and Adjoining States, 1973, The Rising South, 1976, Poisonous Plants and Venomous Animals of Alabama and Adjoining States, 1990. Bd. dirs. Internat. Potato Ctr., 1977—83, chmn., 1982—83; bd. dirs. Internat. Svc. for Nat. Agrl. Rsch., 1985—91. Named Citizen of Yr., City of Tuscaloosa, 1987; recipient Ala. Acad. Honor, 1983, Palmer Mus. Art medal, Coll. Pres.'s award, All-Am. Football Found., 1997, Spl. Recognition award, Assn. for Continuing Higher Edn., 1998. Mem.: Golden Key, Phi Kappa Phi, Omicron Delta Kappa (Laurel Crowned Circle award 2001), Sigma Xi, Phi Beta Kappa. Office: Univ Ala 413 Sci Collections Bldg Tuscaloosa AL 35487-0001 E-mail: jlthomas@dbtech.net.

THOMAS, JOE CARROLL, retired human resources director; b. Belmont, N.C., Nov. 2, 1931; m. Ruth Stone, June 17, 1951; children: Joe (dec.), Jerry, Angela. BA, Belmont Abbey Coll., 1954; MS, Cornell U., 1961; student Exec. Program, U. N.C. Diplomate in profl. counseling. Mgr. terr. sales Gen. Foods Corp., San Antonio, 1954-62; asst. dir. personnel textiles divsn. Kendall Co., Charlotte, N.C., 1962-64; dir. personnel S.E. region Gifford Hill & Co., 1964-71; dir. mgmt. svcs. Ervin Industries, 1971-75; v.p. indsl. rels. Crompton & Knowles, 1975-76; exec. v.p., dir. human resources Barclays Group Inc. (USA), 1976-97; ret., 1997. Mem. adv. coun. Sch. Bus., Western Carolina U., Cullowhee, N.C., 1980-84; mem. bd. arbitrators NASD Dispute Resolution, Inc., 2001. Vice chmn. bd. trustees Belmont Abbey Coll., 1982-88; chmn. fundraising campaign Charlotte chpt. Am. Heart Assn., 1984; mem. bd. visitors mercy Hosp., Charlotte, 1984-87; bd. dirs. mercy Health Svcs., Charlotte, 1988-96; bd. dirs. Jr. Achievement Charlotte, 1985-88; chmn. bd. dirs. INROADS divsn. Charlotte, Inc., 1987-88; bd. visitors Johnson C. Smith Univ., 1989-92. Mem. Soc. Human Resource Mgmt., Employers Assn. (bd. dirs. 1993-99, exec. com. 1995-99), Charlotte Athletic Club (pres. 1982-83), Charlotte Rotary, Charlotte C. of C. (bd. advisors 1992-97). Republican.

THOMAS, JOHN, mechanical engineer, research and development; b. Tiruvalla, Kerala, India, Jan. 2, 1946; came to U.S., 1974; s. Munnencheril Varghese and Rachel (Mathai) T.; m. Mary Parapat Varghese, Apr. 28, 1975; children: Joel George, Sayana Rachel. BSc in Mech. Engring., Birla Inst. Tech., Ranchi, India, 1969; MA Sc in Mech. Engring., U. Waterloo, Ont., Can., 1974. Registered profl. engr., Wis. Lectr. mech. engring. U. Kerala, India, 1970-71; design engr. Combustion Engring., Inc., Springfield, Ohio, 1974-76; mech. engr. Ingersoll-Rand Co., Painted Post, N.Y., 1977-80; engr. Allis-Chalmers Corp., Milw., 1980-82; pvt. practice engring. cons., 1982-84; sr. tech. devel. engr. Cross & Trecker divsn. Kearney & Trecker Corp., 1984-87; prin. John Thomas & Assocs., Brookfield, Wis., 1988-90; sr. product engr. N.W. Water Group, Pub. Ltd. Corp., Waukesha, 1989-94; pres. Thomas Products Co., Brookfield, 1995—; staff engr. Milsco Mfg. Co. unit of Jason Inc., Milw., 1997—. Patentee in field. Mem. Am. Soc. Mech. Engrs., U. Waterloo Alumni Assn. Mem. Mar Thoma Syrian Ch. of Malabar. Avocation: photography. Home: 18330 Benington Brookfield WI 53045-5419 Office: Thomas Products Co PO Box 401 Brookfield WI 53008-0401

THOMAS, JOHN ARLEN, pharmacology educator, health science administrator; b. LaCrosse, Wis., Apr. 6, 1933; s. John M. and Eva Hazel (Nelson) T.; m. Barbara A. Fisler, June 22, 1957; children: Michael J., Jane L. BS in Sci. Edn., U. Wis., 1956; MA in Physiology, U. Iowa, 1958, PhD in Physiology, 1961. Diplomate Am. Acad. Toxicologic Sci. Instr. U. Iowa, Iowa City, 1961; asst. prof. U. Va., Charlottesville, 1961-64; assoc. prof. Creighton U., Omaha, 1964-67, W.Va. U., Morgantown, 1968-69, prof. pharmacology, 1970-80; asst. dean W.Va. Sch. Medicine, 1973-75, assoc. dean, 1973-80; v.p. corp. rsch. Baxter Internat. Travenol Labs., Round Lake, Ill., 1980-87; v.p. acad. svcs. U. Tex. Health Sci. Ctr., San Antonio, 1988-99, prof. emeritus pharmacology dept. toxicology, 1988—. Cons. NIH, Bethesda, Md., 1975, Nat. Libr. Medicine, Bethesda, 1994; bd. dirs. ILSI, Washington, NAS Com., Wash., 1998-, Tex. Soc. Biomed. Rsch., Austin, v.p., 1996; chmn. expert adv. com. Can. Network Toxicol. Ctr., 1999-2002. Author (with M.G. Mawhinney): Synopsis of Endocrine Pharmacology, 1978; author: (with E.J. Keenan) Principles of Endocrine Pharmacology, 1986; editor (with others): Basic and Clinical Toxicology of Lead, 1985; editor: Endocrine Toxicology, 1985, 1996, Drugs Athletes & Physical Performance, 1988, Biotechnicology and Safety Assessment, 1993; editor: (with Roy L. Fuchs) Biotechnicology and Safety Assessment, 3d edit., 2002; editor: Endocrine Methods, 1996, Toxic Substances Mechanism Jour.; contbr. articles to profl. jours. Sgt. U.S. Army, 1951-53. Recipient Cert. Svc. U.S. EPA, 1977; named Outstanding Tchr., W.Va. U., 1971, Outstanding alumnus U. Wis.-La Crosse, 1978, Disting. Alumni, U. Iowa, 1997. Fellow Acad. Toxicol. Sci. (pres. 2001); mem. Endocrine Soc., Soc. Toxicology (councilor, Merit award 1998), Am. soc. Pharmacology and Exptl. Therapeutics, Am. Coll. Toxicology (councilor, pres., Disting. Svc. award), Teratology Soc., Am. Acad. Vet. Pharmacology, Am. Chem. Soc. (pres. chem. toxicology pathology), Tex. Soc. Biomed. Rsch. (bd. sci. advisors 1989-99, Disting. Svc. award 1996, Hall of Excellence 2002). Home: 219 Wood Shadow St San Antonio TX 78216-1633 E-mail: jat-tox@swbell.net.

THOMAS, JOHN CHARLES, lawyer, former state supreme court justice; b. Norfolk, Va., Sept. 18, 1950; s. John and Floretta V. (Sears) T.; m. Pearl Walden, Oct. 9, 1982; children: John Charles Jr., Ruby Virginia, Lewis LeGrant. BA in Am. Govt. with distinction, U. Va., 1972, JD, 1975. Bar: Va. 1975, U.S. Dist. Ct. (ea. and we. dists.) 1976, U.S. Ct. Appeals (4th cir.) 1976, U.S. Supreme Ct. 1979, U.S. Ct. Appeals (D.C. cir.) 1980, U.S. Ct. Appeals (10th cir.) 1991, U.S. Ct. Appeals (11th cir.) 1992. Assoc. Hunton & Williams, Richmond, Va., 1975-82, ptnr., 1982-83, 89—; justice Supreme Ct. of Va., 1983-89. Former mem. adv. con. on appellate rules U.S. Jud. Conf., permanent mem. 4th cir. Hon. dir. U. Va. Law Sch. Found. Master John Marshall Inn of Ct. (exec. com.); fellow Am. Bar Found., Va. Bar Found.; mem. ABA (former co-chair nat. conf. of lawyers and reps. of media, mem. coun. appellate lawyers), Am. Arbitration Assn. (bd. dirs., exec. com.), Am. Acad. Appellate Lawyers, Va. State Bar, Va. Bar Assn., Bar Assn. City of Richmond, Old Dominion Bar Assn., Omega Psi Phi, Sigma Pi Phi. Office: Hunton & Williams Riverfront Plz East Tower PO Box 1535 Richmond VA 23218-1535

THOMAS, JOHN DAVID, musician, composer, arranger, graphic designer, recording engineer, producer; b. Muncie, Ind., Mar. 30, 1951; s. John Charles and Phyllis Lorraine (Wear) T.; m. Rosalie Faith Baldwin, July 27, 1974 (div. 1991); children: Bethany Carol, Mark David. Student, Purdue U., 1969-71, Jordan Coll. of Music, Indpls., 1961-65; BS in Music Theory and Composition, Ball State U., 1976. Musician, composer, 1955—; cellist The Howe String Quartet (with Ann Pinney, Mary Ann Tilford, Anne Wuster), Indpls., 1967-68; keyboardist, vocalist, cellist Fire and The Rebel Kind rock bands, 1967-69, Good Conduct rock band, Muncie, 1972-73; pianist The Pavillion at Olde Towne, Los Gatos, Calif., 1969; radio announcer John David's Late Night Rock Show WCCR-AM, West Lafayette, Ind., 1969-70; photographer Indpls., 1964—84, 1991—2000; budget analyst Office of Comptr. USAFAC, 1976-84; co-leader, keyboardist, composer, arranger, vocalist, sound technician Jetstream band, Carmel, Indpls., Kokomo, Columbus, Bloomington, 1979-83; co-leader, keyboardist, vocalist, sound technician The Thomas Bros., King's Crown Inn, Kokomo, 1979; sound/audio visual technician Valley Cathedral Ch., Phoenix, 1987. Pianist, synthesist Paul Thomas and Night and Day, The Tim Barnett Band, Indpls. Mus. Art, 1992, Radisson Hotel and Broadmoor Country Club, Indpls., 1991, Highland Country Club, Indpls., The Ritz Charles Hotel and Summertrace, Carmel, Ind., Stonehenge Resort, Bedford, Ind., 1991; solo pianist Terranova Mansion, Paradise Valley, Ariz., 1987, Wrigley Mansion, Phoenix, 1988, Boulders Resort, Carefree, Ariz., 1987, Clarion Inn/McCormick's Ranch Resort, Scottsdale, Ariz., 1986, China Gate, Phoenix, 1988, Victor's, Phoenix, 1988, Cascade Club, Everett, Wash., 1990; keyboardist, synthesist, key bassist, The Gulch Gang, Pinnacle Peak Patio, Scottsdale, 1984, Dee Dee Ryan, The Longhorn Saloon, Apache Junction, Ariz., 1984-86, The Last Straw Band, Country City saloon, Mesa, Ariz., 1986; keyboardist, pianist, vocalist with Peter, Paul and John, Anderson (Ind.) Coll., 1977; CEO, owner, composer, arranger, prodr., musician, engr., graphic designer, computer operator, John David Thomas Prodns., Indpls., 1993—; CEO, owner JD Thomas Music Co., 1999—, Monolith Records, 1999-2001, JDT Records, 2001—; rec. artist CD label mp3.com., 2000—, CD label besonic.com (Europe), 2002-, JDT Records, 2001-. Composer, lyricist of over 150 classical, religious, comml., rock, jazz, popular and avante garde/futuristic compositions, including Infinity, 1970-71, Death of Rock and Roll, 1970, Night Visions, 1972, First Things First, 1972, Two Nudes and a Fire Hydrant, 1972-73, Zeitgeist: The Spirit of the Time, 1974, The Little Prince, 1973, When We Dead Awaken, 1973, Pray, 1972, Apogee, 1974, Chinese Baby, 1973, Alabama DA (Top Forty recording), 1973, Angel, 1974, Music for French Horn, Cello, and Piano, 1976, Cruising Beyond, 1979, Jetstream Theme, 1979, Chrissy, 1979, Love Theme in B Minor, 1979, In Your Heart, 1983, Future Music, 1987, The Recurrent New Millenium Orchestral Olympic Disco Festival Dance, 1989, Jubilee in F, 1989, Praise Him, The King Liveth, 1989, Love Flowers: Reflections and Meditations on Beauty and Truth, 1990, Sheena's Theme, 1992, I Want You Forever You're My Miracle, 1992, My Pseudo-Erotic, Sensual, Exotic Musical Fantasy and Romance for Our Heavenly Nocturnal Starry-Skied Carpet Ride to Paradise in Istanbul and Constantinople, 1992, I'm in Love with Someone Beautiful, 1992, Improvisations for Sheena, 1992, Music for Baritone Vocal and String Orch., 1995, Meditations for Pipe Organ and Male Choir, 1996, Trumpet Voluntary in F, 1996, Pathway to Love, 1996, Majestic Brass Music in F#, 1997, J.D.'s Theme, 1998, Love Theme in D, 1972, 98, The Road to Tomorrow, 1999, 32 short compositions, 2000-2001, Let Me Be the One, 2000, God and the Everlasting, 2000, Sunshine, 2000, Love Theme, 2000, Dreaming, 2000, Together, 2000, Love You, 2000, The Road of Life, 2000, Desires of the Heart, 2000, The Open Sky, 2000, Just Me and You, 2000, In the Spirit of Mozart, 2001, From Me to You, 2001, 23 new piano compositions, 2002; (albums) The Journey of Life, Destiny's Calling: Improvisations, 1994, 2002, Musical Essences, 1995, 2002, (cd's) From Me to You, 2002, Desires of the Heart, 2002, Spirit Music, 2002, The Seen and the Unseen, 2000, Potpourri: Music for the World, 2000, Music for the World, vol. 2, 2000, (broadcast) Hometown Hour, Sta. WFBQ-FM, Indpls., 1979-80; performed orginal composition, Someday, WFBM-TV, Indpls., 1969; designer automotive concepts and popular fashions; recordings of over 90 original songs and compositions, Ind., Ariz., Wash., 1970— including Love Theme in D, 1972, 98, Majestic Brass Music in F# for Bethany and Mark, 1997, J.D.'s Theme, 1998; also 59 recordings on CD's, 2001-02; author (poetry with others) Mind, 1993, 96, Poetry.com, 2001. Musician, vocalist, composer Downey Ave. Christian Ch., Indpls., 1961-69, Univ. Presbyn. Ch., West Lafayette, Ind., 1969-71, Castleview Bapt. Ch., Indpls., 1974-84, Valley Cathedral Ch., Phoenix, 1986-87, Edmonds (Wash.) Christian Ch., 1988-90, Edmonds United Meth. Ch., 1989-90; page to speaker Ho. of Reps. Ind. State Legislature, 1963; active All Souls Unitarian Ch., Indpls., 1994-96. GM scholar Purdue U., 1969-70, Hoosier scholar, 1969, Palmer Meml. Music scholar Ball State U., 1971-74; named to Ind. All-State Orch. (cellist), 1968; recipient 1st place award (cellist) Ind. State Music Contest, 1968, God and Country award, 1965, Outstanding Musician award Irvington Music Club, Indpls., 1969, Purdue U. Symphonette, 1970, Hometown Hour award WFBQ-FM Radio Sta., Indpls., 1979. Mem. ASCAP, NARAS, Audio Engring. Soc., Mensa. Avocations: reading, computers, listening to music, dining, photography. Home and Office: 2704 Central Ct Indianapolis IN 46280-1930 Home: PO Box 3593 Carmel IN 46082 Office Fax: 317-574-0580. E-mail: composer@searchking.com., jdtp@searchking.com.

THOMAS, JOHN HOWARD, astrophysicist, engineer, educator; b. Chgo., Apr. 9, 1941; s. William Whitney and Dorothy Loretta (Derris) T.; m. Lois Ruth Moffit, Aug. 11, 1962; children: Jeffrey, Laura. BS in Engring. Sci., Purdue U., 1962, MS in Engring. Sci., 1964, PhD in Engring. Sci., 1966. Lic. profl. engr., N.Y. NATO postdoctoral fellow U. Cambridge, Eng., 1966-67; asst. prof. mech. and aerospace sci. U. Rochester, 1967-73, assoc. prof., 1973-81, prof., 1981—, prof. astronomy, 1986—, assoc. dean for grad. studies Coll. Engring. and Applied Sci., 1981-83, univ. dean grad. studies, 1983-91. Vis. astronomer Nat. Solar Obs., Sunspot, N.Mex., 1971; vis. scientist Max-Planck Inst. for Physics and Astrophysics, Munich, 1973-74, High Altitude Obs., Boulder, Colo., 1985; vis. fellow Worcester Coll, vis. prof. dept. theoretical physics Oxford (Eng.) U., 1987-88; affiliate scientist Nat. Ctr. for Atmospheric Rsch., Boulder, 1989—; vis. prof. Rsch. Ctr. for Theoretical Astrophysics, U. Sydney, Australia, 1991, Sch. Math. and Stats., 1993; vis. fellow Clare Hall; vis. prof. dept. applied math. and theoretical physics U. Cambridge (Eng.), 2002; prin. investigator NASA, NSF, USAF, Office Naval Rsch. Editor: Physics of Sunspots, 1981, Sunspots: Theory and Observations, 1992; assoc. editor Astrophys. Jour., 1993-96, sci. editor, 1996—; author articles on astrophysics, solar physics and fluid dynamics. NSF fellow, 1963-66; Guggenheim fellow, 1993-94. Fellow Am. Phys. Soc.; mem. AAAS, Am. Astron. Soc. (chair solar physics divsn. 1995-97), Internat. Astron. Union, Am. Geophys. Union, Royal Astron. Soc. (UK), Sigma Xi, Tau Beta Pi, Sigma Delta Chi. Office: U Rochester 223 Hopeman Bldg Rochester NY 14627

THOMAS, JOHN MELVIN, retired surgeon; b. Carmarthen, U.K., Apr. 26, 1933; came to U.S., 1958; s. Morgan and Margaret (Morgan) T.; m. Betty Ann Mayo, Nov. 3, 1958; children: James, Hugh, Pamela. MB, BChir, U. Coll. Wales, U. Edinburgh, 1958. Intern Robert Packer Hosp., Sayre, Pa., 1958-59, chief surg. resident, 1963, pres. med. staff, 1968; assoc. surgeon Guthrie Clinic Ltd., 1963-69, chmn. dept. surgery, 1969-91; vice chmn. Guthrie Healthcare System, 1995—. Pres. bd. dirs. Guthrie Clinic Ltd., 1972-89; pres. bd. dirs. Donald Guthrie Found., 1983-95; chmn. Chemung Springwater Co.; trustee

Robert Packer Hosp.; chmn. exec. com. Guthrie Healthcare Sys., 1990-92, dir., 1994—; guest examiner Am. Bd. Surgery, 1979, 81, 85; bd. dirs. Measurement Innovations Corp., Citizen Fin. Bank, Mansfield, Pa., Trianalytics Corp.; cons. The Hunter Group, 1993-96. Bd. dirs. Donald Guthrie Found. for Rsch., pres., 1983-94; bd. dirs. Pa. Trauma Sys. Found., 1984-90, pres., 1988, 89; chmn. licensure and accountability Gov.'s Conf., 1974; bd. dirs. Vol. Hosps. Am., 1993-95; trustee Mansfield (Pa.) U. Found., 1991—; trustee Mansfield Univ. Found., 1991-95. Fellow ACS (gov. 1985-91); mem. AMA, Am. Group Practice Assn., Soc. for Surgery Alimentary Tract, Pa. Med. Soc., Bradford County Med. Soc., Cen. N.Y. Surg. Soc., Internat. Soc. Surgery, Soc. Surgery Alimentary Tract, Ea. Vascular Soc., Ithaca Country Club, Moselem Springs Golf Club, Ft. Lauderdale Country Club. Presbyterian. Home: L'Hermitage I Apt 908 3100 N Ocean Blvd Fort Lauderdale FL 33308 E-mail: jthoma8422@aol.com.

THOMAS, JOHN THIEME, management consultant; b. Detroit, Aug. 21, 1935; s. John Shepherd and Florence Leona (Thieme) T.; m. Ellen Linden Taylor, June 27, 1959; children: Johnson Taylor, Evan Thurston. BBA, U. Mich., 1957, MBA, 1958. Mfg. dept. mgr. Procter & Gamble Co., Cin., 1958-60, brand mgr., 1960-63; sr. cons. Glendinning Cos. Inc., Westport, Conn., 1964-66, v.p. London, 1967-69, exec. v.p. Westport, 1970-74, also bd. dirs.; exec. v.p., chief operating officer Ero Industries, Chgo., 1974-76; v.p. Lamalie Assocs. Inc., 1977-81; pres. Wilkins & Thomas Inc., 1981-87; ptnr. Ward Howell Internat., 1987—, mng. dir., cons. practice, 1992-98, chief of staff, 1995-98; also bd. dirs.; cons. ret. LAI Ward Howell, Chgo., 1999—, El Jefe, Thomas Ent. Inc., 1999. Exec. dir. Proctor & Gamble Alumni Assn., Chgo., 1981—. Pub. Procter & Gamble Mfg. Alumni directory, 1981—; author articles in profl. jours. Chmn. bd. dirs. Winnetka (Ill.) Youth Orgn., 1986—; bd. dirs. No. Ill. Girl Scouts Coun., 2002—; selector Winnetka Town Coun., 1978, 1980, 1984, Winnetka Caucus Exec. Com., 1997—2001. Mem. Nat. Assn. Corp. & Profl. Recruiters, Assn. Exec. Search Cons., Am. Soc. Pers. Adminstrn. Clubs: Fairfield (Conn.) Hunt (treas. 1971-74). Avocations: gardening, music, playing tuba. Home and Office: 525 Ash St Winnetka IL 60093-2601 E-mail: enjthomas@aol.com.

THOMAS, JOSEPH ERUMAPPETTICAL, psychologist; b. Piravom, Kerala, India, Feb. 11, 1937; came to U.S., 1971; s. Iype Erumappettiyil and Kunjamma M. (Padiyil) T.; m. Chinnamma Kavatt, Nov. 23, 1964; children: Joseph Jr., Kurian, Elizabeth. BA, Kerala U., India, 1957, MA, 1960, PhD, 1969. Diplomate Internat. Acad. Behavioral Medicine, Counseling, and Psychotherapy; lic. psychologist; bd. cert. neurotherapist. Lectr. psychology U. Kerala, Trivandrum, India, 1967-70; postdoctoral fellow in psychology Northwestern U. Med. Sch., Chgo., 1971-72; psychologist U. Chgo., 1972-74; instr. psychiatry Northwestern U. Med. Sch., Chgo., 1972-76, asst. prof. dept. psychiatry, 1977-97; psychologist Northwestern Meml. Hosp., 1974-80; pvt. practice psychology, 1980—. Cons. Michael Reese Hosp., Chgo., 1980-86; founding mem. Inst. Psychiatry, Northwestern U., Chgo.; coord. psycho-oncology program Inst. Integrative Cancer Ctr., Evanston, 1995—. Contbr. articles to profl. jours. Mem. Dupage County Health Planning Com., Wheaton, Ill., 1984; founding mem., trustee St. Thomas Ch. Chgo., St. Gregorios Orthodox Ch., Oak Park, Ill. Commonwealth fellow Govt. U.K., U. Glasgow, 1970; sr. fellow Biofeedback Certification Inst. Am. Mem. Am. Psychological Assn., Mental Health Assn. DuPage County (bd. dirs. 1982-84), Biofeedback Soc. Ill. (pres. 1984-85). Home: 16w731 89th Pl Burr Ridge IL 60527-6087 Office: Sallas Ctr 401 N Michigan Ave Ste 818 Chicago IL 60611-4277

THOMAS, JOSEPH FLESHMAN, retired architect; b. Oak Hill, W.Va., Mar. 23, 1915; s. Robert Russel and Effie (Fleshman) T.; m. Margaret Ruth Lively, Feb. 28, 1939 (dec.); children: Anita Carol, Joseph Stephen; m. Dorothy Francene Root, Apr. 29, 1967 (div.); m. Bonnie Abbott Buckley, June 15, 1991 (dec.). Student, Duke, 1931-32; B.Arch., Carnegie-Mellon U., 1938. Practice architecture various firms, W. Va., Va., Tenn., Calif., 1938-49; staff architect Calif. Div. Architecture, Los Angeles, 1949-52; prin. Joseph F. Thomas, architect, Pasadena, Calif., 1952-53; pres. Neptune & Thomas (architects-engrs.), Pasadena and San Diego, 1953-78. Mem. Pasadena Planning Commn., 1956-64, chmn., 1963-64; pres. Citizens Coun. for Planning, Pasadena, 1966-67; mem. steering com. Pasadena NOW, 1970-74; mem. Pasadena Design Com., 1979-86; mem. adv. bd. Calif. Office Architecture and Constrn., 1970-72; mem. archtl. adv. com. Calif. State U. System, 1981-84; mem. adv. coun. Sch. Environ. Design Calif. Poly. Inst., 1983-2002; mem. outreach for architecture com. Carnegie Mellon U., 1989-95, pres.'s devel. com., 1991-95. Prin. works include Meth. Hosp., Arcadia, Calif., Foothill Presbyn. Hosp., Glendora, Calif., master plans and bldgs., Citrus Coll., Azusa, Calif., Riverside (Calif.) Coll., Westmont Coll., Monticeto, Calif., Northrop Inst. Tech., Inglewood, Calif, Indian Valley Coll., Marin County, Calif., Pepperdine U., Malibu, Calif., UCLA, U. Calif., San Diego, Long Beach (Calif.) State U., Calif. Inst. Tech., Pasadena, Calif., other coll. bldgs. Pacific Telephone Co., Pasadena, L.A. County Superior Ct. Bldg., U.S. Naval Hosp., San Diego. Trustee Almansor Edn. Ctr., 1986-92; bd. dirs., co-founder Syncor Internat., 1973-83; founding dir. Bank of Pasadena, 1962-65. Lt. (j.g.) USNR, 1943-46. Recipient Service award City of Pasadena, 1964; Disting. Service award Calif. Dept. Gen. Services, 1972; Gold Crown award Pasadena Arts Council, 1981 Fellow AIA (4 awards honor, 13 awards merit 1957-78, dir. Calif. coun. 1966-68, exec. com. 1974-77, pres. Pasadena chpt. 1967, chmn. Calif. sch. facilities com. 1970-72, mem. nat. jud. bd. 1973-74, nat. dir. 1974-77, treas. 1977-79, exec. com., planning com., chmn. finance com.); mem. Breakfast Forum (chmn. 1983), Annandale Golf Club, Pi Kappa Alpha. Republican. Methodist. Home: 330 San Miguel Rd Pasadena CA 91105-1446

THOMAS, JOSEPH WINAND, lawyer; b. New Orleans, Aug. 2, 1940; s. Gerald Henry and Edith Louise (Winand) T.; m. Claudette Condoll, Aug. 2, 1960 (div. Nov. 1985); children: Jeffery J., Anthony W.; m. Shawn B. Watkins, May 26, 1986 (div. June 1989); children: Adelle, Anne; m. Sandra J. Green, May 17, 1992; children: Winand, Elizabeth, Alice, Shepard, Julia. BS, Loyola U., Chgo., 1967; JD, Loyola U., New Orleans, 1973; MBA, Tulane U., 1984. Bar: La. 1973, U.S. Dist. Ct. (ea. dist.) La. 1973, U.S. Ct. Appeals (5th cir.) 1973, U.S. Supreme Ct. 1976, D.C. 1980. Staff atty. New Orleans Legal Assistance Corp., 1973-74; asst. atty. gen. State of La., 1974-80; pvt. practice New Orleans, 1980—. Pres., bd. dirs. New Orleans Legal Assistance Corp. Active NAACP, New Orleans, 1987-89; bd. dirs. Urban League, New Orleans. Mem. ABA, Louis Martinet Legal Soc., New Orleans Bar Assn., La. Bar Assn. Democrat. Roman Catholic. Office: 2 Canal St New Orleans LA 70130-1408 E-mail: jthomas@jwtlaw.com.

THOMAS, JUDITH BRANCH, music educator; b. Biltmore, N.C., Aug. 16, 1941; d. Herbert Leon and Hazle (Boyle) Branch; m. James Donald Thomas, May 16, 1964; children: Elizabeth Suzanne Thomas Woolwine, Blake Fleming Thomas. BS in Music, High Point U., 1963. Cert. tchr., Va. 8th grade tchr. Franklin County Pub. Schs., Rocky Mountain, Va., 1963-64; 3d grade tchr. Henry County Pub. Schs., Collinsville, 1964-66, 4th grade tchr., 1967-71, music specialist, 1972-97, ret., 1997. Mem. NEA, Va. Edn. Assn., Henry County Edn. Assn., Fairystone Squares. Methodist. Avocations: reading, square dancing. Home: 231 William St Collinsville VA 24078-2291

THOMAS, JUDY JANET, reporter, health services professional; b. Detroit, Feb. 28, 1964; d. J.W. and Geneva Anna Thomas; children: Robert A., Arrelle R. BA, U. of D Mercy, Detroit, MI; Associates, Wayne County Coll., Detroit, MI. Job developer U. D Mercy, Detroit, 1999—2000; mgr. Alstate Glass Co., 2000; reporter Metroplex Newspaper, 2002—; cmty. svc. Doctors Ho. Svc., 2002—. Dir. Sr. Consortium Orgn., Detroit. Mem. NWACP, Detroit, 2001—01. Liberal. Avocations: reading, writing, banking, banking. Home: 19144 Robson Detroit MI 48235 Office: Doctors House Call Service 17117 W 9 Mile Road Southfield MI

THOMAS, KAREN P. composer, conductor; b. Seattle, Sept. 17, 1957; BA in Composition, Cornish Inst., 1979; MusM in Composition and Conducting, U. Wash., 1985. Condr. The Contemporary Group, 1981-85; condr., music dir. Wash. Composers Forum, 1984-86; artistic dir., condr. Seattle Pro Musica, 1987—. Conducting debut Seattle, 1987; composer: Four Delineations of Curtmantle for Trombone or Cello, 1982, Metamorphoses on a Machaut Kyrie for Strong Orch. or Quartet, 1983, Cowboy Songs for Voice and Piano, 1985, There Must Be a Lone Range for Soprano and Chamber Ensemble, 1987, Brass Quintet, 1987, Four Lewis Carroll Songs for Choir, 1989, (music/dance/theater) Boxiana, 1990, Elementi for Clarinet and Percussion, 1991, (one-act children's opera) Coyote's Tail, 1991, Clarion Dances for Brass Ensemble, 1993, Roundup for Sax Quartet, 1993, Three Medieval Lyrics for Choir, 1992, Sopravvento for Wind Quartet and Percussion, 1994, When Night Came for Clarinet and Chamber Orch. or Clarinet and Piano, 1994, Over the City for Choir, 1995, also numerous others. Recipient Composers Forum award N.W. Chamber Orch., 1984, King County Arts Commn., 1987, 90, Artist Trust, 1988, 93, 96, Seattle Arts Commn., 1988, 91, 93, New Langton Arts, 1988, Delius Festival, 1993, Melodious Accord award 1993; fellow Wash. State Arts Commn., 1991; Charles E. Ives scholar AAAI. Mem. Am. Choral Dirs. Assn., Broadcast Music, Am. Music Ctr., Internat. Alliance for Women in Music, Soc. Composers, Chorus Am., Conductors Guild. Office: 4426 1st Ave NW Seattle WA 98107-4306 E-mail: kpthomas1@aol.com.

THOMAS, KARIN RONNEFELDT, interior designer; b. Frankfurt, Fed. Republic Germany, Aug. 23, 1930; d. Adolf Friedrich and Mary Eugenie (von Pistohlkors) R.; m. Charles Davis Thomas, Apr. 20, 1956; 1 child, Cord Alexander. Student, Frankfurt U., 1951-52; diploma, Ecole Guerre-Lavigne, Paris, 1954; postgrad., Parsons Sch. Design, 1974-75. Designer Sonia Gowns, N.Y.C., 1955-57, Jewel Calif., Los Angeles, 1958-59, Marusia, Beverly Hills, Calif., 1959-61, N.Y.C., 1962-66; pvt. practice graphic design Geneva, 1967-68; pvt. practice design N.Y.C., 1969-77; prin. Karin Thomas Interior Design, Camden, Maine, 1979—. Co-editor, designer: Moon: Man's Greatest Adventure, 1970, People of the First Man, 1976. Trustee Maine Coast Artists, 1979—, v.p. 1985-86, pres. 1989-96; trustee Ctr. for Furniture Craftsmanship, Rockport, Maine, 1997—. Mem. Camden Yacht Club, Megunticook Country Club (Rockport, Maine). Office: 57 Megunticook St Camden ME 04843-1643

THOMAS, KATHERINE JANE, magazine and newspaper columnist; b. Bryan, Tex., Mar. 22, 1942; d. William Holt Jr. and Mary Anne (McCasland) Oliver; m. Robert Wayne Thomas, June 1, 1968; children: Jennifer Ann, Michael Frederick. BA, U. Tex., 1964. News reporter Abilene Reporter, Tex., 1964-67; with Ralston Purina Co., 1967-68; journalist The Eagle, Bryan, Tex., 1969-72, Wall St. Jour., Houston Bus. Jour., 1976-80; bus. columnist Houston Post, 1980-95. Sr. bus. columnist; features editor Hart's Energy Markets; electric power editor Oil & Gas Jour. Online. Judge Houston Area Inc. Mag. Entrepreneur of Yr., 1995; vol. judge out-of-state journalism competitions. Recipient Writing awards Tex. Press Assn., 1978-79, AP, 1966, 88, 91, Dallas Press Club Katie Finalist, 1990, 94, Matrix, 1989-90, Press Club of Houston, 1987, 89, 90, 91, 95, 96, Sierra Club of Houston, 1989, St. Louis United Fund, 1968, Abilene C. of C., 1965. Mem. Press Club of Houston (bd. dirs., sec. 1991), Press Club of Houston Ednl. Found. (treas. 1991, bd. dirs.). Episcopalian. Avocations: sailing, entertaining, walking, reading. Office: 1700 West Loop S Ste 1000 Houston TX 77027-3007 E-mail: katet@ogjonline.com.

THOMAS, KEITH VERN, bank executive; b. Provo, Utah, Oct. 21, 1946; s. Vern R. and Lois (Doran) T.; m. Sherrie Hunter, Oct. 7, 1969; children: Genevieve, Joshua, Rachel, William, Rebecca. AA, Dixie Coll., 1969; BS, Brigham Young U., 1971; MBA, St. Mary's Coll., 1980. From examiner to asst. dir. Fed. Home Loan Bank Bd., San Francisco, 1971-85; sr. v.p., dir. exams. and supervision Fed. Home Loan Bank, Seattle, 1985-88; exec. v.p., COO Frontier Savings Assn., Las Vegas, Nev., 1988-89, pres., CEO, dir., 1989-90; sr. v.p. Am. Fed. Savs. Bank, 1991-96; pres., CEO Frontier Fin. Corp., 1996—; chmn. of the bd., pres., CEO U.S. Savings Bank, 1997-99. Bd. dirs., chmn. Nev. Cmty. Reinvestment Corp.; bd. dirs. So. Nev. Housing Corp., Bank of Commerce. Editor: Real Estate Textbook, 1983-84. Trustee Nev. Sch. Arts; mem. fin. com. North Las Vegas Neighborhood Housing Svcs.; mem. cmty. reinvestment and housing com. Western League Savs. Instns.; bd. dirs., asst. coun. com. Boulder Dam Area coun. Boy Scouts Am.; active Leadership Las Vegas; bd. dirs. Nev. Cmty. Found., Local Initiatives Support Corp.; housing coord. Nev. Las Vegas West Mission-LDS Ch., 2001; contract com. United Way; active Leadership Las Vegas Alumni Assn., Clark County Cmty. Housing Adv. Com. Recipient Silver Beaver award Boy Scouts Am., 1997; named Outstanding Instr., Inst. Fin. Edn. 1984. Mem. Nev. Clearing House Assn. (v.p., bd. dirs.), Nat. Assn. Rev. Appraisers and Mortgage Underwriters, Brigham Young Mgmt. Soc., So. Nev. Exec. Coun. (bd. dirs., past pres.), Las Vegas C. of C. (Cmty. Achievement award 1996), Nev. Devel. Authority, So. Nev. Home Builders Assn., Las Vegas S.W. Rotary (bd. dirs.). Republican. Mem. Lds Ch. Avocations: sports, reading, music, family, computers. Office: Frontier Fin Corp PO Box 81796 Las Vegas NV 89180-1796 E-mail: kthomas@lvcm.com.

THOMAS, KENNETH EUGENE, auditor; b. Meridian, Miss., Dec. 27, 1943; s. John and Winnie Adline (White) T. AA, East Miss. Jr. Coll., 1962; BS in Acctg., Miss. State U., 1967. CPA, Miss.; cert. pub. mgr., Miss. Asst. contr. So. Pipe & Supply Co., Meridian, 1967-69, 70-75; plant acct. Quitman (Miss.) Knitting Mills, Inc., 1969-70; corp. contr. Acme Bldg. Supply Co., Meridian, 1977-78; corp. controller Reliable Trucks of Meridian, 1979-80; operating acct. Dept. Housing and Urban Devel., Atlanta, 1980-81; supervisory operating acct. Dept. of Def.-Army, Hinesville, Ga., 1981, sr. auditor Atlanta, 1981-83; fin. planner Miss. Band of Choctaw Indians, Phila., 1984; sr. auditor Dept. of Def.-Army, Lexington, Ky., 1985-87; supervisory operating acct. Dept. of Def. USAF, Blytheville, Ark., 1987-88; comptroller Dept. Corrections, Parchman, Miss., 1989; internal auditor Dept. Mental Health, Meridian, 1989—. Editor: (poetry) The Comforter. MSgt. Miss. Air Nat. Guard, 1967-91. Mem. AICPAs, Miss. Soc. CPAs, Phi Kappa Phi, Phi Theta Kappa. Republican. Methodist. Home: 6826 Valley Rd Meridian MS 39307-9429 E-mail: kenthomascpa@excite.com.

THOMAS, KENNETH GLYNDWR, mining executive; b. Llanelli, Wales, June 25, 1944; arrived in Can., 1980; m. Elizabeth June Hickman, Sept. 25, 1976; children: Louise June, Kelly Jane. BSc in Metallurgy, U. Wales, Cardiff, 1970; MSc in Mgmt. Sci., U. London, 1971; PhD in Tech. Sci., U. of Delft, The Netherlands, 1994. Chartered engr., U.K.; registered profl. engr., Ont., Can. Metallurgist Brit. Steel Corp., Wales, 1959-67, Anglo Am. Corp., Kitwe, Zambia, 1971-75, plant supt. Klerksdorp, South Africa, 1975-80; design metallurgist Kilborn Engring., Toronto, Ont., 1980-85; mill supt. Giant Yellowknife (Can.) Mines Ltd., N.W.T., 1985-87; sr. v.p. metallurgy and constrn. Barrick Gold Corp., Toronto, 1987-95, sr. v.p. tech. svcs., 1995-2001; mng. dir. mining and mineral processing Hatch, Mississauga, Ont., 2001—. Contbr. articles to tech. jours.; co-patentee in field. Fellow Inst. Materials (U.K.); mem. Can. Inst. Mining, Metallurgy and Petroleum (Mill Man of Yr. award 1990, Airey award 1999, Selwyn G. Blaylock medal 2001). Office: Hatch 2800 Speakman Dr Mississauga ON Canada L5K 2R7 E-mail: kthomas@hatch.ca.

THOMAS, KEVIN ANTHONY, biomedical engineer; b. New Orleans, Oct. 22, 1959; s. James E. and Marian (Deffner) T.; children: Samuel Taylor, Philip Matthew. BS in Biomed. Engring. summa cum laude, Tulane U., 1981, MS in Biomed. Engring., 1983, PhD in Biomed. Engring., 1985. Pre-doctoral fellow/post-doctoral fellowship VA Med. Ctr., New Orleans, 1983-85; asst. prof. orthopedic surgery Tulane U. Sch. of Medicine, 1990-92; asst. prof. biomed. engring. Tulane U. Sch. Engring., 1990—; asst. prof. orthopedic surgery La. State U. Med. Ctr., 1991-2000, assoc. prof. orthopedic surgery, 1996-2000; dir. testing and biomechanics MacroPore, Inc., San Diego, 2000—. Contbr. articles to profl. jours. Mem. Am. Soc. Biomechanics, Orthopedic Rsch. Soc., Soc. for Biomaterials, Biomed. Engring. Soc., Orthopedic Trauma Assn., Sigma Xi, Tau Beta Pi. Office: MacroPore Inc 6740 Top Gun St San Diego CA 92121 Office Fax: 858-458-0994. E-mail: kthomas@macropore.com.

THOMAS, LARRY DEE, retired corrections administrator, poet; b. Haskell, Tex., Feb. 23, 1947; s. Roy L. and Edith Ardena Coleman T.; m. Cynthia Ann Zimbal, June 3, 1966 (div. June 1975); 1 child, Deena Kay; m. Lisa Ann Parker, June 11, 1988. BA, U. Houston, 1970. Adult pbation officer Harris County Adult Probation Dept., Houston, 1975-79, unit supr., 1979-83; br. dir. Harris County Cmty. Supv. & Corrections Dept., 1983-98. Author: (poems) The Lighthouse Keeper, 2000, Amazing Grace, 2001, The Woodlanders, 2002; contbr. poetry to profl. jours. Recipient, Tex. Rev. Poetry prize, 2001, Spur award finalist, 2002. Mem. Tex. Campgrounds Club (Galveston) (bd. dirs.). Avocations: classical music, outdoors.

THOMAS, LAURA MARLENE, artist, retired private antique dealer; b. Chico, Calif., Apr. 29, 1936; d. Boyd Stanley Beck and Lois Velma (Behnke) Lyons; m. Charles Rex Thomas (div.); children: Tracy Loraine, Jeffory Norris. AA in Fine Arts, Sacramento City Coll., 1978; BA in Fine Arts, Calif. State U., 1981. Tchrs. asst. Hanford Elem. Sch., Hanford, Calif., 1963-68; asst. dir. RSVP: Retired Sr. Vol. Program, 1971-74; dir. of Art Bank Sacramento City Coll., Sacramento, 1976-78; pub. asst. Student Activities Calif. State Univ., 1978-81; antique dealer pvt. practice, 1981—, arts and crafts bus., 1976-99; ret., 1999; social worker Cath. Social Svcs., Sacramento, 1985-93. Vol. worker Sr. Ctr., 1999—. Artist: weaving, Double Image, 1977, 2nd Place 1977. Charter mem. YWCA, Sacramento, 1972, Folsum Hist. Soc., 1988; vol. Hart Sr. Ctr., Sacramento, Friends for Survival Inc., Sacramento. Cert. of appreciation, Carmellia City Ctr. Adv. Council, Sacramento, 1986. Mem. Internat. New Thought Alliance, Statue of Liberty-Ellis Island Found., 1985, North Shore Animal League (Benefactors award 1985), Calif. State U. Alumni Assn., Hanford Sportsman Club (v.p. 1963-68). Republican. Protestant. Avocations: tennis, needlepoint, gourmet cooking. Home: 2714 E Street #14 Sacramento CA 95816

THOMAS, LAVON BULLOCK, interior designer; b. San Angelo, Tex., Oct. 6, 1929; d. J. T. and Ina (Malone) Bullock; m. W. Grant Thomas, June 9, 1956; children: Lorin Gwen Thomas Tavel, Lance Kevin. BS, Sam Houston State U., 1950; MEd, U. Houston, 1961. Tchr. Houston Ind. Sch., 1950-58; youth dir. St. Paul's Meth. Ch., Houston, 1958-60; designer Grant Thomas, Inc., 1960—, builder, 1994—; real estate broker, 1975—. Unit pres. LWV, Houston, 1990, 91; v.p. Houston Assembly Delphian Chpts., Houston, 1992-93; bd. dirs. Panhellenic, Houston, 1993-94; active Houston UN Assn., 1994; Harris County Forest Landowners Assn. Recipient Cachet award for community svc. Women Helping Women, 1993. Mem. Nat. Assn. Realtors, Tes. Assn. Interior Designers, Tex. Ass. Realtors, Tex. Forestry Assn., Houston Assn. Realtors, Alph Chi Omega (pres. Beta Zeta Beta Chpt. 1994-96). Democrat. Methodist. Avocations: art, music, drama. Home: 15422 Mauna Loa Ln Houston TX 77040-1345

THOMAS, LEONA MARLENE, health information educator; b. Rock Springs, Wyo., Jan. 15, 1933; d. Leonard H. and Opal (Wright) Francis; children: Peter, Paul, Patrick, Alexis. BA, Govs. State U., 1982, MHS, 1986; cert. med. records adminstrn., U. Colo., 1954. Staff assoc. Am. Med. Records Assn., Chgo., 1972-77, asst. editor, 1979-81; statistician Westlake Hosp., Melrose Park, Ill., 1982-84; asst. prof. Chgo. State U., 1984—, acting dir. health info. adminstrn. program, 1991-92; acting dir. health info. Internat. Coll., Naples, Fla., 1994; dir. health info. adminstrn. program Chgo. State U., 1994—. Chairperson Coll. Allied Health Pers., 1986-88; mem. rev. bd. network Newsletter of Assembly on Edn. Liaison Ill. Trauma Registry, 1991; mem. adv. com. Wellness Ctr., mem. adv. com. occupl. therapy program Chgo. State U. Mem. Assembly on Edn., Am. Health Info. Mgmt. Assn., APHA, Ill. Pub. Health Assn., Chgo. and Vicinity Med. Records Assn. (publicity com. 1989-90), Ill. Assn. Allied Health Profls., Gov.'s State Alumni Assn. Democrat. Methodist. Home: 6340 Americana Dr Apt 1101 Oak Brook IL 60527 Office: Chgo State U Coll Health Scis 95th at King Dr Chicago IL 60628

THOMAS, LESTENE, nurse; b. Hampton, Ark., May 1, 1956; d. James Earnest Moore and Alma Lee Moore-Penny; m. Emile Garth Thomas; children: Learie D., Stephen J.R. AAS in Nursing, U. Ark. Little Rock, 1978. RN; notary public, Ark. Nurse U. Hosp., Little Rock, 1978-82, Vets. Hosp., Little Rock, 1982-86, Ctrl. Ark. Home Health Agy., Little Rock, 1986-89, St. Vincent Infirmary, Little Rock, 1989-90, Jefferson Regional Med. Ctr., Pine Bluff, 1990-94, Ark. Convalescent Nursing Home, Pine Bluff, 1996-97, Pulaski County Regional Detention Facility, Little Rock, 1998—. Mem. Nat. Alliance for Mentally Ill, Zeta Phi Beta. Baptist. Avocations: calligraphy, photography, music, international pen-friends. Home: 8501 Dreher Ln Apt 25 Little Rock AR 72209

THOMAS, LEWIS, physicist, researcher; b. Kingston, Pa., Mar. 16, 1924; s. Lewis Clatyon and Marion Hay Thomas; m. Jean Bartle; children: Bart, James, Dwight. BEE, Cornell U., 1949; BSEE, Newark Coll. Engring., 1958; PhD in Physics, MIT, 1960; PhD in Astronomy, London U., 1999. Radar engr. Philco Radio Corp., Phila., 1947-49; mem. tech. staff elec. transmission divsn. Bell Labs., Murray Hill, N.J., 1950-89; cons. in physics Lucent Techs., Murray Hills, 1989—; lectr., tchr. Am. Mus. Natural History, Hayden Planetarium, N.Y.C., 1950-86. Pres. Astrosoft Co., North Plainfield, N.J., 1980—; trustee Amateur Astronomers Inc., Cranford, N.J. Author: Celestial Mechanics, 1992, 2d rev. edit., 1999, Astronomy of Solar System, 1997, Astronomy Beyond Solar System, 2000, Vistas in Astronomy, 2002; patentee in field. Pres. North Plainfield City Coun., 1969-71. Sgt. U.S. Army. Decorated Bronze star; named Ark. Traveler, Gov. of Ark., 1972. Avocations: astronomy, computer science, camping. Home: 236 Watchung Ave North Plainfield NJ 07060

THOMAS, LINDSEY KAY, JR. research ecology biologist, educator, consultant; b. Salt Lake City, Apr. 16, 1931; s. Lindsey Kay and Naomi Lurie (Biesinger) T.; m. Nancy Ruth Van Dyke, Aug. 24, 1956; children: Elizabeth Nan Thomas Cardinale, David Lindsey, Wayne Hal, Dorothy Ann Thomas Brown. BS, Utah State Agrl. Coll., 1953; MS, Brigham Young U., 1958; PhD, Duke U., 1974. Park naturalist Nat. Capital Parks, Nat. Park Svc., Washington, 1957—62, park naturalist (rsch.) Region 6, 1962—63, rsch. park naturalist Nat. Capital Region, 1963—66; rsch. biologist S.E. Temperate Forest Park Areas, 1966, Durham, NC, 1966—67, Great Falls, Md., 1967—71, Nat. Capital Parks, Great Falls, 1971—74, Nat. Capital Region, Triangle, Va., 1974—93, Washington, 1985—93, Nat. Biol. Svc., Washington, Triangle, 1993—96; resource mgmt. specialist Balt.-Washington Pkwy., Greenbelt, Md., 1996, Nat. Capital Parks-East, 1996—98; rsch. ecologist emeritus and cons. Nat. Capital Region, Nat. Park Svc., 1998—. Bd. dirs. Prince William County (Va.) Svc. Authority, 1996—; adj. prof. George Mason U., Fairfax, Va., 1988—, George Washington U., Washington, 1992-98; instr. Dept. Agr. Grad. Sch., 1964-66; aquatic ecol. cons. Fairfax County (Va.) Fedn. Citizens Assns., 1970-71; guest lectr. Washington Tech. Inst. (now U. D.C.), 1976. Contbr. articles to profl. jours. Wildlife mgmt. cons. Girl Scouts Am., Loudoun County, Va., 1958; asst. scoutmaster, scoutmaster, merit badges counselor Boy Scouts Am., 1958—, Scouters Tng. award, 1961. Recipient incentive awards Nat. Park Svc., 1962, Superior Performance award, 1989; rsch. grantee Washington Biologists' Field Club, 1977, 82. Mem. AAAS, Bot. Soc. Washington, Ecol. Soc. Am., George Wright Soc., Nature Conservancy, Soc. Early Hist. Archaeology, So. Appalachian Bot. Soc., Washington Biologists' Field Club, Sigma Xi. Mem. Lds Ch. Home: 13854 Delaney Rd Woodbridge VA 22193-4654 Office: Balt-Washingtn Pky 6565 Greenbelt Rd Greenbelt MD 20770-3207 also: Prince William Forest Park 18100 Park Hdqs Rd Triangle VA 22172

THOMAS, LISA FRANCINE, secondary school educator, assistant principal; b. New Haven, Feb. 15, 1966; d. Fred and Elaine Carolyn (Webb) McCauley; married, Apr. 22, 2001. AA, Mt. Sacred Heart Coll., Hamden, Conn., 1988; BA in History, So. Conn. State U., 1989, MS in History, 1992, 6th yr. cert. advanced grad. studies, 1998. Cert. secondary edn. grades 7-12, Conn. Tchr. St. Lawrence Sch., West Haven, Conn., 1989-95, Wilbur Cross H.S., New Haven, 1996-2001; asst. prin. East Lyme (Conn.) H.S., 2001—. Adj. prof. So. Conn. State U., New Haven, 1993-2001. Vol. Conn. Spl. Olympics, New Haven, 1989—; dist. coord. Nat. History Day, Conn. Hist. Soc., Hartford, 1993-98. Recipient cert. for dedicated svcs. and encouragement of student participation Conn. Hist. Soc., Hartford, 1992, cert. appreciation Jr. Achievement, Wallingford, Conn., 1992; named Outstanding Tchr. of Merit Conn. Hist. Soc., 1997, Best Beginning Educator Support Tchr., 2000. Mem. AAUP, ASCD, Am. Assn. Sch. Adminstrs., Nat. Cath. Edn. Assn., Conn. Coun. for the Social Studies, Conn. and New Haven Hist. Socs., Conn. Geographic Alliance, Conn. Humanities Coun. Congregationalist. Avocations: musician, reading. Home: 81 Main St # 47 Branford CT 06405 E-mail: lisa.thomas@eastlymeschools.org.

THOMAS, LLOYD BREWSTER, economics educator; b. Columbia, Mo., Oct. 22, 1941; s. Lloyd B. and Marianne (Moon) T.; m. Sally Leach, Aug. 11, 1963; 1 child, Elizabeth. AB, U. Mo., 1963, AM, 1964; PhD, Northwestern U., 1970. Instr. Northwestern U., Evanston, Ill., 1966-68; asst. prof. econs. Kan. State U., Manhattan, 1968-72, assoc. prof., 1974-81, prof., 1983—; asst. prof. Fla. State U., Tallahassee, 1973-74. Vis. prof. U. Calif., Berkeley, 1981-82, U. Del., 1993, U. Ind., Bloomington, 1997-98, Adelaide U., 2002; prof., chair dept. econs. U. Idaho, 1989. Author: Money, Banking and Economic Activity, 3d edit., 1986, Principles of Economics, 2d edit, 1993, Principles of Macroeconomics, 2d edit., 1993, Principles of Microeconomics, 2d edit, 1993, Money, Banking and Financial Markets, 1997; contbr. articles to profl. jours.

Mem. Am. Econs. Assn., Midwest Econs. Assn., So. Econs. Assn., Western Econs. Assn., Phi Kappa Phi. Avocations: tennis, classical music. Home: 1501 N 10th St Manhattan KS 66502-4607 E-mail: lbt@ksu.edu.

THOMAS, LOUISE PARRY, medical assistant, educator; b. Cedar City, Utah, Apr. 27, 1937; d. Chauncey Gardner Parry and Helen Clare Daynes; m. John W. Thomas, May 30, 1968; children: Kirk, Chris, William, Marten. Student, U. Utah, 1955-56, Salt Lake C.C., 1992-94; cert., Salt Lake Coll. Med. Arts, 1968. Cert. med. asst. Sec. Charles A. Steen Assn., Moab, Utah, 1958-60; med. asst. Valley West Hosp., Salt Lake City, 1968-70; chief med. asst. Family Practice Assn., 1970-78; instr. Stevens-Henager Coll., Provo, Utah, 1979-86; instr., mem. program adv. bd. Salt Lake C.C., Salt Lake City, 1986-2000, mem. faculty senate, 1995-98. Adj. faculty Dixie State Coll., St. George, Utah. Author: The Alpha Connection to Mind and Body, 1998 (Pres.'s award 1999). Recipient Tchg. Excellence award Salt Lake C.C. Avocations: writing, lecturing, golf. Home: 642 N Sky Mountain Blvd Hurricane UT 84737-3461

THOMAS, LOWELL, JR. writer, lecturer, former lieutenant governor, former state senator; b. London, Oct. 6, 1923; s. Lowell Jackson and Frances (Ryan) T.; m. Mary Taylor Pryor, May 20, 1950; children: Anne Frazier, David Lowell. Student, Taft Sch., 1942; BA, Dartmouth Coll., 1948; postgrad., Princeton Sch. Pub. and Internat. Affairs, 1952. Asst. cameraman Fox Movietone News, S.Am., 1939, Bradford Washburn Alaskan mountaineering expdn., 1940; illustrated lecturer, 1946—; asst. economist, photographer with Max Weston Thornburg, Turkey, 1947, Iran, 1948; film prodn. Iran, 1949; Tibet expdn. with Lowell Thomas, Sr., 1949; field work Cinerama, S.Am., Africa, Asia, 1951-52; travels by small airplane with wife, writing and filming Europe, Africa, Middle East, 1954-55; mem. Rockwell Polar Flight, first flight around the world over both poles, Nov., 1965; mem. Alaska State Senate, 1967-74; lt. gov. State of Alaska, 1974-79; owner Talkeetna Air Taxi, Inc., air contract carrier, Anchorage, 1980-94. Producer series of films Flight to Adventure, NBC-TV, 1956; producer, writer TV series High Adventure, 1957-59; producer documentary film Adaq, King of Alaskan Seas, 1960; producer two films on Alaska, 1962, 63, film on U. Alaska, 1964, South Pacific travel documentary, 1965, film on Arctic oil exploration, Atlantic-Richfield Co., 1969. Author: Out of this World, A Journey to Tibet, 1950, (with Mrs. Lowell Thomas, Jr.) Our Flight to Adventure, 1956, The Silent War in Tibet, 1959, The Dalai Lama, 1961, The Trail of Ninety-Eight, 1962, (with Lowell Thomas Sr.) More Great True Adventures, 1963, Famous First Flights that Changed History, 1968. Past pres. Western Alaska coun. Boys Scouts Am.; bd. dirs. Anchorage unit Salvation Army, Alaska Conservation Found. 1st lt. USAAF, 1943-45. Mem. Nat. Parks and Conservation Assn. (bd. dirs.), Alaska C. of C., Aircraft Owners and Pilots Assn. Clubs: Explorers, Marco Polo, Dutch Treat (N.Y.C.); Rotary, (Anchorage), Press (Anchorage); Dartmouth Outing; American Alpine. Address: 10800 Hideaway Lake Dr Anchorage AK 99507-6139

THOMAS, LOWELL SHUMWAY , JR. lawyer; b. Phila., Aug. 9, 1931; s. Lowell Shumway and Josephine (McVey) T.; m. Judith Evans, Aug. 27, 1955; children: Megan E., Heather McVey, Lowell S., Taylor G. BA, Dartmouth Coll., 1953; JD, U. Pa., 1960. Bar: Pa. 1961, U.S. Tax Ct. 1961, U.S. Dist. Ct. (ea. dist.) Pa. 1961, U.S. Ct. Appeals (3d cir.) 1961. Assoc. Duane, Morris & Heckscher, Phila., 1960-64, Saul, Ewing, Remick & Saul, Phila., 1965-68, ptnr., 1968-96, of counsel, 1997—. Bd. dirs. Boardwalk Securities Corp., Peter Lumber Co., Chestnut Hill Acad., Phila., 1978-86; bd. dirs. Southeastern Pa. ARC, 1975-82, chmn., 1983-86, bd. govs., 1989-95; trustee Beaver Coll. 1987-2000, emeritus trustee, 2001—, chmn., 1989-903. Author: Taxation of Marriage, Separation and Divorce, 1986. Trustee Barra Found., 1999—. Lt. USN, 1953-57. Fellow Am. Coll. Tax Counsel; mem. ABA, Pa. Bar Assn., Phila. Bar Assn., Phila. Bar Found. (trustee 1980-83), Am. Law Inst., Suunybrook Golf Club. Republican. Episcopalian. Office: Saul Ewing Remick & Saul 3800 Centre Sq W Philadelphia PA 19102 E-mail: LST8012@acadia.net.

THOMAS, LYNN MARIE, artist, retired dude ranch owner, operator; b. L.A., Nov. 20, 1939; d. Eugene Leonard and Genevie Juanita (Hupp) Pfeiffer; m. Joe Glen Thomas, Dec. 2, 1969 (div.); children from previous marriage: Beverly Linda Hahn, Deborah Jean Hahn, Michelle Marie Hahn (dec.). Grad h.s., Henderson, Nev. One-woman shows include Burk Gallery, Boulder City, Nev., 1976, 78, Pa-Jo's Western Art Gallery, Pinedale, Wyo., 1976, 80, 89, Bank of Nev., Las Vegas, 1976, 78, Energy Rsch. & Devel. Adminstrn., Las Vegas, 1977, U. Nev., Las Vegas, 1979, Rock Springs (Wyo.) Fine Arts Ctr., 1988, 89, White Mountain Libr., Rock Springs, 1990, 92, Green River (Wyo.) Libr., 1990, 93; group exhbns. include Wyo. Artists Assn. (Best of Show, Artist's Choice, People's Choice, Pres.'s Choice, 4 1st pl., 14 misc. awards), Sweetwater County Art Guild Nat. (Best of Show, People's Choice, 2 1st pl. in profl. divsn., misc. other awards), Seven State Regional (3 awards for 3 pieces), Black Canyon Show (2 1st pl., 3 misc. awards), Cody Western & Wildlife Classic (Purple ribbon), Audubon Nat. Wildlife Art Show (2 1st in oil prizes), Women Artists of West (Artist's Artist, 1987, 1st pl. in oils, 10 misc. awards), Cheyenne Frontier Days Old West Mus. (Beanie Herzog award 1985), Am. Mothers (Sweepstakes award 1979, 83, several misc. awards), Las Vegas Elks Helldorado Show (1st pl. oils 1975, 84, 3 misc. awards), Sublett County Fair (36 1st pl. awards, 10 Best of Show awards, 6 Overall Champion awards, 23 Champion awards, 13 misc. awards), Daisy Patch Gallery, Casper, Wyo., 1996, Savage Gallery, Sioux Falls, S.D., 1996, High Desert Gallery, Rock Springs, Wyo., 1996, ; represented in permanent collections including Las Vegas Rev. Jour., 1st Wyo. Bank, Big Piney, Sublett County Wyo. Libr., Las Vegas Elks Western Art Collection, Rock Springs Fine Arts Ctr., Ft. Huachuca Post Cavalry Mus., Green River Valley Mus., Big Piney; contbr. art to numerous pubs. and profl. jours. Mem. Nat. Cowgirl Hall of Fame, Hereford, Tex., Cowboy Artists of Am. Mus., Kerrville, Tex., Mus. of the Mountain Man, Pinedale, Wyo., Wyo. Coun. on Arts, Flaming Gorge Natural History Assn., Sublette County Hist. Soc., Green River Valley Mus.; charter mem. Nat. Mus. for Women in the Arts, Washington, Nat. Mus. of the Am. Indian, Washington. Mem. Women Artists of the West (emeritus), Pinedale Fine Arts Coun., Sublette County Artists Guild, Mixed Media, Wyo. Artists Registry, Nev. Artists Register, Wyo. Artists Assn. Avocations: photography, outdoors, horses, music, poetry. Home: House on Muddy 105 Richie Rd Boulder WY 82923-9617

THOMAS, MALAYILMELATHETHIL, minister, English language educator; b. Chengannur, Kerala, India, Jan. 26, 1932; came to U.S. 1959; s. Malayilmelathethil Thomas and Rachel (Thomas) Koruthu. BA, Kerala U., 1952; BD, Serampore U., Calcutta, 1956; MTh, Princeton Theol. Sem., 1960; MA, Morehead State U., 1961; EdD, U. Tulsa, 1964. Prin. St. George Mid. Sch., Kizharalloor, Kerala, India, 1952-53; tchr. Catholicate High Sch., Pathanamthitta, 1956-59; asst. prof. English Morehead (Ky.) State U., 1964-65, assoc. prof. English, 1965-67, prof. English, 1967-94, prof. emeritus, 1994—; pastor St. Gregorios Orthodox Ch., Oak Park, Ill., 1994—. Mem. MLA, Ky. Philol. Soc., Coll. Composition and Communication, Nat. Coun. Tchrs. English, Phi Kappa Phi, Phi Delta Kappa, Kappa Delta Pi. Democrat. Mem. Indian Orthodox Ch. Avocations: travel, cooking, gardening. Home: 310 W Sun St Morehead KY 40351-1560 Office: 1121 N Humphrey Oak Park IL 60302

THOMAS, MARGARET ANN, educational administrator, art educator; b. Waukesha, Wis., June 19, 1951; d. Melvin Michael and Elizabeth (Brewer) T.; m. Bruce Fiedler; 1 child, James. BA in Art Edn., Beloit Coll., 1974; MA in Art, U. Wis., Whitewater, 1981, MA in Ednl. Psychology, 1985; MS in Ednl. Adminstrn., U. Wis., 1995, PhD in Ednl. Adminstrn., Ednl. Psychology. Cert. K-12 art tchr., Wis., elem. and H.S. prin., curriculum dir. K-12, supt. Tchr. art Beloit (Wis.) Pub. Schs., 1974—; adj. prof. Beloit Coll., 1992—; prin. Mclenegan Elem. Sch., Beloit, 1999—2001, adminstrator office of grants, 2002—. Muralist instr. Beloit Coll., summers, 1985-91, adj. prof., 1993—; adj. prof. Nat. Louis U., 1994—. Author: Effective Teachers; Effective Schools, 1989; contbr. articles to profl. jours. Bd. dirs. Wis.-Gate Found., 1985-87, Wis. Racquetball Assn., 1986-87, Wis. Future Problem Solving, 1986-87; pres. bd. dirs. YWCA, 1987-91; dir. Beloit and Vicinity Art Show, Beloit Coll., 1982-84, Rock Prairie Showcase Festival; founder Summer Explorers Beloit Coll. Mem. Wis. Coun. for Gifted and Talented (bd. dirs. 1984-87, v.p. 1985-86, pres. 1986-87). Home: 4421 Ruger Ave Janesville WI 53546-9780 E-mail: mathomas@sdb.k12.wi.us.

THOMAS, MARGOT EVA, lawyer; b. Grass Valley, Calif., Apr. 28, 1943; d. Walter Frederick and Edith Louise (Clark) T.; life ptnr. Rose Maloof; children: Matthew E. Albertson Konda, Nicholas E. Albertson, Elizabeth R. Albertson. AB, Brown U., 1965; JD, Western New Eng. Coll., 1981. Bar: Mass. 1981. Field worker So. Christian Leadership Conf., Lisman, Ala., 1965-66; computer programmer Irving Trust Co., N.Y.C., 1966-67; social worker Phila. Dept. Welfare, 1968-70; field dir. Girl Scouts of Delaware County Pa., Upper Darby, 1971-73; project dir. Pioneer Valley Girl Scouts, Springfield, Mass., 1973-74; pvt. practice lawyer Northampton, 1981—. Pres. Northampton (Mass.) Girls Soccer Assn., 1985-91; chair Northampton (Mass.) City Dem. Com., 1989-91. Mem. Women's Bar Assn., Mass. Bar Assn., Hampshire County Bar Assn., Mass. Lesbian and Gay Bar Assn. Office: 2 Maple Ave Ste 22 Northampton MA 01060-4422

THOMAS, MARIANNA, volunteer community activist, writer, speaker; b. Greenville, Ohio, Dec. 9, 1927; d. John Darl and Eva Jane (Hill) Munn; m. Harold D. Krickenbarger, Aug. 31, 1947 (div.); children: Harold Jr., Jane, Maryln, John; m. Lowell J. Thomas, Jan. 5, 1977 (dec.); 1 stepchild Lowell J. *The Munns are descendants of Henry Wolcott who immigrated in 1628 to the colonies. He returned to England and brought his wife, Elizabeth Saunders, to Martha's Vineyard in 1630. A descendent, Silas Wilcott, was an assigned bodyguard to George Washington when mutiny was threatened at Valley Forge. His cousin, Oliver, Governor of Connecticut, signed the Declaration of Independence. The Munns are descendents of King Robert II of Scotland.* Student, Dayton (Ohio) Art Inst.; MA (hon.), Union (Ky.) Coll., 1978. Farmer Holstein Show Herd, Arcanum, Ohio, 1947-68; advt., broadcasting sta. work and writing positions Arcanum Times; sales and decorating positions Lowe Bros., Greenville, Ohio; exec. dir./fundraising Help for Children in the Holy Land/Spafford Children's Ctr., N.Y.C., 1969-76. *"Citizens for Moral War" promoted alternate legislators for election, so presidents and legislators could directly participate in the wars they legislate. "U.S. Civil Responsibilities" was devoted to the responsibilities as well as the rights, and focused on teaching the basic principles of civic law in schools, as well as using phonics to enable students to read.* Author: Catitudes, 1987, The Second Mrs. Lowell Thomas, 2000; mem. bd. contbrs. Dayton Daily News. Founder Citizens for Moral War peace orgn., 1967-70; mem. coun. Freedoms Found. at Valley Forge, 1982-84; nat. bd. dirs. Family Svc. Assocs. Am., N.Y.C., 1979-85, Am. Judicature Soc., 1978-80; founder, chmn. U.S. Civil Responsibilities, Dayton, 1988-93. Mem. Dayton Engrs. Club (hon.). Avocations: oil painting, poetry, swimming, cooking. Home: PO Box 626 Dayton OH 45405-0626 E-mail: MARIANNAMUNN@aol.com.

THOMAS, MARIANNE GREGORY, school psychologist; b. N.Y.C., Dec. 10, 1945; BS, U. Conn., 1985; MS, So. Conn. State U., 1987; cert. advanced studies, ednl. adminstrn., NYU, 1998. Cert. sch psychologist Conn, NY. Sch. psychology intern Greenwich (Conn.) Pub. Schs., 1986-87; sch. psychologist Hawthorne (N.Y.)-Cedar Knolls, U.F.S.D., 1987-88, Darien (Conn.) Pub. Schs., 1988—. Adj. instr. Coll. New Rochelle, 2002. Mem.: APA, NASP (cert), Conn Asn Sch Psychologists, Kappa Delta Pi, Phi Delta Kappa. Home: 154 Indian Rock Rd New Canaan CT 06840-3117

THOMAS, MARJORIE OLIVIENE, health care administrator; b. Spaldings, Jamaica, Sept. 05; came to U.S., 1971; d. Cedrick Milo and Avis Clair (Morgan) West; m. Carol Oswald Thomas, Sept. 10, 1977; children: Chandra, Brian. AA, Kendall Coll., 1973; BS, U. Ill., Chgo., 1975; MPA, Roosevelt U., Chgo., 1977. Asst. to dir. utilization rev. Bellevue Hosp., N.Y.C., 1977-81, risk mgr., 1981-83, assoc. dir., dir. quality assurance, 1983-85; dir. risk mgmt. svcs. Adminstrs. for Professions, Inc., Manhasset, N.Y., 1985-93, v.p. risk mgmt. and underwriting, 1993-99, sr. v.p., 1999—. Fellow Am. Soc. for Healthcare Risk Mgmt. (reg. profl. liability underwriter). Mem. Christ Temple. Avocations: reading, writing, travel. Office: 111 E Shore Rd Manhasset NY 11030-2902

THOMAS, MARK P. conductor, educator; b. Sellersville, Pa., Jan. 6, 1961; s. Russell C. and Pearl Thomas; m. Eileen Brown Thomas; children: Parker M., Pryce M. MS Telecom. (music), Kutztown U., Kutztown, PA, 1989; BS Music Edn., West Chester U., West Chester, PA, 1984. Artistic dir. and condr. Choral Arts Soc. of Upper Perkionen Valley, Red Hill, Pa., 2001—; music and humanities educator Pa, State U., Schuylkill Haven, 2000—; sr. dir. of vocal music Upper Perkiomen Sch. Disrict, Pennsburg, 1999—; music dir. and condr. Schuylkill County Cmty. Chorus, Pottsville, 1986—; sr. high music dir. So. Columbia Sch. Dist., Catawissa, 1992—99; instr. of performing arts Bucks County CC, Newtown, 1989—92; music dir. St. John's Luth. Ch., Spinnerstown, 1988—92. Guest condr. Allentown Diocese Music Festival, Tamaque, Pa., 2002, Ocean Grove Choral Festival Choir, Ocean Grove, NJ, 1998—2001, Schuylkill County Choral Festival, Pine Grove, Pa., 1996. Music dir. and conductor (choral music cd) Holiday Favorites. Mem.: Am. Choral Director's Assn., Pa. Music Director's Assn., Music Educator's Nat. Conf., Columbia Montour County Choral Festival (originator 1996), St. Mark's Luth. Ch., Kappa Kappa Psi (originator 1982). Avocation: coaching basketball. Office: Schuylkill County Community Chorus 1440 Mahantonge Street Pottsville PA 17901 Personal E-mail: mpthomas@mcin.org.

THOMAS, MARY ANN MCCRARY, counselor, school system administrator; b. Washington, Feb. 11, 1935; d. Frank Robert and Mary (Davison) McCrary; m. John Ralph Thomas, Sept. 30, 1961; children: Robert Davison, John Shannon, Kristen Aldridge. BA, U. Calif., Berkley, 1956; MA, UCLA, 1959. Cert. tchr., Calif. Supr. Pacific Bell, San Francisco, 1962-67; advisor gifted, talented San Rafael (Calif.) City Schs., 1973—, counselor, 1973—, dir. student affairs, 1982—. Pres. San Rafael PTA Coun., 1981-84, outstanding svc. award, 1983, 86, 89, San Rafael High Sch. Site Coun., 1985; pres. bd. dirs. Marin Wildlife Ctr., 1979-85. Recipient Golden Bell award, Marin Community Found., 1987, Outstanding Student Activities program state award, 1992; named Pub. Schoolmaster of Yr., 1993. Mem. Calif. Assn. Gifted, Calif. Assn. Tchrs. English. Republican. Episcopalian. Avocations: reading, gardening. Home: 70 Windsor Ave San Rafael CA 94901-1068 Office: Davidson Mid Sch 280 Woodland Ave San Rafael CA 94901-5097

THOMAS, MARY AUGUSTA, library administrator; b. Washington, Mar. 15, 1951; d. Abram Henry and Mary Agnes Rosenfeld; m. George D. Thomas Jr., Nov. 9, 1991. AB cum laude, Mt. Holyoke Coll., 1973; MSLS, Cath. U., Washington, 1978. From rare book libr. to mgr. planning and adminstrn. Smithsonian Librs., Washington, 1976-91, asst. dir., 1991—2002. Editor: Information Imagineering, 1998; contbr. articles to popular mags. Recipient Smithsonian Inst. Sec.'s award for Excellence in Equal Employment Opportunity, 2000. Mem. ALA (chair editl. adv. bd. LA & M, 1998—, councilor 1999—, chair com. on resolutions), D.C. Libr. Assn. (pres. 1999, Disting. Svc. award 2001), Fed. Librs. and Info. Ctrs. (adv. bd. 1997-99), Libr. Adminstrn. and Mgmt. Assn. (chair bus. and fiscal officer discussion group 1998-2000), Beta Phi Mu. Avocations: cooking, writing. Office: Smithsonian Librs Nhb 22 Washington DC 20560-0001

THOMAS, MARY JO, librarian; b. Louisville, Feb. 15, 1952; d. Manuel Edward and Josephine Marie (Smith) Stevens; m. Robert H. Thomas, June 4, 1985; 1 child, Sarah Elizabeth. BA, U. Louisville, 1983; MS, U. Ky., 1985. Govt. documents libr. Ohio State Supreme Ct. Libr., Columbus, 1986; libr. Mercer County Pub. Libr., Harrodsburg, 1987-88; asst. libr. Lindsey Wilson Coll., Columbia, Ky., 1988-92; coll. libr. U. Ark. C.C., Hope, Ark., 1992—99; libr. dir. MacMurray Coll., Jacksonville, Ill., 1999—. Contbr. articles to profl. jours. Judge Odyssey of the Mind, S.W. Ark., 1994. Mem. Ark. Libr. Assn., Ark. Coun. Women in Higher Edn., Sangamon Valley Acad. Libr. Consortium (chmn. 2001-), Ark. Assn. Instructional Media, Phi Beta Lambda. Office: Henry Pfeiffer Libr 447 E College Ave Jacksonville IL 62650

THOMAS, MELISSA P. adult education educator; b. Covington, Ga., May 24, 1965; d. Wesley Ron and Dorothy Camp Palmer; m. David R. Thomas, June 1, 2001; m. Gilbert M. Diaz Jr., June 28, 1986 (div. Oct. 1999); children: Allison Kathleen Diaz, Gilbert M. III Diaz. BS in Edn., U. Ga., 1991; MS in Edn., Brenau U., Gainesville, Ga., 1999. Tchr. Lilburn Mid. Sch., Ga., 1990—99, curriculum chmn., 1997—99; tchr. Gwinnett Tech. Coll., Lawrenceville, 1999—2001, Dacula Mid. Sch., 1999—2002, curriculum chmn., 2000—; tchr. Profl. Career Devel. Inst., Norcross, 2000—. Mem.: Ga. Assn. Educators, Kappa Delta Pi. Baptist. Avocations: reading, writing, running.

THOMAS, MICHAEL EUGENE, electrical engineer, researcher, educator; b. Dayton, Ohio, Apr. 24, 1951; s. Eugene Franklin and Helen Philomena (Lechner) T.; m. Martha Jane Brammer, Mar. 19, 1983; children: Daniel James, Jane Michelle, Alissa Marie, Rebecca Christine, Joseph Michael, Christopher Kyle. MSEE, Ohio State U., 1976, PhD, 1979. Rsch. assoc. Electro Sci. Lab., Ohio State U., Columbus, 1973-79; prin. engr. Applied Physics Lab., Johns Hopkins U., Laurel, Md., 1979—. Rsch. prof. dept. elec. and computer engring. Johns Hopkins U., 1998. Contbg. author: Handbook of Optical Constants of Solids, Vol. II, 1991, Vol. III, 1998, Electro-Optics Handbook, The Infrared and Electro-Optical Systems Handbook, Vol. 2, Atmospheric Propagation of Radiation, OSA Handbook of Optics; contbr. numerous articles to Jour. Infrared Physics and Tech., Jour. Applied Optics, IEEE Jour., Trans. Geosci. and Remote Sensing, Optical Engring. Janney fellow Johns Hopkin's U., 1988, 98, Parsons fellow, 1991-92, postdcotoral fellow Naval Postgrad. Sch., Monterey, Calif., 1982; recipient Walter Berl award Johns Hopkin's U., 1988. Fellow Optical Soc. Am.; mem. IEEE (sr.), Internat. Soc. for Optical Engrs. Achievements include development of mathematical models for describing electromagnetic propagation in the atmosphere of the earth, seawater, and optical window materials. Office: Johns Hopkins U Applied Physics Lab Johns Hopkins Rd Laurel MD 20723 E-mail: michael.e.thomas@jhuapl.edu.

THOMAS, MICHAEL S. software engineer; b. Ft. Benning, Ga., Dec. 11, 1977; s. Timothy Lee and Christine Marie Thomas. Student, Kans. State U., 1996—. Sys. engr. Logicon RDA, Leavenworth, Kans., 1998; sys. software specialist Logicon LAT, Grafenwoehr, Germany, 1999; automation intern Motorola Corp., Austin, Tex., 2000; software engr. Lockheed Martin, 2002—. Mem. NSPE, N.Y. Acad. Scis. Lutheran. Avocations: running, basketball, skiing. Home: 2803 Riverside Pkw Grand Prairie TX 75050 E-mail: Michael_S_Thomas@lycos.com.

THOMAS, MICHELLE AMOR, film company executive; b. Chgo., Mar. 26, 1971; d. Sherman Lee Thomas, Linda LaVerne Brunson; m. Tyrone P. Christian II, Nov. 23, 1991 (div. Jan. 2002); 1 child Crislin Rénee Christian. BA Honors, Columbia Coll., Chgo., 1995. Pres. S.I.P. Prodns., Chgo., 1998—. Admissions counselor Kellogg Sch. Mgmt., Chgo., 1999—. Office: SIP Productions Chicago IL 60623

THOMAS, NOREEN JO, healthcare system educator, writer; b. Hazen, N.D., Dec. 31, 1955; d. Delmont D. and Rachel M. (Hinsz) Sagmiller; m. Lee D. Thomas, Jan. 10, 1987; children: Brita, Evan, Carsten. BS in Food and Nutrition, Microbiology, N.D. State U., 1979. Cert. master gardener; cert. water arthritis aerobics instr. Quality control, rschr. Gen. Mills Nutrition, Fargo, 1979-83; tea taster Celestial Seasonings, Boulder, Colo., 1980-83; lab. technician State of N.D., State Lab., Bismark, 1984-87; rschr. USDA, Fargo, 1987-88; nutritionist Women Infants and Children Program of Clay County, N.D., 1991-97; writer, nutrition educator Dakota Heartland Med. Sys., 1991-97; writer, grant writer, pub., 1997—; grant writer, bd. dirs. gifted learning project. Adv. bd. U. Minn. Author: Caterpillar Scramble and Cantaloupe Boats, 1997 (Best Child's Book award Midwestern Publ., 1997), Dehydrator Delights, 1994, (newsletter) Project Nutrition. Tchr. YMCA, 1994-97, North Buffalo Luth. Ch., Moorhead, Minn., 1996-97; active Youth in Rural Am., Moorhead; chmn. bd. dirs. Am. Heart Assn., 1990-97, Balance Health and Wellness Mag.; pub. rels. coord. Red River Skating Club; advisor Happy Feet 4-H Charity; leader 4-H. Finalist Country Woman of Yr. Farm and Ranch Guide, 1997; recipient Best of Planet People's Choice Awards Task.Company, 1998, Best Child's Book award Great Plains Book, 1997. Mem. Soybean Assn. Avocations: fishing, swimming, scuba diving, travel, gardening. Home: 12506 20th St N Moorhead MN 56560-7230 Office: Noreen Thomas Pub Co PO Box 193 Georgetown MN 56546-0193 E-mail: nthomas8@juno.com.

THOMAS, NORMAN, education educator; b. Edmonton/London, June 1, 1921; s. Bowen and Ada (Redding) T.; m. Rose Matilda Henshaw, Dec. 24, 1942; children: Jill Evelyn, Paula Blodwyn. Hon. fellow, Coll. of Preceptors, U.K., 1988; DLitt (hon.), U. Hertfordshire, 1998. Cert. tchr. Various posts in commerce and industry, London, 1937-47; primary sch. tchr. London, Hertfordshire, 1948-56; head tchr. Longmeadow Primary Sch., Stevenage, Eng., 1956-61; HM inspector of schs. HM Inspectorate, Eng., 1962-69, staff inspector Eng., 1969-73, chief inspector, primary schs. Eng., 1973-81. Chmn. com. of inquiry, primary edn., Inner London, 1984-85; specialist adviser House of Commons, Select Com. on Edn., U.K., 1984-86, 93-97; external examiner Bishop Grosseteste Coll., U. Surrey, Open U., 1982-84, 86-90, 93-96; vis. prof. East London Polytechnic, Univ. Warwick, Nottingham, Hertfordshire, 1984-88, 88—. Author: Primary Education From Plowden to the 1990s, 1990, The Aims of Primary Education in Handbook of Primary Education in Europe, 1989; author articles and profl. papers; contbr. book chpts. to books in field. Comdr. Brit. Empire, HM The Queen, U.K., 1980. Mem. Nat. Assn. for Primary Edn. (life). Avocations: reading, computing, photography. Home: 19 Langley Way Watford Herts WD17 3EJ England E-mail: thomasnr@cwcom.net.

THOMAS, ORVILLE C. retired physician, consultant; b. Haynesville, La., Aug. 23, 1915; children— David, Diane, Cody Pre-med. Student, Marian Mil. Inst., 1932-33, Tulane U., 1933, MD, 1939. Diplomate Am. Bd. Pediatrics. Diplomate Am. Bd. Allergy and Immunology. Intern Shreveport Charity Hosp., La., 1939-40; asst. resident in pediatrics Children's Meml. Hosp., Chgo., 1946-47, resident in pediatrics, 1947, chief resident in pediatrics, 1948; active staff Tex. Children's Hosp., Houston, 1962—, fellow pediatric allergy, 1963-65, chief allergy sect., 1973-78; fellow in pediatric allergy Baylor Coll. Medicine, 1963-65; chief pediatrics Schumpert Meml. Hosp., Shreveport, La, 1958-61, chief of staff, 1958; sr. staff pediatrics Confederate Meml. Hosp., 1948-61; active staff Highland Hosp., 1948-61, North La. Hosp., Shreveport, 1948-61, Physicians and Surgeons Hosp., Shreveport, 1948-61, Ben Taub Gen. Hosp., Houston, 1962—, Hermann Hosp., Houston, 1966-69; hon. staff St. Luke's Hosp., 1962—; cons. staff Meth. Hosp., 1962—, St. Joseph Hosp., Houston, 1966—, Bellaire (Tex.) Gen. Hosp., 1966-86, Rosewood Gen. Hosp., Houston, 1967—, Meml. Bapt. Hosp., Houston, 1968—, Pasadena Bayshore Hosp., Pasadena, Tex., 1970—; instr. pediatrics Northwestern U. Sch. Medicine, Chgo., 1948; assoc. prof. pediatrics La. State U. Postgrad. Sch. Medicine, 1956-61; clin. instr. pediatrics Baylor Coll. Medicine, Houston, 1961-66, asst. clin. prof. pediatrics, 1966-76, assoc. clin. prof. pediatrics, 1977—. Assoc. clin. prof. allergy and immunology U. Tex. Grad. Sch. Biomed. Scis., Houston, 1970—. Book reviewer: Venom Diseases; Aspects of Allergy and Applied Immunology. Contbr. articles to profl. jours. Served to maj. USMC AUS, 1942-46. Fellow Am. Coll. Allergy and Immunology (pediatrics com. 1964—, pres. 1978), Am. Acad. Allergy and Immunology, Am. Assn. Cert. Allergists (bd. govs. 1974, pres. 1979); mem. AMA, Am. Acad. Pediatrics, So. Med. Assn. (chmn. allergy sect. 1970-71), Tex. Allergy Research Found. Houston- (research and edn. com. 1966-86, chmn. sci. adv. council 1973—), Tex. Pediatric Soc., Harris County Med. Soc., Tex. Med. Assn. (chmn. allergy sect. 1976-77), Am. Assn. for Inhalation Therapy (awards com. 1969-72, spl. edn. com. 1969-72), Greater Houston Allergy Soc. (pres. 1977), Joint Council of Allergy and Immunology, Internat. Assn. of Allergology and Clin. Immunology (U.S. rep. 1981-85). Home: 1111 Bering Dr Apt 704 Houston TX 77057-2320

THOMAS, OUIDA POWER, music educator; b. Louisville, Nov. 25, 1939; d. Robert Alvin and Mavis (Simpson) Power; m. Charles Victor Thomas, Aug. 4, 1962; children: Karla Victoria, Sylvia Katharine Thomas White, Charles Gregory. BS in Bus. Edn. with highest honors, Miss. State U., Starkville, 1963; M Music Edn., Delta State U., 1993; postgrad., U. Memphis, 1996—. Nat. cert. tchr. of music. Ind. music tchr. piano and organ, Grenada, Miss., 1963—; classroom gen. music tchr. Kirk Acad., 1977-87. Adjudicator auditions Federated Music Clubs, Oxford, Miss., 1990—. Accompanist musical prodns. Grenada Fine Arts Playhouse, 1979-81; organist, choirmaster All Saints' Episcopal Ch., Grenada, 1977—; mem. music and liturgy com. Episcopal Diocese of Miss., 1996-99. Mem. Am. Guild Organists, Nat. Guild Piano Tchrs. (chmn. local auditions 1977—, adjudicator auditions 1993—), Music Tchrs. Nat. Assn. (cert. in piano and organ), Miss. Music Tchrs. Assn. (cert. in piano and organ, exec. bd. 1993-94, state chair pre-coll. student activities

1995-96, chair state cert. 1999-2000, adjudicator auditions 1993—), Grenada Area Music Tchrs. Assn. (v.p. 1995—). Avocations: gardening, needlework. Home: 1985 Wooded Dr Grenada MS 38901-4073 E-mail: othomas@network-one.com.

THOMAS, PAMELA ADRIENNE, special education educator; b. St. Louis, Oct. 28, 1940; d. Charles Seraphin Fernandez and Adrienne Louise (O'Brien) Fernandez Reeg; divorced, 1977; m. Alvertis T. Thomas, July 22, 1981. BA in Spanish and EdS, Maryville U., 1962; Cert. EdS, U. Ky., 1966-67; MA in Edn., St. Louis U., 1974. Cert. learning disabilities, behavior disorders, educable mentally retarded, Spanish, Mo. Tchr. Pawnee Rock Kans. Sch., 1963-64; diagnostic tchr. Frankfort State Hosp. Sch., Ky., 1964-67; spl. edn. tchr. St. Louis City Pub. Schs., 1968-71, itinerant tchr., 1971-73, ednl. strategist, 1973-74, elem. level resource tchr., 1974-78, secondary resource tchr., dept. head, 1978—, head dept. spl. edn., 1978—, resource tchr., 1998—, dept. head, 1998; ret., 2000. Co-author: Sophomore English Resource for Credit Curriculum Handbook, 1991. Co-author: Teaching Foreign Language to Handicapped Secondary Students, 1990. Pres. Council for Exceptional Children, local chpt. #103, 1982-83, Mo. Division of Mentally Retarded, 1985-87. Mem. Alpha Delta Kappa (St. Louis chpt. pres. 1982-84). Avocations: traveling, reading, swimming, theatre, handicrafts. Home: 4534 Ohio Ave Saint Louis MO 63111-1324

THOMAS, PATRICIA GOODNOW, journalist; b. Framingham, Mass., Dec. 28, 1924; d. Charles Frederick and Dorothy (Eaton) G.; m. Roy Condit Thomas, Oct. 7, 1961. BS, Simmons Coll., 1946; MAT, Rollins Coll., 1971. News reporter-writer Radio Station WCOP, Boston, 1946-52; editorial specialist Central Intelligence Agy., Washington, 1952-54; asst. editor Hood Milk Corp., Boston, 1954-55; sr. writer/editor Voice of America, Washington, 1955-61; writer Orlando Mag., Orlando, Fla., 1964-72; tchr. French, Eng. Oviedo (Fla.) H.S., 1965-66; prof. of journalism Seminole Cmty. Coll., Sanford, Fla., 1972-88; freelance writer Blairsville, Ga., 1988—. Editor: From Sky to Sea, 1993; contbr. articles to profl. jours. Mem. Fla. Freelance Writers Assn., Kappa Delta Pi.

THOMAS, PATRICIA JOANNE, journalist, writer; b. Kenosha, Wis., July 17, 1948; d. Leatrice Shuman Magic and Russell Morton Maxwell(Stepfather); life ptnr. Meriwether Burruss Rhodes. BA, U. of Calif., Berkeley, 1967—69; MA, Stanford U., 1969—70. Vis. scholar, knight ctr. for sci. and med. journalism Boston U., Boston, 2002—; editor, harvard health letter Harvard Med. Sch., 1991—97. Mem., bd. of advisors Am. Bd. of Internal Medicine, Philadelphia, Pa., 1992—98. Author: (non-fiction book) Big Shot: Passion, Politics, and the Struggle for an AIDS Vaccine (Leonard Silk Journalism fellowship, 1998). Elected mem. Town Meeting, Arlington, Mass., 1992—2002. Fellow Knight Sci. Journalism Fellowship, MIT, 1986-1987. Mem.: Nat. Assn. of Sci. Writers. Avocations: tennis, standard poodles. Office: College of Communication Boston Univ 640 Commonwealth Avenue Boston MA 02215 Office Fax: 617-358-2348. Personal E-mail: pthomasauthor@yahoo.com.

THOMAS, PATRICK ROBERT MAXWELL, oncology educator, academic administrator; b. Exmouth, Devon, Eng., Feb. 23, 1943; came to U.S., 1976; s. Christopher Codrington and Aileen Daphne (Gordon) T.; m. Linda Sharon Rich, June 23, 1986 (dec. 1987), m. Geraldine M. Jacobson, Mar. 2, 1996 (div. 1999). Diploma in biochemistry, London U., 1965, MB, BS, 1968. Lectr. Inst. Cancer Rsch., London, 1974-76; assoc. chief clinician Roswell Park Meml. Inst., Buffalo, 1976-79; asst. prof. Washington U., St. Louis, 1979-83, assoc. prof., 1983-89, prof., 1989-90; prof., chmn. Temple U., Phila., 1991-98; radiation oncologist Pinellas (Fla.) Radiation Oncology Assocs., 1998—. Extramural bd. PDQ, Bethesda, Md., 1989—; mem. in-svc. exam. com. Am. Coll. Radiology, Reston, Va., 1990-97; examiner Am. Bd. Radiology, Louisville, 1990—. Mem. editl. adv. bd.: Med. and Pediatric Oncology, 2002—. Fellow Am. Coll. Radiologists, Royal Coll. Physicians of London; mem. Internat. Soc. Pediatric Oncology (sci. com. 2000—). Home: 100 Beach Dr NE Saint Petersburg FL 33701-3965 Office: 3155 N McMullen Booth Rd Clearwater FL 33761

THOMAS, PAUL LINDSLEY, composer, organist, music director; b. N.Y.C., Mar. 18, 1929; s. Richard Banks and Virginia Bartholomew (Carrington) T.; m. Joyce Robertshaw, Sept. 3, 1955; 1 child, Craig Carrington. BA, Trinity Coll., Hartford, Conn., 1950; diploma, Am. Conservatory, Fontainbleau, France, 1954; MusB, Yale U., 1957, MusM, 1958; D of Musical Arts, U. North Tex., 1979. Organist, choirmaster St. George's-by-the-River, Rumson, N.J., 1950-55, St. James Episcopal Ch., West Hartford, Conn., 1955-60; organist Wesleyan U., Middletown, 1958-60; dir. Apollo Glee Club, Yale U., New Haven, 1958-60; instr. in organ So. Meth. U., Dallas, 1960-65; music dir., organist St. Michael and All Angels Ch., 1960-97, composer in residence, music dir. emeritus, 1997—; music dir. Trinity Epis. Ch., 1998—. Chmn. liturgy and music comm. Episcopal Diocese of Dallas, 1995—. Composer (opera) Everyman, 1986; composer ch. anthems and organ music. Named Canon of Ch. Music, Episcopal Diocese of Dallas, 1980; recording grantee Stemmons Found., Dallas, 1995; Joyce and Paul Thomas Music Wing named in his honor St. Michael and All Angels, Dallas, 1994. Fellow Am. Guild Organists (dean Dallas chpt. 1967-69, gen. chmn. nat. conv. 1972, nat. coun. 1972-75); mem. Assn. Anglican Musicians, Am. Choral Dirs. Assn. Republican. Episcopalian. Home: 6822 Northwood Rd Dallas TX 75225-2538 Office: Trinity Episcopal Ch 12727 Hillcrest Rd Dallas TX 75230-2007

THOMAS, PAUL MILTON, retired science educator; b. Sligo, Pa., Dec. 1, 1929; s. Milton Ivan and Maude Hazel Thomas; m. Dorothy Marie McGinnett; children: Mona Lee Callahan. BA, Allegheny Coll., Meadville, PA, 1958; M.Ed., Univ. Mich., Ann Arbor, MI, 1959, MA, 1962, Dr. Philosophy, 1964. Instr., biol. Houghton Coll., Houghton, NY, 1959—62; asst. prof. Point Loma Coll., San Diego, 1964—66; rsch. fellow Calif. Inst. of Tech., Pasadena, 1967—68; vis. prof. Johns Hopkins Univ., Baltimore, 1968; prof., biol./chmn. Edinboro Univ., Edinboro, 1968—90; pastor United Ch. of Christ, Greensburg, 1995—2002. Contbr. articles to profl. jours.; author: (book) W. Edwards Deming: Improving Quality in Colleges and Universities, Easter Urges Us to Look at Death, A Christian Looks at Death, Pennsylvania Fish Commission. Mem. Sch. Bd., Union City, Pa., 1969—75. Mem.: Audubon Soc., Sigma Xi (Caltech), Phi Kappa Phi (Univ. Mich.). R-Conservative. United Church Of Christ. Avocations: hiking, world traveling. Home: 87 West High Street Union City PA 16438-1239 Office: Edinboro University of Pennsylvania Edinboro PA 16444 Home Fax: 814-438-1053. Personal E-mail: pthomas@velocity.net.

THOMAS, PAULETTE SUZANNE, holistic health practitioner, physician assistant; b. Lowell, Mass., Aug. 29, 1948; d. Armand Avila and Lucienne Adrienne (Lanseigne) Sawyer; Philip Edward Thomas Jr., June 9, 1979. AN, No. Essex C.C., Haverhill, Mass., 1972; cert. cardiac care nurse, Merrimack Coll., 1975; student, Boston Coll., 1976, Northeastern U., 1976-78, John A. Burns Sch. Medicine, 1981; D of Naturology, PhD in Naturology, Am. Inst. Holistic Theology, 1997. RN, Mass., Maine, Hawaii, Fla.; registered hypnotherapist; cert. hypnotherapist; diplomate naturopathic physician Am. Naturopathic Med. Cert. & Accreditation Bd. Head nurse insvc. and daycare Solomon Mental Health Ctr., Lowell, 1972-73; charge nurse ICU Las Olas Gen. Hosp., Ft. Lauderdale, Fla., 1973-74, Lemuel Shattuck Hosp., Jamaica Plain, Mass., 1975-76; charge nurse cardiac care unit Bon Secours Hosp., Methuen, 1974-75; supr., medicare coord. Oxford Manor, Haverhill, 1978-79, 84; physician asst. to chief internal medicine Straub Clinic and Hosp., Honolulu, 1980-82; owner managed elderly housing, Haverhill, 1982-87; physician asst. employee/occupl. health Lawrence (Mass.) Gen. Hosp., 1984-87; owner Tuckaway Shores Cabins and Restaurant, Jackman, Maine, 1987—; nursing educator cert. nursing asst. course Kennebec Valley Vocat. Tech. Inst., Fairfield, 1990-94; asst. program dir., dir. nursing svcs., adminstr. Northland Living Ctr., Jackman, 2000—. Mem. profl. policies com., mem. safefy com. Northland Living Ctr., Jackman, 1990-92. Author, editor, pub. Hawaiian Acad. Physician Assts. Newsletter, 1980-82; contbr. biweekly health column to Jackman/Moose River Chronicle, 1988-89. Bd. dirs. Tuckaway Assn., Nottingham, N.H., 1985-87; mem. Conservation Commn., Jackman, 1989; chmn. Main St. '90, Jackman and Moose River, 1989-90; originator, coord. Wellcome Wagon, Jackman and Moose River, 1990-92; mem. Town of Jackman Budget Com., 1991—. Mem. Am. Acad. Physician Assts. (pres. Hawaii chpt. 1980-82), First Nations Coun., Am. Naturopathic Med. Assn., Inst. Holistic Studies, Jackman/Moose River C. of C. Avocations: hiking, dancing, hand-crafts, music, boating. Home and Office: PO Box 44 Jackman ME 04945-9602

THOMAS, PHILIP ROBINSON, management consulting company executive; b. Torquay, Devon, Eng., Dec. 9, 1934; came to U.S., 1963, naturalized, 1969. s. Leslie Robinson and Margaret (Burridge) T.; m. Wayne Laverne Heirtzler, Apr. 6, 1973; children by previous marriage: Martin N.R., Stephen D.R. BSc, U. London, 1959, MSc, 1961, postgrad., 1961064. With Tex. Instruments Corp., 1961-72, ops. mgr., 1963-72, Bedford, Eng., 1961-63; v.p., gen. mgr. MOS/LSI divsn. Gen. Instruments Co., N.Y.C., 1972-73; gen. mgr. MOS Products divsn. Fairchild Camera and Instrument Corp., Mountainview, Calif., 1973-75; v.p. Integrated Circuits divsn. RCA, Somerville, N.J., 1975-78; chmn. bd. dirs., CEO Thomas Group Inc., Dallas, 1978-98. CEO, chmn. bd. dirs. Thomas Group Holding Co., Woodland Lakes LLC, PRT Global; gen. ptnr. Celerity Investment Fund; mng. ptnr. Wealth Enhancement Internat.; spkr. industry confs. Author: Competitiveness Through Total Cycle Time: An Overview for CEOs, 1989, Getting Competitive, 1990, Time Warrior, 1992, Quality Alone is Not Enough, 1993, Survival at Nodulex, 1994; contbr. articles to profl. jours.; patentee semicondrs. Home: # C 3510 Turtle Creek Blvd Dallas TX 75219-5542 Office: PRT Global 2710 N Stemmons Fwy Ste 200 Dallas TX 75207-2215

THOMAS, PHILIP STANLEY, economist, educator; b. Hinsdale, Ill., Oct. 23, 1928; s. Roy Kehl and Pauline (Grafton) Thomas; m. Carol Morris, Dec. 27, 1950; children: Lindsey Carol, Daniel Kyle, Lauren Louise, Gay Richardson. BA, Oberlin Coll., 1950; MA, U. Mich., 1951, PhD, 1961; postgrad., Delhi U., 1953-54. Instr. U. Mich., 1956-57; asst. prof. Grinnell (Iowa) Coll., 1957-63, assoc. prof., 1963-65; assoc. prof. econs. Kalamazoo Coll., 1965-68, prof. econs., 1968-94, prof. emeritus, 1994—. Econ. advisor Pakistan Inst. Devel. Econs., 1963—64, USAID, 1965—68, 1971, Planning Commn., Pakistan, 1969—70, Ctrl. Bank Swaziland, 1974—75, Ministry Planning, Kenya, 1980—81, Kenya, 1983—85, 1986—88, Ministry Fin., Swaziland, 1990, Kenya, 91, Kenya, 92, Ministry Indsl. Devel., Sri Lanka, 1997, Res. Bank Malawi, 1998—99, Jordan-U.S. Bus. Partnership, 2000—01. Contbr. articles to profl. jours. Mem. alumni coun. Oberlin Coll., 1961—63, 1974—76, 1983—86, 1995—2001. With AUS, 1954—56. Fellow Overseas, Ford Found., 1953—54; scholar Fulbright. Mem.: Am. Econs. Assn., Phi Beta Kappa. Home and Office: 313A S Shabwasung St Northport MI 49670-9604 E-mail: pcthomas@traverse.net.

THOMAS, RALPH CHARLES, III, federal official; b. Roanoke, Va., Apr. 10, 1949; s. Ralph C. Jr. and Dorothy (Easley) T. BA, U. Calif., Berkeley, 1975; JD, Harvard U., 1978. Assoc. Bergson, Borkland, Margolis & Adler, Washington, 1978-80; sr. ptnr. Thomas, John & Everett, 1980-85; clin. instr. in Law Sch. George Washington U., 1982-83; exec. dir. Nat. Assn. Minority Contractors, 1985-92; assoc. adminstr. for small/disadvantaged bus. utilization NASA, 1992—. Adj. instr. U. Va., Charlottesville, 1989—91; co-chmn. Fed. Small Bus. Dirs. Interagy. Coun., 2001—. Author: Extreme Flashbacks, 1997; contbr. articles to profl. jours. Mem. Pres.'s Interagy. Working Group on Minority Bus. Devel., 1995. Staff sgt. USAF, 1967-71, Vietnam. Recipient Presdl. Rank for Disting. Exec. award, 2001, Spl. Honor award, World Assn. Small and Medium Enterprises, 1999. Mem. Fed. Bar Assn. (chair govt. contracts sect. 2002--). Office: NASA Small & Disadvantaged Bus Utilization 300 E St SW Code K Washington DC 20546-0005

THOMAS, RALPH H. manufacturing executive; b. Bklyn., July 20, 1921; s. Neal and Genevie Mary Thomas; 4 children. BE, Fairleigh Dickinson U. Dir. packaging Bristol-Myers Co., Hillside, NJ; owner Thomas Packaging Cons., Union. With USN, 1944—45. Recipient award, Packaging Inst. Mem.: Mem. Orgn. Packaging Profls. Achievements include patents for 38 patents on roll-on-ball. Office: Thomas Packaging Cons 2204 Morris Ave #LL6 Union NJ 07083

THOMAS, RANDALL STUART, lawyer, educator; b. Princeton, N.J., Nov. 25, 1955; s. John Bowman and Eleanor (Graefe) T.; m. Cheri D. Ferrari; children: Cameron Stuart, Cortland Andrew, Colin Duncan, Carson F. Thomas. BA, Haverford Coll., 1977; MA, U. Mich., 1979, PhD, 1983, JD, 1985. Bar: Del. 1987, U.S. Dist. Ct. Del. 1987. Economist U. Mich., Ann Arbor, 1979-83; law clk. Fed. Dist. Ct. (ea. dist.) Mich., 1985; assoc. Potter, Anderson & Corroon, Wilmington, Del., 1986, Skadden, Arps, Slate, Meagher & Flom, Wilmington, 1987-90; assoc. prof. law U. Iowa, 1990-94, prof. law, 1994—, Vanderbilt Univ., 2000—. Vis. prof. Boston U. Law Sch., 1995, U. Mich. Law Sch., 1996, Duke U. Sch. Law, 1999. Rackham fellow U. Mich., 1982-83. Mem.: Order of Coif. Democrat. Methodist. Office: Vanderbilt Univ Sch Law 131 21st Ave S Nashville TN 37203-1120

THOMAS, RICHARD, actor; b. N.Y.C., June 13, 1951; s. Richard and Barbara (Fallis) T.; m. Alma Gonzalez, Feb. 14, 1975 (div.); children: Richard F., Barbara, Gwyneth and Pilar (triplets); m. Georgiana Bischoff, Nov. 20, 1995; 1 child, Montana; children from previous marriage: Brooke, Kendra. Student, Columbia U. Owner, prin. Melpomene Prodns. (broadway debut at age 7 in) Sunrise at Campobello, 1958, (regular on children's series) One, Two, Three-Go!, 1961-62, regular (TV series) The Waltons, 1972—77; actor: (films) Strange Interlude, 1962, The Playroom, 1965, Winning, 1969, Last Summer, 1969, You Can't Have Everything, 1970, Red Sky at Morning, 1971, The Todd Killings, 1971, Cactus in the Snow, 1971, You'll Like My Mother, 1972, 9/30/55, 1977, Battle Beyond the Star, 1980, Wonder Boys, 2000, Fortune Hunters, 2000; (stage appearances) Sunrise at Campobello, 1958, Whose Life Is It Anyway?, 1980, The Fifth of July, 1981, The Sea Gull, 1984, The Count of Monte Cristo, 1985, Citizen Tom Paine, 1986, The Front Page, 1986, Hamlet, 1987, Peer Gynt, 1989 , Love Letters, 1989-90, Square One, 1990, Lisbon Traviata, 1990, Danton's Death, 1992, Richard II, 1993, Richard III, 1994, Tiny Alice, 1998, 2000, Measure for Measure, 1999, A Midsummer's Night's Dream, 1999 , ART (west end), 2000, 2001, A Distant Country Called Youth, 2002; author: (poems) Poems by Richard Thomas, Vols. I and 2, 1974; actor: (TV dramatic spl. and movies) The Homecoming-A Christmas Story, 1971, The Red Badge of Courage, 1974, The Silence, 1975, All Quiet on the Eastern Front, 1979, The Hank Williams Jr. Story, 1983, Hobson's Choice, 1984, The Master of Ballantrae, 1984, Getting Married, No Other Love, 5th of July, 1981, Common Ground, Glory!, Glory!, 1990, Andre's Mother, 1990, It, 1990, Mission of the Shark , 1991, Yes, Virginia There Is a Santa Claus, 1991, A Walton's Thanksgiving Reunion, 1993, Death in Small Doses, 1993, Linda, 1993, A Walton Wedding, 1995, A Christmas Box, 1995, What Love Sees, 1996, A Walton Easter, 1998, Swiss Family Robinson, 1997, 1,000 Men and a Baby, 1997, Swiss Family Robinson, 1997, 1,000 Men and a Baby, 1997, Flood: A River's Rampage, 1997, Down Out and Dangerous, 1997, Big and Hairy, 1998, Beyond the Prairie, 2000, In the Name of the People, 2000, It's a Miracle, 1999-2000, The Christmas Secret, 2000, Miracle of the Cards, 2001, Beyond the Grave II, 2002; (host children's spl.) H.M.S. Pinafore, 1973. Nat. chmn. Better Hearing Inst., 1987—. Office: care Springer Assoc 1501 Broadway Ste 1314 A New York NY 10036-5601

THOMAS, RICHARD IRWIN, lawyer; b. Pitts., Jan. 28, 1944; s. Donald Martin and Mary Jane (Smith) T.; m. Karen Sorg (dec. Aug. 1979); children: Amy, Joe, Mike, Jim, Mauri, Mark, John; m. Jacalyn Silagyi, Feb. 1, 1992. Student, Georgetown U., 1961-62; BA, W.Va. Wesleyan Coll., 1965; JD, Duquesne U., 1972. Bar: Pa. 1972, U.S. Dist. Ct. (we. dist.) Pa. 1972, U.S. Ct. Appeals (3d cir.) 1974, U.S. Dist. Ct. (ea. dist.) Pa. 1976, U.S. Supreme Ct. 1977, U.S. Ct. Appeals (6th cir.) 1981, W.Va. 1999. Asst. personnel mgr. Continental Can Co., Pitts., 1966; mgr. labor relations U.S. Steel Corp., 1966-72; ptnr. Thorp, Reed & Armstrong, 1972-97; exec. mem. Burns White & Hickton, 1997—. Adj. prof. Duquesne U., Pitts., 1974-76; jud. mgr. Allegheny County Common Pleas Ct., Pitts., 1985; pres. Four North Shore Assocs., Pitts., 1997—; bd. dirs. Gen. Roofing Co., Bridgeville, Pa. Coach Upper St. Clair (Pa.) Athletic Assn., 1977-85; firefighter Upper St. Clair (Pa.) Vol. Fire Co., 1977-84. Named one of Outstanding Young Men in Am., 1973. Mem. ABA, Pa. Bar Assn., Allegheny Bar Assn. Republican. Roman Catholic. Avocations: skiing, white water rafting, golf, athletics. Home: 283 Mcmurray Rd Pittsburgh PA 15241-1613 Office: Burns White & Hickton 120 5th Ave Ste 2400 Pittsburgh PA 15222-3011 E-mail: rithomas@bwhllc.com.

THOMAS, RICHARD LEE, banker; b. Marion, Ohio, Jan. 11, 1931; s. Marvin C. and Irene (Harruff) T.; m. Helen Moore, June 17, 1953; children: Richard L., David Paul, Laura Sue. BA, Kenyon Coll., 1953; postgrad. (Fulbright scholar), U. Copenhagen, Denmark, 1954; MBA (George F. Baker scholar), Harvard U., 1958. With First Nat. Bank Chgo., 1958—, asst. v.p., 1962-63, v.p., 1963-65; v.p., gen. mgr. First Nat. Bank (London br.), 1965-66; v.p. term loan divsn. First Nat. Bank, Chgo., 1968; sr. v.p., gen. mgr. First Chgo. Corp., 1969-72, exec. v.p., 1972-73, vice chmn. bd., 1973-75, pres., 1975-92, chmn., pres., CEO, 1992-95; chmn. First Chgo. NBD Corp., 1995-96, ret. chmn., 1996. Bd. dirs. Sara Lee Corp., Sabre Holdings Corp., IMC Global Inc., PMI Group Inc., EXELON Corp. Trustee, past chmn. bd. trustees Kenyon Coll., Chgo. Symphony Orch.; trustee Rush-Presbyn.-St. Luke's Med. Ctr., Northwestern U. With AUS, 1954-56. Mem. Chgo. Coun. Fgn. Rels., Sunningdale Golf Club (London), Econ. Club (past pres.), Comml. Club (past chmn.), Chgo. Club, Casino Club, Mid-Am. Club, Indian Hill Club (Winnetka, Ill.), Old Elm Club (Highland Park, Ill.), Phi Beta Kappa, Beta Theta Pi. Office: First Chgo NBD Corp 1 Bank One Plz Ste IL1-0518 Chicago IL 60670-0001 E-mail: richard_l_thomas@bankone.com.

THOMAS, RICHARD O. civilian military employee; b. Boise, Idaho, May 29, 1941; s. Ormond and Mary Lacey T.; m. Linda Hill, Oct. 5, 1963; children: Lauren, Sharon, Steven. BS Aeronautical Engring., Rensselaer Polytech. Inst., 1963; MS Ops. Rsch., George Washington U., 1973; postgrad. program for sr. execs., MIT, 1986. Rschr. David Taylor Rsch. Ctr., Carderock, Md., 1963-68; head support forces, logistic sect. Office Naval Ops., 1969-75; mgr. Am. Mgmt. Systems Inc., 1976-77; dir. Office Policy and Plans Maritime Adminstrn. (U.S. Dept. Commerce, now U.S. Dept. Transp.), Washington, 1978-82; dir. resources and policy evaluation Office Asst. Sec. Navy U.S. Dept. Navy, 1983-90, dep. asst. sec. Shore Resources, 1991—. Office: Installations & Environment 1000 Navy Pentagon Washington DC 20350-1000

THOMAS, RICHARD STEPHEN, financial executive; b. Mason City, Iowa, June 5, 1949; s. H. Idris and Mildred (Keen) T.; m. Pamela Jane Chipka, Sept. 11, 1982. AA, No. Iowa C.C., 1969; BA, U. No. Iowa, 1971, BLS, 1991; MBA, U. Calif., Berkeley, 1991. Cost acct. Boise Cascade, Mason City, Iowa, 1971-72, cost acct. mgr. Shippensburg, Pa., 1973-74; staff acct. Grumman Corp., Williamsport, 1974-76; acctg. mgr. Pullman Power Products, 1976-79; treas, controller Schweizer Dipple Inc., Cleve., 1979-87; treas., corp. controller Langenau Mfg. Co., 1987-92, chief fin. officer, 1987-92; sec.-treas. World Trade Wins Inc., 1987-92; v.p. fin. and CFO Norris Bros. Co., Inc., 1992—. Mem. employer adv. com. Ohio Job Svc., Greater Cleve. Growth Assn., Westlake Ohio Sch. Bd. Mem. Inst. Mgmt. Accts. (contr.'s coun. 1985), Constrn. Fin. Mgmt. Assn. (pres. 1995—, state dir., nat. dir.), Am. Coun. for Constrn. Edn. (accreditation and standards com. 1996—, fin. comm. 1997-98), Constrn. Industry Liason Comm. (chmn.), Cleve. Treas.'s Assn., Cleve. Engring. Soc., Associated Builders and Contractors, Constrn. Employers Assn., Econ. Club Indpls., Cleve. World Trade Assn., Masons (local treas. 1984), York Rite Bodies, City Club of Cleve., Phi Beta Lambda. Republican. Avocations: skiing, photography, sailing. Home: 1663 Settlers Reserve Way Westlake OH 44145-2042 Office: Norris Bros Co Inc 2138 Davenport Ave Cleveland OH 44114-3791 E-mail: rsthomas49@aol.com.

THOMAS, RITCHIE TUCKER, lawyer; b. Cleve., Aug. 12, 1936; s. Myron F. and Marjorie (Ritchie) T.; m. Elizabeth Blackwell Hanes Main, Jan. 1, 1994. BA, Cornell U., 1959; JD, Case-Western Res. U., 1964. Bar: Ohio 1964, U.S. Dist. Ct. (no. dist.) Ohio 1964, U.S. Ct. Appeals (D.C. cir.) 1971, U.S. Ct. Appeals (fed. cir.) 1973, U.S. Ct. Fed. Claims 1973, U.S. Ct. Internat. Trade 1976, U.S. Ct. Appeals (9th cir.) 1985. Assoc. office of gen. counsel U.S. Tariff Commn., Washington, 1964-67; assoc. Squire, Sanders & Dempsey, Cleve., 1967-69, Cox, Langford & Brown, Washington, 1969-74; ptnr. Squire, Sanders & Dempsey, 1974—. Mem. exec. com. Meridian House Internat., Washington, 1977-94; Washington rep. Am. C. of C. in Germany, 1984—; v.p. bd. dirs. Belgian Am. Assn., 1989—. Assoc. editor Western Res. U. Law Rev., 1964; columnist Commerce Germany; contbr. articles to profl. jours. Mem. Waring Prize Com., Western Res. Acad., 1996—. Recipient various book award West Pub. Co., 1964. Mem. Fed. Bar Assn., D.C. Bar Assn., Order of Coif. Home: 6700 Bradley Blvd Bethesda MD 20817-3045 Office: Squire Sanders & Dempsey 1201 Pennsylvania Ave NW PO Box 407 Washington DC 20044-0407 E-mail: rtthomas@ssd.com.

THOMAS, ROBERT EGGLESTON, former corporate executive; b. Cuyahoga Falls, Ohio, July 28, 1914; s. Talbott E. and Jane S. (Eggleston) T.; children: Robert Eggleston, Barbara Ann. BS in Econs, U. Pa., 1936. Asst. to gen. mgr., sec., mgr. r.r. investments Keystone Custodian Funds, Boston, 1936-53; v.p. Pennroad Corp., N.Y.C., 1953-59; chmn. exec. com., dir. M.-K.-T. R.R., 1956-65; mem. exec. com. MAPCO Inc., 1960-84, dir., chief exec. officer, 1960-80, pres., 1960-76, chmn. bd., 1973-84. Adv. bd. BancOkla. Corp. Mem.: Newcomen Soc., Nat. Mining Assn. (hon. dir.), Am. Petroleum Inst. (hon. dir.), Desert Horizons Country Club (Indian Wells, Calif.), San Diego Yacht Club, Summit Club (Tulsa), So. Hills Country Club (Tulsa), Chgo. Club. Episcopalian. Office: Williams Cos PO Box 4679 Tulsa OK 74159-0679

THOMAS, ROBERT L. manufacturing company executive; b. Atlanta, Aug. 1, 1941; s. Orville Kermit Smith and Ina Evelyn (Farris) Peterson; m. Karen Degenhardt, Dec. 4, 1960 (div. Apr. 1978); children: John Harding, Gregory James, Kristen Ann; m. Mary Ellen Seaman, May 2, 1981; children: Lindsey Marian, Mark Gordon. BA in History, Queens Coll., 1968. Buyer J.C. Penney Co. Inc., N.Y.C., 1964-70; sales mgr. Avon Products Inc., Atlanta, 1970-72; pres. Saul Bros. & Co. Inc., 1973—. Bd. dirs. Murphey Candler Little League, Atlanta, 1972, also bd. trustees; bd. dirs. Leukemia Soc., Atlanta, 1988—; mem. Dekalb County Exec. Com. Rep. Party, Atlanta, 1970-74; delegate State Convention Rep. Party, Atlanta, 1972. Established scholarship Michael Daniel and Alexander Tyler Smith Scholarship Found., U. S.C., 1995—. Mem. South East Textile and Apparel Mfrs., U.S. Polo Assn., Atlanta Polo Club, Gulfstream Polo Club (West Palm Beach), N.Y. Athletic Club (N.Y.C.), Country Club of the South (Alpharetta, Ga.). Republican. Roman Catholic. Home: 4095 Big Creek Overlook Alpharetta GA 30005-4213 Office: Saul Bros & Co Inc 5730 Oakbrook Pkwy Ste 105 Norcross GA 30093-1825

THOMAS, ROBERT MORTON , JR. lawyer; b. Kansas City, Kans., Jan. 1, 1941; s. Robert Morton Sr. and Arlowyne Edith (Arganbright) T.; m. Rebecca Ann Myers, Aug. 21, 1965; children: Brooke J., Austin B. BA, U. Kans., 1962; LLB, Harvard U., 1966. Bar: N.Y., U.S. Dist. Ct. (so. dist.) N.Y., U.S. Ct. Appeals (2nd cir.). Local govt. advisor Republic of Botswana, Gaborone, 1966, dist. officer Serowe, 1967, dist. commr. Maun, 1968; assoc. Sullivan & Cromwell, N.Y.C., 1969-75, ptnr., 1975—, ptnr.-in-charge London, 1979-82, mng. ptnr. gen. practice group N.Y.C., 1986-91. Mem. exec. bd. Manhattan coun. Boy Scouts Am.; trustee U. Kans. Endowment Assn. Mem. ABA, N.Y. State Bar Assn., Assn. of Bar of City of N.Y., Internat. Bar Assn., India House, Buck's Club, Harvard Club, Mill Reef Club, Verbank Hunting and Fishing Club (dir., pres.), Knickerbocker Club, Confrerie des Chevaliers de Tastevin. Republican. Presbyterian. Office: Sullivan & Cromwell 125 Broad St New York NY 10004-2498 E-mail: thomasr@sullcrom.com.

THOMAS, ROBERT R. judge; b. Rochester, N.Y., Aug. 7, 1952; m. Maggie Thomas; 3 children. BA in govt., U. Notre Dame, 1974; JD, Loyola U., 1981. Cir. ct. judge DuPage County, 1988, acting chief judge, 1989—94; judge Appellate Ct. Second Dist., 1994—2000; Supreme Ct. justice Ill. State Supreme Ct., 2000—. Mem.: DuPage County Bar Assn., Acad. All-Am. Hall of Fame (life NCAA Silver Ann. Award 1999). Office: Bldg A Rm 207A 1776 S Naperville Rd Wheaton IL 60187*

THOMAS, ROBERT RENE, physician assistant, athletic trainer; b. Santa Monica, Calif., July 19, 1955; s. Erving Robert Thomas and Vertis Lee Sample; adopted parents: Terry and Ann Corrigan. BE, Gonzaga U., 1980; MS in Physician Asst., U. Detroit, 1998. Cert. physician asst. Tchr., Spokane, Wash., 1981-82, Fed. Way (Wash.) Sch. Dist., 1983-90; summer intern Phila. Eagles, 1988, 89; asst. athletic trainer Detroit Lions, 1990-97; physician asst. Henry Ford Hosp., W. Bloomfield, Mich., 1998-2000, Ctr. for Spine and Orthopedic Surgery, Cheyenne, Wyo., 2000-01, Sportsmedicine Fairbanks, Alaska, 2001—. Athletic trainer Goodwill Games, Seattle, 1990, U.S. Womens Soccer, Pontiac, Mich., 1994. Grantee NSF, 1984. Fellow Am. Assn. Physician Assts.; mem. Nat. Athletic Trainers Assn. Democrat. Roman Catholic. Avocations: hunting, fishing, golfing.

THOMAS, ROBERTA MARIE, librarian; b. Chgo., Oct. 10, 1955; d. Donald Earl and Lucile Viola (Halaska) T. BA, Rosary Coll., 1978, MALS, 1980. Circulation dept. head Palatine (Ill.) Pub. Libr. Dist., 1979-94; adminstrv. librarian Grayslake (Ill.) Area Pub. Libr. Dist., 1994—. Mem. ALA, Ill. Libr. Assn., Grayslake Jaycees (pres. 1998-99), Grayslake Woman's Club (pres. 2000—). Office: Grayslake Area Pub Libr Dist 100 Library Ln Grayslake IL 60030-1684

THOMAS, RODNEY BRENT, ecologist, biologist; b. Ft. Smith, Ark., Apr. 13, 1969; s. Norman Ervin and Joyce June (Elder) T.; m. Stephanie Jo Schaffer, June 15, 1990. BS in Biol. Scis., U. Ozarks, 1991; MS in Biol. Scis., S.W. Mo. State U., 1993; postgrad., Miss. State U., 1995—. Social svcs. asst. Cass Job Corp. Ctr., Ozark, 1988-91; adj. faculty S.W. Bapt. U., Springfield, Mo., 1993-94, Ozarks Tech. C.C., Springfield, 1993-94; wildlife biologist Mo. Dept. Conservation, Columbia, 1995; adj. faculty Miss. U. Women, Columbus, 1996. Co-chmn. Miss. Delta region Declining Amphibian Task Force, La., Miss., Ark., 1997—. Contbr. articles to profl. jours. Recreational asst. Boys and Girls Clubs, Springfield, 1994-95. Miss. State U. fellow 1996—. Mem. Soc. Study Amphibians Reptiles, Animal Behavior Soc., Am. Soc. Ichthyologists Herpetologist, Southwestern Assn. Naturalist, Herpetologists League. Avocation: hunting, fishing, martial arts, hiking. Office: Mississippi State Univ Dept Biol Sci PO Drawer GY Mississippi State MS 39762

THOMAS, ROGER MERIWETHER, lawyer; b. Hartford, Conn., Feb. 28, 1930; s. Frederick Metcalf and Helen Meriwether (Lewis) T.; m. Mary Dorothea Wyman, Dec. 4, 1965; children— Donald Wyman, Helen Dorothea AB, Princeton U., 1952; LL.B., Va. U., 1957; LL.M., Boston U., 1964. Bar: N.Y. 1958, Mass. 1960, U.S. Dist. Ct. (Mass) 1965, U.S. Tax Ct. 1965, U.S. Supreme Ct. 1967. Assoc. Angulo, Cooney, Marsh & Ouchterloney, N.Y.C., 1957-60; assoc., then ptnr. Gaston & Snow, Boston, 1960-91; counsel Condit & Assocs., P.C., 1992-94. Outline author and lectr. Mass. Continuing Legal Edn., Inc., Boston; past panelist New Eng. Law Inst. Estate Planning Forums, Boston. Trustee Buckingham Browne & Nichols Sch., Cambridge, Mass., 1967-69. Served to 1st lt. U.S. Army, 1952-54, Korea. Mem. Am. Coll. Trust and Estate Counsel, Boston Bar Assn., Mass. Bar Assn. Avocations: reading; sports; old movies. Home: 40 Byron Rd Weston MA 02493-2229

THOMAS, ROGER WARREN, lawyer; b. South Weymouth, Mass., Sept. 17, 1937; s. Clement Rogers and Beatrice (Merritt) T.; m. Maria Sava Brenner, July 5, 1968; children: Caroline, Andrew, Phillip. BA, U. N.H., 1959; postgrad. (Rotary Internat. fellow), Free U. Berlin, 1960; LLB (Root-Tilden scholar), NYU, 1963, LLM (Ford Found. grantee), 1965; postgrad., U. Chile, Santiago, 1965. Bar: N.Y. 1964. Assoc. Cleary, Gottlieb, Steen and Hamilton, N.Y.C., 1965-66, 69-74, partner, 1974—. Mem. Harvard-Chile Tax Reform Project, 1966-68, head project in Chile, 1968-69; cons. to UN, Santiago, 1969; adj. prof. taxation NYU, 1974-96. Co-author: El Impuesto a la Renta, 1969. Bd. dirs. Spanish Repertory Theatre, Fundacion Chile, UNH Found. Mem. ABA, Am. Fgn. Lawyers Assn., N.Y. State Bar Assn., N.Am.-Chilean C. of C. (pres. 1984-96), Am. Soc., Coun. of Am., Down Town Assn. N.Y.C., Knickerbocker Club. Home: 1150 5th Ave New York NY 10128-0724 Office: 1 Liberty Plz New York NY 10006-1404

THOMAS, SARAH REBECCA, computer science educator; b. East Lansing, Mich., Feb. 2, 1965; d. Stuart Winston and Caroline Thomas; m. Bryan William Van Norden, July 7, 1990; children: Charles Rutherford III, Melissa Caroline. BS, MIT, 1987; PhD, Stanford U., 1993. Asst. prof. U. No. Iowa, Cedar Falls, 1993-95; asst, prof. Marist Coll., Poughkeepsie, N.Y., 1995-2000; assoc. prof. computer sci. Bard Coll., Annandale-on-Hudson, 2000—. Reviewer Spl. Interest Group on Computer Sci. Edn., NIA, 1994—. Author: (with others) Encyclopedia of Computer Science and Technology, 1993, Intelligent Agents, 1995, Foundations of Rational Agency, 1999. Recipient scholarship AT&T Bell Lab. Engring. scholarship, 1983-87, grad. fellowship NSF, 1987-91; grantee: NSF. Mem. Am. Assn. for Artificial Intelligence, Assn. for Computing Machinery, Sigma Xi, Tau Beta Pi. Office: Bard Coll Dept Computer Sci Annandale On Hudson NY 12504-5000

THOMAS, SCOTT E. federal government executive, lawyer; b. Buffalo, Mar. 5, 1953; s. Ralph E. and Bonnie E. Thomas; m. Elena W. King, Apr. 28, 1984. BA, Stanford U., 1974; JD, Georgetown U., 1977. Bar: D.C. 1977, U.S. Ct. Appeals (9th cir.) 1980, U.S. Supreme Ct. 1981. Atty. Office of Gen. Counsel, Fed. Election Commn., Washington, 1977-80, asst. gen. counsel, 1980-83; exec. asst. to commr. Fed. Election Commn., 1983-86, commr., 1986—. Mem. D.C. Bar Assn. Office: Fed Election Commn 999 E St NW Washington DC 20463-0002

THOMAS, SHIRLEY, author, educator, business executive; b. Glendale, Calif. d. Oscar Miller and Ruby (Thomas) Annis; m. W. White, Feb. 22, 1949 (div. June 1952); m. William C. Perkins, Oct. 24, 1969. BA in Modern Lit., U. Sussex, Eng., 1960, PhD in Comm., 1967; diploma, Russian Fedn. Cosmonautics, 1995. Actress, writer, producer, dir. numerous radio and TV stas., 1942-46; v.p. Commodore Prodns., Hollywood, Calif., 1946-52; pres. Annis & Thomas, Inc., 1952—; prof. technical writing U. So. Calif., L.A., 1975—. Hollywood corr. NBC, 1952-56; editor motion pictures CBS, Hollywood, 1956-58; corr. Voice of Am., 1958-59; now free lance writer; cons. biol. scis. communication project George Washington U., 1965-66; cons. Stanford Rsch. Inst., 1967-68, Jet Propulsion Lab., 1969-70. Author: Men of Space vols. 1-8, 1960-68, Spanish trans., 1961, Italian, 1962; Space Tracking Facilities, 1963, Computers: Their History, Present Applications and Future, 1965; The Book of Diets, 1974. Organizer, chmn. City of L.A. Space Adv. Com., 1964-73, Women's Space Symposia, 1962-73; founder, chmn. Aerospace Hist. Soc. Inc.; chmn. Theodore von Karman Postage Stamp Com., 1965—, stamp issued 1992; bd. dirs. World Children's Transplant Fund, 1993—, Achievement Rewards for Coll. Scients. Recipient Aerospace Excellence award Calif. Mus. Found. 1991, Nat. Medal Honor DAR, 1992, Yuri Gagarin Medal Honor, 1995. Fellow Brit. Interplanetary Soc.; mem. AIAA, AAAS, Internat. Acad. Astronautics, Internat. Soc. Aviation Writers, Air Force Assn. (Airpower Arts and Letters award 1961), Internat. Acad. Astronautics, Nat. Aero. Assn., Nat. Asn. Sci. Writers, Soc. for Tech. Communications, Am. Astronautical Soc., Nat. Geog. Soc., Am. Soc. Pub. Adminstrn. (sci. and tech. in govt. com. 1972—), Achievement Awards for Coll. Scientists, Theta Sigma Phi, Phi Beta. Home: 8027 Hollywood Blvd Los Angeles CA 90046-2510 Office: U So Calif Profl Writing Program University Park Waite Phillips Hall 404 Los Angeles CA 90089-0001 E-mail: snowtech@pacbell.net.

THOMAS, SIDNEY, fine arts educator, researcher; b. N.Y.C., Dec. 21, 1915; s. Hyman and Rose (Samilowitz) T.; m. Rae Dinkowitz, May 26, 1940; children: David Phillip, Deborah Rose. BA, CCNY, 1935; MA, Columbia U., 1938, PhD, 1943. Tutor in English CCNY, N.Y.C., 1939-43; instr. English Queens Coll., 1946-54; self-employed as editor, 1954-58; asst. editor Merriam-Webster, Springfield, Mass., 1958-61; assoc. prof. fine arts Syracuse U. (N.Y.), 1961-66, prof., 1966-85, prof. emeritus, 1985—, dir. humanities doctoral program, 1964-72, chmn. dept. fine arts, 1969-73. Bibliographer Shakespeare Assn., N.Y.C., 1949-54 Author: The Antic Hamlet, 1943; co-editor: The Nature of Art, 1964; editor: Images of Man, 1972. Served to sgt., inf. U.S. Army, 1943-45, ETO. Research fellow Folger Shakespeare Library, Washington, 1947-48 Fellow Royal Soc. Arts (London); mem. MLA (life), Shakespeare Assn. Am., AAUP (pres. Syracuse U. chpt. 1974), ACLU, Phi Beta Kappa Office: Syracuse U Dept Fine Arts Syracuse NY 13210

THOMAS, SIDNEY R. federal judge; b. Bozeman, Mont., Aug. 14, 1953; m. Martha Sheehy. BA in Speech-Comm., Mont. State U., 1975, JD cum laude, 1978; D (hon.) , Rocky Mountain Coll., 1998. Bar: Mont. 1978, U.S. Dist. Ct. Mont. 1978, U.S. Ct. Appeals (9th cir.) 1980, U.S. Dist. Ct. (9th cir.) 1980, U.S. Ct. Fed. Claims 1986, U.S. Supreme Ct. 1994. Shareholder Moulton, Bellingham, Longo and Mather, P.C., Billings, Mont., 1978—96; judge U.S. Ct. Appeals 9th Cir., 1996—. Adj. instr. Rocky Mountain Coll., Billings, 1982—95. Contbr. articles to profl. jours. Recipient Gov.'s award for Pub. Svc., 1978, Outstanding Faculty award, Rocky Mountain Coll., 1988. Mem.: ABA, Yellowstone County Bar Assn., State Bar Mont. Office: US Ct Appeals Ninth Circuit PO Box 31478 Billings MT 59107-1478*

THOMAS, STAFFORD TUTT, political scientist, educator; b. Kansas City, Mo., Jan. 13, 1941; s. Edward Sandusky and Dorothy Stafford Thomas; m. Carol Leslie Berg, Dec. 27, 1976. BA, Whittier Coll., 1962; MA, Ga. State U., 1971; PhD, U. Colo., 1975. Def. analyst USN, Pt. Mugu, Calif., 1962—64; sys. analyst Citizens and So. Bank, Atlanta, 1966—68; prodn. mgr. Teledata Corp., 1968—71; grad. asst. U. Colo., Boulder, 1971—76; assoc. prof. Canisius Coll., Buffalo, 1976—84; prof. Calif. State U., Chico, 1984—2002, prof. emeritus, 2002—. Author: The U.S. Intelligence Community, 1984; mem. editl. bd.: Internat. Jour. Intelligence and Counterintelligence, 1999—. Served with U.S. Army, 1964—66. Mem.: Western Polit. Sci. Assn., Am. Polit. Sci. Assn. Avocations: reading, travel. Office: Calif State U Dept Polit Sci Chico CA 95929 Business E-Mail: sthomas@csuchico.edu.

THOMAS, STEPHEN JAY, anesthesiologist; b. Washington, 1943; Intern San Francisco Gen. Hosp., 1968-69; resident in anesthesiology Mass. Gen. Hosp., Boston, 1971-73, fellow, 1973-74; assoc. prof. NYU Med. Ctr.; vice chmn., prof. dept. anesthesiology N.Y. Presbyn. Weill Cornell Ctr., 1989—; pres. American Board of Anesthesiology, 2001—. Office: NY Presbyn Weill Cornell Ctr Dept Anesthesiology 525 E 68th St New York NY 10021-4870*

THOMAS, STEPHEN PAUL, lawyer; b. Bloomington, Ill., July 30, 1938; s. Owen Wilson and Mary Katherine (Paulsen) T.; m. Marianne Sauer, Dec. 7, 1963 (dec. June 1984); 1 child, Catherine Marie; m. Marcia Aldrich Toomey, May 28, 1988; 1 child, Ellen Antonia. BA, U. Ill., 1959; LLB, Harvard U., 1962. Bar: Ill. 1962; cert. naturalist Morton Arboretum, 2001. Vol. Peace Corps, Malawi, Africa, 1963-65; assoc. Sidley & Austin, Chgo., 1965-70, ptnr., 1970-2000. Lectr. on law Malawi Inst. Pub. Adminstrn., 1963-65. Pres. Hyde Park-Kenwood Cmty. Conf., Chgo., 1988-90; trustee Chgo. Acad. for Arts, 1991—, chmn., 1992-97; bd. dirs. Union League Civic and Arts Found., Chgo., 1999—. Recipient Paul Cornell award Hyde Park Hist. Soc., 1981. Mem. ABA, Chgo. Bar Assn., Chgo. Fedn. of Musicians, Lawyers Club of Chgo., Union League Club Chgo., Chgo. Literary Club. Democrat. Roman Catholic. Avocations: jazz piano playing, naturalist studies. Home: 9765 S Longwood Dr Chicago IL 60643-1610 Office: Sidley Austin Brown & Wood 55 W Monroe St Chicago IL 60603-5001 E-mail: sthomas@sidley.com.

THOMAS, SUZANNE WARD, public relations executive, communications educator, radio personality; b. Akron, Ohio, Sept. 21, 1954; d. Kendall Kramer and Margaret Ann (Owen) Ward; m. James Michael Thomas, Oct. 20, 1980; children: Seth Evin, James Kendall. BS in Edn., Miami U., Oxford, Ohio, 1977; MA in Comm., Regent U., Virginia Beach, Va., 1980. Writer, prodr. Sta. WVIZ, PBS, Cleve., 1980-82; dir. pub. rels. Sta. WOAC-TV, Canton, 1982-83, hostess children's show, 1982-84; v.p. Thomas Video Prodns., Canal Fulton, 1987-90; dir. pub. rels., instr. comm. Malone Coll., Canton, 1990—, editor Horizon, 1990—. Author: (children's book) The Miracles of Jesus, 1991, also manuals. Hostess pub. affairs program Community TV Consortium, Canton, 1987; subcom. chmn. Govt. Day, Leadership Canton, 1987; v.p. Right to Life Ednl. Found., Canton, 1990; chmn. pub. rels. Jr. League Canton, 1986-87, rec. sec., 1987-88; bd. dirs. PTO, 1989-90; mgmt. assistance program United Way, 1998-99. Recipient Sparkler award Jr. League Canton, 1986, Pub. Rels. award, 1987, Addy awards Canton Advt. Club, 1992, 96. Mem. Sales and Mktg. Execs. (bd. dirs. Stark County chpt. 1989), Assn. Jr. Leagues Internat., Pub. Rels. Soc. Am. (accredited in pub. rels. 1995, bd. dirs.). Republican. Avocations: reading, tennis, aerobics, golf, writing. Office: Malone Coll 515 25th St NW Canton OH 44709-3823

THOMAS, SYLVIA ELIZABETH, artist; b. Amarillo, Tex., Apr. 18, 1931; d. Orville Alvie and Erah (Cearley) Blankenship; m. Allen Ralph Thomas, June 21, 1953 (dec. Nov. 1984); children: Michael Allen, Melanie Kay Thomas-Singleton, Terry Neal, Kelly Andrew. BA in Fine Art, West Tex. State Coll., 1953. Cert. life tchg. cert., Tex. Jr. H.S. art tchr. Dumas (Tex.) Pub. Schs., 1953; art tchr. Amarillo Pub. Sch. 5, 1973-76. Vol. art tchr. Sr. Citizen Assn., Amarillo, 1992-96. One-woman shows include Lost Circus Gallery, Amarillo, 1989, Carson County Square House Mus., Panhandle, Tex., 1991, 98, XIT Mus. Art Gallery, Dalhart, Tex., 1992, Junction City (Kans.) Arts Coun., 1993, Crabb Art Ctr., Dumas, Tex., 1993, 98, Kathleens Art Cafe, Dallas, 1994; exhibited in group shows at Carson County Sq. House Mus., 1995, Jamboree of Arts, Amarillo, 1995 (Best of Show), Colony Gallery, Amarillo, 1998, numerous others; permanent collections include Carson City Square House Mus., Crabb Art Ctr.; represented in numerous pvt. collections in Tex., Kans., Colo., N.Mex. Mem. Lone Star Pastel Soc. (pres., founder 1995-96), Pastel Soc. S.W. (show chmn. 1983-84, PSA plaque 1984, Gold Grumbacher medal 1989, 2d place award 1994), Artists and Craftsmen, Pastel Soc. Am.(signature mem., Sauter Margulies award 1992), Pastel Soc. N.Mex., Amarillo Fine Arts Assn. (Best of Show award 1986, 2d pl award 1988, 95, 1st place award 1991). Republican.

THOMAS, TARQUIN CRAIG, computer scientist, writer; b. Haslemere, Surrey, Eng., May 7, 1966; s. Leicester Craig and Margaret Lina T. Systems analyst Multisoft Systems Ltd., Alton, Eng., 1984-85; cons. Migration Techs. Ltd., Windsor, Eng., 1987; prin. tech. mgr. TIS Ltd., Bourne End, Eng., 1988-94; cons. Barclays Global Investors, San Francisco, 1995—. Cons. MISYS P.L.C., Eng., 1994. Author: (CD-Rom) EJW-CDR, 1994; contr. articles to profl. jours. Recipient Barclays Chmn.'s award for Cmty. Involvement. Mem. Inst. Data Processing Mgmt., Brit. Mensa. Avocations: art, advocacy child rights and welfare.

THOMAS, TERENCE PATRICK, writer, researcher, electronics design engineer; b. Concord, Ky., Sept. 16, 1942; s. Charles Edwin Thomas and Daisy Merle (Wolfe) Minger. Tchr. Freespace Alternate U., N.Y.C., 1977, The Mannes Coll. Music, N.Y.C., 1978-79, New Sch. for Social Rsch., N.Y.C., 1978; head design engr. NYU, 1978-80; rschr. Thomas Enterprises, Venice, Fla., 1984—. Author: Sound Synthesis (Analog and Digital Techniques), 1990; contbr. to Robotics column Radio/Electronics Mag., Farmingdale, N.Y., 1986. Mem. N.Y. Acad. Scis. Achievements include design of computer-controlled high-speed laser beam modulator; with use of conductive vinyl, development of robotic sensors to enable hand devices to sense slippage and apply only the amount of pressure necessary to lift an object, thus preserving delicate samples. Avocations: tennis, chess, science fiction, music composition, football. Home: 336 Warfield Ave S Venice FL 34292-2657

THOMAS, TERESA ANN, microbiologist, educator; b. Wilkes-Barre, Pa., Oct. 17, 1939; d. Sam Charles and Edna Grace T. BS cum laude, Coll. Misericordia, 1961; MS in Biology, Am. U., Beirut, 1965; MS in Microbiology, U. So. Calif., 1973; cert. in ednl. tech., U. Calif., San Diego, 1998. Tchr., sci. supr., curriculum coord. Meyers High Sch., Wilkes-Barre, 1962-64, Wilkes-Barre Area Public Schs., 1961-66; rsch. assoc. Proctor Found. Rsch. in Ophthalmology U. Calif. Med. Ctr., San Francisco, 1966-68; instr. Robert Coll. of Istanbul (Turkey), 1968-71, Am. Edn. in Luxembourg, 1971-72, Bosco Tech. Inst., Rosemead, Calif., 1973-74, San Diego C.C. Dist., 1974-80; prof. microbiology and ecology Sch. Math Scis. and Engring. Southwestern Coll., Chula Vista, Calif., 1980—; mem. Vecinos Baja Studies EcoMundo team internat. program Southwestern Coll. Pres. acad. senate, 1984-85, del., 1986-89; chmn., coord., steering com. project Cultural Rsch. Ednl. and Trade Exch., 1991-2000, Southwestern Coll.-Shanghai Inst. Fgn. Trade; coord. Southwestern Coll. Great Teaching Seminar, 1987, 88, 89, coord. scholars program, 1988-90; mem. steering com. Southwestern Coll.; mem. exec. com. Acad. Senate for Calif. C.C.s, 1985-86, Chancellor of Calif. C.C.s Adv. and Rev. Coun. Fund for Instrnl. Improvement, 1984-86; co-project dir. statewide, coord. So. Calif. Biotech. Edn. Consortium, 1993-95, steering com., 1993-98; adj. asst. prof. Chapman Coll., San Diego, 1974-83, San Diego State U., 1977-79; chmn. Am. Colls. Istanbul Sci. Week, 1969-71; mem. adv. bd. Chapman Coll. Cmty. Ctr., 1979-80; cons. sci. curriculum Calif. Dept. Edn., 1986-89; pres. Internat. Rels. Club, 1959-61; mem. San Francisco World Affairs Coun., 1966-68, San Diego World Affairs Coun., 1992—; v.p. Palomar Palace Estates Home Owners Assn., 1983-85, pres., 1994-99, v.p., 1999—; presenter in field; mem. Rsch. Conf. on Undergrad. Microbiology Edn., Conn. Coll., 1999; bd. dirs. U.S. Internat. Boundary and Water Commn. Citizens Forum, 2002-. : mem. editl. rev. bd. Jour. Coll. Sci. Teaching, ; mem. editl. rev. bd. NSTA Jour. of Coll. Sci. Tchg., ; mem. editl. rev. bd. U.S. Orgn. Med. and Ednl. Needs, 1968—. Mem. Chula Vista Nature Ctr. (life), Internat. Friendship Commn., Chula Vista, 1985-95, vice chmn., 1989-90, chmn., 1990-92, Chula Vista, Calif., 1987-95; mem. U.S.-Mex. Sister Cities Assn., nat. bd. dirs., 1992-94, gen. chair 30th nat. conv., 1993; mem. City of Chula Vista Resource Conservation Commn., 1996—, chmn. 2002-03; mem. Chula Vista Bd. Ethics, 1999-2000; co-organizer Chula Vista People-to-People Sister City Dels. to Odawara City, Japan, 1991, 94, 99; cmty. adv. com. San Diego Mus. Man, 2000—; mem. County San Diego Solid Waste Hearing Panel, 2000—; mem. citizen's forum bd. U.S. Internat. Boundary and Water Commn., 2002-; mem. citizens adv. bd. San Diego Mus. of Man, 2000—. NSF fellow, 1965; USPHS fellow, 1972-73; recipient Nat. Tchg. Excellence award Nat. Inst. Staff and Orgnl. Devel., 1989; recognized at Internat. Conf. Tchg. Excellence, Austin, 1989; Pa. Heart Assn. rsch. grantee, 1962; named Southwestern Coll. Woman of Distinction, 1987. Hon. Coach Southwestern Coll. Ladies Basketball Apaches, 2001. Mem.: NEA, NIH (mentor Bridges to the Future program Southwestern Coll. and San Diego 1993—98, steering com.), Am. Assn. Cmty. and Jr. Colls., Calif. Tchrs. Assn., Nat. Sci. Tchrs. Assn. (coord. internat. honors exch. lectr. competition 1986, internat. com.), Am. Soc. Microbiology (So. Calif. Microbe Discovery Team 1995—99), Calif. Sci. Tchrs. Assn. (life), Nat. Assn. Biology Tchrs. (life), Chula Vista-Odawara (Japan) Sister Cities Assn. (founding pres. 1994—), San Diego Zool. Soc., Am.-Lebanese Assn. San Diego (1st v.p. 1984—91, pres. 1988—93, chmn. scholarship com.), Am. U. of Beirut Alumni and Friends of San Diego (1st v.p. 1984—91), Japan Soc. San Diego and Tijuana, Am. Lebanese Syrian Ladies Club (pres. 1982—83), Lions Internat. (bull. editor 1991—93, 2d v.p. 1992—93, 1st v.p. 1993—94, editor Roaring Times Newsletter 1993—94, chmn. dist. internat. rels. and cooperations com. 1993—95, pres. S.W. San Diego County chpt. 1994—95, Sweetwater Zone chmn. dist. 4-L6 1996—97, with pub. rels. 1997—98, pub. rels. 1997—98, best bull. award 1992—93, named S.W. San Diego County Lion of Yr. 2000), Phi Theta Kappa, Sigma Phi Sigma, Kappa Gamma Pi (pres. Wilkes-Barre chpt. 1963—64, pres. San Francisco chpt. 1967—68), Alpha Pi Epsilon (life; advisor Southwestern Coll. chpt. 1989—90, founder).

THOMAS, THOMAS DARRAH, chemistry educator; b. Glen Ridge, N.J., Apr. 8, 1932; s. Woodlief and Jean (Darrah) T.; m. Barbara Joan Rassweiler, Sept. 8, 1956; children: David, Steven, Kathleen, Susan. BS, Haverford Coll., 1954; PhD, U. Calif., Berkeley, 1957. Instr. chemistry U. Calif., Berkeley, 1957-58, asst. prof., 1958-59; rsch. assoc. Brookhaven Nat. Lab., Upton, N.Y., 1959-61; asst. prof. Princeton (N.J.) U., 1961-66, assoc. prof., 1966-71; prof. Oreg. State U., Corvallis, 1971-89, disting. prof., 1989-97, chmn. dept. chemistry, 1981-84, dir. Ctr. Advanced Materials Rsch., 1986-91, Disting. prof. emeritus, 1997—. Cons. Los Alamos (N.Mex.) Sci. Lab., 1965. Contbr. articles to profl. jours. Fellow Alfred P. Sloan Found., 1966-68, Guggenheim Found., 1969, U. Liverpool, Eng., 1984-85. Fellow AAAS, Am. Phys. Soc.; mem. Am. Chem. Soc., Sigma Xi, Phi Beta Kappa. Home: 1470 NW Greenwood Pl Corvallis OR 97330-1827 Office: Oreg State U Dept Chemistry 153 Gilbert Hall Corvallis OR 97331-8546 E-mail: thomast@chem.orst.edu.

THOMAS, THORP, lawyer; b. Alexander, Ark., Sept. 15, 1923; s. Howard Norman and Letitia Helen (Miller) T.; m. Kermit Maurice Toombs (dec. Feb. 1998); children: Victoria, Helen, Deborah, Thorp Jr., Terry; m. Marie Elaine Underwood, July 22, 1999. Student, Little Rock Jr. Coll., 1945; JD, U. Ark., 1950. Bar: Ark. 1951, U.S. Dist. Ct. 1951, U.S. Ct. Appeals (8th cir.) Ark. 1953, U.S. Supreme Ct. 1954. Claims examiner Fidelity & Casualty Co. N.Y., Little Rock, 1950-53; asst. atty. gen. Atty. Gen.'s Office, 1953-63; pvt. practice law, 1963—. Chmn. planning commn., Alexander, Ark., 1980—. Mem. ABA, Ark. Bar Assn., Masons. Democrat. Methodist. Avocations: music, art, aviation. Home: 8310 Louwanda Dr Little Rock AR 72205-1666 E-mail: tmthomas@arkansas.net.

THOMAS, TOM, retired plastics company executive; b. Malang, Java, Indonesia, Feb. 15, 1932; arrived in Can., 1954; s. Ferdinand and Elfrieda Emma (Macht) T.; m. Jannie Chine Sneep, Jan. 19, 1956; children: Gregory John, Renée Sonja Elfrieda, Michael Grant, Thomas. Grad. high sch., The Hague, Holland. Jr. mgr. Lever Bros. Ltd., Toronto, Ont., Can., 1954-60; sr. mgr. Impac & Somerville Plastics, Can., 1960-64; founder, C.E.O. Can. Cup Inc., Can., 1964—, also bd. dirs. Can., 1964-93; ret., 1993. Inventor in field. Trustee Frazer Inst., Vancouver, B.C., Can., 1977-93; gov. Massey and Roy Thomson Hall, Toronto, 1991-92; bd. dirs. Toronto Symphony, 1986-92, mem. Maestro's Club, 1984, mem. pres.'s coun. Can. Opera Co., 1980, adv. coun. Toronto Symphony, 1995-2000, pres. Coun. Can. Opera, 1980-95. Avocations: sailing, history, classical music, chess.

THOMAS, TONY, producer; Prodr., ptnr. Witt-Thomas Prodns., L.A., 1976-81; ptnr. Witt-Thomas-Harris Prodns., 1981—. Exec. prodr. (with others) (TV series) Fay, 1975-76, Loves Me, Loves Me Not, 1977, Soap (Emmy award nominations best nighttime and primetime comedy series, 1978, 80, Emmy award best primetime comedy series 1981), Benson, 1979, It's a Living, 1980-81, Making a Living, 1982, It Takes Two, 1982-83, Condo, 1983; exec. prodr. (TV series), The Golden Girls, 1985-92 (Emmy awards best primetime comedy series 1986, 87), Beauty and the Beast, 1987, Empty Nest, 1988-95, Nurses, 1991, Herman's Head, 1991, Blossom, 1991-95, The John Larroquette Show, 1993-97; prod. (TV movies) Bloodsport, 1973, Snatched, 1973, Griffin and Phoenix: A Love Story, 1976; co-exec. prodr. (TV movies) Satan's Triangle, 1975; assoc. prodr. (TV movies) Brian's Song, 1971, No Place to Run, 1972, Home for the Holidays, 1972, The Letters, 1973, A Cold Night's Death, 1973, Remember When, 1974, The Gun and the Pulpit, 1974, High Risk, 1993; co-prodr. (films) Firstborn, 1984, Dead Poets Society, 1989, Final Analysis, 1992. Office: Witt Thomas Harris Prodns # 156 1438 N Gower St Bldg 35 Hollywood CA 90028-8362

THOMAS, VICKIE MUELLER, medical laboratory director; b. Benkelman, Nebr., Apr. 6, 1947; d. Iron Henry Mueller and Ruby Mae Elliott; m. Gary Wayne Thomas, Apr. 24, 1981. AB summa cum laude, Vassar Coll., 1968; PhD, U. Colo., 1974. Diplomate Am. Bd. Clin. Chemistry. Asst. dir. Regional Med. Labs, Inc., Pensacola, Fla., 1975-81; lectr. Med. Tech. Internship, 1976-82; lab. dir. Roche Biomed. Labs, Inc., 1982-83, Sheridan (Wyo.) Med. Lab., 1987—. Faculty assoc., adj. prof. U. West Fla., Pensacola, 1977-82; lab. cons., Laramie, 1984-87; CEO Mueller Enterprises, Inc. (dba Mueller Grain Co.), 1984—; v.p. Iron Mueller, Inc., 1984—, Iron Mueller Farms, Inc., 1984—. Contbr. articles to profl. jours. Officer Albany County Rep. Women, Laramie, 1989-92; vol. Laramie County Rep. Women, Cheyenne, 1994-98. Fellowship Nat. Sci. Found., Nat. Def. Edn. Act, 1969-73. Fellow Acad. of Clin. Biochemistry; mem. Am. Assn. for Clin. Chemistry, Cheyenne Country Club, Am. Contract Bridge League, Phi Beta Kappa. Avocations: duplicate bridge, golf. E-mail: vt300@msn.com.

THOMAS, VIOLETA DE LOS ANGELES, real estate broker; b. Buenos Aires, Dec. 21, 1949; came to U.S., 1967; d. Angel and Lola (Andino) de Rios; m. Jess Thomas, Dec. 23, 1971; 1 child, Victor Justin. Student, Harvard U. and U. Buenos Aires, 1967—73. Mgr. book div. Time-Life, N.Y.C., 1985-94; real estate broker First Marin Realty, Inc., Mill Valley, Calif., 1996-97; assoc. broker Trump Corp., N.Y.C., 1997—, Brown Harris Stevens, N.Y.C., 1997—. Rep. N.Y.C. Bd. dirs. Alliance Francaise, St. Louis, 1995-96, City of Tuburon, Calif., 1987-93, Art and Heritage Commn., Tiburon. Named Woman of Yr., City of Buenos Aires, 1977, Broker of Yr., Marin County and San Francisco, 1987-92. Mem. Principia Coll. Club (pres. 1997—). Office: Brown Harris Stevens 655 Madison Ave Fl 3 New York NY 10021-8056 E-mail: vthomas@bhsusa.com.

THOMAS, WALTER DILL, JR. retired forest pathologist, consultant; b. St. Louis, July 3, 1918; s. Walter D. and Helen (Gardner) T.; m. Dolores B. Thomas, Dec. 31, 1939 (div. May 1984); children: Sandra Thomas Bosworth, Arthur D; m. Nancy McCarthy, Feb. 15, 1985. BS, Colo. State U., 1939; MS, U. Minn., 1943, PhD, 1947. Diplomate Am. Bd. Forensics Examiners. Prof. plant pathology Colo. State U., Ft. Collins, 1947-55; supr. biol. research Chevron Chem. Co., Richmond, Calif., 1955-70; v.p. rsch. Nat. Resource Mgmt., Eureka, 1970-72; pres. Forest Ag Corp., Lafayette, 1972-86; ret., 1999. Coord. bd. forest stewardship Calif. Dept. Forestry and Fire Control, 1990-94; cons. in field, 1986-97. Author: Field Manual of Forest and Shade Tree Diseases, 1947, Not Long Apart, 1965, Mauget Field Manual: Insects and Diseases of Shade Trees, 1995. Commr. Park and Recreation Com., Ft. Collins, 1949-54, Concord, Calif., 1959-65; city forester, Ft. Collins, 1950-55. Comdr. USNR, 1944-80. Fellow AAAS (life); mem. Am. Phytopathol. Soc., Soc. Am. Foresters, Foresters Assn. (Calif. lic.), Pesticide Applicators Profl. Assn., Internat. Soc. Arboriculture, Nat. Forensic Soc., Bd. Forensics Examiners, Assn. Cons. Foresters, Am. Soc. Cons. Arborists, Soc. Tech. Comms. (sr. mem.), VFW, Lions. Republican. Avocations: swimming, writing, music. Home: 2435 Heatherleaf Ln Martinez CA 94553-4337 *It is better to fail humbly while trying to succeed than to never even try.*

THOMAS, WARD J. political science educator; b. Ft. Benning, Ga., Apr. 27, 1963; s. Edward J.F. and JoAnn H. Thomas; m. Kari Thomas, Aug. 15, 1992; children: Jack, Patrick. BA, Coll. William and Mary, 1985; MA, U. Va., JD, 1988; PhD, Johns Hopkins U., 1997. Postdoctoral fellow John M. Olin Inst. for Strategic Studies Harvard U., Cambridge, Mass., 1998-99, assoc., 2000—; asst. prof. Coll. of the Holy Cross, Worcester, 1997—. Young Scholar, Program on Ethics and Pub. Life, Cornell U., Ithaca, N.Y., 2000-01. Author: The Ethics of Destruction: Norms and Force in International Relations, 2001. Mem. Am. Polit. Sci. Assn., Internat. Studies Assn. Office: Coll of the Holy Cross One College St Worcester MA 01610 E-mail: wthomas@holycross.edu.

THOMAS, WAYNE LEE, lawyer; b. Sept. 22, 1945; s. Willard McSwain and June Frances T.; m. Patricia H. Thomas, Mar. 16, 1968; children: Brigitte Elisabeth Williams, Kate Adelaide Culpepper. BA, U. Fla., 1967, JD cum laude, 1971. Bar: Fla. 1971, U.S. Supreme Ct. 1975, U.S. Ct. Appeals (5th cir.) 1975, U.S. Ct. Appeals (11th cir.) 1981, U.S. Ct. Claims 1976, U.S. Dist. Ct. (mid. dist.) Fla. 1973, U.S. Dist. Ct. (so. dist. trial bar) Fla. 1975; cert. mediator and arbitrator. Law clk. U.S. Dist. Ct. (mid. dist.) Fla., 1971-73; assoc. Trenam, Simmons, Kemker, Scharf, Barkin, Frye & O'Neill, PA, Tampa, 1973-77, ptnr., 1978-81; founder, pres. McKay & Thomas, PA, 1981-89; ptnr. Carlton, Fields, Ward, Emmanuel, Smith & Cutler, PA, 1989-95; pvt. practice Tampa, 1995—. Mem. ABA, Fla. Bar (chmn. sect. gen. practice 1981-83, mem. ethics com., vice chmn. unauthorized practice law com. 1994-98, 2000-, vice chmn. fed. practice com. 1995-96, chmn. 1996-97, mem. bd. bar examiners 1986-91, chmn. 1990-91, chmn. unauthorized practice law com. 13A 1998-2001), Nat. Conf. Bar Examiners (multistate profl. responsibility exam. policy com. 1994—), Hillsborough County Bar Assn. (chmn. grievance com. 1985-86), Order of Coif, Fla. Blue Key, Phi Kappa Phi, Omicron Delta Kappa. Democrat. Office: 707 N Franklin St Fl 10 Tampa FL 33602-4430 E-mail: wayne.lee@verizon.net.

THOMAS, WESTLEY, actor, writer; b. Bronx, N.Y., June 15, 1947; s. David and Arlene Clara Thomas; m. Margarita Rosa Thomas, May 23, 1970 (div. Nov. 1977); 1 child Ti'Isha M. ; m. June H. Mobley Tatum, June 26, 1982; 1 child Sean L. Mobley stepchildren: Lawrence D. Mobley, Chad Mobley. AA, Coll. Stafen Island, 1977; BA, Coll. Staten Island, 1980. Author: A Hard Decision; actor: The Rainmaker, Universal Star, Street to Harlem, Victim of Ridicule, No Compassion, The Resurrection of John Henry, The Gospel of The Harlem Renaissance, The Sun People, Tribute To Malcolm X, For the Love of My Black Woman, Black Broadway; dancer Dance to African Drums, Frederick Taylor Dance Co.; actor: (films) Malcom X. Sgt. USMC, 1965—69, Vietnam. Baptist. Avocations: martial arts, creative writing, dancing, body building. Home: 33-47 14th St #3C Long Island City NY 11106

THOMAS, W(ILLIAM) BRUCE, retired steel, oil, gas company executive; b. Ripley, Mich., Oct. 25, 1926; s. William and Ethel (Collins) T.; m. Phyllis Jeanne Smith, June 25, 1950; 1 son, Robert William. BA magna cum laude, Western Mich. U., 1950; JD with distinction, U. Mich., 1952; postgrad., Law Sch., NYU, 1953. Bar: Mich. 1952. With USX Corp. (formerly U.S. Steel) and subs., various locations, 1952-91; tax atty. Oliver Iron Mining Div., Duluth, Minn., 1952-53; tax atty., tax supr., comptroller Orinoco Mining Co., N.Y.C. and Venezuela, 1953-64, dir., v.p. taxes, 1967-70, v.p., asst. treas., 1970-71, v.p., treas., 1971-75; exec. v.p., CFO, dir. USX Corp., Pitts., 1975-82, vice chmn., CFO, dir., 1982-91. Dir. Manufacturer's Hanover Bank, Chem. Bank, Chase Manhattan Bank, Nat. Distillers Corp., Qualitum Chem. Corp., Discount Corp. of N.Y., formerly. Bd. dirs. Duquesne U.; trustee Kenyon Coll. With USAAF, 1943-45. Mem. ABA, Mich. Bar Assn., Fin. Execs. Inst., Order of Coif, Duquesne Club, Pitts. Club, Laurel Valley Golf Club, Rolling Rock Club, Allegheny Country Club, Sky Club, Links, Belleair Country Club, Phi Alpha Delta. Methodist. Home: Blackburn Rd Sewickley PA 15143 Office: USX Corp 600 Grant Building Ste 6200 Pittsburgh PA 15219-2203

THOMAS, WILLIAM GERAINT, museum administrator; b. Columbo, Sri Lanka, June 27, 1931; came to U.S., 1941; s. Cecil James and Iris Katharine (Evans) T.; m. Maria Alcalde, Jan. 2, 1976; 1 child, Laura. BA, U. Calif., Berkeley, 1952. Reporter, editor San Francisco Chronicle, 1952-64; asst. to mayor City of San Francisco, 1964-66; chief cons. majority caucus Calif. State Assembly, Sacramento, 1966-68; adminstrv. asst. U.S. Congressman Phillip Burton, Washington, 1968-70; cons. interior com. U.S. Ho. of Reps., 1970-72; ptnr. Thomas & Iovino, San Francisco, 1972-78; asst. regional dir. Nat. Park Svc., 1978-89; supt. San Francisco Maritime NHP, 1989—. Mem. Nat. Dem. Club; bd. dirs. Nat. Libery Ship Meml., 1978-80. Sgt. U.S. Army, 1952-54, Korea. Mem. Nat. Maritime Mus. Assn., Nat. Maritime Hist. Soc., Press Club of San Francisco (pres. 1973-74, Best News Story 1963). Episcopalian. Avocation: sailing. Office: San Francisco Maritime Bldg E Ft Mason San Francisco CA 94123

THOMAS, WILLIAM GRIFFITH, lawyer; b. Washington, Nov. 1, 1939; s. Henry Phineas and Margaret Wilson (Carr) T.; m. Suzanne Campbell Foster, June 7, 1960. Student, Williams Coll., 1957-59, Richmond Coll., 1960; JD, U. Richmond, 1963. Bar: Va. 1963. Ptnr. Reed Smith LLP, Falls Church, Va., 1999—. Dir. Va. Electric and Power Co., Richmond, 1987-2000. Sec. Va. Dem. Com., 1968-70, chmn., 1970-72. Mem. ABA, Va. State Bar Assn., Alexandria Bar Assn., Am. Law Inst., Am. Coll. Real Estate Lawyers. Home: 4783 Herring Creek Rd Aylett VA 23009 Office: Reed Smith LLP 3110 Fairview Park Dr Ste 1400 Falls Church VA 22042-4503 Fax: 703-641-4340. E-mail: wthomas@reedsmith.com.

THOMAS, WILLIAM JOSEPH, secondary school educator, administrator; b. Orange, N.J., June 1, 1966; s. Willie Thomas and Sandra Thomas; m. Lisa, Dec. 30, 1990; children: William, Sydney, Jordan. BA, Jersey City State Coll., 1993; EdM, St. Peters Coll., 1998; postgrad., Seton Hall U., 1998—. Cert. elem. and secondary tchr., N.J. Dir. summer inst. Roselle (N.J.) Pub. Schs.; math. and sci. staff developer Newark (N.J.) Pub. Schs.; adj. prof. Rutgers U.; vice-prin. Plainfield (N.J.) H.S. Mem. AAUP, Orgn. of African Am. Adminstrs., Plainfield Assn. Supers. and Adminstrs. (pres.), N.J. Prins. and Supers. Assn. Avocations: sailing, gardening, singing. Office: Cedarbrook Elem Sch 1049 Central Ave Plainfield NJ 07060

THOMAS, WILLIAM LEROY, geography educator, cruise lecturer; b. Long Beach, Calif., Mar. 18, 1920; s. William LeRoy and Margaret Lucile (Young) T.; m. Mildred Phyllis Smith, Apr. 10, 1942 (div.); children: Barbara Jean, Lawrence Charles, Virginia Jane, Margaret Joan, Pamela June; m. Loida Ayson Aquino, Aug. 29, 1964 (dec.); children: William John Aquino, Lloyd Aquino; m. Rosalinda Zuñiga Valencia, July 4, 1986; 1 adopted child, Don Valencia. AB, UCLA, 1941, MA, 1948; PhD, Yale U., 1955. Instr. geography Rutgers U., 1947-50; research asst. S.E. Asia studies Yale U., 1949-50; asst. dir. research Wenner-Gren Found. Anthrop. Research, N.Y.C., 1950-57; asst. to assoc. prof. geography U. Calif., Riverside, 1957-63; prof. anthropology and geography Calif. State U., Hayward, 1963-71, chmn. dept. anthropology and geography, 1963-66, prof. geography and Southeast Asian studies, 1971-91, prof. emeritus, 1983—, chmn. dept. geography, 1971-74, assoc. dir. Ctr. for Filipino Studies, 1990-91; v.p. rsch. and devel. Heritage Tours, Ltd., Oakland, Calif., 1981-83; v.p. rsch. and devel., chmn. bd. Geo-Expdns. Internat., Inc., 1981-83; pres. Thomas Opportunity Program Services, 1983-90. Vis. prof. La. State U., spring 1966, U. Hawaii, summer 1966, U. Wis., fall 1966, U. Toronto, Canada, fall 1968, 69, Georgetown U., 1992; vis. research assoc. Inst. Philippine Culture, Ateneo de Manila U., Quezon City, 1970, 76-77; Fulbright lectr. Centre for Research Asian Studies, U. Western Australia, Nedlands, 1974; Fulbright sr. research scholar Mariano Marcos State U., Batac, Ilocos Norte, Philippines, 1984-85; organizer internat. symposium Man's Role in Changing the Face of the Earth, Princeton, N.J., 1955; cons. Nat. Acad. Scis.-NRC, in orgn. of sect. 6th Nat. Conf. UNESCO, 1957; mem. tech. cons. group Calif. Pub. Outdoor Recreation Plan Com., 1958-60; geog. cons. Pacific Missile Range, Pt. Mugu, Calif., 1958-60; organizer geography sect. 10th Pacific Sci. Congress, 1961; foreign field research, Philippines, 1961-62, Philippines, Thailand, Burma, 1970, Australia, Indonesia, 1974, Philippines, 1976-77, 84-85, 86, French Polynesia, 1992, 93, Thailand, Malaysia, Indonesia, Singapore, 1993, Indonesia, 1994, 95 Northern Australia, 1995; mem. ad hoc com. on geography Nat. Acad. Scis.-NRC, 1963-65, cons. effects of herbicides in, Vietnam, 1972-74; chmn. Asian studies council Calif. State Colls., 1971-72; mem. com. internat. symposium earth as transformed by human action Clark U., Worcester, Mass., 1987; invited speaker V.I. Vernadsky anniversary symposium USSR Acad. Scis., Leningrad, Kiev, Moscow, 1988; guest lectr. Cunard Line 'Vistafjord' cruise, Feb. 1992, Royal Viking Line 'Sun' Cruise, 1992, Paquet Cruise Company 'Ocean Pearl' cruise, 1993, Cunard Line 'Sagafjord' cruise, 1993, Seven Seas Cruise Line 'Song of Flower' cruise, 1993-94, Cunard Line 'Vistafjord' Cruise, 1994, Crystal Cruises 'Crystal Harmony' Cruise, 1994, Regency Cruises 'Regent Sea' Cruise, 1994, Orient Line 'Marco Polo' Cruise, 1994, Holland-Am. Line 'Rotterdam' Grand World Voyage Cruise, 1995, Orient Line 'Marco Polo' Cruise, 1995, Royal Caribbean Cruises on Sun Viking, Far East, 1996; edn. specialist Bur. Pvt. Postsecondary and Vocat. Edn., Dept. Consumer Affairs, State of Calif., 1998—. Author: (with J. F. Embree) Ethnic Groups of Northern Southeast Asia, 1950, Land, Man and Culture in Mainland Southeast Asia, 1957, (with J.E. Spencer) Cultural Geography, 1969, Asia, East by South, 2d edit, 1971, Introducing Cultural Geography, 1973, 2d edit., 1978; Editor: (with Anna M. Pikells) International Directory of Anthropological Institutions, 1953, Yearbook of Anthropology, 1955, Current Anthropology, 1956, Man's Role in Changing the Face of the Earth, 1956, Am. Anthrop. Assn. Bull, 1958-60, Man, Time, and Space in Southern California, 1959;paperback series Man-Environment System in The Late 20th Century, 1969-75. Moderator United Ch. Hayward, 1988-90. 1st lt. C.E., AUS, 1942-45. Mem. Assn. Asian Studies, Asian Studies on Pacific Coast (chmn. standing com. 1979-80, conf. chmn. 1980), Pacific Sci. Assn. (U.S. mem. sci. com. on geography), Assn. Am. Geographers (Pacific Coast regional councilor 1971-74, citation for meritorious contbn. to geography 1961, 50 yr. life mem.), Assn. Pacific Coast Geographers (v.p. 1976-77, pres. 1977-78, Disting. Svc. award 1988), Calif. Geog. Soc. (pres. 1967-68, Outstanding Educator award 1986). Democrat. Address: 3257 Brightwood Ct Oceanside CA 92054-7034

THOMAS, WILLIAM MARSHALL, congressman; b. Wallace, Idaho, Dec. 6, 1941; s. Virgil and Gertrude Thomas; m. Sharon Lynn Hamilton, Jan. 1968; children: Christopher, Amelia. BA, San Francisco State U., 1963, MA, 1965. Mem. faculty dept. Am. govt. Bakersfield (Calif.) Coll., 1965-74, prof., 1965-74; mem. Calif. State Assembly, 1974-78, U.S. Congress from 21st Calif. dist., 1979—; chmn. ways and means com., 2001—; chmn. Com. on House Oversight, 1995-2001. Mem. del. to Soviet Union, by Am. Council Young Polit. Leaders, 1977; chmn. Kern County Republican Central Com., 1972-74; mem. Calif. Rep. Com., 1972-80; del. Republican Party Nat. Conv., 1980, 84, 88; mem. Rep. Leader's Task Force on Health Care Reform. Office: House Reps 2208 Rayburn Ho Office Bldg Washington DC 20515-0001*

THOMAS, ZACH MICHAEL, football player; b. Pampa, Tex., Sept. 1, 1973; Student, Tex. Tech, 1996. Linebacker Miami Dolphins, 1996—. Opened health and fitness club Zach's Club 54, Amarillo, Tex. Mem. Crunch on Paralysis team. Recipient Mackey award, 1996, Dolphin's Leadership award, 1998, 99; named to Pro Bowl, All-Madden Team, 1998, first-team All-Pro selection, AP, USA Today, Coll. and Pro Football Weekly, Football Digest; named MVP and Newcomer of Yr., S.Fla. media, 1996, NFL Alumni Assn. Linebacker of Yr. Avocations: weightlifting, basketball. Office: Miami Dolphins Tng Facility 7500 SW 30th St Davie FL 33314*

THOMAS, ZDENĚK, retired civil engineer, researcher; b. Opava, Silesia, Czech Republic, May 11, 1929; s. Alois Kovalčik and Matylda Thomasová; m. Jitka Kadlecová, July 31, 1954; 1 child, Robin. MCE, Tech. U. Brno, Czech Republic, 1954, PhD, 1967; ScD, U. Prague, 1992. Rschr. Water Rsch. Inst., Prague, 1954-91, watercourses sect. chief, 1963-68, sci. worker, 1969-91, ret., 1991. Vis. rschr. Hydraulic Lab., Delft, The Netherlands, 1968-69; vis. scientist U. Stuttgard, Germany, 1989, Inst. Mexicano del Patrol, 1999—; sci. worker czech Acad. Sci., Prague, 1992; vis. scientist U. Autonoma de Mex., Mexico City, 1996-98. Author: Works and Studies No. 127, 1967, Works and Studies No. 134, 1974, Works and Studies No. 140, 1975; patentee in field. With Czech Mil., 1954-56. Deutsche Forschungsgemeinschaft grantee, 1989. Mem. Sci.-Tech. Soc. Prague (sci. conf. com. 1978, 80, 82, 84), Union of Czech Mathematicians and Physicians, Czech Soc. for Chem. Tech. Roman Catholic. Avocations: opera, singing, classical music. Home: Kladenská 19 160 00 Prague 6 Czech Republic Office: Inst Mex Petroleo, Eje Ctrl Lázaro Cárdenas 152 San Bartolo Atepehuacan 07730 Mexico City Mexico

THOMAS-CAPPELLO, ELIZABETH, arts administrator; b. Bridgeport, Conn., Apr. 12, 1970; d. Leon Evan Thomas III and Mary Guccione Olson; 1 child, Chandler John Hunt; m. John Christopher Cappello, Jan. 2, 1999; 1 child, Camille Cappello. BS, So. Ill. U., Carbondale, 1993; MS, U. Ill., Springfield, 1996. Asst. to the dir. Univ. Mus., Carbondale, 1994; asst. dir. Peoria (Ill.) Art Guild, 1995; devel. Springfield Art Assn., 1995; exec. dir. Arts Coun. Orange County, Middletown, N.Y., 1996-97; cons. Dutchess County Arts Coun., Poughkeepsie, 1997—; substiture art tchr. Valley Ctrl. Sch. Dist., Montgomery, 1999—. Bd. dirs. Newburgh Ctr. for the Arts, chair, 1998—; bd. dirs. Museum Village, 1997-99; mem. Leadership Orange, 1998—. Home: 78 Ulster Ave Walden NY 12586-1442

THOMASCH, ROGER PAUL, lawyer; b. N.Y.C., Nov. 7, 1942; s. Gordon J. and Margaret (Molloy) T.; children: Laura Leigh, Paul Butler. BA, Coll. William and Mary, 1964; LLB, Duke U., 1967. Bar: Conn. 1967, Colo. 1974. Assoc. atty. Cummings & Lockwood, Stamford, Conn., 1967-70; trial atty. U.S. Dept. Justice, Washington, 1970-73; ptnr. Roath & Brega, Denver, 1975-87; mng. ptnr. Denver office of Ballard, Spahr, Andrews & Ingersoll LLP, 1987—. Vis. assoc. prof. of law Drake U. Sch. Law, Des Moines, 1973-74; frequent lectr. in field, U.S. and Can.; adj. faculty mem. U. Denver Coll. Law, 1976-80. Recipient Leland Forrest Outstanding Prof. award, Drake U. Sch. Law, 1973. Fellow Am. Coll. of Trial Lawyers, Colo. Bar Found.; mem. ABA, Colo. Bar Assn., Denver County Club, Univ. Club. Office: Ballard Spahr Andrews & Ingersoll LLP 1225 17th St Ste 2300 Denver CO 80202-5535 E-mail: Thomasch@BallardSpahr.com.

THOMASHOW, BYRON MARTIN, pulmonary physician; b. Bklyn., Apr. 19, 1949; s. Alexander Irwin and Emma (Zaslow) T.; m. Laurie Jo Kasoff, July 2, 1972; children: Samantha, Michael. BA, Columbia U., 1970, MD, 1974. Diplomate Nat. Bd. Med. Examiners, Am. Bd. Internal Medicine, subspecialty in pulmonary medicine. Med. intern Roosevelt Hosp., N.Y.C., 1974-75, med. resident, 1975-77, med. chief resident, pulmonary fellow, 1977-78; sr. pulmonary fellow Harlem Hosp., 1978-79; asst. attending physician Presbyn. Hosp., Columbia Presbyn. Med. Ctr., 1979-90, assoc. attending physician, 1991-99, attending physician, 1999—; physician in charge Tbc Clinic Presbyn. Hosp., 1983-90, attending physician Chest Clinic, 1979—; asst. prof. clin. medicine Columbia U., 1979-90, assoc. clin. prof. medicine, 1990-99, clin. prof. medicine, 1999—. Lectr. ACP, 1986-92, Harlem Hosp., 1984, 93, Roosevelt Hosp., 1978, 86, 87, 88, 91, Columbia Presbyn. Hosp., various yrs., N.Y. Trudeau Soc., 1982, Columbia U. Coll. Physicians and Surgeons, 1980-96, Med. House staff Pulmonary Bd. Rev., 1980—, Emergency Med. Course, 1981—; mem. Presbyn. Hosp. Med. Bd., 1995—; med. co-dir. Lung Failure Ctr. Columbia Presbyn. Med. Ctr., 1995—, co-investigator, primary pulmonol. Columbia Ctr., Nat. Emphysema Treatment Trial, NIH; co-investigator FORTE study NIH Feasibility Study of Retinoic Acid Therapy for Emphysema, interferon gamma study IPF. Stony Wold-Herbert Fund fellowship grantee, 1978-79. Fellow ACP, Am. Coll. Chest Physicians; mem. NIH (steering com. 1997), Am. Thoracic Soc., N.Y. Trudeau Soc. (exec. com. 1992-94, chmn. membership com. 1992-94), Soc. Practitioners (exec. com. 1994—, chmn. quality care com. 1995—). Office: 161 Fort Washington Ave New York NY 10032-3713

THOMASHOW, STEVEN ROY, military officer, intelligence officer; b. Bronx, N.Y., Jan. 27, 1957; s. Isaac Tom and Dorothy (Cuillino Bodsky) T. Accredited, U.S. Mil. Acad. Commd. United States of the World, adm., with spl. ops., 1988—; served with Israeli War USN, served with Gulf War. Recipient Pres. Nat. Medal of Patriotism, Am. Police Hall of Fame, 1996. Fellow Nat. Law Enforcement Acad. (hon.); mem. Am. Fedn. Police. Avocations: karate, Torah studies, boxing, reading. Home and Office: 4644 Myrtle Ln West Palm Beach FL 33417-5316 Fax: 561 640-4359.

THOMAS-JOHN, YVONNE MAREE, artist, interior designer; b. Leeton, New South Wales, Australia, Sept. 8, 1944; came to U.S., 1966; d. Percy Edward and Gladys May (Markham) Thomas; m. Michael Peter John, Aug. 20, 1966; children: Michael Christian, Stephen Edwin Dennis. Student, Buenaventura Coll., 1969, U. Calif., Santa Barbara, 1975; cert., United Design Guild, 1975; AA, Interior Design Guild, 1976. Designer Percy Thomas Real Estate, Leeton, 1960-66; cosmetologist, artist Bernard's Hair Stylists, Ventura, Calif., 1966-67, 74-73; cosmetologist Banks Beauty Salon, Chgo., 1968-69; owner, mgr. Yvonne Maree Designs, Ventura and Olympia, Wash., 1978—. Owner, cosmetologist Mayfair Salon, Leeton, 1962-66; owner, mgr. Y.M. Boutique, Griffith, Australia, 1965-66. Contbr. numerous short stories and poems to newspapers; numerous pen and ink drawings, one-woman shows include Royal Mus. Sydney, Australia, 1954, exhibited in group shows at Ventura County Courthouse, 1970, Wash. Women in Art, Olympia, 1990, Timberland Libr., 1990, Maska Internat. Gallery, Seattle, 1991, Nat. Hdqrs. of Am. Soc. Interior Designers, Washington, 1992, Michael Stone Collection, 1992, Funding Ctr., Alexandria, Va., 1992, Mus. Modern Art, Bordeaux, France, 1993, Abbey Galleries, N.Y.C., 1993, Mus. Modern Art, Miami, 1993, Hargus Unique Gallery, Pomona, Calif., 1994, Gallery Brindabella, Oakville, Ont., Can., 1996, Art Comm. Internat., Phila., 1996, World Bank, Washington, 1996—97, UN Fourth World Conf. on Women, Beijing, China, 1995, others, 1st release of ltd. edit. prints, exhibitions include Hargus Unique Gallery, Pomona, Calif., 1994, Represented in permanent collections Royal Mus. Sydney, O'Toole Coll., Melbourne, Nat. Mus. Women in Arts, Washington, Patterson Collection, Mich., Witherow Collection, Washington, Samaniego Collection, Calif., Ronald Reagan Collection, Calif. Artist Ventura County Gen. HOsp. Artist Ventura County Gen. Hosp., 1970's. Recipient Cash and Cert. awards Sydney Newspapers, 1950's, Ribbon awards Sydney County Fairs, 1950's, 1st round winner painting Hathaway Competition, Ventura, Calif., 1970's. Mem. Am. Platform Assn. Avocations: swimming, tennis, walking, books, music. Office: Yvonne Maree Designs PO Box 2143 Olympia WA 98507-2143 E-mail: ymaree@ix.netcom.com.

THOMASON, HARRY JACK LEE, JR. mechanical engineer; b. Washington, Apr. 12, 1953; s. Harry Emmitte and Annie Jeffreys aka Hattie Cornelia (Davis) T.; m. Ema Jean Bulaon, Dec. 15, 1974. AA, Prince Georges C.C., 1973; BS, U. Md., 1975. Cons. Thomason Solar Homes Inc., Ft. Washington, Md., 1975-79, v.p. engring., 1979-84; mech. engr. Naval Surface Weapons Ctr., Dahlgren, Va., 1984-86, White Oak, Md., 1986-87; energy conservation engr., asst. chief ops. Walter Reed Army Med. Ctr., Washington, 1987-88; sr. mech. engr. Armed Forces Inst. of Pathology, 1988-90; mech. engr. U.S. Naval Acad., Annapolis, Md., 1990-95. Instr. solar house heating and cooling, George Washington U., Washington, 1974-75. Contbr. articles to profl. jours. Patentee in field of solar energy; recipient 1st place environ. award Isaac Walton League, 1971, spl. awards Washington Soc. Engrs., 1971, IEEE, 1971, Solar Hall of Fame award, 1992, Internat. Man of Yr. award, 1991-92; named World Intellectual of 1993, named to Millennium Hall of Fame, 1998, named among 2,000 Outstanding Scientists of the 20th Century, 2,000 Outstanding Intellectuals of the 20th Century. Mem. ASME, Wash. Soc. Engrs.

THOMASON, JO, association executive, consultant, educator; b. Chgo., Mar. 7, 1937; d. Clarence Walker Failor and Mary Springer Dotts; m. Tom William Thomason, June 4, 1960. BA, U. Minn., 1958, MS, 1968; EdD, U. N.Mex., 1977. Tchr. Taos (N.Mex.) Pub. Schs., 1958-59, Albuquerque Pub. Schs., 1959-69, coord. spl. edn., 1969-78, asst. dir., 1978-86; cons. Coun. of Adminstrs. of Spl. Edn., 1986-88, exec. dir., 1988—2002. Adj. prof. U. N.Mex., Albuquerque, 1980-97; vis. faculty U. B.C., Vancouver, 1987; cons. numerous univs., 1986-88, Malagasy Republic, Tananarive, Madagascar, 1967. Editor (newsletter) InCASE, 1988-2002; contbg. author: Models for Mainstreaming, 1987; field editor Teaching Excepetional Children, 1984-86. Pres. Albuquerque Women's Christian Assn., Albuquerque, 1985; chairperson Foster Grandparents Adv. Bd., Albuquerque, 1990-93. Mem. Coun. for Exceptional Children (pres. 1981-82, Outstanding Contbr. 1993), N.Mex. Sch. Adminstrs. (exec. com. 1986-88, Outstanding Leadership 1987), Am. Soc. of Assn. Exec., N.Mex. Coun. for Exceptional Children (Jo Thomason award 1993). Democrat. Unitarian Universalist. Avocations: traveling, gardening, reading, needlework. E-mail: thomasonjo@aol.com.

THOMASON, NOLA FAYE, critical care-emergency supervisor; b. East St. Louis, Ill., May 23, 1957; d. Noel Noble and Dorothy Bernice (Burkett) Manring; m. Paul David Thomason, Mar. 23, 1979; children: Paula Faye, Rachel Elisabeth. ADN, Frontier Community Coll., Fairfield, Ill., 1986; Mobile Intensive Care Nurse/Emergency Care RN, Good Samaritan Hosp., Mt. Vernon, 1992; Trauma Nurse Specialist, Carbondale Meml. Hosp., 1996; EMT Basic, Frontier C.C., 1997. Cert. mobile intensive care nurse, mobile intensive care instr., emergency nursing care pediatric core curriculum, 1997. Charge nurse Rest Haven Manor, Albion, Ill., 1986—; staff nurse Kimberly Quality Care, Belleville, 1986-87; staff nurse emergency room Clay County Hosp., Flora, 1987-88; RN, supr. Good Samaritan Hosp., Mt. Vernon, 1990-92, Crossroads Community Hosp., Mt. Vernon, 1988-91; night supr. Fairfield (Ill.) Meml. Hosp., 1993—. Home: RR 3 Box 86 Fairfield IL 62837

THOMASON, TERESA, musician, educator; b. Lake Charles, LA, Jan. 27, 1953; d. Leo and Helen (Carraway) Layssard; m. Timothy Neal Thomason June 16, 1973; children: Jenry Neal, Jody Nolan, Jennifer Nicole, Joy Nerissa. BA in Music, La. Coll., 1991. Cert. tchr. music. Music sec. Horseshoe Drive Baptist Ch., Alexandria, La., 1973-75; clerical typist La. Dept. Employment Security, 1975-76; keyboard cons. La. Baptist Conv., 1978—; pvt. piano tchr., 1978—; tchr. piano, flute Calvary Conservatory of Music, 1994—; tchr. piano Alexandria Country Day Sch., 1991—. Chmn. Sonatina Festival Cenla Piano Tchrs. Assn., 1983-87, 90-94. Accompanist La. Baptist Singing Women, 1998—; pianist Benefit Concert La. Coll. Music. Dept., Pineville, La., 1995, 97; flautist Cenla Symphonic Band, 1977-80, 82; cons. Hymn Playing Festival La. Baptist Conv., 1979—, state festival chmn., 1986—. Recipient Mattie Lee Pate award La. Coll. Music Dept., Pineville, 1991. Mem. Music Tchrs. Nat. Assn., La. Music Tchrs. Assn. (state rally chmn. 1998—, dist. rally chmn. 1997-98), Cenla Piano Tchrs. Assn. (v.p. 1997-98, sec. 1986-87, 89-92, pres. 1992-94). Southern Baptist. Avocations: cross stitching, hand crafts, working with young people, travel. Home: 5613 Bruyninckx Rd Alexandria LA 71303-2202 E-mail: tnt01@linknet.idt.net.

THOMASON-MUSSEN, JANIS FAYE, human services administrator; b. Rome, Oct. 6, 1946; d. Howard Irving and Marjorie Ellen (Thomason) Mussen; children: John Kennedy Pratt, Wendy Jo Pratt Bowen, Amara Jo Pratt. BA in Journalism, Syracuse U., 1983. Reporter, columnist Oneida (N.Y.) Daily Dispatch, 1983-85; editor Coll. Graphic Arts and Photography Rochester (N.Y.) Inst. Tech., 1985-87; freelance writer, editor, photographer Rochester, 1987-88; exec. dir. Come-Unity Ctr., Inc. Wayne County Rural Ministry/Come-Unity Ctr., Inc., Williamson, N.Y., 1988—. Founder Wayne County (N.Y.) Coalition of Migrant Farmworker Svcs., 1991—; mem. Wayne County Task Force on In-Home Svcs. for Elderly, 1989—. Scholarship Gannett News Svc., 1982, 83; named Woman of Excellence Seven Lakes Girl Scout Coun., 1995. Mem. Sigma Delta Chi. Home: PO Box 698 Williamson NY 14589-0698 Office: Wayne County Rural Ministry PO Box 73 Williamson NY 14589-0073

THOMAS-ROBINSON, GREGORY LEON, sales executive; b. Portland, Oreg., Nov. 13, 1964; s. Raydell and Catherine Ann Robinson; m. Martha Ann Moncrief, Aug. 25, 1996; children: Tieavsha Robinson, Lakeisha Harris, Gregory Robinson, Donta Harris, Mia Robinson. Student, Western Oreg. State U., 1983—86; AS, Chemeketa C.C., Salem, Oreg., 1987; AA, United Theol. Sem., 2001. Mgr. Nordstrom, Gaithersburg, Md., 1988—92; sales mgr. Polo Meier & Frank, Portland, 1992—94; customer rep. Wash. Mutual FSB, Vancouver, 1994—96; adminstrv. coord. Legacy Emanuel Hosp., Portland, 1996—97; health svc. rep. Oakdale (La.) Cmty. Hosp., 1997—98; owner Around Town Sounds, 1997—. Coord. G&T Bus. and Consultant, Oakdale, 1997—. Male mentor Urban League, Portland, 1993—; pres. Young Minister's Alliance, 2001—; pastor Dominion and Power House of Prayer, Mount Olive Bapt. Ch., 1998—2001. Republican. Avocations: weight lifting, reading, Biblical research and writing. Home: 4103 NE 10th St Portland OR 97211 Office: Mount Olive Bapt Ch Hwy 432 Oakdale LA 71463

THOMAS-ROOTS, PAMELA M. writer; b. New Haven, May 3, 1965; d. Faith Santos. BA in Biology, Am. U., 1989. Author: You Have One Body. Take Care of It!, 1999, PTR's Educational Fun Booklets, Collection One, 1999, PTR's Educational Fun Booklets, Collection Two, 2000, More Fun with Pamma Lamma, 2002. Avocations: exercise, reading, mystery shows. Home: 1220 E West Hwy Apt 1123 Silver Spring MD 20910-3274

THOMASSEN, PAULINE FRANCES, medical and surgical nurse; b. Cleve., Jan. 19, 1939; d. Henry Clifford and Mabel Pauline (Hill) Nichols; m. Ruben Thomassen, Nov. 10, 1979; children: Rhonda, Terry, Diana, Philipp, Jody, Barbara. AA in Nursing, So. Colo. State Coll., 1974, BA in Psychology with distinction, 1975; BSN magna cum laude, Seattle Pacific U., 1986. RN Wash. Staff nurse III orthopedic unit, clin. spine educator Swedish Hosp. Med. Ctr., Seattle, 1975—, preceptor orientation of RNs and student RNs, 1975—, clin. spine educator, 2000—. Mem. planning task force and faculty Nat. Nurses Conf., The Nurse and Spinal Surgery, Cleve.; lectr. Coll. of Nursing, Raleigh Fitkin Meml. Hosp., Manzini, Swaziland, South Africa, 1999; mem. med. mission to assist in clinic for street children, Satipo, Peru, 2000, Honolulu Police Dept., 2001; guest spkr. degenerative lumbar spinal techniques, cadaver workshop U. Wash., Seattle, 2001; guest spkr. Am. Acad. Orthop. Surgeons, Dallas, 2002, Dallas, 02. Author: Spinal Disease and Surgical Interventions, 1995. Mem.: Nat. Assn. Orthop. Nurses. Office: Swedish Health Center 747 Broadway Seattle WA 98122-4379

THOMASSON, KATHRYN AMBLER, chemistry educator, biophysical researcher; b. Richmond, Va., Nov. 20, 1959; d. John Nelson and Joan (Hollebeck) T. PhD, Iowa State U., 1990. Rsch. assoc. Biosym Techs., Inc., San Diego, 1990-91; Dreyfus postdoctoral fellow Tenn. Technol. U., Cookeville, Tenn., 1991-93; assoc. prof. chemistry U. N.D., Grand Forks, 1993—. Contbr. articles to profl. jours. Mem. Am. Chem. Soc. (Red River Valley sect. bd. dirs. 1999-2000, Sigma Xi (U. N.D. chpt. pres. 1999-2000), Iota Sigma Pi (coord. members-at-large).. Office: Univ ND Dept Chemistry PO Box 9024 Grand Forks ND 58202-9024 Fax: 701 777-2331. E-mail: kthomasson@chem.und.edu.

THOMAS-WILLIAMS, PAMELA RAE, publishing executive, writer; b. La Crosse, Wis., July 30, 1955; d. Dale Richard and Betty Jean (Clark) Thomas; m. Richard G. Williams, Oct. 30, 1987. BA in Journalism, Marquette U., 1977. Pres. Visual Concepts, ltd., La Crosse, 1979-85, Books By Pamela, Ltd., La Crosse, 1985—. Dir. developmental resources Cath. Cmty. Svcs., Las Vegas, Nev., 1990-91; cons., fundraiser Cath. Charities, La Crosse, 1985-91, U.S. Dept. Commerce-Census Bur., 1999—; co-owner Williams Properties. Author: From My Pallet of Winter, Let Me Paint Your Spring, 1978, The Bride's Guide-A Complete Guide on How to Plan Your Wedding, 7th edit., 2000, (Spanish translation Bridal Guide) Guía Nupcial, 1994, Wedding Showers for Couples, 2nd edit., 2000. Mem. area VFW aux., 1992—. Mem. Pub. Rels. Soc. Am., Sigma Delta Chi. Republican. Lutheran. Avocations: reading, collecting antiques and handguns. Office: Books By Pamela Ltd 2820 Leonard St La Crosse WI 54601-

THOME, DENNIS WESLEY, lawyer; b. Yakima, Wash., Feb. 1, 1939; s. Walter John and Vareta Lucille (Voris) T.; m. Penelope Lee Freeman, Aug. 27, 1961; children: Christopher, Geoffrey. BSBA, U. Denver, 1961, JD, 1967. Bar: Colo. 1967, U.S. Dist. Ct. Colo. 1967, Calif. 1971, U.S. Dist. Ct. (cen. dist.) Calif. 1971, U.S. Supreme Ct. 1971, U.S. Ct. Appeals (9th cir.) 1972. Assoc. Pehr & Newman, Westminster, Colo., 1967-69, Juggert, VaVerka & Wayman, Costa Mesa, Calif., 1975-77; house counsel Wycliffe Bible Translators, Inc., Huntington Beach, 1969-73; pvt. practice Newport Beach, 1973-75, Denver, 1977—. Bd. dirs. First Fruit, Inc., Newport Beach, MOPS Internat., Inc., Denver, Reach Internat., Inc., Denver; mem. Centennial Estate Planning Coun., 1977—. Treas. Gibson for Mayor Com., Denver, 1967; bd. dirs. Christian Eye Ministry, Inc., San Diego, 1983-91, World Eye Care, Inc., 1990-91, Christian Legal Soc. Metro Denver, Inc., 1994-98; chmn. Arvada (Colo.) Covenant Ch., 1993-94; bd. dirs., sec. Wycliffe Bible Translators, Inc., Huntington Beach, Calif., 1977-83. Mem. Colo. Bar Assn. (Bill of Rights com. 1977-90, 92—), State Bar Calif., Omicron Delta Kappa. Avocations: city league volleyball. Office: 7515 W 17th Ave Ste C Lakewood CO 80215-3302

THOME, JIM, professional baseball player; b. Peoria, Ill., Aug. 27, 1970; Player Cleve. Indians, 1991—. Office: Cleve Indians 2401 Ontario St Cleveland OH 44115*

THOMFORD, WILLIAM EMIL, engineer, consultant; b. San Francisco, Mar. 15, 1927; s. Emil George and Anna Marie (Robohm) T.; m. Irene Shapoff, Mar. 21, 1948; children: Elaine Margaret, John William. AA, City Coll. San Francisco, 1949; BA, U. Calif., Berkeley, 1951; postgrad., Stanford U., 1967. Registered profl. engr., Calif. Various engring. positions So. Pacific Transp. Co., San Francisco, 1951-80, mgr. research and test, 1981-83; prin. Transp. Cons. Services, Millbrae, Calif., 1983—. Tech. cons. Nippon Sharyo USA, Inc., N.Y.C., 1987—, Assn. Am. R.R.s, 1986—, Transp. Systems Ctr., U.S. Dept. Transp., 1989. Designer Hydra-Cushion, 1954 (Henderson medal Franklin Inst. 1964), Vert-A Pac rail car for 30 autos (Best Design in Steel award Am. Iron and Steel Inst. 1971), double stack car for 10 Internat. Standards Orgn. containers, 1980, fiberglas covered hopper car, 1982. Served with USN, 1944-46. Fellow ASME (rail transp. engring. achievement A. Stucki award 1991); mem. NSPE, Assn. Am. Railroads, Car Dept Officers' Assn. Clubs: Engrs. (San Francisco), Pacific Railway (San Francisco). Lutheran. Avocations: golf, fishing. Home and Office: 1176 Glenwood Dr Millbrae CA 94030-1014

THOMLINSON, RALPH, demographer, educator; b. St. Louis, Feb. 12, 1925; s. Ralph and Ora Lee (Barr) T.; m. Margaret Mary Willits, Dec. 21, 1946; children: Elizabeth Barr, William Lockwood. BA, Oberlin Coll., 1948; postgrad., U. Pitts., 1943-44, Harvard U., 1948; MA, Yale U., 1949; PhD, Columbia U., 1960. Asst. town planner, Montclair, N.J., 1949-50; asst. city planner Paterson, 1950; research asst. Bur. Applied Social Research, N.Y.C., 1952; med. statistics asst. actuarial dept. Met. Life Ins. Co., 1952-53; instr. statistics and population U. Wis., 1953-56; instr. sociology and anthropology Denison U., Granville, Ohio, 1956-59; asst. prof. sociology Calif. State U., L.A., 1959-62, assoc. prof., 1962-65, prof., 1965-88, prof. emeritus, 1988—, chmn. dept. sociology, 1967-69; vis. prof. sociology U. Alta., Can., 1966; vis. prof. biostatistics U. N.C., Chapel Hill, 1972-73; demographic adviser Inst. Population Studies, Chulalongkorn U., Bangkok, Thailand, 1969-71; cons. Nat. Family Planning Program, Thailand, Census of Thailand, 1970-71, Population/Food Fund, 1977-79, also various research centers abroad, 1969-73. Cons. to fourteen book pubs., 1965— ; field assoc. Population Coun., N.Y.C., 1969-71; rsch. adviser Ctr. for Rsch. and Demographic Studies, Rabat, Morocco, 1972-73; acad. visitor Population Investigation Com., London Sch. Econs., 1973; vis. scholar Nat. Inst. Demographic Studies, Paris, 1973-74 Author: A Mathematical Model for Migration, 1960, Population Dynamics, 2d edit, 1976, Sociological Concepts and Research, 1965, Demographic Problems, 2d edit, 1975, Urban Structure, 1969, Thailand's Population, 1971, (with others) The Methodology of the Longitudinal Study of Social, Economic and Demographic Change, 1971; editor: (with Visid Prachuabmoh) The Potharam Study, 1971; adv. editor: Sociol. Abstracts, 1963-67, Sociology Quar, 1978-84; cons. editor: As-Soukan, 1972-73; assoc. editor: Pacific Sociol. Rev, 1976-83; Sociol. Perspective, 1983-85; chmn. editorial bd. Calif. Sociologist, 1981-84; cons.: Dictionary of Modern Sociology, 1969; contbr. to: Dictionary of Demography, 5 vols., 1985-86; books, profl. jours. Served with AUS, 1943-45, ETO. Mem. Population Assn. Am., Internat. Union for Sci. Study Population, Am. Sociol. Assn., Internat. Assn. Survey Statisticians, Assn. Asian Studies. Home: 712 Coronado Ln Foster City CA 94404-2925

THOMOPULOS, GREGS G. consulting engineering company executive; b. Benin City, Nigeria, May 16, 1942; s. Aristoteles and Christiana E. (Ogiamien) T.; m. Patricia Walker, Sept. 4, 1966 (div. 1974); 1 child, Lisa; m. Mettie L. Williams, May 28, 1976; children: Nicole, Euphemia. BSCE with highest distinction, U. Kans., 1965; MS in Structural Engring., U. Calif., Berkeley, 1966; PhD (hon.), Teikyo Marycrest U., 1996. Sr. v.p. internat. div. Stanley Cons., Inc., Muscatine, Iowa, 1978-84, sr. v.p. project divsn., 1984-87; pres., CEO Stanley Consultants, Inc., 1987—; exec. v.p. SC Co., Inc., 1992-98; pres., COO, 1998-99; pres., CEO, 2000—; also bd. dirs. SC Co., Inc., Muscatine; chmn., CEO Stanley Environ., Inc., Chgo., 1991—, also bd. dirs.; chmn., CEO SC Power Devel., Inc., 1992—. Chmn., CEO Stanley Design-Build, Inc., 1995—; bd. dirs. Stanley Cons., Inc., Muscatine, Wellmark, Inc., Blue Cross Blue Shield Iowa and S.D., 1999—; mem. adv. bd. U. Kans. Sch. Engring., 2002—. Mem. adv. bd. Coll. Engring. U. Iowa, 1992-2000, Hydraulics Inst., 2000—. Fellow ASCE, Am. Cons. Engring. Coun.; mem. NSPE, 33 Club (pres. 1987), Rotary. Presbyterian. Avocations: tennis, computers, music. Home: 75 Shagbark Ct Iowa City IA 52246-2786 Office: Stanley Cons Inc 225 Iowa Ave Muscatine IA 52761-3765 E-mail: thomopulos@home.com., :thomopulosg@stanleygroup.com.

THOMPSON, ALAN ERIC, economics educator; b. Sept. 16, 1924; s. Eric Joseph and Florence Thompson; m. Mary Heather Long, 1960; 4 children. MA, U. Edinburgh, 1949, MA with 1st class honors, 1951, PhD, 1953. Asst. in polit. econ. U. Edinburgh, 1952-53, lectr. econs., 1953-59, 64-71; prof. econs. of govt. Heriot-Watt U., Edinburgh, 1972—. Adviser to Scottish TV, 1966-76; Scottish gov. BBC, 1976-79; vis. prof. Grad. Sch. Bus., Stanford U. (Calif.), 1966, 68; chmn. adv. bd. econs. edn. Esmee Fairbairn Rsch. Project, 1970-76. Author: (with others) Development of Economic Doctrine, 1980; contbr. articles to profl. jours. M.P. Labour Party, Dunfermline, 1959-64; mem. Scottish Com. Pub. Schs. Commn., 1969-70; mem. Joint Mil. Edn. Com. Edinburgh and Heriot-Watt Univs., 1969-71, local govt. boundary commn. for Scotland, 1975-82; chmn. No. Offshore Resources Study, 1974-84; chmn. bd. govs. Newbattle Abbey Coll., 1980-82; bd. govs. Leigh Nautical Coll., 1981-87; trustee Bell's Nautical Trust, 1981-87; parliamentary adviser Pharm. Gen. Coun., 1985-2000; bd. dirs. Scottish AIDS Rsch. Found., 1992; adv. Robert Burns Meml. Trust, 1995—; advisor Robert Burns Meml. Trust, 1995—. With Brit. Army, WWII. Carnegie Rsch. scholar, 1951-52. Fellow Royal Soc. Arts, Soc. Antiquaries (Scotland); mem. Assn. Nazi War Camp Survivors (v.p. 1960—), Edinburgh Amenity and Transport Assn. (pres. 1970-75), New Club, Edinburgh Univ. Staff Club, Loch Earn Sailing Club.

THOMPSON, ALLEN JOSEPH, construction executive, civil engineer; b. San Juan, P.R., May 14, 1937; s. Allen Lincoln and Antonia Bartolome (Martin) T.; m. Lucy Elizabeth Stoutenburgh, Oct. 4, 1957 (div. June 1982); children: Lucy An, Cristina Mae, Elizabeth Anne; m. Maria Josefina Moya, Oct. 1, 1987. BS in Civil Engring., The Citadel, 1956; postgrad., N.Y. Polytech. Inst., 1958-59, George Washington U., 1960-61. Registered profl. engr., D.C., Md., Miss., Fla., P.R. Civil engr. Raymond Internat., San Juan, 1956-58; structural designer Buell Engring., N.Y.C., 1958-59; civil engr. Norair Engring., Washington, 1959-62; constrn. mgr. Bechtel Corp., San Francisco, 1962-87; pres. Thompson Martin Assocs., Miami, Fla., 1987—, NCI Constrn., Miami, 1994—. Cons. Bechtel Power Corp., San Francisco, 1987-90; constrn. arbitrator-mediator Am. Arbitration Assn., 1992—. Commr. Boy Scouts Am., Md., 1967. Mem. Am. Soc. Civil Engrs., Nat. Soc. Profl. Engrs., Am. Arbitration Assn. Republican. Roman Catholic. Avocations: pilot, scuba diving, sports car racing. Home: 2333 Brickell Ave Apt 1716 Miami FL 33129-2414 E-mail: ncicmiami@yahoo.com.

THOMPSON, ALVIN W. judge; b. 1953; BA, Princeton U., 1975; JD, Yale U., 1978. With Robinson & Cole, Hartford, Conn., 1978-94; dist. judge U.S. Dist. Ct., 1994—. Mem. ABA, Conn. Bar Assn., Hartford County Bar Assn. Office: US Dist Ct 450 Main St Rm 240 Hartford CT 06103-3022

THOMPSON, ANA CALZADA, secondary education educator, mathematician; b. Sanderson, Tex., Nov. 29, 1940; d. Leopoldo G. and Maria Deo Gracia (Sandoval) Calzada; m. Tommy Salinas Thompson, July 1, 1962; children: Tommy Michael, Anthony Jude, Ana Marie. BS, Sul Ross State U., Alpine, Tex., 1966; MEd, S.W. Tex. State U., 1980. Tchr. Poteet (Tex.) Ind. Sch. Dist., 1965-67, Northside Ind. Sch. Dist., San Antonio, 1967-68; tchr. math. N.E. Ind. Sch. Dist., 1968-97, chmn. dept., 1976-97. Prof. math. St. Philips Coll., San Antonio, 1986—; mem. Region 20 Tchr. Ctr., San Antonio, 1978-82; pres. S.W. Tchr. Ctr., San Marcos, Tex., 1970-82. Contbg. author: Graphing Power, 1995. Sec., La Vernia (Tex.) Ind. Sch. Dist., 1977-87, mem. bd., 1978-87; del. Tex. Dem. Conv., Houston, 1988, Ft. Worth, 1992, Dallas, 1996, El Paso, 2002; del. Guadalupe County Dem. Com., Seguin, Tex., 1988, 92, 96, 2002. Mem. NEA, Nat. Coun. Tchrs. Math., Tex. Tchrs. Assn., Alamo Dist. Coun. Tchrs. Math. Roman Catholic. Avocations: reading, knitting, travel, gardening.

THOMPSON, ANDREW ERNEST, secondary school educator; b. Springfield, Mass., Oct. 17, 1947; s. Richard Ernest and Virginia Laurie (Knight) T.; m. Anne Adams, Apr. 6, 1973; children: Stephanie Anne, Elizabeth Clare, Adam Richard. BA in Maths., Bridgewater State Coll., 1969; M in Maths., Worcester Polytech. Inst., 1988; postgrad., Harvard U., 1988, Mich. State U., 1989-90. Cert. math., secondary edn. and social studies tchr., secondary adminstrn. Test engr. Pratt & Whitney Aircraft Co., 1968; tchr. math. Whitman (Mass.) Pub. Schs., 1969-91, Whitman-Hanson Regl. Sch. Dist., 1991-2001, Wareham (Mass.) Pub. Schs., 2001—; sr. mem. faculty Cambridge (Mass.) Coll., 2000—. Mgr. Dairy Queen Ice Cream, 1976-77; curriculum coord. Horace Mann, 1986-88; curriculum cons. Bridgewater (Mass.) Pub. Schs., 1987-89; scorer Mass. Ednl. Assessment Program, 1990, 92; sr. faculty Cambridge Coll., Mass. Mem. Bridgewater Sch. Com., 1992-95; supt. Ctrl. Sq. Congl. Ch., 1989-90, 92-94; cubmaster Boy Scouts Am., Bridgewater, 1988-92, troop com., 1992-95; mem. Bridgewater-Raynham Sch. Com., 1999-2001. Recipient Harvard U. Practitioner award, 1988; NSF grantee, 1989-90. Mem. ASCD, Am. Math. Soc., Assn. Tchrs. Math. in Mass., Nat. Coun. Tchrs. Math., Math. Assn. Am., Mass. Tchrs. Assn., Plymouth County Edn. Assn. (bd. dirs. 1977-84, chmn. county negotiating com. 1981-83), Whitman Edn. Assn. (pres.-elect 1981, 83, pres. 1982-84, chmn. negotiating com. 1977-80, 90-92), Whitman Hanson Edn. Assn. (pres. 1992-2001). Home: PO Box 419 Bridgewater MA 02324-0419

THOMPSON, ANNE ELISE, federal judge; b. Phila., July 8, 1934; d. Leroy Henry and Mary Elise (Jackson) Jenkins; m. William H. Thompson, June 19, 1965; children: William H., Sharon A. BA, Howard U., 1955, LLB, 1964; MA, Temple U., 1957. Bar: D.C. bar 1964, N.J. bar 1966. Staff atty. Office of Solicitor, Dept. Labor, Chgo., 1964-65; asst. dep. public defender Trenton, N.J., 1967-70; mcpl. prosecutor Lawrence Twp., Lawrenceville, 1970-72; mcpl. ct. judge Trenton, 1972-75; prosecutor Mercer County, Mercer County, Trenton, 1975-79; judge U.S. Dist. Ct. N.J., Trenton, 1979—. Vice chmn. Mercer County Criminal Justice Planning Com., 1972; mem. com. criminal practice N.J. Supreme Ct., 1975-79, mem. com. mcpl. cts., 1972-75; v.p. N.J. County Prosecutors Assn., 1978-79; chmn. juvenile justice com. Nat. Dist. Attys. Assn., 1978-79 Del. Democratic Nat. Conv., 1972. Recipient Assn. Black Women Lawyers award, 1976, Disting. Service award Nat. Dist. Attys. Assn., 1979, Gene Carte Meml. award Am. Criminal Justice Assn., 1980, Outstanding Leadership award N.J. County Prosecutors Assn., 1980, John Mercer Langston Outstanding Alumnus award Howard U. Law Sch., 1981; also various service awards; certs. of appreciation. Mem. Am. Bar Assn., Fed. Bar Assn., N.J. Bar Assn., Mercer County Bar Assn. Democrat. Office: US Dist Ct US Courthouse-4000 402 E State St Trenton NJ 08608-1507

THOMPSON, ANNIE FIGUEROA, academic director, educator; b. Río Piedras, P.R., June 7, 1941; d. Antonio Figueroa-Colón and Ana Isabel Laugier; m. Donald P. Thompson, Jan. 23, 1972; 1 child, John Anthony. BA, Baylor U., 1962; MSLS, U. So. Calif., 1965; AMD, Fla. State U., 1978, PhD, 1980. Educator Mayan Sch., Guatemala City, Guatemala, 1962-63; cataloger libr. system U. P.R., Río Piedras, 1965-67, head music libr., 1967-81, assoc. prof. librarianship, 1981-85, dir. grad. sch. libr. info. sci. Rio Piedras, 1986-93, prof., 1986-96; ret., 1996. Author: An Annotated Bibliography About Music in Puerto Rico, 1975; co-author: Music and Dance in Puerto Rico from the Age of Columbus to Modern Times, An Annotated Bibliography, 1991; contbr. articles to profl. jours.; performed song recitals Inst. of P.R. Culture and U. P.R. Artist Series, 1974-78; soloist with P.R. Symphony Orch., San Juan, 1978; performed in opera, on radio and TV, San Juan, 1968-81 Sec. P.R. Symphony Orch League, San Juan, 1982-84; mem. pub. libr. adv. com. Adminstrn. for Devel. of Arts and Culture, P.R., 1982-84, Pub. Libr. Adv. Bd., 1989-94. Recipient Lauro a la Instrucción Bibliotecaria Sociedad de Bibliotecarios de P.R., 1985, Lauro a la Bibliografía Puertorriqueña, 1993. Mem. Sarasota Rotary (bd. dirs. 2000-02), Sociedad de Bibliotecarios de P.R. (pres. 1994-96), Music Libr. Assn. (bd. dirs. 1982-84, asst. conv. mgr. 2002—), Sigma Delta Kappa, Mu Phi Epsilon, Beta Phi Mu. Episcopalian. Home: 435 S Gulfstream Ave Sarasota FL 34236-6736 E-mail: figarotu@msn.com.

THOMPSON, ANNIE LAURA (ANNE), foreign language educator; b. Henderson, Tenn., July 8, 1937; d. Wesley Sylvester and Letha Irene (Jones) T.; m. Edward L. Patterson, June 7, 1980. BA, U. Ala., 1959; MA, Duke U., 1961; PhD, Tulane U., 1973. Instr. Spanish lang. U. Miss., Oxford, 1960-64; instr. Auburn (Ala.) U., 1964-66; tchg. asst. Tulane U., New Orleans, 1966-70; prof. Spanish lang. Delgado C.C., 1970—. Instr. Spanish for Physicians and Med. Persons Tulane U., La. State U. Med. Eye Ctr., Ochsner Clinic and Hosp. Author: Religious Elements in the Quijote, 1960, The Attempt of Spanish Intellectuals to Create a New Spain, 1930-36, 1973, The Generation of 1898: Intellectual Politicians; asst. editor The Crusader, 1961-64. Rep. candidate for gov. State of La., 1991, 95, for 1st Dist. U.S. Congress, 1992; alt. mem. La. Coastal Commn., 1984—; del. Women's State Rep. Conv., 1987, La. State Rep. Conv., 1990, 93, La. Coastal Adv. Coun., 1988, Pan Am. Commn., 1992-95; v.p. pub. rels. Alliance for Good Govt., 1990; candidate State Senate La., 1994; mem. DAR (Vieux Carré chpt.), 2000. Recipient Outstanding Tchr. award Delgado Coll. Student Govt. Assn., 1974; Woodoow Wilson fellow, 1959-60, NDEA fellow, 1968-69. Mem. AAUP, DAR, Pachyderm Club, Women's Rep. Club, Phi Beta Kappa, Phi Alpha Theta, Sigma Delta Pi. Republican. Mem. Ch. of Christ. Home: PO Box 24399 New Orleans LA 70184-4399

THOMPSON, ANTHONY RICHARD, electrical engineer, astronomer; b. Hull, Yorkshire, Eng., Apr. 7, 1931; came to U.S., 1957; s. George and Ada Mary (Laybourn) T.; m. Sheila Margaret Press, Oct. 12, 1963; 1 child, Sarah Louise. BSc in Physics with honors, U. Manchester, Eng., 1952, PhD, 1955. Engr. E.M.I. Electronics Ltd., Feltham, Eng., 1956-57; rsch. fellow Coll. Obs. Harvard U., Cambridge, Mass., 1957-62; sr. rsch. assoc. Radio Astronomy Inst. Stanford (Calif.) U., 1962-72; head electronics divsn., VLA and VLBA projects Nat. Radio Astronomy Obs., Charlottesville, Va., 1973-92, dep. head Ctrl. Electronics Lab., 1993-99, emeritus scientist, 2001—. Vis. sr. rsch. fellow Owens Valley Radio Obs., Calif. Inst. Tech., Pasadena, 1966-72; mem. Com. on Radio Frequencies NAS, Washington, 1980-91; sec. Interunion Commn. on Frequency Allocations for Radio Astronomy and Space Sci., 1982-88, mem., 1991-99; guest lectr. in radio astronomy Ukrainian Acad. Sci., 1988. Prin. author: (monograph) Interferometry and Synthesis in Radio Astronomy, 1986; contbr. articles to Astrophys. Jour., Astron. Jour., Proceedings of IEEE, Sci., Radiosci. Fellow IEEE; mem. Internat. Telecom. Union (radiocommunication sector, chmn. working group on radio astronomy U.S. Study group 7 1978-99), Am. Astron. Soc., Internat. Astron. Union. Achievements include research in astronomy and contributions to system design of the VLA and VLB array; design of instruments: frequency coordination for radio astronomy. Office: Nat Radio Astronomy Obs 520 Edgemont Rd Charlottesville VA 22903-2454 E-mail: athompso@nrao.edu.

THOMPSON, ANTHONY WAYNE, metallurgist, educator, consultant; b. Burbank, Calif., Mar. 6, 1940; s. William Lyman and Mary Adelaide (Nisbet) T.; m. Mary Ruth Cummings, Aug. 24, 1963; children: Campbell Lyman, Michael Anthony. BS, Stanford U., 1962; MS, U. Wash., 1965; PhD, MIT, 1970. Research engr. Jet Propulsion Lab., Pasadena, Calif., 1962-63; mem. tech. staff Sandia Labs., Livermore, 1970-73, Rockwell Sci. Ctr., Thousand Oaks, 1973-77; assoc. prof. Carnegie Mellon U., Pitts., 1977-79, prof., 1980-94, dept. head, 1987-90; staff scientist Lawrence Berkeley Lab., Berkeley, Calif., 1994-99; rsch. engr. U. Calif., 1995—. Vis. scientist U. Cambridge, Eng., 1983, Risø, Denmark, 1987, U. Calif., 1991; cons. Sandia Labs., 1977—, GE, 1988—. Editor: Work Hardening, 1976, Metall. Transactions, 1983-88; co-editor: Hydrogen in Metals, 1974, Hydrogen Conf. Proc., 1976, 81, 89, 94; mem. editl. bd. Internat. Metals Revs., 1980-88; contbr. articles to profl. jours. Overseas fellow Churchill Coll. Cambridge U., 1982 Fellow Am. Soc. Metals; mem. AAAS, AIME, Sigma Xi Clubs: Sierra, Nat. Model R.R. Assn. Democrat. Home: 2942 Linden Ave Berkeley CA 94705-2328 Office: Lawrence Berkeley Lab Material Sci Divsn Berkeley CA 94720-0001

THOMPSON, ARLENE RITA, nursing educator; b. Yakima, Wash., May 17, 1933; d. Paul James and Esther Margaret (Danroth) T. BS in Nursing, U. Wash., 1966, Masters in Nursing, 1970, postgrad., 1982—. Staff nurse Univ. Teaching Hosp., Seattle, 1966-69; mem. nursing faculty U. Wash. Sch. Nurses, 1971-73; critical care nurse Virginia Mason Hosp., 1973—; educator Seattle Pacific U. Sch. Nursing, 1981—. Nurse legal cons. nursing edn., critical care nurse. Contbr. articles to profl. jours. USPHS grantee, 1969; nursing scholar Virginia Mason Hosp., 1965. Mem. Am. Assn. Critical Care Nurses (cert.), Am. Nurses Assn., Am. Heart Assn., Nat. League Nursing, Sigma Theta Tau, Alpha Tau Omega. Republican. Presbyterian. Avocations: sewing, swimming, jogging, bicycle riding, hiking. Home: 2320 W Newton St Seattle WA 98199-4115 Office: Seattle Pacific U 3307 3rd Ave W Seattle WA 98119-1997

THOMPSON, BARBARA STORCK, state official; b. McFarland, Wis., Oct. 15, 1924; d. John Casper and Marie Ann (Kassabaum) Storck; m. Glenn T. Thompson, July 1, 1944; children— David C., James T. BS, Wis. State U., 1956; MS, U. Wis., 1959, PhD, 1969; L.H.D. (hon.), Carroll Coll., 1974. Tchr. pub. schs., West Dane County, Mt. Horeb, Wis., 1944-56; instr. Green County Tchrs. Coll., Monroe, 1956-57; coordinator curriculum Monroe Pub. Schs., 1957-60; instr. U. Wis., Platteville, 1960; supr. schs. Waukesha County Schs., Wis., 1960-63, supt. schs., 1963-65; prin. Fairview Elem. Schs., Brookfield, Wis., 1962-64; adminstrv. cons. Wis. Dept. Pub. Instrn., Madison, 1964-72, state coordinator, 1971-72; instr. U. Wis., Madison and Green Bay, 1972; supt. pub. instrn. Madison, Wis., 1973—81. Mem. Wis. State Bd. Vocat. Edn., 1973-81, Wis. Edn. Comm. Bd., 1973-81, Univ. Wis. Sys. Bd. Regents, 1973-1981. Author: A Candid Discussion of Critical Issues, 1975; Mem. editorial bd.: The Education Digest, 1975— ; Contbr. articles to profl. jours. Mem. White House Conf. Children, 1970, Gov.'s Com. State Conf. Children and Youth, 1969-70, Manpower Council, 1973-81; bd. dirs. Vocational, Tech. and Adult Edn., 1973-81, Ednl. Communications, 1973-81, Higher Edn. Aids, 1973-81, Agy. Instructional TV, 1975-81; mem. nat. panel on SAT score decline; bd. regents U. Wis., 1973-81 Recipient State Conservation award Madison Lions CLub, 1956; Waukesha Freeman award, 1961 Mem. Nat. Council Adminstrv. Women in Edn. (named Woman of Year 1974), Nat. Council State Cons. in Elementary Edn. (pres. 1974-75), Wis. Assn. Sch. Dist. Adminstrs., Assn. Supervision and Curriculum Devel., Wis. Assn. Supervision and Curriculum Devel., Southwestern Wis. Assn. Supervision and Curriculum Devel., Southeastern Wis. Assn. Supervision and Curriculum Devel. (mem. exec. council 1972-73), Dept. Elementary Sch. Prins., Wis. Elementary Sch. Prins. Assn., NEA, Wis. Edn. Assn. (pres. local chpt. 1970-71); life mem. So. Wis. Edn. Assn., Wis. Ednl. Research Assn., Dept. Elementary-Kindergarten-Nursery Edn., Assn. Childhood Edn. Internat., Assn. Childhood Edn., Council Chief State Sch. Officers, Edn. Commn. of States, Nat. Council State Cons. in Elementary Edn. (pres. 1974-75), Am. Assn. Sch. Dist. Adminstrs. (chmn. policy com. 1963-81), Madison Internat. Lions Club, U. Wis. Alumni Orgn. (Sarasota, Fla. and Madison), U. Wis. League (Madison chpt.), Delta Kappa Gamma, Pi Lambda Theta. Office: Apt 123 325 S Yellowstone Dr Madison WI 53705-4301

THOMPSON, BARRY HAMMOND, medical geneticist; b. Chattanooga, Nov. 13, 1939; s. Harold Deforrest and Ruth (Hammond) T.; m. Jo Ann Bennett, May 30, 1964; children: Christopher, David, Kathryn, Stuart. BA in Biology, The U. of the South, Sewanee, Tenn., 1961; MD, Vanderbilt U., 1965; MS in Med. Genetics, Ind. U., Indpls., 1974. Diplomate Am. Bd. Pediatrics, Am. Bd. Med. Genetics, Am. Bd. Med. Mgmt. Resident in pediatrics Vanderbilt Med. Ctr., Nashville, 1965-68; commd. 2d lt. USAF, 1966, advanced through grades to col., 1980; pediatrician 2795 USAF Hosp., Warner Robin, Ga., 1968-71; dir. med. genetics ctr. USAF Med. Ctr., Keesler AFB, Miss., 1974-85; dir. profl. svcs. Wilford Hall Med. Ctr., San Antonio, 1985-87; comdr. USAF Med. Ctr., Keesler AFB, 1987-91; command surgeon US Air Forces-Europe, Ramstein Air Base, Germany, 1991-95; dir. Ctr. for Genetics Armed Forces Inst. Pathology, Washington, 1995-2001. Cons. in med. genetics Surgeon Gen. USAF, Bolling AFB, Washington, 1980—2001; Dept. Def. rep to NIH, Bethesda, Md., 1997—2001; cons. Nat. Coalition on Breast Cancer, Bethesda, 1996—2001; asst. clin. prof. pediats. Uniformed Svcs. U. Health Scis., 1991—. Contbr. articles to profl. jours.; editl. reviewer Assn. Mil. Surgeons of U.S., Bethesda, 1995—. Fellow Am. Acad. Pediatrics, Am. Coll. Med. Genetics, Am. Coll. Physician Execs.; mem. AAAS, Am. Soc. Law and Medicine, Am. Assn. Bioethics. Episcopalian. Avocations: beekeeping, model railroading, Civil War medicine, agricultural bioterrorism.

THOMPSON, BASIL F. ballet master; b. Newcastle-on-Tyne, Eng., 1937; came to U.S., 1958; Grad., Royal Acad. Dance; studies with, David Lichine, Tania Riabouchinska; student, Sch. Classical. Ballet, 1958-60. Dancer Covent Garden Opera Co., Sadler Wells Opera Co., London, 1954-55, Royal Ballet Eng., London, 1955-58; instr. ballet and character Eugene Loring Sch. Ballet, L.A., 1958-60, Al Gilber Sch. Ballet, L.A., 1958-60; instr. ballet Michael Panaieff Sch. Ballet, 1958-60; soloist Am. Ballet Theatre, N.Y.C., 1960-67; ballet master Joffrey Ballet Co., 1967-79; ballet master, choreographer N.J. Ballet Co., West Orange, 1979-80; mem. faculty ballet and character N.J. Ballet Sch., Morristown/West Orange, 1979-80; ballet master Milw. Ballet, 1981-86, also artistic head; ballet master Pa. and Milw. Ballet; apptd. artistic dir. Milw. Ballet, spring 1995; now prof. dance U. Iowa, Iowa City. Guest ballet instr. Internat. Ballet Inst., Aix-en-Provence, France, 1980; guest instr. character Am. Ballet Co. Sch., 1981. Roles include (prin.) Billy the Kid, Sleeping Beauty, Graduation Ball, La Sylphide, Moon Reindeer, Peter and The

Wolf, Three Cornered Hat, others, (soloist) Rodeo, Fall River Legend, Fire Bird, Coppelia, Swan Lake, Cinderella, La Boutique Fantastic, Undertow, others (opera) Aida; guest appearances include for Dame Margo Fontayne Royal Acad. Gala, Pres. John F. Kennedy, Pres. Lyndon B. Johnson, L.A. Civic Light Opera, Michael Panaieff Ballet Theatre; TV appearances include Bell Telephone Hour Spectacular prodn. Graduation Ball, NBC prodn. Sleeping Beauty and Cinderella; Broadway prodns. On a Clear Day You Can See Forever, Tavarich, Happiest Girl in the World; choreographer La Traviata. Office: Univ of Iowa Dept Dance 107 W Halsey Hall Iowa City IA 52240 E-mail: basil-thompson@uiowa.edu.

THOMPSON, BENNIE G. congressman; b. Bolton, Miss., Jan. 28, 1948; m. London Johnson; 1 child Benda Lonne. BA Polit. Sci., Tougaloo Coll., 1968; MS Ednl. Adminstrn., Jackson State U., Miss., 1972; grad., U. So. Miss. Alderman, Bolton, Miss., 1969—73; mayor, 1973—79; supr. dist. 2 Hinds County Bd., 1980-93; mem. U.S. Congress from 2d dist. Miss., 1993—; mem. agr. com., budget com. Presdl. appointee Nat. Coun. Health Planning and Devel. Bd. trustees Tougaloo Coll.; bd. dirs. So. Regional Coun., Housing Assistance Coun. Mem.: Miss. Assn. Black Suprs. (founding mem.), Miss. Assn. Black Mayors (founding mem.). Democrat. Methodist. Original plaintiff in 1975 Ayers case. Office: 2432 Rayburn House Office Bldg Washington DC 20515-0001*

THOMPSON, BERNADETTE MARIA, poet; b. Oakland, Calif., June 15, 1952; Cert. key punch operator, Healds Coll., 1984. Poet, Calif., 1985—. Composer numerous songs including Guide My Hand; author: (poems) Love, 2001, Oh Faithful Blue Eyes, 2000. Named to Internat. Hall of Fame for Poetry, 1996. Mem. Internation Soc. Poets, Famous Poets Soc. (Muse of Fire trophy 2000). Avocations: reading, tennis, writing, bowling. Home: # 126 2124 Kittredge St Berkeley CA 94704-1436

THOMPSON, BERNIDA LAMERLE, principal, consultant, educator; b. Tuskeegee, Ala., July 5, 1946; d. Berry James Sr. and Doris LaMerle (Askey) T.; m. Rolando Amerson, June 15, 1968 (div. Aug. 1988); children: Afriye Amerson, Mwando Amerson. BS in Elem. Edn., Cen. State U., 1968; MEd in Adminstrn. and Curriculum, Miami U., Oxford, Ohio, 1971; EdD in Early and Mid. Childhood Edn., Nova U., 1992. Classroom elem. sch. tchr. Dayton Pub. Schs.; asst. prin., intern St. James Cath. Sch., Dayton, Ohio; tchr. St. Augustine Cath. Sch., Washington; sci. resource tchr. D.C. Pub. Schs.; prin., co-founder, tchr. Roots Activity Learning Ctr., co-founder, 1977—, Roots Pub. Charter Sch., 1999—. Multicultural advisor HBJ 1992 Reading Textbook. Author: Black Madonnas and Young Lions a Rite of Passage for African American Adolescents, 1992, Africentric Interdisciplinary Multi-Level Hands On Science, 1994; contbr. articles to profl. jours. Mem. Nat. Assn. Edn. Young Children, World Coun. Curriculum Instrn., Coun. Ind. Black Inst., Inst. Ind. Edn., Nat. Black Child Devel. Inst. Office: Roots Pub Charter Sch 15 Kennedy St NW Washington DC 20011-5201

THOMPSON, BERT ALLEN, retired librarian; b. Bloomington, Ind., Dec. 13, 1930; s. James Albert and Dorothy Fern (Myers) T.; m. Martha Ellen Palmer; children— John Carter II, Anne Palmer, Paul Julian. BS, Ball State Tchrs. Coll., 1953; AM, Ind. U., 1960; certificate in archival adm., U. Denver, 1967. Tchr., libr. Ind. pub. schs., 1953-55; ref. asst. Indpls. Pub. Libr., 1956-59; head ref. svc. Mankato (Minn.) State U., 1959-61; instr. Grad. Libr. Sch. No. Ill. U., Dekalb, 1961-63; dir. libs., asst. prof. ednl. media U. Nebr. at Kearney, 1963-69; dir. libr. svc. Benedictine U., Lisle, Ill., 1969-90, spl. collections libr., 1990-92. Mem. exec. bd. Ill. regional Libr. Coun., 1976-79. Recipient 1st Melvin R. George LIBRAS award for Outstanding Svc. to Libr. Cooperation, 1993. Mem. Ill. (de Lafayette Reid Research scholar 1976), Cath. Libr. Assn. (treas. Ill. chpt. 1973-75, nat. sec.-treas. coll./univ. sect. 1981-85, nat. bd. dirs. 1987-93), Nebr. Libr. Assn, chmn. coll. and univ. sect. 1963-64) Episcopalian. Home: 1808 Caxton Dr Wheaton IL 60187-6140

THOMPSON, BERTHA BOYA, retired education educator, antique dealer and appraiser; b. New Castle, Pa., Jan. 31, 1917; d. Frank L. and Kathryn Belle (Park) Boya; m. John L. Thompson, Mar. 27, 1942; children: Kay Lynn Thompson Koolage, Scott McClain. BS in Elem. & Secondary Edn., Slippery Rock State Coll., 1940; MA in Geography and History, Miami U., 1954; EdD, Ind. U., 1961. Cert. elem. and secondary edn. tchr. Elem. tchr., reading specialist New Castle (Pa.) Sch. System, 1940-45; tchr., chmn. social studies Talawanda Sch. System, Oxford, Ohio, 1954-63; assoc. prof. psychology and geography, chair edn. dept. Western Coll. for Women, 1963-74; assoc. prof. edn., reading clinic Miami U., 1974-78, prof. emeritus, 1978—; pvt. antique dealer, appraiser, 1978—. Contbr. articles to profl. jours. Mem. folk art com. Miami U. Art Mus., Oxford, 1974-76; mem. adv. com. Smith libr., Oxford Pub. Libr., 1978-81. Mem. AAUP, Nat. Coun. Geographic Edn. (exec. bd. dirs. 1966-69), Nat. Soc. for Study Edn., Assn. Am. Geographers, Soc. Women Geographers, Nat. Coun. for the Social Studies, Pi Lambda Theta, Zeta Tau Alpha, Pi Gamma Mu, Gamma Theta Upsilon, Kappa Delta Pi. Avocations: antique collecting, reading, travel, tennis. Home: 6073 Contreras Rd Oxford OH 45056-9708

THOMPSON, BETSY PALMER, special health education services professional; b. Gloversville, N.Y., Apr. 24, 1941; d. Joseph James Thompson and Margaret Ruth (Worden) Reeves. BA, Antioch Coll., 1964; postgrad., U. Wis., 1964-65; MAT, U. Mass., 1968; cert. in gardening, Inst. Ecosystem Studies, 2000. Cert. health edn., biology and gen. sci. tchr., N.Y. Tchr.-counselor Otter Lake Conservation Sch., Greenfield, N.H., 1961; asst. to dir. Inst. Animal Behavior, Rutgers U., Newark, 1962; asst. to curator of mammals Chgo. Mus. Natural History, 1963; interpretive naturalist Ward Pound Ridge (N.Y.) Reservation, 1966; edn. aide N.Y. State Edn. Dept., Albany, 1968-77, asst. in sch. health edn., 1977-2000. N.Y. State Edn. Dept. liaison to N.Y. State Coun. Alcohol and Other Drug Addictions, 1985-89; mem. student adv. bd. Dept. Continuing Edn. Inst. of Ecosystem Studies, 2000—. Author: Annotated Resource Guide for Alcohol, Tobacco and Other Drug Abuse Prevention Edn. Programs, elem. level, 1978, secondary level, 1979; co-author: New York State Drug Education Curriculum K-12, 1981. Vol. Valley Presbyn. Hosp., L.A., 1960, Nature Conservancy, George Landis Arboretum, Esperence, N.Y., 1989-90, Berkshire Botanical Garden, 2001-; adv. com. dept. continuing edn. Inst. Ecosystem Studies, 1996—. Recipient Outstanding Person of Yr. award Alcohol Edn. for Youth, Inc., 1983. Mem. Am. Sch. Health Assn., Assn. for Advancement Health Edn., N.Y. State Fedn. Profl. Health Educators (co-chmn. ann. N.Y. state health edn. conf. 1976, 87-89, liaison 1987-90, Dedicated Svc. award 1990, panel reviewer, site reviewer U.S. Drug-Free Schs. Recognition Program, 1993-94, Fed. Child Nutrition Edn. and Tng. Program 1995-96, Comprehensive Sch. Health and Wellness Team, N.Y. State Edn. Dept. 1996-2000, garden designer, garden photographer, gardening instr. and cons. 2000—). Avocations: natural history, classical music.

THOMPSON, BETTY JANE, small business owner; b. Ladysmith, Wis., Nov. 18, 1923; d. Edward Thomas and Mayme Selma (Kratwell) Potter; m. Frederick Sturdee Thompson, Apr. 19, 1945 (div. Apr. 1973); children: Denise Alana, Kent Marshall; m. J.R. Critchfield, Feb. 14, 1977 (div. 1989). Student, Jamestown (N.D.) Coll., 1946-47, U. Calif., Long Beach, 1964-69; AA, Orange Coast Coll., 1976; postgrad., Monterey Peninsula Coll., 1979-80; SBA Cert., Hartnell Coll., 1982. Cert. fashion cons. Owner, mgr., buyer Goodview (Minn.) Food Mart, 1947-50; dist. mgr. Beauty Counselor of Minn., Winona County, 1951-61; Boy Scout liaison J.C. Penney Co., Newport Beach, Calif., 1969-72; dept. mgr. and buyer boyswear At Ease, 1972-77; mgr. Top Notch Boys Wear, Carmel, Calif., 1977-83, buyer, 1984-88; owner, mgr. Top Notch Watch, Sun City, Ariz., 1989-95; editor H&R Block, 1995-98. V.p., chmn. Don Loper Fashion Show, 1967, pres., 1968, bd. dirs., 1969. Co-editor Aux. Antics mag., 1965. Vol. fundraising leadership Family Svc. Assn., Orange County, Calif., 1962-68, other orgns.; chmn. publicity, study group, Sunday sch. tchr., Congl. Ch., Winona, Minn., 1956-58, fellowship pres., Santa Ana, Calif., 1963-65; pres. Goodview Civic Club, 1948; active Wells Fargo and Co. Bank Silver Bullets, Sr. Citizens of the Sun Cities, Phoenix, 1998—; counselor AARP Tax Aide, 1997—; moderator Congl. Christian Fellowship, 1999-2001; sec. Tont Ct. Condominium, 1998—. Recipient Athena award Panhellenic Assn. Orange City, Calif., 1968, El Camino Real Dist. Svc. award Orange Empire coun. Boy Scouts Am., Baden-Powell award, Outstanding Leadership award, El Camino Real Dist., Calif., 1972. Ringling North award, 1949; named Outstanding Svc. Vol. Family Svc. Assn., 1969. Mem. Carmel Bus. Assn. Avocations: travel, photography, ballroom dance, bicycling, skiing. Home and Office: 10048 W Hawthorn Dr Sun City AZ 85351-2829 E-mail: tbjtonto@aol.com.

THOMPSON, BIRGIT DOLORES, civic worker, writer; b. Jamestown, N.Y., Apr. 7, 1930; d. Oscar Einar and Karin Johanna (Videll) Wolff; m. William Andrew Thompson, Jan. 26, 1952 (div. June 1978); children: William A., Christina A., Michael J., Timothy A., Kathleen S., Jeffrey B. AB summa cum laude, SUNY, Fredonia, 1974. Exec. dir. Fenton Hist. Ctr., Jamestown, 1975-82; fin. dir. Amicae, Inc., Fredonia, 1983-90; office mgr. JEM Counseling Ctr., Jamestown, 1990-93; resource/info. person Audubon Nature Ctr., 1993—. Author: Illustrated History of Jamestown and Chautauqua County, 1983; musician Jamestown String Quartet, violist local orchestras, 1970-2000; contbr. articles to newspapers. Historian City of Jamestown, 1978—; bd. dirs., chair scholarship com. Mozart Club, 2001—; play selection com. Lucille Ball Little Theatre of Jamestown, 1976—, pit orch.; bd. dirs. Jamestown YWCA, Chautauqua Regional Youth Symphony, pres., 1996—2001; com. mem. Jamestown Audubon Soc., newsletter editor, 1982—98. Mem. AAUW (chmn. What's New Fair Jamestown 1988-94, legislative breakfast 1995—, bd. dirs., pres. 1988-92, co-pres. 2000—, named gift award 1987), Interclub Coun. Jamestown (treas. 1998—, Woman of Yr. award 1992). Avocations: museums, concerts, reading, gardening. Home: 13 Lamont St Jamestown NY 14701-2021 E-mail: musicat@netsync.net.

THOMPSON, BOBBY GENE, physician; b. Trenton, Tenn., May 4, 1936; s. William Bryan and Grace (Perciful) T.; m. Martha Glenda Boswell; 1 child, Karen René. MD, U. Tenn., 1960. Diplomate Am. Bd. Family Practice. Sec. Franklin County Med. Soc., Benton, Ill., 1978-91; chief staff Union Hosp., West Frankfort, 1989-91, 96-99. Mem. profl. svcs. com. So. Ill. Healthcare, 1997-99; clin. instr. dept. of cmty. medicine and rural health U. N.D., 1999. Bd. dirs. Franklin Cmty. Care Svcs., Benton, 1997-99. Capt. U.S. Army, 1966-68, Vietnam. Fellow Am. Acad. Family Practice. Republican. Baptist. Avocations: tennis, photography, gardening, exercising. Office: Med Clinic 309 W Saint Louis St West Frankfort IL 62896-2099 E-mail: bgtmd@dnamail.com.

THOMPSON, BONNIE RANSA, secondary educator, chemistry educator; b. Charleroi, Pa., Oct. 12, 1940; d. William Edward and Edith Lorraine Ransa; m. Joel E. Thompson, June 15, 1963 (div. Dec. 1980). BA, Seton Hill Coll., Greensburg, Pa., 1963; MEd, Ariz. State U., 1979, postgrad. Cert. in secondary chemistry, anthropology, and gifted edn., Ariz. Tchr. chemistry Scotch Plains (N.J.)-Fanwood High Sch., 1963-74; tchr. chemistry and anthropology Tolleson (Ariz.) Union High Sch., 1974-93; tchr. chemistry Westview High Sch., Phoenix, 1992—; owner Driven Solutions, Inc.-Material Handling Systems, 1996—2000. Instr. anthropology and archaeology Rio Salado CC, Sun City, Ariz., 1981—88; instr. chemistry Glendale CC, Glendale, Ariz., 1988—; mem. Ariz. Reagent and Task Force on Lab. Sci., Tempe, Ariz., 1987; instr. chemistry Estrella Mt. CC, 1996—98; pres. Brite Ednl. Programs, Ltd., Phoenix, 1988—91; tchr., cons. Pitts. SuperComputer Project, Tolleson, Ariz., 1992—; amb. People to People Sci. Exchange summer program, Russia, 1989—92, Australia, 1989—92, New Zealand, 1989—92; rsch. partnership HS/Coll. Flinn Found. Rsch. Corp., 1988—91. Editor: Starting at Ground Zero, 1988, others; editor: Energy Education Kits, 1985; contbr. articles to mags. V.p. Villa Casitas Townhouse Assn., Phoenix, 1991—92, pres., 1993—. Woodrow Wilson fellow, 1983; recipient Golden Bell award Ariz. Sch. Bd. Assn., 1985, 88; recipient Growth Incentives for Tchrs. award GTE Corp., 1987, Tech. Scholar award Tandy Corp., 1990, Excellence in Constrn. Innovative Edn. award Am. Subcontractors Assn. Ariz., 2000; named Outstanding High Sch. Sci. Tchr. Ariz. Coun. for Engring. and Scientific Assocs., 1993. Mem. NEA, Ariz. Edn. Assn., Tolleson Edn. Assn. (pres. 1981-83), Nat. Sci. Tchrs. Assn., Ariz. Sci. Tchrs. Assn., Ariz. Alliance for Math., Sci. and Tech., S.W. Archeol. Team. Avocations: reading, touring motorcycles. Office: Westview High Sch 10850 W Garden Lakes Pkwy Avondale AZ 85323-3799 Address: 5638 S 42 Ave Phoenix AZ 85041 E-mail: brtefg@qwest.net.

THOMPSON, BRADLEY SCOTT, music educator; b. Mechanicsburg, Pa., June 8, 1965; s. Calvin Robert and Zana Lee Thompson; m. Jennifer Keenan, Oct. 18, 1975. BS, Indiana U. of Pa., 1989. Cert. music edn. Tchr., band dir. Steel Valley H.S., Munhall, Pa., 1990—. Music caption head Gen. Butler Vagabonds, Lyndora, PA., 1992—96. Tchr., musician Anne Ashley United Meth. Ch., Munhall, 1998. Mem.: MENC. Home: 202 W Larkspur St Homestead PA 15120 Office: Steel Valley Sch Dist 3113 Main St Homestead PA 15120 Office Fax: 412-464-3609. Personal E-mail: thompsonbradley@hotmail.com. Business E-Mail: thompsonbradley@hotmail.com.

THOMPSON, BRIAN JOHN, university administrator, optics educator; b. Glossop, Eng., June 10, 1932; came to U.S., 1962; s. Alexander William and Edna May (Gould) T.; m. Joyce Emily Cheshire, Mar. 31, 1956; children: Karen Joyce, Andrew Derrick. B of Sci. Tech., U. Manchester, Eng., 1955, PhD, 1959. Demonstrator in physics dept. tech. U. Manchester, 1955-56, asst. lectr. dept. tech., 1957-59; lectr. physics U. Leeds, Eng., 1959-62; sr. physicist Tech. Optics, Inc., Burlington, Mass., 1963-65, dir. dept. optics, 1966-67; mgr. tech. ops. west, tech. dir. Beckman and Whitley, Mountainview, Calif., 1967-68; prof. Inst. Optics U. Rochester, N.Y., 1968-94, dir. Inst. Optics, 1968-75, dean Coll. Engring. and Applied Scis., 1975-84, Wm. F. May prof. engring., 1982-85, provost, 1984-94, provost emeritus, Disting. U. prof., 1994—. Editor Optics and Laser Tech., 1969-96; assoc. editor: Optical Engring., 1972-76, Optics Comm., 1978-86; editor Optica Acta, 1981-85, Optical Engring. Series, vols. 1-73, 1980—; mem. editl. bd. Laser Focus, 1970-84, Particle Characterization, 1984-95, Optics and Lasers in Engring., 1985, Milestone Series of Selected Papers, vols. 1-167, 1984—, Optical Engring., 1991-98; chmn. adv. bd. Marquis Who's Who Directory Optical Scientists and Engrs., 1983-86; contbr. articles to profl. jours. With Brit. Army, 1950-52. Fellow: Inst. Physics and Phys. Soc. (Gt. Britain), Optical Soc. Am. (bd. dirs. 1969—72, exec. com. 1970—73, assoc. editor jour. 1966—77), Soc. Photo-Optical Instrumentation Engrs. (life; pres. 1974—76, editor jour. 1991—98, Pres.'s award 1967, Pezzuto award 1978, Kingslake medal 1978, Gold medal 1986, Dir. award 1998); mem.: AAAS, Am. Phys. Soc. Home and Office: 9 Esternay Ln Pittsford NY 14534-1014

THOMPSON, BYRON GREGORY, neurosurgeon, researcher; b. Kansas City, Mo., Sept. 28, 1959; s. Byron Gregory and Jeanne (Collins) T.; m. Ramona Gatschet; children: Byron Gregory III, Kelsey Anne, Molly Jeanne, Theresa Marie, Peter Joseph. AB, Harvard U., 1982; MD, U. Kans., 1986. Diplomate Am. Bd. Neurol. Surgery. Resident in neurosurgery U. Pitts., 1986-90, chief resident neurosurgery, 1992-93; rsch. fellow NIH, Bethesda, Md., 1990-92; fellow in skull base and neurovascular surgery Phoenix, 1993-94; chief neurovascular surgery dept. neurol. surgery U. Utah Sch. Medicine, Salt Lake City, 1994-98; chief neurovascular surgery U. Mich. Sch. Medicine, Ann Arbor, 1998—. Contbr. articles to profl. jours. Recipient Stroke Young Investigator award Am. Heart Assn., Phoenix, 1992, Galbraith award in cerebrovascular surgery Joint Sect. of Cerebrovascular Surgery, 1992. Mem. AMA, Am. Assn. Neurol. Surgeons (chmn. young neurosurgeons sect. 1999—, bd. dirs. 1999—), Congress Neurol. Surgeons. Avocations: hiking, skiing, cycling. Office: U Mich Dept Neurosurgery Taubman Health Care Ctr 2128 1500 E Medical Center Dr Ann Arbor MI 48109-0005

THOMPSON, C. MICHAEL, congressman; b. St. Helena, Calif., Jan. 24, 1951; s. Charles Thompson and Beverly (Forni) Powell; m. Janet Thompson, Mar. 8, 1982; children: Christopher, Jon. MA, Chico State U. Owner, maintenance supr. Beringer Winery; mem. Calif. State Senate, 1990-99, U.S. Congress from 1st Calif. dist., 1999—; mem. armed svcs. com., agr. com. Former chair select com. on Calif.'s Wine Industry; former chair Calif. Senate budget com.; former vice chair Calif. Senate natural resources com. Staff sgt. U.S. Army, Vietnam. Decorated Purple Heart. Named Freshman Legislator of the Yr. Calif. Sch. Bds. Assn., 1990, Legislatorof the Yr. Calif. Abortion Rights Action League, Legislator of the Yr. Calif. Assn. Persons with Handicaps, Legislator of the Yr. Police Officers Rsch. Assn. Calif., Legislator of the Yr. Disabled in State Svc., 1994, Senator of the Yr. Calif. Assn. Homes and Svcs. for Aging, 1995; Recipient Disting. Svc. award Calif. State Assn. Counties, Disting. Svc. award Calif. Assn. Hosps., Legis. Leadership award Calif. Assn. Health Svcs. Home, 1994, Disting. Svc. award Aids Project L.A., 1995, Outstanding Senator award Planned Parenthood Affiliates Calif., 1996, Outstanding Senator of the Yr. award Calif. Sch. Bds. Assn., 1996, Outstanding Senator of the Yr. award Calif. Profl. Firefighters, 1996 Democrat. Roman Catholic. Office: 119 Cannon House Office Bldg Washington DC 20515-0001*

THOMPSON, CAROL JOYCE HINKLEY, philanthropy consultant, motivational speaker, writer; b. Detroit, Oct. 28, 1939; d. Carl O. and Vivian Louise (Hoover) Hinkley; m. Keith Francis MacKechnie Thompson, Oct. 6, 1962 (div. Aug. 1979); children: Kathryn M. Thompson Timms, Gregory R., Rebecca E. Thompson Cecin, Gwendolynne Thompson Frost, Monica Clare. Student, Mercy Coll. Sch. Nursing, Detroit, 1960-62; BS magna cum laude, Tex. Woman's U., Denton, Tex., 1988. Office nurse Miller & Shore, Boston, 1962; pvt. perinatal educator Cambridge, Dallas, Tulsa, 1965-90; S.W. regional dir. Am. Soc. Psychoprophylaxis in Obs., Inc., Dallas, 1967-71; exec. dir. Family Life Info. Ctr., 1973-81; mgr., co-founder Dallas Chamber Orch., 1979-82; major gifts officer U. North Tex., Denton, 1989-92; pvt. practice, 1992—; chmn., exec. producer LORAC, Inc., Dallas, 1994—. Philanthropic advisor LORAC & Assoc., Internat., Inc., 1982—; founder Paddintaine Publ., 2001-. Originator, lobbyist for passage Child Safety Act U.S. Congress, Washington, 1965-66, The Breast and Ovarian Cancer Treatment Act, 1999; co-founder Stop the Hwy., Tulsa, 1966, Family Life Info. Ctr., Dallas, 1973; trustee Family Counseling and Children's Svcs., Big Bros., Big Sisters, Lenawee County, Mich., Estate and Fin. Planning Coun.; founder Project-Abandoned Mother and Child, Dallas, 1978, Leadership Dallas, Project Outreach Internat.; bd. dirs. YWCA, Richardson, Tex., 1996-97; opened clinics in Dallas for perinatal care, parenting, and teenage pregnancy, 1975-81; created Project! Outreach: Early Breastcare, Edn., Screening and Advocacy, Inc., co-founder Internat. Alliance Breast Cancer Orgn., 2002 (bd. chmn. 2002-), trustee Amberheart Breast Cancer Found., Ltd., 2002-. Mem. Internat. Platform Assn., Nat. Soc. Fund Raising Execs., Internat. Trade Assn., Dallas, Ind. Colls. Advancement Assn., The Dallas 40, Dallas Coun. World Affairs, Univ. Ind., Ctr. on Philanthropy. Avocations: the arts, econ. devel., flying, traveling, history, geneology. Office: LORAC Inc 1316 Seventh St Shallowater TX 79363-5102 E-mail: lorac1957@cox.net.

THOMPSON, CARSON R. retail and manufacturing company executive; b. Feb. 10, 1939; s. Silas and Della (Woods) T.; m. Charlotte Arwine, Dec. 26, 1959; children: Shelley Elaine, Susan Denise. BS, Tex. Wesleyan U., 1962, D Bus. and Fin. (hon.). Leather buyer, mdse. mgr. Tandy Leather Co., Ft. Worth, 1970-74, 74-77; pres. Tex Tan Welhausen Corp., Yoakum, Tex., 1978; v.p. Tandy Brands Corp., Ft. Worth, 1981—, chmn., CEO 1982—. Pres., CEO Bombay Co., Inc. (formerly Tandy Brands, Inc.), 1996—; chmn. bd., pres., CEO CRT Group, Inc., 1991—; chmn., CEO PawnMart, Inc., Tony Jeary High Performance Resources. Home: 1801 Sanguinet St Fort Worth TX 76107-3765

THOMPSON, CATHERINE RUSH, physical therapist, educator; b. Kansas City, Mo., Feb. 26, 1954; d. John Adams and Jacqueline (Richard) Rush; m. Gerald Lathen Thompson, Aug. 4, 1979; children: Richard Lathen, Eric Rush. BS in Phys. Therapy with distinction, U. Colo., Denver, 1976; MS in Spl. Edn. with distinction, U. Kans., 1981; PhD in Psychology and Edn., U. Mo.Kansas City, 2001. Cert. phys. therapist, Kans., Mo. Sch. phys. therapist Easter Seal Soc., Miami, Fla., 1976, Taylor Rehab. Ctr., Cedar Rapids, Iowa, 1977-79; cons. B.W. Shepard State Schs., Kansas City, Mo., 1979-86; pediatric phys. therapist Consol. Sch. Dist. 1, 1986-94, Spina Bifida Clinic-U. Kans. Med. Ctr., Kansas City, Kans., 1991-94; instr. phys. therapy U. Kans. Med. Ctr., 1990-96, Rockhurst Coll., 1997—. Phys. therapy cons. Lakemary Ctr., Paola, Kans., 1991—1995; pediat. phys. therapist, early intervention for Johnson Co. and Leavenworth Co., 2002-; mem. desegregation monitoring com. Kansas City (Mo.) Sch. Dist., 1991—1993; chair Kansas City (Mo.) Pediatric Alliance, 1981-84; adv. com. Ctr. for Devel. Disabled, Kansas City, Mo., 1982-85; pres. Rush Assocs., Inc., 1980-85; spkr. in field. Festival chair Hyde Park Neighborhood Assn., Kansas City, Mo., 1985; parent rep. sch. adv. com. Faxon Montessori Sch., Kansas City, Mo., 1987; summer tchr. Trinity United Meth. Ch., Kansas City, Mo., 1991; grants chair sch. adv. com. Ecole Longan, Kansas City, Mo., 1991. Arthur Mag fellow U. Mo., 1989. Mem. Am. Phys. Therapy Assn. (abstract editor pediatric sect. 1981-83), Kans. Phys. Therapy Assn. (rsch. com. 1989-94), Spina Bifida Assn., Kansas City Soc. Neurosci., Ind. Therapy Svcs. (pres. 1982-86). Avocations: wellness, historic preservation, gardening, poetry. Home: 711 Manheim Rd Kansas City MO 64109-2633 Office: Rockhurst Univ Dept Phys Therapy Edn 108 Van Ackeran Kansas City MO 64110-2561

THOMPSON, CHARLES AMOS, lawyer; b. Rockwood, Tenn., Sept. 30, 1945; s. Amos Carson and Helen (Holloway) T.; m.Deborah Kaye Perdue, June 30, 1973 (div. Oct. 1987). BSBA, U. Montevallo, 1972; JD, Birmingham Sch. Law, 1985. Bar: Ala. 1989, U.S. Dist. Ct. (no. dist.) Ala. 1990. Pvt. practice, Birmingham, Ala., 1989—. Olympic Torch bearer, 1996. Capt. USMC, 1966-69. Mem. Ala. State Bar Assn., Birmingham Bar Assn., Greater Birmingham Criminal Def. Lawyer's Assn., Birmingham Track Club (pub. rels. 1990—, marathon instr. 1986—, Dr. Arthur Black award 1987). Democrat. Methodist. Avocations: running, track and field, automobile-motorcyclehouse maintenance. Home and Office: 3174 Pipe Line Rd Birmingham AL 35243-5241

THOMPSON, CHARLES KERRY, company executive; b. Chgo., Sept. 11, 1943; s. Charles Edward and Rose Elizabeth (Peacock) T.; children: Charles Edward, Tiffany Shaffer, Rebecca Lynn. Student, Parsons Coll., 1961-62. Dept. mgr. Montgomery Ward, Chgo., 1962-65; gen. mgr. Jackie's Smartwear, Inc., Niles, Ill., 1965-76; pres. Am. Woman, Inc., Richardson, Tex., 1976-79; zone mgr. The Southland Corp., Dallas, 1979-86; pres. Printelligence Inc. (formerly Graphic Telesis, Inc.), 1986-92; ptnr. Cybersearch-U.S., Inc., 1995—; mktg. dir. Nova Internet Svcs., Inc., 1996—. Pres. Charles K. Thompson Mktg. and Promotional Cons.; pres. CyberSearch-U.S., Inc. Contbr. articles to profl. jours. Chmn. Muscular Dystrophy, Southland, N. Tex., 1982-86, March of Dimes, 1982-86. Mem. Intertel, Mensa, Jaguar Club (pres. 1972-74). Republican. Home: 14588 Berklee Dr Addison TX 75001-3532

THOMPSON, CHARLES OTIS, lighting designer; b. Dallas, Feb. 5, 1942; s. Truman Charles and Rose Bell (Cox) T.; children from previous marriage: Peter Mitchell, Carla Michelle; m. Frances Delores Hall, Nov. 23, 1977; children: Andrea S. Drew, Barry R. Drew. Degree in Archtl. Engring Tech., Tampa (Fla.) Tech. Inst., 1974. Elec. designer Capell & Clark, Columbia, S.C., 1974-75, Lyles, Bissett, Carlisle & Wolfe, Columbia, 1975-77, Wilbur Smith & Assocs., Columbia, 1977-78, Elec. Design Cons., Columbia, 1978-81; lighting cons. Cotangent Lighting Design, 1981-84; sr. lighting designer Tectonics Engring. Cons., 1984-87; prin., dir. design Charles Thompson Assocs. Lighting Design, 1987—. Cons. S.C. Dept. Trade and Indsl. Edn., Columbia, 1981-84, Lighting Research and Edn. Fund, Atlanta, 1981-82; spkr., presenter in field. Designer archtl. lighting for St. Peter's Ch., Columbia, 1985, Tech. Coll. of the Low Country Learning Resource Ctr., 1987, S.C. Senate Chamber, 1988, Forset Lake Country Club Ballroom, 1989, S.C. Supreme Ct., 1990, NationsBank lobby, Columbia, 1992, Syzygy Restaurant, Raleigh, N.C., 1996, St. John Bapt. Cathedral, Charleston, S.C., 1995, Chatham-Effingham-Liberty Regional Libr., Savannah, Ga., 1997, SRC Corp. Hqrs. and Offices, Columbia, S.C., Lake City Mall, Lake City, Fla., 1999, Silk Hope Plantation, Berkley County, S.C., Red Bone Alley Restaurant Prototype, Sumter, S.C., Blue Ridge Mall, Hendersonville, N.C., 2000, Cross Creek Mall, Greenwood, S.C., 2000, West Ga. Commons Mall, LaGrange, Ga., 2001, Statesboro (Ga.) Mall, 2001, Russell Libr., Ga. Coll. & State U., Milledgeville, 2001, Gov.'s Mansion Landscape Lighting, Columbia, S.C., 2001, Hasty Point Plantation, Georgetown, S.C., 2002, Holy Family Cath. Ch., Hilton Head Island, S.C., 2002, Hatcher Sq. Mall, Milledgeville, Ga., 2002; patentee in field. With U.S. Army, 1959-62. Recipient 7 Edwin F. Guth awards of Merit, Illuminating Engring. Soc. N.Am., 1986-96. Mem. Illuminating Engring. Soc. (sect. pres. 1980-82, 87-88, program chmn. 1979-80, steering com. Piedmont sect. 1981-82), Constrn. Specifications Inst. (Columbia chpt. membership chmn. 1990-92, pres. 1992-93), Quail Valley Swim and Racquet Club. Lutheran. Avocations: reading, tennis, drawing and painting, surf fishing, sailing, hiking. Home: 109 Archers Ln Columbia SC 29212-1601 Office: Charles Thompson Assocs 2500 Devine St Ste C Columbia SC 29205-2400 E-mail: thompson_c_d@msn.com.

THOMPSON, CHARLES WILLIAM SYDNOR See THOMPSON, SYDNOR JR.

THOMPSON, CHARLOTTE ELLIS, pediatrician, educator, author; d. Robert and Ann Ellis; divorced; children: Jennifer Ann, Geoffrey Graeme. BA, Stanford U., 1950, MD, 1954. Diplomate Am. Bd. Pediat. Intern Children's Hosp., San Francisco, 1953-54; resident UCLA, 1960-61, L.A. Children's Hosp., 1962-63; pvt. practice La Jolla, Calif., 1963-75; dir. Muscle Disease Clinic, Univ. Hosp.-U. Calif. Sch. Medicine, San Diego, 1969-80, asst. clin. prof. pediat., 1969—; dir. Ctr. for Handicapped Children and Teenagers, San Francisco, 1981—. Cons. U.S. Naval Hosp., San Diego, 1970-91; dep. dir. Santa Clara County Child Health and Disability, Santa Clara, Calif., 1974-75; dir. Ctr. for Multiple Handicaps, Oakland, Calif., 1976-81; co-dir. Muscle Clinic Children's Hosp., San Diego, 1963-69; dir. muscle program U. Rochester, 1957-60. Author: Raising a Handicapped Child: A Helpful Guide for Parents of the Physically Disabled, 1986, 4th edit., 1991, rev., expanded edit., 2000, Allein leben: Ein umfassendes Handbuch für Frauen, 1993, Making Wise Choices: A Guide for Women, 1993, Raising a Child with a Neuromuscular Disorder, 1999, Raising A Handicapped Child, 1999; contbr. articles to med. jours., including Clin. Pediat., New Eng. Jour. Medicine, Neurology, Jour. Family Practice, Mothering, Jour. Pediatric Orthopedics, Pediatrician, Am. Baby, Pediatric News, also chpts. to books. Mem. Calif. Children's Svc. Com., 1977—. Fellow Am. Acad. Pediat. Avocations: tennis, ice skating, opera. Office: Ctr for Handicapped Children and Teenagers 2001 Union St Ste 482 San Francisco CA 94123 E-mail: cetmd@earthlink.net.

THOMPSON, CHERYL MAE, software consultant; b. Rochester, Minn., Sept. 24, 1951; d. Harold Francis and Lenora Lucy (July) Thompson; m. William Otto Nelson, Sept. 8, 1971 (div. Feb. 1984); m. Christopher Hitchcock Miller, Dec. 9, 1988 (div. Jan. 1993). BS in Organizational Behavior, U. San Francisco, 1987. Legal sec. O'Connor & Hannan, Mpls., 1970-72, Curtin, Emerick & Mahoney, Mpls., 1973-76, Newby, Dodge & Korman, Ltd., Cloquet, Minn., 1977-78; office mgr. North Star Steel Co., Duluth, 1979-84; acctg. mgr. Pillsbury, Madison & Sutro, San Francisco, 1984-92; human resources adminstr. MAMAC Systems, Inc., Mpls., 1992-94; mgr. of adminstrv. svcs. BWBR Architects, St. Paul, 1994-96; regional cons. mgr. Epicor Software Corp., Mpls., 1996—. Bd. dirs., treas. Minn. Women of Today Found., Mpls. Children's Med. Ctr. Aux. Mem. Cloquet Jaycee Women (state del. 1977-78, 80-81, 83-84, pres. 1978-79, treas. 1982-83, v.p. 1983-84, Outstanding Local Mem. 1978-83, Outstanding Local Project Chmn. 1982-83, Outstanding State Project Chmn. 1979-82), Minn. Jaycee Women (dist. dir. 1980-81, state sec. 1981-82, state treas. 1982-83, state parliamentarian 1983-84, state editor Newsletter 1984, key woman 1983, Bronze Key 1983-84, Outstanding State Officer 1981-83, Presdl. award of excellence 1982, Outstanding Dist. dir. 1980-81, Outstanding Young Woman Am. 1983, 84), U.S. Jaycee Women (region V individual devel. program mgr. 1982-83, region V parliamentarian 1983-84, Outstanding State Officer 1982-83, Region V Speak-Up winner 1983), Australian-Am. C. of C. (exec. dir. 1993-94), Key Women Club, Minn. Women Today (pres. 1993-94). Avocations: music, reading, travel, walking. Home: 265 Shelard Pkwy Minneapolis MN 55426-4905 Office: Epicor Software Corp 600 Highway 169 S Minneapolis MN 55426-1205

THOMPSON, CINDY LOU, food service executive; b. Anderson, Ind., Aug. 2, 1963; d. Elmer Delaine and Phyllis Jean Hymer; m. Elmer David Bennett, Jan. 1, 1993 (div.); m. Henry Richard, Nov. 19, 1999. Grad., Madison County H.S., Danielville, Ga. Housekeeper Athens (Ga.) Regional Med. Ctr., 1983—93; cook, chef So. Cross Guest Ranch, Madison, 1993—. Author: An Eternity of Bliss, 2001. Recipient Silver Poet award, World of Poetry, 1986, Golden Poet award, 1991, Editor's Choice award, Internat. Libr. Poetry, 2001. Avocations: writing, crafts, sewing, cooking, gardening. Home: 1670 Bethany Church Rd Madison GA 30650

THOMPSON, CLIFTON C. retired chemistry educator, university administrator; b. Franklin, Tenn., Aug. 16, 1939; s. Clifton C. and Ruby M. (Moore) T.; m. Sarah Ellen Gaunt, Dec. 1, 1978; children: Brenda Kay, Victoria Lea. BS, Middle Tenn. State U., 1961; PhD, U. Miss., 1964. Asst. prof. Rutgers U., New Brunswick, N.J., 1965, Marshall U., Huntington, W.Va., 1965-66; assoc. prof. Middle Tenn. State U., Murfreesboro, 1966-68, Memphis State U., 1968-74; prof. chemistry, dept. head, dean Coll. Sci. and Math., dir. Ctr. for Sci. Rsch., assoc. v.p. for grad. studies and rsch. S.W. Mo. State U., Springfield, 1974-96, prof. emeritus, 1996—; prof. chemistry Cen. Mich. U., Mt. Pleasant, 1996-98. Rsch. assoc. U. Tex., Austin, 1964-65; rschr. Oak Ridge Nat. Lab., 1968; cons. Mid-South Research Assocs., Memphis, 1969-71; mem. med. tech. rev. com. Nat. Accrediting Agy. for Clin. Lab. Sci., Chgo., 1974-80; vis. prof. So. Ill. U., Carbondale, 1995. Author: Ultraviolet-Visible Absorption Spectroscopy, 1974; contbr. articles to profl. jours. Mem. health care com. Springfield C. of C., 1978-79, mem. econ. devel. com., 1983-89; bd. dirs. United Hebrew Congregation, Springfield, 1983-86, United Hebrew Found., Inc., 1994-96. NSF fellow, 1961-64; Sigma Xi grantee-in-aide, 1970; NSF sr. fgn. scientist grantee, 1971; NSF coop-coll. sch. sci. grantee, 1972; Higher Edn. Applied Projects grantee, 1987-90. Mem. Am. Chem. Soc., Royal Soc. Chemistry, Sigma Xi, Phi Kappa Phi. Jewish. Office: SW Mo State U Dept Chemistry Springfield MO 65804 E-mail: thompson@biip.net.

THOMPSON, CRAIG SNOVER, corporate communications executive; b. Bklyn., May 24, 1932; s. Craig F. and Edith (Williams) T.; m. Masae Sugizaki, Feb. 21, 1957; children: Lee Anne, Jane Laura. Grad., Valley Forge Mil. Acad., 1951; BA, Johns Hopkins U., 1954. Newspaper and radio reporter Easton (Pa.) Express, 1954-55, 57-59, Wall St. Jour., 1959-60; account exec. Moore, Meldrum & Assocs., 1960; mgr. pub. relations Cen. Nat. Bank of Cleve., 1961-62; account exec. Edward Howard & Co., Cleve., 1962-67, v.p., 1967-69, sr. v.p., 1969-71; dir. pub. relations White Motor Corp., Cleve., 1971-76; v.p. pub. relations No. Telecom Inc., Nashville, 1976-77, White Motor Corp., Farmington Hills, Mich., 1977-80, v.p. corp. communications, 1980-81; dir. exec. communications Rockwell Internat. Corp., Pitts., 1981-86, El Segundo, Calif., 1986-91, Seal Beach, 1992-97, sr. communications exec., 1997; pres. Craig S. Thompson, Inc., 1997—. Bd. dirs. Shaker Lakes Regional Nature Center, 1970-73. Served to 1st lt., inf. U.S. Army, 1955-57. Mem. Pub. Rels. Soc. Am. (accredited), Alumni Assn. Valley Forge Mil. Acad. (bd. dirs. 1988-94).

THOMPSON, DANIEL EMERSON, vending machine service company executive; b. Fairbanks, Alaska, Jan. 24, 1947; s. George Edmond and Emma Jean (Burns) T.; m. Yvette Clarice Brazeau, Aug. 16, 1980. Student, U. Notre Dame, 1965-67. Vice-pres. Music Inc., Fairbanks, 1965-67; pres. Music Inc. (doing bus. as Alaska Music Co.), 1967-81; sec.-treas. Music Inc. (doing bus. as Alaska Music Co. and TLC Vend), Anchorage, 1981-84; sec. Music Inc. (doing bus. as Vend Alaska-Fairbanks), Fairbanks, 1984-87, pres., 1987—, Vend Inc. (doing bus. as Vend Alaska-Anchorage), Anchorage, 1984—. Bd. dirs. Music Inc., Fairbanks, Vend Inc., Anchorage, Denali State Bank, Fairbanks, FAlaska First Bank & Trust, N.A., Anchorage; ptnr. Thompson Investment Co., Fairbanks, 1976—. Trustee Hi Pow, Fairbanks, 1972—; pres. Fairbanks Downtown Assn., 1987-88, bd. dirs., 1984-94; bd. dirs. Alaska State Devel. Corp., Juneau, 1971-82, Monroe Found., Fairbanks, 1991-2000. Mem. Amusement Music Operators Am., Nat. Automatic Merchandising Assn., N.W. Automatic Vending Assn. (bd. govs. 1983—), Rotary, Fairbanks C. of C. (co-chmn. local govt. com. 1988-90). Roman Catholic. Office: Vend Alaska 1890 Marika Rd Fairbanks AK 99709-5520

THOMPSON, DAVID RENWICK, federal judge; b. 1930; BS in Bus., U. So. Calif., 1952, LLB, 1955. Pvt. practice Thompson & Thompson (and predecessor firms), 1957—85; judge U.S. Ct. Appeals (9th cir.), 1985—98, sr. judge, 1998—. With USN, 1955—57. Mem.: ABA, Am. Bd. Trial Lawyers (sec. San Diego chpt. 1983, v.p. 1984, Pres. 1985), San Diego County Bar Assn. Office: US Ct Appeals 940 Front St Rm 2193 San Diego CA 92101-8919*

THOMPSON, DAVID RUSSELL, engineering educator, academic dean; b. Cleve., Apr. 4, 1944; s. Dwight L. and Ella Caroline (Wolff) T.; m. Janet Ann Schall, Aug. 27, 1966; children: Devin Mathew, Colleen Michelle, Darin Michael. BS in Agrl. Engring., Purdue U., 1966, MS in Agrl. Engring., 1967; PhD in Agrl. Engring., Mich. State U., 1970. Asst. prof. agrl. engring., food sci. and nutrition depts. U. Minn., St. Paul, 1970-75, assoc. prof., 1975-81, prof., 1981-85; prof. agrl. engring., head dept. Okla. State U., Stillwater, 1985-91, assoc. dean Coll. Engring., Architecture and Tech., 1991—. Engr. ops. dept. Green Giant Co., La Sueur, Minn., 1978-79; reviewer Colo. State U., Cooperative State Rsch. Svc., USDA, Ft. Collins, 1989, foods, feeds and prodn. cluster U. Mo., Columbia, 1989, 93, dept. agrl. engring. Pa. State U., University Park, 1990, Tex. A&M U., College Station, 1992, Utah State U., Logan, 1993, USAF, Tyndall, Fla. and San Angelo, Tex., 1994-95, 97, Wash. State U., Pullman, 1995, U. Ga., Athens, 1996, S.D. State U., 1997, U. Fla., 1998, U. Del., 1998, U. Neb., 1999, U. Wis., 2000, U. Idaho, others; reviewer USDA, 1983; vis. scholar Va. Poly. Inst. and State U., Blacksburg. Author: The Influence of Materials Properties on the Freezing of Sweet Corn , 1984, Mathematical Model for Predicting Lysine and Methionine Losses During Thermal Processing of Fortified Foods; contbr. over 50 articles to profl. jours. including Jour. Food Sci. Fellow Am. Soc. Agrl. Engrs. (div. chmn. 1976-77, bd. dirs. 1981-84, 87-89, v.p. 1994-98, stds. coun. chmn. 1997-98, Farm and Indsl. Equip. Inst., Young Rschr. award 1983, Pres.'s citation 1989, 98); mem. ASHRAE, NSPE (chair Okla. mid-north sect. 1994-95), Okla. Soc. Profl. Engrs. (v.p. 2000-2001), Inst. Food Technologists (program com. 1982-85, state officer 1987-89), Am. Soc. Engring. Edn. (chair Midwest sect. 1994-95), Sigma Xi Phi Kappa Phi, Tau Beta Pi, Alpha Epsilon, Phi Eta Sigma, Gamma Sigma Delta. Office: Okla State U Coll Engring Arch & Tech 201 Adv Tech Rsch Ctr Stillwater OK 74078-5010 E-mail: dthomps@okstate.edu.

THOMPSON, DAVID ALFRED, industrial engineer; b. Chgo., Sept. 9, 1929; s. Clifford James and Christobel Eliza (Sawin) T.; children: Nancy, Brooke, Lynda, Diane, Kristy. B.M.E., U. Va., 1951; BS in Indsl. Engring, U. Fla., 1955, MS in Engring, 1956; PhD, Stanford U., 1961. Registered profl. engr., Calif; cert. profl. ergonomist. Research asst. U. Fla. Engring. and Industries Exptl. Sta., Gainesville, 1955-56; instr. indsl. engring. Stanford U., 1956-58, acting asst. prof., 1958-61, asst. prof., 1961-64, asso. prof., 1964-72, prof., 1972-83, prof., asso. chmn. dept. indsl. engring., 1972-73, prof. emeritus, 1983—; mem. clin. faculty occupational medicine U. Calif. Med. Sch., San Francisco, 1985—; pres., chief scientist Portola Assocs., Palo Alto, Calif., 1965—, Incline Village, Nev., 1965—; prin. investigator NASA Ames Rsch. Ctr., Moffatt Field, Calif., 1974-77. 0ons. Dept. State, Fed. EEO Commn., maj. U.S. and fgn. cos.; cons. emergency commn. ctr. design Santa Clara County Criminal Justice Bd., 1974, Bay Area Rapid Transit Control Ctr., 1977, Govt. of Mex., 1978, Amadahl Corp., 1978-79, Kerr-McGee Corp., 1979, Chase Manhattan Bank, 1980, St. Regis Paper Co., 1980-82, Pacific Gas & Electric, 1983-85, Pacific Bell, 1984-86, 89-93, IBM, 1988-91, Hewlett-Packard, 1990-91, 98-99, Reuter's News Svc., 1990-92, Safeway Corp., 1992-94, New United Motors Mfg., 1993-95, Sun Microsys., 1993-94, Microsoft, 1995-00; mem. com. for office computers Calif. OSHA. Dir., editor: documentary film Rapid Answers for Rapid Transit, Dept. Transp., 1974; mem. editorial adv. bd. Computers and Graphics, 1970-85; reviewer Indsl. Engring. and IEEE Transactions, 1972-86; contbr. articles to profl. jours. Served to lt. USNR, 1951-58. HEW grantee, 1967-70 Mem. IEEE, Am. Inst. Indsl. Engrs., Human Factors and Ergonomics Soc. Home: PO Box 6685 Incline Village NV 89450-6685 Address: PO Box 6088 Incline Village NV 89450-6088 E-mail: davidthompson@human-factors.org.

THOMPSON, DAVID WILLIAM, business educator; b. Ft. Wayne, Ind., Sept. 3, 1914; s. William Byron and Georgia Louise (Davis) T.; m. M. Miriam Vollmer, Dec. 21, 1956 (dec.). BS, Ind. U., 1938, MS, 1940. C.P.A., N.Y., Ill., Ind., Va., N.C., N. Mex., La. Prof. Samford U., Birmingham, Butler U., Indpls., 1941-42, Ind. U., Bloomington, 1942-54; cons. Gen. Electric Co., N.Y.C., 1954-56; ptnr. KPMG Peat Marwick, 1956-76; Frank S. Kaulback Jr. prof. commerce McIntire Sch. Commerce U. Va., Charlottesville, 1976—. Chmn. State Bd. Examiners C.P.A.s, N.Y.C., 1966-70, State Bd. Pub. Accountancy, N.Y.C., 1974-76 Dir. Univ. of the Ams., Mexico City, U. of the Ams. Found., San Antonio. Mem. AICPA, Ind. U. Acad. Alumni Fellows, Indpls. Athletic Club, India House Club N.Y.C., Univ. Club N.Y.C., Farmington Country Club Charlottesville Va., Beta Gamma Sigma (dirs. table). Home: Ednam Forest 425 Wellington Dr Charlottesville VA 22903-4746 Office: U Va Monroe Hall McIntire Sch Commerce Charlottesville VA 22903

THOMPSON, DAYLE ANN, management and accounting systems consultant; b. Grand Forks, N.D., Jan. 6, 1954; d. Duane Theodore and Anna Mae (Desautel) T.; m. Michael Gary Sciulla, Aug. 6, 1977 (div. Sept. 1980); m. Manfred Hans von Ehrenfried II, June 11, 1982. Secretarial degree, Aaker's Bus. Coll., Grand Forks, 1973; Masters Cert. in Project Mgmt., George Washington U., 1995. Receptionist U.S. Rep. Norman F. Lent U.S. Ho. of Reps., Washington, 1973-74; office mgr., personal sec. U.S. Rep. Les AuCoin, U.S. Ho. of Reps., 1975-78; bus. mgr., bookkeeper Virgin Islands POST, St.Thomas, USVI, 1978; office and pers. mgr. Internat. Energy Assocs. Ltd., Washington, 1978-82; program support mgr. MSI Svcs. Inc., 1982-84; pres., treas., chief exec. officer Tech. and Adminstrv. Svcs. Corp., 1984-2000; acctg. mgr. Carolyn Kinder, Inc., Clearwater, Fla., 97—; ind. mgmt. and acct. sys. cons. St. Petersburg, 2000—. Hosp. vol. ARC, Arlington, Va., 1987. Recipient Group Achievement award NASA, 1984, 93, Commendation Letter, NASA, 1985, 87, 88, 91, 93, 94, Small Bus. Prime Contractor of Yr. award Small Bus. Adminstrn. Region 3, 1994. Mem. Washington Space Bus. Roundtable (sponsor-benefactor 1990-92). Republican. Roman Catholic. Avocations: boating, fishing, reading. Home and Office: 4250 42d Ave S Saint Petersburg FL 33711-4231 E-mail: dayle.thompson@gte.net.

THOMPSON, DEAN ALLAN, cattleman; b. Peru, Ind., Jan. 29, 1934; s. Paul Franklin and Pauline St. Clair (Thrush) T. Student Purdue U., 1952-54. Mgr. Thompson Farms, breeders registered Hereford cattle, Peru, 1956-69; owner Thompson Farms, Wartrace, Tenn. and Peru, 1970-87, Dean Thompson Prodns., Wartrace, Wartrace Records; chmn. bd. Instant Copy and Printing, Inc., Monterrey, Calif., 1976-86, Trenton Energy Inc., 1977-83, Bloomfield, Ind.; v.p., dir. 5B Cattle Co., Twin Bridges, Mont., 1986-87; ptnr., Brann-Thompson Ltd.; internat. beef cattle judge; dir. Maine Manna, Gorham. Bd. dirs. Thrush-Thompson Found. (formerly H.A. Thrush Found.), Peru; trustee Middle Tenn. State U. Found., 1981-83, 85-89, chmn. fin. com., 1982-83, 85-87, exec. com., 1983-89, sec. 1988, pres.-elect, 1989; precinct committeeman, chmn. Miami County (Ind.) Young Republican Com., 1962-67; elder Presbyn. Ch., 1986-88. With U.S. Army, 1955-56. Mem. Nat. Western (dir.), Ind. (dir. 1958-68, pres. 1960) Polled Hereford Assns., Ind. Cattleman's Assn. (founding dir.), Ind. Livestock Breeders Assn., Am. Hereford Assn. (v.p. pres.'s coun. 1981, pres. 1982), Tenn. Hereford Assn. (dir. 1977-81, 93-97, v.p. 1979, pres. 1980-81, 97), Toastmasters (pres., area gov.), Columbia Club. Home and Office: 900 19th Ave S Apt 1201 Nashville TN 37212-2155

THOMPSON, DENISSE R. mathematics educator; b. Keesler AFB, Miss., Aug. 26, 1954; BA, BS, U. South Fla., 1976, MA, 1980; PhD, U. Chgo., 1992. Cert. tchr., Fla. Tchr. Hernando County Schs., Brooksville, Fla., 1977-82; instr. maths. Manatee C.C., Bradenton, 1982-87; asst. prof. U. South Fla., Tampa, 1991-97, assoc. prof., 1997—. Cons. in field. Author: Fundamental Skills of Mathematics, 1987, Advanced Algebra, 1990, 2d edit., 1996, (with others) Precalculus and Discrete Mathematics, 1992, Nat. Coun. Tchrs. of Math. Yearbook, 1991, 93, 94, 95, 2002; co-editor: Standards-Based School Mathematics: What Are They? What do Students Learn?; contbr. articles to profl. jours. Recipient Carolyn Hoefer Meml. award Pi Lambda Theta, 1988. Mem. ASCD, Math. Assn. Am., Nat. Coun. Tchrs. Math., Nat. Coun. Suprs. Math., Assn. Women in Maths., Phi Delta Kappa, Phi Kappa Phi. Office: U South Fla College of Edn EDU162 Tampa FL 33620

THOMPSON, DENNIS FRANK, political science and ethics educator, consultant; b. Hamilton, Ohio, May 12, 1940; s. Frank and Florence (Downs) T.; m. Carol Thompson, June 22, 1963; children: Eric, David. BA, Coll. of William and Mary, 1962, Oxford U., 1964, MA, 1968; PhD, Harvard U., 1968; LHD (hon.), Coll. of William and Mary, 1990. Instr. govt. Harvard U., Cambridge, Mass., 1967-68, Alfred North Whitehead prof., 1986—, dir. univ. ctr. for ethics and professions, 1986—, assoc. provost, 1996—2002, sr. advisor to the pres., 2002—; asst. prof. politics Princeton U., N.J., 1968-72, assoc. prof., 1972-75, dept. chmn., 1972-73, 76-79, 82-83, prof., 1975-86. Cons. to spl. counsel U.S. Senate Select Com. on Ethics, 1990-91, U.S. Dept. HHS, 1980, FDA, 1993. Author: The Democratic Citizen, 1970, John Stuart Mill and Representative Government, 1976, Political Ethics and Public Office, 1987, Ethics in Congress, 1995, (with A. Gutmann) Democracy and Disagreement, 1996, Ethics and Politics: Cases and Comments, 3d edit., 1997, Just Elections, 2002; mem. edit. bd. Polit. Theory, 1974—, Philosophy and Pub. Affairs, 1971—, Am. Polit. Sci. Rev., 1985-88. Trustee Smith Coll., 1994—. Fellow Am. Acad. Arts and Scis.; mem. Am. Soc. Legal and Polit. Philosophy (v.p. 1977-80, pres. 1986-89). Home: 9 Shady Hill Sq Cambridge MA 02138-2035 Office: Harvard U Ctr for Ethics and Professions 202 Taubman 79 JFK St Cambridge MA 02138-5801

THOMPSON, DENNIS PETERS, plastic surgeon; b. Chgo., Mar. 18, 1937; s. David John and Ruth Dorothy (Peters) T.; m. Virginia Louise Williams, June 17, 1961; children: Laura Faye, Victoria Ruth, Elizabeth Jan. BS, U. Ill., 1957, BS in Medicine, 1959, MS in Physiology, MD, U. Ill., 1961. Diplomate Am. Bd. Surgery, Am. Bd. Plastic Surgery. Intern Presbyn.-St. Lukes Hosp., Chgo., 1961—62; resident in gen. surgery Mayo Clinic, Rochester, Minn., 1964—66, fellow in gen. surgery, 1964—66; resident in gen. surgery Harbor Gen. Hosp., L.A., 1968—70; resident in plastic surgery UCLA, 1971—73, clin. instr. plastic surgery, 1975—82, asst. clin. prof. surgery, 1982—97, assoc. clin. prof. surgery, 1998—. Practice medicine specializing in plastic and reconstructive surgery, L.A., 1974-78, Santa Monica, Calif., 1978—; chmn. plastic surgery sect. St. John's Hosp., 1986-91; mem. staff Santa Monica Hosp., UCLA Ctr. Health Scis.; chmn. dept. surgery Beverly Glen Hosp., 1978-79; pres. Coop. of Am. Physicians Credit Union, 1978-80, bd. dirs., 1980-97, chmn. membership devel. com., 1983-97, treas., 1985-97. Contbr. articles to med. jours. Moderator Congl. Ch. of Northridge (Calif.), 1975-76, chmn. bd. trustees, 1973-74, 80-82; bd. dirs. L.A. Bus. Coun., 1987-90. Am. Tobacco Inst. rsch. grantee, 1959-60. Fellow ACS; mem. AMA (alt. del. 2002-, Physicians Recognition award 1971, 74, 77, 81, 84, 87, 90, 93, 96, 99), Calif. Med. Assn., L.A. County Med. Assn. (chmn. bylaws com. 1979-80, chmn. ethics com. 1980-81, 2000-01, sec.-treas. dist. 5 1982-83, program chmn. 1983-84, pres. 1985-86, councilor 1988-96, 2001-, v.p. 1999-2000), Pan-Pacific Surg. Assn., Am. Soc. Plastic Surgeons, Calif. Soc. Plastic Surgeons (chmn. bylaws com. 1982-83, chmn. liability com. 1983-85, councilor 1988-91, sec. 1993-95, v.p. 1995-96, pres.-elect 1996-97, pres. 1997-98), L.A. Soc. Plastic Surgeons (sec. 1980-82, pres. 1982-97), Lipoplasty Soc. N.Am., UCLA Plastic Surgery Soc. (treas. 1983-84, v.p. 1996-98, pres. 1998-2002), Am. Soc. Aesthetic Plastic Surgery, Internat. Soc. Clin. Plastic Surgeons (bd. dirs. 1999—), Am. Assn. Accreditation of Ambulatory Surg. Facilities (bd. dirs. 1995-97, 2002-, ofcl. observer house del. 1999-2001), Western L.A. Regional C. of C. (bd. dirs. 1981-84, 86-89, chmn. legis. action com. 1978-80), Phi Beta Kappa, Alpha Omega Alpha, Nu Sigma Nu, Phi Kappa Phi, Delta Sigma Delta, Omega Beta Pi, Phi Eta Sigma. Republican. Office: 2001 Santa Monica Blvd Santa Monica CA 90404-2102 E-mail: dthompso@ucla.edu.

THOMPSON, DIDI CASTLE (MARY BENNETT), writer, editor; b. Terre Haute, Ind., Feb. 7, 1918; d. Robert Langley Bennett and Marjorie Rose (Tyler) Castle; student U. Ill., Champaign, 1935-36, U. Ky., 1936-39; m. Jamie Campbell Thompson, Jr., June 24, 1939; children— Jamie III, Julia King Balko, Langley Stewart Ruede. News editor Glen-Echoes, Glencoe, Ill., 1930; columnist Ky. Kernel, U. Ky., Lexington, 1937-39; radio script writer Modern Am. Music, 1940-42; asst. pub. relations dir. Salem Coll., Winston-Salem, N.C., 1945; pub. relations chmn. Barrington (Ill.) Horse Show, 1959-67; staff writer, columnist Barrington Press Newspapers, 1958-84; editor ECHO, Defenders of the Fox River, Inc. newsletter, 1970-80; travel editor Barrington Press Newspapers, 1973-84; columnist The Daily Herald, Paddock Publs., 1984-86; columnist Rapid City (S.D.) Journal, 1990-95; freelance writer, 1943— . Past bd. mem. Barrington chpt. Lyric Opera Guild Chgo., Barrington Sr. Center, Infant Welfare Soc. Chgo., Art Inst. Chgo., Barrington Assos.; elected trustee Village of Barrington Hills, 1969-73, health, pub. relations chmn., 1969-73; mem. Barrington Hills Plan Commn., 1986. Mem. DAR, Women in Communications (past dir.), Citizens for Conservation (past dir.), Barrington Countryside Assn. (past dir.), Barrington Hist. Soc., Spring Creek Basset Hounds Club, Barrington Hills Riding Club (past dir.), Pan Hellenic Coun., Gulf Shore Lit. Soc., Conservancy S.W. Fla. (Naples), Chgo. Press Club, Chi Omega. Episcopalian. Address: 1827 Princess Ct Naples FL 34110-1001

THOMPSON, DONALD CHARLES, electronics company executive, former coast guard officer; b. Hollis, N.Y., Nov. 9, 1930; s. Arthur I. and Gertrude M. (Hauck) T.; m. Jeannie Germaine Kline, Oct. 4, 1952; children: Dennis C., Mitchell L., Sandra J., Janice M., Theresa A., Patrick J. BS, U.S. Coast Guard Acad., 1952; MS (Krannert scholar), Krannert Grad. Sch., Purdue U., 1966. Commd. ensign USCG, 1952, advanced through grades to vice adm., 1986; shipboard navigator and engr., 1952-54; naval flight tng., 1954-55; search and rescue aviator and aircraft maintenance officer Calif., Ill., Alaska and Fla., 1955-65; chief computer-based mgmt. info. div. Elizabeth City, N.C., 1966-70; chief aero. engring. div. USCG Hdqrs., 1970-74; capt. of the port, group comdr., air sta. comdr. San Diego, 1974-76; chief ops. 11th USCG Dist., Long Beach, Calif., 1976-78, chief of staff, 1979; chief office of engring. USCG Hdqrs., Washington, 1979-81, chief office of ops., 1981-82, chief staff, 1984-86, comdr. Atlantic area, 1986-88; comdr. 7th Coast Guard Dist., Miami, Fla., 1982-84; math. instr. Coll. Albermarle, N.C., 1967-70, Nat. U., San Diego, 1975-76; chmn. Interagy. Com. Search and Rescue, 1981-82; ret. USCG, 1988; v.p. strategic devel. R&E Electronics, Inc., Wilmington, N.C., 1990-93; pres. D.C. Thompson Consulting, 1994—. V.p.'s coordinator for S.E. region Nat. Narcotics Border Interdiction System, 1983-84 Contbr. articles to profl. jours. Coordinator White House South Fla. Task Force on Crime, 1983-84. Decorated DSM with two gold stars, Coast Guard Meritorious Service medal, Def. Superior Service medal, Commendation medal with three gold stars, Legion of Merit with gold star Mem. Soc. Am. Mil. Engrs. (dir. 1979-81), Am. Soc. Naval Engrs., Am. Helicopter Soc. (dir. 1981-82), Air Force Assn., Naval Inst. Clubs: Propeller, Nat. Aviation. Roman Catholic. Home and Office: 2213 Tattersall Dr Wilmington NC 28403 E-mail: deeset@wilmington.net.

THOMPSON, DONALD JOSEPH, JR. accountant, computer programmer, consultant; b. West Islip, N.Y., June 4, 1965; s. Donald Joseph and Frances Ann (Koerber) T.; m. Melanie Frank, June 25, 1995. Student, SUNY, Cortland, 1983-85; student, Suffolk County C.C., Brentwood, N.Y., 1992—. Acct. North Atlantic Life Ins. Co. Am., Jericho, N.Y., 1987-88; office supr. East Neck Nursing Ctr., West Babylon, 1988—; income tax preparer/pvt. practice East Islip, 1990—; pres., ptnr. Thompson Assocs. Consultants Inc., North Lindenhurst, 1991-93; computer applications developer/owner Donald J. Thompson Jr. Consulting Svcs., East Islip, 1993—. Cons. Gary J. Warnecke CPA and Co., North Lindenhurst, 1990-92. Author (software) 401(k) Financial Statements Made Easy, 1993. Vol. Babylon Town Rep. Com., 1988, 92. Mem. Am. Inst. Profl. Bookkeepers, SUNY Cortland Men's Athletic Assn. (asst. treas. 1984-85), USA Hockey Inline, Beta Phi Epsilon. Republican. Avocations: reading, skating, hockey, sports card collecting. Office: Donald J Thompson Jr Consulting Svcs 1333 W Cove Dr Gilbert AZ 85233-6632

THOMPSON, DOROTHY BARNARD, elementary school educator; b. Flushing, N.Y., Aug. 14, 1933; d. Henry Clay and Cecelia Minnie Theresa (La Pardo) Barnard; m. Norman Earl Thompson, Aug. 12, 1956; children: Greg, Scot, Henry, Marc, Matthew. BSEd, SUNY, New Paltz, 1953; MS, Hofstra U., 1984. Cert. elem. tchr. K-6th grades, reading specialist K-12th grades, N.Y. Adjunct prof. Suffolk Community Coll., Brentwood, N.Y., 1987—, Nassau Community Coll., Uniondale, 1986—; adjunct prof., instr. Ctr. for Acad. Achievement Long Island U., Greenvale, 1984-92; tchr. reading, 1st and 2nd grades Long Beach (N.Y.) Pub. Schs., 1988—. Mem. founding group Parent/Tchr., The Learning Tree, Garden City, N.Y., 1971; founder parent coop. Happy Day Nursery Sch., Bellmore, N.Y., 1975; parent-tchr. Commonwealth Sch., Bay Shore, Oakdale, 1976-82. Mem. Internat. Reading Assn. E-mal. Office: 456 Neptune Blvd Long Beach NY 11561-2400 Home: PO Box 1065 Bellmore NY 11710-0259 E-mail: anetco01@aol.com.

THOMPSON, DOUGLAS MARSHALL, geomorphologist, educator; b. Winchester, Mass., Sept. 26, 1967; s. William Russell and Judith Francis Thompson; m. Rebecca Anne Nash, July 17, 1993; children: Haley Nash-Thompson. PhD, Colo. State U., 1997, MS, 1994; BA, Middlebury Coll., 1991. Asst. prof. Conn. Coll., New London, 1997—2002. Recipient G.K. Gilbert award, Assn. Am. Geographers, 2000, CAREER award, NSF, 1999. Mem.: Assn. Am. Geographers, Am. Geophysical Union, Geological Soc. Am. Office: Conn Coll 270 Mohegan Ave New London CT 06320 Office Fax: (860) 439-5011. Business E-Mail: dmtho@conncoll.edu.

THOMPSON, DWIGHT ALAN, vocational rehabilitation expert; b. Monterey Park, Calif., Mar. 2, 1955; s. Irvin Edward and Lydia (Busch) T.; m. Irene Anita Arden, June 18, 1977; children: Dwight Christopher, Meredith Irene, Hilda Arden. BA in Social Welfare, U. Wash., 1978, MSW, 1980. Registered vocat. rehab. counselor, Wash.; cert. social worker, Wash.; cert. case mgr.; diplomate Am. Bd. Clin. Examiners in Social Work; cert. disability mgmt. Specialist Commn. Houseparent Parkview Home for Exceptional Children, Seattle, 1976-77; rsch. analyst Wash. State Ho. Reps., Olympia, 1979-81; v.p. The James L. Groves Co., Everett, Wash., 1982-86; exec. dir. Evaluation & Tng. Assocs., Seattle, 1984-86; CEO, owner Rehab. & Evaluation Svcs. Inc., 1986—; v.p., founder Next Generation Technologies, Inc., 1994—. Social work officer 50th Gen. Army Res. Hosp., Seattle, 1982-87, 91-93; med. adminstrv., social worker officer Operation Desert Storm, Riyadh, Saudi Arabia, 1990-91; aide-de-camp 2d Hosp. Ctr., San Francisco, 1987-88, pub. affairs officer, 1988-90; acting commdr. 1972d MED DET-Combat Stress Control, 1993, exec. officer, 1994-97, comdr., 1998-2001, profl. svcs. chief, 2001—. Co-author Correction Study Report, 1981. Conf. pres. St. Vincent de Paul Soc., 1975-78; lt. Thurston County Fire Dist #6, East Olympia, Wash., 1980-83; alumni rep. COS Track Com. U. Wash., 1984-87; primary candidate Dem. Primary for State Rep., Renton, Wash., 1984; mem. Wash. Vocat. Rehab. adv. com. Dept. Labor Industries, 1992-96; tech. advisor Com. on Vocat. Rehab., 1997-2000; pres. Sheridan Beach Cmty. Club, Inc., 1994-95; chair human svcs. commn. City Lake Forest Park, Wash, 1995; mem. city coun., 1996—, mayor protem, 2000—; mem. Girl Scouts of Am.; trustee First Ave Svc. Ctr., 1998—; scoutmaster World Jamboree Western Region Boy Scouts Am., 1999. Fellow Am. Acad. Pain Mgmt. (cert.); mem. NASW (cert.), Internat. Assn. Rehab. Profls. (pvt. sector, Wash. legis. chair), Acad. Cert. Social Workers, Wash. Self-Insurers Assn., Assn. Mil. Surgeons U.S., Res. Officers Assn., Nat. Eagle Scout Assn., Am. Bd. Forensic Examiners, Case Mgmt. Soc. Am., Boy Scouts Am., Internat. Assn. Rehab. Profls. (Kevin Karr award for Most Innovative Rehab. Program 1995), Theta Xi (pres. 1975-77). Roman Catholic. Home: 16270 Beach Dr NE Lk Forest Park WA 98155-6704 Office: Rehab and Evaluation Svcs 226 Summit Ave E Seattle WA 98102-5619

THOMPSON, EARL ALBERT, economics educator; b. L.A., Oct. 15, 1938; s. Hyman Harry and Sue (Field) T.; m. Velma Montoya, June 9, 1961; 1 son, Bret. BA, UCLA, 1959; MA (fellow), PhD, Harvard U., 1961. Asst. prof. econs. Stanford (Calif.) U., 1962-65, UCLA, 1965-68, assoc. prof., 1968-70, prof., 1970—. Grantee NSF, Lily Found., Found. Rsch. in Econs. and Edn. Mem. Am. Econ. Assn. Home: 6970 Los Tilos Rd Los Angeles CA 90068-3107 E-mail: thompson@econ.ucla.edu.

THOMPSON, EDWARD IVINS BRADBRIDGE, biological chemistry and genetics educator, molecular endocrinologist, department chairman; b. Burlington, Iowa, Dec. 20, 1933; s. Edward Bills and Lois Elizabeth (Bradbridge) T.; m. Lynn Taylor Parsons; children: Elizabeth Lynn, Edward Ernest Bradbridge. BA with distinction, Rice U., 1955; postgrad., Cambridge U., 1957-58; MD, Harvard U., 1960. Intern The Presbyn. Hosp., N.Y.C., 1960-61, asst. resident internal medicine, 1961-62; rsch. assoc. Nat. Inst. Mental Health, NIH, Bethesda, Md., 1962-64; rsch. scientist Nat. Inst. Arthritis and Metabolic Diseases, NIH, 1964-68, Lab of Biochemistry, Nat. Cancer Inst., NIH, Bethesda, 1968-73, sect. chief, 1973-84; I.H. Kempner prof. U. Tex. Med. Br., Galveston, 1984, prof., chmn. dept. human biol. chemistry and genetics, 1984—, prof. internal medicine, 1984—, interim dir. Sealy Ctr. for Molecular Sci., 1996—. Attending physician Nat. Naval Med. Ctr., Bethesda, 1978-80; chmn. hormones and cancer task force NIH, Bethesda, 1978-80; co-chmn. Gordon Research Conf., 1980; mem. adv. com. on Biochem. & Chem. Carcinogenesis, Am. Cancer Soc., 1982-86; mem. revision com. Endocrinology adv. panel U.S. Pharmacopoeial Conv., Inc., 1980-85; mem. council for clin. investigation and research awds., Am. Cancer Soc., 1989-93; bd. scientific overseers Pennington Nutrition Rsch. Ctr. La. State U., 199-98—; Fulbright prof., Marburg, Germany. 1992-93; vis. prof. Bristol U., U.K., 1998; vis. prof. U. Bristol, U.K., 1998; mem. edn. bd. Am. Med. and Grad. Depts. Biochemistry, 1999—. Co-editor Gene Expression and Carcinogenesis in Cultured Liver, 1975, Steroid Receptors and the Management of Cancer, 1979, DNA: Protein Interactions and Gene Regulation, other vols. in field; assoc. editor Cancer Rsch. jour., 1976-86; corr. editor Jour. Steroid Biochemistry, 1977-85; founding editor-in-chief Molecular Endocrinology Jour., 1985-92; editor-in-chief Endocrine Reviews,, 2001—; mem. editl. bd. Steroids & WWW Jour. Biology, 1995—, Molecular Endocrinology, 1998; contbr. over 200 sci. articles to profl. jours. Mem. troop com. Girl Scouts U.S., Rockville, Md., 1970-76; mem. PTA, Rockville, 1967-77, Wilderness Soc., Washington, 1964-75; initiator sci. edn. liaison program Galveston Pub. Schs., 1991; mem. pres.'s cabinet U. Tex. Med. Br. Served as med. dir. USPHS, 1962-84. Grantee NIH, Walls Rsch., Nat. Inst. Diabetes and Digestive and Kidney Diseases, Nat. Cancer Inst.; Am. Cancer Soc. scholar, 1992-93; Fulbright scholar; recipient J.G. Sinclair award Sigma Xi, 1997. Mem. Am. Soc. Cell Biology, Am. Assn. Cancer Rsch., Am. Soc. Biol. Chemists, Endocrine Soc. (mem. history com. 1999), Am. Soc. Microbiology, Am. Coll. Med. Genetics (affiliate), S.W. Ennviron. Mutagen Soc., The Yacht Club, Raquet Club, Harvard Club, Pres.'s Clubs of Rice U. and U. Tex. Med. Br., Phi Beta Kappa, Alpha Omega Alpha. Achievements include patent on anti-tumor activity of a modified fragment of glucocorticoid receptor. Office: U Tex Med Br Dept Human Biol Chem & Gene Galveston TX 77555-0001 E-mail: bthompso@utmb.edu.

THOMPSON, EDWARD P. lawyer; b. Ann Arbor, Mich., June 8, 1946; m. N. Terrill Fentress, July 1973 (dec. Apr. 1988); children: Mark S., Carolyn T., Kimberly Anne, Bonnie L. Biggs; m. Terry Lynn Biggs, May, 1993. BA, Kalamazoo (Mich.) Coll., 1968; JD, U. Mich., 1970. Bar: Oreg., 1971, U.S. Fed. Ct., 1972. Clerk to ptnr. Cass, Scott, Woods & Smith, Eugene, Oreg., 1971-83; pvt. practice, 1983—. Bd. dirs. Centro Latino Americano, Eugene, 1993-2000; 1st v.p., bd. dirs. Western Rivers Girl Scouts, Eugene, 1970-83, United Way Lane County, 1985—; active Wesley United Meth. Ch., Eugene, 1975-84. Mem. Eugene Met. Rotary (founder, past pres.). Home: 30316 Fox Hollow Rd Eugene OR 97405-9436 Office: 875 Country Club Rd Eugene OR 97401-2255 Fax: 541-687-1891. E-mail: edpthom@aol.com.

THOMPSON, ELEANOR DUMONT, nurse; b. Derry, N.H., May 26, 1935; d. Louis Arthur and Florence Berthae (Gendreau) D.; m. Carl Hugh Thompson, Aug. 22, 1959; children: Justine, Julie. Student, Dartmouth Hitchock Nur. Sch., 1956; BA, New Eng. Coll., 1977; MS, Drake U., 1984. Registered art therapist. Pediatric instr. Hanover (N.H.) Sch. Practical Nursing, 1958-61; pub. W.B. Sanders Co., Phila., 1962-95; pediatric instr. St. Joseph Hosp., Nashua, N.H., 1978-81; cert. clin. nurse specialist Mercy Hosp. Med. Ctr., Des Moines, 1987-90; clin. nurse specialist Portsmouth (N.H.) Regional Hosp., 1991-2000; pvt. practice Silverman & Assoc., Inc., 1991-93. Puppeteer St. Joseph's Hosp. Sch. Nursing, Nashua, 1981-82; created and conducted shows on hospitalization for children; nursing cons. Hospice Cen. Iowa, Des Moines, 1982-89; cons. art therapy N.H. Hosp., 2001—. Author: Pediatric Nursing An Introductory Text, 1965, 6th edit., 1992, (translations in Spanish, Italian and Portuguese), Introduction to Maternity and Pediatric Nursing, 1990, 2d edit., 1995. Vol. nurse Vietnam Vets. Ctr., Des Moines, 1985-87, Camp Apanda Childrens Cancer Camp Boone, Iowa, 1984-86; organist Holy Trinity Ch. Des Moines, 1982, St. Pius Ch., Des Moines, 1982. Mem. ANA, Am. Art Therpy Assn. (pres.), N.H. Art Therapy Assn., N.H. Nurses Assn. Democrat. Roman Catholic. Avocations: playing piano and organ, travel, fishing, camping. Home: 13 Sherman Ave Brentwood NH 03833-6225 E-mail: edthompson@mediaone.net.

THOMPSON, ELIZABETH JANE, small business owner; b. Ithaca, N.Y., Jan. 11, 1927; d. Merle Godley and Nellie Gray (Trowbridge) T. AB, Syracuse U., 1948, MA, 1962, PhD, 1971. Writer, editor Cornell U., Ithaca, N.Y., 1950-53; dir. pub. rels. Taylor Ward Advt., 1953-54; account exec. Doug Johnson Assocs., Syracuse, N.Y., 1954-58; assoc. in community rels., Youth Devel. Ctr. Syracuse U., 1958-66, grad. asst., 1967-68; from asst. prof. to prof. sociology Shippensburg (Pa.) U., 1968-90, dir. Fashion Archives, 1980-90; owner Timelines & Hemlines Cons. Svc., Shippensburg, 1991—. Bd. dirs. Shippensburg Univ. Fashion Archives; lectr. on costume, fashion and sociology of dress to numerous civic and ednl. groups. Co-editor: Among the People: Studies of the Urban Poor, 1968; contbr. articles on sociology of dress to numerous publs. Mem. Costume Soc. Am. Dutch Reform. Avocations: vintage clothing, photography, travel, Native American art. Home and Office: 19 S Prince St Shippensburg PA 17257-1919 E-mail: ethompson@pa.net., ecottage@aol.com.

THOMPSON, ERIC THOMAS, retail executive; b. Warren, Ohio, July 19, 1962; s. Thomas Leroy Thompson; Eugene (stepfather) and Georgia Kay (Rex) Stafani; m. Susan E. Robertson, 1988; children: Sara Rebecca, Eric Thomas Jr., Katlyn Grace. Student., Youngstown State U., 1981, 83-84, Kent State U., 1982. Outside sales rep., disc jockey WTCL Radio Sta., Warren, Ohio, 1979-80; disc jockey WOKG, 1981-82, WMGZ, Sharon, Pa., 1982-83; sales rep. Custom Sound Co., Warren, Ohio, 1983-86, Litco Internat., Youngstown, 1986-88; admissions rep. Bryant and Stratton Bus. Inst., Cleve., 1988-89; broker Argent Diamond & Gems, Charlotte, N.C., 1983; asst. sales mgr. Gene and Sons Jewelers, Warren, 1986-87; mgr. sales ops. Internat. Graphics Co., Cleve., 1988-89; network coord. The Ohio Desk Co., 1989-90; account executive Alco Office Furniture, 1989-91; high sch. admissions rep. Nat. Edn. Ctr., 1992-93; small bus. owner, operator, ptnr. Satolli Carpet Floor Covering, Warren, Ohio, 1993—. Hometown Mattress and Futon, Warren, 2000—; ptnr., owner/operator Mahoning Ave. Manufactured Housing Cmty., 1997-2000; cable TV talk show host Falls Focus Cmty. Program, 1995-96; v.p., treas. Northeast Ohio Realty Investors, Inc., Warren, 1996—. Disc jockey WSOM-WQXK, Salem, Ohio, 1980-82; comedian, magician, 1981—; host (TV weekly program) Newton Falls Focus, 1995-96; ptnr. Real Estate Holdings Mahoning, 1997-2000; owner, distbr. EcoQuest Internat. Host, Bus. Connections radio show WRRO, Warren; contbr. articles to bus. publs., newspapers and mags. Firefighter and EMT, Newton Falls Fire and Rescue Dept., 2000—; pres. Brooklyn (Ohio) Rep. Club, 1990-93, treas., 1992; team capt. spl. project Am. Heart Assn. N.E. Ohio, 1992; vol. Shoes for Kids, 1991-93, Child Care Task Force, Brooklyn, 1991-93; mem. Greater Cleve. Holiday Lighting Com., 1991-93; st. capt. Mayor's Com. on Recycling, Brooklyn, 1990-93; bd. mem. Trumbull County Govt. Affairs Com., 1996-99; cons. Jr. Achievement, Cleve., 1991-93; mem. Rock and Roll Hall of Fame and Mus. Task Force, Clean-Land Ohio Task Force; dir., com. mem. Newton Falls Bus. Comty. Expo, 1994-96; dir. Broad St. Merchants Group, 1994-95; co-dir., advisor Newton Falls United Meth. Youth Group, 1996-98; bd. trustees Newton Falls United Meth. Ch., 1995-98, liturgist, lay spkr., 1995-2000; mem. bd. July 4th Com., 1995—; mem. Youngstown-Warren Ohio Better Bus. Bur., 1993—, Crescendo Club/Band Boosters, 1997-2002; youth coach Newton Falls (Ohio) Hot Stove Baseball, 1994—; vol. Newton Falls Cmty. Car Show, 1995—, Newton Falls All-Weather Track Com., 1999, Newton Falls Athletic Boosters, 1997—; dir., cubmaster pack 67 Greater Western Res. coun. Newton Falls Boy Scouts, 1997-99; mem. Friends of the Newton Falls Libr., 1995-99; mem. Ohio H.S. Athletic Assn., varsity/jr. varsity baseball umpire, 1998—; ofcl. Continental Am. Baseball Assn., umpire, 1998—; youth league coord., exec. com. Newton Falls Babe Ruth Youth Baseball/Softball Assn., 1998—, umpire in chief, 1999—, Little League Invitational Tournament, Trumbull County, Ohio, 2000. Recipient Outstanding Leadership award Brooklyn Rep. Club, 1990, Coun. of Sml. Bus. Outstanding Effort award, 1991, Comty. Leadership & Bus. Success award U.S. Congress, 1997, Home Town Hero award Cub Scouts/Boy Scouts, 1999; inducted as umpire Am. Youth Baseball Hall of Fame, 2000. Mem. Greater Cleve. Growth Assn. (Outstanding Vol. Svc. award 1991, 93), Greater Cleve. Coun. Smaller Enterprises, Ind. C. of C., Cleve. Zool. Soc., Internat. Customer Svc. Assn., Sale and Mktg. Execs., N.E. Ohio Floor Covering Assn., Eagles Bus. and Profl. Orgn., Internat. Brotherhood Magicians, Soc. Am. Magicians, Fellowship Christian Magicians, Eagles, Soc. Am. Baseball Rsch. (umpire and rules history com. 1999—), Newton Falls C. of C. (pres. 1994, 95, 96, bd. dirs. 1993-96, Disting. Svc. Honor Leadership award 1995), N.E. Ohio Floor Covering Assn., Youngstown Warren C. of C., Kiwanis Club (v.p. 1994-95, chmn. program com. Newton Falls chpt. 1993-94, July 4th festivities com. 1995), Warren Civic Music Assn., Bus. Connections (bd. dirs. 1998), Trumbull County Interscholastic Umpires Assn. (h.s. ofcl. 1998—), Ohio H.S. Athletic Assn. Methodist. Avocations: stand up comedy, magic and illusion, travel, reading. Home: 315 Marshall St Newton Falls OH 44444-1426 Office: 367 High St NE Warren OH 44481-1246

THOMPSON, EUGENE MAYNE, retired minister; b. Oxford, N.S., Can., Jan. 5, 1931; s. Curry Allison and Hortense Essie (Mayne) T.; m. Rhoda Mitchell, May 21, 1955; children: Adrian Calvin, Nancy Lynn, Howard Allison. BA, Acadia U., 1954, BD, 1956, DD, 2000, MDiv, 1976; D of Ministry, So. Bapt. Theol. Sem., 1979. Pastor South End United Bapt. Ch., Dartmouth, N.S., 1954-58; assoc. sec. of Christian Edn. United Bapt. Conv. of Atlantic Provinces, St. John, N.B., 1958-61, exec. min., 1984-96, area min. for West N.S. Middleton, N.S., 1974-84; pastor Immanuel Bapt. Ch., Truro, 1961-65, Hillcrest Bapt. Ch., St. John, N.B., 1965-68; area min. for Man. Bapt. Union of Western Can., 1968-74; ret., 1996. Coun., exec. mem. Can. Bapt. Ministries, Mississauga, Ont.; bd. dirs. Atlantic Bapt. Sr. Citizen Homes, Inc., Moncton, N.B.; bd. govs Atlantic Bapt. Coll., Moncton; trustee Acadia Div. Coll.; mem. Bapt. Found. Author: Baptist Youth Fellowship Handbook, 1958, New Design for a Dynamic Church, 1973. Dir. St. John, N.B., Habitat for Humanity. Avocations: music, gardening, painting. E-mail: emtrt@nbnet.nb.ca.

THOMPSON, EWA M. foreign language educator; b. Kaunas, Lithuania; came to U.S., 1963; d. Jozef and Maria Majewski; m. James R. Thompson. BA in English and Russian, U. Warsaw, Poland, 1963; MFA in Piano, Sopot Conservatory Music, 1963; MA in English, Ohio U., 1964; PhD in Comparative Lit., Vanderbilt U., 1967. Instr. Vanderbilt U., Nashville, 1964-67; asst. prof. Ind. State U., Terre Haute, 1967-68, Ind. U., 1968-70, Rice U., Houston, 1967-73, assoc. prof., 1974-79, prof., 1979—, chair, 1987-90; assoc. prof. U. Va., Charlottesville, 1973-74. Cons. NEH, 1973—, The John D. and Catherine T. MacArthur Found., The John Simon Guggenheim Found., U.S. Dept. Edn.; vis. cons. Tex. A&M U.; seminar dir. NEH Summer Inst., Southeastern La. U., 1990; chair Russian lit. conf. Rice U., 1989; lectr. various colls. and univs. Author: Russian Formalism and Anglo-American New Criticism: A Comparative Study, 1971, Witold Gombrowicz, 1979, Understanding Russia: The Holy Fool in Russian Culture, 1987 (Chinese translation 1995, 2nd Chinese edit. 1998), The Search for Self-Definition in Russian Literature, 1991, Imperial Knowledge: Russian Literature and Colonialism, 2000, Polish translation, 2000; editor the Sarmatian Rev., 1988—; contbr. articles to profl. jours., chpts. to books. Mellon grant, 1990, Rice U. grant 1990, Internat. Rsch. and Exchanges Sr. Scholar grant, 1991; Hoover Inst. fellow, 1988; scholar Vanderbilt U., 1964-67; recipient Silver Thistle award Houston's Scottish Heritage Found., 1988. Roman Catholic. Home: 142 Stoney Creek Houston TX 77024 Office: Rice University 6100 S Main St MS 32 Houston TX 77005-1892 E-mail: ethomp@rice.edu.

THOMPSON, FRANCIS NEAL, financial services consultant; b. Yonkers, N.Y., Oct. 21, 1940; s. Maury Weldon and Mary Temple (Meacham) T.; m. Patricia Jennings Turner, June 12, 1962 (div. 1980); children: Melissa Temple Thompson, Turner Jennings Thompson; m. Sharon Griffin, May 8, 1982. BA in Econs., Lynchburg Coll., 1962; MBA, U. Richmond, 1966. Chartered life underwriter; ChFC; CFP. Stockbroker Mason & Lee (now Legg, Mason & Co.), Lynchburg and Richmond, Va., 1960-63; pension analyst Southwestern Life Ins. Co., Dallas, 1963-68; v.p., mktg. dir. Fidelity Bankers Life Ins. Co., Richmond, 1968-75; v.p., dir., chmn. exec. com. Wheat 1st Union (now First Union Securities), 1975-78; chmn., CEO Corp. Cons. Inc., 1978-84; exec. v.p., dir. Fin. Mgmt. Group, 1984-88; v.p. mktg. dir. Ind. Fin. Mktg. Group, White Plains, N.Y., 1988-89; spl. projects mgr. The Acacia Group, Washington, 1990-91; ins. cons. Blue Cross/Blue Shield of Va. (now Trigon Blue Cross/Shield), Richmond, 1992-93; regional sales mgr. Allmerica Fin., State Mut. Life and Provident Mut., 1993-97; founder Fin. Svcs. Consultants, Inc., Richmond, 1994—. Cons. Signet Ins., Richmond, 1984-88, Funds of Am., Portland, 1988; founding stockholder Fidelity Assurance Assocs. LLC, 2001, Commonwealth Asset Group, 2001. Author: Assessing Individual Managerial Performing, 1967. Bd. dirs. Emergency Shelter Inc., Richmond, 1991-95, Boy Scouts Am.-Robert E. Lee Coun., Richmond, 1984-94. With USN, 1955-58. Recipient Disting. Prof. 20 Yr. Svc. award Coll. for Fin. Planning, 1997. Fellow Life Underwriters Tng. Coun. (Ernest E. Cragg Amb. award 1996); mem. Ctrl. Va. Soc. CFP's (bd. dirs. 1991-97, edn. chmn. 1991-92), Richmond Life Underwriters Assn. (bd. dirs. 1994-97). Presbyterian. Avocations: sailing, tennis. Home: 10006 Bellona Ct Richmond VA 23233-2044 Office: PO Box 29634 Richmond VA 23242-0634 E-mail: peddler804@aol.com.

THOMPSON, FRANK JOSEPH, political science educator; b. New Ulm, Minn., Mar. 21, 1944; s. Joseph Mariem and Alice Louise (Lindquist) T.; m. Benna Miriam, June 15, 1944; children: Samuel, Aliza, Elizabeth. BA in Polit. Sci., U. Chgo., 1966; MA in Polit. Sci., U. Calif., Berkeley, 1967, PhD in Polit. Sci., 1973. Asst. prof. polit. sci. Calif. State U., Long Beach, 1971-72; asst. prof. U. Ga., Athens, 1972-78, assoc. prof., 1978-83, prof., 1983-88, head dept., 1982-87; prof. pub. adminstrn., policy, polit. sci. and pub. health SUNY, Albany, 1987—, dean Grad. Sch. of Pub. Affairs, 1988—, assoc. provost, 1990-97, interim provost, 1997-2000; dean Rockefeller Coll., 2000—. Analyst HEW, Washington, 1968, City Govt. Oakland, Calif., 1968-71; cons. USPHS, 1976-79, 82, U.S. Pres.'s Commn. for Nat. Agenda for 80's, 1980, Am. Pub. Welfare Assn., 1981-83; publ. cons. U.S. Adv. Commn. on Intergovtl. Rels., 1983; mem. task force on exec. and mgmt. devel. U.S. Office Pers. Mgmt., 1990; exec. dir. Nat. Commn. on the State and Local Pub. Svc., 1991-97. Author: Personnel Policy in the City, 1975, Health Policy and the Bureaucracy, 1981, Public Administration: Challenges, Choices, Consequences, 1990; editor: Classics of Public Personnel Policy, 1979, 2d edit., 1991, Revitalizing State and Local Public Service, 1993, Medicaid and Devolution: A View from the States; contbr. articles to profl. jours. Bd. dirs. Upper Hudson Planned Parenthood, 1990-96, Albany-Tula Alliance, 1998—. Pub. adminstrn. fellow U.S. Pub. Health Service, 1975-76, NSF fellow, 1970-71; recipient Simon award Internat. Jour. Pub. Adminstrn., 1981. Fellow Nat. Acad. Pub. Adminstrn.; mem. Am. Pub. Health Assn., Assn. for Pub. Policy Analysis and Mgmt., Am. Soc. for Pub. Adminstrn. (publs. com. 1982-84, William E. Mosher award 1983), Am. Polit. Sci. Assn. (chmn. departmental services com. 1985-87, exec. com. sect. pub. adminstrn. 1985-87, 89, 91, 96—, chair sect. pub. adminstrn. 1990-91, chair Gaus award com. 1991-92), Nat. Assn. Schs. Pub. Affairs and Adminstrn. (peer rev. com. 1984-86, 1st chmn. commn. on peer rev. and accreditation 1986-87, chmn. task force on revitalizing the pub. svc., v.p. 1990-91, pres. 1991-92, chmn. com. advancement of pub. adminstrn. 1996-98), N.Y. State Acad. Pub. Adminstrn. (bd. dirs. 1994—). Home: 9 Harvard Ave Albany NY 12208-2019 Office: SUNY Rockefeller Coll Milne 102 Albany NY 12222-0001 E-mail: thompson@albany.edu.

THOMPSON, FRED, senator; b. Sheffield, Ala., Aug. 19, 1942; BS, Memphis State U., 1964; JD, Vanderbilt U., 1967. Asst. U.S. atty. Mid. Tenn., 1969-72; min. counsel Senate Watergate Com., 1973-74; pvt. practice, 1975-94; spl. counsel U.S. Senate Fgn. Rels. Coms., 1980, Senate Intelligence Com., 1982; atty. Arent, Fox, Kintner, Plotkin & Kahn, 1991-94; U.S. senator from Tenn., 1994—. Chmn. senate govtl. affairs com., 1997-2001. Appeared in 18 films including Hunt for Red October, In the Line of Fire, Cape Fear, 1985-94; author: At That Point In Time, 1975. Office: US Senate 511 Dirksen Senate Bldg Washington DC 20510-0001*

THOMPSON, G. GAYE, lawyer; b. Greensboro, N.C., Sept. 15, 1945; d. O.C. and Jean T.; m. Alvis Layton Barrier, Jr., Aug. 28, 1965 (div. 1988); children: Breton Foster, Amé Rebecca. BA, Southwestern U., 1967; JD, St. mary's U., 1987. Bar: 1987, U.S. Ct. Appeals (5th cir.) 1991, U.S. Supreme Ct. 1991. Psychiat. caseworker Austin (Tex.) State Hosp., 1967-68; counselor, acting dir. counseling Meth. Mission Home Tex., San Antonio, 1968-70; assoc. Irvine & Dial, P.C., Attys. at Law, Seguin, 1987; 1st asst. county atty. Guadalupe County, 1987-90; ptnr. Thompson & Tiemann LLP, Attys. and Counselors at Law, Austin, 1991—. Pres., bd. dirs. Marywood Child and Family Svcs., 1995-97,; pres bd. dirs. Family Eldercare, 1996-97. Mem. AAUW, Nat. Acad. Elder Law Attys. (bd. dirs. Tex. chpt.), Travis County Bar Assn. (bd. dirs. probate and estate planning sect.), Tex. Dist. and County Attys. Assn., Delta Delta Delta. Episcopalian. Avocations: orchids, fly fishing, photography. Home: PO Box 201988 Austin TX 78720-1988 Office: Thompson & Tiemann LLP Attys and Counselors at Law PO Box 201988 Austin TX 78720-1988 E-mail: ggt@elderlawline.com.

THOMPSON, G. KENNEDY, bank executive; b. Rocky Mount, N.C., Nov. 25, 1950; BA in Am. Studies, U. N.C.; MBA, Wake Forest Fu. With 1st Union Corp., Charlotte, NC, 1976—, head S.E. divsn., mgr. mid. market dept., 1999—, mgr. N.Y. loan prodn. office, pres. 1st Union-Ga., sr. v.p., head human resources, pres. 1st Union-Fla., vice chmn. corp., head global capital markets, until 1999, pres., CEO, 1999—2001, Wachovia Corp. (merger of 1st Union and Wachovia Corp.), 2001—. Bd. dirs. Fla. Rock Industries, Inc., VISA Internat.; mem. fin. svcs. roundtable Fin. Svcs. Forum. Bd. visitors U. N.C., Chapel Hill, Babcock Grad. Sch. Mgmt., Wake Forest U.; bd. dirs. N.C. Blumenthal Performing Arts Ctr., Charlotte Latin Sch., so. region Boy Scouts Am., United Way, Charlotte; mem. met. bd. YMCA, Charlotte. Morehead scholar U. N.C. Office: 301 S College St Charlotte NC 28288*

THOMPSON, GENEVA FLORENCE, medical technologist, cytotechnologist; b. Zionsville, Ind., Apr. 5, 1915; d. Alfred Seymour and Grace Viola (Kutz) T. Cert. in cytotechnology, Ohio State U., 1964; BA, Ind. U./Purdue U., Indpls., 1972. Cert. Am. Soc. Clin. Pathologists. Med. technician Noblesville (Ind.) Hosp., 1948-52, Riverview Hosp., Noblesville, 1952-56, med. technologist, 1956-60, Office of Robert Harris, M.D., Noblesville, 1960-64; cytotechnologist Office of Thornton, Haymond, Costin, Buehl & Bolinger, M.D., Indpls., 1965-78, ret., 1978. Active with local church; served with U.S. Army W.A.C., 1944-46. Mem. AAUW (chmn. literature study group), Ind. U. Women's Club of Indpls., Am. Soc. Clin. Pathologists, Noblesville Tourist Club (sec.), Sr. Citizens Orgn., Inc. Republican. Avocations: antique book collecting, bridge, clothing design and construction.

THOMPSON, GEORGE ALBERT, geophysics educator; b. Swissvale, Pa., June 5, 1919; s. George Albert Sr. and Maude Alice (Harkness) T.; m. Anita Kimmell, July 20, 1944; children: Albert J., Dan A., David C. BS, Pa. State U., 1941; MS, MIT, 1942; PhD, Stanford U., 1949. Geologist, geophysicist U.S. Geol. Survey, Menlo Park, Calif., 1942-49; asst. prof. Stanford (Calif.) U., 1949-55, assoc. prof., 1955-60, prof. geophysics, 1960—, chmn. geophysics dept., 1967-86, chmn. geology dept., 1979-82, Otto N. Miller prof. earth scis., 1980-89, dean sch. earth scis., 1987-89. Part-time geologist U.S. Geol. Survey, Menlo Park, 1949-76; cons. adv. com. on reactor safeguards Nuclear Regulation Commn., Washington, 1974-94; mem. bd. earth sci. NRC, 1986-88, vice chmn. Yucca Mountain Hydrology-tectonics panel NRC, 1990-92; mem. exec. com. Inc. Rsch. Inst. for Seismology, Washington, 1990-92; mem. sr. external events rev. com. Lawrence Livermore Nat. Lab., 1989-93; mem. Coun. on Continental Sci. Drilling, 1990-94; cons. Los Alamos Nat. Lab. on volcanotectonic processes, 1993-96, S.W. Rsch. Inst., 1993; chair com. to review sci. issues NRC, Ward Valley, Calif., 1994-95; mem. panel on probabalistic volcanic hazard analysis Geomatrix Cons., Inc., 1995-96. Author over 100 research papers. With USNR, 1944-46. Recipient G.K. Gilbert award in seismic geology, 1964, John Wesley Powell award U.S. Geol. Survey, 1999; NSF postdoctoral fellow, 1956-57; Guggenheim Found. fellow, 1963-64 Fellow AAAS, Geol. Soc. Am. (coun. mem. 1983-86, George P. Woollard award 1983, v.p. 1995, pres. 1996), Am. Geophys. Union; mem. NAS (chair geology sect. 2000-), Seismol. Soc. Am., Soc. Exploration Geophysicists. Avocation: forestry. Home: 421 Adobe Pl Palo Alto CA 94306-4501 Office: Stanford U Geophysics Dept Stanford CA 94305-2215 E-mail: thompson@pangea.stanford.edu.

THOMPSON, GEORGE FREDERICK, JR. public management educator; b. Anderson, Ind., Oct. 29, 1942; s. George Frederick and Ellen Leah (Reuter) T.; m. Sharon O'Rand, Sept. 8, 1968 (div. Nov. 1978); children: MacKendree and Kyrie' O'Rand; m. Ruth Ann Crowley, June 20, 1980; 1 child, Jonathan Crowley. BA, Pomona Coll., 1964; PhD, Claremont Grad. Sch., 1972. Asst. to sr. analyst Dept. Fin. State of Calif., Sacramento, 1972-75; assoc. dep. dir. for fin. and capital outlay planning Calif. Postsecondary Edn. Commn., 1975-76; vis. asst./assoc. prof. U. British Columbia faculty commerce and bus. adminstrn., 1976-77; sr. rsch economist Econ. Coun. Can., Ottawa, Ont., 1978-79; vis. assoc. prof., acting chmn. Grad. Sch. Mgmt. Pub. and Not for Profit Mgmt. Group UCLA, 1981; assoc. prof. Columbia U. Sch. Internat. and Pub. Affairs MPA Program, N.Y.C., 1980-85; Grace and Elmer Goudy Prof. Pub. Mgmt. and Policy Analysis Atkinson Grad. Sch. Mgmt. Willamette U., Salem, Oreg., 1985—. Bd. dirs. Fin. Pub., Inc.; mem. task force on state budgeting Nat. Ctr. for Higher edn. Mgmt. Systems, Boulder, Colo., 1975-76, adv. com. Calif. State Senate Judiciary Com. subcom. on Consumr Affairs, 1980-81, Gov.'s Task Force on Sch. Fin. Reform, Oreg., 1988-89, adv. com. on Tax Reform, Oreg., 1990, Govt. Standards and Practices Commn., Oreg., 1995—; cons. House of Commons Can., on Regulatory Reform, Pub. Svcs. Commn. N.Y. Atty. Gen.'s Office of Consumer Affairs, Defense Sec.'s Commn. on Base Realignment and Closure, Senate Armed Svcs. subcom. on mil. constrn., others Co-author: (with W.T. Stanbury) Regulatory Reform in Canada, 1982, (with L.R. Jones) Regulatory Policy and Practices: Regulating

Better and Regulating Less, 1982, Reinventing the Pentagon, 1994, Public Management: Institutional Renewal for the 21st Century, 1999; translator (with Ruth Crowley) F. Scharpf's Crisis and Choice in European Social Democracy, 1991; editor: Regulatory Regimes in Conflict, 1984; co-editor: (with LeRoy Gramer) Reforming Social Regulation, 1982, (with W.T. Stanbury) Managing Public Enterprises, 1982; editor Internat. Pub. Mgmt. Jour.; contbr. numerous articles, notes, essays, book revs. to profl. jours. Mem. acad. adv. bd. Cascade Policy Inst. Recipient Clara Ihrig Linhardt Traveling fellowship, Mexico, Cen. Am., 1970-71, Mayr Found. Essay award, Lincoln Inst. Pub. Fin., Claremont Grad. Sch., 1973; nominated for Koopman prize of ORSA spl. interest group of defense analysis, 1987. Mem. Assn. for Pub. Policy and Mgmt., ASPA (exec. coun. sect. on pub. budgeting and fin. 1991-97, pres. 1998, sect. on rsch. and theory 1996—, Mosher award 1994, NASPAA/ASPA Disting Rsch. award 2000), Am. Soc. Mil. Controllers (Gold medal 1994), Oreg. Acad. Scis. Home: 540 Tillman Ave SE Salem OR 97302-3786 Office: Willamette Univ Atkinson Grad Sch Mgmt Salem OR 97301 E-mail: fthompso@willamette.edu.

THOMPSON, GEORGE LEE, consulting and retailing company executive; b. Denver, June 12, 1933; s. George H. and Frances M. (Murphy) T.; m. Patricia M. Mackenzie, Sept. 25, 1993; children: Shannon, Tracy, Bradley. BS in Bus., U. Colo., 1957; AMP in advanced mgmt., NYU, 1969. With GTE Sylvania, Danvers, Mass., 1957-65, nat. sales mgr., 1965-67, mktg. mgr., 1967-68; v.p. sales entertainment products Batavia, N.Y., 1968-73; dir. corp. mktg. Stamford, Conn., 1973-74; v.p. mktg. Servomation Corp., N.Y.C., 1974-76, exec. v.p., 1976-78, Singer Co., Edison, N.J., 1978-81, pres., 1981-83; pres. consumer products SCM Corp., N.Y.C., 1983-86; pres., CEO Smith-Corona Corp., New Canaan, Conn., 1986-89, chmn., CEO, 1989-95; chmn. Mackenzie-Thompson Assocs., Essex, 1995—. Bd. dirs. Vol. Products, Inc.; chair Sweet P's, Essex, Conn., 1998—. Chmn. Standards Com. U.S. Dept. Commerce; mem. bus. alumni adv. coun. U. Colo., 1989—94; mem. bd. overseers Sch. Bus. U. Conn., 1993—96; mem. Pres.'s Export Coun., 1991—93; mem. bd. advisors Jr. League; Bd. dirs. Internat. Tennis Hall of Fame; Am. Jr. Golf Found., 1986—89; Am. Jr. Golf Assn., 1986—2000; United Way of New Canaan, 1989—93. Recipient Disting. Bus. Alumni award U. Colo., 1990. Mem. Computer and Bus. Equipment Mfg. Assn. (bd. dirs. 1992-94), Sales and Mktg. Execs. Internat. (trustee), Am. Mgmt. Assn. (trustee, exec. com. chmn., gen. mgmt. coun. 1989-99), St. John Assn. (bd. dirs., pres. 1983-93), Woodway Country Club, Club at Seabrook Island, Wilton Riding Club (bd. govs. 1980-83), Navesink Country Club (bd. govs. 1983-86), Harbour Ridge Yacht and Country Club, Essex Yacht Club, Old Lyme Country Club, Chi Psi. Episcopalian. Office: Mackenzie Thompson Assocs 51 Main St Essex CT 06426-1150 also: Sweet P's LLC Griswold Sq Essex CT 06426 E-mail: Glee13507@aol.com.

THOMPSON, GEORGE LEROY, mechanical engineer; b. Elwood, Nebr., Aug. 2, 1952; s. Leonard and Mary (Tillotson) T.; m. Linda Susan Philo, June 22, 1980; children: Samantha, Diana, David. BSME, U. Nebr., 1976; post-grad., U. No. Iowa, 1979-80, Mercer U., 1990-92. Registered profl. engr., Iowa, Ga. Design engr. Maytag Co., Newton, Iowa, 1977-79, Doerfer div. Container Corp. Am., Cedar Falls, 1979-82; sr. mech. engr. Becton-Dickinson, Columbus, Nebr., 1982-85; sr. engr. Coca-Cola Co., Atlanta, 1985—. Co-inventor proportional flow control valve. Mem. Pi Tau Sigma. Republican. Methodist. Avocations: gardening, woodworking, coin collecting, tennis. Home: 2502 Meadow Glen Trl Snellville GA 30078-5631 Office: The Coca Cola Co PO Box 1734 1 Coca Cola Plz NW Ste 3A Atlanta GA 30301-1734 E-mail: gthompson@NA.KO.com.

THOMPSON, GEORGE RALPH, church administrator; b. Connell Town, Saint Lucy, Barbados, Mar. 20, 1929; s. George Gilbert and Edna (Griffith) T.; m. Imogene Clotilde Barker, July 19, 1959; children: Carol Jean, Linda Mae, Gerald Randolph. BA, Atlantic Union Coll., 1956; MA, Andrews U., 1958, BD, 1962, DDiv (hon.), 1983. Ordained to ministry Seventh-day Adventists, 1959. Evangelist South Caribbean conf. Seventh-day Adventists, Trinidad and Tobago, 1950-53; tchr., ch. pastor, chmn. dept. theology Caribbean Union Coll., Trinidad and Tobago, 1953-54, 59-64; pres. East Caribbean conf. Seventh-day Adventists, Barbados, 1964-70, pres. Caribbean Union conf. Trinidad and Tobago, 1970-75; v.p. Gen. Conf. Seventh-day Adventists, Washington, 1975-80, sec. Silver Spring, Md., 1980-2000; field rep. Ellen G. White Estate, Gen. Conf. Seventh-day Adventists, 2000—. Host radio shows, Barbados. Office: Gen Conf Seventh-day Adventists Ch 12501 Old Columbia Pike Silver Spring MD 20904-6601

THOMPSON, GERALD EVERETT, economics educator; b. Leland, Iowa, Feb. 22, 1924; s. Gilbert Theodore and Clara Marie (Charlson) T.; m. Betty Phyllis Collman, Aug. 26, 1950; 1 child, David Forsyth. BA, U. Iowa, 1947, MA, 1948, PhD, 1953. Asst. prof. econs. U. Toledo, Ohio, 1950-54; from asst. to full prof. econs. U. Nebr., Lincoln, 1954—; vis. assoc. prof. statis. U. Mich., Ann Arbor, 1965-66. Author: Linear Programming, 1971, Statistics for Decisions, 1972, Management Science, 1976, Microeconomics, 2001. 1st lt. U.S. Army Air Corps. Harvard U. Faculty fellow Ford Found., Cambridge, Mass., 1959-60. Mem. Am. Econs. Assn., Am. Statis. Assn. Home: 130 57th Ct West Des Moines IA 50266-2814

THOMPSON, GORDON, JR. federal judge; b. San Diego, Dec. 28, 1929; s. Gordon and Garnet (Meese) T.; m. Jean Peters, Mar. 17, 1951; children— John M., Peter Renwick, Gordon III. Grad., U. So. Calif., 1951, Southwestern U. Sch. Law, Los Angeles, 1956. Bar: Calif. 1956. With Dist. Atty.'s Office, County of San Diego, 1957-60; partner firm Thompson & Thompson, San Diego, 1960-70; U.S. dist. judge So. Dist. Calif., 1970—, chief judge, 1984-91, sr. judge, 1994—. Mem. ABA, Am. Bd. Trial Advocates, San Diego County Bar Assn. (v.p. 1970), San Diego Yacht Club, Delta Chi. Office: US Dist Ct 940 Front St San Diego CA 92101-8994

THOMPSON, GREG ALAN, computer sciences consulting executive; b. Palo Alto, Calif., Sept. 15, 1955; s. Jack Edward and Elaine Irene (Palmer) T.; m. Michelle Marie Barnes, Dec. 26, 1987; children: Amy, Beth, Kimberly. BSEE and Computer Sci., MIT, 1977. Cons. engr. Informatics-PMI Ames Rsch. Ctr. NASA, Moffett Field, Calif., 1975-78; prin. software specialist Digital Equipment Corp., Santa Clara, 1978-83, lead engr. computer aided design-CAM ctr., 1982; lead cons. engr., mgr. Interlink computer Scis., Inc., Fremont, Calif., 1983-93; sr. comm. engr. nCUBE, Foster City, 1993-96, dir. product mgmt. and engring., 1996—. Bank of Am. and Hertz Found. scholar, 1973. Mem. IEEE Computer Soc., Bay Area MIT Alumni. Avocation: sailing. Office: nCUBE 110 Marsh Dr Foster City CA 94404-1121

THOMPSON, GREGORY LEE, social sciences educator; b. Huntington Pk., Calif., June 14, 1946; s. Karl Windsor and Virginia Alice (Hanna) T. AB in Geography, U. Calif., Davis, 1968; M of City Planning, U. Calif., Berkeley, 1970; PhD in Social Scis., U. Calif., Irvine, 1987. Transp. planner City of Edmonton (Alberta) Transit Sys., 1970-72; transp. analyst Can. Transport Commn., Ottawa, Ontario, 1972-73; transp. coord. City of Berkeley (Calif.) Planning Dept., 1973-74; sr. transp. planner San Diego County, 1974-77, Met. Transp. Devel. Bd., San Diego, 1977-80; sr. cons. Mass Transit, Calif. Assembly, Sacramento, 1980-81; rsch. fellow Hagley Mus. & Libr., Wilmington, Del., 1987-88; asst. prof. Fla. State U., Tallahassee, 1988-94, assoc. prof., 1994—. Author: The Passenger Train in the Motor Age: California 1910-1941, 1993; contbr. articles to profl. jours. Organizer, pres. Citizens of Rail Calif., San Diego, 1976-80. Named Advanced Rsch. fellow Andrew W. Mellon/NEH, 1987-88, Disting. Student scholar Sch. Engring. U. Calif., Irvine, 1983. Mem. Am. Planning Assn. (sect. dir. San Diego), Soc. for History of Technology, Econ. History Assn., Bus. History Assn., Planning History Assn., Am. Inst. Cert. Planners. Democrat. Avocations: photography, swimming. Home: 2635 Lucerne Dr Tallahassee FL 32303-2261 Office: Fla State U Dept Urban Regional Pl Tallahassee FL 32306

THOMPSON, HARRY FLOYD, II, research collections and book publications director; b. Albany, N.Y., Mar. 3, 1953; s. Harry Floyd Sr. and Mae Catherine (Bush) T.; m. Ronelle Kay Hildebrandt, Dec. 24, 1976; children: Clarissa Mae, Harry Floyd III. BA in English, Houghton (N.Y.) Coll., 1975; MA in Am. Studies, Baylor U., 1977; MA in Tchg., Colgate U., 1979; MA in English, U. Rochester, 1981; PhD in English, U. S.D., 2000. Cert. in archives adminstrn. Sr. English tchr. Ticonderoga (N.Y.) H.S., 1977-78; instr. English U. Rochester, N.Y., 1979-81; lectr. in English Winthrop Coll., Rock Hill, S.C., 1981-82; pub. rels. writer U. S.C., Lancaster, 1983; instr. English Augustana Coll., Sioux Falls, S.D., 1984-87, archivist, 1984-87, curator rsch. collections, mng. editor book publs., 1987—; dir. rsch. collections and publications, 1999—. Author: Guide to the Archives of the South Dakota Conference of the United Church of Christ, 1987; editor: Guide to Collections Relating to Norwegian-Americans in South Dakota, 1991; prin. editor: A Common Land, A Diverse People: Ethnic Identity on the Prairie Plains, 1987. Bd. dirs. S.D. State Hist. Soc., Pierre, 1989—, v.p., 1998—; bd. dirs. Frontier Heritage Alliance, Sheridan, Wyo., 1998—, Nordland Heritage Found., Sioux Falls, 1992—; conf. dir. Dakota History Conf., Sioux Falls, 1990—; project dir. History of the Arts in S.D., Sioux Falls, 1986-89; mem. bd. edn. Gloria Dei Luth. Ch., Sioux Falls, 1992-93; mem. adv. coun. Minn. Pub. Radio, Sioux Falls, 1994-95; mem. archives adv. coun. Evang. Luth. Ch. in Am., 1998-2001; bd. dirs. Sioux Falls Bd. Preservation, 2000—. Dixon Wecter fellow Baylor U., 1975, Grad. Tuition scholar U. Rochester, 1978, Dorothy Baisch Selz Meml. scholar U. S.D., 1998. Mem. Western History Assn., Western Lit. Assn., Soc. Am. Archivists, Midwest Archives Conf. Avocations: country walking, tennis, museums, family. Office: Augustana Coll Ctr Western studies 2001 S Summit Ave Sioux Falls SD 57197-0001

THOMPSON, HERBERT ERNEST, tool and die company executive; b. Jamaica, N.Y., Sept. 8, 1923; s. Walter and Louise (Joly) T.; m. Patricia Elaine Osborn, Aug. 2, 1968; children: Robert Steven, Debra Lynn. Student, Stevens Inst. Tech., 1949-51. Foreman Conner Tool Co., 1961-62, Eason & Waller GrindingCorp., 1962-63; owner Endco Machined Products, 1966-67, Thompson Enterprises, 1974—. Pres. Method Machined Products, Phoenix, 1967; pres., owner Quality Tool, Inc., 1967-96. Served to capt. USAAF, 1942-46. Decorated DFC, Air medal with cluster. Home: 14009 N 42nd Ave Phoenix AZ 85053-5306

THOMPSON, HERBERT STANLEY, neuro-ophthalmologist; b. Shansi, China, June 12, 1932; arrived in U.S., 1949, naturalized, 1955; s. Robert Ernest and Ellen Thompson; m. Delores Lucille Johnson, June 27, 1953; children: Geoffrey, Peter, Kenneth, Philip, Susan. Student, Methodist Coll., Belfast, No. Ireland, 1947—49; BA, U. Minn., 1953, MD, 1961; MS, U. Iowa, 1966. Diplomate Am. Bd. Ophthalmology (assoc. examiner 1972-88, bd. dirs. 1989-96, chmn. ABO 1996). Intern U. Iowa, Iowa City, 1961—62, resident in ophthalmology, 1962—66; fellow in pupillography Columbia Coll. Physicians and Surgeons, 1962; fellow in clin. neuro-ophthalmology U. Calif., San Francisco, 1966—67; prof. ophthalmology U. Iowa, Iowa City, 1976—97, emeritus prof., 1997—, dir. neuro-ophthalmology unit, 1967—97; practice medicine specializing in neuro-ophthalmology Iowa City, 1967—97. Editor: Topics in Neuro-ophthalmology, 1979; assoc. editor: Am. Jour. Ophthalmology, 1981—84, book rev. editor: , 1984—91, cons.: Stedman's Med. Dictionary, 26th edit. Served with AUS, 1954-55. Recipient rsch. career devel. award, NIH, 1968—72; fellow spl. fellow, 1966—67. Fellow: N.Am. Neuro-ophthalmol. Soc., Am. Acad. Ophthalmology; mem.: Cogan Ophthalmic History Soc. (Charles Snyder lectr. 1995), Am. Ophthalmol. Soc. Avocation: research on movements of the pupil of human eye. Office: U Iowa Dept Ophthalmology Iowa City IA 52242

THOMPSON, HOWARD KING, JR. retired physician, educator; b. Boston, May 19, 1928; s. Howard King and Maude Ellen (Short) T.; m. Christine Slotemaker De Bruine, Apr. 11, 1963 (dec. Feb. 1, 1990); children: Ulrike, Friederike, Howard, III. BA, Yale U., 1949; MD, Columbia U., 1953. Diplomate Am. Bd. Internal Medicine. Inter, jr. asst. resident Bellevue Hosp., N.Y.C., 1953-55; sr. asst. resident, chief resident in medicine Duke U. Med. Ctr., Durham, N.C., 1958-59, 60-61; assoc. prof. medicine Duke U., 1967-71; prof. medicine Baylor Coll. Medicine, Houston, 1971-78, Albany (N.Y.) Med. Coll., 1978-83; physician in charge Permanente Med. Assoc. Tex., Dallas, 1988-94; retired, 1994. Chmn. biotech. resources rev. com., divsn. rsch. resources NIH, Bethesda, Md., 1981. Contbr. over 50 articles to profl. jours. Capt. USAR, 1956-57, Korea. Avocations: music. Home: 67 Balfour Rd West Hartford CT 06117-2936

THOMPSON, HUGH LEE, academic administrator; b. Martinsburg, W.Va., Mar. 25, 1934; s. Frank Leslie and Althea T.; m. Patricia Smith; children: Cheri, Linda, Tempe, Vicki. BS, BA in English and Secondary Edn, Shepherd Coll., Shepherdstown, W.Va., 1956; MS, Pa. State U., 1958; PhD in Higher Edn. Adminstrn, Case Western Res. U., 1969. Mem. faculty Pa. State U., 1957-60, Akron (Ohio) U., 1960-62, Baldwin-Wallace Coll., Berea, Ohio, 1962-70, asst. to pres., 1966-69, dir. instl. planning, asst. to pres., 1969-70; coord. Associated Colls., Cleve., 1970-71; pres. Siena Heights U., Adrian, Mich., 1971-77, Detroit Inst. Tech., 1977-80; chancellor Ind. U., Kokomo, 1980-90; pres. Washburn U., Topeka, 1990-97, Higher Edn. Assocs., Merritt Island, Fla., 1997—; interim v.p. for acad. affairs Clarke Coll., 1999-2000. Former mem. pres.'s adv. coun. Assn. Governing Bds. Univs. and Colls.; Fulbright scholar to China, 1998, to Bulgaria, 2001. Mem. Am. Assn. State Colls. and Univs. (coun. of state reps., steering com. urban and met. univs. coun.), North Ctrl. Assn. (evaluator, cons.). Home and Office: PO Box 542751 Merritt Island FL 32954-2751 E-mail: hughthompson@worldnet.att.net. *I have found that to be successful in any field of endeavor an individual must work very diligently at finding solutions to problems, should be highly goal oriented, honest and forthright, and adhere to the teachings of Christ.*

THOMPSON, HUGH P, state supreme court justice; b. Montezuma, Ga., July 7, 1943; married; 2 children. Grad., Mercer U.; JD, Emory U., 1969. Bar: Ga. 1970. Pvt. practice, Milledgeville, Ga., 1970—71; judge Recorder's Ct. of Milledgeville, 1971—79, Baldwin County Ct., 1973—78; judge, chief judge Superior Ct. of Ga., 1979—94; chief judge Ocmulgee Jud. Cir., 1987—94; assoc. justice Supreme Ct. of Ga., Atlanta, 1994—. Instr. bus. law Ga. Coll., 1971—72; pres. Coun. Superior Ct. Judges, 1993—94. Communicant St. Stephen's Episcopal Ch. Named Outstanding Young Man of Baldwin County, 1972; recipient Disting. Svc. award, Baldwin County Jaycees, 1972, Outstanding Alumnus award, Mercer U. Law Sch., 1994. Mem.: ABA, Ga. Bar Found., State Bar Ga., Charles Longstreet Weltner Family Law Inn of Ct., Old War Horse Lawyers Club, Lawyers Club Atlanta. Avocations: hunting, rose gardening, golf, fishing. Office: Supreme Ct Ga State Judicial Bldg 244 Washington St SW Rm 572 Atlanta GA 30334-9007

THOMPSON, HUNTER STOCKTON, author, political analyst, journalist; b. Louisville, July 18, 1937; s. Jack R. and Virginia (Ray) T.; 1 child, Juan. Carribean corr. N.Y. Herald Tribune, 1959—60; South Am. corr. Nat. Observer, 1961—63; West Coast corr. The Nation, 1964—66; columnist Ramparts, 1967—68, Scanlan's, 1969—70; nat. affairs editor Rolling Stone, 1970—99; global affairs corr. High Times, 1977—82; political columnist San Francisco Examiner, 1985—89; polit. analyst European mags. London Observer, Tempo, Time Out, Das Magazine, Nieuwe Revu, Die Woche, 1988—; "Hey Rube!" columnist ESPN.com, 2000—. Conbr. U.S. pubs. including Time, New Yorker, Esquire, Vanity Fair, men's Health, GQ, Cycle World, Smart, Lexis.com; creative cons. CBS-TV series "Nash Bridges", 1996—2000; screenplay adaptation cons. Where the Buffalo Roam, 1980, Fear & Loathing in Las Vegas, 1998, The Rum Diary; song lyricist music by Warren Zevon, Paul Oakenfold, 2001; judge Nat. Book Awards, 1975. Author: Prince Jellyfish, 1960, Hell's Angels, 1966, Fear and Loathing in Las Vegas, 1972, Fear and Loathing On the Campaign Trail '72, 1973, The Great Shark Hunt, 1979, (with Ralph Steadman) The Curse of Lono, 1983, Generation of Swine, 1988, Songs of the Doomed, 1990, Screwjack, 1991, Better Than Sex, 1993, The Proud Highway, 1997, The Rum Diary, 1998, Fear and Loathing in America, 2000, Kingdom of Fear, 2002; creator Gonzo journalism. Mem. pres.'s task force; mem. nat. adv. bd. Nat. Orgn. for the Reform of Marijuana Laws, 1976—; founder 4th Amendment Found. Recipient Literary Lion award, N.Y. Pub. Libr., 1989. Mem. NRA, ACLU, Athenaeum Lit. Assn., U.S. Naval Inst., Air Force Assn., Hong Kong Fgn. Corrs., Kona Coast Marlin Fisherman's Assn., Vincent Black Shadow Soc., Woody Creek Rod and Gun Club (exec. dir.), Overseas Press Club, Nat. Press Club, Bengal Snow Leopard Breeders, Castlewood A.C. Club, Key West Mako Club.

THOMPSON, J. ANDY, bank executive; b. Ft. Worth, Sept. 21, 1943; s. Fredrick Dickson and Mary Alice (Rhea) T.; m. Nancy Sealy, Jan. 15, 1966; children: J. Andrew Jr., Christopher Sealy. BBA, U. Tex., 1965. Exec. v.p. Internat. Svc. Ins. Co., Ft. Worth, 1968-83, Ctrl. Bancorp. Inc., Ft. Worth, 1984-86, pres., 1986-88, chmn., chief exec. officer, 1988-97, Cen. Bank & Trust, Ft. Worth, 1988-97, North Ft. Worth Bank, 1988-92. Adv. bd. Policy Mgmt. Systems, Columbia, S.C., 1975-83; bd. dirs. Ft. Worth C. of C., 1989-91; chmn., trustee Tex. Health Resources. Mem. adminstrv. bd. First Meth. Ch.; trustee, chmn. Harris Meth. Hosp., Ft. Worth; chmn., trustee Harris Meth. Health System; bd. dirs. Lena Pope Home for Children, James L. West Presbyn. Spl. Care Ctr., Fortworth Mus. Sci. & History. Capt. U.S. Army, 1966-68, Vietnam. Mem. Tex. Banker's Assn., Am. Banker's Assn., Ft. Worth Club (pres. 1993-96, mem. bd. govs.), Rotary Internat. Republican. Methodist. Avocations: tennis, sailing, golf.

THOMPSON, JACK EDWARD, mining company executive; b. Central City, Nebr., Nov. 17, 1924; s. Ray Elbert and Bessie Fay (Davis) T.; m. Maria del Carmen Larrea, May 8, 1948; children: Jack Edward, Ray Anthony, Robert Davis. Student, Northwestern U., 1942-43, Colo. Sch. Mines, 1943-45, D of Engring. (hon.), 1993. V.p. Cía. Química Comercial de Cuba S.A., 1946-60, Cía. de Fomento Químico S.A., 1946-60; with Newmont Mining Corp., N.Y.C., 1960-86, asst. to pres., 1964-67, v.p., 1967-71, dir., 1969-86, exec. v.p., 1971-74, pres., 1974-85, vice chmn., 1985-86, cons., 1986-90. Chmn. bd. trustees Minerals Industry Ednl. Found. Recipient Distinguished Achievement medal Colo. Sch. Mines, 1974 Mem. AIME, Mining and Metall. Soc. Am., Mining Found. of S.W. (past pres., bd. govs.), Tucson Country Club. E-mail: rayonera@aol.com.

THOMPSON, JAMES CHARLES, surgeon; b. San Antonio, Aug. 16, 1928; s. Oscar Augustus and Vera Marie (Powell) T.; children: Patricia A. Thompson Frnka, Jan L. Thompson Brown, Gayle A. Thompson Crocker, James Charles, John W.; 1 stepchild, Laura V. Fargas. BS, A&M Coll. Tex., 1948; MD, U. Tex. Med. Br., Galveston, 1951, MA in Anatomy and Endocrinology, 1952. Diplomate Am. Bd. Surgery (examiner 1978—). Intern U. Tex. Med. Br. Hosps., Galveston, 1951-52, chief of surgery, 1970-95, prof., chmn. dept. surgery, 1970-87, prof. physiology and biophysics, 1975—, John Woods Harris prof., chmn., 1987-95, Ashbel Smith prof. surgery, 1995—; resident in surgery U. Pa. Hosp., Phila., 1952-54, 56-59; assoc. in surgery Sch. Medicine U. Pa., 1959-61, asst. prof. surgery Sch. Medicine, 1961-63; surgeon Pa. Hosp., 1959-63, Harbor Gen. Hosp., Torrance, Calif., 1963-67, chief of surgery, 1967-70; assoc. prof. UCLA, 1963-67, prof., 1967-70. U.S.-USSR health exchange prof., 1973; vis. prof. China Acad. Medicine, 1980, 82, 86, 90; cons. FDA, 1983-86; hon. prof. for life U. Beijing, 1991; elected mem., Inst. Medicine, 2000. Author: Atlas of Surgery and the Stomach, Duodenum and Small Bowel, 1991; also numerous articles on gastrointestinal physiology and clin. surgery in profl. jours.; editor: Gastrointestinal Hormones, 1975; sr. editor: Gastrointestinal Endocrinology, 1987, Gastrointestinal Hormones: Receptors and Post-Receptor Mechanism, 1990. Served with M.C. U.S. Army, 1954-56. Recipient Career Devel. award NIH, 1961-62, Merit award, 1986; Outstanding Clin. Prof. award U. Tex. Med. Br., 1973, Herman Barnett award, 1975, Ashbel Smith Disting. Alumnus award, 1979; NIH grantee, 1960—, program-project grantee, 1985—. John A. Hartford Found. grantee, 1963-73, 77-81. Fellow ACS (chmn. surg. forum com. 1977-78, bd. govs. 1985-91, exec. com. of program com. 1985-94, scholarship com. 1988-94, chmn. com. on rsch. and edn. 1989-94); mem. AAAS, Am. Assn. Surgery of Trauma, Am. Fedn. Clin. Rsch., Am. Gastroenterol. Assn., Am. Physiol. Soc., Am. Surg. Assn. (treas. 1985-90, pres. 1991-92), Endocrine Soc., Pacific Coast Surg. Assn., Soc. for Surgery Alimentary Tract (pres. 1982-83, Founder's medal 1990), Soc. Univ. Surgeons (chmn. com. on edn., mem. exec. coun. 1967-71), So. Surg. Assn. (pres. 1995), Tex. Surg. Soc. (pres. 1993), Surg. Biology Club, Soc. Surg. Chmn. (pres. 1993-94), Transplantation Soc., Cosmos Club, Alpha Omega Alpha. Office: U Tex Med Br Dept Surgery Galveston TX 77555-0001*

THOMPSON, JAMES FRANK, music educator; b. Alhambra, Calif., Dec. 27, 1949; s. William Laun and Mayemma Thompson; m. Linda Christine Wilson, Sept. 6, 1969; children: Adrienne, Christopher. BA, Calif. State U., Los Angeles, CA, 1969—73. Music educator Bonita Unified Sch. Dist., San Dimas, Calif., 1973—86, Monrovia Unified Sch. Dist., Monrovia, 1986—94, Whittier Union H.S., Whittier, 1994—96, Rowland Unified Sch. Dist., Roland Heights, 1996—97, Tustin Unified Sch. Dist., Tustin, 1997—. Adjudicator So. Calif. Sch. Band & Orch. Assn., Anaheim, Calif., 1974—2002; mem. Bellflower Symphony Orch., Bellflower, Calif., 1993—2002. City commr. City of Duarte, Duarte, Calif., 1986—96. Grantee Grant, Tustin Pub. Schools Found., 2000. Mem.: NEA, Internat. Assn. Jazz Edn. Avocations: aviation, music. Office: Hewes Middle School 13232 Hewes Avenue Santa Ana CA 92705 E-mail: jim91010@yahoo.com.

THOMPSON, JAMES HOWARD, historian, library administrator; b. Memphis, Aug. 20, 1934; s. Curtis Barnabas and Clara (Terry) T.; m. Margareta Ortenblad, Nov. 24, 1961; children— Ralph, Anna, Howard. BA in History, Rhodes Coll., Memphis, 1955; MA, U. N.C., Chapel Hill, 1957, PhD in History, 1961; MS in LS, U. Ill., 1963. Teaching fellow U. N.C., Chapel Hill, 1955-56, departmental asst., 1956-57, reference asst., 1959-61, dir. undergrad. library, lectr. in history, 1968-70; circulation asst. U. Ill., 1961-63; asst. Center for Russian Area and Lang. Studies, 1962-63; cataloger Duke U., 1963-65; asst. prof. history U. S.W. La., 1965-66; asst. prof. U. Colo., 1966-68; dir. libraries, prof. history U. N.C., Greensboro, 1970-94; ret., 1994. Bd. dirs. Southeastern Library Network, 1979-82, treas., 1981-82 Contbr. articles, revs. to profl. jours. Ford Found. research fellow, 1957-58; U. Colo. grantee, 1967; U. N.C. at Greensboro grantee, 1977-78, 89. Mem. Phi Beta Kappa (chpt. pres. 1979-80), Beta Phi Mu, Phi Alpha Theta, Chi Beta Phi. Episcopalian. Home: 4020 Crown Hill Dr Durham NC 27707-5393

THOMPSON, JAMES MARTIN, minister, protective services official; b. LaGrange, Ga., Aug. 13, 1943; s. James D. Thompson and Zora B. Hyatt Wheelus; m. Janet L. Thompson, Aug. 8, 1988; children: James M. Jr., Charles J., Barbaretta P.; stepchildren: Michelle Edwards, Kim Turner. AA in Edn., Clayton State Coll., 1972; AA in Bible, Immanuel Bible Coll., 1987; BMin, MMin, Bethany Bible Coll., 1990; D of Ministry, Bethany Theol. Sem., 1991, PhD in Religion, 1993. Ordained to ministry Bapt. Ch., 1960. Pastor numerous chs. including Antioch Bapt. Ch., Woodbury, Ga., 1961—; police officer Clayton County Police Dept., Jonesboro, 1970—. Maj., comdr. Clayton County Drug Enforcement Task Force. Named Outstanding Law Enforcement Officer Clayton County Jaycees, 1976. Mem. Ga. Assn. Police Cmty. Rels. Officers (pres. 1974). Home: 6042 Katherine Rd Rex GA 30273-1122 *Man's ability is not the major thing God looks for in our service; it is our availability to God that is a deciding factor in our success or failure rate.*

THOMPSON, JAMES ROBERT, JR. lawyer, former governor; b. Chgo., May 8, 1936; s. James Robert and Agnes Josephine (Swanson) T.; m. Jayne Carr, 1976; 1 child, Samantha Jayne. Student, U. Ill., Chgo., 1953-55, Washington U., St. Louis, 1955-56; JD, Northwestern U., 1959. Bar: Ill. 1959, U.S. Supreme Ct. 1964. Asst. state's atty., Cook County, Ill., 1959-64; assoc. prof. law Northwestern U. Law Sch., 1964-69; asst. atty. gen. State of Ill., 1969-70; chief criminal div., 1969; chief dept. law enforcement and pub. protection, 1969-70; 1st asst. U.S. atty. No. Dist. Ill., 1970-71, U.S. atty., 1971-75; counsel firm Winston & Strawn, Chgo., 1975-77, ptnr., chmn. exec. com., 1991—; gov. Ill., 1977-91. Chmn. Pres.' Intelligence Oversight Bd., 1989—93; adv. bd. Fed. Emergency Mgmt. Agy., 1991—93; bd. govs. Chgo. Bd. Trade; bd. dirs. FMC Corp., FMC Techs., Inc., Prime Retail Inc., Hollinger Internat., Inc., Prime Group Realty Trust, Navigant Consulting Inc., Maximus, Inc., Chgo. Mus. Contemporary Art, Lyric Opera Chgo., Econ. Club Chgo., Civic Com., Comml. Club Chgo., Execs. Club Chgo. Co-author: Cases and Comments on Criminal Justice, 2 vols, 1968, 74; Criminal Law and Its Adminstration, 1970, 74. Chmn. Ill. Math. and Sci. Acad. Found.; chmn. Rep. Gov's. Assn., 1982, Nat. Gov.'s Assn., Midwest Gov.'s Assn., Coun. Gt. Lakes Gov's., 1985. Mem. ABA, Ill. Bar Assn., Chgo. Bar Assn. Republican. Office: Winston & Strawn 35 W Wacker Dr Ste 4200 Chicago IL 60601-1695

THOMPSON, JAMES W., JR. state official; b. Sidney, Ohio, Feb. 7, 1948; s. James and Margret Louise (Mote) T.; m. Virginia Ann Wilcoxen, June 11, 1976; 1 child, James W. AAS, Lima (Ohio) Tech. Coll., 1978; student, Wittenberg U., Springfield, Ohio, 1973; grad., FBI Nat. Acad., 1981. Dep. sheriff Shelby County Sheriff's Dept., Sidney, Ohio, 1972-75, chief dep., 1976-83; chief of police Botkins (Ohio) Police Dept., 1975-76; chief criminal investigations Ohio Dept. Agr., Columbus, 1983-88; chief investigations Ohio Vet. Med. Bd., 1988—. Disaster svcs. coordinator Ohio Dept. Agr., 1983-88. Charter, mem., v.p., founder Ohio Coun. on Welfare Fraud, Columbus, 1988-89; pres. Botkins Village Coun., 1989, 94, 95; councilman, 1986-90, 92-96; pres. Botkins Pub. Libr., 1989-93; mem. Shelby County Regional

Planning Commn., 1988-93; bd. dirs. Shelby County Red Cross. With USN, 1968-72. Recipient Combat Action ribbon USN, 1969, Legion of Valor award, Buckeye State Sheriff's Assn., 1977; Disting. Pub. Svc. Hon., Am. Police Officers Hall of Fame, 1980. Mem. Am. Soc. Indsl. Security, FBI Assn., Masons. Democrat. Avocations: reading, photography, bird watching, antiques, book plate collecting. Home: PO Box 474 Botkins OH 45306-0474 Office: Ohio Veterinary Med Bd 77 S High St Columbus OH 43215-6108

THOMPSON, JAYNE CARR, public relations and communications executive, lawyer; b. Oak Park, Ill., Apr. 7, 1946; d. Robert Edward and Laurette (Rentner) Carr; m. James R. Thompson, June 19, 1976; 1 child, Samantha Jayne. BA, U. Ill., Chgo., 1967; JD, Northwestern U., 1970; hon. degree, Lincoln (Ill.) Coll., 1991, St. Xavier Coll., Chgo., 1991. Assoc. in litigation McDermott, Will & Emery, Chgo., 1970; asst. atty. gen. State of Ill., 1970-77, chief of criminal appeals divsn., 1972-77, dep. chief prosecution assistance bur., 1975-76, dep. chief criminal divsn., 1976-77, acting chief criminal divsn., 1977; of counsel Brown, Hay & Stephens, Springfield, 1977-78, Silets & Martin, Chgo., 1983-84; house counsel and v.p. devel. Nat. Coll. Edn., Evanston, 1984-85; atty. Lydon & Griffin, Chgo., 1989-91; prin. Dilenschneider Group Inc., 1999-2000, mng. prin., 2000—02; CEO, pres. Jayne Thompson and Assocs. Ltd., 2002—. Contbr. chpt. to book, articles to profl. jours. First Lady of Ill., Springfield, 1977-91; mem. Ill. Commn. on Status of Women, Chgo., 1997-2001; pres. bd. dirs. Chgo. Pub. Libr., 1998—; mem. women's bd. Northwestern U., 1978—; bd. dirs. Chgo. Pub. Libr. Found., 1998—; mem. adv. bd. for Ill. Treas. for Women's Issues, 2002—; mem. chmn.'s adv. coun. Lincoln Pk. Zoo, 2002—; mem. Met. Planning Coun., 2002--. Mem. Ill. State Bar Assn., Execs. Club (Chgo.), Coun. on Fgn. Rels. (Chgo. com.), Econ. Club (Chgo.). Avocations: reading, cooking, tennis. Office: Jayne Thompson & Assocs Ltd 33 N Dearborn St Ste 2200 Chicago IL 60602 E-mail: jthompson@jaynethompson.com.

THOMPSON, JEAN ALLING, librarian; b. Montclair, N.J., Aug. 19, 1950; d. Richard Adams and Ann Chase (Alling) T. BA in English, Juniata Col., 1972; MLS, Rutgers U., 1974. Cataloger, reference librarian West Caldwell (N.J.) Pub. Library, 1974; cataloger, head of acquisitions Tampa-Hillsborough (Fla.) County Pub. Library, 1974-80; librarian Tampa Col., 1980-81; monographic cataloger Fla. Internat. U., Miami, 1981-87; asst. dir. Falmouth (Maine) Meml. Library, 1992-93; monographic cataloger U. Albany, N.Y., 1994-99; coord. tech. svcs., cataloging libr. Owen D. Young Libr., St. Lawrence U., Canton, 1999—. Head Tampa (Fla.) Support Com. of United Farm Workers, 1976-78. Mem.: ALA, N.Am. Serials Interest Group, New Eng. Libr. Assn. Democrat. Jewish. Avocations: hiking, canoeing, folk music, story telling. Home: PO Box 107 Canton NY 13617-0107 Office: St Lawrence U Owen D Young Libr Canton NY 13617 E-mail: jthompson@stlawu.edu.

THOMPSON, JEAN TANNER, retired librarian; b. San Luis Obispo, Calif., June 15, 1929; d. Chester Corey and Mildred (Orr) T.; 1 child, Anne Marie Miller Student, Whitworth Coll., Spokane, Wash., 1946-49; AB, Boston U., 1951; postgrad., U. Wis., Eau Claire, 1964-67; MSL.S., Columbia U., 1973; Ed.M., U. Va., Charlottesville, 1978. Asst. social sci. librarian Univ. Libraries Va. Polytechnic Inst. and State U., Blacksburg, 1973-77, head social sci. dept. Univ. Libraries, 1977-83; head reference dept. Meml. Library U. Wis., Madison, 1983-86, asst. dir. reference and info. svcs., 1986-91, ret. Contbg. editor: ALA Guide to Information Access, 1994; mem. editorial bd. RQ, 1984-89. Mem. ALA, Assn. Coll. and Research Libraries (edn. and behavioral sci. sect. vice chmn. 1985-86, chmn. 1986-87), Wis. Library Assn., Wis. Assn. of Acad. Librarians. Presbyterian. Home: 4929 High Grove Rd Tallahassee FL 32309-2957

THOMPSON, JEANNINE LUCILLE, community health nurse; b. Forest City, Iowa, Oct. 1, 1954; d. Kenneth Hanson and Janice (Gelner) Whitehurst; children: Jill Morehead, Patricia Bitker. ADN, North Iowa Area Community Coll., Mason City, 1975; BSN, Upper Iowa U., 1983; cert. in enterostomal therapy, Abbott N.W. Hosp., 1989. Cert. enterostomal therapy nurse; cert. BLS, breast self-exam. instr. RN St. Joseph Mercy Hosp., Mason City, 1975-83; RN open heart surg. ICU St. Mary's Hosp., Rochester, Minn., 1983-84; night supr., health educator North Iowa Med. Ctr., Mason City, 1984-88; enterostomal therapy nurse Mercy Homecare, 1988—2001, Vis. Nurses Assn., Dallas, 2001—. Vol. Am. Heart Assn., Am. Cancer Soc. Mem. Wound, Ostomy and Incontinence Soc. Nurses (nat. profl. practice com., regional nomination and pub. rels. chairperson, IA govt. affairs chairperson, Nursing in Washington Internship grad., offsite Enterostomal Therapy Nurse Edn. Programs clin. instr., Iowa affiliate pres.-elect), United Ostomy Assn. (advisor). Office: 5213 Sandstone Ln Mc Kinney TX 75070

THOMPSON, JEFFREY CHARLES, lawyer; b. Mpls., June 30, 1966; s. Charles David and Sharon Alice (Hanson) T.; m. Keri Lee Plant, Aug. 10, 1991; children: Drake Jeffrey, Payton Lee, Kazlin Grace. BS in Acctg., Northwestern Coll., 1988; JD, William Mitchell Coll., 1992. Bar: Minn. 1992, Wis. 1992, U.S. Dist. Ct. Minn. 1995. Law clk. to Hon. Judge George O. Petersen Ramsey County Dist. Ct., St. Paul, 1989-92; asst. city atty. criminal divsn. City of St. Paul, 1992-93, asst. city atty. civil divsn., 1993-95; assoc. Vest & Howse, PA, Brooklyn Center, Minn., 1995—. Vice-chmn. Oak Park Cmty. Ch., Blaine, Minn., 1995-97. Republican. Mem. Christian Missionary Alliance. Avocation: golf. Office: Vest & Howse PA 6300 Shingle Creek Pkwy Ste 360 Brooklyn Center MN 55430-2191

THOMPSON, JEREMIAH BEISEKER, international medical business executive, sinologist; b. Harvey, N.D., July 20, 1927; s. Linden Brown and Ferne Althea (Beiseker) T.; m. Paula Maria Ketchum, Feb. 5, 1960; children: Cole, Per, Gover, Susannah. BS, U. Minn., 1949, MD, 1966. Rsch. assoc. U. Colo. Med. Sch., Denver, 1955-56, U. Calif. Med. Sch., San Francisco, 1956-57, Stanford U., 1957-59; applications rsch. scientist Beckman/Spinco Co., Palo Alto, Calif., 1959-61; mgr. Asia and Africa Hewlett Packard Co., 1966-72; med. cons. Alyeska Co., Anchorage, 1973-76; mgr. Asia, Africa, Australasia Corometrics Med. Systems, Wallingford, Conn., 1976-82; dir. internat. ops. Oximetrix (Abbott), Mountain View, Calif., 1982-84, Novametrix Med. Systems, Wallingford, 1984-88; ptnr. TMC Internat., Tokyo and Concord, Calif., 1988—. Advisor, cons. Yokogawa-Hewlett Packard, Tokyo, 1966—70; cons. Kupat Holim, Tel Aviv, 1967—92, Itochu, Tokyo, 1984—2002, Nat. Heart-Lung Inst., Beijing, 1984—2002. Project dir. Comparative Study of Western and Japanese Medicine in Taisho and Showa Eras, 1991—. With USN, 1945-46; PTO. Officer Legion of Honor, France, 1998. Founding fellow Brit. Interplanetary Soc.; assoc. Japan Found., Assn. Asian Studies; mem. Kokusai Bunka Kaikan, Tokyo, World Affairs Coun., Mechanics Inst. Achievements include cancer research, joint Japan/U.S. project screening and evaluation for anti-cancer activity of halogenated methane derivatives, augmentation of irradiation effects by chemotherapy. Home and Office: TMC Internat 3718 Barrington Dr Concord CA 94518-1614

THOMPSON, JESSE ELDON, vascular surgeon; b. Laredo, Tex., Apr. 7, 1919; s. Jesse Eathel and Sara Gail (Bolton) T.; m. Madeleine Jane Curtis, Sept. 18, 1944; children: Sally C., Jesse E., Janet E., Diane B. BA, U. Tex., 1939; MD, Harvard U., 1943; Rhodes scholar, Oxford U., 1949-50. Intern Mass. Gen. Hosp., Boston, 1943, resident in surgery, 1944-48; practice medicine specializing in surgery, tchr. surgery Boston U., 1949-54; practice medicine specializing in surgery, tchr. vascular surgery Baylor Hosp., Dallas, 1954—, chief vascular surgery, 1980-86. Clin. prof. surgery U. Tex. Southwestern Med. Sch., Dallas; attending surgeon Baylor Hosp., 1954-92, hon. surgeon, 1992—, chief surgery Baylor Hosp., Dallas, 1982-86; Mem Ark. and Dist. Rhodes Scholar Selection Coms. Author: Surgery for Cerebrovascular Insufficiency, 1968; mem. editl. bd. Surgery, 1975-89, Jour. Cardiovasc. Surgery, 1975—; sr. editor Jour. Vascular Surgery, 1984-86; contbr. over 200 articles to profl. jours. Served to capt. M.C. AUS, 1945-47. Fulbright sr. fellow, 1949-50 Fellow ACS (treas., pres. N. Tex. chpt. 1961); mem. Am. Surg. Assn., So. Surg. Assn., Tex. Surg. Soc. (pres. 1972), Soc. Vascular Surgery (pres. 1977), Internat. Cardiovascular Soc. (pres. N.Am. chpt. 1973), Internat. Soc. Surgery, So. Assn. for Vascular Surgery (pres. 1986-87), Dallas Country Club, Dallas Petroleum Club. Methodist. Home: 3705 Stanford Ave Dallas TX 75225-7204

THOMPSON, JOEL ERIK, lawyer; b. Summit, N.J., Sept. 15, 1940; s. Maurice Eugene and Charlotte Ruth (Harrington) T.; m. Bonnie Gay Ransa, June 15, 1963 (div. Dec. 1980); m. Deborah Ann Korp, Dec. 24, 1980 (div. Jan. 1987); m. Shandae Emlaw, Apr. 21, 2002; children: Janice Santiesteban, Amber; m. Shandae EmLaw, Apr. 21, 2002. Student, Va. Poly. Inst., 1958, Carnegie Inst. Tech., 1960-61; BSME cum laude, Newark Coll. Engring., 1966; JD, Seton Hall, 1970. Bar: N.J. 1970, Ariz. 1975, U.S. Tax Ct. 1972, U.S. Ct. Claims 1972, U.S. Customs Ct., 1972, U.S. Ct. Mil. Appeals, 1972, U.S. Customs and Patent Appeals 1972, U.S. Dist. Ct. N.J. 1970, Ariz. 1975, U.S. Ct. Appeals (9th cir.) 1975, U.S. Supreme Ct. 1975; cert. specialist criminal law Ariz. Bd. Legal Specialization; lic. profl. engr., N.J. Sr. technician Bell Tel. Labs., Inc., Murray Hill, N.J., 1965-67, patent agent, 1967-70, staff atty., 1970-73; sr. trial atty. N.J. Pub. Defender's Office, Elizabeth, N.J., 1973-74; assoc. Cahill, Sutton and Thomas, Phoenix, 1974-76; trial lawyer Maricopa County Pub. Defender's Office, 1976-80; trial lawyer, criminal law specialist Henry J. Florence, Ltd., 1980-86; pvt. practice, 1987—. Judge Superior Ct. Ariz., Phoenix, 1987-95; instr. Phoenix Regional Police Acad., 1976-80, Glendale C.C., 1977, Ariz. State U. Sch. of Law, 1978, Am. Inst., 1990; pres., CEO Eagle Master Corp., Phoenix, 1995—; pres. Joel Erik Thompson, Ltd., Phoenix, 1987—; bd. dirs. Am. Loans, Inc., San Diego, 1999-; presenter in field. Contbr. articles to profl. jours. Mem. planning com. Camelback East Village, Phoenix, 1992-98, chmn., 1993-96; mayor's select com., Phoenix, 1997, blue ribbon com. Maricopa Assn. Govs., 1996-97. Mem. Ariz. Bar Assn., Nat. Assn. Criminal Def. Lawyers, Ariz. Attys. Criminal Justice (charter), Ariz. Assn. Pvt. Investigators (hon.), Internat. Assn. Identification (hon.), Tau Beta Pi, Pi Tau Sigma. Office: 3104 E Camelback Rd # 521 Phoenix AZ 85016-4502 E-mail: joel.thompson@azbar.org.

THOMPSON, JOHN A. retired literature educator, writer; b. Grand Rapids, Mich., June 14, 1918; s. John Anderson and Grace George Thompson; m. Helen Louise Keeler, June 1943 (div. 1962); children: Louise Steketee, Keeler George, Peter Spaulding(dec.) ; m. Susan Otis Thompson, Dec. 29, 1962. BA magna cum laude, Kenyon Coll., 1940; MA, Columbia U., 1947, PhD, 1957. Instr. English Bard Coll., NY, 1946—47, Sarah Lawrence Coll., 1947—48, Columbia U., N.Y.C., 1949—56; exec. dir. Fairfield Found., 1956—65; prof. English SUNY, Stony Brook, 1965—83, prof. English emeritus, 1983—. Chmn. African Lit. panel L.I. U., NY, 1966; judge for essays The First Am. Anthology, 1968. Author: The Founding of English Meter, 1961, The Talking Girl and Other Poems, 1968; contbr. novels, reviews, essays, poems and stories to publs. Recipient faculty rsch. fellow, Rsch. Found. SUNY, 1967. Home: 418 Central Park West #71 New York NY 10025

THOMPSON, JOHN ALBERT, JR. dermatologist; b. Austin, Tex., June 5, 1942; s. J. Albert Sr. and Elizabeth (Brady) T. BA, Georgetown U., 1963; MD, Bowman Gray Sch. Medicine, 1967; Dermatology Fellowship, U. N.C., 1971-73. Diplomate Am. Bd. Dermatology. Resident in internal medicine N.C. Baptist Hosp., Winston-Salem, N.C., 1967-69; resident in dermatology N.C. Meml. Hosp., Chapel Hill, 1971-73; pvt. practice Charlotte, 1974—; clin. prof. dermatology Dept. Dermatology, U. N.C. Sch. Medicine, Chapel Hill, 1974—. Author profl. papers. Lt. comdr. USNR, 1969-71, Vietnam. Mem. Am. Acad. Dermatology (chmn. subcom. for sch. health edn. 1976-79, task force--nat. health ins.), Carolinas-Va. Dermatology Assn. (adv. bd. council rep. 1976-79), Charlotte Dermatology Assn., Mecklenburg County Med. Soc., N.C. Med. Soc., North Am. Clin. Dermatology Soc. Southern Med. Assn., Southeastern Consortium for Continuing Dermatol. Edn. (steering com. 1983—), South Cen. Dermatol. Congress (organizing com. 1982-86), Am. Soc. Dermatol. Surgery, Am. Dermatol. Soc. Allergy and Immunology, Am. Soc. Laser Medicine and Surgery, Inc. Democrat. Episcopalian. Home: 2633 Richardson Dr Apt 8A Charlotte NC 28211-3346 Office: Dermatol Laser Ctr Dermatologic Laser Ctr 2310 Randolph Rd Charlotte NC 28207-1526

THOMPSON, JOHN DOUGLAS, financier; b. Montreal, Que., Can., Sept. 28, 1934; s. William Douglas and Anne F. (Whebby) T.; children: Jacqueline, Catherine, Peter, Anne Marie, Francois. BEng, McGill U., 1957; MBA, U. Western Ont., 1960. Dep. chmn. bd. Montreal Trustco Inc. Past chmn. bd. dirs. Trust Cos. Assn. of Can., bd. dirs. Domtar Inc., Air Transat, Capital d'Amérique CDPQ Inc., Benvest Capital Inc., Shermag Inc., Nat. Trust Co., Scotia Mortgage Corp., Scotia Life Ins. Co., Scotia Gen. Ins. Co., The Bank of Nova Scotia Trust Co., The Mortgage Ins. Co. of Can, Victoria and Grey Corp. Bd. dirs. MacDonald Stewart Found., Windsor Found., Salvation Army, chmn. Montreal adv. bd.; chmn. Montreal YMCA Found.; mem. audit com. McGill U.; past pres. St. Mary's Hosp. Found.; gov., past pres. St. Mary's Hosp. Ctr. Mem. Assn. Profl. Engrs., Que. and Ont., Mt. Royal Club (Montreal), Royal Montreal Golf Club, Mt. Bruno Country Club Inc., The Forest and Stream Club. Roman Catholic. Office: Montreal Trust 4th Fl 1800 McGill College Ave 4th Fl Montreal QC Canada H3A 3K9

THOMPSON, JOHN HERD, history educator; b. Winnipeg, Man., Can., Sept. 18, 1946; came to U.S. 1989; s. Joseph Whyte and Gladys Kate (Campain) T.; m. Katrin Ann Partelpoeg, Jan. 15, 1977 (div. Sept. 2001); children: Anne Marie, Mark Thomas. BA with honors, U. Winnipeg, 1968; MA, U. Man., 1969; PhD, Queens U., Kingston, Ont., 1975. Faculty Duke U., Durham, N.C., 1989—, chair dept. history, 2000—. Author: Harvests of War, 1978, Decades of Discord: Canada 1922-1939, 1985, Canada and the United States: Ambivalent Allies, 1994, 2d edit., 1997, 3d edit., 2001, Forging the Prairie West, 1998. Mem. Am. Hist. Assn., Can. Hist. Assn., Soc. for Am. Baseball Rsch., Assn. for Can. Studies in the U.S. Avocation: baseball. Home: Duke Univ Dept History Durham NC 27708

THOMPSON, JOHN M. information technology executive; Degree in engring. sci., U. Western Onto.; grad. exec. mgmt. program, U. Western Ont., Northwestern U. Sys. engr. IBM Can., Ltd., Canada, 1966, various mgmt. positions, pres., CEO, 1986; corp. v.p. mktg. and svcs. IBM, White Plains, NY, 1991—93, sr. v.p. server group, 1993—95, sr. v.p., group exec. software group, 1995—2000, vice chmn. bd. dirs., 2000—. Bd. dirs. Toronto-Dominion Bank. Office: IBM 1133 Westchester Ave White Plains NY 10604*

THOMPSON, JOHN W. information technology executive; BBA, Fla. A&M U.; M in Mgmt. Sci., MIT's Sloan School of Mngmt. Various sr. exec. pos. in sales and software devel. IBM; gen. mgr. IBM Ams.; chmn., pres., CEO The Antivirus Guardian Co., Symantec Corp., Cupertino, Calif., 1999—. Bd. dirs. UPS, NiSource, Inc., Seagate, Crystal Decisions. Chmn. Fla. A&M U. Cluster; Ill. Gov's human resource adv. coun.*

THOMPSON, JONATHAN SIMS, army officer; b. Ft. Benning, Ga., Nov. 19, 1947; s. Donald Frederick and Gene Elizabeth (Pierce) T.; m. Dinetha Lynn Richards, Aug. 26, 1979; children: Tracy A., Terry A., Jonathan S. II, Tiffany A. BSME, Tex. A&M U., 1970, M Indsl. Engring., 1978; M Bus. Mgmt., Ctrl. Mich. U., 1980; diploma in program mgmt., Def. Sys. Mgmt. Coll., 1987. Registered profl. engr., Tex. Commd. 2d. lt. U.S Army, 1971, advanced through grades to col., engr. platoon leader 27th Engr. Battalion N.C., 1971-72, staff engr. 5th Spl. Forces Group, 1973-74, engr. instr. Spl. Forces Sch., 1974-75, co. comdr. 2d Engr. Battalion Camp Castle, Korea, 1976-77, project dir. Engr. Strategic Studies Ctr. Rockville, Md., 1978-81, plans and ops. officer 317th Engr. Battalion Eschborn, Germany, 1982-84, engr. staff officer Office of Chief of Staff Washington, 1985-87, ops. rsch. analyst Office of Sec. of Army, 1987-88, battalion comdr. 2d Engr. Battalion Camp Castle, 1989-90, dep. chief of staff Corps. of Engrs. Washington, 1991-92, exec. dir. Office of Chief of Engrs., 1992-93, fellow Ctr. Stratetic/Internat. Studies U.S. Army War Coll., 1993-94, brigade comdr. 20th Engr. Brigade Ft. Bragg, N.C., 1994-96; sr. fellow U.S. Dept. State, 1996-97; chief of staff U.S. Army Criminal Investigations Command, 1997-99; CEO, chmn. Attventure Ltd., 1999—. Editor: Peacetime Defensive Preparations in Europe, 1981 (deMarche award 1985); author govt. study, article in field. Adult leader, asst. scoutmaster Boy Scouts Am., Dale City, Va., 1990-92, chmn. troop advancement com., Ft. Bragg, 1994-96; coun. rep. Recreation Ctr. Bd., Dale City, 1985-89. Decorated Legion of Merit with 2 oak leaf clusters, DSM; fellow, Govt. Affairs Coun. for Excellence in Govt., 1991—92. Fellow Soc. Am. Mil. Engrs. (nat. bd. dirs. 1990-92, post pres. 1994—); mem. NSPE, Army Navy Club, Shriners (life mem., Noble), Masons (Companion, Sir Knight). Presbyterian. Achievements include leading the world's largest military engineering task force into Haiti during Operation Uphold Democracy to restore the government and rebuild the infrastructure; principal deputy to engineer commander of 24th infantry "Hail Mary" task force during Operation Desert Storm and the liberation of Kuwait. Avocations: skiing, golf, parachuting. Home: 9796 Thorn Bush Dr Fairfax Station VA 22039-2538 E-mail: jack@attventure.com.

THOMPSON, JOSHUA A, music educator; b. Steubenville, Ohio, Mar. 30, 1974; s. Albert Wayne Thompson and Janice Marie Panebianco. BM in Music Edn., Youngstown State U., Youngstown, OH, 1979; MM in Music Performance, U. of Ky., Lexington, KY, 1999. Tchg. asst. U. of Ky., Lexington, Ky., 1997—99; orch. dir. Cobb County Pub. Schools, Marietta, Ga., 1999—2002, Plano Ind. Sch. Dist., Plano, Tex., 2002—. Dist. xii orch. chmn. Ga. Music Educators Assn., Manetta, Ga., 2002—; mentor tchr. Cobb Orch. Directors Assn., Marietta, Ga., 2001—. Mem.: Internat. Trumpet Guild, Am. String Teachers Assn., Am. Fedn. of Musicians. Home: 2525 Preston Road Apartment 1121 Plano TX 75093 Personal E-mail: hosway66@yahoo.com.

THOMPSON, JOYCE LURINE, retired information systems specialist; b. White Oak Twp., Mich., Mar. 5, 1931; d. Orla Jacob and Ethel Inita (Thayer) Sheathelm; m. Robert E. Thompson, Dec. 10, 1949 (div. 1972); children: Wendy, Robin, Kristen (dec.). Student, Mich. State U., 1972-78, Lansing (Mich.) Community Coll, 1976-77. Programmer, analyst Mich. State U., East Lansing, 1966-73; tech. programmer Mich. State Police, 1973-77; database coord. Mich. Dept. Treasury, Lansing, 1977-79; systems engr. 4-Phase Systems, Grand Rapids, Mich., 1979-81; mktg. rep. Motorola, 1981-84; data analyst Whirlpool Corp., Benton Harbor, Mich., 1984-88, data adminstr., 1988—; owner, propr. Thompson House, South Haven, 1994—. Activity chmn. Girl Scouts U.S.A., East Lansing; leader 4-H Clubs, East Lansing; vol. Stepping Stones South Haven, ADA Com., Lake Mich. Maritime Mus., Scott Club South Haven, 2000—. Mildred Erickson fellow Mich. State U., EAst Lansing, 1974-78. Mem. Assn. Systems Mgmt. (sec. 1984), Data Adminstrn. Mgmt. Assn. Avocations: photography, music, beach combing, antiques.

THOMPSON, JUDITH KASTRUP, nursing researcher; b. Marstal, Denmark, Oct. 1, 1933; came to the U.S., 1951; d. Edward Kastrup and Anna Hansa (Knudsen) Pedersen; m. Richard Frederick Thompson, May 22, 1960; children: Kathryn Marr, Elizabeth Kastrup, Virginia St. Claire. BS, RN, U. Oreg., 1958, MSN, 1963. RN, Calif., Oreg. Staff nurse U. Oreg. Med. Sch., Eugene, 1957-58, Portland, 1958-61, head staff nurse, 1960-61; instr. psychiat. nursing U. Oreg. Sch. Nursing, 1963-64; rsch. asst. U. Oreg. Med. Sch., 1964-65, U. Calif., Irvine, 1971-72; rsch. assoc. Stanford (Calif.) U., 1982-87; rsch. asst. Harvard U., Cambridge, Mass., 1973-74; rsch. assoc. U. So. Calif., L.A., 1987—. Contbg. author: Behavioral Control and Role of Sensory Biofeedback, 1976; contbr. articles to profl. jours. Treas. LWV, Newport Beach, Calif., 1970-74; scout leader Girl Scouts Am., Newport Beach, 1970-78. Named Citizen of Yr. State of Oreg., 1966. Mem. Soc. for Neurosci., Am. Psychol. Soc. (charter), ANA, Oreg. Nurses Assn. Republican. Lutheran. Avocations: art collecting, travel, tennis. Home: 28 Sky Sail Dr Corona Del Mar CA 92625-1436 Office: U So Calif University Park Los Angeles CA 90089-0001 E-mail: judith@neuro.usc.edu.

THOMPSON, KATHERINE GENEVIEVE, lawyer; b. Bklyn., May 11, 1945; d. George Otway and Marie (Burke) T. BS, Good Counsel Coll., 1966; JD, Bklyn. Law Sch., 1970; LLM, NYU, 1981. Bar: N.Y. 1971, U.S. Dist. Ct. (so. and ea. dists.) N.Y. 1978, U.S. Supreme Ct. 1981. Editor Matthew Bender Pub. Co., N.Y.C., 1970-71; atty. juvenile rights div. Legal Aid Soc., 1971-76, asst. atty. in charge juvenile rights div. N.Y. County office, 1976-77; sole practice, 1977-78; ptnr. Rothenberg, Sherman, Thompson & Halpin, 1978-84, Sherman, Thompson & Halpin, N.Y.C., 1984-87, Beldock, Levine & Hoffman, N.Y.C., 1987—. Mem. appellate div. 1st Dept. Screening Panel, 1981-82, appellate div. 1st Dept. Family Ct. Adv. Com., 1983-90, chmn., 1986-89. Co-author: Adoption Law and Practice, 1988; contbg. editor: Bender's Federal Practice Forms, 1971, Bender's Forms of Discovery, 1971. Bd. dirs. August Aichorn Resdl. Ctr., N.Y.C., 1979-94. Fellow Am. Bar Found., N.Y. State Bar Found.; mem. ABA (family law sect.) N.Y. State Bar Assn. (spl. com. on juvenile justice 1980-87, family law sect. 1980—), Assn. of Bar of City of N.Y. (family ct. and family law com. 1977-80, chmn. 1980-83, lectures and continuing edn. com. 1984-85, matrimonial law com. 1985-88), Womens Bar Assn., N.Y. County Lawyers Assn. (family ct. com. 1978-79). Office: Beldock Levine & Hoffman 99 Park Ave Fl 16 New York NY 10016-1508

THOMPSON, KATHLEEN SHAMBAUGH, family counselor; b. Bakersfield, Calif., Oct. 22, 1945; d. Stephen W. and Marilyn L. Shambaugh; m. John W. Thompson, June 10, 1967 (dec. Mar. 1971); children: Stephen, Charles. BA, U. Colo., 1971; MA, U. Denver, 1976. Lic. marriage and family counselor. Tchr., Denver, 1971—76; marriage, family and child counselor, 1982—. Editor, proofreader, 1978—80. Author: A Life Filled with Poetry, 2000, Coping with Grief and the Death of Loved Ones, 2001, An American Girl in Canada, 2001, Counseling Helps, 2002, I Care for My Cats, 2002, Professional Guides: The Case Study, Human Sexuality in Marriage, Crime and Rehabilitation, Introducing the Gap Theory, 2002, A Car Accident, Different Kinds of Pain, and Surgery 5 Years Later, 2002, A Journey Through the Triangle of Canada, Britain, and America, 2002. Named one of Best Poets of 2000, Internat. Libr. Poetry, 2001. Mem.: Internat. Soc. Poets (Internat. Poet Merit 2000), Delta Delta Delta. Presbyterian. Avocations: stamp collecting, doll collecting, art, collectibles, gardening. Home and Office: 1655 W Ajo Way # 170 Tucson AZ 85713

THOMPSON, KENNETH ROY, management educator; b. Elgin, Ill., Feb. 8, 1948; s. Glen Edward and Margaret Lydia (Johnson) T.; m. Ann Marie Wesley, June 7, 1980; children: Tracey Katherine, Wesley Graham. BS, Elmhurst Coll., 1970; MBA, No. Ill. U., 1972; PhD, U. Nebr., 1977. Instr. of mgmt. and finance Ind. State U., Terre Haute, 1972-75; instr. of mgmt. U. Nebr., Lincoln, 1976-77; asst. prof. U. Notre Dame, Ind., 1977-84, U. Ark., Fayetteville, 1984, dir. ctr. for mgmt. and exec. devel., 1985-86; chmn. dept. mgmt. DePaul U., Chgo., 1986-93, assoc. prof., 1986-98, prof., 1998—. Cons. in quality mgmt., 1977—. Author: Social Issues in Business, 6th edit., 1990, Cases in Management, 1990; contbr. articles to profl. jours. Lead sr. examiner state quality awards Lincoln Found., Chgo., 1997—, examiner, 1996; mem. planning commn. Milton Twp., 1998—, sec. planning commn., 1999—. Mem. Acad. Mgmt. (dir. publ. rels. 1989-97, chair tchg. effectiveness task force 1999—, local arrangement chair 1998-2000), Midwest Acad. Mgmt. (chair bd. dirs. 1995-96, pres. 1990-91, bd. dirs. 1992-98, 99—), Golden Key, Delta Mu Delta, Beta Gamma Sigma. Avocations: railroad travel, civil war reenactment, snow skiing, sailing. Home: 178 Fir Rd Niles MI 49120-9722 Office: DePaul U 1 E Jackson Blvd Chicago IL 60604-2287 E-mail: kthompson@wppost.depaul.edu.

THOMPSON, KENNETH W(INFRED), educational director, author, editor, administrator, social science educator; b. Des Moines, Aug. 29, 1921; s. Thor Carlyle and Agnes (Rorbeck) T.; m. Betty Bergquist (dec.); m. Beverly Bourret (dec.); children: Kenneth Caryle, Paul Andrew, James David, Carolyn Cordry. AB, Augustana Coll., 1943, LHD (hon.), LLD, Augustana Coll., 1986; MA, U. Chgo., 1948, PhD, 1950; LLD, U. Notre Dame, 1964, Bowdoin Coll., 1972, St. Michael's Coll., 1973, St. Olaf Coll., 1974, U. Denver, 1983; L.H.D., W.Va. Wesleyan U., 1970; LHD, Nebr. Wesleyan Coll., 1971. Lectr. social scis. U. Chgo., 1948, asst. prof. polit. sci., 1951-53; from asst. prof. to assoc. prof. polit. sci. Northwestern U., 1949-55, chmn. internat. relations com., 1951-55; asst. dir. social scis Rockefeller Found., 1955-57, from assoc. dir. social scis. to v.p., 1957-73; dir. higher edn. for devel. Internat. Council for Ednl. Devel., 1974-76; Commonwealth prof. govt. and fgn. affairs U. Va., 1975-78, White Burkett Miller prof. govt. and fgn. affairs, 1979-86; J. Wilson Newman prof. govt. and fgn. affairs, 1986—; dir. White Burkett Miller Ctr. Pub. Affairs, 1978-98; sr. scholar Miller Ctr., 1999—. Riverside Meml. lectr. Riverside Ch., N.Y.C., 1958; Lilly lectr. Duke, 1959; James Stokes lectr. N.Y.U., 1962; Rockwell lectr. Rice U., 1965; Ernest Griffith lectr. Am. U.; Andrew Cecil lectr. U. Tex., 1983; Stuber lectr. U. Rochester, 1984; Morgenthau Meml. lectr., N.Y.C., Mike Mansfield Ctr. lectr., U. Mont.; dir. Inst. Study World Politics, N.Y.C., 1975—; cons. in field. Author, editor: Principles and Problems of International Politics, 1951, 82, Man and Modern Society, 1953, Christian Ethics and the Dilemmas of Foreign Policy, 1959, 81, Conflict and Cooperation Among Nations, 1960, Political Realism and the Crisis of World Politics, 1960, 82, American Diplomacy and Emergent Problems, 1962, 82, Foreign Policies in a World of Change, 1964, The Moral Issue in Statecraft, 1966, Reconstituting the Human Community, 1972, Foreign Assistance: A View From Private Sector, 1972, 82, Higher Education for National Development, 1972, Understanding World Politics, 1975, Higher Edn. and Social Change, 1976, World Politics, 1976, Truth and Tragedy, 1977, Ethics and Foreign Policy, 1978, Interpreters and Critics of the Cold War, 1978, Foreign Policy and the Democratic Process, 1978, Ethics, Functionalism and Power, 1979, Morality and Foreign Policy, 1980, Masters of International Thought, 1980, The Virginia Papers, vols. 1-30, 1979-96, The President and the Public Philosophy, 1981, Cold War Theories: World Polarization, 1944-53, Vol. I, 1981,91. Winston S. Churchill's World View, 1983, 89, Toynbees's World Politics and History, 1985, Moralism and Morality, 1985, Theory and Practice of International Relations, 1987, Arms Control and Foreign Policy, 1990, Traditions and Values in Politics and Diplomacy, 1992, Fathers of International Thought, 1994, Schools of Thought in International Relations, 1996; editor: Am. Values Series, Vols. I-XX, Presdl. Nominating Process, Vols. I-IV, Portraits of American Presidents, Vols. I-VII, Herbert Butterfield: The Ethics of History; The American Presidency, Vols. I-XVI, 1982-83, Ethics and International Relations, 1985, Moral Dimensions of American Foreign Policy, 1985, 94, The Credibility of Leadership and Institutions, Vols. I-XX, 1983-86, Rhetoric and Political Discourse, Vols.I-XX, Governance, Vols. I-VII, 1990-97, Constitutionalism, Vols. I-VII, 1989-91, Presidency and Science Advising, Vols. I-VIII, 1986-90, Political Transitions and Foreign Policy, Vols. I-IX, 1985-91, A World in Change, Vols. I-XI, 1989-96, Presidential Disability, Vols. I-IV, 1989-96, A New World Order, Vols. I-VI, 1991-97, Great American Presidents, 1994, Defeated Presidential Candidates, 1994, Statesmen Who Were Never President, 1996; bd. editors Va. Quar. Rev., Society, Ethics and International Affairs, Interpretation, The Rev. of Politics; contbr. articles to profl. jours. Pres. Dist. of Scarsdale and Mamaroneck (N.Y.) Bd. Edn., 1965-68; trustee Union Theol. Sem., 1967-71, Dillard U., 1975-96, Social Sci. Found., U. Denver, 1974-94, Compton Found., 1975-98. 1st lt. AUS, 1943-46. Named Va. laureate, 1981; recipient Phi Beta Kappa and Va. Coll. Stores prizes, Va. Social Sci. Assn. ann. award, English Speaking Union award, medal U. Chgo., 1968, Spl. Edward Weintal prize Georgetown U. Acad. Diplomacy, 1999. Fellow Soc. Religion Higher Edn., Am. Acad. Arts and Scis.; mem. Century Club, Scarsdale Town Club, Raven Soc. (ann. award U. Va.), Phi Beta Kappa (pres.), Omicron Delta Phi. Office: Univ Va Miller Ctr PO Box 400406 Charlottesville VA 22904-4406

THOMPSON, LARRY ANGELO, producer, lawyer, personal manager; b. Clarksdale, Miss., Aug. 1, 1944; s. Angelo and Anne (Tuminello) T.; m. Kelly Ann LeBlanc, 1999. BBA, U. Miss., 1966, JD, 1968. Bar: Miss. 1968, Calif. 1970. In-house counsel Capitol Records, Hollywood, Calif., 1969-71; sr. ptnr. in entertainment law Thompson, Shankman and Bond, Beverly Hills, 1971-77; pres. Larry A. Thompson Orgn., Inc., 1977—. Co-owner New World Pictures, 1983-85; lectr. entertainment bus. UCLA, U. So. Calif., Southwestern U. Law Sch. Author: How to Make a Record Deal and Have Your Songs Recorded, 1975, Prime Time Crime, 1982; producer (TV) Jim Nabors Show, 1977 (Emmy nominee), Mickey Spillane's Margin for Murder, 1981, Bring 'Em Back Alive, 1982, Mickey Spillane's Murder Me, Murder You, 1982, The Other Lover, 1985, Convicted, 1986, Intimate Encounters, 1986, The Woman He Loved, 1988 (Emmy nominee, Golden Globe nominee), Original Sin, 1989, Class Cruise, 1989, Little White Lies, 1989, Lucy and Desi: Before The Laughter, 1990 (Emmy nominee), Broken Promises, 1993, Separated By Murder, 1994, Face of Evil, 1996, Replacing Dad, 1998, The Beat Goes On: The Sonny and Cher Story, 1999 (Emmy nominee), Murder in the Mirror, 2000; (motion pictures) Crimes of Passion, 1984, Fraternity Vacation, 1985, Quiet Cool, 1987, My Demon Lover, 1987, Breaking the Rules, 1992. Co-chmn. Rep. Nat. Entertainment Com.; apptd. by Gov. of Calif. to Calif. Entertainment Commn.; mem. Inauguration of Thompson Ctr. for Fine Arts in Clarksdale, 1986. Served with JAGC, U.S. Army, 1966-72. Recipient Show Bus. Atty. of Yr. award Capitol Records, 1971, Vision award, 1993; named Showman of Yr., U.S. TV Fan Assn., 1997. Mem. ABA, Miss. Bar Assn., Calif. Bar Assn., Inter-Am. Bar Assn., Hon. Order Ky. Cols., Am. Film Inst., Nat. Acad. Rec. Arts and Scis., Acad. TV Arts and Scis. Republican. Roman Catholic. Office: Larry A Thompson Org 9663 Santa Monica Blvd Ste 801 Beverly Hills CA 90210-4303 Home: 1348 Club View Dr Los Angeles CA 90024-5304

THOMPSON, LARRY DEAN, Federal Agency Administrator, Lawyer; b. Hannibal, Mo., Nov. 15, 1945; s. Ezra W. and Ruth L. (Robinson) T.; m. Brenda Anne Taggart, June 26, 1970; children: Larry Dean, Gary E. BA cum laude, Culver-Stockton Coll., Canton, Mo., 1967; MA, Mich. State U., 1969; JD, U. Mich., 1974. Bar: Mo. 1974, Ga. 1978. Indsl. rels. rep. Ford Motor Co., Birmingham, Mich., 1969-71; atty. Monsanto Co., St. Louis, 1974-77, King & Spalding, Atlanta, 1977-82; U.S. atty. U.S. Dist. Ct. (no. dist.) Ga., 1982-86; ptnr. King & Spalding, Atlanta, 1986—; dep. atty. gen. U.S. Dept Justice, Washington, 2001—. Mem. 11th Cir. Commn. on Lawyer Qualifications and Conduct; ind. counsel HUD investigation, 1995; mem. Ga. Bd. Bar Examiners. Editor: Jury Instructions in Criminal Antitrust Cases 1976-80, 1982. Chmn. Atlanta Urban League; mem. Ga. Bd. Edn., 1997; bd. dirs. Ga. Rep. Found. Recipient Outstanding Achievement award FBA, 1992. Mem. ABA, Nat. Bar Assn. Presbyterian. Office: US Dept Justice Dep Atty Gen 950 Pennsylvania Ave NW Washington DC 20530-0001*

THOMPSON, LARRY FLACK, semiconductor equipment company executive; b. Union City, Tenn., Aug. 31, 1944; s. Rufus Russell and Polly (Flack) T.; m. Joan Bondurant, Aug. 30, 1964 (dec.); children: Anthony Scott, Russell Allen. BS, Tenn. Tech. U., Cookeville, 1966; MS, Tenn. Tech. U., 1968; PhD, U. Mo., Rolla, 1970. Mem. tech. staff Bell Labs., Murray Hill, N.J., 1971-80; dept. head AT&T Bell Labs., 1981-94; v.p. product devel., chief tech. officer Integrated Solutions, Inc., Austin, Tex., 1994-97; pres. Ultrabeam Lithography, 1997—, Ultrabeam Lithography Inc. (divsn. of Ultratech Stepper), 1999—. Mem. adv. coun. dept. chem. engring. Cornell U., Princeton U.; chmn. adv. com. to divsn. of chem., biochem. and thermal engring. NSF. Author: Introduction to Microlithography, 1993; patentee in field. Recipient SEMI award for N. Am., 1997. Mem. NAE, Am. Chem. Soc. (bd. dirs. 1993-96, Indsl. Chemistry award 1993, Roy W. Tess award 1993), Am. Inst. Chem. Engring. Avocations: gardening, hunting. Home: 309 Comet St Austin TX 78734

THOMPSON, LARRY JAMES, retired gifted education educator; b. Savannah, Ga., May 14, 1948; s. James Howell and Dorothy (Hendley) T. BA, Armstrong Atlantic State U., 1970; MAT, Tulane U., 1974; EdD, U. Ga., 1986. Cert. tchr., instrnl. supr., adminstr., Ga. Tchr. social studies Chatham County Bd. Edn., Savannah, 1970-71, 75-87, adminstrv. coord. social studies, 1987-97, gifted, talented educator, 1997-2001; ret., 2001. With USNR, 1971-73. Mem. Nat. Coun. Social Studies, Ga. Coun. Social Studies, Profl. Assn. Ga. Educators, Ga. Hist. Soc., Nat. Trust for Hist. Preservation, Phi Delta Kappa. Home: 18 E Deerwood Rd Savannah GA 31410-3171

THOMPSON, LAVERNE ELIZABETH THOMAS, college official; b. Bklyn., July 17, 1945; d. Roscoe Lee and Mary Elizabeth (Blackwell) Thomas (dec.). BA in English, Bluffton Coll., 1967; MS in Ednl. Adminstrn./Supervision, U. Dayton, 1977; PhD in Higher Edn., U. Toledo, 1991. Cert. sch. prin., secondary sch. supr., realtor, Ohio. Tchr. English and speech Piqua (Ohio) Ctrl. H.S., 1967-68; instr. Lima (Ohio) Sr. H.S., 1968-77, Shawnee H.S., Lima, 1977-86; grad. asst. U. Toledo, 1986-91, interim counselor, adminstr. student support svcs., 1989, interim adminstrv. asst. multicultural student devel., 1990; dir. pre-svc. edn./urban tchr. program Wayne County C.C., Detroit, 1996—2002; dean of instrn. N.W. campus Wayne County C.C. Dist., 2002—. Real estate agt. Alberta Lee Realty, Lima, Ohio, 1978-82, Slonaker Realty, Lima, 1982-84, Gooding Co., Lima, 1985-90; substitute English tchr., Maumee (Ohio) City Schs., 1996; adj. prof., acad. coord. alternative edn. Spring Arbor Coll., Lambertville, Mich., 1995-96; reviewer Eisenhower Grants for Higher Edn., Mich. Dept. Edn., 1997, 98, 99, 2000, 01, 02; stakeholder Skillman Found. project Child Care Coord. Coun. Greater Detroit, Wayne County, 1998-2001; exec. bd. mem. Young Educators Soc. of Mich., 1999—. Editor Higher Edn. newsletter, 1987. Participant 17th ann. Nat. Conf. on Citizenship, Washington, 1962; co-chair Brotherhood Dinner Sr. H.S., Lima, 1976; bd. dirs. Lima YWCA, 1971. Mem. Va. Assn. New Homemakers Am. (state pres. 1962, nat. pres. 1963), Nat. Assn. for Edn. of Young Child, Mich. Assn. for Edn. of Young Child, All God's Children Collectors' Club, Belleek Collectors' Internat. Soc., Harmony Kingdom Collectors Club, Boyd's Bears Friends Collectors Club. Avocations: periodical reading, writing, walking. Home: 13851 Sibley Rd Riverview MI 48192-7759

THOMPSON, LAWRENCE HYDE, federal agency official; b. Hamilton, Ohio, Oct. 6, 1943; s. William Hayton and Evelyn (Covault) T.; m. Catherine Crosby, Feb. 3, 1973; children: Bradford Stephen, Sarah Catherine. BS, Iowa State U., 1964; MBA, U. Pa., 1966; PhD, U. Mich., 1971. Economist Office Sec. Health, Edn. and Welfare, Washington, 1974-77, dir. Soc. Security Planning, 1977-79; assoc. commr. Social Security Adminstrn., 1979-81, dir. rsch., 1981-83; chief economist Gen. Acctg. Office, 1983-89, asst. comptroller gen., 1989-93; prin. dep. commr. Social Security Adminstrn., 1993-95; sr. fellow The Urban Inst., Washington, 1996—. Contbr. articles to pubs., books. Mem. Am. Economic Assn., Nat. Acad. Social Ins. (dir. 1985-96, sec. 1997-99, pres. 1999—). Avocations: racquetball, choral singing. Office: The Urban Inst 2100 M St NW Ste 401 Washington DC 20037-1264

THOMPSON, LEE (MORRIS THOMPSON), lawyer; b. Hutchinson, Kans., Nov. 29, 1946; s. Morris J. and Ruth W. (Smith) T.; m. M. Susan Morgan, May 26, 1974; children: Deborah, Erin, Andrew, Christopher. BA, Wichita State U., 1968; MA, Emporia State U., 1970; JD, George Washington U., 1974. Bar: Kans., 1974, U.S. Dist. Ct. Kans., 1974, U.S. Ct. Appeals (10th cir.) 1976, U.S. Supreme Ct., 1978. Instr., lectr. Emporia (Kans.) State U., 1969-70; lctr. in speech George Washington U., Washington, 1970-71; asst. to Senator James Pearson, 1971-75; assoc. Martin, Pringle, et al., Wichita, Kans., 1976-78, ptnr., 1979-89; U.S. atty. for dist. of Kans., Dept. Justice, 1990-93; ptnr. Triplett, Woolf & Garrets, LLC, 1993—2001; mng. mem. Thompson Stout & Goering LLC, 2001—. Treas. Kansans for Kassebaum, Wichita, 1978-88; mem. Kans. State Rep. Cen. Com., Topeka, 1978-79, 88-90; candidate U.S. Ho. of Reps., Kans., 1988; chmn. civil issues subcom. Atty. Gen.'s Adv. Com. of U.S. Attys., 1992-93. Mem. Kans. Bar Assn. (pres. criminal law sect. 1994-95). Methodist. Office: Thompson Stout & Goering LLC 100 N Broadway Ste 710 Wichita KS 67202 E-mail: Lthompson@tslawfirm.com.

THOMPSON, LEONARD RUSSELL, pediatrician; b. Columbus, Ohio, Sept. 29, 1934; s. Oliver Bernard and Christina (Nichols) T.; m. Candice Elizabeth Brisken, Dec. 6, 1980; children: Ryan, Deron, Hillary, Jon, Christina, Lisa. BA, Ohio State U., 1956, MD, 1960. Diplomat Am. Bd. Pediatrics. Intern Fitzsimmons Gen. Hosp., Denver, 1960-61, resident, 1961-63; chief pediatrics Ireland Army Hosp., Ft. Knox, Ky., 1965-66; chmn. dept. pediatrics Fresno (Calif.) Med. Group, 1966-80; pediatrician pvt. practice, Fresno, 1990—; clinical prof. pediatrics UCSF, 1990—. Pres. med. staff Valley Children's Hosp., Fresno, 1992. Maj. U.S. Army, 1960-66. Fellow Am. Acad. Pediatrics. Office: 1187 E Herndon Ave # 104 Fresno CA 93720-3114 E-mail: lrthompson1@att.net.

THOMPSON, LIBBIE MOODY (MRS. CLARK THOMPSON), civic worker; b. Galveston, Tex., Nov. 22, 1897; d. William Lewis and Libbie Rice (Shearn) Moody; student Holton-Arms, Washington, 1915; m. Clark W. Thompson, Nov. 16, 1918 (dec.); children— Clark W., Libbie (Mrs. James I. Stansell) (dec.). Past dir. YWCA, ARC, Galveston; bd. dirs. Nat. Eye Found.; mem. nat. bd. Med. Coll. Pa.; mem. fine arts com. State Dept., Washington; mem. chancellor's council U. Tex.; mem. pres.'s club U. Tex. Med. Br.; founding mem. Jr. Welfare; bd. dirs. Meridian House Internat.; Mem. Plantagenet Soc., Colonial Dames Am., Daus. Republic of Tex., Am. Legion Aux., Am. Newspaper Women's Club, LWV (past dir.), Huguenot Soc., U.D.C., Soc. Sponsors USN (life), Magna Charta Dames, Smithsonian Soc. of Assocs. (life, mem. James Smithson Soc.), Order of Washington, Descs. Most Noble Order of Garter, Salvation Army Aux. Washington, Friends of Kennedy Center, Friends of Rosenberg Library, Galveston, Jr. League (hon.), Friends of LBJ Library, Fine Arts Soc. Tex (dir.), Presidents Assocs. of Med. Coll. Pa., Friends of Am. Philos. Soc., Nat. Preservation Hist. Internat. Fund Monuments, Com. Ireland (charter), Hubert H. Humphrey Leadership Fund, ARC Aux., UN Assn. U.S.A. Clubs: Women's Nat. Democratic, Sulgrave, 1925 F Street (Washington); Georgetown; Galveston Artillery. Home: 1616 Driftwood Ln Galveston TX 77551-1343 also: 3301 Massachusetts Ave NW Washington DC 20008-3610

THOMPSON, LOHREN MATTHEW, oil company executive; b. Sutherland, Nebr., Jan. 21, 1926; s. John M. and Anna (Ecklund) T.; children: Terence M., Sheila M., Clark M. Ed., U. Denver. Spl. rep. Standard Oil Co., Omaha, 1948-56; sales mgr. Frontier REF. Co., 1956-67, v.p. mktg., 1967-68; mgr. mktg. U.S. region Husky Oil Co., Denver, 1968-72; v.p. Westar Stas., Inc., 1967-70; chmn. bd. Colo. Petroleum, 1971—. Served with USAAF, 1944-46 Mem. Colo. Petroleum Council, Am. Petroleum Inst., Am. Legion Clubs: Denver Petroleum, Denver Oilman's,. Lodges: Lions. Lutheran. Home: 2410 Spruce Ave Estes Park CO 80517-7146 Office: Colo Petroleum 4080 Globeville Rd Denver CO 80216-4906

THOMPSON, LOIS JEAN HEIDKE ORE, psychologist; b. Chgo., Feb. 22, 1933; d. Harold William and Ethel Rose (Neumann) Heidke; m. Henry Thomas Ore, Aug. 28, 1954 (div. May 1972); children: Christopher, Douglas; m. Joseph Lippard Thompson, Aug. 3, 1972; children: Scott, Les, Melanie. BA, Cornell Coll., Mt. Vernon, Iowa, 1955; MA, Idaho State U., 1964, EdD, 1981. Lic. psychologist, N.Mex. Tchr. pub. schs. various locations, 1956-67; tchr., instr. Idaho State U., Pocatello, 1967-72; employee/orgn. devel. specialist Los Alamos (N.Mex.) Nat. Lab., 1981-84, tng. specialist, 1984-89, sect. leader, 1989-93; pvt. practice indsl. psychology and healthcare, Los Alamos, 1988—. Sec. Cornell Coll. Alumni Office, 1954-55, also other orgns.; bd. dirs. Parent Edn. Ctr., Idaho State U., 1980; counselor, Los Alamos, 1981-88. Editor newsletter LWV, Laramie, Wyo., 1957; contbr. articles to profl. jours. Pres. Newcomers Club, Pocatello, 1967, Faculty Womens Club, Pocatello, 1968; chmn. edn. com. AAUW, Pocatello, 1969. Mem.: APA, N.Mex. Soc. Adlerian Psychology (pres. 1990, treas. 1991—97, bd. dirs. 1996—), N.Mex. Psychol. Assn. (bd. dirs. divsn. II 1990, 1999, sec. 1988—90, chmn. 1990, 1999—2000). Mem. Lds Ch. Avocations: racewalking, backpacking, skiing, tennis, biking. Home and Office: 340 Aragon Ave Los Alamos NM 87544-3505 *Honesty, dependability, spiritual inspiration, and always doing our best are ingredients that lead to a successful and happy life.*

THOMPSON, LOLA MAY, music educator, volunteer; b. Mpls., Mar. 10, 1931; d. Jens Christian and Lydia Mathilda (Ronsberg) Jensen; m. Wayne Leo Thompson, July 27, 1957; children: Mark Wayne, Scott Christopher. BS, U. Minn., 1953, postgrad., 1953—54. Nationally cert. tchr. of music. Music supr. Little Falls (Minn.) Pub. Schs., 1954-57; music coord. Bloomington (Minn.) Pub. Schs., 1957-61; tchr., owner Thompson Piano Studio, St. Paul, 1961—. Sr. choir dir. Holy Trinity Ch., Mpls., 1953-54, 1st English Luth. Ch., Little Falls, Minn., 1954-57, dir. Jr. Sunday Sch. Choir Cen. Luth. Ch., Mpls., 1970—; benefit co-chmn. Dale Warland Singers, 1989, 95, benefit chmn., 1989-90, benefit honorary chair, 1991; bd. dirs. Friends of Dale Warland Singers; chmn. Thursday Mus. 100th Anniverssary, 1992; organist specializing in wedding music, 1950—. Author: Haarstad, 1992; editor nat. Haarstad newsletter; composer numerous children's songs, choir piece Twenty-Seventh Psalm, 1949 (received award). Pres. Friends of St. Paul Chamber Orch., 1974—77, coun., 1977—; benefit chmn., 1978—80, 1988; gen. chmn. Minn. Orch. and Women's Assn. for Young Artist Competition, 1982—84, repertoire chmn., 1984—; advisor Women's Assn. Minn. Orch., 1986—; benefit chmn. U. Minn. Found., 1984—85; mem. com. for gala opening U. Minn. Mann Performing Arts Ctr., 1993; mem. Minn. Hist. Soc. Women's Orgn.; accompanist Mpls. Choraliers, 1950—54; mem. 1006 Avenue Soc.; spl. events advisor Hamline U., 1990; chmn. 100th Anniversary of Thursday Musical, 35th Anniversary Celebration of The St. Paul Chamber Orch., 1993; co-chair Dale Warland Singers Gala, 1989—90, 1996—2001. Recipient Good Neighbor award Sta. WCCO, 1985, Ultimate Friend award Friends of the St. Paul Chamber Orch., 1999. Mem. AAUW, Music Tchrs. Nat. Assn., Minn. Music Tchrs. Assn. (state chair Student Achievement Fund, grants and funding), Minn. Opera Assn., Sigma Alpha Iota (nat. province v.p. 1979-82, pres. St. Paul-Mpls. chpt. 1969-72, 83-85, Sword of Honor 1969, Rose of Honor 1970, 50 Yr. award 2001) Republican. Lutheran. Avocations: needlepoint, boating, swimming, travel, family history.

THOMPSON, LORAN TYSON, lawyer; b. N.Y.C., Dec. 23, 1947; s. Kenneth Webster and Mary (Tyson) T.; m. Meera Eleanora Agarwal, Apr. 2, 1976. BA magna cum laude, Amherst Coll., 1969; MA, Harvard U., 1970, JD, 1976. Bar: N.Y. 1977, U.S. Tax Ct. 1977. Assoc. Breed, Abbott & Morgan, N.Y.C., 1976-83, ptnr., 1983-93, Whitman Breed Abbott & Morgan LLP, N.Y.C., 1993-2000, Winston & Strawn, N.Y.C., 2000—. Mem. ABA, N.Y. State Bar Assn. (exec. com., tax sect. 1991-98, co-chmn. com. on nonqualified employee benefits 1991-95, co-chmn. com. on qualified plans 1995-98), Assn. Bar of City of N.Y., Phi Beta Kappa. Home: 79 W 12th St Apt 12G New York NY 10011-8510 Office: Winston & Strawn 200 Park Ave New York NY 10166-4193 E-mail: lthompson@winston.com.

THOMPSON, LORING MOORE, retired college administrator, writer; b. Newton, Mass., Feb. 17, 1918; s. Henry E. and Ella (Gould) T.; m. Pearl E. Judiesch, Dec. 30, 1949 (dec. May 2002); children— Bruce C., Douglas P. (dec.). BS in Indsl. Engring, Northeastern U., 1940; MS, U. R.I., 1947; PhD, U. Chgo., 1956. Instr. U. R.I., 1946; asst. to pres. Assn. Colls. Upper N.Y., 1947-49; assoc. prof. U. Toledo, 1952-59, asst. dean acad. adminstrn., 1958-59; dir. univ. planning Northeastern U., Boston, 1959-63, dean adult programs, 1964-66, v.p. planning, 1967-80, emeritus, 1980—; faculty assoc. continuing edn. Ariz. State U., 1982-84. Cons. in field. Author: (with others) Business Communication, 1949; contbr. (with others) articles to profl. publs. Bd. dirs. Back Bay Assn., Boston, 1961-63, v.p., 1963; trustee Huntington Gen. Hosp., Boston, 1970-80; mem. Fenway Project Area Com., 1973-76; mem. Mass. conf. ch. and edn. com. United Ch. of Christ, 1972-78, chairperson, 1973-74, mem. task force on ch. growth, 1978-80; mem. Chandler Area Coun., 1988-89; sec. Interfaith Coun. Greater Sun Lakes, 1993-96. Lt. USNR, 1942-45. Mem. Inst. Noetic Scis., Tau Beta Pi. Home: 25408 S Sedona Dr Sun Lakes AZ 85248-6636

THOMPSON, LOUIS MILTON, agronomy educator, scientist; b. Throckmorton, Tex., May 15, 1914; s. Aubrey Lafayette and Lola Terry (Frazier) T.; m. Margaret Stromberg, July 10, 1937 (dec. Nov. 1972); children: Louis Milton, Margaret Ann, Glenda Ray (dec.), Carolyn Terry, Jerome Lafayette; m. Ruth Hiatt Phipps, July 7, 1990. BS, Tex. A&M U., 1935; MS, Iowa State U., 1947, PhD, 1950. Soil surveyor, Tex., 1935-36, 39-40; instr. Tex. A&M U., 1936-39, 40-42; asst. prof. soils Iowa State U., Ames, 1947-50, prof. soils, head farm operation curriculum, 1950-58, assoc. dean agr. charge resident instrn., 1958-83, emeritus prof. agronomy, 1983—, assoc. dean emeritus, 1984—. Author: Soils and Soil Fertility, rev. edit., 1957, co-author rev. edit., 1978, 83, 93, Russian edit., 1983; contbr. articles on weather-crop yield models and climate change to profl. jours. Elder Presbyn. Ch. With AUS, 1942-46; col. Res. (ret.). Recipient Henry A. Wallace award for Disting. Svc. to Agr., 1982, Faculty citation Iowa State U. Alumni Assn., 1990, Disting. Achievement citation, 1993, Alumni Recognition medal, 1996, Disting. Iowa Scientist award Iowa Acad. Sci., 1991, Agr. Innovator award Iowa State U. Agr. Alumni Soc., 1992, Friends of Agrl. award Iowa Dept. Agr. and Nat. Agrl. Mktg. Assn., 1993, Disting. Svc. to Iowa Agr. award Iowa Farm Bur., 1995, Disting. Svc. to Agr. award Iowa chpt. Am Soc. Farm Mgrs. and Rural Appraisers, 2000; named one of 150 Iowans Who Made a Difference, Iowa Farm Bur., 1996. Fellow AAAS, Am. Soc. Agronomy, Soil Sci. Soc. Am., Soil and Water Conservation Soc. (pres.'s citation); mem. Farm House (hon.), Rotary (past local pres., Paul Harris fellow), Sigma Xi, Alpha Zeta (Tall Corn award 1957), Gamma Sigma Delta (nat. pres. 1956-58), Phi Kappa Phi (pres. 1961, Centennial medal 1997). Home: 414 Lynn Ave Ames IA 50014-7318 *To succeed in an academic community one must become an authority on a subject and be able to communicate it.*

THOMPSON, LOUIS MILTON, JR. association executive, horse breeder; b. Bryan, Tex., Sept. 21, 1938; s. Louis Milton and Margaret (Stromberg) T.; m. Anne Strand, Aug. 5, 1961 (div. Feb. 1992); children: Louis Milton III, Eric Norman, Christopher Scott, Mary Margaret, Mary Elizabeth; m. Laura Russell, Nov. 28, 1992; children: Emily Allan, Helen Aubrey. BS, Iowa State U., 1961, MS with honors, 1969. News editor, anchor Sta. WOI-TV-AM-FM, Ames, Iowa, 1960-61; commd. 2d lt. U.S. Army, 1961, resigned, 1974; advanced through grades to lt. col. USAR, 1981; asst. press sec. The White House, Washington, 1974-75; asst. to pres. Am. Enterprise Inst., 1975-76; dir. pub. affairs Nonprescription Drug Mfrs. Assn., 1976-78; sr. v.p. Nat. Assn. Home Builders, 1978-82; pres., CEO, Nat. Investor Rels. Inst., Vienna, 1982—. Mem. individual investor adv. com. N.Y. Stock Exch., N.Y.C., 1990-92; mem. new founds. working group Harvard U. John F. Kennedy Sch., Cambridge, Mass., 1992-94; mem. consumer affairs adv. com. SEC, Washington, 1996—; mem. adv. bd. Greenlee Sch. Journalism and Comm., Iowa State U., Ames, 1998—, mem. liberal arts and scis. dean's coun., 2001—; mem. Conf. Bd., 1995-96; bd. dirs. Nat. Coun. for Econ. Edn., 2001—. Contbg. author: The Handbook of Investor Relations, 1989; contbr. articles to profl. jours. Va. chmn. U.S. Equestrian Team, Gladstone, N.J., 1978-82; dressage judge Am. Horse Shows Assn., Lexington, Ky., 1979-86. Recipient Disting. Svc. award, Investment Edn. Inst., 1987, Investor Rels. Mag. and Barron's lifetime achievement award in investor rels., 2000, J.W. Schwartz award for disting. svc. in journalism, Iowa State U., 2001. Mem. Investor Rels. Assn., Internat. Investor Rels. Fedn., Am. Hanoverian Soc. (disting. mem., pres. 1988-94), Univ. Club, Phi Kappa Phi. Avocations: equestrian sports, golf, wine collecting. Home: Wanderland Farm 11539 Spicers Mill Rd Orange VA 22960-2103 Office: Nat Investor Rels Inst 8045 Leesburg Pike Ste 600 Vienna VA 22182-2797

THOMPSON, LYLE EUGENE, electrical engineer; b. Pocatello, Idaho, May 16, 1956; s. Clyde Eugene and Doris (Pratt) T.; m. Barbara Mae Dickerson, Dec. 31, 1986. Grad. high sch. Sr. diagnostic engr. Calma/GE, Santa Clara, Calif., 1978-83; mem. tech. staff Telecommunications Tech., Inc., Milpitas, 1983-84; proprietor/cons. Lyle Thompson Cons., Fremont, 1984-87; sys. analyst Raynet Corp., Menlo Park, 1987-88; proprietor/cons. Lyle Thompson Cons., Hayward, 1988-89; mgr. sys. design Raylan Corp., Menlo Park, 1989-90, dir. system design, 1990-91; pvt. practice cons. San Lorenzo, Calif., 1991-96; pres., CEO HelioSoft, Inc., 1996—; instr. U. Calif., Berkeley, 1999—. Cons. in field. Mem.: IEEE, ACM. Achievements include patents in field. Avocations: music, role playing, golf. Home: 664 Paseo Grande San Lorenzo CA 94580-2364 E-mail: lyle@heliosoft.com

THOMPSON, MACK EUGENE, history educator; b. Burley, Idaho, Feb. 24, 1921; s. Eugene and Nora (McFate) T.; m. Helen Goldhamer, Oct. 30, 1945. AB, Queen's Coll., CUNY, 1948; MA, Brown U., 1951, PhD, 1955. Instr. history Brown U., 1954-55; asst. prof. Calif. Inst. Tech., 1955-56, U. Calif. at Riverside, 1956-62, asso. prof., 1962-66, prof., 1966-77; emeritus prof., 1977—; chmn. div. humanities U. Calif. at Riverside, 1961-63, asso. univ. dean acad. planning, 1965-66, dean, div. undergrad. studies, 1971-74; exec dir. Am. Hist. Assn., Washington, 1974-81. Chmn. editorial bd. Experiment and Innovation: New Directions in Edn., U. Calif., 1966-68 Author: The Ward-Hopkins Controversy and the American Revolution in Rhode Island: An Interpretation, 1959, Moses Brown, Reluctant Reformer, 1962, Causes and Circumstances of the Du Pont Family's Emigration, 1969. Bd. dirs. Harry S. Truman Libr. Inst., 1974-81. With AUS, 1942-45. E-mail: thompsono'brien@juno.com. Home: 1378 River Oaks Ct Oldsmar FL 34677-4828

THOMPSON, MARGARET M. physical education educator; b. Merrifield, Va., Aug. 1, 1921; d. Lesley L. and Madeline (Shawen) T. BS, Mary Washington Coll., 1941; MA, George Washington U., 1947; PhD, U. Iowa, 1961. Tchr., supr. phys. edn. Staunton (Va.) City Schs., 1941-44; tchr. jr. high sch. phys. edn. Arlington County, Va., 1944-47; instr. women's phys. edn. Fla. State U., Tallahassee, 1947-51; instr., asst. prof., assoc. prof. phys. edn. Purdue U., Lafayette, Ind., 1951-65, dir. gross motor therapy lab., 1963-65; assoc. prof. phys. edn. U. Mo., Columbia, 1965-68, prof., 1968-71, dir. Cinematography and Motor Learning Lab. Dept. Health and Phys. Edn., 1965-71; prof. phys. edn. U. Ill., Champaign-Urbana, 1971-87, prof. emeritus, 1987—. Vis. prof. Escola de Educacão Fisica, U. de São Paulo, Brazil, 1985; vis. prof. phy. edn. Inst. Bioscis. de Rio Claro, U. Estadual Paulista, Brazil, 1991. Author: (with Barbara B. Godfrey) Movement Pattern Checklists, 1966, (with Chappelle Arnett) Perceptual Motor and Motor Test Battery for Children, 1968, (with Barbara Mann) An Holistic Approach to Physical Education Curriculum: Objectives Classification System for Elementary Schools, 1977, Gross Motor Inventory, 1976, revised edit., 1980, Developing the Curriculum, 1980, Setting the Learning Environment, 1980, Sex Stereotyping and Human Development, 1980; also film strips, articles. Mem. AAHPER, Internat. Assn. Phys. Edn. and Sports for Coll. Girls and Women. Home and Office: 1311 Wildwood Ln Mahomet IL 61853-9770 E-mail: mmthomps@uiuc.edu.

THOMPSON, MARI HILDENBRAND, medico-legal and administrative consultant; b. Washington, Apr. 26, 1951; d. Emil John Christopher Hildenbrand and Ada Lythe (Conklin) Hildenbrand-Kammer; m. R. Marshall Thompson, Sept. 27, 1970 (div. June 1981); 1 child, Jeremy Marshall; m.

Michael R. Pritchard, Apr. 25, 1999. BA in Secondary Edn., BA in Performing Arts, Am. U., 1976. Cert. med. staff coord.; cert. profl. credentialing specialist. Employment interviewer Scripps Meml. Hosp., La Jolla, Calif., 1977-81; office mgr. Jacksina & Freedman Press Office, N.Y.C., 1982-83; staffing coord., med. staff asst. Am. Med. Internat. Clairemont Hosp., San Diego, 1983-85; adminstrv. asst. Am. Med. Internat. Valley Med. Ctr., El Cajon, Calif., 1985-88; med. staff coord. Sharp Meml. Hosp., San Diego, 1988-92; adminstrv. asst. Grossmont Hosp., La Mesa, Calif., 1992-93, coord. Sharp family practice residency program, 1993-94; mgr. Sharp Meml. Hosp. med. staff svcs., San Diego, 1994-96; cons. med. staff svcs. San Diego Rehab. Inst., 1997. Cons. and adminstrv. support for Legal Support, Inc., 1989—, St. Charles Med. Ctr., 1998—; coord. Deschutes Ct. Defenders, 1999—; wardrobe mistress various cmty. theatres, San Diego, 1978-79, actress, San Diego, 1979-81. Co-founder N.Y.C. Playreaders Group, 1981-83, N.J. Shakespeare Theatre, Madison, 1982, Good Humor Improv Co., N.Y.C., 1982-83; contbg. writer to Poetry Revival: An Anthology, 1994. Active Dem. Nat. Com., 1996—; vol. Cmty. Theatre of the Cascades, 1997—. Named one of Outstanding Young Women of Am., 1986. Mem. AFTRA. Democrat. Nichiren Buddhist. Buddhist. Avocations: writing poetry, horseback riding, swimming, gardening, fishing. Home: 22925 Superior Ct Bend OR 97702-9271 E-mail: marutz@buddhist.com.

THOMPSON, MARIAN NELL, poetry, historical, non-fiction and fiction writer, educator, poet; b. Birmingham, Ala., Aug. 30, 1938; d. Euclid Derring and Gena Grace Meadows; m. Claude Thompson, Jr., Aug. 2, 1962; children: Steven Claude, Shirley Nell. BS, Samford U., Homewood, AL, 1959. Salesperson Darling Shoppe, Birmingham, Ala., 1955—56; student asst. Samford Libr., East Lake, 1956—59; youth dir. various churches, Birmingham, Ala., Ocilla, Ga., and Flint, Mich.; educator Atherton Elem. Sch., Flint, Mich., 1959—61; writer, student libr. asst. New Orleans Seminary Libr., New Orleans, 1961—62; educator Chalmette El. Sch., Chalmette, 1962—63; preschool dir. Golden Acres Bapt. Ch., Pasadena, Tex., 1979—88; educator St. Pias Parochial Sch., 1988—89, Richey E & South Shaver Elem. Schools, Pasadena, 1989—98. Substitute tchr. Pasadena Schools, Pasadena, Tex., 1970—74; vol. Golden Acres Sch. Libraries, Pasadena, Tex., 1970—79. Author short stories, (chapbook) Thank God For His Creations, (poetry) Wheels of Thoughts. Sustaining and life membership Rep. Party, 2001. Recipient Life Membership, Internat. Libr. of Photography, 2001. Mem.: Golden Vista Ext. for Home Edn., Tex. State Teacher's Retirement Assn. R-Conservative. Baptist. Avocations: music, reading, writing, photography. Office: Read Writing of MYNE 2722 Randolph Road Pasadena TX 77503-4244 Office Fax: 281-487-3546. E-mail: Marian_Tho@msn.com.

THOMPSON, MARIE ANGELA, computer engineer, consultant; b. Sheffield, Yorkshire, Eng., Aug. 8, 1951; came to U.S., 1979. d. Leslie Arthur and Gloria Mabel (Sheldon) Findley; m. Stephen J. Thompson, Feb. 10, 1990. BS with honors, U. Leeds, 1973; MS, U. Reading, 1975. Software engr. ITT, London, 1975-79, GTE, Northlake, Ill., 1979-80, St. Petersberg, Fla., 1980-82, Reston, Va., 1982-83; dir. rsch. Northcor, Hamden, Conn., 1985-90; mgr. spl. projects SAC of Am., Ridgefield, 1990-98; cons. Universal Solutions 2000, 1998, Thompson, Findley & Co., Hampton Bays, N.Y., 1998—. Cons. Ivy League Corp., Ridgefield, Conn., 1995-98, Digital Network 1, Ridgefield, 1995-98, First Frontier Capital Corp., Great Neck, 1999—, East End Trading Co., Hampton Bays, N.Y., 1999—. Dir. concessions Pop Warner Football, Ridgefield, 1993, 94, dir. registration, 1994, 95, 96, 97, dir. fundraising, 1996-98. Recipient Bob Scalzo Meml. award Ridgefield Pop Warner Football, 1997. Mem. AAUW, AAAS, Am. Inst. Chem. Engrs., Conn. Assn. for the Gifted, N.Y. Acad. Scis., Conn. Business and Industry Assn., Ridgefield C. of C., Mensa. Avocations: tennis, go, computing, skiing, reading. Office: Thompson Findley & Co PO Box 258 Hampton Bays NY 11946-0211

THOMPSON, MARTIN CHRISTIAN, news service executive; b. Council Bluffs, Iowa, Oct. 25, 1938; s. Ross Kenneth and Mary Ellen (Pierce) T.; m. Janet Ann Morrow, Aug. 4, 1962; children: Chris Michael, Sean Martin. BA in Communications, U. Wash., 1960. Newsman Sta. KEDO, Longview, Wash., 1960-61; news dir. Sta. KREW, Sunnyside, 1961-66; newsman AP, Seattle, 1966-68, corr. Reno, 1968-70, newsman San Francisco, 1970-72, news editor, 1972-75, chief of bur., 1975-86, Los Angeles, 1986-88, mng. editor N.Y.C., 1989-92, dir. state news, 1992—. Mem. Beta Rho Tau, Sigma Delta Chi. Methodist. Office: 50 Rockefeller Plz New York NY 10020-1605

THOMPSON, MARTYN PHILIP, political and literary studies educator, translator; b. Hitchin, Gt. Britain and No. Ireland, Nov. 13, 1945; arrived in U.S., 1991; s. Philip John and Doris Primrose Thompson; m. Penelope Ann Burden, Jan. 15, 1972; 1 child, Daniel. BS in Econs., London Sch. Econs., 1967; PhD, London U., 1974; Dr. phil. habil., Tübingen (Germany) U., 1984. Lectr. in polit. studies London U., 1971-74; lectr. Tübingen, 1974-76, asst. prof., 1976-85, assoc. prof., 1985-87, prof. lit. and intellectual history, 1987-91; prof. polit. theory Tulane U., 1991—. Founder, mem. exec. com. German Soc. Study of Polit. Thought, Münster, 1989; vice chmn. Conf. for Study of Polit. Thought, 1991-96, chmn., 1996; mem. nat. screening com. for Fulbright Awards, Inst. Internat. Edn., N.Y.C., 2000—. Author: Ideas of Contract in the Age of John Locke, 1987; editor: Locke and Kant: Historical Reception and Contemporary Relevance, 1991, co-editor Yearbook of German Political Thought, 10 vols., 1991—; contbr. articles to profl. jours. Huntington Libr. and Art Gallery fellow, 1980; fellow commoner Churchill Coll., Cambridge U., Eng., 1985—; recipient Mellon fellowship William Andrews Clark Meml. Libr., UCLA, 1981. Mem. Am. Polit. Sci. Assn., Polit. Studies Assn. Gt. Britain, Inst. Hist. Rsch. U.K., Collingwood Soc. UK (hon. life), Deutsche Gesellschaft zur Erforschung des politischen Denkens (exec. com. 1989-2001). Avocations: travel, chess, non-pedigree dogs. Office: Tulane Univ Dept Polit Sci St Charles Ave New Orleans LA 70118-5698 E-mail: martynpt@aol.com., mpt@tulane.edu.

THOMPSON, MARY B. writer, illustrator; b. Corpus Christi, Tex., Dec. 11, 1929; d. Henry Charles and Marjorie Murray Keller. BA in Psychology, So. Meth. U., 1957; MA in Secondary Edn., MA in Creative Writing, NYU, 1961, ABD in Higher Edn. Adminstrn., 1969. Cert. secondary edn. English N.Y. Rschr. Ruder & Firm ILC, N.Y.C., 1958—60; TV script writer Philco Corp., 1961, Phila., 1961; faculty The New Lincoln Sch., N.Y.C., 1961—64, So. Meth. U., Dallas, 1964—68; freelance writer pub. rels. Albany, NY, 1981—85; author, pub. Melior Press, Leesburg, Fla., 1997—2000; author, illustrator LighthouseEditions.com, Deerfield Beach, 2000—, Booklocker.com, Bangor, Maine, 2000—. Mem. curriculum com. So. Meth. U., Dallas, 1966; vol. tchr. advanced English classes Leesburg H.S. Author: (novella) Closed Circuit, 1961, (book) B.S. Detecting, 1999; (illustrator): B.S. Detecting: Success Possible Communicating, 2000. Mem.: LWV, Nat. Writers Union, Defenders of Wildlife, South Lake Animal League, Sierra Club, Kappa Delta Pi. Avocations: gardening, recreational vehicle travel. Home: 6623 Hopi Trail Leesburg FL 34748

THOMPSON, MARY CECILIA, nurse midwife; b. Georgetown, Guyana; came to the U.S., 1977; d. John Alexander and Monica Eileen (Thorne) T. RN, Southend-on-Sea Sch. Nursing, Essex, Eng., 1973; cert. midwife, Basildon & Thurrock Sch., Essex, Eng., 1975; perinatal nurse practitioner, Cmty. Gen. Hosp., Syracuse, N.Y., 1986; cert. nurse midwife, Frontier Sch. Midwifery, Hyden, Ky., 1990. Cert. nurse midwife. Staff nurse pediatric unit Rochford Hosp., Essex, 1973-74; staff midwife Basildon & Orsett Maternity Units, 1975-76, St. Peter's Hosp. Chertsey, Surrey, Eng., 1976-78; staff nurse pediatric critical care SUNY Health Sci. Ctr., Syracuse, 1978-82; staff nurse pvt. duty nursing Med. Pers. Pool, 1982-83; staff nurse labor and delivery Cmty. Gen. Hosp., 1983-86, perinatal nurse practitioner, 1986-90; pvt. practice cert. nurse midwife, 1990—. Mem. AWHONN, Am. Assn. Nurse Practitioners, Am. Coll. Nurse Midwives. Roman Catholic. Avocations: embroidery, reading, tennis, music, travel. Home: 4904 Razorback Run Syracuse NY 13215-1347 Office: Choices West Med Ctr West W Genesee St Camillus NY 13031-2238

THOMPSON, MARY EILEEN, chemistry educator; b. Mpls., Dec. 21, 1928; d. Albert C. and Blanche (McAvoy) T. BA, Coll. St. Catherine, 1953; MS, U. Minn., 1958; PhD, U. Calif., Berkeley, 1964. Tchr. math. and sci. Derham Hall H.S., St. Paul, 1953-58; mem. faculty Coll. of St. Catherine, 1964-69, prof. chemistry, 1969-2000, chmn. dept., 1969-90, prof. emeritus, 2000—. Project dir. Women in Chemistry, 1984-98. Contbr. articles to profl. jours. Mem. AAAS, Am. Chem. Soc. (chmn. women chemists com. 1992-94, award for encouraging women into chem. scis. careers 1997), Coun. Undergrad. Rsch. (councillor 1991-96), N.Y. Acad. Scis., Chem. Soc. London, Sigma Xi, Phi Beta Kappa (senator 1997—). Democrat. Roman Catholic. Achievements include research interests in Cr(III) hydrolytic polymers, kinetics of inorganic complexes, Co(III) peroxo/superoxo complexes. Office: Coll of St Catherine 2004 Randolph Ave Saint Paul MN 55105-1750 E-mail: methompson@stkate.edu., MTHOM17349@aol.com.

THOMPSON, MARY KOLETA, sculptor, non-profit organization management consultant; b. Portsmouth, Va., Dec. 27, 1938; m. James Burton Thompson, May 5, 1957; children: Burt, Suzan, Kate, Jon. BFA, U. Tex., 1982; postgrad., Boston U.; MA in Philanthropy and Devel., St. Mary's U. Minn., 1999. Cert. fund raising exec., non-profit mgmt. Pres., CEO The Planning Resource People, Lampasas, Tex., 1990—; Tex. fin. devel. specialist ARC Tex., 1994-98; devel. dir. Very Spl. Arts Tex., 1991-92; dir. devel. ARC, Austin, 1992-94; pub. affairs adminstr. Pink Palace Mus. and Memphis Mus. Inc., Memphis, 1998; CEO Lamapasas C. of C., Lampasas, TX, 1998-99; pres., CEO Assn. Non-Profit Orgns., 1998—, Tex. Assn. Bed and Breakfast Innkeepers, 1998; pres. A Little Cottage B&B, 1999—; owner Heritage Sta. Antiques, 1999—. Dir. Tex. Children's Mus., Fredericksburg, 1987-88, Internat. Hdqrs. SHAPE Command Arts and Crafts Ctr., 1985-86; com. chmn. Symposium for Encouragement Women in Math. and Natural Sci., U. Tex., Austin, 1990. Sculptor portrait busts. Bd. dirs. Teenage Parent Coun., Austin, 1990-92, ARC. Named U.S. Vol. of Yr., Belgium, 1986; grantee NEA, 1988. Mem.: AAUW (life; pres. 1990—92), Women in Comm. (co-chmn. SW regional conf.), Lometa Lions Club (pub. rels. com. 1999—), Heritage Station Antique Vehicle Show (founder), Heritage Station Antiques Show and Sale (founder), Leadership Tex. (life), U. Tex. Ex-Student Assn. (life), Heritage Station Antiques Forum (founder), Raleigh Tavern Soc. (founder), Leadership Tex. Alumnae Assn. (bd. dir.), Tex. Hist. Found (life). Avocations: writing, lecturing, meeting and strategic planning. Office: 100 W 190 PO Box 10 Lometa TX 76853-0010

THOMPSON, MAXINE LEAK (GERRY THOMPSON), supply manager, inventory director; b. Brigham, Utah, Nov. 25, 1938; d. Gerald L. and Luetta Grace (Peterson) Leak; m. Gordon Wise Thompson, Sept. 27, 1957; children: Kellee, Kris, Kasey. A in Bus. A in Bus. Adminstrn., A in Mktg., GTE, 1992; BS in Bus. Adminstrn. and Mgmt., U. Phoenix, 1992. Cert. real estate agent, Utah. Plant clk. Contel, Tremonton, Utah, 1977-78, warehouse person, 1978-82, storekeeper, 1982-89, Utah state purchasing/supply agt., 1989-91, GTE, Tremonton, 1992—. Editor: T-P Times, 1970-74. Active LDS Primary Orgn., LDS Mutual Improvement Assn. Orgn., Thatcher-Penrose, Utah, 1960-80; exhibit chmn. Box Elder County Fair, 1969, 74. Recipient award LDS Ch., 1981. Avocations: creative readings, art, bicycling, working out, aerobics. Home: 61 Amber Ave Tremonton UT 84337-2311

THOMPSON, MICHAEL LAURIE, food manufacturing executive; b. Toronto, Ont., Can., July 17, 1947; came to U.S., 1995; 1 child, David Graham; m. Susan Elizabeth McNamara. B of Commerce, Concordia U., Montreal, Que., Can., 1968, MBA, 1974. Dir. purchasing Redpath Sugars Ltd., Montreal, 1971-80; dir. groundfish sales H.B. Nickerson & Sons Ltd., North Sydney, N.S., Can., 1980-81; mktg. mgr. Prince Rupert Fisherman's Coop., Vancouver, B.C., Can., 1981-82; dir. export Dare Foods Ltd., Kitchener, Ont., 1982-90, v.p. internat. markets, 1991-94; v.p., gen. mgr. Dare Foods Inc., Marblehead, Mass., 1995—. Mem.: Internat. Data Corp. (mem. adv. bd. 1999—), Biscuit & Cracker Distbrs. Assn. (pres. 1993—94, Spl. Recognition award 1994), Splty. Food Distbr.'s and Mfrs. Assn. (chmn. mfrs. coun. bd. 1994—95). Office: Dare Foods Inc 5 Bessom St Marblehead MA 01945-2328 E-mail: michael.l.thompson@attbi.com.

THOMPSON, MICHAEL ALAN, political cartoonist; b. Mankato, Minn., Aug. 3, 1964; s. Orrel Edward and Joan Alice (Hopkins) T.; m. Constance Reneé Gosnell, Oct. 12, 1991. BA in Polit. Sci., U. Wis., Milw. Contbg. cartoonist Milw. Jour., 1988-89; cartoonist St. Louis Sun, 1989-90, State Jour.-Register, Springfield, Ill., 1990-98, Detroit Free Press, 1998—. Cartoons syndicated through Copley News Svc. to over 600 newspapers throughout U.S., including Newsweek, Wall Street Jour., N.Y. Times, USA Today, Washington Post, U.S. News & World Report, Nat. Rev. Vol. Big Bros.-Big Sisters, Springfield. Recipient Charles M. Schulz award Scripps Howard Found., 1988, Locher award Assn. Am. Editorial Cartoonists, 1989, Mark of Excellence award Soc. Profl. Journalists, H.L. Mencken Cartooning award, 1994, Sigma Delta Chi award for cartooning Soc. Profl. Journalists, 2000, Clarion award Women in Comm., 2000; named Cartoonist of Yr. Nat. Press Found., 1999, Thomas Nast award for best cartoons on internat. affairs Overseas Press Club, 2001. Avocations: karate, canoeing.

THOMPSON, MICHAEL B.A. physician; b. Eau Claire, Wis., Sept. 20, 1945; s. Alexander and Ruth E. (Berg) T.; m. Mary J. Busacker, June 16, 1968; children: Robert Walter, Stephen Michael, Heather Naomi, David John. BS in Biology, Moorhead State U., 1967; MD, U. Minn., 1972. Diplomate Am. Bd. Family Practice. Intern Hennepin County Med. Ctr., Mpls., 1972-73; family physician Alexandria (Minn.) Clinic P.A., 1973-81; physician Mesa (Ariz.) Luth. Hosp., 1981-83; pvt. practice Alexandria, 1983-97; care provider Rush City (Minn.) Area Clinic, Fairview Lakes Clin., 1997—. Chief of staff Douglas County Hosp., Alexandria, 1976-77; rural physician U. Minn. Med. Sch., Alexandria, 1977-78. Contbr. articles to profl. jours. Mem. Am. Acad. Family Physicians, Alexandria Golf Club. Republican. Lutheran. Avocations: biology, birding, biking, cross-country and downhill skiing. Home: 1004 Bay Ln NE Alexandria MN 56308-9090 Office: Rush City Clin Fairview Lakes 760 W 4th St Rush City MN 55069-9063

THOMPSON, MORLEY PUNSHON, textile company executive; b. San Francisco, Jan. 2, 1927; s. Morley Punshon and Ruth (Wetmore) T.; m. Patricia Ann Smith, Jan. 31, 1953 (dec.); children: Page Elizabeth Tredennick, Morley Punshon; m. Katharine Shaw Wallace. AB, Stanford U., 1948; MBA, Harvard U., 1950; JD, Chase Law Sch., 1969; LLD, Xavier U., 1981. CPA, Ohio. Chmn. Stearns Tech. Textiles Co., Cin., 1985—, Stearns Can., Inc., Cin., 1985—. Bd. dirs. Cin. Inst. Fine Arts. Lt. Supply Corps USNR, 1952-54. Mem. Beta Theta Pi. Office: 100 Williams St Cincinnati OH 45215-4602

THOMPSON, MORRIS MORDECAI, civil engineer, researcher, consultant; b. Jersey City, Feb. 6, 1912; s. Barney and Rachel (Golub) T.; m. Sophia Esther Shapiro, Feb. 29, 1936; 1 child, Robert David. BS in Engring., Princeton U., 1934, CE, 1935. Registered profl. engr., D.C. Topographic engr. U.S. Geol. Survey, Chattanooga, Washington, 1939-65, Atlantic region engr. Arlington, Va., 1966-68, chief rsch. and tech. standards Washington, 1968-76, cons. Reston, Va., 1976-95. Author: Maps for America, 1979, 3d edit., 1988; editor-in-chief: Manual of Photogrammetry, 2 vols., 3d edit., 1966; prodn. editor Manual of Remote Sensing, 2 vols., 2d edit., 1983; also numerous articles, chpt. to book. Active Boy Scouts Am., Binghamton, N.Y., Chattanooga, Arlington, 1937-53. Recipient Disting. Svc. award U.S. Dept. Interior, 1967. Fellow ASCE (life, chmn. surveying and mapping div. 1973-75, Surveying and Mapping award 1977), Am. Congress on Surveying and Mapping (life, bd. dirs. 1958-60, Cartographic Honors award 1980); mem. Am. Soc. Photogrammetry and Remote Sensing (hon., cert. photogrammetrist, publs. cons. 1979-84, chmn. publs. com. 1980-84, Fairchild award 1966). Democrat. Jewish. Home: 7446 Spring Village Dr Apt 109 Springfield VA 22150-4453

THOMPSON, NEAL PHILIP, food science and nutrition educator; b. Bklyn., July 18, 1936; s. Thomas I. and Ellenor (Backie) T.; m. Beverly Ethel Godshall, Oct. 4, 1958; children: Erick, Victor, Clifford, Karen, Stuart. BS, Wheaton Coll., 1957; MA, Miami U., 1962; PhD, Princeton U., 1965. Asst. prof. U. Fla., Gainesville, 1965-70, assoc. prof., 1970-76, prof., 1976—, asst. dean, 1980-86, assoc. dean, 1986-93. Capt. USNR, ret. Home: 27104 NW 203d Pl High Springs FL 32643 Office: U Fla Inst Food & Agrl Scis Food & Environ Toxicology Gainesville FL 32611-0720

THOMPSON, NEIL DANIEL, legal and genealogical researcher, retired lawyer; b. Calexico, Calif., Feb. 21, 1935; s. Francis Marion Thompson and Leah Harriet Howell. AB with honors, UCLA, 1957; PhD, Columbia U., 1963; LLB, Harvard U., 1963. Bar: N.Y. 1964, U.S. Dist. Ct. (so. dist.) N.Y. 1965, U.S. Customs Ct. 1967, U. S. Ct. Appeals (2d cir.) 1971, U.S. Supreme Ct. 1973. Assoc. Jas. Maxwell Fassett, N.Y.C., 1964-65, Doman & Ablondi, N.Y.C., 1965-69, Pollack & Kaminsky, N.Y.C., 1969-80; pvt. practice, 1980-86; rsch. cons. Salt Lake City, 1986—. Author: Family of Bartholomew Stovall, 1993; editor The Genealogist, 1980-96; contbr. articles to profl. jours. Trustee Bd. for Cert. of Genealogists, 1977-89, pres., 1983-86. Fellow Am. Soc. Genealogists (pres. 1992-95), Soc. Genealogists (London), Utah Geneal. Assn. (bd. dirs. 1988-89); mem. Phi Beta Kappa, Phi Mu Alpha. Democrat. Mem. Lds Ch. Avocations: music, philately, book collecting. Home: 255 N 200 W Salt Lake City UT 84103-4545 E-mail: gryphon801@aol.com.

THOMPSON, N(ORMAN) DAVID, insurance company executive; b. Rockville Centre, N.Y., July 30, 1934; s. Norman J. and Laurel H. (Johnson) T.; m. Joyce L. Angeletti, June 7, 1958; children: John L., Jennifer L., Sarah S. BA with distinction, Wesleyan U., 1956; LLB, Columbia U., 1959; postgrad., Harvard U., 1973. Bar: N.Y. Pvt. practice law, N.Y.C., 1961-62; corp. sec. Gen. Reins. Corp., 1964-69, v.p. Greenwich, Conn., 1969, v.p., gen. counsel, sec., 1976-77; exec. v.p. N.Am. Reins. Corp., N.Y.C., 1977-78, pres., 1978-92; chmn., CEO Swiss Reins. Am. Corp. (formerly N.Am. Reins.), 1992-95, Swiss Re Am. Holding Corp. (formerly SwissRe Holding Co.), 1992-97; chmn. SwissRe Group Cos. (U.S.), 1992-95. Dir. Nat. Legal Ctr. for Pub. Interest, chmn., 1992-95; trustee Coll. Ins., 1992, 98. With U.S. Army, 1959-60. Mem. Reins Assn. Am. (chmn. 1982-83), Nat. Assn. Casualty and Surety Execs. (pres. 1986-87), Am. Arbitration Assn. (bd. dirs., chmn. fin. com. 1992-93), Am. Inst. Property and Casualty Underwriters (trustee, 1992-98), Univ. Club (N.Y.C.), Saugatuck Harbor Yacht Club (Westport, Conn.). Home: 47 Kettle Creek Rd Weston CT 06883-2208

THOMPSON, NORMAN WINSLOW, surgeon, educator; b. Boston, July 12, 1932; s. Herman Chandler and Evelyn Millicent (Palmer) T.; m. Marcia Ann Veldman, June 12, 1956; children: Robert, Karen, Susan, Jennifer. BA, Hope Coll., 1953; MD, U. Mich., 1957; MD (hon.), U. Linköping, Sweden, 1995. Diplomate Am. Bd. Surgery. From intern to prof. emeritus surgery U. Mich., Ann Arbor, Mich., 1957—2001, prof. emeritus surgery, 2001—. Contbr. articles to profl. jours. Trustee Hope Coll., Holland, Mich., 1973-88. Fellow Royal Australasian Coll. Surgeons (hon.), Royal Coll. Physicians and Surgeons of Glasgow; mem. ACS (gov. 1979-85), Ctrl. Surg. Assn., Western Surg. Assn. (1st v.p. 1992-93, pres. 1994-95), F.A. Coller Surg. Soc. (pres. 1986), Am. Surg. Assn., Am. Thyroid Assn., Soc. Surg. Alimentary Tract, Internat. Assn. Endocrine Surgeons (pres. 1989-91), Internat. Soc. Surgeons (v.p. 1995—), Am. Assn. Endocrine Surgeons (pres. 1980-81, 81-82), Royal Soc. Medicine, Brit. Assn. Endocrine Surgeons, Assn. French Endocrine Surgeons, Scandanvian Surg. Soc., Soc. Surg. Oncology, Turkish Assn. Endocrine Surgeons, Alpha Omega Alpha. Home: 465 Hillspur Rd Ann Arbor MI 48105-1048 Office: U Mich Med Ctr 2920 Taubman Bldg Ann Arbor MI 48109 Fax: 734 936 5830. E-mail: normant@umich.edu.

THOMPSON, PAMELA PADWICK, public relations executive; b. Columbus, Ohio, June 13, 1943; d. Frank John and Tiami Judith (Bampton) T.; stepfather, James William Bampton; m. Fairman Rogers Thompson, Jan. 10, 1942; children: Ryder McNeal, Darby McNeal. BA, U. Louisville, 1994; MA, U. Dayton, 1998. Ptnr. Crutcher, Kelly and Assocs., Louisville, 1979-83; owner Transl. Co., 1981-83, Technigraphics, Louisville, 1984-87; v.p. dir. individual support Grtr. Louisville Fund for the Arts, 1989-92; dir. comms. John Templeton Found., Radnor, Pa., 1997—. Adj. prof. U. Louisville, 1997. Contbr. articles to profl. jours. including Small Group Behavior. Chair pub. rels. com. Keene Valley Libr., 2000-01; bd. dirs. Louisville Nature Ctr., 1996-97; mem. ad hoc com. State Ky. Biodiversity Coun., Louisville, 1996-97; city commr. City of Rolling Fields, Louisville, 1991-94; alliance bd. dirs. J.B. Speed Art Mus., Louisville, 1986-92. Mem. APA, Soc. for Consumer Psychology, Pub. Rels. Soc. Am., Jr. League Phila., Cosmo. Club Phila. Episcopalian. Avocations: hiking, gardening, tennis, travel. Home: 4 Porter Ln Wallingford PA 19086 Office: John Templeton Found Five Radnor Corp Ctr Ste 100 Radnor PA 19087 Fax: (610) 687-8961. E-mail: thompson@templeton.org.

THOMPSON, PAUL A. business consultant, performance improvement expert; b. Orpington, Kent, Eng., Nov. 16, 1942; came to U.S., 1970; s. William John and Jean Inez Thompson; m. Sarah Jean Erskine, July 15, 1972; 1 child, Alastair Stewart. BA in Econs. with honors, Cambridge (Eng.) U., 1965, MA in Econs., 1969. Sr. analyst Shell Oil, London, 1966-70; bus. analyst Westinghouse Electric, Pitts., 1970-76, site mgr. Richmond, Va., 1976-79; founder Westinghouse Productivity & Quality Ctr., 1979; productivity improvement mgr. Westinghouse Electric, Pitts., 1980-94; internat. bus. cons., 1995—. Advisor to U.S. Congress and fgn. govts., 1980—; cons. to airlines, automobile corps., banks, ins., oil and gas, engring., power, healthcare, postal, comms., armed forces, higher edn., and govt. depts.; founder, chmn. Reengring. Users Group, Pitts., 1992—, dir. productivity & leadership consortium, 1996—; vis. lectr. Carnegie Mellon U., Oakland, Pa., 1992—; lectr. United Arab Emirates Higher Colls. of Tech., 1995-2001; internat. author and seminar leader on productivity and quality, 1995—. Editor Forum mag.; mem. editorial bd. Focus on Change Mgmt., 1994—; contbr. articles to profl. jours. Pres. Children's Festival Chorus, Pitts., 1991-96; program dir. Pitts. Folk Festival, 1980-96; chmn. strategic planning Redstone Presbytery, Westmoreland, Pa., 1990-92; tchr. Royal Scottish Country Dance Soc. Republican. Presbyterian. Avocations: golf, travel, horseback riding, dancing, music/theatre. Home and Office: 127 Surrey Dr Delmont PA 15626-1539 E-mail: pthompson@tqconsultants.com.

THOMPSON, PAUL BROWER, lawyer; b. East Orange, N.J., Feb. 15, 1922; s. Harvey Brower and Agnes (Norman) T.; m. Audrey Hyde, Aug. 17, 1952; 1 child, Paul Brower Jr. BA, Colgate U., 1943; JD, Harvard U., 1948. Bar: N.J. 1949, U.S. Ct. Appeals (3d cir.) 1949, U.S. Dist. Ct. N.J. 1949. Assoc. Markley & Broadhurst, Jersey City, 1949-55, Lamb Langan & Blake, Jersey City, 1955-59; ptnr. Lamb Blake Thompson & Chappell, 1959-74; judge Esssex County Ct., Newark, 1975-79, Superior Ct. N.J., Newark, 1979-85, presiding judge, civil divsn., 1985-91; of counsel Tompkins McGuire Wachenfeld & Barry, 1991—. Editor (compendium) Traps for the Unwary, 1997. With USAF, 1942-46. Fellow Am. Bar Found.; mem. ABA, N.J. Bar Assn., Essex County Bar Assn., Montclair Hist. Soc. (pres. 1980), Harvard Law Sch. Assn. N.J. (pres. 1985), Retired Judges Assn. (pres. 2000—). Republican. Congregationalist. Avocations: golf, gardening. Office: Tompkins McGuire Wachenfeld & Barry 4 Gateway Ctr Newark NJ 07102-4007 Home: 309 North Rd Chester NJ 07930-2333 E-mail: pthompson@tompkinsMcguire.com.

THOMPSON, PAUL HAROLD, university president; b. Ogden, Utah, Nov. 28, 1938; s. Harold Merwin and Elda (Skeen) T.; m. Carolyn Lee Nelson, Mar. 9, 1961; children: Loralyn, Kristyn, Shannyn, Robbyn, Daylyn, Nathan. BS, U. Utah, 1964; MBA, Harvard U., 1966, D Bus. Adminstrn., 1969. Rsch. assoc. Harvard U., Cambridge, Mass., 1966-69, asst. prof., 1969-73; assoc. prof. bus. Brigham Young U., Provo, Utah, 1973-78, prof., 1978-84, asst. dean, 1978-81, dean, 1984-89, v.p., 1989-90; pres. Weber State U., Ogden, 1990—. Cons. Goodyear, Hughes Aircraft, Portland GE, Esso Resources Ltd., GE. Co-author: Organization and People: Readings, Cases, and Exercises in Organizational Behavior, 1976, Novations: Strategies for Career Management, 1986; also articles. Named Outstanding Prof. of Yr., Brigham Young U., 1981; Baker scholar Harvard U., 1966. Mem. Am. Assn. State Colls. and Univs. (com. 1991—), Ogden C. of C. (exec. com. 1990—), Rotary (prograam com. Ogden 1991—, Harris fellow 1992—), Phi Beta Kappa. Office: Weber State U Presidents Office 3750 Harrison Blvd Ogden UT 84408-0001*

THOMPSON, PAUL MICHAEL, lawyer; b. Dubuque, Iowa, Aug. 30, 1935; s. Frank W. and Genevieve (Cassutt) T.; m. Mary Jacqueline McManus, Jan. 30, 1960; children: Anne, Tricia, Paul, Tim, Jim. BA magna cum laude, Loras Coll., 1957; LL.B., Georgetown U., 1959. Bar: Iowa 1959, D.C. 1959, Va. 1966. Atty. appellate ct. br. NLRB, Washington, 1962-66; assoc. Hunton & Williams, Richmond, Va., 1966-71, ptnr., 1971—. Adj. prof. The T.C. Williams Sch. Law, U. Richmond. Served with JAGC, USAF, 1960-62. Mem. ABA, Va. State Bar, Va. Bar Assn., Internat. Bar Assn., Commonwealth Club. Roman Catholic. Office: Office of the Attorney General 900 E Main St Richmond VA 23219 E-mail: pthompson@hunton.com.

THOMPSON, PETER LAYARD HAILEY, SR. landscape and golf course architect, architectural firm executive; b. Modesto, Calif., Apr. 26, 1939; BS in East Asian Studies, U. Oreg., 1962, B in Landscape Architecture, M in Urban Planning, U. Oreg., 1971; postgrad., U. Calif., Berkeley, 1975, Nat. U.

Registered landscape arch., Calif., Oreg., Wash., Nev. With Oreg. Planning Commn., Lane County, 1965-70, commr. Eugene, 1981-83; sr. assoc. Ruff, Cameron, Lacoss, 1971-75; prin. Peter L. H. Thompson & Assocs., 1975-83, John H. Midby & Assocs., Las Vegas, Nev., 1983-86, Thompson-Wihlborg, Ltd., Corte Madera, Calif., 1982-89, Thompson Planning Group (now Thompson Golf Planning), Ltd., Novato, 1989—. With Oreg. Planning Commn., commr., 1981-83, Novato, Calif. Planning Commn., commr. 1989-93, pres. 1989-93; spkr. Oreg. Home Builders Conf., 1980, Pacific Coast Builders Conf., 1984, Tacoma Country Club Pro-Pres. Tournament, 1991, Madrona Links Men's Golf Club, 1991, Twin Lakes Country Club Pro-Pres. Tournament, 1992, Golf Expo, Palm Springs, Calif., 1993, 95, Golf Expo, Nashville, 1993, Golf Expo, Monterey, Calif., 1994, others. Contbr. articles to mags. Mem. citizen's adv. bd. City of Eugene, Oreg., City of Las Vegas. Mem. USGA, Am. Soc. Landscape Archs., Am. Assn. Planners, Nat. Golf Found., Urban Land Inst., Rotary Internat. Office: Thompson Golf Planning Ltd 1510 Grant Ave Ste 305 Novato CA 94945-3146

THOMPSON, RALPH GORDON, federal judge; b. Oklahoma City, Dec. 15, 1934; s. Lee Bennett and Elaine (Bizzell) T.; m. Barbara Irene Hencke, Sept. 5, 1964; children: Lisa, Elaine, Maria. BBA, U. Okla., 1956, JD, 1961. Bar: Okla. 1961. Ptnr. Thompson, Thompson, Harbour & Selph (and predecessors), Oklahoma City, 1961-75; judge U.S. Dist. Ct. for Western Dist. Okla., 1975—; chief judge U.S. Dist. Ct. (we. dist.) Okla., 1986-93. Mem. Okla. Ho. of Reps., 1966-70, asst. minority floor leader, 1969-70; spl. justice Supreme Ct. Okla., 1970-71; tchr. Harvard Law Sch. Trial Advocacy Workshop, 1981—; apptd. by chief justice of U.S. to U.S. Fgn. Intelligence Surveillance Ct., 1990-97; elected to jud. conf. of the U.S., 1997; apptd. to Edward J. Devitt Disting. Svc. Justice award selection com., 1997-99; apptd. by chief justice of U.S. to exec. com. of Jud. Conf. of the U.S., 1998-2000; coord. Long Range Planning for Fed. Judiciary, 1999-2000. Co-author: Bryce Harlow: Mr. Integrity, Bob Burke and Ralph G. Thompson, 2000. Rep. nominee for lt. gov., Okla., 1970; chmn. bd. ARC, Oklahoma City, 1970-72; chmn., pres. Okla. Young Lawyers Conf., 1965; mem. bd. visitors U. Okla., 1975-78. Lt. USAF, 1957-60, col. Res., ret. Decorated Legion of Merit; named Oklahoma City's Outstanding Young Man, Oklahoma City Jaycees, 1967, Outstanding Fed. Trial Judge, Okla Trial Lawyers Assn., 1980; recipient Regents Alumni award U. Okla., 1990, Disting. Svc. award, 1993, Jour. Record Pub. Co. award for Disting. Svc., 2001; inducted Okla. Hall of Fame, 1995; nominee Pulitzer Prize, 2000. Fellow Am. Bar Found.; mem. ABA, Fed. Bar Assn., Okla. Bar Assn. (chmn. sect. internat. law and gen. practice 1974-75), Oklahoma County Bar Assn. (Jud. Svc. award 1988), Jud. Conf. U.S. (com. on ct. adminstrn. 1981-89, com. on fed.-state jurisdiction 1988-91), U.S. Dist. Judges Assn. 10th Cir. (pres. 1992-94), Rotary (hon.), Order of Coif, Am. Inns of Ct. (pres. XXIII 1995-96), Phi Beta Kappa (pres. chpt. 1985-86, Phi Beta Kappa of Yr. 1991), Beta Theta Pi, Phi Alpha Delta. Episcopalian. Office: US Dist Ct 200 NW 4th St Oklahoma City OK 73102-3027

THOMPSON, RALPH NEWELL, former chemical corporation executive; b. Boston, Mar. 4, 1918; s. Ralph and Lillian May (Davenport) T.; m. Virginia Kenniston, Jan. 31, 1942; children: Pamela, Nicholas, Diana. BS, MIT, 1940. Research engr. Middlesex Products Co., Cambridge, Mass., 1940-42; tech. dir. Falulah Paper Co., Fitchburg, 1945-48; staff engr. to v.p., div. gen. mgr. Calgon Corp., Pitts., 1948-70; v.p. mktg., corp. devel. Pa. Indsl. Chem. Corp., Clairton, 1970-74; gen. mgr. chem. div. Thiokol Corp., Trenton, N.J., 1974-76, group v.p.-chem. Newtown, Pa., 1976-82; marine artist, specializing in lighthouses and historic sailing vessels, 1982—. Dir. Mulford Co. Inc., Mass., 1956-82, Thiokol Can. Ltd., 1975-82, Thiokol Chems., Ltd., Eng., 1976-82, Toray Thiokol Co. Ltd., Japan, 1976-82, Nisso-Ventron K.K., Japan, 1977-82, S.W. Chem. Services Inc., Tex., 1978-82, S.W. Plastics Europe (S.A.), Belgium, 1978-82, Dynachem. Corp., Calif., 1979-82, Carstab Corp., Ohio, 1980-82 Patentee in field. Mem. Mt. Lebanon (Pa.) Civic League, 1950-74. Served with USNR, 1942-45. Recipient Goodreau Meml. Fund medal in chemistry, 1936 Fellow Am. Inst. Chemists; mem. TAPPI (contributor monograph series 1950-65), N.Y. Acad. Scis., Soc. Chem. Industry, Nat. Maritime Soc., Am. Soc. Marine Artists, Mil. Order World Wars, Pa. Soc., Soc. Descs. Colonial Clergy. Republican. Presbyterian. E-mail: corbet1006@aol.com.

THOMPSON, RAYMOND EUGENE, JR. education educator; b. Merrillville, Ind., Apr. 19, 1958; s. Mary A. (Be) Thompson. AA, Purdue U., 1979, BS, 1980, MS, 1985. Flight instr. Culver (Ind.) Mil. Acad., 1978; asst. prof. Lewis U., Romeoville, Ill., 1980-81; maintenance supr. Aviation Svcs. FBO, 1981; teaching asst. Purdue U., West Lafayette, Ind., 1979-80, asst. prof. edn., 1982-92, assoc. prof., 1993—. Cons. E. G. Composites, Indpls., 1989—, Am. Trans Air, Indpls., 1990—, Am. Corp. Mfg. Learning Ctr., Stuart, Fla., 1992—; aero. tech. curriculum chair Purdue U., 1997—, coord. student svcs. dept. aviation tech., 1998—. Author: Applied Composite Technology, 1992; editor book chpt.; author curriculum in field. Named Outstanding Maintenance Inst., Aviation Tech. Edn. Coun., 1993. Mem. ASM Internat., Great Lake Aviation Tech. Edn. Coun., Soc. for Advancement of Material and Process Engring., Soc. Mfg. Engrs., Am. Soc. Non-Destructive Testing, Profl. Aircraft Maintenance Assn. Avocations: flying, drama, music, outdoor activities.

THOMPSON, RAYMOND HARRIS, retired anthropologist, educator; b. Portland, Me., May 10, 1924; s. Raymond and Eloise (MacIntyre) T.; m. Molly Kendall, Sept. 9, 1948; children: Margaret Kelsey Luchetta, Mary Frances. BS, Tufts U., 1947; A.M., Harvard U., 1950, PhD, 1955. Fellow div. hist. research Carnegie Instn., Washington, 1950-52; asst. prof. anthropology, curator Mus. Anthropology, U. Ky., 1952-56; faculty U. Ariz., 1956-97, prof. anthropology, 1964—, Riecker Disting. prof., 1980-97, head dept., 1964-80; emeritus, 1997; dir. Ariz. State Mus., 1964-97; emeritus, 1997. Mem. adv. panel program in anthropology NSF, 1963-64, mem. mus. collections program, 1983-85; mem. NSF grad. fellowship panel Nat. Acad. Scis.-NRC, 1964-66; mem. research in nursing in patient care rev. com. USPHS, 1967-69; com. on social sci. commn. edn. in agr. and natural resources Nat. Acad. Scis., 1968-69; mem. anthropology com. examiners Grad. Record Exam., 1967-70, chmn., 1969-70; mem. com. recovery archaeol. remains, 1972-77, chmn., 1973-77; collaborator Nat. Park Service, 1972-76; mem. Ariz. Hist. Adv. Commn., 1966-97, chmn., 1971-74, chmn. hist. sites rev. com., 1971-83; chmn. Ariz. Humanities Council, 1973-77, mem., 1979-85; adv. bd. Ariz. Hist. Recors, 1976-84; mem. research review panel for archaeology NEH, 1976-77, mem. rev. panel for museums, 1978, Ariz. Archaeology Adv. Commn., 1985-97; cons. task force on archaeology Adv. Council on Historic Preservation, 1978. Author: Modern Yucatecan Maya Pottery Making, 1958; editor: Migrations in New World Culture History, 1958, When is a Kiva, 1990; mem. editl. bd. Science, 1972-77. Trustee Mus. No. Ariz., 1969-84, 86-90; bd. dirs. Tucson Art Mus., 1974-77; cons. Nat. Mus. Act Coun., 1984-86. Served with USNR, 1944-45, PTO. Recipient Pub. Svc. award, Dept. Interior, 1990. Fellow AAAS (chmn. sect. H 1977-78), Tree-Ring Soc., Am. Anthrop. Assn. (Disting. Svc. award 1980); mem. Soc. Am. Archaeology (editor 1958-62, exec. com. 1963-64, pres. 1976-77, disting. svc. award 1998), Am. Soc. Conservation Archaeology (Conservation award 1980), Seminario de Cultura Maya, Am. Assn. Museums (accreditation vis. com. 1972, 82-90, cons. mus. assessment program 1983-89, repatriation task force 1987, steering com. mus. data collection program 1988-93), Internat. Coun. Museums (assoc.), Coun. Mus. Anthropology (dir. 1978-79, pres. 1980-83), Assn. Sci. Mus. Dirs. (sec.-treas. 1978-80), Ariz. Acad. Sci., Ariz. Archaeol. and Hist. Soc. (Byron Cummings award 1993), Mus. Assn. Ariz. (pres. 1983, 84), Phi Beta Kappa, Sigma Xi. Office: Univ Ariz Ariz State Museum Tucson AZ 85721-0026

THOMPSON, RICHARD FREDERICK, psychologist, neuroscientist, educator; b. Portland, Oreg., 1930; s. Frederick Albert and Margaret St. Clair (Marr) T.; m. Judith K. Pedersen, May 22, 1960; children: Kathryn M., Elizabeth K., Virginia St. C. BA, Reed Coll., 1952; MS, U. Wis., 1953, PhD, 1956. Asst. prof. med. psychology Med. Sch. U. Oreg., Portland, 1959-63, assoc. prof., 1963-65, prof., 1965-67; prof. psychobiology U. Calif., Irvine, 1967-73, 75-80; prof. psychology Harvard U., Cambridge, Mass., 1973-74, Lashley chair prof., 1973; prof. psychology, Bing prof. human biology Stanford U., Palo Alto, Calif., 1980-87; Keck prof. psychology and biol. scis. U. So. Calif., L.A., 1987—, dir. neuroscience program, 1989—. Author: Foundations of Physiological Psychology, 1967, (with others) Psychology, 1971, Introduction to Physiological Psychology, 1975; Psychology editor (with others), W.H. Freeman & Co. publs., chief editor, Behavioral Neurosci., 1983—; editor: Jour. Comparative and Physiol. Psychology, 1981-83; regional editor: (with others) Physiology and Behavior; contbr. (with others) articles to profl. jours. Fellow AAAS, APA (Disting. Sci. Contbn. award 1974, governing coun. 1974—), Soc. Neurosci. (councilor 1972-76); mem. NAS, Am. Acad. Arts and Scis., Internat. Brain Rsch. Orgn., Am. Philos. Soc., Psychonomic Soc. (gov. 1972-77, chmn. 1976), Am. Psychol. Soc. (pres. 1994-96), Western Psychol. Assn. (pres. 1994-95), Soc. Exptl. Psychology (Warren medal). Office: Univ of So Calif Neuroscis Program HNB 122 Univ Park Los Angeles CA 90007

THOMPSON, RICHARD LEON, pharmaceutical company executive, lawyer; b. Rochester, N.Y., Dec. 5, 1944; s. Leslie L. and Marion (Cosad) T.; m. Catherine Jean Terry, July 6, 1974; children: Kristin Anne, Catherine Elizabeth. AB cum laude, SUNY, Albany, 1966; MA, Syracuse U., 1967; JD, Cath. U., 1975. Staff dir., counsel U.S. Ho. of Reps., Washington, 1973-78; dir. Abbott Labs., 1978-83; v.p. Squibb Corp., 1983-89, Bristol-Myers Squibb Corp., Washington, 1989—2001, sr. v.p. policy and govt. affairs, 2001—. Chmn. legis. adv. com. Proprietary Assn., Washington, 1984; bd. dirs. Bus. Govt. Rels. Coun. Mem. com. on changing enrollments Fairfax (Va.) County Pub. Sch., 1983-84, supts. adv. com., 1984-85, mem., 1988—; mem. Fed. City Coun., 1992; chmn. legis. com. P.R.-U.S.A. Found., 1985—; co-chair Edn. in 2010; bd. dirs. D.C. Hospice, Bryce Harlow Found., 1990-95; bd. dirs., treas. Ford Theater, 2000--; chmn. governance com. Meritian Internat. Ctr. 1st lt. U.S. Army, 1968-69, Vietnam. Named one of Outstanding Young Men of Am., Jaycees, 1976. Mem. ABA, D.C. Bar Assn., Pharm. Mfrs. Assn. (chmn. Washington reps. com.1988), Congl. Country Club, Georgetown Club, City Club. Home: 1005 Woburn Ct Mc Lean VA 22102-2133 Office: Bristol-Myers Squibb Corp 655 15th St NW Ste 300 Washington DC 20005-5717

THOMPSON, RICHARD LLOYD, pastor; b. Lansing, Mich., May 8, 1939; s. Lloyd Walter and Gladys V. (Gates) T.; m. Dianne Lee Tuttle, Nov. 14, 1958; children: Matthew, Beth Anne, Douglas. BA, Azusa Pacific U., 1969; MDiv, Concordia Theol. Sem., 1973; DD, Concordia U., Mequon, Wis., 1997. Aerospace industry test engr. Hycon Mfg. Co., Monrovia, Calif., 1961-69; pastor Trinity Luth. Ch., Cedar Rapids, Iowa, 1973-84, Billings, Mont., 1984-94, Good Shepherd Luth. Ch., Watertown, Wis., 1994—2001. Chmn. mission com. Iowa E. dist. Luth. Ch. Mo. Synod, 1979-81, 2nd v.p. Iowa dist. E., Cedar Rapids, 1981-84, bd. mgr. Concordia plans, St. Louis, 1983-86, bd. dirs., St. Louis, 1986-98, chmn. bd. dirs., 1992-98, mem. commn. on theology and ch. rels., 2001; served on various task forces and coms. dealing with structure and vision setting for chs. at local, dist. and nat. level, 1975—. Mem. Nat. Exch. Club, Cedar Rapids, 1982-84, Billings, 1986. With USN, 1957-61. Mem. Kiwanis. Avocations: attending auctions, yard work, travel, exercise activity. E-mail: rlt50@hotmail.com.

THOMPSON, RICHARD STEPHEN, management consultant; b. Des Moines, Oct. 14, 1931; s. Richard Stephen and Mary Ellen (Dailey) T.; m. Nancy Ann Jensen, Apr. 17, 1954; children— Traci Nan, Gregory Christian, Jonathan Richard BSC, State U. Iowa, 1953; MBA, Ind. U., 1960. Regional dir. Bristol Myers Co., N.Y.C., 1969-75; regional dir. Warner Lambert Co., Morris Plains, N.J., 1975-78; exec. v.p. Milton Bradley Co., Milton Bradley Internat., Inc., Springfield, Mass., 1979-83, pres., 1983-84; sr. v.p. internat., dir. Hasbro, Inc., Pawtucket, R.I., 1984-89; pres. Richard Thompson Assocs., London, 1989—. Served to 1st lt. USAF, 1954-55 Mem.: Chatham Beach Tennis (Mass.); Pilgrims (London and N.Y.); American (London); Roehampton (London). Republican. Avocations: tennis; skiing; hiking; reading.

THOMPSON, RICHARD THOMAS, academic administrator; b. Buffalo, Oct. 11, 1939; m. Nancy A. Streeter, July 29, 1959; children: Elizabeth Thompson Grapentine, Richard Thomas Jr., David Bryant. BA, Ea. Mich. U., 1961, MA, 1963; LLD (hon.), Walsh Coll., 2000. Cert. tchr., Mich. Tchr. Warren (Mich.) Consol. Sch., 1961-66; dean, pres. Highland Lake campus Oakland C.C., Union Lake, Mich., 1966-75, pres. Orchard Ridge campus Farmington, 1975-84, v.p. Bloomfield, 1984-88, vice chancellor, 1988-91, chancellor, 1996—, pres. Auburn Hills campus. Arbitrator Better Bus. Bur., Detroit, 1987—; bd. dirs., past chair Providence Hosp., Southfield, Mich., 1988—; cons. examiner N. Ctrl. Assn. Commn. on Higher Learning, 1988—. Contbr. articles to profl. jours. Pres. Oakway Symphony Orch., Livonia, Mich., 1981-85; chair Oakland Literacy coun., Pontiac, Mich., 1988—. Recipient Leadership award Oakland County C. of C., 1987, Tricounty Disting. Svc. award Detroit Coll. Bus., 1996, Shirley B. Gordon award of Distinction Phi Theta Kappa Internat., 2001. Mem. Phi Delta Kappa. Home: 625 E Commerce St Milford MI 48381-1723 Office: Oakland Community Coll 2480 Opdyke Rd Bloomfield Hills MI 48304-2223

THOMPSON, RICHARD THOMAS, communication company executive; b. Bklyn., Mar. 25, 1948; s. Richard Thomas Sr. and Louise Marguerite (Jackson) T.; m. Kay Childs Bowen, June 16, 1973; children: Thomas Richard, Kenneth Bowen. BSEd, Lock Haven State Coll., 1970. Tchr. St. Mary's County Schs., Lexington Park, Md., 1970-71; reporter St. Mary's Beacon, Leonardtown, 1971; news dir. WESM Radio, Prince Frederick, 1971-72; mng. editor Bowie (Md.) Blade, 1972-80; editor Calvert County Recorder, Prince Frederick, 1980-81; gen. mgr. Custom News, Inc., Bethesda, Md., 1981-89; pres. Thompson Comm., Inc., Prince Frederick, 1989—. Pres. Seabrook Little Theatre, 1974-76, 82-83; bd. dirs. Tidewater Theatre, 1979. Recipient 1st Place News Story award, 1976, 78, 1st Place Editorials award, 1971, 1st Place News Feature Series award, 1973, 74, 78, 2d Place News Feature Story award, 1973, 77, 2d Place Editorials award, 1978, 1st Place Overall Newspaper Design award, 1980, 2d Place Front Page Design award, 1980, others, all from Md.-Del.-D.C. Press Assn. Mem. Soc. Profl. Journalists.

THOMPSON, RICHARD W. retired health facility administrator; b. New Haven, June 12, 1932; s. Hugo W. Thompson, Sibyl L. Thompson; m. Ruth Nash, May 5, 1961; children: Beth Diane, Allison Lynne, Maxwel Tollef. BA, Macalester Coll., 1954; MA, U. Chgo., 1960; MSSA, Case We. Res. U., 1965. Cert. LSW Pa., LISW Ohio. Group worker Cleve. Psychiat. Inst., 1965—67; coord. group svcs. Hill House, Cleve., 1967—79; rsch. assoc. Cmty. Guidance, Inc., 1979—81; coord. intermed. Nova Behavioral Health, Inc., Canton, 1981—89, pres./CEO, 1989—99; ret., 1999. Mobile therapist Stairways, Inc., Erie, Pa., 2001—; cons. WSCMHC, Cuyaga Falls Hosp., Cleve., Akron, Ohio, 1978—79. Contbr. Mem.: IAPSRS, AASWG, NASW. Home: 12191 Angling Rd Edinboro PA 16412-1348

THOMPSON, ROBERT ALLAN, aerospace engineer; b. Cleve., June 10, 1937; s. Roy Henry and Viola Alverta (Nehls) T.; m. Louise Alberta Saari, Nov. 27, 1970. BSEE, Case Western Reserve U., 1958; postgrad. studies, Cleve. State U., 1959, John Marshall Law Sch., 1970; PhD, Union Inst., 1979. Registered profl. engr. Ohio, Wis., Conn., R.I. Tchr. Cleve. Bd. Edn., 1958-65; rsch. engr. Sohio Satellite Tracking Sta., Standard Oil Rsch. Lab., Cleve., 1958-63, acting dir., 1964-65; dir. Warrensville Hghts. (Ohio) Planetarium and Space Sci Program, 1964-65; tchr. spl. programs faculty Case Inst. Tech., Cleve., 1965; dir. planning phase sci. divsn. Cleve. Supplementary Edn. Ctr., 1965-66; dir. James A Lovell Regional Space Ctr., Milw., 1967-73; engring. and edn. cons. Chgo., 1973-78, Mystic, Conn., 1978—; pres., chmn. bd. Spatialworld Corp., 1982—. Chmn. secondary math. curriculum com. Cleve. Pub. Schs., 1963-64; mem. Wis. Aerospace Edn. Com., 1968-71; lectr. U. Wis., Milw., 1968-71; sec. Friends of Space Ctr., 1968-75. Author: The New Egoshell: An Individualized Space Age Realty; co-author (with wife) Egoshell-Planetary Individualism Balanced within Planetary Interdependence, 1987; contbr. articles to encys. and profl. jours. Recipient Leadership award Kiwanis Key Club, 1961; named Goodwin Watson Inst. doctoral fellow, 1978-79. Fellow: Brit. Interplanetary Assn.; mem.: AIAA (chmn. Wis. sect. 1969—70, coun. 1984—85, disting. lectr. 1987—89, sr. mem. Conn. sect.), AAAS (sr.; mem. exec. com.), IEEE (chmn. membership com. Cleve. sect. 1965—66), Cleve. Astron. Soc. (mem. exec. com. 1966—67), Cleve. Engring. Soc., Inst. for Planetary Egology (pres. 1988—), Union Inst. Alumni Assn., Case Alumni Assn. Home: PO Box 624 Mystic CT 06355-0624 Office: PO Box 2001 Mystic CT 06355-0624 E-mail: egoshell@aol.com.

THOMPSON, ROBERT CHARLES, lawyer; b. Council, Idaho, Apr. 20, 1942; s. Ernest Lavelle and Evangeline Montgomery (Carlson) T.; m. Marilyn Anne Wilcox, Jan. 17, 1960 (dec. Mar. 1962); m. Patricia Joan Price, June 1, 1963 (div. 1969); m. Jan Nesbitt, June 29, 1973 (dec. May 1998); m. Shari Lewis, Feb. 7, 1999; children: Tanya, Carrie, Christopher, Eric. AB, Harvard U., 1963, LLB, 1967. Bar: Mass. 1967, Calif. 1983, U.S. Dist. Ct. (ea. dist.) Mass. 1975, U.S. Ct. Appeals (1st cir.) 1976, U.S. Ct. Appeals (9th cir.) 1984, U.S. Dist. Ct. (no. dist.) Calif. 1983, U.S. Dist. Ct. (ea. dist.) Calif., 1996. Assoc. Choate, Hall & Stewart, Boston, 1967-73; asst. regional counsel EPA, 1973-75, regional counsel, 1975-82, assoc. gen. counsel, 1979-82, regional counsel San Francisco, 1982-84; ptnr. Graham & James, 1984-91, LeBoeuf, Lamb, Greene & MacRae LLP, San Francisco, 1992—99, of counsel, 2000—. Contbr. articles to profl. jours. Bd. dirs. Peninsula Indsl. and Bus. Assn., Palo Alto, Calif., 1986-98, chmn. Cambridge (Mass.) Conservation Commn., 1972-74; co-chmn. The Clift Confs. on Environ. Law, 1983-98; assoc. mem. Bay Conservation and Devel. Commn., 1998-2000. John Russell Shaw traveling fellow Harvard Coll., 1963-64; recipient Regional Administrs. Bronze medal EPA, 1976, 84. Mem. ABA (natural resources sect., com. on native Am. natural resources law, spl. com. on mktg.), Human Rights Watch, Phi Beta Kappa. Democrat. Episcopalian. Avocations: personal computers, yoga, antiques, wines, cooking, gardening. Office: LeBoeuf Lamb Greene & MacRae One Embarcadero Ctr San Francisco CA 94111

THOMPSON, ROBERT DOUGLAS, computer science educator, banker, consultant; b. Van Wert, Ohio, Apr. 2, 1944; s. Ernest Clinton and Gertrude Marcele (McBride) T.; m. Gail Joyce Knudson; children: Linda Marie Temple, Cheryl Elizabeth Christensen, Mark Robert. BS summa cum laude, Huntington Coll., 1966; MA, Mich. State U., East Lansing, 1967; student, Wright State U., 1974-90, Bowling Green State U., 1984, U. Dayton, 1985. Cert. tchr., Ohio. Office sec. United Brethren in Christ Denomination Ch., Huntington, Ind., 1963-66; grad. research asst. Mich. State U., East Lansing, 1966-67; instr. Wright State U. Lake Campus, Celina, Ohio, 1976, 93-97, Tri Star Career Compact, Celina, 1984-96; ptnr. Thompson Painting and Carpentry, Rockford, Ohio, 1969-95; tchr., dept. head, tech. coord. St. Henry (Ohio) Consol. Local Schs., 1967-97; asst. v.p., br. mgr. Peoples Bank Co., Rockford, Ohio, 1997—. Author, photographer numerous newspaper articles, 1974—, Business Professionals of America Ohio Association Handbook, 1989. Bd. dirs., pres., v.p. Oscar Figert Guidance Clinic, 1972-75; pres. Mercer County Mental Health Clinic, 1975; fin. chmn. Coldwater United Meth. Ch., 1982-90, 2000—, chmn. adminstrv. bd., 1994-99, lay leader, 1998--; solicitor Coldwater Combined Charities, 1982, 85; PRIDE evaluation svc. rep. State Dept. Edn., 1973, 78; troop treas. Coldwater area Boy Scouts Am., 1989-92; mem. office tech. adv. bd. Wright State U.-Lake Campus, Celina, Ohio, 1991—; gen. chairperson Rockford Combined Charities, 1997-2001; exec. officer Rockford Citizen Crime Awareness, 1998—; trustee Shanes Park, 1999—, Rockford Carnegie Libr., 1999—, v.p. 2001, pres. 2002; pres. Leota Braun Charitable Found., Inc., 2002--. Named super advisor Ohio Office Edn. Assn., 1983, 84, 85; recipient proclamation of excellence, Ohio State Dept. Edn. Mem. NEA, Am. Vocat. Assn., Bus. Profl. Am. (advisor 1973-97, star advisor and honor advisor award), Ohio Bus. Tchrs. Assn. (state exec. bd. 1976-77, 93-98, state conv. chmn. 1995, Western Ohio Bus. Tchr. of Yr. award 1983, 91, 95, Ohio Bus. Tchr. of Yr. 1995, Editor of Publs. 1996-98), Ohio Edn. Assn., St. Henry Edn. Assn. (local pres. 1970-72), Wabash Valley Dartball Assn. (sec. 1978-79, 87-88), Rockford (Ohio) C. of C. (treas. 1998—), Lions (Rockford chpt. v.p. 2001—), Delta Pi Epsilon. Republican. Avocations: travel, computers, choir singing. Home: 405 S Main St PO Box 242 Rockford OH 45882-0242 Office: Peoples Bank Co PO Box 475 101 N Main St Rockford OH 45882-8118 E-mail: rthompson@pbcbank.com.

THOMPSON, ROBERT FRANK, JR. career officer; b. Durham, N.C., Sept. 25, 1959; s. Robert Frank Sr. and Betty Ross (Connelly) T.; m. Vickie Marie Fjone, Nov. 17, 1979; children: Robert Frank III, Kimberly Anne. BA in English and History, Met. State Coll. Denver, 1993. Commd. 2d lt. U.S. Army Nat. Guard, 1989, advanced through grades to maj., 1998; stationed at Panama, Ft. Polk, La., 1983-87; rural rt. carrier U.S. Postal Svc., Brighton, Colo., 1988-93; adminstrv. officer Colo. Army Nat. Guard, Denver, 1993-98, state family program dir., 1999-2000. Defense movement coord, 1998; master fitness trainer Colo. Army Nat. Guard, 1987, advisor work climate improvement program, 1995, facilitator increasing human effectiveness, 1996. Editor The Adv., 1990-91; founder Bob Thompson Freelance Writing and Editing Svcs., 2000; founder, gen. editor The Christian Fine Arts Review, 2000; contbr. poetry to publs. including The bible Advocate mag., The Sound of Poetry CD Set, 2001. Deacon Crossroads Bapt. Ch., Northglenn, Colo., 1997-99. Decorated Army Commendation medal (6); recipient Exceptional Acad. Achievement award ROTC, 1989, Metro State Coll. V.P.'s Honor Roll (3). Mem.: N.G. Assn. U.S., U.S. F.A. Assn. (Hon. Order St. Barbaras 1993), Poetry Soc. Colo., Golden Key Nat. Honor Soc., Pi Gamma Mu, Phi Alpha Theta. Republican. Avocations: freelance writing, traveling, reading, sports. Home: 11305 Nome St Henderson CO 80640-9259 E-mail: bvthom@attbi.com.

THOMPSON, ROBERT JOSEPH, university administrator, educator; b. Portsmouth, Ohio, May 20, 1949; s. Shirley and Patricia Ann Thompson; m. Elaine Ann Wulf, Aug. 7, 1971 (div. Sept. 1993); m. Marie Elizabeth Pokorny, July 5, 1996. BA in Polit. Sci., Miami U., Oxford, Ohio, 1971; MA in Polit. Sci., PhD in Polit. Sci., U. Okla., 1976. Dir. Office Planning and Instnl. Rsch. East Carolina U., Greenville, NC, 1991—, chief staff to chancellor, 1999—2001, interim vice chancellor for acad. affairs, 2001—. Chair dept. polit. sci. East Carolina U., Greenville, 1988-93, asst. prof. polit. sci., 1981-87, assoc. prof. polit. sci.; vis. asst. prof. polit. sci. Tex. A&M U., College Station. Editor: (books) Ethnoterritorial Politics, Policy, and the Western World, 1989, Politica etnoterritorial, 1992; author: (book chpts.) The Spokes of the Wheel in Operation: The Carter Example, 1993, Contrasting Models of White House Staff Organization: The Eisenhower, Ford, and Carter Experiences, 1992, The Home Front: Domestic Policy in the Bush Years, 1992. Mem. exec. bd. United Way Pitt County, Greenville, 2001—, mem. exec. allocations, 1998. Mem. Am. Polit. Sci. Assn., Assn. for Instnl. Rsch., Soc. for Coll. and Univ. Planning, So. Assn. for Instnl. Rsch., Brit. Politics Group. Avocations: travel, gardening, mysteries. Office: East Carolina U 207 Spilman Bldg Greenville NC 27858-4353 Fax: 252-328-6160. E-mail: thompsonro@mail.ecu.edu.

THOMPSON, ROBERT KNOX, surgeon; b. Memphis, Jan. 4, 1957; MD, U. Tenn. Ctr. Health Scis., 1983. Diplomate Am. Bd. Surgery, Am. Bd. Gen. Vascular Surgery. Intern U. Tex., San Antonio, 1983-84, resident in gen. surgery, 1984-88; fellow in vascular surgery Baylor U. Med. Ctr., Dallas, 1988-89; pvt. practice San Antonio. Mem. staff Bapt. Meml. Hosp. Sys., San Antonio, Meth. Hosp., San Antonio; clin. assoc. prof. surgery U. Tex., San Antonio. Fellow ACS; mem. Internat. Soc. Cardiovasc. Surgery, So. Assocs. for Vascular Surgery, San Antonio Vascular Surg. Soc., Peripheral Vascular Surgery Soc., Bexar Conty Med. Soc., Tex. Med. Assn., Tex. Surg. Soc. Office: Peripheral Vascular Assocs 8715 Village Dr Ste 518 San Antonio TX 78217-5501

THOMPSON, ROBERT L., JR. pharmaceutical executive, lawyer; b. St. Paul, Aug. 9, 1944; s. Robert L. and Dorothy R. (Bergstrom) T.; m. Carolyn H. Foss, Aug. 4, 1973; children: Sarah, Kathryn, Jill. BA, Macalester Coll., St. Paul, 1967; JD, U. Oreg., 1973; LLM, NYU, 1988. Bar: Minn. 1973, U.S. Dist. Ct. Minn. 1978, N.Y. 1984. Corp. counsel Northrup King Co., Mpls., 1974-84; assoc. gen. counsel Sandoz Corp., N.Y.C., 1984-88, v.p., gen. counsel, sec., 1989-96; exec. v.p., gen. counsel Novartis Corp., 1997-2001; pres., mng. dir. Novartis India, Ltd., Bombay, 2001—. Mem. adv. bd. FM Global Ins. Co., N.Y.C., 1990-2001; mem. bd. visitors U. Oreg. Law Sch., 1995-2001. 1st lt. U.S. Army, 1968-70. Mem. ABA, Assn. Bar City N.Y. Republican. Presbyterian. Office: Novartis India Ltd Dr Annie Besant Rd Shivagar Worli Mumbai 400 018 India

THOMPSON, ROBERT LEE, agricultural economist, nonprofit executive; b. Canton, N.Y., Apr. 25, 1945; s. Robert M. and Esther Louise (Weatherup) T.; m. Karen Hansen, Aug. 9, 1968; children— Kristina Marie, Eric Robert. BS, Cornell U., Ithaca, N.Y., 1967; MS, Purdue U., West Lafayette, Ind., 1969, PhD, 1974; LLD, Dalhousie U., 1999; DSc honoris causa, Pa. State U., 1999. Vol. agriculturalist Internat. Vol. Service, Pakse and Vientiane, Laos, 1968-70; vis. prof. Fed. Univ. Vicosa, Brazil, 1972-73; prof. Purdue U., West Lafayette, Ind., 1974-93, dean of agr., 1987-93; rsch. scholar Internat. Inst. for Applied Systems Analysis, Laxenburg, Austria, 1983; sr. staff economist Council Econ. Advisers, Washington, 1983-85; asst. sec. econs. U.S. Dept. Agr., 1985-87; pres., CEO Winrock Internat. Inst. Agrl. Devel., 1993-98; sr. advisor World Bank, Washington, 1998-99, dir. rural devel., 1999—2002; sr. advisor Ctr. for Strategic and Internat. Studies, 1998—. Vis. prof. Econ. Rsch. Svc., USDA, 1979-80; bd. dirs. Terra Industries, Inc., Nat. Coop. Bank, Washington, 1985-97, Commodity Credit Corp., Washington, 1985-87, PSI Resources and

P.S.I. Energy, 1987-94; chmn. adv. coun. Nat. Ctr. for Food and Agrl. Policy, Washington, 1987-92; mem. Ind. Commn. on Agr. and Rural Devel., 1989-93, Nat. Commn. on Agrl. Trade and Export Policy, 1985-86, Nat. Commn. Internat. Trade, Devel., and Cooperation, 1996-97; mem. bd. agr. NRC, 1987-92; mem. Internat. Policy Coun. on Agr. and Trade, 1987—, chmn., 2000—; mem. USDA Joint Coun. on Food and Agrl. Scis., 1994-96; cons. USAID, Agr. Can., Ford Found., Brazilian Agr. Ministry, FAO, World Bank, Internat. Food Policy Rsch. Inst., Internat. Maize and Wheat Improvement Ctr., U.S. Feed Grains Coun., Nat. Planning Assn., USIA, Centre for Internat. Econs., Canberra, Club d'Experts en Economie Agricole Internat., Paris, Danish Coun. Rsch. Policy, FAO, Rome. Contbr. numerous articles to profl. publs. Author monographs, book chpts. Bd. dirs. Ind. 4-H Found., Ind. Inst. Agr. Food and Nutrition, 1987-93, Inst. for Sci. in Soc., 1991-93, USDA Grad. Sch., Washington, 1985-87; mem. nat. adv. coun. Minorities in Agr., Natural Resources and Related Sci.; bd. dirs. Farm Found., 1987-92, chmn. 1991-92. Recipient Agrl. Rsch. award Purdue U., 1983, Outstanding Alumni award Cornell U., 1988, Superior Svc. award USDA, 1989, Justin Smith Morrill award, 1995, Nat. 4-H Alumni award, 1992, Chgo. Farmers Agriculturalist of Yr. award, 1992, Bob Pim Agrl. Vision award Nat. Forum Agr., 1997; named Humanitarian of Yr., Am. Coll. Nutrition, 1999. Fellow AAAS, Am. Agrl. Econs. Assn. (editorial coun. 1983-85, quality com. award 1979, 91, 93); mem. Internat. Agribus Mgmt. Assn. (bd. dirs.), Am. Econ. Assn., Internat. Assn. Agrl. Economists (pres. 1993-96), Coun. on Fgn. Rels., Bretton Woods Com., Royal Swedish Acad. Agr. and Forestry (fgn.), Ukrainian Acad. Agrl. Scis., Cosmos Club (Washington), Sigma Xi, Alpha Gamma Rho, Alpha Zeta (Centennial Honor Role award 1997), Gamma Sigma Delta. Republican. Avocation: foreign language study. Office: 1300 Crystal Dr Apt 602 Arlington VA 22202-3234 E-mail: robert_l_thompson2@att.net.

THOMPSON, ROBERT SAMUEL, lawyer; b. Cleve., Nov. 2, 1930; s. Wayne Charles Thompson and Cornelia Irene (Anderson) Thompson Baker; m. Dorothy "JoAnne" Courtney; children: Robert Dale, Richard Wayne. BA, Hamilton Coll., 1953; JD, U. Mich., 1956; postgrad., Air Command and Staff Coll., Montgomery, Ala., 1967-68. Bar: Mich. 1956, Ohio 1962, U.S. Supreme Ct. 1962, Oreg. 1973. Judge advocate USAF, 1956-77; pvt. practice McMinnville, Oreg., 1977-98. Judge mcpl. ct., 1977—. Maj. USAF, 1977. Judge mcpl. ct. 1977—. Maj. USAF. Mem. Oreg. Soc. SAR (pres. 1989-90), Oreg. Mcpl. Judges Assn. (pres. 1992-93), Rotary (bd. dirs. McMinnville chpt. 1989), Am. Legion, Masons. Home and Office: 127 NW 19th St Mcminnville OR 97128-2611

THOMPSON, ROBERT WAYNE, JR. judge, lawyer; b. Sioux Falls, S.D., Feb. 22, 1948; s. Robert Wayne Thompson Sr. and Lawella Mildred Thompson; m. Julie Ann Harris, Aug. 27, 1976; 1 child Huette Brianna. AB, U. S.D., 1970; MUA, U. Colo., 1976; JD, U. Denver, 1983. Bar: Colo. 1984. Bldgs. mgr. trainee Gen. Svcs. Adminstrn., Kansas City, Mo., 1970—71; employment counselor M.N. Nelson & Assoc., Englewood, Colo., 1972—74; employment rep. Colo. Dept. Labor, Denver, 1976—78; analyst, edn. specialist Louisville (Ky.) -Jefferson County, 1979—81; law clk. Ullstrom Law Offices, Denver, 1982—84; pvt. practice, 1984—; adminstrv. law judge State of Colo., 1992—. Co-author: Practitioners Guide to Colorado Employment Law, 1998; author: As Sweet as it Gets, 2002. Commr. Cultural Affairs Commn., Aurora, Colo., 1997—. Mem.: Denver Bar Assn., Colo. Bar Assn. Avocations: sports, reading. Home: 366 S Victor St Aurora CO 80012 Office: Colo State Pers Bd 1120 Lincoln St #1420 Denver CO 80203

THOMPSON, ROBERTA JILL, social worker; b. Chgo., Mar. 30, 1948; d. Obert Osmann and Walma Tuulikki (Martinmaki) T. AB, U. Ill., 1970; MSW, U. Minn., 1976. Cert. social worker; bd. cert. dimpomate social work; lic. ind. clin. social worker, Minn., Ill. Social worker, Minn. case worker Ill. Dept. Pub. Aid, Chgo., 1971-74, summer 1975; acting dir. social svcs. Martha Washington Hosp., 1976-77; social worker IV Fond Du Lac County (Wis.) Social Svcs., 1977-80; social worker VA Med. Ctr., Tomah, Wis., 1980, Germantown (Wis.) Sch.Dist., 1980-81, Zablocki VA Med. Ctr., Milw., 1981-87; supr. social worker VA Lakeside Med. Ctr., Chgo., 1987—. Mem. NASW. Avocations: antique collecting, travel, swimming. Office: VA Lakeside Med Ctr 333 E Huron St Chicago IL 60611-3004

THOMPSON, RODNEY LEE, infectious diseases specialist; b. Kansas City, Mo., Nov. 2, 1941; s. Ernest Arthur and Frances Raymond T.; m. Carol Kindell; children: Rodney L., Jr., Christopher K., Deborah C., Bradley F. BA, Kans. U., 1963, MD, 1967. Diplomate Am. Bd. Internal Medicine. Med. officer U.S. Army, Munich, 1971-74; cons. Mayo Found., Rochester, Minn., 1976—. Fellow ACP; mem. AMA, Soc. Healthcare Epidemiology Am., Am. Practitioners Infection Control. Office: Mayo Clinic 200 1st St SW Rochester MN 55905-0002

THOMPSON, RODNEY MARLIN, computer consultant; b. Ft. Dodge, Iowa, June 27, 1955; m. Deborah Kay Owen; children: Ryan, Thomas. BA, Iowa State U., 1977; MBA, Pa. State U., 1988. Cert. software test engr., cert. in transp. and logistics, cert. project mgmt. profl., cert. profl. logistician, cert. prodn. and inventory mgmt., cert. integrated resource mgmt. Commd. ensign USN, 1977, advanced through grades to comdr., 1992; supply officer USS Batfish, Charleston, S.C., 1978-81, Comsubron Eight, Norfolk, Va., 1981-83; stores officer USS Dwight D. Eisenhower, 1983-86; weapon sys. mgr. Aviation Supply Office, Phila., 1988-91; frt. terminal dir. USN Supply depot, Subic Bay, The Philippines, 1991-92; project mgr. Mil. Traffic Mgmt. Command, Washington, 1992-96; Navy liaison officer-in-chg. NAVTRANS, Norfolk, 1997; ret.; sr. cons. Cap Gemini, St. Louis, 1997-99, Baird, Kurtz & Dobson, St. Louis, 2000-01, MidTec, St. Louis, 2001—. Recipient Cert. of Appreciation, U.S. Customs Svc., 1991; named to Outstanding Young Men of Am., 1987. Mem. Internat. Soc. Logistics, Project Mgmt. Inst., Am. Soc. Transp. and Logistics, Quality Assurance Inst., Am. Prodn. and Inventory Control Soc., Beta Sigma Psi, Phi Alpha Theta. Lutheran. Avocations: reading, writing. Office: MidTec 706 N Jefferson Saint Louis MO 63103

THOMPSON, RONALD EDWARD, lawyer; b. Bremerton, Wash., May 24, 1931; s. Melville Herbert and Clara Mildred (Griggs) T.; m. Marilyn Christine Woods, Dec. 15, 1956; children: Donald Jeffery, Karen, Susan, Nancy, Sally, Claire BA, U. Wash., 1953, JD, 1958. Bar: Wash. 1959. Asst. city atty. City of Tacoma, 1960-61; pres. firm Thompson, Krilich, LaPorte, West & Lockner, P.S., Tacoma, 1961-99. Judge pro tem Mcpl. Ct., City of Tacoma, Pierce County Dist., 1972—, Pierce County Superior Ct., 1972—. Chmn. housing and social welfare com. City of Tacoma, 1965-69; mem. Tacoma Bd. Adjustment, 1967-71, chmn., 1968; mem. Tacoma Com. Future Devel., 1961-64, Tacoma Planning Commn., 1971-72; bd. dirs., pres. Mcpl. League Tacoma; bd. dirs. Pres. Tacoma Rescue Mission, Tacoma Pierce County Cancer Soc., Tacoma-Pierce County Heart Assn., Tacoma Grand Cinema, Tacoma-Pierce County Coun. for Arts, Econ. Devel. Coun. Puget Sound, Tacoma Youth Symphony, Kleiner Group Home, Tacoma C.C. Found., Pierce County Econ. Devel. Corp., Wash. Transp. Policy Inst.; Coalition to Keep Wash. Moving, precinct committeeman Rep. party, 1969-73. With AUS, 1953-55; col. Res. Recipient Internat. Cmty. Svc. award Optimist Club, 1970, Patriotism award Am. Fedn. Police, 1974, citation for cmty. svc. HUD, 1974, Disting. Citizen award Mcpl. League Tacoma-Pierce County, 1985; named Lawyer of the Yr. Pierce County Legal Secs. Assn., 1992. Mem. ATLA, Am. Arbitration Assn. (panel of arbitrators), ABA, Wash. State Bar Assn. Local Hero award 2002), Tacoma-Pierce County Bar Assn. (sec. 1964, pres. 1979, mem. cts. and judiciary com. 1981-82), Wash. State Trial Lawyers Assn., Tacoma-Pierce County C. of C. (bd. dirs., exec. com., v.p., chmn.), Downtown Tacoma Assn. (com. chmn., bd. dirs. exec. com., chmn.), Variety Club (Seattle), Lawn Tennis Club, Tacoma Club, Optimist (Tacoma, internat. pres. 1973-74), Phi Delta Phi, Sigma Nu. Roman Catholic. Home: 3101 E Bay Dr NW Gig Harbor WA 98335-7610 Office: Atty Law PO Box 1189 7525 Pioneer Way Ste 101 Gig Harbor WA 98335-1165 E-mail: retpllc@att.net.

THOMPSON, RONALD MACKINNON, former family physician, artist, writer; b. N.Y.C., Oct. 19, 1916; s. George Harold and Pearl Anita (Hatfield) T.; m. Ethel Joyce Chastant, June 30, 1950; children: Phyllis Anita, Walter MacKinnon, Charles Chastant, Richard Douglas. BS, U. Chgo., 1947, MS, 1948, MD, 1949. Diplomate Am. Bd. Family Practice. Intern U. Mich., Ann Arbor, 1950-51; resident in psychiatry U. Tex., Galveston, 1951-52; pvt. practice, family and internal medicine South Dixie Med. Ctr., West Palm Beach, Fla., 1952-85; ret., 1985. Instr. Anatomy, U. Chgo., 1946-47, Pharmacology, 1948-49. Contbr. more than 300 poems and short stories to lit. mags., also articles to med. jours.; 7 one-man shows (over 30 awards for painting in regional and nat. shows); represented in permanent collections at 6 mus. Former mem. bd. dirs. Norton Mus. of Art, West Palm Beach. With Fla. N.G., 1936-40; cadet USAAF, Force, 1943-44. Over thirty awards for painting in juried regional and nat. shows. Fellow Am. Acad. Family Physicians; mem. AMA, Fla. Med. Assn., Fla. Acad. of Family Physicians, Palm Beach County Med. Soc., Nat. Watercolor Soc., Ariz. Watercolor Soc. Republican. Episcopalian. Avocations: chess, tennis, writing, square and round dancing. Home: 308 Leisure World Mesa AZ 85206-3142

THOMPSON, RONELLE KAY HILDEBRANDT, library director; b. Brookings, S.D., Apr. 21, 1954; d. Earl E. and Maxine R. (Taplin) Hildebrandt; m. Harry Floyd Thompson II, Dec. 24, 1976; children: Clarissa, Harry III. BA in Humanities magna cum laude, Houghton Coll., 1976; MLS, Syracuse U., 1976; postgrad., U. Rochester, 1980, 81; cert., Miami U., 1990. Libr. asst. Norwalk (Conn.) Pub. Libr., 1977; elem. libr. Moriah Ctrl. Schs., Port Henry, NY, 1977—78; divsn. coord. pediat. gastroenterology and nutrition U. Rochester (N.Y.) Med. Ctr., 1978—81, cons., pediat. housestaff libr. com., 1980—81; dir. Medford Libr. U. S.C., Lancaster, 1981—83; dir. Mikkelsen Libr., Libr. Assocs., Ctr. for Western Studies, mem. libr. com. Augustana Coll., Sioux Falls, SD, 1983—, adminstrv. pers. coun., 1989—94, 1997—. Presenter in field. Contbr. articles to profl. jours. Mem. S.D. Symphony, Sioux Falls Civic Fine Arts Assn.; advisor pers. dept. City of Sioux Falls. Recipient leader award YWCA, 1991; Gaylord Co. scholar Syracuse U., 1976; named S.D. Libr. of Yr., 1998. Mem. ALA, AAUW, Assn. Coll. and Rsch. Librs. (nat. adv. coun. coll. librs. sect. 1987—), Mountain Plains Libr. Assn. (chair acad. sect., nominating com. 1988, pres. 1993-94), S.D. Libr. Assn. (chair interlibr. coop. task force 1986-87, pres. 1987-88, chair recommended minimum salary task force 1988, chair local arrangements com. 1989-90, 2002—), S.D. Libr. Network (adv. coun. 1986—, exec. com. 1992-96, 1998-2000, chair adv. coun. 1994-96, 98-2000). Office: Augustana Coll Mikkelsen Libr 29th & Smt Sioux Falls SD 57197-0001 E-mail: ronelle_thompson@augie.edu.

THOMPSON, SALLY ANN, newspaper editor; b. Hillsboro, N.D., Apr. 10, 1943; d. C. Hilman and Blanche E. (Bjerkan) Swenson; m. Arthur G. Thompson, July 1, 1965 (dec. Mar. 1990); 1 child, Laurie Kate Beth. Student, Concordia Coll., Moorhead, Minn., 1961-65. Reporter The Valley Journal, Halstad, Minn., 1979-84; contbg. editor Prairie West Publs., Wahpeton, N.D., 1982-84; editor Hillsboro Banner, Hillsboro, 1984-95, Sun Newspapers, Minnetonka, Minn., 1995—. Lectr. Career Day Mayville State U., N.D., 1985-92. Mem. commns. com. Ea. N.D. Synod ELCA, 1990-93; bd. dirs. Traill County Hist. Soc., 1979-95, Hillsboro Forestry Bd., 1990-93. Recipient numerous journalism awards. Lutheran. Avocations: photography, collages, reading, history. Home: 1805 Highway 101 Apt 203 Plymouth MN 55447-2715 Office: Sun Newspapers 13911 Ridgedale Dr Ste 110 Minnetonka MN 55305-1773 E-mail: sthompson@mnsun.com.

THOMPSON, SANDRA FAY, psychiatrist; b. Takoma Park, Md., Oct. 5, 1961; m. Glynn Mark Thompson. BS in Biology, Columbia Union Coll., Takoma Park, Md., 1984; MD, Loma Linda U., 1990. Resident in psychiatry U. Md., Balt., 1991-96; pvt. practice, Balt. and Bel Air, Md., 1996—. Med. dir. Motor Disorder Clinic, Md. Psychiat. Rsch. Ctr., Catonsville, 1998—. Contbr. article to med. jours. Mem. Am. Psychiat. Assn., Am. Assn. Cmty. Psychiatrists, Md. Psychiat. Soc. Avocations: backpacking, writing poetry. Office: Keypoint Health Svcs 209 Thomas St Bel Air MD 21014-3649

THOMPSON, SANDRA LEE, library administrator; b. Dover, Ohio, Jan. 23, 1968; d. Robert Leonard and Gwendolyn Ruth Stewart; m. Alan McKinney Thompson, Sept. 9, 1990; children: LeeAnna, Alisha, James. BS in Edn., Ohio U., 1989; M of Libr. Info. Sci., U. S.C., 1999. Tchr. Harrison Hills City Sch. Dist., Hopedale, Ohio, 1989-90; asst. dir. Puskarich Pub. Libr., Cadiz, 1990-97, dir., 1998—. Mem. Ohio Libr. Coun., Columbus, 1994—; tech. chairperson Southeastern Ohio Libr. Orgn., Caldwell, 1997—. Office: Puskarich Pub Libr 200 E Market St Cadiz OH 43907-1200 E-mail: thompss2@oplin.lib.oh.us.

THOMPSON, SANDRA ROMAINE, retired corporate facility nurse; b. West Grove, Pa., Mar. 6, 1938; d. Thomas Walter and Florence Elizabeth (Mahan) T. Diploma in nursing, Del. Hosp., 1959. Cert. HIV infection and AIDS, N.Y. State Dept. Health, 1991, cert. HIV counselor, 1991. Staff nurse and charge nurse Mt. View Hosp., Lockport, N.Y., 1960-67; dir. nurses Newfane (N.Y.) Nursing Home, 1967-72; staff nurse Harrison Radiator Div., GM, Lockport, 1972-97; ret., 1997. Vol. AIDS Community Svcs., Buffalo, 1987-94, Ea. Niagra County divsn. Am. Heart Assn., Buffalo, 1987-94, bd. dirs., 1989-94, v.p. bd. dirs., 1991-92, pres. 1992-94; bd. dirs. western N.Y. region, 1991-94, program com., 1989-92; active Niagra Falls chpt. Am. Cancer Soc., 1987, 90-94, bd. dirs. 1990-94; charter mem. Niagra County Healthy Heart Program, 1988-94, mem. task force on smoking cessation and obesity. Recipient Smoking Cessation Achievement award Lakeside Pharm. Co., Lockport, 1988, Program award of Excellence Ea. Niagra County div. Am. Heart Assn., 1988, 89, 90, Program Vol. Yr. award Western N.Y. Region, 1991, 93, Pub. Edn. Life Saver's award Niagra chpt. Am. Cancer Soc., 1988, Pub. Edn. award Am. Cancer Soc., 1989, Vol. award United Way, 1990, Community Svc. award Lockport Community Cable, 1991. Mem. Am. Assn. Occupational Health Nurses, Western N.Y. Assn. Occupational Health Nurses, N.Y. State Occupational Health Nurses, N.Y. State Am. Heart Assn. (profl. mem.). Democrat. Roman Catholic. Avocations: ceramics, antiques, sewing, knitting, reading, writing poetry.

THOMPSON, SANDY MARIA, health and staff development coordinator; b. Ballston Spa, N.Y., May 3, 1953; d. George Andrew and Dorothy (Cooper) Simpson; m. John Michael Thompson, Jr., June 10, 1972; children: John, Matthew, Katie. ADN, No. Va. C.C., 1974; BSN, George Mason U., 1985, MSN, 1990. RN, Va. Staff RN No. Va. Doctors Hosp., Arlington, Va., 1974-84; sch. nurse Alexandria (Va.) City Pub. Schs., 1985-89; health and staff devel. coord. City of Manassas (Va.) Pub. Schs., 1989—. Planner for cmty. summit The Changing Manassas Cmty. Steering Com., 1994; chairperson health adv. bd. City of Manassas Sch., 1992-94, numerous other coms. Author: (with others) Virginia School Health Guidelines, 1992, (booklet) First Aid for School Emergencies, 1991. Recipient Nurses Make a Difference award Am. Orgn. of Nurse Execs. and Am. Hosp. Assn., 1988, Outstanding Contbn. award City of Manassas, 1994, Excellence in Edn. award Va. Poly. Inst. and State U., 1998, VA Tech. Excellence in Edn. award, 1998. Mem. Va. Sch. Nurse Assn. (sec. 1988-89, dir. area 1 1990-91). Roman Catholic. Avocations: cooking, tennis, bridge, golf. Home: 11951 Shenandoah Ct Woodbridge VA 22192-1308 Office: City of Manassas Pub Schs 9000 Tudor Ln Manassas VA 20110-5700

THOMPSON, SARAH ELLEN, not-for-profit developer; b. Springfield, Mo., June 19, 1942; d. Paul Raymond and Beulah Evelyn (Cowen) Gaunt; m. Clifton C. Thompson, Dec. 1, 1978; children: Brenda Kay, Victoria Lea. BS cum laude, S.W. Mo. State U., 1983; MSA, Ctrl. Mich. U., 1994. Instr. chemistry and physiology S.W. Mo. State U., Springfield, 1984-89, dir. sponsored rsch., 1989-95, Ctrl. Mich. U., Mt. Pleasant, 1995-97. Owner Nutrim Nutritional Consulting, Springfield, 1984-89; lectr. Mid-Mich. C.C., Mt. Pleasant, 1997; instr. Alma (Mich.) Coll., 1997; cons. in pvt. practice, Beaver Island, Mich., 1997—. Author: Guide To Dynamic Nutrition, 1988, Proposal Development Workbook, 1993; contbr. articles to profl. jours. Mem. adv. bd. Office of Fed. Programs, Washington, 1995—97; co-chair fundraising com. Beaver Island Preservation Assn., 1999, v.p. bd. dirs., 2000—01. Recipient grant U.S. Dept. HUD, 1990, 93; grantee U.S. Dept. Edn., 1991, 93, Grand Traverse Band of Ottawa and Chippewa Indians, 2002. Mem. ACS, Phi Kappa Phi. Home: 29550 East Side Dr Beaver Island MI 49782 E-mail: thompson@biip.net.

THOMPSON, SHAWN CHESTER, network engineer; b. Pikeville, Ky., Dec. 18, 1968; s. Melvin Chester and Linda Lou (Thacker) T.; m. Kimberly Ann Borders, Mar. 26, 1994. AAS, Prestonsburg C.C., 1988; BSEE, U. Ky., 1992. Chief engr. Intermountain Cable Co., Harold, Ky., 1992-97; elec. engr. rank I Parsons Telecom, Inc., Charlotte, N.C., 1997-2000; elec. engr. BellSouth, Prestonsburg, Ky., 2000, Foothills Rural Telephone Coop., Staffordsville, 2000—. Tchr. Sunday sch. Toms Creek Freewill Bapt. Ch., Nippa, Ky., 1994—. Mem. U.K. Alumni Assn. Republican. Avocations: gardening, hunting, hiking, model building, fishing. Home: HC 83 Box 1240 Ulysses KY 41264-9705 Office: Foothills Rural Telephone Coop PO Box 240 Staffordsville KY 41256

THOMPSON, STANLEY B. church administrator; Pres., CEO, dir. The Free Meth. Found., Spring Arbor, Mich.; chmn., CEO, dir. King Trust Co., N.A.; chmn., dir. Free Meth. Found. Office: Free Methodist Foundation PO Box 580 Spring Arbor MI 49283-0580 E-mail: sbthompson@kingtrust.org.

THOMPSON, STEVE ALLAN, writer; b. Mpls., Sept. 10, 1951; s. John Thomas and Charlotte Joan (Ellis) T.; m. Michele Rae Jones, July 16, 1983; 1 child, Kent Lloyd. Student, U. Minn., 1969-73. Dept. supr. Hennepin County Libr., Edina, Minn., 1973-87; writer, 1987—. Cons. Okefenokee Glee & Perloo Inc., Manassas, Va., 1988—, Waycross/Ware County (Ga.) C. of C., 1990—, Phipps Ctr. for Arts, Hudson, Wis., 1996. Author: Walt Kelly Collector's Guide; co-author: Pogo Files for Pogophiles, 1992; editor The Fort Mudge Most 1988—; editl. bd. of Internatl. Jour. of Comic Art; contbr. articles to profl. jours. Mem. Internat. Soc. for Humor Studies, Bibliographical Soc. Am., Walt Kelly Soc. (pres. 1987—), Lewis Carroll Soc., Baker Street Irregulars, Grand Comics Database Project, Comics Scholars Consortium. Achievements include international recognized on life and career of Walt Kelly. Home: 6908 Wentworth Ave Richfield MN 55423-2363 E-mail: thompson_@s@epi.umn.edu., thomp034@tc.umn.edu.

THOMPSON, STEVEN, zoological park administrator; PhD in Conservation Biology, U. Calif., Irvine. Rschr. Nat. Zool. Pk., Smithsonian Instn. , 1983—90; v.p., Emily and John Alexander chair for conservation and sci. Lincoln Park Zoo, Chgo., 1990—. Office: Lincoln Park Zoo 2001 N Clark St Chicago IL 60614*

THOMPSON, SUE WANDA, small business owner; b. Azle, Tex., Nov. 26, 1935; d. Weldon W. Beasley and Eula Mae Hardee; m. William Henry Clark, Feb. 20, 1952 (div. 1959); children: Gloria, Russ, Bonnie; m. Robert L. Thompson Jr., Sept. 20, 1963; stepchildren: Christene, Lee. Nurse Harris Hosp., Ft. Worth, 1960-62, Denton State Sch., 1962-63; owner, v.p. Dalworth Med. Labs., Ft. Worth, 1963-68; sales leader, trainer Home Interior and Gifts, Dallas, 1970-80; owner, pres. Thompson Enterprises, 1980—; mgr., trainer Jafra Cosmetics, West Lake Village, Calif., 1981-84, Jewels by Park Lane, Chgo., 1984-89, Just Am., Rutlerfordton, N.C., 1989-91; with sales Dyna Tech Nutritionals, Willston Park, N.Y., 1993-94. Dir. parks and recreation City Forest Hills, Tex., 1970. Mem. Beta Sigma Phi (treas. Eta Lambda chpt. 1971-72, pres. 1972-73, Girl of Yr. 1974). Republican. Mem. Ch. Nazarene. Avocations: sports collecting, Gospel singing, crafts. Home: 4717 Applewood Rd Fort Worth TX 76133-7435

THOMPSON, SUSAN DIANE, physician; b. Highland Park, Mich., May 19, 1957; d. George William and Carol Marie (Mitchell) T. BS, U. Mich., 1978, MD, 1982. Diplomate Am. Bd. Internal Medicine, Am. Bd. Infectious Disease. Intern and resident in internal medicine U. Ala. Hosps., Birmingham, 1982-85; fellow UCLA, 1985-89; asst. prof. medicine Wayne State U., Detroit, 1989-94, Mich. State U., East Lansing, 1994-95; med. officer FDA, Rockville, Md., 1996-99; physician, epidemiologist Mich. Dept. Cmty. Health, Lansing, 1999-2001; med. officer FDA, Rockville, Md., 2001—. Mem. AMA, ACP, Am. Soc. for Microbiology, Infectious Disease Soc. Am., Alpha Omega Alpha. Office: FDA CDER DAIDP HFD-520 9201 Corporate Blvd Rockville MD 20850

THOMPSON, SYDNOR, JR. (CHARLES WILLIAM SYDNOR THOMPSON JR.), lawyer, mediator, arbitrator; b. Balt., Feb. 18, 1924; s. Charles William Sydnor Thompson and Helen Josephine Layne; m. Harriette Line, June 2, 1947; children: Darcy T. Kluttz, Charles William Sydnor III, Harriet T. Moore, Brenneman L., Mary Katerine Line T. Kelly. AB, Syracuse U., 1947; LLB, Harvard U., 1950; student, St. Andrews U., Scotland, 1945, Manchester U., Eng., 1950, London Sch. Econs., 1951. Cert.: N.C. Dispute Resolution Commn. (mediator), EEOC, Am. Arbitration Assn. (arbitrator), Nat. Assn. Securities Dealers. Assoc. Davis Polk & Wardwell, N.Y.C., 1951—54; ptnr. Parker Poe Thompson Bernstein Gage & Preston, Charlotte, NC, 1954—94; judge N.C. Ct. Appeals, Raleigh, 1994; of counsel Parker, Poe, Adams & Bernstein, LLP, Charlotte, 1995—; prin. Mediation, Inc., Winston-Salem, 1995—. Author: The Sydnor Family Saga, 2000, A Collection of Ad Hominem Verse, 2002; contbr. articles to law revs. Pres. Charlotte Symphony Orch., 1958—61, Charlotte Opera Assn., 1971—75; vice chair N.C. Arts Coun., Raleigh, 1981—84; pres. Mecklenburg Ministries, 1987—89, Wing Haven Found., 2001—; chmn. Mecklenburg County Dem. Party, 1977—81. Served with U.S. Army, 1943—46, ETO. Decorated Bronze star; scholar Fulbright scholar, 1950, 1951. Master: William H. Bobbitt Inn of Ct.; mem.: ABA (chmn. circuits subcom. 1977—95), Mecklenburg Bar Assn. (pres. 1990), N.C. Bar Assn. (chmn. appellate rules study com. 1989—91, chmn. local bar svcs. com. 1991—93), Old Catawba Soc., Horace Williams Philosophy Club, English Speaking Union, Sporadic Book Club, Charlotte Country Club, Tower Club. Avocations: genealogy, writing, tennis, acting. Office: Parker Poe Adams & Bernstein LLP Ste 3000 401 S Tryon St Charlotte NC 28202

THOMPSON, TERENCE WILLIAM, lawyer; b. Moberly, Mo., July 3, 1952; s. Donald Gene and Carolyn (Stringer) T.; m. Caryn Elizabeth Hildebrand, Aug. 30, 1975; children: Cory Elizabeth, Christopher William, Tyler Madison. BA in Govt. with honors and high distinction, U. Ariz., 1974; JD, Harvard U., 1977. Bar: Ariz. 1977, U.S. Dist. Ct. Ariz. 1977, U.S. Tax Ct. 1979. Assoc. Brown & Bain P.A., Phoenix, 1977-83, ptnr., 1983-92, Gallagher and Kennedy, P.A., Phoenix, 1992—. Legis. aide Rep. Richard Burgess, Ariz. Ho. of Reps., 1974; mem. bus. adv. bd. Citibank Ariz. (formerly Great Western Bank & Trust, Phoenix), 1985-86. Mem. staff Harvard Law Record, 1974-75; rsch. editor Harvard Internat. Law Jour. ,1976; lead author, editor-in-chief: Arizona Corporate Practice, 1996; contbr. articles to profl. jours. Mem. Phoenix Mayor's Youth Adv. Bd. 1968-70, Phoenix Internat.; active 20-30 Club, 1978-81, sec. 1978-80, Valley Leadership, Phoenix, 1983-84, citizens task force future financing needs City of Phoenix, 1985-86; exec. coun. Boys and Girls Clubs of Met. Phoenix, 1990-2000, sr. coun. 2000—; bd. dirs. Phoenix Bach Choir, 1992-94; deacon Shepherd of Hills Congl. Ch., Phoenix, 1984-85; pres. Maricopa County Young Dems., 1982-83, Ariz. Young Dems., 1983-84, sec. 1981-82, v.p. 1982-83; exec. dir. Young Dems. Am., 1985, exec. com. 1983-85; others. Fellow Ariz. Bar Found.; mem. State Bar Ariz. (vice chmn. internt. law sect. 1978, sec. securities law sect. 1990-91, vice chmn. sect. 1991-92, chmn.-elect 1992-93, chmn. 1993-94, exec. coun. 1988-96, sec. bus. law sect. 1992-93, vice chmn. 1993-94, chmn. 1994-95, exec. coun. 1996-98), Nat. Assn. Bond Lawyers, Nat. Health Lawyers, Greater Phoenix Black C. of C. (bd. dirs. 1999-2001), Blue Key, Phi Beta Kappa, Phi Kappa Phi, Phi Eta Sigma. Home: 202 W Lawrence Rd Phoenix AZ 85013-1226 Office: Gallagher & Kennedy PA 2575 E Camelback Rd Phoenix AZ 85016-9225

THOMPSON, TERRIE LEE, graphic designer; b. Myrtle Creek, Oreg., Apr. 22, 1960; d. Claud Willie and Blanche Bernice Thompson. Student, Umpqua C.C., 1983-84; BFA, Pacific N.W. Coll. Art, 1988. Freelance graphic designer Terrie Thompson Design, Portland, 1987-90; graphic designer Promotion Products Inc., 1989-90, L. Grafix Inc., Portland, 1990-91, Warn Industries, Milwaukie, Oreg., 1991-92; pres. Thompson Typographics Inc., Portland, 1990—; typography contractor Nike Inc., Beaverton, Oreg., 1992—. Typography trainer for various design firms and agys., Portland, 1992-98, pres. Seeing Spots, Inc., 1998—. Work published in various design publs., including The Best in Catalogue Design, Comm. Arts Design Ann., How Mag. Computer Art and Design Ann.; creator cartoon character "Spot", 1989. Vol. graphic designer Washington Park Zoo, Portland, 1990; vol. art dir. Portland Mac Users Group, Portland, 1995; vol. beach clean-up crew Stop Oreg. Litter and Vandalism, 1990—. Recipient Bronze award Optima Design Awards, 1995, Digital Art and Design Ann. award Print Mag., 1997, Regional Design Ann. award Print Mag., 1997, Applied Arts Annual, 1997, 98, Good Neighbor award Forest Park Neighborhood Assn., 1999. Avocations: hiking, travel, camping, photography, music. Home and Office: Thompson Typographics Inc PO Box 83327 Portland OR 97283-0327

THOMPSON, THEODIS, retired healthcare executive, health management consultant; b. Palestine, Ark., Aug. 10, 1944; s. Percy and Grozellia Monroves (Weaver) T.; m. Patricia Holley, Sept. 16, 1964; children: Gwendolyn Ware, Theodis E., Omari P. BS, Tuskegee Inst., 1968; MPA, U. Mich., 1969, PhD, 1972. Asst. chemist John T. Stanley Co., N.Y.C., 1964-66; news announcer, disc jockey KATZ Radio Sta., St. Louis, 1966-67; sr. rsch. assoc. U. Mich., Ann Arbor, 1969-71; asst. prof., chmn. Howard U., Washington, 1973-78; assoc. prof., dir. health planning U. So. Calif., L.A., 1978-79; dir. planning and evaluation Memphis Health Ctr., 1979-87, chief operating officer, 1987-88; CEO Bklyn. Plaza Med. Ctr., 1988-99; asst. chemist John T. Stanley Co., 1964-66. Cons. Charles Mathis Assocs., Yonkers, N.Y., 1991—, USPHS, Bethesda, Md., 1993—; mem. adv. bd. N.Y. Urban League, Bklyn., 1991-93; lectr. St. Joseph's Coll., Bklyn., 1998—. Author, editor: Health Policy and Planning, 1975; contbr. articles to profl. jours. Bd. dirs. CHCANYS, Inc., N.Y.C., 1994; vice chair Cmty. Assocs. Devel. Corp., Inc., Bklyn., 1989. Recipient Disting. Svc. award N.Y. State Assn. Black and Puerto Ricans, Inc., 1992; named Disting. Man of Yr., 18th Senatorial Dist., 1996. Mem. APHA.

THOMPSON, THEODORE ROBERT, pediatric educator; b. Dayton, Ohio, July 18, 1943; s. Theodore Roosevelt and Helen (Casey) J.;m. Lynette Joanne Shenk; 1 child, S. Beth. BS, Wittenberg U., 1965; MD, U. Pa., 1969. Diplomate Am. Bd. Pediatrics (Neonatal, Perinatal Medicine). Resident in pediat. U. Minn. Hosp., Mpls., 1969-72, chief resident in pediat., 1971-72, fellow neonatal, perinatal, 1974-75, asst. prof., 1975-80, dir. divsn. neonatology and newborn intensive care unit, 1977-80, assoc. prof., 1980-85, prof., 1985—, co-dir. Med. Outreach, 1988-91, med. dir. med. outreach, 1991-00, assoc. chief of pediat., 1988—; med. dir. outreach U. Minn. Physicians, 1992—, dir. clin. edn. med. students, 1999—. Editor: Newborn Intensive Care: A Practical Manual, 1983. Bd. dirs. Life Link III, St. Paul, 1987—; cons. Maternal and Child Health, Minn. Bd. Health, 1975-94; bd. dirs. Minn. Med. Found., 1995-99. With USPHS. 1972-74. Fellow: Am. Acad. Pediats.; mem.: Gt. Plains Orgn. for Perinatal Health Care (Sioux Falls, SD Kunshe award 1989). Lutheran. Office: MMC 39 420 Delaware St SE Minneapolis MN 55455-0374 E-mail: thomp005@umn.edu.

THOMPSON, THOMAS DANIEL, biology and chemistry educator; b. Danvenport, Iowa, Apr. 22, 1961; s. Thomas James and Mary Alice Thompson. BS in Biology and Chemistry, Regis Coll., Denver, 1983; MA in Tchg. of Biology, Marycrest Internat. U., Davenport, 2001. Sci. info. analyst Chem. Abstracts Svc., Columbus, Ohio, 1985-98; instr. biology and chemistry Marycrest Internat. U., Davenport, 1999—, chem. hygiene officer, 1999—. Rsch. asst. Solar Energy Rsch. Inst., Golden, Colo., 1980-81; tchr. asst. Miami U., Oxford, 1983-85, Regis Coll., Denver, 1980-83. Recipient Am. Inst. Chemists award, 1983. Mem. NEA, Am. Chem. Soc. (10 yr. svc. award 1995), Internat. Union Pure and Applied Chemistry (assoc.), Iowa State Edn. Assn., Nat. Sci. Tchrs. Assn., Nat. Assn. Chem. Hygiene Officers, Lab. Safety Inst., Beta Beta Beta (life, sec. 1999-2001), Alpha Sigma Nu (life). Roman Catholic. Avocations: football, auto racing, American history, American literature.

THOMPSON, THOMAS ADRIAN, sculptor; b. Sidney, Mont., Aug. 28, 1944; s. Vernon Eugene and Helen Alice (Torstenson) T.; m. M. Aileen Braun, June 7, 1968; children: Blair C., Meghann C. BA, Concordia Coll., 1966; postgrad., Mich. State U., 1968-69, Oakland U., 1970-72. Art tchr. Carman Ainsworth Sch. Dist., Flint, Mich., 1966-98; ret., 1998. Chmn. Flint Art Curriculum Com., 1980. Mem. adv. bd. Mich. Equine Artists; mem. Gand Blanc Arts Coun. Mem. NEA, Nat. Art. Edn. Assn., Mich. Art Edn. Assn. (liaison mem.), Internat. Arabian Horse Assn., Arabian Horse Registry. Lutheran. Avocations: painting, sculpture, golf. Home: 1120 Old Town Ct Grand Blanc MI 48439-1622 E-mail: TaThomps@hotmail.com.

THOMPSON, THOMAS MARTIN, lawyer; b. Albion, Pa., Jan. 7, 1943; s. Donald C. and Mabel Louise (Martin) T.; m. Judith E. Daucher; children: Reid, Chad, Matthew, Molly. AB, Grove City Coll., 1965; JD cum laude, Harvard U., 1968. Bar: Pa. 1968. Ptnr. Buchanan Ingersoll, Pitts., 1968—, chair corp. fin. group. Adj. prof. law U. Pitts.; , v.p., dir., past chairperson Pa. Lawyer Trust Acct. Bd. Past pres. Neighborhood Legal Svcs. Assn.; bd. dirs., sec. and past mem. exec. com. Pitts. Pub. Theater. Mem. ABA, Pa. Bar Assn. (vice-chair bus. law coun., Pro Bono award 1989), Allegheny County Bar Assn. (past chmn. pub. svc. com., past chmn. bus. law coun., chair PBA legal opinion steering com.), Assn. for Corp. Growth (past pres. Pitts. chpt.). Democrat. Home: 1142 Dartmouth Rd Pittsburgh PA 15205-1705 Office: Buchanan Ingersoll One Oxford Ctr 301 Grant St Fl 20 Pittsburgh PA 15219-1410 E-mail: thompsontm@bipc.com.

THOMPSON, TIM, music educator; b. Denver, July 11, 1947; s. Ted and Lois Thompson; m. Paulette Ann Nolan, Jan. 30, 1982; children: Todd, Chris Hamilton, Trevor, Justin Hamilton. BS in Music Edn., U. of Wyo., Laramie, Wyoming, 1965—69. Teaching PTSB Wyo., 1969. Tchr./band dir. Sch. Dist. #1 Weston County, Newcastle, Wyo., 1969—. Trustee Wyo. Educators Benefit Trust, Cheyenne, Wyo., 1998—2002. Mem.: NEA (life). R-Consevative. Protestant. Avocations: travel, dining, family. Home: 215 Highland Avenue Newcastle WY 82701 Office: School District #1 Weston County 116 Casper Avenue Newcastle WY 82701 Personal E-mail: tthomps@trib.com. E-mail: tthomps@trib.com.

THOMPSON, TIMOTHY CHARLES, research scientist; b. Indpls., Apr. 9, 1951; s. Charles Avery and Gladys Kathryn T.; m. Sang Hee Park, Feb. 9, 1988; 1 child, Benjamin Paul. AB, Ind. U., 1974; PhD, Colo. U., 1985; postdoctoral fellow, Imperial Cancer Rsch. Fund, London, 1988. Asst. prof. dept. urology and cell biology Baylor Coll. Medicine, Houston, 1988-92, dir. rsch. Scott dept. urology, 1992—, assoc. prof. dept. urology, cell biology and radiology, 1992-96, prof. dept. urology, cell biology and radiology, 1996—. Cons. reviewer for acad. jours. Cancer Rsch., 1991—; mem. pathology B study sect. NIH, Bethesda, Md., 1993-97; cons. Oncor, Inc., Gaithersburg, Md., 1994—, UroCor, Inc., Oklahoma City, 1995—. Contbr. numerous articles to profl. jours. and chpts. to books. Adult class Sun. sch. tchr. Rice Temple Bapt. Ch., Houston, 1992—. Grantee NIH, 1989—. Mem. Soc. Basic Urol. Rsch. (program com. 1989—), CaP CURE (bd. sci. dir. 1993—), Metastasis Rsch. Soc., Keystone Symposia (co-organizer 1996 Symposium). Democrat. Achievements include devel. of in vivo mouse model for prostate cancer; genetic complementation in prostate cancer; rsch. on molecular and cellular determinants of prostate cancer metastasis; patent for seminal vesicle specific markers of invasive prostatic neoplasia. Office: Baylor Coll of Medicine One Baylor Plz Houston TX 77030

THOMPSON, TINA, professional basketball player; b. Feb. 10, 1975; B of Sociology, U. S.C., 1997. Forward WNBA - Houston Comets, 1997—. Played in WNBA All-Star Games (1999,2000,2001). Named Pac-10 Freshman of Yr., 1994, AP All Am. 2d Team, Kodak Dist. All-Am. Team, All- Pac-10 First Team, 1996-97; won 1997, 98, 99 WNBA championship with Houston. Office: Houston Comets 2 E Greenway Plz Ste 400 Houston TX 77046-0202*

THOMPSON, TOMMY GEORGE, federal agency administrator, former governor; b. Elroy, Wis., Nov. 19, 1941; s. Allan and Julia (Dutton) T.; m. Sue Ann Mashak, 1969; children: Kelli Sue, Tommi, Jason. BS in Polit. Sci. and History, U. Wis., 1963, JD, 1966. Polit. intern U.S. Rep. Thomson, 1963; legis. messenger Wis. State Senate, 1964-66; sole practice Elroy and Mauston, Wis., 1966-87; mem. Dist. 87 Wis. State Assembly, 1966-87, asst. minority leader, 1972-81, floor leader, 1981-87; self-employed real estate broker Mauston, 1970—; gov. State of Wis., 1987-2001; Secy Dept HHS, Washington, 2001—. Alt. del. Rep. Nat. Conv., 1976; chmn. Intergovtl. Policy Adv. Commn. to U.S. Trade Rep.; chmn. Natl. Govs. Assn., 1995-96, mem. nat. govs. assn. exec. com.; chmn. bd. dirs., Amtrak, 1998-99. Served with USAR. Recipient med. award for Legis. Wis. Acad. Gen. Practice, Thomas Jefferson Freedom award Am. Legis. Exchange Coun., 1991, Most Valuable Pub. Official award City and State Mag., 1991, Governance award Free Congress Found., 1992, Governing Mag. Public Ofcl. of the Year, 1997, recipient Horatio Alger Awd., 1998, USA Mex. C of C, Good Neighbor Awd., 1999. Mem. ABA, Wis. Bar Assn., Rep. Govs. Assn., Phi Delta Phi. Roman Catholic. Office: Dept HHS Office of the Secy 200 Independence Ave SW Washington DC 20201-0004 Office Fax: 202-690-7203.*

THOMPSON, VENITA BRANT, nutritionist, diet technician; b. Washington, Oct. 7, 1936; d. Kenneth Vernon and Reta Iona (Stephens) Brant; m. Charles R. Blackhurst, Feb. 27, 1954 (div. Nov. 1973); children: Debra Ann Blackhurst Fleming, Terry Alan, Christopher Bryan; m. James Orlando Thompson, Feb. 11, 1989. AS in Bank Mgmt., Hillsborough Communnity Coll., 1962, AA, 1984; AS in Diet Tech., Pa. State U., 1986; BA in Gerontology, U. South Fla., Tampa, 1992; MS in Community Health Administrn. and Wellness, Calif. Coll. Health Scis. Registered diet technician. Asst. cashier Internat. Bank Tampa, 1955-65, asst. v.p., 1965-71; v.p., cashier Carrolwood State Bank, Tampa, 1971-73; dietetic technician St. Joseph Hosp., 1977-86, nutritional ops. mgr., 1986-92, nutritional ops. mgr., purchasing mgr., 1992-95; food svc. dir. Carrollwood Care Ctr., 1995-96; dir. clin. nutrition IHS, Brandon, Fla., 1996—. Mem. Am. Soc. for Hosp. Food Svc. Adminstrs., Am. Dietetic Assn., Tampa Dietetic Assn., Soroptimist Club, Order Rainbow Girls. Democrat. Presbyterian. Avocations: fishing, swimming, travel. Home: 401 W Paris St Tampa FL 33604-6652 Office: IHS of Brandon 702 S Kings Ave Brandon FL 33511-5925 E-mail: vthomp2971@earthlink.net.

THOMPSON, VERN, state senator; b. Maddock, N.D., Aug. 23, 1956; m. Cindy; one child, Will. City councilman; supr.; rep. N.D. State, 1989-91, state senator, 1997—. Chmn. ND Dem. Party. Recipient N.D. Weekly N.D. POl. Figure of the Yr., 1995, Minnewaukan Citizen of the Yr., 1996. Democrat. Office: Dist 12 111 East B Street Minnewaukan ND 58351*

THOMPSON, VETTA LYNN SANDERS, psychologist, educator; b. Birmingham, Ala., Sept. 7, 1959; d. Grover and Vera Lee (King) S.; m. Cavelli Andre Thompson, May 27, 1990; children: Olajuwon, Malik Rashad, Kimberlyn, Assata Iyana. BA, Harvard U., 1981; MA, Duke U., 1984, PhD, 1988. Cert. psychologist and health svc. provider, State of Mo. Com. Psychologists. Psychology intern Malcolm Bliss Mental Health Ctr., St. Louis, 1985-86; psychotherapist, testing coord. Washington U. Child Guidance Clinic, 1986-87; psychologist, treatment team coord. Hawthorn Children's Psychiatric Hosp., 1987-89; asst. prof. U. Mo., 1989-95, assoc. prof., coord. black studies, 1995—. Tchg. asst. Duke U., Durham, N.C., 1982-84, rsch. asst., 1984-85; chair monitoring com. crisis access sys. Ea. Regional Adv. Coun. Dept. Mental Health, St. Louis, 1995-97; chair African Am. Task Force on Mental Health, Jefferson City, Mo., 1995-97; chair budget and planning com. Ea. Regional Adv. Coun., Dept. Mental Health, St. Louis, 1996-97, pres. Ea. Regional Adv. Coun., 1997-99; mem. children's mental health planning group St. Louis Mental Health Bd., 1996-97. Mem. editl. adv. bd. A Turbulent Voyage: Readings in African American Studies, 1995-96; mem. bd. editl. advisors Gt. Plains Rsch.; contbr. articles to profl. jours. Mem. adv. com. on violence prevention and investment in youth Mo. House, Jefferson City, 1995; mem. managed care steering com. Dept. Mental Health, 1995—96, mem. strategic planning adv. com., 1997; mem. Mo. Bd. for Respiratory Care, 1997; mem. state com. for psychologists Mo., 1997—; chair, 2000—02; sec., chair discipline com., 2000—02; bd. dirs. St. Louis Mental Health Assn., sec., 2002, chair planning com., 2002, 2d v.p., 2002. Kellogg Found.-Mo. Youth Initiative fellow, 1991-93; Ctr. for Great Plains Studies fellow U. Nebr., 1995—; recipient Disting. Svc. award Mental Health Assn. St. Louis, 1998, 99. Mem. APA (divsns. 1, 45), Assn. Black Psychologists, Am. Orthopsychiat. Assn. Methodist. Avocations: aerobics, walking, jazz. Office: U Mo 8001 Natural Bridge Rd Saint Louis MO 63121-4401

THOMPSON, WADE FRANCIS BRUCE, manufacturing company executive; b. Wellington, New Zealand, July 23, 1940; came to U.S., 1961, naturalized, 1990. m. Angela Ellen Barry, Jan. 20, 1967; children: Amanda and Charles (twins). B in Commerce, Cert. Acctg., Victoria U., Wellington, 1961; MSc, NYU, 1963. Dir. diversification Sperry & Hutchinson, N.Y.C., 1967-72; v.p. Texstar Corp., 1972-77; chmn. Hi-Lo Trailer Co., Butler, Ohio, 1977—; chmn., pres., chief exec. officer Thor Industries Inc., Jackson Center, 1980—. Trustee Mystic Seaport Mus., Conn., 1984—; trustee Wade F.B. Thompson Charitable Found. Inc., 1985—, Mcpl. Art Soc., N.Y.C., 1993—, Seventh Regiment Armory Conservancy, N.Y.C., 1997—; founder The Drive Against Prostate Cancer. Mem. Union Club, N.Y. Yacht Club (N.Y.C.). Avocations: tennis, collecting contemporary art. Office: Thor Industries Inc PO Box 629 Jackson Center OH 45334-0629

THOMPSON, WADE S. artist, art and design educator; b. Moorhead, Minn., July 30, 1946; s. Roy S. and Nora A. (Hanson) T.; m. Maureen Larkey, June 14, 1975; children: Mora Eileen, Sarah Maria. BA in Art with distinction, Macalaster Coll., 1968; MA, MFA, Bowling Green U., 1972; postgrad., Pratt Inst., 1985. Graphic designer Assoc. Design, St. Paul, 1969-70; asst. prof. art Temple U., Phila., 1972-79; prof. art and design S.W. Mo. State U., Springfield, 1979—, asst. head dept. art and design, 1999—. Lectr. U. Art and Design Helsinki, 1994; vis. prof. U. Minn., Mpls., 1995; organizing chair 1998 Williamsburg Conf., 1996—; organizing chair Color and Design: 21st Century Tech. and Creativity Conf., 1998; organizing chair, moderator Artist and Digital Media Symposium, AIC Color, Rochester, N.Y., 2001; spkr., presenter in field. Contbr. articles to profl. jours.; one or two person shows include Alnico Gallery, N.Y.C., 1977, Nat. Art Ctr., N.Y.C., 1980, Jan Weiner Gallery, Kansas City, Mo., 1986, Peter Drew Galleries, Boca Raton, Fla., 1988, Mary Bell Galleries, Chgo., 1989, Still-Zinsel Contemporary Art, New Orleans, 1990, Aaron Gallery, Washington, 1990, Alexandre Hogue Gallery U. Tulsa, Okla., 1991, The Parthenon Mus., Nashville, 1995, Jack Meier Gallery, Houston, 1997, numerous others; group exhibns. include Provincetown (Mass.) Art Assn., 1976, Portsmouth (Va.) Art Ctr., 1976, The Smithsonian Traveling Exhibn., 1977-79, J.B. Speed Mus., Louisville, Ky., 1981, 84, The Nelson Gallery Atkins Mus., Kansas City, Mo., 1982, George Walter Vincent Smith Art Mus./Mus. Fine Arts, Springfield, Mass., 1984, 86, West Surrey Coll. Art and Design, Farnham, Surrey, Eng., 1984, Lamar Dodd Art Ctr., LaGrange, Ga., 1985, Arlington (Tex.) Mus. Art, 1989, Still-Zinsel Contemporary Fine Art, New Orleans, 1992, The Watkins Gallery Am. U., Washington, 1993, Elliot Smith Gallery, St. Louis, 1996, Keyes Gallery, Springfield, Mo., 1998, Malton Gallery, Cin., 2001, numerous others; featured in Am. Artist mag., catalog Color Archive Collections U. Art and Design Helsinki, The Oak Ridger, New Orleans Art Rev., New Art Examiner, The Kansas City Star, numerous others. Disting. scholar S.W. Mo. State U., 1992; recipient award for acrylic Chautauqua Nat. Exhbn., 1984, Color Archive Collection award U. Art and Design, Helsinki, Finland, 1997; grantee visual arts program Mo. Arts Coun., 1998. Mem. Inter-Soc. Color Coun. (nat. bd. dirs. 1995-98, vice chair art, design, psychology interest group 1992-94, chair art, design, psychology interest group 1994-96). Avocations: music, travel, reading. Home: 1910 E Cardinal St Springfield MO 65804-4329 Office: SW Mo State U Dept Art and Design 901 S National Ave Springfield MO 65804-0088

THOMPSON, WAITE, investment company executive, researcher; b. St. Louis, Nov. 5, 1940; s. Frank Charles Jr. and Jane (Waite) T. BA, Principia Coll., 1962. Polit. cons. Rep. Party of Calif., L.A., 1964-67, 72-74; traveling v.p. Club Universe, 1967-68, 69-72; comml. real estate investor Coldwell Banker, 1974-79; pres. Waite Thompson Inc., Santa Fe, 1979—. Author: The Santa Fe Guide, 1981—. Bd. trustees Hist. Santa Fe Found., 1989-94, Old Santa Fe Assn., 1994-96; mem. City of Santa Fe Hist. Design Review Bd., 1996-99; mem. coun. benefactors Santa Fe Cmty. Found., 1994—; mem. adv. bd. Rep. Nat. Com., Washington, 1964-67, 72-74. Mem. Santa Fe Opera Found., Mus. N.Mex. Found., Nat. Soc. Sons/Daughters of the Pilgrims, Nat. Soc. Sons of Am. Revolution. Republican. Mem. Christian Sci. Ch. Avocations: walking, swimming, reading, tennis, family history. Home and Office: 503 Johnson Ln Santa Fe NM 87505-2865

THOMPSON, WALLACE REEVES, III, physical education educator; b. Atlanta, Oct. 17, 1950; s. Wallace Reeves II and Annie Mae (Neal) T.; m. Sherrilyn Winkfield, Aug. 19, 1976 (div. 1985); 1 child, Sherrilyn M. m. Sandra Hicks, Feb. 28, 1994; 3 children: Garry C., Keneisha R., Ira. BA, Morehouse Coll., 1973. Cert. phys. edn. tchr., Ga. Phys. edn. tchr. Atlanta Pub. Schs., 1974—. Coach Saturday Sch. for the Arts, Atlanta, 1979-81. Vol. Nat. Black Arts Festival, Atlanta, 1990—, Ga. State Games, Atlanta, 1992—; coach Butler St. YMCA, Atlanta, 1982-85, AAU-Jr. Olympics, Atlanta, 1977-82, Centennial Olympics, Sports Video Viewing Room, Atlanta, 1996. Mem. AAHPERD. Baptist. Home: 119 Anderson Ave NW Atlanta GA 30314-1852 Office: Anderson Park Elem Sch 2050 Tiger Flowers Dr NW Atlanta GA 30314-1326

THOMPSON, WALTER DAVID, JR. systems analyst; b. Leakesville, N.C., Sept. 8, 1952; s. Walter David Sr. and Rachel Henderlite (Jones) T. Student, St. Andrews Coll., 1970-75. Beverage distributor N.Y. Seltzer, N.Y.C., 1975-76; restaurant mgr. Fountainhead Cafe, 1976-77; newspaper delivery Greensboro (N.C.) Daily News, 1978-80; computer programmer Gary Brown Assocs., Greensboro, 1980-82; pvt. cons. Thompson Software Systems, 1982-86; asst. treas. corp. trust Bankers Trust, N.Y.C., 1987-88; computer analyst bond funds Merrill Lynch, 1988; team leader, cons. corp. fin. Citibank, 1988-89; v.p., sr. systems analyst Kidder, Peabody & Co., Inc., Manakin-Sabot, Va., 1989-94; dir. MIS James River Capital Corp., 1995—. Rsch. grantee NSF, 1971. Mem. Am. Mensa Ltd. (membership coord. 1990-91). Home: 2236 Rockwater Ter Richmond VA 23233-3622 Office: James River Capital Corp 58 Broad Street Rd Manakin Sabot VA 23103-2213

THOMPSON, WAYNE WRAY, historian; b. Wichita, Jan. 30, 1945; s. Clarence William and Elaine Maxine (Wray) T.; m. Lillian Evelyn Hurlburt, June 28, 1969 (div. 1999); m. Geraldine Kelleher Richter, Dec. 30 2000. BA, Union Coll., Schenectady, 1967; student, U. St. Andrews, Scotland, 1965-66; PhD, U. Calif., San Diego, 1975. Historian USAF, 1975—, Checkmate Air Campaign Planning Group, 1990-91; sr. hist. advisor Gulf War Air Power Survey, 1991-93. Contbr. Congress Investigates (Arthur M. Schlesinger Jr. and Roger Bruns, editors), 1975; editor Air Leadership, 1986; contbr. War in the Pacific (Bernard Nalty, editor), 1991; contbr.: Winged Shield, Winged Sword, 1997; author: To Hanoi and Back, 2000. Served with AUS, 1971-72 Mem. Am. Hist. Assn., Orgn. Am. Historians, Air Force Hist. Found., Air Force Assn., Soc. Historians Am. Fgn. Rels., Soc. for Mil. History, U.S. Commn. on Mil. History, Inter-Univ. Seminar on Armed Forces, Assn. Asian Studies, Asia Soc., World History Assn., Phi Beta Kappa. Home: 2720 N Quincy St Arlington VA 22207 Office: Hdqrs USAF History Washington DC 20332-1111

THOMPSON, WILLARD SCOTT (W. SCOTT THOMPSON), social sciences educator; b. Providence, Jan. 1, 1942; s. Francis Willard and Loretta Belle Thompson; m. Phyllis Arina Nitze, Dec. 28, 1968 (div. May 1982); children: Phyllis Elizabeth Nitze, Nicholas Edwin Scott, Heidi Alexandra Nitze. BA hons., Stanford U., 1963; PhD, Oxford U., Oxford, England, 1967. Assoc. profl. internat. politics Fletcher Sch. Law and Diplomacy, Medford, Mass., 1967—93; asst. to sec. of def. Dept. Def., Washington, 1975—76; assoc. dir. U.S. Info. Agy. U.S. Govt., 1981—84; rsch. adj. prof. internat. politics Fletcher Sch. Law and Diplomacy, Medford, Mass., 2001—. Vis. prof. Asian Inst. Mgmt., Manila, 2001—; chair Universal Trading and Investment Co., Boston, 1993—, Internat. Ctr. for Instnl. Develop., Berkeley, Calif., 2000. Author: (novels) Ghana's Foreign Policy, 1969; co-author (with Nicholas Thompson) The Baobab and The Mango Tree, 2000, The Philippines in Crisis, 1992; contbr. articles to profl. jours. Co-chair Ams. for Effective Pres., Boston, 1980, Mass. Tomorrow, Boston, 1972—78; pres. Inst. Internat. Rels., Stanford U., 1962—63. Fellow Fulbright fellowship, Fulbright Com., Manila, 1989, Danforth fellowship, Danforth Found., 1965—67, fellowship, White House, 1975—76; scholar Rhodes scholarship, Rhodes Inst., 1980. Mem.: Coun. on Fgn. Affairs, Internat. Inst. for Strategic Studies. Avocations: gardening, film, marathons, writing fiction. Home: 14398 Storybook Ln Amissville VA 20106 Office: Policy Ctr Asian Inst Mgmt Paseo de Roxas Makati Philippines Address: Villa Kusuma Seri Sukuwati Indonesia E-mail: thompsonwscott@yahoo.com.

THOMPSON, WILLIAM, JR. engineering educator; b. Hyannis, Mass., Dec. 4, 1936; s. William and Dinella Helen (Szeliga) T.; m. Martha Marion Cate, July 4, 1959; children: Melanie A., Sharon E., Jennifer L., Keith W. SB, MIT, 1958; MS, Northeastern U., 1963; PhD, Pa. State U., 1971. Staff engr. Raytheon Co., Wayland, Mass., 1958-60; sr. engr. Cambridge (Mass.) Acoustical Assocs., 1960-66; rsch. asst. Applied Rsch. Lab., State College, Pa., 1966-72; asst. prof. engring. sci. Pa. State U., University Park, 1972-78, assoc. prof., 1978-85, prof., 1985-2001, prof. emeritus, 2001—. Head transducer group Applied Rsch. Lab., State College, 1971-80; sabbatic leave Naval Rsch. Lab., Orlando, Fla., 1988-89; chairperson IBM Master Tchrs. Team, 1997-98. Contbr. articles to profl. jours.; patentee in field. Bd. dirs., treas., past pres. Nittany Mountain chpt. Am. Diabetes Assn., State College, 1979-92; bd. dirs., asst. treas., treas. Mid-Pa. affiliate, Bethlehem, Pa., 1980-90; bd. dirs. Sight-Loss Support Group of Ctrl. Pa., 1999—, treas. 2000—. Recipient Disting. Svc. citation Mid-Pa. Affiliate Am. Diabetes Assn., 1981, and Affiliate Svc. award, 1988, J.R. Cardenuto award, Sight-loss Support Group of Ctrl. Pa., 1998. Fellow Acoustical Soc. Am. (patent reviewer of soc. jour. 1990—); mem. Soc. Engring. Sci., Lions (pres. State College 1981-82, 89-90, sec.-treas. 1984-88, 90-92, treas. 1992—, dist. diabetes chmn. 1983-88, 94—, chmn. Ctr. Lions Foresight Commn. 1992—, Melvin Jones fellow 1991, internat. leadership award 1998), Cen. Pa. Ballroom Dancers Assn. (pres.-elect 1997-98, pres. 1998-99). Republican. Avocations: sports, reading, photography, ballroom dancing. Home: 1245-62 Westerly Pky State College PA 16801 Office: Pa State U Dept of Engring Sci and Mechanics 203B Earth and Engring Scis University Park PA 16802-6812 E-mail: W1TESM@engr.psu.edu.

THOMPSON, WILLIAM REID, public utility executive, lawyer; b. Durham, N.C., Aug. 13, 1924; s. William Reid and Myrtle (Siler) T.; m. Mary Louise Milliken, Aug. 16, 1952; children: Mary Elizabeth, William Reid III, John Milliken, Susan Siler. BS, U. N.C., 1945; LLB, Harvard U., 1949. Bar: N.C. 1949. Ptnr. Barber and Thompson, Pittsboro, N.C., 1949-58; judge Superior Cts. N.C., 1958-60; assoc. gen. counsel Carolina Power & Light Co., 1960-63, v.p., gen. counsel, 1963-67, exec. v.p., 1967-71; chmn. bd., chief exec. officer Potomac Electric Power Co., Washington, 1971-89, chmn. bd., 1989-92. Adv. dir. Potomac Elec. Power Co. Bd. dirs. Nat. Orgn. on Disability; mem., former chmn. Fed. City Coun., N.C. Gen. Assembly from Chatham County, 1955-57. Served to lt. (j.g.) USNR, 1943-45, PTO. Mem. ABA, Edison Electric Inst. (bd. dirs., past chmn.), Southeastern Electric Exchange (past pres.), Assn. Edison Illuminating Cos. (past pres.), Bus. Coun., Met. Club, Burning Tree Club, Chevy Chase Club, Rotary, Phi Beta Kappa, Delta Kappa Epsilon. Republican. Methodist. Office: Potomac Electric Power Co 1900 Pennsylvania Ave NW Washington DC 20068-0002

THOMPSON, WILLIAM BENBOW, JR. obstetrician, gynecologist, educator; b. Detroit, July 26, 1923; s. William Benbow and Ruth (Locke) T.; m. Constance Carter, July 30, 1947 (div. Feb. 1958); 1 child, William Benbow IV; m. Jane Gilliland, Mar. 12, 1958; children: Reese Ellison, Belinda Day. AB, U. So. Calif., 1947, MD, 1951. Diplomate Am. Bd. Ob-Gyn. Resident Gallinger Mun. Hosp., Washington, 1952-53, George Washington U. Hosp., Washington, 1953-55; asst. ob-gyn. La. State U., 1955-56; asst. clin. prof. UCLA, 1957-64; assoc. prof. U. Calif.-Irvine Sch. Med., Orange, 1964-92, dir. gynecology, 1977-92, prof. emeritus, 1993—, vice chmn. ob-gyn., 1978-89. Assoc. dean U. Calif.-Irvine Coll. Med., Irvine, 1969-73. Inventor: Thompson Retractor, 1976; Thompson Manipulator, 1977. Bd. dirs. Monarch Bay Assn. Laguna Niguel, Calif. 1969-77, Monarch Summitt II A ssn. 1981-83. With U.S. Army, 1942-44, PTO. Fellow ACS, Am. Coll. Ob-Gyn. (life), L.A. Ob-Gyn. Soc. (life); mem. Orange County Gynecology and Obstetrics Soc. (hon.), Capistrano Bay Yacht Club (commodore 1975), Internat. Order Blue Gavel, Dana West Yacht Club. Avocation: boating. Office: UCI Med Ctr OB/GYN 101 The City Dr S Orange CA 92868-3201 E-mail: Benbow1923@aol.com.

THOMPSON, WILLIAM CHARLES, civil engineer; b. Wausau, Wis., Feb. 2, 1954; BS in Civil and Environ. Engring., U. Wis., 1977. Registered profl. engr., Nebr. Staff engr. Union Pacific R.R. Co., Omaha, 1978-80, resident engr., 1980-81, roadmaster Spokane, Wash., 1981-82, asst. divsn. engr. North Platte, Nebr., 1983-84, divsn. engr. Kansas City, Mo., 1984-88, dir. engring. rsch. Omaha, 1989—; asst. mgr. test ops. Assoc. of Am. R.R., Pueblo, Colo., 1982-83. Contbr. articles to profl. jours. Treas. pack 435 Boy Scouts Am., Omaha, 1990-91, asst. scoutmaster, 1991—. Mem. ASCE, Am. Rlwy. Engring. Assn. (bd. dirs. 1995—), Am. Roadmasters and Maintenance of Way Assn., Am. Bridge and Bldg. Assn., Transp. Rsch. Bd. (chmn. com. 1992—). Achievements include patent (with other) for track fastening device. Office: Union Pacific RR Co 1416 Dodge St # 3300 Omaha NE 68179-0002

THOMPSON, WILLIAM DAVID, investment banking executive; b. Pitts., Nov. 30, 1921; s. Ross Ephraim and Blanche (Watson) T. BS, Yale U., 1944. Asst. advt. mgr. Scovill Mfg. Co., Waterbury, Conn., 1945-48; acctg. supr. James Thomas Chirurg, N.Y.C., 1948-52; mgr. mktg. dept. McCann-Erickson, 1951-52; exec. v.p. Young & Rubicam, 1952-89; chmn. Ctr. Devel. Investments, Inc., Greenwich, Conn., 1990-98. Bd. dirs. Marine Bank & Trust Co., Vero Beach, Fla. Mem. found. bd. Indian River Hosp. Found., Vero Beach,

Fla. Mem. Union League (N.Y.C.), Wee Burn Country Club, John's Island Club. Republican. Presbyterian. Avocations: golf, tennis. Home and Office: John's Island 240 Johns Island Dr Vero Beach FL 32963-3237

THOMPSON, WILLIAM DAVID, minister, homiletics educator; b. Chgo., Jan. 11, 1929; s. Robert Ayre and Mary Elizabeth (McDowell) T.; m. Linda Brady Stevenson, Nov. 2, 1968; children— Tammy, Kirk, Lisa, Rebecca, Gwyneth. AB, Wheaton Coll., Ill., 1950; BD, No. Bapt. Sem., 1954; MA, Northwestern U., 1955, PhD, 1960. Ordained to ministry Am. Baptist Ch., 1954. Instr. speech Wheaton Coll., 1952-55; pastor Raymond Baptist Ch., Chgo., 1956-58; assoc. prof. homiletics No. Bapt. Sem., 1958-62; mem. faculty Eastern Bapt. Sem., Phila., 1962-87, prof. preaching, 1969-87; minister 1st Bapt. Ch., 1983-90. Pres. Thompson Comm., 1988—, The Spirited Workplace, 1998—. Author: A Listener's Guide to Preaching, 1966, Recent Homiletical Thought, 1967, Dialogue Preaching, 1969, Preaching Biblically, 1981, Listening on Sunday for Sharing on Monday, 1983, Philadelphia's First Baptists, 1989, Public Speaking for Pleasure and Profit, 1997; editor Abingdon Preachers Libr., 12 vols., Essence of Public Speaking series, 10 vols. Mem. Phila. Hist. Commn., 1984-92. Vis. fellow Cambridge U., 1968-69. Mem. Nat. Speakers Assn., Liberty Bell Speakers Assn. (pres. 1995), Acad. Homiletics (pres. 1973), Religious Speech Comm. Assn. (v.p. 1983, pres. 1984), Union League Club. Democrat. Home: 765 Ormond Ave Drexel Hill PA 19026-2417 E-mail: thompson@spiritedworkplace.com.

THOMPSON, WILLIAM GRANT, management executive; b. Westville, N.S., Can., June 27, 1925; s. Harvey Alden and Jessie (MacGregor) T.; m. Margaret Jean Mackenzie, Sept. 24, 1952; children: Heather, Anne, Andrew, Carole. Degree in bus. edns., Maritime Bus. Coll., Halifax, N.S., 1943. Chartered acct., N.S. Treas. Maritime Steel and Foundries, Ltd., New Glasgow, N.S., 1951-58; v.p, gen. mgr. EMI Elecs. Can., Ltd., Halifax, 1958-69; ptnr. Price Waterhouse, Ltd., 1970-87, v.p., 1977-87; pres. Revenue Mgmt., Ltd., 1987—. Pres. MacCulloch & Co., Ltd., Halifax, 1983-87, Oakwood Investments, Halifax, 1983-87. Mem. Commn. Food Prices Rev. Bd., Ottawa, Ont., 1974-77; chmn. fin. com. Waterfront Devel. Corp., Halifax, 1977-81; chmn. Pine Hill Div. Hall, Halifax, 1974-79, Atlantic Sch. Theology, Halifax, 1982-85, Maritime Bd. Trustees, Sackville, N.B., 1982-88; treas., chmn. investment com. Fin. Svcs. Maritime Conf., 1988—; chmn. Windsor Elms Srs. Home, Windsor, N.S., 1983-87. Fellow Inst. Chartered Accts. N.S., Inst. Chartered Secs. and Adminstrs.; mem. Soc. Mgmt. Accts. N.S., Inst. Mgmt. Cons. Atlantic Can., Can. Litigation Acctg. and Valuation Inst., Saraguay Club. Mem. United Ch. Can. Home: 2184 Connaught Ave Halifax NS Canada B3L 2Z3 E-mail: Rev_Mgmt@istar.ca.

THOMPSON, WILLIAM IRWIN, humanities educator, writer; b. Chgo., July 16, 1938; s. Chester Andrew and Lillian Margaret (Fahey) T.; m. Gail Joan Gordon, Feb. 3, 1960 (div. Jan. 1979); children: Evan Timothy, Hilary Joan, Andrew Rhys; m. Beatrice Madeleine Rudin, Mar. 1, 1979. BA with honors in Philosophy, Pomona Coll., 1962; MA (Woodrow Wilson fellow), Cornell U., 1964, PhD (Woodrow Wilson dissertation fellow), 1966. Instr. humanities MIT, Cambridge, 1965-66, asst. prof., 1966-67, Old Dominion fellow, 1967, assoc. prof. humanities, 1968, York U., Toronto, Ont., Can., 1968-72, prof., 1973. Vis. prof. religion Syracuse (N.Y.) U., 1973; vis. scholar in polit. sci. U. Hawaii, 1981, vis. prof., 1985; vis. prof. Celtic studies U. Toronto, 1984; founding dir. Lindisfarne Assocs., 1972-97. Author: Imagination of an Insurrection: Dublin, Easter 1916, 1967, At the Edge of History, 1971, Passages about Earth, 1974, Evil and World Order, 1976, Darkness and Scattered Light, 1978, The Time Falling Bodies Take to Light, 1981, From Nation to Emanation, 1981, Blue Jade from the Morning Star, 1983, Islands Out of Time, 1985, Pacific Shift, 1986, GAIA: A Way of Knowing, 1987, Imaginary Landscape, 1989, Selected Poems 1959-89; GAIA TWO: Emergence, the New Science of Becoming, 1991, Reimagination of the World, 1991, The American Replacement of Nature, 1991, Coming into Being, 1996, Worlds Interpenetrating and Apart, 1997, Transforming History, 2001. Hon. colleague and Lindisfarne Scholar of the Cathedral of St. John the Divine, N.Y.C., 1972-97. Recipient Obstfelder prize Oslo Internat. Poetry Festival, 1986; Rockefeller scholar Calif. Inst. Integral Studies, 1992-95; Laurance S. Rockefeller fellow, 1992-98. Address: PO Box 381561 Cambridge MA 02238

THOMPSON, WILLIAM MOREAU, radiologist, educator; b. Phila., Oct. 20, 1943; s. Charles Moreau and Aileen (Haddon) T.; m. Judy Ann Seel, July 27, 1968; children: Christopher Moreau, Thayer Haddon. BA, Colgate U., 1965; MD, U. Pa., 1969. Diplomate Am. Bd. Radiology. Intern Case Western Res. U., Cleve., 1969-70; resident in radiology Duke U., Durham, N.C., 1972-75; asst. prof. Duke U. Med. Ctr., 1975—77, assoc. prof., 1977-82, prof. radiology, 1982-86; prof., chmn. dept. radiology, Vilhelmina and Eugene Gedgared chair in Radiology U. Minn. Hosp. and Clinic, Mpls., 1986-2000, prof. radiology, dir. imaging rsch., 2000-01; prof. radiology Duke U. Med. Ctr., 2001—. Contbr. chpts. to books and articles to profl. jours. Served with USPHS, 1970-72. Recipient James Picker Found. Scholar in Acad. Medicine award, 1975-79, Disting. Scientist award, Armed Forces Inst. Pathology, Washington, 2001-02; R&D grantee VA, 1977-86. Fellow Am. Coll. Radiology; mem. AMA, Radiology Soc. N.Am. (program chmn. 1994-97), Minn. Med. Soc., Am. Roentgen Ray Soc., Assn. Univ. Radiologists (pres. 1989-90, Gold medal 2001), Soc. Gastrointestinal Radiology (pres. 1994-95, Cannon medal 2001), Assn. Program Dirs. (pres. 1995, Achievement award 2001), Soc. Chairs of Acad. Radiology Depts. (pres. 1997-98), Sigma Xi. Republican. Presbyterian. Home: 225 Galway Dr Chapel Hill NC 27517-6558 Office: PO Box 3808 Durham NC 27702-3808

THOMPSON, W(ILMER) LEIGH, pharmaceutical company executive, physician, pharmacologist; b. Shreveport, La., June 25, 1938; s. Wilmer Leigh and Mary Bissell (McIver) T.; m. Maurice Eugenie Horne, Mar. 29, 1957; 1 child, Mary Linton Bounetheau. BS, Coll. Charleston, 1958; MS in Pharmacology, Med U. S.C., 1960, PhD, 1963, ScD (hon.), 1994; MD, Johns Hopkins U., 1965. Diplomate Am. Bd. Internal Medicine. Intern Johns Hopkins Hosp., 1965-66, resident, 1966-67, 69-70; staff assoc. NIH, Bethesda, Md., 1967-69; asst. prof. medicine and pharmacology Johns Hopkins U., Balt., 1970-74, dir. critical care medicine and emergency medicine, 1974-82; prof. medicine, assoc. prof. pharmacology Case Western Res. U., Cleve., 1974-82, head critical care and clin. pharmacology, 1974-82; prof. medicine Ind. U., 1985-95; dir. Lilly Rsch. Labs., Eli Lilly & Co., Indpls., 1982, exec. dir., 1982-86, v.p., 1986-88, group v.p., 1988-91, exec. v.p., 1992-93, chief sci. officer, 1993-94; chmn., CEO Profound Quality Resources Cons., Charleston, 1995—. Bd. dirs. BAS, Diabetogen, Guilford Pharms., Depo Med, Inspire, La Jolla Pharms., Sontra, Medarex. Editor: Textbook of Critical Care Medicine, 1984, 89, State of the Art: Critical Care, 1980-83. Served to surgeon USPHS, 1967-69. Recipient Faculty Devel. award Pharm. Mfrs. Assn. Found.; named Disting. Alumnus, Med. U. S.C., 1999; Burroughs Wellcome Fund scholar, 1975-80. Fellow ACP, Am. Coll. Critical Care Medicine; mem. Soc. Critical Care Medicine (pres. 1981-82, hon. life mem. 1987), Ctrl. Soc. Clin. Rsch., Am. Soc. Pharmacology and Exptl. Therapeutics. Episcopalian and Huguenot. Office: Profound Quality Resources Consulting 54 King St Charleston SC 29401-2731 E-mail: electricpotato@jhu.edu.

THOMPSON, YAAKOV, rabbi; b. St. Mary's, Ohio, Dec. 2, 1954; s. Herbert and Carolyn Jean (Gallimore) T.; m. Sarah Jeffery, Dec. 30, 1982; children: Adina Michal, Benjamin Asher. BA, Ohio State U., 1977; MA, Jewish Theol. Sem. Am., 1983, DHL, 1988. Ordained rabbi, 1983. Asst. rabbi Jewish Ctr. Kew Gardens Hills, Flushing, N.Y., 1980-82; rabbi Uniondale Jewish Ctr., N.Y., 1982-84, Suburban Park Jewish Ctr., East Meadow, N.Y., 1984-88, Congregation Benai Israel of Fair Lawn, N.J., 1988-96, Temple Beth Israel, Sunrise, Fla., 1996—. Bd. govs. L.I. Bd. Rabbis, 1985—; lectr. Jewish Welfare Bd. Lecture Bur., N.Y.C., 1986—; asst. prof. Bible Jewish Theol. Sem. Am., 1988—, Rabbinical Assembly, Nassau, Suffolk, L.I., N.Y., 1983—; com. chmn. 1988—; bd. dirs. Fair Lawn Mental Health Ctr., pres. 1993-95. Contbr. articles to profl. jours. Bd. dirs. Fair Lawn Mental Health Ctr. Mem. N.Y. Bd. Rabbis, Soc. Bibl. Lit., Am. Acad. Religion, Assn. for Jewish Studies. Avocations: music, reading, sports. Home: 3905 NW 75th Ter Lauderhill FL 33319-3934 Office: Temple Beth Israel 7100 W Oakland Park Blvd Sunrise FL 33313-1098 E-mail: yaakovt@aol.com. *Life is most meaningful when lived with a sense of being a part of that which is greater than any individual. Let us make the task of religion the construction of new paths to the Holy One and to each other. Such paths can lead all of us to a better world.*

THOMPSON-CURRY, DOROTHY, federal agency administrator; b. Washington, Mar. 24, 1959; d. George and Bernice (Hamlin) Whitaker; m. Wendall Curry, Sept. 21, 1997 (div. Sept. 1999); 1 child Dorothe Bell Tollar-Curry ;1 child Eric D. Thompson. Student, U. D.C. Sec. Dept. of Edn., Washington; mgmt. staffing asst. Dept. of Labor. Author (editor): (book) The Dream Still Lives, 1995; author: (CD) What About the Children?, 1995. Coord. CFC Dept. Labor, 1999; tutor Admidon Elem. Sch., Washington, 1984—88. Avocations: poetry, Karate, sports. Home: 1201 7th St NW #201 Washington DC 20002

THOMPSON-KRAMER, HELEN AMELIA, retired librarian; b. Meadville, Pa., Dec. 28, 1936; d. Donald Chester and Laura Belle Thompson; m. Raymond Louis Kramer, Nov. 24, 1966; children: Lauralyn Ann Rickman, Kurt Alexander Kramer. BS Edn., Clarion State Coll., Clarion, Pennsylvania, 1959. Ch. sec. West Anaheim United Meth. Ch., Anaheim, Calif., 1995—; libr. Brown and Root-Braun Inc., Alhambra, 1989—94, Santa Fe Internat. Corp., Alhambra, 1978—89, St. Vincent Coll., Latrobe, Pa., 1968—70, East Deer - Frazier Jr. and Sr. H.S., Creighton, 1967—68, The Population Coun., New York, NY, 1965—66, Union Theol. Sem., Buenos Aires, Argentina, 1961—64, Conneaut Lake Jr. and Sr. H.S., Conneaut Lake, Pa., 1959—60. Libr. cons. Menonite Sem., Montevideo, Uruguay, 1963. Author: (book) Look Up! Look Around! My World in Poetry. Mem.: ALA. Methodist. Avocations: song writing, song writing, song writing, song writing, choir. Home: 9080 Bllomfield Street #35 Cypress CA 90630-2496 Office: West Anaheim United Methodist Church 2045 West Ball Road Anaheim CA 92804-5414 E-mail: hkramer@seniorexplorer.com.

THOMS, DAVID MOORE, lawyer; b. N.Y.C., Apr. 28, 1948; s. Theodore Clark and Elizabeth Augusta (Moore) T.; m. Susan Rebecca Stuckey, Dec. 16, 1972. BA, Kalamazoo Coll., 1970; M in Urban Planning, Wayne State U., 1975, LLM in Taxation, 1988; JD, U. Detroit, 1979. Bar: Mich. 1980, N.Y. 1995. Planner City of Detroit, 1971-75; atty. Rockwell and Kotz, P.C., Detroit, 1980-87; pvt. practice David M. Thoms & Assocs., P.C., 1987—2002, Miller Canfield Paddock and Stone, P.L.C., 2002—. Adj. assoc. prof. Madonna U., 1993—; presenter NYU Tax Inst. Editor Case and Comment U. of Detroit Law Rev., 1978-79. Mem. program com. Fin. and Estate Planning Coun. Detroit, 1980—; mem. adv. bd., chmn. nominating com., mem. exec. com. Met. Detroit Salvation Army, 1980—, sec.-treas., vice chmn., 1994-95, chmn., 1995-96; bd. dirs. bylaws and property com., mem. nominating com., devel. com., exec. com. Mich. chpt. ARC; bd. dirs. L'Alliance Française de Grosse Pointe, 1980-, pres., 1985-88, 94-95; bd. dirs. French Festival of Detroit, Inc., 1986-89, 91-94, pres.; bd. dirs. Fedn. of Alliances Françaises, 1989-95, 97—, also past treas., v.p., chmn. fin. com., pres., 2000-01; bd. dirs. Detroit Symphony Orch. Hall, Inc., 1996-97; trustee Kalamazoo Coll., 1993-97, mem. exec. com., 1995-97; dir. vis. com. European art DIA, 1995-97. Decorated Officier dans l'Ordre des Palmes Academiques; recipient Prix Charbonnier; Burton scholar U. Detroit, 1979. Mem. ABA (chmn. subcom. on probate and estate planning, mem. charitable trust com.), Fed. Bar Assn., Oakland County Bar Assn., Detroit Bar Assn., State Bar Mich., N.Y. Bar Assn., Bar Assn. of City of N.Y., Am. Planning Assn. (Mich. chpt.), Detroit Athletic Club, Renaissance Club, The Grosse Pointe Club. Mem. United Church of Christ. Avocations: tennis, architectural history, music, travel, art history. Office: 400 Renaissance Ctr Ste 950 Detroit MI 48243-1678 E-mail: thoms@ameritech.net.

THOMS, JEANNINE AUMOND, lawyer; b. Chgo. d. Emmett Patrick and Margaret (Gallet) Aumond; m. Richard W. Thoms; children: Catherine Thoms, Alison Thoms. AA, McHenry County Coll., 1979; BA, No. Ill. U., 1981; JD, Ill. Inst. Tech., 1984. Bar: Ill. 1984, U.S. Dist. Ct. (no. dist.) Ill. 1984, U.S. Ct. Appeals (7th cir.) 1985; cert. mediator 19th Jud. Cir. Ill. Assoc. Foss Schuman Drake & Barnard, Chgo., 1984-86, Zukowski Rogers Flood & McArdle, Crystal Lake and Chgo., 1986-92, ptnr., 1992—. Arbitrator 19th Jud. Ct. Ill., 1991—. Mem. women's adv. coun. to Gov. State of Ill.; mem. McHenry County Mental Health Bd., 1991—98, v.p., 1993—94, pres., 1995—98; mem. governing coun. Good Shepherd Hosp., Barrington, Ill., 2001—. Mem.: LWV, ABA, Acad. Family Mediators (cert.), Am. Trial Lawyers Assn., McHenry County Bar Assn., Chgo. Bar Assn., Ill. State Bar Assn. (coun. trust and estates sect. 2000—01, Ill. legis. dist. scholarship com. 2001, Ill. legis. dist. scholarship com. 2002), Phi Alpha Delta. Office: Zukowski Rogers Flood & McArdle 50 N Virginia St Crystal Lake IL 60014-4126 also: 100 S Wacker Dr Chicago IL 60606-4006

THOMS, JOSEPHINE BOWERS, artist, illustrator; b. Lansing, Mich., Sept. 14, 1922; d. Raymon Lyon and Adele (Hammond) Bowers; m. Bert Thoms, June 4, 1945 (dec.); 1 child, Adele Lucile Thoms; m. Peter Blackford Lauck, May 10, 1983. BA, Hillsdale Coll., 1944; MA, Md. Inst. Coll. Art, 1977. Instr. modern dance Hillsdale (Mich.) Coll., 1943-44; artist-in-residence St. John's Coll., Annapolis, Md., 1953-55, 68-70; instr. art Washington and Jefferson Coll., Washington, 1956, Bethany (W.Va.) Coll., 1963-65; illustrator Md. Dept. Natural Resources, Annapolis, 1977-95. Joint owner Onset Bay Gallery and Studio, Onset, Mass., portrait artist, colorist; instr. Washington Art Assn., 1958-69; art dir. Md. Fedn. Art, Annapolis, 1970-72, pres., 1972-74. Illustrator: Federal Prose, 1947; executed murals: History of Electricity, Hillsdale, 1942, The Harbor at Annapolis, Crownsville, Md., 1989. Mem. Caritas Soc. at St. John's Coll., 1969—, Md. Peace Action, Annapolis, 1983—. Recipient 1st prize for Exhbn. of Nature-Related Art, Adkins Arboretum, Tuckahoe State Pk., Denton, Md., 1995. Mem. Md. Soc. Portrait Painters (cert., exhibits chairperson 1995—), Annapolis Watercolor Club (1st prize 1993). Democrat. Episcopalian. Avocations: swimming, aerobics, piano, needlepoint design. Home: 61 Southgate Ave Annapolis MD 21401-2829

THOMSEN, CHARLES HAKON, real estate company executive, media consultant; b. Keene Valley, NY, May 1, 1930; s. Eric Hakon Thomsen and Althea Payson; m. Joan Robertson Knight; children: Amy Hale Harris, Eric Winslow. MA, Johns Hopkins U., 1950; AB, Harvard U., 1953. Asst. fgn. affairs rep. Gulf Oil Corp., Washington, 1958—63; asst. rep. U.S. Peace Corps, Tunisia and Morocco, 1963—65; vis. fellow Internat. Mktg. Inst., Cambridge, Mass., 1965—67; univ. registrar Brandeis U., Waltham, 1967—74; realtor, real estate trustee The Real Estate Co., East Orleans, 1982—. Cons. U.S. Peace Corps. Pres. Orleans Conservation Trust, East Orleans, 1977—; v.p. Compact Cape Cod Conservation Trusts, Barnstable, 1985—; clk. Assn. for Preservation of Cape Cod, Orleans, 1996—. 1st lt. U.S. Army, 1953—60. Mem.: Harvard Club of Boston. Avocations: sailing, shellfishing. Home: 30 Payson Ln East Orleans MA 02643 Office: The Real Estate Co 207 Main St East Orleans MA 02643

THOMSEN, DAVID ALLEN, lawyer; b. L.A., July 14, 1950; s. Henry Alfred and Ruth Virginia (McKinzie) T.; m. Janet Kay Thomas, June 25, 1972; children: Jennifer Marie, Carl Edward, Daniel Eric. BA, Loma Linda U., 1974; JD, U. Calif., Davis, 1978. Bar: Calif. 1978, N.Mex. 1979. Asst. city atty. City of Farmington, N.Mex., 1979-81, 88-90; city atty. City of Alamogordo, 1981-87; pvt. practice Alamogordo, 1987-88, Ruidoso, N.Mex., 1992-99; village atty. Village of Ruidoso, 1990-92; Children's Ct. atty. State of N.Mex., 1999—. CLE lectr. N.Mex. Mcpl. League, Santa Fe, 1989-90. Active Riverside (Calif.) County Dem. Ctrl. Com., 1973-75. Mem. Ruidoso Noon Lions Club (pres. 1993-94). Home: 2317 Union Ave Alamogordo NM 88310

THOMSEN, DONALD LAURENCE, JR. institute executive, mathematician; b. Stamford, Conn., Apr. 21, 1921; s. Donald Laurence and Linda (Comstock) T.; m. Linda Rollins Leach, June 14, 1958; children: Melinda Rollins, Katherine Thomsen Love, Donald Laurence III. Grad., Phillips Exeter Acad., 1938; BA in Math. magna cum laude, Amherst Coll., 1942; PhD, MIT, 1947. Tchg. fellow MIT, 1942, instr., 1943-47; instr., then asst. prof. Haverford (Pa.) Coll., 1947-50; rsch. fellow, then rsch. engr. Jet Propulsion Lab., Calif. Inst. Tech., 1950-52; asst. prof. Pa. State U., 1952-54; with IBM Corp., 1954-72, spl. asst. to dir. edn., 1961-62, dir. profl. activities, 1963-66, corp. dir. engring. edn., 1967-72; pres. Societal Inst. of Math. Scis., New Canaan, Conn., 1973—, also bd. dirs. Mem. vis. com. Coll. Sci., Drexel Inst. Tech., 1969-71; mem. adv. com. for Individualized sci. instrnl. sys. Coll. Edn., Fla. State U., 1973-75; prin. investigator rsch. studies in environ. pollution and human exposure, 1973—; AIDS rschr., 1988—. Author: Higher Transcendental Functions, 3 vols; contbr. articles to profl. jours. Recipient Spl. cert. Milw. Sch. Engring., 1969. Mem. AAAS, Am. Math. Soc., Am. Statis. Assn., Math. Assn. Am. (chmn. com. insts.), Soc. Indsl. and Applied Math. (pres. 1959, chmn. trustees 1960-72, Merit cert. Inst. Math. and Soc. 1972), Am. Fedn. Info. Processing Socs. (chmn. edn. com. 1965-66, chmn. U.S. com. IFIP Congress 1968, 66-69, bd. dirs. 1969-77, exec. com. 1975-77), Assn. Computing Machinery, Am. Ordnance Assn. (chmn. rsch. divsn.), Internat. Fedn. Info. Processing (chmn. exhibits com. N.Y.C. Congress 1965), Conf. Bd. Math. Scis. (chmn. budget and fin. com.), Internat. AIDS Soc., Internat. Soc. Exposure Analysis, Conn. Acad. Arts and Scis., Cosmos Club (Washington), The Princeton Club (N.Y.C.), Woodway Country Club (Darien, Conn.), Phi Beta Kappa, Sigma Xi, Delta Tau Delta. Presbyterian. Home and Office: Societal Inst Math Scis 73 Oenoke Rdg Apt 106 New Canaan CT 06840-4138

THOMSEN, PEGGY JEAN, educator, mayor, council member; b. St. Louis, Feb. 28, 1940; d. Harold Herman and Crystal Mary (Margolf) Levora; m. John Henry Thomsen, Dec. 1, 1961; children: Dianna, James, Robert. BA, Calif. State U., Fresno, 1961, MA with honors, 1968; PhD, U. Calif., Berkeley, 1997. Gen. secondary credential, Calif. Instr. Ctrl. Tex. Coll., 1980-83, City Colls. Chgo., 1983-86, Heald Colls., San Francisco, 1987; mayor, coun. mem. City of Albany, 1997—. Mem. East Bay Econ. Alliance, 1997—, Nat. Mayors Conf., 1998-99, Alameda County Mayor's Conf., 1998-99; bd. alt. Waste Mgmt. Authority, 1999—; bd. dirs. Alameda County Congestion Mgmt. Agy., 1997—. Editor City of Albany (Calif.) Newsletter, 1987. Mem. sch. bd. Albany Unified Sch. Dist., 1978-97, pres. sch. bd., 1980-81, 85-86; pres. PTA, Albany, 1976-78, 69-71; leader Girl Scouts U.S.A., Albany, 1970-82; mem. fund-raising team YMCA, Albany, 1981-88; bd. dirs., sec. Bay Area chpt. March of Dimes, San Francisco, 1979-88, chmn., 1985-86, chmn. Alameda County chpt., 1985-88; mem. adminstrv. code Rev. com. Calif. Dept. Edn., 1981-83, chmn. sch. improvement program selection panel, 1981, mem. fin. com., 1982, state budget com., 1982; Acorn Br. Assoc. Children's Hosp., Oakland. Recipient Svc. award Jaycees, Albany, 1970, Svc. awards Calif. PTA, 1971, 78, Vol. of Yr. award March of Dimes, Alameda County, 1984; named Sta. KABL Citizen of Day, 1984. Mem. NEA, LWV, Nat. Sch. Bds. Assn., Calif. Sch. Bds. Assn., Calif. Elected Women's Edn. Asn., League Calif. Cities (pres.-bd. mem. East Bay divsn. 1997—), Calif. Elected Women's Assn. for Edn. and Rsch., Congestion Mgmt. Agy. (bd. mem. 1997—), Pi Gamma Mu. Democrat. Avocations: needlework, editing, reading. Home: 757 Pierce St Albany CA 94706-1033 Office: City of Albany 1000 San Pablo Ave Albany CA 94706-2226

THOMSEN, SAMUEL BORRON, non-profit executive, consultant; b. St. Paul, July 10, 1931; s. Samuel W. and Margaret (View) T.; m. Judith Diane Wolf, June 17, 1961; children: Kathryn G., Samuel P.E., Robert J. BA in Polit. Sci., UCLA, 1957; postgrad., Cornell U., 1966-67. With U.S. Dept. State, Washington, 1960-90, U.S. Consul, Hue, Vietnam, 1964-66; polit. advisor U.S. Marines, Vietnam, 1965-66; dir. Office for Internat. Sci. Coop. Dept. State, Washington, 1980-83; dep. pres.'s rep. Office for Micronesian Status Negotiations, 1983-87; amb. U.S. Embassy, Majuro, Marshall Islands, 1987-90; pres. The Micronesia Inst., Washington, 1990—. Mem. commissioning bd. U.S. Info. Agy., Washington, 1980-86; chmn. Washington tradecraft program Fgn. Svc. Inst., Dept. State, 1995-96, dir. Micronesian diplomatic tng. program, 1996-99; cons. The Mustard Seed Found., 2000—. Mem. editl. bd. Fgn. Svc. Jour., 1961-62. Mem. Rotary, Vientiane, Laos, 1968-70, Gaborone, Botswana, 1974-76; trustee Am. Anglican Coun. With U.S. Army, 1951-54. Fellow Assn. Diplomatic Studies and Tng.; mem. Washington Inst. Fgn. Affairs, Diplomatic and Consular Officers Ret. (sec.), Asia Soc., World Affairs Coun. Washington, Am. Fgn. Svc. Assn., Am. Legion. Republican. Episcopalian. Avocations: tennis, gardening, computing. Home: 6502 Kerns Ct Falls Church VA 22044-1402 E-mail: sthomsen@erols.com.

THOMSEN, THOMAS RICHARD, retired communications company executive; b. Avoca, Iowa, July 29, 1935; s. Howard August and Edna Mary (Walker) T.; m. Raylene Alice Tomes, Sept. 1, 1956; children: Jeffrey, Cathy. BSME, U. Nebr., 1958; MS, MIT, 1973. Engr. Western Electric Co., Omaha, 1957-64, mgr. Columbus, Ohio, 1964-72, v.p. Bell Sales West Morristown, N.J., 1979-80; asst. v.p. ops. staff AT&T, Basking Ridge, 1980-81; exec. v.p. Western Electric Corp., N.Y.C., 1981-82; pres. AT&T Tech. Systems, Berkeley Heights, N.J., 1982-90; chmn. bd. dirs. Lithium Tech. Corp., Pa., 1995-99; retired, 1999—. Bd. dirs. EFJ Inc., Ilion Corp.; exec. com. U. Nebr. Tech. Park. Bd. dirs. Tele. Pioneer Found., 1997—. Mem. Telephone Pioneers Am. (former pres.), Pi Tau Sigma, Sigma Tau. Republican. Presbyterian. Avocations: golf, tennis. Home: 26 Bellinghamshire Pl New Hope PA 18938-5657

THOMSON, ALEXANDER BENNETT, JR. financial planner, tax and management consultant; b. Wyandotte, Mich., Sept. 1, 1954; s. Alexander Bennett and Norma Lee (Fields) T.; m. Rita Elizondo, May 8, 1982; 1 child, Luis Joaquin Elizondo. Student Eastern Mich. U., 1972-74, Kalamazoo Coll. 1975-77; MA, Antioch Sch. Law. 1983. Cert. fin. planner; chartered life underwriter, fin. cons.; registered rep., investment adviser, health underwriter. Pres. Thomson Mgmt. Group, Inc., Washington, 1977—; budget dir. The White House Conf. on Small Bus., 1979; asst. treas. Kennedy for Pres. Com. 1980, nat. scheduler, Geraldine A. Ferraro, 1984. Mem. Inst. Certified Fin. Planners, Internat. Assn. Fin. Planners, Nat. Assn. Tax Practitioners, Nat. Assn. Security Dealers. Democrat.

THOMSON, BASIL HENRY, JR. lawyer, university general counsel; b. Amarillo, Tex., Jan. 17, 1945; m. Margaret Shepard, May 4, 1985; children: Christopher, Matthew, Robert. BBA, Baylor U., 1968, JD, 1973. Bar: Tex. 1974, U.S. Ct. Mil. Appeals 1974, U.S. Supreme Ct. 1977, U.S. Dist. Ct. (we. dist.) Tex. 1988, U.S. Ct. Appeals (fed. cir.) 1990. Oil title analyst Hunt Oil Co., Dallas, 1971-73; atty., advisor Regulations and Adminstrv. Law div. Office of Chief Counsel USCG, Washington, 1973-77; dir. estate planning devel. dept. Baylor U., Waco, Tex., 1977-80, gen. counsel, 1980—. Adj. prof. law Baylor U.; lobbyist legis. Ind. Higher Edn., 71st Session of Tex. Legislature; mem. legis. com. Gov.'s Task Force on Drug Abuse; dir. govtl. relations Baylor U.; speaker at meetings of coll. and univ. adminstrs.; assisted in drafting legis. for Texan's War on Drugs Tex. Legislature; mem. legal adv. com. United Educators Ins. Risk Retention Group, 1994-96; mem. legal svcs. rev. panel Nat. Assn. Ind. Colls. and Univs., 1997—, 1st v.p., 2002, Nat. Assn. Coll. and Univ. Attys. Active Heart O'Tex. coun. Boy Scouts Am.; bd. dirs. Longhorn Coun. on Alcoholism and Drug Abuse, 1987-91; mem. bd. adjustment City of Woodway. Recipient Pres.'s award Ind. Colls. and Univs. of Tex., 1994, Dist. award of merit Boy Scouts Am. Fellow Coll. State Bar Tex.; mem. ABA, FBA, Nat. Assn. Coll. and Univ. Attys. (fin., nominations and elections coms. 1994-95, bd. dirs. 1988-91), Tex. Bar Assn., Waco Bar Assn., McLennan County Bar Assn., Owners Assn. of Sugar Creek, Inc. (bd. dirs. 1995-2000). Baptist. Avocations: backpacking, running, environmental concerns. Home: 100 Sugar Creek Pl Waco TX 76712-3410 Office: Baylor U PO Box 97034 Waco TX 76798-7034 E-mail: Basil_Thompson@Baylor.edu.

THOMSON, CAROLINE HELEN, artist; b. Takapuna, New Zealand, Jan. 12, 1945; d. William Harvey Thomson and Phyllis Alwyn Morgan. Artist Provincetown Art Assn. and Mus. One-woman shows include Eye of Horus Gallery, Provincetown, 1993, 94, Bangs Street Gallery, Provincetown, Mass., 1995-99; exhibited in group shows at Bangs Street Gallery, Provincetown, 1995-99, David Armstrong, Susanna Coffey, Jack Pierson, Caroline Thomson, 2000, two person exhbns., Susanna Coffey, Caroline Thomson, 1996-99, Provincetown Art Assn. and Mus., 1999, selections from the permanent collection, juried exbns., Provincetown Art Assn. and Mus., 1989-97, Invitational exhbns., PAAM, 1989-98. Exhbns. include Charles Hawthorne, Varujan Boghosian, Lily Harmon, Provincetown Art Assn. and Mus. Documentary film based on the life of Caroline Thomson, London, 1967, directed by Sheldon Rochlin and Diane Rochlin. Avocations: singer-song writer, wildlife rehabilitation. Fax: 508-349-7922. E-mail: bangst@tiac.net.

THOMSON, DAVID, dancer, vocalist; b. N.Y.C. BA, SUNY Purchase. Mem. Trisha Brown Co., N.Y.C., 1987—93; vis. lectr. Sarah Lawrence Coll., 1994—95; founder, mem. Hot Mouth, Bklyn., 1995—. Cons., database programmer Random House, N.Y.C., 2000—. Recipient Bessie Ward award, 2002. Office: 70 Nevins St #3 Brooklyn NY 11217*

THOMSON, DONALD ARTHUR, education educator; b. Detroit, Apr. 9, 1932; s. Arthur and Theresa Rita (Stasin) T.; m. M. Jenean Gruner, Apr. 6, 1957; children: Erin, Kurt, Lisa, Madelon. BS, U. Mich., 1955, MS, 1957; PhD, U. Hawaii, 1963. Asst. prof., curator of fishes & dir. mar. sci. to prof. U. Ariz., Tucson, 1963-98, prof. emeritus, 1998—. Author: (books) Reef Fishes of the Sea of Cortez, 2000, Fishwater's Guide to the Gulf of California, 1976,

Tide Calendar for the Northern Gulf of California 1967-2001; contbr. articles to profl. jours. Democrat. Avocations: photography, fly fishing, aquaria, dogs. Office: Dept Ecol/Evol Biol Univ Ariz Tucson AZ 85721-0001

THOMSON, GARY, state official; Chmn. Republican Party Va., 2002—. Republican. Office: 115 E Grace St Richmond VA 23219 Business E-Mail: chairman@rpv.org.*

THOMSON, GEORGE BREED, retired urban planner; b. Boston, Jan. 10, 1921; s. Malcolm and Helen May (Breed) Thomson; m. Jeanne Goddard Morrison, Aug. 1, 1942 (dec. Nov. 1993); children: Dale Goddard Thomson Milne, Laurie Breed Thomson DiClerico. SB, Harvard Coll., 1942. Design developer various co., Mass., 1949—78; ret., 1978. Chmn., bd. selectmen Swampscott Town Hall, Mass., 1956—64; rep. Met. Boston area Planning Coun., 1964—78; rep. planning com. Upper Valley Regional Planning Commn., NH, 1979—; rep. Mass. Gen. Ct., Boston, 1958—65. Mem.: Lake Sunapee Country Club, Harvard Faculty Club. Republican. Home: PO Box 1127 New London NH 03257

THOMSON, GEORGE RONALD, lawyer, educator; b. Wadsworth, Ohio, Aug. 25, 1959; s. John Alan and Elizabeth (Galbraith) T. BA summa cum laude, Miami U., Oxford, Ohio, 1982, MA summa cum laude, 1983; JD with honors, Ohio State U., 1986. Bar: Ill. 1986, U.S. Dist. Ct. (no. dist.) Ill. 1986. Teaching fellow Miami U., 1982-83; dir. speech activities Ohio State U., Columbus, 1983-86; assoc. Peterson, Ross, Schloerb & Seidel, Chgo., 1986-87, Lord, Bissell & Brook, Chgo., 1987-94; asst. corp. counsel employment litig. divsn. City of Chgo., 1994—. Adj. prof. dept. comm. De Paul U., Chgo., 1988-90; presenter in field. Contbr. articles to profl. jours. Fundraiser Chgo. Hist. Soc., Steppenwolf Theater Co., AIDS Legal Counsel Chgo., Smithsonian Instn., Washington, 1988-90, U.S. Tennis Assn., 1990—; bd. dirs. Metro Sports Assn., 1992-94, Gerber-Hart Libr. and Archives, 1993-95, Gay and Lesbian Tennis Alliance Am., 1993-95, Team Chgo., 1994-96, Second City Tennis, 1999-2000, 02—; mem. coord. coun. Nat. Gay and Lesbian History Month; mem. Lawyer's Com. for Ill Human Rights; dir. Chgo. Internat. Charity Tennis Classic, 1993, 94, 95, 98. Recipient Spl. Commendation Ohio Ho. of Reps., 1984, 85, Nat. Forensics Assn. award, 1982. Mem. ABA, Chgo. Bar Assn., Lesbian and Gay Bar Assn., Speech Comm. Assn. Am., Mortar Bd., Phi Beta Kappa, Phi Kappa Phi, Omicron Delta Kappa, Delta Sigma Rho-Tau Kappa Alpha, Phi Alpha Delta. Presbyterian. Avocations: tennis, flute, antiques, folk arts and crafts, reading, travel. Home: 2835 N Pine Grove Ave Unit 2S Chicago IL 60657-6109 Office: City of Chgo Dept of Law 30 N La Salle St Ste 1020 Chicago IL 60602-2503

THOMSON, GERALD EDMUND, physician, educator; b. N.Y.C., 1932; s. Lloyd and Sybil (Gilbourne) T.; m. Carolyn Webber; children: Gregory, Karen. MD, Howard U., 1959; DSc (hon.), Morehouse Med. Coll., 1997. Diplomate Am. Bd. Internal Medicine (bd. govs. 1985-92, exec. com. 1988-91, chmn.-elect 1990-91, chmn. 1991-92). Resident in medicine SUNY-Kings County Hosp. Center, 1959-62, chief resident, 1962-63, N.Y. Heart Assn. fellow in nephrology, 1964-65, asst. vis. physician, 1963-70, clin. dir. dialysis unit, 1965-67; practice medicine specializing in internal medicine N.Y.C., 1963-64; attending physician SUNY Med. Bklyn. Hosp., 1966-70; instr. in medicine SUNY, Bklyn., 1963-68, clin. asst. prof. medicine, 1968-70; asso. chief med. services Coney Island Hosp., Bklyn., 1967-70; attending physician Presbyn. Hosp., 1970—; dir. nephrology Harlem Hosp. Center, N.Y.C., 1970-71, dir. med. services, 1971-85, pres. med. bd., 1976-78; assoc. prof. medicine Columbia Coll. Physicians and Surgeons, 1970-72, prof., 1972—, Samuel Lambert prof. medicine, 1980—, Robert Sonneborn prof. medicine, 1997—; exec. v.p. for profl. affairs, chief of staff Columbia-Presbyn. Med. Ctr., 1985-90; sr. assoc. dean Coll. Physicians and Surgeons, Columbia U., N.Y.C., 1990—. Mem. Health Rsch. Coun. City N.Y., 1972-75; mem. med. adv. bd. N.Y. Kidney Found., 1971-82; mem. Health Rsch. Coun., State N.Y., 1975-81; mem. hypertension info. and edn. adv. com. NIH, 1973-74, N.Y. State Adv. Com. on Hypertension, 1977-80; com. on non-pharm. treatment of hypertension Inst. of Medicine, Nat. Acad. Scis., 1980; mem. med. adv. bd. Nat. Assn. Patients on Hemodialysis and Transplantation, 1973-83; mem. adv. bd. Sch. Biomed. Edn., CUNY, 1979-83, Med. News Network, 1993-95; mem. com. on mild hypertension Nat. Heart and Lung Inst., 1976, mem. clin. trials rev. com., 1980-85, mem. rev. panel, 1979; bd. dirs. N.Y. Heart Assn., 1973-81, chmn. com. high blood pressure, 1976-81; bd. dirs. Primary Care Devel. Corp.; chmn. com. hypertension N.Y. Met. Regional Med. Program, 1974-76; mem. adv. com. Heart and Hypertension Inst. of N.Y. State, 1984; mem. N.Y. Gov.'s Health Adv. Coun., 1981-84, pub. Health Coun., N.Y., 1983-95, Joint Nat. Com. High Blood Pressure NIH, 1983-84, 87-88, mem. rev. panel hypertension detection and monitoring bd. study cardiovasc. risk factors in young Nat. Heart, Lung and Blood Inst., 1984-90; mem. panel on receiving and withholding med. treatment ACLU, 1984-88; mem. Grad. Med. Edn. Commn., State of N.Y., 1984-86, mem. Commn. on End-State Renal Disease, 1985, 89-90; pres. Washington Heights-Inwood Ambulatory Care Network Corp., 1986-91; bd. dirs. Primary Care Devel. Corp., 1993—. Mem. adv. bd. Jour. Urban Health, 1974-80, Med. News Network, 1993-94. Chmn. ad hoc com. on access to nursing homes Pub. Health Coun. State of N.Y., 1982-96; pres. Washington Heights-Inwood Ambulatory Care Network Corp., 1986-91; mem. Mayor's Commn. Health and Hosps. Corp.; dir. Harlem Ctr. for Health Promotion and Disease Prevention, 1993-95. Recipient Nat. Med. award Nat. Kidney Found., N.Y., 1984, Outstanding Alumnus award Howard U., 1987, Disting. Alumnus award, 1998, Dean's Outstanding Tchg. award Coll. Physicians and Surgeons Columbia U., 1986. Fellow ACP (Gov.'s coun. downstate region 1982-89, chmn. com. health pub. policy N.Y. chpt. 1982-89, health care professions com. 1987-90, bd. regents 1990-97, chmn. nat. health and pub. policy com. 1993-94, pres.-elect 1994-95, pres. 1995-96), N.Y. Acad. Medicine (mem. com. medicine in soc. 1974-76, chmn. com. medicine in soc. 1997-98); mem. AAAS, N.Y. Soc. Nephrology (pres. 1973-74), Am. Fedn. Clin. Rsch., Federated Coun. for Internal Medicine (chmn. 1991-92, 95-96), Soc. Urban Physicians (pres. 1972-73), Am. Soc. Artificial Internal Organs, Assn. Program Dirs. in Internal Medicine, Pub. Health Assn. N.Y.C. (dir. 1983-86), Physicians for Social Responsibility of N.Y. (dir. 1983), Assn. Acad. Minority Physicians (pres. 1988-90), Inst. of Medicine, Nat. Acad. Scis. Home: Premium Pt New Rochelle NY 10801-5327 Office: Coll Physicians & Surgeons Columbia U New York NY 10032

THOMSON, H. BAILEY, editor, educator; b. Aliceville, Ala., Feb. 4, 1949; s. William Joshua and Attie (Kimbrell) T.; m. Reba Kristi Garrison, Nov. 19, 1977; 1 child, Sarah Rachel. BA, U. Ala., 1972, MA, 1974, PhD, 1995. Copy editor Huntsville (Ala.) Times, 1971-72, staff writer, 1975-77; reporter, copy editor Tuscaloosa (Ala.) News, 1972-75; editorial page editor Shreveport (La.) Jour., 1977-86; chief editorial writer Orlando (Fla.) Sentinel, 1986-91; assoc. editor Mobile (Ala.) Press Register, 1992-96. Phifer vis. prof. journalism U. Ala., 1996-97, assoc. prof. journalism, 1997. Author: Shreveport, 1986; editor, author: Century of Controversy, 2002. Vice chmn. La. Endowment Humanities, 1984-85; bd. dirs. Ala. Citizens for Constl. Reform. Profl. journalism fellow Stanford U., 1981-82; recipient finalist Pulitzer prize for editl. writing, 1995, Green Eyeshade awards, 1988, 1996, Disting. Writing award Am. Soc. Newspaper Editors, 1999, Nat. Disting. Tchg. award Soc. Profl. Journalists, 1999. Mem.: Nat. Conf. Editl. Writers (bd. dirs. 1991—92), Ala. Hist. Assn. (bd. dirs.). Presbyterian. Avocations: gardening, reading, hiking. Office: Col of Communication Dept Journalism PO Box 870172 Tuscaloosa AL 35487-0172 E-mail: thomson@jn.ua.edu.

THOMSON, HELEN LOUISE, artist; b. Lewiston, Ill., Nov. 28, 1928; d. Clyde Arthur Pomeroy and Myrtle Lynch Cluney; m. William Edward Thomson, 1950; children: Persephone Ann, Lucinda Renee, Cynthia Louise. Student, Western Ill. U., 1972, 78, 85, U. Ill., 1972; diploma, North Light Art Sch. Artist, Table Grove, Ill., 1970—. Adj. prof. Western Ill. U., Macomb, 1985-94; mem. spkrs. roster Spoon River Coll., Canton, Ill., 1986-94; exec. dir. Two Rivers Arts Coun., Macomb, 1985-94. Exhibited in numerous one woman and group exhbns.; contbr. art to calendars United Fed. Savs. & Loan, 1980, 86. Pres. Spoon River Coll. Found., Canton, Ill., 1979-85, Fulton County Arts Coun., Canton, 1973-83; bd. dirs. Regional Arts Adv. Coun., Western Ill. U., 1978-85; mem. adv. panel Ill. Arts Coun., Chgo., 1980-83; officer PTA, Table Grove, 1957-85. Recipient Ruth Watts Svc. award Performing Arts Soc., Western Ill. U., 1994, award Two Rivers Arts Coun., 1994; selected for feature stories on pub. TV sta. WMEC, 1997, Canton Dily Ledger, Macomb Jour., Peoria (Ill.) Jour. Mem. PEO Sisterhood (pres., sec., chpalain, v.p.), Ill. Art League (exhbn. awards), Ill. Watercolor Soc., Galesburg Civic Art Ctr. (exhbn. awards), Chgo. Art inst. Avocations: antiques, antique dolls, family history, travel. Home: 404 S Broadway St Table Grove IL 61482-0163

THOMSON, HUGH TALBERT, lawyer; b. San Francisco, Nov. 21, 1944; s. Douglas Hugh and Margaret Rose (Coffen) T.; children: Brian, Kimberly. BA, U. Calif., Berkeley, 1967; JD, U. Calif., Davis, 1970. Bar: Calif. 1971. Sole practice, San Jose, Calif., 1971—. Lectr. Continuing Edn. of Bar, Judge's Conf. Fellow Am. Acad. Matrimonial Lawyers; mem. State Bar Calif. (writer family law specialization exam. 1981, 82, 84, author Family Law News, exec. com. family law sect. 1979-83), Calif. Bd. Legal Specialization for Family Law. Office: 941 W Hedding St San Jose CA 95126-1216 E-mail: httlaw@ev1.net.

THOMSON, JAMES ADOLPH, medical group practice administrator; b. Kansas City, Mo., Feb. 25, 1924; s. Edward Wilkins and Gladys Lucile (Opperman) T.; m. Patricia Jane Herron, Jan. 24, 1943; children: Linda Lee Thomson Schwartz, Kenneth Leroy, James Howard. BBA, Rockhurst U., Kansas City, 1950. Cost acct. Std. Brands, Inc., Kansas City, 1950-52; asst. comptr. Menorah Med. Ctr., 1952-56; comptr. Holzer Hosp. and Clinic, Gallipolis, Ohio, 1956-63; adminstr. Oberlin (Ohio) Clinic, Inc., 1963-71; adminstr. and treas. Thompson, Brumm & Knepper Clinic, Inc., St. Joseph, Mo., 1971-80; bus. mgr. Cin. Neurol. Assocs., Inc., 1980-89, ret., 1989. Cons. med. groups, Ohio, 1968-70. V.p. St. Joseph (Mo.) Area C. of C., 1976-78; pres. Oberlin Health Commn., 1968-69; bd. dirs. St. Joseph Sheltered Workshop, 1978-80. Served with M.C. U.S. Army, 1943-46, ETO. Recipient Disting. Svc. award St. Joseph Area C. of C., 1979. Fellow Am. Coll. Med. Group Adminstrs.; mem. Am. Assn. Hosp. Accts. (charter, pres. 1954-56), Mo. Med. Group Mgmt. Assn. (charter, pres. 1978-79), Med. Group Mgmt. Assn., Ohio Med. Group Mgmt. Assn., Cin. Med. Group Mgmt. Assn. (pres. 1983-84), Rotary (pres. Oberlin and St. Joseph), Lions (pres. 1962-63), KC, Masons, Shriners, Am. Legion. Republican. Episcopalian. Avocations: woodworking, gardening, golf.

THOMSON, JAMES ALAN, research company executive; b. Boston, Jan. 21, 1945; s. James Alan and Mary Elizabeth (Pluff) T.; m. Darlene Thomson; children: Kristen Ann, David Alan. BS, U. N.H., 1967; MS, Purdue U., 1970, PhD, 1972, DSc (hon.), 1992; LLD (hon.), Pepperdine U., 1996. Research fellow U. Wis., Madison, 1972-74; systems analyst Office Sec. Def., U.S. Dept. Def., Washington, 1974-77; staff mem. Nat. Security Council, White House, 1977-81; v.p. RAND, Santa Monica, Calif., 1981-89, pres., chief exec. officer, 1989—. Bd. dirs. L.A. World Affairs Coun., AK Steel Holding Corp., Tex. Biotech. Corp. Contbr. articles to profl. jours. and chpts. to books. Mem. Internat. Inst. for Strategic Studies (coun. 1985-99), Coun. Fgn. Rels. Office: RAND 1700 Main St Santa Monica CA 90401-3297 E-mail: thomson@rand.org.

THOMSON, KEITH STEWART, biologist, author; b. Heanor, Eng., July 29, 1938; s. Ronald William and Marian Adelaide (Coster) T.; m. Linda Gailbreath Price, Sept. 27, 1963; children: Jessica Adelaide, Elizabeth Rose. B.Sc. with honors, U. Birmingham, Eng., 1960; A.M., Harvard U., 1961, PhD (NATO fellow), 1963. NATO postdoctoral fellow Univ. Coll., London U., 1963-65; asst. prof. to prof. biology Yale U., 1965-87, dean Grad. Sch., 1979-87; dir. Peabody Mus. Natural History, 1976-79; pres. Acad. Natural Scis., Phila., 1987-95; disting. scientist-in-residence New Sch Social Rsch., N.Y.C., 1996-98; prof., dir. Mus. Natural History Oxford U., 1998—. Dir. Sears Found. Marine Rsch. and Oceanographic History; hon. rsch. fellow Australian Nat. U., 1967; trustee, mem. corp. Woods Hole Oceanographic Inst.; bd. dirs. Wistar Inst., Ctrl. Phila. Devel. Corp., Wetlands Inst., Phila. Cultural Alliance, Charles Darwin Trust; rschr. in vertebrate evolution. Mem. editl. bd. Paleobiology, Jour. Morphology, 1988, Aspects of Lower Vertebrate Evolution, 1968, Origin of Terrestrial Vertebrates, 1968, Saltwater Fishes of Conn., 1971, 88, Priorities and Needs in Systematic Biology, 1981, Morphogenesis and Evolution, 1988, Living Fossil, 1991, The Common But Less Frequent Loon and Other Essays, 1993, HMS Beagle, 1995. Fellow Linnean Soc. London, Zool. Soc. London; mem. Soc. Vertebrate Palaeontology, Sigma Xi. Office: Oxford U Mus Parks Rd Oxford 0X1 3PW England

THOMSON, KENNETH R. (LORD THOMSON OF FLEET), freelance/self-employed publishing executive; b. Toronto, Ont., Can., Sept. 1, 1923; s. Lord Thomson of Fleet; m. Nora Marilyn Lavis, June 1956; children: David Kenneth Roy, Peter John, Taylor Lynne. Student, Upper Can. Coll., Toronto; BA, MA, U. Cambridge, Eng., 1947. With editl. dept. Timmins Daily Press, 1947; with advt. dept. Cambridge (Galt) Reporter, 1948-50, gen. mgr., 1950-53. Chmn., bd. dirs. The Woodbridge Co. Ltd.; pres., bd. dirs. Thomson Works of Art Ltd.; bd. dirs. The Thomson Corp. With RCAF, World War II. Mem. Granite Club, Hunt Club, Toronto Club, York Club, York Downs Golf Club. Baptist. Avocations: collecting paintings and works of art, walking, golf. Home: 8 Castle Frank Rd Toronto ON Canada M4W 2Z4 Office: Thomson Corp 65 Queen St W Toronto ON Canada M5H 2M8

THOMSON, MABEL AMELIA, retired elementary school educator; b. Lancaster, Minn., Oct. 28, 1910; d. Ernest R. and Sophie Olinda (Rotert) Poore; m. Robert John Thomson, June 20, 1936; children: James Robert, William John. BS, U. Ill., 1933; MEd, Steven F. Austin Coll., Nacogdoches, Tex., 1959. Tchr. La Harpe (Ill.) Sch. Dist., 1930, Scotland (Ill.) Sch. Dist., 1934, Washburn (Ill.) Sch. Dist., 1935-36, Tyler (Tex.) Ind. Sch. Dist., 1959-76; ret., 1976. Substitute tchr. Tyler (Tex.) Ind. Sch. Dist., 1976-86 Past pres. Woman's Soc. Christian Svc. of local Meth. Ch. Mem. AAUW (pres. Tyler chpt. 1947-48), Am. Childhood Edn. (pres. 1960-61), Alpha Delta Kappa (charter Tyler br.), Phi Mu (life). Republican. Methodist. Avocations: reading, gardening, bridge.

THOMSON, MARJORIE BELLE ANDERSON, sociology educator, consultant; b. Topeka, Dec. 4, 1921; d. Roy John and Bessie Margaret (Knarr) Anderson; m. John Whitner Thomson, Jan. 4, 1952 (div. June 9, 1963); 1 child, John Coe. Diploma hostess, Trans World Airlines, 1945; diploma, U.Saltillo, Mex., 1945; BS, Butler U., 1957; MS, Ft. Hays Kans. State U., 1966; postgrad., U. Calif., Santa Barbara, 1968, Kans. State U., 1972-73, Kans. U., 1973. Cert. elem. tchr., Calif., Colo., Ind., Kans., jr. coll. tchr. Tech. libr. N.Am. Aviation, Dallas, 1944-45; flight attendant TWA, Kansas City, Mo., 1945-50; recreation dir. U.S. Govt., Ft. Carson, Colo., 1951-52; elem. tchr. Indpls. Pub. Schs., 1954-57; jr. high tchr. Cheyenne County Schs., Cheyenne Wells, Colo., 1958-59; elem. tchr. Sherman County Schs., Goodland, Kans., 1961-62; lectr. Calif. Luth. U., Thousand Oaks, 1967-69; instr. Ft. Hays Kans. State U., 1969-71; dir. HeadStart Kans. Coun. of Agrl. Workers and Low Income Families, Inc., Goodland, 1971-72; supr. U.S. Govt. Manpower Devel. Programs, Plainville, Kans., 1972-74; bilingual counselor Kans. Dept. Human Resources, Goodland, 1975-82. Leader trainee Expt. in Internat. Living, Brattleboro, Vt., 1967-71; cons. M. Anderson & Co., Lakewood, Colo., 1982—; participant Internat. Peace Walk, Moscow to Archangel, Russia, 1991, N.Am. Conf. on Ecology and the Soviet Save Peace and Nature Ecol. Collective, Russia, 1992, Liberators-The Holocaust Awareness Inst., Denver, 1992; amb. internat. Friendship Force, Tiblisi, Republic of Georgia, 1991, Republic South Africa, 1995, Republic of Turkey, 1996, Republic of Egypt, 1999, Republic of Israel-Kfar Blum Kibbutz, 1999, Republic of Austria, 1999; presenter State Conv. AAUW, Aurora, Colo., 1992, presenter nat. conv. Am. Acad. Audiology, Denver, 1992; cons. Gov.'s Conf. in Libr. and Info. Svc., Vail, Colo., 1992; presenter annual conf. Nat. Emergency Number 911 Assn., Denver, 1996. Docent Colo. Gallery of the Arts, Littleton, 1989; spkr. Internat. Self Help for Hard of Hearing People, Inc., 1990—, mem. state recreation resource com. for Self Help for Hard of Hearing People Internat. Conv., Denver, 1991; mem. Denver Deaf and Hard of Hearing Access Com., 1991—; spkr. Ret. Sr. Vol. Program, Denver, 1992—; dir. Holiday Project, Denver, 1992; mem. Lakewood Access Com., 1994—, Arvada Ctr.'s Women's Voices com., 1995; participant women readers com. Rocky Mountain News, Denver, 1995; trustee Internat. Self Help for Hard of Hearing People, Inc., Bethesda, Md., 1995-98; Deaf Panel spkr. for Deaf Awareness Week, Denver, 1995-98; program co-chair Lakewood Woman's Club, 1996, 97; mem. access adv. com. Arvada Ctr. for Arts and Humanities, 1997; commr. Denver Commn. for People with Disabilities, 1997-98; mem. Colo. State Rehab. Adv. Coun., 1997—, 98, Gov.'s Adv. Coun. for People with Disabilities, 1998—; mem. Lakewood Citizen Police Acad. XIX, 1999; participant Funding Assistive Technology: Where to Turn in Colo. and When, Denver, 1999, Sr. Transp. Summit, Denver, 2000; mem. program com. Wisdom Keepers, Lakewood, 1999-2000; participant Aurora 5 States Assistive Tech. Conf. for Disabled, 1999-2000; mem. Colo. State Sr. Drug Abuse Task Force, 2000-02; apptd. mem. Lakewood Sr. Citizen's Adv. Commn., 2000-. Recipient Svc. award, Mayor of Lakewood, 1995, Honorable Mention Four Who Dare, Colo. Bus. and Profl. Women and KCNC Channel 4, 1995, J.C. Penney Nat. Golden Rule award for cmty. vol. svc., 1996, Cmty. Svc. award, Mayor Denver, 1996, City and County of Denver Proclamation for Marjorie Thomson Day, May Wellington E. Webb, Apr. 8, 1997, Svc. Recognition award, Oticon Co., 1997, Worker of Yr. Recognition award, Dickie Co., 1997, coll. scholarship presented in her name, Alpha Sigma Alpha, 2000; grantee, NSF, 1970, 1971. Mem. AAUW (life; v.p., program chairperson Lakewood br. 1996, Trailblazer award Denver br. 1997, mem. diversity com. Colo. 1997-98), AARP (pres. Denver-Grandview chpt. 1994), VFW Aux. (life), Sociologists for Women in Soc. (participant Gullah Culture, Charleston, S.C. 1997), Bus. and Profl. Woman's Club, Internat. Peace Walkers, Spellbinders, Denver Press Club (Wheat Ridge Grange # 155 1993-98), Lakewood Woman's Club, TWA Internat. Clipped Wings (cert.), Mile High Wings, Order Ea. Star (life), Sons of Norway, UNESCO, Bus. and Profl. Women's Club (com. for Ms. Golden Bus. and Profl. Woman of Yr. 1999), Confederate Air Force (hon. col.), Toastmasters, PHAMALy, Pi Gamma Mu, Alpha Sigma Alpha (life, participant Centennial Conv., Alumni Star). Democrat. Presbyterian. Avocations: photography, traveling, whitewater rafting, storytelling, writing.

THOMSON, RICHARD MURRAY, retired banker; b. Winnipeg, Man., Can., Aug. 14, 1933; s. H.W. and Mary T. BASC in Engring., U. Toronto, 1955; MBA, Harvard U., 1957; fellow course in banking, Queen's U., 1958. With Toronto Dominion Bank, Ont., Can., 1957—, asst. to pres. head office Can., 1963-68, chief gen. mgr. Can., 1968-71, v.p., chief gen. mgr., dir. Can., 1971-72, pres. Can., 1972-77, pres. and CEO Can., 1977-78, chmn. Can., 1978-98, CEO, 1978-97, also bd. dirs., chmn., 1977-98. Bd. dirs. S.C. Johnson & Son Inc., The Prudential Fin., Inc., The Thomson Corp., Inco Ltd., Can. Pension Plan Investment Bd., Ont. Power Generation Inc., The Toronto Dominion Bank, Stuart Energy Sys. Inc., TrizecHahn Corp.; chmn. bd. dirs. Nexen Inc. Office: The Toronto Dominion Bank 55 King St West 10th Fl TD Bank Tower POB 1 Toronto Dominion Ctr Toronto ON M5K 1A2 Canada

THOMSON, THYRA GODFREY, former state official; b. Florence, Colo., July 30, 1916; d. John and Rosalie (Altman) Godfrey; m. Keith Thomson, Aug. 6, 1939 (dec. Dec. 1960); children— William John, Bruce Godfrey, Keith Coffey. BA cum laude, U. Wyo., 1939. With dept. agronomy and agrl. econs. U. Wyo., 1938-39; writer weekly column Watching Washington pub. in 14 papers, Wyo., 1955-60; planning chmn. Nat. Fedn. Republican Women, Washington, 1961; sec. state Wyo. Cheyenne, 1962-86. Mem. Marshall Scholarships Com. for Pacific region, 1964-68; del. 72d Wilton Park Conf., Eng., 1965; mem. youth commn. UNESCO, 1970-71, Allied Health Professions Council HEW, 1971-72; del. U.S.-Republic of China Trade Conf., Taipei, Taiwan, 1983; mem. lt. gov.'s trade and fact-finding mission to Saudi Arabia, Jordan, and Egypt, 1985 Bd. dirs. Buffalo Bill Mus., Cody, Wyo., 1987—; adv. bd. Coll. Arts and Scis., U. Wyo., 1989, Cheyenne Symphony Orch. Found., 1990—. Recipient Disting. Alumni award U. Wyo., 1969, Disting. U. Wyo. Arts and Scis. Alumna award, 1987, citation Omicron Delta Epsilon, 1965, citation Beta Gamma Sigma, 1968, citation Delta Kappa Gamma, 1973, citation Wyo. Commn. Women, 1986; named Internat. Woman of Distinction, Alpha Delta Kappa, Keith and Thyra Honors Convocation in her honor Coll. of Arts and Scis. U. Wyo., 1997. Mem. N.Am. Securities Adminstrs. (pres. 1973-74), Nat. Assn. Secs. of State, Council State Govts. (chmn. natural resources com. Western states 1966-68), Nat. Conf. Lt. Govs. (exec. com. 1976-79) Home: 3102 Sunrise Rd Cheyenne WY 82001-6136

THOMSON OF FLEET, Lord See THOMSON, KENNETH

THONET, JOHN A. environmental planning and engineering consultant; b. Baldwin, N.Y., Aug. 4, 1950; s. John Chester and Grace W. (Keeling) T.; m. Kathi Lynn Blatt, May 1973; children: Hannah, Rebecca. BS in Forest Engring. cum laude, SUNY, Syracuse, 1972, MS, 1975. Registered profl. engr., Mass., N.J., Pa., Mich., W.Va., profl. planner, N.J.. Environ. engr. Power Authority of State of N.Y., N.Y.C., 1973-74; project mgr., civil engr. Tippetts Abbett McCarthy Stratton Engrs. & Architects, 1974-79; assoc. Dresdner Assocs. Environ. Land Use Planning Cons., Summit, N.J., 1979-80; pres. Thonet Assocs., Inc. Environ. Planning & Design Cons., South Orange, 1980—. Contbr. articles to profl. jours. Chmn. S. Orange Environ. Com., adv. coun. Environ. Resources and Forest Engring. Dept., SUNY; trustee N.J. Environ. lobby; mem. adv bd. Engring. and Computer Sci., Syracuse U. Mem. ASCE, Soc. Am. Foresters, N.J. Soc. Profl. Engrs., Nat. Assn. Environ. Profls. Avocations: guitar, tennis. Office: Thonet Assocs Environ Planning & Design Cons 14 S Orange Ave South Orange NJ 07079-1754 E-mail: jthonet@thonetassociates.com.

THONG, TRAN, biomedical company executive; b. Saigon, Vietnam, Dec. 8, 1951; came to U.S., 1969, naturalized, 1980. s. Vy and Vinh-Thi (Nguyen) T.; m. Thuy Thi-Bich Nguyen, Jan.12, 1978. BSEE, Ill. Inst. Tech., 1972; MS in Engring., Princeton U., 1974, PhD, 1975. Rsch. scientist Western Geophys., Houston, 1975-76; computer devel. engr. GE Co., Syracuse, N.Y., 1976-79; dir. electronic system lab. Tektronix, Inc., Beaverton, Oreg., 1980-90; v.p. engring., and digital signal processing gen. mgr. Tektronix Fed. Systems Inc., 1990-93; v.p. systems design and devel. Micro Systems Engring., Inc., Lake Oswego, 1993—; prin. N.W. Signal Processing, Inc. Adj. asst. prof. Syracuse U., 1979-81, Oreg. State U., Corvallis, 1980-83, U. Portland, Oreg., 1981-83; adj. prof. Oreg. Grad. Ctr., Beaverton, 1984—; mem. adv. bd. Biomed. Engring. Inst., U. Erlangen, Germany, 1996—. Author numerous sci papers and U. S. patents. Bd. dirs. S.E. Asia Scholarship Fund, 1994—, Fellow IEEE (com. chmn. 1982-88, assoc. editor Trans. 1979-81, gen. chmn, 1989, exec. v.p. circuits and sys. 1989); mem. Vietnamese Assn. for Computing Engring. Tech. and Sci. (founding mem., chmn. 1994-95, past pres, 1995-96, pres. 1998-99), Sigma Xi, Eta Kappa Nu, Tau Beta Pi. Republican. Office: Micro Sys Engring 6024 Jean Rd Lake Oswego OR 97035-5308

THONGSAK, VAJEEPRASEE THOMAS, business planning executive; b. Udonthani, Thailand, Feb. 10, 1935; came to U.S., 1970; s. Chanmar and Pee Vajeeprasee; m. Somchit; 1 child, Rosarine. BS in Sociology, BA in Philosophy, Mahamakut U., Bangkok, 1968; MA in Edn., Kean Coll. N.J., 1976; MA in Philosophy, NYU, 1989; PhD in Mgmt., AMA Mgmt. Inst., 1987. Cert. cash mgr. Tchr. Machimavas Sch., Udonthani, 1958-65; spl. instr. Chana Songkram Sch., Bangkok, 1965-68; tchrs. staff Thai Sripratoom U., 1968-70; salesman Met. Life of N.Y., 1974-76; rep. Mut. Life of N.Y., 1976-78; agt. Equitable Life Ins., N.Y.C., 1983-84; insp. IBI Security Svc. Inc., L.I., 1979-85; security police insp. Brandeis U., Waltham, Mass., 1985-86; U.S. chief legal investigator, pvt. investigator U.S. Legal Investigation, Inc., U.S. Bur.'s Security Agy., Boston, N.Y.C., Fresno, Calif., 1987—; chmn. Worldwide Bank Assocs. Investment, 2000—. Advisor Thai N.E. Assn., N.Y.C., 1980—, Rep. Nat. Com., Washingotn, 1980—; state advisor U.S. Congl. Adv., Washington, 1980; assoc. mem. Nat. Security Ctr., Citizen's Adv. Coun., Washington, 1989; pres., chief security agt. U.S. Bur. Security Agy., 1991; mem. Pres. Pvt. Sector Survey on Cost Control, Washington, 1989—; adv. bd. Am. Security Coun., Washington, 1983-88. Mem. G.O.P. Republican Conservative Party (recommendation pres. Gerald R. Ford 1977), 1977—, Nat. Republican Congl. Com. Victory Fund, Washington, 1982—, Republican Presdl. Task Force and Comsn. (recommendation chmn. Nat. Republican Senatorial Com. 1982, 93), 1982—, Am. Security Coun. Found., 1978—, Defense Dept., Defense Inst., 1982—, Nat. Rep. Senatorial Com., Washington, Chiefs of Police Nat. Drug Task Force, 1982—, Nat. Law Enforcement Officers Meml. Fund, Washington, 1982—, Natl. Wildlife Fedn., 1982—; apptd. state adviser U.S. Congl. Adv. Bd., 1979, 93; priest asst. U.S.A. Buddhayaram Temple, Bronx, 1970—; pres. S.E. Asia Found., 1970; mem. Citizens Against Govt. Waste, Washington; mem. U.S. Def. Com., Washington, 1982-86; sec. Wat Buddhamonthol United Buddhist Meditation Ctr., 1992—. Recipient Presdl. Seal, Rep. Orgn., 1983, 84, Rep. Presdl. Legion of Merit highest level of Govts. for Lifetime, 1993. Mem. Internat. Assn. Chiefs of Police, President's Club, Senator's Club, Rep. Presdl. Legion of Merit.

'T HOOFT, GERARDUS, physicist, educator; b. Den Helder, The Netherlands, July 5, 1946; s. Hendrik 't Hooft and Margaretha Agnes (van Kampen) t' Hooft; m. Albertha Anje Schik, July 1, 1972; children: Saskia Anne, Ellen Marga. Ed., Utrecht U., The Netherlands; doctoraalexamen Theoretical Physics, Rijksuniversiteit Utrecht, The Netherlands, 1969, PhD, 1972; DSc (hon.) , U. Chgo., 1981, U. Louvain, 1996, U. Bologna, 1998, Eurasian U., Astana, Kazakjstan, 2000, U. Western Cape, South Africa, 2001. Fellow European Ctr. Nuc. Rsch., Geneva, 1972—74; lectr., asst. prof. physics U. Utrecht, The Netherlands, 1974—77, prof. The Netherlands, 1977—. Loeb lectr. Harvard U., Cambridge, Mass., 1976; Fairchild disting. scholar Calif. Inst. Tech., Pasadena, 1981; assoc. +248tranger Acad. des Scis., Paris, 1995. Assoc. editor Nuc. Physics B; contbr. articles to profl. jours. Decorated officer Legion of Honor France, comdr. Order Ned. Leeuw; recipient Dannie Heineman prize, Am. Phys. Soc., 1979, Am. Inst. Physics, N.Y.C., 1979, Wolf prize, Wolf Found., Jerusalem, 1981, Piou XI medal, Pontifica Accademia delle Sci. John Paul II, Vatican City, 1983, Spinoza premium, NWO, 1995, Franklin medal, Phila., 1995, Gian Carlo Wick comm. medal, Lausanne, 1997, HEP prize, European Phys. Soc., 1999, Nobel prize in physics, 1999. Mem.: Koninlijke Nederlandse Academie voor Wetenschappen (Lorentz medal 1986), Am. Acad. Arts and Scis. (hon.), U.S. Nat. Acad. Scis. (assoc.). Office: Spinoza Inst PO Box 80 195 NL3508TD Utrecht Netherlands E-mail: g.thooft@phys.uu.nl.

THOPPIL, CECIL KOSHEY, pediatrician, consultant, educator; b. Trivandrum, India, Aug. 4, 1961; m. Jennifer Carrol Gallego, Apr. 25, 1992; children: Cecilia Ruth, Andrew Obed. Pre-degree, Mar Ivanios Coll., Trivandrum, Kerala, India, 1979; MB, BS, Med. Coll. Hosp., Trivandrum, 1984. Diplomate Am. Bd. Pediat.; cert. instr. neonatal advanced life support, pediat. advanced life support, BLS. Compulsory rotating internship Med. Coll. Hosp., Trivandrum, Kerala, India, 1985-86; postgrad. tng. pediatric medicine dept. child health S.A.T. Hosp., India, 1986-87; postdoctoral rsch. assoc. dept. perinatal pediatrics U. Tex. Med. Br., Galveston, 1987-89; pediatric internship Univ. Hosps. Cleve. Rainbow Babies and Children's Hosp., 1989-90; pediatric residency dept. pediatrics Scott & White Meml. Hosp./Tex. A&M U. Coll. Medicine, Temple, 1990-92; pediatrician Surry County Health Dept., Dobson, N.C., 1992-94, Med. Assocs. of Surry, Novant Health Physicians Divsn. Triad Region, Mt. Airy, 1994—. Physician cons. Mount Airy Sch. Health Adv. Coun., Surry Pre-sch. Interagy. Coun., Surry County Day Care Assn.; pediat. cons. Surry Smart Start Task Force. Contbr. articles to profl. jours. Deacon Haymore Bapt. Ch. Recipient Father Kuncheria Goldmedal for First Rank in Loyola Sch. for Matriculation. Fellow Am. Acad. Pediat.; mem. AMA, N.C. Med. Soc., N.C. Pediat. Soc., Surry-Yadkin Med. Soc. Home: 151 Cross Creek Dr Mount Airy NC 27030-9229 Office: Med Assocs of Surry 865 W Lake Dr Mount Airy NC 27030-2157 Fax: 336-719-7935. E-mail: ckthopill@novanthealth.org.

THOR, PAUL VIETS, computer science educator; b. Schenectady, N.Y., Mar. 10, 1946; s. Donald D. and Eleanor B. (Viets) T.; m. Barbara K. Nelson, Mar. 27, 1982 (div. Dec. 1993). BSME, U. Denver, 1968; MS in Engring. Mgmt., UCLA, 1976; MS in Computer Sci., George Mason U., 1993; DCS, Colo. Tech. U., 1999. Engr. Martin Marietta Corp., Denver, 1968-69; commd. 2d lt. USAF, 1969, advanced through grades to maj., 1982; pilot trainee USAF-Williams AFB, Phoenix, 1970-71; pilot C141A 15 MAS-Norton AFB, San Bernardino, Calif., 1971-75, pilot C141B, 1981-84; communications and computer officer 2044 CG-Pentagon, Washington, 1977-81; air field mgr. 18TFW-Kadena AB, Okinawa, Japan, 1984-86; pilot C12 1402 MAS-Andrews AFB, Washington, 1986-87; comm. and computer officer 7 Comm. Group-Pentagon, 1987-89; cons. George Mason U., Fairfax, Va., 1990-93; pvt. practice cons. Colorado Springs, Colo., 1993—. Wing flight examiner 63 MAW-Norton AFB, San Bernardino, 1981-84; acquisitions officer 7th Comms. Group-Pentagon, 1987-89; assoc. prof. computer sci. Colo. Tech. U., Colorado Springs, 1993-2001, prof., 2001—. Mem. Computer Soc. of IEEE, Assn. Computer Machinery, Air Force Assn. (life), Ret. Officers Assn. Avocations: personal computers, woodworking, crafts, photography, book collector. Home: 3262 Muirfield Dr Colorado Springs CO 80907-7805 Office: Colo Tech U 4435 N Chestnut St Colorado Springs CO 80907-3812 E-mail: pthor@coloradotech.edu., pvthor@earthlink.net.

THORBECKE, ERIK, economics educator; b. Berlin, Feb. 17, 1929; s. William and Madelaine (Salisbury) T.; m. Charla J. Westerberg, Oct. 17, 1954; children: Erik Charles, Willem, Jon. Student, Netherlands Sch. Econs., Rotterdam, 1948-51; PhD, U. Calif., 1957; hon. doctorate, U. Ghent, 1981. Asst. prof. econs. Iowa State U., 1957-60, assoc. prof., 1960-63, prof., 1963-73, Cornell U., 1974—, chmn. dept. econs., 1975-78, H.E. Babcock prof. econs. and food econs., 1978—. Econ. adviser Nat. Planning Inst., Lima, Peru, 1963-64; asso. asst. adminstr. for program policy AID, Washington, 1966-68, mem. research advisory com., 1976-81; sr. economist world employment program Internat. Labor Office, Geneva, 1972-73; vis. prof. Erasmus U., Rotterdam, 1980-81; mem. com. on internat. nutritional programs NRC-NAS, 1979-81; dir. program on comparative econ. devel., Cornell U., 1988—; sr. rsch. fellow USAID Inst. Policy Reform, 1990—. Author: The Tendency Towards Regionalization in International Trade, 1960, (with Irma Adelman) Theory and Design of Economic Development, 1966, (with K. Fox, J. Sengupta) Theory of Quantitative Economic Policy, 1968, Role of Agriculture in Economic Development, 1968, (with G. Pyatt) Planning Techniques for a Better Future, 1976; (with J. Defourny) Structural Path Analysis and Multiplier Decomposition within a Social Matrix, 1984, (with J. Foster, J. Greer) A Class of Decomposable Poverty Measures, 1984, (with J. Lecaillon, C. Morrisson) Economic Policies and Agricultural Performance of Low Income Countries, 1987, Planning Techniques for Social Justice In: The Balance between Industry and Agriculture in Economic Development, vol. 4, 1989, (with I. Adelman) The Role of Institutions in Economic Development, Special Issue of World Development, 1989, (with others) Adjustment and Equity in Indonesia, 1992, (with D. Berrian) Budgetary Rules to Minimize Societal Poverty in a General Equilibrium Context, 1992, (with T. van der Pluijm) Rural Indonesia: Socio-economic Development in a Changing Environment, 1993, (with A. de Janvry and E. Sadoulet) Impact of State and Civil Institutions on the Operation of Rural Market and Non-Market Configurations In: State, Market and civil Organizations: New Theories, New Practices, and Their Implications for Rural Development, 1995, (with A. Parikh) Impact of Rural Industrialization on Village Life and Economy: A Social Accounting Matrix, 1996, (with H-S Jung) A Multiplier Decomposition Method to Analyze Poverty Alleviation, 1996, (with others) Methods of Interregional and Regional Analysis, 1998, (with H. Wan) Taiwan's Development Experience: Lessons on Roles of Government and Market, 1999; contbr. articles to profl. jours. Mem. Am. Econ. Assn., Am. Assn. Agrl. Econs. (Nat. award for best pub. research 1970) Office: Cornell U Dept Econs Ithaca NY 14853 Home: 29601 Highway 20 Fort Bragg CA 95437-8281

THORBECKE, WILLEM HENRY, international company executive, consultant; b. Paris, July 4, 1924; s. Willem Johan Rudolf and Madelaine (Salisbury) T.; m. Sonya Stokowski, June 8, 1946; children; Noel Evangeline, Johan Rudolf, Willem Leif, Christine Louise. BS in Engring., BSBA, MIT, 1948. Exec. Royal Dutch Shell, N.Y.C., London, Tokyo, 1948-60, Mobil Corp., N.Y.C., 1960-69; cons. various cos., N.Y.C., Chgo., Houston, others, 1969-75; pres. Dravo Internat., Pitts., 1975-82, W.H. Thorbecke Assocs., Sewickley, Pa., 1982—. Chmn., chief exec. officer Energy Support Svcs. Inc., Coraopolis, Pa., 1982-87, dir., 1987-90; founder, chmn., CEO Thorbecke Enterprises, Inc., Sewickley, 1996—. Dir. World Affairs Coun., Pitts., 1978—; chmn. MIT Enterprise Forum, Pitts., 1987-89, 93-94. Flight lt. RAF. Named Tri-State Area Entrepreneur of Yr. Venture Mag., Ernst & Young, 1987. Mem. Am. Mgmt. Assn. (internat. coun. 1977-83), Nat. Assn. Corp. Dirs., Duquesne Club (Pitts.), Haagse Club (The Netherlands). Republican. Epsicopalian. Home: Deer Haven Farm Stonedale Rd Sewickley PA 15143 E-mail: whthorbecke@aol.com.

THORBURN, JAMES ALEXANDER, humanities educator; b. Martins Ferry, Ohio, Aug. 24, 1923; s. Charles David and Mary Edna (Ruble) T.; m. Lois McElroy, July 3, 1954; children: Alexander Maurice, Melissa Rachel; m. 2d, June Yingling O'Leary, Apr. 18, 1981. BA, Ohio State U., 1949, MA, 1951; postgrad., U. Mo., 1954-55; PhD, La. State U., 1977. Head English dept. high sch., Sheridan, Mich., 1951-52; instr. English, U. Mo., Columbia, 1952-55, Monmouth (Ill.) Coll., 1955-56, U. Tex., El Paso, 1956-60, U. Mo., St. Louis, 1960-61, La. State U., Baton Rouge, 1961-70; prof. Southeastern La. U., Hammond, 1970-89, ret., named prof. emeritus English and linguistics; testing and cert. examiner English Lang. Inst., U. Mich., 1969—; participant Southeastern Conf. on Linguistics; mem. Conf. Christianity and Lit. Contbg. author: Exercises in English, 1955, also poetry, short stories; book rev. editor: Experiment, 1958-87; editor: Innisfree, 1984-89. With F.A., AUS, 1943-46. Mem. MLA, Linguistic Assn. S.W., Avalon World Arts Acad., Linguistic Soc. Am., Am. Dialect Soc., La. Assn. for Coll. Composition, La. Retired Tchrs. Assn., Internat. Poetry Soc., Internat. Acad. Poets, Sociedad Nacional Hispânica, Sigma Delta Pi, Phi Kappa Phi (named emeritus life), Phi Mu Alpha Sinfonia. Republican. Presbyterian. Home: 602 Susan Dr Hammond LA 70403-3444 Office: Southeastern La U # 739 Hammond LA 70402-0001 *I have always felt that no experience is wasted, if it is not selfish or vicious. Every such experience adds something, I believe, to that inner fund on which one draws, consciously or unconsciously, throughout one's life.*

THORDARSON, SMARI, diagnostic radiologist; b. Buchanan, Mich., Nov. 11, 1961; s. Steinthor and Lilja Thordarson; m. Lori Ann Zbaraschuk, June 23, 1991; children: Erik Michael, Shelby Renee. BA, Andrews U., 1983; MD, Loma Linda U., 1987. Diplomate Am. Bd. Radiology. Resident Loma Linda U., Calif., 1987—91; radiologist LaPorte Hosp. & Health Svcs., Ind., 1991—, chmn. dept. diagnostic imaging, 1994—99. Pres. med. staff LaPorte Hosp., 1999. Bd. dirs. No. Ind. Sch. Radiol. Tech., LaPorte, 1993-96. Mem. AMA, Am. Coll. Radiology, Radiol. Soc. N.Am. (councelor Ind. 1997—2001), Ind. State Med. Assn., LaPorte County Med. Assn. (pres. 1997). Avocations: reading, scuba, travel. Office: LaPorte Radiology Inc 900 I St La Porte IN 46350-5533

THORDARSON, WILLIAM, retired hydrogeologist; b. N.Y.C., Mar. 14, 1929; s. William and Lillian (Hirsch) T. BA, Columbia U., 1950; postgrad., U. Kans., Lawrence, 1953-55; MA, U. Colo., 1987. Hydrogeologist U.S. Geol. Survey, Denver, 1955-94. Author: Perched Groundwater, Nevada, 1965, Hydrogeology of Test Wells, 1975, Hydrogeology of South-Central Great Basin, 1983, Hydrogeologic Monitoring, Nevada, 1985, Hydrogeology of Anhydrite, 1989. Served with U.S. Army, 1950-52. Mem. Nat. Geog. Soc., Colo. Ground Water Assn., Colo. Sci. Soc., Geol. Soc. Wash. Home: 1453 Belcourt Lane Mount Pleasant SC 29466-8103

THORN, BRIAN EARL, Internet company executive; b. Tucson, Oet. 30, 1955; s. Charles Walter and Jacquelyn Grace (Sloat) T.; m. Mary L. Ayala, Nov. 23, 1979 (div. 1981); m. Brenda Anne Benson, Dec. 28, 1983; 1 child, Justin. Student, U. Ariz. Loss prevention mgr. HRT Industries, Tucson, 1977-82; sales mgr. Circuit City, 1982-86, ops. mgr. Calif., 1986-87, divsn. mgr., 1987-90; store mgr. Barnes & Noble, Houston, 1992-97; ops. mgr. Best Buy, The Woodlands, Tex., 1997-99; nat. sales mgr. Aerial/Voicestream Comm., Houston, 1999-2000; mgr. tech. InfoHighway Comms., 2000—. Bd. dirs. Infohighway Comms., Inc.; mem. advt./mktg. com. Woodlands Corp. Mem. planning com. Edn. for Tomorrow Alliance; mem. planning com., 4th of July planning com. Home for the Holidays Planning Com. Mem. Tex. Tech. Forum (treas.), Woodlands C. of C. (bd. dirs., mem. exec. nominating com., mem. affinity com., mem. visioning com.), Woodlands Libr. Guild (bd. dirs.), Montgomery County Sheriff Citizens Acad. Alumni Assn. Avocations: golf, reading, old cars, flying, computers.

THORN, FRANK, vision scientist, educator, researcher; b. N.Y., Apr. 17, 1940; s. Frank and Cathrine Elizabeth (Gundersen) T.; m. Sondra Joy Koonz, May 23, 1959; children: Sondra Joy, Laura Ann, Renee Louise Thorn Magovsky, Cynthia Lynn Thorn Koivisto. BS, Rennselear Polytechnic Inst., 1961; PhD, U. Rochester, 1967; postdoctoral trainee, U. Calif., 1967-69; OD, NE Coll. Optometry, 1979. Rsch. asst. U. Rochester, Rochester, N.Y., 1962-67; assoc. prof. Pacific U. Coll. Optometry, Forest Grove, Oreg., 1969-75; exec. dir. Oreg. Optometric Ctr., 1974-75; rsch. assoc. U. Rochester, 1975-76; assoc. prof. NE Coll. Optometry, Boston, 1979-85; prof., 1985—; dir. rsch. NE Coll. Optometry, Boston, 1985—. Vis. scientist Mass. Inst. Tech., Cambridge, 1982-95; consultant Essilor Internat. Corp., Paris, 1982-88, Bausch & Lomb Co., Rochester, 1985-89; chair Eighth INternat. Conf. on Myopia, 2000. Bd. trustees NE Coll. Optometry, Boston, 1987-88; bd. dirs. Oreg. Zoological Rsch. Ctr., Portland, 1972-75. Recipient Small Project grant Nat. Eye Inst., 1982, Myopia study grant Am. Optometric Found., 1985, TV Captioning grant B & L InVision Inst., 1991, grantee Nat. Eye Inst., 1995—. Mem. Assn. Rsch. Vision & Opthalmology, Am. Assn. Advancement of Sci., Sigma Xi. Achievements include numerous rsch. articles on visual neurophysiology, accommodation, the development of ocular optics, refractive errors, and eye alignment; optical blur and the visual problems of the hearing impaired. Office: New Eng Coll Optometry 424 Beacon St Boston MA 02115-1129

THORN, ROD, professional basketball executive; b. 1941; m. Peggy Thorn; children: Jonathan, Amanda, Jessica. Student, W.Va. U. Player Balt. Bullets, NBA, 1963-64, Detroit Pistons and St. Louis Hawks, NBA, 1964-66, Seattle Supersonics, NBA, 1966-70, asst. coach, 1971-73, N.Y. Nets, Am. Basketball Assn., 1973-75; coach St. Louis Spirits, Am. Basketball Assn., 1975-76; asst. coach N.Y. Nets, 1976-78; gen. mgr. Chgo. Bulls, NBA, 1978-85; v.p. ops. NBA, N.Y.C., 1985-2000; pres. New Jersey Nets, East Rutherford, N.J., 2000—. Office: Nat Basketball Assn Olympic Tower 645 5th Ave Fl 10 New York NY 10022-5986 Address: NJ Nets Nets Champion Ctr 390 Murray Hill Pkwy East Rutherford NJ 07073-2109*

THORN, ROSEMARY KOST, former librarian; b. N.Y.C., Dec. 15, 1954; d. Stephen John and Henrietta (Rosso) K.; m. Michael Thorn; children: Russell, Stephen. BA in Anthropology, Rutgers U., 1977; MLS, U. N.C., 1980. Head libr. U.S. EPA, Research Triangle Park, N.C., 1980-96; EPA. Avocations: running, gardening, travel, Tae Kwon Do (2d degree black belt).

THORN, SUSAN HOWE, interior designer; b. Washington, Apr. 22, 1941; d. James Bennett Cowdin and Lois (Fiesinger) Howe; m. William D. Thorn, June 22, 1963; children: Melissa Ann, William David. Lighting design, Parsons Sch. Design, 1975-77; BA , Syracuse U., 1962; AB, N.Y. Sch. Interior Design, 1995. Owner, designer Susan Thorn Interiors, Inc., Cross River, N.Y., 1965—. Designer total bldg. Cooper Labs, Bedford Hills, N.Y., 1973, total redesign Nycrest Corp., Cold Spring, N.Y., 1973-75, showrooms, model rooms stylist and coordinator France Voiles Co. Inc., N.Y.C., 1976, total design new corp. hdqrs. in Gen. Dynamics Bldg. (with Marjorie Borradaile Helsel), Robert E. Eastman Co., N.Y.C., 1967, Cummin & Friedland Capital Corp., 1982; designer offices, stores, employee areas comml., public, residential clients, including Waccabuc (N.Y.) Country Club, 1969, S. Salem (N.Y.) Library, St. Vincent's Hosp., N.Y.C., 1996; instr. adult edn. dept. John Jay High Sch.; spkr. civic orgns. Mem. Am. Soc. Interior Designers (profl.), Internat. Assn. Lighting Designers (assoc.), Decorators Club, Club of N.Y., Waccabuc Country Club. Episcopalian. Home: 88 N Salem Rd Cross River NY 10518 E-mail: thorninteriors@earthlink.net.

THORN, TERENCE HASTINGS, international energy industry executive; b. Takoma, Md., July 6, 1946; s. John Hastings and Norine R. (Freytag) T.; m. Judith Carol Bailey, Aug. 15, 1970; children: Kristin Lynn, Matthew Hastings. BA, U. Md., 1969, MA, 1973. Dir. congl. rels. Am. Gas Assn., Arlington, Va., 1975-79; dir. govt. rels. J. Walter Thompson Co., Washington, 1979-81; v.p. govt. rels. Houston Natural Gas Co., 1981-85; exec. v.p., chmn. bd. Mojave Pipeline Co., Houston, 1986-89; pres., CEO Transwestern Pipeline Co., 1993—; sr. v.p., exec. mgmt. com. bd. Enron Corp., 1993-98, exec. v.p. internat. govt. rels. and environ. affairs, 1998—2001, mng. dir. Middle East, 2001; cons. Houston Tex. Energy, Environment, Tech. Bd. dirs. Houston Pops, 1989-90, Pin Oak Charities, Houston, 1991-93, Greater Houston chpt. YMCA, 1994; city alderman, 1992-93; mem. Hermann Soc., 1993—, Energy Industry Sector Adv. Com. U.S. Dept. Commerce; prin. liason Pres.'s Coun. Sustainable Devel.; chmn. internat. com. Bus. Coun. of Sustainable Devel.; mem. adv. com. Commn. for Environ. Cooperation; trustee Tomas Rivera Policy Inst.; chmn. Internat. Gas Ctr. Mem. Pacific Coast Gas Assn. (chmn. 1994-95), Internat. Gas Union (chmn. com. 9), U.S. C. of C. (mem. internat. policy com.), Coun. of the Ams. (adv. com.), Wildlife Conservation Soc. (trustee), Nature Conservancy (trustee). Avocation: tennis.

THORNBERRY, MAC, congressman; b. Clarendon, Tex., July 15, 1958; m. Sally Thornberry; 2 children. BA in History summa cum laude, Tex. Tech U., 1980; JD, U. Tex., 1983. Legis. coun. Rep. Tom Loeffler, 1983-85; chief of staff Rep. Larry Combest, 1985-88; dep. asst. sec. legis. affairs U.S. State Dept., 1988-89; def. atty. Peterson, Farris, Doores & Jones, Amarillo, Tex., 1989-94; mem. U.S. Congress from 13th Tex. dist., 1995—; mem. armed svcs. com., resources com., budget com., oil and gas caucus. Family rancher. Mem. Tex. and Southwestern Cattle Raisers Assn. Republican. Office: US House Reps 131 Cannon HOB Washington DC 20515-4313*

THORNBURG, FREDERICK FLETCHER, diversified business executive, lawyer; b. South Bend, Ind., Feb. 10, 1940; s. James F. and Margaret R. (Major) T.; children: James Brian, Charles Kevin, Christian Sean, Christopher Herndon; m. Patricia J. Malloy, Dec. 4, 1981. AB, DePauw U., 1963; postgrad., U. Notre Dame, 1965; JD magna cum laude, Ind. U., 1968. Bar: Ind. 1968, U.S. Tax Ct. 1970, U.S. Ct. Appeals (7th cir.) 1970, U.S. Supreme Ct. 1971. Tchr., coach U.S. Peace Corps, Colombia, 1963-65; law clk. to chief judge U.S. Ct. Appeals (7th cir.), 1968-69; assoc. Thornburg, McGill, Deahl, Harman, Carey & Murray, South Bend, 1969-75, ptnr., 1975-80; v.p. systems and svcs. group The Wackenhut Corp., Coral Gables, Fla., 1981-82, sr. v.p. adminstrn., 1982-86, exec. v.p., 1986-88, also bd. dirs.; pres. Wackenhut Internat. Corp. and Wackenhut Svcs., Inc.; v.p., legal counsel St. Thomas U., 1988-90, adj. prof. law, 1989-90; pres., CEO PropServ, Inc., 1991-94; pres. EPS Ltd., 1995—; CEO Practice Resources Corp., 1996-97; CEO, of counsel Stephens, Lynn, Klien & McNicholas, 1998-2000. Cons. Merayo Med. Arts Group, GMMG, Ltd., MSC, Am. Tel. Corp.; legal and mgmt. cons., mem. bd. advisors Publix Supermarkets, Inc., 1994—95, St. Thomas U., 1990—95; bd. dirs. Doral Park Country Club, RFBD, Inc.; trustee U. Cmty. Hosp. Found., 1991—94; adj. prof. bus. St. Mary's Coll., 1975—78; vis. prof. CTA, 1985—95; vice chmn., pvt. sec. adv. coun. Fla. Sec. of State, 1985—90; mem. ind. ethics oversight com. Miami-Dade County Pub. Sch. Ethics Com., 2002—. Assoc. editor in chief Ind. Law Jour., 1967-68; contbr. articles to legal and bus. jours. Mem. Civic Ctr. Found., 1976—80; pres. Jaycees, 1974; bd. dirs. RFD&D, Inc.; former bd. dirs. Michiana YMCA, Channel 34, Symphony Orch. Assn., 1974—80, Boy Scouts of U.S.A.; bd. dirs. Doral and West Airport C. of C. Fulbright selectee, Halleck scholar. Mem. ABA, Ind. Bar Assn., Greater Miami C. of C. (former corp. rep. trustee), Elks Club, Doral Park Country Club, Order of Coif, Phi Delta Phi, Alpha Delta Sigma. Office: 10005 NW 52nd Ter Miami FL 33178-2608 Fax: (305) 591-6560. E-mail: MrFPT@aol.com.

THORNBURG, LACY HERMAN, federal judge; b. Charlotte, N.C., Dec. 20, 1929; s. Jesse Lafayette and Sarah Ann (Ziegler) T.; m. Dorothy Todd, Sept. 6, 1953; children— Sara Thornburg Evans, Lacy Eugene, Jesse Todd, Alan Ziegler. AA, Mars Hill Coll., 1950; BA, U. N.C., 1951, JD, 1954. Bar: U.S. Dist. Ct. (we. dist.) N.C. Practiced law, Webster, N.C., 1954-67; superior ct. judge State of N.C., 1967-83, atty. gen, 1985-92; emergency judge N.C. Superior Ct., Webster, 1993-94; mem. Nat. Indian Gaming Commn., 1994-95; judge U.S. Dist. Ct. for N.C., Asheville, 1995—. Mem. staff Congressman Taylor, Sylva, N.C., 1960, Congressman David Hall, Sylva, 1959-60; mem. N.C. Ho. of Reps., 1961-65; mem. N.C. Cts. Commn., N.C. Criminal Code Commn., Capital Planning Commn., Raleigh. Chmn. Jackson County Bd. of Health, Sylva, 1965-84; commr. Tryon Palace, New Bern, N.C. Served with U.S. Army, 1947-48. Mem. Lions, Masons, Shriners. Democrat. Avocations: fly fishing, skeet shooting. Office: US Dist Ct 241 US Courthouse 100 Otis St Asheville NC 28801-2611

THORNBURG, LEE ELLIS, film executive, director; b. Houston, Feb. 16, 1942; s. Richard Ellis and Lucyle (Comstock) T.; m. Jane Kaiser (div. 1981); children: Janette Mattas, Deanne Waddell; m. Patricia Ann Kirkham, June 16, 1987. Tech. svc. engr. Dresser Industries, Houston, 1970-76; pres. Lone Star Pictures Internat., Inc., Dallas, 1976—. Bd. dirs. TCI Wholesale. Dir. films including Hollywood High Part II, 1981, 6-Pack, 1991, Southwest, 1996, Memo, 1996; prodr. films including Kings of the Hill, 1976, Mr. Mean, 1978. Mem. Am. Film Market Assn. Republican. Methodist. Office: PO Box 4160 La Puente CA 91747-4160 E-mail: lonestarpictures@aol.com.

THORNBURG, LINDA A. writer; b. Denver, Aug. 8, 1949; d. William J.R. Thornburg and Marjory Smith. BA, U. Colo., 1973. Pres., prin. Word Wizards, Woodbridge, Va., 1990—. Author: (book series) Cool Careers for Girls, 1999—2002; editor: iLinx Society for Human Resource Management, 2000—02. Mem.: AAUW (br. sec. 2000—02), Washington Ind. Writers. E-mail: wordwzrds@aol.com.

THORNBURGH, DANIEL ESTON, retired university administrator, journalism educator; b. Terre Haute, Ind., Sept. 17, 1930; s. Lester D. and Dorothy (Green) T.; m. Adrianne Ames, Aug. 11, 1956; children: Debra Kay Thornburgh Considine, Stewart Beckett, Malcolm Noble. BS, Ind. State U., 1952; MA, U. Iowa, 1957; EdD, Ind. U., 1980. Reporter Terre Haute Star, 1952; publicity dir. Simpson Coll., Indianola, Iowa, 1955-57; info. dir. Marshall U., Huntington, W.Va., 1957-59, Eastern Ill. U., Charleston, 1959-65, chmn., prof. journalism, 1965-84, dir. univ. rels., 1984-92. Vis. prof. U. Hawaii, 1982-83, U. Fla., 1993-94, Millikin U., 1996; mem. Gov.'s Coun. Health and Phys. Fitness, 1987—; pub. Casey Banner Times, Ill., 1967-69. Editor: (with others) Interpretative Reporting Workbook, 1982. Mem. Charleston City Coun., 1973-77; active Ill. Recreation Coun., Springfield, 1979-85; pres. Coles Hist. Soc., Charleston, 1972-74, 92; pres., trustee Five Mile House Found., 1998—; trustee Lincoln and Sargent Farm Found., 1999—; chmn. higher edn. and campus min. com. Meth. Ch., 2000-02. With U.S. Army, 1952—54. Named Outstanding Advisor, Coun. Coll. Publs. Advisors, 1971. Mem. Charleston C. of C. (area man of yr. award 1971), Assn. Edn. Journalism and Mass Comm., Pub. Rels. Soc. Am., Soc. Profl. Journalists, Coun. Advancement and Support Edn. (EIU PRSSA chpt.), Masons (Cmty. Builder award 1997), Elks, Rotary (pres. Charleston 1976-77, dist. gov. 6490 2000-01). Methodist. Avocations: tennis, writing. Home: 1405 Buchanan Ave Charleston IL 61920-2924 Fax: 217-345-8808. E-mail: adthorn@mcleodusa.net.

THORNBURGH, DICK (RICHARD L. THORNBURGH), lawyer, former United Nations official, former United States attorney general, former governor; b. Pitts., July 16, 1932; s. Charles Garland and Alice (Sanborn) T.; m. Virginia Walton Judson, Oct. 12, 1963; children: John, David, Peter, William. B in Engring., Yale, 1954; LLB, U. Pitts., 1957; hon. degrees, from 30 colls. and univs. Bar: Pa. 1958, U.S. Supreme Ct. 1965, D.C. 1998. Atty. Kirkpatrick & Lockhart, Pitts., 1959-69, 77-79, 87-88, 91-92, 94—; U.S. atty. for Western Pa., 1969-75; U.S. asst. atty. gen. Dept. Justice, Washington, 1975-77; gov. State of Pa., Harrisburg, 1979-87; dir. Inst. Politics John F. Kennedy Sch. Govt., Harvard U., 1987-88; U.S. atty. gen. Washington, 1988-91; under-sec.-gen. for adminstrn. and mgmt. UN, N.Y.C., 1992-93. Del. Pa. Constl. Conv., 1967-68; vice chair World Com. on Disability; bd. dirs. Elan Corp. plc, Nat. Mus. Indsl. History, Gettysburg Nat. Battlefield Mus. Found. Mem. Coun. Fgn. Rels., Am. Law Inst.; trustee Urban Inst., U. Pitts. Fellow Am. Bar Found.; mem. Am. Judicature Soc. Republican. Office: Kirkpatrick & Lockhart LLP 1800 Massachusetts Ave NW Washington DC 20036-1800

THORNBURGH, ELAINE MARGARET, musician; b. Key West, Fla., Feb. 15, 1952; d. Charles Harry and Nancy (Golan) T.; children: Andrew Linford, Thomas Linford; m. Tsvi Bar-David, Aug. 1998. MusB, San Francisco Conservatory of Music, 1981, MusM, 1982. Freelance performer on harpsichord, 1971—; freelance performer on forte piano, 1982—; founding pres., dir. Humanities West, San Francisco, 1983-94; harpsichord instr. Stanford (Calif.) U., 1996—. Adj. lectr. harpsichord U. Calif., Santa Cruz, 1981-82; cons. NEH, Washington, 1986 (peer rev. bd.). Solo Recitalist Nat. Endowment for the Arts, 1984-85; touring artist Calif. Arts Coun., 1985—; performer (recs.) 18 Scarlatti Sonatas, 1990, Haydn Songs with Judith Nelson, soprano, Elaine Thornburgh, fortepiano, 1991, William Byrd Grounds and Variations, 1991. Mem. San Francisco Early Music Soc. (v.p., pres., 1982-84). Avocations: hiking, gardening, cooking. Home and Office: 580 Funston Ave San Francisco CA 94118-3636 E-mail: t.bar-david@worldnet.att.net.

THORNBURY, JOHN ROUSSEAU, radiologist, physician; b. Cleve., Mar. 16, 1929; s. Purla Lee and Gertrude (Glidden) T.; m. Julia Lee McGregor, Mar. 20, 1955; children: Lee Allison, John McGregor. AB cum laude, Miami U., Oxford, Ohio, 1950; MD, Ohio State U., 1955. Diplomate: Am. Bd. Radiology. Intern Hurley Hosp., Flint, Mich., 1955-56; resident U. Iowa Hosps., Iowa City, 1958-61; instr., asst. prof. radiology U. Colo. Med. Center, Denver, 1962-63; practice medicine specializing in radiology, 1962-63, Iowa City, 1963-66, Seattle, 1966-68, Ann Arbor, Mich., 1968-79, Albuquerque, 1979-84, Rochester, N.Y., 1984-89, Madison, Wis., 1989-94, Mem. staff U. Wisconsin Hosp., Madison; prof. radiology, chief sect. of body imaging, U. Wis. Med. Sch., 1989-94, prof. emeritus, 1994—; asst. prof. radiology U. Iowa Hosps.,

1963-66, U. Wash. Hosp., Seattle, 1966-68; assoc. prof. radiology U. Mich. Med. Ctr., 1968-71, prof., 1971-79, chief uroradiology section, 1971-79; prof. radiology, chief divsn. diagnostic radiology Sch. Medicine, U. N.Mex., 1979-84; prof. radiology U. Rochester Sch. Medicine, 1984-89, acting chmn., 1985-87; chmn. sci. com. on efficacy studies Nat. Coun. on Radiation Protection, 1980-95; rapporteur/mem. sci. group on indications/limitations of x-ray diagnostic procedures WHO, 1983; cons. com. on efficacy of magnetic resonance nat. health tech. adv. panel Australian Inst. Health, 1986; invited U.S. cons. MRI program, Nijmegen, The Netherlands, 1992; mem. planning group Low Back Pain Collaboratives and Nat. Congress, Inst. for Health Care Improvement, 1997-98; mem. methodologic rsch. issues working group NIH and Pub. Health Svc.-Office of Women's Health, 1998; cons., spkr. Royal Australasian Coll. Radiologists, Melbourne, Australia, 1997; cons. tech. assessment and outcomes rsch., 1994—; cons. to Am. Soc. Neuroradiology, 1995-2000; lectr. in field. Co-author/cons. Clin. Efficacy Assessment Project, Am. Coll. Physicians, 1986-89; assoc. editor: Yearbook of Radiology, 1971-82; mem. editl. bd.: Contemporary Diagnostic Radiology, 1977-84, Urologic Radiology, 1977-84 Bd. dirs. Sally Jobe Found., Denver, 1996—. Capt., M.C. USAF, 1956-58. Recipient Dist. Svc. award Am. Bd. Radiology, 2000, Alumni Achievement award Ohio State U. Coll. Medicine, 2000, Gold medal Assn. Univ. Radiologists, 2002; grantee Agy. Health Care Policy and Rsch., 1986-91, U. Rochester, 1986-89, U. Wis., Madison, 1989-91. Fellow Am. Coll. Radiology (mem. emeritus); mem. Am. Coll. Radiology Imaging Network (outcomes and quality of life subcom., urology com., NIH, 1999-2002), Soc. Uroradiology (pres. 1976-77, dir. 1977-79), Assn. Univ. Radiologists (pres. 1980-81), Radiol. Soc. N.Am., Am. Roentgen Ray Soc. (Caldwell medal 1993), Soc. for Health Svcs. Rsch. in Radiology (adv. com. to bd. dirs. 1998—), Colo. Radiol. Soc., Phi Beta Kappa, Delta Tau Delta, Omicron Delta Kappa, Phi Chi. Republican. Lutheran. Home: 185 Morgan Pl Castle Rock CO 80108 *"Mooring Post" relationships and sharing have been essential to success and achievements in my multi-disciplinary research. "Mooring Post" persons range from expert mentors and stellar colleagues, to the bedrock of a loving and supportive family. Further, to me, Rule One in medicine has always been, "The patient comes first".*

THORNDIKE, EDWARD HARMON, physicist; b. Pasadena, Calif., Aug. 2, 1934; s. Edward Moulton and Louise (Harmon) T.; m. Elizabeth H. Wenger, Sept. 8, 1955; children: Susan Lee, Patricia Lynn, Edward Harmon Jr. AB, Wesleyan U., Middletown, Conn., 1956; MS, Stanford U., 1957; PhD, Harvard U., 1960. Research fellow Harvard U., Cambridge, Mass., 1960-61; mem. faculty U. Rochester, N.Y., 1961—, asso. prof. physics, 1965-72, prof., 1972—. Vis. prof. U. Geneva, 1969-70; vis. scientist CERN, Geneva, 1969-70; mem. adv. coun. Ctr. Environ. Info., Rochester, 1974-93; mem. adv. com. Stanford Linear Accelerator Ctr. Exptl. Program, 1987-89; mem. vis. com. for Fermilab, Univs. Rsch. Assn., 1993-95. Author: Energy and Environment, a Primer for Scientists and Engineers, 1976; contbr. articles to profl. jours. Recipient W.K.H. Panofsky prize, 1999; NSF fellow, 1970, Guggenheim fellow, 1987-88. Fellow Am. Phys. Soc. Office: U Rochester Dept Physics/Astronomy Rochester NY 14627

THORNDIKE, ELIZABETH, educator; m. Edward H. Thorndike; children: Susan Lacy, Patricia Suriel, Edward Jr. BA, Stanford U.; MAT, Harvard U.; PhD, Cornell U. Founder, exec. dir. Ctr. for Environ. Info., Rochester, N.Y., 1974-92; commr. Adirondack Park Agy., 1980-95; pres. E-Collaborative, Ithaca, 1996—. Mem. gov.'s environ. adv. bd. State of N.Y., 1984-94; vis. fellow Cornell U. ctr. for environment Cornell U., 1995-96, dept. natural resources, 1996-98, Coll. of Agr. adv. coun., 1996—, program assoc., 1998—, vis. lectr. dept. city and regional planning, 1999—. Life mem. Girl Scouts Genesee Valley, Rochester, bd. dirs., 1978-85; trustee Energy Rsch. and Devel. Authority, N.Y., 1979-80, 97—. Recipient 15th Anniversary award U.S. EPA, 1975, 86, Environ. Law Sect. ann. award N.Y. State Bar Assn., 1992, Hugh Cumming award Ctr. Environ. Info., 1994. Mem. Assn. for Protection of the Adirondacks (bd. dirs. 1996—), Ctr. for Environ. Info. (bd. dirs.). Avocations: hiking, camping, canoeing. Home: 38 Lake Lacoma Dr Pittsford NY 14534-3953

THORNDIKE, JOHN, writer; b. N.Y.C., Nov. 6, 1942; s. Joseph Jacobs and Virginia Thorndike; m. Clarisa Rubio, Mar. 9, 1969 (dec.); 1 child, Janir Daniel. BA, Harvard U., 1964; MA, Columbia U., 1966. Author: (novels) Anna Delaney's Child, 1986, The Potato Baron, 1989, (memoir) Another Way Home, 1996. Home: 13034 Mcdougal Rd Athens OH 45701-9731 E-mail: jtjt@frognet.net.

THORNE, FRANCIS, composer; b. Bay Shore, N.Y., June 23, 1922; s. Francis Burritt and Hildegarde (Kobbé) T.; m. Ann Cobb, Dec. 9, 1942; children: Ann Boughton (Mrs. William F. Niles), Wendy Oakleigh (Mrs. William H. Forsyth, Jr.), Candace Kobbé (Mrs. Anthony M. Canton). BA in Music Theory, Yale U., 1942. Founder, pres. Thorne Music Fund, Inc., 1965-75; pub. Edward B. Marks Music Corp., 1963—, Gen. Music Pub. Co., 1971—, G. Schirmer/AMP, 1985—, Theodore Presser Co., 1989—. Exec. dir. Lenox Arts Center, 1972-76, Am. Composers Alliance, 1975-85; co-founder, pres. Am. Composers Orch., 1976—. Composer: Elegy for Orch., 1964, Burlesque Overture, 1966, Lyric Variations for Orch., 1967, Symphony No. 1, 1963, No. II, 1966, No. III, 1970, No. IV, 1977, Fortuna, 1961-62, Liebesrock, 1969, Sonar Plexus, 1969, Six Set-Pieces, 1969, Contra Band Music, 1970, Antiphonies, 1970, Simultaneities, 1971, Quartessence, 1971, Fanfare, Fugue and Funk, 1972, Lyric Variations II, 1972, Piano Sonata, 1972, Lyric Variations III, 1973, Cantata Sauce, 1973, Evensongs, 1973, Cello Concerto, 1974, Piano Concerto, 1974, Violin Concerto, 1975, String Quartet 1, 1960, 2, 1967, 3, 1976, 4, 1983, Spoon River Overture, 1976, Grand Duo, 1976, Five Set Pieces, 1976, Love's Variations, 1976, Pop Partita, 1978, The Eternal Light for Soprano and Orchestra, 1979, Divertimento for Flute, Strings and Percussion, 1979, Lyric Variations IV for Solo Violin, 1980, Divertimento 2 for Bassoon and Stringed Instruments, 1980, Eine Kleine Meyermusik, 1980, Gems From Spoon River, 1980, Lyric Variations No. 6 for solo clarinet, 1981, Divertimento No. 3, 1982, Praise and Thanksgiving, 1983, Lyric Variations No. 5 for Orch., 1980-81, Symphony No. 5, 1984, Concerto Concertante, 1985, Rhapsodic Variations, No. 2, 1985, Humoresque for Orch., 1985, Rhapsodic Variations No. 3 for Oboe and Strings, 1986, The Affirming Flame for Soprano and Chamber Ensemble, 1987; seven simple syncopations for Piano solo, 1987, Rhapsodic Variations No. 4 For Viol Solo, 1987, Rhapsodic Variations No. 5 for Violins and Piano, 1988, Money Matters for Tenor and Chamber Ensemble, 1988, Piano Concerto No. 3, 1989, Remembering Dizzy for Brass Quintet, 1990, Pop Partita No. 2 for woodwinds and strings, 1991, Mario and The Magician, opera after Thomas Mann, in Prologue and 1 Act, 1991, Symphony No. 6 for Strings, 1992, Symphony No. 7 Along the Hudson for chorus and orch., 1994, Cello Concerto No. 2, 1995, Echo for Soprano and Mixed Chorus, 1996, Clarinet Concerto, 1997, Rhapsodic Variations No. 7 for Solo Piano, 1998, Lyric Variations No. 8, 1999, Flash Dances for Orchestra, 1999, Oboe Concerto, 1999-2000, (song) To Mark Stand's Poem, 2000, Concerto for Orchestra, 2000-2001; recs. on Composers' Recs., Inc., Serenus, Owl, Louisville Opus One and New World; founder, pres. Am. Composers Orch., 1976. Trustee Am. Symphony Orchestra League, Manhattan Sch. Music, Am. Music Center, MacDowell Colony, Walter W. Naumburg Found., Contemporary Music Soc., Theater Devel. Fund, Group for Contemporary Music., Am. Brass Quintet. Served to lt. USNR, 1942-45. Nat. Endowment Arts grantee, 1966, 73; fellow, 1976, 79; Nat. Inst. Arts and Letters grantee, 1968; N.Y. State Arts Council ballet commn., 1973 Mem. AAAL, BMI, Contemporary Music Soc. (bd. dirs.), Am. Composers Alliance, League Composers. Clubs: Century Assn. (N.Y.C.). Home: 116 E 66th St New York NY 10021-6547 *Having spent ten years as a businessman, I have been privileged to serve my composer colleagues as an administrator for musical organizations. The practical experience has also served me well as a creative artist in having instilled the virtues of discipline. Serving music as composer and administrator gives the highest sense of satisfaction, from participating in this life-giving world in a total comprehensive way.*

THORNE, JAMES M, chemist, educator; Bacheolor Sci., Utah State U., Logan, Utah, 1957—61; PhD, U. Calif. Berkley, Berkley, California, 1961—66. Chemistry prof. Brigham Young U., Provo, Utah, 1966—99; sr. scientist Mortex, Oremi, 1999—.

THORNE, JOHN REINECKE, business educator, venture capitalist; b. Pitts., Mar. 25, 1926; s. John Mueller and Louise (Reinecke) T.; m. Barbara Siebert, Aug. 31, 1951 (dec. Feb. 1995); children: John S., Barbara L., Richard W.; m. Helen L. Totzke, Dec. 29, 1999. BS, Brown U., 1947; MSEE, U. Pitts., 1949; MS in Indsl. Adminstrn., Carnegie Mellon U., 1952. Devel. engr. Westinghouse Elec. Corp., Pitts., 1947-50; mgr. fin. analysis Hughes Aircraft Co., L.A., 1952-54; dir. computer systems lab. Litton Industries, 1954-61; founder, chmn., pres. The Scionics Corp., 1961—69; cons., 1969-72; prof. bus. Carnegie-Mellon U., Pitts., 1972—, Morgenthaler prof. entrepreneurship, 1987—, dir. Donald H. Jones Ctr. for Entrepreneurship, 1990—2000; founder, chmn. Enterprise Corp. Pitts., 1983-98; gen. ptnr. Pitts. Seed Fund, 1985—2000. Contbr. numerous articles on entrepreneurship to profl. jours. Named Fin. Svcs. Adv. of Yr. by SBA, 1988 Mem.: Rolling Rock Club, Duquesne Club. Unitarian Universalist. Home: Furnace Run Laughlintown PA 15655 Office: Dept of Bus Carnegie-Mellon U Pittsburgh PA 15213 E-mail: thorne@andrew.cmu.edu.

THORNE, JOHN WATSON, III, advertising and marketing executive; b. Washington, Jan. 16, 1934; s. John Watson, Jr. and Mary Washington (Tucker) T.; m. Joan Kramer Vail, Mar. 2, 1957; children: Vail Tucker, Tracy Tucker, John Watson, IV. BA in Polit. Sci., George Washington U., 1955; MA in Sociology, New Sch. U., 1974. Asst. account exec. Young & Rubicam, Inc., N.Y.C., 1957-59; advt. mgr. Gen. Electric Co., Decatur, Ill., 1959-63; dir. advt. promotion Brand Names Found., N.Y.C., 1963-66; account exec. Tatham-Laird & Kudner (advt.), 1966-67; v.p., mgmt. supr. Wells, Rich, Greene, Inc., 1973-76; v.p., account supr. Batten, Barton, Durstine & Osborn, Inc., 1967-73, sr. v.p., mgmt. supr., 1976-81, exec. v.p., 1981-87, also dir., mem. operating com.; chmn. Thorne & Assocs., Newtown, Pa., 1987—; pres. Telerx Mktg., Spring House, 1991-95; chmn. Alliance Mktg. Svcs. Group, Inc., Jamison, 1995—. Mem. bus. program com. Proprietary Assn., Washington, 1984-85; adj. prof. advt. Syracuse (N.Y.) U. Pres. Hastings-on-Hudson (N.Y.) Bd. Edn.; bd. dirs. Young Concert Artists, N.Y.C.; mem. communications coms. Nat. Urban League, Carnegie Hall. Served as 1st lt. USMCR, 1955-57. Mem. Buckingham Racquet Club. Republican. Roman Catholic. Home: 100 Stoney Brook Rd Newtown PA 18940-2506 Office: Alliance Mktg Svcs Group 2370 York Rd Bldg B Jamison PA 18929-1031

THORNE, KIP STEPHEN, physicist, educator; b. Logan, Utah, June 1, 1940; s. David Wynne and Alison (Comish) T.; m. Linda Jeanne Peterson, Sept. 12, 1960 (div. 1977); children: Kares Anne, Bret Carter; m. Carolee Joyce Winstein, July 7, 1984. BS in Physics, Calif. Inst. Tech., 1962; A.M. in Physics (Woodrow Wilson fellow, Danforth Found. fellow), Princeton U., 1963, PhD in Physics (Danforth Found. fellow, NSF fellow), 1965, postgrad. (NSF postdoctoral fellow), 1965-66; D.Sc. (hon.), Ill. Coll., 1979; Dr.h.c., Moscow U., 1981; D.Sc. (hon.), Utah State U., 2000, U. Glasgow, 2001; D.H.L. (hon.), Claremont Grad. U., 2002. Research fellow Calif. Inst. Tech., 1966-67, assoc. prof. theoretical physics, 1967-70, prof., 1970—, William R. Kenan, Jr. prof., 1981-91, Feynman prof. theoretical physics, 1991—. Fulbright lectr., France, 1966; vis. assoc. prof. U. Chgo., 1968; vis. prof. Moscow U., 1969, 75, 78, 82, 83, 86, 88, 90, 98; vis. sr. rsch. assoc. Cornell U., 1977, A.D. White prof.-at-large, 1968-92; adj. prof. U. Utah, 1971-98; mem. Internat. Com. on Gen. Relativity and Gravitation, 1971-80, 92-01, Com. on U.S.-USSR Coop. in Physics, 1978-79, Space Sci. Bd., NASA, 1980-83; co-founder, chair steering com. LIGO, 1984-87. Co-author: Gravitation Theory and Gravitational Collapse, 1965, Gravitation, 1973, Black Holes: The Membrane Paradigm, 1986, Black Holes and Time Warps: Einstein's Outrageous Legacy, 1994. Alfred P. Sloan Found. Rsch. fellow, 1966-68; John Simon Guggenheim fellow, 1967; recipient Sci. Writing award in physics and astronomy Am. Inst. Physics, 1969, 94, P.A.M. Dirac Meml. lectureship Cambridge U., 1995, Karl Schwarzschild medal Astron. Soc. Germany, 1996, J. Robert Oppenheimer Meml. lectureship U. Calif., 1999, Charles Darwin Meml. Lectureship Royal Astron. Soc., 2000, Arthur Holly Compton Meml. lectureship Washington U., 2001, Herzberg Meml. Lectureship Can. Assn. Physicists, 2001; Robinson Prize in Cosmology, U. Newcastle, 2002. Fellow Am. Phys. Soc. (Julius Edgar Lilienfeld prize 1996, chair tropical group in gravity 1997-98); mem. Am. Philosophical Soc., Nat. Acad. Scis., Am. Acad. Arts and Scis., Am. Astron. Soc., Internat. Astron. Union, AAAS, Russian Acad. Scis., Sigma Xi, Tau Beta Pi. Office: California Inst Tech 130-33 Theoretical Astrophysics 1200 E California Blvd Pasadena CA 91106

THORNE, RICHARD MANSERGH, physicist; b. Birmingham, Eng., July 25, 1942; s. Robert George and Dorothy Lena (Goodchild) T.; children: Peter Baring, Michael Thomas, Thomas Mansergh. BSc, Birmingham U., 1963; PhD, MIT, 1968. Grad. asst. M.I.T., 1963-68; asst. prof. dept. atmospheric scis. UCLA, 1968-71, asso. prof., 1971-75, prof., 1975—, chmn. dept., 1976-79. Vis. fellow St. Edmund's Coll., Cambridge (Eng.) U., 1986-87, 92; cons. NATO Adv. Group for Aerospace R&D, 1973, Jet Propulsion Lab., Aerospace Corp. Contbr. articles to profl. jours. Recipient numerous grants NSF, NASA, NATO, Jet Propulsion Lab.; Fulbright scholar, 1963-70; fellow Royal Norwegian Coun. for Sci. and Indsl. Rsch., 1973, sr. vis. fellow U. Sussex, 1979-80, rsch. fellow Royal Soc. London, 1986-87. Fellow Am. Geophys. Union; mem. Internat. Union Radio Scis. Home: 10390 Caribou Ln Los Angeles CA 90077-2809 Office: UCLA Dept Atmospheric Scis Los Angeles CA 90095-0001

THORNE, WILLIAM ALBERT, retired lawyer; b. Chgo., Feb. 20, 1924; s. William A. and Irma J. Thorne; m. Elizabeth Lee Douglas, June 19, 1948; children: Deborah, Elizabeth Ann, Margaret, Douglas. JD, Valparaiso U., 1949. Bar: Ind. 1949, U.S. Dist. Ct. (no. and so. dists.) Ind. 1949, U.S. Supreme Ct. 1960. Pvt. practice, Elkhart, Ind., 1949-63; ptnr. Thorne Grodnik, LLP, 1963-95; of counsel Thorne.Grodnik, LLP and predecessor, 1995—2002, ret., 2002. Bd. visitors Valparaiso U. Law Sch., 1990-96; chmn. City of Elkhart Parks and Recreation Bd., 1971-75; chmn. Elkhart Bd. Water Works, 1975-83, No. Ind. Conf. United Meth. Ch., Bd. Higher Edn. and Campus Ministry, 1994-2000; bd. trustees Meth. Theol. Sch. Ohio, 1993—. Cpl. U.S. Army, 1943-46. Fellow Ind. State Bar Assn. (chmn. bankruptcy sect. 1985-86, bd. govs. 1987-88). Democrat. United Methodist. Avocations: golf, reading. Office: Thorne.Grodnik LLP 228 W High St Elkhart IN 46516-3176 E-mail: williamthorne@thornegrodnik.com., tholaw@aol.com.

THORNELL, JACK RANDOLPH, photographer; b. Vicksburg, Miss., Aug. 29, 1939; s. Benjamin O. and Myrtice (Jones) T.; divorced; children—Candice, Jay Randolph. Ed. pub. schs. Photographer Jackson (Miss.) Daily News, 1960-64; with A.P., 1964—, assigned Dominican Republic, 1965, Selma, Ala., 1965, Democratic Nat. Conv., 1968. Served with AUS, 1958-60. Recipient Pulitzer prize for news photography of shooting of James Meredith, 1967; Headliners Photography award, 1967 Home: 6815 Madewood Dr Metairie LA 70003-4529 Office: 3800 Howard Ave New Orleans LA 70125-1429

THORNELL, WILLIAM CLYDE, retired physician; b. Cin., Mar. 9, 1915; AB, U. Cin., 1936, BM, 1939; MD, Cin. Coll. Medicine, 1940; MS, Mayo Found., 1944. Cert. ENT. Intern Cin. Gen. Hosp., 1939-40; pvt. practice Cin., 1945-85; retired, 2000. Staff Mayo Clinic, 1943-45. Bd. dirs. North Side Bank & Trust Co., 1972—. Mayo Found. fellow, Rochester, 1940-43. Fellow: Am. Coll. Allergy (assoc.); mem.: ACS, AAAS, AMA, Triol. Soc., Am. Laryngol. Assn., Am. Acad. Ophthalmology and Otolaryngology. Home: 3516 Traskwood Cir Cincinnati OH 45208-1810

THORNHILL, ARTHUR H., JR. retired book publisher; b. Boston, Jan. 1, 1924; s. Arthur Horace and Mary Josephine (Peterson) T.; m. Dorothy M. Matheis, Oct. 28, 1944; children: Sandra Susanne Thornhill Brushart, Arthur Horace. AB magna cum laude, Princeton U., 1948. With Little, Brown & Co., Inc., Boston, 1948-88, v.p., 1955-58, gen. mgr., 1960-87, chief exec. officer, pres., 1962-87, chmn. bd., 1970-87; chmn., pres., dir. Little, Brown & Co. (Can.), Ltd., 1955-84; v.p. Time, Inc., 1968-87; vice chmn. Time-Life Books, Inc., 1976-86. Mem. adv. council history dept. Princeton U., 1964-85; trustee, treas. Princeton U. Press, 1972-85; chmn. N.Y. Graphic Soc., 1974-79. Trustee Bennington Coll., 1969-76; fellow emeritus Ctr. for Creative Photography U. Ariz.; bd. dirs. Am. Book Pubs. Council, 1964-67. Served to 1st lt. USAAF, World War II. Decorated Air medal; recipient Princeton U. Press medal, 1985, Disting. Alumni award Dwight-Englewood Sch., 1998. Mem. Assn. Am. Pubs. (bd. dirs. 1978-81), Edgartown Yacht Club, Edgartown Reading Room (pres. 1990-92), Union Club (N.Y.C.), Princeton Club (N.Y.C.), Century Club (N.Y.C.), Publs. Lunch Club (N.Y.C.), Union Club (Boston), St. Botolph (Boston). Home: 50 S School St Portsmouth NH 03801-5258

THORNHILL, BARBARA COLE, marketing executive; b. Rahway, N.J., Sept. 4, 1960; d. Clayton Eugene and Margaret (Fitzgerald) Cole; m. Matthew Thomas Thornhill, Oct. 15, 1983 (div. 1996); children: Allison, Clark. BBA in Mktg., Coll. of William and Mary, 1982. Asst. account exec. March Direct/McCann Direct, N.Y.C., 1983-84, account exec., 1984-86, account supr., 1986-87; dir. comml. client divsn. Huntsinger & Jeffer Direct, Richmond, Va., 1987-89; v.p., account supr. The Stenrich Group, 1989-90, sr. v.p., dir. account mgmt., 1990-92, exec. v.p., dir. account mgmt., bd. dirs., 1992-95; exec. v.p. for integrated mktg. comm., mem. exec. com. The Martin Agy., 1995-96, exec. v.p., chief adminstrv. officer, 1996—. Mem. profit sharing com. The Martin Agy., Richmond, 1993—, chair mgmt. com., 1999—. Exec. com. bd. trustees Richmond Children's Mus., 1992-99, dir. bd. trustees, 1991-92; area coord. William and Mary Alum Admissions Network, Richmond, 1988-98; co-chair William and Mary Class of 82 Reunion com., 1997; mem. Leadership Metro Richmond Class of 1997; book fair chairperson Mayberry Elem. Sch., 1997—; cookie chairperson Brownie Troop #292, Girl Scouts U.S., 1996-98; bd. dirs. Arts Coun. Richmond, 1998—; bd. dirs. Leadership of Metro Richmond, 1998—, mem. exec. com., 1999—, also chair devel. com. Recipient Silver Echo award Direct Mktg. Assn., 1991, 94, Richmond Area Marketer of Yr. award Am. Mktg. Assn., 1992, 93, 94, Gold Effie award, 1992, YWCA Outstanding Woman award, 1999. Mem. Willow Oaks C.C., Farmington C.C. Avocations: travel, family, reading, golf. Office: The Martin Agy One Shockoe Plz Richmond VA 23219-4132

THORNHILL, GABRIEL FELDER, III, securities company executive; b. N.Y.C., Mar. 14, 1928; s. Gabriel Felder Jr. and Weta Acker (Ingram) T.; m. Mary Elizabeth Vick, Feb. 26, 1960; children: Gabriel Felder IV, Elizabeth, Mary Ann. BBA, U. Tex., 1948; postgrad. in banking, U. Pa., 1962. Ptnr. Dewar Robertson & Pancoast, Austin, Tex., 1953-68; exec. v.p. Hornblower & Weeks, 1968-74, Rotan Mosle, Austin, 1974-80, Fin. Svcs. Austin, 1980-88; pres. Thornhill Securities, Austin, 1988—. Exec. v.p. FSA Inc., Austin, 1980-89; pres. FSA Capital, Austin, 1982-84; bd. dirs. Austin Trust Co. Vestryman Good Shepherd Episcopal Ch., Austin, 1967-69, mem. endowment fund com., 1988—; treas. Laguna Gloria Art Mus., Austin, 1963, bd. dirs. 1962-64; treas. Child and Family Svc., Austin, 1965, v.p., 1966; chmn. pacesetter div. United Way, Austin, 1967; bd. dirs. Child Guidance Ctr., Austin, 1973-75; mem. Austin Urban Renewal Bd., 1978-82; bd. dirs. Austin History Ctr., 1987-93, v.p., 1989; trustee Westminster Manor, Austin, 1985—, vice chmn., 1989, chmn., 1994. Sgt. U.S. Army, 1950-52, Korea. Mem. Investment Bankers Am. (fin. com. 1954-57), Austin Investment Assn. (founder, bd. dirs. 1963-69, v.p. 1963, pres. 1964), Allegro Club, Headliners Club, Westwood Country Club, Adms. Club (chmn. 1975), Coronet Club (pres. 1969), Tarry House (bd. dirs., v.p. 1989, pres. 1990-92). Avocations: swimming, tennis, hunting, skiing. Home: 3233 Tarryhollow Dr Austin TX 78703-1638 Office: 100 Congress Ave Ste 790 Austin TX 78701-4072

THORNLEY, WENDY ANN, retired educator, sculptor; b. Bolton, Lancashire, Eng., Feb. 28, 1948; came to U.S., 1953; d. Ronald Thornley and Joan Gladys (Hancock) Green. BS, So. Conn. State U., 1970, MS, 1979; MA, Wesleyan U., Middletown, Conn., 1991. Cert. tchr., Conn. Tchr. art New Canaan (Conn.) Pub. Schs., 1970-71, Bristol (Conn.) Pub. Schs., 1972-2001; ret., 2001. Adj. faculty Naugatuck Valley Cmty.-Tech. Coll., 1993—; adj. faculty U. Conn., Waterbury, 2002—; profl. artists residency Oxbow Summer Sch. Art Inst. Chgo., 1994. Exhibited in nat. and regional juried shows, 1978—, including tour Nat. Assn. Women Artists, 1989; commns. include wall relief Reichhold Chem. Co., 1987, Aetna Ins. Co., 1988, Bank of Boston, 1989, Law Office of Halloran, Sage, Phelon and Hagerty, 1990, Pitney-Bowes, Stamford, Pitney-Bowes Corp., 1996. Summer fellow Skidmore Coll., 1986; recipient 1st prize for sculpture Homestead Show, Fairfield, Conn., 1996. Mem. Nat. Art Edn. Assn., Conn. Art Edn. Assn. (Outstanding Secondary Art Educator award 1995), Nat. Assn. Women Artists, Soc. Conn. Crafts (bd. dirs. 1981-88, Best-in-Show award 1982, 84, 91, Best in Fiber award 1990, Master Craftsman award 1994, excellence in mixed media award 1998), Conn. Women Artists (Binney & Smith award 1985, Best Featurerd Artist, 1999, 2000), New Eng. Sculptors Assn. Avocations: photography, reading, travel. Home: 97 Summit Rd PO Box 7094 Prospect CT 06712-0094

THORNLOW, CAROLYN, law firm administrator, consultant; b. Kew Gardens, N.Y., May 25, 1954; 1 child, Johanna Louise Ramm. BBA magna cum laude, Baruch Coll., 1982. Gen. mgr. Richard A. Ramm Assocs., Levittown, N.Y., 1972-78; adminstr. Tunstead Schechter & Torre, N.Y.C., 1978-82, Cowan Liebowitz & Latman, P.C., N.Y.C., 1982-84, Rosenberg & Estis, P.C., N.Y.C., 1984-85; contr. Finkelstein, Borah, Schwartz, Altschuler & Goldstein, P.C., 1986-92; pres. Concinnity Svcs., Hastings, N.Y., 1984—. Instr. introduction to law office mgmt. seminars Assn. Legal Adminstrs., N.Y.C., 1984. Editor: The ABA Guide to Professional Managers in the Law Office, 1996; contbr. numerous articles to profl. jours. Mem. ABA (bd. dirs. law practice mgmt. div. 2000-01), N.Y. Assn. Legal Adminstrs. (v.p. 1982-83), Internat. Assn. Legal Adminstrs. (asst. regional v.p. 1983-84, regional v.p. 1984-85), Nat. Soc. Tax Profls. (cert. tax profl.), Am. Mgmt. Assn., Inst. Cert. Profl. Mgrs. (cert.), ABA, Inst. Cert. Mgmt. Accts., Mensa, Beta Gamma Sigma, Sigma Iota Epsilon. Home and Office: 445 Broadway Hastings On Hudson NY 10706 E-mail: cthornlow@concinnityservices.com., lawbucks@aol.com., CRTinNY@aol.com.

THORNLYRE, PADMA JARED, poet; b. Ft. Collins, Colo., Sept. 22, 1959; s. William Lee Farnsworth, Susan Harleen (Corash) Olson; m. Julie Dyan McKinney-Thornlyre, May 1, 1995; m. Tassana Maria Isarankura, Feb. 12, 1982 (div. Feb. 1984); 1 child Circe Morganna. BA in English, Coe Coll., Cedar Rapids, Iowa, 1981. Adminstrv. asst. Colo. Dept. Edn., Denver, 1990—94; pub. mgr. Rocky Mountain Ctr. for Health Promotion and Edn., Lakewood, 1994—. Author: (poetry chapbook) Fire Witch, 1989, (poetry book) My Guru, My Midwife, 1994, Angel Flesh, 1998. Vol. Jesse Jackson Presdl. Campaign, Denver, 1988, Gary Hart Presdl. Campaign, Denver, 1984. Recipient Hon. Mention, New Millenium Writings, 2000. Mem.: The Ancient Order of the Fire Gigglers (pper 1992—). Green Party. Buddhist. Avocations: reading, hiking, performance art promotion, art appreciation. Home: 30803 Hilltop Dr Evergreen CO 80439

THORNSBERRY, WILLIS LEE, JR. chemist; b. Sturgis, Ky., Aug. 10, 1940; s. Willis Lee and Jane (Hall) T.; m. Mary Elizabeth Gaswint, June 19, 1965; children: Brian, Michele. BS, Murray State U., 1963; MS, U. Ark., 1967; PhD, Tulane U., 1974. Rsch. chemist Freeport-McMoran Inc., Belle Chasse, La., 1967-74, sr. rsch. chemist, 1974-92; pres. Tech. Devel. Svcs. Inc., Sturgis, Ky., 1995—. Contbr. articles to profl. jours. Coach, leader for youth groups Jefferson Parish Playgrounds, Gretna, La., 1970-84, Boy Scouts Am., Gretna, 1975-82. 1st lt. U.S. Army, 1963-65. Mem. Am. Chem. Soc. (sect. chmn. 1982), Sigma Xi (nominating com. 1967—). Democrat. Achievements include numerous patents for process for uranium recovery from phosphoric acid, recovery of silica from hydrofluorosilicic acid, stabilization of gypsum for construction purposes, preparation and use of fertilizer additives. Office: 1024 N Main St Sturgis KY 42459-1245 E-mail: mwthorns@bellsouth.net.

THORNSBURY, MICHAEL, judge; b. Williamson, W.Va., July 6, 1956; s. John and Maggie Z. (Thocker) T.; m. Dreama K. Keith, June 25, 1977; children: Melissa, Matthew, Elizabeth Ann. BA, Pikeville (Ky.) Coll., 1977; JD summa cum laude, U. Ky., 1980. Bar: Ky. 1980, W.Va. 1980, U.S. Dist. Ct. (so. dist.) W.Va. 1980, U.S. Dist. Ct. (ea. dist.) Ky. 1980, U.S. Appeals 1988. Chief legal aid dept. Fed. Correctional Instn., Lexington, Ky., 1978-80; pvt. practice Williamson, 1980-96; city atty. Town of Gilbert, W.Va., 1985-90; cir. judge Mingo 30th Jud. Cir., Williamson, 1997-98. Re-elected to eight-yr. term 2000; asst. pros. atty. County of Mingo, Williamson, 1981-85; special justice W.Va. Supreme Ct. Appeals; bd. trustees Pikeville Coll, 2000—. Mem. Mingo County Dep. Sheriff's Civil Svc. Commn., 1983-85. Recipent Amb. award Belfry H.S., 2000, Delbarton 2000 Cmty. Svc. award; Presdl. scholar Pikeville Coll., 1974. Mem. Assn. Trial Lawyer Am., Ky. Bar Assn., W.Va. Bar Assn., W.Va. Trial Lawyers Assn., W.Va. Jud. Assn., Ky. Trial Lawyers Assn., Mingo County Trial Lawyers Assn. (pres. Williamson chpt. 1986-88), Pike Coll. Alumni Assn. (bd. dirs.), Moose, Tug Valley Shriners (pres. 1999-2000),

Kiwanis (bd. dirs. 1997—, pres. 2000-01), O'Brien Lodge 101, Scottish Rite, Temple Aide Beni Kedem Temple. Democrat. Methodist. Home: 1717 W 4th Ave Williamson WV 25661-3014 Office: Mingo Cir Judge PO Box 1198 75 E 2d Ave Williamson WV 25661

THORNTON, ANTHONY L, aerospace engineer; b. Fairfield, Calif., Mar. 19, 1956; s. Alfred Edward and Shirley Jean (Holbert) T. BS Aerospace Engring. Scis., U. Colo., 1978; MS Engring., Stanford U., 1980; PhD Aeronautics and Astronautics, Purdue U., 1992. Sr. mem. tech. staff Sandia Nat. Labs., Albuquerque, 1980-93, mgr., Univ. Outreach, 1993-94, dir., Diversity Leadership and Edn. Outreach, 1994-97; sr. rsch. and devel. engr. Lockheed Martin Skunk Works, Palmdale, CA, 1997—. Contbr. articles to profl. technical publs. Steering com. mem. NSF funded Utah, Colo., Ariz., N. Mex. Rural Systemic Initiative, 1994-97; charter mem. and adv. Norwest Bank Leadership Coun., 1995-96. Lt. USN-Reserve, Albuquerque, NM, 1983-86. Recipient Boeing Aircraft scholarship, 1974, 75, 76, Sandia award for excellence Sandia Nat. Labs., 1992, Disting. Engring. Achievement award Engring. Indsl. Coun., Inc., 2000; named Black Engr. of Yr. in Profl. Achievement U.S. Black Engr. & Info. Tech. mag., 2001; grantee SACHS Found., 1974-78, 1984-88; fellow Com. on Institutional Coop., Purdue U., 1984-89. Sr. mem. Am. Inst. Aeronautics and Astronautics. Independent. Baptist. Avocations: chess, track and field, investments. Office: PO Box 748 Fort Worth TX 76101 Fax: (661) 572-7157. E-mail: Anthony.Thornton@lmco.com., lcesaint@aol.com.

THORNTON, ARLAND, sociologist, educator; b. Boise, Idaho, July 18, 1944; s. Lavar and Alzina Thornton; m. Shirley Dray; children: Richard, Blake; children: Rebecca, Amy. PhD, U. Mich., 1975. Sr. rsch. scientist Survey Rsch. Ctr., U. Mich., Ann Arbor, 1975—; prof. sociology U. Mich., 1977—; sr. rsch. scientist Population Studies Ctr., U. Mich., 1983—. Mem. population rsch. subcommittee Nat. Inst. Child Health and Human Develop., Bethesda, 1996—2000; mem. Family and Child Well-Being Rsch. Network, Nat. Inst. Child Health and Hum Devel., Bethesda, 1993—99; mem. social scis. and population study sect. NIH, Bethesda; assoc. dir., acting dir. Population Studies Ctr., U. Mich., Ann Arbor. Author: (book) Social Change and the Family in Taiwan, 1994 (Otis Dudley Duncan Book award and Goode Disting. Book award, 1995); editor: Ties That Bind, 2000, The Well Being of Children and Families: Research and Data Needs, 2001; contbr. articles to profl. jours. and chpts. to books. Lt. (j.g.) U.S. C.G., 1968—71. Recipient MERIT award, National Inst. Child Health and Human Devel., 2001. Mem.: Nat. Coun. on Family Rels., Am. Sociol. Assn. (various offices in population, family, and children sects., Disting. Career award family sect. 2000), Population Assn. Am. (pres. 2001). Avocations: bicycling, hiking, travel, sports. Office: U Mich Inst for Social Rsch Ann Arbor MI 48106 Business E-Mail: Arlandt@umich.edu.

THORNTON, CAMERON MITCHELL, financial planner; b. L.A., Sept. 30, 1954; s. H. Walter and Naomi L. (Brown) T.; m. Jane Kubasak, June 18, 1978; children: Mitchell, Kathryn, Andrew. BA, U. So. Calif., L.A., 1976; MBA, U. La Verne, 1983. CFP. Planner Lockheed Calif. Co., Burbank, 1980-84; adv. assoc. Fin. Network Investment Corp., 1983—, fin. cons., 1983—, prin., br. mgr., 1997—; prin. Cameron Thornton Assocs., 1982—; prin. lic. charitable gift planner Renaissance Inc., 1992-99. Author: (manual) Computer Aided Planning System, 1982-83. Mem., vice chair St. Joseph Med. Ctr. Found., 1988-92, chmn. planned giving dept., 1991-92; mem. planned giving dept. Mater Dolorosa Passionist Retreat Ctr., Sierra Madre, Calif., 2000-; mem., chair Burbank Police Commn., 1981-85, Burbank Planning Commn., 1989-93; with ARC, Burbank, 1984-88, chmn. 1985-87; asst. scoutmaster troop 209 Boy Scouts of Am., Burbank, 1994-97, scoutmaster, 1997-2000. Named Friend of Campfire, Camp Fire Coun., Pasadena, Calif., 1989, 92; named to Bloomberg's Top Wealth Mgr. List, 2001. Mem. Fin. Planning Assn., Cert. Fin. Planner Bd. Standards, Burbank C. of C. Republican. Roman Catholic. Avocations: fishing, reading, snow skiing, water skiing. Office: Cameron Thornton Assocs 290 E Verdugo Ave Ste 205 Burbank CA 91502-1342 E-mail: cameron@cameronthornton.com.

THORNTON, CHARLES VICTOR, metals executive; b. Salt Lake City, Feb. 8, 1915; s. Charles Victor and Winnie May (Fitts) T.; m. Margaret Louise Wiggins, Apr. 17, 1937; children: Charles Victor III, Carolyn Louise (Mrs. John J. Moorhouse), David Frank. BS in Civil Engring., U. Utah, 1935; HHD, Ind. Inst. Tech., 1972. Registered profl. engr., Ohio, Tex. Engr. Truscon Steel Co., Youngstown, Ohio, 1935-37, dist. engr. Washington, 1937-40; chief engr. So. Iron Works, Inc., Alexandria, Va., 1940-45; pres. Thornton Industries, Inc., Ft. Worth, 1945-75, chmn. bd., 1975-88. Bd. dirs. Bank Commerce and Comml. Fin. Corp.; chmn. bd. dirs. Southview Corp. Author: American Association of Private Railroad Car Owners Roster of Private R.R. Cars, 1991, Autobiography, 1993, Charlie, 1994, Winnie, 1994. Chmn. bd. Southview Corp., 1980—, chmn. emeritus Shriners Hosps. for Children; mem. nat. adv. coun. U. Utah, 1985-96; chmn. investment com. Longhorn coun. Boy Scouts Am., 1985-88; v.p. campaign chmn. Ft. Worth Arts United, 1989; v.p. Tarrant County Arts Coun., 1989; pres. Tarrant County Water Bd., 1984-88; mem. policy com. Dallas-Ft. Worth Railtran, 1991-98; pres. Ft. Worth chpt. Internat. Good Neighbor Coun., 1991-92; bd. dirs. Ft. Worth Opera, 1997—; mem. World Affairs Coun. Ft. Worth, 1996, bd. dirs., 1997—, treas., 1998. Recipient Salesman of Yr. award Ft. Worth Sales and Mktg. Execs., 1984, Good Neighbor of Yr. award Internat. Good Neighbor Coun., 1984, Merit of Honor award U. Utah, 1986; holder airplane speed record Dallas to Wichita, Kans., 1969. Mem. ASCE (life) (Tex. sect. Svc. to People award 1995), Tex. Assn. Bus. (life), Ft. Worth C. of C. (pres. 1960), Am. Assn. Pvt. R.R. Car Owners (pres. 1982-83), Petroleum Club, Fort Worth Club, City Club, Exch. Club of Fort Worth (past pres.), La Cima Club, Oxford Club, Grand Coun. (Fort Worth chpt. Confrerie Saint Etienne), Masons (33 degree s.r.), Shriners (past imperial potentate), Kiwanis (past pres.), Elks, Petroleum Club, Tau Beta Pi. Office: PO Box 136397 Fort Worth TX 76136-0397 Fax: 817-237-0100.

THORNTON, CLARENCE GOULD, electronics engineering executive; b. Detroit, Aug. 3, 1925; s. Lorenzo C. and Violet (Gould) T.; m. Gloria Fuchs, June 18, 1949; children: Susan Carol, Richard Scott. BS, U. Mich., 1949, MS, 1950, PhD, 1952. Project engr. Sylvania Electric Co., Woburn, Mass., 1951-52; sect. head to dir. Semiconductor div. Philco Corp., Lansdale, Pa., 1952-60; dir. R&D Philco Corp., Blue Bell, 1960-72; dir. Electronics Technology and Devices Lab., U.S. Army, Fort Monmouth, N.J., 1972-92; directorate exec. Army Rsch. Lab., 1992-95. Mem. Commn. on Engring. and Tech. Sys. Bd. on Army Sci. and Tech., Nat. Rsch. Coun., 1995—; sci., tech., bus. cons. 1995—. Contbr. articles to profl. jours.; patentee in field of electronics. Mem. Colts Neck Bd. Health, 1974-79. Served with USN, 1944-46. Recipient Local Svc. award Boy Scouts Am., 1963, Sci. Conf. award Dept. Army, 1976, Rsch. and Devel. Achievement award, 1976, Lab. of Yr. award, 1980, 83, 88, Lab. Excellence award, 1981, 85, 86, Sr. Exec. award, 1980-93, Gold medal Armed Forces Comms. and Electronics Assn., 1983, Handicapped Adv. Coun. award of achievement, 1985, Exceptional Civilian Svc. medal Dept. Army, 1985, Presdl. Rank award of Meritorious Svc., 1986, Presdl. Rank award of Disting. Sr. Exec., 1987, Crozier award, 1990, Superior Civilian Svc. medal, 1995, Exceptional Civilian Svc. medal, 1995. Fellow IEEE (Centennial medal 1994, Third Millennium medal 2000, Engring. Leadership Recognition award 1994, Joint Logistics Comdrs. award 1994); mem. AAAS, Nat. Def. Indsl. Assn., Assn. U.S. Army, Armed Forces Electronics Assn., Sr. Execs. Assn. (Exec. Achievement award 1994), Am. Defense Preparedness Assn., Alpha Chi Sigma, Phi Kappa Phi, Phi Lambda Upsilon. Mem. Reformed Ch. Home: 28 Glenwood Rd Colts Neck NJ 07722-1015 Office: AMSRL-EP Fort Monmouth NJ 07703

THORNTON, BILLY BOB, actor, director; b. Hot Springs, Ariz., Aug. 4, 1955; Actor (films) U-Turn, 1997, A Thousand Miles, 1997, A Simple Plan, 1997, Primary Colors, 1997, Homegrown, 1997, The Apostle, 1997, Pushing Tin, 1998, A Gun, A Car, A Blonde, 1998, Primary Colors, 1998, Homegrown, 1998, Armageddon, 1998, Simple Plan, 1998, Monster's Ball, 2001, ; writer (screen plays) For the Boys, 1991, Indecent Proposal, 1993, Tombstone, 1993, Trouble Bound, 1993, Floundering, 1994, On Deadly Ground, 1994, Some Folks Call It a Slingblade, 1994, Don't Look Back, 1996, A Family Thing, 1996, The Gift, 2000; guest appearence (TV episode) Ellen, 1997, (series), Hearts A Fire, 1992; dir., actor, writer, Sling Blade (AA Best Adapted Screen Play), 1996. Office: Rogers & Cowan 1888 Century Park East Ste 500 Los Angeles CA 90067*

THORNTON, D. MCCARTY, lawyer; b. Wilmington, Del., Sept. 6, 1947; m. Molly F. Carr, July 7, 1996. BA, Stanford U., 1969, JD, 1972. Bar: Calif., D.C. Trial atty., then dep. asst. dir. FTC, Washington, 1972-78; prosecutor Criminal Fraud sect. U.S. Dept. Justice, 1978-82; assoc. Cole & Corette, 1982-83; chief of litigation Office of Insp. Gen., U.S. Dept. HHS, 1983-90, chief counsel, 1990—. Founder, chmn. bd. W.Va. Rivers Coalition, Elkins, 1989-97. Mem. The Potomac Conservancy (founder, chair 1992-95, vice chair 1995-99), Am. Health Lawyers Assn. (bd. dirs. 1991-97). Avocation: whitewater kayaking. Office: US Dept HHS Rm 5065 330 Independence Ave SW Washington DC 20201-0003 E-mail: dthornto@os.dhhs.gov.

THORNTON, D. WHITNEY, II, lawyer; b. Miami, Fla., Oct. 17, 1946; s. Dade Whitney and Hilda (Bryan) T.; m. Jane Collis, Nov. 27, 1971; children: Bryan Whitney, Elizabeth Jane, Virginia Anne. BA, Washington and Lee U., 1968, JD cum laude, 1970. Bar: Va. 1970, D.C. 1976, U.S. Ct. Appeals (4th cir.) 1978, U.S. Supreme Ct. 1980, Calif. 1987, U.S. Ct. Appeals (9th cir.) 1987. Atty. Naval Air Sys. Command, Dept. Navy, Washington, 1970-73; asst. counsel to comptr. Dept. Navy, 1973-74, asst. to gen. counsel, 1974-76; assoc. Sullivan & Beauregard, Washington, 1976-77, ptnr., 1977-81, Bowman, Conner, Touhey & Thornton, Washington, 1981-83; pres. Continental Maritime Industries, Inc., San Francisco, 1983-87; ptnr. Dempsey, Bastianelli, Brown & Touhey, 1987-91, Seyfarth Shaw, San Francisco, 1992—. Contbr. articles to profl. jours. Mem. ABA (pub. contract law sect., chmn. suspension and debarment com. 1977), FBA (vice chmn. govt. contracts coun., Disting. Svc. award 1981), Washington Golf and Country Club (Arlington, Va.), Blackhawk Country Club (Danville, Calif.). Republican. Methodist. Office: Seyfarth Shaw 101 California St Ste 2900 San Francisco CA 94111-5858 E-mail: wthornton@sf.seyfarth.com.

THORNTON, DEAN DICKSON, retired airplane company executive; b. Yakima, Wash., Jan. 5, 1929; s. Dean Stoker and Elva Maud (Dickson) T.; m. Joan Madison, Aug. 25, 1956 (div. Apr. 1978); children— Steven, Jane Thornton; m. Mary Shultz, Nov. 25, 1981; children— Volney, Scott, Peter, Todd Richmond BS in Bus., U. Idaho, 1952. C.P.A., Wash. Acct. Touche, Ross & Co., Seattle, 1954-63; treas., controller Boeing Co., 1963-70, various exec. positions, 1974-85; pres. Boeing Comml. Airplane Co., 1985-94, retired, 1994; sr. v.p. Wyly Co., Dallas, 1970-74. Bd. dirs. Flow Internat., Cray Inc. Bd. dirs. YMCA, Seattle, 1966-68, Jr. Achievement, Seattle, 1966-68; chmn. Wash. Council on Internat. Trade, Seattle, 1984-87, Seattle Art Mus., 1994-96. 1st lt. USAF, 1952-54. Named to U. Idaho Alumni Hall of Fame. Mem. Phi Gamma Delta. Clubs: Rainier, Seattle Tennis, Seattle Yacht, Conquistadores de Cielo. Republican. Presbyterian. Avocations: skiing; sailing; fishing. Home: 1602 34th Ct W Seattle WA 98199-3906

THORNTON, EDMUND B. philanthropist; b. Chgo., Mar. 9, 1930; s. George A. and Suzanne W. Thornton; children from previous marriage: Thomas, Jonathan, Susan, Amanda; m. Susan Feldhaus; 1 child, Taylor. BA, Yale U., 1954. With No. Trust Co., Chgo., 1957-59; asst. sec., asst. treas. Ottawa (Ill.) Silica Co., 1959-61, v.p. corp. devel., 1961-62, pres., CEO, 1962-75, chmn. bd., CEO, 1975-83, chmn. bd., 1983-86; dir., v.p. Ottawa Nat. Bank. Author various articles on historic preservation, history and military subjects. Del. Rep. Nat. Conv., 1964--, precinct committeeman, 1978-92; chmn. LaSalle County Rep. Ctrl. Com., 1980-92, Ill. and Mich. Canal Nat. Heritage Commn., 1985—; pres. Ottawa Silica Co. Found., Edmund B. Thornton Found., Ottawa, 1986— 1st lt. USMC, 1954—56. Recipient Conservation Svc. award U.S. Dept. Interior, 1973. Mem. Nat. Assn. Mfrs., U.S. C. of C., Nat. Indsl. Sand Assn. (dir. 1968-73), Ill. Mfrs.' Assn. (dir. 1969-75, chmn. 1975), Ill. State C. of C. (dir. 1972-78), Explorers Club, Univ. Club (Chgo.), Elks. Republican. Congregationalist. Home: PO Box 1 Ottawa IL 61350-0001 Office: PO Box 949 Ottawa IL 61350-0949

THORNTON, ELAINE SERETHA, oncology clinical nurse specialist; b. N.Y.C., Mar. 25, 1967; d. Jerry Richard and Shelia (Beckford) T. BS, Syracuse U., 1990; MSN, Columbia U., 1997. Cert. in gerontology. Staff nurse, clin. nurse I New Rochelle (N.Y.) Hosp. Med. Ctr., 1990-92, staff nurse, clin. nurse II, 1993-96, staff nurse drug and alcohol detoxification unit, 1996-97, oncology clin. nurse specialist, 1997-99; breast svc. coord. Robert and Helen Appell Comprehensive Breast Svc., 1997-99; nurse educator III Dept. Vets. Affairs/N.Y. Harbor HealthCare Sys., N.Y.C., 1999—; oncology clin. nurse specialist Wyckoff Heights Med. Ctr., 2002—. RN lab. asst. Sch. Nursing Coll. New Rochelle, 1992-97; adj. prof. Coll. New Rochelle, Borough Manhattan C.C., N.Y.C., 1995-97, adj. asst. prof. Iona Coll. Sch. Nursing, New Rochelle, adj. assoc. prof., 1998; vol. Am. Cancer Soc. Vol. Cancer Info. Svc., N.Y.C., 1991-92, Clinton/Gore Presdl. campaign, 1992; vol. providing cancer screening, blood pressure screening Pelham (N.Y.) Sr. Ctr., 1992; pub. info. rep. to economically disadvantaged Am. Cancer Soc., bd. dirs. Westchester divsn., 1993-95, 95-97, pres. So. unit; organizer 1st & 2d ann. Cmty. Health Fair, New Rochelle. Recipient Orthobiotech. Spkrs. Bur. Quality of Life award, Pub. Educator award Westchester divsn. Am. Cancer Soc. Mem. Oncology Nursing Soc. (Hudson Valley chpt., nominating com. 1992-93, treas. 1993-94, pres. elect Hudson Valley chpt. 1995-97), Oncology Nursing Soc. (corr., pres. Hudson Valley chpt. 1998-2000), CTME (nat. membership). Republican. Home: 109 Kensington Rd #8 Bronxville NY 10708

THORNTON, GEORGE WHITELEY, investment company executive; b. York, Pa., Aug. 11, 1936; s. Henry Moser and Virginia (Whiteley) T.; m. Dianne Fay George, Sept. 9, 1961; children: Sandra Whiteley, William Foster. BA, U. Va., 1958. Asst. to pres. mfg. Dentsply Internat., York, Pa., 1963-69, v.p. mfg., 1969-79, sr. v.p., 1979-85; pres., bd. dirs. Thornton Group Ltd., 1985—; chmn., chief exec. officer Thornton-White Inc., Charleston, S.C., 1986-92. Bd. dirs. Dentsply Internat., York, Commonwealth Nat. Bank (York region). Bd. dirs. United Way, York County, 1974-76; exec. com. Nat. Alliance Businessman, York, 1972-73, chmn., York metro, 1974-75; bd. dirs. Pennsylvanians for Right to Work, 1979-81; bd. trustees Right to Work Def. and Edn. Found., 1979-81. Recipient Dirksen Meml. award Pennsylvanians for Right to Work, 1979, Employer of Yr. award. Mem.: The Club at Pelican Bay (Fla.), Country Club of York (Pa.), Delta Phi. Republican. Presbyterian. Home: 1040 Box Hill Ln York PA 17403-4436

THORNTON, IVAL CRANDALL, interior architect; b. American Falls, Idaho, Apr. 28, 1932; s. Crandall Dunn and Enid Rosalie (Walker) T.; m. Bonnie Jean Larson, June 10, 1951 (div. May 1961); children: Blake, Brek; m. Cheryl Lynn Bader, July 13, 1974; 1 child, Anne Bader. Student, Weber State Coll., 1956-58, Colo. Inst. Art, 1959-60, Art Ctr. Sch. of Design, L.A., 1963-64. Artist Richard Daly Art Studio, Salt Lake City; illustrator Victor Gruen & Assocs., L.A., Carlos Diniz Assocs., L.A.; sr. assoc. Arthur Gensler Assocs., San Francisco, 1972-75. Prin. works include Investment Mortgage Internat., San Francisco (design award 1984), Mountain Bell Tng. Ctr., Denver (design award), Denver Sporting House Interior (1st pl.), Caesar's Palace Forum Shops and Gateway, Internat. Cruise Ships and Corp. Aircraft Interiors, including SS U.S. Cruise Vessel, Elitch's Amusement Pk., Denver, Princess Cruises Grand Princess 97, Prince Fahd's Summer Palace interior, Saudi Arabia, Hall of Fame Colo. Inst. Art, 1995, painted murals in Salt Lake Temple, 1962. With USMC. Republican. Mem. Lds Ch. Avocations: skiing, sailing, painting, golf, music.

THORNTON, J. RONALD, technology center director; b. Fayetteville, Tenn., Aug. 19, 1939; s. James Alanda and Thelma White (McGee) T.; m. Mary Beth Packard, June 14, 1964 (div. Apr. 1975); 1 child, Nancy Carole; m. Martha Klemann, Jan. 23, 1976 (div. Apr. 1982); 1 child, Trey; m. Bernice McKinney, Feb. 14, 1986; 1 child, Paul Leon. BS in Physics and Math., Berry Coll., 1961; MA in Physics, Wake Forest Coll., 1964; postgrad., U. Ala., 1965-66, Rollins Coll., 1970. Rsch. physicist Brown Engring. Co., Huntsville, Ala., 1963-66; sr. staff engr. Martin Marietta Corp., Orlando, Fla., 1966-75; dep. dir. NASA, Washington, 1976-77; exec. asst. Congressman Louis Frey, Jr., Orlando, 1978; pres. Tens Tec, Inc., 1978-79; dir. So. Tech. Applications Ctr. U. Fla., Gainesville, 1979—. Bd. dirs., treas. North Fla. Tech. Innovation Ctr., 1994—; mem. light wave tech. com. Fla. High Tech. and Indsl. Coun., Tallahassee, 1986-93, NASA Tech. Transfer Exec. Com., Washington, 1987—, Javits Fellowship Bd., Washington, 1986-91, Gov.'s New Product Award Com., Tallahassee, 1988—, Fla. K-12 Math., Sci. and Computer Sci. Edn. Quality Improvement Adv. Coun., 1989-92, Fla. Sci. Edn. Improvement Adv. Com., 1991-92; bd. dirs. Fla.-NASA Bus. Incubation Ctr., North Fla. Enterprise Corp., 2001. Pres. Orange County Young Rep. Club, Orlando, 1970-71; treas. Fla. Fedn. Young Reps., Orlando, 1971-72; chmn. Fla. Fedn. Young Reps., Orlando, 1972-74; pres. Gainesville Area Innovation Network, 1988-89. Named Engr. Exhibiting Tech. Excellence and Accomplishment cen. Fla. chpt. Fla. Engring. Soc., 1975, Achievement award NASA, 1977. Mem. IEEE, Soc. Mfg. Engrs., Tech. Transfer Soc. (pres. 1999, bd. dirs. 1996—, Thomas Jefferson award 1999), Nat. Assn. Mgmt. and Tech. Assistance Ctrs. (bd. dirs. 1988, pres. 1992). Republican. Avocations: music, travel, reading. Home: 17829 NW 20th Ave Newberry FL 32669-2143 Office: U Fla So Tech Applications Ctr 1900 SW 34th St Gainesville FL 32608-1202 E-mail: brthorn@quixnet.net., r-thornton@ufl.edu.

THORNTON, JOHN WILLIAM, SR. lawyer; b. Toledo, July 3, 1928; s. Cletus Bernard and Mary Victoria (Carey) T.; m. Mary Feeley, Mar. 10, 1951; children: John W. Jr., Jane Thornton Mastrucci, Deborah Thornton Hasty, Michael; m. Gabriela Marin, 1994. AB magna cum laude, U. Notre Dame, 1950, LLB summa cum laude, 1956, JD, 1969. Bar: Fla. 1956, U.S. Dist. Ct. (no., mid. and so. dists.) Fla. 1956, U.S. Ct. Appeals (5th cir.) 1956, U.S. Ct. Appeals (11th cir.) 1982; cert. civil mediator Fla. Supreme Ct., arbitrator Fla. Supreme Ct. Assoc. area def. firm, Miami, Fla.; ptnr. Dixon, DeJarnette, et al, 1956-67, Stephens, Demos, Magill & Thornton, Miami, 1968-76; pvt. practice Thornton & Mastrucci, P.A. and predecessor firm, 1976—. Chairperson legis. com. Fla. Med. Malpractice Claims Coun., Inc., 1984—, legis. and adminstrv. code rep. on hosp. risk mgrs. qualifications, rules and liability and nursing home rules and liability, 1986—; lectr. Fla. tort ins. law hosp. and physician series on risk mgmt. Am. Inst. Med. Law, U. Miami Sch. Trial Techniques; lectr. South Fla. Hosp. Risk Mgmt. Soc.; legis. atty. Fla. Sch. Bd. Assn.; presenter legal, healthcare and ins. industry confs.; lectr. in field. Contbr. articles to profl. publs. Mem. Dade County Sch. Bd., 1967—. Lt. USN, 1950-53, Korea. Mem. ABA (vice chmn. torts and ins. practice sect., chair sr. issues law com., torts and ins. practice sect., 1999—, active sr. lawyers divsn. 2001-02), ATLA, Internat. Assn. Def. Counsel (chmn. med. malpractice com. 1975-76, chmn. profl. errors and omissions com. 1987—, chair excess, surplus lines and reins. law com. 1988), Def. Rsch. Inst. (chmn. practice and procedure com. 1976-77), Fedn. Ins. and Corp. Counsel (chmn. auto and casualty ins. sect. 1987—, chmn. legis. com. 1984-88, vice chmn. ethics com. 1990-94, mem. task force on nursing home liability 1998—), Fla. Def. Lawyers Assn. (bd. dirs. 1976), Internat. Assn. Ins. counsel (chmn. med. malpractice 1972-74, com. 1975-99, def. counsel com. 1976-91, reins. excess and surplus lines com. 1980-99, spkr. and presenter 1966-2000), Dade County Def. Bar Assn., Fed. Ins. Corp. Counsel (casualty ins. law com. 1972—, med. malpractice com. 1974-99, excess surplus and reins. com. 1976—, publs. com. 1976-87), Maritime Law Assn. U.S., Fla. Def. Lawyers Assn. (bd. dirs., chmn. legis. com. 1974-77), Internat. Law Soc., Broward County Bar Assn., Am. Judicature Soc., Am. Health Care Assn., Congress Romanian Ams., Coral Gables Club, Ocean Reef Club, Riviera Country Club, Sapphire Valley Country Club. Roman Catholic. Home: 7898 SW 57 Terr Miami FL 33143 Office: Ste 230 4601 Ponce de Leon Blvd Coral Gables FL 33146-1905 Fax: 305-668-0400. E-mail: J.ThorMas@aol.com.

THORNTON, JOSEPH SCOTT, research institute executive, materials scientist; b. Sewickley, Pa., Feb. 6, 1936; s. Joseph Scott and Evelyn (Miller) T.; divorced; children: Joseph Scott III, Chris P. BSME, U. Tex., 1957, PhD, 1969; MSMetE, Carnegie Mellon U., 1962. Engr. Walworth Valve Co., Boston, 1958; metall. engr. Westinghouse Astronuclear Lab., Large, Pa., 1962-64; instr., teaching assoc. U. Tex., Austin, 1964-67; group leader Tracor Inc., 1967-69, dept. dir., 1973-75; dept. mgr. Horizons Rsch., Inc., Cleve., 1969-73; chmn., chief exec. officer Tex. Rsch. Internat., Inc. (formerly Tex. Rsch. Inst., Inc.), Austin, 1975—. Contbr. numerous tech. papers to profl. publs.; editor: WANL Materials Manual, 2 vols., 1964; patentee in field. Recipient IGS award, 2002; fellow Alcoa, Austin, 1964, RC Baker Found., 1967. Mem.: ASTM, Internat. Geosynthetics Soc., Adhesion Soc., Am. Soc. Metals Internat. (exec. com. 1965—66). Office: Tex Rsch Internat Inc 9063 Bee Caves Rd Austin TX 78733-6201

THORNTON, LARRY LEE, psychotherapist, author, educator, minister; b. Lake, Miss., Nov. 9, 1937; s. Harvey L. and Onzell (Goodson) T.; children: Matt Alan, Leigh Ann, Pamela; m. Helen Louise Thornton. BA, Miss. Coll., 1959; MDiv, New Orleans Bapt. Theol. Sem., 1963, MA, 1964; MS, U. So. Miss., 1966, PhD, 1969; postgrad., Harvard U., 1985. Dir. admissions Miss. Coll., Clinton, 1961; sr. prof. psychology Delta State U., Cleveland, Miss., 1968-99, prof. psychology emeritus, 1999—; founder, dir. Lic. Profl. Counseling, Assocs., Cleveland, 1988-98; pvt. practice Jackson, Miss., 1999—. Adj. prof. psychology Miss. Coll., Clinton, 1999—, New Orleans Bapt. Theol. Sem., 2000—; chmn. Miss. Bd. Lic. Profl. Counselors, 1992-93. Author: Insights into Human Development, 2002. Charter mem. Internat. Devel. Coun., Bapt. Theol. Sem., Rûschlikon, Zurich, Switzerland, 1992. Recipient Panhellenic Outstanding Faculty award, 1996, S.E. Kossman Outstanding Tchr. award, 1991. Mem. APA, ACA. Avocations: golf, tennis, walking. Home and Office: PO Box 13475 Jackson MS 39236 E-mail: thorntonlh@aol.com.

THORNTON, MARK CHRISTOPHER, economist; b. Geneva, June 7, 1960; s. Carroll Francis and Constance Katherine (Ryan) T. BS in Econs., St. Bonaventure U., Olean, N.Y., 1982; PhD in Econs., Auburn (Ala.) U., 1989. O.P. Alford asst. prof. econs. Ludwig von Mises Inst. and Auburn U., 1989—; acad. dir. Auburn C. Ctr. Ludwig Von Mises Inst., 1987—; asst. supt. of banking and economist Office of Gov. of Ala., 1997—. Con. Ekelund and Assocs., Auburn, 1986—. Author: The Economics of Prohibition, 1991; editor: Austrian Econ. Newsletter, 1984-92; contbr. articles to profl. jours. Constable Dist. 79 Lee County, Ala., 1988—; dist. rep. Ala. Libertarian Party, 1983-85, fin. chmn., 1987-89, vice chmn., 1985-86, chmn., 1996; U.S. congl. candidate 3d Dist., 1984; U.S. senate candidate, Ala., 1996. Office: Auburn U Dept Econs Coll Bus Auburn AL 36849

THORNTON, MAURICE, retired academic administrator; b. Birmingham, Ala., Dec. 31, 1930; s. William Cullen and Alberta (Jones) T.; m. Elizabeth Ann McDonald, Apr. 15, 1961; children: Karen, Susan, Christopher. BS, Ala. State U., 1952; MEd, Cleve. State U., 1973; EdD, Nova-Southeastern U., 1981; golden diploma (hon.) , Ala. State U., 2002. Investigative caseworker, supr. title V Cuyahoga County Welfare Dept., Cleve., 1958-67, coord. neighborhood youth corps, asst. dir. pers. dept., 1958-67; equal employment officer, minority recruiter Cuyahoga C.C., 1967-82, dir. equal opportunity, 1967-82; dir. affirmative action compliance SUNY, Albany, 1982—; dir. affirmative action program SUNY Sys. Adminstrn., 1982-97. Sec. Capital Dist. Human Rights Adv. Com., Albany; N.Y. mid-Hudson coord. Am. Assn. Affirmative Action Officers, Albany; univ. coord. Capital Dist. Black and Puerto Rican Caucus, Albany; participant Leadership Devel. Program, Cleve. and Albany; adj. prof. SUNY, Albany, 1998—. Contbr. articles to profl. jours. Active NAACP; fundraiser United Negro Coll. Fund., Albany and Cleve., loaned exec. program United Way, Albany and Cleve.; exec. adv. bd. Boy Scouts Am. Scholar State of Ala., State of Ohio. Mem. VA (nat. v.p. 369th), 100 Black Men (charter, adv. com. on restoration and display of N.Y. State's mil. battle flags-commn.), Omega Psi Phi, Sigma Pi Phi (charter). Avocations: walking, reading, golf, traveling, history buff. Home: 7 Keith Rd Delmar NY 12054-4006 Office: SUNY State University Albany Albany NY 12203 E-mail: maurice@empireone.net.

THORNTON, MICHAEL B. federal judge; Judge U.S. Tax Ct., Washington, 1998—. Office: US Tax Ct 400 2D St NW Washington DC 20217-0001

THORNTON, PAULINE CECILIA MARIE, special education educator; b. L.A., July 1, 1951; d. John Woodrow Thornton and Pauline Lucia DeWolfe; children: Patrick Ellis Hooker-Wafford, Damien Charles Wafford. Student, L.A. City Coll., 1969—71; B in English, UCLA, 1975; MA in Spl. Edn., postgrad., Calif. State U., Bakersfield, 2002—. Profl. clear multiple-subjects credential/profl. clear learning Calif. State Dept. Edn. Reading tutor L.A. Unified Sch. Dist., 1970—71, instrnl. asst., 1975, tchrs. asst., 1975—78; childcare worker Children's Home Soc. Bakersfield, 1981—84; instnl. technician Nat. Assn. for People with Disabilities, 1981—85; instrnl. aide I Bakersfield City Sch. Dist., 1981—85, substitute tchr., 1985—94, cert. spl. edn. tchr., 1994—; +. Mem.: AARP, Folgers Shakespeare Libr., Am. Acad. Poets, Internat. Soc. Poets, Nat. Writers' Union, others, The Wisdom Fund, Amnesty Internat., ACLU Alumni, Nuc. Peace Orgn., Muslim Peace Fellowship, Peace and Freedom Party, Internat. Soc. for Krishna Consciousness, United Lodge Theosophists, Sigma Tau Delta. Roman Catholic. Avocations: science fiction, jazz, philosophy, movies. Home: 5805 Hartman Bakersfield CA 93309

THORNTON, RAY, state supreme court justice, former congressman; b. Conway, AR, July 16, 1928; s. R.H. and Wilma (Stephens) Thornton; m. Betty Jo Mann, Jan. 27, 1956; children: Nancy, Mary Jo, Stephanie. BA, Yale U., 1950; JD, U. Ark., 1956. Bar: Ark. 1956, U.S. Supreme Ct. 1956. Pvt. practice in, Sheridan and Little Rock, 1956—70; atty. gen., 1971—73; mem. 93d-95th Congresses from 4th Ark. dist.; exec. dir. Quachita Bapt. U./Henderson State U. Joint Ednl. Consortium, Arkadelphia, Ark., 1979—80; pres. Ark. State U., Jonesboro and Beebe, 1980—84, U. Ark. Sys., Fayetteville, Little Rock, Pine Bluff, Monticello, 1984—89; mem. 102nd-104th Congresses from 2d Ark. dist., 1991—96; assoc. justice Ark. Supreme Ct., 1997—. Chmn. Ark. Bd. Law Examiners, 1967—70; del. 7th Ark. Constl. Conv., 1969—70. Chmn. pres.'s devel. coun. Harding Coll., Searcy, Ark., 1971—73. Served with USN, 1951—54, Korea. Mem.: AAAS (chmn. com. on sci., engring. and pub. policy 1980). Office: 625 Marshall St, 120 Justice Building Little Rock AR 72201*

THORNTON, ROBERT JAMES, SR. economics educator, author; b. Chgo., Oct. 3, 1943; s. John Clifford and Mary Bridget (Fuest) T.; m. Julie A. Roske, Aug. 12, 1967; children: Jennifer, Robert J. Jr. AB, Xavier U., 1965; MA, U. Ill., 1967, PhD, 1970. Rsch. asst. Brookings Instn., Washington, 1969-70; prof. econs. Lehigh U., Bethlehem, Pa., 1970—, chmn. econs., 1984-93, MacFarland prof., 1991—. Pvt. cons., Bethlehem, 1970—. Author: Lexicon of Intentionally Ambiguous Recommendations, 1988, 2nd edit., 1998; editor: Reindustrialization: Implications for U.S. Industrial Policy, 1984, Forging New Relationships Among Business, Labor and Government, 1986, Canada at the Crossroads, 1988, Economic Aspects of Regional Trade Arrangments, 1989, Global Protectionism, 1991, Litigation Economics, 1993, Economic Consequences of American Education, 1993; contbr. numerous articles to econ. jours. Mem. Nat. Assn. Forensic Economists (pres. 1988-90), Am. Econ. Assn. Avocations: handball, baseball. E-mial. Home: 305 W Wabash St Allentown PA 18103-5024 Office: Rauch Business Ctr Lehigh Univ 621 Taylor St Bethlehem PA 18015-3117 E-mail: rjt1@Lehigh.edu.

THORNTON, SPENCER P. ophthalmologist, educator; b. West Palm Beach, Fla., Sept. 16, 1929; s. Ray Spencer and Mae (Phillips) T.; m. Annie Glenn Cooper, Oct. 6, 1956; children: Steven Pitts, David Spencer, Ray Cooper, Beth Ellen. BS, Wake Forest Coll., 1951, MD, 1954. Diplomate: Am. Bd. Ophthalmology. Intern Ga. Bapt. Hosp., Atlanta, 1954-55; resident gen. surgery U. Ala. Med. Center, 1955-56; resident ophthalmology Vanderbilt U. Sch. Medicine, 1960-63; practice medicine specializing in ophthalmic surgery Nashville, 1960—; med. dir. Thornton Eye Ctr., 1995-99; disting. vis. prof. dept. ophthalmology U. Tenn., 2001. Mem. staff Bapt. Hosp., chief ophthalmology svc., 1982-87; guest prof., vis. lectr. U. Toronto, 1990, 91, 92, U. Paris, 1989, Rothchilds Inst., Paris, 1992, 94, U. Pretoria, 1991, 93, others; instr. Moscow Inst. Eye Microsurgery, 1981; instr. ophthalmic surgery Am. Acad. Ophthalmology Ann. Courses; lectr. lens implant symposiums Eng., Spain, Australia, Switzerland, Can., Sweden, Greece, Germany, France, Republic of South Africa, Japan; Berzelius lectr. U. Lund, Sweden, 1992; P.J. Hay Gold medal lectr., North of Eng. Ophthal. Soc., Scarborough, 1992. King Features syndicated newspaper columnist, 1959-60, feature writer, NBC radio and TV, 1958-60; author, co-author textbooks on cataract and refractive surgery; mem. editl. bd. Jour. Refractive and Corneal Surgery, Jour. Cataract and Refractive Surgery, Video Jour. Ophthalmology, Ocular Surgery News (Ophthalmologist of Yr. 1996), Ophthalmic Practice (Can.), Eye Care Tech. Mag. (Lifetime Achievement award 1996); contbr. articles to profl. jours.; inventor instruments and devices for refractive and lens implant surgery. Named among Outstanding Young Men of Yr., U.S. Jaycees, 1965; recipient Honor award Can. Implant Assn., 1993, Outstanding Achievement award Bowman Gray Sch. Medicine, 1995. Named 1 of 100 Best Ophthalmologists in Am., Ophthalmology Times mag., 1996. Fellow: ACS (life), Am. Coll. Nutritional Medicine (pres. 2000—), Am. Acad. Ophthalmology (honor award 1995); mem.: Am. Soc. Cataract and Refractive Surgery (pres. 1997—99), Can. Implant Soc. (life), South African Intraocular Implant Soc. (life), Am. Med. Soc. Vienna (life), Internat. Refractive Surgery Club (v.p. 1994), Delta Kappa Alpha, Phi Rho Sigma. Baptist. Home and Office: 5070 Villa Crest Dr Nashville TN 37220-1425 E-mail: spthornton@comcast.net.

THORNTON, SUE BONNER, former librarian; b. Fairfield, Tex. d. John Carder and Mary (Bonner) T. AB, U. Okla., 1920, AB in L.S, 1938, Mus.B. in Piano, 1921; MA, Columbia U., 1932; postgrad., U. Hawaii, summer 1936. Music supr. Okla. pub. schs., 1921-25; head music dept. Northeastern State Coll., Tahlequah, Okla., 1925-32, librarian, 1932-64. Author: The Bonner Family History. Mem. Central Area, Freestone County, B-RI museums; chmn. bd. trustees Freestone County (Tex.) Mus. Mem. NEA, ALA, Daus. Am. Colonists, Colonial Dames of 17th Century, Tahlequah C. of C., League Women Voters, United Ch. Women Tahlequah (chmn. 1960), D.A.R. (chmn. good citizens com. for Okla. 1958-60), Magna Charta Dames, Ams. Royal Descent, Plantagenet Soc., Soc. Descs. Knights Garter, Nat. Soc. U.S. Daus. 1812, Huguenot Soc. S.C., P.E.O., Order Washington Daus. Colonial Wars, Colonial Order of Crown, Tex. and Southwestern Cattle Raisers Assn., Pan Am. Round Table, Alpha Gamma Delta. Clubs: History (Fairfield, Tex.); Harvey Woman's (Palestine, Tex.); Soroptimist, Freestone County Country. Democrat. Presbyterian. Home: 351 Fm 833 E Fairfield TX 75840-5104

THORNTON, THOMAS NOEL, publishing executive; b. Marceline, Mo., Apr. 23, 1950; s. Bernard F. and Helen F. (Kelley) T.; m. Cynthia L. Murray, Nov. 26, 1971; children: T. Zachary, Timothy. B.J., U. Mo., 1972. Asst. to editor Universal Press Syndicate, Kansas City, Mo., 1972, v.p., 1974, dir. mktg., 1976; v.p., dir. mktg. Universal Press Syndicate and Andrews McMeel Pub., Kansas City, 1976-87; pres., COO Andrews McMeel Pub., 1987—. Bd. dirs. Andrews McMeel Universal. Office: Universal Press Syndicate 4520 Main St Ste 700 Kansas City MO 64111-7701 E-mail: tthornton@amuniversal.com.

THORNTON, WAYNE ALLEN, naval officer, engineer, political scientist; b. Manchester, Conn., Dec. 17, 1952; s. Warren George and Dorothy Marie (Brooks) T. BS in Ocean Engring. with honors, U.S. Naval Acad., 1974; MS in Mech. Engring., Stanford U., 1980; MA in Nat. Security Studies, Georgetown U., 1991; Grad. with highest distinction, Naval War Coll, 1996; student, MIT, Cambridge, 1999—2001; postgrad., Harvard U., 2002—. Commd. ensign USN, 1974, advanced through grades to capt., 1995; naval liaison officer to U.S. Senate, Office of Legis. Affairs, Washington, 1974; elec./reactor controls officer, main propulsion asst., radiological controls officer, combat sys. officer USS Barb, San Diego, 1976-79; rsch. asst. Stanford U., 1980-81; engring. officer USS Gurnard, San Diego, 1981-84; engring. officer submarine group five staff, 1984-86; engring. officer submarine squadron 11 staff, 1986; exec. officer USS Pollack, 1987-88; br. head undersea manpower, staff ACNO for undersea warfare Washington, 1988-91; commdg. officer USS Drum, San Diego, 1991-94; Fed. Exec. fellow Hoover Inst., Stanford U., 1994-95; dept. head undersea warfare Office of Naval Intelligence, Washington, 1995-97; commdg. officer submarine base San Diego, 1997-98; commdg. officer naval base point Loma, asst. chief staff for environment occupl. safety and pub. safety Navy Region S.W., 1998-99; ret., 1999; rsch. asst. MIT, 1999-2001, Harvard, 2001—. Mem. ASME, AIAA, Soc. Naval Architects and Marine Engrs., Stanford Alumni Assn., Georgetown Alumni Assn., Porsche Club of Am., Armed Forces Commns., Electronics Assn., Sigma Xi. Avocations: foreign language, foreign travel, scuba diving, underwater photography, military history. Office: Dept of Govt Harvard U Cambridge MA 02138

THORNTON, YVONNE SHIRLEY, physician, author, musician; b. N.Y.C., Nov. 21, 1947; d. Donald E. and Itasker F. (Edmonds) T.; m. Shearwood McClelland, June 8, 1974; children: Shearwood III, Kimberly Itaska. BS in Biology, Monmouth Coll., 1969; MD, Columbia U., 1973, MPH, 1996. Resident in ob-gyn Roosevelt Hosp., N.Y.C., 1973-77; fellow maternal-fetal medicine Columbia-Presbyn. Med. Center, 1977-79; commd. lt. comdr. M.C. USN, 1979; asst. prof. ob-gyn Uniformed Svcs. U. Health Scis., 1979-82; assoc. prof. Cornell U. Med. Coll., N.Y.C., 1989-92; dir. clin. svcs. dept. ob-gyn N.Y. Hosp.-Cornell Med. Center, 1982-88; asst. attending N.Y. Lying-In Hosp., 1982-89; assoc. clin. prof. ob-gyn. Columbia P&S, 1995-98; clin. prof. ob-gyn. U. Medicine and Dentistry N.J., 1998-2000. Dir. Chorionic Villus Sampling Program, 1984-92; dir. perinatal diagnostic testing ctr. Morristown Meml. Hosp., 1992-2000, divsn. maternal-fetal medicine St. Luke's Roosevelt Hosp. Ctr., 2000—; staff Nat. Naval Med. Center, Bethesda, Md.; saxophonist Thornton Sisters ensemble, 1955-76; vis. assoc. physician The Rockefeller U. Hosp., 1986-96; Diplomate Am. Bd. Ob-Gyn, examiner 1997—. Author: The Ditchdigger's Daughters, 1995, (named best books for young adults ALA, Excellence in Lit. award, N.J. Edn. Assn.) Primary Care for the Obstetrician and Gynecologist, 1997, Woman to Woman, 1997. Recipient Excellence in Literature award, N.J. Edn. Assn., 1996, winner Daniel Webster Oratorical Competition, Internat. Platform Assn., 1996. Fellow: ACOG, ACS; mem.: AMA, Am. Fedn. Musicians, Soc. Maternal-Fetal Medicine, Assn. Women Surgeons, N.Y. Acad. Medicine. Democrat. Baptist. Office: 1000 10th Ave New York NY 10019-1147

THORNTON-ARTSON, LINDA ELIZABETH, psychiatric nurse; b. Balt., Dec. 27, 1956; d. Herbert and Helen (Thornton) Powell; m. Michael C. Artson, Oct. 28, 1983; children: Michelle Cherise, Mia Charmain. AA in Psychology, Community Coll. of Balt.; BSN, Coppin State Coll. Cert. gerontol. nurse; cert. psychiat. nurse; cert. nurse cons. in case mgmt.; cert. med.-legal cons. Charge nurse Melchor Nursing Home, 1973-83; med./surg. nurse North Charles Gen. Hosp., Balt., 1975-80; psychiat. nurse Wyman Park Psychiat. Hosp., 1980-84; dir. nurses Lebran Nursing Home, Cin., 1984-85, George A. Martin Gerontology Ctr., Cin., 1983-84; staff nurse Walter P. Carter Psychiat. Hosp., Balt., 1986-90; pvt. cons. Woodbridge, Va. Expert witness in elderly abuse, head injury, and myofacial pain syndrome; instr. for med. tech. nursing assistance counrse in cert. nursing assts. for Va.; med.-legal cons. for Suder & Suder Lar Firm; lectr. in field psychiat. nursing and gerontology nursing; cons. long-term care; cons. for law firms, nursing students, case mgmt. for ins. cos.; mem., supporter AIDS Fuond., Whitman-Walker Clinic Inc., Washington; v.p. Artson Ent., 1985—. Co-author: Warehouse of the Living Dead, 1989; appeared on nat. TV as expert on elderly abuse; contbr. articles to profl. jours. Mem. NAFE, ANA, Nat. League for Nursing, Am. Heart Assn., Md. Nurses Assn., WHO, Nat. Found. for Depressive Illness Inc., Nat. Headache Found., Nat. Cleft Palate Soc., Psychiat. Nurse Soc., Back Pain Assn. Am., Am. Pain Soc., Am. Acad. Pain Mgmt., Am. Chronic Pain Assn., Pain Found., Arthritis Found., Head Injury Found., Va. Nursing Assn., Head Injury Svc. Partnership, Fibromyalgia Assn. Washington, Coppin State Coll. Alumni Assn., Brain Injury Assn. of Va., Am. Chronic Pain Assn. (leader Woodbridge Va. chpt.), Head Injury Partnership Va., Am. Bd. Forensic Nursing (diplomate), Am. Coll. of Forensic Examiners. Avocations: reading, cooking, art, travel, head injury advocacy. Address: PO Box 5150 Woodbridge VA 22194

THORNTON-ERMES, LUCIE ELIZABETH, lawyer; b. Mena, Ark., Apr. 26, 1957; d. Oris Bryant and Carolyn (Cox) T.; m. Frank E. Lamothe (div.); children: Victorine Day Lamothe, Julien Guy Lamothe; m. Peter A. Thornton Ermes, Oct. 6, 2001. BA, Centenary Coll., Shreveport, La., 1979; JD, Tulane U., 1982. Bar: La. 1983, U.S. Dist. Ct. (ea. dist.) La. 1983. Law clk. 1st Cir. Ct. Appeals, Baton Rouge, 1982-83; assoc. Law Offices of Charles E. Hamilton III, New Orleans, 1983-85; law clk. Civil Dist. Ct. New Orleans, 1985-92; pvt. practice New Orleans, 1992-2000; ptnr. Hemelt and Foshee, LLP, 2000—. Mem. editorial bd. La. Appellate Ct. Handbook, 1982—. Mem. La. Adv. Com. on Child Care Facilities and Child Placing Agys., 1994-98; active Jr. League of New Orleans, 1988-98, Greater Covington Jr. Svc. League, 1994-96; trustee La. Children's Mus., 1992-96; bd. dirs. Save Our Cemeteries, 1992-96, Youth Svc. Bd., 1997-99; vestrywoman Christ Episcopal Ch., 1996-98, dir. Christian Formation, 1999-2000; sustainer Jr. League New Orleans, Greater Covington Jr. Svc. League. Mem. La Bar Assn. (CLE com. 1986-87, bench-bar liaison com. 1991-94), Chi Omega. Republican. Home: 126 Live Oak Mandeville LA 70448 Office: Hemelt and Foshee LLP 717 W 17th Ave Covington LA 70433

THORON, GRAY, lawyer, educator; b. Danvers, Mass., July 14, 1916; s. Ward and Louisa Chapin (Hooper) T.; m. Pattie Porter Holmes, Dec. 30, 1971 (dec. 2000); children from previous marriage: Claire, Louisa, Grenville C., Molly D., Thomas G. AB, Harvard U., 1938, LLB, 1941. Bar: N.Y. 1942. Assoc. Sullivan & Cromwell, N.Y.C., 1941-42, 45-48; assoc. prof. law U. Tex., 1948-50, prof. law, 1950-56; dean Law Sch. Cornell U., Ithaca, N.Y., 1956-63, prof. law, 1956-87, prof. emeritus, 1987—. Vis. prof. law summers U. Mich., 1951, U. Tex., 1970; mem. faculty Salzburg Seminar in Am. Studies, summer 1959; asst. to solicitor gen. Dept. Justice, Washington, 1954-56; mem. N.Y. State Laporte Legis. Ethics Com., 1964; spl. asst. atty. gen. N.Y. State, 1965. Del. Rep. Nat. Conv., 1952; trustee Concord Acad., 1958-61. Served with inf. AUS, 1942-45. Decorated silver star, bronze star, purple heart with oak leaf cluster. Fellow Am. Bar Found. (life); mem. Am. Law Inst. (life), Am. Jud. Soc., ABA, N.Y. State Bar Assn. (chmn. spl. com. to rev. code of profl. responsibility 1974-77, com. profl. ethics 1965-87, vice chmn. 1973-83, emeritus 1987—), Am. Arbitration Assn. (arbitrator 1965-90), Assn. Bar City N.Y., Lawyers Com. Civil Rights Under the Law (trustee 1965-97), Phi Alpha Delta, Phi Kappa Phi, Century Assn., Harvard Club (N.Y.C.). Office: Cornell U Law Sch Myron Taylor Hall Ithaca NY 14853

THORP, BENJAMIN A., III, paper manufacturing company executive; b. Albany, N.Y., May 31, 1938; s. Benjamin A. Jr. and Anna C. (Head) T.; m. Barbara Sue Tellock, Aug. 1, 1964 (div. Mar. 1986); 1 child, Benjamin A. IV; m. Laurie Diane Murdock, Oct. 25, 1987. Student in elec. engring., Rensselaer Poly. Inst., 1956-61, postgrad. in mgmt., 1967-68; BS in Physics, U. Md., 1964; postgrad. in engring., U. Bridgeport, 1966; postgrad. in mktg., U. Tenn., 1970. Product devel. mgr. Huyck Formex div. Huyck, Greenville, Tenn., 1969-71, mktg. mgr., 1971-73, v.p., gen. mgr., 1973-75, Huytech Systems div., Wake Forest, N.C., 1975-78; v.p., dir. research Huyck Corp., Rensselaer, N.Y., 1978-80; pres. Benjamin A. Thorp Inc., Albany, 1980-82, POYRY-BEK Inc., Raleigh, N.C., 1982-84; v.p. engring. BE&K Inc., Birmingham, Ala., 1984-85, James River Corp., Richmond, Va., 1984-95; v.p. mfg. tech. Chesapeake Corp., 1996-97; dir. pulp and paper engring. Ga. Pacific, Atlanta, 1998—. Mem. exec. com. Pulp and Paper Found. Bd., Ga. Inst. Tech., 1991-95, pres., 1993-95; mem. indsl. adv. bd. Forest Web.com, 2000—, MTCI, Balt., Md., 2001—, Peregrine Energy, Greenville, S.C., 2002—. Tech. editor Paper Machine Operations, Vol. 7, 3d edit., 1991; contbr. more than 100 articles to profl. jours.; patentee in field. Bd. dirs. Richmond Math. and Sci. Ctr., 1987-93, Sic. Mus. of Va. Found., 1989-98; chmn. papermaking project adv. com. Inst. Paper Sci. and Tech., 1990-94. Fellow TAPPI (chmn. appermakers com. 1984-86, vice chmn. paper and bd. divsn. 1988-90, chmn. 1990-92, bd. dirs., Leadership award 1994); mem. Paper Industry Mgmt. Assn. (Glen T. Rinnegar award 1999, pres. 1996-97, chmn. bd. trustees 1999—), Exptl. Aircraft Assn., Meadowbrook Estates Civic Assn. (bd. dirs. 1996-98). Presbyterian. Office: Ga Pacific PO Box 105605 Atlanta GA 30348-5605

THORP, EDWARD OAKLEY, investment management company executive; b. Chgo., Aug. 14, 1932; s. Oakley Glenn and Josephine (Gebert) T.; m. Vivian Sinetar, Jan. 28, 1956; children: Raun, Karen, Jeffrey. BA in Physics, UCLA, 1953, MA, 1955, PhD in Math., 1958. C.L.E. Moore instr. MIT, Cambridge, Mass., 1959-61; asst. prof. N.Mex. State U., 1961-63, assoc. prof. math., 1963-65, U. Calif., Irvine, 1965-67, prof. math., 1967-77, prof. fin., 1977-82, regents lectr., 1992-93. Vis. prof. UCLA, 1991; chmn. Oakley Sutton Mgmt. Corp., Newport Beach, Calif., 1972-91; mng. gen. ptnr. Princeton/Newport Ptnrs., Newport Beach, 1969-91, OSM Ptnrs., MIDAS Advisors, Newport Beach, 1986-89; gen. ptnr. Edward O. Thorp & Assocs., L.P., Newport Beach, 1989—, Ridgeline Ptnrs., Newport Beach, 1994—; portfolio mgr., cons. Glenwood Investment Corp., Chgo., 1992-94; prin., cons. Grosvenor Capital Mgmt., Chgo., 1992-93; pres. Noesis Corp., 1994—. Author: Beat the Dealer: A Winning Strategy for the Game of Twenty-One, 1962, rev. edit., 1966, Elementary Probability, 1966, The Mathematics of Gambling, 1984; co-author: Beat The Market, 1967, The Gambling Times Guide to Blackjack, 1984; columnist Gambling Times, 1979-84, Wilmott 2001. Grantee NSF, 1954-55, 62-64, Air Force Office Sci. Rsch., 1964-73. Fellow NSF, Inst. Math. Stats.; mem. Phi Beta Kappa, Sigma Xi. Avocations: astronomy, distance running. Office: Edward O Thorp & Assocs LP 610 Newport Center Dr Ste 1240 Newport Beach CA 92660-6436

THORP, PATRICIA ANN, public relations executive; b. Anchorage, Dec. 25, 1955; d. Howard Richard Thorp and Mary Virginia Cooperider Thorp. BS in Journalism, U. Fla., 1982. Gen. mgr. Edelman Worldwide, Miami, Fla., 1982-86; v.p., pub. rels. svcs. Group 3hree, 1986-87; owner, pres. Thorp & Co., Coral Gables, Fla., 1988—. Author: A PR Manual for Business Managers, 1994. Pro bono cons. Children's Home Soc., Miami, 1992-94, Habitat for Humanity, Miami, 1994-96; mktg. com. chair Miami City Ballet, Miami Beach, 1997-98. Mem. Nat. Investor Rels. Inst., Counselors Acad. of Pub. Rels. Soc. Am., Internat. Advt. Assn. (bd. dirs. 1996-98), Greater Miami C. of C. (trustee 1998—), Alliance for Ethical Govt. (convening chair comm. 1999). Avocations: scuba diving, skiing, reading, travel. Office: Thorp & Co 150 Alhambra Cir Ste 900 Coral Gables FL 33134-4534

THORPE, GARY STEPHEN, chemistry educator; b. Los Angeles, Mar. 9, 1951; s. David Winston and Jeanette M. (Harris) T.; m. Patricia Marion Eison, Apr. 13, 1949; children: Kristin Anne, Erin Michelle. BS, U. Redlands, 1973; MS, Calif. State U., Northridge, 1975. Tchr. L.A. Schs., 1975-80, L.A. Community Colls., 1976-81, Beverly Hills (Calif.) High Sch., 1980—; instr. chemistry Coll of the Canyons, Santa Clarita, Calif., 1998—. Author: AP Chemistry Study Guide, 1993, Barron's AP Environmental Science Preparation Guide, 2002. Res. police officer L.A. Police Dept., 1991; CEO For Our Kids Found., L.A., 1999—. Recipient Commendation L.A. County Bd. Suprs., 1983, 84, Beverly Hills City Coun., 1983, 84, City of L.A., 1995, Resolution of Commendation State of Calif. Senate and Assembly, 1983, 84, Cert. of Appreciation L.A. County Bd. Edn., 1984-85, Gov. George Deukmejian, Sacrament, 1984-85. Mem. Am. Chem. Soc. (exec. dir. So. Calif. divsn. 1995—, bd. dirs. 1998—, selected as Outstanding Chemistry Tchr. of So. Calif. 1989, 92), NEA, Calif. Tchrs. Assn., Phi Delta Kappa. Lodges: Masons. Republican. Lutheran. Avocations: ham radio, computer application. Home: 6127 Balcom Ave Encino CA 91316-7207

THORPE, JAMES, humanities researcher; b. Aiken, S.C., Aug. 17, 1915; s. J. Ernest and Ruby (Holloway) T.; m. Elizabeth McLean Daniells, July 19, 1941; children: John D., Sally Jans-Thorpe. AB, The Citadel, 1936, LL.D., 1971; MA, U. N.C., 1937; PhD, Harvard U., 1941; Litt.D., Occidental Coll., 1968; L.H.D., Claremont Grad. Sch., 1968; H.H.D., U. Toledo, 1977. Instr. to prof. English Princeton, 1946-66; dir. Huntington Libr., Art Gallery and Bot. Gardens, San Marino, Calif., 1966-83; sr. research assoc. Huntington Libr., 1966-99. Author: Bibliography of the Writings of George Lyman Kittredge, 1948, Milton Criticism, 1950, Rochester's Poems on Several Occasions, 1950, Poems of Sir George Etherege, 1963, Aims and Methods of Scholarship, 1963, 70, Literary Scholarship, 1964, Relations of Literary Study, 1967, Bunyan's Grace Abounding and Pilgrim's Progress, 1969, Principles of Textual Criticism, 1972, 2d edit., 1979, Use of Manuscripts in Literary Research, 1974, 2d edit., 1979, Gifts of Genius, 1980, A Word to the Wise, 1982, John Milton: The Inner Life, 1983, The Sense of Style: Reading English Prose, 1987, Henry Edwards Huntington: A Biography, 1994, H.E. Huntington: A Short Biography, 1996, A Pleasure of Proverbs, 1996, Proverbs for Friends, 1997, Proverbs for Thinkers, 1998, The Gutenberg Bible, 1999, Poems Written at the Huntington Library, 2000. Served to col. USAAF, 1941-46. Decorated Bronze Star medal.; Guggenheim fellow, 1949-50, 65-66 Fellow Am. Acad. Arts and Scis., Am. Philos. Soc.; mem. MLA, Am. Antiquarian Soc., Soc. for Textual Scholarship. Clubs: Zamorano. Democrat. Episcopalian. Home: 20 Loeffler Rd Apt T320 Bloomfield CT 06002-2277

THORPE, JANET CLAIRE, lawyer; b. Bklyn., Dec. 8, 1953; d. Burton Walter and Phyllis Claire (Read) T.; m. David Frank Palmer, Aug. 26, 1978 (div. Aug. 1988); children: Katherine Elaine, Jennifer Claire; m. James Francis Box, June 29, 1991; children; Melissa Richelle, Maergrethe Cashel. Student, Boston U., 1972-74; BA in Polit. Sci. & History with honors, Union Coll., 1975; postgrad., Western New Eng. Sch. Law, 1975-76; JD, Emory U., 1978. Bar: Ga. 1978, U.S. Ct. Appeals (5th and 11th cirs.) 1978, 80, Fla. 1987, U.S. Dist. Ct. (mid. dist.) Fla. 1987. Law clk. to judge U.S. Dist. Ct., Atlanta, 1978; regional atty. Comptroller of Curency, 1978-80; assoc. corp. counsel Trust Co. Ga., 1980-86; dir. Trusco Properties, Inc., 1981-86; gen. counsel, corp. sec. SunTrust Banks Fla., Inc., Orlando, 1986-2000; gen. counsel SunTrust Bank Ctrl. Fla. N.A., 1986-2000; group v.p. SunTrust Banks, Inc., 1995-2000; cir. ct. judge State of Fla. (9th cir.), Orlando, Fla., 2000—. Mem. Coun. Battered Women, Atlanta, 1983-86, bd. dirs., 1986; bd. visitors Cornell Mus. Fine Art, Rollins Coll., 1990-96; mem. bd. zoning variances City of Orlando, 1996-99; bd. dirs. Orange County Cmty. Alliance, 2000--. Mem. Ga. Bar Assn., Fla. Bar Assn., Assn. Bank Holdings Cos (lawyers com. 1983-90), Am. Corp. Counsel Assn. (bd. dirs. ctrl. Fla. chpt. 1991-99), Am. Diabetes Assn. (bd. dirs. Fla. chpt. 1989-97), Leadership Orlando. Episcopalian. Avocations: gardening, child rearing, house renovation, photography. Office: Juvenile Justice Ctr 2000 E Michigan St Orlando FL 32806-4941

THORPE, SAMUEL STANLEY, JR. artist; b. Stoneham, Mass., July 15, 1933; m. Louise Harwood Gove; children: Michael, Scott, Craig, Heidi. Student, Sch. of Mus. of Fine Art, Boston. Represented in permanent collections at MBNA Am. Banks Corp. Collections, Aubuchon Hardware Corp., Nashua Fed. Savs. Bank, Indianhead Bank, Gardner Savs. Bank, Pepperell Bus. Assn., USA Distbg., Attys. Watnik & Watnik, PC, numerous pvt. collections including Ambassador and Mrs. Wylie T. Buchanan and Pres. and Mrs. George H.W. Bush; illustrator Cameo Greetings, Maine, Doehler Card Corp., N.H., Marion Health Greetings, Mass., Airmar Corp., N.H. Mem. So. Vt. Art Assn., Chaffee Art Ctr. (Rutland, Vt.), Artists Guild of the Kennebunks, Leominster Art Assn., New Haven Paint and Palette Club, Salmagundi Club (N.Y.C.), Copley Soc. (Boston). Home: 30 Elm Cir Townsend MA 01469-1236

THORSEN, JAMES HUGH, retired aviation director, retired airport manager; b. Evanston, Ill., Feb. 5, 1943; s. Chester A. and Mary Jane (Currie) T.; m. Nancy Dain, May 30, 1980. BA, Ripon Coll., 1965. FAA cert. comml. pilot, flight instr. airplanes and instruments. Bd. dirs. Internat. Northwest Aviation Coun. Pres. Thorsen Aviation Cons. Recipient Region Safety award FAA N.W. Mountain. Mem. Am. Assn. Airport Execs. (past pres. N.W. chpt., Disting. Svc. award 1999), Mensa, Idaho Falls W. Rotary Club (pres. 2002), Quiet Birdmen, Sigma Alpha Epsilon. Home: 334 Westmorland Dr Idaho Falls ID 83402-4607

THORSEN, MARIE KRISTIN, radiologist, educator; b. Milw., Aug. 1, 1947; d. Charles Christian and Margaret Josephine (Little) T.; m. James Lawrence Troy, Jan. 7, 1978; children: Katherine Marie, Megan Elizabeth. BA, U. Wis., 1969; MBA, George Washington U., 1971; MD, Columbia Coll. Physicians and Surgeons, 1977. Diplomate Am. Bd. Radiology. Intern. Columbia-Presbyn. med. Ctr., N.Y.C., 1977-78, resident dept. radiology, 1978-81; asst. prof. radiology Med. Coll. Wis., 1982-84, assoc. prof., 1984-89, prof., 1989-94; dir. computed tomography Waukesha Meml. Hosp., 1994—. Contbr. articles to profl. jours. Fellow computed body tomography Med. Coll. Wisc., Milw, 1981-82; Am. Coll. Radiology, Radiol. Soc. N. Am., Wis. Radiologic Assn. (sec., treas. 2001—). E-mail: mkthoren@aol.com.

THORSETT, PETER E. logistics management executive, consultant; b. Houston, Oct. 5, 1973; s. Eugene D. and Ruth Ann (Kehir) T. BS, U. Tenn., 1996. Sr. project adminstr. Athena Neuroscis., Inc., So. San Francisco, 1992-94; regional Mgmt. Info. Systems mgr. QLM Advertising, Atlanta, 1996; supr. Call Ctr. Turner Broadcasting, 1997; mgr. ops. Adair-Greene, 1997—. Cons. Mgmt. Info. Sys., Atlanta, Ga., 1996—. Mem. adv. bd. FBLA-PBL Profl. Divsn., Atlanta, 1992—; mem. Human Rights Campaign, Atlanta, 1992— Alumni Svc. award AAUW, Half Moon Bay, Calif., 1994 Alumni Svc. award Tenn. Intrcollegiate State Legis., Knoxville, Tenn., 1996, Prudential Peer award, 1996. Mem. Project Mgmt. Inst., Am. Soc. for Public Adminstrn., Internat. Facility Mgmt. Assn. Democrat. Roman Catholic. Avocations: reading, cinema, golf, hiking. Office: Adair-Greene 200 Atlanta Tech Ctr 1575 Northside Dr NW Atlanta GA 30318-4235

THORSNESS, JULIA MARIE, hospice administrator; b. Yakima, Wash., Apr. 8, 1958; d. Edward Gerhard William Rosin and Margaret Julia Franke; m. James Ray Thorsness; children: Rebecca, Timothy. BA in Social Work, Pacific Luth. U., 1980. Pub. rels. coord. Our Lady of Compassion Care Ctr., Anchorage, 1985-88; cmty. rels. mgr. Covenant Ho. Alaska, 1989-95; devel. dir. Camp Fire Boys and Girls, 1995-99; exec. dir. Hospice of Anchorage, 1999—. Editor, contbr. Hospice of Anchorage Newsletter, 2000— (awards). Mem. Pub. Rels Soc. Am. (bd. mem. Alaska chpt. 1996-98), Assn. Fundraising Profls. (past pres. Anchorage chpt.), Nat. Soc. Fund Raising Execs. (pres. Alaska chpt. 2000, Philanthropy Day chair 1997), Anchorage Lions Club (pres. 1998-99), Foraker Group (ops. bd. mem.). Lutheran. Home: 1161 W 77th Ave Anchorage AK 99518 Office: Hospice of Anchorage 500 W Int Airport Rd # C Anchorage AK 99518 E-mail: hospice@ak.net.

THORSON, JOHN MARTIN, JR. electrical engineer, consultant; b. Armstrong, Iowa, Dec. 16, 1929; s. John Martin and Hazel Marguerite (Martin) T.; m. Geraldine Carol Moran, Apr. 21, 1956 (dec. 1975); children— John Robert, James Michael; m. Lee Houk, Sept. 24, 1977 BSE.E., Iowa State U., 1951. Transmission engr. No. States Power Co., Mpls., 1953-58, system operation relay engr., 1962-74, telephone engr. Minot, N.D., 1958-62; utility industry mktg. mgr. Control Data Corp., Mpls., 1974-77, product/program mgr. utilities, 1977-84, sr. cons. energy mgmt. systems, 1984-90; pres. Thorson Engrs., Inc., Chanhassen, Minn., 1991—. Inductive coordination cons. SNC Corp., Oshkosh, Wis., 1985—; tech. cons. Power Technologies, Inc., Schenectady, N.Y., 1991—, Control Corp., Osseo, Minn., 1992-93, Control Data, Plymouth, Minn., 1991-92, Hathaway, Denver, 1992-93, Scottish Hydro-Electric, PLC, Perth, Scotland, 1992—, NRG Energy Inc., Mpls., 1993—, Stanford Rsch. Inst., 1995—, Univ. Online, Inc., 1995—, GE, 1996—, No. States Power Co., 1998-2000, Siemens, 2000—; head U.S. nat. com. Internat. Electrotech. Com., TC57, 1985-2001. Contbr. tech. papers to profl. jours. Dist. commr. Boy Scouts Am., Minn., 1954-58, 64-65, coun. commr. N.D., Mont., 1959-62; mem. coun. St. Philip Luth. Ch., Wayzata, Minn., 1968-69; county del. Rep. Com., Chanhassen, Minn., 1980-82. 1st lt. USAF, 1951-53. Recipient Alumni Service award Iowa State U., 1972 Fellow IEEE (life mem., bd. dirs. 1981-82, dir. region 4, 1981-82, mem. U.S. activities bd. 1981-82, regional activities bd. 1981-82, Centennial medal 1984); mem. Internat. Conf. on Large High Voltage Electric Sys. (Atwood assoc. 2000), Iowa State U. Alumni Assn. (v.p., pres. 1963-66). Independent. Avocations: canoeing, back packing, mountain climbing. Home and Office: 7320 Longview Cir Chanhassen MN 55317-7905

THORSON, LEE A. lawyer; b. Seattle, Nov. 10, 1949; s. Theodore Arthur and Irene Mary (Dakers) T.; m. Elizabeth Clayton Hay, June 7, 1975; children: Kirk Hunter, Alex Peter. BA, U. Wash., 1971; JD, U. Pacific, Sacramento, 1975; LLM Taxation, Boston U., 1976. Atty. Dahlgren & Dauenhauer P.S., Seattle, 1976-79, Lane Powell Spears Lubersky, Seattle, 1980-93; shareholder Birmingham Thorson & Barnett, P.C., 1993—; affiliate prof. U. Wash. Grad. Program in Taxation, 1995—. Mem. ABA (health law forum), Internat. Found. Employee Benefits, Employee Benefits and Health Law coms., Wash. State Bar Assn. Avocations: bicycling, skiing. Office: Birmingham Thorson Barnett 601 Union St Ste 3315 Seattle WA 98101-4018 E-mail: lthorson@btbpc.com.

THORSON, STEVEN GREG, lawyer; b. Van Nuys, Calif., Feb. 7, 1948; s. Robert G. and Ruth C. T.; m. Patricia Lynn LaPointe, Aug. 3, 1974; 1 child, Kai Johannes. BA, St. Olaf Coll., 1977; JD, Hamline U., 1980. Bar: Minn. 1980, U.S. Dist. Ct. Minn. 1980, U.S. Tax Ct. 1980, U.S. Ct. Appeals (8th cir.) 1980. Pres. Thorson & Berg, Maple Grove, Minn., 1990-99; with Barna, Guzy & Steffen, Ltd. Attys. at Law, Mpls., 1999—. Lectr. continuing legal edn., 1986—; apptd. to Minn. State Bar Assn. Commn. on Unauthorized Practice of Law, 1990-92; atty. for Columbus Twp. (Anoka County), 1981-96; mem. residential real estate com. Minn. State Bar Assn., 1992—. Mem. ch. coun. Peace Luth. Ch. Named a Super Lawyer, Minn Law and Politics Mag., 2000, 2001, 2002; named one of Minn. Top Lawyers, Mpls./St. Paul mag., 1998, 2000, 2001, 2002. Mem. ABA, Minn. State Bar Assn. (real property coun., chair publs. com. 2001—), Hennepin County Bar Assn. (chmn. purchase agreement com. 1986-88), Anoka County Bar Assn. (pres. real estate sect. 1988). Avocations: alpine and nordic skiing. Home: 12071 Norway St NW Minneapolis MN 55448-2243 Office: 400 Northtown Fin Plz 200 Coon Rapids Blvd NW Ste 400 Minneapolis MN 55433-5894 E-mail: sthorson@bgslaw.com.

THORSTEINSSON, GUDNI, physiatrist; b. Vestmannaeyjar, Iceland, Aug. 5, 1941; came to U.S., 1971; s. Thorsteinn and Asdis Gudbjörg Einarsson; m. Elin Klein, Apr. 10, 1965; children: Arnar Karl, Asdis Thora. BS, Reykjavik (Iceland) Coll., 1961; candidatus med. et chirurg., U. Iceland, Reykjavik, 1968; MS, U. Minn., 1976. Diplomate Am. Bd. Phys. Medicine and Rehab. Dist physician Icelandic Govt., Djupivogur, 1970-71; resident dept. phys. medicine and rehab. Mayo Found., Rochester, Minn., 1972-75, mem. consulting staff, 1975-80; chair dept. Nat. Hosp., Reykjavik, 1980-81; dir. rehab. Mayo Clinic/St. Mary's Hosp., Rochester, 1981-85; dir. out-patient rehab. Mayo Clinic, 1985-88, chair dept., 1987-91, chair dept. phys. medicine and rehab. Jacksonville, Fla., 1991-99. Physiatrist cons. Mayo Clinic, Rochester, 81-91, Jacksonville, 1991—. Author: (with others) Efficacy of Transcutaneous Electrical Stimulation, 1977, Placebo Effect of Transcountaneous Electrical Stimulation, 1978, Electrical Stimulation for Anagesia, 1983, Management of Post Polio Syndrome, 1997. Mem. AMA, Am. Acad. Phys. Medicine and Rehab., Fla. Med. Assn. Office: Mayo Clinic Jacksonville 4500 San Pablo Rd S Jacksonville FL 32224-1865

THORSTENBERG, LAURENCE (JOHN L. THORSTENBERG), oboe and English horn player; b. Salt Lake City, Dec. 6, 1925; s. Laurence Nathaniel and Alys Josephine (Blomquist) T. MusB, Curtis Inst. Music, Phila., 1951. Instrumental tchr., 1975-96, New Eng. Conservatory, Boston U., 1980-96; mem. Symphony Orch. Balt., 1951-52, Dallas Symphony Orch., 1952-54, Chgo. Symphony Orch., 1954-63, Boston Symphony Orch., 1964-93. Appeared summers, Marlboro (Vt.) Music Festival, 1952-54. With U.S. Army, 1944-46, ETO. Mem. Internat. Conf. Symphony and Opera Musicians (emeritus).

THOTTUPURAM, KURIAN CHERIAN, priest, college director, educator; b. Cherianad, Kerala, India; came to U.S., 1971; s. Cherian Koruth and Eliamma (Kandanavila) T.; m. Susan Grace Kompady, Dec. 29, 1969; children: Cherian, Kurian Jr., Theodore-George. BA, St. Joseph's Coll., India, 1964; grad. diploma in theology, Sem. of Lateran U., 1966; MA, Karnatak U., 1970, Mundelein Coll., Chgo., 1973; MEd, Loyola U., Chgo., 1979, PhD, 1981; DD, Notre Dame de Lafayette U., 1993. Ordained subdeacon, 1967, deacon, 1970, priest, 1970, chorbishop, 1986. Tchr. Mt. Tabor Monastery Coll., Pathanapuram, India, 1966-70; founder Malankarese Orthodox Syrian Ch., Chgo., 1971—; pastor St. John's Syrian Orthodox Ch., 1971-72; founder, pastor St. Thomas Orthodox Ch., 1972-80, St. Mary's Orthodox Ch., 1982—; counseling psychologist Incentives Inst., Des Plaines, Ill., 1974-76; dir. social svc. Millardogden Ctr., Chgo., 1976-77; ednl. adminstr. ednl. program Chgo. Housing Authority, 1977-81; ecumenical officer Malankarese Orthodox Diocese, Chgo., 1981-85; dir. program planning and devel. Malcolm X Coll., Chgo. City Coll. System, 1985-91; english faculty Truman Coll., 1991-92; exec. dir. International Edn. Cons. and Evaluators of Ill., 1992; dir. curriculum/instrn. S.E.A. Ctr., 1993-94; mem. philosophy faculty Daley Coll., 1993-95, Triton Coll., 1995—. Pioneer Malankarese Orthodox Chs., 1971-81; adj. prof. philosophy Coll. of Lake County, 1995-96; pres. Am. Acad. Comparative-Internat. Edn., Chgo., 1993—; mem. Sch. Bd. Coun., 1991-93. Author: Dhyanamitram, 1966, Kalari, 1967, Perumpepadam, 1968, Foundations of Kerala Education, 1981, Bible Reading Guide of the Malankara Orthodox Church, Education and Social Change, 1987, The Mystery of Man, 1971, Personality of a Child: A Constant Process of Dualistic Eruption into Monism, 1972, Incarnation: A Theologico-mystical Study, 1981, Holy Spirit: The Life Giver, 1981, An Orthodox Introduction to Sacraments, 1983, The Book of Common Prayer of the Syrian Orthodox Ch., 1985, Book of Ordinations of the Syrian Orthodox Ch., 1987, Marriage After the Holy Priesthood, 1985, Contraception and Orthodox Theology, 1990, The Orthodox Christian Priesthood: An Anthology of Patristic Writings, 1995, Pre-British European Educational Activities in India, 1989; chief editor: Voice of Orthodoxy, 1986. Chmn. social action Diocese of Niraram, India, 1967-71; mem. Zonal coun. Diocese of Am., 1975-78, Diocesan Coun.; bd. regents Lafayette U., Aurora, Colo., 1989-95; exec. mem. Alleppey DT Kerala Congress, India, 1967-71; pres. Ecumenical Coun. Kerala Chs. Chgo., 1983-97; founder Voice of Orthodox Found., Chgo., 1995. Recipient Taylor award for High Achievement, Greek Orthodox Archdiocese, Schmitt Found. award, 1977, Pub. Svc. award Citizens Cultural Found., 1985. Mem. Am. Ednl. Studies Assn., Midwest History of Edn. Soc., Am. Assn. Biofeedback Clinicians, Internat. Assn. of Mission Studies, Germany. Mem. Eastern Orthodox Ch. Avocations: music, philanthropic work.

THOULESS, DAVID JAMES, physicist, educator; b. Bearsden, Scotland, Sept. 21, 1934; came to U.S., 1979; U.S. citizen, 1994; s. Robert Henry and Priscilla (Gorton) T.; m. Margaret Elizabeth Scrase, July 26, 1958; children: Michael, Christopher, Helen. BA, U. Cambridge, Eng., 1955, ScD, 1986; PhD, Cornell U., 1958. Physicist Lawrence Berkeley Lab., Calif., 1958-59; rsch. fellow U. Birmingham, Eng., 1959-61, prof. math. physics Eng., 1965-78; lectr., fellow Churchill Coll. U. Cambridge, Eng., 1961-65; prof. physics Queen's U., Kingston, Ont., Can., 1978; prof. applied sci. Yale U., New Haven, 1979-80; prof. physics U. Wash., Seattle, 1980—. Author: Quantum Mechanics of Many Body Systems, 2d edit., 1972, Topological Quantum Numbers in Nonrelativistic Physics, 1998. Recipient Maxwell medal Inst. Physics, 1973, Holweck prize Soc. Francaise de Physique-Inst. Physics, 1980, Fritz London award for Low temperature physics, Fritz London Meml. Fund, 1984, Wolf prize in physics, 1990, Paul Dirac medal Inst. Physics, 1993, Lars Onsager prize Am. Phys. Soc., 2000; Edwin Uehling disting. scholar U. Wash., 1988-98. Fellow Royal Soc., Am. Acad. Arts and Scis., Nat. Acad. Sci. Office: U Wash PO Box 351560 Seattle WA 98195-1560 E-mail: Thouless@phys.washington.edu.

THOW, GEORGE BRUCE, surgeon; b. Toronto, Mar. 24, 1930; came to U.S., 1965; s. George and Helen Bruce (Smith) T.; m. Marion Bernice Perry, Sept. 7, 1956; children— Deborah, George, Helen, Catherine MD, U. Toronto, 1954. Diplomate Am. Bd. Gen. Surgery, Am. Bd. Colon and Rectal Surgery (pres. 1983-84, adv. coun. 1989—, sr. examiner 1989—). Intern Toronto East Gen. Hosp., 1954-55; gen. practice medicine Toronto, 1955-56; instr. anatomy U. Toronto; resident in gen. and colon and rectal surgery Mayo Postgrad. Sch. Medicine, Rochester, Minn., 1957-63; gen., colon and rectal surgeon Lockwood Clinic, Toronto, 1963-65; founder and dir. colon and rectal residency program U. Ill. Med. Sch. and Carle Found. Hosp., Urbana, 1974-85; dir. dept. colon and rectal surgery Carle Clinic Assocs., Ill., 1974-85; clin. assoc. Sch. Basic Med. Scis., U. Ill., 1973-77; clin. asst. prof. Coll. Medicine, U. Ill., Urbana-Champaign, 1975-78, clin. assoc. prof., 1978-85; prof. clin. nutrition, dept. food sci. U. Ill., Urbana, 1981-85; practice medicine specializing in colon and rectal surgery Chattanooga, 1985—. Vice chmn. Residency Rev. Bd. in Colon and Rectal Surgery, 1980-82; active Am. Bd. Med. Specialties, 1979-84; mem. interspecialty bd. AMA, Chgo., 1974-80 Assoc. editor Diseases of the Colon and Rectum Jour., 1978—; contbr. chpt. to book, numerous articles to profl. publs.; inventor Thow tube, Colovage operative irrigation tube. Cmty. coord. Urbana conv. Inter-Varsity Christian Fellowship, Ill., 1967-84. Recipient Med. Edn. award Carle Found., 1982 Fellow Royal Coll Surgeons (Can.) (cert. 1963), ACS (credentials com. 1980-82); mem. Priestley Surg. Soc., Mid-West Colon and Rectal Surg. Soc. (pres. 1985-86), Can. Assn. Gen. Surgeons, Am. Bd. of Colon and Rectal Surgery (chmn. exam. com.1980-83, pres. 1983-84, adv. coun. 1989), Soc. Surgery Alimentary Tract, Am. Cancer Soc. (pres. Champaign County unit 1975-77, Ill. Top Ten award 1973-74), United Ostomy Assn. (founding mem. Champaign-Urbana chpt.) Presbyterian. Home: 7142 Revere Cir Concord Highlands Chattanooga TN 37421-1205 Office: Univ Surg Assocs Inc Med Ctr Plz North 979 E 3rd St Ste 300 Chattanooga TN 37403-2187

THOYER, JUDITH REINHARDT, lawyer; b. Mt. Vernon, N.Y., July 29, 1940; d. Edgar Allen and Florence (Mayer) Reinhardt; m. Michael E. Thoyer, June 30, 1963; children: Erinn Thoyer Rhodes, Michael John. AB with honors, U. Mich., 1961; LLB summa cum laude, Columbia U., 1965. Bar: N.Y. 1966, D.C. 1984. Law libr. U. Ghana, Accra, Africa, 1963-64; assoc. Paul, Weiss, Rifkind, Wharton & Garrison, N.Y.C., 1966-75, ptnr., 1975—. Mem. TriBar Opinion Com., 1995—. Bd. visitors Law Sch. Columbia U., N.Y.C., 1991—; bd. dirs. Women's Action Alliance, N.Y.C., 1975-89, pro bono counsel, 1975-97; mem. Women's Coun. Dem. Senatorial, campaign com., 1993-97; organizing com. Alumnae Columbia Law Sch., 1996—. Mem. N.Y. County Lawyers Assn. (mem. securities and exchs. com. 1976-98), Assn. of Bar of City of N.Y. (mem. securities regulation com. 1976-79, mem. recruitment of lawyers com. 1980-82, mem. spl. com. on mergers, acquisitions and corp. control contests 1996—). Home: 1115 5th Ave Apt 3B New York NY 10128-0100 Office: Paul Weiss Rifkind Et Al 1285 Ave of Americas New York NY 10019-6028

THRAILKILL, DANIEL B. lawyer; b. Sept. 21, 1957; BSBA, U. Ark., 1979; JD, Univ. Ark., 1981. Bar: Ark. 1982, Tex. 1988, U.S. Dist. Ct. (eas. and we. dists.) Ark. 1982, U.S. Dist. Ct. (ea. dist.) Okla. 1995, U.S. Ct. Appeals (8th cir.) 1983, U.S. Supreme Ct. 1985. Ptnr. Page, Thrailkill & McDaniel, P.A., Mena, Ark., 1981—. Assoc. prof., lectr. rich Mountain C.C.; assoc. justice Ark. Supreme Ct., 1996—; city atty. Cities of Mena and Hatfield. Mem.: ABA, ATLA, Ark. Trial Lawyers Assn., Ark. Bar Assn. (bd. govs., tenured del.), Lions Club, Phi Alpha Delta. Methodist. Home: 200 Craig St Mena AR 71953-2427 Office: Page Thrailkill & McDaniel 311 DeQueen St Courthouse Sq W Mena AR 71953

THRAILKILL, ROBERT WILLIAM, physician; b. Lakeland, Fla., Oct. 13, 1952; s. Wayne Hochstetler and Dorothy (Stallings) T.; m. Nancy Natalie Chery, June 23, 1979; children: Matthew, Lauren, Allison, Joshua. BS, Duke U., 1974; MD, U. Miami, 1978. Diplomate Am. Bd. Internal Medicine. Physician Orlando (Fla.) Regional Med. Ctr., 1981-91, Meml. Hosp., Modesto, Calif., 1992-94, St. Jospeh's Hosp., Stockton, 1994—. Mem. AMA.

THRALL, ARTHUR ALVIN, artist, educator; b. Milw., Mar. 18, 1926; s. Irving and Helen (Fabich) T.; m. Winifred Rogers, 1960; children: Grant, Wade, Sara, Jay. BS, Milw. State Tchrs. Coll., 1950; MS, U. Wis., Milw., 1954; postgrad. (fellow), U. Ill., 1954-55. Tchr. art Lincoln Jr. High Sch., Kenosha, Wis., 1951-54; asst. prof. SUNY, Geneseo, 1955-56; assoc. prof. Milw.-Downer Coll., 1956-64; prof., Farrar-Marrs prof. fine arts Lawrence U., Appleton, Wis., 1964-90, prof. emeritus, 1990—. One-man shows include Smithsonian Instn., 1960, U. Dubuque, Iowa, 1993, Mt. Mary Coll., Milw., 1994, St. Norbert Coll, De Pere, Wis., 1995, Cardinal Stritch U., Milw., 1998, also others; group shows include Corcoran bienials, Washington, 1951, 53, 55, 57, 62, Bklyn. Mus. annuals, Mus. Modern Art, N.Y.C., NAD, N.Y.C, Audubon Artists, N.Y.C., 1985, S.A.G.A., N.Y.C., 1985, Charles Allis Art Mus., Milw., 1996, Miller Art Ctr., Sturgeon Bay, Wis., 1997, Elvehem Mus. Art, Madison, Wis., 1998, 99, Fairfield Gallery, Sturgeon Bay, Wis., 2001; represented in permanent collections Tate Gallery, Victoria and Alberta Mus., Brit. Mus., all London, Phila. Mus., Seattle Mus., Art Inst. Chgo., Bklyn. Mus., others. Served with U.S. Army, 1944-46, ETO. Recipient Bklyn. Mus. print awards 1952, 64; Pa. Acad. Arts award 1960; NAD awards 1956, 68); Louis Comfort Tiffany fellow, 1963 Mem. AAUP, Boston Printmakers (awards 1963, 65), Soc. Am. Graphic Artists (awards 1951, 52, 60, 78, 2000), Audubon Artists Inc. (award 1977). Home: 4225 N Woodburn St Milwaukee WI 53211-1504

THRALL, EILEEN FOWLER, real estate broker, government staff official; b. Washington, July 20, 1943; d. Edward Earl and Violet Wells (Ashford) Fowler; m. William Anthony Thrall, Feb. 2, 1963; children: James Edward, Jennifer Dianne, John Joseph. AS in Bus. Adminstrn., Am. U., 1964; BSBA, George Mason U., 1985. Cert. real estate broker. Girl Friday property mgmt. rental cashier The Carey Winston, Co., Washington, 1964-65; adminstrv. asst., asst. rental mgr. Reston, Va., Inc., 1965-67; cmty. columnist Potomac News, Woodbridge, Va., 1981-85; realtor, salesperson Old Mill Properties ERA Tatum, Inc., Prince William, 1985-92; realtor, assoc. broker ERA Tatum, Inc., Better Homes Realty, 1992—2002; asst. to chmn. bd., county supr. Prince William County Govt., 1992-99. Bd. dirs. Prince William County Pub. Schs., 1991-92; mem. magisterial dist. chair Prince William County Dem. Com., 1975-2001; mem. steering com. No. Va. C.C. Tech. Consortium, Woodbridge, Va., 1991-98; mem. various offices Dumfries Meth. Ch., 1977—; mem. Bd. Zoning Appeals, 2002-, Prince William. Mem. Nat. Assn. Realtors, Va. Assn. Realtors, Prince William Assn. Realtors. Democrat. Methodist. Avocations: reading, bicycling, boating, camping, cooking. Home: 18312 Possum Point Rd Dumfries VA 22026-2817 Office: Better Homes Realty Inc 16150 Country Club Dr Dumfries VA 22026-1633

THRALL, GORDON FISH, lawyer; b. Jamestown, N.Y., July 28, 1923; s. Clyde Lowell and Beulah Mae (Fish) T.; m. Betty Jane Roberts, Sept. 24, 1964; 1 dau., Jenifer Jane. A.B. in History and Polit. Sci., Alfred U., 1949; J.D., Baylor U., 1953. Bar: Tex. 1953, U.S. Supreme Ct. 1957, D.C. 1958, U.S. Ct. Appeals (D.C. cir.) 1958, U.S. Ct. Mil. Appeals 1958, U.S. Dist. Ct. (ea. dist.) Tex. 1976, U.S. Ct. Appeals (5th cir.) 1986. Law clk. U.S. Dist. Ct. (ea. dist.) Tex., 1953-54; asst. prosecutor Dallas County Dist. Atty., 1954-55; assoc. firm Phinney & Hallman, Dallas, 1955-56; asst. Tex. Atty. Gen., 1957; adviser, examiner ICC, Washington, 1957-59; asst. gen. counsel Tex. State Bar, Austin, 1959-61; county atty. Reagan County, Big Lake, Tex., 1961-72; ptnr. Norman, Thrall, Angle & Guy, L.L.P., Jacksonville, Tex., 1972— . Mem. exec. com. Tex. Baptist Gen. Conv., 1965-70, adminstrv. bd., 1991-95; deacon So. Bapt. Ch.; chmn. Permian Basin dist. Concho Valley council Boy Scouts Am., Big Lake, 1965-66; chmn. Jacksonville United Fund Drive, 1987, pres., 1989; pres. Cherokee County Health Facilities Devel. Corp., 1982—; v.p., bd. dirs. Travis Towers Retirement Facility, Jacksonville, 1980—; co-trustee Summers A. Norman Found., 1988—; mem. Nan Travis Meml. Hosp. Found. Bd., 1994—. Mem. Tex. State Bar, Tex. Bar Found. (vice chmn. UPL com. 1964), Big Lake C. of C. (pres. 1963, 67), Jacksonville C. of C. (pres. 1979), Cherokee Country Club, (dir. 1981-83), Kiwanis (pres. 1978, lt. gov. div. 34 1982), Big Lake Lions (pres. 1969), Masons (32 degree). Republican. Home: 702 Fort Worth St Jacksonville TX 75766-2610 Office: Norman Thrall Angle & Guy LLP 215 E Commerce St Jacksonville TX 75766-4955

THRALL, RICHARD CAMERON, JR. broadcasting executive; b. Delaware, Ohio, Nov. 13, 1929; s. Richard Cameron and Pauline (Taylor) T.; m. Nancy Burrows, June 7, 1952 (div. Jan. 1962); children: Vallerie E. Alm, Cynthia L. Graser; m. Shirley Annette Sturgeon, Oct. 6, 1962; children: Laurie Jo Woodward, James W. Hochberg. BA, Miami U., Oxford, Ohio, 1951. Producer, dir. Sta. WBNS-TV, Columbus, Ohio, 1951-57, Sta. KDKA-TV, Pitts., 1957-59, pub. affairs dir., 1959-63, asst. program dir., 1963-67; program mgr. Sta. WLWC, Columbus, 1967-68; mgr. corp. TV Avco Broadcasting, Cin., 1968-70, mgr. TV programming, 1970-76; v.p. programming Multimedia Broadcasting., 1976-82; sr. v.p. Multimedia Entertainment, 1982-84; sr. v.p., gen. mgr. Multimedia Entertainment of Tenn., Nashville, 1984-88; sr. v.p. ops. and adminstrn. Multimedia Entertainment, N.Y.C., 1988-94, sr. v.p. programming, 1994-96; ret., 1996. Freelance prodr., writer, program cons., 1996—. Writer numerous TV scripts and songs. Served with USN, 1947-48. Recipient Outstanding Country Special award Music City News, Nashville, 1983-87; named to Hon. Order Ky. Cols. Mem. Country Music Assn., NATAS (pres. Columbus/Dayton/Cin. chpt. 1980-83, bd. govs. 1985-87, chmn. nat. awards com. 1989-2002, winner regional Emmys and Emmy cert.). Congregationalist. Avocations: fishing, boating, skiing, travel.

THRAPP, MARK STEPHEN, executive search consultant; b. Cheyenne, Wyo., Dec. 2, 1949; s. Thomas Albert and Zona Beth Thrapp; divorced; 1 child, Jan Lauren. BS in Psychology, Ga. State U., 1973. Personnel mgr. Davison's R.H. Macy & Co., Inc., Atlanta, 1973-74, Marriot Hotels, Chgo., Boston, 1974-76; cons. Roth Young Am., Atlanta, 1976-78; dir. recruitment Federated Dept. Stores, N.Y.C., 1978-81; v.p. search cons. R.H. Macy & Co., Inc., 1981-94; mng. dir. Exec. Search Cons. Internat., 1994-2000, Endeavor Capital, N.Y.C., 1997-2000; dir. nat. recruiting Hay Group, Phila., 2000—02; COO Globalwrap Inc., 2002—. Ptnr. Endeavor Capital Fin. Adv. Firm, N.Y.C., 1997-2000 Avocations: antiques, restoration of Victorian homes. E-mail: mark_thrapp@haygroup.com.

THRASH, JOHN CURTIS, JR. petroleum engineer, executive; b. Harris County, Tex., Feb. 9, 1925; s. John Curtis and Alicia May (Lindsey) T.; m. Patricia Ruth Francis, Dec. 21, 1949; children: Denise S., John F., Allison E. BS in Petroleum Engring., U. Tex., 1947. Registered profl. engr., Tex. Prodn. engr. Tex. Co., Odessa, 1947-50; dist. engr. Forest Oil Corp., Tex., 1950-55, Brit. Am. Oil Co., Dallas, Oklahoma City, 1955-63; cons. profl. engr. Bart De Coat & Assocs., Houston, 1963-65; v.p. Houston Pipe Line Co., 1965-81; pres. Thrash Oil and Gas Co., 1979-90, Togco Gas Storage Corp., Houston, 1985-90, e-Corp and Togco Natural Gas Storage Corp., Houston, 1991—. Contbr. articles to profl. jours. Chmn. Houston chpt. Am. Petroleum Inst., 1975-76. Lt. USNR, 1942-47, 51-54, Korea, World War II. Mem. Am. Petroleum Inst. (chmn. Houston chpt. 1975-76), Tex. Ind. Producers Assn., Ind. Producers Assn. of Am., Soc. Petroleum Engrs. Nat. Soc., Am. Gas Assn., Houston C. of C. (air and water conservation com.). Avocations: flying, golf, tennis. Home: 10105 Longwood Ct Houston TX 77024-5633 Office: eCorp and Togco Natural Gas Storage Corp 3131 W Alabama St Ste 500 Houston TX 77098-2035

THRASH, PATRICIA ANN, educational association administrator; b. Grenada, Miss., May 4, 1929; d. Lewis Edgar and Weaver (Betts) T. BS, Delta State Coll., 1950; MA, Northwestern U., 1953, PhD, 1959; cert. Inst. Edn. Mgmt., Harvard U., 1983; EdD (hon.) , Vincennes U., 1997; DHL, Drake U., 1997, Adrian Coll., 1998. Tchr. high sch. English, Clarksdale, Miss., 1950-52; head resident Northwestern U., 1953-55, asst. to dean women, 1955-58, asst. dean women, 1958-60, lectr. edn., 1959-65, dean women, 1960-69, assoc. prof. edn., 1965-72, assoc. dean students, 1969-71; asst. exec. sec. Commn. on Instns. Higher Edn., North Central Assn. Colls. and Schs., 1972-73, assoc. exec. dir., 1973-76, assoc. dir., 1976-87, exec. dir., 1988-96; exec. dir. emeritus, 1997—. Mem. adv. panel Am. Coun. on Edn., MIVER program evaluation mil. base program, 1991-94; mem. nat. adv. panel Nat. Ctr. Postsecondary Tchg., Learning & Assessment, 1991-95. Author (with others): Handbook of College and University Administration, 1970; editor Jour. Northwestern U. Inst. for Learning in Retirement, 2000-02; contbr. articles to ednl. jours. Bd. dirs. Delta State U. Found., 2000—. Mem. Nat. Assn. Women Deans and Counselors (v.p. 1967-69, pres. 1972-73), Ill. Assn. Women Deans and Counselors (sec. 1961-63, pres. 1964-66), Am. Coll. Pers. Assn. (editl. bd. jour. 1971-74), Coun. Student Pers. Assns. in Higher Edn. (program nominations com. 1974-75, adv. panel Am. Coll. Testing Coll. Outcome Measures project 1977-78, staff Coun. on Postsecondary Accreditation project for evaluation nontraditional edn. 1977-78, mem. editl. bd. Jour. Higher Edn. 1975-80, guest editor Mar.-Apr. 1979, co-editor NCA Quar. 1988-96, vice-chair regional accrediting dirs. group 1993, exec. com. Nat. Policy Bd. for Higher Edn. Inst. 1993-95), Mortar Bd. (hon.), Phi Delta Theta, Pi Lambda Theta, Alpha Psi Omega, Alpha Lambda Delta. Methodist. Home: 2337 Hartrey Ave Evanston IL 60201-2552

THRASHER, DIANNE ELIZABETH, mathematics educator, computer consultant; b. Brockton, Mass., July 11, 1945; m. George Thomas Thrasher, Jan. 28, 1967; children: Kimberly Elizabeth, Noelle Elizabeth. BA in Math., Bridgewater State Coll., 1967, postgrad., 1984-87. Cert. secondary math., history tchr. Tchr. math. Plymouth/Carver Regional Schs., Plymouth, Mass., 1976-78, Alden Sch., Duxbury, 1980-82, Marshfield (Mass.) H.S., 1982-84; computer cons. TC2I-Thrasher Computer Cons. and Instrn., Duxbury, Mass., 1988—; dir., owner Internat. Ednl. Franchise, 1991-95; owner Duxbury Math. Ctr. K-Adult, 1995—. Owner New Eng. Regional Kumon Ednl. Franchise, 1991-95, www.sumizumi.com, 2000—; Mass. State approved profl. point devel. provider for tchr. cert., 1996. Active U.S. Figure Skating Assn., Colorado Springs, 1978-85; 2d reader First Ch. Christ Scientist, Plymouth, 1971-73; bd. govs. Skating Club of Hingham, Mass., 1978-85, pres., 1983-85, dir. Learn to Skate program, 1983-85; mem. First Ch. Christ Scientist, Boston, 1964—; with New Eng. Regional Kumon Franchise Owners, 1991-95; charter mem. Nat. Adv. Coun. of the U.S. Navy Meml. Found., 1992, Mary Baker Eddy Libr. for the Betterment of Humanity, Boston, 2002. Recipient Presdl. Nomination for Excellence in Tng. Math., NSF, 1992, Ed Taylor Meml. Vol. Svc. award Skating Club Hingham, 1995, Amateur Photo award Internat. Libr. Photography, 1999. Mem. NAFE, AAUW, Math. Assn. Am., Nat. Coun. Tchrs. Math, Duxbury Bus. Assn., Bostonian Soc., Nat. Hist. Trust & Preservation Soc., Smithsonian, Internat. Soc. Photographers (Amateur Photo award 1999). Avocations: antiques, bicycling, skating, sailing. Home: 140 Toby Garden St Duxbury MA 02332-4945 E-mail: sumizumi@aol.com.

THRASHER, JACK DWAYNE, toxicologist, researcher, consultant; b. Nashville, Aug. 13, 1936; s. Harold A. and Margaret E. (Bolin) T.; m. Diane L. Walton, June 29, 1963; children: Traci L., Kristen I. BS, Longbeach State U., 1959; PhD, UCLA, 1964. Asst. prof. U. of Colo. Sch. of Medicine, Denver, 1964-66, UCLA Sch. of Medicine, L.A., 1966-72; application specialist Millipore Corp., Bedford, Mass., 1973-75; cons. Thrasher and Assocs., L.A., 1975-92, Alto, N.Mex., 1992-96; mem. faculty E. N. Mex. U., Ruidoso, 1992-97; mentor Columbia Pacific U., San Rafael, Calif., 1992-96. Bd. dirs., chmn. Internat. Inst. Rsch. for Chem. Hypersensitivity, Alto, N. Mex., 1991-94; advisor Chem. Impact Project Mill Valley, Calif., 1993—. Author: (books) Cellular and Molecular Renewal in the Mammalian Body, 1971, The Poisoning of our Homes and Work Places, 1990; editor-in-chief Informed Consent, 1993-94. Grantee: USPHS, NIH, 1966-69. Avocations: golf, fishing, wood working. Home and Office: Sam-1 Trust PO Box 874 110 Raven Court Alto NM 88312 E-mail: sam-1trust@zianet.com.

THRASHER, JOHN, lawyer, former state legislator; b. Columbia, S.C., Dec. 18, 1943; BS, Fla. State U., 1965, JD with honors, 1972. Bar: Fla. Mem. Fla. Ho. of Reps., 1992—2001; co-chmn. rules, resolutions and ethics com.,

1996-97; mem. utilities and comms., edn. appropriations coms., 1996-97; mem. civil justice and claims, ednl. facilities coms., 1996-97; attorney Smith, Hulsey & Busey, 2001—. Chmn. Clay County Del., 1993; mem. com. Rep. Caucus Policy, 1992, 93; v.p. Govtl. Affairs Clay County C. of C., 1989, 91, 92; mem. sch. bd. Clay County, 1986-90, chmn. 1989-90, vice chmn., 1988; mem. adv. bd. Children's Haven, Quigley House, 1993-94; bd. dirs. Clay Police Athletic League, Clay YMCA. Capt. U.S. Army, 1966-70, Germany, Vietnam. Decorated Bronze Star with oak leaf cluster; recipient Raymond B. Stewart Gavel of Authority award, Fla. Assn. Sch. Adminstrs., 1994; named 1st term Legislator of Yr., Fla. Sch. Bd. Assn., 1993, Ho. of Reps. Legislator of Yr., 1994. Republican. Presbyterian. Avocations: golf, basketball. Office: Smith, Hulsey & Busey 225 Water St, Ste 1800 Jacksonville FL 32202*

THRASHER, ROSE MARIE, critical care and community health nurse; b. Urbana, Ohio, Jan. 19, 1948; d. Jesse and Anna Frances (Clark) T. Student, Mercy Med. Ctr. Sch. Med. Tech, Springfield, Ohio, 1966-67, Wittenberg U., 1969-70; BSN, Ohio State U., 1974, BA anthropology, 1994, BA art history, 1997, BA geography, 2002. RN, Ohio; bd. cert. cmty. health nurse ANA; bd. cert. provider BCLS and ACLS, Am. Heart Assn., CCRN, AACN; cert. asthma mgmt. edn. Am. Lung Assn. Ohio. Pub. health nurse Columbus (Ohio) Health Dept., 1977-78; critical care nurse VA Med. Ctr., San Francisco, 1981, Staff Builders Health Care Svc., Oakland, 1975-76, 81-85; supr., case mgr., home health nurse, passport program and intermittent care program Interim Health Care (formerly Med. Pers. Pool), Columbus, 1976-77, 85—, chart reviewer, 1996-98; IRP nurse Ohio State U. Hosps. East, 1999—; ind. home health nurse, provider med. svcs. State of Ohio Dept. Human Svcs., 1999—. Chart reviewer Interim Health Care Support Svcs., Columbus, 1997. Acad. scholar Wittenberg U., Ohio State U. Mem. AACN, ANA (coun. cmty. health nursing), AAUW, AAAS, Internat. Union Anthropl. and Ethnol. Scis., N.Y. Acad. Scis., Ohio Nurses Assn., Intravenous Nurses Soc., Ohio State U. Alumni Assn., Am. Anthropol. Assn., Midwest Art History Soc., Coll. Art Assn., Nat. Mus. Women in Arts, Nat. Women's Hall of Fame, Ohio Acad. Sci., Ohio State U. Coll. of Nursing Alumni Soc. E-mail: thrasher.2@osu.edu.

THRASHER-LIVINGSTON, KARA SCOTT, program director; b. Richmond, Va., Dec. 30, 1964; d. James Winfield and Janet Marie (Geldard) Thrasher; m. Clifford Joseph Livingston, Aug. 8, 1988; children: Wolfgang Clifford, Thor Maximus. BA, Rutgers, 1986. Mgr. The Futon Shop, Emeryville, Calif., 1990-93; arts cons. Blaine's Art and Graphic Supply, Anchorage, 1993-95; tech. asst. Sheila Wyne, Sculptor, 1995-96; art program dir. The Arc of Anchorage, 1996, cmty. inclusion program dir., 1996—. Mem. Grandview Gardens Curatoral Com., Anchorage, 1995-96; art educator Very Spl. Arts Alaska, Anchorage, 1996, Artists in Schs., Anchorage, 1996—; mem. jury for Pub. Art Program, 1998. One-person shows include Harmonics, 1995; writer, musician Parallax 1, 1995—, (stage performance) Trial By Fire, 1997, Archeo/logic, 1998. Graphics cons. Dem. Party, Anchorage, 1994; vol. art educator The Arc of Anchorage, 1995, exhibit cons. The Arc of Anchorage, 1996. Democrat. Avocations: jewelry making, sewing, photography, film making, painting. Office: The Arc of Anchorage 2211 Arca Dr Anchorage AK 99508-3475 E-mail: kthrasher-livingston@arc-anchorage.org.

THREADCRAFT, JOSEPH LEE, civil engineer; b. Morgan, Ga., Jan. 22, 1961; s. Nursey Lee and Florence (Brackins) T.; m. Angeline Thomas, Jan. 10, 1983 (div. Nov. 1994); 1 child, Joseph Lee; m. Sharon McKinney, Aug. 15, 1997; 1 child, Alexis Leanne. BS in Civil Engring. Tech., Fla. A&M U., 1990; MBA, Albany (Ga.) State U., 1998. Engr., estimator D.L. Kirby Inc., Miami, Fla., 1995; civil engring. technician Ga. Dept. Transp., Macon, 1995; asst. city engr. City of College Park, Ga., 1996-97; engr. City of Albany, 1994-96, sr. engr., 1997—; pres., mng. dir. JSE, LLC, Albany, 1998-2000. Mem. ASCE (sec. 1989, pres. 1990), Delta Mu Delta.

THREATT, ROBIN MICHELLE, pharmaceutical executive; b. Omaha, July 1, 1970; d. Edward Dewayne and Wanda Faye T.; 1 child, Guyon D. Shipman. BS, U. Wis., 1993; MS, 1995. Profl. sales rep. DuPont Agrl. Products, Madison, Wis., 1995—98; cardiovasc. specialist DuPont Pharms., Indpls., 1998—; basketball player Seattle Storm, 2000—01; advanced therapeutic sales specialist Aventis Pharms., Indpls., 2002—. Mem. Delta Sigma Theta. E-mail: rchelles@hotmail.com.

THREATTE, GREGORY ALLEN, pathology educator, academic director; b. Smithdale, Pa., Aug. 28, 1947; s. James Hylton T. and Thelma Elizabeth (Wilson) Youngblood; m. Stephanie Ruth Mills, May 13, 1948; children: Leah Ruth, Renee Ruth, Lonnie Taylor. BA, Colgate U., 1969; MD, SUNY, Upstate, 1973. Diplomate Am. Bd. Pathology. Intern U. Hosp., Syracuse, N.Y., 1973-74; resident in anatomic pathology W. Penn Hosp., Pitts., 1974-76; resident in clin. pathology U. Calif., San Francisco, 1976-78; fellow Lawrence Berkeley Lab, Berkeley, Calif., 1978-81; asst. prof. Georgetown U., Washington, 1981-86; assoc. prof. pathology SUNY Upstate Med. U., Syracuse, 1986-98, prof. pathology, 1998—, interim chmn., 2001—. Contbr. chpt. to book. Trustee Univ. United Meth. Ch., Syracuse, N.Y., 1990-98, Syracuse Urban League, 1990-95, Colgate U., 1993-2002. Recipient Pres. award Affirmative Action, 1992, Excellence in Tchg. award, 1998. Mem. Am. Assn. Clin. Chemistry, Am. Soc. Hematology, Coll. Am. Pathologists, Assn. Academic Minority Profs. Methodist. Avocations: skiing, golf. Office: SUNY Upstate Med U 750 E Adams St Syracuse NY 13210-2306 E-mail: threatte@upstate.edu.

THREEFOOT, SAM ABRAHAM, physician, educator; b. Meridian, Miss., Apr. 10, 1921; s. Sam Abraham and Ruth Frances (Lilienthal) T.; m. Virginia Rush, Feb. 6, 1954; children: Barbara Jane Stockton Mattingly, Ginny Ruth Threefoot Lindberg, Tracyann Threefoot Esenstad, Shelley Ann Threefoot Cowan. BS, Tulane U., 1943, MD, 1945. Diplomate: Am. Bd. Internal Medicine. Intern Michael Reese Hosp., Chgo., 1945-47; asst. vis. physician Charity Hosp. New Orleans, 1947-50, vis. physician, 1950-57, sr. vis. physician, 1957-69, cons., 1969-70, 76-91; clin. asst. dept. medicine Touro Infirmary, New Orleans, 1953-56, jr. asst., 1956-60, sr. asst., 1960-63, dir. med. edn., 1953-63, dir. research, 1953-70, sr. dept. medicine, 1963-70; fellow dept. medicine Tulane U., 1947-49, instr., 1948-53, asst. prof., 1953-59, asso. prof., 1959-63, prof., 1963-70, 76-91, prof. emeritus, 1991—, asst. dean, 1979-91, adj. prof. emeritus Sch. Pub. Health & Tropical Medicine, 1993—; chief of staff VA Hosp. (Forest Hills div.), Augusta, Ga., 1970-76; assoc. chief staff VA Hosp., New Orleans, 1976-79, chief of staff, 1979-91, cons., 1991—; asst. dean Med. Coll. Ga., 1970-76, prof. medicine, 1970-76. Cons. physician Lallie Kemp Charity Hosp., Independence, La., 1951-53 Editor: Lymphology, 1967-70; Contbr. articles profl. jours. Served with AUS, 1943-45. La. Heart Assn. grantee, 1953-55; John A. Hartford Found. grantee, 1956-74; Am. Heart Assn. grantee, 1959-61; USPHS grantee, 1953-66 Fellow A.C.P., Am. Coll. Cardiology, N.Y. Acad. Sci.; mem. Am. Heart Assn. (v.p. 1970, fellow council on circulation), Central Soc. Clin. Research, So. Soc. Clin. Investigation (pres. 1967), AAAS, Internat. Soc. Lymphology, Soc. Exptl. Biology and Medicine, Soc. Nuclear Medicine, Microcirculatory Conf., Inc., Am. Fedn. Clin. Research, La. Heart Assn. (pres. 1967), Nat. Assn. VA Chiefs of Staff (pres. 1987-88), Phi Beta Kappa, Sigma Xi. Jewish. Home: Apt 302 1750 St Charles Ave New Orleans LA 70130 E-mail: s3fta@tulane.edu. *I am one of those fortunate individuals who has been able to approach goals set early in life. Although my achievements are far short of my aspirations, at least I have had the opportunity. In dealing with both people and things, I have always felt that no detail was too small to receive attention.*

THREET, JACK CURTIS, oil company executive; b. Dundas, Ill., Aug. 16, 1928; s. Ivy Clemon and Daryl (Curtis) T.; m. Catherine Irene Hall, Mar. 24, 1951; children— Linda Sue, Judith Ann. BA in Geology, U. Ill., 1951. Geologist, dist. geologist, div. exploration mgr., area exploration mgr. Shell Oil Co., various locations including Oklahoma City, Amarillo, Tex., Denver, Pitts., Lafayette, La., Billings, Mont., N.Y.C., L.A., 1951-69; gen. mgr. exploration and prodn. Shell Australia Ltd., Melbourne, 1969-71; v.p. exploration and prodn. Shell Can., Calgary, Alta., 1972-74, Shell Oil Co., New Orleans, 1974-75; v.p. internat. exploration and prodn. Houston, 1975-78, corp. v.p. exploration, 1978-87, ret., 1987; v.p., dir., co-founder Energy Exploration Mgmt. Co., Houston, 1989-92; pres., owner Threet Energy, Inc., 1989—, Threet, Inc., Houston, 1995—. Served with U.S. Army, 1953-55. Mem. Am. Assn. Petroleum Geologists, Lakeside Country Club (Houston), Rotary. Republican. Methodist.

THRELKEL, ROBERT HAYS, pediatrician; b. Beaver Dam, Ky., June 20, 1940; s. Frank Hays and Kathryn Taylor (Bentley) T.; m. Mireille Clivas Smith, May 24, 1995. BA magna cum laude, Vanderbilt U., 1962; MD, Duke U., 1966. Diplomate Am. Bd. Pediatrics. Physician/officer U.S. Army, 1964-71; intern in pediatrics Vanderbilt U. Hosp., Nashville, 1966-67, chief resident in pediatrics, 1968-69; ptnr. Carithers, Threlkel et al., Jacksonville, Fla., 1971—; trustee Wolfson Childrens Hosp., 1997—. Chief of staff Wolfson's Children's Hosp., Jacksonville, 1991-92. Maj. U.S. Army, 1969-71. Mem. Am. Bd. Pediatrics (ofcl. examiner 1987-93), Am. Acad. Pediatrics (alt. dist. chmn. 1989-94, Fla. chpt. chmn. 1981-85), Duval County Med. Soc. (pres. 1984), Phi Beta Kappa, Alpha Omega Alpha. Office: Drs Carithers Threlkel PA 2121 Park St Jacksonville FL 32204-3811

THRELKELD, LOIS ELAINE ISENSEE, process management specialist; b. St. Louis, June 11, 1947; d. Fred John and Vera Marie (Laumann) Isensee; m. H. Ray Threlkeld Jr., Sept. 6, 1969; children: Thomas Justin, Christopher Ray. AB in Chemistry, U. Mo., 1969; BSCE, U. Tenn., Knoxville, 1977, MS in Indsl. Engring., 1994. Registered profl. engr., Tenn.; cert. project mgmt. profl. Civil engr. TVA, Knoxville, 1977-86, project mgr., 1986-88, engring. specialist, 1989-90, project control mgr. Watts Bar Nuclear Plant Spring City, 1990-93, quality mgr. Knoxville, 1994-95, bus. ops. mgr., 1995-96, process mgmt. specialist Norris, Tenn., 1997—98, performance team leader Knoxville, 1998—2001, bus. process analysis mgr., 2001—. Recipient Woman of Distinction award, TVA, 2002. Mem.: ASCE, Project Mgmt. Inst. (pres. 2000—). Episcopalian. Home: 518 Tanasi Cir Loudon TN 37774-3126 Office: TVA 400 W Summit Hill Ave Knoxville TN 37902

THRELKELD, MARY HELEN, accountant; b. East St. Louis, June 8, 1960; d. James John and Charlette Ann (Mongan) T. BBA, Tex. Christian U., 1982; MBA, U. Chgo., 1990. CPA. Software analyst Tandy Corp./Radio Shack, Ft. Worth, 1981-84; cons. supr. Coopers & Lybrand, Austin, Tex., 1985-88; cons. mgr. Coopers & Lybrand Europe, Brussels, Belgium, 1990-92; strategic analyst Software Spectrum, Inc., Garland, Tex., 1993-94, internat. acct., 1994—. Avocations: travel, reading, music. Office: Software Spectrum 2140 Merritt Dr Garland TX 75041-6184

THRELKELD, RICHARD DAVIS, broadcast journalist; b. Cedar Rapids, Iowa, Nov. 30, 1937; s. Robert M. and Lou Jane (Davis) T.; m. Sharon A. Adams, June 11, 1960 (div. 1983); children: Susan Anne, Julia Lynn; m. Betsy Aaron, May 15, 1983. BA, Ripon Coll., 1959; MS in Journalism, Northwestern U., 1961; LHD (hon.), Ripon Coll., 1989. Editor Sta. WHAS-TV, Louisville, 1961; reporter Sta. WMT-TV, Cedar Rapids, Iowa, 1961-66; corr. CBS News, N.Y.C. and San Francisco, 1966-82, nat. corr., 1989-96; chief corr. ABC News N.Y., N.Y.C., 1982-89; Moscow corr. CBS News, 1996-98, ret., 1998. Author: Dispatches From the Former Evil Empire, 2001; corr.: TV news documentary Defense of America, 1981 (Emmy award); TV news report Rhodesia Remembered, 1980 (Overseas Press Club award), TV news report Vietnam Remembered, 1985 (Emmy award), TV news series Status Reports, 1984 (Dupont award), TV new report Lebanon-Grenada 1983 (Overseas Press Club award). CBS News fellow, 1964 Mem. AFTRA, Sigma Delta Chi

THRELKELD, STEVEN WAYNE, civil/environmental engineer; b. La Jolla, Calif., Feb. 22, 1956; s. Willard Wayne and Sylvia Eileen (Daugherety) T.; m. Sheree Leslie Chabot, Nov. 17, 1984; children: Tristan David, Kayla Lee. BS in Geol. Scis., San Diego State U., 1985. Geophys. trainee Western Geophys., Bakersfield, Calif., 1985; civil engr. Dee Jaspar & Assocs., 1986, Bement, Dainwood & Sturgeon, Lemon Grove, Calif., 1987, Calif. Dept. Transp., San Diego, 1988—. Comml. scuba diver, San Diego, 1987-88. Photo editor Montezuma Life Mag., San Diego, 1981; portrait photographer Coast Prodns., San Diego, 1975. Mem. Profl. Engrs. in Calif. Govt. (San Diego chpt.), Union Concerned Scientists, Concord Coalition, Inst. Noetic Sciences, Nat. Resources Def. Coun., Planning and Conservation League. Avocations: traveling, writing, scuba diving, hiking, photography. Home: 4262 Bancroft Dr La Mesa CA 91941-6744

THRIFT, ASHLEY ORMAND, lawyer; b. Charlotte, N.C., Aug. 29, 1946; s. William Johnson Thrift Sr. and Katherine Roberta Ormand; m. Julianne Fickling Still, Aug. 3, 1974; children: Lindsay Still Thrift, Laura Still Thrift. AB in History, U. N.C., 1968; JD, U. S.C., 1972. Acting dean campus rels. U. S.C., Columbia, 1971-72, asst. dean Law Sch., 1972-74, assoc. counsel, 1974-75; legis. counsel Rep. James R. Mann U.S. Ho. of Reps., Washington, 1976-77, assoc. counsel subcom. on criminal justice judiciary com., 1977; legis. dir., counsel Senator Ernest F. Hollings U.S. Senate, 1977-84, chief of staff, counsel Senator Ernest F. Hollings, 1984-92; of counsel Womble Carlyle Sandridge & Rice PLLC, Winston-Salem, N.C., 1992-94, ptnr., 1994—. Advisor Clinton-Gore Com. on Transition, 1992-93; bd. visitors Winston-Salem State U., 1995—; chair bd. dirs. N.C. Partnership for Children, Raleigh, N.C., 1995—; vice-chair bd. trustees U. N.C. Ctr. for Pub. TV, Research Triangle Park, N.C., 1995-00, chair, 2000—; bd. dirs. Assn. Ams. Pub. TV Stas., 2000—; chair govt. affairs com. Lex Mundi, 1999—. With USAR, 1968-74. Recipient Holderness-Weaver award, U. N.C.-Greensboro, 2000, The Order of the Long Leaf Pine, 2000, 2001, James and Carolyn Hunt award, Child Care Assn. N.C., Humanitarian award, N.C. Assn. Black Elected Ofcls., 2001, Champion for Children award, N.C. Partnership for Children, 2002. Mem. Soc. Internat. Bus. Fellows. Democrat. Presbyterian. Home: 723 S Main St Winston Salem NC 27101-5330 Office: Womble Carlyle Sandridge & Rice PLLC 200 W 2nd St Ste 1600 Winston Salem NC 27101-4048 E-mail: athrift@wcsr.com.

THRIFT, JULIANNE STILL, academic administrator; b. Barnwell, S.C. m. Ashley Ormand Thrift; children: Lindsay, Laura. BA, MEd, U. S.C.; PhD in Pub. Policy, George Washington U. Formerly asst. exec. dir. Nat. Assn. Coll. and Univ. Attys.; ombudsman U. S.C.; exec. dir. Nat. Inst. Ind. Colls. and Univs., 1982-88; exec. v.p. Nat. Assn. Ind. Colls. and Univs., Washington, 1988-91; pres. Salem Acad. and Coll., Winston-Salem, N.C., 1991—. Office: Salem Coll Office of the President Winston Salem NC 27108-0548

THRO, WILLIAM EUGENE, lawyer, university administrator; b. Elizabethtown, Ky., Nov. 8, 1963; s. Ernest Guernsey and Joan (Young) T.; m. Mary Ellen Edwards, Dec. 30, 1989; children: Sandra Lucinda Grace Edwards-Thro, William Thomas Daniel Edwards-Thro, Noah Christopher James Edwards-Thro. BA, Hanover Coll., 1986; MA, U. Melbourne, Australia, 1988; JD, U. Va., 1990. Bar: Ky. 1990, Colo. 1991, Va. 1998, U.S. Dist. Ct. (we. dist.) Ky. 1990, U.S. Dist. Ct. Colo. 1991, U.S. Ct. Appeals (6th and 10th cirs.) 1991, U.S. Ct. Appeals (3d cir.) 1993, U.S. Supreme Ct. 1993, U.S. Ct. Appeals (4th cir.) 1997, U.S. Dist. Ct. (ea. dist.) Va. 1998, U.S. Dist. Ct. (we. dist.) Va. 1998, U.S. Ct. Appeals (D.C. cir.) 1999, U.S. Bankruptcy Ct. (ea. and we. dists.) Va. 1999. Jud. clk. Judge Ronald E. Meredith, U.S. Dist. Ct. (we. dist.) Ky., Louisville, 1990-91; asst. atty. gen. State of Colo., Denver, 1991-97, Commonwealth of Va., Richmond, 1997-99; gen. counsel Christopher Newport U., Newport News, Va., 2000—; dept. state solicitor Commonwealth Va., 2002—. Mem. authors' com. West's Edn. Law Reporter, St. Paul, 1992—. Author: Why You Cannot Sue State U: A Guide to Sovereign Immunity, 2001; mem. editl. bd., Jour. Coll. and Univ. Law, 2000—; contbr. articles to scholarly jours. Mem. gen. counsel adv. bd. NCAA. U.S. Senate Youth scholar Hearst Found., 1982; Harry S Truman scholar Truman Scholarship Found., 1984, Rotary Internat. Ambassadorial scholar, Melbourne, 1987. Mem. Ky. Bar Assn., Nat. Assn. Coll. and Univ. Attys., Federalist Soc., Nat. Eagle Scout Assn., Inst. for Justice, Human Human Action Network, Honorable Order of Ky. Cols, Rotary Club Oyster Point (Va.). Republican. Home: 615 St Michaels Way Newport News VA 23606 Office: Christopher Newport U 1 University Pl Newport News VA 23606 E-mail: wthro@cnu.edu.

THROCKMORTON, JOAN HELEN, direct marketing consultant; b. Evanston, Ill., Apr. 11, 1931; d. Sydney L. and Anita H. (Pusheck) T.; m. Sheldon Burton Satin, June 26, 1982 (dec. Feb. 2002). BA with honors, Smith Coll., 1953. Mktg. exec. Lawrence Chait & Co., N.Y.C., 1965; mktg. exec. Cowles Communications, Inc., 1968-69; founder, chief exec. officer Throckmorton Assocs., Inc., 1970-83; pres. Joan Throckmorton, Inc., Pound Ridge, N.Y., 1983—. Lectr. in field; instr. Direct Mktg. Assn., Sch. Continuing Edn., NYU, N.Y.C., 1985; mem. corp. Culinary Inst. Am., 2000. Author: Winning Direct Response Advertising, 1986, 2d edit., 1996. Trustee Halle Ravine Com. Nature Conservancy, 2001; mem. expedition com. Outward Bound, 1980-83. Recipient Edward N. Mayer Jr. award, Direct Mktg. Edn. Found., 1996, Andi Emerson award John Caples Internat. Awards, Inc., 1996, E.F. Sisk award for vision Direct Mktg. Assn. Washington, 2001; named Direct Mktg. Women of the Yr., 1986; named to Direct Mktg. Assn.'s Hall of Fame, 1997. Mem. Women's Dir. Response Group (founding mem.), Dir. Mktg. Assn. (bd. dirs. 1971-77, exec. com. 1972-77, mem. long-range planning com. 1977-78), Women's Forum, Dir. Mktg. Idea Exchange, Dir. Mktg. Creative Guild (bd. dirs. 1984-85), Jr. League Mexico City, Jr. League N.Y.C., Phi Beta Kappa. Office: Joan Throckmorton Inc PO Box 452 Pound Ridge NY 10576-0452

THROCKMORTON, PETER EUGENE, retired organic chemist, consultant; b. St. Paul, Jan. 20, 1927; s. James and Carla Margaret (Strim) T.; m. Phyllis Marie McGrew, June 30, 1948; children: Ann Marie, Carla Louise, Peter Eugene Jr. BSChemE, U. Minn., 1948, MS in Chemistry, 1955; PhD in Organic Chemistry, Kansas State U., 1960. Rsch. engr. Tainton Products Co., Balt., 1948-49; mfg. rsch. engr. Glenn L. Martin Aircraft Co., Middle River, Md., 1949-52; rsch. chemist Gen. Mills Rsch., Inc., Mpls., 1952-56; petroleum fellow Petroleum Rsch. Inst. Kans. State U., Manhattan, 1957-58; assoc. chemist Midwest Rsch. Inst., Kansas City, Mo., 1960-65; sr. rsch. chemist Archer-Daniels-Midland Co., Mpls., 1965-67; sr. rsch. chemist II Ashland Chem. Co. (formerly Archer-Daniels-Midland Co.), Columbus, Ohio, 1967-86; prin. Throckmorton Cons., Plain City, 1986-95; cons. Teltech, Inc., Mpls., 1991-96. Assoc. chmn. 15th Ann. Kansas City Chemistry Conf., 1963; mem. People's Republic China-U.S. Sci. Exchange Program, Beijing and Shanghai, 1984. Contbr. over 27 articles to profl. jours. including Modern Plastics, Jour. Am. Chem. Soc., Jour. Elastoplastics, Jour. Am. Oil Chemists Soc., Inorganica Chimica Acta. Recipient Best Paper award Reinforced Plastics Div. of Soc. Plastics Industry, 1963. Fellow Am. Inst. Chemists (bd. dirs. 1987-89); mem. AAAS, Am. Chem. Soc. (chmn. tech. program Columbus sect. 1979-80), Am. Oil Chemists Soc. (editl. reviewer 1986-91), Sigma Xi, Phi Lambda Upsilon. Democrat. Achievements include 17 patents, including patent for trimethylene sulfide chemical derivative that when chemically reacted into a well-known plastic provided a substance highly resistant to deterioration by strong radiation, such as gamma rays; derivation of new, effective, very biodegradable surfactants from cornstarch and a fatty substance; novel, highly effective palladium-lead acetate complex oxidation catalyst for aromatics; new blend of melamine and polyol chemicals for fire retardant plastic. Home: 114 Colchester Drive Normal IL 61761-2775

THROCKMORTON, SPENCER S., III, art dealer; b. Halifax, Va., Oct. 29, 1948; s. Spencer S. Throckmorton II and Lila Ruth Petty. BFA, Va. Commonwealth U., 1972. Pres. Throckmorton Fine Art Inc., N.Y.C., 1980—. (editor, pub.): (rsch. exhbn.) Enduring Art of Jace Age China, 2001. Named to Ams. Elite 1000, London, 2000, 2001. Mem.: ADATA, AOPA, NAOD, Antique Tribal Art Dealers Assn. Inc., Nat. Assn. Dealer in Ancient Oriental Art. Office: Throckmorton Fine Art 153 E 61st St Fl4 New York NY 10021-8123

THRODAHL, MARK CRANDALL, medical technology company executive; b. Charleston, W.Va., Mar. 31, 1951; s. Monte Cordon and Josephine (Crandall) T.; m. Sudie Kenton, Oct. 21, 1978; children: Mary Elizabeth, Anne Katherine, Andrew Kenton. AB, Princeton U., 1973; MBA, Harvard U., Boston, 1975. Various positions Mallinckrodt, Inc., St. Louis, 1975-88; dir. corp. planning Becton Dickinson & Co., Franklin Lakes, N.J., 1988-91, pres. Nippon Becton Dickinson, Tokyo, 1991-94, sector pres. Franklin Lakes, 1994-95, sr. v.p., 1995-2001; CEO Bespak Plc, London, 2001—. Mem. Old Warson Country Club, Ivy Club. Republican. Episcopalian. Home: 38 Carteret Rd Allendale NJ 07401-1850 Office: Bespak Plc 4 Stanhope Gate London W1K 1AQ England

THROESCH, DAVID, lawyer; b. Pocahontas, Ark., Feb. 24, 1951; s. Roy and Kathleen Throesch; m. Leslie Throesch; children: Melodie, Amber. BA, Ark. State U., Jonesboro, 1973; JD, U. Ark., 1975. Bar: Ark. 1975. Pvt. practice, Pocahontas and Randolph, Ark., 1976—; pros. atty. Pocahontas and Randolph County, 1979—. Mem. Ark. Trial Lawyers Assn. (adminstrv. law chair). Democrat. Roman Catholic. Avocation: coin collection. Home: 3722 Pyburn Ext Pocahontas AR 72455-1347 Office: PO Box 463 Pocahontas AR 72455-0463

THROGMARTIN, DIANNE, educational foundation executive; b. Indpls., May 3, 1964; d. Roy Don and Suzzane (Jackson) T. Cert., Landmark Coll., 1988, Motivation Inst., 1991; BS in Edn., Butler U., 1992; cert., Fund Raising Sch., Indpls., 1992-93. Product mgr. H.H. Gregg, Indpls., 1982-85, salesperson, trainer, 1988-90; substitute tchr. Camp Delafield Lakeview Temple, 1990-91; gen. asst. Robo Group Internat., 1992-93, Indpls. Jaycees, 1993-94; pres., founder Dyslexia Ednl. Found. Am., Indpls., 1994—. Pres. bd. Ind. Hugh O'Brian Youth Found., Indpls., 1992-95, Leadership America, 1996. Recipient Cmty. Svc. award Landmark Coll., 1988, 87. Mem. Jaycees (dir. Indpls. chpt. 1993-95, Mem. of Month 1992, Outstanding Com. chmn. 1993, 94, Dir. of Month 1993, Dir. of Yr. 1994, Mgmt. Devel. award 1994), Indpls. C. of C. Republican. Avocations: movies, cooking, spending time in the country, camping, walking. Home: 3100 N Ocean Blvd Apt 309 Fort Lauderdale FL 33308-7188 Office: Dyslexia Ednl Found Am 4181 E 96th St Ste 120 Indianapolis IN 46240-3814

THRONDSON, EDWARD WARNER, residential association administrator; b. Woodland, Calif., May 22, 1938; s. Edward J. and Arden Warner (Law) T.; m. Marjorie Jean Waite, June 25, 1960 (div. 1993); children: Mark Edward, Kimberly Anne, Sulin Marget; m. Mary Jo Riddell Law, Jan. 13, 1994. BS, Stanford U., 1960; MBA, Harvard U., 1962. Profl. Community Assn. Mgr., Community Assn. Inst. Asst. br. mgr. Pacific Delta Gas, Santa Rosa, Calif., 1962-65, corp. staff asst. San Jose, 1965-72; regional mgr. Pargas, 1972-86; gen. mgr., COO The Villages Golf and Country Club, 1986-93; sr. v.p. West Coast Community Assocs., Campbell, Calif., 1994-95; assn. mgr. Cmty. Assns. Consulting, Napa, 1996-97, Oakmont Village Assn., Santa Rosa, 1997—. Mem. Cmty. Assns. Inst. (com. chair 1991—, Pres.'s Appreciation award 1991), Calif. Assn. Cmty. Mgrs. (cert., founding mem., com. chair 1992—, author course 1992, 94, 96). Avocations: golf, stamp collecting, geneology.

THRONER, GUY CHARLES, JR. engineering executive, scientist, engineer, inventor, consultant; b. Mpls., Sept. 14, 1919; s. Guy Charles and Marie (Zechar) T.; m. Jean Holt, Dec. 5, 1943; children— Richard, Carol Anne, Steven BA, Oberlin Coll., 1943; postgrad., UCLA, 1960, 61. Registered profl. engr., Calif. Br. head Naval Weapon Ctr., China Lake, Calif., 1946-53; mgr. ordnance div., mgr. weapon systems div. Aerojet Gen. Corp., Azusa, 1953-64; v.p., div. mgr. FMC Corp., San Jose, 1964-74; research dir. Vacu Blast Corp., Belmont, 1976-78; v.p., devel. mfg. Dahlman, Inc., Braham, Minn., 1978-79; mgr. ordnance systems & tech. Battelle Meml. Inst., Columbus, Ohio, 1979-85; pres. Guy C. Throner & Assocs., tech. and mgmt. cons., 1985—. Dir. Omron Corp. Am., Chgo., 1976-77 Inventor, patentee indls., med. and mil. systems design Served as officer USNR, World War II Recipient Am. Order St. Barbara medal U.S. Army Arty, 1983, IR-100 award Indsl. Research Mag., Chgo., 1971, Congl. Commendation, 1985, Commendation, State of Ohio Ho. of Reps., 1995, also various commendations Mem. AIAA, Am. Def. Preparedness Assn. (Bronze medal 1974, Simon Silver medal 1985), Lake Wildwood Country Club, Sigma Xi. Republican. Avocations: astronomy, photography, golf. Home and Office: 17992 Jayhawk Dr Penn Valley CA 95946-9205 E-mail: guytlww@nccn.net.

THRUSH, THOMAS CLARK, lawyer; b. Kansas City, Mo., Nov. 18, 1948; s. Roy Thrush and Margaret Clark; m. Elizabeth A. Prescott, Sept. 7, 1984; children: Christopher, Ryan. AA, Foothill Coll., Los Altos, Calif., 1968; BA, Calif. State U., San Francisco, 1970; JD, U. Denver, 1976. Pvt. practice, Denver, 1976—. Nat. ski patrol mem., Denver, 1972—. Mem. Cherry Creek Gun Club (pres. 1996-98). Office: 1750 Gilpin St Denver CO 80218-1206

THUAN, TRINH XUAN, astrophysicist, educator; b. Hanoi, Vietnam, Aug. 20, 1948; arrived in U.S., 1967; s. Trinh Xuan Ngan and Le Thi Nghia. BS in Physics, Calif. Inst. Tech., 1970; PhD, Princeton U., 1974. Postdoctoral fellow Calif. Inst. Tech., Pasadena, 1974—76; prof. astronomy U. Va., Charlottesville, 1976—, U. Paris, 1993—94, 1999—2000. Bd. advisors John Templeton Found., Radnor, Pa., 2002—; mem. UNESCO Coun. on the Future, Paris, 1999—. Author: The Birth of the Universe, 1993, The Secret Melody, 1994, Chaos and Harmony, 2000, The Quantum and the Lotus, 2001; contbr. numerous articles to profl. jours. Recipient Asia Lit. prize, French Writers Assn., 2000; scholar, Fulbright Found., 1987—88. Mem.: Internat. Astron.

Union, Am. Astron. Soc. (Henri Chretien award 1992). Avocations: tennis, swimming. Office: U Va Dept Astronomy PO Box 3818 University Sta Charlottesville VA 22903 Fax: 434-925-3104. E-mail: txt@virginia.edu.

THUEME, WILLIAM HAROLD, educator; b. St. Clair, Mich., Sept. 4, 1945; s. Harold Arthur and Delphine Betty (Buhl) Thueme; m. Katheen Koning, May 8, 1971 (div.); children: Benjamin William, Rebecca Kathleen, Jeffery William, Sarah Kathleen. Student, Port Huron Jr. Coll., 1963-64; BA, Mich. State U., 1967, MA, 1969; PhD in Counseling, Universal Life Ch., 1997; postgrad., Oakland U., 1971, U. Mich., 1970-77, San Francisco State U., 1975, U. Hawaii, 1975; student, Spring Arbor Coll., 1968; PhD in Motivation, Progressive Universal Life Ch., 1997. Cert. tchr., Mich. Ordained min. Universal Life Ch. Tchr. pub. schs., Charlotte, Mich., 1967-69, Ann Arbor, 1969—. Fgn. travel coord.-Ambs. Abroad Program, Amsterdam, The Netherlands, 1968—; regional driver coord. for Southeastern Mich. Avis Rent-a-Car, 1983—. Author: (poetry) The Ideal Teacher Should Posess, 1987. Active UN Children's Found., Mich. Sheriffs Ednl. Found., Woods Rd. Assn., Normal Pk. Neighborhood Assn., U.S. Legal Found., Found. for Nicaraguan Democracy, Nat. Coun. Better Edn., participant Skyhook II Project; elections coord. Eaton County (Mich.) Rep. Party, 1968, mem. nat. com., 1968—, mem. nat. senatorial com.; mem. troop com. Coun. Boy Scouts Am., Ypsilanti, counselor for reading, 1988-89; cub scout summer camp instr. Wolverne Coun., 1987, merit badge counselor, 1988-89; coach of the angels Ypsilanti Am. Little League, 1988; parent adv. bd. The Childrens Devel. Lab. Ea. Mich. U., 1988-89; active Mich. United Conservation Clubs, Big Bros. Am., Charlotte, Mich., Human Rights Watch, Nat. Security Caucus U.S., 1988—, Heritage Found., 1988—, ofcl. sponsor Mandate for Leadership III, Policy Strategies for 1990's Project, Project Save Our Schs., 1988—, Citizens United for Better Edn., World Awareness, Inc., Group 61 Amnesty Internat., Legal Affairs Coun., Coun. for Inter-Am. Security, Nicaraguan Resistance Edn. Found., Nat. Right to Work Legal Def. Found., Citizens Against Govt. Waste, Citizens Commn. for Ethics in Govt., Citizens for Decency Through Law, Inc., Participating Parents for Progress in Ypsilanti Pub. Schs.; parents adv. bd. Chapelle Elem. Sch., Ypsilanti, 1989-90, West Mid. Sch., Ypsilanti, 1991-92, Ypsilanti Pub. Schs., 1990—, Ypsilanti H.S.; charter sponsor Victory over Communism Project; nominated charter mem. Presdl. Task Force; participant The Imperial Congress: Crisis in the Separation of Powers Project, line-item veto project The Heritage Found., 1989, campaign to revise medicare catastrophic coverage law project Nat. Assn. Uniformed Svcs., 1989, repeal of catastrophic coverage act program Conservative Caucus Inc., 1989, Srs. Coal. Against the Tax, 1989; nat. adv. coun. Citizens Com. for Right to Bear Arms; jr. and sr. choir, Sunday sch. tchr. St. Paul's Luth. Ch., 1959-64 (Perfect Attendance award 8 yrs.), Marine city, Mich., 1960-63; youth Sunday sch. tchr., dir. youth min. coun. Lawrence Ave. Meth. Ch., Charlotte, Mich., 1967-69, life ELCA Evang. Luth. Ch. in Am., Treas. St. Paul's Luther League, 1960. Recipient Spl. Recognition award Richard Nixon, 1968-79, Gerald Ford, 1974-76, Ronald Reagan, 1971-88, George Bush, 1988-92, Spl. Recognition award Reagan Presdl. Campaign, 1981, Bush Presdl. Campaign, 1988, Citizen of Yr. award Citizens Com. for Right to Bear Arms, 1988, cert. recognition U.S. Justice Found., 1991, Hale Found., Am. Security Coun. 30th Anniversary Spl. Recognition cert., cert. appreciation award 2d Amendment Found., 1988, Appreciation of Devoted and Valuable Svc. award Chapelle Elem. Sch., 1988-89, Merit Badge, Wolverine Coun.; Internat. Peace prize, United Cultural Conv., 2002, One Thousand Great Ams., Internat. Biographical Ctr., England, 2002, Lifetime Achievement award, 2001, Teaching Intellectuals of the World, Am. Biog. Inst.,2001, Outstanding contributions to Literacy, Edn., Humanitarians and Peace, 2002; named One of Most Outstanding People of 20th Century, IBC, Cambridge, Eng., 1997, Internat. Man of Yr., IBC, 1998, Outstanding Intellectuals of 21st Century, award letters from First Lady Nancy Regan, Mich. Gov. John Engler, Nelson Mandella, award from The Am. Biog. Inst. for Literacy and Peace Contbn., 2001 Mem. NEA, NRA (life, endowment), The Lincoln Inst. for Rsch. Edn., United Conservatives of Am. (participant citizens against the catastrophic health act tax 1989), Mich. Edn. Assn., Internat. Reading Assn., Mich. Sheriffs Assn. (assoc.), Police Marksmanship Assn., Washtenaw Reading Coun., Southeastern Mich. Reading Assn., Mich. Reading Assn., Mich. Assn. for Supervision and Curriculum Devel., Ann Arbor Edn. Assn., Am. Security Coun., Am. Def. Inst., Found. for Christian Living, Am. Family Assn., Nat. Geog. Soc., Am. Film Inst., Internat. Freelance Photographers Orgn. (life), Taxpayers Edn. Lobby, Gun Owners Am., Nat. Assn. Federally Lic. Firearms Dealers, Conservative Caucus, Inc., Ams. for Freedom, Tri-County Sportsman League, Mich. United Conservation Clubs, Mich. State U. Alumni Assn. (Blue Water chpt.), Mich. State U. Coll. Comm. Arts Alumni Assn., Mich. State U. Coll. Social Sci. Alumni Assn., Ft. Gratiot, Lions Club (v.p. 1998—), Lions Club Internat., Washtenaw Sportsmen's Club (Ypsilanti), Internat. Optimist Club (v.p., bd. dirs. 1975-78) (Ann Arbor), Port Huron Noon Optimist Club, Judo Black Belt Fedn. Am., Sigma Alpha Eta. Lutheran.

THUESEN, GERALD JORGEN, industrial engineer, educator; b. Oklahoma City, July 20, 1938; s. Holger G. and Helen S. T.; m. Harriett M. Thuesen; children: Karen E., Dyan L. BS, Stanford U., 1960, MS, 1961, PhD, 1968. Engr. Pacific Tel. Co., San Francisco, 1961-62, Atlantic Richfield Co., Dallas, 1962-63; asst. prof. indsl. engring. U. Tex., Arlington, 1963, 67-68; assoc. prof. indsl. and sys. engring. Ga. Inst. Tech., Atlanta, 1968-76, prof., 1976-96, prof. emeritus, 1996—. Author: Engineering Economy, 4th edit., 1971, 5th edit., 1977, 6th edit., 1984, 7th edit., 1989, 8th edit., 1993, 9th edit., 2001, Economic Decision Analysis, 1974, 2nd edit., 1980, 3rd edit., 1998; assoc. editor: The Engring. Economist, 1974-80, editor, 1981-91. NASA/Am. Soc. Engring. Edn. summer faculty fellow, 1970 Fellow Inst. Indsl. Engrs. (dept. editor Trans. 1976-80, v.p. publs. 1979-80, divsn. dir. 1978-80, Wellington award 1989, Publs. award 1990, bd. trustees 1979-87), Am. Soc. Engring. Edn. (bd. dirs. 1977-79, Eugene L. Grant award 1977, 91); mem. Sigma Xi. Office: Ga Inst Tech Sch Indsl & System Engring Atlanta GA 30332-0205

THUESON, DAVID OREL, pharmaceutical executive, researcher, educator, writer; b. Twin Falls, Idaho, May 9, 1947; s. Orel Grover and Shirley Jean (Archer) T.; m. Sherrie Linn Lowe, June 14, 1969; children: Sean, Kirsten, Eric, Ryan, Todd. BS, Brigham Young U., 1971; PhD, U. Utah, 1976. Postdoctoral fellow U. Tex. Med. Br., Galveston, 1976-77, asst. prof., 1977-82; sr. rsch. assoc. Parke-Davis Pharms., Ann Arbor, Mich., 1982-88; dir. pharmacology Immunetech Pharms., San Diego, 1988-90; dir. immunopharmacology Tanabe Rsch. Labs., 1990-92; v.p. discovery Cosmederm Techs., 1992-97. Contbr. articles to profl. jours.; patentee in field. Scout leader Boy Scouts Am., Mich., Tex. and Calif., 1979—. NIH grantee, 1978-81. Mem. Am. Acad. Allergy and Clin. Immunology, Am. Assn. Immunologists, Am. Thoracic Soc. Republican. Mem. Lds Ch. Avocations: water skiing, tennis, scuba diving. Home: 1356 Winchester Ave Mckinleyville CA 95519-8801 Office: 2330 Central Ave Ste 3 Mckinleyville CA 95519-3696 E-mail: thueson@reninet.com.

THULEAN, DONALD MYRON, symphony conductor; b. Wenatchee, Wash., June 24, 1929; s. Elmer Edward and Mary (Myron) T.; m. Meryl Mary Parnell, Mar. 17, 1951; children— Dorcas Marie, Mark Myron, William Norton. BA, U. Wash., 1950, MA in Music, 1952; Mus.D. (hon.), Whitworth Coll., 1967. Faculty Pacific U., 1955-62; dean Pacific U. (Sch. Music), 1957-62. Assoc. conductor Portland (Ore.) Symphony, 1961-62, conductor, music dir. Spokane Symphony, 1962-84; v.p. profl. and artistic svcs. Am. Symphony Orch. League, 1983-99, condr. emeritus, 1998—; asst. conductor Seattle Symphony, 1966-69, chorus master, Aspen Music Festival, 1957-61; artistic cons. Title III project in performing arts, Wash., 1966-68, music dir. Tamarack Music Festival, 1971. Bd. dirs. Seattle Symphony, 2000—, Seattle Youth Symphonies, 2002--; mem. vis. com. U. Wash. Sch. Music, 2000--. Served with AUS, 1953-55. Unitarian (trustee).

THULIN, ADELAIDE ANN, design company executive, interior designer; b. Chgo., Nov. 15, 1925; d. Martin Evold and Kathleen Marie (Glennon) Peterson; m. Frederick Adolph Thulin, Jr., Aug. 18, 1945; children: Frederick, Kristin, Mary, Margaret, Francis, Peter, Andrea, Charles, Joseph, Kathleen, James, Suzanne, Patricia. Student, Northwestern U., 1943—47; AA in Interior Design, Harper Coll., 1977. Registered interior designer. Asst. prodn. mgr. Cruttenden & Eger, Chgo., 1946; editor Mt. Prospect (Ill.) Independent, 1960; real estate salesperson Homefinders, Northwest Chgo. and suburbs, 1965, 69-70; asst. v.p. advt. Littelfuse, Des Plaines, Ill., 1966-67; owner, pres. Applied Design Assocs., Mt. Prospect, 1977—; ptnr., sec. Applied Design Internat. Ltd., 1992—. Career day spkr. local high schs., 1982—; bd. dirs. Works subs. Pvt. Industry Coun. Author, editor monthly newsletter Women's Archtl. League, 1983-85, The Binnacle, CYC, 1979-81. Organizer, Mothers March of Dimes, Mt. Prospect, 1953-54, Vols. for Stevenson, 1952, 56, Citizens for Douglas, 1954, Citizens for Kennedy, 1960; mem. Fair Rev. Coun., Chgo., 1983-84; mem. 13th Congl. Dist. Dem. Women's Club, publicity chmn., 1957-58; mem. Chgo. Symphony Orch. Chorus, 1972; del. Ill. Statehouse Conf. on Small Bus., 1984, 85; bd. dirs. Arts Coun. Mt. Prospect, 1986-931 organizer Mt. Prospect chpt. Internat. Sister Cities Program; chmn. Mt. Prospect Sign Rev. Bd.; mem. renovation com. Mt. Prospect Hist. Soc., 1988—; pres. cmty. edn. coun. H.S. Dist. 214, 1994-96; bd. dirs. Cmty. Edn. Foun.; reader for print-handicpped CRIS RAdio, 1982-92. Mem. AIA (profl. affiliate Chgo. chpt.), Am. Women Internat. Understanding, Nat. Small Bus. United (bd. dirs., v.p. state govt. affairs 1994), Ill. Coalition for N.Am. Free Trade Agreement, Women's Archt. League (publicity chmn. 1964-65), Mt. Prospect C. of C., Chgo. Women in Arch., Soc. Design Adminstrn., Disting. mem. Internat. Soc. Poets, Gamma Alpha Chi. Roman Catholic. Avocation: choral singing, poetry writing. Home: 4 S Owen St Mount Prospect IL 60056-3309 Office: Applied Design Assocs Ltd 800 E Northwest Hwy Mount Prospect IL 60056-3457 E-mail: appldzn@aol.com.

THUMMA, SAMUEL ANDERSON, lawyer; b. Emmetsburg, Iowa, May 2, 1962; s. H. Russell and Lanore Ava (Anderson) T.; m. Barbara J. Dawson. BS, Iowa State U., 1984; JD, U. Iowa, 1988. Bar: Iowa 1988, Ill. 1990, D.C. 1990, Ariz. 1992. Broadcaster Sta. WOI-AM, Ames, Iowa, 1982-84; print journalist Iowa Dept. Agr., Des Moines, 1985; law clk. to Hon. David R. Hansen, U.S. Dist. Ct. for No. Dist. Iowa, Cedar Rapids, 1988-90; assoc. Arnold & Porter, Washington, 1990-92; law clk. to Hon. Stanley G. Feldman, Ariz. Supreme Ct., 1992-93; mem. Brown & Bain, P.A., Phoenix, 1996. Adj. prof. Ariz. State U. Coll. Law, 2000. Contbr. articles to profl. jours. Ex officio bd. mem. and spl. transp. svcs. com. chair Grand Canyon chpt. ARC, 1998-99, bd. dirs., 1999--, chmn. bd., 2002--; bd. dirs., chair nat. conv. cabinet vice chair blood related activities ARC, 2000-2002; bd. dirs., purchasing coord. Gifts for Homeless, Inc., Washington, 1991-93; mem. study affairs devel. adv. coun. Iowa State U., 1993-96; mem. Paradise Valley Village Planning Com., 1994-96, sec., 1995-96; judge Nat. Chpt. award and Proficiency award Ariz. FFA, 1996-99, 2001. Harry S. Truman Found. scholar, 1982-87. Mem. ABA, State Bar of Ariz. (fee arbitration com. 1994—, chair 1997-2002, civil practice and procedure com. 1997—, vice chair 2001-2002, chair 2002—), Maricopa County Bar Assn. (task force on recruitment and retention of women and minorities 1999-2002, CLE com. 1995-99, barristers ball com. 1997-99), Ill. Bar Assn., D.C. Bar Assn., Iowa Bar Assn., Ariz. Bar Assn., Order of Coif. Republican. Methodist. Avocations: photography, travel, cooking. Office: Brown & Bain PA PO Box 400 2901 N Central Ave Ste 2000 Phoenix AZ 85012-2788

THUMMEL, ROSA, artist; b. Des Moines, Apr. 17, 1916; d. Sposeto Frank and Victoria Jaquinta; m. John W. Thummel-Senneich (dec. Mar. 1988); children: Randolph, Carl, Gabriella Student, Drake U., U. Iowa. One woman shows include Swiss Ctr. Gallery, N.Y.C., 1975, Nat. Art Ctr., N.Y.C., 1979, Tosta Gallery, Coconut Grove, Fla., 1980-83, Corridor Gallery, Summit, N.J., 1981; exhibited in group shows at Montclair (N.J.) Pub. Libr., 1976, Summit Art Ctr., 1978, 80, 82 (Beth Born Portrait award 1978, Best in Show 1980, First prize 1982), Painters & Sculpters Soc., N.Y.C., 1976-79, N.J., 1980-83, Bergen County (N.J.) Artist Guild, 1980, Sheila Nussbaum Gallery, Millburn, N.J., Lever House, N.Y.C., 1984, others; represented in pvt. collections. Home: 72 Holton Ln Essex Fells NJ 07021-1709

THUMS, CHARLES WILLIAM, designer, consultant; b. Manitowoc, Wis., Sept. 5, 1945; s. Earl Oscar and Helen Margaret (Rusch) T. B. in Arch., Ariz. State U., 1972. Ptnr., Grafic, Tempe, Ariz., 1967-70; founder, prin. I-Squared Environ. Cons., Tempe, Ariz., 1970-78; designer and cons. design morphology, procedural programming and algorithms, 1978— . Author: (with Jonathan Craig Thums) Tempe's Grand Hotel, 1973, The Rossen House, 1975; (with Daniel Peter Aiello) Shelter and Culture, 1976; contbg. author: Tombstone Planning Guide, 5 vols., 1974. Office: PO Box 3126 Tempe AZ 85280-3126

THUNE, JOHN, congressman; b. Murdo, S.D., Jan. 7, 1961; m. Kimberley Thune; children: Brittany, Larissa. BBA, MBA, U. S.D. Legis. asst. Senator James Abdnor, 1985-87; dep. staff dir. to the ranking rep. Senate Small Bus. Com., 1987-89; exec. dir. South Dakota Rep. Party, 1989-91; state railroad dir. Gov. George Mickelson, 1991-93; exec. dir. S.D. Mcpl. League, 1993-96; mem. U.S. Congress from S.D., 1997—. Mem. agr. com., transp. and infrastructure com., small bus. com. Avocations: basketball, pheasant hunting.*

THURA, PETER, emergency physician; b. Mandalay, Myanmar, Apr. 30, 1949; came to U.S., 1976; s. Hla Aung and Khin Khin; m. Jennifer Ahad, June 4, 1983; children: Farhan, Nadia and Soraiya (twins). MB, BChir, Inst. Medicine 1, Rangoon, Myanmar, 1973. Diplomate Am. Bd. Internal Medicine. Resident house physician/surgeon Mandalay Gen. Hosp., 1973-74; pvt. practice Rangoon, 1974-76; intern in gen. surgery Monmouth Med. Ctr., Long Branch, N.J., 1978-79; intern in internal medicine Good Samaritan Hosp., Balt., 1979, D.C. Gen. Hosp., 1980-81, resident in internal medicine, 1981-83, emergency medicine physician, 1983—2001; primary care physician Nat. Health Plan, Washington, 1983-88; emergency medicine physician Walter Reed Army Med. Ctr., 1992-95; gen. med. officer St. Elizabeth Hosp., 2001—. Scholar Burmese Govt. Ministry of Edn., 1966-73. Mem. ACP. Moslem. Avocations: walking, yard work, reading National Geographic magazines, basketball, soccer. Home: 6512 Walters Woods Dr Falls Church VA 22044-1425 Office: St Elizabeth Hosp 2700 Martin Luther King Jr Ave SE Washington DC 20032-2601 E-mail: thura@cox.net.

THURBER, EMILY FORREST, political consultant; b. Chgo, Oct. 31, 1930; d. Maulsby and Harriette (Reichmann) Forrest; m. James Perry Thurber, Jr., Aug. 8, 1950. BA, Stanford U., 1964. Legis. aide Sen. Alan Cranston U.S. Senate, Washington, 1974-78, 82-83; fundraiser Cranston for Pres., 1983-84; program dir. Fgn. Student Coun., 1984-86; polit. cons. EJT Assocs., Los Altos, Calif., 1991—; campaign mgr. Sher for Senate, 1996-2000. Bd. dirs. Sempervirens Fund; vice chair Santa Clara County Commn. on the Status of Women. Mem., dir. polit. outreach Santa Clara County Dem. Ctrl. Com., Calif., 1992—; mem. Calif. State Dem. Ctrl. Com., 1992—; exec. com. Calif. Dem. Com., 1995—, mem. resolutions com.; del. Dem. Nat. Com., 1996, 2000; bd. dirs. Los Altos Cmty. Found.; treas. Peninsula Dem. Coalition, 1996-98; sec. Los Altos Sister Cities Inc., 1995-96, membership chmn., 1997-2002; sec. Mid-Peninsula YWCA, 1995-96, v.p. pub. policy, 1996-2000; polit. dir. Mid-Peninsula NAACP, 1993-95; newsletter editor Los Altos History Mus. Mem. Phi Beta Kappa. Avocations: tennis, hiking. Home and Office: 694 Benvenue Ave Los Altos CA 94024-4013 E-mail: ejt@thurberfamily.com.

THURBER, JAMES CAMERON, law enforcement officer, consultant, author; b. Boynton Beach, Fla., Oct. 3, 1965; s. John Cameron and JeanAnn (Bridgeman) T. AA, Palm Beach CC, 1986; BS in Criminology, Fla. State U., Tallahassee, 1988, MPA, 1991. Cert. Police Officer, EMT. EMT Atlantic Ambulance Svc., West Palm Beach, 1984-88, Bethesda Ambulance Svc., Boynton Beach, Fla., 1988-92; police officer Lake Worth (Fla.) Police Dept., 1992-94; law enforcement investigator Fla. Divsn. Ins. Fraud, 1994—. Vol. aux. police officer Lake Worth Police Dept., 1985-92; cons. Fla. C. of C., Tallahassee, 1991, Fla. Div. Emergency Mgmt., Tallahassee, 1991; intern. Fed. Bureau of Prisons, Tallahassee, 1990, Fla. Dept. Law Enforcement, Pompano Beach, 1987. Contbr. articles to profl. jours. Mem. Lake Worth Pioneer Assn., West Palm Beach, 1965-94, Hist. Soc. Palm Beach County, 1993—; squadron emergency svcs. officer CAP, Lantana, Fla., 1983-89. Recipient Outstanding Academic Achievement award Fraternal Order of Police, Lake Worth, 1992. Mem. Am. Soc. Pub. Adminstrn., Lake Worth Scottish Rite, Masons (Boynton Lodge @ 236), Lambda Chi Alpha, Palm Beach County Seminole Boosters. Episcopalian. Office: Ste 704 1655 Palm Beach Lakes Blvd West Palm Beach FL 33401-2208

THURBER, JOHN ALEXANDER, lawyer; b. Detroit, Nov. 9, 1939; s. John Levington and Mary Anne (D'Agostino) T.; m. Barbara Irene Brown, June 30, 1962; children: John Levington II, Sarah Jeanne. AB in History, U. Mich., 1962, JD, 1965. Bar: Ohio 1965, Mich. 1968. Assoc. Hahn, Loeser and Parks, Cleve., 1965-67, Miller, Canfield, Paddock and Stone, Birmingham, Mich., 1967-73; sr. mem. Miller, Canfield, Paddock and Stone, P.L.C., Troy, 1974—. Treas. Birmingham Community House, 1971-73; pres. Birmingham Village Players, 1983-84; bd. dirs. Oakland Parks Found., Pontiac, Mich., 1984—, pres., 1989-92; mem. capital com. Lighthouse Found.; trustee Oakland Land Conservancy. Avocations: reading, theater, walking, sports. Office: Miller Canfield Paddock & Stone PLC 840 W Long Lake Rd Ste 200 Troy MI 48098-6358 E-mail: thurberj@millercanfield.com.

THURBER, JOHN PETER, academic administrator, lawyer; b. N.Y.C., June 21, 1954; s. Lucius Newton and Constance T.; m. Constance Elaine Cloonan; children: Patrick Newton, Elizabeth Ann. BA, Hampshire Coll., 1976; JD summa cum laude, Rutgers U., 1982. Bar: N.J. 1983, N.Y. 1983. Law clk. to Hon. Harold A. Ackerman U.S. Dist. Ct. N.J., 1982-84; asst. dep. pub. advocate N.J. Dept. Pub. Advocate, Trenton, 1984-91; exec. dir. Inst. Pub. Policy Thomas Edison State Coll., 1991-96; v.p. Thomas Edison State Coll., 1996—. V.p. Trenton Downtown Assn., 2000—; mem. urban edn. adv. com. N.J. Dept. Edn., Trenton, 1998—; bd. trustees Greater Princeton Youth Orchestra, 1998—; mem. cmty. rels. com. Capital Health Sys. Bd. Dirs., Trenton, 1998—; chmn. bd. mgrs. Am. Cancer Soc. Mercer Unit, Lawrence, N.J., 1997-99. Mem. Rotary Club (Princeton, chmn. internat. svc. com. 1999—, fellow leadership N.J., 1992). Home: 4396 Province Line Rd Princeton NJ 08540 Office: Thomas Edison State Coll 101 W State St Trenton NJ 08608

THURBER, PETER PALMS, lawyer; b. Detroit, Mar. 23, 1928; s. Cleveland and Marie Louise (Palms) T.; m. Ellen Bodley Stites, Apr. 16, 1955; children: Edith Bodley, Jane Chenoweth, Thomas, Sarah Bartlett BA, Williams Coll., 1950; JD, Harvard U., 1953. Bar: Mich., 1954. With Miller, Canfield, Paddock and Stone, Detroit, 1953-93, of counsel, 1994—. Trustee McGregor Fund, Detroit, 1979—. Bd. dirs. Detroit Symphony Orch., Inc., 1974-93; trustee Community Found. for Southeastern Mich., 1990-2000, Coun. Mich. Founds., 1991-2000. With U.S. Army, 1953-55. Fellow Am. Bar Found.; mem. ABA, Mich. Bar Assn. Clubs: Country of Detroit (Grosse Pointe Farms, Mich.). Roman Catholic. Avocations: reading; traveling; athletics. Home: 28 Provencal Rd Grosse Pointe Farms MI 48236-3038 Office: Miller Canfield Paddock & Stone 150 W Jefferson Ave Ste 2500 Detroit MI 48226-4416

THUREAU, LANI CAROLE, speech and language pathologist; b. Jacksonville, Fla., Sept. 23, 1948; d. Samuel Howard and Joan (Miller) Zeigler; m. Donald Douglas Thureau, June 14, 1969; 1 adopted child, Christina Marie. BA, U. Miami, 1970; MA, Kent State U., 1979; postgrad., Johns Hopkins Hosp. and John F. Kennedy Inst., 1982. Cert. clin. competence Am. Speech-Lang. Assn.; cert. tchr., Del.; lic. speech-lang. pathologist, Del. Speech therapist Vanguard Sch., Miami, Fla., 1970-71, Marian Ctr., Opa-Locka, 1971-73; speech-lang. pathologist Beechwood Sch., Wilmington, Del., 1979-80; speech-lang. pathologist, supr. Del. Curative Workshop, 1980-86; speech-lang. pathologist Pilot Sch., Inc., 1986—. Cons. Del. Curative Workshop, 1986-88, Pilot Sch., 1986—. Co-author, advisor (film) Del.: A Place to be Somebody, 1990. Exec. chmn. United Way, Wilmington, 1986—94; host mother Au Pair Home Stay, 1993—95; active Jewish Cmty. Ctr. Winterthur; fundraiser Arthritis Found., 1999; camp unit leader Brownie and Girl Scouts U.S., 2000, 2001, 2002. Recipient Adult Ice Dance Silver level U.S. Figure Skating Assn., 1990, Pres.'s award, 1994, Woman of Yr., 1996, Internat. Woman of Yr., 2001. Mem. Am. Speech-Lang.-Hearing Assn., Del. Speech, Lang. and Hearing Assn. (exec. coun., chair job bank), Nat. Audubon Soc., Skating Club Wilmington (10 badge improvement 1985, Improvement award 1988), Del. Art Mus., Del. Adoption Support Group, Jewish Cmty. Ctr., Winterthur, Gourmet Dinner Group, The Dance Group, People to People, Delta Gamma. Avocations: ice dancing, ballroom dancing, world travel, bird watching, piano. Home: 740 Taunton Rd Wilmington DE 19803-1723 E-mail: godon@zdial.com.

THURM, KEVIN L. bank executive; b. Brooklyn, Apr. 5, 1961; BA Tufts, 1983, MA Oxford, 1986, JD Harvard Law Sch., 1989. Assoc. Cahill, Gordon & Reindel, 1989—91; deputy sec. Dept. Health & Human Svcs, Washington, 1996—2000; first dir. strategic planning, consumer div. Citigroup, Inc., 2001—.*

THURMAN, ADDISON EUGENE, JR. urologist; b. Pawnee, Okla., Apr. 27, 1943; s. Addison Eugene and Cathleen Lee (Irwin) T.; m. Eileen Lee Ittmann, Aug. 10, 1968; children: Scott Addison, Sally Ann. BS, Southwestern State Coll., Weatherford, Okla., 1965; MS, Tulane U., 1967; D. of Medicine, U. Okla., Oklahoma City, 1971. Diplomate Am. Bd. Urology. Intern in surgery Bexar County Hosp. Dist., San Antonio, 1971—72, resident in urology, 1972—77; maj., dept. urology USAF Carswell AFB Hosp., Ft. Worth, 1977—79; pvt. practice in urologic surgery, 1979—85; mem. staff Ft. Worth Urol. Clinic, 1985—; chief dept. surgery St. Joseph Hosp., Ft. Worth, 1989—90; chief, divsn. urology Harris Meth. Hosp., 1999—. Maj. USAF, 1977-79. Fellow ACS, Tex. Surg. Soc.; mem. AMA, Am. Urol. Assn., Tex. Med. Assn., Alpha Omega Alpha. Home: 2111 Pembroke Dr Fort Worth TX 76110-1239 Office: Fort Worth Urol Clinic 1300 W Terrell Ave Ste 405 Fort Worth TX 76104-2810

THURMAN, ANDREW EDWARD, lawyer; b. Raleigh, N.C., May 11, 1954; s. William Gentry and Peggy Lou (Brown) T.; m. Patricia Thurman, May 19, 1979 (dec. 1989); children: Gentry Brown, Harrison Beauchamp, Andrew Guilford; m. Tracy Fletcher, Nov. 16, 1991; 1 child, Spencer Lee. BA, Columbia U., 1976; JD, Coll. William and Mary, 1979; MPH, U. Okla., 1984. Bar: Va. 1979, Okla. 1980, U.S. Ct. Appeals (10th cir.) 1981, U.S. Supreme Ct. 1985, Pa. 1988. Staff atty. Dept. of Human Services, Oklahoma City, 1979-80; counsel State of Okla. Teaching Hosps., 1980-84; mem. Miller, Dollarhide, Dawson & Shaw, 1984-87; ptnr. Berkman, Ruslander, Pohl, Lieber & Engel, Pitts., 1988-89; of counsel Buchanan Ingersoll, 1989; sr. v.p. and gen. counsel Forbes Health System, 1989-96; sr. counsel Allegheny Health Edn. & Rsch. Found., 1997-98; dep. gen. counsel Allegheny U. Hosps. West, 1998-99; asst. gen. counsel W. Penn. Allegheny Health Sys., 1999—; assoc. prof. Carneige-Mellon U., 2000—. Pres. Council of Neighborhood Assns., Oklahoma City, 1984, Lincoln Terr. Neighborhood Assn., Oklahoma City, 1984; trustee Rader Trust, Oklahoma City, 1980—; treas. Bd. dirs. State Okla. Tchg. Hosps. Found., Oklahoma City, 1984-87, Newman Meml. Hosp., 1983-87, Willowview Hosp., Spencer, Okla., 1985-87, Allegheny U. Med. Ctrs., 1997—, AUMC/Cannonsburg Ambulance Svc., 1997—, Allegheny U. Hosps. West, 1998—, Diversified Health Group, 1998-99, Allegheny Med. Practices Network, 1999—, Allegheny Speciality Practice Network, 1999—; chair HCWP Ethics Task Force, 1993-2000. Fellow Am. Health Lawyers Assn.; mem. St. Anthony Hall Club of N.Y.C. (pres. 1976), Rivers Club. Democrat. Presbyterian. Avocation: reading detective novels. Home: 106 Richmond Dr Pittsburgh PA 15215-1039 Office: Allegheny Gen Hosp 320 E North Ave Pittsburgh PA 15212-4756 E-mail: athurman@wpahs.org., andy@thurmans.net.

THURMAN, KAREN L. congresswoman; b. Rapid City, S.D., Jan. 12, 1951; d. Lee Searle and Donna (Altfillisch) Loveland; m. John Patrick Thurman, 1973; children: McLin Searl and Liberty Lee. BA, U. Fla., 1973. Mem. Dunnellon City Coun. (Fla.), 1975—83; mayor of Dunnellon Dunnellon, 1979-81; mem. Monroe Regional Med. Ctr. Governancy Com., Comprehensive Plan Tech. Adv. Com., Fla. State Senate, 1983—93, U.S. Congress from 5th Fla. dist., 1993—, ways and means com ., 1996—, House agrl. comm., comm. on gov. reform and oversight. Del. Fla. Dem. Conv., Dem. Nat. Conv., 1980; mem. Regional Energy Action com. Recipient Svc. Above Self award Dunnellon C. of C., 1980, Regional Coun. Appreciation for Svc. award. Mem. Dunnellon C. of C. (dir.), Fla. Horseman's Children's Soc. (charter). Episcopalian. Office: US Ho of Reps 201 CannonHo Office Bldg Washington DC 20515-0905*

THURMAN, ROBERT, philosophy, religious studies educator; m. Nena von Schlebrugge. Co-founder Am. Inst. Buddhism, 1973—; founder Tibet House, N.Y., 1987—; scholar, activist, chair religion dept. Columbia U., N.Y.C., 1988—, prof. religion dept. Named One of the Most Influential Americans, Time Mag. Office: Columbia U 1140 Amsterdam Ave New York NY 10027-7003

THURMAN, VIRGIL LEON, voice educator; b. Knoxville, Tenn., Nov. 4, 1940; s. Virgil Lee and Marie Campbell T. BA, David Lipscomb Coll., Nashville, 1962; MS, U. Ill., Urban-Champagne, Ill., 1965, EdD, 1977. K-12 vocal music educator Harlan (Ky.) County Schs., 1962-64; 4-12 vocal music educator North Royalton (Ohio) City Schs., 1965-68; grad. teaching asst. U. Ill., Urbana-Champaign, Ill., 1968-70; chorister Norman Luboff Choir, N.Y.C., 1970-71; announcer WILL-AM & FM Pub. Radio, Urbana-Champaign, Ill., 1971-73, 76-78; asst. prof. voice, choral music, music edn. Yankton (S.D.) Coll., 1973-76; instr. voice and choral music MacPhail Ctr. for the Arts, Mpls., 1977-86; artist-in-residence Mpls. Pub. Schs., 1977-78; vocal advisor Minn. Boychoir, 1981-86; sole proprietor, ptnr., specialist voice educator The Voice Ctr., Mpls., 1986-95; specialist voice educator Fairview Voice Ctr. Fairview-Univ. Med. Ctr., 1995—. Bd. dirs., pres. Minn. chpt. Nat. Assn. Tchrs. of Singing, 1980-81, 84-86; assoc. dir. Interdisciplinary Voice Colloquium, U. Minn., Mpls., 1981-84' voice dept. asst. coord. MacPhail Ctr. for the Arts U. Minn., 1982-86; founder, bd. dirs., prin. faculty The VoiceCare Network, 1982—; mem. adv. bd. Ctr. Advanced Studies Music Edn., U. Surrey Roehampton, London; guest presenter, Am. Choral Dirs. Assn., Music Educators Nat. Conf., Internat. Soc. for Music Edn., The Choristers Guild, Voice Found. Am., N.Y.C., Alberta Music Conf., Assn. for Prenatal and Perinatal Psychology and Health, Am. Orff-Schulwerk Assn., Assn. Can. Choral Condrs., Orgn. Am. Kodaly Educators, Suzuki Assn. of the Ams., Internat. Soc. for Prenatal and Perinatal Psychology and Medicine, Austria, 1986, voice symposium Brit. Voice Assn., 1989, European Coun. Internat. Schs., 1992, Festival 500: Sharing the Voices, St. Johns, Nfld., Can., 1997, Internat. Symposium: The Phenomenon of Singing, Meml. U. of Nfld., Can., 1997, interdisciplinary voice seminar Utah State U., 1999, Internat. Conf. Music Perception and Cognition, 2000, Minn. Music Tchrs. Assn., 2002, Early Childhood Music & Movement Assoc., 2002; vis. instr. U. Ill., Roosevelt U., Chgo., Queensland State Schs., Australia, 1988, Middle Tenn. State U., U. St. Thomas, St. Paul, U. Hartford, 1991, 93, 94, U. Iowa, 1987, U. Nebr., 2001, U. Alta., 1998, U. Queensland and Queensland Conservatorium, 1988, Westminster Choir Coll., Princeton, N.J., N.D. State U., U. Nebr., 2001. Author, co-editor: Bodymind and Voice: Foundations of Voice Education, 1997, 2000; contbr. articles to profl. jours.; mem. editl. bd. Internat. Jour. Rsch. in Choral Singing. Music dir., conductor Betty Marin Hobby Singers, Mpls., 1977-80, Skyway Singers, Mpls., 1983-87, Choral Soc. Tri-Cities, Cumberland, Benham, Lynch, Ky., 1962-64; dir., actor Royalton Players Cmty. Theatre, North Royalton, Ohio, 1965-68; chorister Cleve. Orchestra Chorus, 1965-67, Cleve. Orchestra Chamber Chorus, 1967. Mem. ASCD, AAAS, Actors Equity Assn., Am. Choral Dirs. Assn., Am. Choral Dirs. Assn. of Minn., Am. Guild of Musical Artists, Am. Fedn. TV and Radio Artists, Assn. Canadian Choral Conductors, Assn. for Prenatal and Perinatal Psychology and Health, European Soc. for Cognitive Scis. of Music, Internat. Music Soc. for Prenatal Devel., Internat. Soc. for Music Edn., Nat. Assn. of Tchrs. of Singing, Music Educators Nat. Conf., N.Y. Acad. Scis., The Schubert Club, Thursday Musical, Voice and Speech Trainers Assn., The VoiceCare Network, Early Childhood Music and Movement Assn. Avocations: walking, jogging. E-mail address. Office: Fairview Voice Ctr 2450 Riverside Ave Minneapolis MN 55454-1450 E-mail: lthurma1@fairview.org.

THURMAN, WALTER N. economics educator; b. Palo Alto, Calif., July 28, 1955; s. Samuel David Jr. and Emeline (Nebeker) T.; m. Rita D. Thurman, Dec. 29, 1979; children: Hannah P., Lydia S., Abigail D. BA in Environ. Studies, Utah State U., Logan, 1976; MS in Econs., Mont. State U., Bozeman, 1977; PhD in Econs., U. Chgo., 1984. Prof. agrl. and resource econs., prof. econs. N.C. State U., Raleigh, 1983—, dir. grad. program in econs., 1996-99. Author: Assessing the Environmental Impact of Farm Policies, 1995; reviewer, contbr. articles to profl. jours. Mem. Am. Agrl. Econs. Assn. (sr. assoc. editor jour. 1993-97, Quality Rsch. Discovery award 1996). Office: NC State U Agrl & Resource Econs PO Box 8109 NCSU Raleigh NC 27695-8109

THURMOND, JOHN PETER, II, bank executive, rancher, archaeologist; b. Elk City, Okla., Apr. 22, 1955; s. Arthur Leslie and Dorothea Jean (Lee) T.; m. Susan Ide Smith, June 7, 1979; children: Katherine Anne, Allison Lee, Patrick Andrew. BA, U. Tex., 1976, MA, 1979. Pres., chmn. First Nat. Bank of Leedey, Okla., 1984-92, Leedey Bancorporation, Inc., 1984-92, Thurmond Ranch, Inc., Cheyenne, Okla., 1982—. Pres., chmn. Dempsey Divide Rsch. Found., Inc., 2001—; vis. rsch. assoc. Sam Noble Okla. Mus. Natural History, U. Okla., 2001—; vice chmn. 1st Nat. Bank & Trust Co., Elk City, 1992—. Author: Archeology of the Cypress Basin, NE Texas, 1981, Late Paleoindian Utilization of the Dempsey Divide, 1990. Emergency med. technician, sec. Leedey Ambulance Svc., Inc., 1981-88. Recipient Hist. Preservation award Okla. Hist. Soc., 1991, 97, Goodyear Conservation award, 2000. Mem. Okla. Anthrop. Soc. (sec., treas. 1988—, Disting. Svc. award 1999), Tex. Archeol. Soc., Plains Anthrop. Soc., Am. Quaternary Assn., Geol. Soc. Am., Okla. Cattlemen's Assn., Okla. Hist. Soc., Cum Laude Soc., Phi Beta Kappa, Phi Kappa Phi. Republican. E-mail: dempseydiv@aol.com.

THURMOND, STROM, senator; b. Edgefield, S.C., Dec. 5, 1902; s. John William and Eleanor Gertrude (Strom) T.; m. Jean Crouch, Nov. 7, 1947 (dec. Jan. 1960); m. Nancy Moore, Dec. 22, 1968; children: Nancy Moore (dec.), J. Strom, Jr., Juliana Gertrude, Paul Reynolds. BS, Clemson Coll., 1923; 34 hon. degrees. Bar: S.C. 1930. Tchr. S.C. schs., 1923-29; city atty., county atty., supt. edn. Edgefield County, 1929-33; state senator, 1933-38; circuit judge, 1938-46; gov. of S.C., 1947-51; chmn. So. Govs. Conf., 1950; practiced in Alken, S.C., 1951-55; U.S. senator from S.C., 1954—; pres. pro tem, 1981-87, 1995—2001. Del. Nat. Democratic Conv., 1932, 36, 48, 52, 56, 60; chmn. S.C. dels., armed svcs. com.; mem. Judiciary VA com.; mem. Dem. Nat. Com., 1948; States Rights candidate for Pres. U.S., 1948; del. Nat. Republican Conv., 1968, 72, 76, 80, 84, 88, 92, 96. Bd. dirs. Ga.-Carolina council Boy Scouts Am. Served with AUS; attached to 82d Airborne Div. for D-Day invasion 1942-46, Europe; maj. gen. Res. Decorated Legion of Merit with oak leaf cluster, Bronze Star with V, Purple Heart, Croix de Guerre France; Cross of Order of Crown Belgium; others; recipient Congl. Medal Honor Soc. Nat. Patriots award, 1974, Presdl. Medal of Freedom, 1993. Mem. S.C. (past v.p.), ABA, Clemson Coll. Alumni Assn. (past pres.), also numerous def., vets., civic, fraternal and farm orgns. Baptist. Office: US Senate 217 Russell Senate Office Bldg Washington DC 20510-0001

THURNER, AGNES H. retired art association administrator, retired executive secretary; b. Manistique, Mich., July 21, 1934; d. Joseph and Elise Kaulfuerst; m. James C. Wegner, June 5, 1954 (div. 1969); children: Robin, Leonard; m. Maximilian Franz Joseph Thurner, May 29, 1993. Pres. Sq. Dance Assn., Milw., 1987-2000; ret., 2000. Author: Square Dancing in Wisconsin, 1998. Pollworker Ozaukee County, Mequon, Wis., 1995—. Mem. Wis. Regional Writers Assn. Lutheran. Avocations: reading, music, crafts, dancing, composer/lyricist.

THURNER, HENRY, retired writer; b. Ulm, Germany, Mar. 3, 1924; s. Charles and Charlotte Thurner; m. Trudy Cecilia Eder, Apr. 9, 1945; children: Claudia, Ritchie. BA cum laude, Syracuse U., Syracuse, NY, 1947—53. Counter intelligence agt. US War Dept., Various, Various Overseas, 1945—47; tech. writer / editor GE, Syracuse, NY, 1950—69. Author: (novels) The Man Who Knew God, GECKO. Sgt. US Army, 1946—50, France / Germany. Decorated Cert. of Appreciation Electronic Systems Divsn., Air Force Systems Command. Avocations: oil painting, wood carving, wood carving, wood carving, wood carving.

THURSBY, JERRY GILBERT, economics educator, consultant; b. Camp Le Jeune, N.C., Aug. 6, 1947; s. Gilbert Earl and Mary Kathleen (Bailey) T.; m. Marie Sloan Currie, Mar. 11, 1972; children: James, Mary. AB, U. N.C., 1969, PhD, 1975. Asst. prof. Syracuse (N.Y.) U., 1975-78; from asst. to assoc. prof. Ohio State U., Columbus, 1978-88; prof. Purdue U., West Lafayette, Ind., 1988-01; prof. econs., chmn. dept. Emory U., Atlanta, 2001—. Contbr. articles to profl. jours. With U.S. Army, 1969-71. edu. Home: 910 Springdale Rd NE Atlanta GA 30306-4620 Office: Emory U Dept Econs Rich Meml Bldg Atlanta GA 30322 E-mail: jthursb@emory.edu.

THURSBY, MARIE CURRIE, economics educator; b. Durham, N.C., July 27, 1947; d. James Sloan and Virginia (Spruill) Currie; m. Jerry Gilbert Thursby, Mar. 11, 1972; children: James, Mary. AB in Econs. cum laude, Mt. Holyoke Coll., 1969; PhD in Internat. Econs., U. N.C., 1974. Vis. asst. prof. N.C. State U., Raleigh, 1974-75; asst. prof. Syracuse (N.Y.) U., 1975-78, Ohio State U., Columbus, 1978-82, assoc. prof., 1981-88; prof. econs. Purdue U., West Lafayette, Ind., 1988—2002; Hal and John Smith chair entrepreneurship Ga. Tech, Atlanta, 2002—. Vis. assoc. prof. U. Mich., 1986-88; rsch. assoc. Nat. Bur. Econs. Rsch., Cambridge, Mass., 1987—; presenter in field; referee numerous econ. jours., including Am. Econ. Rev., Am. Jour. Agrl. Econs., Can. Jour. Econs.; reviewer NSF. Co-author: Economics of World Grain Trade, 1978; assoc. editor Jour. Internat. Econ., 1998—, Mgmt. Sci., 2001—; mem. editorial adv. bd. Studies in Internat. Trade Policy; contbr. numerous articles to profl. jours. Co-recipient Mershon Nat. Security award, 1981; grantee GE, 1980, NSF, 1985-88, 2000—, Ford Found. and Nat. Bur. Econ. Rsch., 1987, 89. Mem. Am. Econ. Assn. Home: 144 Creighton Rd West Lafayette IN 47906-2102 Office: Ga Tech DuPree Coll Mgmt 955 Ferst Dr Atlanta GA 30332-0520

THURSFIELD, FRED FALCONER, II, foundation administrator; b. Rochester, N.Y., Mar. 13, 1950; s. Richard Emmons and Alice (Hedges) T.; m. Kathi Suzanne Heathcote, Jan. 22, 1972 (div. Dec. 1996); children: Amy Christine Humphreys, Jennifer Anne; m. Sara Garland Barr, Sept. 2, 1997; 1 stepchild, Shelby Blair Forde. BA, U. Md., 1972. Agt., sales rep. Life of Va. Ins. Co., Washington, 1972-78; dir. alumni fund Johns Hopkins Med. Instns., Balt., 1978-82; major gift officer, dir. acad. programs Duke U., Durham, N.C., 1982-92, asst. dir. devel. Sch. Environ, 1992-94; dir. ann. and capital programs Geisinger Found., Danville, Pa., 1994-95; exec. dir. devel. Washington Hosp. Found., 1995-97; exec. dir. Peninsula Regional Found., Salisbury, Md., 1997—2001, Health First Found., Melbourne, Fla., 2001—. Mem. coun. Wildlife Preservation Trust, Internat., 1991, 94-99, mem. bd., 1991-94, regional sec.-treas., 1998-99, chair-elect, 1999-2000, chair, 2000-2001. Mem.: Nat. Soc. Fundraising Execs., Assn. Healthcare Philanthropy, U. Md. Alumni Assn. and Terrapin Club, Eau Gallie Yacht Club, Rotary. Republican. Methodist. Avocations: philately, golf, reading. Home: 2666 Lowell Cir Melbourne FL 32935 Office: Health First Found 1355 S Hickory Ste 203 Melbourne FL 32901 E-mail: fthursfi@health-first.org.

THURSTON, DONALD ALLEN, broadcasting executive; b. Gloucester, Mass., Apr. 2, 1930; s. Joseph Allen and Helen Ruth (Leach) T.; m. Oralie Alice Lane, Sept. 9, 1951; children: Corydon Leach, Carolie Lane. Grad., Mass. Radio and Telegraph, 1949; HHD (hon.), North Adams (Mass.) State Coll., 1977; LHD (hon.), Emerson Coll., 1995. Announcer, engr. Sta. WTWN, St. Johnsbury, Vt., 1949-52; v.p., gen. mgr. Sta. WIKE, Newport, 1952-60; v.p., treas., gen. mgr. Sta. WMNB, North Adams, 1960-66; pres., treas. Berkshire Broadcasting Co., Inc., 1966—. Bd. dirs. Broadcast Capital Fund, Inc., 1980-96, chmn. bd., 1981-89; bd. dirs. Broadcast Music, Inc., N.Y.C., 1990—, chmn. bd., 1994-97. Pres. No. Berkshire Indsl. Devel. Corp., 1965-67; commr. Mass. Cmty. Antenna TV Commn., 1972-74; trustee Mass. Coll. Liberal Arts, 1991-2000, vice chmn. bd. trustees, 1993-96, chmn., 1996-2001. Recipient Laymen's award Vt. Tchrs. Assn., 1958; Laymen's award Mass. Tchrs. Assn., 1962; Abe Lincoln Merit award So. Baptist Radio and TV Commn., 1975; named Man of Yr. Vt. Assn. Broadcasters, 1978 Mem. North Adams C. of C. (Hayden award 1967, pres. 1964-67), Nat. Assn. Broadcasters (dir. 1965-69, 73-77, chmn. radio 1976-77, chmn. bd., chmn. exec. com. 1977-79, Disting. Svc. award 1980), Mass. Broadcasters Assn. (pres. 1964, Disting. Svc. award 1964, 71, 78), Taconic Golf Club (Williamston, Mass.; bd. dirs. 1975-89). Republican. Methodist. Office: 466 Curran Hwy North Adams MA 01247-3919 *My goals have been to better my community, profession and life in general because I was a positive participant, and to provide independence, a sense of responsibility and a love of humanity for my family.*

THURSTON, ETHEL HOLBROOKE, retired music educator, foundation executive; b. Mpls., Oct. 30, 1911; d. Edward Sampson and Florence Chapman (Holbrooke) T. BA, Vassar Coll., 1933; diploma in organ, Fontainebleau Music Sch., France, 1930, 38; diploma in Gregorian chant, Pius X Sch., N.Y.C., 1945; PhD, NYU, 1954. Lectr. Coll. St. Catherine, St. Paul, 1945-46; prof. Hunter Coll., N.Y.C., 1953-59, St. John's U., Jamaica, N.Y., 1959-66; chmn. music history Manhattan Sch. Music, N.Y.C., 1966-81; ret., 1981. Editor facsimile edition The Music in the St. Victor Manuscript, 1959; editor music and text: The Works of Perotin, 1970, The Conductus Collections in Ms. Wolfenbuttel 1099 (3 vols.), 1980; contbr. articles on 13th century polyphony and manuscript transcription to various publs. Chair Beauty Without Cruelty USA, N.Y.C., 1972—; trustee Am. Fund for Alternatives to Animal Rsch., N.Y.C., 1977—. Mem. Am. Musicological Assn., Music Libr. Assn., Internat. Musicological Assn., Phi Beta Kappa, Mu Phi Epsilon, Mu Sigma. E-mail: alt2animals@aol.com., beautywocruelty@aol.com.

THURSTON, GEORGE BUTTE, mechanical and biomedical engineering educator; b. Austin, Tex., Oct. 8, 1924; s. Rudolph D. and Olivia Ruth (Lester) T.; m. Carol A. McWharter, Apr. 5, 1947; children— John Douglas, Mary Elizabeth. BS, U. Tex., Austin, 1944, MA, 1948, PhD, 1952. Registered profl. engr., Tex. Supr. hydroacoustics sect. Def. Research Lab., U. Tex., Austin, 1949-52; asst. prof. physics U. Wyo., Laramie, 1952-53, U. Ark., Fayetteville, 1953-54; physicist Naval Ordnance Test Sta., Inyokern, Calif., 1954-55; assoc. prof. Okla. State U., Stillwater, 1954-59; research physicist U. Mich., Ann Arbor, 1958-59; prof. Okla. State U., 1959-68; vis. scientist Centre de Recherche sur les Macromolecules, Strasbourg, France, 1963-64; prof. mech. engring. and biomed. engring. U. Tex., Austin, 1968—; pres. Vilastic Scientific, Inc. Vis. prof. Helmholtz Inst. fur Biomedizinische Technik, Aachen, West Germany, 1975-76; cons. for govt., industry. Contbr. articles to profl. jours. Recipient Brown U. Calculus prize, 1942; Alexander von Humboldt Found. Sr. U.S. Scientist award, 1975; NSF faculty fellow, 1963-64; numerous grants. Fellow Am. Phys. Soc., Acoustical Soc. Am.; mem. ASME, Soc. Rheology, Internat. Soc. Biorheology, Brit. Soc. Rheology, Sigma Xi, Sigma Pi Sigma. Home: 1000 Madrone Rd Austin TX 78746-4320 Office: U Tex Dept Mech Engring Austin TX 78712 E-mail: thurston@mail.utexas.edu.

THURSTON, JOHN THOMAS, university advancement official; b. Lockport, N.Y., Oct. 24, 1948; s. John Henry and Helen Lenore (Shaffert) Mahar. BA in English and Journalism, So. Ark. U., 1971. Ednl. affairs writer SUNY, Buffalo, 1972-74, sci. editor, 1974-76, news editor, 1976-77, assoc. dir. Univ. New Burs., 1977-78, dir., 1979-83, assoc. dir. pub. affairs, 1983-86, staff assoc. Univ. Rels., 1987-92, budget and pers. officer dept.Univ. Advancement and Devel., 1992-99, grant writer, 2000—. Communications instr., freelance writer, cons. Hockey coach, ofcl., youth baseball, basketball and football, pres. Western N.Y. High Sch. Club, 1983-85; pres. Lockport Tigers Youth Hockey Assn., 1996—. Recipient nat. award Coun. Advancement and Support of Edn., 1975, 78; named Lockport Sportsman of Yr., 1984. Mem. Coun. Advancement and Support Higher Edn., Nat. Assn. Sci. Writers, Constrn. Writers Am., Pub. Rels. Soc. Am., USA Hockey, Prof. Com. Western N.Y. Republican. Roman Catholic. Home: 4 Rogers Ave Lockport NY 14094-2520 Office: SUNY 318 Wende Hall Buffalo NY 14214 E-mail: jtt13@adelphia.net.

THURSTON, TINA LYN, archaeologist, educator; b. N.Y.C., Sept. 11, 1958; d. Ted Thurston and Danya Krupska; m. Nestor Enrique Zarragoitîa. BA, MA in Anthropology, CUNY, 1990; PhD in Anthropology, U. Wis., 1996. Archaeologist Wis. State Hist. Soc., Madison, 1994—96; asst. prof. Millsaps Coll., Jackson, Miss., 1997—99; dir. Thy Archaeol. Project, Thisted, Denmark, 1998—; asst. prof. Baylor U., Waco, Tex., 1999—2002, dir. Inst. of Archaeology, 2000—02; asst. prof. SUNY, Buffalo, 2002—. Author: Landscapes of Power, Landscapes of Conflict, 2001. Fellow, NSF, 1990—92; grantee, 1992—93, 1998, 2000—02. Mem.: North Atlantic Biocultural Orgn., Am. Anthrop. Assn., Soc. Am. Archaeology.

THURSTON, WILLIAM CECIL, flight engineer; b. Lexington, Ky., Mar. 3, 1945; s. Cecil Ballard and Ruth Eloise (Pickett) T.; m. Seher Demir, Oct. 24, 1992; children: Tammy Lynn Dill, Wendy JoAnn Collins, Oyku. BS, So. Ill. U., 1968; M in Aeronautics, Columbia U., 1994, PhD in Aviation Tech., 1998. Pilot USAF, Travis AFB, Calif., 1968-80; flight engr. Saudia/TWA, Jeddah, Saudi Arabia, 1980-87, IASCO, Burlingame, Calif., 1987—. Capt. USAF, 1968-80. Decorated Disiting. Flying Cross, 1968, Air Medal, 1968. Mem. AOPA, Masons (grand master Albert Pike Masonic Lodge, Wichita, Kans. 1978). Republican. Baptist. Avocations: golf, fishing. Home: 4321 Heart Pine Cir Pensacola FL 32504-7833

THURSTON, WILLIAM RICHARDSON, oil and gas industry executive, geologist; b. New Haven, Sept. 20, 1920; s. Edward S. and Florence (Holbrooke) T.; m. Ruth A. Nelson, Apr. 30, 1944 (div. 1966); children: Karin R., Amy R., Ruth A.; m. Beatrice Furnas, Sept. 11, 1971; children: Mark P., Stephen P., Douglas P., Jennifer P. AB in Geol. Sci. with honors, Harvard U., 1942. Field geologist Sun Oil Co., Corpus Christi, Tex., 1946-47, asst. to div. geologist Dallas, 1947-50; chief geologist The Kimbark Co., Denver, 1952-59; head exploration dept. Kimbark Exploration Co., 1959-66; co-owner Kimbark Exploration Ltd., 1966-67, Kimbark Assocs., Denver, 1967-76, Hardscrabble Assocs., Denver, 1976-80; pres. Weaselskin Corp., Durango, Colo., 1980—. Bd. dirs. Denver Bot. Gardens, 1972-99, Crow Canyon Ctr. for Archaeology, Cortez, Colo., 1980-92. Comdr. USNR, World War II, Korea. Decorated D.F.C. with 2 gold stars, air medal with 10 gold stars. Mem. Am. Assn. Petroleum Geologists, Denver Assn. Petroleum Landmen, Rocky Mountain Assn. Petroleum Geologists, Four Corners Geol. Soc. Republican. Avocations: photography, gardening, reading. Office: Weaselskin Corp 12995 Highway 550 Durango CO 81303-6674

THURSWELL, GERALD ELLIOTT, lawyer; b. Detroit, Feb. 4, 1944; s. Harry and Lilyan (Zeitlin) T.; m. Lynn Satovsky, Sept. 17, 1967 (div. Aug. 1978); children: Jennifer, Lawrence; m. Judith Linda Bendix, Sept. 2, 1978 (div. May 1999); children: Jeremy, Lindsey. LLB with distinction, Wayne State U., 1967. Bar: Mich. 1968, N.Y. 1984, D.C. 1985, Colo. 1990, Ill. 1992, U.S. Dist. Ct. (ea. dist.) Mich. 1968, U.S. Ct. Appeals (7th cir.) 1968, U.S. Supreme Ct. 1994. Student asst. to U.S. Atty. Eas. Dist. Mich., Detroit, 1966; assoc. Zwerdling, Miller, Klimist & Maurer, 1967-68; st. prnt. The Thurswell Law Firm. Southfield, Mich. Arbitrator Am. Arbitration Assn., Detroit, 1969—; mediator Wayne County Cir. Ct., Mich., 1983—, Oakland County Cir. Ct. Mich., 1984—, also facilitator, 1991; twp. atty. Royal Oak Twp., Mich., 1982—; lectr. Oakland County Bar Assn. People's Law Sch., 1988. Pres. Powder Horn Estates Subdivsn. Assn., West Bloomfield, Mich., 1975, United Fund, West Bloomfield, 1976. Arthur F. Lederly scholar Wayne State U. Law Sch., 1965; Wayne State U. Law Sch. grad. profl. scholar, 1965, 66. Mem. ATLA (treas. Detroit met. chpt. 1986-87, v.p. 1989-90, pres. 1991-93), Mich. Bar Assn. (investigator/arbitrator grievance bd., atty. discipline bd., chmn. hearing panel), Mich. Trial Lawyers Assn. (legis. com. on govtl. immunity 1984), Detroit Bar Assn. (lawyer referral com., panel pub. adv. com. jud. candidates), Oakland County Bar Assn., Skyline Club (Southfield). Office: The Thurswell Law Firm 1000 Town Ctr Ste 500 Southfield MI 48075-1221

THYDEN, JAMES ESKEL, diplomat, educator, lecturer; b. L.A., Apr. 10, 1939; s. Eskel A. and Mildred Aileene (Rock) T.; m. Patricia Irene Kelsey, Dec. 15, 1959; children: Teresa Lynn, Janice Kay, James Blaine. BA in Biology, Pepperdine U., 1961; MA in Scandinavian Area Studies, U. Wash., 1992. Cert. secondary tchr., Calif., Wash. Tchr. Gompers Jr. High Sch., L.A., 1962-64; fgn. svc. officer U.S. Dept. State, Washington, 1964-90; rschr. U. Wash., Seattle, 1992-93; exec. dir. Seattle chpt. UN Assn., 1993-96. Travel lectr. Cunard Lines' Royal Viking Sun, 1995, and Royal Caribbean's Splendour of the Seas, 1997. Editor govt. report, ann. human rights reports, 1983-86; author, editor in-house govt. reports, documents. Dir. Office of Human Rights, 1983-86; counselor Embassy for Polit. Affairs, Am. Embassy, Oslo, Norway, 1986-90; bd. mem. Edmonds Libr. Named Outstanding Young Man Am., 1969, Alumnus of Yr., Pepperdine U., 1984. Mem.: Edmonds Libr. Bd., Soc. Advancement of Scandinavian Studies, World Affairs Coun. Seattle, Am. Fgn. Svc. Assn. Avocations: travel, reading, gardening. Home: 5631 153rd Pl SW Edmonds WA 98026-4239 E-mail: jethyden@aol.com.

THYSEN, BENJAMIN, biochemist, health science facility administrator, researcher; b. N.Y.C., July 27, 1932; s. Bernard and Clara (Linietsky) Tissenbaum; m. Joan Albin; children: Julie Ann, Gregory Eden. BS, CCNY, 1954; MS, U. Mo., 1963; PhD, St. Louis U. Med. Sch., 1967. Instr. biochemistry and ob-gyn. depts. St. Louis U. Med. Sch., 1967-68; sr. rsch. scientist Technicon Instrument Corp., Ardsly, N.Y., 1968-69, group leader Tarrytown, 1969-70; asst. prof. lab., med., and ob-gyn depts. Albert Einstein Coll. Medicine, Bronx, 1971-86, assoc. prof. lab. med. and ob-gyn depts., 1986-2001, assoc. prof. epidemioogy and ob-gyn. depts., 2001—, dir. endocrine labs., 1971-2001, dir. andrology labs., 1997-2001; lab. dir. Park Ave. Fertility, N.Y.C., 2001—. Cons. Technicon Instrument Corp., Tarrytown, 1979-81; mem. spl. study sect. Nat. Inst. Environ. Health Sci., 1986. Contbr. articles to profl. jours. Served with U.S. Army, 1956-58. Recipient Cancer Research award St. Louis U., 1967-68; fellow NIH, 1963-67. Mem. AAAS, Fed. Am. Socs. Exptl. Biology, Assn. Clin. Scientists, Soc. Study of Reprodn., Endocrine Soc., Sigma Xi. Office: Albert Einstein Coll Med 1300 Morris Park Ave Bronx NY 10461-2659 E-mail: thysen@aecom.yu.edu.

TIA, MANG, civil engineering educator; b. Phnom-Penh, Cambodia, Aug. 31, 1953; came to U.S., 1972; s. Chhay and You (Khou) T.; m. Liang Tsi Maria Mao, May 25, 1980; children: Samuel Q., Luke L., Timothy J. BSCE, BSME, MIT, 1976; MSCE, Purdue U., 1978, PhD in Civil Engring., 1982. Registered profl. engr., Fla. Vis. asst. prof. La. Tech. U., Ruston, La., 1982; vis. rsch. assoc. prof. Nat. Ctrl. U., Taiwan, 1989-90; asst. prof. U. Fla., Gainesville, 1982-87, assoc. prof., 1987-92, prof. civil engring., 1992—. Cons. in field. Contbr. articles to Jour. Asphalt Paving Technologists, ACI Material Jours., ASCE Transp. Jour., Transp. Rsch. Record. Deacon Gainesville Chinese Christian Ch., 1990—. Mem. ASCE, ASTM, Am. Concrete Inst., Am. Soc. Engring. Edn., Assn. Asphalt Paving Technologists, Transp. Rsch. Bd. Achievements include patent for Field Permeability Test Apparatus for Concrete. Home: 8214 NW 63rd Pl Gainesville FL 32653-6806

TIAHRT, W. TODD, congressman, former state senator; b. Vermillion, S.D., June 15, 1951; s. Wilbur E. and Sara Ella Marcine (Steele) T.; m. Vicki Lyn Holland, Aug. 14, 1976; children: Jessica, John, Luke. Student, S.D. Sch. Mines & Tech., Rapid City, 1969-72; BA, Evangel Coll., 1975; MBA, S.W. Mo. State U., 1989. Property estimator Crawford & Co., Springfield, Mo., 1975-78; project engr. Zenith Electronics, 1978-81; cost engr. Boeing, Wichita, Kans., 1981-94, proposal mgr., 1991-94; state senator State of Kans., Topeka, 1993—95; mem. U.S. Congress from 4th Kans. dist., Washington, 1995—; mem. appropriations com., 1997—. Chmn. 4th dist. Rep. party, 1990-92; exec. com. Kans. Rep. party, 1990-92, nat. security com., sci. com. Mem. Pachyderm (bd. dirs. 1991-92), Delta Sigma Phi. Republican. Home: 1329 Amity St Goddard KS 67052-9133 Office: 401 Cannon HOB Washington DC 20515-1604*

TIAN, XIUCHUN, research scientist; b. Beijing, Mar. 21, 1963; came to US, 1986; s. Zhentong Tian and Rongzhen Ma; m. Xiangzhong Yang, Jan. 5, 1986; 1 child, Andrew Yang. BS, Beijing Agrl. U., 1985; MS, Cornell U., 1989, PhD, 1994. Postdoct. assoc. Cornell U., Ithaca, N.Y., 1995-96; rsch. assoc. U. Conn., Storrs, 1996—, asst. prof., 2002—. Contbr. articles to scientific jours.; patentee in field. Co-organizer U. Conn. Chinese Sch., Storrs, 1999. Overseas fellow Chinese Edn. Commn., 1985; rsch. grantee Conn. Invention, Inc., 1999; recipient Nat. Rsch. Svc. award NIH, 1995, 2001, USDA, 2001. Mem. Internat. Embryo Transfer Soc., N.Y. Acad. Scis., Phi Kappa Phi. Avocation: internat. travel. Office: U Conn 3636 Horsebarn Rd Ext Storrs Mansfield CT 06269

TIANO, ANTHONY STEVEN, television producer, book publishing executive; b. Santa Fe, Mar. 27, 1941; s. Joseph A. and Marian (Adlesperger) T.; m. Kathleen O'Brien, Dec. 29, 1972; children: Mark A., A. Steven. BA, U. N.Mex., 1969, MA, 1971; LittD (hon.), Calif. Sch. Profl. Psychology, 1985. Dir. programming Sta. KNME-TV U. N.Mex., Albuquerque, 1968-72; sta. mgr. Sta. WHA-TV U. Wis., Madison, 1972-76; exec. dir. Sta. KETC-TV, St. Louis, 1976-78; pres., CEO KQED, Inc., San Francisco, 1978-93; chmn., CEO Santa Fe Ventures, Inc., 1993—. Vice-chair bd. dirs. Calif. Sch. Profl. Psychology, San Francisco, 1985-90. Mem. Nat. Assn. Pub. TV Stas. (vice chair bd. dirs. 1986). Office: Santa Fe Ventures 999 16th St 9 San Francisco CA 94107-2468

TIBBITTS, BARRICK FRANK, engineer; b. Annapolis, Md., Sept. 24, 1934; s. Frank Pixley T. and Kathryn Jane (Barrick) Rice; m. Marcia Slayton Coughlin, Apr. 30, 1989; children from previous marriage: Tamara, Felisa, Christopher. BS, U.S. Naval Acad., 1956; MS, MIT, 1965. Commd. ensign USN, 1956, advanced through grades to capt., 1976, retired, 1990; chief systems engr. John J. McMullen Assocs., Arlington, Va., 1991—. Comdr. David Taylor Rsch. Ctr., 1981-84; prof. naval constrn. MIT, Cambridge, Mass., 1987-90. Co-author: (chpts.) Aircraft Carriers, 1963, Naval Vessels, 1968, Naval Submarines, 1968. Fellow Royal Inst. Naval Architects; mem.

Am. Soc. Naval Engrs., Soc. Naval Architects & Marine Engrs. (ship design com. 1995—). Home: 6908 Pacific Ln Annandale VA 22003-5935 Office: JJMA 4300 King St Alexandria VA 22302

TIBBLE, DOUGLAS CLAIR, lawyer; b. Joliet, Ill., May 26, 1952; BA, DePaul U., 1974; JD, Syracuse U., 1977, MPA, 1978. Bar: Ill., U.S. Dist. Ct. (no. dist.) Ill., U.S. Ct. Appeals (7th cir.), U.S. Supreme Ct. Ptnr. McBride, Baker & Coles, Oakbrook Terrace, Ill., 1996—. Mem. ABA, DuPage County Bar Assn., Chgo. Bar Assn. Office: McBride Baker & Coles 1 Mid America Plz Ste 1000 Oakbrook Terrace IL 60181-4710 E-mail: tibble@mbc.com.

TIBBS, MARTHA JANE PULLEN, civic worker; b. Memphis, Feb. 12, 1932; d. John Thomas Jr. and Martha Frances (Gragg) Pullen; m. Eugene Edward Tibbs; children: Martha Katherine, Eugene Edward Jr. BSBA, U. Tenn., 1953; MA Edn., U. Memphis, 1958. Cert. tchr., social worker, Tenn. Tchr. Lausanne Sch., Memphis, 1954-55, Millington H.S., Memphis, 1955-56, Presbyn. Day Sch., Memphis, 1956-57, St. Mary's Episcopal Sch., Memphis, 1958-60; social worker Tenn. Dept. Pub. Welfare, 1962-63. Author geneal. works. Mem. Memphis Vol. Svc. Bd., 1963-64; mem. Shelby County Hist. Comm., 1983-97, commr., 1983—; block worker Cancer, Kidney and Heart Fund, Memphis, 1984—. Mem.: DAR (past chpt. regent, sec.-treas. regents coun.), AAUW, NEA, Tenn. Geneal. Soc., Tenn. Tchrs. Assn., Planetgenet Soc., Sovereign Colonial Soc. Ams. Royal Descent, Tenn. State Dames of Ct. of Honor (historian, nat. def. chmn., 1st v.p.), Colonial Dames Am., Cleve. Jr. Aux., Cleve. Med. Aux. (sec./treas.), West Tenn. Hist. Soc., Chicasaw Dist. DAR Sch. (Tenn. state vice chmn. DAR schs., parliamentarian Zachariah Davies chpt., chmn. Zachariah Davies chpt.), Nat. Registrar Daus. of Founders and Patriots Am. (v.p. Tenn. chpt. , past Tenn. state registrar), Tenn. State Registrar Founders and Patriots, Nat. Soc. Colonial Dames XVII Century (2d v.p. past treas. Chucaqua chpt.), Nat. Soc. So. Dames Am. (past pres. Memphis chpt., past state pres., historian 2001—02), Tenn. State DAR (transp. chmn. 2001—), Colonial Order of Crown, Soc. Descendants of Knights Most Noble Order of Garter, Am. Clan Gregor Soc., Family of Bruce Soc., Memphis Scottish Soc., Am. Clan Donald Soc., Nat. Soc. Magna Charta Dames and Barons (past Magna Carta sec. West Tenn. chpt. 2001—02), Cleve. Garden Club (past pres.), U. Club Memphis, Early Settlers Shelby County (registrar 1988, bd. dirs. 1992—, sec. 1998—, pres. 2002—), Nineteenth Century Club (newsletter editor 1985—88, sec. 1993—95, corr. sec. 1999—), Racquet Club, Cleve. Women's Club, Alpha Omega Pi. Republican. Presbyterian. Avocations: art, genealogy, computers, dancing, tennis. Home: 2008 Massey Rd Memphis TN 38119-6404

TIBERI, PAT, former state legislator, congressman; m. Denice Tiberi. BA, Ohio State Univ. Asst. dist. mgr. Congressman John Kasich; rep. from dist. 26 Ohio Ho. Reps., 1993—2001, majority fl. leader, mem. ins. and vets. affairs coms.; mem. U.S. Congress from 12th Ohio dist., 2001—, Armed Svcs. Com., Small Bus. Com. Pres. Windsor Terrace Learning Ctr. Mem. adv. bd. Columbus chpt. ARC, Columbus Italian Cultural Ctr., Com. Edn. & Workforce, Fin. Svcs.; past pres. Forest Park Civic Assn.; former rep. Northland Community Coun.; pres., co-founder Windsor Terrace Learning Ctr. Recipient Pres.'s award Northland Cmty. Coun., Vet. Admin Commendation award, Svc. award Am. Red Cross, Watchdog of Treas. award United Conservatives of Ohio. Mem. Sons of Italy. Home: 5208 Honeytree Loop W Columbus OH 43229-4631 Office: 508 Cannon Ho Office Bldg Washington DC 20515 also: Dist Office 2700 E Dublin Granville Rd Ste 525 Columbus OH 43231*

TIBLIER, FERNAND JOSEPH, JR. municipal engineering administrator; b. New Orleans, Mar. 11, 1960; s. Fernand Joseph and Dorothy May (Bosworth) T.; m. Janine Therese Cousineau, Sept. 1, 1990; children: Amanda, Christine. BA in Chemistry, Biology, Drury Coll., 1982; MS in Environ. Engring., U. Cen. Fla., 1986. Registered profl. engr., Fla. Rsch. asst. U. Cen. Fla., Orlando, 1983-86; asst. city engr., then acting city engr. City of Longwood, Fla., 1986-92, city engr., 1992-94, dir. pub. works, city engr., 1994-96; city engr., dir. pub. works City of Deltona, 1996-2000; engring. project mgr. McKim & Creed, P.A., 2000—. Mem. road impact fee com. Seminole County Citizen Adviser, Sanford, Fla., 1988-89; mem. water resources task force Seminole County Tech. Adviser, Sanford, 1992; advisor Pub. Works Acad. Oak Ridge High Sch., Orlando, 1996—; mem. Dean of Engring. adv. coun. U. Cen. Fla.; mem. tech. adv. com. Volusian Water Alliance. Lector, youth minister Nativity Ch., Lake Mary, Fla., 1987—; team capt. City of Longwood March of Dimes, 1992; mem. City of Longwood Planning Agy., 1997-98. Mem. ASCE, NSPE, Am. Pub. Works Assn., Am. Water Works Assn., Fla. Engring. Soc. (sec. Daytona Beach chpt. 2002), Volusia Assn. Mcpl. Engrs. Republican. Roman Catholic. Avocations: home improvement, photography, travel, cooking, reading. Home: 407 Parson Brown Way Longwood FL 32750-4020 Office: McKim & Creed 1901 Mason Ave Ste 102 Daytona Beach FL 32117-5105

TIBREWALA, SUSHIL, physician; b. Mukundgarh, Rajasthan, India, Feb. 11, 1953; s. Shantidevi and M.P. T.; m. Neelam Tibrewala, Feb. 20, 1981; children: Anjan, Neha. MBBS, U. Bombay, 1977, MS. Resident in internal medicine to chief resident U. Health Scis./Chgo. Med. Sch., 1987-90; fellow in gastroenterology Univ. Health Scis./Chgo. Med. Sch., 1990-92; gastroenterologist Carbondale (Ill.) Clinic, 1992-99; med. dir. Carbondale Clinic Ambulatory Surgery Ctr., 1996-99; chair dept. medicine Carbondale Clinic, 1997-99; gastroenterologist Gastroenterology Care So. Ill., Herrin, 1999—. Chair Meml. Hosp. of Carbondale, 1995-97. Contbr. articles to profl. jours. Fellow Am. Coll. Physicians; mem. India Assn. of So. Ill. (bd. dirs. 1995-97), Assn. of Am. Physicians of Indian Origin (regional dir. 1997-98). Avocations: tennis, swimming. Office: Gastroenterolgy Care So Ill 3305 Logan Dr Herrin IL 62948-3730 Fax: 618-998-8886.

TIBSHRAENY, JAY, former mayor; b. Chandler, Ariz. m. Karen Tibshraeny; 1 child, Lauren. BS in Acctg., Ariz. State U. Owner property mgmt. firm, Chandler; citrus grower; mem. Chandler City Coun., 1986—; vice mayor City of Chandler, 1990—94, mayor, 1994—2002. Chmn. Regional Pub. Transp. Authority, City of Chandler; mem. Maricopa Assn. Govts. Regional Coun., Greater Phoenix Econ. Coun., Ariz. Mcpl. Water Users Assn., Ariz. League of Cities and Towns Resolutions Com., Williams Air Force Redevel. Partnership, Nat. League of Cities Transp. and Comm. Com. Mem. Chandler Friends of the Libr.; adv. bd. Chandler-Gilbert Assn. for Retarded Citizens, Child Crisis Ctr., Chandler; mem. City Coun. Pub. Safety com., Chandler Pub. Safety Retirement Sys. Bd., Chandler Vol. Firemen Pension bd. Mem. Chandler Hist. Soc., Chandler C. of C. (bd. dirs.).*

TICE, BRADLEY SCOTT, humanities educator; b. Palo Alto, Calif., Oct. 6, 1959; s. Lilburn Trent and Paula Nanette (Osborne) T. AA, De Anza Coll., Cupertino, Calif., 1983; BA in History, San Jose State U., 1987; AA, De Anza Coll., Cupertino, Calif., 1995; PhD in Chemistry, Fairfax U., Baton Rouge, 1996; Diploma in Ayurvedic Medicine, The Ayurvedic Inst.; Diploma in Stress therapy, Internat. Yoga Sch.; LittD in Tchg., St. Clements Univ., The Carribean, 1998; DD (hon.), 1999; Doctor Philosophy in Comparative Religion, Am. Coll. Metaphysical Theology, Minn., 2001; PhD in Elec. Engring., Cambridge State U., 2001; PhD in Metaphysics, Am. Coll. of Metaphysical Theology, 2002. Cert. Cmty. Emergency Response Tng., Cupertino, Calif.; ordained to ministry Protestant Ch. Mem. staff Stanford Linear Accelerator Ctr., 1981-87; prof. Pacific Lang. Inst., Cupertino, Calif., 1992—; dir. rsch. Advanced Human Design, 1992—; CEO Tice Pharms., San Jose; intern Ames Rsch. Ctr. NASA, Moffett Field, Calif., 1997-98, mission specialist astronaut candidate, 2001; substitute instr. Palo Alto (Calif.) Unified Sch. Dist., 2001. Substitute libr. Robert Crown Law Libr. Stanford U., 1989; substitute instr. San Jose Unified Sch. Dist., 2002; adj. prof. Sch. Arts and Scis. Nat. U., San Jose, 2000—01; adj. prof. Nat. Hispanic U., San Jose, 2000—02, mem. faculty senate; grand awards judge engring. Intel Internat. Sci. and Engring. Fair, Louisville, 2002; mem. staff San Jose Giants Baseball Club, 2002. Editor: Jour. Pacific Lang. Inst., 1995—96; mem. editl. bd. The Story of Life.; contbr. articles to profl. jours. Vol. De Young Mus., San Francisco, 1990, Mus. Modern Art, San Francisco, 1990, Calif. Acad. Scis., San Francisco, 1990; vol. guide Monterey Bay Aquarium, 1990; elected mem. Cupertino Pub. Safety Comm., 2000—02; mem. Santa Clara County Sheriff's Citizens Acad., San Jose, 2002; block leader tng. program Cupertino, 2002; mem. spl. events patrol dept. pub. safety Stanford U., 2001; candidate for bd. trustees Foothill-De Anza CC Dist., Los Altos Hills, 2002; neighborhood accountability bd. vol. Count of Santa Clara Probation Dept. Restorative Justice Program, Juvenile Probation Dept., San Jose, 2001; grand awards judge in chemistry Intel Internat. Sci. and Engring. Fair, 2001; investor in preservation Computer History Mus., Moffett Field, 2001. Recipient Pres.'s award Nat. Author's Registry, 1996, editor's choice award (3), The Nat. Libr. of Poetry, 1995, (2), 1996, Cert. Merit for essay, Pharmacia Biotech and Sci. prize for young scientists, 1997, Commemorative Medal Honor, Hallmark, 2000, Jr. Engr. award A.G. Spalding and Bros., 1965; elected Order of Internat. Ambs., 1999, Internat. Man of the Year (medal of hon.), 1996, 97, Man of the Year (commemorative medal award), 1997, Internat. Order Merit, 2000, Commemorative medal of honor Hallmark, 2000, Noble Prize Outstanding Achievement and Contbns. to Humanity, United Cultural Conv., Raleigh, N.C., 2001. Fellow Am. Coll. Metaphys. Theology; em. ACS, IEEE, AIAA, COSPAR (mem. com. space rsch.), Am. Physical Soc., N.Y. Acad. Scis., Assn. Computing Machinery, Am. Soc. Microbiology, Internat. Assn. Tchrs. English as a Fgn. Lang., Internat. Soc. Poets, Mars Soc. (found. mem.), Calif. Assn. for Health, Phys. Edn., Recreation and Dance (v.p. elect for recreation 1999), Internat. Pankration Assn. (founder). Avocations: weight training, fencing, bicycling, swimming, scuba diving. Office: Pacific Language Inst PO Box 2214 Cupertino CA 95015-2214

TICE, CAROL HOFF, intergenerational specialist, consultant; b. Ashville, N.C., Oct. 6, 1931; d. Amos H. and Fern (Irvin) Hoff; m. (div.); children: Karin E., Jonathan H. BS, Manchester Coll., North Manchester, Ind., 1954; MEd, Cornell U., 1955. Cert. tchr., Mich., N.Y., N.J. Tchr. Princeton (N.J.) Schs., 1955-60; tchr. Ann Arbor (Mich.) Schs., 1964—; dir. intergenerational programs Inst. for Study Children and Families Eastern Mich. U., Ypsilanti, 1985-96. Founder, pres. Lifespan Resources, Inc., Ann Arbor, 1979—; presdl. appointee to U.S. Nat. Commn. Internat. Yr. of the Child, Washington, 1979-81; del. to White House Conf. on Aging, Washington, 1995. Innovator; program, Tch. Learning Intergenerational Communities, 1971; author: Guide Books and articles, Community of Caring, 1980; co-producer, Film, What We Have, 1976 (award, Milan, Italy Film Festival 1982). Trustee Blue Lake Fine Arts Camp, Twin Lake, Mich., 1975—; dir. Visual Arts Colony, 1990—. Recipient Program Innovation award, Mich. Dept. Edn., 1974—80, C.S. Mott Found. award, 1982, Nat. Found. Improvement in Edn. award, Washington, 1986, Disting. Alumni award, Manchester Coll., 1979, A+ Break the Mold award, U.S. Sec. of Edn., 1992, Ann Arbor Sch. Supts. Golden Apple award, 1999, Disting. Svc. award, Mich. Art Edn. Assn., 2001; fellow Ford Found. fellow, Ithaca, N.Y., 1955. Mem. AAUW (agt. 1979, Agent of Change award), Generations United (hon. com. for Margaret Mead Centennial 2001, 1998—, Pioneer award 1989), Mich. Edn. Assn. (hon. mention Program Innovation 2000), Optimist Club (Humanitarian award). Democrat. Presbyterian. Office: Scarlett MS 3300 Lorraine St Ann Arbor MI 48108-1970

TICE, DOUGLAS OSCAR, JR. federal bankruptcy judge; b. Lexington, N.C., May 2, 1933; s. Douglas Oscar Sr. and Lila Clayton (Wright) T.; m. Janet N. Capps, Feb. 28, 1959 (div. Sept. 1976); children: Douglas Oscar III, Janet E.; m. Martha Murdoch Edwards, June 8, 1996. BS, U. N.C., 1955, JD, 1957. Bar: N.C. 1957, U.S. Ct. Appeals (4th cir.) 1964, Va. 1970, U.S. Dist. ct. (ea. dist.) Va. 1976, U.S. Bankruptcy Ct. (ea. dist.) Va. 1976. Exec. sec. N.C. Jud. Coun., Raleigh, 1958-59; assoc. Baucom & Adams, 1959-61; trial atty. Office Dist. Coun., IRS, Richmond, Va., 1961-70; corp. atty. Carlton Industries, Inc., 1970-75; ptnr. Hubard, Tice, Marchant & Samuels, P.C., 1975-87; judge U.S. Bankruptcy Ct. (ea. dist.), Richmond, Norfolk, Alexandria, Va., 1987-99, chief judge, 1999—. Co-author: Monument & Boulevard, Richmond's Grand Avenues, 1996; contbr. articles to profl. jours. Vice pres. Richmond Pub. Forum, 1976-80, com. chmn. Richmond Forum, Inc., 1986-2001; past pres. Richmond Civil War Roundtable, mem., 1965—; bd. dirs. Epilepsy Assn. Va., Inc., 1976-87. Capt. USAR, 1957-66. Mem. ABA, Va. Bar Assn., City of Richmond Bar Assn., Am. Bankruptcy Inst., Nat. Conf. Bankruptcy Judges, So. Hist. Assn., Va. Hist. Soc., Old Dominion Sertoma (pres. Richmond chpt. 1967). Home: 5 Foxmere Drive Richmond VA 23233 Office: US Bankruptcy Ct 1100 E Main St Ste 339 Richmond VA 23219-3538 E-mail: home:dotice@aol.com., bus.douglas_tice@vaeb.uscourts.gov.

TICE, GEORGE A(NDREW), photographer; b. Newark, Oct. 13, 1938; s. William S. and Margaret T. (Robertson) T.; m. Joanna Blaylock, 1958; m. Marie Tremmel, 1960; children: Christopher, Loretta, Lisa, Lynn, Jennifer. Instr. photography New Sch. Social Research, 1970-98. Photographer (one-man shows) Witkin Gallery, 1970, Met. Mus. Art, 1972, (group shows) Whitney Mus. Am. Art, 1974, Mus. Modern Art, 1979, (permanent collections), Met. Mus. Art, Art Inst. Chgo., Bibliotheque Nationale, Nihon U., Tokyo, books include Fields of Peace, 1970, Fields of Peace, reissued, 1998, Goodbye River, Goodbye, 1971, Paterson, 1972, Seacoast Maine, 1973, George A. Tice Photographs, 1953-73, 1975, Urban Landscapes, 1975, Artie Van Blarcum, 1977, Urban Romantic, 1982, Lincoln, 1984, Hometons, 1988, Stone Walls, Grey Skies, 1991, George Tice: Selected Photographs, 1953-1999, 2001, photographer (one-man shows) Internat. Ctr. Photography, 2002, books include George Tice: Urban Landscapes, 2002. Served with USN, 1956-59. Recipient Grand prix for best photography book of Year Arles, France, 1973; Guggenheim Found. fellow, 1973-74, Nat. Endowment for Arts fellow, 1973—; Bradford fellow, Eng., 1990-91, N.J. State Coun. on the Arts fellow, 1998. Address: 581 Kings Hwy East Atlantic Highlands NJ 07716-2825 Fax: 732-706-3586.

TICE, KIRK CLIFFORD, health care facility executive; b. Jersey City, July 3, 1954; s. Clifford Cromwell and Anneke Meta (Vanderveer) T.; m. Judith Elizabeth Sheppard, Oct. 15, 1988; children: Brian Clifford, Jonathan Robert. AAS, Bergen Community Coll., 1976; BA, M Profl. Svcs., New Sch. Social Rsch., 1987. Asst. dir. clin. svcs. Rahway (N.J.) Hosp., 1982-84, dir. clin. svcs., 1984-88, dir. bus. devel., 1987-88, v.p. clin. svcs., 1988-93, sr. v.p., 1993-94, interim pres., 1994; pres., CEO, 1994—. Bd. dirs. Rahway Geriatric Ctr., chmn., 1993—; bd. dirs. QualCare Preferred Providers. Mem.: Sr. Healthcare Execs. N.J. (sec.-treas. 1991, v.p. 1991—92, pres. 1993), N.J. Hosp. Assn., Am. Hosp. Assn., Am. Coll. Healthcare Execs., Rahway Kiwanis (v.p. 1989—90, pres.-elect 1990—91, pres. 1991—92). Home: 16 Swans Mill Ln Scotch Plains NJ 07076-3406 Office: Rahway Hosp 865 Stone St Rahway NJ 07065-2797 E-mail: ktice@rahwayhospital.com.

TICE, LAURIE DIETRICH, lawyer; b. Houston, Apr. 9, 1959; d. Donald Vernon and June (Reagan) Dietrich; m. Michael Dean Tice, Feb. 25, 1984 (div. May 1991); children: Rachel Michele, Rebekah Leigh. ABA approved, Southwestern Paralegal Inst., Houston, 1989; BA in History with highest honors, U. Tex., El Paso, 1994; JD, U. Tex., 1997. Bar: Tex. 1997. Legal sec. Gant & Juarez, Carlsbad, N.Mex., 1979-80; dep. clk. 5th Jud. Dist. Ct. N.Mex., 1980-82; legal asst. Hinkle, Cox, Eaton, Coffield & Hensley, Roswell, N.Mex., 1982-86, Kemp, Smith, Duncan & Hammond, El Paso, Tex., 1986-92; assoc. McGinnis, Lochridge & Kilgore L.L.P., Austin, 1997-99, Rogers & Whitley, L.L.P., Austin, 1999—. Elder, chair resource and planning com., Univ. Presbyn. Ch., Austin, 2000-; mem. UPC Hard Knox Tennis Team. Franklin Myers Endowed Presdl. scholar, 1994-95, Judge Wilson Cohen Endowed Presdl. scholar, 1995-96, Israel Dreeben Endowed Meml. scholar, 1995-96. Mem. ABA, Tex. Bar Assn., Travis County Bar Assn. (dir. real estate sect.), Travis County Women Lawyers Assn. (membership com., dir., treas. 2001-02), Austin Young Lawyers Assn., Golden Key, Mortar Board (pres.), Beta Sigma Phi (rec. sec. 1984-85), Alpha Lambda Delta, Phi Alpha Theta (pres., sec.), Alpha Chi. Democrat. Home: 4404 Travis Country Cir Apt A2 Austin TX 78735-6601 E-mail: ltice@rwllp.com.

TICE, PAMELA PARADIS, scientific editor, writer; b. Hutchinson, Minn., Sept. 1, 1955; d. Paul Edward, Sr. and Mary LaVerne (Hebert) Paradis; m. Jeffrey Johns Powell, June 17, 1977 (div. July 1982); m. Christopher Allen Tice, Aug. 25, 1997. BA, Coll. of St. Scholastica, 1977. Statis./sec. U. Tex. M.D. Anderson Cancer Ctr., Houston, 1978-87; data coord. Baylor Coll. Medicine, 1987-88, editl. asst., 1988-90, sr. editor, 1992-2000, rsch. assoc., 2000—; dept. editor U. Tex. Med. Sch., 1990-91; editor, Houston medicine HCA Ctr. for Health Excell., 1991-92; exec. asst. U. Tex. Sch. Nursing, 1991-92. Mem. scope and mandate task force, Coun. of Sci. Editors, Chgo., 1996. Editor-in-chief: Am. Med. Writers Assn. Jour., 1992-95 (Apex awards 1995, 96, 97, Matrix award 1996, 2000, 2001, others). Mem. AAAS, Am. Med. Writers Assn. (chpt. sec. 1989-90, chpt. treas. 1990-92, chpt. pres.-elect 1992-93, chpt. pres. 1993-94, chpt. past pres. 1994-95, chpt. dir.-at-large 2001—, Chpt. Svc. award 1994, Assn. Pres. award 1993, Assn. Leadership award 1995), Coun. of Sci. Editors, Bd. of Editors in the Life Scis. (diplomate 2002), Assn. for Women in Comm. Office: Baylor Coll Medicine Dept Family & Cmty Medicine 5615 Kirby Dr Ste 610 Houston TX 77005-2489 E-mail: pptice@bcm.tmc.edu.

TICE, RAPHAEL DEAN, army officer; b. Topeka, Dec. 4, 1927; s. Arthur Taylor and Mamie (McDonald) T.; m. Eunice Miriam Suddarth, Dec. 23, 1946; children: Karen Ann Tice Claterbos, William Dean. BS in Mil. Sci., U. Md., 1963; MSBA, George Washington U., 1970. Served as enlisted man U.S. Army, 1946-47; commd. 2d lt., 1947; advanced through grades to lt. gen., 1981; platoon leader and co. comdr. 1st Inf. div., W.Ger., 1949-52; co. comdr., regimental adj. 8th Inf. divsn., 1955-56; tng. advisor Vietnam, 1956-57; mem. staff Office of Dep. Chief of Staff for Pers., Dept. Army, 1960-63; chief pers. mgmt. divsn. Office of Under Sec. of Army, 1963-64; plans Officer So. Command, Panama, 1965-67; dep. comdr. 3rd Brig., 4th Inf. Divsn., 1967; comdr. 2nd Bn., 12th Inf. of 25th Inf. divsn., Vietnam, 1968; exec. for pers. procurement Office of Sec. Def. for Manpower and Res. Affairs, 1968-69; comdr. 1st Brig., 1st Inf. divsn., 1970, chief of staff, 1971; dep. dir. mil. pers. mgmt. Dept. Army, 1972-73; comdg. gen. Berlin Brigade, 1974-76; dep. chief of staff personnel U.S. Army Europe, 1976-77; comdg. gen. 3rd. Inf. divsn., 1977-79; dep. asst. sec. def. for mil. pers. and force mgmt. Dept. Def., 1979-85; exec. dir. Nat. Recreation and Pk. Assn., 1986—. Spl. adviser Pres.'s Coun. on Phys. Fitness and Sports Decorated Silver Star, Legion of Merit with 2 oak leaf clusters, Air medal with V and 7 oak leaf clusters, Bronze Star with V, Vietnam Cross of Gallantry with Palm, Purple Heart., Def. Disting. Service medal, Army Disting. Service medal Mem. Assn. U.S. Army, Am. Chess Found. (hon. pres.) Home: 18077 Clendenning Cir Round Hill VA 20141-2580 Office: Nat Recreation and Pk Assn 22377 Belmont Ridge Rd Ashburn VA 20148-4501 E-mail: rdt509@aol.com., d.tice@nrpa.org.

TICER, PATRICIA, state senator; m. Jack Ticer; 4 children. Grad., Sweet Briar Coll. Councilwoman City of Alexandria, Va., 1982-84, vice mayor, 1984-90, appointed mayor, 1991-92, mayor, 1992-95; state senator Commonwealth of Va., 1995—. Mem. Agrl., Conservation and Natural Resources Com., Rehab. and Social Svcs. Com., Local Govt. Com., 1995—; vice chair, Joint Com. on Tech. and Sci., former chair Metro Washington Coun. of Govts.; bd. dirs. No. Va. Transp. Commn., chmn., 1994; bd. trustees Land Conservation Found. commn. on Early Childhood and Child Day Care Programs. Mem. Commn. on Access and Diversity in Higher Edn. in Va. Office: City Hall 301 King St Alexandria VA 22314-3211 Also: Va Senate 429 Gen Assembly Bldg Richmond VA 23219 E-mail: patsy@tidalwave.net.

TICHENOR, CHARLES BECKHAM, III, operations research analyst; b. Balt., Mar. 10, 1950; s. Charles Beckham II and Suzanne Nelson (Stevens) T.; m. Alison P. Walton, May 29, 1971; 1 child, Charles Beckham IV. BSBA, Ohio State U., 1972; MBA, Va. Tech., 1990; PhD in Bus., Berne U., 1999. Asst. prodn. supr. Champale Products, Norfolk, Va., 1977-80; ops. rsch. analyst IRS, Washington, 1989-93, tech. adv. info. sys. performance mgmt. office. Adj. faculty Strayer U., Balt. Lt. col. USAR, ret. Mem. Mensa. Roman Catholic. Avocations: Tae Kwon Do (black belt), amateur astronomer. Home: 6207 Cardinal Brook Ct Springfield VA 22152-1516 Office: Def Security Coop Agy Jefferson Davis Hwy Ste 203 Alexandria VA 22301 E-mail: charley.tichenor@osd.pentagon.mil.

TICHENOR, JAMES ROBERT, III, retired career officer; b. Louisville, May 30, 1938; s. James Robert Jr. and Mary Elizabeth T.; m. Loralyn Joan Higgins, July 3, 1961 (div. Aug. 1969); children: Mark Owen, Dana Lynn, Eric Russell; m. Patricia Ann Dawson, June 13, 1970. BS, U.S. Mil. Acad., 1960; MS (with distinction), U.S. Naval Postgrad. Sch., 1967. Commd. 2nd lt. U.S. Army, 1960, advanced through grades to col., 1981, platoon leader, asst. S3 11th armored cav regiment Germany, 1961-62, co. comdr. 87 ordinance battalion Nellingen, Germany, 1963-64, co. comdr. 725th maintenance battalion Cu Chi, Republic Vietnam, 1967-68, battalion comdr. 708th maintenance battalion Baumholder, Germany, 1978-80; sr. readiness officer U.S. Army Europe, Heidelberg, Germany, 1976-78; logistics assistance officer U.S. Army Tng. and Doctrine Command, Hampton, Va., 1984-86; innkeeper, viticulturalist Fassifern Bed and Breakfast and Oak Spring Farm, Lexington, 1986-96; co-founder Bed and Breakfasts of the Historic Shenandoah Valley, 1987. Co-founder Imagine Rockbridge Citizens Visioning Group, Lexington, 1997—; chmn. Rockbridge Area Info. Line, 2001—. Builder log house Better Homes & Gardens, 1992-94 (Merit award 1997). Commr. Ctrl. Shenandoah Planning Dist. Commn., Staunton, Va., 1995, Rockbridge County Planning Commn., Lexington, 1996—. Decorated Legion of Merit with oak leaf cluster, Bronze Star. Mem. Retired Officers Assn. Republican. Avocations: candlemaking, winemaking. Home: 1997 Timber Ridge Rd Buena Vista VA 24416-4105 Office: Imagine Rockbridge 1997 Timber Ridge Rd Buena Vista VA 24416-4105 Fax: 810-277-7531. E-mail: jtichiii@yahoo.com.

TICHMAN, NADYA ERICA, violinist; b. Freeport, N.Y., June 12, 1958; d. Herbert L. and Ruth Tichman. MusB, Curtis Inst. Music, 1980. Violinist, Aspen Music Festival 1975, 76, Opera Co. Phila. 1978, 79, Concerto Soloists of Phila. 1979-80, Santa Fe Opera Orch. 1979-81, San Francisco Symphony 1980—, assoc. concertmaster, 1990—, Grand Teton Music Festival 1982—, Chamber Music West, 1986, Midsummer Mozart Festival, New Albion Records; numerous solo and chamber music recitals; co-dir. Chamber Music Sundaes, San Francisco, Olympic Music Festival, Music in the Vineyards, Sir Georg Solti's World Orch.

TICKLE, PHYLLIS ALEXANDER, writer, publisher; b. Johnson City, Tenn., Mar. 12, 1934; d. Philip Wade and Mary Katherine (Porter) Alexander; m. Samuel Milton Tickle, June 17, 1955; children: Nora Katherine, Mary Gammon, Laura Lee, John Crockett II, Samuel Milton Jr., Philip Wade, Rebecca Rutledge. BA, East Tenn. State U., 1955; MA, Furman U., 1961. Tchr. Latin, English Memphis City Schs., 1955-57; fellow Furman U., Greenville, S.C., 1959-61; lectr. English Rhodes Coll., Memphis, 1961-64; dean humanities Memphis Coll. Art, 1964-71; mng. editor St. Luke's Press, Memphis, 1975-82; sr. editor St. Luke's Press, Iris Press, 1982-85, Peachtree Pubs., Atlanta, 1988-90; dir. trade pub. group The Wimmer Cos., Memphis, 1990-92; religion editor Publishers Weekly, 1992-96; contbg. editor Pubs. Weekly, editor-at-large PW's Religion Bookline, 1996—. Mem. editl. bd. The Ch. News, Memphis, 1987-99; poet-in-residence Brooks Meml. Gallery, 1981-89; poetry coord. Cumberland Valley Writer's Conf., 1977-83; mem. adv. bd. Iris Press, Servant Publs., PBS Religion and Ethics Newsweekly, Forward Movement Publs., Mary Baker Eddy Libr., Garrett-McDill Ctr., Christy Awards, Dykes Found. Author: Syntactical Patterns in Indo-European Speech, 1968, The Story of Two Johns, It's No Fun to be Sick, 1976, On Beyond Koch, 1981, On Beyond Ais, 1982, The City Essays, 1982, What the Heart Already Knows, Stories for Advent, Christmas and Epiphany, 1985, Final Sanity: Stories of Lent, Easter and the Great Fifty Days, 1987, And Ordinary Time: Stories of the Days Between Ascensiontide and Advent, 1988, The Tickle Papers: Parables and Pandemonium, 1989, (dramas) Figs and Fury, 1976, Tobias and the Angels, 1983, Children of Her Name, 1987, (monograph) Of Snakes and Their Skins, 1980, (narrative poem) American Genesis, 1976, 3d edit., 1984, (poetry) Selections, 1984; contbg. author: Upper Room devotional, Disciplines, 1989, 365 Meditations for Women, 1990, 365 More Meditations for Women, 1992; gen. editor, contbr.: Confessing Conscience: Church Women on Abortion, 1990, Re-Discovering the Sacred: Spirituality for America, 1995, My Father's Prayer: A Remembrance, 1995; gen. editor: Home Works: An Anthology of Tennessee Writers, 1996; contbr. The Reader's Companion to "Crossing the Threshold of Hope," 1996, God-talk in America, 1997, The Divine Hours-Prayers for Summertime (Doubleday-Top Ten Books of Yr. 2000), 2000, The Divine Hours-Prayers for Autumn and Wintertime, 2000, The Shaping of a Life-A Spiritual Landscape, 2001, The Divine Hours-Prayers for Springtime, 2001; poetry has appeared in Cumberland Poetry Rev., Front St. Trolley, Images, Kudzu, Mid-South Writer, Nexus, Old Hickory Rev., Painted Bride, Poets on, X-A Jour. of the Arts, Velvet Wings, others; also anthologized; columnist Dixie Flyer; writer mags. including Feminist Digest, Newsletter for Ctr. of So. Folklore, Ctr. City, The Tenn. Churchman, The Episcopalian, Alive Now!, John Milton mag., others. Chair lit. panel Tenn. Arts Commn., Nashville, 1990-92, mem. panel, 1978-82, past chair artists in edn., 1986-89; mem. exec. bd. Tenn. Humanities Coun., Nashville, 1986-90; vestrywoman St. Anne's Ch., Millington, 1988-92, 93-95; lay eucharistic min. Episcopal Ch., 1996—. Recipient Int. Artist fellowship in lit. Tenn. Arts Commn., Nashville, 1985, Polly Bond award of excellence

Episc. Comm., N.Y.C., 1988, Books of Excellence award Body, Mind and Spirit mag., 1996, Book of Yr. 1995 Catholic Press Assn., Mays award for lifetime contbn. to publ., 1996. Mem. Pubs. Assn. of the South (bd. dirs. 1986—, pres., chair 1985-86), Southeastern Booksellers Assn. (bd. dirs. 1986-91), Tenn. Lit. Arts Assn. (pres. 1984-86). E-mail: tickrel@aol.com., thi:farmlnLucy@aol.com.

TIDBALL, CHARLES STANLEY, computer scientist, educator; b. Geneva, Switzerland, Apr. 15, 1928; (parents Am. citizens); s. Charles Taylor and Adele (Desmaison) T.; m. Mary Elizabeth Peters, Oct. 25, 1952. BA, Wesleyan U., 1950; MS (Univ. scholar), U. Rochester, 1952; PhD, U. Wis., Madison, 1955; MD (Shattuck fellow, Van Noyes scholar), U. Chgo., 1958; LHD (hon.), Wilson Coll., 1994; DSc (hon.), Hood Coll., 1999. Rotating intern Madison (Wis.) Gen. Hosp., 1958-59; physician I Mendota State Hosp., Madison, 1959; asst. research prof. physiology dept. George Washington U. Med. Center, Washington, 1959-63, USPHS spl. fellow, 1960-61, asso. prof., acting chmn. dept., 1963-64, prof., 1964-65, chmn. dept., 1964-71, Henry D. Fry prof., 1965-84, research prof. med., 1972-80; dir. Office Computer Assisted Edn. George Washington U. Med. Ctr., 1973-75, dir. Office Computer Assisted Edn. and Svcs., 1975-78; Lucie Stern disting. vis. prof. natural scis. Mills Coll., 1980; prof. edn. George Washington U., 1982-84, dir. ednl. computing tech. program Sch. Edn., 1982-84, prof. computer medicine Med. Ctr., 1984-92, prof. emeritus computer medicine, 1992, prof. neurol. surgery, 1990-92, prof. emeritus neurol. surgery, 1992; civil surgeon Immigration and Naturalization Svc., Dept. Justice, Washington, 1986-89; disting. rsch. scholar, co-dir. Tidball Ctr. for Study Ednl. Environments Hood Coll., Frederick, Md., 1994—. Trustee in residence Skidmore Coll., 1995. Author: (with others) Consolidated Index to For Thy Great Glory, 1993, (with others) Taking Women Seriously, 1999; editor: (with M. C. Shelesnyak) Frontiers in the Teaching of Physiology: Computer Literacy and Simulation, 1981; mem. editorial bd.: Jour. Applied Physiology, 1966-69, Jour. Computer-Based Instrn., 1974-89, Am. Jour. Physiology; assoc. editor physiology tchr. sect.; The Physiologist, 1979-85; contbr. articles to profl. jours. Trustee Cathedral Choral Soc., 1976-79, Wilson Coll., 1983-92, Everitt-Pomeroy, 1993-96, Population Reference Bur., 1987-94, 96—, chmn. bd. trustees, 1992-94, sec., 1994-97; lay reader St. Albans Parish, 1965-67, Washington Nat. Cathedral, 1967-94, lay eucharist minister, 1994—, clergy asst., 1968—, homilist, 1977—, info. sys. specialist, 1986-93, vol. mgr. info. sys. program, 1993—; mem. commn. Episcopal Diocese Washington, 1976-78; mem. com. mgmt. YMCA Camp Letts, 1968-96, chmn., 1972-75, dir., chmn. Endowment Fund, 1977-96; bd. dirs. Met. YMCA, Washington, 1972-84, trustees coun., 1984-91, fin. com., 1972-93, v.p. internat. program, 1974-75, asst. treas., 1975-77, v.p., treas., 1977-79, vice chmn., 1979-80, chmn., 1980-82, pres. of found., 1991-93; bd. dirs., treas. Woodley Ensemble, 1993—; bd. dirs. Mid-Atlantic Region YMCA, 1974-83; bd. dirs., vice-chmn. Cathedral West Condo., 1983-84, chmn., 1984-87, 91-93, fin. com., 1979-94; bd. dirs. Buckingham's Choice Residents' Assn., 2000—, chmn. resident svcs. com. Recipient award Washington Acad. Scis., 1967, Leader of Yr. award Met. YMCA, Washington, 1974, Red Triangle award, 1976, Service award, 1979; Dakota Indian name Am. Youth Found., 1976; Research Career Devel. award USPHS, 1961-63 Mem. Am. Physiol. Soc. (emeritus). Home: 3200 Baker Cir #I-235 Adamstown MD 21710 E-mail: ctidball@gwu.edu.

TIDBALL, JANE ALISON, judge; b. Helena, Mont. Bar: Colo. 1984, U.S. Dist. Ct. Colo. 1987, U.S. Dist. Ct. Ariz. 1992. d. Eugene Clayton and Marcia Ann Tidball; m. Dan A. Sciullo, Aug. 22, 1987; children: Jordan Lee Tidball-Sciullo, Cameron James Tidball-Sciullo. BA, U. Colo., 1980, JD, 1984. Law clerk Hon. Aurel Kelly, Colo. Ct. Appeals, Denver, 1984-85; pvt. practice, 1985-91; lawyer FDIC/RTC, 1991-95; magistrate 20th Jud. Dist., Boulder, 1995-99; dist. ct. judge 1st Jud. Dist., Golden, Colo., 1999—. Mem. Phi Beta Kappa.

TIDBALL, LEE FALK, elementary education educator; b. Waukon, Iowa, Feb. 26, 1955; s. John Harlow and Katherine Jane (Falk) T.; m. Catherine Susan Cooper, June 14, 1975 (div. Aug. 1982); children:: Aaron Matthew, Jonathan Michael. BS, Le Tourneau U., Longview, Tex., 1979. Cert. elem. tchr., Calif. Youth dir. Centenary Meth. Ch., Modesto, Calif., 1979-80; recreation dir. Crestwood Manor Hosp., 1980; substitute tchr. Modesto City Schs., 1981-83; 7th grade tchr. Orangeburg Christian Sch., Modesto, 1983-84; 5th & 6th tchr. Bret Harte Elem., 1984-91, gifted edn. tchr., 1991-97; tchr. 6th grade Beard Elem. Sch., 1997—. Author: (juvenile fiction) Windfork Secrets, 1998, Hidden Talents: Ginah's Journals #2, 2000. Head coach Silverwings Track Club, Modesto, 1982—2000, pres., 1982—2000; actor Modesto Performing Arts, 1994—98; founder Modesto Kids on Stage (non-profit children's theater co.), 2000—. Named Outstanding Young Religious Leader, Mason City (Iowa) Jaycees, 1976. Mem.: NEA, Soc. Children's Book Writers and Illustrators, Modesto Tchrs. Assn. Avocations: singing, writing, running. Office: Beard Elem Sch 915 Bowen Ave Modesto CA 95350-3096 Home: Apt 1 501 Rose Ave Modesto CA 95355-4336 E-mail: leesius@netzero.net.

TIDBALL, M. ELIZABETH PETERS, physiologist, educator, research director; b. Anderson, Ind., Oct. 15, 1929; d. John Winton and Beatrice (Ryan) Peters; m. Charles S. Tidball, Oct. 25, 1952. BA, Mt. Holyoke Coll., 1951, LHD, 1976; MS, U. Wis., 1955, PhD, 1959; MTS summa cum laude, Wesley Theol. Sem., 1990; ScD (hon.), Wilson Coll., 1973; DSc (hon.), Trinity Coll., 1974, Cedar Crest Coll., 1977; ScD (hon.), U. of South, 1978, Goucher Coll., 1979; DSc (hon.), St. Mary-of-The-Woods Coll., 1986; LittD (hon.), Regis Coll., 1980, Coll. St. Catherine, 1980, Alverno Coll., 1989; HHD (hon.), St. Mary's Coll., 1977, Hood Coll., 1982; LLD (hon.), St. Joseph Coll., 1983; LHD (hon.), Skidmore Coll., 1984, Marymount Coll., 1985, Converse Coll., 1985, Mt. Vernon Coll., 1986. Teaching asst. physiology dept. U. Wis., 1952-55, 58-59; research asst. anatomy dept. U. Chgo., 1955-56, research asst. physiology dept., 1956-58; USPHS postdoctoral fellow NIH, Bethesda, Md., 1959-61; staff pharmacologist Hazleton Labs., Falls Church, Va., 1961; assoc. in physiology George Washington U. Med. Ctr., 1960-62; cons. Hazleton Labs., 1962; asst. research prof. dept. pharmacology George Washington U. Med. Ctr., 1962-64, assoc. research prof. dept. physiology, 1964-70, research prof., 1970-71, prof., 1971-94, prof. emeritus, 1994—; asst. dir. M of Theol. Studies program Wesley Theol Sem., 1993-94; disting. rsch. scholar Hood Coll., Frederick, Md., 1994—, co-dir. Tidball Ctr. for Study of Ednl. Environments, 1994—. Lucie Stern Disting. vis. prof. natural scis. Mills Coll., 1980; scholar in residence Coll. Preachers, 1984, Salem Coll., 1985, Wesley Theol. Sem., 1992; Disting. scholar in residence So. Meth. U., 1985; vis. trustee prof. Skidmore Coll., 1995; cons. FDA, 1966-67, assoc. sci. coord. sci. assocs. tng. programs, 1966-67; com. on NIH tng. programs and fellowships Nat. Acad. Scis., 1972-75; faculty summer confs. Am. Youth Found., 1967-78; founder, dir. Summer Seminars for Women Am. Youth Found., 1987-95; cons. for instl. rsch. Wellesley Coll., 1974-75; exec. sec. com. on edn. and employment women in sci. and engring. Commn. on Human Resources, NRC/NAS, 1974-75, vice-chmn., 1977-82; cons., staff officer NRC/Nat. Acad. Scis., 1974-75; cons. Woodrow Wilson Nat. Fellowship Found., 1975-99, NSF, 1974-91; bd. mentor Assn. Governing Bds. of Univs. and Colls., 1991—, Gale Fund for the Study of Trusteeship Adv. Comm., 1992—1998; cons. Women's Coll. Coalition Rsch. Adv. Com., 1992—; Single Gender Schooling Working Group, U.S. Dept. Edn., 1992-94, women's colls. roundtable, 1998; rep. to D.C. Commn. on Status of Women, 1972-75; nat. panelist Am. Coun. on Edn., 1983-90; panel mem. Congl. Office of Tech. Assessment, 1986-87; fellows selection com., fellows mentor Coll. Preachers, 1992—. Lead author: Taking Women Seriously, 1999; columnist Trusteeship, 1993-95; mem. editl. bd. Jour. Higher Edn., 1979-84, cons. editor, 1984—; mem. editl. bd. Religion and Intellectual Life, 1983—; contbr. articles to profl. jours. Trustee Mt. Holyoke Coll., 1968-73, vice chmn., 1972-73, trustee fellow, 1988—; trustee Hood Coll., 1972-84, 86-92, exec. com., 1974-84, 89-92, trustee emerita, 1997—; overseer Sweet Briar Coll., 1978-85; trustee Cathedral Choral Soc., 1976-90, pres. bd. trustees, 1982-84, hon. trustee, 1991—; trustee Skidmore Coll., 1988—, mem. exec. com., 1993—; mem. governing bd. Coll. of Preachers, 1979-85, chmn., 1983-85; mem. governing bd. Protestant Episcopal Cathedral Found., 1983-85, mem. exec. com., 1983-85; bd. vis. Salem Coll., 1986-93; ctr. assoc. Nat. Resource Ctr., Girls Club Am., 1983-90; mem. governing bd. Buckinham's Choice Residents' Assn., 1999—2002. Named Outstanding Grad., The Penn Hall Sch., 1988; recipient Alumnae medal Honor, Mt. Holyoke Coll., 1971, Outstanding Svc. award, Am. Youth Found., 1975, Valuable Contbns. Gen. Alumni Assn. award, George Washington U., 1982, 1987, Pres.'s medal, 1999, Chestnut Hill medal Outstanding Achievement, Chestnut Hill Coll., Phila., 1987, Lifetime Svc. and Schoalrship award, Bd. Women's Coll. Coalition and Nation's Women's Coll. Presidents, 1998, Order of Merit, Cathedral Choral Soc., 2000; fellow Shattuck fellow, 1955—56, Mary E. Woolley fellow, Mt. Holyoke Coll., 1958—59, postdoctoral fellow, USPHS, 1959—61. Mem. AAAS, Am. Physiol. Soc. (chmn. task force on women in physiology 1973-80, com. on coms. 1977-80, mem. emeritus 1994—), Am. Assn. Higher Edn., Mt. Holyoke Alumnae Assn. (dir. 1966-70, 76-77), Histamine Club, Sigma Delta Epsilon, Sigma Xi. Episcopalian. Home: 4100 Cathedral Ave NW Washington DC 20016-3584 also: 3200 Baker Cir # I-235 Adamstown MD 21710

TIDWELL, GEOFFREY MORGAN, medical company executive; b. San Diego, Aug. 16, 1958; s. Morgan Alfred and Dorothy (Doolittle) T. BA in Psychology, U.S. Internat. U., 1991; MBA in Health Care Adminstrn., Nat. U., 1996. Rsch. asst. San Marcos (Calif.) Clinic, 1988-91; area svc. mgr. Nat. Med. Sys., Frederick, Md., 1993-94, Life Med. Svcs., San Diego, 1994-95; intern San Diego County Med. Soc., 1995-96; adminstrn. resident dept. interventional radiology U. Calif., San Diego, 1995-96; v.p., dir. clin. svcs. M&G Med. Svc., 1995—. Vis. scholar U. Calif. Sch. Medicine, San Diego, 1996, 97, 98; radio personality Sta. KOWF, Escondido, Calif., 1989-90, Sta. KKYY, San Diego, 1990-91, Sta. KRMX, San Diego, 1990-91, Sta. KGB, San Diego, 1991-97; clin. svcs., v.p. sales and mktg. M&G Med. Svc., San Diego, 1995—; dir. client svcs. Calif. Anti-Aging Inst., Encinitas, Calif., 1999—. Co-author chpts. Podiatry Today, vol. 10 # 7, 1997. Vol. telethon Muscular Dystrophy Assn., San Diego, 1991, Easter Seals, San Diego, 1991. Mem. Am. Coll. Healthcare Execs. (assoc.), Med. Group Mgmt. Assn. (assoc.), Emergency Med. Assembly (assoc.), Healthcare Coalition San Diego County (assoc.), Psi Chi. Republican. Methodist. Avocations: fitness training, horseback riding, target shooting, reading, guitar. Office: M&G Med Svcs 4198 Convoy St San Diego CA 92111-3702 E-mail: gmtidwell@pol.net.

TIDWELL, ROY ROBINSON, SR. television producer, consultant; b. Tampa, Fla., Apr. 11, 1953; s. Arthur Kenneth and Alice (Correy) T.; m. Christine Rogers, Aug. 14, 1976; children: Roy Robinson Jr., Heather Christine. BA, Liberty U., Lynchburg, Va., 1976. Cert. broadcast technologist. Prodn. dir. So. Teleprodns., Orlando, Fla., 1976-81; prodr. Liberty Broadcasting Net, Lynchburg, 1981-88; dir. mktg. Freedom Village, USA, Lakemont, N.Y., 1988-91; gen. mgr. Am. Portrait Films, Cleve., 1991—. Cons. Save the Manatee Club, Maitland, Fla., 1988—, The Rutherford Inst., Charlottesville, Va., 1990—. Prodr. Jerry Falwell Live, 1987; exec. prodr. videos Child Abuse "Maddness," 1989 (Angel award 1989), The Mountain, 1989 (Angel award 1989). Mem. Soc. Broadcast Engrs. (program chmn. 1987-88, technologist award 1987). Republican. Avocations: theater, gardening, fishing. Home: 3809 Royal Oak Dr Brunswick OH 44212-3577 Office: Am Portrait Films 503 E 200th St Cleveland OH 44119-1575

TIEDE, TOM ROBERT, journalist; b. Huron, S.D., Feb. 24, 1937; s. Leslie Albert and Rose (Allen) T.; children: Kristina Anne, Thomas Patrick. BA in Journalism, Wash. State U., 1959. Mem. staff Kalispell (Mont.) Daily Interlake, 1960-61, Daytona Beach (Fla.) News Jour., 1961-63; war corr. Newspaper Enterprise Assn., N.Y.C., 1964—. Lectr. in field., 1965— Author: Your Men at War, 1965, Coward, 1968, Calley: Soldier or Killer?, 1971, Welcome to Washington, Mr. Witherspoon, 1979, The Great Whale Rescue, 1986, American Tapestry: Eye Witness Accounts of the 1900's, 1988, The Man Who Discovered Pluto, 1990, Fosser, 1994, Self Help Nation, 2001. Served as lt., inf. AUS, 1960. Recipient Ernie Pyle Meml. award, 1965; Freedoms Found. award, 1966; George Washington medal, 1972 Mem. Internat. Platform Assn., Sigma Delta Chi, Lambda Chi Alpha. Clubs: Overseas Press, National Press, Nat. Headliners (award 1966 Atlantic City). Roman Catholic. Achievements include work collected by Boston U. Library. Office: NEA 1090 Vermont Ave NW Washington DC 20005-4905 also: PO Box 1783 Charlottesville VA 22902-1783

TIEDEMAN, DAVID VALENTINE, education educator; b. Americus, Ga., Aug. 12, 1919; s. Walter Dohlen and Edna M(arie) (Komfort) T.; m. Marjorie I(da) Denman, Sept. 26, 1942 (div. Jan. 2, 1973); children— David Michael, Jeffrey Denman; m. Anna Louise Miller, Jan. 6, 1973. AB, Union Coll., Schenectady, 1941; AM, U. Rochester, 1943; EdM, Harvard, 1948, EdD, 1949. Staff mem. NRC com. selection and tng. aircraft pilots U. Rochester, 1941-43; staff mem. test constrn. dept. Coll. Entrance Exam. Bd., 1943-44; assoc. head statistics div. Manhattan Project, 1944-46; Milton teaching fellow, instr. edn. Harvard Grad. Sch. Edn., 1946-48, Sheldon travelling fellow, 1948-49, instr. edn., 1949-51, asst. prof. edn., 1951-52, from lectr. edn. to prof., 1952-71, assoc. dir., research assoc. Center for Research in Careers, 1963-66, also chmn. exec. com., info. system for vocat. decisions, 1966-69; prin. research scientist Palo Alto office Am. Insts. for Research, 1971-73; prof. edn. No. Ill. U., DeKalb, 1973-80; dir. ERIC Clearinghouse in Career Edn., 1973-76; coordinator Office Vocat., Tech., and Career Edn., 1978-80; prof. career and higher edn. U. So. Calif., Los Angeles, 1981-84, prof. emeritus, 1984—; exec. dir. Nat. Inst. Advancement of Career Edn., 1981-84; pres. Internat. Coll., 1985-86; v.p. Lifecareer Found., 1985—; provost William Lyon U., 1988-91; faculty Walden U., 1992—. Mem. Adv. Council on Guidance Dept. Edn. Commonwealth Mass., 1957-63; chmn. commn. on tests Coll. Entrance Exam. Bd., 1967-70; mem. advisory screening com. in edn. Council Internat. Exchange of Scholars, 1975-79, chmn., 1978-79 Co-author 8 books.; editorial assoc.: Jour. Counseling Psychology, 1957-63, Personnel and Guidance Jour., 1960-63, Character Potential: A Record of Research, 1977-82, Jour. Career Edn., 1979-85; contbr. articles to profl. jours., chpts. to books. Bd. dirs. Mass. Com. Children and Youth, 1961-63. Fellow Ctr. for Advanced Study in Behavioral Scis.; spl. fellow NIMH, 1963-64 Fellow Am. Psychol. Soc., APA (prs. divsn. counseling psychology 1965-66); mem. ACA, Nat. Career Devel. Assn. (pres. 1965-66, Eminent Career award 1979), Nat. Coun. Measurement in Edn. (pres. 1962-63), Phi Beta Kappa, Sigma Xi, Phi Delta Kappa, Phi Kappa Phi. Fax: 760-724-0083. E-mail: annamt1@home.com.

TIEDEMANN, ALBERT WILLIAM, JR. retired chemist; b. Balt., Nov. 7, 1924; s. Albert William and Catherine (Madigan) T.; m. Mary Therese Sellmayer, Apr. 6, 1953; children: Marie Therese, Donna Elise, Albert William III, David Lawrence. BS, Loyola Coll., Balt., 1947; MS, NYU, 1949; PhD, Georgetown U., 1958. Tchg. fellow NYU, 1947-50; instr. chemistry Mt. St. Agnes Coll., 1950-55; chief chemist Emerson Drug div. Warner Lambert Pharm. Co., Balt., 1955-60; analytical supr. Hercules Powder Co., Allegany Ballistics Lab., Cumberland, Md., 1960-68; tech. svc. supt. Hercules Inc., Radford, Va., 1968-72; dir. Va. Div. Consol. Labs., Richmond, 1972-78; vice-chmn. Va. Toxic Substances Adv. Council, 1978-92; dep. dir. for labs. Va. Dept. Gen. Svcs., 1978-92, cons. 1992-98; ret . Mem. sci. adv. com. Longwood Coll., 1983-90. Served to lt. (j.g.) USNR, 1943-46; capt. Res., 1946—. Fellow Am. Inst. Chemists, Soc. Advancement Mgmt. (chpt. v.p. 1983-84, chpt. pres. 1984-85), Am. Soc. Quality Control (chmn. Richmond sect. 1975-76, councilor biomed. divsn. 1978-80), U.S. Naval Inst., Naval Res. Assn. (dist. pres. 1954-57; nat. v.p. 1962-63, 65-69; nat. chmn. Navy Sabbath Program 1969-75, Nat. Meritorious Svc. award 1971, Twice a Citizen award 1978), Cen. Atlantic States Assn. Food & Drug Ofcls. (exec. bd. 1977-84, v.p. 1981-82, pres. 1982-83, CASA award 1986), Nat. Assn. Food & Drug Ofcls. (chmn. sci. and tech. com. 1981-85, sec.-treas. 1985-87), Internat. Assn. Ofcl. Analytical Chemists (editl. bd. 1986-88, bd. dirs. 1987-90), Analytical Lab. Mgrs. Assn., Royal Acad. Pharmacy (elected acad. fgn. mem. Barcelona, Spain 1989—). Home: 10511 Cherokee Rd Richmond VA 23235-1008

TIEDGE, HENRI, neuroscientist, educator, researcher; b. Stade, Germany, Feb. 16, 1954; came to U.S., 1986; m. Ellen Hsu. PhD, U. Hannover, Germany, 1986. Rsch. assoc. Luebeck (Germany) Med. Sch., 1983-86, Columbia U. Coll. P&S, N.Y.C., 1986-88, Mt. Sinai Sch. Medicine, N.Y.C., 1988-90, rsch. asst. prof., 1990-93; asst. prof. pharmacology and neurology SUNY Health Sci. Ctr., Bklyn., 1994-97, assoc. prof. pharmacology and neurology, 1997-99, assoc. prof. physiology, pharmacology and neurology, 1999—. Contbr. chpts. to books, articles to profl. jours. Mem. Soc. Cell Biology, Soc. for Neurosci. Office: SUNY Health Sci Ctr Bklyn Dept Physiol/ Pharmacology 450 Clarkson Ave Brooklyn NY 11203-2056

TIEDGE-LAFRANIER, JEANNE MARIE, editor; b. N.Y.C., July 24, 1960; d. Richard Frederick and Joan Jean (Gerardo) Tiedge; m. John Daniel Lewis Lafranier, Oct. 8, 1989; children: Katelyn Ellen, John Richard. BA, Drew U., 1982. Asst. Denise Marcil Lit. Agy., N.Y.C., 1982-84; sr. editor New Am. Libr., 1984-87, Warner Books, N.Y.C., 1987-95; editor corp. comm. Disticor, Ajax, Ont., Can., 1995—. Avocation: marathoner, equestrian.

TIEFEL, VIRGINIA MAY, librarian; b. Detroit, May 20, 1926; d. Karl and June Garland (Young) Brenkert; m. Paul Martin Tiefel, Jan. 25, 1947; children: Paul Martin Jr., Mark Gregory. BA in Elem. Edn., Wayne State U., 1962; MA in Library Sci., U. Mich., 1968. Librarian Birmingham Schs., Mich., 1967-68; librarian S. Euclid-Lyndhurst Schs., Cleve., 1968-69; acquisitions-reference librarian Hiram Coll., Ohio, 1969-77; head undergrad. libraries Ohio State U., Columbus, 1977-84, dir. library user edn., 1978-95, faculty outreach coord., 1995-98. Contbr. articles to profl. jours. Recipient Disting. Alumnus award U. Mich. Sch. Info. and Libr. Studies, 1993. Mem. ALA (v.p. Ohio sect. 1973-74, pres. 1974-75, Miriam Dudley Bibliographic Instrn. Librarian of Yr. 1986), Acad. Library Assn. Ohio (Outstanding Ohio Acad. Librarian 1984), Assn. Coll. and Research Libraries (chmn. bibliographic instrn. sect. com. on research 1983-84, chmn. com. on performance measures 1984-90). Lutheran. Home: 4711 Oak Bluff Ct Eau Claire WI 54701 E-mail: vtiefel@aol.com.

TIEFEL, WILLIAM REGINALD, hotel company executive; b. Rochester, N.Y., Mar. 30, 1934; s. William Reginald and Mary Hazel (Cross) T.; m. Vada Morell, Dec. 30, 1985 (dec. Apr. 1999); m. Norma Gewirz Kline, Nov. 25, 2000. Student, Williams Coll., 1952-54; BA with honors, Mich. State U., 1956; postgrad., Harvard Bus. Sch.; DBA in Hospitality Mgmt. (hon.), Johnson and Wales U. Gen. mgr. Marriott Hotels, Arlington, Va., 1964-65, Saddle Brook, N.J., 1966-69, Newton, Mass., 1969-71, regional v.p. Washington, 1971-80; corp. v.p. Marriott Corp., 1976-89; exec. v.p. Marriott Hotels and Resorts, 1980-88; pres. Marriott Hotels, Resorts and Suites, 1988-92; exec. v.p., mem. exec. and growth coms. Marriott Corp., 1988—; pres. Marriott Lodging Group, 1992-98; vice chmn. Marriott Internat., 1998—2002; chmn. Ritz-Carlton Hotel Co, 1998—2002, chmn. emeritus, 2002; dir. Bulgari Hotels and Resorts, 2001—. Bd. visitors Valley Forge Mil. Acad. and Jr. Coll., 1976-79, chmn., 1979, trustee, 1982-88, 89-92; chmn. Campaign for Valley Forge, 1985-88, chmn. com. on trustees, 1989-91, hon. life trustee. Mem. Am. Hotel and Lodging Assn. (dir. Ednl. Inst., Arthur Landstreet award 1997), Corp. Hotelier of the World, 1996. Republican. Roman Catholic. Home: 236 Via Las Brisas Palm Beach FL 33480-1643 Office: Marriott Internat Inc 1 Marriott Dr Washington DC 20058 E-mail: william.tiefel@marriott.com.

TIEFENBRUNN, ALAN JAMES, medical educator; b. St. Louis, Aug. 26, 1948; s. Kenneth Sylvester and Margaret Ann (Smith) T.; m. Sharon Kay Frost, June 3, 1972; children: Theresa, Curtis. AB cum laude, Washington U., St. Louis, 1970, MD, 1974. Intern, resident U. Calif., San Diego, 1974-77; fellow in cardiology Washington U., St. Louis, 1977-79, asst. prof. medicine, 1980-86, assoc. prof. medicine, 1986—, asst. prof. radiology, 1980—; assoc. physician Barnes Hosp., 1980—. Mem. adv. bd. Nat. Registry Myocardial Infarction, 1991—; cons. in field. Contbr. articles to profl. jours. Fellow Am. Coll. Cardiology, Am. Heart Assn. (coun. clin.cardiology), Alpha Omega Alpha. Avocations: skiing, SCUBA diving. Home: 6255 Wydown Blvd Saint Louis MO 63105-2306 Office: Washington U Box 8086 660 S Euclid Ave Saint Louis MO 63110-1093 E-mail: atiefenb@im.wustl.edu.

TIEFENWERTH, ELEANOR GERTRUDE, foundation executive; b. Bayonne, N.J.; m. William J. Tiefenwerth, Apr. 27, 1947; 1 child, William J. B.A. in Edn., Jersey City State Coll., 1946; student in parliamentary law Jersey City State Coll., 1964-66; student in pub. speaking Douglass Coll., 1966-68. Exec. dir. Bayonne Econ. Opportunity Found., N.J., 1976— ; mem. exec. bd. Community Action Programs Exec. Dirs. Assn., Trenton, 1982— . Editor: Learning Together At Project HeadStart, 1984. Parliamentarian, Pavonia council Girl Scouts U.S., 1978-84; pres. Hudson County council PTA, N.J., 1978-80; sec. Bayonne Mayor's Adv. Com., 1981-83; chairperson Ambulance Study for City of Bayonne, 1982; site chairperson Holocaust Com. Meml., Bayonne, 1985-86. Mem. Community Action Dirs. Assn. State of N.J. (by-laws chairperson 1985-86), Headstart Dirs. Assn., Nat. Assn. Female Execs., Am. Legion Aux. Lodge: Women of Moose (sr. regent, Red Stole Collegiate award 1981). Avocations: reading; baking; travel. Office: Bayonne Econ Opportunity Found 555 Kennedy Blvd Box 10 # 32 Bayonne NJ 07002

TIEFENWERTH, WILLIAM PHILIP, university program director; b. Bklyn., June 25, 1951; s. William Frederick and Catherine Florence (Klotz) T.; m. Karen Taylor, Aug. 15, 1977; 1 child, Casey Elizabeth. BS in Philosophy and Religion, Towson, U., 1973. Tchr., dept. dir. St. Mark Sch., Catonsville, Md., 1975-79; asst. to chaplain Johns Hopkins U., Balt., 1979-92, dir. vol. svcs., 1992-96, dir. cmty. rels., 1996—. Acad. advisor Johns Hopkins U., 1997, co-chairperson Mid-Atlantic region Am. Reads Regional Conf., 1997. Co-designer area mural (Balt.'s Best Mural award City Paper 1997). Founder cmty. ctr. Safe & Smart, 1994; bd. dirs. Homewood Literacy Adv., Balt., 1997, Charles Village Ben. Dist., Balt., 1996—; advisor Learn and Serve, Met. Balt., 1997, St. Paul St. Libr. Project, Balt., 1997; recruitment advisor Balt. Mentoring Partnership, 1997. Recipient award for Best Usage of Urban Property for Cmty. Use, 1994, 941st Point of Light award U.S. Pres. George Bush, Washington, 1992, Learning Loft award Abell Found., Balt., 1994. Mem. Md. Coun. Dirs. of Vol. Svcs., Student Affairs Adminstrs. Higher Edn. Democrat. Roman Catholic. Avocations: jazz, gardening, contemporary literature. Home: 2204 Grey Fox Ct Bel Air MD 21015-8905 Office: Johns Hopkins Univ 3400 N Charles St Baltimore MD 21218-2680

TIELENS, STEVEN ROBERT, information specialist; b. Orlando, Fla., Mar. 8, 1953; s. James D. and Nancy A. (Caffie) T.; m. Cynthia A. Bradley, June 4, 1976. AS, Jones County Jr. Coll., Ellisville, Miss., 1986. Elec. foreman IBEW Local 474, Memphis, 1976-83; telecommunications adminstr., asst. ops. mgr. Forrest Gen. Hosp., Hattiesburg, Miss., 1984-87; dir. info. svcs. JFK Med. Ctr., Atlantis, Fla., 1987-91; info. tech. cons. West Palm Beach, 1991; mgr. user support Racal-Datacom, Inc., Sunrise, 1992—. Jones County Jr. Coll. acad. scholar. Mem. Data Processing Mgmt. Assn., Internat. Platform Assn., Phi Theta Kappa, Phi Beta Lambda (pres., 1st place state competition in data processing I and II, 3rd place nat. in data processing II, 1986). Office: Racal Datacom Inc 1601 Harrison Pkwy Sunrise FL 33323-2834 Home: 39 Lancaster Dr Greenacres FL 33463-1739

TIELKE, JAMES CLEMENS, retail and manufacturing management consultant; b. St. Helena, Nebr., May 15, 1931; s. Joseph Hubert and Catherine Josephine (Schmidt) T.; m. Betty Merle Adams, Apr. 18, 1953; children: P.J., Michael J., Dawn M. BS in Bus. Adminstrn., U. S.D., 1959, MA in Speech and Econ., 1960. Partner, Tielke Motors, Yankton, S.D., 1952-54; owner Ft. Collins Motors, Colo., 1954-56; grad. tchg. asst. U. S.D., 1959-60; corp. buyer and mgr. auto, lawn/garden, paint, electronics Montgomery Ward, Chgo., 1960-77, v.p. mdse. adminstrn., 1978-81; pres. Midwest div. Structured Approaches, Inc., 1981-82; v.p. nat. accounts Dupli-Color Products, Elk Grove Village, Ill., 1983-85; pres. Black Leaf Products Co., 1985-89; v.p. Hysan Corp., Des Plaines, Ill., 1985-89; v.p. ice melter sales Koos, Inc., IMC Vigoro, Kenosha, Wis., 1989-97; pres. J.C. Tielke Assocs., Inc., 1997—. Participant NICB Pers. Mgmt. Conf., 1966, Am. Mgmt. Assn. Sr. Mgmt. Conf., 1977. Chmn. Chgo. Minority Bus. Opportunities Fair Devel. Commn.; bd. dirs. Chgo. Youth Ctrs., 1979-82. Recipient Honors award U. S.D. Sch. Bus., 1977 Mem. Internat. San. Supply Assn.

TIEMANN, JEANNINE E. music educator, educator; b. Florissant, Mo., Nov. 24, 1970; d. Lambert Owen and Janet Evelyn T. BA in Music Edn., So. Ill. U. Edwardsville, 1994, MA in Music Edn., 1996. Cert. special tchr. K-12. Pvt. piano/voice instr. So. Ill. U., Edwardsville, 1991-99; choral dir. Edward A. Fulton Jr. High, O'Fallon, Ill., 1996—. Mem. Am. Choral Dirs. Assn., Music Educators Nat. Conf., Ill. State Music Tchrs. Assn., Ill. Music Educators Assn. (chmn. dist. 6 1999—), Sigma Alpha Iota (mem. award 1994, sword of honor 1994, sec. 1992-93, treas. 1993-94, v.p. mem. 1998-2000, sec. 2000-). Republican. Luth. Avocations: bowling, counted cross stitch. Office: Edward A Fulton Jr High 307 Kyle Rd O'Fallon IL 62269-6611 E-mail: jtiemann@ofallon90.net.

TIEMEYER, CHRISTIAN, conductor; m. Pattie Farris; children: Jeanie, Hank, Elisa. Grad., Peabody Conservatory; D of Musical Arts, Cath. U. of Am. Assoc. condr. Dallas Symphony, 1978-83; interim artistic dir., prin. guest condr. Omaha Symphony; music dir. Cedar Rapids Symphony, 1982—; founder Symphony Sch. of Music, 1986. Chmn. string and conducting faculties U. Utah; faculty Brigham Young U.; founding condr. Snowbird Summer Arts Inst.; founder Bear Lake Music Festival, 1992; guest condr. Preucil Orch. Prin. cellist Utah Symphony. Avocations: fly fishing, boating, outdoor activities. Office: Cedar Rapids Symphony Orch 205 2nd Ave SE Cedar Rapids IA 52401-1213*

TIEMSTRA, JOHN PETER, economics educator; b. Chgo., July 15, 1950; s. Peter John and Margaret (Lamont) T.; m. Suzanne Spicer, Dec. 28, 1985; 1 stepchild: Remi Spicer Rakipi. AB, Oberlin Coll., 1971; PhD, MIT, 1975. Asst. prof. econs. Calvin Coll., Grand Rapids, Mich., 1975-81, assoc. prof., 1981-85, prof., 1985—. Vis. prof. Potchefstroom U., South Africa, 1992. Author: Economics: A Developmental Approach, 1999; editor, co-author: Reforming Economics, 1990; contbr. articles to profl. jours. Dean Grand Rapids Am. Guild of Organists, 1990-91; pres. West Mich. Irish Heritage Soc., Grand Rapids, 1988-91, Forest Hills Condo Assn., Cascade, Mich., 1988—; organist St. Paul's Epicopal Ch., Grand Rapids, 1990—. Mem. Assn. for Social Econs., Assn. of Christian Economists, Am. Econ. Assn. Christian Reformed. Avocation: folk and church music. Office: Calvin Coll 3201 Burton St SE Grand Rapids MI 49546-4301 *Simple competence or skill is usually easy to find or at least to develop. What is much harder is to find a basis in shared values that can lead to a powerful relationship.*

TIEN, CHARLES P, political scientist, educator; b. Pittsburgh, PA, Feb. 10, 1965; s. Tseng-Ying Tien, Chin-Kai Tien; m. Kari R Olson; children: Madeline, Kaia. PhD, University of Iowa, Iowa City, IA, 1992—97; BA, University of Michigan, Ann Arbor, 1983—88. Legislative Assistant United States House of Representatives, Washington, 1988—91; Associate Professor Hunter College, CUNY, New York, NY, 2002—. Fulbright Scholar Lecturer People's University, Beijing, 1999—2000. Author: (journal article) "Representation, Voluntary Retirement, and Shirking in the Last Term." , 2001, "American Ambivalence Toward China." , 2001, . "Do Differences Matter? The Impact of Women in Congress." , 2002, "The Future in Forecasting: Prospective Presidential Models.", 1996, "Voters as Forecasters: A Micromodel of Election Prediction.", 1999. Mem.: American Political Science Association. Avocation: tennis, travel. Office: Hunter College, CUNY 695 Park Avenue New York NY 10021 Business E-Mail: ctien@hunter.cuny.edu.

TIEN, DAVID ROBBINS, physician; b. Phila., July 3, 1955; s. H. Ti Tien and Joseleyne Slade; m. Alexandra Meyer, May 18, 1996; children: Caroline, Julian, Christopher. BA, Mich. State U., 1978; cert. advanced study, Beijing U., 1979; MD, U. Mich., 1983. Diplomate Am. Bd. Ophthalmology, Nat. Bd. Med. Examiners. Intern Presbyn. U. Pa. Med. Ctr., Phila., 1983-84; resident NYU Med. Ctr., N.Y.C., 1986-88, chief resident in ophthalmology, 1988-89; fellow Manhattan Eye, Ear & Throat Hosp., 1989-90; clin. prof. Brown U., Providence, 1991—; dir. ophthalmology Hasbro Children's Hosp., 1994—. Author: Vision Screening Guidelines for School Nurses, 1992; contbr. articles to profl. jours. Fellow Internat. Strabismological Assn., Am. Assn. Pediat. Ophthalmology Strabismus, Am. Acad. Ophthalmology; mem. R.I. Soc. Eye Physicians Surgeons, R.I. Med. Soc., Phi Beta Kappa. Avocations: tennis, languages, string band. Office: 2 Dudley St Ste 505 Providence RI 02905-3249 E-mail: rtien@lifespan.org.

TIEN, JAMES M. engineering educator, consultant; b. N.Y.C., Mar. 27, 1945; s. Yu-Shih Tien and Tien-Lun Li; m. Ellen S. Weston, Aug. 27, 1981; children: Lee, Rex. BEE, Rensselaer Poly. Inst., 1966; SM, MIT, 1967, PhD, 1972. Mem. tech. staff Bell Labs., Holmdel, N.J., 1966-69; rsch. project dir. Rand Corp., N.Y.C., 1970-73; area dir. Urban Sys. Rsch. & Engring., Cambridge, Mass., 1973-75; prin., v.p. Structured Decisions Corp., 1975—; prof., chair Rensselaer Poly. Inst., Troy, N.Y., 1977—. Fellow IEEE (Joseph G. Wohl Oustanding Career award 1998, Major Ednl. Innovation award 2000), Nat. Acad. Engring. Office: Rensselaer Poly Inst 110 Eighth St Troy NY 12180-3590 E-mail: tienj@rpi.edu.

TIENKEN, ARTHUR T. retired foreign service officer; b. Yonkers, N.Y., Aug. 5, 1922; BA, Princeton U., 1947, MA, 1949. With U.S. Fgn. Svc., 1949-87, dep. chief mission Tunisia, 1973-75, Addis Ababa, Ethiopia, 1975-77; Ambassador to Gabonese Republic and Democratic Republic of Sao Tome and Principe, Libreville, Gabon, 1978-81; dir. Fgn. Svc. Assignments and Career devel. Dept. State, 1981-85, sr. insp., 1985-87, ret., 1987. Diplomat-in-residence Marquette U., 1972-73 Served with U.S. Army, 1943-46. Mem. Diplomatic and Consular Officers Ret. (bd. govs. 1999—).

TIERNEY, BILL, university athletic coach; Head coach Princeton Tigers, 1988—. NCAA Divsn. 1A Champions, 1992, 94, 96, 97, 98; named Morris Touchstone Divsn. 1A Coach of the Yr.; elected to L.I. Lacrosse Hall of Fame, 1995. Office: Princeton U Dillon Gym Princeton NJ 08544-0001

TIERNEY, CATHERINE MARIE, librarian; b. Woodbury, N.J., July 11, 1947; d. William John and Marie Cecilia (Oakes) Morgan; m. Phillip A Tierney, Aug. 9, 1969. BA, Cardinal Stritch Coll., 1969; MLS, Kent State U., 1974. Reference libr. Akron Beacon Jour., Ohio, 1974—76, chief libr., 1976—2001; dir. news rsch. St. Louis Post-Dispatch, 2001—. Mem. Spl. Librs. Assn. Republican. Episcopalian. Office: St Louis Post-Dispatch New Rsch 900 N Tucker Blvd Saint Louis MO 63101

TIERNEY, GORDON PAUL, real estate broker, genealogist; b. Ft. Wayne, Ind., Oct. 17, 1922; s. James Leonard and Ethele Lydia (Brown) T.; m. Carma Lillian Devine, Oct. 17, 1946; 1 child, Paul N. Student, Ind. U., 1940-41, Cath. U. Am., 1941-42; coll. tng. detachment, Clemson U., 1943. Br. mgr. Bartlett-Collins Co., Chgo., 1956-84; prin., broker Kaiser-Tierney Real Estate, Inc., Palatine, Ill., 1984-89; pres. Tierney Real Estate, Newburgh, Ind. Author: Burgess/Bryan Connection, 1978; assoc. editor Colonial Genealogist Jour., 1976-85. Served in USAC, 1943-45, China. Decorated Legion of Honor; named Ky. Col. Fellow Am. Coll. Genealogists (pres. 1977-2000); mem. SAR (v.p. gen. 1984-85, genealogist gen. 1981-83, Silver and Bronze medals 1978-80, Patriot medal 1976, Meritorious Svc. award 1983, Minutemen award 1984), Huguenot Soc. Ill. (state pres. 1978-80), Huguenot Soc. S.C., Nat. Huguenot Soc., Huguenot Soc. Ind. (pres. 1993-95), Nat. Geneal. Soc., Ind. Hist. Soc., Soc. Ind. Pioneers, First Families Ohio, Ohio Geneal. Soc., Va. Geneal. Soc., Md. Geneal. Soc., Augustan Soc., Gen. Soc. War 1812 (state pres. 1985), Sons. and Daus. Pilgrims, Descs. Old Plymouth Colony, Mil. Order Stars and Bars, Soc. Descs. Colonial Clergy, Sons of Union Vets., Sons of Confederate Vets., Pioneer Wis. Families, Welcome Soc. Pa., Pa. Geneal. Soc., Nat. Soc. Archivists, Soc. Colonial Wars in Ill., Soc. Colonial Wars in Ind. (gov. 1992-94), Soc. Colonial Wars in Commonwealth Ky. (life), Sons of Am. Colonists (nat. v.p. 1971-74), Mil. and Hospitalier Order St. Lazarus of Jerusalem, Clan Johnston/e in Am., Order Descs. Ancient Planters, Hump Pilots Assn., Nat. Bd. Realtors, Ill. Bd. Realtors, Sword Bunker Hill, Tri-State Geneal. Soc., Jamestowne Soc., Baronial Order Magna Charta, Royal Order Scotland, Masons, Shriners, Rolling Hill Country Club, Legion of Honor (comdr. 2001-02). Republican. Presbyterian. Home and Office: 8766 Hanover Dr Newburgh IN 47630-9327

TIERNEY, JOHN F. congressman, lawyer; b. Salem, Mass., Sept. 18, 1951; m. Patrice Tierney. BA, Salem State Coll., 1973; JD, Suffolk U., 1976. Ptnr. Tierney, Kalis, and Lucas, North Shore, Mass.; mem. U.S. Congress from 6th Mass. dist., 1997—; mem. com. edn. and workforce, com. gov. reform. Pres. Salem C. of C. Democrat. Office: US House Reps 120 Cannon House Office Bldg Washington DC 20515-0001*

TIERNEY, JOHN WILLIAM, chemical engineering educator; b. Oak Park, Ill., Dec. 29, 1923; s. John William and Agnes (Shea) T.; m. Patricia A. O'Neill, June 21, 1952; children: John, Patrick, Joseph, Paul. BS in Chem. Engring., Purdue U., 1947; MS in Chem. Engring., U. Mich., 1948; PhD in Chem. Engring., Northwestern U., 1951. Sr. research engr. Pure Oil Co., Crystal Lake, Ill., 1948-53; asst. prof. Purdue U., West Lafayette, Ind., 1953-56; mgr. dept. Remington Rand Univac, St. Paul, 1956-60; assoc. prof. chem. engring. U. Pitts., 1960-62, prof., 1962—, W.K. Whiteford prof. chem. engring., 1991-94, prof. emeritus, 1995—. Vis. prof. U. Técnica Federico Santa Maria, Valparaiso, Chile, 1960-62; lectr. U. Barcelona (Spain), 1968-69. Fellow AIChE (chmn. Pitts. sect. 1982, McAfee award Pitts. sect. 1995); mem. Am. Chem. Soc., Am. Soc. Engring. Edn. Home: 1330 N Sheridan Ave Pittsburgh PA 15206-1760 Office: U Pitts 1230 Benedum Hall Pittsburgh PA 15261-2212

TIERNEY, MICHAEL EDWARD, lawyer; b. N.Y., July 16, 1948; s. Michael Francis and Margaret Mary (Creamer) T.; m. Alicia Mary Boldt, June 6, 1981; children: Colin, Madeleine. BA, St. Louis U., 1970, MBA, JD, St. Louis U., 1978. Bar: Mo. Assoc., law clk. Wayne L. Millsap, PC, St. Louis, 1977-80; staff atty. Interco. Inc., 1980-83; textile divsn. counsel Chromalloy Am. Corp., 1984-87; v.p., sec. P.N. Hirsch & Co., 1983-84; sr. counsel, asst. sec. Jefferson Smurfit Corp., 1987-92, v.p., gen. counsel, sec., 1993-99, Kinexus Corp., St. Louis, 1999—2002. Adv. bd. St. Louis Area Food Bank, 1980—. U.S. Army Security Agy., 1970-73. Mem. Racquet Club St. Louis, Old Warson Country Club. Republican. Roman Catholic. Avocations: sailing, squash. Home: 10 Twin Springs Ln Saint Louis MO 63124-1139 Address: Kinexus Corp 18500 Edison Ave Chesterfield MO 63005-3629

TIERNEY, MICHAEL JOHN, mathematics and computer science educator; b. St. Louis, Feb. 19, 1947; s. John Thomas and Alice Marie (Krieger) T.; m. Edith L. Echelmeyer, Nov. 21, 1975 (div. Sept. 1984); 1 child, John E.; m. Virginia Lee Christian, Apr. 6, 1985. BS, St. Louis U., 1969, MS, 1971, PhD, 1974; MS, U. Va., 1995. Prof. math. and actuarial sci. Maryville Coll., St. Louis, 1974-83; prof. math. and computer sci. Va. Mil. Inst., Lexington, 1983—; dept. chair, 1995—. Mem. AAUP, AAAS, Am. Math. Soc., Math. Assn. Am., Soc. Indsl. and AppliedMath., Assn. Computing Machinery, Sigma Xi. Presbyterian. Avocations: tennis, landscaping. Home: 819 Gwynne Ave Waynesboro VA 22980-3342 Office: Va Mil Inst Lexington VA 24450 E-mail: Tierney@vmi.edu.

TIERNEY, THOMAS J. business management consultant; b. San Francisco, Mar. 5, 1954; s. Ralph Thomas and Eleanor Faye (Walker) T.; m. Joy Karen McGee, Sept. 23, 1984; children: Colin McGee, Braden Thomas. BA in Econs. with distinction, U. Calif., Davis, 1976; MBA with distinction, Harvard, 1980. Field engr. Bechtel Internat., Azrew, Algeria, 1976-78; cons. Bain & Co., San Francisco, 1980-82, mgr., 1982-83, v.p., 1983-87, mng. ptnr., 1987-92; pres. Bain & Co. Worldwide, 1992-2000, CEO, 1993-2000; founder & chmn. Bridgespan Group, 2000—; dir. Bain & Co., 2000—. Co-author: Aligning the Stars, 2002. Bd. dirs. Inst. for Higher Edn., Cath. Charities; trustee Woods Hole Oceanographic Inst., The Hoover Inst., WGBH, New England Acquarium, Harvard Bus. Sch., Harvard Bus. Sch. Social Enterprise; former bd. dirs. Nature Conservancy, U. Calif.-Davis Alumni Assn., Bay Area United Way, United Way Mass. Bay, Stanford Bus. Sch. Recipient Winslow Meml. award U. Calif. Davis, 1976. Mem. U. Calif. Davis Alumni Assn. (dir. 1984-88), Harvard Bus. Sch. Alumni Assn. Roman Catholic. Avocations: fishing, politics, non-profit sector. Home: 45 Old Farm Rd Wellesley MA 02481-1423

TIERNEY, VICTORIA HODGETTS, artist; b. White Plains, N.Y., Sept. 29, 1942; d. Lawrence R. and Helen (Beling) Kahn; m. Craig E.W. Hodgetts, Jan. 26, 1964 (div. 1972); 1 child, Blake Christopher; m. Mark Julian Tierney, Dec. 22, 1980; stepchildren: Martin Grant, Mark Jr. BFA, U. Calif., Berkeley, 1963; postgrad., Calif. Inst. Arts, 1970-71. Advt. artist Cost Plus Imports, San Francisco, 1964-65; art dir. New Haven (Conn.) Register Mag., 1965-66; asst. art dir. N.Y. Mag., Manhattan, 1968-69; West Coast corr. N.Y. Village Voice, N.Y.C., L.A., 1972-76; art dir. Camouflage Prodns., L.A., 1972-74; freelance writer and illustrator, 1972-77; asst. curator Bandon (Oreg.) Hist. Mus., 1979-81; profl. painter Bandon, 1981—. Owner Chgo. St. Gallery Communication Graphics. Author, illustrator: Story of Pregnancy, 1977, Dream of the Dinosaurs, 1978, Composer Comix, 1994-96; curator Shadows: 2000, Cats & Dragons, 2000 Coos Art Mus.,; co-creator (with Corrie Gant) The Last Flapper, 1999, Moliere By the Sea, 1999, Book Follies, Waiting for Godot, 2000. Pres., bd. dirs. Bandon Playhouse, 1983-97; bd. dirs. Oreg. Coun. for Humanities, Portland, 1990-94, Coos Art Mus., Coos Bay, Oreg., 1996-97; chair, bd. dirs. South Coast Coun. Arts and Humanities, Coos and Curry Counties, Oreg., 1990-92. Named Woman of Yr. Delta Kappa Gamma., 1995. Mem. Watercolor Soc. Oreg., Womynspirit Continuum. Avocations: drumming, theater, photography. Home: PO Box 827 Bandon OR 97411-0827 E-mail: victory@harbovside.com.

TIERNEY, WILLIAM MICHAEL, internist, educator; b. Detroit, July 2, 1951; s. Thomas John and Joan Rosemary (Lynch) Tierney; m. Mary Menzies, Aug. 12, 1972; children: Ryan Menzies, Adam Taylor. BA, Ind. U., 1973, MD, 1976, postgrad., 1976-79. Chief resident internal medicine Wishard Meml. Hosp., Ind. U. Med. Ctr., Indpls., 1979-80; fellow Regenstrief Inst. Health Care, 1980-82; asst. prof. dept. medicine Ind. U. Sch. Medicine, Indpls., 1980-86, assoc. prof., 1986-91, prof., 1991—; chmn. divsn. gen. internal medicine and geriatrics Ind. U. Med. Ctr., 2000—. Assoc. dir. computer sci. rsch. sect. Regenstrief Inst., 1987-93, dir. quality assessment and improvement sect., 1993—, dir. Regenstrief-Moi (Kenya) Informatics Fellowship, 1998—; mem. divsn. gen. internal medicine Roudebush VA Med. Ctr., 1996—, assoc. dir. health svcs. rsch. program, 1996—, dir. ambulatory care fellowship program., 1997—; chair large-scale database task force Nat. Heart Attack Alert Program, 1997—; mem. steering com. ambulatory quality improvement program Dept. Vets. Affairs, 1997-99, mem. steering com. vets. health study, 1995-97, mem. health svcs. rsch. large grants rev. bd., 1993; mem. steering Federated Coun. for Internal Medicine, 1997-98; expert witness Office of Hearing and Appeals, Social Security Adminstrn., 1981-92; mem. spl. study sect. NIH, 1989; med. malpractice reviewer Ind. Atty. Gen.'s Office, 1991-93; interim dir. U. Ctr. Health Svcs. Rsch., 2001—. Contbr. articles to profl. jours. Founder, dir. med. support team Wishard Meml. Hosp., 1982-90; chmn. med. manpower com. Pan Am. Games, Indpls., 1985-87, sports medicine officer, 1987; vol. physician Indpls. Horizon House Ctr. for Homeless Persons, 1993-98; mem. Ind. Alliance for Preventive Health, Ind. State Dept. Health, 1993-96; co-founder Parents for Acad. Challenge, 1994-95; mem. coord. com. cmty. health access project Marion County Dept. Health; mem. Ind. Commn. on Health Care for the Working Poor, 1995-98; mem. steering com. Ind. U. Parents Fund, 1996-2000; mem. clin. performance team Clarian Health Care, mem. data repository subcom. info. sys. com., 1997; mem. evaluation subcom. Ind. Children's Health Care Ins. Program, 1998. Recipient Vitae bonae award for outstanding contbns. in fitness and health awareness Senator Richard Lugar, 1987; grantee NCHSR, PHS, NIH, AHCPR, Glaxo Pharms., Indpls. Found., Indpls. Health Found., Regenstrief Inst., Ind. State Dept. Health, Boehringer-Mannheim Pharms. Corp., Caremark, Inc., Eli Lilly Co., Dept. Vets. Affairs, NLM, NIH/Fogarty Internat. Ctr., Dept. Vets. Affairs, Ind. U., CDC, Bristol-Myers-Squibb, NIMH. Fellow: ACP (mem. med. informatics com. 1991—92), Am. Med. Informatics Assn. (founding fellow, chair ambulatory health care area nat. symposium 1993, bd. dirs. 1996—99, nominations com. 1998), Am. Coll. Med. Informatics; mem.: APHA (co-editor Med. Care, med. nat. leadership med. care sect. 1997—2001), Ams. for Better Care for Dying, Assn. Health Svcs. Rsch., Soc. Med. Decision Making, Ctrl. Soc. Clin. Rsch., Am. Fedn. Med. Rsch., Soc. Gen. Internal Medicine (pres., membership chair midwestern region 1987, program chair nat. meeting 1989, fin. com. 1989—93, mem. com. 1989—93, nominating com. midwestern region 1990, nat. coun. mem. 1990—93, chair fin. com. 1991—92, chair mgmt. com. 1991—92, nat. sec.-treas. 1991—92, mem. ethics com. 1992—94, nat. coun. mem. 1995—97, chair ethics com. 1993—94, long-range planning com. 1993—96, edn. com. 1994—96, Glaser award com. 1995, pres. 1996—97, devel. com. 1997—99, chair devel. com. 1997—98, comms. com. 1998—2000, rsch. awards com. 1998—), Assn. of Am. Physicians. Avocations: running, tennis. E-mail: wtierney@iupui.edu.

TIERNO, PHILIP MARIO, JR. microbiologist, educator, researcher; b. Bklyn., June 5, 1943; s. Philip M. and Phyllis (Tringone) T.; m. Josephine Martinez, Apr. 2, 1967; children: Alexandra Lorraine, Meredith Anne. BS, L.I. U., 1965; MS, NYU, 1974, PhD, 1977. Microbiologist Luth. Med. Ctr., Bklyn., 1965-66; chief rsch. microbiologist hemodialysis unit VA Hosp., Bronx, N.Y., 1966-70; dir. microbiology divsn. NYU Med. Ctr. Goldwater Meml. Hosp., F.D. Roosevelt Island, 1970-81; assoc. and cons. microbiologist Maimonides Med. Ctr., Bklyn., 1970-79; dir. microbiology dept. Tisch-Univ. Hosp., NYU Med. Ctr., 1981—. Adj. asst. prof. CUNY, 1974—76, Bloomfield (N.J.) Coll., 1975—82; assoc. prof. microbiology and pathology NYU Med. Sch., 1981—; cons. Office Atty. Gen. N.Y. State, NIH, Coll. of Am. Pathologists, Dept. Health City of New York, 1981—; mem. Mayoral Task Force on Bioterrorism, N.Y.C. Author: The Secret Life of Germs: Observations and Lessons from a Microbe Hunter, 2001; contbr. articles to profl. jours., chapters to books; author: Protect Yourself Against Bioterrorism, 2002. Pres. Flushing Taxpayers Assn., 1973-77; bd. dirs. Comprehensive Health Planning Agy. City N.Y., 1974-75, Norwood Bd. Adjustment, N.J., 1978-83, 86-98, Norwood Bd. Edn., 1983-86; chmn. Norwood Environ. Commn., 1986-98; co-founder, bd. dirs. Found. Sci. Rsch. in Pub. Interest, S.I., N.Y., 1985—. Mem. AAAS, N.Y. Acad. Scis., Am. Acad. Microbiology, Am. Pub. Health Assn., Am. Soc. Microbiology, Optimists (v.p. Norwood 1978-95), Knights of Malta (Knighthood). Home: 102 Harbor Cove Piermont NY 10968 Office: Tisch Hosp-Microbiology Dept NYU Med Ctr 560 1st Ave New York NY 10016-6402

TIESZEN, RALPH LELAND, SR. internist; b. Marion, S.D., Sept. 21, 1928; s. Bernard D. and Hulda J. (Thomas) T.; m. Florence Morrill Johnson, July 25, 1952; children: Ralph Leland Jr., Stuart Carl, Stephan Lee. Student, Freeman Jr. Coll., 1946-48; BS, Wheaton Coll., 1950; postgrad., U. S.D., 1950-52; MD, Loma Linda U., 1954. Diplomate Am. Bd. Internal Medicine, Am. Bd. Geriatric Medicine. Intern L.A. County Hosp., 1954-55, resident TB and Chest, 1955-56; commd. 2d lt. med. corps. USAF, 1956, advanced through grades to maj., 1964, chief medicine hosp., 1962-64, ret., 1979; resident in internal medicine Mayo Found., Rochester, Minn., 1957-60; mem. active staff dept. internal medicine Carraway Meth. Med. Ctr., Birmingham, 1964—, dir. resident program, 1968-72, trustee, 1972-77, pres. staff, 1973-75, exec. com., fin. com., 1974-77, dir. geriatrics, 1989—; pvt. practice Carraway Internal Medicine Assocs., Ala.; asst. clin. prof. medicine Med. Coll. Ala., 1965-69, asst. clin. prof. dept. endocrinology, 1969-70, clin. assoc. prof. medicine, 1970-81, clin. prof. medicine, 1981—; clin. prof. gerontology and geriatric medicine U. Ala., Birmingham, 1999—; med. dir. Community Hosp., 1989—. Mem. faculty joint commn. accreditation hosps., 1974-78; exec. com. Birmingham Regional Health Systems Agy.; investigator numerous clin. trials. Contbr. articles to profl. jours. Chmn. Birmingham String Quartet, 1970-74; v.p. ticket sales Ala. Symphony Assn., 1979, exec. com.; sec. men's com. Ala. Symphony, 1986-88, pres. 1990-91. Gen. Med. Officer USAR, 197984, comdr. U.S. Army Hosp., Birmingham, 1984-88, col., chief profl. svcs. 5th med. group, Birmingham, 1988-92, ret., 1992. Fellow ACP; mem. AMA, Am. Thoracic Soc. (sr.), Med. Assn. State Ala., Jefferson County Med. Soc. (past bd. censors, del. to state med. assn.), Birmingham Acad. Medicine (pres. 1987-88), Birmingham Internists Soc. (pres. 1972-73). Democrat. Avocations: opera, symphony, philosophy, medical ethics, astronomy. Office: Carraway Internal Medicine Assocs 1600 Carraway Blvd Ste 302 Birmingham AL 35234

TIETENBERG, THOMAS, economist, department chairman; b. Oct. 21, 1942; s. Harry Hall and Florence Elaine (Moxley) Tietenberg; m. Gretchen Ethel Sprague, Oct. 28, 1967; children: Heidi Leigh, Eric Justin. BS with distinction, U.S. Air Force Acad., 1964; MA in Econs., U. of East, Manila, 1965; MS in Econs., U. Wis., 1970, PhD in Econs., 1971. Asst. prof. econs. Williams Coll., Williamstown, Mass., 1971—77; assoc. prof. econs. Colby Coll., Waterville, Maine, 1977—84, prof. econs., 1984—, chmn., dept. econs., 1985—88, 1993—95, chmn., environ. studies program, 2000—, C.A. Johnson disting. tchg. prof., 1990—93, Mitchell Family prof. econs., 1993—. Mem. sci. adv. bd. environ. econs. com. U.S. EPA, 1993—96; editl. bd. Land Econs. Mgmt., 1981—, Jour. Environ. Econs. and Mgmt., 1992—, Resource and Energy Econs., 1993—. Author: Emissions Trading: An Exercise in Reforming Pollution Policy, 1985, Environmental Economics and Policy, 2000, Environmental and Natural Resource Economics, 2002. Lay leader Pleasant St. United Meth. Ch., Waterville, 1964—68. Served from 2d lt. to capt. USAF, 1964—68. Fellow Gilbert T. White Resources for Future, Inc., 1984, econ. policy, Brookings Inst., 1974; scholar Fulbright, Inst. Internat. Edn., 1964. Mem.: Assn. Environ. and Resource Economists (pres. 1987—88). Avocations: golf, tennis. Home: 2616 W River Rd Sidney ME 04330-2732

TIETJEN, JOHN HENRY, retired biology and oceanography educator; b. Jamaica, N.Y., June 19, 1940; s. Reinhard L. and Emma (Wilkomm) T.; m. Theresa Mary Martin, Aug., 24, 1968; children: Theresa Emma, Mary Elizabeth. BS, CCNY, 1961; PhD, U. R.I., 1966. Asst. prof. biology CCNY, N.Y.C., 1966-71, assoc. prof., 1971-75, prof., 1975-98, prof. emeritus, 1998—; ret. Ecol. cons. Tex. Instruments, Dallas, 1977-79, S.W. Rsch. Inst., Houston, 1978-80, Henderson and Bodwell Engrs., Bethpage, N.Y., 1982, N.E. Utilities, Hartford, Conn., 1968—, North Atlantic Energy Svc., Seabrook, N.H., 1994—, Dominion Resources, Inc., Waterford, Conn., 2001—; rsch. assoc. Am. Mus. Natural History, 1993—. Contbr. over 70 articles to profl. jours. V.p., pres. Leonia (N.J.) Bd. Edn., 1977-86. Rsch. grantee NSF, Office Naval Research, Dept. Energy, NOAA. Mem. Estuary Rsch. Found., Sigma Xi. Roman Catholic. Avocations: outdoor activities, reading, travel. Office: AMNH divsn Invert Zool New York NY 10024 E-mail: jhtcc@cunyvm.cuny.edu., tietjen@amnh.org.

TIETJEN, SCOTT PHILLIPS, computer programmer, analyst; b. West Haven, Conn., May 14, 1960; s. Henry Louis and Ruth Evelyn (Haupt) T. BS in Applied Math. and Computer Sci., Carnegie-Mellon U., 1982; MS in Computer Sci., Marist Coll., 1991. Staff programmer IBM Corp., Poughkeepsie, N.Y., 1982-93; cons. personal computer technician Aerotek, Inc., N.Y.C., 1993; cons. programmer/analyst Data-Based Devel. Sys., East Providence, R.I., 1994; cons. data security analyst Atlantic Search Group, Inc., Stamford, Conn., 1994-95; cons. programmer/analyst Maxim Group, Shelton, 1995; sr. cons., programmer/analyst Keane, Inc., Danbury and Rocky Hill, 1996-99; sr. cons. programmer/analyst Compyter Horizons Corp., Glastonbury, 1999-2001. Treas. Aid Assn. for Luths. Br. 6981. Mem. IEEE (computer soc.), Assn. Computing Machinery, Tall Clubs Internat. (club del.), Tri-County Talls of N.Y. and Conn. (newsletter editor), Rivercity High Soc. (Evansville, Ind.), Atlanta Sky-Hi Club, Atlantic Tall Club. Republican. Lutheran. Avocations: theatrical and architectural lighting design. Office: 500 Winding Brook Dr Glastonbury CT 06033-4336 E-mail: stjen@ieee.org.

TIETJEN, SUZANNE DAVENPORT, critical care nurse; b. Newport News, Va., Apr. 13, 1953; d. William Whitney and Camille Louise (Humes) Davenport; m. Michael Ray Tietjen, June 16, 1973; children: Michael Asher, Zachary Neil, Bethany Lynne. BA, U. of South Fla., 1973; BSN, Columbus (Ga.) Coll., 1987. RN, Ill., Ga.; CCRN; cert. in neonatal intensive care Assn. Women's Health, Obstetrics and Neonatal Nurses. Staff nurse high risk nursery The Med. Ctr., Columbus, 1987-88; staff nurse neonatal ICU Hosp. of Good Samaritan, Watertown, N.Y., 1988-91; staff/transport nurse neonatal ICU Children's Hosp. of Ill. Saint Francis Med. Ctr., Peoria, 1991-96, neonatal nurse practitioner, 1996—. Contbr. articles to nursing jours. Mem. AACN, ANA, Ill. Nurses Assn., Nat. Assn. Neonatal Nurses. Office: Children's Hosp of Ill St Francis Med Ctr 530 NE Glen Oak Ave Peoria IL 61637-0001 E-mail: cotswold9@home.com.

TIETKE, WILHELM, gastroenterologist, educator; b. Niengraben, Germany, Oct. 15, 1938; came to U.S., 1969, naturalized, 1979; s. Wilhelm and Frieda (Schmeding) T.; m. Imme Schmidt, Oct. 15, 1965; children: Cornelia, Isabel. MD, U. Goettingen, Germany, 1968. Diplomate Am. Bd. Internal Medicine, Am. Bd. Gastroenterology. Intern Edward W. Sparrow Hosp., Lansing, Mich., 1970; resident in internal medicine Henry Ford Hosp., Detroit, 1971-73, fellow in gastroenterology, 1973-75; practice medicine specializing in gastroenterology Huntsville, Ala., 1975—. Mem. vol. faculty, cons. U. Ala., Huntsville, 1976; clin. assoc. prof. internal medicine, 1979—; v.p. Huntsville Gastroenterology Assocs., P.C., 1979—. Fellow Coll. Gastroenterology; mem. AMA, ACP, Ala. Med. Soc., Am. Soc. Gastrointestinal Endoscopy, Rotary. Lutheran. Home: 2707 Westminister Way SE Huntsville AL 35801-2241 Office: 119 Longwood Dr Huntsville AL 35801 also: PO Box 2169 Huntsville AL 35804-2169

TIETZ, DIETMAR JUERGEN, computer Web engineer, scientist; b. Berlin, Jan. 19, 1951; s. Alfred Georg Paul and Gertrud Klara (Schulz) T. m. Angelina (Osorio Ugalde). PhD, Hamburg U., 1982. Lectr. U. Hamburg, 1977-82; sr. scientist macromolecular analysis NIH, Bethesda, Md., 1983-93; pres., CEO, chmn. mktg. Forty Plus Greater Washington, 1992-93; sci. project mgr. dept. biostats. Justus-Liebig U., Giessen, Germany, 1993-95; web engring. team lead, software arch. Aerotek Md., NASA EOSDIS govt. project Raytheon Systems, 1996-99; dir. product devel. Dynamic Diagrams subs. Cadmus Profl. Comm., 1999—. Editor: Nucleic Acid Electrophoresis Lab Manual, 1998; mem. editl. bd. Electrophoresis Jour., VCH Weinheim, Germany, 1994-96.

Mem. Am. Chem. Soc., Assn. German Naturforscher and Aerzte. Lutheran. Avocations: nature, computers, photography, electronic keyboard. Office: Cadmus Profl Comm 940 Elkridge Landing Rd Linthicum Heights MD 21090 E-mail: djt@his.com.

TIETZ, JOEL FORD, management consultant, professional engineer; b. Somerville, N.J., July 21, 1961; s. Roy Henry and Myrna Gwen (Ford) T.; m. Cathy McGrath, Aug. 20, 1988; children: Roy Wesley, Celeste Elizabeth. BS in Mech. Engring., U. Notre Dame, 1983. Computer programmer Am. Telephone, Basking Ridge, N.J., 1983-84; mgr. of engring. The Cahill Ptnrship., Far Hills, 1984-88; project mgr. Yannaccone Assocs., Chester, 1988, Bellemead Devel., Roseland, 1988-91; asst. v.p. Chubb Svcs. Corp., Warren, 1991—. Speaker in field. Inventor in field. Vice chmn. Piscataway (N.J.) Indsl. Commn., 1990-93. Recipient Mulligan award U. Notre Dame, South Bend, Ind., 1983. Mem. ASME, NSPE, N.J. Soc. Profl. Planners, Disaster Recovery Inst. Republican. Avocations: outdoor sports, music, reading. Home: 4 Trotwood Dr Franklin NJ 07416 Office: Chubb Svcs Corp 25 Independence Blvd Warren NJ 07059-2706

TIETZ, NORBERT WOLFGANG, clinical chemistry educator, administrator; b. Stettin, Germany, Nov. 13, 1926; s. Joseph and Anna (Kozalla) T.; m. Gertrud Kraft, Oct. 17, 1959; children— Margaret, Kurt, Annette, Michael Student, Tuebingen, Germany, 1945-46; D.Sc., Tech. U., Stuttgart, W.Ger., 1950. Chmn. dept. chemistry Reid Meml. Hosp., Richmond, Ind., 1956-59; prof., dir. clin. chemistry Mt. Sinai Med. Ctr. and Chgo. Med. Sch., Chgo., 1959-76, U. Ky. Med. Ctr., Lexington, 1976-96; prof. pathology U. Calif., San Diego, 1996—. Research fellow and asst. U. Munich, W.Ger., 1951-54; research fellow dept. pathology U. Chgo. and St. Luke's Hosp., Chgo., 1955-56, Rockford Meml. Hosp., Ill., 1954-55; cons. Ill. Dept. Pub. Health, 1967-76, VA Hosp., Hines, Ill., 1974-76; prof. biochemistry and pathology Rush Med. Coll., Chgo., 1975-76; vol. cons. VA Hosp., Lexington, 1976-96; cons. Dept. VA Med. Ctr., San Diego, 1997—. Editor: Fundamentals of Clinical Chemistry, 1970, 76, 87, Clinical Guide to Laboratory Tests, 1983, 90, 95, Textbook of Clinical Chemistry, 1986, A Study Guide to Clinical Chemistry, 1987, Applied Laboratory Medicine, 1992; assoc. editor: Dictionary and Encyclopedia of Laboratory Medicine and Technology, 1983; contbr. numerous articles to profl. jours. Recipient A. Dubin award Nat. Acad. Clin. Biochemistry, 1995, Disting. Internat. Svc. award Internat. Fedn. Clin. Chemistry, 1996. Fellow Acad. Clin. Lab. Physicians and Scientists, Am. Inst. Chemists; mem. Am. Assn. Clin. Chemistry (clin. chemist award 1971, award for outstanding efforts in edn. and tng. 1976, Disting. Alumnus award 1977, Steuben Bowl award 1978, Bernard F. Gerulat award N.J. chpt. 1988, award for Outstanding Contbns. to Clin. Chemistry 1989, Donald D. Van Slyke award N.Y. Met. chpt. 1989), AAAS, Am. Chem. Soc., Am. Soc. Clin. Pathologists, Man. Soc. Clin. Chemists (ann. Lectureship award 1987), Sigma Xi. Roman Catholic. Home: 7472 Caminito Rialto La Jolla CA 92037-3957 Office: U Calif Dept Pathology 9500 Gilman Dr La Jolla CA 92093-0612 E-mail: ntietz@ucsd.edu.

TIETZ, REINHARD, economics educator; b. Frankfurt am Main, Fed. Republic Germany, July 28, 1928; s. Edwin and Gerda (Broesel) T.; m. Ursula Naujoks, 1964; children: Christiane, Susanne. Student, U. Mainz, 1958-59, U. Muenchen, 1959-60, U. Frankfurt, 1960-63, diploma in bus., 1963, D. in Polit. Sci., 1971. Lab. technician, sales engr. chem., paper, printing industry, 1951-58; univ. asst. U. Frankfurt, 1963-73, lectr. computer programming, 1970-73, asst. prof. econs., 1973-74, prof. econs., 1974-95. Cons. OECD, 1973-74; guest prof. U. Innsbruck, 1994, 96, 99, 2001; exam. contr. European Bus. Sch., Oestrich-Winkel, 1999-2000. Author: Anspruchsanpassungsorientiertes Wachstums-und Konjunkturmodell, 1973; editor: Wert-und Praeferenzprobleme in den Sozialwissenschaften, 1981, Aspiration Levels in Bargaining and Economic Decision Making, 1983; co-editor: Sozialwissenschaften im Studium des Rechts, 1977, Bounded Rational Behavior in Experimental Games and Markets, 1988; mem. editorial bd. Jour. Behavioral Decision Making, 1987-94. Mem. Am. Econ. Assn., Internat. Assn. for Rsch. in Econ. Psychology, Verein für Socialpolitik (chmn. com. for social scis. 1976-81), Gesellschaft fuer experimentelle Wirtschaftsforschung (chmn. 1982-95—), Gesellschaft fuer Wirtschafts- und Sozialkybernetik (bd. dirs. 1977-2000), Econ. Sci. Assn. Home: Steinhausenstrasse 23 D 60599 Frankfurt am Main Germany E-mail: tietz@wiwi.unifrankfurt.de.

TIFFANY, JOSEPH RAYMOND, II, lawyer; b. Dayton, Ohio, Feb. 5, 1949; s. Forrest Fraser and Margaret Watson (Clark) T.; m. Terri Robbins, Dec. 1, 1984. AB magna cum laude, Harvard U., 1971; MS in Internat. Relations, London Sch. Econs., 1972; JD, U. Calif., Berkeley, 1975. Bar: U.S. Dist. Ct. (no. dist.) 1975, U.S. Dist. Ct. (ea. dist.) 1977, U.S. Ct. Appeals (9th cir.) 1982. Assoc. Pillsbury, Madison & Sutro, San Francisco, 1975-82, ptnr., 1983-2001, Pillsbury Winthrop LLP, San Francisco, 2001—. Mem. ABA (antitrust, intellectual property, litigation sects.), Calif. Bar Assn., Harvard Club. Office: Pillsbury Winthrop LLP 2550 Hanover St Palo Alto CA 94304-1115 E-mail: jtiffany@pillsburywinthrop.com.

TIFFANY-CASTIGLIONI, EVELYN, biomedical science educator, researcher; b. El Paso, Tex. d. Robert Samuel and Frances James Tiffany; m. Aldo Joseph Castiglioni Jr., Dec. 28, 1977; children: Anna Tiffany, Peter Vincent. BS in Biology, U. Tex., El Paso, 1975; PhD, U. Tex. Med. Branch, Galveston, 1979. Postdoc. fellow U. Calif., L.A., 1980-82; asst. prof. Tex. A&M U., College Station, 1982-87, assoc. prof., 1987-94; vis. assoc. prof. U. Tex. Health Sci. Ctr., San Antonio, 1989-90; prof. Tex. A&M U., College Station, 1994—; asst. dean for undergrad. edn. Coll. of Vet., Medicine Tex. A&M U., 1996-98, assoc. dean for undergrad. edn., 1998—, head dept. vet. anatomy and pub. health, 1999—. Editl. bd. Neurotoxicology, 1999—, Internat. Jour. Neurosci. Rsch., 2000—; exec. com. mem. U. Tex. Med. Branch Grad. Sch. of Biomed., Galveston, 1999—. Author: (poems) Perspectives in Biology and Medicine, 1990; contbr. articles to profl. jours. Recipient Faculty Disting. Achievement Award for Rsch., Tex. A&M U. Assn. of Former Students, 1998; grantee Investigator-initiated rsch. grant, Nat. Inst. Health, 1993-97, rsch. grant Environ. Protection Agy., 1985-89. Mem. Soc. Toxicologists, Am. Soc. Neurochemistry, Soc. for Neuroscience, Phi Kappa Phi. Avocations: harpist, accordionist. E-mail address. Office: Dept Vet Anatomy and Pub Health Texas A&M University College Station TX 77843-0001 Fax: (979) 847-8981. E-mail: ecastiglioni@cvm.tamu.edu.

TIFFORD, ARTHUR W. lawyer; b. Bklyn., July 7, 1943; s. Herman and Dorothy (Kessler) T.; m. Barbara J. Sinreich, Aug. 15, 1965; children: Melissa Beth, Alexandra Lynn. BA, CUNY, 1965; JD, Bklyn. Law Sch., 1967. Bar: N.Y. 1967, Fla. 1967, U.S. Dist. Ct. (so. dist.) Fla. 1968, U.S. Ct. Mil. Appeals 1968, U.S. Ct. Appeals (5th cir.) 1971, U.S. Dist. Ct. (mid. dist.) Fla. 1979, U.S. Ct. Appeals (10th cir.) 1979, U.S. Ct. Appeals (1st cir.) 1982, U.S. Ct. Appeals (9th cir.) 1982, U.S. Ct. Appeals (11th cir.) 1981, U.S. Ct. Appeals (fed. cir.) 1985, U.S. Ct. Appeals (4th cir.) 1998, U.S. Claims Ct. 1985, U.S. Tax Ct. 1988. Rschr., mgr. clk. Cravath, Swaine & Moore, N.Y.C., 1967; asst. U.S. atty. U.S. Dept. Justice (so. dist. Fla.), Miami, 1971-72; pvt. practice, 1972—. With USMC, 1968-71, USMCR, 1971-92, ret. col. Mem. ABA, Am. Trial Lawyers Assn., Fla. Trial Lawyers Assn., Nat. Assn. Criminal Def. Lawyers, N.Y. Bar Assn., Fla. Bar Assn., Marine Corps Res. Officers Assn. (pres. Greater Miami chpt. 1978-79, 81-82, 84-85, nat. bd. dirs. 1987-89). Democrat. Avocations: writing, photography, parachuting, scuba diving, running. Home: 9980 SW 128th St Miami FL 33176-5632 Office: 1385 NW 15th St Miami FL 33125-1621 Fax: 305-325-1825. E-mail: tiffordlaw@aol.com.

TIFFT, WILLIAM GRANT, astronomer, educator; b. Derby, Conn., Apr. 5, 1932; s. William Charles and Marguerite Howe (Hubbell) T.; m. Carol Ruth Nordquist, June 1, 1957 (div. July 1964); children: Jennifer, William John; m. Janet Ann Lindner Homewood, June 2, 1965; 1 child, Amy, stepchildren: Patricia, Susan, Hollis. AB, Harvard Coll., 1954; PhD, Calif. Inst. Tech., 1958. Nat. sci. postdoctoral Australian Nat. U., Canberra, 1958-60; rsch. assoc. Vanderbilt U., Nashville, 1960-61; astronomer Lowell Obs., Flagstaff, Ariz., 1961-64; assoc. prof. U. Ariz., Tucson, 1964-73, prof., 1973—2002, prof. emeritus, 2002—. Joint author: Revised New General Catalog, 1973; joint editor: Modern Mathematical Models of Time and Their Applications to Physics and Cosmology, 1997; contbr. over 100 articles to profl. jours. NSF Predoctoral fellow, 1954-58, NSF Postdoctoral fellow, 1958-60; grantee NASA, NSF, ONR, Rsch. Corp. Fellow Am. Astron. Soc.; mem. Internat. Astron. Union. Achievements include discovery of redshift quantization and correlations relating to it, including variability; first to detect voids in mapping of large scale supercluster structure; investigations of three-dimensional time in cosmology and particle physics. Office: U Arizona Dept Astronomy Tucson AZ 85721-0001 E-mail: wtifft@as.arizona.edu.

TIFT, MARY LOUISE, artist; b. Seattle, Jan. 2, 1913; d. John Howard and Wilhelmina (Pressler) Dreher; m. William Raymond Tift, Dec. 4, 1948. BFA cum laude, U. Wash., 1933; postgrad., Art Ctr. Coll., L.A., 1945-48, U. Calif., San Francisco, 1962-63. Art dir. Vaughn Shedd Advt., L.A., 1948; asst. prof. design Calif. Coll. Arts & Crafts, Oakland, Calif., 1949-59; coord. design dept. San Francisco Art Inst., 1959-62. Subject of cover story, Am. Artist mag., 1980, studio article, 1987; one-woman shows, Gumps Gallery, San Francisco, 1977, 1986, 90, Diane Gilson Gallery, Seattle, 1978, Oreg. State U., 1981, Univ. House, Seattle, Frye Art Mus., Seattle, 2000; exhibited in group shows including Brit. Biennale, Yorkshire, Eng., 1970, Grenchen Triennale, Switzerland, 1970, Polish Biennale, Crakow, 1972, Nat. Gallery, Washington, 1973, Madrid Biennale, 1980, U.S.-U.K. Impressions, Eng., 1988; represented in permanent collections, Phila. Mus. Art, Bklyn. Mus., Seattle Art Mus., Library Congress, Achenbach Print Collection, San Francisco Palace Legion of Honor, San Diego Mus. Art, U.S. Art in Embassies. Served to lt. USNR, 1943-45. Mem. Print Club Phila., World Print Council, Calif. Soc. Printmakers, Phi Beta Kappa, Lambda Rho. Christian Scientist. Studio: 4400 Stone Way N Apt 521 Seattle WA 98103-7487

TIGANI, BRUCE WILLIAM, lawyer; b. Wilmington, Del., May 10, 1956; s. J. Vincent Jr. and Josephine C. (DeAngelis) T.; m. Janice Rowe, Sept. 25, 1982; children: Jessica Lynne, Bruce William Jr. Student, Georgetown U., 1974-75; BBS, U. Del., 1978; JD, Villanova U., 1981. Bar: Del. 1981, Pa. 1982, U.S. Dist. Ct. Del. 1982, U.S. Dist. Ct. (ea. dist.) Pa. 1982, U.S. Tax Ct. 1982. Assoc. Lord & Mulligan, Media, Pa., 1981-84, resident atty. Wilmington, 1984-87, ptnr., 1987-88; mng. ptnr. Werb, Tigani, Hood & Sullivan, 1988-99, Tigani & Hood LLP, Wilmington, 2000—. Del. to IRS, Mid. Altantic Regional liason. Mem. lay adv. bd. The Little Sisters of Poor; active Rep. Com. of State Del. Mem. ABA, Del. State Bar Assn. (chmn. tax sect. 1991-92, real estate sect., chair trusts and estates sect. 1997-98, lectr. bus. and tax seminars), Wilmington Tax Group (chmn. 1994-95), Del. State C. of C. (commerce tax com.), Estate Planning Coun. Del., Inc. (bd. dirs. 1993-95), Concord Country Club, Univ. and Whist Club Wilmington, Blue and Gold Club. Avocations: golf, softball. Office: Tigani & Hood LLP PO Box 1471 1801 Mellon Bank Ctr 919 Market St Wilmington DE 19899-1471 E-mail: btigani@TiganihoodLaw.com.

TIGAR, MICHAEL EDWARD, law educator; b. Glendale, Calif., Jan. 18, 1941; s. Charles Henry and Margaret Elizabeth (Lang) T.; m. Pamet Ayer Jones, Sept. 21, 1961 (div. Mar. 1973); children: Jon Steven, Katherine Ayer; m. Amanda G. Birrell, Feb. 16, 1980 (div. Aug. 1996); 1 child, Elizabeth Torrey; m. Jane E. Blanksteen, Aug. 22, 1996. BA in Polit. Sci., U. Calif., Berkeley, 1962, JD, 1966. Bar: D.C. 1967, U.S. Ct. Appeals (2d, 4th, 5th, 6th, 7th, 8th, 9th, 10th, 11th, fed. and D.C. cirs.), U.S. Tax Ct., U.S. Supreme Ct. 1972, N.Y. 1993. Assoc. Williams & Connolly, Washington, 1966-69; editor-in-chief Selective Svc. Law Reporter, 1967-69; acting prof. law UCLA, 1969-71; pvt. practice law Grasse, France, 1972-74; assoc. William & Connolly, Washington, 1974, ptnr., 1975-77, Tigar & Buffone, Washington, 1977-84; prof. law U. Tex., Austin, 1984-87, Joseph D. Jamail Centennial prof. law, 1987-98; of counsel Haddon, Morgan & Foreman, Denver, 1996-98; prof. law, and Edwin A. Mooers, Sr., Scholar Am. U. Washington Coll. Law, Washington, 1998—. Reporter 5th Cir. Pattern Jury Instrns., Austin, 1988-90. Author: Practice Manual Selective Service Law Reporter, 1968, Law and the Rise of Capitalism, 1977, (with Jane B. Tigar) Federal Appeals: Jurisdiction and Practice, 3d edit., 1999, Examining Witnesses, 1993, Persuasion: The Litigator's Art, 1999; contbr. articles to profl. jours. Mem. ABA (vice chair 1987-88, chair elect 1988-89, chair 1989-90 sect. litigation). Avocations: sailing, cooking. Office: Washington Coll Law 4801 Massachusetts Ave NW Washington DC 20016-8196

TIGER, IRA PAUL, lawyer; b. Bklyn., Jan. 31, 1936; s. Sidney and Rebecca (Frankel) T.; m. Rosalind Silverman, July 4, 1957 (dec. Nov. 1972); children: Ruth, Lori; m. Ann Mae Gersh, May 5, 1974; stepchildren: Jimmie, Randy, Richard Riesenberg. BS in Econs., U. Pa., 1956, JD magna cum laude, 1959. Bar: Pa. 1960, U.S. Dist. Ct. (ea. dist.) Pa. 1960, U.S. Ct. Appeals (3d cir.) 1960, U.S. Supreme Ct. 1971, U.S. Ct. Appeals (7th cir.) 1996. Law clk. 3d cir., 1959-60; assoc. Schnader, Harrison, Segal & Lewis, Phila., 1960-67, ptnr., 1968—, chmn. litigation dept., 1986-90, chmn. standing com. on profl. conduct, 1992—. Judge pro tem Phila. Ct. Common Pleas, 1994—; mediator U.S. Dist. Ct. (ea. dist.) Pa., 1991—. Rsch. editor U. Pa. Law Rev., 1958-59. Pres. Temple Sinai Synagogue, 1989-91, Elkins Park House Coun., 1996-98; mem. Planning Adv. Bd. Upper Dublin Twp., 1982-87, mem. ednl. adv. com., 1976-78; legal counsel Phila. Jr. C. of C., 1963-64, bd. dirs., 1962-66, sec. Jewish campus activities bd., 1971-73. Mem. ABA, Am. Judicature Soc., Inst. Jud. Adminstrn., Pa. Bar Assn., Phila. Bar Assn. (chmn. fed. cts. com. 1985), Lawyers Club Phila., Order of Coif (exec. com. Pa. chpt. 1981-83), Beta Alpha Psi, Beta Gamma Sigma. Democrat. Office: Schnader Harrison 1600 Market St Ste 3600 Philadelphia PA 19103-7286 Fax: (215) 972-7266. E-mail: itiger@schnader.com.

TIGER, LIONEL, social scientist, anthropology consultant; b. Montreal, Que., Can., Feb. 5, 1937; s. Martin and Lillian (Schneider) T.; m. Virginia Conner, Aug. 19, 1964; 1 child, Sebastian Benjamin. BA, McGill U., 1957, MA, 1959; PhD, U. London, 1963. Instr. anthropology U. Ghana, Accra, 1960; asst. prof. dept. anthropology and sociology U. B.C., Vancouver, Can., 1963-68; assoc. prof. anthropology Rutgers U., New Brunswick, N.J., 1969-74, prof. anthropology, 1974—, Charles Darwin prof. anthropology, 1990—. Cons., rsch. dir. Harry F. Guggenheim Found., N.Y.C., 1972-84; chmn. bd. social scientists U.S. News and World Report, 1986-88; sci. adv. bd. Am. Wine Inst., San Francisco; sr. rsch. assoc. Nat. Inst. Pub. Policy. Author: Men in Groups, 1969, 2d edit., 1987, (with Robin Rox) The Imperial Animal, 1971, 3d edit., 1998, (with Joseph Shepher) Women in the Kibbutz, 1975, Optimism: The Biology of Hope, 1979, 2d edit., 1994, China's Food, 1985, The Manufacture of Evil: Ethics, Evolution and the Industrial System, 1987; editor: Female Hierarchies, 1978, (with Michael Robinson) Man and Beast Revisited, 1992, The Pursuit of Pleasure, 1992, 2d edit., 2000, The Decline of Males, 1999, The Apes of New York, 2002; mem. editl. bd. Social Sci. Info., Ethology and Sociobiology jour., Jour. of Social Distress and the Homeless. Bd. advisors David R. Graham Found., Toronto; cultural laureate N.Y.C. Landmarks Found., 1999. Recipient W.I. Susman award for excellence in tchg., 1985, McNaughton prize for creative writing; Guggenheim fellow, 1969, rsch. fellow ASDA Found., 1985, Can. Coun., fgn. area tng. fellow Ford Found., Can. Coun.-Killam fellow for interdisciplinary rsch., Rockefeller fellow Aspen Inst., 1979, H.F. Guggenheim Found, fellow, 1988-891 Inst. for Law and Behavioral Rsch. fellow. Mem. PEN (mem. exec. bd., treas. 1988-91, v.p. 1991-94), Am. Anthrop. Assn., Internat. Humanist Assn. (humanist laureate), Can. Humanists Assn. (hon.), Soc. for Study of Evolution, Century Assn. Home: 248 W 23rd St Fl 4 New York NY 10011-2304 also: RR 2 Millbrook NY 12545-9802 Office: Rutgers U 131 George St New Brunswick NJ 08901-1414 E-mail: ltiger@rcl.rutgers.edu.

TIGER, MADELINE J. writer, educator; b. N.Y.C., Nov. 17, 1934; d. Howard Lang and Elinor Hamburg T.; children: Randall, Barbara Joan, Joseph, Timothy, Homer. BA, Wellesley Coll., 1956; MAT in Tchg. Eng., Harvard U., 1957; MFA, Columbia U., 1986. Tchr. Watchung Hills (N.J.) Regional H.S., 1957-58, Columbia H.S., Maplewood, N.J., 1959-60; artist-in-residence N.J. State Coun. on Arts, Trenton, 1973—; instr. Upward Bound Seton Hall U., South Orange, N.J., 1975-83; adj. instr. Upsala Coll., East Orange, 1982-88; poetry facilitator Geraldine R. Dodge Found., Madison, 1986—. Author: (poetry) The Chinese Handcuff, 1975, Keeping House in This Forest, 1977, Toward Spring Bank, 1982, My Father's Harmonica, 1991, Mary of Migdal, 1991, Water Has No Color, 1992, White Owl, 2000. Mem. Poets, Essayists, Novelists Am. Ctr., Poetry Soc. Am., Poets House. Democrat. Jewish. Avocations: reading, gardening, biking. Home and Office: 126 Beverly Rd Bloomfield NJ 07003 E-mail: mtiger126@yahoo.com.

TIGERMAN, STANLEY, architect, educator; b. Chgo., Sept. 20, 1930; s. Samuel Bernard and Emma Louise (Stern) T.; m. Margaret I. McCurry; children: Judson Joel, Tracy Leigh. Student, MIT, 1948-49; BArch, Yale U., 1960, MArch, 1961. Archtl. draftsman firm George Fred Keck, Chgo., 1949-50, Skidmore, Owings and Merrill, Chgo., 1957-59, Paul Rudolph, New Haven, 1959-61, Harry Weese, Chgo., 1961-62; partner firm Tigerman & Koglin, 1962-64; prin. firm Stanley Tigerman & Assos., 1964-82; ptnr. Tigerman Fugman McCurry, 1982-88, Tigerman McCurry, 1988—. Prof. architecture U. Ill.-Chgo., 1967-71, 80-93, dir. Sch. Architecture, 1985-93; vis. lectr. Yale U., 1974, Cornell U., Ithaca, N.Y., 1963, Cooper Union, 1970, U. Calif. at Berkeley, 1968, Cardiff (Wales) Coll., 1965, Engring. U., Bangladesh, 1967; chmn. AIA com. on design, coordinator exhbn. and book Chicago Architects, 1977; Charlotte Shepherd Davenport prof. architecture Yale U., 1979; architect-in-residence Am. Acad. in Rome, 1980; vis. prof. architecture Harvard U., 1982; William Henry Bishop Chair. prof. architecture Yale U., 1984, Sarrinen prof., 1993; dir. post-professional grad. program U. Ill.-Chgo.; co-founder Archeworks, Design Lab., Chgo., 1993; mem. adv. com. Princeton U., 1997. Prin. works include The Ounce of Prevention Educare Ctr., Chgo., Fukuoka Apt. Complex, Japan, The Power House, Zion, Ill., The Chgo. Children's Adv. Ctr.; author: Versus, 1982, Architecture of Exile, 1988, Stanley Tigerman: Buildings and Projects, 1966-89, 1989; contbr. , , , , articles;exhibitions include Venice Biennale, 1976, 1980, Calif. Condition, 1982; , author essay;exhibitions include Chicago Architecture, The New Zeitgeist: In Search of Closure, 1989, 1989; author: (catalog) Chicago Architecture, The New Zeitgeist: In Search of Closure, 1989. Pres. Yale Arts Assn., 1969-70; mem. advisory com. Yale Archtl. Sch., 1976—; bd. dirs. Bangladesh Found. Served with USN, 1950-54. Recipient Alpha Rho Chi medal, Yale, 1961, Archtl. Record award, 1970, Masonry award, 1974, Masonry gold medal, 1974, Alumni Art award, Yale U., 1985, Design award for Art Inst. Chgo. Schinkel Exhbn., Am. Soc. Interior Designers, 1995, Humanitarian award, Holocaust Meml. Found. Ill., 2001, Grand award of Excellence, NAHB, 2001, 2002; grantee Advanced Studies in Fine Art, Graham Fedn., 1965. Fellow AIA (chmn. com. design 1976-77, adv. com., Disting. Svc. award Chgo. chpt. 1983, Chgo. Honor awards 1977-79, Nat. Honor award 1982, 84, 87, 91, 98, Nat. Modern Income Housing award 1970, Nat. Homes for Better Living award 1974, 75, Ill. award 1976, Nat. award of Merit 1970, 74, 75, named to Hall of Fame 1990, Disting. Bldg. award for pvt. residence Chgo. chpt. 1991, Chgo. Interior Archtl. Award of Excellence 1981, 83, 87, 91, 92, Nat. Interior Archtl. Award of Excellence 1992-93, Chgo. Disting. Bldg. award 1971, 73, 75, 77, 79, 81, 82, 84, 85, 86, 91, 94, Italian Ceramic Tile Design award 1995, Fukuoka Urban Beautification award 1995, 6 citations of merit Chgo. chpt. 1994, Interior Design award for A.I.C. Schinkel Exhibit 1996, Chgo. Interior Architecture award 1997, Chgo. Chpt. Arch. award 1998, Nat. Interior Architecture award 1998, Louis Sullivan award 2000); mem. Arts Club of Chgo., Yale Club of N.Y.C., Century Assn. Club, Phi Kappa Phi. Office: Tigerman & McCurry Ltd 444 N Wells St Ste 206 Chicago IL 60610-4522

TIGGES, JOHN THOMAS, writer, musician, lecturer; b. Dubuque, Iowa, May 16, 1932; s. John George and Madonna Josephine (Heiberger) T.; m. Kathryn Elizabeth Johnson, Apr. 22, 1954; children: Juliana, John, Timothy, Teresa, Jay. Student, Loras Coll., 1950-54, 57, U. Dubuque, 1960. Night club entertainer, 1950-52; clk. John Deere Tractor Works, Dubuque, 1957-61; agt. Penn Mut. Life Ins. co., 1961-97; bus. mgr., bd. dirs. Dubuque Symphony Orch., 1960-68, 71-74; v.p., sec. Olson Toy and Hobby, Inc., 1964-66; pres. JKT, Inc., 1978-82; rsch. specialist Electronic Media Svcs. (Scripp-Howard), 1983-85; violinist. Tchr. continuing edn. creative writing N.E. Iowa C.C., 1975-98; tchr. writing U. Wis. Outreach Program's Ednl. Teleconf. Network, summer writing workshop U. Iowa; tchr. Rhinelander Sch. of the Arts, 1997-98; mem. faculty S.W. Writers Workshop, 1998; co-founder Dubuque Symphony Orch., 1960; founder Julien Strings, 1972, Dubuque Sch. of Novel, 1978, N.E. Iowa Writers Workshop, 1981; co-host Big Broadcast Radio Program, WDBQ Radio, 1979-82; founder Sinipee Writers Workshop, 1985, dir. emeritus, 1997; founder Sinipee Critiquing/Editl. Svcs., 1988; faculty Southwest Writers Workshop, 1998. Author: (novels) The Legend of Jean Marie Cardinal, 1976, Garden of the Incubus, 1982, Unto the Altar, 1985, Kiss Not the Child, 1985, Evil Dreams, 1986, The Immortal, 1986, Hands of Lucifer, 1987, As Evil Does, 1987, Pack, 1987, Venom, 1988, Vessel, 1988, Slime, 1988, Book of the Dead, 1989, From Below, 1989, Comes the Wraith, 1990, Breed, 1990, Mountain Massacre, 1990, Blood on the Rails, 1990, One Man Jury, 1991, The Curse, 1993, Monster, 1995, (book of short stories) Nightales, 1990, (plays) No More-No Less, 1982, We Who Are About to Die, 1983, Remember When...?, 1997; contbg. author Murder for Father, 1994, The New Amazons, 1997; author: (radio plays) Valley of Deceit, 1978, Rockville Horror, 1979, The Timid, 1982, All Bets are Down, 1991, 20th Century in Review, 2000, (TV drama) An Evening with George Wallace Jones, 1983, (biographies) George Wallace Jones, 1983, John Plumbe Jr., 1983; prodr.: (TV series) The Loneliest Job, 1989; co-author: (nonfiction) The Milwaukee Road Narrow Gauge: The Bellevue, Cascade & Western, Iowa's Slim Princess, 1985, They Came from Dubuque, 1983, Milwaukee Road Steam Power, 1994, Dubuque in the 19th Century, 2000, Dubuque in the 20th Century, 2000, Dubuque-Then and Now, 2000, The Mississippi River: Father of the Waters, 2000, Nightfeeders, 2002; editl. asst.: Julien's Jour.; contbg. editor: Over 49 News and Views; co-author, editor: A Cup and a Half of Coffee, 1977; ; interviewer, spl. reporter: Editl. Assocs., 1982—84; columnist Memory Lane, What's the Difference, Telegraph Herald, syndicated columnist Tough Trivia Tidbits, Remember When..?, The 20th Century in Review; author: 2500 articles. Founder, bus. mgr. Dubuque Pops Orch., 1957; founder Better Quality Writing Pubs., 1996. Recipient Nat. Quality award, 1966-70, Carnegie-Stout Libr. World of Lit. honors award, 1981; John Tigges Writing contest named in his honor, John T. (and Kathryn E.) Tigges endowment scholarship for Writing Majors named in his honor, Loras Coll., Dubuque. Fellow World Lit. Acad.; mem. Horror Writers Am., Western Writers Am., Iowa Authors, Internat. Platform Assn., Toy Train Collectors Club, Dubuque Rails Model Railroad (co-founder 1987). Roman Catholic. Home: 2240 Coates St Dubuque IA 52003-7108

TIGGES, MICHAEL GERARD, veterinarian, government medical officer; b. Carroll, Iowa, Nov. 15, 1960; s. Leon Alva and Ruth Ann Tigges. DVM, Iowa State U., 1986; MS, Tex. A&M U., 1991. Veterinarian, Canistota, S.D., 1986-87; rsch. assoc. Tex. Agrl. Experiment Sta., College Station, 1987-91; vet. med. officer USDA-FSIS, Sioux City, Iowa, 1993-98, supervisory vet. med. officer Dakota City, Nebr., 1998—2002, SVMO circuit supr. St. Louis, 2002—. Mem. AAAS, Nat. Assn. Fed. Vets., Am. Vet. Med. Assn., Iowa Vet. Med. Assn., Iowa State U. Alumni Assn., Phi Kappa PHi.

TIGHE, THOMAS JAMES GASSON, JR. healthcare executive; b. Malden, Mass., July 11, 1946; s. Thomas J. G. and Barbara (Buckland) T.; m. Carolyn Payne, Mar. 29, 1969; children: Jessica, Chelsea, Alexandra. BA, Bates Coll., 1968; MSc, Columbia U., 1970; MPH, Johns Hopkins U., 1973. Adminstr. asst. Boston U. Med. Ctr. U. Hosp., 1970-71, asst. adminstr., 1971-72; asst. dir. Mary Imogene Bassett Hosp., Cooperstown, N.Y., 1973-80, Cen. Maine Med. Ctr., Lewiston, 1980-86; exec. v.p. Cen. Maine Healthcare Corp., 1986—. Lectr. U. Maine, Augusta, 1987-88, St. Joseph's Coll., Windham, Maine, 1990—; corporator Androscoggin Savs. Bank, Lewiston, 1990—. Bd. dirs. Maine Hosp. Assn., 1990-94, Maine Acting Co., Lewiston, 1986-88, Auburn (Maine) Pub. Libr., 1987-90, LA Arts, Lewiston, 1988-94. Fellow Am. Coll. Healthcare Execs. (bd. govs. 1993—, coun. regents 1986-92); mem. Am. Hosp. Assn., Soc. Healthcare Planning, Mktg., Maine Hosp. Assn.

TIGHE-MOORE, BARBARA JEANNE, electronics executive; b. Wadsworth, Ohio, Jan. 12, 1961; d. Norton Raymond and Laura Alida (Frank) Tighe; m. Derek William Moore, June 26, 1982. Student, Hocking Tech. Coll., 1981, Sinclair Coll., 1986; BBA Honors Coll. magna cum laude, Kent State U., 1988. Lic. amateur radio operator. Tech. writer computer dept. Sinclair Coll., Dayton, Ohio, 1983; project mgr. O'Neil & Assocs., 1983-84; biomed., bio-acoustic real-time flight simulation tempest developer Systems Rsch. Labs., 1984-86; computer specialist Kent State U. Press, 1987-88; mgmt. analyst Electronic Warfare Frontier Engring. Inc., 1988-89; supr. small computer tech. svcs. Frontier Engring., Inc., 1989-90, project engr., 1990-92; ptnr., bd. dirs. MKCC, Dayton, 1990—, SDCC, Dayton, 1992—; regional mgr. User Tech. Assocs., 1993-96; pres., owner Lida Ray Techs., 1978—. Mem. graphics steering com., mem. sanctioned UNIX software adv. team Aero. Sys.

Divsn.; program chair IEEE Internat. Wireless LAN Conf.; mem. Engring. Application Support Environ. Security Working Group, pres., 2000; proceedings chmn. Nat. Aerospace & Electronics Conf., 1995, 96, 97, bd. dirs., pres., 2000; bd. dirs. MKCC, Dayton, 1993—, Cin. Digital Women, SDCC; pres, bd. dirs. NAECON, 2000; spkr. Govt. Land Mobile Commn. Conf., 1993, Internat. Engring. Mgmt. Cons., 1994, Wireless '93, Calgary, Alta., Nat. Aerospace & Electronics Conf., 1995, 96, 97. Author: Job Search Strategies for the 90's, 1993, Through the Glass Ceiling, 1997, Riding the 5:15, 2000; co-author: Women on a Wire, 1996, Women on a Wire, vol. 2, 2001; editor: Graphics Directions, 1990—91; pub.: Team Advisor, SDCC Cleaning Times, IEEE Update; contbr. , ; author: Convergence of Socio-Economic and Technology Factors, 2001. Counselor Kwam's Kinder Kamp; tchr. Bible Sch.; cook Meals on Wheels; organizer/cook funeral Svcs. Dinners. Recipient Vol. Citizen award Wadsworth C. of C, 1979, Ohio Essayist award, 1979, Virginia Perryman award, 1979, Disting. Leadership award, 1990, 91. Mem.: IEEE (former treas., sec. Dayton sect., bd. dirs. 1995—97, chmn. bd. dirs. Dayton sect. 1999, region 2 chpt. coord. 2000—), Equestrian Team (point rider 1977—87), Armed Forces Comms. and Electronics Assn. (judge sci. fair western dist. 1992—), Internat. Film Soc. (pres. 1986—88), Assn. Internat. Students Econs. & Commerce (pres. 1986—87), Def. Planning Analysis Soc. (exec. bd.), Assn. Computer Machinery, Data Processing Mgmt. Assn., Tech. and Soc. of IEEE, Engring. Mgmt. Soc. of IEEE, Computer Soc. of IEEE (sec. 1991—92, vice chmn. 1992—93, chmn. 1994—95), Mortar Bd., Fencing Club, Beta Gamma Sigma, Omicron Delta Kappa, Phi Theta Kappa. Avocations: travel, investing, equestrian show jumping, soccer. Home: 729 Kyle Dr Tipp City OH 45371-1435 Business E-Mail: bjmoore@lidaray.com. E-mail: lidaray@siscom.net.

TIGHT, DEXTER CORWIN, lawyer; b. San Francisco, Sept. 14, 1924; s. Dexter Junkins and Marie (Corwin) T.; m. Elizabeth Callander, Apr. 20, 1951; children: Dexter C. Jr., Kathyrn Marie Loken, Steven M., David C. AB, Denison U., 1948; JD, Yale U., 1951. Bar: Calif. 1951. Assoc. Pillsbury, Madison & Sutro, San Francisco, 1953-60; gen. atty. W.P. Fuller & Co., 1960-61; gen. counsel Schlage Lock Co., 1961-77; dir. govt. affairs Crown Zellerbach Corp., 1977-78; sr. v.p., internat. and gen. counsel The Gap Inc., San Bruno, Calif., 1978-90; cons. in field, 1990-99; gen. coun. The Nature Co., 1990-96. Bd. dirs. Shaw-Clayton Plastics, San Rafael, Calif., Granite Rock Co., Watsonville, Calif., Boys and Girls Club of the Peninsula; mem. World Affairs Coun., Internat. Diplomcay Coun.; chmn. That Man May See, San Francisco, 1997, 98. Trustee Denison U., 1978-99, chmn. capital fund dr., 1988-94; trustee Calvary Presbyn. Ch., 1968, 73, elder, 1969-90; elder Valley Presbyn. Ch., 1992—; vol. Internat. Exec. Svc. Corps. 1st lt. U.S. Army, 1943-45, 51-52. Mem. ABA, Calif. Bar Assn., San Francisco Bar Assn. (chmn. various coms.), Commonwealth Club Calif. (past bd. dirs., exec. com.), Menlo Country Club, Bohemian Club (San Francisco), Guardsman Club (1st v.p. 1961), Phi Beta Kappa. Republican. Presbyterian. Avocations: horseback riding, fishing, tennis, golf, photography. Home: 170 Wildwood Way Redwood City CA 94062-2352

TIGUE, VIRGINIA BETH (GINNY TIGUE), volunteer; b. Owosso, Mich., Sept. 10, 1945; d. Joseph Frederick and Florence Marion Sahlmark; m. Joseph James Tigue Jr., Aug. 12, 1967; children: James Christopher, Molly Elizabeth. BS, cert. in phys. therapy, U. Mich., 1967. Registered phys. therapist, Mich., Calif. Phys. therapist at hosps., rehab. ctrs. and pvt. practice. Co-owner Tigue Property Co.; former co-owner Tex. Toyota of Grapevine. Councilman Pl. 5 City of Colleyville, 1998—, mayor pro tem, 2000—, bond steering com., 1991, master plan revision com., 1997-98, chmn. cmty. ctr. adv. com. 1998; mem. Art Coun. Ft. Worth and Tarrant County Bd., Ft. Worth, 1997—, Tarrant County College Found. Bd., 2001-; founding bd. dirs. Grapevine-Colleyville Ind. Sch. Dist. Edn. Found., 1998—; chmn., bd. dirs. Colleyville C. of C., 1994; founding chmn. Harris Hosp., 1992, 93, mem. women's adv. bd., 1992—, bd., HEB Hosp. trustees, 1999—, bd. Methodist Health Harris Found. 2001-; bd. dirs. Arts Coun. N.E. Tarrant, 1991-98, chmn., 1995-96; bd. dirs. Origins Mus., 1998—, v.p. 2000—; bd. dirs. Vol. Ctr. of Tarrant County, 1998—, chmn. 2000; bd. dirs. Dallas Mus. Art League, 1999—, United Way of Met. Tarrant County, 2000; bd. dirs. N.E Leadership Forum, 1999—; sustaining mem. Dallas Jr. League, 1991—; founding bd. dirs. Tarrant County Coll., 2001—; sr. advisor Nat. Charity League, 1994,; bd. dirs. N.E. Tarrant County divsn. Am. Heart Assn., 1993-94, co-chmn. gala 1997; fund raising chmn. Friends of Colleyville Libr., 1992-94; home tour com. Colleyville Women's Club, 1990, 93, 96, fashion show chmn., 1996; mem. adv. bd. Women's Shelter, 1996—; mem. Women Leader's Summit, Washington, 1995, 96, 98, 99; mem. Women's Policy Forum, 1999—, Women's Found. of Tarrant County, 2000—; chmn.-vol. Ctr. of Tarrant County. Named Most Influential Bus. Woman, The Bus. Press, 1997, Vol. of Yr., City of Colleyville, 1997, Colleyville Citien of Yr., 2001; recipient Legacy of Women award The Women's Shelter, 1995, Herman J. Smith Leadership award Colleyville C. of C., 1994, Proclamation as Outstanding Citizen of Colleyville, 1995. Mem. Colleyville Area C. of C. (bd. dirs. 1990-98, pres.-elect 1993, pres. 1994, vice-chmn. membership devel. 1997, vice-chmn. cmty. devel. 1998, Citizen of Yr. 2001), Tex. Congress Parents and Tchrs. (hon. life mem.). Republican. Methodist. Avocations: golf, traveling, reading, the arts. Home: 4415 Meandering Way Colleyville TX 76034-4513

TIHANYI, LASZLO, finance educator, researcher; b. Tata, Komarom, Hungary, Oct. 17, 1962; s. Mihaly Tihanyi and Iren Koczian; m. Emese Kiraly; children: Orsi, Daniel. BSc, Janus Pannonius U., Pecs, Hungary, 1986; Doctorate, Budapest U. Econ. Scis., 1989; cert. gen. mgmt., Harvard U., 1992; PhD, M of Bus., Ind. U., 1996. Asst. prof. Budapest U. Econ. Scis., 1986—92; vis. scholar Fuqua Sch. Bus. Duke U., Durham, NC, 1989—90; asst. prof. Calif. State U., Fullerton, 1996—99; vis. prof. Kelley Sch. Bus. Ind. U., Bloomington, 1999—2000; asst. prof. M.F. Price Coll. Bus. U. Okla., Norman, 2000—. Contbr. Recipient McKinsey/SMS Best Conf. Paper prize hon. mention, McKinsey & Co. and Strategic Mgmt. Soc., 2001; scholar George F. Baker Found. scholar, Harvard Bus. Sch., 1992, Know How Fund scholar, London Bus. Sch., 1991, George Soros scholar, George Soros Found., 1989. Mem.: Harvard Business School Alumni Association, Ind. U. Alumni Assn., European Group for Orgl. Studies, Strategic Mgmt. Soc., Acad. Internat. Bus., Acad. Mgmt., Beta Gamma Sigma. Office: U Okla 307 W Brooks AH 206 Norman OK 73019-4006 Office Fax: 405-325-1957.

TIJMANN, WILLEM BERT, civil engineer, consultant; b. Semarang, Java, Indonesia, Oct. 19, 1929; came to the U.S., 1956; s. Johan Hendrik and Alida Catharina (Deylius) T.; m. Martha Vanderlaan, Oct. 21, 1958 (div. 1986); children: Sonya Maria, John (dec.); m. Mirna Aeschlimann, Aug. 18, 1991. BS, Poly. Coll., Amsterdam, The Netherlands, 1953, M in Civil Engring., 1955. Registered profl. engr., Europe. Sr. hydraulics engr. Olarte, Ospina Arias y Payan Ltda, Civil Engrs., Bogotá, Colombia, 1955-56; soils and materials engr. Fay Spofford, Boston, 1956-62; sr. project engr. Dames & Moore, San Francisco, 1962-76; v.p. Slope Indicator Co., Seattle, 1976-87; pres. E&T Instrumentation, Stoneham, Mass., 1987—, W.B.T. Cons., Edmonds, Wash., 1987—. Inventor: holds 4 patents in U.S. and Can. Mem. ASCE (hon.), ASTM (sr.), Internat. Soc. Soil Mechanics and Engring. Found., Assn. Engring. Geologists (affiliate). Avocations: certified professional diver, diving, sailing, tennis, hiking. E-mail: tijmann. Home: 101A Pond St Stoneham MA 02180-2804 Office: PO Box 2367 Woburn MA 01888-0667 E-mail: 70@yahoo.com.

TIKARE, SATYANARAYANA K. retired internist; b. Shimoga, Karnataka, India, Apr. 9, 1934; came to U.s., 1974; s. Khanderao M. and Sunderabai Tikare; m. Sneha Bondade, May 10, 1963; children: Veena, Seema. B Medicine B Surgery, Mysore (India) Med. Coll., 1958; MD, M.A. Med. Coll., New Delhi, 1963. Diplomate Am. Bd. Internal Medicine, Am. Bd. Geriatrics. Assoc. prof. medicine Goa Med. Coll., Panjim, India, 1969-74; staff physician VA Med. Ctr., Lake City, Fla., 1975-79, Augusta, Ga., 1979-97; ret., 1997. Pres. Hindu Temple Soc., Augusta, 1988-89, chmn. bd. trustees, 1998-99. Recipient cert. of merit, pub. svc. award Geico, 1987. Fellow ACP, Am. Heart Assn. (stroke coun.). Avocations: gardening, reading, travel. Home: 2418 Woodbluff Ct Augusta GA 30909-2074 E-mail: stikare@comcast.net.

TIKKALA, WILLARD RICHARD, forester; b. Wakefield, Mich., July 25, 1925; s. Herman and Hilja (Frigord) T.; m. JoAnne King, June 25, 1950; children: Richard, Deborah, David, Kathryn, Michael. BS in Forestry, U. Mich., 1949. Cert. secondary sch. tchr., Mich. Jr. h.s. tchr. Washington Jr. H.S., Pontiac, 1950-51; ranger dist. positions forest svc. USDA, Calif., 1951-57, dist. ranger, 1957-60, forester timber mgmt. Milw., 1960-63, branch chief coop. fire dept., 1963-66, dir. coop. fire control Upper Darby, Pa., 1966-70, dir. coop. fire protection Washington, 1970-80; spl. projects forester Am. Forests, 1982—2000. Fellow Soc. Am. Forests. Lutheran. Avocations: gardening, woodworking. Home: 6714 Reynard Dr Springfield VA 22152-2760

TIKOSH, MARK AXENTE, lawyer; b. Arad, Banat, Romania, Aug. 17, 1955; came to U.S., 1981; s. Axente and Elena Ticosh; m. Mary Victoria Rotarescu, Sept. 10, 1979. BBA in Acctg. summa cum laude, Calif. State U., Fullerton, 1989; JD, U. of the Pacific, 1992, LLM, 1993. Bar: Calif. 1993. Acct., auditor II Orange County Probation Dept., 1984-88; pvt. practice Sacramento, 1993-94, Long Beach, 1994—. Cons. U. Banat Acad. Found., Timisoara, Romania, 1997—, mem. CATO Inst. Editor The Transnational Lawyer, 1991. Mem. Cato Inst. Scholarship McGeorge Legal Edn. Endowment Found., 1989-90, Dana Found., 1992-93. Mem. Calif. State Bar Assn. (estate planning trust and probate law sect.), L.A. County Bar Assn. (litigation sect.), Cato Inst., Beta Gamma Sigma. Republican. Avocations: travel, history, philosophy. Office: 800 E Ocean Blvd Ste 100 Long Beach CA 90802-5463

TILAK, AVINASH G. industrial engineer, management consultant; s. Gangadhar S. and Indumati G. Tilak; m. Vasanti A. Pendse, Jan. 4, 1980; children: Gaurie, Hershed. B in Tech., Indian Inst. of Tech., 1972; MS in Indsl. Engring., Tex. Tech U., 1974, PhD, 1977. Registered Profl. Engr., 1988. Asst. prof. N.C. A&T State U., Greensboro, NC, 1977—81; mgr. AT&T, Basking Ridge, NJ, 1981—84; pres. Advanced Tech. Decisions Inc., Denville, 1985—. Bd. adv. City Harvest, N.Y.C., 1984—90; adj. faculty State U. N.J., New Brunswick, NJ, 1986—. Treas. Boy Scouts, Denville, NJ, 1998—. Named to Acad. of Indsl. Engring., Tex. Tech U., 2002. Mem.: Inst. for Ops. Rsch. & Mgmt. Sci. (pres. 1983—84), India Assn. (pres. 1978—79), Sigma Xi, Alpha Pi Mu, Tau Beta Pi. Office: Advanced Technology Decisions Inc 22 N Ridge Road Denville NJ 07834 E-mail: avi@atdinc.com.

TILBE, LINDA MACLAUCHLAN, nursing administrator; b. Bangor, Maine, Mar. 1, 1950; d. John and Ruby Mae (Dorr) MacLauchlan; married; children: William, Robert, Grant. BSN, U. Maine, 1973; M in Healthcare Adminstrn., Quinnipiac Coll., 1988. RN, Conn., Fla. Ob-gyn. staff nurse Yale New Haven Hosp., 1973-79, med. ICU nurse, 1979-83, post anesthesia staff nurse, 1983-88; adminstrv. mgmt. intern Shirley Frank Found., New Haven, 1987-88; clin. nurse adminstr. pain mgmt. Yale U., 1988-92; nurse mgr., arthritis and pain ctrs. North Broward Med. Ctr., 1992-95; dir. Doctors Hosp. Sarasota (Fla.), 1995-99; sr. cmty. health nurse Manatee County Health Dept., Bradenton, Fla., 2000; ICU nurse Jackson Hosp., Marianna, 2000—. Author: A Manual for Acute Postoperative Pain Management, 1992; author and editor: Acute Pain Mechanisms and Management, 1992; contbr. articles to profl. jours. Mem. Internat. Assn. Study of Pain, Am. Pain Soc., Am. Soc. Post Anesthesia Nurses, Am. Soc. Pain Mgmt. Nurses (founder). Home: 5405 Ezell St Apt 102 Graceville FL 32440-1808 E-mail: pjtservant@lycos.com.

TILBERG, ANNA FAE, biology educator, researcher; b. Lewisburg, Pa., Sept. 13, 1944; d. Murray Norman and Blanche Elizabeth Maurer; m. Frederick James Tilberg, Sept. 6, 1969; children: Todd Edward, Wendy Ann, Amy Elizabeth. BA, U. Pa., 1969; MS, Millersville U., 1982. Clin. chemistry technician Hosp. U. Pa., Phila., 1964-69; rsch. asst. Pa. State U., University Park, 1970-71; biology instr. Gettysburg (Pa.) Coll., 1971-76, Pa. Jr. Coll. Med. Arts, Harrisburg, 1976-80; rsch. assoc. Coll. Medicine Pa. State U., Hershey, 1983—. Adj. prof. Harrisburg Area C.C., Lebanon, Pa., 1993—, Lebanon Valley Coll., Annville, 1982—. Contbr. articles to profl. jours. Leader Girl Scouts USA, Palmyra, Pa., 1980s; tchr. Ch. Sch., Palmyra, 1980-90. Mem. U. Pa. Alumni Club (sec. Grtr. Harrisburg chpt. 1994—), Rotary Women's Club (pres. 1989-92). Republican. Lutheran. Avocations: travel, reading, writing, photography. Home: 1319 Mill Pond Way Palmyra PA 17078 Office: Hershey Med Ctr-Surgery 500 University Dr Hershey PA 17033 E-mail: atilberg@psu.edu.

TILCHIN, WILLIAM NEAL, educator; b. Detroit, Nov. 1, 1950; s. Asher N. and Jeannette K. T.; m. Carol T. Giliberto, May 29, 1977; children: Benjamin, Elizabeth. BA, Mich. State U., 1973, MA, 1976; PhD in History, Brown U., 1992. Prof. Boston (Mass.) U., 1994—. Author: Theodore Roosevelt and the British Empire: A Study in Presidential Statecraft, 1997. Office: Boston U Coll Gen Studies 871 Commonwealth Ave Boston MA 02215

TILDEN, RALPH FULTON, retired music educator, organist; b. High Point, N.C., Feb. 10, 1930; s. Thomas Alphonso and Ruth Eugenia (Fulton) T. BMus, Cin. Conservatory Music, 1952, MMus, 1954. Tchr., Fla. Prof. organ Cin. Conservatory Music, 1954-60; tchr. music, theology Cathedral Sch., Orlando, 1960-65; prof. Edison C.C., Ft. Myers, Fla., 1966-95. Organist, choirmaster Calvary Ch., Cin., 1954-60, St. Luke's Cathedral, Orlando, 1960-65, St. Luke's Ch., Ft. Myers, 1965-95; organ recitalist, U.S.A., France, Eng. Composer (choral works) Come, Holy Spirit, Come, 1987, His Voice as the Sound, 1997, Assumpta Est Maria, 2000. Vol., activist ACLU, 1960—, Nat. Gay & Lesbian Task Force, 1960—, Mtn. AIDS Support Coun., Boone, N.C., 1999. Mem. Am. Guild Organists (dean), Assn. Anglican Musicians, Organ Hist. Soc., Liturgy & Music Commn., Diocese of Western N.C. Democrat. Episcopal. Avocations: antique collecting, gardening. Home: 960 Meadow Ave Banner Elk NC 28604-9401

TILDEN, WESLEY RODERICK, writer, retired computer programmer; b. Saint Joseph, Mo., Jan. 19, 1922; s. Harry William and Grace Alida (Kinnaman) T.; m. Lorraine Henrietta Frederick, June 20, 1948 (dec. Mar. 1999). Grad., Navy Supply Corps Sch., 1945; BS, UCLA, 1948; BA, Park Coll., Mo., 1990. Purchasing agent Vortox Co., Claremont, Calif., 1951-61; lang. lab. dir. Mount San Antonio Coll., Walnut, 1962-65; computer programmer, operator General Dynamics, Pomona, 1967-70; ret., 1970. Author: (book) Scota, The Egyptian Princess, 1994, Merit-Sekhet: Foster Mother of Moses?, 1996; photographer, textbooks, mags., newspaper, catalogs. Historian Claremont Sister City Assn., 1963-66. Lt. USNR, 1942-46 PTO. Recipient with Lorraine Tilden People to People award Reader's Digest Found., 1963-64, 1964-65; named Hon. Citizen Guanajuato, Mexico, 1963. Mem. Soc. Mayflower Descendants, Scottish Clans, UCLA Alumni Assn., Park Coll. Alumni Assn., Univ. Club of Claremont, The Scituate (Mass.) Hist. Soc. Republican. Avocations: history, genealogy, photography, gardening. Home: 351 Oakdale Dr Claremont CA 91711-5039

TILFORD, TRICIA J. accountant; B in Bus. Adminstrn. with high honors, U. Notre Dame, 1993. CPA, Ariz. Experienced mgr. Arthur Andersen, N.Y.C., 1993—2002. Leader Girl Scouts, N.Y.C., 1996—, Manhattan assn. chair, 1997—2000, mem. Britenstool scholarship com., 1998—, mem. nat. coun. 48th conv. del., 1999—2002, mem. legis. network, 2000—, World Conf. del., 2002, trainer, 1996—2002, mem. world fin. com., 2002—. Recipient Gold and Silver awards, Girl Scouts, 1989, Outstanding Vol. award, 2001. Mem.: AICPA, Olave Baden-Powell Soc.

TILGER, JUSTINE THARP, research director; b. New Point, Ind., Sept. 11, 1931; d. Joseph Riley and Marcella Lorene (King) Tharp; m. Clarence A. Tilger II, Aug. 22, 1959 (div. Nov. 1972); children: Evelyn Mary, Clarence Arthur III, Joseph Thomas. AB, U. Chgo., 1951; BA, St. Mary's Coll., Notre Dame, Ind., 1954; MA, Ind. U., 1962, PhD, 1971. Mem. Sisters of the Holy Cross, Notre Dame, 1954-58; teaching fellow Ind. U., Bloomington, 1959-61; asst. editor Ind. Mag. History, 1962-64; bookkeeper Touche Ross, Boston, 1974-77; mgr. account services Harvard U., Cambridge, Mass., 1977-81; dir. research and records Bentley Coll., Waltham, 1982-84; dir. support services Sta. WGBH-TV, Boston, 1985; dir. research Tufts U., Medford, Mass., 1986—. Cons. Laduke Assocs., Framingham, Mass., 1972-74, New Eng. Ballet, Sudbury, Mass., 1981-82. V.p. Potter Rd. Sch. Assn., Framingham, 1968-69; chmn. vols. St. Anselm's, Sudbury, 1970-71. Mem. Coun. for Advancement and Support Edn., Assn. Records Mgmt. Adminstrs., Am. Prospect Rsch. Assn., New Eng. Devel. Rsch. Assn., Mass. Bus. and Profl. Women (sec. 1981-82), Mensa. Roman Catholic. Avocations: dramatics, travel. Home: 142 Maynard Rd Apt 303B Framingham MA 01701-2512 Office: Tufts U Dept of Research Packard Hall Medford MA 02155

TILGHMAN, RICHARD GRANVILLE, banker; b. Norfolk, Va., Sept. 18, 1940; s. Henry Granville and Frances (Fulghum) T.; m. Alice Creech, June 28, 1969; children: Elizabeth Arrington, Caroline Harrison BA, U. Va., 1963. Asst. cashier United Va. Bank-Seaboard Nat., Norfolk, Va., 1968-70, asst. v.p., 1970-72, United Va. Mortgage Corp., Norfolk, 1972, v.p., 1972-73, pres., chief exec. officer, 1974-76, United Va. Leasing Corp., Richmond, 1973-74; sr. v.p. bank related United Va. Bankshares, Inc., 1976-78; pres., chief adminstrv. officer United Va. Bank, 1978-80; exec. v.p. corp. banking United Va. Bankshares, Inc., 1980-84, vice chmn., 1984-85; pres., chief exec. officer United Va. Bankshares, Inc., now Crestar Fin. Corp., 1985-99; chmn. SunTrust Bank-Mid-Atlantic (formerly Crestar Fin. Corp.), 1986-2000. Bd. dirs. Chesapeake Corp., Richmond, 1986—; chmn. Va. Pub. Bldg. Authority, Richmond, 1982-87; prin. Va. Bus. Coun., 1987-2000; mem. Fed. Adv. Coun., 1994-97, pres. 1996-97. Chmn. bd. dirs. Richmond Symphony, 1984-85; bd. dirs., mem. gen. adv. coun. Sheltering Arms Hosp., Richmond, 1981-89; bd. dirs. Va. Free, 1989-90, Richmond Symphony Found., 1989-91, Va. Found. Ind. Colls., 1988—, bd. trustees, Norfolk Acad., 2001—, bd. dirs., Richmond Cmty. Found., 2002—,Va. Literacy Found., 1986-89; bd. govs. St. Catherine's Sch., 1989-95; bd. dirs. Va. Mus. Found., 1986-92, trustee, 1994—; trustee Randolph Macon Coll., 1985-93, Richmond Renaissance, 1986-99, Colonial Williamsburg Found., 1994—, founding trustee VCU Sch. Engring. Found., 1995—; co-chmn. NCCJ. 1st lt. U.S. Army, 1963-66. Mem. Bankers Rountable (dir. 1996-99), Am. Bankers Assn., Va. Bankers Assn. (bd. dirs. 1991-98, pres. 1996-97). Clubs: Commonwealth, Country of Va. Episcopalian. Office: SunTrust Bank Mid-Atlantic PO Box 26665 919 E Main St Richmond VA 23261-6665

TILGHMAN, SHIRLEY MARIE, academic administrator, biology educator; PhD in biochemistry, Temple U., 1975. Prof. molecular biology Princeton (N.J.) U., 1986—, Howard A. Prior prof. in life scis., pres., 2001—. Investigator Howard Hughes Med. Inst. Co-editor: Gene Expression & Its Control, 1991, Genes & Phenotypes, 1991, Genetic & Physical Mapping, 1991, Genome Maps & Neurological Disorders, 1993, Genome Rearrangement & Stability, 1993, Regional Physical Mapping, 1993. Office: Princeton U One Nassau Hall Princeton NJ 08544-0001*

TILININ, IGOR STANISLAVOVICH, physicist, educator; b. Vladivistock, Russia, Dec. 2, 1952; came to U.S., 1996; s. Stanislav Vladislavovich and Elena Andreevna Tilinin; m. Nadezhda Nikolaevna Yaroshuk, Aug. 7, 1980. MSc with distinction, Moscow Inst. Physics/Engring., 1976, PhD, 1981, DSc, 1994. Engr. Moscow Inst. for Physics and Engring., 1976-78, 81-83, asst. prof., 1983-90; rsch. fellow Inst. Phys. Chemistry, Polish Acad. Scis., Warsaw, 1994-96, docent, 1996; vis. scientist Lawrence Berkeley Nat. Lab., Berkeley, Calif., 1996-98; software engr. D.W. Smith & Assocs., San Mateo, 1998-2000; cons. DHL Sys., Inc., Burlingame, 2000—. Vis. scientist Odense (Denmark) U., 1994, 95; guest prof. Charles U., Prague, Czech Republic, 1995; guest prof., vis. scientist U. Tech., Vienna, 1992-93. Author: Qualitative Problems on Atomic Physics with Solutions, 1990; co-author: Surface Analysis by Particle Backscattering, 1985. Recipient 2nd prize for best sci. paper Inst. Phys. Chemistry, Warsaw, 1995, 2nd prize for best rsch. work Moscow Inst. for Physics and Engring., 1982, 1st prize for best sci. paper Inst. Phy. Chemistry, Warsaw, 1997. Mem. AAAS, European Microbeam Analysis Soc., N.Y. Acad. Scis., Am. Phys. Soc. Christian. Home: 3135 Campus Dr Apt 320 San Mateo CA 94403-3138 Office: DHL Sys Ste 300 700 Airport Blvd Burlingame CA 94010 E-mail: itilinin@systems.dhl.com.

TILKIAN, ARA GARABED, cardiologist; b. Syria, Dec. 7, 1944; came to U.S., 1968; s. Garabed G. and Nevart N. T.; m. Elizabeth Zereyohanes. BS, Am. U. Beirut, Lebanon, 1966; MD, U. Ill., 1970. Co-dir. dept. cardiology Holy Cross Med. Ctr., Mission Hills, Calif., 1975-88; dir. dept. cardiology Providence Holy Cross Med. Ctr., 1989—; asst. clin. prof. medicine-cardiology UCLA Med. Ctr., 1975—. Cons., reviewer CHEST-Cardio pulmonary jour., Archives Internal Medicine, Chgo., 1980—, Annals Internal Medicine, Phila., 1980—. Contbr. articles to cardiology books. Fellow Am. Coll. Cardiology, Soc. Cardiac Angiography; mem. Am. Heart Assn., Am. Soc. Echocardiography, Alpha Omega Alpha. Avocations: writing, travel, reading, sports. Office: Cardiovascula Cons 15243 Vanowen St Ste 301 Van Nuys CA 91405-3646 E-mail: atilkian@aol.com.

TILL, BEATRIZ MARIA, international business consultant, translator; b. Havana, Cuba, Sept. 27, 1952; came to U.S., 1961; d. Thomas Emanuel and Gladys Manuela (Loret de Mola) Alexander; m. John Edwin Till, Oct. 30, 1976. Student, U. Fla., 1970-71, 72-74, U. Ariz., 1988. Translating sales sec. Rozier Machinery, Tampa, Fla., 1976-78; paralegal, interpreter-translator, 1979-83; pres. Beatriz M. Till Translations, 1983—. Interpreter-translator Office of Worker's Compensation, State of Fla., Tampa, pvt. attys., 1979—; spl. advisor to Sec. of Commerce, State of Fla.; surveillance audio/video transcription specialist Fed. Ct. State of Fla. (middle dist.); interpreter for Pres. Ronald Reagan, 1983; also, expert witness on tape recording transcriptions and translations. Active World Trade Ctr.; adv. bd. mem. Neighborhood Justice Ctr. Mem. Internat. Platform Assn., Nat. Assn. Judiciary Interpreters and Translators, Fla. C. of C., Riverview C. of C., Tampa Bay Internat. Trade Coun.,Fla. Coun. Internat. Devel. Republican. Avocations: reading, photography, cooking, gardening. Home: 12301 Pathway Ct Riverview FL 33569-4122 Office: Beatriz M Till Translations 12301 Pathway Ct Riverview FL 33569-4122 E-mail: bmtilltran@aol.com.

TILL, JAMES EDGAR, medical educator, researcher; b. Lloydminster, Sask., Can., Aug. 25, 1931; s. William and Gertrude Ruth (Isaac) T.; m. Marion Joyce Sinclair, June 6, 1959; children: David William, Karen Sinclair, Susan Elizabeth. BA, U. Sask., 1952, MA, 1954; PhD, Yale U., 1957. Mem. physics divsn. Ont. Cancer Inst., Toronto, 1957-67, with divsn. biol. rsch., 1967-89, divsn. head, 1969-82, with divsn. epidemiology and stats., 1989—; assoc. dean U. Toronto, 1981-84, univ. prof., 1984-97, univ. prof. emeritus, 1997—. Contbr. articles on biophysics, cell biology and cancer control research to sci. jours. Recipient Gairdner Found. Internat. award, 1969, Order of Can., 1994. Fellow Royal Soc. Can., Royal Soc. London. Home: 182 Briar Hill Ave Toronto ON Canada M4R 1H9 Office: 610 University Ave Toronto ON Canada M5G 2M9 E-mail: till@uhnres.utoronto.ca. *Albert Einstein said: "The most beautiful thing we can experience is the mysterious. It is the source of all true art and science." He also believed that concern for humanity must always form the chief interest of all technical endeavors— "in order that the creations of our mind shall be a blessing and not a curse to mankind." Is there a more eloquent summary of standards for the scientist than this?.*

TILL, ROBERT E. psychology educator; b. Washington, Dec. 9, 1947; BA, U. San Francisco, 1969; PhD, U. Minn., 1974. Instr. Davidson (N.C.) Coll., 1974-76; asst. prof. So. Meth. U., Dallas, 1976-80; assoc. prof., chair U. N.D., Grand Forks, 1981-87, prof., 1987-2000; prof., chair No. Ariz. U., Flagstaff, 2000—. Author: (book) Adulthood and Aging, 3d editl., 1998; author, editor: (book chpt.) Comparing Short-Term Recall of Item, Temporal, and Spatial Information in Children and Adults, 1991; contbr. articles to profl. jours. Predoctoral fellow Ctr. for Rsch. in Human Learning, U. Minn., 1971-73. Mem. APA, Psychonomic Soc., Soc. for Text and Discourse, Rocky Mountain Psychol. Assn. Avocations: hiking, skiing, travel, family history. Office: No Ariz U PO Box 15106 Flagstaff AZ 86011-5106 Office Fax: 520 523 6777. E-mail: robert.till@nau.edu.

TILLAR, THOMAS CATO, JR. university alumni relations administrator, consultant; b. Radford, Va., Sept. 9, 1947; s. Thomas Cato Sr. and Ruth (Wiemer) T. BS in Biology, Va. Poly. Inst., 1970, MA in Edn., 1973, EdD, 1978. Cert. fund raising executive. Program director Va. Poly. Inst., Blacksburg, 1970-73, coord. student programs, 1973-74, grad. teaching asst., 1974-75, dir. alumni svcs., 1975-78, dir. corp. foundn. prog., 1978-80, dir. ann. giving, 1980-90, dir. alumni rels., 1990-95, v.p. alumni rels., 1996—. Cons. Colo. State U., Fort Collins, 1982, Va. Mil. Inst., Lexington, 1983, Datatel Minicomputer Co., Alexandria Va., 1985-86. Editor: (book) A Pictorial History of Virginia Tech, 1984. Bd. dirs. Montgomery Reg. Hosp., 1998—, Blacksburg Shelter Home; pres. Smithfield Preston Found., 1999—. Mem. Nat. Soc. Fund Raising Execs., Nat. Edn. Alumni Trust (bd. dirs.), Coun. Advancement and Support of Edn., Alumni Assn. Execs. (mem. coun.), Rotary (pres. 1990-91), Pi Kappa Alpha (pres., trustee edn. found., Memphis, 1991-93). Presbyterian (elder). Avocations: running, golf, traveling. Home: 3010 Stradford Ln Blacksburg VA 24060-8176

TILLER, DOYLE, state agency administrator; s. Beauford and Lilla Mae Tiller. BS in Mining Engring. Tech., W.Va. Inst. of Tech., 1986. Cert. indoor air quality profl. Indoor air quality program mgr. State of Del., Dover, 1995—, indsl. hygienist/environ. health specialist. Project engr. II BCM Engineers,

Washington, 1986—92. Vol. Dept. of Fish and Wildlife, Smyrna, Del., 1989—92. Mem.: ASHRAE, Bldg. Officials Code Assn., Assn. of Energy Engineers, Am. Indsl. Hygiene Assn. Office: State of Delaware 149 Transportation Cir Dover DE 19901 Office Fax: 302-739-3037. E-mail: dtiller@state.de.us.

TILLER, J(OHN) HOWELL, physician; b. Milton, Fla., Oct. 12, 1953; m. Ruth Josephine (Allan) T. BS, U. West Fla., 1975; MS, U. Louisville, 1977, MD, 1980. Diplomate Am. Bd. Plastic Surgery. Staff, plastic surgeon USN, Nat. Naval Med. Ctr., Bethesda, 1985-88; gen. surgery resident Greenville (S.C.) Hosp. System, 1980-93; plastic surgery resident U. Louisville, 1983-85; pvt. practice Watergate Cosmetic Surgery, Washington, 1988-95, South Beach Cosmetic Surgery, Miami Beach, Fla., 1995—. Comdr. USN, 1985-88. Mem. Am. Soc. Aesthetic Plastic Surgery, So. Med. Assn., The Lipoplasty Soc., Beach Rep. Club. Methodist. Office: South Beach Laser and Cosmetic Surgery 1674 Meridian Ave Ste 402 Miami Beach FL 33139-2800

TILLER, LAUREL LEE, lawyer; b. Morton, Wash., Jan. 11, 1938; s. Edgar L. and Edna (Ball) T.; m. Priscilla Sue Prouty, Dec. 22, 1962; children: Peter B., Rachael M. BA, Willamette U., 1960; JD, U. Wash., 1963. Bar: Wash. 1963, U.S. Dist. Ct. (we. dist.) Wash. 1965, U.S. Dist. Ct. (ea. dist.) 1986, U.S. Ct. Appeals (9th cir.) 1982. Asst. atty. gen. State of Wash., Olympia, 1963-65; pvt. practice Tiller, Wheeler & Tiller, Centralia, Wash., 1965—. Mcpl. ct. judge City of Centralia, 1968-78. Mem. Wash. Bar Assn. (numerous coms. 1965—). Home: PO Box 58 Centralia WA 98531-0058 Office: Tiller Wheeler & Tiller Corner Of N Rock E Pine Centralia WA 98531

TILLER, OLIVE MARIE, retired church worker; b. St. Paul, Dec. 13, 1920; d. Otto William and Myrtle Alice (Brougham) Foerster; m. Carl William Tiller, June 21, 1940; children: Robert W., Jeanne L. Peterson; m. Edward J. Alo, Dec. 15, 2001. BS, U. Minn., 1940. Spl. edn. tchr., Prince Georges County, Md., 1955-63; spl. asst. for profl. svcs. Kendall Demonstration Elem. Sch., Gallaudet Coll., Washington, 1971-78; spl. asst. for program Ch. Women United, N.Y.C., 1979-80; exec. asst. to gen. sec. Nat. Coun. Chs. of Christ in U.S.A., 1981-87; dep. gen. sec. for coop. Christianity Am. Bapt. Chs. of U.S.A., Valley Forge, Pa., 1987-88. Author: (with Carl W. Tiller) At Calvary, 1994. Mem. Human Rels. Commn., Prince George's County, 1967-73; v.p. Am. Bapt. Chs. U.S.A., Valley Forge, 1976-77; bd. dirs. Am. Leprosy Missions, Greenville, S.C., 1981-95, Bapt. Peace Fellowship of N.Am., Charlotte, N.C., 1984-95; mem. Nat. Interreligious Svc. Bd. for Conscientious Objectors, 1991-98, treas., 1994-98, sec., 1997-98; mem. nat. coun. Fellowship of Reconciliation, 1985-88, 96-97, Study Commn. on Human Rights, Baptist World Alliance, 1995-2000, Study Commn. on Freedom and Justice, 2000—, World Aid Com., 2000—. Recipient Dahlberg Peace award Am. Bapt. Chs., 1991, Valiant Woman award Ch. Women United, 1978, Meeker award Ottawa U., 1995, Luke Mowbray Ecumenical award, Am. Bapt. Chs., 1999. Baptist. Home: 283 Norman Dr Cranberry Township PA 16066-4235 E-mail: olivet@nauticom.net.

TILLERY, BILLY CAREY, writer, poet; b. Electric Mills, Miss., Nov. 12, 1927; s. Herbert Carey and Marie (Madison) T.; m. Helen Marie Scheibert, Dec. 27, 1948; children: Bruce Carey, Martha Karen Tillery Jacobs. AA in English, U. Louisville, 1952, BS in Econs., 1954. Radio/TV announcer, dir., prodr., writer various orgns., various locations, 1947-50, 56-59, assn. exec., 1951-55, mgmt. cons., 1960-64; creator, editor, pub. audiotaped med. jour. Med. Monitor, Edina, Minn., 1968-70; mng. editor Modern Medicine, N.Y. Times Co., 1970-77; mgr. sci. publs. Vicks Rsch. Ctr., Richardson-Vicks, Proctor & Gamble Inc., Shelton, Conn., 1977-82; med. editor-in-chief Cordis Rsch. Corp., Miami, Fla., 1982-90; freelance writer Eagan, Minn., 1990-93; freelance writer, cmty. activist Citrus Springs, Fla., 1993—. Cons. in field. Contbr. poetry and stories to lit. publs.; contbr. over 600 articles to profl. jours. and conf. procs. With USN, 1945-47. Named Ky. Col., Gov. of Ky., 1978, Col., Confederate Air Corps, 1959. Mem. Internat. Poetry Hall of Fame, Masons. Republican. Avocations: music, woodworking, creative writing. Home and Office: 10163 N Pearl Way Citrus Springs FL 34434-3062

TILLETT, M. PATRICK C. urban designer; b. U.K., Apr. 27, 1943; came to U.S., 1982; s. John Edwin and Margaret Cameron Tillett; m. Bryony Elizabeth Gray, June 11, 1983; children: Marcus Robert Gray, Chloë Julia Gray. Diploma in arch., Oxford (Eng.) Sch. Arch., 1969; M of Civic Design, Liverpool (Eng.) U., 1972. Registered arch. Archt. Registration Bd. U.K., NCARB, State of Oreg. Arch., planner Wilson & Womersley, London, 1973-74, Greater London Coun., 1974-80; pvt. cons. London, Germany, Nigeria, 1980-82; dir. planning and urban design Zimmer Gunsul Frasca Partnership, Portland, Oreg., 1982—. Chair Willamette Light Brigade, Portland, 1987—. Fellow AIA, Am. Inst. Cert. Planners (cert. planner), Royal Town Planning Inst. (registered town planner), Inst. for Urban Design; mem. Royal Inst. Brit. Archs. (registered arch.), City Club of Portland (pres. 2001—). Avocations: ocean racing, fly fishing, skiing. Office: Zimmer Gunsul Frasca Partnership 320 SW Oak St Ste 500 Portland OR 97204-2737 E-mail: ptillett@zgf.com.

TILLEY, BARBARA, statistician, consultant; BA in Math., Calif. State U., 1972; MS in Biomathematics, U. of Wash., 1975; PhD in Biometry, U. of Tex., 1981. Biostatistician, coord. Mayo Clinic and Mayo Found., Rochester, Minn., 1974—77; faculty assoc. U. of Tex. Sch. of Pub. Health, Houston, 1978—80; sect. head M.D. Anderson Hosp. & Tumor Inst., 1980—82; adj. asst. prof. U. of Mich., Ann Arbor, Mich., 1983—87; divsn. head Henry Ford Health Sci. Ctr., Detroit, 1983—97; adj. assoc. prof. U. of Mich., 1988—97; dir. Ctr. for Med. Treatment Effectiveness Programs in Diverse Populations and Resource Ctr. on African Am. Aging Rsch., Detroit, 1994—98; full prof. with tenure Case Western Res. U., Cleveland, Ohio, 1998—99; dept. chair Henry Ford Health Sci. Ctr., Detroit, 1997—99; prof, chmn. Med. U. of S.C., Charleston, SC, 1998—. Grantee Nat. Ctr. for Health Svc. R & D Traineeship, U. of Wash. Mem.: APHA (Profl. Merit award Statistics Sect. 1993), Soc. for Clin. Trials, Caucus for Women in Stats. (pres. 1993—94), Biometric Soc., Am. Statis. Assn., Assn. for Women in Sci. Office: Medical University of South Carolina 135 Cannon Street Suite 303 Charleston SC 29425 Office Fax: 843-876-1127. E-mail: tilleybc@musc.edu.

TILLEY, CAROLYN BITTNER, technical information specialist; b. Washington, July 29, 1947; d. Klaud Kay and Margaret Louise (Hanson) Bittner; m. Frederick Edwin Dudley, June 18, 1985 BS, Am. U., 1975; M.L.S., U. Md., 1976. With NIH, 1965-71; statis. research asst. Health Manpower Edn., Bethesda, Md., 1971-72; tech. info. specialist Nat. Libr. Medicine, 1972-81, head medlars (med. lit. analysis and retrieval system) mgmt. sect., 1981—. Mem. editorial bd.: Med. Reference Services Quar. Mem. Nat. Fed. Abstracting and Info. Svc. Editl. Com. Recipient Merit award NIH, 1984, Rogers award Nat. Libr. Medicine, 1991. Mem. Med. Libr. Assn. Presbyterian. Avocation: horseback riding. Office: Nat Libr Medicine 8600 Rockville Pike Bethesda MD 20894-0002

TILLEY, DAVID RONALD, retired science educator; b. Fuquay Springs, N.C., Mar. 10, 1930; s. Bennehan Cameron and Willa Ferrell Tilley; m. Anne Mae Wooten; children: David. BS in Physics, U. N.C., 1952; MS in Physics, Vanderbilt U., 1953; PhD in Physics, Johns Hopkins U., 1958. Jr. instr. physics Johns Hopkins U., Balt., 1953—58; rsch. assoc. nuc. physics Duke U., Durham. NC, 1958—61, asst. prof. physics, 1961—66; assoc. prof. physics N.C. State U., Raleigh, 1966—72, prof. physics, 1972—98, emeritus prof. physics, 1998—; mem. rsch. faculty Triangle Univs. Nuc. Lab., Durham, 1966—. Undergrad. coord. dept. physics N.C. State U., 1990—97; evaluator, compiler nuc. data U.S. Nuc. Data Network and Triangle Univs. Nuc. Lab., Durham, 1990—. Contbr. articles to profl. jours. Mem.: AAAS, Am. Phys. Soc., Phi Eta Sigma, Phi Beta Kappa, Sigma Xi. Democrat. Baptist. Avocations: sailing, American history. Personal E-mail: ron_tilley@ncsu.edu. Business E-Mail: ron_tilley@ncsu.edu.

TILLEY, SHERMAINE ANN, investment company executive; b. Shawnee, Okla., Feb. 22, 1952; d. Cecil Fern and Zona Emma (Evans) T. BA in Chemistry summa cum laude, Okla. City U., 1973; PhD in Biochemistry, The Johns Hopkins U., 1980; MBA in Investment Banking/Corp. Fin., U. Toronto, 2000. Rsch. assoc. Albert Einstein Coll. Medicine, Bronx, 1980-85; rsch. asst. prof. NYU Sch. Medicine, N.Y.C., 1985-94, rsch. assoc. prof., 1994-2000; asst. mem. Pub. Health Rsch. Inst., 1985-93, assoc. mem., 1994-2000. Ad hoc reviewer SBIR grants NIH, 1989-98; sec., staff coun. adv. com. Pub. Health Rsch. Inst., N.Y.C., 1990-95; pres's. appointee bd. dirs. Pub. Health Rsch. Inst., 1993-95, Drug Royalty Corp., Toronto, 2000—. Contbr. articles to profl. jours.; patentee in field. Recipient Letzeiser medal, Okla. City U., 1973; Nat. Arthritis Found. fellow, 1982-85; Life and Health Ins. Med. Rsch. Fund grantee, 1986-89; NIH grantee, 1988-99; Canadian credit mgmt. found. fellow, 1998-99. Mem. AAAS, Am. Assn. Immunologists, Am. Soc. Microbiology, Licensing Exec. Soc., Assn. U. Tech. Transfer Mgrs., Canadian Healthcare Licensing Assn., Toronto Biotech. Initiative. Achievements include demonstration of synergistic neutralization of HIV-1 by human monoclonal antibodies against the V3 loop and CD4 binding site of gpl20; completion of a $US 4.4 M deal for a royalty interest in Remicade, a major new drug for arthritis and Crohn's disease, as part of a five-member management team. Office: Drug Royalty Corp 8 King St E Ste 202 Toronto ON Canada M5C 1B5

TILLEY, TANA MARIE, pharamaceutical executive, registered nurse; b. Athens, Ga., Dec. 28, 1955; d. Harry Sanford Pierce and Shirley Joanne Webster; m. Scott David Tilley, Aug. 28, 1977; children: Christopher Scott, Lauren Brooke. AD in Nursing, U. S.C., 1980, BS in Nursing cum laude, 1990. Asst. mgr. Brook's Fashions, 1975-78; staff nurse labor and delivery Spartanburg Regional Hosp., 1980-84, head nurse labor and delivery, 1984-89, staff nurse emergency rm., 1989-90; pharm. sales rep. L'Nard & Assocs., 1989-90, TAP Pharm., 1990-92, regional hosp. liaison, 1992-95, dist. mgr., hosp. acct. execs., 1995-96, dist. mgr., 1996, 1997-2000, regional sales mgr., 2000—. Methodist. Home: 11342 Colonial Country Ln Charlotte NC 28277 Office: TAP Pharmaceuticals 1050 Crown Point Ste 1445 Atlanta GA 30338 E-mail: tanatilley@tap.com.

TILLINGHAST, CHARLES CARPENTER, III, marketing company executive; b. N.Y.C., Nov. 16, 1936; s. Charles C. Carpenter, Jr. and Lisette (Micoleau) T.; m. Cynthia Branch, Sept. 28, 1974; children by previous marriage: Avery D., Charles W., David C. BS in Mech. Engring, Lehigh U., 1958; MBA, Harvard U., 1963. Asst. to dir. devel. Lehigh U., Bethlehem, Pa., 1958-61; adminstrv. asst. Boise Cascade Corp., Portland, Oreg., 1963, asst. to v.p. Boise, Idaho, 1964-65, gen. mgr. office supply div., 1965-67, gen. mgr. paper distbn. div., 1966, v.p. bus. products, 1967-69, sr. v.p. housing group, 1969-71, sr. v.p., 1971-73; pres. CRM div. Ziff-Davis Pub. Co., Inc., Del Mar, Calif., 1971-75; pres., treas. Value Communications, Inc., La Jolla, 1975-76; pres. Oak Tree Publs., Inc., San Diego, 1976-81, Advanced Mktg. Services Inc., San Diego, 1982-94, chmn., 1994—. Served to 2d lt. AUS, 1959. Home: 1762 Nautilus St La Jolla CA 92037-6413 Office: Advanced Mktg Svcs Inc 5880 Oberlin Dr Ste 400 San Diego CA 92121-4794

TILLINGHAST, DAVID ROLLHAUS, lawyer; b. N.Y.C., Feb. 25, 1930; s. Charles Carpenter and Josephine Dorothy (Rollhaus) T.; m. Phyllis Van Horn, Sept. 24, 1955 (div. Jan. 1984); m. Lisa Sewell, Feb. 25, 1984; children: Gregory Barrett Sewell, Lauren Alexa. AB cum laude, Brown U., 1951; LLB cum laude, Yale U., 1954. Bar: N.Y. 1955, Oreg. 1956, U.S. Supreme Ct. 1978. Assoc. Hughes, Hubbard & Reed, N.Y.C., 1954-55, 57-61, ptnr., 1961-62, 65-90; assoc. King, Miller, Anderson, Nash & Yerke, Portland, Oreg., 1955-57; spl. asst. for internat. tax affairs U.S. Dept. Treasury, Washington, 1962-65; ptnr. Chadbourne & Parke, N.Y.C., 1990-99, Baker & McKenzie, N.Y.C., 1999—. Adj. prof. Sch. Law, NYU, 1977-87; cons. UN Ctr. on Transnat. Corps., 1978-87; reporter Am. Law Inst. Project on Internat. Aspects of U.S. Income Taxation, 1982-91; cons. to reporters Am. Law Inst. Revision of Restatement of Fgn. Relations Law of U.S., 1982-83. Author: Tax Aspects of Internat. Transactions, 1978, 2d edit., 1984; contbr. articles to profl. publs. Mem. transition team Sec. of Treasury W. Michael Blumenthal, 1977. Estab. David L. Tillinghast lectr. on internat. taxation NYU Sch. Law. Mem.: Coun. Fgn. Rels., Tax Forum, Internat. Bar Assn. (vice chmn. com. on taxation bus. law sect. 1984—86), Internat. Fiscal Assn. (v.p. U.S. br. 1983—2000, permanent sci. com. 1983—2000, vice chmn. 1993—95, chmn. 1995—2000), Assn. of Bar of City of N.Y. (chmn. com. on taxation 1981—83). Democrat. Avocations: golf; tennis. Office: Baker & McKenzie 805 3rd Ave New York NY 10022-7513 E-mail: david.r.tillinghast@bakernet.com.

TILLINGHAST, JOHN AVERY, utilities executive; b. N.Y.C., Apr. 30, 1927; s. Charles C. and Dorothy J. (Rollhaus) T.; m. Mabel Healy, Sept. 11, 1948; children: Katherine Brickley, Susan Trainor, Abigail Ryan. BSME, Columbia U., 1948, MS, 1949. Registered profl. engr., Ky., Ind., Mich., N.Y., Ohio, Va., W.Va., N.H. With Am. Elec. Power Service Corp., N.Y.C., 1949-79, exec. v.p. engring. and constrn., 1967-72, sr. exec. v.p., vice chmn. engring. and constrn., 1972-79; sr. v.p. tech. Wheelabrator-Frye Inc., Hampton, N.H., 1979-83, Signal Advanced Tech. Group, The Signal Cos., Hampton, 1983-85; sr. v.p. Allied-Signal Internat., 1985-86, Sci. Applications Internat. Corp., San Diego, 1986-88; pres. TILTEC, Portsmouth, N.H, 1987-94; CEO, Great Bay Power Corp., Dover, 1994-97; CEO BayCorp Holdings, Ltd., 1997-98, chmn. bd. Portsmouth, 1998—. Patentee generating unit control system. Elder Reformed Ch., 1976-79. Served with USN, 1944-46. Fellow ASME; mem. IEEE, NAE, Sigma Xi, Tau Beta Pi. Office: Great Bay Power Corp 20 International Dr Portsmouth NH 03801-6809

TILLINGHAST, JON DALTON, public health physician; b. Oklahoma City, Sept. 4, 1940; s. Henry Virgil and Elizabeth (Walker) T.; m. Alice Marie Gaidaroff, Aug. 16, 1963; children: Timothy Dale, Daniel Todd, Tamara Ruth. BS, Okla. Bapt. U., 1962; MD, U. Okla., 1965, MPH, 1977. Diplomate Am. Bd. Preventive Medicine and Pub. Health. Missionary physician Fgn. Mission Bd., SBC, Yemen Arab Rep., 1972-79; occupl. medicine physician Tinker AFB, Midwest City, Okla., 1979-80; acute care physician AM-PM clinic, Oklahoma City, 1980; pvt. practice, 1980-84; med. dir. Okla. Dept. Corrections, 1985-89; med. dir., CEO City-County Health Dept. Okla. County, 1989-93; tuberculosis control officer Okla. State Dept. Health, 1993—. Capt. USAF, 1966-68. Recipient Outstanding Contbn. Pub. Health award Okla. Pub. Health Assn., 1994. Baptist. Office: Oklahoma State Dept Health 1000 NE 10th St Oklahoma City OK 73117-1207 Fax: 405-271-6680. E-mail: JonT@health.state.ok.us.

TILLMAN, BARBARA ANN, education educator, consultant; b. Waterbury, Conn., Oct. 20, 1945; d. Jehue and Carrie Lee Tillman. BSBA, Loyola, Paris, 1978; MA in Behavior Sci., Calif. State U., Dominguez Hills, 1994. Program mgr. Barclay Career Schs., New Port Beach, Calif., 1984-90, dir. edn. L.A., Cypress, 1984-90; vocat. rehab. counselor Am. Interant. Health and Rehab., L.A., 1990-92, Cascade Rehab. Co., Inc., L.A., 1992-94, Career Transition Ctr., Long Beach, Calif., 1994-96; instr. Nat. U., Costa Mesa, 1996—; ednl. cons. Fred Jefferson Foster Agy., Compton, 1996—. Cons. County L.A. Mem. Nat. Rehab. Assn., Internat. Assn. Personnel Employment Security, So. Calif. Mediation Soc. Democrat. Roman Catholic. Avocations: story telling, cooking. Office: Nat U 3390 Harbor Blvd Costa Mesa CA 92626-1502 Fax: 714-773-4644.

TILLMAN, JOSEPH NATHANIEL, engineering executive; b. Augusta, Ga., Aug. 1, 1926; s. Leroy and Canarie (Kelly) T.; m. Alice Lavonia Walton, Sept. 5, 1950 (dec. 1983); children: Alice Lavonia, Robert Bertram; m. Areerat Usahaviriyakit, Nov. 24, 1986. BA magna cum laude, Paine Coll., 1948; MS, Northrop U., 1975, MBA, 1976; DBA, Nova U., 1989. Dir. Rockwell Internat., Anaheim, Calif., 1958-84; pres. Tillman Enterprises, Corona, 1985—. Guest lectr. UCLA, 1980-85. Contbr. articles to profl. jours. Capt. USAF, 1948-57, Korea. Recipient Presdl. Citation Nat. Assn. for Equal Opportunity in Higher Edn., 1986. Mem. Acad. Mgmt. (chmn. 1985-86), Soc. Logistics Engrs. (pres. 1985-86), Paine Coll. Alumni Assn. (v.p. 1976—), NAACP (pres. 1984-88). Avocations: duplicate bridge, travel, swimming, skiing, hiking. Office: Tillman Enterprises 1550 S Rimpau Ave Spc 45 Corona CA 92881-3206 E-mail: areetman@yahoo.com.

TILLMAN, JUNE TORRISON, musician; b. Mpls., June 11, 1917; d. Odvin Olai and Anne Johanne (Andersen) Torrison; m. Jean Paul Tillman, July 19, 1941; 1 child, Paula Jeanne Tillman Morrow. BA, Macalester Coll., 1940; postgrad., MacPhail Coll Music, 1952-55, U. Minn., 1944-45; student, Dr. Hoch's Konservatorium, Frankfurt am Main, 1956-57. Cert. piano tchr., Fla., Mo. Clk. auditing dept. The Dayton Co., Mpls., summer 1935; tchr., libr. Howard Lake H.S., Minn., 1941; prin. clk. Army Office Chief of Fin., Washington, 1942-43; gold acct. Gen. Refineries, Inc., Mpls., 1944-45; asst. acct. First Acceptance Corp., 1946-47, 51; property acct. clk. Army Quartermaster Commissary, Camp Wolters, Tex., 1959-61; music tchr. various orgns., 1953—. Nat. com. chmn. Music Tchrs. Nat. Assn., Ind. Music Tchrs. Forum Studio Policies, 1975-77; state conv. chmn. Fla. State Music Tchrs., Ft. Lauderdale, 1978; auditions ctr. chmn. Nat. Guild Piano Tchrs., Ft. Lauderdale, 1975-87; sponsor, tchr. Mus. Arts Jr. Club of Fla. Fedn. Music Clubs, Wilton Manors, 1976-87, Springfield, Mo., 1988-91, sr. club mem., 1987, pres., 1990-92, state conv. accompanist, 1988-90, v.p. S.W. region of Mo., 1989-91; organist, choir dir. various mil. chapels and civilian chs., U.S., Germany and Japan, 1935-65. Composer numerous works, 1958-87; reviewer (books, records, choral arrangements) 1978-86; editor Fla. Fedn. Music Clubs Publs., 1975-77, 81-84; music editor 12 Choral Octavos, 1981; composer, panelist state convention Minn. Fedn. Music Clubs, Bloomington, 1984; Soprano, Alto, Tenor, Bass, Organ anthem performed by Moramus Chorale at Moravian Music Festival, Winston-Salem, N.C., 1978; prodr., dir., accompanied Menotti's The Old Maid and the Thief, 1965, Argento's The Boor, 1966. Chmn. 10-piano concerts Broward County Music Tchrs., Plantation, Fla., 1969, 71;life mem. Women's Div. Boys Clubs of Broward, Fla., Ft. Lauderdale Symphony Soc.; organist, choir dir. Coral Ridge Moravian Ch., Ft. Lauderdale, 1966-85. Mem. Music Tchrs. Nat. Assn., Nat. Fedn. of Music Clubs (life, dist. pres. 1983-85, young artists auditions com. 1993-97), Morning Musicale of Ft. Lauderdale, Inc. (hon., life, pres. 1970-72), Am. Guild Organists (treas. 1967), Phi Beta (founder, pres. Pi Alpha Rho chpt., life, honor bracelet, scrolls 1971, 76, 83, citations 1988), Order Ea. Star (Richfield, Minn. chpt.), Masons (Fla. Grand chpt. Cmty. Svc. award 1987), Springfield Piano Tchrs. Forum, Toastmasters (gov. S.W. Mo. area 1988-89). Avocations: reading (especially biographies), crossword puzzles, langs. Home and Office: 845 Nottingham Dr Princeton IL 61356-2858

TILLMAN, KAREN SUE, lawyer; b. Garland, Tex., June 21, 1962; d. Franklin Willard and Mary Ruth Wright; m. Massie Tillman, July 2, 1993. BA, Baylor U., 1984, JD, 1986. Bar: U.S. Dist. Ct. (no. dist.) Tex. Law clk. U.S. Bankruptcy Ct., Ft. Worth, 1987-89; assoc. Hill & Gilstrap, Arlington, Tex., 1989-90; litigation atty. Radio Shack Corp., Ft. Worth, 1990—. Mem.: Ft. Worth Club. Republican. Baptist. Avocation: piano. Office: Radio Shack Corp 100 Throckmorton St Ste 1700 Fort Worth TX 76102-2847 E-mail: karen.tillman@radioshack.com.

TILLMAN, MARY LOU, elementary school educator; b. Phila., Oct. 19, 1951; d. Joseph Michael Tillman and Malvina Leona Szabo. BA in Music, Chestnut Hill Coll., 1983; MEd, Millersville U., 1995. Cert. tchr. Pa., N.J. 1st grade tchr. Immaculate Heart of Mary Parochial Sch., Phila., 1973—74; 1st, 4th, and 7th grade tchr. and music dir./tchr. Visitation Parochial Sch., 1974—78; 7th grade tchr., parish choir dir. Ambler Cath. Elem. Sch./St. Joseph's Parish, 1978—80; 7th and 8th grade tchr. St. Peter Celestine Parochial Sch., Cherry Hill, NJ, 1980—90; 7th and 8th grade social studies/reading tchr. Annville-Cleona Mid. Sch., Annville, Pa., 1993—. Author: (book) Sense of a Cat, 2000. Mem.: NEA, Pa. State Edn. Assn., Annville-Cleona Edn. Assn. Avocations: theater , travel, fishing, reading, music. Office: Annville-Cleona Sch Dist 500 S White Oak St Annville PA 17003 Business E-Mail: marylou_tillman@acsd.k12.pa.us.

TILLMAN, MARY NORMAN, urban affairs consultant; b. Atlanta, Jan. 31, 1926; d. Mary Nellie Shehee; m. James A. Tillman Jr., Apr. 11, 1952; children: James A., Gina G. BA, Morris Brown Coll., 1947; postgrad., U. Minn., 1964, Old Dominion U., 1975—. Asst. bus. mgr. Morris Brown Coll., Atlanta, 1947-53; race rels. and urban affairs cons. Tillman Assocs. Cons. Social Engrs., Atlanta and Syracuse, N.Y., 1963—, sr. ptnr., treas., from 1965, now pres. Bd. dirs. The Tillman Inst. of Human Rels., Inc.; clin. prof. United Theol. Sem., New Brighton, Minn.; adj. prof. Gordon-Conwell Theol. Sem., South Hamilton, Mass. Author: What is Your Racism Quotient?, 1964, A Common Sense Approach to Racism and Other Exclusivities, 1998, (with James A. Tillman, Jr.) Why America Needs Racism and Poverty, 1972, Black Intellectuals, White Liberals and Race Relations: An Analytic Overview, 1973; What is your Exclusivity Quotient, 1978, A Common Sense Approach to Racism and Other Exclusivities, 2001; also articles. Mem. adv. coun. to urban ministries dept. So. Bapt. Conv., Cmty. Rels. Commn., Atlanta; bd. dirs. Christian Coun. Met. Atlanta, Tillman Inst. Human Rels. Mem. Tidewater Assn. Pub. Adminstrs. (dir.), Am. Acad. Cons., Nat. Black Writers Consortium (v.p.), Joint Ctr. for Polit. Studies. Office: 1765 Glenview Dr SW Atlanta GA 30331-2307

TILLMAN, MASSIE MONROE, mediator, retired federal judge; b. Corpus Christi, Tex., Aug. 15, 1937; s. Clarence and Artie Lee (Stewart) T.; m. Karen Wright, July 2, 1993; children: Jeffrey Monroe, Holly. BBA, Baylor U., 1959, LLB, 1961. Bar: Tex. 1961, U.S. Dist. Ct. (no. dist.) Tex. 1961, U.S. Ct. Appeals (5th cir.) 1969, U.S. Supreme Ct. 1969; bd. cert. Personal Injury Trial Law, Tex. Ptnr. Herrick & Tillman, Ft. Worth, 1961-66; pvt. practice, 1966-70, 79-87; ptnr. Brown, Herman et al, 1970-78, Street, Swift et al, Ft. Worth, 1978-79; U.S. bankruptcy judge Ft. Worth divsn. No. Dist. Tex., 1987-2001; mediator, 2001—. Author: Tillman's Trial Guide, 1970; comments editor, case notes editor; mem. editl. bd. Baylor Law Rev., 1960-61. Mem. Ft. Worth Symphony League. Fellow Am. Bd. Trial Advocates, Tex. Bar Found.; mem. Ft. Worth/Tarrant County Bar (bd. dirs. 1969-70, v.p. 1970-71), Trial Attys.'s of Am., Nat. Conf. of Bankruptcy Judges, Am. Bankruptcy Inst., Tex. Trial Lawyers Assn. Republican. Baptist. Avocations: competition shotgun shooting, quail hunting. Address: PO Box 20213 Fort Worth TX 76102

TILLMAN, ROBERT L. home improvement company executive; With Lowe's Cos., Inc., Wilkesboro, NC, 1962—, pres., CEO, chmn., 1996—, chmn. bd. dirs., 1988—. Office: Lowes Cos Inc 1605 Curtis Bridge Rd Wilkesboro NC 28697-2246*

TILLMAN, WILLIAM MORRIS, JR. theology educator; b. McAlester, Okla., Dec. 30, 1946; s. William Morris and Evelyn Dorris Tillman; m. Leta Ruth Tillman, July 25, 1974; children: William Andrew, Glenn Michael. BS in Edn., Southeastern State Coll., 1968, MEd, 1972; MDiv, Southwestern Bapt. Theol. Sem., 1974, PhD, 1978. Biology and chemistry tchr. McAlester (Okla.) H.S., 1968-72; dir. rsch. and editl. svcs. Christian Life Commn., Nashville, 1977-81; asst. prof., 1981-90; assoc. prof. Christian ethics Southwestern Sem., Ft. Worth, 1990-98; coord. theol. edn. Bapt. Gen. Conv. of Tex., Dallas, 1998-2000; T.B. Maston prof. Christian ethics Hardin-Simmons U., Abilene, Tex., 2000—. Author: The Bible and Family Relations, 1983, Christian Ethics: A Primer, 1986, AIDS: A Christian Response, 1990, Understanding Christian Ethics, 1988; contbr. over 200 articles and reviews to profl. jours. Bd. dirs. Drug Prevention Resources, Dallas, 1989-97, Christian Life Commn., Dallas, 1984-90, T.B. Maston Found., Dallas, 1987-98; com. mem. ethics com. Cook-Ft. Worth Children's Med. Ctr., 1994-99; precinct chair Tarrant County, Ft. Worth, 1985-93, election judge, 1985-87, 90-93; mem. bioethics com. Hendrick Med. Ctr., Abeline. Mem. So. Bapt. Hist. Soc., Soc. of Christian Ethics, Nat. Assn. of Bapt. Profs. of Religion, Bapt. Ctr. for Ethics (assoc. 1991-94), Am. Acad. of Religion (chair S.W. region ethics sect. 1992-93), Kappa Delta Pi. Democrat. Baptist. Avocations: reading, photography, outdoor recreation, travel, writing. E-mail: btillman@hustx.edu.

TILLMON, JOEY E. chief of police; b. Victoria, Tex., Mar. 1, 1953; s. Lawrence Eugene and Florence Ann Tillmon; m. Jill A. Tillmon, Feb. 29, 1980; children: Logan, Haven, Brandy. BA in Sociology and Psychology, Tex. A & I U., 1975; A in Criminal Justice, Clark County C.C., North Las Vegas, Nev., 1983, A in Arts and Humane Letters, 1998. Police officer North Las Vegas Police Dept., 1980—, police sgt., 1990-96, police lt., 1996-97, dep. chief of police, 1997, chief of police, 1997—. Chair Law Enforcement Chiefs Com., Nev., 1997—; mem. bd., So. Nev. Women's Prison Facility Cmty. Rels., 1997—; mem. Command Coll. curriculum com., 1997—. Mem. for Police Explorers, Boy Scouts Am., North Las Vegas, 1997—; mem. advocate Missing & Exploited Children, 1997—, State Dept. Domestic Violence, 1997—. With USAF, 1975-79. Mem. Internat. Assn. Chiefs of Police, Nev. Sheriffs & Chiefs Assn., Nat. Orgn. Black Law Enforcement, Injured Police Officers Fund. Avocations: softball, basketball, golf, '74 Chevy restoration. Office: North Las Vegas Police Dept 1301 E Lake Mead Blvd North Las Vegas NV 89030

TILLSON, JOHN BRADFORD, JR. newspaper publisher; b. Paris, Dec. 21, 1944; s. John Bradford Sr. and Frances (Ragland) T.; m. Patricia Hunt, June 14, 1966 (div. June 1978); children: John, Karen; m. Cynthia Wornom, Oct. 10, 1981. BA, Denison U., Granville, Ohio, 1966. Reporter Charlotte (N.C.) News, 1969-71, Dayton (Ohio) Daily News, 1971-76, city editor, 1977-80, asst. mng. editor, 1980-82, mng. editor features, 1982-84; editor Dayton Daily News and Jour. Herald, 1984-88, pub., 1988—; pres., CEO Cox Pub., 1996—. Lectr. Am. Press Inst., Reston, Va., 1980-84. Chair Inventing Flight/2003 Com., 1998—; mem. Centennial of Flight Commn., 1998—; chair Miami

Valley Econ. Devel. Coalition, 1999-2001; pres. Dayton Art Inst., 1990-96; chair Alliance for Edn., 1992-94. Mem. Oio Newspaper Assn. (treas. 2000—), Newspaper Assn. Am. Episcopalian. Office: Cox Ohio Pub 45 S Ludlow St Dayton OH 45402-1810*

TILLY, NANCY MCFADDEN, writer, retired educator; b. Atlanta, June 8, 1935; d. Bradford McFadden and Sarah Fischer Davis; m. Eben Fletcher Tilly Jr., July 27, 1963; 1 child, John Eben Bradford. BA in Creative Writing with honors, U. N.C., 1957, MA in English Lit., 1959; MA in Divinity, U. Chgo., 1961. Instr., assoc. prof. humanities City Colls., Chgo., 1961-71; writer, 1971-89; assoc. editor N.C. Homes and Gardens mag., 1990-91, contbg. editor, 1991-92; vis. lectr. in English N.C. State U., 1990—. Author: Golden Girl (Juvenile Lit. award 1986); contbr. short stories and articles to profl. publs. Bd. trustees N.C. Writers Network, Chapel Hill, 1985-89; lit. cons. Dept. of Social Svcs., Chapel Hill, 2000—; vol. Estes Hills Elem. Sch., Chapel Hill, 1976-82. Fellowship Bread Loaf Writers Conf., 1985, Divinity Sch., U. Chgo., 1959-61, Innovations Ctr. City Coll. Chgo., 1968. Mem. Soc. of Children's Book Writers and Illustrators, Phi Beta Kappa, Alpha Lambda Delta. Episcopalian. Avocations: reading, cooking, walking. Home: 628 Kensington Dr Chapel Hill NC 27514 E-mail: nmtilly@juno.com.

TILNEY, NICHOLAS LECHMERE, surgery educator; b. N.Y.C., Oct. 19, 1935; s. Robert Wallace and Olive van Rensallaer (Gawtry) T.; m. Henriette Beatrice Loudon, Sept. 20, 1958 (div. 1975); children: Rebecca, Louise Moore, Victoria; m. Mary Johanna Graves, June 17, 1978; 1 child, Frances. AB, Harvard U., 1958; MD, Cornell U., 1962. Surg. resident Peter Bent Brigham Hosp., Boston, 1962-71; rsch. fellow U. Oxford, Eng., 1968-69, 71-72; surg. registrar U. Glasgow, Scotland, 1972-73; asst. prof. surgery Harvard Med. Sch., Boston, 1974-76, assoc. prof. surgery, 1977-82, prof. surgery, 1983—, Francis D. Moore prof., 1992—, dir. Surg. Rsch. Lab., 1975—. Dir. transplant svcs. Brigham & Womens Hosp., Boston, 1976-92, Transplant Rsch. Ctr., 1992—. Contbr. articles to profl. jours. Lt. comdr. USN, 1966-68. Fellow ACS, Royal Coll. Physicians and Surgeons (Glasgow); mem. Am. Soc. Transplant Surgeons (pres. 1995), Am. Surg. Assn., Phi Beta Kappa. Avocation: boating. Office: Brigham and Womens Hosp 75 Francis St Boston MA 02115-6106

TILSON, DOROTHY RUTH, word processing executive; b. Bloomsburg, Pa., Mar. 24, 1918; d. Roy Earl and Mary Etta (Masteller) Derr; m. Irving Tilson, Sept. 1949. BS, Bloomsburg U., 1940. Tchr. Madison Consol. Sch., Jerseytown, Pa., 1940-42; gage checker Phila. Ordinance Gage Lab., 1942-43; tabulating asst. Remington Rand, Phila., N.Y.C., 1943-46; copy writer Sears Roebuck, 1946-48; statis. asst. Ford Internat., N.Y.C., 1949-56; word processing adminstrv. asst. Coopers & Lybrand, 1956-91. Life mem. Rep. Senatorial Inner Circle, Washington, 1987—. Mem. Am. Movement for World Govt. (sec. 1991—), N.Y. Theosophical Soc. (libr. 1969—), UN Assn.-USA (mem. global policy project which includes internat. econ. governance and human rights). Home: 435 W 119th St # 9G New York NY 10027-7110

TILSON, HUGH HANNA, epidemiologist; b. New Kensington, Pa., Jan. 6, 1940; s. Donald Heath and Ann Coe T.; m. Judith Scullin, June 10, 1961; children: Hugh, Richard S., Ann C., Alice H. BA, Reed Coll., 1963; MD, Washington U., 1964; MPH, Harvard U., 1969, DPH, 1972. Diplomate Am. Bd. Preventive Medicine (trustee 1986-95, vice chmn. pub. health & preventive medicine, 1988-95). Intern Yale-New Haven Med. Center, 1964-65; resident in preventive medicine Harvard Sch. Pub. Health, 1968-72; research mem. John F. Kennedy Inst. Politics, 1969-70; research assoc. Health Services Research Ctr., U. N.C., Chapel Hill, 1970-81; asst. prof. preventive medicine and pub. health U. Oreg. Med. Sch., 1971-74, assoc. prof., 1974-76, clin. prof., 1976-78; asst. health officer Multnomah County, Oreg., 1971-75, health officer, dir. div. health services, 1975-76, health officer, dir. dept. human services, 1976-78; dir. div. health services State of N.C., Raleigh, 1979-81; with Burroughs Wellcome Co., Research Triangle Park, N.C., 1981-96, internat. v.p. surveillance, epidemiology and econ. rsch., 1994-96. Adj. prof. epidemiology U. N.C. Sch. Pub. Health, clin. prof. family medicine U. N.C. Med. Sch., 1981—, sr. advisor to dean, 1997—; cons. in field; examiner Am. Bd. Preventive Medicine, 1974-75; cons. Nat. Center for Health Services Research, HEW, 1975-89; mem. external adv. bd. Health Services Research Center, U. Wash. Sch. Public Health, 1977-80; mem. public health standards work group USPHS, 1977-92; chmn. external adv. bd. Health Services Research Center, U. N.C., 1979-93, mut. adv. bd. , 1993—; mem. med. adv. bd. Planned Parenthood of Portland, 1973-79, Planned Parenthood Greater Raleigh, 1986-95; bd. dirs. N.W. Oreg. Health Systems Agy., 1976-79; vice chmn. policy adv. bd. Joint Commn. on Accreditation of Hosps., 1980-81; mem. adv. bd. AIDS Svc. Agency; bd. health promotion and disease prevention Inst. Medicine, 1993-99, mem. study panels, 1990—. Mem. editl. bd. Am. Jour. Pub. Health, 1980-85, assoc. editor, 1985-99, sr. advisor, 2000-01; mem. editl. bd. Jour. Community Health, 1977-86, Jour. Public Health Policy, 1979-87, Jour. Clin. Rsch. and Pharmacoepidemiol., 1986-89, Am. Jour. Preventive Medicine, 1987--. Bd. dirs. United Way Columbia-Willamette, Oreg., 1977-78, Portland Opera Assn., 1977-79, Raleigh Chamber Music Guild, 1981-96, Partnership for Prevention, 1993—, Coun. on Linkages, 1995—; mem. Research Triangle Internat. Visitors Ctr., 1981—, bd. dirs., v.p., 1981-85. With M.C. U.S. Army, 1963-68. Fellow Am. Coll. Preventive Medicine (regent 1988-92, pres.-elect 1993-95, pres. 1995-97, chair devel. 1997—); mem. Nat. Assn. County Health Officers (pres. 1977-79), N.C. Med. Soc., English Speaking Union, N.C. Pub. Health Assn., APHA, Wake County Med. Soc. (v.p. 1981-82), AMA (alt. del. 2002--), Assn. Tchrs. Preventive Medicine, Pharm. Mfrs. Assn (med. sect. steering com. 1988—, sec. 1989-92, vice chmn. 1992—, chmn. 1994—), Internat. Soc. Pharmacoepidemiology (founding co-pres. 1990-91), Internat. Soc. Pharmacoecons. Outcomes Rsch. (founding mem., chmn. policy bylaws 1996--), Ctrs. for Edn. and Rsch. in Therapeutics (chmn. nat. steering com. 1999--), Wake County Med. Soc., Harvard Sch. Pub. Health Alumni Assn., Am. Acad. Pharm. Physicians (bd. dirs. 1994—, hon. life mem. 1994—, policy com. chair 1996—). Democrat. Episcopalian. Home: 1612 Oberlin Rd # 5 Raleigh NC 27608 Office: U NC Sch Pub Health Chapel Hill NC 27599-7400

TILSWORTH, TIMOTHY, retired environmental/civil engineering educator; b. Norfolk, Nebr., Apr. 6, 1939; s. Brooke and Mildred (Palmer) T.; m. Joanne Novak, Apr. 19, 1966 (div. Jan. 1984); children: Craig Scott, Patrick Joseph; m. Debbie J. May, July 20, 1984. BSCE, U. Nebr., Lincoln, 1966, MSCE, 1967; PhD, U. Kans, 1970. Registered profl. engr., Alaska; diplomate Inst. Hazardous Materials Mgmt. Instr. U. Nebr., Lincoln, 1967; prof. environ. quality and civil engring. U. Alaska, Fairbanks, 1970-94, dir. program environ. quality engring. and sci., 1972-76, 78-94, asst. to pres. for acad. affairs, 1976-78, head dept. civil engring, 1990-91, chmn. grad. coun., chmn. chancellor search com., 1990-91, prof. emeritus civil engring. and environ. quality engring., 1994—; co-owner Raven Press Pub. Co., Fairbanks, 1990—; with NSF Antarctic Rsch. McMurdo, 1991—92. Pres. faculty senate U. Alaska, 1992-93; owner Alaska Arctic Environ. Svcs., Fairbanks, 1972-99, DJT's Shelties Delight, Fairbanks, 1985-99, T2 Antiques, 1994-99; project mgr. superconducting super collider proposal State of Alaska, Fairbanks, 1987-88. Chmn. exec. com. Cowper for Gov. Alaska, Fairbanks, 1986. Recipient commendation State of Alaska, 1988. Mem. Assn. for Environ. Engring. Profs., ASCE (Outstanding Service award 1975), Am. Water Works Assn. Water Pollution Control Fedn., Fairbanks Golf and Country Club (bd. dirs. 2000-01), Chi Epsilon. Roman Catholic. Home and Office: 1900 Raven Dr Fairbanks AK 99709-6661 E-mail: fftt@uaf.edu.

TILTON, DAVID LLOYD, savings and loan association executive; b. Santa Barbara, Calif., Sept. 21, 1926; s. Lloyd Irving and Grace (Hart) T.; m. Mary Caroline Knudtson, June 6, 1953; children: Peter, Jennifer, Michael, Catharine. AB, Stanford U., 1949, MBA, 1951. With Santa Barbara Savs. & Loan Assn., 1951-90, pres., 1965-84; now pres. Fin. Corp., Santa Barbara. Trustee, chmn. Calif. Real Estate Investment Trust, 1988. Served with USNR, World War II. Mem. Calif. Savs. and Loan League (dir. 1980), Delta Chi. Home: 630 Oak Grove Dr Santa Barbara CA 93108-1402 Office: Fin Corp Santa Barbara 1187 Coast Village Rd Ste 1-322 Santa Barbara CA 93108-2761 E-mail: dtilton@earthlink.net.

TILTON, GEORGE ROBERT, geochemistry educator; b. Danville, Ill., June 3, 1923; s. Edgar Josiah and Caroline Lenore (Burkmeyer) T.; m. Elizabeth Jane Foster, Feb. 7, 1948; children— Linda Ruth, Helen Elizabeth, Elaine Lee, David Foster, John Robert Student, Blackburn Coll., 1940-42; BS, U. Ill., 1947; PhD, U. Chgo., 1951; D.Sc. (hon.), Swiss Fed. Inst. Tech., Zurich, 1984. Phys. chemist Carnegie Instn., Washington, 1951-65; prof. geochemistry U. Calif.-Santa Barbara, 1965-91, emeritus, 1991—, chmn. dept. geol. scis., 1973-77. Guest prof. Swiss Fed. Inst., Zurich, 1971-72; prin. investigator NSF research grant, 1965— ; mem. earth scis. panel NSF, 1966-69, 82-85 Assoc. editor Jour. Geophys. Research, 1962-65, Geochimica et Cosmochimica Acta, 1973— ; contbr. articles to profl. jours. Served with AUS, 1942-45 Decorated Purple Heart; recipient Sr. Scientist award Alexander von Humboldt Found., 1989. Fellow AAAS, Am. Geophys. Union, Geol. Soc. Am.; mem. Nat. Acad. Scis., Geochem. Soc. (pres. 1981), Sigma Xi. Episcopalian. Home: 2661 Tallant Rd Apt 512 Santa Barbara CA 93105-4807 Office: U Calif Dept Geol Scis Santa Barbara CA 93106

TILTON, GLENN F. oil company executive; b. Washington, Apr. 9, 1948; BA in Internat. Rels., U. S.C., 1970. Sales trainee U.S. mktg. ops. Texaco Inc., Washington, 1970, various assignments, 1970-76, div. supr. mktg. East Brunswick, N.J., 1976-78, area mgr. resale N.Y. div. N.Y.C., 1978, asst. to gen. mgr. northeastern region, 1978-79, mktg. mgr. resale Phila. div., 1979-81, staff coord. corp. planning and econs. dept. N.Y., 1981-83; asst. gen. mgr. sales Texaco Europe, 1983-84, gen. mgr. mktg., 1984-87; v.p. mktg. Texaco U.S.A., Houston, 1987-88; pres. Texaco Refining and Mktg. Inc., 1988-91; v.p. Texaco Inc., 1989; chmn. Texaco Ltd., 1991-92; pres. Texaco Eruope, 1992-94, Texaco USA, Houston, 1994—; sr. v.p. Texaco Inc., 1995—; CEO Texaco, White Plains, NY, 2001; chmn., pres., CEO UAL Corp. and United Airlines, 2002—. Office: UAL PO Box 66100 Chicago IL 60666*

TILTON, JAMES CHARLES, computer engineer; b. Burlington, Wis., July 1, 1953; s. Charles Edwin and Mary Jean (Robinson) T.; m. Hac Hua, June 12, 1982; children: Man, Thoa, Phuong, Nancy. BA, MEE, Rice U., 1976; MS, U. Ariz., 1978; PhD, Purdue U., 1981. Sr. engr. Computer Scis. Corp., Silver Spring, Md., 1982-83, Sci. Applications Rsch., Riverdale, 1983-85; computer engr. NASA Goddard Space Flight Ctr., Greenbelt, 1985—. Editor workshop procs.; contbr. articles to profl. jours. Mem. ch. coun. The Greenbelt Community Ch., 1991-92. Mem. IEEE (geosci. and remote sensing soc. adminstrv. com. 1992-96; assoc. editor Transactions on Geosci. and Remote Sensing 1996—), Internat. Assn. for Pattern Recognition (chair tech. com. 7 1990-92). Mem. United Ch. of Christ. Office: NASA Goddard Space Flight Ctr Mail Code 935 Ctr Greenbelt MD 20771-0001

TILTON, JOHN ELLSWORTH, ceramic artist; b. Red Bank, N.J., Nov. 8, 1944; s. Ellsworth Nollner and Virginia Caroline (Loog) T.; m. Anne Kathryn Bowers, Jan. 5, 1993. BS in Math., U. Fla., 1966, MS in Math., 1969; MFA in Ceramics, U. South Fla., 1972. Artist, Alachua, Fla., 1972—. Developer art glazes of the matte crystalline variety, specific porcelain forms to use with glazes. Avocations: music, yoga, meditation. Home and Office: 16211 NW 88th Ter Alachua FL 32615-5012 Fax: 386-462-2762. E-mail: tilton@atlantic.net., john@tiltonpottery.com.

TILTON, JOHN ELVIN, mineral economics educator; b. Brownsville, Pa., Sept. 16, 1939; s. John Elvin Sr. and Margaret Julia (Renn) T.; m. Elizabeth Martha Meier, June 18, 1966; children: Margaret Ann, John Christian. AB, Princeton U., 1961; PhD in Econs., Yale U., 1965. Staff analyst Office of Sec. of Def., Washington, 1965-67; rsch. assoc. Brookings Inst., 1967-70; asst. prof. econs. U. Md., College Park, 1970-72; assoc. prof. mineral econs. Pa. State U., University Park, 1972-75, prof., 1975-85; Coulter prof. Colo. Sch. Mines, Golden, 1985—, dir. Divsn. Econs. and Bus., 1987-98. Officer econ. affairs commodities divsn. UN Conf. on Trade and Devel., Geneva, 1977; leader rsch. Internat. Inst. Applied Systems Analysis, Laxenburg, Austria, 1982-84; vice chmn. bd. mineral and energy resources NRC, Washington, 1980-83, mem. nat. materials adv. bd., 1987-89; vis. prof. Pontifica Cath. U., Santiago, Chile, 1998-99. Author: International Diffusion of Technology, 1971, The Future of Nonfuel Minerals, 1977, On Borrowed Time? Assessing the Threat of Mineral Depletion, 2002; editor: Material Substitution, 1983, World Metal Demand, 1990, Mineral Wealth and Economic Development, 1992, View from the Helm, 1995; co-editor: Economics of Mineral Exploration, 1987, Competitiveness in Metals, 1992. Capt. U.S. Army, 1965—67. Fulbright scholar Ecole Nat. Supérieure des Mines de Paris, 1992. Mem. Am. Econ. Assn., Am. Inst. Mining Metall. and Petroleum Engrs. (Mineral Econs. award 1985), Mineral Econs. and Mgmt. Soc. (pres. 1993-94), Mining and Metall. Soc. Am. Avocations: skiing, hiking. Office: Colo Sch Mines Divsn Econs & Bus Golden CO 80401 E-mail: jtilton@mines.edu.

TILTON, MARK CAMPBELL, educator; b. Oakland, Calif., Aug. 9, 1956; s. Glenn Walter and Crystal Lee (Campbell) T.; m. Patricia Ann Boling, Sept. 19, 1981 (div.); children: Ellen Crystal, Clio Catharine, Andrew. BA, U. Calif., Berkeley, 1979, MA, 1982, PhD, 1990. Rsch. assoc. U. Tokyo, 1987-88; asst. prof. Purdue U., West Lafayette, Ind., 1990-96, assoc. prof., 1996—. Author: Restrained Trade: Cartels in Japan's Basic Materials Industries, 1996, Is Japan Really Changing Its Ways? Regulatory Reform and the Japanese Economy, 1998. Rsch. grantee Japan-U.S. Friendship Commn., 1995-96, 97—; Abe fellow Social Sci. Rsch. Coun., N.Y., 1996—, Fulbright fellow, Tokyo, 1986-87; Nat. Merit scholar, 1974. Mem. Am. Polit. Sci. Assn., Japan Policy Rsch. Inst., Japan Info. Access Project, Internat. House Japan, Assn. Asian Studies, Assn. Japanese Bus. studies. Democrat. Episcopalian. Avocations: church choir, swimming, languages. Office: Purdue U Dept Polit Sci LAEB 1363 West Lafayette IN 47907

TILTON, WEBSTER, JR. contractor; b. St. Louis, Sept. 11, 1922; s. Webster and Eleanor (Dozier) T.; student St. Marks Prep. Sch., 1936-40, Pawling Prep. Sch., 1940-42; master brewers degree, U.S. Brewers Acad., 1949; m. Grace Drew Wilson, Feb. 14, 1948 (div. Oct. 1959); 1 son, Webster III; m. 2d, Nancy McBlair Payne, Jan. 5, 1963. Asst. brewing technologist F&M Schaffer Brewing Co., Bklyn., 1948-52; factory sales rep. Cole Steel Equipment Co., N.Y.C., 1957-68; dist. sales mgr. Scantlin Electronics, Inc., Washington, 1968-70; sales rep. Comml. Washer & Dryer Sales Co., Washington, 1970-72; propr. Webster Tilton, Jr., contractor, Washington, 1972-86. Served from cadet to chief mate Mcht. Marine Res.-USNR, 1942-45. Episcopalian. Home: 309 Briar Hill Rd Cooperstown NY 13326-3905

TILY, STEPHEN BROMLEY, III, bank executive; b. Phila., July 7, 1937; s. Stephen Bromley Jr. and Edith Helen (Straub) T.; m. Janet Anita Walz, July 10, 1965; children: Deborah Powell, Stephen Bromley IV, James Charles II. BS in Econs., Washington and Jefferson Coll., 1960; postgrad., Temple U. Sch. Law, 1963. Trust officer Indsl. Valley Bank & Trust Co., Phila., 1968-71; v.p. Farmers Bank of Delaware, Wilmington, 1971-77; exec. officer G&T, Inc., Ltd., 1977-80; pres., COO DCG&T Co., 1977-91, chmn., CEO, 1991-93, chmn. emeritus, 1993—. Chmn. The Declaration Group, Conshohocken, Pa., 1985-97; trustee Declaration Fund, 1988-99; tchr. Am. Inst. Banking, 1970-79. Capt. USAR, 1960-61. Mem. Fin. Analysts of Phila., Barnegat Light Yacht Club (commodore 1988-89, trustee 1989-92), Kimberton Fish and Game Assn., Waynesborough Country Club, John's Island Golf Club, Merion Golf Club, Ducks Unltd. Republican. Episcopalian.

TIMBERG, SIGMUND, retired lawyer; b. Antwerp, Belgium, Mar. 5, 1911; came to U.S., 1916, naturalized, 1921; s. Arnold and Rose (Mahler) T.; m. Eleanor Ernst, Sept. 22, 1940; children: Thomas Arnold, Bernard Mahler, Rosamund and Richard Ernst (twins). AB, A.M., Columbia U., 1930, LL.B., 1933. Bar: N.Y. 1935, U.S. Supreme Ct. 1940, D.C. 1954. Sr. atty., solicitors' office Dept. Agr., 1933-35, chief, soil conservation sect., 1935-38; staff mem. Temporary Nat. Econ. Com., 1938-39; sr. atty. SEC, 1938-42; chief, property relations and indsl. orgn. div., reoccupation br. Bd. Econ. Warfare and Fgn. Econ. Adminstrn., 1942-44; spl. asst. to atty. gen., antitrust div. Dept. Justice, 1944-45, chief judgments and judgment enforcement sect., 1946-52; sec. UN Com. on Restrictive Bus. Practices, 1952-53; cons. UN, 1953-55, 62-64; pvt. law practice, 1954-88. Prof. law Georgetown U. Law School, 1952-54; faculty Parker Sch. Comparative Law, Columbia U., 1967-80; spl. counsel Senate Mil. Affairs Subcom. on Surplus Property Legislation, 1944; mem. Mission for Econ. Affairs, Am. Embassy, London, 1945; del. Anglo-Am. Telecommunications Conf., Bermuda, 1945, Geneva Copyright Conf., 1952; cons. Senate Patents Subcom., 1961, UN Patents Study, 1962-64, OAS, 1970; mem. adv. com. on fed. policy on indsl. innovation, patent and info. policy sub com., 1978-79, adv. com. on internat. investment, tech. and devel., 1979-85. Contbr. articles on antitrust, intellectual property and internat. law to legal periodicals. Mem. ABA, D.C. Bar Assn., Internat. Bar Assn., Internat. Law Assn., Am. Soc. Internat. Law, Washington Fgn. Law Soc., Am. Law Inst., Assn. Bar City N.Y., Copyright Soc. Am., Cosmos Club (Washington), Philosophy Club (Washington). Home: 3519 Porter St NW Washington DC 20016-3177

TIMBERLAKE, CHARLES EDWARD, history educator; b. South Shore, Ky., Sept. 9, 1935; s. Howard Ellis and Mabel Viola (Collier) T.; m. Patricia Alice Perkins, Dec. 23, 1958; children: Mark Brewster, Daniel Edward, Eric Collier BA, Berea Coll., 1957; Calif. State Teaching Credential, Claremont Grad. Sch., 1958, MA, 1962; PhD, U. Wash., 1968. Tchr. Barstow H.S., Calif., 1959-60, Claremont City Sch., 1960-61; tchg., rsch. asst. U. Wash., Seattle, 1961-64; asst. prof. history U. Mo., Columbia, 1967-73, assoc. prof., 1973-81, prof., 1981—, Byler disting. prof., 1996, chmn. dept., 1996—2000, asst. dir. Honors Coll., 1988-90. Exch. prof. Moscow State U., 1985, U. Manchester, England, 1987—88; hon. prof. history Lanzou U., China, 1991; dir. edn. svcs. Leisure Voyages, 1992—2000; vis. prof. Joensuu (Finland) U., 1996, 98, 2000. Author: The Fate of Russian Orthodox Monasteries and Convents Since 1917, 1995; editor: Essays on Russian Liberalism, 1972, Detente: A Documentary Record, 1978, Religious and Secular Forces in Late Tsarist Russia, 1992, Profiles of Finland series, 1991-94, (microfiche) The St. Petersburg Collection of Zemstvo Publs., 1992—; contbr. chpts. to books, articles to profl. jours. Mem. Citizens Alliance for Progress, Columbia, Mo., 1969—75, pres., 1969—70; founding mem. High Edn. Rescue Operation, 1983—91; mem. Columbians Against Throw-Aways, 1980—83. Recipient Disting. Alumnus award Berea Coll., 2002; Fgn. Area fellow, 1965-66, fellow Internat. Rsch. and Exchs. Bd., 1971, 95, 2001, Am. Coun. Learned Socs., 1978-79, Fulbright-Hays fellow, 1995; grantee NEH, 1972, 79, 87. Mem. Am. Assn. Advancement Slavic Studies (bd. dirs. 1980-82, 84-86, chmn. council regional affiliates 1981-82, 85-86, chmn. permanent membership com. 1981-84), Western Slavic Conf., Am. Hist. Assn. (exec. council Conf. on Slavic and East European History 1987-89), Central Slavic Conf. (sec.-treas. 1967-68, pres. 1968-69, 76-77, 83-84, 88-89, 2001-02, exec. bd. 1972— , custodian archive 1972—), Mo. Conf. History (pres. 1992, sec.-treas. 1996-2000), State Hist. Soc. Mo., Fulbright Assn. (pres. Mo. chpt. 1997-2000). Avocations: hiking, travel. Home: 9221 S Rt N Columbia MO 65203-9312 Office: U Mo Dept History Columbia MO 65211-0001 E-mail: timberlakec@missouri.edu.

TIMBERLAKE, MARSHALL, lawyer; b. Birmingham, Ala., July 25, 1939; s. Landon and Mary (Perry) T.; m. Rebecca Ann Griffin, Aug. 22, 1987; children: Sumner Timberlake Starling, Jane Ellison. BA, Washington and Lee U., 1961; JD, U. Ala., 1970. Bar: Ala. 1970, U.S. Supreme Ct. 1970, U.S. Dist. Ct. (no., so. and mid. dists.) Ala. 1970, U.S. Supreme Ct. 1976, U.S. Ct. Appeals (11th and 5th cirs.) 1981, U.S. Ct. Appeals (D.C. cir.) 1991. Assoc. Balch & Bingham Law Firm, Birmingham, 1970-76, ptnr., 1976—. Pres. Legal Aid Soc., Birmingham, 1980-81; chmn. Ala. Supreme Ct. Commn. on Dispute Resolution, 1994-96, commr., 1996—; trustee Ala. Dispute Resolution Found., 1995—, vice chmn., 1997—. Pres. Ala. Alcohol and Drug Abuse Coun., 1994-95, dir., 1989—; v.p. Assn. Atty. Mediators, 1994-97; co-chair Gov.'s Task Force on State Agy. Alternative Dispute Resolution, 1998—; bd. dirs. Partnership Assistance to the Homeless, 1998—, chmn. endowment fund com., 1999—. Capt. U.S. Army, 1962-66, Vietnam. Recipient Ann. award Dispute Resolution Inst., 1998; hon. fellow State Agy. ADR Program, 2001. Fellow Ala. Law Found.; mem. ABA, Ala. State Bar (chmn. corp. banking and bus. law sect. 1981-82, chmn. state bar task force on alternative dispute resolution 1992-94, State Bar Merit award 1995, co-chmn. state bar com. on ADR 1996-97, mem. state bar task force on jud. selection 1996-98), Birmingham Bar Assn. (mem. and co-chmn. grievance com. 1972-74, chmn. ethics com. 1975-76, chmn. unauthorized practice of law com. 1976-77, chmn. spl. projects com. 1994-95, co-chmn. com. on jud. and legal reform 1996-97, chmn. com. on jud. and legal reform 1997-98), Am. Arbitration Assn. (state adv. com.), Ala. Acad. Atty. Mediators (co-founder), Redstone Club (bd. govs. 1977 -78), Rotary (Birmingham chpt., chmn. civic club found. 1984), Beaux Arts Krewe, Mountain Brook Club. Republican. Presbyterian. Avocations: tennis, thoroughbred racing, photography. Office: Balch & Bingham 1901 6th Ave N Birmingham AL 35203-2618 Home: 3349 Brookwood Rd Birmingham AL 35223-2020

TIMBERLAKE, WILLIAM DAVID, psychology educator; b. San Francisco, Nov. 19, 1942; s. William Burman Timberlake and Lynn Louzelle Spradling; m. Kathleen Marie Nagy, Dec. 20, 1969 (div.); m. Susan Holly Stocking, Apr. 20, 1980; children: Anne Elizabeth, William Ryder. BA cum laude, Pomona Coll., 1964; MA, U. Mich., 1967, PhD in Exptl. Psychology with honors, 1969. From tchg. asst. to hon. faculty assoc. dept. psychology U. Mich., Ann Arbor, 1965-69; from lectr. to assoc. prof. psychology Ind. U., Bloomington, 1969-82, prof., 1982—, co-dir. Ctr. for Integrative Study Animal Behavior, 1992—. Hon. rsch. assoc. Harvard U., Cambridge, Mass., 1977-78; vis. assoc. prof. U. Calif., San Diego, 1978; adj. faculty mem. in cognitive and neural scis. Ind. U., 1987, adj. prof. biology, 1992—; vis. prof. zoology sub-dept. animal behavior Kings Coll., U. Cambridge, Eng., 1994-95, core faculty mem. cognitive sci., 1995—, core faculty mem. neural sci., 2000—; vis. prof. behavioral neuroscience Oreg. Health Scis. U., 2000-01; vis. scholar Reed Coll., 2000-01. Editor spl. issue Learning and Motivation, 1984; assoc. editor jour. Animal Learning and Behavior, 1992-94, 94-96, 97—; mem. editl. bd. Jour. Exptl. Psychology, Animal Behavior Processes, Behavioural Processes, Behavior and Philosophy, Jour. of Exptl. Analysis of Behavior contbr. articles to profl. jours. Bd. advisors Theatre Cir., Bloomington, 1993-2000; mem. Bloomington Chamber Singers, 1995—; bd. fellows Poynter Ctr. for Study of Ethics and Am. Instns., Ind. U., 1993—. Recipient FACET award for tchg. excellence Ind. U., 1999, James M. Catell Found. Sabbatical award, 2000; grantee NSF, 1979—, NIH, 1984—; NSF predoctoral fellow, 1965-68. Fellow APA (mem. coun. divsn. 6 1996-98, 2001—, divsn. 1, 3, 6 and 25), Am. Psychol. Soc.; mem. AAAS, Animal Behavior Soc., Psychonomic Soc., Soc. for Rsch. Biol. Rhythms, Soc. for Study of Ingestive Behavior, Ea. Psychol. Assn., Midwestern Psychol. Assn., Assn. for Behavior Analysis, Internat. Soc. for Behavioral Ecology, Behavioral Brain Scis. Assocs., Am. Soc. Mammalogists, Soc. Neuroscience, Phi Beta Kappa, Phi Kappa Phi, Sigma Xi. Avocations: music, writing. Office: Ind U Psychology Dept 1101 E 10th St Bloomington IN 47405-7007 E-mail: timberla@indiana.edu.

TIMBERS, JUDITH ANN, academic administrator, writer; b. Elmhurst, Ill., Dec. 10, 1946; d. James G.W. and Betty Timbers; children: Brandy, Pica. BA, U. Ill., 1968; MEd, U. Hawaii, 1972, EdD, 1982; MA, Forest Inst. Profl. Psychology, 1992; PsyD, Am. Sch. Profl. Psychology, 1999. Cert. tchr., Hawaii. Instr. U. Hawaii, Honolulu, 1974-76, coord., 1976-86, asst. prof., 1984-87; pres., founder, dir. Competency Tutoring Ctr., 1974—. Varsity Internat. Sch., Honolulu, 1980—. Grant writer to federally and locally funded grants; presenter in field. Contbr. articles to profl. jours. Active Pacific and Asian Affairs Coun. U.S. HEW fellow, 1971-72; recipient Profl. Svc. award State of Hawaii, 1984. Mem. NEA, NAFSA, Nat. Assn. Secondary Sch. Prins., Hawaii Assn. Children with Lea Avocations: Japanese culture, golfing, traveling, reading. Office: Varsity Internat Sch 2617 S King St Ste 3D Honolulu HI 96826-3274

TIMCENKO, LYDIA TEODORA, biochemist, chemist; b. Beograd, Yugoslavia, July 4, 1951; arrived in U.S., 1975; d. Teodor Pavle and Branislava (Spasojevic) Timcenko; m. Ghazi Youssef, June 16, 1980 (div. Oct. 1989); children: Ali Alexander Youssef, Kareem Misha Youssef; m. Peter Porzio, Mar. 11, 1996. BS in Chemistry, U. Belgrade, Yugoslavia, 1975; MS, Wayne State U., 1977, PhD, 1984. Grad. asst. Wayne State U., Detroit, 1976-78, 81-84, rsch. assoc., 1986-88, lectr. in chemistry, 1989; postdoctoral fellow Mich. Cancer Found., 1985; postdoctoral fellow Sch. Medicine Wayne State U., 1986-88; lectr. in chemistry Lawrence Tech. U., Southfield, Mich., 1989, 90-91; biochemist Strohtech, Inc., Detroit, 1990-91; prof. chemistry Sussex County Coll., Newton, N.J., 1997-98; asst. prof. chemistry N.Y. Techol. Coll., City U. Bklyn., 1999—; sci. tchr. New Milford (NJ) H.S., 2002—. Prin. investigator, rsch. scientist ICN Galenika Inst., Clin. Ctr. Serbia, Belgrade, 1991—96; rsch. scientist, mktg. cons. Huet Biol. , Birmingham, Mich., 1987—91; adj. prof. chemistry Kean Coll.; adj. prof. dept. chemistry and chem. biology Stevens Inst. Tech., Castle Point on Hudson, Hoboken, NJ; adj. assoc. prof. organic chemistry Pace U., N.Y.C., 2002. Contbr. articles to profl. jours. Mem.: Am. Chem. Soc., Am. Soc. Microbiology, Phi Lambda Upsilon. Achievements include research in in shigella toxin in shigella and E. coli;

mitoch GPO in advenal cortex; liberation of labile sufur from ferredoxins; adhesion shigella to HCTH and HELA; localization of GST and GP in adrenal. Home: 306 State Route 94 Columbia NJ 07832-2771 E-mail: ltim51@cs.com.

TIMCHAK, LOUIS JOHN, JR. lawyer, real estate executive; b. Johnstown, Pa., June 7, 1940; s. Louis John and Edna Ann Timchak; m. Susan Truesdale Mueller; children: Louis John, Alexander Mueller, Christopher Truesdale. AB, Georgetown U., 1962; JD, U. Pitts., 1965. Bar: Pa. 1965, D.C. 1966, Fla. 1970, N.Y. 1973, Ga. 1980; lic. real estate broker, N.Y., Fla. Sole practice, Johnstown, 1968-69; real estate atty. Marriott Corp., Washington, 1969-73; assoc. Finley, Kumble, Wagner, Heine & Underberg, N.Y.C., 1973-74; v.p., corp. counsel Phipps Land Co., Atlanta, 1974-76; regional v.p. IDR Mgmt., Inc., 1976-79; real estate cons. Boothe Fin. Corp., 1980; v.p., gen. counsel The Bankers Land Co., Palm Beach Gardens, Fla., 1980-83; v.p., mgr. corp. devel. Merrill Lynch Realty Inc., Stamford, Conn., 1983-84; Scott, Royce, Harris & Bryan, Palm Beach, Fla., 1984-85; sr. v.p. Turner Devel. Corp., North Palm Beach, 1985-86; pres., dir. Turner Real Estate Group Inc., 1986-88; sole practice, 1988-97, 99—; pres. Timchak Real Estate Group II, Inc., 1988-97; v.p., gen. counsel, sec. Jumbo Sports, Inc., Tampa, Fla., 1997-99. Bd. advisors Proudfoot Cons. Co., West Palm Beach, 2000—. Founding dir., past pres. Palm Beach County Devel. Bd., bd. dirs., 1984-86; bd. dirs. Palm Beach County chpt. Am. Heart Assn., 1983-91, sec., 1984, 1st v.p., 1985, pres., 1987, chmn. bd. dirs., 1988-90; mem. Leadership Palm Beach County. Served to lt. JAGC, USNR, 1965-68, Vietnam. Mem. ABA, D.C. Bar Assn., Hillsborough County Bar Assn., Urban Land Inst., Nat. Assn. Corp. Real Estate Execs., North Palm Beach County C. of C. (bd. dirs. 1981-83, 84—, treas. 1983, v.p. 1985). Club: City Tavern (Washington). Office: 18810 Place Antibes Lutz FL 33558-5341

TIMENES, NICOLAI, policy analyst; b. Waterbury, Conn., Aug. 21, 1938; s. Nicolai Sr. and Margit (Bjornsgaard) T. BA, Yale U., 1960, MA, 1962. With U.S. Dept. of Interior, Washington, 1970-75, 82-85; dep. asst. dir. Congl. Budget Office, 1975-77; with U.S. Dept. of Energy, Washington, 1977-82, Ctr. for Naval Analyses, Arlington, Va., 1962-70; prin. dir. mil. pers. policy Office of Sec. of Def., Washington, 1991-95; cons., 1996—. Vis. prof. environ. studies Dartmouth Coll., Hanover, N.H., 1979-80. Home: 5208 Albemarle St Bethesda MD 20816-1829

TIMINS, BONITA LEA, interior decorator; b. Scranton, Pa., Nov. 26, 1951; d. Edward Joseph and Mary Loretta (Lake) T. BS in Art Edn., Kutztown U., 1973; MA in Art Edn. magna cum laude, Marywood Univ., 1976, MA in Psychology magna cum laude, 1990; PhD in Metaphysics, Am. Internat. U., 1994. Art tchr. Scranton Sch. Dist., 1974-77; prodn. asst. Garan, Inc., N.Y.C., 1977-78, Marty Gutmacher, Inc., N.Y.C., 1979-81, R.R.J. Industries, N.Y.C., 1981-82; prodn. mgr. Double Dutch Sportswear, 1982-84; MR/CLA supr. Allied Svcs., Scranton, 1984-86; home health care coord., 1986-95; interior decorator Kurlancheek Furniture Gallery, Clarks Summit, Pa., 1995—; self-employed rsch. writer. Rsch. data analysis, Scranton, 1992-94; chemistry tutor U. Scranton, 1994-95. Contbr. articles to profl. jours. Com. woman Dem. Party, Scranton, 1994; fundraiser Am. Cancer soc., Scranton, 1993; mem. Nat. Coun. for Geocosmic Rsch. Recipient Nightingale award Pa. Hosp. Assn., 1995, Outstanding Assoc. Mem. Cmty. Svc. award Lackawanna County Young Dems., 1996, Excellence award Sigma Theta Tau Internat. Nursing Soc., 1995. Mem. Art Student's League N.Y.C. (life), Psi Chi, Kappa Pi. Roman Catholic. Avocations: travel, costume design, oil painting. Home and Office: 2108 Jackson St Scranton PA 18504-1610

TIMINSKY, DALE, academic administrator; Pres. Sierra Nev. Coll., Incline Village, Nev. Office: Sierra Nevada Coll 999 Tahoe Blvd Incline Village NV 89451*

TIMLIN, JAMES CLIFFORD, bishop; b. Scranton, Pa., Aug. 5, 1927; s. James C. and Helen E. (Norton) T. AB, St. Mary's Sem., Balt., 1948; S.T.B., Gregorian U., Rome, Italy, 1950. Ordained priest Roman Catholic Ch., 1951; asst. pastor St. John the Evangelist Ch., Pittston, Pa., 1952-53, St. Peter's Cathedral, Scranton, 1953-66; asst. chancellor, sec. Diocese of Scranton, 1966-71, chancellor, 1971-77, aux. bishop, vicar gen., 1976-84; pastor Ch. of Nativity, Scranton, 1979-84; bishop Diocese of Scranton, 1984—. Address: 300 Wyoming Ave Scranton PA 18503-1285

TIMLIN, ROBERT J. judge; b. 1932; BA cum laude, Georgetown U., 1954, JD, 1959, LLM, 1964. Atty. Douglas, Obear and Campbell, 1960-61, Law Offices of A.L. Wheeler, 1961; with criminal divsn. U.S. Dept. Justice, 1961-64; atty. U.S. Atty. Office (ctrl. dist.) Calif., 1964-66, Hennigan, Ryneal and Butterwick, 1966-67; city atty. City of Corona, Calif., 1967-70; prin. Law Office of Robert J. Timlin, 1970-71, 75-76; ptnr. Hunt, Palladino and Timlin, 1971-74, Timlin and Coffin, 1974-75; judge Mcpl. Ct., Riverside, Calif., 1976-80, Calif. Superior Ct., Riverside, 1980-90; assoc. justice Calif. Ct. Appeals, 1990-94; judge U.S. Dist. Ct. (ctrl. dist.) Calif., L.A., 1994—. Part-time U.S. Magistrate judge Ctrl. Dist. Calif., 1970-74. Served U.S. Army, 1955-57. Mem. Calif. Judges Assn. Office: US Dist Ct Central District of Calif Eastern Divsn 3470 12th St Riverside CA 92501

TIMM, DEBORAH A. critical care nurse; b. Sandusky, Ohio, Nov. 8, 1953; d. Eugene and Shirley F. (Lane) Lentz; m. Thomas R. Timm, June 17, 1973; children: Dawn Marie, Rebecca Lynn. AA in Bus., Bowling Green State U., Huron, Ohio, 1974; lic. practical nurse, Sandusky Sch. Practical Nursing, 1978; diploma, Providence Hosp. Sch. Nursing, Sandusky, 1990; BSN, Bowling Green State U., Med. Coll. Ohio, 1997. RN, Ohio; cert. advanced cardiac life support. Emergency rn. nurse Fireland Regional Med. Ctr. Mem. Emergency Nurses Assn., Bowling Green State U. Alumni Assn., Providence Hosp. Sch. Nursing Alumni Assn.

TIMM, ROGER K. lawyer; b. Bay City, Mich., May 21, 1947; BS, U. Mich., 1969; JD, Harvard U., 1972. Bar: Mich. 1972. Mem. Dykema Gossett, Detroit. Mem. ABA, State Bar Mich. Office: Dykema Gossett 400 Renaissance Ctr Detroit MI 48243-1668 E-mail: rtimm@dykema.com.

TIMM, WALTER WILLIAM, lawyer; b. St. Louis, Sept. 11, 1956; s. Walter F. and Lois B. Timm; m. Jacquelyn Ann Timm, Nov. 30, 1979; children: Robert, Elizabeth. BSBA, U. Mo., St. Louis, 1978; MBA, Western Ill. U., 1983; JD, No. Ill. U ., 1990. Bar: Mo. 1990, Ill. 1991. Assoc. atty. Thompson & Mitchell (not Thompson Coburn), St. Louis, 1990—94; corp. counsel Angelica Corp., Chesterfield, 1994—96, asst. gen. counsel, 1997—99, Purina Mills Inc., Brentwood, 1999—2001, gen. counsel, 2001—02; ptnr. The Lowenbaum Partnership, LLC, Clayton, 2002—. Chmn. bd. edn. Salem Luth. Sch., 1995-99; nat. bd. dirs. Nat. Family Partnership, Miami, Fla. Office: The Lowenbaum Partnership LLC 222 S Central Ave #901 Clayton MO 63105 Fax: 314-746-4848. E-mail: wwt@lowenbaumlaw.com.

TIMMCKE, ALAN EDWARD, physician and surgeon; b. Madison, Wis., July 7, 1949; s. Wesley Eugene Timmcke; m. Deborah Cameron Brosseau (div.); m. Teresa Ann Watkins, Dec. 31, 1977; children: Gretchen Kristine, Alan Edward Jr. BS, Dickinson Coll., 1971; MD with honors, Temple U., 1975. Diplomate Am. Bd. Surgery, Am. Bd. Colon and Rectal Surgery; lic. physician, Pa., Maine, Mo., La. Intern in surgery Nat. Naval Med. Ctr., Bethesda, Md., 1975-76, resident in gen. surgery, 1976-79; rsch. fellow in colon and rectal surgery Jewish Hosp./Washington U. Med. Ctr., St. Louis, 1985-86, clin. fellow in colon and rectal surgery, 1986-87; asst. in surgery Washington U. Sch. Medicine, 1985-87; staff colon and rectal surgeon Ochsner Clinic, New Orleans, 1987—. Staff surgeon Nat. Naval Med. Ctr., Bethesda, 1979, Naval Regional Med. Ctr., Newport, R.I., 1979-82, dept. colon and rectal surgery Lahey Clinic Med. Ctr., Burlington, Mass., 1984-85; staff surgeon Rumford (Maine) Community Hosp., 1982-84, med. staff v.p., 1983-84; instr. surgery Uniformed Svcs. U. of Health Scis., Bethesda, 1978-79; lectr. in field. Contbr. articles and abstracts to profl. jours. Lt. comdr. M.C., USN, 1975-82. Recipient Harry E. Bacon Found. award for best original paper, 1987; NIH Summer Rsch. fellow, 1972. Fellow ACS, Am. Soc. Colon and Rectal Surgeons; mem. New Orleans Surg. Soc., Surg. Assn. of La., Internat. Soc. Univ. Colon and Rectal Surgeons, Soc. of Am. Gastrointestinal Endoscopic Surgeons, Am. Soc. Gastrointestinal Endoscopy, Alpha Omega Alpha. Office: Ochsner Clinic Dept Colon/Rectal Surgery 1514 Jefferson Hwy New Orleans LA 70121-2483

TIMMER, BARBARA, United States Senate official, lawyer; b. Holland, Mich., Dec. 13, 1946; d. John Norman and Barbara Dee (Folensbee) T. BA, Hope Coll., Holland, Mich., 1969; JD, U. Mich., 1975. Bar: Mich. 1975, U.S. Supreme Ct., 1995. Assoc. McCrosky, Libner, VanLeuven, Muskegon, Mich., 1975-78; apptd. to Mich. Women Commn. by Gov., 1976-79; staff counsel subcom. commerce, consumer & monetary affairs Ho. Govt. Ops. Com., U.S. Ho. of Reps., 1979-82, 85-86; exec. v.p. NOW, 1982-84; legis. asst. to Rep. Geraldine Ferraro, 1984; atty. Office Gen. Counsel Fed. Home Loan Bank Bd., 1986-89; gen. counsel Com. on Banking, Fin. and Urban affairs U.S. Ho. of Reps., Washington, 1989-92; asst. gen. counsel, dir. govt. affairs ITT Corp., 1992-96; ptnr. Alliance Capitol, 1994—; sr. v.p., dir. govt. rels. Home Savs. of Am., Irwindale, Calif., 1996-99; ptnr. Manatt, Phelps & Phillips, Washington, 1999—; gen. counsel MyPrimeTime, Inc., San Francisco, 2000-01; asst. sec. U.S. Senate, 2001—. Editor: Compliance With Lobbying Laws and Gift Rule Guide, 1996. Bd. dirs. Women's HIgh Tech Coalition. Recipient Affordable Housing award Nat. Assn. Real Estate Brokers, 1990, Acad. of Women Achievers, YWCA, 1993. Mem. ABA (bus. law sect., electronic fin. svcs. subcom.), FBA (chair, exec. coun. banking law com.), Exchequer Club, Women in Housing and Fin. (bd. dirs. 1992-94, gen. counsel 1994-98), Supreme Ct. Bar Assn., Supreme Ct. Hist. Soc., Mich. Bar Assn., Bar of D.C. Episcopalian. Address: PO Box 21777 Washington DC 20009-9777 E-mail: btimmerdc@earthlink.net.

TIMMER, CHARLES PETER, agricultural and development economist; b. Troy, Ohio, July 29, 1941; s. Thomas Gerhart and Rose Marie (Hoffman) T.; m. Carol Falb, Aug. 31, 1963; children: Anne Carol, Ashley Susan. AB in Econs. magna cum laude, Harvard U., 1963, PhD in Econs, 1969. Commodity analyst W.R. Grace and Co., N.Y.C., 1964-66; asst. prof. econs. Food Research Inst., Stanford U., 1968-74, assoc. prof., 1974-75; econ. adv. Indonesian Nat. Planning Agy., Harvard Adv. Group, Jakarta, 1970-71; H.E. Babcock prof. food econs. Cornell U., 1975-77; prof. econs. of food and agr. Sch. Public Health Harvard U., Cambridge, Mass., 1977-80, John D. Black prof. agr. and bus., 1980-86, prof. devel. studies at large Bus. Sch., 1986-88, Thomas D. Cabot prof. devel. studies, at large, 1988-98; dean Grad. Sch. Internat. Rels., prof. devel. studies U. Calif., San Diego, 1998-2000. Hibbard lectr. U. Wis., 1993; cons. on food and agr. Author: (with others) Choice of Technology in Developing Countries, 1975, (with Perkins et al) Small Scale Rural Industry in the People's Republic of China, 1977, (with Falcon and Pearson) Food Policy Analysis, 1983, (with Nelson et al) Food Aid and Development, 1981, Getting Prices Right: Scope and Limits of Agricultural Price Policy, 1986; editor, contbg. author: Rice Policy in Indonesia, 1974, The Political Economy of Rice in Asia, 1976, The Corn Economy of Indonesia, 1987, Agriculture and the State: Growth, Employment, and Poverty in Developing Countries, 1991; guest editor, contbg. author to Food Policy, 1995. Recipient Bintang Jasa Utama medal Govt. Indonesia, 1992; named San Diego Citizen-Diplomat of Yr., 2000; John Harvard scholar, 1960-63; Fulbright fellow, 1963-64; NSF fellow, 1966-68 Mem. Am. Econ. Assn., Am. Agrl. Econs. Assn., AAAS, Phi Beta Kappa. E-mail: ptimmer@ucsd.edu.

TIMMER, DAVID HART, civil engineer; b. Omaha, May 30, 1953; s. Donald Hendrik and Imogene Agnes (Hart) T.; m. Sharon Kathryn Fussnecker, May 11, 1974; children: Donald H., Douglas H., Karen M., Gerrit J. BA in History and Edn., Eastern Ky. U., 1975; BSCE, Ohio State U., 1976. Registered profl. engr., Ohio, Ind. W. Va., Mich., Pa. Drafter survey crew Richland Engring. Ltd., Mansfield, Ohio, 1969-76, bridge inspector, 1976, civil engr., 1976-78, structural engr., 1978-80, design engr., 1980-88, chief bridge insp., 1984-88, project engr., 1989-95, assoc. ptnr., 1996-98, sr. ptnr. structures sect., 1999—. CCD instr. Resurrection Parish, Lexington, Ohio, 1986-88; coun. pres., asst. Webbs leader Cub Scout Pack 126, Bellville, Ohio, 1988-89, tiger cub leader, 1987-88. Mem.: ASCE, NSPE, Assn. Bridge Contractors and Designers, Internat. Assn. Bridge and Structural Engrs. Republican.

TIMMER, MARGARET LOUISE (PEG TIMMER), educator; b. Osmond, Nebr., July 4, 1942; d. John Henry and Julia Adeline (Schilling) Borgmann; m. Charles B. Timmer, May 23, 1964 (div. June 1990); children: Jill Marie, Mark Jon. AA, N.E. Community Coll., Norfolk, Nebr., 1987; BA in Edn., K-12 art endorsement, Wayne (Nebr.) State U., 1988; MEd, Bank Street Coll./Parsons Sch. Design, N.Y.C., 1992. Cert. tchr., Nebr. Bookkeeper Goeres Electric, Osmond, 1960-61; tel. operator Northwestern Bell, Norfolk, 1961-64; with want advt. dept. Washington Post, 1964-65; saleswoman Jeannes Fashion Fabrics, Norfolk, 1970-72, Tripps, Norfolk, 1986-87; office and fin. mgr. Tim's Plumbing & Heating Inc., 1972-86; tchr. art Norfolk Cath. Schs., 1988—, mem. bd., 1985-88. Instr. art history N.E. Community Coll., 1992—; mem. youth art bd. Norfolk Art Ctr., 1988—. One-woman show Uptown Restaurant, Norfolk, 1993, Norfolk Art Ctr., 1996; exhibited in group shows Sioux City (Iowa) Art Ctr., 1988, Columbus (Nebr.) Art Ctr., 1993. Mem. choir St. Mary's Cath. Ch., Norfolk, 1991—; mem. Norfolk Community Choir, 1991; bd. dirs. Norfolk Community Concerts Assn., 1984-87; treas. Norfolk Cath. Booster Club, 1985-86; leader 4-H, Madison County, 1973-78; judge art show Laurel (Nebr.) Women's Club, 1988. Named outstanding profl. vol. Norfolk Art Ctr., 1996; recipient Crystal Apple award Norfolk (Nebr.) C. of C., 1999. Mem. N.E. Nebr. Art Assn., Nebr. Art Edn. Assn. (3d place award 1988). Avocations: watercolor and oil painting, gardening, reading, gourmet cooking, sewing. Home: Rte 2 Box 239 55380 Warnerville Dr Norfolk NE 68701-9758 Office: Norfolk Cath Schs 2300 Madison Ave Norfolk NE 68701-4456 E-mail: ptimmer57@yahoo.com.

TIMMER, SHARON PHYLLIS, marketing communications consultant, writer, artist; b. Detroit, July 7, 1934; d. Manuel M. and Evelyn (Goldis) Nidorf; m. John J. Timmer, Apr. 9, 1965; 1 child, Stacy A. V.p. Wexton Adv. Agy., N.Y.C., 1955-58; acct. exec., v.p. Nides-Cini Advt., L.A., 1958-67; founder, owner operator Timmerco, 1967-73, corp. v.p., pres., CEO Santa Monica, Calif., 1981—. V.p. spl. events Vidal Sassoon, L.A., 1978-79, pres. of internat., 1979-80, corp. v.p., 1980-81; lectr. in field. Contbr. articles to popular mags. Bd. dirs. L.A. Arts Coun. Recipient Merit award Advt. and Editl. Art in the West, Indsl. Graphics Internat., Arts Dirs. Club L.A., Outstanding Contribution award YWCA. Mem. Nat. Womens Forum (founding mem. L.A. chpt.).

TIMMERHAUS, KLAUS DIETER, chemical engineering educator; b. Mpls., Sept. 10, 1924; s. Paul P. and Elsa L. (Bever) T.; m. Jean L. Mevis, Aug. 3, 1952; 1 dau., Carol Jane. BS in Chem. Engring, U. Ill., 1948, MS, 1949, PhD, 1951. Registered profl. engr., Colo. Process design engr. Calif. Rsch. Corp., Richmond, 1952-53; extension lectr. U. Calif., Berkeley, 1952; mem. faculty U. Colo., Boulder, 1953-95, prof. chem. engring., 1961-95, asso. dean engring., 1963-86, dir. engring. rsch. ctr. coll. engring., 1963-86, chmn. aerospace dept., 1979-80, chmn. chem. engring. dept., 1986-89, Patten Chair Disting. prof., 1986-89, presdl. teaching scholar, 1989—. Chem. engr. cryogenics lab. Nat. Bur. Standards, Boulder, summers 1955,57,59,61; lectr. U. Calif. at L.A., 1961-62; sect. head engring. div. NSF, 1972-73; cons. in field. Bd. dirs. Colo. Engring. Expt. Sta., Inc., Engring. Measurements Co., both Boulder Editor: Advances in Cryogenic Engineering, vols. 1-25, 1954-80; co-editor: Internat. Cryogenic Monograph Series, 1965— . Served with USNR, 1944-46. Recipient Disting. Svc. award Dept. Commerce, 1957, Samuel C. Collins award for outstanding contbns. to cyrogenic tech., 1967, Meritorious Svc. award Cryogenic Engring. Conf., 1987, Disting. Pub. Svc. award NSF, 1984; named CASE Colo. Prof. of Yr., 1993, Disting. Lectr., L-T Fan, 2001. Fellow AAAS (v.p. 1985, pres. 1986, Southwestern and Rocky Mountain divsn. Pres.'s award 1989), Internat. Inst. Refrigeration (v.p. 1979-87, pres. 1987-95, U.S. nat. commn. 1983—, pres. 1983-86, W.T. Pentzer award 1989), AIChE (v.p. 1975, pres. 1976, Alpha Chi Sigma award for chem. engring. rsch., 1968, Founders award 1978, Eminent Chem. Engr. award 1983, W.K. Lewis award 1987, F.J. Van Antwerpen award 1991, Inst. Lecture award 1995), Am. Soc. for Engring. Edn. (bd. dirs. 1986-88, George Westinghouse award 1968, 3M Chem. Engring. divsn. award 1980, Engring. Rsch. Coun. award 1990, Delos Svc. award 1991); mem. NAE, Am. Astron. Soc., Austrian Acad. Sci., Cryogenic Engring. Conf. (chmn. 1956-67, bd. dirs.), Internat. Cryocooler Conf. (bd. dirs. 1980—), Soc. Automotive Engrs. (Ralph Teetor award 1991), Sigma Xi (v.p. 1986-87, pres. 1987-88, bd. dirs. 1981-89), Verein Deitschner ingenieure, Cryogenic Soc. Am., Sigma Tau, Tau Beta Pi, Phi Lambda Upsilon. Home: 905 Brooklawn Dr Boulder CO 80303-2708 E-mail: klaus.timmerhaus@colorado.edu.

TIMMERMAN, DORA MAE, community volunteer, art advocate; b. Wichita, Kans., Mar. 28, 1931; d. George M. and Effie (Stevens) Branham; m. Lewin E. Timmerman, Oct. 30, 1949 (dec. 1990); children: Curt E., Kyle A. Student, Wichita State U., 1948-50, 73-75. Legal sec., Wichita, 1948-55; mgr. Wichita Art Mus. Shop, 1977-81; owner, mgr. Rubbing Renaissance, Wichita, 1981—. Co-chair Greater Wichita Save Outdoor Sculpture Project Smithsonian Instn.'s Nat. Mus. Am. Art, Nat. Inst. Conservation Cultural Property, 1992-97, chair, 1997—; presenter workshops on brass and stone rubbing, lectr. and program presenter mus., coll., libr. and sch. orgns.; lectr. and tour guide for Wichita's outdoor sculpture and pub. art; dir. pub. adv. bd. Unified Sch. Dist. 259 Interactive Sculpture Project Wichita, 1995—. Pres., bd. dirs. Wichita Bar Assn. Aux., 1961-62, Kos Harris PTA, 1963-64, Twentieth Century Cornelias, 1966-68, Met. Arts Bd., 1980, Lands and Peoples Club, 1982-83; bd. dirs. Project Beauty, Inc., 1968-99, women's divsn. Inst. Logopedics, YWCA, UNICEF adv. coun., 1985; founding mem. Wichita Pub. Arts Task Force, 1988-90, Wichita Pub. Art Adv. Bd., 1990-2000, chmn. 1992—; chmn. Friends of Soldiers & Sailors Civil War Monument; charter and exec. bd. mem. Friends of Campbell Castle, 1993-95; exec. bd. mem. Sedgwick County Cmty. Image Task Force, 1993-2000; pres., vol. svcs. bd. Wichita Art Mus., 1975-77; active Wichita Ctr. for Arts, Wichita-Sedgwick County Arts and Humanities Coun., Edwin A. Ulrich Mus. Wichita State U., Wichita-Sedgwick County Hist. Mus., Project Concern Internat., 1978-85, various youth and charitable orgns.; chair Friends of Wichita Art Mus., 1999-2000; trustee Wichita Art. Mus., 1999-2000; bd. dirs. Wichita Greyhound Charities, Inc., 1999—; mem. mus. policy com. Mid-Am. All-Indian Ctr., 2000, others. Recipient many awards from: Project Beauty, Inc., Kans. State Hist. Soc., City of Wichita Pub. Art Adv. Bd., 1996 Good Apple award Wichita Pub. Schs.; recipient Smithsonian SOS! Achievement award; recognition award for restoration of soldiers and sailors civil war monument, Sedgwick County Bd. Commrs. Mem. Monumental Brass Soc. Eng., Friends of Botanica (charter), Internat. Platform Assn., Stock Markettes Investment Club, Present Day Club, PEO. Presbyterian. Avocations: calligraphy, reading, bridge, travel, art. Home: 6606 Magill St Wichita KS 67206-1344

TIMMERMANN, ALLAN GILLING, economics educator; b. Skovlund, Denmark, Oct. 9, 1964; came to U.S., 1994; s. Viggo Nielsen and Gyda Bente (Gilling) T.; m. Solange Maria Ferelli Fortes, Feb. 1, 1992. MS, London Sch. Econs., 1988; PhD, U. Cambridge, England, 1992. Lectr. fin. econs. U. London, 1991-94; asst. prof. U. Calif., San Diego, 1994-98, assoc. prof., 1999—2001, prof., 2001—. Cons. Barclay's Global Investors, San Francisco, 1998—; prof. fin. London Sch. Econs., 1998-99. Columnist Internat. Broker, London, 1992; contbr. articles to profl. jours. Hellman Faculty fellow, U. Calif., San Diego, 1997; British Coun. scholar, London, 1987; recipient Tress prize U. London, 1993. Mem. Am. Fin. Assn., Neural Networks Capital Markets (organizing com.), Ctr. Econ. Policy Rsch. (rsch. fellow), Econometric Soc. Avocations: long distance running, tennis. Office: U Calif 9500 Gilman Dr La Jolla CA 92093-5004 E-mail: atimmerm@ucsd.edu.

TIMMERMANN, SANDRA, educational gerontologist, communication specialist; b. Orange, N.J., Mar. 25, 1941; d. Bernhard and Matilda (Schaaf) T.; m. George W. Bonham. BA with honors, U. Colo., 1963; MA, Columbia U., 1967, EdD, 1979. Account exec. Rowland Co., N.Y.C., 1964-67; dir. pub. info. The N.Y. TV Network/SUNY, 1967-72; assoc. Hoefer/Amidei Pub. Rels./Mktg., 1972-74; assoc. dean Inst. Lifetime Learning, AARP, Washington, 1974-76, dir. Inst., 1976-84, dir. geriatric edn., 1984-86; exec. dir. Peninsula Ctr. for the Blind, Palo Alto, Calif., 1986-88; dir. western states region Am. Found. for the Blind, San Francisco, 1988-90; dir. edn. Am. Soc. on Aging, 1990-94, SeniorNet, San Francisco, 1995-97. Dir. Mature Market Inst., Met. Life Ins. Co., Westport, Conn., 1997—; bd. dirs. Calif. Coun. of Gerontology and Geriatrics, 1988-90; mem. tng. com. Nat. Ctr. for Black Aged; mgr. older adults sect. HEW Lifelong Learning Project; cons. Brookdale Ctr. on Aging, Hunter Coll.; cons. to bus. and industry; mem. adv. com. nat. project on counseling older people Am. Pers. and Guidance Assn.; mem. nat. adv. com. vocat. edn. and older adults U.S. Dept. Edn.; bd. dirs. Am. Soc. on Aging, 2000—; chair LEARN, 2000—. Fin. gerontology columnist Jour. Fin. Svc. Profls.; contbr. articles to profl. jours. and newspapers. Trustee, chmn. adv. com. on later yrs. Am. Found. for the Blind; commr., v.p. Commn. on Status of Women, San Mateo County, Calif.; pres. bd. dirs. Sr. Coastsiders; chmn. youth and edn. Cmty. United Meth. Ch., Half Moon Bay, Calif.; mem. Nat. Adv. Coun. on Injury Prevention in Aging, 1998—; mem. exec. com., bd. dirs. Bridgeport (Conn.) YMCA, 1997—. Mem. Southwestern Conn. Agy. of Aging (bd. dirs. 1998—), Am. Assn. Adult and Continuing Edn. (editor Edn. and Aging newsletter, chmn. commn. on aging, bd. dirs.), Bus. Forum on Aging (governing coun. 1999—), Coalition Adult Edn. Orgns. (dir., pres, 1984-85), Capital Spkrs. Club, Pi Beta Phi, Pi Lambda Theta, Kappa Delta Pi, Phi Delta Kappa. Home: 555 Hill Farm Rd Fairfield CT 06430-2149

TIMMINS, EDWARD PATRICK, lawyer; b. Denver, June 8, 1955; s. M. Edward and Elizabeth Jean (Imhoff) T.; m. Mary Joanne Deziel, Dec. 27, 1985; children: Edward Patrick Jr., Joan Deziel. BA with honors, Harvard U., 1977; JD magna cum laude, U. Mich., 1980. Bar: Colo. 1981, U.S. Ct. Appeals (D.C. and 9th cirs.) 1982, U.S. Dist. Ct. Colo. 1984, U.S. Ct. Appeals (10th cir.) 1984. Law clk. to cir. justice U.S. Ct. Appeals (7th cir.), Chgo., 1980-81; trial atty. U.S. Dept. Justice, Washington, 1981-84; asst. U.S. atty. Denver, 1984-88; dir. Otten, Johnson, Robinson, Neff & Ragonetti P.C., 1985-96; pres. Timmins & Assocs., LLC, 1996—. Sr. editor U. Mich. Law Rev., 1979-80. Bd. dirs., vice chair Colo. Easter Seals; bd. dirs., chair Denver Pub. Schs. Found.; bd. dirs., chmn. career exploring com. Boy Scouts Am.; bd. dirs. March of Dimes, Am. Ireland Fund. Harvard Nat. scholar, 1976. Mem. ABA, Colo. Bar Assn. (exec. coun. jud. sect.), Colo. Bar Found., Denver Bar Assn., Order of Coif, Friends of Harvard Rowing. Avocations: skiing, golf. Office: Timmins & Assocs LLC 1625 Broadway Ste 300 Denver CO 80202-4739

TIMMINS, JAMES DONALD, venture capitalist; b. Hamilton, Ont., Can., Oct. 3, 1955; came to U.S., 1979; s. Donald G. and Myrna L. (Seymour) T. BA, U. Toronto, 1977; law degree, Queen's U., 1979; MBA, Stanford U., 1981. Investment banker Wood Gundy, Toronto, 1980, Salomon Bros., San Francisco, 1981-84; mng. dir., CEO McKewon & Timmins, San Diego, 1984-87; ptnr. Hambrecht & Quist, San Francisco, 1987-90, Redwood Ptnrs., Menlo Park, Calif., 1991-98, NIF Ventures, Palo Alto, 1998—. Bd. dirs. AcceLight Networks, Inc., Pitts., Escend Technologies, San Mateo, Calif., Harmony Software, Inc., San Mateo, Calif., SpectraSwitch Inc., Santa Rosa, Calif., Ancore Corp., Santa Clara, Simpata, Inc., Folsom, Calif., Kanisa, Inc., Cupertino, Calif., StatisFusion, Inc., Long Beach, Calif., Vpacket Comm., Inc., Milpitas, Calif., NetContinuum, Santa Clara. Mem. bd. advs. Fuller Sem. of No. Calif., Menlo Park. Mem. Olympic Club of San Francisco. Home: 2131 Manzanita Ave Menlo Park CA 94025-6539 Office: NIF Ventures USA Inc 5 Palo Alto Sq 3000 El Camino Real 9th Fl Palo Alto CA 94306-2155 E-mail: timmins@nifusa.com.

TIMMINS, MARYANNE, real estate accountant, educator; b. Hackensack, N.J., Feb. 15, 1975; d. Paul Langerfeld and Loretta Timmins. BS, Rutgers U., 1997. CPA Am. Inst. CPA's. Personal banking rep. PNC Bank, Hackensack, 1996-97, personal banking rep. supr. Lyndhurst, N.J., 1997-98; auditor Valley Nat. Bank, Wayne, 1998-99, Summit Bancorp, Ridgefield Park, 1999-2000; fin. instr. Ctr. Fin. Tng., Clifton, 1999—; sr. acctg. assoc. Prudential Real Estate Investors, Parsippanny, NJ, 2000—. Religious instr. Queen of Peace Ch., North Arlington, N.J., 1997—. Samuel and Marcella S. Geltman scholar Rutgers U., 1997. Mem. AICPA, N.J. Soc. CPAs. Avocations: computers, step aerobics, reading, gardening. Home: 74 Birchwood Dr North Arlington NJ 07031-5130 Office: Prudential Investment Mgmt 8 Campus Dr 4th Fl Parsippany NJ 07054-4409 E-mail: maryanne.timmins@prudential.com.

TIMMINS, MICHAEL JOSEPH, communications services company executive; b. Jersey City, Feb. 14, 1952; s. Michael Joseph and Eva Marie (Corti) T.; m. Janice Rose Markham, May 12, 1973; children: Keith Dylan, Christopher Michael, Chelsea Victoria. BA in Econs., Jersey City State Coll., 1977. Securities clk. N.Y. Stock Exch., N.Y.C., 1971-73; rsch. analyst Metro Containers, Kraft Foods, Lyndhurst, N.J., 1973-77; mktg. rep. Infonet div. Computer Scis. Corp., N.Y.C., 1977-80, sales mgr. Hackensack, N.J., 1980-82, multinat. mgr., 1982-88, dir. for Europe, 1985-88; v.p. Europe, Africa and Middle East Infonet Svcs. Corp., 1988-91, corp. v.p. internat., 1991-92, exec. v.p. internat. ops., exec. v.p. software sales/svcs., 1992—, exec. v.p. global bus. devel., 1993—. Bd. dirs. Interpac Belgium, S.A., vice chmn., Brussels,

Infonet Oy, Helsinki, vice chmn., Infonet/CSCL Ltd., Toronto, vice chmn. Infonet Svenska AB, Stockholm, vice chmn., Osiware, S.A., Paris, chmn., Infonet Nederland B.V., Infocom Joint Venture, Moscow. Mem. Internat. Computers and Communications (planning coord. 1989—). Roman Catholic. Avocation: golf. Home: 677 Palmer Ave Maywood NJ 07607-1521 Office: Infonet Svcs Corp 201 Route 17 Rutherford NJ 07070-2574

TIMMINS, PATRICK FARRELL, III, gynecologic oncologist; b. Columbus, Ohio, Mar. 16, 1966; s. Patrick Farrell Jr. and Elizabeth Flavin T.; m. Victoria Louise Ketz, July 20, 1991; children: Alejandra I., Patrick B. BS in Biochemistry, Ohio State U., 1988, MD cum laude, 1992. Resident in obgyn. Magee Women's Hosp. U. Pitts., 1992-96; gyn. oncology fellow Albert Einstein Coll. Medicine/Montefiore Med. Ctr., Bronx, N.Y., 1996-99; dir. gyn. oncology Albany (N.Y.) Med. Coll., 1999—. Recipient Merit award for young investigators ASCO, 1997. Mem. ACOG (rsch. award in gyn. infections and their complications 1997, rsch. award in menstrual health 1997), AMA, Am. Assn. Cancer Rsch. (young investigator award 1997), Soc. Gynecol. Oncologists. Home: 10 Klaasen Way Loudonville NY 12211 Office: 317 S Manning Blvd STe 280 Albany NY 12208 Fax: 518-458-1390. E-mail: patrick.timmins@usoncology.com.

TIMMINS, WILLIAM JOHN, human resources executive; b. Phila., Dec. 13, 1955; s. William John and Theresa Christine (Sullivan) T.; m. Holly Blake, Jan. 2, 1982; children: Brendan, Genevieve. B.Mus., Temple U., 1978, MBA in Human Resources, 1993; BBA in Econs., U. Pa., 1986. Mem. Mcpl. Orch. of Caracas, Venezuela, 1981-83; mgr. compensation/benefits Okidata Corp., Mt. Laurel, N.J., 1983-86; mgr. pers./ops. Phila. Orch. Assn., 1986-87; mgr. wage/salary State of Del., Wilmington, 1987-88; sr. compensation analyst ICIA Inc., 1988-90; mgr. compensation (N.Am.) ICI/Zeneca Ag Products, Zeneca Inc., 1990-95; dir. human resources AgrEvo USA, 1995—. Adv. bd. Agrochem. Human Resources Forum, 1988—; lectr. in field. Adv. bd. Ashland Nature Ctr., Del., 1988-91, Del. Heart Assn., 1989-92. Mem. Am. Compensation Assn., Employee Benefits Assn., Friendly Sons of St. Patrick, Sigma Kappa Phi, Beta Gamma Sigma. Roman Catholic. Avocations: reading, music, swimming, family activities.

TIMMONS, BARBARA ALICE, retired geriatrics nurse; b. Muncie, Ind., Dec. 11, 1932; d. John and Audrey Muriel (Halleck) Schumacher; m. Jerry Alyn Timmons, Apr. 7, 1951; children: Gary Alyn, Karen, Benjamin. Diploma in nursing, Muncie Sch. Practical Nursing, 1983. LPN. Charge nurse Maple Village Nursing Home, Middletown, Ind., 1983-84, Millers Merry Manor, Middletown, 1984-85, Sylvesters Nursing Home, Muncie, 1985-87; dir. nursing Countryside Healthcare, 1987-90, med. records, 1990-91; nursing adminstrn. Liberty Village, 1991-95; PRN sch. nurse Daleville (Ind.) Cmty. Schs., 1999—. Mem. Ind. Health Care Assn. Dirs. Nursing (legis. lobbying com. 1989-90).

TIMMONS, EVELYN DEERING, pharmacist; b. Durango, Colo., Sept. 29, 1926; d. Claude Elliot and Evelyn Allen (Gooch) Deering; m. Richard Palmer Timmons, Oct. 4, 1952 (div. 1968); children: Roderick Deering, Steven Palmer. BS in Chemistry and Pharmacy cum laude, U. Colo., 1948. Chief pharmacist Meml. Hosp., Phoenix, 1950-54; med. lit. rsch. librarian Hoffman-LaRoche, Inc., Nutley, N.J., 1956-57; staff pharmacist St. Joseph's Hosp., Phoenix, 1958-60; relief mgr. various ind. apothecaries, 1960-68; asst. then mgr., dir. compounding Profl. Pharmacies, Inc., 1968-72; mgr. Mt. View Pharmacy, 1972-76, owner/mgr., 1976—; pres. Ariz. Apothecaries, Ltd., 1976—. Mem. profl. adv. bd., bereavement counselor Hospice of Valley, 1983-96; mem. profl. adv. bd. Upjohn Health Care and Svcs., Phoenix, 1984-86; bd. dirs. Am. coun. on Pharm. Edn., Chgo., 1986-92, v.p., 1988, 89, treas., 1990-91; mem. expert adv. bd. compounding pharms. U.S. Pharmacoepial Conv., 1992—; preceptor U. Ariz., 1965—, Midwestern Coll. Pharmacy, Ariz. Campus, 1998—; lectr. on NHRT. Author poetry; contbr. articles to profl. jours. Mem. Scottsdale (Ariz.) Fedn. Rep. Women, 1963-68; various other offices Rep. Fedn.; mem. platform com. State of Ariz., Nat. Rep. Conv., 1964; asst. sec. Young Rep. Nat. Fedn., 1963-65; active county and state Rep. coms.; adv. bd. Internat. Jour. of Pharm. Compounding, 1996-2001; fin. chmn. Internat. Leadership Symposium: Women in Pharmacy, London, 1987; treas. Leadership Internat. Women Pharmacy, 1991-2001; mem. founders circle Gladys Taylor McGarey Med. Found., 1996—. Named Outstanding Young Rep. of Yr., Nat. Fedn. Young Reps., 1965, Preceptor of Yr., U. Ariz./Syntex, 1984; recipient Disting. Pub. Svc. award Maricopa County Med. Soc., 1962, Disting. Alumni award Wasatch Acad., 1982, Career Achievement award Kappa Epsilon, 1983, Leadership and Achievement award Upjohn Labs., 1985-86, Outstanding Achievement in Profession award Merck, Sharp & Dohme, 1986, award of Merit Kappa Epsilon, 1988, Disting. Coloradoan award U. Colo., 1989, Vanguard award Kappa Epsilon, 1991, Unicorn award Kappa Epsilon, 1993, Compounding Pharmacist of the Yr. award Profl. Compounding Corp. of Am., 1994, 96, Healing Heart award Gladys Taylor McGarey Found., 1998, 50 Yr. Certificate U. Colo., 2000. Fellow Am. Coll. of Apothecaries (v.p. 1982-83, pres. elect 1983-84, pres. 1984-85, chmn. bd. dirs. 1985-86, adv. coun. 1986-92, Chmn. of Yr. 1980-81, Victor H. Morganroth award 1985, J. Leon Lascoff award 1990), Internat. Acad. of Compounding Pharmacists (bd. dirs. 1993-2000); mem. Ariz. Soc. of Hosp. Pharmacists, Am. Pharm. Assn. (Daniel B. Smith award 1990), Ariz. Pharmacy Assn. (Svc. to Pharmacy award 1976, Pharmacist of Yr. 1981, Bowl of Hygeia 1989, 1st Innovative Pharmacy award 1994, 50 Yr. Practice and Membership award 2001), Maricopa County Pharmacy Assn. (pres. 1977, Svc. to Pharmacy award 1977), Am. Soc. of Hosp. Pharmacists, Am. Aircraft Owners and Pilots Assn., Air Safety Found., Nat. Assn. of Registered Parliamentarians, Civinettes (pres. Scottsdale chpt. 1960-61), Kappa Epsilon (recipient Career Achievement award 1986, Vanguard award 1991, Unicorn award 1993). Avocations: flying, skiing, swimming, hiking, writing. Office: Mt View Pharmacy 10565 N Tatum Blvd Ste B-118 Scottsdale AZ 85253-1095 E-mail: evelyn@mountainviewpharmacy.com.

TIMMONS, GERALD DEAN, pediatric neurologist; b. Rensselaer, Ind., June 1, 1931; s. Homer Timmons and Tamma Mildred (Spall) Rodgers; 1 child, Deanna Lynne; children from previous marriage: Jane Christina Timmons Mitchell, Ann Elizabeth, Mary Catherine. AB, Ind. U., 1953, MD, 1956. Diplomate Am. Bd. Psychiatry and Neurology. Intern Lima (Ohio) Meml. Hosp., 1956-57; resident Ind. U. Hosp., Indpls., 1957-59, 61-62; instr. neurology dept. Ind. U., 1962-64; practice medicine specializing in psychiatry and neurology, 1962-64; practice medicine specializing in pediatric neurology Akron, Ohio, 1964—; chief pediatric neurology Children's Hosp. Med. Ctr., 1964—2000; chmn. neurology subcouncil Coll. Medicine Northeastern Ohio Univs., Rootstown, 1978-99. Sr. examiner Am. Bd. Neurology and Psychiatry. Contbr. articles to profl. and scholarly jours. Served to capt. USAF, 1959-61. Mem. Summit County Med. Soc., Ohio Med. Soc., AMA, Am. Acad. Pediatrics, Am. Acad. Neurology (practice com. 1980-86, sec. child neurology sect. 2000—), Child Neurology Soc. (chmn. honors and awards com. 1978-88), Am. Soc. Internal Medicine, Am. Electroencephalographic Soc. Republican. Methodist. Office: Akron Pediatric Neurology 300 Locust St Ste 460 Akron OH 44302-1804

TIMMONS, GORDON DAVID, economics educator; b. Elbert, Tex., May 21, 1919; s. Walter James and Ella Mae (McCarson) T.; m. Jean Betty Kulhanek, Feb. 11, 1947; children: Kathy, Linda, Scott, Jim, Tamara, Dallas, Timothy, Kelly, Susanna. Student, U. Tex., 1937-40, U. Mont., 1961-64; BS, Utah State U., 1955; MS, Mont. State U., 1958. Enlisted USAF, 1939, advanced through grades to col., ret., 1961; instr. Columbia Basin Coll., Pasco, Wash., 1966-86. Pres. Assn. Higher Edn., 1969-72. Decorated Legion of Merit, Croix de Guerre (France). Mem. Acad. Polit. Sci., N.W. Econ. Conf. Democrat. Avocation: horse breeding. Home and Office: Star Rte Box 39-A Olney TX 76374-0039 E-mail: Timmons@brazosnet.com.

TIMMONS, SHARON L. retired elementary education educator; b. South Kansas City, Mo., July 25, 1949; d. Clyde George and Sarah Ethyl (Thrift) Manley; m. Joseph D. Timmons, June 6, 1970; children: Stacia, Matt. BSE, U. Kans., 1972; MA, U. Mo., Kansas City, Mo., 1980. Cert. elem., jr. high tchr., Mo; elem. tchr., Kans. Elem. team tchr. Loretto Acad., Kansas City, Mo., 1976-80; team tchr. 8th grade Ctr. Sch. Dist. 58, 1980-94; ret., 1994. Author: (Title II grants) For Indivdualized Math Program, Kansas City Rep. for Scientific Literacy. Mem. NEA, Assn. Women in Sci., Nat. Sci. Tchrs. Assn., CEA, Sigma Kappa,

TIMMONS, WILLIAM EVAN, corporate executive; b. Chattanooga, Dec. 27, 1930; s. Owen Walter and Doris (Eckenrod) T.; m. Mimi Bakshian, Sept. 28, 1966; children: Karen Leigh, Kimberly Anne, William Evan. Grad., Baylor Mil. Acad., Chattanooga, 1949; BS in Fgn. Svc., Georgetown U., 1959; postgrad., George Washington U., 1959-61. Aide to U.S. Senator Alexander Wiley, 1955-62; adminstrv. asst. to U.S. Rep. William Brock, 1963-69; dep. asst. to Pres. Richard M. Nixon, 1969-70, asst., 1970-74; asst. to Pres. Gerald R. Ford, 1974; pres. Timmons & Co. Inc., 1975-86, chmn. exec. com., 1986—. Mem. Fed. Property Rev. Bd., 1972-75, Pres.'s Trade Adv. Com., 1975-80; U.S. del. to Internat. Conf. on Viet Nam, Paris, 1973. Presdl. appointee U.S.-Japan Adv. Commn., 1983—85; nat. conv. dir. Reagan for Pres. Com., Detroit, 1980, Dallas, 1984, nat. polit. dir., 1980; exec. dir. Tenn. Rep. Com., 1962; mgr. Brock campaigns, 1962, 1964, 1966, 1968; dir. congl. rels. Nixon-Agnew campaign, 1968; coord. Nixon for Pres.; active Rep. Nat. Conv., Miami, Fla., 1968, 1972, dir. Pres. Ford com. Kansas City, 1976; mem. adv. com. Rep. Nat. Com. Conv., New Orleans, 1988, San Diego, 1996; mem. exec. com. Nat. Young Reps., 1965—67; dep. dir. for transition Office of Pres.-Elect, 1980—81; mem. faculty Nat. REp. campaign workshops, 1963—69; sr. adviser Bush for Pres. Com., New Orleans, 1988, Dole for Pres. Com., 1996; mem. adv. com. Bush for Pres., Rep. Nat. Conv., Phila., 2000; adviser Bush-Cheney Transition, 2000—01; bd. dirs. Radio Free Europe/Liberty, 1975—82, Georgetown U. Ctr. Strategic and Internat. Studies, 1982—85. With USAF, 1951—55. Named Outstanding Young Rep. of Year Nat. Rep. Com., 1965; recipient 1970 Ann. Achievement award Georgetown Alumni Club; citation for Disting. Service Baylor Mil. Acad. Alumni Assn., 1970 Mem. SCV, SAR, Soc. of the Cin., Columbia Country Club, George Towne Club, City Club, St. Alban's Tennis Club, Masons (33d degree). Home: 4426 Garfield St NW Washington DC 20007-1142 Office: Timmons & Co 1850 K St NW Ste 850 Washington DC 20006-2241 E-mail: BTimmons@aol.com.

TIMMONS, WILLIAM MILTON, producer, freelance writer, retired cinema arts educator, publisher, film maker; b. Houston, Apr. 21, 1933; s. Carter Charles and Gertrude Monte (Lee) T.; m. Pamela Cadorette, Dec. 24, 1975 (div. 1977). BS, U. Houston, 1958; MA, UCLA, 1961; PhD, U. So. Calif., 1975. Child actor Houston Jr. Theater, 1945-46; staff announcer Sta. KMCO, Conroe, Tex., 1951-52; prodn. asst. Sta. KUHT-TV, Houston, 1953-54, 56-57; teaching fellow UCLA, 1960-61; ops. asst. CBS-TV, Hollywood, Calif., 1961-62; prof. speech and drama Sam Houston State U., Huntsville, Tex., 1963-67; chmn. dept. cinema Los Angeles Valley Coll., Van Nuys, Calif., 1970-91, ret., 1992. Prodr. Sta. KPFK, L.A., 1959-60, 83-95; pub. Acad. Assocs., L.A., 1976-2000; proofreader, cons. Focal Press Pub. Co., N.Y.C., 1983-92; mem. ind. investigations group Ctr. for Inquiry; lectr. Ctr. for Inquiry-West. Author: Orientation to Cinema, 1986, Everything About the Bible That you Never Had Time to Look Up, 2002; contbr. articles to mags.; prodr., dir.: (radio programs) Campus Comments, 1963-67, numerous ednl. films, 1963—; prodr. ednl. series for cable TV, 1993—. With USNR, 1954-56. Named Hon. Tex. Ranger, State of Tex., Austin, 1946; U. Houston scholar, 1957. Mem. Mensa, U. So. Calif. Cinema-TV Alumni Assn., Red Masque Players, Secular Humanists L.A., Alpha Epsilon Rho, Delta Kappa Alpha. Democrat. Avocations: reading, writing, viewing movies. E-mail: miltonimmons@adelphia.net.

TIMMRECK, THOMAS C. health sciences and health administration educator; b. Montpelier, Idaho, June 15, 1946; s. Archie Carl and Janone (Jensen) T.; m. Ellen Prusse, Jan. 27, 1971; children: Chad Thomas, Benjamin Brian, Julie Anne. AA, Ricks Coll., 1968; BS, Brigham Young U., 1971; MEd, Oreg. State U., 1972; MA, No. Ariz. U., 1981; PhD, U. Utah, 1976. Program dir. Cache County Aging Program, Logan, Utah, 1972-73; asst. prof. div. health edn. Tex. Tech U., Lubbock, 1976-77; asst. prof. dept. health care adminstrn. Idaho State U., Pocatello, 1977-78; dept. chair, asst. prof. health services program No. Ariz. U., Flagstaff, 1978-84; cons., dir. grants Beth Israel Hosp., Denver, 1985; prof. dept. health scis. and human ecology, coordinator grad. studies, coordinator health adminstrn. and planning Calif. State U., San Bernardino, 1985—; pres. Health Care Mgmt. Assocs., 1985—. Presenter at nat. confs.; dept. chair health and wellness dept., faculty Loretto Heights Coll., Denver; adj. faculty Dept. Mgmt. U. Denver, Dept. Mgmt. and Health Adminstrn. U. Colo., Denver, dept. bus. adminstrn. U. Redlands (Calif.), U. So. Calif., L.A., Chapman U. Author: Dictionary of Health Services Management, rev. 2d edit., 1987, Health Services Cyclopedic Dictionary, 3d edit., An Introduction to Epidemiology, 1994, 2d edit., 1998, Planning and Program Development and Evaluation: A Handbook for Health Promotion, Aging, and Health Services, 1995; mem. editl. bd. Jour. Health Values, 1986—, Basic Epidemiological Methods and Biostats., Dictionary of Epidemiology and Public Health, 1996; contbr. numerous articles on health care adminstrn., behavioral health, gerontology and health edn. to profl. jours. Chmn., bd. dirs. Inland Counties Health System Agy.; mem. strategic planning com. chmn. Vis. Nurses Assn. of Inland Counties; bd. dirs. health svc. orgns. With U.S. Army, 1966-72, Vietnam. Mem. Assn. Advancement of Health Edn., Am. Acad. Mgmt., Assn. Univ. Programs in Health Care Adminstrn., Healthcare Forum. Republican. Mem. Lds Ch. Office: Calif State U Dept Health Scis & Human Ecology San Bernardino CA 92407

TIMMS, MICHELE, retired professional basketball player; b. Australia, June 28, 1965; Guard Australia's Women's Nat. Basketball League - Bulleen Boomers, 1984-85, Nunawading Spectres, 1985, Lotus Munchen, Germany, 1989-90, Perth Breakers, Australia, 1991-92, Basket Firenze, Italy, 1993-94, Sydney Flames, Australia, 1995, WTV Wuppertal, Germany, 1995-96, Phoenix Mercury, 1997—2001. Named WNBL Player of Yr., 1995, 96. Avocations: tennis, golf.*

TIMONEY, PETER JOSEPH, veterinarian, virologist, educator, consultant; b. Dublin, Ireland, June 5, 1941; came to U.S., 1983; s. John Francis and Evelyn Norah (Whittle) T.; m. Katherine Mary Murphy, Sept. 11, 1971; children: Peter, Caroline, Sarah, David. MVB, Nat. U., Dublin, 1964; MS, U. Ill., 1966; PhD, U. Dublin, 1974. Rsch. assoc. U. Ill., Urbana, 1964-66; rsch. officer Vet. Rsch. Lab., Abbotstown, Ireland, 1966-72; sr. rsch. officer equine diseases sect. Veterinary Rsch. Lab., Ireland, 1972-79; assoc. prof. diagnostic lab., dept. microbiology Cornell U., Ithaca, N.Y., 1979-81; sci. dir. Irish Equine Ctr., Johnstown, Ireland, 1981-83; assoc. prof. virology vet. sci. dept. U. Ky., Lexington, 1983-87, prof. virology, assoc. chair for rsch., 1987-89, Frederick Van Lennep chair, 1988—, acting chair, 1989-90, chair, 1990-99, 2002—; bd. dirs. Gluck Equine Rsch. Ctr., 1990—. Cons. Daryl Labs., Inc., Santa Clara, Calif., 1981-86, Ft. Dodge (Iowa) Animal Health Lab., 1986-92, 94—. Fellow Royal Coll. Vet. Surgeons, World Equine Vet. Assn. (pres. 1995-99); mem. AAAS, Am. Assn. Equine Practitioners, Am. Soc. Microbiology, Am. Soc. Virology, U.S. Animal Health Assn. Avocations: reading, gardening. Office: Gluck Equine Rsch Ctr 108 Gluck Ctr Lexington KY 40506-0001 E-mail: ptimoney@uky.edu.

TIMOUR, JOHN ARNOLD, retired librarian, medical bibliography and library science educator; b. Hartford, Conn., Jan. 20, 1926; s. John Alfred and Karin Elizabeth (Levin) T.; m. Betty Jo Lord, Mar. 23, 1952; children— Jon, David, Alan BA, Miami U., Oxford, Ohio, 1951; postgrad., Fla. State U., 1951-52; MA, George Washington U., 1960; M.L.S., U. Md., 1969. Tng. and Med. Lit. Analysis and Retrieval System liaison officer Nat. Library of Medicine, Bethesda, Md., 1966-69; dir. library services Conn. Regional Med. Program-Yale U., New Haven, 1969-73; dir. Mid-Eastern Med. Library Service Coll. Physicians of Phila., 1973-75; univ. librarian Thomas Jefferson U., Phila., 1975-87. Instr. U.S. Army Reserve, Hamden, Conn., 1970-73; lectr. library sci. So. Conn. State Coll., New Haven, 1970-71; adj. prof. library sci. Drexel U., Phila., 1976-78 Contbr. articles to profl. jours. Served to RM2-c USN, 1943-46, PTO; 2d lt. USAF, 1951-53, lt. col. USAR, ret. Mem. Assn. Acad. Health Sci. Libr. Dirs., Am. Med. Writers Assn. (pres. Phila. chpt. 1986-87), Med. Libr. Assn. (bd. dirs. 1978-81, Eliot prize 1974), Acad. of Health Info. Profls. (disting. mem.), Spl. Librs. Assn. (pres. Phila. chpt. 1979-80), Conn. Assn. Health Sci. Librs. (hon. life), Sigma Xi (bull. editor Jefferson chpt. 1980-86, recognition cert. 1982), Beta Phi Mu. Clubs: Washington Yacht and Country. Episcopalian. Avocations: golfing, chess, Macintosh computers. Home: 6000 River Rd Apt 10 Washington NC 27889 E-mail: jtimour@coastalnet.com.

TIMPANE, PHILIP MICHAEL, education educator, policy analyst; b. Troy, N.Y., Nov. 27, 1934; s. Philip Thomas and Rita (Killeen) T.; m. Genevieve LaGrua, Nov. 30, 1957; children: Michael J., Joseph T., Paul J., David A. AB, Cath. U. Am., 1956, MA, 1964, LLD (hon.), 1991; MPA, Harvard U., 1970; LittD (hon.), Wagner Coll., 1986. Historian Joint Chiefs of Staff Dept. Def., 1961-65; spl. asst. civil rights Office of Sec. Def., 1965-68; edn. policy planner HEW, 1968-72; sr. fellow Brookings Instn., 1972-74; dir. edn. policy ctr. RAND Corp., 1974-77; dep. dir. Nat. Inst. Edn., Washington, 1977-80, dir., 1980-81; prof. edn. Columbia U. Tchrs. Coll., N.Y.C., 1981—, dean, 1981-84, pres., 1984-94; mem. Aspen Inst. Edn. Program, 1974-77, 87—; v.p. and sr. scholar Carnegie Found. for Advancement Tchg., Princeton, N.J., 1994-97; sr. adv. for edn. policy RAND, Washington, 1997—. Author: Corporate Interest in Public Education in the Cities, 1982; co-author: Youth Policy in Transition, 1976, Business Impact on Education and Child Development Reform, 1991, Rhetoric Versus Reality: What We Know and What We Need to Know about Vouchers and Charter Schools, 2001; co-editor: Planned Variation in Education, 1975, Work Incentives and Income Guarantees, 1975, Ethical and Legal Issues in Social Experimentation, 1975, Higher Education and School Reform, 1998, Rediscovering the Democratic Purposes of Education, 2000; editor: Federal Interest in Financing Schooling, 1978. Mem. Arlington (Va.) Sch. Bd., 1972-76, chmn., 1973-74; bd. dirs. Children's TV Workshop, 1989-99, Jobs for the Future, 1995—, So. Edn. Found., 1995—, Inst. for Ednl. Leadership, 1999—. Democrat. Roman Catholic. Office: Aspen Inst Edn Program 1 Dupont Cir Ste 700 Washington DC 20036 E-mail: mike.timpane@aspeninst.org.

TIMPANI, NANCY EVELYN, elementary school educator; b. Jackson, Miss., Oct. 26, 1952; d. Charlie and Joyce N.; m. Tim Timpani, June 15, 1974; children: Melody, John. BS, Stephen F. Austin State U., 1974. Cert. elem. tchr., Tex. Tchr. North Shore Elem. Galena Park (Tex.) Ind. Sch. Dist., 1974-77, 86—. Mem. adv. bd. Houston Chronicle, 1999-2000. Liaison Mus. Health and Med. Sci., Houston, 1995—; mem. PTA, Tex. Mem. Assn. Tex. Profl. Educators (bldg. rep. 1990-95, 98—), Tex. Sci. Tchr. Assn. Avocations: music, reading. Office: North Shore Elem 14310 Duncannon Dr Houston TX 77015-2514

TIMPE, RONALD ERNEST, insurance company executive; b. Atkinson, Kans., July 9, 1939; BS Math., Lewis & Clark Coll., 1961; grad. advanced mgmt. program, Harvard U., 1979. CLU. With Standard Ins. Co., Portland, Oreg., 1968—, asst. actuary, 1973—, asst. v.p., actuary, 1980—, v.p. group pensions, sr. v.p. group ins. and corp. fin. svcs., pres., CEO, 1993—, chmn., pres., CEO, also bd. dirs. Bd. dirs. Oreg. Bus. Coun., Oreg. Ind. Coll. Found., Oreg. Symphony. Fellow Soc. of Actuaries; mem. Portland Met. C. of C. (past chmn.). Office: StanCorp Fin Group Inc 1100 SW 6th Ave Portland OR 97204

TIMPERLAKE, EDWARD THOMAS, writer; b. Perth Amboy, N.J., Nov. 22, 1946; s. James Elwood Timperlake Jr. and Joan Dorothy (Conkling) Maurer; m. Barbette Runckel, Aug. 10, 1969 (div. 1993); children: Tara, Kimberly; m. Cathryn Porcelli, Apr. 8, 2000. BS, U.S. Naval Acad., 1969; MBA, Cornell U., 1977. Commd. 2d lt. USMC, 1969, advanced through grades to lt. col., 1985, ret., 1993; asst. venture mgr. Exxon Enterprise, N.Y.C., 1977-78; sect. mgr. T.A.S.C., Arlington, Va., 1978-81; dep. dir. Nat. Dir. Vietnam Vets. Leadership Program, Action Agy., Washington, 1981-83; dir. mobilization plans and requirements Office of Sec. Def., 1984; campaign staff George Bush for Pres., 1988; asst. sec. Dept. Vets. Affairs, Washington, 1989-93; pres. T-9 Group, 1993-95; profl. staff rules com. U.S. House of Reps., Washington, 1996-99. Author: Year of the Rat, 1998, Red Dragon Rising, 1999; contbr. numerous articles to profl. jours. Bd. dirs. Louis Puller Vietnam Children's Fund. Mem. Naval Acad. Alumni Assn., Army-Navy Club, N.Y. Yacht Club. Home: 1027 22d St Arlington VA 22202

TIMPTE, ROBERT NELSON, secondary school educator; b. Mpls., Dec. 4, 1925; s. Oscar William and Mildred Marie (Nelson) T. BS in Edn., U. Minn., 1949, postgrad., 1955-73; MA in History, U. Iowa, 1956. Jr. high english, social studies tchr. Bloomington (Minn.) Pub. Schs., 1955-63, secondary schs. social studies coord., 1963-65, K-12 social studies coord., 1965-73, jr. high sch. social studies tchr., 1973-85. Condr. insvc. in field. Editor curriculum guides and catalogs Bloomington K-12 Social Studies Guides, 1963-73, Human Rels. Guide: Inter and Intracultural Education, 1974; creator Realia (Material Culture Kits) Asia and Africa, 1966-73. Cons. Human Rights Commn., Bloomington, 1970—73; City Hall tour guide City of Bloomington, 1963—73; treas., bd. dirs. Hidden Village Townhomes, Golden Valley, Minn. India Inst. grant, 1966; recipient Omar Bonderud Human Rights award Bloomington Human Rights Commn., 1974, WCCO Radio Good Neighbor award, 1974. Mem. Am. Fedn. Tchrs., Minn. Ret. Tchrs. Assn., Minn. Coun. for Social Studies (treas., conv. arrangements chmn.). Democrat. Avocations: travel, the Arts, American Indian culture research.

TIMS, ROBERT AUSTIN, data processing official, pilot; b. Seattle, Dec. 21, 1942; s. Robert Mitchell Tims and Winifred Eileen (Dorgan) Bristol; m. Jane Moore, June 6, 1980. Student, Pacific Union Coll., 1960-61, Alpha Aviation Sch., 1976-77; BS in Computer Info. Sys. with honors, Ark. State U., 1998. Lic. comml. and instrument pilot; cert. flight instr. Engring. technician Tex. Instruments, Inc., Ridgecrest, Calif., 1966-67, various projects, Conn., N.Y. and N.J., 1967-70; homesteader Leslie, Ark., 1970-77; chief pilot/flight instr. Sharp Aviation Co., Jonesboro, 1977-79; chief pilot Pizza Inn of Ark., 1979-83; data processing mgr., chief pilot Realty Assocs. Brokerage, Inc., 1983-91, microanalyst, 1991-94. Pres., owner ABS Logic, Inc., computers and programming cons., Jonesboro, 1985—; programmer Jimco Lamp Mfg., Bono, Ark., 1998—99; programmer, analyst TEK Systems, Memphis, 2000—. Served with USN, 1962-66. Recipient Nat. Collegiate Bus. Merit award. Mem. CAP (squadron comdr. Jonesboro 1986-93), Am. Philatelic Soc., Planetary Soc., Nat. Space Soc., SETI Inst., Beta Gamma Sigma. Avocation: philately. Home and Office: 1616 Alonzo St Jonesboro AR 72401-4802

TINAGLIA, MICHAEL LEE, lawyer; b. Chgo., Dec. 21, 1952; s. Michael Leo and Josephine (Esposito) T.; m. Lucia Yolando Guzzo, Oct. 14, 1978; children: Laura, Lisa, Elena. BA, Northwestern U., 1974; JD, DePaul U., 1977. Bar: Ill. 1977, U.S. Dist. Ct. (no. dist.) Ill. 1978, U.S. Dist. Ct. (ea. dist.) Wis. 1986. Assoc. Arnold & Kadjan, Chgo., 1977-79; ptnr. Leader & Tinaglia, 1979-86; assoc. Laser, Schostok, Kolman & Frank, 1987-92; prin. Law Office of Michael Lee Tinaglia Ltd., 1992-93, 2000—; equity ptnr. DiMonte & Lizak, Park Ridge, Ill., 1994-99. V.p., corp. counsel Tiara Med. Sys., Inc., Oak Forest, Ill. Contbr. articles to profl. jours. Alderman City Coun., Park Ridge, 1997—, mem. pub. safety com., 1997—, mem. procedures and regulations com. Mem. Ill. Bar Assn., Chgo. Bar Assn. Roman Catholic. Avocations: skiing, guitar. Office: Law Offices of Michael Lee Tinaglia 161 N Clark St Ste 2550 Chicago IL 60601-3246

TINDALL, GEORGE BROWN, historian, educator; b. Greenville, S.C., Feb. 26, 1921; s. Goin Roscoe and Nellie Evelyn (Brown) Tindall; m. Carliss Blossom McGarrity, June 29, 1946; children: Bruce McGarrity, Blair Alston Mercer. AB, Furman U., 1942, LittD, 1971; MA, U. N.C., 1948, PhD, 1951. Asst. prof. history Eastern Ky. State Coll., 1950-51; asst. prof. U. Miss., 1951-52; asst. prof. Woman's Coll. U. N.C., Chapel Hill, 1952-53, assoc. prof., 1958-64, prof., 1964-69, Kenan prof., 1969-90, Kenan prof. emeritus, 1990—; asst. prof. La. State U., 1953-58. Vis. prof. Coll. Charleston, 1951, Kyoto Am. Studies Sem., 1977; Fulbright guest prof. U. Vienna, 1967—68; mem. Inst. Advanced Study, 1963—64, Ctr. Advanced Study Behavioral Scis., 1979—80. Author: (book) South Carolina Negroes 1877-1900, 1952, The Emergence of the New South, 1913-1945, 1967 (Jules F. Landry award, 1968, Mayflower Cup, 1968, Lillian E. Smith award, 1968, Charles S. Syndor award, 1968), The disruption of the Solid South, 1972, The Persistent Tradition in New South Politics, 1975, The Ethnic Southerners, 1976, America: A Narrative History, 1984; author: (with David Shi) America: A Narrative History, 5th edit., 1999; author: Natives and Newcomers: Ethnic Southerners and Southern Ethnics, 1995; editor: The Pursuit of Southern History, 1964, A Populist Reader, 1966. Fellow Guggenheim, 1957—58, Social Sci. Rsch. Coun., 1959—60, Ctr. Advanced Study Behavioral Scis., 1979—80. Mem.: So. Hist. Assn. (pres. 1973), Orgn. Am. Historians, N.C. Lit. and Hist. Soc., Hist. Soc. N.C. (pres. 1990), Am. Hist. Assn. Home: Carol Woods 750 Weaver Dairy Rd Apt 242 Chapel Hill NC 27514 E-mail: tindall@email.unc.edu., historymill@nc.rr.com.

TINDALL, JON W. research scientist; b. Trenton, N.J., May 21, 1940; s. John William and Virginia K. (Snell) T.; m. Linda Mae Tindall, Apr. 21, 1983; children: William, Christine, Matthew. BA in Math., Claremont Men's Coll., Calif., 1972; MS in Indsl. Engring., UCLA, 1978; postgrad., U. So. Calif., 1975-77. Dept. mgr. Aerojet Gen., Azusa, Calif., 1965-69; staff engr. TRW, Redondo Beach, 1970-81; prin. investigator McDonald Douglas, Seal Beach, 1981-86; assoc. fellow Nichols Rsch., Newport Beach, 1986-93, fellow, sr. prin. investigator Colorado Springs, Colo., 1993—2000; chief engr. Millennium Engring., 2000—. Tech. project mgr. CSC/Nichols Rsch., Colorado Springs, 1997-2000; data fusion working group USAF, Colorado Springs, 1996-98, infared discrimination group, Newport Beach, Calif., 1990-94; radar systems analyst TRW, L.A., 1980-86. Designer: (realtime software) Engagement Coordination System, 1998; author tech. publs. in field. Recipient medal for acquisitions and technology Jacques Gansler, 1999. Mem. AIAA. Avocations: golf, bowling, computer games. Office: Millennium Enging 5450 Tech Center Dr Colorado Springs CO 80919 E-mail: tindallJ@nichols.com.

TINDALL, ROBERT EMMETT, lawyer, educator; b. N.Y.C., Jan. 2, 1934; s. Robert E. and Alice (McGonigle) T.; children: Robert Emmett IV, Elizabeth. BS in Marine Engring., SUNY, 1955; postgrad., Georgetown U. Law Sch., 1960-61; LLB, U. Ariz., 1963; LLM, NYU, 1967; PhD, City U., London, 1975. Bar: Ariz. 1963. Mgmt. trainee GE, Schenectady, N.Y., Lynn, Mass., Glens Falls, N.Y., 1955-56, 58-60; law clk. Haight, Gardner, Poor and Havens, N.Y.C., 1961; prin., mem. Robert Emmett Tindall & Assocs., Tucson, 1963—; assoc. prof. mgmt. U. Ariz., 1969—. Vis. prof. Grad. Sch. of Law, Soochow U., China, 1972, Grad. Bus. Ctr., London, 1974, NYU, 1991—; dir. MBA program U. Ariz., Tucson, 1975-81, dir. entrepreneurship program, 1984-86; investment cons. Kingdom of Saudi Arabia, 1981—; lectr. USIA, Eng., India, Mid. East, 1974; lectr. bus. orgn. and regulatory laws Southwestern Legal Found., Acad. Am. and Internat. Law, 1976-80. Actor cmty. theatres, Schenectady, 1955-56, Harrisburg, Pa., 1957-58, Tucson, 1961-71; appeared in films Rage, 1971, Showdown at OK Corral, 1971, Lost Horizon, 1972; appeared in TV programs Gunsmoke, 1972, Petrocelli, 1974; author: Multinational Enterprises, 1975; contbr. articles on domestic and internat. bus. to profl. jours. Served to lt. USN, 1956-58. Fellow Ford Found., 1965-67; grantee Asia Found., 1972-73. Mem. Strategic Mgmt. Soc., State Bar of Ariz., Acad. Internat. Bus., Screen Actors Guild, Honourable Soc. of Mid. Temple (London), Phi Delta Phi, Beta Gamma Sigma, Assn. Corp. Growth, Royal Overseas League (London). Home: PO Box 42196 Tucson AZ 85733-2196 Office: Coll Bus & Public Adminstrn U Ariz Dept Mgmt & Policy Tucson AZ 85721-0001

TING, ALBERT CHIA, bioengineering researcher; b. Hong Kong, Sept. 7, 1950; came to U.S., 1957; s. William Su and Katherine Sung T.; m. Shirley Roung Wang, July 30, 1988. BA, UCLA, 1973; MS, Calif. State U., L.A., 1975, Calif. Inst. Tech., 1977; PhD, U. Calif., San Diego, 1983. Rsch. asst. Calif. Inst. Tech., Pasadena, 1975-77, U. Calif., San Diego, 1982-83; sr. staff engr. R&D Am. Med. Optics, Irvine, 1983-86; project engr., rsch. Allergan Med. Optics, 1987-89, sr. project engr., rsch., 1989-92, sr. project engr., enging., 1993-94; bioengr. cons. Pharmacia Iovision, Inc., 1995-97; sr. engr. D & E, 1997, sr. engr., project mgr., 1998-99; rsch. and devel. mgr., surg. Bausch & Lomb, Irvine, 1999—2001; R & D mgr. Visiogen, Inc., 2001—02, sr. R & D mgr., 2002—. Inventor med. and optical devices, recipient patent awards 1988, 89, 91, 92, 93, 95; contbr. articles to sci. jours. Mem. AAAS, Biomed. Engring. Soc., Assn. for Rsch. in Vision and Ophthalmology, Biomed. Optics Soc. Office: Visiogen Inc 4 Jenner St # 180 Irvine CA 92618

TING, JOSEPH K. mechanical engineer; b. Manila, Jan. 23, 1950; s. Manuel and Lourdes (Co) T.; m. Monique Crenn, Sept. 2, 1978; children: Audrey Adrienne, William Alexander. BSME, De La Salle U., Manila, 1972; MSc, MIT, 1974; MBA, U. Ottawa, Ont., Can., 1986. Registered profl. engr., NY, Mass., Ont., Can. Product engr. Brier Mfg. Co., Providence, 1974-75; plant mgr. Nemo Brier Ltd., Hull, Que., Can., 1975; assoc. engr., asst. rsch. officer Nat. Rsch. Coun., Ont., 1975-86; sr. mech. engr., supr. Dormitory Authority/State of NY, Delmar, 1986—2001; v.p. engring. svcs. Integrated Faculty Systems, Syracuse, 2002—. Adj. prof. Rensselaer Polytechnic Inst., Troy, N.Y., 1993—; ednl. counselor MIT Admissions, Cambridge, Mass., 1993-2000. Contbg. author: Canadian Financial Managment, 1983, Essentials of Engineering Economics, 1983, Computer Aided Design Drafting, 1987, ASHRAE Std. 15-1992, 1992; inventor Rolls-Royce RB211 jet engine into a gas pumping engine. Pres. Chinese Am. Comm. Ctr., Albany, N.Y., 1993-94, bd. dirs. 1993-2002, chmn. facility devel. and mgmt. com., 1997-2000; bd. dirs. Habitat for Humanity, 2001—. Grantee E.I. DuPont Co.; recipient Disting. Svc. award Chinese Am. Comm. Ctr., 1991, Outstanding Svcs. award, 1996. Mem.: ASHRAE (chpt. pres. 1991—92, chmn. refrigeration com. 1993—94, regional chmn. northeastern U.S. 1994—97, bd. dirs. Atlanta 1994—97, asst. regional chmn. 1992—94, 2000—01, nominating com. 1997—98, 2000—, regional vice-chmn. rsch. promotion 1998—99, govtl. affairs mem. tech., energy and govtl. activities com. 1999—2000, hist. com. 2000—, Black Ink award 1990, Golden Gavel award 1992, Disting. Svc. award 1997, Regional award of Merit 1998), U.S. Energy Assn. (Pub. Svc. Energy award 2001), Gen. Soc. Mechanics and Tradesmen, N.E. Tae Kwon Do Assn. (black belt 2001), MIT Alumni Club (pres. 1992—94, bd. dirs. 1992—2000, fin. dir. 1996—98). Roman Catholic. Avocations: tennis, swimming, organizing seminars and confs., martial arts (Tae Kwon Do Black Belt). Home: PO Box 234 Delmar NY 12054-0234 Office: Integrated Facility Systems 459 Burnet Ave Syracuse NY 13203- E-mail: jting@integratedfacilitysys.com., tingj@rpi.edu.

TING, ROBERT YEN-YING, physicist; b. Kwei-yang, China, Mar. 8, 1942; came to U.S. 1965; s. Chi-yung and Shou-feng (Yang) T.; m. Teresa Yen-chun Ting, June 3, 1967; children: Paul H., Peggy Y. BS, Nat. Taiwan U., 1964; MS, MIT, 1967; PhD, U. Calif., San Diego, 1971. Rsch. engr. U.S. Naval Rsch. Lab., Washington, 1971-77, supervisory engr., 1977-80, supervisory physicist Orlando, Fla., 1980-97; prof. dept. chemistry and dept. materials engring. U. Ctrl. Fla., 1997—. Prof. George Washington U., 1972-80. Contbr. over 100 articles in rheology, polymer and acoustics to profl. jours. Fellow Acoustical Soc. Am.; mem. Am. chem. Soc., Am. Ceramics Soc., Am. Inst. Chem. Engrs. Office: U Central Fla Dept Chemistry Dept Chem and Mech Engring Orlando FL 32816-2366 E-mail: rting@pegasus.cc.ucf.edu.

TING, SAMUEL CHAO CHUNG, physicist, educator; b. Ann Arbor, Mich., Jan. 27, 1936; s. Kuan H. and Jeanne (Wong) Ting; m. Susan Carol Marks, Apr. 28, 1985; children: Jeanne Min, Amy Min, Christopher M. BS in Engring., U. Mich., 1959, MS, 1960, PhD in Physics, 1962, ScD (hon.), 1978, Chinese U. Hong Kong, 1987, U. Bologna, Italy, 1988, Columbia U., 1990, U. Sci. and Tech., China, 1990, Moscow State U., 1991, U. Bucharest, Romania, 1993. Ford Found. fellow CERN (European Orgn. Nuc. Rsch.), Geneva, 1963; instr. physics Columbia U., 1964, asst. prof., 1965—67; group leader Deutsches Elektronen-Synchrotron, Hamburg, Germany, 1966; assoc. prof. physics MIT, Cambridge, 1967—68, prof., 1969—; Thomas Dudley Cabot Inst. prof. M.I.T., 1977—. Program cons. divsn. particles and fields Am. Phys. Soc., 1970; hon. prof. Beijing Normal Coll., 1987, Jiatong U., Shanghai, 1987, U. Bologna, Italy, 1988. Assoc. editor Nuc. Physics B, 1970, editl. bd. Nuc. Instruments and Methods, Mathematical Modeling; contbr. articles to profl. jours. Recipient Nobel prize in Physics, 1976, De Gasperi prize in Sci., Italian Republic, 1988, Ernest Orlando Lawrence award, U.S. Govt., 1976, Gold medal in Sci., City of Brescia, Italy, 1988, Golden Leopard award, Town of Taormina, 1988, Forum Engelberg prize, 1966, Pub. Svc. medal, NASA, 2001; fellow Am. Acad. Arts and Scis., 1975. Mem.: NAS, Seutsche Acad. Naturforscher Leopoldina, Russian Acad. Sci., Acad. Sinica, Pakistani Acad. Sci. Office: MIT Dept Physics 51 Vassar St Cambridge MA 02139-4308

TING, SHAO KUANG, artist, educator; b. Beijing, Oct. 7, 1939; came to U.S., 1980; s. Jun Sheng and Shiang Jun (Lee) T.; m. Daxi Zhang, Oct. 8, 1968 (div. Oct. 1987); children: Angelina, Li. B degree, Ctrl. Acad. Arts & Design, Beijing, 1962. Prof. Yunnan Inst. Arts, Kunming, Peoples Republic of China, 1962-80; lectr. dept. visual arts UCLA, 1983; profl. artist Beverly Hills, Calif., 1980—. Prof. Ctrl. Acad. Arts & Design, Beijing, 1992—, U. Shanghai (People's Republic of China), Sch. Fine Arts, 1992—, U. Shan Xi, Taiyuan, People's Republic of China, 1992—, Yunan Inst. Arts, 1992—. One-man shows include Ginza Art Mus., Tokyo, 1988, Studio 47 Gallery, N.Y.C., 1989, Bernheim Gallerr, Paris, 1990, Historical Mus., Beijing, 1992; exhibited in group shows at Internat. Art Expo, 1986-94, Floriade Artist, Amsterdam, The Netherlands, 1991, Exhbn. by Chinese Artists in USA, Taipei, Taiwan, 1994; prin. works include mural The Great Hall of the People, People's Republic of China, 1989-90, Mus. Shanghai, Mus. Beijing, Matsuzakaya Gallery, Nagoya, Japan. Artist World Fedn. of UN, 1993, 94, 95; artist, donator UNICEF Charity Art Bazar, Tokyo, 1990, Midwest Inundation, L.A., 1993. Recipient Best of Show award U. So. Calif., 1984; recipient Outstanding Chinese Am. Role Model award Chinese Cultural Club Orange County, 1993, Pan Pacific Performing Arts, Internat., 1993; Ting Shao Kuang Day proclaimed by Mayor of Sante Fe, 1993; recipient Golden Image award Transpacific, Face and XO mags., 1994. Mem. Chinese Artists Assn. (pres. 1992—), Pang Xunqin Art Mus. (hon. curator 1992—). Avocations: music, literature, movies. Home: 707 N Alpine Dr Beverly Hills CA 90210-3305

TING, YU-CHEN, science educator, researcher; b. Hsia-Yi Hsien, China, Oct. 3, 1920; arrived in U.S., 1948; s. Jin-yung Ting and Yi-ying Wang; m. Jovina Chen, June 25, 1959; children: Andrew, Claire. BS, Nat. Henan U., Kaifeng, China, 1945; MS in Agr., Cornell U., 1951; PhD, La. State U., 1954. Tchg. asst. Nat. Henan U., 1944—48; rsch. asst. La. State U., Baton Rouge, 1951—54; postdoctoral rschr. Harvard U., Cambridge, Mass., 1954—58, rsch. fellow, 1958—62; asst. prof. Boston Coll., Chestnut Hill, 1962—64, assoc. prof., 1964—66, prof., 1966—91, prof. emeritus, 1991—. Cons. Cetus, Madison, Wis., 1982—85, Sci. Press of China, N.Y.C., 1992—; advisor Gerson and Lehrman, N.Y.C., 2001—. Author: Chromosomes of Maize-Teosinte Hybrids, 1964; contbr. articles to profl. jours. Com. mem. Nat. Assn. Chinese-Ams., Boston, 1975—86. Fellow sr. fellow, NAS, 1978; grantee rsch. grantee, NSF, 1983, Pioneer Hi-Bred Internat., Ames, Iowa, 1979. Fellow: AAAS. Achievements include discovery of meiosis and chromosome number of sweet potato plant; proposal that abnormal chromosome 10 in maize was originated by A-B translocation; investigation of inversion polymorphism of teosintes and maize; study of chromosome fine structures, anther culture and cloning of maize. Avocations: swimming, volleyball. Home: 230 Bonad Rd Chestnut Hill MA 02467 Office: Dept Biology Boston Coll 144 Commonwealth Ave Chestnut Hill MA 02467 Fax: 617-552-2011. E-mail: tiny@bc.edu.

TINGELSTAD, JON BUNDE, retired physician; b. McVille, N.D., Jan. 15, 1935; s. Sophus B. and Mabelle (Bunde) T.; m. Marcia Ayers, Dec. 17, 1960; children: Paul, Catherine, David. BA, U. N.D., 1957, BS, 1958; MD, Harvard U., 1960. Diplomate Am. Bd. Pediatrics. Intern Children's Hosp. Med. Ctr., Boston, 1960-61, resident, 1961-62, U. Colo. Med. Ctr., Denver, 1962-63; fellow in pediatric cardiology Children's Hosp., Buffalo, 1965-67; asst. prof. pediatrics Med. Coll. Va., Richmond, 1967-71, assoc. prof., 1971-76; prof., vice chmn. pediatrics East Carolina U. Sch. Medicine, Greenville, N.C., 1976-77, prof., chmn. pediatrics, 1977-2000. Mem. Greenville City Bd. Edn., 1978-82, chmn., 1981-82. Served to capt. USAF, 1963-65. Fellow Am. Acad. Pediatrics, Am. Coll. Cardiology; mem. Am. Bd. Pediatrics, Phi Beta Kappa, Phi Eta Sigma. Home: 103 Providence Pl Chocowinity NC 27817-8940 Office: E Carolina U Sch Med Dept Pediatrics Greenville NC 27858-4354 E-mail: JonBTing1@msn.com.

TINGLE, AUBREY JAMES, pediatric immunologist, research administrator; b. St. Paul, Can., June 28, 1943; s. Cyril Nisbet Tingle and Margaret Lucy (Fraser) Tarbuck; m. Valerie Jean Anderson, Nov. 2, 1968; children: Heather Lynn, Brian James. MD, U. Alta., Edmonton, 1967; PhD, McGill U., Montreal, Que., Can., 1974. Asst. prof. dept. pediatrics U. B.C., Vancouver, Can., 1974-79, head div. immunology dept. pediatrics Can., 1974-86, assoc. prof. Can., 1979-86, prof. Can., 1986—, prof. dept. pathology Can., 1986—; dir. rsch. B.C. Rsch. Inst. for Children's and Women's Health, 1992-2001; asst. dean rsch. Faculty of Medicine, U. B.C., 1992-2001; v.p. rsch. & edn. Children's & Women's Health Ctr B.C., 1997-2001; pres., CEO Michael Smith Found. for Health Rsch., 2001—. Fellow Royal Coll. Physicians and Surgeons Can., Soc. Pediatric Research, Am. Acad. Pediatrics; mem. Western Soc. Pediatric Research. Office: Michael Smith Found 1285 W Broadway Vancouver BC Canada V6H 3X8 E-mail: atingle@msfhr.org.

TINGLE, JAMES O'MALLEY, retired lawyer; b. N.Y.C., June 12, 1928; s. Thomas Jefferson and Mercedes (O'Malley) T. BS, U. Mont., 1950, BA, LL.B., U. Mont., 1952; LL.M., U. Mich., 1953, S.JD, 1958. Bar: Calif. 1959, Mont. 1952, N.Y. 1961. Asst. prof. law U. Mont., Missoula, 1955-56; atty. Shell Oil Co., N.Y.C., 1957-62; assoc. Pillsbury, Madison & Sutro, San Francisco, 1962-68, ptnr., 1969-2000. Author: The Stockholder's Remedy of Corporate Dissolution, 1959; editor: State Antitrust Laws, 1974. Served to 1st lt. USAF, 1953-55. William W. Cook fellow U. Mich. Mem. Mont. Bar Assn., Calif. Bar Assn., ABA Democrat.

TINGLEY, FLOYD WARREN, retired physician; b. Charlotte, N.C., Nov. 22, 1933; s. Floyd Warren Sr. and Janie (Suggs) T.; m. Sandra Carpenter, Aug. 20, 1955 (div. Dec. 1984); children: Sheryl Tingley Hagen, David Alan; m. Johnette Hill, Apr. 5, 1985. BA in English, Emory U., 1955, MD, 1959. Diplomate Am. Bd. Internal Medicine (bd. govs. 1986-92). Intern USAF Hosp., Lackland AFB, Tex., 1959-60; resident in internal medicine Parkland Meml. Hosp., Dallas, 1963-65, fellow in cardiology, 1965-66; pvt. practice specializing in internal medicine Arlington, Tex., 1966-88; med. dir. southwestern region Met. Life Ins. Co., Irving, 1988-90; regional practice leader William M. Mercer Inc., 1990-91; v.p., sr. med. dir. Provident Life and Accident Co., Chattanooga, 1991-92; v.p., nat. med. dir. Travelers Ins. Cos., Hartford, Conn., 1992-94; sr. v.p., chief med. officer Kemper Nat. Svcs., Plantation, Fla., 1995-2000, ret., 2000. Apptd. Tex. Commn. on Health Care Reimbursement Alternatives, 1987; bd. dirs. Riverside Nat. Bank, Grand Prairie, Tex. Contbr. articles to profl. jours. Pres. Arlington YMCA, 1971; chmn. budget com. Family Services, Ft. Worth, 1973; participant Health Policy Agenda for Am. People, Chgo., 1984-87; trustee Tex. Med. Liability Trust, Austin, 1987-88. Capt. USAF, 1958-63. Fellow ACP (pres. Tex. chpt. 1981); mem. AMA (chmn. sect. coun. internal medicine, 1979-88), Am. Soc. Internal Medicine (pres. 1986-87), Tex. Med. Assn. (treas. 1978-85, alt. del. to AMA 1985-91, commendation 1985), Tarrant County Med. Soc. (pres. Arlington br. 1974, del. to Tex. Med. Assn., Community Svc. award 1983). Presbyterian. Avocations: photography, sailing, gardening, computer hobbies. Home: 2709 Park Place Ct Arlington TX 76016-5891

TINGLEY, WALTER WATSON, computer systems manager; b. Portland, Maine, July 24, 1946; s. Edward Allen Tingley and Ruth Annie (Howard) Tuttle; m. Elizabeth A. Fletcher, May 1970 (div. 1975); m. Carol S. Gadoury, Dec. 1998. BS, U. Md., 1974. Programmer analyst U.S. Ry. Assn., Washington, 1974-80, Digital Equipment Corp., Maynard, Mass., 1980-81, Interactive Mgmt. Sys., Belmont, 1981; sys. designer Martin Marietta Data Sys., Greenbelt, Md., 1982-84; mgr. computer ops. Genex, Rockville, 1984; sys. mgr. Applied Rsch. Corp., Landover, 1985; programmer analyst Input/Output Computer Svcs., Washington, 1986-87, Lockheed Engring. and Scis., Las Vegas, Nev., 1987-91, Los Alamos (N.Mex.) Nat. Lab., 1992-96, Miller Internat., Denver, 1997-99, Ferrell Ventures, Denver, 1999—. Author tech. book revs., software revs. With USAF, 1964-68. Mem. Computer Soc. of IEEE, Assn. Computing Machinery. Avocations: skiing, hiking, swimming. Home: 8271 Johnson Ct Arvada CO 80005-2155

TINGWALD, GEORGE RUHL, architect, healthcare planner, physician; b. Cleve., June 2, 1955; s. Fred Ruhl and Helen Marie (Reeves) T.; m. Ellen Louise Henderson, May 12, 1989; children: Karl Fredrick, Mark Edward. BA, U. Chgo., 1977; MD, Ohio State U., 1981; M in Arch., Columbia U., 1987. Architect Skidmore, Owings & Merrill, N.Y., 1988-89, San Francisco, 1989-91, Anshen & Allen, San Francisco, 1991-93; dir. healthcare design Skidmore, Owings & Merrill, L.L.P., 1993—. Sect. leader Ctr. for Healthcare Design, Martinez, Calif., 1995—. Contbr. articles to profl. jours. Mem. AIA, AMA, Am. Hosp. Assn., Am Coll. Healthcare Architects (founding mem.). Avocations: painting, gynmastics. Office: Skidmore Owings & Merrill LLP One Front St San Francisco CA 94111

TINKER, AVERILL FAITH, special education educator; b. Rochester, N.Y., May 7, 1953; d. George Douglas and Adele (Page) M.; m. William Dean, Sept. 17, 1977 (div. Dec. 1989); children: Paul, David. B in Music Edn., Baldwin-Wallace Coll., 1975; M in Music Therapy, So. Meth. U., 1978; cert. in spl. edn., Tex. Women's U., 1984; postgrad., Notre Dame Coll., 1996. Cert. spl. edn. Music therapist Terrell (Tex.) State Hosp., 1978-79, Ft. Worth State Sch., 1979-84, spl. edn. tchr., 1985-86, Sch. Adminstrv. Unit 43, Newport, N.H., 1986-93, Hartford High Sch., White River Junction, Vt., 1993-94, Dothan Brook Elem. Sch., White River Junction, 1994—. Organist, choir dir. St. Paul's Episc. Ch., White River Junction, Vt., 1988-99, organist West Lebanon Congregational Ch., 1999—; vol. Spl. Olympics, N.H., 1987-88; den mother Cub Scouts, Vt., 1988. Mem. Coun. for Exceptional Children, Am. Guild Organists, Am. Guild English Handbell Ringers, Kappa Delta Pi, Mu Phi Epsilon. Democrat. Avocations: swimming, hiking, attending concerts. E-mial. Home: 6 College Ave Lebanon NH 03766-2504 E-mail: averill.tinker@valley.net.

TINKER, MICHAEL, technical researcher; b. N.Y.C., Feb. 22, 1945; s. Ralph and Josephine (Seewald) T.; m. Agnes Lee Zitelli, Apr. 30, 1966; children: Megan Hope, Elizabeth Larson. BA, U. Pitts., 1966; MA, U. Wis., 1967, PhD, 1975. Asst. prof. Tex. A&I, Kingsville, 1970-78; tech. writer, sr. programmer Data Gen., Durham, N.C., 1978-83; engr. Exxon, Princeton, N.J., 1983-85; mem. tech. staff RCA Rsch. Labs., 1985-88; mgr. algorithms Intel, 1988-93; head video and entertainment Sarnoff Corp., 1993—. U.S. del. Moving Pictures Experts Group of Internat. Stds. Orgn., Geneva,1990-92. Author: (play) A Feast of Angels, 1991, Cain, 1997; contbr. chpt. to book, articles to profl. jours. Mem. IEEE, Assn. Computing Machinery, SMPTE (vice chair digital cinema compression subcom.). Avocations: creative writing, sailing, acting. Home: 35 Highland Dr Yardley PA 19067-2701 Office: Sarnoff Corp CN 5300 Princeton NJ 08543

TINKHAM, MICHAEL, physicist, educator; b. Green Lake County, Wis., Feb. 23, 1928; s. Clayton Harold and LaVerna (Krause) T.; m. Mary Stephanie Merin, June 24, 1961; children: Jeffrey Michael, Christopher Gillespie. AB, Ripon (Wis.) Coll., 1951, Sc.D. (hon.), 1976; MS, MIT, 1951; PhD, 1954; MA (hon.), Harvard, 1966; DSc (hon), ETH Zurich, 1997. NSF postdoctoral fellow at Clarendon Lab., Oxford (Eng.) U., 1954-55; successively research physicist, lectr., asst. prof., asso. prof., prof. physics U. Calif. at Berkeley, 1955-66; Gordon McKay prof. applied physics Harvard U., 1966—, prof. physics, 1966-80, Rumford prof. physics, 1980—, chmn. physics dept., 1975-78. Cons. to industry, 1958—; participant internat. seminars and confs.; mem. commn. on very low temperatures Internat. Union Pure and applied Physics, 1972-78; vis. Miller rsch. prof. U. Calif.-Berkeley, 1987; vis. prof. Technical Univ., Delft, The Netherlands, 1993. Author: Group Theory and Quantum Mechanics, 1964, Superconductivity, 1965, Introduction to Superconductivity, 1975, 2d edit., 1996; contbr. articles to profl. jours. Served USNR, 1945-46. Recipient award Alexander von Humboldt Found. U. Karlsruhe, W. Ger., 1978-79; NSF sr. postdoctoral fellow Cavendish lab.; vis. fellow Clare Hall Cambridge (Eng.) U., 1971-72; Guggenheim fellow, 1963-64 Fellow Am. Phys. Soc. (chmn. div. solid state physics 1966-67, Buckley prize 1974, Richtmyer lectr. 1977), AAAS; mem. Am. Acad. Arts and Scis., Nat. Acad. Scis. Home: 98 Rutledge Rd Belmont MA 02478-2633 Office: Harvard Univ Physics Dept Lyman Lab of Physics 326 Cambridge MA 02138 E-mail: tinkham@RSJ.harvard.edu.

TINKLE, THERESA L. language educator; b. Stockton, Calif., Apr. 28, 1954; d. Mary Ellen Zawilla; m. John Edward Kotoski, May 1, 2000. BS in Elem. Edn., Oreg. Coll. Edn., 1981; MA in English, Ariz. State U., 1984; PhD in English, UCLA, 1989. From asst. to Arthur F. Thurnau prof. U. Mich., Ann Arbor, 1989—. Author: Medieval Venuses: Sexuality, Hermeneutics, and English Poetry, 1996; author, editor The Iconic Page in Manuscript, Print, and Digital Culture, 1998. Recipient Van Courtlandt Elliott prize, Medieval Acad. Am., 1989. Mem.: MLA (exec. com. on bibliography 2000—), Medieval Assn. of Pacific, New Chaucer Soc., Soc. Textual Scholarship (exec. com. 2002—). Office: Univ Mich Dept English 3224 Angell Hall Ann Arbor MI 48109

TINNER, FRANZISKA PAULA, social worker, artist, designer, educator, entrepreneur; b. Zurich, Switzerland, Sept. 18, 1944; arrived in U.S., 1968; d. Siegfried Albin and Gertrude Emilie (Sigg) Maier; m. Rolf Christian Tinner, Dec. 19, 1976; 1 child, Eric Francis. Student, U. Del., 1973-74, Va. Commonwealth U., 1974; BFA, U. Tenn., 1984; BA of Arts, U. Ark., Little Rock, 1991, postgrad. Lic. real estate broker. Dominican nun, Ilanz, Switzerland, 1961-67; waitress London, 1967-68; governess Bryn Mawr, Pa., 1969; saleswoman, 1970-90; model, 1983; artist, designer Made For You, Kerrville, Tex. and Milw., 1984-90; realtor Century 21, Milw., 1987-91; owner, entrepreneur Exquisite Treasures by Swiss Miss, 1998—. Intern Birch Community Ctr., 1992-93. Designer softsculptor doll Texas Cactus Blossom, 1984; author: (poems) The Gang (recorded by Nat. Libr. of Poetry), 1996, Cry Out for Help, 1998 (pres. choice award 1999), Springtime, 2000 (contest finalist). Ombudsman Action 10 Consumerline, Knoxville, Tenn., 1983—84; foster mother Powhatan, Va., 1976—81; vol. ARC, Knoxville, 1979; Va. Home for Permanently Disabled, 1975; vol., counselor Youth of Understanding-Fgn. Exch., Powhatan, 1975—77; tchr. pager/archiving host, mentor, area expert on Am. On Line, 1992—98; vol. Interactive Ednl. Svc., Ark., 1999—; vol. infant intensive care Ark. Children's Hosp., 1999—; vol. Online Internet Emotional/Psych Support BB (WWW), 1999—. Recipient Art Display award U. Knoxville, 1983, Prof. Choice of Yr. award, 1983, Outstanding Achievemnt award TV Channel 10, Knoxville, 1984, 1st place award for paintings and crafts State Fair Va., Tenn., 1st place award Nat. Dollmakers, 1985, finalist Best of Coll. Photography, 1991, Achievement award Coll. Scholar at Am., 1991, Achievement cert. in technique of anger therapy, 1993, Achievement cert. in crisis response team tng., 1994, Editors' Choice award, Internat. Poetic Soc., 1997, Achievement cert. vol. work tchg. AOL; named One of Outstanding 1000 Women, 1995, Woman of Yr. Internat. Biog. Inst., 1995; nominated Poet of Yr., Internat. Soc. Poets, 1997. Mem. NASW, NAFE, Milw. Bd. Realtors, Homemakers Club (pres. 1979-80), Newcomers Club, Bowlers Club (v.p.), Internat. Platform Assn. Avocations: art, cooking, teaching, writing, helping disabled and mentally ill. E-mail: elfqueenz@aol.com.

TINNEY, THOMAS MILTON, SR. genealogical research specialist; b. Waynesville, Ohio, Aug. 10, 1941; s. Prentice Thomas and Hazel Kathleen (Greene) T.; m. Sheila Mary Foxon, Feb. 10, 1961 (div. May 1971); children: Jennifer Sheila, Andrew Thomas, Phillip Alexander, Sylvia May, Cynthia Anne; m. Kim Barrett, July 29, 1971 (div. 1985); children: Teresa Ruth Anne, Michael Thomas, David Seth Ahlish, Nelson Mahonri Moriancumer; m. Vicki Rae Chris Baker, Apr. 8, 1986; children: Rebecca Sarah, Matthew Abraham, Thomas Milton Jr., Michelle Gabrielle, Jonathan Ray Elijah. Student, Utah Tech. Coll., 1968-71; BS in Econs., U. Utah, 1979, postgrad., 1979-85. Clk., carrier U.S. Postal Svc., 1961-69, 80-81; staff engr. Anthony B. Cassedy & Assocs., Ridgefield, Conn., 1980; lic. ins. agt. Colo., 1980-82; housing project mgr. Fort Douglas, Utah, 1981-84, Missoula, Mont., 1981-84; mgr., owner Tinney GenSearch Cons., 1971—. Contbr. articles to profl. jours. Served with Utah N.G. and Army Res. Mem. SAR, Jewish Geneal. Soc. Sacramento, Calif. Aggie Alumni Assn., Davis Genealogy Club and Libr. Mem. Lds Ch. Avocation: matching scholarly record sources with Mormon family history library systems, classical music, bicycling, swimming. Home: 2814 Tiber Ave Davis CA 95616-2959 E-mail: vctinney@dcn.org.

TINOCO, PATRICIA ANN, elementary education educator; b. Belleville, Ill., Dec. 1, 1950; d. Jesse Salvador and Audrey May (Wild) T.; m. Howard Lee Boller, June 14, 1990; 1 stepchild, Kimberly Boller Pope. BSBA in Elem. Edn. and Spanish, So. Ill. U., 1972, MS in Secondary Edn., 1976. Cert. tchr., Ill., middle sch. endorsement. 2nd grade tchr. High Mount Sch. 116, Swansea, Ill., 1972-79, 5th grade tchr., 1979-81, jr. high sch. tchr., 1981—, 5th through 8th grade programming instr., 1983-94, speech coach, 1983-94, lead tchr., 1993—, curriculum coord., 2000—01. Evaluator Belleville Area Presch. Testing, 1977-80; mem. Belleville Area Effective Teaching Cadre, 1987-88; instr. children's Spanish program Belleville Area Coll., 1991-93; cons. Computer Gender Equity, 1991—. Bd. dirs. Pine Tree, 1983-85, 93, sec.-treas., 1982, v.p., 1987-89. Grantee Women's Action Alliance, Inc., 1991-92, 92-93, Ill. Power Edn. grantee, 1996-97, ICONnect grantee, 1996-97, L.I.T.E.S. project grantee, 2002—; recipient Those Who Excel Edn. award State of Ill., 1995-96, Emerson Electric Excellence in Tchg. award, 1998, Eisenhower award. Mem. High Mount Fedn. Tchrs. (treas. 1988-89, sec. 1978-80, 86-97, pres. 1980-84, 90-91). Roman Catholic. Avocations: swimming, travel, foreign languages. Office: High Mount Sch 116 1721 Boul Ave Belleville IL 62226-4294 E-mail: ptinoco@highmountschool.com.

TINSLEY, ADRIAN, college president; b. N.Y.C., July 6, 1937; d. Theodore A. and Mary Ethel (White) Tinsley. AB, Bryn Mawr Coll., 1958; MA, U. Wash., 1962; PhD, Cornell U., 1969. Asst. prof. English U. Md., College Park,

1968-72; dean William James Coll., Grand Valley State, Allendale, Mich., 1972-80; assoc. vice chancellor acad. affairs Minn. State U., St. Paul, 1982-85; exec. v.p., provost Glassboro (N.J.) State Coll., 1985-89; pres. Bridgewater (Mass.) State Coll., 1989—2002, pres. emerita, 2002—. Coord. women higher edn. adminstrn. Bryn Mawr & Hers Summer Inst., Bryn Mawr, Pa., 1977—. Editor: Women in Higher Education Administration, 1984. Office: Boyden Hall Bridgewater State Coll Bridgewater MA 02325-0001

TINSLEY, HOWARD ELIJA ANTHONY, psychology educator, researcher, photographer; b. Iola, Kans., July 20, 1940; s. Howard Moran and Fannie Jane (Gasche) T.; m. Diane Evelyn Johnson, Dec. 16, 1967; children: Kelly Anne, Laurel Jeanne. BA in Psychology, Western Wash. U., 1965, MA in Psychology, 1966; PhD in Psychology, U. Minn., 1971. Lic. psychologist, Ill.; diplomate Am. Bd. Vocat. Experts. With dept. counseling psychology U. Oreg., Eugene, 1971-73; with dept. psychology So. Ill. U., Carbondale, 1973-98, U. Fla., Gainesville, 1998—. Vis. prof. dept. ednl. psychology U. Tex., Austin, 1979—80, U. Minn., 1987—88, U. Wash., 1994—95; mem. disting. educator's tour USAF, 1987; cons. editor Ency. Career Decision and Work Issues, 1989—91; mem. editl. adv. bd. The Test Corp. Am., Kansas City, 1987—89; prof. WLRAInternat. Ctr. of Excellence, also dept. leisure and environments Wageningen U. , Netherlands, 1991—. Guest editor Jour. Counseling Psychology, 1993-98, Jour. Leisure Rsch., 1980-83, Jour. Vocat. Behavior, 1999—; editor Jour. Vocat. Behavior, 1989-98. With USMC, 1958-61. Recipient rsch. award Am. Rehab. Counselors Assn., 1976, Allen V. Sapora rsch. award 1991. Fellow APA (chair program com. 1976-77, chair fellows com. 1993-94, 00-01), Acad. Leisure Scis. (pres. 1988-89, sec.-treas. 1999-2001), Western Psychol. Assn., Am. Psychol. Soc.; mem. Coun. Counseling Psychology Tng. Programs (bd. dirs. 1980-83), Am. Coll. Pers. Assn. (directorate chair commn. on assessment 1981-83), Assoc. Artists Gallery (sec. 1989-92). Office: Dept of Psychology Univ Fla Gainesville FL 32611-2250 E-mail: tinsley@ufl.edu.

TINSLEY, JACKSON BENNETT, newspaper editor; b. Ewing, Tex., Dec. 14, 1934; s. Henry Bine and Sallie Alberta (Jackson) T.; m. Claudia Anne Miller, Oct. 3, 1965; children: Ben, Anna. BS, Sam Houston State U., 1958. Editor Diboll News-Bull., 1953-54, Corrigan Times, 1954; reporter Lufkin News, 1952, 56; news editor Port Lavaca Wave, 1955; mem. staff Ft. Worth Star-Telegram, 1959—60, 1962—2000, Sunday editor, 1967-71, asst. mng. editor, 1971-74, asst. to editor, 1974-75, exec. editor, 1975-82, v.p., exec. editor, 1982-86, v.p., editor, 1986-90, sr. v.p., editor, chmn., 1990—; info. asst. S.W. Bell Telephone Co., 1960-62. Part time instr., editor Tex. Christian U., 1971-72 Com. chmn. United Way Tarrant County, 1970-87, gen. chmn. Tex. Gridiron Show, 1981, 93-95; bd. dirs. Safety Coun. Ft. Worth, 1975-80; pres., bd. dirs. Parenting Guidance Ctr., 1989-90. 2d lt. U.S. Army, 1959. Recipient Nat. Writing award Edn. Writers Assn., 1965, citation Tex. Conf. AAUP, 1965; named Disting. Alumnus, Sam Houston State U., 1984; named to C.E. Shuford Journalism Hall of Honor, U. North Tex., 1987, his bust in U. Tex. Wall of Honor; established Jack B. Tinsley/Fort Worth Star Telegram endowed journalism scholarship. Mem. Soc. Profl. Journalists (pres. Ft. Worth chpt. 1991-92, chmn. journalism adv. com. U. North Tex. and Sam Houston State U. 1988-93), Am. Soc. Newspapers Editors, AP Mng. Editors Assn., Tex. AP Mng. Editors Assn. (pres. 1979-80), Press Club Ft. Worth (pres. 1970-71), Colonial Country Club, Ft. Worth Club, Rotary (v.p. Ft. Worth 1981, pres. 1983-84). Home: 3550 Wind River Ct Fort Worth TX 76116-9329 Office: Ft Worth Star-Telegram 400 W 7th St Fort Worth TX 76102-4793 E-mail: tinsley@star-telegram.com.

TINSLEY, JENNIFER, ballerina; b. Dallas; Student, Brookhaven CC, Nancy Schoeffenburg Ballet Sch., Dallas Ballet, Dallas Met. Ballet; student (summer), Sch. Am. Ballet, 1983—88, student, 1988—90. Apprentice N.Y.C. Ballet, 1990—91, mem. corps de ballet, 1991—99, soloist, 1999—. Guest tchr. N.Y., Tex.; guest performer Vt., Portugal, Argentina, Eng. Featured dancer (CD-ROM) Ballet is Fun by Bill Atkinson, dancer (PBS broadcast) Balanchine Celebration, Live from Lincoln Ctr: Swan Lake, (films) The Nutcracker, 1993, Accent on the Offbeat, (ballets) Jewels, Ballo Della Regina, Chaconne, La Sonnambula, Fearful Symmetries, Jeu De Cartes, Slavonic Dances, Polyphonia, many others. Office: NYC Ballet NY State Theatre 20 Lincoln Ctr Plz New York NY 10023-6913*

TINSLEY, NIKKI LEE, federal agency administrator; b. Apr. 23, 1948; BS in Bus. Admin., Ohio State U./Virginia Commonwealth U., 1970; MS in Bus. Admin., U. Colorado.U/Northern Colorado, 1981. Ednl. prog. asst. Office of Edn., Wash., D.C., 1971; bookstore mgr. U.S. Govt. Printing Office, Denver, 1971-76; auditor U.S. Gen. Acctg. Office, 1976-82; supervisory auditor Dept. of Interior, Minerals Mgmt. Svc., Lakewood, 1982-90; divisional inspector general Environ. Protection Agency, Kansas City, KS, 66101, Dep. Inspector General Wash., D.C., 1995-96, acting inspector general, 1997-98, inspector general, 1998—. Recipient, Bronze medal for commendable svc., Environ. Protection Agency, 1995. Mem., Assn. of Govt. Accts., 1992—, Inst. of Internal Auditors, 1995—, Colo. Soc. CPAs, Coun. on Integrity and Efficiency (pres.). Office: EPA MC 2410 1200 Pennsylvanis Ave NW Washington DC 20460-0001

TINSTMAN, DALE CLINTON, food products company consultant; b. Chester, Nebr., May 19, 1919; s. Clinton Lewis and Elizabeth Golashin (Gretzinger) T.; m. Jean Sundell, Oct. 1, 1942; children: Thomas C., Nancy Tinstman Remington, Jane C. Tinstman Kramer. BS, U. Nebr., 1941, JD, 1947. Bar: Nebr. 1947. Asst. sec., asst. mgr. investment dept. First Trust Co., Lincoln, Nebr., 1947-48; v.p., asst. treas. Securities Acceptance Corp., Omaha; fin. v.p., treas. Ctrl. Nat. Ins. Group, 1958-60; pres., treas. Tinstman & Co., Inc., Lincoln, 1960-61; exec. v.p. First Med Am., Inc., 1961-68, pres., 1968-74, fin. cons., 1974—; pres., dir. Iowa Beef Processors, Inc., 1976-77, vice chmn., 1977-82, co-chmn., 1982-83, dir., cons., 1983—; chmn., dir. Eaton Tinstman Druliner, Inc., 1983—2000. Bd. dirs. IBP, Inc.; past chmn. Nebr. Investment Coun. Trustee, chmn. U. Nebr. Found.; trustee Lincoln Found., Nebr. Coun. Econ. Edn. Served with USAAF World War II, Korea; to col. Nebr. Air N.G. Mem. Nebr. Bar Assn., Nebr. Diplomats, Newcomen Soc. N.Am., Am. Legion, Nebr. State C. of C., Firethorn Country Club, Alpha Sigma Phi, Phi Delta Phi. Republican. Presbyterian (elder). Home and Office: 3500 Faulkner Dr B206 Lincoln NE 68516-6638

TINTLE, CARMEL JOSEPH, public relations executive; b. Paterson, N.J., Sept. 25, 1924; s. Herbert J. and Agnes (Merna) T.; m. Alice M. Hayes, Sept. 1, 1948; children: Joseph, Alice Maureen. BS, Fordham U., 1951; postgrad., NYU. Editl. asst. Newsweek mag., N.Y.C., 1946-50; news editor Beverage Retailer Weekly, 1950-52; city editor Paterson Sunday Eagle, 1950-52; staff writer Carl Byoir & Assocs., Inc., N.Y.C., 1952-59, asst. account exec., 1959-64, assoc. account exec., 1964; account supr. Grey Pub. Rels., Inc., 1964; v.p. Schenley Affiliated Brands Corp., subs. Schenley Industries, 1964-72, sr. v.p., 1972-74; v.p. corp. affairs Am. Distilling Co., 1974—80; v.p. Banfi Vintners, Old Brookville, NY, 1980—90; CEO Vinum Comm., Inc., 1980-90; cons. corp. comm. Banfi Vinters, 1990—. Publicity dir., Jumby Bay Island, a Banfi resort property, Antigua, 1985-95. Ensign U.S. Maritime Svc., 1943-46. Mem. N.Y. Press Club, SAR, KC, St. Patrick Guard of Honor N.J., U.S. Mcht. Marine Vets., Irish-Am. Cultural Inst., Fordham Univ.'s Golden Rams. Home and Office: Winding Way East Convent Station NJ 07960

TINTURIN, NOËLLE COMPINSKY, pianist, music educator; b. L.A., Feb. 20, 1948; d. Manuel and Dorothy Marie (Atwood) Compinsky; m. Charles Douglas Russell, June 21, 1969 (div. Sept. 1976); 1 child, Celine Reneé Russell; m. Glenn Tinturin, Apr. 25, 1987. Student, U. So. Calif., 1964, Calif. State U., Northridge, 1969, Mt. St. Mary's Coll., L.A., 1972. Pvt. instr. piano, L.A., 1967-93, Lake Arrowhead, Calif., 1993—; owner Tinturin Music Studio, 1993—; mem. numerous chamber music ensembles, 1967—; mem. (with Glenn Tinturin) Tinturin Duo (piano and guitar), 1990—. Mem. chamber music faculty Idyllwild Sch. Music and Arts, U. So. Calif., 1967; oboist Mt. St. Mary's Cmty. Orch., L.A., 1964-69; founding mem. Am. Youth Symphony, L.A., 1965-69; accompanist for various choruses, vocalists, instrumentalists, 1970—. Piano soloist compact disc Romantic Miniatures, 1999, Romantic Minatures II, 2000; performer Tinturin Duo compact disc Romancero Gitano, 1994; arranger 14 classical works for Tinturin Duo; prodr. Mountain Musicales concert series, Lake Arrowhead, Calif., 1994—; prodr. Concert Master Series for Arrowhead Arts Assn., 2001— Dir. classical music festival Arrowhead Arts Assn., Lake Arrowhead, 1998-99, bd. dirs., 1998—. Mem. ASCAP, Music Tchr.'s Nat. Assn., Music Tchr.'s Assn. Calif., Musician's Union (local 47, L.A.), Lake Arrowhead C. of C. Avocations: dancing, concerts, sailing, boating. Home: PO Box 1773 Lake Arrowhead CA 92352-1773 E-mail: noelle@tinturinmusic.com.

TIÓ, ADRIAN RICARDO, artist, art educator; b. Ft. Wayne, Ind., Jan. 13, 1951; BA, Temple U., Phila., 1974; student, Tyler Sch. Art, Rome, 1975-76; MFA, U. Cin., 1979. Founds. coord. Sch. Art Bowling Green (Ohio) State U., 1979-87, drawing head, 1989-94, assoc. dir., 1991-94, assoc. dean arts and scis., 1994-96; chair dept. art Ind. State U., Terre Haute, 1996-2000; chmn. sch. art No. Ill. U., Dekalb, 2000—. Cons. for migrant edn. Pa. Dept. Edn., Harrisburg, 1986-87; grant reviewer pub. artworks Ohio Arts Coun., Columbus, 1995-2000, artists/orgn. grants Arts Commn. Greater Toledo, Ohio, 1995-96. One-person shows include Artreach Gallery, Columbus, Ohio, 1984, Currents Gallery, Bowling Green, 1989, ARC Gallery, Chgo., 1991, C.A.G.E. Gallery, Cin., 1992; exhibited in group shows at Latino Arts Gallery, Chgo., 1990, Machine Shop Gallery, Emery Ctr., Cin., 1990, Canton (Ohio) Art Inst., 1990, Holland (Mich.) Area Arts Coun., 1991, Bertoncini Gallery, Chgo., 1991, Carnegie Arts Ctr., Covington, Ky., 1991, Mansfield (Ohio) Art Ctr., 1992, Ford Gallery Eastern Mich. U., Ypsilanti, 1992, 93, Hopkins Hall Gallery, Ohio State U., Columbus, 1992, Index Gallery, Clark Coll., Vancouver, Wash. 1992, Sweet Briar (Va.) Coll., 1992, Artspace, Lima, Ohio, 1993, Hugh N. Ronald Meml. Gallery, Portland, Ind., 1993, Temple U. Gallery, Phila., 1993, Purdue U. Galleries, West Lafayette, Ind., 1993, Jewish Cmty. Ctr., Louisville, 1994, Emison Art Ctr., DePauw U., Greencastle, Ind., 1995, Artemisia Gallery, Chgo., 1995, Doshi Ctr. Contemporary Art, Harrisburg, Pa., 1995, Multicultural Ctr. Gallery, U. Toledo, Ohio, 1995, African-Am. Cultural Ctr., U. Ill., Chgo., 1995, Corcoran Gallery Art, Washington, 1995, Stocker Ctr. Gallery, Lorain, Ohio, 1996, 20 North Gallery, Toledo, 1996, others; represented in permanent collections at Afro-Am. Mus. and Cultural Ctr., Chgo., Andy Warhol Found. Visual Arts, N.Y.C., Elvehejm Mus., U. Wis., Madison, Nat. Endowment for Arts, Washington, Ohio Arts Coun., Columbus, Rockefeller Found., N.Y.C., Toledo Mus. Art, White House, Washington, U. Cin., Villa Taverna Found., Washington, others; also pvt. collections. Bd. mem. Arts Illiana, Terre Haute, 1997-2000, Arts Commn. Greater Toledo, 1995-96. Recipient award new Partnerships for Artists, Arts Midwest/Nat. Endowment Arts, Mpls., 1990, new forms regional grant Nat. Endowment Arts, Chgo., 1992, individual artists fellowship Ohio Arts Coun., Columbus, 1994, Arts Endowment award Ind. State U., Terre Haute, 1997, Individual Artists grant Ind. Arts. Commn., 2000. Mem. Coll. Art Assn., Nat. Coun. Arts Adminstrs., Founds. in Art, Edn. and Theory (pres. 1984-86, editor 1982-86), Chgo. Artists Coalition, Can. Bookbinders and Book Artists Guild, Chgo. Hand Bookbinders, Coll. Art Assn., Mid-Am. Print Coun., Mid-Am. Coll. Art Assn. Office: School of Arts Northern Ill U Dekalb IL 60115-2854 E-mail: artio@niu.edu.

TIPIRNENI, TIRUMALA RAO, metallurgical engineer; b. Gudivada, India, 1948; came to U.S., 1973; s. Subrahmanyam and Vasumathi (Bobba) T.; m. Pavani Rathnam, Idupuganti, Mar. 1, 1978; children: Renuka, Anita, Vijay Srinivas. BS in Chem., Physics and Math., Andhra U., India, 1966; B Metall. Engring., Nagpur U., India, 1971; MS in Metallurgy, Stevens Inst. Tech., Hoboken, N.J., 1975. Chief metallurgist Structure Probe, Inc., Metuchen, N.J., 1975-78; lab. dir. Consolidated Testing Labs, Inc., New Hyde Park, N.Y., 1978-85; pres. L.I. Testing Labs, Inc., North Babylon, 1985—. Pres. Telugu Literary and Cultural Assn., N.Y., 1978-79, chmn., 2000—; trustee TANA Found., 1999—. Mem. ASM Internat. (chmn. L.I. chpt. 1986-87, 93-94), ASTM, N.Y. Acad. Scis., Soc. Automotive Engrs., Am. Soc. for Quality, Am. Welding Soc. Office: Long Island Testing Labs 243A Wyandanch Ave North Babylon NY 11704-1501 E-mail: rao@litlab.com.

TIPLER, FRANK JENNINGS, III, physicist; b. Andalusia, Ala., Feb. 1, 1947; s. Frank Jennings Jr. and Anne (Kearley) T.; m. Jolanta Rokicka; children: Allison Anne, Caroline Nicole. S.B., MIT, 1969; PhD, U. Md., 1976. Rsch. mathematician U. Calif., Berkeley, 1976-79; sr. rsch. fellow Oxford (Eng.) U., 1979; rsch. assoc. U. Tex., Austin, 1979-81; assoc. prof. physics and math. Tulane U., New Orleans, 1981-87, prof., 1987—. Vis. sr. scientist Max-Planck Inst. Astrophysics, Munich, 1987; vis. fellow U. Sussex, Brighton, Eng., 1987; vis. prof. Inst. Astrophysics, Liege, Belgium, 1988, U. Bern, Switzerland, 1988, U. Vienna, Austria, 1992. Author: l'Homme et le Cosmos, 1984, The Anthropic Cosmological Principle, 1986, The Physics of Immortality, 1994; editor: Essays in General Relativity, 1980; contbr. articles to profl. jour. Rsch. grantee NSF, 1984, 86. Libertarian.

TIPPING, HARRY A. lawyer; b. Bainbridge, Md., Nov. 2, 1944; s. William Richard and Ann Marie (Kelly) T.; m. Kathleen Ann Palmer, July 12, 1969; 1 child, Christopher A. B.A., Gannon U., 1966; J.D., U. Akron, 1970. Bar: Ohio. Asst. law dir. City of Akron, Ohio, 1971-72, chief asst. law dir., 1972-74; ptnr. Gillen, Miller & Tipping, Akron, 1974-77, Roderick, Myers & Linton, Akron, 1977-87; prin., COO Harry A. Tipping Co. L.P.A., Akron, 1987—. Mem. Fairlawn Charter Rev. Commn., 1990—; chmn. bd. Assessment Equalization for the City of Fairlawn, 1989, 90, 97; chmn. Bd. of Tax Appeals, City of Fairlawn, Ohio, 1979-81, mem. merger com., 1980-82. With USCGR, 1966-72. Mem. ABA, Am. Bd. Trial Advocates (advocate), Akron Bar Assn., Ohio Bar Assn., Def. Rsch. Inst., Am. Arbitration Assn., Fedn. Ins. & Corp. Counsel. Republican. Roman Catholic. Clubs: Fairlawn Country (Ohio), Catawaba Island (Ohio), Firestone County (Akron, Ohio). Office: 1 Cascade Plz Ste 2200 Akron OH 44308-1135

TIPPING, WILLIAM MALCOLM, social services administrator; b. Oak Park, Ill., Mar. 31, 1931; s. William McKinley and Evelyn Amelia (Freier) T.; m. Lois A. Grife, Sept. 18, 1954 (dec. May 1986); children: William, Barbara, Robert; m. Babette J. Cumming, Oct. 10, 1987; children: Christopher Cumming, Courtney Barone. BA, Carleton Coll., Northfield, Minn., 1954. Sales rep. Gen. Mills, Inc., Mpls., 1954-56; account exec. Campbell Mithun, Inc., 1956-63, v.p. mgmt., supr. Mpls. and Chgo., 1965-76; account supr., v.p. Lennen & Newell, Inc., N.Y.C., 1963-65; ptnr., mgr. Heidrick & Struggles, Inc., Chgo., 1976-88; exec. v.p., chief exec. officer Am. Cancer Soc., Atlanta, 1988-91; pres. Tipping and McRae, Inc., 1991-93; mng. dir. Ward Howell Internat., Inc., 1993-97. Trustee Carleton Coll., 1986-90; bd. dirs. Nat. Health Coun., N.Y.C., Ga. Conservancy, Families First; mem. fin. com. UICC, Geneva, 1990-91. Recipient Disting. Svc. award Carleton Coll., 1984. Mem. Capital City Club (Atlanta), Quechee (Vt.) Club, Comerce Club (Atlanta). Republican. Episcopalian.

TIPPINS, SUSAN SMITH, elementary school principal; b. Jacksonville, Fla., Jan. 4, 1961; d. Arthur Thomas and Kathleen May (Blake) Smith; m. John Malcolm Tippins Jr., Apr. 21, 1984; children: Matthew Scott, Paul Blake. AA, Fla. Jr. Coll., Jacksonville, 1980; BA in Edn., U. North Fla., 1983, MEd, 1993. Cert. tchr., Fla. 6th grade tchr. Duval County Sch. Sys., Jacksonville, 1984-87; 3rd grade tchr. Nassau County Sch. Sys., Callahan, Fla., 1987-88, tchr. specific learning disabilities, 1990-92, 1st grade tchr., 1992-96, adminstrv. intern, 1995-96; prin. Bryceville (Fla.) Elem. Sch., 1997—. Mem. ASCD, Internat. Reading Assn., Fla. Reading Assn., Fla. Assn. Computer Edn., Alpha Delta Kappa (pres. 1996), Kappa Delta Pi. Avocation: crafting. Home: Rt 2 Box 1413 Bryceville FL 32009 Office: Bryceville Elem Sch PO Box 3 Bryceville FL 32009-0003

TIPPS, GREGORY PAUL, music educator; b. Woodstock, Ill., Aug. 5, 1953; s. Robert Lee Elden and Helen Louise Tipps; m. Beverly Ann Jarosch; children: Bryan, Jamie. MusB in Edn., No. Ill. U., 1976, Masters in Music Edn., 1983, postgrad., 1983—86, Vander Cook Coll., Chgo., 1998—2000. Cert. music educator K-12 Ill. Band dir. Schaumburg (Ill.) H.S., 1976—. Choir dir. Congl. Ch. of Algonquin, Ill., 1991—98; trumpet player Playboy Club Orch., Lake Geneva, Wis., 1974—79, Vito Buffalo Orch., Algonquin, 1982—; free lance trumpet player, Chgo., 1979—; assoc. condr. Crystal Lake (Ill.) Cmty. Band, 1998—. Composer: (jazz composition) Fly By Night, 1976. Trustee Congl. Ch. of Algonquin, 2001—; bd. dirs. Musicians Union Local 48, Elgin, 1983—88. Mem.: Music Educator's Nat. Conf. Home: 1425 Saddlebrook Cir Algonquin IL 60102-1948 Office: Schaumburg HS 1100 W Schaumburg Rd Schaumburg IL 60194 Personal E-mail: trumpetdude53@yahoo.com.

TIPTON, CHARLES L. musician; b. Big Spring, Tex., Oct. 3, 1960; s. Billy K. and Stella M. Tipton; m. Suzanne Leba Cotton, June 18, 1988; children: William Andrew, Savannah Marilyn. BMus Edn., Ea. N.Mex U., Dortoles, NM, 1983. Music tchr. , grades 4-12 Post ISD, Post, Tex., 1983—84; choir dir., grades 7-9 Yucca Jr. High, Clovis, N.Mex., 1984—90; music tchr., grades k-6 Mesa Elem., 1991—2002; choir dir. Clovis H.S., 2002—. Mem.: MENC, Phi Alpha Smfonia. Avocations: golf, woodworking, composing.

TIPTON, CLYDE RAYMOND, JR. communications and resources development consultant; b. Cin., Nov. 13, 1921; s. Clyde Raymond and Ida Marie (Molitor) T.; m. Marian Gertrude Beushausen, Aug. 6, 1942; children: Marian Page Ashley, Robert Bruce. BS, U. Ky., 1946, MS, 1947. Research engr. Battelle Meml. Inst., Columbus, Ohio, 1947-49, sr. tech. adviser, 1951-62, coordinator corporate communications, 1969-73, v.p. communications, 1973-75, asst. to pres., 1978-79, v.p., corp. dir. communications and pub. affairs, 1979-86; ret.; staff mem. Los Alamos Sci. Lab., 1949-51; dir. research Basic, Inc., Bettsville, Ohio, 1962-64; asst. dir. Battelle Pacific N.W. Labs., Richland, Wash., 1964-69; pres., trustee Battelle Commons Co. for Community Urban Redevel., Columbus, 1975-78; cons. bus. communications and devel., 1986—. Secretariat U.S. del. 2d Internat. Conf. on Peaceful Uses Atomic Energy, Geneva, 1958; cons. U.S. AEC in Atoms for Peace Program, Tokyo, 1959, New Delhi, 1959-60, Rio de Janeiro, Brazil, 1961. Author: How to Change the World, 1982; editor: Jour. Soc. for Nondestructive Testing, 1953-57, The Reactor Handbook, Reactor Materials, vol. 3, 1955, vol. 1, 1960, Learning to Live on a Small Planet, 1974; patentee in field. Past pres. Pilot Dogs, United Way of Franklin County, Greater Columbus Arts Coun.; bd. dirs., treas. Pilot Guide Dog Found.; pres. emeritus Archs. Soc. Ohio. Served with U.S. Army Air Corp., 1943. Named to U. Ky. Engring. Hall of Distinction, 1997; U. Ky. Haggin fellow, 1947; Otterbein Coll. Sr. fellow, 1978. Fellow NSPE (past pres., Outstanding Svc. award 1992); mem. Am. Soc. Metals, Ohio Soc. Profl. Engrs. (past pres., award of distinction, Uncommon Man award, Outstanding Svc. award 1993, 98), Lions Club, Sigma Xi, Alpha Chi Sigma. Episcopalian. Home and Office: 2218 Aschinger Blvd Columbus OH 43212-4620

TIPTON, E. LINWOOD, trade association executive; b. Adrian, Mo., Nov. 19, 1934; s. Harlow Acklin and Mary Catherine (Lacy) T.; m. Marjorie A. Wolford, Dec. 17, 1955 (div. June 1983); children: Kelly A., Mark A.; m. Constance E. Eaton Broadstone, Oct. 8, 1983. BS in Agriculture, U. Mo., 1955, MS in Agriculture and Econs., 1956. Economist USDA Fgn. Agrl. Svc., Washington, 1956-57, Eastern Milk Prodrs., Syracuse, N.Y., 1960-62; exec. dir. Coop. Dairy Econ. Svc., Boston, 1962-65; v.p., exec. v.p., pres., chief exec. officer Internat. Dairy Foods Assn., Washington, 1965—. Founder Nat. Economist Club, Washington, treas., chmn. bd., 1967-73; founder Nat. Economist Ednl. Found., Washington, treas., chmn. bd., 1969-74; chmn. bd. Petlin, Inc., Washington; expert witness congl. coms., regulatory agencies; founder Internat. Sweetener Colloquium; apptd. to Nat. Commn. Agrl. Trade and Export Policy, 1984; advisor Sec. Agriculture, U.S. Trade Rep.; co-founder, chmn. bd. restaurant/motel chain, 1967—; chmn. The Food Group, The Ice Cream and Milk Polit. Action Com., Food Processors Steering Com. on Wage and Price Stability; elected to governance bd. dirs. Winn-Boll-Dann, Moscow, 2002. 1st lt. Army Fin. Corp., 1957-60. Recipient Citation of Merit U. Mo. Alumni Assn., 1988. Avocations: tennis, golf. Office: Internat Dairy Foods Assn 1250 H St NW Ste 900 Washington DC 20005-3952

TIPTON, GARY LEE, retired services company executive; b. Salem, Oreg., July 3, 1941; s. James Rains and Dorothy Velma (Dierks) T. BS, Oreg. Coll. Edn., 1964. Credit rep. Standard Oil Co. Calif., Portland, Oreg., 1964-67; credit mgr. Uniroyal Inc., Dallas, 1967-68; ptnr., mgr. bus. Tipton Barbers, Portland, 1968-94; ret., 1994. Mem. Rep. Nat. Com., 1980—, Sen. Howard Baker's Presdl. Steering Com., 1980; dep. dir. gen. Internat. Biog. Ctr., Cambridge, Eng., 1987—; mem. U.S. Congl. adv. bd. Am. Security Coun., 1984-93; mem. steering com. Coun. on Fgn. Rels. Portland Com., 1983-84, chmn. 1984-86, mem. exec. com., 1988-90, bd. dirs., 1990-91. Recipient World Culture prize Accademia Italia, 1984, Presdl. Achievement award, 1982, cert. Disting. Contbn. Sunset High Sch. Dad's Club, 1972, 73, Cert. of Perfection award Tualatin Valley Fire and Rescue Dist., 1994, Cert. of Recognition, Rep. Nat. Com., 2002. Fellow Internat. Biog. Assn. (life, Key award 1983, U.K.); mem. Sunset Mchts. Assn. (co-founder, treas. 1974-79, pres. 1982-83), Internat. Platform Assn., Smithsonian Assocs., UN Assn. (steering com. UN day 1985), World Affairs Coun. of Oreg., City Club of Portland.

TIPTON, HARRY BASIL, JR. state legislator, physician; b. Salida, Colo., Mar. 14, 1927; s. Harry Basil Sr. and Nina Belle (Hailey) T.; m. Dorothy Joan Alexander, Sept. 16, 1950; children: Leslie Louise, Harry Basil III, Robert Alexander. BA, U. Colo., 1950, MD, 1953. Diplomate Am. Bd. Family Practice. Postgrad. med. tng. Good Samaritan Hosp., Phoenix., Ariz., Maricopa County Hosp., Phoenix; ptnr., dir. Lander (Wyo.) Med. Clinic, 1954—; mem. Wyo. Ho. Reps., Cheyenne, 1981—, chmn. judiciary com., 1986-98, speaker pro tem, 1999-2001, mem. appropriations com., 2001—. Cons. Indian Health Svc., Ft. Washakie, Wyo., 1968—; dir NOWCAP Family Planning, Worland, Wyo., 1975-90. Mem., pres. Fremont County Sch. Dist. # 1, Lander, 1958-78. With USMC, 1945-46, capt. USNR Med. Corps, 1950-87. Recipient Dr. Nathon Davis award, AMA, 1999; named Capt. Med. Corps. USNR, 1974. Fellow Am. Coll. Ob.-Gyn., Am. Assn. Family Practice (charter); mem. Wyo. Med. Soc. (Physician of Yr. 1989), Rotary (pres. 1960-61), Elks. Republican. Avocations: fishing, skiing, bird hunting, military history. Office: Lander Med Clin PC 745 Buena Vista Dr Lander WY 82520-3431

TIPTON, KENNETH WARREN, agricultural administrator, researcher; b. Belleville, Ill., Nov. 14, 1932; s. Roscoe Roy and Martha Pearl (Davis) T.; m. Barbara Adds, Mar. 2, 1957; children: Kenneth Warren Jr., Nancy Tipton O'Neal. BS, La. State U., 1955, MS, 1959; PhD, Miss. State U., 1969. Asst. prof. Agrl. Ctr., La. State U., Baton Rouge, 1959-70, assoc. prof., 1970-75, prof., 1975—, supt. Red River Rsch. Sta., La. Agrl. Expt. Sta. Bossier City, 1975-79, assoc. dir. La. Agrl. Expt. Sta. Baton Rouge, 1979-89, dir. La. Agrl. Expt. Sta., vice chancellor, 1989-96, vice chancellor, dir. emeritus, 1996—. Mem. com. nine USDA/Coop. State Rsch. Svc., 1986-88; Expt. State Com. Orgn. Policy, 1988-91. Contbr. articles to Agronomy Jour., Jour. Econ. Entomology, Grain Sorghum Conf. Coach baseball program Am. Legion, 1969-74; scoutmaster Boy Scouts Am., Baton Rouge, 1970-75. Capt. USAF, 1955-58. Mem. Am. Soc. Agronomy, Crop Sci. Soc. Am., Coun. Agrl. Sci. Tech. Achievements include research on inheritance of fiber traits in cotton, resistance of grain sorghum hybrids to bird damage, tannin content of grain sorghum and effects of phosphorus on growth of sorghum. Home: 732 Baird Dr Baton Rouge LA 70808-5916 E-mail: barkentip@aol.com.

TIPTON, MARTHA JOHNSON, communications educator; b. Newton, Miss., Jan. 5, 1944; d. Herbert Henry and Florene Mildred (Rhodes) Johnson; m. Jon Paul Tipton, Dec. 29, 1968; children: Nicole, Paula. AA, East Ctrl. C.C., Decatur, Miss., 1964; BS, U. So. Miss., 1966; MA, Auburn U., 1967; PhD, Ohio U., 1970. Instr. Ohio U., Athens, 1970; host quiz show Sta. WTAP TV, Parkersburg, W.Va., 1975-81; mem. adj. faculty Marietta (Ohio) Coll., 1975-95, asst. prof., 1995—. Summer asst. Nat. 4-H Found., Washington, 1965; congrl. intern U.S. Ho. of Reps., Washington, 1966. Mem. PEO Sisterhood, Speech Comm. Assn. Ohio, Pi Kappa Pi. Republican. Lutheran. Avocations: reading, travel. E-mail. Home: 101 Meadow Ln Marietta OH 45750-1345 Office: Marietta Coll Speech Comm and Leadership 215 5th St Marietta OH 45750-4033 E-mail: tiptonm@marietta.edu.

TIPTON, SHEILA KAY, lawyer; b. Martins Ferry, Ohio, Aug. 4, 1951; d. Donald Duane and Elizabeth Julia T.; m. Orrin Frink, Nov. 2, 1973 (div.); m. William Llewellyn Dawe III, Dec. 6, 1985; children: Nicholas Albert, Alexander McNeill; stepchildren: William Llewellyn IV, Christopher Michael. BS, Ohio U., 1973; JD, Drake U., 1980. Bar: Iowa 1980, U.S. Dist. Ct. (no. and so. dists.) Iowa 1980, U.S. Ct. Appeals (8th cir.) 1980. Assoc. Bradshaw, Fowler, Proctor & Fairgrave, P.C., Des Moines, 1980-85; ptnr., shareholder Bradshaw, Fowler, Proctor & Fairgrave, 1985-99; ptnr. Dorsey & Whitney LLP, 1999—. Presenter in field. Contbr. articles to profl. jours. Pres. Polk County Legal Aid Soc., 1991-92; bd. dirs. Youth Home Mid-Am., 1990-97, sec., 1994-96, v.p., 1996-97; bd. dirs. des Moines Metro Opera Found., 1993-98, pres., 1997-98; bd. dirs. Des Moines Metro Opera, 1991-92, v.p. devel., 1994-95, pres.-elect, 1995-96, pres., 1996-97, v.p. long range planning com., 1998-99; bd. counselors Drake U. Law Sch., 1996-98. Recipient State of Iowa Govs. Vol. award, 1996. Mem. Iowa State Bar Assn. (adminstrv. law sect. coun. 1989-91, mem. bus. law sect. coun. 1993-97, co-chmn. quality life task force 1993-96, chair internat. trade com. 1992-94), Rotary (chmn. scholar com. 1994-95, bd. dirs. 1996—, sgt.-at-arms, 1997-98, sec.-treas. 1998-99, v.p. 1999-2000, pres.-elect 2000-01, pres. 2001—). Avocations: opera, cooking, reading, golf, travel. Home: 13074 Lincoln Ave Des Moines IA 50325-7413 Office: Dorsey & Whitney LLP 801 Grand Ave Ste 3900 Des Moines IA 50309-2790 E-mail: tipton.sheila@dorseylaw.com., sheilatepton@aol.com.

TIPTON, THOMAS WESLEY, retired aerospace engineer; b. Okmulgee, Okla., May 12, 1952; s. John Melvin and Norma Dean (Boyd) T.; children: Samuel Lawrence, Stacy Lynn; m. Evelyn Marie Harzinski, Sept. 17, 1988; 1 child, Jonathan Clark. Student, William Penn Coll., Oskaloosa, Iowa, 1970-72. Enlisted U.S. Navy, 1972; div supr. Fighter Squadron 101, Naval Air Sta., Oceana, Va., 1973-76; quality assurance Naval Air Sta., Keflavik, Iceland, 1976-79; drill instr. Recruit Tng. Ctr., Great Lakes, Ill., 1980-83; flight engr., evaluator Patrol Squadron 26, Brunswick, Maine, 1983-89; flight engr., test and evaluation Force Warfare Naval Air Warfare Ctr. Aircraft Div., Patuxent River, Md., 1989-94; maintenance control profl. U.S. Air Express, 1993-94; with DynCorp Aerospace, Egress/Environ. Sys. Tech. Naval Air Warfare Ctr. Quality Control Divsn. (IN), 1994—. Mem. NRA (life), Smithsonian Air and Space Mus., Friends of the Kennedy Ctr., Nat. Geographic Soc. Avocations: reading, woodworking, wildlife conservation, cycling. Home: 436 Council Bluffs Ct Lusby MD 20657-3313 Office: Force Warfare Directorate Naval Air Sta Patuxent River MD 20670-5000

TIQUIA, SONIA MARAYA, microbiologist; b. Olongapo City, Zambales, Philippines, Mar. 1, 1970; d. Angelo Bais Tiquia, Zenaida Maraya Tiquia. Grad. cum laude, Ctrl. Luzon State U., 1991; PhD Environ. Microbiology, U. Hong Kong, 1996. Rsch. asst. City Poly Hong Kong, Kowloon Tong, China, 1991—93; grad. asst. U. Hong Kong, Pokfulam, 1993—96; rsch. scientist Ohio State U., Wooster, Ohio, 1999—2001, Oak Ridge Nat. Lab., Oak Ridge, Tenn., 2001—. Vis. scientist Iowa State U., Ames, 1998—99. Co-author: The Science of Composting , 1996, Microbiology of Composting, 2002; mem. editl. bd.: Process Biochem., 2001—, mem. editl. bd.: Bioresource Tech., 2002—; contbr. articles to profl. jours. Fellow, Weed Sci. Soc. Philippines, 1988—91, City U. of Hong Kong, 1996—98, Oak Ridge Inst. Sci. & Edn., 2001—; grantee Young Scientist grantee, Fedn. European Microbiol. Socs., 2000. Mem.: AAAS, The Sci. Adv. Bd., Internat. Soc. Microbial Ecology, Am. Soc. Microbiology. Avocation: travel. Office: Oak Ridge Nat Lab ESD Bldg 1505 Rm 350 MS 6038 Oak Ridge TN 37919

TIRANA, BARDYL RIFAT, lawyer; b. Geneva, Dec. 16, 1937; s. Rifat and Rosamond English (Walling) T.; m. Anne Prather, June 22, 1985; children by previous marriage: Kyra, Amina. AB, Princeton U., 1959; LL.B., Columbia U., 1962. Bar: D.C. 1962, Md. 1986, N.Y. 1986, Va. 1986, Pa. 1992. Trial atty. Dept. Justice, 1962-64; assoc. Amram, Hahn & Sundlun, Washington, 1965-68, ptnr., 1969-72; dir., sec. Exec. Jet Aviation, Inc., Columbus, Ohio, 1970-77, Technics, Inc., Alexandria, Va., 1971-77; ptnr. Sundlun, Tirana & Scher, Washington, 1972-77; dir. def. civil preparedness agy. Dept. Def., 1977-79, mem. armed forces policy coun., 1977-79; chmn. bd. Technics, Inc., San Jose, Calif., 1979-85; of counsel Silverstein and Mullens, Washington, 1982-84, ptnr., 1984-90; pvt. practice law, 1991—. Mem.-at-large D.C. Bd. Edn., 1970-74; trustee Jimmy Carter Inaugural Trust, Washington, 1977-87; co-chmn. 1977 Presdl. Inaugural Com., 1976-77; mem. exec. adv. coun. Calif. Commn. Indsl. Innovation, 1981-82; pres. China/USA Edn. Fund, Inc., Washington, 1981—; trustee, sec. The Waltz Group of Washington, 2000--; dir. Rocky Mountain Inst., Snowmass Colo., 1982-95. Recipient medal for disting. pub. svc. Dept. Def., 1979, Fuess award Phillips Acad., 1991, Svc. Commendation award YWCA of Nat. Capital Area, 1991. Mem. N.Y.C. Racquet and Tennis Club, D.C. Met. Club. Home: 3550 Tilden St NW Washington DC 20008-3121 E-mail: btirana@aol.com.

TIRARD, JEAN-MARC, lawyer, educator; b. Tunis, Tunisia, Aug. 10, 1948; s. Marc Tirard and Jeanne Robinet; m. Martine Delamare, Aug. 6, 1968; children: Anne-Mathilde, Marc-Antoine, Marie-Amélie. Licence en Droit, Faculty de Droit, Dijon, France, 1969, Maitrise en Droit, 1970; grad., Ecole Nat. des Impôts, Clermont Ferrand, France, 1970. Bar: 1976. Tax inspector Ministry France, Paris, 1970—76; tax assoc. Ernst & Whinney, 1976—80, tax ptnr., 1980—89, Clifford Chance, Paris, 1989—97; ptnr. Tirard, Naudin, 1997—. Assoc. prof. U. Burgundy, Dijon, 1981—. Author: Corporate Taxation in EU Countries, 5th edit., 2000. Mem.: Soc. Trust and Estate Practioners (chmn. French br. 2000), Internat. C. of C. (co-chmn. tax commn. 1990—). Office: Tirard Naudin 10 rue Clement Marot 75008 Paris France

TIRAS, HERBERT GERALD, engineering executive; b. Houston, Aug. 11, 1924; s. Samuel Louis and Rose (Seibel) T.; m. Aileen Wilkenfeld, Dec. 14, 1955; children— Sheryle, Leslie. Student, Tex. A. and M. U., 1941-42; attended, Houston U., 1942-65, student, Nat. Defence U., 1986. Registered profl. engr., Calif. Cert. mfg. engr. in gen. mfg.; robotics; mfg. mgmt; gen. mgmt. Engr., Reed Roller Bit, Houston, 1942-60; pres. Tex. Truss, Houston, 1960-77; chief exec. officer Omnico, Houston, 1977— ; Nat. Defense exec. res. resources officer, Region VI Fed. Emergency Mgmt. Agy., 1982— . Served to 1st lt. CAP, 1954-61. Mem. Machine Vision Assn., Nat. Defense U. Found., Am. Assn. Artificial Intelligence, Soc. Mfg. Engrs., Robot Inst. Am., Robotics Internat., Marine Tech. Soc., Coll. and Univ. Mfg. Ednl. Council (nat. dir.), Assn. of the Indsl. Coll. of the Armed Forces. Lodge: Masons, Shriners. Home: 9703 Runnymeade Dr Houston TX 77096-4219 Office: PO Box 2872 Houston TX 77252-2872 E-mail: H.Tiras@att.net.

TIRELLA, DAVID THEODORE, lawyer; b. Miami, Fla., Apr. 12, 1962; s. Alfred Lewis and Julia (Papparo) T.; m. Patricia Ellen Smith, Jan. 2, 1987; children: Peter N., Carolyn S. BS in Polit Sci., Fla. State U., 1986; JD, Cumberland Sch. Law, 1989. Bar: Fla. 1989, U.S. Dist. Ct. (mid. dist.) Fla. 1990, U.S. Ct. Appeals (11th cir.) 1994. Asst. state atty. Hillsborough County State Atty.'s Office, Tampa, Fla., 1989-92; ptnr. Tirella & Tirella, 1993-96; assoc. Eaton & Gordon, now Cohen, Jayson & Foster, 1996—. Apptd. spl. prosecutor Hillsborough County State's Atty.'s Office, Tampa, 1991-92; spl. pub. defender Hillsborough County Pub. Defender's Office, Tampa, 1993-95; instr. Am. Inst. Paralegals, Tampa, 1995. Mem. pub. spkrs. bur. Am. Cancer Soc., Tampa, 1996—. Mem.: ATLA, Hillsborough County Bar Assn., Fla. Acad. Trial Lawyers, Fla. Bar Assn. (grievance com. Tampa 1999—2002), Million Dollar Advocates Forum, Ferguson White Inns of Ct., Phi Alpha Delta. Avocations: public speaking, travel. Office: Cohen Jayson & Foster Ste 1000 201 E Kennedy Blvd Tampa FL 33602

TIRELLI, MARIA DEL CARMEN S. retired realtor; b. Rio Grande, P.R., Apr. 8, 1919; d. Carmelo Sieca Pacheco and Luisa Guzman Berrios; m. Francesco Tirelli, Dec. 20, 1947; children: Rose, Frank, Marie, Angelo. BS, U. P.R., 1941; MS, U. Chgo., 1944; JD, InterAm. U., 1978. Cert. home econs. tchr., N.Y., Spanish tchr., N.Y.C.; registered dietitian/nutritionist; cert. realtor, counselor. Home econs. tchr. Dept. Edn., San Juan, P.R., 1941-43; nutritionist USDA, 1944-45, Dept. Health, San Juan, 1946-47; sch. lunch supr. III & IV Dept. Edn., 1948-55; dietitian Good Samaritan Hosp., West Islip, N.Y., 1961-62; food svc. dir. N.Y. Dept. Mental Hygiene, Islip, 1964-74; sch. lunch dir. North Babylon (N.Y.) Schs., 1964-74; realtor C-21, Watson, Coldwell Banker, Brandon, Fla., 1982-00; realtor, assoc. Coldwell Banker, 1985-00; retired, 2000—. Pres. P.R. Dietetic Assn., San Juan, 1951-52, L.I. (N.Y.) Dietetic Assn., 1973; cons. dietitian various nursing homes, L.I., 1973-75; ad honorem lectr. U. P.R., Rio Piedras, 1955. Contbr. articles to profl. jours. Mem. Nativity Ch. Chorale, 1982-00. Recipient scholarship U. P.R., San Juan, 1943, grant U. Chgo., 1943. Mem. Nat. Assn. Realtors, Fla. Assn. Realtors., Tampa Board of Realtors (realtor assoc., mem. legis. title com. 1983), Legion of Mary (Brandon, sec. 1983-91). Republican. Roman Catholic. Avocations: music, piano, chorale. Home: PO Box 667 Valrico FL 33595-0667

TIRRELL, JOHN ALBERT, organization executive, consultant; b. Boston, Feb. 11, 1934; s. George Howard and Helen Sarah (Hitchings) T.; m. Helga Ruth Eisenhauer, Jan. 29, 1966; children: Steffanie Ruth, Sabina Lisette, Monica Susanne. BA in Psychology, The King's Coll., Briarcliff Manor, N.Y., 1961; MEd, U. Ariz., 1975. Various positions for several orgns., 1962-68; analyst instrnl.-ednl. systems GE, Daytona Beach, Fla., 1969-72; dir. curriculum and program devel. Brookdale C.C., Lincroft, N.J., 1972; dir. learning and faculty resources Pima C.C., Tucson, 1972-76; dir. human resources planning and devel. Miami divsn. Cyprus Copper Co., Claypool, Ariz., 1976-79; exec. dir. Calvary Missionary Fellowship, Tucson, 1983-85; interim pastor Sagauro Evang. Ch., 1985-86; pastor Midvale Evangelical Ch., 1986-87; founder, pres. The Jethro Consultancy, Birmingham, Mich., 1979—; v.p. mgmt. svc. AA Gage, Ferndale, 1987-88; pastor Desert Hills Bapt. Ch., Tucson, 1993-95. Mem. adv. bd. UIM Internat., Flagstaff, Ariz., 1983-92, mem. fin. com., 1983-94, sec. support svcs. field bd., 1993-01, sec. bus. and devel. field bd., 2002--, sec. pers. com., 1997—, sec., 1998—, also bd. dirs., 1993—; assoc. faculty mem. Gila Pueblo Campus Ea. Ariz. Coll., Globe, 1978; adj. prof. Montclair State Coll., Upper Montclair, N.J., 1972; chmn. mgmt. and pers. com. Wildwood Ranch, Inc., Howell, Mich., 1989-92; interim pres., v.p. programs, v.p. devel. Detroit Rescue Mission Ministries, 1990-92; v.p. corp. planning, tng., productivity George Instrument Co., Royal Oak; mem. mgmt., comm., sociology So. Ariz. Campus U. Phoenix, 1997—, area chair for social scis., 2001—; adj. faculty mem. psychology Pima County C.C., 1999—. Contbr. articles to profl. jours. Mem. Ariz. Coun. for Econ. Conversion, 1992-94; mem. facilities task force Grace Evang. Free Ch., Birmingham, 1989-90, chmn. bylaws revision com., 1989-90, chmn. property devel. com., 1990-92; interim pastor Desert Hills Bapt. Ch., Tucson, 1992-93; elder 1st Evang. Free Ch., Tucson, 1979-81, 86-87, 97, supt. Sunday sch., 1981-84, supr. adult Sunday sch., 1992-93, chmn. gen. bd., elder bd., 1979-82, short-term missions coord., missions bd., 1992-93; bd. dirs. S.W. Border dist. Evang. Free Ch. Am., 1996-00, mem. comm. com., 1996-01, chmn. comm. com., 1998-99; bd. dirs. Clearing House of Operational Resources for Christian Orgns., Royal Oak, Mich., 1991; bd. dirs. Shadow Roc Homeowners Assn., 1996-98, treas., 1997; v.p. parent-tchr. fellowship Palo Verde Christian Sch., Tucson, 1980-81. Staff sgt. USAF, 1952-56. Mem. ASTD (treas., Old Pueblo chpt. 1982, bd. dirs.-at-large 1983, Human Resources Devel. award Valley of the Sun chpt. 1977), Birmingham-Bloomfield C. of C. (mem. profl. devel. edn. com. 1987-91, mem. pub. rels. mktg. com. 1989), King's Coll. Alumni Assn. (class gov. 1988-95, 2000--). Republican. Avocations: photography, Bible teaching. Home and Office: 1205 E Deer Canyon Rd Tucson AZ 85718-1069 Fax: (253) 681-8198. E-mail: jack.tirrell@att.net.

TIRRO, FRANK PASCALE, music educator, author, composer; b. Omaha, Sept. 20, 1935; s. Frank and Mary Carmela (Spensieri) T.; m. Charlene Rae Whitney, Aug. 16, 1961; children: John Andrew, Cynthia Anne. B.M.E., U. Nebr., 1960; M.M., Northwestern U., 1961; PhD, U. Chgo., 1974. Chmn. lab. schs. U. Chgo., 1961—70; fellow of Villa I Tatti Harvard U., Florence, Italy, 1971—72; lectr. U. Kans., Lawrence, 1972—73; asst. prof. music Duke U., 1973—74; dir. Southeastern Inst. Medieval and Renaissance Studies, Durham, NC, 1978—80; chmn., assoc. prof. music Duke U., 1973—80; prof. Yale U., New Haven, 1980—, dean, 1980—89. Reader, cons. several univ. presses; jurist Parisot Internat. Cello Competition, Sao Paolo, Brazil, 1981. Author: Jazz: A History, 1977, rev. edit., 1993, Renaissance Choirbooks in the Archive of San Petronio in Bologna, 1986, Living With Jazz, 1996, (with others) The Humanities: Cultural Roots and Continuities, 1980, 6th edit., 2000; editor: Medieval and Renaissance Studies No. 9, 1982; mem. editl. bd. Wittenberg Rev.; composer American Jazz Mass, 1960; assoc. editor Am. Nat. Biography, 1994—. Bd. dirs. New Haven Symphony, 1980-89, Neighborhood Music Sch., New Haven, 1982-89, Chamber Orch. New Eng., 1980-82, Ctr. for Black Music Rsch., 1985—. Recipient Standard Composer award Am. Soc. Composers, Authors and Pubs., 1966, 99, 2000, 01, Gustavus Fine Arts medal, 1988, Duke Ellington Fellow medal, 1989; travel grantee Am. Coun. Learned Socs., 1967; rsch. grantee Duke U., 1978; named to Omaha Ctrl. H.S. Hall of Fame, 2002. Mem. Am. Musicol. Soc. (council 1978-80), Coll. Music Soc. (council 1980-82, mem. exec. bd. 1984-86), Nat. Assn. Schs. of Music, Internat. Soc. Jazz Research, Renaissance Soc. Am., Mory's Club, Yale Club (N.Y.C.). Republican. Lutheran. Office: Yale U Sch Music PO Box 208246 New Haven CT 06520-8246 E-mail: frank.tirro@yale.edu.

TIRSCHWELL-NEWBY, KATHY ANN, theater producer; b. Hudson, Wis., Jan. 8, 1961; d. Walter Haskell and Doris Hilda (Dornfeld) T. DDS (hon.), Roth/Williams Ctr., 1993. Traffic dir. Sta. KRKC, King City, Calif., 1978-79; office mgr. Cable TV of King City/Greenfield, 1979-82; lead cashier Del Webb's High Sierra Hotel & Casino, Lake Tahoe, Nev., 1982-84; acctg. analyst Hyatt Hotels, Burlinghame, Calif., 1984-87; v.p., owner Computer Diagnostic Info Inc., Burlingame, 1987-93; exec. dir. Roth/Williams Ctr., 1990-93; event support mgr. Stuart Rental Co., Sunnyvale, Calif., 1994-96, Cheskin & Masten/ImageNet, Redwood Shores, 1996; adminstr. Bayshore Animal Hosp., San Mateo, 1996-97; event sales mgr. Stuart Rental Co., Sunnyvale, 1997-2000; prodr. sports and corp. events E2k/Olmstead Prodns., Palo Alto, Calif., 2000—. Pres. Jr. Fairboard, Salinas Valley Fair, King City, Calif., 1979-80. Office: e2k/Olmstead Prodns 801 High St Palo Alto CA 94301 E-mail: katjtn@aol.com.

TIRYAKIAN, EDWARD ASHOD, sociology educator; b. Bronxville, N.Y., Aug. 6, 1929; s. Ashod Haroutioun and Keghinee (Agathon) T.; m. Josefina Cintron, Sept. 5, 1953; children: Edmund Carlos, Edwyn Ashod. BA summa cum laude, Princeton U., 1952; MA, Harvard U., 1954, PhD, 1956; PhD (hon.), U. Rene Descartes, Paris, 1987. Instr. Princeton U., 1956-57, asst. prof., 1957-62; lectr. Harvard U., 1962-65; assoc. prof. Duke U., Durham, N.C., 1965-67, prof., 1967—, chmn. dept. sociology and anthropology, 1969-72, dir. internat. studies, 1988-91. Vis. lectr. U. Philippines, 1954-55, Bryn Mawr Coll., 1957-59; vis. scientist program Am. Sociol. Assn., 1967-70; vis. prof. Laval U., Quebec City, Que., Can., 1978, Inst. Polit. Studies, Paris, 1992, Free U., Berlin, 1996; summer seminar dir. NEH, 1978, 80, 93, 89, 91, 96; lectr. Kyoto Am. Studies Summer Seminar, 1985, project leader Fulbright New Cent. Scholars Program, 2002—. Author: Sociologism and Existentialism, 1962; Editor: Sociological Theory, Values and Sociocultural Change: Essays in Honor of P.A. Sorokin, 1963, The Phenomenon of Sociology, 1971, On the Margin of the Visible: Sociology, the Esoteric, and the Occult, 1974, The Global Crisis: Sociological Analyses and Responses, 1984; co-editor: Theoretical Sociology: Perspectives and Developments, 1970; New Nationalisms of the Developed West, 1985. Fellow Ctr. for Advanced Study in Behavioral Scis., 1997-98; recipient Fulbright rsch. award, 1955; Ford faculty rsch. fellow, 1971-72, fellow Ctr. for Advanced Study in Behavioral Scis., 1997-98, Disting. New Century scholar Fulbright Scholar Program, 2002-03. Mem. Am. Sociol. Assn., African Studies Assn., Am. Soc. for Study Religion (co uncil 1975-78, pres. 1981-84), Assn. Internationale des Sociologues de Langue Française (v.p. 1985-88, pres. 1988-92), Soc. for Phenomenology and Existential Philosophy, Phi Beta Kappa. Clubs: Princeton, Century Assn. (N.Y.C.). Home: 16 Pascal Way Durham NC 27705-4924 *As a sociological researcher, I have sought to understand on a comparative basis the dynamics of social consciousness in the process of historical change. As a teacher, I have sought to encourage in students—undergraduates, graduates, and postgraduates— a gusto for intellectual curiosity in exploring the myriad of linkages that make up social reality, our human patrimony.*

TISCH, JAMES SOLOMON, diversified holding company executive; b. Atlantic City, Jan. 2, 1953; s. Laurence A. and Wilma (Stein) T.; m. Merryl Hiat; children: Jessica, Benjamin, Samuel. BA, Cornell U., 1975; MBA, Wharton Grad. Sch., U. Pa., 1976. With Loews Corp., N.Y.C., 1977—, exec. v.p., 1987-94, pres., COO, 1994-99, pres., CEO, 1999—, also mem. mgmt. com. Chmn., CEO Diamond Offshore Drilling, Inc.; bd. dirs. CNA Fin., Vail Resorts, Inc., Loews Corp. Bd. dirs. Fedn. Employment and Guidance Svc., N.Y.C., 1985—; trustee Mt. Sinai Med. Ctr./NYU Med. Ctr., N.Y.C., 1988—; pres.-elect UJA Fedn. N.Y. Office: Loews Corp 667 Madison Ave Fl 7 New York NY 10021-8087*

TISCH, PRESTON ROBERT, finance and sports executive; b. Bklyn., Apr. 29, 1926; s. Abraham Solomon and Sayde (Brenner) T.; m. Joan Hyman, Mar. 14, 1948; children: Steven E., Laurie M., Jonathan M. Student, Bucknell U., 1943-44; BA, U. Mich., 1948. Co-chmn., dir. Loews Corp., N.Y.C., 1960—; postmaster gen. U.S. Postal Svc., Washington, 1986-88; chmn., co-CEO, half owner N.Y. Football Giants, 1990—. Bd. dirs. CNA Fin. Corp., Bulova Watch Co., Hasbro Corp., Loews Corp. Chmn. emeritus N.Y. Conf. and Visitors Bur., Nat. Dem. Conv., 1976, 80; trustee NYU; mem. Quadrennial Commn. on Exec., Legis. and Jud. Salaries, 1988; mem. Gov.'s Bus. Adv. Coun. for N.Y. State; pres. Citymeals on Wheels, chmn. With AUS, 1943-44. Mem. Century Country Club, Sigma Alpha Mu. Office: Loews Corp 667 Madison Ave Fl 7 New York NY 10021-8087 also: NY Giants Giants Stadium East Rutherford NJ 07073

TISCHLER, HERBERT, geologist, educator; b. Detroit, Apr. 28, 1924; s. Louis and Hermina (Leb) T.; m. Annette Zeidman, Aug. 10, 1954; children— Michael A., Robert D. BS, Wayne U., 1950; MA, U. Calif.-Berkeley, 1955; PhD, U. Mich., 1961. Instr. Wayne State U., Detroit, 1956-58; assoc. prof. No. Ill. U., DeKalb, 1958-65; prof. dept. earth scis. U. N.H., Durham, 1965-97, chmn. dept., 1965-90, prof. emeritus dept. earth scis., 1997—; co-dir. No. New Eng. Jr. Sci. and Humanities Symposium, 1979-2001, mem. nat. adv. com., 1989-92. Trustee Mt. Washington Observatory, 1980-92. With USCG, 1943-46. Fellow Geol. Soc. Am. (sr.). Home: 36 Oyster River Rd Durham NH 03824-3029 Office: U NH Dept Earth Scis James Hall Durham NH 03824 E-mail: herbtischler@attbi.com.

TISCHLER, JUDITH BLANCHE, retired music publishing executive, educator; b. N.Y.C., May 14, 1933; d. Max and Anna (Drescher) Zucker; m. Alfred Tischler, Dec. 14, 1958; children: Marva, Mira, Gary. MA, CCNY, 1975; PhD, Jewish Theol. Sem., 1989. Editor, dir. Transcontinental Music Publs., N.Y.C., 1981—. Prof. music Jewish Theol. Sem., H.L. Miller Cantorial Sch. French hornist various concerts worldwide, 1952-71. Office: HL Miller Cantonal Sch Jewish Theol Sem of Am 3080 Broadway New York NY 10027 E-mail: tisch33@netvision.net.il., judithtischler@hotmail.com.

TISCHMAN, MICHAEL BERNARD, lawyer; b. Elizabeth, N.J., Oct. 8, 1937; s. Nathan and Ann (Goldberg) T.; m. Elinor Cohen, Aug. 16, 1959; children: David F., Susan F. BA, U. Pa., 1959; LLB, Harvard U., 1963; LLM in Taxation, NYU, 1968. Bar: N.J. 1964, Fla. 1979, N.Y. 1984. Law sec. Judge Walter J. Freund N.J. Appellate Div., 1963-64; assoc. Schiff, Cummis & Kent, Newark, 1964-67; ptnr. Cummis, Kent, Radin & Tischman, 1968-70, Sills, Beck, Cummis, Radin & Tischman, Newark, 1971-87, Sills, Cummis, Radin, Tischman, Epstein & Gross, Newark, 1988—. Panel chmn. fee arbitration com. N.J. Supreme Ct. Dist. Essex County, 1987-91; mem. health law and policy program adv. bd. Seton Hall Law Sch., 1997—. Mem. Mayor's Performing Arts Ctr. Task Force, Newark, 1988-96. Mem. N.J. Bar Assn. (com. on ltd. partnership act revisions 1983-88), Phi Beta Kappa. Home: 8 Wedgewood Way Scotch Plains NJ 07076-2727 Office: Sills Cummis Radin Tischman Epstein & Gross One Riverfront Pla Newark NJ 07102 E-mail: mtischman@sillscummis.com.

TISDALE, DOUGLAS MICHAEL, lawyer; b. Detroit, May 3, 1949; s. Charles Walker and Violet Lucille (Battani) T.; m. Patricia Claire Brennan, Dec. 29, 1972; children: Douglas Michael Jr., Sara Elizabeth, Margaret Patricia, Victoria Claire. BA in Psychology with honors, U. Mich., 1971, JD, 1975. Bar: Colo. 1975, U.S. Dist. Ct. Colo. 1975, U.S. Ct. Appeals (10th cir.) 1976, U.S. Supreme Ct. 1979. Law clk. to chief judge U.S. Dist. Ct. Colo., Denver, 1975-76; ptnr. Brownstein Hyatt Farber & Strickland, P.C., 1976-92; shareholder Popham, Haik, Schnobrich & Kaufman, Ltd., 1992-97, dir., 1995-97; ptnr. Baker & Hostetler LLP, Denver, 1997—2002; owner Tisdale & Assocs. Dir. Vail Valley Med. Ctr., 1990—; chmn. bd. dirs. Eagle Health Care Ctr., Inc., 2001—. City councilman Cherry Hills Village, Colo., 2000—. Home: 4662 S Elizabeth Ct Cherry Hills Village CO 80110-7106 Office: Tisdale & Assocs LLC Ste 3150 370 17th St Denver CO 80203

TISDALE, GREGORY BROKAW, artist; b. Newark, May 8, 1946; s. Lawrence Tisdale and Nancy Johanna Smith; m. Kathy Maschmeyer, July 20, 1991. Student, Ctr. for Creative Studies, Detroit, 1965-69. Comml. artist various advt. agys., Detroit, 1965-69; graphic artist Smith Henchman Grills, 1974-75; art dir. Klock Advt., 1975-84; freelance artist, 1984—. Lectr. in field. Paintings featured in publs. including Best of Watercolor, 1995, In Watercolor Places, 1996, Dictionary of Sea Painters, 1997, Painting in Light and Shadow, 1997; painting of Edmund Fitzgerald declared only ofcl. painting by Mariners Ch.; State of Mich. Senate Resolutions No. 191 for artistic contrbns. to the cmty., 1987. Staff sgt. USAF, 1969-73. Mem. Internat. Guild Fine Artists (v.p. 1996—), Am. Soc. Marine Artists (artist mem.), Grosse Pointe Boat Club (commodore 1995). Avocations: sailboat racing, skiing, scuba diving, motorcycles, cruising boats. Home: 35 Briarwood Pl Grosse Pointe MI 48236-3773

TISDALE, JAMES EDWARD, pharmacy educator, pharmacotherapy researcher; b. Winnipeg, Man., Can., Apr. 23, 1960; came to U.S., 1986; s. Charles Edward Murray and Helen Joan (Millar) T. BSc in Pharmacy, U. Man., 1983; PharmD, SUNY, Buffalo, 1988. Bd. cert. pharmacotherapy specialist. Pharmacist Health Scis. Ctr., Winnipeg, 1984-86; fellow cardiovascular therapeutics Hartford (Conn.) Hosp., 1988-90; clin. asst. prof. U. Conn., Storrs, 1988-90; adj. clin. instr. Mass. Coll. Pharmacy and Allied Health Scis., Springfield, 1988-90; asst. prof. Coll. Pharmacy and Health Scis. Wayne State U., Detroit, 1990-96, assoc. prof. Coll. Pharmacy and Health Scis., 1996—2002; coord. edn. and tng. dept. pharmacy Henry Ford Hosp., 1990—2002; assoc. prof. Sch. of Pharmacy and Pharmacal Sci. , Purdue Univ., Indpls., 2002—. Mem. cardiology item writing panel Specialty Coun. Bd. Pharm. Specialties, 1994-98; mem. expert panel Am. Soc. Health Sys. Pharmacists, 1994-96. Author 3 book chpts.; contbr. articles to profl. jours. Mem.: Am. Soc. Health-Sys. Pharmacists, Am. Pharm. Assn., Am. Soc. Clin. Pharmacology and Therapeutics, Am. Heart Assn. Mich. (chmn. profl. edn. com. 1993—95, mem. clin. cardiology coun. 1994—), Am. Coll. Clin. Pharmacy (chmn. publs. com. 1993—94, chmn. rsch. affairs com. 1995—97, chmn. ann. meeting program com. 1997—99, chmn. constn. and bylaws com. 1999—2000, bd. regents 2001—). Achievements include research in area of antiarrhythmic drug pharmacokinetics and pharmacotherapy, drug therapy of atrial fibrillation and cardiac arrhythmias induced by drugs. Avocations: guitar, music, sports, travel, football officiating. Office: Dept of Pharmacy Practice Purdue Univ D711 Myers Bldg WHs 101 W 10th St Indianapolis IN 46202 E-mail: jtisdale@iupui.edu.

TISE, LARRY EDWARD, association executive, historian; b. Winston-Salem, N.C., Dec. 6, 1942; s. Russell Edward and Lena Irene (Norman) T.; children: Larry Edward, Nicholas Allen, William Zane. AB, Duke U., 1965, M.Div., 1968; PhD (Ford Found. fellow, 1970, Research Triangle fellow, 1971), U. N.C., 1974. Part-time editor John Fries Blair, Pub., Winston-Salem, 1969-72; teaching fellow history dept. U. N.C., Chapel Hill, 1971, instr., 1972-73; dir. hist. publs. N.C. Bicentennial Com., 1973-74; asst. dir. N.C. Div. Archives and History, Raleigh, 1974-75, dir., 1975-81, N.C. State Hist. Preservation officer, 1975-81; exec. dir. Pa. Hist. and Mus. Commn., 1981-87; Pa. State Hist. Preservation officer, 1981-87; dir. Am. Assn. for State and Local History, Nashville, 1987-89; exec. dir. Benjamin Franklin Nat. Meml., Phila., 1989-97; pres., CEO Internat. Congress of Disting. Awards, 1997—. Adj. prof. grad. sch. fine arts U. Pa., 1984-87; vis. prof. Vanderbilt U., 1988-89, Temple U., 1989-91; Willbur Orville Wright vis. disting. prof. E. Carolina U., 2000; mem. Nat. Hist. Publs. and Records Commn., 1982-88 Author, co-author writings in fields of archives, hist. preservation, hist. sites and museums, history, society, religion; author: The Southern Experience in the American Revolution, 1978, The Monitor: Its Meaning and Future, 1978, Writing North Carolina History, 1979, A House Not Made with Hands, 1966, The Yadkin Melting Pot: Methodism and the Moravians in the Yadkin Valley, 1750-1850, 1968, Proslavery: The Defense of Slavery in America, 1987, A Book About Children, 1992, The American Counterrevolution, 1998, Keep on Running, 1998, Benjamin Franklin and Women, 2000; gen. editor: writings in fields of archives, hist. preservation, hist. sites and museums, history, society, religion including Winston-Salem in History, 13 vols, 1976; edit. bd. The Public Historian, 1980-86; editor N.C. Hist. Rev., 1974-81, Pa. Heritage, 1981-87, History News, 1987-89, Franklin Gazette, 1989-97; contbr. articles to books, newsletters, publs. Recipient William R. Davie History award, 1979, Herbert L. Feis award, Am. Hist. Assn., 1989, Benjamin Franklin Nat. Meml. awards 1990, Best New Book in History, Ind. Book Pubs., 1999; Nat. Endowment for the Humanities fellow, 1992-93; faculty fellow NASA-Langley, 2000, 2001. Mem. Am. Hist. Assn. (various coms.), Orgn. Am. Historians (chmn. coms.), So. Hist. Assn., Am. Assn. State and Local History (mem. coun. and coms.), Nat. Assn. State Archives and Records Adminstrs. (pres. 1980-81), Nat. Conf. State Hist. Preservation Officers (bd. dirs. 1976-79, pres. 1979-81), Nat. Coun. on Pub. History (bd. dirs., exec. com. 1979-83, pres. 1983-85), N.C. Hist. Commn. (sec. 1975-81), N.C. Lit. and Hist. Assn. (sec., treas. 1977-81), Pa. Fedn. Hist. Socs. (sec. 1981-87), Friends of Franklin, Inc. (exec. sec. 1989-97). Methodist.

TISHKEVICH, FRANCES MARY, mathematics educator; b. Worcester, Mass., Dec. 23, 1953; d. Edward Gregory and Theresa (Siminski) T.; children: Joseph Gorgol, David Gorgol. BS in Math. Edn., Plymouth State Coll., 1975; MA in Gifted Edn., Norwich U., 1989; postgrad., Calif. Coast U. Cert. experienced educator, N.H. Math. tchr. West H.S., Manchester, N.H., 1975-81; prof. math. N.H. Coll., 1989-98; assoc. prof. math. Notre Dame Coll., 1991—2002; instr. math. Plymouth State Coll., 1998. Regional problem coord., judge N.H. Odyssey of the Mind, N.H., 1987-95. Author: N.H. Mensa's Gifted Children's Handbook, 1987. Coach East Soccer League, Manchester, 1994; math.-sci. coord. Swift Water Girl Scout Coun., Nashua, N.H., 1995-96; active Norwich U. Parent Assn., 1999—; founder Norwich U. Soccer Parents Assn., 2000—. Mem. Nat. Coun. Tchrs. Math., N.H. Tchrs. of Math, Mensa (gifted childrens coord. 1985-93, Gifted Childrens Coord. of Yr. 1990). Avocations: hiking, skiing, needlework, reading. E-mail.

TISHLER, WILLIAM HENRY, landscape architect, educator; b. Baileys Harbor, Wis., June 22, 1936; s. William John and Mary Viola (Sarter) T.; m. Betsy Lehner, Sept. 23, 1961; children: William Phillip, Robin Elizabeth. BS in Landscape Architecture, U. Wis., 1960; M in Landscape Architecture, Harvard U., 1964. Urban planner City of Milw., 1961-62; mem. faculty dept. landscape architecture U. Wis., Madison, 1964—; assoc. Hugh A Dega & Assocs. (Landscape Archs.), 1964-66; prin. Land Plans Inc. (Land and Hist. Preservation Planning Cons.), Madison, 1966—. Advisor emeritus Nat. Trust for Hist. Preservation; bd. dirs. The Hubbard Ednl. Trust. Author: American Landscape Architecture: Designers and Places, 1989, Midwestern Landscape Architecture, 2000; contbr. articles to profl. jours. With C.E., U.S. Army, 1960. Recipient Design Arts Program award NEA, 1981, Hawthorn award Friends of The Clearing, 1997, Outstanding Educator award Coun. Educators in Landscape Architecture, 1998; Attingham (Eng.) Program fellow Soc. Archtl. Historians, 1980; Dumbarton Oaks sr. fellow, 1990. Fellow Am. Soc. Landscape Archs. (Horace Cleve. vis. prof. U. Minn. 1993, nat. merit award 1971, 97, 99, honor award 1980, 89, Wis. chpt. Lifetime Achievement award 2000); mem. Assn. Preservation Tech., Wis. Acad. Arts, Letters and Scis., Pioneer Am. Soc. (Henry Douglas award) , Hist. Madison (hon.), Vernacular Architecture Forum (past pres.), Madison Trust for Hist. Preservation, Alliance for Hist. Landscape Preservation (founder), The Clearing Landscape Inst. (founder, dir.), Phi Kappa Phi, Sigma Lambda Alpha, Sigma Nu. Lutheran. Home: 3925 Regent St Madison WI 53705-5222 Office: U Wis Dept Landscape Architecture Dept Landscape Architecture Madison WI 53706 E-mail: wtishler@facstaff.wisch.edu.

TISINGER, DAVID HARVEY, lawyer; b. Carrollton, Ga., May 8, 1937; s. Robert D. and Naomi E. Tisinger; m. sharon Inman, Feb. 3, 1975; children: John David, Joel Wesley. BS, Ga. Inst. Tech., 1958; LLB, U. Ga., 1963. Bar: Ga. 1962. Ptnr. Tisinger Vance & Greer, Carrollton, 1963—. Instr. law U. Ga., Athens, 1964; chmn. bd. Carrollton State Bank, 1974-78. Mem. bd. regents U. Sys. of Ga., Atlanta, 1972-79. Lt. USNR, 1958-60. Fellow Am. Coll. Trial Lawyers; mem. ATLA, Def. Rsch. Inst. Avocations: farming, sailing. Office: Tisinger Tisinger Vance & Greer 100 Wagon Yard Plz Carrollton GA 30117-3490

TISMA, MARIJA STEVAN, artist; b. Indjija, Serbia, Yugoslavia, Aug. 22, 1950; s. Stevan Ilija and Djurdjinka Steva (Tubic) T.; m. Nenad Ante Rukavina, May 24, 1989; 1 child, Dane. BArch, Belgrade U., 1983. Pres. ARDIUM.com, BBS for Art & Architecture, Belgrade, 1995—. One-man shows at Libertas Gallery, Dubrovnik, Croatia, 1977, Mostar RU Gallery, Bosnia-Hercegovina, 1980, Can. Embassy Gallery, Belgrade, Yugoslavia, 1987, Lazar Vozarevic Gallery, Yugoslavia, 1988, City Mus., Kraljevo, Yugoslavia, 1988, Singidunum Gallery, Belgrade, 1993, others; group shows include Oct. Salon, Belgrade, 1976-87, May Salon, Belgrade, 1977-87, Serbian Contemporary, Brussels, 1978; included in collections at Hotels Intercontinental, Belgrade, McDonald's Corp., Novi Sad, Yugoslavia. Yugoslav Ministry of Edn. grantee, 1978. Fellow Yugoslav Inst. Artists (Grand prize 1979, Great prize 1989); mem. Yugoslav Inst. Architects. Avocations: travel, books. Home: 15 Excelsior Pl Butler NJ 07405-1511

TISMANEANU, VLADIMIR, political science educator, researcher; b. Brasov, Romania, July 4, 1951; s. Leonte and Hermina Tismaneanu; m. Mary Frances Sladek, Nov. 22, 1991; 1 child, Adam Volo. BA, MA, U. Bucharest, Romania, PhD, 1980. Rsch. assoc. Fgn. Policy Rsch. Inst., Phila., 1983-90; lectr. U. Pa., 1985-90; sr. asst. prof. U. Md., Coll. Pk., 1990-92, assoc. prof., 1992-97, prof., 1997—. Mem. E. Europe com. Am. Coun. Learned Socs., N.Y.C., 1997—. Author: Crisis of Marxist Ideology in Eastern Europe, 1988, Reinventing Politics, 1992, Fantasies of Salvation, 1998, Slowly, Towards Europe, 2000; editor: Revolutions of 1989, 1999, Between Past and Future, 2000; mem. Jour. Democracy, 1996—; jour. editor East European Politics and Society, 1998—. Bd. dirs. Internat. Forum Dem. Studies, Washington, 1997—. Recipient Vis. Disting. Lectr. award U.S. Dept. State, 1994; Book award Romanian-Am. Acad. Arts and Scis., 1998, award Romanian Cultural Found., 2000. Mem. Am. Assn. Advancement Slavic Studies, Am. Polit. Sci. Assn. Office: U Md Dept Govt & Politics Tydings Hall College Park MD 20742 Fax: 202-686-5131.

TISSER, DORON MOSHE, lawyer, educator; b. Tel Aviv, Israel, Mar. 3, 1955; came to U.S., 1958; s. Leon Tisser and Livia H. (Lorber) S.; m. Laurie J. Satnick, Nov. 18, 1978; children: Benjamin A., Jeremy N. BA in Polit. Sci., UCLA, 1978; JD cum laude, Southwestern U., 1981; LLM in Taxation, NYU, 1982. Bar: Calif. 1981, U.S. Dist. Ct. (cen. dist.) Calif. 1982, U.S. Tax Ct. 1982, U.S. Ct. Appeals (9th cir.) 1982. Pvt. practice, Woodland Hills, Calif., 1987—. Instr. Coll. Continuing Edn., U. So. Calif., Los Angeles, 1984-85, dept. bus. and mgmt. UCLA, 1985-88, Calif. Luth. U., Thousand Oaks, 1985-87; panel mem. pro se program U.S. Tax Ct., 1984—; lectr. to profl. orgns., 1985—. Contbg. editor (taxation) Calif. Bus. Law Reporter, 1986—; contbr. articles to legal publs. Mem. steering com. Warner Ctr. bus. and profl. div. San Fernando Valley region Jewish Fedn. Coun. Greater Los Angeles, 1987—. Mem. ABA, Calif. State Bar (cert. taxation specialist), Phi Alpha Delta. Democrat. Jewish. Avocation: running.

TISSOT, JOHN NORMAN, elementary school educator, artist, writer; b. Riverside, Calif., May 31, 1926; s. Alden Francis and Francyl Reseda Tissot; m. Beatriz Elena Carvajal, July 30, 1953; 1 child Janet Elaine Tissot-Kirk. BA, U. Calif., Berkeley; postgrad., U. Calif., L.A. Tchr. Los Molinos (Calif.) H.S., Jackson (Calif.) H.S., Carpinteria (Calif.) H.S.; instr. U. Calif., Santa Barbara. Author: The Ultimate Lie, 1980, The Button and the Blood, 1999, Around the World on a Breakfast Tray, 1999, (plays) Five with I.E. Clark; contbr. short story , juvenile fiction and non-fiction to various publs. Mem. Bd. Edn., Carpinteria. With USN. Mem.: Dyslexia Awareness and Resource Ctr., Santa Barbara Artists' Assn. Home: PO Box 1107 Carpinteria CA 93014-1107

TISSUE, MIKE, medical educator, respiratory therapist; b. Garfield, Wash., Aug. 24, 1941; s. Altha Lester and Fern Adeline (Willard) T.; m. Marjorie Lena Atkinson, Feb. 24, 1961 (div. June 1991); children: Sue Tipton, Pam Kromholtz, Paul, Donna; m. Mary Emma Napier, Aug. 24, 1998. AAS (4 degrees) with honors, Spokane (Wash.) C.C., 1985; BS in Respiratory Therapy cum laude, Loma Linda (Calif.) U., 1987; MS in Respiratory Care, Ga. State U., 1999. Registered cardiovasc. technologist (invasive and non-invasive), Nat. Soc. Cardiopulmonary Technol./Cardiovasc. Credentialing Internat.; registered respiratory therapist, pulmonary function technologist, perinatal/pediatric specialist NBRC; registered respiratory care practitioner, Calif., Ga.; diplomate sr. disability analyst Am. Bd. Disability Analysts. Respiratory intern, Level III NICU Therapist Loma Linda (Calif.) U. Med. Ctr., 1985-87; educator, therapist Riyadh (Saudi Arabia) Armed Forces Hosp., 1987-91; dept. head respiratory care Security Forces Hosp., Riyadh, 1991-93; asst. prof., dir. clin. edn. respiratory therapy program Morehead (Ky.) State U., 1993-94; program dir. assoc. degree respiratory therapy Chattahoochee Tech. Inst., Marietta, Ga., 1994-98; clin. instr. Ga. State U., Atlanta, 1999-2001; dir. respiratory therapy program Nat. Inst. Tech., 2001—. Pres., founder Riyadh Cardiorespiratory Soc., 1988-93; rschr. Loma Linda U., 1987, Riyadh Armed Forces Hosp., 1988; instr. and affiliate faculty ACLS Wash. State Heart Assn., 1983-85, Calif. Heart Assn., 1985-87, Saudi Heart Assn., 1985-87, Ky. Heart Assn., 1993-94, Ga. affiliate, 1994—; instr. and affiliate faculty pediatric advanced life support Saudi Heart Assn., 1987-93; instr. and affiliate faculty basic life support/CPR Wash. State, 1974-85, Calif., 1985-87, Saudi Heart Assn., 1987-93, Ky. Heart Assn., 1993-94, Ga. affiliate, 1994—; cons. ARC, Tacoma, Wash., 1984, instr. advanced 1st aid, standard 1st aid, CPR, 1975—, Inland Empire Chpt., Spokane, Wash., 1975-94, San Bernardino/Redlands Svc. Ctr., Loma Linda, 1985-87, Am. Cmty. Svcs. U.S. Embassy, Riyadh, 1991-93, U.S. Mil. Operation Desert Storm, Riyadh, 1991-93, Ga. affiliate Cobb County chpt., Marietta, 1994—; instr. Freedom From Smoking Clinic Program Am. Lung Assn., Calif., 1985-87, Saudi Arabia, 1987-93, Smyrna, Ga., 1994—; mem. Instl. Effectiveness Com., Campus Computer Com. Chattahoochee Tech. Inst., 1994—. Contbr. articles to profl. jours. Bd. dirs. Am. Heart Assn., Spokane, 1976-83, chair fin. com., 1981-83; chair spkrs. bur. ARC, Inland Empire Chpt., Spokane, 1982-85, chair pub. rels., 1983-85; mem. Calif. affiliate San Bernardino Chpt., Loma Linda, 1985-87, Ga. affiliate Cobb County Chpt., Marietta, 1994—; chair programming and spkrs. bur. Am. Lung Assn., Smyrna, Ga., 1994—, chmn. bd. dirs., 1995—; sec. Cobb County Cmty. Coun., Marietta, 1995-96, spkr., 1995, v.p., 1996, pres. 1997; vol. Ga. Internat. Cultural Exch., 1995; registry exam. sr. proctor Cardiovascular Credentialing Internat./Nat. Bd. Cardiovascular Technologists, Riyadh, 1987-90; commr. Boy Scouts Am., Spokane, 1973-82, wood badge, 1977, commrs. key, 1977, scouters key, 1979. Named Citizen of Day KGA Radio, Spokane, 1983. Mem. AAUP (legislature com. Atlanta 1995—), Am. Assn. Respiratory Care (therapist driven protocol rev. com. 1994, ad hoc com. on patient-driven-protocol rev. com. 1996, ad hoc com. for sects. rev. 1995, 96), Alliance of Cardiovas. Profls., Ga. Soc. Respiratory Care (bd. dirs. 1994—, edn. com., smoking and health com.), Phi Delta Kappa (Alpha Nu chpt. Morehead, Ky. 1993-94, Kennesaw Mountain chpt. Atlanta 1994—, pub. rels. Com. 1995—). Roman Catholic. Avocations: photography, travel. Home: 1881 Arnold Dr SW Austell GA 30106-2907 Office: Nat Inst Tech Respiratory Therapy Program 1706 Northeast Pkwy Atlanta GA 30329 E-mail: tissue@5pillars.com.

TITCOMB, CALDWELL, music and theatre historian; b. Augusta, Maine, Aug. 16, 1926; s. Samuel and Lura Elizabeth (Smith) T. AB summa cum laude, Harvard U., 1947, MA, 1949, PhD, 1952. Univ. organist Brandeis U., Waltham, Mass., 1953-70, dir. undergrad. studies music, 1956-84, curator creative arts, library, 1961-64, co-chmn. music dept., 1977-84, from instr. to prof. music, 1953-88, prof. emeritus, 1988—. Drama critic Harvard Crimson, 1953-82, Bay State Banner, 1975—, This Month on Stage, 1996-99, Totaltheater.com, 2000—; trustee Charles Playhouse, Boston, 1966-71 Editor: The Art of Fine Words, 1965, The Furies (Lucien Price), 1988; co-editor: Varieties of Black Experience at Harvard, 1986, Blacks at Harvard: A Documentary History of African-American Experience at Harvard and Radcliffe, 1993; contbr. articles to profl. jours., ency.; composer stage and film music scores. Bd. dirs. Cambridge Civic Symphony Orch., Mass., 1959-70; exec. bd. Mus. Fine Arts Friends Music, Boston, 1959-65; panelist Mass. Commn. Arts and Humanities, 1981-83; mem. selection com. Theater Hall of Fame, 1980—; juror Elliot Norton awards, 1985—; pres. Boston Theater Critics Assn., 1994—. With U.S. Army, 1944-46, PTO; with Mil. Intelligence Res., 1946-50. Mem. AAUP, Coll. Music Soc., Am. Theatre Critics Assn. (charter), New Eng. Theatre Conf. (adv. coun. 1961-81, coll. fellows 1981—), Am. Guild Organists, Am. Musicol. Soc. (coun. 1965-67), Soc. for Ethnomusicology, Hist. Brass Soc., Signet Soc., Sonneck Soc., Phi Beta Kappa (sec. Mu chpt. Mass. 1984—). Avocations: philology, Afro-American history and culture. E-mail: caldwell67@aol.com.

TITE, JOHN GREGORY, secondary school educator; b. Southbridge, Mass., Sept. 20, 1941; s. Gregory Louca and Androniq (Zhidro) T. BS, U. Mass., 1963; MEd, Worcester (Mass.) State Coll., 1966; MS, Clarkson Coll. Tech., 1971. Instr. math. Grafton (Mass.) Pub. Schs., 1963-67, math. dept. chairperson, calculus instr., 1967—. Adj. prof. calculus Anna Maria Coll., Paxton, Mass., 1986-88; in-svc. instr. metrics for h.s. and elem. tchrs., 1974-76; spkr. in field. Grantee NSF, 1965, 67, 75, Computer Assisted Math Project grant U. Mass., 1985-86. Mem. Assn. of Tchrs. of Math. in Mass. (pres., exhibits chmn. 1970), Nat. Coun. Suprs. of Math., Nat. Coun. of Tchrs. of Math. (chmn. films and filmstrips com. 1973, chmn. sales of materials 1976), Neighborhood Assn. of Math. Dept. Heads (bd. dirs. 1976-79). Avocations: reading, traveling, walking. Home: 12 Arrowhead Ave Auburn MA 01501-2302 Office: Grafton Pub Schs 24 Providence Rd Grafton MA 01519-1178

TITLEY, LARRY J. lawyer; b. Tecumseh, Mich., Dec. 9, 1943; s. Leroy H. and Julia B. (Ruesink) T.; m. Julia Margaret Neukom, May 23, 1970; children: Sarah Catherine, John Neukom. BA, U. Mich., 1965, JD, 1972. Bar: Va. 1973, Mich. 1973. Assoc. Hunton & Williams, Richmond, Va., 1972-73, Varnum, Riddering, Schmidt & Howlett, Grand Rapids, Mich., 1973—. Trustee Friends Pub. Mus., 1985—94; bd. dirs. Pub. Mus. Found., 1988—97, pres., 1992—95; bd. dirs. Camp Optimist YMCA, 1993—98, Peninsular Club, 1994—, pres., 1997. Mem. ABA, Mich. Bar Assn., Grand Rapids Bar Assn. Home: 520 Roundtree Dr NE Ada MI 49301-9707 Office: Varnum Riddering Schmidt & Howlett Bridgewater Pl PO Box 352 Grand Rapids MI 49501-0352 E-mail: ljtitley@vrsh.com.

TITLEY, ROBERT L. lawyer; b. Tecumseh, Mich., Dec. 15, 1947; AB, U. Mich., 1970; JD, Duke U., 1973. Bar: Wis. 1973, Mich. 1974. Ptnr. Quarles & Brady, Milw. Mem. editorial bd. Duke Law Jour., 1972-73. Mem. State Bar Mich., State Bar Wis., Order of Coif. Office: Quarles & Brady 411 E Wisconsin Ave Milwaukee WI 53202-4497

TITONE, VITO JOSEPH, state supreme court justice; b. Bklyn., July 5, 1929; s. Vito and Elena (Ruisi) T.; m. Margaret Anne Viola, Dec. 30, 1956; children: Stephen, Matthew, Elena Titone Hill, Elizabeth. BA, NYU, 1951; JD, St. John's U., 1956, LL.D., 1984. Bar: N.Y. 1957, U.S. Dist. Ct. (ea. and so. dists.) N.Y., 1962, U.S. Supreme Ct. 1964, U.S. Ct. Appeals N.Y. 1985. Ptnr. Maltese & Titone, N.Y.C., 1957-65, Maltese, Titone & Anastasi, N.Y.C., 1965-68; assoc. counsel to pres. pro tem N.Y. State Senate, 1965; justice N.Y. State Supreme Ct, N.Y.C., 1969-75; assoc. justice appellate div. 2d dept., 1975-85; judge N.Y. State Ct. Appeals, Albany, 1985—; of counsel Mintz & Gold LLP, N.Y.C., 1998—. Adj. prof. Coll. S.I., CUNY, 1969-72, St. John's U., Jamaica, N.Y., 1969-85. Bd. editors N.Y. Law Jour., 1999; contbr. articles to law jour. Bd. govs. Daytop Village Inc., N.Y.C.; bd. dirs. Boy Scouts Am.; bd. trustees The Am. Parkinson Disease Assn. With U.S. Army, 1951-53, to col. N.Y. State Guard. Named Citizen of Yr. Daytop Village, N.Y.C., 1969, Disting. Citizen Wagner Coll., S.I., 1983, Outstanding Contbr. Camelot Substance Abuse Network, 1983; recipient citation of merit S.I. Salvation Army Adv. Bd., 1983, Rapollo award Columbian Lawyers Assn., 1983, Disting. Judiciary award Cath. Lawyers Guild Diocese of Bklyn., 1991, Disting. Svc. award N.Y. State Lawyers Assn., Justice William Brennan award N.Y. Assn. Criminal Def. Lawyers, 1993, Life Achievement award N.Y. Conf. Italian Am. State Legislators, 1994, Ellis Island Medal of Honor, 1997, gold medal Bklyn. Bar Assn., 1997. Mem. ABA, N.Y. State Bar Assn., Richmond County Bar Assn., Supreme Ct. Justice Assn., VFW, Am. Legion (past comdr.), Charles C. Pinckney Tribute Def. Assn. of N.Y., Justinian Soc., K.C. Roman Catholic. Office: Mintz and Gold LLP 444 Park Ave S New York NY 10016-7321

TITRUD, OLIVER GEORGE, retired medical educator; b. Clarissa, Minn., May 11, 1926; s. Geroge Marius Titrud and Gunda Gjerstad; m. Dorothy Selma Lindborg, Oct. 9, 1949; children: Kermit Oliver, Cheryll Lu, Douglas Glenn, Bethine Joy, Debrah Lynn, Timothy Craig, Howard George, Rebecca Ann. BS, Bemidji (Minn.) State U., 1948; MS, U. Denver, 1951; MEdn, Macalester Coll., 1958; D of Chiropractic, L.A. Coll. Chiropractic, 1963; cert. advanced studies, No. Ill. U., 1972. Assoc. prof. Northwestern Coll., Roseville, Minn., 1952-57, Pasadena (Calif.) Coll., 1957-60; prof. biology Azusa (Calif.) Pacific U., 1960-63, Warner Pacific Coll., Portland, Oreg., 1963-69; prof. anatomy Nat. Coll. Chiropractic, Lombard, Ill., 1969-72; mem. faculty Can. Meml. Chiropractic Coll., Toronto, Ont., 1972-73; acad. dean, prof. anatomy Western States Chiropractic Coll., Portland, 1973-79; mem. faculty Palmer Coll. Chiropractic, San Jose, Calif., 1979-89; prof. Naturopathic Coll., Portland, 1989-93. Chmn. test com. Nat. Bd. Chriopractic Examiners, Denver, 1975-78. Author: Titrud's Method of Human Dissection, 1977. With USN, 1944-46. Grantee Western Mich. U., 1960. Avocations: studying languages, public speaking. Home: 1969 Camellia Way Woodburn OR 97071

TITTLE, DOLORES, dental hygienist, artist; b. Lockport, N.Y., Apr. 8, 1930; d. Leo and Bertha (Plews) Ryszka; m. Cecil Deforest Tittle, July 26, 1958; children: Bernadine Allen, Mark, Blair. AAS, Erie County Tech. Coll., Buffalo, N.Y., 1957. Comml. artist Moore Bus. Forms, Niagara Falls, N.Y., 1948-51; dental asst. VA Hosp., Buffalo, 1953-55; dental hygiene tchr. Bd. Edn., Niagara Falls, 1957-59; dental hygienist various dental offices Niagara Falls and Lewiston, 1959—. Exhbns. include local arts shows. With USNR, 1973-90. With USN, 1951-53. Republican. Roman Catholic. Avocations: painting, travel, plays, classical music, reading. Home: 780 Oneida St Lewiston NY 14092

TITTMANN, BERNHARD RAINER, engineering science and mechanics educator; b. Moshi, Tanganjika, East Africa, Sept. 15, 1935; came to U.S., 1950, naturalized, 1956; s. Gustav and Hermine Marie (Polland) T.; m. Katharine Shower, Dec. 17, 1966; children: Christine M., Heidi E., Raymond J., Monica M., Brian P.F. BS, George Washington U., 1957; MS, UCLA, 1961, PhD, 1965. Mem. staff Hughes Aircraft Co., Culver City, Calif., 1957-65; asst. prof. UCLA, 1965-66; mem. staff Rockwell Internat., Thousand Oaks, Calif., 1966-79, dept. mgr., 1979-89; Schell prof. engrng. Pa. State U., University Park, 1989—. Co-author 6 books; contbr. over 300 articles to profl. jours.; patentee in field. George Washington fellow George Washington U., 1953, Howard Hughes fellow Hughes Aircraft Co., 1957, Fulbright fellow, 1998. Fellow IEEE (administrv. com. for ultrasonics, ferrolectrics, frequency control, major awards chmn. 1999—, disting. lectr. 1998-99), Acoustical Soc. Am., KC (4th degree); mem. Phi Beta Kappa. Home: 2466 Sassafras Ct State College PA 16803-3366 Office: Pa State U 212 Earth Engring Sci Bldg University Park PA 16802-6804

TITTSWORTH, CLAYTON (CLAYTON MAGNESS TITTSWORTH), lawyer; b. Tampa, Fla., Nov. 8, 1920; Student, U. Tampa, 1939-42; LLB, Stetson Law Sch., 1951. Bar: Fla. 1951. Ptnr. Tittsworth & Tittsworth, Tampa, 1951-65, Brandon, Fla., 1964-73, pvt. practice, 1973-83, Tittsworth and Curry, PA, Brandon, 1983-87, 1987—. Mem.: Fla. Bar Assn. Office: 1021 Hollyberry Ct Brandon FL 33511-7657 E-mail: cmt20@msn.com.

TITUS, ANN SCHIEWETZ, social worker, nurse; b. Dayton, Ohio, Feb. 6, 1932; d. Herbert Jacob and Grace Marie (Kurtz) Schiewetz; m. William Edward Duellman, Feb. 6, 1953 (div. Jan. 1965); children: Beverly Ann Duellman Heumann, Deborah Lee Duellman Shimkus; m. William Hart Titus, Oct. 10, 1987. BSN, U. Mich., 1955; MSW, Ohio State U., 1968. Lic. social worker, Mich., Colo.; RN. Staff nurse neuropsychiat. unit U. Mich. Hosp., Ann Arbor, 1955-57; office nurse Dr. Russell Frink, Lawrence, Kans., 1965-66; social worker El Paso County Sch. Dist. #11, Colorado Springs, Colo., 1968-91; ret., 1991—. Field instr. U. Denver, Colorado Springs, 1978-79; chairperson Dept. Social Work Sch. Dist. #11, 1989-91; mem. High Risk Intervention Task Force, Colorado Springs, 1989-91. Contbr. articles to profl. jours. Mem. Nat. Assn. Social Workers. Republican. Lutheran. Avocations: golf, gardening, sewing, music.

TITUS, BRUCE EARL, lawyer; b. N.Y.C., June 5, 1942; BA, Coll. William and Mary, 1964, JD, 1971. Bar: Va. 1971, D.C. 1972, Md. 1984. Asst. dir. torts br., civil divsn. U.S. Dept. Justice, 1971-82; mem. Jones, Waldo, Holbrook and McDonough, Washington; ptnr. Venable, Baetjer and Howard, LLP, McLean, Va., 1986-976; prin. Rees, Broome & Diaz P.C., Vienna, 1997—. Exec. editor William & Mary Law Review, 1970-71. Mem. ABA, Va. State Bar, D.C. Bar, Fairfax Bar Assn. (pres. 1999-2000), Md. State Bar, Phi Delta Phi, Omicron Delta Kappa. Office: Rees Broome & Diaz PC 9th Fl 8133 Leesburg Pike Vienna VA 22182-2706

TITUS, EDWARD DEPUE, psychiatrist, administrator; b. N.Y.C., May 24, 1931; s. Edward Kleinhans and Mary (Brown) Chadbourne; m. Virginia Van Den Steenhoven, Mar. 24, 1963 (div.); m. Catherine Brown, Apr. 22, 1990. BA, Occidental Coll., 1953; MS, U. Wis., 1955; MD, Stanford U., 1962; PhD, So. Calif. Psychoanalytic Inst., 1977. Mng. ptnr. Hacker Clinic Assn., Lynwood, Calif., 1968-90; chief psychiatrist parole outpatient clinic region III Calif. Dept. Corrections, L.A., 1991-2001; asst. clin. prof. psychiatry U. So. Calif., 1993—; cons. psychiatrist Gateways FCTP, L.A., 2001—. Chmn. dept. psychiatry St. Francis Hosp., Lynwood, 1979-80. Fellow Am. Psychiat. Assn.; mem. Calif. Med. Assn. (ho. of dels. 1981-95), So. Calif. Psychiat. Soc. (sec. 1984-85, 98-99, pres.-elect 2002-03), L.A. County Med. Assn. (dist. pres. 1980-81, pres. sect. psychiatry 1990-92). Avocations: photography, backpacking. Office: Gateways FCTP 621 S Virgil Ave Ste 300 Los Angeles CA 90005

TITUS, JACK L. pathologist, educator; b. South Bend, Ind., Dec. 7, 1926; s. Loren O. and Rutha B. (Orr) T.; m. Beverly Harden, June 18, 1949; children—Jack, Elizabeth Ann Titus Engelbrecht, Michael, Matthew, Joan, Marie Titus Davis. BS, Notre Dame U., 1948; MD, Washington U., St. Louis, 1952; PhD, U. Minn., 1962. Practice medicine, Rensselaer, Ind., 1953-57; fellow in pathology U. Minn., 1957-61; assoc. prof. pathology Mayo Grad. Sch., Rochester, Minn., 1961-72; prof. pathology Mayo Med. Sch., 1971-72, coordinator pathology tng. programs, 1964-72; W.L. Moody Jr. prof., chmn. dept. pathology Baylor Coll. Medicine, Houston, 1972-87; chief pathology service Meth. Hosp., 1972-87; pathologist-in-chief Harris County Hosp. Dist., 1972-87; chmn. dept. pathology Med. Ctr. Hosp., Conroe, Tex., 1982-87, Woodlands Community Hosp., 1984-87; dir. registry for cardiovascular diseases United Hosp., 1987-95, 97—, sr. cons. registry, 1996-97, dir., 1997—; prof. pathology U. Minn., 1987—. Adj. prof. pathology Baylor Coll. Medicine, 1987—; sr. cons. in pathology U. Tex. System Cancer Ctr., Houston, 1974—. Mem. editl. bd. Circulation, 1966-72, Am. Heart Jour., 1972-77, Modern Pathology, 1987-95, Human Pathology, 1988—, Am. Jour. of Cardiovascular Pathology, 1987-94, Cardiovascular Pathology, 1991—, Advances in Pathology, 1998—; contbr. articles to med. jours. Served with U.S. Army, 1945-47. Recipient Billings gold medal AMA, 1968, Hoektoen gold medal, 1969, Disting. Achievement award Soc. Cardiovascular Pathology, 1993, Scholarly Achievement award Houston Soc. Clin. Pathology, 1993. Mem. Internat. Acad. Pathology, Am. Assn. Pathologists, Am. Soc. Clin. Pathologists, AAAS, AMA, Am. Heart Assn., Coll. Am. Pathologists, Minn. Med. Assn., Minn. Heart Assn., Minn. Soc. Clin. Pathologists, Minn. Acad. Medicine (pres. 1998-99), Ramsey County Med. Soc., Soc. for Cardiovascular Pathology (pres. 1995-97), Sigma Xi, Alpha Omega Alpha. Methodist. Office: 333 Smith Ave N Ste 4625 Saint Paul MN 55102-2518 E-mail: jtitus@allina.com.

TITUS, JON ALAN, lawyer; b. Milw., Oct. 6, 1955; s. Mary Elna Irwin; m. Laura Jean Newman, Sept. 5, 1982; children: Katherine, Derek. BA, U. Ariz., 1977; JD, Ariz. State U., 1980. Bar: Ariz. 1980, U.S. Dist. Ct. Ariz. 1980; cert. real estate specialist. Pres. Titus, Brueckner & Berry, P.C., Scottsdale, Ariz., 1980—. Mem. Ariz. Kidney Found., 1984—, pres., 1991-92. Recipient Alumni Achievement award Ariz. State U., 1996. Mem. Ariz. Bar Assn. (chmn. securities regulation sect. 1986-87), Maricopa County Bar Assn., Scottsdale Bar Assn. (dir. 1993-95). Office: Titus Brueckner & Berry PC 7373 N Scottsdale Rd Ste B-252 Scottsdale AZ 85253-3513

TITUS, ROGER WARREN, lawyer; b. Washington, Dec. 16, 1941; s. George R. and Margaret (Merithew) T.; m. Catherine Mary Gaughen, Aug. 16, 1961; children: Paula Titus Laboy, Richard Roger, Mark William. BA, Johns Hopkins U., 1963; JD, Georgetown U., 1966. Bar: Md. 1966, D.C. 1966, U.S. Dist. Ct. Md. 1966, D.C. Dist. 1966, U.S. Ct. Appeals (4th cir.) 1966, U.S. Supreme Ct. 1970. Ptnr. Titus & Glasgow, Rockville, Md., 1966-88, Venable, Baetjer & Howard, Rockville, 1988—. Asst. city atty. City of Rockville, 1966-69, city atty., 1970-82; spl. asst. Md. State Bd. of Law Examiners, 1969-72; adj. prof. law Georgetown U., Washington, 1972-78; mem. inquiry com. Atty. Grievance Commn., Annapolis, Md., 1975-80; mem. Trial Cts. Judicial Nominating Commn. Montgomery County, 1979-91; mem. standing com. on rules of practice and procedure Ct. of Appeals of Md., 1989—; mem. Appellate Jud. Nominating Commn., 1991-99. Trustee Suburban Hosp., Inc., Bethesda, Md., 1986-2000, chmn. bd., 1997-2000. Fellow: Am. Acad. Appellate Lawyers, Md. Bar Found. (bd. dirs. 1987—93, v.p. 1990—91, pres. 1991—93), Am. Bar Found., Am. Coll. Trial Lawyers; mem.: ABA (del. 1987—95), Montgomery County Bar Assn. (exec. com. 1983—84), Md. Mcpl. Attys. Assn. (pres. 1975), Am. Judicature Soc. (bd. dirs. 1995—2001), Md. Bar Assn. (sec. 1984—87, pres. 1988—89), Nat. Conf. Bar Pres. (mem. exec. coun. 1990—93), City Tavern Club. Office: Venable Baetjer & Howard PO Box 1906 1 Church St Ste 1000 Rockville MD 20850-4158

TITZL, MARY TRUEHEART, social work educator, consultant; b. Memphis, Jan. 12, 1921; d. Ross Alexander Williamson and Katherine Roberta Sharman; m. Robert Joseph Titzl, Nov. 20, 1943. AB, U. Louisville, 1942, MSSW, 1944; PhD, U. Chgo., 1968. Cert. social worker. Intake supr. Family Svc. Orgn., Louisville, 1946-51; dir. ct. svcs. Domestic Relations Ct., 1952-54; planning dir. Health & Welfare Coun., 1954-63; assoc. prof. social work U. Louisville, 1965-66; prof. and dean Sch. Profl. Psychology and Social Work Spalding U., Louisville, 1969-87; ret. Adv. coun. Ky. Coun. for Social Svcs., Frankfort, 1981-93; v.p. Coun. on Social Work Edn., N.Y.C., 1982-85; chmn. Assn. of Baccalaureate Program Dirs., 1975-77, Task Force on Human

Needs, Louisville, 1981-83. Recipient Svc. Recognition award Spalding U., 1999. Mem. Louisville Geneaol. Assn. (v.p.), Pi Beta Phi. Episcopalian. Avocation: genealogy. Home: 7606 Dudley Square Dr Louisville KY 40222

TIUMAN, ERICH LIM, textile company executive; b. Manila, Philippines, Nov. 20, 1935; s. Guat Ngo and Aytee Lim; m. Sofia Lu Tiuman, Dec. 25, 1960; children: Siegfried L., Luzono L. B Music Composition and Conducting, Centro Escolar U. Sch Music, Manila, 1968, M Music Composition, 1969. Prodn. mgr. Bee Lam Shirt Factory, Manila, 1954-63; pres. Peng Kong Grand Mason Band, 1954-63; dir., rsch. conductor China Youth Symphony Orchestra, Taipei, 1964-66; owner Tiuman Textile Distributors, Manila, 1968-75; pres., gen. mgr. Tiuman & Co., 1968-75; chmn., gen. mgr. Tiuman Ent. MLA, 1985-91; pre gen. mgr. Philtai Internat., 1985-88; owner Yecy Mfg., 1993—; with Izhu Inc., N.Y.C., 1995—. Composer orchestra lit., Symphony # 2, 1971, Tainoko Ballet Music, 1971. Recipient Philippine Swimming Championship/2nd pla., Philippines Athletic Assn., Manila, 1951, Chung Shan awards for Lit. and Arts, Csala Found., Taipei, 1971, Pres. Chiang Kai Sek Cultural award, MLA Literay Club, Manila, 1971. Mem. Asian Composers League/Philippines, Asian Pacific Ethnomusicology Soc. Avocations: swimming, rsch. in humanities, travel, composing, phy. tng. Home: Apt 40 B 1 Central Park W New York NY 10023 Office: 3-A Sta Agueda Ave Sto Niño Parañague Manila 1704 Philippines also: Izhu Inc 295 Greenwich St Apt 6P New York NY 10007-1052

TIVENAN, CHARLES PATRICK, lawyer; b. Newark, Feb. 20, 1954; s. Gerard Charles and Mary Jo (Vogel) T.; m. Mary Katherine Herlihy, Aug. 2, 1980; children: Moire Kathleen, Sean Patrick, Liam Francis, Michala Maureen. BA in Govt., Seton Hall U., 1975, JD, 1980. Bar: N.J. 1982, U.S. Dist. Ct. N.J. 1982, U.S. Supreme Ct. 1995. Law clk. Essex County Prosecutor's Office, Newark, summer 1978, Dwyer Connell & Lisbona, Attys., Montclair, N.J., 1978-79; legal rsch. asst. Inst. Continuing Legal Edn., Newark, 1979; jud. law clk. to Hon. John J. Dios Superior Ct., 1980—81; assoc. Timothy J. Provost, Atty., Freehold, 1981—85, Arthur Stein & Assocs., Forked River, N.J., 1985-92; sole practice Bricktown, 1992—. Mediator, Early Settlement panelist Superior Ct. N.J/Ocean County, Toms River, N.J., 1987—, roster of N.J. Superior Ct. Approved Mediators, 2001—. Mem. juvenile conf. com. South Orange (N.J.) JCC, 1974-81; condemnation commr. Ocean County, Toms River, 1986—; conflict atty. Brick Twp., 1994—, planning bd. atty., 2002--; conflict pub. defender Brick Twp. Mcpt. Ct., Bricktown, 1994—; candidate Brick Twp. Coun., 1992; active Bricktown Dem. Club, trustee 1995-98, v.p. 1999—; commr. Brick Twp. Housing Authority, Brick, 1997-2001, Municipal Utilities Authority, 2001—; atty. advisor Brick Twp. Trial Moot Ct., 1998—. Recipient Cert. of Appreciation, Ocean County Superior Ct., 1987—, certs. of appreciation various orgns., 1985—. Mem. ABA, N.J. Bar Assn. (gen. practice, family law 1985—), Am. Trial Lawyers Assn. (N.J. affiliate, lectr. 1985—), Ocean County Bar Assn. (family law com. 1985—), KC (3d degree), Epiphany Coun. Roman Catholic. Avocations: reading, current events/politics, running, computers. Office: Godfrey Lake Profl Bldg 426 Herbertsville Rd Brick NJ 08724-1310 E-mail: cptesq@aol.com.

TIZARD, BARBARA, education and child development researcher; b. London, Apr. 16, 1926; d. Herbert and Elsie (Kirk) Parker; m. Jack Tizard, Dec. 20, 1947 (dec. Aug. 1979); children: Bill, John (dec.), Jenny, Martin (dec.), Lucy. BA with honors, Oxford (Eng.) U., 1948; PhD in Psychology, U. London, 1957. Ednl. psychologist Child Guidance Clinic, London Hosp., 1957-60; lectr. dept. exptl. neurology Inst. Psychiatry U. London, 1963-67, research officer dept. child devel. Inst. Edn., 1967-71, sr. rsch. fellow, 1971-77, reader in edn., 1978-80, prof. edn., 1980—; dir. Thomas Coram rsch. unit Inst. Edn., 1980-90. Cons. WHO, 1984—. Author: Early Childhood Education, 1975, Adoption: A Second Chance, 1977, (with others) Involving Parents in Nursery and Infant Schools, 1981, Young Children Learning, 1984, Young Children at School in the Inner City, 1988, Black, White or Mixed Race, 1993; co-editor: The Biology of Play, 1977; mem. editl. bd. Jour. Child Psychology and Psychiatry, 1979-90, Social Devel., 1990—; contbr. numerous articles to profl. jours. Fellow Brit. Psychol. Soc., Brit. Acad. (sr.). Office: U London Thomas Coram Research 27 Woburn Square London WC1N OAA England E-mail: tcrul@ioe.ac.uk.

TIZZIO, THOMAS RALPH, brokerage executive; b. Elmont, N.Y., Jan. 9, 1938; s. Anthony Thomas and Ann Marie (Pascale) T.; m. Mary Ann Gentile, Aug. 26, 1962; children: Anthony, Vincent, Thomas. BBA, Bklyn. Coll., 1962. Underwriter W.J. Roberts & Co., N.Y.C., 1957-65; sr. underwriter Atlantic Mut. Ins. Co., 1965-67; various positions AIG Am. Home Assurance Co., N.Y.C., 1967-74, sr. v.p. property underwriting, 1974-78; exec. v.p. AIG Transatlantic Reins. Co., 1978-80, pres., bd. dirs., 1980-82; sr. v.p. reins. Am. Internat. Group, Inc., 1982-85, pres. domestic brokerage divsn., 1985-91, pres. Brokerage divsn., 1986-91, pres., 1991-97, sr. vice chmn., 1997—. Mem. Am. Inst. for Property and Liability Underwriters (trustee), Ins. Inst. Am. (trustee). Office: Am Internat Group Inc 175 Water St New York NY 10038-4918

TJOFLAT, GERALD BARD, federal judge; b. Pitts., Dec. 6, 1929; s. Gerald Benjamin and Sarita (Romero-Hermoso) Tjoflat; m. Sarah Marie Pfohl, July 27, 1957 (dec.); children: Gerald Bard, Marie Elizabeth; m. Marcia Penman Parker, Feb. 21, 1998. Student, U. Va., 1947—50, U. Cin., 1950—52; LLB, Duke U., 1957; DCL (hon.) , Jacksonville U., 1978; LLD (hon.) , William Mitchell Coll., 1993. Bar: Fla. 1957. Pvt. practice, Jacksonville, Fla., 1957—68; judge 4th Jud. Cir. Ct. , 1968—70, U.S. Dist. Ct. Mid. Dist. , Jacksonville, 1970—75, U.S. Ct. Appeals 5th Cir., Jacksonville, 1975—81, U.S. Ct. Appeals 11th Cir., Jacksonville, 1981—, chief judge, 1989—96. Mem. Adv. Corrections Coun. U.S., 1975—87, Jud. Conf. of U.S., 1989—, Fed. Jud. Ct. Com. on Sentencing, Probation an dPretrial Svcs., 1988—90; mem. com. adminstrn. probation system Jud. Conf. of U.S., 1972—87, chmn., 1978—87; U.S. del. 6th and 7th UN Congress for Prevention of Crime and Treatment of Offenders. Hon. life mem., bd. visitors Duke U. Law Sch., 2000; pres. North Fla. coun. Boy Scouts Am., 1976—85, chmn., 1985—90; trustee Jacksonville Marine Inst., 1976—90, Episc. H.S., Jacksonville, 1975—90; mem. vestry St. Johns Cathedral, 1969—71, 1973—75, 1977—79, 1981—83, 1985—87, 1993, 1995—96, sr. warden, 1975, 1983, 1987, 1991, 1992. With U.S. Army, 1953—55. Recipient Merit award, Duke U., 1990, Fordham-Stein prize, 1996. Mem.: ABA, Am. Judicature Soc., Am. Law Inst., Fla. Bar Assn. Episcopalian. Office: US Ct Appeals US Courthouse PO Box 960 311 W Monroe St Rm 539 Jacksonville FL 32201*

TKACHUK, KEITH, professional hockey player; b. Melrose, Mass., Mar. 28, 1972; With Phoenix Coyotes formerly Winnipeg (Canada) Jets, 1992—2001, St. Louis Blues, 2001—. Named to Hockey East All-Rookie team, 1990-91, NHL All-Star second team, 1994-95, Sporting News All-Star team, 1996. Office: St. Louis Blues Savvis Center Saint Louis MO 63103*

TKACIK, MICHAEL PATRICK, political science educator, lawyer; b. Balt. s. Charles Thomas and Jacqueline Lee Tkacik; m. Theresa Marie Vendetti, Aug. 7, 1999; 1 child, Paulina. JD, Duke U., 1989; MA in Polit. Sci., Columbia U., 1993; PhD in Polit. Sci., U. Md., 1999. Instr. George Mason U., Fairfax, Va., 1996-99, U. Md., College Park, 1996-99; asst. prof. polit. sci. Stephen F. Austin State U., Nacogdoches, Tex., 1999—. Author: (book chpt.) Evolutionary Theory and Its Critics, 2001; contbr. articles to profl. jours. Vis. Scholar fellow Social Sci. Rsch. Coun.-MacArthur Found., 1996. Mem. Internat. Studies Assn., Am. Polit. Sci. Assn., S.W. Assn. Am. Geographers, Calif. State Bar Assn. Office: Stephen F Austin State U Box 13045-SFA Station Nacogdoches TX 75962-3045 Fax: (936) 468-2732. E-mail: mtkacik@sfasu.edu.

TKACZUK, NANCY ANNE, cardiovascular services administrator; b. Cambridge, Mass., Nov. 17, 1949; d. Ralph Aubrey and Eleanor Mae (Goding) Bedley; m. John Paul Tkaczuk, Apr. 9, 1977 (div. Apr. 1983); children: Timothy Aubrey, James Paul. AS in Social Svc., Endicott Coll., 1969; ADN, Clayton Coll., 1975. Coronary care nurse New England Meml. Hosp., Wakefield, Mass., 1975; cardiac cath lab nurse Saint Josephs Hosp., Atlanta, 1976-79; dir. cardiovascular svcs. Northside Hosp., 1979—. Founder Mitral Valve Prolapse Support, Atlanta, 1986—; BCLS instr., trainer Am. Heart Assn., 1976—, instr. ACLS, 1990—, pub. spkr., 1975—. Author: Mitral Valve Prolapse, The Heart With A Different Beat, 1986. Mem. Am. Coll. Cardiovascular Adminstrs., Atlanta Health Care Alliance, Am. Heart Assn., Ga. Hosp. Assn., Ga. Soc. Ambulatory Care. Methodist. Avocations: tennis, golf. Home: 715 Cranberry Trl Roswell GA 30076-2377 Office: Northside Hosp Cardiology Dept 1000 Johnson Ferry Rd NE Atlanta GA 30342-1611 E-mail: nancy.tkaczuk@northside.com.

TLOU, JOSIAH S. education educator, educator; b. Zimbabwe, Dec. 31, 1935; s. Litsila and Mothateho T.; m. Litha T., Sept. 3, 1959; children: Lee, Hla, Joy B., Leeto. BA, Luther Coll., 1968; MA, Ill. State U., 1969; EdD, U. Ill., 1976. Cons. curriculum Glencoe (Ill.) Pub. Schs.; specialist social studies USAID U. Botswana, Gaborone; prof. Va. Tech., Blacksburg; civic curriculum planner for U.S. AID project Creative Assocs. Internat./Harvard Inst. Internat. Devel., Malawi, 1996-98; dir. USAID/Malawi Govt. Projects UPIC, 1998—. Cert. tchr., Zimbabwe. Contbr. articles to profl. jours. Recipient Disting. Svcs. award Luther Coll.; Luce-Bergeson rsch. grantee, African-Am., Scholars Coun. grantee, Creative Univ. Rsch. grantee, 1991-92, 94-95. Mem. ASCD, WCCI, Nat. Coun. Social Studies, ASA, AAPRDTW, Botswana Edn. Rsch. Assn., Phi Delta Kappa. E-mail: tlou@vt.edu.

TOAL, JAMES FRANCIS, academic administrator; b. N.Y.C., June 7, 1932; s. John Joseph and Catherine (Whyte) T. MA, St. John's U., 1966; PhD, Fordham U., 1976. Cert. elem. tchr., N.Y. cert. supt., adminstrn. and supervision, English 7-12. Athletic dir., tchr. English St. Francis Prep. High Sch., N.Y.C., 1957-60; tchr. Bishop Ford High Sch., 1960-66, chmn. dept. English; prin. St. Francis Central Summer High Sch., 1966-73, St. Francis Prep. High Sch., N.Y.C., 1966-73; exec. v.p., assoc. prof. dept. edn. adminstrn. and supervision Grad. Sch. St. Bonaventure U., N.Y., 1976-83; pres., prof. Quincy U., Ill., 1983-97; v.p. Siena Coll., Loudonville, N.Y., 1997—; also bd. trustees. Mem. Springfield Diocesan Bd. of Edn., Provincial Bd. of Edn., Franciscan Friars of Chgo. and St. Louis. Trustee Siena Coll., Loudonville, N.Y., 1977-83; bd. advisors Jamestown Community Coll., Olean, N.Y., 1979-83; bd. dirs. Am. Cancer Soc., Olean, 1981-83; mem. Mental Health Assn., 1981-83; mem. state legis. com. Commn. of Ind. Colls. and Univs., Albany. N.Y., 1980-83; mem. bd. trustees Padua Franciscan High Sch. Grantee Colgate U., 1967; grantee SUNY-Plattsburg, 1968, St. Bonaventure U., 1980 Mem. Am. Coun. on Edn., Associated Colls. of Ill., Ill. Bus. and Edn. Forum, Assn. of Governing Bds., West Ctrl. Ill. Ednl. Telecomm. Corp. (bd. dirs. exec. com., fin. com., pers. com.), Fedn. Ind. Ill. Colls. and Univs. (pub. rels. com.), Mid. States Accrediting Assn. (assoc., evaluation team for higher edn.), Nat. Assn. Secondary Sch. Prins., North Ctrl. Accrediting Assn. (evaluation team for higher edn., chair evaluation team 1986—), Soc. Coll. and U. Planning, Quincy C. of C. (transp. com. 1985-96, computer com. 1996—), Rotary, Univ. Club, KC, Phi Delta Kappa. Office: Siena Coll Office of VP Loudon Rd Loudonville NY 12211

TOAL, JEAN HOEFER, state supreme court chief justice; b. Columbia, S.C., Aug. 11, 1943; d. Herbert W. and Lilla (Farrell) Hoefer; m. William Thomas Toal; children: Jean Hoefer Eisen, Lilla Patrick. BA in Philosophy, Agnes Scott Coll., 1965; JD, U. S.C., 1968; LHD (hon.), Coll. Charleston, 1991; LLD (hon.), Columbia Coll., 1992, The Citadel, 1999, Francis Marion U., 1999. Bar: S.C. Assoc. Haynsworth, Perry, Bryant, Marion & Johnstone, 1968-70; ptnr. Belser, Baker, Barwick, Ravenel, Toal & Bender, Columbia, 1970-88; assoc. justice S.C. Supreme Ct., 1988-00, chief justice, 2000—. Mem. S.C. Human Affairs Commn., 1972-74; mem. S.C. Ho. of Reps., 1975-88, chmn. house rules com., constitutional laws subcom. house judiciary com.; mem. parish coun. and lector St. Joseph's Cath. Ch.; chair S.C. Juvenile Justice Task Force, 1992-94; chair S.C. Rhodes Scholar Selection Com., 1994. Mng. editor S.C. Law Rev., 1967-68. Bd. visitors Clemson U., 1978; trustee Columbia Mus. Art; bd. trustees Agnes Scott Coll., 1996—. Named Legislator of Yr. Greenville News, Woman of Yr., U. S.C.; recipient Disting. Svc. award S.C. Mcpl. Assn., Univ. Notre Dame award, 1991, Algernon Sydney Sullivan award U. S.C., 1991. Mem. John Belton O'Neill Inn of Ct., Phi Beta Kappa, Mortar Bd., Order of the Coif. Office: Supreme Ct SC PO Box 11330 Columbia SC 29211-2456*

TOALE, THOMAS EDWARD, school system administrator, priest; b. Independence, Iowa, Aug. 30, 1953; s. Francis Mark and Clara R. (DePaepe) T. BS in Biology, Loras Coll., 1975, MA in Ednl. Adminstrn., 1986; MA in Theology, St. Paul Sem., 1980; PhD in Ednl. Adminstrn., U. Iowa, 1988. Ordained priest Roman Cath. Ch., 1981; cert. tchr., supt., Iowa. Tchr. St. Joseph Key West, Dubuque, Iowa, 1975-77, Marquette High Sch., Bellevue, 1981-84, prin., 1984-86; assoc. supt. Archdiocese of Dubuque, 1986-87, supt. schs., 1987—. Assoc. pastor St. Joseph Ch., Bellevue, 1981-84; pastor Sts. Peter and Paul Ch., Springbrook, Iowa, 1984-86, St. Peter, Temple Hill, Cascade, Iowa, 1986—. Mem. Nat. Cath. Edn. Assn. (pres., chief adminstrn. Cath. edn.). Office: Archdiocese of Dubuque 1229 Mount Loretta Ave Dubuque IA 52003-7826

TOAN, BARRETT A. health products executive; BA, Kenyon Coll.; MBA, U. Pa. Commr. divsn. social svcs. State of Ark., 1979—81; dir. dept. social svcs. State of Mo., 1981—85; exec. dir., COO Sanus Health Plan of St. Louis, 1985—91; pres., CEO Express Scripts, Maryland Heights, Mo., 1992—, chmn., 2000—. Names Entrepreneur of Yr. Inc. Mag., 1994. Office: Express Scripts 13900 Riverport Dr Maryland Heights MO 63043-4827*

TOAY, THELMA M. columnist; b. Anamosa, Iowa, Feb. 22, 1915; d. Frank Leroy and Edna May Stoughton. Student, St. Lukes Sch. Nursing, Davenport, IA, 1933, Highland Coll., 1966—67, Famous Writer's Course, Westport, CT, N.E. Iowa C.C., Peosta, 1996, U. Iowa, 1998—2002. Contbr. various newspapers, Freeport, Ill., 1962—95; contbr. Julien's Jour., Dubuque, Iowa, 1995—; columnist Manchester (Iowa) Press, 2002—, Dyersville (Iowa) Comml., 2002—. Author: (Book) Bittersweet, 1979, (book) Places for the Heart - Profiles of Life, 2001. Scholar, U. Iowa, 1997—2001. Avocations: humanitarian efforts, theater , music.

TOBE, STEPHEN SOLOMON, zoology educator; b. Niagara-on-the-Lake, Ont., Can., Oct. 11, 1944; s. John Harold and Rose T. (Bolter) T.; m. Martha Reller. BSc, Queen's U., Kingston, Ont., 1967; MSc, York U., Toronto, Ont., 1969; PhD, McGill U., Montreal, Que., Can., 1972. Rsch. fellow U. Sussex, Eng., 1972-74; asst. prof. U. Toronto, 1974-78, assoc. prof., 1974-78, prof., 1982—, assoc. dean scis., faculty arts and sci., 1988-93, vice dean faculty arts and sci., 1995-96. Vis. prof. U. Calif., Berkeley, 1981, Nat. U. Singapore, 1987, 1993-94, U. Hawaii, 1988; mem. animal biology grant selection com. Natural Scis. and Engring. Rsch. Coun. Can., 1986-89, chair, 1988-89; lectr. Internat. Congress Entomology, Vancouver, B.C., Can., 1988; cons. in hydroponics. Editor Insect Biochemistry, 1987; mem. editl. bd. Jour. Insect Physiology, 1980—, Physiol. Entomology, 1985—, Life Scis. Advances, 1987—, Gen. and Comparative Endocrinology, 1995—; contbr. chpts. to books and articles to profl. jours. Recipient Pickford medal in comparative endocrinology, 1993; E.W.R. Steacie fellow Natural Scis. and Engring. Rsch. Coun. Can., 1982-84. Fellow Royal Soc. Can., Royal Entomol. Soc.; mem. AAAS, Entomol. Soc. Can. (C. Gordon Hewitt award 1982, gold medal 1990), Soc. Exptl. Biology. Avocations: amateur radio, gardening, hydroponics. Home: PO Box 695 Virgil ON Canada L0S 1T0 Office: U Toronto Dept Zoology 25 Harbord St Toronto ON Canada M5S 3G5 E-mail: stephen.tobe@utoronto.ca.

TOBER, BARBARA D. (MRS. DONALD GIBBS TOBER), editor; b. Summit, N.J., Aug. 19, 1934; d. Rodney Fielding and Maude Starkey; m. Donald Gibbs Tober, Apr. 5, 1973. Student, Traphagen Sch. Fashion, 1954-56, Fashion Inst. Tech., 1956-58, N.Y. Sch. Interior Design, 1964. Copy editor Vogue Pattern Book, 1958-60; beauty editor Vogue mag., 1961; dir. women's services Bartell Media Corp., 1961-66; editor-in-chief Bride's mag., N.Y.C., 1966-94; chmn. Am. Craft Mus.; pres. Acronym, Inc., N.Y.C., 1995—, The Barbara Tober Found., 1995—. Sec.-treas., dir. Sugar Foods Corp.; adv. bd. Traphagen Sch.; coord. SBA awards; Am. Craft Coun., 1983—, benefit food com. chmn., 1984-87. Author: The ABC's of Beauty, 1963, China: A Cognizant Guide, 1980, The Wedding . . . The Marriage . . . And the Role of the Retailer, 1980, The Bride: A Celebration, 1984 Mem. Nat. Council on Family Relations, 1966; nat. council Lincoln Center Performing Arts, Met. Opera Guild; mem. NYU adv. bd. Women in Food Service, 1983; NYU Women's Health Symposium: Steering Com., 1983—. Recipient Alma award, 1968, Penney-Mo. award, 1972, Traphagen Alumni award, 1975, Diamond Jubilee award, 1983, Disting. Women award Northwood U., 1997. Mem. Fashion Group, Internat. Furnishings and Design Assn. (v.p., program chmn.), Am. Soc. Mag. Editors, Am. Soc. Interior Designers (press mem.), Intercorporate Group, Women in Communications (60 yrs. of success award N.Y. chpt. 1984), Nat. Assn. Underwater Instrs., Pan Pacific and S.E. Asia Women's Assn., Asia Soc., Japan Soc., China Inst., Internat. Side Saddle Orgn., Millbrook Hounds, Golden's Bridge Hounds, Wine and Food Soc., Chaines des Rotisseurs (chargée de press) (bd. dirs.), Dames d'Escoffier, Culinary Inst. Am. Home and Office: 620 Park Ave New York NY 10021-6591

TOBER, STEPHEN LLOYD, lawyer; b. Boston, May 27, 1949; s. Benjamin Arthur Tober and Lee (Hymoff) Fruman; m. Susan V. Schwartz, Dec. 22, 1973; children: Cary, Jamie. Grad., Syracuse U., 1971, JD, 1974. Bar: N.H. 1974, U.S. Dist. Ct. N.H. 1974, U.S. Supreme Ct. 1978, N.Y. 1981. Assoc. Flynn, McGuirk & Blanchard, Portsmouth, N.H., 1974-79; sole practice, 1979-81; ptnr. Aeschliman & Tober, 1981-91; prin. Tober Law Offices, P.A., 1992—. Lectr. Franklin Pierce Law Ctr., Concord, N.H., 1978-80. Contbr. articles to law jours. Mem. Portsmouth Charter Commn., 1976, Portsmouth Planning Bd., 1977-81; del. N.H. Constl. Conv., Concord, 1984; city councilman, Portsmouth, 1977-81. Fellow: Am. Bar Found.; mem.: ATLA (gov. 1980—86), ABA (state del., chair credentials and admissions com., mem. standing com. on fed. judiciary), New H. Bd. Bar Examiners, N.H. Trial Lawyers Assn. (pres. 1977), N.H. Bar Assn. (pres. 1988—89, chair com. to redraft code of profl. responsibility, Disting. Svc. award 1986, 1994), New Eng. Bar Assn. (bd.dirs. 1988—91). Democrat. Jewish. Avocations: reading, tennis. Home: 55 T J Gamester Ave Portsmouth NH 03801-5871 Office: Tober Law Offices PA PO Box 1377 Portsmouth NH 03802-1377 Business E-Mail: stober@toberlaw.com.

TOBEY, MARTIN ALAN, cardiologist; b. Dallas, Sept. 24, 1947; s. Nathan Gene and Rose Marcus T.; m. Judith Helane Ross, Mar. 10, 1974; children: Daniel, Rachel. BS with highest distinction, Pa. State U., 1968; MD, Jefferson Med. Coll., 1970. Diplomate Am. Bd. Internal Medicine, Am. Bd. Cardiovascular Diseases, Am. Bd. Interventional Cardiology. Intern Phila. Gen. Hosp., 1970-71; resident in internal medicine Parkland Meml. Hosp., Dallas, 1971-74; fellow in cardiology U. Tex. Southwestern Med. Sch., 1976-78; cardiologist Cardiology Assocs. of Fort Worth, Tex., 1978—. Mem. med. bd. Harris Hosp. Meth., Ft. Worth, 1988-90, chmn. cardiology divsn., 1988-90. Author (software) Workshops in Coronary Angioplasty, 1984. Major U.S. Army, 1974-76. Fellow Am. Coll. Cardiology (regional rep. Tex. chpt. 1996—), Am. Heart Assn., Alpha Omega Alpha. Avocations: classical music, bicycling, computers. Office: Cardiology Assocs Ft Worth 1300 W Rosedale St Fort Worth TX 76104-2802

TOBIA, RONALD LAWRENCE, lawyer; b. Newark, Oct. 25, 1944; s. Salvatore and Marie (Melillo) T.; m. Sandra A. Boutsikaris, June 15, 1969; children: Jill, Alisandra, Joseph. BA, Lafayette Coll., 1966; JD, U. Miami, 1969. Bar: Fla. 1969, N.J. 1970, U.S. Dist. Ct. (so. dist.) N.Y. 2000, U.S. Dist. Ct. (ea. dist.) N.Y. 2000. Legal asst. region 22 NLRB, Newark, 1967, 68; jud. clk. to presiding justice N.J. Superior Ct., Passaic County, 1969-70; hearing officer N.J. Pub. Employment Rels. Com., Trenton, 1970—71; sr. ptnr. Schwartz, Tobia, Stanziale, Sedita & Campisaro, PA, Montclair, 1972—. Contbr. articles to profl. jours. Fin. co-chmn. N.J. Rep. Com. With JAGC, U.S. Army, 1967-68. With JAGC U.S. Army, 1967—68. Mem. ABA, N.J. Bar Assn., Fla. Bar Assn., Essex County Bar Assn., Indsl. Rels. Rsch. Assn. Republican. Roman Catholic. Avocations: skiing, tennis. Home: 48 Old Indian Rd West Orange NJ 07052-3226 Office: Schwartz Tobia Stanziale Sedita & Campisano PA 22 Crestmont Rd Montclair NJ 07042

TOBIAS, BENJAMIN ALAN, portfolio manager, financial planner; b. Bklyn., June 4, 1951; s. Joseph M. and Alma Ruth (Schneider) T.; m. Barbara Anne Biller, July 31, 1977; children: Daniel, Rachel. BBA, CUNY, 1973. CPA Fla.; cert. investment mgr. analyst. Sr. acct. Deloitte & Touche, N.Y.C., Miami, 1973-79; pres. Tobias Fin. Advisors, Plantation, Fla., 1980—. Mem. adj. faculty Rollins Coll., 1996, Nova Southeastern U., 1997-99, Fla. State U., 2000; mem. CFP Bd. Profl. Rev., Denver, 1999—. Author weekly newspaper column, Sun Newspapers, 1988-89. Bd. trustees Jewish Cmty. Found. of Broward County, 1998—; chmn. investment com. Jewish Found. of Broward County. Named One of Best Fin. Advisors in U.S., Worth Maz., 1996, 2002, One of Best Fin. Advisors for Doctors, Med. Econs., 1997, 1998, 1999, 2000, One of 100 Gt. Fin. Planners, Mut. Funds mag., 2001. Mem. AICPAs, Fla. Inst. CPAs, South Fla. Cert. Fin. Planners (pres. 1992-93, chmn. 1993-94), Inst. Cert. Fin. Planners (mem. nat. com. 1994-95), Rotary (Pembroke Pines chpt., pres. 1986-87). Office: Tobias Fin Advisors 8211 W Broward Blvd Ste Ph2 Plantation FL 33324-2745 E-mail: ben@tobiasfinancial.com.

TOBIAS, CHARLES HARRISON, JR. lawyer; b. Cin., Apr. 16, 1921; s. Charles Harrison and Charlotte (Westheimer) T.; m. Mary J. Kaufman, June 15, 1946; children— Jean M., Thomas Charles, Robert Charles. BA cum laude, Harvard U., 1943, LL.B., 1949. Bar: Ohio 1949. Assoc. firm Steer, Strauss and Adair, Cin., 1949-56; ptnr. firm Steer, Strauss, White and Tobias, 1956-90; mem. Kepley MacConnell & Eyrich, 1990-93; mediator U.S. Ct. Appeals (6th crct.), 1993—. Bd. dirs. Cin. City Charter Com., 1955-75; mem. Wyoming (Ohio) City Council, 1972-77, vice mayor, 1974-77; bd. govs., past chmn. Cin. Overseers, Hebrew Union Coll.-Jewish Inst. Religion; pres. Met. Area Religious Coalition of Cin., 1977-80, Jewish Fedn. Cin., 1972-74; mem. nat. bd. govs. Am. Jewish Com., 1981-87. With USN, 1943-46. Mem. Cin. Bar Assn., Losantiville Country Club. Office: US Ct Appeals Potter Stewart US Courthse 5th and Walnut St Cincinnati OH 45202 Home: 2115 Evergreen Ridge Dr Cincinnati OH 45215-5713

TOBIAS, JOHN MICHAEL, electronics engineer; b. Somerville, N.J., Dec. 7, 1965; s. John Nicholas and Katherine (Polak) T.; m. Carol Ann Schmidt, July 22, 1989; children: Sarah Elaine, Rachel Grace, Daniel Paul. BS, Seton Hall U., 1987; MS, U. Md., 1992. Registered profl. engr., N.J. Electronics engr. U.S. Dept. Army, Ft. Monmouth, N.J., 1992—; owner ElectroQuest, LLC, 2000—. Contbr. articles to profl. publs.; inventor surface ground device and radial surface ground electrode. Prin. lightning protection com. Nat. Fire Protection Assn., 1995; dep. tech. advisor U.S. Nat. Com. of the Internat. Electrotechnical Commn. Mem. IEEE. Office: US Army Comm-Electrncs Cmd 2539 Laboratory Rd Fort Monmouth NJ 07703 E-mail: john.tobias@att.net.

TOBIAS, JUDY, university development executive; b. Pitts. d. Saul Albert Landau and Bess (Previn) Kurzman; m. Seth Tobias (dec. May 1983); children: Stephen Frederic, Andrew Previn; m. Lewis F. Davis, 1990. Student, Silvermine Artists Guild, 1951-55; BA (hon.) (hon.) , New Coll. of Calif., 1989. Art cons. Westchester Mental Health Asn., White Plains, N.Y., 1968-69; cons. sch. social work NYU, 1973-74, devel. exec., 1976—. Conf. coord. Today's Family: Implications for the Future, N.Y.C., 1974-75; cons. Playschools, Inc., N.Y.C., 1975; majority counsel mem. Emily's List, 1991—. Mem. Gov.'s Commn. on Continuing Edn., Albany, N.Y., 1968-70, Nat. Coun. on Children and Youth, Washington, 1974-75, Manhattan Inter-Hosp. Group on Child Abuse, 1975-76; chmn. N.Y. met. com. for UNICEF, 1976-77; mem. exec. com. Town Hall Found., N.Y.C., 1979—, vice chmn., 1986-90; founder, bd. dirs. N.Y. chpt. WAIF, Inc., 1961-99, nat. pres., 1978-82, nat. bd. dirs., 1978—; pres. emeritus, 1993-99; bd. dirs. Citizen's Com. for Children, City of N.Y., 1975—, v.p., 1983-90, 97-99; bd. dirs. Am. br. Internat. Social Svc., 1965-80; bd. dirs. Andrew Glover Youth Program, 1986-89, mem. adv. coun., 1989—; bd. dirs. Goddard Riverside Cmty. Ctr., 1985—, Dance Mag. Found., 1986-92, St. John's Place Family Ctr., 1987-93, Capitol Hall Preservation Corp., 1989-93, chmn. bd. Inst. for Cultural Diversity, steering com., The Leadership Connection, 1992—. Recipient Nat. Humanitarian award, WAIF, 1990, Millennium Honoree award, NYU Sch. Social Work, 2000. Mem. Child Study Assn. Am. (bd. dirs. 1963-71, pres. 1969-71, bd. dirs. Wel-Met Inc. 1972-85), Brookings Instn. (coun. mem. 1998—), Emily's List (majority coun. 1990—). E-mail: ajtdavis@aol.com.

TOBIAS, KAL, transportation executive; b. Bklyn., Feb. 1, 1946; m. Karen Liberty, Mar. 11, 1967; children: Kristopher, Kirk. BA, CUNY, Bklyn., 1967. Mgr. dealer devel. Volkswagon Can., Toronto, Ont., 1967-72; pres. cons. firm Can., 1972-78; v.p. Burmah Oil Group, Can., 1978-83; pres., CEO DHL Internat. Express Ltd., Can., 1983—, also bd. dirs. Can., 1983—. Bd. dirs DHL Customs Brokerage, Toronto, Skyhawk Trans., Toronto, Can. Courier Assn., pres., CEO, 1987—. Office: DHL Internat Express Ltd 6205 Airport Rd Ste 400 Mississauga ON Canada L4V 1E1 E-mail: ktobias@ca.dhl.com.

TOBIAS, LESTER LEE, psychological consultant; b. Bklyn., Oct. 11, 1946; s. Nathan and Charlotte T.; m. Andrea Furmanek, July 10, 1977; children: Lauren A., Julia E. AB, Grinnell Coll., 1967; AM, U. Ill., 1971, PhD, 1972. Diplomate Am. Bd. Profl. Psychology. Instr. dept. univ. extension U. Ill., Urbana, 1970-72, intern Psychol. and Counseling Ctr., 1970-71, clin. counselor, 1971-72; psychologist Jefferson County (Colo.) Mental Health Ctr., Denver, 1972-73, team leader, psychologist, 1973-74;; psychol. cons. to Denver OEO Colo. Dept. Social Svcs., 1973-74; instr. Denver Community Coll., 1973-74; cons. psychologist Nordli, Wilson Assocs., Westborough, Mass., 1974-81; ptnr., cons. psychologist, 1981—. Pres. Psychol. Svcs. Internat., Inc., Westborough, 1983—. Author: Psychological Consulting to Management, 1990; contbr. articles to profl. and bus. publs. Bd. dirs. Worcester Big Bros., 1976, PMCS, 1983—. Meuhlstein Found. scholar, 1964-67; USPHS trainee, 1967-68. Fellow APA; mem. Nat. Psychol. Cons. to Mgmt. (Excellence award 1991), Mass. Psychol. Assn. Home: 6 John St Westborough MA 01581-2511 Office: Nordli Wilson Assocs Ste 212 18 Lyman St Westborough MA 01581-1474

TOBIAS, PAUL HENRY, lawyer; b. Cin., Jan. 5, 1930; s. Charles H. and Charlotte (Westheimer) T.; 1 child, Eliza L. AB magna cum laude, Harvard U., 1951, LLB, 1958. Bar: Mass. 1958, Ohio 1962. Assoc. Stoneman & Chandler, Boston, 1958-61, Goldman & Putnick, Cin., 1962-75; ptnr. Tobias, Kraus and Torchia, 1976—. Instr. U. Cin. Law Sch., 1975-77. Author: Litigating Wrongful Discharge Claims, 1987; co-author: Job Rights and Survivor Strategies, a Handbook for Terminated Employees, 1997; contbr. articles to profl. jours. Mem. Cin. Bd. of Park Commrs., 1973-81, Cin. Human Rels. Commn., 1980-84, Cin. Hist. Conservation Bd., 1990-91. With U.S. Army, 1952-54. Mem. ABA, Nat. Employment Lawyers Assn. (founder), Nat. Employee Rights Inst. (chmn.; editor-in-chief Employee Rights quar. 2000—), Ohio State Bar Assn., Cin. Bar Assn. (past chmn. legal aid com.), Phi Beta Kappa. Home: 15 Hill And Hollow Ln Cincinnati OH 45208-3317 Office: Tobias Kraus Torchia 911 Mercantile Libr Bldg Cincinnati OH 45202

TOBIAS, RANDALL LEE, retired pharmaceutical company executive; b. Lafayette, Ind., Mar. 20, 1942; m. Marilyn Jane Salyer, Sept. 2, 1966 (dec. May 1994); children: Paige Noelle, Todd Christopher; m. Marianne Williams, July 15, 1995; stepchildren: James Russell Ullyot, Kathryn Lee Ullyot. BS in Mktg., Ind. U., 1964; LLD (hon.), Galuedette U.; D of Engring. (hon.), Rose Hulman Inst. Tech., Sagamore of the Wabash, Ind.; LLD (hon.), Ind. U., 1997. Numerous positions Ind. Bell, 1964-77, Ill. Bell, 1977-81; v.p. residence mktg. sales and service AT&T, 1981-82, pres. Am. Bell Consumer Products, 1983, pres. Consumer Products, 1983-84, sr. v.p., 1984-85; chmn., CEO AT&T Comm., N.Y.C., 1985-91, AT&T Internat., Basking Ridge, N.J., 1991-93; vice chmn. bd. AT&T, N.Y.C., 1986-93; chmn., CEO Eli Lilly & Co., Indpls., 1993-98, chmn. emeritus, 1999. Bd. dirs. Kimberly-Clark, Knight-Ridder, Phillips Petroleum. Chmn. bd. trustees Duke U.; trustee Colonial Williamsburg Found.; bd. govs. Indpls. Mus. Art; bd. dirs. Indpls. Symphony Orch., Ind. U. Found. (hon.), Econ. Club Indpls. Named one of Top 25 Mgrs. of Yr., Bus. Week, 1997, Family Champion, Working Mothers Mag., 1997. Mem. Bus. Coun., Indpls. Corp. Cmty. Coun., Coun. Fgn. Rels., Meridian Hills Country Club (Indpls.), Woodstock Club (Indpls.), Columbia Club (Indpls.), Athletic Club (Indpls.), Univ. Club (Indpls.), Amwell Valley Conservancy (N.J.), Theta Chi. Avocations: skiing, fly fishing, shooting. Office: Eli Lilly & Co 500 E 96th St Ste 110 Indianapolis IN 46240-3733

TOBIAS, ROBERT MAX, labor leader, lawyer; b. Detroit, Aug. 4, 1943; BA, U. Mich., 1965, MBA, 1968; JD, George Washington U., 1969. Lawyer Nat. Treasury Employees Union, Washington, 1968-70, gen. counsel, 1970-79, exec. v.p. and gen. counsel, 1979-83, pres., 1983-99; disting. adj. prof. pub. adminstrn., dir. Inst. for Study of Pub. Policy Implementation, Am. U., 1999—. Lectr. George Washington U. Law Sch., Washington, 1970-90; mem. IRS oversight bd., 2000—. Contbr. articles to law revs. Pres. Fed. Employee Edn. and Asst. Fund, Washington, 1986—. Mem. ABA, Soc. for Labor Relations Profls. (1st Annual Union Leader award, 1987), Fed. Bar Assn. Democrat. Episcopalian. Office: Am U Sch Pub Affairs 4400 Massachusetts Ave Washington DC 20016-8070 E-mail: rtobias@american.edu.

TOBIAS, SHEILA, writer, educator; b. N.Y., Apr. 26, 1935; d. Paul Jay and Rose (Steinberger) Tobias; m. Carlos Stern, Oct. 11, 1970 (div. 1982); m. Carl T. Tomizuka, Dec. 16, 1987. BA, Harvard Radcliffe U., 1957; MA, Columbia U., 1961, MPhil, 1974; PhD (hon.) , Drury Coll., 1994, Wheelock Coll., 1995; PhD (hon.) , SUNY, Potsdam, 1996, Mich. State U., 2000, Worcester Polytech, 2002. Journalist, W. Germany, U.S. and Fed. Republic Germany, 1957-65; lect. in history C.C.N.Y., N.Y.C., 1965-67; univ. adminstr. Cornell U., Wesleyan U., 1967-78; lect. in women's studies U. Calif., San Diego, 1985-92; lect. in war, peace studies U. So. Calif., 1985-88. Author: Overcoming Math Anxiety, 1978, rev. edit., 1994, Succeed with Math, 1987, Revitalizing Undergraduate Science: Why Some Things Work and Most Don't, 1992, Science as a Career: Perceptions and Realities, 1995; co-author: The People's Guide to National Defense, 1982, Women, Militarism and War, 1987, They're Not Dumb, They're Different, 1990, (with Carl T. Tomizuka) Breaking the Science Barrier, 1992, Rethinking Science as a Career, 1995, (with Jacqueline Raphael) The Hidden Curriculum, 1997, Faces of Feminism, 1997. Fellow AAAS; mem. Am. Assn. Higher Edn. (bd. dirs. 1993-97), Coll. Sci. Tchrs. Assn., Nat. Women's Studies Assn., Phi Beta Kappa. Avocations: outdoor hiking, skiing. E-mail: Sheila@SheilaTobias.com.

TOBIAS, STEPHEN C. rail transportation executive; b. Bogota, Colombia, Dec. 11, 1944; BA in History, Citadel, 1967. Jr. engr. Pocahontas divsn. Norfolk and Wester Rlwy. Co., 1969-70, asst. roadmaster Scioto divsn., 1970, asst. trainmaster Pitts. divsn., 1970-71, gen. yardmaster Pitts. divsn., 1971-73, trainmaster Bellevue terminal, 1973-74, asst. supt. Bellevue terminal, 1974-79, supt. Pitts. divsn., 1979-81, asst. gen. mgr. lake region, 1981, asst. gen. mgr. supt. eastern region, 1981-84; gen. mgr. eastern region Norfolk (Va.) So. Corp., 1984, gen. mgr. western region, 1984-89, v.p. transp., 1989-92, v.p. strategic planning, 1992-93, sr. v.p. ops., 1993-94, exec. v.p. ops., 1994-98; vice chmn. and COO Norfolk (Va.) So. Corp. , 1998—. Trustee Norfolk Acad.; prin. Va. Bus. Coun.; bd. dirs. Plum Creek Timber Co., TTX Co., Inc. Dir. Va. law Enforcement Found.; mem. exec. adv. coun. Commonwealth Musical Stage. Capt. U.S. Army, 1967-69. Mem. Assn. Am. R.R.s. Office: Norfolk So Corp 3 Commercial Pl Norfolk VA 23510-2108

TOBIASSEN, BARBARA SUE, systems analyst consultant, educator, Peace Corps volunteer; b. Bklyn., Feb. 22, 1950; d. Vincent and Esther Alice (Hansen) M. BA in Math Edn., Rider Coll., 1972; postgrad., Montclair State U., 1973. Cert. secondary tchr., N.J. Math tchr. Westwood (N.J.) H.S., 1973-80; programmer Prudential Ins. Co., Roseland, N.J., 1980-81; programmer, analyst Grand Union, Paramus, 1981-82; cons. Five Techs., Montvale, 1987-90; project mgr. Info. Sci., Inc., 1982-84, cons., project mgr., 1987-90; pres. B. Maxwell Assoc., Inc., Westwood, N.J., 1990—; vol. Peace Corps; mem. Peace Corps., 2001—02. Guest spkr. Info. Sci., Best of Am., Computer Assocs. B.A.C. Contbr. articles to profl. jours. Vol. Peace Corps, 2001—02. Mem.: APA (v.p. N.J. chpt. 1996), NAFE, Am. Payroll Assn., N.J. Info., Westwood Heritage Soc. Republican. Lutheran. Avocations: travel, reading, gardening, hiking.

TOBIN, AILEEN WEBB, educational administrator; b. Milford, Del., July 9, 1949; d. Wilson Webster Webb and Dorothy Marie (Benson) Rust; m. Thomas Joseph Tobin, Jr., July 31, 1971. BA cum laude, U. Del., 1971, MEd, 1975, PhD, 1981. Cert. tchr. secondary edn., cert. reading specialist, cert. reading cons., Del. Dir. Del. Tutoring Ctr., Wilmington, 1971-74; grad. teaching asst. U. Del., Newark, 1974-81, instr. Coll. Edn., 1978-82; ednl. specialist U.S. Army Ordnance Ctr. & Sch., Aberdeen Proving Ground, Md., 1982-85, chief internal eval. br., 1985-88, chief evaluation divsn., 1988, chief standardization and analysis div., 1988-90, dir. quality assurance, 1990-94, dir. tactical support equipment dept., 1994-98, dir. command planning office, 1998—. Cons. Dorchester County Sch. Dist., Dorchester County, Md., 1977-80; rsch. assoc., Ctr. for Ednl. Leadership, Newark, 1981-82; staff assoc., Rsch. for Better Schs., Inc., Phila., 1981-84. Author: (book chpt.) Approaches Informal Eval. of Reading, 1982, Dialogues in Literary Research, 1988, Cognitive & Social Perspectives for Literary Research & Instruction, 1989; contbr. articles to profl. jours. Recipient Silver award Fed. Exec. Bd., 1992, Comdr.'s award for Civil Svc. Dept. Army, 1994, 96, Order of Samuel Sharpe award Ordnance Corps Assn., 1994, Superior Civil Svc. award Dept. Army, 1995, 98. Mem. Internat. Reading Assn., Nat. Reading Conf., Am. Ednl. Rsch. Assn., Am. Evaluation Assn., Ordnance Corps Assn., Kappa Delta Pi. Methodist. Avocations: travel, reading, tennis, sailing. Home: 4839 Plum Run Ct Wilmington DE 19808-1715 Office: US Army Ordnance Ctr & Sch ATSL CP Aberdeen Proving Ground MD 21005

TOBIN, BRUCE HOWARD, lawyer; b. Detroit, July 17, 1955; s. Marshall Edward and Rhoda Maureen (Milman) T.; m. Kathleen Tobin; children: Benjamin Stewart, Jenna Rose, Lainie Nicole. BA in Social Sci., Mich. State U., 1978; JD, Detroit Coll. Law, 1982; LLM in Taxation, NYU, 1983. Bar: Mich. 1982, Fla. 1982, Nebr. 1983, U.S. Dist. Ct. (ea. dist.) Mich. 1982, U.S. Tax Ct. 1983. Assoc. Kutak, Rock & Campbell, Omaha, 1983-85; ptnr. Lebow & Tobin P.L.L.C., West Bloomfield, Mich., 1985—. Pres. West Bloomfield Sch. Bd. Mem. ABA, Fla. Bar Assn., Mich. Bar Assn. (tax com. 1985—), Nebr. Bar Assn. Jewish. Office: Lebow & Tobin PLLC 7001 Orchard Lake Rd Ste 312 West Bloomfield MI 48322-3607 Fax: (248) 851 4303. E-mail: btobin@lebowardtobin.com.

TOBIN, CALVIN JAY, architect; b. Boston, Feb. 15, 1927; s. David and Bertha (Tanfield) T.; m. Joan Hope Fink, July 15, 1951; children— Michael Alan, Nancy Ann. B.Arch., U. Mich., 1949. Designer, draftsman Arlen & Lowenfish (architects), N.Y.C., 1949-51; with Samuel Arlen, 1951-53, Skidmore, Owings & Merrill, N.Y.C., 1953; architect Loebl, Schlossman & Bennett (architects), Chgo., 1953-57, v.p., 1953-57, Loebl, Schlossman & Hackl, 1957—; retired, 1998. Chmn. Jewish United Fund Bldg. Trades Div., 1969; chmn. AIA and Chgo. Hosp. Council Com. of Hosp. Architecture, 1968-76 Archtl. works include Michael Reese Hosp. and Med. Ctr., 1954—, Prairie Shores Apt. Urban Redevel., 1957-62, Louis A. Weiss Meml. Hosp., Chgo., Chgo. State Hosp., Ctrl. Cmty. Hosp., Chgo., Gottlieb Meml. Hosp., Melrose Park, Ill., West Suburban Hosp., Oak Park, Ill., Thorek Hosp. and Med. Ctr., Chgo., Water Power Pl., Chgo., Christ Hosp., Oak Lawn, Greater Balt. Med. Ctr., Shriners Hosp. for Crippled Children, Chgo. Hinsdale (Ill.) Hosp., South Chgo. Cmty. Hosp., Chgo., Mt. Sinai Med. Ctr., Chgo., Alexian Bros. Med. Ctr., Elk Grove Village, Ill., Luth. Gen. Hosp., Park Ridge, Ill., Evanston (Ill.) Hosp., Resurrection Med. Ctr., Chgo., New Cook County Hosp., Chgo., also numerous apt., comml. and cmty. bldgs. Chmn. Highland Park (Ill.) Appearance Rev. Commn., 1972-73; mem. Highland Park Plan Commn., 1973-79; mem. Highland Park City Coun., 1974-89, mayor pro-tem, 1979-89; mem. Highland Park Environ. Control Commn., 1979-84, Highland Park Hist. Preservation Commn., 1982-89; bd. dirs. Highland Park Hist. Soc., Young Men's Jewish Coun., 1953-67, pres., 1967; bd. dirs. Jewish Community Ctrs. Chgo., 1973-78, bd. dirs., 1989-93; Ill. Coun. Against Handgun Violence, 1989-94; trustee Ravinia Festival Assn., 1990-98; bd. govs. Highland Park Cmty. House, 1994—; v.p Kohl Children's Mus. Wilmette, Ill., 1999—. With USNR, 1945-46. Fellow AIA (2d v.p. Chgo. chpt.); mem. U. Mich. Alumni Soc. Coll. Architecture and Urban Planning (bd. govs. 1989-95), U. Mich. Alumni Assn. (bd. govs. 1990-95, v.p. 1993-95, pres. 1997-99, Disting. Alumni Svc. award 1996), Std. Club, Ravinia Green Country Club, Pi Lambda Phi. Jewish. Home: 814 Dean Ave Highland Park IL 60035-4749

TOBIN, CRAIG DANIEL, lawyer; b. Chgo., Aug. 17, 1954; s. Thomas Arthur and Lois (O'Connor) T. BA with honors, U. Ill., 1976; JD with high honors, Ill. Inst. Tech., 1980. Bar: Ill. 1980, U.S. Dist. Ct. (no. dist.) Ill. 1980, U.S. Dist. Ct. (no. dist.) Ind. 1986, U.S. Ct. Appeals (7th cir.) 1986, U.S. Supreme Ct. 1987. Trial atty. Cook County Pub. Defender, Chgo., 1980-82; trial atty. homicide task force Pub. Defender, 1982-84; ptnr. Craig D. Tobin and Assocs., 1984—. Lectr. Ill. Inst. for Continuing Legal Edn., Cook County Pub. Defender, Chgo., 1983, 92, Ill. Pub. Defender Assn., 1987; instr. Nat. Inst. Trial Advocacy. Named One of Outstanding Young Men in Am., 1985. Mem. ABA, Chgo. Bar Assn., Nat. Assn. Criminal Def. Lawyers. Roman Catholic. Office: Craig D Tobin & Assocs 3 First National Plz Chicago IL 60602

TOBIN, DENNIS MICHAEL, lawyer; b. Chgo., June 3, 1948; s. Thomas Arthur and Lois (O'Connor) T.; m. Sue Wynn Henslee, June 14, 1969 (div. 1977); m. Karen Thompson, Oct. 11, 1980; children: Kyle James, Daniel Patrick BA with honors, U. Ill., 1971; JD, Loyola U., Chgo., 1976. Bar: Ill. 1976, U.S. Dist. Ct (no. dist.) Ill. 1976, U.S. Ct. Appeals (7th cir.) 1985, U.S. Supreme Ct. 1985, Wis. 1989. Trial atty. Cook County Homicide Task Force, Chgo., 1976-84; prin. Dennis M. Tobin & Assocs., 1984—. Gen. counsel Forest Health Systems and Found., Ill., Miss., Hawaii, 1986—. Manages Behavioral Care Inc., Psychiat. Ins. Co. Am. Dir. Forest Health Systems Found.; mem. Chgo. Coun. on Fgn. Rels. Mem. ABA (forum on health law), Nat. Assn. Criminal Def. Attys., Chgo. Bar Assn. (com. on health law), Am. Soc. Law and Medicine, Ill. Assn. Criminal Def. Attys. (v.p. 1984-87), Ill. Attys. for Criminal Justice, Wis. Bar Assn., Ill. Assn. Hosp. Attys., Nat. Health Lawyers Assn., U.S. Sporting Clays Assn., Nat. Sporting Clays Assn., Gateway Gun Club. Roman Catholic. Office: 18-3 E Dundee Rd Barrington IL 60010-5292

TOBIN, GARY ALLAN, cultural and community organization educator; b. St. Louis, July 26, 1949; BA in History, Washington U., 1971; PhD in City and Regional Planning, U. Calif., Berkeley. Pres. Inst. for Jewish and Cmty. Rsch., San Francisco; dir. Abramson Program in Jewish Policy Rsch. U. Judaism, L.A.; former dir. Cohen Ctr. for Modern Jewish Studies Brandeis U., Waltham, Mass. Rsch. on antisemitism, racial and ethnic diversity, Jewish orgn. planning and philanthropy in Jewish Cmty. and Jewish Family Founds. Author: Jewish Perceptions of Antisemitism, Church and Synagogue Affiliation, Opening the Gates: How Proactive Conversion Can Revitalize the Jewish Community, Rabbis Talk About Intermarriage. Office: Inst Jewish & Cmty Rsch 3198 Fulton St San Francisco CA 94118

TOBIN, ILONA LINES, psychologist, marriage and family counselor, educator, media consultant; b. Trenton, Mich., Apr. 15, 1943; d. Frank John and Marjorie Cathalean (Lines) Kotyuk; m. Roger Lee Tobin, Aug. 20, 1966. BA, Ea. Mich. U., 1965, MA, 1968, Mich. State U., 1975; EdD, Wayne State U., 1978. Diplomate Am. Bd. Sexology, lic. marriage & family therapist, cert. sex educator & counselor, sex therapist, lic. psychologist. Tchr., counselor Willow Run Pub. Schs., Ypsilanti, Mich., 1966-72; prof. Macomb County C.C., Mt. Clemens, 1974-79; psychotherapist Identity Ctr., Inc., 1974-79; dir. treatment Alternative Lifestyles, Inc., Orchard Lake, Mich., 1979-80; psychologist Profl. Psychotherapy and Counseling Ctr., Farmington Hills, 1980-83; pvt. practice clin. psychology Birmingham, 1983—. Lectr. Wayne State U., Detroit, 1977—88; tchr. med. edn. St. Jospeh's Hosp., Pontiac, Mich., 1993—98; recruitment dir. Upward Bound Ea. Mich. U., Ypsilanti, Mich., 1969—72. Creator Doc's Dolls. Co-chmn. Birmingham Families in Action, 1982—83; mem. exec. bd., v.p. pres. Birmingham Cmty. Women's Ctr., 1984—85, also bd. dirs.; mem. adv. bd. Woodside Med. Ctr. for Chemically Dependent Women, 1984—86; mem. Ronald Reagan Rep. Ctr. Founder's Wall, Rep. Presdl. Round Table/Founders Wall, Washington, 2001; bd. dirs. HAVEN-Oakland County's Phys. and Sexual Abuse Ctr. and Oakland Area Counselors Assn., 1984—85. NIMH fellow, 1976-78; Wayne State U. scholar, 1976-78. Mem. ASCD, APA, Mich. Psychol. Assn. (mass media cons. 1983—, mem. crisis intervention network, legis. com. 1992-94), Am. Assn. Sex Educators, Counselors and Therapists, Pi Lambda Theta, Phi Delta Kappa. Jewish. E-mail: Imdoctobin@aol.com.

TOBIN, JAMES MICHAEL, lawyer; b. Santa Monica, Calif., Sept. 27, 1948; s. James Joseph and Glada Marie (Meisner) T.; m. Kathleen Marie Espy, Sept. 14, 1985. BA with honors, U. Calif., Riverside, 1970; JD, Georgetown U., 1974. Bar: Calif. 1974, Mich. 1987. From atty. to gen. atty. So. Pacific Co., San Francisco, 1975-82; v.p. regulatory affairs So. Pacific Communications Co., Washington, 1982-83; v.p., gen. counsel Lexitel Corp., 1983-85; v.p., gen. counsel, sec. ALC Communications Corp., Birmingham, Mich., 1985-87, sr. v.p., gen. counsel, sec., 1987-88; of counsel Morrison & Foerster, San Francisco, 1988-90, ptnr., 1990—. Mem. ABA, Calif. Bar Assn., Mich. Bar Assn., Fed. Communications Bar Assn. Republican. Unitarian Universalist. Avocations: carpentry, travel. Home: 3134 Baker St San Francisco CA 94123-1805 Office: Morrison & Foerster 425 Market St Ste 3100 San Francisco CA 94105-2482 E-mail: jtobin@mofo.com.

TOBIN, LOIS MOORE, home economist, educator, retired; b. Johnstown, Pa., Oct. 8, 1928; d. William B and Ida L. (Diehl) Moore; m. Warner E. Tobin, June 7, 1953 (dec.); children: Brian W., Robert E. BS, Indiana State Tchrs. Coll., Pa., 1951; postgrad., U. Pitts., 1952, U. Colo., 1953; MEd, Pa. State U., 1967; postgrad., Indiana U. of Pa., 1977-85. Tchr. Allegheny Valley Joint Sch. Dist., Springdale, Pa., 1951-53, Kittanning (Pa.) Sch. Dist., 1953-55, Carlisle (Pa.) Joint Sch. Dist., 1964-66, State Coll. (Pa.) Sch. Dist., 1967-73; mem. faculty dept. food and nutrition Indiana U. of Pa., 1974, 76-77, mem. faculty home econs. edn., 1979-82, coord. Single Parent-Homemaker Svc. Ctr. Vocat. Pers. Prep., 1984-91. Mem. adv. com. Indiana Area Vocat.-Tech. Sch., 1981-94; presenter in field. Author: (booklet) Home Economics Education Bibliography on Special Needs, 1982, Teaching Special Needs Individuals in Home Economics, 1982; contbr. articles to profl. newsletters. Sec. Indiana County Human Svcs. Coun., 1990—91; vol. Bloodmobile, 1986—; tour guide Breezedale Restoration, 1986—; pres. Calvary Ch. Women's Club, 1975—76, Indiana County Newcomers Club, 1974, 1975; elder, session mem. Calvary Presbyn. Ch., 1996—2002. Grantee Dept. Edn. Bur. Vocat. Edn., 1980-82, 86-91, Human Svcs. Devel. Fund, 1989-91. Mem. Am. Vocat. Assn., Pa. Vocat. Assn., Nat. Trust for Hist. Preservation, Indiana County Hist. and Geneal. Soc., Indiana U. of Pa. Ret. Faculty Assn. (treas. 1998—), Indiana County Alumni Assn. (bd. dirs.), Pa. Home Econs. Assn. (treas. 1975-77), Pa. Vocat. Home Econs. Educators (sec. 1990-91). Avocations: swimming, travel, church choir. Home: 896 White Farm Rd Indiana PA 15701-1254

TOBIN, MARGARET ANN, cardiac medical critical care nurse; b. Oakland, Calif., Dec. 10, 1959; d. William Leroy Jones Sr. and Barbara Kay (Rains) Carter; m. Wesley Vernon Keene, June 21, 1977 (div. June 1984); m. James Edward Tobin, Aug. 15, 1985; 1 child, Nicholas William. ADN, Ctrl. Tex. Coll., 1983; BSN, U. Mary Harden Baylor, 1994; MSN, Tex. A&M U., Corpus Christi, 1997. RN, Tex.; cert. med.-surg. nurse ANCC; cert. BCLS, BCLS instr., ACLS, ACLS instr. Grad. nurse surg. fl. Olin E. Teague VA Ctr., Temple, Tex., 1983-84, staff nurse cardiac med. ICU, 1984-95, nurse mgr. surg. ICU, 1995-96, nurse mgr. cardiac med. ICU, 1996, clin. instr., 1996—. Mem. Tar Wars Kids Against Tobacco, Temple, 1993—. Mem.: AACN (cert. edn. nurse 2001, pres.-elect 1993—94, pres. 1994—95), Sigma Theta Tau. Baptist. Home: 4307 Sunflower Ln Temple TX 76502 E-mail: mtobin@vvm.com., margaret.tobin@med.va.gov.

TOBIN, MARLA JANEEN, family physician; b. Independence, Mo., Feb. 12, 1954; d. Howard I. and Doris M. (Farmer) Tobin; m. Ronald G. Bowman, June 22, 1985. BA in Biology, U. Mo., 1975, MD, 1980. Diplomate Am. Bd. Family Practice. Family practice resident Duke U., Durham, N.C., 1980-83; family physician Kelling Clinic, Waverly, Mo., 1983-85, Family Practice Assocs., Higginsville, 1985-97; pres. Family Practice Assn. West Ctrl. Mo., 1987-97; med. dir. Aetna U.S. Healthcare, 1997—2002. Speaker in field. Mem. editorial bds. various publs.; contbr. chpts. to books, articles to profl. jours. Vol. sch. and civic projects. Fellow Am. Acad. Family Physician (Mead Johnson award 1982); mem. Am. Med. Women's Assn., Mo. State Med. Soc., Assn. Reproductive Health Profls., Mo. Acad. Family Physicians (pres. 1993-94). Avocations: horseback riding, skiing, gardening, travel.

TOBIN, MARTIN JOHN, pulmonary and critical care physician; b. Kilkenny, Ireland, Apr. 23, 1951; came to U.S., 1980; s. Edmund and Johanna (Brennan) T.; m. Sareen Boland, Sept. 13, 1974; children: Damien, Kate, Kieran. MD, U. Coll., Dublin, Ireland, 1975. Diplomate Am. Bd. Internal Medicine, Am. Bd. Pulmonary Disease, Am. Bd. Critical Care Medicine. Resident in internal medicine U. Coll. and Trinity Coll., Dublin, Ireland, 1975-79; fellow Kings Coll. Med. Sch., London, 1978-80, Mt. Sinai Med. Ctr., Miami, 1980-82, U. Pitts., 1982-83; asst. prof. U. Tex. Med. Sch., Houston, 1983-88, assoc. prof., 1988-90; prof. medicine Loyola U. Chgo. Sch. Medicine, Maywood, Ill., 1990—, chief pulmonary and critical care, 1992, dir. fellowshp tng. program, 1990—. Chief pulmonary and critical care Hines VA Hosp., Hines, Ill., 1990; 1996 lectr. in Pulmonary and Critcal Care Medicine, Harvard Med. Sch., Boston, D.H. Simmons lectr. UCLA Med. Sch., L.A., 1997; Balfour lectr. Mayo Clinic, Rochester, Minn.; Egan lectr. Am. Assn. Respiratory Care, Las Vegas, 1999; Wellcome lectr. Royal Soc. Medicine, London, 2000. Author: Principles and Practices of Mechanical Ventilation, 1994, Principles and Practice of Intensive Care Monitoring, 1998 and 5 other books; contbr. numerous articles to profl. internat. jours.; assoc. editor Am. Jour. Respirator Critical Care Medicine, 1992-99; N. Am. editor Intensive Care Medicine, Berlin, 1993-99; editor in chief Am. Jour. Respiratory & Critical Care Medicine, 1999—. Recipient Forrest M. Bird Achievement award, Am. Respiratory Care Found., Cin., 2000, Hon. Fellowship award of Faculty of Medicine, Univ. Coll. Dublin, Ireland, 2002. Mem. Am. Thoracic Soc. (bd. dirs. chair critical care assembly 1997-99). Avocations: reading, music. Office: Loyola U Chgo 2160 S 1st Ave Maywood IL 60153-3304

TOBIN, PAUL EDWARD, JR. naval officer; b. Detroit, Oct. 24, 1940; s. Paul Edward and Mary Margaret (Atkinson) T.; m. Lynne Dawson Carter, June 12, 1963; children: Mary Elizabeth, Patricia Carter. BS in Naval Sci., U.S. Naval Acad., 1963; MS in Computer Sys., U.S. Naval Postgrad. Sch., 1969. Commd. ensign USN, 1963, advanced through grades to rear adm., 1988; commdg. officer USS Tattnall (DDG-19), 1979-81; chief engr. USS Forrestal (CV-59), 1981-83; commdg. officer USS Fox (CG-33), 1984-86, Surface Warfare Officers Sch., 1986-88; dir. USN Info. Sys. Mgmt., 1988-90; commdr. Surface Group Western Pacific, Subic Bay, The Philippines, 1990-92; asst. chief naval pers. USN, Washington, 1992-94, vice commdr. naval edn. and tng. Pensacola, Fla., 1994-96, oceanographer, 1996-98, ret., 1998; v.p. edn. Armed Forces Comms. and Electronics Assn., 1998—. Decorated D.S.M., Legion of Merit (4), Bronze Star. Mem. U.S. Naval Inst., Surface Navy Assn., Army Navy Country Club. Presbyterian. Avocations: classical music, running, computers, boating. Home: 114 Riverton Pl Edgewater MD 21037-1800 Office: $D 4400 Fair Lakes Ct Fairfax VA 22033-3801

TOBIN, ROBERT EDWIN, regional director; b. Carlisle, Pa., Sept. 18, 1959; s. Dr. Warner E. and Lois Moore T.; m. Linda Drew, June 21, 1986; children: Emily May, Drew Warner. BA, Ind. Univ. of Pa., 1982; MBA, George Mason Univ., 1993. Rest. mgr. Pizza Hut, Myrtle Beach, S.C., 1982-85, area mgr. Fairfax, Va., 1985-91, divsn. tng. mgr. Washington, 1991-93, proj. mgr. Atlanta, 1993-94, dir. ops., 1994-97, Kansas City, 1997-98; reg. dir. ops. Denny's Restaurants, Pitts., 1998—. MBA mentor George Mason U., Fairfax, 1995-97. Dist. commr. Boy Scouts Am., Myrtle Beach, S.C., 1983-85; Sunday sch. tchr., mem. vestry and fin. com., Ch. of Ascension, Pitts., 1999—. Mem. Edgewood Club. Republican. Home: 135 W Swissvale Ave Pittsburgh PA 15218-1630 E-mail: R_Tobin@Advantica-Dine.com.

TOBIN, TARY JEANNE, educational consultant, researcher; b. Des Moines, Sept. 18, 1940; d. Deam Hunter and Merle Bonne (Wildey) Ferris; m. David William Tobin, June 8, 1968; children: Robert, Jean, Mary Sue, Joseph, Anastasia, Teresa, Rebekah. BSc, U. Oreg., 1970, MEd, 1990, PhD, 1996. Cert. elem. tchr., tchr. of learning impaired, Oreg. Tchr. elem. sch. St. Mary's Cath. Sch., Eugene, Oreg., 1962-68; tchr. elem. and jr. high sch. St. Paul's Cath. Sch., 1969-70, 72-74; mgr. adult foster care home Sr. and Disabled Svcs., 1983-90; tchr. spl. edn. elem. sch. Springfield (Oreg.) Sch. Dist., 1991; rsch. assoc. U. Oreg., 1997—. Contbr. articles to profl. jours. Mem.: Am. Evaluation Assn., Coun. for Children with Behavioral Disorders, Coun. Exceptional Children. Avocations: digital photography, flower arranging, bicycling. Home: 1055 W 18th Ave Eugene OR 97402 Office: Coll Edn 1235 U Oreg Eugene OR 97403-1235

TOBIN, THOMAS EDWARD, JR. civil engineer; b. Butte, Mont., May 10, 1939; s. Thomas Edward and Helen Augusta (Trask) T.; m. Barbara Sayler Burrell, Dec. 24, 1962; children: Thomas Alexander, Elizabeth Marie, Catherine Louise. BSCE, U. Colo., 1965; MS in Mgmt., So. Nazarene U., 1990. Registered profl. engr., Colo., Okla., Tex., Utah, profl. land surveyor, Colo., Okla. Project and resident engr. Nelson, Haley Patterson & Quirk, Greeley, Colo., 1968-72; city and county engr. City and County of Gunnison (Colo.), 1972-76; chief engr. and surveyor Tom Tobin P.E. & L.S., Gunnison, 1976-79; county engr. LaPlata County, Durango, Colo., 1979-81; project engr. Rea Engring., Oklahoma City, 1981-82; city engr. City of Bethany (Okla.), 1983-90; chief engr. and surveyor Agape (Tobin) Engring., Tulsa, 1990-93; hwy. engr. Bur. Indian Affairs, Muskogee, Okla., 1993—. Project engr. Nova Inc., Edeco Inc., Tulsa, 1990-91; cons. engr., Gunnison, 1972-79. Author profl. reports. Precinct chmn. Laplata County Republican Party, Durango, 1980-81. Fellow ASCE; mem. NSPE (const. state gov. 1987-95), Am. Pub. Works Assn. (state exec. com.), Kiwanis. Episcopalian. E-mail (office) Email (home).

Office: Bur Indian Affairs 101 N 5th St Ste 506 Muskogee OK 74401-6205 Home: 1030 N F St Muskogee OK 74403-2613 E-mail: thomastobin@bia.gov., tom_tobin@hotmail.com.

TOBIN, THOMAS F. lawyer; b. Chgo., Apr. 12, 1929; BSS, John Carroll U., 1951; JD, Loyola U., 1954. Bar: Ill. 1954. Ptnr. Connelly Robert and McGivney, Chgo. Office: Connelly Robert and McGivney 1 N Franklin St Ste 1200 Chicago IL 60606-3447

TOBIN, VINCENT MICHAEL, professional football coach, former sports team executive; b. Burlington Junction, Mo., Sept. 29, 1943; BE, U. Mo., 1965, M in Guidance and Counseling, 1966. Def. ends coach Missouri, 1967-70, def. coord., 1971-76, Brit. Columbia Lions CFL, 1977-82, Phila./Balt. Stars USFL, 1983-85, Chgo. Bears NFL, 1986-92, Indpls. Colts NFL, 1994-95; head coach Ariz. Cardinals, 1996—2000.*

TOBIS, JEROME SANFORD, physician; b. Syracuse, N.Y., July 23, 1915; s. David George and Anna (Feinberg) T.; m. Hazel Weisbard, Sept. 18, 1938; children: David, Heather, Jonathan. BS, CCNY, 1936; MD, Chgo. Med. Sch., 1943. Diplomate: Am. Bd. Phys. Medicine and Rehab. Intern Knickerbocker Hosp., 1943-44; resident Bronx VA Hosp., 1946-48; med. dir. state fever therapy unit USPHS, Brookhaven, Miss., 1944-46; practice medicine N.Y.C., 1948-70; prof. dir. dept. phys. medicine and rehab. N.Y. Med. Coll., Flower and Fifth Av. Hosps., 1948-61; prof. rehab. medicine Albert Einstein Coll. of Medicine, 1963-70; chief div. rehab. medicine Montefiore Hosp., 1961-70; dir. vis. physician Met., Bird S. Coler hosps., 1952-61; prof., chmn. dept. phys. medicine and rehab. Calif. Coll. Medicine, U. Calif. at Irvine, 1970-82, prof., dir. program in geriatric medicine and gerontology, 1980-86; mem. adv. com. Acad. Geriatric Resource program, 1984-86, 95—. Mem. expert med. com. Am. Rehab. Found., 1961-70; cons. Dept. Health, N.Y.C., Long Beach VA Hosp., 1970—, Fairview State Devel. Ctr., 1976—; mem. adv. coun. phys. medicine and rehab. for appeals com. Calif. Med. Assn., 1971-74, adv. com. U. Calif. Acad. Geriatric Resource Program, 1995—; NIH Internat. Fogarty fellow, hon. lectr., dept. geriatric medicine U. Birmingham, 1979-80; chair ethics com. U. Calif.-Irvine Med. Ctr., 1986—; mem. rev. panel musculoskeletal diseases NIH, 1996; rsch. prof. dept. phys. medicine & rehab. U. Calif., Irvine, 1986—, chair med. ethics com., 1986—; mem. Ctr. Health Policy Rsch. U. Calif., Davis, 1996—. Mem. editorial bd.: Heart and Lung, 1973-76, Geriatrics, 1975-80, Archives of Phys. Medicine and Rehab, 1958-73. Named Physician of the Year, 1957; recipient Distinguished Alumnus award Chgo. Med. Sch., 1972, Acad. award Nat. Inst. on Aging, 1981-86; named hon. faculty mem. Calif. Zeta chpt. Alpha Omega Alpha, 1981; Leavitt Meml. lectureship Baylor Coll. Medicine, 1983, Griffith Meml. lectureship Am. Geriatric Soc., 1984; Australian Coll. Rehabilitation Medicine, 1984; Jerome S. Tobis Ann. Conf. on Geriatric Medicine established in his name, U. Calif. at Irvine, 1986. Fellow ACP, Am. Coll. Cardiology; mem. AMA (mem. residency rev. com. Coun. Med. Edn. 1973), AAAS, Am. Acad. Cerebral Palsy, Am. Acad. Phys. Medicine and Rehab. (Disting. Clinician award 1993), Am. Congress Rehab. Medicine (pres. 1962), Calif. Coun. Gerontology and Geriatrics (bd. dirs. 1980-86, pres. 1985), N.Y. Acad. Medicine, N.Y. Acad. Sci., Orange County Med. Soc., Assn. U. Calif. Irvine (chair emeritae/i 1996-97). Home: 1115 Goldenrod Ave Corona Del Mar CA 92625-1508 E-mail: jstobis@uci.edu.

TOBISMAN, STUART PAUL, lawyer; b. Detroit, June 5, 1942; s. Nathan and Beverly (Porvin) T.; m. Karen Sue Tobisman, Aug. 8, 1965; children: Cynthia Elaine, Neal Jay. BA, UCLA, 1966; JD, U. Calif., Berkeley, 1969. Bar: Calif. 1969. Assoc. O'Melveny & Myers, L.A., 1969-77, ptnr., 1977—. Contbr. articles to profl. jours. Trustee L.A. County Bar Assn., 1983-84. With USN, 1961-63. Fellow Am. Coll. Trust and Estate Counsel; mem. Phi Beta Kappa, Order of Coif. Office: O'Melveny & Myers LLP 1999 Avenue Of The Stars Los Angeles CA 90067-6035

TOBLER, WILLIAM DONN, neurosurgeon; b. Cin., Apr. 7, 1952; s. Robert and Ruth Virginia Tobler; m. Therese Rohde, Aug. 15, 1981; children: William, Blair, Hillary. BA, U. Notre Dame, 1974; MD, U. Cin., 1978. Intern Good Samaritan Hosp., Cin., 1978-79; resident U. Cin., 1980-85, prof. neurosurgery, 1985—; vice chmn. Mayfield Clinic, Cin., 1992—; v.p. Ohio Med. Instrument Co., 1994—. Neurosurg. cons. Cin. Bengals; mem. adv. bd. Midmark Corp., Versailles, Ohio, 1998, Gliodel-Rohn Polenc rohrer, 1999, Gliatech, Cleve.; bd. dirs. Ohio Med. Instrument Corp., Basco Mfg. Corp., Mason, Ohio, OutWest Resorts, Hartsel, Colo. Home: 18 Garden Pl Cincinnati OH 45208-1001 Office: Mayfield Clinic 506 Oak St Cincinnati OH 45219-2507 E-mail: toblermd@aol.com.

TOBON, HECTOR, gynecologic pathologist, educator; b. Aranzazu, Colombia, Sept. 20, 1934; came to U.S., 1962; MD, Univ. de Caldas, S.Am. Diplomate Am. Bd. Pathology. Intern Hosp. San Juan de Dios Armenia; resident Inst. Nat. Cancer, Hosp. San Juan de Dios Bogota; resident in pathology Meml. Hosp., Danville, Va., 1962-65, Presbyn. U. Hosp./U. Pitts. Med. Ctr., 1965-66; assoc. prof. pathology U. Pitts., 1967—2000, prof. emeritus, Sch. Medicine, 2000—. Assoc. chief pathology Magee Womens Hosp., Pitts., 1986-99 Office: Magee Womens Hosp 300 Halket St Ofc 4410 Pittsburgh PA 15213-3180

TOBORG, ALFRED, history educator; b. Bklyn., Nov. 9, 1932; s. Willy Carl Heinrich Toborg and Gertrud Weck; m. Linda Onsruth, Aug. 17, 1963; children: Katherine Ann Toborg Franko, Louise Elaine Toborg Merrigan, William Lindell, Mary Elizabeth Toborg Boe. BA in History and German, Columbia U., 1954, PhD in History, 1965; MA in History, Xavier U., 1957. Lectr. in history Queens (N.Y.) Coll., 1959-60, Hunter Coll., N.Y.C., 1960; grad. asst. in history Columbia U., 1959-60; prof. history Lyndon State Coll., Lyndonville, Vt., 1960-99, prof. history emeritus, 2000—. Lectr. in history L.I. U., Bklyn., summer 1961, U. Vt., Lyndonville br., summer 1963-65, 68. Contbr. articles, book revs. to profl. jours. Mem. Vt. Rep. State Com., 1999-; chmn. Lyndon Rep. Town Com., 1970-73;mem. Lyndonville, 1968—, Caledonia County Rep. Com., 1969-79, 81-83, 97-, vice chmn., 1971-73; chmn. Lyndon Town History Adv. Com., Lyndonville, 1993—; acad. assoc. Atlantic Coun. of U.S., Washington, 1987-99; deacon St. Elizabeth Ch., Lyndonville, 1990—; moderator Village of Lyndonville, 1999—. With U.S. Army, 1954—56, with U.S. Army, 1962—62. Humanities scholar Vt. Coun. on Humanities, 1985—. Fulbright scholar, 1958-59; Lyndon State Coll. grantee 1979-82, 85, 87, 92, 94-95, 98; Vt. State Colls. faculty fellow, 1989-90; recipient Appreciation award Lyndon State Coll. Alumni Assn., 1999, Vt. Pub. Svc. award Vt. Sec. of State, 1999. Mem. Am. Hist. Assn., Am. Cath. Hist. Assn., Am. Soc. 18th Century Studies, Vt. Cursillo (treas. 1978-80), Vt. Hist. Soc., Lyndon Hist. Soc. (pres. 1975-77), KC (4th deg. knight). Roman Catholic. Avocations: reading, writing, gardening, church activities, research. Home: 143 South St Lyndonville VT 05851-0272 E-mail: altoborg@together.net.

TOBY, JACKSON, sociologist, educator; b. N.Y.C., Sept. 10, 1925; s. Phineas and Anna (Weissman) T.; m. Marcia Lifshitz, Aug. 1, 1952 (dec. Jan. 1997); children: Alan Steven, Gail Afriat. BA, Bklyn. Coll., 1946; MA in Econs, Harvard U., 1947, MA in Sociology, 1949, PhD in Sociology, 1950. Rsch. assoc. Lab. Social Relations, Harvard, 1950-51; mem. faculty Rutgers U., 1951—2002, prof. sociology, chmn. dept., 1961-68, dir. Inst. for Criminological Rsch., 1969-94. Cons. Youth Devel. Program, Ford Found., 1959-63 Author: (with H.C. Bredemeier) Social Problems in America, 1960, 2d edit., 1971; Contemporary Society, 1964, 2d edit., 1971; contbr. numerous articles to profl. jours., pub. policy jours., N.Y. Times, Wall St. Jour., L.A. Times, Chgo. Tribune, Washington Post, The Weekly Standard, Nat. Rev., Sociol. Rsch. Cons., Pres.'s Commn. Law Enforcement and Adminstrn. Justice, 1966; trustee NAMI-N.J., 1997-2000. Recipient numerous research grants Mem. Am. Sociol. Assn., Am. Soc. Criminology, Nat. Assn. Scholars. Achievements include spl. research adolescent delinquency in U.S., Sweden, Japan, other countries, on violence and dropouts in Am. public schools. Home: 17 Harrison Ave Highland Park NJ 08904-1813 Office: Rutgers U Dept Sociology Lucy Stone Hall Livingston Campus New Brunswick NJ 08903 E-mail: jtoby@rci.rutgers.edu.

TOCCI, NEIL MICHAEL, marketing and corporate communications executive, educator; b. Boston, Feb. 15, 1949; s. Nildo Neil and Irene Marie (Rioux) T.; m. Marlene Perscheid, Apr. 22, 1972; 1 child, Margaux. BS, Boston Coll., 1971; MBA in Mktg., Fairleigh Dickinson U., 1976; MA, Seton Hall U., 1999. Pres. Carrera Graphic Assocs. Inc., Newark, 1976-94, Carrera Digital, Newark, 1994-97; digital color specialist AOE Ricoh, Fairfield, N.J., 1997-99; mgr., mktg. and corp. comm. Kyocera Mita Am. Inc., 1999—. Adj. prof. psychology William Paterson U., Wayne, N.J., 2000—; mem. panel, cons. mktg. strategy Essex County Coll., Newark, 1990; mem. panelist, cons. comms. skills Seton Hall U., South County, N.J., 1992. Mem. Wyckoff YMCA, 1999—, coach recreation league, Wycoff, 2002—. Mem. ACA, N.J. Psychol. Assn., High Mountain Golf Club. Roman Catholic.

TOCCO, ELAINE KAY, insurance policy specialist; b. Columbus, Ohio, May 20, 1957; d. Arthur Gene and Nancy Louise Lanker; m. Peter Joseph Tocco; children: Nicholas, Alexander; children: Zachary. BA, Brescia U., 1981. Program cons. Disability Determination Svcs., Indpls., 1983—98; social ins. specialist Social Security Adminstrn., Balt., 1999—. Webelos leader Boy Scouts Am., Columbia, 1999—2001; coord. support group Multiple Sclerosis Soc., Indpls., 1985—86. Mem.: Nat. Assn. Disability Examiners, Psy Chi, Alpha Chi. Roman Catholic. Avocations: reading, gardening. Home: 6048 Misty Arch Run Columbia MD 21044 Office: Social Security Adminstrn 6401 Security Blvd Baltimore MD United States Personal E-mail: elaine_tocco@hotmail.com. Business E-Mail: elaine.tocco@ssa.gov.

TOCCO, JAMES, pianist; b. Detroit, Sept. 21, 1943; s. Vincenzo and Rose (Tabbita) T.; 1 child, Rhoya. Prof. music Ind. U., Bloomington, 1977-91; eminent scholar, artist-in-residence U. Cin. Coll.-Conservatory Music, 1991—; prof. Musikhochschule, Lübeck, Ger., 1990—; artistic dir. Great Lakes Chamber Music Festival, 1994—. Debut with orch., Detroit, 1956, since performed with symphony orchs. including Chgo. Symphony, Los Angeles Philharmonic, Cin. Symphony, Detroit Symphony, Nat. Symphony, Balt. Symphony, Atlanta Symphony, Denver Symphony, Montreal Symphony, London Symphony, London Philharm., BBC Orch., Berlin Philharm., Moscow Radio-TV Orch., Amsterdam Philharmonic, Munich Philharmonic, Bavarian Radio Orch., Royal Concertebouw Orch., also recitals, U.S. and abroad, and performances, CBS and NBC networks; guest performer, White House; Recs. include the complete preludes of Chopin, collected piano works of Leonard Bernstein, complete piano works of Charles Tomlinson Griffes, 4 piano sonatas of Edward MacDowell, selected piano works of Aaron Copland, complete Bach-Liszt organ transcriptions, piano works of John Corigliano. Recipient Bronze medal Tchaikovsky Competition, Moscow 1970, Bronze medal Queen Elisabeth of Belgium Competition, Brussels 1972, 1st prize Piano Competition of Americas, Rio de Janeiro 1973, 1st prize Munich Internat. Competition 1973. Office: U Cin Coll Conservatory Musi Cincinnati OH 45221-0001

TOCHO, LEE FRANK, mechanical engineer; b. New Orleans, Sept. 21, 1955; s. John Reaves Jr. and Grace Felice (Weekley) T.; m. Linda Varela, May 13, 1989; 1 child, Alexander Varela. BSME, Auburn U., 1977. Mech. engr. NOPSI, New Orleans, 1978-91, HC&S, Puunene, Hawaii, 1991—. Gov. Hawaii Sugar Technologists, Aiea, 1994-98, pres., 1998. Dir. Riverland Credit Union, New Orleans, 1987-91. Mem. ASME, NFPA, Maui Engring. Soc. Libertarian. Mem. Lds Ch. Achievements include invention of shrouded condenser entrance, direct contact de-superheater and power plant condenser automatic cleaner. Home: PO Box 814 Makawao HI 96768-0814 Office: Hawaiian Comm & Sugar Co PO Box 266 Puunene HI 96784-0266

TOCKLIN, ADRIAN MARTHA, insurance company executive, lawyer; b. 1951; m. Gary Tocklin. BA, George Washington U.; JD, Seton Hall U. Sr. v.p. Continental Corp., 1988-92, exec. v.p., 1992-94; pres. diversified ops. CNA Ins., Chgo., 1995-98; CEO, pres. Tocklin & Assocs., 1998—; with Continental Corp., 1974—95. Bd. dirs. Underwriters Adjusting Co., Arbitration Forums, Inc., Tarrytown, NY, Continental Ins. Co., Sonat Corp., 1st Ins. Co. of Hawaii; dir. CNA Surety, 1997—, El Paso Energy Corp., 1999—2001. Named Ins. Women of Yr. APIW, 1998. Mem.: Nat. Assn. Ins. Women (Outstanding Ins. Woman in N.Y.C.), YWCA Acad. Women Achievers. Democrat. Lutheran.

TOCZYNSKI, JANET MARIE, oncological nurse; b. Toledo, Sept. 21, 1953; d. William J. and Patricia B. (Daugherty) Meyer; m. Daniel J. Toczynski, May 21, 1988; children: Aaron, Stephanie, Christie; children by previous marriage: Brooke, Shana. Diploma, St. Vincent's Sch. Nursing, 1974. RN, Ohio. Float nurse ICU, CCU, burn care ctr. St. Vincent Med. Ctr., Toledo, 1974-80, head nurse orthopedics, 1980-83, ops. analyst, 1983-87; staff nurse Mercy Hosp., 1987-92; oncology nurse Med. Coll. Ohio, 1992-97, documentation specialist health info. mgmt., 1997-2001, mgr. health info. mgmt. record completion, 2001—. Mem. Intravenous Nursing Soc., Toledo Area Oncology Nurses Soc., St. Vincent Alumni Assn. Home: 2160 Kingston Dr Maumee OH 43537-1153 Office: Med Coll Ohio 3000 Arlington Ave Toledo OH 43614-2595 E-mail: jtoczynski@mco.edu.

TODA, TADASUMI, business consultant; b. Morioka, Iwate Prefecture, Japan, Apr. 15, 1946; s. Tadakuni and Fuji (Horiai) T.; m. Shizue Yamaguchi, May 10, 1970; children: Rikiya, Yusuke, Shimpei. B. degree, Yokohama City U., 1969. Asst. mgr. Yamashita-Shinnihon Steamship Co., Ltd., Tokyo, 1979-88; bus. cons. Bus. Cons. Inc., Tokyo, 1988—. Avocation: soccer. Home: 176 Karibacho Hodogaya-Ku Yokohama 240 Japan Office: Bus Cons Inc 2-7-2 Yaesu Chuo-Ku Tokyo 104 Japan

TODARO, MICHAEL PAUL, economics educator, consultant; b. May 14, 1942; s. George Joseph and Annette (Piccini) Todaro; m. Donna Renee Crickenberger, June 17, 1974; 1 child Lenora Jean. BA, Haverford Coll., 1964; MPhil, Yale U., 1966, PhD, 1967. Vis. lectr. Makerere U. Uganda, 1964—65; vis. sr. lectr. U. Nairobi, Kenya, 1968—70, Kenya, 1974—76; assoc. dir. Rockefeller Found., N.Y.C., 1968—76; vis. prof. U. Calif., Santa Barbara, 1976—77; dep. dir. Population Coun., N.Y.C., 1977, sr. assoc., cons., 1978—; prof. econs. NYU, 1977—97. Cons. Fund for Peace (Inst. for Study of World Politics), N.Y.C., 1979—. Author: Internal Migration in Developing Countries, 1976, Economics for a Developing World, 1991, Economic Development in the Third World, 2000; co-author: Economic Theory, 1969; mem. editl. bd.: Population and Devel. Rev., 1976—. Fellow, Woodrow Wilson Found., 1966, NDEA, 1966; grantee, Compton Found., 1981—84. Mem.: Population Assn. Am., Internat. Union for Sci. Study of Population, Am. Econ. Assn., Coun. on Fgn. Rels., Phi Beta Kappa. Roman Catholic. Home: PO Box 432 York Harbor ME 03911 Office: Population Coun 1 Dag Hammarskjold Plz New York NY 10017

TODD, ANDREW CHRISTIAN, research scientist, consultant; b. Birmingham, Eng., Dec. 6, 1964; s. Robert Derrick and Rita T. BS, U. Birmingham (Eng.), 1986; phD, 1989. Chartered physicist. Vis. prof. U. Md., Balt., 1990-92; asst. prof. Mt. Sinai Sch. Medicine, N.Y.C., 1992-2000, assoc. prof., 2001—. Adj. asst. prof. Johns Hopkins U., Balt., 1995—. Contbr. numerous articles to profl. jours. Mem. Am. Assn. Physicists in Medicine, Inst. Physics., Inst. Phyisics and Engring. in Medicine. Avocations: music, photography. Office: The Mt Sinai Med Ctr Box 1057 One Gustave L Levy Pl New York NY 10029-6574 Fax: (212) 423-9313. E-mail: andrew.todd@mssm.edu.

TODD, EDWARD FRANCIS, JR. risk management consultant, insurance broker; b. N.Y.C., Mar. 18, 1956; s. Edward Francis and Alberta (Meyer) T.; m. Catherine Theresa Mangino, Oct. 22, 1977; children: Edward Michael, Kristen Ann. BBA, Coll. Ins., N.Y.C., 1979; MBA, Seton Hall U., 1992. CPCU; cert. Assoc. in Risk Mgmt., Assoc. in Claims. With Atlantic Mut., N.Y.C., 1972-79; sr. risk analyst Continental Ins. Co., 1979-82; supervising underwriter Hartford Ins. Co., 1982-84; staff cons. Blades & Macaulay, Union, N.J., 1984-88; sr. mgr., risk mgmt. Ernst & Young, Phila., 1988-95; sr. v.p. Frenkel & Co., Inc., N.Y.C., 1995—. Mem. Am. Inst. CPCUs. Home: 23 Carter Rd East Brunswick NJ 08816-4603 E-mail: etodd@frenkel.com.

TODD, EDWARD WILLIAM, insurance analyst; b. Tagbilaran, Bohol, The Philippines, Nov. 7, 1948; came to U.S., 1951; s. Edward Todd and Doris Julia Crozier-Todd; m. Janice Lynn Gustafson, July 2, 1983; children: Erin Kathleen, Kelsey Michelle. BA in Polit. Sci., Seattle Pacific U., 1970. Credit ctrl. supr. Sears, Seattle, Portland, Oreg., 1969-74; cost acct. Peerless Industries, Tualatin, 1974-75; personal lines underwriter SAFECO Ins. Cos., Lake Oswego, 1975-79, area underwriting mgr., 1979-96, cmty. involvement chmn., 1985—2002, sr. analyst, diversity mktg. coord., 1999—2002; N.W. region diversity mktg. specialist SAFECO Ins. Co., 2002—. Mem. session, elder, trustee Lake Grove Presbyn. Ch., 1989—92, mem. bd. deacons, 1986—89; bd. dirs. Lake Oswego C. of C., 1989—93, pres., 1992—93; co-founder Cmty. Cultural Diversity Week, 1997; bd. dirs., co-pres. Samaritan Counseling Ctr., 1997—98; co-chair legal budget com. Lake Oswego Sch. Dist., 1997—; bd. dirs. Lake Oswego Sch. Dist. Found., 1997—, pres., 1999—2000. Recipient Cmty. Leader of Year award, Lake Oswego C. of C., 2001. Democrat. Avocations: community service, walking, reading, gardening. Fax: 503-697-6676.

TODD, FRANCES EILEEN, pediatrics nurse; b. Hawthorne, Calif., Aug. 20, 1950; d. James Clark and Jean Eleanor (McGinty) Nailen; m. Steven Charles Todd, Oct. 25, 1975; 1 child, Amanda Kathryn. ASN, El Camino Jr. Coll., 1974; BSN, Calif. State Coll., Long Beach, 1982, postgrad.; M in Health Adminstrn., U. La Verne, Calif., 2000. RN, Calif.; cert. pub. health nurse, Calif.; cert. PNP; cert. provider pediat. advanced life support, Am. Heart Assn. Nursing attendant St. Earne's Nursing Home, Inglewood, Calif., 1973; clinic nurse I Harbor-UCLA Med. Ctr., Torrance, 1974-77, evening shift relief charge nurse, clinic nurse II, 1977-85, pediatric liaison nurse, 1984-90, pediatric nurse practitioner, 1985—. Steward Local Union 660, 1995—; tutor Compton (Calif.) C.C., 1988, clin. instr., 1987-88; lectr. faculty dept. pediatrics UCLA Sch. Medicine, 1980—; lectr. in field. Co-author: Judges and Stewards Handbook, 1992; contbr. articles to profl. jours. Past co-chairperson parent support group Sherrie's Schs., Lomita, Calif. Mem. Nat. Assn. Pediat. Nurse Assocs. and Practitioners, L.A. Pediat. Soc., Emergency Nurses Assn., Local 660 (shop steward), Svc. Employees Int. Union, local 660 (union steward), Peruvian Paso Horse Registry N.Am. (co-chair judge's accreditation com. 1989-98, judge's Andalusian horses). Avocations: Peruvian Paso horses, orchids, jewelery design. Office: Harbor UCLA Med Ctr 1000 W Carson St Torrance CA 90502-2004

TODD, HAROLD WADE, retired association executive, retired air force officer; b. Chgo., Jan. 17, 1938; s. Harold Wade and Jeanne (Fayal) T.; m. Wendy Yvonne Kendrick, July 12, 1981; children by previous marriage: Hellen J. Wilson, Kenneth J., Stephen D., Joseph M., Michelle M. Adams, Mark A.; stepchildren: Jamie Y. White, James K. Mills, Timothy S. Emerson. BS, U.S. Air Force Acad., 1959; grad., Nat. War Coll., 1975. Commd. 2d lt. U.S. Air Force, 1959, advanced through grades to maj. gen., 1982; aide to comdr. (2d Air Force (SAC)), Barksdale AFB, La., 1970-71; exec. aide to comdr.-in-chief U.S. Air Forces Europe, Germany, 1971-74; spl. asst. chief of staff USAF, 1975-76; chief Concept Devel. Divsn., 1976-77; chief Readiness and NATO Staff Group, Hdqrs. USAF, 1977-78; exec. asst. to chmn. Joint Chiefs Staff Washington, 1978-80; comdr. 25th region N. Am. Aerospace Def. Command McChord AFB, Wash., 1980-82; chief staff 4th Allied Tactical Air Force Heidelberg, 1982-85; commandant Air War Coll., 1985-89; vice comdr. Air U., 1985-89, ret., 1989; ind. cons. Colorado Springs, Colo., 1989-95; pres., CEO, Nat. Stroke Assn., Englewood, 1995-00. Founder, pres. Bossier City (La.) chpt. Nat. Assn. for Children with Learning Disabilities, 1970-71. Decorated Def. DSM, Air Force DSM (2), Legion of Merit (2), DFC, Air medal (8), Air Force Commendation medal. Mem. Air Force Assn., USAF Acad. Assn. Grads., Nat. War Coll. Alumni Assn. Home: 1250 Big Valley Dr Colorado Springs CO 80919-1015

TODD, J. C. See COOPER, JANE TODD

TODD, JAMES DALE, federal judge; b. Scotts Hill, Tenn., May 20, 1943; s. James P. and Jeanette Grace (Duck) T.; m. Jeanie M. Todd, June 26, 1965; 2 children. BS, Lambuth Coll., 1965; M Combined Scis., U. Miss., 1968; JD, Memphis State U., 1972. Bar: Tenn. 1972, U.S. Dist. Ct. (we. dist.) Tenn. 1972, U.S. Ct. Appeals (6th cir.) 1973, U.S. Supreme Ct. 1975. Tchr. sci., chmn. sci. dept. Lyman High Sch., Longwood, Fla., 1965-68, Memphis U. Sch., 1968-72; ptnr. Waldrop, Farmer, Todd & Breen, P.A., 1972-83; cir. judge div. II 26th Jud. Dist., Jackson, Tenn., 1983-85; judge U.S. Dist. Ct. (we. dist.) Tenn., 1985-2001, chief judge, 2001—. Recipient Lifetime Achievement award Lambuth U., 2001; named Alumnus of Yr. Lambuth Coll. Alumni Assn., 1985. Fellow Tenn. Bar Found.; mem. Fed. Judges Assn. (bd. dirs. 1998-2002), Fed. Bar Assn., Jackson Madison County Bar Assn. (pres. 1978-79), Dist. Judges Assn. of 6th Cir. (pres. 2000-2001). Methodist. Office: US Dist Ct 111 S Highland Ave Jackson TN 38301-6107

TODD, JAMES HIRAM, II, management consultant, educator; b. Oklahoma City, Nov. 2, 1942; s. Prentiss Oliver and Itillious Vener (Jackson) T.; m. Unzerlo Vergínia General, June 19, 1963; 1 child, Mark A. BA, U. Okla., 1972, MA, 1986; PhD, Western Inst. Social Rsch., Berkeley, Calif., 1990. Health adminstr. Mary Mahoney Health Ctr., Spencer, Okla., 1973-76; spl. project dir. North Tulsa Ambulatory Care System, 1976-78; clin. nurse Bapt. Med. Ctr., Oklahoma City, 1979-83; pres., CEO Ednl. Resource Devel. Group, 1983-94; regional mgr. STAT Nursing Svcs., Oakland, Calif., 1986-88; rsch. prof. San Francisco State U., 1988—. Adv. com. San Francisco Unified Sch. Dist., 1989-94; White House Conferee, 1975. Author: Our Home is Not the Ghetto, 1995. Fin. com. United Way, Oklahoma City, 1973-76; scout master Boy Scouts Am., Norman, Okla., 1970-72; v.p. Nat. Black Child Devel. Inst., San Francisco, 1990—; bd. dirs., congrl. cons. Nat. Assn. Cmty. Health Ctrs., Washington, 1973-78; bd. dirs. Emergency Med. Svcs. Auth., Tulsa, 1976-78. With U.S. Army, 1960. Recipient Cert. Commendation, City of Tulsa, 1978, Cert. Appreciation, U.S. Dept. Edn., 1991, proclamation award Mayor San Francisco, 1990. Mem. AAUP, Nat. Assn. Black Sch. Educators, Calif. Commonwealth, Calif. Acad. Sci., World Future Soc., Ernest W. Lyons Lodge. Democrat. Avocations: travel, reading, photography, bowling. Office: San Francisco State U 8 Tapia Dr San Francisco CA 94132-1717

TODD, JAY MARLYN, retired editor; b. Granger, Utah, July 28, 1936; s. Kenneth Christian and Gertrude A. (Viehweg) T.; m. Janet Cutrer Todd, Mar. 20, 1964; children: Deborah, Jay Randall, Deanna, Jason Cutrer, Sarah Janet. BS, U. Utah, 1961. Staff writer Deseret News, Salt Lake City, 1960-61; tchr. Ch. Edn. Sys., various cities in Utah, Idaho, 1961-65; asst. editor, asst. mng. editor Improvement Era, Salt Lake City, 1966-70; mng. editor New Era, 1971-72, Ensign, Salt Lake City, 1972-2001. Author: Curtain Time USA: Ambassador of Inspiration, 1965, Saga of the Book of Abraham, 1968, (booklets) The Creed Haymond Story, 1979, A Historical Walking Tour of Holladay, 1996; editor: A Treasury of Edward J. Wood, 1983.

TODD, JOE LEE, historian; b. Bartlesville, Okla., Sept. 28, 1946; s. Harold Albert and Mildred Viola Todd. Student, Okla. State U., 1964-66; BA in Anthropology, U. Okla., 1974; postgrad. in Anthropology, U. Tex., Austin, 1979-81. Curator of collections Okla. Hist. Soc., Oklahoma City, 1971-76; dir. 45th Infantry div. mus., 1976-78; curator Ft. Hood (Tex.) Mus., 1978-82; oral historian, archivist Okla. Hist. Soc., Oklahoma City, 1982—. Cons. Confederate Air Force, Midland, Tex., 1990—, Andersonville (Ga.) POW Ctr., 1991—. Author: Pipe-Tomahawks in the Oklahoma Historical Society, 1976, Native American Interveiws, oral histories, 1985, USS Oklahoma, Remembrance of a Great Lady, 1990. Bd. dirs. Sacred Heart (Okla.) Indian Mission, 1989-95. With U.S. Army, 1966-69, Okla. Nat. Guard, 1975-78, Tex. Nat. Guard, 1978-83, USAR, 1983-96. Decorated Air medal; recipient Humanitarian Svc. medal U.S. Army, 1992, Vietnam Svc. medal, 1969, Kuwaiti Liberation medal, 1991. Republican. Episcopalian. Office: Okla Hist Soc 2100 N Lincoln Blvd Oklahoma City OK 73105-4907 Home: RR 5 Box 415 Bartlesville OK 74003-9315

TODD, JOHN DICKERSON, JR. retired lawyer; b. Macon, Ga., June 30, 1912; s. J.D. and Hazel (McManus) T.; m. Mellicent McWhorter, Mar. 7, 1943; children— Rosalind (Mrs. Jack Harding Tedards, Jr.), John D. Student, Va. Mil. Inst., 1930-32; LLB, U. Ga., 1935. Bar: S.C. 1935. With firm Hingson & Todd, 1935-51; partner firm Leatherwood, Walker, Todd & Mann, Greenville, S.C., 1952-2000; sr. partner; judge Greenville City Ct., 1939; atty. County of Greenville, 1948-56; mem. bd. bar examiners State of S.C.; ret. Chmn. S.C. Judicial Study Commn., 1995. Served to maj. AUS, 1941-45. Mem. ABA, Am. Coll. Trial Lawyers, Am. Bar Found., 4th U.S. Cir. Jud. Conf., S.C. Bar Assn. (bd. govs., pres. 1978—), Greenville Jr. C. of C. (pres.), Greenville County Bar (past pres.), Greenville Kiwanis (past pres.), Greenville Country Club (past pres.), Summit Club, Poinsett Club, Phi Delta Phi, Sigma Nu. Baptist. Home: 200 Riverside Dr Greenville SC 29605-1133

TODD, JOHN JOSEPH, lawyer; b. St. Paul, Mar. 16, 1927; s. John Alfred and Martha Agnes (Jagoe) T.; m. Dolores Jean Shanahan, Sept. 9, 1950; children: Richard M., Jane E., John P. Student, St. Thomas Coll., 1944, 46-47; B.Sci. and Law, U. Minn., 1949, LL.B., 1950. Bar: Minn. bar 1951. Practice in, South St. Paul, Minn., 1951-72; partner Thuet and Todd, 1953-72; asso.

justice Minn. Supreme Ct., St. Paul, 1972-85; sole practice West St. Paul, 1985-92; of counsel Brenner & Glassman Ltd., Mpls., 1992-99, Orme & Assoc., Eagan, Minn., 1999—. Served with USNR, 1945-46. Mem. state bar assns., VFW. Home: 6689 Argenta Trl W Inver Grove Heights MN 55077-2208 Office: Orme & Associates 3140 Neil Armstrong Blvd Eagan MN 55121-2273 E-mail: jtodd@ormelaw.com., jjbtodd@aol.com.

TODD, KENNETH S., JR. parasitologist, educator; b. Three Forks, Mont., Aug. 25, 1936; s. Kenneth S. and Anna Louise (Seeman) T. BS, Mont. State U., 1962, MS, 1964; PhD, Utah State U., 1967. Asst. prof. U. Ill., Urbana, 1967-71, assoc. prof., 1971-76, prof. vet. parasitology, 1976-94, chmn. div. parasitology, 1983-90, asst. head vet. pathobiology, 1984-87, prof. vet. programs in agr., 1984-94, acting head vet. pathobiology, 1987-90, head, 1990-94; prof. emeritus, 1994. Affiliate scientist Ill. State Natural History Survey, 1987-94; adj. prof. microbiology Mont. State U., 1994—. Served with USAF, 1954-58. NSF grad. fellow, 1966-67 Mem. AVMA, Am. Assn. Vet. Parasitologists, Am. Micros. Soc., Am. Soc. Parasitologists, Am. Soc. Tropical Medicine and Hygiene, Helminthologic Soc. Washington, Midwest Conf. Parasitologists, Wildlife Disease Assn., Soc. Protozoologists, Mont. Acad. Scis., Rocky Mountain Conf. Parasitologists, World Assn. for Advancement of Vet. Parasitology. Office: Mont State U Dept Microbiology Bozeman MT 59715 E-mail: kstoddjr@hotmail.com.

TODD, LINDA MARIE, nutrition researcher, financial consultant, pilot; b. L.A., Mar. 30, 1948; d. Ithel Everette and Janet Marie Fredricks; m. William MacKenzie Cook, Jan. 11, 1982 (div. Oct. 1989); m. Robert Oswald Todd, Apr. 8, 1990; 1 child, Jesse MacKenzie Todd. BA in Psychology and Sociology, U. Colo., 1969; student Psychology Grad. work, U. No. Colo., 1970. Pilot lic., weather cert., FCC lic., Calif. life ins. lic., coll. teaching credential; registered with Nat. Assn. Securities Dealers. Counselor Jeffco Juvenile Detention Ctr., Golden, Colo., 1969-71; communications Elan Vital, Denver, 1971-81; legal sec. Fredman, Silverberg & Lewis, San Diego, 1980-82; escrow supr. Performance Mktg. Concepts, Olympic Valley, 1982-85; mgmt. commn. instr. Sierra Coll., Truckee, 1986-87; regional mgr. Primerica Fin. Svcs., Reno, 1987-91; air traffic, weather advisor Truckee (Calif.) Tahoe Airport Dist., 1986-96; dist. mgr. Sierra Sun & Tahoe World Newspapers, 2001—. Student tour leader, air show organizer Truckee (Calif.) Tahoe Airport, 1986-96; fin. cons. Primerica Fin. Svcs., Truckee, 1987-91; gen. agt. TTS Fin., 1992—; co-founder Todd Nutrition, 1995—; co-owner Todd Aero, 1990—; bd. dirs. Pacific Crest Fin. Corp., 1996—. Editor: (newsletter) Communications, 1975. Chorus mem. operas and musicals, 1960s-70s; prodn. crew mem. Lake Tahoe Summer Music Festivals; sec. gen. Arapahoe H.S. Model UN, Littleton, Colo., 1965; del. State Model UN, Colo., 1966; conv. del. Elan Vital, The Ninety-Nines, Inc.; mem. Civil Air Patrol. Recipient Univ. scholarship Littleton (Colo.) Edn. Assn., 1966, flight scholarship The Ninety-Nines Inc., Reno, 1990; named Recruiter of Month, Al Williams Primerica, Reno, 1987. Mem. CAP, Elan Vital, Plane Talkers, The Ninety Nines, Planetary Soc. Avocations: hiking, skiing, swimming, flying, soaring. Home and Office: PO Box 1303 Truckee CA 96160-1303 E-mail: m2wlindatodd@hotmail.com.

TODD, NORMA ROSS, retired government official; b. Butler, Pa., Oct. 3, 1920; d. William Bryson and Doris Mae (Ferguson) Ross; m. Alden Frank Miller, Jr., Apr. 16, 1940 (dec. Feb. 1975); 1 child, Alden Frank III; m. Jack R. Todd, Dec. 23, 1977 (dec. Sept. 1990). Student, Pa. State U., 1944-46, Yale U., 1954-57. Exec. mgr. Donora (Pa.) C. of C., 1950-57, pres., 1972; exec. mgr. Donora Cmty. Chest, 1950-57; office mgr. Donora Golden Jubilee, 1951; staff writer Donora Herald-American, 1957, city editor, 1957-70; assoc. editor Daily Herald, Donora, 1970-73; svc. rep. Pitts. Telesvc. Ctr., Social Security Adminstrn., HHS, 1977-83. Mem. Mayor's Adv. Coun., Donora, 1965-69, Citizens' Adv. Coun., Donora, 1965-69; mem. Donora Bd. Edn., 1954-60, pres., 1960; mem. Donora Borough Coun., 1970-72; bd. dirs. Mon Valley chpt. ARC, 1964-99, sec. bd., 1964-97, chmn. bd. dirs., 1997-99, mem. lifetime adv. bd., 2000; bd. dirs. Washington County Tourism Agy., 1970-90, sec., 1972-90; bd. dirs. Washington County History and Landmarks Found., 1971-80, 91-92, sec., 1975-80, 91-93, hon. life mem., 1996; bd. dirs. Mon Valley YMCA, 1960-66, Mon Valley coun. Camp Fire Girls, 1965-79, Mon Valley Drug and Alcoholism Coun., 1971-78; hon. life mem. Pa. Congress PTAs; bd. dirs. United Way Mon Valley, 1973-82, chmn. pub. rels., 1973-74. Recipient Fine Arts Festival of Pa. Poetry first prize award Fedn. of Women's Clubs, 1987, 1st and 2nd pl. awards for photography Washington County Fine Arts Festival, County Fedn. Women's Clubs, 1990, Disting. Svc. award Donora Rotary Club, 1997, Millenium Peace award, India, 2001; published in Best Poems of 1995 Nat. Libr. of Poetry, Best Poems of 1996, Best Poems of 1997, Outstanding Poets of 1998, and numerous anthologies in U.S., Italy and India. Mem. AAUW, Svc. Corps Retired Execs. (sec. 1998—), Pa. Soc. Newspaper Editors, Pitts. Press Club, Donora C. of C. (pres. 1971-72), DAR (regent Monongahela Valley chpt. 1974-77, treas. 1992-2001), Internat. Platform Assn., World Poetry Soc. Internat., Internat. Poets Acad., U.S. Poets, Metverse Muse, Washington County Poetry Soc. (pres. 1967-69), Donora Hist. Soc. (curator 1990—), Family of Bruce Soc. (descendants of King Robert the Bruce of Scotland 1987—), Washington County Fedn. Women's Clubs (rec. sec. 1964-66, pub. rels chmn. 1990-92), Order Ea. Star (worthy matron 1966-67, treas. 1986-94, 98—, bd. dirs. Western Pa. Eastern Star Home 1997-98, adv. bd. Masonic Eastern Star Home-West 1998-2000), White Shrine of Jerusalem (high priestess 1973-74, treas. 1995-2001), Order of Amaranth (royal matron 1966, dist. dep. 3 times, grand rep. W.Va. 1979-80), Donora Forecast (pres. 1957-59), Donora Unidon (pres. 1965-66, 56-57), Clan Ross Assn. U.S. Avocation: genealogy. Home: Overlook Ter Donora PA 15033 also: 1310 Mckean Ave Donora PA 15033-2200

TODD, ROBERT FRANKLIN, III, oncologist, educator; b. Granville, Ohio, Apr. 16, 1948; m. Susan Erhard, 1977; children: Currier Nathaniel, Andrew Joseph. AB, Duke U., 1970, PhD, 1975, MD, 1976. Diplomate Am. Bd. Internal Medicine. Intern Peter Bent Brigham Hosp., Boston, 1976-77, resident, 1977-78; fellow in oncology Sidney Farber Cancer Inst., 1978-80; clin. fellow in medicine Harvard Med. Sch., 1978-81; postdoctoral fellow divsn. tumor immunology Sidney Farber Cancer Inst., 1979-81; asst. prof. medicine Harvard Med. Sch., 1981-84; assoc. prof. internal medicine U. Mich., Ann Arbor, 1984-88, assoc. prof. cellular and molecular biology, 1985-88, assoc. dir. divsn. hematology-oncology internal medicine, 1987-91, prof. internal medicine, 1988—, assoc. chair for rsch. dept. internal medicine, 1989-91, assoc. chair dept. internal medicine, 1991-93, chief divsn. hematology-oncology dept. internal medicine, 1993—, assoc. v.p. rsch., 1999—, Frances and Victor Ginsberg prof. hematology/oncology, 1999—. Attending physician U. Mich. Hosps., 1984—; chmn. hematology/oncology subsplty chpt. Ctrl. Soc. for Clin. Rsch., 1995-97. Contbr. numerous articles to profl. jours.; patentee in field. Mem.: The Microcirculatory Soc., Am. Soc. for Clin. Investigation, S.W. Oncology Group, Ctrl. Soc. for Clin. Rsch. (councilor 1997—, pres. 2001—), Am. Fedn. for Clin. Rsch. (councilor midwest chpt. 1986—89), Am. Soc. Hematology, Soc. Leukocyte Biology (councilor 1996—99), Am. Soc. Clin. Oncology, Am. Assn. for Cancer Rsch., Am. Assn. Immunologists, ACP, Alpha Omega Alpha, Phi Beta Kappa. Office: U of Mich Med Sch 1500 E Med Ctr Dr 7216 CCGC Ann Arbor MI 48109-0948

TODD, RONALD GARY, lawyer; b. Spokane, Wash., Dec. 12, 1946; s. Theodore H. and Dorothea I. (Swanson) T.; m. Natalie A., June 16, 1973; children: Russell E., Brian N., David E. AB, Cornell U., 1969; JD, Columbia U., 1972. Bar: N.Y. 1973, U.S. Dist. Ct. (so. and ea. dists.) N.Y. 1975, U.S. Ct. Appeals (2nd cir.) 1975, U.S. Supreme Ct. 1976, D.C. 1993. Atty. Dewey Ballantine, N.Y.C., 1973-79, Simpson Thacher & Bartlett, N.Y.C., 1980-82; atty., ptnr. Golenbock & Barell, 1982-89; ptnr. Reid & Priest (now Thelen Reid & Priest LLP), 1989-2000; chief counsel J.P. Morgan Title Agy. LLC, 2000—; asst. gen. counsel JP Morgan Chase & Co., 2000—. Instr., guest lectr. NYU Sch. Continuing Edn., 1983-90; adv. bd. Commonwealth Land Title and TransAm. Title Ins. Co., N.Y.C., 1992-97. Contbr. articles to profl. jours. Pres., bd. dirs. Seven Bridges Field Club, 1982-85. Mem. ABA (real property sect. 1973—), N.Y. Bar Assn. (real property sect. 1973—), D.C. Bar Assn. (real property sect. 1992—). Avocations: instrumental music, tennis. Office: JP Morgan Title Agy LLC 261 Madison Ave New York NY 10016-2303

TODD, SHIRLEY ANN, school system administrator; b. Botetourt County, Va., May 23, 1935; d. William Leonard and Margaret Judy (Simmons) Brown; m. Thomas Byron Todd, July 7, 1962 (dec. July 1977). B.S. in Edn., Madison Coll., 1956; M.Ed., U. Va., 1971. Cert. tchr., Va. Elem. tchr. Fairfax County Sch. Bd., Fairfax, Va., 1956-66, 8th grade history tchr., 1966-71, guidance counselor James F. Cooper Mid. Sch., McLean, Va., 1971-88, dir. guidance, 1988-96; chmn. mktg. Lake Anne Joint Venture, Falls Church, Va., 1979-82, mng. ptnr., 1980-82. Del. Fairfax County Republican Conv., 1985, 96. Fellow Fairfax Edn. Assn. (mem. profl. rights and responsibilities commn. 1970-72, bd. dirs. 1968-70), Va. Edn. Assn. (mem. state com. on local assns. and urban affairs 1969-70), NEA, No. Va. Counselors Assn. (hospitality and social chmn., exec. bd. 1982-83), Va. Counselors Assn. (exec. com. 1987), Va. Sch. Counselors Assn., Am. Assn. for Counseling and Devel., Women's Golf Assn. (pres. 1997-98), Chantilly Nat. Golf and Country Club (v.p. social 1981-82, Centreville, Va.). Baptist. Avocations: golf, tennis. Home: 6543 Bay Tree Ct Falls Church VA 22041-1001

TODD, STEPHEN MAX, lawyer; b. Kansas City, Mo., Oct. 22, 1941; s. Louis O. and A. Maxine (Mittag); m. Carlene Harre; children: Stephanie A., Louis P. BA, Kans. State U., 1963; JD, U. Kans., 1966. Bar: Kans. 1966, U.S. Dist. Ct. Kans. 1966, U.S. Ct. Appeals (10th cir.) 1967, U.S. Supreme Ct. 1971, Mo. 1973. Assoc. Schroeder, Heeney, Groff & Spies, Topeka, 1966-72; office counsel Chgo. Title Ins. Co., Kansas City, 1973-78, regional counsel, 1978—. Author: Missouri Foreclosures of Deeds of Trust, 1983, 4th edit. 2001; contbr., editor books. Mem. Kans. Bar Assn., Mo. Bar (chmn. property law com. 1990-92), Am. Coll. Real Estate Lawyers, Kiwanis (pres. Topeka Downtown Club 1971-72, lt. gov. Mo.-Ark. dist. 1976-77, pres. Kansas City South Platte Club 1979-80), Phi Delta Phi. Home: 5519 N Woodhaven Ln Kansas City MO 64152-4319 Office: Chgo Title Ins Co PO Box 26370 Kansas City MO 64196-6370 E-mail: todds@ctt.com., stoddinkc@kc.rr.com.

TODD, STEVEN A. judge; b. Portland, Oreg., Dec. 27, 1955; s. Horace E. and Lois M. Todd; m. Sherry Poole, Jan. 30, 1987; 1 child, Andrew Poole. BA in Music and Polit. Sci., Northwestern U., 1978; JD, Lewis and Clark Coll., 1981. Bar: Oreg. 1981. Law clk. U.S. Dist. Ct., Portland, 1981-82, Multnomah County Cir. Ct., Portland, 1982-83; dep. dist. atty. Columbia County, St. Helens, Oreg., 1983-87, Multnomah County, Portland, 1987-97; cir. ct. judge pro tem Multnomah County Cir. Ct., 1997—. Office: Multnomah County Cir Ct 1021 SW 4th Ave Portland OR 97204-1123

TODD, THOMAS ABBOTT, architect, urban designer, city planner; b. North Stonington, Conn., May 5, 1928; s. James Arnold and Isabel Nisbet (Downs) T.; m. Carol Roberts, July 7, 1956; children: Christopher, Suzannah, Cassandra. BA, Haverford Coll., 1950; MCP, MArch with honors, U. Pa., 1959. Designer Geddes Brecher Qualls Cunningham, Phila., 1961; chief designer Eshbach Pullinger Stevens Bruder, 1962; ptnr. Grant & Todd, 1963, Wallace McHarg Roberts Todd, Phila., 1963-79, Wallace Roberts & Todd, Phila., 1979-91, Warner, Todd Gaffney, Jamestown, R.I., 1993-01. Prin. works include The master plan for Abuja, capitol city of, Nigeria; urban design concept, master plan and public architecture for Balt. Inner Harbor; master plan U.S. Capitol Grounds, McKeldin Sq., Balt., Norfolk waterfront master plan, (Va.), Atlantic City Conv. Ctr./Rail Terminal, Lower Manhattan Plan, N.Y.C., Downtown L.A. devel. Plan, plan for State facilities, Annapolis, Md., master plan Haverford Coll., 6th St Market Place, Richmond, Va., Tredegar Galleries Valentine Mus., Richmond, Waterside Festival Market, Norfolk, Liberty State Pk., Jersey City, N.J., Wiggins Waterfront State Pk., Camden, N.J., Downtown Buffalo master plan, Quadrangle Life Care Community, Haverford, Pa., Liberty Pl. master plan, Phila., long range devel. plan U. Pa., Performing Arts Ctr., Haverford Coll., Assembly Hall, Germantown Friends Sch., plan for downtown Westerly, R.I., Newport, R.I., Harborfront and South Thames Street Demonstration Plan, Newport, also numerous pvt. residences, landscape plans, instl. and pub. master plans; contbr. articles to profl. jours. Bd. dirs. Germantown Friends Sch., Phila., 1972-74, Green St. Friends Sch., Phila., 1973-75, Phila. Maritime Mus., 1986-90, Philomel Ancient Instruments, Phila., 1986-91, Maxwell Mansion, Phila., 1983-86, Save the Bay, Naragansett Bay, 1997, Grow Smart R.I., 1997; v.p. Haverford Coll. Arboretum, 1983; chmn. ann. giving Haverford Coll., 1987; mem. Jamestown (R.I.) Planning Bd.; advisor Ft. Adams Found., Newport. Theophilus Parsons Chandler fellow, 1959; recipient numerous design awards. Fellow AIA; mem. Am. Inst. Cert. Planners. Independent. Quaker. Home: 118 Highland Dr Jamestown RI 02835-2900

TODD, VIRGIL HOLCOMB, clergyman, religion educator; b. Jordonia, Tenn., June 22, 1921; s. George Thurman and Nellie Mai (Dutton) T.; m. Irene Rolman, Sept. 21, 1941; 1 child, Donald Edwin. BA, Bethel Coll., 1945; BD, Cumberland Presbyn. Sem., 1947; MA, Scarritt Coll., 1948; PhD, Vanderbilt U., 1956. Ordained to ministry Presbyn. Ch., 1944. Minister Cumberland Presbyn. Chs., Tenn. and Ky., 1943-52; assoc. prof. Bethel Coll., McKenzie, Tenn., 1952-54; prof. of Old Testament Memphis Theol. Sem., 1954-2001, ret., 2001. Interim minister Presbyn. chs. in Tenn., Ky. and Miss., 1952—; vice-moderator Gen. Assembly Cumberland Presbyn. Ch., 1984-85, moderator, 1985-86. Author: Prophet Without Portfolio (2d Isaiah), 1972, A New Look at an Old Prophet (Ezekiel), 1977, Biblical Eschatology, 1985. Active Shelby (County) United Neighbors, Memphis, 1973-74, United Way of Greater Memphis, 1974-82. Mem. Soc. Bibl. Lit., Memphis Ministers' Assn. Lodges: Civitan (chaplain, bd. dirs. local chpt.). Democrat. Avocations: travel, golf. Home: 3095 E Glengarry Rd Memphis TN 38128-2911

TODD, WILLIAM MICHAEL, lawyer; b. Cleve., Dec. 13, 1952; s. William Charles and Jennie Ann (Diana) T. BA, U. Notre Dame, 1973; JD, Ohio State U., 1976. Bar: Ohio 1976, U.S. Dist. Ct. (so. dist.) Ohio 1977, U.S. Supreme Ct. 1987. Assoc. Porter, Wright, Morris & Arthur, Columbus, Ohio, 1976-82, ptnr., 1983-93, Squire, Sanders & Dempsey, Columbus, 1993—. Trustee Callvac Svcs., Columbus, 1985-91, pres. 1988. Mem. ABA (governing com. forum on health law 1988-91), Ohio Bar Assn., Columbus Bar Assn., Am. Soc. Med. Assn. Counsel, Am. Bd. Trial Advocates, Ohio Soc. Healthcare Attys. (pres. 1999-2000), Am. Health Lawyers Assn., Worthington Hills Country Club, Columbus Athletic Club. Roman Catholic. Avocations: music, recreational sports. Office: Squire Sanders & Dempsey 41 S High St Columbus OH 43215-6101

TODD, ZANE GREY, retired utilities executive; b. Hanson, Ky., Feb. 3, 1924; s. Marshall Elvin and Kate (McCormick) T.; m. Marysnow Stone, Feb. 8, 1950 (dec. 1983); m. Frances Z. Anderson, Jan. 6, 1984. Student, Evansville Coll., 1947-49; BS summa cum laude, Purdue U., 1951, DEng (hon.), 1979; postgrad., U. Mich., 1965; DHL, U. Indpls., 1993. Fingerprint classifier FBI, 1942-43; electric system planning engr. Indpls. Power & Light Co., 1951-56, spl. assignments supr., 1956-60, head elec. system planning, 1960-65, head substation design div., 1965-68, head distbn. engring. dept., 1968-70, asst. to v.p., 1970-72, v.p., 1972-74, exec. v.p., 1974-75, pres., 1975-81, chmn., chief exec. officer, 1976-89, dir., chmn. exec. com., 1989-94, chief exec. officer, 1981-89; chmn., pres. IPALCO Enterprises, Inc., Indpls., 1983-89, dir., chmn. exec. com., 1989-94; chmn. bd., chief exec. officer Mid-Am. Capital Resources, Inc. subs. IPALCO Enterprises, Inc., 1984-89, also bd. dirs., 1984-94. Gen. mgr. Mooresville (Ind.) Pub. Svc. Co., Inc., 1956-60; bd. dirs. Nat. City Bank Ind. (formerly Mchts. Nat. Corp.), 1975-94, Am. States Ins. Co., 1976-94; hon. dir. 500 Festival Assocs., Inc., pres. 1987. Originator probability analysis of power system reliability; contbr. articles to tech. jours. and mags. Past pres. adv. bd. St. Vincent Hosp.; bd. dirs. Commn. for Downtown, YMCA Found., Crime Stoppers Cen. Ind., Corp. Community Coun.; past chmn., bd. trustees Ind. Cen. U. (now U. Indpls.); Nat. and Greater Indpls. adv. bds. Salvation Army, 1984-96; bd. govs. Associated Colls. of Ind., 1979-92. Sgt. AUS, 1943-47. Recipient William Booth award Salvation Army, 1994; named Disting. Engring. Alumnus Purdue U., 1976, Outstanding Elec. Engr. Purdue U., 1992, Knight of Malta, Order of St. John of Jerusalem, 1986. Fellow IEEE (past chmn. power sys. engring. com.); mem. ASME, NSPE, Power Engring. Soc., Ind. Fiscal Policy Inst. (bd. govs.), Ind. C. of C., Indpls. C. of C., Mooresville C. of C. (past pres.), PGA Nat. Country Club, Ulen Country Club, Columbia Club, Indpls. Athletic Club (past bd. dirs.), Meridian Hills Country Club (past bd. dirs.), Skyline Club (bd. govs.), Newcomen Soc. (past chmn. Ind.), Rotary, Lions (past pres.), Eta Kappa Nu, Tau Beta Pi. Home: 7645 Randue Ct Indianapolis IN 46278-1565

TODD COPLEY, JUDITH A. materials and metallurgical engineering educator; b. Wakefield, West Yorkshire, Eng., Dec. 13, 1950; came to U.S., 1978; d. Marley and Joan Mary (Birkinshaw) Booth; m. David Michael Todd, June 17, 1972 (div. June 1981); m. Stephen Michael Copley, Aug. 3, 1984; 1 child, Amy Elizabeth. BA in Materials Sci., Cambridge (Eng.) U., 1972, MA, PhD in Metall./Materials Sci., 1977. Research asst. Imperial Coll. Sci. and Tech., London, 1976-78; research assoc. SUNY, Stonybrook, 1978; research engr. U. Calif., Berkeley, 1979-81; asst. prof. materials sci. and mech. engring. U. So. Calif., L.A., 1982—90; assoc. prof. metall. and materials engring. Ill. Inst. Tech., Chgo., 1990-97, assoc. chairperson mech. materials and aerospace engring., 1995—, prof. materials and mech. engring., 1997—, assoc. dean rsch. Armour Coll. Engring. and Sci., 2001—. Mem. task force Materials Property Coun., N.Y.C., 1979—89; prof. Iron and Steel Soc., 1996—2002; mem. editl. bds. Contbr. articles to profl. jours.; patentee in field. Recipient Brit. Univs. Student Travel award, 1972, Brit. Fedn. Univ. Women award, 1972, Faculty Rsch. award Oak Ridge (Tenn.) Nat. Lab., 1986, Vanadium award British Inst. Materials, 1990; Kathryn Kingswell Meml. scholar, 1972, Julia Beveridge Award, IIT, 1998, Cert. Appreciation Am. Soc. Mech. Engrs., 1995, 97, Forging Industry Ednl. Rsch. Found., 1993, Booz-Allen and Hamilton Award for Tchg. and Svc., Ill. Inst. Tech., 1996, Mary Ewart Traveling Scholarship, Cambridge Univ., 1972, Sci. Rsch. Coun. Fellowship and Overseas Travel Award, 1972. Fellow ASME Internat. (chmn. materials and fabrication com. exec. com. 2001-, pressure vessel and piping divsn. 1993-97, membership chair, PVP div., 1997-2001, assoc. editor Jour. Pressure Vessel and Piping Tech. 1994, v.p. mfg. group 2002, bd. on women and miniorites award 1997-), Assn. Women in Sci., ASM Internat. (chmn. L.A. chpt. 1986-87, coun. mem. materials sci. divsn. 1984-89); mem. AIME (Rsch. award 1983), ASTM, Soc. Women Engrs. (sr.), Electron Microscopy Soc., Hist. Metallurgy Soc., Nat. Soc. Corrosion Engrs. (Seed grant award 1983), Microbeam Analysis Soc., Soc. Mfg. Engr., Am. Assn. Univ. Women, Instn. Metall., Chartered Engr. Status, Minerals, Metals, Materials Soc. of the Am. Inst. Mining, Metall. Petroleum Engrs., Am. Soc. Mech. Engr., Am. Soc. Testing and Materials, Am. Ceramics Soc., Ill. Microscopical Soc. Avocation: archaeometry. Fax: 312-567-7018. E-mail: jtodd@iit.edu.

TODER, ERIC JAY, economist; b. N.Y.C., Mar. 16, 1944; s. Saul and Rose (Cohen) T.; m. Susan C. Cote, Aug. 2, 1980. BS, Union Coll., 1964; MA in Econs., U. Rochester, 1967, PhD in Econs., 1971. Asst. prof. econs. Tufts U., Medford, Mass., 1968-73; sr. rsch. assoc. Charles River Assocs., Cambridge, 1973-76; fin. economist U.S. Dept. Treasury, Washington, 1976-83; dir. fin. and tax analysis U.S. Dept. Energy, 1980-81; dep. dir. Office Tax Analysis, U.S. Treasury, 1983-84; dep. asst. dir. Congl. Budget Office, 1984-88, 91-93; cons. New Zealand Treasury, Wellington, 1988-91; dep. asst. sec. tax analysis U.S. Dept. Treasury, Washington, 1993-96; vis. prof. econs. U. Mich., 1997; sr. fellow Urban Inst., Washington, 1998—2001; dir. rsch. IRS, 2001—. Author: Trade Policy and U.S. Auto Industry, 1978; contbr. to econs. publs. Mem. Am. Econ. Assn., Nat. Tax Assn., Assn. Pub. Policy Analysis and Mgmt., Washington Tax Economists Forum. Jewish. Avocations: travel, hiking, music. bus. Office: IRS 1111 Contitution Ave NW N ADC R R Washington DC 20224- E-mail: etoder@his.com., eric.j.toder@irs.gov.

TODHUNTER, JOHN ANTHONY, toxicologist, consultant; b. Cali, Valle, Colombia, Oct. 9, 1949; s. John Arthur and Teresa Maria (Torres) T.; divorced, 1986; children: Jennifer, Julia; m. D. Holli Wilson, Apr. 19, 1986; 1 child, Jacqueline Rose. BSc, UCLA, 1971; MSc, Calif. State U., 1973; PhD, U. Calif., Santa Barbara, 1976. Diplomate Am. Bd. Toxicology, Am. Bd. Forensic Examiners; regulatory affairs cert. Instr. Calif. State U., L.A., 1972-73; rsch. asst. U. Calif., Santa Barbara, 1973-76; fellow Roche Inst. Molecular Biology, Nutley, N.J., 1976-78; asst. prof. Cath. U. Am., Washington, 1978-81, chmn. Biochemistry Program, 1980-81; asst. adminstr. U.S. EPA, 1981-83; cons. Sci. Regulatory Svcs. Internat., 1983-91; pres. SRS Internat. Corp., 1991—, SRS Internat. Health Care Group, 1995—. Expert advisor European regional office WHO, Stockholm, 1984; mem. Hazardous Waste Siting Bd., Annapolis, Md., 1980-81. Contbr. articles to profl. jours. Bd. dirs. Reagan Alumni Assn., Washington, 1985—; vol. Am. Cancer Soc., Washington, 1988—; mem. Presdl. Transition Team, Washington, 1980. U. Calif. Bd. Regents fellow, 1975, B.R. Baker Meml. fellow dept. chemistry U. Calif., Santa Barbara, 1976. Fellow Am. Inst. Chemists (dir. at large 1989-92, vice chmn. bd. 1992); mem. Soc. of Toxicology, Am. Chem. Soc., Soc. for Risk Analysis, N.Y. Acad. Sci. Office: SRS Internat 1625 K St NW Ste 1000 Washington DC 20006-1619 E-mail: todhunter@srsinternational.com.

TODOROVIC, JOHN, chemical engineer; b. Madison, Wis., Mar. 28, 1961; s. Radmilo A. and Lillian Todorovic; m. Nadja P., June 29, 1991. BSChemE, Tex. A&M U., 1984; MSChemE, Rose-Hulman Inst. Tech., 1987. Process engr. GE Plastics, Pittsfield, Mass., 1989-90; sr. product devel. engr. Rexam Image Products, South Hadley, 1991—. Pres. Brazos Valley Amateur Soccer Leauge, College Station, 1984. B. Rankovich scholarship B. Rankovich Found., 1986. Mem. AIChE (pres. student chpt. 1985), Sigma Xi, Tau Beta Pi, Alpha Chi Sigma, Chi Omega. Serbian Orthodox. Achievements include implementation of new die coating technology that enabled a specialized product to be coated efficiently after several previous unsuccessful attempts. Office: PO Box 854 Pittsfield MA 01202-0854

TODREAS, NEIL EMMANUEL, nuclear engineering educator; b. Peabody, Mass., Dec. 17, 1935; s. David and Anna (Gendleman) T.; m. Carol S. Schonberg, June 19, 1958; children: Timothy, Ian. BSM.E., MS, Cornell U., 1958; Sc.D. in Nuclear Engring., MIT, 1966. Asst. prof. dept. nuclear engring. MIT, Cambridge, 1970-71, assoc. prof., 1971-75, prof., 1975—, Kepco prof. nuclear engring. and prof. mech. engring., 1992—, head dept. nuclear engring., 1981-89. Served to lt. (j.g.) USN, 1958-62. Named Disting. Tchr., Ruth and Joel Spira award MIT Sch. Engring., 1995. Fellow ASME, Am. Nuclear Soc. (Arthur Holly Compton award for outstanding educators in nuclear engring. 1995, Tech. Achievement award for outstanding contbns. to thermal hydraulics 1994); mem. Nat. Acad. Engring., Sigma Xi, Tau Beta Pi, Pi Tau Sigma. Office: MIT Bldg Rm 219 77 Massachusetts Ave #24 Cambridge MA 02139-4307

TODSEN, DANA ROGNAR, health care executive; b. St. Petersburg, Oct. 8, 1947; s. Birger Rognar and Elsie (Ewing) T.; m. Janis Hellman, June 13, 1970; children: Matthew Kristian, Jennifer Alana. BA, U. South Fla., 1970, MA, 1976. Assoc. dir. So. Health Found., Tampa, Fla., 1976-78; dir. U. Tampa, 1978-82; mng. dir. St. Anthony's Health Care Found., St. Petersburg, 1982-85; dir. devel. Moffitt Cancer Ctr., Tampa, 1985-91; CEO Meml. Health Trust, 1991-98. Found. cons. Quorum Health Resources, Brentwood, Tenn., 1997—; pres., CEO Bapt. Health Found., Birmingham, Ala., 1998—; pres. Todsen & Assocs., Savannah, Ga., 1997—; adj. instr. Hillsborogh C.C., 1978, U. South Fla., 1980; assoc. faculty the Kaiser Inst., Colo., 2001; keynote spkr. in field. Contbr. articles to profl. jours. Bd. trustees Cmty. Found. Greater Tampa; bd. dirs. Savannah Maritime Festival, 1991-98, Ga. Nonprofit Resource Ctr. Ala., 1998—, Ga. Med. Soc. Growing Health Partnership, 1996-98, Pres.'s Summit for Am.'s Future, The Alliance for Youth, 1997-98, Ptnrs. for Cmty. Health, 1996-98, Ronald McDonald House Charities of the Coastal Empire, 1992-98, St. Andrew's Prep. Sch., 1993-96, United Way of the Coastal Empire, 1993, Centennial Olympic Games Yachting Com., 1993-96, Children's Home Soc., 1983-91, Leadership, Tampa Bay, 1987—, bd. dirs., 1987-91, pres., 1990-91; mem. Leadership Tampa, 1981—; cons. Coffeeville (Kans.) Health Found., Monroe Health Found., Monroeville, Ala., Hubbard Regional Hosp., Webster, Mass., Gibson Meml. Hosp., Gibson City, Ill., Jordan Health Sys., Plymouth, Mass., Hickory (N.C.) Day Sch., Beaufort (S.C.) Acad., Spring of Tampa Bay, McLaughlin Rsch. Inst., Great Falls, Mont., Big Bros./Big Sisters Tampa, Met. Ministries, Tampa Cmty. Health Ctr., Suicide and Crisis Ctr., Exec. Svc. Corp. Tampa. Fellow AHA Health Forum, 2000. Mem. Am. Coll. Healthcare Execs., Nat. Soc. Fund Raising Execs. (cert., bd. dirs. 1992—, pres. 1992—), Assn. Am. Med. Coll., Nat. Ctr. for Nonprofit Bd., Acad. for Health Svc. Mktg., Am. Mktg. Assn., Assn. for Healthcare Philanthropy (cert.), Am. Coll. Healthcare Mktg., Sales & Mktg. Execs. Internat., Mil. Affairs Coun., Coun. for Advancement and Support Edn., Philanthropic Action Coun., Savannah Area C. of C. (mil. and civilian affairs coun.), Greater Tampa C. of C., Tampa Tiger Bay, Greystone Country Club, Summit Club, Savannah Yacht Club, Chatham Club, First City Club, Rotary Club Birmingham, Alpha Tau Omega. Democrat. Methodist. Home: 3705 Wyngate Cv Birmingham AL 35242-4218 Office: Bapt Health Found PO Box 830605 Birmingham AL 35283-0605

TOEKES, BARNA, chemical engineer, polymer consultant; b. Budapest, Hungary, Oct. 12, 1923; came to U.S., 1949; s. Barna and Jusztina (Szatmári) Tőkés; m. Ida Maria Kálmán, Aug. 24, 1948 (div. 1966); m. Georgianna D. Doyle, Aug. 26, 1967; 1 child, C. Justin. BS in Engring., UCLA, 1955, postgrad., 1955-57. Rsch. engr. Stauffer Chem. Co., Richmond, Calif., 1955-60; sr. rsch. engr. Rexall Chem. Co., Paramus, N.J., 1960-69, Holyoke, Mass., 1960-69; plant mgr., gen. mgr. Southern Petrochemicals, Channelview, Tex., 1969-73; mgr. process engring. and devel. Polysar Resins, Inc., Leominster, Mass., 1973-77; system engring. mgr. Sperry Rsch. Ctr., Sudbury, 1978-82; prin. process engr. C. F. Braun & Co., Alhambra, Calif., 1982-85; cons. engr. Dart Container Corp., Mason, Mich., 1987—. Cons. B. Toekes Cons., Baytown, Tex., 1977-78, Mason, Mich., 1985—. Contbg. author: Aromatic Fluorine Compounds, 1962, Fire Safety Aspects of Polymeric Materials, 1978; editor, co-author: Organic Working Fluid Properties, 1982, System Component Compatibility, 1982; contbr. articles to profl. jours. Mem. AIChE, Am. Chem. Soc., Soc. Plastics Engrs., Plastics Pioneers Assn. Achievements include 6 U.S. and 19 foreign patents in field of precesses for polymerization, depolymerization and devolatilization of polyvinyl aromatic compounds, equipment for polymerization processes. Home: 1148 Okemos Rd Mason MI 48854-9314 Office: Dart Container Corp 432 Hogsback Rd Mason MI 48854-9599 E-mail: toekes@voyager.net.

TOENSING, VICTORIA, lawyer; b. Colon, Panama, Oct. 16, 1941; d. Philip William and Victoria (Brady) Long; m. Trent David Toensing, Oct. 29, 1962 (div. 1976); children: Todd Robert, Brady Cronon, Amy Victoriana; m. Joseph E. diGenova, June 27, 1981. BS in Edn., Ind. U., 1962; JD cum laude, U. Detroit, 1975. Bar: Mich. 1976, D.C. 1978. Tchr. English, Milw., 1965-66; law clk. to presiding justice U.S. Ct. Appeals, Detroit, 1975-76; asst. U.S. atty, U.S. Atty.'s Office, 1976-81; chief counsel U.S. Senate Intelligence Com., Washington, 1981-84; dep. asst. atty. gen. criminal div. Dept. Justice, 1984-88; spl. counsel Hughes Hubbard & Reed, 1988-90; ptnr. Cooter and Gell, 1990-91; ptnr., co-chmn. nat. white collar group Manatt, Phelps and Phillips, 1991-95; founding ptnr. diGenova & Toensing, Wasington, 1996—. Mem. working group on corp. sanctions U.S. Sentencing Commn., 1988-89; co-chairperson Coalition for Women's Appts. Justice Judiciary Task Force, 1988-92; spl. counsel for Teamsters investigation, U.S. Ho. of Reps., Subcom. on Oversight and Investigations of com. on Edn. and the Workforce, 1997-98. Author: Bringing Sanity to the Insanity Defense, 1983, Mens Rea: Insanity by Another Name, 1984; contbg. author: Fighting Back: Winning The War Against Terrorism, Desk Book on White Collar Crime, 1991; contbr. articles to profl. jours. Founder, chmn. Women's Orgn. To Meet Existing Needs, Mich., 1975-79; chmn. Republican Women's Task Force, 1979-81; bd. dirs. Project on Equal Edn. Rights, Mich., 1980-81, Nat. Hist. Intelligence Mus., 1987-95, America's Talking Legal Analyst, 1995; MSNBC legal analyst, 1998-99. Recipient spl. commendation Office U.S. Atty. Gen., 1980, agy. seal medallion CIA, 1986, award of achievement Alpha Chi Omega, 1992; featured on cover N.Y. Time Mag. for anti-terrorism work, April 1991. Mem. ABA (mem. standing com. on law and nat. security, mem. coun. criminal justice sect., mem. adv. com. complex crimes and litigation, vice chmn. white collar crime com., chmn. subcom. on corp. criminal liability).

TOEPFER, THOMAS LYLE, district judge; b. Hays, Kans., Oct. 4, 1950; s. Anthony Lyle and Mary Alice (Clark) T.; m. Mary M. Glassman; 1 child, Russell Thomas. AB in Econs. summa cum laude, Ft. Hays State U., 1972; JD, Washburn U., 1975. Bar: Kans. 1975, U.S. Dist. Ct. Kans. 1975, U.S. Ct. Appeals (10th cir.) 1982, U.S. Supreme Ct. 1999. Assoc. Dreiling, Bieker & Kelley, Hays, 1975-83; prosecutor City of Hays, 1977-2000; spl. adminstrv. law judge Workers Compensation, 1992-2000; sole practice Hays, 1984-2000; dist. judge, 2001—. Mem. Hays Bd. Edn., 1985-93; treas. Ellis County Dems., Hays, 1980; pres. St. Nicholas Ch. Parish Coun., Hays, 1985-86; trustee Hays Med. Ctr., Hays, 1987-2000, Cancer Coun. Ellis County. Mem.: Ellis County Bar Assn. (pres. 1984—85), Kans. Bar Assn. Democrat. Roman Catholic. Office: 1204 Fort Hays KS 67601

TOEPLITZ, GIDEON, symphony society executive; b. Tel Aviv, Nov. 18, 1944; s. Erich and Ruth (Loeb) T.; m. Gail Ransom, Sept. 2, 1978. B.A., Hebrew U., Jerusalem, 1969; M.B.A., UCLA, 1973. Flutist, Israel Philharm. Orch., 1969-71; asst. mgr. Rochester Philharm., 1973-75; asst. mgr. Boston Symphony, 1975-79, orch. mgr., 1979-81; exec. dir. Houston Symphony Soc., 1981-87, exec. v.p., mng. dir. Pitts. Symph. Orch., 1987—; active Am. Symphony Orchestra League. Mem. Nat. Acad. Rec. Arts and Scis., Am. Jewish Com. (bd. dirs.), Penn S.W. Assn. (bd. dirs.). Home: 2087 Beechwood Blvd Pittsburgh PA 15217-1705

TOEPPE, WILLIAM JOSEPH, JR. retired aerospace engineer; b. Buffton, Ohio, Feb. 27, 1931; s. William Joseph Sr. and Ruth May (Hipple) T. BSEE, Rose-Hulman Inst. Tech., Terre Haute, Ind., 1953. Engr. Electronics divsn. Ralph M. Parsons Co., Pasadena, Calif., 1953-55; pvt. practice cons. Orange, 1961-62; engring. supr. Lockheed Electronics Co., City of Commerce, 1962-64; staff engr. Interstate Electronics Corp., Anaheim, 1957-61, engring. supr., 1964-89, ret., 1989. Author: Finding Your German Village, 1990, Gazetteers and Maps of France for Genealogical Research, 1990, German Geneal. Soc. Am. Library User's Guide, 1995, Sandusky County, Ohio, Births, Infant-Name Soundex Index, 1997, Osnabrück Farm Histories, 1999, GCSA Libr. Shelf List Catalog, 1999. Pres. Golden Cir. Home Owners' Assn., Orange, 1989-95. With U. S. Army, 1955-57. Mem. Ohio Geneal. Soc. (life), So. Calif. Geneal. Soc., German Geneal. Soc. Am. (bd. dirs. 1993-97). Avocations: genealogy, music. Home: 700 E Taft Ave Apt 19 Orange CA 92865-4400

TOERING, DOUGLAS L. lawyer; BA with high honors, Grand Valley State Coll., 1979; JD cum laude, Wayne State U., 1982. With legal staff GM, Detroit, 1984-91; ptnr. Bowman and Brooke, 1991-93, Grassi & Toering PLC, Troy, Mich., 1993—. Adj. lectr. U. Mich., Dearborn. Mem. ABA (mem. internat. litig. com., mem. pretrial practice and discovery com., mem. automotive law com., mem. comml. torts com., mem. internat. tort com., mem. ins. law and practice com.), ATLA, State Bar Mich., Mich. Trial Lawyers Assn., Oakland County Bar Assn., Christian Legal Soc. Avocations: walking, tennis, classical music. Office: Grassi and Toering PLC Ste 750 888 W Big Beaver Rd Troy MI 48084-4745 Fax: 248-269-2025. E-mail: dlt@grassiandtoering.com.

TOEVS, ALDEN LOUIS, management consultant, researcher; b. American Falls, Idaho, Jan. 25, 1949; s. Alden Louis and Wilma Christen (Coffee) T. BS, Lewis and Clark Coll., 1971; PhD, Tulane U., 1975. NSF fellow MIT Energy Lab., Boston, 1975-76; prof. econs. La. State U., Baton Rouge, 1976-77, U. Oreg., Eugene, 1978-83; dir. mortgage rsch. Morgan Stanley and Co., N.Y.C., 1983-90; exec. v.p. First Manhattan Cons. Group, 1990—. Vis. scholar Fed. Home Loan Bank, San Francisco, 1983, Fed. Reserve Bank, 1982; dir. capital market research U. Oreg., Eugene, 1982-83; instnl. investor All-Am. Rsch. Team, 1990. Author: Innovations in Bond Portfolio Managements, 1983, Winning Over the Credit Cycle, 1998; bd. dirs. Fin. Analysts Jour., Jour. Portfolio Mgmt.; contbr. articles to profl. jours. Bd. trustees Orch. St. Lukes, 1990—. Recipient Graham and Dodd scroll Fin. Analysts Fed., 1983.

TOFANY, VICTOR JOSEPH, retired anesthesiologist; b. Rochester, N.Y., May 8, 1921; BS, St. Bonaventure U., 1942; MD, U. Rochester, 1950. Diplomate Am. Bd. Anesthesiology. Intern St. Mary's Hosp., Rochester, 1950-51, resident in anesthesiology, 1951-52, Wayne State U., Detroit, 1952-53; ret., 1991. Attending anesthesiologist St. Mary's Hosp., Rochester, 1953-91, rochester Gen. Hosp., 1988-91, Park Ridge Hosp., Rochester, 1980-86, Lakeside Meml. Hosp., Brockport, N.Y., 1975-91; cons. Arnold Gregory Meml. Hosp., Medina, N.Y., 1975-89, Genesee Hosp., Rochester, 1970-78; cons. BC-BS, 1972-91. Mem. AMA, Am. Soc. Anesthesiology.

TOFEL, RICHARD JEFFREY, communication executive; b. N.Y.C. s. Robert Leonard and Carol T.; m. Jeanne Helen Straus, Feb. 26, 1983; children: Rachel Straus, Colin Straus. AB, Harvard U., 1979; MPP, JFK Sch. Govt., 1983; JD, Harvard U., 1983. Bar: N.Y. 1984, U.S. Dist. Ct. (so. and ea. dists.) N.Y. 1984, U.S. Ct. Appeals (2d cir.) 1987, U.S. Dist. Ct. (no. dist.) N.Y. 1988, U.S. Supreme Ct. 1990. Assoc. Patterson, Belknap, Webb & Tyler, N.Y.C., 1983-86; exec. dir. Mayor's Commn. Human Svcs. Reorganization, 1984-85; assoc. Gibson, Dunn & Crutcher, 1986-89; counsel Dow Jones & Co., 1989-91, asst. gen. counsel, 1991-92; asst. mng. editor Wall Street Jour., 1992-95; dir. internat. devel. and adminstrn. Dow Jones & Co., 1995-97, v.p. corp. comm., 1997-2000, v.p., asst. to publ. Wall Street Jour., 2000—02, v.p., asst. publ. Wall Street Jour., 2002—. Bd. dirs. Wildcat Svc. Corp. Author: A Legend in the Making: The New York Yankees in 1939, 2002; contbr. articles to profl. jours. Democrat. Jewish. Home: 5205 Sycamore Ave Bronx NY 10471-2835 Office: Dow Jones & Co 200 Liberty St 12th Fl New York NY 10281-1003 E-mail: dick.tofel@dowjones.com.

TOFF, NANCY ELLEN, book editor; b. Greenburgh, N.Y., Aug. 29, 1955; d. Ira N. and Ruth (Bluthenthal) T. AB, Harvard U., 1976. Editor, prodr. Music Minus One, N.Y.C., 1973-75; rschr. Time-Life Books, Alexandria, Va., 1976-80; editor, asst. prodr. Time-Life Music, 1980-84; prodn. mgr. Vanguard Recording Soc., N.Y.C., 1984-86; editor Grove's Dictionaries of Music, 1984-85; v.p., editor-in-chief Chelsea House Pubs., 1986-89, v.p., dir. book devel., 1990; editl. dir. Julian Messner/Silver Burdett Press, Englewood Cliffs, N.J., 1990-91; editl. dir. children's and young adult books Oxford U. Press, N.Y.C., 1991-98, editl. dir. trade and young adult reference, 1998—, v.p., 1999—. Editorial cons., Music Div. Lib. of Congress, 1983; hist. cons., Dept. of Musical Instruments, Met. Mus. of Art, N.Y.C., 1986. Author: The Development of the Modern Flute, 1979, The Flute Book, 1985, 2d edit., 1996, Georges Barrère and the Flute in America, 1994; cons. editor Flutist Quar., 1990-99; contbr. articles to profl. jours.; curator Georges Barrère and the Flute in America, N.Y. Pub. Libr., 1994. Bd. dirs., Radcliffe Coll. Alumnae Assn. 1979-80. Recipient Dena Epstein award Music Libr. Assn., 1997; Sinfonia Found. rsch. grantee, 1999. Mem. Nat. Flute Assn. (asst. sec. 1988-89, sec. 1989-90, bd. dirs. 1990-92), N.Y. Flute Club (bd. dirs. 1986—, sec. 1991-92, 98-2000, pres. 1992-95, 1st v.p. 1995-98). Home: 425 E 79th St Apt 6F New York NY 10021-1011 Office: Oxford U Press 198 Madison Ave New York NY 10016-4341 E-mail: net@oup-usa.org.

TOFF, RUTH BLUTHENTHAL, editor; b. St. Louis; d. Alvin Freiberg and Jeannette (Kohn) Bluthenthal; m. Ira Newton Toff, Apr. 2, 1953; 1 child, Nancy. AB with honors, Wellesley Coll., 1944. Rsch. sec. Coun. Social Agencies, Memphis, 1944-45; rsch. assoc. Cmty. Chests and Couns. of Am., Inc., N.Y.C., 1945-52; editor Edgemont Sch. Dist., Scarsdale, N.Y., 1969—. Bd. dirs., former pres. Ft. Hill Assn., Scarsdale; 1st v.p., treas. Wellesley-in-Westchester, 1966-79; chmn. Edgemont Cmty. Com. on Edn., Scarsdale, 1971-73; v.p. Greenburgh Nature Ctr., Scarsdale, 1995-97, sec., 1998; bd. dirs., former coord. sec. Edgemont Scholarship Coun., Scarsdale; bd. dirs. Westchester Philharmonic, 1999—, sec., 2002—. Recipient Silver Box Greenville Cmty. Coun., 1979. Mem. Nat. Assn. Social Workers (cert.). E-mail: rtoff@email.msn.com. Home: 277 Beverly Rd Scarsdale NY 10583-1513

TOFFEL, ALVIN EUGENE, corporate executive, business and governmental consultant; b. Los Angeles, July 14, 1935; s. Harry and Estelle Charlotte Toffel; m. Neile McQueen; children: Stephanie, Elizabeth, Michelle; stepchildren: Terry (dec.), Chad. BA, UCLA, 1957. Dir. mgmt. systems and organizational planning Rockwell Internat., 1963-69; Exec. Office for the Pres. White House, Washington, 1969-70; nat. chmn., campaign dir. McCloskey for Pres., 1971-72; polit. cons., 1971—. Cons. personal bus. and govt. Norton Simon and Norton Simon, Inc., Los Angeles, 1972-80; pres. Norton Simon Found., Pasadena, Calif., 1977-80; cons. exec. asst. to pres. Twentieth Century Fox Film Corp., 1980; bd. dirs. Geometrics, Inc.; pres. So. Shellfish Inc., Atlantic Internat. Ins. Ltd., Toffel Thoroughbred Racing; lectr. mgmt. UCLA, Stanford U. Pres. Norton Simon Mus. Art, Pasadena; vice chmn. U.S. Pension Svcs., Inc. With SAC USAF, 1958-63. Recipient White House Interchange Exec. Outstanding Achievement, 1971; recipient Achievement Am. Advtg. Council, 1972 Mem. Ky. Cols., Presdl. Interchange Execs. Assn., Assn. Old Crows Achievements include developing standard U.S. govt. program performance measurement system, aerospace engring. techniques of program mgmt., aerospace manuals. Home and Office: 2323 Bowmont Dr Beverly Hills CA 90210-1808 *My legacy derives from my grandparents leaving the familiar to come to America. Here, anything can be accomplished if one honestly defines what he wants. It then becomes a matter of choosing among the many ways to accomplish anything. The character of the individual can be seen by the choices he makes.*

TOFIAS, ALLAN, accountant; b. Boston, Apr. 13, 1930; s. George I. and Anna (Seidel) T.; m. Arlene Shube, Aug. 30, 1981; children: Bradley Neil, Laura Jean Silver. BA, Colgate U., 1951; MBA, Harvard U., 1956. CPA, Mass. Sr. acct. Peat, Marwick, Mitchell & Co., Boston; mng. ptnr. Tofias, Fleishman, Shapiro & Co., P.C., 1960-96; chmn. bd., 1996-97. Bd. dirs. Rowe Cos., One Price Clothing Stores, Inc.; trustee Gannett, Welch & Kotler Mut. Funds. Mem. Brookline (Mass.) Town Meeting, 1970-77, mem. fin. adv. bd., 1975-81; mem. New Eng. Bapt. Health Care Corp., 1985—, trustee, chmn. fin. com., 1998—; bd. dirs. West Newton YMCA, 1986-89; mem. exec. com. Boston Aid to Blind, bd. dirs., 1988-97, pres., 1993-94. Lt. USNR, 1951-54. Mem. AICPA (coun. 1995-99), Mass. Soc. CPA's (pres. 1995-96), Nat. CPA Group (exec. com. 1983-88, vice chmn. 1985-88), BKR Internat. (world bd. dirs. 1988-97, chmn. 1994-96), Wightman Tennis Club (treas. 1974-76), Newton Squash and Tennis Club (bd. dirs. 1966-99), Masons. Home: 59 Monadnock Rd Wellesley MA 02481-1334 Office: 2044 Beacon St Waban MA 02468-1445

TOFIGHI, MOHAMMAD-REZA, engineer, researcher; b. Mazandaran, Iran, Jan. 14, 1967; s. Jafar Tofighi and Zibandeh Zorofi; m. Afsaneh Ebrahimi; children: Golnaz, Tannaz. BSEE, Sharif U. of Tech., Tehran, Iran, 1989; MSEE, Iran U. of Sci. and Tech., Tehran, 1993; MS, Temple U., 1998; PhD, Drexel U., 2001. Microwave engr. Telecomm. Rsch. Ctr., Tehran, 1990—91; lectr. Air U., 1993—95; rsch. asst. Drexel U., Phila., 1989—2001, postdoctoral rsch. assoc., 2001—. Cons. Daryoush GEMS Inc., Bryn Mawr, Pa., 2001. Recipient Best Poster-Session Paper award, IEEE Sarnoff Symposium in Advances in Comm. Tech., Sarnoff Corp., 2000. Mem.: IEEE. Office: Drexel U 3141 Chestnut St Rm 7-506 Philadelphia PA 19104 E-mail: mtofighi@ece.drexel.edu.

TOFLE, RUTH BRENT, design educator, researcher, educator; b. Washington, Sept. 11, 1951; d. Clarence Frank and Dorothy May (Horstick) Stumpe; m. Edward Everett Brent, May 14, 1972 (div. Mar. 1999); 2 children ; m. Marvin Tofle, Nov. 17, 2001. BS cum laude, U. Mo., 1972; MA, U. Minn., 1974, PhD, 1978. Cert. of qualification Nat. Coun. Interior Design Qualification; registered comml. interior designer, Mo., 2000. Postdoctoral fellow in socio-clin. geriatrics NIMH, 1978-79; asst. prof. U. Mo., Columbia, 1981-86, assoc. prof. design, 1986-92, prof., 1992—, acting dept. chair, 1984-85, chair environ. design dept., 1985—. Project dir. Adminstrn. on Aging Grant, 1979-81; v.p. Idea Works, Inc., Columbia, 1981-99; chair campus planning com. for facilities and grounds, U. Mo., Columbia, 1993—. Co-author: (computer software) Home-Safe-Home, 1989; co-editor: Popular American Housing, 1995, Aging, Autonomy and Architecture: Advances in Assisted Living, 1999; dep. editor: Jour. Housing for Elderly; assoc. editor: Jour. Archtl. and Planning Rsch.; contbr. articles to profl. jours. Active Mayor's Task Force, Columbia Low-Income Housing, 1984-85; mem. Main St. adv. coun. dept. econ. devel. State of Mo., 1989-90; regional chairperson dists. 84 and 85 United Way, Columbia, 1989, 90, 98, 99, 2000, 2001; mem. adv. bd. Pub. Housing Authority, Columbia, 1984-85; chairperson North Cen. Region-54 Agrl. Expt. Sta. Rsch., 1989-91; mem. Columbia Regional Home Health and Hospice Adv. Bd., Columbia Regional Hosp., 1993-2000; mem. pub. bldg. devel. and fin. com. City of Columbia, 2000—; bd. trustees The Mo. 4-H Found., 1997—, co-chair mktg. and pub. rels. com.; chair campus planning com. for facilities and grounds U. Mo., 1993—. Grantee Adminstrn. on Aging, 1979-81, VA, 1981, Am. Home Econs. Assn., 1981-82, 2 Joel Polsky Found. Interior Design Rsch. grantee, 1986, 87; recipient Fulbright award Chinese History and Culture, 1988, exch. faculty award Prince of Sonkla U., Thailand, 1990, Chonnam U., Korea, 1992; Fulbright fellow to Morocco and Tunisia, 1993. Mem. Am. Home Econs. Assn. (chmn. art/design sect. 1984-87, New Achievers award 1987), Am. Assn. Housing Educators, Am. Soc. Interior Designers (allied mem., chmn. position papers com. 1988-90, Presdl. citation 1990), Interior Design Educators Coun., Nat. Coun. for Interior Design (cert.), Environ. Design Rsch. Assn., Illuminating Engring. Soc. (participant workshop for tchrs.), Gerontol. Assn., Mo. Fulbright Alumni Assn. (membership chmn. 1989-90, v.p. 1990-92, pres. 1992-94), Univ. Club Inc. (pres. 1991-92, bd. dirs., sec. 1993-95, U. Mo. faculty alumni award 1992), Gamma Sigma Delta (pres. 1993-94, Disting. Adminstrn. award 1997), Omicron Nu, Phi Upsilon Omicron. Home: 1805 Cliff Dr Columbia MO 65201 Office: U Mo Dept Environ Design 137 Stanley Hall Columbia MO 65211-7700 E-mail: TofleR@missiour.edu.

TOFT, THELMA MARILYN, secondary school educator; b. Balt., Sept. 15, 1943; d. George Edward and Thelma Iola (Smith) Trageser; m. Ronald Harry Toft, Aug. 27, 1966 (div. 1998); 1 child, Joanna Lynn. BS in Med. Tech., Mt. St. Agnes Coll., Balt., 1965; BSE, Coll. Notre Dame, Balt., 1972; MEd, Pa. State U., 1983. Recreation dir. Villa Maria, Balt., 1961-65; blood bank supr. Wayman Park NIH, 1965-68; tchr. Sacred Heart, St. Mary's Govan's, 1968-74, Lincoln Intermediate Unit # 12, Adams County, Pa., 1979-80, York (Pa.) City Sch. Dist., 1980—; curriculum dir. M.O.E.S.T. Pa. State U., 1991-93. Mem. Pa. State Consortium-Pa. Team for Improving Math. and Sc.; grant writer, spkr. in field; writer Project Connections curriculum. Active Girl Scouts USA, Hanover, 1988-92, leader, 1984-87; mgmt. bd. Agrl. Indsl. Mus. Mem. ASCD, AAUW, Nat. Ptnrs. in Edn., Am. Bus. Women's Assn. (edn. com. 1992, sec. 1993, Chpt. Woman of Yr. 1994, York County Woman of Yr. 1995), Phi Delta Kappa. Democrat. Roman Catholic. Avocations: writing, marketing. Home: 30 Panther Dr Hanover PA 17331-8888

TOFTELAND, CURT L. producer, director; b. Martin, N.D., Apr. 30, 1952; s. Donald Morris and Jona Georgine (Goodman) T.; m. Marcia Tarbis, May 30, 1981; 1 child, Joshua Tarbis. BFA in Music, U. N.D., 1974; MFA, U. Minn., 1978. Actor Asolo Touring Theater, Sarasota, Fla., 1978-79; assoc. artistic dir. Stage One, Louisville, 1979-85; pres. Joshua Prodns., 1985-89; producing dir. Ky. Shakespeare Festival, 1989—. Adj. faculty U. Louisville, 1987—, Ind. U. S.E., 1993—, Bellarmine Coll., 1994—; cons. Ky. Arts Coun., Frankfort, 1985—, Ky. Humanities Coun., Lexington, 1988, Very Spl. Arts Ky., Frankfort, 1987—. Playwright six plays. Al Smith fellow, 1988. Mem. Ky. Allinace for Arts in Edn., Ky. Citizens for the Arts, Actors' Equity Assn. Office: Ky Shakespeare Festival 1114 S 3rd St Louisville KY 40203-2902

TOFTNER, RICHARD ORVILLE, engineering executive; b. Warren, Minn., Mar. 5, 1935; s. Orville Gayhart and Cora Evelyn (Anderson) T.; m. Jeanne Bredine, June 26, 1960; children: Douglas, Scott, Kristine, Kimberly, Brian. BA, U. Minn., 1966; MBA, Xavier U., 1970. Registered environ. assessor, Calif. Sr. economist Federated Dept. Stores, Inc., Cin., 1967-68; dep. dir. EPA, Washington and Cin., 1968-73; mgmt. cons. environ. affairs, products and mktg., 1973-74; prin. PEDCo Environ., Cin., 1974-80; trustee PEDCo trusts, 1974-80; pres. ROTA Mgmt., Inc., Cin., 1980-82; gen. mgr. CECOS, 1982-85; cons., 1985—; v.p. Smith, Stevens & Young, 1985-88; real estate developer, 1980—. Pres., CEO Toxitrol Internat., Inc., 1988-89; dir. Environ. Svcs. Belcan Enging. Group, Inc., Cin., 1989-92; prin. exec. cons. Resource Mgmt. Internat., Inc., 1994—; adj. prof. environ. engring. U. Cin., 1975-86; lectr. Grad. fellowship rev. panel Office of Edn., 1978-79; advisor, cabinet-level task force Office of Gov. of P.R., 1973; pvt. investor, 1991—; bd. dirs. EnviroAudit Svcs., Inc., pres., CEO, 1992—; mem. legis. com. Ohio Chem. Coun., 1995—; v.p. environ. engring. CSA Architects & Engrs., 1996-2001; client svc. mgr. Weston Solutions, Inc. Environ. Cons., 2001—; subcom. Nat. Safety Coun., 1972; mem. exec. environ. briefing panels Andersen Consulting, 1991-92; nominee commr. PUCO, Ohio; chmn. Cin. City Waste Task Force, 1987-88; co-chair Hamilton County Resource Recovery Com., 1989—. Contbr. articles on mgmt. planning and environ. to periodicals, chpts. to books; inventor, developer Toxitrol Waste Minimization; inventor EnviroAudit. With AUS, 1954-57. Mem. USTA, Nat. Registry Environ. Profl. Rep., Engring. Soc. Cin., Assn. Corp. Environ. Execs., Cin. C. of C., Global Assn. Corp. Environ. Execs. (charter), U.S. Tennis Assn. Republican. Lutheran. Home: 9175 Yellowwood Dr Cincinnati OH 45251-1948 Office: 4100 Executive Park Dr Ste 11 Cincinnati OH 45241-4026

TOFTNESS, CECIL GILLMAN, lawyer, consultant; b. Glasgow, Mont., Sept. 13, 1920; s. Anton Bernt and Nettie (Pedersen) T.; m. Chloe Catherine Vincent, Sept. 8, 1951. AA, San Diego Jr. Coll., 1943; student, Purdue U., Northwestern U.; BS, UCLA, 1947; JD cum laude, Southwestern U., 1953. Bar: Calif. 1954, U.S. Dist. Ct. (so. dist.) Calif. 1954, U.S. Tax Ct. 1974, U.S. Supreme Ct. 1979. Pvt. rpactice, palos Verdes Estates, Calif., 1954—. Chmn. bd., pres., bd. dirs. Fishermen & Mchts. Bank, San Pedro, Calif., 1963-67; v.p., bd. dirs. Palos Verdes Estates Bd. Realtors, 1964-65; participant Soc. Expdn. through the Northwest Passage. Chmn. capital campaign fund Richstone Charity, Hawthorne, Calif., 1983; commencement spkr. Glasgow H.S., 1981. Served to lt. (j.g.) USN, 1938-46, ETO, PTO, commdg. officer USS Ptarmigan, 1941-45. Decorated Bronze Star; mem. Physicians for Prevention of Nuclear War which received Nobel Peace prize, 1987; named Man of Yr., Glasgow, 1984. Mem. South Bay Bar Assn., Southwestern Law Sch. Alumni Assn. (class rep. 1980—), Themis Soc.-Southwestern Law Sch., Schumacher Founders Cir.-Southwestern Law Sch. (charter), Kiwanis (sec.-treas. 1955-83, v.p., pres., bd. dirs.), Masons, KT. Democrat. Lutheran. Home: 2229 Via Acalones Palos Verdes Peninsula CA 90274-1646 Office: 2516 Via Tejon Palos Verdes Estates CA 90274-6802 E-mail: cgtoftness@aol.com.

TOGA, ARTHUR W. neurologist, educator, lab director; b. Mass., July 19, 1952; s. Carl and Elayne Toga; m. Deborah Toga; children: Nicholas, Elizabeth, Rebecca. BS, U. Mass., Boston, 1974; MS, PhD, St. Louis U., 1978. Rsch. asst. prof. neurology Washington U., St. Louis, 1980—87; assoc. prof. neurology UCLA, 1987—93, asst. chmn. rsch. affairs, 1987—, prof. neurology, 1993—. Mem. campus network users com. UCLA, 1988—, mem. exec. adv. com. BRI, 1990—, mem. promotions com. dept. neurology, 1995—2000, mem. advising com. Crump Inst., 1995—, mem. info. tech. planning bd., 2000—. Editor: Three Dimensional Neuroimaging, 1990, Brain Mapping: The Methods, 1996, 2d edit., 2002, Brain Warping, 1999; The Rhesus Monkey in Stereotactic Coordinates, 1999, Brain Mapping: The Systems, 2000, Brain Mapping: The Disorders, 2000, MRI Atlas of the Human Cerebellum, 2000. Named Silver finalist for nat. med. video, Axiem Awards, 1999; recipient 1st prize for cum laude paper, SPIE Med. Imaging, 1997, Outstanding Sci. Rsch. award, Giovanni DiChiro, 1997, award for sci. video, The Comm. Award, 1998, award for sci. innovation, Smithsonian, 1999, award for excellence, The Videographic Award, 1999. Mem.: AAAS, APA, Nat. Computer Graphics Assn., Soc. for Neurosci., Orgn. for Human Brain Mapping (sci. bd. of directors). Office: UCLA Sch Medicine Rm 4238 710 Westwood Plz Los Angeles CA 90095 Office Fax: 310-206-5518. Business E-Mail: toga@loni.ucla.edu.

TOGASAKI, SHINOBU, computer scientist; b. San Francisco, Aug. 17, 1932; s. Kikumatsu and Sugi (Hida) T.; m. Toshiko Kawaguchi, Nov. 24, 1959; children: John Shinobu, Ann Mariko. BS in Math., Duke U., 1954; postgrad., Stanford U., 1954-56. Math. programmer IBM, 1956-69, sr. programmer, 1970-87; mgr. applications devel. Service Bur. Corp., 1961-64, sr. analyst, 1964-68, systems architect devel. lab. San Jose, Calif., 1968-70; chief fin. officer Robin Hood Ranch, Inc., 1976-86; mgr. architecture & strategy Hewlett Packard Corp., Cupertino, Calif., 1987-89, mgr. strategic planning, 1989-93; chief architect MFA Hewlett Packard, 1993—. Mem. Am. Mgmt. Assn., AAAS, Am. Statis. Assn., Assn. Computing Machinery, Inst. Mgmt. Sci., Sigma Pi Sigma. Home: 2367 Booksin Ave San Jose CA 95125-4705 Office: 19447 Pruneridge Ave Cupertino CA 95014-0609 E-mail: bob_togasaki@hp.com.

TOGERSON, JOHN DENNIS, computer software company executive, retired; b. Newcastle, England, July 2, 1939; arrived in Can., 1949; s. John Marius and Margaret (McLaughlin) T.; m. Donna Elizabeth Jones, Oct. 3, 1964 (div. 1972); children: Denise, Brenda, Judson; m. Patricia Willis, May 5, 1984. BME, GM Inst., Flint, Mich., 1961; MBA, York U., Toronto, Ont., 1971. Sr. prodn. engr. GM of Can., Oshawa, Ont., 1961-69; with sales, investment banking Cochran Murray, Toronto, 1969-72; pres. Unitec, Inc., Denver, 1972-79, All Seasons Properties, Denver, 1979-81, Resort Computer Corp., Denver, 1981—; mng. dir. VCC London (subs. of Resort Computer Corp.), 1992; retired, 1996. Bd. dirs. VCC London (sub. of 1st Nat. Bank U.K.), London, 1989—, mng. dir., 1992; pres., bd. dirs. Resort Mgmt. Corp., Dillon, Colo., 1980-81; presenter Assn. of Resort Developers Nat. Conv., 1993, Internat. T.S. Found. Think Tank, 1993, and others; cons for computer sys., including Expert Witness assignment; internat. bus. devel. cons. Contbr. articles to profl. jours. Avocations: mountain biking, ice hockey, international business development consulting.

TOGNINO, JOHN NICHOLAS, financial services executive; b. N.Y.C., Sept. 20, 1938; s. Gennaro and Catherine (Barbieri) T.; m. Norma Lucille Borrelli, Nov. 7, 1959; children: Katherine Ann, John Nicholas Jr., Michael A. BA in Econs. summa cum laude, Fordham U., 1975. Instnl. sales trader A.G. Becker & Co., N.Y.C., 1970-72; trader Merill Lynch, 1957-69, instnl.

salesman, 1972-74, mgr. over-the-counter sales trading, 1974-83, dir. over-the-counter dept., 1983-87, dir. unlisted trading, 1987-88, mng. dir. non-dollar equities London, 1988-91, mng. dir. global equities, ret. N.Y.C., 1991-93; exec. v.p. Charles Schwab & Co., Inc., Jersey City, 1993-96; pres., CEO Security Traders Assn., N.Y.C., 1996-99, EVP NASDAQ, 1999—2001; chmn., CEO Pepper Fin. Group, 2001—. Bd. dirs. Nat. Assn. Security Dealers Automated Quotations Inc. Contbg. author: Market Maker Sponsorship: A Synergistic Package of Services, 1987. Mem. Ardlsey Bd. Edn., 1977—84, pres., 1979; v.p. Ardsley Sch. Dist. Bd., 1978, 1981; trustee, vice chmn. St. Barnabas Hosp., Bronx, 1996—; mem. health sci. adv. coun., Coll. of Phys. and Surgeons Columbia Presbyn. Med. Ctr., 1998—; pres. Ardsley Rep. Club, 1967—68; mem. exec. com. of laity Archdiocese of N.Y.C., 1988; trustee Fordham U., 2000—; dir. Muscular Dystrophy Assn., 2000—; bd. dirs. Bus. Coun. for Internat. Understanding, 2000—01. Named Trader of Yr., Security Traders Monthly mag., 1984, Over-the-Counter Man of Yr., Equities mag., 1986; recipient lifetime achievement award Chgo. Stock Exch., 1997. Mem. Nat. Security Traders Assn. (various offices 1981-88, chmn. fin. com. Found. 1992—), Nat. Assn. Security Dealers (bus. conduct com. 1984-86), Security Traders Assn. N.Y. (various offices 1973-83, pres. 1980-81), St. Andrews Golf Club (Hastings, N.Y.), Grey Oaks Country Club (Naples, Fla.), Alpha Sigma Lambda, Alpha Sigma Nu. Republican. Roman Catholic. Avocations: jogging, tennis, golf. Home: Two Stoneleigh Plz Apt 4H Bronxville NY 10708 Office: Pepper Fin Group 2 Hollyhock Ln Bedford NY 10506

TOGUT, TORIN DANA, lawyer; b. N.Y.C., Apr. 24, 1951; s. Benjamin Morris and Millicent (Friedman) T.; m. Emily Jane Greenberg, July 27, 1975 (dec. Oct. 1985); m. A. Teresa Romasco, Oct. 20, 1990. BS, Cornell U., 1973; JD, LaVerne U., 1976. Bar: Ga. 1977. Pvt. practice, Decatur, Ga., 1977—84; atty. Ga. Legal Svcs. Program, Atlanta, 1984—; exec. dir. Vt. Protection and Advocacy, Inc., 2001—02. Atty. trainer Advocacy Ctr., Inc., Tallahassee, 1990. Chair Citizens Adv. Coun. Brook Run, Atlanta, 1992-93; bd. dirs. Mental Health Assn. Ga., Atlanta, 1987-90, mem. protection and advocacy com., 1986-87; mem. task force on mentally ill State Bar Ga., 1988-89; mem. task force on forensic mental health svcs. Ga. Dept. Human resources, 1990; mem. human rights com. ARC/Ga., 1986-88; bd. dirs. GARAL, 1994-95; v.p. ACLU Ga.; bd. dirs. PEPP (Parents Educating Parents and Profls.) adv. bd. North Fulton County chpt. Children and Adults with ADD, 2000—. Recipient Phil Heiner award Atlanta Bar Assn., 1997, 20-Yr. Svc. award Atlanta Vol. Lawyers Found., 1997; named Prof. of Yr., ARC/Ga., 1992. Mem. ABA, ACLU (bd. dirs. 1989—, co-chair legal com. 1988-90, v.p. Ga. 1999-01), North Fulton Bar Assn. Avocations: sports, reading, cooking, photography, gardening. Home: 24 French St Barre VT 05641 E-mail: tandt@mindspring.com.

TOH, CHAI, information science educator; b. Singapore, Singapore, Dec. 19, 1965; Diploma in Elec. Engring., Singapore Poly., 1986; B in Engring., Manchester (Eng.) U., 1991; PhD, Cambridge U., 1996. Network specialist Archive Singapore, Singapore, 1991-92; tech. staff/project leader Info. Tech. Inst., Nat. Computer, 1992-93; lab. supr. Cambridge U., Cambridge, Eng., 1993-96; project leader Hughes Rsch. Labs., Malibu, Calif., 1996-98; prof. Ga. Tech. U., Atlanta, 1998—2000; dir. rsch. TRW Systems, Carson, Calif., 2002—. Tech. bd. mem. Convergence Corp., Norcross, Ga., EBA Systems, San Francisco. Author: Wireless ATM & Ad Hoc Networks, 1996, 98, 99, 2000; author, editor: Wireless Computer Networks, IEEE Network Mag., 1996-99; feature editor: Mobile Comm. & Computing, ACM Mobile Computing and Comm. Rev., 1996—; editor: Computer Sci., Personal Techs. Jour., 1996—; patentee in field. Hon. Cambridge Commonwealth Trust scholar, 1993-96; fellow Cambridge Commonwealth Soc., 1993; fellow Cambridge Philos. Soc., 1994; prin. investigator NSF, 1999; recipient Assn. Computing Machinery Recognition of Svc. award, Svc. Appreciation award Korean Inst. Comm. Scis., tchg. fellow award, 2000. Mem. IEEE (sr.; tech. chmn. Conf. on Broadband Wireless, 1999, tech. co-chmn. Workshop on Ad Hoc Mobile Networking, 1999, chmn. subcom. Ad Hoc Mobile Networks 2000—, guest editor Jour. on Selected Areas in Comm., 1999, editor 2000—, chmn. Atlanta Ctr. 2000—, Disting. Lectr., chmn. tech. com. on computer comms.), Sigma Xi. Office: TRW Systems 1800 Glenn Curtis St DH4/1423 Carson CA 90746

TOHAMY, SOUMARA M. economist, educator; b. Cairo, Egypt, May 28, 1966; arrived in U.S., 1988; d. Mohamed Tohamy and Suzanne Elibiary; m. Ahmed H. Omar, May 9, 1997; 1 child Adam. BA, Am. U. Cairo, 1988; PhD, Emory U., 1994. Cons. World Bank, Washington, 1993—95; vis. asst. prof. Emory U., Atlanta, 1995—97; asst. prof. Berry Coll., Mount Berry, 1997—. Member of editorial board Business Quest, 2000—. Mem. editl. bd.: Bus. Quest, 2000—. Recipient Teaching award, Emory University, 1992—93. Mem.: Am. Econ. Assn., Sigma Beta Delta, Omicron Delta Epsilon. Office: Berry Coll Mount Berry GA 30149 Business E-Mail: stohamy@campbell.berry.edu.

TOIFEL, RONALD CHARLES, librarian; b. Mobile, Ala., June 4, 1933; s. Leopold Francis and Thelma Teresa (Eckert) T.; m. Peggy Suzanne White, Jan. 15, 1972; children: Ronald Charles Jr., Mark, Lance. BS, Miss. So. Coll., 1957; MSLS, La. State U., Baton Rouge, 1966; EdD in Higher Edn., Fla. State U., 1990. Head bookmobile divsn. Davis Ave. Br. Libr.; asst. head reference dept., head circulation dept. Internat. Trade Ctr. Libr., Mobile Pub. Libr., 1966-68; asst. libr. dir. Gadsden (Ala.) Pub. Libr., 1968-69; libr. U. West Fla., Pensacola, 1969—. Contbr. articles to profl. jours. Mem. Bagdad Village Preservation Assn., Santa Rosa County Hist. Soc.; chmn. Libr. Faculty Coun., 1994-96. With USAF,1958-65. Mem. ALA (ednl. and behavioral scis. sect./bibliog. instr. for edn. com., com. on problems of assessment and control of curriculum materials), Southea. Libr. Assn. (sec. online svcs. roundtable), West Fla. Libr. Assn. (pres. 1971-72), Gulfcoast Online and Automated Librs. (pres. 1983-84). Democrat. Avocations: education, civil war history. Home: 6029 Players Pl Milton FL 32570-8769 Office: University of West Florida John C Pace Libr 11000 University Pkwy Pensacola FL 32514-5750

TOIRAC, S(ETH) THOMAS, software engineering executive, consultant; b. Ft. Wayne, Ind., May 17, 1951; s. Florent D. and Dorothy M. (Lee) T.; m. Martha J. Rife, Dec. 20, 1969 (div. 1979); m. Linda Diane Benecke, Aug. 2, 1987 (div. 1999); m. Deborah L. Schiller, Nov. 16, 2001; children: Kristina M., Danielle Shari, Anthony David. Student, Grace Coll., 1970. Computer operator United Telephone Co., Warsaw, Poland, 1968-69; programmer-analyst GTE Data Svcs., Ft. Wayne, 1970-76, systems programmer, 1976-79, systems supr., 1979-82; mgr. software N.Am. Van Lines, 1982-84, dir. computing svcs., 1984-90; founder, exec. dir. Pioneer Missionary, Inc., 1990-94; CFO Pillar Pub., New Carlisle, Ind., 1990-94; exec. v.p. Kessington Network, Indpls., 1990-91; info. mgmt. cons., 1991-95; sr. consulting engr. Lexis-Nexis, Inc., Dayton, Ohio, 1995-98, mgr. devel. svcs., 1998—2001, mgr. sys. support, 2001—. Chmn. GTE Tech. Adv. Group, 1978-79; cons. in field. Sec.-treas. bd. dirs. Greater Ft. Wayne Crime Stoppers, 1986-91; lay min. Wesleyan Meth. Ch., Ft. Wayne, 1974-75; mem. Share, Inc., 1976-81. Republican. Avocations: photography, personal computers. E-mail: tom.toirac@lexisnexis.com.

TOKAR, BETTE LEWIS, economics educator; b. Phila, Mar. 26, 1935; d. Howard H. and Irma Rhodes (Pixton) Lewis; m. Jacob John Tokar, Oct. 1, 1955; children: Teresa, Bonnie, Michael, Robert. Student, Ursinus Coll., 1953-55; BA in Polit. Economy, Holy Family Coll., 1967, MA in Econs., Temple U., 1973, EdD, 1993. Lectr. Holy Family Coll., Phila., 1972-75, instr., 1975-78, asst. prof., 1978-82, dept. chair, 1977-85, assoc. prof., 1982-96, prof., 1996—; lectr. La Salle Coll., Phila., 1977, Cmty. Coll. Phila., 1986-90; assessor CLEO, Phila., 1979-85. Candidate for auditor, Lower Southampton Township, Bucks County, Pa., 1967, 69; Dem. committeewoman Lower Southampton Township, Bucks Co., 1968; treas. Dem. Club Lower Township, Bucks Co., 1968, bd. dirs. Pine Tree Farms Assoc., Feasterville, Pa., 1968. Mem. MENSA, Acad. Internat. Bus., Assn. social Econ., Nat. Bus. Edn. Assn., Am. Acctg. Assn., Am. Econ. Assn., Am. Management Assn., Internat. Trade & Fin. Assn., Fin. Mgmt. Assn., Delta Pi Epsilon, Pi Gamma Mu. Episcopalian. Office: Holy Family Coll Grant And Frankford Ave Philadelphia PA 19114-2094

TOKARZ, MICHAEL THEODORE, merchant banker; b. Chgo., Nov. 3, 1949; s. Ted and Lorraine Tokarz; m. Nancy C. Tokarz, Sept. 20, 1975; children: Andrew M., Justin T. BA in Econs., U. Ill., 1971, MBA, 1973. CPA, N.Y. Various exec. positions Continental Ill. Nat. Bank and Trust Co., N.Y.C. and Miami, Fla., 1973-85; from assoc. to mem. Kohlberg Kravis Roberts & Co., N.Y.C., 1985—2002; with The Tokarz Group LLC, Purchase, 2002—. Bd. dirs. Evenflo Co., Inc., Vandalia, Ohio, IDEX Corp., Northbrook, Ill., KAMAZ, Inc., Naberezhnye Chelny, Tatarstan, Russia, Spalding Holdings Cpr., Chicopee, Mass., Walter Industries, Inc., Tampa, Fla., Nexstar Fin. Corp., St. Louis, Lomonosov Porcelain Corp., St. Petersburg, Russia., U.F. Holdings, Inc., Niles, Mich. Trustee Rye (N.Y.), YMCA, 2001—; bd. dirs. U. Ill. Found., Champaign, 1997—, bd. mgrs. U. Ill. I-Venture LLC, 2000—. Office: The Tokarz Group LLC 287 Bowman Ave Purchase NY 10577

TOKER, FRANKLIN K. art history educator, archaeologist, foundation executive; b. Montreal, Apr. 29, 1944; came to U.S., 1964; naturalized, 1983; s. Maxwell Harris and Ethel (Herzberg-Serchuk) T.; m. Ellen Judith Burack, Sept. 3, 1972; children: Sarah Augusta, Maxwell, Jeffrey. BA, McGill U., Montreal, 1964; AM in Fine Arts, Oberlin Coll., 1966; PhD in Fine Arts, Harvard U., 1973. Instr. Boston Sch. Architecture, 1967; archaeol. dir. Florence (Italy) Cathedral excavations, 1969-74; A.W. Mellon vis. prof. Carnegie-Mellon U., Pitts., 1974-76, assoc. prof., 1976-80; assoc. prof. fine arts U. Pitts., 1980-87, prof., 1987—. Vis. prof. U. Florence, 1988-89, U. Rome, 1991—, U. Reggio Calabria, 1996; preservation cons. The Carnegie, Pitts., 1981-83; bd. dirs. Allegheny Survey, Pitts. History and Landmarks Found., 1980-85; mem. Inst. for Advanced Study, Princeton, N.J., 1985; fellow Com. to Rescue Italian Art, Florence, 1969; fellow I Tatti-Harvard U. Ctr. for Italian Renaissance Studies, Florence, 1972. Author: Notre Dame in Montreal, 1970 (Alice Davis Hitchcock award 1971), French edit., 1981, 2d English edit., 1991, S. Reparata: l-Antica Cattedrale Fiorentina, 1974, Pittsburgh: An Urban Portrait, 1986 (Pitts. History and Landmarks Found. award 1987), 2d edit., 1995; contbr. articles to profl. jours. Mem. econ. devel. com. Allegheny Conf. Community Devel., Pitts., 1983-85. Kress fellow, 1965; Can. Coun. fellow, 1966; Guggenheim fellow, 1979; NEH grantee 1979, 92, NEH sr. fellow, 1985, fellow Bellagio Study and Conf. Ctr., Rockefeller Found., 1994. Mem. Coll. Art Assn. (life, Arthur Kingsley Porter prize 1980), Medieval Acad. (life), Soc. Archtl. Historians (pres., 1993-94, life mem., bd. dirs. 1985-88), Archaeol. Inst. Am., Internat. Ctr. for Medieval Art. Avocations: creative writing, photography, cycling. Home: 1521 Denniston Ave Pittsburgh PA 15217-1449 Office: U Pittsburgh Dept History Art Architecture Pittsburgh PA 15260

TOKERUD, ROBERT EUGENE, electrical engineer; b. Great Falls, Mont., Aug. 30, 1936; s. Fred Eugene Tokerud and Helen A. (Tadevich) Thomas; m. Marsha Kay Tokerud; children: Pamela, Torri, Marc, Camille, Corinne, David, Jeramie, Autumn, Melanie. BSEE, U. Calif., Berkeley, 1959; cert. Inst. Mgmt., Northwestern U., 1975. Sr. project engr. Sperry Utah Co., Salt Lake City, 1959-65; mgr. infosystems Lockheed Electronics Co., Houston, 1965-69; mgr. earth resources Lockheed Engring. and Sci. Co., 1969-74, asst. dir. sci. and applications, 1974-79, dir. bus. devel., 1980-87, life sci. program mgr. Washington, 1987-89; pres. Lockheed Martin Logistics Mgmt., Arlington, Tex., 1989-97; v.p. Lockheed Corp., 1993-97; exec. v.p. Lockheed Martin Aircraft and Logistic Ctrs., 1997; ret., 1997. Cons. Aerospace, 1997-2000; pres., CEO Operational Tech. Inc., 2000-2002. Author conf. procs., other profl. publs. Commr. Tex. Strategic Mil. Planning Commn., 1997—2002; bd. dir. El Lago Water and Waste Mgmt. Dist., El Largo, Tex., 1974. Office: 4100 NW Loop 410 San Antonio TX 78229-4253 Fax: 210-731-3458. E-mail: rtokerud@gte.net.

TOKHEIM, ROBERT EDWARD, physicist; b. Eastport, Maine, Apr. 25, 1936; s. Edward George and Ruth Lillian (Koenig) T.; m. Diane Alice Green, July 1, 1962; children: Shirley Diane, William Robert, David Eric, Heidi Jean. BSEE, Calif. Inst. Tech., 1958, MSEE, 1959; Degree of Engr., Stanford U., 1962, PhD in Elec. Engring., 1965. Rsch. asst. Hansen Labs Physics Stanford (Calif.) U., 1960—65; microwave engr. Watkins-Johnson Co., Palo Alto, 1965—73, head ferrimagnetic R&D dept., 1966—69; sr. physicist SRI Internat., Menlo Park, 1973—, assoc. dept. dir., 1998—. Co-author: Tutorial Handbook on X-ray Effects on Materials and Structures, 1992; contbr. articles to Jour. Applied Physics, IEEE Transactions on Magnetics, conf. proceedings on shock compression, and others. Mem. IEEE (sr. mem.), Am. Phys. Soc., Toastmasters, Tau Beta Pi, Sigma Xi. Achievements include discovery of nonreciprocal line-coupled microwave ferrimagnetic filters, optimum thermal compensation axes in YIG and GaYIG ferrimagnetic spheres, development of various shock wave equation-of-state computational models and computational debris modeling for large laser and plasma-radiation-source machines. Office: SRI International 333 Ravenswood Ave Menlo Park CA 94025-3453 E-mail: robert.tokheim@sri.com.

TOKIOKA, JUDITH KIKUNO, executive secretary; b. Honokaa, Hawaii, Sept. 25, 1947; d. Juro and Mieko Kawakami Kaku; m. Alexander K. Tripp, May 3, 1969 (div. Nov. 20, 1971); m. Robert M. Jr. Tokioka, Feb. 14, 1981 (div. Sept. 18, 1999). Grad. H.S., Honolulu. Office mgr. Roofers Union Local 221, Honolulu, 1970—. Treas., mgr Roofer FCU, Honolulu, 1975—92. Democrat. Mem. Lds Ch. Avocations: crafts, gardening, reading, writing, cooking. Home: 1364 Mahiole St Honolulu HI 96819

TOKOFSKY, JERRY HERBERT, film producer; b. N.Y.C., Apr. 14, 1936; s. Julius H. and Rose (Trager) T.; m. Myrna Weinstein, Feb. 21, 1968 (div.); children: David, Peter; m. Fiammetta Bettuzzi, 1970 (div.); 1 child, Tatianna; m. Karen Oliver, Oct. 4, 1981. BS in Journalism, NYU, 1956, LLD, 1959, M in Am. Lit., 1999. Talent agt. William Morris Agy., N.Y.C., 1953-59, v.p. L.A., 1959-64; exec. v.p. Columbia Pictures, 1964-69; v.p. Paramount Pictures, London, 1970; exec. v.p. MGM, 1971; pres. Jerry Tokofsky Prodns., L.A., 1972-82; exec. v.p. Zupnik Enterprises, 1982-92; pres. Jerry Tokofsky Entertainment, Encino, Calif., 1992—; CEO TKO Comm. Prof. Sch. TV and Film U. So. Calif. Sch. Bus. Prodr. films: Where's Poppa, 1971, Born to Win, 1972, Dreamscape, 1985, Fear City, 1986, Wildfire, 1988, Glengarry Glen Ross, 1992, The Grass Harp, 1995, American Buffalo, 1995, Double Down, 1997, Life on Mars, 1998, Alibi Store, 2000, John Steinbecks In Dubious Battle, 2001, Constellation, 2002, Buck 50, 2002, Puccini, 2002--. With U.S. Army, 1959, res. 1959-63. Named Man of Yr. B'nai B'rith, 1981; recipient L.A. Resolution City of L.A., 1981. Mem. Variety Club Internat. Avocations: skiing, tennis, golf, chess. *Passion for family, life, work, with patience and intelligence and you have a chance to grab that winning ring.*

TOKUHATA, GEORGE K. retired medical educator, epidemiologist, consultant; b. Matsue, Japan, Aug. 25, 1924; arrived in U.S., 1951; s. Yujiro and Hama Tokuhata; m. Sumiko Matsui, June 10, 1949. BA, Keio U., Tokyo, 1950; MA, Miami U., Oxford, Ohio, 1952; PhD, U. Iowa, 1955; Dr.PH, Johns Hopkins U., 1962. Chief epidemiology chronic disease div. USPHS, Washington, 1961—64; assoc. prof. preventive medicine U. Tenn., Memphis, 1965—67; dir. rsch. Pa. Dept. Health, Harrisburg, 1968—89; prof. behavioral sci. Pa. State U. Coll. Medicine, Hershey, 1970—95; prof. epidemiology U. Pitts., Pitts., 1970—90; ret. Cons. product safety U.S. FDA, Washington, 1970—73; cons. maternal child health rsch. U.S. Children's Bur., 1974—77; cons. rsch. grant svcs. Nat. Cancer Inst., 1982—86. Contbr. chapters to books, articles to numerous profl. jours. Grantee, USPHS, U.S. FDA. Fellow: APHA, Am. Coll. Epidemiology; mem.: Fgn. Policy Assn. (bd.dirs. 1995—2000), Torch Club (bd.dirs. 1999—2002). Achievements include first to find genetic role played in lung cancer; research in radiation, stress and health. Avocations: classical music, landscape design, gardening. Home: 410 Rupley Rd Camp Hill PA 17011

TOKUNAGA, EMIKO, dancer; b. San Francisco, Sept. 28, 1939; d. Shigao and Utako (Seiki) T. BFA, U. Utah, 1961; MA, NYU, 1966. Co-dir. Tokunaga Dance Ko, N.Y.C., 1967—; faculty Boston Conservatory, 1971—, Harvard U. and Radcliffe Coll., Cambridge, Mass., 1986—92, dance program coord., 1995—98. Over 40 residencies in U.S., Japan and Norway. Choreographer 60 modern and Japanese dances; dancer: over 2000 performances in theaters and ednl. instns. in U.S., Norway and Japan. Nat. Endowment for the Arts grantee, Japan-U.S. Friendship Commission, N.Y.C. Dept. of Cultural Affairs; fellow Harvard U., 1995-96. Office: Tokunaga Dance Ko 1 Sheridan Sq New York NY 10014-6825 E-mail: emikotokunaga@es.org.

TOKUNO, KENNETH ALAN, college administrator, poet; b. Tokyo, Nov. 2, 1947; came to U.S., 1948; s. Shiro and Asako (Maida) T.; m. Diane Emi Nushida, July 7, 1979; children Chelsea Kiyoko Alana and Jamie Asako Nalani (twins). AA, Am. River Coll., 1967; BS, U. Calif., Davis, 1969, MS, 1973; PhD, U. Hawaii, 1977. Lectr. U. Hawaii, Honolulu, 1978-80, asst. prof., 1980-85; acad. counselor U. Wash., Seattle, 1985-87, dir. student svcs. dept. sociology, 1987-89, dir. curriculum and programs, 1989-93; dean student svcs. Leeward C.C., Pearl City, Hawaii, 1993-99, acting provost, 1995; acad. affairs program officer U. Hawaii at Manoa, Honolulu, 1999—2000; interim asst. grad. dean U. Hawaii, Manoa, 2002—. Cons. devel. gen. edn. arch. U. Mo., Columbia, 1992; mem. selection com. Am. Acad. Achievement, 1990-93. Reviewer: Jour. of Freshman Yr. Experience, 1992—; textbook reviewer Worth Pub. Co., Houghton-Mifflin Co., Charles Merrill Pub. Co., 1983-91; proposal reviewer Biennial Meeting of the Society for Research in Child Development, 1983, Social and Devel. Psychology Program, NSF, 1982-85; cons. editor: Child Development, 1979-81; contbr. poetry to anthologies and mags., 1987-99. Mem. Nat. Assn. Student Pers. Adminstrs. (exec. bd. Hawaii state chpt. 1994-98), Nat. Resource Ctr. for Freshman Yr. Experience and Students in Transition (nat. adv. bd. 2002), Western Assn. Schs. and Colls. (accreditation evaluator 2000—). Avocations: classical guitar, reading. Office: U Hawaii at Manoa 105 Bachman Hall Honolulu HI 96822 E-mail: toluno@hawaii.edu.

TOKUTANI, MASAO, risk management educator; b. Tokyo, Nov. 1, 1940; s. Takeo and Matsu (Hagiwara) T. B, Chuo U., 1964, Dr., 1978; Mr., Waseda U., 1967. CPA, Tokyo. Asst. prof. Chiba U. Commerce, 1967-73; assoc. prof. Seikei U., Tokyo, 1974-78, full prof., 1979-2001, prof. emeritus, 2001—; prof. Grad. Sch. Internat. Acctg. Chuo U., 2002. Cons. in field. Author: Corporate Social Accounting, 1977, Risk Management, 1983. Mem. Japan Acctg. Assn., Secom Sci. and Tech. Found. (Risk Measurement and Bus. Behavior award 1983), Asian-Pacific Rsch. Ctr. Seikei U. Avocations: golfing, fishing. Home: 63-25 Isshiki Hayama Miuragun, Kanagawa 240-0111 Japan Office: 1-19-403 Sakaecho-Kanagawku Yokohama 221-0052 Japan E-mail: mt@miraisitu.com.

TOLAN, ROBERT WARREN, pediatric infectious disease specialist; b. Bowling Green, Ohio, Nov. 20, 1960; s. Robert Warren Tolan and Margaret Delores (Petter) Cardwell. BA, Ind. U., 1982, MA, 1983; MD, Washington U., St. Louis, 1987. Diplomate Nat. Bd. Med. Examiners, Am. Bd. Pediatrics, sub-bd. of pediat. infectious diseases. Resident in pediat. Riley Hosp. for Children, Indpls., 1987-90; fellow in infectious diseases St. Louis Children's Hosp., 1990-94; pvt. practice pediatrics and pediatric infectious diseases, 1994—; clin. instr. pediat. Washington Univ. Sch. Med., 1994—98; clin. asst. prof. pediats. MCP-Hahnemann U. Sch. Medicine, 1999—2001, clin. assoc. prof. pediat., 2002—; clin. asst. prof. MCP Hahnemann U. Sch. of Med., 1999—2001; clin. assoc. prof. Drexel U. Coll. Medicine, 2002—. Co-author: Fever of Unknown Origin in Children, 1991; contbr. articles to Clin. Infectious Diseases, Pediatric Infectious Diseases Jour., Infection and Immunity, Jour. Clin. Microbiology. Nat. Merit scholar Pitts. Plate Glass, 1978; Pediatric Scientist Devel. Program fellow, 1990-94. Fellow Am. Acad. Pediatrics; mem. AMA, Am. Soc. Microbiology, Infectious Diseases Soc. Am., Pediatric Infectious Diseases Soc., Soc. for Preservation and Encouragement of Barbershop Quartet Singing in Am., Physicians for Social Responsibility. Democrat. Episcoplian. Achievements include patent for a cloned outer membrane protein from Haemophilus influenzae type b which is being developed as a vaccine candidate; reviews of surgical management of pediatric endocarditis and of toxic shock syndrome and influenza; description of systemic pseudomalignant form of cat-scratch disease in normal children, the cloning of an outer membrane protein from Haemophilus influenzae type b, the lack of epidemiologic utility of analysis of lipopolysaccharide from the same organism. Office: St Christopher's Hosp for Children Specialty Care at Capitol Health Sys 416 Bellevue Ave Trenton NJ 08618-4502

TOLAND, CLYDE WILLIAM, lawyer; b. Iola, Kans., Aug. 18, 1947; s. Stanley E. and June E. (Thompson) T.; m. Nancy Ellen Hummel, July 27, 1974; children: David Clyde, Andrew John, Elizabeth Kay. BA, U. Kans., 1969, JD, 1975; MA, U. Wis., 1971. Bar: Kans. 1975, U.S. Dist. Ct. Kans. 1975, U.S. Supreme Ct. 1980. Ptnr. Toland and Thompson LLC, Iola, 1975—. Author: Samuel Franklin Hubbard and Permelia Caroline (Spencer) Hubbard: Pioneer Settlers in 1857 of Allen County, Kansas Territory, and their Descendants, 1985, (with others) Clark and Eliza (Wright) Toland: Their Ancestors and Descendants, 1984, David Wilson and Charlotte Elizabeth (Cooper) Wilson, 1830-1961, and Their Ancestors and Descendants, 1988. Mem. exec. com. Friends of Libr., U. Kans., 1977-92, pres., 1988-91; pres. Allen County Hist. Soc., Inc., 1990-95; founder Annual Buster Keaton Celebration, Iola, Kans., co-chmn., 1993-97; leader restoration Frederick Funston Boyhood Home, 1991-95. Co-recipient with U.S. Sen. Nancy Kassebaum First Alumni Disting. Achievement award Coll. Liberal Arts and Scis. U. Kans., 1996. Fellow Kans. Bar Found.; mem. ABA, Kans. Bar Assn. (Outstanding Svc. award 1988), Allen County Bar Assn., U. Kans. Alumni Assn. (Strickland award 1969), Phi Beta Kappa, Order of Coif, Omicron Delta Kappa (presdl. plaque 1969). Republican. Prsbyterian. Avocations: speaking on estate planning and history; historical field trips. Home: 211 S Colborn St Iola KS 66749-3405 Office: PO Box 404 Iola KS 66749-0404

TOLAND, JOHN ROBERT, lawyer; b. Iola, Kans., Oct. 7, 1944; s. Stanley E. and June Elizabeth (Thompson) T.; m. Karen Alice Jeffries, Apr. 26, 1980; children: Carol Jane, Mark Charles, Scott Robert, Kent William. BA with highest distinction, U. Kans., 1966, JD, 1969. Bar: Kans. 1969, U.S. Dist. Ct. Kans. 1969, U.S. Ct. Appeals (10th cir.) 1969, U.S. Supreme Ct. 1976. Ptnr. Toland and Thompson, LLC, Iola, 1973—. City atty., Yates Center, Kans., 1976-82; spkr. in field. Editor-in-chief Kans. Law Rev., 1968-69; mem. bd. editors Kans. Bar Assn. Jour., 1988-92. Trustee Allen County Hosp., Iola, 1979-82; bd. dirs. Iola Pub. Library, 1980-88, pres., 1983-88; bd. dirs. United Fund of Iola Inc., 1975-79, treas., 1975-77; bd. dirs. Iola Area Symphony Orch., 1994-97; ruling elder 1st Presbyn. Ch., Iola, 1983-85, 97-98; mem. Allen County Hist. Soc., Kans. State Hist. Soc., The Friends of the Eisenhower Found., U. Kans. Alumni Assn.; mem. com. on ministry John Calvin Presbytery, Presbyn Ch. (USA), 1986-88; mem. Permanent Jud. Commn., 1998—; coach Boys Basketball Youth League. Capt. JAGC, U.S. Army, 1969-73, Vietnam. Decorated Bronze Star, Army Commendation medal with oak leaf cluster; John Ise scholar in Econ., 1965-66, Summerfield scholar, U. Kans., 1962-66, Nat. Merit scholar, 1962-66. Fellow Kans. Bar Found.; mem. ABA, Kans. Bar Assn., Kans. Sch. Attys. Assn. (bd. dirs. 1989-93, spkr. at sch. law seminars), Allen County Bar Assn. (pres. 1980-81), Am. Legion, Rotary (pres. Iola chpt. 1980-81, Paul Harris fellow 1986), Order of Coif, VFW, Phi Beta Kappa, Phi Delta Phi, Beta Theta Pi, Sigma Pi Sigma. Home: PO Box 312 Iola KS 66749-0312 Office: Toland and Thompson LLC 103 E Madison St Iola KS 66749-3330 E-mail: jrtoland@aceks.com.

TOLBERT, BERT MILLS, biochemist, educator; b. Twin Falls, Idaho, Jan. 15, 1921; s. Ed and Helen (Mills) T.; m. Anne Grace Zweifler, July 20, 1959; children— Elizabeth Dawn, Margaret Anne, Caroline Joan, Sarah Helen. Student, Idaho State U., 1938-40; BS, U. Calif. at Berkeley, 1942, PhD, 1945; postgrad., Fed. Inst. Tech., Zurich, Switzerland, 1952-53. Chemist Lawrence Radiation Lab., Berkeley, 1944-57; faculty U. Colo., Boulder, 1957-89, prof., 1961-89, prof. emeritus, 1989—, assoc. chmn. dept. chemistry and biochemistry, 1980-88. Bd. dirs. Hauser Chem. Rsch., Boulder, 1983-99; dir. Hauser Inc., Boulder, 1983-99, vis. prof. IAEA, Buenos Aires, Argentina, 1961-62; Biophysicist U.S. AEC, Washington, 1967-68; cons. pvt. cos, govt. agys. Author: (with others) Isotopic Carbon, 1948; contbr. (with others) articles to profl. jours. Fellow AAAS; mem. Am. Chem. Soc., Am. Soc. Biochemistry and Molecular Biology, Radiation Rsch. Soc., Soc. for Exptl. Biology and Medicine. Achievements include rsch. on organic chemistry, including use of isotopes in chemistry and biochemistry, radiation chemistry, radiation effects in protein, intermediary metabolism, metabolism of ascorbic acid, nutritional biochemistry, instrumentation in radioactivity. Home: 444 Kalmia Ave Boulder CO 80304-1732

TOLBERT, BETH WILLDEN, real estate company executive, broker; b. Delta, Utah, Apr. 7, 1935; d. Delbert B. and Mildred (Twitchell) Willden; m. Stanley Tolbert, May 12, 1955; children: Keven, Tracy, Troy. Student, Brigham Young U., 1953-54. Cert. residential specialist. Realtor Harding Realty, Am. Fork, Utah, 1976-82; associate broker Pine Valley Realty, Alpine, 1982-97; prin., owner Beth Tolbert Realty Group, St. George, 1997—. Apptd. Utah Real Estate Commn., Salt Lake City, 1993—, chair 1993-94; bd. trustees Utah Valley State Coll., Orem, 1991—, chair 1996-97; pres. Nat. Womens Coun. Realtors, 1994; bd. trustees Leadership Dixie, 2000-01. Recipient

Realtor of Yr. award Utah Assoc. Realtors, 1984, Distinguished Svc. award 1994, 97, Realtor of Yr. award Utah County Bd. Realtors, 1984. Home: 656 Country Ln Santa Clara UT 84765-5471

TOLBERT, CHARLES MADDEN, II, sociology educator; b. Jackson, Miss., Oct. 30, 1952; s. Charles M. and Jean (Furr) T.; m. Patricia Hesterly, Dec. 30, 1972; children: Rachel, Patrick. BA in Sociology, Baylor U., 1973, MA in Sociology, 1975; PhD in Sociology, U. Ga., 1980. Vis. asst. prof. Emory U., Atlanta, 1980-81; asst. prof. Fla. State U., Tallahassee, 1982-88, assoc. prof., chair dept. sociology, 1988-91; prof. sociology and rural sociology La. State U., Baton Rouge, 1992-2000, chair dept. sociology, 1998-2000, head dept. rural sociology, 1998-2000; prof. and chair dept. sociology Baylor U., Waco, Tex., 2000—. Rsch. assoc. ctr. econ. studies U.S. Bur. Census, 1998—. Author: Introduction to Computing, 1985, Work in the Fast Lane, 1992; contbr. articles to profl. publs. Deacon Univ. Presbyn. Ch., Baton Rouge, 1996-99. Mem. Am. Sociol. Assn., So. Sociol. Soc. (v.p. 1997-98), Southwestern Sociol. Assn. (exec. com. 1996-97), Population Assn. Am., Rural Sociol. Soc. Avocation: cooking. Office: Baylor U Dept Sociology PO Box 97326 Waco TX 76798-7326 Fax: 254-710-1175. E-mail: charlie_tolbert@baylor.edu.

TOLBERT, CLINTON JAME, army officer, machinist; b. Auburn, Ala., Dec. 22, 1953; s. Clinton and Rosia Love (Fillmore) T.; m. Gloria Jean Fitzpatrick, Sept. 23, 1974; children: Christopher, Mark, Marcella. BS, Tukegee U., 1983; MBA, Troy State U., 1987, MS, 1990; AS in Applied Sci., So. U., Opelika, Ala., 1996. EMT U.S. Army, Fort Benning, Ga., 1972-75; machine operator West Point Pepperll, Inc., Valley, Ala., 1975-82; 1st lt. Army Nat. Guard, Roanoke, 1982-86, capt., 1986-92, major Montgomery, Ala., 1992-96; machinist Falk Corp., Auburn, Ala, 1996—. Elder Methodist Ch., Auburn, Ala., 1996— Named All- Am. Scholar, U.S. Achievement Acad., Lexington, Ky., 1996; recipient Minority Leadership award, U.S. Achievement Acad., Lexington, 1996. Mem. Nat. Guard Assn. Democrat. Avocations: reading, golf. Home: 989 Fitzpatric Rd Auburn AL 36830

TOLBERT, DANNY LEE, music producer, songwriter; b. Ft. Pierce, Fla., Dec. 7, 1961; s. Nathaniel and Jessie Mae Tolbert; m. Mary Anne Tolbert, June 5, 1982; children: Danny Lee Jr., Joshua. Student, Lyndon B. Johnson Acad., Franklin, N.C. Min. of music Living White Throne, Ft. Pierce, 1972—78; pastor Harvest Deliverance Temple, Okeechobee, 1994—96; CEO, songwriter, prodr. Dra Music Prodns. Studio, 1996—. Songwriter: Handwriting on the Wall, 2001. Vol. spiritual guidance NAACP, Okeechobee, 1995; vol. artist support World AIDS Day Com., Ft. Pierce, 1996; hon. chmn. Economy Stimulant Program Nat. Rep. Congl. Com., 2001. Mem.: Okeechobee County C. of C. Avocations: reading, music. Home: 1605 NW 7th Ave Okeechobee FL 34972 Office: Dra Music Prodns Studio 414 NW 3d St 34972 Fax: 863-763-9727. E-mail: dannyt@dramusic.com.

TOLBERT, MARGARET ELLEN MAYO, laboratory administrator; b. Suffolk, Va., Nov. 24, 1943; d. Clifton Jessie and Martha Taylor (Artis) Mayo; divorced; 1 child, Lawson Kwia Tolbert. BS in Chemistry, Tuskegee U., 1967; MS in Analytical Chemistry, Wayne State U., 1968; PhD in Biochemistry, Brown U., 1974. Asst. prof. chemistry Tuskegee U., Tuskegee Institute, Ala., 1973-76; assoc. prof., assoc. dean Sch. Pharmacy, Fla. A&M U., Tallahassee, 1977-78; dir. Carver Rsch. Found., asso. provost R&D, prof. chemistry Tuskegee, 1979-88; sr. planner, sr. budgets and control analyst BP Am., Inc., Warrensville Heights, Ohio, 1987-90; dir. rsch. Improvement in Minority Instns. program NSF, Arlington, Va., 1990-93; cons. scientist Howard Hughes Med. Inst., 1994; dir. divsn. ednl. programs Argonne (Ill.) Nat. Lab., 1994-96; dir. New Brunswick Lab. U.S. Dept. Energy, Argonne, 1996—. Cons., panelist NSF, NIH, NRC; chair com. visitors Acad. Rsch. Insts. program NSF, 1995; spkr. in field. Contbr. numerous articles to profl. jours. Recipient numerous honors and awards for sci. contbns. and cmty. svc. Fellow AAAS; mem. Am. Chem. Soc., Inst. for Nuclear Materials Mgmt., N.Y. Acad. Scis., Chgo. Chemists Club, Sigma Xi. Office: New Brunswick Lab 9800 S Cass Ave Argonne IL 60439-4899 E-mail: margaret.tolbert@ch.doe.gov.

TOLCHIN, JOAN GUBIN, psychiatrist, educator; b. N.Y.C., Mar. 10, 1944; d. Harold and Bella (Newman) Gubin; m. Matthew Armin Tolchin, Sept. 1, 1966; 1 child, Benjamin. AB, Vassar Coll., 1964; MD, NYU, 1972. Diplomate Am. Bd. Gen. Psychiatry, Am. Bd. Child Psychiatry. Rsch. asst. Albert Einstein Coll. Medicine, N.Y.C., 1964-68; instr. psychiatry med. coll. Cornell U., 1977-78, clin. instr., 1978-86, clin. asst. prof., 1986—. Contbr. articles to profl. jours. Fellow: Am. Acad. Child and Adolescent Psychiatry; mem.: NY Coun. Child and Adolescent Psychiatry (bd. dirs. 1992—96, pres. 1994—95, bd. advisors 2001—), Am. Acad. Psychoanalysis (sec. 1998—2001), Alpha Omega Alpha (mem. disaster psychiatry outreach). Office: 35 E 84th St New York NY 10028-0871

TOLCHIN, MARTIN, newspaper reporter, author; b. N.Y.C., Sept. 20, 1928; s. Charles T. and Evelyn (Weisman) Tolchin; m. Susan Jane Goldsmith, Dec. 23, 1965; children: Charles, Karen. Student, U. Utah, 1947-49; LL.B., N.Y. Law Sch., 1951. Reporter N.Y. Times, N.Y.C., 1954-94; publisher and editor-in-chief The Hill, Washington, 1994—. Author (with Susan Jane Tochin): To The Victor, 1971; author: Clout-Woman Power and Politics, 1974, Dismantling America-The Rush to Deregulate, 1983, Buying Into America: How Foreign Money is Changing the Face Of Our Nation, 1988, Selling Our Security-The Erosion of American's Assets, 1992, Glass Houses: Congressional Ethics and the Politics of Venom, 2001. Served with U.S. Army, 1951-53. Recipient Schaeffer Gold Typewriter award E.M. Schaeffer Co., 1967; recipient Page One award Newspaper Guild N.Y., 1967, 69, 73, Citizens Budget Commn. award, 1967, Sigma Delta Chi award, 1973, Everett M. Dirksen award for disting. reporting of Congress, 1983 Mem. Nat. Press Club (Washington), Univ. Club. Jewish. Home: 3525 Winfield Ln NW Washington DC 20007-2378 Office: The Hill 733 15th St NW Washington DC 20005-2112 E-mail: mtolchin@aol.com.

TOLCHINSKY, PAUL DEAN, organization design psychologist; b. Cleve., Sept. 30, 1946; s. Sanford Melvin and Frances (Klein) T.; m. Laurie S. Schermer, Nov. 3, 1968 (div. Jan. 1982); m. Kathy L. Dworkin, June 19, 1988; children: Heidi E., Dana M. BA, Bowling Green State U., 1971; PhD, Purdue U., 1978. Asst. br. mgr., tng. instr. Detroit Bank and Trust, 1971-73; mgr. tng. and devel. nuclear divsn. Babcock and Wilcox Co., Barberton, Ohio, 1973-75; internal cons. food products divsn. Gen. Foods Corp., West Lafayette, Ind., 1975-77; grad. tchg. asst. Krannert Grad. Sch. Mgmt. Purdue U., 1975-78; asst. prof. mgmt. Coll. Bus. Adminstrn. Fla. State U., Tallahassee, 1978-79, U. Akron, Ohio, 1979-81; pres. Performance Devel. Assocs., Cleve., 1975—; ptnr. Dannemiller Tyson Assocs., 1994-99; mng. ptnr. Performance Devel. Assocs., 2000—. Contbr. articles to profl. publs. Bd. dirs. Temple Tiferth Israel, Cleve., 195. With U.S. Army, 1966-69, Vietnam. Mem. APA, Acad. Mgmt. Democrat. Jewish. Avocations: running, travel. Office: Performance Devel Assocs 50 Fox Glen Rd Moreland Hills OH 44022

TOLEDANO, JAMES, lawyer; b. N.Y.C., Apr. 26, 1944; s. Ralph Robert Toledano and Nora (Romaine) Toledana; m. Peggy Cashman, Dec. 18, 1971 (div. Dec. 2001); 1 child Gwyn Alcock Toldeano ;1 child Michael Howard Toldeano. AB in Polit. Sci., U. Calif., Riverside, 1968; JD, U. Calif., Berkeley, 1971. Bar: Calif. 1972. Sole practice, Irvine, Calif., 1976-88; lawyer mgr. ptnr. Toledano & Wald, 1988-98; pvt. practice, 1998—. Bd. dirs., pres. U. Calif. Riverside Alumni Assn., 1972-90; alumni regent U. Calif., 1985-87; candidate Calif. State Assembly, 1992, 94; chair Orange County Calif. Dem. Party, 1995-97. Democrat. Mem. Religious Soc. of Friends. Avocations: stamp collecting, working out, reading, writing, hiking. Office: 200 E Sandpointe Ave Ste 750 Santa Ana CA 92707-5777

TOLEDANO, RALPH DE, columnist, author, poet; b. Internat. Zone of Tangier, Aug. 17, 1916; s. Hayim and Suzanne (Nahon) de T.; m. Nora Romaine, July 6, 1938 (div. 1964); children: James, Paul Christopher; m. Eunice Marshall, Apr. 19, 1979 (dec. Aug. 1999). BA, Columbia Coll., 1938; postgrad., Cornell U., 1943. Founder, co-editor Cross-Town, 1932-33; Founder, co-editor Jazz Info., 1938-39; assoc. editor The New Leader, 1941-43; editor The Standard, 1946; mng. editor Plain Talk, 1946-47; pub. dir. Dress Joint Bd., Internat. Ladies Garment Workers Union, 1947-48; asst. editor Newsweek, 1948, nat. reports editor, 1950-60, asst. chief Washington Bur., 1956-60; syndicated columnist King Features, 1960-71, Nat. News Research Syndicate, 1971-74, Copley News Service, 1974-89, Heritage Features Syndicate, 1989-91, Creators Syndicate, 1991-98; editor House Republican Leadership report Am. Mil. Strength and Strategy; chief Washington Bur., Taft Broadcasting Co., 1960-61; dir. polit. intelligence Goldwater Presdl. Campaign Com., 1963-64; contbg. editor Nat. Rev., 1960—; pres. Nat. News-Rsch., 1960—, Anthem Books, 1970; editor-in-chief Washington World, 1961-62. Vice-chmn. Am. Conserva-Union, 1965-66; mem. 20th Century Fund Task Force on Freedom Press, 1971-72. Author: Seeds of Treason, 1950, Spies, Dupes and Diplomats, 1952, Day of Reckoning, 1955, Nixon, 1956, Lament for a Generation, 1960, The Greatest Plot in History, 1963, The Winning Side, 1963, The Goldwater Story, 1964, RFK: The Man Who Would be President, 1967, America, I-Love-You, 1968, One Man Alone: Richard M. Nixon, 1969, Claude Kirk: Man and Myth, 1970, Little Cesar, 1971, J. Edgar Hoover: The Man in His Time, 1973, Hit and Run: The Ralph Nader Story, 1975, Let Our Cities Burn, 1975, Poems: You & I, 1978, Devil Take Him, 1979, The Apocrypha of Limbo (poems), 1994, Notes from the Underground: The Chambers-Toledano Letters, 1997, Cry Havoc: The Assault on America, 2001; editor: Frontiers of Jazz, 1947, Mark Twain on Practically Anything, 2001; co -editor: (with Melvin Laird) The Conservative Papers, 1962,; editor-in-chief: Political Success, 1968-69; mem. editl. bd. Yale Lit. Mag, 1981-86; contbr. articles to mags. Bd. dirs. Americans for Constitutional Action, 1966-67, Constructive Action, 1990—. With OSS, AUS, 1943-46. Recipient Freedoms Found. award, 1950, 61, 74; Americanism award VFW, 1953; Heritage Found. Disting. Journalism fellow. Mem. Internat. Mark Twain Soc., Bibl. Archeology Soc., Dutch Treat Club (N.Y.), Nat. Press Club, Naval and Mil. Club (London), Am. Legion (comdr. Pershing post), Sigma Delta Chi. Office: 500 23rd St NW Washington DC 20037-2828

TOLEDANO, STUART ROBERT, pediatrics educator; b. N.Y.C., Mar. 27, 1947; s. Solomon and Jeanne Toledano. BS, CUNY, 1968; MD, SUNY, Buffalo, 1972. Diplomate Am. Bd. Pediat., subbd. Hemetology/Oncology. Intern in pediat. Montefiore Hosp., Bronx, 1972-73, resident in pediat., 1973-75, fellow in pediat. hemetology/oncology, 1974-75, Children's Hosp. of Phila., 1977-79; prof. pediat. U. Miami (Fla.) Sch. Medicine, 1981—. Prin. investigator Pediatric Oncology Group, Miami, 1982—; cons. children's med. svcs. Fla. Dept. Health, 1987—; mem Cancer Control and Adv. Bd., Fla., 1994—. Contbr. articles to med. jours., including Internat. Jour. Cancer, Med. Pediatric Oncology, Jour. Pediatric Hematology-Oncology. Maj. M.C., USAF, 1975-77. Mem. Am. Acad. Pediat., Am. Soc. Pediatric Hematology and Oncology, Am. Soc. Hematology, Fla. Med. Assn., Fla. Pediatric Soc., Greater Miami Pedatric Soc. Office: U Miami Sch Medicine PO Box 016960 (R-131) Miami FL 33101

TOLEDO, ANDREW ANTHONY, obstetrician, gynecologist; b. Tampa, Fla., June 24, 1955; MD, U. South Fla., 1979. Diplomate in ob-gyn. and reproductive endocrinology Am. Coll. Ob-Gyn. Intern U. Louisville, 1979-80, resident in ob-gyn., 1980-83, fellow in reproductive endocrinology, 1983-85; active staff Northside Hosp., Atlanta, 1990—, Piedmont Hosp., Atlanta, 1992—; cons. staff Dunwoody (Ga.) Med. Ctr., 1992—; asst. clin. prof. ob-gyn. Emory U. Sch. Medicine, Atlanta. Mem. N.Am. Soc. Pediat. and Adolescent Gynecology, Am. Coll. Ob-Gyn., Am. Fertility Soc., N.Am. Soc. for Adolescent Gynecology. Office: Reproductive Biology Assocs Ste 400 1150 Lake Hearn Dr Atlanta GA 30342-1717 E-mail: andrew.toledo@rba-online.com.

TOLEDO, FREDERICO GRANCHI STEIDEL, physician, scientist; b. Rio de Janeiro, Brazil, Jan. 21, 1972; s. Jose Augusto Toledo and Francisca Granchi. MD, U. Fed. Rio de Janeiro, 1996. Rsch. trainee U. Fed. Rio de Janeiro, 1990-93; spl. project assoc. Mayo Clinic, Rochester, Minn., 1994, rsch. fellow, 1996-98; resident in internal medicine U. Miami, 1999—2002; endocrinology fellow U. Pitts., 2002—. Mem.: Am. Assn. Clin. Endocrinologists, Endocrine Soc. Avocations: computers, movies, art, science. Office: 17980 NE 31st Ct Apt 1226 Aventura FL 33160

TOLEDO, VICTOR, educational consultant; b. N.Y.C., Jan. 8, 1932; s. Joseph Jacob and Esther (Ben-Ezra) T.; m. Alix-Marie Hall, Oct. 14, 1982. BA magna cum laude, CUNY, 1967, grad. in psychology, 1967-73. Draftsman S.J. Pehel Naval Architecture, N.Y.C., 1950-52; human resources exec. Argo Personnel, 1953-56; founder AAA Contracting Co., 1960-67; dir. Office Instnl. Rsch., Hunter Coll.-CUNY, 1969-74; dir., CEO Nat. Tng. and Evaluation Ctr., Inc., 1974—. Founder, dir. Search for Young Scholars, N.Y.C., 1980-84; vol. cons. Anderson Program for Gifted, N.Y.C., 1989—; spkr. workshop leader MENSA, N.Y.C., 1990, 92. Founder, adminstrv. dir. Am. Dance Theatre, N.Y.C., 1957-59. Mem. Phi Beta Kappa, Psi Chi. Avocations: reading, gardening, music, conservation, theater.

TOLENTINO, CASIMIRO URBANO, lawyer; b. Manila, May 18, 1949; came to U.S., 1959; s. Lucio Rubio and Florence (Jose) T.; m. Jennifer Masculino, June 5, 1982; 2 children: Casimiro Masculino, Cristina Cecelia Masculino. BA in Zoology, UCLA, 1972, JD, 1975. Bar: Calif. 1976. Gen. counsel civil rights divsn. HEW, Washington, 1975-76; regional atty. Agrl. Labor Relations Bd., Fresno, Calif., 1976-78; regional dir. Sacramento and San Diego, 1978-81; regional atty. Pub. Employment Relations Bd., L.A., 1981; counsel, west divsn. Writers Guild Am., 1982-84; dir. legal affairs Embassy TV, 1984-86; pvt. practice, 1986-87. Mediator Ctr. Dispute Resolution, Santa Monica, Calif., 1986-87; asst. chief counsel Dept. of Fair Employment and Housing, State of Calif., 1986-92, adminstrv. law judge dept. social svcs., 1992—. Editor: Letters in Exile, 1976; contbr. articles and revs. to Amerasia Jour. Chmn. adv. bd. UCLA Asian Am. Studies Ctr., 1983-90; chmn. bd. Asian Pacific Legal Ctr., L.A., 1983-93 (Decade award); pres. bd. civil svc. commrs. City of L.A., 1984-85, 90-93; bd. dirs. met. region United Way, 1987-95; bd. dirs. Rebuild L.A., 1992-97; mem. Asian-Pacific Am. adv. coun. L.A. Police Commn., 1995-97; adv. coun. L.A. Children's Scholarship Fund, 1998-2000. Mem. Nat. Asian-Am. Legal Consortium (bd. dirs. 1991—), State Bar Calif. (exec. com. labor law sect. 1985-88), Los Angeles County Bar Assn., Minority Bar Assn. (sec. 1984-85), Philippine Am. Bar Assn. (chmn. bd. 1988, award of merit 1999), Philippine Lawyers of So. Calif. (pres. 1984-87, award of merit 1982), Philippine-Am. Alumni Assn. (Cmty. Svc. award 2001). Democrat. Roman Catholic. Avocations: history, photography, travel.

TOLER, RANDALL DOUGLAS, computer consultant; b. Elgin, Ill., May 4, 1956; s. Ralph Douglas and Barb (Schuyler) T.; m. Alicia Kirk, Jan. 3, 2001; 1 child, Kellie. BS in Pub. Adminstrn., U. Mo., 1978. Founder U.S. Green Party, Niles, Mich., 1973—. Author: Green Party Newsletter, 1980—. Candidate for U.S. Congress, Orange County, Calif., 1983, for Pres., 1992, for mayor, Aurora, Ill., 1997. Avocations: skiing, jogging, basketball. Office: Green Party Nat Newsletter 461 N Lake St Apt 209 Aurora IL 60506-4158

TOLES, THOMAS GREGORY, editorial cartoonist; b. Buffalo, Oct. 22, 1951; s. George Edward and Rose Elizabeth (Riehle) T.; m. Gretchen Amanda Saarnijoki, May 26, 1973; children: Amanda Laurel, Seth August. BA in English, SUNY-Buffalo, 1973. Artist Buffalo Courier-Express, 1973-80, cartoonist, 1980-82, Buffalo News, 1982—2002, UPS, 1982—, The New Republic, 2000—02, U.S. News & World Report, 1994-99, Washington Post, 2002—. Author: (fiction) My School Is Worse than Yours, 1997; (cartoon collections) The Taxpayer's New Clothes, 1985, Mr. Gazoo: A Cartoon History of the Reagan Era, 1987, At Least Our Bombs Are Getting Smarter: A Cartoon Preview of the 1990's, 1991, My Elected Representatives Went to Washington, 1993, Duh, 1996; creator (comic strip) Curious Avenue, 1992-94; creator (comic panel) Randolph Itch, 2a.m., 2000-02. Recipient John Fischetti Editorial Cartoon award Columbia Coll., Chgo., 1984, Pulitzer Prize for editorial cartooning, 1990. Mem. Am. Assn. Editorial Cartoonists Home: 75 Central Ave Hamburg NY 14075-6219 Office: Buffalo News PO Box 100 Buffalo NY 14240-0100

TOLF, ROBERT WALTER, writer; b. Chgo., Aug. 3, 1929; s. Carl Oscar and Margaret Emilia (Zeltner) T.; m. Nancy Ellen List, Aug. 9, 1952; 1 child, Carolyn Anne. BA cum laude, Harvard U., 1951; PhD, U. Rochester, 1957. Attache, 2d sec. U.S. Dept. State, various locations, 1957-70; editor Fla. Trend, St. Petersburg, 1973—; columnist, critic Sun-Sentinel, Ft. Lauderdale, Fla., 1975—; exec. dir. Phileas Soc., 1988—; producer, writer, narrator Columbus Documentaries, 1989-92. Author: The Russian Rockefellers, 1976, Addison Mizner, 1983, Chicago Sketch Book, 1988, Paris Sketch Book, 1990, Discover Florida, 1982, Country Inns of the Old South, 1978, 83, Country Inns of New York State, 1984, Country Inns of the Mid-Atlantic, 1986, Florida Weekends, 1990, 94, Florida's Best Beach Vacations, 1992, Florida Country Inns, 1993, 96, Destination Florida--Sanibel and Captiva, 1993, Destination Florida--South Beach Miami, 1993, 14 Florida Restaurant Guides, 1973-96, Trumpy, 1996, others; editor: Columbus Documents, 1992; author, prodr. narrator 15 videos in The Great Explorers Series. Lt. U.S. Army, 1954-57. Mem. Harvard Varsity Club, Fox Club, Harvard Club Broward County. Office: 3100 S Ocean Blvd Apt 422 Highland Beach FL 33487

TOLFORD, FRANK STEFAN, bookstore executive; b. Bremen, Germany, June 30, 1949; came to U.S., 1955; s. Charles Lawrence and Marta Sophia Tolford. AA, St. Johns River Jr. Coll., Palatka, Fla., 1973; BA, U. North Fla., Jacksonville, 1976. Warehouse mgr. Smith & Royals Elec. Svc. Co., Jacksonville, 1977-80; gen. mgr. Chamblin Bookmine, 1981—. Donor Fla.-Ga. Blood Alliance, Jacksonville, 1982—. Mem. Fla. Antiquarian Booksellers Assn. (v.p. 1990-91, pres. 1991-94). Republican. Episcopalian. Avocations: stamps, chess, books. Office: Chamblin Bookmine 4551 Roosevelt Blvd Jacksonville FL 32210-3314

TOLHURST, FIONA CATHERINE, English language educator; b. N.Y.C., Feb. 25, 1968; d. H. Desmond and Patricia Anne (Maddock) T.; m. Christoph John Neuendorf, Sept. 1, 1991. BA, Rice U., 1990; MA, Princeton U., 1994, PhD, 1995. Asst. prof. English Tex. A&M Internat. U., Laredo, 1995-96, Alfred (N.Y.) U., 1996-2001, assoc. prof., 2001—. Reviewer: Arthuriana, 1995—, guest editor spl. issue, 1998. Advisor Women's Issues Coalition, Alfred U., 1997-2001. Mellon fellow in humanities, 1990; Alfred U. summer rsch. grantee, 1997, 98. Fellow Soc. for Values in Higher Edn. (bd. mem.); mem. MLA, Pearl-Poet Soc. (v.p. 1995-97, pres. 1997-98), Phi Beta Kappa, Phi Kappa Phi. Democrat. Avocations: hiking, piano, choir, gardening. Office: Alfred U Divsn English Saxon Dr Alfred NY 14802 E-mail: ftolhurst@alfred.edu.

TOLIA, BHUPENDRA MANILAL, urologist; b. Jamnagar, India, Dec. 21, 1936; came to U.S., 1967; s. Manilal Premji and Prabhavati Manilal (Mehta) T.; m. Chandrika J. Lakhani, Jan. 7, 1967; children: Nameeta B., Chirag B. MB BS, Med. Coll. Baroda, India, 1962; MS, Med. Coll. Baroda, 1966. Diplomate, Am. Bd. Urology. Resident in gen. surgery SSG Hosp., Baroda, India, 1962-66, Nazareth Hosp., Phila., 1967-68; resident in urology Thomas Jefferson U. Hosp., 1968-71; spl. fellow in urology Meml. Sloan-Kettering Cancer Ctr., N.Y.C., 1971-72; spl. trainee spinal cord injury svc. VA Hosp., Bronx, N.Y., 1972-73; dir. urology clinic Bronx Mcpl. Hosp. Ctr., 1973-80; attending urologist Albert Einstein Hosp., Bronx, 1973—; clin. instr. urology, then asst. prof. urology Albert Einstein Coll. Medicine, 1973-80, assoc. prof. urology, 1980-91, assoc. clin. prof. urology, 1991—; attending urologist Westchester Sq. Med. Ctr., 1992—, Our Lady of Mercy Med. Ctr., 1992—. Cons. urologist, Dr. Martin Luther King Jr. Health Ctr., Bronx. Fellow ACS (Bronx chpt. treas. 1988-90, pres.-elect 1990-91, pres. 1991-92), N.Y. Acad. Medicine, Internat. Coll. Surgeons; mem. Am. Urol. Assn., Soc. Univ. Urologists, Societe Internat. d'Urologie. Republican. Jain. Office: 1695 Eastchester Rd Ste 306 Bronx NY 10461-2375

TOLIA, VASUNDHARA K. pediatric gastroenterologist, educator; b. Calcutta, India; came to U.S., 1975; d. Rasiklal and Saroj (Kothari) Doshi; m. Kirit Tolia, May 30, 1975; children: Vinay, Sanjay. MBBS, Calcutta U., 1968-75. Intern, resident Children's Hosp. Mich., Detroit, 1976-79, fellow, 1979-81, dir. pediat. endoscopy unit, 1984-90, dir. pediat. gastroenterology and nutrition, 1990—; instr. Wayne State U., 1981-83, asst. prof., 1983-91, assoc. prof., 1991-97, prof., 1997—. Mem. editl. bd. Inflammatory Bowel Diseases, 1999— Am. Jour. Gastroenterology, 1999, Rev. of World Lit. in Pediatrics, 1999—; contbr. articles to profl. jours. Named Woman of Distinction, Mich. chpt. Crohn's and Colitis Found. Am., 1991. Fellow Am. Coll. Gastroenterology (chair ad-hoc com. pediat. gastroenterology 1998-2000), Am. Acad. Pediats.; mem. Am. Gastroenterology Assn., N.Am. Soc. Pediat. Gastroenterology and Nutrition, Soc. Pediat. Rsch. Office: Children's Hosp of Mich 3901 Beaubien St Detroit MI 48201-2119

TOLIAS, LINDA PUROFF, music educator; b. Dearborn, Mich., Nov. 26, 1954; d. Nick Puroff and Milka Stoycheff; m. Peter Elias Tolias, June 26, 1988. MusB in Music Edn. with honors, U. Mich., 1976; MusM in Music Performance, Wayne State U., 1992. Tchr. music El Dorado (Ark.) Pub. Schs., 1976-77, Ferndale (Mich.) Pub. Schs., 1979-83; tchr. bands and orch. Dearborn Pub. Schs., 1983—. Founder, condr. El Dorado Youth Symphony, 1976-77; instr. Oakland U. Summer Music Camp, Rochester, Mich., 1982-84; condr., string clinician Oakland U. Youth Orch., Rochester, 1982-84; string clinician Dearborn Pub. Schs., 1983-96, Farmington Pub. Schs., 1994-96; music performer Detroit Symphony Orch., 1978-83, Mich. Opera Theatre, 1977-90; prin. violinist U. Mich. Philharm. Orch., 1975-77, South Ark. Symphony, 1976-77, Detroit Symphony Civic Orch., 1977-79; mem. Las Palmas Internat. Opera Orch. '76 Tour; mem. Internat. Musicians Local 5, 1978. Sponsor City Beautiful Commn., Dearborn, 1983—. Fellowship U. Mich., 1975-76; recipient Roberta Siegel award for Opera, 1975-76, Music Educator of Yr. award 1998. Mem. NOW, Mich. Educator's Nat. Conf., U. Mich. Alumni Assn., Am. String Tchrs. of Am. Democrat. Greek Orthodox. Avocations: music, reading, dancing, cooking. Home: 32267 Auburn Dr Beverly Hills MI 48025-4234

TOLINS, ROGER ALAN, lawyer; b. Bklyn., Jan. 25, 1936; s. Albert and Claire (Rothstein) T.; m. Doris Levine, May 15, 1960; children: Fran, Jonathan. AB with distinction, Dartmouth Coll., 1956; LLB, NYU, 1959, LLM in Taxation, 1961. Bar: N.Y. 1959. Assoc. Brennan, London & Buttenwieser, N.Y.C., 1961-67; ptnr. Goldfeld, Charak, Tolins & Lowenfels, 1967-74, Tolins & Lowenfels, N.Y.C., 1975—. Guest lectr. in securities law Seton Hall U. Sch. Law, 1989—. With U.S. Army, 1959-60. Mem. ABA (sect. on taxation), N.Y. State Bar Assn.

TOLINS-KAUFMAN, SELMA L. psychologist; b. Flushing, N.Y., Aug. 6, 1930; d. Emanuel Leifer and Sally Lillian Weinstock; m. David B. Tolins, Jr., May 30, 1951 (div. June 1984); children; Madeline Tolins-Schlitt, Andrew M.; m. David Kaufman, July 28, 1984. BA, Queens Coll., 1952; MEd, Temple U., 1967. Lic. psychologist, Pa. Tchr. East Meadow (N.Y.) Sch. Dist., 1952-55, Tchr. Tng. Sch. P.S. 201, Flushing, 1955-56, Centennial Sch. Dist., Warminster, Pa., 1962-63, guidance counselor, 1963-66, psychologist, 1966-70; dir. guidance and psychology Upper Moreland Sch. Dist., Willow Grove, Pa., 1970-78; dir. pupil pers. svcs. Methacton Sch. Dist., Fairview Village, 1978-90; pvt. practice consulting psychologist Maple Glen, 1975—. Author children's plays. Mem. Nat. Assn. Pupil Svcs., Pa. Pupil Svcs. Assn., Pa. Psychol. Assn., Spl. Edn. Assn. Avocations: tennis, bridge, travel, opera, theatre. Home: 1881 Dillon Rd Maple Glen PA 19002-3104 E-mail: seldav@webtv.net.

TOLIVER, LEE, mechanical engineer; b. Wildhorse, Okla., Oct. 3, 1921; s. Clinton Leslie and Mary (O'Neall) T.; m. Barbara Anne O'Reilly, Jan. 24, 1942 (dec. Jan. 1999); children: Margaret Anne, Michael Edward. BSME, U. Okla., 1942. Registered profl. engr., Ohio. Engr. Douglas Aircraft Co., Santa Monica, Calif., 1942, Oklahoma City, 1942-44, Los Alamos (N.Mex.) Sci. Lab., 1946; instr. mech. engring. Ohio State U., Columbus, 1946-47; engr. Sandia Nat. Labs., Albuquerque, 1947-82; instr. computer sci. and math. U. N.Mex., Valencia County, 1982-84; number theory researcher Belen, N.Mex., 1982—. Author: (computer manuals with G. Carli, AF. Schkade) Experience with an Intelligent Remote Batch Terminal, 1972; (with C.R. Borgman, T.I. Ristine) Transmitting Data from PDP-10 to Precision Graphics, 1973, Data Transmission-PDP-10/Sykes/Precision Graphics, 1975; Relations Between Prime and Relatively Prime Integers, 1998. With Manhattan Project (Atomic Bomb) U.S. Army, 1944-46. Achievements include devel. of 44 computer programs with manuals. Home: 206 Howell St Belen NM 87002-6225

TOLL, BARBARA ELIZABETH, art gallery director; b. Phila., June 8, 1945; d. Joseph M. and Evelyn Toll BA, Goucher Coll., 1967; MFA, Pratt Inst., 1969. Asst. dir. jr. coun. Mus. Modern Art, N.Y.C., 1969-70; dir. Hundred Acres Gallery, 1971-76; curator David Rockefeller Collection, 1975-81; pres., dir. Barbara Toll Fine Arts, 1981-94, dir., 1994—. Mem. Corp. Yaddo; curator Focus: Donald Judd Furniture, Parrish Art Mus. Southampton, N.Y., 1996, Friendships in Arcadia: Writers and Artists at Yaddo in the 90s, 2000, Follies: Fantasy in the Landscape, Parrish Art Mus., 2001. Nat. bd. dirs. ArtTable, 2001—; bd. dirs. Parks Coun., N.Y.C., 1995—2002. Avocation: gardening. Office: 138 Prince St New York NY 10012-3135

TOLL, DANIEL ROGER, corporate executive, civic leader; b. Denver, Dec. 3, 1927; s. Oliver W. and Merle D'Aubigne (Sampson) T.; m. Sue Andersen, June 15, 1963; children: Daniel Andersen, Matthew Mitchell. AB magna cum laude (Pyne prize), Princeton U., 1949; MBA with distinction, Harvard U., 1955. With Deep Rock Oil Corp., Tulsa, 1949-51, asst. mgr. product supply and distbn.; with Helmerich & Payne, 1955-64, roughneck, landman, exploration mgr., pipeline constrn. mgr., v.p. fin., 1961-64; with Sunray DX Oil Co., 1964-69, treas., v.p. corp. planning and devel.; v.p. Sun Oil Co., 1969; with Walter E. Heller Internat. Corp., Chgo., 1970-85, sr. v.p. fin., dir., 1970-80, pres., dir., 1980-85, corp. and civic dir., 1985—. Bd. dirs. Mallinckrodt, Inc. (formerly IMCERA Group Inc.), Kemper Nat. Ins. Co., Lincoln Nat. Income Fund, Inc., Lincoln Nat. Convertible Securities, Inc. Vice chmn. Tulsa Cmty. Chest, 1964-66; v.p., bd. dirs. Tulsa Opera, 1960-69; bd. dirs. Tulsa Little Theatre, 1963-69, Internat. House, Chgo., 1984-87; bd. dirs. Inroads, Inc., 1973-95, nat. vice chmn., 1982-95; bd. dirs. Chgo. Area coun. Boy Scouts Am., 1976-94, pres., 1981-83; mem. Kenilworth (Ill.) Sch. Bd. Dist. 38, 1975-81, pres., 1978-81; bd. dirs., mem. exec. com., chmn. fin. and hosp. affairs coms. Evanston (Ill.) Northwestern Healthcare, Inc., 1982—; bd. dirs. Chgo. Met. Planning Coun., 1989—, pres., 1991-94; bd. dirs. Northwestern Healthcare Network, Inc., 1995-99; trustee Princeton U., 1990-94. Lt. (j.g.) USNR, 1951-52. Baker scholar Harvard U., 1955. Mem. Chgo. Assn. Commerce and Industry (bd. dirs. 1979-86), Chgo. Club, Comml. Club, Econ. Club, Harvard Bus. Sch. Club (past pres., bd. dirs. 1971-91), Indian Hill Club (bd. govs. 1987-90), Princeton Club (past pres., bd. dirs. 1985—), Phi Beta Kappa. Home: 1005 Mount Pleasant Rd Winnetka IL 60093-3614 Office: Ste 300 560 Green Bay Rd Winnetka IL 60093-2242

TOLL, DAVID, pediatrician; b. Cleve., May 6, 1925; s. Herman I. and Mollie (Neuger) T.; m. Bridget Ann Fryer; children: Job, Abel, Seth. BA, Harvard U.; MD, Western Res. U., 1948. Intern Children's Hosp., Boston, 1948-50; resident in pediatrics Mass. Gen. Hosp., 1951-52; practice medicine specializing in pediatrics St. Johnsbury, Vt., 1952; med. dir. Child Health Ctr., 1952—. Cons. Vt. Health Dept., N.H. Health Dept., 1952— ; adj. asst. prof. pediatrics Dartmouth Med. Sch.; preceptor Stanford, Dartmouth, Case Western Res., U. Vt. med. schs. Contbg. editor Am. Acad. Pediatrics Grand Rounds. Mem. AMA, Vt. Med. Assn., Am. Acad. Pediatrics, New Eng. Pediatric Soc., Am. Acad. Med. Dirs. Home and Office: 1394 Main St Saint Johnsbury VT 05819-1829

TOLL, JOHN SAMPSON, university president, physics educator; b. Denver, Oct. 25, 1923; s. Oliver Wolcott and Merle d'Aubigne (Sampson) T.; m. Deborah Ann Taintor, Oct. 24, 1970; children: Dacia Merle Sampson, Caroline Taintor. BS with honors, Yale U., 1944; AM, Princeton U., 1948, PhD, 1952; DSc (hon.), U. Md., 1973, U. Wroclaw, Poland, 1975; LLD (hon.), Adelphi U., 1978; PhD (hon.), Fudan U., Peoples Republic China, 1987; LHD (hon.), SUNY, Stony Brook, 1990; LLD (hon.), U. Md., Eastern Shore, 1993. Mng. editor, acting chmn. Yale Sci. mag., 1943-44; with Princeton U., 1946-49, proctor fellow, 1948-49; Friends of Elementary Particle Theory Research grantee for study in France, 1950; theoretical physicist Los Alamos Sci. Lab., 1950-51; staff mem., assoc. dir. Project Matterhorn, Forrestal Rsch. Ctr., Princeton U., 1951-53; prof., chmn. physics and astronomy U. Md., 1953-65; pres., prof. physics SUNY, Stony Brook, 1965-78, U. Md., 1978-88, chancellor, 1988-89, chancellor emeritus, prof. physics, 1989—; pres. Univs. Rsch. Assn., Washington, 1989-94, Washington Coll., Chestertown, Md., 1995—. 1st dir. SUNY Chancellor's Panel on Univ. Purposes, 1970; physics cons. to editl. staff Nat. Sci. Tchrs. Assn., 1957-61; U.S. del., head sci., secretariat Internat. Conf. on High Energy Physics, 1960; mem.-at-large U.S. Nat. Com. for Internat. Union of Pure and Applied Physics, 1960-63; chmn. rsch. adv. com. on electrophysics to NASA, 1961-65; mem. gov. Md. Sci. Resources Adv. bd., 1963-65; mem., chmn. NSF adv. panel for physics, 1964-67; mem. N.Y. Gov.'s Adv. Com. Atomic Energy, 1966-70; mem. commn. plans and objectives higher edn. Am. Coun. Edn., 1966-69; vis. prof. Nordic Inst. Theoretical Physics, Niels Bohr Inst., Denmark, U. Lund, Sweden, 1975-76; mem. Hall of Records Comm., 1979-88; mem., chmn. adv. coun. Princeton Plasma Physics Lab, 1979-85; mem. Adv. Coun. of Pres.'s, Assn. of Governing Bds., 1980-88, So. Regional Edn. Bd., 1980-90; mem. exec. com. Washington/Balt. Regional Assn., 1980-89, Nat. Assn. State Univs. and Land Grant Colls., 1980-88, Ctr. for the Study of the Presidency, 1983-84; mem. univ. programs panel of energy rsch. bd. Dept. Energy, 1982-83; mem. SBHE Adv. Com., 1983-89, Md. Gov.'s Chesapeake Bay Coun., 1985; mem. resource com. State Trade Policy Coun. Gov.'s High Tech Roundtable Md. Dept. Econ. Devel., 1986-89; marine divsn. chmn. NASULGC, 1986; bd. trustees Aspen Inst. for Humanities, 1987-89; mem. Commn. on Higher Edn. Middle States Assn. Colls. and Schs., 1987; chmn. adv. panel on tech. risks and opportunities for U.S. energy supply and demand U.S. Office Tech. Assessment, 1987-91; chmn. adv. panel on internat. collaboration in def. tech., U.S. Office Tech. Assessment, 1989-91; mem. Math. Scis. Edn. Bd. NAS, 1991-93;mem. Sea Grant Rev. Panel U.S. Dept. Commerce, 1992—, chair, 1996-97, Com. on Financing Higher Edn. Nat. Assn. Independent Colls. Univs., 1996-98; bd. govs. Chesapeake Bay Maritime Mus., 1996—; dir. Hodson Scholarship Found., 1996—; mem. Md. Gov.'s Blue Ribbon Citizens Pfiesteria Action Commn., 1997; mem. governing coun. Wye Faculty Seminar, 1997—; dir. Eastern Shore Assn. Coll. Pres., 1998—, mem. bd. dirs. Md. Ctr. Agro-ecology, Inc., 1999—; hon. bd. mem. Radcliffe Creek Sch., 2000—. Contbr. articles to profl. jours. Mem. Adv. Coun. Boy Scouts Am. De-Mar-Va Coun., 1999; bd. mem. Mid-Shore Cmty. Found., 2002-. Recipient Benjamin Barge prize in math. Yale U., 1943, George Beckwith medal for Proficiency in Astronomy, 1944, Outstanding Citizen award City of Denver, 1958, Outstanding Tchr. award U. Md. Men's League, 1965, Copernicus award govt. of Poland, 1973, Stony Brook Found. award for disting. contbns. to edn., 1979, Disting. Svc. award State of Md., 1981, Silver medal Sci. U. Tokyo, 1994, Internat. Landmark award U. Md., 1994, first recipient Lifetime Achievement award Md. Assn. for Higher Edn., 2000, Chief Exec. Leadership award Coun. for Advancement and Support Edn., 2000; named Washingtonian of Yr., 1985, Citizen of Yr. Chestertown Optimist Club, 1997; John Simon Guggenheim Meml. Found. fellow Inst. Theoretical Physics U. Copenhagen, U. Lund, Sweden, 1958-59. Fellow AAAS, Am. Phys. Soc., Washington Acad. Scis. (pres. 1995-96), N.Y. Acad. Scis.; mem. NSTA, Am. Coun. Edn. (bd. dirs. 1986-89, NAACP (life), Am. Assn. Physics Tchrs., Fedn. Am. Scientists (chmn. 1961-62), Philos. Soc. Washington, Assn. Higher Edn., Yale U. Sci. and Engring. Assn. (award for disting. contbns. 1996), Cosmos Club, Hamilton St. Club, Baltimore, Univ. Club (Washington and N.Y.), Phi Beta Kappa, Phi Kappa Phi (disting., Marylander of Yr. 2000 award), Sigma Xi (Sci. Achievement award 1965), Omicron Delta Kappa (hon.), Sigma Pi Sigma. Achievements include research on elementary particle theory, scattering. Office: U Md Dept Physics College Park MD 20742-4111 also: Washington Coll Pres's Office Chestertown MD 21620 E-mail: johntoll@physics.umd.edu., president.toll@washcoll.edu. *Throughout my life I have tried mainly to do whatever seemed most important and useful.*

TOLL, PERRY MARK, lawyer, educator; b. Kansas City, Mo., Oct. 28, 1945; s. Mark Irving and Ruth (Parker) T.; m. Mary Anne Shottenkirk, Aug. 26, 1967; children: Andrea Lynne, Hillary Anne. BS in Polit. Sci. and Econs., U. Kans., 1967, JD, 1970. Bar: Mo. 1970 1970, U.S. Dist. Ct. (we. dist.) Mo. 1970, U.S. Tax Ct. 1979, U.S. Supreme Ct. 1979. With Shughart, Thomson & Kilroy P.C., Kansas City, 1970—, pres., 1995—, chmn. bus. dept., 1999—. Asst. prof. deferred compensation U. Mo., Kansas City, 1979-83; bd. dirs., pres. Heart of Am. Tax Inst., Kansas City, 1975-87. Mem., chmn. Prairie Village (Kans.) Bd. Zoning Appeals, 1977-95. Mem. ABA, Mo. Bar Assn., Nat. Health Lawyers Assn., Am. Agr. Law Assn., Mo. Merchants and Mfrs. Assn., Greater Kansas City Med. Mgrs. Assn., Lawyers Assn. Kansas City, East Kans. Estate Planning Coun. (bd. dirs., pres.), Phi Kappa Tau (bd. dirs. Beta Theta chpt.). Office: Shughart Thomson & Kilroy 12 Wyandotte Plz 120 W 12th St Ste 1500 Kansas City MO 64105-1929

TOLL, SEYMOUR I. lawyer, writer, educator; b. Phila., Feb. 19, 1925; s. Louis David and Rose (Eisenstein) T.; m. Jean Marie Barth, June 25, 1951; children: Emily Barth, Elizabeth Terry, Martha Anne, Constance Nora Frances. BAmagna cum laude, Yale U., 1948, LLB, 1951. Bar: N.Y. 1953, U.S. Dist. Ct. (ea. dist.) Pa. 1955, Pa. 1956, U.S. Ct. Appeals (3d cir.) 1956, U.S. Dist. Ct. (so. dist.) N.Y. 1958, U.S. Supreme Ct. 1958, U.S. Ct. Appeals (5th cir.) 1970. Law clk. U.S. Dist. Ct. (so. dist.), N.Y.C., 1951-52; from assoc. to ptnr. Richter, Lord, Toll & Cavanaugh, Phila., 1955-65, 69; sole practice, 1965-68, 69-74; ptnr. Toll, Ebby, Langer & Marvin, 1975-2001; of counsel Marvin, Larsson, Henkin & Scheuritzel, 2001—. Vis. lectr. U. Pa. Law Sch., 1978-86. Author: Zoned American, 1969, A Judge Uncommon, 1993 (Athenaeum Literary award 1995); jour. editor: The Retainer, 1972-73, A Court's Heritage, 1984-88; jour. assoc. editor: The Shingle, 1970-78, editor, 1979-80; contbr. numerous articles to profl. jours. Pres. Phila. Citizen's Coun. on City Planning, 1967-69; pub. dir., mem. exec. com. Phila. Housing Devel. Corp., 1967-72; bd. dirs. The Libr. Co. Phila. (pres. 1992-98). Grantee Am. Philos. Soc., 1968. Mem. ABA, Pa. Bar Assn., Phila. Bar Assn. (Fidelity Bank award 1984), Am. Coll. Trial Lawyers, 3d Cir. Jud. Conf. (permanent del.), Jr. Legal Club, Phi Beta Kappa. Clubs: The Franklin Inn (pres. 1981-84), Yale (Phila.). Democrat. Jewish. Avocations: music, sailing, travel. Home: 453 Conshohocken State Rd Bala Cynwyd PA 19004-2642 Office: Marvin Larsson Henkin & Scheuritzel Centre Sq West Ste #3510 1500 Market St Philadelphia PA 19102 E-mail: stoll@marvinlarsson.com.

TOLL, SHELDON SAMUEL, lawyer; b. Phila., June 6, 1940; s. Herman and Rose (Ornstein) T.; m. Roberta Darlene Pollack, Aug. 11, 1968; children: Candice Moore, John Maitland, Kevin Scott. Bar: Pa. 1967, Mich. 1972, Ill. 1990, Tex. 1990, U.S. Dist. Ct. (ea. dist.) Pa. 1968, U.S. Ct. Appeals (3d cir.) 1970, U.S. Supreme Ct. 1971, Mich. 1972, U.S. Dist. Ct. (ea. dist.), U.S. Ct. Appeals (6th cir.) 1973, U.S. Ct. Appeals (5th cir.) 1978, U.S. Dist. Ct. (no. dist.) Calif. 1986, U.S. Ct. Appeals (9th cir.) 1987, U.S. Dist. Ct. (ea. dist.) Wis. 1989. Assoc. Montgomery, McCracken et al, Phila., 1967-72; sr. ptnr. Honigman Miller Schwartz and Cohn, Detroit, 1972—. Panelist Bankruptcy Litigation Inst., N.Y.C., 1984-94. Author: Pennsylvania Crime Codes, 1972, Bankruptcy Litigation Manual, 1988. Bd. dirs. Southeastern Mich. chpt. ARC, Detroit. Mem. Fed. Bar Assn. (past pres. Detroit chpt.), ABA, Pa. Bar Assn., Phila. Bar Assn., Detroit Bar Assn., Am. Bankruptcy Inst. (cert. bus. bankruptcy law specialist), Franklin (Mich.) Hills Country Club, Phi Beta Kappa. Democrat. Jewish. Office: Honigman Miller Schwartz & Cohn 2290 1st National Bldg Detroit MI 48226

TOLLAKSEN, THOMAS WILLIAM, village manager; b. Racine, Wis., Dec. 9, 1949; s. Gordon Keith and Marcella (Mockler) T.; m. Margaret Frances Cherf, Dec. 20, 1980; 1 child, David Michael. AB in Govt., U. Notre Dame, 1972; JD in law, Marquette U., 1975. Bar: Wis. 1975. Asst. corp. counsel County of Racine, 1975-77; atty. Thomas W. Tollaksen, S.C., Racine, 1977-86; ptnr. Foley, Dye, Foley & Tollaksen, S.C., 1986-92; village adminstr., atty. Village of West Milw., 1992-96; village mgr. Village of River Hills, Wis., 1996—. Exec. dir. West Milw. Cmty. Devel. Authority, 1992-96, River Hills Civic Improvement Found., 1996—. Mem. Internat. City/County Mgmt. Assn., Wis. State Bar Assn., Wis. City/County Mgmt. Assn., Milw. Met. Employers Assn. (chair 1997). Avocation: golf. Office: Village of River Hills 7650 N Pheasant Ln River Hills WI 53217-3000 Fax: 414-247-2308. E-mail: TTollaksen@aol.com.

TOLLE, GORDON J. political scientist; b. South Bend, ind., Dec. 1, 1942; s. Wilmer H. and L. Jeannette Tolle; m. Mary Louise Crow, Aug. 6, 1977; children: Jay E., Steven. AB, Oberlin Coll., 1965; MA in Govt., U. Notre Dame, 1967; PhD in Polit. Sci., U. Colo. Instr. SD State U., Brookings, 1967—71, 1973—75, asst. prof., 1975—79, assoc. prof., 1979—84, prof. polit. sci., 1984—87, 1988—; prof. Ariz. State U., Tempe, 1987—88. Bd. dirs. Upper Midwest Honors Coun., 1977—81, 1982—85; coord. European Studies Program, Brookings, 1981—. Author: Human Nature Under Fire: The Political Philosophy of Hannah Arendt, 1982; contbr. articles, book revs. to profl. publs. Recipient Merit Tchg. award, Regents of SD, 1985. Mem.: L.Am. Studies Assn., Am. Polit. Sci. Assn. Avocations: biking, trombone. Office: SD State U Polit Sci Dept Scobey Hall Box 504 Brookings SD 57007

TOLLE, MELINDA EDITH, engineer, scientist; b. N.Y., Aug. 8, 1964; d. Robert Dale and Mildred Elva Tolle. BS in Physics, BS in Geophysics, U. Utah, 1986, MS in Mech. Engring., 1988. Cert. quality engr. Am. Soc. for Quality; cert. quality mgr. Am. Soc. for Quality. Engr. assoc. Thiokol, Brigham City, Utah, 1987-88, sr. engr. assoc., 1988-90, engr., 1990-92, sr. scientist, sr. engr., 1992-98, prin. scientist, prin. engr., 1998-2000; sr. prin. scientist, sr. prin. engr. Alcoa, 2000—. Adj. instr. Weber State U., Ogden, Utah, 1996—. Mem. AIAA (regional dep. dir. Meb 2000—, Utah sect. chair-elect 1998-99, chair 1999—), Am. Soc. for Quality (sect. chair 1997-98, mem. chair 1995-96, vice chair 1996-97, strategic mgmt. plan chair 2000—), Am. Nuc. Soc., Utah Engring. Coun. (bd. dirs. 1998—), Alpha Nu Sigma (pres. 1988). Office: Thiokol PO Box 707 Brigham City UT 84302-0707

TOLLE, SUSAN W. internist, educator, educational administrator; b. Nov. 21, 1951; BS, Lewis & Clark Coll., Portland, Oreg., 1973; MD, Oreg. Health Sci. U., 1977. Chief resident U. Calif., San Diego, 1977-81; gen. internal medicine faculty Oreg. Health Sci. U., Portland, 1981—, dir. Ctr. for Ethics in Health Care, 1989—. Fellow in Ethics U. Calif., 1988—89. Contbr. articles to profl. jours. Mem. Task Force to Improve the Care of Terminally Ill Oregonians. Office: Ctr for Ethics in Health Care UHN-86 Oreg Health Sci Univ Portland OR 97201

TOLLENAERE, LAWRENCE ROBERT, retired industrial products company executive; b. Berwyn, Ill., Nov. 19, 1922; s. Cyrille and Modesta (Van Damme) T.; m. Mary Elizabeth Hansen, Aug. 14, 1948; children: Elizabeth, Homer, Stephanie, Caswell, Mary Jennifer. BS in Engring., Iowa State U., 1944, MS in Engring., 1949; MBA, U. So. Calif., 1969; LLD (hon.), Claremont Grad. Sch., 1977. Specification engr. Alumninum Co. Am., Vernon, Calif., 1946-47; asst. prof. indsl. engring. Iowa State U., Ames, 1947-50; sales rep. Am. Pipe and Constrn. Co. (now AMERON), South Gate, Calif., 1950-53, spl. rep. S.Am., 1952-54, 2nd v.p., mgr. Columbian divsn. S.Am., 1955-57, divsn. v.p., mgr. Calif., 1957-63, v.p. concrete pipe ops., 1963-65, pres. corp. hdqrs., 1965-67; pres., CEO Ameron Inc., Monterrey Park, 1967-89, CEO, pres. Pasadena, 1989-93, chmn. bd. dirs., 1989-94, ret., 1994. Trustee The Huntington Library, Art Gallery and Bot. Gardens; emeritus mem. bd. fellows Claremont U. Ctr.; bd. gov.'s Iowa State U. Found. Mem. Newcomen Soc. N.Am., Calif. C. of C. (bd. dirs. 1977-92), Calif. Club (past pres.), Jonathan Club, Bohemian Club, San Francisco Club, Commanderie de Bordeaux Club, L.A. Confrerie des Chevaliers du Tastevin Club, Twilight Club, Lincoln Club, Beavers Club (past pres., hon. dir.), Valley of Montecito Club, Alpha Tau Omega. Republican. Avocations: fishing, hunting, equestrian, philately. Home: 1400 Milan Ave South Pasadena CA 91030-3930 Office: 750 E Green St Ste 301 Pasadena CA 91101-2134

TOLLES, BRYANT FRANKLIN, JR. history and art history educator; b. Hartford, Conn., Mar. 14, 1939; s. Bryant Franklin and Grace Frances (Ludden) T.; m. Carolyn Coolidge Kimball, Sept. 15, 1962; children: Thayer Coolidge, Bryant Franklin III. BA, Yale U., 1961, MA in Teaching, 1962; PhD, Boston U., 1970. Instr. history King Sch., Stamford, Conn., 1962-63; tchr. history St. George's Sch., Newport, R.I., 1963-65; instr., asst. dean Tufts U., Medford, Mass., 1965-71; asst. dir., libr., editor publs. N.H. Hist. Soc., Concord, 1972-74; exec. dir., libr. Essex Inst., Salem, Mass., 1974-84; dir. mus. studies program, prof. history and art history U. Del., Newark, 1984—, chmn. art conservation dept., 1997-2000. Mem. Com. for a New England Bibliography, Inc. Author: New Hampshire Architecture, 1979, Architecture in Salem, 1983, The Grand Resort Hotels of the White Mountains: A Vanishing Architectural Legacy, 1998, Summer Cottages in the White Mountains: The Architecture of Leisure and Recreation, 1870-1930, 2000; editor: Leadership for the Future, 1991; contr. articles and book revs. to profl. jours. Trustee Mt. Washington Obs., N.H., N.H. Hist. Soc. Ford. Found. fellow Yale, 1962 Mem. Colonial Soc. Mass., Orgn. Am. Historians, Soc. Archtl. Historians, Soc. Indsl. Archaeology, Am. Assn. Mus., New Eng. Mus. Assn., Mid-Atlantic Mus. Assn., Am. Assn. for State and Local History, Wilmington Rowing Club, Appalachian Mountain Club, Univ. Barge Club (Phila.). Home: 1002 Kent Rd Wilmington DE 19807-2820 Office: U Del Mus Studies Program 301 Old Coll Newark DE 19716 E-mail: bftolles@udel.edu.

TOLLEY, AUBREY GRANVILLE, physician, hospital administrator; b. Lynchburg, Va., Nov. 15, 1924; married. Student, Duke U., 1942-43, U. Va., 1946-48, MD, 1952. Diplomate Am. Bd. Psychiatry and Neurology. Intern St. Elizabeths Hosp., Washington, 1952-53; asst. resident psychiatry U. Va. Hosp., Charlottesville, 1953-54; resident psychiatry VA Hosp., Roanoke, Va., 1955-56; instr. U. N.C. Sch. Medicine, 1956-61, asst. prof., 1961-66, clin. asst. prof. psychiatry, 1966-72, clin. assoc. prof., 1972-76, clin. prof., 1976—; dir. psychotherapy Dorothea Dix Hosp., Raleigh, 1962-67, dir. hosp., 1973-88. Dir. resident tng. John Umstead Hosp., Butner, N.C., 1966-67; dir. profl. tng. and edn. N.C. Dept. Mental Health, Raleigh, 1967-72, asst. dir., 1972-73; Prin. investigator USPHS grant, 1957-59; cons. VA Hosp., Fayetteville, N.C., 1957-78; sr. cons., supervising faculty, community psychiatry sect. dept. psychiatry U. N.C. Sch. Medicine, 1971-88; exec. sec. Multiversity Group, 1968-73 Trustee Found. Hope, Raleigh, N.C., 1984—. Served with USNR, 1943-46. Fellow Am. Psychiat. Assn. (assembly rep. N.C. Dist. br. 1969-82, 86-2000, mem. joint commn. on pub. affairs 1984-87, mem. constl. membership com. 1990-96, mem. commn. on subspecialization 1990-94, Warren Williams award 1987), Am. Coll. Psychiatrists; mem. N.C., Durham-Orange County med. socs., N.C. Psychiat. Assn. (pres. 1984-85, lifetime disting. svc. award 1999), N.C. Hosp. Assn. (life), George C. Ham Soc. (Disting. Alumni award 1992). Home and Office: 110 Laurel Hill Rd Chapel Hill NC 27514-4323

TOLLEY, EDWARD DONALD, lawyer; b. San Antonio, Jan. 31, 1950; s. Lyle Oren and Mary Theresa Tolley; m. Beth Dekle Tolley; 1 child, Edward Spencer. BBA, U. Ga., 1971, MBA, 1974, JD, 1975. Bar: Ga. 1975, U.S. Dist. Ct. (5th cir.) 1976, U.S. Supreme Ct. 1978, U.S. Ct. Appeals (11th cir.) 1981. Ptnr. Cook, Noell, Tolley Bates and Michael and predecessor firms, Athens, Ga., 1975—. Lectr. various colls., univs., civic and profl. groups. Mem. Family Counseling Assn. of Athens, Inc., mem. Gov.'s Commn. on Criminal Sanctions and Correctional Facilities, 1988-90; past bd. dirs. Am. Cancer Soc.; pres. Clarke County Bd. Edn., 1992-93. Recipient award for cmty. svc. Chief Justice Ga. Supreme Ct., 2000. Fellow Ga. Bar Found., Am. Bd. Criminal Lawyers (bd. dirs. 1987, pres. 1996); mem. Fed. Bar Assn. (sec. 1983, treas. 1985, pres. Macon chpt. 1997-98), Ste Bar Ga. (chmn. law office and econ. com., bd. govs. 1985—, formal adv. opinion bd.), Ga. Trial Lawyers (v.p.), Ga. Assn. Criminal Def. Lawyers (pres. 1985, Indigent Def. award 1983, 88), Athens Bar Assn. (past pres.), Am. Judicature Soc., Order of Barristers (Cmty. Svc. award Chief Justice Ga. Supreme Ct., 2000). Office: Cook Noell et al 304 E Washington St Athens GA 30601-2751

TOLLEY, JERRY RUSSELL, university administrator; b. Goldsboro, N.C., Nov. 6, 1942; s. Elva Russell Tolley and Clara (Smith) Tolley-Bunch; m. Joan Morrison, June 8, 1965; children: Jerry R. Jr., Justin Clay. BS, East Carolina U., 1965, MEd, 1966; EdD, U. N.C., Greensboro, 1982; exec. mgmt. courses, Duke U. Tchr., coach Fayetteville (N.C.) Sr. High Sch., 1966; asst. football coach, head track and tennis coach Elon Coll., N.C., 1967-77, head football coach, 1977-81, dir. athletic sholarship fund, 1982, dir. corp. and ann. resources, 1983, coordinator Pride II Capital Campaign, 1984, assoc. dir. devel., 1985, officer corp. and major gifts, maj. gifts officer, 1999, dir. ann. giving, 2001; asst. v.p. tng., nat. dir. tng. & pub. affairs Lab. Corp. of Am., Burlington, N.C., 1986—. Author: Intercollegiate History of Athletics and Elon College, 1982, American Football Coaches Guidebook to Championship Football Drills, 1985; contbg. author: 101 Winning Plays, 1977, Leadership Education: A Source Book, 1989; contbr. articles to profl. jours. Treas. Town of Elon Coll., 1984-87, mayor protem, 1988, mayor, 1990-98, mayor emeritus, 1998—, chmn. recreation commn.; convenor City County Govt. Assn., 1987-98, Alamance County, N.C., 1986—; mem. exec. bd. dirs. Cherokee Coun. Boy Scouts Am., 1986, Thomas E. Powell Jr. Biology Found., Alamance Found.; exec. bd. N.C. Health & Fitness Found.; visitors Elon Coll.; mem. exec. com. Alamance County Ptnrs. in Edn.; bd. govs. 2 Those Who Care; dir. Alamance Edn. Alliance; bd. dirs. Cmty. Found. Greensboro; chmn. Citizens for Schs.; mktg. advisory com. Village of Brookwood; bd. advisors Morris Plan Bank. Named one of Outstanding Young Men Am., 1980, Internat. Men of Achievement, 1990, Cmty. Leaders Am., 1990, Mayors Hall of Fame, 1995; recipient Dwight D. Eisenhower award Nat. Football Hall of Fame, 1980, 81, Nat. Collegiate Football Championship award Eastman Kodak, Meritorious Svc. award Tom Sawyer-Huck Finn Tennis Classic, 1986, Order of the Long Leaf Pine, 1997, Laurel Wreath award State of N.C., 2002; named Nat. Football Coach of Yr., Nat. Assn. Intercollegiate Athletics, 1980, Elon Coll. Sports Hall of Fame, East Carolina U. Athletic Hall of Fame, 1991. Mem. Am. Football Coaches Assn., Coun. for Advancement of Edn., Phi Delta Kappa, Sigma Delta Psi. Avocations: writing, racquet sports, jogging. Home: Box 463 1322 Westbrook Ave Elon College NC 27244-9358 Office: Elon Coll 2600 Campus Box # 2600 Elon College NC 27244-2010

TOLLEY, JIM, not-for-profit developer; b. Jackson, Tenn., Apr. 9, 1962; s. Connie Way Tolley and Modena Laverne Baker. AS in Info. Mgmt., Jackson State Coll., 1991; BS in Social Work, Union U., 1992. Lic. alcohol and drug abuse counselor; nat. cert. addictions counselor level II; cert. criminal justice specialist. Dir. quality assurance KADDIS Mfg. Corp., Parsons, Tenn., 1983-88; psychiat. social worker Jackson Psychiat. Hosp., 1989-91; family therapist Jackson Area Coun. on Alcoholism, 1991-94; dir. treatment svcs. Memphis Recovery Ctrs., Inc., 1997-98, program dir., 1994-97; exec. dir. Family Counseling Svcs., Inc., Jackson, 1998—; accreditation mgr. Serenity Recovery Ctrs., Inc., Memphis, 1999-2000; human resources dir., compliance officer Whitehaven S.W. Mental Health Ctr., 2001—. Pvt. cons. Freshstart, West Tenn., 1997—2000; bd. dirs. A Vision For You, Inc., Jackson; radio show host. Regional coord. Am.-Scandinavian Student Exchange, Helsinki, Finland, 1984-86. Mem. ASPA, Nat. Assn. Alcohol and Drug Abuse Counselors, West Tenn. Assn. Alcohol and Drug Abuse Counselors. Libertarian. Presbyterian. Avocations: cultural anthropology, antiques, bridge. Office: Family Counseling Svcs Inc 3363 N Highland Ave Jackson TN 38305-3487 E-mail: fcsjackson@msn.com.

TOLLEY, STEPHEN GREGORY, oceanographer; b. Huntington, W.Va., July 4, 1958; s. Gary Maurice and Wanda Gordon (Chain) T. BS, Marshall U., 1980; PhD, U. So. Fla., 1994, knight fellow, 1987-92. Rsch. asst. U. So. Fla., St. Petersburg, 1983-86; mgr., curator The Pier Aquarium, 1988-89; rsch. assoc. U. So. Fla., 1989-94, asst. prof., 1995—. Cons. The Pier Aquarium, 1988, Natural History Mus., N.Y.C., 1988, Mote Marine Lab., Sarasota, Fla., 1985; treas. bd. dirs. Pier Aquarium, Inc., 1989-96. Contbr. articles to profl. jours. Judge Ann. State Sci. and Engring. Fair, 1990-96; exhibit adv. St. Petersburg Hist. Mus., 1986, Hands On, Inc., 1996; bd. dirs. Friends of Weedon Island, 1996. Mem. Am. Soc. Ichthyologists & Herpetologists, Am. Fisheries Soc., Oceanography Soc., Am. Inst. Fisheries Rsch. Biologists, Sigma Xi, Omicron Delta Kappa, Phi Kappa Phi. Office: Florida Gulf Coast Univ 19501 Benhill Griffin Park Fort Myers FL 33965-0001 Address: 7121 Golden Eagle Ct Apt 621 Fort Myers FL 33912-1745

TOLLIFSON, THOMAS GERALD, retired art education consultant, teacher; b. Albert Lea, Minn., Feb. 4, 1925; s. Virgil Irving and Lucile Katherine Tollifson; m. Jeannine May Dill, Aug. 10, 1952. BS in Art Edn., U. Minn., 1950; MA in Art Edn., Ohio State U., 1952. Art tchr. Columbus (Ohio) State Sch. for Mentally Retarded, 1951-52; art helping tchr. Arlington (Va.) Elem. Schs., 1952-54; art tchr. Washington Lee H.S., Arlington, 1954-56; art edn. instr. Am. U., Washington, 1953-54; art tchr. Jones Jr. H.S., Upper Arlington, Ohio, 1956-66; state art edn. cons. Ohio Dept. Edn., Columbus, 1966-94; ret., 1994. Art edn. instr. Ohio State U., 1950-51, 59-60, U. Va., Arlington, 1954-55—. Author (art edn. TV series guides) Images and Things, Nat. Instrn. TV, 1971, The Big A, 1986, Sta. KCTS-TV, Seattle, In Touch, Tollifson's Art Attack (series) in Art Line, Ohio Edn. Assn.; co-author, actor (TV program) What's an Art Curriculum for Anyway?", 1980; editor (art curriculum guide) Planning a Balanced Comprehensive Art Curriculum, Ohio Dept. Edn., 1970, 87, 92; co-prodr.: (ednl. TV program) Making Connections, 1995; co-author: Comprehensive Arts Education Curriculum Framework for Ohio Schools, 1991, Ohio Plan for Comprehensive Arts in Education, 1978; art exhbn. Fitton Art Ctr., Hamilton, Ohio, 1997, Michelle's Art Gallery, Columbus, Ohio, 2002. Founder Ohio Gov.'s Youth Art Exhbn., Columbus, 1969—, Ohio Alliance for Arts Edn., 1974, Ohio Youth Art Month, 1973, Ohio Arts Criticism Invitational and Open, 1989; advisor Getty Ctr. for Arts in Edn., L.A., 1987, Joint Coun. State Bd. Regents and State Bd. Edn., 1999—, Coalition for Equity and Adequacy, Columbus, 1999—; art judge, Ohio PTA. Sgt., U.S. Army Inf., 1943-45, ETO. Named Gov.'s Arts Educator of Yr., Ohio Arts Coun., 2000; recipient Grand Nat. Youth Art Month award, 1974; Jerry Tollifson Ohio Mid. Sch. Art Criticism Open Contest named in his honor, 2000. Fellow: Ohio Art Edn. Assn. (advisor Ohio arts edn., adv. com. 1994—, Outstanding Ohio Art Educator of Yr. 1984); mem.: Columbus Mus. Art, WWII Roundtable, Nat. Assn. State Dirs. Art Edn. (founder, chmn. 1967—70), Nat. Art Edn. Assn. (nat. art adminstr./supr. award 1995, Disting. Svc. award 1990), PBS. Avocations: drawing, painting, sculpture, architecture, landscape design. Home: PO Box 24352 Columbus OH 43224-0352

TOLLINCHE, CHARLES R. physician; b. Bayamon, P.R., Aug. 16, 1942; s. Felix and Beba (Portell) T.; m. Maria Pilar Bartolomé; children: Maria, Charles, Luis, Evelyn, Felix. BA, Inter.-Am. U., San German, P.R., 1963; MD, U. Zaragoza, Spain, 1972. Diplomate Am. Bd. Surgery. Intern Mayaguez Med. Ctr., 1972-73, resident in gen. surgery, 1973-74, San Juan Mcpl. Hosp., 1974-77; chief surg. svcs. 4th Med. Group Seymour Johnson AFB, N.C., 1995—. Mem. Am. Soc. Gen. Surgeons, KC.

TOLLIVER, GLENDA REEDER, social worker; b. Tyler, Tex., May 12, 1949; d. Nathaniel and Jessie Mae Reeder; m. Cletis Frank Tolliver, Feb. 23, 1985; 1 stepchild Cletis K. Student in psychology, Tyler Jr. Coll., 1967—69, Tex. So. U., 1969—71, student in psychology, 1975—77. LCSW. Day care counselor Neighborhood Ctr., Inc., Houston, 1973—77; child protective svc. specialist Tex. Dept. Protective and Regulatory Svcs., 1977—99, supr., child protective svcs., 1999—. Adv. mem. 5th Ward Enrichment Program, Houston, 1992. Mem.: NAACP, Nat. Black Child Devel., Inc. (pub. rels. 1981—, Pres. award, Houston chpt. 1994), Nat. Coun. Negro Women (v.p. Houston chpt. 1982—83), Toastmasters (pin), Gamma Phi Delta (pres. 1985—91). Avocations: sign language, writing poetry and novellas, piano, reading, studying cultures.

TOLLNER, ERNEST WILLIAM, agricultural engineering educator, agricultural radiology consultant; b. Maysville, Ky., July 14, 1949; s. Ernest Edward and Ruby Geneva (Henderson) T.; m. Caren Gayle Crane, Sept. 27, 1987. BS, U. Ky., 1972; PhD, Auburn (Ala.) U., 1981. Registered profl. engr., Ga. Rsch. specialist U. Ky., Lexington, 1972-74, rsch. engr., 1974-76; teaching asst. Tex. A&M U., College Station, 1976-77; rsch. specialist Auburn U., 1977-80; asst. prof. U. Ga., Griffin, 1980-85, assoc. prof., 1985-90, prof., 1990—, grad. coord., 2000—. Chmn. Coll. Faculty Coun., U. Ga., chmn. Coll. Agr. Faculty Coun., 1998; cons. to govtl. agys. and pvt. indusry; mem. Ga. State Acad. Panel addressing stream sediment transport issues. Author: Introduction to Natural Resource Engineering; contbr. 70 articles to profl. jours. Treas. Condominium Assn., Peachtree City, 1988-91. Mem. Am. Soc. Agrl. Engrs., Am. Soc. Engring. Edn., Sigma Xi (pres. U. Ga. chpt. 1997-98, grad. program coord. 1999). Achievements include first to use an x-ray tomographic scanner devoted solely to agricultural research tasks; pioneered research into the use of vegetative filterstrips for sediment control; pioneered alternative, nonaerobic composting process for farm and municipal wastes; coordinated bioconversion laboratory construction at University of Georgia. Home: 1010 Rogers Rd Bogart GA 30622-2723 Office: U Ga Dept Biology and Agrl Engring Driftmier Engring Ctr Athens GA 30602 E-mail: btollner@engr.uga.edu.

TOLMACH, JANE LOUISE, community activist, municipal official; b. Havre, Mont., Nov. 12, 1921; d. Robert Francis and Veronica (Tracy) McCormick; m. Daniel Michael Tolmach, Sept. 9, 1946; children: James, Richard, Eve Alice, Adam, Jonathan. AB, UCLA, 1943; M in Social Scis., Smith Coll., 1945; JD, S. We. U., L.A., 1981. Social worker ARC Field Svcs. Corona Naval Hosp., Norco, Calif., 1945-46; chmn. bd. dirs. Camarillo (Calif.) State Hosp., 1959-68; mem. bd. trustees Oxnard (Calif.) Union High Sch. Dist., 1965-72; mem. state reclamation bd. Calif., 1981-82; mem. bd. govs. Calif. C.C., 1982-87; mem. bd. St. John's Regional Hosp., Oxnard, 1986-89; mem. bd. of assessment appeals County of Ventura, Ventura, Calif., 1992—2002, transp. commr., 2002—. Chmn. fin. com. Ventura County Grand Jury, 1958; mem. Oxnard (Calif.) Planning Commn., 1957-62; exec. mem. So. Calif. Assn. Govts., L.A., 1975-76. Author: Smith Studies, 1945. Chmn. Ventura County Dem. Com., 1959-62; alternate or del. Dem. Nat. Convs., 1960, 68, 76, 88, 92, alt. 1956, 64; Women'schm. S. Calif. Dem. Com., 1966-70; nominee state assembly, 36th dist., Ventura, Calif., 1976; elected Oxnard City Coun. 1970-78, mayor, 1973-74. Home: 656 Douglas Ave Oxnard CA 93030-4614

TOLMACHOFF, WILLADENE, accountant, auditor; b. Mt. Vernon, Ky., July 13, 1945; d. Willie and Wanda Thacker; m. Innokenty Tolmachoff, July 27, 1968. MS, George Washington U., 1978; M. in Gen. Adminstrn., U. Md., 1994. Cert. fin. mgr. Audit mgr. USDA, Washington, 1987-97; dir. performance audits Office of Inspector Gen., 1998-2000; cash mgmt. dep. project mgr. Office of Fin. and Sys., 2000—01, internal audit/internal security audit mgr., 2001—. Adj. prof. Strayer U., 1997—. Mem.: Assn. Govt. Accts. Avocations: walking, bicycling, reading. Home: 1010 Rhode Island Ave NE Washington DC 20018 Office: Rm 367 810 1st St NE Washington DC 20002 E-mail: tolmachev@aol.com.

TOLMAN, RICHARD ROBINS, zoology educator; b. Ogden, Utah, Dec. 1, 1937; s. Dale Richards and Dorothy (Robins) T.; m. Bonnie Bjornn, Aug. 18, 1964; children: David, Alicia, Brett, Matthew. BS, U. Utah, 1963, MSEd, 1964; PhD, Oreg. State U., 1969. Tchr. sci. Davis County Sch. Dist., Bountiful, Utah, 1964-66; instr. Mt. Hood C.C., Gresham, Oreg., 1968-69; staff assoc., project dir. Biol. Scis. Curriculum Study, Boulder, Colo., 1969-82; prof. zoology Brigham Young U., Provo, Utah, 1982—, chair dept. of zoology, 1994-98, assoc. dean Coll. Biology and Agrl., 1998—2001, clin. dept. physiology & develop. biology, 2001—. Contbr. articles to profl. jours. Scoutmaster Boy Scouts Am., Orem, Utah, 1992. With USAR, 1956-63. Alcuin fellow Brigham Young U., 1991. Mem. Nat. Sci. Tchrs. Assn., Utah Sci. Tchrs. Assn. (exec. sec. 1991—), Nat. Assn. for Rsch. in Sci. Teaching, Nat. Assn. of Biology Tchrs. Mem. Ch. of LDS. Avocations: whitewater rafting, hunting, fishing, hiking. Home: 174 E 1825 S Orem UT 84058-7836 Office: Brigham Young Univ Dept Zoology Provo UT 84602 E-mail: richard_tolman@byu.edu.

TOLMAN, VERNA ANN, music educator; b. Worland, Wyo., Sept. 20, 1953; d. George and Anna (Brill) Bashford; m. Craig H. Tolman; children: Joshua, Amber, April, Ben, Zachary, Nikalous. Pvt. music tchr., Riverton, Wyo., 1976—. Stake young women's pres. Ch. Jesus Christ of Latter-Day Saints, Riverton, 1995—; coord. Riverton Youth Soccer Assn., 1993-97; pres. Riverton H.S. Booster Club, 1995-97; den leader Boy Scouts Am., 1991-95, pack com. chmn., 1983-85. Recipient Disting. Den Leader award Boy Scouts Am., 1995. Mem. Riverton Music Tchrs. Assn. (pres. 1991—). Avocations: sewing, reading, walking.

TOLMIE, KENNETH DONALD, artist, author; b. Halifax, N.S., Can., Sept. 18, 1941; s. Archibald and Mary Evelyn (Murray) T.; m. Ruth MacKenzie, Aug. 11, 1962; children: Sarah Katherine, Jane Marianna. B.F.A., Mt. Allison U., 1962. Owner Tolmie Film Prodns., Kendog Films, Tolmie Gallery, Toronto. Chmn. Visual Arts Ottawa, 1975-76; founding mem. Bridgetown and Area Hist. Soc., James House Mus. Author: (children's book) Tale of an Egg, 1974, (art book) A Rural Life: An Artist's Portrait, 1986; 3 TV documentary films produced on his work by CBC and by TV-Ont.; one-man shows include Dorothy Cameron Gallery, Toronto, 1963, Beckett Gallery, Hamilton, 1986, Kaspar Gallery, Toronto, 1988; Mt. Allison Univ. solo cross Can. touring exbn. Bridgetown Series, 1982-84; group shows include Banfer Gallery, N.Y.C., 1963, Nat. Gallery Can., Watercolors Prints and Drawing, 1964, 66, London Art Mus., Ont., 1966, Can. Soc. Graphic Art, 1973, Art Gallery N.S., 1980, 81, N.S. Art Bank, 1981; represented in permanent collections Nat. Gallery Can., Ottawa, Montreal Mus. Fine Arts, N.S. Art Bank, Art Gallery N.S., Confedn. Centre for Arts, Hirshhorn Collection, Washington, Owens Art Gallery, Mt. Allison U., Dofasco Ltd., Husky Oil Ltd., Procter & Gamble Ltd., Slater Steels Ltd., Crownx Ltd. Bd. dirs. Art Gallery N.S., 1979-81. Recipient prodn. grant Nova Scotia Film Devel. Corp., 1999. Mem. Writer's Union Can. (hon. life mem.), Writers Fedn. N.S., Visual Arts N.S., Visual Arts Ont., Visual Arts Ottawa (chmn. 1975-76), Bridgetown Hist. Soc. (hon. life) Address: 30 Morrow Ave Ste 201 Toronto ON Canada M6R 2J2 Fax: (416) 534-2913. E-mail: ken@kentolmie.com.

TOLOR, ALEXANDER, psychologist, educator; b. Vienna, Austria, Oct. 21, 1928; s. Stanley and Josephine (Kellner) T.; m. Belle Simon, Sept. 2, 1951; children: Karen Beth, Lori Ann, Diana Susan. BA, NYU, 1949, MA, 1950, PhD, 1954. Diplomate Am. Bd. Profl. Psychologists. Grad. asst. NYU, 1950-52; intern Neurol. Inst., N.Y.C., 1952-53, clin. psychologist, 1953-55; sr. clin. psychologist Inst. of Living, Hartford, Conn., 1957-59; dir. psychol. services Fairfield Hills Hosp., Newtown, 1959-64; clinic dir. Kennedy Center, Bridgeport, 1964-65; dir. Inst. Human Devel., Fairfield U., 1965-77, assoc. prof. psychology, 1965-68, research prof. psychology, 1968-75, prof. psychology, 1975-89, dir. school psychology div., 1975-77, dir. sch. and applied psychology program, 1982-86, prof. emeritus, 1989—; practice psychology Danbury, Conn., 1960-96; clin. instr. psychology Yale U., 1963-67. Cons. West Haven VA Hosp., 1962-66, Bridgeport Bd. Edn., Silver Hill Found., 1972-75, Fairfield Hills Hosp., 1973-94, Hallbrooke Hosp., 1975-92. Author: (with H.C. Schulberg) An Evaluation of the Bender-Gestalt Test, 1963, (with G.G. Brannigan) Research and Clinical Applications of the Bender-Gestalt Test, 1980, (with M. Deignan) Adjustment Problems in Children, 1984; editor: Effective Interviewing, 1985; adv. editor Jour. Cons. and Clin. Psychology; cons. editor Personality: An Internat. Jour.; contbr. articles to profl. jours. Served to 1st lt. USAF, 1955-57. Fellow Am. Psychol. Assn., Soc. Personality Assessment, Conn. Psychol. Assn. (mem. council 1964, pres. 1984); mem. Eastern Psychol. Assn., Psi Chi, Delta Phi Alpha, Beta Lambda Sigma, Phi Delta Kappa Home: 6 Brittania Dr Danbury CT 06811-2606 E-mail: atbt51@aol.com.

TOLPYGO, VLADIMIR K. materials scientist, researcher; b. Kiev, Ukraine, Jan. 12, 1958; s. Kirill B. Tolpygo, Yelena I. Tolpygo; m. Irina V. Ryzhova, Aug. 19, 1977; children: Elena, Anastassia. M in Metall. Engring., Steel and Alloys Inst., Moscow, Russia, 1980; PhD in Materials Sci., Bardin Ctrl. Rsch. Inst. for Ferrous Metallurgy, Moscow, Russia, 1991. Post-doctoral fellow Max Planck Inst., Duesseldorf, Germany, 1994—95; engr., rsch. scientist Bardin Ctrl. Rsch. Inst. for Ferrous Metallurgy, Moscow, 1980—93; rschr. materials dept. U. Calif., Santa Barbara, 1995—. Recipient Outstanding Paper award, Scripta Metallurgica et Materialia, 1994. Office: U Calif Materials Dept Santa Barbara CA 93106 Office Fax: 805-893-8971. Business E-Mail: tolpygo@engineering.ucsb.edu.

TOLSON, JOHN J. writer, editor; b. Montgomery, Ala., June 28, 1948; s. John J. and Margaret Jordan (Young) T.; m. Mary Irene Bradshaw; 1 child, Benjamin Bradshaw. AB, Princeton U., 1972; MA, Am. Univ., 1977. Instr. English and history Asheville (N.C.) Sch., 1972-74, Landon Sch., Bethesda, Md., 1974-77; free-lance writer, critic Washington, 1977-81; lit. editor The Wilson Quar., 1981-89, editor, 1989-98; sr. writer U.S. News and World Report, 1999—. Author: Pilgrim in the Ruins: A Life of Walker Percy (So. Book Nonfiction award 1992-93, Hugh Holman prize for best work of criticism and scholarship 1992), 1992; editor: The Correspondence of Shelby Foote and Walker Percy; contbr. essays and criticism to The New Republic, The Nation, The Scis., Washington Post, The Times Lit. Supplement, Civilization, other publs. Independent Scholars fellow NEH, Washington, 1989. Mem. Nat. Book Critics Circle. Home: 2010 N Lincoln St Arlington VA 22207-3729 Office: US News & World Report Ste 150 1050 Thomas Jefferson St NW Washington DC 20007-3817

TOLSTOY, NIKOLAJ THEODORSSON, civil engineer, consultant; s. Theodor and Ulla (Key) T.; m. Gunnel De Geer, Sept. 19, 1975; children: Theodor, Georg. MS in Civil Engring., Chalmers U. Tech., Gothenburg, Sweden, 1973; PhD, Royal Inst. Tech., Stockholm, 1994. Site rschr. Inst. Testing Materials and Products, Stockholm, 1973-75; info. engr. Bldg. Centre, Gothenburg, 1975-78; rschr. Swedish Inst. Bldg. Rsch., Gavle, 1978-94; bldg. cons. AB Jacobson & Widmark, Stockholm, 1994—. Capt. Swedish Navy, 1966-69. Mem. CIB Bldg. Pathology. Avocations: sailing, reading, skiing. Office: AB Jacobson & Widmark Arenavägen 7 121 88 Stockholm-Globen Sweden

TOLU, TOLU, foundation administrator; b. Washington; BBA, BS in Bus. Mgmt. Radiation Therapy Tech., Howard U. Lic. real estate broker; former lic. ins. broker, gen. agent. Fin. planner, life ins. broker, agt. recruiter and trainer EWW Fin. Svcs., 1977-86; br. mgr. Medox Health Care Svcs., 1982-83; founder, exec. dir. Tolu Found., 1986—; pres., broker EWW Real Estate, Inc., 1990-96. Pub. spkr. in field, 2001—. Author: Why and How Women Are Exploited By Men Worldwide, 1999. Mem. Internat. Toastmistress. Avocations: body building, anthropology, world politics, travel, gender bias issues. Home: PO Box 48331 Washington DC 20002-0331 E-mail: tolu2@aol.com.

TOLUIE, KAMRAN, cardiologist, electrophysiologist; b. Tehran, Iran, June 29, 1961; came to U.S., 1991; s. Kiumars Toluie and Shahin Noor Bakhsh; m. Fereshteh Salim Shahshahani, June 14, 1990; children: Sherwin, Ava. MD, Tabriz (Iran) U., 1986. Diplomate Am. Bd. Internal Medicine, Am. Bd. Cardiovascular Diseases, Am. Bd. Cardiac Electrophysiology. Resident in internal medicine SUNY, Bklyn., 1993-96; cardiology fellow Metrohealth Med. Ctr./Mt. Sinai Med. Ctr., Cleve., 1996-98; electrophysiology fellow Hosp. of U. of Pa., Phila., 1998-2000. Transl.: Introduction to ECG, 1990, Manual of Medical Procedures; contbr. chpt. to book. Fellow Am. Coll. Cardiology; mem. ACP. Avocation: tennis. Home: 4325 Beaver Hollow SE Cedar Rapids IA 52403 Office: 1002 4th Ave SE Cedar Rapids IA 52403-2425 E-mail: ktoluie@pol.net.

TOLZMANN, DON HEINRICH, curator, educator; b. Granite Falls, Minn., Aug. 12, 1945; s. Eckhart Heinrich and Pearl (Lundeberg) T.; m. Patricia Ann Himebaugh, Mar. 20, 1971; children: Anna, Katherine, Christian. BA, U. Minn., 1968; MDiv, United Theol. Sem., 1972; MA, U. Ky., 1973; PhD, U. Cin., 1983. Sr. libr., dir. German-Am. studies program U. Cin., 1974—. Author: German-Americana, 1975, America's German Heritage, 1976, German-American Literature, 1977, Festschrift, 1982, The Cincinnati Germans After the Great War, 1987, Spring Grove and its Creator, 1988, The Frist Description of Cincinnati, 1988, The Catalog of the German-Americana Collection, 1990, The First Mayor of Cincinnati, 1990, The German-American Experience, 2000. Mem. German-Am. tricentennial com. Ohio German Heritage Coun., Cin., 1983, chmn., 1990—; chmn. Ohio German Heritage Coun., 1990—; pres. German-Am. Citizens League, 1995—. Recipient Cert. of Appreciation, Pres. of U.S., 1972, Friendship award, Fed. Rep. Germany, 1986, Fed. Svc. Cross, 1991, Ohiana Humanities Citation, 1995. Mem. Soc. German-Am. Studies (pres. 1981—, award 1973). Home: 6829 Westin Rdg Cleves OH 45002-9412

TOM, C. F. JOSEPH, economics educator; b. Guangzhou, Guang Dong, People's Republic of China, May 30, 1922; came to U.S., 1939; s. Y.S. Tom and K.H. Chan; m. Grace Moy, Feb. 14, 1948. BA, Hastings Coll., 1944; MA, U. Chgo., 1947, PhD, 1963. Instr. econs. Beloit (Wis.) Coll., 1948-54; asst. prof. Lebanon Valley Coll., Annville, Pa., 1954-64, assoc. prof., 1964-67, chmn. dept. econs. and bus. adminstrn., 1964-74, prof., 1967-89, prof. emeritus, 1989—. Author: The Entrepot Trade and the Monetary Standards of Hong Kong, 1964, Monetary Problems of an Entrepot: The Hong Kong Experience, 1989. Econs.-in-Action grantee Republic Steel Corp., Case Western Res. U., Cleve., 1953; Ford Found. faculty grantee U. Pa., summer 1960; Gen. Electric Found. faculty grantee U. Va., summer 1963, UCLA, summer 1969; Econs. Seminar grantee Stel Industry, U. Chgo., 1975. Mem. Am. Econ. Assn., Hong Kong Econ. Assn. Avocations: travel, chess, golf, reading, music. Home: PO Box 125 Cornwall PA 17016-0125 Office: Lebanon Valley Coll Annville PA 17003 E-mail: tom@lvc.edu.

TOM, HOWARD S. company executive; b. N.Y.C., June 23, 1952; s. Hall Bing and Yvonne Quan Tom; m. Elena Nieves, Jan. 22, 1994. AB, Columbia U., 1974, MBA, 1976; MSSM, U. So. Calif., 1982; postgrad., Columbia U. Cert. LAN. Cost adminstr. AIL div. Eaton Corp., Deer Park, N.Y., 1984-85; fin. cons. Equitable, Citibank, J. Gregory, N.Y.C., 1986-95; tech. cons. Green Star Enterprises, Inc., L.I., 1997; v.p. contracts RK Group, Inc., N.Y.C., 1998; v.p. tech. cons. Concepts in Staffing, 1999; in bus. devel. franchisexchange-.com, 2000-01; account exec. Konica Office Products, Inc., 2001, Salience Assocs. Inc., 2001—. Lt. USN, 1976-82. Mem. Columbia Bus. Sch. Alumni Club, Guggenheim Mus., Met. Mus. Art. Republican. Roman Catholic. Avocations: opera, ballet, classical music, modern dance. Home: 229 E 12th St Apt 21 New York NY 10003-9120 E-mail: hstom@msn.com.

TOM, JAMES ROBERT, accountant; b. Odessa, Tex., Apr. 21, 1939; s. George Ellison and Mattie Inez (Zimmerman) T.; m. Frances Kay Mackey, Sept. 16, 1961; children: Susan Kay, James Robert Jr., Emily Christian. Student, Tex. A&M U., 1957; BBA in Acctg., Tex. Tech. U., 1961; postgrad., Colo. State U., 1961-62. CPA, Tex. Jr. acct. Peat, Marwick, Mitchell & Co., Midland, Tex., 1965; asst. trust officer 1st City Nat. Bank, 1966-67; sr. acct. Main Hurdman, 1967-68; v.p., trust officer 1st City Nat. Bank, 1969-72; pres. Gibson Mfg. Co., 1972-73; exec. v.p., CEO, Teraco, Inc., 1974-75; fin. cons., 1975-76; acct., 1976—. Bd. dirs. Am. Heart Assn., Midland, 1966, Arthritis Found., Midland, 1971-72, 75, Midland County Livestock Assn., Midland, 1966-72, ARC, Midland, 1970-80, Boys Club, Midland, 1971-72. 1st lt. U.S. Army, 1963-65. Mem. AICPAs, Tex. Soc. CPAs, Permian Basin CPAs. Republican. Roman Catholic. Avocations: fishing, hunting, reading. Home: 3104 Humble Ave Midland TX 79705-8207 Office: 1010 W Texas Ave Midland TX 79701-6170

TOM, LAWRENCE, engineering executive; b. L.A., Jan. 21, 1950; BS, Harvey Mudd Coll., 1972; JD, Western State U., San Diego, 1978; spl. diploma, U. Calif., San Diego, 1991. Design engr. Rockwell Internat., L.A., 1972-73, Goodrich Corp. (formerly Rohr, Inc.), Chula Vista, Calif., 1973-76, sr. design engr., 1980, computer graphics engring. specialist, 1980-83, chief engring. svcs., 1989-91, chief engring. quality, 1991-93, project mgr., 1993-98, info. tech. specialist, 1998—2002. Sr. engr. Rohr Marine, Inc., Chula Vista, 1977-79; chief exec. officer Computer Aided Tech. Svcs., San Diego, 1983-87; software cons. Small Systems Software, San Diego, 1984-85; computer graphics engring. specialist TOM & ROMAN, San Diego, 1986-88; dir. Computervision Users Group, 1986-88, vice chmn. 1988-91, pres., 1991-93, exec. chmn., 1992-94; bd. dirs. Exec. Program for Scientists and Engrs.-Alumni Assn. U. Calif., San Diego, 1991—; CFO Global Peregrine Users Group, 2001—; pres. Art to Art, San Diego, 1994-99; pres. SGL Computer Profls., San Diego, 1999—; cons. in field. George H. Mayr Found. scholar, 1971, Bates Found. Aero. Edn. scholar, 1970-72. Mem. Nat. Mgmt. Assn. (chpt. v.p.), Aircraft Owners and Pilots Assn., Infiniti Club. Office: 7770 Regents Rd Ste 113-190 San Diego CA 92122-1967 E-mail: larry.tom@sglpro.com.

TOM, LAWRENCE WAH-CHAN, pediatric otolaryngologist; b. Honolulu, Oct. 21, 1949; s. Kam Sung and Marjorie (Chun-Hoon) T.; m. Mary Shaffer, May 23, 1981; children: Christopher, Kathryn, Nicholas. BS in Biology, Trinity Coll., 1971; MD, Tulane U., 1975. Diplomate Am. Bd. Otolaryngology. Intern U. Pa., 1975-76, resident in internal medicine, 1976-80; otolaryngologist Thomas Jefferson Hosp., Phila., 1980-81, Danbury (Conn.) Hosp., 1982-86; asst. surgeon Children's Hosp. Phila., 1986—; asst. prof. U. Pa. Sch. Medicine, Phila., 1988-96, assoc. prof., 1996—. Asst. prof. Sch. Med. Thomas Jefferson U., Phila., 1980-81, U. Pa., 1988—; mem. program adv. com. Nat. Inst. on Deafness and other Comm. Disorders of NIH, Bethesda, Md., 1991—. Author: (with others) Cosmetic Occuloplastic Surgery, 1982; contbr. articles to profl. jours. Mem. Yellowstone Assn., 1993. Recipient Physician's Recognition award AMA, 1993, 1996, 1999. Fellow Am. Acad. Otolaryngology (head and neck surgery 1981), ACS, Am. Soc. Pediatric Otolaryngology; mem. Am. Laryngological, Phinological and Otological Soc., Phila. Country Club. Avocations: golf, squash. Office: Childrens Hosp Phila 3400 Civic Center Blvd Philadelphia PA 19104-4303 E-mail: tom@email.chop.edu.

TOMA, RAMSES B. food scientist, educator; b. Cairo, Nov. 9, 1938; arrived in U.S., 1968; s. Bassoum and Fieka Toma; m. Rosette Toma, Nov. 7, 1969; children: Nasmer Tomy, Kamy Tomy. BS, Ain Shams U., Cairo, 1959; MS, Ain Shams U., 1965; MS and PhD, La. State U., 1971; MPH, U. Minn., 1980. Food inspector Min. of Food Supplies, Cairo, 1961—68; quality control staff Crystal Foods, New Orleans, 1969; grad. asst. La. State U., Baton Rouge, 1969—71; dir. R&D St. Martinville Food, 1972; from asst. to assoc. prof. and chair dept. food sci. U. N.D., Grand Forks, 1972—84; prof. food sci. and nutrition Calif. State U., Long Beach, 1984—. Cons. in field; vis. prof. various univs. Contbr. Named Disting. Prof., Calif. State U., 1991, Best Advisor of the Yr., 2001. Mem.: Am. Dietetic Assn., Inst. of Technologists, Am. Chem. ., Am. Assn. Cereal Chemists, Am. Inst. Chemists. Republican. Christian Orthodox. Office: California State Univ 1250 Bellflower Blvd Long Beach CA 90840

TOMAIN, JOSEPH PATRICK, dean, law educator; b. Long Branch, N.J., Sept. 3, 1948; s. Joseph Pasquale and Bernice M. (Krzan) T.; m. Kathleen Corcione, Aug. 1, 1971; children: Joseph Anthony, John Fiore. AB, U. Notre Dame, 1970; JD, George Washington U., 1974. Bar: NJ, Iowa. Assoc. Giordano & Halleran, Middletown, N.J., 1974-76; from asst. to prof. law Drake U. Sch. Law, Des Moines, 1976-83; prof. law U. Cin. Coll. Law, 1983—, acting dean, 1989-90, dean, 1990—, Nippert prof. law, 1990—. Vis. prof. law U. Tex. Sch. Law, Austin, 1986-87. Author: Energy Law in a Nutshell, 1981, Nuclear Power Transformation, 1987; co-author: Energy Decision Making, 1983, Energy Law and Policy, 1989, Energy and Natural Resources Law, 1992, Regulatory Law and Policy, 1993, 2d edit., 1998, Energy, The Environment and the Global Economy, 2000. Bd. trustees Ctr. for Chem. Addictions Treatment, Cin., Vol. Lawyers for Poor, Cin.; mem. steering com. BLAC/CBA Round Table, Cin.; chair KnowledgeWorks Found. Served with USAR, 1970-76. Mem. ABA, Am. Law Inst., Ohio State Bar Assn. (del.), Cin. Bar Assn. (bd. trustees). Roman Catholic. Home: 3009 Springer Ave Cincinnati OH 45208-2440 Office: U Cin Coll Law Office Dean PO Box 210040 Cincinnati OH 45221-0040 E-mail: joseph.tomain@uc.edu.

TOMAINO, JOSEPH CARMINE, former retail executive, former postal inspector; b. Danbury, Conn., Dec. 12, 1948; s. Joseph and Lena Marie (LaCava) T.; m. Eileen M. Pulver (div. Feb. 1978); m. Ann C. Underriner, Sept. 20, 1986; children: Joseph Richard, Robert John. BS, Western Conn. State U., 1970; MBA, Roosevelt U., 1978, MS in Acctg., 1986. Cert. fraud examiner; diplomate of American Bd. of Law Enforcement, Am. Coll. Forensic Examiners; expert, lic. pvt. investigator, Ill. Post office clk. U.S. Postal Svc., Ridgefield, Conn., 1970-71, postal inspector Chgo., 1971-80, supervisory postal inspector, 1980-93; mgr. western ops. loss prevention dept. Walgreen Co., Deerfield, 1993-96; sr. mgr. litigation svcs. Altschuler, Melvoin & Glasser CPAs, 1996-98; dir. litigation svcs. Altschuler, Melvoin & Glasser/Am. Express Co., Chgo., 1999-2000; ptnr. Altschuler, Melvoin & Glasser CPAs, 2000—; mng. dir. Am. Express Tax & Bus. Svcs., 2000—02, Citigate G.I.S., Chgo., 2002—. Bd. dirs. Ill. State Crime Commn. Mem. Am. Soc. Indsl. Security, Fed. Law Enforcement Officers Assn., Nat. Assn. Chiefs Police, Ill. Chiefs Police, Spl. Agts. Assn., Ill. Police Assn., Nat. Soc. Pub. Accts., Assn. Cert. Fraud Examiners, Am. Coll. Forensic Examiners, Ill. Soc. CPAs. Office: Citigate GIS PO Box 966 Chicago IL 60690

TOMAIUOLO, NICHOLAS GREGORY, librarian, educator; b. Hartford, Conn., June 30, 1955; s. Carmen Peter and Victoria Lucy (DeLuca) T.; children: Benjamin David, Kristin Elizabeth. BS, U. Conn., 1977; MLS, So. Conn. State U., 1988. Cert. tchr. secondary English, Conn. Electronic resources libr. U. Conn. Health Ctr. Libr., Farmington, 1988-94; libr., bibliographic instr., assoc. libr. reference dept. Ctrl. Conn. State U., New Britain, 1994—. Instr. adult edn. Town of Wethersfield, Conn., 1995—; world wide web and bibliographic database search cons. Co-editor newsletter Elihu Burritt Libr., Ctrl. Conn. State U., 1994—. Contbr. articles to profl. publs. Mem. Conn. Libr. Assn. (at large), Beta Phi Mu (life). Republican. Roman Catholic. Home: 11 Buckland Rd Wethersfield CT 06109-1204 Office: Ctrl Conn State Univ Elihu Burritt Libr Stanley St New Britain CT 06050

TOMAJCZYK, S(TEPHEN) F(RANCIS), communications company executive, author; b. Newport, R.I., Mar. 30, 1960; s. Charles F. and Gretchen (Mintz) T.; m. Joyce J. Welch, June 21, 1991. BS in Natural Resources, U. Mich., 1982; Diploma in Profl. Photography, N.Y. Inst. Photography, 1999; grad., FEMA Emergency Mgmt. Inst., 2002. Editor IDG/CW Comms., Peterborough, N.H., 1982-83; assoc. pub. SoftSide Comms., Milford, 1983-84; mktg. dir. Ultimate Press, Inc., Nashua, 1984-88; pub. info. officer N.H. Divn. Pub. Health, Concord, 1988-96; pres. Turning Point Comm., 1996—. Sr. lectr. Franklin Pierce Coll., Nashua, N.H., 1985-88, Rivier Coll., Nashua, 1988-91; comms. cons. Ctrs. for Disease Control and Prevention, Atlanta, 1989-96; literary agent Vigliano Assocs., N.Y.C.; photo agent Check Six/Code Red, San Francisco; guest speaker in field. Author: Eyes on the Gold, 1985, The Children's Writer's Marketplace, 1987, Dictionary of the Modern United States Military, 1996, U.S. Elite Counterterrorist Forces, 1997, Bomb Squad!, 1999, 101 Ways to Survive the Y2K Crisis, 1999, Carrier Battle Group, 2000, Modern US Navy Destroyers, 2001, U.S. Counterterrorist Forces, 2002; mng. editor Am. Jour. Health Comms., 1995—; editor-in-chief DisasterMag.com, 2001--, contbr. to 6 nat. comms. manuals including Public Health Communications Workbook, 1995, HIV/AIDS Mass Communications Handbook, 1989; columnist Running Shorts, 1983-85; contbr. numerous articles to writers and popular mags. and newspapers including People, Yankee, Writer's Digest, Sportscape, Pico, Lost Treasure, SWAT mag., The Telegraph, Treasure Facts, inCider, Commodore; poetry published in poetry jours. and Am. Poetry Assn. Anthology; pub., editor-in-chief DISASTER! Mag., 2001—. Judge Harbinger awards Women in Comm., Inc., Nashua, N.H., 1991; exec. bd. mem. Nat. Pub. Health Info. Coalition, 1993-96, v.p., 1995, pres., 1995-96; mem. com.

Author's Guilds' Freedom of Expression Com., 1994—; mem. media com. Partnership for a Drug Free N.H., 1994—; mem. steering com. Nat. Pub. Health Week, 1995—. Recipient numerous awards for pub. svc. print and video including 1st Place award Pub. Svc. Print Creative Club N.H., 1990, 1st Place award NH Graniteer Awards, 1993, 94, 96, Telly award, 1993, Golden Mike award, 1994, Silver award 22d Graniteer awards, 1997. Mem. Author's Guild (freedom of expression com. 1994—), Nat. Writers Union, Nat. Pub. Health Info. Coalition (v.p. 1995, pres. 1995-96, region I rep., mem. exec. bd., 1993-96, 1st pl. prize state produced TV 1992, 1st pl. splty. item 1993-94, 1st pl. poster 1994, 1st pl. print info campaign 1995, 1st pl. pub. info. campaign 1996), Author's League Am., Soc. Profl. Journalists, Am. Med. Writers Assn., Am. Soc. Media Photographers, Internat. Assn. Counterterrorism and Security Profls., Nat. Press Photographers Assn., Internat. Assn. Emergency Mgrs. Home: 120 Hemlock Hill Dr Loudon NH 03307-0703

TOMALTY, DEREK JAMES, writer; b. Potsdam, N.Y., June 15, 1969; s. Melvin David and Sandra Jean Tomalty. Student, SUNY, Binghamton, 1988—89; BA, Potsdam Coll., 1993. Movie projectionist The Roxy, Potsdam, 1988; salesperson Radio Shack/Tandy Co., Inc., Ogdensburg, N.Y., 1989, Household Merit, Gouverneur, 1989-90; food svc. staff Potsdam Coll., 1994-95; with Confidential Svc., Canton, N.Y., 1997, No. Border Indsl., Ogdensburg, 1999—; writer The Transition box, 1999—; employee, peer advocate Step-By Step, 2000—01. Mem. World Federalist Assn., Nat. Alliance for the Mentally Ill, St. Lawrence Valley; vol./mentor North Country Self-Help, 1999. Mem.: Internat. Assn. Near-Death Studies. Unitarian Universalist. Avocations: walking, classical music, philosophy. E-mail: bach32@nothrnet.org.

TOMAN, MARY ANN, federal official; b. Pasadena, Calif., Mar. 31, 1954; d. John James and Mary Ann Zajec T.; m. Milton Allen Miller, Sept. 10, 1988; 1 child, Mary Ann III. BA with honors, Stanford U., 1976; MBA, Harvard U., 1981. Mgmt. cons. Bain and Co., Boston, 1976-77; brand mgr. Procter & Gamble Co., Cin., 1977-79; summer assoc. E.F. Hutton, N.Y.C., 1980; head corp. planning The Burton Group, PLC, London, 1981-84; pres., founder Glenclair Ltd., 1984-86; pres. London Cons. Group, London, Beverly Hills, Calif., 1987-88; mem. U.S. Presdl. Transition Team, Bus. and Fin., 1988-89; dep. asst. sec. commerce, automotive affairs, consumer goods U.S. Dept. Commerce, Washington, 1989-93; commr., chmn. L.A. Indsl. Devel. Authority, 1993-95; dep. treas. State of Calif., Sacramento, 1995-99. Bd. dirs. U.S. Coun. of Devel. Fin. Agencies, 1994-97. Founder, chair Stanford U. Fund-raising, London, 1983-88; chair Reps. Abroad Absentee Voter Registration, London, 1983-88; bd. dirs. Harvard Bus. Sch. Assn., London, 1984-87; vol. Bush-Quayle Campaign, 1988; trustee Bath Coll., Eng., 1988—; apptd. by Gov. Wilson to State of Calif. Econ. Devel. Adv. Coun., 1994-97, Jobs Tng. Coordinating Coun., 1998-2000; first vice chmn. Rep. Party L.A. County, 1996-99; chmn. Republican Party Los Angeles County, 1999—; mem. exec. bd. Coun. Calif. County Chairmen, 1999—; mem. U.S. Presdl. Transition Team, 2000-2001; Rep. candidate for Calif. State Treas., 2002. Named Calif. Mother of Yr., 1997. Mem. Stanford Club U.K. (pres. 1983-88), Harvard Club N.Y., Harvard Club Washington, Nat. Assn. of Urban Rep. County Chmn. Roman Catholic. Home: 604 N Elm Dr Beverly Hills CA 90210-3421 Office: PO Box 71483 Los Angeles CA 90071-0483

TOMANIC, JOSEPH P(AUL), retired research scientist; b. Danbury, Conn., Nov. 18, 1943; s. Joseph A. and Helen M. (Drusik) T.; m. Helen G. Brown Gannon, Apr. 15, 1967; children: Sharon A., Karen S. BEE, U. Bridgeport, 1972. Electronic technician Manson Labs., Wilton, Conn., 1964-66; assoc. rsch. scientist Schlumberger-Doll Research, Ridgefield, 1966-99; ret., 1999. Contbr. articles to profl. jours. Mem. Inst. Elec. and Electronic Engrs. Roman Catholic. Home: 36 Deepwood Dr Bethel CT 06801 E-mail: jhtomanic@netscape.net.

TOMAO, PETER JOSEPH, lawyer; b. Bklyn., Feb. 11, 1951; s. Joseph Louis and Marie A. Tomao; m. Kathryn Carter Reed, Oct. 15, 1978. BA, St. John's U., Queen's, N.Y., 1973; JD, Columbia U., 1976. Bar: N.Y. 1977, D.C. 1980, U.S. Dist. Ct. D.C., 1980, U.S. Ct. Appeals (2d cir.), 1983, U.S. Dist. Ct. (ea. dist.) N.Y. 1985, U.S. Dist. Ct. (so. dist.) N.Y. 1997. Trial atty. antitrust div. U.S. Dept. Justice, Washington, 1976-82; asst. U.S. atty. U.S. Dist. Ct. (ea. dist.) N.Y., Bklyn., Uniondale, and Garden City, N.Y., 1982-97; ptnr. Del Gadio & Tomao, Uniondale, 1997-99; pvt. practice Garden City, 1999—. Mem. Nassau County Bar Assn. (fed. cts. chair 1996-97, 99-2001, environ. law chair 2001—), N.Y. Bar Assn., Theodore Roosevelt Am. Inn of Ct. (pres. 1996-97). Office: 226 Seventh St Ste 302 Garden City NY 11530-1666 E-mail: ptomao@justice.com.

TOMAR, RICHARD THOMAS, lawyer; b. Camden, N.J., Mar. 4, 1945; s. William and Bette (Brown) T.; children: Lindsay, Leanne Meryl, Daniel Gregory. AB, Columbia Coll., 1967; JD, U. Pa., 1970. Bar: D.C. 1971, N.J. 1971, Md. 1976. Pvt. practice, Washington, 1971-73; ptnr. Philipson, Mallios & Tomar, P.C., 1973-89, Margolius, Mallios, Davis, Rider & Tomar, LLP, Washington, 1989—. Mem. D.C. Trial Lawyers Assn. (bd. dirs. 1980-89). Office: Margolius Mallios Davis Rider & Tomar LLP 1828 L St NW Ste 500 Washington DC 20036-5127 E-mail: rtomar@mmdrt.com.

TOMAR, RUSSELL HERMAN, pathologist, educator, researcher; b. Phila., Oct. 19, 1937; s. Julius and Ethel (Weinreb) T.; m. Karen J. Kent, Aug. 29, 1965; children: Elizabeth, David. BA in Journalism, George Washington U., 1959, MD, 1963. Diplomate Am. Bd. Pathology, Am. Bd. Allergy and Immunology, Am. Bd. Pathology, Immunopathology. Intern Barnes Hosp., Washington U. Sch. Medicine, 1963-64, resident in medicine, 1964-65; asst. prof. medicine SUNY, Syracuse, 1971-79, assoc. prof., 1979-88, assoc. prof. microbiology, 1980-84, prof., 1984-88, asst. prof. pathology, 1974-76, assoc. prof., 1976-83, prof., 1983-88, dir. immunopathology, 1974-88, attending physician immunodeficiency clinic, 1982-88, acting dir. microbiology, 1977-78, 82-83, interim dir. clin. pathology, 1986-87; prof. pathology and lab. medicine U. Wis. Ctr. for Health Scis., Madison, 1988—; dir. div. lab medicine U. Wis., 1988-95, dir. immunopathology and diagnostic immunology, 1995-98, prof. preventive medicine, 1999—; chair dept. pathology Cook County Hosp., Chgo., 1999—. Past mem. numerous coms. SUNY, Syracuse, U. Wis., Madison; mem. exec. com., chair and med. cons. AIDS Task Force Cen. N.Y., 1983-88. Assoc. editor Jour. Clin. Lab. Analysis; contbr. articles, rev. to profl. jours. Mem. pub. health com. Onondaga County Med. Soc., 1987-88. Lt. comdr. USPHS, 1965-67. Allergy and Immunology Div. fellow U. Pa. Fellow Coll. Am. Pathologists (diagnostics immunology rsch. com. 1993—, stds. com. 1995-97, commn. on clin. pathology 1997—), Am. Soc. Clin. Pathology (com. on continuing edn. immunopathology 1985-91, pathology data presentation com. 1976-79), Am. Acad. Allergy (penicillin hypersensitivity com. 1973-77); mem. AAAS, Am. Assn. Immunologists, Am. Assn. Pathology, Acad. Clin. Lab. Physicians and Scientists (com. on rsch. 1979-81, chairperson immunology 1979), Clin. Immunology Soc. (clin. lab. immunology com., chair coun. 1991-96). Office: Cook County Hosp Dept Pathology 627 S Wood St Ste 229 Chicago IL 60612-3810 Fax: 312-633-3364. E-mail: rtomar@hektoen.org.

TOMAR, SCOTT LANCE, dentist; b. Phila., Jan. 6, 1959; s. Robert and Jeannette L. T.; m. Jill S. Yaffe, July 12, 1981; children: Joshua, Aviel S. BA, Temple U., 1980; DMD, Temple U. Sch. of Dentistry, 1984; MPH, Columbia U. Sch. Pub. Health, 1989; DrPH, U. Mich. Sch. Pub. Health, 1993. Cert. Dental Pub. Health. Gen. dentist, Phila., 1984-88; rsch. asst. Columbia U. Sch. Pub. Health, N.Y., N.Y., 1988-89; dental pub. health res. U. Mich. Sch. Pub. Health/Mich. Dept. Pub. Health, Ann Arbor, Lansing, Mich., 1989-90; rsch. fellow U. Mich. Sch. Pub. Health, Ann Arbor, 1990-93; Epidemic Intelligence Svc. officer Ctrs. for Disease Control and Prevention, Atlanta, 1993-95, epidemiologist Office of Smoking and Health, 1995-96; asst. prof. U. Calif. San Francisco Sch. of Dentistry, 1996-98; epidemiologist/dental officer Ctrs. for Disease Control and Prevention/Divsn. Oral Health, Atlanta, 1998—2000; assoc. prof. U. Fla. Coll. Dentistry, 2000—. Dental cons. Calif. Dept. of Corps., Sacramento, 1997-99. Editor Jour. Pub. Health Dentistry, 2000—; contbr. articles to prof. jours. Mem. ADA, APHA, Am. Assn. Pub. Health Dentistry (exec. coun. 1996—, Grad. Student Merit award 2nd place 1990), Am. Assn. for Dental Rsch. Home: 5904 SW 89th Dr Gainesville FL 32608-5572 Office: U Fla Coll Dentistry Divsn Pub Health Svcs/Rsch 1600 SW Archer Rd Rm D8-38 Gainesville FL 32610-0404 Fax: 352-846-1643. E-mail: stomar@dental.ufl.edu.

TOMAR, WILLIAM, lawyer; b. Camden, N.J., Oct. 10, 1916; s. Morris and Katie (Sadinsky) T.; m. Bette Brown, Nov. 28, 1942; children: Richard T., Dean Jonathon. LLB cum laude, Rutgers U., 1939. Bar: N.J. 1940, U.S. Ct. Appeals (3d cir.) 1953, U.S. Supreme Ct. 1953, Fla. 1975, D.C. 1978. Sr. ptnr. Tomar, O'Brien, Kaplan, Jacobi & Graziano, Haddonfield, N.J., 1958—. Mem. faculty Ctr. Trial and Appellate Advocacy, Hastings Coll. Law, U. Calif., 1971-86, Nat. Coll. Advocacy, Harvard U. Law Sch., 1973-75. Mem. UN Speakers Bur., UNICEF, 1960—; mem. adv. bd. Salvation Army, 1967-84, Inst. Med. Rsch., 1967—, N.J. Capital Punishment Study Commn., 1972-73, Touro Law Sch., 1981; mem. adv. bd. N.J. Student Assistance Bd., 1987-98, vice chmn., 1992-98; bd. dirs. South Jersey Assn. Performing Arts, Haddonfield Symphony Soc., 1985—; bd. dirs., pres. 1992-99; mem. exec. bd. So. N.J. Coun. Boy Scouts Am., 1985—, pres. 1992—, Disting. Citizen award, 2001; vice chmn., mem. bd. trustees Cooper Hosp., Univ. Med. Ctr. 1979-97, bd. mem. emeritus 1998; mem. planning com. World Peace Through Law Ctr., 1970—; trustee Cooper Med. Ctr., 1979—. Recipient Disting. Alumni award Rutgers U. Sch. Law, 1996, Neighbor of Yr. award N.J. chpt. ARC, 1999; honored at Juvile Diabetes Found. South Jersey ann. gala, 2000. Fellow Am. Coll. Trial Lawyers; mem. ABA, Assn. Trial Lawyers Am. (assoc. editor jour. 1962-68, gov. 1963-64, nat. parliamentarian 1964-70, nat. exec. com. 1964-70, chmn. seminars 1965 lectr. student adv. program 1968—), World Jurist Assn. (founding mem. 1974—), N.J. Bar Assn. (fee arbitration com. 1972-74, 75-77), Trial Lawyers of N.J. (cert. by Supreme Ct. of N.J. as civil trial atty, Trial Bar award 1977), N.J. Workers Compensation Assn. (trustee 1958-83), N.Y. Trial Attys. Assn., Phila. Trial Lawyers Assn., Camden County Bar Found. (bd. trustees 1986—), Camden County Bar Assn., (com. on rels. of bench and bar 1964—, adult edn. com. 1975—). Office: 20 Brace Rd Cherry Hill NJ 08034-2634

TOMASELLI, ANTHONY ALLEN, lawyer; b. Madison, Wis., Dec. 12, 1961; s. Louis Mark and Patricia Rose (Fenske) T.; m. Lori Lynn Zoha, May 8, 1993; children: Olivia Patrice, Antonia Grace. BS, U. Wis., 1984, JD, 1988. Bar: Wis. 1988, U.S. Dist. Ct. (we. and ea. dists.) Wis. 1988, U.S. Ct. Appeals (7th and Fed. cir.), 1990. Law clk. Wis. Supreme Ct., Madison, 1988-89; assoc. Quarles & Brady LLP, 1989-97, ptnr., 1997—. Office: Quarles & Brady LLP 1 S Pinckney St Madison WI 53703-2892 E-mail: aat@quarles.com.

TOMASELLI, RENZO, railroad locomotive engineer; b. Superior, Wyo., Aug. 18, 1925; s. Chiliano and Maria (Valandro) T.; m. Phyllis Emma Fronk, Nov. 21, 1953; 1 stepchild, Michael Scott Burroughs. Student, U. Nev., 1946-47, Utah State U., 1948-50. Sect. hand So. Pacific R.R., Montello, Nev., 1942-44, machinist, helper Ogden, Utah, 1946-49, locomotive firemen, 1950-73, locomotive engr., 1973—. Pres. Brotherhood Locomotive Firemen and Enginemen, 1970-73; sec.-treas. Brotherhood Locomotive Engrs., 1977-90; mem. Ogden City planning commn. for restoration of Weber County Office Bldg., fire sta. and police sta., 1996. With USN, 1944-46. Mem. Lds Ch. Home: 3515 Madison Ave Ogden UT 84403-1002

TOMASH, DIANE, painter, educator; b. Elizabeth, N.J., Aug. 12, 1955; d. George Joseph and Catherine Agnes (Kennedy) Tomash. Grad., Newark Sch. Fine and Indsl Art, 1977; Cert., Pa. Acad. Fine Arts, 1995. Woven design colorist Dan River Co., N.Y.C., 1977-78; textile designer and colorist Covington Fabrics Co., 1978-80; freelance wallpaper designer and colorist Norman Blumenthal Inc., 1980-87, Pinkerton Prints Inc., Paterson, N.J., 1980-87; instr. art workshops Atlantic C.C., Mays Landing, 1990-95, adj. instr. art, 1997; instr. art Cygnus Creative Arts Ctr., English Creek, 1995-97. Artist in residence monotype workshop Noyes Mus., Oceanville, NJ, Stockton State Coll. Teen Arts Festival, Pomona, NJ; instr. oil painting Long Beach Island Found. Arts and Scis., Loveladies, NJ, 2002, Long Beach Island Found. of Arts. Exhibited in solo shows at Ocean County Artists Guild, Island Heights, N.J., Pine Shores Art Assn., Mamahawkin, N.J.; group shows at Woodmere Art Mus., Salmagundi Club, N.Y.C., Nat. Arts Club, N.Y.C., Pastel Soc. Am., The Hahn Gallery, Phila., Watermark Gallery, Tuckertown, N.J., numerous others; represented in collections at Pa. Acad. Fine Arts, Rohm and Haas Corp. Recipient Rohm and Haas Fine Arts Achievement award, 1995, Pres.'s award, Catherine Lorillard Wolfe Art Club, 1997, Anita E. Kertzer award, Pastel Soc. Can., 1999, Charlotte Dunwiddie Meml. award, Catherine Lorillard Wolfe Art Club, 1999, Cecilia Cardman Meml. award, 2000, Placide Daues Schriever Meml. award, Catherine Lorillard Wolfe Art Club, 2001, award of merit, Long Beach Island Found. Arts and Scis., 2002, 3d Nat. Juried Competition award of merit, Long Beach Island Found. of Arts and Sci., 2002. Fellow: Pa. Acad. Fine Arts; mem.: Creative Artists Network Phila., Creative Artists Network (Phila.), Pine Shores Art Assn., Am. Artists Profl. League (bd. dirs. 1996—97), Catherine Lorillard Wolfe Art Club (bd. dirs.). Avocation: hiking in the Catskill Mountain region and the protected N.J. Pine Barrons.

TOMASH, ERWIN, retired computer equipment company executive; b. St. Paul, Nov. 17, 1921; s. Noah and Milka (Ehrlich) T.; m. Adelle Ruben, July 31, 1943; children: Judith Sarada Tomash Diffenbaugh, Barbara Ann Tomash Bussa. BS, U. Minn., 1943; MS, U. Md., 1950. Instr. elec. engring. U. Minn., 1946; assoc. dir. computer devel. Univac div. Remington Rand Corp., St. Paul, 1947-51; dir. West Coast ops. Univac div. Sperry Rand Corp., L.A., 1953-55; pres. Telemeter Magnetics, Inc., 1956-60; v.p. Ampex Corp., 1961; founder, pres. Dataproducts Corp., 1962-71, chmn. bd., 1971-80, chmn. exec. com., 1980-89; chmn. bd., dir.. Newport Corp., Irvine, Calif., 1982-94. Founder, trustee, dir. Charles Babbage Found., U. Minn.; dir. and nat. gov. Coro Found., L.A. Served to capt. Signal Corps AUS, 1943-46. Decorated Bronze Star; recipient Outstanding Grad. award U. Minn., 1983. Mem. IEEE (sr., computer entrepeneur award 1988), Am. Soc. for Technion, History of Sci. Soc., Soc. for History of Tech., Assn. Internationale du Bibliophile. Home: 110 S Rockingham Ave Los Angeles CA 90049-2514 E-mail: etomash@ieee.org.

TOMASI, DONALD CHARLES, architect; b. Sacramento, Oct. 24, 1956; s. Thomas M. and Anita (Migliavacca) T.; m. Loretta Elaine Goveia, Feb. 1, 1986; children: Jeffrey, Genna, Michael. AB in Architecture with honors, U. Calif., Berkeley, 1979; MArch, U. Wash., 1982. Registered architect, Calif. Project mgr. Robert Wells and Assocs., Seattle, 1982-84, Milbrandt Architects, Seattle, 1984, T.M. Tomasi Architects, Santa Rosa, Calif., 1984-86; prin. Tomasi Architects, 1986-93, TLCD Architecture, Santa Rosa, 1993—. Grad. Leadership Santa Rosa, 1992; mem. design rev. com. Sonoma County, 1988-90; chmn. Santa Rosa Design Rev. Bd., 1990-97. Recipient Honor award Coalition for Adequate Sch. Housing, 1991, 93, 96, 99, Merit award, 1991. Mem. AIA (chpt. bd. dirs. 1990-91, 98, v.p. 1999, pres. 2000, Calif. Coun. bd. dirs. 2002-, Merit award 1986). Avocations: snow skiing, wine, travel.

TOMASI, THOMAS B. cell biologist, administrator; b. May 24, 1927; s. Thomas B. and Ivis (Ratazzi) T.; m. Barbara Betzold, May 27, 1995; children: Barbara, Theodore, Anne. AB, Dartmouth Coll., Hanover, N.H., 1950; MD, U. Vt., Burlington, 1954; PhD, Rockefeller U., 1965. Intern, resident, chief resident Columbia Presbyn. Hosp., N.Y.C., 1954-58, instr. medicine, 1958-60; prof., chmn. div. exptl. medicine U. Vt., Burlington, 1960-65; prof. medicine, dir. immunology SUNY, Buffalo, 1965-73; prof., chmn. immunology dept. Mayo Med. Sch., Rochester, Minn., 1973-81; dir. Cancer Ctr., Disting. Univ. prof., chmn. dept. cell biology U. N. Mex., Albuquerque, 1981-86; pres., CEO Roswell Park Cancer Inst., Buffalo, 1986-96, chmn. dept. molecular medicine, 1986-97, prof. microbiology, 1997—, prof. immunology, 1997—. Author: The Immune System of Secretions, 1976; contbr. over 200 articles to profl. jours. Served with USN, 1945-46 Mem. Am. Soc. Cell Biology, Am. Assn. Immunologists, Am. Assn. Cancer Research, Am. Soc. Clin. Investigation, Am. Fedn. Clin. Research, Assn. Am. Physicians Roman Catholic. Avocations: skiing, tennis, hunting, fishing, gardening. Office: Roswell Park Cancer Inst Elm And Carlton St Buffalo NY 14263-0001

TOMASKO, EDWARD A. financial planner; b. Stafford Springs, Conn., Sept. 18, 1943; s. Edward A. Sr. and Gertrude Ann (Burr) T.; m. Helen F. Flanagan, Oct. 18, 1969; children: Felicia, Joy. BA, Quinnipac Coll., 1966; MBA, Am. U., 1968. CFP. Direct mktg. & sales Iroquois Brands, Stamford, Conn., 1979-81; owner Tomasko Bus. Cons., Bethel, 1981-82; v.p. mktg. & consulting Excell Mktg., New Canaan, 1982; market mgr. Stauffer Chem., Westport, 1982-85; direct mktg. & sales Folz Vending, L.I., N.Y., 1986; registered rep. Moseley Securities, New Haven, 1987-88, Fahnestock & Co. Inc., Danbury, Conn., 1988-90; prin. Titan Value Equities, Hamden, 1990—. V.p. bd. govs. Quinnipac Coll.; chmn. pension and ins. commn. Town of Bethel, Conn. Mem. FPA (pres. So. Conn. chpt. 1993-96, chmn. state conf. 1992-93, adv. coun. 1997—). Republican. Avocations: photography, choir singing. Home: 20 Spring Hill Ln Bethel CT 06801-2726 Office: Mut Svc Corp Fin Strategies Investment Advisors Svc LLP 2600 Dixwell Ave Ste 1 Hamden CT 06514-1833 E-mail: EdTomasko@attglobal.net.

TOMASKY, SUSAN, corporate officer; b. Morgantown, W.Va., Mar. 29, 1953; m. Ron Ungvarsky; 1 child, Victoria. BA cum laude, Univ. Ky., 1974; JD (hons.), George Washington Univ., 1979. Staff mem. House Com. Interstate and Fgn. Commerce, Washington, 1974—76; with FERC's Office of Gen. Counsel., 1979—81; assoc. Van Ness, Feldman & Curtin, 1981—86; ptnr. Van Ness, Feldman & Curtis, 1986—93; gen. coun. Federal Energy Regulatory Commn., 1993—97; 1997ptnr. 1998Hogan & Harts, 1997-98; senior v.p., gen. coun. & Sec. Am. Electric Power Svc. Corp., Columbus, Ohio, 1998—2000, exec. v.p., gen. counsel, sec., 2000—01, exec. v.p., CFO, 2001—02. Staff mem. George Washington U. Law Rev., 1979. Trustee Columbus Symphony Orch., Columbus Sch. for Girls; co-chair Keystone Energy Bd. Mem. Greater Columbus C. of C., Phi Beta Kappa.

TOMASULA, STEVEN ANTHONY, literature educator, writer; b. Aug. 12, 1954; s. Paul and Genowefa Tomasula; m. Maria Carolina Tomasula; children: Alba Tomasula y Garcia, Ava Tomasula y Garcia. PhD, U. Ill., Chgo., 1995. Asst. prof. English U. Notre Dame, Ind., 2002—. Author: (novel) VAS: An Opera in Flatland, 2002; contbr. short fiction, art/culture criticism to jours. in field; editor: Electronic Book Rev., 1996—. Recipient Iowa prize for best lit. work in any genre, The Iowa Rev., 2000. Office: U Notre Dame English/356 O'Shaughnessy Hall Notre Dame IN 46556 E-mail: Tomasula.4@nd.edu.

TOMASULO, VIRGINIA MERRILLS, retired lawyer; b. Belleville, Ill., Feb. 10, 1919; d. Frederick Emerson and Mary Eckert (Turner) Merrills; m. Nicholas Angelo Tomasulo, Sept. 30, 1952 (dec. May 1986); m. Harrison I. Anthes, Mar. 5, 1988. BA, Wellesley Coll., 1940; LLB (now JD), Washington U., St. Louis, 1943. Bar: Mo. 1942, U.S. Ct. Appeals (D.C. cir.) 1958, Mich. 1974, U.S. Dist. Ct. (ea. dist) Mo. 1943, U.S. Supreme Ct. 1954, U.S. Tax Ct. 1974, U.S. Ct. Appeals (6th cir.) 1976. Atty. Dept. of Agr., St. Louis and Washington, 1943-48; Office of Solicitor, Chief Counsel's Office IRS, Washington and Detroit, 1949-75; assoc. Baker & Hostetler, Washington, 1977-82, ptnr., 1982-89, of counsel, 1989, ret., 1989. Sec. S.W. Day Care Assn., Washington, 1971—73; state bd. mem., mem. exec. com. Fla. Life Care Residents Assn., 2002; mem. adv. bd. Brede-Wilkins Scholarship Found. Mem.: FBA, ABA, Mo. Bar, Village on the Green Residents Assn. (chair health care com. 1999—2001, mem. fin. com., mem. coun. 1998—2000), Wellesley Club (Ctrl. Fla.). Episcopalian. Home: 570 Village Pl Apt 300 Longwood FL 32779-6037

TOMASZEK, THOMAS RICHARD, manufacturing executive; b. Blackstone, Mass., Jan. 12, 1952; s. Adolph Paul and Genevieve Barbara (Tycks) T.; m. Joyce Christine Lockwood, Dec. 18, 1952. BA, R.I. Coll., 1973; tech. cert., O'Keefe Tech., Framingham, Mass., 1979. Cert. sec. tchr., R.I. Technician, sales rep. Rockwell Internat., Charlotte, N.C., 1973-76; sales correspondent Nelmor Co., North Uxbridge, Mass., 1976-78, gen. sales mgr., 1979-87; sales mgr. Rapid Granulator Co., Rockford, Ill., 1978-79; sales, mktg. mgr. Eaglebrook East Plastics Corp., Middletown, N.Y., 1987-88; mgr. recycling ops. Plastics Again, Leominster, Mass., 1988-90; pres. N.Am. Plastics Recycling Corp., Ft. Edward, N.Y., 1990-93; v.p., gen. mgr. Nelmor Co., Inc., SBU Operations, An AEC Co., North Uxbridge, Mass, 1993-96; v.p. of sales and bus. devel. Discas, Inc., Waterbury, Conn., 1996-99; pres. DMG Mktg. divsn. of Discas; assoc. Plastic Solutions, Inc., Charlton, Mass., 1999—. Guest lectr. North Smithfield (R.I.) Hist. Soc., 1982-86, Plastics Recycling Retec, Charlotte, N.C., 1989; bd. dirs. Selectech, Inc., Taunton, Mass., Discas, Waterbury, Conn., Soc. of Plastics Engrs. recycling divsn., Discas, Inc., Waterbury, Christie Products, Inc., Waterbury; cons. plastic redesign project sponsored by EPA and 26 states, 1998—. Inventor in field. Recipient Sen. Pell award, State of R.I., 1969, Appreciation award IML Tech., Inc., North Brook, N.J., 1986. Mem. ASTM, Soc. Plastics Engrs. (sr. mem., regional dir. recycling divsn., bd. dirs. recycling divsn., Appreciation awards Chgo., 1984, Phoenix, 1979), Assn. Post-Consumer Plastics Recyclers (founding mem., voting meeting soc. of the plastics industry, tech. advisor EPA/Recycling World Plastics Recycling Study, task force to address concerns with SPI Resin Code), Founding mem./ptnr. Blackstone Ptnrs., 2002, Evergreen Partnering Group, 2001, Mass. Audubon Soc., Exch. Club. Republican. Roman Catholic. Avocations: owner of antique retail/wholesale store. Office: Plastic Solutions Inc 90 Worcester Rd Charlton MA 01507-1351 Home: PO Box 185 Blackstone MA 01504-0185 Fax: (508) 248-2022. E-mail: thomast447@aol.com.

TOMASZESKI, JOSEPHINE GALLAS, retired nursing educator; b. Manchouli, Manchuria, China, Jan. 18, 1919; d. Paul Fedorovich Kislitzin and Barbara Matveevna (Borodeev) Kislitzin-Meisel; m. John Joseph Gallas, Jan. 22, 1953 (dec. Feb. 1966); m. Julian Stephen Tomaszeski, June 10, 1972; stepchildren: Julie Ann, Mary Jane, Wayne Michael (dec.), John William. Student, Mary Washington Coll., 1937; diploma, St. Mary's Coll. Nursing, 1941; BS in Pub. Health Nursing, Cath. U. Am., 1943; MSN, U. Calif., Berkeley and San Francisco, 1960. RN, Calif.; cert. pub. health nurse, tchr., Calif. Nurse, charge nurse Children's Hosp., Washington, 1941-43; pub. health nurse Dept. Pub. Health, 1943-45; dir. outpatient clinic, nurse instr. Mary's Help Hosp., San Francisco, 1946-49; nurse, pub. health nurse, nurse instr. VA Med. Ctr. and Gen. Clinics, 1949-54; nurse instr. St. Mary's Hosp., 1954-55; asst. prof. nursing U. San Francisco, 1954-72; medicine and treatment nurse Schutz Am. Sch., Alexandria, Egypt, 1972-73; newspaper corr. Representative, Calmar, Alta., Can., 1975-81; medicine and treatment nurse Hillhaven Convalescent Hosp., San Rafael, Calif., 1982. Vol. nurse County Health Dept., Sausalito, Calif., 1956-63; vol. pollworker City of Sausalito, 1962-65; vol. city coun. campaigns, Sausalito, 1962-65; vol. Santa Venitia Cmty. Orgn., San Rafael, Calif.; vol. Ladies Aux. Can. Legion; substitute tchr. religious classes. Fed. Nursing grant Cath. U. Am., 1942-43; Fed. scholar U. Calif., Berkeley, 1959-60. Mem. ANA, AAUP, Nursing Alumni Bd. U. San Francisco (voting vol. 1982-94), NLN (sec. 1956-60), Ch. Womens Club, Colmar Royal Can. Legion Women's Aux. (exec. com. 1999--), Sigma Theta Tau, Alpha Phi Sigma. Republican. Roman Catholic. Avocations: music, reading, oil painting, fishing, writing. Home: 5114 49 Ave PO Box 444 Calmar Alberta Canada TOC 0V0

TOMASZEWSKI, KATHLEEN BERNADETTE, social worker, educator; b. Detroit, Jan. 31, 1945; d. Thomas Joseph and Margaret Rice Gilmore; m. Kenneth Patrick Tomaszewski, July 30, 1966; children: Kenneth Anthony, Kara Patricia, Kristyn Alisa, Kraig Matthew. BS, Wayne State U., 1981; MEd, U. Toledo, 1983; MSW, U. Mich., 1984. Cert. social worker, Mich. Social worker hemophilia-obstetrics, child abuse and neglect N.W. Ohio Ctr. for Women & Children, Toledo, 1984-87; social worker nephrology Hosp. for Sick Children, Toronto, Ont., Can., 1987-90; social worker cystic fibrosis and craniofacial Childrens Hosp., Phila., 1990-91; dir. placement svcs. Childrens Bur. of Del., Wilmington, 1991-92; pvt. practice in adoption and counseling Beijing, 1993-94; social worker Crittenton Hosp., Rochester Hills, Mich., 1995-97; therapist Cath. Social Svc., Flint, 1998—. Tchr. NYU, Toronto, 1991; bd. dirs. Nat. Hemophilia Assn., Toledo. Contbr. to profl. publs. Rsch. grantee Can. Kidney Assn., 1991. Mem. NASW (cert.), Am. Assn. Marriage and Family Therapists (cert., clin. assoc.), Am. Assn. Play Therapists. Avocations: writing, photography, gardening, travel. Home: 16171 Meredith Ct Linden MI 48451-9095 Fax: 232-7599.

TOMASZEWSKI, RICHARD PAUL, market representation executive; b. Flushing, N.Y., Jan. 8, 1958; s. Francis Richard and Agatha Jean (Corsaro) T.; m. Joann L. Turone, Aug. 2, 1980; children: Elizabeth Jean, Annamaria Concetta. BA in Econs. and Polit. sci. cum laude, Union Coll., Schenectady, N.Y., 1980; MBA in Mktg., Fin., Syracuse U., 1982. Grad. asst. Syracuse (N.Y.) U., 1981; field ops. analyst Ford Motor Co., Charlotte, N.C., 1982-83, zone mgr., 1983-93, mkt. representation specialist Atlanta, 1993-98, nat. employee involvement rep. Atlanta region, 1994-98, mkt. representation mgr., 1998—. Mem. Ford Motor Co. Polit. Action Com., Atlanta, 1993, Cmty. Rels. Com., 1999—. Recipient Tidmarsh scholarshp Union Coll., Schenectady, 1977; co-recipient Total Market Representation award, 1997, 99, 2000, 2001. Mem. Union Coll. Alumni Assn., Syracuse U. Alumni Assn., U.S. Tennis Assn., Atlanta Lawn Tennis Assn., Omicron Delta Epsilon, Alpha Mu Alpha.

Republican. Roman Catholic. Avocations: tennis, swimming, basketball, chess, bicycling. Office: Ford Motor Co 1455 Lincoln Pkwy E Ste 530 Atlanta GA 30346-2288 E-mail: rtomasze@ford.com.

TOMAZI, GEORGE DONALD, retired electrical engineer; b. St. Louis, Dec. 27, 1935; s. George and Sophia (Bogovich) T.; m. Lois Marie Partenheimer, Feb. 1, 1958; children: Keith, Kent. BSEE, U. Mo., Rolla, 1958, Profl. EE (hon.), 1970; MBA, St. Louis U., 1965, MSEE, 1971. Registered profl. engr., Mo., Ill., Wash., Ohio, Calif. Project engr. Union Electric Co., 1958-66; dir. corp. planning Gen. Steel Industries, 1966-70; exec. v.p. St. Louis Research Council, 1970-74, Hercules Constrn. Co., St. Louis, 1974-75; dir. design and constrn. div. Mallinckrodt, Inc., 1975-93; ret., 1993. Author: P-Science: The Role of Science in Society, 1972, The Link of Science and Religion, 1973. Active Nat. Kidney Found.; bd. dirs. U. Mo. Devel. Council, St. Louis Artists Coalition, Citizens for Modern Transit; elder Luth. Ch.; v.p. Coun. Luth Chs., St. Louis; mem. adv. com. grad. sch. U. Mo., Columbia, mem. pres.'s role and scope commn.; dir. Coun. Luth. Chs. Greater St. Louis; mem. bldg. com. Humane Soc. Mo.; pres. coun. Luth. Ch. of the Living Christ. Served with U.S. Army, 1959-61. Recipient award Acad. Elec. Engrs., U. Mo., Rolla, Achievement award Humane Soc. of Mo., special award, 1998. Mem. NSPE, IEEE (chmn. state govt. activities com. 1990-93), Japan-Am. Soc., AAAS, AIChE, Profl. Engrs. in Industry, Mo. Soc. Profl. Engrs. (Profl. Engr. in Industry 1989, pres. St. Louis chpt.), Profl. Engrs. and Land Surveyors (chmn. Mo. bd. for architects 1989-95), Am. Def. Preparedness Assn., U. Mo. Alumni Assn. (bd. dirs. 1972-78), Engrs. Club (pres. 1985-86, Achievement award 2002), Mo. Athletic Club, Rotary, Sigma Pi. Address: #44 Jamestown Farm Dr Florissant MO 63034-1405 Office: 44 Jamestown Farm Dr Florissant MO 63034-1405 E-mail: G-L-Tomazi@worldnet.att.net.

TOMB, DIANE LENEGAN, federal agency administrator; Grad., Mt. St. Mary's, Md. Assoc. dir. Office Bus. Liaison U.S. Dept. Commerce, 1991—93, dir. pub. affairs for Internat. Trade Adminstrn.; dir. pub. affairs practice, mktg. dir. Washington regional office Burson-Marsteller, 1994—97; sr. v.p. for comm. Fannie Mae Found.; asst. sec. for pub. affairs Dept. HUD, Washington, 2002—. Office: Dept HUD Pub Affairs 451 7th St SW Washington DC 20410-9000*

TOMBACK, JAY LOREN, lawyer; b. Chgo., Aug. 4, 1953; s. Seymour and Marilyn Lee (Klein) T.; m. Nancy Jo Corey, July 8, 1984; 1 child, Jarrett. BS in Acctg., U. Ill., 1976; JD, John Marshall Sch. Law, 1979. Bar: Ill. 1979, Ariz. 1980, U.S. Dist. Ct. Ariz. 1980, U.S. Tax Ct. 1980. Assoc. Robert L. Lane, Ltd., Phoenix, 1980-82; prin., bd. dirs. Lane & Tomback, Ltd., 1982-84, Lane, Tomback & Ehrlich, Ltd., Phoenix, 1984-89, Jay L. Tomback Ltd., Phoenix, 1989—. Mem. Western Pension Conf., Phoenix, 1982-92. Mem. Valley Estate Planners, Phoenix, 1980-82. Fellow Ariz. Bar Found.; mem. ABA, Internat. Assn. Fin. Planning, Am. Judicature Soc., Ill. Bar Assn., State Bar Ariz., Maricopa County Bar Assn. Office: Jay L Tomback Ltd 4000 N Central Ave Ste 1430 Phoenix AZ 85012-3506 Fax: (602) 274-1090.

TOMBAUGH, DOROTHY ELVE, retired secondary school educator, author, lecturer; b. Newark, Mar. 19, 1917; d. John E. and Edith Deming Elve; m. Roy Wilson Tombaugh, Aug. 10, 1940; children: Sandra Tombaugh Ehrman, Karen Tombaugh Dean. BS, Alfred U., 1938, DSc, 1983; MAT, Siena Heights U., 1965, DHL (hon.), 1982. Cert. med. technologist, Am. Soc. Clin. Pathologists. Med. technologist Rochester (N.Y.) Gen. Hosp., 1938-39, Sage Meml. Hosp., Ganado, Ariz., 1940, Cedars of Lebanon Hosp., L.A., 1941; spectographer, rsch. asst. Applied Rsch. Labs., Glendale, Calif., 1942-44; tchr. chemistry and biology Euclid (Ohio) H.S., 1963-79; lectr. NSF Grant, 1979-81, mainstreamed blind students in biology classes and labs, 1970-75. Judge for state and internat. sci. fairs N.E. Ohio, So. Ariz., 1965-98; lectr. NSF Chatauqua for Coll. Tchrs., 1977-80; lectr. in field. Author: Biology for the Blind, 1973; contbr. articles to profl. jours. Troop leader Girl Scouts, Eagle Rock, Calif., 1943-44, Bethel Park, Pa., 1954-55, Dayton, Ohio, 1957-59; deacon Presbyn. Ch., North Elmonte, Calif., 1947-50, Tucson, 1990-93; fin. com. YWCA, Pitts., 1954-56. Named Outstanding Biology Tchr., Nat. Assn. Biology Tchrs., Ohio, 1975. Presbyterian. Avocations: greenhouse and gardening. Home: 2341 S Circle X Pl Tucson AZ 85713-6703

TOMBAUGH, RICHARD LEE, financial aid consultant; b. Warsaw, Aug. 16, 1938; s. Wayne Hurst and Trella Marie (Kuhn) T.; m. Phyllis Cook, 1960 (div. 1967); children: Brian, Bradley; m. C. Jeannie Tombaugh, Apr. 10, 1976; children: Randall, Meagan. B of Phys. Edn., Purdue U., 1960, MS in Edn., 1961; postgrad. in higher edn., Mich. State U., 1965. Asst. unit mgr. residence halls U. Wis., Madison, 1961-63; head resident advisor Mich. State U., 1963-65; asst. dir. admissions, dir. student loans and fin. aid Purdue U., West Lafayette, Ind., 1965-72; from assoc. dir. to dir. fin. aid George Washington U., Washington, 1972-74; exec. sec. Nat. Assn. Student Fin. Aid Adminstrs., 1972-75; exec. dir. Nat. Inst. Fin. Aid Adminstrn., 1972-75; pres. Edni. Methods, Inc., Denver and Washington, 1975-79; v.p. mktg. Sys. Rsch. Inc., Washington and L.A., 1979-80; dir. Student Fin. Assistance Tng. Program, Nat. Assn. Student Fin. Aid Adminstrs., others, 1980-82; sr. program analyst Advanced Tech., Inc., Reston, Va., 1983-84; coord. market devel., mgr. ednl. svcs. Nat. Computer Sys., Inc., Englewood, Colo., 1984-88; cons., dir. need analysis svcs., dir. mktg. CSX Comml. Svcs., Jacksonville, Fla., 1989-92; pres., CEO, Edn. Fin. Cons. Group, 1992—. Columnist Greatree Gazette; contbr. articles to profl. publs. Scoutmaster Boy Scouts Am., 1956-60. Mem. Nat. Assn. Student Fin. Aid Adminstrs. (nat. coun. 1968-70, 70-75, Hall of Honor inductee, Disting. Svc. award 1975), Midwest Assn. Student Fin. Aid Adminstrs. (Disting. Svc. award 1975), DC/Del./Md. Assn. Student Fin. Aid Adminstrs. (life), Fla. Assn. Student Fin. Aid Adminstrs. Home: 2311 Barefoot Trce Atlantic Beach FL 32233-6604 Office: Edn Fin Cons Group Inc 6440 Southpoint Pkwy Ste 280 Jacksonville FL 32216-8003 E-mail: rltefcg@sprynet.com.

TOMBLIN, EARL RAY, state legislator; b. Logan County, W.Va., Mar. 15, 1952; s. Earl and Freda (Jarrell) T.; m. Joanne Jaeger, Sept. 8, 1979; 1 child, Brent Jaeger. BS, W.Va. U.; MBA, Marshall U.; postgrad., U. Charleston. Former sch. tchr.; businessman; mem. W.Va. Ho. Dels., 1974-80, W.Va. State Senate, 1980—, pres., 1995—; lt. gov. State of W.Va., Charleston, 2000—. Chmn. So. Legis. Conf. Former pres., bd. dirs. Appalachia Ednl. Lab., Inc.; mem. Logan County Devel. Authority. Mem. Kappa Alpha. Democrat. Presbyterian. Office: Capitol Bldg Rm 229M Charleston WV 25305 Address: PO Box 116 Chapmanville WV 25508-0116*

TOMBRELLO, THOMAS ANTHONY, JR. physics educator, consultant; b. Austin, Tex., Sept. 20, 1936; s. Thomas Anthony and Jeanette Lilian (Marcuse) T.; m. Esther Ann Hall, May 30, 1957 (div. Jan. 1976); children: Christopher Thomas, Susan Elaine, Karen Elizabeth; m. Stephanie Carhart Merton, Jan. 15, 1977; 1 stepchild, Kerstin Arusha. BA in Physics, Rice U., 1958, MA, 1960, PhD, 1961; Doctoral Degree (hon.), Uppsala (Sweden) U., 1997. Rsch. fellow in physics Calif. Inst. Tech., Pasadena, 1961-62, 64-65, asst. prof. physics, 1965-67, assoc. prof., 1967-71, prof., 1971—, William R. Kenan Jr. prof., 1997—, tech. assessment officer, 1996—, chair divsn. physics, math. and astronomy, 1998—; asst. prof. Yale U., New Haven, 1963. Cons. in field; disting. vis. prof. U. Calif.-Davis, 1984; v.p., dir. rsch. Schlumberger-Doll Rsch., Ridgefield, Conn., 1987-89; mem. U.S. V.P.'s Space Policy Adv. Bd., 1992; mem. sci. adv. bd. Ctr. of Nanoscale Sci. and Technology, Rice U., 1995—; bd. dirs. Schlumberger Tech. Corp., Schlumberger Found. Assoc. editor Nuc. Physics, 1971-91, Applications Nuc. Physics, 1980-89, Radiation Effects, 1985-88, Nuc. Instruments and Methods B, 1993-96. Recipient Alexander von Humboldt award von Humboldt Stiftung, U. Frankfurt, Germany, 1984-85; named Disting. Alumnus, Rice U., 1998; NSF fellow Calif. Inst. Tech., 1961-62, A.P. Sloan fellow, 1971-73. Fellow Am. Phys. Soc.; mem. AAAS, Materials Rsch. Soc., Phi Beta Kappa, Sigma Xi, Delta Phi Alpha. Democrat. Avocations: reading, jogging. Office: Calif Inst Tech Dept Physics Mail Code 200 36 Pasadena CA 91125-0001

TOMBROS, PETER GEORGE, pharmaceutical company executive; b. Oak Hill, W.Va., June 12, 1942; s. George P. and Mary Jane (Boliski) T.; m. Ann Riblett Cullen, June 12, 1965. BS, Pa. State U., 1964, MS, 1966; MBA, U. Pa., 1968. Mktg. asst. Pfizer Labs. div. Pfizer Inc., N.Y.C., 1968; asst. product mgr. Pfizer Inc., 1969, product mgr., 1970-71, group product mgr., 1972-74, v.p. mktg., 1975-80; sr. v.p., gen. mgr. Roerig div. Pfizer Inc., 1980-86; exec. v.p. Pfizer Pharms. div. Pfizer Inc., 1986-90, v.p. corp. strategic planning, 1990-94; also corp. officer Pfizer Inc.; ret. pres., CEO Enzon, Inc., Piscataway, 1994—2001, also bd. dirs.; chmn., CEO VivoQuest Inc., 2001—, also bd. dirs.; dir. Cambrex Corp., East Rutherford. Alumni fellow Penn State, 1993; bd. dirs. Pfizer Pharm. Inc., 1986-1992, Alpharma Inc., Oslo, Norway, NPS Pharm., Inc., Salt Lake City. Bd. dirs. Am. Found. for Pharm. Edn., North Plainfield, N.J., 1980-2001, past chmn.; trustee Fisk U., Nashville, 1986-96, Dominican Coll., Orangeburg, N.Y., 1987—2002; trustee Bklyn. Borough Hall Restoration, 1987-92; mem. corp. devel. com. Cen. Park Conservancy, N.Y.C., 1986-94; bd. dirs. Vote America, 1990; bd. dirs. Cancer Care. Mem. Pharm. Mfrs. Assn. (past chmn. mktg. steering com., 1986-1992), Links Club, Blind Brook Club, Masons. Avocations: marathon running, golf, tennis, skiing, bridge. Office: VivoQuest Inc 711 Executive Blvd Valley Cottage NY 10989

TOMEH, AMIN ADNAN, geotechnical engineer, consultant; b. Damascus, Syria, Apr. 17, 1971; came to U.S., 1986; s. Adnan and Souad (Idlibi) T.; m. Rula Edilbi. BSCE, U. Pitts., 1990; MSCE, Ga. Inst. Tech., 1992. Registered profl. engr., Ga., N.C. Grad. team leader researcher U. Pitts., Pitts., 1989-90; grad. rsch. asst. Ga. Inst. Tech., Atlanta, 1991-92; sr. project engr. R&D Testing & Drilling, Inc., 1992-94, dept. mgr. constrn. svcs., 1994-95; prin. Matrix Engring. Group, 1995—. Civil engring. tutor U. Pitts., 1989; project mgr. law/R&D joint venture Atlanta Fed. Ctr., Olympic Equestrian Venue, Atlanta Olympic Stadium, Olympic Shooting Venue; project engr. Hartsfield Atlanta Internat. Airport Concourse "E" project; project mgr. South Gobb Water Reclamation Facility Expansion project. Mem. ASTM, Ga. Tech. Geotech. Soc. (founding, constn. com. 1991—) Achievements include replacement up to 50% of the cement used in normal weight concrete with an oil shale ash (by-product) without affecting the compressive strength; defined aggregate breaking patterns under compaction devices. Home: 3212 Trace Views Ct Norcross GA 30071-1494 Office: 6298 Oakwood Cir Norcross GA 30093-1629

TOMEK, WILLIAM GOODRICH, agricultural economist; b. Table Rock, Nebr., Sept. 20, 1932; s. John and Ruth Genevieve (Goodrich) T. BS, U. Nebr., 1956, MA, 1957; PhD, U. Minn., 1961. Asst. prof. Cornell U., Ithaca, N.Y., 1961-66, NSF fellow, 1965, assoc. prof. agrl. econs., 1966-70, prof., 1970-99, grad. sch. prof., 2000—, chmn. dept. agrl. econs. N.Y., 1988-93. Vis. econ. USDA, 1978-79; vis. fellow Stanford U., 1968-69, U. New Eng., Australia, 1988; mem. adv. panel Rev. Agrl. Econs., 1996-98. Author: Agricultural Product Prices, 1990; editor: Am. Jour. Agrl. Econs., 1975-77; co-editor: Chgo. Bd. Trade Rsch. Symposia, 1993—; mem. editl. bd. Jour. Futures Markets, 1992-95; contbr. articles to profl. jours. Served with U.S. Army, 1953-55. Recipient Earl Combs Jr. award Chgo. Bd. Trade Found. Mem. Am. Agrl. Econs. Assn. (pres. 1985-86), Am. Econ. Assn., Econometric Soc., Northeastern Agrl. Econs. Assn., Am. Agrl. Econs. Assn. (awards 1981, 89, 97, fellow), Gamma Sigma Delta (rsch. award 1994). Democrat. Methodist. Office: Cornell U Warren Hall Ithaca NY 14853-7801 E-mail: wgt1@cornell.edu.

TOMEY, ANN LOUISE MARRINER, nursing educator; b. Holdrege, Nebr., Jan. 25, 1943; d. Wilbur Dodge and Arlene Mae (Hanni) Clawson; m. Gerald Lynn Marriner, Feb. 10, 1964 (div. 1985); m. H. Keith Tomey, Feb. 14, 1987. BSN, U. Colo., Boulder, 1967; MSN, U. Colo., Denver, 1970; PhD, U. Colo., Boulder, 1975. RN, Colo., Ind. Instr. U. Tex., San Antonio, 1970-71; asst. prof. N.Y. State U., Plattsburgh, 1971-72; lectr. Humboldt State U., Arcata, Calif., 1973-74; pub. health nurse, supr. Humboldt County Health Dept., Eureka, 1974-75; assoc. prof. nursing U. Colo., Denver, 1975-80; prof. nursing Ind. U., Indpls., 1980-92, Ind. State U., Terre Haute, 1991—. Gen. duty nurse Boulder Meml. Hosp., 1964-67; pub. health nurse Tri-County Health Dept., Aurora, Colo., 1966-67, sch. nurse Boulder City and County Health Dept., 1968-70; ind. cons., 1975—; peer mentor, S. Am., 1999—. Editor: Current Perspectives in Nursing Management, 1979 (Book of Yr.), Dimensions of Nursing Administration, 1989 (Book of Yr.); author, editor: 40 books; contbr. chapters to books, over 65 articles to profl. jours. Mem. adv. com. Ind. U. Sch. Medicine, Terre Haute, 1992-98, Ivy Tech State Coll., Terre Haute, 1992-98; mem. rev. panel United Way, Terre Haute, 1994—; chair adv. com. Midwest Ctr. for Rural Health, Terre Haute, 1996-98. Disting. lectr. Sigma Theta Tau, 1988—. Fellow: Am. Acad. Nursing; mem.: Ind. Nurses Found. (PAC chair 2001—, treas. 1996—99, 2001—), Ind. Nurses Assn. (2d v.p. 1985—89, 1st v.p. 1989, pres. 1989—91), Phi Kappa Phi (pub. rels. officer 2001—02). Avocations: reading, writing, cooking, gardening, walking. Home: 3939 S Willowbrook Ct Terre Haute IN 47802-8842 Office: Ind State U 8th And Chestnut Terre Haute IN 47809-0001 E-mail: A-Tomey@indstate.edu.

TOMEZSKO, GEORGE ANTHONY, writer; b. Philadelphia, Pa., Sept. 17, 1949; s. George Anthony and Dorothy Theresa Tomezsko. BA, La Salle Coll., Philadelphia, PA, 1971; MA, Temple U., Philadelphia, PA, 1974. Tech. writer Biosis, Philadelphia, Pa., 1976—99; editor Merck & Co., Inc., West Point, 1999—2001; tech. writer McNeil Pharm., Ft. Washington, 2002—. Author: (book) Civil War Fragments. Recipient Mem., Coll. Four Chaplains. Mem.: KC. Roman Catholic. Avocations: history, philosophy, coin collecting. Home: 808 Huntingdon Pike Hollywood PA 19046-4439

TOMHAVE, BEVERLY KORSTAD, corporate executive; b. St. Paul, Feb. 17, 1947; d. William Bernard and Dorothy Ann (Danielson) Korstad; m. Jonathan F. Tomhave, Oct. 15, 1977; children: Anna M., William D. Stefan. BA, Grinnell Coll., 1969; postgrad., U. Minn., 1974-76; student, various schs., India, Japan, Thailand, Ethiopia. Researcher Devel. Rsch. Corp., Mpls., 1965-66; researcher dept. biology Grinnell (Iowa) Coll., 1966-69; with dist. office Northwestern Bell, St. Paul, 1969-72, dist. traffic inst. Mpls., 1972-74; v.p., pres. Jonathan Studios, Plymouth, Minn., 1974—. Treas. Korridor Capital Investment, Mpls., 1986-95; bd. dirs E.D. Properties; v.p. Woodhurst Properties, LLC, 2000—. Active Human Rights Commn., St. Paul, 1969, United Fund Commn., St. Paul, 1972; adviser Jr. Achievement, St. Paul, 1973. Recipient Spectrum award Ceramic Tile Distbrs. Assn., 1988. Mem. Minn. State Hist. Soc., Sci. Mus. Minn., Minn. Bus. and Profl. Women. Avocations: genealogical research, travel, historic preservation. Office: Jonathan Studios PO Box 693 Long Lake MN 55356-0693

TOMHAVE, ROGER DOYLE, art educator; b. Fergus Falls, Minn., Jan. 7, 1955; s. Muriel Elaine Swenson Lundsetter and Doyle Earl Tomhave; m. Kristi Johnson, Aug. 11, 1979 (div.); children: Stacy Marie, Stephanie Rae. BA, U. of Wis., River Falls, WI, 1978; MA, U. of Minn., Minneapolis, MN, 1990, Ph. D, 2000. Teaching Minn., 1978, Va., 1990. Educator Stillwater Pub. Schools, Stillwater, Minn., 1977—78, Mahnomen Pub. Schools, Mahnomen, 1978—89; supr. student teachers U. of Minn., Minneapolis, 1989—91; art specialist Fairfax County Pub. Schools, Fairfax, Va., 1991—98, fine arts coord., 1998—. Rsch. asst. J Paul Getty Inst., Los Angeles, Calif., 1989—91; cons. Minn. DBAE Consortium, Minneapolis, Minn., 1990—93. Editor: (jour.) Sch. Arts Mag.; co-author: (book) Fine Arts Standards of Learning; author: Portfolio Assessment in the Visual Arts. Ednl. adv. coun. mem. Nat. Gallery of Art, Washington, 1999—99; metro supervisors Kennedy Ctr. for Performing Arts, 1990; nat. selection com. Am. Tchr. Awards, 1994—97. Recipient Supervision And Adminstrn. Art Educator Of The Yr., Nat. Art Edn. Assn., 1999, Art Educator Of The Yr., Va. Art Edn. Assn., 1997. Mem.: Virginians for the Arts, Music Educators Nat. Conf., Nat. Art Edn. Assn. (supr. 2001). Avocations: art, songwriting, theatrical performance. Office: Fairfax County Public Schools 7423 Camp Alger Avenue Falls Church VA 22042 E-mail: rogtomhave@aol.com.

TOMICH, LILLIAN, lawyer; b. L.A. d. Peter S. and Yovanka P. (Ivanovic) T. AA, Pasadena City Coll., 1954; BA in Polit. Sci., UCLA, 1956, cert. secondary tchg., 1957, MA, 1958; JD, U. So. Calif., 1961. Bar: Calif., U.S. Ct. Appeals (9th Cir.) 1978. Sole practice, 1961-66; house counsel Mfrs. Bank, L.A., 1966; assoc. Hurley, Shaw & Tomich, San Marino, Calif., 1968-76, Driscoll & Tomich, San Marino, 1976—. Dir. Continental Culture Specialists Inc., Glendale, Calif. Trustee St. Sava Serbian Orthodox Ch., San Gabriel, Calif. Recipient Episcopal Gramata award Serbian Orthodox Met. of Midwestern Am., 1993, Episcopal Gramata award Serbian Orthodox Bishop of Western Am., 1996; Charles Fletcher Scott fellow, 1957; U. So. Calif. Law Sch. scholar, 1958. Mem. ABA, Calif. Bar Assn., Los Angeles County Bar Assn., Women Lawyers Assn., San Marino C. of C., UCLA Alumni Assn., Town Hall and World Affairs Coun., Order Mast and Dagger, Iota Tau Tau, Alpha Gamma Sigma, Pi Kappa Delta. Office: 2460 Huntington Dr San Marino CA 91108-2643

TOMICH-BOLOGNESI, VERA, educator; b. L.A. d. Peter S. and Yovanka (Ivanovich) T.; m. Gino Bolognesi, July 12, 1969. AA, John Muir Jr. Coll., Pasadena, Calif., 1951; BA in Polit. Sci., UCLA, 1953, MEd, 1955, EdD, 1960. Cert. secondary tchr., Calif.; cert. secondary sch. adminstrn., Calif.; cert. jr. coll. tchr., Calif. Tchg. asst. dept. edn. UCLA, 1956; tchr., dept. chmn. Culver City (Calif.) Unified Sch. Dist., 1956-91; rschr., writer U.S. Dept. Edn., Washington, 1961, del. to Yugoslavia, 1965; co-owner, exec. Metrocolor Engring., San Gabriel, Calif., 1973—. Cons., Continental Culture Specialists, Inc., Glendale, Calif., 1985-92; rsch. asst. Law Firm of Driscoll & Tomich, San Marino, Calif., 1989—. Author: Education in Yugoslavia and the New Reform, 1963, Higher Education and Teacher Training in Yugoslavia, 1967; screenplay editor 1996—. Bd. trustees St. Sava Serbian Orthodox Ch., San Gabriel, 1975—, mem., 1960—. Recipient Episcopal Gramata, Serbian Orthodox Ch. of Western Am., 1996; named in Outstanding Young Women of Am., 1966. Mem. NEA (life), Calif. Tchrs. Assn., UCLA Alumni Assn., Alpha Gamma Sigma, Pi Lambda Theta. Home: 100 E Roses Rd San Gabriel CA 91775-2343 Office: Metrocolor Engring 5110 Walnut Grove Ave San Gabriel CA 91776-2026

TOMIKAWA, SOJI, educational institute administrator; b. Nagoya, Aichi-Ken, Japan, July 13, 1918; came to U.S., 1953; s. Tatsujiro and Yuki (Kojima) T. Law degree, Tohoku U., Sendai, Japan, 1942; MA in pub. adminstrn., Syracuse U., 1955, PhD in polit. sci., 1966. Mem. facilities subcom. Admin. Agreement U.S.-Japan Security Treaty Prime Minister's Office Japanese Govt., Tokyo, 1950-53; chief procurement officer UN Hdqs., N.Y.C., 1960-80; officer-in-charge UN Peace Keeping Emergency Force Middle East, Jerusalem, 1973-74; exec. sec. Japanese Edn. Inst. N.Y., N.Y.C., 1982-90, spl. adv. coun. for founding Greenwich Japanese Sch. Greenwich, Conn., 1990—. 1st lt. Japanese Navy, 1942-46. Decorated Order of Rising Sun, Gold and Silver Rays, H.M. Emperor Hirohito of Japan, 1994; recipient Fulbright Exchange Program scholarship, 1953-57, 46th Yomiuri Shimbun Press cert. of excellence in edn., 1997, 23rd Internat. Contribution award Kokokai exclusive cultural soc. Gtr. Nagoya Area Japan, 2000. Mem. U.S.-Japan Fulbright Alumni Assn. N.Y.C., Japan Soc. Fairfield County (Conn., chair adv. bd.), Nippon Club N.Y.C. (bd. dirs.), The Japanese Am. Assn. N.Y. Avocations: golf, swimming, hiking. Home: 68-28A 136th St Flushing NY 11367 Office: Japanes Ednl Inst 15 The Ridgeway Greenwich CT 06831-3712

TOMINAGA, MASATOSHI, anthropologist, consulting company executive; b. Tokyo, Oct. 17, 1960; came to U.S., 1991; s. Masao and Mieko Tominaga. BA, Keio U., Tokyo, 1984; MA in Adminstrn. and Policy Analysis, Stanford U., 1993. Cons. fin. and corp. loan divsn. The Mitsubishi Bank, Tokyo, 1984-85; exec. v.p. The Tokyo Indsl. Corp., Kanagawa, Japan, 1985-91; lectr. U. Penn., Phila., 1997. Editor-in-chief: Ronso, 1982-82. Mem. Am. Edn. Rsch. Assn., Am. Anthropological Assn. Home: 1815 Jfk Blvd Apt 821 Philadelphia PA 19103-1707 E-mail: tominaga@stanfordalumni.org.

TOMITA, TATSUO, pathologist, educator, diabetes researcher; b. Tokyo, Apr. 20, 1939; came to U.S., 1970; s. Tatsusaburo and Haru (Hiraga) T. MD, Tokyo Med. and Dental U., 1965; PhD, Yokohama (Japan) City U., 1970. Diplomate Am. Bd. Pathology. Asst. resident Barnes Hosp. and Washington U., St. Louis, 1970-73; resident Jewish Hosp. St. Louis, 1973-74; fellow Med. Ctr. U. Kans., Kansas City, 1974-75, asst. prof., 1975-80, assoc. prof., 1980-85, prof., 1985—. Mem. editorial bd. Internat. Assn. Pancreatology, Omaha, 1985-88; contbr. articles to Diabetes, Endocrinology, Am. Jour. Pathology, Diabetologia. Grantee NIH, 1979-84, Am. Heart Assn., 1985-87, 89-91. Mem. AAAS, Am. Assn. Pathologists, Am. Diabetes Assn. (grantee 1983-85), Sigma Xi. Achievements include in vitro analysis on diabetogenic effects of alloxan, pancreatic polypeptide producing islet cell tumors of the pancreas, pancreatic polypeptide secretion in exptl. diabetes. Home: 4707 W 65th Ter Shawnee Mission KS 66208-1360 Office: U Kans Med Ctr 39th And Rainbow Blvd Kansas City KS 66103

TOMIYASU, KIYO, consulting engineer; b. Las Vegas, Nev., Sept. 25, 1919; s. Yonema and Toyono (Kawamura) T.; m. Eiko Nakamizo, Aug. 31, 1947. BS, Calif. Inst. Tech., 1940; MS, Columbia U., 1941; M.E.S., Harvard U., 1947, PhD, 1948. Instr. Harvard U., 1948-49; head engring. sect. Sperry Gyroscope Co., Gt. Neck, N.Y., 1949-55; with GE, 1955-93; cons. engr. microwave techniques GE Valley Forge Space Ctr., Phila., 1969-93; with Martin Marietta Corp., 1993-95, Lockheed Martin Corp., Phila., 1995—. Author: The Laser Literature-An Annotated Guide, 1968; articles; patentee in field. Exec. bd. Friendship Hill Civic Assn., Paoli, Pa., 1972-73, pres., 1973. Recipient Steinmetz award Gen. Electric Co., 1977; Mgmt. and Data Systems fellow Martin Marietta Corp., 1993; established Tomiyasu Meml. ann. scholarship Calif. Inst. Tech., 1977. Fellow IEEE (life, hon. life mem. Microwave Theory and Techniques Soc. 1973, tech. activities bd., awards bd., publs. bd., bd. dirs. div. IV 1985-86, ednl. activities bd. 1987-88, Microwave Career award, 1981, Centennial medal 1984, Millennium medal 2000, established Kiyo Tomiyasu award 2000), Geosci. and Remote Sensing Soc. (hon. life; Geosci. and Remote Sensing Outstanding Svc. award 1986, Microwave Disting. Svc. award 1987); mem. Am. Phys. Soc. Home: 366 Hilltop Rd Paoli PA 19301-1211 Office: Lockheed Martin Corp PO Box 8048 Philadelphia PA 19101-8048

TOMIZUKA, MASAYOSHI, mechanical engineering educator, researcher; b. Tokyo, Mar. 31, 1946; came to U.S., 1970; s. Makoto and Shizuko (Nagatome) T.; m. Miwako Tomizawa, Sept. 5, 1971; children: Lica, Yumi. MS, Keio U., Japan, 1970; PhD, MIT, 1974. Rsch. assoc. Keio U., 1974; asst. prof. U. Calif., Berkeley, 1974-80, assoc. prof., 1980-86, prof., 1986—, Roscoe and Elizabeth Hughes prof., 1996-97, Cheryl and John Neerhout Jr. disting. prof., 1998—. Assoc. editor: Internat. Fedn. Automation Control Automatica, 1993-2000; contbr. more than 150 articles to profl. jours. NSF grantee, 1976-78, 81-83, 86-89, 93—, State of Calif. grantee, 1984-86, 88-93. Fellow ASME (chmn. dynamic systems and control divsn. 1986-87, tech. editor Jour. Dynamic Systems Measurement and Control, 1988-93), IEEE (assoc. editor IEEE control sys. mag. 1986-88, editor-in-chief IEEE/ASME Transactions on Mechatronics 1997-99), Soc. Mfg. Engrs. (mem. sci. com. 1993—). Office: U Calif Dept Mech Engring Berkeley CA 94720-0001 E-mail: tomizuka@me.berkeley.edu.

TOMJANOVICH, RUDOLPH, professional athletic coach; b. Hamtramck, Mich., Nov. 24, 1948; Scout Houston Rockets, 1981-83, asst. coach, 1983-92, head coach, 1992—. Named to Sporting News All-Am. first team, 1970; coach NBA championship team, 1994-95. Office: Houston Rockets Two Greenway Plz Ste 400 Houston TX 77046-3865*

TOMKA, PETER, Slovakian diplomat; b. Banská, Bystrica, Slovakia, June 1, 1956; s. Ján and Kornélia (Plai) T.; m. Zuzana Halgasová, June 30, 1990. Grad., Charles U., Prague, Czechoslovakia, 1979; PhD in Internat. Law, Charles U., 1985. Lectr. Law Sch., Charles U., Prague, 1980-86, assoc. lectr. in internat. law, 1986-91; asst. legal advisor Fed. Ministry of Fgn. Affairs, Czechoslovakia, 1986-90, head pub. internat. law divsn. Czechoslovakia, 1990-91; counsellor, legal advisor Permanent Mission to UN, N.Y.C., 1991-92, amb., dep. permanent rep. of Slovakia, 1993-97, charge d'affaires, 1994-97; legal advisor Ministry Fgn. Affairs, Bratislava, Slovakia, 1997-98, dir. gen. legal and consular affairs Slovakia, 1998-99; permanent rep. of Slovakia to UN, N.Y.C., 1999—. Agt. of Slovakia Internat. Ct. of Justice in Gabcikovo-Nagymaros Project Case, Hungary/Slovakia; mem. Permanent Ct. Arbitration, 1995; chmn. UN Legal Com., 1997; vice chair com. legal advisors Coun. of Europe, 1998-99, chmn. com. legal advisors, 2001—; mem. UN Internat. Law Commn., 1999—, vice chmn., 2000. Office: Perm Mission of Slovakia UN 866 U N Plz Rm 494 New York NY 10017-1822

TOMKEWITZ, MARIE ADELE, elementary school educator; b. San Antonio, Feb. 26, 1965; d. David Eugene and Marie Frances (Sergi) T. BS in Elem. Edn., S.W. Tex. State U., 1988. Tchr. 2nd grade Sinclair Elem. Sch. East Ctrl. Ind. Sch. Dist., San Antonio, 1990—, chmn. 2nd grade, 1992-93, tchr. 2nd grade Sinclair Elem. Sch. Mem. Holy Spirit Cath. Ch., San Antonio, 1965—. Mem. Kappa Delta Pi, Alpha Phi. Avocations: reading, tennis. Home: 1119 Melissa Dr San Antonio TX 78213-2028 Office: Sinclair Elem Sch 6126 Sinclair Rd San Antonio TX 78222-2400

TOMKINS, CALVIN, writer; b. Orange, N.J., Dec. 17, 1925; s. Frederick and Laura (Graves) T.; m. Grace Lloyd Fanning, Sept. 11, 1948; children: Anne Graves, Susan Temple, Spencer; m. Judy Johnston, Nov. 11, 1961 (div. Feb. 1981); m. Susan Cheever, Oct. 1, 1981; 1 child, Sarah Liley Cheever; m.

Dodie Kazanjian, May 28, 1988. BA, Princeton U., 1948. Assoc. editor Newsweek mag., N.Y.C., 1955-57, gen. editor, 1957-59; staff writer The New Yorker, 1960—. Author: The Bride and The Bachelors, 1965, Merchants and Masterpieces, 1970, Living Well Is the Best Revenge, 1971, Off the Wall, 1980, Post- to Neo-, 1988, (with Dodie Kazanjian) Alex: The Life of Alexander Liberman, 1993, Duchamp: A Biography, 1997. Bd. dirs. Cunningham Dance Found., N.Y.C., 1963-90. With USN, 1944-46. Guggenheim fellow, 1978 Mem. Authors League Am. Inc., Pen Am. Ctr. Clubs: Century (N.Y.C.). Home: 145 E 74th St New York NY 10021-3225 Office: New Yorker Mag 4 Times Sq New York NY 10036-6561

TOMKOS, IOANNIS, research scientist, communications educator; b. Athens, Greece, Mar. 15, 1973; s. Vagelis and Despina (Tsivitzi) T. BSc in Physics, U. Parma, Greece, 1994; MSc, U. Athens, 1996, postgrad., 1998—. Rschr. U. Paris, 1996; prof. Tech. Sch., Athens, 1996—; rschr. U. Athens, 1996—. Cons. in field. Contbr. articles to profl. jours. Hellenic Nat. Inst. Scholarships grant, 1991-93. Mem. IEEE, Greek Physicist Union. Greek Orthodox.

TOMKOVICZ, JAMES JOSEPH, law educator; b. L.A., Oct. 10, 1951; s. Anthony Edward and Vivian Marion (Coory) T.; m. Nancy Louise Abboud, June 27, 1987; children: Vivian Rose, Michelle Evelene, Henry James. BA, U. So. Calif., 1973; JD, UCLA, 1976. Bar: Calif. 1976, U.S. Dist. Ct. (so. dist.) Calif., U.S. Ct. Appeals (9th and 10th cirs.), U.S. Supreme Ct. Law clk. to Hon. Edward J. Schwartz, San Diego, 1976-77; law clk. to Hon. John M. Ferren Washington, 1977-78; atty. U.S. Dept. Justice, 1979-80; assoc. prof. law U. Iowa, Iowa City, 1982-86, prof., 1986—. Vis. prof. U. Iowa, Iowa City, 1981, U. Mich., Ann Arbor, 1992; adj. prof. UCLA, 1981-82. Author: (casebook) Criminal Procedure, 4th edit. (with W. White), 2001, (book) The Right to the Assistance of Counsel, 2002; (outline) Criminal Procedure, 1997; contbr. articles to profl. jours. Mem. Order of Coif, Phi Beta Kappa. Democrat. Roman Catholic. Avocations: running, softball, creative writing. Office: U Iowa Coll Law Melrose & Byngton Iowa City IA 52242 E-mail: james-tomkovicz@uiowa.edu.

TOMKOW, GWEN ADELLE, artist; b. Detroit, May 16, 1932; d. Galen A. and Edythe Christine (Barr) Roberts; m. Michael Tomkow, Nov. 14, 1953; children: Eric Michael, Thomas Edward, Nikola Christine, Kit Adair. A of Bus., Detroit Bus. Inst., 1952; student, Birmingham Bloomfield Art Assn., Assn., Mich., 1985-87, Visual Art Assn., Livonia, Mich., 1984-89. Tchr. watercolor Visual Art Assn., Livonia, 1989—; tchr. watercolor workshop Village Fine Art Assn., Milford, Mich., 1996; tchr. workshop Ella Sharp Mus. Jackson Civic Art, 1996-2001; slide lectr. Livonia Artist Club, 1995, Palette and Brush Club, Southfield, Mich., 1995, Pontiac (Mich.) Oakland Artists, 1995, Ea. Mich. U. Watercolor Soc., 1994; tchr. watercolor workshop Ann Arbor Women Painters U. Mich. Art Sch., 1997; slide lectr. Western Ohio Water Color Soc., 1999. Artist-in-residence Farmington Art Comm., Farmington Hills, 1988; slide lectr. Springfield (Ohio) Art Mus. Contbr. articles and photos to books including, , ;exhibitions include Cary Gallery, 1995, 1997, Joppich's Bay St. of Northport, 1988—98, 2000—02, Art Corridor, 1998, Represented in permanent collections E. Carothers Dunnegan Gallery of Art Mus., Bolivar, Mo. Recipient Purchase awards U.S.A. Springfield (Mo.) Art Mus., 1990, 93, 94, Watercolor U.S.A., 1999, 1st prize Helen de Roy Competition, Oakland C.C., Farmington, Mich., 1988, 92, Grumbacher Gold medal Farmington Artists Club, 1992, 2001, Farmington Hills, Mich., 1995, 98. Mem. Nat. Watercolor Soc. (signature, Alex Nepote Meml. award 1998), Mich. Watercolor Soc. (Meml. award 1992), Farmington Art Assn. (pres. 1987-89), Detroit Soc. Women Painters Sculptors (sec. 1994-95, award 1999), Palette and Brush (v.p. 1982-83), Founders Soc. Detroit Inst. Arts, Nat. Mus. Women in the Arts. Presbyterian. Avocations: tennis, golf, choir singer, theater.

TOMLIN, JAMES MILTON, lawyer; b. Springfield, Ill., July 16, 1942; s. Bernard A. and Iona M. T.; m. Carol L. Wandell, Dec. 23, 1966 (div. Mar. 1994); children: Brian, Brad, Mitch; m. Barbara Soldwedel, Aug. 24, 1998. BS, U. Ill., 1964, JD, 1967. Bar: Ill. 1968, U.S. Dist. Ct. (no. dist.) Ill. 1973. Judge adv. gen. corps. USN, 1968-71, USNR, 1971-91; atty. Westervest, Johnson, Nicol & Keller, Peoria, Ill., 1971-73; asst. corp. counsel City of Peoria, 1973-74; pvt. practice Peoria, 1974—. Mem. law adv. bd. Ctrl. Ill. C.C., Peoria, 1990-94. Bd. dirs. Neighborhood House Assn., Peoria, 1985—, former pres., Tower Pk., Peoria Heights, 1974-84; former pres. Forest Pk. Found., Peoria, bd. dirs. Lt. USN, 1968-71, capt. USNR, 1971-92, ret. Recipient Cmty. Svc. award, Ill. State Bar Assn., 2001. Avocations: skiing, golfing, bicycling. Office: 5823 N Forest Park Dr Peoria IL 61614-3559 Fax: 309-688-7581. E-mail: jtomlinlaw@aol.com.

TOMLIN, JEANNE BRANNON, real estate broker, small business owner; b. Carroll, Iowa; d. James Leonard and Mary Agnes (Cavenaugh) Brannon; widowed; children: David, Elizabeth; m. James W. Tomlin; stepchildren: Angela, Julie, Lori, Fran. A in Archtl. Tech., Ind. U. Purdue U., Indpls., 1970, student. Lic. real estate broker. Salesperson F.C. Tucker, Indpls.; mgr. Dan Nichols Builder, Greenwood, Ind.; asst. mgr. Carpenter Better Homes and Gardens, Carmel, sales broker, 1989-92, Tomlin Realtors, Greenwood, 1992-97, pres., CEO, 1997—. Mem. com. Nat. Handicapped Sports, Indpls., 1986-88; mem tech. task force Met. Indpls. Bd. Realtors, 1993-94, mem. comm. com., 1998—. Mem. Indpls. C. of C., Greenwood C. of C., Golden Key Nat. Honor Soc., Alpha Sigma Lambda. Avocations: scuba diving, skiing. Office: Tomlin Realtors 243 S Madison Ave Greenwood IN 46142-3123

TOMLIN, NANCY BARNES, tool and die maker, artist; b. Salem, Ohio, July 19, 1960; d. Teddy Lee and Shirley Ruth Barnes; m. Beth Anne Tomlin. AS in Elec. Engrng. Tech., Kent State U., Salem, 1993. In resource and prodn. Land O'Lakes, Kent, Ohio, 1993-94; designer elec. control sys. for prototype indsl. machinery Astro Tech. Svcs., Warren, 1994-98; tool and die maker Delphi Packard Electric, 1998—. Contbg. author: Voices: A Collection of Essays, Stories, and Poems on the Female Experience, 1992, The Best of the Bad Poems, 1976-99, 1999; painter. Mem. Internat. Union Elec. Workers.

TOMLIN-HOUSTON, LISA, foundation consultant; b. Bklyn., Apr. 6, 1965; d. George L. and Joan J. (Hill) Tomlin; m. Anthony Houston, Feb. 2, 1991. BA in Psychology, Oberlin Coll., Ohio, 1987; MEd in Counseling Psychology, Rutgers U., 1990. Career counselor U. Pa., Phila., 1990-93; dir. career svcs. H. John Heinz III Sch. of Public Policy and Mgmt., Carnegie Mellon U., Pitts., 1993-95; cons. The Ford Found., 1995—. Mem. Middle Atlantic Placement Assn. (com. mem. profl. devel. commn. 1990-91, chairperson new profl. com. 1991-92). Avocations: reading, travel, woman's issues. Office: The Ford Found 320 E 43rd St New York NY 10017-4890

TOMLINSON, ALEXANDER COOPER, investment banker, consultant; b. Haddonfield, N.J., May 13, 1922; s. Alexander Cooper and Mary (Buzby) T.; m. Elizabeth Anne Brierley, Jan. 10, 1953 (div.); children: William Brierley, Deborah T. Marple, Alexander Cooper III; m. Margaret L. Dickey, Nov. 15, 1986. BS, Haverford Coll., 1943; postgrad., London Sch. Econs. and Polit. Sci., 1947-48; MBA, Harvard U., 1950; LLD (hon.), Haverford Coll., 1995. With Morgan Stanley & Co., N.Y.C., 1950-76, ptnr., 1958-76, mng. dir., 1970-76; dir., pres. Morgan Stanley Can. Ltd. div., Montreal, Que., 1972-76; chmn. exec. com. First Boston, Inc., N.Y.C., 1976-82, dir., 1976-88; pres. Nat. Policy Assn., Washington, 1982-85; exec. dir. Ctr. for Privatization, 1985-88; pres. Hungarian-Am. Enterprise Fund, 1990-93; chmn. Fund for Arts and Culture in Ctrl. and Ea. Europe, 1994-97. Mem. U.S. adv. bd. Que. Hydro, 1984-95. Trustee Incorp. Village, Cove Neck, N.Y., 1958-72, 76-82, Cold Spring Harbor Lab., 1976-87, N.Y. Infirmary-Beekman Downtown Hosp., 1968-82, East Woods Sch., Oyster Bay, N.Y., 1962-70, Nature Conservancy, L.I., N.Y., 1970-82, Salisbury Sch., Conn., 1976-87, Carnegie Found. for Advancement Tchg., 1984-90; bd. mgrs. Haverford Coll., 1979—; bd. dirs. Nat. Bldg. Mus., 1987-94, Nat. Policy Assn., 1982-90, Decatur House Coun., 1990-94; chmn. Am. Friends Can., Inc., 1982-91, Harvard Bus. Sch. Fund, 1981-83. Lt. USNR, 1943-46. Mem. Coun. on Fgn. Rels., Metropolitan Club (Washington), Links (N.Y.). Home: 3314 P St NW Washington DC 20007-2701

TOMLINSON, GARY ALFRED, music educator, department chairman; b. West Point, N.Y., Dec. 4, 1951; s. John Gibson and Norma (Cerino) T.; m. Lucy Eve Kerman, June 15, 1977; children: David, Laura, Julia. BA, Dartmouth Coll., 1973; MA, U. Calif., Berkeley, 1975, PhD, 1979. Asst. prof. music U. Pa., Phila., 1979-84, assoc. prof., 1984-89, prof., 1989-96, Annenberg prof. humanities, 1996—, chmn. dept. music, 1986-89, 98—. Vis. prof. Duke U., 1983, Princeton U., 1993, Folger Shakespeare Libr., 1993; Housewright eminent vis. scholar Fla. State U., Tallahassee, 1994; vis. scholar Phi Beta Kappa 1997-98. Author: Monteverdi and the End of the Renaissance, 1987 (Deems Taylor award ASCAP 1988), Music in Renaissance Magic: Toward a Historiography of Others, 1993, Metaphysical Song: An Essay on Opera, 1999; co-author: (with Joseph Kerman) Listen, 2000; editor: (series) Italian Secular Song, 1606-1636, 7 vols., 1988-89, Strunk's Source Readings in Music History: The Renaissance, 1998, (series) New Cultural Studies; mem. editl. bd. Cambridge Opera Jour., Repercussions, music jour. Guggenheim fellow, 1982-83, fellow MacArthur Found., 1988-93. Mem. Am. Musicological Soc. (exec. bd. 1988-90, Alfred Einstein award 1982)), Renaissance Soc. Am. (exec. bd. 1989-91). Office: U Pa Dept Music 201 S 34th St Philadelphia PA 19104-6313 E-mail: gatomlin@sas.upenn.edu.

TOMLINSON, GEORGE HERBERT, retired industrial company research executive; b. Fullerton, La., May 2, 1912; emigrated to Can., 1914; s. George Herbert and Irene Loretta (Nourse) T.; m. Frances Fowler, July 17, 1937; children: Peter George, David Lester, Susan Margaret Tomlinson Goff. BA, Bishop's U., 1931; PhD, McGill U., 1935; DCL (hon.), Bishop's U., 1986. Chief chemist Howard Smith Chem. Ltd., Cornwall, Ont., Can., 1936-39; research dir. Howard Smith Paper Mills Ltd., 1939-61, Domtar Ltd., Montreal, Que., 1961-70, v.p. research and environ. tech., 1970-77, sr. sci. adv., 1977-90. Active in forestry problems in Europe and N.Am. Author book; contbr. articles to profl. jours.; patentee in field. Recipient Gov. Gen.'s Gold medal, 1931; Laureate of UN Environ. Programme Global 500, June, 1987. Fellow Royal Soc. Can., Internat. Acad. Wood Sci., Chem. Inst. Can., TAPPI (dir. 1976-79, medal 1969, hon. life mem.); mem. Am. Chem. Soc. (emeritus), Can. Pulp and Paper Assn. (hon. life mem.), Chemists Club (N.Y.). Anglican. Home: Kendal at Hanover #326 80 Lyme Rd Hanover NH 03755-1225

TOMLINSON, GERALD ARTHUR, writer, publisher, editor; b. Elmira, N.Y., Jan. 24, 1933; s. Arthur William and Margaret Delphene (Loomis) T.; m. Alexis Usakowski, Mar. 13, 1967; children: Eli Theodore, Matthew Akim. BA, Marietta (Ohio) Coll., 1955; postgrad., Columbia U., 1959-60. Jr. high tchr. Watkins Glen (N.Y.) H.S., 1955-56, Horseheads (N.Y.) Jr. H.S., 1958-59; assoc. editor Prentice Hall, Englewood Cliffs, N.J., 1960-63, Harcourt Brace Jovanovich, N.Y.C., 1963-66; sr. editor Holt, Rinehart and Winston, 1966-69; exec. editor Silver Burdett Ginn, Morristown, N.J., 1969-82; freelance writer, editor Lake Hopatcong, 1982—. Pres. Home Run Press, Lake Hopatcong, 1984—. Author: On a Field of Black, 1980, Speaker's Treasury of Political Stories, Anecdotes, and Humor, 1990; (short stories) Ellery Queen, etc., 1974—, Murdered in Jersey, 1994, Fatal Tryst, 1999, Seven Jersey Murders, 2003. Pres. Unitarian Universalist Fellowship Sussex County, Newton, N.J., 1988-90, 99-2001. With U.S. Army, 1956-58. Mem. Mystery Writers Am., Soc. for Am. Baseball Rsch., Omicron Delta Kappa, Phi Alpha Theta. Avocations: reading, photography, theater. Home and Office: 19 Harbor Dr Lake Hopatcong NJ 07849-1332 E-mail: gerrytom@juno.com.

TOMLINSON, HERBERT WESTON, lawyer; b. Upland, Pa., Feb. 11, 1930; s. Herbert Elmer and Hilda Josephine (Schlosbon) T.; m. Mary Jean Litwhiler, Oct. 27, 1961. BS, Pa. State U., 1952, postgrad., 1956-57; JD, Dickinson Sch. Law, 1960; postgrad., Temple U. Law Sch., 1969-73; BA with highest distinction, Pa. State U., 1994. Bar: Pa. 1961, U.S. Supreme Ct. 1968; lic. pilot. Law clk., pres. Delaware County Bar Assn., 1960-61; assoc. DeFuria Larkin Defuria, Chester, Pa., 1960-62, Hodge & Balderston, Chester, 1962-65, Edward McLaughlin, Chester, 1965-67; exec. dir. Legal Svcs. Program, Deleware County, 1967-69; atty. pvt. practice, Media, Pa., 1969—; sr. staff atty. Delaware County Pub. Defender's Office, 1969—. Prof. bus. law Pa. State U., 1969-75, Widener U., 1971-76, 78-80, Delaware County C.C., 1971-75; arbitrator Am. Arbitration Assn. Actor in TV commercials, 1998—. Legal counsel Disabled Vets Am.; county dir. Delaware County March of Dimes, 1966-71; rep. candidate U.S. Ho. Reps., 1976; rep. committeeman, 1966—, treas. 168th Legis. Dist., 1975-81; chmn. Media Rep. Com., 1975-76, Media Borough Auditor, 1975-79; nat. dir. Jaycees, 1965-66. Capt. USMCR, 1952-56. Named Outstanding Young Men Am. U.S. Jaycees, 1966. Mem. AAUP, ABA, Am. Assn. Trial Lawyers, Nat. Assn. Securities Dealers, Am. Arbitration Assn., Pa. Bar Assn., Pa. Trial Lawyers Assn., Delaware County Bar Assn., Delaware County Real Estate Bd., Delaware County Med. Soc. (dir. pub. health fund 1967—), Aircraft Owners and Pilots Assn., Kiwanis, Masons, Shriners, Rotary, Phi Theta Kappa (past pres.), Phi Kappa Phi, Alpha Sigma Lambda), Screen Actors Guild. Republican. Presbyterian. Home: 103 Kershaw Rd Wallingford PA 19086-6311 Office: Rm 20 247 N Middletown Rd Media PA 19063-4535 E-mail: westontomlinson@msn.com.

TOMLINSON, IAN, software engineer; b. St. Johns, Antigua, Sept. 2, 1964; s. Lydia C. (Davis) Ross; m. Averil V. Archibald, Oct. 24, 1992; children: Akil Ian, Jameel Ian. BA in Bus. Adminstrn., cert in data processing, U. V.I., 1988; MS in Info. Systems, Am. U., 1992; postgrad., George Mason U., 1994—. Database adminstrr., programmer V.I. Water and Power Auth., 1988-90; programmer, analyst, task leader Data Tree, Inc., 1990-92; sr. cons. Booz-Allen and Hamilton, Inc., 1992—; pres. Omni Systems, Inc., 1993—. Joseph and Jenny Alexander scholar, 1983; Gail E. Boggs Data Processing scholar, 1987. Mem. Assn. for Computing Machinery. Avocations: volleyball, scuba diving, motorcycles. Office: Omni Sys Inc 6255 Brandon Ave Ste 260 Springfield VA 22150-2510

TOMLINSON, J. RICHARD, engineering services company executive; b. Newtown, Pa., Mar. 26, 1930; s. Robert K. and Margaret (Wright) T.; m. Barbara Elizabeth Brazill, Apr. 30, 1955; children: Karin Kathleen Tomlinson Pizzitola, Kimberly Ann Tomlinson Donahue. BA, Swarthmore Coll., 1952; postgrad., George Washington U., 1952-53, U. Mich., 1955-57, Drexel Inst. Tech., 1954-57, Am. U., 1965. Mgmt. analyst Dept. State, Washington, 1952-53; with Old Republic Life Ins. Co., 1953-54; supr. financial analysis Ford Motor Co., Detroit, 1954-61; cons. McKinsey & Co., Washington, 1961-65; v.p. finance, dir. passenger svcs. Reading Co., Phila., 1965-69; v.p. finance Rollins Internat., Inc., 1969-71; exec. v.p. Amtrak, Washington, 1972-74; ptnr. L.T. Klauder and Assocs., 1974-75, 79-83; exec. v.p. Penn Central Transp. Co., 1975-78; pres. LTK Engring. Svcs., 1984-95; retired. Named Man of Month, Phila. C. of C., 1967 Mem. Union League, Aronimink Golf and Country Club, Phila. Aviation Country Club. Home: 451 Inveraray Rd Villanova PA 19085-1139

TOMLINSON, JAMES FRANCIS, retired news agency executive; b. Long Beach, Calif., Oct. 18, 1925; s. Lilburn Jesse and Margaret (Roemer) T.; m. Sally JoAnne Ryan, Aug. 12, 1967; children— Elizabeth Anne, Victoria Alexandra. BA, U. Va., 1950; student, Harvard U., Grad. Sch. Arts and Scis., 1950-51; grad., Advanced Mgmt. Program, Harvard U., 1977. With A.P., 1951-92, chief bur., 1957-63, bus. news editor N.Y.C., 1963-67, dep. treas., 1967-68, treas., 1968-87, v.p., 1972-92, sec., 1978-92, asst. to pres., 1987-92. Served with AUS, 1943-46, ETO. Mem. Phi Beta Kappa, Phi Eta Sigma. Clubs: N.Y. Athletic (N.Y.C.), Harvard (N.Y.C.). Home: 222 E 71st St New York NY 10021-5164

TOMLINSON, JAMES LAWRENCE, mechanical engineer; b. Detroit, Sept. 12, 1935; s. James Emmet and Ethel Pearl (Williams) T.; m. Marilyn Joyce Peterson, Aug. 24, 1957; children: James, Mary, Robert, Susan. BSME, Mich. Tech., 1957. Registered profl. engr., Mich. Design engr. Buick Motor div. GMC, Flint, Mich., 1960-61, project engr., 1961-66, sr. project engr., 1966-71; staff analysis engr. GM Corp., Warren, 1971-82, sr. staff analysis engr., 1983-88; pres. Eastport (Mich.) Engring., 1989—. Mayor City of Grand Blanc, 1985-89, city councilman, 1969-84, police liaison/commr., 1971-82, planning adv. bd., 1978-80, planning commn., 1985-89; nat. coun. mem. Boy Scouts Am., 1979-90, 93—, regional bd. mem., 1995—, coun. commr., 1979-84, coun. v.p., 1984—, nat. camp sch. staff, 1986-88, regional camp inspector/accreditation team, 1988—, subcamp chief nat. jamboree, 2001; vice chmn. Genesee County Sml. Cities and Villages Assn., 1986, chmn., 1987; bd. dirs. Three Lakes Assn., Inc., 1997—. Capt. USAF, 1958-60. Recipient Silver Beaver Tall Pine coun. Boy Scouts Am., 1980, Silver Antelope Ctrl. region, 1996. Mem. NSPE (treas. Flint chpt. 1968-72, Engr. of the Yr. Flint chpt. 1990), SAE (mem. com. 1992-94, 96-98), ASME (exec. bd. Saginaw Valley chpt. 1968-70), Friends of Torch Lake Twp., Inc. (pres. 1994—). Mem. Congl. Ch. Home: PO Box 25 Eastport MI 49627-0025

TOMLINSON, JOHN EDWARD, secret service agent; b. Alexandria, Va., Oct. 7, 1949; s. John Edward and Mary Frances (Higgins) T.; m. Suzanne Miller, Dec. 14, 1979; children: Jessica, C. Samantha, David, Timothy. BS, Va. Commonwealth U., 1971; MS, Ea. Ky. U., 1972; MS in Strategic Planning (hon.), Nat. War Coll., 1993. Grad. fellow dept. edn. Ea. Ky. U., 1971-72; officer, detective Wilmington (Del.) Bur. Police, 1972-78; spl. agt. U.S. Secret Svc., Phila., 1978-79, N.Y.C., 1979-85, Washington, 1985—. Mem. adj. faculty Brandywine Coll., Wilmington, 1972-74, Wilmington Coll., 1974-76, Salem (N.J.) C.C., 1975-77. Author: Protective Ops. Manual, 1993-94 (Treas. award 1995). Mem. Gift of Peace Charity, 1988—. Recipient Spl. Act award U.S. Dept. of Treas., 1985. Mem. Nat. War Coll. Alumni Assn. (life), U. Md. "M" Club, Alpha Phi Sigma (past sec.), Phi Theta Pi (past sec., v.p.). Roman Catholic. Avocations: jogging, basketball, racquetball, travel. Home: 9421 Copenhaver Dr Potomac MD 20854-3025

TOMLINSON, KEITH, state claims examiner; b. Jersey City, Aug. 26, 1943; s. Elmer R. and Helen S. (Saxton) T. BA, Trenton State U., 1970. File clk. N.J. Jud., Trenton, 1972-75; claims examiner Disability Ins./N.J. Labor, 1975-80, sr. claims examiner, 1980—. Mem. Camp Olden Civil War R.T., Ctrl. Jersey Genealogy Club (newsletter editor). Avocations: genealogy rsch., index records for club.

TOMLINSON, MARGARET LYNCH, lawyer; b. Cleve., June 21, 1929; d. John Joseph and Margaret (Stevenson) Lynch; m. Alexander C. Tomlinson. AB, Smith Coll., 1950; JD, N.Y. Law Sch., 1963. Bar: N.Y. 1963, D.C. 1971, U.S Ct. Appeals (D.C. cir.) 1971. Staff officer Dept. of State, 1950-55; U.S. Del. UN Gen. Assembly, N.Y.C., 1964-68; asst. legal adviser U.S. Mission to the UN, 1963-69; asst. to Sen. Claiborne Pell, Washington, 1969-71; sr. adviser U.S. Del. to the Law of the Sea Conf., 1972-78; ptnr. Dickey, Roadman & Dickey, Washington, 1978-82; cons. office gen. counsel CIA, 1987-93. Cons. Law of the Sea; bd. dirs. Coun. Ocean Law, Washington, 1984—, vice-chmn., 1994—; U.S. del. spl. session UN Gen. Assembly, 1994. Contbr. articles to profl. jours. Mem. ABA (internat. law sect., chmn. law of the sea com.), Am. Soc. Internat. Law, Internat. Law Assn., D.C. Bar Assn., Nat. Press Club, Sulgrave Club. Home: 3314 P St NW Washington DC 20007-2701

TOMLINSON, RICHARD GILES, author, consultant; b. Lima, Ohio, Mar. 20, 1936; s. Leland W. and Annie (Paulding) T.; m. Judith A. Jancy, Mar. 17, 1962; children: Ann, Amy. BS, Case Western Res. U., 1958, MS, 1960; PhD, Ohio State U., 1964; MBA, Rensselaer Poly. U., 1979. Rsch. assoc. Case Western Res. U., Cleve., 1959-60; rsch. assoc. Electrosci. Lab. Ohio State U., Columbus, Ohio, 1960-65; rsch. scientist UTC Rsch. Lab., East Hartford, Conn., 1965-80; mgr. sys. devel. UTC Bldg. Sys. Co., Hartford, 1980-85; v.p. strategic planning UTC Comms. Co., 1985-86; founder, pres. Conn. Rsch., Glastonbury, 1986—. Dir. Convergent Comms., Inc., 1997—. Author, contbg. author to 5 books in field; contbr. articles to profl. jours.; patentee in field of lasers and optics; editor, pub. newsletter Report on Competitive Telecomms., 1993-96; author, pub. Local Telecom. Competition, 1989-96. Mem. IEEE (sr.), Conn. Soc. Genealogists, Inc. (bd. govs. 1969-99, treas. 1970-99, pres. 1973-74). Avocation: genealogy. Office: Conn Rsch PO Box 1379 Glastonbury CT 06033-1027

TOMLINSON, WILLIAM HOLMES, management educator, retired army officer; b. Thornton, Ark., Apr. 12, 1922; s. Hugh Oscar and Lucy Gray (Holmes) T.; m. Dorothy Payne, June 10, 1947 (dec.); children: Jane Axtell, Lucy Gray, William Payne; m. Florence Mood Smith, May 1, 1969 (div.); m. Suzanne Scollard Gill, Mar. 16, 1977. Student, Centenary Coll., 1938-39; BS, U.S. Mil. Acad., 1943; grad., Field Arty. Sch., 1951, Air Command Staff Coll., 1958; MBA, U. Ala., 1960; MS in Internat. Affairs, George Washington U., 1966; grad., U.S. Army War Coll., 1966, Indsl. Coll. Armed Forces, 1968; PhD in Bus. Adminstrn., Am. U., 1974; grad. Advanced Mgmt. Program, Harvard U., 1968, 69. Commd. 2d lt. U.S. Army, 1943, advanced through grades to col., field arty., 1966; combat svc. in Leyte and Cebu Philippines 246 Field Arty. Bn. Americal Divsn., 1945; aide de camp to comdg. gen. Robert Eichelberger 8th U.S. Army, Japan, 1945-48; exec. officer 34 FA Bn, ops. officer 9th Divsn. Arty. Germany and Ft. Carson, Colo., 1954-57; with Office of Undersec. Army, The Pentagon, Washington, 1961-64; comdr. 2d Bn. 8th Arty. and 7th Divsn. Arty. UN Comd. South Korea, 1964-65; mem. faculty Indsl. Coll. Armed Forces, Ft. McNair, Washington, 1966-72, ret., 1973; mem. faculty U. North Fla., Jacksonville, 1972—2002, prof. mgmt., 1993—. Vis. prof. U. Glasgow, Scotland, fall 1987; vis. lectr. Moscow Linguistics U., Plekhanov Econ. U., Ulyanovsk U., Russia, fall 1993; mem. Nat. Def. Exec. Res., Fed. Emergency Mgmt. Agy., 1976—. Author: Assessment of the National Defense Executive Reserve, 1974; co-author: International Business, Theory and Practice, 1991, Business Policy and Strategy, 2000; contbr. articles to profl. jours. Mem. exec. bd. Jacksonville Campus Ministry, 1991—, pres., 2002--. Decorated Bronze Star, Legion of Merit, Philippine Liberation medal, Japanese Occupation, Asiatic Pacific with Invasion Arrow; recipient Freedom Found. award, 1967-71, Sr. Profl. in Human Resources, Tchg. Incentive award State Univ. Sys., 1994-95. Mem. SAR, Sons Confederate Vets., Soc. Human Resource Mgmt., Acad. Mgmt., Indsl. Rels. Rsch. Assn., Acad. Internat. Bus., European Internat. Bus. Assn., Internat. Trade and Fin. Assn., Exec. Svc. Corp. Bd., Co. Mil. Historians, Nat. Eagle Scout Assn., N.E. Fla. Employee Svcs. Mgmt. Assn. (charter pres. 1987-89), West Point Soc. North Fla. (pres. 1976-77), Mil. Order Stars and Bars (comdr. 1980-90), Army Navy Club, Fla. Yacht Club, Masons, Shriners, Rotary, Beta Gamma Sigma (pres. 1988-89), Kappa Alpha. Presbyterian (elder). Home: 1890 Shadowlawn St Jacksonville FL 32205-9430 Office: 1890 Shadowlawn St Jacksonville FL 32205-9430 E-mail: wtomlins@attbi.com.

TOMLINSON-KEASEY, CAROL ANN, university administrator; b. Washington, Oct. 15, 1942; d. Robert Bruce and Geraldine (Howe) Tomlinson; m. Charles Blake Keasey, June 13, 1964; children: Kai Linson, Amber Lynn. BS, Pa. State U., 1964; MS, Iowa State U., 1966; PhD, U. Calif., Berkeley, 1970. Lic. psychologist, Calif. Asst. prof. psychology Trenton (N.J.) State Coll., 1969-70, Rutgers U., New Brunswick, N.J., 1970-72; prof. U. Nebr., Lincoln, 1972-77, U. Calif., Riverside, 1977-92, acting dean Coll. Humanities and Social Scis., 1986-88, chmn. dept. psychology, 1989-92, vice provost for academic planning and pers. Davis, 1992-97, vice provost for academic initiatives, 1997-99, chancellor, 1999—. Author: Child's Eye View, 1980, Child Development, 1985; also numerous chpts. to books; articles to profl. jours. Recipient Disting. Tchr. award U. Calif., 1986. Mem. APA, Soc. Rsch. in Child Devel., Riverside Aquatics Assn. (pres.). Office: PO Box 2039 Merced CA 95344

TOMLJANOVICH, ESTHER M. state supreme court justice; b. Galt, Iowa, Nov. 1, 1931; d. Chester William and Thelma L. (Brooks) Moellering; m. William S. Tomljanovich, Dec. 26, 1957; 1 child, William Brooks. AA, Itasca Jr. Coll., 1951; BSL, St. Paul Coll. Law, 1953, LLB, 1955. Bar: Minn. 1955, U.S. Dist. Ct. Minn. 1958. Asst. revisor of statutes State of Minn., St. Paul, 1957-66, revisor of statutes, 1974-77, dist. ct. judge Stillwater, 1977-90; assoc. justice Minn. Supreme Ct., St. Paul, 1990-98. Mem. adv. bd. women offenders Minn. Dept. Corrections, 1999—; mem. leadership com. So. Minn. Legal Svcs. Corp., 1999—. Former mem. North St. Paul Bd. Edn., Maplewood Bd. Edn., Lake Elmo Planning Commn.; trustee William Mitchell Call Law, 1995—, Legal Rights Ctr., 1995—, pres., 1999; trustee So. Minn. Legal Svcs. Corp.; bd. dirs. Itasca C.C. Found., 1996—, Medica Health Ins. Co., 2001—. Recipient Centennial 2000 award William Mitchell Coll; named one of One Hundred Who Made a Difference William Mitchell Coll. Law Mem. Minn. State Bar Assn., Bus. and Profl. Women's Assn. St. Paul (former pres.), Minn. Women Laywers (founding mem.). Office: Supreme Ct MN 423 Minnesota Judicial Center 25 Constitution Ave Saint Paul MN 55155-1500

TOMME, CURTIS RABON, lawyer; b. Brady, Tex., Feb. 18, 1956; s. William Rabon Tomme and Hannah Mae Curtis; m. Elizabeth Ann Watson, Nov. 1, 1997. BS in Indsl. Distribution, Tex. A&M U., 1978; JD, Tex. Tech U., 1988. Bar: Tex. 1989. Asst. dist. atty. Taylor County, Abilene, Tex. Bd. dirs. Salvation Army, Abilene, 1998—, sec., 1999—; staff Rdy Issard for Congress Camp, Abilene, 1995-96. Mem. Abilene Bar Assn., Abilene C. of C., Abilene A&M Club (pres. 2000). Office: Taylor County Criminal Dist Atty 400 Oak St Ste 110 Abilene TX 79602-1527

TOMMEY, CHARLES ELDON, retired surgeon; b. Nashville, Jan. 13, 1922; s. William Robert and America Anna (Compton) T.; m. Clara Blair Newman, Aug. 28, 1948; children: Robert, Jean, Phillip, Dale, Scott. Student,

Henderson State Tchrs. Coll., 1940-42; BSM, U. Ark. Sch. Medicine, 1944, MD, 1945. Diplomate Am. Bd. Surgery. Intern City Hosp., Columbus, Ga., 1945-46; surg. resident Bapt. Hosp., Little Rock, 1948-49, VA Hosp., Cleve., 1950-54; pvt. practice surgery El Dorado, Ark., 1954-95; ret., 1995. Asst. clin. instr. surgery U. Ark. Coll. Medicine. Capt. U.S. Army Med. Corps, 1943-45, 46-48. Fellow ACS. Baptist. Avocations: golf, photography. Home: 123 Glenridge Pky El Dorado AR 71730-3117

TOMOEDA, CHERYL KUNIKO, academic researcher; b. Honolulu, Sept. 24, 1958; d. Charles Kunio and Doris Masue (Takehara) T. BS, U. Hawaii, 1980; MS, U. Ariz., 1982. Cert. speech-lang. pathology. Speech pathologist Amphitheater Pub. Schs., Tucson, 1983-84; rsch. asst. U. Ariz., 1982-83, rsch. asst. II, 1984-86, rsch. coord., 1985-91, sr. rsch. specialist, 1991—. Author: (test) Ariz. Battery for Comm. Disorders of Dementia, 1991, The Functional Linguistic Communication Inventory, 1994, (book) The ABC/s of Dementia, 1993, Improving Function in Dementia, 1997; prodr. videoconf. series Telerounds. Recipient U. Ariz. Asian Am. Faculty, Staff and Alumni Assn. award, 1999, Cert. of Recognition for spl. contbns. in multicultural affairs Am. Speech-Lang.-Hearing Assn., 2000. Mem. Acad. Neurologic Communication Disorders and Scis. (acting sec. 1991, sec. 1992-93), Internat. Neuropsychol. Soc., Am. Speech-Lang.-Hearing Assn. Office: U Ariz Nat Ctr Neurogenic Comm Disorders Dept Speech & Hearing Scis Tucson AZ 85721-0001

TOMOMATSU, HIDEO, chemist; b. Tokyo, June 8, 1929; arrived in U.S., 1959; s. Shinsai Nasu and Suma T.; m. Yuko Ito, Nov. 12, 1967; 1 child, Tadao. BSChemE., Waseda U., 1952; MS in Chemistry, U. of the Pacific, 1960; PhD in Chemistry, Ohio State U., 1964. Registered profl. engr., Tex., U.S. patent agt. Chem. Hodogaya Chem. Co., Tokyo, 1952-59, Texaco Chems. Co., Austin, Tex., 1964-72; Quaker fellow Quaker Oats Co., Barrington, Ill., 1972-96; cons. Functional Food Resources, Inc., Escondido, Calif., 1996—. Contbr. articles to profl. jours.; patentee in field. Mem. Am. Chem. Soc., Am. Assn. Cereal Chemists, Inst. Food Technologists. Home: 2555 Seascape Gln Escondido CA 92026-3862 E-mail: hitomoyuko@earthlink.net.

TOMOVIC, MILETA MILOS, mechanical engineer, educator; b. Belgrade, Yugoslavia, Dec. 29, 1955; came to U.S., 1979; naturalized, 1995; s. Milos Nedeljko and Danica Dane (Lemaic) T.; m. Cynthia Lou Bell, Apr. 15, 1994; children: Adriane, Milos, Senja. BS, U. Belgrade, 1979; MS, MIT, 1981; PhD, U. Mich., 1991. Rsch. asst. MIT, Cambridge, Mass., 1979-81, 83-85; design engr. Foundry Belgrade, 1982-83; sys. engr. Energoproject, Belgrade, 1985-86; assoc. prof. Purdue U., West Lafayette, Ind., 1991—; v.p. Metalcasting Engring., Inc., 1996—. Cons. Tech. Assistance Program, 1993—; mem. adv. bd. Engineered Casting Solutions. Assoc. editor Foundry, 1995—, also conf. procs. in field; author textbook on materials and mfg. processes. Grantee Purdue Rsch. Found., 1994, 95, 2001—; named Key prof. Foundry Edn. Found., 1991—; recipient Rep. Gold Medal award 2002, Dir.'s award Metal Casting Consortium, 2002. Mem. ASME (chpt. bd. dirs. 1993-95), Am. Soc. Metals (chpt. chmn. 1994-95), Am. Soc. Engring. Educators, Am. Foundrymen Soc. (chpt. bd. dirs. 1995—). Christian Orthodox. Achievements include patents in areas of metalcasting refiner plates for pulp and paper industry, mill balls for cement and metal extraction industry; research on wear and impact resistant materials, new metalcasting technologies, welding processes. Avocations: tennis, skiing, swimming. Home: 3344 Dubois St West Lafayette IN 47906-1199 Office: Purdue U MET Dept Knoy Hall West Lafayette IN 47907

TOMPANE, MARY BETH, management consultant; b. Hollywood, Calif. d. Richard F. and Mary Elizabeth (McGregor) Goss; m. Eugene F. Tompane (dec. Mar. 2001); children: Michael, Richard, Donald, John. MBA, U. Calif., Riverside, 1973; postgrad., Stanford U., 1981. Cert. mgmt. cons.; cert. vol. adminstr. Dept. head Boswell Hosp., Sun City, Ariz.; prin., owner Tompane Consulting, Phoenix & Tempe, Carlsbad, Calif. Active Girl Scouts USA, 1972—. Named Phoenix Woman of Yr., Phoenix Ad Club, 1965. Mem. LWV, Assn. Vol. Adminstrs. Home and Office: 2855 Carlsbad Blvd #N214 Carlsbad CA 92008-2902 Fax: 760-435-2590. E-mail: tomcons@earthlink.com.

TOMPERT, JAMES EMIL, lawyer; b. Battle Creek, Mich., July 21, 1954; s. James Russell and Marjorie Mary (Storkan) T. BA, Duke U., 1976; JD, U. Mich., 1981. Bar: D.C. 1981, Md. 1985, Va. 1986. Legis. asst. to congressman U.S. Ho. of Rep., Washington, 1977-78; assoc. Baker & Hostetler, 1981-84, Cooter & Gell, Washington, 1984-86, ptnr., 1987-94, Cooter Mangold Tompert & Wayson LLC, Washington, 1995—. Mem. Arts Club Washington, 1989—, Univ. Club of Washington, 1997—. Mem. ABA, D.C. Bar Assn. Office: Cooter Mangold Tompert & Wayson LLC 5301 Wisconsin Ave NW Washington DC 20015-2015 E-mail: jtompert@cootermangold.com.

TOMPKINS, CHRISTOPHER ROBIN, director, educator; b. Mt. Kisco, N.Y., Apr. 2, 1967; s. John Roger Tompkins, Sr. and Marie Helen Tompkins; m. Katherine Ann Ide Tompkins, July 31, 1993; children: Hannah Elizabeth Ide, Phoebe Neet DeVoe. BA, Colby Coll., 1989; MSSc, Syracuse U., 2000. History tchr. Wellington Sch., Columbus, Ohio, 1989—90, Greens Farms Acad., Greens Farms, Conn., 1990—93; tchr., coll. counselor Acad. Cotopax, Quito, Ecuador, 1993—94; dir. admission South Kent Sch., Kent, Conn., 1994—96; dir. admission and fin. aid St. Andrews Sewanee Sch., Sewanee, Tenn., 1996—99; asst. headmaster Canterbury Episcopal Sch., DeSoto, Tex., 1999—2000; dir. admission and fin. aid Mercersburg Acad., Mercersburg, Pa., 2000—. Chair admission com. Colby Alumni Coun., Waterville, Maine, 1997—2001; bd. dirs. Chambersburg Montessori Sch., Chambersburg, Pa. Author: (novels) Croton Dams and Aqueduct, 2000. Founding dir. Southeastern Assn. of Boarding Schs., 1997; Active St. Johns Episcopal Ch., Hagerstown, Md., 2000—. Mem.: Fountain Head C.C., Yorktown Sportsman's Club. Avocations: model railroading, stamps, golf, cross country skiing, hiking. Home and Office: 300 E Seminary St Mercersburg PA 17236-1550 Fax: 717-328-6319. E-mail: ct3408@hotmail.com.

TOMPKINS, CURTIS JOHNSTON, university president; b. Roanoke, Va., July 14, 1942; s. Joseph Buford and Rebecca (Johnston) T.; m. Mary Katherine Hasle, Sept. 5, 1964; children: Robert, Joseph, Rebecca. *Wife, Kathy, is executive director of the Pine Mountain Music Festival with opera, symphony, chamber, jazz and ensemble performances in four Upper Peninsula (Mich.) cities each summer. Son, Robert, earned BA and law degrees at Washington & Lee University and is an attorney with Patton Boggs in Washington, D.C. Son, Joseph, is a percussionist in New York City, having earned degrees from the Eastman School of Music and the Manhattan School of Music and served as principal percussionist of the Tenerife Symphony Orchestra. Daughter, Rebecca earned a degree in flute performance at West Virginia University. Brother, Deal is a consultant in planned giving. Brother, Joseph, is a partner in the law firm of Sidley, Austin,Wood & Brown.* BS, Va. Poly. Inst., 1965, MS, 1967; PhD, Ga. Inst. Tech., 1971. Indsl. engr. E.I. DuPont de Nemours, Richmond, Va., 1965-67; instr. Sch. Indsl. and Systems Engring., Ga. Inst. Tech., Atlanta, 1968-71; assoc. prof. Colgate Darden Grad. Sch. Bus. Adminstrn., U. Va., Charlottesville, 1971-77; prof., chmn. dept. indsl. engring. W.Va. U., Morgantown, 1977-80, dean Coll. Engring., 1980-91; pres. Mich. Technol. U., Houghton, 1991—, also bd. dirs. Mem. engring. accreditation commn. Accreditation Bd. for Engring. and Tech., 1981-86; mem. exec. bd. Engring. Deans Coun., 1985-89, vice chmn., 1987-89; mem. engring. adv. com., chmn. of planning com. NSF, 1988-91, chm. Mich. Univs. pres. coun., 1996-98; bd. dirs. Oak Ridge Assoc. Univs., 1996-99, Mich. Technologies, Inc., 1998-99; Pres. Coun. Assn. Governing bds. 1996—, Gov's. Workforce Commn., 1996-2002; mem. engring. adv. bd. U. Cin., 1996-99 *After serving as dean of engineering at West Virginia University for eletven years, Curt Tompkins became eighth president of Michigan Technological University (MTU) in 1991. The $44 million Dow Environmental Sciences and Engineering Building was dedicated in August, 1998, and the $20 million Rozsa Performing Arts Center, and $10 million Center for Ecosystems Sciences were dedicated in October,2000. Founded in 1885 in Houghton, Michigan, Michigan Tech is the Upper Midwest's only public, nationally ranked, doctorate-granting technological university, currently enrolls 6,500 students from more than 70 countries and has an annual operating budget of $150 million.* Author: (with L.E. Grayson) Management of Public Sector and Nonprofit Organizations, 1983, (with others) Maynard's Industrial Engineering Handbook, 1992; contbr. chpt. to Ency. of Profl. Mgmt, 1978, 83. Co-chmn. W.Va. Gov.'s Coun. on Econ. Devel.; bd. dirs. Pub. Land Corp. W.Va., 1980-89; mem. faculty Nat. Acad. Voluntarism, United Way Am., 1976-91; mem. Morgantown Water Commn., 1981-87, Morgantown Utility Bd., 1987-91; mem. steering com. W.Va. Conf. on Environ., 1985-89; chmn. Monogalia County United Way, 1989-90; campaign chmn. Copper Country United Way, 1995-96. Named to Com. of 100 Va. Tech. Coll., Disting. Alumni Acad. dept. indsl. engring; recipient Frank and Lillian Gilbreth Indsl. Engring. award Inst. Indsl. Engrs., 1998. Fellow Inst. Indsl. Engrs. (life mem., trustee 1983-90, pres. 1988-89), Am. Soc. Engring. Edn. (pres. 1990-91), Mich. Soc. Profl. Engrs.; mem. Am. Assn. Engring. Soc. (bd. govs. 1987-90, exec. com. 1987-90, sec.-treas. 1989-90), Jr. Engring. Tech. Soc. (bd. dirs. 1988-91), Nat. Soc. for Sci., Tech. and Society (bd. dirs. 1991-94), Internat. Hall of Fame of Sci. and Engring. (hon. trustee), Ga. Tech. Coll. Engring. Disting. Alumni Acad., Ga. Tech. Sch. Indsl. and Sys. Engring. Disting. Alumni Acad., W.Va. U. Dept. Indsl. Engring. Disting. Alumni Acad. (hon.), Mich. C. of C. (bd. dirs 1997—), Blue Key (hon.), Sigma Xi, Phi Kappa Phi, Tau Beta Pi, Alpha Pi Mu. Methodist. Home: 21680 Woodland Rd Houghton MI 49931-9746 Office: Mich Technol U 1400 Townsend Dr Houghton MI 49931-1200 E-mail: curt@mtu.edu.

TOMPKINS, DWIGHT EDWARD, lawyer; b. Toledo, June 29, 1952; s. Leonard Charles and Amanda Virginia (Bunce) T.; m. Marilyn Vergara, June 15, 1974; children: Jason, Kristin. BA in Anthropology, San Diego State U., 1974; MPA, Long Beach State U., 1981; JD, Loyola U., L.A., 1990. Bar: Calif. 1990, U.S. Dist. Ct. (ctrl. dist.) Calif. 1990, U.S. Dist. Ct. (so. dist.) Calif. 1991. Analyst City of Long Beach, 1985-89; law clk. Ching, Kurtz & Blix, Santa Ana, Calif., 1989-90; assoc. Ching & Assocs., 1990-91; pvt. practice Downey, Calif., 1991—. Bd. dirs. Gladius, Inc., Las Vegas, Nev., Ontrack Mgmt. Systems, Inc., Downey, Calif. Recipient Am. Jurisprudence Trial Advocacy award, 1990. Mem. Rotary (pres. 1997-98). Office: 9530 Imperial Hwy Ste E Downey CA 90242-3041

TOMPKINS, JOSEPH BUFORD, JR. lawyer; b. Roanoke, Va., Apr. 4, 1950; s. Joseph Buford and Rebvecca Louise (Johnston) T.; m. Nancy Powell Wilson, Feb. 6, 1993; children: Edward Graves, Claiborne Frobes; 1 stepchild, Clayton Tate Wilson. BA in Politics summa cum laude, Washington and Lee U., 1971; M Pub. Policy, JD, Harvard U., 1975. Bar: Va. 1975, U.S. Ct. Appeals (D.C. cir.), U.S. Ct. Appeals (5th cir.), 1977, U.S. Supreme Ct. 1977, U.S. Dist. Ct. D.C. 1982, U.S. Ct. Appeals (11th cir.) 1982, U.S. Ct. Appeals (3d cir.) 1983, U.S. Ct. Appeals (6th cir.) 1985, U.S. Ct. Appeals (7th cir.) 1991, U.S. Ct. Appeals (4th cir.) 1993. Assoc. Sidley & Austin (now Sidley Austin Brown & Wood), Washington, 1975-79, ptnr., 1982—; assoc. dir. Office Policy and Mgmt. Analysis criminal divsn. U.S. Dept. Justice, 1979-80, dep. chief fraud sect. criminal divsn., 1980-82. Contbr. articles to legal publs. Mem. Va. Bd. Health Professions, Richmond, 1984-92, vice chmn., 1984-86, chmn., 1986-88, 90-91. Mem. ABA (white collar crime com. criminal justice sect. 1980—, chmn. task foce on computer crime 1982-92), FBA, Va. Bar Assn., D.C. Bar Assn., Phi Beta Kappa, Home: 8146 Wellington Rd Alexandria VA 22308-1214 Office: Sidley Austin Brown & Wood LLP 1501 K St NW 8th Fl Washington DC 20005 Fax: 202-736-8711. E-mail: jtompkins@sidley.com.

TOMPKINS, RAYMOND EDGAR, lawyer; b. Oklahoma City, July 13, 1934; s. Charles Edgar and Eva Mae (Hodges) T.; m. Sue Anne Sharpe, June 10, 1963; children: Matthew Stephen, Christopher T., Katherine Anne. BS, Okla. State U., 1956; JD, U. Okla., 1963. Bar: Okla. 1963, U.S. Dist. Ct. (no. dist.) Okla. 1963, U.S. Dist. Ct. (we. dist.) Okla. 1964, U.S. Ct. Appeals (10th cir.) 1965, U.S. Supreme Ct. 1968, U.S. dist. Ct. (ea. dist.) Okla. 1969, U.S. Ct. Appeals (9th cir.) 1981, U.S. Ct. Appeals (4th cir.) 1986. Adminstrv. asst. U.S. Congress, 1966-68; ptnr. Linn & Helms, Oklahoma City, 1980-90, Daughery, Bradford, Haught & Tompkins, P.C., Oklahoma City, 1990-94; shareholder Conner & Winters, P.C., 1994—. Past chmn. bd. trustees Okla. Ann. Methodist Conf., St. Luke's United Meth. Ch.; past chmn. adminstrv. bd.; mem. Okla. Bur. Investigation Commn., past chmn.; past gen. counsel Rep. State com., Interstate Oil Compact. Maj. USAR. Recipient award of Honor Oklahoma City Bi-Centennial Commn., 1976. Fellow Am. Coll. Civil Trial Mediators; master William S. Holliway Am. Inns of Ct. (emeritus, pres.), Robert J. Turner Am. Inn of Ct. (pres.); mem. ABA, Okla. County Bar Assn. (Pres.'s award 1988), Okla. Bar Assn. (chmn. bench and bar com. 1995-97, chmn. ADR sect., Law Day award), Am. Arbitration Assn. (mediator/arbitrator), NASD (mediator, arbitrator), Am. Judicature Soc., Assn. Atty.-Mediators (past pres. Okla. chpt., nat. dir. and sec., Nat. President's award 2000), Blue Key, Lions (pres. Oklahoma City chpt.). Home: 3148 Birch Bark Ln Oklahoma City OK 73120 Office: 211 N Robinson Ave Ste 1700 Oklahoma City OK 73102-7136

TOMPKINS, RONALD K. surgeon; b. Malta, Ohio, Oct. 14, 1934; s. Kenneth Steidley and Mildred Lillian (Loomis) T.; m. Suzanne Colbert, June 9, 1956; children: Gregory Alan, Teresa Susan, Geoffrey Stuart. BA, Ohio U., 1956; MD, Johns Hopkins U., 1960; MS, Ohio State U., 1968; DSc (hon.), U. Bordeaux, 1995. Diplomate: Am. Bd. Surgery. Intern in surgery Ohio State U., 1960-61, resident in surgery, 1964-68, adminstrv. chief resident in surgery, 1968-69, NIH trainee in acad. surgery, instr. physiol. chemistry, 1966-69; asst. prof. surgery UCLA, 1969-73, asso. prof., 1973-79, prof., 1979-2001; prof. emeritus, 2001—; chmn. basic surg. tng. program UCLA, 1970-79, asst. dean student affairs, 1979-82, chief div. gen. surgery, 1982-88, chief gastrointestinal surgery, 1986-97, assoc. dean, 1988-91, dir. surg. edn., 1996—. Cons. VA Hosps. Editor-in-chief World Jour. Surgery, 1993— With M.C. USAF, 1961-64. Recipient Disting Alumni award, Ohio U. Arts & Scis., 2001; fellow, Royal Soc. Medicine Eng., 1976—77; grantee, NIH, 1968—70, John A. Hartford Found., 1970—79. Fellow ACS; mem. Am. Surg. Assn., Am. Gastroenterol. Assn., Am. Fedn. Clin. Rsch. Am. Inst. Nutrition, AMA, Assn. Acad. Surgery, Pacific Coast Surg. Assn. (recorder 1986-91, pres. 1995), Soc. Clin. Surgery, Soc. Surgery Alimentary Tract (sec. 1982-85, pres.-elect 1985, pres. 1986, chmn. bd. trustees 1987), Soc. Univ. Surgeons, Societe Internationale de Chirurgie (U.S. chpt. sec. 1990-94, pres. 1996-98), Internat. Biliary Assn. (pres. 1979-81), Bay Surg. Soc., L.A. Surg. Soc. (pres. 1981), ACS (So. Calif. chpt. pres. 1987), Robert M. Zollinger/Ohio State U. Surg. Soc. (pres. 1988-90), Longmire Surg. Soc. (pres. 1997-99), Phi Beta Kappa, Sigma Xi, Alpha Omega Alpha, Delta Tau Delta. Republican. Achievements include research numerous publs. in gastrointestinal surgery and gastrointestinal metabolism and biochemistry. Office: U Calif Dept of Surgery Los Angeles CA 90024

TOMPKINS, SHARON LEE, primary education educator; b. Catskill, N.Y., Oct. 27, 1961; d. Harold Emory and Joan (Phillips) T. BA in Theatre and English, Potsdam Coll. Arts and Scis., 1983; cert. in edn., Potsdam Coll., 1985; MS in Edn., Cortland Coll., 1990. Cert. primary edn. tchr., N.Y. Kindergarten educator Camden (N.Y.) Cen. Schs., 1985-89; pre 1st grade educator Catskill (N.Y.) Ctrl. Schs., 1989-94, modified 1st grade educator, 1994-95, 1st grade educator, 1995-99, 2nd grade educator, 1999—. Mem. Greene County (N.Y.) Ladies Aux., 1985—; mem. Hose Co. 1 Ladies Aux., Catskill, 1979—, sec., 1990-94; pres. Catskill Rescue Squad, 1994-95, 1st lt., 1995-96, treas. 1996-98; vice chair bd. dirs. Catskill Valley EMS, Inc., 2001-02. Mem. Catskill Tchrs. Assn. (sec. 1990-93, pres. 1993-99), DAR, Order of Eastern Star, Gamma Sigma Sigma (nat. v.p. 1989-91, chpt. pres. 1990, nat. pres. 1991-93, dist. 3 dir. 1995-97, mem. Empire Alumnae Chap., nat. parliamentarian 1999). Democrat. Methodist. Avocations: travel, reading, computer and desk top publishing, crafts. Home: 134 Park Ln Leeds NY 12451-1624 Office: Catskill Ctrl Schs Irving 1 Academy St Catskill NY 12414-1304 E-mail: sltomp@aol.com.

TOMPSON, MARIAN LEONARD, professional society administrator; b. Chgo., Dec. 5, 1929; d. Charles Clark and Marie Christine (Bernardini) Leonard; m. Clement R. Tompson, May 7, 1949 (dec. 1981); children: Melanie Tompson Kandler, Deborah Tompson Frueh, Allison Tompson Fagerholm, Laurel Tompson Davies, Sheila Tompson Doucet, Brian, Philip. Student public and parochial schs., Chgo. and Franklin Park, Ill. Co-founder La Leche League (Internat.), Franklin Park, 1956, pres., 1956-80, dir., 1956—, pres. emeritus, 1990—; exec. dir. Alternative Birth Crisis Coalition, 1981-85; co-founder, pres., exec. dir. AnotherLook, Inc., 2001—. Cons. WHO; bd. dirs. N.Am. Soc. Psychosomatic Ob-Gyn, Natural Birth and Natural Parenting, 1981-83; mem. adv. bd. Nat. Assn. Parents and Profls. for Safe Alternatives in Childbirth, Am. Acad. Husband-Coached Childbirth; mem. adv. bd. Fellowship of Christian Midwives; mem. profl. adv. bd. Home Oriented Maternity Experience; guest lectr. Harvard U. Med. Sch., UCLA Sch. Pub. Health, U. Antioquia Med. Sch., Medellín, Columbia, U. Ill. Sch. Medicine, Chgo., U. W.I., Jamaica, U. N.C., Nat. Coll. of Chiropractic, Am. Coll. Nurse Midwives, U. Parma, Italy, Inst. Psychology, Rome, Rockford (Ill.) Sch. Medicine, Northwestern U. Sch. Medicine, NGO Forum/4th World Conf. on Women, Beijing; mem. family com. Ill. Commn. on Status of Women, 1976-85; mem. perinatal adv. com. Ill. Dept. Pub. Health, 1980-83; mem. adv. bd. Internat. Nutrition Comm. Svc., 1980—; bd. cons. We Can, 1984—; exec. adv. bd. United Resources for Family Health and Support, 1985-86; mem. internat. adv. coun. World Alliance of Breast Feeding Action, 1996. Author: (with others) Safe Alternatives in Childbirth, 1976, 21st Century Obstetrics Now!, 1977, The Womanly Art of Breastfeeding, 6th edit., 1997, Five Standards for Safe Childbearing, 1981, But Doctor, About That Shot..., 1988, The Childbirth Activists Handbook, 1983; author prefaces and forwards in 11 books; columnist La Leche League News, 1958-80; columnist People's Doctor Newsletter, 1977-88, mem. adv. bd., cons., 1988-92; assoc. editor Child and Family Quar., 1967—; mem. med. adv. bd. East West Jour., 1980—; also articles. Mem. adv. bd. Shelters for Healthy Environments, 1998, Shelders for H.E., 1998-2002, The Beginning Project, 2000. Recipient Gold medal of honor Centro de Rehabilitacao Nossa Senhora da Gloria, 1975, Night of 100 Stars III Achiever award Actors Fund Am., 1990, N.Y. Soc. Ethical Culture Ethical Humanist award, 1999, 100 Women Making a Difference Today's Chgo. Woman. Mem. Nat. Assn. Postpartum Care Svcs. (adv. bd.), Chgo. Cmty. Midwives (adv. bd.), World Alliance for Breast Feeding Action (mem. internat. adv. coun. 1997). Office: 1400 N Meacham Rd Schaumburg IL 60173-4808 E-mail: m.tompson@attbi.com.

TOMS, BARBARA DELORES, lawyer, state agency administrator; b. Nashville, Mar. 16, 1949; children: Carla Martin, Jonathan Toms. JD, U. Dayton, 1983. Bar: Tenn. 1983. Pvt. practice, Nashville, 1990-93; dep. registrar Davidson County Election Commn., 1993-95; dir. divsn. of charitable solicitations State of Tenn., 1996—. Commr. Metro Bd. of Traffic and Parking, Nashville, 1999—. Mem. Tenn. Bar Assn., Napier-Looby Bar Assn. Office: Office of Sec of State 312 Eighth Ave N 8th Fl Nashville TN 37243 Fax: 615-253-5173. E-mail: Barbara.Toms@state.tn.us.

TOMS, MICHAEL ANTHONY, broadcast journalist, editor, writer, producer; b. Washington, June 7, 1940; s. Austin Herman Toms and Margaret Dorothy (Pitcher) Slavinsky; m. Justine Willis, Dec. 16, 1972; children: Michael Anthony, Robert Welch. Student, U. Miami, 1959-60, U. Va. Extension, 1961-63; postgrad., Calif. Inst. Integral Studies, San Francisco, 1973-75; DrTheology, Sem. St. Basil the Great, Sydney, Australia, 1981; DHL (hon.), U. Humanistic Studies, San Diego, 1983. Field govt. rep. VariTyper Corp., Washington, 1960-64, sales mgr. San Francisco, 1964-67, regional sales mgr. San Bernardino, 1967-68; pres. Creative Mktg. Assocs., San Francisco, 1968-73; chmn. bd. The Response Mktg. Group, 1971-73; CEO Michael A. Toms & Assocs., 1973-76; pres. New Dimensions Found., 1973—. Sr. acquisitions editor Harper Collins, San Francisco, 1989-95; exec. prodr., host nat. pub. radio interview series New Dimensions, 1980—, on-line radio series Spirit of the Times, 1999—; chmn. bd. emeritus Calif. Inst. Integral Studies, San Francisco, 1979-83; exec. dir. Audio Inds., Inc., San Francisco, 1981-83; adj. prof. Marylhurst Coll. Grad. Sch. of Bus., 1993—, Union Grad. Sch., 1994—; founder, CEO New Dimensions Broadcasting Network, 1994—; exec. editor New Dimensions Book Series, 1993—; mem. bd. dirs. KQED, Inc., San Francisco, 1980-83, Green Earth Found., 1989-95, KZYX-FM, Mendocino County, Calif., 1989-91; mem. bd. adv. The Great Round, 1989-95. Author: Worlds Beyond, 1978, The New Healers, 1980, An Open Life, 1988, At The Leading Edge, 1991, Wise Words, 1997, The Power of Meditation and Prayer, 1997, The Well of Creativity, 1997, The Soul of Business, 1997, Roots of Healing, 1997, Money, Money, Money, 1998, Buddhism in the West, 1998; co-author: True Work, 1998; exec. prodr.: Spirit of the Times, Deep Ecology for the 21st Century; editor The Inner Edge newsletter, 1997—. Mem. Task Force to Promote Self Esteem and Personal and Social Responsibility, Mendocino County, Calif., 1988-89; mem. internat. adv. bd. Radio for Peace Internat., 1988—; bd. dirs. Human Potential Audio Found., 1994-97; mem. adv. bd. New Road Map Found., 1991—. Mem. Internat. Assn. for Socially Responsible Radio (founding dir. 1991—). Avocations: travel, writing, reading, birdwatching. Home: PO Box 1029 Ukiah CA 95482-1029 Office: New Dimensions Found PO Box 569 Ukiah CA 95482-0569

TOMSKY, JUDY, fundraiser and event planner, importer; b. Oklahoma City, Nov. 28, 1959; d. Mervin and Helen (Broude) T. Student, Hebrew U. of Jerusalem, 1979-80; BA in Liberal Studies, Sonoma State U., 1981. Telemktg. supr., mktg. and advt. coord. The Sharper Image, San Francisco, 1983-85; br. mgr., acct. exec. advt. Marin Express Ltd., Corte Madera, 1986; spl. events coord., fundraiser Sausalito, 1987; Pacific N.W. regional dir. Jewish Nat. Fund, San Francisco, 1987-90; event mgmt., mktg. and promotion specialist, 1990-93; devel. dir. Insight Meditation West, Woodacre, Calif., 1993-94; propr. import/wholesale bus. Sonoma, 1994—. Avocations: beading, travel, hiking, vipassana meditation.

TOMSON, JON SCOTT, business professional; b. Rochester, N.Y., Dec. 13, 1948; s. Peter and Genevieve Helen Tomson; m. Carol Neuman, June 24, 1973; children: Brett Neuman, Christopher William. B of Indsl. Engring., Kettering U., 1971; M of Urban Planning, CUNY, 1974. Asst. dir. N.J. Dept. Higher Edn., Trenton, 1974—77; dir. human resources N.J. Dept. Human Svcs., 1977—81; dir. sales and mktg. Getinge Internat., Lakewood, NJ, 1981—90; prin. CUH2A, Inc., Princeton, 1990—. Trustee Forum Inst. for Pub. Policy , Princeton, 1999—, Friends of Old Yellow Meeting House, Allentown, N.J., 1980—. Mem.: Internat. Soc. Pharm. Engring. (officer 1995—, chmn. bd. 2002, Mem. of Yr. 1995), Soc. Coll. and Univ. Planning, Soc. Mktg. Profl. Svcs., Am. Inst. Cert. Planners. Avocations: soccer, skiing, scuba diving. Office: CUH2A Inc 211 Carnegie Ctr Princeton NJ 08540

TONDEL, LAWRENCE CHAPMAN, lawyer; b. N.Y.C., Apr. 9, 1946; s. Lyman Mark and Jean (Basch) T.; m. Sharyn A. Smith, Aug. 3, 1974; children: Michael Lawrence, Kathryn Chapman. Student, The Lawrenceville Sch., 1964; AB, Wesleyan U., 1968; JD, U. Mich., 1971. N.Y. 1972. Assoc. Brown & Wood LLP, N.Y.C., 1971-79, ptnr., 1980-97, sr. ptnr., 1997-2001; ptnr. Sidley Austin Brown & Wood LLP, 2001—. Chmn. Internat. Bus. Comm. Ann. Internat. Forum on Offshore Funds, 1993-2000. Trustee Elisabeth Morrow Sch., Englewood, N.J., 1988-93; mem. Washington U. St. Louis Exec. Com. Parents Coun., 2000-2002. Mem. ABA, Am. Law Inst., Am. Bar Found., Assn. Bar City N.Y. Republican. Roman Catholic. E-mail: ltondel@sidley.com.

TONDEUR, PHILIPPE MAURCIE, mathematician, educator; b. Zurich, Switzerland, Dec. 7, 1932; came to U.S., 1964, naturalized, 1974; s. Jean and Simone (Lapaire) T.; m. Claire-Lise Ballansat, Dec. 20, 1965. PhD, U. Zurich, 1961. Rsch. fellow U. Paris, 1961-63; lectr. math. U. Zurich, 1963-64, U. Buenos Aires, 1964, Harvard U., Cambridge, Mass., 1964-65, U. Calif., Berkeley, 1965-66; asso. prof. Wesleyan U., Middletown, Conn., 1966-68; assoc. prof. U. Ill., Urbana, 1968-70, prof., 1970—2002, prof. emeritus, 2002—, chair dept. math., 1996-99. Vis. prof. Auckland U., 1968, Eidg. Techn. Hochschule U. Heidelberg, 1973, U. Zurich, 1987, U. Rome, 1984, Ecole Poly., Paris, 1987, U. Santiago de Compostela, Spain, 1987, Max Planck Inst., 1987, U. Leuven (Belgium), 1990, Keio U., Yokohama, Japan, 1993; assoc. mem. Ctr. Advanced Study U. Ill., 1977—78, 1991—92; dir. divsn. math. sci. NSF, 1999—2002. Contbr. articles to profl. jours. Recipient DMS Govtl. Math. award; fellow Swiss Nat. Sci. Found., Harvard U., U. Ill. Mem.: Math. Assn. Am., Soc. Indsl. and Applied Math. (Frederick A. Howes pub. svc. award), Soc. Math. France, Schweiz Math. Gesellschaft, Am. Math. Soc. Office: U Ill Math Dept Urbana IL 61801

TONEGAWA, SUSUMU, biology educator; b. Nagoya, Japan, Sept. 5, 1939; arrived in U.S., 1963; s. Tsutoma and Miyoko T. (Masuko) Tonegawa; m. Mayumi Yoshinari, Sept. 28, 1985; children: Hidde, Hanna, Satto. BS, Kyoto U., Japan, 1963; PhD, U. Calif., San Diego, 1968. Rsch. asst. U. Calif., San Diego, 1963—64, teaching asst., 1964—68; mem. Basel (Switzerland) Inst. Immunology, 1971—81; prof. biology MIT, Cambridge, 1981—. Investigator Howard Hughes Med. Inst., 1988—; dir. MIT Ctr. for Learning and Memory, 1994—; professorship Amgen, Inc., 1994. Mem. editl. bd. Immunity. Decorated Order of Culture Emperor of Japan; co-recipient Albert Lasker Med. Rsch. award, 1987; named Person with Cultural Merit, Japanese Govt., 1983; recipient Cloetta prize, 1978, Avery Landsteiner prize, Gesselschaft fur

Immunologie, 1981, Louisa Gross Horwitz prize, Columbia U., 1982, Gardiner Found. Internat. award, Toronto, Ont., Can., 1983, Robert Koch Found. prize, Bonn, Germany, 1986, Nobel prize in Physiology or Medicine, 1987. Mem.: NAS (fgn. assoc.), Scandinavian Soc. Immunology (hon.), Am. Assn. Immunologists (hon.). Office: MIT Rm E17-353 77 Massachusetts Ave Cambridge MA 02139-4307*

TONELLI, GIOVANNA MARIE, professional development consultant, social worker; b. Phila., Nov. 13, 1951; d. Peter Paul and Mary Rita (Campagna) T. AAS, Community Coll. of Phila., 1972; B of Social Work, Temple U., 1974, MSW, 1981. Lic. social worker, Pa. Med. social worker Bio-Med. Applications, Phila., 1976-79; with foster care program Tabor Children's Svcs., Doylestown, Pa., 1981, with adoption program, cons., 1982; social worker City of Phila., 1982; program dir. Italian Home for Children, Boston, 1983-87; trainer, cons. Temple U., Phila., 1987; social worker Support Ctr. for Child Advocates, 1987-88; trainer/ cons. profl. devel. Becoming, 1987—. Mem. exec. bd. Today's Child, Boston, 1985-87 ; mem. network speakers USA, Inc., Pigeon Forge, Tenn., 1991; convenor Gathering Bus. Women in South Phila., 1991—. Vol. Boston Dept. Social Svcs., 1986-87; adv. Nat. Abortion Rights Action League, Phila. and Boston, 1974-89. Recipient Achiever award Success Motivation Inst., Inc., Waco, Tex., 1988. Mem. Nat. Assn. Social Workers (mem. child welfare task force 1984-87), NAFE, Bus. Women's Network. Avocations: reading, theater, music, hiking. Home and Office: Becoming 905 Mountain St Philadelphia PA 19148-1117

TONELLO-STUART, ENRICA MARIA, political economist; b. Monza, Italy; d. Alessandro P. and Maddalena M. (Marangoni) Tonello; m. Albert E. Smith; m. Charles L. Stuart. BA in Internat. Affairs, Econs., U. Colo., 1961; MA, Claremont Grad. Sch., 1966, PhD, 1971. Sales mgr. Met. Life Ins. Co., 1974-79; pres., CEO, ETS R&D, Inc., Palos Verdes Peninsula, Calif., 1977—. Dean internat. studies program Union U., L.A. and Tokyo; lectr. internat. affairs and mktg. UCLA Ext., Union U. Pub., editor Tomorrow Outline Jour., 1963—, The Monitor, 1988; pub. World Regionalism-An Ecological Analysis, 1971, A Proposal for the Reorganization of the United Nations, 1966, The Persuasion Technocracy, Its Forms, Techniques and Potentials, 1966, The Role of the Multinationals in the Emerging Globalism, 1978; developed the theory of social ecology and econsociometry. Organizer 1st family assistance program Langley FB Tactical Air Command, 1956-58. Recipient vol. svc. award VA, 1956-58, ARC svc. award, 1950-58. Mem. Corp. Planners Assn. (treas. 1974-79), Investigative Reporters and Editors, World Future Soc. (pres. 1974-75), Asian Bus. League, Soc. Environ. Journalists, Chinese Am. Assn. (life), Japan Am. Assn., L.A. World Trade Ctr., Palos Verdes C. of C. (legis. com.), L.A. Press Club (bd. dirs.), Zonta (chmn. internat. com. South Bay), Pi Sigma Alpha. Avocations: writing, collecting old books and maps, community service, travel.

TONER, MICHAEL F. journalist; b. LeMars, Iowa, Mar. 17, 1944; s. Francis F. and Mary Ann (Delaney) T.; m. Patricia L. Asleson, Aug. 28, 1966; children: Susan Michelle, Sharon Lynn. BA cum laude, U. Iowa, 1966; postgrad., U. Okla., Peru; MS cum laude, Northwestern U., 1967. Reporter UPI, Chgo., 1966-67; bur. chief Miami Herald, Key West, Fla., 1967-68, reporter, 1968-69, asst. city editor, 1970-72; sci./environ. writer Miami (Fla) Herald, 1973-84; sci. editor Atlanta Journal and Constitution, 1984-91, sci. writer, 1991—. Co-author: Florida by Paddle and Pack, 1979; contbr. articles to mags. Recipient Pulitzer Prize for explanatory journalism, 1993; Stanford U. profl. journalism fellow, 1973. Avocations: hiking, swimming, photography, stamp collecting, cooking. Office: Atlanta Journal and Constn 72 Marietta St NW Atlanta GA 30303-2804

TONEY, ANGELA M. medical administrator and educator; b. Southbridge, Mass., June 1, 1970; d. Alvin Darryl Toney; 1 child, Meghan. BS i Biology, BA in English, Harvard U., 1993, MPH, 1996. Med. asst., Boston, 1989-96; emergency med. technician EMT-I Boston EMS, 1991-95; rschr. Premier Rsch. Worldwide, Phila., 1997-98; med. instr. Star Tech. Inst., Upper Darby, Pa., 1997—, asst. dir., 1997-98, med. dir., 1998—, U. Pa., 1998—. Advisor Delaware County Intermediate Unit, 1997—; Disaster Health Svcs. vol. ARC, Phila., 1998—, vol. trainer, 1997—; med. exam. proctor NCCT, Overland Park, Kans., 1997—. Mem. Am. Assn. Med. Assts., Internat. Congress Med. Profls., Am. Soc. Clin. Lab. Sci., Tri-County Chpt. Med. Assts., Delaware County Computer Assn. (dir. pub. rels. 1998—), Delaware County C. of C., Alpha Beta Kappa Delta Pa. Democrat. Ropman Catholic. Avocations: black and white photography, travel, classical literature, foreign films. Office: Star Tech Inst 1570 Garrett Rd Upper Darby PA 19082-4500 also: U Pa 3400 Spruce St Philadelphia PA 19104-4206 E-mail: Angeland45@yahoo.com.

TONEY, BRIAN MICHAEL, music educator; b. Yakima, Wash., Sept. 29, 1977; s. Stanley Raymond and Carol Lynn T.; m. Amy Christine Schoeller, May 20, 2000. MusB in Edn., Grove City Coll., Grove City, Pa., 2000. Cert. music tchr. K-12 Pa. Dir. of bands, music tchr. Frederick County Pub. Schools, Frederick, Md., 2000—01, Palmyra Area H.S., Palmyra, Pa., 2001—. Mem.: Music Educators Nat. Conf. Christian. Avocations: travel, tennis, spending time with family. Office: Palmyra Area High Sch 1125 Park Dr Palmyra PA 17078 Office Fax: 717-838-7915. Personal E-mail: phscougarband@yahoo.com. E-mail: toney@palmyra.k12.pa.us.

TONEY, KELLY LYNNE SMITH, violinist, educator; b. Tulsa, Sept. 23, 1959; d. Frederick Lloyd and Harriet Elizabeth (Powell) Smith; m. Gregory Ashby Toney, Jan. 3, 1987; 1 child, Claire. BM, Juilliard Sch., 1982, MusM, 1983. Soloist Gulf Coast Symphony Orchestra, Biloxi, Miss., 1983; 1st violinist, asst. concertmaster Singapore Symphony Orchestra, 1983-85; concertmaster, asst. concertmaster Singapore Symphony Chamber Orchestra & Recording Group, 1983-85; concertmaster, soloist La. Sinfonietta Chamber Orchestra, Baton Rouge, 1985—; first violinist Campanile String Quartet, 1986—; guest soloist La. State U. New Music Ensemble, New Orleans, 1986, N.Y.C., 1987, Baton Rouge, 1990, Nicholls State U., Thibodaux, La., 1990, 92; recitalist Music Club of Baton Rouge, 1987—; rotating 1st violinist Valcour String Quartet, Baton Rouge, 1986-88; first violinist Baton Rouge Symphony Orchestra, 1986—. Judge scholarship auditions Music Club of Baton Rouge, 1988—; judge string div. Solo and Ensemble Festival, Baton Rouge, 1988; judge violin All-Parish Orch. Audition, Baton Rouge, 1986-87, Student Div. Award La. Fedn. Music Clubs, Baton Rouge, 1986; state chair Crusade for Strings and Chamber Music, La. Fedn. Music Clubs, 1990-93; guest soloist La. United Meth. Ann. Conf., Shreveport, 1992; founding mem. Zenaida Chamber Group, Baton Rouge. Mem. Cherokee Indian Tribe; mem. Capital Area Network, Baton Rouge, 1992-93. Recipient 2nd Place Student Div. award Nat. Fdn. Music Clubs, 1983, 1st Place Biennial Student award Dixie Dist. Fedn. Music Clubs, 1983, 1st. Place Student Div. award La. Fedn. Music Clubs, 1983, 2nd Place Young Artist award La. Fedn. Music Clubs, 1989. Mem. Music Tchrs. Nat. Assn., La. Music Tchrs. Assn. (state chair. string rally, 1992-94), Music Club Baton Rouge, Juilliard Sch. Alumni Club. Methodist. Avocation: singing in church choir. Home and Office: 611 Chippenham Dr Baton Rouge LA 70808-5612

TONG, ALEX WAIMING, immunologist; b. Hong Kong, Apr. 8, 1952; came to U.S., 1970; s. Robert S. and Agnes M. (Cheng) T.; m. Susan J. Radtke, May 23, 1980 (div. Mar. 1988); 1 child, Nicole L.; m. S. Quay Mercer, May 13, 1995; children: Alexander C., Caitlyn Y., Madeleine H. BA in Biology, U. Oreg., 1973; PhD in Microbiology and Immunology, Oreg. Health Scis. U., 1980. Undergrad. teaching asst. biology dept. U. Oreg., Eugene, 1972-73; rsch. asst. dept. microbiology and immunology Oreg. Health Scis. U., Portland, 1975-80, teaching asst. Sch. Medicine, 1977-78, rsch. assoc. dept. micrology and immunology, 1981-82; postdoctoral fellow Surg. Rsch. Lab. Portland VA Med. Ctr., 1980-82; rsch. assoc. in immunology Charles A. Sammons Cancer Ctr., Baylor U. Med. Ctr., Dallas, 1982-86; assoc. dir. immunology lab. Baylor U. Med. Ctr., 1986—2000; asst. prof. Inst. Biomed. Studies, Baylor U., Waco, 1988-97, assoc. prof., 1997—2001, prof., 2002—; scientific dir. molecular & cell processing ctr., U.S. oncology rsch. Ctr., 2002—. Prin. investigator Nat. Cancer Inst., Bethesda, Md., 1994—; adj. assoc. prof. immunology grad. studies program U. Tex. Southwestern Med. Ctr., Dallas, 1982—. Contbr. articles to profl. jours. Tatar rsch. fellow Med. Rsch. Found. Oreg., Portland, 1981-83. Mem. Am. Assn. Immunologists, Am. Assn. Cancer Rsch., Am. Soc. Hematology, Clin. Immunology Soc., Japan Karate Assn. Dallas (dir.), Internat. Traditional Karate Fedn. (cert. coach 1990—, cert. referee 1988—), Am. Amateur Karate Fedn. (dir. S.W. region). Democrat. Avocations: traditional karate, alpine skiing, scuba diving. Office: Baylor U Med Ctr Cancer Immunology Rsch Lab 3500 Gaston Ave Dallas TX 75246-2096

TONG, CHILING, trade and commerce administrator; b. Taipei, Taiwan, Mar. 19, 1958; d. Ping Tong and Shin-Mei Shui; m. Joel Szabat. BA in English Lit., Chinese Cultural U., Taipei, 1981; MBA, Calif. State U., Long Beach, 1985-87. Dir. pub. affairs Am. Chinese Bus., L.A., 1988-89; employer rep. Employment Devel. Dept., Sacramento, 1989-92, comt. rels. profl., 1992-94; dir. Calif. Office in Taipei, 1994—; asst. sec. Trade & Commerce, Sacramento, 1998. Pub.: (newsletter) CA Connection, 1994—; transl.: Crown Book, 1988. Commr. Sacramento Arts Commn., 1994; chairperson L.A. County Comty. Action Bd., 1992; v.p. Comty. Rels. Commn., Monterey Park, Calif., 1991; bd. dirs. El Sereno (Calif.) Luther Day Care Ctr., 1988. Named Hon. Treas., Miss. State, 1995; recipient Outstanding Women award YWCA, 1993, Outstanding Svcs. award, 1992, Outstanding Achievement award Monte Jade Sci., 1997; fellow CORO Found., 1984—. Mem. Global Fedn. of Chinese Bus. Women, Am. State Office Assn. (v.p. 1995—), Friends of Calif. Assn. (hon. chmn. 1995—), Am. C. of C. in Taipei, Rotary Club Taiwan, Taiwan's Srs. Jaycee Club, Asian C. of C. Lutheran. Office: Calif Office Trade/Investment 5 Hsin Yi Rd Sect 5 Taipei 110 Taiwan

TONG, HING, mathematician, educator; b. Canton, China, Feb. 16, 1922; s. Shen-Beu and Fung-Kam (Cheng) T.; m. Mary Josephine Powderly, Aug. 19, 1956; children— Christopher Hing, Mary Elizabeth, William Joseph, Jane Frances, James John. AB, U. Pa., 1943; PhD, Columbia, 1947; MA (hon.), Wesleyan U., Middletown, Conn., 1961. NRC postdoctoral fellow Inst. Advanced Study, Princeton, 1947-48; lectr. Canton (China) U., 1949; Cutting travelling fellow Inst. Henri Poincare, Paris, France, 1950-51; asst. prof. Reed Coll., 1952-53; vis. asst. prof. Barnard Coll., 1953-54; mem. faculty Wesleyan U., 1954-67, prof. math., 1960-67, chmn. dept., 1962-64; prof. math. Fordham U., Bronx, N.Y., 1966-84, chmn. dept., 1967-74. Mem. U.S. subcom. World Orgn. Gen. Systems and Cybernetics. Contbr. profl. jours. Mem. Phi Beta Kappa, Sigma Xi. Home: 725 Cooper Ave Oradell NJ 07649-2334

TONG, LOUIS LIK-FU, information scientist; b. Kowloon, British Hong Kong, June 15, 1962; came to U.S., 1980; naturalized, 1994; s. Yu-Tung and Chen (Yao) T. BS, U. Houston, 1985; M Libr. and Info. Sci., U. North Tex., 1992. Info. asst. Houston Acad. Medicine, Tex. Med. Ctr. Libr., Houston, 1990-93; rsch. libr. svcs. specialist Internat. Facility Mgmt. Assn., 1993-98; knowledge and info. mgr. Brown & Root Svcs., 1998-99; web content adminstr. Halliburton Co., 1999—. Mem.: Tex. Bldg. Energy Inst. (exec. com. 1997—98), Japan-Am. Soc. Houston, Spl. Librs. Assn. (Houston local planning chair 2000—02, sec. Tex. chpt. 2001—02), Med. Libr. Assn. (minority scholar 1992), Internat. Facility Mgmt. Assn. (chmn. codes and regulations com. 1994—98, founding dir. environ., health and safety coun. 1998—2002), Tex. State Rifle Assn. (life), NRA (life). Republican. Home: PO Box 230453 Houston TX 77223-0453 Office: Halliburton Co 4100 Clinton Dr Houston TX 77020-6237 E-mail: louis@louistong.com.

TONG, ROSEMARIE, medical humanities and philosophy educator, consultant and researcher; b. Chgo., July 19, 1947; d. Joseph John and Lillian (Nedued) Behensky; m. Paul Ki-King Tong, Aug. 15, 1971 (dec. Apr. 1988); children: Paul Shih-Mien Tong, John Joseph Tong; m. Jeremiah Putnam, Aug. 1, 1992. BA, Marygrove Coll., 1970; MA, Cath. U., 1971; PhD, Temple U., 1978; LLD (hon.), Marygrove Coll., 1987; LHD (hon.), SUNY, Oneonta, 1993. Asst. and assoc. prof. philosophy Williams Coll., Williamstown, Mass., 1978-88; vis. disting. prof. humanities Davidson (N.C.) Coll., 1988-89, Thatcher Prof. in med. humanities and philosophy, 1989-99; prof. humanities and philosophy U. N.C., Charlotte, 1999—. L. Stacy Davidson vis. chair in liberal arts U. Miss., Oxford, 1998; Louise M. Olmstead vis. prof. philosophy and women's studies, Lafayette Coll., Easton, Pa., 1993; disting. prof. health care ethics U. N.C., Charlotte, 1999—; manuscript reviewer Wadsworth Pub. Co., 1985-92; curriculum reviewer philosophy dept. Carlton and Bowdoin Colls., 1986; honors examiner Hobart and William Smith Colls., 1990; dissertation dir., adj. faculty The Union Inst., 1992-93; cons., awards judge, panelist, organizer and speaker in field; mem. numerous U. coms. Author: Women, Sex and the Law, 1984, Ethics in Policy Analysis, 1985, Feminist Thought: A Comprehensive Introduction, 1989, Feminist Philosophies: Problems, Theories, and Applications, 1991, Feminine and Feminist Ethics, 1993, Feminist Thought: A More Comprehensive Introduction, 1998, (with Larry Kaplan) Controlling Our Reproductive Destiny, 1994, Feminist Philosophy: Essential Readings in Theory, Reinterpretation and Application, 1994, Feminist Bioethics, 1997, Feminist Thought: A More Comprehensive Ethics, 1998, Globalizing Feminist Bioethics: Crosscultural Perspectives, 2000; contbr. numerous articles to profl. jours.; mem. various editl. bds. Project reviewer Annenberg/CPB Project, Washington, 1986; policy writer dvsn. health svcs. rsch. and policy U. Minn., 1988, Frank Graham Porter Early Childhood Ctr., U. N.C. Chapel Hill, 1988; mem. Charlotte task force Congl. Task Force Health Care, Congressman Alex McMillan, 1991, standards and ethics com. Hospice N.C., 1991, resource and ethics comms. McMillan-Spratt Task Force Health Care Policy, 1992, pastoral care com. Carolinas Med. Ctr., 1990—, ethics com. Presbyn. Hosp., 1990—, N.E. Regional Hosp., 1991, Nat. Adv. Bd. Ethics in Reproduction, Washington, 1993; active Hastings Ctr. Project Undergrad. Values Edn., Briarcliff Manor, N.Y., 1993, N.C. Found. Humanities and Pub. Policy; mem. bioethics Resource Group, 1992—; mem. feminist approaches to bioethics network, 1996—; dir. med. humanities program Davidson Coll., 1988-98. Named Prof. of Yr., Carnegie Found. and Coun. Advancement and Support of Edn., 1986. Mem. Internat. Assn. for Feminist Approaches to Bioethics Network (coord. 1999—), Am. Assn. for Bioethics and Humanities, Am. Cath. Philos. Assn., Am. Philos. Assn. (ad hoc com. computers, pub. and role of Am. Philos. Assn. 1984, adv. com. to program com. 1986-88, nomination com. 1989-91, nat. com. on status of women 1989-93), Am. Legal Studies and Assn., Am. Soc. Pol. and Legal Philosophy, Am. Soc. Law and Medicine, Nat. Coun. Rsch. on Women, Nat. Women Studies Assn., Internat. Assn. Philosophy of Law and Social Philosophy, Assn. Practical and Profl. Ethics, Society Christian Ethics, Soc. Women in Philosophy, Soc. Philosophy and Tech., Soc. Philosophy and Pub. Affairs, Soc. Study of Women Philosophers, Network Feminist Approaches to Bioethics, The Hastings Ctr., Triangle Bioethics Group, So. Soc. Philosophy and Psychology. Avocations: aerobics, boating, hiking.

TONG, SIU WING, computer programmer; b. Hong Kong, May 20, 1950; came to U.S., 1968; BA, U. Calif., Berkeley, 1972; PhD, Harvard U., 1979; MS, U. Lowell, 1984. Rsch. assoc. Brookhaven Nat. Lab., Upton, N.Y., 1979-83; software engr. Honeywell Info. Systems, Billerica, Mass., 1984-85; sr. programmer, analyst Hui Computer Cons., Berkeley, Calif., 1985-88; sr. v.p. devel., chief fin. officer Surgicenter Info. Systems, Inc., Orinda, 1989-94; sr. sys. specialist Info. Sys. Divsn. Contra Costa County Health Svcs., Martinez, 1995-97, info. tech. supr. Info. Sys. Divsn., 1997—. Vol. tchr. Boston Chinatown Saturday Adult Edn. Program of Tufts Med. Sch., 1977-79. Muscular Dystrophy Assn. fellow, 1980-82. Mem. AAAS, IEEE, Assn. Computing Machinery, N.Y. Acad. Scis. Home: 17 Beaconsfield Ct Orinda CA 94563-4203 Office: Contra Costa County Health Svcs 595 Center Ave Ste 210 Martinez CA 94553-4634 E-mail: swtong@hsd.co.contra-costa.ca.us.

TONGATE, DARREL EDWIN, accountant; b. Hopkinsville, Ky., Nov. 4, 1943; s. Forrest L. and Christine (Martin) T.; m. Judy Jean Harrell, Dec. 20, 1964; children: Jean Rená, Scott Alan, John Edwin, Tammy Michelle. BS in Acctg., David Libscomb U., Nashville, 1965. CPA, Tenn., Ky. Staff acct. Smith & Smith, Nashville, 1965-67; asst. controller Nauta Line Houseboat Mfg. Co., Hendersonville, Tenn., 1968-70; acct., proprietor Darrel E. Tongate CPA, Madison, 1971-73, Nashville, 1980-86; mng. ptnr. Tongate & Ryan, 1974-76; CPA Tongate, Ryan, Connelly & Shaub, 1977-80; dir.-in-charge James R. Meany & Assocs., 1986-87; v.p. fin. Hydra Sports, Inc., 1987-88; pres. Vision Boats, Inc., Old Hickory, Tenn., 1988-93; acct. Goodlettsville, 1994—; exec. dir. Tenn. State Bd. Accountancy, Nashville, 1994—. Deacon Hendersonville Ch. of Christ, 1974-89, 91-97, elder, 1997—, treas., 1974—. Fellow Tenn. Soc. CPAs (pres. 1990-91, treas. polit. action com. 1980-81, pres. polit. action com. 1986-87, sec. Nashville chpt. 1975-76, v.p. 1976-78, pres. 1978-79, bd. dirs. 1984-92), Nashville City Club, Kiwanis (bd. dirs. 1972-73). Home: 119 Cima Dr Goodlettsville TN 37072-2005

TONGUE, PAUL GRAHAM, financial executive; b. Phila., Dec. 30, 1932; s. George Paul and Florence Amelia (Kogel) T.; m. Marjorie Joan Meyers, May 26, 1954; children: Suzanne Marjorie, Douglas Paul BS in Commerce, Drexel U., 1957; MBA, NYU, 1965. With Chase Manhattan Bank, N.Y.C., 1957-87; chmn. Plus Systems Inc., Denver, 1985; pres. Eppley-Tongue Assocs., Inc., Towson, Md., 1988—; exec. v.p. Veritas Venture Inc., Scotch Plains, N.J., 1990-91. Pres. Our Saviour Luth. Ch., Manhasset, N.Y., 1984; pres. 1st Night of Williamsburg, Inc.; bd. dirs. Ronald Reagan Club, Ford's colony Homeowners' Assn., Williamsburg Area Civic and Cultural Ctr., Inc., Sr. Exec. Resource Corps, Coll. William and Mary. Mem. Ford's Colony Country Club. Avocations: golf, classical music.

TONGUE, WILLIAM WALTER, economics and business consultant, educator emeritus; b. Worcester, Mass., May 24, 1915; s. Walter Ernest and Lena (Brown) T.; m. Beverly Harriet Cohan, Dec. 26, 1936; children— Barbara Tongue Duggan, Kathleen Tongue Alligood. AB, Dartmouth, 1937, M.C.S., 1938; PhD, U. Chgo., 1947. Jr. acct. Price, Waterhouse & Co. (C.P.A.'s), N.Y.C., 1938; instr. Coe Coll., Cedar Rapids, Iowa, 1941-42; spl. cons. OSS, 1942; fin. economist Fed. Res. Bank Chgo., 1942-44; economist Jewel Companies, Inc., Chgo., 1944-64; prof. econs. and finance U. Ill. Chgo. , 1965-80. Prof. emeritus, 1980—; econ. cons. LaSalle Nat. Bank, Chgo., 1968-91; mem. com. CNA Fin. Separate Fund B.; dir. St. Joseph Light & Power Co., Mo., 1965-86; trustee Signode Employees' Savs. and Profit Sharing Trust Fund, 1980-89. Author articles; contbr.: to books including How We Can Halt Inflation and Still Keep Our Jobs, 1974. Bd. dirs., v.p. rsch. and stats. Chgo. Assn. Commerce and Industry, 1968-69. Mem. Nat. Assn. Bus. Economists (pres. 1962-63), Conf. Bus. Economists, Am. Statis. Assn. (pres. Chgo. chpt. 1951-52), Econ. Club Chgo., Investment Analysts Assn. Chgo., Inst. Chartered Fin. Analysts (chartered fin. analyst 1963), Midwest Fin. Assn. (pres. 1972-73). Home and Office: 1220 Village Dr Apt 427 Arlington Heights IL 60004-8123 E-mail: williamtongue@msn.com.

TONINI, LEON RICHARD, sales professional; b. Pittsfield, Mass., May 16, 1931; s. John Richard and Mabel Grayce (Rushbrook) T.; m. Helen Jo, Aug. 15, 1966; 1 son, John Richard II. BA in Mgmt., U. Md., 1951. Enlisted in U.S. Army, 1947, advanced through grades to master sgt., 1968; service in W.Ger., Korea and Vietnam; ret., 1974; dir. vets. employment and assistance Non-Commd. Officers Assn., San Antonio, 1974-75; supr. security Pinkerton's Inc., Dallas, 1975-78; gen. mgr. civic ctr. Travelodge Motor Hotel and Restaurant, San Francisco, 1978-85; sales rep. Vernon Co., 1985—. Chmn. San Francisco Vets. Employment Com., 1981. Served as sgt. maj. Calif. N.G., res. Decorated Bronze Star, Republic Vietnam Honor medal, 2d class. Mem. Non-Commd. Officers Assn. (dir. Calif. chpt.), Am. Legion, Assn. U.S. Army Res. Officers Assn., Amvets, Patrons of Husbandry, Masons. Baptist. Home and Office: 205 Collins St Apt 9 San Francisco CA 94118-3429 E-mail: lrtonini@compuserve.com. *Personal philosophy: You can be what you want to be, go beyond the rest.*

TONJES, MARIAN JEANNETTE BENTON, education educator; b. Rockville Center, N.Y., Feb. 16, 1929; d. Millard Warren and Felicia E. (Tyler) Benton; m. Charles F. Tonjes (div. 1965); children: Jeffrey Charles, Kenneth Warren. BA, U. N.Mex., 1951, cert., 1966, MA, 1969; EdD, U. Miami, 1975. Dir. recreation Stuyvesant Town Housing Project, N.Y.C., 1951-53; tchr. music., phys. edn. Sunset Mesa Day Sch., Albuquerque, 1953-54; tchr. remedial reading Zia Elem. Sch., 1965-67; tchr. secondary devel. reading Rio Grande High Sch., 1967-69; rsch. asst. reading Southwestern Coop. Ednl. Lab., 1969-71; assoc. dir., vis. instr. Fla. Ctr. Tchr. Tng. Materials U. Miami, 1971-72; asst. prof. U.S. Internat. U., San Diego, 1972-75; prof. edn. Western Wash. U., Bellingham, 1975-94, prof. emerita, 1994—; dir. summer study at Oriel Coll. Oxford (Eng.) U., 1979-94. Adj. prof. U. N.Mex., Albuquerque, 1995—, reading supr. Manzanita Ctr., 1968; vis. prof. adult edn. Palomar (Calif.) Jr. Coll., 1974; vis. prof. U. Guam, Mangilao, 1989-90; spkr., cons. in field; invited guest Russian Reading Assn., Moscow, 1992. Author: (with Miles V. Zintz) Teaching Reading/Thinking Study Skills in Content Classroom, 3rd edit., Secondary Reading, Writing and Learning, 1991, (with Roy Wolpow and Miles Zintz) Integrated Content Literacy, 1999. Trustee The White Mountain Sch., 2000—; tour assoc. In the Footsteps of Dickens, England, 2001; mem. read by three com. Albuquerque Bus. and Edn. Compact. Tng. Tchr. Trainers grantee, 1975; NDEA fellow Okla. State U., 1969. Mem.: Am. Reading Forum, Internat. Reading Assn., PEO (past chpt. pres.), World Congress in Reading Buenos Aires (spkr. 1994), European Coun. Internat. Schs. (The Hague, spkr. 1993), European Conf. in Reading (spkr. Berlin 1989), UK Reading Assn. (spkr. 1977—93, spkr. Edinburgh 1991, spkr. Malmo 1993, spkr. Budapest 1995), Internat. Reading Assn. (mem. non-print media and reading com. 1980—83, workshop dir. S.W. regional confs. 1982, mem. travel, interchange and study tours com. 1984—86, mem. com. internat. devel. N.Am. 1991—96, Outstanding Tchr. Educator award 1988—), Am. Reading Forum (chmn. bd. dirs. 1983—85), Albuquerque Tennis Club, Internat. Soc. Rwy. Travelers, Delta Delta Delta. Avocations: miniatures, tennis, bridge, art, travel.

TONKENS, REBECCA ANNETTE, maternal/women's health nurse; b. Searcy, Ark., Dec. 17, 1943; d. William T. and Velda M. (Goodloe) McAfee; m. Richard E. Morris, June 24, 1960 (div. Nov. 1980); children: Terri L. Morris Bomar, Toni L. Morris Carroll; m. Solvin W. Tonkens, Dec. 22, 1986. LPN, Area Vocat. Tech. Sch., Kansas City, Kans., 1973; ADN, Kansas City C.C., 1980; BSN, Webster U., 1992. RN, Kans., Mo. Area Vocat. Tech. Sch.; staff nurse Providence-St. Margaret Hosp., Kansas City, 1973-80; indsl. nurse, office mgr. Kansas City Indsl. Clinic, 1980-81; staff nurse Bethany Med. Ctr., Kansas City, 1981-1999; retired, 1999; outreach nurse specialist Quintiles Phase I Svcs., 2000—. Active community rels. diabetes unit Bethany Med. Ctr., 1983-86. Officer, v.p., bd. dirs. Cambridge Townhouse Assn., Leawood, Kans., 1989-92; chaperone Rose Bud (Ark.) Band at Presdl. Inauguration, Washington, 1992; mem. adv. bd. Kansas City Kans. C.C. Day Care Ctr.; vol. Habitat for Humanity, Salvation Army, others. Recipient Cert. of Appreciation, Salvation Army, 1994, Korean Am. Sr. Citizen Soc. Kans. City, 2001, Ctrs. for Medicare and Medicaid Svc., 2002. Mem. ANA, Am. Coll. Occupational and Environ. Medicine (aux.), Mo.-Kans. Assn. Medicine Shoppes, Inc. (flu prevention coord.), Assn. Osteo. Physicians and surgeons (aux.). Episcopalian. Home and Office: 12861 Cambridge Ter Leawood KS 66209-1634 E-mail: flunurse@aol.com.

TONKIN, HUMPHREY RICHARD, academic administrator, educator; b. Truro, Cornwall, Eng., Dec. 2, 1939; came to U.S., 1962; s. George Leslie and Lorna Winifred (Sandry) T.; m. Sandra Julie Winberg, Mar. 9, 1968 (div. 1981); m. Jane Spencer Edwards, Oct. 1, 1983; 1 child, Sebastian George. BA, St. John's Coll., Cambridge, Eng., 1962, MA, 1966; AM, PhD, Harvard U., 1966; DLitt (hon.), U. Hartford, 1999. Asst. prof. English U. Pa., Phila., 1966-71, assoc. prof., 1971-80, prof., 1980-83, vice-provost undergrad. studies, 1971-75, coord. internat. programs, 1977-83, master Stouffer Coll. House, 1980-83; pres. State Univ. Coll., Potsdam, N.Y., 1983-88, U. Hartford, Conn., 1989-98, prof. humanities, pres. emeritus, 1998—; vis. fellow Whitney Humanities Ctr. Yale U., 1998-99. Vis. prof. English Columbia U., N.Y.C., 1980-81; exec. dir. Ctr. Rsch. and Documentation on World Lang. Problems, Rotterdam and Hartford, 1974—. Editor: Lang. Problems and Lang. Planning; author: (bibliography) Sir Walter Raleigh, 1971, Esperanto and International Language Problems, 4th edit., 1977, Spenser's Courteous Pastoral, 1972, (with Jane Edwards) The World in the Curriculum, 1981, The Faerie Queene, 1989; editor: (with Allison Keef) Language in Religion, 1989, Esperanto, Interlinguistics and Planned Language, 1997; editor, translator: Esperanto: Language, Literature and Community (Piere Janton), 1993, Maskerado: Dancing Around Death in Nazi Hungary (Tivadar Soros), 2000; contbr. articles to profl. jours. Pres. Pa. Coun. Internat. Edn., 1980-81; bd. dirs. World Affairs Coun. Phila., 1979-83, Zamenhof Found., 1987-94, Hartford Symphony Orch., 1989-98, World Affairs Coun. Conn., 1989—, Greater Hartford Arts Coun., 1989-96, Can.-U.S. Found. Ednl. Exchange, 1997—, chmn. 1999-2000; bd. dirs. World Learning, 1998—; chmn. Coun. Internat. Exch. Scholars, 1988-94, Esperantic Studies Found., 1991—, Partnership for Svc.-Learning, 1991-96, v.p., 2001—; bd. dirs. Am. Forum, 1985—, chmn., 1998—. Recipient Lindback award for disting. teaching, 1970; Frank Knox fellow Harvard U., 1962-66; Guggenheim fellow, 1974 Fellow Acad. Esperanto; mem. Universal Esperanto Assn. (pres. 1974-80, 86-89, rep. to UN 1974-83, hon. com. 1995—), Spenser Soc. (pres. 1983-84, former dir.), Internat. Acad. Scis. San Marino, Conn. Acad. Arts and

Scis., Cosmos Club. Home: 279 Ridgewood Rd West Hartford CT 06107-3542 Office: U Hartford Mortensen Libr 200 Bloomfield Ave West Hartford CT 06117-1599 E-mail: tonkin@mail.hartford.edu.

TONKIN, INA LYNN DYER, cardiovascular radiologist, educator; b. Louisville, Apr. 26, 1944; d. Robert S. and Nancy E. (Camp) Dyer; m. Allen K. Tonkin, June 29, 1968; children: Allison Elizabeth-Ann, Kieth Allen. BA, DePauw U., 1966; MD, U. Louisville, 1970. Diplomate Am. Bd. Radiology, Am. Bd. Vasc. Interventional Radiology, Am. Bd. Pediatric Radiology. Pediatric intern U. Fla., Gainesville, 1970-71, resident in radiology, 1971-73, fellow in cardiovascular radiology, 1974-75; asst. prof. U. Ariz. Health Sci. Ctr., Tucson, 1975-77, U. Ala.-Birmingham, 1977-79; assoc. prof. radiology U. Tenn., Memphis, 1979-84, prof., 1984—, prof. pediatrics, 1985—. Exec. com. LeBonheur Children's Med. Ctr., Memphis, 1981-85, chief of med. staff, 1987; disting. scientist Armed Forces Inst. of Radiologic Pathology, Washington, 1992-93; prof. radiology & pediat. U. Tenn. Hlth. Sci. Ctr., Memphis. Editor: (book) Pediatric Cardiovascular Imaging, 1992; contbr. chpts. to books, rsch. articles to profl. jours. Recipient Disting. Alumnus award U. Louisville Med. Sch., 1999. Fellow Am. Heart Assn. (exec. com. Coun. Cardiovascular Radiology 1980—), Soc. Interventional Radiology, Am. Coll. Radiology; mem. Soc. Pediatric Radiology (treas.), Jour. Rev. Club of Memphis (sec. 1984, pres. 1985), Soc. Interventional Radiology, N.Am. Soc. Cardiac Imaging (pres.). Methodist. Home: 3415 Chambers Chapel Rd Lakeland TN 38002-9573 Office: LeBonheur Children's Med Ctr 50 N Dunlap St Memphis TN 38103-4909 E-mail: Drs.Tonkin@mindspring.com.

TONKIN, LEO SAMPSON, educational foundation administrator; b. Suffern, N.Y., Apr. 2, 1937; s. Leo S. and Ann (Petrone) T. AB, Johns Hopkins, 1959; postgrad., Sch. Advanced Internat. Studies, 1962-63; JD, Harvard, 1962; Dr. Pedagogy, SUNY, 1973. Legis. asst. to U.S. Congressman; then Sen. Charles McC. Mathias, Jr., of Md., 1962-63; asso. counsel U.S. Ho. of Reps. Select Com. on Govt. Research, 1964; spl. cons. Ho. Spl. Subcom. on Edn., 1965-66; exec. dir. Commrs. Council on Higher Edn., Washington, 1965-66; pres. Leo S. Tonkin Assos., Inc., 1966—; founder, dir., chmn. bd. Washington Workshops Found., 1967—; pres. Travel Seminars, Ltd., 1999—. Mem. White House Conf. on Edn., 1965, White House Conf. on Youth, 1971; spl. asst. to chmn. U.S. Ho. of Reps. Select Com. on Crime, 1972; mem. bd. plebe sponsors U.S. Naval Acad., 1977— ; v.p. London Fedn. Boys' Clubs, 1980— ; mem. adv. panel Nat. Commn. for Protection of Human Subjects of Biomed. and Behavioral Research, HEW, 1976-77; bd. dirs. Star Scientific, Inc., 1998—; nat. adv. coun. Retinitis Pigmentosa Found., 1999—. Contbr. articles to mags. Bd. dirs. Washington Choral Arts Soc., 1971-73, Nat. Coordinating Council on Drug Edn., 1973, Nat. Student Ednl. Fund, 1974— ; chmn. Wall Street Seminar Found., 1978— ; chmn. bd. trustees St. Thomas Aquinas Coll., 1966-73, continuing trustee, 1973-78, trustee, chmn. emeritus, 1978— ; chmn. bd. trustees City of Phila. Govt. Honors Program; trustee Southeastern U., 1966-73; asso. bd. trustees Immaculata Coll., 1966-73; mem. advisory bd. Pub. Affairs and Govt. Degree Program, Mt. Vernon Coll., 1971-74; bd. dirs. YMCA, Washington, 1969-71. Recipient Americanism award, Valley Forge Freedoms Found, 1973 Mem. Johns Hopkins Alumni Assn. of Washington (pres. 1969-72) Clubs: Georgetown (Washington), City Tavern (Washington), Nat. Press (Washington), Capitol Hill (Washington), Capitol Yacht (Washington); Harvard (N.Y.C.). Home: 4368 Sunset Ct Warrenton VA 20187-3584 Office: 3222 N St NW Washington DC 20007-2849

TONKS, ROBERT STANLEY, pharmacology and therapeutics educator, former university dean; b. Aberystwyth, Wales; emigrated to Can., 1973; s. Robert Patrick Dennis and Prudence Violet (Williams) T.; m. Diana Mary Cownie; children: Pamela Mary, Julia Rosalind, Robert Michael, Sara Katharine. Student, U. Coll. of South Wales, Welsh Coll. Pharmacy; B.Pharm., PhD, Welsh Nat. Sch. Medicine, Cardiff. Organon postdoctoral fellow Med. Sch., Cardiff, Nat. Health Service postdoctoral fellow; Nat. Health Service sr. fellow Cardiff and Nevill Hall Hosp., Abergavenny; lectr. pharmacology U. Wales, Cardiff, 1958-72; vis. fellow Claude Bernard Research Assn., Faculté de Medicine, Paris, 1959; sr. lectr. pharmacology and therapeutics Med. Sch. and U. Wales Hosp., Cardiff, 1972-73; dir., prof. Coll. Pharmacy, Dalhousie U., Halifax, N.S., Can., 1973-77, dean Faculty of Health Professions Can., 1977-88, prof. geriatric pharmaco-therapeutics Can., 1988—, acting head divsn. geriatric medicine Can., 1991-94. Cons. pharm. industry in U.K., Govt. of N.B., Can., Health and Welfare Dept. Can.; advisor health manpower Govt. of N.S.; coordinator N.E. Can./Am. Health Coun. co-chmn., 1974-91; emeritus chmn., mem. Health and Welfare Personnel Career Rev. Com., 1991—; pharm. scis. grants com. Med. Rsch. Council Can., chmn.; mem. rev. com. health protection br. fed. govt. div. pharm. chemistry, Can.; chmn. advisory com. N.B. Minister of Health; mem. joint com. on devel. rsch. in nursing Med. Rsch. Coun.-Nat. Health Rsch. Devel. Program; mem. nat. adv. panel on risk/benefit mgmt. of drugs.; adv. com. on restructuring Health Canada's Personnel Career Awards; trustee Lakeridge Health Corp., Oshawa, Ont., 2001—. Contbr. articles on pharmacology and pathology to profl. jours. Fellow: Inst. Biology, Pharm. Soc. Gt. Britain; mem.: Welsh Cultural Soc. (past pres.), Med. Soc. N.S. (task force on pharmacare), N.S. Pharm. Soc. (coord. drug and med. supplies Ethiopia airlift, cert. of merit), Can. Geriatrics Soc., Can. Soc. Hosp. Pharmacy (hon.), N.B. Pharm. Soc. (hon.), Am. Soc. Clin. Pharm. and Therapeutics, Canadian Soc. Clin. Investigation, Internat. Soc. Thrombosis and Haemostasis, Brit. Pharmacol. Soc. Anglican. Mailing: 6 Tom Edwards Dr Whitby ON Canada L1R 2R4 Office: Dalhousie U Coburg Rd Halifax NS Canada E-mail: bobtonks@is.dal.ca.

TONN, ELVERNE MERYL, pediatric dentist, dental benefits consultant, forensic odontologist; b. Stockton, Calif., Dec. 10, 1929; s. Emanuel M. and Lorna Darlene (Bryant) T.; m. Ann G. Richardson, Oct. 28, 1951; children: James Edward, Susan Elaine Tonn. AA, La Sierra U., Riverside, Calif., 1949; DDS, U. So. Calif., 1955; BS, Regents Coll., U. State N.Y., 1984. Lic. dentist; diplomate Am. Bd. Forensic Dentistry, Am. Bd. Quality Assurance and Utilization Rev. Physicians; cert. dental benefits cons. Pediatric dentist, assoc. Walker Dental Group, Long Beach, Calif., 1957-59, Children's Dental Clinic, Sunnyvale, 1959-61; pediatric dentist in pvt. practice Mountain View, 1961-72; pediatric dentist, ptrn. Pediatric Dentistry Assocs., Los Altos, 1972-83; pediatric dentist, ptnr. Valley Oak Dental Group, Manteca, 1987—; from clin. instr. to assoc. prof. U. Pacific, San Francisco, 1964-84; assoc. prof. U. Calif., 1984-86. Pediat. dental cons. Delta Dental Plan, San Francisco, 1985—; chief dental staff El Camino Hosp., Mountain View, 1964—65, Mountain View, 1984—85; dental cons. Interplast program Stanford U. Sch. Medicine; lectr. in field. Weekly columnist Manteca Bull., 1987-92; producer 2 teaching videos, 1986; contbr. articles to profl. jours. Capt. U.S. Army, 1955—57. Fellow Am. Coll. Dentists, Internat. Coll. Dentists, Am. Acad. Pediatric Dentistry, Royal Soc. Health (Eng.), Acad. of Dentistry for Handicapped, Pierre Fauchard Acad., Acad. Dental Materials, Am. Soc. Dentistry for Children; mem. ADA, Internat. Assn. Pediatric Dentistry, Internat. Assn. Dental Rsch., Am. Acad. Forensic Scis., Am. Soc. Forensic Odontology, Fedn. Dentaire Internationale, Am. Assn. Dental Cons., Calif. Dental Assn., Calif. Soc. Dentistry for Children (pres. 1968), Calif. Soc. Pediatric Dentists, N.Y. Acad. Scis., Calif. Acad. Sci., Rotary Internat., Nat. Assn. for Healthcare Quality, Am. Coll. Med. Quality. Republican. Avocations: photography, travel, medieval history. Home: 374 Laurelwood Cir Manteca CA 95336-7122 Office: Valley Oak Dental Group Inc 1507 W Yosemite Ave Manteca CA 95337-5182 Fax: 209-823-7836. E-mail: emtonn@aol.com.

TONN, ROBERT JAMES, retired entomologist; b. Watertown, Wis., June 23, 1927; s. Harry James and Elise (Foogman) T.; m. Noemi C. Tonn; children: Sigrid M., Monica E. BS, Colo. State U., 1949, MS, 1950; MPH, Okla. Med. Sch., 1963; PhD, Okla. State U., 1959. Rsch. assoc La. State U., Costa Rica/New Orleans, 1961-63; dir. Taunton Field Sta., Taunton, Mass., 1963-65; chief PMO unit WHO, various locations, 1965-87. Adj. prof. of parasitology U. Tex.-El Paso, 1988—; cons. USAID/VBC, 1987—. Contbr. numerous articles to profl. jours. Mem. Am. Soc. Tropical Medicine, Soc. Vector Ecology (pres. 1984), Am. Mosquito Control Assn., U.S./ Mex. Border Health Assn., Royal Soc. Tropical Medicine and Hygiene, Masons. Congregationalist. Home: 4247 Winchester Rd Las Cruces NM 88011 E-mail: stonn@zianet.com.

TONSO, WILLIAM RAE, retired sociology educator, freelance writer; b. Herrin, Ill., Sept. 26, 1933; s. Joe and Eva (Martoglio) T.; m. Beverley Jean Davis, June 9, 1973. BS, So. Ill. U., 1955, MS, 1966, PhD, 1976. With NorgeBorg-Warner, 1959-60, Allen Industries, 1960-61; supr. handicapped Employment Tng. Ctr. So. Ill. U., 1964-66; prof. sociology U. Evansville, Ind., 1969-99, prof. emeritus, 1999—. Author: Gun and Society, 1982; editor, contbg. author: The Gun Culture and Its Enemies, 1990; contbr. numerous articles to profl. jours. and popular publs. and newspapers. 1st lt. USAF, 1955-58, capt. USAFR. Recipient James Madison award Second Amendment Found., 1985. Mem. NRA, Nat. Assn. Scholars, Red Brush Rifle Range. Avocations: reading and writing, guns and shooting, nature watching. Home: 3303 Bayard Park Dr Evansville IN 47714-0503

TONTIRUTTANANON, CHANNARONG, electrical engineer, researcher; b. Muang, Surin, Thailand, 1971; B Engring, Chulalongkorn U., Bangkok, Thailand, 1992; MS, Auburn U., 1997, PhD, 1998. Instr. Assumption U., Bangkok, 1992—95; grad. rsch. asst. Auburn (Ala.) U., 1995—98; postdoctoral rsch. fellow U. Iowa, Iowa City, 1999—99; sr. mem. sci. staff Nortel Networks Inc., Richardson, Tex., 1999—. Contbr. articles to profl. jours. Mem.: IEEE, Am. Math. Soc., Phi Kappa Phi, Eta Kappa Nu. Achievements include patents for overload control system and method for a telecommunication system. E-mail: ctont@nortelnetworks.com.

TOOBIN, JEFFREY ROSS, writer, legal analyst; b. N.Y.C., May 21, 1960; s. Jerome and Marlene Sanders T.; m. Amy Bennett McIntosh, May 31, 1986; children: Ellen Frances, Adam Jerome. AB, Harvard U., 1982, JD, 1986. Bar: N.Y. 1987. Law clerk Hon. J. Edward Lumbard, N.Y.C., 1986-87; assoc. counsel Indep. Counsel Lawrence Walsh, Washington, 1987-89; asst. U.S. Atty. Ea. Dist. N.Y., Bklyn., 1990-93; legal analyst ABC News, N.Y.C., 1996—2002; staff writer The New Yorker, 1993—; legal analyst CNN, 2002—. Author: Opening Arguments: A Young Lawyer's First Case-United States v. Oliver North, 1991, The Run of His Life: The People v. O.J. Simpson, 1996, A Vast Conspiracy: The Real Story of the Sex Scandal that Nearly Brought Down a President, 2000, Too Close To Call: The Thirty Six Day Battle To Decide the 2000 Election, 2001; contbr. articles to The New Yorker. Office: The New Yorker 4 Times Sq New York NY 10036-6592

TOOHEY, BRIAN FREDERICK, lawyer; b. Niagara Falls, N.Y., Dec. 14, 1944; s. Matthew and Marilyn (Hoag) T.; m. Mary Elizabeth Monihan; children: Maureen Elizabeth, Matthew Sheridan, Margaret Monihan, Mary Catherine, Elizabeth Warner. BS, Niagara U., 1966; JD, Cornell U., 1969. Bar: N.Y. 1969, N.Mex. 1978, Ohio 1980. Ptnr. Cohen, Swados, Wright, Hanifin & Bradford, Buffalo, 1973-77; pvt. practice Santa Fe, 1977-79; of counsel Jones, Day, Reavis & Pogue, Cleve., 1979-80, ptnr., 1981—. Mem. Citizens League Greater Cleve., 1982—. Lt. JAG Corps, USNR, 1970-73. Mem. ABA, N.Y. State Bar Assn., State Bar N.Mex., Ohio State Bar Assn., Greater Cleve. Bar Assn. Roman Catholic. Home: 25 Pepper Creek Dr Cleveland OH 44124-5279 Office: Jones Day Reavis & Pogue N Point 901 Lakeside Ave E Cleveland OH 44114-1190 E-mail: bftoohey@jonesday.com.

TOOHEY, EDWARD JOSEPH, financial services company executive, retired; b. Jersey City, Jan. 15, 1930; s. John Joseph and Estelle Anita (Hudson) T.; m. Ruth Phyllis Scheidecker, Mar. 13, 1948; 1 child, Phyllis Karen. BA, Yale U., 1953. From with to mgr. dir. Merrill Lynch, Pierce, Fenner & Smith, Inc., N.Y.C., 1956—94, mgr. dir. instl. nat. sales, 1994—2001, ret., 2001. Pres. Bunbury Co., N.Y.C. Trustee Windham Found., Grafton, Vt., 1978—; vice chmn. Peddie Sch., Highstown, N.J., 1981—, trustee, 1976—; bd. dirs. N.Y.C. Ballet, 1993-96, emeritus, 1996—. Maj. USMC, 1953-55. Mem. Canoe Brook Country Club (Summit, N.J.), Yale Club, Sky Club, Univ. Club (N.Y.C.), Georgetown Club (Washington). Home: 1 Gracie Ter New York NY 10028-7955 E-mail: etoohey@exchange.ml.com.

TOOHEY, PHILIP S. lawyer; b. 1943; BA, Hamilton Coll., 1965; JD, Cornell U., 1968. Bar: N.Y. 1968. Law clk. Hon. Louis M. Greenblatt Appellate Divsn., 1968-69; assoc. Phillips, Lytle, Hitchcock, Blaine & Huber, 1969-74, ptnr., 1975-84; sr. bank counsel Marine Midland Banks, Inc., Buffalo, 1984-88, dep. gen. counsel, 1988-91, gen. counsel, sec., 1991-2000; sr. exec. v.p., gen. counsel, sec. HSBC Bank USA, 2000—. Mem. N.Y. State Bar Assn. (chmn. bus. law com. of banking, corp. & bus. law sect. 1985-88, sec. bus. law sect. 1988-89, vice chmn., treas. bus. law sect. 1989-90, 1st vice chmn. bus. law sect. 1990-91, chmn. bus. law sect. 1991-92). Office: HSBC Bank USA 1 Hsbc Ctr Buffalo NY 14203-2840

TOOKER, GEORGE, artist; b. Bklyn., Aug. 5, 1920; s. George Clair and Angela Montejo (Roura) T. BA, Harvard U., 1942; student, Art Students League, N.Y.C., 1943-44. Instr. Art Students League, N.Y., 1965-68. One man shows include Edwin Hewitt Gallery, 1951, 55, Robert Isaacson Gallery, 1960, 62, Durlacher Bros., 1964, 67, Hopkins Center at Dartmouth Coll., 1967, Fine Arts Mus., San Francisco, 1974, Mus. Contemporary Art, Chgo., 1974, Whitney Mus., N.Y.C., 1975, Indpls. Mus. Art, 1975; exhibited in group shows at Whitney Mus., 1947-50, 53, 55-58, 61, 64, 65, 67, 75, Venice Biennale, 1956, Art Inst. Chgo., 1951, 52, 54, 59, Inst. Contemporary Arts, London, 1950, Va. Mus., 1954, 62, Pa. Acad., 1966, Marisa Del Re Gallery, 1985, 88, 92, Spoleto Festival, Gibbes Mus. Art, Charleston, S.C., 1987, Robert Hall Fleming Mus. U. Vt., 1987, Marsh Gallery, U. Richmond, Va., 1989, Addison Gallery of Am. Art, 1994; represented permanent collections at Smithsonian Nat. Mus. of Am. Art, Smithsonian Hirshhorn Mus., Whitney Mus., Dartmouth Coll., Met. Mus., Walker Art Center, Mus. Modern Art, S.C. Johnson & Sons, Inc., Art, U.S.A., Sara Roby Fund Collection Am. Art, Addison Gallery, Ariz. State Univ. Gallery, Bklyn. Mus. Columbus (Ohio) Mus. Recipient Vt. gov.'s award for excellence in arts, 1983; Grantee Nat. Inst. Arts and Letters, 1960 Mem. NAD., Acad. Arts and Letters Address: PO Box 385 Hartland VT 05048-0385 Office: care DC Moore Gallery 724 5th Ave New York NY 10019-4106

TOOKES, JAMES NELSON, real estate investment company executive; b. Tallahassee, Sept. 16, 1934; m. Hortense Latricia James, June 22, 1958; 1 child, Gerald Ray. BS, Fla. A&M U., 1955, MEd, 1956. Tchr. Griffin Elem. Sch., Tallahassee, 1957-58, Douglas Elem. Sch., Wabasso, Fla., 1958-59, Barrow Hill Sch., Tallahassee, 1959-60, prin., 1960-67; tchr. various sch. ctrs. Leon County Dist., 1960-65; prin. Pineview Elem. Sch., 1967-73. Pres. Geray Petroleum, Inc., Tallahassee, 1980—, J.N.T. Properties, Inc., Tallahassee, 1973-77; broker Tookes Realty, Tallahassee, 1973-85; adv. bd. Barnett Bank of Tallahassee, 1977-79; bd. dirs. Marine State Bank. Bd. dirs. Tallahassee Youth Ctr., 1952-54, Tallahassee Meml. Regional Med. Ctr., 1977-82; chmn. divsn. United Fund campaign, 1962; trustee Tallahassee C.C., 1974-82, chmn. bd., 1976-77. Recipient Sch. Adminstr. Svc. award Pineview Elem. Sch. Student Coun., 1967-73, commednation award Bert Roger's Sch. Real Estate, 1973, Contbns. to Cmty. award Phi Beta Lambda, 1974; named One of 5 Most Outstanding Black Businessmen in State of Fla., Fla. A&M U. Sch. Bus. and Industry, 1974. Mem. Phi Delta Kappa, Kappa Alpha Psi (Man of Yr. 1973). Home: 925 E Magnolia Dr Apt 5C Tallahassee FL 32301-6606 Office: JNT Properties Inc 525 John Knox Rd Tallahassee FL 32303 E-mail: tookesj@jntprop.com.

TOOKEY, ROBERT CLARENCE, consulting actuary; b. Santa Monica, Calif., Mar. 21, 1925; s. Clarence Hall and Minerva Maconachie (Anderson) T.; m. Marcia Louise Hickman, Sept. 15, 1956; children: John Hall, Jennifer Louise, Thomas Anderson. BS, Calif. Inst. Tech., 1945; MS, U. Mich., 1947. With Prudential Ins. Co. Am., Newark, 1947-49; assoc. actuary in group Pacific Mut. Life Ins. Co., L.A., 1949-55; asst. v.p. in charge reins. sales and svc. for 17 western states Lincoln Nat. Life Ins. Co., Ft. Wayne, Ind., 1955-61; dir. actuarial svcs. Peat, Marwick, Mitchell & Co., Chgo., 1961-63; mng. prin. So. Calif. office Milliman & Robertson, cons. actuaries, Pasadena, 1963-76; pres. Robert Tookey Assocs., Inc., 1977—. Committeeman troop 501 Boy Scouts Am., 1969-72. Served to lt. (j.g.) USNR, 1943-45, 51-52. Fellow Soc. Actuaries, Conf. Consulting Actuaries; mem. Am. Acad. Actuaries, Pacific Ins. Conf., Rotary Club (Pasadena), Union League Club (Chgo.). Home and Office: PO Box 646 La Canada CA 91012-0646

TOOLAN, BRIAN PAUL, newspaper editor; b. Carbondale, Pa., June 29, 1950; s. Walter William and Elizabeth (Cleary) T.; m. Maureen Ellen Connolly, Sept. 7, 1974; children: Brendan, Seamus, Bridget, Colin, Molly. BA in English, St. Bonaventure U., Olean, N.Y., 1972. Reporter Scranton (Pa.) Tribune, 1972-79; copy editor Dayton (Ohio) Jour. Herald, 1979-81; layout editor Balt. News Am., 1981; copy editor Phila. Daily News, 1982-84, sports editor, 1984-89, asst. mng. editor, 1989-91, mng. editor, 1991-98; editor Hartford (Conn.) Courant, 1998—. Mem. AP Mng. Editors, Am. Soc. Newspaper Editors, Pa. Soc. Newspaper Editors (dir. 1989-92). Roman Catholic. Office: Hartford Courant 285 Broad St Hartford CT 06115-2510*

TOOLE, BRUCE RYAN, retired lawyer; b. Missoula, Mont., June 21, 1924; s. John Howard and Marjorie Lee (Ross) T.; m. Loris Knoll, Sept. 29, 1951; children: Marjorie, Ryan, Allan. JD, U. Mont., 1949. Bar: Mont., U.S. Ct. Appeals (9th & Fed. cirs.), U.S. Supreme Ct., U.S. Claims Ct. Sole practice, Missoula, 1950; dep. county atty. Missoula County, 1951; ptnr. Crowley Law Firm, Billings, Mont., 1951-92, of counsel, 1992—; ret. Editor Mont. Lawyer, 1979-83. Mem. Mont. Com. for Humanities, Missoula; v.p. Billings Preservation Soc.; precinctman Yellowstone County Reps. With U.S. Army, 1944-45, ETO. Fellowship grantee NEH, Harvard U., 1980. Fellow Am. Coll. Trial Lawyers, Am. Bar Found.; mem. Am. Bd. Trial Advs., State Bar Mont. (pres. 1977-78), Yellowstone County Bar (pres. 1973, chmn. com. on mediation 1992), Internat. Assn. Def. Counsel. Avocations: politics, history, photography, metal work. Home: 3019 Glacier Dr Billings MT 59102-0711 Office: Crowley Law Firm 490 N 31st St Ste 500 Billings MT 59101-1288 E-mail: crowley@crowleylaw.com.

TOOLE, JOHN HARPER, lawyer; b. Johnson City, N.Y., Apr. 4, 1941; s. Edward Joseph and Anne (Junius) T.; m. Lamar Sparkman, May 30, 1969; children: John Carter, Lucy Bland. BS, U. Va., 1963; JD, Washington Coll. of Law, 1971. Bar: Va. 1971, D.C. 1972. From assoc. to ptnr. Lewis, Mitchell & Moore, Tysons Corner, Va., 1971-77; ptnr. Watt, Tieder, Killian, Toole & Hoffar, 1978-82; of counsel, ptnr. McGuire, Woods, Battle & Boothe, 1983-90, McLean, Va., 1990-99; ptnr. Cooley Godward LLP, Reston, 2000—. 1st Lt. U.S. Army, 1963-66. Mem. ABA, Va. State Bar, Va. Bar Assn., D.C. Bar Assn. Office: Cooley Godward LLP 11951 Freedom Dr Reston VA 20190-5601 Fax: 703 456-8100. E-mail: jtoole@cooley.com.

TOOLE, WILLIAM WALTER, lawyer; b. Phila., Feb. 17, 1959; s. James Francis and Patricia (Wooldridge) T.; m. Claudina Ghianni, May 20, 1989; 1 child, Lauren Marie. BA, Haverford Coll., 1982; MBA, JD, Wake Forest U., 1989. Bar: N.C. 1989, Md. 1990, U.S. Dist. Ct. Md. 1990, U.S. Ct. Appeals (4th cir.) 1991, Va. 1992. Journalist Rural Hall (N.C.) Ind., 1983-84; comml. fisherman Destin, Fla., 1984-85; law clk. to Hon. Louis B. Meyer N.C. Supreme Ct., Raleigh, 1989-90; atty. Piper & Marbury, Balt., 1990-93, Robinson, Bradshaw & Hinson PA, Charlotte, N.C., 1993-98; ptnr. Robinson, Bradshaw & Hinson, PA, 1999—. Adj. prof. UNC, Charlotte. Editor-in-chief Md. Environ. Law Newsletter, 1990-93; contbr. chpt. to Md. Environ. Law Handbook. Bd. dirs. Gaston Day Sch., Carolina Raptor Ctr.; action team leader Water Quality Protection Bd. Mem. Haverford Alumni Assn. (regional rep. 1990-98). Office: 101 N Tryon St Charlotte NC 28246-0100 E-mail: wtoole@rbh.com.

TOOLEY, CHARLES FREDERICK, communications executive, consultant; b. Seattle, Sept. 29, 1947; s. Creath Athol and Catherine Ella (Wainman) T.; m. Valerie Adele Gose, Mar. 7, 1981 (dec. Feb. 1991); children: Paige Arlene Chytka, Marni Higdon Tooley; m. Joan Marie Stapleton, Feb. 21, 1998. BA, Lynchburg Coll., 1968. Producer, stage mgr., tech. dir. various theatre cos. and performing arts orgns., 1965-74; field underwriter N.Y. Life Ins. Co., Billings, Mont., 1974-77; market adminstr. Mountain Bell Telephone Co., Butte and Billings, 1978-83; pres. BCC Inc., Billings, 1983—. Dir. Mont. Elec. and Gas Alliance, 2000—. Mem. Mont. Arts Coun., 1982-92; mem. divsn. of overseas ministries Christian Ch. Disciples of Christ, 1997—; elder Ctrl. Christian Ch., Billings, 1983—; del. Dem. Nat. Conv., 1980; mem. Mont. Dem. Exec. Bd., 1982-87; mem. adv. bd. Salvation Army, Billings, 1984—; mem. Billings City Coun., 1988-94, mayor pro tem, 1992-94; mayor City of Billings, 1996—; mem. Common Global Ministries Bd., 1997—; chair U.S. Com. Mayors on Resource Conservation and Population, 1999—; bd. dirs. The Population Inst., 2002--. Sgt. U.S. Army, 1969-72, Vietnam. Recipient communication and leadership award Toastmasters Internat., 1999. Mem. Masons, Shriners, Elks. Mem. Christian Ch. (Disciples Of Christ). Avocations: theatre productions.

TOOLEY, LOWELL JAMES, city manager; b. Sauk County, Wis., July 21, 1923; m. Marceil Sprecher, July 9, 1949; children: David Son, Paul Wayne, Mary Lynn, Jeanne Louise. BS, U. Wis., 1953. Registered profl. engr., N.Y., Wis. Engr., mgr. Shorewood Hills (Wis.), 1949—56; asst. mgr. Scarsdale (N.Y.), 1956—61, mgr., 1961—95; v.p. ops. Grand Ctrl. Partnership, 34th St. Partnership and Bryant Pk. Restoration Corp., 1995—98; exec. v.p., asst. sec. Grand Ctrl. Partnership, 1999—2001. Chmn. adv. coun. Inst. for Local Govt. Westchester CC, 1965—85; mem. NY Lt. Gov.'s Roundtable, 1983—84. Bd. dirs. Coun. on Mcpl. Performance, 1985—87; chmn. recycling adv. com. County of Westchester, 1988—94; mem. Model Cities Charter Task Force, 1986—89. Named named Citizen of Yr., Scarsdale C. of C., 1992; recipient outstanding svc. award, Scarsdale Village Bd., 1986, Entered in Congl. Record, 1986. Mem.: N.Y. State Soc. Profl. Engrs. (Westchester County chpt. sec. 1987—91, pres. 1991—92, Outstanding Engr. in Govt. Westchester County chpt. 1983), Nat. Council on Pub. Works Improvement (discussion participant), Am. Water Works Assn., Am. Pub. Works Assn. (Edward P. Decher award N.Y.-N.J. Met. chpt. 1982), Nat. Soc. Profl. Engrs. (govt. adv. group 1982—86), Westchester County Village Ofcls. Assn. (exec. bd.), Am. Soc. Pub. Adminstrn. (dir. 1980—83, named Man of Yr. Lower Hudson Valley chpt. 1979), N.Y. State Conf. Mayors (legis. com. 1962—95), N.Y. State Mcpl. Mgmt. Assn. (pres. 1964—65), Internat. City Mgmt. Assn. (v.p. 1980—82, chmn. ethics com. 1982, 40 yr. svc. award 1989), Westchester 2000 (chmn. intergovtl. relations com. 1987—95), Westchester County Assn., Nat. Mcpl. League (coun. advisors 1986—89). E-mail: ltooley2@aol.com.

TOOMAJIAN, WILLIAM MARTIN, lawyer; b. Troy, N.Y., Sept. 26, 1943; s. Leo R. and Elizabeth (Gundrum) T.; children: Andrew, Philip. AB, Hamilton Coll., 1965; JD, U. Mich., 1968; LLM, N.Y.U., 1975. Bar: N.Y. 1968, Ohio 1978. Mem. firm Cadwalader, Wickersham & Taft, N.Y.C., 1971-77, Baker & Hostetler, Cleve., 1977—. Served to lt. USCG, 1968-71. Mem. ABA, Ohio Bar Assn., Cleve. Bar Assn., Cleve. Tax Club. Home: 3582 Lytle Rd Cleveland OH 44122-4908 Office: Baker & Hostetler 3200 National City Ctr 1900 E 9th St Ste 3200 Cleveland OH 44114-3475

TOOMAN, STEPHANIE, performing arts educator; BFS, Julliard Sch.; MFA, Purchase Coll. Rehearsal dir. Neta Pulvermacher, Errol Grimes, The Purchase Dance Corps; dancer, rehearsal dir. Kazuko Hirabayashi, Tokyo; tchr. dance Alvin Ailey Am. Dance Ctr., the Netherlands Dance Theatre, 1st and 2d Cos., the Hague, Netherlands, The Rotterdam Dance Acad., The Inst. del Theatre, Barcelona; with Merian Soto/Pepatian, EarlMosley Diversity of Dance, Nathan Trice, Errol Grimes Dance Group; collaborator, dancer Reggie Wilson, 1989—.*

TOOMBS, KENNETH ELDRIDGE, librarian; b. Colonial Heights, Va., Aug. 25, 1928; s. Garnett Eldridge and Susie W. (Bryant) T.; m. Ada Teresa Hornsby, Aug. 29, 1949; children— Susan Elizabeth Shealy, Cheri Lynn Morris, Teresa Ann Heilman. AA, Tenn. Wesleyan Coll., 1950; BS, Tenn. Poly. Inst., 1951; MA, U. Va., 1955; MLS, Rutgers U., 1956; student, La. State U., 1961-63. Reference asst. Alderman Library, U. Va., 1954-55; research asst. Grad. Sch . Library Sci., Rutgers U., 1955-56; mem. staff and faculty La. State U., 1956-63, asst. dir. charge pub. services, 1962-63; dir. libraries, prof. library sci. U. Southwestern La., 1963-67; dir. libraries U. S.C., Columbia, 1967—; bd. dirs. Southeastern Library Network, 1967-88; disting. dir. of librs. emeritus U. S.C., Columbia, 1988—; vice chmn. Southeastern Library Network, 1973-74, 83-84, chmn., 1974-75, treas., 1984-85. Libr. cons. for bldgs. and adminstrn. for 60 colls. and univs. in past 30 yrs.; chmn. librarians sect. La. Coll. Conf., 1965-67; mem. Bd. La. Libr. Examiners, 1966-67; participant Libr. Mgmt. Inst., U. Wash., Seattle, 1969, Libr. Bldg. Problems Inst., UCLA, 1970; co-founder Southeastern Libr. Network with John Gribbin. Contbr. articles to profl. jours.; editor: Bull. La. Library Assn, 1959-62; mng. editor: SW La. Jour, 1963-67; adv. bd.: Linguistic Atlas Am. Treas. Wesley Found.; v.p. Am. Field Services Internat. Scholarships; bd. dirs. U. S.C. Ednl. Found., 1975-82; Danforth assoc., 1967—; AIA/ALA Bldg. Awards Jury, 1987. Served to 1st lt. AUS, 1946-47, 51-53. Mem. ALA (life), La. Library Assn. (parliamentarian 1962-63, 66-67), Southeastern Library Assn. (Life mem., exec. bd. 1981-85, Rothrock award 1978), Southwestern Library Assn., S.C. Library Assn. (Life mem., pres. 1976, exec. bd. 1981-85), Assn. Southeastern Research Libraries (chmn. 1973-75, adv. com. to OCLC 1979-84), AAUP (sec.), La. Hist. Assn., La. Tchrs. Assn., Soc. Tympanuchus Cupido Pinnatus,

South Caroliniana Soc., Nat. Library Bldg. Consultants List (chmn. 1981-84), Tenn. Squire (Ky. col.), Assn. of S.C. Retirees (bd. dirs. 1995—), Omicron Delta Epsilon. Clubs: Mason (Shriner), Kiwanis. Methodist. Home: 16 Garden Springs Rd Columbia SC 29209-1716

TOOMBS, RUSS WILLIAM, laboratory director; b. Troy, N.Y., July 11, 1951; s. George John and Olive Catherine (Blodgett) T.; m. Patrice Ann De Paul, Aug. 19, 1972; children: David Christopher, Mark Patrick. BS, Cornell U., 1973. Environ. scientist Wapora, Inc., Washington, 1973-74; bacteriologist N.Y. State Dept. Health, Wadsworth Ctr. for Labs. and Rsch., Albany, N.Y., 1974-76, sr. bacteriologist, 1976-78, assoc. bacteriologist, 1978-86, dir. ops., 1986-90, assoc. dir., 1990-96; asst. dir. Wadsworth Ctr. for Labs. and Rsch., NY, 1996—2001; project and facilities mgr. Charitable Leadership Found., 2001—. Contbr. articles to profl. jours. Bd. dirs. Albany Ctr. Gallery. Mem. AAAS, Am. Soc. Microbiology, N.Y. Acad. Scis., Assn. Pub. Health Labs., Am. Assn. Clin. Chemistry, Am. Biol. Safety Assn., Saratoga Performing Arts Ctr. Roman Catholic. Home: 65 Huntleigh Dr Albany NY 12211-1175 Office: Ctr for Medical Science 150 New Scotland Ave Albany NY 12208 E-mail: rtoombs@charitableleadership.org.

TOOMBS, WILLIAM EDGAR, professor; b. Phila., Feb. 2, 1920; s. Edgar and Cordelia (Parry) T.; m. Jean I. Buckley, Mar. 8, 1943; children: W. Scott, Gwenyth, David E. BS, West Chester U., 1942; AM, U. Pa., 1949; PhD, U. Mich., 1971. Dean of men, assoc. prof. Drexel U., Phila., 1953-66; asst. to dean, Horace Rackham Sch. U. Mich., Ann Arbor, 1967-71; assoc. prof., sr. rschr. Pa. State U., State Col., 1971-81, dir., prof. Ctr. Study Higher Edn., 1981-86, prof., 1986-89, prof. emeritus, 1989—. Cons. TAS Assocs., State Col., Pa., 1989—. Bd. dirs. Westminster Found., Phila., 1961-63; trustee African Scholarship Program: Am. Us., Cambridge, Mass., 1963-67. Capt. USN, 1942-46. 50-53, ret. USNR. Recipient Howard Bowen award Assn. for Study of Higher Edn., 1995. Presbyterian. Avocations: nature study, photography. Home: 130 Outer Dr State College PA 16801-7927

TOOMER, CYNTHIA YVONNE, information systems administrator; b. Camden, N.J., Nov. 9, 1947; d. Nathaniel and Dorothy (Hudson) T. BA, Brandeis U., 1969; MS, Simmons Coll., 1973. Reference librarian Boston U. Mugar Library, Boston, 1973-77; head reference dept. Harvard U. Lamont Library, Cambridge, Mass., 1977-84; sr. proposal writer CLSI, Inc., Newton, 1984-87; tech writer, analyst Index Tech., Cambridge, 1987; dir. devel. info. sys. Radcliffe Inst. Harvard U., 1988—. Mem. Mensa. Independent. Avocations: photography, travel, language study, genealogy. Home: 253 Norfolk St Cambridge MA 02139-1451 Office: Radcliffe Inst Devel Office 10 Garden St Cambridge MA 02138-3600 E-mail: toomer@mediaone.net.

TOOMEY, JEANNE ELIZABETH, animal activist; b. N.Y.C., Aug. 22, 1921; d. Edward Aloysius and Anna Margaret (O'Grady) Toomey; m. Peter Terranova, Sept. 28, 1951 (dec. 1968); children: Peter Terranova, Sheila Terranova Beasley. Student, Hofstra U., 1938-40; student law sch., Fordham U., 1940-41; BA, Southampton Coll., 1976; postgrad., Monmouth Coll., 1978-79. Reporter, columnist Bklyn. Daily Eagle, 1943-52; with The Fitzgeralds, NBC Radio, N.Y.C., 1952-53; reporter, writer King Features Syndicate, 1953-55; reporter, columnist N.Y. Jour.-Am., 1955-61; newsman AP, 1963-64; stringer; columnist News Tribune, Woodbridge, N.J., 1976-86; editor Calexico (Calif.) Chronicle, 1987-88; editor community sect. Asbury Park (N.J.) Press, 1988; pres., dir. Last Post Animal Sanctuary, Falls Village, Conn., 1989—. Author: Murder in the Hamptons, 1994, Assignment Homicide, 1998. Named Woman of the Yr. N.Y. Women's Press Club, 1960. Mem. Newswomen's Club of N.Y., Overseas Press Club, N.Y. Press Club, Silurians. Roman Catholic. Address: PO Box 259 Falls Village CT 06031-0259 Fax: 860-824-5460.

TOOMEY, PATRICK J. congressman; b. Providence, 1962; m. Kris.; 1 child, Bridget. BS cum laude, Harvard U. Investment banking Chem. Bank N.Y.; v.p., dir. U.S. subsidiary British merchant bank; co-founder internat. fin. svcs. consulting firm; founder Toomey Enterprises, Inc., Allentown, Pa.; mem. U.S. Congress from 15th Pa. dist., 1999—. Serves on Banking and Fin. Svcs., Budget and Small Bus. coms. Elected to Allentown Govt. Study Commn., 1994. Elected in 1998 to U.S. Ho. Reps. seat vacated by retiring Rep. Paul McHale. Served an internship with Sen. John Chafee (R-R.I.). Republican. Achievements include Toomey Enterprises, Inc., a family restaurant bus., operates 2 Rookies Restaurants located in Allentown and Lancaster, Pa. Office: 224 Cannon Hob Washington DC 20515-0001 : 2020 Hamilton Street Allentown PA 18104*

TOOMEY, SISTER STEPHANA, space designer, nun; b. Wilmington, Del., Nov. 19, 1930; d. Hugh Jeremiah and Ellen (Vahey) Toomey. BS in Art Edn., Moore Coll. Art, Phila., 1952; MEd in Art, Temple U., 1960; cert., Internat. Ctr. Glass-Mosaics, Ravenna, Italy, 1975; postgrad., Paros (Greece) Sch. Fine Arts, 1975. Lic. lic. liturgical cons. and designer; joined Dominican Order, Roman Cath. Ch., 1956. Tchr. art pub. schs., Camden, N.J., 1952-54, Oak Grove, Del., 1954-56; founder, pres. Efharisto Studio Inc., worship space design studio, Balt., 1976—. Cons., mem. liturgical adv. com. Archdiocese of Balt., 1986—91. Contbr. articles and photogs. to various publs.; 5 nat. TV documentaries produced on her work; Represented in permanent collections Nat. Mus. Women in Arts. Mem. New Ventures. Named winner for stained glass in chs., Bene Competition, San Jose, 2000—01; recipient hon. mention for stained glass in chs., 1991, 1993, 1998. Mem.: Domican Order's Internat. Inst. Arts (founding mem. Dominican Inst. Arts 1997, Fra Angelico Life Achievement award 1999), Balt. Writers Alliance, Form Reform, Faith and Form of AIA, Constrn. Specifications Inst., Art Architecture of AIA, Interfaith Forum Religion. Avocations: being with nature, classical music, assisting all religious traditions in design of worship space, liturgical appointments, stained glass. Office: Efharisto Studio Inc 5130 Franklintown Rd Baltimore MD 21207 Fax: 410-448-3259.

TOOMEY, THOMAS MURRAY, lawyer; b. Washington, Dec. 9, 1923; s. Vincent L. and Catherine V. (McCann) T.; m. Grace Donohoe, June 22, 1948; children: Isabelle Marie Toomey Hessick, Helen Marie, Mary Louise, Thomas Murray. Student, Duke U., 1943-44, Catholic U. Am., 1942-43, 47-49, JD, 1949. Bar: D.C. 1949, Md. 1952. Sole practice, Washington and Md., 1949—. Bd. dirs. Allied Capital Corp, Washington, Chgo., Detroit, San Francisco, Atlanta, Frankfurt, Germany, Fed. Ctr. Plz. Corp., Nat. Capital Bank, Washington. Chmn. aviation and transp. coms. Met. Washington Bd. Trade, 1954-76, bd. dirs., 1962-77; chmn. dedication Dulles Internat. Airport, 1962; trustee Cath. U. Am., 1981—; founding trustee Heights Sch. Served to 1st lt. USMC, 1942-46, 50-52. Recipient Ann. Alumni Achievement award, Cath. U., 1977, Most. Disting. Alumnus award, St. John's Coll. H.S. D.C., 1994, 1st Bishop Thomas J. Shahan award, Cath. U., 2001. Mem. ABA, D.C. Bar Assn., Md. Bar Assn., Bar Assn. D.C., Am. Judicature Soc., Comml. Law League Am., Friendly Sons St. Patrick (pres. 1983), Sovereign Mil. Order of Malta (Fed. Assn. U.S.A.), Congl. Golf and Country Club, Kenwood Golf and Country Club, Univ. Club, Army and Navy Club (Washington), Tower Club, Lago Mar Beach Club (Ft. Lauderdale, Fla.). Home: 6204 Garnett Dr Chevy Chase MD 20815-6618 Office: 4701 Sangamore Rd Bethesda MD 20816-2508 also: 2000 S Ocean Dr Fort Lauderdale FL 33316-3804

TOOMEY, WILLIAM SHENBERGER, retired wire manufacturing company executive; b. Windsor, Pa., Feb. 6, 1935; s. Harold DeWitt and Ruth Evelyn Belle (Shenberger) T.; m. Nancy Antoinette Mangin, Oct. 13, 1962; children: William, Michael, John. BS in Metall. Engring., Lehigh U., 1957. Supervising metallurgist primary rolling mills LTV Steel Corp., Aliquippa, Pa., 1972-73, gen. supr. heat treating shipping and invoice, 1973-76, supervising metallurgist rod wire and tubular, 1976-77, mgr. product quality rod and wire, 1977-78, mgr. product quality tubular, 1978-85; mgr. product quality and product devel. Fostoria (Ohio) div. Seneca Wire & Mfg. Co., 1986, plant mgr., 1986, gen. mgr., 1986-87, corp. tech. dir., 1987-91; cons. Am. Spring Wire, Bedford Heights, Ohio, 1991, new product devel. mgr., 1992-98; ret., 1998. With USN, 1958. Mem. Am. Wire Assn., Am. Soc. Nondestructive Testing. Republican. Avocations: fishing, hunting, reading. Home: 280 Ash Grove Cir Aurora OH 44202-8470

TOOMRE, ALAR, applied mathematician, theoretical astronomer; b. Rakvere, Estonia, Feb. 5, 1937; came to U.S., 1949, naturalized, 1955; s. Elmar and Linda (Aghen) T.; m. Joyce Stetson, June 15, 1958; children: Lars, Erik, Anya. BS in Aero. Engring., BS in Physics, MIT, 1957; PhD in Fluid Mechanics, U. Manchester, Eng., 1960. C.L.E. Moore instr. math. dept. MIT, Cambridge, 1960-62, asst. prof. applied math., 1963-65, assoc. prof., 1965-70, prof., 1970—; fellow Inst. for Advanced Study, Princeton, N.J., 1962-63. Contbr. articles to profl. jours. Guggenheim fellow, 1969-70, MacArthur fellow, 1984-89; Fairchild scholar, 1975, Marshall scholar, 1957-60 Fellow AAAS; mem. Am. Astron. Soc. (Dirk Brouwer award 1993), Internat. Astron. Union, Am. Acad. Arts and Scis., Nat. Acad. Scis. Office: MIT 77 Massachusetts Ave Rm 2-371 Cambridge MA 02139-4307

TOON, MALCOLM, former ambassador; b. Troy, N.Y., July 4, 1916; s. George and Margaret Harcomb (Broadfoot) T.; m. Elizabeth Jane Taylor, Aug. 28, 1943; children: Barbara, Alan, Nancy. AB, Tufts U., 1937, LL.D. (hon.), 1977; MA, Fletcher Sch. Law and Diplomacy, 1938; student, Middlebury Coll., 1950, Harvard U., 1950-51; LL.D. (hon.), Middlebury Coll., 1978, Drexel U., 1980, Am. Coll. Switzerland, 1985, Grove City Coll., 1990. Fgn. service officer, 1946-79; assigned successively Warsaw, Budapest, Moscow, Rome, Berlin, Washington, 1946-60; assigned Am. embassy, London, 1960-63, counselor political affairs Moscow, 1963-67; with Dept. of State, Washington, 1967-69; ambassador to Czechoslovakia, 1969-71; to Yugoslavia, 1971-75; to Israel, 1975-76; to USSR, 1976-79. Mem. U.S. del. Nuclear Test Conf., Geneva, 1958-59, Four Power Working Group, Washington, London, Paris, 1959, Fgn. Ministers Conf., Geneva, 1969, Ten Nation Disarmament Com., Geneva, 1960; mem. SALT II del., 1977-79, U.S.-Soviet Summit Conf., Vienna, 1979; Brennen prof. U. N.C., Asheville, 1981; Finch prof. Miami U., Oxford, Ohio, 1982; Allis-Chalmers chair Marquette U., Milw., 1982 Trustee emeritus Tufts U.; bd. overseers Fletcher Sch. Law and Diplomacy, 1992; former chmn. U.S. Delegation to Joint U.S. Russian Commn. on POW's, MIA's. Served from ensign to lt. comdr. USNR, 1942-46. Decorated Bronze Star with combat V; recipient Freedom Leadership award Hillsdale Coll., 1980, Valley Forge Freedom award, 1981, Disting. Honor award Dept. State, 1980, Wallace award, 1984, Gold medal Nat. Inst. of Social Scis., 1987, Degree of Prof., Acad. Natural Scis. of the Russian Fedn., 1996, Silver medal, 1996. Home: 375 Pee Dee Rd Southern Pines NC 28387-2118

TOOR, HERBERT LAWRENCE, chemical engineering educator, researcher; b. Pitts., June 22, 1927; s. Matthew G. and Jean (Mogul) T.; m. Elizabeth Margaret Weir, Dec. 1950; children: Helen Mary, John Weir, William Ramsay. BS, Drexel U., 1948; MS, Northwestern U., 1950, PhD, 1952. Rsch. chemist Monsanto Chems., Ltd., 1952-53; asst. prof. Carnegie Mellon U., Pitts., 1953-57, assoc. prof., 1957-61, prof., 1961—, head chem. engring dept., 1967-70, dean Carnegie Inst. Tech., 1970-79, Mobay prof. chem. engring., 1980-92, Mobay prof. chem. engring. emeritus, 1992-95, engring. univ. prof. emeritus, 1997—. Vis. UNESCO prof. U. Madras, India, 1962-63. Contbr. numerous articles to tech. jours. With USNR, 1944-45. Recipient merit award Northwestern U. Alumni, 1973. Fellow AAAS, Am. Inst. Chem. Engrs. (Colburn award 1964); mem. NAE.

TOOTHACKER, WILLIAM SANFORD, III, physics educator; b. Washington, Mar. 23, 1943; s. William Sanford Jr. and Grace (Nelson) T. BS, Purdue U., 1965; MA, Wayne State U., 1970; PhD, U. Mich., 1977. Rsch. asst. Edsel B. Ford Inst. for Med. Rsch., Detroit, 1966-72; instr. physics Wayne County C.C., 1972-83; asst. prof. physics Pa. State U., Mont Alto, 1984-89, assoc. prof. physics, 1989-96, prof. physics, from 1996. Vis. lectr. The Open U., Eng., 1981-82; vis. scientist Fermi Nat. Lab., Chgo., 1990-91, Deutsches Elektronen-Synchrotron Lab., Germany, 1997-98. Reviewer Am. Jour. Physics, 1990—; contbr. more than 60 articles to profl. jours. Mem. Am. Phys. Soc., Am. Assn. Physics Tchrs. Home: Chambersburg, Pa. Died May 16, 2000.

TOOTHE, KAREN LEE, elementary and secondary school educator; b. Seattle, Dec. 13, 1957; d. Russell Minor and Donna Jean (Drolet) McGraw; m. Edward Frank Toothe, Aug. 6, 1983; 1 child, Kendall Erin. BA in Psychology with high honors, U. Fla., 1977, MEd in Emotional Handicaps and Learning Disabilities, 1979. Cert. behavior analysis Fla. Dept. Profl. Regulation, behavior analyst Nat. Behavior Analyst Bd. Alternative edn. self-contained tchr. grades 2 and 3 Gainesville Acad., Micanopy, Fla., 1979; emotional handicaps self-contained tchr. Ctr. Sch. Alternative Sch., Gainesville, 1979-80; learning disabilities resource tchr. grades 2 and 3 Galaxy Elem. Sch., Boynton Beach, 1980-81, learning disabilities self-contained tchr. grades 1-3, 1981, varying exceptionalities self-contained tchr. grades 3-5, 1981-83, chpt. one remedial reading tchr. grades 3 and 4, 1982-83; sec. and visual display unit operator Manpower, London, 1983-84; dir. sci./geography/social studies program Fairley House Sch., 1984-86, specific learning difficulties self-contained tchr. ages 8-12, dir. computing program, 1984-89; specific learning difficulties resource tchr. ages 8-16 Dyslexia Inst., Sutton Coldfield, Eng., 1990; behavior specialist, head Exceptional Student Edn. dept. Gateway High Sch., Kissimmee, Fla., 1990, behavior specialist, head ESE dept., 1991, resource compliance specialist, head ESE dept., 1991-93, tchr. summer youth tng. and enrichment program, 1993, Osceola High Sch., Kissimmee, 1992; resource compliance specialist, program specialist for mentally handicapped, physically impaired, occupational and phys. therapy programs St. Cloud (Fla.) Mid. Sch., 1993-96, local augmentative/assistive tech. specialist, 1995—; resource compliance specialist, program specialist physically impaired occupl./phys. therapy programs, local augmentative/assistive tech. specialist Hickory Tree Elem. Sch., 1996-97, program specialist assistive tech., occpl., and phys. therapy, physically impaired programs, 1997-99, program specialist assistive tech., 1999—. Sch. rep. CREATE, Alachua County, Fla., 1979-80, Palm Beach County South Area Tchr. Edn. Ctr. Coun., 1980-83, chmn., 1982-83; mem. writing team Title IV-C Ednl. Improvement Grant, Palm Beach County, Fla., 1981; mem. math. curriculum writing team Palm Beach County (Fla.) Schs., 1983; mem., co-dir. Fairley House Rsch. Com., 1984-90; co-founder, dir. Rsch. Database, London, 1984-89; co-chmn. computer and behavior/social aspects writing teams Dyslexia Inst. Math., Staines, Eng., 1990; lectr., course tutor Brit. Dyslexia Assn., Crewe, Eng., 1990; mem. Vocat.-Exceptional Com., 1991-93; mem. Osceola Reading Coun., 1991-98; mem. sch. adv. com. Gateway High Sch., 1991-93, St. Cloud Mid. Sch., 1993-96; mem. sch. adv. com. Hickory Tree Elem. Sch., 1999-2000; presenter in field. Named Mid. Sch. Profl. of Yr. Osceola chpt. Coun. Exceptional Children, 1995, 96, Profl. Recognised Spl. Educator, 1997,; winner Disney's Teacherific Spl. Judges award, 1997. Mem. CEC (named local chpt. Mid. Sch. Profl. of Yr. 1995, 96, exec. com. 1997—, C.A.N. rep. 1997-99, pres.-elect 1999-2000, pres. 2000-2001), Fla. Soc. for Augmentative and Alt. Comm., Fla. Profl. Assn. Staffing Specialists, 1992-97, Phi Beta Kappa. Avocations: traveling, reading, physical fitness, scuba diving, arts and crafts. Home: 2175 James Dr Saint Cloud FL 34771-8830 Office: Osceola Dist Schs ESE Adminstrv Annex 805 Bill Beck Blvd Kissimmee FL 34744-4492 E-mail: toothek@osceola.k12.fl.us.

TOP, FRANKLIN HENRY, JR. physician, researcher; b. Detroit, Mar. 1, 1936; s. Franklin Henry Sr. and Mary (Madden) T.; m. Lois Elizabeth Fritzell, Sept. 23, 1961; children: Franklin H. III, Brian N., Andrew M. BS, Yale U., 1957, MD cum laude, 1961. Diplomate Am. Bd. Pediatrics. Intern, resident, infectious diseases fellow U. Minn. Hosps., Mpls., 1961-66; commd. officer U.S. Army, advanced through grades to col.; med. officer, dept. virus diseases Walter Reed Army Inst. Research, Washington, 1966-70, chief dept. virus diseases, 1973-76, dir. div. communicable diseases and immunology, 1976-79, dep. dir., 1979-81, dir. and comdt., 1983-87; chief dept. virology Seato Med. Research Lab., Bangkok, 1970-73; comdr. U.S.A. Med. Research Inst. of Chem. Def., Aberdeen Proving Ground, Md., 1981-83; ret. U.S. Army, 1987; sr. v.p. Praxis Biologics Inc., Rochester, N.Y., 1987-88; exec. v.p., med. dir. MedImmune, Inc., Gaithersburg, Md., from 1988. Contbr. over 40 articles to med. jours. Decorated Legion of Merit with 2 oak leaf clusters. Fellow Am. Acad. Pediatrics, Infectious Diseases Soc. Am.; mem. AMA, Alpha Omega Alpha. Avocation: ornithology.

TOPALIAN, NAOMI GETSOYAN, writer; b. Beirut, Lebanon, Jan. 26, 1928; came to the U.S., 1953; d. Avedis S. and Zarouhi T. (Yezegelian) G.; m. Paul G. Topalian, Sept. 18, 1954; children: Andrew P., Janet Z. Topalian Moffatt. Diploma, Am. U. Hosp. Sch. Nursing, Beirut, 1952; BS, Boston U., 1967. RN, Mass. Pediat. nurse Children Med. Ctr., Boston, 1954-55; inservice edn. supr. Winchester (Mass.) Hosp., 1967-70; tchr. nursing Northeastern Vocat. H.S., Wakefield, Mass., 1970-72; med. and surg. nurse various tchg. hosps., Boston, 1973-87. Author: Dust to Destiny, 1986, People, Places and Moultonborough, 1989, Legacy of Honor, 1995; contbr. Personality and Presidency: A Scientific Inquirey, 1998, Breaking the Rock of Tradition, 2000; contbr. articles to profl. jours. Supt. primary divsn., Sunday sch. tchr., mem. pulpit com., co-pres. couples club Armenian Meml. Ch., Watertown, Mass.; Armenian lang. tchr. First Armenian Ch. of Belmont; active Belmont Coun. Chs., chair religious edn. com.; pres. Armenian Women's Edn. Club. Mem. Armenian Internat. Womens Assn. Avocations: needle work, knitting, counseling the bereaved. Home: 46 Circle Rd Lexington MA 02420-2926

TOPEL, DAVID GLEN, agricultural studies educator; b. Lake Mills, Wis., Oct. 24, 1937; BS, U. Wis., 1960; MS, Kans. State U., 1962; PhD, Mich. State U., 1965. Assoc. prof. animal sci. and food tech. Iowa State U., Ames, 1967-73, prof. animal sci. and food tech., 1973-79, dean Coll. Agr., 1988-2000, dir. agr. and home econs. experiment sta., 1988-2000, M.E. Ensminger chair animal sci., 2000—; prof., head dept. Auburn U., 1979-88, M.E. Ensminger endowed chair animal sci., 2000—. Cons., presenter, lectr. in field; mem. Gov. of Iowa's Sci. Adv. Coun., 1990-2000, Gov. of Iowa's Livestock Revitalization Task Force, 1993-98; chair Gov.'s Environ. Agr. Com., 1994; mem. Iowa Corn Promotion Bd.; mem. faculty Royal Vet. and Agrl. U., Denmark, 1971-72, 90; vis. prof. Nat. Taiwan U., 1972. Author: The Pork Industry - Problems and Progress, 1968. Secretariat World Food Prize, Iowa State U., Ames, 1991-96. Fulbright-Hays scholar Royal Vet. and Agrl. U., 1971-72; recipient award of merit Knights of Ak-Sar-Ben, 1973, Commr.'s award Agrl. Commr. Republic of China, 1977, disting. Achievement award Block and Bridle Club, 1979, Ala. Cattlemen's Assn.,1 984, Hon. State Farmer Degree, Ala., 1986, Harry L. Rudnick Educator's award Nat. Assn. Meat Purveyors, 1989, USDA Honor award, 1999, Hon. Prof. award Gyöngyös Coll., Hungary, 2000; named hon. prof. Ukrainian State Agrl. U., 1993. Fellow Am. Soc. Animal Sci. (Disting. Rsch. award in meat sci. 1979); mem. Am. Meat Sci. Assn., Inst. Food Tech., Iowa Crop Improvement Assn., Extension and Tchg. (pres. North Ctrl. Region 1992), Nat. Assn. State Univs. and Land-Grant Colls. (chair bd. agr. 1993, mem. commn. on food, environ. and renewable resources 1992-99), Ukrainian Acad. Agrl. Scis., Sigma Xi (Outstanding Achievement award Iowa chpt. 1993), Alpha Zeta, Gamma Sigma Delta (Internat. award). Presbyterian. Avocations: fishing, golf. Home: 2630 Meadow Glen Rd Ames IA 50014-8239 Office: Iowa State U Coll Agriculture 2374 Kildee Hall Ames IA 50011-0001

TOPELIUS, KATHLEEN ELLIS, lawyer; b. July 15, 1948; BA, U. Conn., 1970; postgrad., U. Md., 1971-74; JD, Cath. U. Am., 1978. Bar: D.C. 1978, U.S. Supreme Ct. 1988. Atty. office of gen. counsel Fed. Home Loan Bank Bd., 1978-80; ptnr. Morgan, Lewis & Bockius, Washington, 1985-93, Bryan Cave, Washington, 1993—. Recipient Alpha award Fed. Home Loan Bank Bds., 1979. Office: Bryan Cave 700 13th St NW Fl 7 Washington DC 20005-5921 Business E-Mail: ktopelius@bryancave.com.

TOPETZES, FAY KALAFAT, retired school guidance counselor; b. Auburn, Ind., July 13, 1923; d. Alexander Christ and Andromache Basiliou Kalafat; m. Nick John Topetzes, Jan. 31, 1953; children: Andrea Topetzes Mann, John Nick, Sophia Angela. BS in Acctg. and English, Ind. U., 1945; cert. tchr., Marquette U., 1969, MS in Guidance and Counseling, 1973. Cert. tchr., Wis. Acct. Dana Corp., Auburn, Ind., 1945-47; mgr. theaters Kalafat Bros., 1947-53; tchr. Univ. Sch. of Milw., 1962-64, Spencerian Bus. Coll., Milw., 1959-62, Milw. Pub. Schs., 1962-69; counselor, dir. guidance West Allis (Wis.) Ctrl. H.S., 1969-86; ret., 1986. Charter pres., mem. Ind. U. of Greek Am. Student Assn., 1942-45; bd. dirs. Gov.'s Tourism Coun. of Wis., Milw., 1990—, FLW Heritage Bd., Madison, Wis., 1990—; vol. for many charitable orgns.; active in ch., ednl., cultural and art orgns. Mem. APA, AAUW (past pres., pub. policy chairperson, Nat. award 1994-95), Wis. Pers. and Guidance Assn., Wis. Assn. Sch. Counselors, Milw. Found. for Women, Daus. of Penelope (dist. gov. 2 dists., nat. chmn. various coms. 1994-96, Penelope of Yr. award), numerous Hellenic orgns. Home: 9119 N White Oak Ln Bayside WI 53217-6203

TOPHAM, LEE EVANS, lawyer; MBA, Plymouth State Coll., 1988; JD, Franklin Pierce Law Ctr., Concord, N.H., 1991. Bar: N.H. 1991, U.S. Dist. Ct. N.H. 1991. Staff atty. N.H. Pub. Defender, Keene, 1991-93, Concord, 1993-95, mng. atty., 1995-2000; assoc. McSwiney, Semple, Bowers & Wise, P.C., New London, 2000—01; staff atty. N.H. Pub. Defender, 2001—. Town moderator Town of Wilmot, N.H., 1998—. Mem. N.H. Bar Assn., N.H. Assn. Criminal Def. Lawyers., Kearsarge Lodge No. 81 F.& A.M. Office: 117 N State St Concord NH 03301 E-mail: let@nl.msbwnl.com.

TOPHAM, SALLY JANE, ballet educator; b. N.Y.C., June 2, 1933; d. William Holroyd Topham and Marian Phyllis (Thomas) Topham Halligan; m. Joseph Vincent Ferrara, Dec. 27, 1958 (div. 1977); children: Gregory Paul, Mark Edward. Student Ballet Theatre Sch., Royal Acad. Dance, London; trained in Europe. Freelance profl. dancer ballet, opera ballet, summer stock, 1956-59; founder, dir. Monmouth Sch. Ballet, N.J., 1963-83; dir. Shore Ballet Theatre Sch., 1986-95; freelance tchr., choreographer, 1996—. Tchr., dir. Mount Allison U. Summer Sch., New Brunswick, Canada, 1973—77; dir. Westfield Sch. Ballet, NJ, 1976—77; artistic dir. Shore Ballet Co., 1977—; prof. ballet Monmouth Coll., West Long Branch, NJ, 1981—83; founder Ctrl. Jersey Acad. Ballet, Red Bank, NJ, 1983—85; dir. Acad. of Shore Ballet, 1995—2000; cons. formulation dance curriculum for N.J. pub. schs. State Bd. Edn., 1997; tchr. Colts Neck Dance Acad., 2000—. Choreographer (ballet) Coppelia, 1981, 90, 96, Shubert Songs, 1980, Homage to Bournonville, 1977, Nutcracker, 1985, Cinderella, 1988; staged many ballets and opera ballets. Bd. dirs. Monmouth Arts Found., Red Bank, 1972—, Shore Ballet Co., Red Bank, 1976—; founder, bd. dirs. Monmouth Civic Ballet, Red Bank, 1972-75. Mem.: English Speaking Union, Am. Acad. Ballet (assoc.), Royal Acad. Dance (assoc.; reg. tchr., advanced tchg. diploma 1979). Avocations: sailing, theater, music, books. Office: Shore Ballet Co 8 Hunt St Rumson NJ 07760-1428 E-mail: Stshore@juno.com.

TOPIK, STEVEN CURTIS, history educator; b. Montebello, Calif., Aug. 6, 1949; s. Kurt and Gertrude Irene (Kriszanich) T.; m. Martha Jane Marcy, Feb. 3, 1979; children: Julia, Natalia. BA, U. Calif., San Diego, 1971; MA, U. Tex., 1973, PhD, 1978. Asst. prof. Universidade Fed. Fluminense, Rio de Janeiro, 1978-81, vis. prof., 1984—; asst. prof. Colgate U., Hamilton, N.Y., 1981-84; vis. prof. Univ. Ibero Americana, Mexico City, 1982; prof. U. Calif., Irvine, 1984-96, chair history dept., 1996-2000; vis. prof. Ecols des Hautes Etudes en Sci. Social, Paris, 1990, London Sch. Econs., 2002. Cons. in field; mem. editorial com. U. Calif. Press, Berkeley, 1987-89. Author: The Political Economy of the Brazilian State, 1987, Trade and Gunboats, The United States and Brazil in the Age of Empire, 1996; co-author (with Allen Wells) The Second Conquest of Latin America, 1998, (with Kenneth Pomerany) The World Trade Created, 1999; co-editor: (with Dorothy Solinger and David Smith) States and Sovereignty in the Global Economy, 1999, (with William Clarence-Smith) The Global Coffee Economy in Africa, Asia and Latim America 1500-1989, 2003; contbr. articles, revs. to profl. publs. Mem. Mayor's Adv. Bd. on Sister Cities, Irvine, 1989-90; mem. adv. bd. Orange County (Calif.) Com. on Latin Am., 1989-90. Fellow NEH, 1987, 89-90, Rockefeller Found., 1977, Social Sci. Rsch. Coun. Mexico City, 1982-83, Fulbright-Hayes Found., 1978-79, 84, U. Calif., 1988-89. Mem. L.Am. Studies Assn., Am. Hist. Assn., Conf. L.Am. History (com. on hist. statistics, com. on projects and pubs., chair Brazilian studies com. 1988-90), Pacific Coast Coun. on L.Am. Studies (bd. govs. 1987-90). E-mail: sctopik@uci.edu.

TOPJON, ANN JOHNSON, librarian; b. Los Angeles, Dec. 2, 1940; d. Carl Burdett and Margaret Elizabeth (Tildesley) Johnson; m. Gary M. Topjon, 1963; children: Gregory Eric and Cynthia Elizabeth (twins); m. Philip M. O'Brien, 1990. BA, Occidental Coll., 1962; MLS, UCLA, 1963. Reference asst. Whittier (Calif.) Pub. Libr., 1973-78; pub. svc. and reference libr., assoc. prof. Whittier Coll., 1981—. Bibliography: Carl Larsson, 1992 (portions published in catalogs 1992, 97), Carland Karin Larsson. Creators of the Swedish Style, 1997; contbr. articles to profl. publs. Faculty rsch. grantee Whittier Coll., 1987-88, 91-92, 95-96, 2000-01; grantee The Am.-Scandinavian Found., N.Y., 1991. Mem. Calif. Acad. and Rsch. Librs. (liaison at Whittier Coll. 1990—), AAUW (Whittier br. 1968-77, Brea-La Habra br., Calif. 1977—, chmn. lit. group, 1977—, chmn. scholarship fund raising 1988-89). Office: Whittier Coll Wardman Libr 7031 Founders Rd Whittier CA 90608 E-mail: atopjon@whittier.edu.

TOPKIS, WILLIAM MORRIS, financial planner; b. Wilmington, Del., Feb. 11, 1939; s. J. Henry an Alice G. Topkis; m. Judith Lange, Apr. 30, 1961; children: Nicole Topkis Pickles, Julie Topkis Scanlan. BSBA, U. Del., 1960. ChFC, CLU. Assoc. James & Schnaars & Assocs. Provident Mut. Life Ins.

Cos., 1963-69, sales mgr., 1969-72; pres. Topkis Assocs., 1972-78, Topkis Fin. Group, 1978-84, Wilmington Fin. Group, 1984-92; ptnr. Daniels Daniels Topkis & McDermott, 1992-99, Topkis & McDermott LLP, 1999—. Mem. exec. bd. Del-Mar-Va Coun. Boy Scouts Am., 1990—; trustee Del. Cmty. Found., 1993-2001; bd. dirs. Wellness Cmty., 1999—; co-chmn. Small Bus. Alliance Del. State C. of C., 2000—. Lt. U.S. Army, 1960-62. Disting. Eagle Scout Boy Scouts Am. Office: Topkis & McDermott LLP 900 Foulk Rd Ste 202 Wilmington DE 19803 E-mail: wtopkis@wealthguide.org.net.

TOPLITT, GLORIA H. voice educator, singer, actress; b. St. Louis, May 22, 1925; d. Wade Fitzgerald Hamilton and Neyneen Farrell Pires; m. James Parnell, 1942 (div. July 1949); 1 child, Dennis James Parnell; m. Abraham Toplitt, Aug. 19, 1968. Student, Guy Bates Post Acad. Dramatic Arts, L.A., 1941-43. Stage performer, N.Y.C., 1944-59; dir. entertainment Holland Am. Lines, 1959-61; tchr. voice North Hollywood (Calif.) Conservatory, 1965-67; pvt. voice tchr. North Hollywood, 1968-95; music specialist outreach program NASA Space Sci. and Tech., Inc., Springfield, Va., 1997—. Dir. Workshop Theatre Program, North Hollywood, 1968-78; coach for impaired voices, North Hollywood, 1968—. Author, composer: Parade of Planets, 1998, Space Challenge, 1999 actor: (plays, N.Y. stage prodns.) appeared as leading lady Oklahoma, Chocolate Soldier, Lend an Ear, Courtin' Time, Showboat, Take Me Along, Auld Lang Syne, Three Musketeers, Carousel, Oh! Captain, Brigadoon, Guys and Dolls, Hit the Deck, Finian's Rainbow, others. Mem. election bd. Office of Voter Registrar, North Hollywood, 1996-98. Avocations: poetry, travel, theatre, elderhostel classes, reading. Home: 4405 Carpenter Ave North Hollywood CA 91607-4110

TOPLITZ, GEORGE NATHAN, lawyer; b. Winsted, Conn., June 13, 1936; s. Morris and Rose (Dolinsky) T.; m. Janet S. Strauss, July 30, 1961 (div.); children: Jill, Wendy, Anna; m. Kimilene A. Snead, Nov. 25, 1979. BA, U. Conn., 1958; LLB, Boston U., 1961. Bar: N.Y. 1964, U.S. Dist. Ct. (so. dist.) N.Y. 1968, U.S. Dist. Ct. (ea. dist.) N.Y. 1968, U.S. Ct. Appeals (2d cir.) 1986, U.S. Supreme Ct. 1987. Claims atty. Royal-Globe Ins. Co., surety dept., N.Y.C., 1963-65; surety atty. Transam. Inst. Co., N.Y.C., 1965-67; assoc. Max E. Greenberg, Cantor, Reiss, N.Y.C., 1967—, ptnr., 1974-88; ptnr. Max E. Greenberg, Cantor, Trager, Toplitz, 1988—; lectr. Am. Mgmt. Assn., 1974-76, Am. Assn. Cost Engrs., 1974-75, Sch. Continuing Edn. NYU, 1975; NW Ctr. Profl. Edn., 1988. With U.S. Army, 1961-63. Recipient Letter of Commendation for acting vol. spl. master Supreme Ct. N.Y., 1982, 84, 85, 86, 87, 88, 89, 90, Fed. mediator, U.S. Dist. Ct. (ea. dist.), N.Y., 1992. Mem. ABA, N.Y. State Bar Assn., N.Y. County Lawyers Assn., Assn. Trial Lawyers Am., Internat. Platform Assn. Home: Fort Lee, NJ. Died Mar. 13, 2002.

TOPOL, ROBERT MARTIN, retired financial services executive; b. N.Y.C., Mar. 9, 1925; s. Morris and Pearl Topol; m. D'Vera Greene, Oct. 10, 1948; children— Clifford M., Gail S., Martha E. BA, NYU, 1948. Ptnr. Greene & Co., N.Y.C., 1948-71; dir. Harris Upham & Co, 1971-76; exec. v.p., dir. Shearson Lehman Bros., 1976-94; ret., 1995. Served with USMC, 1943-46 Mem. Security Traders N.Y., Nat. Security Traders Assn., N.Y. Security Dealers Assn. (gov. 1961-77), Securities Industry Assn. (v.p. 1981-94), Investment Co. Inst., Chevalier Chaine de Rotisseurs, Hampshire Country Club. Republican. Jewish. Home: 825 Orienta Ave Mamaroneck NY 10543-4314

TOPOL, ROBIN APRIL LEVITT, lawyer; b. N.Y.C., Apr. 02; d. Anatole Roy and Phyllis Patricia (Redman) Levitt; m. Clifford Miles Topol, Oct. 23, 1982. Student, Stanford U., Eng., 1974; BA, Barnard Coll., 1976; JD, NYU, 1979; postgrad. exec. mgmt. program, Yale U., 1987. Bar: N.Y. 1980, Fla. 1981. Ptnr. real estate dept., comml. real estate and leasing Kurzman Eisenberg Corbin Lever & Goodwin LLP, White Plains, NY, 1996—. Trustee alumni bd. dirs. Yale U. Sch. Mgmt., 1987-88. Mem. ABA (vice chmn. real property com. 1986-90), N.Y. County Bar Assn. (real estate com. 1986-96), Women's Bar Assn. (chmn. real estate com. 1980-96). Avocations: tennis, golf, running. Office: Kurzman Eisenberg Corbin Lever & Goodman LLP 1 N Broadway White Plains NY 10601-2310

TOPP, ALPHONSO AXEL, JR. environmental scientist, consultant; b. Indpls., Oct. 15, 1920; s. Alphonso Axel and Emilia (Karlsson) T.; m. Mary Catherine Virtue, July 7, 1942; children: Karen, Susan, Linda, Sylvia, Peter, Astrid, Heidi, Eric, Megan, Katrina. BS in Chem. Engring., Purdue U., 1942; MS, UCLA, 1948. Commd. 2d lt. U.S. Army, 1942, advanced through grades to col., 1966, ret., 1970; environ. protection scientist radiation protection sect. State of N. Mex., Santa Fe, 1970-78, program mgr. licensing and registration sect., 1978-81, chief radiation protection bur., 1981-83, cons., 1984—. Decorated Legion of Merit, Bronze Star with 2 oak leaf clusters, U.S. Army. Mem. Rotary, Triangle, Sigma Xi. Republican. Presbyterian. Home and Office: 1200 Calle Cordoniz Los Osos CA 93402-4428 E-mail: alphons188@aol.com.

TOPP, SUSAN HLYWA, lawyer; b. Detroit, Oct. 9, 1956; d. Michael Leo and Lucy Stella (Rusak) Hlywa; m. Robert Elwin Topp, July 25, 1985; children: Matthew, Sarah, Michael and Jamie (triplets). BS in Edn. cum laude, Ctrl. Mich. U., 1978; JD cum laude, Wayne State U., Detroit, 1991. Bar: Mich. 1992, U.S. Dist. Ct. (ea. dist.) Mich. 1992. Conservation officer Mich. Dept. Natural Resources, Pontiac, 1980-88, environ. conservation officer Livonia, 1988-93; pvt. practice Gaylord, Mich., 1993; ptnr. Rolinski & Topp, PLC, 1993; assoc. Plunkett & Cooney, PC, 1995—. Adj. faculty Audubon Internat. Active Rocky Mountain Mineral Law Found., Urban Land Inst. Recipient Am. Jurisprudence award Wayne State U., 1987, Trial Advocacy award, 1988. Mem. ABA (nat. resources and environ. law com.), AAUW, Mich. State Bar Assn. (environ. law sect. coun. mem. 1999), Mich. C. of C. Roman Catholic. Avocations: backpacking, skiing, scuba diving, back-country camping, canoeing. Office: Plunkett & Cooney PC 123 W Main St Gaylord MI 49735-1397 E-mail: toppsu@plunkettlaw.com.

TOPPETA, WILLIAM JOHN, insurance company executive, lawyer; b. N.Y.C., Sept. 18, 1948; s. John Francis and Rita Ann (Carretta) T. BA, Fordham u., 1970; JD, NYU, 1973, ML, 1977. Bar: N.Y. 1974, U.S. Supreme Ct. 1977. Atty. Met. Life, N.Y.C., 1973-79, asst. v.p., 1979-81, asst. gen. counsel, 1981-82, assoc. gen. counsel, 1982-83, v.p., assoc. gen. counsel, 1983-92; pres., CEO MetLife Can. Ops., 1993-95, sr. v.p. corp. re-engring., 1995-97, exec. v.p., 1995-97; sr. exec. v.p. Met. Life, 1997-99, pres., chief admin. officer, 1999—, pres. internat., 2001—. Adj. prof. Pace U. Law Sch., White Plains, N.Y., 1984—, Bklyn. Law Sch., 1985—. Mem. ABA (vice-chairperson com. on trial techniques 1986—), N.Y. State Bar Assn., Assn. Bar of City of N.Y. Democrat. Roman Catholic. Office: Met Life 1 Madison Ave New York NY 10010-3603 E-mail: btoppeta@metlife.com.

TOPPING, AUDREY RONNING, photojournalist, author; b. Camrose, Alta., Can., May 21, 1928; came to U.S., 1967; d. Chester Alvin and Inga Marie (Horte) Ronning; m. Seymour Topping, Nov. 10, 1949; children: Susan, Karen, Lesley, Robin, Joanna. Student, Augustana Univ., Camrose, 1943-46, Nanking (China) U., 1947-48, Berlin Art Sch., 1956-58, U. B.C., 1949-50; D of Arts (hon.), Rider Coll., N.J., 1983. Freelance journalist N.Y. Times Mag., N.Y.C., 1966—; writer, photographer Nat. Geographic, Washington, 1971-79; columnist Earth Times, N.Y.C., 1996—; spl. corr. Houston Chronicle, 1997—. Advisor U.S.-China Arts Exch., 1997—. Author: Dawn Wakes In the East, 1972, The Splendors of Tibet, 1981, Charlie's World, 2000; photographer: A Day in the Life of Canada, 1986, 2 children's books; photo essays for N.Y. Times, Nat. Geographic, Readers Digest, Time, Life, Geo, Sci. Digest, Earth Times, others; photos exhibited at Royal Ont. Mus., Toronto, 1980, Hallmark Gallery, N.Y.C., 1973, Overseas Press Cub, N.Y.C., 1975, Westchester C.C., 1989, others; scriptwriter: (TV documentations) China Mission, 1975, Great Wall Across The Yangtze, 2000; commentator, writer (PBS documentary) Great Wall Across The Yangtze. Recipient Alumni award Augustana Univ. Coll., 1989, Medallion award Westchester C.C., 1989, Greenway Winship award Internat. Ctr. Journalists, 2000. Mem. Fgn. Policy Assn. (dir. 1975-85), Soc. Woman Geographers, Coun. Fgn. Rels., Asia Soc., Jr. Fortnightly, Scarsdale Golf Club. Avocations: sculpture, painting, tennis, skiing, exploring. Home and Office: 5 Heathcote Rd Scarsdale NY 10583-4413 E-mail: topaud@aol.com.

TOPPING, EVA CATAFYGIOTU, writer, lecturer, educator; b. Fredericksburg, Va., Aug. 23, 1920; d. Themistocles John and Katherine (Polizou) Catafygiotu; m. Peter Topping, June 20, 1951; 1 child, John T. BA, Mary Washington Coll., 1941; MA in Classics, Radcliffe Coll., 1943; postgrad., U. Athens, 1950-51. Trustee Greek Orthodox Ch. of Fredericksburg, Va., 1990—; bd. dirs. Orthodox Christian Laity, Chgo., 1988-92, bd. advisors, 1992—; exec. coun. Ch. Women United, N.Y.C., 1981-85. Author: Sacred Stories from Byzantium, 1977, Holy Mothers of Orthodoxy, 1987, Saints and Sisterhood, 1990, Sacred Songs: Studies in Byzantium Hymnography, 1997; contbg. editor The Greek American, N.Y.C., 1991-99; author numerous articles on women's studies, Greek Am. history, Philhellenism, Byzantine liturgical poetry, modern Greek poetry, Byzantine hagiography. Mem. xec. bd. Greek Am. Womens Network, N.Y.C., 1990-94; adv. com. Helen Z. Papanikolas Trust, Salt Lake City, 1989-94. Recipient Am. Hellenic Achievement award Hellenic Spirit Found., 1992, Lifetime Achievement award Am. Hellenic Inst., 1993; Fulbright scholar U.S. Ednl. Found., N.Y.C., 1950. Mem. NOW, Am. Hellenic Inst., Philoptochos Womens Soc., Peace Action, Greek Am. Womens Network (co-founder), U.S. Nat. Com. Byzantine Studies, ACLU, Common Cause, Athenaeum Univ. Club, Phi Beta Kappa. Democrat. Greek Orthodox. Home: 1823 Rupert St Mc Lean VA 22101-5434 *Given the ambiguities, uncertainties and complexities of life today, in our search for peace and justice most of us need inspiration and reasons for hope. These I find in the spirituality and Christian humanism of the Eastern Orthodox Church (into which I was born). It is good to have the support of Orthodoxy's long experience and ancient traditions.*

TOPPING, PETER, historian, educator; b. Milw., May 13, 1916; s. William P. and Anastasia (Makris) Topitzes; m. Eva V. Catafygiotu, June 20, 1951; 1 son, John Themis. BA, U. Wis., 1937, MA, 1938; postgrad., U. Cin., 1939-40; PhD, U. Pa., 1942. Instr. history U. Wis., 1943-44, Northwestern U., 1944-45; asst. prof. history U. Calif.-Santa Barbara, 1948-53; librarian Gennadeion Am. Sch. Classical Studies, Athens, Greece, 1953-60, mem. mng. com. Greece, 1961—; vis. assoc. prof. history, library cons. U. Pa., 1960-61; assoc. prof. history, later Greek studies U. Cin., 1961-64, prof., 1964-67, Charles Phelps Taft prof., 1967-78; fellow Grad. Sch., 1972—78; sr. research assoc. Dumbarton Oaks Rsch. Libr. and Collection, Washington, 1978-84; mem. bd. scholars Dumbarton Oaks Center for Byzantine Studies, 1972-74, mem. sr. fellows, 1979-86, hon. sr. research assoc., 1984—. Interpreting officer U.S. staff Allied Mission to Observe Greek Elections, 1946; mem. exec. com. Frank L. Weil Inst. in Religion and Humanities, 1964-78 Author: Feudal Institutions as Revealed in the Assizes of Romania, 1949, (with Jean Longnon) Documents sur le régime des terres dans la principauté de Moreé au XIVme siècle, 1969, Studies on Latin Greece A.D. 1205-1715, 1977; contbr. articles, revs. to hist. jours. Advanced fellow Belgian Am. Edn. Found., 1947-48; Fulbright sr. research awardee Greece, 1950-51; sr. fellow NEH, 1974-75 Mem. Am. Hist. Assn., Mediaeval Acad. Am., Soc. Byzantine Studies (Athens, Greece) (hon.), Modern Greek Studies Assn., Phi Beta Kappa. Democrat. Mem. Greek Orthodox Ch. Home: 1823 Rupert St Mc Lean VA 22101-5434

TOPPING, SEYMOUR, publishing executive, educator; b. N.Y.C., Dec. 11, 1921; s. Joseph and Anna (Seidman) Topolsky; m. Audrey Elaine Ronning, Nov. 10, 1949; children: Susan, Karen, Lesley, Rebecca, Joanna. BJ, U. Mo., 1943; LittD (hon.), Rider Coll., 1983. With I.N.S. (China civil war), 1946-47; with AP, 1948-59, corr., 1957-59; mem. staff N.Y. Times, 1959-93, chief corr., 1960-63, S.E. Asia, 1963-66, fgn. editor, 1966-69, asst. mng. editor, 1969-76, dep. mng. editor, 1976-77, mng. editor, 1977-86; dir. editl. devel. N.Y. Times Regional Newspapers, 1987-93; chmn. New Directions for News, 1990-91; pres. Am. Soc. Newspaper Editors, 1992-93; prof. Grad. Sch. Journalism Columbia U., N.Y.C., 1993—, adminstr. Pulitzer Prizes, 1993—2002, Sanpaolo prof. emeritus dept. internat. journalism, 1994—. Adviser Internat. Ctr. for Journalists, Found. Am. Comm.; juror Pulitzer Prize com.; lectr. in field. Author: Journey Between Two Chinas, 1972, The Peking Letter, A Novel of the Chinese Civil War, 1999. Spl. advisor to Sec.-Gen. UN to Earth Summit, Rio de Janeiro, 1992; mem. Nat. Com. U.S.-China Rels.; bd. dirs. Lamont-Doherty Earth Obs. Served with inf. AUS, 1943-46, PTO. Recipient Greenway-Winship award for contbns. to internat. journalism, 2000. Mem. Coun. Fgn. Rels., Asia Soc., Am. Soc. Newspaper Editors, Internat. Press Inst., Century Assn. Home: 5 Heathcote Rd Scarsdale NY 10583-4413

TORABI, MOHAMMAD R. health education educator; b. Nahavard, Iran, Feb. 19, 1951; s. Mohammad Ibrahim Torabi and Malous Malekey; children: Ali, Amir. BS, Tehran U., 1975, MSPH, 1978; PhD, Purdue U., 1982; MPH, Ind. U., 1984. Teaching asst. Purdue U., West Lafayette, Ind., 1980-82; postdoctoral fellow Ind. U., Bloomington, 1982-84, asst. prof. Health Edn., 1984-89, assoc. prof. Health Edn., 1989-93, prof., 1993—, chancellors prof., 1997—, chair dept. applied health sci., 1999—. Co-author (book) Healthy Lifestyle Education, 1984; editor Health Education Monograph series; contbr. numerous articles to profl. jours. Bd. dirs. Am. Cancer Soc., Bloomington, 1984-86, Assn. Advancement Health Edn.; pres. Am. Lung Assn./Ind., 1990-91. Recipient Nat. Disting. Svc. award, Ind. U., 1993, Disting. Teaching award, Disting. Alumnus award Purdue U., Auerbach medal Lung Assn., Scholar award Am. Assn. for Health Edn., 2000. Mem. APHA, Am. Sch. Health Assn. (chair rsch. coun. 1990-91, Howe award 2001), Phi Delta Kappa (Ind. U. pres. 1989-90). Office: Ind U 116 Hper Bloomington IN 47404 E-mail: torabi@indiana.edu.

TORABI-POUR, NASSIM NASROLLAN, medical researcher; b. Tehran, Iran, Mar. 21, 1974; s. Mohmad and Hidie Torabi-Pour. PhD, London U., London, United Kingdom, 2001, MSc, 1995; BSc, Greenwich U., London, United Kingdom, 1994. Pharmaceutical Certificate Royal Pharm. Soc., UK, 2001. Rsch. fellow Mayo Clinic, Rochester, Minn., 2001—; rsch. asst. Jena U., Jena, Germany, 1997—98, London U., London, United Kingdom, 1996—97. Contbr. articles in professional journals. Recipient Bartholomew's Cancer Award, Orchid Cancer Rsch., London, UK, 2000-2001, Gene Therapy Award, Ministry of Def., London, UK, 1996-1997. Mem.: Royal Pharm. Soc., Drug Delivery Soc., Immunology Soc. Avocations: soccer, chess, badminton, swimming. Home: 34 Patterson Court London EC1V 9EX England

TORAK, ELIZABETH LICHTENSTEIN, artist; b. N.Y.C., Apr. 12, 1959; d. Immanuel and Nancy (Rabi) Lichtenstein; m. Thomas John Torak, Jan. 5, 1985. BA in Math., U. Chgo., 1981; postgrad., Art Students League N.Y., 1981-85. One-woman shows include Capricorn Galleries, Bethesda, Md., 1993, G.C. Lucas Gallery, 1999; two-person shows include Tilting at Windmills Gallery, Manchester, Vt., 1998, G.C. Lucas Gallery, Indpls., 1995-98, So. Vt. Art Ctr., Manchester, 1995, Clapp & Tuttle Galley, Woodbury, Conn., 1992, N.J. Mus. Agr., New Brunswick, 1992; exhibited in group shows at Butler Inst. Am. Art, Youngstown, Ohio, 1992-95, 97-99, Conn. Valley Hist. Mus., Springfield, Mass., 1996, Wiregrass Mus. Art, Dothan, Ala., 1996, Arlington (Tex.) Mus. Art, 1991, San Diego Art Inst., 1989, First Ch. Gallery, Court Square, Springfield, 1997, 93, Salmagundi Club, N.Y.C., 1993-99, Francesca Anderson Fine Art, Lexington, Mass., 1994, 96-98, Nat. Arts Club, N.Y.C., 1993-96, Greenhouse Gallery of Fine Art, San Antonio, 1995-96, Copley Soc. Boston, 1994, Gallery 128, N.Y.C., 1994, Wyckoff (N.J.) Gallery, 1994; represented in permanent collections Pierre Hotel, Reliance Nat. Ins. Co., Miss. Chem. Corp.; commd. by Fatima Retreat House, Indpls., Our Lady of Grace Ch., Bronx. Mem. Am. Artists Profl. League, Acad. Artists Assn., Oil Painters Am., Audubon Artists. Democrat. Avocations: reading, gardening, hiking.

TORAL, MIGUEL A, customer service administrator, actor; b. Washington, May 16, 1959; s. Ruben E. and Elizabeth B. Toral; m. Nilo Del Consuelo Gomez, Apr. 29, 2001; children: Cefira Nilais. BA Spanish, U. NC, Charlotte, NC, 1981. Home tchr. / acting coach Pvt. Family With Child Actors, Los Angeles, Calif., 1992—93; prodr. / writer McNerd, Inc., 1991—96; star westwood after sch. counselor City of LA, 1995—96; bilingual interpreter LA Med. Ctr., 1990—95. Gen. mem. SAG, Los Angeles, Calif., 1992—. Author: (children's book) Babu Goes Back to the Zoo. Vol. Presbyn. Hosp., Charlotte, NC, 1985—85. Recipient Membership, Nat. Spanish Honor Soc., 1976, Finalist, NC Laugh Off Competition, 1987, Funniest Person in Charlotte, NC Competition, 1985-1986, Semi-Finalist, Johnny Walker Comedy Competition, 1988. Roman Catholic. Avocations: latin dancing, latin dancing, latin dancing, latin dancing. Home: 5355 SE 30th Pl #A Ocala FL 34471 Personal E-mail: mikeltoral@hotmail.com.

TORBAT, AKBAR ESFAHANI, investment advisor, economics educator; b. Esfahan, Iran, Nov. 29, 1945; came to U.S., 1972; s. Ali and Gohar Soltan Torbat E.; m. Fleur Taher Tehrani, June 16, 1997. MS in Engring., Tehran Poly., 1969; MS in Indsl. Engring., U. Tex., Arlington, 1974; MA in Polit. Economy, U. Tex., Dallas, 1980, PhD in Polit. Economy, 1987. Registered investment advisor. Indsl. engr. Long Star Gas Co., Dallas, 1974-77; lectr. Richland Coll., 1987-88, UCLA, L.A., 1990, Calif. State U., L.A., 1989-97, Northridge, 1994-97, U. So. Calif., L.A., 1996-97, Calif. State U. Dominguez Hills, Carson, 1998—; pres. Investek Co., Anaheim, Calif., 1992-2000. Cons. in field; lectr. Calif. State U., Fullerton, 2000—; mem. Ctr. for Iranian Rsch. and Analysis. Mem. Am. Econ. Assn., Network Iranian Profl. Orange County, Internat. Studies Assn. Avocations: chess. Home: 6066 E Butterfield Ln Anaheim CA 92807-4844

TORBERT, BARTON DOUGLAS, music educator; b. Hillsboro, Oreg., Feb. 12, 1959; s. Douglas Eugene and Dale Adayre Torbert; m. Laurie Jean Torbert, Aug. 16, 1980; children: Nicholas, Meghan, Mitchell. BA Music Edn., No. State U., Aberdeen, South Dakota, 1980. Choir dir. Sturgis Brown H.S., Sturgis, SD, 2000—; music specialist Rapid City Area Schools, Rapid City, 1999—2000; music and choral educator Gettysburg Schools, Gettysburg, 1990—99, band dir., 1982—90; music educator Bristol Pub., Bristol, 1981—82. Mem.: SD Music Educator's Nat. Conf., Am. Choral Director's Assn. (conf. host 2002). Evangelical Free. Home: 3207 Simpson Drive Rapid City SD 57702 Office: Sturgis Brown High School 12930 East Highway 34 Sturgis SD 57785 Personal E-mail: torbinrapid@yahoo.com.

TORBERT, MEG BIRCH, artist, design and color consultant; b. Faribault, Minn., Sept. 30, 1912; d. William Alfred and Lucille Birch; m. Arnnold Clair, Aug. 30, 1937 (dec.); m. Donald Torbert, Aug. 12, 1940 (dec. 1985); 1 child, Stephanie B.; m. Arthur Hopmans, Feb. 22, 2000. BA, U. Minn., 1934; MA, U. Iowa, 1938. Prof. Kans. Wesleyan U., Salina, 1934-35, U. Mont., Dillon, 1937-38; assoc. prof. U. Minn., Mpls., 1939-49; curator, editor Walker Art Ctr., 1950-63; film dir. NSF, 1963-68; freelance color cons., 1968-78. Editor Design Quar., 1950-63; dir. (films): Vectors, 1967, Equidecomposable Polygons, 1968; one-woman shows: Hutchins Gallery, Cambria, Calif., 1986, 88, 90, Elizabeth Fortner, Santa Barbara, Calif., 1987, 88, 90, 91, Santa Barbara Art Co., 1992, Lacuna Gallery, Santa Barbara, 2000. Carnegie fellow U. Iowa, 1935-37. Home: 3775 Modoc Rd Apt 123 Santa Barbara CA 93105-4468

TORBET, LAURA, writer, artist, photographer, graphic designer; b. Paterson, N.J., Aug. 23, 1942; d. Earl Buchanan and Ruth Claire (Ehlers) Robbins; m. Bruce J. Torbet, Sept. 9, 1967 (div. 1971); m. Peter H. Morrison, June 19, 1983 (dec. Nov. 1988); m. Salam Habibi, Aug. 23, 1995 (div. 2000). BA, BFA, Ohio Wesleyan U., 1964. Mng. editor Suburban Life mag., East Orange, N.J., 1964-65; asst. pub. rels. dir. United Funds N.J., Newark, 1965-67; art dir. Alitalia Airlines, N.Y.C., 1967-69; propr. Laura Torbet Studio, 1969-84. Author: Macrame You Can Wear, 1972, Clothing Liberation, 1973, Leathercraft You Can Wear, 1975, The T-Shirt Book, 1976, The Complete Book of Skateboarding, 1976, How To Do Everything with Markers, 1977; (with Doug McLaggan) Squash: How to Play, How to Win, 1977, The Complete Book of Mopeds, 1978; (with Luree Nicholson) How to Fight Fair With Your Kids...and Win!, 1980; editor: Helena Rubenstein's Book of the Sun, 1979, The Encyclopedia of Crafts, 1980; (with George Bach) A Time for Caring, 1983, The Inner Enemy, 1983; (with Hap Hatton) Helpful Hints for Hard Times, 1982, The Virgin Homeowners Handbook, 1984, Helpful Hints for Better Living, 1984; (with James Braly) Dr. Braly's Optimum Health Program, 1985; (with Bernard Gittelson) Intangible Evidence, 1987; (as writer for Harville Hendrix) Keeping the Love Your Find, 1992, The Couples Companion, 1994, The Personal Companion, 1996, (as writer for Peter Lambrou and George Pratt) Instant Emotional Healing, 1999; editor, ghostwriter, co-author books. Pres., bd. dirs. The Living/Dying Project. Mem. Boss Ladies. Home and Office: 503 The Alameda San Anselmo CA 94960 E-mail: lulutorbet@aol.com.

TORBETT, GARY BURL, telephone company executive; b. Beaumont, Tex., Sept. 16, 1942; s. John Crittendon and Gladys (Porter) T.; m. Sandra Louise Vessels, Mar. 21, 1972; 1 child, Brooke Sheneen. BSBA, Auburn U., 1971. Mgr. Grayson (Ala.) Tel. Co., 1971-73, McClellanville (S.C.) Tel. Co., 1973-76; mgr. S.E. region comml./mktg. Tel. & Data Systems, Inc., Leesburg, Ala., 1976-81, western region network mgr. Madison, Wis., 1981-89; pres., gen. mgr. Okla. Comm. Systems, Inc., Choctaw, 1989—, also bd. dirs.; Okla./Ark. area mgr. TDS Telecom., 1995. Mem. adv. com. Ea. Okla. County Vocat. Tech. Sch., Choctaw, 1992, bd. edn., 1994. With U.S. Army, 1965-67, Korea. Mem. Ind. Tel. Pioneer Assn, Okla. Tel. Assn. (bd. dirs.), Choctaw C. of C. (v.p. 1996), Am. Legion. Methodist. Avocations: golf, walking, reading. Home: 14295 Whippoorwill Vis Choctaw OK 73020-7027 Office: Okla Comm Systems Inc 2495 Main St Choctaw OK 73020

TORCHILIN, VLADIMIR PETROVICH, biochemist, researcher; b. Moscow, Sept. 13, 1946; came to U.S., 1991; s. Piotr Konstantinovich and Faina Volfovna (Dimand) T.; m. Vera Ivanovna Korovkina, Feb. 14, 1970; 1 child: Ekaterina Vladimirovna. BS, Moscow State U., 1966, MS, 1968, PhD, 1971, DSc, 1980. Jr. rschr. Moscow State U., 1971-73; from. sr. rschr. to lab. head USSR Cardiology Rsch. Ctr., Moscow, 1974-91, prof., 1985-91; assoc. chemist Mass. Gen. Hosp., Boston, 1991-93, chmn. chmistry program Ctr. for Imaging and Pharm. Rsch., 1994—; assoc. prof. radiology Harvard Med. Sch., 1994—98; prof. and chmn. dept. of pharm. scis. N. Ea. U., 1998—. Author: Immobilized Enzymes in Medicine, 1991, over 300 papers and book chpts. in field; editor: Targeted Delivery of Imaging Agents, 1995; patentee in field. Polit. analyst "Novoye Russkoye Slovo", N.Y.C., 1991—. Recipient Lenin prize in science, Coun. of Mins. of USSR, Moscow, 1982. Mem. Russian Acad. Biotechnology (full academician), Am. Chem. Soc., Soc. Nuclear Medicine, Controlled Release Soc. (Outstanding Pharm. Paper 1993, Outstanding Paper of 1993 Jour. of Controlled Release), Fellow Am. Inst. Med. and Biol. Engring., 2002, mem. European Acad. of Scis., 2002. Avocations: Russian books, art collecting. Office: Dept Pharm Sci N Ea Univ 360 Huntington Ave Boston MA 02129-2020

TORDOFF, HARRISON BRUCE, retired zoologist, educator; b. Mechanicville, N.Y., Feb. 8, 1923; s. Harry F. and Ethel M. (Dormandy) T.; m. Jean Van Nostrand, July 3, 1946; children: Jeffrey, James. BS, Cornell U., 1946; MA, U. Mich., 1949, PhD, 1952. Curator Inst. of Jamaica, Kingston, 1946-47; instr. U. Kans., 1950-52, asst. prof., 1952-57, assoc. prof., 1957; asst. prof. U. Mich., 1957-59, assoc. prof., 1959-62, prof., 1962-70; former dir. Bell Mus. Natural History; prof. ecology U. Minn., Mpls., 1970-91, dean coll. biol. scis., 1986-87. Contbr. articles in ornithology to profl. jours. Served with USAF, 1942-45. Decorated D.F.C., 17 Air medals. Fellow Am. Ornithologists Union (pres. 1978-80); mem. Nature Conservancy (chmn. bd. Minn. chpt. 1975-77), Wilson Ornithol. Soc. (editor 1952-54), Cooper Ornithol. Soc. Office: 100 Ecology 1987 Upper Buford Cir Saint Paul MN 55108-1051 Home: 189 11th St Lake Placid FL 33852-9460 E-mail: tordoff@ecology.umin.edu.

TOREN, BRIAN KEITH, futures, multimedia, management consultant; b. St. Paul, Jan. 8, 1935; s. Clarence August and Anna (Penner) T.; divorced; children: Sean Marshall, Kisten Kaye. BSBA, U. Minn., 1970. Programmer Sperry Corp., Mpls., 1957-67, sales support staff, 1968-71, site mgr. Atlantic City, 1972-76, mktg. cons. Mpls., 1976-83, comm. svc. support cons., 1983-86; telecom. network developer, 1983-91; pres., cons. Internat. Robot, Mpls., 1982-94; mgr. quality analysis and support Unisys, 1986-91, comm. project mgr., 1987-91; v.p. Anticipatory Scis. Inc., St. Paul, 1991—, also bd. dirs. Assoc. project mgr., workshop guide multimedia tng. developer for Fissure Corp., 1994—; faculty Met. State U., Mpls., 1999—. Contbr. articles to encys. including MacMillan's Ency. of Future. Bd. dirs. Minn. Citizens on Line. Mem. Soc. Gen. Systems Rsch. Minn. (contbr. monthly column 1981-88), Minn. Futurists (past pres., 1986-88, contbr. monthly column 1986—, bd. dirs.). Avocations: computer and history research, photography, writing, speaking, management education. Home and Office: 2441 Dupont Ave S Minneapolis MN 55405-2725 E-mail: bktoren@visi.com.

TOREN, MARK, state official, econometrician; b. Warsaw, Poland, Dec. 7, 1950; s. Jacob Toren and Assia (Hanukayeva) Merson; m. Angela Aleksandrovna, July 12, 1997; children: Alexander Michael, Anna A. Cert., U. Cologne, Fed. Republic Germany, 1974; AA, AAS, SUNY, Suffern, 1972; BA, SUNY, New Paltz, 1975; MA, SUNY, Albany, 1976; MS, Rensselaer Poly. Inst., 1983, PhD, 1992. Sr. statistician Triad Data Scis., Albany, N.Y., 1980-84; sr. economist N.Y. State Dept. Taxation and Fin., 1984-85; econometrician N.Y. State Dept. Social Svcs., 1985-92, N.Y. State Dept. of Health, Albany, 1992-97. Faculty bus. mgmt. and econs. SUNY, Empire State Coll., Saratoga Springs, N.Y., 1994-98, cons. Calay Sys. Inc., Newport Beach, Calif., 1998—;

rschr. N.Y. State Dept. Health, Albany, 1999—. Author: Cost Efficiency in Nursing Homes: A Stochastic Frontier Approach, 1994, Hospital Cost and efficiency in a Regime of Stringent Regulation, 1996, Economics Macro/Micro, 1996, Economics of Government Regulation and the Market, 1996. Served with U.S. Army, 1969-71. Mem. Am. Econ. Assn., Am. Statis. Assn., Health Econs. Rsch. Orgn., Micro-Computer Users Group, Internat. Platform Assn., Omicron Delta Epsilon. Avocations: lit., art, music, photography. Office: NYS Dept of Health 1970 Corning Tower Albany NY 12237-0001 E-mail: mxt10@health.state.ny.us.

TORG, JOSEPH STEVEN, orthopaedic surgeon, educator; b. Phila., Oct. 25, 1934; m. Barbara Jane Groenendaal, May 23, 1959; children: Joseph Steven, Elisabeth, Jay Michael. AB, Haverford Coll., 1957; MD, Temple U., 1961. Diplomate: Am. Bd. Orthopaedic Surgeons. Intern San Francisco Gen. Hosp., 1961-62; resident in orthopaedic surgery Temple U. Hosp., Phila., 1964-68, Shriners Hosp. for Crippled Children, Phila., 1966-67; asst. surgeon Episcopal Hosp., 1968-70; surgeon Shriners Hosp. Crippled Children, 1970-78; mem. staff Temple U. Hosp., 1970-78, instr. orthopaedic surgery, 1968-70, asst. prof., 1970-75, assoc. prof., 1976-78; dir. Center for Sports Medicine and Sci., 1974-78; chief orthopaedic sect. St. Christopher's Hosp. for Children, Phila., 1971-74, mem. staff, 1974—; active staff St. Joseph's Hosp., 1977—; prof. U. Pa., 1978—, active staff hosp., 1978—; dir. Sports Medicine Center, 1978—; prof. orthopaedic surgery Temple U., 1995. Mem. active staff Children's Hosp., Phila., 1978; med. cons. Pres.'s Council on Phys. Fitness and Sports Mem. editorial bd. Sports Medicine, Yearbook of Sports Medicine, Contemporary Orthopaedics, Jour. Clin. Sport Medicine, Am. Jour. Knee Surgery, Orthopaedic Rev.; contbr. articles to profl. jours. Served with M.C. U.S. Army, 1962-64. Recipient Layman Honor award Pa. State Assn. Health, Phys. Edn. and Recreation, 1970, Grad. Honor award, 1975; Commendation of Merit Phila. Public High Sch. Football Coaches, 1974 Fellow Am. Acad. Orthopaedic Surgeons, Am. Coll. Sports Medicine (trustee 1975-78), Phila. Coll. Physicians; mem. AMA, Eastern Orthopaedic Soc., Am. Orthopaedic Soc., Sports Medicine, Phila. County Med. Soc., Phila. Orthopaedic Soc., Pa. State Med. Soc., Pa. State Orthopaedic Soc. Home: 401 Conestoga Rd Wayne PA 19087-4811 Office: Temple U Sch Medicine 3401 N Broad St Philadelphia PA 19140

TORGERSEN, PAUL ERNEST, academic administrator, educator; b. N.Y.C., Oct. 13, 1931; s. Elnar and Frances (Hansen) T.; m. Dorothea Hildegarde Zuschlag, Sept. 11, 1954; children: Karen Elizabeth, Janis Elaine, James Einar. BS, Lehigh U., 1953, DEng, 1994; MS, Ohio State U., 1956, PhD, 1959. Grad. tchg. asst. Ohio State U., Columbus, 1957, instr., 1957-59; asst. to assoc. prof. Okla. State U., Stillwater, 1959-66; prof., dept. head, dean Coll. Engring. Va. Tech, Blacksburg, 1967-93, pres., 1993-2000, John W. Hancock chair of engring. Dir. Roanoke (Va.) Electric Steel, 1986—, Luna Innovations, 2000—, EDD, 1996—. Author 5 books. Mem. Gov. Mark Warner's Coommn. on Bd. of Visitor Appts., Richmond, Va., 2002--; So.State Energy Bd., Richmond, 1986-90. 1st lt. USAF, 1953-55. Fellow Am. Soc. Engring. Edn. (Lamme medal 1994), Inst. Indsl. Engring (Frank and Lillian Gibreth award 2001); mem. Nat. Acad. Engring. (coun. 1999--). Avocation: tennis. Office: Va Tech 302A Whittemore Blacksburg VA 24061-0118

TORGERSEN, TORWALD HAROLD, architect, designer; b. Chgo., Sept. 2, 1929; s. Peder and Hansine Malene (Hansen) T.; m. Dorothy Darlene Peterson, June 22, 1963. BS in Archtl. Engring. with honors, U. Ill., 1951. Lic. architect Ill., D.C., real estate broker, Ill., interior designer, Ill.; registered architect Nat. Coun. Archtl. Registration Bds. Ptnr. Coyle & Torgersen (Architects-Engrs.), Washington, Chgo. and Joliet, Ill., 1955-56; project coord. Skidmore, Owings & Merrill, Chgo., 1956-60; corp. architect, dir. architecture, constrn. and interiors Container Corp. Am., 1960-86; prin. in charge of orgn. and adminstrn. Jack Train Assocs. Inc., 1987-88; cons. Torwald H. Torgersen, AIA, FASID, 1988—. Guest lectr. U. Wis. Capt. USNR, 1951-82. Recipient Top Ten Design award Factory mag., 1964 Fellow Am. Soc. Interior Designers; mem. AIA, Naval Res. Assn., Ill. Naval Militia, Am. Arbitration Assn., Am. Soc. Mil. Engrs., Paper Industry Mgmt. Assn. (hon.), Sports Car Club Am., Nat. Eagle Scout Assn. Clubs: 20 Fathoms. Home and Office: 3750 N Lake Shore Dr Chicago IL 60613-4238

TORGERSON, LARRY KEITH, lawyer; b. Albert Lea, Minn., Aug. 25, 1935; s. Fritz G. and Lu (Hillman) T. BA, Drake U., 1958, MA, 1960, LLB, 1963, JD, 1968; MA, Iowa U., 1962; cert., The Hague Acad. Internat. Law, The Netherlands, 1965, 69; LLM, U. Minn., 1969, Columbia U., 1971, U. Mo., 1976; PMD, Harvard U., 1973; EdM, 1974. Bar: Minn. 1964, U.S. Dist. Ct. Minn. 1964, Wis. 1970, Iowa 1970, U.S. Dist. Ct. (no. dist.) Iowa 1971, U.S. Tax Ct. 1971, U.S. Supreme Ct. 1972, U.S. Dist. Ct. (ea. dist.) Wis. 1981, U.S. Ct. Appeals (8th cir.) 1981. Asst. corp. counsel 1st Bank Stock Corp. (88 Banks), Mpls., 1963-67, 1st Svc. Corp. (27 ins. agys., computer subs.), Mpls., 1965-67; v.p., trust officer Nat. City Bank, 1967-69; sr. mem. Torgerson Law Firm, Northwood, Iowa, 1969-87; trustee, gen. counsel Torgerson Farms, 19677—, Redbirch Farms, Kensett, Iowa, 1987—, Sunburst Farms, Grafton, 1987—, Gold Dust Farms, Bolan, 1988—, Torgerson Grain Storage, Bolan, 1988—, Indian Summer Farms, Bolan, 1991—, Sunset Farms, Bolan, 1992—, Sunrise Farms, Grafton, 1994—. CEO, gen. counsel Internat. Investments, Mpls., 1983-96, Transoceanic, Mpls., 1987-96, Torgerson Capital, Northwood, 1996—, Torgerson Investments, Northwood, 1984—, Torgerson Properties, Northwood, 1987—, Torgerson Ranches, Sundance, Wyo., 1998—, Hawaiian Investments Unltd., Maui, Hawaii, 1998—, Internat. Investments Unltd., San Pedro, Belize, 1999—. Recipient All-Am. Journalism award Thomas Arkle Clark Outstanding Achievement award, 1958, Dennis E. Brumfield Outstanding Achievement award, 1958, Johnny B. Guy Outstanding Leadership award, 1958; named to Outstanding Young Men of Am., U.S. Jaycees; Hagen scholar, Honor scholar. Mem. ABA, Am. Judicature Soc., Iowa Bar Assn., Minn. Bar Assn., Wis. Bar Assn., Hennepin County Bar Assn., Mensa, Drake Student-Faculty Coun., Drake Student Alumni Coun. (chmn.), Jaycees, Harvard Bus. Sch. Study (pres., exec. com., univ. editor in chief), Psi Chi, Circle K (pres. local chpt.), Phi Alpha Delta, Omicron Delta Kappa (pres. local chpt.), Pi Kappa Delta (pres. local chpt.), Alpha Tau Omega (pres. local chpt., Silver Bullet Outstanding Leadership award, 1965, 66), Pi Delta Epsilon (founder, chpt. pres.), Alpha Kappa Delta, Alpha Scholastic Hon. (U. editor-in-chief), Harvard Bus. Sch. Exec. Com. (U. editor-in-chief). Lutheran.

TORGERSON, LINDA BELLE, music educator; b. Sioux City, Iowa, Dec. 16, 1951; d. Fredric William and Clara Jeanette Wilson; m. Peter Kinsey Torgerson; children: Christopher, Patricia. Diploma, Ctrl. H.S., 1971; MusB Edn., Morningside Coll., 1976; MEd, City U., 1999. Cert. Iowa tchr., tchr. Mont., Washington. Choral dir. First United Meth. Ch., Sioux City, Iowa, 1974—76, First Presbyn. Ch., Kalispell, Mont., 1976—80; pvt. music instr. Self-employed, 1976—80; music tchr. St. Matthews Sch., 1976—77; music dir., coord. Flathead County Rural Schools, 1979—85; music dir. Clarkston Sch. Dist., Clarkston, Wash., 1985—. Treas. Clarkston Edn. Assn., Clarkston, Wash., 1988—90, v.p., Wash., 1990—92, pres., Wash., 1991—92; sec. Wash. uniserv polit. action com. Wash. Edn. Assn., Olympia, Wash., 1992—93; bldg. rep. Clarkston Edn. Assn., Clarkston, Wash., 1993—94; jazz band dir. Lincoln Mid. Sch., Clarkston, Wash., 1996—; bldg. rep. Clarkston Edn. Assn., Clarkston, Wash., 2000—01, v.p., Wash., 2001—; co-director for asotin county teens against smoking Asotin County Devel. Services, Clarkston, Wash., 2001—02. Singer (composer): (commercial) Flathead County Milk Music Ad for the Radio, 1981; contbr. articles to profl. jours. Mem. U-Pac bd. for SE Wash. Edn. Assn., Kennewick, Wash., 1992—93. Grantee Dist., Clarkston Sch. Dist., 1994, 1995. Mem.: NEA, Clarkston Edn. Assn. (v.p. 2001), Clarkston Edn. Assn. (bldg. rep. 1992—94), Clarkston Edn. Assn. (pres./past pres. 1991—92), Clarkston Edn. Assn. (v.p. 1989—91), Clarkston Edn. Assn. (treas. 1987—89), SE Wash. Music Educators Assn., Wash. Music Educators Assn., Music Educators Nat. Conf. Home: 1505 8th St Clarkston WA 99403 Office: Lincoln Mid Sch 1945 4th Ave Clarkston WA 99403 Office Fax: 509-758-7838 5245. Personal E-mail: ltorgerson@clarkston.com. E-mail: ltorgers@jawbone.clarkston.wednet.edu.*

TORGET, ARNE ODMUND, retired electrical engineer; b. Cathlamet, Wash., Oct. 10, 1916; s. John B. and Anna J. (Olson) T.; m. Dorothy M. Lackie, Aug. 30, 1941; children: Kathleen, James, Thomas. BSEE, U. Wash., 1940. Registered profl. elec. engr., Calif. Design engr. Boeing, Seattle, 1940-41, asst. group engr., 1941-46; design specialist N.Am. Aviation, L.A., 1946-50, 60-64, elec. supr., 1950-55, design specialist Rocketdyne Canoga Park, Calif., 1955-60; design specialist Space Div. Rockwell Internat., Downey, 1964-79; commr. Wahkiakum Count Pub. Utility, Cathlamet, 1985-96; ret., 1996. Bd. dirs. Wash. Pub. Utility Dist. Utility Systems, Seattle, 1985-96, Wash. Pub. Power Supply System, Richland, 1987-96, Wash. Pub. Utility Dist. Assn., Seattle, 1985-96. Mem. AAAS, IEEE, Elks. Republican. Roman Catholic. Home: 10928 Kings Rd Ventura CA 93004-1034 E-mail: aotorget@msn.com.

TORGOW, EUGENE N. electrical engineer; b. Bronx, N.Y., Nov. 26, 1925; s. Frank and Blanche Anita (Revzin) T.; m. Cynthia Silver, Mar. 19, 1950; children: Joan, Martha, Ellen. BSEE, Cooper Union, 1946; MSEE, Poly. Inst. Bklyn., 1949; Engr. in E.E., Poly. Inst. N.Y., 1980; postgrad., UCLA, 1983. Rsch. assoc., sect. leader Microwave Rsch. Inst., Poly. Inst. Bklyn., 1947-51, 53-60, instr., 1954-59; mgr. microwave lab. A.B. Dumont Labs, East Paterson, N.J., 1951-53; chief engr., mgr. microwave products Dorne & Magolin, Inc., Westbury, L.I., N.Y., 1960-64; chief engr., dir. rsch., dir. mktg. Rantec divsn. Emerson Electric, Calabasas, Calif., 1964-68; with Missle Sys. Group, Hughes Aircraft Co., Canoga Park, 1968-85, assoc. labs. mgr., 1981-85. Cons. various electronics firms, N.Y.C., 1956-59; cons., 1986—; cons. Exec. Svc. Corps of So. Calif., 1996—; pres. Cons. Adv. Coun., 1999-2000; lectr. Calif. State U., Northridge, 1986-91. Contbr. articles to profl. jours.; patentee in field. Mem. Fair Housing Coun. San Fernando Valley, L.A., 1967—, L.A. Co. Mus. Assn., 1976—2001; trustee Amiotropic Lateral Sclerosis Assn. So. Calif., 1999—. Served with USAAF, 1946—47. Recipient Engr. '85 Merit award San Fernando Valley Engrs. Coun., 1985. Fellow IEEE, Inst. for Advancement Engring.; mem. WINCON (bd. dirs. 1984-89, chmn. bd. dirs. 1988-89), Microwave Theory and Techniques Soc. of IEEE (pres. 1966, mem. adminstrn. com. 1962-72, Svc. award 1978), Accreditation Bd. Engring. and Tech. (mem. engring. accreditation com. 1994-99) Hughes Mgmt. Club (edn. chmn. 1979-80), Sigma Xi. Democrat. Office: 9531 Donna Ave Northridge CA 91324-1816

TORIANI, DENISE MARIA, legal administrator; b. Oakland, Calif., Dec. 30, 1954; d. David and Doris Elizabeth (Cantrell) Eirich; m. Robert Joseph Turocy, Dec. 30, 1972 (div. 1976); children: Robert Justin, Shannon James; m. Oscar Quiroga DeLaRosa, May 1, 1983 (div. 1992); m. Dennis James Toriani, June 22, 1996. AAS, Truman Coll., 1983; BABA, DePaul U., 1987. Legal adminstr. Taylor, Miller, Sprowl, Hoffnagle & Merletti, Chgo., 1985-91, Leonard M. Ring & Assocs., Chgo., 1991-93, Boehm, Pearlstein & Bright, Ltd., Chgo., 1994-95, Purcell & Wardrope Chartered, Chgo., 1995-99; coord. emergency medicine residency dept. Resurrection Med. Ctr., 2000—. ESL tutor Literacy Vols., Chgo, 1985-86. Mem. Germans frm Russia Heritage Soc., Am. Hist. Soc. Germans from Russia, Alliance of Grandparents Against SIDS Tragedy. Democrat. Roman Catholic. Office: 7435 W Talcott Ave Chicago IL 60631-3717 E-mail: dtoriani@reshealthcare.org.

TORIBARA, MASAKO ONO, voice educator; b. Fresno, Calif., Sept. 8, 1925; d. Mataichi Harry and Sawo Ono; m. Taft Y. Toribara, Aug. 28, 1948; children: Lynne Suzanne, Neil Willard. B Music Edn. magna cum laude, U. Mich., 1946, MusM in Voice, 1949. Instr Bowling Green (Ohio) State U., 1946-48, Hochstein Music Sch., Rochester, N.Y., 1965-66; instr. to lectr. Eastman Sch. Music, 1965—, prof. emerita, 1999—. Mem. Opera Under the Star, Rochester, 1954-56; judging panel Rochester Philharmonic Young Artist Audition, 1986, 98, 99; adjudicators various competitions. Soprano soloist Dewey Ave. Presbyn. Ch., Rochester, 1953-59, 1st Bapt. Ch. Rochester, 1961-77, Ars Antigua, Rochester, 1961-65. Den mother Brownie Scouts, Rochester, 1959; co-pres. Jr. High Family Faculty Forum in Mid. Sch. in Gates Sch., Rochester, 1964-66. Mem. Music Tchrs. Nat. Assn. (state and nat. cert.), Nat. Assn. Tchrs. Singing, Pi Kappa Lambda, Phi Beta Kappa, Phi Kappa Phi, Mu Phi Epsilon. Avocations: reading, travel, attending musical events, cooking. Home: 54 Timpat Dr Rochester NY 14624-2928 Office: Eastman Sch Music 26 Gibbs St Rochester NY 14604-2599

TORIBARA, TAFT YUTAKA, radiation biologist, biophysicist, chemist, toxicologist; b. Seattle, Apr. 10, 1917; s. Minekichi and Hisano (Miyata) T.; m. Masako Ono., Aug. 28, 1948; children— Lynne Suzanne, Neil Willard. BS in Chem. Engring. summa cum laude, U. Wash., 1938, MS in Chem. Engring, 1939; PhD, U. Mich., 1942. Rsch. chemist dept. engring. rsch. U. Mich., 1942-48; from asst. prof. to prof. radiation biology and biophysics Sch. Medicine and Dentistry, U. Rochester, N.Y., 1948-89, prof. emeritus toxicology in biophysics, 1989-93; prof. emeritus dept. environ. medicine, 1993—. Cons. in field. Editor: Modern Techniques for the Detection and Measurement of Environmental Pollutants, 1978, Polluted Rain, 1980; contbr. articles to profl. jours. Chmn. advancement com. Boy Scouts Am., 1964-67; pres. Jr. High Family Faculty Forum, 1964-66; mem. Gates Library Bd., 1965-75, pres., 1972-74. NIH Spl. Rsch. fellow, 1960-61. Mem. Am. Chem. Soc., AAAS. Inventor ultrafiltration apparatus, 1953. Home: 54 Timpat Dr Rochester NY 14624-2928 Office: EHSC U Rochester Med Ctr Rochester NY 14642-0001 *My life might be summarized by the statement, "Adversity is not always bad".*

TORKILDSEN, PETER G. state agency administrator; b. Milw., Jan. 28, 1958; s. Robert Allan and Mary Ellen (Hill) T.; m. Gail Bloomgarden, Jan. 1996. BA, U. Mass., 1980; MPA, Harvard U., 1990. Mem. Mass. House of reps., 1985-91, 103rd and 104th Congress from 6th Mass. dist., 1993-97; pres. Thunder Hill Inc., Peabody, Mass., 1997—; commr. Mass. Labor Rels. Commn., Boston. Mem. Danvers Town Meeting, 1983-85, Mass. Rep. State Com., Boston, 1984-93. Mem. Am. Legis. Exchange Council, Mass. Legislator's Assn., Nat. Rep. Legislator Assn. Lodges: Sons of Norway. Roman Catholic. Home: 12 Spruce St Danvers MA 01923-2613 Office: 399 Washington St 4th Fl Boston MA 02108

TORKILDSON, RAYMOND MAYNARD, lawyer; b. Lake City, S.D., Nov. 19, 1917; s. Gustav Adolph and Agnes (Opitz) T.; m. Sharman Elizbeth Vaughn, Sept. 8, 1956; children: Stephen, Thomas. S.B., U. S.D., 1946; JD, Harvard U., 1948. Bar: Calif. 1949, Hawaii 1950. Assoc. James P. Blaisdell, Honolulu, 1949-52; ptnr. Moore, Torkildson & Rice and successors, 1955-64; exec. v.p. Hawaii Employers Council, 1964-67; ptnr. Torkildson, Katz, Fonseca, Jaffe, Moore & Hetherington and predecessors, 1967-72; sr. ptnr., 1972-92; of counsel, 1993—. Mem. mgmt. com. Armed Forces YMCA, Honolulu, 1971; treas. Hawaii Republican Com. 1977-83. Served with U.S. Army, 1941-46; lt. col. Res. ret. Mem. ABA, Hawaii Bar Assn. Clubs: Oahu Country, Pacific (Honolulu). Roman Catholic.

TORME, MARGARET ANNE, public relations executive, communications consultant; b. Indpls., Apr. 5, 1943; d. Ira G. and Margaret Joy (Wright) Barker; children: Karen Anne, Leah Vanessa. Student, Coll. San Mateo, 1961-65. Pub. rels. mgr. Hoefer, Dieterich & Brown (now Chiat-Day), San Francisco, 1964-73; v.p., co-founder, creative dir. Lowry & Ptnrs., 1975-83; pres., founder Torme & Co., 1983—. Cons. in communications. Mem. Coun. Pub. Rels. Firms, San Francisco C. of C. (Outstanding Achievement award for Women Entrepreneurs 1987), Jr. League (adv. bd.), Pub. Rels. Orgn. Internat. (v.p., dir.). Office: 847 Sansome St San Francisco CA 94111-2908

TORMEY, JEROME MARSHALL, human services administrator; b. Des Moines, Apr. 18, 1948; s. Thomas Carmody Tormey and Catherine Alexandra Reinig; m. Patricia Marie Doody, Mar. 19, 1982; children: Callahan. BA in Sociology, St. Mary of the Plains, Dodge City, Kans., 1970. Staff supr. Fifth Jud. Dist., Des Moines, 1972—75; assoc. dir. Westminster Ho. Inc., 1980—2000; v.p. Behavioral Health Resources, 2000—. Charter mem. Healthy Polk 2010, Des Moines, 1995—; bus. alliance chairperson Grand View Coll. / Human Svc. Adv., Des Moines, 1995—; coord. Ctrl. Iowa Health Care Providers Group, Des Moines, 1988—. Bd. dirs. Urbandale Cmty. Sch. Dist., Iowa, 2001, Urbandale Cmty. Theatre, 2001. Mem.: Soc. Human Resource Mgrs. Avocations: photography, genealogy, antiques, skiing, calligraphy. Home: 3308 Melanie Dr Des Moines IA 50322-6854 Personal E-mail: stormey@juno.com.

TORMOLLAN, GARY GORDON, health facility administrator, physical therapist; b. Plainfield, N.J., Feb. 23, 1954; s. Gordon William and Doris Evelyn (Palmer) T.; m. Stacey Lee Cole, Aug. 20, 1983; children: Brian, Kristin. BS in Health Edn., Trenton (N.J.) State Coll., 1976; cert. in phys. therapy, Hahnemann U., 1982; MEd, Trenton State Coll., 1987. Lic. phys. therapist, Maine, Pa.; lic. athletic trainer, N.J. Athletic trainer Princeton (N.J.) High Sch., 1976-81; phys. therapist Holy Redeemer Hosp., Huntington Valley, Pa., 1982-83, Phys. Therapy of Princeton, 1984-86; sports medicine coord. Omni-Fit, Mt. Laurel, N.J., 1986-87; dir. rehab. svcs. Med. Coll. of Pa., Phila., 1987-90; dir. phys. therapy Mid-Maine Med. Ctr., Waterville, 1990-92; pres., CEO Maine Phys. Therapy, 1993—. Cons. Burnt Mill Med. Ctr., Cherry Hill, N.J., 1983; mem. clin. faculty Temple U., Phila., 1989-90; cons., mem. adv. bd. phys. therapy asst. program Kennebec Valley Tech. Coll., Fairfield, Maine, 1990-94. Deacon Ewing (N.J.) Presbyn. Ch., 1989; coach Waterville Little League, Waterville (Maine) Youth Soccer Assn. Mem. Waterville Rotary, Greater Boston Labrador Retriever Club. Congregationalist. Avocation: golf, dogtraining. Home: 42 Messalonskee Ave Waterville ME 04901-5352 Office: Maine Physical Therapy 28 College Ave Waterville ME 04901-6105 Personal E-mail: tormollan@adelphia.net.

TORNABENE, RUSSELL C. communications executive; b. Gary, Ind., Sept. 18, 1923; s. Samuel Tornabene and Marion LaVorci Roush; m. Audrey F. Shankey, June 21, 1952; children: Joseph, Leigh, David, Lynn. AA, Gary Jr. Coll., 1941, 46-47; BA, Ind. U., 1949, MA, 1950. Radio, TV newswriter WRC-AM-TV, Washington, 1951-55; network supr. NBC Network News, 1955-61, network gen. mgr. NYC, 1961-75; v.p. NBC News, 1975-81; exec. officer Soc. Profl. Journalists, Chgo., 1981-87; Midwest dir. Exec. TV Workshop, 1987-96; pres. Russell Communications Cons., 1996—. Bd. dirs. LifeLine Pilots. Contbr. articles on news to mags. and newspapers Mem. N.Y. Catholic Archdiocese Sch. Bd., N.Y.C., 1972 Recipient Disting. Service award, Sigma Delta Chi, 1949; Ernie Pyle scholar, 1949 Mem. Acad. TV Arts and Scis., Radio TV News Dirs. Assn. Clubs: Overseas Press (former v.p.). Avocation: photography. Office: 626 Sheridan Sq Apt 2 Evanston IL 60202

TORNBLOM, CLAUDIA L. civilian military employee; BSc, Iowa State U.; MPA, U. Minn.; graduate, Nat. Defense U., 1992. From fiscal programs mgmt. officer to dep. asst. sec. U.S. Army Civil Works Program, Washington, dep. asst. sec. mgmt. & budget. Office: Office of Secretary of Army for Civil Works Army Pentagon Washington DC 20310-1500*

TORNEDEN, CONNIE JEAN, bank officer; b. Tonganoxie, Kans., Sept. 14, 1955; d. Byron Calvin and Edna Jeannette (Keck) Swain; m. Lawrence Dale Torneden, Sept. 18, 1976; 1 child, James Milton. Bus. cert., Kansas City (Kans.) C.C., Kans., 1974; student, Nat. Compliance Sch., Norman, Okla., 1984; Mortgage Lending Diploma, ABA Am. Inst. Banking, 1997. Adminstrv. sec. to chmn. of bd., pres. First State Bank and Trust, Tonganoxie, 1974-80, asst. cashier, 1981-83, asst. v.p. and compliance officer, 1984-97, bank security officer, 1989-95, loan ops. officer, 1998, loan prodn. specialist, 1999—2002, loan asst., 2002—. Lobbyist, treas. 24-40 Hwy. Task Force, Leavenworth, Kans., 1989-91; bd. dirs. sec. Reno Cemetery Assn., Tonganoxie, 1986—; co-founder Tonganoxie Days, chmn., 1986, 88-93, 95-2002; grad. So. Leavenworth County Leadership Devel., 1991; sec.-treas. Maple Grove Cemetery Assn., 1995—, Reno Twp. Fire Dept., 1996—. Mem. Am. Bus. Women's Assn. (treas. 1986-87, sec. 1997-98, 2001-2002, 2002-, Woman of Yr. award Twilight chpt. 1994), Mid-Am. Dairymen Assn. (sec. 1978-80), Nat. Assn. Old West Gunfighter Teams (nat. champions 1989, 90), Linwood Grange (5th and 6th degrees 1978), Tonganoxie C. of C. (sec. 1983-86, 92-94, pres. 1986, 88, 89, 96, v.p. 1995, treas. 1997, Mem. of Yr. award 1990, 92, Citizen of Yr. award 2001), Tonganoxie Jaycees (sec. 1991). Democrat. Mem. Soc. Of Friends. Avocations: music, fossil collecting, stamp collecting, coin collecting, writing poetry and short stories. Office: First State Bank and Trust PO Box 219 Tonganoxie KS 66086-0219

TORNETTA, FRANK JOSEPH, anesthesiologist, educator, consultant; b. Norristown, Pa., Jan. 22, 1916; s. Joseph F. and Maria (Ciaccio) T.; m. Edith Galullo, Nov. 21, 1941 (dec. 1952); m. Norma Zollers, July 16, 1957; children: Frank Jr., David A., Mark A. BS, Ursinus Coll., 1938; MA, U. Pa., 1940; PhD, NYU, 1943; MD, Hahnemann Med. Coll., 1946. Diplomate Am. Bd. Anesthesiology, 1953. Instr. U. Md., College Park, 1940, Hofstra Coll., Hempstead, N.Y., 1941; teaching fellow NYU, N.Y.C., 1941-43; asst. instr. Med. Sch. U. Pa., Phila., 1949-50; dir. dept. anesthesiology. dir. Sch. Anesthesia, founder Montgomery Hosp. Med. Ctr., Norristown, Pa., 1950-91; clin. assoc. prof. Sch. Medicine Temple U., Phila., 1985-91. Lectr. Grad. Sch. St. Joseph's U., Phila., 1987-91. Contbr. articles to profl. jours. Chmn. task force Montgomery County Health Dept., Norristown, 1989-91; active Valley Forge chpt. Boy Scouts Am., Norristown, 1982. Lt. USN, 1943-50. Fellow Am. Coll. Chest Physicians, Am. Coll. Anesthesiologists, Coll. Physicians Phila.; mem. Pa. Soc. Anesthesiologists (pres. 1970), Montgomery County Med. Soc. (pres. 1969), Montgomery Hosp. Med. Staff Assn. (pres. 1960), Hahnemann Med. Coll. Alumni Assn. (v.p. 1982), KC. Republican. Roman Catholic. Home: 307 Anthony Dr Plymouth Meeting PA 19462-1109 Office: Montgomery Hosp Med Ctr 1300 Powell St Norristown PA 19401-3324

TORNOW, BARBARA, academic administrator; b. Buffalo, Feb. 17, 1943; d. Elmer Henry and Elizabeth Jane S. Tornow; m. Charles Jack Sheehan, Sept. 1987 (dec. 1992); stepchildren: Charles, Jacquelyn. BA summa cum laude, William Smith Coll., 1965; MA in Polit. Sci., U. Pa., 1966, postgrad., 1966-70. Residence dir. Phila. Coll. Art, 1969-72, asst. dir. fin. aid./housing, 1972-77; dir. fin. aid Clark U., Worcester, Mass., 1977-79, Brandeis U., Waltham, 1979-86; dir. fin. assistance Boston U., 1986-96, exec. dir. fin. assistance, 1996—2002, sr. advisor, v.p. enrollment, 2002—. Trustee, admissions com. chair Hobart and William Smith Colls., Geneva, 1994—; bd. dirs. TERI , Boston, chmn., 1985—88. Chair Action Ctr. Ednl. Svcs. & Scholarships, Boston, 1998-99, mem., 1986-99; participant U.S. Dept. Edn. Negotiated Rulemaking, Washington, 1999, Project EASI, 1996-98. Mem.: Student Loan Mktg. Assn. (adv. com.), Mass. Assn. Student Fin. Aid Adminstrs. (pres. 1982—83, chair 1994—96, Svc. to Profession 1991), Nat. Assn. Student Fin. Aid Adminstrs. (dir. bd. 1994—97), Phi Beta Kappa. Democrat. Avocations: horseback riding, travel. Office: Boston U 881 Commonwealth Ave Boston MA 02215-1300 E-mail: btornow@bu.edu.

TORNOW, L. WILLIAM, musician; b. Devils Lake, N.D., Feb. 1, 1949; s. E. Edward and Ellen Naomi Tornow. BMus in Pub. Sch. Music, Concordia Coll., Moorhead, Minn., 1971; MA in Music, Trinity U., San Antonio, 1978; DMA in Piano Performance, U. Minn., Mpls., 1983. Artist in residence Cmty. Music Ctr., Fargo, ND, 1978—79; organist Our Saviour's Evang. Luth. Ch., Cannon Falls, Minn., 1984—85, St. George's Episc. Meml. Ch., Bismarck, ND, 1985—86. Composer: Symphony No. 1 for Chamber Orch., 1989, Symphony No 2 for Piano and Orch., 2002, Elegy, 1971. Spl. 4 (E-4) U.S. Army, 1971—74, Germany and Tex. Fellow: Nat. Music Tchrs. Assn.; mem.: Am. Guild of Organists. Avocations: fishing, golf. Home and Studio: 1107 W Capitol Ave Apt 62 Bismarck ND 38501

TORNQVIST, ERIK GUSTAV MARKUS, chemical engineer, research scientist; b. Lund, Sweden, Jan. 13, 1924; came to U.S., 1951; s. Gustav Ivar and Anne Marie (Lassen) T.; m. Linnéa Dagmar Lindborg, June 28, 1969; children: Gunvor, Karin, Carl-Erik. MSChemE, Royal Inst. Tech., Stockholm, 1948; MS in Biochemistry, U. Wis., 1953, PhD in Biochemistry/Organic Chemistry, 1955. Registered engr., Sweden. 1st rsch. asst. div. food chemistry Royal Inst. Tech., 1949-51; rsch. asst. dept. biochemistry U. Wis., Madison, 1951-55; rsch. chemist chem. divsn. Esso Rsch. and Engring. Co., Linden, N.J., 1955-58, rsch. assoc., 1958-66, sr. rsch. assoc., 1966-72, Exxon Chem. Co., Tech., Linden, 1972-86; internat. cons. Watchung, NJ, 1986—90, 2002—; pres. PolymErik, Inc., 1990—2002. Vis prof. Royal Inst. Tech., 1987; invited prin. speaker Scandinavian Day, Chautauqua (N.Y.) Instn., 1983, 87; invited speaker, chmn. numerous nat. and internat. meetings. Co-editor: Polymer Chemistry of Synthetic Elastomers, 2 vols., 1968, 69; patentee in field; contbr. articles to profl. jours., chpts. to books. Treas. United Swedish Socs., N.Y.C., 1972-86, Swedish Sch. Assn. N.J., 1988-91; bd. govs. Am. Swedish Hist. Mus., Phila., 1974-89; trustee New Sweden Co., Bridgeton, N.J., 1986-89, Kalmar Nyckel Found., Wilmington, Del., 1987-96, hon. trustee, 1996; bd. dirs. Watchung Hills Soccer Assn., Watchung/Warren, N.J., 1989-95. Recipient award 1st Nat. Inventors Day, 1973, gold Bicentennial medal King of Sweden, 1980, John Hanson award for excellence in pub. svc. Am.-Swedish Cultural Found., Mpls., 1981, citation Swedish Coun. of Am., 1983, cert. of appreciation Swedish New Sweden '88 Com., 1989; grad. fellow Roos' Found., Stockholm, 1949, 51, Govt. of Sweden, 1948, State Coun. for Technol. Rsch., Stockholm, 1949, Adelsköld fellow Royal Acad. Sci., 1951, 53, Univ. fellow Sweden-Am. Found., Stockholm, 1951. Fellow: Swedish Colonial Soc. (hon. gov. Ad Vitam 1982, gov. 1977—82, 1986—89); mem.: John Ericcson Soc., Internat. Union Pure and Applied Chemistry (affiliate),

Swedish Assn. Grad. Engrs., Am. Soc. Swedish Engrs. (life; sec. 1965—68, pres. 1968—72, John Ericsson Gold medal 1984), Swedish Soc. Chem. Engrs., Am. Chem. Soc., NY Acad. Scis., Schlaraffia, Wis. Alumni Assn. (life), Svensk I Varlden (life), Am.-Scandinavian Soc., KTH Alumni, Swedish-Am. C. of C., Swedish Ski Club (pres. 1972—74), Vasa Order Am. (co-cultural leader NJ Dist. 6, 1997, chmn. Lodge Skandia 2000—), Sigma Xi, Phi Lambda Upsilon. Lutheran. Achievements include invention and development of numerous catalysts for polymerization of olefins and dienes, especially the catalyst for making most of the isotactic polypropylene over a period of more than 20 years (from about 1958) and still in large-scale use, having resulted in production of billions of dollars worth of polymer, also, elucidation of many aspects of the mode of action of these and other catalysts and the preparation of numerous novel polymers. Avocations: skiing, music, photography, historical research and writing. Home and Office: 38 Mareu Dr Watchung NJ 07069-5025

TOROK, MARGARET LOUISE, insurance company executive; b. Detroit, June 22, 1922; d. Perl Edward Ensor and Mary (Seggie) Armstrong; m. Leslie A. Torok, Aug. 14, 1952; 1 child, Margaret Mary Ryan. Lic. Ins. Agy. From ins. agt. to corp. officer Grendel-Wittbold Ins., Southgate, Mich., 1961-72, pres. of corp., 1972—2001. Bd. dirs. Ind. Ins. Agts. of Mich., Lansing, 1984-92, Ind. Ins. Agts. of Wayne County, Dearborn, 1967—, pres. 1978. Bd. dirs. So. Wayne County C. of C., Taylor, 1975—, CEO, chmn. bd. dirs., 1997-98; bd. dirs. City of Southgate Tax. Increment Fin. Authority Dist. and Econ. Devel. Commn., 1987—, YMCA, Wyandotte, 1978—, Downriver Cmty. Alliance, 1990-94; chmn. Leadership, 1980-88; lay chmn. Cath. Svc. Appeal for Archdiocese of Detroit, 1989; co-chair fundraiser Sacred Heart Ch.; mem. bd. MESC Employers Com., 1991-95; com. mem., bd. dirs. New Workforce Devel. Com., gov. appt., charter mem.; hon. chmn. Art Ambience, 2002. Recipient Capital award Ind. Ins. Agts. of Mich., 1988, Lifetime Achievement award, Amb. award, 1994, Woman of Yr. AAUW, 1994, Salute to Excellence award Downriver Coun. of Arts, 1993-94, Chmn. of Yr. award MESC Job. Svc. Employers Com., 1991, Robert Stewart award Wyandotte Svc. Club Coun., 1994, Partnership award The Info. Ctr., 1996, 2001, W.O. Hildebrand award Mich. Assn. Ins. Agts., 1997; named to Ins. Hall of Fame, Olivet Coll., 1998. Mem.: Mich. Assn. Ins. Agts., Soroptimist Club of Wyandotte Southgate Taylor (pres. 1984—86, Advancing Status Women award 1988, Soroptimist of Yr. award 1993—94), Wyandotte Yacht Club. Roman Catholic. Office: Grendel Wittbold Agy Inc 12850 Eureka Rd Southgate MI 48195-1344

TOROP, PAUL, psychiatrist; b. N.Y.C., Oct. 18, 1940; s. Ralph and Betty Torop; m. Karen Torop, Dec. 19, 1965; children: Jonathan, Daniel. BA, Yale U., 1962; MD, Harvard U., Boston, 1966. Diplomate Am. Bd. Psychiatry and Neurology. Intern Mt. Zion Hosp., San Francisco, 1966-67; resident McLean Hosp., Belmont, Mass., 1967-70; instr. psychiatry Harvard Med. Sch., 1970; psychiatrist Underclift Mental Health Ctr., Meriden, Conn., 1972-73; asst. clin. prof. psychiatry Yale U., New Haven, 1973—; pvt. practice psychiatry Middletown, Conn., 1973—. Sr. attending psychiatrist Middlesex Hosp., Middletown, Conn., 1973—; psychiatrist Wesleyan U. Student Mental Health Svc., Middletown, Conn., 2000—. Contbr. articles to profl. jours., chpts. to books. Pres., bd. dirs. Gilead Cmty. Svcs., Middletown, 1991-94. Maj. USAF, 1970-72. Fellow Am. Psychiat. Assn.; mem. AMA, Conn. Psychiat. Assn. (New Haven/Middlesex br. pres. 1987-88). Office: 267 William St Middletown CT 06457

TORPEY, ROBIN LEE, computer science and information systems educator; b. Cuba, N.Y., Oct. 30, 1958; s. Charles E. and Betty L. Torpey; m. Laurie Ann Alaimo, Nov. 23, 1979; children: Gwendolyn, Megan. AAS in Avionics Tech., C.C. of Air Force, 1984; AS in Office Mgmt., Park Coll., 1991; BS in Interdisciplinary Studies, SUNY, Alfred, 1995. Cert. in microcomputer tech. Lectr. computer sci. and computer info. sys. SUNY Alfred State Coll., 1991—. Cons. Cuba Circulating Libr. Staff sgt. USAF, 1981-84. Mem. ALA. Methodist. Avocations: travel, photography. Office: SUNY Alfred State Coll 408 EJ Brown Hall Alfred NY 14802 Fax: 978-334-5587. E-mail: torpeyrl@alfredtech.edu.

TORPEY, SCOTT RAYMOND, lawyer; b. Detroit, July 4, 1955; s. Raymond George and Carmela Rose (Aquaro) T. BA in English, Wayne State U., 1978; JD, U. Detroit, 1982. Bar: Mich. 1984, D.C. 1985, N.Y. 1990, Ill. 1990, Calif. 1991, U.S. Dist. Ct. (ea. and we. dist.) Mich., U.S. Dist. Ct. (so., we., no. and ea. dists.) N.Y. 1990, U.S. Dist. Ct. (no., cen. and so. dists.) Ill. 1990, U.S. Dist. Ct. (D.C. dist.) 1989, U.S. Dist. Ct. (cen., so., no. and ea. dists.) Calif., 1991, U.S. Tax Ct., U.S. Ct. Appeals (D.C., fed., 2d, 6th, 7th and 9th cirs.), U.S. Supreme Ct. 1988. Ligitation ptnr. Jaffe, Raitt, Heuer and Weiss, PC, Detroit, 2000—; assoc. Long & Levit, San Francisco, 1982-83, Keating, Canham & Wells, Detroit, 1983-85; ligitation ptnr. Kohl, Secrest, Wardle, Lynch, Clark & Hampton, Farmington Hills, Mich., 1985-2000. Editor Tax Law Jour., 1981, Corp., Fin. and Bus. Law Jour., 1982. Mem. ABA, Fed. Bar Assn., Lawyer-Pilots Bar Assn., Bar Assn. San Francisco, Mich. State Bar Assn. (chmn. aviation torts com. of aviation law sect. 1992—). Republican. Avocations: sports, music, sports cars. Office: Jaffe Raitt Heuer & Weiss 1 Woodward Ave Ste 2400 Detroit MI 48226

TORPY, KATHLEEN ANN, educational association administrator; b. Wellsboro, Pa., July 17, 1950; d. Quentin Ward and Sophia Lucille (Tacka) T. AB, Wilson Coll., 1972; MBA, Shippensburg U., 1990. Mgr. The Naturalist, Exton/Plymouth Meeting, Pa., 1973; asst. mgr. Doubleday Bookstore, Bala Cynwyd, 1974-75; acctg. supt. and contracts adminstr. Ducon Fluid Transport Inc., King of Prussia, 1975-79; dir. budget and planning Wilson Coll., Chambersburg, 1979-88; assn. sec., bus. mgr. Middle States Assn. Colls. and Schs., Phila., 1988—. Cons. Coll. Misericordia Alumnae Assn., Dallas, Pa., 1984, Cedar Crest Coll. Alumae Assn., Allentown, Pa., 1981. Mem. Nat. Assn. Coll. and Univ. Bus. Officers, Am. Soc. Assn. Execs., Nat. Women's Studies Assn., Greater Chambersburg C. of C. (sec. bd. dirs. 1984-85), NOW. Democrat. Avocations: tennis, reading. Home: Creek Dr Wayne PA 19087-5216

TORQUATO, SALVATORE, materials science and chemistry educator; b. Falerna, Calabria, Italy, Feb. 10, 1954; came to U.S., 1955; s. Vincent and Palma (Vaccaro) T.; m. Kim Tracey Hoberock, Nov. 8, 1975; children: Michelle, Lisa. BSME, Syracuse U., 1975; MSME, SUNY, Stony Brook, 1977, PhD in Mech. Engring., 1980. Rsch. engr. Grumman Aerospace Corp., Bethpage, N.Y., 1975-78; rsch. asst. dept. mech. engring. SUNY, Stony Brook, 1978-80; asst. prof. dept. mech. engring. GM Inst., Flint, Mich., 1981-82; from asst. to assoc. prof. depts. mech., aerospace & chem. engring. N.C. State U., Raleigh, 1982-90, prof. depts. mech., aerospace & chem. engring., 1991-92; prof. Civil Engring. Princeton (N.J.) U., 1992-99, prof. chemistry, 2000—. Vis. prof. Courant Inst. Math. Scis., N.Y.C., 1990-91; cons. Eastman Kodak, Rochester, N.Y., 1989—; mem. Inst. Advanced Study, 1998-99. Contbr. articles to profl. jours. Grumman Masters fellow, 1975-77; fellow Guggenheim, 1998; grantee NSF, 1982—, U.S. Dept. Energy, 1986—; recipient Engring. Rsch. Achievement award Alcoa Co., 1987, Disting. Engring. Rsch. award, 1989, Gustus L. Larson Meml. award, 1994. Fellow ASME; mem. Am. Inst. Chem. Engrs., Am. Phys. Soc., Soc. Engring. Sci., Soc. for Indsl. and Applied Math. Avocations: racquetball, reading, music. Office: Princeton U Princeton Materials Inst Dept Chemistry Princeton NJ 08544-0001

TORRACO, STEPHEN FRANCIS, priest, theologian, educator; b. Watertown, Mass., Nov. 25, 1953; s. Italo and Clorinda Antoinette (Dimare) T. BA Theology/Philosophy summa cum laude, St. Francis de Sales Coll., 1975; MA in Theology, Boston Coll., 1977; MDiv magna sum laude, Harvard U., 1979; PhD in Theology, Boston Coll., 1986. Prof. Theology Boston Coll., Chestnut Hill, Mass., 1980-86, 88, Stonehill Coll., North Easton, 1986-88, Assumption Coll., Worcester, 1988—, dir. Inst. Study of Magisterial Teaching of Ch. Cons. Pope Paul VI Ctr. for Study of Human Reproduction, Omaha, 1994—. Author (book) Priests as Physicians of Souls, 1991; editor (jour.) Catholic International, 1993—; contbr. articles to profl. jours. Assoc. mem. Cath. Commn. on Intellectual and Cultural Affairs; mem. Fellowship of Cath. Scholars, Soc. of Cath. Social Scientists, Am. Acad. Natural Family Planning. Republican. Roman Catholic. Office: Assumption Coll 500 Salisbury St Worcester MA 01609-1265

TORRE, JOSEPH JOHN, endocrinologist; b. Plainfield, N.J., Sept. 16, 1946; s. Salvatore Frank and Rose Mary (Patrissi) T.; m. Elise Augusta Lampazzi, Oct. 30, 1971; children: Vincent Salvatore, Christina Angela. BA in Chemistry cum laude, Cornell U., 1968; MD, Boston U., 1972. Diplomate Am. Bd. Internal Medicine, Am. Bd. Endocrinology and Metabolism. Intern, then resident St. Luke's Hosp. Ctr., N.Y.C., 1972-74, fellow in endocrinology and metabolism, 1974-76; rsch. fellow MIT Arteriosclerosis Ctr., Cambridge, Mass., 1976-77; physician North River Med. Assn., Hanover, 1977-91; endocrinologist Buffalo (N.Y.) Med. Group, P.C., 1991—; asst. clin. prof. medicine SUNY, Buffalo, 1995—. Cons. Buffalo Gen. Hosp., 1991—, Roswell Park Cancer Inst., 1991—. Fellow ACP, Am. Coll. Endocrinology; mem. Am. Assn. Clin. Endocrinologists (chmn. chpt. 1997—), Endocrine Soc., Am. Diabetes Assn. Roman Catholic. Office: Buffalo Med Group 85 High St Buffalo NY 14203-1149

TORRE, JOSEPH PAUL (JOE TORRE), professional baseball team manager; b. Bklyn., July 18, 1940; m. Alice Torre; children: Michael, Lauren, Tina, Andrea Rae. Profl. baseball player Milw. Braves, 1960-69, St. Louis Cardinals, 1969-74, N.Y. Mets, 1974-77, player-mgr., 1977-82; mgr. Atlanta Braves, 1982-84; TV broadcaster Calif. Angels, 1984-90; mgr. St. Louis Cardinals, 1990-94, N.Y. Yankees, 1995—. Named Nat. League's Most Valuable Player, Baseball Writers Assn. Am., 1971, Player of Yr., Sporting News, 1971, AP Mgr. of Yr., 1982; named to All-Star Team, 1963-67, 70-73, Sporting News All-Star Team, 1964-66, 71; recipient Gold Glove award, 1965; hit for cycle, 1973; winner World Series N.Y. Yankees Greatest Win Percentage 127 Regular Season Wins, 1998. Office: New York Yankees Yankee Stadium E 161 St & River Ave Bronx NY 10451*

TORREGIAN, SOTÈRE, poet; b. June 25, 1941; Grad., Rutgers U., 1963. Asst. in Afro-Am. studies, writer-in-residence Stanford (Calif.) U., 1969-73; poet, 1965—. Scholar, lectr. in field. Author: (poetry collections) Song for Woman, 1965, The Golden Palomino Bites the Clock, 1966, The Wounded Mattress, 1968, City of Light, 1971, The Age of Gold, 1976, Amtrak, 1979, Always for the First Time, 1999, (poem-play) Pantograph, 2001, (poems) Selected Poems and Other Works 1957-2000. Recipient Frank O'Hara award for Poetry, 1968, Gotham Book Mart Author of Yr. award 1976. Home and Office: 999 Porter Ave Apt 28 Stockton CA 95207-4278 E-mail: jamesgus@yahoo.com.

TORRENCE, BILLY HUBERT, minister; b. Lynchburg, Va., Aug. 29, 1949; s. Charles Hubert and Mabel (Pillow) T.; m. Linda P. Pool, Apr. 1, 1972; children: Joseph Scott, Susan Marie Richards. Grad., Ctrl. Va. C.C., 1993, Wesley Sem., Washington, 1997, Duke U., 2000. Ordained assoc. mem. Va. Annual Conf., 2000; c.p.e. Bapt. Hosp. Wake Forest. Foreman, crew leader Va. Dept. Transp., Lynchburg, 1987-90; local pastor Meth. Ch., Va., 1990-93, Staunton, 1993-95, Providence UMC, Danville Dist., Patrick Springs, 1995-98; bookkeeper Va. Dept. Hwys., 1992-93, 1992-93; foreman, crew leader Va. Dept. Transp., Lynchburg, 1987-90; local pastor Mt. Bethel Ch. UMC, Martinsville, Va., 1998—; dir. Camp Overlook Property, Keezletown, 2000—. With U.S. Army, 1968-72, Vietnam. Mem. Ruritan (zone gov. Peaks of Otter chpt. 1983, lt. dist. 1984-86, dist. gov. 1985, 87, Ruritan of Yr. 1984), Phi Theta Kappa. Home and Office: 76 Dodson Dr Lynchburg VA 24501-7466 Office: 76 Dodson Dr Lynchburg VA 24501-7466 E-mail: torrencebill@aol.com. *I have found that a person is never to old to learn the ways of God for their life. Seek God in the morning, evening and all day long for continuing guidance. Take everyday as a journey. learn from it and move on. Each obstacle offers opportunity for learning. Thank God for them.*

TORRENCE-THOMPSON, JUANITA LEE, public relations executive; b. Brockton, Mass., Nov. 08; d. James Lee Torrence and Zylpha Odyselle Mapp-Robinson; m. Hugh Warren Thompson, Dec. 19, 1965; 1 child, Derek Rush. BS in Bus. & Comm., Empire State Coll., Old Westbury, N.Y., 1983; MA in Comm., Fordham U., 1989. Newsletter editor UN Internat. Sch., 1976-77; pub. rels., editl. asst. Nat. Assn. Theatre Owners, 1979-80; asst. acct. exec. Richard Weiner, Inc., 1984; newsletter editor SUNY Empire State Coll., 1985-87; editor Dorf & Stanton Comm., Inc., 1987-88; pub. rels. exec. pvt. practice, 1988—. Adj. prof. pub. rels. Coll. New Rochelle, N.Y., 1997. Author: Spanning The Years, Wings Span to Eternity; contbr. articles, poems, short stories, essays to mags., newspapers & newsletters. Bd. dirs. So. Queens Park Assn., Jamaica, N.Y., 1988-91; mem. parent faculty soc. UN Internat. Sch., N.Y.C., 1976-80; pub. rels. cons. UN Coll. Fund, N.Y.C., 1994. Recipient Feature Article award Writers Digest, 1985, Meritorious Svc. award United Negro Coll. Fund, 1994, Editors Choice award Nashville Newsletter, 1994, Robins Nest Mag., 1996, First prize N.Y. Pub. Libr. Contest, 1996, Outstanding Achievement award SUNY, Empire State Coll., Old Westbury, honoree SUNY, Margaret A. Walker Short Story Competition award 1999, 2000. Mem. AAUW, Nat. Assn. Black Journalists, Pub. Rels. Soc. Am., Poetry Soc. Am., Acad. Am. Poets, Native Am. Journalists Assn., Black Pub. Rels. Soc., Black Women in Pub., Poets & Writers, Fresh Meadows Poets. Avocations: travel, theatre, films, poetry, concerts. Office: PO Box 751205 Forest Hills NY 11375-8805

TORRENS, DANIEL, lawyer; b. Phila., Oct. 30, 1969; BA, Ariz. State U., 1992; JD, U. Nebr., 1996. Bar: Ariz. 1996, Colo. 1997, U.S. Dist. Ct. Ariz. 1996, U.S. Ct. Appeals (9th cir.) 1997. Assoc. Struckmeyer & Wilson, Phoenix, 1996-98, Turley, Swan & Childers, Phoenix, 1998—. Mem. ABA, Ariz. Bar Assn., Colo. Bar Assn., Def. Rsch. Inst., Delta Theta Phi. Office: Turley Swan & Childers 3101 N Central Ave Ste 1300 Phoenix AZ 85012-2656 E-mail: dtorrens@tsc-law.com.

TORRENZANO, RICHARD, public affairs executive; BS, N.Y. Inst. Tech., 1972, LittD (hon.), 1990; postgrad., Stanford U., 1986. With N.Y. Stock Exch., 1981-90, sr. v.p., mgmt. and exec. coms., chief spokesman; sr. v.p., dir. corp. affairs, mgmt. com. SmithKline Beecham, London, 1990-94; chmn., CEO, The Torrenzano Group, 1995—. Coord. Pres. Reagan's Bd. Advisors on Pvt. Sector Initiatives, Washington, 1986—89; pvt. sector adv. com. USIA, Washington, 1983—92; coord. program USSR-USA Conf. on Stock Markets, Moscow, 1989, PRC-USA Conf. on Stock Markets, Beijing, 1986; lectr. in field. Contbr. articles to profl. jours. Trustee, mem. exec. com. N.Y. Inst. Tech., 1985—; trustee John Cabot U., Rome, 1998. Decorated Knight of Malta, Knight cmdr. of Holy Sepulchre, Knight of Savoy Orders of Saints Maurice and Lazarus, Comdr. Constantinian Order of St. George; recipient Silver Anvil award, Pub. Rels. Soc. Am., Ellis Island Medal of Honor, 1997. Mem.: Royal Soc. Medicine (London), N.Y. Press Club, Nat. Press Club Washington. Office: The Torrenzano Group 551 Fifth Ave Ste 1400 New York NY 10176-1400 Fax: 212-681-6961. E-mail: richard@torrenzano.com.

TORRES, ART, former state legislator; b. L.A. children: Joaquin, Danielle. AA, East L.A. C.C.; BA, U. Calif., Santa Cruz; JD, U. Calif. John F. Kennedy teaching fellow Harvard U.; with State Assembly, 1973—81; former senator state legislator State of Calif., L.A., 1982—93; chmn. Calif. Dem. Party, 1996—. Chmn. Senate Com. Ins., Claims and Corps., Assembly Health Com., Senate Toxics and Pub. Safety Mgmt. Com., Select Com. Pacific Rim, Senate Spl. Rask Force on New L.A.; founder Calif. EPA; sr. mem. Senate Edn. Com.; author 1992 Immigrant Workforce Preparation Act; mem. Nat. Conf. State Legislatures Coalition on Immigration, Senate Appropriations Com., Senate Energy and Pub. Utilities Com., Senate Govtl. Orgn. Com., Senate Judiciary Com., Senate Natural Resources Com., Senate Transp. Com., chmn. California Dem. Party. Mem. Coun. Fgn. Rels., N.Y., Nat. Commn. Internat. Migration and Econ. Devel.; participant IVth Nobel Prizewinners Meeting Nova Spes Internat. Found., Vatican, Rome, 1989—. Recipient Legislator of Yr. award Calif. Orgn. Policy and Sheriffs, 1990, Outstanding Legislator of Yr. award Calif. Sch. Bd. Assn., 1990, Outstanding Alumnus award U. Calif. Santa Cruz, Dreamer award Boys and Girls Club Am., 1990, Achievement award Latin Am. Law Enforcement Assn., 1992. Office: 911 20th St Sacramento CA 95814-3115 Address: 1401 21st St Ste 100 Sacramento CA 95814*

TORRES, BARBARA WOOD, technical services professional; b. Coudersport, Pa., Sept. 18, 1945; d. Ken and Myrna Wood; m. James Torres, July 3, 1965; children: James C, William D. BS in Physics, U. N.Mex., 1969, MS in Physics, 1972. Mem. staff Quantum Systems, Inc., Albuquerque, 1967-72, EG&G, Albuquerque, 1972-76, Mission Rsch. Corp., Albuquerque, 1977-78; from staff mem. to v.p. test engring. BDM, 1978-97; dir. test engring. TRW, 1998-2000, divsn. dir. compliance programs, 2001—. Mem. N.Mex. State Sci. and Tech. Commn., 1983—86; mem. com. NEWTEC Joint Venture, N.Mex., 1998—. Mem. adv. bd. N.Mex. Comprehensive Regional Ctr. Minorities, 1993—96; judge N.Mex. Regional and State Sci. Fair, 1986—; bd. dirs. N.Mex. Network for Women in Sci., 1988—92. Named Outstanding Grad, Rio Grande HS, 1995; recipient Gov Award for Outstanding NMex Women, 1988. Mem.: Int Electronic and Elec Engrs, Int Test and Eval Asn, Am Bus Women's Asn (dist vpres 1995—96, nat secy 1996—97, One of Top 10 Bus Women 1982), Am Physical Soc. Avocations: travel, mystery and spy novels, walking. Home: PO Box 1660 Tijeras NM 87059-1660 Office: TRW 6001 Indian School Rd NE Albuquerque NM 87110-4182 E-mail: barbara.torres@trw.com.

TORRES, ESTEBAN EDWARD, former congressman, business executive; b. Miami, Ariz., Jan. 27, 1930; s. Esteban Torres and Rena Baron (Gomez) T.; m. Arcy Sanchez, Jan. 22, 1955; children: Carmen D'Arcy, Rena Denise, Camille Bianca, Selina Andre, Esteban Adrian. Student, East Los Angeles Coll., 1960, Calif. State U., Los Angeles, 1963, U. Md., 1965, Am. U., 1966; PhD (hon.), Nat. U., 1987; DHL (hon.), Whittier Coll., 2001. Chief steward United Auto Workers, local 230, 1954-63, dir. polit. com., 1963; organizer, internat. rep. United Auto Workers (local 230), Washington, 1964; asst. dir. Internat. Affairs Dept., 1975-77; dir. Inter-Am. Bureau for Latin Am., Caribbean, 1965-67; exec. dir. E. Los Angeles Community Union (TELACU), 1967-74; U.S. ambassador to UNESCO, Paris, 1977-79; chmn. Geneva Grp., 1977-78; chmn. U.S. del. Gen. Conf., 1978; spl. asst. to pres. U.S., dir. White House Office Hispanic Affairs, 1979-81; mem. 98th-103rd Congresses from 34th Dist. Calif., 1983-98; mem. appropriations com., subcom. fgn. ops., subcom. transp. Campaign coordinator Jerry Brown for Gov., 1974; Hispanic coordinator Los Angeles County campaign Jimmy Carter for Pres., 1976; mem. Sec. of State Adv. Group, 1979-81; v.p. Nat. Congress Community Econ. Devel., 1973-74; pres. Congress Mex.-Am. Unity, 1970-71, Los Angeles Plaza de la Raza Cultural Center, 1974; dir. Nat. Com. on Citizens Broadcasting, 1977; cons. U.S. Congress office of tech. assessment, 1976-77; del to U.S. Congress European Parliament meetings, 1984; ofcl. congl. observer Geneva Arms Control Talks; chmn. Congl. Hispanic Caucus, 1987; speaker Wrights Del. to USSR, 1987; Dem. dep. Whip, 1990; chmn. Nat. Latino Media Coun. Contbr. numerous articles to profl. jours. Co-chmn. Nat. Hispanic Dems., 1988—; chmn. Japan-Hispanic Inst. Inc.; bd. visitors Sch. Architecture UCLA, 1971-73; bd. dirs. Los Angeles County Econ. Devel. Com., 1972-75, Internat. Devel. Conf., 1976-78; chmn. Congrl. Hispanic Caucus, 1985-86; pres. Plaza de la Raza Cultural Ctr., 1972-73; trustee Am. Coll. Paris, 1977-79; mem. Calif. Transp. Commn., Sacramento. Served in AUS, 1949-53, ETO. Recipient Congrl. award Nat. Leadership award 1997. Mem. Americans for Dem. Action (exec. bd. 1975-77), VFW Post 6315, Pico Rivera, Calif., Am. Legion, Smithsonian Inst. (regent 1997—), S.W. Voter Inst., Calif. Transp. Commn. Address: 908 E Lucille Ave West Covina CA 91790-5221

TORRES, HUGO R. financial analyst, international credit analyst, telecommunications analyst; b. Bogotá, Colombia, Nov. 29, 1963; arrived in U.S., 1979; s. Juan B. and Beatriz (Vanegas) T.; m. Michelle L. Hartman, Dec. 31, 1989; children: Brandon, Allison. BA in Bus. Adminstrn. and Econs., Hope Coll., 1988. Telecomm. analyst Metromedia Long Distance, East Rutherford, N.J., 1988-93; acct. analyst Cantor Fitzgerald Sec., N.Y.C., 1993-95; internat. credit analyst Whirlpool Corp., Miami, 1996-97; internat. fin. analyst Lotus/IBM Corp., 1998—. Author: Ira Guia Hispana de Como Iniciar un Negocio, 1994. Co-founder, gen. sec., mem. Asocomercol, Jersey City, N.J., 1993-95; vol. CASA, Miami, 1995-96, Hispanic Orgn. of BC, Hackensack, N.J. Republican. Avocations: swimming, running, international business. Home: 12121 SW 94th St Miami FL 33186-2073 Office: Lotus Corp 5201 Blue Lagoon Dr Ste 800 Miami FL 33126-2092

TORRES, JUDITH, lab administrator; b. N.Y.C. d. Benigno Rodriguez and Luz Maria Ruiz; m. William Rodriguez Torres, Dec. 29, 1991; 1 chld, William Elijah. BS in Indsl. Chemistry, U. P.R., 1985; postgrad. student, McCrone Rsch. Inst., Chgo., 1987-92. Analytic chemist Bristol Meyers Squibb, Humacao, P.R., 1984-88, supr. quality control, 1988-91; pharm. chemist Eli Lilly and Co., Indpls., 1991-95, head dept. quality control labs., 1998—. Office: Eli Lilly and Co Lilly Corp Ctr Drop Code 5532 Indianapolis IN 46256 Fax: (317)276-5727. E-mail: torres_judith@lilly.com.

TORRES, LOUIS, editor, writer; b. Orange, N.J., Jan. 22, 1938; s. Allah and Lillian (Bougeois) T.; m. Eva Korycanova, Aug. 17, 1973 (div. Apr. 1980); m. Michelle Marder Kamhi, Aug. 28, 1987. BA in Psychology, Rutgers U., 1960; postgrad., U. Minn., 1960—61; MA in Tchg. English, Columbia U., 1971. Elem. tchr. Eatontown (N.J.) Pub. Sch., 1966-67; tchr. English, Franklin Sch., N.Y.C., 1967-69; tchr. English and humanities Indian Hills H.S., Oakland, N.J., 1969-80; mng. dir. William Carter Dance Ensemble, N.Y.C., 1980-82; tchr. English and esthetics Am. Renaissance Sch., White Plains, N.Y., 1981-84; founder, editor, pub. Aristos, N.Y.C., 1982-92, co-editor, pub., 1992—. Co-founder, chmn. The Aristos Found., N.Y.C., 1986—. Co-author: What Art Is: The Esthetic Theory of Ayn Rand, 2000; contbr. articles to profl. jours. With USNR, 1961-63. Mem. Am. Philos. Assn., Am. Soc. for Aesthetics, Ayn Rand Soc., Assn. for Art History, Assn. Lit. Scholars and Critics. Office: The Aristos Found 147 W 94th St New York NY 10025-7016

TORRES, MILTON JOHN, industrial engineering educator; b. N.Y.C., July 28, 1931; s. Milton and Vitalia (Cabrera) T.; m. Dorothy Spaugh (div. Feb. 1971); children: Milton J. III, Geoffrey, Vicky L. Lopez; m. Dorothy Roberts. BS in Gen. Engring., U. Okla., 1963, M Aerospace Engring., 1964; DArts in Mech. Engring., U. Miami, 1989. Commd. 2d lt. USAF, 1954, advanced through grades to maj.; chief test control br. Ops. Directorate Air Force Ea. Test Range, Cape Kennedy, Fla., 1968-71; ret. USAF, 1971; indsl. engr., sr. indsl. engr. Pan Am. World Airways, Inc., Miami, Fla., 1972-73; plant supt. Am. Panel Corp., 1973-77; plant mgr. Dyplast of Fla., 1977-83; asst. prof. indsl. systems dept. Fla. Internat. U., 1983-87, rsch. scientist, lectr. dept. indsl. engring., 1987-94. Contbr. articles to profl. jours., patentee in field. Decorated DFC, Air medal (13), Air Force Meritorious Svc. medal, Air Force Commendation medal. Mem. Tau Beta Pi, Sigma Tau, Sigma Gamma Tau, Alpha Pi Mu. Home: 11200 SW 99th Ct Miami FL 33176-4123

TORRES, ROBERT ALVIN, dancer, singer, actor, sign language interpreter; b. Camden, N.J., Apr. 4, 1960; s. Pedro Juan and Nora Hilda (Cesfallanos) T.; m. Karen Lea Dearborn, Nov. 21, 1987; children: Ariane Lea, Ryan Alexander. A of Liberal Arts, LeHigh Carbon C.C., 1999; BS in Info. Sys., Muhlenberg Coll., 2001. Dancer Burlington (N.J.) Ballet Co., 1976-78; soloist Harkness Dancers, N.Y.C., 1979; ind. dancer, singer, 1982—; prin. dancer Rod Rogers Dance Co., 1985, Louis Johnson Dancers, 1986; dance tchr. Muhlenberg Coll., 1993—, Hartford Ballet Sch., 1993—; tchr. Muhlenberg Coll., 1993-94, adaptive tech. specialist, 2001—. Sign lang. interpreter, 1992—; guest tchr. master classes Mount Holyoke Coll., 1987, Conn. Coll., 1992, Pa. Youth Theatre, 1993, Ethel Walker Sch., 1993, Dance Forum Lehigh Valley, 1994; dance tchr. Cedar Crest Coll. Allentown Acad. Arts; tchr. Lehigh Valley Ballet Guild; guest tchr. Muttlenberg Coll. H.S. Summer Dance Camp, 1996-99; webmaster Muttlenberg Coll., 2000—. Choreographer (restaged) Sundazy by Sandra Machala, 1979, Midsummer Night's Dream, 1990, On The Town, 1991, Peter Pan, 1994, Wake Up The Moon, 1994, Keep on Walking, 1995, Evita, 1995, A Chorus Line, 1995, Keep on Twalking, 1995, Switching Stations, 1996, Seasonal Alliances, 1996, Follow the Beacon, 1996, My Partner, Myself, 1997, Can You See the Bull..., 1997, In Search of..., 1998, Conversations, 1998, Shadow Play, 1998, Connected Isolation part IV, 1999, Cogs in the Machine, 1999, Deep Down, 1999; dancer Busch Gardens, 1980, Kiss Me Kate with Robert Goulet, 1981; dancer, singer Evita nat. tours III and IV, 1982-84, Barnum, 1986, Cats nat. tour IV, 1987, The Star Dust Road Workshop, 1988, Carousel, 1988, Golden Boy, 1988, West Side Story, 1989, My Fair Lady, 1989, The Chocolate Soldier, 1990; dance capt. Evita, 1985, A Chorus Line, 1986; acrobatic cons. A Christmas Carol, 1989, dance capt., 1989, 90; asst. choreographer, actor A Christmas Carol, 1990, Here's Love, 1991; guest artist with the Decatur Dekalb Ballet, 1979, Virginia Beach Ballet, 1980, St. Petersburg Ballet, 1980, Miss. Ballet Theatre, 1980, Rio Grande Valley Co., 1980-81; choreographer, dance capt., dancer, singer Here's Love, 1991, co-choreographer, Oliver; sign lang.-based movement choreographer Trojan Women; fight dir. Oliver, 1996; sign lang. performance interpreter Come Back to the Five and Dime, Jimmy Dean, Jimmy Dean, 1997, In Search of Cinderella, 1997, Sleeping Beauty, 1999; performance interpreter Alice in Wonderland, American Beauty., Mother Hicks, 2000; composer: Homage to

Bobby, 1999. Recipient 3d place award N.J. Scholastic State Gymnastic Tournament, 1978. Mem. Actors' Equity Assn. Republican. Avocations: hang gliding, skiing, skating, diving, auto repair. Office: care Torres Family 514 Cambridge Dr Mount Laurel NJ 08054-2804 E-mail: ratorres@muhlenberg.edu.

TORRES, RUDY ARNOLD, artist; b. L.A., Dec. 21, 1957; s. Benjamin Tiburcio and Josephine Irene Torres. Student, East Los Angeles Coll., 1981—83, Pacific Inst. Comml. Art, 1984—85, Otis Parsons Sch. Design, 1985—86. Artist, co-owner Echo Park Gallery, L.A., 1989—91. One-man shows include Minus Zero Gallery, L.A., 1990, Mary Norton Clapp Libr., Occidental Coll., 2000, exhibitions include Alpha Contemporary Exhibits, 1983—86, Mac Houston Art Gallery, Pasadena, Calif., 1986, Grand Libr. Art Gallery, Glendale, Calif., 1987, Design Ctr. L.A., 1987, L.A. Photography Ctr., 1987, 1989, L.A. Mcpl. Gallery, 1989, L.A. Art Assn., 1989, 1990, Minus Zero Gallery, Torrance, Calif., 1990, Echo Park Gallery, L.A., 1990—91, Boathouse Gallery, 1992, Weingart Gallery, 1992, Atrhut Coons Gallery, 1992, Galeria Las Americas, 1992—94, 1996, Art & Barbee Art Gallery, Hollywood, Calif., 1993, Hilles Libr. at Harvard U., 1995, Palette Des Artists, Pasadena, 1996, Galeria Otravez, East Los Angeles, Calif., 1996, 2001, Olvera St. Gallery, L.A., 1996, Long Beach (Calif.) Gallery, 1998, Calif. State U. Fresno grand Ctrl. Art Ctr., Santa Ana, 2001, Guggenheim Gallery, Chapman U., Orange, Calif., 2001, Huntington Beach (Calif.) Gallery, 2002, Coll. of Brea (Calif.) Gallery, 2002, Showcase North Gallery, Santa Ana, 2001—02. Recipient cert. of appreciation for mural in Herman Dist., 14th Dist. City of L.A., 1986. Avocations: body building, swimming, jogging, camping, fishing. Home: 700 W La Veta Ave # R5 Orange CA 92868

TORRES, TERRY TEROL, mechanical engineer, general contractor; b. N.Y.C., Apr. 27, 1946; s. Angel M. and Flor E. (Lozada) T.; 1 child, Tuesday Lee; m. Mary Hunter Stevens, July 4, 1980; children: Laura Diana, Anna Maria. BS in Mech. Engring., Va. Poly. Inst. and State U., 1969. State cert. gen. contractor, lic. real estate broker, Fla. Tech. sales engr. Westinghouse Elec., N.Y.C., 1969-70; project engr. Southern Bell AT&T, Miami, 1970-75; supervising engr. Am. Bell, Inc., San Juan, P.R., 1975-76; chmn., CEO Atlantic Aluminum Dist., Ft. Pierce, Fla., 1977-82, Cosmos Developing Assn., Vero Beach, 1976—; pres., CEO Cosmos Contracting Corp., 1981—, Watershed Environ. Technologies, Inc., Vero Beach, 1995—. Tech. cons. P.R. Telephone Co., San Juan, 1975-76; solar engring. and design, MIT, Cambridge, Mass., 1975; chmn. govt. affairs Indian River Co. Bd. Realtors, Vero Beach, 1990; environ. cons. Vero Beach, 1995-96. Designer and contractor vent-skin walls with radiant barrier for bldg. constrn., 1986, high-performance homes and bldgs., 1986—; designer and developer ventilation systems for indoor firing ranges, Ft. Benning, Ga., 1972; designer, chief engr. bomb disposal trailers and portable units, Miami, 1973-74. Project supr. and contractor Habitat for Humanity, Very Beach, 1996. Lt. U.S. army Inf., 1970-72. Recipient Five-Star Energy award City of Vero Beach, 1988, Energy Efficiency award Fla. Power and Light Co., Ft. Pierce, 1987, cert. achievement Indian River Bd. Realtors, 1989. Mem. Nat. Assn. Realtors, Nat. Geographic Soc., Aircraft Owners and Pilots Assn., Fla. Assn. Realtors. Republican. Episcopalian. Office: Watershed Environ Techs Inc PO Box 3808 Vero Beach FL 32964

TORRESE, DANTE MICHAEL, prosthodontist, educator; b. Yonkers, N.Y., Feb. 12, 1949; s. Dante Angelo and Matilda (Dal Lago) T.; m. Camille Patricia DiPaola, Aug. 7, 1982. BS in Biology, Manhattan Coll., 1971; DDS, Columbia U., 1975; prosthodontic cert., NYU, 1983. Resident in dentistry Presbyn. Hosp., N.Y.C., 1975-76; clin. instr. dentistry Columbia U., 1976-78, asst. clin. prof. dentistry, 1978—; pvt. practice dentistry Yonkers, N.Y., 1976—. Attending dentist Presbyn. Hosp., N.Y.C., 1976-86; lectr. in field. Recipient Am. Acad. Oral Pathology Grad. award 1975, Densply Corp. award for removable prosthodontics, 1975, Psi Omega Scholastic Achievement award, 1975. Fellow Am. Coll. of Dentists, Royal Soc. Health; mem. NRA (life), Yonkers Dental Soc., 9th Dist. State Dental Soc., Invested Baker St. Irregular, Sherlock Holmes Wireless Soc., Single Action Shooting Soc. (life), Yonkers Amateur Radio Club, Westchester Astronomy Club, Exch. Club (sec. 1979—), Three Garridebs of Westchester, Priory Scholars of N.Y.C. Club, Montague Street Lodgers of Bklyn. Club, Omicron Kappa Upsilon. Office: 984 N Broadway Ste 503 Yonkers NY 10701-1308

TORRES-GIL, FERNANDO M. federal official, academic administrator; b. Salinas, Calif., June 24, 1948; BA in Polit. Sci., San Jose State U., 1970; MSW, Brandeis U., 1972, PhD, 1976. Spl. asst. to sec. Dept. Health, Edn. and Welfare, Washington, 1978-79, Dept. Health and Human Svcs., Washington, 1979-80, asst. sec. for aging, 1993—; prof. gerontology and pub. adminstrn. U. So. Calif., 1981-91, assoc. dir. Nat. Resource Ctr. on Minority Aging Populations, 1988-92, prof. social welfare, 1991-93; assoc. dean Sch. Pub. Policy and Soc. Rsch. UCLA. Staff dir. Select Com. on Aging, U.S. Ho. of Reps., Washington, 1985-87. Contbr. articles to profl. jours. White House fellow, 1978-79. Mem. Am. Soc. Aging (pres. 1989-92). Office: UCLA Sch Pub Plicy & Social Rsch Box 951656 3250 Public Policy Blvd Los Angeles CA 90095-1656

TORRES-LABAWLD, JOSE DIMAS, institutional research director, service company executive, educator; b. Luquillo, P.R., Mar. 25, 1932; s. Antonio Torres Herrera and Maria S. (Labawld) Torres; m. Patricia Ann Zaccaria, Apr. 18, 1959; children: Peter, Michelle, Mary E., Patrick, David, Gwendolyn, Christopher. BA cum laude, Inter-Am. U., San German, P.R., 1957; MPA, Syracuse U., 1959; postgrad., U. Notre Dame, 1961-62; PhD, Ohio State U., 1973; postgrad., Dartmouth Coll., 1995-96. Mgmt. ofcl., adminstr. U.S. state dept. Point IV program Office of Pers., Office of Gov., San Juan, P.R., 1959-61; lectr. Ind. U., South Bend, 1963-64; lectr. NDEA Knox Coll., Galesburg, Ill., 1965; instr. Ohio U., Athens, 1965-69; rsch. assoc. Mershon Ctr. Ohio State U., Columbus, 1970-71; dir. dept. gen. studies Hocking Coll., Nelsonville, Ohio, 1973-75, dir. instl. rsch., 1975—2002, emeritus, 2002—; pres. IMSA, Inc., Athens, 1981—. Bus. cons. IMSA, Inc., 1981—. Coord. youth for understanding internat. exchg. program U.S. State Dept., 1966-70; cand. Athens County Cen. Com. Dem., 1974; chmn. fin. com. Ohio U. Christ the King Parish, 1992—; dir. Transnational Bus. Program, U.S., Mexico, Can., 1995—. Cpl. U.S. Army, Korea, 1951-53. Commonwealth of P.R. fellow Syracuse U., 1959; Hocking Coll. scholar, 1990. Mem. Am. Arbitration Assn., Assn. for Instnl. Rsch., U.S. Hispanic C. of C., World Trade Club, Columbus Area C. of C., VFW, Lions (pres. Athens chpt. 1984), Am. Legion, Phi Alpha Theta. Roman Catholic. Avocations: tennis, golf, piano, painting, chess. Home: 15 Grand Park Blvd Athens OH 45701-1438 E-mail: pepe@frognet.net.

TORRESYAP, PEARL MARIE, surgical nurse; b. Cleve., Oct. 1, 1930; d. Clyde E. and Pearl C. (Flanagan) Callender; m. Fortunato Torresyap, Oct. 30, 1953; children: Joy, Gay, Fay. Diploma, Luth. Hosp. Sch. Nursing, 1951. Cert. nurse in oper. rm. Staff nurse Lakewood (Ohio) Hosp., 1951-54, Choate Hosp., Woburn, Mass., 1976-78; thoracic charge nurse Boston VA Med. Ctr., 1979-94, orthopedic charge nurse in oper. rm., 1994-96, ret., 1996. Contbr. articles to jours. in field. Vol. Mus. Sci. Human Body Connection, 1996—. Mem. ANA, Assn. Oper. Rm. Nurses (pres. Mass. chpt. 1988-89, book reviewer for jour.), Mass. Coun. Nursing Orgns. (rep. 1989-93), Mass. Nurses Assn., Internat. Toastmasters (treas. 1989-90). E-mail: beanblossom@aol.com.

TORREY, BARBARA BOYLE, research council administrator; b. Pensacola, Fla., Nov. 27, 1941; d. Peter F. and Elsie (Hansen) Boyle; m. E. Fuller Torrey, Mar. 23, 1968; children: Michael, Martha. BA, Stanford U., 1963, MS, 1970. Vol. Peace Corps, Tanzania, 1963-65; fiscal economist Office Mgmt. and Budget, Washington, 1970-80; dept. asst. sec. HHS, 1980-81; dir. Ctr. for Internat. Rsch. Census Bur., 1984-92; pres. Population Reference Bur., 1992-93; exec. dir. Commn. on Behavioral and Social Scis. and Edn. NRC, NAS, 1993—. Bd. dirs. Luxembourg Income Study. Co-editor: The Vulnerable, 1987, Population and Land Use, 1992; contbr. articles to profl. jours. Fellow AAAS; mem. Population Assn. Am. (bd. dirs. 1993—). Office: NRC 2101 Constitution Ave NW Washington DC 20418-0007

TORREY, CLAUDIA OLIVIA, lawyer; b. Nashville, June 10, 1958; d. Claude Adolphus and Rubye Mayette (Prigmore) T. BA in Econ., Syracuse U., 1980; JD, N.Y. Law Sch., 1985. Bar: N.Y. State 1988. Legal intern Costello, Cooney & Fearon, Syracuse, N.Y., 1979; legal clk. First Am. Corp., Nashville, 1981; legal asst. James I. Meyerson, N.Y.C., 1982-85; jud. law clk. N.Y. State Supreme Ct., 1985; interim project supr., legal asst. CUNY Ctrl. Office, 1985-86; legal analyst Rosenman & Colin Law Firm, N.Y.C., 1986-87; asst. counsel N.Y. State Legis., Albany, 1988-90; atty., cons. pvt. practice, Nashville, Cookeville, Tenn., 1991—. Bd. dirs. Children's Corner Day Care Ctr., Albany, N.Y., 1989-90, PDS/USN Aumni Bd., Nashville, 2001--. Author column Health Law Jour. of N.Y. State Bar Assn., 1996—. Ch. rep. FOCUS exec. coun. Westminster Presbyn. Ch., Albany, 1990; v.p. dormitory coun., flr. rep. Syracuse U., 1977-79; bd. mem. PDS/USN Alumni Bd., Nashville, 2001--; chair Synod of Living Waters COR Com., Presbyn. Ch. (U.S.A.), 2002--. Mem. ABA (young lawyers divsn. liaison to ABA forum on health law 1994-96), Internat. Platform Assn., N.Y. State Bar Assn. (chmn. health law sect. study group on health info., privacy and confidentiality 1998-99), Alpha Kappa Alpha. Avocations: singing, reading, harp, travel, art. Home and Office: PO Box 150234 Nashville TN 37215-0234 E-mail: jewel3@prodigy.net.

TORREY, DAVID LEONARD, investment banker; b. Ottawa, Ont., Can., Oct. 6, 1931; s. Arthur Starratt and Josephine Edith (Leonard) T.; divorced; children: Heather Torrey Murphy, John Winthrop, Diana Bruce, Arthur Bruce, David Molson. BA in Econs., St. Lawrence U., 1953; diploma, Grad. Sch. Bus., U. Western Ont., 1954. With Pitfield Mackay Ross Ltd., Toronto, Ont., Can., 1954-84, v.p., 1963-73, sr. v.p., 1973-80, vice chmn., 1980-82, pres., 1982-84, also bd. dirs.; vice chmn. Dominion Securities, Inc., 1984-88, RBC Dominion Securities, Inc., 1988-91. Chmn. Montreal Stock Exch., 1971-73, Phillips Cables Ltd., 1991-96; bd. dirs. Wajax Ltd., 1963-2002, Can. Stebbins Engring. and Mfg. Co. Ltd.; mem. coun. Montreal Bd. Trade, 1971-72. Chmn. Montreal Downtown YMCA, 1972-74; trustee St. Lawrence U.; bd. dirs. Montreal Gen. Hosp. Found. Mem. Investment Bankers Assn. (gov. 1971-72), Securities Industries Assn. (bd. govs. 1972-73), Multiple Sclerosis Can. (past pres., bd. dirs.), Royal Montreal Golf Club, Mt. Royal (Montreal) Club, Toronto Club, Saifish Club Fla. (Palm Beach), Beta Theta Pi. Home: 389 Carlyle Ave Montreal QC Canada H3R 1T3 Office: PO Box 6001 1 Pl Ville Marie 7S Montreal QC Canada H3C 3A9

TORREY, JAMES D. mayor, communications executive, consultant; b. Drayton, N.D., July 16, 1940; s. Howard J. Torrey and Gertrude (Carpenter) Steenson; m. Katherine Joann Kowal, Sept. 2, 1958; children: Tamara, Timonthy (dec.), Teresa, Todd. Student, U. Oreg., 1959-61. Mgr. Waldport (Oreg.) Food Market, 1959-67; dist. mgr. Obie Outdoor Advt., Aberdeen, Wash., 1967-68; dir. sales Obie Media Corp., Eugene, Oreg., 1968-71, exec. v.p., 1971-78, pres., CEO, 1980-88, Total Comm., Inc., Eugene, 1989-91; N.W. area market mgr. 3M Nat. Advt., 1978-80; dir. mktg. State Accident Ins. Fund, Salem, 1988-89. Mem. exec. com. affiliate bd. Mut. Broadcasting, 1981-87. Pres. Waldport City Coun., 1962-67; coach Eugene Kidsports, 1968-92, Am. Softball Assn. Girls Softball Team, 1988; mem. adv. com. 4 J Sch. Dist., 1988-90; bd. dirs. Lane County United Way, 1983-86, dir., 1992, Lane County Goodwill Industries, 1989-90; mem. Eugene City Budget Com., 1992-94, Eugene City Coun., 1994-97; mayor City of Eugene, Oreg., 1997—. Named JCI senator, Oreg. State Jaycees, 1966, Citizen of Yr., City of Waldport, 1967, Outstanding Vol., City of Eugene, 1991. Mem. Oreg. Outdoor Advt. Assn. (pres. 1971-80), Oreg. Assn. Broadcasters (dir. 1984-87), Eugene C. of C. (bd. dirs., pres. 1991-92), Eugene Rotary (dir., pres. 1984, Paul Harris fellow 1985). Republican. Roman Catholic. Avocation: youth coaching. Office: Mayor's Office 777 Pearl St Ste 105 Eugene OR 97401-2720*

TORREY, RICHARD FRANK, utility executive; b. Saratoga Springs, N.Y., Dec. 31, 1926; s. Reginald Frank and Marian (Currey) T.; m. Betty Louise Stetson, July 2, 1949; children: Patricia Ann Torrey, Carol Louise Torrey Kress, Barbara Jean Torrey Friedman. BA cum laude, Syracuse U., 1951. News reporter, Syracuse (N.Y.) Post Standard, 1947-51; pub. rels. account exec. Syracuse, 1951-53; home sec. 35th Congl. Dist., 1952-53; exec. sec. to mayor Syracuse, 1954-58; dir. area devel. Niagara Mohawk Power Corp., Syracuse, 1958-66, comml. v.p. Buffalo, 1966-68, adminstrv. v.p., 1968-72, v.p., gen. mgr., 1972-76, sr. v.p., 1976-88, ret., 1988; pres. Can. Niagara Power Co. Ltd., Niagara Falls, Ont., Can., 1968-88, dir. Can., 1968-89. Pres., dir. Caragh Investments Ltd., 1981-85; pres. Opinac Investments Ltd., Toronto, 1982-88, bd. dirs., 1982-89; pres. Opinac Energy Ltd., Calgary, Alta., 1983-88, bd. dirs., 1983-89. Pres. Syracuse USO, 1959-61, mem. nat. coun., 1959-62, 68-74; co-chmn. Ctrl. N.Y. Interim Coun. Regional Planning, 1965-66; gen. chmn. Dunbar-Huntington Bldg. Fund, Syracuse, 1963; state campaign chmn. N.Y. Job Devel. Authority, 1961; gen. chmn. United Way of Buffalo and Erie County, 1971; mem. Syracuse U. Corp. Adv. Coun., 1972-76; trustee Elmcrest Children's Ctr., 1962-63, Camp Good Will, Syracuse, 1964-66, Syracuse Area Coun. Chs., 1959-64; bd. dirs. United Way Buffalo and Erie County, 1967-76, Greater Buffalo Devel. Found., Kenmore Mercy Hosp., 1970-76, Crouse Irving Meml. Hosp. Found., 1978-87, Nat. Kidney Found., 1987-89, Bon Secours-Venice (Fla.) Hosp. Found., 1992-98, vice chmn. 1995-96, chmn. 1996-98; bd. dirs. Plantation Cmty. Found., Venice, 1989, pres., 1990-93, pres. emeritus, 1993—; mem. bd. adv. Sisters of St. Joseph, 1967-76; elder Trinity Presbyn. Ch., Venice, 1992-94; assoc. mem. Dewitt Cmty. Ch. Served with Air Corps U.S. Army, 1944-47. Recipient Syracuse Young Man of Yr. award, 1962; Outstanding Citizen award Buffalo Evening News, 1973. Mem. Empire State (v.p., bd. dirs. 1963-80), Buffalo Area (v.p. 1968-72, bd. dirs. 1968-76, pres. 1972-73, chmn. bd. 1973-74, Man of Yr. 1974) C. of C., Associated Industries of N.Y. (bd. dirs. 1978-80), Bus. Coun. N.Y. (bd. dirs. 1980-82), Mfrs. Assn. Cen. N.Y. (bd. dirs. 1977-88), Augusta Villa Assn. (bd. dirs. 1989-92), Buffalo Club (past 2d v.p., dir.), Syracuse Century Club (gov. 1980-83), Onondaga Golf Club, Plantation Golf and Country Club, Automobile Club Western N.Y.(bd. dirs. 1971-73, pres. 1973), N.Y.S. Automobile Assn. (dir. 1975-76), Venice Yacht Club. Home and Office: 705 Carnoustie Ter Venice FL 34293-4349

TORREY, WILLIAM ARTHUR, professional hockey team executive; b. Montreal, Que., Can., June 23, 1934; BS, St. Lawrence U., 1957. From dir. pub. rels. to bus. mgr. Pitts. Hornets Am. Hockey League team, 1960-68; exec. v.p. Calif. Golden Seals, 1967-72; gen. mgr. N.Y. Islanders, 1972-93, pres., 1980-89, chmn. bd., 1989-92, cons., 1993; pres. Fla. Panthers, Ft. Lauderdale, 1993—. N.Y. Islanders NHL Stanley Cup Champions, 1980-83. Office: Florida Panthers Hockey Club Nat Car Rental Ctr 1 Panther Pkwy Sunrise FL 33323-5315

TORRIANI-GORINI, ANNAMARIA, microbiologist, educator; b. Milan, Italy, Dec. 19, 1918; came to U.S., 1955, naturalized, 1962; d. Carlo and Ada (Forti) Torriani; m. Luigi Gorini (dec. Aug. 1976); 1 child, Daniel. PhD, U. Milan, Italy, 1942. Research assoc. Istituto Ronzoni Chimica-Biochimica, Milan, 1942-48; charge de recherche Institut Pasteur, Paris, 1948-56; research assoc. NYU, 1956-58, Harvard U., Cambridge, Mass., 1958-60, MIT, Cambridge, 1960-71, assoc. prof. microbiology, 1971-76, prof., 1976—; prof. emerita, 1989. Recipient NIH Career award, 1962-72; Fulbright fellow, 1956-58. Mem. Am. Soc. Microbiology, Soc. Française de Microbiologie (hon.). Home: 115 Longwood Ave Brookline MA 02446-6625 Office: MIT Dept of Biology 68-371 Cambridge MA 02139 E-mail: Pho@mit.edu.

TORRICELLI, ROBERT G. senator; b. Franklin Lakes, N.J., Aug. 26, 1951; BA, Rutgers U., 1974, JD, 1977; MPA, Harvard U., 1980. Bar: N.J. 1978. Dep. legis. counsel Office Gov. N.J., 1975-77; counsel to V.P. Mondale, Washington, 1978-81; pvt. practice, 1981-82; mem. 98th-104th Congresses from 9th Dist. N.J., 1983-96, sci., space and tech. com., fgn. affairs com., select com. on intelligence, chmn. Western Hemisphere subcom., 1992-94; U.S. senator from N.J., 1996—. Mem. rules, govt. affairs, judiciary and fgn. rels. coms. Bd. govs. Rutgers U., 1977-83. Mem. ABA, N.J. Bar Assn. Democrat. Office: US Senate 113 Dirksen Senate Ofc Bldg Washington DC 20510-0001*

TORRIERI, DON JOSEPH, electronics engineer, mathematician, researcher; b. Balt., Nov. 19, 1942; s. Peter and Mary Torrieri; m. Nancy Karen Weir, Jan. 27, 1971; children: Karen Marisa, Peter. BS, MIT, 1964; MS, Poly. U., Farmingdale, N.Y., 1966, U. Md., 1969, PhD, 1971. Electronics engr. Naval Rsch. Lab., Washington, 1971-77; mathematician Dept. of the Army, Adelphi, Md., 1977—. Faculty George Washington U., Washington, 1988-92, Johns Hopkins U., Balt., 1993—. Author: Principles of Military Communication Systems, 1981, Principles of Secure Communication Systems,1985, 2d edit., 1992; contbr. chpt. to book, articles to profl. jours. Coach boys soccer and basketball Calverton Recreation Coun., Silver Spring, Md., 1990-94; coach girls softball Montgomery County, Md., 1993-94; coach boys baseball Burtonsville (Md.) Athletic Assn., 1995-97; coach various soccer, basketball, baseball & softball youth teams, 1990-2000. Mem. IEEE (sr., Best Paper award Mil. Comms. Conf. 1991), Sigma Xi. Achievements include authorship of a textbook that is the standard in the field. Home: 2204 Hidden Valley Ln Silver Spring MD 20904-5240 Office: Army Rsch Lab 2800 Powder Mill Rd Adelphi MD 20783-1138 E-mail: dtorr@arl.army.mil.

TORRUELLA, JUAN R. federal judge; b. San Juan, P.R., June 7, 1933; BS in Bus. and Fin., U. Pa., 1954; LLB, Boston U., 1957; LLM, U. Va., 1984; MPA, U. P.R., 1984; LLD (hon.) , St. John's U., 1995, Roger Williams U., 1995. Judge U.S. Dist. Ct. P.R., San Juan, 1974—82, chief judge, 1982—84; judge U.S. Ct. Appeals (1st cir.), 1984—94, 2001—, chief judge, 1994—2001. Former mem. jud. conf. com. on the Adminstrn. of the Fed. Magistrate Sys.; mem. jud. conf. exec. com. on Internat. Jud. Reform. Mem.: FBA, ABA, P.R. Bar Assn., D.C. Bar Assn., Assn. Labor Rels. Practitioners P.R. and V.I. Office: John J Moakley US Courthouse 1 Courthouse Ste 2500 Boston MA 02210*

TORSTRICK, REBECCA LEE, anthropologist, educator; b. Louisville, Dec. 17, 1954; d. Donald Lee Torstrick and Dolores King; m. Jeffrey David Sutter; children: Maia Sutter. AB, U. Ill., 1972—76; MEd, Wash. U., 1979—81, PhD, 1984—93. From asst. prof. to assoc. prof. Ind. U., South Bend, Ind., 1996—2002, assoc. prof., 2002—. Vis. asst. prof. Wash. U., St. Louis, 1994—96. Author: (book) The Limits of Coexistence: Identity Politics in Israel, 2000. Mem.: Assn. Rsch. Motherhood, Am. Ethnol. Soc., Assn. Polit. and Legal Anthropology, Am. Anthrop. Assn., Mid. E. Sec.- AAA. Office: Ind U South Bend 1700 Mishawaka Ave South Bend IN 46634-7111

TORTI, FRANK MICHAEL, physician, healthcare administrator; BA, MA, Johns Hopkins U., 1969; MPH, Harvard U., 1973, MD, 1974. Diplomate in internal medicine and med. oncology Am. Bd. Internal Medicine. Asst. prof. medicine Stanford (Calif.) U., 1979-84, clin. assoc. prof. medicine, 1984-86, assoc. prof. medicine, 1986-93; head sect. hematology/oncology Wake Forest U. Sch. Medicine, Winston-Salem, N.C., 1993-98, prof. medicine, 1993—, dir. Comprehensive Cancer Ctr., 1993—, chmn. dept. cancer biology, 1993—. Chair N.C. Gov.'s Commn. on Cancer Coordination and Control, 1993—; v.p., founding mem. Nat. Bladder and Prostate Cancer Found., 1990—; mem. study sect. Am. Inst. for Cancer Rsch., Bethesda, Md., 1989—. Mem. Am. Assn. for Cancer Rsch., Am. Soc. Clin. Oncology, Am. Soc. Cell Biology, Internat. Soc. Interferon Rsch., Am. Fedn. for Clin. Rsch., Soc. for Biol. Therapy. Office: Wake Forest U Sch Medicine Medical Center Blvd Winston Salem NC 27157-1082 E-mail: ftorti@wfubmc.edu.

TORTO, RAYMOND GERALD, economist; b. Lynn, Mass., Dec. 16, 1941; s. Edward Dante and Lucy (Petrucci) T.; m. Linn Torto; children: Stephanie, Pamela, Nathaniel. AB, Boston Coll., 1963, MA, 1967, PhD, 1969. Prof. econs. U. Mass., Boston, 1970-96; spl. asst. to mayor for tax policy City of Boston, 1976-80, commr. assessing, 1980-82; pres. Torto Wheaton and Assocs., Boston, 1982-86; prin. CB Comml./Torto Wheaton Rsch., 1987—. Sr. fellow., dir. McCormack Inst. U. Mass., Boston, 1984-95; bd. dirs. Boston Mcpl. Rsch. Bur., Assoc. Ind. of Mass., Real Estate Rsch. Inst. Author: The Rich Get Richer and the Rest Pay Taxes, 1974, Money and Financial Institutions, 1981, Property Tax Reevaluation, 1983. Chmn. fiscal issues study group Commonwealth of Mass., 1988-90. Mem. Am. Soc. Real Estate Councilors (Homer Hoyt fellow), Am. Real Estate Soc., Lambda Alpha Soc., Corinthian Yacht Club. Avocations: sailing, squash, gardening. Home: 38 Foster St Marblehead MA 01945-3645 Office: CB Comml/Torto Wheaton Rsch 200 High St Boston MA 02110-3036

TORTOLANI, ANTHONY JOHN, surgeon, educator; b. Eastchester, N.Y., Oct. 15, 1943; s. Salvatore Paul and Yolanda (Vecciarelli) T.; m. Beth Callahan, Dec. 15, 1967 (dec. Oct. 1993); children: Julia Sue, Paul Justin; m. Katherine Gormley, Sept. 25, 1999. BS, Fordham U., 1965; MD, George Washington Sch. Medicine, 1969. Diplomate Am. Bd. Surgery, Am. Bd. Thoracic Surgery. Chief divsn. cardiovascular & thoracic surgery North Shore U. Hosp., Manhasset, N.Y., 1978-90, chmn. dept. surgery, 1988-96, chmn. med. bd., 1994-96, chmn. dept. surgery Glen Cove, 1990-96; John D. Mountain chair surgery North Shore U. Hosp.- Cornell U. Med. Coll., Manhasset, 1989-96, program dir. surg. residency program, 1992-96; prof. surgery Cornell U. Med. Coll., N.Y.C., 1993-97, prof. cardiothoracic surgery, 1997-99; mem. staff N.Y. Hosp., 1997-99; dir., prof. cardiothoracic surgery Jack D. Weiler Hosp./Montefiore Med. Ctr. Albert Einstein Coll. of Medicine, 1999-2001; prof. clin. cardiothoracic surgery Weill Med. Coll., Cornell U., 2001—. Vice chmn. N.Y. Presbyn. Cornell Cardiothoracic Surgery Network. Active Columbus Citizens Found., N.Y.C. Maj. USAF, 1974-76. Roman Catholic. Avocation: breeding Arabian horses. Office: NY Presbyn Hosp 525 E 68th St Rm M-404 New York NY 10021

TORTORELLO, NICHOLAS JOHN, public opinion and market research company executive; b. Maspeth, N.Y., Dec. 1, 1948; s. John Anthony and Verla Jean (Odel) T.; m. Joan Elizabeth King, Jan. 13, 1973; children: Kerry Ann, Jennifer Joan. BA in Polit. Sci. with highest honors, Williams Coll., 1971; M Religious Studies, St. Joseph's Sem., Yonkers, N.Y., 1988. Vice pres. Louis Harris & Assocs., N.Y.C., 1971-73, sr. v.p., 1973-79; exec. v.p. DMT Inc., 1979-83; pres. Tortorello Corp., Pearl River, N.Y., 1983-85; pres. Tortorello group Market Facts Inc.-N.Y., N.Y.C., 1985-86; v.p. Total Rsch. Corp., Princeton, N.J., 1986-88; chmn. Rsch. and Forecasts Inc., N.Y.C., 1989-93; sr. v.p. Roper Starch Worldwide Inc., 1993-98; pres. Guideline Consulting, 1998—. Editor, author Tortorello Trendline, 1983-85, Rsch. and Forecasts Trendline, 1989-91. Trustee Riverdale (N.Y.) Country Sch., 1982-90, v.p., 1986-89; trustee Marymount Manhattan Coll., N.Y.C., 1986-88; lectr., tchr. religion St. Anthony's Ch., Nanuet, N.Y., 1984-86; mem. CARA Bd. Georgetown U., Washington, 1992-98, rsch. adv. coun., 2000—; mem. Hosp. Chaplaincy Bd., 1991-97; v.p. Class of '71, Williams Coll., 2001. Recipient Am. Legion award for leadership, scholarship, honor and svc., 1967, Disting. Alumnus of Yr. award Riverdale Country Sch., 1984. Mem. Am. Dirs. Inst. (trustee 1984-87), Coun. Am. Survey Rsch. Orgn. (chmn. bd. dirs. 2001, chmn. publs. com. 1991-94, chmn. pub. rels. com. 1995-97, chmn. mktg. and comms. com. 1997-99, bd. dirs., chmn. 1999 ann. conf., chmn. bd. dirs. 1999, chmn. bd. trustees 2001, chmn. nominating com. 2002), Am. Assn. Pub. Opinion Rsch., Williams Club. Democrat. Avocations: collecting Lionel trains, collecting stereo equipment, softball, golf, collecting American coins. Office: Guideline Cons 3 W 35th St Fl 7 New York NY 10001-2284 E-mail: ntorbrello@guidelineresearch.com.

TORTORICI LUNA, JOANNE MARIE, counseling psychologist, consultant, educator; b. Bklyn., Nov. 28, 1949; d. Michael Anthony and Anna Loretta T.; m. Julio Cesar Luna Molina; 1 child, Martin Julio Luna. BA, Calif. State U., L.A., 1980; MA, U. Calif., L.A., 1986; PhD, U. Southern Calif., L.A., 1988. Reg. dance movement therapy Am. Dance Therapy Assn.; credential Pupil Personnel Counseling, Calif. Prof. child psychotherapy Ctrl. Am. U., Managua, Nicaragua, 1988; regional coord. mental health svcs. Min. Health, Nicaragua, 1988-89; nat. coord. Child Victim's of War, Nicaragua, 1989-91; cons. Internat. Cath. Child Bur., Managua, Nicaragua, 1991-93, UNICEF, Managua, Nicaragua, 1993-94; faculty Antioch U. Southern Calif., Marina Del Rey, 1994—, Calif. State U. Long Beach, Long Beach, Calif., 1997—; sch. counselor Woodrow Wilson H.S., 1994-98; violence prevention coord. Long Beach Unified Sch. Dist., 1998—2000, cons., 2000—. Tech. cons. UN Children's Fund, 1990—, WHO, 1990—; cons. Mercy Corps, 2001--; trainer, cons. N.Y.C. Schs. Post 9/11 Recovery, 2001--. Author: UN Children's Fund's First Country Program for South Africa, 1992, First Peace Education Program for Nicaragua, 1993, Violence in American Schools: Practical Guidelines for Counselors, 2000, Faces of Violence, Psychological Correlates, Concepts and Intervention, 2000; co-author: Children in War A Guide to the Provision of Services, 1993. Mem. Ref. Group on Child Soldiers, Inst. Henry Dunant, Geneva, Switzerland, 199 2; adv. Goldstone Commn. for Prevention of Polit. and Pub. Violence, South Africa, 1993—, Min. of Edn., UN Children's Fund, Managua, Nicaragua, 1993; co-chair Counseling Reform Launch Initiative, Long Beach, Calif., 1998-2001. Recipient Faculty Commendation, Bouggess-White Scholarship Found., Long Beach, Calif., 1997, Safe Schools award Calif. State Atty. Gen., Long Beach, Calif., 1998; named EDUCARE scholar U. Southern Calif., L.A., 1988. Mem. APA, Am. Counseling Assn., Assn. Counselor Educators, Am. Sch. Counselor Assn. Avocations: music, dance. Office: Calif State U ED PAC 1250 Bellflower Blvd Long Beach CA 90840 Fax: 562-985-4534. E-mail: jtortori@csulb.edu.

TORUÑO, RHINA M. Literature educator, researcher, writer; b. San Salvador, El Salvador; came to U.S., 1981; d. Juan Felipe and Juana (Contreras) Toruño; m. Henriquez Trujillo, Nov. 4, 1967 (div.); children: Mario Felipe, José Rodrigo; m. Hector-Neri Castañeda (dec.). Grad., Santa Ines Coll., Nueva San Salvador, El Salvador, 1961; BA in Philosophy, Nat. U .El Salvador, 1971; MA in Philosophy, Cath. U. Louvain, Belgium, 1973, PhD in French Contemporary Philosophy, 1978; MA in Hispanic and Latin Am. Lit., Nat. U. Paris/Sorbonne, 1976; PhD in Latin Am. Lit., Ind. U., Bloomington, 1994. Tchr. asst. Nat. U. El Salvador, San Salvador, 1968-71, prof. philosophy, 1976-81; vis. scholar Sch. Edn. Stanford U., Palo Alto, Calif., 1981-82; vis. asst. prof. Fla. State U., 94-95; asst. prof. U. Tex. of the Permian Basin, Odessa, 1995-97, assoc. prof., 1997-00, prof., 01—, Kathlyn Cosper Dunagan prof. humanities, Spanish area coord., 1997—. Cons. for edn. com. Mexican-Am. Network of Odessa, 1997—. Author: Time, Destiny and Oppression on the Work of Elena Garro, 1996, 2d edit., 1998; assoc. editor Chiricu, Ind. U., Bloomington, 1985-90, Third Woman, Berkeley U., 1986-87; author more than 50 articles on literary criticism in English, French, Spanish. Recipient Ednl. Rshc. award, Pan Am. Round Table, Odessa, Tex., 1996, Internat. Prize Emmanuel Mounier, French Assn. of Friends of Emmanuel Mounier, Paris, 1974, Damas de Oro, Odessa, Tex., 2000; grantee U Tex., Odessa, 2000; fellow Internat. Fedn. Univ. Women, Geneva, 1981-82. Mem. Soc. des Amis d'Emmanuel Mounier, Fedn. Internat. des Femmes Deplomees de Univs. Internat., Salvadoran Acad. Scis. (1st female mem.), Salvadoran Acad. Spanish Lang., Pan Am. Round Table, Spanish Book Club (pres. 1996—), Hispanic C. of C. Democrat. Roman Catholic. Avocations: reading short stories for children, aerobics, gardening, travel. Home: 4305 Buck Pl Odessa TX 79762-4650 Office: U Tex Permian Basin 4901 E University Blvd Odessa TX 79762-0001 E-mail: toruno_r@utpb.ed.

TORVALDS, LINUS (BENEDICT), application developer; b. Helsinki, Finland, Dec. 28, 1969; married; children: Patricia Miranda, Daniela. Developer Transmeta Corp., Santa Clara, Calif. Achievements include invention of Linux operating system. Office: Transmeta Corp 3940 Freedom Cir Santa Clara CA 95054*

TORZ, RICHARD J. economics and finance educator; b. N.Y.C., May 10, 1956; s. Florian and Halyna (Stanislawski) T. BA in Econs., Queens Coll.-CUNY, 1980, MA in Econs., 1988; M.Phil. in Econs., CUNY, N.Y.C., 1990, PhD in Econs., 1993. Grant teaching asst. Queen Coll. CUNY, 1980-84, adj. lectr. Queens Coll., 1984-89, adj. lectr. Queensborough Community Coll., 1988-89, instr. Lehman Coll., 1989-91; instr. C.W. Post Campus L.I. U., Brookville, N.Y., 1991, asst. prof. C.W. Post Campus, 1993; asst. prof. St. Joseph's Coll., Bklyn. and Patchogue, 1993—. Reviewer book: Macroeconomics: Private and Public Choice, 1988. Rsch. assistantship, CUNY, 1985, grad. assistantship, 1985. Mem. Am. Econ. Assn., Eastern Econ. Assn., Nat. Assn. Bus. Economists, N.Y. State Econs. ASsn., Omicron Delta Epsilon. Avocations: reading, analyzing financial markets. Home: 57-81 79th St 1st Fl Elmhurst NY 11373-5309 Office: St Joseph's Coll Bklyn Campus 245 Clinton Ave Brooklyn NY 11205-3602 also: St Joseph's Coll Suffolk Campus 155 W Roe Blvd Patchogue NY 11772-2325

TOSATO, GIOVANNA, researcher; b. Vicenza, Italy, Mar. 20, 1949; came to U.S., 1976; d. Egidio and Cecilia (Di Valmarana) T.; m. Robert Yarchoan, Nov. 7, 1981; children: Mark, John. MD, State U. Rome, 1973. Asst. prof. Cath. Univ. of Rome (Italy) Med. Sch., 1974-76; vis. fellow NIH, Bethesda, Md., 1976-80, expert, 1980-83; sr. staff fellow Ctr. for Biologics Evaluation and Rsch., FDA, 1983-84, lab. chief, 1984-93; chief Divsn. of Hematologic Products, FDA, 1993-99; head sect. exptl. transplantation and immunology br. NIH, 1999—. Reviewer scientific jours., 1980-99; contbr. numerous articles to profl. jours. Office: NIH 8800 Rockville Pike Bethesda MD 20892-0001 E-mail: tosatog@mail.nih.gov.

TOSCANO, JAMES VINCENT, medical institute administration; b. Passaic, N.J., Aug. 8, 1937; s. William V. and Mary A. (DeNigris) T.; m. Sharon Lee Bowers; children: Shawn Truelson, Lauren Bjorklund, David Brendan, Dania Toscano Miwa. AB summa cum laude, Rutgers Coll., 1959; MA, Yale U., 1960. Lectr. Wharton Sch., U. Pa., 1961-64; chief opinion analyst Pa. Opinion Poll, 1962-64; mng. dir. World Press Inst., St. Paul, 1964-68, exec. dir., 1968-72; dir. devel. Macalester Coll., St. Paul, 1972-74; v.p. resource devel. and public affairs Mpls. Soc. Fine Arts, 1974-79; pres. Minn. Mus. Art, 1979-81; exec. v.p. Park Nicollet Med. Found., 1981-95; corp. sec. Park Nicollet Clinic, 1983-86; sr. v.p. Am. Med. Ctrs., Inc., 1985-87; exec. v.p. Park Nicollet Inst., Mpls., 1996—. Adj. prof. sch. of mgmt. U. St. Thomas, 1989—; co-chair prin. practices nonprofit excellence com. MCN, 1994-98. Author: The Chief Elected Official in the Penjerdel Region, 1964; co-author, co-editor: The Integration of Political Communities, 1964. Bd. dirs., exec. com., sec., World Press Ins., 1972—; bd. dirs., chmn. Southside Newspaper Mpls., 1975-79; chmn. com. to improve student behavior St. Paul Pub. Schs., 1977-79; bd. dirs. Planned Parenthood St. Paul, 1965-72, Mpls. Action Agy., 1976-79; emeritus dir. Help Enable Alcoholics Receive Treatment; mem. St. Paul Heritage Preservation Commn., 1979-82, vice chmn., 1981; mem. Citizens Adv. Com. on Cable Comm.; bd. dirs. Citizens League, 1980, Park Nicollet Med. Found., 1981-95, Park Nicollet Inst., 1996—2000, African-Am. Culture Ctr., 1979-82, Am. Composers Forum, 1981-85, St. Paul Chamber Orch., 1976-80, 83-89, United Theol. Sem., 1985-88; dir. emeritus Minn. Citizens for the Arts; bd. dirs., mem. exec. com., chmn. Med. Alley Assn., 1986-96; mem. task force on tech. assessment Med. Alley, 1992-93; mem. health affairs adv. com. Acad. Health Ctr. U. Minn., 1988-95; bd. dirs. Mother Cabrini House, 1985-92, Minn. Civil Justice Coalition, 1987-91, also chmn.; chmn. Gov.'s Task Force on Health Care Promotion, 1985-86, mem. Gov.'s Com. Promotion Health Care Resources, 1986-87; chmn. bd. Minn. Fin. Counseling Svcs., Inc., 1990-93; mem. task force cost effectiveness Med. Alley, 1994-95; bd. dirs. Meml. Blood Bank, 1995—2001, mem. exec. com., 1996—; bd. dirs. Bakken Mus., 1997—, Stevens Square Cmty. Orgn., 1997-99, Rainbow Rsch., Inc., 2002-. Woodrow Wilson Nat. fellow, 1960. Mem. Minn. Newspaper Found. (bd. dirs. 1987-92), Minn. Coun. Nonprofits (bd. dirs. 1989-95, 97—, bd. mem. Plymouth Music series 1993-96, alt. Minn. Healthcare Commn., 1993-95, mem. Minn. Healthcare Commn., 1995-97, chair task force on med. edn. and rsch. costs 1994-96; mem. com. on med. rsch. and edn. costs, 1996—, chair 1996-99; liaison health tech. adv. com. 1993-97; pres. bd. dirs. Summit Ave Residential Preservation Assn., 2000—), Skylight Club, Informal Club. Address: 1982 Summit Ave Saint Paul MN 55105-1460 Office: Pk Nicollet Inst 3800 Park Nicollet Blvd Minneapolis MN 55416-2527 E-mail: Toscaj@ParkNicolkt.com., jvt2@attbi.com.

TOSCANO, OSCAR ERNESTO, lawyer; b. Ecuador, Jan. 24, 1951; s. Hugo and Maruja (Lopez) T.; children: Marina, Tracy, Oscar Emerson, Jacob, Nicole, David. BA, UCLA, 1975; JD, Loyola U., L.A., 1978. Bar: Calif. 1978, U.S. Dist. Ct. (9th dist.) Calif. 1978. Pvt. practice, Glendale, 1978—. Mem. Assn. Consumer Attys. of L.A., Consumer Attys. of Calif., Los Angeles County Bar, Mex.-Am. Bar Assn., State Bar Calif., Glendale Bar Assn., Hispanic Alumni Scholarship Found. Avocations: tennis, chess, trial work. Office: 625 W Broadway Glendale CA 91204-1058

TOSCO, LORENZO A. priest, educator; b. Pinerolo, Italy, Nov. 12, 1942; arrived in U.S., 1974; s. Tommaso Tosco and Caterina Garis. SSL, Pontifical Biblical Inst., Rome, 1973, SSD, 1983. Dir. CSJ House of Study, Cleve., 1975—80; assoc. Holy Rosary Ch., 1977—88; provincial superior Congregation of St. Joseph, 1982—88; prof. scripture St. Mary Sem., Wickliffe, 1974—. Treas. U.S.-Mexico Province Congregation of St. Joseph, 2000—. Author: (novels) Pietro e Pietro Ministri Del Giudrio, 1989. Coord. Bldg. Youth Retreat Ctr., 1998. Mem.: Italian Biblical Assn., Cath. Biblical Assn. Roman Catholic. Avocations: gardening, wine making, bicycling, mountain climbing. Home: 4076 Case Rd Avon OH 44011 Office: St Mary SEm and Grad Sch Theology 28700 Euclid Ave Wickliffe OH 44092-2527 Home Fax: 440-934-6270. Personal E-mail: lato@aol.com.

TOSHACH, CLARICE OVERSBY, real estate developer, former computer executive; b. Firbank, Westmoreland, Eng., Nov. 21, 1928; came to U.S., 1955; d. Oliver and Nora (Brown) Oversby; m. Daniel Wilkie Toshach, July 30, 1965 (dec. Aug. 1992); 1 child, Duncan Oversby Toshach; 1 child from previous marriage, Paul Anthony Beard. Textile designer Storeys of Lancaster, Eng., 1949-55; owner, operator Broadway Lane, Saginaw, Mich., 1956-70; pres., owner Clarissa Jane Inc., 1962-70, Over-Tosh Computers, Inc. dba Computerland, Saginaw and Flint, Mich., 1983-95; mgr., ptnr. Mich. Comml. Devel. L.L.C., Saginaw, 1995—. Trustee Saginaw Gen. Hosp., 1977-83, Home for the Aged, 1978-80; bd. dirs. Vis. Nurse Assn., pres., 1981-83; bd. dirs. Hospice of Saginaw, Inc., v.p., 1981-83; mem. long range planning com. United Way of Saginaw, 1982-83; cmty. advisor Jr. League of Saginaw, 1982-83; pres. Saginaw Gen. Hosp. Aux., 1972-82, pres., 1976-77.

TOSHEFF, JULIJ GOSPODINOFF, psychiatrist; b. Svishtov, Bulgaria, July 3, 1925; came to U.S., 1968; s. Gospodin P. and Mara A. (Karaivanova) T.; m. Finnie I. Kancheva, Feb. 10, 1927; 1 child, Deana. MD, Higher Med. Inst., Sofia, Bulgaria, 1952. Resident Higher Inst. Specialization of Physicians, Sofia, Bulgaria, 1953-56, 59-62, staff physician Bulgaria, 1957-59, staff psychiatrist clinic psychiatry Bulgaria, 1962-67; staff internist Gen. City Hosp., Tetovo, Yugoslavia, 1967; rsch. assoc. dept. psychiatry Johns Hopkins U. Sch. Medicine, Balt., 1968-69, instr. behavioral biology, dept. psychiatry, 1969-72; intern South Baltimore Gen. Hosp., 1972-73; resident L.I. Jewish Med. Ctr., Hillside Hosp., Glen Oaks, N.Y., 1973-76, staff psychiatrist, 1976—. Contbr. articles to profl. jours. Lt. Bulgarian Army. Mem. APA. Avocations: classical music, opera, reading. Office: 45 N Station Plz Great Neck NY 11021-5011

TOSI, LAURA LOWE, orthopaedic surgeon; b. N.Y.C., Mar. 25, 1949; d. Jerome Richard T. and Deborah Thornton (Prouty) Rogers; m. David S.C. Chu, Apr. 1, 1978. BA, Boston U., 1971; MD, Harvard U., 1977. Orthop. surgeon Children's Nat. Med. Ctr., Washington, 1984—, chief pediat. orthop. surgery, 2000—; assoc. prof. orthop. surgery George Washington U., 1984—. Bd. trustees Orthopaedic Rsch. and Edn. Found., 1995-2002, sec. bd. trustees, 2000-2002. Fellow: Am. Acad. Orthopedic Surgeons (bd. dirs. 1994—95), Am. Acad. Cerebral Palsy and Devel. Medicine; mem.: Ruth Jackson Orthopaedic Soc. (treas. 1987—90, v.p. 1990—91, pres. 1991—92), Pediat. Orthopedic Soc. N.Am. (bd. dirs. 1990—91, sec. 2001—, sec. elect 2000), Acad. Orthopaedic Surgeons (bd. dirs. 1998—), Am. Orthopaedic Assn. Office: Children's Nat Med Ctr 111 Michigan Ave NW Washington DC 20010-2916

TOSTE, ANTHONY PAIM, chemistry educator, researcher; b. Mountain View, Calif., June 26, 1948; BS in Chemistry with honors, Santa Clara (Calif.) U., 1970; PhD in Biochemistry and Chemistry, U. Calif., Berkeley, 1976. Rsch. fellow Cardiovascular Rsch. Inst., San Francisco, 1977-79; rsch. scientist Battelle Meml. Inst. Pacific N.W. Nat. Lab., Richland, Wash., 1980-88; asst. prof. S.W. Mo. State U., Springfield, 1988-94, assoc. prof., 1994-99, full prof., 1999—. Cons. Mitsubishi Metal Corp., Tokyo, 1984-87, Dow Chem., Tex., 1994-96; presenter in field. Contbr. articles to jours. in field, cmty. svc. presentations. Bd. dirs. Mid Columbia Arts Coun., Richland, 1987-88, Bot. Soc. S.W. Mo., Springfield, 1997—; pres. bd. dirs. Springfield Sister Cities Assn., 1993-96; co-founder, leader Internat. Friendship Delegations to Japan, 1996, 99, 2001. Rsch./equipment grantee NSF, 1990; recipient Diverse Cmty. award Sister Cities Internat., Boston, 1996. Mem. Am. Chem. Soc. (treas. Ozark sect. 1989-91, chmn.-elect 2000, chmn. 2000-01), Am. Nuc. Soc. (Best Poster award 1987), Assn. Ofcl. Analytical Chemists (program chair 1986, 90), Mo. Acad. Sci. (program chair 1997, 2002). Avocations: picture framing, collecting fine art, woodworking, reading, cinema. Home: 2113 E Woodhaven Pl Springfield MO 65804-6767 Office: SW Mo State U Dept Chemistry 901 S National Ave Springfield MO 65804-0088 E-mail: anthonytoste@smsu.edu.

TOSTENGARD, JILL ELLEN, artist; b. Milw., Aug. 20, 1971; d. Jon Edwin and Mary Ellen DeGlopper; m. Karl Nelson Tostengard; children: Troy. Exhibited in group shows at James Store Gallery, 2001. Home: 64 S Maple St Oconomowoc WI 53066 Personal E-mail: jillellenart@aol.com.

TOSTERUD, ROBERT JAMES, economist, educator; b. Chgo., July 21, 1946; s. Orval H. and Dorothy J. Tosterud; m. Karen Renee Lechner; children: Robert, Jr., Jonathan J. PhD, U. Man., Winnipeg, 1973. Staff dir. Joint Econ. Com. U.S. Congress, Washington, 1984—89; econs. program officer The Ford Found., N.Y.C., 1989—91; prof. and Freeman chmn. of entrepreneurship sch. Bus., U. S.D., Vermillion, 1991—. Founder Coun. of Entrepreneurship Chairs, Vermillion, 1995—98. Dir. Cmty. and Family Ent. (CAFE), Vermillion, 1992—. Named Tchr. of the Yr., Students of the U. S.D., 1992, 2000, Top-10 Nat.l Entrepreneurship Educator of the Yr., Kauffman Found. Inc. Mag., 1994; recipient Leavey award, for outstanding entrepreneurship educator, Freedom's Found. at Valley Forge, 1994; scholar vis. scholar in econ. growth and entrepreneurship, Libr. of Congress, Washington, 1998. Mem.: Acad. of Mgmt. (chmn. disting. chmns. com. 1997—99). Home: 25 S University Vermillion SD 57069 Office: University of South Dakota School of Business Vermillion SD Personal E-mail: Tosterud@dtgnet.com. Business E-Mail: btosteru@usd.edu.

TOSTESON, DANIEL CHARLES, physiologist, medical school dean emeritus; b. Milw., Feb. 5, 1925; s. Alexis H. and Dilys (Bodycombe) T.; m. Penelope Kinsley, Dec. 17, 1949 (div. 1969); children: Carrie Marias, Heather Tosteson, Tor, Zoe Losada; m. Magdalena Tieffenberg, July 8, 1969; children: Joshua, Ingrid. Student, Harvard U., 1942-44, MD, 1949; DSc (hon.), U. Copenhagen, 1979; Dr. hon. causa, U. Liege, 1983; DSc (hon.), Med. Coll. Wis., 1984, NYU, 1992; DHL (hon.), Johns Hopkins U., 1993; Dr. honoris causa, Cath. U. Louvain, 1996, Duke U., 1996, Emory U., 1996. Fellow physiology Harvard Med. Sch., 1947-48; intern, then asst. resident medicine Presbyn. Hosp., N.Y.C., 1949-51; research fellow medicine Brookhaven Nat. Lab., 1951-53; lab. kidney and electrolyte metabolism Nat. Heart Inst., 1953-55, 57, research fellow biol. isotope research lab., 1955-56; research fellow Physiol. Lab., Cambridge, Eng., 1956-57; assoc. prof. physiology Washington U. Sch. Medicine, St. Louis, 1958-61; prof., chmn. dept. physiology and pharmacology Duke U. Sch. Medicine, 1961-75, James B. Duke Distinguished prof., 1971-75; dean div. biol. scis., dean Pritzker Sch. Medicine U. Chgo., Lowell T. Coggleshall prof. med. scis., v.p. for Med. Center, 1975-77; dean, Caroline Shields Walker prof. cell biology Harvard Med. Sch., Boston, 1977-97, dean emeritus, Caroline Shields Walker prof., 1997—, pres. Med. Ctr., 1977-97. Mem. molecular biology panel NSF, 1959-62; cons. sci. rev. com. NIH, 1964-67, nat. adv. gen. med. scis. coun., 1982-86; mem. U.S. Office Tech. Assessment, 1976; ethics adv. bd. HEW, 1977-80; nat. adv. gen. med. scis. coun. NIH, 1982—; mem. governing bd. NRC, 1977; mem. sci. com. Found. pour l'Etude du Systeme Nerveux Central et Peripherique, 1982—; nat. adv. com. biomed. scis. PEW Scholars Program, 1984-87. Mem. Inst. Medicine NAS (coun. 1975-78, adv. bd. PEW scholars program 1984-85), AAAS, Acad. Arts and Scis. (pres. 1997-00), Am. Physiol. Soc. (council 1967-75, pres. 1973-74), Soc. Gen. Physiologists (pres. 1968-69), Biophys. Soc. (council 1970-73), Assn. Am. Med. Colls. (chmn. coun. acad. socs. 1969-70, chmn. assembly 1973-74, chmn. physician supply task force 1988-90, Abraham Flexner award 1991), Assn. Am. Physicians, Am. Acad. Arts and Scis. (pres. 1997-2000), Red Cell Club, Soc. Health and Human Values, Danish Royal Soc. (fellow), Alpha Omega Alpha. Achievements include spl. research cellular transport processes, red cell membranes. Office: Harvard Med Sch Goldenson Bldg B-243 220 Longwood Ave Boston MA 02115-5701

TOSTI, DONALD THOMAS, psychologist, consultant; b. Kansas City, Mo., Dec. 6, 1935; s. Joseph T. Tosti and Elizabeth M. (Parsons) Tosti Addison; m. Carol J. Curless, Jan. 31, 1957 (dec. 1980); children: Rene, Alicia, Roxanna, Brett, Tabitha, Todd Marcus; m. Annette Brewer, Dec. 29, 1989. BSEE, U. N.Mex., 1957, MS in Psychology, 1962, PhD in Psychology, 1967. Chief editor Tchg. Machines, Inc., Albuquerque, 1960-64; divsn. mgr. Westinghouse Learning Corp., 1964-70; founder, sr. v.p. Ind. Learning Sys., San Raphael, Calif., 1970-74, pres., 1974-76; chmn. bd. Omega Performance, San Francisco, 1976-77; pres. Operants, Inc., San Rafael, 1978-81; v.p. Forum Corp., 1981-83; mng. ptnr. Vanguard Cons. Group, San Francisco, 1983—. Author: Basic Electricity, Advanced Algebra, Fundamentals of Calculus, TMI Programmed Mathematics Series, 1960-63, Behavior Technology, 1970, A Guide to Child Development, Tactics of Communication, 1973; co-author: Learning Is Getting Easier, 1973, Indtroductory Psychology, 1981, Usibility Factors in Hardware and Software Design, 1982, Comparative Usibility, 1983, Performance Based Management, Positive Leadership, 1986, Strategic Alliances, 1990, The Professional Manager, 1995, Power and Governance, 1996, Global Fluency, 1999, Organizational Alignment, 2000, Internal Branding, 2000, Principles of Performance Consulting, 2001. Mem. APA, Internat. Soc. for Performance Improvement (v.p. rsch. 1983-85, treas. 1997-99, Outstanding Mem. award 1984, Life Membership award 1984, Outstanding product award 1974). Home: 41 Marinita Ave San Rafael CA 94901-3443

TOSTI, JEANNE MARIE, lawyer; b. Chgo., Sept. 6, 1948; BSN cum laude, St. John Coll. Cleve., 1970; MSN, Kent State U., 1985; JD, Cleve. Marshall Coll. Law, 1992. Bar: Ohio 1992, U.S. Dist. Ct. (no. dist.) Ohio 1998. Assoc. atty. Becker & Mishkind L.P.A., Cleve., 1992—. Mem. Assn. Trial Lawyers Am., Ohio Assn. Trial Lawyers, Ohio State Bar Assn., Cleve. Bar Assn. Office: Becker & Mishkind Co LPA 1660 W 2d St Ste 660 Cleveland OH 44113

TOSTI, SALLY T. artist, educator; b. Scranton, Pa., Jan. 21, 1946; d. Ivan and Helen (Odell) Thompson; m. Robert Matthew Tosti, May 3, 1974; 1 child, Jennifer Marie. BS in Art Edn., Ind. (Pa.) U., 1967; postgrad., Tyler Sch. Art, 1969-70; MFA in Drawing and Painting, Marywood Coll., 1985. Art tchr. Bristol Twp. Schs., Levittown, Pa., 1967-69, Ctrl. Bucks Schs., Doylestown, 1971. Adj. faculty Marywood Coll., Scranton, Pa., 1986-87; art coord. Keystone Coll., LaPlume, Pa., 1991-96, adj. faculty, 1995—. Exhbns. include San Diego Art Inst., 1993-94, Allentown (Pa.) Art Mus., Abercombie Gallerie, 1994, Lakeview Mus., 1995, U. Tex., Tyler, 1995-96, Linder Art Gallery, 1994—, Haggin Mus., Stockton, Calif., 1996, Fla. Printmakers Soc. Traveling Exhbn., 1995-97, So. Graphics Traveling Exbhn., 1996—, Elon Coll., N.C., 1997, Moss-Thorns Gallery Art, 1997, others. Active Countryside Conservancy, Waverly, Pa. Grantee Pa. Coun. Arts, 1995; F. Lammot Belin Arts scholar, 1996. Mem. Waverly Womans Club, Print Ctr. Phila., So. Graphics Coun., Am. Print Alliance, Womens Studio Workshop, Everhart Mus. Democrat. Home: PO Box 776 Waverly PA 18471-0776

TOTENBERG, NINA, journalist; b. N.Y.C., Jan. 14, 1944; d. Roman and Melanie (Shroder) T.; m. Floyd Haskell, Feb. 3, 1979 (dec.); m. H. David Reines, 2000. Student, Boston U.; LLD (hon.), Haverford Coll., Chatham Coll., Gonzaga U., Northeastern U., St. Mary's, SUNY; LHD, Lebanon Valley Coll., Westfield State Coll., Pa. State U., Pine Manor Coll., De Paul U., Simmons Coll. Reporter Boston Record Am., 1965, Peabody Times, 1967, Nat. Observer, 1968-71, Newtimes, 1973, Nat. Pub. Radio, Washington, 1974—, Inside Washington, 1992—; reporter Nightline ABC, 1993-98. Contbr. articles to N.Y. Times Mag., Harvard Law Rev., Christian Sci. Monitor, N.Y. Mag., Parade. Recipient Sidney Hillman award, 1983, Alfred I. Dupont award Columbia U., 1988, 91, George Foster Peabody award, 1991, George Polk award, 1991, Joan Barone award, 1991, Silver Gavel award ABA, 1968-98, Woman of Courage award Women in Film, 1991, Athena award, 1994, Presdl. Commendation, Radcliffe Coll., 1998; named outstanding broadcast journalist of yr. Nat. Press Found., 1999. Mem. Sigma Delta Chi (award 1991). Office: NPR 635 Massachusetts Ave NW Washington DC 20001-3740

TOTER, KIMBERLY MROWIEC, nurse; b. Chgo., Apr. 22, 1956; d. A. Kenneth and Megan Dawson (Schiefer) Mrowiec; m. William Frank Toter, Dec. 16, 1978; children: William Kenneth, Kimberly Helen, Tod Frank, Matthew Jonathan, Haley Victoria, Toria Megan. BS in Biology, Millikin U., 1978; cert. sch. nursing, Decatur (Ill.) Meml. Hosp., 1978. RN, Ill.; cert. operating room nurse. Oper. room nurse Riddle Meml. Hosp., Media, Pa., 1979-89; pres., chief exec. officer Towic Med., Inc., Park Ridge, Ill., 1986—; staff nurse oper. room Luth. Gen. Hosp., 1991; perioperative nurse, 1991—. Instr. Delaware Community Coll., Media, 1986; reviewer, cons. Perioperative Nursing Care Planning; speaker laparoscopy seminar Luth. Gen. Hosp., 1992, 93; cheerleading coach St. Paul of the Cross, 1993-96, volleyball coach, 1997—. Contbg. author: Decision Making in Perioperative Nursing, 1987; also articles; patentee gastric drainage system. Cheerleading coach St. Paul of the Cross, 1993-96, volleyball coach, 2000—. Recipient Young Alumnus of Yr. award Millikin U., 1991. Mem. Assn. Operat. Rm. Nurses (v.p. Southeast Pa. chpt. 1983-85, pres.-elect 1985-86, pres. 1986-87, ednl. chmn. 1983-85, chmn. bylaw and policy com. 1987—, bd. dirs. 1983-89, chmn. 1987-88, bd. dirs. NW suburban chpt. 1995—), Pa. Coun. Oper. Rm. Nurses, Am. Tech Mgmt. (bd. dirs. 1989), Pi Beta Phi. Roman Catholic. Avocations: jogging, swimming, aerobic dance, photography, volleyball.

TOTH, GEZA, mathematician; b. Budapest, Hungary, Aug. 12, 1968; s. Laszlo Toth and Erika Lakatos; m. Natalia Zagyva; children: Lilla, Sara. PhD, NYU, 1997. Postdoctoral rsch. fellow DIMACS Ctr., Rutgers U., Piscataway, NJ, 1997—98; math. instr. MIT, Cambridge, Mass., 1998—2001; assoc. prof. Alfred Renyi Inst. Math., Budapest, 2001—. Mem.: Janos Bolyai Math. Soc. (Grunwald prize 1998). Office: Alfred Renyi Inst Math Realtanoda u 13-15 Budapest 1053 Hungary Home Fax: 36 1 4838333; Office Fax: 36 1 4838333. Personal E-mail: geza@renyi.hu. Business E-mail: geza@renyi.hu.

TOTH, JÓZSEF, diplomat; b. Budapest, Hungary, Apr. 10, 1961; s. József and Józsefné Toth; m. Mária Urbánszki, July 20, 1985; children: Anita, Agnes. MBA, U. Econs., Budapest, 1985. Desk officer Germany Ministry Fgn. Affairs, Budapest, 1985-89; diplomat Embassy of Hungary, London, 1989-94; head office of polit. state sec. Ministry Fgn. Affairs, Budapest, 1994-97; min., DCM Embassy of Hungary, Washington, 1997—. Office: Embassy of Hungary 3910 Shoemaker St NW Washington DC 20008 E-mail: hembwegy@aol.com.

TOTH, ROBERT ALLEN, research scientist; b. Richmond, Ind., Aug. 10, 1939; AB, Earlham U., 1962; PhD, Fla. State U., 1969. Physicist Nat. Bur. Stds., Washington, 1962—64; instr. physics Earlham Coll., Richmond, 1966—67; rsch. scientist Jet Propulsion Lab., Pasadena, Calif., 1967—. Postdoctoral rsch. assoc. Fla. state U., Tallahassee, 1969—70; staff NASA Hdqs., Washington, 1979—80. Author: (scientific publications) spectroscopy, 65-. Recipient Am. Men Sci. award, 1975; fellow Oak Ridge fellow, 1964-1966, Epply Found. fellow, 1966-1969. Avocations: golf, piano. Home: 3075 Foothill Blvd #117 La Crescenta CA 91214 Personal E-mail: toth@dracula.jpl.nasa.gov.

TOTH, ROBERT CHARLES, retired polling consultant, journalist, writer; b. Blakely, Pa., Dec. 24, 1928; s. John and Tillie (Szuch) T.; m. Paula Goldberg, Apr. 12, 1954; children: Jessica, Jennifer, John. BS in Chem. Engring., Washington U., St. Louis, 1952; MS in Journalism, Columbia U., 1955; postgrad., Harvard U., 1960-61. Started as engr. in Army Ordnance Dept., 1952—54; reporter Providence Jour., 1955—57; sci. reporter N.Y. Herald Tribune, 1957—62, N.Y. Times, 1962—63; mem. staff Los Angeles Times, 1963—93, bur. chief, 1965—70, diplomatic corr. Moscow, 1970—71, White House corr. Washington, 1972—74, bur. chief Moscow, 1974—77, nat. security corr. Washington bur., 1977—93; ret. Cons. opinion poll in U.S. and abroad by Times Mirror Ctr. (now Pew Rsch. Ctr.) for People and Press, 1990, sr. assoc., 1993-98. Co-author: The Dimishing Divide, Religion's Changing Role in American Politics, 2000. Served with USMC, 1946-48. Recipient Overseas Press Club award, 1977, Sigma Delta Chi award, 1977, George Polk award in Journalism for fgn. reporting L.I. U., 1978, Columbia U. Alumni award, 1978, Wienthal award Fgn. Service Inst., Georgetown U., 1986, Edwin N. Hood award Nat. Press Club, 1986; Pulitzer Travelling scholar, 1955; Nieman fellow Harvard U., 1960-61 Mem. Coun. on Fgn. Rels. Home: 21 Primrose St Chevy Chase MD 20815-4228 E-mail: tothrc@aol.com.

TOTH, SUSAN SMITH, investment executive; b. N.Y.C., Dec. 30, 1964; d. John Brewster and Ida (Hawa) Smith. BA in English, Tex. A&M U., 1986; MA in Journalism, Ind. U., 1988; MBA, U. N.C., Wilmington, 1997. Parachutist and broadcast journalist 1st Special Ops. Command, Ft. Bragg, N.C., 1989-91; media rels. journalist U.S. Army Parachute Team - Golden Knights, 1991-92; TV reporter Sta. WLTX-TV, Columbia, S.C., 1992; bus. writer The Herald, Rock Hill, 1992-94; plant comms. specialist Brunswick Nuclear Plant Carolina Power & Light, Southport, 1994-97; fin. advisor Morgan Stanley Dean Witter, Wilmington, NC, 1997—2001; investment exec. Ferris, Baker, Watts, Inc., 2001—. With U.S. Army, 1988-92, Panama, Persian Gulf. Recipient South Korean Jump Wings Republic of Korea Spl. Warfare Ctr., 1989. Mem. VFW, Wilmington E. Rotary, Wilmington Jaycees (treas. 2000). Presbyterian. Avocations: running, the outdoors. Home: 3917 Mayfield Ct Wilmington NC 28412-0965 Office: Ferris Baker Watts Inc 1410 Commonwealth Dr Ste 201 Wilmington NC 28403-1623 E-mail: sbtoth@msn.com.

TÓTH-OROWAN, LÓRÁNT MIKLÓS, civil engineer; b. Geneva, Switzerland, Apr. 14, 1932; s. Béla (Vojtech) and Kornélia (Orowan) T. Degree, U. for Bldg. and Transp., Budapest, Hungary, 1956; postgrad., Tech. U. Budapest, 1968-70, PhD, 1973. Asst. engr. steel structures dept. Enterprise for Bridge

Bdlg., Budapest, 1954-56; design engr. Mcpl. Planning Enterprise, 1956-80; sr. design engr. Mcpl. Planning Office, 1980-92; cons. engr. Mcpl. Civil Engring. Consultancy, 1992-99. Contbr. papers to profl. jours. Mem. N.Y. Acad. Scis., Hungarian Chamber of Engrs. Avocations: etymology, Latin and ancient Greek languages, mythology, amateur radio, cats. Home: Kosztolányi Dezso tér 5 II 24 H-1113 Budapest Hungary Office: Felsozöldmáli út 1/A H-1025 Budapest Hungary Fax: 36-1-325-9114. E-mail: dr.toth.lorant@axelero.hu.

TOTMAN, CONRAD DAVIS, history educator; b. Conway, Mass., Jan. 5, 1934; s. Raymond Smith and Mildred Edna (Kingsbury) T.; m. Michiko Ikegami, Jan. 21, 1958; children: Kathleen Junko, Christopher Ken. BA, U. Mass., 1958; MA, Harvard U., 1960, PhD, 1964. Asst. prof. U. Calif., Santa Barbara, 1964-66; asst. prof. Northwestern U., Evanston, Ill., 1966-68, assoc. prof., 1968-72, prof. Japanese history, 1972-84, chmn. dept. history, 1977-80; prof. Japanese history Yale U., New Haven, 1984-97, prof. emeritus, 1997—, acting chmn. Dept. History, 1989-90; prof. Kyoto Ctr. for Japanese Studies, 1992-93. Vis. prof. Stanford U., 1997, Yale U., 1999. Author: Politics in the Tokugawa Bakufu 1600-1843, 1967, paperback edit., 1988, The Collapse of the Tokugawa Bakufu 1862-1868, 1979 (John K. Fairbank prize Am. Hist. Assn. 1981), Japan Before Perry: A Short History, 1981, Tokugawa Ieyasu: Shogun, 1983, The Origins of Japan's Modern Forests, 1985, The Green Archipelago: Forestry in Preindustrial Japan, 1989, paperback edit., 1998 (Japanese translation 1998), Early Modern Japan, 1993, paperback edit., 1995, The Lumber Industry in Early Modern Japan, 1995, A History of Japan, 2000. Served with U.S. Army, 1953-56. Recipient Carstensen prize for essay Agrl. History Soc., 1982; Woodrow Wilson nat. fellow, 1958-59; Social Sci. Research Council-Am. Council Learned Socs. fellow, 1968-69; NEH sr. fellow, 1972-73; Fulbright-Hays research grantee, 1968-69; Japan Found. grantee, 1981-82 Mem. Assn. Asian Studies (N.E. Asia coun. 1977-80, chmn. 1978-80, exec. com. 1978-80, pres. New Eng. Conf. 1985-86, coun. of confs. 1992-95), Forest History Soc. Office: Yale U Dept History New Haven CT 06520

TOTO, MARY, elementary and secondary education educator; b. Phila., Mar. 12, 1922; d. John and Piacentina (Rossi) T. BS in Edn., Temple U., 1943; MS in Edn., U. Pa., 1951; MS in LS, Villanova U., 1963. Cert. elem. and secondary tchr., Pa. Tchr. Phila. Sch. Dist., 1943-81. Mem. Dem. Nat. Com., 1995-98. Mem. NEA, AAUW, LWV, Phila. Fedn. Tchrs., Columbus Forum Lodge, Nationalities Svc. Ctr. of Phila., Italian Folk Art Fedn. of Am., Nat. Assn. Retired Tchrs., Pa. Assn. Sch. Retirees, Pa. Edn. Assn., Womens Internat. League Peace and Freedom, United We Stand Am. Roman Catholic. Avocations: needlework, interior decorating, folk dancing, travel. Home: 1210 W Ritner St Philadelphia PA 19148-3524

TOTOSY DE ZEPETNEK, STEVEN, editor, educator; b. Budapest, Nov. 22, 1950; s. Istvan Töttössy, Magdolna Maria Haidekker; m. Joanne E. Totosy de Zepetnek, Dec. 11, 1976; children: Chantal, Julia. BA, U. Western Ont., London, Ont., Can., 1980; MA, Carleton U., Ottawa, Ont., 1983; BEd, U. Ottawa, 1984; PhD, U. Alta., Edmonton, 1989. Adj. prof., dir., editor U. Alta., Edmonton, Canada, 1989—2000; editor Purdue Univ. Press, West Lafayette, Ind., 2000—. Prof. comparative media studies U. Halle-Wittenberg, 2002; assoc. dir. Rsch. Inst. for Comparative Lit. U. Alta., 1995—99; vis. prof. Peking U., China, 1996, Jozsef Attila U., Szeged, Hungary, 1995. Contbr. over 100 articles, book chpts., bibliographies and ency. entries to profl. jours.; author: Comparative Literature: Theory, Method, Application, 1998, Legitimizing the Study of Literature. A New Pragmatism: The Systemic Approach to Literature and Culture, 1997, The Social Dimensions of Fiction: On the Rhetoric and Function of Prefacing Novels in the Nineteenth-Century Canadas, 1993; editor: Comparative Literature and Comparative Cultural Studies, 2002, Comparative Central European Culture, 2002; co-editor: Comparative Literature Now: Theories and Practice, 1999, Canadian Culture and Literatures: And a Taiwan Perspective, 1998, The Systemic and Empirical Approach to Literature and Culture as Theory and Application, 1997, East Asian Cultural and Historical Perspectives: Histories and Society/Culture and Literatures, 1997; editor: International Perspectives on Reading, 1996, various articles in profl. jours.; series editor Books in Comparative Cultural udies, 2001—; editor: CLCWeb: Comparative Literature and Culture: A WWWeb Jour., 1999; assoc. editor CRCL/RCLC: Canadian Rev. of Comparative Lit., 1989—97. Mem.: MLA, Internat. Assn. Empirical Aesthetics, Am. Comparative Lit. Assn., Internat. Comparative Lit. Assn. (life), Can. Comparative Lit. Assn. (life). Home: 8 Sunset Rd Winchester MA 01890

TOTTEN, ARTHUR IRVING, JR. retired metals company executive, consultant; b. Laurel, Del., Mar. 15, 1906; s. Arthur Irving and Lena Meade (Fowler) T.; m. Margaret Ross, Nov. 10, 1934 (dec. Mar. 1988); children: Margaret Totten Peters, Fitz-Randolph Fowler, Eleanor Totten Shumaker. BS in Chemistry, Union Coll., Schenectady, 1928. Rsch. chemist E.I. du Pont de Nemours & Co., Inc., Parlin, N.J., 1928-32, prodn. supt., 1932-37, rsch. chemist Phila., 1937-42; dir. packaging rsch. Reynolds Metals Co., Richmond, Va., 1946-71; exec. v.p. rsch. Reynolds Rsch. Corp., 1966-71; ret., 1971. Cons. Nat. Inventors Coun., Washington, 1940-46; presenter in field, U.S., Can., Eng., France; pres. Rsch. & Devel. Assocs., N.Y.C., 1965-67, chmn. bd., 1967—. Contbr. articles to profl. jours. Pres. River Rd. Citizens Assn., 1949; head comml. divsn. Richmond chpt. ARC, 1954, bd. dirs., 1955-58; trustee Va. Inst. Sci. Rsch., 1970—; emeritus dir. Adult Care Svcs., Richmond, 1995—; pres. Westham Green Citizens Assn., 1982; sr. warden Episc. Ch., 1952, 60, 66. Lt. col. Chem. Warfare Svc., U.S. Army, 1942-46. Recipient Cert. of Appreciation U.S. Army Natick Lab., 1971, Humanitarian award Adult Devel. Ctr., 1992. Mem. Am. Inst. Chemists (life, past chpt. pres.), Rsch. and Devel. Assn. (life, past pres., cert. of appreciation, 1971), Packaging Inst. (pres. 1971, Profl. award 1968), N.Am. Packaging Inst. (pres. 1971), World Packaging Inst. (v.p. 1971), Inst. Food Tech. (Indsl. Achievement award 1978), Packaging Edn. Found. (Hall of Fame 1973), Country Club Va., Richmond Engrs. Club (past bd. dirs.), Soixante Plus, Masons, Sigma Phi. Achievements include patents for camouflage coatings for aircraft and other military equipment in World War II; for caustic soluble inks for beer labels. Home: 1600 Westbrook Ave Apt 729 Richmond VA 23227-3398

TOTTEN, GEORGE EDWARD, materials science engineer, researcher; b. Toledo, June 26, 1945; s. George William and Alva May Alta (Creller) T.; m. Alice Joan Totten, Apr., 1967 (dec. Mar. 1993); m. Alice Wong, Apr. 1994. AAS, Broome Tech. C.C., Binghamton, N.Y., 1970; BS, Farleigh Dickinson U., 1974, MS, 1978; PhD, NYU, 1989. Sr. rsch. scientist Union Carbide Corp., Tarrytown, N.Y., 1970—. With U.S. Army, 1963-66, Vietnam. Fellow ASM Internat. (trustee 1994-97); mem. ASTM (mem. com. publs., 1986—), SAE (mem. fluid power com. 1986—), ASME, Soc. Tribologists and Librication Engrs. (hydraulics tools sect.), Am. Chem. Soc. Home: 9 Gilmore Dr Stony Point NY 10980-1005 Office: Union Carbide Corp Ste 205 771 Old Saw Mill River Rd Tarrytown NY 10591-6799 Fax: 914-345-5314. E-mail: GETotten@aol.com.

TOTTEN, GEORGE OAKLEY, III, political science educator; b. Washington, July 21, 1922; s. George Oakley Totten Jr. and Vicken (von Post) Börjesson Totten Barrois; m. Astrid Maria Anderson, June 26, 1948 (dec. Apr. 26, 1975); children: Vicken Yuriko, Linnea Catherine; m. Lilia Huiying Li, July 1, 1976; 1 child, Blanche Maluk Lemes. *Wife, Lilia Huiying Li, BA Yenching, MA equivalent University of Hong Kong, journalist and writer in Chinese, publsihed in Hong Kong, Mainland China, Taiwan, Europe, and America. Her career started with her leading Hong Kong businesswomen to Beijing in 1956 where she publicly met Chairman Mao Zedong. She had married a prominent Hong Kong doctor who died in 1963. After marrying Dr. Totten, she retained her maiden name, became an East Asian Studies Center Fellow at the University of Southern California in 1976 and founded the China Seminar in 1985 to promote peaceful relations between Taiwan and Mainland China.* Cert., U. Mich., 1943; AB, Columbia U., 1946, AM, 1949; MA, Yale U., 1950, PhD, 1954; docentur i japanologi, U. Stockholm, 1977. Lectr. Columbia U., N.Y.C., 1954-55; asst. prof. MIT, Cambridge, 1958-59, Boston U., 1959-61; assoc. prof. U. R.I., Kingston, 1961-64, Mich. State U., 1964—65; assoc. prof. polit. sci. U. So. Calif., L.A., 1965-68, prof., 1968-92, chmn. dept., 1980-86, prof. emeritus, 1992—96, disting. prof. emeritus, 1996—. Dir., founder Calif. Pvt. Univs. and Colls. Yr.-in-Japan program Weseda U., 1967-73; 1st dir. East Asian Studies Ctr., 1974-77; 1st dir. USC-UCLA Joint East Asian Studies Ctr., 1976-77; sr. affiliated scholar Ctr. for Multiethnic and Transnat. Studies, 1993-98; chair USC Korea Project, 1998—; vis. prof. U. Stockholm, 1977-79, 1st dir. Ctr. Pacific Asia Studies, 1986-89, sr. counselor bd. dirs., 1989—; hon. pres. Huaxiu Pvt. Sch., Anyang City, Henan Province, China, 1999—; vis. prof. Ctr. for Japanese Studies, U. Hawaii, Manoa, 1992-93. *In his career, he came to know personally numerous statesmen through conversations, interviews, or socially: (1) Four presidents of South Korea (Chun, Roh, Kim, and Kim Dae-Jung-the latter a long-time friend), two prime ministers (Chung Il-Kwan and Dr. Kang Young-Hoon-his student and friend), four mayors of Seoul and a National Assembly Speaker, (2) North Korean Party Secretary Hwang Jang-Yop, (3) Five premiers of Japan (Katayama, Yoshida, Tanaka, Miki, Nakasone), (4) Two premiers of China (Zhao Ziyang, Li Peng) and Madame Zhou Enlai, (5) High Taiwan officials, and (6) three premiers of Sweden (Palme, Carlsson, Bildt), and King Carl XVI Gustaf.* Author: Social Democratic Movement in Prewar Japan, 1966, Chinese edit., 1987, Korean edit., 1997; co-author: Socialist Parties in Postwar Japan, 1966, Japan and the New Ocean Regime, 1984, Japan in the World, the World in Japan, Fifty Years of Japanese Studies at Michigan, 2001; editor: Helen Snow's Song of Ariran, 1973, Korean edit., 1991, Chinese edit., 1993, Kim Dae-jung's A New Beginning, 1996, Lee Hee-ho's (Mrs. Kim Dae-jung's) Praying for Tomorrow: Letters to My Husband in Prison, 1999; author, co-editor: Developing Nations: Quest for a Model, 1970, Japanese edit., 1975, China's Economic Reform: Administering the Introduction of the Market Mechanism, 1992, Community in Crisis: The Korean American Community After the Los Angeles Civil Unrest of April 1992, 1994; co-translator: Ch'ien Mu's Traditional Government in Imperial China, 1982, 1st paperback edit., 2000; contbr. The Politics of Divided Nations, 1991, Chinese edit., 1995, Japanese edit., 1997; editl. bd. Acta Koreana, 1997—. Mem. U.S.-China People's Friendship Assn., Washington, 1974—, World Feds., 1962—; mem. Com. on U.S.-China Relations, N.Y.C., 1975—; chmn. L.A.-Pusan Sister City Assn., L.A., 1976-77; bd. dirs. L.A.-Guangzhou Sister City Assn., 1990—; mem. nat. adv. com. Japan Am. Student Conf., 1984—, Assn. Korean Polit. Studies in N.Am., 1992—, v.p. 1996-98; bd. dirs. Assn. for the Study of Korean Culture and Identity, Korea, 1999-2000; mem. coun. China Soc. for People's Friendship Studies, Beijing, 1991—. 1st lt. AUS, 1942-46, PTO. Recipient Plaque for program on Korean studies Consulate Gen. of Republic of Korea, 1975, Disting. Emeritus award U. So. Calif., 1996; Social Sci. Rsch. Coun. fellow, 1952-53; Ford Found. grantee, 1955-58, NSF grantee, 1979-81, Korea Found. grantee, 1993, Rebuild L.A. grantee, 1993, Philippine Liberation medal, 1994. Mem.: U. So. Calif. Faculty Ctr., European Assn. Japanese Studies, Japan-Am. Soc. Calif. (bd. dirs. 1990—94), Japanese Polit. Sci. Assn., Internat. Studies Assn., Internat. Polit. Sci. Assn., Asia Soc., Am. Polit. Sci. Assn., Assn. Asian Studies, Swedish Club of L.A., Phi Beta Delta (founding mem. Beta Kappa chpt. 1993—). Episcopalian. Home: 5129 Village Green Los Angeles CA 90016-5205 Office: USC Korea Project Dept Polit Sci VKC 327 Los Angeles CA 90089-0044 E-mail: totten@usc.edu.

TOTTEN, GLORIA JEAN (DOLLY TOTTEN), real estate executive, financial consultant; b. Port Huron, Mich., Sept. 23, 1943; d. Lewis Elmer and Inez Eugenia (Houston) King; m. Donald Ray Totten, Feb. 5, 1961 (div. Apr. 1981); children: D. Erik, Angela J. Totten Sales, Kymberly D. Totten DiVita. Student, instr., Patricia Stevens Modeling Sch., Detroit, 1976-79; student, Gold Coast Sch., West Palm Beach, Fla., 1988; degree in mktg., St. Clair County Coll., Port Huron, Mich., 1979. Lic. real estate saleswoman, Fla., Mich.; registered real estate appraiser, Fla. Demonstrator, saleswoman Hoover Co., 1969-75; instr., promoter Port Huron Sch. Bus., 1973-75; real estate broker Select Realty, Port Huron, 1979-81, Earn Keim Realty, Port Huron, 1981-83, Schweitzer's Better Homes and Gardens, Marysville, Mich., 1983-86, Coldwell Banker Property Concepts Corp., North Palm Beach, Fla., 1986-94; pres., broker, owner Dolly Totten Real Estate Inc., West Palm Beach, 1994—; travel agt. Global Access, Lake Park, 1997—; registered real estate appraiser State of Fla. Model, instr. Patricia Stevens Modeling Sch., Troy, Mich., 1972-75; beauty cons. Mary Kay Cosmetics, 1982—; ind. travel agt. Global Access Internat., 1997. Grantee Mich. State U., 1972. Mem. Nat. Assn. Realtors, North Palm Beach Bd. Realtors, Million Dollar Club, Women's Coun. Realtors (co-founder Port Huron chpt.). Avocations: singing, acting, dancing, horticulture, crafts. Home and Office: 118 E 24th St Riviera Beach FL 33404-4555

TOTTEN, MARY ANNE, internist; b. Topeka, May 22, 1946; d. Frederick Eugene Totten and Mildred Roberta (Johnson) Black. BA in Microbiology, U. Kans., 1968, MD, 1972; MPH, Boston U., 1984. Diplomate Am. Bd. Internal Medicine with added qualifications in geriatrics, Nat. Bd. Med. Examiners, cert. med. dir. in long term care. Intern in internal medicine Hosp. of St. Raphael, New Haven, 1972-73; resident New Eng. Deaconess Hosp., Boston, 1973-75; fellow in endocrinology and metabolism Lahey Clinic Found., Burlington, 1975-76; fellow in diabetes Joslin Clinic, Boston, 1976-77; instr. medicine Boston U. Med. Ctr., 1977-83, asst. clin. prof., 1983-84; staff physician in gen. internal medicine Boston City Hosp., 1977-80; staff physician endocrinology Boston Hosp., 1977-84; dir. diabetes treatment and rehab. unit Mattapan (Mass.) Hosp., 1982-84; staff physician St. Joseph's Hosp., Parkersburg, W.Va., 1984—2002, chmn. dept. internal medicine, 1989-91, med. dir. skilled nursing unit, 1992—97, 2000—02, advisor to diabetes care task force, 1994-97, pres. med. staff, 1995-97; fellow in geriatrics UMPC Shadyside Hosp., Pitts., 1998-2000; specialist in geriatrics rehabilitation Health South Rehab Hosp., Parkersburg, W.Va., 2000—02. Attending physician Health South, Parkersburg, 2000-2002; med. dir., Elliot Hosp. Sr. Health Ctr, Manchester, NH, 2002-; mem. del. diabetes educators People to People Tour, USSR and China, 1987, med. dir. Sr. Health Primary Care, Manchester, 2002—. Author, editor: Case Studies for Nurses and Nurse Practitioners, 1990; contbr. articles to med. jours. Bd. dirs., mem. YWCA, Parkersburg, 1986-87. Recipient Physician Recognition award, AMA, 1987, 1990, 1997, 2001, Trailblazing Women of the Yr. award, YWCA and Altrusa, 1988, Leadership Devel. award, Parkersburg C. of C., 1990. Fellow ACP (mem. Gov.'s Coun. W.Va. 1990-91); mem. Am. Med. Dirs. Assn., Am. Diabetes Assn. (bd. dirs. W.Va. 1987-89), Am. Geriatrics Soc., W.Va. Med. Assn., Parkersburg Area Diabetes Assn. (pres. 1988-90, bd. dirs. 1991-92), Parkersburg Acad. Medicine. Methodist. Avocations: swimming, bicycling, photography, music. Office: Senior Health Primary Care 138 Webster St Manchester NH 03104-4027 E-mail: mtotten@elliot-hs.org.

TOTTIE, THOMAS J.H. librarian; b. Waxholm, Sweden, July 3, 1930; s. John and Gerda (Willers) T.; m. Marianne Sandels, 1972; children: John, Henry; children from previous marriage: Louise, Sophie. Lic. in Philosophy, Stockholm U., 1961; PhD (hon.), Uppsala (Sweden) U., 1994. Asst. libr. Royal Libr., Stockholm, 1961; sec. Swedish Coun. Rsch. Librs., 1966-73; dep. dir. Stockholm U. Libr., 1975-76; dir., chief libr. Libr. of Royal Caroline Med. Surg. Inst., Stockholm, 1976-78; chief libr. Uppsala U., 1978-96. Author 2 books; contbr. articles to profl. jours. Capt. Swedish Artillery, 1955-85. Home: Kyrkogårdsg 5A Se-75310 Uppsala Sweden Office: Uppsala Univ Libr Uppsala Univ Libr Box 510 SE-75120 Uppsala Sweden E-mail: thomas.tottie@ub.uu.se.

TOUBA, NUR ALI, electrical engineer; b. Edina, Minn., July 8, 1968; s. Ali R. and Ase Touba; m. Martha Jean Barone; 1 child Amanda. BSEE, U. Minn., 1990; MS, Stanford U., 1991, PhD, 1996. Assoc. prof. U. Tex., Austin, 1996—. Recipient Early Faculty CAREER award, NSF, 1997. Mem.: IEEE. Achievements include patents for altering bit sequences to contain predetermined patterns. Office: U Tex Engring Sci Bldg Austin TX 78712-1084 Office Fax: 512-471-5532. Personal E-mail: touba@ece.utexas.edu. Business E-Mail: touba@ece.utexas.edu.

TOUBORG, MARGARET EARLEY BOWERS, museum executive; b. Rome, Aug. 12, 1941; d. George Thomas and Margaret Earley (Brown) Bowers; m. Jens Touborg, Sept. 9, 1961 (div. 1985); children: Margaret Earley Touborg-Jebsen, Anne Touborg Zimmer, Sarah, Peter Nicolai. AB magna cum laude, Radcliffe Coll., 1965; MEd, Harvard U., 1984. Asst. to pres. Radcliffe Coll., Cambridge, Mass., 1984-86, exec. asst. to pres., 1986-87, dir. corp. and found. relations, 1988-89; pres. U. Cape Town Fund, Inc., N.Y.C., 1989-2000; sr. project dir. Open Soc. Scholars Fund, 1989-2000; spl. adv. to dir. The Frick Collection, 2000—. Dir. Instituto Empresa Funo, 2001; acad. fellow Carnegie Corp., 2001. Mem. Harvard Club N.Y.C., Phi Beta Kappa (Iota chpt. chmn. com. hon. membership 1976-94), Cosmpolitan Club (N.Y.C.). Episcopalian. E-mail: touborg@frick.org.

TOUBY, KATHLEEN ANITA, lawyer; b. Miami Beach, Feb. 20, 1943; d. Harry and Kathleen Rebecca (Hamper) T.; m. Joseph Thomas Woodward; children: Mark Andrew, Judson David Touby. BS in Nursing, U. Fla., 1965, MRC in Rehab. Counseling, 1967; JD with honors, Nova U., 1977. Bar: Fla. 1978, D.C. 1978. Counselor Jewish Vocat. Svc., Chgo., 1967-68; rehab. counselor Fla. Dept. Vocat. Rehab., Miami, 1968-70; spl. asst., asst. U.S. atty. U.S. Dept. Justice, 1978-80; assoc. Pyszka & Kessler, P.A., 1980-83; ptnr. Touby & Smith, P.A., 1983-89, Touby, Smith, DeMahy & Drake, P.A., Miami, 1989-94, Touby & Woodward, P.A., Miami, 1994—. Chmn. adv. exec. bd. Paralegal Edn. program Barry U., 1986-87; lectr. Food and Drug Law Inst., 1987-89, 91; lectr. environ. law Exec. Enterprises, 1987-88; lectr. trial techniques, Hispanic Nat. Bar Assn., St. Thomas Law Sch.; adj. prof. product liability Can. Govt., U.S. Trade and Mktg. Dept., 1989-95. Co-author: The Environmental Litigation Deskbook, 1989; contbr. chpts. to books, articles to profl. jours. Mem. ABA, Am. Inns of Ct. (pres. 1998-99, pres.-elect St. Thomas Law Sch. chpt. 1997-98, pres. 1998-99), Dade County Bar Assn. (legal aid, pub. svcs. com. 1988), Fed. Bar Assn. (bd. dirs. 1989—, v.p. 1991-92, pres.-elect So. Fla. chpt. 1992-93, pres. 1993-94), Phi Delta Phi (province pres. 1982-85, bd. dirs. 1985-87). Roman Catholic. Home: 450 Sabal Palm Rd Miami FL 33137-3352 Office: Touby & Woodward PA 250 Bird Rd Ste 308 Miami FL 33146-1424

TOUCH, JOSEPH DEAN, computer scientist, educator; b. Bristol, Pa., Apr. 20, 1963; s. Ralph Benjamin and Filomena (Cianfrani) T. BS in Biophysics and Computer Sci., U. Scranton, 1985; MS in Computer Sci., Cornell U., 1987; PhD in Computer Sci., U. Pa., 1992. Cons., indsl. undergrad. rsch. participation program student GTE Labs., Inc., Waltham, Mass., 1983-85; cons. The Software Engring. Inst., Pitts., 1986; rsch. asst. Cornell U., Ithaca, N.Y., 1985-87; cons. Bell Comm. Rsch., Morristown, N.J., 1987-88; grad. rsch. fellow, AT&T Bell Labs. Rsch. assistantship U. Pa., Phila., 1988-92; cons. NASA Goddard Space Flight Ctr., Greenbelt, Md., 1992; computer scientist, dir. Postel Ctr. Exptl. Networking U. So. Calif. Info. Scis. Inst., Marina del Rey, Calif., 1992—; rsch. asst. prof. U. So. Calif., L.A., 1994—. Mem. U. Scranton Acad. Computing Adv. Coun., 1983-85; univ. coun. com. on comm. U. Pa., 1989-90, com. on rsch. policy, 1990-91, acad. planning and budget com., 1990-91; reviewer various jours.; lectr. in field. Contbr. articles to profl. jours.; patentee in field. Mem. IEEE, Assn. for Computing Machinery (chpt. pres. 1984-85), IEEE Comm. Soc. (tech. program com. 1993), U. Scranton Phila. Alumni Soc. (v.p. 1990-91), Sigma Xi, Alpha Sigma Nu, Sigma Pi Sigma, Upsilon Pi Epsilon. Democrat. Roman Catholic. Avocations: rollerblading, volleyball, guitar, bicycling, sketching. Office: USC Info Scis Inst Ste 1001 4676 Admiralty Way Marina Del Rey CA 90292-6601 Home: 1101 John St Manhattan Beach CA 90266-4929 E-mail: touch@isi.edu.

TOUCHTON, CYNTHIA VILLARREAL, interior designer; b. Tampa, Fla., Mar. 19, 1949; d. Jose Garza and Maria (Jordon) Villarreal; m. Robert Allen Touchton, Dec. 2, 1972 (div. Dec. 1975). BS, Fla. State U., 1971. Interior designer Ethan Allen Carriage House, Pinellas Park, Fla., 1971-72, Jame Interiors, St. Petersburg, 1972-75; design dir. Whitehall Interiors, Inc., Largo, 1975-79; pres. Archtl. Interior Designers, Palm Harbor, 1979—. Adv. bd., instr., prof. St. Petersburg Jr. Coll., Clearwater, Fla., 1973-83. Big sister Big Bros./Big Sisters of Pinellas County, Largo, 1987; mem. St. Petersburg Symphony Guild. Mem. Am. Soc. Interior Designers. Avocations: French cooking, skiing, nautilus, beach activities.

TOUCHY, DEBORAH K.P. lawyer, accountant; b. Pasadena, Tex., Dec. 9, 1957; d. Donald Carl and Bobbie Jo (Jackson) Putzka; m. Harry Roy Touchy, Jr., Feb. 23, 1980. BBA, Baylor U., 1979; JD, U. Houston, 1988. Bar: Tex. 1989; CPA, Tex.; cert. in estate planning and probate law Tex. Bd. Legal Specialization. Sr. mgr. tax KMPG Peat Marwick, Houston, 1980-86; assoc. Fizer Beck Webster & Bentley, 1989-90; pvt. practice law, 1990—; chmn. spl. events Jr. League Houston, 1997-98. Editor Houston Law Rev., 1988-89. Chmn. ticket sales incentives Chi Omega, Houston, 1985; active ticket sales Mus. Fine Arts, Houston, 1984; facilities chmn. Woodland Trails West Civic Orgn., Houston, 1982-83; pres. Women Attys. in Tax & Probate, 1994-95; bd. dirs. Episcopal Ch. Women at St. John the Divine; active St.John's Sch., 1999—. Recipient Outstanding Alumni award, Beta Alpha Psi, 1997. Mem. ABA (estate-probate sect. 1989—, vice chmn. commn. property com. 1994—), AICPA (taxation sect., estate and gift tax com. 1992-95, 98-2000), Tex. Soc. CPAs (bd. dirs. 1995—, chmn. tax inst. com. 1996-97, estate planning com. 1990-94, 96—), Houston Chpt. CPAs (chmn. taxpayer edn. 1985-86, chmn. membership com. 1992-93, v.p. 1993-94, 96-97, chmn. tax forums 1994-95, long range planning com. 1995-96, chmn. leadership devel. 1997-98, treas. 1998-99, chmn. ann. charity event 1999-2000, bd. dirs. 1999-2000, 2002-03, pres. 2001-02), Houston Bar Assn. (estate-probate sect. 1989—), State Bar Tex. (estate-probate sect. 1989—, mem. elder law com. 1991-97), Houston Estate and Fin. Forum, Baylor U. Women's Assn. (treas. 1993-94, chmn. fin. com. 1994-95, parliamentarian 1995-96, sec. 1996-97, pres. 1997-98, chmn. audit com. 1999-2000), Chief Justice-Advocates, Tex. Bd. Legal Specializations (cert. estate planning, probate law 1994), Order of Coif, Omicron Delta Kappa, Phi Delta Phi, Beta Alpha Psi (Outstanding Alumni 1997). Office: PO Box 130122 Houston TX 77219-0122

TOUGIAS, MARK A. artist; b. Springfield, Mass., Nov. 1, 1957; s. Arthur E. and Geraldine M. (Loncrini) T. BA in Edn., U. Mass., 1979. One-person shows include Cambridge Gallery, Worcester, Mass., 1988, Clarke Gallery, Stowe, Vt., 1991, 99, Ivory Treasures Gallery, Montreal, 1993, So. Vt. Art Ctr., Manchester, Vt., 1995, 98, Blue Heron Gallery, South Burlington, Vt., 2000, Gallery of Graphic Arts, N.Y.C., 2000; exhibited in small group shows Hardcastles Gallery, Wilmington, Del., 1993, Gallery of Graphic Arts, N.Y.C., 1999, Mary Bryan Gallery, Jeffersonville, Vt., 1994—, Noroton Gallery, Darien, Conn., 2000; large group exhbns. include Springfield (Mass.) Mus. Fine Arts, 1985-88, Whistler House Mus., Lowell, Mass., 1988, Cape Cod Art Assn., Barnstable, Mass., 1989, Salmagundi Club, N.Y.C., 1993, Stratton (Vt.) Arts Festival, 1995-98, North Shore Arts Assn., Gloucester, Mass., 1998—; co-author: Autumn Rambles of New England, 1998. Mem. Am. Soc. Marine Artists, No. Vt. Artist Assn. (Harold Knight award 1996, Best in Oils 1996, 2000), North Shore Arts Assn. (Guild of Boston Artists-Roger Curtis award for excellence 1998), Helen Day Art Ctr. (artist mem., Artists' Choice award 1999), So. Vt. Art Ctr. Avocations: travel, cultural studies, music.

TOUHILL, C. JOSEPH, environmental engineer; b. Newark, Aug. 27, 1938; s. Charles J. and Caroline A (Lesaius) T.; m. Helen Elizabeth O'Malley, June 11, 1960; children: Gregory Joseph, Stephen Mark, Christopher Alan, Kathleen Elizabeth. BCE, Rensselaer Poly. Inst., 1960, PhD in Environ. Engring., 1964; SM, MIT, 1961. Diplomate Am. Acad. Environ. Engrs. Mgr. water and land resources dept. Battelle Meml. Inst., Richland, Wash., 1964-71; pres. Baker/TSA Inc., Pitts., 1977-90; group sr. v.p. ICF Kaiser Engrs. Inc., 1990-94; exec. v.p. EG&G Environ. Inc., 1994-97; pres. Touhill Tech. Mgmt. Corp., 1997-99; discipline lead for process and environ. engring. Foster Wheeler Environ. Corp., Langhorne, Pa., 1999—. Cons. various engring. firms, Washington and Pitts., 1971-77; trustee Am. Acad. Environ. Engrs., Annapolis, 1971-77, 83-86, Kappe lectr., 1992; chmn. bd. Pennwood Bancorp, 1998-2000. Co-author: Hazardous Materials Spills Handbook, 1982, Hazardous Waste Management Engineering, 1987; editor: Resource Management in the Great Lakes Basin, 1971; mem. editorial bd. Environ. Progress Jour., 1979-93. Bd. dirs. Suburban Gen. Hosp., Pitts., 1986-96, Pennwood Bancorp, Pitts., 1991-2000, chmn. bd., 1998-2000; vice chmn. Franklin Park (Pa.) Authority, 1977-96, chmn. adv. com., dept. Environ. and energy Engring., Rensselaer Polytech Inst., 1996-98, mem. adv. bd. Dept. Civil and Environ. Engring., 2000-. Recipient fellow award Rensselaer Alumni Assn., 1994. Fellow ASCE, AIChE (chmn. environ. engring. div. 1977, Inst. fellow 2000), Am. Chem. Soc. (editl. adv. bd. 1975-77), Am. Water Works Assn. (life), Water Environment Fedn. (life). Office: Foster Wheeler Environ Corp One Oxford Valley Ste 200 2300 Lincoln Hwy East Langhorne PA 19047

TOULMIN, PRIESTLEY, retired geologist; b. Birmingham, Ala., June 5, 1930; s. Priestley and Catharine Augusta (Carey) T.; m. Martha Jane Slason, Aug. 30, 1952; children: Catharine Bosier (Mrs. Robert G. Gibson), Priestley Chewning. AB, Harvard U., 1951, PhD, 1959; MS, U. Colo., 1953. With U.S. Geol. Survey, Washington, 1953-56, 57-89, staff geologist for exptl. geology, 1966, chief br. exptl. geochemistry, 1966-71, geologist geologic div., 1971-89, Reston, Va., 1974-89, ret., 1989; also leader inorganic chemistry team NASA (Viking Project). Adj. prof. Columbia U., 1966; research asso. in geochemistry

Calif. Inst. Tech., 1976-77; vis. lectr. Am. Geol. Inst.; dir. petrogenesis and mineral resources program NSF, 1985; bd. dirs., treas. 28th Internat. Geol. Congress, 1985-86 Mng. sci. editor Geochemistry Internat., 1965-68; assoc. editor Am. Mineralogist, 1974-76; contbr. articles to profl. jours. Mem. advisory com. spl. edn., Alexandria, Va., 1977-80. Recipient Exceptional Service medal NASA, 1977; Meritorious Service award U.S. Dept. Interior, 1978 Fellow Geol. Soc. Am., Mineral Soc. Am. (bd. assoc. editors 1974-76), Soc. Econ. Geologists; mem. AAAS, Geol. Soc. Washington (2d v.p. 1977, councillor 1973-74, 90-91, 1st v.p. 1981, pres. 1982), Am. Geophys. Union, Soc. Mayflower Descs., S.R., SAR, Soc. Colonial Wars (D.C.), Aztec Club of 1847, St. Andrews Soc. (Washington), Cosmos Club (pres. 1993-94, found. trustee 1994—, chmn. 1996-2001), Sigma Xi, Sigma Gamma Epsilon. Home: 418 Summers Dr Alexandria VA 22301-2449 Office: PO Box 183 Alexandria VA 22313-0183

TOULMIN, STEPHEN EDELSTON, humanities educator, educator; b. London, Mar. 25, 1922; BA in Math. and Physics, King's Coll., Cambridge, Eng., 1942; PhD, King's Coll., 1948; D Tech. (hon.), Royal Inst. Tech., Stockholm, 1991. Lectr. in philosophy of sci. Oxford U., Eng., 1949-55; prof., chmn. dept. of philosophy U. Leeds, Yorkshire, Eng., 1955-59; dir. unit for history of ideas Nuffield Found., London, 1960-65; prof. history of ideas and philosophy Brandeis U., Waltham, Mass., 1965-69; prof. philosophy Mich. State U., East Lansing, 1969-72; prof. humanities U. Calif., Santa Cruz, 1972-73; prof. com. social thought U. Chgo., 1973-86; Avalon prof. humanities Northwestern U., Evanston, Ill., 1986-92, Avalon prof. emeritus, 1992—; Henry R. Luce prof.Ctr. Multiethnic and Transnational Studies U. So. Calif., L.A., 1993-2001, prof., 2001—. Vis. prof. U. Melbourne, Australia, 1954-55, Stanford U., 1959, Columbia U., N.Y.C., 1960, Hebrew U., Jerusalem, 1964, U. South Fla., 1972, Dartmouth Coll., 1979, SUNY, Plattsburgh, 1980, Colo. Coll., 1980, 82, MacMaster U., 1983, Harvard Project Physics Grad. Sch. Edn., Harvard U., 1965; counselor Smithsonian Inst., Washington, 1967-77; cons., staff mem. Nat. Commn. Protection Human Subjects Biomed. Behavioral Rsch., 1975-78; sr. vis. scholar, fellow Inst. Soc. Ethics and Life Scis., Hastings-on-Hudson, N.Y., 1981-2001; regent's lectr. U. Calif. Med. Sch., Davis, 1985; Mary Flexner lectr. Bryn Mawr Coll., 1977; Reyerson lectr. U. Chgo., 1979, John Nuveen lectr., 1980; Tate-Wilson lectr. So. Meth. U., 1980; Or Emet lectr. Osgoode Hall Law Sch., 1981; McDermott lectr. U. Dallas, 1985; lectr. Sigma Xi, 1965-66, Phi Beta Kappa, 1978-79, Phi Beta Kappa-AAAS, 1984, Thomas Jefferson lectr. NEH, Washington, 1997; Tanner lectr. Clare Hall, Cambridge U., 1998; guest prof. social and human scis. Wolfgang Goethe Universitat, Frankfurt, Germany, 1987; vis. fellow Internationales Forschungszentrum Kulturwissenschaften (IFK), Vienna, 1995. Author: The Place of Reason in Ethics, 1949, The Philosophy of Science: an Introduction, 1953, The Uses of Argument, 1958, Foresight and Understanding, 1961, Human Understanding, vol. 1, 1972, Knowing and Acting, 1976, The Return to Cosmology, 1982, Cosmopolis, 1989; (with J. Goodfield) The Fabric of the Heavens, 1961, The Architecture of Matter, 1963, The Discovery of Time, 1965; (with A. Janik) Wittgenstein's Vienna, 1973; (with R. Rieke and A. Janik) An Introduction to Reasoning, 1978; (with A. Jonsen) The Abuse of Casuistry, 1987; (with B. Gustavsen) Beyond Theory, 1996, Return to Reason, 2001; contbr. numerous sci. articles to profl. jours. Recipient Honor Cross 1st class (Austria), 1991; Getty Ctr. for History of Art and Humanities scholar, 1985-86, First Book of the Year prize Am. Soc. Social Philosophy, 1992; Ctr. for Psychosocial Studies fellow, 1974-76. Fellow Am. Acad. Arts and Scis.

TOULOUSE, MARK GENE, religion educator; b. Des Moines, Feb. 1, 1952; s. O. J. and Joan (VanDeventer) T.; m. Jeffica L. Smith, July 31, 1976; children: Joshua Aaron, Marcie JoAnn, Cara Lynn. BA, Howard Payne U., 1974; MDiv, Southwestern Bapt. Theol. Sem., 1977; PhD, U. Chgo., 1984. Instr. Ill. Benedictine Coll., Lisle, 1980-82, asst. prof., 1982-84, Grad. Sem., Phillips U., Enid, Okla., 1984-86; prof., dean Brite Div. Sch. Texas Christian U., Ft. Worth, 1986—. Author: The Transformation of John Foster Dulles, 1985, Joined in Discipleship: The Maturing of an American Religious Movement, 1992, Joined in Discipleship: The Shaping of Contemporary Disciples Identity, 1997; co-editor: Makers of Christian Theology in America, 1997, Sources of Christian Theology in America, 1999; editor: Walter Scott: A Nineteenth Century Evangelical, 1999; contbr. articles to religious jours. Henry Luce III fellow Theol., 1997-98; Theol. scholar, rsch. award Assn. Theol. Schs., 1990-91. Mem. Am. Acad. Religion (jr. scholar S.W. region 1990-91), Am. Soc. Ch. History. Home: 4129 Alava Dr Fort Worth TX 76133-5462 Office: Brite Divinity Sch TCU Box 298130 Fort Worth TX 76129-0001 E-mail: m.toulouse@tcu.edu.

TOUPIN, HAROLD OVID, retired chemical company executive; b. Hibbing, Minn., Jan. 21, 1927; s. Ovid Pascal and Ellen (Holt) T.; m. Edna F. Sallila, Feb. 8, 1948 (div. Feb. 1973); m. Colleen Beverly Lange, Apr. 18, 1981; children: James, Ronald. BS, U. Minn., 1954, MA, 1955, postgrad, 1968; PhD (hon.), Internat. Acad. Color, Las Vegas, Nev., 1982, U. Mont., 1990. Mgr. Firestone Tire Co., East Los Angeles, Calif., 1948-51; dir. vocat. edn. Hopkins (Minn.) Pub. Schs., 1955-75; with research and devel. Powero-Peat Co., Gilbert, Minn., 1956-67; chief exec. officer, cons. Color Specialties Inc., Mpls., 1976-98; ret., 1999. Pres., founder travel, meeting planners svc. co., 1990; founder internat. office for color specialties, 1994; bd. dirs. Vu-tek Inc., St. Paul, Airport Auto Sales, St. Paul Color Specialties of Nev., Las Vegas, Instant Air Inc., Mpls., Freedom Fin.; cons. Runs Hot Cons. Svc., 1966-75; ptnr. Vermes Jewelry, Mpls., 1956-80. Contbr. articles to profl. jours. Bd. dirs. Hopkins Jaycees, 1958-60. Served with USAAF, 1944-47. Mem. Am. Assn. Mfrs., Internat. Assn. Color, Nat. Ret. Tchrs. Assn., Am. Assn. Self Employed, Met. Area Dist. Edn. Instrs. Assn. (pres.), Mpls. C. of C. (Super Bowl com. 1992), Am. Legion, VFW. Lodges: Lions (sec. Hopkins club 1956-76). Democrat. Roman Catholic. Avocations: traveling, golfing, writing. Home: 14582 Summit Shores Dr Burnsville MN 55306-5801

TOURETZKY, MURIEL WALTER, nursing educator; b. Elizabeth, N.J., Jan. 9, 1944; d. Robert Harry and Marian Elizabeth (Bannan) Walter; m. Simeon Jacob Touretzky, Jan. 24, 1982. BS in Med. Tech., Rutgers U., 1966; MS in Biology, U. Mo., St. Louis, 1977; BSN, Rutgers U., 1986. RN, N.J.; cert. tchr., N.J., cert. health edn. specialist, cert. sch. nurse ANA, cert. sch. nurse, N.J. Lead nurse pediatric unit St. Michael's Med. Ctr., Newark, 1986-89; instnl. supr. Woodbridge (N.J.) Devel. Ctr., 1989; sch. nurse Regional Sch. Union Campus, Scotch Plains, N.J., 1989—; part-time instr. scis. practical nursing program Middlesex County Vocat. and Tech. Schs., East Brunswick, 1989—. Mem. ANA, Am. Sch. Health Assn. (mem. sch. nurse com.), Nat. Assn. Sch. Nurses, Am. Assn. Blood Banks, Sigma Theta Tau. Home: 592 Madison Dr # B Jamesburg NJ 08831-4330 Office: 1524 Terrill Rd Scotch Plains NJ 07076-2914

TOURIN, PETER TANNY, computer scientist, educator; b. Fairfield, Ohio, Feb. 20, 1945; s. Jack and Jeanne (Tanenbaum) T.; children: Jaime, Mischa. BS in Psychology, U. Mich., 1967; postgrad., Yale U., New Haven, Conn., 1970. Apprentice Hubbard Harpsichords, Waltham, Mass., 1967-68, Donald Warnock luthier, Princeton, 1970-71; prin. Tourin Musica, Jericho Ctr., Vt., 1972—; computer application devel. Cool Wind Ventilation Corp., Long Island City, N.Y., 1985—. Co-dir. Ensemble Soleil, New London, N.H., 1995—. Technical dir. multimedia theatrical events, 1999; author: Comprehensive Catalogue of Extant Viole da Gamba in Public and Private Collections, 1979. Tax appraiser town govt., Duxbury, Vt., 1984-87. Grantee Vt. State Coun. on Arts, 1975, NEA, 1982. Mem. Vt. Cons. Network (founding), Viola da Gamba Soc. Am. (bd. dirs. 1984-89). Avocations: bluegrass and folk music, sailing, skiing, kayaking, woodworking. Office: Tourin Musica PO Box 1048 Jericho Center VT 05465

TOURLITSAS, JOHN CONSTANTINE, radiologist; b. Cavala, Greece, Oct. 4, 1926; came to U.S., 1956; s. Constantine Nacos and Marica Constantine (Athanasiou) T. MD, U. Athens, Greece, 1955. Diplomate Am. Bd. Radiology. Intern Sioux Valley Hosp., Sioux Falls, S.D., 1956-57; resident Midway Hosp., Mpls.-St. Paul, 1957-59, New Eng. Deaconess Hosp./Harvard U., Boston, 1959-60, Mass. Meml. Hosps./Boston U., 1960-61, Toronto (Ont., Can.) Western Hosp.-U. Toronto, 1961-62; rsch. fellow in radiology Postgrad. Rsch. Inst. Hosp for Sick Children, U. Toronto, 1962; resident Sunnybrook VA Hosp.-U. Toronto, 1963, Royal Victoria Hosp., McGill U., Montreal, 1963-65; attending radiologist, vis. radiologist Maimonides Med. Ctr., Coney Island Hosp., Bklyn., 1966-68; attending, cons. radiologist Bronx (N.Y.)-Lebanon Hosp. Ctr.-Albert Einstein Coll. Med., 1968-95; ret., 1995. Instr. radiology Albert Einstein Coll. Medicine, 1972-77. Joslin Clinic fellow, Boston, 1959-60. Fellow Am. Coll. Chest Physicians; mem. AMA, Am. Coll. Radiology, Am. Roentgen Ray Soc., Radiol. Soc. N.Am., N.Y. State Med. Soc. Avocations: reading, walking, traveling. Home: 372 Fifth Ave Apt 8C New York NY 10018-8109

TOURNIER, JEAN-PIERRE, consultant company executive; b. Jemmapes, Algerie, Feb. 15, 1943; came to Can., 1965; s. Alexandre and Maria (Lamouille) T.; m. Angeline Nadon, June 24, 1967; children: Pierre-Yves, Jean-Philippe, Alexandre, Marie-Sophie. Pub. Works Engr., Ecole Speciale des Travaux Pub, Paris, 1965; M Applied Scis., Ecole Polytechnique, Montreal, Que., Can., 1966; PhD in Civil Engring., U. Sherbrooke, Can., 1971. Soils mechanics engr. Hydro-Que., Montreal, 1971-75; dep. mgr. geotech. dept. Le Groupe LGL, 1975-77, mgr. geotech. dept., 1977-81, v.p. internat. affairs, 1988-92; pres., gen. mgr. La Societe D'Expertise et D'ingenierie LGL S.A., Port-Au-Prince, Haiti, 1981-88; pres. LGLSA, Haiti, 1981-92; tech. cons. Societé d'Energie de la Baie James, Montreal, Can., 1992-97; pres. Groupe Conseil Promumdo, Sherbrooke, Que., 1992—; mgr. geotech. & hydraulic dept. Hydro-Quebec, 1997—, chief engr. engring. dept., 2000—. Bd. dirs. Immobiliere Colasi; v.p. Sea-Shores Mgmt., Panama, 1991-92; mem. Geotech. Standards Commn. Que., 1995—. Contbr. numerous articles to tech. jours. Gov. Fondation de Recherches en Administration, Faculty of Mgmt., U. Sherbrooke, 1989—. Mem. ASCE, Ordre des Ingenieurs du Que., Internat. Commn. Large Dams, Can. Geotech. Soc., Internat. Soc. Soils Mechanics and Found. Engring., Societe des Ingenieurs Diplomes E.T.P. Paris. Roman Catholic. Home: 283 Ave Putney Saint-Lambert QC Canada J4P 3B3 Office: Hydro-Quebec 855 St Catherine E Montreal QC Canada H2L 4M8 E-mail: tournier.jean-pierre@hydro.qc.ca.

TOURTELLOTTE, CHARLES DEE, physician, educator; b. Kalamazoo, Aug. 28, 1931; s. Dee and Helen May (Lotz) T.; m. Barbara Richwine, June 25, 1955; children: Daniel DeWitt, Elizabeth Anne, William Charles, Scott David. AB, Johns Hopkins U., 1953; MS in Biochemistry, MD, Temple U., 1957. Diplomate Am. Bd. Internal Medicine. Intern, resident in medicine U. Mich. Hosp., Ann Arbor, 1957-60; fellow in rheumatology Temple U. Hosp., Phila., 1960-61; fellow in biochemistry Rockefeller U., N.Y.C., 1961-63; faculty Sch. Medicine, Temple U., 1963—, prof. medicine, 1972-97, prof. emeritus, 1997—; chief rheumatology Temple U. Hosp., 1994-97, pres. med. staff, bd. govs., 1984-86. Dir. Greater Delaware Valley Arthritis Control Program, 1974-77; pres. Eastern Pa. chpt. Arthritis Found., 1972-74; mem. active/cons. staff 10 area and regional hosps. Contbr. chpts. to textbooks, articles to profl. jours.; Editorial Bd.: Arthritis and Rheumatism, 1969-77, 19th-24th Rheumatism Revs, 1969-81. Mem. Haddonfield (N.J.) Bd. Edn., 1968-74, pres., 1974; mem. Borough of Haddonfield Environ. Comm., 1975-87, chmn., 1977-85; mem. Haddonfield Civic Assn., 1963—; South N.J. chmn. Johns Hopkins U. Alumni Schs. Com., 1975-90; trustee Bobby Fulton Meml. Fund, 1979—, 1st Presbyn. Ch. of Haddonfield, 1998-2000. With AUS, 1953-61. Helen Hay Whitney Found. fellow, 1962-63; Arthritis Found. fellow, 1963-66 Fellow ACP, Phila. Coll. Physicians, Am. Coll. Rheumatology (founding fellow); mem. Pa. Med. Soc., Phila. County Med. Soc., Babcock Surg. Soc., Phila. Rheumatism Soc. (pres. 1968-69), Pa. Rheumatology Soc. (founding pres. 1985-86), N.J. Soc. of Pa., Huguenot Soc. Pa., Temple U. Med. Alumni Assn. (pres. 1997-99), Tavistock County Club (N.J.), Little Egg Harbor Yacht Club, Med. Club of Phila. (bd. dirs., pres. 1998-99), Sigma Xi, Alpha Omega Alpha, Delta Upsilon, Phi Chi. Presbyterian. Home: 6 Lane Of Acres Haddonfield NJ 08033-3505 Office: Temple Univ Hosp Dept Rheumatology Philadelphia PA 19140-5192 E-mail: cd_tourte@prodigy.net.

TOURTELLOTTE, MILLS CHARLTON, mechanical and electrical engineer; b. Great Falls, Mont., Dec. 16, 1922; s. Nathaniel Mills and Frances Victoria (Charlton) T.; m. Dorothy Elsie Gray, Sept. 16, 1947 (dec. 1994); children: Jane Tourtellotte Collins, Kathryn Tourtellotte Bauman, Thomas; m. Linda M. Merritt, July 1, 1995. BS, Ill. Inst. Tech., 1947, MS, 1952. Registered profl. engr., Ill., Mich., Tex. Engr. Automatic Electric Co., Chgo., 1947-49, Inland Steel Co., East chicago, Ind., 1952-56; sr. project engr. Gulf States Tube divsn. Vision Metals, Rosenberg, Tex., 1956—2001; fallout shelter analyst Fed. Emergency mgmt., Washington, 1970—; dealer Amsoil, 1977—; pres. Fabricators, Inc., Rosenberg, Tex. Substitute tchr. Lamar Consol. Ind. Sch. Dist., Rosenberg, 2001—. Contbr. articles to profl. jours.; patentee mech. and elec. devices. Election judge Ft. Bend County Republican party, 1965; chmn. 4H Adult Leaders Assn., 1968. With USN, 1944-46, WWII. Named Friend of 4H, Ft. Bend County Extension Svc., 1968. Mem. NSPE, ASME (life), Tex. Soc. Profl. Engrs. (edn. chmn. 1969), Fluid Power Soc., Am. Soc. for Engring. Edn. (industry chmn. 1969), Assn. Iron and Steel Engrs. (life), Mich. Soc. Profl. Engrs., Ill. Soc. Profl. Engrs., VFW (life, quartermaster 1984), Am. Legion, Houston Inventors Assn., Handyman Club Am. Office: Fabricators Inc PO Box 242 Rosenberg TX 77471 Fax: 281-232-0813.

TOURTELLOTTE, WALLACE WILLIAM, neurologist, educator; b. Great Falls, Mont., Sept. 13, 1924; s. Nathaniel Mills and Frances Victoria (Charlton) T.; m. Jean Esther Toncray, Feb. 14, 1953; children: Wallace William, George Mills, James Millard, Warren Gerard. PhB, BS, U. Chgo., 1945, PhD, 1948, MD, 1951. Intern Strong Meml. Hosp. U. Rochester (N.Y.) Sch. Medicine and Dentistry, 1951-52; resident in neurology U. Mich. Med. Ctr., Ann Arbor, 1954-57, asst. prof. neurology, 1957-59, assoc. prof., 1959-66, prof., 1966-71; prof. dept. neurology UCLA, 1971—, vice chmn. dept. neurology, 1971-98, emeritus vice chmn. dept. neurology, 1998; chief neurology svcs. VA Wadsworth, West Los Angeles, Calif., 1971-99, emeritus, 1991-99, emeritus dir. tng. program, 1991—, staff neurologist, neuroscientist, 1991—. Vis. assoc. prof. Washington U., St. Louis, 1963-64; hon. mem. med. adv. bd. Nat. Multiple Sclerosis Soc., 1968—, 1994—, So. Calif. Multiple Sclerosis Socs., 1972—; dir. Multiple Sclerosis Rsch. and Treatment Ctr., Human Brain and Spinal Fluid Resource Ctr., 1971—. Co-editor (with Cedric Raines, Henry McFarland): Multiple Sclerosis, Clinical and Pathogenetic Basis, 1997; mem. editorial bd. Jour. Neurol. Sci., Revue Neurologica, Italian Jour. Neurol. Sci., Multiple Sclerosis Jour.; dedicated The Wallace W. Tourtellotte Clin. and Neurosci. Libr., 1999; called the 13th most quoted neurologist in USA, 1999. Lt. (j.g.) M.C., USNR, 1952-54. Recipient Disting. Alumni Service award U. Chgo., 1982. Fellow Am. Acad. Neurology (S. Weir Mitchell Neurology Reseach award 1959); mem. Am. Assn. Univ. Neurol. Prof. (emeritus), Am. Neurol. Assn. (counselor 1982—, v.p. 1992), World Fedn. Neurology (founding mem.), Am. Assn. Neuropathologists, Internat. Soc. Neurochemsitry (founding mem.), Am. Soc. Pharmacology and Exptl. Therapeutics, Am. Soc. Neurochemistry (founding mem.), Soc. Neurosci., Confrerie de la Chaine des Rotisseur, Argentier du Baillage de Los Angeles (vice chanceller, comdr.), Ordre Mondial des Gourmets Degustateurs Etats-Unis Chevalier, Pasadena Wine and Food Soc., Physician Wine & Food Soc., Soc. Med. Friends of Wine, Sigma Xi. Republican. Presbyterian. Home: 1140 Tellem Dr Pacific Palisades CA 90272-2244 Fax: 310-454-7650. E-mail: wtourtel@ucla.edu.

TOURTET, CHRISTIANE ANDRÉE, writer, human rights activist, photo journalist, reporter; b. Grenoble, France, June 18, 1945; came to U.S., 1965; d. André and Maria Tourtet. Cert. completion humanistic psychology, Fla. Jr. Coll., Jacksonville, 1969, AS with high honors, 1973, AA with high honors, 1974; BA, Jacksonville U., 1975. Hostess interpreter-translator Credit Lyonnais, Grenoble, 1963-65; instr. French Albany (N.Y.) Acad. for Girls, 1965-66; instr. French, asst. lang. lab. Coll. of St. Rose, Albany, 1966-67; instr. French Bartram Sch., Jacksonville, 1970; instr. French and modeling Fla. Jr. Coll., 1971-74; producer-dir., radio personality ednl. French program Sta. WFAM FM radio, 1977-79; interpreter, translator French Lang. Bank, 1980-83. Tutor pvt. and small group classes in French; model for publicity ads, brochures in major mags., newspapers; lectr. in field. Author: Fruits of Life (Silver medal Arts Scis. Letter, Paris, 1977); editor, contbr. publs. New Leaf News, Fla. Flambeau, Back to School Mag.; editor, pub., contbr. Environ. Med. and Disability Corner, Tallahassee Area Ch. News, FSView, AARP Newsletter, Tallahassee Alliance with Disabilities Newsletter; recs. Flamingo Studios, Tallahassee, Fla., 1986-87; paintings exhibited in France, Monte Carlo and U.S.; photography exhibited in galleries, pub. in mags. including Today's Photographer; participant in over 28 TV commls. Pres. Le Cercle Francais, Albany, 1965. Recipient 1st prize Solfège Artistic Competition, 1957, 1st prize Accordion Acad. Grenoble, 1958, Gold medal Cup of France, 1959, Cup of Europe, 1959, 2d prize Singing Competition City of Grenoble, 1961, medal of City of Grenoble, France, 1977, medal of Dauphine County, 1977, medal of Chevalier of Order of Merit, Paris, 1976, medal of Chevalier of French Courtesy, Paris, 1977, medal of Nat. Merit, Paris, 1976, crowned twice by Romanian Prince Paltin Sturdza, Princess Cornelia Sturdza and Prince Michael Sturdza, U.S. flag flown over Capitol, Washington in her honor, 1999, 2000, 2001. Mem. NAFE, APHA, Am. Acad. Environ. Medicine (assoc.), Environ. Illness Assn. Tallahassee (founder, pres. 1989—), Nat. Ctr. Environ. Strategies, Share, Care, Prayers, H.E.A.L., Am. Med. Writers Assn., Internat. Platform Assn., Nat. Assn. Sci. Writers, Freelance Media Svcs., India Assn. Tallahassee (publicity officer), Internat. Freelance Photographers Orgn., Am. Image Press, Phi Theta Kappa. Address: PO Box 20517 Tallahassee FL 32316-0517 E-mail: tourtet@yahoo.com.

TOUS DE TORRES, LUZ M. banker; b. San Juan, P.R., Apr. 23, 1944; d. Rafael Tous Cortes and Iris Fernos; m. Manuel A. de Torres, Jr., Feb. 17, 1967; children: Rosa Iris, Lara Sofia. BBA magna cum laude, U. P.R., 1965; MBA summa cum laude, Interam. U., 1976; also P.R. Sch. Banking, 1976. With Banco Popular, San Juan, 1965—, sr. v.p. corp. real estate adminstrn., 1987—. Co-founder P.R. Indsl. Editors Assn., pres., 1970-72; dir. bank's blood program for ARC, 1972—, dir. bank's personnel donors program United Fund, 1981—; trustee BPPR Found., 1986-87; dir. Greater San Juan Com., 1993. Recipient Outstanding Acad. Achievement award Interam. U., 1976. Mem. NAFE, Soc. Human Resources Mgmt. (accredited profl. in human resources), Internat. Facility Mgmt. Assn. (cert. facility mgr.), Internat. Assn. Corp. Real Estate Execs., Bldg. Owners Mgmt. Assn., Urban Land Inst., Met. Mus. of Art (N.Y.), Mus. Contemporary Art, P.R. Mus. of Art, Corp. Devel. Hato Rey Fin. Ctr. (pres. 2000-01), Santurce Rotary (sec. 2000). Office: PO Box 362708 San Juan PR 00936 E-mail: lucy_tous@bppr.com.

TOUSIGNANT, JACQUES, human resources executive, lawyer; b. Montreal, Que., Can., Sept. 20, 1948; JD, Sherbrooke U., Que., 1975. Assoc. law firm Pouliot Mercure & Assocs., Montreal, Que., 1975-85; dir. assoc. law firm Montreal Trans. Soc., 1985-87; v.p. La Presse Ltee, 1987—. Mem. Can. Bar Assn., Que. Bar Assn. Office: La Presse 7 Rue St Jacques Montreal QC Canada H2Y 1K9 E-mail: jtousign@lapresse.ca.

TOUSLEY, RUSSELL FREDERICK, lawyer; b. New Haven, Nov. 19, 1938; s. Russell F. and Della (Ermer) T.; m. Sarah Morford, July 23, 1963; children: Ellen Elizabeth, Kenneth Morford. BA cum laude, Yale Coll., 1960; JD, U. Wash., 1967. Bar: Wash. 1967. Assoc. Davis Wright, Seattle, 1967-69; v.p. Safecare Co., Inc., 1969-78, Winmar Co., Inc., Seattle, 1977-78; ptnr. Tousley Brain Stephens PLLC, 1978—. Trustee Seattle Opera Assn., 1980—, pres., chmn. bd., 1985-87; trustee Seattle Chamber Music Festival, 1990-93; moderator Plymouth Congl. Ch., Seattle, 1975-77, 83-85, trustee, 1969-93, adminstrn., property and fin. bd., 1999-2001. Lt. (j.g.) USN, 1960-64. Mem. ABA, Wash. State Bar Assn., Seattle-King County Bar Assn., Internat. Coun. Shopping Ctrs. (assoc.), Rainier Club, Seattle Tennis Club, Rotary. Avocations: opera, reading, collecting mint U.S. regular issue stamps. Office: Tousley Brain Stephens PLLC Key Tower 56th Flr 700 5th Ave Ste 5600 Seattle WA 98104-5056 E-mail: rtousley@tousley.com.

TOUSSAINT, CHRISTOPHER ANDRE, video producer, director, editor, writer; b. Balt., Aug. 27, 1953; s. Andre Jean and Genevieve Stella Toussaint. BA in Speech and Dramatic Arts, U. Md., 1975. Film editor Am. Nat. Enterprises, Hollywood, Calif., 1979; editor In Search Of, Alan Landsburg Prodns., West Los Angeles, 1980; film editor Joy Renchers Editl., Hollywood, 1988; sales mgr. 20/20 Video, Santa Monica, Calif., 1986-88; exec. dir., prodr. The Prodrs. Consortium, L.A., 1986-92; dir., prodr. Only New Age Music, 1988-91; editor, prodn. asst. Smith-Hemion Prodns., 1990-91; dir. acquisitions Lightworks Audio and Video, 1992-95; prodr., dir. Harry DeLigter Prodns., 1993-97; owner, prodr. Free Spirit Prodns. Prodr., dir.: (video programs) Starflight, 1990 (Silver award Houston Film Festival 1990), Opening to Angels, 1994 (Telly award 1996, Angel award Excellence in Media 1995, award of Excellence, Film Adv. Bd. 1995), Free Energy: The Race to Zero Point, 1997 (Telly award 1997, Aurora Gold award 1998), Roswell: The UFO Un Coverup, 1998 (EBE award, Telly award finalist 1999), Cold Fusion-Fire From Water, 1999 (Aurora Platinum award 1999, Telly award 2000), (video short) Columbus Go Home, 1992, (video documentary) Future Options, 1989. Mem. Internat. Documentary Assn., Union of Concerned Scientists, Cambridge, Mass. Mem. Green Party. Avocations: photography, hiking, reading. Home: 11720 La Maida St Valley Village CA 91607 Office: Free Spirit Prodns 11720 La Maida St Valley Village CA 91607-3226 E-mail: c2saint@aol.com.

TOUSSAINT, MAURICIO, painter; b. Guadalajara, Jalisco, Mex., June 3, 1960; s. Rene Eduardo Toussaint, Maria Eugenia Villaseñor. Degree, Universidad Autónoma de Guadalajara, 1985. Asst. to curator Inst. Cultural Cabañas, Guadalajara, Mexico, 1986—88; asst. Barbara Gillman Gallery, Miami, Fla., 1996—97. Exhibited in group shows at VII Salon de Octubre, 1995 (1st pl. in painting, 2d pl. in drawing), Imagen de Zapopan, 1984 (Acquisition award). Personal E-mail: desertbuddah@earhtlink.net.

TOUSSIE, MICHAEL ISAAC, accountant; b. Bklyn., Dec. 10, 1949; s. Isaac Samuel and Marie (Sasson) T.; m. Deborah Etta Kaplan, June 13, 1985; children: Danielle, Isaac. BBA cum laude, CCNY, 1970. CPA, N.Y. Staff acct. J.K. Lasser & Co., CPA's, N.Y.C., 1970; sr. acct. Arthur Andersen & Co., CPA's, 1970-71; pvt. practice Michael I. Toussie CPA/PFS, 1971—. V.p., dir. Levitt House, Inc., Medford, N.Y., 1976-78; adj. lectr. acctg. Queen's (N.Y.) Coll., 1979-80; CFO Pitkin Bargain Ctr., Inc., Bklyn., 1981—; CFO, v.p. Jenel Mgmt. Corp., N.Y.C., 1985—. Bd. mem., treas. Murray Hill Mews Owners Corp., N.Y.C., 1989—. Mem. AICPA (accredited personal fin. specialist), N.Y. State Soc. CPA's, Mensa, Beta Gamma Sigma, Beta Alpha Psi. Democrat. Jewish. Avocations: skiing, sailboarding, running, waterskiing, bicycling. Home: 160 E 38th St Apt 19E New York NY 10016-2611 Office: Jenel Mgmt Corp 275 Madison Ave Ste 702 New York NY 10016-1101 E-mail: toussie@aol.com.

TOUSTER, SAUL, law educator; b. Bklyn., Oct. 12, 1925; s. Ben and Bertha (Landau) T.; m. Helen Davidson, Nov. 23, 1954 (div. 1967); children: Natasha Ann, Jonathan Bach; m. Irene Tayler, Jan. 14, 1978. AB magna cum laude, Harvard U., 1944, JD, 1948. Bar: N.Y. 1949. Practiced in , N.Y.C., 1949-55; prof. law SUNY-Buffalo, 1955-69, asst. to pres., 1966-68, mem. adj. faculty in medicine, edn., psychology, 1964-69; prof. law and social scis. State Coll. at Old Westbury, 1969-71; prof., provost, acad. v.p. CCNY, 1971-73; acting pres. Richmond Coll. City U. N.Y., 1973-74; prof. law CUNY Grad. Sch. also John Jay Coll. of Criminal Justice, 1974-80; prof., dir. legal studies, humanities, professions programs Brandeis U., Waltham, Mass., 1980-93, prof. emeritus, 1993. Legis. cons. N.Y. State Law Rev. Commn., 1956-61; vis. prof. U. Brussels, summer, 1968, Boston Coll. Law Sch., 1994. Author: Still Lives and Other Lives, 1966; editor, author introduction: A Survivors' Haggadah, 1998, editor, author introduction: Beyond Words: A Holocaust History in Sixteen Woodcuts done in 1945 by Miklos Adler, A Hungarian Survivor , 2001; contbr. articles. Served to lt. (j.g.) USNR, 1944-46. NEH fellow, 1978; Am. Bar Found. Legal History fellow, 1977-78 Mem. Internat. Inst. Boston (bd. advisors), Phi Beta Kappa. Home: 180 Beacon St Boston MA 02116-1408 E-mail: stouster@mac.com.

TOUTANT, STEVEN MICHAEL, neurosurgeon; b. Eau Claire, Wis., Apr. 30, 1949; s. Steven Joseph and Nona Ann (Murphy) T.; m. Nina Tucker, Oct. 4, 1980; children: Jay, Peter, Alec. BA, U. St. Thomas, 1971; MD, Loyola U., Chgo., 1974; postgrad., Dartmouth Coll., 1981. Bd. cert. neurol. surgery. Intern Dartmouth Affiliated Hosps., 1975-76, resident in gen. surgery, 1976-77, resident in neurosurgery, 1977-81; asst. prof. neurosurgery U. Calif., San Diego, 1981-83; staff neurosurgeon Dean Med. Ctr., Madison, Wis., 1983—. Dir. helmet safety program Dean Med. Ctr., Madison, 1990—; bd. dirs. Dean Health Sys., Madison, Dean Health Plan, Madison. Mem. Internat. Neurosurg. Soc., Wis. Neurosurg. Soc., Wis. Med. Soc., Congress Neurol. Surgeons. Office: Dean Med Ctr 1313 Fish Hatchery Rd Madison WI 53715-1911

TOUTANT, SYLVAIN, retail executive; Pres., CEO Réno-Dépôt/Bldg. Box Inc, Montreal, Canada. Office: Réno Dépôt 1011 Rue du Marche-Central Montreal QC Canada H4N 3J6

TOUTONGHI, MICHAEL, information technology executive; Steel worker; jewelry designer; co-founder Sunny Hill Software, CAD Innovations; dir. software devel. SOTA Tech.; dir. R&D Gibson Rsch. Corp.; from mem. staff to corp. v.p. Microsoft, Redmond, Wash., 1992, corp. v.p. Office: One Microsoft Way Redmond WA 98052-6399

TOVAR, ELIZABETH, economist; b. Caracas, Venezuela, Mar. 13, 1950; came to U.S., 1982; d. Silvestre A. Tovar and Elizabeth (Degwitz) T.; children— Cristina, Andres. Student Escuela Nacional Agrotecnica, 1980; D.Agronomy, Florence U., 1968. Dir., gen. mgr. Trassa S.A., Puerto La Cruz, Venezuela, 1978-82; pres. Trassa Internat., Miami, Fla., 1982-87; v.p. 60 Magic Minutes, Miami, 1982-86; v.p. Ultra Internat., Miami, 1984-86; pres. E-Z Mail...Etc., Miami, 1987—; bd. dirs. Trans 28 Corp., Curacao, N.A. Founder Orquesta Nacional Juvenil de Venezuela, Caracas, 1967-68, Airclubs Barcelona, Zaraza, Caroni, Venezuela, 1979-80. Served with 1st Res. Force, Venezuelan Air Force, 1980-82. Named Person of Yr., Venezuelan Fedn. Gen. Aviation/Transport Minister, 1981. Mem. Internat. Bottled Water Assn., Nat. Assn. Female Execs., Coral Gables C. of C., Greater Miami C. of C. Roman Catholic. Avocations: pilot; sailing; reading; golf; tennis. Office: E-Z Mail Etc 7936 SW 8th St Miami FL 33144-4209

TOVAR, NICHOLAS MARIO, mechanical engineer; b. Ogden, Utah, Jan. 18, 1960; s. Gerdo and Alice (Martinez) T.; m. Suzanne Oxborrow, Sept. 17, 1982; children: Ashley, Nicholas Brock, Clinton Gregory, Lance Edward, Marshall Prescott, Jarrett Stanley, Hathaniel William. BSME in Logistics Engring., Weber State U., 1986; BSME in Mech. Engring. and Mfg., Nat. U., 1990. Logistics contr. Utah-Idaho Supply Co., Salt Lake City, 1985-86; sr. manufacturing engr. Aerojet Propulsion div. GenCorp., Sacramento, 1986-93; sr. quality engr. BP Chems. Adv. Materials Divsn., Stockton, 1993-94; dir. quality engring. Indsl. Testing Internat., Lincoln, 1994-95; quality assurance mgr. Siemens Transp. Systems, Sacramento, 1996-98; v.p. quality assurance Precision Components Group - RPMI, 1998—. Republican. Mem. Lds Ch. Avocations: athletics, wargames, history, music. Home: 11428 Sabalo Way Gold River CA 95670-6207 Office: Precision Comppnent Group - RPMI 4180 Duluth Ave Rocklin CA 95765-1400 E-mail: nmtovar@rocklinprecision.com.

TOVEY, JOSEPH, investment banker; b. Tel Aviv, Nov. 5, 1938; came to U.S., 1940, naturalized, 1947; s. Samuel and Rachel (Weiman) T.; m. Anita Beverly Losice, Feb. 20, 1961; children: David, Debra, Nissan Chaim, Seth Reuven, Shaina Nava. BS summa cum laude, Bklyn. Coll., 1959; MBA, NYU, 1961, PhD, 1969. CPA. Staff acct. Machtiger Green & Co., N.Y.C., 1959-60, Loeb & Troper, N.Y.C., 1960-61; tax rschr. Lybrand, Ross Bros. & Montgomery, 1961-63; planning assoc. Mobil Oil Corp., N.Y.C., 1963-67; asst. v.p. A.G. Becker & Co., N.Y.C., 1967-70; assoc. Roth, Gerard & Co., N.Y.C., 1970-73; v.p. Faulkner, Dawkins & Sullivan, Inc., 1973-76, Shields Model Roland, Inc., N.Y.C., 1976-77; ptnr. Tovey & Co., 1977—. Pres. Joint Trading Ltd., 1977-83, Tovey & Co., Inc., 1978-96, Midwood Petroleum Corp., 1980-91, Joint Trading (Del.) Ltd., 1984-96; chmn. Midwood Asset Mgmt. Co., Inc., 1985-96; CEO Terra Link Comm. Corp., 1997—. Mem. exec. bd. Agudath Israel Am., 1963-67; CEO Healthside Comm. Ltd. LLC, 1998—. Author: (with H.C. Smith) Federal Tax Treatment of Bad Debts and Worthless Securities, 1964; assoc. editor Tax Letter, 1961-66; contbr. articles to profl. jours. Mem. Am. Newcomen Soc., Am. Fin. Assn., Am. Inst. CPAs, Fgn. Policy Assn., NYU alumni Assn., Bklyn. Coll. Alumni in Fin. Home: 1170 E 19th St Brooklyn NY 11230-4902 Office: PO Box 934 40 Wall St New York NY 10268-0934

TOVI, MURRAY, futurist, research scientist; b. N.Y.C., Mar. 18, 1937; s. Louis Tovi and Jean Cohen; m. Joan Granoff; children: Rosanna. BBA, CCNY, 1961. Exec v.p. Tovi and Perkins Inc., N.Y.C., 1969—73; pres. Murray Tovi Designs, Inc., 1975—78, Concepts in Art and Sci. Inc., Colorado Springs, 1982—89, Transflectors, Inc., Colorado Springs, 1988—90, Theoretical Optics Inc., Colorado Springs, 1988—90, Tovi Scis., Ocala, Fla., 1991—. Cons. Am. Soc. Interior Designers, N.Y.C., 1985—86. Author: Introduction to Neo-Classical Physics, 2001; inventor. Recipient Best Booth award, N.Y. Ski Show, 1965, Most Meritorious Exhibit of Equipment or Supplies award, Internat. Assn. Amusement Parks, 1969. Mem.: Internat. Orgn. Physicists (assoc.). Office: Tovi Scis PO Box 116 Sparr FL 32192 Office Fax: 352-369-1861. Business E-Mail: ToviSciences@aol.com.

TOVLIN, JOSEPH GERARD, engineer; b. Homestead, Pa., June 15, 1963; s. Joseph William and Bernadette (Kundravi) T. AA in Mech. Engring., Tex. State Tech. Coll., Waco, 1983; BS in Mech. Engring. Tech., Tex. Tech. U., Lubbock, 1986. Cert. automotive svc. excellence master. Svc. tech. Associated Supply, Lubbock, 1985-86; product engr. Wynn's Climate, Ft. Worth, 1987-88; tech. writer RDT Svcs., Houston, 1988; project engr. MTU N. Am., Sugarland, Tex., 1989-95; project engr. Mark-V Soccom program Stewart & Stevenson, Houston, 1995—. Author: (books) Diesel Engine Tech, 1988, Gasoline Engine Tech, 1988, Hydraulic Tech, 1988. Mem. ASHRAE, Soc. Automotive Engrs., Soc. Mfg. Engrs., Am. Welding Soc. Avocations: fishing, golf, hunting, automotive work. Home: 4700 Kendall Rd Baytown TX 77520-8338

TOW, BRUCE LINCOLN, computer software architect, consultant; b. Pasadena, Calif., Jan. 6, 1952; s. Philip Samuel and Lois Mary (Rogers) T.; m. Lois Mary Gadway, June 22, 1974; 1 child, Emily Winona. BA in Math., Dartmouth Coll., 1973. Systems programmer Dartmouth Coll., Hanover, N.H., 1971-73; systems rep. Honeywell Info. Systems, Manchester, 1973-77, sr. systems rep. Evansville, Ind., 1977-78, sr. systems cons. Phoenix, 1979-82; product mgr. Walker Intractive Products, San Francisco, 1982-85; software cons., 1985; dir. application architecture Oracle Corp., Redwood Shores, Calif., 1985-93; v.p. architecture Ten Fold Corp., Draper, Utah, 1993—. Prin. Synovation, San Francisco, 1990—; presenter Software Monterey Conf., 1992; multi-disciplinary cons.; CEO, founder synthesis Inst. Mem. Synthesis Inst. (founder), N.Y. Acad. Scis. Avocation: hiking. Home: 455 Hazelwood Ave San Francisco CA 94127-2129

TOWBIN, A(BRAHAM) ROBERT, investment banker; b. N.Y.C., May 26, 1935; s. Harold Clay and Minna (Berlin) T.; m. Jacqueline de Chollet; children: Minna Joyce Pinger, Abraham Robert Jr., Zachary Harold. BA, Dartmouth Coll., 1957. With Asiel & Co., N.Y.C., 1958-59; with L.F. Rothschild, Unterberg, Towbin Holdings, Inc. (merged with C.E. Unterberg, Towbin Co. 1977), 1959-86, vice chmn., 1961-86; mng. dir. Lehman Bros. (formerly Shearson Lehman Bros., Inc.), N.Y., 1987-94; pres. Russian Am. Enterprise Fund., Moscow and N.Y.C., 1994-95; vice chmn. U.S. Russian Investment Fund, 1995; mng. dir. C.E. Unterberg, Towbin, N.Y.C., 1995—99, co-chmn., 1999—2002; dir. Globecomm Systems, 1997; mng. dir. Stephens Fin. Group, 2002—. Bd. dirs. Gerber Sci. Inc., Globalstar Telecom. Ltd., K&F Industries. Hon. mem. N.Y. State Coun. Arts., bd. dirs.; trustee, N.Y. State Hist. Soc.; trustee, South St. Seaport. Mem. Securities Industry Assn., Bond Club N.Y., Stock Exch. Luncheon Club, Harmonie Club (N.Y.C.), Nat. Golf Links Am., N.Y. Yacht Club (bd. trustees), Antigua Yacht Club, Chelsea Art Club (London), Century Assn. Office: Stephens Inc # 2471 10 E 50th St New York NY 10022-6831 Business E-Mail: rtowbin@stephens.com.

TOWE, A. RUTH, museum director; b. Circle, Mont., Mar. 4, 1938; d. David and Anna Marie (Pedersen) James; m. Thomas E. Towe, Aug. 21, 1960; children: James Thomas, Kristofer Edward. BA, U. Mont., 1960, MA, 1970; postgrad., Am. U., 1964. Bookkeeper, copywriter Sta. KGVO, Missoula, Mont., 1960-61; grad. asst. Sch. of Journalism U. Mont., 1961-62; editorial asst. Phi Gamma Delta mag., Washington, 1964; reporter The Chelsea (Mich.) Standard, 1965-66; dir. Mont. Nat. Bank, Plentywood, 1966-73; bookkeeper, legal sec. Thomas E. Towe, Atty. of Law, Billings, Mont., 1967-68; dir. Mont. Nat. Bank, Browning, 1972-73; mus. exec. dir. The Moss Mansion Mus., Billings, 1988—. Bd. dirs. Billings Depot, Inc., sec., 1999—. Mem. Mont. Coun. of Family Rels. & Devel., 1970; pres. Mont. Assn. of Symphony Orchs., 1987-88; sheriff Yellowstone Corral of Westerners, Billings, 1993; pres. Yellowstone Hist. Soc., 1998-2000; vice-chmn. Yellowstone Dem. Ctrl. Com., Billings, 1983-84; mem. Billings Friends Mtg., 1986—. Mem. AAUW, PEO, Mont. Assn. Female Execs., Mus. Assn. Mont. (pres. 1990-92, bd. dirs. 1989-96), Jr. League, Theta Sigma Phi (hon.). Avocation: gardening. Office: The Moss Mus 914 Division St Billings MT 59101-1921 E-mail: ruth@mossmansion.com., rtowe@attbi.com.

TOWE, THOMAS EDWARD, lawyer; b. Cherokee, Iowa, June 25, 1937; s. Edward and Florence (Tow) T.; m. Ruth James, Aug. 21, 1960; children: James Thomas, Kristofer Edward. Student, U. Paris, 1956; BA, Earlham Coll., 1959; LLB, U. Mont., 1962; LLM, Georgetown U., 1965. Ptnr. Towe, Ball, Enright, Mackey & Sommerfeld, Billings, Mont., 1967—; legislator Mont. House of Rep., 1971-75, Mont. State Senate, Billings, 1975-87, 91-94. Served on various coms. Mont. Senate, 1975-87, 91-94. Contbr. articles to law revs. Mem. Alternatives, Inc., Halfway House, Billing, 1977-99, pres., 1985-86; mem. adv. com. Mont. Crime Control Bd., 1973-78, Youth Justice Coun., 1981-83; mem. State Dem. Exec. Com., 1969-73; candidate for Congress, 1976; bd. dirs. Mont. Consumer Affairs Coun., Regl. Cmty. Svcs. for the Devel. Disabled, 1975-77, Rimrock Guidance Found., 1975-80, Vols. of Am., Billings, 1984-89, Youth Dynamics Inc., 1989-96, Zoo Mont., 1985-2001, Inst. for Peace Studies, 1993—, Mont. State Parks Assn., 1993—. Capt. U.S. Army, 1962-65. Named as one of 100 Most Influential Montanans in 20th Century, Missoulian newspaper. Mem. Mont. Bar Assn., Yellowstone County Bar Assn., Am. Hereford Assn., Billings C. of C. Mem. Soc. Of Friends. Avocation: outdoor recreation. Home: 2739 Gregory Dr S Billings MT 59102-0509 Office: 2525 6th Ave N Billings MT 59101-1358 E-mail: t.towe@attbi.com.

TOWE, VIOLET, writer; b. Porterdale, Ga., Sept. 15, 1942; d. Annie Conner; m. Ulysses Towe; children: Jeffrey Harrison, Tammy Helton, Anthony, Michael. Grad., Monroe Ga. Comprehensive H.S., 1963. Author: The Evil Stalker, 2001, Death by Bad Magic, 2002. Mem.: Ga. Writers Assn. (assoc.). Personal E-mail: vladytoe@aol.com.

TOWER, ALTON G., JR. pharmacist; b. Buffalo, Jan. 16, 1927; m. Nan R. Spinner, Aug. 15, 1953; children: Adrienne, Michele, Renee. BS in Pharmacy, U. Buffalo, 1953. Registered pharmacist. Pharmacist Woldmans Drug Store, Buffalo, 1946-53; med. svc. rep. Strasenburgh Lab., Rochester, N.Y., 1953-66; pharmacist, mgr. Eckerd Drugs, Clearwater, Fla., 1966—. Bd. dirs. Am. Cancer Soc. Pinellas County, Fla., 1976—, pres., 1988-89, Life Saver award, 1988, life mem., 1995—, dir. cmty. affairs Pinellas Pharmacist Soc.; charter mem. Smoke Free Class of 2000, Pinellas County, 1988—. Recipient Vol. of Yr. award Am. Cancer Soc. Pinellas County, 1987, 97, Life Saver award Am. Cancer Soc. Pinellas County, 1988, James Beal award Pharmacist of the Yr., Fla. Pharm. Assn., 1992; named Hon. Life Mem., Am. Cancer Soc. Pinellas County Unit, 1995, Vol. of Yr., Am. Cancer Soc., 1997, Pharmacist of Yr. Pasco Hernando Pharmacy Assn., 2001.. Mem. Am. Pharm. Assn., Fla. Pharmacy Assn. (bd. dirs. 1981-85, speaker ho. of dels. 1986, chmn., bd. trustees, R.Q. Richards award 1989, Bowl of Hygeia award 1990, Sid Simkowitz Involvement award 1991), Pinellas County Pharmacy Soc. (life; dir. 1968-73, 78-81, 89-91, pres. 1973, 88, Pharmacist of Yr. 1973), Fla. Pharmacy Assn. Found. (pres. 1999), Phi Lambda Sigma. Avocations: gardening, hiking, travel. Office: Eckerds # 2332 Pinellas Park FL 33782

TOWER, LEONARD HARRY, JR. systems programmer; b. Astoria, N.Y., June 17, 1949; s. Leonard Harry and Dorothy Anne (Clouse) T. SB, MIT, 1971. Programmer TE Corp., Boston, 1981-84; system programmer Inter Metrics, Cambridge, Mass., 1984-86; asst. GNUisance, 1986-87; system programmer Boston U., 1987—. Bd. dirs. Free Software Found., Cambridge, 1985—. Co-designer software CNU C-Compiler, 1986. Home: 36 Porter St Somerville MA 02143-2313 Office: Boston U 111 Cummington St Boston MA 02215-2411

TOWER, RONI BETH, psychologist; b. Akron, Ohio, Dec. 11, 1943; d. Arnold Edward Weinstein and Elva Hermoine (Gross) MacRae; children: Jennifer, Daniel. BA, Barnard Coll., N.Y.C., 1964; MS, Yale U., 1977, M in Philosphy, 1979, PhD, 1980. Lic. in clin. psychology, Conn.; diplomate Clin. Psychology Am. Bd. Profl. Psychology. Psychologist Silver Hill Found., New Canaan, Conn., 1979-81; pvt. practice Westport, 1981-97; rsch. affiliate dept. epidemiology Yale U., New Haven, 1995—. Lectr. in psychology Yale U., New Haven, 1981-89, Am. Bd. Profl. Psychology seminar, Washington, 1990; adj. asst. prof. Tchrs. Coll., Columbia U., N.Y.C., 2002—; cons. in field. Cons. editor Jour. of Imagination Cognition and Personality, 1983—; contbr. numerous articles to profl. jours. Active Yale Alumni Fund Bd. Recipient Traineeship award USPHS, 1979-80; postdoctoral fellow Yale Sch. Epidemiology and Pub. Health, 1992-95. Mem.: APA, Internat. Assn. for Relationship Rsch., Gerontol. Soc. Am. Avocations: hiking, travel. Office: 186 Indian Trail Rd New Milford CT 06776

TOWER, SUE WARNCKE, artist; b. Seattle, Mar. 25, 1940; d. Edgar Dean and Ione Althea (Smith) T.; m. Donald Frank Speyer, Dec. 31, 1958 (div. June 1968); children: Stacy, Monte. BFA, Pacific N.W. Coll. Art, 1982. Vis. artist So. Oreg. State Coll., 1996; performing artist (slide presentation) Oreg. Arts Commn. Arts-in-Edn. Program, Salem region, 1996-98; featured artist Oreg. Symphony's Composer Program Cover Art Project, 1997. One woman exhibits include Jacobs Gallery Hult Ctr. Performing Arts, Eugene, Oreg., 1993, Littman Gallery, Portland (Oreg.) State U., 1994, BICC Libr., Oreg. Health Scis. U., 1994, City of Las Vegas Reed Whipple Cultural Ctr., 1996; group exhibits inlcude Bellvue Art Mus., 1992, Galerie Bratri Capku and The Okresni Mus., Prague and Jicin, Czech Republic, 1995, State Capital, Salem, Oreg., 1995, Maryhill Mus. of Art, Goldendale, Wash., 1998, Blackfish Gallery, 1998, Orange County Art Ctr., 1998, Beaverton Arts Commn., 1998, Wheeler (Oreg.) Gallery, 1999, 20th anniversary catalog and exhbn. Blackfish Gallery, 1999. Fundraiser, donor Blackfish Gallery, Pacific N.W. Coll. Art, 1994; donor Cascade AIDS Project Benefit Art Auction, 1996. Avocations: ballet. Office: Apt 213 520 SE Columbia River Dr Vancouver WA 98661-8033 E-mail: towers@ohsu.edu.

TOWER-HARRIS, TABATHA AUMETRA, auditor, writer; b. Lorain, Ohio, Feb. 10, 1967; d. Peter George and Clara Louise Tower; life ptnr. Major Daniel Cole; children: Marcellus Harris, Pharoah Harris. BBA, Tiffin U., 1990; MA, Ball State U., 2000. Auditor Auditor of State of Ohio, Columbus, Ohio, 1990—93; office asst. Ohio EPA, 1996; reporter intern Anderson Herald Bull., Anderson, Ind., 1999; reporter Killeen Daily Herald, Killeen, Tex., 2000; copy editor, reporter, intern Belo, Dallas, 2000—01; auditor Tex. Dept. of Mental Health & Mental Retardation, Austin, 2001—. (Publ. award, 2001); author: Within Your Reach, 2002. Sec. Nat. Assn. Black Acct., Columbus, Ohio, 1992; mem. S.a.v.e., 1994—95. Mem.: Inst. of Internal Auditors, Sigma Delta Sigma. Republican. Baptist. Office: TxD Mental Health & Mental Retardation 909 W 45th Street Bldg 5 Austin TX 78711 Personal E-mail: Teestar@myexcel.com. Business E-Mail: Tabatha.Tower-Harris@mhmr.tx.state.us.

TOWERS, BERNARD LEONARD, medical educator; b. Preston, Eng., Aug. 20, 1922; s. Thomas Francis and Isabella Ellen (Dobson) T.; m. Carole Ilene Lieberman (div. 1992); 1 child, Tiffany Sabrina; children from previous marriage: Helena Marianne, Celia Marguerite, Julie Carole. M.B., Ch.B., U. Liverpool, 1947; MA, U. Cambridge, 1954. House surgeon Royal Infirmary, Liverpool, 1947; lectr. U. Bristol, 1949-50, U. Wales, 1950-54, Cambridge U., 1954-70; fellow Jesus Coll., 1957-70, steward, 1961-64, tutor, 1964-69; dir. med. studies, 1964-70; prof. pediatrics UCLA, 1971-84, prof. anatomy, 1971-91, prof. psychiatry, 1983-91, prof. emeritus anatomy and psychiatry, from 1991, convenor, moderator medicine and soc. forum, 1974-89; pvt. practice integrative medicine, 1991-98; ret., 1998. Co-dir. Program in Medicine, Law and Human Values, 1977-84; cons. Inst. Human Values in Medicine, 1971-84; adv. bd. Am. Teilhard Assn. for Future of Man, 1971-98; v.p. Teilhard Centre for Future Man, London, 1974-98. Author: Teilhard de Chardin, 1966, Naked Ape or Homo Sapiens?, 1969, Concerning Teilhard, 1969; also articles, chpts. on sci. and philosophy.; Editor anat. sect.: Brit. Abstracts Med. Scis, 1954-56, Teilhard Study Library, 1966-70; adv. bd.: Jour. Medicine and Philosophy, 1974-84. Served to capt. RAMC, 1947-49. NIH grantee, 1974-78; NEH grantee, 1977-83 Fellow Cambridge Philos. Soc., Royal Soc. Medicine; mem. Brit. Soc. History of Medicine, Soc. Health and Human Values (pres. 1977-78), Anat. Soc. G.B., Worshipful Soc. Apothecaries London, Am. Assn. for Study Mental Imagery, Western Assn. Physicians, Societe Europeene de Culture Venise. Home: Pacific Palisades, Calif. Died Aug. 19, 2001.

TOWERS, KENNETH DALE, journalism educator; b. Chgo., July 4, 1935; s. Albert M. and Irene D. Towers; m. Rita Kennedy, Feb. 28, 1959 (dec. Nov. 1993); m. Susan J. Culliton, May 13, 2000. B of Philosophy, Northwestern U., 1960. Editor, mng. editor, city editor, reporter Chgo. Sun-Times, 1955-90; exec. dir. Ill. Ins. Info. Svc., Chgo., 1990-92; journalism prof. Northwestern U., Evanston, Ill., 1994—. Staff sgt. U.S. Army, 1957-63. Mem. Soc. Profl. Journalists (regional dir. 1980), Chgo. Coun. Fgn. Rels., Internat. Press Club, Chgo. Press Club (pres. 1976), Chgo. Headline Club (pres. 1972). Roman Catholic. Avocations: reading, writing, spectator sports. Home: 444 W Oakdale Chicago IL 60657 E-mail: k.towers@attbi.com.

TOWERS, ROBERT, restaurant executive; b. N.Y.C., Feb. 24, 1947; s. Albert and Ronnie Torriani; m. Arlene Monash, June 25, 1970; 1 child, Brian. BBA in Acctg., St. Francis Coll., Bklyn., 1968; MS in Acctg., L.I.U., 1972. Acct. Keller & Steinmuller CPAs., N.Y.C., 1968-69; div. controller CBS, Inc., 1969-72; controller B. Lippman Inc., 1972-74; exec. v.p., chief fin. officer Blanchard Mgmt. Corp., 1974-82; exec. Rivers Food, Moonachie, N.J., 1982-83; exec. v.p., COO, dir. ARK Restaurants, N.Y.C., 1983—. Home: 37 Marbourne Dr Mamaroneck NY 10543-1044 Office: ARK Restaurants Corp 85 5th Ave New York NY 10003-3019

TOWERY, CURTIS KENT, lawyer; b. Hugoton, Kans., Jan. 29, 1954; s. Clyde D. and Jo June (Curtis) Towery. BA, Trinity U., 1976; JD, U. Okla., 1979; LLM in Taxation, Boston U., 1989. Mem. Curtis & Blanton, Pauls Valley, Okla., 1980-81; lawyer land and legal dept. Trigg Drilling Co., Oklahoma City, 1981-82; adminstrv. law judge Okla. Corp. Commn., 1982-85; counsel Curtis & Blanton, Pauls Valley, 1985-88; adminstrv. law judge Okla. Dept. Mines, Oklahoma City, 1985-88, assoc. gen. counsel, 1989-92; contracts and purchasing adminstr., atty. Okla. Turnpike Authority, 1992-93; asst. gen. counsel Okla. Corp. Commn., 1993-97; spl. judge City of Oklahoma City, 1997—2000; adminstrv. law judge Okla. Dept. of Labor, 1998, 2002—; v.p., trust officer Bank One Trust, Oklahoma City, 1998-2000; mgr. Cherokee Capital Holdings, 2000—. Assoc. bd. Okla. Mus. Art, 1985—88, Okla. Symphony Orch., 1987—92, Ballet Okla., 1987—92, sec., 1990—91, v.p., 1988—89; mem. Oklahoma City Estate Planning Coun., Ruth Bader Ginsburg Am. Inn. of Ct., 1999—2002. Mem.: ABA, Okla. Bar Assn., Tex. Bar Assn., Faculty Ho., Elks, Rotary, Sigma Nu, Phi Alpha Delta. Democrat. Presbyterian. Avocations: flying, golf, travel, investment analysis. Office: PO Box 14891 Oklahoma City OK 73113-0891 Home: 11300 N Pennsylvania Ave Oklahoma City OK 73120

TOWERY, JAMES E. lawyer; b. Los Alamos, N.Mex., July 12, 1948; s. Lawson E. and Irma (Van Apeldorn) T.; m. Kathryn K. Meier, July 20, 1991; 1 child, Mark J. BA, Princeton U., 1973; JD, Emory U., 1976. Assoc. Morgan Beauzay Hammer, San Jose, Calif., 1977-79; ptnr. Morgan & Towery, 1979-89; assoc. Hoge Fenton Jones & Appel, 1989-90, ptnr., 1990—. Chmn. bd. trustees Alexian Bros. Hosp., San Jose, Calif., 1995-98. Mem. ABA (ho. of dels. 1989-98, standing com. client protection 1996—, chair 1998-00), State Bar Calif. (v.p. and chair discipline com. 1994-95, pres. 1995-96, bd. govs. 1992-96, pres. 1995-96, presiding arbitrator, fee arbitration program 1990-92), Santa Clara County Bar Assn. (counsel 1984-85, treas. 1987, pres. 1989). Office: Hoge Fenton Jones 60 S Market St San Jose CA 95113-2351

TOWLE, LAIRD CHARLES, book publisher; b. Exeter, N.H., Sept. 13, 1933; s. Gerald Charles and Wilma Lois (Buzzell) T.; m. Marlene Ann Towne, Apr. 14, 1956; children: Karen Lee, Joel Andrew, Glenn Corbett, Leslie Kim. BS in Physics, U. N.H., 1955, MS in Physics, 1958; PhD, U. Va., 1962. Rsch. physicist AVCO Corp., Wilmington, Mass., 1962-63, Allis Chalmers Corp., West Allis, Wis., 1963-67; section head Naval Rsch. Lab., Washington, 1967-77, project mgr., 1977-81; chief exec. officer Heritage Books, Inc., Bowie, Md., 1981—. Author: N.H. Genealogical Research Guide, 1973, The Descendants of William Brown and Isabella Kennedy, 1992; editor: Genealogical Periodical Annual Index, 1974—; contbr. articles to profl. jours. Pres. NRL Fed. Credit Union, Washington, 1970-71, treas., 1972-84; pres. Prince George's County General Soc., Bowie, 1970-71; mem. Bowie Adv. Planning Bd., 1987-91. Mem. Nat. Geneal. Soc., N.E. Historic Geneal. Soc., Prince George's County General Soc., Sigma Xi. Avocations: genealogical research, sailing, gardening. Home: 3602 Maureen Ln Bowie MD 20715-2936 Office: Heritage Books Inc 1540 Pointer Ridge Pl Ste E Bowie MD 20716-1800

TOWLE, LELAND HILL, retired government official; b. Boston, Mar. 29, 1931; s. Leland and Bertha Mary (Hill) T.; m. Carol Peterson, June 5, 1953; children— Peter Kimball, Gretchen Towle Maynard, Michele. BS, U. N.H., 1952; MS, M.I.T., 1953; Cert. in Bus. and Mgmt, U. Calif., Berkeley, 1962. Nuclear chemist Stanford Research Inst., Menlo Park, Calif., 1956-59, community systems economist, economist, nuclear economist, 1959-68, mgr. health scis. research, 1968-74; asst. dir. Nat. Center for Alcohol Edn., Arlington, Va., 1974-75. Cons. Medicine in the Pub. Interest, Washington, 1975, Internat. Ctr. for Alcohol Policies, 1995-98—; vis. scientist Nat. Inst. on Alcohol Abuse and Alcoholism, Rckville, Md., 1975-76, dep. dir. office of program devel. and analysis, 1976-77, assoc. dir. office of program devel. and analysis, 1977-81, dir. internat. and intergovtl. affairs, 1981-95; dir. LHT Assocs., Inc., 1995-98. Contbr. articles to profl. jours. Bd. dirs. Med. Resources Found., Palo Alto, Calif., 1972-73. Served with USAF, 1952-56. Mem. Am. Pub. Health Assn., Sci. Research Soc. Am., Am. Nuclear Soc., Am. Chem. Soc., Sigma Xi, Phi Kappa Phi. Home: PO Box 516 Burgess VA 22432

TOWLE, TONY, poet, editor; b. N.Y.C., June 13, 1939; s. Erwin Weible and Mary Rigg T.; children: M. Scott, Rachel L. Student, Georgetown U., 1957-58, NYU, 1962, Columbia U., 1963. Adminstrv. asst. Universal Ltd. Art Editions, West Islip, N.Y., 1964-81; editor, adminstr. asst. Ctr. Entrepreneurial Mgmt., N.Y.C., 1982-85; copy editor Arts Mag., 1988-92; sr. staff writer Nat. Found. Tchg. Entrepreneurship, 1986—. Author: (poetry books) North, 1970 (Frank O'Hara award 1970), New and Selected Poems, 1983, Some Musical Episodes, 1992, The History of the Invitation: New and Selected Poems 1963-2000, 2001. Fellow N.Y. State Coun. Arts, 1975, NEA, 1979, Ingram-Merrill Found., 1982; recipient Avant-Garde poetry prize Gotham Book Mart, 1963, Frank O'Hara award. Avocation: history, making postcards. Home: 75 Hudson St Apt 2 New York NY 10013-2865 E-mail: ttowlepoet@aol.com.

TOWLES, DONALD BLACKBURN, retired publishing executive; b. Lawrenceburg, Ky., Sept. 10, 1927; s. Joseph Sterling and Marjorie (Blackburn) Towles; m. Geraldine Gooch, Dec. 20, 1947 (dec. Nov. 1980); children: Sally Blackburn Towles Clark, Rebecca Neale Towles Brown; m. Julia Mason, Dec. 3, 1981. AB in Journalism, U. Ky., 1948. Asst. dir. publicity, editor In Ky. Mag. Commonwealth of Ky., Frankfort, 1948-55; pub. svc. mgr. Courier-Jour. and Louisville Times Co., Louisville, 1956-66, dir. pub. service and promotion, 1966-71, v.p., 1974-92, v.p., dir. circulation, 1971-76, v.p., dir. pub. affairs, 1976-92. Author: (book) The Press of Kentucky 1787-1994; editor: Newspaper Promotion Handbook, 1983. Chmn. Louisville area chpt. ARC, 1987—89; mem. adv. bd. Salvation Army, 1982—97; elder emeritus Discple of Christ; chmn. program adv. com. Louisville Devel. Program, 1971—80; bd. dirs. Louisville Med. Ctr., 1982—97; pres. Heritage Corp. Louisville, 1982—85; chmn. Thos. D. Clark Found., 2000—; adv. bd. Christian Ch. Homes Ky., 1992—96; chmn. Sr. Citizens East, 1996—97. With U.S. Army, 1952—54, Korea. Named Outstanding Chpt. Vol., Louisville area ARC, 1993, Outstanding State Vol., 1994; named to Ky. Journalism Hall of Fame, 1992; recipient Cmty. Svc. award, Louisville Devel. Com., 1980. Mem.: Soc. Profl. Journalists (pres.Louisville chpt. 1991—92), Ky. Press Assn. (pres. 1982, Pres.'s Cup Leadership 1982, Disting. Svc. award 1987), Internat. Newspaper Promotion Area (pres. 1980—82, Silver Shovel 1983), Journalism Alumni Assn. U. Ky. (pres. 1979—94, Outstanding Alumnus award 1976, All-Am. Alumni award 1994). Democrat. Home: 3536 Norbourne Blvd Louisville KY 40207-3753

TOWLES, STOKLEY PORTER, commercial and investment banking executive; b. St. Louis, Dec. 12, 1935; s. Harold Robert Towles and Margaret (Salmon) Derrick; m. Eleanor Hollingsworth, June 19, 1960 (div. 1983); children: Stokley Porter, Amor Hollingsworth, Holly Kimbrough; m. Jeanne Glass, Dec. 28, 1983. AB, Princeton U., 1957; MBA, Harvard U., 1960. With Brown Bros. Harriman & Co., Boston, 1960—, asst. mgr., 1964-67, dep. mgr., 1967-69, mgr., 1969-78, ptnr., 1978—. Bd. dirs. Groveland Mutual Ins. Co., Auto-HomePage Ins. Agy., Dorchester Mut. Ins., Dedham, Brown Bros. Harriman S.A., Luxembourg, Brown Bros. Harriman Trustee Svcs. (Ireland) Ltd., Dublin; corporator Dedham Instn. for Savs.; mem. Dean's Com. Internat. Devel. John F. Kennedy Sch. Govt. Harvard U. Overseer Boys and Girls Clubs, Boston, 1965, Vincent Meml. Hosp., Boston, 1978, Noble and Greenough Sch., Dedham, 1985, Mus. Fine Arts, Boston; treas. St. Philip's

Ch.; trustee Sears Found., Com. for Econ. Devel. Mem. Somerset Club, The Country Club (Brookline, Mass; gov. 1967-73), Phi Beta Kappa. Avocations: tennis, golf, jogging, reading. Office: Brown Bros Harriman & Co 40 Water St Boston MA 02109-3661

TOWNE, ALAN RAYMOND, neurologist, educator; b. Malden, Mass., July 9, 1948; s. Allen Newman and Carmelia (Foskin) T.; m. Elizabeth Ann Hull. BA, Hobart Coll., 1970; Cert. d'etudes in French Lit., U. d'Anger, France, 1972; MD with honors, U. Aix-Marseille, France, 1981. Diplomate Am. Bd. Psychiatry and Neurology; lic. MD, Va. Intern in neurology Hosp. Ste. Anne, Toulon, France, 1979-80; fellow in neuroimaging and neurophysiology U. Aix-Marseille, France, 1980-81; rotating intern Med. Coll. Va., Richmond, 1981-82, resident in neurology, chief resident in neurology, 1982-85, 84-85, fellow in neurophysiology, 1985-86, asst. prof. neurology dept. neurology, 1986-94, assoc. prof. neurology, 1994—, co-dir. clin. neurophysiology labs., 1994-97, chmn. divsn. clin. neurophysiology, divsn. adult neurology, 1997—2001, chmn. divsn. clin. neurophysiology, 1997—2001, dir. ambulatory EEG svc. monitoring lab., 1988—2001, attending physician epilepsy monitoring unit, 1988—, dir. status epilepticus rsch. program, 1988—, chmn. dept. neurology, 2001—; co-dir. Med. Coll. of Va. Headache Ctr., 1995—; dir. epilepsy program McGuire VA Hosp., 1997—. Chmn. dept. neurology residency recruitment program Med. Coll. of Va., 1989—2000; guest reviewer Epilepsia; guest lectr. in field. Contbr. articles to profl. publs. and chpts. to books. Usher com. Episcopal Ch. of the Redemmer, 1988—, spl. events com., 1992—; organizing com. Boy Scouts Am., Robert E. Lee Coun., 1992; com. chmn. Pack 811, Boy Scouts Am., 1992-98. Grantee, NIH, 1987—, Burrough Wellcome, 1989—90, 1990—, Janssen Rsch. Found., 1989—91, Abbott Labs., 1990, 1991—93, 1992—93, 1992—. Merrell Dow Pharms. Inc., 1990—92, Marion Merrell Dow, 1991—92, 1992—93, Carter-Wallace Labs., 1992—93, 1992—94, Dainippon Pharm. Co., 1993—95, VA, 1997—, Ortho-McNeil, 1998—. Mem. Am. Assn. for Study of Headache, Am. Acad. Neurology, Richmond Acad. Medicine, Am. Epilepsy Soc., Va. Neurol. Soc., Soc. for Neurosci., Am. Electroencephalographic Soc., Am. Acad. Clin. Neurophysiology. Episcopalian. Avocations: swimming, cycling, reading. Home: 2120 Christendom Dr Midlothian VA 23113-6010 Office: Va Commonwealth U Med Coll Va Dept Neurology Box 599 Richmond VA 23298 E-mail: atowne@hsc.vcu.edu.

TOWNE, EDGAR ARTHUR, theologian, educator; b. Albany, N.Y., Feb. 27, 1928; s. Arthur Bethuel and Margaret (Shug) T.; m. Sara Jean Wright, June 14, 1952 (div. 1961); children: Mary Michal, Jonathan Wright, Nathan Arthur; m. Marian Kleinsasser, Dec. 18, 1961; 1 child, Stephen Edgar. BA, Coll. Wooster, 1949; BD, Pitts. Theol. Sem., 1952; MA, U. Chgo., 1962, PhD, 1967. Ordained to ministry Presbyn. Ch. (USA), 1952. Assoc. prof. systematic theology Winebrenner Theol. Sem., Findlay, Ohio, 1962-67; prof. philosophy and religion Findlay Coll., 1967-70; min. Hyde Park Union Ch., Chgo., 1971-75; prof. theology Christian Theol. Sem., Indpls., 1975-93, prof. theology emeritus, 1993—. Vis. prof. theology Christian Theol. Sem., Indpls., 1970-71; vis. scholar Grad. Theol. Union, Berkeley, Calif., 1981-82, Pitts. Theol. Sem., 1988-89; co-moderator com. on pub. ministry Synod of Lincoln Trails, Ind., Ill., 1986-88. Author: Two Types of New Theism: Knowledge of God in the Thought of Paul Tillich and Charles Hartshorne, 1997. Mem. ethics com. Meth. Hosp. Ind., Indpls., 1985-90 Mem. Am. Theol. Soc. (pres. Midwest div. 1986-87), Am. Acad. Religion, Ctr. Process Studies, Soc. Christian Ethics, Highlands Inst. for Am. Religious and Philos. Thought. Democrat. Home: 5129 N Illinois St Indianapolis IN 46208-2613

TOWNES, BOBBY JOE, travel agency executive; b. Pickens, S.C., Aug. 29, 1932; s. James Harold and Coda Lenora (Nations) T.; m. Addie Elise Ray, May 2, 1956; children: John William, Robert Scott. Assoc. BA, Mars Hill (N.C.) Jr. Coll., 1952; BA, Furman U., Greenville, S.C., 1955; diploma, Grad. Sch. Banking, Rutgers U., 1969. V.p. Peoples Nat. Bank, Greenville, 1954-73; exec. v.p. Community Bank, 1973-76; pres. Piedmont Travel, Inc., 1976-93, chmn., 1993—; mng. ptnr. Long Beach Properties, 1992—, Pawleys Promise, Pawleys Island, S.C., 1998—. Chmn. Greenville World of Travel, 1976-80; pres. Piedco Assocs., Greenville, 1973—; mng. ptnr. Cutter Joint Ventures, Hilton Head, S.C., 1972—; pres. Piedco II, 1992—; chmn. Boutique Ltd., 1971-75; instr. Am. Inst. Banking, 1964-70, Charter Life Underwriters, Greenville, 1968; mem. adv. com. KLM Dutch Airlines, Atlanta, 1982, System One Automation, Miami, Fla., 1980, Eastern Airlines, Miami, 1983-87; mem. adv. bd. Mars Plus Data Systems, Miami, 1976-79. Author: Independent Bank Survival, 1968, Townes and Allied Families, 1995. Chmn. United Way, Greenville, 1973; v.p. ARC, Greenville, 1970, Cancer Soc., Greenville, 1966; v.p. Furman U. Alumni Bd., Greenville, 1968-70, Furman U. Paladin Bd., Greenville, 1972-74; mem. Furman U. Com. for Self Study, Greenville, 1976; com. Gov.'s Econ. Coun., Columbia, S.C., 1972; v.p., mem. founders com. Cmty. Concerts, Greenville, 1976; pres. YMCA Youth Guides, Greenville, 1970; v.p., organizer Centurian Club, 1978; mem. nat. alumni bd. Mars Hill Coll., 1998. Recipient Sertoma Internat. Disting. Club Pres. award, 1967, Outstanding Young Mem. of Am. award, 1968, Finalist Ernst & Young Entrepreueur of Yr., 2000. Mem. Am. Inst. Banking (pres. 1964, bd. dirs. 1966), Young Bankers S.C. (bd. dirs. 1965), S.C. Bankers Assn. (bd. dirs. 1969), Greenville Wine Soc. (pres., organzer 1968, 72), S.C. Hist. Soc., Greenville County Hist. Soc., Poinsett Club, Commerce Club, Colonial Club (v.p. 1989, pres. 1991), Sertoma (v.p. 1982, Gold Honor club 1967). Republican. Episcopalian. Avocation: genealogy. Home: 14 Selwyn Dr Greenville SC 29615-1727

TOWNES, CHARLES HARD, physics educator; b. Greenville, S.C., July 28, 1915; s. Henry Keith and Ellen Sumter (Hard) Townes; m. Frances H. Brown, May 4, 1941; children: Linda Lewis, Ellen Screven, Carla Keith, Holly Robinson. BA, BS, Furman U., 1935; MA, Duke U., 1937; PhD, Calif. Inst. Tech., 1939. Mem. tech. staff Bell Telephone Lab., 1939—47; assoc. prof. physics Columbia U., 1948—50, prof. physics, 1950—61; exec. dir. Columbia Radiation Lab., 1950—52, chmn. physics dept., 1952—55; provost and prof. physics MIT, 1961—66, Inst. prof., 1966—67; v.p., dir. research Inst. Def. Analyses, Washington, 1959—61; prof. physics U. Calif., Berkeley, 1967—86, 1994, prof. physics emeritus, 1986—94, prof. grad. sch., 1994—. Guggenheim fellow, 1955—56; Fulbright lectr. U. Paris, 1955—56, U. Tokyo, 1956; dir. Enrico Fermi Internat. Sch. Physics, 1963; Richtmeyer lectr. Am. Phys. Soc., 1959; Scott lectr. U. Cambridge, 1963; Centennial lectr. U. Toronto, 1967; Lincoln lectr., 1972—73; Halley lectr., 1976; Krishnan lectr., 92; Nishina lectr., 92; Weinberg lectr. Oak Ridge (Tenn.) Nat. Lab., 1997; Rajiv Gandhi lectr., 97; Henry Norris Russell lectr. Am. Astron. Soc., 1998; dir. Gen. Motors Corp., 1973—86; dir. Perkin-Elmer Corp., 1966—69; mem. Pres.'s Sci. Adv. Com., 1966—69, vice chmn., 1967—69; chmn. sci. and tech. adv. com. for manned space flight NASA, 1964—70; mem. Pres.'s Com. on Sci. and Tech., 1976; rschr. on nuclear and molecular structure, quantum electronics, interstellar molecules, radio and infrared astrophysics. Author (with A.J. Schawlow): Microwave Spectroscopy; author: Making Waves, 1996, How the Laser Happened. Adventures of a Scientist, 1999; author, co-editor Quantum Electronics, 1960, Quantum Electronics and Coherent Light, 1964, editl. bd. Rev. Sci. Instruments, 1950—52, Phys. Rev., 1951—53, Jour. Molecular Spectroscopy, 1957—60, Procs. NAS, 1978—84, Can. Jour. Physics, 1995—, contbr. articles to sci. publs., patentee masers and lasers. Mem. corp. Woods Hole Oceanographic Instn.; bd. mem. Calif. Inst. Tech., Carnegie Instn. Washington, Ctr. for Theology and Natural Scis., Mount Wilson Inst. Decorated officier Légion d'Honneur (France); named to Nat. Inventors Hall of Fame, 1976, Engring. and Sci. Hall of Fame, 1983; recipient numerous hon. degrees and awards including Nobel prize for Physics, 1964, Stuart Ballantine medal, Franklin Inst., 1962, Thomas Young medal and prize, Inst. Physics and Phys. Soc., Eng., 1963, Disting. Pub. Svc. medal, NASA, 1969, Wilhelm Exner award, Austria, 1970, Niels Bohr Internat. Gold medal, 1979, Nat. medal of Sci., 1982, Berkeley citation, U. Calif., 1986, Common Wealth award, 1993, ADION medal, Obs. Nice, 1995, Mendel award, Villanova U., Frank Annunzio award, Christopher Columbus Fellowship Found., 1999, Rabindranath Tagore Birth Centenary plaque, Asiatic Soc., 1999. Fellow: IEEE (life medal of honor 1967), Calif. Acad. Scis., Indian Nat. Sci. Acad., Optical Soc. Am. (Mees medal 1968), Am. Phys. Soc. (pres. 1967, Plyler prize 1977, Frederick Ives medal 1996); mem.: NAE (founders award 2000), NAS (coun. 1968—72, 1978—81, chmn. space sci. bd. 1970—73, Comstock award 1959, Carty medal 1962), N.Y. Acad. Scis., Max-Planck Inst. Physics and Astrophysics (fgn. mem.), Pontifical Acad. Scis., Russian Acad. Scis. (fgn. mem., Lomonosov medal 2000), Royal Soc. (fgn. mem.), Am. Acad. Arts and Scis., Am. Astron. Soc., Am. Philos. Soc. Office: U Calif Dept Physics 366 Leconte # 7200 Berkeley CA 94720-0001 E-mail: cht@sunspot.ssl.berkeley.edu.

TOWNS, DONALD LIONEL, engineering executive; b. Sioux City, Iowa, Mar. 8, 1935; s. William Lionel and Violet V. (Robinson) T.; m. Joyce Harper, June 18, 1960; children: Jean Linda, Erik Donald. BChemE, Ga. Inst. Tech., 1957; PhD, U. Wis., 1962; cert. in bus. mgmt., Harvard U., 1985. Rsch. engr. FMC Corp., Princeton, N.J., 1962-73, team leader Balt., 1973-74, operating supr. Middleport, N.Y., 1974-80; project mgr. Herzog Hart Corp., Boston, 1990-93; engring. mgr. Carlson Process Co., Cochituate, Mass., 1985-88; mgr. engring. Facility Group, Framingham, 1988-90; project mgr. Herzog Hart Corp., Boston, 1990-93, Facility Engrs. Inc., Smyrna, Ga., 1994-97, ret., 1997. 1st lt. U.S. Army, 1958. Mem. Am. Chem. Soc., Am. Inst. Chem. Engrs., Chem. Soc. London. Home and Office: 112 Studley Rd South Yarmouth MA 02664-2906

TOWNS, EDOLPHUS, congressman; b. Chadbourn, N.C., July 21, 1934; m. Gwendolyn Forbes, 1960; children: Darryl, Deidra. BS, N.C. A & T State U., Greensboro, 1956; MSW., Adelphi U., Garden City, N.Y., 1973; PhD (hon.), N.C. A&T, Shaw U. Tchr. Medgar Evers Coll., Bklyn., N.Y.C. Pub. Schs.; dep. hosp. adminstr., 1965-71; dep. pres. Borough of Bklyn., 1976-82; mem. U.S. Congress from 11th N.Y. dist. Washington, 1983—91; mem. U.S. Congress from 10th N.Y. dist., 1992—; mem. energy and commerce com., govt. reform com. Mem. adv. council Boy Scouts Am.; active Salvation Army. Served with U.S. Army, 1956-58. Named to Acad. of Distinction Adelphi U. Mem. Kiwanis, Phi Beta Sigma. Democrat. Office: US Ho of Reps 2232 Rayburn Ho Office Bldg Washington DC 20515-0001*

TOWNSEND, ALAIR ANE, publisher, municipal official; b. Rochester, N.Y., Feb. 15, 1942; d. Harold Eugene and Dorothy (Sharpe) T.; m. Robert Harris, Dec. 31, 1970 (div. 1994). BS, Elmira Coll., 1962; MS, U. Wis., 1964; postgrad., Columbia U., 1970-71. Assoc. dir. budget priorities Com. on Budget, U.S. Ho. of Reps., Washington, 1975-79, dep. asst. sec. for budget HEW, 1979-80, asst. sec. for mgmt. and budget, 1980-81; dir. N.Y.C. Office Mgmt. and Budget, 1981-85; dep. mayor for fin. and econ. devel. City of N.Y., 1985-89; pub. Crain's N.Y. Bus., N.Y.C., 1989—. Bd. dirs. Armor Holdings, Inc.; bd. overseers Tchrs. Ins. and Annuity Assn.-Coll. Retirement Equities Fund; former mem. adv. bd. Ford Motor Credit Corp. Former vice-chmn., trustee Elmira Coll.; former mem. Coun. Fgn. Rels.; former bd. govs. Am. Stock Exch.; chmn. Am. Woman's Econ. Devel. Corp.; former chmn. N.Y.C. Sports Commn.; former chmn. Consol. Corp. Fund of Lincoln Ctr.; bd. dirs. Lincoln Ctr. Mem. Women's Forum (bd. dirs.), N.Y.C. Partnership C. of C., N.Y. State Bus. Coun. (past vice chmn.), Econ. Club N.Y. (bd. dirs.). Office: Crain's NY Bus 711 3d Ave New York NY 10017

TOWNSEND, ALVIN NEAL, artist; b. Rock Island, Tex., Oct. 26, 1934; s. Archie Lee and Synthia Ellen (Westbook) T.; m. Phyllis Virginia Keyes (div.); 1 child, Phyllis Lynn; m. Betsy Rose Brown; children: Brita, Lissi, Shana, Kristinn. BFA, U. N.Mex., 1961, MA, 1962. Base crafts dir. U.S. Civil Svc., Sandia Base, N.Mex., 1962-69, post crafts dir. Ft. Belvoir, Va., 1969-70; prof. art edn. U. N.Mex., 1970-91, prof. emeritus, 1991. Artist-in-residence Otago Polytech., Dunedin, New Zealand, 1988; vis. prof. art. No. Ariz. U., Flagstaff, 1984; vis. artist New Zealand Soc. of Potters, New Zealand, 1988. More than 250 exhbns., including Mus. of Internat. Folk Art, 1959, 60, 62, 66, Mus. of Fine Arts, U. N.Mex., 1968, Tweed Mus., Duluth, Minn., 1975, Salzbrand, Galerie Handwerkskammer, Koblenz, Germany, 1983, 86, 89, 93, IX Bienne de Ceramique d'Art, Vallauris, France, 1984, Fletcher Brownbuilt Exhbn., Auckland, New Zealand, 1982, Clay Az Art, Rotorua, New Zealand, 1987, As 220 Exchange, Providence, R.I., 1997, Free Spirits Mus. of the Horse, Ruidoso, N.Mex., 1998, Durango Art Ctr., Durango, Colo., 1999, Harwood Art Ctr., Albuquerque, N.Mex., 1999. Named Artist of Month Binney & Smith, Inc., 1997; faculty rsch. grant U. N.Mex., 1986-87, 82-83, 79-80. Democrat. Avocations: camping, fishing. Home: 2583 Ramirez Rd SW Albuquerque NM 87105-4149

TOWNSEND, ANN VAN DEVANTER, foundation administrator, art historian; b. Washington, June 20, 1936; d. John Ward and Ellen Keys (Ramsey) Cutler; m. Willis Van Devanter, Dec. 27, 1958 (div. May 1974); 1 child, Susan Earling Van Devanter (Mrs. John Philip Newell); m. Lewis Raynham Townsend, Dec. 10, 1983. BA, Brown U., 1958; MA, George Washington U., 1975. Grantsmanship ctr. cert. Guest curator Balt. Mus. Art, 1971-77; dir. cultural affairs Chevy Chase (Md.) Savs. & Loan, Inc., 1978-81; dir. spl. partnership projects NEA, Washington, 1982-83; founding pres. The Trust for Mus. Exhbns., 1984—. Organizer over 60 nat. and internat. mus. exhbns. for more than 240 mus. Co-author: Self-Portraits of American Artists, 1670-1973, 1974; author: Anywhere So Long As There Be Freedom, 1975, Two Hundred Years of American Painting, 1976; contbr. articles to mags. U.S. commr. Cagnes-Sur-Mer Internat. Afts Festival, France, 1977, 78; mem. women's com. Washington Opera, 1993—; bd. dirs. Friends of Corcoran Gallery of Art, Washington, 1975-76, Strathmore Hall Arts Ctr., Rockville, Md., 1978-80, Am. Swedish Hist. Mus., Phila., 1987-89, U.S. Com. World Fedn. Friends of Mus., 1995—. Acad. grad. fellow Johns Hopkins Sch. Advanced Internat. Studies, 1958. Mem. Nat. Soc. Arts & Letters, Am. News Women's Club, Soc. Women Goegraphers, Sulgrave Club, Cosmos Club. Episcopalian. Avocations: backgammon, gourmet cooking, ballroom dancing. Office: The Trust for Mus Exhbns 1424 16th St NW Ste 600 Washington DC 20036-2239

TOWNSEND, BARBARA, actress; b. Oakland, Calif. d. Charles Edward Townsend and Anna Woodworth Kalkman; m. John Jackson Shaffer III, June 25, 1938 (dec. 1944); 1 child, Sandra Shaffer Van Doren; m. William Louis Wheeler Jr., May 27, 1958 (dec. 1969). BA, U. Calif., Berkeley; student, Am. Acad. Dramatic Arts, N.Y.C. Tchr. Sch. of Drama, Nairobi, Kenya, 1970-75. Actress appearing in feature films Hard to Kill, Say Anything, Motel Vacancy, Good Cop, (TV shows) Star Trek, Divorce Court, Nikki and Alexander, After Mash, Murder She Wrote, Aaron's Way, Hunter, St. Elsewhere, Mr. Belvedere, Highway to Heaven, Remington Steele, Little House on the Prairie, Streets of San Francisco, As the World Turns, Guiding Light, Quantum Leap, Civil Wars, Northern Exposure, Sisters, (Broadway shows) The Rose Tatoo, Best of Spirits, As You Like It, (theatre) Children's World Theatre, Am. Theatre Wing, Orpheus Descending, Ann of Green Gables, Nairobi, Talk Back Taper II, L.A. Vol. recorder Braille Inst., L.A., 1978-94; vol. Bedside Network, N.Y.C., 1960-69; reader to Headstart children, handicapped adults in retirement home, 1994—; rschr. Spl. Women's Aux. of Navy, Washington, 1941-44; mentor for reading in elem. sch., 1996—. Mem. Actors Equity Assn., Screen Actors Guild, Am. Fedn. Radio and TV Artists. Democrat. Avocations: attending opera, symphony, ballet, reading. Office: Artists Group Inc 10100 Santa Monica Blvd Los Angeles CA 90067-4003

TOWNSEND, BYRON EDWIN, lawyer; b. Louisville, Feb. 27, 1956; s. Julius Charles III and Jeryl Townsend; m. Vicki L. Stolberg, Apr. 4, 1987. BA, U. Fla., 1977, JD, 1980. Bar: Fla. 1981, U.S. Dist. Ct. (mid. dist.) Fla. 1985; bd. cert. Fla. Bar Worker's Compensation. Assoc. Blake & Assocs., Tampa, Fla., 1982-84; staff counsel Aetna Casualty & Surety Co., 1984-87; pvt. practice, 1987-90; ptnr. Barrs, Willamson, Stolberg Townsend Gonzalez, P.A., 1990—. Mem. ABA, Fla. Bar Assn., Hillsborough County Bar Assn. (bar workers compensation sect., trial lawyers sect.), Assn. Trial Lawyers Am., Assn. Fla. Trial Lawyers. Avocations: volleyball, tennis, stamp collecting. Home: 248 Blanca Ave Tampa FL 33606-3328 Office: 2503 W Swann Ave Tampa FL 33609-4017

TOWNSEND, CHRISTOPHER GORDON, lawyer; b. New Bedford, Mass., June 9, 1947; s. Christopher Gordon and Rita Mary (Fitzgerald) T.; m. Christine P. Davis, June 17, 1972; children: Christopher IV, Jessica C. BA, Providence Coll., 1969; JD, Georgetown U., 1975. Bar: D.C. 1975. Jud. clk. Supreme Ct. Del., Wilmington, 1975-76; atty. U.S. Dept. Justice, Washington, 1976-77, U.S. SEC, Washington, 1977-82; asst. gen. counsel Marriott Corp., Bethesda, Md., 1982-93; dep. gen. counsel Host Marriott Corp., 1993-96, gen. counsel, 1996-01; ptnr. Patton, Boggs LLP, 2001—. Editor: Am. Criminal Law Rev., 1974-75. Lt. USN, 1969-72. Mem. ABA. Office: Patton Boggs LLP 8484 Westpark Dr Mc Lean VA 22102

TOWNSEND, EARL C., JR. lawyer, writer; b. Indpls., Nov. 9, 1914; s. Earl Cunningham and Besse (Kuhn) T.; m. Emily Macnab, Apr. 3, 1947 (dec. Mar. 1988); children: Starr, Vicki M., Julia E. (Mrs. Edward Goodrich Dunn Jr.), Earl Cunningham III, Clyde G. Student, De Pauw U., 1932-34; AB, U. Mich., 1936, JD, 1939. Bar: Ind. 1939, Mich. 1973, U.S. Supreme Ct. 1973, U.S. Ct. Appeals (4th, 5th, 6th, 7th cirs.), U.S. Dist. Ct. (no. and so. dists.) Ind., U.S. Dist. Ct. (ea. dist.) Va., U.S. Dist. Ct. (ea. dist.) Mich. Sr. ptnr. Townsend & Townsend, Indpls., 1941-64, Townsend, Hovde & Townsend, Indpls., 1964-84, Townsend & Townsend, Indpls., 1984—. Dep. prosecutor, Marion County, Ind., 1942-44; radio-TV announcer WIRE, WFBM, WFBM-TV, Indpls., 1940-53, 1st TV announcer Indpls. 500 mile race, 1949, 50; Big Ten basketball referee, 1940-47; lectr. trial tactics U. Notre Dame, Ind. U., U. Mich., 1968-79; chmn. faculty seminar on personal injury trials Ind. U. Sch. Law, U. Notre Dame Sch. Law, Valparaiso Sch. Law, 1981; mem. Com. to Revise Ind. Supreme Ct. Pattern Jury Instrns., 1975-83; lectr. Trial Lawyers 30 Yrs. Inst., 1986; counsel atty gen., 1988-92. Author: Birdstones of the North American Indian, 1959; editor: Am. Assn. Trial Lawyers Am. Jour., 1964-88; contbr. articles to legal and archeol. jours.; composer (waltz) Moon of Halloween. Trustee Cathedral High Sch., Indpls., Eiteljorg Mus. Am. Indian and Western Art, Cale J. Holder Scholarship Found. Ind. U. Law Sch.; life trustee, bd. dirs., mem. fin. and bldg. coms. Indpls. Mus. Art; life trustee Ind. State Mus.; founder, dir. Meridian St. Found.; mem. dean's coun. Ind. U.; founder, life fellow Roscoe Pound/Am. Trial Lawyers Found., Harvard U.; fellow Meth. Hosp. Found. Recipient Ind. Univ. Writers Conf. award, 1960, Hanson H. Anderson medal of honor Arsenal Tech. Schs., Indpls., 1971; named to Coun. Sagamores of Wabash, 1969; Rector scholar, 1934, Ind. Basketball Hall of Fame; hon. chief Black River-Swan Creek Saginaw-Chippewa Indian tribe. Fellow Internat. Acad. Trial Lawyers, Internat. Soc. Barristers, Ind. Bar Found. (life trustee, disting. fellow award); mem. ASCAP, ABA (com. on trial techniques 1964-76, aviation and space 1977—), Assn. Trial Lawyers Am. (v.p.), Ind. State Bar Assn. (Golden Career award 1989), Indpls. Bar Found. (disting. charter 1986), Ind. Trial Lawyers Assn. (pres. 1965, pres. Coll. Fellows 1984-90, Lifetime Achievement award 1992), Am. Bd. Trial Advs. (diplomate, pres. Ind. chpt. 1980-86), Am. Arbitration Assn. (nat. arbitrators panel), Am. Judicature Soc., State Bar of Mich. (Champion of Justice award 1989), Roscommon County Bar Assn., 34th Jud. Cir. Bar Assn., Bar Assn. 7th Fed. Cir. (bd. govs. 1966-68), Mich. Trial Lawyers Assn., Soc. Mayflower Descendants (gov. 1947-49), Ind. Hist. Soc., Marion County/Indpls. Hist. Soc. (bd. dirs.), U. Mich. Pres. Club, U. Mich. Victors Club (founder, charter mem.), Trowel and Brush Soc. (hon.), Genuine Indian Relic Soc. (founder, pres., chmn. frauds com.), The Players Club, Key Biscayne Yacht Club, Columbia Club, Masons (33 degree), Shriners, Delta Kappa Epsilon, Phi Kappa Phi. Republican. Methodist. Avocations: art, Indian relics. Home: 5008 N Meridian St Indianapolis IN 46208-2624

TOWNSEND, EDWARD ALLEN, banker; b. Brazil, Mar. 9, 1942; came to U.S., 1954; s. Charles H.T. and Elsa (Seiffert) T., Jr.; m. Patricia Nulty, June 26, 1965 (div. 1984); children: Jennifer, Leslie, Lara; m. Barbara Ann Newman, May 25, 1985; children: Hilary, Lainey. BA in Econs., U. Tex., 1964, BBA in Fin., 1965, MBA in Fin, 1967. Chmn., pres., chief exec. officer Local Fed. and Local Am. Bank, Okla., 1985—; formerly with First Nat. Bank in Dallas, v.p., 1970-73, sr. v.p., 1973-79, exec. v.p., 1979, chief fin. officer, 1979, vice chmn., chief fin. officer, 1984; vice chmn., chief adminstrv. officer, pres. Houston Citizens Bank, 1979-83, chmn., chief exec. officer, 1983-84. Bd. dirs. Fed. Home Loan Bank Topeka. Chmn. United Way Oklahoma City; bd. dirs. Last Frontier coun. Boy Scouts Am., Presbyn. Health Found., Am. Hearth Assn. Mem. Oklahoma City C. of C. (vice chmn.). Address: 910 E 38 1/2 St Austin TX 78751-5217

TOWNSEND, HAROLD GUYON, JR. publishing company executive; b. Chgo., Apr. 11, 1924; s. Harold Guyon and Anne Louise (Robb) T.; AB, Cornell U., 1948; m. Margaret Jeanne Keller, July 28, 1951; children: Jessica, Julie, Harold Guyon III. Advt. salesman Chgo. Tribune, 1948-51; gen. mgr. Keller-Heartt Co., Clarendon Hills, Ill., 1951-62; pub. Santa Clara (Calif.) Jour., 1962-64; chmn. bd. dirs., pub. Dispatch-Tribune newspaper Townsend Communications, Inc., Kansas City, Mo., 1964-99. Chmn., Suburban Newspaper Research Commn., 1974-99; dir. Certified Audit Bur. of Circulation, 1968-72. del. Rep. Nat. Conv., 1960; chmn. Mission Hills Rep. Com., 1966-77; bd. dirs. Kansas City Jr. Achievement, 1966-68, Kansas City council Girl Scouts U.S.A., 1969-71, Kansas City council Boy Scouts Am., 1974, Kansas City chpt. ARC, 1973-79, Kansas City Starlight Theater, Clay County (Mo.) Indsl. Commn.; treas., trustee Park Coll., Parkville, Mo., 1970-78. Mem. adv. com. North Kansas City Hosp.; bd. dirs. Taxpayers Research of Mo., 1978—, Nelson Gallery Friends of Art, 1980-85. Served with inf. AUS, World War II. Mem. Kansas City Advt. and Sales Club, Kansas City Press Club, Suburban Press Found. (pres. 1969-71), Suburban Newspapers Am. (pres. 1976-77), Kansas City Printing Industries Assn. (pres., dir.), Printing Industries of Am. (pres. non-heatset web sect. 1980-82), North Kansas City C. of C. (dir., pres. 1964-70), Univ. Assocs. (treas. 1977-80), Sigma Delta Chi, Pi Delta Epsilon, Phi Kappa Psi. Clubs: University (treas. 1977); Indian Hills Country; Hinsdale (Ill.) Golf; Field (Sarasota, Fla.). Deceased. Home: Prairie Vlg KS

TOWNSEND, IRENE FOGLEMAN, accountant, tax specialist; b. Birmingham, Ala., May 29, 1932; d. James Woods and Virginia (Martin) Fogleman; m. Kenneth Ross Townsend, Mar. 18, 1951; children: Marietta Irene, Martha Shapard, Kenneth Ross Jr., Elizabeth Buchanan. BSBA, East Carolina U., 1980. CPA, N.C., Va. Acct. Norwood P. Whitehurst & Assocs., Greenville, N.C., 1981-86; asst. v.p. Tenet Healthcare Corp., Vienna, 1995—; v.p. NME Psychiatric Hosps., Inc., 2001—. Fellow AICPA, N.C. Assn. CPAs, D.C. Inst. CPAs, Va. Soc. CPAs; mem. DAR, N.C. Soc. Daus. of Colonial Wars, Colonial Dames 17th Century. Democrat. Episcopalian (lay reader, chalice bearer). Avocations: bicycling, genealogy. Home: 2521 Paxton St Lake Ridge VA 22192-3414 Office: Tenet Healthcare Corp 501 Church St NE Ste 301 Vienna VA 22180-4734 E-mail: irene_townsend@hotmail.com.

TOWNSEND, JAMES DOUGLAS, accountant; b. Kokomo, Ind., May 20, 1959; s. Lemon Dale and Diamond Sue (Turner) T.; m. Ariane Antonia Atkins, May 7, 1983 (div. July 1992); 1 child, Bradley Alan; m. Mildred Ann Kurtz, Oct. 18, 1992; children: Heather Marie, Tyler Neil. Student, Ind. U., 1977, Ind. State U., 1977-78; BS in Acctg. summa cum laude, Ball State U., 1980. CPA, Ind., Colo.; cert. mgmt. acct. Acctg. intern Chevrolet Motor Div. Gen. Motors Corp., Muncie, Ind., 1979; staff acct. Price Waterhouse, Indpls., 1980-83, sr. acct., 1983-85, mgr., 1985-88, sr. mgr., 1988-89; contr. Raffensperger, Hughes & Co., Inc., 1989-92, asst. treas., 1991-95, asst. v.p., 1991-92, v.p. fin., 1992-95; sr. v.p., chief adminstrv. officer Nat City Investments, Inc., 1995-99; pres. Fin. Mgmt., Inc., 1994—; sr. v.p. Madison Ave. Capital Group LLC, 1999-2000; CFO Colo.'s Ocean Journey, 2000-01, exec. v.p., COO, 2001—; pres., CEO Colo.'s Ocean Journey , 2001—. Coord. Seek Program Ind. U., Indpls., 1985-86; cons. project bus. Jr. Achievement, Indpls., 1986; treas., asst. sec. Sagamore Funds Trust, 1991-94; treas. Raffensberger Hughes Capitol Corp., 1991-94, RHGP, Inc., 1993-95. Baseball coach Pike Twp. (Ind.) Youth League, 1986-87; cubmaster Pike Twp. Coun. Boy Scouts Am., 1987-88; mem. Pike Twp. Sch. Bd., 1988-92, v.p., 1989-90, pres., 1990-92; bd. dirs. Project I-Star, 1992-94, Crooked Creek Villages Homeowners Assn., 1998-99; fin. com. Highlands Ranch Cmty. Assn., 2000—. Fellow Life Mgmt. Inst.; mem. AICPA, Inst. Mgmt. Accts., Ind. CPA Soc. (vice chmn. edn. com. 1988-89, chmn. 1989-90, chmn. govt. rels. com. 1999), Colo. Soc. CPAs, Indpls. C. of C. (SKLA exec. coun. 1992-94), Swallow Hill Music Assn. Republican. Avocations: boating, golf, guitar, chess. Home: 10011 S Heywood Ln Highlands Ranch CO 80130-8860

TOWNSEND, JAMES WILLIS, computer scientist; b. Evansville, Ind., Sept. 9, 1936; s. James Fredrick and Elma Elizabeth (Galloway) T.; m. Leona Jean York, Apr. 20, 1958; 1 child, Eric Wayne. BS in Arts and Scis., Ball State U., 1962; PhD, Iowa State U., 1970. Rsch. technologist Neuromuscular div. Mead Johnson, Evansville, 1957-60; chief instr. Zoology dept. Iowa State U., Ames, 1965-67; asst. prof. Ind. State U., Evansville, 1967-72; cons. electron microscopy Mead Johnson Rsch. Ctr., 1971-73; mgr. neurosci. Neurosci. Lab., Kans. State U., Manhattan, 1974-76; head electron microscopy Nat. Ctr. for Toxicology Rsch., Jefferson, Ark., 1976-82; dir. electron microscopy U. Ark. Med. Sci., Little Rock, 1982-87; dir. computer ops. pathology dept. Univ. Hosp., 1987-99, sr. analyst clin. info. sys., 1999-2000; sr. cons. Soft Computer Consultants, Palm Harbor, Fla., 2000—. Workshop presenter Am. Soc. Clin. Pathology, 1980-81, Nat. Soc. Histotechnologists, 1984-88. With USAF, 1957.

Contbr. articles to profl. jours.; reviewer Scanning Electron Microscopy, 1977-78. Nat. Def. fellowship NDEA, Iowa State U., 1962-65; recipient Chgo. Tribune award Chicago Tribune, 1955. Mem. Sigma Xi, Sigma Zeta. Baptist. Avocations: genealogy, American Civil War, scuba. Home and Office: 116 Trelon Way Little Rock AR 72223

TOWNSEND, JERRIE LYNNE, librarian; b. Pine Bluff, Ark., July 19, 1951; d. Charles Ray Sr. and Billie Jean (Morgan) Jones; m. Dennis Ewell Townsend, June 15, 1975 (dec. June 1980). BS, Ark. State U., 1973; MLIS, U. Okla., 1987. Cert. profl. sec. Sec. divsn. art Ark. State U., Jonesboro, 1973-74; adminstrv. sec. Steelship Corp., Pine Bluff, Ark., 1974; tchr. 5th grade Coleman Middle Sch., 1974-75; sec. I Mgmt. Devel. Ctr. U. Tulsa, Okla., 1975-76; sec. II City of Tulsa, 1976-78, adminstrv. sec., 1978-80; exec. sec. Hilti, Inc., Tulsa, 1980, statis. asst., 1980-82, sales promotion, mktg. analyst, 1982-87, mngr. sales planning, 1987-96; office asst. White River Irrigation Dist., Stuttgart, Ark., 1997-98; librarian Phillips C.C. of U. of Ark., 1998—. Mem. Citizen's Com. MTTA/City of Broken Arrow (Okla.) Bus. Svc., 1977-79, Office Sci. Adv. Com. Tulsa Jr. Coll., 1980-83, Civic Ctr. Com., Broken Arrow, 1988-90, Broken Arrow City Coun., 1990-97, Spl. Transp. Adv. Com., Tulsa, 1995-96; pres. Friends of Broken Arrow Libr., 1984-85; bd. dirs. Indian Nation Coun. Govts., Tulsa, 1992-97; sec. bd. trustees Broken Arrow Comty. Playhouse, 1992-94; vice mayor Broken Arrow, 1992-97; v.p. Broken Arrow Hist. Soc., 1992-93, pres., 1994-95; libr. Broken Arrow Geneal. Soc., 1985, sec., 1992-94; mem. Grand Prairie Hist. Soc.; pres. Grand Prairie Geneal. Soc., 1998—; treas. United Meth. Women First United Meth. Ch., Stuttgart, 1999—. Named Competent Toastmaster, Out-to-Lunch Toastmasters, Tulsa, 1985; elected to Broken Arrow Hall of Fame, 1996. Mem. Profl. Secs. Internat. (rec. sec. Tulsa chpt. 1979-80, pres. 1980-81, Outstanding Mem. of Yr. 1983), Stuttgart Bus. and Profl. Women (sec. 1998—), Chi Omega (philanthropic chair Grand Prairie Alumni chpt.) Democrat. Methodist. Avocations: genealogy, historical research.

TOWNSEND, JOHN MICHAEL, lawyer; b. West Point, N.Y., Mar. 21, 1947; s. John D. and Vera (Nachman) T.; m. Frances M. Fragos, Oct. 8, 1994; children, James E., Patrick M. BA, Yale U., 1968, JD, 1971. Bar: N.Y. 1972, U.S. Dist. Ct. (so. and ea. dists.) N.Y. 1975, U.S. Ct. Appeals (2nd cir.) 1975, U.S. Supreme Ct. 1975, U.S. Ct. Appeals (8th cir.) 1982, U.S. Ct. Appeals (7th and 10th cirs.) 1986, D.C. 1990, U.S. Dist. Ct. D.C. 1990, U.S. Ct. Appeals (D.C. cir.) 1990, U.S. Ct. Appeals (4th cir.) 1991, U.S. Ct. Appeals (fed. cir.) 2000, U.S. Ct. Appeals (11th cir.) 2001, U.S. Ct. Fed. Claims, 2000. Assoc. Hughes Hubbard & Reed, LLP, N.Y.C., 1971-73, 75-80, ptnr., 1980—; assoc. Hughes Hubbard & Reed, Paris, 1973-74. Bd. dirs., exec. com., chair law com. Am. Arbitration Assn.; trustee U.S. Coun. Internat. Bus. Editl. bd. ADR Currents. 1st lt. USAR, 1971-75. Mem. ABA, Am. Law Inst., Internat. Bar Assn., Assn. Bar City N.Y., Union Internat. des Avocats, Univ. Club, Yale Club (N.Y.C.). Democrat. Episcopalian. Office: Hughes Hubbard & Reed LLP 1775 I St NW Washington DC 20006-2401 Fax: (202) 721-4646. E-mail: townsend@hugheshubbard.com.

TOWNSEND, JOHN WILLIAM, JR. physicist, retired federal aerospace agency executive; b. Washington, Mar. 19, 1924; s. John William and Elenore (Eby) T.; m. Mary Irene Lewis, Feb. 7, 1948; children: Bruce Alan, Nancy Dewitt, John William III, Megan Lewis; m. JoAnn C. Clayton, Sept. 17, 1996. BA, Williams Coll., 1947, MA, 1949, ScD, 1961. With Naval Research Lab., 1949-55, br. head, 1955-58; with NASA, 1958-68, dep. dir. Goddard Space Flight Ctr., 1965-68; dep. adminstrn. Environmental Scis. Services Adminstrn., 1968-70; asso. adminstr. Nat. Oceanic and Atmospheric Adminstrn., 1970-77; pres. Fairchild Space and Electronics Co., 1977-82; v.p. Fairchild Industries, 1979-85; pres. Fairchild Space Co., 1983-85; sr. v.p. Fairchild Industries, 1985-87; chmn. bd. Am. Satellite Co., 1985, sr. v.p., exec. aerospace group, 1987, exec. v.p., 1987; dir. NASA Goddard Space Flight Ctr., 1987-90; ret., 1990. Mem. U.S. Rocket, Satellite Rsch. Panel, 1950-60; chmn. space applications bd. NRC, 1985-87; bd. dirs., trustee Telos Corp., 1990-92; mem. adv. bd. Loral Corp., 1990-92; mem. coms. NRC, 1990—; bd. dirs CTA, Inc., 1990-98. Author numerous papers, reports in field. Pres. town council, Forest Heights, Md., 1951-55. Served with USAAF, 1943-46. Recipient Profl. Achievement award Engrs. and Architects Day, 1957; Meritorious Civilian Service award Navy Dept., 1957; Outstanding Leadership medal NASA, 1962; Distinguished Service medal, 1971, 90; recipient Arthur S. Fleming award Fed. Govt., 1963, Edward A. Flinn III award, 1999. Fellow AIAA, AAAS, Am. Meteorol. Soc.; mem. NAE (com. 1990-93), Am. Phys. Soc., Am . Geophys. Union. (fin. com. 1991-98, Edward A. Flinn III award, 1999), Internat. Astronautical Fedn. (mem., tru stee internat., acad. astronautics), Sigma Xi. Home: 6532 79th St Cabin John MD 20818-1201

TOWNSEND, JUNE H. foreign language educator; b. Dunbar, W. Va. d. Lawrence Hobart and Naomi Jane Hickman; m. Horace Raymond Townsend; children:Horace Raymond III, Timi Jane, Thomas Lawrence, Christopher Randolph. MEd, Xavier U., Cin., 1973; MA, Ohio State U., 1988, PhD, 1993. Tchr. pub. schs. of Ohio, 1960-84; tchg. assoc. Ohio State U., Columbus, 1986-89; prof. of Spanish Wilmington (Ohio) Coll., 1989—. Spkr. Congress Internat., Madrid, 1995, U. Louisville, 1994, 1993, U. Cin., 1993, Duquesne U., Pitts., 1993, AATSP Ann. Mtg., Cancun, Mexico, 1992, E. Carolina U., Greenville, N.C., 1991. Contbg. author: Ency., 1999; author: The Influence of William Faulkner in the Spanish Post Civil War Novel, 2000. Mem. Am. Assn. of Tchrs. of Spanish and Portuguese, Assn. Internat. Hispanica de las Humanidades (sec. 1995), MLA, Soc. Nat. Honoraria Hispanica, Ohio Humanities Coun. Directory of Scholars, Sigma Delta Pi. Mem. Soc. Of Friends. Avocations: travel, reading, music. Office: Wilmington Coll 25 Ludovic St Wilmington OH 45177 E-mail: june_townsend@wilmington.edu.

TOWNSEND, KATHLEEN KENNEDY, lieutenant governor; b. Greenwich, Conn., July 4, 1951; d. Robert F. and Ethel S. Kennedy; m. David Townsend; children: Meaghan, Maeve, Kate, Kerry. BA cum laude, Harvard U., 1974; JD, U. N.Mex., 1978. Instr. Dundalk C.C., 1985-86, Essex C.C., 1986-87, U. Pa., 1987-88; exec. dir. Md. Student Svcs. Alliance, State dept. of Edn., 1987—93; dep. asst. atty. gen. U.S. Dept. Justice, Washington, 1993-94; lt. gov. State of Md., 1995—. Chair so. region Nat. Conf. Lt. Govs., chair oversight com. Johns Hopkins U., Peabody Inst., 1995-96; nat. adv. bd. Export-Import Bank U.S.; bd. advs. Johns Hopkins U. Sch. Advanced Internat. Studies, Inst. Human Virology U. Md; chair, State House Trust, 1995-, Adv. Bd., After-School Opportunity Programs, 1999-, co-chair, Safe Schools Interagency Steering Com., 1999-. Delegate, Dem. Party Nat. Convention, 1988, 1996, 2000; chair, Dem. Caucus of Lt. Govs. Editor U. N.Mex. Law Rev.; contbr. articles to profl. jours. and newspapers. Founder Robert F. Kennedy Human Rights award; chair Cabinet Coun. Criminal and Juvenile Justice, 1995—; chair Cabinet Coun. for Bus. and Econ. Devel.; chair Md. del. Pres.'s Summit Am.'s Future, 1997; chair State Sys. Reform Task Force for Children and Youth Reform, 1996, Task Force to study increasing availability of substance abuse programs, 1998-2001, Gov's. Yr. 2000 Pub. Info.; chair adv. bd. after sch. opportunity programs; co-chair Md. Family Violence Coun.; bd. dirs. John F. Kennedy Libr. Found., Nat. Inst. Women's Policy Rsch.; chair external adv. bd. Kennedy Krieger Inst. Early Infant Transition Ctr.; sr. advisor, Appropriations Com., House of Delegates, 1984-85; asst. atty. gen., Maryland, 1985-86; bd. ptnrs. Radcliffe Coll. Recipient 4 hon. degrees; Visionary Leadership award, Healthy Families America, 2000, Clinton Center award for Leadership, Dem. Leadership Coun., 2002. Mem., Economic Devel. Commn., Baltimore County, 1987, Gov.'s Exec. Coun., Gov.'s Commn. on Service and Volunteerism, 1998-. Office: Lt Gov State House 100 State Cir Annapolis MD 21401-1924 Office Fax: 410-974-5882. Business E-Mail: ltgovernor@gov.state.md.us.*

TOWNSEND, LINDA LADD, mental health nurse; b. Louisville, Apr. 26, 1948; d. Samuel Clyde and Mary Elizabeth Ladd; m. Stanley Allen Oliver, June 7, 1970 (div. 1978); 1 child, Aaron; m. Warren Terry Townsend Jr., Jan. 1, 1979; children: Mark, Amy, Sarah. Student, Catherine Spalding Coll., 1966-67; BSN, Murray State U., 1970; MS in Psychiat./Mental Health Nursing, Tex. Woman's U., 1976. RN, Tex., Ky.; lic. advanced practice RN, profl. counselor, marriage and family therapist, Tex.; cert. group psychotherapist. Charge nurse med. and pediatric units Murray (Ky.)-Calloway County Hosp., 1970-71; team leader surg./renal transplant unit VA Hosp., Nashville, 1971-73; team leader, charge nurse gen. med.-surg. unit Providence Hosp., Waco, Tex., 1973-74; outpatient therapist Mental Hygiene Clinic, Ft. Hood, 1975-76; outpatient nurse therapist Ctrl. Counties Ctr. for Mental Health/Mental Retardation, Copperas Cove & Lampasas, 1977-80; psychiat. nurse clin. specialist, marriage/family therapist Profl. Counseling Svc., Copperas Cove, 1979—. Cons. Metroplex Hosp. and Pavilion, Killeen, Tex., 1980—. Founding mem. Family Outreach of Coryell County, 1986—, past pres. and past sec.; founding memd. Partnership for a Drug and Violence-Free Copperas Cove; advocate Tex. Peer Assistance Program for Nurses, Walk to Emmaus, 1993; disaster mental health svc. counselor ARC, 1998. Recipient Mary M. Roberts Writing award Am. Jour. of Nursing, 1970; named Mem. of Yr.-Vol., Family Outreach of Coryell County. Mem. ANA (cert. clin. specialist in adult psychiat. and mental health nursing, cert. clin. specialist in child and adolescent psychiat. and mental health nursing), Tex. Nurses Assn., Am. Group Psychotherapy Assn. (cert.), Inst. for Humanities at Salado, Sigma Theta Tau. Democrat. Methodist. Avocations: genealogy, camping, nature activities, music, sports. Home: 3276 Arista Rueda Kempner TX 76539 Office: Profl Counseling Svc 806 E Avenue D Ste F Copperas Cove TX 76522-2231

TOWNSEND, MARJORIE RHODES, aerospace engineer, business executive; b. Washington, Mar. 12, 1930; d. Lewis Boling and Marjorie Olive (Trees) Rhodes; m. Charles Eby Townsend, June 7, 1948; children: Charles Eby Jr., Lewis Rhodes, John Cunningham, Richard Leo. BEE, George Washington U., 1951. Electronic scientist Naval Rsch. Lab., Washington, 1951-59; rsch. engr. to sect. head Goddard Space Flight Ctr.-NASA, Greenbelt, Md., 1959-65, tech. asst. to chief systems divsn., 1965-66, project mgr. small astronomy satellites, 1966-75, project mgr. applications explorer missions, 1975-76, mgr. preliminary systems design group, 1976-80; aerospace and electronics cons. Washington, 1980-83; v.p. systems devel. Space Am., 1983-84; aerospace cons. Washington, 1984-90; dir. space systems engring. BDM Internat., Inc., 1990-91; dir. space applications BDM ESC, 1991-92; sr. prin. staff mem. BDM Fed., Inc., 1992-93. Aerospace cons., Washington, 1993—. Patentee digital telemetry system. Decorated Knight Italian Republic Order, 1972; recipient Fed. Women's award, 1973, EUR award for Culture, 1974, Engr. Alumni Achievement award George Washington U., 1975, Gen. Alumni Achievement award George Washington U., 1976, Exceptional Svc. medal NASA, 1971, Outstanding Leadership medal NASA, 1980, Eye-of-the-Needle award NASA, 1991. Fellow IEEE (chmn. Washington sect. 1974-75), AIAA (chmn. nat. capitol sect. 1985), AAAS (coun. del. 1985-88), Washington Acad. Sci. (pres. 1980-81); mem. Internat. Acad. Astronautics, Am. Geophys. Union, Soc. Women Engrs., Wing of Aerospace Med. Assn., Inc. (hon.), DAR, Daus. Colonial Wars, Mensa, Sigma Kappa, Sigma Delta Epsilon (hon.). Republican. Episcopalian. Home and Office: 3529 Tilden St NW Washington DC 20008-3122

TOWNSEND, MILES AVERILL, aerospace and mechanical engineering educator; b. Buffalo, Apr. 16, 1935; s. Francis Devere and Sylvia (Wolpa) T.; children: Kathleen Townsend Hastings, Melissa, Stephen, Joel, Philip. BA, Stanford U., 1955; BS MechE, U. Mich., 1958; advanced cert., U. Ill., 1963, MS in Theoretical and Applied Mechanics, 1967; PhD, U. Wis., 1971. Registered profl. engr., Ill., Wis., Tenn., Ont. Project engr. Sundstrand, Rockford, Ill., 1959-63, Twin Disc Inc., Rockford, 1963-65, 67-68; sr. engr. Westinghouse Electric Corp., Sunnyvale, Calif., 1965-67; instr., fellow U. Wis., Madison, 1968-71; assoc. prof. U. Toronto, Ont., Can., 1971-74; prof. mech. engring. Vanderbilt U., Nashville, 1974-81; Wilson prof. mech. and aerospace engring. U. Va., Charlottesville, 1981—, chmn. dept., 1981-91. Ptnr., v.p. Endev Ltd., Can. and U.S., 1972—; cons. in field. Contbr. numerous articles on dynamics, design dynamical systems, controls and optimization to profl. jours.; 7 patents in field. Recipient numerous research grants and contracts. Fellow ASME, AAAS; mem. N.Y. Acad. Scis., Sigma Xi, Phi Kappa Phi. Pi Tau Sigma. Avocations: running, reading, music. Home: 212 Alderman Rd Charlottesville VA 22903-1704 Office: U Va Dept Mech and Aerospace Engring Thornton Hall Charlottesville VA 22903-2442 E-mail: mat@virginia.edu.

TOWNSEND, PAMELA GWIN, business educator; b. Aug. 24, 1945; d. William Thomas and Doris (Gwin) T. BA in Econs. with distinction, U. Mo., Kansas City, 1977, MBA, 1980; postgrad., U. Kans., 1982-90. CPA, Kans. Real estate sales assoc. KEW Realtors, Austin, Tex., 1967-70; staff mktg. asst. Lincoln Property Co., Dallas, 1970-72; dir. mktg. Commonwealth Devel. Co., 1972-73; v.p. market analysis Fin. Corp. N.Am., Kansas City, 1973-75; asst. prof., dir. dept. acctg. Park Coll., Parkville, Mo., 1980-86; co-founder Irie Prodns., 1990-92. Columnist Tax Tips, Platte County Gazette, 1981. Univ. scholar U. Mo., 1977. Mem. AICPA (tax divsn.), Kans. Soc. CPAs, Mo. Soc. CPAs, Am. Acctg. Assn., Nat. Assn. Accts., Nat. Tax Assn., Am. Fin. Assn., Beta Alpha Psi Alumnae (pres. 1982), Beta Gamma Sigma, Phi Kappa Phi, Omicron Delta Epsilon, Alpha Chi Omega, Mortar Bd. Home: 7106 Westlake Ave Dallas TX 75214-3546

TOWNSEND, RICHARD MARVIN, government insurance executive, city manager, consultant; b. White Plains, N.Y., Dec. 28, 1933; s. Benjamin Richter and Frances (Mills) T.; m. Joanne Schwartz; children: Drue, Brent, Merric. BA, Cornell U., 1955, MPA with distinction, 1956. Adminstrv. aide, analyst City of Corpus Christi, Tex., 1956-58, budget and rsch. analyst, 1958-59, adminstrv. asst. III, 1959-60, asst. city mgr., 1960-67, city mgr., 1968-81, City of Laredo, 1982-89; dep. dir. Tex. Mcpl. League Intergovtl. Risk Pool, Austin, 1990-91, exec. dir., 1991—. Facilitator Future of a Region Conf., San Antonio, 1986. Contbr. articles to profl. jours. Mem. mobile home performance bd. State of Tex., Austin, 1971-76; bd. dirs. Legend Oaks Homeowners Assn., Austin, 1992-2001, United Way Bd., Laredo, 1984-89. Named one of Outstanding Young Men of Am., Corpus Christi Jr. C. of C., 1968. Mem. ASPA, Tex. City Mgmt. Assn. (pres. 1980), Internat. City Mgmt. Assn., Phi Kappa Phi. Home: 8008 Isaac Pryor Dr Austin TX 78749-1862 Office: 1821 Rutherford Ln Austin TX 78754-5128 E-mail: mtownsend@tmlirp.org.

TOWNSEND, SANDRA LYNNETTE, nurse; b. Boise, Idaho, Nov. 16, 1957; d. Edward Elmo and Betty Jean (Maus) Letney; m. Richard Wayne Townsend, Apr. 2, 1982; 1 child, Mallory Jean. BSN, Boise State U., 1992. CNA, cert. oncology nurse. From claims approver to internal auditor, asst. supr. John Hancock Ins. Co., 1978-88; oncology/BMT unit nurse St Luke's Regional med. Ctr., Boise, 1993—, patient care coord. oncology unit, 1995-98, clin. instr. oncology, 1998—, adminstrv. supr., 2001—. Singer-dancer Mayors and Minors, Nampa, Idaho, 1988. Mem. Idaho Nurses Assn. (membership dir. 1993, treas. 1994-95), Oncology Nurses So. Idaho (pres. 1995-96). Republican. Avocations: power boating, reading, water-skiing. Home: 11101 Hummingbird Dr Boise ID 83709-1371

TOWNSEND, SUSAN ELAINE, religious organization officer; b. Phila., Sept. 5, 1946; d. William Harrison and Eleanor Irene (Fox) Rogers; m. John Holt Townsend, May 1, 1976. BS in Secondary Edn., West Chester State U., 1968; MBA, Nat. U., 1978; PhD in Human Behavior, La Jolla U., 1984. Biology tchr. Methacton Sch. Dist., Fairview Village, Pa., 1968-70; bus. mgr., analyst profl. La Jolla Research Corp., San Diego, 1977-79; pastoral asst. Christ Ctr. Bible Therapy, 1980-82, also bd. dirs.; v.p., pub. relations World Outreach Ctr. of Faith, 1981-82, also bd. dirs.; owner, pres., cons. Townsend Research Inst., 1983-89. Teaching assoc. La Jolla U. Continuing Edn., 1985-86, adminstr., assoc. registrar, adj. faculty, 1990. Author: Hostage Survival-Resisting the Dynamics of Captivity, 1983; contbr. articles to profl. jours. Instr. USN Advanced Survival Evasion Resistance Escape Sch., 1986-89; security officer Shield Security, San Diego, 1991-92; COO Matthew 25:34-40 Ministries, San Diego, 2000—; bd. dirs. Christ Fellowship Ch. of San Diego, 1987-96, music dir., 1992-2000; religious vol. Met. Correctional Ctr., San Diego, 1983-89; vol. San Diego County Jail Ministries, 1978-2000, scheduling coord., 1993-99, sec., 1998-2000. Comdr. USN, 1970-76, USNR, 1976-93. Mem. Naval Res. Assn. (life), Res. Officers Assn.(outstanding Jr. Officer of Yr. Calif. chpt. 1982), Navy League U.S. (life), West Chester U. Alumni Assn., Nat. U. Alumni Assn. (life), La Jolla U. Alumni Assn., Gen. Fedn. Women's Club (pres. Peninsula Women's Club 1983-85, 94-96, pres. Parliamentary Law Club 1984-86, 96-98, rec. sec. Past Pres.' Assn. 1994-96, pres. 2000-02), Calif. Fedn. Women's Clubs (v.p.-at-large San Diego dist. 25 1982-84, rec. sec. 1994-96, 1st v.p./dean of chmn. 1996-98, pres. 1998-2000).

TOWNSEND, TERRY, publishing executive; b. Camden, N.J., Dec. 14, 1920; d. Anthony and Rose DeMarco; m. Paul Brorstrom Townsend, Dec. 8, 1961; 1 child, Kim. BA, Duke U., 1942; LHD (hon.), Dowling Coll., 1991. Pub. rels. dir. North Shore U. Hosp., Manhasset, N.Y., 1956-68; pres. Theatre Soc., L.I., 1967-70, Townsend Comm. Bur., L.I., 1970-98; ptnr. L.I. Communicating Svc., Bellport, 1977—. Pub. L.I. Bus. News, 1979-98, pub. emeritus, 1998—; v.p. ParrMeadows Racetrack, Yaphank, N.Y., 1977. Columnist, writer L.I./Bus., Ronkonkoma, 1970-75. Assoc. trustee North Shore U. Hosp., 1968—; bd. govs. Adelphi U. Friends Fin. Edn., 1978-85; chmn. ann. archtl. awards competition N.Y. Inst. Tech., 1970-83; trustee Dowling Coll., 1984-2000; trustee L.I. Fine Arts Mus., 1984-85; pub. broadcasting PBS Sta. WLIW TV, Garden City, L.I., N.Y., 1990-93; bd. dirs. Family Svc. Assn. Nassau County, 1982-92; dinner chmn. L.I. 400 Ball, 1987; trustee L.I. Mus. Art, 1994—. Recipient Media award 110 Ctr. Bus. & Profl. Women, 1977, Enterprise award Friends of Fin. Edn., 1981, L.I. Loves Bus. Showcase Salute, 1982, Cmty. Svc. award N.Y. Diabetes Assn., 1983, Disting. Long Islander in Comm. award L.I. United Epilepsy Assn., 1984, Spl. award Dowling Coll. Spring Tribute, 1989, Disting. Svc. award Episcopal Health Svcs., 1989, Disting. Citizen award Dowling Coll., 1991, Gilbert Tilles award Nat. Assn. Fundraising Execs., 1994, Hadassah Cmty. Svc. award, 1996, Golden rule award Little Village Sch., 1997, Lifetime Achievement award L.I. Assn., 1998, Promote L.I. Achievement award, 1998, Lifetime Achievement award Advancement for Commerce & Industry, 1999; named 1st Lady of L.I., L.I. Pub. Rels. Assn., 1973, L.I. Woman of Yr. L.I. Assn. Action Com., 1989. Office: LI Communicating Svcs PO Box 915 Bellport NY 11713-0915 E-mail: terytowns@aol.com.

TOWNSEND, THOMAS PERKINS, former mining company executive; b. Bryn Mawr, Pa., Mar. 28, 1917; s. John and Mildred (Perkins) T.; m. Laura M. Trench, Sept. 14, 1940; children: Joanne Townsend Taber, Hunter, Elizabeth Macdonald. BS in Econs., U. Pa., 1939; postgrad., Harvard U., 1944. C.P.A., Pa. Sr. acct. Price Waterhouse & Co., 1945-48; treas., dir. Fox Products Co., 1948-53, Wilcolator Co., 1953-55; staff acct. Tex. Gulf Sulphur Co., N.Y.C., 1955-57, asst. treas., 1958-61, v.p., controller, 1961-62, v.p., treas., 1962-64, v.p. internat. ops., 1964-68; exec. v.p. Bosco Middle East Oil Corp., Greenwich, Conn., 1968-69; pres. Conn. Real Estate Corp., 1969-70, also bd. dirs., 1969—; v.p. finance Rosaria Resources Corp., N.Y.C., 1970-81; treas. Unidyne Corp., 1984-85. Cons. AMAX, Inc., 1981-85; bd. dirs. Thermal Exploration Corp., Carlin Gold Co. Chmn. nat. com. for employment youth Nat. Child Labor Com., 1968-70; trustee, pres. South Kent Sch.; trustee Soc. to Advance Retarded, Norwalk, Conn.; bd. dirs. United Way of Tri-State, Denison Pequotsegos Nature Ctr.; mem. New Canaan Bd. Fin., Conn., 1985-89 . Served to lt. (s.g.) Supply Corps, USNR, World War II. Mem. Am. Inst. Accts., N.Y. State Soc. CPAs, Fin. Execs. Inst., Mason's Island Yacht Club, Off Soundings Club. Episcopalian (treas., vestryman 1960-72, 87-95). E-mail: ttownsend@sprintmail.com. *The principal goal in my life has been to be a straight dealer, to be honest in thought, word and deed. It has paid off for me. Crooked dealing may make more money, but it does not lead to a happier life. One must live by his God.*

TOWNSEND, WILLIAM JACKSON, lawyer; b. June 4, 1932; s. Robert Glenn and Lois Juanita (Jackson) T. BS, Wake Forest U., 1954; student, U. Ky., 1957, U. Louisville, 1958; JD, U. N.C., 1960. Lawyer; b. Grayson, Ky., June 4, 1932; s. Robert Glenn and Lois Juanita (Jackson) T. BS, Wake Forest U., 1954; Student U. Ky., 1957, U. Louisville, 1958, U. N.C., 1960. Bar: N.C. 1965. Claims adjuster State Farm Ins. Co., 1963; sole practice, Fayetteville, N.C., 1965—; pub. adminstr. Robeson County, N.C., 1966; dir., treas. Colonial Foods, Inc., St. Paul, N.C., 1959—; tax atty. City of Lumberton, 1966-67 . Served as 1st lt. U.S. Army, 1954-56. Mem. N.C. Bar Assn., N.C. State Bar, Cumberland County Bar Assn., N.C. Bar Assn., Scabbard and Blade (pres.), Delta Theta Phi. Presbyterian. Club: Kiwanis (treas. Fayetteville 1973-82). Office: PO Box 584 2109 Elvira St Apt 806 Fayetteville NC 28302

TOWNSEND-BUTTERWORTH, DIANA BARNARD, educational consultant, author; b. Albany, N.Y., Dec. 12; d. Barnard and Marjorie (Bradley) Townsend; m. J. Warner Butterworth, Jan. 23, 1969; children: James, Diana. AB, Harvard-Radcliffe Coll., 1960; MA, Tchrs. Coll., Columbia U., 1971. Tchr. St. Bernard's Sch., N.Y.C., 1963-78, head of lower sch. English, 1965-71, head of jr. sch., 1971-78; assoc. dir. Early Care Ctr., 1984-87; acad. advisor Columbia Coll., 1987-88; ednl. cons., lectr., 1988—. Dir. parent involvement initiative Ctr. Ednl. Outreach & Innovation, Tchrs. Coll., Columbia U., 1996, chmn. devel. com. alumni coun. Tchrs. Coll., 1994-98; chmn. sub-com. Harvard schs. com. Harvard Coll., Cambridge, Mass., 1975—. Author: Preschool and Your Child: What You Should Know, 1995, Your Child's First School, 1992 (Parent's Choice award 1992), (book chpt.) Handbook of Clinical Assessment of Children and Adolescents; contbr. articles to ednl. publs. and jours. Mem. women's health symposium steering com. N.Y. Hosp., N.Y.C., 1988—. Mem. Assn. Lower Sch. Heads (co-founder 1975), Alumni Coun. Tchrs. Coll. (com. chair 1993-98), Harvard Faculty Club. Avocations: skiing, hiking, swimming, theatre, reading. Home: 1170 5th Ave New York NY 10029-6527

TOWSNER, CYNTHIA MERLE, educator, administrator; b. Washington, Apr. 23, 1939; d. A. Philip and Edith Towsner; (div. Oct. 1987); 1 child, Scott David Garrison; m. Karl R. Katterjohn, June 10, 1996; 1 stepchild, Katrina L. BS, U. Md., 1961, postgrad., 1964-65, Am. U., 1987. Adv. cert. contracting officer's tech. rep. U.S. Dept. Edn. Tchr. Montgomery County Pub. Schs., Rockville, Md., 1961-66, 72-80; spl. asst. to commr. rehab. svcs. adminstrn. U.S. Dept. Edn., Washington, 1981-85, spl. asst. to the dir. Office Intergovtl. & Interagy. Affairs, 1985-87, acting dir. intergovtl. affairs office, 1987, ednl. program specialist Office Bilingual Edn. & Minority Languages Affairs, 1987-93, edn. program specialist Bilingual Vocat. Tng., 1993-96, nat. coord. family literacy and literacy vols. for adults, 1996—. Pres. Office Vocat. Adult Edn., U.S. Dept. Edn., Educare Programs, Inc., Chevy Chase, Md., 1988—; cons. R.J. Comer Comm., Inc., Jacksonville, Fla., 1995-97; v.p. Dalmahoy Group Internat., Chevy Chase, 1997-99. Photographer Project Education Reform: Time for Results, vol. 1, 1987. Vol. Holy Cross Hosp., Silver Spring, Md., 1969-74; asst. to pres. for edn. issues, chair nominating com., chair cmty. directory Rock Creek Hills Civic Assn., Kensington, 1968-85; v.p. D.C., Md. and Va. region, chair youth rally, chair radiothon publicity St. Jude's Children's Rsch. Hosp., Aiding Leukemia Stricken Am. Children, Memphis, 1969-81; chair internat. festival Larchmont Elem. Sch. PTA, Montgomery County, MD, 1976-78; bd. dirs., mem., chair Citizens for Edn., Montgomery County, Md., 1977-82; active Renaissance Women, Washington, 1983-87; chair corp. and bus. contbns. Hosp. Relief Fund for the Caribbean, Chevy Chase, 1989-91, annual ball com., 1989-94; vol. tutor Laubach Literacy Action and Literacy Vols. Am., Chevy Chase, 1989-93. Recipient Meritorious Svc. medal Am. Automobile Assn., Washington, 1952, Honors award Rock Creek Hills Civic Assn., Kensington, Md., 1979, Pres.'s award Combined Fed. Campaign, Washington, 1987, Hammer award V.P. of the U.S., Washington, 1996, 1st place ribbon in photography Montgomery County Agrl. Fair, Gaithersburg, Md., 1998, 1st, 2nd and 3rd place ribbons in photography Montgomery County Agrl. Fair, Gaithersburg, 1999, 1st and 2nd place ribbons in photography Md. State Fair, Timonium, 1999, 1st pl. award Md. State Fair, 2000. Mem. AAUW, Internat. Freelance Photographers Orgn. (named Master Photographer 2002), Assn. for Career and Tech. Edn., Soc. Govt. Meeting Profls., Nat. Trust for Scotland, Nat. Mus. Women in the Arts (founding mem.). Avocations: photography, reading, traveling. Home: 4620 N Park Ave Apt 1404E Chevy Chase MD 20815-4563 E-mail: cindytk@starpower.net.

TOY, CHARLES DAVID, lawyer; b. N.Y.C., June 29, 1955; s. Frank H.F. and Louise S.K. (Louie) Toy; m. Sandra Lynn Youla, Mar. 10, 1984; 1 child Alana May Youla. BA cum laude, Harvard U., 1977, JD, 1980. Bar: NY 1981, DC 2001. Assoc. Milbank, Tweed, Hadley & McCloy, N.Y.C., 1980-84, Kaye, Scholer, Fierman, Hays & Handler, Hong Kong, 1984-88, ptnr. Hong Kong, 1989-91, N.Y.C., 1991-93; v.p., gen. counsel Overseas Pvt. Investment Corp., Washington, 1993-2001, v.p. fin., 1995-96, v.p. investment funds, 1998-99; ptnr. Wilmer, Cutler & Pickering, 2001—. Spkr. seminars Bus. Internat., 1985, Cookson Asia Conf., 1988, Korea Fgn. Trade Assn., 1989, 90, World Trade Inst., 1992, U. Pa., 1993, 94, 95, Washington Internat. Trade Assn., 1993, ABA, 1993, 94, 95, 97, 98, 99, Am. Conf. Inst., 1994, 95, 96, 98, Am. Soc. Internat. Law, 1994, 96, 97, Small Bus. Exporters Assn., 1994, Inst. for Infrastructure Fin., 1995, Assn. Bar City of N.Y., 1995, 2000, Infocast, 1995, Calif. Coun. Internat. Trade, 1995, World Econ. Devel. Congress, 1995, 96, Baker & McKenzie Ann. Mtg. Client Conf., 1995, Ctr. for Bus. Intelligence, 1995, Corp. Legal Times Roundtable, 1996, Com. of 100, 1996, Asian Am. Bar Assn., 1996, Asian Bus. Assn., 1996, Asian Pacific Am. Bar Assn., 1996, 97, Forbes, 1997,; profile subject Internat. Fin. Law Rev., 1996, Avenue Asia, 1996, 97, Adam Smith Inst., 1998, Jerome Levy Econs. Inst. of Bard Coll.,

1998, Asian Pacific Am. Inst. for Congl. Studies, 1998, Embassy of South Africa, 1998, Harvard Inst. for Internat. Devel., 1998, 99, Insight Info., 1998, 99, Nat. Asian Pacific Am. Bar Assn., 1998. U. Fla. Levin Coll. Law, 1999, CNA/Schinnerer Conf., 1999, Case We. Res. U. Sch. Law, 1999, Practising Law Inst., 1999, 2000, U. Iowa Tippie Sch. Mgmt., 2000, Met. Corp. Counsel Interview, 2000, Internat. Project Fin. Assn., 2000, Am. Corp. Counsel Assn., 2000, U.S. Inst. of Peace, 2001. Contbg. editor Taxes and Investment in Asia and the Pacific, 1985, Tax News Svc., 1986—, Bull. for Internat. Fiscal Documentation, 1986—; bd. editors Strategic Alliance Alert, 1994-95. Bd. trustees Lower East Side Tenement Mus., 1994-98. Mem. ABA, N.Y. State Bar Assn., Assn. Bar City of N.Y., Nat. Asian Pacific Am. Bar Assn., Asian Pacific Am. Bar Assn., Harvard Law Sch. Assn., Am. Club (Hong Kong), Ladies Recreation Club (Hong Kong), Phi Beta Kappa Democrat. Roman Catholic. Office: Wilmer Cutler & Pickering 2445 M St NW Washington DC 20037-1420 E-mail: ctoy@wilmer.com.

TOY, MARY L. music educator; b. Wenatchee, Wash. d. Hugh Albert and Lina Katharina (Stolte) Teeter. Tchr. Toy Piano Studio; chmn. piano divsn. Wash. State Creative Arts Program, Spokane, 1972; chmn. N.W. divsn. Nat. H.S. Auditions-Music Tchr. Nat. Assn., 1975-82; faculty Acad. of Music N.W., Seattle, 1997—. Adjudicator, clinician Can. Music Festivals, Trail, Alberta, Vancouver, B.C., Can., 1980. Mem. adv. bd. Seattle Young Artist Music Festival, 1998, Greater Spokane Music and Allied Festival Arts, 1975-97. Named to Hall of Fame, WSMTA, 2002. Mem. Music Tchrs. Nat. Assn. (master cert., lectr., panel mem., exec. bd. 1986-90, Tchr. Recognition award 1973, 74-75, 76-77, adjudicator Eastside chpt. 1999), Wash. State Music Tchrs. Assn. (adjudicator 1975—, v.p. Spokane chpt. 1982-84, exec. bd.), Seattle Music Tchrs. Assn. (lectr.), Eastside Music Tchrs. Assn. (workshop lectr. Snohomish chpt. 1999). Home and Office: 108 2d Ave S Apt 101 Kirkland WA 98033-6582

TOYODA, SHOICHIRO, automobile company executive; b. Nagoya, Japan, Feb. 27, 1925; s. Kiichiro and Hatako Toyoda; m. Hiroko Mitsui, Nov. 30, 1952; children: Atuko, Akio. B in Engring., Nagoya U., 1947, D in Engring., 1955. Dir. Toyota (Japan) Motor Co., Ltd., 1952-61, mng. dir., 1961-67, sr. mng. dir., 1967-72, exec. v.p., 1972-81; pres. Toyota Motor Sales Co., Ltd., 1981-82, Toyota Motor Corp., 1982-92, chmn., 1992-99, hon. chmn., 1999—. Bd. dirs. Denso Co., Ltd., Nagoya Broadcasting Network; chmn. bd. dirs. Inst. Internat. Econ. Studies. Chmn. Keidanren, Tokyo, 1994-98; hon. chmn. KDDI, 2000; consul gen. Honorario de Costa Rica, Nagoya, 1984—. Recipient Medal with Dark-Blue Ribbon, Govt. of Japan, 1972, The Deming Prize, 1980, Medal with Blue Ribbon, Govt. of Japan, 1984, FISITA medal, France, Medal of Isabel la Cath., King of Spain, 2000; decorated knight comdr. Most Noble Order of the Crown (Thailand), gran cruz Order Nacional al Merit, Colombia, knight comdr. Brit. Empire, grand cordon Order of the Sacred Treasure (Japan), Order Francisco de Miranda First Class (Venezuela), Ordem Nat. do Cruzeiro do Sul (Brazil), Order of Merit (Turkey), comdr. Legion of Honor (France), Grande Ufficiale, Govt. of Italy, hon. companion Gen. divsn. Order of Australia, grand decoration of honor in gold with star, Austria. Office: Toyota Motor Corp 1 Toyota-cho Toyota 471-8571 Japan

TOZER, ELIZABETH FARRAN, interior and floral designer, philanthropist; b. Cleve., Jan. 25, 1942; d. Charles and Irma (Gaensslen) Farran; m. W. James Tozer Jr., July 30, 1965; children: Farran Tozer Brown and Katherine Tozer Roddy. BFA, Ohio Wesleyan U., 1964. Residential and comml. interior and floral designer Elizabeth Farran Tozer Design, N.Y.C., 1982—. Interior design cons. N.Y. Found. for Sr. Citizens, N.Y.C., 1982—; pres. The Flower Svc. Store, N.Y.C., 1972-92; spokesperson Am. Florists Mktg. Coun., 1987; appeared in numerous radio, TV, and newspaper interviews in eleven maj. U.S. cities. Author: The Art of Flower Arranging, 1981; contbr. articles to profl. publs. Chmn. N.Y. Flower Show, 1996; mem. exec. com., mem. nominating com. Mus. of the City of N.Y., 1994—; vice chmn., chmn. nominating com., bd. dirs. N.Y. Found. for Sr. Citizens, 1980-; mem. nominating com. Sch. Am. Ballet, Lincoln Ctr., 1977—; chmn. more than 30 maj. fundraising events in N.Y.C. and Dutchess County, N.Y., 1977—; mem. adv. bd. Nat. Acad. Design, 1999-; chmn. Inst. Ecosys. AldoLeopold Soc., 2001-. Recipient award Mcpl. Arts Soc., 1997, award YWCA Acad. Women Achievers, 1995, Pillars of Industry award, Best Srs. Mid-Rise Bldg. award Nat. Assn. Home Builders, 1995, Spl. Merit award Associated Builders and Owners of Greater N.Y., 1993. Mem. N.Y. Hort. Soc. (nominating com.). Avocation: raising miniature horses. Office: EFT Design Ltd 1112 Park Ave # 6A New York NY 10128-1235

TOZER, W. JAMES, JR. investment company executive; b. Salt Lake City, Feb. 9, 1941; s. W. James and Virginia (Somerville) T.; m. Elizabeth Farran, July 30, 1965; children: Farran Virginia, Katharine Coppins. BA cum laude, Trinity Coll., 1963; MBA, Harvard U., 1965. Investment officer First Nat. City Overseas Investment Corp., N.Y.C., 1965-70; v.p. corp. devel. Citicorp, 1970-71; sr. v.p. and head Citicorp Subs. Group, 1971-74; sr. v.p., gen. mgr., head Merchant Banking Group, 1974-75, sr. v.p., gen. mgr. N.Y. banking div., 1975-77; sr. exec. v.p., dir. and head investment banking div. Shearson Hayden Stone, Inc., N.Y.C., 1978-79; sr. exec. v.p. Marine Midland Bank and Marine Midland Banks, Inc., 1979-80, sr. exec. v.p. ops., fin. and strategic staff units, 1980-85, mem. office of chmn., sector exec. corp., instl. and internat. banking, 1985-87; chmn. Mountain West Banking Corp., Denver, 1988-89; pres., chief operating officer Prudential-Bache Securities, Inc., N.Y.C., 1989-90; pres., CEO Lincolnshire Mgmt., Inc., 1993-94; mng. dir. Vectra Mgmt. Group, 1990—. Bd. dirs. Lending Tree, Inc.; chmn. exec. com. Draper Bancorp, dir. traction. Chmn. bd. Fellows Trinity Coll., 1972-78; trustee, treas. Community Service Soc., 1976-87; trustee, treas. The Sch. for Field Studies, 1995—; mem. Citizens Budget Commn., 1986—; adv. council Atlanta U. Sch. Bus. Adminstrn., 1985-89; bd. Episcopal Charities. Mem. N.Y. State Bankers Assn. (legis. policy com. 1981-87), Assn. Res. City Bankers (govt. rels. com. 1984-87), Am. Bankers Assn. (govt. rels. coun. 1985-87), Economic Club, University Club, Bond of N.Y. Club, Millbrook Club, Mashomack Club, River Club (N.Y.C.), Alta Club, (S.L.C). Home: 1112 Park Ave New York NY 10128-1235 Office: 65 E 55th St 31st Fl New York NY 10022-3219

TOZER, WILLIAM EVANS, entomologist, educator; b. Binghamton, N.Y., July 7, 1947; s. William Evans and Gertrude Genevieve (Lewis) T. BS in Natural Sci., Niagara U., 1969; MS in Biology, Ball State U., 1979; PhD in Entomology, U. Calif., Berkeley, 1986. Cert. C.C. biology and zoology tchr. Calif. Jr. H.S. sci. and English tchr. St. Patricks Sch., Corning, N.Y., 1969-71; tchg. asst. biology Ball State U., Muncie, Ind., 1974-76; pvt. practice biol. eviron. cons. Berkeley, Calif., 1976-79, 86-88; rsch. asst. U. Calf., 1979-86; dept. head edn. and tng. USN Disease Vector Ecology and Control Ctr., Poulsbo, Wash., 1988—. Mem., acting chmn. San Francisco Bay Area Mosquito Control Coun., Alameda, 1988-96; chmn. com., mem. Armed Forces Pest Mgmt. Bd., Washington, 1994—; bd. dirs. Cert. and Tng. Assessment Group, EPA/USDA, 2001--. Editor (field handbook) Navy Environmental Health Center, 1994; contbr. articles to profl. jours. With U.S. Army, 1971-73. Mem. Am. Entomol. Soc., Sigma Xi. Achievements include first to publish evidence for underwater behavioral thermoregulation in adult insects. Avocations: photography, tennis, hiking, bicycling, softball. Home: 1407 NW Santa Fe Ln Apt 304 Silverdale WA 98383-7915 Office: USN Disease Vector Ecol Control Ctr 2850 Thresher Ave Silverdale WA 98315- E-mail: William.tozer@ndvecc.navy.mil.

TOZZER, JACK CARL, civil engineer, surveyor; b. Marion, Ohio, Jan. 5, 1922; s. Carl Henry and Henrietta (Schellenbaum) T.; children: Brent Jack, Hal Jack; m. Aleta C. Lehner, July 14, 1974. BCE, Ohio No. U., 1944. Registered profl. engr., Ohio, Fla., registered surveyor, Ohio. Pres. firm Tozzer & Assocs. Inc., Marion, 1948-85; county engr. Marion County, Ohio, from 1964. City engr. Marion, 1959, Galion, Ohio, 1960-85; cons. civil engr. Mem. cons. bd. Coll. Engring. Ohio No. U., 1970; v.p. Marion Community Improvement Corp.; mem. Marion County Regional Planning Commn. Served with USNR, 1944-46. Recipient Order of Engr. Coll. Engring. Ohio No. U., 1971. Fellow ASCE; mem. NSPE, Marion C. of C., Cons. Engrs. Ohio, Profl. Land Surveyors Ohio, Ohio Hist. Soc., Marion County Hist. Soc. (past dir.), Elks, Delta Sigma Phi. Lutheran. Home: Marion, Ohio. Died Nov. 24, 2001.

TRAAS, PIETER J. civilian military employee; b. The Netherlands; BSEE, U. Md., 1973; MSEE, Fla. Inst. Tech. Student trainee, then sr. project engring. Electronic Sys. Engring. Activity, 1968—80; head SATCOM Naval Telecomms. Command, 1980—83; with MILSATCOM Def. Comms. Agy., 1984; dep. dir., tech. advisor opers. divsn. Naval Space Command, Dahlgren, Va., 1984—87, tech. dir.; head SATCOM br. SHAPE Tech. Ctr. NATO, 1987—91, head techs. and techniques br., 1987—91. Office: Naval Space Command Pub Affairs 5280 4th St Dahlgren VA 22448-5300*

TRABITZ, EUGENE LEONARD, aerospace company executive; b. Cleve., Aug. 13, 1937; s. Emanuel and Anna (Berman) T.; m. Caryl Lee Rine, Dec. 22, 1963 (div. Aug. 1981); children: Claire Marie, Honey Caryl; m. Kathryn Lynn Bates, Sept. 24, 1983; 1 stepchild, Paul Francis Rager. BA, Ohio State U., 1965. Enlisted USAF, 1954, advanced through grades to maj.; served as crew commdr. 91st Stragetic Missile Div., Minot, S.D., 1968-70; intelligence officer Fgn. Tech. Div., Dayton, Ohio, 1970-73; dir. external affairs Aero Systems Div., 1973-75; program mgr. Air Force Armament Div., Valparaiso, Fla., 1975-80; dir. ship ops. Air Force Ea. Test Range, Satellite Beach, 1980-83; dep. program mgr. Air Force Satellite Text Ctr., Sunnyvale, Calif., 1983-84; ret., 1984; sr. staff engr. Ultrasystems Inc., 1984-86; pres. TAWD Systems Inc., Palo Alto, Calif., 1986-92, Am. Telenetics Co., San Mateo, 1992—. Cons. Space Applications Corp., Sunnyvale, 1986-87, Litton Computer Svcs., Mountain View, Calif., 1987-91, Battelle Meml. Inst. Columbus, 1993—. V.p. Bd. County Mental Health Clinic, Ft. Walton Beach, Fla., 1973-75. Decorated Bronze Star. Mem. DAV (life), Nat. Def. Indsl. Assn., Armed Forces comms. and Electronics Assn., Am. Soc. for Indsl. Security, U.S. Space Found. (charter), Air Force Assn. (life), Nat. Sojourners, Masons (32 degree). Avocations: golf, tennis, racketball, sailing, bridge. Home: 425 Anchor Rd Apt 317 San Mateo CA 94404-1058

TRABOCCO, RONALD EDWARD, engineer; b. Phila., Feb. 10, 1939; s. Joseph and Amelia (Di Sario) T.; m. Mary Louise Roselli, Aug. 19, 1961; children: Stefanie M., Veronica A., Maria C., Joseph S. BS in Metall. Engring., Drexel U., 1961, MS in Materials Engring., 1966. Registered profl. engr., Pa. Metallurgist Naval Air Materials Ctr., Phila., 1961-71; materials engr., supervisory materials engr. Naval Air Devel. Ctr., Warminster, Pa., 1971—. Cons. MacWilliams Engring., Trenton, N.J., 1976-80; tech. govt. cons. Nat. Materials Adv. Bd., Washington, 1984-87; tech. cons. Export Control, Washington, 1986-88; mem. materials in systems panel Tech. Cooperation Program, Washington, 1985—. Inventor explosive welding composites, portable polymer viscosity device; 2 patents pending; contbr. numerous articles to profl. jours. Organizer, officer Gloucester Twp. Taxpayers Assn., Camden County, N.J., 1965-70; active participant Indian Guides/YMCA, Ambler, Pa., 1976-78; coach Little League Soccer, Softball and Baseball, Whitpain Twp., Pa., 1978-83. Recipient NADC award for scientific Achievement, 1986. Mem. ASTM, AIAA, Am. Soc. for Metals, Soc. for Advancement of Materials and Process Engrs. (fall conf. gen. chmn.), Naval Civilian Mgmt. Assn., Toastmasters. Republican. Roman Catholic. Avocations: fishing, hunting. Office: Naval Air Devel Ctr Code # 6064 Warminster PA 18974

TRACANNA, KIM, elementary and secondary physical education educator; b. Washington, Nov. 3, 1960; d. Frank and Mary Lou (Nardi) T. BSEd in Health and PE, Slippery Rock U., 1982; MS, U. N.C., 1985. Cert. health and physical edn. tchr. K-12, Fla., CPR, Advanced First Aid, ARC. Instr. PE Young World, Inc., Greensboro, N.C.; instr. PE and Health Beth-Ctr. Elem. Sch., Fredericktown, Pa.; rsch. asst. Physical Edn. Dept. U. N.C., Greensboro; instr. phys. edn., health coord. Lakeside Elem. Sch., Orange Park, Fla., 1986—. Mem. exec. bd. dirs. Fla. Striders CORE Team Curriculum Coun. Active in civic orgns., bd. dirs. Clay County Tchrs. Acad. Excellence, 1994—. Recipient World Fellowship award for Outstanding Young Scholar, 1987, cert. of Outstanding Achievment in Elem. PE, 1987, Supt.'s Cert. of Achievement Clay County Sch. Bd., 1987, Gov.'s Leadership award, 1988, Unsung Hero of Yr. award, Jacksonville Track Club, 1989; named to Young Profl. Hall of Fame, 1987; named Tchr. of Yr. Lakeside Elem. Sch., 1995, Fla. Phys. Edn. Tchr. of Yr., 1999-2000, Model Phys. Edn. Program of Yr., Fla., 2000; dist finalist for Tchr. of Yr., Clay County Schs., 1995. Mem. AAHPERD, Fla. Alliance for Health, Phys. Edn., Recreation and Dance (Profl. Recognition awards 1995, 2001), Am. Running and Fitness Assn., Clay County Reading Coun., Clay County Edn. Assn., Nat. Assn. for Edn. of Young Children, Nat. Assn. for Sports and Phys. Edn., Nat. Assn. for Girls and Women in Sports, Phi Epsilon Kappa (Outstanding PE Major award 1982), Sigma Sigma Kappa.

TRACEY, EDWARD JOHN, physician, surgeon; b. Norwalk, Conn., July 26, 1931; s. Edward John and Clara (Hammond) T.; m. Ann Marie Schenk, Sept. 7, 1957; children: Sharon, Scott. BA, Yale U., 1954; MD, N.Y. Med. Coll., N.Y.C., 1958. Diplomate Am. Bd. Surgery. Intern Bellevue Hosp., N.Y.C., 1958-59; resident in surgery NYU-Bellevue Med. Ctr., 1958-63; attending surgeon Norwalk (Conn.) Hosp., 1965-2000, cons. staff, 2000—, asst. dir. dept. surgery, 1975-82, chief of staff, 1982-85, chief sect. gen. surgery, 1989-95, trustee, 1982-85, 92-97, dir., physician support svcs., 1995-99. Acting exec. dir. Norwalk Hosp. Found., 1999-2000. Lt. comdr. USNR, 1963-65. Mem. ACS, Conn. Med. Soc., Fairfield County Med. Soc., Norwalk Med. Soc. (pres. 1976-77), Cath. Club (pres. 1974-75), Shore and Country Club (Norwalk). Clubs: Cath. (Norwalk, Conn., pres. 1974-75), Shore and country (Norwalk, Conn.). Office: 124 East Ave Norwalk CT 06851-5713

TRACEY, TERENCE JOHN, psychology educator; b. Washington, Mar. 2, 1952; s. Gerald A. and Virginia R. Tracey; m. Cheelan Bo Linn, Aug. 11, 1979 (div. 1990; children: Beilee, Erin, Cameron; m. Cynthia Glidden, Jan. 1, 1995; 1 child, Trevor. BA, Cornell U., 1974; MS in Edn., U. Kans., 1977; PhD, U. Md., 1981. Registered psychologist, Ill., N.Y. Psychologist SUNY, Buffalo, 1981-83; prof. ednl. psychology and psychology U. Ill., Champaign, 1983-99, acting assoc. chair dept. ednl. psychology, 1986-89, assoc. chair, dept. ednl. psychology, 1995-97, dir. tng. divsn. counseling psychology, 1988-91, 98-99; prof., dir. tng. counseling psychology, inerim assoc. dean Coll. Edn., Ariz. State U., 1999—. Therapist Psychol. Clinic, Champaign, 1984-99; cons. VA Med. Ctr., Danville, ill., 1985-99. Assoc. editor Jour. Counseling Psychology; contbr. over 100 articles to profl. jours., chpts. to books. Fellow APA, Am. Psychol. Soc., Am. Assn. Applied and Preventative Psychology; mem. Am. Ednl. Rsch. Assn. (com. chair 1987-89, Outstanding Rsch. award 1989, 97). Avocation: squash. Office: Ariz State U PO Box 870611 Tempe AZ 85287-0611

TRACEY, TIMOTHY NEAL, technology company executive; b. Washington, June 21, 1954; s. Gerald A. and Virginia R. (Roscoe) T.; m. Mary Elizabeth Askegaard, Jan. 1, 1986; children: Derek Alexander, Miles Vaughn. BA, Columbia U., 1976; MBA, Harvard U., 1980. Ops. mgr. AT&T, N.Y.C., 1976-78; sr. mktg. mgr. Honeywell, Mpls., 1980-88; dir. Microrim, Redmond, Wash., 1988; pres. Nat. Payment Corp., Tampa, Fla., 1989-94; v.p. LeFebure, Cedar Rapids, Iowa, 1994-96; COO SAC Technologies, Inc., Edina, Minn., 1997-98; CEO IZEX Technologies, Inc. NetRehab.com, Golden Valley, 1999—2001, Finch Partners, Mpls., 2001—. Author: Roosevelt and Churchill: The Unique Alliance, 1976. Mem. Coun. of Growing County, Mpls., 1997; leader Boy Scouts Am., Mpls., 1997-2000; coach AYSO Soccer, Mpls., 1997; mem. Nat. Ski Patrol, 1982-85. Mem. Am. Mktg. Assn., Harvard Bus. Sch. Club. Lutheran. Avocations: travel, skiing, golf, sailing. Home: 150 Lakeview Ln Wayzata MN 55391-1521 Office: 5812 Amy Drive Minneapolis MN 55436 E-mail: tntracey@scc.net.

TRACHE, LIVIUS-MARIAN, physicist, research scientist, educator; b. Padureti, Arges, Romania, Dec. 10, 1952; s. Paul and Ioana Trache; children: Monica, Ileana-Mihaela, Mircea; m. Andreea Apostol. BS in Physics, U. Bucharest (Romania), 1976; PhD in Physics, Ctrl. Inst. Physics, Bucharest, 1987. Physicist Inst. Physics and Nuclear Engring., Bucharest, 1978-87, sr. researcher, 1987-94; rsch. scientist Cyclotron Inst. Tex. A&M U., College Station, 1993—. Spkr. in field. Contbr. over 90 articles to profl. jours. Recipient Physics prize Romanian Acad., 1988. Mem. Am. Phys. Soc. Avocations: tennis, classical music, mountain hiking, books. Office: Cyclotron Tex A&M U MS 3366 College Station TX 77843-3366

TRACHEVSKI, LISA ANN, human resources executive; b. Columbus, Ohio, Nov. 15, 1956; d. Donald Henry and Joan Mary (Morbitzer) Bryant; m. George Joseph Trachevski, Mar. 16, 1979. Student, Ohio State U., 1977. Cert. temporary staffing specialist. File/payroll clk. Olsten of Columbus, Inc., 1974-75, placement coord., 1975-78, office supr., 1978-80, office mgr., 1980-84, v.p. ops., 1984-88, v.p. adminstrn., 1991—; v.p., bd. dirs. Olsten Health Care Svcs., Columbus. Cons. Intensive Office Edn., Grove City, Ohio, 1986—; facility security officer Olsten of Columbus, 1979—. Mem. Nat. Assn. Personnel Cons., Ohio Temporary Svc. Assn. (sec. 1992—), Workforce Basics Consortium (advisor 1991). Roman Catholic. Avocations: reading, landscaping, dogs. Home: 6306 Home Rd Delaware OH 43015-9238 Office: Olsten of Columbus Inc 88 E Broad St Ste 630 Columbus OH 43215-3506

TRACHT, ALLEN ERIC, electronics executive; b. Bethesda, Md., Aug. 14, 1957; s. Myron Edward and Diane Serena (Goldberg) T.; m. Donna June Carothers, Sept. 14, 1986; children: Michael, Diane, Daniel. BS in Physics and Elec. Engring., MIT, 1979; MSEE, Calif. Inst. Tech., 1980. Biomed. rschr. Case Western Res. U., Cleve., 1980-85; exec. engr. IOtech. Inc., 1985-2000; lead engr. Spinnaker Networks, Pitts., 2000—02, prin. engr., 2002—. Cons. engring. Keithley Instruments, Cleve., 1985. Contbr. articles to profl. jours. NIH grantee Case Western Res. U., 1982. Mem. IEEE, Assn. for Computing Machinery, Sigma Xi, Tau Beta Pi, Eta Kappa Nu. Home: 48 Woodland Farms Rd Pittsburgh PA 15238-2020 E-mail: allent@spinnakernet.com.

TRACHTENBERG, HOWARD ALAN, retired medical center administrator, educator; b. N.Y.C., June 9, 1935; s. Harold Bernard and Anne (Krug) T.; m. Carol Ann Goodman, June 27, 1956; children: Helaine Sheri, Fay Robin, David Charles. SB, MIT, 1956; MD, NYU, 1960. Diplomate Am. Bd. Anesthesiology. Attending anesthesiologist Mass. Gen. Hosp., Boston, 1962-67; vice chmn. anesthesiology Beth Israel Hosp., 1967-70; vice-chmn. anesthesiology Baystate Med. Ctr., Springfield, Mass., 1970-85, chmn., 1985-97; asst. prof. anesthesiology Harvard Med. Sch., Boston, 1967-70, Tufts U. Sch. Medicine, Boston, 1975-85, prof., 1985-97; ret., 1998. Trustee Baystate Med. Ctr., 1995-97. Fellow Am. Coll. Anesthesiology; mem. Am. Soc. Anesthesiologists, New Eng. Soc. Anesthesiologists (pres. 1994), Mass. Soc. Anesthesiologists, Sigma Xi. E-mail: tberg@alum.mit.edu.

TRACHTENBERG, MATTHEW J. bank holding company executive; b. N.Y.C., June 20, 1958; s. Mark Trachtenberg and Joanne Horne. BA magna cum laude, NYU, 1974; JD, Bklyn. Law Sch., 1977; MBA in Fin., Fordham U., 1982. Bar: N.Y. 1979. Mgmt. trainee Mfrs. Hanover Trust Co., N.Y.C., 1977-78, credit analyst, 1978-79, corp. banking rep., 1979-80, asst. sec., 1980-82, asst. v.p., 1982, v.p., 1982-86, v.p., corp. sec., 1987-92, Mfrs. Hanover Corp., N.Y.C., 1987-92; dir. Mfrs. Hanover Found., 1987-92; v.p., sec. regional bd. Chem. Bank, N.Y.C., 1992-96; v.p., dep. corp. sec. Chem. Banking Corp., 1992-96, Chem. Bank, 1992-96; sec. Chem. Bank Regional Bd., 1992-96; v.p. Chem. Bank, 1992-96, Chem. Banking Corp., 1992-96; v.p. asst. corp. sec. Chase Manhattan Corp., N.Y.C., 1996-98, Chase Manhattan Bank, N.Y.C., 1996-98. Sec. Chase Manhattan Regional bd., 1996-98; v.p. PNC Bank, N.Y.C., 1999-2000, sr. pvt. banker, 1999-2000; v.p. Fleet Bank, N.Y.C., 2000—, sr. pvt. banker, 2000—. Bd. dirs., pres. Nat. Orch. Assn.; bd. dirs., treas. N.Y. Eye and Ear Infirmary; bd. dirs., past pres. U.S.O. of Met. N.Y.; mem. adv. edn. com. Lighthouse for the Blind. N.Y. State Regents scholar. Mem. N.Y. State Bar Assn., Am. Soc. Corp. Secs., Phi Beta Kappa, Pi Sigma Alpha. Avocations: music, fishing, painting, writing. Office: Fleet Bank 60 E 42d St 3d Fl New York NY 10165

TRACHTENBERG, STEPHEN JOEL, university president; b. Bklyn., Dec. 14, 1937; s. Oscar M. and Shoshana G. (Weinstock) Trachtenberg; m. Francine Zorn, June 24, 1971; children: Adam Maccabee, Ben-Lev. BA, Columbia U., 1959; JD, Yale U., 1962; M in Pub. Adminstrn., Harvard U., 1966; LHD (hon.) , Trinity Coll., 1986; HHD (hon.) , U. Hartford, 1989; LLD (hon.) , Hanyang U., Seoul, 1990; DPA (hon.) , Kyonggi U., Seoul, 1994; LLD (hon.) , Richmond Coll., London, 1995; MD (hon.) , Odessa State Med. U., Ukraine, 1996; LLD (hon.) , Mount Vernon Coll., 1997; LHD (hon.) , Boston U., 1999, Gratz Coll., 1999; LLD (hon.) , So. Conn. State U., 2001, U. New Haven, 2002. Bar: N.Y. 1964, U.S. Supreme Ct. 1967. Atty. AEC, 1962—65; legis. asst. to Congressman John Brademas of Ind., Washington, 1965; tutor law Harvard Coll.; tchg. fellow edn. and pub. policy J.F. Kennedy Grad. Sch. Govt., Harvard U., 1965—66; spl. asst. to U.S. edn. commr. Office of Edn., HEW, Washington, 1966—68; assoc. prof. polit. sci. Boston U., 1969—77, assoc. dean, 1969—70, dean, 1970—76, v.p. acad. svcs., 1976—77; pres., prof. pub. adminstrn. U. Hartford, Conn., 1977—88, George Washington U., Washington, 1988—. Adv. bd. The Presidency; mem. Fed. City Coun.; bd. dirs. Consortium of Univs. Washington Met. Area, Riggs Bank, Greater Washington Bd. Trade, Nat. Edn. Telecom. Orgn., Washington Rsch. Libr. Consortium, DC Com. to Promote Washington; exec. adv. coun. SCT Edn. Sys. Contbr. articles to profl. jours. Trustee Al-Akhawayn U., Morocco, Com. for Econ. Devel.; active 2001 U.S. Savs. Bonds Vol. Com.; chmn. Md./DC Selection Com., 1998—2002, Rhodes Scholarships; active D.C. Mayor's Bus. Adv. Coun.; exec. panel Chief Naval Ops.; bd. overseers List Coll. Jewish Theol. Sem. Am.; bd. dirs. Urban League, Washington. Decorated Grand Officier du Wissam Al Alaoui King Mohammed VI of Morocco; named Outstanding Young Person, Boston Jr. C. of C., 1970, Alumnus of Yr., James Madison H.S., 1982, Washingtonian of Yr., Washingtonian Mag., 2000, Jan. 22, 1998 Stephen Joel Trachtenberg Day, D.C. City Council, Feb. 2, 1999 Stephen Joel Trachtenberg Day, Mayor of San Francisco; named one of 100 Young Leaders, Acad. Am. Council Learning, 1978, Fifty Outstanding Alumni Problem Solvers, Harvard's John F. Kennedy Sch. Govt., 1987; recipient Myrtle Wreath award, Hadassah, 1982, Scopus award, Am. Friends of Hebrew U., 1984, Human Rels. award, NCCJ, 1987, NAACP award, 1988, Conn. Bar Assn. citation, 1988, Univ. medal of highest honor, Kyung Hee U., Korea, 1990, Martin Luther King, Jr. Internat. Salute award, 1992, Hannah G. Solomon award, Nat. Coun. Jewish Women, 1992, Father of Yr. award, Washington Urban League, 1993, Univ. Pres. medal, Kyonggi U., Korea, 1993, Merit award, Am. Czech and Slovak Assn., 1993, John Jay award, Columbia U., 1995, Spirit of Democracy award, Am. Jewish Congress, 1995, Newcomen Soc. award, 1995, Disting. Achievement medal, Greenberg Ctr. for Judaic Studies U. Hartford, 1995, Humanitarian award, B'nai B'rith, 1996, Disting. Pub. Svc. award, U.S. Dept. of State Sec.'s Open Forum, 1997, Tree of Life award, Jewish Nat. Fund, 1999, High Twelve Internat. Founders award, 2000, Key of Life award, Egypt's Inernat. Econ. Forum, 2001, medal of merit, U.S. Dept. Treasury, 2001; fellow Winston Churchill fellow, eng., 1969, Hon. Wolcott fellow, 1999, Morse Coll. Yale U. Fellow: Am. Acad. Arts and Scis.; mem.: Bus.-Higher Edn. Forum, Ind. Retail Cattleman's Assn. (adv. coun.), Sr. Soc. Sachems, Coun. Fgn. Rels., Newcomen Soc. U.S. (life; trustee), Am. Coun. Learned Soc. (assoc.), Internat. Assn. Univ. Pres. (N.Am. coun.), N.Y. Acad. Scis., Am. Assn. Univ. Adminstrs. (pres. 1998—2000, Disting. Svc. award 1996), Hannibal Club, Nat. Press Club, Cosmos Club, Harvard Club, Tumble Brook Country Club, Univ. Club, George Washington U. Club, Masons (33d degree, Grand Cross award), Phi Beta Kappa. Office: George Washington U Office of Pres 2121 Eye St N W Rm 802 Washington DC 20052-0001*

TRACHTMAN, JERRY H. lawyer; b. Phila., Aug. 10, 1945; BSEE, Pa. State U., 1967; JD, U. Fla., 1976. Bar: Fla. 1976, U.S. Dist. Ct. (mid. dist.) Fla. 1978, U.S. Supreme Ct. 1980, U.S. Ct. Appeals (11th cir.) 1989; cert. aviation law. Elec. engr. N.Am. Aviation, Columbus, Ohio, 1967-68, Apollo spacecraft systems engr. Kennedy Space Ctr., Fla., 1968-71; Skylab project engr. Martin Marietta, 1971-74; pvt. practice Satellite Beach, Fla., 1976-80; atty., mng. ptnr. Trachtman, Henderson and Futchko, P.A., Melbourne, 1980—. Adj. prof. aviation law Fla. Inst. Tech., Melbourne, 1983-90; mem. adv. bd. Kaiser Coll., Melbourne, 1994—. Pres. Jewish Fedn. Brevard County, 2000—, bd. dirs. 1996—. Recipient Apollo achievement award NASA. Mem. ATLA, Fla. Bar Assn. (chmn. aviation law com. 1995-96, vice chmn. 1993-95), Lawyer-Pilots Bar Assn., NTSB Bar Assn. (founder 1984—), Acad. Fla. Trial Lawyers. Office: Ste #300 1735 W Hibiscus Blvd Melbourne FL 32901-2616 E-mail: jtrachtman@thf-law.com.

TRACI, KATHLEEN FRANCES, librarian; b. Chgo., Jan. 13, 1943; d. William Henry and Mary Teresa (O'Connor) Kammien; m. Paul A. Traci, Nov. 25, 1965; children: Sean, Meg, Beth, Patricia. MLS, U. Wis., 1975; EdS, Butler U., 1991; EdD, Ind. U., 1998. Libr. media specialist Waukesha (Wis.) Elem. Sch., 1976-84, Butler Middle Sch., Waukesha, 1984-86; libr. Marian Coll., Indpls., 1987-88; libr. media specialist Noblesville (Ind.) Middle Sch., 1990-91, Decatur Ctrl. High Sch., Indpls., 1991—98; dir. libr. media svcs. Rockford (Ill.) Pub. Schs. #205, 1999—. Pres. Friends of Hussey-Mayfield Libr., Zionsville, Ind.; bd. dirs. Rock Valley C.C. Libr., Rockford Pub. Libr. Found. Mem. ALA, ASCD, Am. Assn. Sch. Librs., Ill. Sch. Libr. Media Assn., Ind. U. Sch. Adminstrs. Assn. Avocations: swimming, exercising, reading, storytelling, fishing. Home: 2640 Saddlebrook Dr Naperville IL 60564-4623 Office: Libr Media Svcs Dept/Sterling Holley Ctr Rockford Pub Schs 2000 Christina St Rockford IL 61104 E-mail: tracik@rps205.com.

TRACKMAN, PHILIP CHARLES, biochemist, researcher; b. Montclair, N.J., July 15, 1953; s. John C. and Irene (Boveri) T.; m. Susan Kirkpatrick Troxler, Oct. 24, 1979; children: Louisa, Eric. BA in chem., Coll. of Wooster, 1975; PhD, Boston Univ., 1980; post doctoral rsch., Brandeis Univ., 1980-83. Staff scientist Novo Labs., Wilton, Conn., 1983-85, team leader, 1985-86; rsch. asst. prof. Boston Univ., 1987-92; asst. prof. Boston U. Goldman Sch. Dental Medicine, Boston, 1992-2000, assoc. prof., 2000—. Contbr. articles to profl. jours. Recipient First award Nat. Inst. Health, 1994, fellowship Am. Cancer Soc., 1981. Mem. Am. Chem. Soc. (assoc.), Sigma Xi. Protestant. Achievements include first to demonstrate that non-peptidyl amines are substates for lysyl oxidase and used this to develop a new assay. First to clone lysyl oxidase cDNA; first to study lysyl oxidase regulation by growth factors in osteoblastic cells; and in gingival fibrolasts; first to identify intermediates in a methionine salvage pathway; research in regulation of extracellular matrix biosynthesis in mineralized and non-mineralized tissues in health and disease; patentee in field. Avocation: playing flute. Office: Boston U Goldman Sch Dental Medicine 700 Albany St # 201 Boston MA 02118-2518

TRACT, MARC MITCHELL, lawyer; b. N.Y.C., Sept. 20, 1959; s. Harold Michael and Natalie Ann (Meyerowitz) T.; m. Sharon Beth Widrow; children: Melissa Hope, Harrison Michael, Sarah Michelle. BA in Biology, Ithaca Coll., 1981; JD, Pepperdine U., 1984. Bar: N.Y. 1985, N.J. 1985, D.C. 1986. Assoc. Kroll & Tract, N.Y.C., 1985—90, ptnr., 1990—94, Rosenman & Colin LLP, N.Y.C., 1994—2002, Katten Muchin Zavis Rosenman, N.Y.C., 2002—. Bd. dirs. Rampart Ins. Co., Western Continental Ins. Co, N.Y.C., Navigators Group Inc., N.Y.C., MAPFRE Reins. Corp., Florham Park, N.J., AXA Nordstern Art Ins. Corp., N.Y.C., Fortress Ins. Co., Rosemont, Ill. Bd. dirs. Italian Acad. Found. Decorated Order of Merit of Savoy. Mem. ABA, Assn. of Bar of City of N.Y., N.Y. State Bar Assn., N.J. State Bar Assn., N.Y. County Lawyers Assn., Am. Coun. Germany, Old Westbury Golf and Country Club, Met. Club, Econ. Club N.Y. Republican. Office: KMZ Rosenman 575 Madison Ave Fl 11 New York NY 10022-2511

TRACTENBERG, CRAIG R. lawyer; b. Phila., Dec. 5, 1956; s. Jerome and Diane (Epstein) T.; m. Anna P. McDonald, June 9, 1981; children: David, Jeremy. BA, La Salle Coll., Phila., 1979; JD, Temple U., 1981. Bar: Pa. 1981, N.J. 1983, U.S. Dist. Ct. (ea. dist.) Pa. 1981, U.S. Dist. Ct. N.J. 1983, U.S. Ct. Appeals (2d cir.) 1983, U.S. Ct. Appeals (3rd cir.) 1990, U.S. Supreme Ct. 1987. Assoc. Abraham, Pressman & Bauer, P.C., Phila., 1981-87, ptnr., 1987-97; shareholder Buchanan Ingersoll, Profl. Corp., 1998—. Bd. dirs. Rita's Water Ice Franchising, Inc., ALS Assn. and Camp Ramah; judge pro tem Phila. Ct. Common Pleas. Contbg. editor Franchise Law Quar., Franchise Law Digest, U. Mich. Jour. Law Rev., Franchise Update, Sum., 1991; articles editor ABA Franchise Law Jour.; contbr. articles to law jours. and profl. publs. Trustee Har Zion Temple, Penn Valley, Pa., 1988—. Mem. ABA, Pa. Bar Assn. (chmn. com. on franchising), Phila. Bar Assn., N.J. Bar Assn., Internat. Franchise Assn. Republican. Home: 249 Ithan Creek Rd Villanova PA 19085-1339 Office: Buchanan Ingersoll Profl Corp 1835 Market St 14th Fl Philadelphia PA 19103-2985

TRACY, ALAN THOMAS, trade association administrator; b. Janesville, Wis., May 3, 1947; s. Robert Elmer and Frances Dina (Daane) T.; m. Kris Cunningham; children: Chad, Paul, Sarah. BS in Agrl. Econs., Cornell U., Ithaca, N.Y., 1969; MBA, U. Wis., 1970. With Tracy & Son Farms, Inc., Janesville, Wis., 1970-81, v.p., 1973-76, pres., 1976-81; gen sales mgr., assoc. adminstr. Dept. Agr., Washington, 1981-82, dep. undersec. for internat. affairs and commodity programs, 1982-85, dep. asst. sec. dor mktg. and inspection services, 1985-86; spl. asst. to pres. for agrl. trade and food assistance The White House, 1986-89; sec. Wis. Dept. Agr., Trade and Consumer Protection, Madison, 1990-97; pres. U.S. Wheat Assocs., Washington, 1997—. Dir. Heritage Bank, Beloit, Janesville, 1978-81; pres. Mid. Am. Intrnat. Agrl. Trading Coun., 1994, Nat. Assn. State Depts. Agr., 1995-96. Trustee Beloit Coll., Wis., 1980-83; chmn. Republican party Rock County, 1972-74. Named Outstanding Young Farmer Wis. Wis. Jaycees, 1980; Nat. Merit scholar, 1965 Mem. Janesville C. of C. (chmn. agribus. com. 1978-79) Lodges: Rotary-Janesville (dir. 1980-81). Methodist. Office: US Wheat Assocs 1620 I St NW Ste 801 Washington DC 20006-4005

TRACY, ALLEN WAYNE, management consultant; b. Windsor, Vt., July 25, 1943; s. J. Wayne and Helen (Bernard) T.; m. Karla Noelte, Dec. 14, 1969; children: Tania, Tara. BA, U. Vt., 1965; MBA cum laude, Boston U., 1974. Retail salesman Exxon Corp., Boston, 1965-72; mgr. mfg. Leonard Silver Mfg. Co., Inc., 1974-78, v.p. ops., 1979-81; pres. OESM Corp., N.Y.C., 1978-81; pres., bd. dirs. Gold Lance Inc., Houston, 1981-91; v.p. ops. Town & Country Corp., 1989-92; sr. v.p. L.G. Balfour Co., 1990-92; asst. to pres. Syratech Corp., Boston, 1993; dir. ops. Goldman-Kolber Co., Inc., Norwood, Mass., 1994; exec. v.p., COO, George H. Fuller & Son Co., Inc., Pawtucket, R.I., 1994-97; COO, BioMatrix Techs., Inc., Lincoln, 1997-98; mgmt. cons. IPA, Buffalo Grove, Ill., 1998—. Bd. dirs. Verilyte Gold, Inc., L.G. Balfour Co., Inc. Mem. Ashland Bd. Selectmen, 1977-78; chmn. Ashland Study Town Govt. Com., 1976-77; vice chmn. ch. coun. Federated Ch. Ashland, 1979-80, chmn., 1981; bd. dirs. Nottingham Forest Civic Assn., 1886. With U.S. Army, 1965-68. Mem. Nottingham Forest Club (bd. dirs. Houston 1986), Beta Gamma Sigma. Home: 118 Lakeview Dr Nokomis FL 34275 Office: IPA 1250 Barclay Blvd Buffalo Grove IL 60089-4500

TRACY, CAROL COUSINS, association executive, former educator; b. N.Y.C., Jan. 31, 1943; d. James Franklin and Ruth (Hubbard) Cousins; m. William Ferber Tracy, Feb. 14, 1963; children: Lisa, Scott, Jennifer. BA, Duke U., 1965. Cert. educator, math. Tchr. Thrasher Sch., Signal Mountain, Tenn., 1967-69; tchr., math. Girls Prep. Sch., Chattanooga, 1980-91; exec. dir., founder Psi Beta, 1981—; fin. officer Psi Chi, 1991-98. Vol., bd. dirs. Jr. League, Chattanooga, 1973-83; tutor Inner City, Chattanooga, 1974-75, 88-90; sec., vol. Allied Arts, Chattanooga; publicity LWV; v.p., pres. Chattanooga Ballet Bd., 1991-98; sec., bd. dirs. Signal Mountain Libr.; sec., bd. dirs. Scenic Land Sch., 2000-. Avocations: skiing, reading, roller blading. Home: 1027 Westbridge Ln Chattanooga TN 37405-4274 Office: Psi Beta 1027 Westbridge Ln Chattanooga TN 37405-4274

TRACY, DAVID, theology educator; b. Yonkers, N.Y., Jan. 6, 1939; Licentiate in Theology, Gregorian U., Rome, 1964, Doctorate in Theology, 1969; hon. doctorate, U. of the South, 1982, Cath. Theol. Union, 1990; LHD (hon.), Rosary Coll., 1992, Fairfield U., 1993, Williams Coll., 1994, Fontbonne Coll., 1995, St. Xavier U., 1996. Instr. theology Cath. U. Am., Washington, 1967-69; prof. theology Divinity Sch., U. Chgo., 1969—, prof. com. analysis of ideas and methods, 1981—, Disting. Svc. prof., 1985, Andrew Thomas Greeley and Grace McNichols Greeley Disting. Svc. prof. Cath. studies, 1987, prof. com. social thought, 1990—. Lectr. Beijing Inst. Sci. Study of Religion, Trinity Coll., Dublin, Gregorian U., Rome, World Coun. Chs., Geneva, Cath. U., Leuven, Belgium, Union Theol. Sem., Princeton Theol. Sem., numerous U.S. univs. including Harvard, Yale, Fordham, Notre Dame, Vanderbilt, So. Meth., Xavier, Marquette. Author: The Achievement of Bernard Lonergan, 1970, Blessed Rage for Order: The New Pluralism in Theology, 1975, The Analogical Imagination: Christian Theology and the Context of Pluralism, 1981, Plurality and Ambiguity: Hermeneutics, Religion and Hope, 1987, Religion and the Public Realm, 1987, Dialogue with the Otter, 1990, On Naming the Present, 1994; co-author: (with John Cobb) Talking About God, 1983, (with Stephen Happel) The Catholic Vision, 1983, (with Robert M. Grant) A Short History of the Interpretation of the Bible, 1984; co-editor: (with Hans Küng and Johann Baptist Metz) Towards Vatican III: The Work That Needs to be Done, (with H. Küng) Theologie-Wohin?. German edit., 1983, English edit., 1985, (with Hans Küng) Paradigm Change in Theology, 1989; editor or co-editor various spl. vols. for Jour. Religion, Concilium jour.; co-editor Jour. Religion, Religious Studies Rev., Commonweal; past mem. editorial bd. Jour. Am. Acad. Religion, Theol. Studies jour.; current editorial bd. Theology Today, Jour. Pastoral Psychology; contbr. articles to scholarly and popular jours. including Jour. Religion, Theology Today, Critical Inquiry, Daedalus, Jour. Am. Acad. Religion, New Republic, N.Y. Times Book Rev., Christian Century Mem. Am. Acad. Arts and Scis., Am. Acad. Religion, Am. Theol. Soc., Cath. Theol. Soc. Am. (pres. 1977-78). Office: U Chgo The Divinity Sch 1025 E 58th St Chicago IL 60637-1509

TRACY, HAROLD DEWAYNE, secondary education educator, retired; b. Midwest, Wyo., Nov. 10, 1928; s. Lester Otto and Edith Grace (Fraley) Tracy; m. June A. Burch, Sept. 9, 1950 (div.); children: Kim D., Todd R., Lisa A.; m. Barbara Ann Schurman; children: Matthew D., Elizabeth L. AA in Edn., North Idaho Jr. Coll., 1952; BA in Edn., Whitworth Coll., 1954; postgrad., San Francisco State U., 1959. Tchr. Coeur D'Alene (Idaho) Sch., 1952-54, Oswego (Oreg.) Sch. Dist., 1954-60, D.O.D., Subic Bay, The Phillipines, 1960-64, Forest Grove (Oreg.) Dilley, 1964-66; ins. rep. Northwestern Marsh, Portland, 1966-71; pres. Red Barn Rest Corp., Redmond, Oreg., 1971-79; owner, mgr. Thrifty Ads, Bend, 1979-87. Sgt. USAF, 1946-49. Democrat. Presbyterian. Avocations: flying, hunting, fishing, reading, traveling. Home: 2720 Roberts Rd Medford OR 97504

TRACY, JAMES, history educator, headmaster; b. Stoughton, Mass., Jan. 18, 1961; s. Edward and Dorothy (O'Connor) T.; m. Janet Sargent; 1 child, Forrest. BA, U. Mass., 1984; MA, Stanford U., 1988, PhD, 1993; postgrad., Boston U., 2002—. Instr.history Hotchkiss Sch., Lakeville, Conn., 1993-99; instr., assoc. Inst. Writing & Thinking, Bard Coll., Annandale-on-Hudson, NY, 1995—99; asst. to chancellor Boston U., 1999—2000; headmaster Boston U. Acad., 2000—. Adj. lectr. Stanford (Calif.) U., 1992; adj. instr. Foothills Coll., Palo Alto, Calif., 1993, Deanza Coll., Santa Rosa, Calif., 1993; spkr., cons. and presenter in field. Author: Direct Action, 1996; co-editor, contbr. Christmas Unwrapped, 2001. Trustee Cambridge Friends Sch., 2002--. Nat. Archives grantee, 1992-93; vis. fellow Yale U., New Haven, Conn., 1994-95. Mem. Am. Hist. Assn. Democrat. Mem. Soc. Of Friends. Avocations: writing poetry, chess, astronomy. Office: Boston U Acad 1 University Rd Boston MA 02215-1407

TRACY, JAMES DONALD, historian, educator; b. St. Louis, Feb. 14, 1938; s. Leo W. and Marguerite M. (Meehan) T.; m. Nancy Ann McBride, Sept. 6, 1968 (div. 1993); children: Patrick, Samuel, Mary Ann; m. Suzanne K. Swan, May 2, 1997. BA, St. Louis U., 1959; MA, Johns Hopkins U., 1960, Notre Dame U., 1961; PhD, Princeton U., 1967. Instr. U. Mich., 1964-66; instr. to prof. history U. Minn., Mpls., 1966—, dept. chmn., 1988-91. Vis. prof. U. Leiden, Netherlands, spring 1987, U. Paris IV, 2001. Author: Erasmus: The Growth of a Mind, 1972, The Politics of Erasmus: A Pacifist Intellectual and His Political Milieu, 1979, True Ocean Found; Paludanus' Letters on Dutch Voyages to the Kara Sea, 1980, A Financial Revolution in the Habsburg Netherlands: Renten and Renteniers in the County of Holland, 1515-1565, 1985, Holland under Habsburg Rule: The Formation of a Body Politic, 1506-1566, 1990, Erasmus of the Low Countries, 1996, Europe's Reformations, 1450-1650, 1999, Emperor Charles V, Impresario of War, 2002; editor: Luther and the Modern State in Germany, 1986, The Rise of Merchant Empires: Long Distance Trade in the Early Modern Era, 1350-1750, 1990, The Political Economy of Merchant Empires: Long Distance Trade and State Power in the Early Modern World, 1991, (with T.A. Brady and H.A. Oberman) Handbook of European History in the Late Middle Ages, Renaissance and Reformation, Vol. 1, 1994, Vol. 2, 1995, City Walls: The Urban Enceinte in Global Perspective, 2000; mem. editl. bd. Sixteenth Century Jour., 1979—; co-editor Jour. Early Modern History, 1997-2000, editor, 2000—. Guggenheim fellow, 1972-73; NEH summer grantee, 1977, 85; Fulbright rsch. grantee, Belgium, 1979, Netherlands, 1980; resident fellow Netherlands Inst. for Advanced Studies, 1993-94. Mem. Am. Cath. Hist. Soc. (pres. 1999-00), Soc. Reformation Rsch. (pres. 1995-97), 16th Century Studies Conf. (pres. 1985-86). Republican. Roman Catholic. Home: 757 Osceola Ave # 2 Saint Paul MN 55105-3327 Office: U Minn 614 Social Sci Bldg Minneapolis MN 55455 E-mail: tracy001@tc.edu.

TRACY, JAMES JARED, JR. accountant, law firm administrator; b. Cleve., Jan. 17, 1929; s. James Jared and Florence (Comey) T.; m. Elizabeth Jane Bourne, June 30, 1953 (div. 1988); children: Jane Mackintosh, Elizabeth Boyd, James Jared IV, Margaret Gardiner; m. Judith Anne Cooper, Feb. 18, 1989. AB, Harvard U., 1950, MBA, 1953. CPA, Ohio. Acct., mgr. Price Waterhouse & Co., Cleve., 1953-65; treas., CFO Clevite Corp., 1965-69; asst. treas. Republic Steel Corp., 1969-70, treas., 1970-75; v.p., treas. Johns-Manville Corp., Denver, 1976-81; v.p., treas., CFO I. T. Corp., L.A., 1981-82; exec. dir. Hufstedler, Miller, Carlson & Beardsley, 1983-84, Shank, Irwin & Conant, Dallas, 1984-85, Pachter, Gold & Schaffer, L.A., 1985-86; v.p., sr. cons. Right Assocs., 1987-91; dir. adminstrn. Larson & Burnham, Oakland, Calif., 1991-95; ret., 1995; adminstrv. dir. Law Offices of Thomas E. Miller, Newport Beach, Calif., 1996-97; human resources adminstr. Baker & McKenzie, San Francisco, 1997-98; dir. adminstrn. Wartnick, Chaber, Harowitz, Smith & Tigerman, 1998-2000, Kasdan, Simonds, & Epstein, Irvine, 2000—. Trustee and v.p. Miss Hall's Sch., Pittsfield, Mass., 1970-78; dir. Union Commerce Bank, Cleve., 1971-76; adv. bd. mem. Arkwright-Boston Ins. Co., Boston, 1976-81. Trustee and v.p. Cleve. Soc. for Blind, 1965-76; trustee Western Res. Hist. Soc., Cleve., 1972-76; treas. St. Peters by the Sea Presbyn. Ch., Palos Verdes, Calif., 1981-91, Newport Beach (Calif.) Pub. Libr. Literacy Coun., 2002—. Recipient Alumni award Harvard U., Denver, 1981. Mem. AICPA, Ohio Soc. CPAs, Assn. Legal Adminstrs., Piedmont Montclair Rotary Club (pres. 1995-96), Harvard Radcliffe Club So. Calif. Avocations: sailing, golf, gardening. Home: 2204 Fortuna Newport Beach CA 92660 E-mail: jtracy@kasdansimonds.com.

TRACY, JAMES LEON, artist; b. Bloomington, Ind., Sept. 19, 1950; s. James Allen Tracy and Wilma Jean Pate; children: James Patrick, Michael Evan. Student, Vincennes U., 1970, Ind. U. S.E., New Albany, 1989—90, U. N.Mex., 1991, Ind. U., Bloomington, 1992—94. Illustrator, graphic designer Ind. U. Radio/TV Ctr., Bloomington, 1984—88; dir. design Brucie Fox, Inc., New Albany, 1988—90; art dir. Midtown Screenprinting, Albuquerque, 1990—92, Apparel Design Group, Bloomington, 1992—. Bd. dirs. Ind. Heritage Arts, Nashville, 1999—2000. Exhibitions include Alliance Gallery, Indpsl. Mus. Art, Bloomington Hosp. Purchase Exhbn., The Hoosier Salon, Ind. State Mus., Indpls., 1975, 1986, 1996, 1997 (Outstanding Traditional Painting in Any Media, 1997), 1998, Ind. Heritage Arts Exhbn., Nashville, Ind., 1998 (3 merit awards), 2000, Floyd County Mus., New Albany, 1988, Indpls. Mus. Art, Columbus (Ind.) Gallery, So. Ind. Artists Exhbn., Bloomington, Wabash Valley Exhbn., Sheldon Swope Art Mus., Terre Haute, Ind., 1987, one-man shows include Brown County Art Gallery, Nashville, Ind., McCaughan & Burr Fine Art, St. Louis. Home and Studio: PO Box 1095 Nashville IN 47448

TRACY, JANET RUTH, legal educator, librarian; b. Denison, Iowa, July 16, 1941; d. L. M. and Grace (Harvey) T.; m. Rodd Mc Cormick Reynolds, Feb. 15, 1975 (dec. June 1993); children: Alexander, Lee. BA, U. Oreg., 1963; ML, U. Wash., 1964; JD, Harvard U., 1969. Bar: N.Y. 1970. Reference libr. Harvard Coll. Librs., Cambridge, Mass., 1964-66; assoc. Kelley Drye & Warren, N.Y.C., 1969-71; dir. data base design Mead Data Ctrl., Inc., 1971-75; dir. rsch. Mvpl. Employees Legal Svc. Fund, 1975-76; from asst. to assoc. prof. N.Y. Law Sch., 1976-82; asst. libr. dir. Law Libr. Columbia U., 1982-86; prof., law libr. dir. Fordham U., 1986—. Chmn. Conf. Law Librs. Jesuit Univs., 1988-89. Co-author: Professional Staffing and Job Security in Academic Law Libraries, 1989. Recipient Catalog Automation award Winston Found., 1990, 91, 92. Home: 285 Riverside Dr New York NY 10025-5276 Office: Fordham U Sch of Law 140 W 62nd St New York NY 10023-7407 E-mail: jtracy@law.fordham.edu.

TRACY, JIM, professional sports team executive; m. Debra Tracy; children: Brian, Chad, Mark. Attended, Marietta Coll. Bench coach, coord. all on-field activities L.A. Dodgers; mgr. Midwest League Single-A Peoria, Cubs' affiliate , 1987; minor league mgr. Chgo. Cubs, Cin. Reds, Expos, 1987—91, 1993—94; with Reds, 1989—91, minor league field coord., 1992; mgr. Triple-A Ottawa, Montreal's affiliate , 1994; bench coach Felipe Alou, Montreal Expo mgr. , 1993—; interim mgr. L.A. Dodgers, 2000, mgr., 2000—. Named The Sporting News' Mgr. of Yr., 1993, Ea. League's Mgr. of Yr., 1993, NCAA Divsn. III All-Am. selection, Marietta Coll., Ohio. Mem.: Marietta Coll. Sports Hall of Fame. Office: LA Dodgers 1000 Elysian Park Ave Los Angeles CA 90012*

TRACY, JOHN MICHAEL, small business owner, composer; b. Elmira, N.Y., Jan. 11, 1957; s. John Richard and Nancy Anita Tracy; m. Debra Ann Tracy, Dec. 10, 1977; children: Seth Charles, Matthew John. Grad., Chenango Forks (N.Y.) H.S., 1975. Gas sta. attendant Rotary Gas, Whitney Point, NY, 1975—76; owner Ace Cleaning Co., Marathon, 1976—77; printer assembler IBM, Boca Raton, Fla., 1977—78; auto mechanic Van Brunt Datsun-Cadillac, Elmira, 1978; owner Custom Custodial Enterprises, 1978—82, Custom Colour and Vinyl Repair, Elmira, 1982—89, John Tracy's Paintless Dent Removal, Raleigh, NC, 1989—. Creator Road Pizza Pancake Pets; , composer over 200 songs. Mem.: Songwriters Guild of Am., Nashville Songwriters Assn., Tarheel Tigers GTO Club. Avocations: fishing, classic cars, drawing, painting, hunting. Office: John Tracy's Paintless Dent Removal 6200B Daimler Way Raleigh NC 27607

TRACY, MARK E. gaming executive; b. Alhambra, Calif., Aug. 27, 1956; s. Walter S. Tracy and Jean E. Steers; children: Brandon. BA in Social Ecology, U. Calif., Irvine, 1974—78. Owner WeddingJubilation.com. Author: The Casino Management Handbook, 1995. Achievements include invention of Pyramid-Style Video Game Method and Device; Air-Activated Fish Feeder. Avocations: skiing, hang-gliding, fishing.

TRACY, MICHAEL CAMERON, choreographer, performer, educator; b. Florence, Italy, Feb. 1, 1952; s. Stanley B. and Elizabeth Lee (McIntosh) T. BA Magna cum laude, Dartmouth Coll., 1973. Adj. faculty Yale U., New Haven, 1992—. Artistic dir. Pilobolus Dance Theatre, Washington, Conn., 1974—; choreographer Die Zauberflöte, European prodn. with John Eliot Gardiner's Monteverdi Choir and English Baroque Soloists, 1995; co-choreographer: Ciona, 1974, Monkshood's Farewell, 1975, Untitled, 1976, Day Two, 1980, Pyramid of the Moon, 1996, Aeros, 1996, Elysian Fields, 1997, Apoplexy, 1998, The Hand That Mocked, The Heart That Fed, 1998, A Selection, 1999, Sweet Dreams, 2000, Symbiosis, 2001, The Brass Ring, 2002; choreographer Curiouser and Curiouser Nat. Theatre of Deaf, 1996. Recipient Berlin Critics award, 1975, New Eng. Theatre Conf. prize, 1977, Brandeis award, 1978, Excellence in Arts award Conn. Commn. on the Arts, 1981, Emmy award 1997, Scripps award, 2000; sr. fellow Dartmouth Coll., 1973. Mem. Dartmouth Players. Office: PO Box 388 Washington Depot CT 06794-0388 E-mail: mtracy@pilobolus.com.

TRACY, PATRICIA ELLA, dietitian, consultant; b. Springfield, Mo., May 12, 1940; d. Henry Francis and Helen Irene Meeth; m. Robert Barnetté McPherson, Sept. 10, 1966 (dec. Aug. 1994); children: Patricia Heather, Robert Meeth; m. Larry W. Tracy, Apr. 21, 2001. AB, BS, Drury Coll., Springfield, Mo., 1963. Registered dietitian. 5th and 6th grade tchr. St. Francis Xavier Grade Sch., Sikeston, Mo., 1963-64; dietetic intern Good Samaritan Hosp., Cin., 1964-65; dir. nutrition Mo. Rehab. Ctr., Mt. Vernon, 1965-95; cons. St. Vincent's Hosp., Monett, Mo., 1980-85, Ash Grove (Mo.) Nursing, 1980-85, Sandoz Nutrition, Mo., 1996—. Substitute tchr. Mt. Vernon Pub. Sch. Sys., Monett (Mo.) Pub. Schs. With Parents as 1st tchrs. Mt. Vernon Elem., 1980—; elder First Presbyn. Ch., Mt. Vernon. Mem. Mo. Heart Assn. (mem. bd. state planning com.), Lawrence County Heart Assn. (pres. 1990-93), Mo. Dietetic Assn. (bd. dirs. 1970-72), Kiwanis. Republican. Presbyterian. Avocations: handwork, theater, music, reading. Home: 11998 Lawrence 1106 Mount Vernon MO 65712-8339

TRACY, RICHARD E. medical educator; b. Klamath Falls, Oreg., Apr. 30, 1934; BA, U. Chgo., 1955, MD, PhD, 1961. Diplomate Am. Bd. Anatomic Pathology, Am. Bd. Forensic Pathology. Prof. Sch. Medicine La. State U., New Orleans, 1967. Office: Sch of Medicine La State U Health Sci Ctr New Orleans LA 70112

TRACY, ROBERT (ROBERT EDWARD TRACY), English language educator, poetry translator; b. Woburn, Mass., Nov. 23, 1928; s. Hubert William and Vera Mary (Hurley) T.; m. Rebecca Garrison, Aug. 26, 1956; children: Jessica Janes, Hugh Garrison, Dominick O'Donovan. AB in Greek with honors, Boston Coll., 1950; MA, Harvard U., 1954, PhD, 1960. Teaching fellow Harvard U., Cambridge, Mass., 1954-58; instr. Carleton Coll., Northfield, Minn., 1958-60; from asst. prof. English, to assoc. prof., then prof. U. Calif., Berkeley, 1960-89, prof. English and Celtic Studies, 1989—, assoc. dir. Dickens Project, 1994-95. Vis. prof., Bruern fellow in Am. studies U. Leeds, Eng., 1965-66; vis. prof., Leverhulme fellow Trinity Coll., Dublin, 1971-72; vis. Kathryn W. Davis prof. slavic studies Wellesley (Mass.) Coll., 1979; Charles Mills Gayley lectr. U. Calif., Berkeley, 1989-90; vis. prof. Anglo-Irish lit. Trinity Coll., 1995-96. Author: Trollope's Later Novels, 1978, The Unappeasable Host: Studies in Irish Identities, 1998; translator (poems by Osip Mandelstam): Stone, 1981, 2d edit., 1991; editor J.M Synge's The Aran Islands, 1962, The Way We Live Now (Anthony Trollope), 1974, The Macdermots of Ballycloran (Anthony Trollope), 1989, Nina Balatka and Linda Tressel (Anthony Trollope), 1991, In A Glass Darkly (Sheridan Le Fanu) 1993, Rhapsody in Stephen's Green (Flann O'Brien), 1994; adv. editor The Recorder, 1985—, LIT (Lit., Interpretation, Theory), 1989—, Dickens Studies Annual, 2001--; contbr. articles and revs. to numerous jours. including Shakespeare Quarterly, So. Rev., Nineteenth-Century Fiction, Irish Univ. Rev., Eire-Ireland, Irish Literary Supplement, others; poetry translations in New Orleans Rev., Poetry, N.Y. Rev. of Books, Ploughshares, others. Appointed mem. cultural panel San Francisco-Cork Sister City Com. Fulbright travel grantee, 1965-66; recipient humanities research fellowships U. Calif., Berkeley, 1962, 69, 78, 81, 86 , 92; Guggenheim fellow, 1981-82. Mem. MLA, Philol. Assn. Pacific Coast, Am. Conf. for Irish Studies, Internat. Assn. for Study of Irish Lit. Avocation: exploring western Ireland and no. Calif. Office: U Calif Dept English Berkeley CA 94720-0001

TRACY, SUSANNE MARY, nurse educator; b. Rochester, N.Y., June 9, 1945; d. Edward and Ann (Bihun) Koszalka; m. Daniel A. Tracy, III, June 17, 1967; children: Lisa, Michael, Scott, Erin. BSN, Niagara Univ., 1967; MN, Univ. S.C., 1975; postgrad., Univ. R.I., 1996—; MA, Rivier Coll., 1992. Registered nurse, N.H., Mass. Navy nurse U.S. Navy, Niagara Falls/Pensacola, N.Y./Fla., 1966-68; instr. of nursing Columbus State Univ., Columbus, Ga., 1975-77; asst. prof. nursing Jefferson Cmty. Coll., Watertown, N.Y., 1977-81; asst. head nurse of rehab. Penrose Hosp., Colorado Springs, Colo., 1981-82; edn. cons. Penrose & St. Mary Corwin Hosp., Colorado Springs, Pueblo, 1982-85; asst. prof. nursing Rivier Coll., Nashua, N.H., 1985-91, assoc. prof. nursing, 1991—. Contbr. articles to profl. jours. Decorated Nat. Svc. medal U.S. Navy, 1967; named Outstanding Young Women of Am. Nat. Awards Program, 1977. Mem. Eastern Nursing Rsch. Soc., New Eng. Edn. Assessment Network (bd. dirs. 1995—), Am. Assn. Higher Edn., Sigma Theta Tau, Nat. League for Nsg. Avocations: research, travel. E-mail: olsldr@aol.com.

TRACY, THOMAS MILES, international health organization official; b. Great Barrington, Mass., July 8, 1936; s. Thomas Paul and Marion (Miles) T.; m. June Betts, June 17, 1967; children: Miles Christopher, Keir Thomas John. BA, Colgate U., 1958; MA, Stanford U., 1959; MBA, Columbia U., 1973. Fgn. service officer Dept. State, Washington, 1960-84; counselor Am. Embassy, Moscow, 1975-78, Bonn, Germany, 1978-79; asst. sec. Dept. State, Washington, 1979-83; chief adminstrn. Pan Am./WHO, 1983-98. V.p. Pan-Am. Health and Edn. Found., treas. Trustee, vice chmn. Chelsea Sch., 1988—. With U.S. Army, 1959-60. Recipient Superior Honor award Dept. State, 1978 Mem. Am. Fgn. Svc. Assn. (dir. 1970-72), Am. Fgn. Svc. Protective Assn. (dir. 1988—, v.p. 1997—), Am. Fgn. Svc. Protective Found. (sec., treas.). Home: 5902 Devonshire Dr Bethesda MD 20816-3416

TRACY, TRACY FAIRCLOTH, special education educator; b. Washington, Aug. 22, 1961; d. James Claybert and Esther (Harrell) Faircloth; m. Charles Randall Tracy, Aug. 16, 1986; children: James Wren, Corissa Estelle. BS in Spl. Edn.-Mental Retardation, Old Dominion U., 1983. Tchr. Newport News (Va.) Pub. Schs., 1983—, cmty.-based instrn. specialist, 1992—2000, cmty.-based program adminstr., 2001—. Leader Camp Fire, Inc., Newport News, 1983—92; vol. Newport News Spl. Olympics, 1984—, treas., 1987—; active Va. PTA, Nat. PTA. Named to Outstanding Young Women Am., 1988; recipient Outstanding Svc. award, Newport News Spl. Olympics, 1986, 1988, 1990, Citizenship award, Denbigh Kiwanis, 1988, Appreciation award, Hampton-Newport News Cmty. Svcs. Bd., 1989. Mem.: Student Coun. Exceptional Children (pres. 1982—83), Coun. Exceptional Children, Assn. Retarded Citizens, Alpha Chi, Kappa Delta Pi (Nu Eta chpt.). Democrat.

Methodist. Avocations: arts and crafts, swimming, walking. Home: 4708 Harlequin Way Chesapeake VA 23321-1247 Office: Enterprise Acad 813 Diligence Dr Ste 110 Newport News VA 23606-4237 E-mail: ctracywin@cox.net.

TRACY, WILLIAM FRANCIS, II, lawyer; b. Decatur, Ill., Mar. 7, 1947; s. William Francis and Agnes Madonna (Ryan) Tracy; m. Elaine Baxter, Jan. 23, 1970; children: Katherine, Colleen, Ryan. AB, St. Louis U., 1969; JD, Northwestern U., 1972. Bar: Mo. 1972, Ill. 1977. Law clk. U.S. Dept. of Justice, Washington, 1971; jr. ptnr. Bryan, Cave, McPheeters & McRoberts, St. Louis, 1972—77; assoc. Doss, Simpson & Tracy, Monticello, Ill., 1977—78; ptnr. Miller, Tracy, Braun, Funk & Guenther, 1978—. Spl. asst. atty. gen. State of Ill., Monticello, 1980—83; pub. adminstr., conservator, guardian Piatt County, Ill., 1978—90. Pres. Cmty. Coun., Bement, Ill., 1979. Mem.: ABA, Piatt County Bar Assn., Ill. Bar Assn., Mo. Bar Assn., Monticello Golf Club (treas., bd. dirs. 1982—84), Lions (pres. 1981), KC (adv. 1981—82), Rotary (treas. 1983—84). Home: 807 N State St Monticello IL 61856-1145

TRADER, JOSEPH EDGAR, orthopedic surgeon; b. Milw., Nov. 2, 1946; s. Edgar Joseph and Dorothy Elizabeth (Senzig) T.; m. Janet Louise Burzycki, Sept. 23, 1972 (div. Nov. 1987); children: James, Jonathan, Ann Elizabeth; m. Rhonda Sue Schultz, May 26, 1990. Student, Marquette U., 1964-67; MD, Med. Coll. Wis., 1971. Diplomate Am. Bd. Orthopaedic Surgery. Emergency rm. physician columbia, St. Joseph's Hosps., Milw., 1972-76; orthopaedic surgeon Orthopaedic Assn., Manitowoc, Wis., 1978—. Mem. exec. com. Holy Family Meml. Med. Ctr., Manitowoc, 1985-96, chief-of-staff, 1994-96, ethics com., 1995—, chair instnl. rev. com. Former pres., bd. dirs. Holy Innocents Mens Choir; county del. State Med. Soc. Charitable Sci. and Edn. Found. Fellow Am. Acad. Orthopaedic Surgeons (orthopaedic rsch. and edn. found. state com.), ACS; mem. AMA, Wis. State Med. Soc., Wis. Orthopaedic Soc., Midwest Orthopaedic Soc., Milw. Orthopaedic Soc., Phi Delta Epsilon, Psi Chi, Crown & Anchor. Clubs: Manitowoc Yacht. Roman Catholic. Avocations: singing, piano, scuba diving, tennis, skiing, sailing. Home: 1021 Memorial Dr Manitowoc WI 54220-2242 Office: Orthopaedic Assocs 501 N 10th St Manitowoc WI 54220-4039

TRAFFORD, ABIGAIL, columnist, editor, writer; b. N.Y.C., July 14, 1940; d. William Bradford and Abigail (Sard) T.; children: Abigail Brett Miller, Victoria Brett. BA cum laude, Bryn Mawr Coll., 1962. Researcher Nat. Geog. Soc., Washington, 1964-67; tchr. Hermansberg Mission, Northern Ter., Australia, 1967-68; spl. corr. Time mag., The Washington Post, Houston, 1969-74; writer, asst. mng. editor U.S. News & World Report, Washington, 1975-86; health editor The Washington Post, 1986-00, columnist Second Opinion, 2000—. Author: Crazy Time: Surviving Divorce and Building a New Life, 1982, revised edit., 1992. Journalism fellow Harvard Sch. Pub. Health, 1980. Mem. Washington Press Club Found. (bd. mem. 1989—, pres. 1993-95). Home: 2600 Upton St NW Washington DC 20008-3826 Office: The Washington Post 1150 15th St NW Washington DC 20071-0002

TRAFICANTE, DANIEL DOMINICK, chemist; b. Hoboken, N.J., Nov. 20, 1933; s. Paul and Mary T.; m. Doris Marilyn Poley, Aug. 20, 1955 (div. 1983); children: Daniel D., Mark S., Christopher, Dawn; m. Margaret Mary Kelly, May 19, 1984; children: Paul C., Katrina A.M. BS, Syracuse U., 1955; PhD, MIT, 1962. Commd. 2d lt. USAF, 1956, advanced through grades to capt., 1960, resigned, 1967; dir. undergrad. labs. MIT, Cambridge, 1968-70, dir. nuclear magnetic resonance lab., 1970-78, Yale U., New Haven, 1978-81; dir. Nuclear Magnetic Resonance Inst., Cranford, N.J., 1981-83; dir. chem. instrumentation NSF, Washington, 1983-85; pres. Nuclear Advancement Corp., Kingston, R.I., 1976—. Rsch. fellow, dir. life scis. nuclear magnetic resonance consortium Monsanto Co., Chesterfield, Mo., 1985-86; mem. sci. adv. bd. Inst. Clin. Applications, Boston, 1991-93; dir. Nuclear Magnetic Resonance Concepts; dir. nuclear magnetic resonance rsch. lab. and prof. chemistry U. R.I., 1986—. Author: Chemistry, 1978; editor-in-chief Concepts in Magnetic Resonance jour., 1989—, Jour. of Magnetic Resonance Engring.; mem. edit. bd. Annals of Magnetic Resonance; contbr. articles to profl. jours. Recipient Letter of Commendation Syracuse U., 1987; named Man of Yr. Societa Italiana, 1991 Mem. Am. Chem. Soc. E-mail: nmr_concepts@chm.uri.edu.

TRAFIMOW, DAVID A. psychology educator; b. Ft. Campbell, Ky., May 12, 1962; s. Jordan H. and Alice Trafimow; m. Sabine C. Trafimow, June 14, 1987. BA, U. Ill., 1984, PhD, 1993; MA, Ind. U., 1988. Asst. prof. Va. Tech., Blacksburg, 1992-94, N.Mex. State U., Las Cruces, 1994-98, assoc. prof., 1998-2001, prof., 2001—. Contbr. articles to profl. jours. Mentor McNair Program, New Mex. State U., 1997, 98, 99. Named one of Outstanding Young Men of Am., 1998. Mem. Social Psychol. Attitude Rschrs. Avocations: reading, opera, running, travel. Office: N Mex State U Dept Psychology MSC 3452 PO Box 30001 Las Cruces NM 88003-8001

TRAFIMOW, JORDAN HERMAN, orthopedist; b. Chgo., Nov. 4, 1935; s. Jack and Florence (Silver) Trafimow; m. Alice Emma Lewis, July 11, 1959; children: David, Alan, Janet. BS in Med., U. Ill., 1957, MD, 1958. Orthopedic surgeon Permanente Med. Group, L.A., 1966-69, Elmhurst (Ill.) Clin., 1969-86; asst. prof. Rush St. Luke Presbyn. Med. Ctr., Chgo., 1986—. Contbr. articles to profl. jours. Capt. U.S. Army, 1960-62. Fellow Am. Acad. Orthopedic Surgeons, N.Am. Spine Soc. Jewish. Avocation: chess. Office: Neurodiagnostics 640 E Saint Charles Rd Ste 202 Carol Stream IL 60188-2600

TRAFTON, LAURENCE MUNRO, astronomer, researcher; b. Boston, July 31, 1938; s. Herbert Meara and Vesta Estelle Trafton. BS, Calif. Inst. Tech., 1960, MS, 1961, PhD, 1965. Assoc. scientist Jet Propulsion Lab., Pasadena, Calif., summers 1961-62; project officer Kirtland AFB, Albuquerque, 1968, project scientist, 1968-69; spl. rsch. assoc. dept. astronomy U. Tex., Austin, 1969-72, rsch. scientist dept. astronomy, 1972-93, sr. rsch. scientist McDonald Obs., 1993—. Mem. editl. bd. Icarus, 1976-79, assoc. editor, 1980—; contbr. over 160 articles to sci. jours. 1st lt. USAF, 1965-68. Fellow AAAS; mem. Am. Astron. Soc. (com. mem. div. planetary sci. 1977-80, meeting program chmn. 1976), Internat. Astron. Union. Office: Univ Tex Austin Dept Astronomy Austin TX 78712 E-mail: lmt@astro.as.utexas.edu.

TRAGANAS, ELENI, concert pianist, artist; b. N.Y.C., June 18, 1951; d. Constantine Georgiou and Ioanna Traganas. Studied with, Paul Badura-Skoda, Nadia Reisenberg, Beveridge Webster, Mieczyslaw Horszowski, Eugene List; studied chamber music with, Felix Galimir; diploma, Sch. of Performing Arts, N.Y.C., 1969; MusB, The Juilliard Sch., 1975, MusM, 1976; master classes, Volkwang Musikhochschule, Essen, Germany, 1979—80; internat. master classes, Lucerne Conservatory, Switzerland, 1984. Solo debut Carnegie Recital Hall, N.Y.C., 1978; debut Wigmore Hall, London, 1980, Town Hall, N.Y.C., Am. Music Week Festival, Bonn, Germany; soloist No. State Orch., Salonika, Greece, 1980, Athens (Greece) State Orch., 1989. Condr. master classes and seminars, Greece, 1987—92; lectr., recitalist Mystery and Turbulence: Music of Imperial Russia, U.S., 1996—2002; lectr. on Russian music; guest artist NY Pub. Libr. Lecture-Concerts, 1997—2002. Soloist: Greek nat. TV and radio, 1987—93, soloist: The Israel Sinfonietta, soloist: Chamber Orch. of Salonika, soloist: Nat. Music Week Symphony Orch., rec. artist: WQXR, WNYC, WDR-West German Broadcasting Co., others, 1993, soloist: Rachmaninoff Commemorative Concerts, 1994, CD rec.: The Jewish Mus. Greece, 1994, , ; author (mus. scores): Rachmaninoff-Traganas Isle of the Dead for Piano Solo, 1993, Cadenzas to Mozart's Concerto D-Minor for Piano, 1994, poetry, fiction; contbr. to lit. publs. Recipient Sauter & Margulies award for excellence Hudson Valley Art Assn., 1997, N.J. Watercolor Soc. award, 1998; winner Palma D'Oro Internat. Piano Competition, Italy, 1982. Mem. Am. Soc. Bot. Artists (exhibitor), Catharine Lorillard Wolfe Art Club, Inc. (exhibitor), others. Greek Orthodox.

TRAGEN, IRVING GLENNE, consultant; b. May 18, 1922; m. Eleanor May Dodson, Aug. 7, 1947. AB, U. Calif., Berkeley, 1943; LLM, U. Chile, Santiago, 1946; JD, U. Calif., 1945. Personnel officer Mex.-U.S. Commn. Eradicate Foot & Mouth Disease, Mex., 1948-49, WHO/Pan Am. Sanitary Bur., Washington, 1950-53; with U.S. Dept. State & AID, El Salvador, Chile, Peru, Venezuela, 1953-63; dir. L.Am. bur. instl. devel. AID, 1963-65; dir. AID Mission, La Paz, Bolivia, 1965-68; country dir. Argentina, Paraguay, Uruguay U.S. Dept. State, Washington, 1969-71; v.p. Inter-Am. Found., Rosslyn, Va., 1971-73; chief Ctrl. Am. Regional Office U.S. Dept. State & AID, Guatemala, 1973-75; dir. USAID & econ. counselor U.S. Embassy U.s. Dept. State & AID, Panama, 1975-77; deputy U.S. rep. U.S. Mission fo OAS, U.S. Dept. State, Washington, 1977-80; exec. dir. Inter-Am. ECOSOC, 1980-84; exec. sec. Inter-Am. Drug Abuse Control Commn., 1984-94; prin. advisor Regional C.Am. Legal Devel., San Jose, Costa Rica, 1995-97; cons. L.Am./European Orgns. on Drug Trafficking, Hanford, Calif., 1999—. Mem. adv. bd. U. Pacific, Stockton, Calif., 2000. Mem. editl. bd. (Spanish edit.) Money Laundering Alert Internat., 2000. Trustee emeritus Museo de las Americas, Denver, 2000. Home and Office: 925 Greenfield Ave Hanford CA 93230-3506

TRAGER, D. DAVID, retired pharmacist, general consultant; b. Napa, Calif., Oct. 4, 1931; s. Louis D. (dec.) and Frances Amanda (Brose) T. (dec.); m. Ruth Pacovsky, June 15, 1952 (div. Sept. 1978); children: Louis, Solomon; m. Sarah Ann Brancato, Dec. 28, 1983 (dec. May 2000); children: Daryl, Randy, Missi Hasnas; m. Phyllis Baldwin Douglas, Oct. 7, 2001; 1 child, Robert Gordon Douglas. BS in Pharmacy, U. Calif., San Francisco, 1953; postgrad. in clin. pharmacy, U. So. Calif., 1976, postgrad. in drug action, 1978. Registered pharmacist, Calif. Pharmacist multiple locations, 1953-59; pharmacist, pharmacy mgr. Longs Drugs, West Covina, Calif., 1959-60; pharmacist Bay Pharmacy, Pacific Palisades, 1960-65; pharmacist, v.p. PalisadesDrug Co., 1965-67; pharmacist Bi-Rite, Westwood and Santa Monica, Calif., 1967-68; pharmacist, owner Trager, Pacific Palisades, 1968-72; pharmacist Kaiser Found. Hosp. Pharmacy, Panorama City, Calif., 1973-90, Woodland Hills, 1990-98; ret., 1998. Per diem overnight pharmacist Kaiser Permanente Pharmacy, Woodland Hills, Calif., 2001—; mentor first year pharmacy students U. Pacific, 1998—; patient cons., 1969—; script cons., 1963—; tech. lit. cons., 2001—; proprietor P-I-E Software, 1995—. Mem.: Am. Pharm. Assn. (active ret. emeritus), Royal Arch Masons (life), Shriners, Masons (life), Scottish Rite Rsch. Assn. (life), Scottish Rite, Kappa Psi. Republican. Jewish. Avocations: computers, medical research, reading, Masonic research. Home: 1531 Yosemite Ave Simi Valley CA 93063-4548 Fax: 805-582-1844. E-mail: ddt@consultant.com.

TRAGER, DAVID G. federal judge; b. Mt. Vernon, N.Y., Dec. 23, 1937; s. Sol and Clara (Friedman) T.; m. Roberta E. Weisbrod, May 2, 1972; children: Mara Emet, Josiah Samuel, Naomi Gabrielle. BA, Columbia Coll., 1959; LL.B., Harvard U., 1962. Bar: N.Y. Assoc. Berman & Frost, 1963-65, Butler, Jablow & Geller, 1965-67; asst. corp. counsel Appeals Div. City of N.Y., 1967; law clk. Judge Kenneth B. Keating, N.Y. State Ct. Appeals, 1968-69; asst. U.S. atty. chief, appeals div., 1970-72; U.S. atty. Ea. Dist. N.Y., Bklyn., 1974-78; prof. Bklyn. Law Sch., 1972-94, dean, 1983-94; judge U.S. Dist. Ct. (ea. dist.) N.Y., Bklyn., 1994—; mem. adv. com. on criminal rules Jud. Conf. U.S., 2000—. Chmn. Mayor's Com. on Judiciary, 1982-89, N.Y. State Temp. Commn. on Investigation, 1983-90. Mem. N.Y.C. Charter Rev. Commn., 1986-89. With USAR, 1962-65, USNR, 1965-69. Mem.: Am. Law Inst., Fed. Bar Coun. (pres. 1986—88). Office: US Courthouse 225 Cadman Plz E Brooklyn NY 11201-1818

TRAGER, GARY ALAN, endocrinologist, diabetologist; b. N.Y.C., July 30, 1950; s. Jacob Morris and Elena (Tanzer) T.; m. Marie-Christine Nicole Lachal, Dec. 26, 1976; children: Ashley Audrey, Brendon Alden. BA in Biology and Anthropology, SUNY, Binghamton, 1972; MD, U. Cen. del Este, Dominican Republic, 1980. Subintern-rotating Jamaica (N.Y.) Hosp., 1979-80; intern and resident medicine Bklyn.-Cumberland Med. Ctr., 1980-83; fellow endocrinology SUNY, Stony Brook, 1983-85, clin. asst. instr., 1983-85; asst. attending Huntington (N.Y.) Hosp., 1985-90, assoc. attending, 1990-97, sr. attending, 1997—. Adv. bd. Sankyo-Park Davis, Merck & Co., Bayer Pharms., Hoechst Marion Roussel, Boehringer Mannheim, Eli Lilly & Co., Park Davis, Pratt Pharms., Upjohn, Johnson and Johnson, Pfizer, Inc. and Roerig Divsn.; nat. adv. bd., nat. speaker bureaus Parke Davis, Novodisc, Sherring-Plough, spkr. Forest Pharms., Ciba Geisy, Knoll; mem. nutrition com. Huntington Hosp., 1987—, dir. diabetes club, 1985—; mem. Nassau-Suffolk Hosp. Coun. on Diabetes, with Nat. Diabetes Ednl. Initiative, lab com. H.H., 1997—, pharm. and therapy com., 1998— Mem. profl. edn. com. Am. Diabetes Assn., Long Island, Melville, N.Y., 1985—; mem. Am. Diabetic Assn. Fund, Long Island, N.Y., 1989—; ad hoc mem. Eaton's Neck Emergency Squad, Long Island, 1985-89; I.P.R.O. Nassau-Suffolk Counties, 1998—. Mem. AMA, Am. Fertility Soc., Am. Diabetes Assn., Am. Soc. Internal Medicine, Am. Soc. Andrology, Am. Assn. Clin. Endocrinologists, Peripheral Neuropathy Inst., An. Soc. Hypertension, Adrenal Soc. Office: 158 E Main St Huntington NY 11743-2988

TRAGER, LILLIAN, anthropologist, educator; b. Princeton, N.J., Apr. 15, 1947; d. William and Ida Trager; m. Richard Ammann, July 9, 1977. AB, Cornell U., 1969; MA, U. Wash., 1971, PhD, 1976. Asst. prof. U. Wis.-Parkside, Kenosha, 1975—83, assoc. prof., 1983—91; asst. rep., program dir. The Ford Found., N.Y.C., 1985—87; prof. U. Wis.-Parkside, 1991—. Cons. The Ford Found., 1988, The World Bank, Washington, 1989. Author: The City Connection, 1988, Yoruba Hometowns, 2001. Pres. bd. dirs. Southside Revitalization, Racine, Wis., 2002—. Recipient Fulbright scholar, Dept. of State, 2001—02; grantee, NIMH, 1978—79, NSF, 1992—96. Fellow: Royal Anthrop. Inst., Am. Anthrop. Assn.; mem.: Soc. Econ. Anthropology (bd. dirs. 1998—2001). Achievements include research on migration, hometown linkages and local development amoung the Yoruba of Southwestern Nigeria; informal economy of Africa and U.S.; contemporary African art. Office: Univ Wis Parkside Wood Rd Kenosha WI 53141

TRAGER, MICHAEL DAVID, lawyer; b. N.Y.C., Feb. 15, 1959; s. Philip and Ina (Shulkin) T.; m. Mariella Gonzalez, Sept. 12, 1987; children: Nicholas, Alexander. BA, Wesleyan U., Middletown, Conn., 1981; JD, Boston U., 1985. Bar: Mass. 1985, Conn. 1986, Fla. 1988, D.C. 1989. Staff atty. enforcement divsn. Securities & Exchange Com., Washington, 1985-87; assoc. Morgan, Lewis & Bockius, Miami, Fla., 1987-88; participating assoc. Fulbright & Jaworski, Washington, 1989-92; ptnr. Trager & Trager, 1992-93; of counsel Fulbright & Jaworski, 1993-94, ptnr., 1995—, co-head securities litigation and enforcement. Bd. dirs. Jewish Nat. Fund-Mid-Atlantic Region, 1993-97; officer Horace Mann PTA, 1997-99. Mem. ABA (bus. law sect. fed. regulation securities com. and civil litigation and SEC enforcement matters subcom., litigation sect. securities litigation com. and SEC enforcement subcom., class action and derivative litigation com. and securities litigation subcom., task force on SEC's insider trading and selective disclosure rules), Assn. SEC Alumni, Securities Industry Assn. (legal and compliance divsn.), D.C. Bar (corp., fin. and securities law sect. corp. counsel and planning group for broker-dealer programs 1992-94, broker-dealer regulation com., task force on SEC's proposed insider trading and selective disclosure rules), Mass. Bar, Fla. Bar., Conn. Bar., Bond Market Assn. (litigation adv. com.), Wesleyan Univ. Club of Washington (chair 2001--), Wesleyan U. Alumni Assn. (exec. com. 2001--). Office: Fulbright & Jaworski 801 Pennsylvania Ave NW Fl 3-5 Washington DC 20004-2623

TRAGER, WILLIAM, biology educator; b. Newark, Mar. 20, 1910; s. Leon and Anna Emilfork T.; m. Ida Sosnow, June 16, 1935; children: Leslie, Carolyn, Lillian. BS, Rutgers U., 1930, Sc.D. (hon.), 1965; MA, Harvard U., 1931, PhD, 1933; Sc.D. (hon.), Rockefeller U., 1987. Fellow Rockefeller Inst., Princeton, NJ, 1934—35; mem. faculty Rockefeller U., N.Y.C., 1935—, assoc. prof., 1950—64, prof. biology, 1964—81, prof. emeritus, 1981—. Guest investigator West African Inst. Trypanosomiasis Research, 1958—59, Nigerian Inst. Trypanosomiasis Research, 1973—74; vis. prof. Fla. State U., 1962, U. P.R. Med. Sch., 1963, U. Mex. Med. Sch., 1965; mem. study sect. parasitology and tropical medicine Nat. Inst. Allergy and Infectious Diseases, 1954—58, 1967—70, mem. tng. grant com., 1961—64, mem. microbiology and infectious diseases adv. com., 1978—79; mem. malaria commn. Armed Forces Epidemiol. Bd., 1965—73; mem. study group parasitic diseases Walter Reed Army Inst. Research, 1977—79; chmn. sci. adv. council Liberian Inst. Tropical Medicine, 1965—66; rapporteur 6th, 7th Congresses Tropical Medicine; pres. Am. Found. for Tropical Medicine, 1966—69; mem. steering com. Malaria Immunology Group, WHO, 1977—80; cons. WHO, Bangkok, 1978, Panama, 79, Shanghai, 79; hon. pres. Asia and Pacific Conf. on Malaria, 1985. Author: Symbiosis, 1970, Living Together: The Biology of Animal Parasitism, 1986; editor: Jour. Protozoology, 1954—65; contbr. articles to profl. jours. Capt. AUS U.S. Army, 1943—45. Recipient Darling medal, WHO, 1980, Leuckart medal Deutsche Gesellschaft fur Parasitologie, 1982, First Rameshwardas Birla Internat. award in Medicine, 1982, Manson medal, Royal Soc. Tropical Medicine and Hygiene, 1986, Prince Mahidol award in Med. Sci., 1994; fellow, NRC, 1933—34, Guggenheim Found., 1973—74, Avivah Zuckerman fellow, Kuvin Ctr. Infections and Tropical Diseases, Hebrew U., 1982. Fellow: AAAS, N.Y. Acad. Scis.; mem.: NAS, Am. Soc. Tropical Medicine and Hygiene (pres. 1978—79, Le Prince medal 1991), Soc. Protozoologists (pres. 1960—61), Am. Soc. Parasitologists (council 1956—57, v.p. 1973, pres. 1974). Office: Rockefeller U York Ave At 66th St New York NY 10021 E-mail: trager@rockvax.rockefeller.edu.

TRAGOS, GEORGE EURIPEDES, lawyer; b. Chgo., July 15, 1949; s. Euripedes G. and Eugene G. (Gatziolis) T.; m. Donna Marie Thalassites, Nov. 18, 1978; children: Louise, Gina, Peter. BA, Fla. State U., 1971, JD, 1974. Bar: Fla., U.S. Dist. Ct. (mid., so. dists.) Fla., U.S. Dist. Ct. (we. dist.) Tenn., U.S. Ct. Appeals (5th, 11th cirs.). Legis. aide Fla. Ho. of Reps., 1972-73; tax analyst tax and fin. com., 1973-74; chief, felony asst. states atty. State of Fla., Clearwater, 1974-78; partner firm Case, Kimpton, Tragos & Burke, P.A., Clearwater Beach, 1978-83; chief criminal div. U.S. Atty.'s Office for Middle Dist. Fla., Tampa, 1983-85; lead trial asst. Pres. Organized Crime Drug Enforcement Task Force, 1985; sole practice Clearwater, 1985—. Contbr. articles to profl. jours. and frequent lectr. Mem. Clearwater Bar (pres. 1994), Fla. Bar Assn. (chmn. fed. practice com. 1986, chmn. criminal law sect. 2000, chmn. bar evidence com. 1990), Fla. Assn. Criminal Def. Lawyers (pres. 1991), Fla. State U. Alumni Assn. Law Sch. (bd. dirs.), Tampa Bay Fed. Bar Assn. (v.p. 1989), Clearwater Beach Jaycees (pres. 1979), Fla. U. Gold Key Club (pres. 1972), Ahepa. Mem. Greek Orthodox Ch. Avocations: boating, tennis. Office: 600 Cleveland St Ste 700 Clearwater FL 33755-4158 E-mail: greeklaw@verizon.net.

TRAHAN, ELIZABETH WELT, retired comparative literature educator; b. Berlin, Nov. 19, 1924; came to U.S., 1947; d. Albert and Selma (Silberstein) W.; m. Donald H. Trahan, Aug. 31, 1957 (div. Aug. 1975); 1 child, Jennifer. BA, Sarah Lawrence Coll., 1951; MA, Cornell U., 1953; PhD, Yale U., 1957. Instr. German and Russian lang. and lit. U. Mass., Amherst, 1956-60; asst. to assoc. prof. U. Pitts., 1960-66; assoc. prof., then prof. Monterey (Calif.) Inst. Internat. Studies, 1968-89; vis. prof. SUNY, Binghamton, 1983, Amherst (Mass.) Coll., 1985-88, vis. lectr., 1988-93; ret., 1989. Bd. dirs./sec. exec. com. Nat. Coalition Ind. Scholars, 1993-99; ind. scholar and lectr., 1989—. Author: (in German) Walking With Ghosts: a Jewish Childhood in Wartime Vienna, 1996 (in English 1998, 2000); editor: Die Stillste Stunde, 1961, 75, Gruppe 47: Ein Querschnitt, 1969, 75; editor, translator: Gogol's Overcoat, 1982; book rev. editor Ind. Scholar, 1993-97. Charles E. Merrill Rsch. fellow Univ. Pitts., 1962. Mem. MLA, Nat. Coalition Ind. Scholars, Nat. Writers Union. Democrat. Avocations: theater, art, music, nature. Home: 222 N East St Apt 1 Amherst MA 01002-1676

TRAHAN, HAROLD PAUL, military officer; b. Rapid City, S.D., Aug. 2, 1964; s. Edward John and Linda Fay Trahan; m. Melanie Virginia Wood; children: Benjamin, Andrew. BA, Ea. Wash. U., Cheney , 1996; MPA, U. Okla., 2000; AA, C.C. of USAF. Squadron tng. supt. 961 Airborne Air Control Squadron, Japan, 1998—2000; squadron ops. supt. 16 Airborne Command And Control Squadron, Robins AFB, Ga., 2000—01; wing plans supt. 93 Air Control Wing, 2001—02. Sr. master sgt. USAF, 1983—2002, Virginia, Washington, New York, Oklahoma, Japan, Georgia. Decorated Meritorious Svc. Medal USAF, Outstanding Vol. Svc. Medal. Mem.: ASPA.

TRAHAN, JANET MARIE, artist, former gallery owner; b. Rockville Centre, N.Y., May 28, 1951; d. James Joseph and Dorothy Agnes Ball; m. Scott Trahan, Feb. 10, 1973; children: Mandy A., Kate M. Student, C.W. Post Coll., 1970-71, Suffolk C.C., 1972. Ptnr., owner, artist Bellport (N.Y.) Ln. Art Gallery, 1996-2000; adminstrv. asst. Gateway Performing Arts, 1999—2001; bus. owner Janet M. Trahan, Artist, 1994—; represented by Art Reps., Calif., 2001—, InterContinental Greetings, Ltd., N.Y.C., 2002—. Exhbns. at Longwood Libr., Middle Island, N.Y., 1996, Bald Hill Gallery, L.I., N.Y., 1996, Salmagundi Club, N.Y.C., 1996, 97, 99, 2000, 01, 02 (A.E.S. Meml. award 1996), Fed. Hall, N.Y.C., 1996, Hutchings Gallery, Brookville, N.Y., 1997, Woodbury (N.Y.) Cmty. Ctr., 1997, Bayport Blue Point (N.Y.) Libr., 1997, 98, 99, 2000, 01, 02, Nat. Art League Open Art Exhbn., Douglaston, N.Y., 1997, Stage Gallery, Merrick, N.Y., 1997, Islip (N.Y.) Art Mus., 1996, 97, 98, 99 (1st Pl. Oil 1999), 2000, 01, Nat. Soc. Painters in Casein and Acrylics, Inc., N.Y.C., 1996—, Huntington (N.Y.) Arts Coun., 1998, Heckscher Mus. Art, Huntington, 1998, Houston Watercolor Soc., 2000, Watermedia, 2000, A Victorian on the Bay, Eastport, N.Y., 1998-, Chrysalis Gallery, Southampton, N.Y., 2001—. Grants and awards judge Sayville (N.Y.) Mus. Boosters for Arts, 1998—; costumer designer Ballet L.I., Bohemia, N.Y., 1987-90, set designer, 1989-90; costumer designer Sayville Mid. Sch., 1996, 97. Recipient 1st pl. oil and acrylic category West Hampton Beach Annual Outdoor Show, 1998, North Shore Art League 1st place in acrylics, Most Popular award and Hon. Mention, Arts Coun. E.I. Pub. Libr. Signature mem. Nat. Soc. Painters in Casein and Acrylics (A.E.S. Peterson Meml. award 1996, Antonio Cirino Meml. award 1996, Hon. Mention award 1997), Audubon Artist Assn. (assoc.), Art League of L.I. (hon. mention), South Bay Art Assn. (1st prize acrylic 1997, hon. mention 1999, Best in Show 2001), Wet Paints Studio Group (1st pl. oil 1998, hon. mention 1998, 2d pl Acrylic 1999). Roman Catholic. Avocations: art, music, theater, travel. Home: 22 John St Sayville NY 11782-1308 E-mail: artjmt5285@aol.com.

TRAHAN, WILLIAM L. investment executive; b. Providence, Feb. 13, 1957; s. Robert E. and Anne H. Trahan; m. Lisa R. (Meares) T., Nov. 28, 1981; children: Jessica R., Chason W., Bradley C. BS, U. Cen. Fla., 1979; MA, Appalachian State U., 1981. CFP; cert. fund specialist. Dir. City of Jacksonville Beach, Fla., 1983-85; fin. planner IDS Fin. Svcs. (Am. Express Fin. Svcs.), Jacksonville, 1985-86, Charlotte, N.C., 1986-89; sr. v.p. investments Consol. Planning, Inc., 1989—; pres. CP Adv. Svcs., 1997—. Mem. corp. com. Appalachian State U., 1995-96; com. mem. Harris YMCA Capital Campaign, 1996; mem. fin. com. St. Stephens United Meth. Ch., 1994-95. Mem. Internatl Assn. Fin. Planners (bd. dirs. 1991-96, pres. 1996-97), Inst. CFPs (bd. dirs. 1991-96), Carmel Country Club (jr. golf com., bd. dirs. 1997—, swim team com., co-chmn. 1998). Methodist. Avocation: golf. Home: 4502 Carmel Valley Rd Charlotte NC 28226-7408 Office: 6000 Fairview Rd Ste 415 Charlotte NC 28210-2225

TRAHER, WILLIAM GEORGE, automotive model maker, retired; b. St. Clair Shores, Mich., Jan. 16, 1938; s. William Tye and Mildred (Martuza) T.; m. Betty Marie Flisnik, Sept. 14, 1963. Student, Macomb Coll. Model maker, retired Gen. MTRS Corp. Tech. Ctr., Warren, Mich., 1960-94. V.P. Huron Pointe Homeowners Assn., Harrison Twp., Mich. Lt. Mt. Clemens Power Squadron; with USN, 1955-63. Roman Cath. Avocations: boating, travel, sports, cooking, gardening. Address: Sunset House North 240 Seaview Ct # 401 Marco Island FL 34145

TRAICOFF, GEORGE, retired college president; b. Elyria, Ohio, May 16, 1932; s. George and Lena (Szaroff) T.; m. Diane C. Schneider, Dec. 28, 1965; children: George Scott, Paula Jane, Amy Jo. BS, Miami U., Oxford, Ohio, 1954; MEd, Kent State U., 1959; EdD, Ind. U., 1967. Tchr. bus. LaGrange (Ohio) High Sch., 1956-57, Elyria High Sch., 1957-59; instr., coord. Ind. U., 1959-60, Ohio State U., 1960-63; prof., head dept. No. Mich. U., Marquette, 1963-66, dir. program gen. studies, 1966-67; dean cmty. svcs. Cuyahoga C.C., Cleve., 1967-73; pres. North Shore C.C., Danvers, Mass., 1973-99; ret. Pres. New Eng. Jr. Cmty. and Tech. Coll. Coun.; vice chmn. regional employment bd. Pvt. Industry Coun. With U.S. Army, 1954-56. Mem. Am. Assn. Cmty. and Jr. Colls., Nat. Coun. Cmty. (past pres.), Mass. Adminstrs. C.C.s, Mass. C.C. Assn. (treas.). Episcopalian.

TRAIL, MARGARET ANN, employee benefits company executive, beef cattle producer; b. Bryan, Tex., July 17, 1941; d. Louis Milton and Margaret (Stromberg) Thompson; m. Robert A. Rosemier, Aug. 25, 1962 (div. Feb. 1973); 1 child: Gretchen Elisabeth; m. Newt Shands Trail, Dec. 4, 1989. BSN, U. Iowa, 1963; MS, No. Ill. U., 1971. Cert. Prof. in Healthcare Quality (CPHQ). Instr. Cooley Dickinson Hosp., Northampton, Mass., 1964-65; dir. nursing De Kalb (Ill.) Pub. Hosp., Kishwaukee Community Hosp., 1972-76, Terre Haute (Ind.) Regional Hosp., 1976-78; from mgr. clin. systems to dir. spl. projects Hosp. Corp. Am., Nashville, 1978-86; from dir. med. mgmt. to v.p. Equicor, 1986-90; divsn. v.p. The Travelers Ins. Co., Hartford, Conn.,

1990-93; asst. v.p. health svcs. quality mgmt. Aetna, 1993—. Mem. LWV (pres. DeKalb chpt. 1970-72), Nat. League Nursing. Avocation: gardening. Office: Aetna US Healthcare 930 Harvest Dr Blue Bell PA 19422-1959 E-mail: trailma@aetna.com.

TRAILL, DAVID ANGUS, classics educator; b. Helensburgh, Scotland, Jan. 28, 1942; came to U.S., 1965; s. Angus Nicolson and Elizabeth Blyth (Wilson) Trail. MA, U. St. Andrews, Scotland, 1964; PhD, U. Calif., Berkeley, 1971. Lectr. classics McGill U., Montreal, Que., Can., 1964-65; tchg. asst. U. Calif., Berkeley, 1965-68, asst. prof. Davis, 1970-78, assoc. prof., 1978-85, prof., 1985—. Cons. prodn. documentaries on Schliemann and Troy, Brit. Broadcasting Corp., London, 1980-81, 84, Nat. Geographic, 1999. Author: Walahfrid Strabo's Visio Wettini: Text, Translation and Commentary, 1974; co-editor: Myth, Scandal, and History: The Heinrich Schliemann Controversy, 1986, Excavating Schliemann, 1993, Schliemann of Troy: Treasure and Deceit, 1995; contbr. articles to profl. jours. Mem. Am. Philol. Assn., Archaeol. Inst. Am., Medieval Acad. Am. Home: 1351 Monarch Ln Davis CA 95616-1636 Office: Classics Dept U Calif Davis CA 95616 E-mail: datraill@ucdavis.edu.

TRAIN, HARRY DEPUE, II, retired naval officer; b. Washington, Nov. 5, 1927; s. Harold Cecil and May (Philipps) T.; m. Catharine Peck Kinnear, July 8, 1950; children: Louise Lucas, Catharine Philipps, Elizabeth Langdon, Cecilia Spencer. BS, U.S. Naval Acad., 1949. Commd. ensign U.S. Navy, 1949, advanced through grades to adm., 1978; comdr. Cruiser-Destroyer Flotilla 8, 1971-72; dir. internat. security affairs East Asia and Pacific Region Office Asst. Sec. Def., 1972-73; dir. Systems Analysis Div., Office Chief Naval Ops., 1973-74; dir. joint staff Orgn. Joint Chiefs of Staff, 1974-76; comdr. U.S. 6th Fleet, 1976-78; comdr.-in-chief U.S. Atlantic Fleet and supreme allied comdr. Atlantic, 1978-82, ret., 1982. Mgr. Hampton Rds. Ops. Sci. Applications Internat. Corp. Bd. dirs. Am. Cancer Soc., Inc.; mem. U.S. Commn. on Nat. Security/21st Century. Decorated D.S.M. with 3 gold stars, Def. Disting. Svc. medal, Legion of Merit with 3 gold stars, Meritorious Svc. medal, Joint Svcs. Commendation medal, Navy Commendation medal; comdr. Order Republic of Tunisia; Order Naval Merit Brazil; Pedro Campbell medal Uruguay; Order of Pres. of Republic Chile; decorated Portuguese Mil. Order Christ; Netherlands Order Orange-Nassau; German Order Merit; French Legion of Honor; Colombian Naval Order Admiral Padilla; Mex. Order Spl. Merit; sr. fellow Joint and Combined Warfighting Sch., Joint Forces Staff Coll. Mem. U.S. Naval Inst., Coun. on Fgn. Rels., Def. Sci. Study Group (sr. mentor). Clubs: Columbia Country (Chevy Chase, Md.), Town Point (chmn. bd. govs.). Home: 401 College Pl Apt 10 Norfolk VA 23510-1130

TRAIN, JOHN, investment counselor, writer, government official; b. N.Y.C., May 25, 1928; s. Arthur Cheney and Helen (Coster) T.; m. Maria Teresa Cini di Pianzano, 1961 (div. 1976); children: Helen, Nina, Lisa; m. Frances Cheston, July 23, 1977. BA magna cum laude, Harvard U., 1950, MA, 1951. Founder, mng. editor Paris Rev., 1952-54; staff Asst. Sec. Army, Washington, 1954-56; assoc. de Vegh & Co., 1956-58; chmn. Train, Babcock Advisors (and predecessor firms), N.Y.C., 1958-94, chmn. emeritus, 1995—; co-chmn., then hon. dir. ICAP, S.A., Athens, 1964—; chmn. Montrose Group, N.Y.C., 1992—; pres. Chateau Malecasse, Lamarque-Margaux, Bordeaux, France, 1970-81; columnist Forbes mag., 1977-83, Harvard mag., 1983-95, Wall St. Jour., 1984—, Worth Mag., Boston, 1991-93, Town and Country mag., 1994-95, Fin. Times, London, 1994-99, Strategic Rev., 1998—. Bd. dirs. African Devel. Found., Washington, 1988-94; bd. dirs. Bulgarian-Am. Enterprise Fund, Washington, Genesis Funds, London, Internat. Rescue Com., N.Y.C.; chmn. Northcote Parkison Fund, 1988—; bd. govs. East-West Ctr., Hawaii, 1993-96; overseer Nat. Endowment for Democracy Internat. Forum for Democratic Studies, 1995—. Author: Dance of the Money Bees, 1973, Remarkable Names, 1977, Even More Remarkable Names, 1979, Remarkable Occurrences, 1978, Remarkable Words, 1980, The Money Masters, 1980, Remarkable Relatives, 1971, Preserving Capital and Making it Grow, 1983, Famous Financial Fiascos, 1984, John Train's Most Remarkable Names, 1985, The Midas Touch, 1987, The New Money Masters, 1989, Valsalva's Maneuver, 1989, John Train's Most Remarkable Occurences, 1990, Wit, 1991, Love, 1993, The Craft of Investing, 1994, Crazy Quilt, 1996, Oriental Rug Symbols, 1997, Investing and Managing Trusts under the New Prudent Investor Rule, 1999; contbr. articles to profl. publs. Chmn. Italian Emergency Relief Com., 1976-77; pres. Afghanistan Relief Com., 1986-95; trustee Harvard Lampoon, Cambridge, Mass., 1974-90, World Monuments Fund, 1988-92; chmn. Free Elections Project, 1990, Brit. Mus. Nat. Hist. Internat. Trust, 1990—, Northcote Parkinson Fund, 1990—; trustee Am. U. Bulgaria, 1996—. With U.S. Army, 1954-56. Decorated commendatore Ordine del Merito della Repubblica, commendatore Ordine Della Solidarieta, medal Provincia di Udine (Italy); recipient Disting. Grotonian award, 1996, Queen's Birthday honors Order of St. John, 1997. Mem.: Internat. Inst. Strategic Studies (London), Coun. on Fgn. Rels., Order Colonial Lords of Manors, The Pilgrims, Racquet & Tennis Club, Met. Club (Washington), Century Club. Office: 667 Madison Ave New York NY 10021-8029

TRAIN, RUSSELL ERROL, environmentalist; b. Jamestown, R.I., June 4, 1920; s. Charles R. and Errol C. (Brown) T.; m. Aileen Bowdoin, May 27, 1954; children— Nancy, Emily, Bowdoin, Errol. AB, Princeton U., 1941, LL.D. (hon.), 1970; JD, Columbia U., 1948, LL.D. (hon.), 1970, Bates Coll., 1970, Drexel U., 1970; D.E. (hon.), Worcester Poly. Inst., 1970, U. Md., 1975; Sc.D. (hon.), St. Mary's Coll., 1970, Clarkson Coll. Tech., 1973, Salem Coll., 1975, Southwestern U., 1976, Mich. State U., 1976; D.C.L. (hon.), U. of South, 1973; D public svc., Washington Coll., 1996. Bar: D.C. bar 1949. Atty. staff joint com. on internal revenue taxation U.S. Congress, 1949-53; chief counsel Ways and Means Com., U.S. Ho. of Reps., 1953-54, minority adviser, 1955-56; asst. to sec., head legal adv. staff Treasury Dept., 1956-57; judge U.S. Tax Ct., 1957-65; pres. Conservation Found., 1965-69; also trustee; undersec. Dept. Interior, 1969-70; chmn. Council on Environ. Quality, 1970-73; adminstr. EPA, Washington, 1973-77; sr. assoc. Conservation Found., 1977; pres., chief exec. officer World Wildlife Fund, Washington, 1978-85, chmn. bd., 1985-94, chmn. emeritus, 1994—; chmn. bd. Conservation Found., 1985-90; chmn. Nat. Commn. on the Environment, 1991-93; chmn. Nat. Coun. World Wildlife Fund, Washington, chmn. emeritus. Mem. Washington Nat. Monument Assn.; mem. Nat. Water Commn., 1968; head U.S. del. UN Conf. Human Environment, 1972; rep. Internat. Whaling Commn., 1972, other internat. confs.; mem. Pres.'s adv. com. on trade and trade negotiations, 1991-93. Author: The Bowdoin Family, 2000, The Train Family, 2000, A Memoir, 2000. Trustee emeritus African Wildlife Found.; adv. trustee Rockefeller Bros. Fund. Decorated Order of Golden Ark (The Netherlands); recipient Albert Schweitzer medal Animal Welfare Inst., 1972; Aldo Leopold medal Wildlife Soc., 1975; Conservationist of Yr. award Nat. Wildlife Fedn., 1974; John and Alice Tyler Ecology award, 1978; Freese award ASCE, 1978; Public Welfare award Nat. Acad. Scis., 1981; Elizabeth Haub prize in internat. environ. law, 1981, Lindbergh award, 1985, Environ. Law Inst. award, 1986; conservationist of yr. award.Nat. Wildlife Fedn., 1986; Presidential Medal of Freedom, 1991, Heinz award, 2001. Mem. Coun. Fgn. Rels., Atlantic Coun., Am. Acad. Arts and Sci. Office: World Wildlife Fund 1250 24th St NW Fl 6 Washington DC 20037-1193

TRAINA, ALBERT SALVATORE, publishing executive; b. Bklyn., Apr. 30, 1927; s. Salvatore and Guilia (LeBarbara) T.; m. Vail Devereux, June 27, 1957; children— Caroline Vail, Robert Brooks. BS (N.Y. State War Service scholar), Seton Hall U., 1950; postgrad., Columbia U., 1950-51; MBA, NYU, 1954. Circulation promotion advt. space salesman Fairchild Publs., N.Y.C., 1951-53; Eastern advt. mgr. Modern Bride mag. Ziff-Davis, 1953-58; advt. mgr. Bride and Home mag. Hearst Mags., 1958-60, pub. Bride and Home mag., 1960-64; pub. Sports Afield mag., 1964-65, Town and Country mag., 1965-67, Harpers Bazaar mag., 1967-70; pres., chief exec. officer Bartell Media Corp., 1970-74; pres. Ziff-Davis Pub. Network, 1974-76, group v.p., 1976-78; sr. v.p. Ziff-Davis Pub. Co., 1978-81; pres. Ziff-Davis Consumer Mag., 1981-85; exec. v.p. mags. CBS, N.Y.C., 1985; pres. Traina Assocs., 1985—. Mem. Scarsdale Bi-Partisan Com., 1975-78; bd. dirs. Crane Berkeley Assn., 1978-88, pres., 1983-84; mem. nat. bd. dirs., chmn. comms. com., treas. Goodwill Industries of Am., 1979-92, chmn. bd., 1988-92; chmn. bd. trustees Chebeague Island Libr., 1997—; pres. bd. dirs. Chebeague Recreation Ctr., 1998—. With USNR, 1945-46. Mem. NYU Grad. Sch. Bus. Adminstrn. Alumni Assn., NYU Alumni Fedn. (comms. com. 1970-73), Fox Meadow Tennis Club (Scarsdale), Union League Club (N.Y.C.). Home: RR 1 Box 201 Chebeague Island ME 04017-9723

TRAINES, ROSE WUNDERBAUM, sculptor, educator; b. Monroeville, Ind., Sept. 13, 1928; d. Louis and Leah (Fogel) Wunderbaum; m. Robert Jacob Traines, June 25, 1949; children: Claudia Denise Traines Lang, Monica Rae Traines Martin. Student, Ind. State Tchr.'s Coll., 1946-48, Mich. State U., 1948-49; BS, Cen. Mich. U., 1951. Lectr. in field. One person shows include Cen. Mich. U., Mt. Pleasant, 1964, Alma Artmobile, Mich., 1972, Ctrl. Mich. Homecoming, Mount Pleasant, Mich., 1982, Inst. Scrap Iron and Steel, Inc., Washington, 1983, Fontainebleau Hotel, Miami Beach, Fla., 1983, Elliott Mus. Art Gallery, Stuart, Fla., 1988, 98, Walt Kuhn Gallery, Cape Neddick, Maine, 1988, Coll. Club of Boston, 1990, Brass Latch Gallery, Montpelier, Ind., 1991, 96, 98, Vero Beach Ctr. for the Arts, Fla., 1992, Maritime and Yachting Mus., Stuart, Fla., 1997, Mid-Mich. Regional Med. Ctr., Healing Arts Gallery, Midland, 1997, Commerco Bank Art Series, Palm Beach Gardens, 2002,Gallery Five, Tequesta, Fla., 2002, Park Library Gallery, Michigan U., 2002; two-person shows include Gallery One, North Palm Beach, 1973, Midland Ctr. for the Arts, Mich., 1976, Springfield Art Mart, Ohio, 1977, Hillel Student Ctr. Gallery-U. Cin., 1993, others; exhibited in numerous group shows including Saginaw Mus. Art, Mich., 1965, Grand Rapids Mus., Mich., 1966, Kalamazoo Mus., Mich., 1967, Kellogg/Kresge Art Ctr., Mich. State U., East Lansing, Mich., 1967, Art Reach Mid-Mich., Mount Pleasant Mich., 1987, Salmagundi Club, N.Y.C., 1988, 91, 92, 96, Copley Soc., Boston, 1990, 95, Allied Artists of Am., Inc., N.Y.C., 1995, 96, Self Family Arts Ctr., Hilton Head Island, S.C., 1996, 97, others; represented in permanent collections at Dow-Corning Corp. Collection, Midland Ctr. for the Arts, Elliott Mus., Stuart, Fla., The Walt Kuhn Gallery, Maine, Pullen Elem. Sch., Isabella Bank and Trust Co., Ctrl. Mich. U., Ctrl. Mich. Cmty. Hosp., Northwood U., The Vets. Meml. Libr., The Brass Latch Gallery, others. Tchr. Jewish Sunday Sch., Mt. Pleasant, 1955-70; officer Child and Youth Study Clubs, Mt. Pleasant, 1963-73; mem. City Recreation Commn., Mt. Pleasant, 1963-73, Area Health Planning Coun., Mt. Pleasant, 1974-80; pres., vol. Hosp. Aux. Med. Care, Red Cross Blood Bank, United Fund Cancer Dr., Mt. Pleasant, 1960-80; storyteller pub. libr., Mt. Pleasant, 1957-79. Mem.: Brass Latch Gallery, Art Reach of Mid-Mich., Hilton Head Art League S.C. (Lifetime of Creative Excellence award 1998), Copley Soc. Boston (signature mem.), Allied Artists of Am. (Mems. award of merit 1996, Raymond H. Brumer Meml. award 1999), Nat. Mus. of Women in Arts (charter), Salmagundi Club (Philip Isenberg award 1993, Pamela Singleton award 1997, Elliot Liskin Meml. award 1998, Anonymous award 1998, Peters Sculpture Materials award 2001, Thumb-Box Exhbn.Salmagundi Club 2001 Alphaeus P. Cole Meml. award 2001). Jewish. Avocations: lecturing, community work, tennis, presenting humorous programs, drums. Home: 1217 North Dr Mount Pleasant MI 48858-3226

TRAINOR, BERNARD EDMUND, retired military officer; b. N.Y.C., Sept. 2, 1928; s. Joseph Patrick and Ann Veronica (Whelan) T.; m. Margaret Ann Hamilton, June 13, 1959; children: Kathleen Marie, Theresa Ann, Eileen Cecile, Claire Hamilton. BS, Coll. of Holy Cross, 1951; MA, U. Colo., 1963, postgrad., 1970-73; ed., Air War Coll., Montgomery, Ala., 1969-70. Commd. 2nd lt. USMC, 1951, advanced through grades to lt. gen., 1983, inf. comdr. Korea, 1952, assigned to USS Columbus, 1953-55, mem. staff Marine Corps Hdqrs., 1955-58, with exch. office Royal Marine Commandos, 1958-59, inf. comdr. 1st Marine divsn., 1959-61; asst. prof. naval sci. U. Colo., Boulder, 1961-64; assigned to Marine Corps Command and Staff Coll., 1964-65; adv. Republic of Vietnam, 1965-66; instr. Marine Corps Command and Staff Coll., 1966-69; bn. comdr. Vietnam, 1970-71; staff officer Hdqrs. Marine Corps, Washington, 1970-71; dir. First Marine Corps Dist., N.Y.C., 1974-76; asst. depot comdr. Marine Corps Recruit Depot, Parris Island, S.C., 1976-78; dir. Edn. Ctr., Quantico, Va., 1978-81; dep. chief of staff for plans, policies and ops. Hdqrs. Marine Corps, 1981-85; ret., 1985; mil. corr. N.Y. Times, 1986-90; dir. nat. security program Kennedy Sch. Govt. Harvard U., Cambridge, Mass., 1990-96, assoc. Ctr. Sci. and Internat. Affairs, 1996—; sr. fellow nat. security Coun. on Fgn. Rels., 1999—. Retired USMC, 1985. Author: History of the U.S. Marine Corps, 1968, The Generals' War, 1995; contbg. author: American Defense Annual, 1990, 2d edit., 1996, Defense Beat, 1991, After the Storm, 1992, The Almanac of Seapower, 1993, Newsmen and National Defense, 1991, Perspectives on Warfighting, 1992; mem. editl. adv. bd. Naval War Coll. Rev.; bd. of vis. Air Univ.; contbr. articles to profl. jours. Mil. analyst NBC News; rsch. bd. dirs. Inst. for Fgn. Policy Analysis. Decorated D.S.M., Legion of Merit with Combat V and two stars, Bronze Star with Combat V, Navy Commendation medal with Combat V and two gold stars, others; recipient Anderson Meml. award Air War Coll., 1970. Mem. Naval Inst., Internat. Inst. Strategic Studies, Marine Corps Assn., Coun. Fgn. Rels., World Affairs Coun. (bd. dirs.), Army-Navy Club, Wardroom Club Boston. Roman Catholic. Home: 80 Potter Pond Lexington MA 02421-8247 E-mail: mc151rvn@aol.com.

TRAINOR, JOHN FELIX, retired economics educator; b. Mpls., Dec. 1, 1921; s. James Patrick and Myra Catherine (Pauly) T.; m. Margaret Dolores Pudenz, July 3, 1965 (dec. 1977); children: John Anthony, Patrick James. BA cum laude, Coll. St. Thomas, 1943; MA, U. Minn., 1950; PhD, Wash. State U., 1970. Instr. high sch., Mpls., 1946-47; instr. Coll. St. Thomas, 1949-50; v.p. Trainor Candy Co., Mpls., 1949-56; instr., asst. prof. econs. Rockhurst Coll., Kansas City, Mo., 1956-62; instr. Wash. State U., Pullman, 1966-67; asst. prof. Minn. State U., Moorhead, 1967—70; assoc. prof. econs. Moorhead (Minn.) State U., 1971-87, prof. econ., 1988-89, chmn. dept. econs., 1981-89; prof. emeritus, 1989—. Pres. Minn. Econs. Assn., 1976—77. Author (with Frank J. Kottke) The Nursing Home Industry in the State of Washington, 1968. Ensign to Lt. (j.g.) USNR, 1943-46, ETO. Mem. Assn. Social Econs., Omicron Delta Epsilon. Roman Catholic. Avocations: hiking, crossword puzzles, reading. Home: 1333 4th Ave S Moorhead MN 56560-2971

TRAINOR, LILLIAN (MIDGE TRAINOR), elections official, campaign consultant; b. Oct. 30, 1936; d. Loenell Lesley and Lillie Ara (Kenyon) Barber; m. Arthur James Trainor, Mar. 9, 1959; children: Michael, Arthur, Lynn Marie. Student pub. schs., Pleasantville, N.J. Chair Burlington County Bd. Elections, Mount Holly, N.J., 1978-81, commr. of registration, 1981-83, chair, 1983-90; dir. N.J. Divsn. Elections, 1990-94. Vice chair, mem. exec. bd. Burlington County Dem. Com., 1977-90, 94-2002; chair Southampton Twp. Dem. County Com., 1976-79, 94-2002; bd. dirs. County Canvassers, Burlington County, 1978-90; v.p. Southeastern Dem. Coalition, 1977-87; mgr. Florio for Gov. Campaign, N.J., 1981, Carter for Pres. Campaign, Burlington County area, 1980; del. Dem. Nat. Conv., 1984, 88; coord. Women for Florio Gubanatorial campaign, 1989. With WAC, 1955-57. Mem. Nat. Assn. State Election Dirs., N.J. State Assn. Election Ofcls., VFW Aux., Big Six Club (pres. 1973-79). Avocations: accordian, piano, painting, birdwatching. Home: 20 Pleasant St Vincentown NJ 08088

TRAISAK, SAM, internist; b. Bangkok, 1949; MD, Siriraj Hosp. U., 1973. Diplomate Am. Bd. Internal Medicine, Am. Bd. Critical Care Medicine, Am. Bd. Cardiovasc. Medicine, Am. Bd. Pathology, Am. Bd. Anatomic Pathology, Am. Bd. Clin. Pathology, Am. Bd. Geriatrics. Intern Faculty Medicine Siriraj Hosp., Bangkok, 1973-74; resident in pathology Carney Hosp., Boston, 1977-81; resident in internal medicine United Hosp. Med. Ctr., Newark, 1982-85; fellow in cardiology Kingsbrook Jewish Med. Ctr., Bklyn., 1985-87; mem. staff Colers Meml. Hosp., N.Y.C. Mem. ACP.

TRAISMAN, HOWARD SEVIN, pediatrician; b. Chgo., Mar. 18, 1923; s. Alfred Stanley and Sara (Sevin) T.; m. Regina Gallagher, Feb. 29, 1956; children: Barry D. Lifschultz, Edward S., Kenneth N. BS in Chemistry, Northwestern U., 1943, MB, 1946, MD, 1947. Intern Cook County Hosp., Chgo., 1946-47; resident in pediatrics Children's Meml. Hosp., 1949-51, attending physician div. endocrinology, 1951—; mem. faculty Med. Sch. Northwestern U., Evanston, Ill., 1951—, prof. pediatrics, 1973—, pres., 1999—. Author articles in field, chpts. in books. Capt. M.C. AUS, 1943-46, 47-49. Recipient Northwestern U. Alumni Merit award, 1995. Mem. Am. Diabetes Assn. (Disting. Service award 1976), Am. Pediatric Soc., Am. Acad. Pediatrics, Endocrine Soc., Lawson Wilkins Pediatric Endocrine Soc., AMA, Midwest Soc. Pediatric Research, Ill. Med. Soc., Chgo. Pediatric Soc., Chgo. Med. Soc., Inst. Medicine Chgo. Democrat. Jewish. Office: 1325 Howard St Evanston IL 60202-3766 Fax: 847-869-4330.

TRAKAS, DENO P. English studies educator, writer; b. Charlotte, N.C., Apr. 23, 1952; s. Pedro Nicholas and Anna (Patterson) T.; m. Kathy Jackson, Aug. 10, 1974; children: Hayley Kathleen, Dylan Reed. BA, Eckerd Coll., 1974; MA, U. Tulsa, 1978; PhD, U. S.C., 1981. Women's tennis coach Wofford Coll., Spartanburg, S.C., 1986-2000, asst. prof. English, 1981-98, prof. English, 1998—. Author: (poetry) Shuffle of Wings, 1990, Human and Puny, 2001, (short stories) New Southern Harmonies, 1998 (Best Book Ind. Fiction award 1998). Youth soccer coach AYSO, Spartanburg, 1988-98; youth basketball coach Advent Ch., Spartanburg, 1990-97. Recipient S.C. Fiction Project prize S.C. Arts commn., 1985, 93, 94, 2000, S.C. fellow in fiction, 1992. Avocations: tennis, basketball, art. Office: Wofford Coll 429 N Church St Spartanburg SC 29303

TRALDI, LORENZO, mathematician, educator; b. Rome, Italy, May 22, 1955; arrived in U.S., 1955; s. Giuseppe Alberto Traldi, Ila Dawson Little, Charles Little (Stepfather); m. Sharon Richter; children: Arthur, Matthew, Oliver, Rebecca. BA, CUNY, Flushing, NY, 1976; PhD, Yale U., 1980. Asst. prof. Lafayette Coll., Easton, Pa., 1980—86, assoc. prof., 1986—94, prof., 1994—2001, Marshall R. Metzgar prof. math., 2001—. Contbr. articles and revs. to profl. jours. Grantee, Lafayette Coll., 1983, 1987, 1991, 1996, 1997, 2000, 2001, USAF Office Sci. Rsch., 1991—92, rsch. experience for undergrads. grants, NSF, 1994, 2001. Mem.: IEEE, Am. Math. Soc. Independent. Home: 725 Coleman St Easton PA 18042 Office: Dept Math Lafayette Coll Easton PA 18042 Personal E-mail: traldil@lafayette.edu. Business E-Mail: traldil@lafayette.edu.

TRAMBERT, JONATHAN JACOB, physician, educator; b. N.Y.C., Oct. 27, 1951; s. Harry Louis Trambert and Maxima Marguerite David; m. Dovelet Shashou, Sept. 1, 1985; children: Steven, Emily. BS, U. Conn., 1974; MD, N.Y. Med. Coll., 1977. Diplomate Am. Bd. Radiology (cert. in vascular and interventional radiology). Intern in medicine St. Vincent's Hosp., N.Y.C., 1977-78; resident in diagnostic radiology Bronx (N.Y.) Mcpl. Hosp.-Albert Einstein Coll. Medicine, 1980-83; fellow in vascular and interventional radiology U. Pitts. Med. Ctr., 1983-84, U. Tex.-M.D. Anderson Cancer Inst., Houston, 1984-85; clin. dir. vascular and interventional radiology Hosp. Albert Einstein, 1985—; asst. prof. Albert Einstein Coll. Medicine, 1989-94, assoc. prof., 1994—. Contbr. author: Principles and Practice of Vascular and Interventional Radiology, 2001. Mem. Soc. Cardiovasc. and Interventional Radiology. Avocations: cycling, skiing. Office: Albert Einstein Coll Hosp 1805 Eastchester Rd Bronx NY 10461

TRAMMELL, HERBERT EUGENE, physicist, laboratory executive; b. Laurel, Miss., Apr. 19, 1927; s. Homer Lee and Evie Louisa (Breazeale) T.; m. Jane Walker, Dec. 28, 1948; children— Carmen, Bert, Lisa, Brian. BA in Physics, U. Miss., 1947, MA, 1948. With Nuclear div. Union Carbide, Oak Ridge, 1949-89, mgr. barrier devel. programs, 1967-69, dir. gaseous diffusion devel. div., 1969-77; dir. engring. tech. div. Oak Ridge Nat. Lab., 1977-89, ret., 1989; with Martin Marietta Energy Systems, 1983-89. Bd. dirs. Emory Valley Sch. for Retarded Children, 1962-68, v.p., 1966-68; mem. Tenn. Med. Malpractice Rev. Bd., 1974-80; active PTA. Served with U.S. Navy, 1944-45. Mem.: Rotary (pres. 1980-81). Methodist. Home: 901 Johnson St Key West FL 33040-4745 E-mail: htrammell@webtv.net.

TRAMMELL, JOHN KENT, educator; b. Berea, Ky., Jan. 23, 1964; s. Richard Louis and Carol Sue T.; m. Kathleen J., Aug. 8, 1986; children; Alec, Madeline, Hannah. BA, Grove City Coll., 1986; MEd, Va. Commonwealth U., 1991. Learning specialist, writer Randolph Macon Coll., Ashland, Va., 1993—. Instr., adj. prof. U. Richmond, Va., 1999—. Author: The Saints Departed, 1997, Return to Treasure Island, 1999, Gray, 2000; author of poems. Mem. Poetry Soc. Va., Poets and Writers. E-mail: jtrammel@pen.k12.va.us.

TRAMONTANA, MARIE, guidance counselor; b. Stamford, Conn., July 17, 1943; d. Richard Anthony and Mary Concetta (Gesualdi) T. BA, Marymount Coll., 1965; MA, Fairfield U., 1968; Cert. of Advanced Study, So. Conn. State U., 1984. Cert. secondary edn. tchr., Conn., sch. counselor, Conn. Tchr. St. Aloysius Sch., New Canaan, Conn., 1967-74; guidance counselor Norwalk (Conn.) Pub. Schs., 1974-75, Westbrook (Conn.) Pub. Schs., 1976-78; writer Career Life Cycle Pub. Co., Darien, Conn., 1977-79; guidance counselor The Morgan Sch., Clinton, 1978—. Mem. Coalition for Ams. with Disabilities, New Haven, 1990—; founder Clinton Youth Family Svc. Bur., 1987, Morgan Student Assistance, 1993—; chairperson Dist. Student Assistance Team, 1996—; developer, designer Crisis Intervention Team and Plan. Mem. Am. Assn. Sch. Counselors, Conn. Sch. Counselors Assn. (com. chair 1980-82), South Cen. Area Guidance Assn. (pres. 1978-80, 82-86, v.p. 1980-82, sec./treas. 1990-92, program coord. 1996—). Roman Catholic. Avocations: watercolor painting, pottery, gardening, graphic design. Office: The Morgan Sch Rt 81 27 Killingworth Turnpike Clinton CT 06413

TRAMONTE, JAMES ALBERT, lawyer; b. New Orleans, Mar. 6, 1951; s. August Joseph and Genevieve Tramonte; m. Stephanie Thomas, Aug. 12, 1972; children: James Albert Jr., Karen Elizabeth, David August, Patrick Thomas, Mark Joseph. Student, U. Miss., 1968-70; BS in Acctg., La. State U., New Orleans, 1973; JD, Tulane U., 1976; LLM in Taxation, NYU, 1977. CPA La.; bar: La. 1976, U.S. Tax T. 1977, U.S. Ct. Claims 1978, U.S. Ct. Appeals (5th and 11th cirs.) 1981, Ga. 1989, cert.: La. (tax atty.). Ptnr. Hurt, Richardson, Garner, Todd & Cadenhead, Atlanta, 1988-92; gen. counsel Ctrl. Health Svcs., Inc., 1993-96, Simione Ctrl. Holdings, Inc., Atlanta, 1993-97; exec. v.p., chief legal officer LDC Direct, Ltd. Co., 1998-99; exec. v.p. R.S. Andrews Enterprises, Inc., 1999—2002; of counsel Gorby, Reeves and Peters, PC, 2002—. Author: (book) Estate Planning for Divorced and Remarried Persons, 1986; co-author: Loyola Law Rev. 5th Cir. Symposium, 1986. Mem.: AICPA, ABA (sect. on taxation), State Bar of Ga. (corp. coun. sect.), Ga. State Soc. CPAs (taxation com. 1989), La. State Bar Assn. (sec. on taxation, chmn. formularly com. 1981—82, chmn. liaison com. with dist. dir. IRS 1982—83). Roman Catholic. Home: 5509 Mount Vernon Way Dunwoody GA 30338-2815 Office: Gorby Reeves and Peters PC Resurgens Plz 21st Fl 945 E Paces Ferry Rd Atlanta GA 30326 Business E-Mail: jtramonte@grpb.com.

TRAMONTE, MICHAEL ROBERT, education educator; AB in Sociology, Boston Coll., 1960; EdM, Boston State Coll., 1963; Cert. Advanced Edn. Specialization, Boston Coll., 1971; Comprehensive Cert. in Paralegal Studies, Bentley Coll., 1982; EdD in Human Devel. and Edn., Boston U., 1986. Lic. psychologist, ednl. psychologist Mass., cert. social worker Mass., cert. health svc. provider Mass., tchr. social studies grades 5-9, grades 9-12, moderate spl. needs tchr., sch. psychologist, supt., asst. supt., guidance counselor, supr., dir., secondary sch. prin. Mass., nat. cert. sch. psychologist, cert. sch. psychologist N.H., Mass. Substitute tchr. Medford (Mass.) Pub. Schs., 1960-61, jr. H.S. tchr. social studies, 1961-68; instr. psychology and edn. Anna Maria Coll., 1968-69; adj. instr. psychology Mass. Bay C.C., 1972-80, Middlesex C.C., 1977—; sch. psychologist Lowell (Mass.) Pub. Schs., 1970-98; assoc. prof. edn. Rivier Coll., Nashua, N.H., 1998—. Adj. prof. edn. Rivier Coll., 1983, 87-98; spkr. in field. Chmn. Medford chpt. Greater Boston Assn. Retarded Children, 1969-70; vol. spkr. support groups Mass. chpt. Nat. Multiple Sclerosis Soc., 1971-88; mem. ARC Disaster Svcs. Human Resources Sys. Recipient certificate Medford Mental Health Assn., 1968, certificate Medford chpt. Greater Boston Assn. Retarded Children, 1970, certificate Mass. chpt. Nat. Multiple Sclerosis Soc., 1979, Faculty award for Secondary Edn., Rivier Coll., 1994, cert. of recognition ARC of Mass. Bay, 1999. Fellow Am. Acad. Experts in Traumatic Stress. Home: 24 Erie St Woburn MA 01801-4532 E-mail: mtramonte@rivier.edu.

TRAMONTI, JOHN, JR. lawyer; b. Providence, Dec. 24, 1930; s. John and Patricia Tramonti. BA, Providence Coll.; JD, Boston Coll., 1952. Bar: R.I. 1952. Sole practitioner, Providence. Mem. Am. Bd. Trial Advocates, R.I. Assn. Trial Attys., R.I. Assn. Criminal Def. Attys. Office: 15 Westminster St Ste 808 Providence RI 02903-2415

TRAMONTINE, JOHN ORLANDO, retired lawyer; b. Iron Mountain, Mich., Sept. 21, 1932; s. Orlando F. and Susan M. (Hollar) Tramontine; m. Nancy A. McCabe, July 14, 1956; 1 child Margaret A. BSChemE, U. Notre Dame, 1955; postgrad., Georgetown U., 1956—58; LLB, NYU, 1960. Bar:

N.Y. 1960, U.S. Dist. Ct. (no. dist.) Ill. 1963, U.S. Dist. Ct. (so. and ea. dists.) N.Y. 1965, U.S. Ct. Appeals (2d and 5th cirs.) 1967, U.S. Supreme Ct. 1970, U.S. Ct. Appeals (8th cir.) 1970, (3d cir.) 1973, (7th cir.) 1976, (fed. cir.) 1979, U.S. Dist. Ct. (we. dist.) N.Y. 1981. Examiner U.S. Patent Office, 1956-58; patent agt. Arthur, Dry & Dole, N.Y.C., 1958-60; assoc. Arthur, Dry, Kalish, Taylor & Wood, 1960-62, Wolfe, Hubbard, Voit & Osann, Chgo., 1962-63, Fish & Neave, N.Y.C., 1963-70, ptnr., 1970-2000. 2nd lt. USMCR, 1955. Fellow Am. Coll. Trial Lawyers, Am. Bar Found.; mem. ABA, Assn. of Bar of City of N.Y. (chmn. patent com. 1974-77), Fed. Cir. Bar Assn., N.Y. Intellectual Property Law Assn. (pres. 1985-86), St. Andrews Golf Club (sec. 1981-83). Office: Fish & Neave 1251 Avenue of the Americas New York NY 10020-1105

TRAMUTOLA, JOSEPH LOUIS, lawyer, educator; b. Union City, N.J., Mar. 6, 1931; s. Joseph Emil and Elda (Brioli) T.; m. Mary Ann Banull, Sept. 4, 1965; children Karen, Kim, Karla. BA, St. Peter's Coll., Jersey City, 1953; JD, Fordham U., 1959. Bar: N.J. 1961. Atty. Toolan, Haney, Romand, Perth Amboy, N.J.; prof. law Fairleigh Dickinson U., Madison, 1965—, creator, dir. ednl. program for older persons, 1972-2001, ret., 2001. Pre-legal advisor Silberman Coll. bus., Fairleigh Dickinson U.; cons. Am. Coun. on Edn., Washington, Am. Edn. Assn., Washington, Thomas Edison Coll., Trenton, N.J., Chartered Pub. Underwriters, East Orange, N.J., USDA; adj. faculty U. Mich., dir. Fairleigh Dickinson U. Patent Inst.. dir. ednl. seminars on student law; seminar dir. student law, Calif., Ill., Mass., N.Y., Ga. Author: Guide Book for Student Rights, Legal Perspective for Student Personal Administration, Legal Overview of the New Student; dir. CPA Law Rev. With U.S. Army, 1955-57. Named Outstanding Educator Outstanding Educators Inc., 1973, 1974, Commendation for Civic Contb. N.J. Legis., 1993. Roman Catholic. Avocations: Bonsai, clock making, gardening, zymology, music. Home: 12 Browning Ct Mendham NJ 07945-3301 Fax: 973-543-6621. E-mail: jltram@earthlink.net.

TRAN, HENRY BANG Q. social work case manager; b. Binh Dinh, Vietnam, Dec. 28, 1952; came to U.S., 1975; s. Mau Dinh and Ho Thi Tran; m. Thuhong T. Ngo; children: John, Michael, Robert, Richard, Jennifer. BA, Northeastern Ill. U., 1977, MA, 1978. Cert. social worker, real estate broker. Social worker Tex. Dept. Human Svcs., Houston, 1980-96; founder, pres. Texo Properties, Inc., 1984-85; pres. N.E.W.S. Properties, 1985—; case mgr. Tex. Workforce Commn., 1996—. Instr. math. City Colls. Chgo., 1977, Vietnamese lang. U. Houston, 1985, pres. H Trans Corp. V.p. Buddhist Assn. for Services of Humanity in Am., Houston, 1985—; pres. Quang Trung Mut. Assistance Assn., Houston, 1984—. Fellow U. Miami, 1979. Mem. Nat. Assn. Realtors, Tex. Pub. Employee Assn., Dalat U. Alumni Assn., Asia Soc., Houston Vietnam Lions Club (pres. 1991). Avocations: tennis, soccer, jogging.

TRAN, JACK NHUAN NGOC, gas and oil reservoir engineer; b. Quang Binh, Vietnam, Sept. 21, 1933; came to U.S., 1975; s. Dieu Ngoc and Ly Thi (Nguyen) T.; m. Christine Quang Huynh; children: Quoc Dung, Ann Nga Huyen, Ephram Anh Dung, John Hung Dung. BS, U. San Francisco, 1977, MBA, 1978. With Republic of Vietnam Mil., 1952-67; cadet Rep. Vietnam Mil. Acad., Dalat, 1952-53; 1st lt., co. comdr. 1st Republic of Vietnam Bn., South Vietnam, 1953-54; editor-in-chief Republic of Vietnam Revs., Saigon, 1955-57; commandant Republic of Vietnam Aerial Photo Ctr., 1958-61, Republic of Vietnam Mil. Intelligence Sch., Caymai and Saigon, 1962-67; mem. Republic of Vietnam Senate, 1967-73; v.p. The Meteco Corp., Saigon, Vietnam, 1971-72; pres., chmn. bd. Meteco-Vinaseco Co., 1972-75; air photo analyst Std. Oil Co., San Francisco, 1975-79; gas and oil engr. Chevron Oil Co., 1980—; col. U.S. Intelligence, Calif., 1980-90. Author: Flower in the Battle Field, 1956, Geological Survey of the Kndu, CA, 1982, Beluga River Oil Development, 1984, The Military Life, 1992; editor-in-chief Chien-Si Quoc-Gia Mag. Recipient Hon. Key of the City, City of Omaha, Nebr., 1989, Hon. Citizen City of Fayetteville, N.C., 1969; Resolution of Recognition, Senate of State of Hawaii, 1969, Senate of State of Tex., 1969. Mem. The U. of San Francisco Alumni Assn., Rotary Internat. Roman Catholic. Avocations: swimming, music, reading, traveling. Home: 1418 Lundy Ave San Jose CA 95131-3310

TRAN, JOHN KIM-SON TAN, chemical senses executive, research administrator; b. Quang-Binh, Vietnam, Oct. 4, 1945; Came to U.S., 1975. s. Dong Tan Tran and Chieu Thi Nguyen;m. Ann Xuyen Thi, July 30, 1972; children: Joseph Quoc-Bao Tan, Michael Quoc-Binh Tan, Regina Thuy-Quyen Tan, John Quoc-An Tan. Baccalaureate degree, Nat. Exam. Bd., Saigon, Vietnam, 1966; student, U. Saigon, 1966-70; grad., Republic of Vietnam Army Acad., 1971; BBA, U. Pa., 1976-80, postgrad., 1981-83; MS in Polit. Sci. and Pub. Adminstrn., So. Ill. U., Edwardsville, 1989. Cert. rsch. adminstr. Journalist Saigon bur. Tokyo Broadcasting Sys., 1968-75; tchr. English Cao-Nguyen Jr. Mil. Acad., Pleiku, Vietnam, 1971-75; bookkeeper, budget asst. U. Pa., Phila., 1976-81, bus. admins., 1981-84; bus. mgr., treas. Blackburn Coll., Carlinville, Ill., 1984-87; sec.-treas., adminstr. Monell Chem. Senses Ctr., Phila., 1987-94, dir. for fin. and adminstrv. svcs., sec.-treas, 1994-99, dir. fin. and adminstrv. svcs., treas., 1999—. Sec. gen. Young Christian Students Movement, Saigon, 1969-71; warrant officer, 1971-73; v.p. Vietnamese Cath. Community Archdiocese Phila., 1976-82; treas., bd. trustees Blackburn Coll., Carlinville, Ill., 1984-87. Lt. Republic of Vietnam Army (South), 1973-75. Mem. Nat. Coun. Univ. Rsch. Adminstrs., Soc. Rsch. Adminstrs., Assn. Ind. Rsch. Insts. (primary rep.). Roman Catholic. Avocations: classical music, travel. Home: 1482 Huntingdon Rd Abington PA 19001-2104 Office: Monell Chem Senses Ctr 3500 Market St Philadelphia PA 19104-3360 E-mail: tran@monell.org.

TRAN, LAWRENCE DELANO, family physician, educator; b. Hue, Vietnam, Nov. 20, 1945; came to U.S., 1975; s. Tu Duc and Con Thi (Mac) T.; m. Stephanie Doan, Apr. 8, 1977; children: Tiffany Doan, Sabrina Doan, Helena Doan. MD, U. Hue, 1972. Diplomate Am. Bd. Family Practice. Intern Jackson Meml. Hosp., Mount Sinai Med. Ctr. Greater Miami, VA Hosp., Miami, Fla., 1977—78; resident dept. family medicine U. Miami Sch. Medicine and Affiliated Hosps., 1978—79, UCLA Affiliated San Bernardino (Calif.) County Med. Ctr., 1979—80; family physician Burbank Family Care, Burbank, Calif., 2000—; asst. clin. prof. UCLA Sch. Medicine, 1996—. Fellow Am. Acd. Family Physicians; mem. Soc. Tchrs. Family Medicine. Avocations: photography, sculpture, tennis, travel, investment. Office: Burbank Family Care 2211 W Magnolia Blvd Burbank CA 91506

TRAN, LONG TRIEU, industrial engineer; b. Saigon, Vietnam, Oct. 10, 1956; came to U.S., 1973; s. Nguyen Dinh and Thiet Thi (Nguyen) T.; m. Khanh Thi-Hong Phan, Aug. 3, 1988. BS in Mech. Engrng. with honors, U. Kans., 1976; MS in Mech. Engrng., MIT, 1980; MBA in Bus. Adminstrn. with honors, U. Louisville, 1993. Cert. quality engr.; cert. mfg. engr.; cert. project mgmt. profl. Tchg. asst. U. Kans., 1975-76, U. Calif., Berkeley, 1977; rsch. asst. Lawrence Berkeley Labs., 1977, MIT, 1977-80; libr. staff Harvard U. Med. Sch. Libr., 1977-78; mem. staff New England Deaconess Hosp., Boston, 1978-80; prodn. programming engr. GE, Cleve., 1980-81, advanced mfg. engr. Louisville, 1981-82, quality sys. engr., 1982-84, quality control engr., 1984-86, sr. quality info. equipment engr., 1986-89, sr. quality indsl. engr., 1990-94, sr. supplier tech. assistance engr., 1995-96, sr. advanced supplier quality engr., 1996-98, program mgr. purchased material quality, 1999, combo blackbelt leader supplier quality, 1999-2000, six sigma program mgr., 2000—. Exec. advisor Jr. Achievement Inc., Louisville, 1983-84; monitor/reader Rec. for the Blind, 1994—; fundraiser The Dream Factory Inc., 1994—. Vol. NCCJ, 1994—, Clothe-A-Child, 1993—, Dare-To-Care, 1994—, Ronald McDonald House, 1994—. Mem. AAAS, ASME, Am. Soc. Quality Control, Computer and Automated Sys. Assn. (charter), Am. Prodn. and Inventory Control Soc., Robot Inst. Am., Robotics Internat. (charter), Soc. Mfg. Engrs. (sr.), Instrument Soc. Am. (sr.), Am. Mgmt. Assn., N.Y. Acad. Scis., Internat. Platform Assn., Indsl. Computing Soc. (founding), Project Mgmt. Inst., Nat. Pks. Conservation Assn., U.S. Libr. Congress Assocs. (founding), Sigma Xi, Pi Tau Sigma, Tau Beta Pi, Phi Kappa Phi, Beta Gamma Sigma. Republican. Achievements include research on grinding processes and material surface analysis, also manufacturing project management. Home: 3642 Windward Way Louisville KY 40220-1818 Office: Gen Electric Co Appliance Park AP2-117 Louisville KY 40225-0001

TRAN, NAM VAN, health education specialist; b. Saigon, Vietnam, July 29, 1943; came to U.S., 1983; s. Giap Van Tran and Thai Thi Nguyen; m. Hien Quy Pham; children: Kelly, Peter, Linda. MD, U. Saigon, 1969; MPH, U. Hawaii, 1987. Instr. U. Saigon Sch. Medicine, 1968-70; attending physician, chief dermatology dept. Naval Hosp., Saigon, South Vietnam, 1970-75; attending physician, dermatology Venereology Hosp., Ho Chi Minh City, 1977-83; asst. project dir. Health is Gold U. Calif., San Francisco, 1988-90; health edn. specialist Santa Clara Valley Health and Hosp. Sys., San Jose, 1990—. Pub. health cons. Asian Am. Cmty. Involvement, San Jose, Calif., 1990-94, Alexian Brothers Hosp., San Jose, 1992—. Author: How to Stop Smoking, 1990, How to Protect Your Health, 1992, Delivery: Easily & Pleasantly, 1995, Health is Gold, 1996. Recipient commendation City of San Jose, 1990. Mem. APHA, Vietnamese Physicians Assn. No. Calif. (bd. dirs. 1992-96, award 1994, 1996), Vietnamese Physicians Assn. of Free World, Vietnamese Physicians Assn. of USA. Avocations: reading, listening to music. Home: 884 Coventry Way Milpitas CA 95035-3587 Office: Santa Clara Valley Health and Hosp Sys 595 Millich Dr Ste 100 Campbell CA 95008-0550

TRAN, NANG TRI, electrical engineer, physicist; b. Binh Dinh, Vietnam, Jan. 2, 1948; came to the U.S., 1979, naturalized, 1986; s. Cam Tran and Cuu Thi Nguyen; m. Thu-Huong Thi Tong, Oct. 14, 1982; children: Helen, Florence, Irene, Kenneth. BSEE, Kyushu Inst. Tech., Kitakyushu, Japan, 1973, MSEE, 1975; PhD in Materials Sci./Solid State Device, U. Osaka Prefecture, Sakai, Japan, 1979. Rsch. assoc. U. Calif. Irvine, 1979; engr., rsch. scientist Sharp Electronics, Irvine, 1979-80; sr. rsch. scientist Arco Solar Industries, Chatsworth, Calif., 1980-84; sr. rsch. specialist, group leader 3M Co., St. Paul, 1985-96; staff scientist Imation Corp., Oakdale, Minn., 1996—; exec. Khanti Inc. Adj. prof. Inst. Tech., U. Minn., Mpls.; cons., lectr. Japan industry mgmt.; reviewer NSF. Author: (poetry) My Journey; contbr. articles to profl. jours.; inventor direct digital x-rays, transparent conducting zinc oxide doped with group III elements, thin film transistors on flexible substrate, structured phosphors; patentee in field. Mem. tech. com. various internat. confs. Recipient R&D awards, Photonic Cir. Excellence award; fellow, Govt. South Vietnam, Japan, USAID, Rotary Internat., 1968—79. Mem. IEEE (sr.), Japan Soc. Applied Physics, N.Y. Acad. Scis. Achievements include patents for; research in different types of thin film displays; amorphous silicon solar cells; image sensors; solid state memory; photoconductors; CD; high density data storage media; transparent conducting oxide films. Office: Imation Corp Materials Media Devel 1 Imation Pl Discovery 1D-20 Oakdale MN 55128-3414 E-mail: nttran@imation.com.

TRAN, NGUYET T. accountant; b. Hanoi, Vietnam, Sept. 23, 1930; came to U.S., 1964; d. Huong Van and Chin Thi Tran; divorced; 1 child, Minh C. Nguyen. BSBA, San Francisco State U., 1980; MBA, U. Phoenix, 1987. Lang. tchr. U.S. Dept. Def., Presidio of Monterey, Calif., 1966-71; bookkeeper Nathan B. Siegel, CPA, San Francisco, 1971-76; sr. acct. Nat. Med. Enterprises, San Francisco/San Rafael, Calif., 1976-80; staff acct. Hillhaven Inc., Tacoma, 1980-93; acct., bus. mgr. Guardian Med. Hill Rehab. Ctr., Oakland, Calif., 1993—, dir. adminstrv. svcs., acct., 1998—. Sec. to ambassador Vietnam Mission to UN, N.Y.C., 1964-66; press and info. sec. govt. Ministry of Fgn. Affairs, Saigon, Vietnam, 1956-64. Mem. NAFE, AARP, Nat. Notary Assn., Smithsonian Inst. (assoc.), Am. Cancer soc. Republican. Buddhist. Avocations: reading, gardening, knitting. Home: 2 Davenport Hercules CA 94547-3626 Office: Amer Baptist Homes of the West Piedmont Gardens 110 41st St Oakland CA 94611-5250

TRAN, QUI-PHIET, English educator; b. Dalat, Vietnam, Jan. 6, 1937; came to U.S., 1972; s. But Qui and Anh Nguyen Thi Tran; m. Ngan Vo Thi, Aug. 30, 1963; children: Hung, Thuy, Long, Kien. BA, U. Hue, Vietnam, 1960; MA, U. Tex., 1974, PhD, 1977. English tchr. Votanh H.S., Nhatrang, Vietnam, 1960-64, Petrus Ky H.S., Saigon, Vietnam, 1964-65; instr. English U. Hue, 1965-72, U. Tex., Austin, 1977-78; resource specialist Arlington (Va.) Pub. Schs., 1980-81; asst. prof., then assoc. prof. Schreiner U., Kerrville, Tex., 1982-90; prof. English Schreiner Coll., 1990—. Document analyst Congl. Info. Svc., Washington, 1979-80; refugee resettlement cons. Ctr. for Applied Linguistics, Washington, 1980-81, Action, U.S. Govt., Washington, 1982; Fulbright lectr. Nat. U. Vietnam, Ho Chi Minh City, 1999-2000. Author: William Faulkner, 1980; contbr. articles to profl. publs. Advisor Vietnamese Parents Assn., Arlington, 1980-81. Grantee Mellon Found., 1983, NEH, 1983, 89, Am. Coun. Learned Socs., 1984-85. Mem. MLA, Fulbright Assn. Avocation: gardening. Home: 2100 Memorial Blvd Kerrville TX 78028-5611 Office: Schreiner U 2100 Memorial Blvd Kerrville TX 78028-5611 E-mail: ptran@schreiner.edu.

TRANI, EUGENE PAUL, university president, educator; b. Bklyn., Nov. 2, 1939; s. Frank Joseph and Rose Gertrude (Kelly) T.; m. Lois Elizabeth Quigley, June 2, 1962; children: Anne Chapman, Frank. BA in History with honors, U. Notre Dame, 1961; MA, Ind. U., 1963, PhD, 1966. Instr. history Ohio State U., Columbus, 1965-67; asst. prof. So. Ill. U., Carbondale, 1967-71, assoc. prof., 1971-75, prof., 1975-76; asst. v.p. acad. affairs, prof. U. Nebr., 1976-80; prof., vice chancellor acad. affairs U. Mo. Kansas City, 1980-86; prof., v.p. acad. affairs U. Wis. System, 1986-90; pres. Va. Commonwealth U., 1990—; pres. bd. dirs. Va. Biotech Rsch. Park, 1992-97, chmn., 1997—; pres., chmn. VCU Health Sys., 2000—. Vis. asst. prof. U. Wis., Milw., 1969; bd. dirs. Met. Richmond SunTrust Mid-Atlantic Bank, Innovative Tech. Authority, Universal Corp., Envera, LandAm. Fin. Group, Inc.; cons. various univ. presses, jours., govtl. agys.; mem. commn. Internat. Edn. Am. Coun. Ed., 1991—; bd. gov. Ctr. Russian Am. Bus., Washington, 1993—; mem. adv. coun. Coun. on Grad. Studies and Rsch., U. Notre Dame, 1994—. Author, editor: Concerns of a Conservative Democrat, 1968, The Treaty of Portsmouth: An Adventure in American Diplomacy, 1969, The Secretaries of the Department of the Interior, 1849-69, 1975, (with David Wilson) The Presidency of Warren G. Harding, 3d edit., 1989; contbr. articles to profl. jours., newspapers; book reviewer. Permanent mem. Coun. Fgn. Rels., N.Y.C., 1979—; bd. dirs. Richmond Ballet, 1991-96, NCCJ, Richmond, 1991-94, Va. Spl. Olympics, 1991-96, YMCA of Greater Richmond, 1992—, Richmond Renaissance, 1992-96, Met. Found., 1992—; mem. U.S. Savs. Bond Vol. Com., chmn. higher edn. area, 1992, 93; adv. bd. Greater Richmond chpt. ARC, 1992—; mem. Gov.'s Commn. Info. Tech. in Va.; bd. dirs. Richmond Renaissance, 2001—, chmn., 2001—; bd. dirs. Qatar Found. for Edn., Sci. Comm. Devel., Collegiate Sch. Fellow Russian and East European Inst., 1964-65, Nat. Hist. Publs. Commn., 1969-70, Woodrow Wilson Internat. Ctr. Scholars, 1972-73, So. Ill. U. Sabbatical Leave, 1975-76, Coun. Internat. Exchange Scholars, 1981, U. Mo. Faculty, 1981; grantee U.S. Dept. Interior Rsch., 1965, 66, So. Ill. U. Office Rsch. and Projects, 1967-74, Am. Philos. Soc., 1968, 72, So. Ill U. Summer Rsch. 1970, 72, 75, Lilly Endowment, 1975-76, Sloan Commn. Govt. and Higher Edn., 1978, USIA Am. Participants Program, 1984, 85, 86, 88, 90; Inst. for U.S. Studies fellow U. London, 1995, fellow commoner St. John's Coll., Cambridge, 1998; recipient Younger Humanist award NEH, 1972-73, Leadership and Achievement award Ctrl. Richmond Assn., 1992, Biotech. Leadership award Va. Biotech. Assn., 1999; named among 100 Top Ricmonders of Century, Richmonder of Yr., Style Mag., 1998. Mem. Internat. Inst. Strategic Studies, Am. Assn. Advancement Slavic Studies, Orgn. Am. Historians, Soc. Historians Am. Fgn. Rels., Greater Richmond C. of C. (bd. dirs. 1991-96, chmn. 1997-98), Phi Kappa Phi. Roman Catholic. Avocations: reading, travel, basketball, golf. Office: Va Commonwealth U Box 842512 910 W Franklin St Richmond VA 23284-2612 E-mail: etrani@vcu.edu.

TRANK, DOUGLAS MONTY, rhetoric and speech communications educator; b. Lincoln, Nebr., Sept. 8, 1944; s. Walter John and Hazel Elaine (Stegeman) T.; children: Heather Nicole, Jessica Celeste; m. Christine Marie Quinn, 1992. BA in English, U. Nebr., Kearney, 1967, MS in Comm., 1970; PhD in Comm., U. Utah, 1973. Tchr. Ogallala (Nebr.) High Sch., 1967-70; teaching fellow in communications U. Utah, Salt Lake City, 1970-72; prof. communications Old Dominion U., Norfolk, Va., 1972-74; prof. rhetoric and edn. U. Iowa, Iowa City, 1974—, chmn. rhetoric dept., 1984-89, 2001—. Chmn. bd. control athletics, faculty senate, mem. ednl. policy com., faculty adv. com., faculty assembly, exec. com. U. Iowa. Author 3 books; editor Communication Edn., 1993-96; assoc. editor Communication Studies; contbr. numerous articles to profl. jours. Recipient Admiral award Ace Adventures, Inc., Iowa, 1987, Hemingway prize, 1992. Mem. Speech Communication Assn., Iowa Communication Assn. (pres. 1980-82, editor 1977-81, mem. jour. editorial bd.), Cen. States Communication Assn. (pres. 1990-91), Fedn. Iowa Speech Orgns. (pres. 1977-79), Iowa City Optimist Club (dir. 1982-89, pres. 1987-88). Democrat. Avocations: ice sailing, hunting, fishing, canoeing. Office: U Iowa Dept Rhetoric Iowa City IA 52242 E-mail: douglas-trank@uiowa.edu.

TRANMER, BRUCE IAN, neurosurgeon; b. Cobourg, Ont., Can., Mar. 15, 1954; came to U.S., 1995; s. William and Lois (Nellist) T.; m. Sandra McCormick, Sept. 7, 1984; children: Alexandra, Andrew. MD, Queen's U., Kingston, Ont., 1979. Diplomate Am. Bd. Neurosurgery. Intern Kingston Gen. Hosp., 1979-80; resident in neurosurgery U. Toronto, 1980-86; assoc. prof. U. Calgary, 1988-95; prof., chief neurosurgery Albany (N.Y.) Med. Coll., 1995-99; prof., chmn. neurosurgery U. Vt., Burlington, 1999—. Contbr. articles to profl. jours. Bd. dirs. N.E. chpt. Am. Heart Assn. Fellow Royal Coll. Physicians (Can.). Office: Fletcher Allen Health Care Neurosurgery Fletcher 5 111 Colchester Ave Burlington VT 05401 E-mail: bruce.tranmer@vtmednet.org.

TRANOVICH, MARK, orthopedic surgeon; b. Wheeling, W.Va., Aug. 2, 1956; s. John and Margaret Elizabeth (Robatisin) T.; m. Sharon Elizabeth Takacs, Aug. 27, 1989; 1 child, Alexander Joseph. BS, Ohio State U., 1978, MD, 1981. Diplomate Am. Bd. Orthop. Surgery. Intern Mercy Hosp., Pitts., 1981-82, resident in gen. surgery, 1982-83, Marshall U., Huntington, W.Va., 1983-84; resident in orthop. surgery U. Pitts., 1984-87; pvt. practice orthop. surgery Uniontown, Pa., 1987-88; orthop. surgeon Bone and Joint Surg. Assocs., 1988-95, Wooster (Ohio) Clinic, 1995-97, chmn. dept. surgery, 1998—, mem. exec. com., 2000—; orthop. surgeon Cleve. Clin. Found., 1998—. Mem. adv. bd. Arthritis Found., Uniontown, 1991-95; chmn. infection control com. The Uniontown Hosp., 1992-95; mem. strategic planning group Ohio Acad. Sci., Columbus, 1996; chmn. X-ray com. The Wooster Clinic, 1997-99. Football team physician The Uniontown H.S., 1987-94; vol. med. divsn. United Way, Uniontown, 1989-92; judge State Sci. Day, Ohio Acad. Sci., Delaware, 1996-99; treas. Wayne County Ohio State Alumni, Wooster, 1996-98. Maj. Ohio Army Nat. Guard. Fellow Am. Acad. Orthop. Surgeons; mem. AMA, Am. Coll. Sports Medicine, Ohio Acad. Sci., Ohio Orthop. Soc., Ohio State Med. Assn., Wayne County Med. Soc., McKenzie Inst. Office: Cleve Clin Found 1740 Cleveland Rd Wooster OH 44691-2204

TRANQUADA, ROBERT ERNEST, medical educator, physician; b. Los Angeles, Aug. 27, 1930; s. Ernest Alvro Tanquada and Katharine (Jacobus) Tranquada; m. Janet Martin, Aug. 31, 1951; children: John Martin, Katherine Anne, James Robert. BA, Pomona Coll., 1951; MD, Stanford U., 1955; D.Sc. (hon.) , Worcester Poly. Inst., 1985. Diplomate Am. Bd. Internal Medicine. Intern in medicine UCLA Med. Center, 1955—56, resident in medicine, 1956—57; resident Los Angeles VA Hosp., 1957—58; fellow in diabetes and metabolic diseases UCLA, 1958—59; fellow in diabetes U. So. Calif., 1959—60, asst. prof. medicine, 1960—63, assoc. prof., 1964—68, chmn. dept. community medicine, 1967—70; med. dir. Los Angeles County/U. So. Calif. Med. Center, 1969—74; regional dir. Central Region, Los Angeles County Dept. Health Services, 1974—76; assoc. dean UCLA Sch. Medicine, 1976—79; chancellor and dean U. Mass. Med. Sch., 1979—86; dean U. So. Calif. Sch. Medicine, 1986—91; prof. medicine U. So. Calif., L.A., 1956—92, Norman Topping/Nat. Med. Enterprises prof. med./pub. policy, 1992—97; prof. emeritus, 1997—. Mem, chair L.A. County Task Force on Health Care Access, 1992—94. Corporator Worcester Art Mus., 1980—86; mem. Ind. Commn. on L.A. Police Dept., 1991—92; mem. governing bd. L.A. County Local Initiative Health Authority, 1994—, chmn., 2001—; bd trustees Pomona Coll., 1969—, vice chmn., 1971—79, chmn., 1991—2000; bd. fellow Claremont U. Ct., 1971—79, 1991—2000; chmn. bd. overseers Claremont U. Consortium, 2000—; bd. trustees Keck Grad. Inst. Applied Life Scis., 1997—, vice-chmn., 1997—2000; bd. dirs. Nat. Med. Fellowships, Inc., 1973—, chmn., 1980—85; bd. trustees Charles Drew U. Med. and Sci., 1968—79, 1986—95, Orthopaedic Hosp., 1986—91, Barlow Hosp., 1987—89; bd. dirs. Worcester Acad., 1984—86, U. So. Calif. Univ. Hosp., 1988—91, Alliance for Childrens Rights, 1991—95, Good Hope Med. Found, 1994—, Ralph M. Parsons Found., 2000—. Fellow Milbank faculty, 1967—72. Fellow: Am. Antiquarian Soc., AAAS; mem.: Inst. Medicine, Calif. Med. Assn., L.A. Acad. Medicine, L.A. County Med. Assn., Am. Diabetes Assn., AMA, Alpha Omega Alpha, Sigma Xi, Phi Beta Kappa.

TRANQUILLA, RONALD E. English language educator; b. Latrobe, Pa., May 14, 1941; s. Edward Ned and Martha LaVerne (Shaffer) T.; m. Penny Seaton, Aug. 10, 1963; 1 child, Ryan Eric. BA, Allegheny Coll., 1963; MA, U. Pitts., 1964, PhD, 1973. From instr. to asst. prof. English St. Vincent Coll., Latrobe, 1964-82, prof., 1982—. Hunger-action enabler Synod of Trinity, 1980-81, Redstone Presbytery, 1986-93. Recipient Fern Chertkow Meml. fiction award Gt. Stream Rev., 1988, nat. bronze medal 1989 prof. of yr. program Coun. for Advancement and Support Edn., 1990. Presbyterian. Office: St Vincent Coll Dept English Latrobe PA 15650

TRANSUE, BROOKE MULLEN, occupational assessment and career specialist; b. Traverse City, Mich., Dec. 14, 1942; d. Donald Maurice and Alberta Blanche (Thom) Mullen; m. Frank Max Transue, June 13, 1964; children: Donald, Paul, Elizabeth. BA, U. Mich., 1964, MA, 1970; EdD, No. Ill. U., 1986. Mem. teaching faculty Judson Coll., Elgin, Ill., 1973-83; assessment specialist Sch. Dist. # 46, 1985-87; owner, pres. Assessment Svcs. Ltd., 1987—. Allied health profl. St. Joseph Hosp., Elgin, 1987—. Author: A Quick Start Guide to Implementing Title I Employment Americans with Disabilities Act, 1990. Bd. dirs. Well Child Conf., Elgin, 1988—, Jane Shrover East Seal Ctr., Elgin, 1990—. Recipient Leadership Ill. Com. award, 1992; Trublood scholar U. Mich., 1965. Mem. Am. Vocat. Assn., Ill. Vocat. Assn., Nat. Rehab. Assn., Kappa Delta Pi (bd. dirs. 1987—), Delta Epsilon (bd. dirs. 1987-93). Episcopalian. Avocations: travel, reading, boating. Home: 176 Oakmont Dr Elgin IL 60123-4931 Office: 1730 Larkin Ave Elgin IL 60123-5947

TRANTER, TERENCE MICHAEL, lawyer; b. Cin., Nov. 26, 1944; s. John Lawrence and Florence Ellen (McGann) T.; m. Doris Ann Tepe, June 22, 1968; children— Amy, Terry, Michael, Christopher. A.B., Georgetown U., 1966; J.D., U. Cin., 1969. Bar: Ohio 1969, U.S. Dist. Ct. (so. dist.) Ohio 1969, U.S. Ct. Appeals (6th cir.) 1969. Asst. atty. gen. State of Ohio, Cin., 1970-71; sole practice law, Cin., 1969— ; mem. Ohio Ho. of Reps., Columbus, 1976-92; referee Domestic Relations Ct., Hamilton County, Ohio, 1975. Vice chmn. Hamilton County Democratic Exec. Com., Cin., 1984— ; mem. Ohio Dem. Cen. Com., Columbus, 1984-92; mem. city council Golf Manor, Ohio, 1971-76. Mem. ABA, Ohio Bar Assn., Cin. Bar Assn., Ohio Bd. Realtors, Cin. Bd. Realtors. Democrat. Roman Catholic. Lodges: K.C., Eagles. Avocation: fishing. Home: 7303 Fair Oaks Dr Cincinnati OH 45237-2923 Office: 606 American Bldg Cincinnati OH 45202

TRANTHAM, EMILY, association administrator; b. Nashville; d. Jack Lawrence and Bernita (Weinstein) Laribe; m. Richard Franklin Trantham, Feb. 20, 1963. BA, U. Tex., 1970, MA, 1972. Dir. svcs. to mil. families and vets. ARC, Ft. Worth, 1972-76; adminstrv. mgr. Houston Gen. Ins. Co., 1976-80; exec. dir. NCCJ, 1980—. Dir. Martin Luther King Bd., Ft. Worth, 1985-89, 95—, Tarrant County Youth Collaboration, Ft. Worth, 1985—; mem. Forum Ft. Worth, 1985—; com. mem. Tex. Conf. Chs., Austin, 1995—. Recipient Pride in Tarrant County award Ft. Worth Star-Telegram, 1989, Adopt-A-Sch. award, 1992, Models of Unity award Spiritual Assembly of Baha'is, 1994. Mem. Nat. Soc. Fundraising Execs. (cert.). Home: 903 Mission Dr Southlake TX 76092-6210 Office: NCCJ 500 W 7th St Ste 1707 Fort Worth TX 76102-4739

TRANUM, JEAN LORRAINE, freelance writer; b. Staten Island, N.Y., Apr. 8, 1935; d. William Frederik and Jennie Marguerite (Nye) Stuart; m. John Emil Tranum Sr., June 5, 1954; children: John Emil Jr., Karen Jean Yeisley, William Karl, Jeannette Aileen Zaza. Grad. high sch., Staten Island, N.Y., 1953. Freelance writer, Sacramento, 1968—. Guest speaker for schs. on writing, 1988; rsch. on book in Denmark for biography on John Tranum, stuntman for movies including Wings, Hell's Angels, 1990, On Borrowed Time, 1995. Author: (with Gladys Stuart Pucillo) The Winant House (pseudonym Billie Stuart), On Borrowed Time, 1997, Beneath the Surface, 1998. Active in PTA, Sacramento, 1968-72, Nat. Endowment of the Arts, 1989; pres. United Meth. Women. Mem. Writers Critique Group Freelancers, Sisters in Crime Orgn.

(mem. Sacramento chpt.), Sacramento Suburban Writers. Democrat. Methodist. Avocations: making porcelain dolls, making cut eggs, miniatures, needlework, genealogy. Home: 168 Redondo Ave Sacramento CA 95815-1031 E-mail: Jltjet@worldnet.att.net.

TRAP, JENNIFER JOSEPHINE, special education administrator; b. Columbus, Ohio, Jan. 29, 1951; d. Thomas D. and Sylvia (Gridelli) T.; m. Randall Lee Porter, July 1, 1978 (div. 1983); 1 child, Matthew Aaron Porter. BS, Cen. Mich. U., 1972, MA, 1975; PhD, Ohio State U., 1977; postdoctoral study, Ea. Mich. U., 1988—. Tchr. Vassar (Mich.) Pub. Schs., 1972-73; tchr., tchr. cons. Southgate (Mich.) Community Schs., 1973-75; asst. prof. No. Ky. U., Highland Heights, Ky., 1977-78; spl. edn. specialist Region V Edn. Svc. Agy., Parkersburg, W.Va., 1978-80; asst. prof. Ohio State U., Columbus, 1980-87, Marietta (Ohio) Coll., 1982-83; supr. Jackson County Intermediate Sch. Dist., Jackson, Mich., 1987—. Adapted aquatics instr. ARC, 1969-90; trainer Nat. Crisis Prevention Inst., Milw., 1987—. adv. com. Comty. Mental Health, Jackson, 1991. Contbr. to profl. publs. Vol. Mitten Bay coun. Girl Scouts U.S., 1989-91; tchr. religion St. John's Parish, Jackson, 1989-99. Mem. Coun. Exceptional Children (v.p. chpt. 24 1994-98, pres. divsn. for career devel. and transition 1998-2000). Republican. Roman Catholic. Avocations: swimming, camping, quilting. Home: PO Box 366 Spring Arbor MI 49283-0366 Office: Jackson County Intermediate Sch Dist 6700 Browns Lake Rd Jackson MI 49201-8379

TRAPANI, JANET LEIGH, physical therapist; b. Auburn, N.Y., Sept. 13, 1962; d. Michael A. and Bernadette C. (Beyer) T. BS in Phys. Therapy, Daemen Coll., 1984. Temporary phys. therapist Auburn Meml. Hosp., 1984, asst. dir. phys. therapy, phys. therapist, 1986-92; staff phys. therapist Parkview Med. Ctr., Pueblo, Colo., 1984-86, Swedish Med. Ctr., Englewood, 1985-86; phys. therapist Healthcare Everywhere, Arlington, Va., 1992, Cayuga Orthopedic and Sports Therapy, Auburn, 1992—. Mem. Am. Phys. Therapy Assn., McKenzie Inst. (credentialed therapist 1995). Avocations: skiing, boating, listening to music, swimming, photography. Home: 23 Beardsley St Auburn NY 13021-2809 Office: # 103 37 W Garden St Auburn NY 13021-2657

TRAPANI-HANASEWYCH, MARYBETH ANN, speech language pathologist; b. Pitts., Dec. 3, 1956; d. Dominic Carmen and Patricia Ruth (Konopelski) Trapani; m. John Hanasewych, Aug. 1, 1980; 1 child, Patrick John. BS, California U. Pa., 1977; MS, Indiana U. Pa., 1981. Speech-lang. profl. Jefferson Ctr. Hosp., Pitts., 1977, Baker (Mont.) Pub. Schs., 1978-79, Joint Sch. Dist. #192, Glenns Ferry, Idaho, 1979-80; screener No. Audiological Svcs., Pitts., 1980-81; speech lang. pathologist Valley Cmty. Svcs., Cheswick, Pa., 1981-85; staff speech-lang. pathologist The Rehab. Inst. Pitts., 1986-87, clin. specialist neurodevelopmental treatment, 1989-90, clin. cons., 1991-92, supr. pediat., 1991-96, clin. mgr., 1997-2000, dir., 2000—. Speech-lang. profl. Cameron Manor Nursing Home, Indiana, Pa., 1981, Nursing Svcs./Home Cars, Inc., Pitts., 1983-84, Head Start Program, New Kensington, Pa., 1983-85, United Cerebral Palsy Infant Stimulation Program, Butler, 1984-99, Family Home Health Svcs., 1984-86, Vis. Nurses' Assn., Tarentum, Pa., 1985-87, Allegheny Valley Mental Health/Mental Retardation, New Kensington, 1985-88; cons. Pa. Assn. for Retarded Citizens-Cmty. Living Arrangements, Butler, Pa., 1984-96; presenter in field. Inventor in field; contbr. articles to profl. jours. Mem. adv. team to sch. bd. New Kensington (Pa.) Adv. Bd., 1991-93. Mem. Am. Speech Hearing Assn. (cert. clin. competence), Pa. Speech and Hearing Assn., Neurodevelopmental Treatment Assn., Southwestern Pa. Speech and Hearing Assn. Avocation: golf. Home: 1733 Kensington St New Kensington PA 15068-4006 Office: Childrens Inst Pitts 6301 Northumberland St Pittsburgh PA 15217-1396

TRAPASSO, ROBERT LOUIS, surgical pathologist; b. Litchfield, Ill., Oct. 27, 1951; s. Louis J.A. and Leota M. (Newell) T.; m. Jean Carolyn Barley Chaka, June 1989. BA, Rice U., 1973; MD, SUNY, Syracuse, 1976. Diplomate Am. Bd. Pathology. Resident anatomic and canical pathology Duke U. Med. Ctr., Durham, N.C., 1976-80; med. dir. Richmond Meml. Hosp., Rockingham, 1980-91; staff pathologist Suburban Hosp., Bethesda, Md., 1991-95, Dianon Systems, Stratford, Conn., 1995—. Med. dir. Met. Washington Blood Bank, Silver Spring, Md., 1992-93. Fellow Am. Soc. of Clin. Pathologists, Coll. of Am. Pathologists. Office: Dianon Systems 200 Watson Blvd Stratford CT 06615-7166

TRAPOLIN, FRANK WINTER, retired insurance executive; b. New Orleans, Jan. 29, 1913; s. John Baptiste and Florence Bertha (Winter) T.; m. Thelma Mae Mouledoux, Oct. 27, 1937; children: Timothy, Patricia Couret, Jane Oaksmith, Anne Britt. BS in Econs., Loyola U., New Orleans. cert. ofcl. U.S.A. Track and Field. Agt. Godchaux & Mayer, New Orleans, 1935-42m 46-51; pres. Trapolin-Couret Ins. Agy., Inc., 1953-92; v.p. Gillis, Ellis & Baker, Inc., 1993-94; ret., 1994. Mem. faculty Loyola U., 1938-40; TV lectr., instr. seamanship USCG Aux., New Orleans. Former pres. Cath. Human Rels. Commn. Greater New Orleans, Associated Catholic Charities, Maryland Drive Homeowners Assn., Loyola U. Alumni Assn; former chmn. adv. bd. Ursuline Nuns New Orleans, New Orleans Juvenile Cts.; past scoutmaster Boy Scouts Am., former chmn. troop com.; former v.p. Cmty. Rels. Coun. Greater New Orleans, New Orleans Jr. C. of C.; former v.p. La. Interch. Conf., now treas. emeritus; former trustee United Fund Greater New Orleans Area; dir. emeritus Cath. Book Store Found.; tng. officer 8th USCG Aux.; former mem. adv. bd. Coll. Bus. Adminstrn., Loyola U., Mother-house Sisters of Holy Family, Immaculate Conception Cath. Ch.; group capt. Manresa Retreats, 1947-97; former bd. dirs. St. John Berchman Orphanage, New Orleans Interfaith Conffn.; St. Elizabeth's Home for Girls, Manresa Retreat House; mem. adv. bd. New Orleans Track Club; founder Serra Run for Vocations; bd. dirs. Aubudon Blvd. Assn.; participant U.S. Sr. Olympics, 1997; lector Cath. Ch., 1964-87, eucharist min., 1986—. With USN, 1942-46, 51-53; capt. USNR ret. Decorated Order of St. Louis; recipient merit cert. City of New Orleans, 1972; winner 80 and over category La. Sr. Olympics 5000 meter walk, 1995, 96. Mem. La. Assn. Ins. Agts., Nat. Assn. Ins. Agts., New Orleans Ins. Exch., Navy League, Mil. Order World Wars, Greater New Orleans Execs. Assn. (hon. life, pres. 1985, Exec. of Yr. award 1985), New Orleans Photog. Soc., New Orleans Runners Assn., World Trade Ctr. New Orleans (hon.), Serra Club (pres. New Orleans 1973-74), Sertoma Club (pres. New Orleans 1955-56), Internat. House, New Orleans Track Club, New Orleans Yacht Club, Pass Christian Yacht Club, KC (4th degree), Blue Key. Democrat. Achievements include patents for gunnery, training and machinery devices for the U.S. Navy. Home: 119 Audubon Blvd New Orleans LA 70118-5538

TRAPP, JAMES MCCREERY, lawyer; b. Macomb, Ill., Aug. 11, 1934; BA, Knox Coll., 1956; JD, U. Mich., 1961. Bar: Ill. 1961. Ptnr. McDermott, Will & Emery, Chgo., 1961-98, sr. counsel, 1998—. Chmn. Ill. Inst. Continuing Legal Edn., 1978-79, bd. dirs. 1980-86, pres., 1984-85. Fellow Am. Coll. Trust and Estate Coun. (Ill. chmn. 1980-83, nat. regent 1983—, treas. 1989-90, sec. 1990-91, v.p. 1991-92, pres.-elect 1992-93, pres. 1993-94, exec. com. 1986-94), Am. Bar Found., Ill. Bar Found.; mem. ABA, Ill. State Bar Assn., Chgo. Bar Assn. (chair trust law com. 1972-73, com. on coms. 1972-74), Internat. Acad. Estate and Trust Law, Am. Law Inst. (pres.), Chgo. Estate Planning Coun. Office: McDermott Will & Emery 227 W Monroe St Chicago IL 60606-5096

TRAPP, PETER JARL RUDOLF, investment manager, farmer; b. Darlington, Eng., Oct. 5, 1945; came to U.S., 1971; s. Jarl Rudolph and Olive Lindsay (Fairley) T.; m. Regina Antoinette Thomas, Sept. 6, 1969 (div. Dec. 1986); children: Sophia Antoinette, Alexander Rudolf, Olivia Henrietta Elizabeth. Mi-Lic, Fribourg U., Switzerland, 1971; MBA, Columbia U., 1973. V.p. First Boston Corp., N.Y.C., 1973-78, Goldman Sachs & Co., N.Y.C., 1978-81; mgr. dir. Dean Witter Reynolds Inc., 1982-84; mgr. dir., exec. officer Marine Midland Bank N.A., 1985-89; sr. v.p. Gerard Klauer Mattison & Co., 1990-94; mgr. dir. Needham & Co., 1994—; exec. v.p., portfolio mgr. Needham Investment Mgmt., 1998—. Cadet sgt. Swedish Army, 1968-69. Mem.: Coral Beach Club (Bermuda), Annabel's Club (London), The Leash and Doubles Club (N.Y.). Avocations: skiing, fishing, shooting, farming. Home: Bean Creek Farm Box 948 Pine Plains NY 12567-0948 Office: Needham & Co 445 Park Ave New York NY 10022-2606 E-mail: pt@needhamco.com.

TRASK, JOHN MAURICE, JR. property owner; b. Wilmington, N.C., Oct. 12, 1935; s. John Maurice and Flora Murphy (Graham) T.; m. Caroline Whitehead Clark, Apr. 15, 1961; children: John III, Caroline, Clark, Patrick. BA, Davidson Coll., 1958; MBA, Harvard U., 1964. Asst. alumni dir. Davidson (N.C.) Coll., 1959-60; pres. Beaufort (S.C.) Broadcasting Co., 1960-70, 1st Carolina Bank, Beaufort, 1970-77; assoc. adminstr. U.S. SBA, Washington, 1977-79; pres. 1st Carolina Corp., Beaufort, 1979—. Bd. dirs. Blue Cross-Slue Shield S.C., S.C. Coastal Conservation League; past trustee Davidson Coll., Episcopal H.S.; founder Beaufort County Open Land Trust, 1971; del. Dem. Nat. Conv., 1968, 76, 80, 88, 92. 1st lt. U.S. Army, 1958-59. Avocations: landscape architecture, history, travel.

TRASK, ROGER R. historian; b. Erie, Pa., Sept. 14, 1930; s. Hugh Archie Trask and Martha Ruth Miller; m. Dorothy Arlene Buettner, Jan. 14, 1956; children: Julianne, Laurence, Carolyn. BA, Thiel Coll., Greenville, Pa., 1952; MA, Pa. State U., University Park, Pa., 1954, PhD, 1959. Asst. prof. history Upsala Coll., East Orange, NJ, 1959—62; asst. assoc. prof. history Thiel Coll., Greenville, Pa., 1962—64; asst. to prof. history Macalester Coll., St. Paul, 1964—74; prof. history U. South Fla., Tampa, 1974—81; chief historian U.S. Nuclear Regulatory Commn., Washington, 1977—78; dep. chief historian U.S. Dept. Def., 1980—87, cons., 1994—; chief historian U.S. Gen. Acctg. Office, 1987—93. Author: The United States Response to Turkish Nationalism and Reform, 1914-1939, 1971, Defender of the Public Interest: The General Accounting Office, 1921-66, 1996; co-author: The Department of Defense, 1947-1997: Organization and Leaders, 1997; contbr. articles. SP 3 U.S. Army, 1945—55, Korea. Grantee grant, Am. Philosoph. Soc., 1960, Ford Found., 1970—71. Mem.: Soc. History Am. Fgn. Rels. (mem. coun. 1982—85), Soc. History in Fed. Govt. (pres. 1990—91, Pres. award 1994), Orgn. Am. Historians, Am. Historian Assn., Am. Polar Social (adv. bd. oral history 1999—). Democrat. Avocations: golf, home remodeling, reading. Home: 340 Birchside Cir Locust Grove VA 22508-9554 Office: US Dept Def OSD Hist Office 1777 N Kent St Ste 5000

TRASK, THOMAS EDWARD, religious organization administrator; b. Brainard, Minn., Mar. 23, 1936; m. Shirley Burkhart; children: Kimberly, Bradley, Todd, Tom. BA, North Ctrl. Bible Coll., 1956, DDiv (hon.), 1994. Ordained min. Assemblies of God, 1958. Pastor First Assembly of God, Hibbing, Minn., 1956-60, pastor Vicksburg, Mich., 1960-64; Mich. dist. youth Sunday sch. dir. Assembly of God, 1964-68; pastor First Assembly of God, Saginaw, Mich., 1968-73, Brightmoor Tabernacle, Southfield, 1976-88; supt. Mich. Dist. Coun., Dearborn, 1973-76; gen. treas. The Gen. Coun. Assemblies of God, Springfield, Mo., 1988-93, gen. supt., 1993—. Co-author: Back to the Altar: A Call to Spiritual Awakening, 1994, Back to the Word, A Call to Biblical Authority, 1996, The Battle: Defeating the Enemies of Your Soul, 1997, The Blessing: Experiencing the Power of the Holy Spirit Today, 1998, The Choice: Embracing God's Vision in the New Millennium, 1999, The Fruit of the Spirit, 2000, Ministry for a Lifetime, 2001. Office: Assemblies of God 1445 N Boonville Ave Springfield MO 65802-1894

TRASK-TYRELL, NANCY, management company executive; b. Deer Lodge, Mont., June 1, 1936; arrived in Eng., 1969; d. Frank S. and Cora Isabelle (Nichols) Trask; m. William James Paul, Sept. 17, 1960 (div. 1982); children: William James, Elisa Anne, Michael Justin; m. David Alan Tyrell, Apr. 11, 1992. BA, U. Mont., 1958, MA, 1962. Assoc. Mgmt. Facilitation Inst., London, 1977-80; owner Paul Mgmt. Assn., 1980-87; mng. ptnr. Excel Internat., 1987—. Author: Right To Be You, 1985; co-author: Principles of Project Management, 1989; author (video) Making Meeting Work, 1989; contbr. articles to profl. jours. Mem. Internat. Inst. Transactional Analysis, Inst. Transactional Analysis (founder, v.p. 1982-85), Renaissance Group (founder). Episcopalian. Avocations: antique porcelain, mountain climbing, gardening, skiing, people. Office: Excel Internat 2810 Contour Rd Missoula MT 59802-3376

TRAUB, J(OSEPH) F(REDERICK), computer scientist, educator; b. June 24, 1932; m. Pamela Ann McCorduck, Dec. 6, 1969; children: Claudia Renee, Hillary Anne. BS, CCNY, 1954; PhD, Columbia U., 1959; DSc (hon.), U. Cen. Fla., 2001. Tech. staff Bell Labs., Murray Hill, N.J., 1959-70; prof. computer sci. and math., head dept. computer sci. Carnegie-Mellon U., Pitts., 1971-79; Edwin Howard Armstrong prof. computer sci., chmn. dept., prof. math. Columbia U., 1979-86; prof. computer sci. Princeton (N.J.) U., 1986-87; pres. John Von Neumann Nat. Supercomputer Ctr., Consortium for Sci. Computing, Princeton, 1986-87; Edwin Howard Armstrong prof., chmn. dept. computer sci., prof. math. Columbia U., N.Y.C., 1987-89, Edwin Howard Armstrong prof. computer sci., math., 1989—; external prof. Santa Fe Inst., 1995-98; fellow Biosgroup, 1998—. Dir. N.Y. State Ctr. Computers and Info. Systems, 1982-88; disting. lectr. MIT, 1977; vis. Mackay prof. U. Calif., Berkeley, 1978-79; cons. Hewlett-Packard, 1982, IBM, 1984, Schlumberger, 1986, Signet Bank, 1994, Lucent Techs., 1996, Bios Group, 1998—; mem. pres.'s adv. com. computer sci. Stanford U., 1972-75, chmn., 1975-76; adv. com. Fed. Jud. Center; mem. sci. council I.R.I.A., Paris, 1976-80; central steering com., computing sci. and engring. research study NSF, also liaison to panel on theoretical computer sci. and panel on numerical comp., 1974-80; mem. adv. com. Carnegie-Mellon Inst. Research, 1978-79; mem. applied math. div. rev. com. Argonne Nat. Lab., 1973-75; mem. adv. com. math. and computer sci. NSF, 1978-80; chmn. computer sci. and tech. bd. NRC, 1986-90; chmn. computer sci. and telecommunications bd. NRC, 1990-92; trustee Columbia U. Press, 1983-85; founding chair Spl. Interest Group on Numerical Math., 1965-71. Author: Iterative Methods for the Solution of Equations, 1964, Russian edit., 1985; (with H. Wozniakowski) A General Theory of Optimal Algorithms, 1980, Russian edit., 1983, Chelsea, 1998; (with G. Wasilkowski and H. Wozniakowski) Information, Uncertainty, Complexity, 1983, Information-Based Complexity, 1988; (with A.G. Werschulz) Complexity and Information, 1998; editor: Complexity of Sequential and Parallel Numerical Algorithms, 1973, Analytic Computational Complexity, 1976, Algorithms and Complexity: New Directions and Recent Results, 1976, Jour. Assn. Computing Machinery, 1970-76, Transactions on Math. Software, 1974-76, Jour. Computer and Sys. Scis., 1973-86, Internat. Jour. on Computers and Math. with Applications, 1974—, Cohabiting With Computers, 1985; (with P. Hut and D. Ruelle) Fundamental Sources of Unpredictability, 1997; founding editor Jour. Complexity, 1985—, Ann. Rev. Computer Sci., 1986-92; assoc. editor Complexity, 1995—. Sherman Fairchild Disting. scholar Calif. Inst. Tech., 1991, 92; recipient Award for Disting. Svc. to Computing Rsch. Computer Rsch. Assn., 1992, Lezione Lincee Acad. Nazionale dei Lincei, 1993, Sr. Scientist award Alexander Von Humboldt Found., 1992-98, City of N.Y. Mayor's award for excellence in sci. and tech., 1999. Fellow AAAS (coun. 1971-74), ACM (chmn. award com. 1974-76), N.Y. Acad. Scis.; mem. IEEE (Emanuel R. Piore Gold medal 1991), NAE (membership com. for computer sci., elec. engring. and control 1986-87, membership com. for computer sci. and engring. 1987-91, presdl. search com. 1993-94), Conf. Bd. Math. Scis. (coun. 1971-74), Soc. Indsl. and Applied Math., Am. Math. Soc. Office: Columbia University Dept Computer Sci 1214 Amsterdam Ave #MC0401 New York NY 10027-7003 E-mail: traub@cs.columbia.edu.

TRAUB, LANCE WAYNE, research engineer, lecturer; b. Johannesburg, South Africa, May 11, 1968; came to U.S., 1994; m. Angela Amber Traub, Aug. 8, 1998. BSc, U. Witwatersrand, South Africa, 1989, MSc, 1992; PhD, Tex. A&M U., 1999. Rsch. engr. U. Witwatersrand, Johannesburg, 1992-94; rsch. asst. Tex. A&M U., College Station, 1994-98, rsch. assoc., lectr., 1999—. Cons. Drytech Pty. Ltd., Johannesburg, 1980-94. Contbr. articles to profl. jours. Regents Grad. fellow Tex. A&M U., 1994-95; grantee U. Witwatersrand, 1989-92, Found. for R&D, 1989-92. Mem. AIAA, Royal Aero. Soc. Avocations: archery, plastic modelling. Home: 1508 Arctic Cir College Station TX 77840-4443 Office: Tex A&M U 701 Hr Bright Bldg College Station TX 77843-0001 E-mail: LWT1@tamu.edu.

TRAUB, RICHARD KENNETH, lawyer; b. Lakewood, N.J., Aug. 4, 1950; s. Harold W. and Muriel N. (Zurlin) T.; m. Barbara Lynn Wright, July 9, 1972; children: Russell S., Melissa L. BBA, U. Miami, Coral Gables, Fla., 1972, JD cum laude, 1975. Bar: Fla. 1975, N.Y. 1976, N.J. 1976, U.S. Dist. Ct. N.J. 1976, U.S. Supreme Ct. 1979, U.S. Dist. Ct. (ea. & so. dists.) N.Y. 1981. Ptnr. Wilson, Elser, Moskowitz, Edelman & Dicker, N.Y.C., 1975-95, Traub Eglin Lieberman Straus, Hawthorne, N.Y., 1996—. Ptnr. Time for Patty Stables, N.J., 1992—; officer, dir. X-Ray Duplications, Inc., N.J.; ptnr., founder Fractured Greetings, N.J.; mem., lectr. Fedn. Ins. and Corp. Counsel, 1993—, mem. admissions com., industry cooperation ins. coverage and alt. dispute resolution coms.; lectr. Inst. for Internat. Rsch., Washington, 1988, Engring. News Record Constrn. Claims Conf., 1991. Author: Legal and Professional Aspects of Construction Management, 1990, The Year 2000 and Potential Liabilities and Otherwise, 1999, Litigating Year 2000 Cases, Chapter 8, Insurance Coverage, 1999, Practical Environmental Forensics--Process and Case Histories, 2000; contbr. articles to profl. jours. Mem. ABA (forum com. on constrn. industry 1989, tort and ins. practice sect. 1985—, computer litigation sect.), N.Y. State Bar Assn., N.J. Bar Assn., Fla. Bar Assn., Fedn. Ins. and Corp. Counsel (spkr. The Millenium Bug ins. coverage sect., vice chair ins. coverage and Y2K sects., chair tech. and e-commerce sect., vice chair tech. com., editor The Roster), Def. Rsch. Inst. Office: Traub Eglin Lieberman Straus Mid-Westchester Exec Park Three Skyline Dr Hawthorne NY 10532 also: 505 Main St Hackensack NJ 07601-5900 E-mail: rtraub@tels.com.

TRAUB, RONALD MATTHEW, municipal administrator; b. Shaker Heights, Ohio, Apr. 20, 1951; s. George Spencer and Nina (May) T.; m. Susan Gail Wallack, June 23, 1973; children: Amy, Robyn, Evan. BA in Environ. Studies, Earlham Coll., 1973; M in City and Regional Planning, Ohio State U., 1975. Project mgr. Ohio Conservation Found., Cleve., 1980-82; planner Gould/Assocs., Inc., 1982-85; dir. profl. svcs. N.E. Ohio Areawide Coordinating Agy., 1985-89; dir. cmty. devel. City of Mentor, Ohio, 1989—. Active Leadership Lake County; mem. planning com. United Way Lake County; mentor Performing Concert Series Found. Mem. Am. Planning Assn., Mentor Area C. of C., Rotary Internat. Office: 8500 Civic Center Blvd Mentor OH 44060-2418

TRAUBE, VICTORIA GILBERT, lawyer; b. L.A., Sept. 3, 1946; d. Shepard and Mildred (Gilbert) T. BA, Radcliffe Coll., 1968; MA, Harvard U., 1970; JD, U. Pa., 1974. Bar: N.Y. 1975, U.S. Dist. Ct. (so. dist.) N.Y. 1975, U.S. Ct. Appeals (2d cir.) 1975. Assoc. Paul, Weiss, Rifkind, Wharton & Garrison, N.Y.C., 1974-81; from assoc. counsel to dir. bus. affairs Home Box Office Inc., 1981-85; counsel Stults & Marshall, 1985-86; v.p. bus. affairs Reeves Entertainment Group, L.A., 1986-87, Internat. Creative Mgmt., N.Y.C., 1987-95; sr. v.p., gen. counsel Rodgers & Hammerstein Orgn., 1995—. Adj. prof. Cardozo Law Sch., N.Y.C., 1986. Trustee God Bless Am. Fund, 2001—; bd. dirs. Stage Dirs. and Choreographers Found., 2002—. Mem. Assn. of Bar of City of N.Y. (chair entertainment law com. 1998-2000). Office: Rodgers & Hammerstein Orgn 1065 Ave of Americas New York NY 10018 E-mail: vtraube@rnh.com.

TRAUDT, MARY B. elementary education educator; b. Chgo., Jan. 1, 1930; d. Lloyd Andrews Haldeman and Adele Eleanor (MacKinnon) Haldeman-Oliver; m. Eugene Peter Traudt, Dec. 6, 1952 (dec.); 1 child, Victoria Jean. BS, Cen. Mich. U., 1951; MA, Roosevelt U., 1978; postgrad., U. Ill., 1982. Asst. editor Commerce Clearing House, Chgo., 1951-53; tchr. Cleve. Elem. Sch., 1954-56, Chgo. Sch. System, 1956-57, Community Consolidated # 54, Hoffman Estates, Ill., 1957-64, Avoca Elem. Sch., Wilmette, 1964—; ret., 1995. Recipient Computer award Apple Computer Co. Mem. NEA (life), Ill. Assn. of Ret. Tchrs. (life), North Shore Assn. of Ret. Tchrs. (life), Avoca Edn. Assn. (v.p. 1986-91), Alpha Psi Omega. Presbyterian. Avocations: reading, sewing, music, travel, gardening. Home: 1 W Superior St Apt 1601 Chicago IL 60610

TRAUGER, ALETA ARTHUR, judge; BA in English magna cum laude, Cornell Coll., Iowa, 1968; MAT, Vanderbilt U., 1972, JD, 1976. Tchr., Tenn., Eng., 1970-73; assoc., law clk. Barrett, Brandt & Barrett, P.C., Nashville, 1974-77; asst. U.S. atty., first asst., chief of criminal divsn. Mid. Dist. Tenn., 1977-82, No. Dist. Ill., 1979-80; assoc. Hollins, Wagster & Yarbrough, P.C., Nashville, 1983-84; legal counsel Coll. of Charleston, S.C., 1984-85; counsel, ptnr. Wyatt, Tarrant, Combs, Gilbert & Milom, Nashville, 1985-91; judge Tenn. Ct. of the Judiciary, 1987-93; chief of staff Mayor's Office, Nashville, 1991-92; bankruptcy judge U.S. Bankruptcy Ct. (mid. dist.) Tenn., 1993-98; dist. judge U.S. Dist. Ct. (mid. dist.) Tenn., 1998—. Mem. hearing panel bd. profl. responsibility Tenn. Supreme Ct., 1983-84, mem. adv. com. on rules of civil and appellate procedure, 1989-96; lectr. Vanderbilt U. Sch. Law, 1986-88, mem. Law Sch. alumni bd., 1989-92; master of bench Harry Phillips Am. Inn of Ct., 1990-94; mem. Internat. Women's Forum, 1993—, v.p. Tenn. chpt., 1996-97; mem. Nat. Conf. Bankruptcy Judges, 1994-98, chmn. ethics com., 1994-98; trustee Cornell Coll., 1998—. Bd. dirs. Nashville Inst. for Arts, 1992-99, Miriam's Promise (adoption agy.), 1995-98, Renewal House, 1996-98. Fellow: Nashville Bar Found., Tenn. Bar Found. (life), Am. Bar Found. (life); mem.: FBA (v.p. 1983—84, 1985—86), ABA (vice chmn. com. on bankruptcy judges jud. adminstrn. divsn.), Fed. Judges Assn., Nat. Assn. Women Judges (liaison to commn. on the status of women in the profession 2000—01, vice chair fed. judges com. 2001—), Tenn. Lawyers Assn. for Women (v.p. 1988—89, pres. 1989—90, bd. dirs. 1990—91), Lawyers Assn. for Women (pres. 1982—83, bd. dirs. 1983—84, 1986—88), Nashville Bar Assn. (bd. dirs. 1984, 1989—91). Office: 825 US Courthouse 801 Broadway Nashville TN 37203-3816

TRAUGER, DONALD BYRON, nuclear engineering laboratory administrator; b. Exeter, Nebr., June 29, 1920; s. Charles C. and Ethel L. (Downey) T.; m. Elaine Causey, Sept. 2, 1945; children: Byron Roscoe, Thomas Charles. AB, Nebr. Wesleyan U., 1942, D.Sc. (hon.), 1974; postgrad., Columbia U., 1942-46, U. Tenn., 1946-49; D.Sc. (hon.), Tenn. Wesleyan Coll., 1977. Supr. test equipment devel. Manhattan Dist. Project, 1942-46; supr. Devel. Lab., Oak Ridge Gaseous Diffusion Plant, 1946-54; with Oak Ridge Nat. Lab., 1954-93, assoc. dir. nuclear and engring. technologies, 1970-84, sr. staff asst. to dir., 1984-93; cons. in energy tech., 1993—. Bd. dirs. Gene Rsch. Access Corp. Editorial advisor Anns. Nuclear Engring, 1973—; design features editor sect. IV Nuclear Safety Jour., 1989-98. Mem. Oak Ridge Bd. Edn., 1961-67; pres. Oak Ridge PTA Coun., 1969-70, Oak Ridge Parents Adv. Coun., 1958-59; chmn. exec. com., trustee Tenn. Wesleyan Coll., 1976-81, chmn. bd. govs., 1986-90, chmn. bd. trustees, 1990-93. Recipient Alumni Achievement award Nebr. Wesleyan U., 1962 Fellow Am. Nuclear Soc. (chmn. planning com. 1981-83); mem. AAAS, Am. Phys. Soc., Sigma Xi (pres. Oak Ridge chpt. 1987-88), Sigma Pi Sigma. Clubs: Rotary. Methodist.

TRAUGH, DONALD GEORGE, III, secondary education educator; b. Tucson, Aug. 5, 1950; s. Donald G. Jr. and Leatrice (Rhodes) Traugh-Long; m. Brenda Kay Kreischer, June 14, 1975; children: Jonathan P., Brandon M. AB in Edn., Fairmont (W.Va.) State U., 1974; MEd in Social Studies, Bloomsburg (Pa.) State U., 1980. Cert. tchr., Pa. Tchr. social studies Bloomsburg Area Sch. Dist., 1974—, chmn. dept. social studies, 1978—. Adj. prof. Bloomsburg U., 1999—; co-chair social studies curriculum staff Bloomsburg Area Sch. Dist., 1984—. Vol. firefighter Catawissa (Pa.) Hose Co. 1, 1969—, chief dept., 1987—; mem. Catawissa Borough Coun., 1977-89, v.p., 1987-89. Mem. NEA, Pa. Edn. Assn., Bloomsburg Area Edn. Assn., Nat. Coun. Social Studies, Mid. States Assn. Social Studies, Pa. Coun. Social Studies, Internat. Assn. Fire Chiefs, Nat. Fire Prevention Assn., Nat. Fire Protection Assn., Keystone State Fire Chiefs Assn., Pi Gamma Mu, Delta Sigma Phi. Democrat. Lutheran. Avocations: coaching football, hunting, fishing, scouting, gardening. Home: 503 E Main St Catawissa PA 17820-1030 Office: Bloomsburg HS 1200 Railroad St Bloomsburg PA 17815-3613 E-mail: dtraugh@bloomhs.k12.pa., firewalk@ptdprolog.net.

TRAUGHBER, DEBRA L. nonprofit agency executive; b. Joliet, Ill., Oct. 30, 1950; 1 child, Lara Michelle Ziebarth. BA in French, Ea. Ill. U., Charleston, 1972, MS in Counseling, 1975. Cert counselor supr., Ala.; lic. profl. counselor, Ala. Pres., CEO Family Svcs. Ctr., Inc., Huntsville, 1995—. Mem. Madison County Children's Policy Coun.; coord. vols. disaster mental health svcs. Madison County chpt. ARC, 1999—. Mem. United Way Exec. Dirs. Assn. (chmn. Huntsville 1999), Huntsville Ski Club. Avocations: skiing, hiking, reading, volunteering. Office: Family Svcs Ctr Inc 600 St Clair Ave Bldg 3 Huntsville AL 35801 E-mail: ceo@fsc-hsu.org.

TRAUGOTT, ELIZABETH CLOSS, linguist, educator, researcher; b. Bristol, Eng., Apr. 9, 1939; d. August and Hannah M. M. (Priebsch) Closs; m. John L. Traugott, Sept. 26, 1967; 1 child Isabel. BA in English, Oxford U., Eng., 1960; PhD in English lang., U. Calif., Berkeley, 1964. Asst. prof. English U. Calif., Berkeley, 1964-70; lectr. U. East Africa, Tanzania, 1965-66, U. York, Eng., 1966-67; lectr., then assoc. prof. linguistics and English Stanford (Calif.) U., 1970-77, prof., 1977—, chmn. linguistics dept., 1980-85, vice provost, dean grad. studies, 1985-91, mem. grad. record examinations bd., 1989-93, mem. test of English as a fgn. lang. bd., 1989-91, chmn. test of English as a fgn. lang. bd., 1991—92. Mem. higher edn. funding coun. Eng. Assessment Panel, 1996, 2001. Author: (book) A History of English Syntax, 1972; author: (with Mary Pratt) Linguistics for Students of Literature, 1980;

author: (with Paul Hopper) Grammaticalization, 1993; editor (with ter Meulen, Rielly, Ferguson): On Conditionals, 1986; editor: (with Heine) Approaches to Grammaticalization, 2 vols., 1991; editor: (with Dasher) Regularity in Semantic Change, 2002; series co-editor: Topics in English Linguistics; contbr. articles to profl. jours. Fellow Am. Coun. Learned Soc., 1975—76, Guggenheim, 1983—84, Ctr. Advanced STudy Behavioral Scis., 1983—84. Fellow: AAAS; mem.: AAUW, AAUP, MLA, Internat. Pragmatics Assn. (bd. dirs. 2000—), Internat. Soc. Hist. Linguistic (pres. 1979—81), Linguistics Soc. Am. (pres. 1987, sec.-treas. 1994—98). Office: Stanford Univ Dept Linguistics Bldg 460 Stanford CA 94305-2150 Business E-Mail: traugott@stanford.edu.

TRAUPMAN, ARNOLD FRANK, ophthalmologist, educator; b. Allentown, Pa., Nov. 19, 1947; s. Arnold and Katherine (Didovitz) T.; m. Barbara Zylwitis, Aug. 1, 1970; children: Jonathan, Matthew, C. Gabriel, Emily. BS, St. Joseph's U., 1969; MD, Thomas Jefferson U., 1973. Diplomate Am. Bd. Ophthalmology. Intern Chestnut Hill Hosp., Phila., 1973-74; ophthalmology resident Thomas Jefferson U., 1974-77; ophthalmologist St. Luke's Hosp., Bethlehem, Pa., 1977—, chief ophthalmologist, 2000—. Instr. Thomas Jefferson U., Phila., 1977—; mem. adv. bd. Lehigh Valley Lung Assn., Allentown, 1980-83. Dist. chmn. Boy Scouts Am., 1988-92; v.p. Minsi Trails Coun., Lehigh Valley, Pa., 1992-97, coun. commr., 1998-2000, pres.-elect 2000, pres., 2001—; bd. dirs. Northampton Cmty. Blind Assn., Bethlehem, 1978-81. Recipient Silver Beaver award Boy Scouts Am., 1991, St. George award Cath. Com. Scouting, 1988, Knight, Equestrian Order of the Holy Sepulchre, 2001. Fellow Am. Acad. Ophthalmology; mem. Pa. Med. Soc., Northampton County Med. Soc. (bd. trustees 2000—), Pa. Acad. Ophthalmology, Lehigh Valley Ophthalmology Soc. (treas. 1983-88, pres. 1999-2000). Democrat. Roman Catholic. Avocations: hiking, reading, philately, ham radio, collecting scouting memorabilia. Office: 1313 Center St Bethlehem PA 18018-2502

TRAUTH, DAVID E. dairy company executive; b. Covington, Ky., Oct. 8, 1946; s. Louis J. Jr. and Mary B. Trauth. BBA, U. Cin., 1970. V.p. Louis Trauth Dairy Inc., Newport, Ky., 1972-80, pres., CEO, 1981-2000, Louis Trauth Dairy/Suiza Foods, Newport, 2000—. Bd. dirs. Holly Hill Children's House, Alexandria, Ky., 1998—. Mem. Cin. Dairy Tech. Soc. (pres. 1982-83), No. Ky. C. of C. (bd. dirs. 1990-96, Entrepreneur of Yr. 1986), Quail Unltd., Ducks Unltd., Ruffed Grouse Soc., Wild Turkey Fedn., Ohio Valley Beagle Club (sec. 1974—). Office: Louis Trauth Dairy Dean Foods PO Box 1770 Newport KY 41071

TRAUTLEIN, JOSEPH J. medical administrator; b. N.Y.C., Apr. 15, 1940; s. Eugene Charles and Margaret Agnes (Dorney) T.; m. Joan Marie Starosta, Sept. 10, 1966; children: Ann Margaret, Thomas, Robert. BA, Fordham Coll., 1962; MD, N.Y. Med. Coll., 1966. Cert. Diplomate Am. Bd. Internal Medicine, Am. Bd. Allergy and Immunology, Am. Bd. Quality Assurance and Utilization Review Physicians. Med. dir. Health Pass PPA, Pa., 1986-93, Health Am. Northcentral, 1993—. Mem. bd. dirs. Bur. Profl. & Occupational Affairs, Harrisburg, 1992-95. Editor: Aerosols Airways and Asthma, 1978; mem. editl. bd. Jour. Quality Assurance, Harrisburg, Pa., 1986-2000; editor-in-chief Jour. of Am. Bd. Quality Assurance, 2001—. Pres. Lions, Harrisburg, 1985. Capt. USAF, 1968-70. Fellow ACP, Am. Bd. Quality Assurance and Utilization (1st v.p. 1992-2001, Openshaw award 1992), Am. Acad. Allergy and Immunology, Am. Coll. Allergy and Immunology. Mem. Byzantine Catholic Ch. Avocations: medical history, golf. Home: 6430 Colchester Ave Harrisburg PA 17111-3920 Office: Health America 2575 Interstate Dr Harrisburg PA 17110-9339 E-mail: jtrautlein@cvty.com.

TRAUTMAN, ALTA LOUISE, nurse, funeral director, author; b. McKeesport, Pa., Oct. 30, 1954; d. Ernest Bernhardt and Eleanor Jeannette (Runge) Trautman. AAS in Nursing, Cmty. Coll. Allegheny County, West Mifflin, Pa., 1974; Diploma Grad. Funeral Dir., Pitts. Inst. Mortuary Sci., 1989. RN Pa.; lic. funeral dir. Pa. Staff nurse U. Pitts. Med. Ctr., McKeesport, 1974-80, emergency room nurse, 1981-2001; flight nurse Allegheny Gen. Hosp., Pitts., 1980-81; arranger, embalmer D.J. Heatherington Funeral Home, 1990-91; funeral dir. Teichart-Gracan Funeral Home, 1999; quality assurance and process improvement coord. Three Rivers Family Hospice, White Oak, Pa., 2000—01; staff nurse, emergency dept. Nurse Finders; asst. recovery of flight 93 Shanksville , Pa., 2001. Lutheran. Avocations: cooking, needlecrafts, altar designs.

TRAUTMAN, HERMAN LOUIS, lawyer, educator; b. Columbus, Ind., Sept. 26, 1911; s. Theodore H. and Emma (Guckenberger) T.; m. Marian Lucille Green, Sept. 1, 1940; children: Stephen M., Pamela C.; LLB with distinction Ind. U., 1937, BA, 1946, JD with distinction, 1946; postgrad., NYU, 1953, Ford Found. faculty fellow, Harvard U., 1954-55. Bar: Ind. 1937, U.S. Tax Ct., U.S. Ct. Appeals (6th cir.) Tenn. Sole practice, Evansville, Ind., 1937-43; pres. Crescent Coal Co., Evansville, 1941-43; prof. law U. Ala. Tuscaloosa, 1946-49; prof. law Vanderbilt U., 1949—, prof. law emeritus, 1977; NYU vis. prof., 1955, U. Mich., Ann Arbor, 1963-64; ptnr. Trautman & Trautman, Nashville, 1976-85; sole practice, Nashville, 1986—. Served to lt. comdr. USN, 1943-46. Mem. ABA, Am. Law Inst., Tenn. Bar Assn., Nashville Bar Assn., Nat. Conf. Jud. Adminstrs., Estate Planning Coun., Order of Coif, Phi Gamma Delta, Belle Meade Club, Univ. Club, Kiwanis. Methodist. Address: PO Box 150862 Nashville TN 37215-0862

TRAUTMAN, NED RICHARD, music educator; b. Lebanon, Pa., Oct. 31, 1947; s. Arthur George and Mildred Anna Trautman; m. Lareen Noel Zito, Nov. 26, 1971; children: Christopher, Darren. BS, Adams State Coll., Alamosa, CO, 1971; M.Ed., Edinboro State Univ., Edinboro, PA, 1973. Music educator Cameron County Sch. Dist., Emporium, Pa., 1969—71, Millcreek Twp. Sch. Dist., Erie, 1971—. Dir. McDowell Marching Band, Erie, Pa., 1973—78, Zem Zem Shrine Band, Erie, Pa., 1985—90. Past pres./bd. mem. Penn State Alumni Assn., Erie County Chpt., Erie, Pa., 1980; bd. mem. Alumni Blue Band Assn., University Park, 1998. Mem.: PA State Educators Assn., PA Music Educators Assn., Masonic Lodge, Scottish Rite, Shrine. Avocations: woodworking, reading, golfing, traveling, traveling. Home: 4849 Woodbury Drive Erie PA 16510-6407

TRAUTMAN, WILLIAM ELLSWORTH, lawyer; b. San Francisco, Nov. 27, 1940; s. Gerald H. and Doris Joy (Tucker) T.; m. Dorothy Williamson, June 17, 1962; children: Darcey, Torey. AB, U. Calif., Berkeley, 1962, LLB, 1965. Bar: Calif. U.S. Supreme Ct., Calif. Dist. Ct., U.S. Ct. Appeals (9th and fed. cirs.). Assoc. Chickering & Gregory, San Francisco, 1965-71, ptnr., 1972-81, Brobeck, Phleger & Harrison, San Francisco, 1981—, mng. ptnr., 1992-96, litigation dept. chair, 1984-91. Pres. Oakland (Calif.) Mus. Assn., 1981-83; mem. profl. ethics com. State Bar Calif., 1974-77. Fellow: Am. Coll. Trial Lawyers; mem.: Barrister's Club of San Francisco (v.p. 1973), Calif. Barristers (bd. dirs., v.p.), Bar Assn. San Francisco (bd. dirs. 1972—73), Legal Aid Soc. (bd. dirs. 1982—93, pres. 1985—88), U. Calif.-Berkeley Found. (trustee 1998—2000), Boalt Hall Alumni Assn. (bd. dirs. 1993—99, pres. 1997—98). Office: Brobeck Phleger & Harrison 1 Market St San Francisco CA 94105-1420 E-mail: wtrautman@brobeck.com.

TRAUTMANN, FREDERIC, retired communications educator, translator, author, editor; b. Plymouth, Ohio, Aug. 25, 1936; s. William Frederick and Doris Julia (Lutz) T.; m. Bethel Delano Whiteman, July 12, 1974. BS, U. Wis., River Falls, 1962; MS, Purdue U., 1964, PhD, 1966. Asst. prof., assoc. prof. Temple U., Phila., 1966-96, prof. emeritus, 1996; ret. Author, editor, translator essays and books; contbr. articles to profl. jours., chpts. to books. With U.S. Army, 1956-59. Recipient numerous awards, prizes, fellowships, and grants. Avocations: reading, walking, photography, shooting, history of art and ideas. Home: 300 Cherry Ln Glenside PA 19038-3308

TRAUTMANN, PATRICIA ANN, communications educator, storyteller; b. Hot Springs, S.D., Jan. 6, 1932; d.. Forest Houston and Clara Ruth (Allen) Doling; m. Robert D. Trautmann, Aug. 11, 1954; children: Kurt, Elaine, Sarah, Cynthia, Gretchen. BA, Jamestown Coll., 1954; MA, U. No. Colo., 1962; PhD, Vanderbilt U., 1984; postgrad., Ga. So. U., 1992-93. Tchr. various schs., Colo., N.D., Mich., 1954-67; part-time instr. English Kans. State Coll., Pittsburg, 1967-70; part-time instr. English, children's lit. Baldwin-Wallace Coll., Berea, Parma, Ohio, 1970-73; part-time instr. children's lit., reading, lang. arts U. Tenn., Nashville, 1973-78; English instr. Valdosta (Ga.) H.S., 1978-82; assoc. prof. English, Speech, Langs., asst. dir. programs Ga. Mil. Coll., Milledgeville, 1982-86; assoc. prof. English, art, humanities, langs. South Ga. Coll., Douglas, 1986-94; chair humanities, 1988-94; assoc. prof. English, comm. skills Isothermal C.C., Spindale, N.C., 1995—. Cons. for reading, children's books in schs. and other instns., Kans., Ohio, Tenn., Ga., N.C., 1964—. Storyteller, spkr., internat. lore, poetry, children's lit., world mythology, 1967—. Recipient Humanities award South Ga. Coll., 1993. Mem. AAUW, Music Club. Democrat. Avocations: drawing, painting, singing, gardening, hiking. Home: 257 N Washington St Rutherfordton NC 28139-2405 Office: Isothermal C C Dept English nd Comm Skills Spindale NC 28139 E-mail: ptrautma@isothermal.cc.nc.us.

TRAUTMANN, THOMAS ROGER, history and anthropology educator; b. Madison, Wis., May 27, 1940; s. Milton and Esther Florence (Trachte) T.; m. Marcella Hauolilani Choy, Sept. 25, 1962; children: Theodore William, Robert Arthur. BA, Beloit Coll., 1962; PhD, U. London, 1968. Lectr. in history Sch. Oriental and African Studies, U. London, 1965-68; asst. prof. history U. Mich., Ann Arbor, 1968-71, assoc. prof., 1971-77, prof., 1977—, Richard Hudson rsch. prof., 1979, prof. history and anthropology, 1984—, chmn. dept. history, 1987-90, Steelcase rsch. prof., 1993-94, dir. Inst. Humanities, Mary Fair Croushore prof. humanities, 1997—2002, Marshall D. Sahlins coll. prof. history and anthropology, 1997—. Author: Kautilya and the Arthasastra, 1971, Dravidian Kinship, 1981, Lewis Henry Morgan and the Invention of Kinship, 1987; author: (with K.S. Kabelac) The Library of Lewis Henry Morgan, 1994; author: (edit. with Diane Owen Hughes) Time: Histories and Ethnologies, 1995, Aryans and British India, 1997; author: (edit. with Maurice Godelier and Franklin Tjon Sie Fat) Transformations of Kinship, 1999; editor: Comparative Studies in Society and History, 1997—; contbr. articles on India, kinship and history of anthropology. Sr. Humanist fellow NEH, 1984. Mem. Am. Anthrop. Assn., Assn. Asian Studies, Am. Inst. Indian Studies (mem. exec. com. trustee, sr. rsch. fellow in India 1985, 97), Phi Beta Kappa. Office: U Mich Dept History Ann Arbor MI 48109-1003

TRAUTNER, JOHN JAMES, real estate executive; b. Simpson, Minn., Dec. 4, 1935; s. John Sylvester and Oridena Francis (Baker) T.; m. Donna L. Jones, June 1960 (div. Dec. 1969); m. Carol Lee Rowberry, July 12, 1974 (div. May 1981); 1 child, Lindsey D.; m. Kathy N. Bucy, July 19, 1992; children; Theresa, Carrie, John; 1 stepchild, Victor. BA, Anchorage C.C., 1968; BBA, U. Alaska, 1970, MBA, 1998. Adminstr., pub. affairs RCA Svc. Co., Anchorage, 1965-70; dir. adminstrn. & pub. rels. Alaska Resort, Inc., Girdwood, 1970-71; mgmt. cons. State of Alaska, 1972-73; exec. dir. City of Lost River (Alaska), 1973-74; v.p., gen. mgr. C. Bruce Ficke Investments, Girdwood, 1974-76; pres., gen. mgr. Gateway, Inc., 1976-85; CEO Alyeska Mgmt. Svcs., Inc., 1985—. Mem. MD49 Coun. Govs., Fairbanks, Alaska, 1996-97, chmn., 1999-2000; marriage commr. 3d Jud. Dist., Anchorage, 1973-93. Patentee in field. Chmn., mem. Girdwood Bd. Suprs., 1992-95; fire chief Girdwood Fire Dept., 1972-75; chmn. Girdwood Cmty. Coun., 1976-78, Jr.-Inter-Fraternity Coun., Seattle, 1957-58. Sgt. U.S. Army, 1953-64. Melvin Jones fellow, chgo., 1993-94. Mem. N.Am. Nature Photographers Assn., Am. Legion, Lions, Disabled VFW, Alaska Airmens Assn., San Francisco Tennis Club. Republican. Roman Catholic. Avocations: photography, music, fine art, humanitarianism. Office: Alaska Mgmt Svcs Inc PO Box 909 Girdwood AK 99587-0909 E-mail: outsidermining@msn.com.

TRAUTWEIN, GEORGE WILLIAM, conductor, educator; b. Chgo., Aug. 5, 1927; s. William Jacob and Hilda (Martin) T.; m. Barbara Wilson, Jan. 20, 1955; children: Paul Martin, Matthew Richard. MusB, Oberlin Conservatory, Ohio, 1951; MusM, Cleve. Inst. Music, 1955; MusD, Ind. U., 1961. Mem. faculty U. Minn., U. Tex., Austin, Armstrong (Ga.) State Coll.; arts cons. Nat. Endowment Arts; dir. internat. study program for Wake Forest U. at Tokai U., Japan, 1995. Violinist Indpls. Symphony Orch., 1947-48, Balt. Symphony Orch., 1951-52, Nat. Symphony Orch., Washington, 1952-53, Cleve. Orch., 1953-57, Chautauqua Symphony Orch., N.Y., 1953-59, Camerata Acad., Salzburg, 1957-58, Mozarteum Orch., Salzburg, 1958 (Fulbright grantee 1958), assoc. condr. Dallas Symphony Orch., 1962-66, Mpls. Symphony, 1966-73; music dir. S.D. Symphony, 1971-75, Internat. Congress Strings, Ohio, 1973-75; music dir., condr. Savannah (Ga.) Symphony Orch., 1974-77; music adv., prin. guest condr. Evansville (Ind.) Philharm., 1979-80; music dir., condr. RIAS Edn. Network, Berlin, 1979, Tucson Symphony Orch., 1977-81; artistic dir., condr. Piedmont Chamber Orch.; prin. condr. Internat. Music program; dir. orchestral programs, N.C. Sch. of Arts, 1981-83; dir. instrumental ensembles, Wake Forest U., 1983-96, dir. Artists series, 1985-98; guest appearances with orchs., U.S., Germany, Sweden, France, Rumania, Jugoslavia, Portugal, Hong Kong, India, P.R., Mex. Adv. bd. Avery Fisher Found., N.Y.C. Served with USN, 1948-49. Recipient Orpheus award Phi Mu Alpha, 1971, ASCAP award, 1979, 82, World Peace award Ministry of World Harmony, 1983; Fulbright grantee Mozarteum, Salzburg, 1958; Sr. Fulbright lectr., India, 1989-90. Mem. Am. Fedn. Musicians, Chamber Music Soc. Am., Sir Thomas Beecham Soc., Erich Wolfgang Korngold Soc., Wilhelm Furtwaengler Soc., Literacy Initiative Assn. Avocations: string quartet, art reproduction, British cuisine, W.B. Yeats, James Joyce. Office: Wake Forest U PO Box 7411 Winston Salem NC 27109-7411

TRAUTWEIN, MARK WALTER, music educator, financial consultant; b. St. Louis, Jan. 21, 1948; s. Norman Howard and Grace Anita Trautwein; m. Donna Elizabeth Wynn, Apr. 1, 1978; children: Christopher Steimel, Niki. MusB Edn., Southeast Mo. State U., Cape Girardeau, 1971; MA in Ednl. Processes, Maryville U., St. Louis, 1991. Instrumental music educator Marissa Cmty. Unit Sch. Dist., Marissa, Ill., 1971—80, Hillsboro R-3 Sch. Dist., Hillsboro, Mo., 1980—. Contbr. articles to profl. jours. Mem. of session Grace Presbyn. Ch., Crystal City, Mo.; bd. of edn. Crystal City Sch. Dist. # 47. Recipient Tchr. Appreciation Award, Mo. Fine Arts Acad., Mo. Dept. of Elem. and Secondary Edn., 2000, 2001, 2002, Mo. Scholars Acad., Mo. Dept. of Elem. and Secondary Edn., 2000, 2002, Tchr. of the Yr., Hillsboro R-3 Sch. Dist., 2002. Mem.: NEA (pres., sec., bldg. rep.Hillsboro, Mo. chpt.), Nat. Bandmasters Assn., Mo. Bandmasters Assn., Internat. Assn. of Jazz Educators, Mo. Music Educators Assn., Music Educators Nat. Conf., Ill. Edn. Assn., Phi Mu Alpha Sinfonia (chpt. pres. 1970—71, Best Active Award 1971), Phi Beta Mu. Presbyterian. Avocations: music, travel. Home: 203 Jefferson Ave Crystal City MO 63019

TRAVAGLINI, JOSEPH, educational consultant; b. Phila., Sept. 17, 1932; m. Marilyn Irene Gordon, Dec. 26, 1956; children: Mark D., David H. BSBA, Drexel U., 1955; M of Govtl. Adminstrn., U. Pa., 1960; PhD, U. Md., 1974. Dir. personnel svcs. Antioch Coll., Yellow Springs, Ohio, 1960-65; mgr. adminstrv. svcs. U. Chgo., 1965-66; asst. bur. chief Pa. State Dept. Edn., Harrisburg, 1966-67; asst. to pres. Essex C.C., Baltimore County, Md., 1967-75; program mgr. individualized degree programs Ctrl. Mich. U., Mt. Pleasant, 1975-88; dean grad. and external programs Coll. Santa Fe, 1988-89; assoc. dean, dir. The Union Inst., San Diego Ctr., Cin., 1989-92; ednl. cons. San Diego, 1993—. Co-chair accreditation study Essex C.C., 1969-70; team leader program learning seminar U. Mich., Ann Arbor, 1982; reviewer Calif. Postsecondary Edn. Commn., Sacramento, 1990-91; cons. to pres. La Jolla U., San Diego, 1993. Author: (chpt.) Personalized Instruction in Education Today, 1970; co-author: (chpt.) The University and the Inner City, 1980. Pres. Joppatowne (Md.) Civic Assoc., 1969-74; county coun. candidate Harford County, Bel Air, Md., 1974; alumni amb. Drexel U., Phila., 1997—; vol. auditor Balboa Pk. Japanese Friendship Garden, San Diego, 1995—. With U.S. Army, 1955-57. Recipient Samuel S. Fels scholarship U. Pa., 1958-60, fellowship U. Colo., 1968. Mem. Wharton Alumni Club So. Calif., Sierra Club, World Wildlife Fund, Nature Conservancy, Phi Delta Kappa (emeritus). Democrat. Avocations: environment, international travel, jogging, music, politics. Home: 3375 Date St San Diego CA 92102-1635

TRAVELSTEAD, CHESTER COLEMAN, former educational administrator; b. Franklin, Ky., Sept. 25, 1911; s. Conley and Nelle (Gooch) T.; m. Marita Hawley, Aug. 1, 1936; children: Coleman, Jimmie. AB, Western Ky. State Coll., Bowling Green, 1933; M of Music, Northwestern U., 1947; PhD, U. Ky., 1950; HHD, Morehead (Ky.) State U., 1975; PhD, John F. Kennedy U., Buenos Aires, 1975; LHD, U. N.Mex., 1980. Tchr., prin. rural and consol. schs., Mecklenburg County, Va., 1931-32, 33-35; tchr. gen. sci., math., music Picadome H.S., Lexington, Ky., 1935-37; dir. music Henry Clay H.S., 1937-42; personnel supr. Lexington Signal Dept., Dept. War, 1942-43; supr. music Lexington pub. schs., 1945-47; rep. Investors Diversified Services, Inc., 1947-48; coordinator in-service tchr. edn. Ky. Dept. Edn., 1950-51; asst. prof. edn., asst. dean Coll. Edn., U. Ga., Athens, 1951-53; dean Sch. Edn., U. S.C., Columbia, 1953-56; dean Coll. Edn. U. N.Mex., Albuquerque, 1956-68, v.p. acad. affairs, 1968-76, provost, 1976-77. Mem. Nat. Council Accreditation Tchr. Edn., 1960-66, chmn., 1963-65 Author books; contbr. articles in field to profl. jours. Pres. bd. dirs. N.Mex. Symphony Orch., 1977-78, 84-85; treas. U.S. Senator Jeff Bingaman's re-election campaign, 1988-93; mem. N.Mex. Jud. Stds. Commn., 1995-96. With USNR, 1943-45; PTO. Mem. AAUP, NEA, Nat. Soc. Study Edn., Nat. Assn. Scholars, Soc. Advancement Edn., Phi Kappa Phi, Phi Delta Kappa., Kappa Delta Pi. Home: Montebello # 128 10500 Academy Rd NE Albuquerque NM 87111-7306

TRAVER, COURTLAND LEE, lawyer; b. New Haven, Sept. 20, 1935; s. Courtland L. Sr. and Bertha (Wilmott) T.; (div.); children: Lee, Kim, Amy. BA, U. Conn., 1957; LLB, Georgetown U., 1966. Bar: D.C. 1966, Va. 1967. Law clk. to presiding justice Ct. of Gen. Sessions, Washington, 1965-66; clk. U.S. Ct. Appeals (D.C. cir.), 1966-67; ptnr. McGuire, Woods, Battle & Boothe (now McGuire Woods), McLean, 1967—2001. Contbr. articles on real estate law to jours. Lt., pilot USN, 1957-63. Mem. ABA (various coms.), Va. State Bar Assn. (chmn. real estate com.). D.C. Bar Assn., Va. Bar Assn. (chmn. real estate sect.). Office: World Trade Ctr 101 W Main St Ste 9000 Norfolk VA 23510-1655 E-mail: ctraver@mcguirewoods.com.

TRAVER, NOEL ALLEN, small business owner, creative director; b. New Brunswick, N.J., Nov. 12, 1959; s. Thomas Gordon Sr. and Arline (Yurkunas) T.; m. Jayne Louise Brickner, Mar. 3, 1984. BA, Ohio State U., 1982. Dir. Jeffery Shaw Communications, Columbus, 1982-85; desktop pub. Inacomp Computer Ctrs., Worthington, Ohio, 1985-90; pres., chmn. bd. D'pix, Inc., Columbus, 1990-94, Amber Prodns., Inc., Columbus, 1985—; founder, owner Think Big Color, 1997—. Co-founder, pres., chmn. bd. The Creative Network Inc., Columbus, 1996—; adj. faculty Franklin U., Columbus, 1991-93; lectr. Journalism Assn. of Ohio Schs., Broadcast Designers Assn., Nat. Broadcast Promotion Execs., Marion Advt. and Sales Club, Internat. Assn. Bus., Communicators, The Mac Show, numerous others, 1985—; founder, owner Wooden Universe, 2000—. Recipient Honorable Mention Best Visual Resource, MacUser mag., 1991, Honorable Mention Best Logo and two merit awards, How mag., 1992, Best Computer Art and Design award Computer Graphics, 1992; named to Top 10 List, Clip Art Products-MacWorld Mag., 1994. Mem. Nat. Assn. Desktop Pub., Ohio State U. Alumni Assn., Ohio State U. Sch. Journalism Alumni Assn., Advt. Fedn. Columbus, MacDesigner, Columbus Soc. Communicating Arts, Digital Designers Group. Republican. Achievements include being the founder of high-resolution photography CD-ROM industry. Home: PO Box 572 Columbus OH 43216-0572 also: Wooden Universe 250 S Hamilton Rd Columbus OH 43213-2024 E-mail: amber@infinet.com.

TRAVER, ROBERT WILLIAM, SR. management consultant, author, lecturer, engineer; b. Waterbury, Conn., Oct. 13, 1930; s. Alfred Matthew Sr. and Dorothy Viola (Thomson) T.; m. Eleanor Jean Finnemore (div. Feb. 1963); children: Robert William Jr., Jeffrey Matthew, Elizabeth; m. Valarie Jane Mason. B in Mech. Enginrg., Clarkson U., 1955; MBA, U. Mass., 1963. Registered profl. engr., N.Y. Quality control engr. Gen. Electric Co., Pittsfield, Mass., 1955-62; mgr. reliability and quality assurance Tansitor Electronics, Inc., Bennington, Vt., 1962-65; sr. cons. Rath & Strong, Inc., Lexington, Mass., 1965-70; regional mgr. TAC, Inc., Albany, N.Y., 1970-72; dist. mgr. IDS, Inc., 1972-81; v.p. Reddy, Traver & Woods, Inc., Lexington, 1981-96; owner Traver Assocs., Averill Pk., N.Y., 1996—. Participant in ednl. exch. with Peoples Republic of China, 1985, Australia and New Zealand, 1986. Author: Manufacturing Solutions for Consistent Quality and Reliability; contbr. articles to profl. jours. Chmn. lake com. Crooked Lake Improvement Assn., Averill Park, N.Y., 1973-74; v.p. Sand Lake (N.Y.) Businessmen's Assn., 1974-76. With U.S. Army, 1950. Fellow Am. Soc. for Quality; mem. Trout Unltd. Republican. Congregationalist. Avocations: fishing, gardening. Home and Office: 184 Eastern Union Tpke Averill Park NY 12018-9563 E-mail: rwtraver@aol.com.

TRAVERS, JUDITH LYNNETTE, human resources executive; b. Buffalo, Feb. 25, 1950; d. Harold Elwin and Dorothy (Helsel) Howes; m. David Jon Travers, Oct. 21, 1972; 1 child, Heather Lynne. BA in Psychology, Barrington Coll., 1972; cert. in paralegal course, St. Mary's Coll., Moraga, Calif., 1983; postgrad., Southland U., 1982-84. Exec. sec. Sherman C. Weeks, P.A., Derry, N.H., 1973-75; legal asst. Mason-McDuffie Co., Berkeley, Calif., 1975-82; paralegal asst. Blum, Kay, Merkle & Kauftheil, Oakland, 1982-83; CEO, bd. dirs. Dela Pers. Svcs. Inc., Concord, 1983—; pres. All Ages Sitters Agy., 1986-95; CEO, bd. dirs. Guardian Security Agy., Calif., 1992—. Sec., bd. dirs. Per Diem Staffing Systems, Inc., Securicorp. Vocalist record album The Loved Ones, 1978. Vol. local Congl. campaign, 1980, Circle of Friends, Children's Hosp. No. Calif., Oakland, 1987—; mem. Alameda County Sheriff's Mounted Posse, 1989, Contra Costa Child Abuse Prevention Coun., 1989; employer adv. coun. Ctrl. Contra Costa County, 1993—; Carondelet/De La Salle H.S. Adult Choir, 1998— Mem. NAFE, Am. Assn. Respiratory Therapy, Soc. for Human Resource Mgmt., Am. Mgmt. Assn., Gospel Music Assn., Palomino Horse Breeders Am., DAR, Barrington Oratorio Soc., Commonwealth Club Calif., Nat. Trust Hist. Preservation, Alpha Theta Sigma. Republican. Baptist. Avocations: boating, horses. Home: 3900 Brown Rd Oakley CA 94561-2664 Office: Delta Pers Svcs Inc 1820 Galindo St Ste 3 Concord CA 94520-2447

TRAVERS, SCOTT ANDREW, numismatist; b. N.Y.C., Nov. 12, 1961; s. Harvey Charles and Barbara Joan (Goldman) T. BA in Politics, Brandeis U., 1983. Pres. Scott Travers Rare Coin Galleries, Inc., N.Y.C., 1979—; gov. Am. Numis. Assn., 1995-97, v.p., 1997-99. Authenticator, grader Numismatic Guaranty Corp., 1987-90, grading standards cons., 1987-94; bd. govs. Adelphi U. Inst. Numismatic and Philatelic Studies, 1980-86; state advisor U.S. Congl. Adv. Bd., 1983—; expert cons. FTC, 1992; lectr. and mem. bd. overseers Numismatic Inst. of N.Am.; internat. writing competition coord. Numismatic Literacy Guild; interviewed on various radio and TV programs. Author: The Coin Collector's Survival Manual, 1984 (Book of Yr.), 2d edit., 1988 (Investment and Consumer Protection award), 3d edit., 1995, CD-ROM edit., 1998, 4th edit., 2000, Rare Coin Investment Strategy (Book of Yr.), The Investor's Guide to Coin Trading, 1989 (Investment Book Yr.), Travers' Rare Coin Investment Strategy, 1990, One Minute Coin Expert, 1991, 3d edit., 1998, 4th edit., 2001, The Insiders' Guide to U.S. Coin Values, 1993—(Extraordinary Merit), How to Make Money in Coins Right Now, 1996 (Book of Yr. award), 2nd edit., 2001 (Investment Book of Yr. award), Scott Travers' Top 100 Coins Over $100, 1998 (Investment Book Yr.); contbg. editor COINage mag.; author: (intro.) How to Grade U.S. Coins; author: (chpt.) Comprehensive U.S. Silver Dollar Encyclopedia; editor: Official Guide To Coin Grading and Counterfeit Detection; author (foreword) The New York Times Guide to Coin Collecting; video host: The Future of The Rare Coin Marketplace; host radio talk show Coin Expert Sta. WALE-AM, 1994-95; contbr. foreword to book, articles to profl. jours. and coin website. Liquidator Bd. Gold Coins, El Salvador, 1989. Mem. Am. Numismatic Soc., Am. Numismatic Assn. (gov. 1995-97, v.p. 1997-99, conv. spkr., consumer protection and edn. coms., Outstanding Young Numismatist, Adult Advisor of Yr., Ray Byrne Lit. award, Glenn B. Smedley Disting. Cmty. Svc. award 1992, 99, Nat. Club Coords. award, Clery Lifetime Achievement award), Numismatic Lit. Guild, Am. Israel Numismatic Assn., Ctrl. State Numismatic Soc., Mich. Numismatic Soc., New Eng. Numismatic Assn., Fla. United Numismatists, Numismatics Internat., Profl. Numismatists Guild. Office: PO Box 1711 New York NY 10150-1711 E-mail: travers@pocketchangelottery.com.

TRAVERS, W. LAWRENCE, healthcare executive; b. Syracuse, N.Y., Nov. 1, 1943; s. Walter Roy and Elizabeth Laurene (Hicks) T. BS, Coll. of Emporia, Kans., 1965; MSW, Syracuse U., 1972. Diplomate in clin. social work N.Y.; cert. addictions counselor. Cons. alcoholism treatment Hutchings Psychiat. Ctr. N.Y. State, Office of Mental Health, Syracuse, 1972-73, program dir. alcoholism rehab. unit, 1973-76, program dir. psychogeriatric day treatment/outpatient svcs., 19976-80, mental health outpatient svc., 1980-86, program dir. mentally ill chem. abuse sr. adv. panel, 1986-91; rehab. coord. Capital Dist. Psychiat. Ctr., Albany, N.Y., 1991-94; edn. and tng. cons., 1994-97; cons. to med. dir. managed care N.Y. State/Office of Mental Health, Albany, 1997-98, dir. co-occurring psychiat. and addictive disorders, 1998-2000, dir. health systems transition, 2000—; cons. N.Y.C. Office of Mental Hlth., 2000—; pvt. practice Albany, N.Y. Dir. Health Systems Teransition, Albany,NY, bd. dirs. Franklin Med. Lab. Sch., Westbury, N.Y., 1980. Dem. Party ofcl., 1974-76. Recipient Sci. Achievement award Chem. Rubber Co.,

1965. Fellow Am. Orthophychiat. Assn.; mem. NASW (clin. register), Acad. Cert. Social Workers (diplomate), Am. Coll. Addiction Treatment Adminstrs., Am. Bd. Examiners in Clin. Social Work, Nat. Assn. Drug Abuse and Alcoholism Commn. (master addiction counselor), Am. Coll. Health Care Execs. Presbyterian. Home: Empire View 204 196 Morton Ave Albany NY 12202-1474 Office: NY State Office Mental Health 44 Holland Ave Albany NY 12208-3411 E-mail: lawrencetravers@compuserve.com.

TRAVIS, ALICE DIMERY, journalist; b. Kingstree, S.C., Sept. 23, 1943; d. Virgil Cornelius Dimery and Mary Agnes (Fassitt) Dimery-Murphy; m. William Daniel Travis, Sept. 9, 1967 (div. July 1973); m. Antonio Maugeri, Oct. 30, 1980; 1 child, Alexander Virgil. AB in Sociology, Immaculata Coll., 1965; postgrad., U. Pa., 1965-66, Temple U., 1966-69. Staff technician, mgmt. trainee Bell Telephone Co. of Pa., Phila., 1965-68; dir. tng. comprehensive health svcs. Temple U., 1968-70; co-host Panorama Metromedia TV, Washington, 1970-73; co-host AM New York ABC TV/WABC, N.Y.C., 1973-75; rsch. cons. Paterson, Michael, Jones, London, 1975-76; host Gerber Carter Comm., N.Y.C., 1977-78; comm. cons. Alice Travis, Inc., 1976-88; rsch. journalist Mahopac Falls, N.Y., 1988—. Comm. cons. J. Ray McDermott, Bell Labs., 1977—; tng. analyst Ciba Geigy, Hooker Chem., 1988. Author: Cognitive Evolution: The Biological Imprint of Applied Intelligence, 1995; moderator 26 programs, You series, U.S. Dept. HEW, 1972, 73; host, creator spl. programming People, 1973. Recipient Annie E. Gorman award in sociology Immaculata Coll., 1965, Comm. award Inst. Fgn. Svc., U.S. Dept. State, 1971, media awards Fed. Editors Assn., 1973, Am. Women in Radio and TV, 1973, AAUW, 1975; named Media Woman of the Yr., Nat. Assn. Media Women, 1978, numerous others; keys to cities of Savannah, Ga., West Orange, N.J. Roman Catholic. Avocations: fashion designing, real estate development. Office: PO Box 365 Mahopac Falls NY 10542-0365

TRAVIS, DAVID M. physician; b. Nashville, June 6, 1926; s. Emmet Alexander and Bessie Ethel (Page) T.; m. Jeanne Claire Dorais, Feb. 14, 1953; children: Anne, William. Claire. BA, Vanderbilt U., 1947, MD, 1951. Diplomate Am. Bd. Internal Medicine. Intern, then resident Harvard Med. Svc., Boston, 1951-54; rsch. fellow Harvard Peter Bent Bringham Hosp., 1956-58; from asst. to assoc. prof. U. Fla., Gainesville, 1958-70, prof., 1970-80, U. N.D., Fargo, 1980-91; chief med. svc. VA Med. Ctr., 1980-91; staff physician VA Clinic, Worcester, Mass., 1991-94, 97-00. Corp. mem. Marine Biol. Lab., Woods Hole, Mass., 1962—. Capt. USAF, 1954-56. Recipient Rsch. award Borden Co., 1951, Sr. Rsch. fellow. Nat. Inst. of Health, 1971-72. Fellow Am. Coll. of Physicians, Am. Coll. of Chest Physicians; mem. Am. Physiol.Soc., Am. Soc. for Pharm. and Exptl. Therapectics, Soc. for Gen. Physiologists, Am. Thoracic Soc. (pres. Fla. chpt. 1965-66). Home: 19 High St Woods Hole MA 02543-1221

TRAVIS, DEMPSEY JEROME, author, real estate executive and developer; b. Chgo., Feb. 25, 1920; s. Louis and Mittie (Strickland) T.; m. Moselynne Hardwick, Sept. 17, 1949. BA, Roosevelt U., 1949; grad., Sch. Mortgage Banking, Northwestern U., 1969; D.Econs., Olive Harvey Coll., 1974; D.BA (hon.), Daniel Hale Williams U., Chgo., 1976; PhD (hon.), Kennedy-King Coll., 1982; DHL (hon.), Governor State U., 2001. Cert. property mgr.; cert. real estate counselor. Pres. Travis Realty Co., Chgo., 1949—, Urban Rsch. Press, 1969—. Author: Don't Stop Me Now, 1970, An Autobiography of Black Chicago, 1981, An Autobiography of Black Jazz, 1983, An Autobiography of Black Politics, 1987, Real Estate is the Gold in Your Future, 1988, Harold: The People's Mayor, 1989, Racism: American Style a Corporate Gift, 1990, I Refuse to Learn to Fail, 1992, Views From the Back of the Bus During World War II and Beyond, 1995, The Duke Ellington Primer, 1996, The Louis Armstrong Odessey: From Jazz Alley to America's Jazz Ambassador, 1997, Racism: Revolves Like a Merry Go 'Round: 'Round 'n 'Round It Goes, 1998, They Heard a Thousand Thunders, 1999, The Life and Times of Redd Foxx, 1999, The Victory Monument: The Beacon of Chicago's Bronzeville, 1999, J. Edgar Hoover's FBI Wired the Nation, 2000, The FBI Files on the Tainted and the Damned, 2001, An American Story: In Red, White and Blue, 2002, Norman Erani The White Moses of Black Jazz, 2003. Trustee Northwestern Meml. Hosp., Chgo., Chgo. Hist. Soc., Auditorium Theater, Chgo., Roosevelt U.; bd. dirs. Columbia Coll. With AUS, 1942-46. Recipient award Soc. Midland Authors, 1982, Chgo. Art Deco Soc., 1985, The Human Rights award The Gustavus Myers Ctr. for Study of Human Rights in N.Am., 1995, Humanitarian award Kennedy-King Coll., 1997, Art Deco award, 1983, Soc. Midland Authors award for nonfiction, 1981; named to Jr. Achievement Chgo. Bus. Hall of Fame, 1995; named embedded in sidewalk of Bronzeville Walk of Fame, Chgo; inductee Internat. Literary Hall of Fame, Chgo. State U., 2000. Mem. United Mortgage Bankers Assn. Am. (pres. 1961-74), Dearborn Real Estate Bd. (pres. 1957-59, 70-71), Nat. Assn. Real Estate Brokers (1st v.p. 1959-60), Inst. Real Estate Mgmt., Soc. Profl. Journalists, Soc. Midland Authors (pres. 1988-90), NAACP (pres. Chgo. 1959-60), Econs. Club, Forty Club Chgo., Assembly Club, Cliff Dwellers, The Caxtons Club. Office: Travis Realty Co 840 E 87th St Chicago IL 60619-6298 E-mail: travisDT88@aol.com.

TRAVIS, JOYCE MARIE, real estate executive; b. Lamar, Colo., Jan. 29, 1947; d. Morris Eugene and Mildred Marie (Neary) T.; m. Richard d. Copess, Sept. 19, 1970 (divorced). BA in Tech. Journalism, Colo. State U., 1969; postgrad., U. No. Colo., 1969-72, Ill. State U., 1976-81. Editor, mgr. State Farm Ins., Bloomington, Ill., 1972-82; staff v.p. Inst. Real Estate Mgmt., Chgo., 1982—. Mem. ASTD, Am. Soc. Assn. Execs., Pub. Rels. Soc. Am. Office: Inst Real Estate Mgmt 430 N Michigan Ave Chicago IL 60611-4011

TRAVIS, LAWRENCE ALLAN, accountant; b. Bloomington, Ill., Sept. 17, 1942; s. Willard Burns and Florence May (Harvey) T.; m. Katy Quinones, Apr. 16, 1965 (div. Feb. 1978); children: Lawrence Allan Jr., Matthew B.; m. Kathleen Lucas, May 20, 1995. BS in Bus. Edn., Ill. State U., 1968; MA in Pub. Adminstrn., U. Ill., Springfield, 1976. CPA, Ill. Staff acct. Alexander Grant & Co., Chgo., 1969; internal auditor State Farm Ins., Bloomington, 1969-73; dep. dir. Ill. Dept. Ins., Springfield, 1973-74; audit mgr. Ill. Auditor Gen., 1974-81; pres. Lawrence Travis & Co., P.C., CPAs, Virden, Normal, Springfield and Jacksonville, Ill., 1979—, also bd. dirs.; registered rep. Terra Securities, 1994—. Pres., bd. dirs. Travco, Inc., Virden; v.p., bd. dirs. Ka-Lar Enterprises, Inc., Springfield, Miller Comm., Inc. Mem. Ill. Common Cause, Springfield. Mem. AICPA, Assn. Govt. Accts., Ill. CPA Soc., Internat. Platform Assn., Nat. Space Soc., Smithsonian Assocs., World Future Soc., Internat. Traders. Democrat. Roman Catholic. Avocation: sports. Home: 2409 Idlewild Dr Springfield IL 62704-5403 Office: Lawrence Travis & Co PC 1700 S 1st St Springfield IL 62704-3902

TRAVIS, MARLENE O. healthcare management executive; b. Edmonton, Alta., Can. Came to U.S. 1959. d. LeRoy David and Della Jessie (Campbell) T.; m. Gary T. McIlroy, Aug. 20, 1962; children: Jennifer Renee, Montgomery Travis. Student (mass comms.), St. Cloud State U., 1974-76; cert. exec. edn., U. Pa., 1989-92. Cert. exec. edn. Owner Travis Comms., 1975—; co-founder, operating officer Midwest Lab. Assoc., Mpls., 1977-80; dir., corp. v.p. Meidinger-HRM (MHRM), 1981-83; co-founder, exec. v.p., bd. dirs. Health Risk Mgmt. Inc., 1977-2001, dir., pres., 1986—2001. Chair of bd., CEO HRM Ltd. (Can.), 1989-99; founder, chair CEO Inst. Healthcare Quality, Mpls., 1991-2001; vice-chair Med. Alley, 1994-98, bd. dirs.; pres. Travis-McIlroy Found., 1997—; mem. Twin Cities adv. coun. Bank of Am., 2001-2002. Co-author Self Health Guide to Laboratory Tests, 1982; author: (chpt.) Guide to Managed Care Strategies, 1999; pub. Quality FIRST Index, 1998-99. Chmn. Minn. Task Force on Battered Women, 1977-79; bd. dirs., exec. com. Minn. Task Force on Sexual Assault, 1974-76; co-founder, chair Mid Minn. Women's Ctr. Brainerd, 1975; incorporator, founder, chair Crow Wing County Task Force on Sexual Assault, Brainerd, 1974-77; founder Crow Wing County Task Force to Support Battered Women, 1974; mem. Minn. Commr. of Edn.'s Task Force to Eliminate Sexism in Edn., 1973-74; mem. leadership group Amnesty Internat., 1990—, Com. of 200, 1991—; patron Minn. Orch., 1998—, Mpls. Inst. Art, 2002; charter mem. Nat. Women's History Mus., 2002; mem. mus. coun. Nat. Mus. Women in the Arts, 2002. Named Cornerstone Leader in Giving, United Way Mpls., 1992—2001; named one of City Bus. Most Innovative Women, 2000. Mem. AAUW, NOW (convenor Marshfield, Wis. chpt. 1972, Brainerd area chpt. 1974), C-200 Found. (mentor contbr.), Nat. Assn. Corp. Dirs., Toastmasters (sponsor 1988), Greater Mpls. C. of C. (bd. dirs. 1996-2001). Avocations: skiing, photography, travel, women's studies, piano. E-mail: mtravis@bitstream.net.

TRAVIS, MARTIN BICE, political scientist, educator; b. Iron Mountain, Mich., Sept. 22, 1917; s. Martin Bice and Helen (Carrett) T.; m. Olivia Brewster Taylor, Nov. 29, 1942; children: Elizabeth Nichols (Mrs. Usama Mugharbil), Helen Willard. AB, Amherst Coll., 1939; student, Heidelberg (Germany) U., 1937; MA, Fletcher Sch. Law and Diplomacy, 1940; PhD, U. Chgo., 1948. Asst. prof. internat. relations Syracuse U., 1948-49; asst. prof. polit. sci. Duke U., 1949-52; asst. prof., then asso. prof. polit. sci. Stanford U., 1953-61; prof. polit. sci. SUNY-Stony Brook, 1961-92; coordinator SUNY Program Am. U., Beirut, Lebanon, 1972-73; chmn. dept., 1961-68; dir. Inst. Am. Studies SUNY-Stony Brook, 1965-93. Vis. prof. Sch. Internat. Affairs, Columbia, 1956-57; vis. summer prof. U. Guadalajara, Mex., 1959, 62, U. Wash., 1961; Bd. dirs. State U N.Y. Inst. Am. Studies in France, 1966-77; cons. to industry. Author: (with E.E. Robinson) Powers of the President in Foreign Affairs, 1966; Co-editor, contbr.: (with Philip W. Buck) Control of Foreign Relations in Modern Nations, 1957; bd. editors: Western Polit. Quar, 1956-58; adv. bd.: Almanac of Current World Leaders, 1957— ; editorial critic for book pubs. Mem. sch. bd., Cold Spring Harbor, N.Y., 1965-71, v.p. 1967-68, pres. 1968-69; trustee Village of Laurel Hollow, 1983-95, police com., 1983-85, mayor, 1985-95; established Martin B. Travis Scholarship fund for pre-law majors at SUNY, Stonybrook, 1995. Grantee Ford Found. 1960-61; recipient Hugh Cleland Meml. Outstanding Prof. award Alumni Assn. SUNY Stony Brook, 2000. Mem. Coun. Fgn. Rels., Phi Delta Theta, Phi Delta Kappa. Home: 533 Cold Spring Rd Syosset NY 11791-1206 Office: Dept Polit Science Suny Stony Brook NY 11794-0001

TRAVIS, RANDY BRUCE, musician; b. Monroe, N.C., 1959; married. Musician Country City U.S.A., 1977-82, Nashville Palace, 1982-85; recording artist, 1986—. Rec. artist Warner Bros. Records, 1985-97, DreamWorks Records, 1997-2000, Inspirational Journey Warner Bros. and Atlantic Christian Music Divsn. (Dove award 2001); albums include debut Storms of Life, 1986 (Album of Yr., Acad. Country Music 1987, Album of Yr., Music City News 1987), Always & Forever, 1987 (Album of Yr., Country Music Assn. 1987), Old 8x10, 1988, No Holdin' Back, 1989, An Old Time Christmas, 1989, Heroes and Friends, 1990, High Lonesome, 1991, Greatest Hits, 1992, Wind in the Wire, 1993, This is Me, 1994, Full Circle, 1996, You And You Alone, 1998, Man Ain't Made of Stone, 1999; songs include On the Other Hand (Best Song, Acad. Country Music 1987, Best Single, Acad. Country Music 1987, Single of Yr., Music City News 1987), Diggin' Up Bones, No Place Like Home, Forever and Ever, Amen (Single of Yr., Song of Yr.,Country Music Assn. 1987, Best Country Record, AMOA Jukebox 1987), I Won't Need You Anymore, No Holding Back, 1989, Full Circle, 1996, You and You Alone, 1998 (Dove award 2001, Best Blue Grass album), Baptism (Best Country song); film appearances include: Frank and Jesse, 1994, Wind in the Wire, 1994, A Holiday to Remember, 1995, The Legend of O.B. Taggart, 1995, Edie & Pen, 1996, Boys Will Be Boys, 1996, Fire Down Below, 1997, Steel Chariots, 1997, The Rainmaker, 1997, White River Kid, 1998, Texas Rangers, 1999, John John In The Sky, 1999, Major Reno, 1999, Trial Of Old Drum, 2000, Fathers Of Our Country, 2000, (animated children's movie) Annabelle's Wish, 1997, The Shooter, 1997, T-N-T, 1998, Black Dog, 1998, Baby Geniuses, 1998, Casper's Christmas, 2000, (TV Movie) A Holiday To Remember, 1995 (TV mini series) Texas, 1994, Touched by an Angel, 1994, 95, 97, 2001, Matlock, 1992, 93; (TV movie) Dead Man's Revenge, 1994, At Risk, 1993; (TV spl.) Down Home, 1990, Happy Trails, 1990. Named Top Male Vocalist, Acad. Country Music, 1987, Male Vocalist of Yr., Music City News, 1987, Star of Tomorrow, Music City News, 1987, Male Vocalist of Yr., Country Music Assn., 1987, Entertainer of Yr. Music City News, 1988, Male Artist of Yr., 1988, Favorite Entertainer, Favorite Entertainer, Nashville Network Viewers Choice Awards, 1988; recipient Horizon award Country Music Assn., 1986, Grammy award, 1987, Am. Music award, best country album, 1988, Am. Music award, best country single, 1988, Country Music Assn. best male vocalist, 1988. Mem. Grand Ole Opry. E-mail: traviscorp@home.com.

TRAVIS, VANCE KENNETH, petroleum business executive; b. Coriander, Sask., Can., Jan. 30, 1926; s. Roy Hazen and Etta Orilla (Anderson) T.; m. Louise Mary, Nov. 30, 1948 (div. 1979); children: Stuart, Shirley, Gordon, Donald, Marian; m. Mildred Elaine, June 29, 1979; stepchildren: Susan, Nancy, Gordon, Sandra, Karen. Chmn. bd. Turbo Resources Ltd., 1970-83, Challenger Internat., 1977-83, Bankeno Mines Ltd., 1977-83, Queenston Gold Mines Ltd., Toronto, Ont., Can., 1977-84, Health Risk Mgmt. Inc., Mpls., 1984-86, Triad Internat. Inc., 1985—; dir. Health Resource Mgmt. Ltd., Edmonton, 1990-97. Bd. dirs. Vencap Equities Alta. Ltd., Edmonton, 1981-86, L.K. Resources Ltd., Calgary, 1973-84. Mem. Young. Pres.'s Orgn., Calgary, 1964-76, World Pres. Orgn. Recipient Presdl. pin Jr. Achievement, 1963, Best Pitcher award Petroleum Fastball League, 1955. Mem.: Calgary Petroleum, Ranchmen's. Office: Triad Internat Inc 3030 Sunridge Way NE Ste 21 Calgary AB Canada T1Y 7K4 E-mail: kentravis@telus.net.

TRAVISANO, THOMAS JOSEPH, English language educator; b. Livingston, N.J., Dec. 14, 1951; s. Frank Peter and Nancy (Drees) T.; m. Elsa Kathryn Thompson, May 23, 1981; children: Michael Coulliette, Emily Claire. BA, Haverford Coll., 1973; MA, U. Va., 1975, PhD, 1981. Asst. prof. English Coll. of William and Mary, 1980-82, Hartwick Coll., Oneonta, N.Y., 1982-86, assoc. prof. English, 1987-94, prof. English, 1994—, Cora A. Babcock prof. English, 1995-98. Lectr. The Am. Century, Oneonta, 1992—; dir. Am. Century Project N.Y., 1995-97; lectr. in field. Author: Elizabeth Bishop: Her Artistic Development, 1988—97, Midcentury Quartet: Bishop, Lowell, Jarrell, Berryman and the Making of a Postmodern Aesthetic, 1999; editor: Elizabeth Bishop Bull., 1991—97; co-editor: Gendered Modernisms: American Women Poets and Their Readers, 1996, The New Anthology of American Poetry: Vol. One, Beginnings to 1900, 2002; contbg. editor: Listener mag., 1995—; contbr. articles. NEH grantee 1983, 88, 94, Hartwick Coll. grantee 1983, 85, 87, 89, 92, 96-97, 2000-2001; Win Wandersee Scholar in Residence, 1999-2000; Dupont fellow, 1976-79; Hartwick Coll. faculty rsch. summer fellow, 1989. Mem. MLA, ALA, Elizabeth Bishop Soc. (mem. organizing com. 1991—, editor newsletter 1992—, pres. 1997—), MUG One: Macintosh Users Group of Oneonta (pres. 1991-94). Avocation: classical music. Home: 28 State St Oneonta NY 13820-1311 Office: Hartwick Coll 218 Clark Hall Oneonta NY 13820

TRAVOLTA, JOHN, actor; b. Englewood, N.J., Feb. 18, 1954; s. Salvatore and Helen (Burke) T.; m. Kelly Preston; children: Jett, Ella Bleu. Appeared in TV series Welcome Back Kotter, 1975-77; TV movies: The Boy in the Plastic Bubble, 1976; films: Carrie, 1976, Saturday Night Fever, 1977 (Best Actor award Nat. Bd. Rev., 1977, Best Actor Acad. award nominee 1977, Best Actor 1st runner up Nat. Soc. Film Critics 1977, Best Actor 2nd runner up N.Y. Film Critics Circle 1977), Grease, 1978 (Golden Globe World Film Favorite 1978), Moment-By-Moment, 1979, Urban Cowboy, 1980, Blow Out, 1981, Staying Alive, 1983 (Male/Box Office Star of Yr., Nat. Assn. Theatre Owners Show East 1983), Two of a Kind, 1983, Perfect, 1985, The Dumb Waiter, 1987, The Experts, 1989, Chains of Gold, 1980, Look Who's Talking, 1989 (Male/Box Office Star of Yr., Nat. Assn. Theatre Owners ShowEast 1989), Look Who's Talking Too, 1990, The Tender, 1991, Shout, 1991, Look Who's Talking Now, 1993, Pulp Fiction, 1994 (Best Actor Acad. award nominee 1994, Best Actor award nominee Brit. Acad. Film and TV Arts 1994, Golden Globe Best Actor award nominee 1994, Best Actor award nominee SAG 1994, Best Actor award nominee Chgo. Film Critics 1994, Best Actor award nominee Comedy awards 1994, Best Actor award L.A. Film Critics 1994, Best Actor award Stockholm Film Festival 1993, Best Actor award London Film Critics Cir. 1994), Get Shorty, 1995, White Man's Burden, 1995, Broken Arrow, 1995, Phenomenon, 1996, Michael, 1996, Face Off, 1997, Mad City, 1997, Primary Colors, 1998 (Golden Globe nominee), A Civil Action, 1998, General's Daughter, 1999, Battlefield Earth, 2000, Lucky Numbers, 2000, Swordfish, Domestic Disturbance; author: Staying Fit, 1984, Propeller One Way Night Coach; rec. artist album, 1976, 77. Recipient Best Male Vocalist Billboard award, 1976, Best Male Vocalist award Record World and Music Retail mag., 1976, Best Actor Golden Apple award Cue mag., Juno award Can. Acad. Rec. Arts and Scis., 1978, Golden Apple award 1998, Lifetime Achievement award British Acad. Film and TV Assn., 1998, Chgo. Internat. Film Festival, 1998, Palm Springs Internat. Film Festival, 1999, Alan J. Pakula award U.S. Broadcast Film Critics Assn., 1999,; nominated Best New Male Star Women's Press Club, 1976; named Man of Yr., Hasty Pudding Club, Harvard U., 1981.

TRAXLER, BUCK, newspaper editor; b. Missoula, Mont., Jan. 9, 1948; s. Jack Eugene and Dorothy (Shepherd) T.; m. Elizabeth Marie Traxler, Apr. 15, 1972 (div. 1984). Degree in photography, San Diego City Coll., 1974. Editor Phillips County News, Malta, Mont., 1985-86, Independent Observer, Conrad, 1986—. Mem. Conrad City Coun., 1998-00; ctrl. committeeman Rep. Party, Conrad, 1988—. With USN, 1966-72. Decorated Meritorious Unit commendation, Nat. Def. Svc. medal, Combat Action ribbon. Mem. Conrad C. of C. (pres. 1991, 93), Conrad Crimestoppers (sec. 1988-91), Pondera Golf Club (v.p., dir. 1990-93, sec. 1998—), Lions (sec. 1995—), Moose, VFW. Avocations: golf, hunting. Home: 616 S Delaware St Conrad MT 59425-2511 Office: Independent Observer PO Box 966 Conrad MT 59425-0966

TRAXLER, EVA MARIA, marketing administrator; b. Phorzheim, Germany, June 1, 1955; d. Wayne Delmar and Ruth Lydia (Mischak) Frasure; m. Richard John Traxler, Mar. 25, 1986. BS, U. Minn., 1980; MBA, U. St. Thomas, 1987. Ops. control planner Gen. Mills, Mpls., 1981; asst. prodn. planner Pillsbury, 1982-87, planning specialist, 1987-88; new products planner Land O'Lakes, 1988-89, mktg. asst., 1989-90; sr. product mgr., mgr. mdse. svcs. Anchor Hocking Plastics, St. Paul, 1990-94; mktg. mgr. Jostens, Mpls., 1995-96; brand mgr. Metacom, 1996-98; mgr. sml. bus. mktg. Am. Express, 1998—, advice mgr., 2001—. Big sister Big Bros./Big Sisters, St. Paul, 1982-89, bd. mem., 1986-92, Courage Ctr., 1998—. Avocations: fitness, travel, old house renovation. E-mail: evatraxler@hotmail.com.

TRAXLER, WILLIAM BYRD, JR. federal judge; b. Greenville, S.C., May 1, 1948; s. William Byrd and Bettie (Wooten) Traxler; m. Patricia Alford, Aug. 21, 1972; children: William Byrd III, James McCall. BA, Davidson Coll., 1970; JD, U. S.C., 1973. Assoc. William Byrd Traxler, Greenville, 1973—75; asst. solicitor 13th Jud. Ct., 1975—78, dep. solicitor, 1978—81, solicitor, 1981—85, resident cir. judge, 1985—92; U.S. Dist. judge Dist. of S.C., 1992—98; judge U.S. Ct. of Appeals (4th cir.), 1998—. Recipient Outstanding Svc. award, Solicitors Assn., S.C., 1987, Leadership award, Probation, Parole & Pardon Svcs., S.C., 1990. Office: PO Box 10127 Greenville SC 29603-0127

TRAYLOR, ANGELIKA, stained glass artist; b. Munich, Germany, Aug. 24, 1942; Came to U.S., 1959; d. Walther Artur Ferdinand and Berta Kreszentia (Boeck) Klau; m. Lindsay Montgomery Donaldson, June 10, 1959 (div. 1970); 1 child, Cameron Maria Greta; m. Samuel William Traylor III, June 12, 1970. Student, Pvt. Handelsschule Morawetz Jr. Coll., Munich, 1958. Freelance artist, 1980—. Works featured in profl. jours. including the Daylily Jour., 1987, Design Jour., South Korea, 1989, The Traveler's Guide to American Crafts, 1990, Florida Mag., 1991, Florida Today, 1993, Adventures in Art, vol. 3, 1993, Melbourne Times, 1994, The Orbiter, 1996, The Glass Collector's Digest, 1996, (TV appearances) Focus on History, 1993, Focus, 1998, Space Coast Press, 1999, Weekend Decorating Projects - Women's Day, 1999, Pen Women, 1999, Stained Glass for the First Time, 2000; represented in permanent collections White House Christmas Ornament Collection, 1993, 97, Holmes Regional Med. Ctr., Melbourne, Fla., other pvt. and corp. collections. Recipient Fragile Art award Glass Art mag., 1982, 1st Yr. Exhibitor award Stained Glass Assn. Am., 1984, 2d pl. Non-figurative Composition award Vitraux des USA, 1985, Best of Show Stained Glass Assn. Am., 1989, 3d pl., 1989, Merit award George Plimpton All-Star Space Coast Art Open, 1994; named Hist. Woman of Brevard, Brevard Cultural Alliance, 1991, one of 200 Best Am. Craftsmen Early Am. Life mag., 1994, 95, 97, 98, 2000. Home and Office: 100 Poinciana Dr Indian Harbor Beach FL 32937-4437

TRAYLOR, CHET D. state supreme court justice; b. Columbia, La., Oct. 12, 1945; s. John Hardy and Bernice (Bogan) T.; children: Mary Therese, Leigh Ann, Anna Marie. BA in Govt., N.E. La. State U., 1969; JD, Loyola U., 1974. Bar: La. Judge 5th Jud. Dist. Ct., Franklin, Richland and West Carroll Parishes, La., 1985-97; assoc. justice La. Supreme Ct., 1997—. Past legal advisor La. State Police; past investigator La. Dept. Justice; asst. dist. atty., Franklin Parish, 1975-76. Founding bd. mem. Winnsboro Econ. Devel. Found.; mem. Rocky Mountain Conservation Fund. With U.S. Army. Mem. ABA, La. Bar Assn., La. Dist. Judges Assn., NRA (life), Franklin Parish Mental Health Assn. (past bd. dirs.), Winnsboro Lions Club (past bd. dirs.), Greenwings (founder John Adams chpt.). Methodist. Office: Supreme Ct 301 Loyola Ave New Orleans LA 70112-1814*

TRAYLOR, DONALD REGINALD, mathematics educator; b. Shreveport, La., Aug. 14, 1937; s. Guy Kirby and Eva (Hunt) T.; m. Jacqueline Rose Pearson, June 4, 1959; children: Chapman Parker, Kirby Russell, Pearson Hunt. BA, U. Tex., 1959; MS, Auburn U., 1960, PhD, 1962. Asst. prof. Auburn (Ala.) U., 1962-63, U. Houston, 1963-66, assoc. prof., 1966-71, pres., prof., 1972-77; fellow Am. Coun. on Edn., Washington, 1971-72; pres. Traylor Products & Svcs., San Antonio, 1977-90; prof. math. U. of the Incarnate Word, 1990—, interim v.p. acad. affairs, 1993-95, acting dean Sch. Math., Nursing and Sci., 1995-96, dean Sch. Grad. Studies and Rsch., 1996—, v.p. for extended acad. programs, 1999—. Mem. adv. coun. Auburn U., 1966-96, St. Mary's U., San Antonio, 1978-85. Author: Advanced Calculus, 1970, Creative Teaching: Heritage of R.L. moore, 1972; editor: Proceedings of Topology Conference, 1968; inventor tactile drawing and writing device. Grantee NASA, 1964, NSF, 1965-67, NIH, 1985-89, NSF and Eisenhower, 1992—. Office: U of the Incarnate Word 4301 Broadway St San Antonio TX 78209-6318 E-mail: traylor@universe.uiwtx.edu.

TRAYLOR, ORBA FOREST, economist, lawyer, educator; b. Providence, June 16, 1910; s. Eddie Ewing and Dillie (Stuart) T.; m. Josephine Zananiri, Nov. 17, 1945; children— Joseph Marion, Robert Forest, John Christopher. BA, Western Ky. U., 1930; MA, U. Ky., 1932, PhD, 1948; JD, Northwestern U., 1936. Bar: Ky. 1941. Head dept. econs. Ashland Coll., 1935-36; legal asst. trust dept. 1st Nat. Bank, Chgo., 1936-37; assoc. prof. econs., sociology Western Ky. U., 1938-40; research asst. Bur. Bus. Research, U. Ky., 1939; research dir. Ky. Legislative Council, 1939-41; dir. research and statistics Ky. Dept. Welfare, 1941; assoc. econ. analyst div. tax research U.S. Treasury Dept., 1942; acting chief acctg. UNRRA, Balkan Mission, 1944-45; asst. prof. econs. and bus. U. Denver, 1946-47, U. Mo., 1947-50; tax specialist, asst. econ. commr. ECA, Greece, 1950-53; coordinator exec. devel. programs Ordnance Corps, Dept. Army, 1954; pub. fin. expert UN; lectr. fin. adminstrn. Inst. Pub. Adminstrn., Egypt, 1954-56; exec. asst. to lt. gov. Ky. Legislative Research Commn., Frankfort, 1956-58; commr. fin. State of Ky., 1958-59; dir. finance Office High Commr., Ryukyu Islands, 1960-64, dir. econ. affairs, 1964-65; prof. econs. and pub. adminstrn. U. Ala., Huntsville, 1965-75, chmn. dept. bus. and pub. adminstrn., 1966-68, chmn. econs., 1968-70; vis. prof. pub. adminstrn. San Diego State U., 1975-76, Western Ky. U., 1976-77; fin. economist AID, U.S. State Dept., 1977-78; adj. prof. Ala. A&M U., 1978-81, N.Y. U. and Rider Coll., 1981-82, Columbia Coll., 1982—; cons. economist Am. Tech. Services, Inc., 1982-91. Cons. ops. research Johns Hopkins U., 1957-61; fiscal cons. various orgns.; vis. lectr. econs. various univs. and colls.; lectr. U. Md. Far East Div., 1960-65, Ala. A&M U., 1976-77, Fla. Inst. Tech., 1977; sr. adv. Bank of Ryukyus, 1960-65, Joint Fgn. Investment Bd., 1964-65; chmn. bd. Ryukyuan Devel. Loan Corp., 1960-65, Joint Petroleum Bd., 1960-65; counsellor Oak Ridge Asso. Univs., 1966-67 Mem. editorial bd.: Public Adminstrn. Rev, 1973-79; contbr. articles to profl. publs. Mem. Ala. Edn. Study Commn. Fin. Task Force, 1968-69; chmn. fin. com. Top of Ala. Health Planning Agy., 1974-75; mem. adv. com. Ala. Legislature, 1981-94. With AUS, 1942-46; lt. col. Res. (ret.). Mem. Am., So. econs. assns., Am. Soc. for Pub. Adminstrn. (council 1973-75), Am., Ky. bar assns., Nat. Tax Assn. (dir. 1971-74), local C. of C., Res. Officers Assn., Mil. Order World Wars, Beta Gamma Sigma, Delta Sigma Pi. Clubs: Rotary. Democrat. Baptist. Address: 216 Westmoreland Ave SE Huntsville AL 35801-2726

TRAYLOR, ROBERT ARTHUR, lawyer; b. Syracuse, N.Y., Jan. 15, 1949; s. Robert Arthur and Julia Elizabeth (McNulty) T.; m. Bonita Lynn Schmidt, Nov. 26, 1977. BS, LeMoyne Coll., 1970; JD cum laude, Syracuse U., 1975. Bar: N.Y., U.S. Dist. Ct. (no. dist.) N.Y., U.S. Tax Ct. Assoc. Love, Balducci & Scaccia, Syracuse, N.Y., 1976-77; estate tax atty. IRS, 1977-81; assoc. Scaccia Law Firm, 1981—. Contbr. articles to profl. jours. Of counsel St. Ann Sch., Syracuse, 1981—, mem. coordinating com. Vision 2000 1994—, mem. bd., 1998—. With U.S. Army, 1970-72. Mem. ABA, Onondaga County Bar Assn. (vol. lawyer program 1993—, Vol. Lawyer of Month 1994), World

Wildlife Fedn. Republican. Roman Catholic. Avocations: motorsports, military history, Catholic education. Home: 112 Knowland Dr Liverpool NY 13090-3130 Office: Scaccia Law Firm State Tower Bldg Ste 402 Syracuse NY 13202-1798

TRAYLOR, WILLIAM ROBERT, publisher; b. Texarkana, Ark., May 21, 1921; s. Clarence Edington and Seba Ann (Talley) T.; m. Elvirez Sigler, Oct. 9, 1945; children: Kenneth Warren, Gary Robert, Mark Daniel, Timothy Ryan. Student, U. Houston, 1945-46, U. Omaha, 1947-48. Div. mgr. Lily-Tulip Cup Corp., N.Y.C., 1948-61; asst. to pres. Johnson & Johnson, New Brunswick, N.J., 1961-63; mgr. western region Rexall Drug & Chem. subs. Dart Industries, L.A., 1963-67; pres. Prudential Pub. Co., Diamonds Springs, Calif., 1967—. Cons. to printing industry, 1976-98; syndicated writer (under pseudonym)s. Bill Friday's Bus. Bull., 1989—. Author: Instant Printing, 1976 (transl. into Japanese), Successful Management, 1979, Quick Printing Encyclopedia, 1982, 8th edit., 1998, How to Sell Your Product Through (Not to) Wholesalers, 1980; pubr. Professional Estimator and Management Software for Printing Industry, 1997, Small Press Printing Encyclopedia, 1994. With USCG, 1942-45. Named Man of Yr. Quick Printing Mag., 1987. Mem. Nat. Assn. Quick Printers (hon. lifetime), C. of C., Kiwanis, Toastmasters. Democrat. Avocations: snow skiing, boating.

TRAYNELIS, STEPHEN FRANCIS, neuroscientist, educator; b. South Bend, Ind., Mar. 3, 1962; s. Vincent John and Elaine Anne T.; m. Janice Faye Jernigan, Nov. 26, 1988; children: Joshua Laine, Ruth Anne, James Vincent, John Francis. BS in Chemistry summa cum laude, W.Va. U., 1984; PhD in Pharmacology, U. N.C., 1988. Rschr. dept. pharmacology U. Coll. London, 1989-91; rschr. molecular neurobiology lab. Salk Inst., La Jolla, Calif., 1992-94; asst. prof. dept. pharmacology Emory U., Atlanta, 1994-2000, assoc. prof., 2000—. Grant rev. bds., ad hoc grant revs. including Civilian Rsch. and Def. Found., NIH, 1996—97, 2001—02, pvt. and English granting agys., 1996; lectr. seminars SFB Kolloquium, Goettingen, 1995, Ciba-Geigy, Basel, Switzerland, 1995, SIBIA, Inc., La Jolla, 1995, Rush U., Chgo., 1995, NIH, 1996, NYU, 1996, U. Minn., 1997, Cornell U., 1999, Yale U., 1999, CNRS , Caen, France, 2000, Montpelier, France, 00, L'Ecole Normale Supieure, France, 2000, Albert Einstein U., 2002, U. Fla., others. Mem. editl. bd. Molecular Pharmacology, 1996-99; contbr. articles to profl. jours.; developer Modified Diffusional analysis softwared, 1988, Synaptic Analysis Software, 1991-94, Ion Channel Kinetic Modeling Software, 1996—, Synaptic/single channel modelling-Analysis Software, 1996—, Channelab Software. Recipient Nat. Rsch. Svc. award NIH, 1989, 90, 92; predoctoral fellow NSF, 1984, fellow Am. Epilepsy Soc., 1993, John Merck Fund, 1995-99, Emory U. Tchg. Fund, 1997; John Merck scholar, 1995, John Moore chemistry scholar, 1980, W.Va. achievement scholar, 1980-84; grantee Epilepsy Found. Am., 1995, NIH-NINDS, 1995, 96, 98, 2000, 02, Emory U. Rsch. Com., 1995, 98, 2002, travel grantee Wellcome Trust, Brain Trust Am. Epilepsy Soc., 1990-94, Burroughs-Wellcome, 1998, Ind. Investigators grantee Nat. Alliance for Rsch. in Schizophrenia and Depression. Mem. AAAS, Am. Soc. Pharmacology and Exptl. Therapeutics, Biophys. Soc., Soc. Neurosci. (councilor exec. com. Atlanta chpt. 1995-96, pres. Atlanta chpt. 1997), ASPET, Phi Beta Kappa, Phi Kappa Phi, Golden Key. Office: Emory U Dept Pharmacology 1510 Clifton Rd NE Atlanta GA 30322-4218 E-mail: strayne@emory.edu.

TRAYNHAM, JAMES GIBSON, chemist, educator; b. Broxton, Ga., Aug. 5, 1925; s. James G. and Eddie Louise (Greer) T.; m. Margaret A. Egert, 1948; children: David F., Peter C.; m. Gresdna A. Doty, 1980. Student, South Ga. Coll., 1942-43; BS, U. N.C., 1946; PhD, Northwestern U., 1950. Instr. Northwestern U., 1949-50; asst. prof. Denison U., 1950-53; mem. faculty La. State U., Baton Rouge, 1953—, prof. chemistry, 1963-88, prof. emeritus, 1988—, chmn. dept. chemistry, 1968-73, vice chancellor for advanced studies and rsch., dean Grad. Sch., 1973-81. Postdoctoral research fellow Ohio State U., 1951-53; oral history cons. Chem. Heritage Found., 1997—. Author: Organic Nomenclature: A Programmed Introduction, 1966, 5th edit., 1997; editor: Essays on the History of Organic Chemistry, 1987; contbr. articles to profl. jours. Bd. dirs. Council Grad. Schs. in U.S., 1981. Recipient Petroleum Research Fund-Am. Chem. Soc. Type D award Eidg. Technische Hochschule, Zurich, Switzerland, 1959-60; Charles E. Coates award Baton Rouge sects. Am. Chem. Soc. and Am. Inst. Chem. Engrs., 1965; NATO sr. fellow in sci. Universität des Saarlandes, Saarbrücken, Fed. Republic Germany, 1972 Mem. Am. Chem. Soc. (councilor, past chmn. Baton Rouge sect., chmn. divsn. history of chemistry 1988), La. Acad. Sci., Internat. Union Pure and Applied Chemistry (former titular mem. commn. on nomenclature of organic chemistry, sec. 1994-99), Phi Beta Kappa, Sigma Xi, Phi Lambda Upsilon, Phi Kappa Phi (past pres. La. State U. chpt.). Home: 122 Highland Trace Dr Baton Rouge LA 70810-5061 Fax: 225-769-2162. E-mail: jimtraynham@msn.com.

TRAYNOR, DANIEL M. state representative; Postgrad in law, U.N.D., 1997. Lic.: N.D. (Law). Elected state chmn. N.D. Rep. party, 2001—; law clerk N.D. Supreme Court. District 15 chmn.; vol. Political Campaigns, 1988; dir. N.D. Rep. Party Election, 1992; mem., delegate rules com. Rep. Nat. Convention, Phila., 2000. Republican. Office: PO Box 1917 Bismarck ND 58502-1917*

TRAYNOR, GARY EDWARD, association administrator; b. Ponca City, Okla., Aug. 7, 1944; s. Paul Edward and Berniece Dolores (Hanon) T. Diploma, Ponca City Bus. Coll., 1963. Acctg. supr. Army Air Force Exch. Svc., Norton AFB, Calif., 1966-94; charities chmn. Fraternal Order Eagles, 1995-2000, sec. San Bernardino (Calif.) Aerie 506, 1996—. Mem. Am. Philatelic Soc., Smithsonian Instn. (assoc.). Republican. Baptist. Avocations: stamp collecting, computers, decorating. Home: 7706 Golondrina Dr San Bernardino CA 92410-4623 Office: San Bernardino Aerie 506 Fraternal Order Eagles 895 E 9th St San Bernardino CA 92410-4011

TRAYNOR, JOHN MICHAEL, lawyer; b. Oakland, Calif., Oct. 25, 1934; s. Roger J. and Madeleine (Lackmann) Traynor; m. Shirley Williams, Feb. 11, 1956; children: Kathleen Traynor Millard, Elizabeth Traynor Fowler, Thomas. BA, U. Calif., Berkeley, 1955; JD, Harvard U., 1960. Bar: Calif. 1961, U.S. Supreme Ct. 1966. Dep. atty. gen. State of Calif., San Francisco, 1961-63; spl. counsel Calif. Senate Com. on Local Govt., Sacramento, 1963; assoc. firm Cooley Godward, LLP, San Francisco, 1963-69, ptnr., 1969—. Adviser 3d Restatement of Unfair Competition, 1988—95, 3d Restatement of Torts, Products Liability, 1992—97, Apportionment, 1994—99, 2d Restatement of Conflict of Laws revs., 1988, 3d Restatement of Restitution and Unjust Enrichment, 1997—; lectr. Boalt Hall Sch. Law U. Calif., Berkeley, 1982—89, 1996—98; chmn. EarthJustice Legal Def. Fund (formerly Sierra Club Legal Def. Fund), 1989—91, pres., 1991—92, trustee, 1974—96. Mem. bd. overseers Inst. for Civil Justice The RAND Corp., 1991—97; bd. dirs. Environ. Law Inst., 1991—97, 2000—; Sierra Legal Def. Fund. Canada, 1990—96. 1st lt. USMC, 1955—57. Fellow: Am. Bar Found. (life), Am. Acad. Arts and Scis.; mem.: Bar Assn. San Francisco (pres. 1973), Am. Law Inst. (coun. 1985—, pres. 2000—). Home: 3131 Eton Ave Berkeley CA 94705-2713 Office: Cooley Godward LLP 1 Maritime Plz Ste 2000 San Francisco CA 94111-3580 E-mail: mtraynor@cooley.com.

TREACY, GERALD BERNARD, JR. lawyer; b. Newark, July 29, 1951; s. Gerald B. Sr. and Mabel L. (Nesbitt) T.; m. Joyce M. Biazzo, Apr. 6, 1974. BA summa cum laude, Rider Coll., 1973; JD, UCLA, 1981. Bar: Calif. 1981, Wash. 1982, D.C. 1995. Tchr. English Arthur L. Johnson Regional High Sch., Clark, N.J., 1973-77; assoc. Gibson, Dunn & Crutcher, L.A., 1981-82; ptnr. Perkins Coie, Bellevue, Wash., 1982-94, McGuire Woods Battle & Boothe, McLean, Va. and Bellevue, Va., 1994-96, Egger, Betts, Austin, Treacy, Bellevue, Wash., 1996-98; mem. Treacy Law Group, 1998—; of counsel Montgomery Purdue Blankenship and Austin, Seattle, 2000—. Chmn. bd. dirs. estate planning adv. bd. U. Wash., Seattle, 1990-92; presenter TV Seminar, Where There's a Will, PBS affiliate. Author: Washington Guardianship Law, Administration and Litigation, 1988, supplemented, 1991, 3d edit. supplemented, 2002, Supporting Organizations, 1996, 2d edit., 2002. Mem. endowment fund com. United Way, Seattle, 1987-89, exec. com. Washington Planned Giving Coun., 1993-94, 96-98; bd. dirs., mem. adv. bd. ARC, Seattle, 1985-89, Arthritis Gift, 1987-89, Seattle Symphony, 1992, Seattle U., 1996. Mem. Eastside King County Estate Planning Coun., Order of Coif. Avocations: photography, hiking, ethnic and classical music, poetry, host/writer Gilbert & Sullivan radio show. Office: PO Box 712 Keyport WA 98345 E-mail: gbtreacy@aol.com.

TREACY, SANDRA JOANNE PRATT, art educator, artist; b. New Haven, Aug. 5, 1934; d. Willis Hadley Jr. and Gladys May (Gell) P.; m. Gillette van Nuyse, Aug. 27, 1955; 1 child, Jonathan Todd. BFA, R.I. Sch. Design, 1956; student, William Paterson Coll., 1973-74. Cert. elem. and secondary tchr., N.J. Tchr. art and music Pkwy. Christian Ch., Ft. Lauderdale, Fla., 1964-66; developer Pequannock Twp. Bd. of Edn., Pompton Plains, N.J., 1970-72, tchr. art, 1972-76; vol. art tchr. Person County Bd. of Edn., Roxboro, N.C., 1978-80, tchr. art, 1980-91, So. Jr. High Sch., Roxboro, 1989-91, Woodland Elem. Sch., Roxboro, 1989-93; tchr. Helena Elem. Sch., Timberlake, N.C., 1991-93. Tchr. elem. art Bethel Hill Sch., Roxboro, 1974-79, vol. art tchr., 1979-80; tchr. basic art, vol. all elem. schs. Person County, Roxboro, 1977-80; tchr. arts and crafts, summers 1981-882; tchr. art home sch. So. Mid. Sch., 1993—, Person H.S., 1993-94. Artist, illustrator. Mem. Roxboro EMTs, 1979-81; bd. dirs. Person County Arts Coun., 1980--81, 93-95, pres., 1981-82; piano and organ choir accompanist Concord United Meth. Ch., 1981—; leader Morgan Trotters, 1992-94, asst. dir., 1993-96, bd. dirs.; coach, horseback riding for handicapped. Mem. NEA, Nat. Mus. of Women in the Arts (continuing charter), Smithsonian Assocs., N.C. Assn. Arts Edn., N.C. Assn. Educators, N.C. Art Soc. Mus. of Art, Internat. Platform Assn., Womans Club (tchr. Pompton Plains chpt. 1974-79), Person County Saddle Club (rec. sec. 1981-84), Puddingston Pony Club (dist. sec. 1974-75), Roxboro Garden Club (continuing, commr. 1980-82, pres. 1982-84, 87—, sec. 1993-94, 97-98, v.p. 1993-95, pres. 1995—), Roxboro Woman's Club (arts dept.). Republican. Avocations: horseback riding, swimming, sailing, reading, playing piano and organ. Home: 1345 Kelly Brewer Rd Leasburg NC 27291-9622

TREACY, VINCENT EDWARD, lawyer; b. Mass., Jan. 30, 1942; AB, Boston Coll., 1964; JD with honors, George Washington U., 1971. Bar: Va. 1972, D.C. 1973, Md. 1999; U.S. Supreme Ct. 1976. Atty. Fed. Labor Rels. Coun., Washington, 1971-73; legis. atty. Am. law divsn. Congrl. Rsch. Svc., Libr. Congress, 1973-98; sole practitioner, 1998—. Legis. cons. Romanian Legal Analysis and Legis. Drafting Conf., Senate and Chamber Duputies Romania, Bucharest, 1996. Mem. law rev. staff George Washington Law Rev., 1970. Mem. ABA, George Washington Law Alumni Assn. (pres. Capitol Hill chpt. 1986-87), Order of Coif.

TREACY, WILLIAM JOSEPH, electrical and environmental engineer; b. N.Y.C., Jan. 16, 1959; s. William Joseph and Angela Bridget (Keane) T.; 1 child, Denise Marie. BSEE, Manhattan Coll., 1981; M in Aero. Sci., Embry-Riddle U., 1987. Registered profl. engr., N.Y. Commd. 2d lt. USAF, 1981, advanced through grades to capt., project mgr. Calif., 1981-84, dept. chief Netherlands GLCM program office Ramstein, Germany, 1984-88, chief engr. Soesterberg, The Netherlands, 1988-91, heavy repair supt. Plattsburgh, 1991-92, CFO N.Y., 1992-94, chief environ. engr., 1994-95; bldg. systems supr. Plattsburgh Airbase Redevel. Corp., 1995—. Computer technician, Plattsburgh, 1992—. Active Red Cross, Plattsburgh, 1992. Decorated Meritorious Svc. medal, Air Force Commendation medal with one oak leaf cluster, others; USAF ROTC Program Acad. scholar, 1978. Mem. IEEE, ASHRAE, NSPE, Nat. Fire Protection Assn., Internat. Assn. Elec. Insps., Assn. for Facilities Engring., Aircraft Owners and Pilots Assn., Friends of Ft. Ticonderoga, Am. Legion. Republican. Roman Catholic. Avocations: flying, star trek memorabilia, cross-country skiing. Home: 60 Leonard Ave Plattsburgh NY 12901-2565 Office: Plattsburgh Airbase Redevel Corp 426 Us Oval Ste 1000 Plattsburgh NY 12903-3976 E-mail: billt@parc-usa.com.

TREADWAY, JAMES CURRAN ERIK CORBETT, lawyer, investment company executive, former government official; b. Anderson, S.C., May 21, 1943; s. James C. and Maxine (Hall) T.; m. Susan Pepper Davis, Sept. 6, 1969; children: Elizabeth Pepper Hall, Caroline Worrell Harper Corbett. AB summa cum laude, Rollins Coll., 1964; JD summa cum laude, Washington and Lee U., 1967. Bar: Ga. 1967, Mass. 1968, D.C. 1970. Assoc. Candler, Cox, McClain & Andrews, Atlanta, 1967-68, Gadsby & Hannah, Boston and Washington, 1968-72; ptnr. Dickstein, Shapiro & Morin, Washington, 1972-82; commr. SEC, 1982-85; ptnr. Baker & Botts, 1985-87; exec. v.p., chmn. merchant banking dept., exec. com. Paine Webber Group Inc., N.Y.C., 1987—. Chmn. Nat. Commn. on Fraudulent Fin. Reporting, 1985—87; chmn. bds. dirs. Washington & Lee U. Sch. Law, 1992—94; dir. U. So. Calif., Sch. of Acctg. and Fin. Disclosure, 1985—93; mem. planning com. Garret Securities Law Inst., Northwestern U., 1985—92; spl. expert adviser, witness various U.S. congl. coms.; lectr. and author in field. Editor-in-chief Wash. & Lee U. Law review, 1966-67. Recipient Wildman Medal Am. Acctg. Assn., 1989. Mem. Mass. Bar Assn., Ga. Bar Assn., D.C. Bar Assn., Chevy Chase (Md.) Club, Bedford (N.Y.) Golf and Tennis Club, City Tavern Club, Met. Club, Univ. Club (Washington), Verbank Hunting and Fishing Club (Uniondale N.Y.; dir. 1995—), Order of Coif, Phi Beta Kappa, Omicron Delta Kappa. Home: Laurel Ledge Farm RD 4 Croton Lake Rd Bedford Corners NY 10549-4227 Office: PaineWebber Group Inc 1285 Ave of Americas New York NY 10019-6028

TREADWAY, SANDRA GIOIA, library director; b. Jersey City, Jan. 15, 1950; d. Robert Peter and Essey Grace (Graham) Gioia; m. John David Treadway, Sept. 4, 1976; 1 child, Robyn Grace. BA in History, Manhattanville Coll., 1971; MA in History, U. Va., 1972, PhD in History, 1978. Instr. history Va. Polytech Inst. & State U., Blacksburg, 1976-78; editor Va. State Libr., Richmond, 1978-91, dir. pubs., 1991-96; deputy dir. Libr. Va., 1996—. Author: Women of Mark, 1995; co-author: The Common Wealth: Treasures from the Collections of the Library of Virginia, 1997; co-editor: Dictionary of Virginia Biography, vol. 1, 1999, vol. 2, 2001. Mdm. bd. St. Mary Sch., Richmond, 1988-96. Mem. Am. Hist. Assn., Orgn. Am. historians, So. Historical Assn., So. Assn. Women Historians (pres. 2002), Va. Hist. Soc., Va. Libr. Assn., Serra Internat. (bd. dirs. 1985—). Roman Catholic. Avocations: reading, travel. Home: 8201 Gaylord Rd Richmond VA 23229-4121 Office: Libr LVa 800 E Broad St Richmond VA 23219-1905

TREADWAY, SUSAN MARIE, technical writer; b. West Palm Beach, Fla., June 14, 1951; d. Karl Paul and Margaret Elizabeth (Ross) Casseur; m. Oscar Gaines Owen, June 7, 1969 (div. 1979); 1 child, Angela (dec.); m. Ronald Jay Treadway, Nov. 22, 1980 (div. 1989); children: Cassandra Erin, Kimberly Dawn. Student, Craven Community Coll., Havelock, N.C., 1981, Mid. Ga. Tech. Inst., Warner Robins, 1987-89. NDI radiographer Space Sci. Services, Inc., Riviera Beach, Fla., 1968-69; with Hayes Internat. Corp., Napier Field, Ala., 1970-71; oper. room technician Flowers Hosp., Dothan, 1971-75; inventory programmer Barr Co., Niles, Ill., 1985-86; tech. writer Jana, Inc., Warner Robins, Ga., 1987-89; prodn. assoc. McDonnell Douglas, 1989; tech. writer HEBCO, Inc., Macon, Ga., 1989-94, C Sys., Inc., Dayton, Ohio, 1994-95; tech. data mgr. Advanced Testing Technologies, Inc., Robins AFB, Ga., 1995-99; data analyst IIT Rsch. Inst., Rome, 1999—. Author: Reflections of Feelings, 1980, poems. Family services asst. coord. USAF, 1987. Sgt. USMC,1978-83. Mem. NAFE, Internat. Platform Assn., Assn. Old Crows. Clubs: Mensa. Presbyterian. Avocations: gardening, drafting, architecture. Home: 111 Hillside Dr Oriskany NY 13424-4707 Office: IIT Rsch Inst 201 Mill St Rome NY 13440-6916 E-mail: streadway@iitri.org.

TREADWAY-DILLMON, LINDA LEE, athletic trainer, actress, stuntwoman; b. Woodbury, N.J., June 4, 1950; d. Leo Elmer and Ona Lee (Wyckoff) Treadway; m. Randall Kenneth Dillmon, June 19, 1982. BS in Health, Phys. Edn. & Recreation, West Chester State Coll., 1972, MS in Health and Phys. Edn., 1975; postgrad., Ctrl. Mich. U., 1978; Police Officer Stds. Tng. cert. complaint dispatcher, Goldenwest Coll., 1982. Cert. in safety edn. West Chester State Coll.; cert. EMT, Am. Acad. Orthopaedic Surgeons. Grad. asst., instr., asst. athletic trainer West Chester (Pa.) State Coll., 1972-76; asst. prof., program dir., asst. athletic trainer Ctrl. Mich. U., Mt. Pleasant, 1976-80; police dispatcher City of Westminster, Calif., 1980-89; oncology unit sec. Children's Hosp. Orange County, Orange, 1989-96; control clk. food & beverage Marriott Hotel, Anaheim, 1996—. Stuntwoman, actress United Stunt Artists, SAG, L.A., 1982—; dancer Disneyland, Anaheim, Calif., 1988—; contbr. articles to profl. jours. Athletic trainer U.S. Olympic Women's Track and Field Trials, Frederick, Md., 1972, AAU Jr. World Wrestling Championships, Mt. Pleasant, Mich., 1977, Mich. Spl. Olympics, Mt. Pleasant, 1977, 78, 79. Recipient bronze and gold Spirit of Disneyland Resort awards, 1997; named Outstanding Phys. Educator, Delta Psi Kappa, Ctrl. Mich. U., 1980, Outstanding Young Woman of Am., 1984; named to Disneyland Entertainment Hall of Fame, 1995. Mem. SAG, Nat. Athletic Trainers Assn. (cert., women and athletic tng. ad hoc com. 1974-75, placement com. 1974-79, program dirs. coun. 1976-80, ethics com. 1977-80, visitation team 1978-80, 25 Yr. award 1997), U.S. Field Hockey Assn. (player), Pacific S.W. Field Hockey Assn. (player, Nat. Champion 1980, 81, 82), L.A. Field Hockey Assn. (player), Swing Shift Dance Team (dancer). Presbyterian. Avocations: flying, piano, athletics, stitchery, travel. Home: 18073 Scanlan Ct Fountain Valley CA 92708-5865

TREADWELL, ALEXANDER F. former state official, political party chairman & leader; b. London, Mar. 25, 1946; m. Libby, 1970; children: Carrie, Zach. BA, U. N.C. Former chmn. Essex Cty. Rep. Committee; vice chmn. NY St. Rep. Party, 1989; sec. of state State of N.Y., 1995—2001; chmn. Rep. State Com., 2001—. Reporter & freelance journalist, Sports Illustrated, writer, Classic Magazine, NY Magazine. Author: The World of Marathons, Stewart, Tabori & Chang, 1987. NY Army Natl. Guard, 1968-74. Office: New York Republican State Committee 315 State Street Albany NY 12210*

TREADWELL, HUGH WILSON, publishing executive; b. Waurika, Okla., Nov. 21, 1921; s. Hugh and Jessie Ellen (Cogdell) T.; m. Edith Albena Doolittle, June 20, 1959; children— Pamela, Hugh, Cynthia. BA, U. Okla., 1949, MA, 1952; diploma in French Studies (Rotary Found. fellow), Institut de Touraine, U. Poitiers, France, 1950. Asst. editor internat. lit. quar. Books Abroad, U. Okla., 1952-53; field rep. coll. dept. The Macmillan Co., 1953-60, Holt, Rinehart & Winston, Inc., Okla. and Tex., 1960-62, mgr. coll. programs in fgn. lang. dept., 1962-67; sr. editor coll. dept. Random House-Knopf, 1967-72; dir. U. N.Mex. Press, Albuquerque, 1973-80, Tex. Western Press, U. Tex., El Paso, 1981-85; pvt. practice cons., 1985—; field rep. coll. dept. W.W. Norton & Co., Tex., N.Mex., Okla., 1988-93; instr. ESL El Paso C.C., 1994—. Instr. French U. Okla., 1952-53; Industry rep. Nat. Com. Support of Fgn. Langs., 1971, freelance translator (French-English), 1996—. Pres. El Paso Coun. for Internat. Visitors, 1987-88. With USAAF, 1943-46. Decorated Air medal. Mem. Phi Beta Kappa. Clubs: Alliance Francaise (El Paso). Democrat. Home: 6832 La Cadena Dr El Paso TX 79912-2810 *In my mind, the pursuit of happiness has always been bound up with the pursuit of knowledge—knowledge not in a purely abstract sense, but purposeful knowledge humanely applied. The professions of teaching and publishing, if practiced in the light of the highest ethical standards associated with each, make this pursuit possible and offer the greatest satisfaction to those who view life as I do. I consider myself fortunate to have served in both of these professions.*

TREADWELL, MARJORIE CLARKE, medical educator; b. Detroit, Aug. 26, 1956; d. Donald Hugh and Marjorie Helen (Lee) T. BS, U. Mich., 1978, MD, 1984; MS, Wayne State U., 1980. Diplomate Nat. Bd. Med. Examiners; diplomate in ob-gyn. and in maternal-fetal medicine Am. Bd. Ob-Gyn. Clin. instr. dept. ob-gyn. Wayne State U., Detroit, 1988-90, asst. prof., 1990-97, assoc. prof., 1997—. Dir. obstetric ultrasound dept. ob-gyn. Hutzel Hosp., Detroit, 1991-93, dir. quality assurance, 1995—; dir. obstetric ultrasound Detroit Med. Ctr., 1993—. Contbr. articles to profl. jours., chpts. to books. Named one of Best Drs. in Midwest Woodward/White, Inc., 1996-97. Fellow: Am. Coll. Ob-Gyn.; mem.: Soc. Maternal-Fetal Medicine, Soc. Perinatal Obstetricians, Am. Inst. Ultrasound in Medicine, AMA. Office: Dept Ob-Gyn 4707 Saint Antoine St Detroit MI 48201-1427 E-mail: mtread@med.wayne.edu.

TREANOR, BETTY MCKEE, interior design educator; b. Tooele, Utah, Oct. 2, 1938; d. Oscar Hart and Mable Genevieve (Smith) McK.; m. James Treanor, Dec. 27, 1978. BA, Brigham Young U., 1966; MA, Iowa State U., 1970. Instr. Brigham Young U., Provo, Utah, 1966-68; grad. teaching asst. Iowa State U., Ames, 1968-70; instr. Ariz. State U., Tempe, 1972-74; asst. prof. U. Tex., Austin, 1974-80; assoc. prof. S.W. Tex. State U., San Marcos, 1980—. Freelance designer, artist craftsman, 1972—; comml. interior designer, Phoenix, 1970-72; interior design program coord., S.W. Tex. State U., 1998-. Editor: Comprehensive Bibliography for Interior Design, 1984, 87. Fellow Interior Design Educators Coun. (southwest regional chair 1977-88), Internat. Interior Design Assn., Am. Soc. Interior Designers, Found. for Interior Design Edn. Rsch. (chmn. bd. 1990, 92, trustee 1986-94, accreditation com. 1979-86), Irish Georgian Soc., Tex. Assn. for Interior Design (edn. rep. 1985-90). Home: 10806B Pinehurst Dr Austin TX 78747-1621 Office: SW Tex State U FCS 601 University Dr San Marcos TX 78666-4685

TREANOR, CHARLES EDWARD, scientist; b. Buffalo, Oct. 22, 1924; s. William Michael and Margaret Mary (Powers) T.; m. Ruth Ziegelmaier, Jan. 28, 1950; children: Timothy, John, Peter, Michael, Melissa. BA, U. Minn., 1947; PhD, U. Buffalo, 1952-53. Instr. physics U. Buffalo, 1952-53; physicist Cornell Aero Lab., Buffalo, 1954-68, head aerodynamic rsch. dept., 1968-78; v.p. phys. sci. group Calspen Corp., 1978-83, v.p., chief scientist, 1983-90; pres. CTSA, Inc., 1990—. Contbr. articles to profl. jours.; patentee in field. Served to lt. U.S. Army, 1943-46. Recipient C.C. Furnas award SUNY, Buffalo, 1989. Fellow Am. Phys. Soc. (div. chmn. 1977), AIAA (com. chmn. 1975-76, 87-89, Fluid and Plasma Dynamics award 1978); mem. NAE. Home: 535 Seabrook Drive Buffalo NY 14221-1919 Fax: (716) 633-6540. E-mail: ctreanor@aol.com.

TREANOR, WILLIAM MICHAEL, law educator; b. Morristown, N.J., Nov. 16, 1957; s. William Joseph and Margaret Treanor; m. Allison Derivaux Ames, Oct. 15, 1994; children: William Paul Ames, Katherine Derivaux. BA, Yale U., 1979, JD, 1985; AM in History, Harvard U., 1982. Spl. asst. to dep. commr. U.S. Office Edn., Washington, 1979-80; speechwriter to sec. U.S. Dept. Edn., 1980; law clk. to Hon. James L. Oakes U.S. Ct. Appeals, 2d Cir., Brattleboro, Vt., 1985-86; spl. asst. to chmn. Com. on Govt. Integrity, N.Y.C., 1987; spl. asst. U.S. atty. U.S. Atty.'s Office, Washington, 1990; assoc. counsel Office of Ind. Counsel, 1987-90; assoc. prof. law Fordham U., N.Y.C., 1991-98, prof. law, 2001—; dep. asst. atty. gen. office of legal counsel United States Dept. Justice, 1998-2001. Vis. prof. Univ. Paris I, Pantheon-Sorbonne, 1998, 2000. Contbr. articles to profl. jours. Democrat. Office: Fordham Law Sch 140 W 62nd St New York NY 10023 E-mail: wtreanor@fordham.edu.

TREAS, JUDITH KAY, sociology educator; b. Phoenix, Jan. 2, 1947; d. John Joseph and Hope Catherine (Thomas) Jennings; m. Benjamin C. Treas II, May 14, 1969; children: Stella, Evan. BA, Pitzer Coll., Claremont, Calif., 1969; MA, UCLA, 1972, PhD, 1976. Instr. U. So. Calif., L.A., 1974-75, asst. prof., 1975-81, assoc. prof., 1981-87, dept. chair, 1984-89, prof., 1987-89, U. Calif., Irvine, 1989, dept. chair, 1989-94. Bd. overseers Gen. Social Survey, 1986-88; cons. social sci. and population study sect. NIH, 1989-92. Contbr. articles to profl. jours. Trustee Pitzer Coll., 1977-79. Recipient Rsch. award NSF, 1978-81, 84-91, NIH, 1979-81; Univ. scholar U. So. Calif., 1982-83. Fellow Gerontological Assn. Am.; mem. Golden Key (hon.), Am. Sociol. Assn., Population Assn. Am. Office: U Calif Dept Sociology Irvine CA 92697-0001

TREASTER, JOSEPH B. (JOSEPH BLAND TREASTER), journalist; b. Mt. Union, Pa., May 19, 1941; s. Ellsworth F. and Anna Katherine (Chalupka) T.; m. Barbara A. Gluck, June 6, 1970 (div. Aug. 1976); m. Barbara J. Dill, Feb. 24, 1990; 1 child, Chloe Qiao Xing. BA, U. Miami, 1965; student, Sorbonne, Paris, 1971, San Francisco de Marroquin, Guatemala, 1988; MS, Columbia U., 1996. Reporter Miami (Fla.) Herald, 1963; staff asst. Saigon bur. N.Y. Times, 1965-67, Vietnam corr., 1968-69, 72-74, reporter, 1969-70, chief Conn. bur., 1970-72, investigative reporter N.J. bur., 1974-75, crime/youth violence writer, 1975-76, rewrite desk and spl. assignments to Washington, L.Am. and Mid. East, 1976-84, chief Caribbean bur., 1984-90, drug policy corr. spl. assignments Latin Am., Mid-East, Europe, Baltic States, 1990-95, fin. writer, 1996—. Freelance corr. Atlantic Monthly, Rolling Stone, The Nation, others; fellow Poynter Inst., St. Petersburg, Fla., 1993, U. Nev. Bus. Journalism, 1995; Knight-Bagehot fellow in econs. and bus. Columbia U., 1995-96; Poynter fellow Yale U., 1975. Co-author: No Hiding Place: Inside Report on the Hostage Crisis (in Iran), 1981; contbg. author: Ency. Brit., Insight Guide to Caribbean, Youth Violence, 1992, Writing About Business, 2000, The New York Times What's Doing Around the World, 2001. Served with U.S. Army, 1963-65, Vietnam. Recipient Page One award N.Y. Newspaper Guild, 1977, 79; Tom Wallace award Inter-Am. Press Assn., 1980, citation and awards Overseas Press Club Am., 1977, 80, 85, News Analysis award Soc. of Silurians, 1993, Casey medal for meritorious journalism U. Md., 1995, others. Mem. Mystery Writers Am. Avocations: skiing, sport fishing, running, bicycling. Office: NY Times 229 W 43d St New York NY 10036-3959 E-mail: treaster@nytimes.com.

TREASTER, RONALD G. small business owner; b. Ft. Benning, Ga., May 29, 1942; s. George O. and Joyce A. T.; m. Michelle K., Nov. 5, 1983; 1 child, Aimee D. Student, Harding Coll., 1960-62. Salesman, mgr. Orkin Exterminating, Little Rock, Hot Springs, Ark., 1970-73; salesman, announcer KGUS Radio, Hot Springs, 1973-75; announcer, dir. opers. KZNG Radio, 1975-77; various sales positions Shadow Security Svcs., 1978-81, owner, 1981-94, The Mop Squad, Hot Springs, 1983—. Author: (play) Star Sailor, 1977. City dir. City of Hot Springs, 1999—. Sgt. USAF, 1962-69. Mem. Ark. Security Assn. (pres. 1987, 93, 94). Republican. Office: The Mop Squad 2008 7th St Hot Springs National Park AR 71913-5861

TREASURE-TERRELL, SUZANNE MARIE, marketing and sales professional, writer, poet, lyricist; b. Chgo., Aug. 18, 1963; d. James Allen Olejarz and Christeen Joy Lindblom; adopted by James DuWayne and Mary Frances (Urban) T.; m. Kenneth Dwayne Terrell, Apr. 1, 2000. Student part time, Dallas Bapt. U., 1988-99. Toll assistance operator Southwestern Bell Tel./AT&T, Dallas, 1982-88; bus. office clk. Southwestern Bell Tel., 1988-93, drafting clk., 1993-94, svc. rep., 1994-2000; ret., 2000; customer svc. rep. Blockbuster Video, Dallas, 1994-95; sales rep. Up in Smoke Tobacco Shop, 1995-96; sec. bd. Irving Writers Connection, 1994. Telefundraiser Stephen Dunn & Assoc., Myerson Symphony Ctr., Dallas, 1992-93; mem. V.I.P. security staff Tex. Rangers Ballpk., Arlington, 1993-94; job steward Comm. Workers of Am., Dallas, 1982-2000, ret. mem., 2000—; cons., advisor participative mgmt. and employee interactive com., Dallas, 1991-93; owner Treasured Thoughts; co-owner The Revolving Door Inn. Contbr. poetry to Amherst Soc., Am. Poetry Ann. (Poetic Achievement award 1994); contbr. articles to newsletters, Alzheimer's Assn., Tex. Scottish Rite Hosp. for Children, Irving Writers Connection, SBC PM/EI Com.; lyricist for Fatal Fate. Fundraiser United Way, Dallas, 1992-93; cert. ct. appointed advocate Dallas CASA, 1992—; cert. tel. counselor Contact 214, Dallas, 1995-97; press ops. rep. World Cup USA 94, Dallas. Recipient award of merit World of Poetry, Sacramento, 1987, 91, Editor's Choice award The Nat. Libr. of Poetry, Owings Mills, Md., 1998, Commendation Letter Pres. Bill Clinton for positive contbns. and dedication to volunteerism in local cmty., Dallas, 1993; named Famous Poet for 1998, 99, Famous Poets Soc., Hollywood, Calif., 1998, 99; nominee Golden Rule award JC Penney, Dallas, 1993. Mem. Comm. Workers of Am. (job steward 1982-2000, CWA-COPE Platinum Quorum 1993-96, Outstanding Contbn. award 1994, CWA-COPE Triple Quorum 1996-97, Outstanding Contbn. award 1996, 99), Tel. Pioneers of Am. (life mem.), Irving Writers Connection (sec. bd. 1994), Allen Area Rep. Women's Club. Methodist. Avocations: writing poetry and short stories, arts and crafts, volunteering for children-oriented organizations, illness-related orgns. and nat. events. Home: 42348 Norwood Rd Gonzales LA 70737-7521 E-mail: treasured_angel@hotmail.com.

TREAT, JAMES, theology studies educator, writer; b. Anadarko, Okla., Sept. 13, 1962; s. Jimmie Lee and Marcia Ann Treat. BS, S.D. Sch. Mines and Tech., 1984; MA, Pacific Sch. Religion, Berkeley, Calif., 1989; PhD, Grad. Theol. Union, Berkeley, 1993. Asst. prof. Am. studies dept. U. Calif., Santa Cruz, 1992—95, U. N.Mex, Albuquerque, 1996—2000; reach excellence asst. prof. Honors Coll. U. Okla., Norman, 2000—. Editor: (book) Native and Christian: Indigenous Voices on Religious Identity in the United States and Canada, 1996, For This Land: Writings on Religion in America by Vine Deloria, Jr., 1999. Office: U Okla Honor Coll 1300 Asp Ave Norman OK 73019-6061 E-mail: treaty@ou.edu.

TREAT, JOHN ELTING, entrepreneur; b. Evanston, Ill., June 20, 1946; s. Carlin Alexander and Marjorie Ann (Mayland) T.; adopted s. Howard Elting Jr.; m. Barbara Laflin, May 27, 1984; children: Charles, Luli, Tyler, Tucker, Mayland. BA, Princeton U., 1967; MA, Johns Hopkins U., 1969. Legis. asst. U.S. Senate, 1966; assoc. ops. officer Office of Sec., U.S. Dept. State, 1971-73; research coordinator Presdl.-Congressional Commn. on Orgn. of Govt. for Conduct of Fgn. Policy, Washington, 1973-74; dir. research trade U.S. Fed. Energy Adminstrn., 1974-78; dep. asst. sec. U.S Dept. Energy, 1979-80; staff mem. Nat. Security Council, 1980-81; sr. v.p. N.Y. Merc. Exchange, N.Y.C., 1981-82, pres., 1982-84; ptnr. Bear Stearns & Co., Los Angeles, 1984-85; exec. pub. Petroleum Intelligence Weekly, N.Y.C., 1985-87; pres. Regent Internat., Washington and The Hague, 1987-89; v.p., ptnr. Booz, Allen & Hamilton, Inc., San Francisco, 1989—2001; chmn. Sanctuary Devel. LLC, 2001—. Chmn. spl. gifts Am. Cancer Soc., 1983; chmn. bd. dirs. Mirror Repertory Co., 1987—90; trustee, mem. exec. com., chmn. corp. rels. com. No. Calif. World Affairs Coun.; mem. San Francisco Fgn. Rels. com.; bd. trustees Am. U. of Cairo; trustee Yosemite Nat. Insts., 2001—. With USNR, 1969—71. Decorated AF Commendation medal; Ford Found. European Area Travel grantee, 1972; Woodrow Wilson fellow, 1967; McConnell fellow, 1966 Mem. Coun. Fgn. Rels., Internat. Assn. for Energy Econs. Clubs: Colonial (Princeton, N.J.), St. Francis Yacht Club, Bankers (San Francisco). Democrat. Unitarian Universalist. Home: 1149 Manor Dr Sonoma CA 95476 E-mail: treat_john@bah.com.

TREBING, DAVID MARTIN, automotive executive; b. Lincoln, Nebr., June 2, 1961; s. Harry Martin and Joyce Alice (Christie) T. BA in Mktg., Mich. State U., 1984; MBA in Fin., Wake Forest U., 1986. Project mgr. mktg.-sales Gilbarco div. Exxon Corp., Greensboro, N.C., 1984-86; cash mgmt. analyst Chrysler Fin. Corp., Troy, Mich., 1986-87; sr. corp. fin. specialist Chrysler Corp., Auburn Hills, 1987-92, mgr. activity-based costing implementation Detroit, 1993-96, mgr. Asia-Pacific Sales Fin., 1996-98; v.p. fin. and adminstrn. Daimler Chrysler Taiwan Co. Ltd., 1998—2001; sr. corp. mgr. regional govt. affairs Daimler Chrysler Corp., Auburn Hills, Mich., 2001—. Mem. Internat. Armed Forces Coun., Detroit, 1987-92, Detroit Hist. Soc., Jr. Coun./Detroit Inst. Arts, St. George's Soc. N.Y., N.Y.C.; mem. exec. com., bd. dirs. Meadow Brook Theatre and Festival; Chgo. com. Coun. on Fgn. Rels.; bd. dirs. devel. fund Mich. State U. Lt. (j.g.) USNR, 1987-90. Inst. fellow Inst. Pub. Utilities, 1983. Mem. Econ. Club Detroit, Detroit Com. on Fgn. Rels., Army and Navy Club, Detroit Athletic Club, Church Club of N.Y., Vet. Corps Arty. State N.Y., SAR (pres. Detroit chpt. 1987-89), Soc. War 1812, Soc. Colonial Wars (chmn. grants and awards com., dep. gov. gen. Mich. Soc.), English-Speaking Union, Am. C. of C. in Taipei (bd. suprs.), Pres. Club Mich. State U., Colonial Order of Acorn, Chgo. Yacht Club. Avocations: skiing, tennis, travel, skeet/trap shooting. Office: Daimler Chrysler Corp CIMS 485-10-95 1000 Chrysler Dr Auburn Hills MI 48326-2766 E-mail: DMT@dcx.com.

TREBON, THOMAS, academic administrator; m. Scottie Trebon. B magna cum laude, Seattle U.; M, PhD, U. Denver. Tchr., adminstr. Seattle U.; acad. dean Coll. Arts and Scis. Rockhurst Coll. , Kansas City; provost, v.p. acad. affairs Sacred Heart U., Trumbull, Conn.; with St. Norbert Coll., 1995—2001; v.p. acad. affairs, dean Carroll coll., Helena, Mont.; pres. Carroll Coll., 2001—. Office: Carroll Coll 100 N East Ave Waukesha WI 53186*

TRECEK, TIMOTHY SCOTT, lawyer; b. Racine, Wis., Sept. 26, 1968; s. Robert Thomas and Mona Marie Trecek; m. Karyn Marie Kwiatkowski, Aug. 27, 1994; children: Gabrielle Grace, Danielle Terese. BS in Polit. Sci., Marquette U., 1990, JD, 1993. Bar: Wis. 1993, U.S. Dist. Ct. (ea. dist.) Wis. 1993. Atty. Kasdorf, Lewis & Swietlik, Milw., 1993—95, Habush, Habush & Rottier, S.C., Milw., 1995—. Mem. ABA, Wis. Acad. of Trial Lawyers (com. mem. bd. attys. profl. responsibility), Wis. State Bar Assn., Assn. of Trial Lawyers of Am. Roman Catholic. Avocations: golfing, family. Office: Habush Habush & Rottier 777 E Wisconsin Ave 2300 Milwaukee WI 53202-5381 E-mail: ttrecek@habush.com.

TRECIOKAS, ALODIA DICIUTE, mezzo-soprano, educator; b. Kaunas, Lithuania, Sept. 15, 1905; d. John and Eugenia (Rinkevich) Dicius; came to U.S., 1947, naturalized, 1953; diploma Lithuanian State Sch. of Music, 1930; student of Mme. Gladkaja, Paris, France, 1928-30, Mme. Edwige Ghibaude, Rome, Italy, 1937-38; m. Joseph Treciokes, Oct. 10, 1925; 1 son, Leopold John. Debut in opera as Zibeland Marta in Faust, Lithuanian State Opera, 1930, debut as Carmen, 1935, debut as Delilah in Samson and Delilah, 1938; mem. Lithuanian (Kaunas) State Opera, 1930-44, leading roles in Samson and Delilah, Carmen, Tiefland, Boris Godunov, Prince Igor, Pericola, Faust; appeared as concert soloist numerous concerts Lithuania, Estonia, Germany, U.S.A. including Lithuania Radio Symphony, Lithuania State Opera Orch., Chgo. Symphony Orch.; appeared as soloist in various radio programs in Lithuania, 1923-44, Estonia, 1936— , Germany, 1946-47, U.S., 1949-75; Am. debut as Carmen in Carmen-Bizet, 1949; soloist in recital, Kimball Hall, Chgo., 1951; debut as Catherine in Joan of Arc at the Stake, Orchestra Hall, Chgo., 1952; concert soloist with Nordic Philharmonic Orch., Chgo., 1959; pvt. tchr. voice and opera, Chgo., 1950-65, Tinley Park, Ill., 1963— ; dir. opera theatre class Am. Conservatory of Music, Chgo., 1957; recording artist Webb Recording Co., RCA records. Mem. Nat. Assn. Tchrs. of Singing, Nat. Ret. Tchrs. Assn., Musician Club of Women in Chgo. Roman Catholic. Address: 2021 Santa Monica Blvd # 616E Santa Monica CA 90404-2208

TRECKELO, RICHARD M. lawyer; b. Elkhart, Ind., Oct. 22, 1926; s. Frank J. and Mary T.; m. Anne Kosick, June 25, 1955; children: Marla Treckelo Buck, Mary Treckelo Lucchesi. AB, U. Mich., 1951, JD, 1953. Bar: Ind. 1953, U.S. Dist. Ct. (no. and so. dists.) Ind. Pvt. practice, Elkhart, 1953-70; ptnr. Barnes and Thornburg, Elkhart, South Bend, others, 1971-91, of counsel, 1992—. Sec. Skyline Corp., Elkhart, 1959-94, bd. dirs., 1961-91. Bd. dirs. Elkhart Gen. Hosp. Found., Elkhart Park Found.; co-chmn. Elkhart Constl. Bicentennial Commn. Served with USAF, 1945-46. Mem. ABA, Elkhart City Bar Assn. (pres. 1975), Ind. Bar Assn., Elkhart County Bar Assn., Pres.'s Club (U. Mich.), Christiana Country Club, Michiana Club (chmn., U. Mich. Elbel Scholarship award), Rotary. Republican. Office: Barnes & Thornburg 121 W Franklin St Ste 200 Elkhart IN 46516-3200

TREDENNICK, STEVEN BURROUGHS, lawyer; b. Newport News, Va., June 26, 1943; s. John C. and Jacqueline (Burroughs) T.; m. D. Diane French, June 11, 1966; children: Steven Randolph, Christopher Scott. BA, U. Tex., El Paso, 1965; JD, U. Va., 1968; cert., Coll. for Fin. Planning, 1984. Bar: Va. 1968, Tex. 1970, N.Mex. 1984. Assoc. Goodman, Hallmark & Akard, El Paso, Tex., 1972-74; pvt. practice Steven Tredennick, P.C., 1974-79; sr. shareholder Mayfield and Perrenot, P.C., 1979-05; atty. Steven Tredennick Atty. at Law, Round Rock, Tex., 1996—. Mem. U.S.-Mex. task force Atlantic coun. of U.S., Washington, 1985. Editor newsletter Franchising in the Americas. Chmn. Sun Bowl luncheon Rotary Club of El Paso, 1993-94; chmn. Tex. Lyceum Assn., 1989; chmn. various coms. U. Tex., El Paso, 1980—; sponsor, spkr., writer The Franchise Ctr., 1993-95. Capt. U.S. Army, 1968-72. Recipient Rising Star of Tex. award Tex. Bus. Mag., 1983; named to Best Lawyers in Am., Woodward/White, Inc., 1995—. Fellow Tex. Bar Found. (life); mem. ABA, El Paso Bar Assn. (past program chair 1972—), State Bar of Va. (assoc.). Episcopalian. Avocations: music, reading, golf, volunteer work. Home and Office: 4028 Sable Oaks Dr Round Rock TX 78664-6251

TREDINNICK, ARTHUR FRED, private detective; b. Darby, Pa., Apr. 7, 1944; s. Albert Fred and Agnes (Hunter) T.; m. Marcia Jane Campbell, Jan. 27, 1968; 1 child, Megan Elizabeth. AA, Lehigh County C.C., Schnecksville, Pa., 1973; BA, Alvernia Coll., Reading, Pa., 1976; AAS, Delaware County C.C., Media, Pa., 1982; MS, St. Joseph's U., Phila., 1987. Cert. fire and explosion investigator, fraud examiner. Patrol trooper Pa. State Police, Fogelsville, 1968-75, crime trooper Bethlehem, 1975-85, Fogelsville, 1985-90, from patrol cpl. to crime sgt. Bethlehem, 1990-95; dir. Associated Investigative Svcs., Inc., Allentown, Pa., 1995—. Bd. dirs. Hidden Harbour III Condominium Assn., Ocean City, Md., 1995; disaster assistance employee, security specialist FEMA, Washington, 1995—; adj. faculty Lehigh County C.C., 1997. Author: Fire Protection Master Plan-Lower Macungie Township, Lehigh County, Pa., 1979. Mem. Pub. Safety Commn., Lower Macungie Township, 1989-95; dep. dir. Emergency Mgmt., Lower Macungie Township, 1991-95. With U.S. Army Res., 1971-95. Mem. Am. Soc. Indsl. Security, Internat. Assn. Arson Investigators, Pa. Assn. Arson Investigators (charter), Nat. Assn. Fire Investigators, Nat. Assn. Investigative Splst., Assn. Cert. Fraud Examiners, Pa. Assn. Lic. Investigators (charter), Assn. Christian Investigators. Avocations: golf, fishing. Office: Associated Investigative Svcs Inc 3140B W Tilghman St Ste 175 Allentown PA 18104-4222

TREDINNICK, LAUREL CHRISTINE, social worker; b. Edwardsville, Ill., Nov. 13, 1959; d. Melvin L. and Marian C. (Krejci) Utechtt; m. Don G. Tredinnick, May 26, 1990; 1 chld, Edward Don. BS with honors, Western Ill. U., 1981; MSW, U. Ill., 1988. Lic. clin. social worker. Tchr. spl. edn. Tazewell-Mason Counties Spl. Edn. Assn., Pekin, Ill., 1981-83; case mgr. Mo. Dept. Mental Health, Hannibal, 1983-85; youth svc. counselor Human Svc. Ctr., Peoria, Ill., 1985-87; sch. social worker intern Knox-Warren Counties Spl. Edn. Assn., Galesburg, 1987-88; sch. social worker Guilford County Schs., Greensboro, N.C., 1988—. Supr. interns U. N.C. at Chapel Hill, Greensboro, 1989-91. Contbr. articles to Sch. Social Work Jour. Mem. NASW, Acad. Cert. Social Workers. Avocation: reading. Office: 5813 Lake Brandt Rd Greensboro NC 27455-1207 E-mail: tredinl@guilford.k12.nc.us.

TREDWAY, THOMAS, college president; b. North Tonawanda, N.Y., Sept. 4, 1935; s. Harold and Melanya (Scorby) T.; m. Catherine Craft, Jan. 12, 1991; children: Daniel John, Rebecca Elizabeth. BA, Augustana Coll., 1957; MA, U. Ill., 1958; BD, Garrett Theol. Sem., 1961; PhD, Northwestern U., 1964. Instr. history Augustana Coll., Rock Island, Ill., 1964-65, asst. prof., 1965-69, assoc. prof., 1969-71, prof., 1971—, v.p. acad affairs, 1970-75, pres., 1975—. Vis. prof. ch. history Waterloo Lutheran Sem., 1967-68 Mem. Phi Beta Kappa, Omicron Delta Kappa Lutheran. Office: Augustana Coll Office of President 639 38th St Rock Island IL 61201-2210

TREE, MICHAEL, violinist, violist, educator; b. Newark, Feb. 19, 1934; s. Samuel and Sada (Rothman) Applebaum; m. Johanna Kreck, Sept. 8, 1966; children: Konrad Efrem, Anna Louise. Diploma, Curtis Inst. Music, Phila., 1955; DFA (hon.), U. South Fla., 1975, SUNY, Binghamton, 1983. Faculty Harpur Coll., Binghamton, 1965-70, Curtis Inst. Music, 1970—, U. Md., College Park, 1981—, St. Louis Conservatory Music, 1982-88, Rutgers U., 1988—2000, Manhattan Sch. Music, 1993—, Juilliard Sch., NYC, 2002—. Co-artistic dir. Phila. Chamber Orch., 1985-88; Misha Elman chair Manhattan Sch. Music, 1991. Violin recital debut at Carnegie Hall, 1954; soloist with major orchs. and at maj. internat. festivals, 1958—; founding mem. Guarneri String Quartet, 1964—, rec. artist for Philips, RCA, Columbia, Nonesuch, Vanguard, Sony Classics, Arabesque records. Recipient Seal of Recognition City of N.Y., 1982. Avocations: hiking, tennis. Home: PO Box 193 Marlboro VT 05344-0193 Office: care Herbert Barrett Mgmt Inc 1776 Broadway Ste 1610 New York NY 10019-2002

TREECE, JAMES LYLE, lawyer; b. Colorado Springs, Colo., Feb. 6, 1925; s. Lee Oren and Ruth Ida (Smith) T.; m. Ruth Julie Treece, Aug. 7, 1949 Idiv. 1984); children: James (dec.), Karen Pelletier, Teryl Wait, Jamilyn Smyser, Carol Crowder. Student, Colo. State U., 1943, Colo. U., 1943, U.S. Naval Acad., 1944-46; BS, Mesa Coll., 1946; JD, U. Colo., 1950; postgrad., U. N.C., 1976-77. Bar: Colo. 1952, U.S. Dist. Ct. Colo. 1952, U.S. Ct. Appeals (10th cir.) 1952, U.S. Supreme Ct. 1967. Assoc. Yegge, Hall, Treece & Evans and predecessors, 1951-59, ptnr., 1959-69; U.S. atty. Colo., 1969-77; pres. Treece & Bahr and predecessor firms, Littleton, 1977-91; mcpl. judge, 1967-68; mem. faculty Nat. Trial Advocacy Inst., 1973-76, Law-Sci. Acad., 1964. Chmn. Colo. Dept. Pub. Welfare, 1963-68; chmn. Colo. Dept. Social Svcs., 1968-69; mem. Littleton Bd. Edn., 1977-81. Served with USNR, 1944-46. Recipient awards Colo. Assn. Sch. Bds., 1981, IRS, 1977, FBI, 1977, DEA, 1977, Fed. Exec. Bd., 1977. Mem. Fed. Bar Assn. (pres. Colo. 1975, award 1975), Colo. Bar Assn. (bd. govs.), Denver Bar Assn. (v.p., trustee). Republican. Episcopalian. Home: 12651 N Pebble Beach Dr Sun City AZ 85351-3327 E-mail: jltreece@juno.com.

TREECE, JOSEPH CHARLES, insurance broker; b. Loma Linda, Calif., Sept. 1, 1934; s. Roy G. and Jeane L. (Reade) T.; m. Sandra Larkins; children: Debbie, Mike, David. BA, Chapman Coll., 1956. Cert. Ins. Counselor, Assoc. in Risk Mgmt. Comml. banker Security Pacific Nat. Bank, Hemet, Calif., 1959-72; ins. broker H.I.S./Kent & Hamilton, 1972-89, Russell & Kaufmann, Hemet, 1989-96, Sawyer, Cook & Co., Redlands, Calif., 1996—. Dir. YMCA, Hemet. Lt. USN, 1956-59. Recipient Associate Achievement award Am. Assn. Mng. Gen. Agts., 1991, Disting. Svc. award Cert. Profl. Ins. Agents Soc., 1995. Mem. Ramona Pageant Assn. (life, chmn.-supr. 1962—), Profl. Ins. Assn. (state dir. 1988-91), Profl. Ins. Agts. (pres. Riverside and San Bernardino, Calif. 1989-90), Joint Ins. Assn. (pres. Riverside and San Bernardino 1991), Ind. Ins. Agts. (pres.), Cert. Profl. Ins. Agts. (nat. pres. 1992, Disting. Svc. award 1995), Hemet C. of C. (pres. 1970), Kiwanis Club (life, Hemet chpt. pres. 1971, lt. gov. divsn. 6 Cal-Na-Ha 1972), Sage Soc. of San Jacinto Valley (co-founder, pres. 2000—). Avocations: golf, camping, fishing, canoeing. Home: 839 Don Dr Hemet CA 92543-3729 Office: Sawyer Cook & Co 1 E State St Redlands CA 92373-4729 E-mail: joe.treece@verizon.net.

TREECE, RANDY LIONEL, lawyer; b. Paducah, Ky., Apr. 16, 1956; s. Franklin William and Leona Marie (Kelley) T.; m. Devonda Kaye Corzine, May 30, 1976; children: Natalie, Elliot, Tifanie, Savanah. AA, Paducah C.C., 1976; BSBA in Profl. Acctg., So. Ill. U., 1977; JD, Vanderbilt U., 1984. Bar: Ky. 1984, Ill. 1990, U.S. Dit. Ct. (ea. dist.) Ky. 1985, U.S. Dist. Ct. (we. dist.) Ky. 1987, U.S. Tax Ct. 1990. Staff acct. Ernst & Young, St. Louis, 1977-79, sr. acct. Denver, 1979-81; assoc. Stoll, Keenon & Park, Lexington, Ky., 1984-86; ptnr. Whitlow, Robert, Houston & Straub, Paducah, 1986—. Coauthor: Kentucky Tax Law, 1990, 2d edit., 1994; contbr. articles to profl. jours. Mem. ABA (small bus. com. 1992-95), Ky. Bar Assn., AICPA, Ky. Soc. CPAs (small bus. com. 1991-95). Office: Whitlow Roberts Houston & Straub 300 Broadway St Paducah KY 42001-0733

TREFFERT, DAROLD ALLEN, psychiatrist, author, hospital director; b. Fond du Lac, Wis., Mar. 12, 1933; s. Walter O. and Emma (Leu) T.; m. Dorothy Marie Sorgatz, June 11, 1955; children: Jon, Joni, Jill, Jay. BS, U. Wis., 1955, MD, 1958. Diplomate: Am. Bd. Psychiatry and Neurology. Resident in psychiatry U. Wis. Med. Sch., 1959-62, assoc. clin. prof. psychiatry, 1965—; chief children's unit Winnebago (Wis.) Mental Health Inst., 1962-64, supt., 1964-79, Central State Hosp., Waupun, Wis., 1977-78; dir. Dodge County Mental Health Center, Juneau, 1964-74; mem. staff St. Agnes Hosp., Fond du Lac, 1963—; exec. dir. Fond du Lac County Mental Health Center, 1979-92. Chmn. Controlled Substances Bd. Wis.; mem. critical health problems com. Wis. Dept. Pub. Instrn., med. examining bd. State of Wis. Author: Extraordinary People: Understanding Savant Syndrome, 1989, re-issued, 2000, edits. in U.S., U.K., Italy, Japan, The Netherlands, Sweden; autism cons. (movie) Rainman, 1988. Fellow Am. Coll. Psychiatrists; mem. AMA, Wis. Med. Soc. (pres. 1979-80), Wis. Psychiat. Assn. (pres.), Am. Assn. Psychiat. Adminstrs. (pres.), Alpha Omega Alpha. Home: W 4065 Maplewood Ln Fond Du Lac WI 54935-9562 Office: 430 E Division St Fond Du Lac WI 54935-4560 E-mail: dtreffert@pol.net. *People often spend too much time regretting what they are not and far too little time savoring that which they are.*

TREFNY, JOHN ULRIC, academic administrator, dean; b. Jan. 28, 1942; s. Ulric John and Mary Elizabeth (Leech) T.; m. Sharon Livingston, 1992; 1 child from previous marriage, Benjamin Robin. BS, Fordham U., 1963; PhD, Rutgers U., 1968. Rsch. assoc. Cornell U., Ithaca, N.Y., 1967-69; asst. prof. physics Wesleyan U., Middletown, Conn., 1969-77, Colo. Sch. Mines, Golden, 1977-79, assoc. prof., 1979-85, prof., 1985—, assoc. dean rsch., 1988—90, head physics dept., 1990—95, v.p. for acad. affairs, dean faculty, 1995—2000, pres., 2000—. Dir. Amorphous Materials Ctr. Colo. Sch. Mines, 1986-90; cons. Solar Energy Rsch. Inst., Golden, Energy Conversion Devices, Troy, Mich., others. Contbr. articles to profl. jours. Recipient Tchg. award AMOCO Found., 1984, Friend of Sci. Edn. award, 1990. Mem. Colo. Assn. Sci. Tchrs. (bd. dirs. 1986-88), Sigma Xi (N.W. region co-dir. 1994—), Sigma Pi Sigma. Avocations: golfing, traveling, whiskey. Home: 1722 Illinois St Golden CO 80401-1836*

TREFRY, ROBERT J. healthcare administrator; b. Springfield, Vt., Mar. 29, 1947; married. Bachelors' degree, Ga. Inst. Tech., 1970; Masters' degree, George Washington U., 1974. With Greater Southeast Community Hosp., Washington, 1973, adminstrv. asst., 1973-74, asst. adminstr., 1974-79; sr. v.p. North Kansas City (Mo.) Community Hosp., 1979-83; exec. v.p., chief exec. officer St. Agnes Hosp., White Plains, N.Y., 1983-88; exec. v.p., chief operating officer Carle Found. Hosp., Urbana, Ill., 1988-91; exec. v.p., chief oper. officer Bridgeport (Conn.) Hosp., 1991-94, pres., CEO, 1994—. With U.S. mil. 1970-71. Office: Bridgeport Hosp 267 Grant St Bridgeport CT 06610-2870

TREFTS, JOAN LANDENBERGER, retired educator, administrator; b. Pitts., Jan. 31, 1930; d. William Henry III and Eleanore (Campbell) Landenberger;m. Albert Sharpe Trefts Sr., June 20, 1952 (dec.); children: Dorothy, Albert Jr., William, Deborah, Elizabeth. AB, Western Coll. for Women, 1952; M., John Carroll U., 1982, M., 1984. Lic. and cert. home economist, cert. prin., N.Y., Ohio, supr., biol. sci., econs., voact. edn., pre-kindergarten edn. Summer sch. prin. John Adams H.S., Collinwood and South High, Cleve., 1972-95. Cons. Cleve. Partnership Program. Trustee Chautauqua Literacy and Sci. Cir., Presbyn. Assn. Chautauqua, NY. Named Tchr. of Yr., Cleve., 1994. Mem.: DAR (state officer 2000—), Ohio Vocat. Assn. (bd. dirs.), Am. Vocat. Assn. (nat. com.), Am. Home Econs. Assn., Presbyn. Assn. (trustee), Dames of Ct. of Honor (pres. gen. 2001—), Colonial Daus. of 17th Century (nat. officer), Daus. Am. Colonists (state officer), Nat. Officers Colonial Clergy (nat. officer, chancellor), Colonial Dames Am. (pres. chpt. 18, nat. officer ct. honor), U.S. Daus. of 1912, Colonial Dames of XVII Century, New Eng. Soc. of Western Res. (pres.), Clearwater Country Club, Cleve. Skating Club, Union Clubs. Republican. Presbyterian. Avocations: curling, rug hooking, needlepoint. Home: 20101 Malvern Rd Shaker Heights OH 44122-2825

TREFZGER, RICHARD CHARLES, surgeon; b. Peoria, Ill., Jan. 27, 1948; s. John Dennis and Marilyn Lestilie (Wilson) Trefzger; m. Nancy Ellen Guy, Dec. 19, 1971; children: Emily Jean, Michael Guy. BS, U. Ill., 1970, MD, 1973. Diplomate Am Bd Surgery. Intern in surgery Med. Coll. Wis., Milw., 1973-74, resident in surgery, 1974-75, Presbyn.-St. Luke's Hosp., Chgo., 1975-78; instr. surgery Rush Med. Coll., 1977-78; med. dir. Westminster Village Retirement Ctr., Bloomington, 1980-84, St. Joseph's Trauma Ctr., Bloomington, 1986-96, BroMenn Regional Trauma Ctr., Normal, Ill., 1994-96; chief surgery Bromenn Regional Med. Ctr., 1987-88, 94-96, St. Joseph's Med. Ctr., Bloomington, 1989-91, pres. med. staff, 1991-92. Clin. instr. U. Ill. Coll. Medicine, 1980—; chmn. bd. dirs. BroMenn Physician Hosp. Orgn., 1995—96; sec. med. staff BroMenn Regional Med. Ctr., 1998, v.p., 99, bd. dirs., 1999—, pres. med. staff, 2000—02. Mem Ill State Univ Civic Chorale, Normal, 1991—98; bd dirs Community Cancer Ctr, Bloomington, 1996—, pres, 2000; vpres ofcl bd First Christian Ch, 1981, 1999—2002, elder, 1980—; rector Cursillo in Christianity, 2001; bd dirs Barton Stone Christian Home, Jacksonville, Ill., 1979—82. Fellow: ACS (councilor Ill. chpt. 1986—88, mem. Ill. chpt. com. trauma 1996—); mem.: AMA, Ill. Surg. Soc. (gov. 1990—94, v.p. elect 1997, v.p. 1998, pres. elect 1999, pres. 2000, trustee 2001—), Danvers Cmty. Band-Saxophone, Scottish Rite, Rotary (dir. 1982—85, 1994—99, sec. 1995—96, v.p. 1996—97, pres. 1997—98, band-saxophone, Paul Harris fellow 1989), Masons, Alpha Omega Alpha. Avocations: marathon running, skiing, music, travel. Home: 41 Pendleton Way Bloomington IL 61704-6243 Office: Surg Assocs 1404 Eastland Dr Bloomington IL 61701-3532 E-mail: DoctorT@SABLimited.com., MENDR2@aol.com.

TREGAY, SUSAN WEBB, artist, educator; b. Concord, N.H., Nov. 12, 1946; d. Reuel W. and Natalie (Stevens) Webb; m. George W. Tregay, Sept. 9, 1967; children: Steven W., Sarah B. BS in Edn., Wheelock Coll., 1968; MS, SUNY, Buffalo, 1975. Artist, Buffalo, 1982—; pvt. art educator, 1987—. Instr. Mich. Tech., Gibsons (B.C.) Art Assoc., U. So. Ala., Mobile, Wheelock Coll., Boston, NCCC, Niagara Falls, N.Y. One-woman shows include Kleinhan's Music Hall, Buffalo, 1987, Art Dialogue Gallery, Buffalo, 1991, Impact Gallery, Buffalo, 1994, 96, Roberta Wood Gallery, Syracuse, N.Y., 1995, CAA Gallery, Chautauqua, N.Y., 1996, Adams Art Gallery, Dunkirk, N.Y., 1996, Local Color Art Gallery, Oswego, N.Y., 1997, Wyoming Coun. Arts, Perry, N.Y., 1997, Towne Art Gallery, Wheelock Coll, Boston, 1998; exhibited in group shows at Hallwalls Gallery, Buffalo, 1982, 94, Roberta Wood Gallery, Syracuse, 1993, Brea (Calif.) Art Gallery, 1993, 95, Castellani Art Mus., Lewiston, N.Y., 1993, 96, Anderson Gallery, Buffalo, 1994, Octagonal Art Gallery, Westfield, N.Y., 1995, Brand Art Gallery, Glendale, Calif., 1993, 95, Neville Mus., Green Bay, Wis., 1993, 95, Riverside Art Mus., 1997, Springfield (Mo.) Art Mus., 1996, Madison Art Gallery, Germantown, Tenn., 1996, West Bend (Wis.) Art Mus., 1997, Carnegie Art Assn.; cover art for Buffalo Philharm. Programs, 1986-87, Artist Mag., 1997; included in Best of Watercolor, 1995, Fresh Flowers: The Best of Flower Painting, 1996, Best of Acrylic Painting, 1996, Exploring Color, 1998, Painting Composition, 1998, Creative Inspiration, 1998, Best of Watercolor # 3, 1999; contbr. articles to Artist Mag., Watercolor Magic, and Art Calendar. Recipient First Place and Best of Show awards, Puget Sound award N.W. Watercolor Soc. Nat. Exhbn., 1993, NEWS award N.Am. Open Exhbn., 1994; N.Y. Coun. for the Arts grantee, 1999, Mich. Tech. grantee, 1999, Vis. Women and Minority Scholar grantee, 1999. Mem. Midwest Watercolor Soc. (signature status, Dillman Creative Workshop award 1993, Arches Paper award of merit 1995), Watercolor West (assoc., Arches and Rives Paper award 1993), Niagara Frontier Watercolor Soc. (signature mem., Napa Valley award 1994), Nat. Watercolor Soc. (signature status). Home: Webb Tregay Studio 470 Berryman Dr Snyder NY 14226-4640 E-mail: swtregay@aol.com.

TREGENZA, NORMAN HUGHSON, investment banker; b. Morristown, N.J., Feb. 1, 1937; s. Norman J. and Marion Esther (Hughson) T.; m. Alyce Virginia Bruene, Aug. 27, 1966; children: Norman Arthur, Suzanne Carol. BA, St. Lawrence U., 1959; MBA, NYU, 1963. Sr. investment officer Tchrs. Ins. and Annuity Assn., N.Y.C., 1960-71; sr. v.p. Republic Funding Corp., 1971-82; pres. Convent Capital Corp., 1982—. Bd. dirs. Powertrusion Internat., Inc., Scottsdale, Ariz. Chmn. stewardship com. Presbyn. Ch., Morristown, 1978, ruling elder, 1979, pres. bd. trustees, 1982; trustee St. Lawrence U., Canton, N.Y., 1983-95, Gill/St. Bernards Sch. (hon.), 1982-96, The Morris Mus., Morristown, 1983—. Mem. St. Lawrence U. Alumni Assn. N.J. (pres. 1970-72), Nat. Coun. USS Constitution Mus. Clubs: Baltusrol Golf, Park Ave., Indian Mound Golf. Home and Office: West Shore Dr Silver Lake NH 03875

TREGURTHA, JAMES, retired career officer, engineer; b. Orange, N.J. s. James D. Sr. and Dorothy Elizabeth (Clinton) T.; m. Gloria Dealey, Dec. 27, 1955; children: Diane Elizabeth Churchyard, Catherine Elizabeth Galusha. BS in Life Scis., BS in Naval Scis. and Engring., Cornell U., 1950; diploma, U.S. Naval Submarine Sch., 1953; MS in Bus. Mgmt. & Personnel Adminstrn., U.S. Naval Post Grad. Sch., 1971. Commd. ensign USN, 1950, advanced through grade to capt., 1971; lt. (j.g.) Destroyer Force, 1950-53; lt. USS Becuna, 1953—55, Guided Missle Unit, 1956-58, USS Grayback, 1958-60; lt. comdr. USS Razorback, 1960-61, USS Rasher, 1961-63; lt. Seventh Fleet Subrep., 1963—66; comdr., submarine rep. fleet ops. Pentagon, Washington, 1966-68; comdr. cheif of staff officer submarine squadron eight, 1968-69; comdr. Submarine Dvsn. Eighty One, 1969; capt., chief staff officer Submarine Flotilla Seven, 1971-72; capt., comdr. USS Durham, 1972-74; capt., commodore Amphibious Squadron, 1974-76; capt. head amphibious ship Pentagon, Washington, 1976—78, capt., dep. dir. ships acqisition, 1978-79; capt., chief staff Eastern Pacific Fleet Amphibious Forces, 1979-80; ret. USN, 1980. Dir. phys. plant svcs. and biomedical engring. Anaheim (Calif.) Meml. Hosp., 1980-83, dir. plant engring. and biomedical engring. St. John's Hosp. & Health Ctr., Santa Monica, Calif., 1983-89; asst. chief engr., Long Beach State U., 1989-94. Decorated Legion of Merit. Mem. Retired Officers Assn. (medal, pres. 1998-2002), Submarine Vets. WWII (assoc.), Naval Submarine League, Navy League.

TREGURTHA, PAUL RICHARD, marine transportation company executive; b. Orange, N.J., 1935; married BSME, Cornell U., 1958; MBA, Harvard U., 1963. Contr., v.p. Brown & Sharpe Mfg. Co., 1969-71; v.p. fin. Moore McCormack Resources, Inc., Stamford, Conn., 1971-73, exec. v.p. fin., 1973-78, pres., COO, from 1978, pres., CEO, chmn., 1987-88; chmn., CEO, co-owner Mormac Marine Group, Inc., 1988—. Vice chmn., co-owner The Interlake Steamship Co., 1988; chmn., CEO Moran Transp. Co., 1994—; bd. dirs. Fleet Fin. Corp., FPL Group, Inc., Alliance Resource Mgmt. Group. Trustee emeritus Cornell U., Ithaca, N.Y.; trustee Tchrs. Ins. and Annuity Assn. 1st lt. USAF, 1958-61. Named Baker Scholar, Harvard U., 1963. Office: Mormac Marine Group Inc One Landmark Sq Stamford CT 06901-2608

TREIBLE, KIRK, college president; b. Newton, N.J., Mar. 29, 1941; s. William Bryan and Grace Almond T.; 1 cons, Todd. BS, W.Va. Wesleyan Coll.; MBA, W.Va. U.; LLD, LaGrange Coll. Bus. mgr. Parkersburg (W.Va.) C.C., 1969-71; devel. officer W.Va. Wesleyan Coll., 1972-75, acting treas., 1975-77; v.p. fin. Southwestern U., Georgetown, Tex., 1977-88; pres. Andrew Coll., Cuthbert, Ga., 1988—. Bd. dirs. Citizen Bank, Geogetown, Tex., 1978-88; bd. dirs. Regions Bank, Cuthbert, Ga., 1989-99; cons. Nebr. Wesleyan U.; cons. So. Assn. Schs. and Colls. Chmn. adminstrv. bd. First United Meth. Ch., 1983-85, univ. senate; mem. W.I.H. and Lula E. Pitts Found., Peed scholarship Trust, United Meth. Ch. Served with USAF, 1966-69. Mem. Assn. Pvt. Colls. and Univs. Ga. (pres. dir.), Nat. Assn. Schs. and Colls. Methodist. Home: 408 N Lumpkin St Cuthbert GA 31740-1115 Office: Andrew Coll 413 College St Cuthbert GA 31740-1313 E-mail: ktreible@andrewcollege.edu.

TREICH, RICHARD D. communication executive; b. Morristown, N.J., Oct. 9, 1953; s. Robert F. and Jeannette Treich; m. Nancy S. Dimatteo, Aug. 9, 1981; children:Cameron, Branden. BS in Bus. Adminstrn., Susquehanna U., 1975. Mgr. Ebasco, Dallas, 1975-82; dir. Coopers & Lybrand, 1982-84; prin. KPMG Peat Marwick, Denver, 1984-95; v.p. regulation TCI Comm., Englewood, Colo., 1995—. Office: TCI Comm 5619 Dtc Pkwy Englewood CO 80111-3013

TREICHEL, HELMUTH W.A. technology executive; b. Hessberg, Germany, Aug. 26, 1953; s. Otto Treichel, Elise Treichel; m. Ursula M. Fischer; children: Nicola. BSChemE, Acad. Sci. and Tech., Isny, Germany, 1986. Process devel. engr. Siemens AG, Munich, 1986—92; lead engr. Siemens Components, Burlington, Vt., 1992—94; dept. mgr. multilevel metallization, pilot prodn. mgr. Fraunhofer Inst. for Solid State Tech., Munich, 1994—97; sr. engring. mgr. Lam Rsch. Corp., Fremont, Calif., 1997—2000; dir. tech. Novellus Sys., Inc., San Jose, 2000—02. Presenter in field. Contbr. articles to profl. jours. Mem.: Materials Rsch. Soc. Achievements include patents in field. Home: 859 Pheland Ct Milpitas CA 95035 Home Fax: 408-262-5975; Office Fax: 408-570-7530. Personal E-mail: treichel@yahoo.com. Business E-Mail: helmuth.treichel@novellus.com.

TREIGER, IRWIN LOUIS, lawyer; b. Seattle, Sept. 10, 1934; s. Sam S. and Rose (Steinberg) T.; m. Betty Lou Friedlander, Aug. 18, 1957; children: Louis H., Karen I., Kenneth B. BA, U. Wash., 1955, JD, 1957; LLM in Taxation, NYU, 1958. Bar: Wash. 1958, D.C. 1982, U.S. Dist. Ct. (we. dist.) Wash., U.S. Ct. Appeals (9th cir.), U.S. Supreme Ct. Assoc. Bogle & Gates, Seattle, 1958-63, ptnr., 1964-99, chmn., 1986-94; ptnr. Dorsey & Whitney LLP, 1999—. Pres. Jewish Fedn. Greater Seattle, 1993-95; chmn. Mayor's Symphony Panel, 1986, Corp. Coun. for the Arts, 1987-88; pres. Seattle Symphony Found., 1986—; trustee, co-chmn. Cornish Coll. of the Arts, 1990-96; trustee The Seattle Found., 1992—, vice chair, 1999—; trustee Samis Found., 1989—; chmn. King County Baseball Pk. Commn., 1995. Fellow Am. Coll. Tax Counsel; mem. ABA (chmn. taxation sect. 1988-89, sect. del. 1990-96, bd. govs. 2000—), Wash. State Bar Assn. (chmn. taxation sect. 1975, co-chmn. nat. conf. lawyers and accts. 1997-2000), Greater Seattle C. of C. (chmn. 1993-94), Seattle Rotary (trustee 1998-2000), Seattle Rotary Svc. Found. (v.p. 1995-96, pres. 1996-97). Jewish. Office: Dorsey & Whitney LLP 1420 5th Ave Ste 3400 Seattle WA 98101-4010 E-mail: treiger.irwin@dorseylaw.com.

TREINAVICZ, KATHRYN MARY, software engineer; b. Nov. 25, 1957; d. Ralph Clement and Frances Elizabeth (O'Leary) T. BS, Salem State Coll., Mass., 1980. Tchr. Brockton Pub. Schs., 1980-81; instr. Quincy CETA Inc., Mass., 1981-82; programmer Systems Architects Inc., Randolph, 1982; programmer analyst Dayton, Ohio, 1982-84; sr. programmer analyst System Devel. Corp., 1984-86; project mgr. Unisys Inc., 1986-87; software engr. Computer Scis. Corp. (formerly Systems & Applied Corp. 1988), 1987-89; project mgr. Computer Sci. Corp. (formerly Atlantic Rsch. Corp. 1994), Fairborn, Ohio, 1989-96; dept. mgr., 1996-98; sr. test analyst, 1998—. Mem. NAFE. Democrat. Roman Catholic. Avocations: Steven King novels, needlepoint, knitting, crocheting.

TREISCH, PATRICIA C. foundation administrator; b. Galion, Ohio, Jan. 4, 1929; d. Wilbert Russell and Bertha Coral (Eusey) Eckstein; m. George J. Treisch, July 15, 1951; children: Terrence L., Jeffrey D. BS, Miami U. of Ohio, 1950. Lifeguard, head lifeguard Galion Mcpl. Pool, 1946-48; waterfront dir. Girl Scouts USA, Cin., 1949, Rhinelander, Wis., 1950; health, physical edn. and recreation dir. YWCA, Warren, Ohio, 1950-58; health and safety dir. ARC, Trumbull County chpt., 1971—. Bd. mem. Healthwise, Warren, 1982—. Organizer 4th Grade Swim Program, Warren, 1951, City and County Swim Programs, Warren, 1953—, Adapted Aquatics Programs, Warren, 1961—, Warren City Schs. Parent Boosters for Swimming, Warren, 1968, Trumbull Canoe Trails, Warren, 1970; dean waterfront ARC Nat. Aquatic Schs., Warren, 1969-71; mem. YWCA, 1950—; bd. mem. Urban League, 1950—, v.p. 1951-76, Trumbull Canoe Trails, pres., v.p., treas., 1970—. Mem. AAUW. Democrat. Lutheran. Home: 366 Willard Ave SE Warren OH 44483-6238 Office: Am Red Cross/Trumbull Count 661 Mahoning Ave NW Warren OH 44483-4607

TREISTER, GEORGE MARVIN, lawyer; b. Oxnard, Calif., Sept. 5, 1923; s. Isadore Harry and Augusta Lee (Bloom) T.; m. Jane Goldberg, Jan. 24, 1946; children: Laura, Neil, Adam, Dana. BS, UCLA, 1943; LL.B., Yale U., 1949. Bar: Calif. 1950. Law clk. to chief justice Calif. Supreme Ct., 1949-50; law clk. to Assoc. Justice Hugo L. Black U. S. Supreme Ct., 1950-51; asst. U.S. atty. So. Dist. Calif., 1951-53; dep. atty. gen. Calif., 1953; practiced in Los Angeles, 1953—; mem. Stutman, Treister and Glatt, 1953—; instr. U. So. Calif. Law Sch., 1954-98, Stanford U. Law Sch., 1977-81. Mem., former vice chmn. Nat. Bankruptcy Conf.; former mem. adv. com. on bankruptcy rules Jud. Conf. U.S. Contbr. articles to profl. jours. Served with USNR, 1943-46. Mem. Am. Law Inst., Am. Judicature Soc. Home: 1201 Neil Creek Rd Ashland OR 97520-9778 Office: 3699 Wilshire Blvd Los Angeles CA 90010-2719

TREJOS, FRANKLIN ANTHONY, physician assistant; b. Spokane, Wash., July 6, 1955; s. Frank Trejos and Lloydene Louise (Small) Mielbrecht; m. Felicia Jo Cote, May 27, 1994; children: Cerena, Cebrena, Alyssa. Student in med. assistance, Western Coll. Med. Dental Asst, 1978; grad. physician asst., U. Utah Coll. Medicine, 1984. Advanced EMT Kootenai County Emergency Med. Rescue Svc., Coeur d'alene, Idaho, 1980—82; phys. asst. Franklin Park Minor Emergency Ctr., Spokane, Wash., 1984—85; phys. asst. family practice Cigna Health Plan, Mesa, Ariz., 1985—87; phys. asst. gen. surgery, orthoped. surgery, neurosurgery Mayo Clinic Scottsdale, 1987—97; faculty physician asst. program Midwestern U., Glendale, 1997—2000; physician asst. Sonoran Med. Ctrs., Phoenix, 2001—02; with The Pain Mgmt. Clinic, Scottsdale. Faculty physician asst. program Midwestern U., Glendale, Ariz., 1997—2000. Fellow Am. Acad. Physician Assts. Avocations: waterskiing, mountain biking, astronomy, photography, marine life. Home: 2122 E Behrend Dr Phoenix AZ 85024-1256 Office: The Pain Mgmt Clinic 9787 N 91st St Ste 100 Scottsdale AZ 85258 E-mail: ftrejos@t-3.cc.

TRELEASE, ALLEN WILLIAM, historian, educator; b. Boulder, Colo., Jan. 31, 1928; s. William, Jr. and Helen (Waldo) T.; children— William C. (dec. 1990), Mary E., John A. AB, U. Ill., 1950, MA, 1951; PhD, Harvard U., 1955. Mem. faculty Wells Coll., Aurora, N.Y., 1955-67, prof. history, 1965-67, chmn. dept. history and govt., 1963-67; prof. history U. N.C., Greensboro, 1967-94, head dept., 1984-92, prof. emeritus, 1994—. Author: Indian Affairs in Colonial New York: The Seventeenth Century, 1960, White Terror: The Ku Klux Klan Conspiracy and Southern Reconstruction, 1971, Reconstruction: The Great Experiment, 1971, The North Carolina Railroad, 1849-1871, and the Modernization of North Carolina, 1991, Changing Assignments: A Pictorial History of the U. of N.C. at Greensboro, 1991. Mem. Am., So. Hist. assns., Orgn. Am. Historians, Hist. Soc. N.C. (pres. 1986-87), AAUP, Phi Beta Kappa, Phi Kappa Phi, Phi Eta Sigma, Phi Kappa Psi.

TRELFA, RICHARD THOMAS, paper company executive; b. Alpena, Mich., July 5, 1918; s. Fred R. and Mable (Hagen) T.; m. Heidi Brigitte Ruckstuhl (dec. 1996); children: Thomas W., Barbara E. (dec.), Jeffrey C., Michael F.; m. Jennifer Thorlby Trelfa, Jan. 30, 1999. BS, U. Mich., 1940. With Hercules Powder Co., 1941-52, Watervliet Paper Co., Mich., 1952-58; exec. v.p., treas., dir. Perkins-Goodwin Co., Inc., N.Y.C., 1958-70, v.p., treas., CFO, 1970, sr. v.p., 1974-82; chmn. bd. Elcon, Inc., Houston, 1983-91; vice-chmn. bd. B.S. & W Whiteley Ltd., Eng., 1983-88, also bd. dirs. Treas., dir. Kennebec River Pulp & Paper Co., Madison, Maine, 1967-69, chmn. bd., treas., 1969-72, chmn. bd., mem. exec. com., 1972-73, dir., mem. exec. com., 1973-75; pres. Castle & Overton (Can.) Ltd., 1971-82; chmn. bd. EHV Weidmann Industries, Inc., St. Johnsbury, Vt., 1974-84, Franconia Paper Co. Inc., Lincoln, N.H., 1978-80; N.H. State rep. to Gen. Ctr., 1990-98; water commr. Lisbon, N.H., 1990-97, selectman, Lisbon, 1995-2002. Fellow Am. Soc. Quality Control, TAPPI (past divsn. chmn., dir.); mem. Paper Industry Mgmt. Assn. (past divsn. chmn.), Am. Inst. Chem. Engrs., Am. Chem. Soc., Soc. Rheology, Masons, Univ. Mich. Club. Republican. E-mail: (personal). Home: 245 Northey Rd Lisbon NH 03585-7016 E-mail: rttrelfa@aol.com.

TRELKA, JANICE MARGARET NACE, retired secondary school educator; b. Cleve., Nov. 9, 1944; d. Allen Samuel and Ethel (Pinhard) Nace; m. Martin Frank Trelka, June 24, 1978. Student, Merrill-Palmer Inst., Detroit, 1965; BE, Ashland Coll., 1966, health tchr. cert., 1985; MEd, Cleve. State U., 1976. Supr. indsl. cafeteria Republic Steel, Cleve., 1967-68; bank teller Cen. Nat. Bank, 1968-69; tchr. home econs. Lorain (Ohio) City Schs., 1969-98; ret., 1998. Speaker Cleve. Ctr. for Econ. Edn., 1975, Ohio Home Econs. Conf., 1984, 86, 88, 89, 93, Ohio Edn. Assn., 1985; mem. impact home econs. curriculum guide task force State Dept. Edn., Columbus, Ohio, 1977, mem. mid. sch. resource guide devel., 1988. Tchr. Sunday sch., Cleve., 1967-74; treas. PTA Hawthorne-Boone Sch., Lorain, 1971-74; mem. state bd. Women's Commn., Columbus, 1978-86; mem. bd. Christian edn., Lorain, 1982-88; mem. Sexually Transmitted Disease Task Force, Lorain, 1989-92, Vocat. Task Force, Lorain, 1990-93; mem. choir. State Recognition for Martha Holden Jennings Grant Implementation, 1984; recipient Curriculum Writing Contest 3d Pl. award Ohio Coun. on Econ. Edn., 1984, 1st Pl. award, 1985, Nat. Cert. of Merit award Joint Coun. on Econ. Edn., 1986. Mem. NEA, Am. Vocat. Assn., Am. Home Econs. Assn. (cert.), Ohio Edn. Assn., Ohio Vocat. Assn., Ohio Home Econs. Assn., Lorain Edn. Assn., Lorain County Home Econs. Assn. Avocations: letter writing, needlework, cooking, reading. Home: 2611 Denver Ave Lorain OH 44055-1457 also: 15610 Cashmere Ln Tampa FL 33624 E-mail: jtrelka@aol.com.

TRELSTAD, ROBERT LAURENCE, pathology educator, cell biologist; b. Redding, Calif., June 16, 1940; s. Bertram Laurence and Dorothy (Axt) T.; m. Barbara Stanton Henken, Aug. 27, 1961; children: Derek, Graham, Brian, Jeremy. BA, Columbia U., 1961; MD, Harvard U., 1966. From asst. to assoc. prof. Harvard Med. Sch., Boston, 1972-81; chief pathology Shriners Burns Inst., 1975-81; staff pathologist Mass. Gen. Hosp., 1972-81; prof., chair pathology Robert Wood Johnson Med. Sch., Piscataway/New Brunswick, N.J., 1981-98; acting dir. Child Health Inst. of N.J., 1998—, Paz chair devel. biology, 1999—. Mem. study sect. NIH, Bethesda, Md., 1971-75, 86-90; mem. adv. coun. Nat. Inst. Child Health and Human Devel., 1993-97; chmn. health professions adv. com. Princeton U., 2002—. Co-founder, editor-in-chief: Keyboard Publishing, Inc., 1990; past mem. editorial bd. various profl. jours. including Jour. Cell Biology, Am. Jour. Pathology, Devel. Biology, Devel. Dynamics. Lt. comdr. USPHS, 1967—69. Helen Hay Whitney Found. fellow, 1969-72; recipient Rsch. Faculty award Am. Cancer Soc., 1972-76, Disting. Tchr. in Basic Scis. award Alpha Omega Alpha and Assn. Am. Med. Colls., 1992. Mem. Am. Soc. Cell Biology (sec. 1982-88), Soc. Devel. Biology (pres. 1983). Home: 35 Westcott Rd Princeton NJ 08540-3038 Office: Robert Wood Johnson Med Sch Child Health Inst New Brunswick NJ 08901

TREMAIN, ALAN, hotel executive; b. Kent, England, Aug. 18, 1935; came to U.S., 1966; s. Archibalt and Elizabeth (Morris) T.; m. Ingrid K. Olbrich, Dec. 1997; 1 child, Warren; m. Ingrid Kay Olbrich. Grad., Westminster Hotel Sch., 1952, Canterbury Sch. Econs., 1962; LL.B., La Salle Sch., Chgo., 1971. Chef de Pertie Grosvenor House, London, 1954-55; food and beverage mgr. Peninsula, Hong Kong, 1956-57; gen. mgr. Warners Hotel, also The Russley, Christchurch, New Zealand, 1958-64, Menzies, Sydney, Australia, 1964-65, Empress Hotel, Vancouver, B.C., Can., 1966-69; pres. Planned Food Facilities (Internat.) Ltd., Toronto, 1970-72; resident mgr. Sheraton Boston, 1972; mng. dir. Copley Plaza Hotel, Boston, 1972—. Chmn. Hotels of Distinction, Inc., Boston; dir. The China Fund, Inc., 1992, chmn., 1999—. Author: A Guide to the Fine Art of Living, 1963, A Meal for To-Night, 1965. Decorated officer Order Brit. Empire (U.K.); recipient Culinary Merit award from Cercle Epicurien Mondel, Paris, 1956. Fellow Hotel and Catering Inst. (U.K.); founding mem. Internat. Soc. Chefs de Cuisine (chmn. 1954) Clubs: Mason, Montreal Badminton and Squash, The Beach Club, Palm Beach, Les Ambs., London, Rolls Royce Owners. Address: Hotels of Distinction Inc 380 S County Rd Ste 200 Palm Beach FL 33480-6526 E-mail: ATREMAIN@AOL.COM.

TREMAINE, H. STEWART, lawyer; b. St. Paul, Mar. 17, 1919; s. Hugh Milner and Sally (Fox) T.; m. Harriet Lupton, July 10, 1948; children: Sally, Victoria, Katherine. BA, U. Wash., 1940; LLB, Yale U., 1946. Bar: Oreg. 1947, Wash. 1947. Ptnr. Davis Wright Tremaine, Portland, Oreg., 1947—. Capt. USMC, 1942-45. Decorated Purple Heart (2). Mem. Arlington Club, Waverley Club, Multnomah Athletic Club (pres.). Republican. Presbyterian. Avocations: golf, hiking, climbing, fishing, bridge. Office: Davis Wright Tremaine 1300 SW 5th Ave Ste 2200 Portland OR 97201-5667

TREMAINE, SCOTT DUNCAN, astrophysicist; b. Toronto, May 25, 1950; s. Vincent Joseph and Beatrice Delphine (Sharp) T. BSc, McMaster U., Hamilton, Ont., 1971; PhD, Princeton U., 1975. Postdoctoral fellow Calif. Inst. Tech., Pasadena, 1975-77; rsch. assoc. Inst. Astronomy, Cambridge, Eng., 1977-78; long-term mem. Inst. for Advanced Study, Princeton, N.J., 1978-81; assoc. prof. MIT, Cambridge, 1981-85; prof., dir. Can. Inst. for Theoretical Astrophysics U. Toronto, 1985-96; dir. program in cosmology and gravity Can. Inst. Advanced Rsch., Toronto, 1996—2002; prof. Princeton U., 1997—, chair dept. astrophys. scis., 1998—. Author: Galactic Dynamics, 1987; contbr. articles to profl. jours. E.W.R. Steacie fellow Natural Scis. and Engring. Rsch. Coun., 1988; recipient H.B. Warner prize Am. Astron. Soc., 1983, Steacie prize, 1989, C.S. Beals award Canadian Astron. Soc., 1990, Rutherford medal Royal Soc. Can., 1990, Heinemann prize for Astrophysics, 1997, Brouwer award, 1997. Fellow Royal Soc. London, Royal Soc. Can.; mem. Am. Acad. Arts and Scis. (fgn. hon.), Nat. Acad. Scis. Office: Princeton U Dept Astrophys Sci Peyton Hall Princeton NJ 08544-1001

TREMBLAY, ANDRE GABRIEL, lawyer; b. Jonquiere, Que., Can., Nov. 10, 1937; s. Jean-Charles Tremblay and Julienne (Tremblay) Laberge; children: Jean-Francois, Frederic, Alexandre Reynold. BA, U. Laval-Que. Can., 1959, LL.L., 1962; LLM, U. Ottawa-Ont. Can., 1964, LL.D., 1966. Bar: Que 1963. Asst., law U. Ottawa, 1966-70; assoc. U. Montreal, Que., 1970-75, prof. law, 1972—, pres. Gen. Assn. Profs. Que.; dir. Pub. Law Ctr., 1972-76, vice dean Law, 1982-86; v.p.. Com. on Human Rights, Montreal, 1981-83; legal adv. to bar, govts., law firms, 1972—. Sr Const advisor to Que Govt, 1986—92; pres Prof's Union Univ Montreal, 1995—98; co-counsel Int Criminal Tribunal Rwanda, UN. Author: (book) Les competences legislatives, 1967 (1st Prize Govt Que, 1968), Precis de droit municipal, 1973, Precis de droit constitutionnel, 1982, Droit Constitutionnel-Principles, 1993, Droit Constitutionnel-Principles, 2d ed, 2000, La Revision Constitutionnelle, 1997, Droit Constitutionnel-Documents, 1999; contbr. chapters to books, articles to profl jours. Mem observer's mission Int Comn Jurists, Geneva, 1981—. Mem.: Asn Can Law Teachers. Office: Faculty Law U Montreal CP 6228 succ A Montreal QC Canada H3C 3J7 Fax: 450-243-1795. E-mail: agtremblay@videotron.ca.

TREMBLAY, ANDRÉ-MARIE, physicist; b. Montreal, Que., Can., Jan. 2, 1953; m. Marié à Guylaine Séguin; children: Noémie, Rachel. BSc, U. Montreal, 1974; PhD, MIT, 1978. With Energie Atomique du Can. Limitée, 1973-74, MIT, Boston, 1974-75, Inst. de Recherche de l'Hydro-Que., 1976, Cornell U., Ithaca, N.Y., 1978-80; prof. physics U. Sherbrooke, Que., 1980—, dir. Rsch. Ctr. Physics of Solids, 1991-99. Cons. Cornell U., 1981, Ohio State U., 1982, IBM, 1984; vis. scientist Cornell U., 1986-87; vis. rsch. physicist Inst. for Theoretical Physics, Santa Barbara, Calif., 1989, 96, 2000; vis. scientist Brookhaven (N.Y.) Nat. Lab, 1984; assoc. prof. U. Provence, France, 1982, 83, 97, 99, 2000; Can. Rsch. chair in condensed matter physics, 2000—. Contbr. over 100 articles to profl. publs. Recipient Herzberg medal Can. Assn. Physics, Steacie prize Natural Scis. and Engring. Rsch. Coun., 1987; Killam fellow, 1992-94, CAP-CRM prize in Theoretical and Math. Physics, 2001. Mem. Can. Inst. Advanced Rsch. Office: Sherbrooke U Dept Physics Sherbrooke QC Canada J1K 2R1

TREMBLAY, JANINE MARIE, psychologist; b. Cambridge, Mass., Aug. 11, 1949; d. Henry Joseph and Marie Therese (Fradette) T.; m. George Royal Albert Johns, Nov. 20, 1993. PhD, St. John's U., 1983; postdoctorate, Adelphi U., 1994; BSN, Felician Coll., 2001; postgrad., SUNY Stony Brook, 2001—. Lic. psychologist, N.J., Fla., N.Y. Staff psychologist Rahway State Prison, Avenel, N.J., 1978-81; from staff psychologist to dir. psychology Greystone Park (N.J.) Hosp., 1981-91; pvt. practice psychology Morristown, N.J., 1985—. Cons. Johnstone Tng. & Rsch., Bordentown, N.J., 1979-85; supr. Contemporary Ctr. for Advanced Psychoanalytic Studies, 1995-2001. Mem. editl. bd. N.J. Psychologist, 1981-93, Bd. dirs. Mental Health Assn. Morris County, 1995—2001. Mem. APA, N.J. Acad. Psychology (trustee 1991-94), N.J. Psychol. Assn. (com. mem. 1987-93). Avocations: golf, travel, fitness, reading. Home and Office: 150 Madison Ave Morristown NJ 07960-6015 E-mail: Jantre6767@aol.com.

TREMBLAY, MARC ADÉLARD, anthropologist, educator; b. Les Eboulements, Que., Can., Apr. 24, 1922; s. Willie and Laurette (Tremblay) T.; m. Jacqueline Cyr, Dec. 27, 1949; children: Geneviève, Lorraine, Marc, Colette, Dominique, Suzanne. AB, U. Montreal, 1944, L.S.A., 1948; MA, Laval U., 1950; PhD, Cornell U., 1954; PhD (hon.), Ottawa U., 1982, Guelph U., 1983, U. N. B.C., 1994, Carleton U., 1995, U. Ste. Anne, 1997, McGill U., 1998. Research asso. Cornell U., 1953-56; mem. faculty Laval U., 1956-93, prof. anthropology, 1963-68, 81-93, prof. emeritus, 1994, vice dean social scis., 1968-71, dean Grad. Sch., 1971-79, also mem. univ. council.; pres. Quebec Coun. Social Rsch., 1987-91. Dir. Inuit and Circupolar Study Group Laval U., 1991—93; mem. Nunavik Commn., 1999—2001. Author 25 books and monographs in social scis., about 200 articles. Decorated officer Order of Can., gt. officer Order of Que.; recipient Que. Lit. prize, 1965, Innis-Gerin prize Royal Soc. Can., 1979, Molson prize Can. Coun., 1987, Prix Marcel Vincent ACFAS, 1988, Contbn. exceptionnelle Societé de sociologie et d'anthropolotie, 1990, Esdras Minville award Soc. St.-Jean Baptiste, 1991; named to Internat. Order of Merit, Internat. Biog. Inst., Cambridge, Eng., 1990. Mem. Royal Soc. Can. (pres. 1981-84), Acad. des Scis. Morales et Politiques (sec.), Rsch. Inst. Pub. Policy, Am. Anthrop. Assn. (past fellow), Am. Sociology Soc. (past fellow), Can. Soc. Applied Anthropology, Can. Sociology and Anthropology Assn. (founding pres.), Can. Ethnology Soc. (past pres.), Assn. Can. Univs. for Northern Studies (past pres.), Assn. Internat. Sociology, Societe des savants et sci. Can. (v.p., pres. nat. order Quebec 1998-2000). Home: 835 N Orléans St Sainte Foy QC Canada G1X 3J4 Office: Laval Univ Dept Anthropology Quebec QC Canada G1K 7P4 Fax: (418) 653-9865. E-mail: matrem@microtec.net.

TREMBLAY, RICHARD ERNEST, psychology educator; b. Nov. 23, 1944; BA, U. Ottawa, Can., 1966; MPsed, U. Montreal, 1970; PhD, U. London, 1976. Asst. prof. U. Montreal, 1976-81, assoc. prof., 1981-86, prof., 1986—, Can. Rsch. chair in child devel., 2001—, dir. Ctr. of Excellence for Early Child Devel., 2001—; clinician St. Charles Psychiat. Hosp., Joliette, Can., 1966-69, Boscoville, Montreal, Can., 1967-70, Phillippe Pinel Psychiat. Inst., Montreal, 1970-73. Chmn. Sch. of Psycho-Edn., Faculty of Arts and Scis., U. Montreal, 1986-90; invited prof. ethology lab. U. Rennes I, 1993-94, dept. psychology U. Jyväskylä, Finland, 1991; invited scientist psychophysiology lab. U. Franche-Com., 1982-83; presenter in field. Author (with others): Face to Face with Giftedness , 1983, Ethologie et Development de l'enfant, 1985, Le Traitement des Adolescents Delinquants, 1985, Les Relations Entre Enfants, 1988, Human Development and Criminal Behavior: New Ways of Advancing Knowledge, 1991, Famille, Inadaption et Intervention, 1991, Les enfants agressifs: Perspective Development Interculturelle, 1991, Preventing Antisocial Behavior from Birth to Adolescence , 1992, Juvenile Crime, Juvenile Justice, 2001. Molson fellow Can. Inst. of Advanced Rsch. Fellow Royal Soc. of Can., Can. Psychol. Assn.; mem. AAAS, Internat. Soc. for the Study of Behavioral Devel. (exec. com. 1994—), Internat. Soc. for Rsch. on Agression (coun. mem. 1992-96), Am. Soc. of Criminology, Assn. Canadienne-Française pour l'Avancement des Scis., European Assn. for Psychology and Law, Internat. soc. for Human Ethology, N.Y. Acad. Scis., Soc. for Rsch. in Child Devel.

TREMBLAY, RODRIGUE, economics educator; b. Matane, Que., Can., Oct. 13, 1939; s. George and Germaine (St. Louis) T.; m. Carol Howard, Sept. 5, 1964; children: Jean-Paul, Alain, Joanne. BA, Laval U., Quebec City, 1961; BS in Econs., U. de Montreal (Que.), 1963; MA in Econs., Stanford U., 1965, PhD in Econs., 1968. Prof. Univ. de Montreal, 1967—. Mem. nat. assembly Parliament of Que., 1976-81; min. industry and commerce Govt. of Que., 1976-79; mem. arbitrage panel Can.-U.S. Free Trade Agreement Ottawa (Can.) and Washington, 1989—. Woodrow Wilson Found. fellow, 1964-65. Mem. N.Am. Econs. and Fin. Assn. (pres. 1986-87), Assn. Internat. des Econ. de Langue Francaise. Office: U Montreal Dept Econs Montreal QC Canada H3C 3J7 E-mail: rodrique.tremblay@umontreal.ca.

TREMBLAY, WILLIAM ANDREW, English language educator, writer; b. Southbridge, Mass., June 9, 1940; s. Arthur Achille and Irene (Fontaine) T.; m. Cynthia Ann Crooks, Sept. 28, 1962; children: William Crooks, Benjamin Philip, John Fontaine. BA, Clark U., 1962, MA, 1969; MFA in Poetry, U.

Mass., 1972. English tchr. Southbridge (Mass.) High Sch., 1962-63, Sutton (Mass.) High Sch., 1963-65, Tantasqua Regional High Sch., Sturbridge, Mass., 1965-67; asst. prof. Leicester (Mass.) Jr. Coll., 1967-70; teaching asst. U. Mass., Amherst, 1970-72; instr. Springfield (Mass.) Coll., 1972-73; prof. English Colo. State U., Fort Collins, 1973—, dir. MFA program in creative writing. Fulbright-Hays lectureship, Lisbon, Portugal, 1979, NEH summer program, 1981; mem. program dirs. coun. Associated Writing Programs, 1984-86. Author: The June Rise: The Apocryphal Letters of Antoine Janis, 1994, (poetry) Rainstorm Over the Alphabet, 2001, Duhamel: Ideas of Order in Little Canada, 1986, Second Sun: New and Selected Poems, 1985, Home Front, 1978, The Anarchist Heart, 1977, Crying in the Cheap Seats, 1971; editor-in-chief: Colo. Rev., 1983-91. Summer writing fellow Corp. of Yaddo, 1989, Creative Writing fellow Nat. Endowment for Arts, 1985; recipient Pushcart prize Pushcart Prize Anthology, 1987. Mem.: Puerto del Sol (bd. advisors, John F. Stern Dist. Prof. award 2002), Am. Acad. Poetry, Poudre Wilderness Vol. Home: 3412 Lancaster Dr Fort Collins CO 80525-2817 Office: Colo State U Dept English Fort Collins CO 80523-0001

TREMBLEY, MARK MICHEL, geographer, educator; b. Glendale, Calif., Apr. 21, 1941; s. Stanley Alexander and Elaine Blanche (Rendahl) T.; m. (div.); 1 child, Kirsten Perri. BA in Geography, Calif. State U., Northridge, 1964; MA in Geography, U. Calif., Berkeley, 1970, M in Landscape Arch., 1975. City planner City of Hayward, Calif., 1968-71; instr. earth sci. Fresno (Calif.) City Coll., 1971-73; pvt. practice environ. planner Berkeley, Calif., 1975-79; dir. grad. program in urban and regional planning Antioch U., 1978-81; project mgr. Edaw, Inc., San Francisco, 1981-85; sr. assoc. EIP Assoc., 1985-90; prof. urban geography San Diego Mesa Coll., 1990—. Developer AS degree program in geog. info. sys. San Diego Mesa Coll., 1999-2000; cons. in field. Vol. County Dem. Party, 1996-97. Beatrix Ferrand fellow U. Calif./Oreg. State U., 1973; Nat. Sci. Found. grant Nat. Sci., 1973, Chancellors grant for innovative edn. San Diego C.C. Dist., 1998. Mem. Assn. Am. Geographers, Nat. Coun. for Geographic Edn., Am. Soc. Landscape Architects. Democrat. Unitarian Universalist. Avocations: fly fishing, history, community theater. Home: 3424 Sixth Ave San Diego CA 92103 Office: San Diego Mesa Coll 7250 Mesa Coll Dr San Diego CA 92111 E-mail: mtremble@sdccd.net.

TREMBLEY, PAUL GERARD, communications executive, announcer; b. Pittsfield, Mass., Jan. 9, 1953; s. Paul Gerard and Evelyn Mary (Kavey) T.; m. Carol Margaret Jacques, Sept. 2, 1978. BA in Communications, U. Mass., 1978. Announcer Sta. WBEC-AM, Pittsfield, 1970-74, Sta. WTIC-AM, Hartford, Conn., 1978; radio personality Sta. WHAM, Rochester, N.Y., 1979-80; announcer Satellite Music Network, Mokena, Ill., 1980-81, Sta. WLAK-FM, Chgo., 1981-84; owner Downtown Sound Prodns., Valencia, Calif., 1974—. Voice announcer numerous radio and TV commls.; promotions announcer Disney, CBS-TV, 20th Century Fox; narrator PBS, IBM. Avocations: Rotary, dining, golf.

TREML, VLADIMIR GUY, economist, educator; b. Kharkov, USSR, Mar. 27, 1929; came to U.S., 1950, naturalized, 1953; s. Guy Alexey and Lydia Vladimir (Timofeev) T.; m. Emma Miro, July 12, 1952; children— Irene Treml Cagney, Tatiana, Alexey. BA in Econs, Bklyn. Coll., 1955; MA in Econs, Columbia U., 1956; PhD in Econs, U. N.C., 1963. Dept. supr. Bache & Co., N.Y.C., 1953-58; research asso. Inst. for Social Scis., U. N.C., Chapel Hill, 1958-61; asso. prof. econs. Franklin and Marshall Coll., 1961-66; research asso. Inst. Study USSR, Munich, Germany, 1966-67; prof. econs. Duke U., 1967—; dir. Ctr. for Slavic Studies U.S. Dept. Edn. of Duke U., 1991—. Cons. in field; expert Dept. Commerce, The World Bank, other fed. agys., 1971—; vis. Ford research prof. U. Calif., Berkeley, 1984-85; vis. research prof. U. Hokkaido, Sapporo, Japan, 1985. Author: (with others) Structure of the Soviet Economy, 1972, Input-Output Analysis and the Soviet Economy, 1975, Western Sovietology in the Soviet Union, 1999; contbr. reports to publs. of Joint Econ. Com., U.S. Congress; contbr. articles to profl. publs.; editor: Soviet Economic Statistics, 1972; editor, contbg. author: Studies in Soviet Input-Output Analysis, 1977, Alcohol in the USSR, 1982; contbg. editor: Soviet Economy Jour. Trustee Nat. Council for Soviet and East European Research, Inc., Washington, 1978-84. Served with USMC, 1951-53. Ford Found. grantee, 1972-81, Dept. Def.-Advanced Rsch. Project Agy. grantee, 1975-76, Dept. State grantee, 1976-77, Dept. Def. grantee, 1985-90, Georgetown U. grantee, 1984-86, Olin Found. grantee, 1989, Internat. Rsch. and Exch. Bd. grantee, 1993-96, Nat. Coun. for Eurasian Rsch. grantee, 1996-98; Fulbright fellow Moscow U., 1992. Mem. So. Econ. Assn., Am. Econ. Assn., Assn. Comparative Econ. Studies (exec. com. 1972-74), Am. Assn. Advancement Slavic Studies, So. Conf. on Slavic Studies (pres. 1977-78), Phi Beta Kappa. Democrat. Eastern Orthodox. Home: 603 Longleaf Dr Chapel Hill NC 27517-3039

TRENARY, MICHAEL, chemistry educator; b. L.A., July 8, 1956; s. Bernard Elroy and Jean Ann (Morris) T.; m. Wendy Greenhouse, June 10, 1984; children: Eleanor Jane, Russell Jack. BS, U. Calif., Berkeley, 1978; PhD, MIT, 1982. Rsch. asst. prof. U. Pitts., 1982-84; asst. prof. U. Ill., Chgo., 1984-89, assc. prof., 1989-92, prof., 1992—. Contbr. articles to sci. jours., including Jour. Chem. Physics, Jour. Am. Chem. Soc., Surface Sci., Phys. Rev. Letters. Recipient Dreyfus Tchr.-Scholar award Henry and Camille Dreyfus Found., 1989, U.Ill. Scholar award U. Ill. Found., 1990. Fellow Am. Vacuum Soc.; mem. Am. Chem. Soc., Am. Vacuum Soc., Am. Phys. Soc. E-mail: mtrenary.uic.edu. Office: U Ill at Chgo Dept Chemistry 845 W Taylor St Chicago IL 60607-7056

TRENBEATH, THOMAS L. state legislator, lawyer; b. Neche, N.D., July 23, 1948; m. Rose Trenbeath; children: Ian, Britta. BS, U. N.D., 1970, JD, 1978. Underwriting atty. Chgo. Title Ins. Co., Denver, 1981-84; v.p. Ticor Title Ins. Co., 1984—86; ptnr. Fleming, DuBois & Trenbeath, Attys., 1986-97; city adminstr., atty., 1997—; mem. N.D. Senate from 10th dist., 2001—. Mem. ct. svcs. adminstrn. com. N.D. Supreme Ct., 1995—; dir. Red River Regional Coun., 1999—. Capt. USAR, 1971-78. Mem. N.D. Assn. Mcpl. Power Sys. (v.p. 1999—), N.D. Bar Assn., N.D. Humanities Coun. Republican. Lutheran. Office: PO Box 361 Cavalier ND 58220-0361 E-mail: rosentom@polarcomm.com., ttrenbea@state.nd.us.

TRENBERTH, KEVIN EDWARD, atmospheric scientist; b. Christchurch, New Zealand, Nov. 8, 1944; came to U.S., 1977; s. Edward Maurice and Ngaira Ivy (Eyre) T.; m. Gail Neville Thompson, Mar. 21, 1970; children: Annika Gail, Angela Dawn. BSc with honors, U. Canterbury, Christchurch, 1966; ScD, MIT, 1972. Meteorologist New Zealand Meteorol. Service, Wellington, 1966-76, supt. dynamic meteorology, 1976-77; assoc. prof. meteorology U. Ill., Urbana, 1977-82, prof., 1982-84; scientist Nat. Ctr. Atmospheric Research, Boulder, Colo., 1984-86, sr. scientist, 1986—, leader empirical studies group, 1987, head sect. climate analysis, 1987—; dep. dir. climate and global dynamics divsn. Nat. Ctr. Atmospheric Rsch., 1991-95. Mem. joint sci. com. for world climate rsch. programme, com. climate changes and the ocean Tropical Oceans Global Atmosphere Program Sci. Steering Group, 1990-94; mem. Climate Variability and Predictability Sci. Steering Group, 1995—, co-chair, 1996-99; mem. joint sci. com. World Climate Rsch. Program, 1999—. Editor: Climate System Modeling, 1992, Earth Interactions, 1996-98; contbr. Intergovernmental Panel on Climate Change, 1990, 92, lead author, 1995, 2001; contbr. articles to profl. jours. Grantee NSF, NOAA, NASA. Fellow Am. Meteorol. Soc. (editor sci. jour. 1981-86, com. chmn. 1985-87, Editor's award 1989, Jule G. Charney award 2000), AAAS (coun. del. sect. atmosphere and hydrosphere sci. 1993-97), Royal Soc. New Zealand (hon.); mem. NAS (earth scis. com. 1982-85, tropical oceans global atmosphere adv. panel 1984-87, polar rsch. bd. 1986-90, climate rsch. com. 1987-90, global oceans atmosphere land sys. panel 1994-98, panel on reconciling temperature observations, 1999-2000, com. on global change rsch. 1999-02), Meteorol. Soc. New Zealand. Home: 1445 Landis Ct Boulder CO 80303-1122 Office: Nat Ctr Atmospheric Rsch PO Box 3000 Boulder CO 80307-3000 E-mail: trenbert@ucar.edu.

TRENCH, WILLIAM FREDERICK, mathematics educator; b. Trenton, N.J., July 31, 1931; s. George Daniel and Anna Elizabeth (Taylor) T.; m. Lucille Ann Marasco, Dec. 26, 1954 (div. Dec. 1978); children: Joseph William, Randolph Clifford, John Frederick, Gina Margaret; m. Beverly Joan Busenshut, Nov. 22, 1980. BA in Math., Lehigh U., 1953; AM, U. Pa., 1955, PhD, 1958. Applied mathematician Moore Sch. Elec. Engring., U. Pa., 1953-56; with GE Corp., Phila., 1956-57, Philco Corp., Phila., 1957-59, RCA, Moorestown, N.J., 1957-64; assoc. prof. math. Drexel U., Phila., 1964-67, prof., 1967-86; Andrew G. Cowles disting. prof. math. Trinity U., San Antonio, 1986-97, prof. emeritus, 1997—. Author: Advanced Calculus, 1978; co-author: (with Bernard Kolman) Elementary Multivariable Calculus, 1971, Multivariable Calculus with Linear Algebra and Series, 1972, Elementary Differential Equations, 2000, Elementary Differential Equations with Boundary Value Problems, 2001; contbr. rsch. articles in numerical analysis, ordinary differential equations, smoothing, prediction and spl. functions to profl. jours. Mem. Am. Math. Soc., Soc. Indsl. and Applied Math., Internat. Linear Algebra Soc., Phi Beta Kappa, Eta Kappa Nu, Pi Mu Epsilon. Achievements include development of Trench's Algorithm for inversion of finite Toeplitz matrices, of fast algorithms for computing eigenvalues of structured matrices, of asymptotic theory of solutions of nonlinear functional differential equations under mild integral smallness conditions, of Trench's canonical form for disconjugate differential operations. Home: 95 Pine Ln Woodland Park CO 80863-9535 E-mail: wtrench@trinity.edu.

TRENERY, MARY ELLEN, librarian; b. Conran, Mo., Jan. 10, 1939; d. John Herman and Stella Cecelia (Durbin) Hulshof; m. Frank E. Trenery, June 10, 1967. BA in Classics, Coll. New Rochelle, 1962; MALS, Rosary Coll., River Forest, Ill., 1966; postgrad., Fla. Atlantic U., Boca Raton, 1986-89. Tchr. grades 6, 8 Archdiocesan Sch. System, St. Louis, 1962-64; serials and acquisition libr. U. Ill., Chgo., 1966-69; acquisitions, circulation and cataloging libr. Rosary Coll., River Forest, Ill., 1964-66, 70-72; libr. media specialist St. Coleman Cath. Sch., Pompano Beach, Fla., 1973-94. Coord. for self study St. Coleman Schs., 1982, 83, 89, 90; cons. Pompano Beach City Libr. Author: Policies and Procedures for School Libraries, 1976, UICC Call Number (founding editor), 1967-68, NIUCLA Newsletter (editor 1969-72). Fed. Funding liaison with Broward County Sch. Bd., 1974-94. Mem. Ill. Libr. Assn. (rsch. and tech. svcs. div. chair 1967-69), Cath. Libr. Assn. (No. Ill. unit chair, sec. 1969-72).

TRENKLER, TINA LOUISE, nuclear engineer; b. Poughkeepsie, N.Y., Nov. 11, 1964; d. Irene Elfrede Rockelmann Donahue. BS in Nuclear Engring., U. Cin., 1987; postgrad., U. Ariz., 1987-88, Ga. Inst. Tech., 1994-96; MBA, U. Wash., 2001. Engring. aide U.S. Nuclear Regulatory Commn., Washington, 1984-86; mgr. environ. health physics Foster Wheeler Environ., Bellevue, Wash., 1988-96; v.p. trading card games Wizards of the Coast, Renton, 1996—; v.p. Kirner Cons., Olympia, 1996—. Spkr. in field. Vol. Chicken Soup Brigade, Seattle, 1990-97, Master Home Environmentalist Program, Seattle, 1996—. Scholar Inst. Nuclear Power Ops., 1984. Mem. Health Physics Soc., Am. Nuclear Soc., Soc. for Risk Analysis, NOW. Office: Wizards of the Coast PO Box 707 Renton WA 98057-0707

TRENNEL, LAWRENCE WILLIAM, accountant, educator; b. East Cleveland, Ohio, May 21, 1955; s. Anthony John and Jennie (Perko) T.; m. Bette Lou Witherspoon, May 12, 1984; children: Lauren Ivana, Erica Kathleen. BBA, Cleve. State U., 1977; MA in Human Resource Mgmt., Pepperdine U., 1981. CPA, Ohio. Commd. 2d lt. USMC, 1974, advanced through grades to capt., resigned, 1981, active Res., 1981-91, internal auditor Japan, 1977-78, comptroller, budget officer New Orleans, 1979-81; internal auditor Med. Mutual div. Blue Shield, Cleve., 1981-82, supr. cost and budget, 1982-84; fin. analyst Cleve. Pneumatic, 1984-85; ptnr. Varner, LaCorte & Trennel, Willoughby, Ohio, 1985-88; pvt. practice acctg., 1988—. Instr. Los Angeles Community Coll., Okinawa, 1978, Harding Bus. Coll., Maple Heights, Ohio, 1985-86, MTI Bus. Sch., Cleve., 1987—. Mem. AICPA, NRA, Gun Owners Am., Am. Soc. Mil. Comptrollers, Ohio Soc. CPAs, Am. Legion, Euclid Rifle and Hunting Club (trustee 1985-88, fin. sec. 1988—), Slovene Nat. Benefit Soc. (sec., treas. 1984-88, pres. 1989—, fin. sec. 1990), Amvets, Ashtabula Rod & Gun Club. Republican. Episcopalian. Avocations: baseball, soccer, golf, running, camping, investments. Office: Lawrence W Trennel CPA 4139 Erie St Willoughby OH 44094-7806

TRENNEPOHL, GARY LEE, university administrator, finance educator; b. Detroit, Dec. 6, 1946; s. Leo Donald and Wilma Mae (Tiesnvold) T.; m. Sandra K. Yeager, June 9, 1968; children: Paige E., Adrienne A. BS, U. Tulsa, 1968; MBA, Utah State U., 1971; PhD, Tex. Tech U., 1976. Asst. prof. aero studies Tex. Tech. U., Lubbock, 1972-74; asst./assoc. prof. fin. Ariz. State U., Tempe, 1977—82; prof. U. Mo., Columbia, 1982-86, dir. Sch. Bus., 1984-86; prof., head dept. fin. Tex. A&M U., College Station, 1986-91, assoc. dean Coll. Bus., 1991-93, Peters prof. fin., 1992-95, exec. assoc. dean, 1994-95; dean Coll. Bus. Okla. State U., Stillwater, 1995-99; pres. Okla. State U.-Tulsa, 1999—. Mem. faculty Options Inst., Chgo. Bd. Options Exch., 1987—. Author: An Introduction to Financial Management, 1984, Investment Management, 1993; assoc. editor Jour. Fin. Rsch., 1983-96; contr. chpts. Encyclopedia of Investments, Options: Essential Concepts; contbr. articles to profl. jours. Capt. USAF, 1968-72. Decorated Commendation medal with oak leaf cluster. Mem. Fin. Mgmt. Assn. (v.p. program 1993, pres. 1993-94), So. Fin. Assn., Southwestern Fin. Assn. (bd. dirs. 1983-84, pres. 1986), Midwest Fin. Assn. (bd. dirs. 1985-89). Lutheran. Office: Okla State U Tulsa 700 N Greenwood Ave Tulsa OK 74106-0702 E-mail: garyt@osu-tulsa.okstate.edu.

TRENNER, NELSON RICHARDS, JR. communications executive, writer; b. Plainfield, N.J., Aug. 3, 1948; s. Nelson Richards and Kathryn Theresa (Farrell) T.; m. Annabelle Clare Radcliffe, June 24, 1988; children: Miles Richards Radcliffe, Winslow Radcliffe. AB, Princeton U., 1970; MA, Rutgers U., 1978. Mng. editor Princeton (N.J.) Packet Newspapers, 1971-72; mgr. trade sales promotion Little, Brown & Co., Boston, 1972-73; assoc. curator New England Hist. Geneal. Soc., 1974-76; mng. editor Del. Valley News, Flemington, N.J., 1976-77; pres. Advanced Communication Tng., Princeton, 1981—. Cons. AT&T Labs., Murray Hill, N.J., 1981—; lectr., dir. writing program Woodrow Wilson Sch. Public and Internat. Affairs Princeton U., 1987-88, 91—; sr. comms. cons. Pharm. Rsch. Inst. Bristol-Myers Squibb, Princeton, N.J., 1996—. Author: The Bell Labs Writer, 1985; co-author: The Bell Labs Editor, 1986, The Bell Labs Style Guide, 1988 (internat. award for excellence 1989); co-author, editor: E. L. Doctorow, 1983; asst. editor Ontario Rev., 1980, 82-83. Campaign worker House and Senate Campaigns, N.J., Mass., 1974, 76, 78, 80, 82, 84, 92; com. chmn. Coalition for Nuclear Disarmament, N.J., 1980—; campaign staff writer Millicent Fenwick for U.S. Senate, N.J., 1981-82; admissions assoc. Princeton U., 1981-83; fellow Blue Mountain Ctr., Blue Mountain Lake, N.Y., 1983-87, 95, Millay Colony for the Arts, Austerlitz, N.Y., 1985, Va. Ctr. for the Creative Arts, Sweet Briar, 1986, 95; trustee Starfish Found. Children with AIDS, Inc., 1997—, Youth Found., Princeton, N.J., 1997—; com. chair Planned Parenthood, Mercer County, 1997—. Rutgers U. fellow, Columbia U. fellow; recipient Adirondack Fiction award Blueline Mag., 1986. Democrat. Episcopalian. Avocations: book collecting, photography, journalism, hiking. Home: 4590 Province Line Rd Princeton NJ 08540-2212 Office: Princeton U W Wilson Sch Pub & Internat Affairs Robertson Hall Princeton NJ 08544

TRENT, BERTRAM JAMES, real estate executive; b. N.Y.C., Apr. 14, 1918; s. Gustave K. and Florence (Wertheimer) T.; m. Geraldine Eliza Jacobs, July 20, 1947; children: Bruce L., David P. (dec.), Michael S. Student, Yale U., 1939; BA, U. Va., 1940. Lic. real estate broker, N.Y. Ptnr. Bert Mfg. Co., N.Y.C., 1940-57; v.p. Bert Mfg. Co., Inc., Irvington, N.Y., 1957-69, pres., 1969-72, Bert Realty Co., Inc., Irvington, 1972—. Del. Rep. Nat. Conv., Kansas City, 1976; treas. Scarsdale (N.Y.) Rep. Town Com., 1957-74, chmn., 1974-77; asst. treas. Westchester County Rep. Com., White Plains, N.Y., 1976-78, del. nat. convs., 1960, 68, 72, 84, 88; mem. various coms. Town Club Scarsdale, 1954—. Served with U.S. Army Signal Corps, 1943-46, Aleutian Islands. Mem. Nat. Assn. Mfrs. (internat. rels. com. 1946-49), Palm Beach (Fla.) Condominium Assn. (v.p.), Exch. Club (pres. 1975, 85), Scarsdale Golf Club, Breakers Golf Club, Yale Club N.Y.C., Club Colette (Palm Beach), Palm Beach Rep. Club., Palm Beach Yacht Club. Republican. Avocations: golf, swimming, photography. Office: Bert Realty Co Inc Trent Bldg Irvington NY 10533 E-mail: bertfla@com.

TRENT, CHARLES H., JR. social work educator; b. Abingdon, Va., Sept. 25, 1939; s. Charles Howard Sr. and Sue Sheffey (Coffee) T.; m. Gina Fiering, May 30, 1993. BA, Pace U., 1972; MSW, NYU, 1974; PhD, Fordham U., 1985. Admissions counselor Cooper Union, N.Y.C., 1969-74; supr. II social worker Rapid Intervention Project, 1974-75; coord. SSI Advocacy Ctr., Hempstead, N.Y., 1975-77; dir. Project Life, N.Y.C., 1977-88; exec. dir. East Harlem Com. on Aging, Inc., 1977—; asst. prof. Yeshiva U., 1985-88, assoc. prof., 1985—. Adj. instr., assoc. prof. Fordham U., N.Y.C., 1983—; bd. dirs. Welfare Rsch. Inc., Albany, N.Y. With USAF. Fellow NIMH, 1972-74, Coun. on Social Work Edn. fellow NIMH, 1981-85; Brookdale Inst. scholar, 1981. Mem. NASW, Soc. for Study of Social Problems, Coun. on Social Work Edn., Soc. for Social Work Rsch., Assn. Cmty. Organizers and Social Adminstrs., Fifth Ave. Com. Avocations: writing, reading, computers, sports. Home: 270 5th St Apt 1J Brooklyn NY 11215-7422 Office: Yeshiva U 2495 Amsterdam Ave New York NY 10033-3312 E-mail: CO925S@aol.com.

TRENT, DONALD STEPHEN, thermo fluids engineer; b. Cloverdale, Oreg., Mar. 29, 1935; s. James Charles and Emma (Bauer) T.; (div. Jan., 1986); children: Steve, Lynn Trent Wooldridge, Greg; m. Alta Mae Brown, Aug. 20, 1994. BSAE, Oregon State U., 1962, MSME, 1964, PhD in Mech. Engring., 1972. Chief scientist (emeritus) Battelle Meml. Inst., Richland, Wash., 1965-96; retired, 1996; cons., 1996—. Cons. in field, 1996—; courtesy prof. Oreg. State U., Corvallis, 1987—; rsch. affiliate MIT, Cambridge, Mass., 1990—; mem. tchg. staff Wash. State U., Richland, 1991—; vis. U. Md., College Park, 1995—. Sgt. U.S. Army, 1958-61. Recipient Fed. Lab. Consortium award, 1992. Mem. ASME, Phi Kappa Phi, Sigma Xi. Achievements include patent on a heat pipe; 2 copyrights on computational fluid dynamics software. Home: 1225 Country Ridge Dr Richland WA 99352-7763 Address: 1225 Country Ridge Dr Richland WA 99352-7763

TRENT, JAMES ALFRED, city official; b. Bklyn., May 25, 1946; s. Alfred and Helen (Vanasco) T. Assoc. deg. Applied Sci., SUNY, Farmingdale, 1966; B.Landscape Architecture, U. Ga., 1969. Jr. landscape architect Dept. Design & Constrn., N.Y.C., 1969-70, asst. landscape architect, 1970-79, chief profl. contracts, 1979-84, asst. to dir. Bur. Bldg. Design, 1984-87, dep. chief profl. contracts mgmt. sect., 1987-92; project mgr. Archtl. Specialties, 1992-94; chief profl. contracts sect., 1994—. V.p. Joint Bellerose Bus. Dist. Devel. Corp., Inc., 1997—. Art editor Civil Svc. Merit Coun. Inc., 1972-81., 86. Pres., Creedmoor Civic Assn. Inc., Bellerose, N.Y., 1970-80, v.p., 1980-84, exec. mem., 1984-94, treas., 1989—; mem. ornamental hort. adv. commn. Occupational Edn. Adv. Coun., N.Y.C. Bd. Edn., 1973-85; founder, pres. Queens County Farm Mus., 1975—; pres. Profl. Svc. Ctrs. for the Handicapped, Inc., 1980-81; 1st v.p. Eastern Queens Civic Coun., 1975-97; treas. Queens Civic Congress, 1997—; mem. Queens County Com. Rep. Party, 1968—; v.p. Midland Rep. Club, N.Y. 23d Assembly Dist., 1970-80, pres., 1981-93, grants disbursement judge Queens Coun. on Arts, 1982-86; chmn. bd. dirs. Queens Village Rep. club., 1993—. Named Grad. of Yr., SUNY at Farmingdale Alumni Assn., 1966; Humanitarian of 1977, 105th Police Precinct Community Coun. Mem. Met. Hist. Structures Assn. (dir. 1982—), Poppenhusen Inst. (bd. dirs. 1991-95, v.p. 1995—), Mcpl. Engrs. City of N.Y. (bd. dirs. 1995—, asst. editor jour. 1995-97). Roman Catholic. Home: 24233 90th Ave Bellerose NY 11426-1115 Office: Rm 4-018 30-30 Thomson Ave Long Island City NY 11101 E-mail: JTrent8830@aol.com.

TRENT, JOHN THOMAS, JR. lawyer; b. Hammond, Ind., Mar. 11, 1954; s. John Thomas and Sally (Ritter) T.; m. Laura Marie Nelson, Aug. 5, 1978; children: Lauren, Valerie, Alex. AB, Wabash Coll., 1976; JD, Vanderbilt U., 1979. Bar: Tenn. 1979, U.S. Dist. Ct. (mid. dist.) Tenn. Mng. dir. Boult, Cummings, Conners & Berry P.L.C., Nashville, 1979—. Spkr., panelist real estate and other groups. Chmn. adminstrv. bd. and other coms. and offices West End United Meth. Ch., Nashville, 1983—99; bd. dirs. Cumberland Sci. Mus., 1997—, Jr. Achievement Middle Tenn. Fellow Nashville Bar; mem. ABA, Nat. Assn. Indsl. and Office Parks (past bd. dirs. Nashville chpt.), Tenn. Bar Assn., Nashville Bar Assn., Nat. Assn. Bond Lawyers, Assn. Attys. and Execs. in Corp. Real Estate. Office: Boult Cummings Conners & Berry PLC 414 Union St Ste 1600 Nashville TN 37219-1744

TRENT, ROBERT HAROLD, retired business educator; b. Norfolk, Va., Aug. 3, 1933; s. Floyd Murton and Myrtle Eugenia (White) T.; m. Joanne Bell, Aug. 17, 1951; 1 child, John Thomas BS, U. Richmond, 1963; PhD, U. N.C., 1968. Asst. prof. U. N.C., Chapel Hill, 1968-69; assoc. prof. commerce McIntire Sch. Commerce U. Va., Charlottesville, 1970-74, prof. commerce, 1975-84, Ralph A. Beeton prof. free enterprise, 1985-91; C. & P. Telephone Co. prof. commerce U. Va., 1991-98, prof. commerce emeritus, 1998—. Co-author: Marketing Decision Making, 1976, 4th edit., 1988; editor: Developments in Management Information Systems, 1974 Mem. Beta Gamma Sigma, Omicron Delta Kappa.

TRENT, WARREN C. mechanical engineer; b. Boswell, Okla., Feb. 22, 1921; s. Clem and Fannie Edora (Greer) T.; m. Ruth Magdalene Potts, Apr. 2, 1948; 1 child, Paul Dudley. BSME, Okla. State U., 1943; MSME, Purdue U., 1948. Engr. Boeing Airplane Co., Seattle, 1943-45; instr. Okla. State U., Stillwater, 1946-47; rsch. engr. Kans. State U., Manhattan, 1948-51; mgr. sect. LTV Aerospace, Dallas, 1951-65; dir. engring. tech. McDonnell Douglas, St. Louis, 1965-77; owner Trent Assocs., Tyler, Tex., 1977-93; CEO Trent Techs., Inc., 1993—. Cons. Rockwell Internat., El Segundo, Calif., 1982-87; lectr. Navy Aviation Exec. Inst., Washington, 1973-76; evaluator ABET, 1983-89. Patentee in field. Arbitrator Better Bus. Bur., Tyler, 1985—. With USN, 1945-46. Fellow AIAA (assoc.); mem. ASHRAE, Tex. Profl. Engrs., Mo. Profl. Engrs. Republican. Baptist. Avocations: bridge, golf. Home: 1410 Woodlands Dr Tyler TX 75703-5718 Office: Trent Techs Inc 777 S Broadway Ave Ste 200 Tyler TX 75701-1662 Fax: 903-561-1882. E-mail: warren@trenttech.com.

TRENTANELLI, JOHN ANTHONY, educational administrator; b. Cleve., Oct. 18, 1939; s. Frank Joseph and Marie Theresa Trentanelli; m. Barbara Kay Trentanelli, Apr. 30, 1977; 1 child, Angela Rose. BS in Edn., S.E. Mo. State U., 1969; postgrad., Cleve. State U., 1980-81; M. Edn. and Adminstrn., Prarie View A&M U., Tex., 1987. Substitute tchr. Parma (Ohio) Pub. Sch. Dist., 1977-78; social studies tchr., Am. Fedn. Tchrs. rep. Cleve. Pub. Schs., 1978-81; social studies tchr., dept. chmn. Houston Ind. Sch. Dist., 1981-87, asst. prin., 1987-99, Yonkers (N.Y.) Pub. Sch. Dist., 1999—. Editor Galveston Bay Power Squadron, Bay Breeze, 1999. Treas. Galveston Bay Power Squadron, Clear Lake, Tex., 1999. Mem. ASCD, Pi Kappa Alpha (pres. Dist. 15, 1972-73). Avocation: power and sail boating. Home: 149 Nob Hill Dr Elmsford NY 10523 Office: Lincoln H S 375 Kneeland Ave Yonkers NY 10704 E-mail: jtrentanelli@yonkerspublicschool.org.

TREPP, LEO, rabbi; b. Mainz, Germany, Mar. 4, 1913; s. Maier and Selma (Hirschberger) T.; m. Miriam de Haas, Apr. 26, 1938 (dec. Dec. 15, 1999); 1 child, Susan Trepp Lachtman. PhD, U. Wurzburg, Germany, 1935, U. Oldenburg, 1989; DD, Hebrew Union Coll., 1985; postgrad., Harvard U., 1944-45; PhD (hon.), U. Wurzburg, 1985. Ordained rabbi, 1936. Rabbi various temples, various locations, 1940-51; part-time rabbi Santa Rosa, Calif., 1951-61, Eureka, 1961-90; rabbi emeritus, 1990; Jewish chaplain Vets. Home of Calif., Yountville, 1954-98; prof. philosophy Napa Valley Coll., 1951-83, prof. emeritus, 1983—; prof. Judaic studies U. Mainz, 1983—. Author: Eternal Faith, Eternal People - A Journey into Judaism, 1962, Judaism, Development and Life, 1966, 4th edit., 2000, A History of the Jewish Experience, 1974, 2d edit., 2001, The Complete Book of Jewish Observance, 1980, Judaism and the Religions of Humanity, 1985, What if Shylock were a Marrano, 1985, The Controversy between Samson Raphael Hirsch and Seligmann Baer Bamberger—Halakhical and Societal Implications, 1991, Yamim Nora'im: The Traditional Liturgy and "Gates of Repentance", 1991; author numerous books in other langs.; major works include Die Juden, 1982, 2d edit., 1998, Jüdische Ethik, 1988, Der jüdische Gottesdienst—Form und Entfaltung, 1991, Die Amerikanischen Juden—Profil einer Gemeinschaft, 1991, Jüdisches Denken im 20 Jahrhundant, 1992; (with G. Mayer) Abriss der jüdischen Geschichte, 1992; Gerchichte der Deutschen Juden, 1996, Das Vermächtnis der deutschen Juden, 2000, Liturgical Chants of the Synagogue at Mainz, 2001, Niguney Magenza, 2001; contbr. articles to profl. jours. Mem. Napa Planning Commn., 1964-69. Recipient Great Seal, City of Oldenburg, 1971, George Washington Honor medal, Freedoms Found., 1979; hon. freeman City of Oldenburg, 1990, Hon. Senator, U. Mainz, 1996, Gutenberg Plaquette, City of Mainz, 1993, Cross of Merit 1st class Germany, 1997; new Jewish chapel named in his honor Vets. Home Calif., 1997; commendation Assembly Calif. Legis., 1998. Mem. Ctrl. Conf. Am. Rabbis, Rabbinical Assembly, Am. Philos. Assn., Am. Acad. Religion, No. Calif. Bd. Rabbis. Home: 820 Mission Ave Apt 9 San Rafael CA 94901-3251 E-mail: leotrepp@worldnet.att.net.

TREPPLER, IRENE ESTHER, retired state senator; b. St. Louis County, Mo., Oct. 13, 1926; d. Martin H. and Julia C. (Bender) Hagemann; student Meramec Community Coll., 1972; m. Walter J. Treppler, Aug. 18, 1950; children: John M., Steven A., Diane V. Anderson, Walter W. Payroll chief USAF Aero. Chart Plant, 1943-51; enumerator U.S. Census Bur., St. Louis, 1960, crew leader, 1970; mem. Mo. Ho. of Reps., Jefferson City, 1972-84; mem. Mo. Senate, Jefferson City, 1985-96; chmn. minority caucus, 1991-92. Active Gravois Twp. Rep. Club, Concord Twp. Rep. Club; alt. del. Rep. Nat. Conv., 1976, 84; mem. Mo. Adv. Coun. on Hist. Preservation, 1998—; gov. apptd. Mo. Adv. Coun. on Hist. Preservation, 1998—. Recipient Spirit of Enterprise award Mo. C. of C., 1992, appreciation award Mo. Med. Assn., Nat. Otto Nuttli Earthquake Hazard Mitigation award, 1993, Disting. Legislator award Cmty. Colls. Mo., 1995; named Concord Twp. Rep. of Yr., 1992. Mem. Nat. Order Women Legislators (rec. sec. 1981-82, pres. 1985), Nat. Fedn. Rep. Women. Mem. Evangelical Ch.

TRESCOTT, KATHLEEN MARIE, cultural association administrator; b. Wausau, Wis., Apr. 3, 1941; d. Albert Owen and Ruth Marie (Pauls) Colcord; m. Martin Victor Carroll, June 16, 1962 (div. Apr. 1968); 1 child, Marie Ellen; m. Paul Barton Trescott, Aug. 15, 1982. BS, U. Wis., Stevens Point, 1963; MS, U. Ill., 1970, advanced cert., 1982; postgrad., So. Ill. U., 1984-92. Cert. tchr., Ill. Tchr. elem. and jr. high sch. Blue Island (Ill.) Schs., 1963-68; tchr. mid. sch. Champaign (Ill.) Sch. Dist. #4, 1969-82; tchr. English Peking U., Beijing, 1983-84, 92, 99, Tourism Coll., Beijing, 1992, 99; vol. dir., also tchr. Ctr. for Tchg. About China, Carbondale, 1988—. Edn. advisor Peking U. Key Sch., Beijing, 1982, tchr. English, Shantou, China, 1999. Supr. Sunday sch. and Bible sch., Carbondale, 1985-92; tchr. 1st Presbyn. ch., Carbondale, 1984—; violin player John A. Logan Ensemble Orch., Carterville, Ill., 1997—; leader Girl Scouts Am., Wausau, 1959-60, Champaign, 1972-80; dir. family activities Parents Without Ptnrs., Champaign, 1974-82. Mem. Girl Scouts Am. (life), U.S.-China Peoples Friendship Assn. (midwest rep. 1989-93, 99-2002, pres. 1988-98, treas. 1986-88, 98-2001). Avocations: violin, dancing, travel, bridge, sewing. Home: 1214 W Schwartz Carbondale IL 62901 Office: US-China Peoples Friendship Assn 1214 W Schwartz Carbondale IL 62901 E-mail: trescott@midwest.net.

TRESCOTT, PAUL BARTON, educator; b. Bloomsburg, Pa., Nov. 22, 1925; s. Paul Henry and Stella Henrietta (Potts) T.; children by previous marriage: Jeffrey A., Jill V., Andrew B.; m. Kathleen Colcord, Aug. 15, 1982. BA, Swarthmore Coll., 1949; MA, Princeton U., 1951, PhD, 1954. Reporter Evening Bulletin, Phila., 1948; instr. in econ. Princeton (N.J.) U., 1952-54; asst. assoc. prof. Kenyon Coll., Gambier, Ohio, 1954-67; prof. in econs. Miami U., Oxford, 1967-69; prof. in econs., history So. Meth. U., Dallas, 1969-76; prof. in econs. So. Ill. U., Carbondale, 1976—. Vis. prof. in econs. Thammassat U., Bangkok, 1965-67, People's U., Beijing, 1992; vis. prof. in fin. U. Ill., Champaign and Urbana, 1981; acad. adv. commn. to Thailand U.S. Dept. State, Washington, 1968-70. Authors: Money, Banking and Economic Welfare, 1960, 2d edit., 1965, Financing American Enterprise, 1963, rep., 1982, The Logic of the Price System, 1970, Thailand's Monetary Experience, 1971. Sgt. U.S. Army, 1944-46. Rsch. grantee Brookings Inst., Washington, 1961-62; Fulbright scholar U.S. Govt., Peking U., China, 1983-84, Tech. U., Czestockowa, Poland, 1996. Mem. Am. Econs. Assn., History Econs. Soc. Avocations: music, traveling. Office: So Ill U Dept Econs Carbondale IL 62901

TRESCOTT, SARA LOU, water resources engineer; b. Frederick, Md., Nov. 17, 1954; d. Norton James and Mabel Elizabeth (Hall) T.; m. R. Jeffrey Franklin, Oct. 8, 1983. AA, Catonsville C.C., Balt., 1974; BA in Biol. Sci., U. Md., Balt., 1980. Sanitarian Md. Dept. Health & Mental Hygiene, Greenbelt, 1982; indsl. hygienist Md. Dept. Licensing & Regualtion, Balt., 1982-85; from water resources engr. to chief dredging div. Md. Dept. Natural Resources, Annapolis, 1985-92, chief navigation div. Stevensville, 1992-96, chief ops. & maintenance, 1996, dir. maintenance engring. ops., 1996—. Chair adv. bd. EEO, Annapolis, 1990-92; tech. com. Nat. Mgmt. Info. Systems, Balt., 1983. Contbr. articles to profl. jours. Mem. ASCE, County Engrs. Assn. Md. Democrat. Achievements include research in beneficial uses of dredged material; development of technology for hydrographic surveying, providing Md. with an improved waterway transportation network. Home: PO Box 22 Woodbine MD 21797-0022 Office: DNR 580 Taylor Ave Annapolis MD 21401

TRESHAM, AARON KEITH, mathematician; b. McMinnville, Oreg., July 15, 1977; s. Roger Alan and Joyce Aileen Tresham. BA, Lewis and Clark Coll., 1999; MS, postgrad., U. Oreg., 2002—. Fellow in math. U. Oreg., Eugene, 1999—. Scholar Barbara Hirschi Neely scholar, Lewis and Clark Coll., 1995—99. Mem.: Am. Math. Soc., Phi Kappa Phi, Phi Beta Kappa. Avocation: reading. Home: 2250 Patterson St #52 Eugene OR 97405 Office: Univ Oreg Math Dept 1222 Univ Oreg Eugene OR 97403 Personal E-mail: atresham@oregon.uoregon.edu.

TRESSLAR, NOLA V. artist, retired foundation administrator, marketing professional; b. Tacoma, Mar. 10, 1942; d. Arthur and Viola Mafalda (Sirianni) De Caro; m. Lloyd E. Montgomery, Dec. 8, 1961 (div. 1971); children: Gina N. Montgomery, Melissa R. Montgomery; m. Walter B. Swain, Mar. 11, 1977 (div. 1994); m. Guy E. Tresslar, May 16, 1997. Student, U. Puget Sound, 1959-62. First woman cert. real estate appraiser Wash. Appraiser/assessor Pierce County Assessors Office, Tacoma, 1971-77; chief appraiser Otero Savs. & Loan, Colorado Springs, 1977-78; pvt. fee appraiser, co-owner N.W.S. & Assocs., 1978—. Pres., designer N.V.S. Enterprises, Colorado Springs, 1980-89; dir. mktg. U S WEST Edn. Found., Seattle, 1990-92, exec. dir. Northwest Baby Talk, 1993-95, fund devel., pub. rels. mgr. Child Abuse Prevention Resources, 1995—. Designer numerous gift items. Recipient Women at Work award Council on Working Women, 1985, Pub. Service award Colorado Springs Assn. Life Underwriters, 1985, Salesman With a Purpose Club Booster of Yr. award, 1986. Mem. NAFE, NOW, Urban League, Tacoma Jr. League (cmty. adv. bd.), Soc. Real Estate Appraisers (candidate, treas. 1978, bd. dirs. 1982-84), Chi Omega Alumnae. Democrat. Avocations: traveling, sumi painting, crafts, photography, volunteering.

TRETTIN, ROSEMARY ELIZABETH, fraternal organization administrator; b. Appleton, Wis. d. August W. and Elizabeth C. (Etten) T. BA, Mt. Mary Coll., Milw., 1945. Tchr., forensic coach Pulaski (Wis.) High Sch., 1947-51, Freedom (Wis.) High Sch., 1951-60, St. Mary Cen. High Sch., Menasha, Wis., 1960-79; forensic coach Xavier High Sch., Appleton, 1979-86; pres. St. Mary Ct. Nat. Catholic Soc. Foresters, 1953-86, 91—, nat. dir., 1974-78, nat. v.p., 1978-86, pres., 1986-90; sec. Green Bay (Wis.) Diocesan Assn., 1974-78, pres., 1978-86. Mem. Nat. Cath. Communications Found., N.Y.C., nat. dir., 1986-89, exec. v.p., 1989-90; dir. Wis. Fraternal Congress, 1982-83, Ill. Fraternal Congress, 1989-90; co-leader Fish Community Svc., Civic Leaders Am. Eucharistic min. St. Mary Ch., coord. leisure club. Named to Hall of Fame, Wis. Forensic Coaches Assn., 1994. Mem. Nat. Cath. Forensic League (sec., pres.), Nat. Forensic League (Double Diamond Key award 1983), Cath. Daus. Am., Outagamie County Hist. Soc., Monté Alverno Retreat Guild (treas. and pres.), Optimist (Neenah-Menasha Breakfast Club), St. Joseph Fraternity of Secular Franciscans (sec.), Christ Child Soc. Roman Catholic. Avocations: gardening, travel.

TRETZ, CHRISTOPHE ROBERT, electrical engineer; b. Strasbourg, France, Mar. 22, 1968; came to the U.S., 1991; s. Philippe and Liliane (Gué) T. Diplôme d'Ingénieur, Ecole Nationale Supérieure d'Electronique, d'Electrotechnique, d'Informatique, d'Hydraulique de Toulouse, Toulouse, France, 1991; MS, Columbia U., 1992, PhD, 1997. Rsch. asst. Columbia U., N.Y.C., 1992-97; adv. engr. IBM Rsch., Yorktown Heights, N.Y., 1997-2000, rsch. staff mem. NY, 2000; mem. tech. staff design engr. Advanced Micro Devices, Sunnyvale, Calif., 2000. Rsch. mentor Semiconductor Rsch. Corp., Durham, N.C., 1997—. Mem. IEEE (tech. com. internat. soi conf. 1998-2001, pub. rels. and publicity chair internat. soi conf. 2001-02, sr. com. internat. soi conf. 2001—, short course chair internat. soi conf. 2002). Roman Catholic. Achievements include inventor reduction of hysteresis in soi cmos circuits, method and system to tune integrated circuit, method and system for selecting sizes of components for integrated circuits. Avocations: skiing, golf, wine-tasting, gourmet cooking. Home: 235 Briar Ridge Dr San Jose CA 95123-2667 Office: Advanced Micro Devices One AMD Pl MS 365 PO Box 3453 Sunnyvale CA 94088-3453 E-mail: christophe.tretz@amd.com.

TREU, JESSE ISAIAH, venture capitalist; b. N.Y.C., Apr. 10, 1947; BS, Rensselaer Poly. Inst., 1968; MA, Princeton U., 1971, PhD, 1973. Physicist, liaison sci. components, materials group Gen. Electric Co., Schenectady, N.Y., 1973-77; tech. dir. Technicon Corp., Tarrytown, 1977-82; v.p. Channing Weinberg-CW Ventures, N.Y.C., 1982-85; gen. ptnr. Domain Assocs., Princeton, N.J., 1986—. Office: Domain Assocs 1 Palmer Sq Princeton NJ 08542-3718

TREUMANN, WILLIAM BORGEN, university dean; b. Grafton, N.D., Feb. 26, 1916; s. William King and Dagny Helen (Borgen) T.; m. Mildred Elizabeth Jenkins, Aug. 14, 1948; children— Richard Roy, Robert Evan, Beverly Kay. BS, U. N.D., 1942; MA, U. Ill., 1944, PhD, 1947. Teaching asst. chemistry U. Ill., 1942-45, teaching asst. math., 1945-46, vis. prof., summers 1948-50; from asst. prof. to prof. chemistry N.D. State U., 1946-55; mem. faculty Minn. State U. Moorhead, 1960—, prof. chemistry, 1962—, asso. dean acad. affairs, 1968-70, dean faculty math. and sci., 1970—. Contbr. to profl. jours. Research Corp. Am. grantee, 1954; Minn. U. Bd. grantee, 1967 Fellow Am. Inst. Chemists; mem. Am. Chem. Soc., Am. Assn. U. Profs., Minn. Acad. Sci., Fedn. Am. Scientists, Phi Beta Kappa, Sigma Xi. Home: One 2nd St S Apt 5-204 Fargo ND 58103-1921 Office: Math Dept Moorhead State U Moorhead MN 56560

TREUTING, EDNA GANNON, retired nursing administrator; b. New Orleans, Dec. 16, 1925; d. Alphonse Joseph and Clara Josephine (David) Gannon; m. August Raymond Treuting, Sept. 4, 1948 (dec.); children: Keith, Karen Treuting Stein, Madeline Treuting LeBlanc, Jaime Treuting Gonzales, Jay (dec.). Diploma, Charity Hosp. Sch. Nursing, New Orleans, 1946; BS in Nursing Edn., La. State U., 1953; MPH, Tulane U., 1972, DPH, 1978. RN, La.; cert. family nurse practitioner Tulane U. Head nurse premature nursery Charity Hosp., New Orleans, 1946-47, head nurse pediatrics, 1947-49; instr. pediatrics Charity Hosp. Sch. Nursing, 1949-52, 54, instr., LPN, 1953; pvt. duty Touro, Hotel Dieu, 1957-59; instr. maternal and child health La. State U. Sch. Nursing, 1960, 65, 69-71; from instr. to prof., sect. head Tulane Sch. Pub. Health and Tropical Medicine, 1972-83; dean, prof. Our Lady Holy Cross Coll. Nursing Div., 1983-84; chief nurse Dept. Health and Hosp., 1987-94. Region IV nurse practitioner Baylor U., Health Edn. and Welfare, 1974-76; citizen amb. to South Am. People to People, 1979; presentor U. Hawaii Pub. Health and Nursing, 1977; planner, advisor, reviewer continuing edn. U. Tenn., Memphis, 1990-95. Author, editor: Occupation Health Nursing, 1979; sect. head, prin. investigator Practitioner Programs Family and Pediatric, 1973-83; item writer Nurse Practitioners, Community Health and Occupational Nursing, 1974-80; mem. editl. bd. to sci. jours. and Nurse Practitioner Jour. Pres. Oti-Mrs. Internat., New Orleans, 1955-68; sponsor bd. dirs. Holy Cross H.S. Treuting Scholarship, New Orleans, 1966—; hurricane and disaster nurse ARC, New Orleans, 1966-77; v.p. Pandora Carnival Club, New Orleans, 1968-78; alternate state health dept. Commn. Nursing Supply and Demand by Legislation, 1991-94; planner, presentor La. State Rsch. Day, 1990-92. Named outstanding woman in the mainstream world's fair women of achievement, 1984. Mem. New Orleans Dist. Nurses Assn. (First J.B. Hickey Meml. Community award 1985, Great 100 Nurse-First Yr. 1987), La. Pub. Health Assn. (Dr. C.B. White Merritorious Diligent Svc. 1990), La. Nurse Practitioners Assn.(Edna Treuting scholarship named in her honor), Tulane U. Alumni Assn. (past pres.), Tulane Med. Alumni Assn. (past pres.), Delta Omega (past pres. nat.,Eta chpts.), Sigma Theta Tau (Epsilon Nu chpt.). Republican. Roman Catholic. Avocations: traveling, dancing, swimming, photography, reading. Home: 1914 Marlin Dr Mandeville LA 70448-1069

TREVENA, JOHN HARRY, lawyer; b. Dunedin, Fla., Dec. 28, 1961; s. Ernest Lewis and Lenora Geraldine (Adelson) T.; m. Susan Lee Corris, Nov. 23, 1988; 1 child, Samuel Alan. BA in criminal justice, Univ. S. Fla., 1982; Fla. Police standards, Pinellas Police Acad., 1982; JD, Stetson Univ., 1985. Bar: Fla., U.S. Dist. Ct. (mid. dist.) Fla. 1986; bd. cert. criminal trial lawyer, Fla. Pvt. practice, Largo, Fla. Editorial bd. Fla. Bar Jour., Fla. Bar News, 1990-93. Mem.: Tampa Bay Cath. Lawyers Guild, Inc., Am. Judicature Soc., Nat. Assn. Criminal Def. Lawyers, Pinellas County Criminal Def. Lawyers Assn., Pinellas County Trial Lawyers Assn., Fla. Bar Assn., Clearwater and Am. Bar Assn., Fla. Assn. Criminal Def. Lawyers (life). Roman Catholic. Democrat. Home: 423 Buttonwood Ln Largo FL 33770-4060 Office: 801 W Bay Dr Ste 509 Largo FL 33770-3220 E-mail: trevenalaw@aol.com.

TREVES, SAMUEL BLAIN, geologist, educator; b. Detroit, Sept. 11, 1925; s. Samuel and Stella (Stork) T.; m. Jane Patricia Mitoray, Nov. 24, 1960; children: John Samuel, David Samuel. BS, Mich. Tech. U., 1951; postgrad., U. Otago, New Zealand, 1953-54; MS, U. Idaho, 1953; PhD, Ohio State U., 1959. Geologist Ford Motor Co., 1951, Idaho Bur. Mines and Geology, 1952, Otago Catchment Bd., 1953-54; mem. faculty U. Nebr., Lincoln, 1958—, prof. geology, 1966—, chmn. dept., 1964-70, 74-89, assoc. dean Coll. Arts and Scis., 1989-96. Curator geology Nebr. State Mus., 1964—; participant expdns. to Antarctica and Greenland, 1960, 61, 63, 65, 70, annually 72-76. Rsch. and publs. on geology of igneous and metamorphic rocks of Idaho, New Zealand, Mich., Antarctica, Nebr., Can., Greenland with emphasis on origin of Precambrian granite complexes and basaltic volcanic rocks. Fulbright scholar U. Otago, New Zealand, 1953-54. Fellow Geol. Soc. Am.; mem. Am. Mineral Soc., Am. Geophys. Union, Sigma Xi, Tau Beta Pi, Sigma Gamma Epsilon. Home: 1710 B St Lincoln NE 68502-1524

TREVILLIAN, WALLACE DABNEY, economics educator, retired dean; b. Charlottesville, Va., May 1, 1918; s. Robert Carr and Mary Anna (Perry) T.; m. Mary Lou McEachern, Nov. 28, 1963 (dec. Dec. 2002); children: Malcolm McEachern, Edward Dabney. BS, U. Va., 1940, MA, 1947, PhD, 1954; postgrad., U. Calif., 1950-51. Mem. faculty Clemson (S.C.) U., 1947—, successively instr. econs., asst. prof., assoc. prof., 1947-55, prof. econs., head dept. indsl. mgmt., 1955-63, founding dean Coll. Commerce and Industry, 1963-80, prof., dean emeritus, 1983—. Vis. scholar U. Sussex, Eng., 1980—; mem. Regional Export Expansion Council, 1965-77; sec. commn. on edn. for bus. professions Nat. Assn. State Univs. and Land-Grant Colls., 1975-77; pres. Nat. Council for Textile Edn., 1978-80. Master sgt. AUS, 1941-45. Econ. in Action fellow Case Inst. Tech., 1958. Mem. St. Andrews Soc. Upper S.C., Newcomen Soc., Thomas Jefferson Soc. of Alumni U. Va., Piedmont Econs. Club, Poinsett Club (Greenville, S.C.). Episcopalian. Home: 305 Jones Ave Greenville SC 29605-2862

TREVISAN, MAURIZIO, epidemiologist, researcher; b. Naples, Italy, Jan. 31, 1952; came to U.S., 1979; s. Ilario and Bianca (Bruni) T.; m. Lisa Monagle, Dec. 22, 1983; children: Simona, Alessia, Stefan. MD magna cum laude, U. Naples, Italy, 1977; MS, SUNY, Buffalo, 1989. Cert. in medicine and surgery, Italy, 1977, diabetes and metabolic disease, Italy, 1980. Resident dept. internal medicine Med. Sch. U. Naples, 1977-79; rsch. fellow dept. community health and preventive medicine Med. Sch. Northwestern U., 1979-82; cons. dept. medicine U. Naples, 1983-85; asst. prof. dept. social and preventive medicine SUNY, Buffalo, 1985-88, clinical asst. prof. dept. family medicine, 1988-89, assoc. prof. dept. social and preventive medicine, 1988-92, clinical assoc. prof. nutrition program, 1989-94, assoc. prof. dept. family medicine, 1989-94, interim chair dept social and preventive medicine, 1991-92, prof. and chmn. dept. social and preventive medicine, 1993—, prof. dept. family medicine, 1994—, interim dean Sch. Health Related Professions, 2001—; prin. investigator Women's Health Initiative WNY Vanguard Clin. Ctr., 1993—. Vis. physician dept. physiology Harvard Med. Sch., 1982; adj. asst. prof. dept. cmty. health and preventive medicine Northwestern U. Med. Sch., 1987-96; adj. prof. nutrition program SUNY, Buffalo, 1994—, dir., health in housing, SUNY, Buffalo, 1996—; adj. prof. dept. cmty. health and preventive medicine Northwestern U. Med. Sch., 1996—. Fellow Am. Heart Assn. Coun. on Epidemiology. Recipient Rsch. Career Devel. award NIH, 1989-94. Fellow, Am. Coll. of Epidemiology; mem. Am. Epidemiol. Soc. Achievements include population-based epidemiological investigation of ion transport abnormalities as risk factors for essential hypertension and coronary heart disease. Office: SUNY Buffalo Dept Social & Preventive Medicine 270 Farber Hall Buffalo NY 14214-3000 E-mail: trevisan@buffalo.edu.

TREVISANI, EDMUND THOMAS, JR. company executive, consultant; b. Utica, N.Y., Aug. 4, 1949; s. Edmund Thomas and Rose Mary (Graziano) T.; m. Marina Trevisani, June 28, 1997; children: Edmund, Marc, Antonio. BS in Physics, Niagara U., 1971; MS in Engring. Physics, U. Va., 1973; MBA in Fin./Strategy, Wharton Sch., 1993. Plant mgr. GE, 1981-83, project mgr., 1983-85, mgr. plant ops., 1985-89, mgr. employee tech. devel., 1989-91; cons., pres. P.T. Internat., Ltd., 1991-93; mng. cons. Price Waterhouse & Coopers, 1993—. Leader YMCA, N.Y.C.; asst. scoutmaster Boy Scouts Am., N.Y.C.; lectr., tchr. local ch. Mem. Am. Mgmt. Assn., Nat. Assn. Tng. and Devel., Am. Physics Assn., Am. Entrepenur Assn., Albany C. of C., Toastmasters (pres. 1984-86, speakers award 1986). Avocations: pub. speaking, golfing, racquetball, skiing. Home: 419 Conestoga Rd Radnor PA 19087-4811 Office: Price Waterhouse & Coopers 2400 Eleven Penn Ctr Philadelphia PA 19103

TREVITHICK, RONALD JAMES, underwriter; b. Portland, Oreg., Sept. 13, 1944; s. Clifford Vincent and Amy Lois (Turner) T.; m. Delberta Russell, Sept. 11, 1965; children: Pamela, Carmen, Marla, Sheryl. BBA, U. Wash., 1966. CLU, CPA, ChFC, accredited estate planner. Mem. audit staff Ernst & Ernst, Anchorage, 1966, 68-70; pvt. practice acctg. Fairbanks, Alaska, 1970-73; with Touche Ross & Co., Anchorage, 1973-78, audit ptnr., 1976-78. Exec. v.p., treas., bd. dirs. Veco Internat., Inc., 1978-82; pres., bd. dirs. Petroleum Contractors Ltd., 1980-82; bd. dirs. P.S. Contractors A/S, Norcon, Inc., OFC of Alaska, Inc., V.E. Systems Svcs., Inc., Veco Turbo Svcs., Inc., Veco Drilling Inc., Vemar, Inc., 1978-82; with Coopers & Lybrand, Anchorage, 1982-85; field underwriter, registered rep. New York Life Ins., 1985-2000, Princor, 2000—, Prin. Fin. Group, 2000—; instr. acctg. U. Alaska, 1971-72; lectr. acctg. and taxation The Am. Coll., 1972, 97, instr. adv. sales Life Underwriters Tng. Coun., 1988-89; bd. dirs. Ahtna Devel. Corp., 1985-86. Divsn. chmn. United Way, 1975-76, YMCA, 1979; bd. dirs., fin. chmn. Anchorage Arts Coun., 1975-78, Am. Diabetes Assn., Alaska affiliate, 1985-91, chmn. bd. 1988-89, chmn. hon. bd. 1992-96, Am. Heart Assn., Alaska affiliate, 1986-87, Anchorage dist. com., 1994-96, treas. 1996-98, Alaska State Youth Soccer Assn.; mem. Anchorage Estate Planning Coun., 1996-2000, treas., 1998-99, sec. 1999-2000. With U.S. Army, 1967-68. Mem. Fin. Execs. Inst. (pres. Alaska chpt. 1981-83), Soc. Fin. Svcs. Profs. (v.p. Alaska chpt. 1993-94, pres. 1994-96), Alaska Assn. Life Underwriters (sec., treas. 1987-90), Alaska Goldstrikers Soccer Club (pres. 1992-93, youth coach 1985-95, Ina K tournament dir. 1992-98), Petroleum Club (treas. 1996-2000), Beta Alpha Psi. Home: 4421 Huffman Rd Anchorage AK 99516-2211 Office: 1600 A St Ste 110 Anchorage AK 99501-5146 E-mail: ron4berta@aol.com.

TREVOR, ALEXANDER BRUEN, computer company executive; b. N.Y.C., Apr. 12, 1945; s. John B. Jr. and Evelyn (Bruen) T.; m. Ellen Ruth Armstrong, Sept. 21, 1974; children: Anne Wood, Alexander Jay Bruen. BS, Yale U., 1967; MS, U. Ariz., 1971. Rsch. asst. U. Ariz., Tucson, 1971; systems analyst CompuServe Inc., Columbus, Ohio, 1971-73, dir. systems, 1973-74, v.p., 1974-81, exec. v.p., chief tech. officer, 1981-96, also bd. dirs., 1985-96; pres. Nuvocom, Inc., 1996—. Bd. dirs. Applied Innovation, Inc., Dublin, Ohio, CMHC Sys., Dublin. Author (software program) CB Simulator, 1980. Trustee Trudeau Inst., Saranac Lake, N.Y., Aviation Safety Inst., Worthington, Ohio. 1st lt. Signal Corps, U.S. Army, 1968-70, Vietnam. Decorated Bronze Star. Mem. IEEE, SAR (N.Y.), Union Club (N.Y.). Republican. Episcopalian. Office: Box 340876 Worthington OH 43234-0876

TREVOR, BRONSON, economist; b. N.Y.C., Nov. 12, 1910; s. John Bond and Caroline Murray (Wilmerding) T.; A.B., Columbia Coll., 1931; m. Eleanor Darlington Fisher, Nov. 8, 1946; children— Eleanor, Bronson, Caroline. Own bus., 1931— ; dir., asst. sec. Northwestern Terminal R.R., 1952-58; chmn. bd. Texinia Corp., 1959-92. Former dir. chmn. fin. com. Gen. Hosp. of Saranac Lake mem. Council for Agrl. and Chemurgic Research, Am. Forestry Assn. Mem. Republican County Com. of N.Y. County, 1937-39; leader in primary election campaigns N.Y. County, 1937, 38, 39 to free local Rep. party orgn. from leftwing affiliations. Served with U.S. Army, 1942, World War II. Mem. S.A.R., Soc. Colonial Wars. Clubs: Union, Knickerbocker, Racquet and Tennis, Piping Rock, Bath and Tennis. Author: (pamphlet) The United States Gold Purchase Program, 1941; also numerous articles on econ. subjects. Home: 18 Heron Ln Paul Smiths NY 12970 Office: PO Box 182 Oyster Bay NY 11771-0182

TREVOR, KIRK DAVID NIELL, orchestra conductor, cellist; b. London, Feb. 8, 1952; Student, Dartington Coll., 1968-69; grad. with distinction, Guildhall Sch. Music and Drama, 1974; student, N.C. Sch. Arts, 1975-77. Asst. condr. Guildhall Opera Sch., 1973-74; music dir. Youth Symphony of Carolinas, 1978-82; music dir., condr. Knoxville (Tenn.) Symphony Orch., 1985—; chief condr. Martinu Philharmonic Czech Rep., 1995—; assoc. condr. Charlotte (N.C.) Symphony Orch., 1978-82, Exxon Art Endowment and Dallas Symphony, 1982-85; former resident condr. Dallas Symphony; dir. music Indpls. Chamber Orch., 1988—; asst. prof. U. Tenn., 1985—. Guest condr. U.S., S.Am., USSR, Czech Republic, Poland, Romania, Switzerland; tchr. Condrs. Symphonic Workshop in Zlin, Czech Republic, 1991—, Artistic Dir. Recipient Libottom Meml. prize, 1972, Kappilis Condr. prize, 1974, Toussant prize, 1974; winner Am. Condrs. Program, 1990; Fulbright Exchange grantee U.K. and U.S. Dept. State, 1975, Am. Condrs. Program grantee, 1990. Mem. Condrs. Guild, Am. Symphony Orch. League. Office: Knoxville Symphony Orch 406 Union Ave, Ste 100 Knoxville TN 37902*

TREW, REBA CLAIR, artist; b. Tenn., Dec. 4, 1925; d. Gideon Morgan Jiles and Harriet Jane Brown; m. Buford O. Trew; 1 child, Leland J. Student, Ky. Wesleyan Coll. Prin. works include design of War Meml. Park, Greenville, Ky. Avocations: duplicate bridge, swimming, cooking. Home: 1218 King Arthur Rd Chattanooga TN 37421-4020

TREXLER, EDGAR RAY, minister, editor; b. Salisbury, N.C., Sept. 17, 1937; s. Edgar Ray and Eula Belle (Farmer) T.; m. Emily Louise Kees, Aug. 21, 1960; children: David Ray, Mark Raymond, Karen Emily. AB, Lenoir-Rhyne Coll., 1959, LittD, 1978; MDiv, Luth. Theol. So. Sem., 1962; MA, Syracuse U., 1964; postgrad., Boston U., 1960, Luth. World Fedn. Study Project, Geneva, 1977, 81; LittD (hon.), Midland Coll., 1990; DD, Wittenberg U., 1994. Ordained to ministry United Luth. Ch. Am., 1962; pastor St. John's Luth. Ch., Lyons, N.Y., 1962-65; features editor Luth. Mag., Phila., 1965-72, assoc. editor, 1972-78, editor, 1978-87, Chgo., 1988-99. Sec. Commn. Ch. Papers, Luth. Ch. Am., 1971-72, mem. staff team comm., 1972-78; chmn. Interch. Features, 1971-76; chmn. postal affairs com. Assoc. Ch. Press, 1983-90, Work Group on New Ch. Periodical, 1985-86; Evangelical Luth. Ch. Am. Cabinet of Execs., 1988-99. Author: Ways to Wake Up Your Church, 1969, Creative Congregations, 1972, The New Face of Missions, 1973, Mission in a New World, 1977, LWF/6, 1978, Anatomy of a Merger, 1991; mem. editl. adv. bd. The New World, Roman Cath. Archdiocese of Chgo., 1994-96. Pres. Lyons Coun. Chs., 1964; trustee Lenoir Rhyne Coll., 1975-84, 97—. Recipient Disting. Alumnus award Lenoir-Rhyne Coll., 1991, Disting. Svc. award Newberry Coll., 1992, Bachman award for disting. leadership Luth. Theol. So. Sem., 1993, Mauney Leadership Awd., Luth. Theol. So. Seminary (alumni awd.), 1999, award of merit for editls. Assoc. Ch. Press, 1991, 98, award of merit for articles in mission mags. Assoc. Ch. Press, 1974, hon. life mem., Assoc. Ch. Press, 1999. Mem. Nat. Luth. Editors Assn. (pres. 1975-77). Home: 2504 Carriage Falls Ct Hendersonville NC 28791-1816 E-mail: etrexler@bellsouth.net.

TREXLER, JOHN PETER, retired geology educator, researcher; b. Allentown, Pa., Nov. 8, 1926; s. Robert William and Hilda (Seip) T.; m. Virginia Hamilton, Jan. 29, 1950; children: Margaret T. Hessen, Virginia P. Trexler-Myren. BA, Lehigh U., 1950, MS, 1953; PhD, U. Mich., 1964. Indsl. geologist Lehigh Portland Cement Co., Allentown, Pa., 1950, 51; geologist U.S. Geol. Survey, 1953-62; mem. faculty, prof. Juniata Coll., Huntingdon, Pa., 1962-89, founder, developer geol. dept., chmn. geology dept., 1962-79, emeritus prof. geology, 1989—. Author, co-author numerous articles, reports, and maps. With USNR, 1945-46. Fellow NSF, 1970-71. Fellow Geol. Soc. A.; mem. Rotary (pres. 1972). Republican. Presbyterian. Avocations: horseback riding, sailing, reading, writing. Home: RR 2 Box 294 Huntingdon PA 16652-9113

TREYBIG, EDWINA HALL, sales executive; b. Ft. Worth, Dec. 12, 1949; d. George Edward and Lillian Wanita (Herring) Hall; m. Jerry Kenneth Treybig, Sept. 20, 1980; children: Allison Lindsey, Gifford Carl, Brick Edward. BS in Home Econs., Tex. Tech U., 1972. Office mgr. Am. Internat. Rent-A-Car, Dallas, 1973, gen. mgr., 1973-74; sales rep. Martinez Mud Co., Denver, 1977-80, Am. Mud Co., Denver, 1980-83, Robinson Construction Co., Denver, 1983-87, Dig-It, Inc., N.Y.C., 1987-88; sales rep., corp. sec. Treybig Enterprises, Littleton, Colo., 1984—. Organizer Mile High Golf Tournament, Denver, 1980-84; mem. subcom. Colo. Devel. Disabilities Planning coun., Denver, 1989-90; mem. Coalition to Insure the Uninsurable,

Denver, 1989-90; founder Littleton Acad., 1996-97; founder, pres. governing bd. Littleton Prep. Charter Sch., 1998-2001. Mem. Soc. Petroleum Engrs. (organizer golf tournament), Internat. Assn. Drilling Contractors, Ind. Producers Assn. Mountain States, Assn. Retarded Citizens, Denver Petroleum Club (organizer golf tournament), Alpha Chi Omega (social chmn. 1970-72). Republican. Mem. Ch. of Christ. Avocations: doll and bear collecting, down-hill skiing. Home and Office: 7397 S Fillmore Cir Littleton CO 80122-1942

TREYBIG, JOEL ANDREW, musician, educator; b. Berea, Ohio, Aug. 28, 1969; s. David Louis and Linda Nell Treybig; m. Carolyn Marie Totaro, Sept. 10, 1994. MusB in Edn., Baldwin-Wallace Coll. Conservatory, 1992; MusM, U. Akron, 1994; postgrad., Royal No. Coll. Music, Manchester, Eng., 1994—99; D in Musical Arts, U. Tex., 1999. Instr. trumpet Bowling Green (Ohio) State U., 1999—2000; prof. U. So. Miss., Hattiesburg, 2000—. Editor: (sheet music) F.J. Haydn (arr. Treybig) - Concerto in E-flat, 2001, Walter Dignam (arr. Treybig) - Hope Told a Flattering Tale, 2001; musician: recitals, concerts; musician: (1st trumpet) So. Arts Brass Quintet, 2000—. Mem.: Music Tchrs. Nat. Assn., Miss. Music Tchrs. Assn., Coll. Music Soc., Internat. Trumpet Guild. Office: U So Miss Box 5081 Hattiesburg MS 39406-5081 E-mail: joel.treybig@usm.edu.

TREYNOR, JACK LAWRENCE, financial advisor, educator; b. Council Bluffs, Iowa, Feb. 21, 1930; s. Jack Vernon and Alice (Cavin) T.; m. Elizabeth Glassmeyer, Aug. 29, 1968; children: Elizabeth Childs, Wendy F.C., Thomas Pirrie V. BA, Haverford Coll., 1951; MBA with distinction, Harvard U., 1955; postgrad., MIT, 1962-63. Jr. faculty Harvard U. Sch. Bus., Cambridge, Mass., 1955-56; ops. research staff Arthur D. Little, 1956-66; mgr. computer applications Merrill Lynch, N.Y.C., 1966-69; editor Fin. Analysts Jour., 1969-81; chief investment officer Treynor-Arbit Assocs., Chgo., 1981-85; assoc. vis. prof. dept. of fin. and bus. econs. U. So. Calif., Los Angeles, 1985-88; pres. Treynor Capital Mgmt., Palos Verdes Estates, Calif. Gen. ptnr., trustee, dir. certain mutual funds Eaton Vance, 1970—. Author: (with Patrick Regan and William Priest) The Financial Reality of Pension Funding Under ERISA, 1976; mem. editl. bd. Fin. Analysts Jour., 1969—; co-author and contbr. numerous articles in fin. jours. (Graham and Dodd Scroll award 1968, 82, twice in 1987, Graham and Dodd Plaque for best paper in Fin. Analysts Jour. 1981, Graham & Dodd Scroll award 1998, 99). Trustee Fin. Analysts Research Found., 1970-85; mem. vis. com. Grad. Sch. Bus. Adminstrn. U. Chgo., 1984-89. Served with U.S. Army, 1951-53. Recipient James R. Vertin award Fin. Analysts Rsch. Found., 1997, Lillywhite award Employee Benefit Rsch. Inst., 1997. Fellow Inst. for Quantitative Rsch. in Fin. (disting. fellow, bd. dirs. 1970—); mem. Fin. Analysts Fedn. (Nicholas Molodovsky award 1985), Am. Fin. Assn. (bd. dirs. 1979-81), Haverford Varsity Club, Longwood Cricket Club (Chestnut Hill, Mass.), N.Y. Athletic Club, Manursing Island Club (Rye, N.Y.), Winter Club (Lake Forest, Ill.),), Palos Verdes Tennis Club, Palos Verdes Beach and Athletic Club. Episcopalian. Avocations: jazz piano, sports cars, antique trains.

TREZZA, ALPHONSE FIORE, librarian, educator; b. Phila., Dec. 27, 1920; s. Vincent and Amalia (Ferrara) T.; m. Mildred Di Pietro, May 19, 1945; children: Carol Ann Trezza Johnston, Alphonse Fiore. BS, U. Pa., 1948, MS, 1950, postgrad.; LHD (hon.), Rosary Coll., 1997. Page Free Library, Phila., 1940-41, 45-48, library asst., 1948-49; cataloger, asst. reference librarian Villanova U., 1949-50, instr., 1956-60; head circulation dept. U. Pa. Library, 1950-56; lectr. Drexel Inst. Sch. Library Sci., 1951-60; editor Cath. Library world, 1956-60; exec. sec. Cath. Library Assn., 1956-60; assoc. exec. dir. ALA, exec. sec. library adminstrn. div., 1960-67, assoc. dir. adminstrv. services, 1967-69; dir. Ill. State Library, Springfield, 1969-74; lectr. Grad. Sch. Library and Info. Sci., Cath. U., 1975-82; exec. dir. Nat. Commn. on Libraries and Info. Scis., Washington, 1974-80; dir. intergovt. library Cooperation Project Fed. Library Com./Library of Congress, 1980-82; assoc. prof. Sch. Library and Info. Studies Fla. State U., Tallahassee, 1982-87, prof., 1987-93, emeritus prof., 1993—. Mem. Ill. Library LSCA TITLE I-II Adv. Commn., 1963-69; mem. network devel. com. Library of Congress, 1977-82; bd. visitors Sch. Library and Info. Sci., U. Pitts., 1977-80; cons. Becker & Hayes, Inc., 1980-84, King Research, Inc., 1981-82; mem. planning com and steering com. Fla. Gov.'s Conf. on Library and Info. Svcs., 1988-91. Nat. chmn. Cath. Book Week, 1954—56; pres. Joliet Diocesan Bd. Edn., 1966—68; auditor Borough of Norwood, Pa., 1958—60; mem. patron's bd. Fla. State U. Sch. Theater, 2000—; bd. mem. Lafayette Oaks Home Assn., 2002—; Dem. committeeman Lombard, Ill., 1961—69; Eucharistic min. Blessed Sacramento Cath. Ch., 1984—, mem. parish coun., 2000—. 1st lt. USAAF, 1942—45. Decorated Air medal; recipient Ofcl. commendation White House Conf. on Libr. and Info. Svc., 1979, citation State Libr. Agys., 1994, Silver award Commn. Libr. Info. Sci., 1996. Mem. ALA (coun. 1973-82, 88-92, mem. exec. bd. 1974-79, chmn. stats. coordinating com. 1970-74, mem. pub. com. 1975-78, 81-83, 87-89, chmn. adv. com. interface, 1979-83, chmn. membership com. 1983-84, chmn. nominating com. 1988-89, mem. legis. com. 1989-91, adv. bd. ALA Yearbook 1976-91, Assn. Specialized and Coop. Library Agys. legis. com., 1987-89, ad hoc com. White House Conf. on Libr. and Info. Svcs. 1989-91, chmn. awards com. 1990-92, Exceptional Achievement award 1981, J.B. Lippincott award 1989), Cath. Library Assn. (life, adv. coun. 1960—), Ill. Library Assn. (chmn. legis.-library devel. com. 1964-69, mem. exec. bd., libr's. citation 1974), Fla. Library Assn. (bd. dirs. 1987-93, pres. 1991-92, intellectual freedom com., chmn. com. on Fla. Librs. publ., editor, publ. com., planning com., 1991, site com.), Continuing Libr. Edn. Network and Exchange (pres. 1982-83), Internat. Fedn. Library Assns. and Institutions (statistics standing com. 1976-85, planning com.), Coun. Nat. Library Assns. (chmn. 1959-61), Assn. Coll. and Research Librarians (pres. Phila. chpt. 1953-55), Drexel Inst. Library Sch. Alumni Assn. (pres. 1955-56, exec. bd. 1956-60, chmn. chief officers State Library Agys. 1973-74), Chgo. Library Club (pres. 1969), Assn. Library and Info. Sci. Edn. (govt. relation com. 1985-87), Drexel U. Alumni Assn. (Outstanding Alumnus award 1963), Kappa Phi Kappa (chpt. pres. 1948), Beta Phi Mu (hon.). Lodges: K.C. E-mail: atrezza@mailer.fsu.edu. *You can't do anything alone. You need support and you need opposition. Opposition provides you with challenge. Challenge brings out the best in you.*

TRIANA, GLADYS, artist; b. Camaguey, Cuba, Nov. 17, 1937; came to U.S., 1974; d. Jose Daniel Triana and Francisca Maria Perez; m. Manuel Angel Malleiro, Apr. 11, 1974. Student, Oriente U., Santiago de Cuba, 1957; B in Art summa cum laude, Mercy Coll., 1976; MEd, L.I. U., 1977. Art educator N.Y.C. Bd. Edn., 1978—. Exhbn. cons. Salute to Bklyn.'s Creative Youth Exhbn., The Bklyn. Art Coun., Children's Gallery at Bklyn. Mus., 1986—; created and implemented Children Expressions Mural Program at Cmty. Sch. Bd. Dist. #2, N.Y.C., 1987—. One women shows include Lyceum Gallery, Havana, Cuba, 1962, 63, Tramontana Gallery, 1971, Intar Gallery, 1975, Cuban Mus. Art and Culture, Miami, Fla., 1988, Mus. Contemporary Hispanic Art, N.Y., 1990, Mus. Modern Art, Santo Domingo, 1991, Nader Gallery Fine Arts, Santo Domingo, Bronx Mus. Arts, 1995, Jeux De Memoire, Espace Nesle, Paris, Trapecio Gallery, Lima, Peru, 1997; exhibited in group shows at Palacio de Bellas Artes Mus., 1962, 91, Sala de Arte Gallery, Madrid, 1971, Mus. Sci., Chgo., 1975, Inst. de Cultura Puertorriquena, Museo de Ponce, P.R., 1976, 92, Queens Coll., 1979, Meeting Point Gallery, Miami, 1982, Todd Capp Gallery, N.Y., 1986, Mus. Contemporary Hispanic Art, N.Y., 1988, Warehouse Gallery, N.Y.C., 1989, Stratus Gallery, N.Y.C., 1989, L.I. U., 1989, Mus. Contemporary Art, Caracas, Venezuela, 1990, Discovery Mus., Bridgeport, Conn., 1990, Modern Art Latin Am., Washington, 1990, Humphrey Gallery, N.Y.C., 1992, Paine Weber Art Gallery, N.Y.C., 1992, Artspace, New Haven, Conn., 1992, Adriana Landon Gallery, N.Y.C., 1993, Sotavento Gallery, Caracas, 1995, Nat. Libr. Can., Ottawa, Ont., 1996, Mexic-Art Mus., Austin, Tex., 1997, Espace Nesle, Paris, Trapeeio Gallery, Lima, 1998, Tampa Mus. Art; contbr. articles to profl. publs.; illustrator in field. Mem. Mus. of Women, Washington, 1990—, Women of Caucus, N.Y.C., 1992—, Ctr. for Books of Art, N.Y.C., 1993—. Recipient Art Competition 3rd prize Ateneo de Marianao Gallery, Havana, Cuba, 1964, Ednl. scholarship Nat. Clairol Loving Care Art Program, 1974, Hon. mention Mus. of Sci., Chgo., 1975, Spl. mention The N.Y.C. Bd. Edn. Masters and Apprentices Exhibit, 1990, Outstanding Achievement in Visual Arts award The Queens Borough Pres. of City of N.Y., 1990, Cintas fellowship, 1993. Mem. NOW, Mus. Modern Art, Met. Mus. Avocations: music, ballet, opera, tennis, bicycling.

TRIANDIS, HARRY CHARALAMBOS, psychology educator; b. Patras, Greece, Oct. 16, 1926; s. Christos Charalambos and Louise J. (Nikokavouras) T.; m. Pola Fotitch, Dec. 23, 1966; 1 child, Louisa. B.Engring., McGill U., 1951; M.Commerce, U. Toronto, Ont., Can., 1954; PhD, Cornell U., 1958; Doctorate (hon.), U. Athens, Greece, 1987. Asst. prof. U. Ill., Champaign, 1958-61, assoc. prof., 1961-66, prof. psychology, 1966-97; cons. USIA, 1970-75, NSF, 1968-75; prof. emeritus, 1997—. Author: Attitudes and Attitude Change, 1971, The Analysis of Subjective Culture, 1972, Varieties of Black and White Perception of the Social Environment, 1975, Interpersonal Behavior, 1977, Culture and Social Behavior, 1994, Individualism and Collectivism, 1995; editor: Handbook of Cross-Cultural Psychology, Vol. 1-6, 1980-81, Handbook of Industrial and Organizational Psychology, Vol. 4, 1994; editorial cons.; Jour. Personality and social Psychology, 1963-71, Jour. Applied Psychology, 1970-79, Sociometry, 1971-74, Jour. Cross-Cultural Psychology, 1974—, others. Chmn. fgn. grants com. Am. Psychol. Found., 1968-90. Sr. fellow Ford Found., 1964-65; Guggenheim fellow, 1972-73; grantee USPHS, 1956-60, 62; grantee Office Naval Research, 1960-68, 80-85; grantee Social and Rehab. Service, HEW, 1968-73; grantee Ford Found., 1973-75; recipient award Interam. Soc. Psychology, 1981 Mem. Soc. for Psychol. Study of Social Issues (pres. 1975-76), Internat. Assn. Cross-Cultural Psychology (pres. 1974-76), Interam. Soc. Psychology (pres. 1985-87), Soc. for Exptl. Social Psychology (chmn. 1972-74), Soc. for Personality and Social Psychology (pres. 1976-77), Internat. Assn. Applied Psychology (pres. 1990-94). Home: 1 Lake Park Rd Champaign IL 61822-7101 Office: 603 E Daniel St Champaign IL 61820-6232

TRIANTAFYLLOU, MICHAEL STEFANOS, ocean engineering educator; b. Athens, Greece, Oct. 27, 1951; came to U.S., 1974; s. Stefanos M. and Penelopi I. (Koutras) T.; m. Joan L. Kimball, Sept. 22, 1985; children: Stefanos R., Kimon K. MS in Ocean Engring., MSME, MIT, 1977, ScD, 1979. Rsch. assoc. MIT, Cambridge, Mass., 1978-79, asst. prof., 1979-83, assoc. prof., 1983-86, tenured assoc. prof., 1986-90, prof., dir. ocean engring. testing tank, 1990—. Vis. scientist Woods Hole (Mass.) Oceanographic Inst., 1990—; com. chair MIT/Woods Hole Joint Program in Oceanography. Featured cover Scientific American; contbr. articles to profl. jours. Rsch. grantee OFfice NAval Rsch., Office Naval Tech., NSF, Doherty Found. Dept. Commerce, 1979—. Mem. Internat. Soc. Offshore and Polar Engrs. (founding mem.), Soc. Naval Architects and Marine Engrs. (papers com., vice chmn. OC-2 com.), Am. Phys. Soc. Office: MIT 77 Massachusetts Ave Rm 5-323 Cambridge MA 02139-4307

TRIBBLE, RICHARD WALTER, brokerage executive; b. San Diego, Oct. 19, 1948; s. Walter Perrin and Catherine Janet (Miller) T.; m. Joan Catherine Sliter, June 26, 1980. BS, U. Ala., Tuscaloosa, 1968. Grad. Gulf Coast Sch. Drilling Practices, U. Southwestern La., 1976. Registered rep. ITT-Hamilton, Woodridge, Va., 1969-71; stockbroker Shearson, Loeb & Rhoades and Co., Washington, 1971-76; ind. oil and gas investment sales Falls Church, Va., 1976-77; pres. Monroe & Keusink, Inc., 1977-87; instnl. investment officer FCA Asset Mgmt., Columbus, Ohio, 1983-85; fin. cons. Merrill Lynch Pierce Fenner & Smith, Inc., Phoenix, 1987—, cert. fin. mgr., 1989—, sr. fin. cons., 1992—, asst. v.p., 1993—2002, v.p., 2002—. Mem. adv. bd. Samaritan Found., 1999—. With USMC, 1969-70. Mem. Ariz. Fiduciary Assn. (membership com. 1999), Ctrl. Ariz. Estate Planning Coun., Investment Mgmt. Cons. Assn. Republican. Methodist. Office: # 900 2555 E Camelback Rd Phoenix AZ 85016-4219 E-mail: richard_tribble@ml.com.

TRIBLE, PAUL SEWARD, JR. former United States senator; b. Balt., Dec. 29, 1946; s. Paul Seward and Katherine (Schilpp) T.; m. Rosemary Dunaway; children: Mary Katherine, Paul Seward III. BA, Hampden-Sydney Coll., 1968; JD, Washington and Lee U., Lexington, Va., 1971. Bar: Va. 1971. Law clk. to U.S. dist. judge Albert V. Bryan, Jr., 1971-72; asst. U.S. atty. Office U.S. Atty. Eastern Dist. Va., 1972-74; commonwealth's atty. Essex County, Va., 1974-76; U.S. Congressman 1st Va. Dist., Washington, 1976-82; U.S. Senator from Va., 1982-89; of counsel Laxalt, Washington, Perito & Dubuc, Washington, Shuttleworth, Ruloff & Giordano, Va., 1989-95, Laxalt, Washington, Washington, 1989—95; pres. Jefferson Group, 1991-95, Christopher Newport U., Newport News, Va., 1996—. Mem.: Washington and Lee Law Rev. Republican. Episcopalian. Office: Christopher Newport Univ Office of President 1 University Pl Newport News VA 23606-2998

TRIBUS, MYRON, retired quality counselor, engineer, educator; b. San Francisco, Oct. 30, 1921; s. Edward and Marie D. (Kramer) T.; m. Sue Davis, Aug. 30, 1945; children— Louanne, Kamala. BS in Chemistry, U. Calif. at Berkeley, 1942; PhD in Engring, U. Calif. at Los Angeles, 1949; D.Sc. (hon.), Rockford (Ill.) Coll., 1965, Oakland (Mich.) U., 1971. Registered profl. engr., Mass. Instr. to prof. engring. U. Calif. at Los Angeles, 1946-61; dir. aircraft icing research U. Mich., 1951-54; dean engring. Thayer Sch. Engring., Dartmouth Coll., 1961-69; asst. sec. sci. and tech. Dept. Commerce, Washington, 1969-70; sr. v.p. tech. and engring. info. tech. group Xerox Corp., Rochester, N.Y., 1970-74; dir. Center for Advanced Engring. Study, Mass. Inst. Tech., Cambridge, 1974-86; cons. in quality mgmt., 1986—; dir. rsch., co-founder Exergy, Inc., Hayward, Calif., 1987-99. Cons. heat transfer Gen. Electric Co., 1950; cons. Fed. Office Saline Water; tech. adv. bd. Dept. Commerce; adviser to NATO, 1953; mem. Nat. Adv. Com. Oceans and Atmosphere, 1971-72. Author: Thermostatics and Thermodynamics, 1961, Rational Descriptions, Decisions and Designs, 1969; Contbr. articles to profl. jours. Bd. govs. Technion, Haifa, Israel, 1973-84. Served to capt. USAAF, 1942-46. Recipient Thurman H. Bane award Inst. Aero. Scis., 1945, Wright Bros. medal Soc. Automotive Engrs., 1945; Alfred Noble prize Engring. Socs., 1952, Robert Fletcher awrd Thayer Sch. Engring., Dartmouth Coll., 1994; named UCLA Alumnus of Yr., 1972. Mem. ASME, IEEE, NSPE. Home: 350 Britto Ter Fremont CA 94539-3824 E-mail: mtribus@earthlink.net.

TRICE, MARY SUE WILLIAMS, guidance counselor; b. Marietta, Ga., Aug. 9, 1950; d. Pembroke Whitfield and Virginia Swanson Williams; m. Richard Alan Trice, Dec. 15, 1972; 1 child, Mary Katherine. BA in Art Edn., West Ga. Coll., 1971, MEd, 1972. Guidance counselor, art tchr. Monroe Acad., Forsyth, Ga., 1975-78; art tchr. Gwin Oaks Elem. Sch., Lawrenceville, 1978-79; h.s. counselor Ctrl. Gwinnett H.S., 1979-89, Berkmar H.S., Lilburn, 1989—. Bd. dirs. Ga. Edn. Articulation Com., Atlanta. Girl Scout leader Northwest Ga. Girl Scouts, Suwanee, 1981-2002, svc. unit dir., 1997-2002. Mem. Am. Sch. Counselor Assn., Girl Scouts Am. (life), Ga. Sch. Counselors Assn., Atlanta Yacht Club. Home: 5155 Meadowbrook Cir Suwanee GA 30024-1964

TRICHEL, MARY LYDIA, middle school educator; b. Rosenberg, Tex., Feb. 2, 1957; d. Henry John and Henrietta (Jurek) Pavlicek; m. Keith Trichel, Aug. 8, 1981; children: Daniel, Nicholas. BS cum laude, Tex. A & M U., 1980. Cert. tchr., Tex. Social studies tchr. grades 6, 7 and 8 St. Francis de Sales, Houston, 1980-81; English tchr. grades 7 and 8 Dean Morgan Jr. High, Casper, Wyo., 1983-86; English and journalism tchr. grades 9 and 11 Tecumseh (Okla.) High Sch., 1987; English tchr. grade 6 Christa McAuliffe Middle Sch., Houston, 1988-92; tchr. Tex. history grade 7, journalism grade 8 Lake Olympia Middle Sch., Missouri City, Tex., 1991-92; tchr. social studies 6th grade Lake Olympia Mid. Sch. Ft. Bend Ind. Sch. Dist., 1993-96; tchr. social studies 6th grade Atascocita Mid. Sch. Humble Ind. Sch. Dist., 1997—. Recipient teaching awards. Mem. Nat. Coun. Tchrs. English, Nat. Coun. Tchrs. Social Studies, Am. Fedn. Tchrs. Avocations: desktop publishing, scuba diving, traveling. Home: 14306 Hartshill Dr Houston TX 77044-5066

TRICHOPOULOS, DIMITRIOS VASSILIOS, epidemiologist, educator; b. Volos, Greece, Dec. 9, 1938; s. Vassilios Konstantinou and Alexandra Dimitrios (Kataropoulou) T.; m. Antonia Athanasiou Polychronopoulou, June 17, 1967. MD, Athens U., Greece, 1963, PhD, 1971; MS, Harvard Sch. Pub. Health, 1968; MD honoris causa, Uppsala (Sweden) U., 1994. Diplomate Am. Coll. Epidemiology. Lectr. preventive medicine U. Athens Med. Sch., 1965-67, prof., chair preventive medicine, 1972—; lectr. epidemiology Harvard Sch. Pub. Health, Boston, 1969-70, prof. cancer prevention and epidemiology, 1989—; prof., dir. Harvard Ctr. Cancer Prevention, 1994-97. Chmn. health group Coun. European Union, Brussels, 1988. Editor: Teaching Epidemiology, 1992; contbr. numerous articles to profl. jours. Decorated officier Ordre Palmes Academiques (France), Commdr. of Honor, Greece. Mem. Acad. of Athens, Royal Acad. Medicine Belgium (corr., fgn.), Nat. Acad. Medicine France (corr., fgn.), Harvard Club, Athens Club. Greek Orthodox. Office: Harvard Sch Pub Health 677 Huntington Ave Boston MA 02115-6096

TRICKEY, SAMUEL BALDWIN, physics educator, researcher, university administrator; b. Detroit, Nov. 28, 1940; s. Samuel Miller and Betty Irene (Baldwin) T.; m. Lydia Hernandez, Dec. 28, 1962 (div. June 1981); children: Matthew J., Phillip J.; m. Cynthia Karle, Aug. 13, 1983. BA in Physics, Rice U., 1962; MS, Tex. A&M U., 1966, PhD in Theoretical Physics, 1968. Rsch. scientist Mason & Hanger-Silas Mason Corp., 1962-64; asst. prof. physics U. Fla., Gainesville, 1968-73, assoc. prof., 1973-77, prof. physics and chemistry, 1979—, dir. Quantum Theory Project, 1999—. Dir. J.C. Slater Meml. Computing Lab., 1981-93, Computer and Comm. Resources Coll. Liberal Arts and Scis., 1986-90, exec. dir. info. techs. and svcs. Office of Provost, 1991-96, prof. physics, chmn. physics and engring. physics Tex. Tech. U., Lubbock, 1977-79; cons. Redstone Arsenal Ala., 1972-76; vis. rsch. scholar Mich. Tech. U., 1982-92; vis. scientist IBM Rsch. Ctr., San Jose, Calif., 1975-76; assoc. or dep. dir. Sanibel Symposia; cons. Los Alamos Nat. Lab., 1984—; vis. scientist Max Planck Inst. für Astrophysik, Munich, 1985-94; internat. collaborator Technische U. München Inst. für Theoretische Chemie, 1995—. Contbr. articles to profl. jours. Exec. v.p. U. Fla. chpt. United Faculty of Fla., 1981-83. Named Tchr. of Yr. Coll. Arts and Scis. U. Fla., 1973-74. Fellow Am. Phys. Soc.; mem. Am. Assn. Physics Tchrs., Nat. Assn. Hispanic Physicists, Nat. R.R. Hist. Soc., Gulf Atlantic Yacht Club, Organ Hist. Soc., San Juan 21 Class Assn., S.W. R.R. Hist. Soc., Laser 28 Class Assn., Onigaming Yacht Club, Phi Kappa Phi, Sigma Xi, Sigma Pi Sigma. Democrat. Presbyterian. Home: 723 NW 19th St Gainesville FL 32603-1102 Office: Univ Fla Quantum Theory Project PO Box 118435 Gainesville FL 32611-8435 E-mail: trickey@qtp.ufl.edu.

TRICOLES, GUS PETER, electromagnetic engineer, physicist, consultant; b. San Francisco, Oct. 18, 1931; s. Constantine Peter and Eugenia (Elias) T.; m. Beverly Mildred Ralsky, Dec. 20, 1953 (dec. Dec. 1974); children: Rosanne, Robin; m. Aileen Irma Aronson, Apr. 1, 1980 (div. June 1980). BA in Physics, UCLA, 1955; MS in Applied Math., San Diego State U., 1958; MS in Applied Physics, U. Calif., San Diego, 1962, PhD in Applied Physics, 1971. Engr. Convair divsn. Gen. Dynamics, San Diego, 1955-59, engr. Electronics divsn., 1962-75, engring. mgr. Electronics divsn., 1975-89, sr. engring. staff specialist, 1989-95, Tracor, 1995-99; engr. Smyth Rsch. Assn., San Diego, 1959-61; rsch. asst. Scripps Instn. Oceanography, La Jolla, Calif., 1961-62; sr. engring. staff specialist G.D.E. Systems, Inc., San Diego, 1992—, BAE Sys., 1999—. Engring. staff specialist B&M Sys., 2000; cons. Ga. Inst. Tech., Atlanta, 1972, 79-80, Transco Industries, L.A., 1973, Aero Geo Industries, San Antonio, 1980-82, Vantage Assocs., San Diego, 1988; rsch. reviewer NRC, NAS, Boulder, Colo., 1986-88. Author: (with others) Radome Engineering Handbook, 1970, Antenna Handbook, 1988; contbr. articles to profl. jours.; 19 patents in field. With USN, 1952-53. Fellow IEEE (antenna standards com. 1980—, advancement com. 1988), Optical Soc. Am. (local sect. v.p. 1966); mem. N.Y. Acad. Scis., Am. Geophys. Union. Avocations: woodworking, photography. Home: 4633 Euclid Ave San Diego CA 92115-3226 Office: PO Box 509009 San Diego CA 92150-9009

TRIEBER, EDWARD J. lawyer, psychologist; b. N.Y.C., Mar. 12, 1946; s. William and Edith T.; m. Jo Renee Fine, Apr. 12, 1981; 1 child. JD, NYU, 1969, PhD, 1983. Bar: N.Y. 1970; cert. in psychoanalysis. Pvt. practice, N.Y.C., 1971—; pvt. practice in psychology, 1981—; mng. dir. Harris Rothenberg Internat. LLC, 1993—. Advisor to bd. dirs. Knoa.net, N.Y.C., 2000—. Calder Found. fellow, 1979-80. Mem. Employee Assistance Profls. Assn., Assn. of Work Life Profls., N.Y. State Bar Assn., Nat. Psychol. Assn. for Psychoanalysis. Home: 55 West 16th St New York NY 10011

TRIECE, ANNE GALLAGHER, magazine publisher; b. Bklyn., July 1, 1955; d. Anthony J. and Mary Ann (Clines) Gallagher; m. David Mark Triece, Nov. 3, 1990; 1 child, Elizabeth Renee. BBA cum laude, CUNY, 1978. Media planner Isidore Lefkowitz Elgort, N.Y.C., 1978-80; sr. media supr. Ted Bates Advt., 1980-83; account mgr. Prevention mag., 1983-85; N.Y. mgr. Home mag., 1985-92; assoc. pub. Met. Home mag., 1992—. Coord. Arts Program for Homeless, N.Y.C., 1994. Recipient advt. excellence award Knapp Comm., 1985. Mem. Advt. Women N.Y. (commendation 1985). Roman Catholic. Avocations: scuba diving, tennis, skiing.

TRIENENS, HOWARD JOSEPH, lawyer; b. Chgo., Sept. 13, 1923; s. Joseph Herman and Myrtle (Wilsberg) T.; m. Paula Miller, Aug. 27, 1946; children: John, Thomas, Nancy. BS, Northwestern U., 1945; JD, 1949. Bar: Ill. 1949, N.Y. 1980, U.S. Dist. Ct. (no. dist.) Ill. 1949, U.S. Dist. Ct. (so. and ea. dists.) N.Y. 1980, U.S. Ct. Appeals (2d, 3d, 7th, 8th, 10th, 11th and D.C. cirs.), U.S. Supreme Ct. 1954. Assoc. firm Sidley, Austin, Burgess & Harper, Chgo., 1949-50; law clk. to Chief Justice Vinson, 1950-52; assoc. Sidley, Austin, Burgess & Smith, Chgo., 1952-56; ptnr. Sidley Austin Brown & Wood, 1956—; v.p., gen. counsel AT&T, 1980-86. Trustee Northwestern U., 1967—. With USAAF, 1943-46. Mem. ABA, Ill. Bar Assn., Chgo. Bar Assn., N.Y. State Bar Assn., Am. Coll. Trial Lawyers, Lawyers Club (Chgo.), Chgo. Club, Casino Club (Chgo.), Mid-Day Club, Skokie Country Club, Shoreacres Club, Glen View Club (Golf, Ill.), Met. Club (Washington), Old Elm Club, Sigma Chi. Democrat. Home: 690 Longwood Ave Glencoe IL 60022-1761 Office: Sidley Austin Brown & Wood Apt 605 425 W Surf St Chicago IL 60657-6139 E-mail: htrienens@sidley.com.

TRIER, JERRY STEVEN, gastroenterologist, educator; b. Frankfurt, Germany, Apr. 12, 1933; came to U.S., 1938, naturalized, 1943; s. Kurt J. and Alice L. (Cahn) T.; m. Laurel M. Bryan, June 8, 1957; children: Stanley, Jeryl, Stephen. MD, U. Wash., 1957; MA (hon.), Harvard U., 1973. Diplomate: Am. Bd. Internal Medicine. Intern U. Rochester, N.Y., 1957-58, resident in medicine, 1958-59; clin. asso. Nat. Cancer Inst., Bethesda, Md., 1959-61; trainee in gastroenterology U. Wash., Seattle, 1961-63; asst. prof. medicine U. Wis., Madison, 1963-67; asso. prof. U. N.Mex., Albuquerque, 1967-69, Boston U., 1969-73, Harvard U. Med. Sch., Cambridge, Mass., 1973-76, prof., 1976—. Sr. physician Brigham and Women's Hosp.; cons. Dana Farber Cancer Ctr., Brockton VA Hosp., W. Roxbury VA Hosp. Nat. Inst. Diabetes and Digestive and Kidney Disease; adv. coun. NIH, 1986-90. Editor: Internal Medicine; mem. editorial bd.; Anatomical Record, 1969-98, Gastroenterology, assoc. editor, 1971-77, mem. editorial bd., 1967-71, 78-83, 93-98, chmn., 1988-93, Am. Jour. Medicine, 1978-87, Current Opinion in Gastroenterology, 1990—; contbr. articles to profl. jours.; contbr. chpts. to books. Served as surgeon USPHS, 1959-61. USPHS/NIH grantee, 1963-94. Mem. Am. Soc. Clin. Investigation, Assn. Am. Physicians, Am. Gastroent. Assn. (pres. 1985-86, Julius Friedenwald medal 1999), Am. Soc. Cell Biology, Am. Fedn. Clin. Research. Office: Brigham and Women's Hosp 75 Francis St Boston MA 02115-6110

TRIERWEILER, ROBERT LOUIS, rehabilitation counselor; b. Springfield, Ill., Nov. 24, 1950; m. Jean M. Laughlin. BA, Western Ill. U., 1972, MS in Edn., 1981; postgrad., No. Ill. U., 2001—. Diplomate Am. Bd. Disability Analysts; cert. rehab. counselor; lic. clin. profl. counselor. Work adjustment case mgr. Assn. for Individual Devel., Aurora, Ill., 1979-80, profl. vocat. specialist, 1980-82, coord. vocat. svcs., 1987-88, crisis intervention worker, 1988-90; dir. Fox Valley Evaluation Ctr., Geneva, 1982-85, Elgin (Ill.) Rehab. Ctr., 1985-87; rehab. counselor in pvt. practice Geneva, 1987—; rehab. counselor Marianjoy Rehab. Hosp., Wheaton, Ill., 1988-93; sr. vocat. rehab. specialist Rehab. Inst. Chgo., 1993—, vocat. rehab. counselor, 1999—. Adj. faculty Northwestern U. Med. Sch. Prosthetic-Orthotic Ctr., Chgo., 1996-98; vocat. expert U.S. Dept. Health and Human Svcs., Office of Hearings and Appeals, Chgo., 1989—; grant reviewer Rehab. Svcs. Adminstrn., Washington, 1991—; adv. com. Marianjoy Rehab. Hosp., 1995-99. Cub scout dean leader Boy Scouts Am., Geneva, 1994-97, asst. scoutmaster, 1996-99, 2001—, scoutmaster, 1999-2001. Mem. Ill. Rehab. Counseling Assn. (membership chair, bd. dirs. 1993-95), Nat. Rehab. Counseling Assn. (chair task force 1994-96), Chgo. Assn. Vocat. Experts, Nat. Rehab. Assn. Avocations: camping, bicycling, photography. Home: 217 Oak St Geneva IL 60134-2825 Office: Rehab Inst of Chicago 326 W Illinois St Chicago IL 60610-4113 E-mail: rtrierweil@rehabchicago.org.

TRIEWEILER, TERRY NICHOLAS, state supreme court justice; b. Dubuque, Iowa, Mar. 21, 1948; s. George Nicholas and Anne Marie (Oastern) T.; m. Carol M. Jacobson, Aug. 11, 1972; children: Kathryn Anne, Christina

Marie, Anna Theresa. BA, Drake U., 1970, JD, 1972. Bar: Iowa 1973, Wash. 1973, U.S. Dist. Ct. (so. dist.) Iowa 1973, U.S. Dist. Ct. (we. dist.) Wash. 1973, Mont. 1975, U.S. Dist. Ct. Mont. 1977. Staff atty. Polk County Legal Services, Des Moines, 1973; assoc. Hullin, Roberts, Mines, Fite & Riveland, Seattle, 1973-75, Morrison & Hedman, Whitefish, Mont., 1975-77; sole practice, Whitefish; justice Mont. Supreme Ct., Helena, 1991—; lectr. U. Mont. Law Sch., 1981—; mem. com. to amend civil proc. rules Mont. Supreme Ct., Helena, 1984, commn. to draft pattern jury instrns., 1985; mem. Gov.'s Adv. Com. on Amendment to Work Compensation Act, adv. com. Mont. Work Compensation Ct. Mem. ABA, Mont. Bar Assn. (pres. 1986-87), Wash. Bar Assn., Iowa Bar Assn., Assn. Trial Lawyers Am., Mont. Trial Lawyers Assn. (dir., pres.). Democrat. Roman Catholic. Home: 1079 Woodbridge Dr Helena MT 59601-5477 Office: Mont Supreme Ct 215 N Sanders St Rm 410 PO Box 203001 Helena MT 59620-3001*

TRIFOLI-CUNNIFF, LAURA CATHERINE, psychologist, consultant; b. L.I., N.Y., June 8, 1958; d. Peter Nicholas and Susan Maria (Graziano) T.; m. John Kevin Cunniff, June 6, 1992; children: James Peter, Capri Susan. BA, Hofstra U., Uniondale, N.Y., 1980, MA, 1982, PhD, 1986. Founder, prin. Quality Cons., West Islip, N.Y., 1980-87; sr. tng. officer Norstar Bank, Garden City, 1985-87; asst. v.p. mgmt. devel. First Boston Corp., N.Y.C., 1986-90; mgr. exec. devel. Merrill Lynch, 1990-91; pres. The Exec. Process, 1991—. Cons. Am. Mgmt. Assn., N.Y.C., 1981-83, AT&T, Basking Ridge, N.H., 1982-83, The First Boston Corp., 1991—, Goldman Sachs, 1991—, Merrill Lynch & Co., 1991—, Union Bank of Switzerland, 1991—, Sanford C. Bernstein & Co., 1992—, Alexander & Alexander, 1993—, S.G. Warburg, 1994; instr. dept. psychology Hofstra U., 1983-85. Author: Vietnam Veterans: Post Traumatic Stress and its Effects, 1986; contbr. articles to profl. publs. Shift coord. Islip Hotline, 1976-78; eucharistic min. Hofstra U. Cath. Soc., 1980-85, Good Samaritan Hosp., West Islip, N.Y., 1988—. Scholar, Hofstra U., 1978-81, fellow, 1980, 81. Mem. Am. Psychol. Assn., Am. Soc. Tng. and Devel., Nat. Psychol. Honor Soc., Internat. Platform Soc. Roman Catholic. Avocations: equestrian sports, art, music. Office: 2906 Bree Hill Rd Oakton VA 22124-1212

TRIGG, GLYN RAY, guidance counselor, educational administrator, customer service representative; b. Canton, Miss., Apr. 21, 1964; s. Bruce L. and Eunice W. (Davis) T. BS in Social and Rehabilitative Svcs., U. So. Miss., 1991. Alcohol-drug counselor, intervention-prevention counselor S.W. Miss. Mental Health, McComb, 1992-93; guidance counselor, tchr. phys. edn., coach Porter's Chapel Acad., Vicksburg, Miss., 1993-95, interim headmaster, 1994—. Bell ringer Salvation Army, Vicksburg, 1993; organizer, activities chmn. Eagle Fest, Porter's Chapel Patron's Club, 1994. Named Jaycee of Month, Hattiesburg Jaycees, 1991, recipient cert. of merit, Jacke Eckerd svc. award. Mem. Jackson Jaycees (2d dir. 1990-92, Jaycee of Month 1992), Kiwanis (faculty advisor Key Club 1993-94). Baptist. Home: 6675 Old Canton Rd Apt 2047 Ridgeland MS 39157-1334 Office: Skyte 1 Comms 3450 Highway 80 W Jackson MS 39209-7201

TRIGGER, BRUCE GRAHAM, anthropology educator; b. Cambridge (formerly Preston), Ont., Can., June 18, 1937; s. John Wesley and Gertrude Elizabeth (Graham) T.; m. Barbara Marian Welch, Dec. 7, 1968; children: Isabel Marian, Rosalyn Theodora. BA, U. Toronto, 1959; PhD, Yale U., 1964; DSc (hon.), U. N.B., 1987; LittD (hon.), U. Waterloo, 1990; LLD, U. Western Ont., 1995, McMaster U., 1999. Asst. prof. Northwestern U., 1963-64, McGill U., 1964-67, assoc. prof., 1967-69, prof. anthropology, 1969—, chmn. dept., 1970-75, bd. govs., 1996—2001, James McGill prof., 2001—. Mem. bd. govs. McGill-Queen's U. Press, 1988—; trustee McGill Inst. for the Study of Can., 1996—; Harry Hawthorn Disting. lectr., 1988; Disting. lectr. in archaeology Am. Anthrop. Assn., 1990; Disting. vis. prof. Am. U. in Cairo, 1992; lectr. context and human soc. Boston U., 1997. Author: History and Settlement in Lower Nubia, 1965, Beyond History, 1968, The Huron: Farmers of the North, 1969, 2d edit., 1990, Cartier's Hochelaga, 1972, Nubia Under the Pharaohs, 1976, The Children of Aataentsic, 1976, Time and Traditions, 1978, Gordon Childe: Revolutions in Archaeology, 1980, Natives and Newcomers, 1985, A History of Archaeological Thought, 1989, Early Civilizations, 1993, Sociocultural Evolution, 1998; vol. editor: Handbook of North American Indians, Vol. 15, 1978; editor Native and Northern Series; co-editor: Cambridge History of the Native Peoples of the Americas, North America Volume, 1996. Recipient Can. Silver Jubilee medal, 1977, Cornplanter medal, 1979, John Porter prize, 1987, Prix Victor-Barbeau Acad. Canadienne-Française, 1991, Prix Leon-Gérin (Prix du Québec), 1991, James R. Wiseman Book award Archaeol. Inst. Am., 1991; Woodrow Wilson fellow, 1959-60, Woodrow Wilson dissertation fellow, 1962-63, Can. Coun. Leave fellow, 1968-69, 76-77, Killam rsch. fellow Can. Coun., 1970-71, 90, 91, leave fellow Social Scis. and Humanities Rsch. Coun. of Can., 1983; named officier, Ordre nat. du Quebec, 2001. Fellow Royal Soc. Can. (Innis-Gerin medal 1985), Soc. Antiquaries of Scotland (hon.); mem. Prehistoric Soc. U.K. (hon.), Huron Great Turtle Clan (adopted), Sigma Xi. Home: Apt 603 3495 Mountain St Montreal QC Canada H3G 2A5 Office: McGill U Dept Anthropology 855 Sherbrooke St W Montreal QC Canada H3A 2T7 E-mail: btrigg1@po-box.mcgill.ca.

TRIGGLE, DAVID JOHN, university dean, consultant; b. U.K., Apr. 5, 1935; came to U.S., 1962; s. William John and Maud F. (Henderson) T.; m. Ann. M. Jones, Sept. 22, 1959; children: Andrew B., Jocelyn A. BSc in Chemistry, U. Southampton, United Kingdom, 1956; PhD, U. Hull, United Kingdom, 1959. Sch. fellow U. Ottawa, Ont., Can., 1959-61; rsch. fellow U. London, 1961-62; asst. prof. SUNY Sch. of Pharmacy, Buffalo, 1962-65, assoc. prof., 1965-69, prof., 1985-95, chmn. dept., 1971-85, dean, 1985-95, Disting. prof., 1987—, vice-provost for grad. edn., 1995-2001, dean Grad. Sch., 1995-2001, provost, 2000-01, univ. prof., 0200—. Cons. to pharm. industry, 1980—. Author: Chemical Aspects of Autonomic Nervous System, 1965, Neurotransmitter-Receptor Interactions, 1971, Chemical Pharmacology of the Synapse, 1976. Recipient Volwiler Rsch. Achievement award Am. Assn. Colls. Pharmacy, 1988, 89, George Koepf award Biomed. Rsch. Med. Found. Buffalo, 1994. Fellow AAAS; mem. Am. Chem. Soc., Am. Soc. Pharmacology and Therapeutics (Otto Krayer award 1995), Soc. Neurosci., Brit. Pharmacology Soc., Am. Pharm. Assn., Rho Chi (Rho Chi award 1998). Office: SUNY Sch of Pharmacy 457 Hochstetter Buffalo NY 14260-0001 E-mail: triggle@buffalo.edu.

TRIGIANO, LUCIEN LEWIS, physician; b. Easton, Pa., Feb. 9, 1926; s. Nicholas and Angeline (Lewis) T.; children: Lynn Anita, Glenn Larry, Robert Nicholas. Student, Tex. Christian U., 1944-45, Ohio U., 1943-44, 46-47, Milligan Coll., 1944, Northwestern U., 1945, Temple U., 1948-52. Diplomate Am. Bd. Phys. Medicine & Rehab. Intern Meml. Hosp., Johnstown, Pa., 1952-53; resident Lee Hosp., 1953-54; gen. practice, 1953-59; med. dir. Pa. Rehab. Ctr., 1959-62, chief phys. medicine & rehab., 1964-70; fellow phys. medicine & rehab. N.Y. Inst. Phys. Medicine & Rehab., 1962—64; dir. rehab. medicine Lee Hosp., 1964-71, Ralph K. Davies Med. Ctr., San Francisco, 1973-75, St. Joseph's Hosp., San Francisco, 1975-78, St. Francis Meml. Hosp., San Francisco, 1978-83, Rehab. Ctr. Nev., Las Vegas, 1998—2000. Asst. prof. phys. medicine and rehab. Temple U. Sch. Medicine; founder Disability Alert. Served with USNR, 1944-46. Mem. AMA, Am. Coll. Physicians, Pa. Med. Soc., San Francisco County Med. Soc., Am. Acad. Phys. Medicine & Rehab., Am. Congress Phys. Medicine, Calif. Acad. Phys. Medicine, Nat. Rehab. Assn., Babcock Surg. Soc. Home and Office: 1421 Casa Del Rey Ct Las Vegas NV 89117-1538 E-mail: lltmdmd@aol.com.

TRIGILIO, JOHN PATRICIO, priest, parochial vicar; b. Erie, Pa., Mar. 31, 1962; s. John Eugene and Elizabeth Louise (Lagner) T. BA, Gannon U., 1983; MDiv, Mary Immaculate Coll., 1988; PhD, LaSalle U., 1998. Ordained priest Roman Cath. Ch., 1988. Deacon St. Gregory the Great Ch., Lebanon, Pa., 1987-88; parochial vicar St. Joseph Ch., Mechanicsburg, 1988-92, St. John the Bapt. Roman Cath. Ch., 1992-94; judge instr. Marriage Tribunal of Diocese of Harrisburg, 1994-95; Cath. hosp. chaplain Polyclinic Med. Ctr., Harrisburg Hosp., 1994-95; parochial vicar St. Joan of Arc, Hershey, Pa., 1995-98. Parochial vicar Seven Sorrows of the B.V.M., Middletown, Pa., 1998—. Asst. editor Confraternity of Cath. Clergy newsletter, 1996-97, exec. editor., 1997—; contbr. articles to profl. jours. Chaplain Cath. War Vets., Mechanicsburg, 1989-91; founder, pres. Fraternity of Mary, Queen of the Clergy, Inc., 1996—. Mem. Cath. Conservative Clergy (pres. 1991—), St. Gregory Latin Liturgy Assn., Canon Law Soc. Am., Confraternity of Cath. Clergy, Sons of Italy (chaplain 1991), KC (chaplain 1990-91). Republican. Office: St Joseph Roman Cath Ch PO Box 60542 Harrisburg PA 17106-0542

TRIIPAN, MAIVE, library director; b. Virumaa County, Estonia, Jan. 4, 1942; d. Osvald and Minna (Olesk) Triipan; m. Kalle Dobkevich, Mar. 6, 1971 (div. June 4, 1974); 1 child, Raul. B. of Librarianship, Tartu U., 1967. Rsch. mgmt. asst. Libr. of Estonian Acad. Scis., Tallinn, 1967-74, asst. dir. rsch. work, 1974-84, dir., 1984—. Mem. State Libr. Coun., Tallinn, 1974-87, State Libr. Coun. at Dept. of Culture and Edn., Tallinn, 1989—, Tech. U. Coun., Tallinn, 1993—, Estonian Nat. Libr. Coun., Tallinn, 1994—; fin. mgr. Merelaug, 1998-99; project mgmt. Scis. Dept. Estonian Inst. Pub. Adminstrn. Editl. bd. Estonian Retrospective, 1975; mng. pub. National Bibliography 1525-1940, 1993. Mem. Estonian Librs. Assn. Avocations: literature, music, art.

TRIKHA, AJIT, psychiatrist; b. Madras, India, Oct. 14, 1952; MB BS, Armed Forces Coll. Poona U., 1974. Diplomate Am. Bd. Psychiatry and Neurology, Geriatric Psychiatry, Am. Bd. Forensic Medicine. Intern Montefiore Med. Ctr.-Albert Einstein Coll. Medicine, Bronx, N.Y., 1988-89; resident psychiatry Goodmayes-St. Bartholomew's-The Royal London Hosps., 1982-86, Watford Gen. Hosp., Hertfordshire, Eng., 1986-87; fellow psychiatry Washington U., St. Louis, 1987-88; med. dir. Mid-America Behavioral Healthcare, Inc., Belleville, Ill., 1992-98, Rock Creek Partial Hospitalization Program, Cahokia, 1996-98; mgr. St. Mary's Partial Hospitalization Program, 1998-00. Med. dir. Counseling Ctr., Belleville, 1998-2000. Mem. AMA, Am. Psychiat. Assn. Office: 6915 W Main St Belleville IL 62223-3029 E-mail: trxhlthsys@aol.com.

TRILLIN, CALVIN, writer; b. Kansas City, Mo., Dec. 5, 1935; s. Abe and Edyth T.; m. Alice Stewart, Aug. 13, 1965 (dec.); children: Abigail, Sarah Stewart. BA, Yale U., 1957; DLitt (hon.), Beloit Coll., 1987; LHD (hon.), Albertus Magnus Coll., 1990; DLitt (hon.), SUNY, 1996, U. N.C., 1998, Susquehanna U., 1999; DLitt. (hon.) , Long Island U., 2002. Reporter, writer Time mag., 1960-63; staff writer New Yorker mag., 1963—; columnist Nation mag., 1978-85; syndicated columnist, 1986-95; columnist Time mag., 1996-2001. Trustee N.Y. Pub. Libr. Author: An Education in Georgia, 1964, Barnett Frummer is an Unbloomed Flower, 1969, U.S. Journal, 1971, American Fried, 1974, Runestruck, 1977, Alice, Let's Eat, 1978, Floater, 1980, Uncivil Liberties, 1982, Third Helpings, 1983, Killings, 1984, With All Disrespect, 1985, If You Can't Say Something Nice, 1987, Travels With Alice, 1989, Enough's Enough, 1990, American Stories, 1991, Remembering Denny, 1993, Deadline Poet, 1994, Too Soon to Tell, 1995, Messages From My Father, 1996, Family Man, 1998, Tepper Isn't Going Out, 2002; author, performer one-man show Calvin Trillin's Uncle Sam, Am. Place Theatre, N.Y.C., 1988, Calvin Trillin's Words, No Music, Am. Place Theatre, 1990. Office: care New Yorker 4 Times Sq New York NY 10036-6522

TRILLING, GEORGE HENRY, physicist, educator; b. Bialystok, Poland, Sept. 18, 1930; came to U.S., 1941; s. Max and Eugenie (Walfisz) T.; m. Madeleine Alice Monic, June 26, 1955; children: Stephen, Yvonne, David. BS, Calif. Inst. Tech., Pasadena, 1951, PhD, 1955. Research fellow Calif. Inst. Tech., Pasadena, 1955-56; Fulbright post-doctoral fellow Ecole Polytechnique, Paris, 1956-57; asst. to assoc. prof. U. Mich., Ann Arbor, 1957-60; assoc. to prof. dept. physics U. Calif., Berkeley, 1960-94, prof. emeritus, 1994—. Fellow Am. Phys. Soc., Am. Acad. Arts and Scis.; mem. NAS. Achievements include: research in high energy physics. Office: Lawrence Berkeley Nat Lab Berkeley CA 94720-0001

TRILLING, LEON, aeronautical engineering educator; b. Bialystok, Poland, July 15, 1924; came to U.S., 1940, naturalized, 1946; s. Oswald and Regina (Zakhejm) T.; m. Edna Yuval, Feb. 17, 1946; children: Alex R., Roger S. BS, Calif. Inst. Tech., 1944, MS, 1946, PhD, 1948. Research fellow Calif. Inst. Tech., 1948- 50; Fulbright scholar U. Paris, 1950-51, vis. prof., 1963-64; mem. faculty MIT, Cambridge, 1951—, prof. aeros. and astronautics, 1962-94, prof. emeritus, 1994—, mem. coun. on primary and secondary edn., 1992—. Mem. Program in Sci. Tech. and Society, Engring. Edn. Mission to Soviet Union, 1958; vis. prof. Delft Tech. U., 1974-75; vis. prof. engring. Carleton Coll., 1987 Pres. Met. Com. Ednl. Opportunity, 1967-70, Council for Understanding of Tech. in Human Affairs, 1984— Guggenheim fellow, 1963-64 Fellow AAAS. Home: 180 Beacon St Boston MA 02116-1408 Office: MIT 77 Massachusetts Ave Cambridge MA 02139-4307

TRIM, DONALD ROY, consulting engineer; b. Saginaw, Mich., June 23, 1937; s. Roy E. and Agnes (Kontranowski) T.; m. Dorothy Mae Franek, Aug. 11, 1962; children: Jeffrey D., Gregory S., Christopher M. BS in Civic Engring., U. Mich., 1959. Registered profl. engr., Mich., Ohio, Fla.; registered land surveyor, Mich. Engr. Francis Engring., Saginaw, 1959-64, Edwin M. Orr, Inc., Dearborn, Mich., 1964-66; pres. Wade-Trim Group, Plymouth, 1966-96, CEO, 1996-99, chmn., 1999—. V.p. Plymouth Canton Basketball Assn., 1980-84; bd. govs. Greater Mich. Found., Lansing, 1983-85. Mem. Nat. Soc. Profl. Engrs., Cons. Engrs. Coun. Mich. (dir. 1972-73, Pres. 1983-84), Am. Cons. Engrs. Coun. (v.p. 1986-88, pres. 1998-99), Am. Waterworks Assn. Roman Cath. Office: Wade-Trim Group 400 Monroe St Ste 310 Detroit MI 48226-2962 E-mail: dtrim@wadetrim.com.

TRIMBLE, BERNARD HENRY, tour guide, former trade association executive; b. McKeepsport, Pa., Sept. 19, 1930; s. John Francis and Louise Esther (McKenna) T.; m. Jo McDonald, Nov. 26, 1959; children: Jeanne, Daniel Bernard. BA, St. Vincent COll., 1953; postgrad., Georgetown U., 1953-55, Sophia U., Tokyo, 1957. Dirs. staff FBI, Washington, 1953-55; asst. prof. U. Tex., Austin, 1958-60; market devel. mgr. Reuben H. Donnolley Corp., Washington, 1960-64; mktg. svcs. mgr. Nat. Elec. Contractors Assn., 1964-68, dirs. svcs., 1968-70, sec., treas., 1970-73, sec., mgr. Atlanta, 1973-78; exec. dir. Nat. Assn. Mfg., Washington, 1978-94; pres. Henry McKenna Co., 1994—. Pres. Product Design Inst., Austin, 1959-60, Constrn. Industry Found., Washington, 1968-70. Lt. USN, 1955-60. Acad. Elec. Contracting fellow, Washington, 1975. Mem. VFW, KC, Am. Legion. E-mail: henrymck@erols.com.

TRIMBLE, JAMES T., JR. federal judge; b. Bunkie, La., Sept. 13, 1932; s. James T. Sr. and Mabel (McNabb) T.; m. Murel Elise Biles, Aug. 18, 1956; children: Elise Rumsey, Mary Olive Beacham, Martha McNabb Elliott, Sarah Trimble Moritz. Student, U. La., Lafayette, 1950-52; BA in Law, La. State U., 1955, JD, 1956. Bar: La. 1956. With Gist, Murchison & Gist (now Gist, Methvin, Hughes & Munsterman), 1959-78, Trimble, Percy, Smith, Wilson, Foote, Walker & Honeycutt, 1979-86; U.S. magistrate U.S. Dist. Ct. (we. dist.) La., 1986-91, judge, 1991—. Lt. USAF, 1956-59. Mem. Fed. Judges Assn., Southwest La. Bar Assn., La. Bar Assn., La. Bar Found. Avocations: jogging, gardening, tennis. Office: 611 Broad St Ste 237 Lake Charles LA 70601-4380

TRIMBLE, KATHLEEN LOUISE, library director; b. Reading, Pa., Oct. 10, 1949; d. Melvin Blackburn and Ruth Louise (Kreitz) T.; m. Richard Harvey Greenberg, May 20, 1984; children: Max, Jacob. BA, U. Toledo, 1972, MLS, 1979. Librarian II Toledo Blade, 1971-75, librarian I, 1975-78, asst. head librarian, 1976-78, head librarian, 1978-82; mgr. library info. U.S. News and World Report, Washington, 1982-83, library dir., 1983-97, dir. editl. adminstrn., 1997—. Recipient Henebry award News Divsn., 1993. Mem. Spl. Libraries Assn. (dir. newspaper div. 1978-80, sec.-treas. 1979-81). Jewish. Office: US News & World Report Ste 150 1050 Thomas Jefferson St NW Washington DC 20007-3817

TRIMBLE, PRESTON ALBERT, retired judge; b. Salina, Okla., Aug. 27, 1930; s. James Albert and Winnie Louella (Walker) T.; m. Patricia Ann Beadle; children: Todd, Beth, Amy. BA, U. Okla., 1956, LL.B., 1960. Bar: Okla. 1960. Practice law, 1960; asst. county atty. Cleveland County, Okla., 1960-62; county atty., 1962-67; dist. atty., 1967-79; dist. judge, 1979-91. Spl. instr. S.W. Center Law Enforcement Edn.; cons. prosecution mgmt. Mem. Jud. Council Okla.; chmn. Okla. Corrections Workshop; mem. planning com. Nat. Inst. Crime and Delinquency; mem. com. on multi-agy. problems in criminal justice Appellate Judges Conf. Bd. dirs. Okla. U. Crisis Ctr., 1970—, ARC, Lake Murray Conservation Assn.; trustee Nat. Assn. Pretrial Svc. Agys. Resource Ctr., Sarkeys Found., 1994—. With USNR, 1948-52; col. USAFR. Mem. Okla., Cleveland County bar assns., Nat. Dist. Attys. Assn. (past pres.), Okla. Dist. Attys. Assn. (past pres.), Nat. Coll. Dist. Attys. (bd. regents), Am. Legion. Clubs: Lion. Democrat. Methodist. Home: 1886 Trailview Dr Norman OK 73072-6655 Office: 231 S Peters Ave Norman OK 73069-6035 *An elected public official must remember that the people own his position and he only holds it in trust for them.*

TRIMBLE, SANDRA ELLINGSON, lawyer; b. Buffalo, May 10, 1952; d. Andrew C. and Edna E. Ellingson; children: Samuel James, Stephen Joseph. BA with highest distinction, Colo. State U., 1974; MEd, Sul Ross State U., 1977; JD cum laude, Georgetown U., 1989. Bar: Md. 1989, D.C. 1990. Contract specialist USAF, Pope AFB, N.C., 1979-81; purchasing rep. Damson Oil Corp., Houston, 1982-86; summer assoc. Fried Frank Harris Shriver & Jacobson, Washington, 1988; law clk. Sullivan & Cromwell, 1988-89; assoc. Cleary Gottlieb Steen & Hamilton, 1989-97; of counsel Orrick Herrington & Sutcliffe LLP, 1997—. Assoc. notes editor Georgetown Law Jour., 1988-89. Recipient Disting. Achievement in Advocacy award Internat. Acad. Trial Lawyers, 1989; Nat. Merit scholar, 1970; law fellow Georgetown U. Law Ctr., 1987-88. Mem. ABA, Phi Beta Kappa. Office: Orrick Herrington & Sutcliffe LLP 3050 K St NW Ste 200 Washington DC 20007-5135 E-mail: strimble@orrick.com.

TRIMBLE, STANLEY WAYNE, hydrology and geography educator; b. Columbia, Tenn., Dec. 8, 1940; s. Stanley Drake and Clara Faye (Smith) T.; m. Alice Erle Gunn, Aug. 16, 1964; children: Alicia Anne, Jennifer Lusanne. BS, U. North Ala., 1964; MA, U. Ga., 1970, PhD, 1973. Asst. prof. hydrology and geography U. Wis., Milw., 1972-75; from assoc. prof. to prof. UCLA, 1975—. Vis. asst. prof. U. Chgo., 1978, vis. assoc. prof., 1981, vis. prof. environ. geography, 1990—, vis. prof. U. Durham (Eng.), 1998; vis. lectr. U. London, 1985; hydrologist U.S. Geol. Survey, 1974-84; vis. prof. U. Vienna, 1994, 99; Frost lectr. Brit. Geomorphological Rsch. Group, Durham, Eng., 1994; vis. rsch. lectr. Oxford U., 1995; Fulbright scholar in U.K., 1995; vis. fellow Keble Coll., Oxford U., 1995, Hatfield Coll. U. Durham, 1998. Author: Culturally Accelerated Sedimentation on the Middle Georgia Piedmont, 1971, Man-Induced Erosion on the Southern Piedmont, 1700-1970, 1974, Soil Conservation and the Reduction, 1982, Sediment Characteristics of Tennessee Streams, 1984; joint editor-in-chief: Catena, 1995—; contbr. articles to profl. jours. Served to 1st lt. U.S. Army, 1963-65. Grantee U.S. Geol. Survey, Washington, 1974-79, Wis. Dept. Natural Resources, Madison, 1978, 82, 93, 94, 95, NSF, Washington, 1976, Agrl. Rsch. Svc. of USDA, Washington, 1972, Nat. Geographic Soc., 1993. Mem. NAS-NRC (com. on watershed mgmt. 1996-98), Assn. Am. Geographers, Am. Geophys. Union, Soil Conservation Soc. Am., Brit. Geomorphol. Rsch. Group, Sigma Xi. Republican. Avocations: historic houses, documentation and restoration. Office: UCLA Dept Geography 405 Hilgard Ave Los Angeles CA 90095-9000 E-mail: trimble@geog.ucla.edu.

TRIMBLE, THOMAS JAMES, retired utility company executive, lawyer; b. Carters Creek, Tenn., Sept. 3, 1931; s. John Elijah and Mittie (Rountree) T.; m. Glenna Kay Jones, Sept. 3, 1957; children: James Jefferson, Julie Kay. BA, David Lipscomb U., 1953; JD, Vanderbilt U., 1956; LLM, NYU, 1959. Bar: Tenn. 1956, Ariz. 1961, U.S. Dist. Ct. Ariz. 1961, U.S. Dist. Ct. D.C. 1963, U.S. Ct. Appeals (10th cir.) 1971, U.S. Supreme Ct. 1972, U.S. Ct. Appeals (9th cir.) 1975. From assoc. to ptnr. Jennings, Strouss & Salmon, Phoenix, 1960-85, mng. ptnr., 1985-87; sr. v.p., gen. counsel, corp. sec. S.W. Gas Corp., Las Vegas, Nev., 1987-96, gen. counsel, 1987-92; corp. sec. Primerit Bank, 1990-92, pres., 1994-96; exec. v.p. Energy Ins. (Bermuda) Ltd., 1992-94, bd. dirs., 1992-97. Bd. dirs. Energy Ins. Mut. Ltd., 1988-97, vice chmn., 1992-94, chmn., 1994-96. Mem. editorial bd. Vanderbilt U. Law Rev., 1954-56. Mem. Pepperdine U. Bd. Regents, Malibu, Calif., 1981—, sec., 1982-2000, chmn., 2000—, mem. exec. com., 1982-89, 95—; bd. visitors Pepperdine Sch. Law, Malibu; trustee Okla. Christian U., Oklahoma City, 1994—; pres. Big Sisters Ariz., Phoenix, 1975, bd. dirs., 1970-76; chmn. Sunnydale Children's Home, Phoenix, 1966-69, bd. dirs., 1965-75; pres. Clearwater Hills Improvement Assn., Phoenix, 1977-79, bd. dirs., 1975-80; trustee Nev. Sch. of Arts, 1988-92, chmn., 1989-90. 1st lt. JAGC, USAF, 1957-60. Fellow Ariz. Bar Found. (editl. bd. Jour. 1975-80), Am. Gas Assn. (legal sect. mng. com. 1987-96), Order of Coif, Southshore Golf Club (Las Vegas), Kiwanis (pres. Phoenix 1972-73), Phi Delta Phi. Republican. Mem. Ch. Christ. Home: 10 Rue Du Ville Way Henderson NV 89011-2200

TRIMBLE, VANCE HENRY, retired newspaper editor; b. Harrison, Ark., July 6, 1913; s. Guy L. and Josephine (Crump) T.; m. Elzene Miller, Jan. 9, 1932; 1 dau., Carol Ann. Student pub. schs., Wewoka, Okla. Cub reporter Okemah (Okla.) Daily Leader, 1928; worked various newspapers in Okmulgee, Muskogee, Tulsa and, Okla.; successively reporter, rewrite man, city editor Houston Press, 1939-50, mng. editor, 1950-55; news editor Scripps-Howard Newspaper Alliance, Washington, 1955-63; editor Ky. Post and Times-Star, Covington, 1963-79. Author: The Uncertain Miracle, 1974, Sam M. Walton, 1990, (biography) E.W. Scripps, 1992, Frederick Smith of Federal Express, 1993, An Empire Undone: Rise and Fall of Chris Whittle, 1995; co-author: Happy Chandler Autobiography, 1989; editor: Scripps-Howard Handbook, 1981. Trustee Scripps-Howard Found., 1974-79. Recipient Pulitzer prize for nat. reporting, 1960, Raymond Clapper award, 1960, Sigma Delta Chi award for disting. Washington correspondence, 1960, Frank Luther Mott award for journalism book rsch. U. Mo., 1993; named to Okla. Journalism Hall of Fame, 1974. Mem. Am. Soc. Newspaper Editors, Nat. Press Club (Washington, Press Club (Houston), Wewoka Country Club. Clubs: Nat. Press (Washington); Press (Houston);Wewoka Country. Baptist. Home: 25 Oakhurst Rd Wewoka OK 74884-3714 E-mail: vhtrimble@aol.com.

TRIMBLE, WILLIAM CATTELL, JR. lawyer; b. Buenos Aires, Argentina, Feb. 7, 1935; s. William Cattell and Nancy Gordon (Carroll) Trimble; m. Barbara Janney, June 19, 1960; children: William C, Margery M Kennelly. AB, Princeton U., 1958; LL.B., U. Md., 1964. Bar: Md 1965. With firm Ober, Grimes & Shriver, Balt., 1965-87, ptnr., 1970-87, mng. ptnr., 1973-77; counsel Semmes, Bowen & Semmes, 1987-2000; mem. Gov.'s Commn. to Revise Annotated Code of Md., 1975-83. Hon consul, The Netherlands, 1986—; pres bd trustees Valley Sch, 1968—73; trustee Garrison Forest Sch, 1975—95, Gilman Sch, 1980—84. Lt USNR, 1958—61. Mem.: ABA, Baltimore Bar Asn, Md Bar Asn, Soc Cincinnati, Greenspring Valley Hunt Club, Colonial Club (Princeton). Episcopalian. Office: Semmes Bowen Semmes PC 16th Fl 250 W Pratt St Fl 16 Baltimore MD 21201-2423 E-mail: wtrimble@msn.com.

TRIMMIER, ROSCOE, JR. lawyer; b. Charlotte, N.C., July 22, 1944; s. Roscoe and Susie Elizabeth (Stitt) T.; divorced; 1 child, Leigh Snowden. AB, Harvard U., 1971, JD, 1974. Bar: Mass. 1974, U.S. Dist. Ct. Mass. 1975, U.S. Ct. Appeals (1st cir.) 1975, U.S. Supreme Ct. 1979, U.S. Claims Ct. 1983. Assoc. Ropes & Gray, Boston, 1974-83, ptnr., 1983—. Mem. hearing com. Bd. Bar Overseers, 1983-89; bd. dirs., v.p. Family Counseling & Guidance Ctr., Inc., Boston, 1980-93; gov. Mus. of Sci., 1981-93; mem. exec. com. Jud. Nominating Commn., 1991-96; corp. mem. Mass. Gen. Hosp., 1992—; overseer N.E Med. Ctr. Hosps., 1992—; mem. Mass. Bd. Registration in Medicine, 2001--. 1st lt. U.S. Army, 1965-68. Fellow: Am. Coll. Trial Lawyers, Mass. Bar Found. (life), Am. Bar Found. (life); mem.: ABA (chair standing com. on fed. judiciary), Am. Law Inst., Boston Bar Assn., Mass. Black Lawyers Assn. (life), Mass. Bar Assn. Home: 1265 Beacon St Brookline MA 02446-5200 Office: Ropes & Gray 1 International Pl Boston MA 02110-2624

TRINCHE, PETER JAMES, music educator; b. Glen Cove, Ny, May 8, 1955; s. Albert Arthur and Frances Lyden Trinche; m. Arline Hinkson, July 14, 1990 (div. May 2, 2002). BS, Ball State U., Muncie, IN, 1973—78; MA, U. of Ill., Champaign-Urbana, IL, 1978—82. Cert.: NY (Paralegal). Adj. prof. of trumpet Suffolk CC, Selden, NY, 1982—83; asst. prof. of trumpet Molloy Coll., Rockville Centre, 1983—92; music tchr. Westbury MFSD, Westbury, 1986—87, Lawrence CSD, Lawrence, 1987—88, Garden City UFSD, Garden City, 1988—90, Oyster Bay CSD, Oyster Bay, 1990—96, Longwood Ctrl. Sch. Dist., Middle Island, 1996—. Co-chairperson Suffolk County Music Educators, Huntington, NY, 1999—2001. Chmn. Bayville Environ. Comm., Bayville, NY, 1994—98. Fellow Leadership Fellow, LI Leadership Acad., 2001-2002; scholar scholarship, U. of Ill., 1979-1980. Fellow: LI Leadership Acad.; mem.: Local 802 AF of M. Lutheran. Home: 40 Perry Ave Bayville NY 11709 Personal E-mail: ptrinche@hotmail.com.

TRINCHERO, AGNES THERESA, social services consultant, administrator, educator; b. Niles, Calif. d. Louis Jacob and Theresa Marie (DeMattei) T. BA, San Jose State U.; MSW, U. Calif., Berkeley; DSW, U. So. Calif., L.A. Lic. social worker, Calif. Fulbright lectr. U.S. Dept. of State, Italy; pvt. practice Laguna Beach, Calif., 1993—. Bd. dirs. Calif. Social Welfare Archives, Sch. Social Work U. So. Calif. Recipient Silver medallion YWCA of North Orange County, Child Advocacy award Child Welfare League Am. Mem. NASW (Daniel Koshland Leadership award Calif. chpt.), Laguna Art Mus., L.A. County Mus. Art, Nat. Cathedral Assn. Democrat. Roman Catholic. Avocations: travel, theater, dance, writing, gardening.

TRINDER, RACHEL BANDELE, lawyer; b. Ibadan, Nigeria, Feb. 21, 1955; came to U.S., 1977; d. Victor William John and Margaret (Almond) T. BA with honors, Oxford U., 1977, MA, 1994; LLM, U. Va., 1978. Bar: D.C. 1979, U.S. Dist. Ct. 1979, U.S. Ct. Appeals (D.C. cir.) 1980, U.S. Supreme Ct. 1986. Assoc. Zuckert, Scoutt & Rasenberger, LLP, Washington, 1978-85, ptnr., 1985—. V.p. aviation spl. interest chpt. Transp. Rsch. Forum, 1988-90, exec. v.p., 1990-91, gen. counsel, 1989-91; mem. bd. advisors 3d Ann. Symposium on Law and Outer Space, 1991, program dir., mem. bd. advisors, 4th Ann., 1991-92. Contbr. articles to legal jours. Bd. govs. Internat. Student House, 1986-93, mem. exec. com., asst. treas., 1987-88, mem. bd. advisors, 1993-97. Fellow English Speaking Union, 1977. Mem. ABA, FBA (chair space law com. 1990-94, chair internat. law sect. 1994-96), Internat. Bar Assn., Fed. Bar Assn., Internat. Inst. Space Law (life), Internat. Aviation Women's Assn. (dir.-at-large 1996-98), Internat. Inst. Air and Space Law (bd. govs., exec. com. 1992—), Internat. Aviation Club (bd. govs. 1984-86, pres. 1986), Aero Club (bd. govs. 1993—, pres. 2000), Nat. Aeronautic Assn. (bd. govs. 2000—). Home: 1266 Dartmouth Ct Alexandria VA 22314-4784 Office: Zuckert Scoutt & Rasenberger LLP 888 17th St NW Washington DC 20006-3939 E-mail: rbtrinder@zsrlaw.com.

TRINGALE, ANTHONY ROSARIO, insurance executive; b. Syracuse, N.Y., Apr. 20, 1942; s. Anthony and Susan Marie Tringale; children: Anthony William, Michael Paul, Mark David, Amber Marie. BSFS, Georgetown U., 1967. CLU. Office mgr. trainee N.Y. Life Ins. Co. N.Y., 1965-66, office mgr. Va., 1966, field underwriter, 1966-68; mgmt. asst. home office N.Y. Life Ins. Co., N.Y.C., 1973, gen mgr. Pitts., 1973-76; gen. mgr. Acacia Mut. Life Ins. Co., Annandale, Va., 1976-83, fin. and ins. planner, mgmt. and mktg. cons., 1983-86; from field rep. to mktg. com. Acacia Mut. Life, Anandale, Va., 1983-86; prin. Ins. Consulting Group/Benefits-By-Design, Fairfax, 1986—; pres. Acacia Prodn. Clubs, 1984, 86. Lectr. estate and employee and exec. fringe benefit plans and retirement programs, bus. ins. and comm.; mem. steering com. Entrepreneurship Forum, Washington, 1980—; nat. adv. bd. Entrepreurship Inst., Columbus, Ohio, 1985—; mem., chmn. Mktg. Edn. Adv. Coun., Commonwealth of Va. Supts. Bus. and Industry Adv. Coun., 1989—; mktg edn. adv. bd. Fairfax County Pub. Schs., 1980—; chmn. 1983-84, 90-91. Contbr. articles in field of personal and bus. fin. strategies to Md. Bus. Observer, Washington Bus. Jour., NALU's Life Assoc. News; radio host Basically Bus. Sta. WGMS-FM, Washington. Trustee SME-1 Accreditation Inst. U. Memphis, 1990—99, Syracuse U., 1995—99; past liaison rep. Am. Soc. CLUs, Bryn Mawr, Pa., 1988—98; arbitrator Fairfax County Dept. Consumer Affairs; v.p., sec., bd. dir., exec. com. The Jeane Dixon Children to Children Found.; chmn. VIP panel D.C. and No. Va., 1988—92; pres. VIP panel, 1992—94, Birch Pond Homeowners Assn., 1998—2000; bd. dir., exec. com. United Cerebral Palsy of D.C. and No. Va., 1985—; pres. D.C. Fairfax County Salvation Army Corps., 2002—, United Cerebral Palsy of D.C. and No. Va., 2002; founding vice chmn. Fairfax Orgn. Christians/Jews United in Svc.; lector, extraordinary minister Basilica Nat. Shrine Immaculate Conception, 1980; bd. dir., v.p. exec. com., chmn. grants com. No. Va. Cmty. Found.; bd. dir. Summer Opera Theater Co., 1996—98, Nat. Cath. Cmty. Found., 1996—97. Recipient 2000 Crystal award No. Va. Cmty. Found. Mem. No. Va. Soc. CLUs (past pres.), Am. Soc. CLUs, No. Va. Assn. Life Underwriters (treas. 1972, nat. com. 1997-99, Pres.' Cup 1991-92), Assn. Advanced Life Underwriting, Sales and Mktg. Execs. Met. Washington (pres. 1979-80, 95-97, treas. 1989-92, bd. dirs. 1990—, sr. v.p. profl. devel. 1993-95, Man of Yr. 2000), Nat. Assn. Life Underwriters (Nat. Mgmt. award Gen. Agts. and Mgrs. Conf. 1976-83, exec. com. 1984-85, life qualifying), No. Va. Estate Planning Coun. (exec. com. 1985-92, pres. 1990-91), Internat. Platform Assn. (trustee, bd. govs. 1990—), No. Va. Gen. Agts. and Mgrs. Assn. (pres. 1980-81, dir. 1982-83), Greater Washington Area Health Underwriters, Fairfax County C. of C. (dir. small bus. 1989-90, dir. membership 1990-91, exec. com. dir. at large 1991-92, Small Bus. Adv. of Yr. award 1990), Nat. Christopher Columbus Quincentary Jubilee Adv. Bd. (dir. at large 1995—), Nat. Italian-Am. Found. Coun. of 1000 and Italian Am. Leaders Com. Venture Clinic (chmn., pres. 1989-94, TV interviewer, host The Venture Game), Million Dollar Round Table (life, qualified), John Carroll Soc. Ins. Club Washington (pres. 1997-98), Birch Pond Homeowners Assn. (pres. bd. dirs. 1998-2000). Office: Ins Cons Group 12813 Dogwood Hills #222 Fairfax VA 22033-3249

TRINGALI, JOSEPH, financial planner, accountant; b. Balt., May 8, 1960; m. Tina L. Shifflett, Oct. 24, 1987; children: Alex R., Eric M., Crystal N. BS in Acctg., U. Balt., 1982. CFP; CPA, Md.; lic. Nat. Assn. Securities Dealers. Asst. legis. auditor Md. State Div. of Audits Dept. of Fiscal Svcs., Balt., 1983-84; sr. acct. Jay Leikin, CPA, Columbia, Md., 1984-88; ptnr. Friedman & Assocs., PA, Balt., 1988—. Scholarship Comml. Credit Corp., 1981. Mem. AICPA, Md. Assn. of CPAs (chmn. CFP Pub. Awareness com. 1990-92), Internat. Bd. of Standards and Practices for CFP, Inc., Delta Mu Delta. Republican. Roman Catholic. Avocations: scuba diver, skiing, dancing, computers, reading. Office: Friedman & Assocs PA 1700 Reisterstown Rd Ste 222 Baltimore MD 21208-2920

TRINH, EUGENE H. astronaut; b. Saigon, Vietnam, Sept. 14, 1950; arrived in U.S., 1968; m. Yvette Fabry. BS in Mech. Engrng.-Applied Physics, Columbia U., 1972; MS, Yale U., 1974, MA in Philosophy, 1975, PhD in Applied Physics, 1977. Rschr. NASA, 1979—; alternate payload specialist Spacelab 3 Mission (NASA), 1985; rsch. task mgr., project scientist Drop Physics Module flight experiments, NASA; investigator in fluid physics, biotech., and materials sci. NASA; astronaut Space Shuttle Columbia, STS-50/U.S. Microgravity Lab.-1 (USML-1) Spacelab mission. Contbr. articles to profl. jours. Mem.: ASME, AIAA, Am. Phys. Soc., Sixma Xi Rsch. Soc., Acoustical Soc. Am. Avocations: house remodeling, music, theater, tennis, swimming. Office: Astronaut Office/CB NASA Johnson Space Ctr Houston TX 77058*

TRINH, VICTOR, small business owner; b. Vientiane, Laos, Apr. 7, 1941; came to U.S., 1975; naturalized, 1981. s. Thu and Mao (Nguyen) T.; m. Tuyet Mai Nguyen, Jan. 19, 1972; children: Nancy H., Wiliam Q. Grad. high sch., Vientiane. Electronic assembler Anilam Electronics, Miami, Fla., 1978-80; owner Kim-Do Food, Pitts., 1981-85, Jensen Food Mart, Houston, 1986—; pub. Vic Pub., 1993—. Author: Student Assignments Notebook, 1993. Avocations: biking, swimming. Home and Office: 11735 Teaneck Dr Houston TX 77089-6118

TRINKAUS, ERIK, anthropologist, educator; b. New Haven, Dec. 24, 1948; s. John Philip Trinkaus, Galina Ivanovna Gorokhoff; m. Kathryn Maurer Maurer; children: Alexander Yuri. BA, U. Wis., 1970; MA, U. Pa., 1973, PhD, 1975. Asst. to assoc. prof. Harvard U., Cambridge, Mass., 1975—83; assoc. to full prof. U. of N.Mex., Albuquerque, 1983—97; prof. Washington U., St. Louis, 1997—. Author: The Shanidar Neandertals, 1983, The Neandertals: Changing the Image of Mankind, 1993, The People of the Pavlovian, 2000. Mem.: NAS. Office: Washington Univ. Dept Anthropology 1 Brookings Dr Saint Louis MO 63130 Office Fax: 314-935-5207. Personal E-mail: trinkaus@artsci.wustl.edu. Business E-mail: trinkaus@artsci.wustl.edu.

TRINKAUS, JOHN WILLIAM, management educator; b. Mt. Vernon, N.Y., July 17, 1925; s. Bernard and Elsie (Kelly) T.; m. Irene Klimowski, July 31, 1954; children: Joanne Trinkaus Dillon, Robert John, John William. BEE, NYU, 1952, PhD, 1976; MBA, CCNY, 1961. Registered profl. engr., Mass. Engr. Bendix Aviation Corp., Teterboro, N.J., 1947-52, Curtis Wright Corp., Carlstadt, 1952-53, Sperry Corp., Great Neck, N.Y., 1953-68; prof. CUNY Baruch Coll., N.Y.C., 1968-81, assoc. dean, 1981-93, prof. emeritus, 1993—. Engrng. cons. Electronic Industries Assoc., Washington, 1960-68, USAF, Washington, 1965-68; mgmt. cons. Ford Found., N.Y.C., 1980-82, Interracial Coun. for Bus. Opportunity, N.Y.C., 1983-93; vis. disting. prof. St. John's U., N.Y.C., 1993-96. Chmn., rsch. comm. Am. Acad. Profl. Law Enforcement, Mineola, N.Y., 1978-79; cons. N.Y.C. Vol. Urban Con. Group, 1979-84. Sgt. U.S. Army, 1945-46. Recipient 1st prize for paper Nat. Fedn. Ind. Bus., Washington, 1992. Mem.: Soc. Bus. Ethics, Assn. Pvt. Enterprise Edn., U.S. Assn. Small Bus. and Enterpreneurship, Acad. Mgmt., Inst. Supply Mgmt. Home: 1 Linden St New Hyde Park NY 11040-2311 Office: Baruch Coll CUNY 1 Bernard Baruch Way New York NY 10010-5518

TRINKAUS-RANDALL, GREGOR, librarian, archivist; b. Balt., Jan. 10, 1946; s. John Phillip and Galina Ivanovna (Gorokhoff) T.; m. Vickery Edith Trinkaus-Randall, May 22, 1976; children: Jennifer Alison, Christopher Erik. B.A., U. Wis., 1968, M.A., 1973, M.L.S., 1980. Archival asst./accessioner State Hist. Soc. Wis., Madison, 1977-81; libr. limnology dept. U. Wis., Madison, 1977-80; conservation/preservation intern Yale U. Libr., New Haven, 1981; asst. curator USS Constitution Mus., Boston, 1981-82; archivist Computer Mus., Marlborough, Mass., 1982; libr./archivist-Peabody Mus. of Salem, Mass., 1983-88; collection mgmt./preservation specialist Mass. Bd. of Libr. Commrs., Boston, 1988—; cons. libr., archives, and preservation affairs, 1981—. Contbr. articles to profl. jours. Mem. adv. com. Northeast Document Conservation Ctr., 1989—; preservation adv. com. NELINET, 1991—; co-chair Mass. Task Force on Theft and Mutilation, 1989-90; chair Mass. Task Force on Permanent Paper, 1989-90. Mem. Nat. Ski Patrol, 1966—, Devil's Head Ski Patrol, Merrimack, Wis., 1976-81, regional tng. advisor, Madison, Wis., 1978-81, Nashoba Valley Ski Patrol, Westford, Mass., 1981—, training advisor, 1982—; evaluator Sr. Winter Emergency Care, 1990—; tchr. Royal Scottish Country Dance Soc., Boston, 1976—; instr. first aid, CPR, ARC, Lowell, 1966—, instr. winter emergency care, 1988—. Fellow Soc. Antiquaries of Scotland; mem. Soc. Am. Archivists, Midwest Archives Conf., New Eng. Archivists, Acad. of Cert. Archivists, Mass. Libr. Assn., New Eng. Libr. Assn., New Eng. Hist. Geneal. Soc. (mem. preservation com. 1994—), Phi Kappa Phi. Avocations: dancing, skiing, cycling, tennis, soccer. Office: Mass Bd Libr Commrs 648 Beacon St Boston MA 02215-2013

TRINKUS, LAIMA MARY, special education educator; b. Chgo., Mar. 6, 1950; d. Steven and Antonia (Ambrasas) Trinkus. BS in Sociology, Daemen Coll., Buffalo, 1974; MS in Behavioral Sci. Spl. Edn., SUNY, Buffalo, 1987. Cert. spl. edn. tchr., N.Y. Tchr. aide Cantalician Ctr. for Learning, Buffalo, 1975-78, tchr. spl. edn., 1978-85, Erie I Bd. Coop. Edn. Svcs., Lancaster, N.Y., 1985—. Vol. Spl. Olympics, Buffalo, 1976—. Home: 9821 Greiner Rd Clarence NY 14031-1237

TRIOLO, PETER, advertising agency executive, marketing educator, consultant; b. N.Y.C., Feb. 20, 1927; s. Antonino and Cira T.; m. Audrey Sullivan, Aug. 7, 1954; children— Stuart, Bruce, Ellen, Leslie. AB, Adelphi U., Garden City, N.Y., 1952; exec. program, Columbia U. Grad. Sch. Bus., 1966. Vice pres. Ogilvy & Mather, Inc., N.Y.C., 1958-64; sr. v.p. Ketchum, MacLeod & Grove Inc., Pitts. and N.Y.C., 1964-68; founder, exec. v.p. Marketronics Inc., N.Y.C., 1968-72; chief adminstrv. officer Rosenfeld, Sirowitz & Lawson Inc., 1972-76; sr. v.p., media dir. William Esty Co., Inc., 1976-87; cons. Internat. Exec. Svc. Corps, Stamford, Conn., 1987—. Adj. prof. mktg. Baruch Coll., City U. N.Y., 1980-86, Fordham U., N.Y.C., 1987—. Guest editor: Mktg. and Media Decisions, 1967. Served with USAAF, 1945-47. Mem. Assn. Nat. Advertisers (TV workshops), Advt. Age Media Workshops Faculty, Mktg. and Media Decisions Faculty.

TRIPATHI, GORAKH NATH RAM, physical chemist; b. Gorakhpur, India, Jan. 1, 1944; came to U.S., 1977; s. Vishwanath and Ramdasi (Devi) T.; married, June 8, 1962; children: Pratibha, Pradeep, Amit. PhD, U. Gorakhpur, 1968. Asst. to assoc. prof. U. Gorakhpur, 1964-76; sr. acad. staff fellow U. Manchester, U.K., 1976-77; scientist, rsch. faculty Notre Dame Radiation Lab., Ind., 1978—. Editl. adv. bd. Asian Jour. of Physics, 1992—; contbr. over 130 articles to profl. publs. Achievements include research in the field of time-resolved resonance Raman scattering studies of structure and reactivity of chemical intermediates. Home: 53075 Berwick Dr South Bend IN 46635-1410 Office: Notre Dame Radiation Lab Notre Dame South Bend IN 46635

TRIPATHI, RAM KISHORE, physicist, researcher; b. Rae Bareli, India, Jan. 1, 1942; came to the U.S., 1966; s. Shiva Kumar and Devi Mani Tripathi; m. Pushpa Shukla Tripathi, May 26, 1966; 1 child, Sanjay. BS, U. Lucknow, 1961, MS, 1963; PhD, U. kans., 1970. Asst. prof. U. Ky., Lexington, 1970-71; scientist Kern Forschungsanlage, Juelich, Germany, 1971-73; sr. faculty fellow U. Sussex, Brighton, Eng., 1973-75; fellow Tata Inst. Fundamental Rsch., Bombay, 1975-78; assoc. prof. Dept. of Energy/Inst. Physics, Bhubaneswar, India, 1978-85; prof. U. Tuebingen, Germany, 1980-82, U. Liege, Belgium, 1985-86, U. Ky., Lexington, 1986-87; radiation physicist NASA Langley Rsch. Ctr., Hampton, Va., 1987—. Contbr. numerous articles to profl. jours. Pres. internat. cultural activities U. Kans., Lawrence, 1966-68. Fulbright fellow U.S. Info. Agy., Washington, 1966-70, Sr. NRC fellow NAS, Washington, 1999; grantee NASA, Dept. of Def., Dept. of Energy, NSF. Fellow AIAA (assoc.); mem. AAAS, Am. Nuc. Soc. (life), Am. Phys. Soc. (life). Avocations: jogging, traveling, anthropology. Home: 13 Natalie Dr Hampton VA 23666-5565 Office: NASA Langley Rsch Ctr Ms 188 B Hampton VA 23681-0001

TRIPI, VINCENT JAMES, physician; b. South Euclid, Ohio, Apr. 19, 1926; m. Cynthia Tripi, 1976; 5 children. BS, Kent State U., 1952; DO, Chgo. Coll. Osteo. Medicine, 1957; MD, U. Calif., 1962. Diplomate Am. Osteo. Bd. Surgery; bd. cert. in gen. surgery Am. Osteo. Bd. Surgery. Intern Forest Hills Hosp., 1957-58; resident in gen. surgery Green Cross Gen. Hosp., 1957-61; chief of staff, chief of surgery Harborside Hosp., Fla., 1984-89. Author: New Approach to Pediatric Internal Surgery, 1964. With U.S. Army, 1944-46, ETO. Recipient award of appreciation Zephyr-Haven Nursing Home, 1999. Mem. DAV, Am. Coll. Osteo. Surgeons, Am. Osteo. Assn., Ohio Osteo. Soc. Surgeons (pres. 1974), Fla. Osteo. Med. Assn. Address: 1521 E Memorial Blvd Lakeland FL 33801-2222

TRIPLEHORN, CHARLES A. entomology educator, insects curator; b. Bluffton, Ohio, Oct. 27, 1927; s. Murray E. and Alice Irene (Lora) T.; m. Wanda Elaine Neiswander, June 12, 1949 (dec. Nov. 1985); children: Bradley Alyn, Bruce Wayne; m. Linda Sue Parsons, July 11, 1987. B.Sc., Ohio State U., 1949, MS, 1952; PhD, Cornell U., 1957. Asst. prof. entomology U. Del., Newark, 1952-54; teaching asst. entomology Cornell U., Ithaca, N.Y., 1954-57; asst. prof. entomology Ohio Agrl. Research and Devel. Ctr., Wooster, Ohio, 1957-61, Ohio State U., Columbus, 1961-62, assoc. prof. entomology, 1962-66, prof. entomology, 1966-92, prof. emeritus, 1992—. Econ. entomologist U.S. AID/Brazil, Piracicaba, Sao Paulo, 1964-66; vis. curator Field Mus. Natural History, Chgo., 1974, Can. Nat. Collection, Ottawa, Ont., 1977, Am. Mus. Natural History, N.Y.C., 1982, U. Mich., 1989, U. Ariz., 1989, Nat. Mus. of Natural History, 1998, Cornell U., 1999, Colo. State U., 2000, Brigham Young U., 2000. Co-author: Introduction to the Study of Insects, 6th edit., 1989. Cubmaster Boy Scouts Am., Wooster, Ohio, 1959-60, scoutmaster, Columbus, 1971-72; football coach Upper Arlington Football Assn., Ohio, 1968-71 Grantee Am. Philos. Soc., 1963, NSF, 1979, 85, 92. Mem. Entomol. Soc. Am. (pres. 1985), Coleopterists Soc. (pres. 1976), Royal Entomol. Soc. London, Entomol. Soc. Washington, Sigma Xi, Gamma Sigma Delta Clubs: Wheaton (pres.). Republican. Methodist. Avocations: sports; music; reading; writing. Home: 3943 Medford Sq Hilliard OH 43026-2219 Office: Mus Biol Diversity Div Insects The Ohio State University 1315 Kinnear Rd Columbus OH 43212-1157 E-mail: triplehorn.1@osu.edu.

TRIPLETT, ARLENE ANN, management consultant; b. Portland, Oreg., Jan. 21, 1942; d. Vincent Michael and Lorraine Catherine (Starr) Jakovich; m. William Karrol Triplett, Jan. 27, 1962; children: Stephen Michael, Patricia Ann. BA, U. Calif., Berkeley, 1963. Budgets and reports analyst Cutter Labs., Berkeley, 1963-66; controller Citizens for Reagan, 1975-76; dir. adminstrn. Republican. Nat. Com., 1977-80; asst. sec. Dept. Commerce, Washington, 1981-83; assoc. dir. mgmt. Office Mgmt. and Budget, Exec. Office of Pres., 1983-85; prin. assoc. McManis Assocs., Inc., 1985-87, v.p., 1987-89, sr. v.p., 1989-93; from v.p. to exec. v.p. Am. Tours Internat., Inc., L.A., 1993-97; prin. McManis Assoc., Manhattan Beach, Calif., 1997-98, IBM, Manhattan Beach, 1999—2002; mgmt. cons. Simon for Gov., 2002—. Roman Catholic.

TRIPLETT, E. EUGENE, editor; b. LaJolla, Calif., Mar. 12, 1949; s. Erbin Eugene Triplett and Marjorie Ann (Aldrich) Heath; m. Vannie Carol Crow, July 19, 1968; 1 child, Aaron Eugene. BA in Journalism, Ctrl. State U., 1975. Reporter, columnist The Okla. Jour., Oklahoma City, 1976-80; entertainment editor The Daily Oklahoman, 1981-85, asst. city editor, 1985-89, city editor, 1989-99, sr. feature writer, columnist, 1999—. Bd. dirs. Crime Stoppers Oklahoma City; mem. comm. com. Okla. Heart Assn., 1989-92. With U.S. Army, 1969-71, Vietnam. Recipient 1st pl. Feature Writing award Soc. Profl. Journalists, 1987, 97-98, 2d pl., 1999-2000. Mem. AP/Okla. News Exec. (pres.-elect 1994-95, pres. 1995-96, 2nd pl. Feature Writing award 1988). Democrat. Avocations: collecting recorded music, feature films, vintage TV shows. Home: 8116 NW 118th St Oklahoma City OK 73162-1113 Office: The Daily Oklahoman 9000 Broadway Ext Oklahoma City OK 73114-3799 E-mail: etriplett@oklahoman.com., geneoat@cox.net.

TRIPLETT, KIRK ALLEN, golfer; b. Moses Lake, Wash., Mar. 29, 1962; Named winner, Alberta Open, 1988, Nissan Open, 2000. Office: c/o PGA Tour 112 PGA Tour Blvd Ponte Vedra Beach FL 32082

TRIPODES, JAMES G. environmental regulatory affairs professional; b. San Francisco, Mar. 12, 1954; s. George J. Tripodes and Daisy Natsoulas Pimentel; m. Nham T. Tripodes, Nov. 5, 1983. BS in Environ. Planning and Mgmt., U. Calif., Davis, 1978. Registered hazardous substances profl. Nat. Environ. Health Assn.; registered environ. assessor Calif. EPA. Envir. health/safety technician, cyclotron health physicist U. Calif., Davis, 1972-79, health physics mgr. Irvine, 1979-89, assoc. dir. envir. health/safety for envir. reg. affairs, 1989-2001, acting dir. environ. health and safety, 2001—02; dep. dept. head environ. protection Lawrence Livermore Nat. Lab., Livermore, Calif., 2002—. Co-founder, oversight chmn. Internat. Conf. on Incineration and Thermal Treatment Techs., 1980-2000; prin. investigator, project mgr. U.S. Dept. Energy and Calif. Dept. Health Svcs., 1982-95. Editor: (book and CD-ROM) Proceedings of International Conferences on Incineration and Thermal Treatment Technologies, 1985-2000; guest editor spl. issue: Health Physics Jour., 1991. Mem. govt. affairs coun. Irvine C. of C., 1995—2002; patron Heritage Found., Washington, 1995—. Fellow Acad. Polit. Sci.; mem. AAAS, ASME, Health Physics Soc. (Elda E. Anderson award 1994), Am. Soc. for Quality, Ctr. for Study of the Presidency, N.Y. Acad. Scis. Republican. Avocations: fine art and music appreciation, public affairs. Office: Lawrence Livermore Nat Lab 7000 East Ave L 626 Livermore CA 94550 E-mail: tripodes2@llnl.gov.

TRIPOLD, DAVID MICHAEL, music educator; b. Long Branch, Nj, Jan. 24, 1959; s. Edward Anthony and Lois Marie Tripold; m. Margaret Anne Spence, Nov. 6, 1982; children: Amy Christine, Gregory David. BA Music, Westminster Choir Coll. of Rider Univ., Princeton, NJ, 1981; MA Music, Westminster Choir Coll. (Rider Univ.), Princeton, NJ, 1996. Music Comprehensive 2100 Teaching Cert. Certifying Orgn.?, 1981. Admissions counselor Westminster Choir Coll., Princeton, NJ, 1981—82; music educator Sayreville Bd. of Edn., Parlin, 1982—85; fin. analyst US Army, Fort Monmouth, 1985—99; music instr. Monmouth Univ., West Long Branch, 1999—. Organist/choir dir. Colts Neck Ref. Ch., Colts Neck, NJ, 1995—. Contbr. book, hymnal supplement. Mem.: Am. Choral Directors Assn., Music Educators Nat. Conf., Commn. on Worship, Nat. Music Honors Soc., Phi Kappa Lamda. Reformed Church In America. Avocations: golfing, playing tennis, playing tennis. Home: 32 Village Lane Colts Neck NJ 07722-1649 Office: Monmouth Univ Cedar Ave West Long Branch NJ 07764 E-mail: dtripold@monmouth.edu.

TRIPOLI, MASUMI HIROYASU, financial consultant and diplomat; b. Fukuyama, Japan, Apr. 23, 1956; d. Yoshimi and Suzuko Hiroyasu; 1 child, Mona Lisa Tripoli. BA cum laude, U. Wash., 1978; MA, Sophia U., Tokyo, 1981; MBA, Ecole des Hautes Etudes Comml, Jouy-en-Josas, France, 1983. CFP; chartered fin. cons. Corp. planning mgr. Kowa Corp., Osaka, Japan, 1983-85; internat. bond trader Banque Baribas, Tokyo, 1985-86, Westpac Bank, Tokyo, 1987-88; fin. cons. Masumi Tripoli and Assocs., Glendale, Calif., 1989—, Sagemark Cons./Lincoln Fin. Advisors, Glendale, 1989—; anchor newscaster United TV, L.A., 1989-92. Condr. seminars in field. Contbr. articles to profl. jours. Grantee Sophia U., 1979, H.E.C., 1983. Mem. Internat. Bd. Cert. Fin. Planners. Avocations: child education, horseback riding. Office: Masumi Tripoli & Assocs Crossroads Corp Ctr 3200 Barranca Pkwy Ste 220 Irvine CA 92606 E-mail: masumiusa@hotmail.com.

TRIPOLITIS, ANTONIA, religion, classics and comparative literature educator; b. Phila. PhD, U. Pa., 1971. Rsch. assoc. Inst. for Antiquity and Christianity, Claremont, Calif., 1971—; asst. dean acad. affairs Rutgers U., New Brunswick, N.J., 1975-76, assoc. dean acad. affairs, 1976-79, chair, grad. dir. classical studies, 1979-87, assoc. prof. classics, comparative lit. and religion, 1987—; dir. modern Greek Studies Rutgers Univ., 1995—. Author: Doctrine of Soul in Thought of Plotinus and Origen, 1978, Origen: A Critical Reading, 1985, Kassia: The Legend, The Woman, and Her Work, 1991, Religions of the Hellenistic-Roman Age, 2001; contbr. numerous articles to profl. jours. Nat. Geographic Soc. grantee, 1968-69. Mem. AAUW (fellowship 1969-70), Am. Literary Translators Assn., Am. Soc. Ch. History, Am. Acad. Religion, Soc. Bibl. Lit., Soc. for Neoplatonic Studies, N.Am. Patristic Soc. Office: Rutgers U Dept Modern Greek Studies 223 Scott Hall College Ave New Brunswick NJ 08901

TRIPP, DAVID ENDERS, numismatist, art historian, cartoonist, author; b. N.Y.C., Aug. 24, 1951; s. Paul and Ruth Beatrice (Enders) T.; m. Susan Turner Gerwe, June 9, 1977. BA, NYU, 1972; MA, London U., 1973. Dir. coins and medals Sotheby Parke Bernet, N.Y.C., 1973-75, asst. v.p., dir. coins, tapestries, musical instrument, 1976-79, Balt. rep. Balt., 1979-80; pvt. practice numismatic and fine art cons. N.Y.C., 1980—. Archaeologist, photographer Brit. Sch. at Rome/Cambridge U., Narce, Italy, 1969-71, Her Majesty's Govt., Braughing, Eng., 1971-72; guest lectr. NYU, Johns Hopkins U., Sotheby's Inst., N.Y.C., 1978—. Cartoonist (cartoon strip) Sadie-Cat Fancy Mag., 1985—, (panel cartoons) Punch Mag., 1987; contbg. cartoonist: The Companion Cat, 1990; guest columnist The Rockland Ind., 1965; contbr. chpts. to books; contbg. photographer various books, articles and brochures; appeared in (TV) Mike and Buff, 1953, On the Carousel, 1954-59, Birthday House, 1963-68, (films) The Christmas That Almost Wasn't, 1965, Tubby the Tuba, 1977. Recipient Excellence in History award DAR, Calif., 1963, Extraordinary Merit award Numismatic Lit. Guild, 1991, 2000; named Outstanding Young Man of Am., 1982, Cmty. Leader of Am., 1983. Fellow Royal Numismatic Soc.; mem. Am. Numismatic Soc. (standing libr. com.), Swiss Numismatic Soc., Friends of the Am. Wing Balt. Mus. Art, Am. Friends of the Brit. Mus., Player's Club (life), Nat Cartoonists Soc. Avocations: archaeology, antiquities and classical civilizations, paleontology, wildlife conservation, film history. Office: PO G Stuyvesant NY 12173

TRIPP, FREDERICK GERALD, investment advisor; b. Chgo., Oct. 1, 1936; s. Gerald F. and Kathryn Ann (Siebold) T.; m. Terry Anne Shull, Aug. 26, 1967; children: Mark A., Karin M. Coburn, Tracy L. Clark, Tricia L., Patrick G. BS in Econs., Purdue U., 1958; MBA, Lehigh U., 1964; PhD, The Am. U., 1972. Sr. v.p. CRI, Inc., Rockville, Md., 1979-82, Security Pacific, Inc., Seattle, 1982-83; pres. Frederick G. Tripp & Assocs., Inc., Rockville, 1983—. Instr. Troy State U., 1965-67, Am. U., 1975-77, Indsl. Coll. Armed Forces, 1975-80; mem. pres.'s coun. Investment Mgmt. and Rsch., Inc., 1985-97; chmn. coun. Raymond James Fin. Svcs., Inc., 1998—. Pres. Doctoral Assn., The Am. U., 1973. Maj. U.S. Army, 1958-67, Vietnam. Mem. Fin. Planning Assn., Investment Mgmt. Cons. Assn., Sigma Pi. Methodist. Avocations: skiing, boating, racquetball, flying. Office: Frederick G Tripp & Assocs 2400 Research Blvd Ste 300 Rockville MD 20850-3243 E-mail: fred.tripp@trippinvest.com.

TRIPP, KAREN BRYANT, lawyer; b. Rocky Mount, N.C., Sept. 2, 1955; d. Bryant and Katherine Rebecca (Watkins) Tripp; m. Robert Mark Burleson, June 25, 1977 (div. 1997); 1 child, Hamilton Chase Tripp Barnett. BA, U. N.C., 1976; JD, U. Ala., 1981. Bar: Tex. 1981, U.S. Dist. Ct. (so. dist.) Tex. 1982, U.S, Ct. Appeals (fed. cir.) 1983, U.S. Dist. Ct. (ea. dist.) Tex. 1991, U.S. Supreme Ct. 1994, U.S. Dist. Ct. (no. dist.) Tex. 1998, U.S. Ct. Appeals (5th and 9th cirs.) 2000, U.S. Ct. Appeals (3d cir.) 2001. Law clk. Tucker, Gray & Espy, Tuscaloosa, Ala., 1978-81; law clk. to presiding justice Ala. Supreme Ct., Montgomery, summer 1980; atty. Exxon Prodn. Rsch. Co., Houston, 1981-86, coord. tech. transfer, 1986-87; assoc. Arnold, White and Durkee, 1988-93, shareholder, 1994-98; shareholder, head intellectual property sect. for Houston office Winstead, Sechrest & Minick, Attys. at Law, 1998; pres. Blake Barnett & Co., 1996—; pvt. practice, 1999—. Creator, program planner, master of ceremonies 1st and 2d intellectual property law confs. for women corp. counsels. Editor Intellectual Property Law Rev., 1995-2002; contbr. articles to profl. jours. Chair U. Houston and Houston intellectual Property Law Assoc. Fall CLE Inst. on Intellectual Property, 2000. Mem. ABA (intellectual property law sect., ethics com. 1992-96), Houston Bar Assn. (interprofl. rels. com. 1988-90), Houston Intellectual Property Law Assn. (outstanding inventor com. 1982-84, chmn. 1994-95, sec. 1987-88, treas. 1991-92, bd. dirs. 1992-94, 98-2000, nominations com. 1993, 96, chmn. fall CLE Inst. 2000), Tex. Bar Assn. (antitrust law com. 1984-85, chmn. internat. law com. intellectual property law sect. 1987-88, internat. transfer tech. com. 1983-84), Tex. Exec. Women, Women's Fin. Exch., Am. Intellectual Property Lawyers Assn. (patent law com. 1995), Intellectual Property Owners Assn. (copyright com.), Women in Tech. (founder), Lil Eli's Club (founder), Phi Alpha Delta. Republican. Episcopalian. Office: PO Box 1301 Houston TX 77251-1301 E-mail: ktripp@tripplaw.com.

TRIPP, KEVIN FRANCIS, priest; b. New Bedford, Mass., May 17, 1942; s. Philip Francis and Helen Catherine (FitzGerald) T. BA, St. John's Sem., Brighton, Mass., 1964, MDiv., 1968; postgrad., Notre Dame U., 1965-68. Ordained priest Roman Cath. Ch., 1968. Parish priest Diocese of Fall River (Mass.), 1968-74; dir. religious ministries St. Luke's Hosp., New Bedford, Mass., 1974-83; dir. clin. pastoral edn. Our Lady of the Lake Regional Med. Ctr., Baton Rouge, 1983-87; dir. chaplain svcs. St. Mary's Hosp. and Med. Ctr., San Francisco, 1987-93; pres. SpiritHealth, 1994—; exec. dir. Marin Interfaith Coun., 1997—. Contbr. articles to profl. jours. Recipient Disting. Svc. award Mass. Jaycees, Fall River, 1970. Mem. Nat. Assn. Cath. Chaplains (Disting. Svc. award 1987, 95, pres. elect 1991, pres. 1993-95). Avocations: sailing, reading, playing piano, listening to classical music. Home: 14551 Redwood Ln Guerneville CA 95446-9662 Office: Marin Interfaith Coun 845 Olive Ave Ste 110 Novato CA 94945-2478

TRIPP, LEONARD LEE, software engineer; b. L.A., Oct. 21, 1941; s. Leonard Henry and Allie Marie (Haws) T.; m. Celia Frank, Nov. 28, 1963; children: Valerie, Monica, Allyson, Justin, Mary Esther, Lee. BS, Brigham Young U., 1965, MS, 1967. Sci. programmer Boeing Co., Seattle, 1967-75, computer scientist, 1975-85, sr. computer scientist, 1985-91, assoc. tech. fellow, 1991—. Chair U.S. tech. adv. group to Internat. Orgn. for Stds./Internat. Electrotech. Commn./Joint Tech. Com. 1/SC7 software engring. Contbr. to profl. publs. Mem. Boy Scouts Am.; commr. King County Water Dist. 124, Federal Way, Wash., 1977-82, Lakehaven Sewer Dist., Federal Way, 1979-82, Federal Way Water and Sewer Bd., 1983-84. Recipient Silver Beaver award Boy Scouts Am., 1984. Mem. IEEE (vice-chair computer soc. std. activity bd. 1989-93, v.p. stds. activity computer soc. 1994-95, chair IEEE software engring. stds. com. 1993—, stds. bd. dirs. 1993—), Assn. Computing Machinery, Math. Assn. Am. Achievements include participation in development of standard taxonomy of software engineering standards. Office: Boeing Comml Airplane PO Box 3707 # 6H Tw Seattle WA 98124-2207 Home: 16113 SE 45th St Issaquah WA 98027-9019

TRIPP, LUKE SAMUEL, educator; b. Atoka, Tenn., Feb. 6, 1941; s. Luke Samuel and Dorothy Mae (Watson) T.; m. Hedwidge Mary Bruyns, Aug. 21, 1989; children: Ruth, Azania, Comrade. BS, Wayne State U., 1966; MA, U. Mich., 1974, PhD, 1980. Computer programmer No. Elec. Co., Montreal, Que., Can., 1966-68; tchr. elem. sch. math. Santa Maria Edn. Ctr., Detroit, 1969-70; instr. black studies Wayne County C.C., 1971-72; tchr. secondary sch. sci. Cmty. Skills Ctr., Ann Arbor, Mich., 1971-73; dir. grad. rsch. U. Mich., 1977-80; asst. prof. U. Ill., Champaign, 1981-82, So. Ill. U., Carbondale, 1982-89; from asst. prof. to prof. social sci. St. Cloud (Minn.) State U., 1989-95, prof., 1995—. Co-founder, coord. Faculty/Staff Color Caucus, St. Cloud, 1989—; founder, dir. Human Rights Coputhon, St. Cloud, 1989-91, So. Ill. Anti-Aparthied Coalition, Carbondale, 1984-87. Dir. polit. edn. Nat. Black Ind. Polit. Party, Ann Arbor, 1980-81; co-founder, mem. exec. bd. Labor Defense League, Detroit, 1970-71, League Revolutionary Black Workers, Detroit, 1968-70; coord. Nat. Black Econ. Devel. Conf., Detroit, 1969-70; student activist SNCC, Detroit, 1960-65. Mem. Nat. Coun. Black Studies, Assn. Study Afro-Am. Life and History. Office: St Cloud State U 720 4th Ave S Saint Cloud MN 56301-4498 E-mail: ltripp@stcloudstate.edu.

TRIPP, MARIAN BARLOW LOOFE, retired public relations company executive; b. Lodgepole, Nebr., July 26; d. Lewis Rockwell and Cora Dee (Davis) Barlow; m. James Edward Tripp, Feb. 9, 1957; children: Brendan Michael, Kevin Mark. BS, Iowa State U., 1944. Writer Dairy Record, St. Paul, 1944-45; head product promotion divsn., pub. rels. dept. Swift & Co., Chgo., 1945-55; mgmt. supr., v.p. pub. rels. J. Walter Thompson Co., N.Y.C. and Chgo., 1956-76, v.p. consumer affairs Chgo., 1974-76; pres. Marian Tripp Communications Inc., 1976-94. Mem. Am. Inst. Wine and Food, Confriere de la Chaine des Rotisseriers (officer Chgo. chpt.), Mayflower Soc., Daughters of the Am. Revolution. Episcopalian. Office: 100 E Bellevue Pl Chicago IL 60611-1157 E-mail: mbtripp.@aol.com.

TRIPP, MICHAEL WINDSOR, accountant; b. Fall River, Mass. s. Frederick and Elizabeth (Azevedo) T.; m. Ella Charlene Middlebrooks, May 24, 1966; children: Sandra Lee, Wendy Ann. Cert. computer programming with honors, Plus Sch. Bus., Providence, 1971; BSBA in Acctg. cum laude, Bryant Coll., 1975. CPA, R.I.; diplomate Am. Bd. Forensic Acctg. Fin. mgr. trainee I.T.T. Aetna Fin., Pawtucket, R.I., 1969-70; computer programmer B.A. Ballou & Co., Inc., East Providence, 1970-72; adminstrv. asst. Manasett Corp., Providence, 1972-74; profl. staff Peat, Marwick & Mitchell, 1974-76; ptnr. Turosz, Maccarone, Keenan & Tripp, East Providence, 1976-88; adminstr. Licht & Semonoff, Providence, 1988-89; pvt. practice East Providence, 1989—. Dir. A New Leaf, Providence, 1988-96; mem. LaSalle Acad. bd. regents, 1999—. Vice-chmn., clk. Barrington (R.I.) Sch. Com., 1980-88; active Rep. Town Com., Barrington, 1980—; treas. Hampden Meadows PTA, Barrington, 1976-80, Rhode Islanders for Chafee, Providence, 1976. With USMC, 1965-69, Vietnam. Decorated Purple Heart, Air medal, Navy Commendation medal with combat V. Fellow AICPA; mem. R.I. Soc. CPAs, Manny Moniz Meml. Hockey League (treas. 1992—), Barrington Yacht Club (treas. 1992-93), Narragansett Bay Yachting Assn., Am. Coll. Forensic Examiners, Bryant Coll. Alumni Assn. (exec. dir., treas. 1977-80), La Salle Acad. Alumni Assn. (phonathon chmn. 1992-93), Appalachian Mountain Club, U.S. Sailing Assn. Republican. Roman Catholic. Avocations: sailing, hockey, mountain climbing. Home: 40 Lamson Rd Barrington RI 02806-2643 Office: 589 Warren Ave Ste 3 East Providence RI 02914-2800 E-mail: mtripp@mwt-cpa.coxatwork.com.

TRIPP, NORMAN DENSMORE, lawyer; b. Binghamton, N.Y., Apr. 11, 1938; s. Merritt Frederick and Eleonore Graves (Satterley) T.; m. Jane Grace Mighton, June 15, 1962; children: Jennifer, Norman, Christine, Michael. BA, U. Miami, 1962; JD magna cum laude, Cleve. State U., 1967. Bar: Ohio, Fla. Chmn. Tripp Scott P.A., Fort Lauderdale, Fla.; gen. counsel Cert. Tours (Delta Dream Vacations). Past mem. bd. adjustment City of Ft. Lauderdale; past chair Ft. Lauderdale Downtown Devel. Authority; mem. City of Ft. Lauderdale Downtown Devl. Bd.; past bd. trustees, vice chmn. State of Fla. C.C. Sys.; trustee Fla. Atlantic U., vice chmn.; mem. South Fla. Annenberg Challenge, Broward County. Mem. Am. Soc. Travel Agts., ABA, Broward County Bar Assn., Fla. Bar Assn., Ocean Reef Club (Key Largo), Fort Lauderdale Yacht Club, Grande Oaks Golf Club. Office: Tripp Scott PA PO Box 14245 Fort Lauderdale FL 33302-4245

TRIPP, SUSAN GERWE, museum director; b. Balt., Dec. 28, 1945; d. Earl Joseph and Maria Elizabeth (Wise) Gerwe; m. David Enders Tripp, June 9, 1977. BS, U. Md., 1967. Home econs. tchr. Balt. County Pub. Sch. Sys., 1967-74; curator of art Johns Hopkins U., Balt., 1974-76, curator of art, archivist, 1976-78, instr. evening coll., 1978-84, dir. univ. collections, 1979-91; supr., instr. art history Goucher Coll., Notre Dame U., Balt., 1977-86; dir. docent tng. Homewood Mus., 1987-89; exec. dir. Old Westbury (N.Y.) Gardens, 1992-96; writer Stuyvesant, N.Y., 1996—. Dir. Homewood Restoration Adv. Com., 1983-92, Evergreen Restoration Adv. Com., 1988-92, Advancement Basilica Hist. Trust, Inc., 2000-2001; lectr. in field. Co-author: The Garrett Collection of Japanese Art, 1993 (NEA Grant 1980), Contbr. articles to profl. jours. Dir. Columbia County Hist. Soc., 1996—, pres. bd. dirs., 1997—; bd. trustees Regional and Cmty. Historic Preservation Benefit Plan, 2002-. Recipient Hist. Preservation award Balt. Heritage, Inc., 1988, 91, Rsch. award Am. Soc. Interior Designers, 1991. Mem. Brit. Mus. Soc., Oriental Ceramic Soc., Balt. Mus. Art, So. Garden Hist. Soc., Furniture History Soc., N.Y. Zool. Soc., Am. Assn. Mus. Columbia County Hist. Soc. (bd. dirs. 1997—), Am. Numismatic Soc. (standing com., libr.), John Hopkins U. Faculty Club., Omicron Nu. Avocations: architecture, archaeology, Chinese ceramics, historical restoration. Office: PO Box G Stuyvesant NY 12173-0009

TRIPPENSEE, GARY ALAN, aerospace executive, retired; b. Jefferson City, Mo., May 23, 1940; s. Walter Anton and Juanita (Schneider) T.; m. Concha Elvira Perez, Aug. 18, 1981; children: Jena, Darin. BSME, U. Mo., Rolla, 1962; AA in Bus., Antelope Valley Coll., Lancaster, Calif., 1974. Lic. airframe and powerplant mechanic, FAA; single/multi-engine comml. aircraft lic. land & sea, Inst.; cert. flight instr., instrument. Aircraft flight test engr. McDonnell Douglas, St. Louis, 1965-79; project mgr. NASA/Dryden Flight Rsch. Ctr., Edwards, Calif., 1979—2001, project mgr. F14, 1983-84, project mgr. F15, 1984-85, project mgr. X-29, 1985-91, project mgr. X-31, 1991-92, internat. test. orgn. dir. X-31, 1993-95, project mgr. X-33, 1996-2000, project mgr. X-37, 2000-01, ret., 2001. Capt. U.S. Army C.E., 1962-65, Vietnam. Recipient Laurels award for aeronautics/propulsion Aviation Week & Space Tech., 1990, 93, Outstanding Alumni award U. Mo.-Rolla, 2000. Mem. EAA, Acad. Mech. Engrs. Avocations: flying, fishing, R/C models. Home: 357 Airport Dr Grove OK 74344

TRISCO, ROBERT FREDERICK, church historian, educator; b. Chgo., Nov. 11, 1929; s. Richard E. and Harriet Rose (Hardt) T. BA, St. Mary of Lake Sem., Mundelein, Ill., 1951; STL, Pontifical Gregorian U., Rome, 1955, Hist. Eccl.D., 1962; LHD (hon.), Belmont Abbey Coll., 1992. Ordained priest Roman Catholic Ch., 1954. Faculty Cath. U. Am., Washington, 1959-2000, prof. ch. history, 1975-2000, Kelly-Quinn disting. prof. ch. history, 1999-2000, prof. emeritus ch. history, 2000—. Expert 2d Vatican Coun., 1962-65; pres. Am. subcom. Internat. Commn. Comparative Ch. History, 1978-80, assesseur, 1980—; mem. subcoms. Nat. Conf. Cath. Bishops, 1966-76, 87-92; mem. Pontifical Com. Hist. Scis., 1982—; hon. mem. Accademia di San Carlo (Milan), 1986—; hon. prelate (monsignor), 1992; mem. Internat. Joint Commn. for Theol. Dialogue between Cath. Ch. and Orthodox Ch., 1999—; mem. adv. com. Assn. Friends of the Archives of Congregation for Doctrine of the Faith (Holy See), 1999—. Author: The Holy See and Nascent Church in the Middle Western U.S., 1826-1850, 1962, Bishops and Their Priests in the United States, 1988; co-author: A Guide to American Catholic History, 2d edit., 1982; editor: Catholics in America, 1976; editor CAth. Hist. Rev., 1963—; co-editor, contbr.: Studies in Catholic History in Honor of John Tracy Ellis, 1985; contbr. articles to profl. jours. Decorated knight Equestrian Order of the Holy Sepulchre of Jerusalem, 1993, knight comdr., 1998. Mem. Am. Hist. Assn., Am. Soc. Ch. History (coun. 1980-82), Am. Cath. Hist. Assn. (exec. sec. 1961—, sec., treas. 1983—), Can. Cath. Hist. Assn., Cath. Commn. on Intellectual and Cultural Affairs. Office: Cath U Am Mullen Library Rm 318 Washington DC 20064-0001 E-mail: trisco@cua.edu.

TRISKA, JAN FRANCIS, retired political science educator; b. Prague, Czechoslovakia, Jan. 26, 1922; came to U.S., 1948, naturalized, 1955; s. Jan and Bozena (Kubiznak) T.; m. Carmel Lena Burastero, Aug. 26, 1951; children: Mark Lawrence, John William. JUD, Charles U., Prague, 1948; LLM, Yale U., 1950, JSD, 1952; PhD, Harvard U., 1957. Co-dir. Soviet treaties Hoover Instn., Stanford, Calif., 1956-58; lectr. dept. polit. sci. U. Calif., Berkeley, 1957-58; asst. prof. Cornell U., Ithaca, N.Y., 1958-60; assoc. prof. Stanford U., Calif., 1960-65, prof. polit. sci., 1965-89, assoc. chmn. dept., 1965-66, 68-69, 71-72, 74-75, prof. emeritus, 1990—. Cons. Inst. State and Law, Czech Acad. Scis., Prague, 1995—. Co-author: (with Slusser) The Theory, Law and Policy of Soviet Treaties, 1962; (with Finley) Soviet Foreign Policy, 1968; (with Cocks) Political Development and Political Change in Eastern Europe, 1977; (with Ike, North) The World of Superpowers, 1981, (with Gati) Blue Collar Workers in Eastern Europe, 1981, Dominant Powers and Subordinate States, 1986, The Great War's Forgotten Front, 1998 (Czech, German, Slovene & Italian edits.); mem. editl. bd. East European Quar. Comparative Politics, Internat. Jour. Sociology, Jour. Comparative Politics, Studies in Comparative Communism, Soviet Statutes and Decisions, Documents in Communist Affairs. Recipient Rsch. award Ford Found., 1963-68, Josef Hlavka Commemorative medal Czechoslovak Acad. Scis., 1992, M.A. Comenius 1592-1992 Meml. medal Czechoslovak Pedagogical Mus., Prague, 1991; fellow NSF, 1971-72, Sen. Fulbright fellow, 1973-74, Woodrow Wilson fellow Internat. Ctr. for Scholars, 1980-81. Mem. Am. Polit. Sci. Assn. (sec. pres. conf. on communist studies 1970-76), Assn. Advancement Slavic Studies (bd. dirs. 1975-83), Am. Soc. Internat. Law (exec. coun. 1964-67), Czechoslovak Soc. Arts and Scis. (pres. 1978-80, 90-92), Inst. for Human Scis. Vienna (acting for Commn. European Communities, Brussels, com. experts on transformation of nat. higher edn. and rsch. system in Ctrl. Europe, Brussels 1991—), Fly Fishers Club (Palo Alto, Calif.). Democrat. Home: 720 Vine St Menlo Park CA 94025-6154 Office: Stanford U Dept Polit Sci Stanford CA 94305 E-mail: triska@stanford.edu.

TRITES, DONALD GEORGE, human service consultant; b. Boston, Sept. 26, 1941; s. George Herman and Ada Christena (Patten) T.; m. Ruth Ann Lewis, June 15, 1963 (div. 1987); children: Sarah Jeanne, Amy Bray; m. Beverly Jean Baker, Apr. 8, 1989; children: Erica Christena, Philip Jameson Granville. AB, Colgate U., 1963; EdM, Tufts U., 1964; PhD, Syracuse U., 1976. Thcr., then chair history dept. Hamilton (Mass.)-Wenham Regionial H.S., 1964-70; instr. divsn. ednl. studies Emory U., Atlanta, 1973-76, asst. prof. ednl. studies, 1976-81, vis. faculty, 1981-86; exec. dir. Ga. Advocacy Office, Inc., 1981-86, Devel. Svcs. Strafford County, Inc., Dover, N.H., 1986-95; founder, pres. Jebdas Consulting, Eliot, Maine, 1995—; program mgr. Mental Retardation Svcs. State of Maine, Augusta, 1996-2000, clin. dir. Mental Retardation Svcs., 2000, dir. rsch., 2000—. Cons. in human svc. mgmt. and evaluation, U.S. and Europe, 1978—. Editor, author: The College and A Human Future, 1986; contbr. articles to profl.publs. Bd. dirs. Ashwood Waldorf Sch., Rockport, Maine; deacon, First Bapt. Ch., Melrose, Mass., 1968-69, Syracuse, N.Y., 1972-73; deacon, Ctrl. Congl. Ch., Atlanta, 1984-86. Mem. Assn. for Persons with Severe Handicaps, Delta Upsilon. Democrat. Mem. United Ch. of Christ. Avocations: reading, gardening. Home: 351 Gardiner Rd Jefferson ME 04348-4000 Office: Dept Mental Health & Mental Retardation 40 State House Sta Augusta ME 04333-0040 E-mail: don.trites@state.me.us.

TRITLE, LAWRENCE ALAN, history educator; b. Glendale, Calif., Oct. 13, 1946; s. Robert Charles Jr. and Dorothy (Brown) T.; m. Margaret Burlington, Jan. 31, 1970. BA, UCLA, 1968; MA, U. S. Fla., 1972; PhD, U. Chgo., 1978. Prof. Loyola Marymount U., L.A., 1978—, Marie Chilton chair humanities, 1988. Vis. prof. Loyola U. Chgo., 1981-82, 90-91, UCLA, 1992. Author: Phocion the Good, 1988, From Melos to My Lai. War & Survival, 2000; editor: The Greek World in the Fourth Century BC, 1997, Balkan Currents, 1998, Text and Tradition: Studies in Greek History & Histiography, 1999. Lt. U.S. Army, 1968-71, Vietnam. NEH fellow U. Pa., 1979. Mem. Am. Philol. Assn. (chair com. ancient history 1997-99), Am. Hist. Assn., Assn. Ancient Historians, Soc. Mayflower Descendants (So. Calif. chpt.). Democrat. Home: 7222 W 78th St Los Angeles CA 90045-2516 Office: Loyola Marymount U 7900 Loyola Blvd Ste 1 Los Angeles CA 90045-2699

TRITSCH, GEORGE LEOPOLD, biochemist, educator, retired biomedical researcher; b. Vienna, Austria, Apr. 8, 1929; arrived in U.S., 1940; s. Robert James and Edith Mary Tritsch; m. Norma Elsie Tritsch, June 16, 1951; children: George L., Margaret Ellen, Douglas Evan. BA, NYU, 1948; MS, U. Md., 1951; PhD, Purdue U., 1954. Rsch. assoc. Cornell Med. Coll., N.Y.C., 1954—56, Rockefeller U., N.Y.C., 1956—59; cancer rsch. scientist Roswell Pk. Cancer Inst., Buffalo, 1959—95, cancer. rsch. sci. emeritus, 1995—; from asst. rsch. prof. to prof. emeritus SUNY, 1961—; prof. biochemistry Niagara U., Niagara Falls, 1961—. Vis. prof. dept. biochemistry Dartmouth Med. Sch., 1968, Purdue Cancer Ctr., W. Lafayette, Ind., 1983; mem. grant rev. panel nat. prostatic cancer project NIH, Bethesda, Md., 1975—85; symposium organizer adenosine deaminase N.Y. Acad. Scis., 1984; invited spkr. in field. Editor, author Axenic Mammalian Cell Reactions, 1969, Adenosine Deaminase, 1985; contbr. articles to profl. jours. Bd. dirs. N.Y. State Health Rsch. Coun., Buffalo, 1975—80. Grantee, USPHS, 1960—90, Am. Cancer Soc., 1961—69. Mem.: Soc. Exptl. Biology, Am. Assn. Cancer Rsch., Am. Soc. Pharmacological and Exptl. Therapeutics, Am. Inst. Nutrition, Am. Soc. Biochemistry and Molecular Biology, Harvey Soc., Sigma Xi, Alpha Chi Sigma, Phi Lambda Upsilon. Avocations: playing piano, water sports. Office: Roswell Pk Cancer Inst 666 Elm St Buffalo NY 14263-0001

TRITT, LINCOLN C. writer, educator, musician; b. Salmon River, Alaska, Oct. 18, 1946; s. Isaac Albert and Naomi (Peter) T. Grad., Mt. Edgecombe H.S., 1966; student, U. Alaska, 1972, 84-87; student electricity and electronics, student radioman class A sch., Naval Tng. Ctr., 1967; studied with traditional tchrs. Exploration worker, driver, driller asst. Kandik Oil Field Parker Exploration, Fairbanks, Alaska, 1977; negotiator Venetie (Alaska) Tribal Govt., 1980, heavy equipment operator, 1982; phone survey rep. Mental Health Program and U. Alaska, 1984; curriculum developer Yukon Flats (Alaska) Sch. Dist., 1985; laborer Peter Kewitt and sons, Deadhorse, Alaska, 1985; bookkeeper Tanana Chiefs Conf., Inc., on-site supr., 1985; translator fed. Indian law Fed. Indian Law workshop, Venetie, Alaska, 1986; grant contract negotiator with fed. agys., 1987; grant adminstr., overall project dir. Arctic Village Traditional Coun., 1988-89; liaison, coord. U.S. Geophys. Inst./U. Alaska, Fairbanks, 1989; instr. rural coll. U. Alaska, 1990; tribal adminstr. Native Vill. Venetie (Alaska), 1994-95. Carpenter Bur. Indian Affairs Sch., Arctic Vill., Alaska, 1970; postal clk. U.S. Postal Svc., Fairbanks, Alaska, 1971, substitute postmaster, 1984—; tchr. Gwich'in lang., 1974; store mgr. Midnight Sun Native Store, Arctic Village, Alaska, 1975. Author screenplay on Native Am. alcohol experience; contbr. essays, stories to Raven Tells Stories: An Anthology of Alaska Native Writings, Coyote Bark, Alaska Mag., Alaskan Epiphany, All Alaska Weekly, Talking Leaves, Tundra Times, The Turtle Quarterly, The Council, Nimrod; columnist Fairbanks Daily News Miner, Northland News; composer (song) Belief; mem. of cast: Earth and the Great Weather, 1993, 95, 97; performed at Athabascan Old-Time Fiddling Festival, Summer Folk Festival, Fairbanks Folk Festival, Plate and Palate Restaurant, Native Village at Alaskaland; cons. (videos, films) Wisdom of the Elders, Caribou People. Firefighter Dept. Natural Resource, Fairbanks, Alaska, 1984; lobbyist Gwich'in People, 1986-87; mem. restructuring com. Howard Luke Alternative Sch., 1993, 94; Rural Campuses U. Alaska, 1990; coord. first Gwich'in Gathering in Arctic Village, Alaska, 1988; mem. coun. Native Village of Venetie (Alaska) Govt., 1974-86; mem. Arctic Village Traditional Coun., 1973-89, chief, 1987-89; mem. sch. bd. Arctic Village, 1974-76. Served with USN, 1966-70, Vietnam. Mem. Native Writers Circle of Ams., Internat. Conf. Higher Edn. Indigenous People, Internat. Conf. Hunting and Gathering Socs., Alaska Native Viet Nam Vets, Fairbanks Folk Fest. Avocations: music, photography, recording, space science, history. Home: PO Box 22016 Arctic Village AK 99722-0016

TRITTEN, JAMES JOHN, national security educator; b. Yonkers, N.Y., Oct. 3, 1945; s. James Hanley and Jennie (Szucs) Tritten; m. Kathleen Brattesani (div. 1983); children: Kimberly, James John Jr.; m. Jasmine Clark, Dec. 29, 1990. BA in Internat. Studies, Am. U., 1971; MA in Internat. Affairs, Fla. State U., 1978; AM in Internat. Rels., U. So. Calif., L.A., 1982, PhD in Internat. Rels., 1984. Commd. officer USN, 1967, advanced through grades to commdr., 1981; joint strategic plans officer Office of the Chief of Naval Ops., Washington, 1984-85; asst. dir. net assessment Office of the Sec. of Def., 1985-86; chmn. dept. nat. security affairs Naval Postgrad. Sch., Monterey, Calif., 1986-89; ret. USN, 1989; assoc. prof. nat. security affairs Naval Postgrad. Sch., Monterey, 1989-93; spl. asst. to comdr. Naval Doctrine Command, Norfolk, Va., 1993-96; chief policy and plan divsn. U.S. Joint Forces Command, Suffolk, 1996-01, mem. joint doctrine divsn., 2001—02; chief tng. and inspectors divsn. Def. Threat Reduction Agy., Albuquerque, 2002—. Cons. Rand Corp., Santa Monica, Calif., 1982—84; with Nat. Security Rsch., Fairfax, Va., 1992, AmerInd, Alexandria, Va., 1996. Author: (book) Soviet Naval Forces and Nuclear Warfare, 1986, Our New National Security Strategy, 1992 (George Washington Honor medal, 1991), A Doctrine Reader, 1996; contbr. chapters to books, articles to profl. jours. Mem. Adv. Bd. on Alcohol Related Problems, Monterey, 1987—90; bd. dirs., officer Leadership Monterey Peninsula, 1989—92, Carmel Valley (Calif.) Property Owners Assn., 1989—91; commr. Airport Land Use Commn., Monterey County, 1990—93. Decorated Def. Superior Svc. medal Sec. Def., Washington, Meritorious Svc. medal Sec. Navy, Navy Civillian Supr. Svc. medal; recipient Joint Meritorious Civilian Svc. award, Chmn. Joint Chiefs Staff, 1998, Alfred Thayer Mahan award for literary achievement, Navy League U.S., 1986. Mem.: Mil. Ops. Rsch. Soc. (v.p. 1990—91), U.S. Naval Inst. (Silver and Bronze medals), Naval Order U.S., Pi Gamma Mu, Pi Sigma Alpha. Republican. Presbyterian. Avocations: hiking, camping. Office: Def Threat Reduction Agy-CST 1680 Texas St SE Kirtland AFB NM 87117 E-mail: tritten@jfcom.mil.

TRITTER, DANIEL F. lawyer, writer; b. N.Y.C., Jan. 20, 1934; s. Maurice J. and Hermina (Ronay) T.; m. Rita Frances Shane, June 22, 1958; 1 child, Michael Shane. BA, Williams Coll., 1954; MA, Columbia U., 1957; cert., Inst. on East Cen. Europe, 1957; JD, Benjamin N. Cardozo Sch. Law, 1982. Bar: N.Y. 1984, U.S. Dist. Ct. (so. dist., ea. dist.) 1984, U.S. Supreme Ct. 1987. Writer, exec. Diener & Dorskind, Inc., N.Y.C., 1960-71, M.L. Grant, Inc., N.Y.C., 1971-79; pvt. practice, 1984—. Adj. prof. Williams Coll., 1984, Touro Law Sch., 1989, Benjamin N. Cardozo Sch. Law, 1999. Contbr. essays to profl. jours. Bd. govs. N.Y. chpt. Arthritis Found., 1985-90. Spl. agt. CIC, U.S. Army, 1957-60. Mem. Assn. Trial Lawyers Am., Law and Humanities Inst. (pres. 1986-91, v.p. 1991—), Williams Club. Democrat. Avocations: classical music, writing, sports. Office: 330 W 42nd St Fl 32 New York NY 10036-6902

TRITTER, RICHARD PAUL, strategic planning consulting executive; b. Boston, Sept. 30, 1945; s. Herman Louis and Rose (Greenblatt) T.; 1 child, Melissa Rosanne; m. Marcy Lynn Kroll, June 17, 1984; children: Matthew Alexander, Rachel Danielle, Adam Levi. AB, Columbia Coll., N.Y.C., 1967; JD, Northea. U., 1976. Bar: Mass. 1977, U.S. Supreme Ct. 1980. Mktg. mgr./cons. Digital Equipment Corp., Merrimack, N.H., 1979-86; pres. Video/Demo Ctrs., Inc., Burlington, Mass., 1986-88; v.p. bus. devel. Info. Resources, Inc., Boston, 1988-91; dir. facilitation consulting svcs. Arthur Andersen LLP, Boston, Chgo., 1991-96. Panelist MIT Enterprise Forum, Cambridge, 1983-89; ptnr., mng. dir. Horn of Africa Fishing Partnership, 1998. Author: Control Self-Assessment: Experience, Current Thinking and Best Practices, 1996, Control Self Assessment—A Guide to Facilitation-Based Consulting,, 2000; creator software application testing svc. in coop. with KPMG Peat Marwick, Compliance Testing and Verification, 1981. UN rep. Jubaland Relief and Rehab. Soc., Somalia; dir. Save Somalia Livestock Campaign, 1993. Recipient Better Govt. award Pioneer Inst. for Pub. Policy Rsch., Boston. Achievements include facilitating meetings between opposing clans in the Juba region of southern Somalia; initiated lobster export project with cooperation of Gen. Omar Jess, Col. Ahmed Hashi and other Somali leaders. Home: c/o Chaffell 11 Orchard St Mapleton Depot PA 17052 E-mail: rtritter@ix.netcom.com.

TRITTON, THOMAS RICHARD, academic administrator, biology educator; b. Lakewood, Ohio, Dec. 20, 1947; s. William Frank and Margie Jean (Galbraith) T.; m. Louise Meschter Tritton; children: Lara, Christiana. BA, Ohio Wesleyan U., 1969; PhD, Boston U., 1973. Asst. prof. Yale Med. Sch., New Haven, 1975-80; assoc. prof. Yale U., 1980-85; prof. U. Vt., Burlington, 1985-97, vice provost, 1991-97; pres. Haverford (Pa.) Coll., 1997—. Mem. NIH Exptl. Therapeutics Study Sect., 1988-92. Editor books; mem. editl. bd. several profl. jours.; contbr. numerous sci. papers to profl. jours. Rsch. grantee NIH, Am. Cancer Soc. Mem. Am. Assn. Cancer Rsch. (com. mem.), Am. Soc. Biol. Chemists. Mem. Soc. Of Friends. Avocations: music, tennis. Office: Haverford Coll 370 Lancaster Ave Haverford PA 19041-1336 E-mail: ttritton@haverford.edu.

TRIVEDI, HARSH MAHENDRA, technical associate, educator, writer; b. Ahmedabad, India, Feb. 2, 1969; came to U.S., 1987; s. Mahendra Ravishankar and Mandakini Mahendra Trivedi; m. Nirali H. Trivedi. BSc in Biology magna cum laude, L.I. U., 1990, MSc in Cell Biology, 1992; MSC in Molecular Biology & Biochemistry, U. Medicine & Dentistry, 1994. Student asst. Flushing (N.Y.) H.S., 1990-91; grad. asst. L.I. U., Greenvale, N.Y., 1990-92, U. Medicine & Dentistry, Piscataway, N.J., 1992-94; master tchr. Princeton (N.J.) Rev., 1992—; assoc. scientist Ortho Diagnostic, Raritan, NJ, 1996—99; rsch. scientist Colgate-Palmolive, Piscataway, 1996—99, sr. rsch. scientist, 1999—2002, tech. assoc., 2002—. Tchr., trainer, author Examkrackers, 2002—; tchr. trainer Princeton Rev., 1996—, cons., 1994—; math. tutor;

instr. ESL. Contbr. articles to profl. jours. Mem. Am. Soc. Materials, N.Y. Acad. Scis. Achievements include implementation of PCR to categorize diferent hepatitis and human immune deficiency viruses; genome size determination of G-vaginallis; contribution to G-protein studies in yeast, specifically the N-end rule pathway; sequenced novel gene in drosophilla; working on anti adhesion, antibacterial, biofilm and Quorum sensing research. Home: 134 Grantham Dr Somerset NJ 08873

TRIVEDI, HITESH K. research scientist; BSME, Sardar Petel U., India, 1984; MSMAE, Ill. Inst. Tech., 1990. Lectr. Birla Vishwakarma Mahavidyalaya Eng. Coll., Vallabh-Vidyanagar Nagar, India, 1984-88; rsch. asst. IIT, Chgo., 1988-90; program mgr. UES, Inc, Dayton, Ohio, 1991—. Contbr. articles to profl. jours. Mem. ASME, Soc. Tribology & Lubrication Engrs. (chmn. aerospace coun. 1996, chmn. Dayton chpt. 1997, Capt. Alfred Hunt award 1999), Soc. Automotive Engrs. Office: UES Inc 4401 Dayton Xenia Rd Dayton OH 45432-1805 E-mail: hitesh.trivedi@wpafb.af.mil.

TRIVEDI, MADHUKAR H. psychiatrist; b. Baroda, India, Sept. 22, 1957; came to U.S., 1986; s. Hariprasad and Jyoti T.; m. Beena Madhukar, Aug. 12, 1990; children: Hersh M., Ashesh M. Student, U. Baroda, 1974-76, MB, BChir, 1980. Diplomate Am. Bd. Psychiatry & Neurology. Intern S.S. Gen. Hosp., Baroda, India, 1980-81; resident in radiology Baroda Med. Coll., 1982, resident in psychiatry U. Gen. Hosp., 1982-85; resident in psychiatry Henry Ford Hosp., Detroit, 1986-90, chief resident, 1989-90; rsch. fellow U. Tex. S.W. Med. Ctr., Dallas, 1990-92, NIMH fellow, 1991-93, instr. depression rsch. clinic, 1992-93, dir. depression and anxiety program, 1993-95. Dir. depression module U. Tex. S.W. Med. Ctr., Dallas, 1996—, assoc. prof., 1998—; depression guideline panel Agy. for Health Care Policy and Rsch.; chmn. World Wide Web Conf., Internat. Psychopharmacology Algorithm Project, 1997. Editor Internat. Depression-Neurosci. Rev. Group, 1996—; mem. editl. bd. Depressive Disorders Index & Reviews; contbr. articles to profl. jours. Recipient Young Investigator award Nat. Alliance for Rsch. on Schizophrenia and Devel., 1992-94, New Investigator award NIMH, 1993, Cert. Excellence award Indo-Am. Soc. Biol. Psychiat., 1994. Mem. Am. Psychiat. Assn., Soc. Nuclear Medicine (program chmn. 1990), World Psychiat. Assn. (com. mem. 1995-97), Neuroimaging Adv. Com., Tex. Soc. Psychiat. Physicians (com. mem. 1995-98). Office: UTSW/St Paul Hosp POB 1 Ste 600 5959 Harry Hines Blvd Dallas TX 75390-9101 E-mail: madhukar.trivedi@utsouthwestern.edu.

TRIVELPIECE, ALVIN WILLIAM, physicist, educator, consultant; b. Stockton, Calif., Mar. 15, 1931; s. Alvin Stevens and Mae (Hughes) Trivelpiece; m. Shirley Ann Ross, Mar. 23, 1953; children: Craig Evan, Steve Edward, Keith Eric. BS, Calif. Poly. Coll., San Luis Obispo, 1953; MS, Calif. Inst. Tech., 1955, PhD, 1958. Fulbright scholar Delft (Netherlands) U., 1958—59; asst. prof., then assoc. prof. U. Calif. at Berkeley, 1959—66; prof. physics U. Md., 1966—76; on leave as asst. dir. for research div. controlled thermonuclear research AEC, Washington, 1973—75; v.p. Maxwell Labs. Inc., San Diego, 1976—78; corp. v.p. Sci. Applications, Inc., La Jolla, 1978—81; dir. Office of Energy Research, U.S. Dept. Energy, Washington, 1981—87; exec. officer AAAS, 1987—88; dir. Oak Ridge (Tenn.) Nat. Lab., 1989—2000; v.p. Martin Marietta Energy Systems, 1989—95, Lockheed Martin Energy Systems, 1995; pres. Lockheed Martin Energy Rsch. Corp., 1996—2000; pvt. cons. Oak Ridge, 2000—. Head del. joint NAS and Soviet Acad. Scis. mtg. and conf. on energy and global ecol. problems USSR, 1989; chmn. math. scis. ednl. bd. NAS, 1990—93; chmn. coordinating coun. for edn. NRC, 1991—93, chmn. com. small innovative firms in Russian nuclear cities, 2001; mem. Commn. on Phys. Scis., Math. and Applications, 1993—96, com. on tech. issues related to the comprehensive test ban treaty NAS, 2000—02, Tenn. Sci. and Tech. Adv. Commn., 1993—96, chmn., 1996—99, adv. com. Fedn. Networking Coun., 1992—96; chmn. and pres. Tenn. Tech. Devel. Corp., 1998—2000. Author: Slow Wave Propagation in Plasma Wave Guides, 1966, Principles of Plasma Physics, 1973; contbr. articles to profl. jours. Named Disting. Alumnus, Calif. Poly. State U., 1978, Calif. Inst. Tech., Pasadena, 1987; recipient U.S. Sec. of Energy's Gold medal for disting. svc., 1986, Disting. Assoc. award, 2000, Tenn. Outstanding Svc. commendation, Senate Joint Resolution #530, 2000; fellow Guggenheim, 1966. Fellow: IEEE (Outstanding Engr. award region 3 1995), AAAS, Am. Phys. Soc.; mem.: NAE, AAUP, Am. Assn. Physics Tchrs., Am. Nuc. Soc., Nat. Press Club, Capital Hill Club, Tau Beta Pi, Sigma Xi. Achievements include patents in field. Home and Office: 8 Rivers Run Way Oak Ridge TN 37830-9004

TRIVELPIECE, CRAIG EVAN, computer electronics executive; b. Pasadena, Calif., Apr. 23, 1957; s. Alvin William and Shirley Ann T. Student, Calif. Inst. Tech., 1974-75; BA in Physics, U. Md., 1979. Scientist Maxwell Labs, San Diego, 1979-81; design engr. Rockwell Internat., Costa Mesa, 1981-83; mgr. engring. Tex. Instruments, Irvine, 1983-84; owner, pres. CST Engings Inc., 1984-91, Circuit Plus, Inc., 1990-2000, 4 Every Wall, Inc., 1990-92, Transnational Telecom Inc., 1995-98; dir. advanced tech. Encryptix, Inc., 2000—01; sr. product mgr. Day Software, Inc., 2001—. Cons. Payview Ltd., Hong Kong, 1985-88, Airmedia, Inc., 1996-98. Co-inventor: Video Scrambling System, 1985, home video product with Smart Card Access, 1992, Interactive Video System, 1997, Interactive Video System, 2002. Republican. Avocations: karate, judo, running. Home: 124 46th St Newport Beach CA 92663-2515 Office: Day Software Inc 1 Corporate Plz Newport Beach CA 92660 E-mail: craigtrivelpiece@day.com.

TRIX, FRANCES, linguistic anthropologist, consultant; b. Bellefont, Pa., Aug. 17, 1948; d. Herbert Phelps and Gertrude Aileen Trix; 1 child, Ramsay Ilyas. Student, Middleburg Coll., 1966-68; BA, U. Mich., 1970, MA, 1972, MA, 1976, PhD, 1988. Lectr. U. Mich., Dearborn, 1973-74, vis. asst. prof. linguistics Ann Arbor, 1988-89, vis. asst. rsch. scientist, 1989-90; lectr. Mercy Coll., Detroit, 1976-77; dir. bilingual program Dearborn Pub. Schs., 1977-80; asst. prof. anthropology Wayne State U., Detroit, 1990-97, assoc. prof., 1997—. Cons. U.S. Agy. for Internat. Devel., Yemen, 1978, CMS Energy Corp., Jackson, Mich., 1997, NASA, 2000; rsch. assoc. Ctr. Mid. Ea. and N. African Studies U. Mich., Ann Arbor, 1993—, rsch. assoc. Ctr. Russian and E. European Studies, 1996—, U. Mich. Author: Spiritual Discourse, 1993, Albanians in Michigan, 2001; contbr. articles to profl. jours. Coord. Ann Arbor com. Save Bosnia, 1992—; mem. Commn. Albanian-Am., Taylor, Mich., 1994—; mem. steering com. Interfaith Coun. Peace and Justice, Ann Arbor, 1995-96. Woodrow Wilson Found. fellow U. Mich., 1970-71, Internat. Rsch. and Exch. Bd. fellow IREX, 1987-88, Humanities Ctr. Faculty fellow Wayne State U., Detroit, 1998. Mem. Middle East Studies Assn., Turkish Studies Assn., Linguistic Soc. Am., Am. Anthrop. Assn. Avocations: English country dancing, traveling. Home: 645 Riverview Dr Ann Arbor MI 48104-1853 Office: Wayne State U 906 W Warren Ave Detroit MI 48202

TROCK, WARREN LEIGH, agricultural and natural resource economics educator; b. Pratt, Kans., June 30, 1926; s. Elmer and Lottie Marie (Lemons) T.; m. Bette Jene Sloan, Aug. 15, 1949; children: Daniel Leigh, Rebecca Ann, David Alan. BS in Agrl. Adminstrn., Kans. State U., 1950, MS in Agrl. Econs., 1957, PhD in Agrl. Econs., 1965. Extension economist Mont. State U., Bozeman, 1957-64; from asst. prof. to prof. agrl. econs. Tex. A&M U., College Station, 1964-73; extension economist Colo. State U., Ft. Collins, 1973—95; ret., 1995. Contbr. articles to profl. jours. Served as cpl. U.S. Army, 1944-46, 50-51. Recipient Hildreth award for achievement in pub. policy edn., 2002. Democrat. Avocations: fishing, photography. Home: 1725 Essex Dr Fort Collins CO 80526-1616

TROEN, PHILIP, physician, educator; b. Portland, Maine, Nov. 24, 1925; s. Ben and Gertrude (Cope) T.; m. Betty Ann Zelig, Mar. 22, 1953 (dec.); children: Mark Lawrence, Bruce Robert, Gail Sheri. AB, Harvard U., 1944, MD, 1948. Diplomate: Nat. Bd. Med. Examiners, Am. Bd. Internal Medicine. Intern Boston City Hosp., 1948-49, asst. resident in medicine, 1949-50; resident in medicine Beth Israel Hosp., Boston, 1950, 52-53, chief resident, 1953-54, asst. in medicine, 1955-56, USPHS research fellow, 1955-56, assoc. in med. research, 1956-64, assoc. in medicine, 1956-58, asst. vis. physician, 1959-64; teaching fellow Harvard Med. Sch., 1952-53, asst. in medicine, 1953-54, research fellow, 1955-56, instr. medicine, 1956-59, asso. in medicine, 1959-60, asst. prof., 1960-64; prof. medicine U. Pitts. Sch. Medicine, 1964—, assoc. chmn. dept. medicine, 1969-79, vice chmn. dept. medicine, 1979-90, interim chief divsn. of endocrinology and metabolism, 1995-97, physician in chief Montefiore Univ. Hosp., 1964-90, physician in chief emeritus, 1990—. Sci. counselor NIH, key cons. contraceptive devel. br., 1980; sci. counselor rev. Intramural Reproductive Biology Program, Nat. Inst. Child Health and Human Devel., 1977; cons. male fertility and infertility Nat. Inst. Occupational Safety and Health, 1977; mem. med. res. service merit rev. bd. in endocrinology VA, 1979-82; mem. contract rev. com. Nat. Inst. Child Health and Human Devel., 1975-84, chmn., 1976-89, reviewer intramural site visit devel. endocrinology br., 1983, 87; mem. endocrinologic and metabolic drugs adv. com. FDA, 1984-88, chmn. 1987-88; mem. expert advisor panel on occupational health, WHO, 1987-96. Mem. editorial bd. Jour. Andrology, Jour. Clin. Endocrinology and Metabolism, Internat. Jour. Andrology, Andrologia; contbr. articles to profl. jours. Served to capt. M.C., AUS, 1950-52. Fellow in endocrinology and metabolism Mayo Clinic, Rochester, Minn., 1954-55; Kendall-Hench research fellow, 1955; Ziskind teaching fellow, 1956-59; Med. Found. Greater Boston research fellow, 1959-63; Guggenheim fellow Stockholm, 1960-61 Mem. AAAS, Assn. Am. Physicians, Am. Soc. Clin. Investigation, Am. Soc. for Biochemistry and Molecular Biology, Am. Fedn. Med. Rsch., Am. Soc. Andrology (program and publs. com., exec. coun., 1977-79, v.p. 1979-80, pres. 1980-81, chmn. publ. com. 1990-93, Disting. Andrologist award 1991, Disting. Svc. award 1996), Internat. Soc. Andrology (sec. 1981-89, pres. 1989-93, newsletter publisher and editor 1989—), Endocrine Soc. (publ. com. 1984-90, chmn. 1987-90), N.Y. Acad. Scis., Ctrl. Soc. Clin. Rsch., Soc. Study of Reprodn., Japan Soc. Andrology (hon.), Japan Soc. for Fertility and Sterility (hon.). Office: U Pitts Med Ctr 3601 5th Ave Rm 580 Pittsburgh PA 15213-3403

TROESTER, DENNIS LEE, physical education educator; b. McCook, N.C., June 28, 1948; s. Carl Christopher and Maria Anna (Carolina) Troester. BA in Edn., Kearney State, 1971. Physical edn. educator Rep. Valley Schs., Indianola, Nebr., 1971—, athletic dir., 2001—. Recipient Women's Coach of Yr. award, State Farm Ins., 1998. Mem.: Nebr. Schs. Interscholastic Activities Athletic Assn., Nebr. Coaches Assn. (adv. com. volleyball 1996—, Nebr. volleyball coach of yr. award 1998), Nebr. Edn. Assn., Nat. Edn. Assn. Republican. Lutheran. Avocations: hunting, fishing. Home: RR1 Indianola NE 69034 Office: Republican Valley Schools Box 80 A Indianola NE 69034 Fax: 308-364-2508. E-mail: dtroeste@esu15.org.

TROESTER, WALTRAUD, artist, graphic designer, consultant; b. Wilhelmshaven, Germany, June 26, 1942; came to U.S., 1987; d. Johannes and Gertrud (Mueller) T. Diploma, Higher Comml. Sch., Opladen, Germany, 1961; student, U. Tex.-Pan Am., Edinburg, 1988-90; student of reflexology, 1997. Exec sec. Dresdner Bank AG, Lueckenhaus Co., Hermanns Co., others, Germany, 1961-86; multi-media artist including fine art, graphic design, lettering, McAllen, Tex., 1990—. Reflexologist, Mc Allen, Tex., 1997—. Exhibited in solo exhbns. at McAllen Internat. Mus., 1995, South Tex. Symphony Assn., McAllen, 1996, U. Tex.-PanAm, 1998; exhibited in numerous nat. and internat. juried exhbns.; works include X-ray series, hand-lettered portraits. Recipient Best of Show and Purchase awards. Mem. Internat. Inst. Reflexology, Phi Kappa Phi. Home: 304 Eagles Nest Dr Wimberley TX 78676

TROFFKIN, HOWARD JULIAN, lawyer, diversified company executive; b. Port Chester, N.Y., Jan. 30, 1937; s. Irving and Frieda Troffkin; m. Rhea Dorothy, May 12, 1963; children: Stephen, Barbara. BS in Chemistry, St. Lawrence U., 1959; postgrad., Columbia U., 1959-60; JD, Georgetown U., 1970. Bar: Va. 1971, D.C. 1972. Rsch. chemist Am. Cyanamid Co., 1961-66, legal trainee, 1966-67, patent agt., 1967-71; assoc. Pennie, Edmonds, Morton, Taylor & Adams, Washington, 1971-77; patent atty. W.R. Grace & Co., Columbia, Md., 1977-86, sr. patent counsel, 1987-98; pvt. practice, 1998—; sec., counsel Concrete Corrosive Adhibitor Trade Assn. Patentee in chemistry field. Mem. Willerburn Civic Assn., 1971-75. Served with AUS, 1960-61. Mem. ABA, Va. Bar Assn., D.C. Bar Assn., Washington Patent Lawyers Assn., Md. Patent Law Assn. (pres. 1981-83), Am. Intellectual Property Law Assn., Am. Chem. Soc., Concrete Corrosion Inhibitors Assn. (sec./counsel). Jewish. Avocations: woodcrafting, travel. Home and Office: 7808 Ivymount Ter Potomac MD 20854-3218 E-mail: Troffkin@aol.com.

TROFIMENKO, SWIATOSLAW, chemist, researcher, consultant; b. Lviv, Ukraine, Dec. 15, 1931; came to U.S., 1950; s. Clement and Lydia (Hopanchuk) T.; m. Martha M.A. Babych, Feb. 9, 1962; 1 child, Zoya Lidia. BA, Wesleyan U., Middletown, Conn., 1955; PhD, Northwestern U., Evanston, Ill., 1958; postgrad., Columbia U., 1959. Rsch. chemist Du Pont Co., Wilmington, Del., 1959-76, office dir. Warsaw, Poland, 1977-80, sr. rsch. assoc. Parkersburg, W.Va., 1980-85, Wilmington, 1986-96; vis. scholar U. Del., Newark, 1997—. Richard Merton vis. prof. Münster (Germany) U., 1973. Author: Scorpionates: The Coordination Chemistry of Polypyrazolylborate Ligands, 1999; contbr. over 130 articles to profl. jours.; patentee in field. Wilsmore fellow U. Melbourne, Australia, 1995. Avocations: etymology, linguistics, chess. Home: 515 Brentwood Dr Wilmington DE 19803-4309 Office: Dept Chemistry and Biochemistry U Del Newark DE 19716 E-mail: trofimenko@dol.net., trofimen@udel.edu.

TROJACK, JOHN EDWARD, lawyer; b. St. Paul, Mar. 30, 1946; s. Albert G. and Eleanor (Mader) T.; m. Mary Jo LaNasa, Oct. 12, 1979; 4 children. BA, U. Minn., 1968; JD, William Mitchell Coll. Law, St. Paul, 1976. Bar: Minn. 1976, U.S. Dist. Ct. Minn. 1976, U.S. Ct. Appeals (8th cir.) 1980, U.S. Supreme Ct. 1980. Assoc. John E. Daubney, St. Paul, 1976-78; ptnr. Wagner, Rutchick & Trojack, P.A., 1978-83; sole practice, 1983—. Conciliation Ct. referee Ramsey County Dist. Ct., St. Paul, 1979—; vol. atty. So. Minn. Legal Svcs. Corp., St. Paul, 1982—; arbitrator Hennepin County Dist. Ct., 1986—, Am. Arbitration Assn., 1988—. Served with USN, 1968-72, capt. USNR. Mem.: Naval Res. Assn., Ramsey County Bar Assn., Minn. Bar Assn., Nat. Network of Estate Planning Attys., The Harvesters Club, Phi Alpha Delta. Address: 1549 Livingston Ave Ste 101 Saint Paul MN 55118-3415 E-mail: jetlawoffice@aol.com.

TROLANDER, HARDY WILCOX, engineering executive, consultant; b. Chgo., June 2, 1921; s. Elmer Wilcox and Freda Marie (Zobel) T.; m. Imogen Davenport, July 3, 1946 (dec.); children: Megan, Patricia. BS in Engring., Antioch Coll., 1947. Instr. Antioch Coll., Yellow Springs, Ohio, 1947-48; co-founder, CEO Yellow Springs Instrument Co., Inc., 1948-86. Dir., co-founder Cook Design Ctr., Dartmouth Coll., Hanover, N.H., 1975-88; bd. dirs. Deban Inc., Yellow Springs, Camax Tool co., Arvada, Colo.; mem. evaluation panel Inst. Basic Stds., Nat. Bur. Stds., 1977-79. Contbr. articles to profl. jours.; patentee in field. Co-founder, trustee Yellow Springs Community Found., 1974-83; trustee Autioch Coll., 1968-74, chmn. bd., 1972-74; trustee Engring. and Sci. Found., Dayton, 1982-96, Engrs. Club Dayton Found., 1994—, Engring. and Sci. Hall of Fame, 1994—; mem. adv. bd. Coll. Engring. and Computer Sci. Wright State U., 1993—; bd. dirs. united Way Greater Dayton Area, 1984-92. 1st lt. USAF, 1943-46. Named Outstanding Engr., Dayton Affiliate Socs., 1967, 89. Fellow Dayton Engrs. Club, Am. Inst. for Med. and Biol. Engring.; mem. ACLU, Nat. Acad. Engring., Am. Inst. Biol. Scis. (bioinstrumentation adv. , coun. 1969-75), Internat. Orgn. of Legal Metrology (tech. advisor, sec. 1975-82), Amnesty Internat. Democrat. Home and Office: 1475 President St Yellow Springs OH 45387-1326

TROLLER, FRED, graphic designer, painter, visual consultant, educator; b. Zurich, Switzerland, Dec. 12, 1930; came to U.S., 1961; s. Albert and Katherina (Iseli) T.; m. Beatrice Stocklin, Nov. 22, 1952; children— Simon, Meret BA in Graphic Design, Kunstgewerbeschule, Zurich, 1950. Art dir. Geigy Corp., Ardsley, N.Y., 1961-66; pres. Fred Troller Assoc., Visual Communications Cons., Rye, 1966—; chmn., prof. design div. design Sch. Art and Design N.Y. State Coll. Ceramics at Alfred U., 1991—. Author and illustrator articles. Served to pvt. 1st class Inf. Swiss Army, 1949-60 Mem. Am. Inst. Graphic Arts, Alliance Graphique Internationale, Phi Kappa Phi (Alfred U. chpt.). Home and Office: Fred Troller Assocs 12 Harbor Ln Rye NY 10580-2213

TROMBLEY, EDWARD FRANCIS, III, educational administrator; b. Oneida, N.Y., Sept. 24, 1964; s. Edward F. Jr. and Sharonlee (Sterling) T. BA, SUNY, Oswego, 1986, MS, 1996. Cert. secondary English tchr., N.Y. Adj. instr. Bryant & Stratton Bus. Inst., Liverpool, N.Y., 1993-96, gen. studies dept. coord., 1996, evening and weekend coll. coord., 1996-98; homebound student tutor North Syracuse (N.Y.) Sch. Dist., 1994-96; assoc. dean instrn. Bryant & Stratton Bus. Inst., Liverpool, 1998-2000, dean adminstrn., 2000—01; registrar DeVry U., Arlington, Va., 2001—. Mem. adv. bd. East Syracuse-Minoa Sch. Dist., 1996-97; sch./bus. partnership Cicero-North Syracuse Sch. Dist., 1997; conf. del. Assn. Proprietary Colls., Cooperstown, N.Y., 1997, Saratoga, N.Y., 1998; media cons. Bryant and Stratton Bus. Inst., Liverpool, 1997. Mem. AACRAO, VACRAO, Ctrl. N.Y. Coalition Adult and Continuing Edn. (bd. mem., rec. sec. 2000-01), Trick of the Tail Club (rec. sec. 1995—). Office: DeVry Univ Crystal City Campus 2341 Jefferson Davis Hwy Arlington VA 22202

TROMBLEY, MICHAEL JEROME, lawyer; b. Bay City, Mich., Dec. 10, 1933; s. Clare F. and Sarah I. (Ingersol) T.; m. Anna K. Simons (div. 1963); children: Peter, Tad; m. Sandra V. Bybee (dec. 1980); children: Christine, Jacques; m. Sherry V. Cribbs, June 10, 1981. A.A., Menlo Coll., 1953; B.A., Stanford U., 1955; LL.B., U. Mo., 1960. Bar: Mo. 1960, Fla. 1974; bd. cert. elder law. Sole practice, Columbia, Mo., 1960-68; ptnr. Alexander, Wayland, Trombley, Butcher, Columbia, Mo., 1964-68; sole practice, 1969-79; ptnr. Trombley, Matheny & Schommer, Sebring, Fla., 1980-84, Trombley, Lobozzo, Schommer, Disler & Accorsi, Sebring, 1984— . Charter pres. Estate Planning Council of Highlands County, Fla., 1979-80. Served to 1st lt. USMCR, 1955-57. Mem. Am. Judicature Soc., Acad. Fla. Trial Lawyers, Nat. Acad. Elder Law Attys., Nat. Acad. Fla. Elder Law Attys. (past chmn. cert. com.). Republican. Episcopalian. Clubs: Masons, Shriners, Elks. Office: 329 S Commerce Ave Sebring FL 33870-3607

TRONE, JACQUELYN LEE, artist; b. York, Pa., Apr. 16, 1941; d. John and Bernice (Garvick) Trone; m. Thomas D. White; children from previous marriage: Theodore Trone Butera, John Andrew Butera. BA in Interior Design, Pa. State U., 1963. Antiques dealer Colonial Yard, Audubon, Pa., 1971-97. One-woman shows include Mus. Am. Folk Art, N.Y., Sturbridge Village Mus., Mass., Mercer (Pa.) Mus., Landis Valley Mus., Pa., Gallery Americana, Tex., Eldred Wheeler, Houston, exhibited in group shows at Am. Craftsmen, Wilton, Conn., Historic Waterfor Found., Va., Designer Craftsman, Pa., Williamsburg (Va.) Designer Show, 1989—96, Spring Colonial Yard, 1990—, Winter Colonial Yard, Pa., 1992—, Country Living Mag., 1995, 1996, 2001, Celebration Am. Artists, Downingtown, Pa., 1996—, The Highlands, Blue Bell, Pa., 1997, Home and Garden TV Network "Country at Home" series, 1997—98, Wilmington Hist. Soc. Show, 1999, Winatheur Mus. Art Show, 2001, pvt. permanent collections; contbr. articles to profl. jours. Pres. Audubon Women's Club, 1978; active Lower Providence Twp. Libr. Named one of 200 Best Traditional Craftsmen, Early Am. Life Mag., 1989—. Mem.: Nat. Assn. Artisans and Craftsmen (bd. dirs. 1991—98), Herb Gatherers (com. head 1990—94). Avocations: herb gardening, gourmet cooking, antiques, antique dolls, garden design. Home: 500 S Park Ave Audubon PA 19403-1921

TRONOLONE, TRACEY ANN, social worker; b. N.Y.C., June 25, 1964; d. John A. and Claire C. (Coleman) T. BA, George Washington U., 1987; MSW, Hunter Coll., 1992. Cert. sch. social worker, N.J.; cert. social worker, N.Y.; lic. social worker, N.J. Social worker Luth. Cmty. Svcs., N.Y.C., 1987-88, Children's Aid Soc., N.Y.C., 1988-92, Legal Aid Soc., Bklyn., 1992-93; foster care supr. St. Joseph Svcs. for Children & Families, 1993-96; asst. dir. Battered Women's Shelter Henry St. Settlement, N.Y.C., 1996-97; supr. Graham Windham Svcs., 1997-98; dir. social work Children's Law Ctr., 1998—. Vol. sister Vols. in Protective Svcs., Hackensack, N.J., 1988—. Office: The Children's Law Ctr 1 Boerum Pl Brooklyn NY 11201-5101

TROOP, PAUL MELVIN, public relations executive, journalist; b. Jersey City, May 13, 1942; s. Bernard Lazarus and Ruth (Weiss) T.; m. Maxine Rubin, Dec. 6, 1970; 1 child, Wendy. BA, U. State of N.Y., 1980. Reporter L.I. Press, Jamaica, N.Y., 1965-66; political editor Suffolk Sun, Deer Park, 1966-67; asst. news dir. L.I. Network News, Freeport, 1967; asst. editor Am. Sch. & U., N.Y.C., 1967-68; acct. exec. Ruder & Finn, 1967-70; mng. editor L.I. Comml. Rev., Syosset, N.Y., 1970; bus. writer Atlanta Jour.-Constn., 1970-78; pres. Fin. Comm. Co., Atlanta, 1978—. Cpl. NJNG, 1965-71. Newspaper Fund scholar, 1961, Banking Sch. of the South fellow, 1975. Office: Fin Comm PO Box 29243 Atlanta GA 30359-0243

TROOST, BRADLEY TODD, neurologist, educator; b. Mankato, Minn., July 5, 1937; s. Henry Bradley and Elizabeth (Todd) T.; m. Elizabeth Gail Godet, Apr. 17, 1976; children: Elizabeth Claire, Laurie Anne. BS with honors in Biophysics, Yale U., 1959; MD, Harvard U., 1963. Diplomate Am. Bd. Psychiatry and Neurology. Intern, Colo. Gen. Hosp., Denver, 1963-64; resident in neurology U. Colo., Denver, 1966-69; NIH fellow in neuro-ophthalmology U. Calif.-San Francisco, 1969-70; asst. prof. U. Miami (Fla.), 1970-76; assoc. prof. U. Pitts., 1976-80; prof. Case Western Res. U., Cleve., 1980-83; prof., chmn. dept. neurology Wake Forest U. Sch. Medicine, Winston-Salem, N.C., 1983—; chief dept. neurology VA med. ctrs., Pitts., Cleve. Bd. dirs. Greater Miami Epilepsy Found., 1973-76. Served to capt. U.S. Army, 1964-66. Fellow Am. Acad. Neurology; mem. Am. Neurol. Assn., Am. Assn. Univ. Profs. Neurology (pres.-elect), Barany Soc. Republican. Episcopalian. Contbr. numerous articles to profl. publs.

TROPEZ-SIMS, SUSANNE, pediatrician, educator; b. New Orleans, Apr. 13, 1949; d. Maxwell Sterling and Ethel (Ross) Tropez; m. James Carnell White, Apr. 10, 1971 (div. 1992); children: Lisa, Janifer, James Carnell; m. Michael Milroy Sims, Feb. 18, 1995. BS, Bennett Coll., 1971; MD, U. N.C., 1975, MPH, 1982. Diplomate Am. Bd. Pediatrics. Resident in pediatrics N.C. Meml. Hosp., Chapel Hill, 1975-76, 77-79; pediatrician Darnell Army Hosp., Ft. Hood, Tex., 1976-77; acting dir. pediat. day clinic Wake County Med. Ctr., Raleigh, N.C., 1979-82, dir. pediat. day clinic, 1980-88; dir. pediatric day clinic, asst. prof. U. N.C., Chapel Hill, 1982-88; asst. prof. pediats. La. State U., New Orleans, 1982-88; prof. pediats. U. N.C., Chapel Hill, 1982-88; assoc. prof. pediats. La. State U. Med. Ctr., New Orleans, 1988-97; dir. divsn. pediat. emergency rm. La. State U., New Orleans, 1988-89, chief divsn. ambulatory care, 1989-92; chmn. dept. pediat. Meharry Med. Coll., Nashville, 1997—. Clin. dir. maternal and child health units New Orleans Health Dept., 1992-97, chief divsn. cmty. pediatrics and adolescent medicine, 1992-97; pediatrician Shelly Child Devel. Ctr., Raleigh, 1981-88, child med. examiner program, 1979-88; chair sch. health com. local chpt. AAP, 1993-96; mem. Nat. Com. Sch. Health, 1992-99; chair Meharry Med. Service Found., 2001—. Contbr. articles to profl. jours. Adminstrv. bd. chair Cornerstone U.M.C., 1993-96, chair edn. com., 1991-92; mem. United Meth. Women, Walnut Terr. Child Devel. Ctr., Raleigh, 1981-83, chmn., 1982-83; chmn. pastor parish com. Longview Ch., Raleigh, 1982-84, 87-88, chmn. membership care com.; chair Nat. Edn. Assn.-Health Info. Network Bd., 2000-2002, chair of bd. of trustee, Clark U.M.C., 2002—. Fellow preventive medicine, 1979-82, Faculty Devel. fellow U. N.C. Sch. Medicine, 1985-87. Fellow Am. Acad. Pediatrics (mem. sch. health com.); mem. N.C. Pediatric Soc. (com. child abuse and neglect, adolescent pregnancy), La. Pediatric Soc., Ambulatory Pediatric Assn., Adolescent Pregnancy Coalition United Way, Bennett Coll. Alumnae Assn. Democrat. E-mail: stsims@mmc.edu.

TROPIANO, JOANN ALMA, librarian, library director; b. Bridgeton, N.J., Mar. 7, 1947; d. Herbert Robert and Estenna Dolores (Bell) Gould; m. Robert Lee Carney, June 24, 1970 (div. 1981); children: Robert Christian, Jacqueline Estenna; m. Anthony Tropiano, Jr., May 28, 1990 (dec. Jan. 1995). BA, Glassboro State Coll., 1970; MLS, Rutgers U., 1981. Cert. profl. libr., permanent tchr., ednl. media specialist, N.J. Elem. sch. libr. Nutley (N.J.) Pub. Schs., 1970-77, high sch. libr., 1977—2001; dir. Nutley Free Pub. Libr., 1996—, trustee, 1987-96. Mem. Nutley Mcpl. Alliance, 1997. Recipient Outstanding Educator award Nutley Jaycees, 1995. Mem. ALA, N.J. Edn. Assn., Essex County Edn. Assn., Edn. Assn. Nutley, rep., sec. 1970-72), Rutgers-Sch. Comm. Info. and Libr. Svcs. Alumni Assn., N.J. Libr. Assn., Essex County Libr. Dirs. Assn., Nutley Rotary Club, LWV (webmaster Nutley area). Democrat. Episcopalian. Avocations: travel, reading. Office: Nutley Free Pub Libr 93 Booth Dr Nutley NJ 07110-2706

TROSCLAIR, KATTINA T. graphics designer; b. New Iberia, La., Feb. 19, 1973; d. Melvin Anthony Trosclair, Sr. and Theresa Ann (Schouest) Trosclair; 1 child Jeremiah Paul Gachassin. Student, So. Tech. Coll., Lafayette, La., 1991—92. Libr. clk. St. Mary Parish Libr., Franklin, La., 1989—90; owner, operator Iberia Desktop Publ., New Iberia, 1992—93; ad designer Key West (Fla.) Citizen, 1995; graphics cons. Minuteman Press of South La., Houma, La., 1999; v.p. Blueline Arts, Franklin, 2000—. Author: poems; contbr. articles magazine; editor: (newsletter) The Chatter Bug, 1994; contbr. articles newspaper, magazine. Participant 4-H Alumni, Franklin, 1987—90; vol. Sager-Brown Ctr., Baldwin, 1993—97. Non-Denominational Christian. Avocations: art, music, service to people. Home: 1358 La Hwy 319 Franklin LA

70538-7706 Office: Blueline Arts 1362 La Hwy 319 Franklin LA 70538-7706 Home Fax: 337-867-4102; Office Fax: 337-867-4102. Personal E-mail: tiarafalls@hotmail.com. Business E-Mail: service@blueline-arts.com.

TROSPER, ORVILLE WENDELL, education educator; b. Corbin, Ky., Oct. 18, 1918; s. William E. and Zora B. Trosper. Student, Berea Coll., 1938-40; BA, U. Ky., 1942; postgrad., Cin. Conservatory, 1948, Marseille Conservatory, France, 1946, Nice Conservatory, 1946; M.Mus., VanderCook Coll. Music, 1953; MA, Columbia U., 1958, EdD, 1962; postgrad., Northwestern U., 1965-70, Cin. Conservatory, Marshall U., Marseille Conservatory, France, Nice Conservatory. Tchr. music Harlan County (Ky.) Schs., 1946-48; band dir., tchr. history Huntington (W.Va.)-Cabell County Schs., 1948-55; band dir., instrumental and gen. music tchr. Croton-on-Hudson (N.Y.) Sch., 1955-64; assoc. prof. music Berea Coll., 1964-66, VanderCook Coll. Music, Chgo., 1966—, chmn. dept. edn., 1967-74. Owner, pres. Trosper Ednl. Cons., Chgo., 1968-74; ret. agt. FBI. Author: The Principles and Practice of Producing Vibrato in Brass Instruments. Deacon, 1st Bapt. Ch., Ossining, N.Y., 1963-64. With USAAF, 1942-46, ETO. Mem. AAUP, NEA, VFW, MEA, Coll. Band Dirs. Assn., Masons (32 deg., 50 Yr. Membership 1998), Am. Legion, Shriners, Phi Mu Alpha, Kappa Delta Pi, Phi Delta Kappa, Alpha Sigma Phi. Home: Hillcrest Nursing Home American Greeting Card Rd PO Box 556 Corbin KY 40702-0556

TROST, BARRY MARTIN, chemist, educator; b. Phila., June 13, 1941; s. Joseph and Esther T.; m. Susan Paula Shapiro, Nov. 25, 1967; children: Aaron David, Carey Daniel. BA cum laude, U. Pa., 1962; PhD, MIT, 1965; D (hon.), U. Claude Bernard, Lyons, France, 1994, Technion, Israel, 1997. Mem. faculty U. Wis., Madison, 1965—, prof., chemistry, 1969—, Evan P. and Marion Helfaer prof. chemistry, from 1976, Vilas rsch. prof. chemistry; prof. chemistry Stanford U., 1987—, Tamaki prof. humanities and scis., 1990, chmn. dept., 1996—. Cons. Merck, Sharp & Dohme, E.I. duPont de Nemours.; Chem. Soc. centenary lectr., 1982 Author: Problems in Spectroscopy, 1967, Sulfur Ylides, 1975; editor-in-chief Comprehensive Organic Synthesis, 1991—, ChemTracts/Organic Chemistry, 1993—; editor: Structure and Reactivity Concepts in Organic Chemistry series, 1972—; assoc. editor Jour. Am. Chem. Soc., 1974-80; mem. editl. bd. Organic Reactions Series, 1971—, Chemistry A European Jour., 1995—, Sci. of Synthesis, Houben-Weyl Methods of Molecular Transformations, 1995—; contbr. numerous articles to profl. jours. Named Chem. Pioneer, Am. Inst. Chemists, 1983; recipient Dreyfus Found. Tech.-Scholar award, 1970, 1977, Creative Work in Synthetic Organic Chemistry award, 1981, Baekland medal, 1981, Alexander von Humboldt award, 1984, Guenther award, 1990, Janssen prize, 1990, Roger Adams award, Am. Chem. Soc., 1995, Presdl. Green Univ. Challenge award, 1998, Nicholas medal, 2000, Yamada prize, 2001, Yamada Prize, 2001, ACS Nobel Laureate Signature award, Graduate Ed. Chemistry, 2002; fellow, NSF, 1963—65, Sloan Found., 1967—69, Am. Swiss Found., 1975—, Zencca, 1997; scholar Cope scholar, 1989. Mem.: NAS, AAAS, Chem. Soc. London, Am. Acad. Arts and Scis., Am. Chem. Soc. (award in pure chemistry 1977, Roger Adams award 1995, Herbert C. Brown award for creative rsch. in synthetic methods 1999, Nobel Laureate Signature award for grad. edn. in chemistry 2002). Office: Stanford U Dept Chemistry Stanford CA 94305

TROST, CARLISLE ALBERT HERMAN, retired naval officer; b. Valmeyer, Ill., Apr. 24, 1930; s. Elmer Herman and Luella Caroline (Hoffman) T.; m. Pauline Louise Haley, May 1, 1954; children— Carl, Laura Lee, Steven, Kathleen. Student, Washington U., St. Louis, 1948-49; BS, U.S. Naval Acad., 1953; Olmsted scholar, U. Freiburg, W. Ger., 1960-62. Commd. ensign U.S. Navy, 1953, advanced through grades to adm., 1985; exec. officer U.S.S. Scorpion, 1962-63, U.S.S. Von Steuben, 1963-65; mil. asst. to Dep. Sec. Def., 1965-68; comdg. officer U.S.S. Sam Rayburn, 1968-69; staff Comdr. Sub Force Atlantic, 1969-70; exec. asst. to Sec. Navy, 1970-73; comdr. Submarine Group Five, 1973-74; asst. chief Bur. Naval Personnel, 1974-76; dir. systems analysis div. Office Chief Naval Ops., Washington, 1976-78; dep. comdr.-in-chief U.S. Pacific Fleet, 1978-80; comdr. U.S. Seventh Fleet, 1980-81; dir. Navy program planning Office Chief Naval Ops., 1981-85; comdr.-in-chief U.S. Atlantic Fleet, 1985-86, chief naval ops., 1986-90. Bd. dirs. Lockheed Martin Corp., Gen. Pub. Utility Corp., GPU Nuclear Corp., Bird-Johnson Co., Gen. Dynamics Corp., Precision Components Corp. Trustee U.S. Naval Acad. Found. Decorated Def. D.S.M. with cluster, Navy D.S.M. with 2 clusters, Army D.S.M., Air Force D.S.M., Legion of Merit with 2 oak leaf clusters, Navy Achievement medal, Def. Disting. Svc. medal; named Outstanding Young Man of Am. Nat. Jr. C. of C., 1964 Mem. U.S. Naval Inst., U.S. Naval Alumni Assn. Episcopalian. Home: 11 Compromise St Annapolis MD 21401-1806

TROST, EILEEN BANNON, lawyer; b. Teaneck, N.J., Jan. 9, 1951; d. William Eugene and Marie Thelma (Finlayson) Bannon; m. Lawrence Peter Trost Jr., Aug. 27, 1977; children: Lawrence Peter III, William Patrick, Timothy Alexander. BA with great distinction, Shimer Coll., 1972; JD cum laude, U. Minn., 1976. Bar: Ill. 1976, U.S. Dist. Ct. (no. dist.) Ill. 1976, Minn. 1978, U.S. Tax Ct. 1978, U.S. Supreme Ct. 1981. Assoc. McDermott, Will & Emery, Chgo., 1976-82, ptnr., 1982-93; v.p. No. Trust Bank Ariz. N.A., Phoenix, 1993-95; ptnr. Sonnenschein Nath & Rosenthal, Chgo., 1995—. Mem. Am. Coll. Trust and Estate Coun., Minn. Bar Assn., Internat. Acad. Estate and Trust Law, Chgo. Estate Planning Coun. Roman Catholic. Office: Sonnenschein Nath & Rosenthal 8000 Sears Tower Chicago IL 60606 E-mail: etrost@sonnenschein.com.

TROST, LOUIS FREDERICK, JR. banker, financial planner; b. Kansas City, Mo., Dec. 11, 1926; s. Louis Frederick and Roberta Ford (Broadus) T.; m. Ann Horner Tillma, Mar. 23, 1951 (div. Oct. 1978); children: Louis Frederick III, Scott Tillma; m. Charlotte Granville Graham, Nov. 15, 1984. BBA, U. Okla., 1951; postgrad., grad. Bell Sys. Execs. program, Northwestern U. , 1960; grad., Sch. Banking of South, Baton Rouge, 1968, Coll. Fin. Planning, Denver, 1979. Cert. fin. planner. Divsn. mgr. South Western Bell Tel. Co., Oklahoma City, 1951-64; sr. v.p. Liberty Nat. Bank & Trust Co., 1964-91; pres., CEO, Lincoln Nat. Bank, 1991-95, vice chmn., 1995—, also bd. dirs. Bd. dirs. Fed. Home Loan Bank, Topeka, 1995-2001; advisor Bapt. Found. Okla., Oklahoma City, 1994—; bd. rep., mem. exec. com. Coun. Fed. Home Loan Banks, Washington, 1998—; mem. gov.'s Cmty. Devel. Capital Formation Task Force, 1998—. Pres. Travelers Aid, Oklahoma City, 1962; treas. Okla. Symphony Orch., 1983-87; pres., bd. dirs. Mental Health Assn., Oklahoma City, 1996; mem. Gov.'s Cmty. Devel. Capital Formation Task Force, 1998—. Master sgt. U.S. Army, 1945-46, PTO. Named Outstanding Young Man in Oklahoma City, Oklahoma City Jaycees, 1960; named Ky. Col., Gov. of Ky., 1970; recipient letter of commendation Mental Health Assn., 1996. Mem. Am. Bankers Assn., Ind. Bankers Assn. Am., Okla. Bankers Assn. (sr. mgmt. com. 1995—), Oklahoma City Golf and Country Club (bd. dirs. 1989-91), Petroleum Club Oklahoma City (v.p., treas., bd. dirs. 1979-81), The Assocs. (U. Okla.), Faculty Club, Masons, Scottish Rite, Shriners, Royal Order Jesters, Kiwanis (past pres. Oklahoma City), Phi Gamma Delta (treas., bd. dirs. Ednl. Found. 1989-97, Wall of Fame award 1997). Baptist. Avocations: gardening, reading, travel. Home: 1601 Queenstown Rd Oklahoma City OK 73116-5522 Office: Lincoln Nat Bank 1111 N Lincoln Blvd Oklahoma City OK 73104-2897

TROTT, DENNIS C(HARLES), lawyer; b. Ft. Wayne, Ind., Oct. 31, 1946; s. Charles and Eileen (Collins) T.; m. Nancy J. Servis, Aug. 4, 1973; children: Eileen Susanne, Duncan Eric. AB, Ind. U., 1968; JD, U. Mich., 1973. Bar: N.Y. 1974, U.S. Dist. Ct. (so. dist.) N.Y. 1974, U.S. Ct. Appeals (2d cir.) 1974, U.S. Dist. Ct. (ea. dist.) N.Y. 1978, U.S. Ct. Mil. Appeals 1985, U.S. Ct. Internat. Trade 1986, U.S. Tax Ct. 1986, U.S. Supreme Ct. 1986, U.S. Ct. Claims 1988, U.S. Ct. Appeals (fed. cir.) 1990, U.S. Ct. Appeals (3rd and 6th cirs.) 1991. Assoc. Haight, Gardner, N.Y.C., 1973-75, Breed, Abbott, N.Y.C., 1975-77; pres., chief exec. officer Luke Enterprises, Inc., 1988—; ptnr. Trott & Appel, 1989-91; pvt. practice, 1991—. Bd. dirs. Neighborhood Housing Services of N.Y.C., 1985-89. Served with U.S. Army, 1968-70. Mem. N.Y. County Lawyers Assn. Home: 304 Sherman St Brooklyn NY 11218-1507 Office: 305 Broadway Ste 700 New York NY 10007-1109

TROTT, EDWARD ASHLEY, reproductive endocrinologist; b. Apr. 6, 1961; s. Edward Wilbur and Patricia Dorothy (White) T.; m. Andrea Marie Steede, June 21, 1986; children: Kiley Edward, Kory Ashley. BS with honors, U. Calif., 1983; MD, Jefferson Med. Coll., 1990. Diplomate Nat. Bd. Med. Examiners. Intern Hahnemann U. Hosp., Phila., 1990—91; resident Med. Ctr. of Del., Newark, 1991—94; fellow, instr. Med. Coll. of Ga., Augusta, 1994—96; dir. Del. Inst. for Reproductive Medicine, Newark, 1996—2000; assoc. dir. clin. R&D, Wyeth Rsch., Radnor, Pa., 2000—. Cons. Univ. Hosp., Augusta, 1994-96; ad hoc reviewer Fertility and Sterility, Rochester, 1996; surg. skills instr. Med. Coll. of Ga., 1994-96. Author: Handbook for Primary Care in Ob/Gyn., 1996; contbr. articles to profl. jours. Recipient Tap Pharms. Resident award Tap Pharms., 1992. Mem. AMA, ACS, Nat. Med. Assn., Med. Assn. of Ga., Am. Soc. of Reproductive Medicine, Phi Beta Sigma, Phi Zeta Kappa. Methodist. Avocations: soccer, fishing, kite flying. Office: 500 Arcola Rd Collegeville PA 19426 E-mail: trotte@wyeth.com.

TROTT, JUSTINA A. physician, medical association administrator, internist, medical educator; b. Bridgeport, Conn., Jan. 22, 1948; d. Dominick and Irene Trott; 1 child, Arianna. BA, N.Y. U., 1970; MD, Med. Coll. Pa., 1974. Cert. med. doctor. Dir. Women's Health Svcs. Family Care & Counseling Ctr., Santa Fe. Dir. Santa Fe Nat. Cmty. Ctr. of Excellence in Women's Health. Mem. Am. Coll. Physicians, Am. Coll. Women's Health Physicians (bd. dirs. 1999—, pres. 2001—). Avocations: music, hiking, traveling, cooking. Home: 7506B Old Santa Fe Trl Santa Fe NM 87505-9358

TROTT, SABERT SCOTT, II, marketing professional, consultant; b. Concord, N.C., Nov. 21, 1941; s. Sabert Scott and Mary Welker (Crooks) T.; m. Brenda Lee Bost, Nov. 27, 1964; children— Sabert Scott III, David Lee BS in Textile Tech., N.C. State U., 1964; MBA, U. N.C., 1969. Mgr. trainee Cannon Mills Co., Kannapolis, N.C., 1969-70, mktg. mgr., 1970-75, v.p. mktg., 1975-82, sr. v.p. mktg., 1982-86, dir. telemktg. and premium sales, 1987-89; mgr. spl. markets, mktg. & sales Fieldcrest Cannon Inc., mktg. mgr., telemarketing sales mgr., 1989-92; v.p. mktg. and sales Spencer's Inc., Mt. Airy, N.C., 1992-93; v.p. mktg. Carpenter Co., Richmond, Va., 1994—. Chmn. Cabarrus-Rowan Parks and Recreation Commn., N.C., 1982-86; mem. Cabarrus County Parks and Recreation Commn., N.C., 1980-88; Rep. candidate County Commr., Cabarrus County, 1990; bd. dirs. Cabarrus Meml. Hosp., 1992, N.C. Ctr. for Applied Textile Tech.; vestryman local Episcopal ch., 1988-93. Capt. U.S. Army, 1965-70. Decorated Commendation medal (2) Mem.: Rotary. Republican. Avocations: canoeing; rafting; golf; basketball; racquetball. Home: 2607 Helmsley Ct Midlothian VA 23113-6497 Office: Carpenter Co 5016 Monument Ave Richmond VA 23230-3620 E-mail: sstrott@mciworld.com.net.

TROTT, STEPHEN SPANGLER, federal judge, musician; b. Glen Ridge, N.J., Dec. 12, 1939; s. David Herman and Virginia (Spangler) Trott; m. Carol C. Trott; children: Christina, Shelley. BA, Wesleyan U., 1962; LLB, Harvard U., 1965; LLD (hon.) , Santa Clara U., 1992; LLD (hon.), U. Idaho, 2001. Bar: Calif. 1966, U.S. Dist. Ct. (cen. dist.) Calif. 1966, U.S. Ct. Appeals (9th cir.) 1983, U.S. Supreme Ct. 1984. Guitarist, mem. The Highwaymen, 1958—; dep. dist. atty. L.A. County Dist. Atty.'s Office, L.A., 1966—75, chief dep. dist. atty., 1975—79; U.S. dist. atty. Central Dist. Calif., 1981—83; asst. atty. gen. criminal divsn. Dept. Justice, Washington, 1983—86; faculty Nat. Coll. Dist. Attys., Houston, 1973—; chmn. central dist. Calif. Law Enforcement Coord. Com., 1981—83; coord. L.A.-Nev. Drug Enforcement Task Force, 1982—83; assoc. atty. gen. Justice Dept., Washington, 1986—88; chmn. U.S. Interpol, 1986—88; judge U.S. Ct. of Appeals (9th cir.), Boise, Idaho, 1988—. Trustee Wesleyan U., 1984—87; adv. council Big Brothers, Big Sisters S.W. Idaho, 2001—; bd. dirs., pres. Children's Home Soc., Idaho, 1990—; bd. dirs. Boise Philharm. Assn., 1995—, v.p., 1997—99, pres., 1999—. Recipient Gold record as singer-guitarist for Michael Row the Boat Ashore, 1961, Disting. Faculty award, Nat. Coll. Dist. Attys., 1977. Mem.: Am. Coll. Trial Lawyers, Idaho Classic Guitar Soc. (founder, pres. 1989—), Internat. Brotherhood Magicians, Magic Castle, Idaho Racing Pigeon Assn., Brentwood Racing Pigeon Club (pres. 1977—82), Wilderness Fly Fishers Club (pres. 1975—77). Republican. Office: US Ct Appeals 9th Cir 667 US Courthouse 550 W Fort St Boise ID 83724-0101

TROTT, WILLIAM MACNIDER, lawyer; b. Raleigh, N.C., July 30, 1946; s. Graham Foard and Cornelia (McKimmon) T.; m. Holly Wooten, Oct. 17, 1970 (div.); children: Hollister Wooten, James McKimmon; m. Jean Little, Aug. 11, 1984; children: Elizabeth Yost, William MacNider. AB, U. N.C., 1968, JD, 1971; LLM with highest honors, George Washington U., 1971. Bar: N.C. 1971, U.S. Dist. Ct. (ea., mid. and we. dists.) N.C. 1975, U.S. Supreme Ct. 1975. Assoc. Young, Moore and Henderson, Raleigh, 1975-78; ptnr., mem. Young, Moore & Henderson, 1978—. Mem. N.C. Law Rev., 1969-71; lectr., author N.C. Bar Assn., 1984, 85, 87, Am. Law Firm Assn., 1999, 2000, Lorman Ednl. Svcs., 2000, 2001. Pres. Capital Area Soccer League, Raleigh, 1984-85; bd. dirs. N.C. Tennis Assn., Greensboro, 1987-94, N.C. Tennis Found., 1994—, v.p. ; mem. Wake County Pks. and Recreation Commn., Raleigh, 1988-97, vice chmn., then chmn.; mem. sch. health adv. commn. Wake County Bd. Edn., 1997-99; sec., v.p. Raleigh Tennis Found., 1996—. Lt. JAGC, USNR, 1971-75. Morehead scholar U. N.C., 1964-68, Wettach scholar U. N.C. Law Sch., 1968-71; state tennis age group doubles champion, 1963, 64, 98. Mem. ABA, N.C. Bar Assn., Wake County Bar Assn., Execs. Club, Carolina Country Club (bd. dirs. 2001--). Episcopalian. Office: Young Moore & Henderson PO Box 31627 Raleigh NC 27622-1627

TROTTA, FRANK P., JR. lawyer; BA, SUNY, Albany; JD, Union U., Albany; LLM, NYU; MBA, Columbia U. Bar: N.Y. U.S. Dist. Ct. (no. and we. dists.) N.Y., U.S. Ct. Mil. Appeals, U.S. Dist. Ct. (so. and ea. dists.) N.Y., U.S. Ct. Internat. Trade, U.S. Tax Ct., U.S. Supreme Ct., U.S. Ct. Appeals (D.C. cir.), U.S. Ct. Customs and Patent Appeals, D.C., Conn., Pa. Assoc. Weil, Gotshal & Manges, N.Y.C.; pvt. practice Washington, N.Y.C., New Rochelle, Greenwich, Conn. Former mem. bd. govs. Fund for Justice and Edn., ABA; mem. faculty Practicing Law Inst.; governing mem. Nat. Jud. Coll., Am. Bar Endowment, ABRA Pension Fund; chmn. bd. advisors Columbia U. Grad. Sch. Bus., Inst. for Non-for-Profit Mgmt. Chmn. New Rochelle Rep. Party; mem., bd. dirs. Boys Town of Italy.

TROTTA, MARCIA MARIE, librarian, consultant, education educator; b. Meriden, Conn., Nov. 12, 1949; d. Salvatore Dominic and Teresa Stella (Fuda) Marando; m. Carmine Joseph Trotta, Oct. 23, 1971; 1 child, Christopher Michael. AB, Albertus Magnus Coll., 1971; MLS, So. Conn. State U., 1979. Tchr. St. Mary's Sch., Meriden, 1971-73; circulation libr. Meriden Pub. Libr., 1973-74, asst. children's libr., 1974-76, reference libr., 1976-81, dir. children's libr., 1981-91, asst. dir., 1992—, dir., 1994—. Adj. prof. So. Conn. State U., New Haven, 1987—, Albertus Magnus Coll., 1996—; cons. Pfizer Metall. Libr., Wallingford, Conn., 1987, Woodbridge Town Libr., 1987-89, Conn. Assocs. for Counseling, Wilton, 1988—. Author: (books) Managing Outreach Programs, 1992, Successful Staff Development, 1995, Special Events Program, 1997; editor: CDA Manual, Outreach Services for Children and Youth, 1992, Librarian's Facilities Management Handbook, 2000. Mem. coun. Day Care Adv. Com. Meriden, 1990-95, coun. Student Drug and Alcohol Abuse Prevention, Meriden, 1990-94; pres. Conn. Jaycee Women, 1984-85. Named one of Outstanding Women of Am., U.S. Jaycees Women, 1983; Outstanding Alumna Nat. Cath. Edn. Assn., 1997; Paul Harris fellow Rotary, 1997; recipient Steve Little award, 1986, YWCA Outstanding Profl. Woman award, 1995, Greater Meriden C. of C. Cmty. Partnership award, 1996, Faith Hecktoen award, Conn. Libr. Assn. Mem. ALA, Conn. Libr. Assn. (pres. 1991-92, Outstanding Libr. 1986, 93), New Eng. Libr. Assn., Rotary Internat. (Rotarian of Yr. 1994, Disting. Svc. award 1998, pres. Meriden Rotary 2000-01). Democrat. Roman Catholic. Avocations: writing, gourmet cooking, puppetry, children's book collector. Home: 28 Goff St Meriden CT 06451-2838 Office: Meriden Pub Libr 105 Miller St Meriden CT 06450-4213

TROTTA, RIC CHARLES, aerospace company executive, consultant; b. N.Y.C., Mar. 7, 1942; s. Sigmund Robert and Anita Delores (La Penna) T.; m. Carolyn Carey Bealle Trotta, May 29, 1965; children: Bradley Charles, Ric Charles Jr., Lauren Carey. Student in elec. engring., U. Va., 1959-62; BA in Physics, NYU, 1966; MBA in Mktg., Hofstra U., 1977; postgrad., Carnegie Mellon U., 1987. Engr. Grumman Aerospace Corp., Bethpage, N.Y., 1966-68, asst. to v.p., 1968-70, advanced programs mgr., 1970-78, mgr. advanced planning, 1978-81, asst. dir. advanced systems, 1981-83; dir. corp. ind., rsch. and devel. Grumman Corp., 1983-86, dir. corp. devel. and resources, 1986-94; pres. Trotta Assocs., Cons. to Govt. and Industry, 1994—. Sr. player global war games U.S. Naval War Coll., Newport, RI, 1985—; mem. resources working group Fed. Emergency Mgmt. Agy., Washington, 1991—; vice-chair nat. adv. coun. Fed. Lab. Consortium, 1999—, vice chmn., 2000, chmn., 01. Author: Industry Independent Rsch. and Devel. Study, 1996, Assessing the Impact of Regulatory and Legislative Changes to the DOD Independent Research and Developement Program, 1997, Maritime Industry Definition and Structure- A Workbook for Assessing Organization Capabilities Versus Industry Needs, 1997; Contbg. author: Public Control of Medical Care, 1978, National Security Assessment of the U.S. Maritime INdustry Surveys: Building and Repairing of Ships, Boats and other Marine Platforms, Maritime Research Development and Education, 2000, Nat. Security Assesment of Shipbldg. and Repair Ind., 2001. Bd. dirs. Community Sch., Centerport, N.Y., 1985; com. on sch. utilization Harborfield Sch. Dist., Greenlawn, N.Y., 1984. Recipient Community Svc. award Town of Huntington, N.Y., 1985. Mem. Nat. Security Indsl. Assn., Electronic Industries Assn., Mine Warfare Assn. (bd. dirs. 1997), Assn. Nat. Def. and Emergency Resources, Sigma Nu (historian 1961). Avocations: fishing, tennis, sailing, cooking. Home and Office: 21 Little Bull Ct Centerport NY 11721-1450 E-mail: RTrotta@TrottaAssociates.com., RicTrotta@aol.com.

TROTTA, VINCENT JOHN, transportation executive; b. Huntingdon, Pa., May 7, 1965; s. Vincent Paul and Mary Jane (Stanko) T.; m. Melanie Dawn Wood, June 15, 1991. BS, W.Va. U., 1987. Elec. engr. GE Transp. Systems, Erie, Pa., 1987-91, program mgr., 1991-93, mgr. sales/svc., 1993-96; pres., dir. GE Lokomotif Indonesia, Jakarta, Indonesia, 1997; gen. mgr. GE Transp. Systems, Belo Horizonte, Brazil, 1998-2000; master black belt GE Aircraft Engines, Cin., 2000-2001, gen. mgr. global accessories sales, 2001—. Avocations: travel, golf. Office: 1 Neumann Way Cincinnati OH 45215-1915 E-mail: vincent.trotta@ae.ge.com.

TROTTER, GWENDOLYN DIANE NELSON, choral and vocal educator, music publisher; b. Little Rock, Nov. 13, 1950; d. Milton Donaghey and Dora Elizabeth (Gillespie) N. BBA, U. Ark., 1972; MBA, Calif. State U., Dominguez Hills, 1979, postgrad. in voice/piano, 1980-81; postgrad. in audio recording, Calif. State U., Dominquez Hills, 1993-96; postgrad. in acctg., UCLA, 1973-84. Adminstrv. asst. Ark. Plan, Inc., Little Rock, 1969-73; acct. Hughes Aircraft Co., L.A., 1973-80, ops. auditor, 1986-90, property mgmt. specialist, 1990-93; dir. music dept. Baldwin Hills Baptist Ch., 1979-94; choral, vocal instr. Crossroads Acad. Arts and Sci., 1994-97; with By Faith Cons. & Pub., Inglewood, Calif., 1997—; music specialist L.A. Unified Sch. Dist., 1996—. Auditor Baldwin Hills Baptist Ch., 1983-96; cons. LAUSO Saturday Fine Arts Conservatory, 1995-97; Internet mktg. cons.; moderator for Urban Black Gospel E-mail Discussion List. Author music: (Christian mus. drama) Wings Like Eagles, 1988, mus. dir., L.A., 1988-89; playwright: Dissin' Your Body, 1993; invited speaker seminars and workshops; vocal dir. Guys and Dolls Washington High Performing Art Magnet; clinician conducting music workshops to promote multicultural understanding. Founder, exec. dir. Christian Action Now Is Good Econs., a visual and performing arts orgn. for at-risk youth, 1993; founder, pres. By Faith Cons. and Publishing, 1993; exec. dir. Change, performing arts orgn. for at-risk youth; moderator Urban Black Gospel E-Mail Discussion list. Named Outstanding Tchr. of Yr., ECLA, 2001. Mem. Am. Choral Dirs. Assn., Heritage Music Found., Mu Phi Epsilon, Alpha Kappa Alpha (grad. advisor 1978-79, del. 1980-81). Home: 14563 Saddle Peak Ct Fontana CA 92336

TROTTER, HERMAN EAGER, JR. (HERMAN TROTTER), retired music critic; b. Providence, Sept. 25, 1925; s. Herman Eager, Sr. and Shelley Fern (Jones) T.; m. Johanne Marguerite Haberstro, Sept. 22, 1956 (div. Apr. 1996); children: Kim Avery. Holly Anne. Joy Caroline; m. Rosa Spillane Whetzle, July 22, 1996. BA, Yale U., 1946. Pub. utility sec. analyst Mass. Mut. Life Ins. Co., Springfield, 1947-51; sales engr., mgr. Buffalo office B-I-F Industries, Providence, 1951-56; asst. sec. Buffalo Batt and Felt Co, Depew, N.Y., 1956-68; account exec. Harold Warner Advt., Buffalo, 1968-77; freelance music critic Buffalo News, 1968-77, staff music critic, 1977—2001, music critic emeritus, 2002. Contbr. articles to profl. and popular jours., and to New Grove Dictionary of Music. Program annotator Buffalo Philharm., 1964-70. Lt. (j.g.) USN, 1943-46, PTO. Mem. Music Critics Assn. (v.p. 1988-93, sec. 1999-2001). Avocations: travel, record collecting. Home: 107 Oakland Pl Buffalo NY 14222-2047 E-mail: herros72296@aol.com.

TROTTER, IDE PEEBLES, financial planner, investment manager; b. Colombia, Mo., Oct. 27, 1932; s. Ide Peebles and Lena Ann (Breeze) T.; m. Luella Ruth Haupt, June 9, 1956; children: Ruth Elizabeth, Arrenia Ann, Catherine Suzanne. BS, Tex. A&M U., 1954; MA, Princeton U., 1957, PhD, 1960. Various tech. positions Exxon Research & Enging. Co., 1958-65, sect. head Tex., 1965-67; advisor refining hdqrs. and corp. planning Exxon Co. USA, Houston, 1967-70, tech. supt. Billings, Mont., 1970-72, process supt., 1972-74; sr. advisor logistics Exxon Corp., N.Y.C., 1974-78; gen. mgr. logistics Esso Sekiyu, Tokyo, Japan, 1978-81; mgr. feedstock & energy Exxon Chem. Internat., Brussels, Belgium, 1981-86; dean Coll. Mgmt. & Free Enterprise Dallas Bapt. U., 1986-89, prof. fin., 1989-90; pres. Trotter Capital Mgmt. Inc., Duncanville, Tex., 1990—. Patentee in field. Chmn. Met. Bapt. Ministries, N.Y.C., 1976—78, bd. dirs., 1976—78, Visionwalk Internat. Ministries, 1997, chmn., bd. dirs., 2000—02; bd. dirs. Dallas Life Found., 1996—, vice-chmn., 2001. 1st lt. U.S. Army, 1960. NSF fellow, 1954; recipient Profl. Progress award Soc. Profl. Chemists & Engrs., 1964. Mem. Am. Inst. Chem. Engrs., Am. Chem. Soc., Am. Fin. Assn. Republican. Baptist. Avocations: skiing, hiking, fishing, camping, jogging. Home and Office: 1215 Rock Springs Rd Duncanville TX 75137-2839

TROTTER, LESLIE EARL, operations research educator, consultant; b. Muskogee, Okla., Nov. 17, 1943; s. Leslie Earl and Sylvia Helene (Freeze) T.; m. Jomi Tuggle, July 19, 1968 (div. Dec. 1995); children: Colleen Nicole, Eamonn Scott; m. Jeannine Rouch, July 7, 2000. AB in Math., Princeton U., 1965; MS in Indsl. and Systems Engring., Ga. Inst. Tech., 1971; PhD in Ops. Rsch., Cornell U., 1973. Sci. computer programmer Lockheed-Ga. Co., Marietta, 1965-68; computer applications analyst Control Data Corp., Atlanta, 1968-70; postdoctoral rsch. assoc. Math. Rsch. Ctr., U. Wis., Madison, 1973; asst. prof. Yale U. Sch. Orgn. and Mgmt., New Haven, 1974-75; assoc. prof. ops. rsch. Cornell U. Sch. Ops. Rsch. and Indsl. Enging., Ithaca, N.Y., 1975-84, dir. of Sch., 1983-87, 98—, prof., 1984—; dir. Advanced Computational Optimization Lab. Cornell Theory Ctr., 1995—. Vis. prof. Bonn (Germany) U., 1977-79, math. dept. E.P.F.L., Lausanne, Switzerland, 1984-85, 91-92, 2000, Math. Inst., Augsburg (Germany) U., 1987-88; vis. cons. Bell Labs., Holmdel, N.J., 1981. Editor optimization area Jour. Ops. Rsch., 1982-87; contbr. numerous articles to profl. jours. Recipient tchg. excellence awards Cornell U., 1977, 81, 93, 94, 98, sr. U.S. scientist award Alexander von Humboldt Found., Germany, 1988; numerous rsch. grants NSF, 1974—, including High Performance Computing and Comms. Grand Challenge award, 1995—. Mem. Ops. Rsch. Soc. Am., Math. Programming Soc. (treas. 1988-94), Soc. for Indsl. and Applied Math. Avocations: fitness, hiking, music. Home: 161 Highgate Rd Ithaca NY 14850-1469 Office: Cornell U Sch Ops Rsch Engring Rhodes Hall Ithaca NY 14853 E-mail: ltrotter@cs.cornell.edu.

TROTTER, SHIRLEY ANN, retired computer specialist; b. Oklahoma City, Nov. 30, 1934; d. Charles George and Bessie Lee (Armstrong) Huber; BS in Bus. Edn. beta gamma, Oklahoma City U., 1961, MEDin Math., 1973; m. George Monroe Hilton Trotter, Jr., Oct. 11, 1980; children: Darrell Lynn, Darren Lee Smith; stepchildren: David, Paige. Tchr. math. and bus., Putnam City Schs., Oklahoma City, 1961, 69-79; adminstrv. asst. Nat. Assn. Mature People, Oklahoma City, 1979; instr. FAA, Oklahoma City, 1979-81; co-founder, pres. DocuWrite, Inc., Bethany, Okla., 1981-83; CBT analyst First Data Mgmt. Co., Oklahoma City, 1981-83; mgr. Interactive Product Devel., Advanced Systems, Inc., Arlington Heights, Ill., 1983-84; computer specialist, analyst Computer Data Systems Inc., Rockville, Md., 1984-85, Office of Naval Research, Arlington, Va., 1985, Booz, Allen & Hamilton, Inc., Arlington, 1985-87, Applied Sci. Assocs., Inc. Landover, Md., 1987-88; asst. dir. of spl. programs, U. Md. Univ. Coll., College Park, 1988, cons., 1989-94; analyst Technology Planning, Inc., FAA Tech. Ctr., Atlantic City Internat. Airport, N.J., 1989, FAA Tech. Ctr. Operational Support Svc. (AOS-550), 1989-94; cons. Tech. Planning, Inc., Rockville, Md., 1994-95, Electronic Learning Facilitators Inc., Bethesda, Md., Clear Springs Inc., Great Falls, Va.; adj. faculty El Reno (Okla.) Jr. Coll., Okla. State U. Tech. Inst. Mem. alumni bd.

Oklahoma City U., 1963-64; past pres. The Lakes Property Owners; active First Presbyn. Ch. of Palm Bay. Mem. AARP, Greater Palm Bay Sr. Ctr., Mensa. Democrat. Home and Office: 2430 Alicia Ln Melbourne FL 32935-3664

TROTTER, THOMAS ROBERT, lawyer; b. Akron, Ohio, Apr. 11, 1949; s. Fred and Josephine (Daley) T. BA, Ohio U., 1971; JD, Tulane U., 1975. Bar: Ohio 1975, D.C. 2000, U.S. Dist. Ct. (no. dist.) Ohio 1975. Assoc. Squire, Sanders & Dempsey, Cleve., 1975-80; mem. Buckingham, Doolittle & Burroughs, Akron, 1980—. Chair taxation and legis. com. Akron Regional Devel. Bd., 1988-95. Trustee Akron Symphony Orch., 1984-93, Cascade CDC, Inc., Akron, 1983—, Akron-Summit Solid Waste Mgmt. Authority, 1994-97; trustee Weathervane Cmty. Playhouse, 1996—, pres., 1999-2001. Mem. ABA, Ohio Bar Assn. (chair local govt. law com.), Akron Bar Assn., Nat. Assn. Bond Lawyers, Sigma Alpha Epsilon. Democrat. Home: 589 Avalon Akron OH 44320-2048 Office: Buckingham Doolittle & Burroughs PO Box 1500 50 S Main St Akron OH 44308-1828 E-mail: ttrotter@bdblaw.com.

TROTTER-STEWART, AVA MARIE, educator; b. Baton Rouge, July 15, 1958; d. Albert and Julia (Harrell) Trotter; m. Polite Donald Stewart, Dec. 19, 1981. BS, So. U., Baton Rouge, 1979, MEd, 1984, Columbia U., 1987, EdD, 1989. Speech tchr. East Baton Rouge Parish Sch. Bd., 1980-81; teaching asst. So. U., Baton Rouge, 1983-84; tchr. English sci. and tech. enrichment program Columbia U., N.Y.C., 1986-88; adj. instr. Coll. of New Rochelle, N.Y., 1987-89, dir. English, 1989—. Mem. Nat. Coun. Tchrs. English, Kappa Delta Pi. Avocations: reading, knitting. Office: Coll New Rochelle Rosa Parks Campus 144 W 125th St New York NY 10027-4423

TROTZ, BARRY, professional hockey coach; Asst. coach U. Manitoba, 1984; head coach, gen. mgr. Dauphin Kings Jr. Hockey Club, 1985-87; head coach U. Manitoba, 1987; chief western scout Washington Capitals, 1988, asst. coach, 1991, head coach, 1992-95, U.S. Team at AM. Hockey League All Star Game, 1996, Nashville Predators Hockey Team, 1997—. Office: Nashville Predators 501 Broadway Nashville TN 37203-3932*

TROUNSTINE, JEAN ROLLMAN, humanities educator, writer; b. Cin., Dec. 11, 1946; d. Henry Philip and Amy Joseph Trounstine; m. Robert Wald, Apr. 17, 1988. BA with honors, Beloit (Wis.) Coll., 1969; MFA, Brandeis U., 1975. Tchr. Concord (Mass.) Assabet Sch., 1984-86, Duxbury (Mass.) H.S., 1986-88, Nashoba Regional H.S., Bolton, Mass., 1988-89; prison prof. Framingham Women's Prison, 1986-95; prof., prin. leader Changing Lives Through Lit., Boston, 1992—; humanities prof. Middlesex C.C., Lowell, Mass., 1989—. Caucus adv. bd. women in prison Mass. Legis. Com., Boston, 1992-94; lectr. in field, 1992—. Author: Changing Lives Through Literature, 1999, Shakespeare Behind Bars: The Power of Drama in a Women's Prison, 2001, Almost Home Free, 2002; contbr. articles to profl. jours. Dir. theatre troupe Middlesex. C.C., Lowell, 1991—. Recipient Women who Care Women in Philanthropy, 1993; grantee Mass Found. for Humanities, 1988-90; fellowship NE Humanities, 1987. Mem. NEA, Am. Assn. of Probation and Parole, Internat. Correctional Ednl. Assn., Am. Correctional Assn., Nat. Writers Union. Avocations: cooking, reading, plays, aerobics. Office: Middlesex CC 33 Kearney Sq Lowell MA 01852-1901 E-mail: trounstinej@middlesex.cc.ma.us.

TROUNSTINE, PHILIP JOHN, communications consultant, institute administrator; b. Cin., July 30, 1949; s. Henry P. and Amy May (Joseph) Trounstine; children: Jessica, David; m. Deborah Williams, May 1, 1993; children: Amy, Ryan, Patrick Wilkes. Student, U. Vt., 1967-68, Stanford U., 1968-70; BA in Journalism, San Jose State U., 1975. Graphic artist Eric Printing, San Jose, Calif., 1972-75; reporter Indpls. Star, Ind., 1975-78, San Jose Mercury News, Calif., 1978-83, editl. writer, 1983-86, polit. editor, 1986-99; ednl. cons. Teen Recovery Strategies, 1995-99; comms. dir. Gov. Gray Davis, Calif., 1999-2001, comm. cons., 2001—; dir. Survey and Policy Rsch. Inst. at San Jose State U. Co-author: Movers & Shakers: The Study of Community Power, 1981. Creator, writer SPJ Gridiron Show, San Jose, 1981-91. Pulliam fellow, 1975, Duke U., 1991, J.S. Knight fellow Stanford U., 1993-94. Mem. Soc. Profl. Journalists (mem. nat. ethics com. 1993-96). Jewish. Avocations: golf, fishing. Home: 620 Middlefield Dr Aptos CA 95003 E-mail: phil@trounstine.com.

TROUPE, MARILYN KAY, educational administrator; b. Tulsa, Sept. 30, 1945; d. Ernest Robinson and Lucille (Andrew) T. BA in History, Okla. State U., 1967, MA in History, 1976, EdD, 1993; lic. in cosmetology, Troupe's Beauty Sch., 1970. Cert. tchr. Okla., Tenn. Tchr. social studies Maragret Hudson Prog., Tulsa, 1969-81; tutor Tulsa Indian Youth, 1971-72; instr. cosmetology McLain-Tulsa Pub. Schs., 1982-94; instrnl. devel. specialist Okla. Dept. Vocat. and Tech. Edn., Stillwater, 1987-94; asst. prof., coord. tchr. prep. prog. chair divsn. liberal studies and edn. Lane Coll., Jackson, Tenn., 1995-97; dir. divsn. educator preparation and internship Ky. Edn. Profl. Stds. Bd., Frankfort, 1997-·. Vis. lectr. Okla. State U., 1980-81; cons., lectr. cosmetology. Bd. dirs., mem. adv. bd. Stillwater Park and Recreation, Stillwater Cmty. Rels. and Fair Housing, 1991-94; bd. dirs. Adult Day Care Ctr., 1990-94, Early Childhood Profl. Devel. Coun.; v.p. Okla. Recreation and Park Soc., 1994; judge Okla. Sch. Sci. and Math., 1994; mem. Leadership Stillwater, 1990; vol. Spl. Olympics State Games, Meals on Wheels, United Way, Frankfort Soup Kitchen; mem. women's adv. coun. Jackson Regional Hosp.; mem. adv. com. Okla. Task Force: Goals for Tomorrow, Roman Cath. Ch., Tulsa, 1985-86; mem. Ky. Early Childhood Profl. Devel. Coun.; grad. Leadership Ky., 2001; mem. Ky. Literacy Partnership. Recipient numerous awards for profl. and civic contbns. including Woman of the Yr. award Zeta Phi Beta, 1985, Salute award Gov. Okla., 1985, Outstanding Cmty. Svc. cert. WomenFest, 1985. Mem. AAUW, ASCD, Nat. Coun. Accredition Tchr. Edn. (bd. examiners), Okla. Assn. Advancement of Black Ams. in Vocat. Edn. (Golden Torch award 1994), Ky. Assn. Black Sch. Educators, Vocat. Indsl. Clubs Am. (dist. adv. 1985-86, Appreciation award 1985), Am. Vocat. Assn., Okla. Vocat. Assn., Okla. State Beauty Culturalists League (pres. 1979-85, Outstanding Svc. award 1985), Nat. Assn. Bus. and Profl. Women's Club (charter mem., past pres.), Stillwater C. of C. (bd. dirs.), Langston Alumni Assn., Frankfort-Lexington Links, Cath. Daus. Am., Phi Alpha Theta, Theta Nu Sigma, Alpha Kappa Alpha (Soror of the Yr. 1993), Iota Lambda Sigma, Phi Delta Kappa, Alpha Kappa Alpha. Democrat. Avocations: travel, reading, collecting antiques, volunteer work, shopping.

TROUSDALE, STEPHEN RICHARD, newspaper editor; b. L.A., May 29, 1963; s. Richard Gardner Trousdale and Geraldine Barbara Wisdom. AB, Stanford U., 1985. News editor L.A. Daily Commerce, 1986—87; edit. page editor L.A. Daily Jour., 1987—89, mng. editor, 1989—96; bus. editor Copley L.A. Newspapers, 1996—97; dep. bus. editor Contra Costa Times, 1997—2000, bus. editor, 2000—. Mem. Soc. Profl. Journalists (past pres. L.A. chpt.), AP Mng. Editors, Calif. Soc. Newspaper Editors, Soc. Am. Bus. Editors and Writers. Avocations: skiing, karate. Home: 1820 Virginia St Apt B Berkeley CA 94703-1345 Office: Contra Costa Newspapers 2640 Shadelands Dr Walnut Creek CA 94598-2513 E-mail: strousdale@cctimes.com.

TROUT, CHARLES HATHAWAY, historian, educator; b. Seattle, Nov. 3, 1935; s. Charles Whyron and Elizabeth (Hathaway) T.; m. Margot Stevens, Dec. 30, 1961 (div. 1983); children: Nicholas H., Benjamin C.; m. Katherine Taylor Griffiths, Oct. 6, 1984. BA, Amherst Coll., 1957; MA, Columbia U., 1961, PhD, 1972. History instr. Hill Sch., Pottstown, Pa., 1958-59, Philips Exeter Acad., (N.H.), 1960-69; prof. history Mt. Holyoke Coll., South Hadley, Mass., 1969-80; provost, dean faculty Colgate U., Hamilton, N.Y., 1980-90; pres. Washington Coll., Chestertown, Md., 1990-95; tchr. Tchr. for Africa, Korongoi, Litein, Kenya, 1996-97. Vis. prof. U. Mass. Labor Rels. and Rsch. Ctr., 1974-80; interim pres., Harcum Coll., Bryn Mawr, Pa., 2002-. Author: Boston, The Great Depression, and the New Deal. Chmn. bd. World Edn. Inc.; trustee Sultana Projects, Inc. Columbia U. Pres.'s scholar, 1959-60; NEH rsch. fellow, 1975-76; Charles Warren fellow Harvard U., 1978-79. Democrat. Episcopalian. Home: 211 N Queen St Chestertown MD 21620-1627 Office: Washington Coll Office of President Chestertown MD 21620-1197

TROUT, KEITH WILLIAM, electrical engineer; b. Alton, Ill., Oct. 21, 1967; s. Sheldon Keith and Dorothy Evelyn (Hooper) T.; m. Joy Marie Hardman, Jan. 7, 2000. BSEE, So. Ill. U., 1995. Intern elec. engr. Anheuser Busch Cos., St. Louis, 1993-94; from sys. mfg. technician to sys. devel. engr. Domino Control Sys., Glen Carbon, Ill., 1995-97; project engr. Barry-Wehmiller, St. Louis, 1997—. Office: Barry Wehmiller 8020 Forsyth Blvd Saint Louis MO 63105-1707 E-mail: Keith.Trout@BWDesignGroup.com.

TROUT, LINDA COPPLE, state supreme court chief justice; b. Tokyo, Sept. 1, 1951; BA, U. Idaho, 1973, JD, 1977; LLD (hon.), Albertson Coll. Idaho, 1999. Bar: Idaho 1977. Judge magistrate divsn. Idaho Dist. Ct. (2d jud. divsn.), 1983-90, dist. judge, 1991-92, acting trial ct. adminstr., 1987-91; justice Idaho Supreme Ct., 1992—, chief justice, 1997—. Instr. coll. law U. Idaho, 1983, 88. Mem. Idaho State Bar Assn., Clearwater Bar Assn. (pres. 1980-81).

TROUT, MARGIE MARIE MUELLER, civic worker; b. Apr. 27, 1923; d. Albert Sylvester and Pearl Elizabeth (Jose) Mueller; m. Maurice Elmore Trout, Aug. 24, 1943; children: Richard Willis, Babette Yvonne. Student, Webster Coll., 1944-45. Cert. genealogist Bd. Cert. Genealogy. Sec. offices Robertson Aircraft Corp., St. Louis, 1942; speed lathe and drill press operator Busch-Selzer Diesel Engine Co., 1942-43; Cub Scout den mother Vienna, Austria, 1953-55, Mt. Pleasant, Mich., 1955, London, 1956-57; leader Nat. Capitol coun. Girl Scouts U.S.A., Bethesda, Md., 1963-65; co-chmn. Am. Booth YWCA and Red Cross Ann. Bazaars, Bangkok, 1970-72; worker ARC, Vientiane, Laos, 1959-60, Bangkok, 1970-72; activities co-chmn., exec. bd. mem. Women's Club Armed Forces Staff Coll., Norfolk, Va., 1975-77. Mem. Am. Women's Clubs, Embassy Clubs, Internat. Women's Clubs Vienna, 1952-55, London, 1956-59, Vientiane, 1959-61, Munich, Germany, 1965-69, Bangkok, 1969-72, Norfolk, 1975-77. Crochet articles exhibited Exhbn. of Works of Art by the Corps Diplomatique, London, 1958. Home: 6203 Hardy Dr Mc Lean VA 22101-3114

TROUT, MAURICE ELMORE, diplomat; b. Clifton Hill, Mo., Sept. 17, 1917; s. David McCamel and Charlotte Temple (Woods) T.; m. Margie Marie Mueller, Aug. 24, 1943; children— Richard Willis, Babette Yvonne. BA, Hillsdale Coll., 1939; MA in Pub. Adminstrn, St. Louis U., 1948, PhD in Polit. Sci, 1950. Joined U.S. Fgn. Service, 1950; assigned Paris, France, 1950-52, Vienna, Austria, 1952-55, London, Eng., 1955-59, Vientiane, Laos, 1959-61; with Office Exec. Dir. Bur. Far Eastern Affairs, Dept. State, Washington, 1961-65; Am. consulate gen. Munich, Germany, 1965-69; 1st sec., consul Am. embassy, Bangkok, Thailand, 1969-72; dep. office dir. Bur. Politico-Mil. Affairs, Dept. State, Washington, 1972-75; Dept. State advisor Armed Forces Staff Coll., Norfolk, Va., 1975-77. Bd. dirs. Internat. Sch., Bangkok, 1970-72. Served with USCG, 1939-45; capt. USAFR, 1951-55. Recipient Achievement award diplomacy and internat. affairs Hillsdale Coll., 1962 Mem. Am. Fgn. Service Assn., Diplomatic and Consular Officers Ret., Delta Tau Delta, Delta Theta Phi, Pi Gamma Mu. Home: 6203 Hardy Dr Mc Lean VA 22101-3114

TROUT, MONROE EUGENE, hospital systems executive; b. Harrisburg, Pa., Apr. 5, 1931; s. David Michael and Florence Margaret (Kashner) T.; m. Sandra Louise Lemke, June 11, 1960; children: Monroe Eugene, Timothy William. AB, U. Pa., 1953, MD, 1957; LLB, Dickinson Sch. of Law, 1964, JD, 1969; LLD (hon.), Dickinson Sch. Law, 1996, Bloomfield Coll., 1994. Intern Great Lakes (Ill.) Naval Hosp., 1957-58; resident in internal medicine Portsmouth (Va.) Naval Hosp., 1959-61; chief med. dept. Harrisburg State Hosp., 1961-64; dir. drug regulatory affairs Pfizer, Inc., N.Y.C., 1964-68; v.p., med. dir. Winthrop Labs., 1968-70; med. dir. Sterling Drug, Inc., 1970-74, v.p., dir. med. affairs, 1974-78, sr. v.p., dir. med. affairs, bd. dirs., mem. exec. com., 1978-86; pres., CEO Am. Healthcare Sys., Inc., 1986-95, chmn., 1987-95; also bd. dirs. Am. Healthcare Systems, Inc.; chmn. emeritus Am. Healthcare Sys., Inc., 1995—; interim CEO Cytran Inc., 1996. Bd. dirs. Baxter Internat., SAIC, West Pharm. Svcs., Inc.; chmn. bd. dirs. Cytyc Inc., Ineed MD, Inc., Am. Excess Ins. Ltd., 1990—95; adj. assoc. prof. Bklyn. Coll. Pharmacy; spl. lectr. legal medicine, trustee Dickinson Sch. Law, 1970—73; trustee Ariz. State U. Sch. Health Adminstrn., 1988—91; mem. rsch. bd. Sterling Winthrop, 1977—86; mem. Joint Commn. Prescription Drug Use, 1976—80; sec. Commn. on Med. Malpractice, HEW, 1971—73, cons., 1974; co-chmn. San Diego County Health Commn., 1992—94. Mem. editl. bd. Hosp. Formulary Mgmt., 1969-79, Forensic Sci., 1971—, Jour. Legal Medicine, 1973-79, Reg. Tox. and Pharmac, 1981-87, Med. Malpractice Prevention, 1985—; editl. reviewer Annals of Internal Medicine; contbr. articles to profl. jours. Exec. com. White House Mini Conf. on Aging, 1980; Rep. dist. leader, New Canaan, Conn., 1966-68; mem. Nat. Health Adv. Bd. AAA, N.Y. State Commn. Substance Abuse, 1978-80, Town Coun., New Canaan, 1978-86, vice chmn., 1985-86; bd. dirs. New Canaan Interchurch Svc. Com., 1965-69, Athletes Kidney Found., Circle in Sq. Theatre Inc., 1984-86, Knoxville Symphony Soc., Knoxville Opera Co; trustee Cleve. Clinic, 1971-87, Albany Med. Coll., 1977-86, St. Vincent DePaul Ctr. for the Homeless, 1987-90, U. Calif.-San Diego Thornton Hosp. and Med. Ctr., 1990-97, San Diego Mus. Art, 1996-98, Bapt. Health Sys. Found., Knoxville, Tenn., 1999—; trustee, vice chmn. Morehouse Med. Sch., 1980-89; assoc. trustee U. Pa.; bd. visitors U. Pa. Sch. Nursing, 1988-92; pres. bd. trustees U. Calif. San Diego Found., 1994-97; vice chmn. Med. Commn. for Food and Shelter, Inc.; chmn. bd. Am. Coll. Legal Medicine Found., 1983-87; chmn. Internat. B'nai B'rith Dinner, 1989, 94. Recipient Alumni award of merit U. Pa., 1953, Disting. Alumni award Dickinson Sch. Law, 1989, Nat. Healthcare award Internat. B'nai B'rith, 1991, Entrepreneur of Yr. award San Diego, 1994, Horatio Alger award, 1995, Salvation Army Tradition of Caring award, 1996, Cívis Universitatus award U. Calif. San Diego, 1997, Gold Medal award, Am. Coll. Legal Medicine, 1999. Fellow Am. Coll. Legal Medicine (v.p., pres., bd. govs.); mem. AMA (Physician's Recognition awards 1969, 72, 76, 82, 85, 88, 92), Med. Execs. (pres. 1975-76), Delta Tau Delta (Alumni Achievement award 1996, Named to 100 Most Influential Delts of Twentieth Century 2000). Lutheran. Office: 2110 Cove View Way Knoxville TN 37919

TROUTMAN, GEORGE WILLIAM, geologist, petroleum geological advisor; b. Aug. 8, 1949; s. George I. and Ellen G. Troutman; m. Marcia Lyn Roseman, Aug. 14, 1971; children: Nancy, Anthony, Janet, David, Barbara, Jonathan. Student, Murray State U., 1967-68; BS in Geology, Western Ky. U., 1974. Geophys. engr. Birdwell divsn. Seismograph Svc. Corp., Ohio, Pa., W.Va., 1974-77; geologist Consol. Natural Gas, Clarksburg, W.Va., 1977-79; exloration geologist Mountain Fuel Supply Corp., Denver, 1979-80; regional exploration geologist Al-Aquitaine Exploration, Ltd., 1980-81; sr. staff geologist Resources Investment Corp., 1981-82; geol. mgr. Petro-Lewis Corp., MCR, Oklahoma City, 1982-84; pres., geologist Troutman Geol. & Assocs., Edmond, Okla., 1984-2000; geol. advisor Devon Energy, Oklahoma City, 2000—. With USN, 1968-70. Mem. Am. Assn. Petroleum Geologists (cert.), Soc. Profl. Well Log Analysts, Oklahoma City Geol. Soc. (exec. com. 1985-86, editor Shale Shaker Digest XI 1982-85, treas. 1987-88, v.p. 1988-89, pres.-elect 1996-97, pres. 1997-98), Ardmore Geol. Soc., New Orleans Geol. Soc., Computer Oriented Geol. Soc., Geophys. Soc. of Oklahoma City. Republican. Mem. Lds Ch. Office: Devon Energy Corp 20 N Broadway Ste 1500 Oklahoma City OK 73102 E-mail: troutman@geologist.com., george.troutman@dvn.com.

TROUTNER, JOANNE JOHNSON, school technology administrator, educator, administrator, consultant; b. Muncie, Ind., Sept. 9, 1952; d. Donal Russel and Lois Vivian (Hicks) Johnson; m. Lary William Troutner, May 17, 1975. BA in Media and English, Purdue U., 1974; MS in Edn., 1976. Media spls. Lafayette (Ind.) Sch. Corp., 1974-77, 81-83; computer resource tchr., 1983-84; media splst. Tippecanoe Sch. Corp., Lafayette, Ind., 1984-85; ednl. support, 1985-87; coord. instrl. support, 1988-94; dir. tech. and media, tchr. English Minot (N.D.) Pub. Schs., 1978-79; media splst., 1979-81. Vis. prof. cont. edn. U. S.C., Columbia, summer 1983, U. N.D.; instr. Purdue U., West Lafayette; software selector Elem. Sch. Libr. Collection. Author: The Media Specialist, The Microcomputer and the Curriculum, 1983, World Desk-Classroom Internet Guide, 1998, The Internet: A Curriculum Oriented Guide, 1998, Using the Internet and Technology to Strengthen Learning in English/Language Arts and Social Studies, 1999, Integrating Technology and the Internet into English and Social Studies Classrooms, 1999, Strengthening Your Social Studies Classroom, 2002; contbr. materials rev. column Sch. Libr., Media Quar.; computer literacy columnist Jour. Computers in Math. and Sci. Tchg.; computer software columnist Tchr. Libr., 1989—, internet columnist, 1995—; editor newsletter Ind. Computer Educators. Active Greater Lafayette Leadership Acad. Alumni Group, 1983—; bd. dirs. Tippecanoe County Pub. Libr., pres., 1994—95, trustee, 1990—2000; bd. dirs. Lafayette Family Svc. Agy., 1987—89. Mem. ALA, Ind. Assn. Media Educators (chmn. computer div. 1982-84), Am. Assn. Sch. Librarians (sec. 1983-84, 2nd v.p. 1985-86), Internat. Coun. for Computers in Edn. (interactive video spl. interest group newsletter editor 1986-87), Ind. Computer Educators (bd. dirs. 1986-92, pres. 1990-91), Internat. Soc. Tech. Educators, Assn. Supr. and Curriculum Devel., Phi Beta Kappa, Kappa Delta Gamma, Phi Delta Kappa (v.p. programs 1987-88, v.p. memberships 1988-89, pres. 1989-90). Home: 4001 Penny Packers Mill Rd Lafayette IN 47909-3557 Office: Tippecanoe Sch Corp 21 Elston Rd Lafayette IN 47909-2899 E-mail: troutner@mindspring.com.

TROUTWINE, GAYLE LEONE, lawyer; b. Kansas City, Mo., Feb. 26, 1952; BS, N.W. Mo. State U., 1973; JD with honors, U. Mo., 1978. Bar: Mo. 1978, Oreg. 1983, U.S. Dist. Ct. (we. dist.) Mo., Wash. 1984, U.S. Ct. Appeals (9th cir.), U.S. Dist. Ct. (we. dist.) Wash., U.S. Supreme Ct., Hawaii 1995. Ptnr. Williams & Troutwine, P.C., Portland, Oreg., 1986—. Speaker in field. Contbr. articles to profl. jours. Steering com. mem. Breast Implant Litigation, 1992—, Tobacco Litigation; bd. mem. Portland Area Women's Polit. Caucus, 1992-95, Oreg. Women's Polit. Caucus, 1996—; mem. Jud. Steering com., 1994. Named Queen of Torts Wall St. Jour., 1996. Mem. ATLA (bd. govs.), Hawaii State Bar, Mo. Bar, Oreg. State Bar (exec. bd. litigation sect. 1984-88, chmn. 1987-88, procedure and practice com. 1985-88, bd. govs. 1990-93), Wash. State Bar, Oreg. Trial Lawyers Assn. (bd. govs. 1987-91), Calif. Trial Lawyers Assn., Hawaii Trial Lawyers Assn., Wash. Trial Lawyers Assn., Women Lawyers Assn., Greater Kansas City (sec. 1981-82), Western Trial Lawyers Assn. (bd. govs. 1992—). Democrat.

TROVER, DENIS WILLIAM, microcomputer company executive; b. Columbus, Ohio, Feb. 1, 1945; s. Kenneth Harold and Virginia June (Denis) T.; B.S. in Physics, Mich. State U., 1967; M.B.A., Coll. William and Mary, 1972; M.S. in Physics, Vassar Coll., 1973; m. Florence Ellen Lloyd, June 12, 1971; 1 dau., Florence Emma. Optical physicist IBM, Fishkill, N.Y., 1967-71; staff assoc., systems programmer Rockwell Internat. Sci. Center, Thousand Oaks, Calif., 1974-78; pres., dir. Sonix Systems, Inc., Thousand Oaks, 1978-86; pvt. practice small bus. computer cons., Camarillo, Calif., 1986—. Mem. energy task force Conejo Future Found., 1975— , chmn., 1980-81. Club: Vassar So. Calif. (bd. dirs. 1982—), Market Analysts of So. Calif. Home: 11355 Presilla Rd Camarillo CA 93012-9230

TROVER, ELLEN LLOYD, lawyer; b. Richmond, Va., Nov. 23, 1947; d. Robert Van Buren and Hazel (Urban) Lloyd; m. Denis William Trover, June 12, 1971; 1 dau., Florence Emma. AB, Vassar Coll., 1969; JD, Coll. William and Mary, 1972. Asst. editor Bancroft-Whitney, San Francisco, 1973-74; owner Ellen Lloyd Trover Atty.-at-Law, Thousand Oaks, Calif., 1974-82; ptnr. Trover & Fisher, 1982-89; pvt. practice law, 1989-98; mng. ptnr. The Lloyd-Trover Partnership, 1998—. Editor: Handbooks of State Chronologies, 1972. Trustee Conejo Future Found., Thousand Oaks, 1978—91, trustee emeritus, 1992—, vice chmn., 1982—84, chmn., 1984—88; pres. Zonta Club Conejo Valley Area, 1978—79; trustee Hydro Help for the Handicapped, 1980—85, Atlantis Found., 1994—; pres. Vista Santa Rosa Assn., 2001—. Mem. State Bar Calif., Va. State Bar, Phi Alpha Delta. Democrat. Presbyterian. Home: 11355 Presilla Rd Camarillo CA 93012-9230 Office: 1107E E Thousand Oaks Blvd Thousand Oaks CA 91362-2816 E-mail: etrover@yahoo.com.

TROWBRIDGE, ALEXANDER BUEL, JR. business consultant; b. Englewood, N.J., Dec. 12, 1929; s. Alexander Buel and Julie (Chamberlain) T.; m. Eleanor Hutzler, Apr. 18, 1981; children by previous marriage: Stephen C., Corrin S., Kimberly. Grad., Phillips Acad., Andover, Mass., 1947; AB cum laude, Princeton U., 1951; LLD (hon.), D'Youville Coll., 1967, Hofstra U., 1968, Hobart Coll., William Smith Coll., 1975. With Calif. Tex. Oil Co., 1954-59; ops. mgr. Esso Standard Oil S.A. Ltd., Panama C.Z., 1959-61, div. mgr. El Salvador, 1961-63; pres. Esso Standard Oil Co., P.R., 1963-65; asst. sec. commerce for domestic and internat. bus. U.S., 1965-67; sec. of commerce, 1967-68; pres. Am. Mgmt. Assn., N.Y.C., 1968-70, The Conf. Bd., Inc., N.Y.C., 1970-76; vice chmn. bd. Allied Chem. Corp., 1976-80; bd. dirs. NAM, Washington, 1978—, pres., 1980-90. Mem. Pres.'s Task Force on Pvt. Sector Initiatives, Nat. Commn. on Social Security Reform, 1982; mem. Nat. Commn. on Exec., Legis. and Jud. Salaries, 1985, Nat. Commn. on Pub. Svcs.; mem. Competitiveness Policy Coun., 1991. With USMCR, 1951-53, maj. Res. Decorated Bronze Star with combat V; recipient Arthur Flemming award, 1966, Pres.'s E cert. for export service, 1968, Bryce Harlow award for Bus.-Govt. Rels., 1988. Mem. Coun. Fgn. Rels., Met. Club, Georgetown Club, Univ. Club. Home: 1823 23rd St NW Washington DC 20008-4030 Office: 1317 F St NW Ste 500 Washington DC 20004-1105

TROWBRIDGE, DALE BRIAN, educator; b. Glendale, Calif., May 17, 1940; s. Dale Beverly and Alison Amelia (Goldsborough) T.; m. Helen Elaine Turner, July 2, 1966; children: Katelin Elizabeth, David Brian. BA, Whittier Coll., 1961; MS, U. Calif., Berkeley, 1964, PhD, 1970. Chemist Aerojet Gen., Azusa, Calif., 1961-62; chemistry tchr. Berkeley H.S., 1964-66; prof., chemistry dept. chmn. Sonoma State U., Rohnert Park, Calif., 1969—; vis. prof. chemistry U. Calif., Berkeley, 1970-74, 88; rsch. assoc. Cambridge U., 1978. Contbr. articles to profl. jours. Mem. AAAS, Am. Chem. Soc., Internat. Platform Assn., Sigma Xi. Home: 6039 Elsa Ave Rohnert Park CA 94928-2246 Office: Sonoma State U 1801 E Cotati Ave Rohnert Park CA 94928-3609 E-mail: dale.trowbridge@sonoma.edu.

TROWBRIDGE, JOHN PARKS, physician; b. Dinuba, Calif., Mar. 24, 1947; s. John Parks and Claire Dovie (Noroian) Trowbridge; children: Sharla Tyann, Lyndi Kendyll. AB in Biol. Scis., Stanford U., 1970; MD, Case Western Res. U., 1976; postgrad., Fla. Inst. Tech., 1983-85. Diplomate in Preventive Medicine, Am. Bd. Chelation Therapy (examiner for bd. 1987—, protocol coun. 1996-98), Am. Bd. Biologic Reconstructive Therapy (examiner for bd. 1994-97), Am. Bd. Anti-Aging Medicine, 1998, Nat. Bd. Med. Examiners. Intern in gen. surgery Mt. Zion Hosp. & Med. Ctr., San Francisco, 1976-77; resident in urol. surgery U. Tex. Health Sci. Ctr., Houston, 1977-78; pvt. med. practice health recovery unit, pain relief unit, life long health unit Life Celebrating Health Assn., Humble, 1978—. Chief corp. med. cons. Tex. Internat. Airlines, Houston, 1981-83; indsl. med. cons. to several heavy and light mfg. and svc. cos., Houston, 1979-84; immunology research asst. Stanford U. Med. Ctr., Stanford, Calif., 1967-70; night lab. supr. Kaiser Found. Hosp., Redwood City, Calif., 1971-72; advisor to bd. dirs. Am. Inst. Med. Preventics, Laguna Hills, Calif., 1988-90; featured lectr. profl. and civic orgns., U.S., 1983—; sr. aviation med. examiner FAA, 1983-96. Co-author: The Yeast Syndrome, 1986, Chelation Therapy, 1985, 2d edit., 1990, Yeast Related Illnesses, 1987, Do What You Want to Do, 1996, The Rumble in Humble: Heart Surgery and All That Jazz, 1997, Living Well Past 50: Rejuvenate Your Heart and Arteries, 1998; contbr. Challenging Orthodoxy: America's Top Medical Preventives Speak Out, 1991; edit. adv. bd. mem. nat. health and wellness newsletters, and jours., 1990—; contbr. articles to profl. jours. Adv. bd. mem. Tex. Chamber Orchestra, Houston, 1979-80; med. dir. Humble unit Am. Cancer Soc., 1980-81; med. cons. personal fitness program Lake Houston YMCA, 1981-83. Nat. Merit scholar, 1965-69, Calif. State scholar, 1967-69; recipient Resolution of Commendation house of dels., 1974 Am. Podiatry Assn., Spl. Profl. Svc. Citation bd. trustees, 1976, Am. Podiatry Students Assn. Mem.: Internat. Coll. Integrative Medicine (bd. dirs. 2000—, editor newsletter 2000—01), N.Am. Cervicogenic Headache Soc., The Royal Soc. Medicine (London, sect. orthopaedics), Soc. for Orthomolecular Medicine, Great Lakes Coll. Clin. Medicine (bd. dirs. 1991—93, med. rsch. instnl. rev. bd., v.p. 1993—94, pres. 1994—95, program chair Advanced Tng. Seminar in Heavy Metal Toxicology 1996—98, bd. dirs. 1999—2000), Huxley Inst. for Biosocial Rsch., Inst. Health Freedom (bd. dirs. 1997—2001), The Arthritis Trust Am. (med. adv. bd. 1995—), Internat. Acad. Bariatric Medicine, N.Y. Acad. Scis., Aerospace Med. Assn., Houston Acad. Medicine, Harris County Med. Soc., Tex. Med. Assn., Am. Acad. Anti-Aging Medicine, Assn. Am. Physicians and Surgeons. Avocations: private piloting, computer applications, personal watercraft. Office: Life Celebrating Health Assn 9816 Memorial Blvd Ste 205 Humble TX 77338-4206 E-mail: info@healthCHOICESnow.com.

TROWBRIDGE, MARK ALAN, cultural organization administrator; b. Toledo, May 8, 1968; s. Edgar William and Mary Lou Trowbridge. BS, U. Fla., 1990, MEd, 1992. Residence coord. U. Miami, Fla., 1992-95, dir. student activities, 1995-98; vol. coord. South Fla. Super Bowl XXXIII Host Com., Miami, 1998-99; asst. dir. S. Fla. Breeder's Cup Host Com., Fla., 1999—, Ocean Race Miami, Inc., 2000; pres. Switchboard of Miami, Inc., 2000—.

Pres. So. To Speak, Inc., Miami, 1995—. Conf. chmn. Leadership Miami, 1996—; bd. dirs. Turner Tech. Inst., Miami, 1998—; bd. dirs., chmn. fundraising Switchboard of Miami, 1998-2000; pres. Sigma Alpha Epsilon Alumni Adv. Bd., 1996-2000. Named Adminstr. of Yr., Panhellenic Assn., 1997, Outstanding Adminstr., U. Miami Student Govt., 1997. Mem. U.S. Tennis Assn. (umpire 1998—), Fla. Blue Key, Iron Arrow. Avocations: travel, tennis, reading, films, stand-up comedy. Home: 1208 S Douglas Rd Apt 2 Coral Gables FL 33134-3444 E-mail: MATGator1@aol.com.

TROWBRIDGE, PHILLIP EDMUND, surgeon, educator; b. Hartford, Conn., Oct. 17, 1930; s. John Henry and Isabelle Story (Warner) T.; m. Fay Elaine Russell, June 23, 1956; children: Kimberly, Heather, Allison, John, David. BA, Trinity Coll., 1952; postgrad., Harvard U., 1955; MD, Tufts Med. Sch., 1959. Diplomate Am. Bd. Surgery. Intern Hartford Hosp., 1959-60, resident in gen. surgery, 1960-65, from mem. surg. staff to sr. surgeon, 1965-97; clin. asst. prof. Surgery U. Conn. Med. Sch., Farmington, 1986-97; adj. asst. prof. Surgery Dartmouth Med. Sch., Hanover, N.H., 1986-97. Contbr. 17 articles to profl. jours. Corporator Hartford Sem., Hartford, 1975-77, 86-98, trustee, 1977-86; dir. West Hartford Street Ministry, 1974-79. With USAF, 1952-54. Mem. ACS, Hartford Med. Soc. (pres. 1988, trustee 1989-93, Loving Cup award 1994), Am. Soc. Gen. Surgeons (chmn. Conn. chpt. 1993-97), New Eng. Surg. Soc., New Eng. Cancer Soc., Internat. Surg. Soc., Soc. for Surgery Alimentary Tract. Republican. American Baptist. Avocations: golf, tennis, skiing, photography, painting. Home: 10 Upper Heatherwood Cromwell CT 06416-2708 E-mail: petmd@earthlink.net.

TROWBRIDGE, THOMAS, JR. mortgage banking company executive; b. Troy, N.Y., June 28, 1938; s. of Thomas and Elberta (Wood) T.; m. Delinda Bryan, July 3, 1965; children: Elisabeth Tacy, Wendy Bryan. BA, Yale U., 1960; MBA, Harvard U., 1965. V.p. James W. Rouse & Co., Balt., 1965-66, Washington, 1966-68, San Francisco, 1968-73, 76-78; pres. Rouse Investing Co., Columbia, Md., 1973-76, Trowbridge, Kieselhorst & Co., San Francisco, 1978-97, CEO, chmn., 1997-2000; ret., 2000. Bd. dirs. Columbia Assn., 1975-76; trustee, treas. The Head-Royce Sch., Oakland, Calif., 1980-84; trustee, pres. Gen. Alumni Assn. Phillips Exeter Acad., 1984-90. Lt. USNR, 1960-63. Mem. Urban Land Inst., Calif. Mortgage Bankers Assn. (bd. dirs. 1991-98, pres. 1996-97), Mortgage Bankers Assn. Am. (bd. govs. 1993-2000), Olympic Club, Pacific Union Club, Lambda Alpha Internat. Republican. Presbyterian. Avocation: golf. Home: 4 Ridge Ln Orinda CA 94563-1318

TROWER, WILLIAM KEVIN, lawyer; b. Pitts., Aug. 16, 1958; s. William Harvey and Clara Belle Trower; 1 child, Richard. BA, Point Park Coll., Pitts., 1981; JD cum laude, Duquesne U., 1992. Bar: Pa. 1992. Dir. affiliate rels. Sheridan Broadcasting, Pitts., 1979-91; dir. media rels. United Way, 1991-93; mgr. pub. affairs WTAE-TV, 1993-95; atty. Law Offices of Byrd R. Brown, 1993—2001. Mem. Law Rev., Duquesne U., 1991. Mem. Kappa Alpha Psi. Office: 715 N Negley Ave Pittsburgh PA 15206-2008

TROWN, PATRICK WILLOUGHBY, biopharmaceutics company executive; b. Birmingham, Eng., Mar. 17, 1937; came to U.S., 1962; s. Ronald Hugh and Evelyn Mary (Willoughby) T.; m. Marie-Clarie Allain Labbé, Aug. 19, 1962; children: Christopher Mark, Nicolas Bruce. BA in Chemistry, Oxford (Eng.) U., 1960, DPhil, 1962. Sr. rsch. scientist Lederle Labs., Pearl River, N.Y., 1964-69; rsch. group chief Hoffmann-La Roche, Nutley, N.J., 1969-76, asst. dir. chemotherapy, 1976-78, dir. immunotherapy, 1978-81, dir. exptl. oncology, 1981-86; v.p. preclin. sci. Xoma Corp., Berkeley, Calif., 1986-95; v.p. product devel. ONYX Pharms., Richmond, 1996-2000; biopharm. cons., 2000—. Cons. Hoffmann-La Roche, Nutley, 1986-87; biopharm. cons. in field of biopharms, 2000-02. Contbr. articles to profl. jours. State scholar U.K. Govt., 1955, Open Harrison scholar Oriel Coll., Oxford U., 1956; NATO fellow, 1962. Mem. Am. Assn. Cancer Rsch. Achievements include 4 patents in field; avocations: tennis, skiing, hiking. E-mail: patrick@pwtrown.com.

TROXEL, DAVID B. president; b. Elgin, Ill., 1936; MD, Northwestern U., 1962. Pres. Am. Bd. of Pathology, trustee; clinical prof. Divsn. of Health & Med. Sci.; residency Presbyn. Hosp., Denver, 1966—68, Mayo Clinic Found., Rochester, 1963—64; intern Chgo. Wesley Meml. Hosp., 1962—63. Cons., govr. Doctors Ins. Com. Contbr. articles to jours. Office: Am Bd Pathology PO Box 25915 Tampa FL 33622-5915*

TROXEL, DONALD EUGENE, electrical engineering educator; b. Trenton, N.J., Mar. 11, 1934; s. Shirley Monroe and Emma Ruth Troxel; m. Eileen Millicent Cronk, Aug. 23, 1963; children: Gregory, Jocelyn, Andrea. BS, Rutgers U., 1956; SM, MIT, 1960, PhD, 1962. Ford Found. postdoctoral fellow, asst. prof. MIT, Cambridge, Mass., 1962-64, asst. prof. dept. elec. engring., 1964-67, assoc. prof., 1967-85, prof. elec. engring., 1985—; asst. prof. Tufts U., Medford, 1963. Bd. dirs. ECRM, Inc., Tewksbury, Mass. 1st lt. U.S. Army, 1956-58. Mem. IEEE (sr. mem., Leonard G. Abraham Prize Paper award 1971), Assn. for Computing Machinery, Sigma Xi, Tau Beta Pi, Eta Kappa Nu, Pi Mu Epsilon. Home: 4 Madison St Belmont MA 02478-3536 Office: MIT 77 Massachusetts Ave # 36-287 Cambridge MA 02139-4307

TROXEL, RANDY, lawyer; s. Ronald and Ann Troxel; 1 child Sean. BS, Colo. State U., 1974; JD, Golden Gate U., 1994. Bar: Calif. 1995, U.S. Dist. Ct. (no. dist.) Calif. 1995, U.S. Ct. Appeals (9th cir.) 1995. Assoc. Baker and McKenzie, San Francisco, 2000—01, McCutchen Doyle Brown and Enersen LLP, San Francisco, 2001—. Mem.: ABA (intellectual property sect.), Bar Assn. of San Francisco (intellectual property sect.), San Francisco Intellectual Property Law Assn., Internat. Trademark Assn. Office: McCutchen Doyle Brown and Enersen LLP 25th Fl 3 Embarcadero Center San Francisco CA 94111 E-mail: rtroxel@mdbe.com.

TROXELL, LUCY DAVIS, management consultant; b. Cambridge, Mass., Apr. 25, 1932; d. Ellsworth and Mildred (Enneking) Davis; m. Charles DeGroat Bader, June 13, 1952 (div. Aug. 1974); children: Christie P. Walker, Mary Ellsworth Bader, Charles D. Bader Jr., David Bradford Bader; m. Victor Daniel Shirer Troxell, Aug. 1974. BA, Smith Coll., Northampton, Mass., 1952. Cert.: (paralegal); employee benefit specialist, assoc. in risk mgmt. Paralegal O'Melveny & Myers, L.A., 1976-77; acct. exec. Olanie Hurst & Hemrich, 1977-78; asst. to trustee Oxford Ins. Mgmt., 1978-80; dir. corp. svcs., asst. corp. sec. Consolidated Elec. Distbrs., Inc., Westlake Village, 1980-93; pres. MONMAK LDT, 1993—. Vol. ARC; clk. St. Mathew's Parish Vestry, Pacific Palisades, Calif., 1988, sr. warden, 1989—90; lic. lay eucharistic min. Episcopal Ch.; sustaining bd. dirs. Jr. League, Hartford, Conn., 1952—, L.A., 1952—; bd. dirs. Smith Coll. Club, Hartford, 1952—, Nat. Charity League, L.A., 1964—68, Theatre Palisades, 1960—74; bd. dirs., treas. HOA Lakeshore Cmty. Assn., 1999. Scholar Sophia Smith. Fellow: Risk and Ins. Mgmt. Soc. (program chmn. L.A. chpt. 1985—86), Internat. Soc. Cert. Employee Benefit Specialists (bd. dirs., sec., treas. 1988—89, pres. 1989—90, edn. chmn. L.A. chpt. 1986—88). Republican. Avocations: finance, acting, music, art. Home: 450 Puerto Del Mar Pacific Palisades CA 90272-4233 Office: MONMAK LDT 32001 Viewlake Ln Westlake Village CA 91361

TROXLER, CAROLE WATTERSON, historian, educator; b. LaGrange, Ga., Feb. 22, 1943; d. Eugene Price and Virginia (Knight) W.; m. George Wesley Troxler, Aug. 25, 1967; children: Heidi, Lydia. AB, U. Ga., 1964; MA, U. N.C., 1966, PhD, 1974. Instr. Davidson County C.C., Lexington, N.C., 1966-68; asst. prof. history Elon (N.C.) U. (formerly Elon Coll.), 1970-81, assoc. prof., 1981-87, prof., 1988—. Author: The Loyalist Experience in North Carolina, 1976, Shuttle & Plow: A History of Alamance County, N.C., 1999; (video) Ambush on Cane Creek: The Battle of Lindley's Mill, 1981 (Gertrude Carraway award 1982); editor: Deloise C. Browning, Here for a Season, 2002; contbr. chpt. to books: Loyalists and Community in North America, 1994; Moving On: Black Loyalists in the Afro-Atlantic World, 1999; contbr. numerous articles to profl. publs., including Jour. So. History, N.C. Hist. Rev., others. Active Haw River Assembly, Bynum, N.C., 1984—, Conservation Coun. N.C., Raleigh, 1982-90; precinct officer North Boon Precinct, Dem. Party, Alamance County, N.C., 1974-84. Recipient H.C. Bradshaw award SAR, 1981; Woodrow Wilson fellow, U. N.C., 1964-65, tchg. fellow Woodrow Wilson Nat. Fellowship Found., 1965-66; faculty devel. program grantee Can. Embassy, 1982, rsch. grantee North Caroliniana Soc., 1992. Fellow Royal Nova Scotia Hist. Soc., Isle of Man Natural History and Antiquarian Soc.; mem. Am. Hist. Assn., N.Am. Conf. British Studies, Assn. Can. Studies in U.S., So. Hist. Assn., Internat. Coun. Can. Studies, Hist. Soc. N.C. (bd. dirs., pres., program chmn. 1986—), N.C. Lit. and Hist. Assn., Trading Path Preservation Assn. (bd. dirs. 2001—), So. Conf. British Studies, N.Am. Manx Assn. (life), Manx Heritage (life), Alpha Delta Kappa (v.p., sec. 1982—, rsch. grantee 1982, 99), Phi Alpha Theta (faculty advisor 1979-94). Avocation: music of the British Isles and Upland South. Home: 2748 Amick Rd Elon NC 27244 Office: Elon U 2145 Campus Box Elon NC 27244 E-mail: carole.troxler@elon.edu.

TROXLER, RAYMOND G. pathologist, preventive medicine physician; b. New Orleans, Sept. 21, 1939; s. Ferdinand Arthur and Marjorie T.; m. Barbara J. Keefe, Aug. 10, 1963; children: Karen, Pamela. BS, U. Southwest La., 1960; MD, La. State U. Sch. Medicine, 1964; MPH, U. Tex. Health Sci. Ctr., 1987. Intern Wilford Hall USAF Hosp., San Antonio, 1964-65; flight surgeon USAF, Myrtle Beach, S.C., Vietnam, 1965-67; resident in pathology Wilford Hall USAF Hosp., 1967-71; chief clin. pathology USAF Sch. Aerospace Medicine, San Antonio, 1971-83; pvt. practice in preventive cardiology, 1984—; chief univ. lipid clinic U. Tex. Health Sci. Ctr., 1992—. Mem. APHA, Am. Heart Assn., Tex. Med. Assn., Bexar County Med. Soc. Avocations: medical informatics, medical complications of obesity, writing.

TROY, ANTHONY FRANCIS, lawyer; b. Hartford, Conn., Apr. 16, 1941; children: Anthony John, Francis Gerard II. BA in Govt., St. Michael's Coll., Vt., 1963; LLB, U. Richmond, Richmond, Va., 1966. Bar: Va. 1966, D.C. 1972, U.S. Dist. Ct. (ea. dist.) Va. 1966, U.S. Dist. Ct. (we. dist.) Va. 1967, U.S. Ct. Appeals (4th cir.) 1967, U.S. Supreme Ct. 1969. Asst. atty. gen. Commonwealth of Va., Richmond, 1966-72, atty. gen., 1977-78; assoc. Colson & Shapiro, Washington, 1972-74; ptnr. Troutman, Sanders LLP, Richmond, 1978—. Conard Mattox Disting. adj. prof. chair law U. Richmond Law Sch. Contbr. articles to profl. jours. Trustee Sci. Mus. Va. Fellow Am. Law Found., Va. Law Found. Home: 308 N Lombardy St Richmond VA 23220-3532 Office: Troutman Sanders LLP PO Box 1122 Richmond VA 23218-1122 E-mail: tony.troy@troutmansanders.com.

TROY, FREDERIC ARTHUR, II, medical biochemistry educator; b. Evanston, Ill., Feb. 16, 1937; s. Charles McGregor and Virginia Lane (Minto) T.; m. Linda Ann Price, Mar. 23, 1959; children: Karen M., Janet R. BS, Washington U., St. Louis, 1961; PhD, Purdue U., 1966; postdoctoral, Johns Hopkins U., 1968. Asst. prof. U. Calif. Sch. Medicine, Davis, 1968-74, assoc. prof., 1974-80, prof., 1980—, chmn., 1991-94; vis. prof. Karolinska Inst. Med. Sch., Stockholm, 1976-77. Cons. NIH, Bethesda, Md., 1974—, NSF, Washington, 1975—, Damon Runyon Cancer Found., N.Y.C., 1980-81, VA, Washington, 1984-88, U.S. Army Breast Cancer Study Sect., 1999—. Mem. editl. bd. Jour. Biol. Chem., 1988—, Glycobiol., 1990—; contbr. articles to profl. jours. Recipient Research Cancer Devel. award Nat. Cancer Inst., 1975-80; Eleanor Roosevelt Internat. Cancer fellow Am. Cancer Soc., 1976-77. Mem. AAAS, Am. Soc. Biol. Chemistry and Molecular Biology, Am. Assn. Cancer Rsch., Am. Chem. Soc., Am. Soc. Enologists, Biochemistry Soc., Biophysics Soc., Am. Fedn. for Clin. Rsch., N.Y. Acad. Scis., Soc. for Glycobiol. (pres. 1991-92), Am. Med. and Grad. Sch. Dept. Biochem. (pres.-elect 1995—), Sigma Xi. Office: U Calif Sch Medicine Davis CA 95616

TROY, PAUL JAMES, technology scientist; b. Bklyn., Jan. 30, 1961; s. John Anthony and Mary Ann Hudyma. BS, SUNY, Albany, 1983; PhD, U. Hawaii, 1995. Rsch. asst. oceanography U. Hawaii, Honolulu, 1995-99; sr. scientist Sci. and Tech. Internat., 1999—. Contbr. articles to profl. jours. Mem. SPIE, Am. Soc. Limnology and Oceanography, Sigma Xi. Office: Sci and Tech Internat Makai Tower Ste 3100 733 Bishop St Honolulu HI 96813 Office Fax: 808-540-4850. E-mail: paul@sti-hawaii.com.

TROY, RONALD LAWRENCE, social worker; b. Chgo., Apr. 21, 1937; s. Lawrence Alfred and Geraldine Mary (Hoffman) Troy; m. Margaret Ann Swanson, May 1, 1971; 1 child Eric Ronald ; m. Rosalie Ann Beane, June 7, 1959 (div. Feb. 4, 1971). BA in Social Studies, Drake U., 1959; MSW, U. Iowa, 1966. Admitting clk. Broadlawns Hosp., DesMoines, 1960—62; pub. welfare worker Fayette County Welfare, West Union, 1962—64; pub. welfare supr. State of Iowa, Des Moines, 1966—68; exec. dir. Big Bros., 1968—71, Big Bros.-Big Sisters, Omaha, 1971—87; sch. social worker Western Hills Area Edn. Agy., Sioux City, Iowa, 1987—. Union pres. Profl. Staff Assn., Sioux City, 1993—95. Vol. Big Bros., Des Moines, 1985—87; pres.-elect Kiwanis Club, Denison, 1992. Mem.: NASW, Acad. Cert. Social Workers, Sioux City Chess Club (pres. 1995—97, sec.-treas.). Avocations: chess, reading, walking, dogs. Home: 15009 Westchester Cir Omaha NE 68154 Office: Western Hills Area Edn Agy 1520 Morningside Ave Sioux City IA 51106

TROYANOVICH, STEPHEN JOHN, educational program director, poet; b. Wheeling, W.Va., Dec. 18, 1947; s. Andrew Joseph and Rosalie Miklovic T.; m. Magdalena del Rosario Coronel, Apr. 15, 1972; children: Esteban Fernando. Student, Rio Grande Coll., 1969; BA in Journalism, Riverside U., 1970; MA in Corrections, Montclair State Coll., 1974. Cert. secondary tchr., N.J., behavior modification, pub. mgr., supervision. Vol. Peace Corps, Ecuador, 1970-72; intern N.J. Tchr. Corps Project, Edison, N.J., 1973-74; tchr. corrections N.J. Dept. Corrections, Bordentown, 1974-76, program dir. Skillman, 1977-82, asst. supr. edn. vocational Bordentown, 1982-83, asst. supr. edn. acad., 1983-84, dir. edn. Delmont, 1984—. Author: Dream Dealers and Other Shadows, 1978, In the West of Ireland, 1994; editor: N.J. Corrections Quarterly, 1995—, bd. dirs., 1997—; co-editor: Omniumgathum, 1976. Active Habitat for Humanity, Monmouth County, N.J., 1998, Art Festival; charter mem. Nat. Mus. Am. Indian; mem. Defenders of Wildlife. Mem. Internat. Assn. Jazz Educators, Am. Correctional Assn., Poetry Soc. Am., Writers and Poets, Inc., Jazz Found. Am. Avocation: jazz. Office: So State Correctional Facility PO Box 150 Rte 47 Delmont NJ 08314

TROYER, ALVAH FORREST, agriculture executive, plant breeder; b. LaFontaine, Ind., May 30, 1929; s. Alvah Forrest and Lottie (Waggoner) T.; m. Joyce Ann Wigner, Sept. 22, 1950; children: Anne, Barbara, Catherine, Daniel (dec.). BS, Purdue U., 1954; MS, U. Ill., 1956; PhD, U. Minn., 1964. Rsch. assoc. U. Ill., Urbana, 1955-56; rsch. fellow U. Minn., St. Paul, 1956-58; rsch. sta. mgr. Pioneer Hi-Bred Internat., Inc., Mankato, Minn., 1958-65, rsch. coord., 1965-77; dir. R & D, Pfizer Genetics, St. Louis, 1977-81, v.p. and dir. R & D, 1981-82; v.p. R & D, DeKalb (Ill.) Plant Genetics, 1982-93; cons. Hybrid Seed divsn. Cargill, Mpls., 1993-98; adj. prof. crop sci. dept. U. Ill., 1998—. Rschr. corn breeding, econ. botany, crop physiology, increasing genetic diversity, recent corn evolution. Contbr. articles to numerous publs.; developer of popular corn inbred lines and hybrids. Master sgt. U.S. Army, 1951-53, Korea. Recipient Nat. Coun. Comml. Plant Breeders Genetics and Plant Breeding award, 1992, Outstanding Achievement award U. Minn., 1998, nat. award for agrl. excellence Nat. Agrl. Mktg. Assn., 1999. Fellow AAAS, Am. Soc. Agronomy, Crop Sci. Soc. Am.; mem. Am. Genetic Assn., Genetic Soc. Am., N.Y. Acad. Scis., CAST, VFW, Masons, Sigma Xi, Gamma Sigma Delta (Award of Merit 1996), Alpha Zeta, Lambda Chi Alpha, Gamma Alpha. Methodist. Home: 611 Joanne Ln Dekalb IL 60115 E-mail: atroyer@uiuc.edu.

TROYER, LEROY SETH, architect; b. Middlebury, Ind., Nov. 23, 1937; s. Seth and Nancy (Miller) T.; m. Phyllis Eigsti, May 24, 1958; children: Terry, Ronald, Donald. BArch, U. Notre Dame, 1971. Founder, pres., CEO LeRoy Troyer and Assocs., South Bend, 1971; sr. ptnr. The Trouer Group, Inc. (formerly LeRoy Troyer and Assocs.), Mishawaka, Ind., 1988—; pres. Southfield, Inc., 1988—. Bd. dirs. Lead Devel., Inc. Author numerous documents; contbr. numerous papers and articles to publs. Past pres., chair Environic Found. Internat., Inc.; bd. dirs. Habitat for Humanity Internat. Americus, Ga., 1987-93, Coun. of Christian Colls. and Univs., 1991-96, Habitat for Humanity St. Joseph County, Ind., 1992-99, 2001—; bd. dirs. Bethel Coll., 1988-97, Mishawaka, Housing Devel. Corp., South Bend, CONNECT, South Bend; bd. dirs., exec. com. Fourth Freedom Forum Internat., 1996—; bd. dirs. Evangelicals for Social Action, Wynnewood, Pa., 1997—; chmn. Miracle of Nazareth Internat. Found., 2000--. Recipient numerous local, state and nat. awards and honors. Fellow AIA (practice mgmt. com., chmn. 1983-84), Ind. Soc. Architects, Mennonite Econ. Devel. Assn. Internat. (chmn. bd. 1987-91). Avocations: photography, travel, reading, art, woodworking. Home: 1442 Deerfield Ct South Bend IN 46614-6429 Office: The Troyer Group Inc 550 Union St Mishawaka IN 46544-2346 E-mail: leroy@troyergroup.com.

TROYER, THOMAS ALFRED, lawyer; b. Omaha, Aug. 15, 1933; s. Robert Raymond and Dorothy (Darlow) T.; m. Sally Jean Brown, June 28, 1958; children: Kenneth D., Robert C., Virginia D., Thomas C. BA, Harvard U., 1955; JD, U. Mich., 1958. Bar: Colo. 1958, U.S. Ct. Appeals (D.C. cir.) 1967. Assoc. Holme, Roberts, More & Owen, Denver, 1958-61; USAF, 1961-62; trial atty. U.S. Dept. Justice, Washington, 1962-64; legal staff Asst. Sec. Treasury for Tax Policy, 1964-66; assoc. tax legis. counsel U.S. Dept. Treasury, 1966-67; mem. Caplin & Drysdale, 1967—. Pres. Stern Fund, N.Y.C., 1985—86; bd. dirs. Children's Def. Fund, Washington, Mineral Policy Ctr., Washington; mem. bd. trustees Natural Resources Def. Coun., N.Y.C., 1977—, Carnegie Corp., N.Y.C., 1983—91, Cmty. Found. Nat. Capital Region, 1992—2000; chairperson Charity Lobbying in Pub. Interest, Washington. Contbr. numerous articles to profl. jours. Bd. dirs. Common Cause, Washington, 1980-83; mem. Treasury Adv. Commn. on Pvt. Philanthropy and Pub. Needs, Washington, 1976-77; mem. adv. group to Commr. Internal Rev., Washington, 1978-80; mem. com. of visitors U. Mich. Law Sch., Ann Arbor, 1982—; mem. IRS Commr.'s Exempt Orgn. Adv. Group, Washington, 1987-90. Fellow Am. Bar Found., Am. Coll. Tax Counsel; mem. ABA (vice chmn. govt. rels. tax sect. 1989-91, comm. on homelessness and poverty 1992-94), Coun. for Excellence in Govt., Am. Law Inst. Democrat. Home: 5514 Cedar Pkwy Chevy Chase MD 20815-3444 Office: Caplin & Drysdale Chartered 1 Thomas Cir NW Ste 1100 Washington DC 20005-5894

TROZZOLO, ANTHONY MARION, chemistry educator; b. Chgo., Jan. 11, 1930; s. Pasquale and Francesca (Vercillo) T.; m. Doris C. Stoffregen, Oct. 8, 1955; children: Thomas, Susan, Patricia, Michael, Lisa, Laura. BS, Ill. Inst. Tech., 1950; MS, U. Chgo., 1957, PhD, 1960. Asst. chemist Chgo. Midway Labs., 1952-53; assoc. chemist Armour Rsch. Found., Chgo., 1953-56; tech. staff Bell Labs., Murray Hill, N.J., 1959-75; Charles L. Huisking prof. chemistry U. Notre Dame, 1975-92, Charles L. Huisking prof. emeritus, 1992—; asst. dean U. Notre Dame Coll. Sci., 1993-98; P.C. Reilly lectr. U. Notre Dame, 1972, Hesburgh Alumni lectr., 1986, Disting. lectr. sci., 1986. Vis. prof. Columbia U., N.Y.C., 1971, U. Colo., 1981, Katholieke U. Leuven, Belgium, 1983, Max Planck Inst. für Strahlenchemie, Mülheim/Ruhr, Fed. Republic Germany, 1990; vis. lectr. Academia Sinica, 1984, 85; Phillips lectr. U. Okla., 1971; C.L. Brown lectr. Rutgers U., 1975; Sigma Xi lectr. Bowling Green U., 1976, Abbott Labs., 1978; M. Faraday lectr. No. Ill. U., 1976; F.O. Butler lectr. S.D. State U., 1978; Chevron lectr. U. Nev., Reno, 1983; J. Crano lectr. U. Akron, 2000; plenary lectr. various internat. confs.; founder, chmn. Gordon Conf. on Organic Photochemistry, 1964; trustee Gordon Rsch. Confs., 1988-92; cons. in field. Assoc. editor Jour. Am. Chem. Soc., 1975-76; editor Chem. Revs., 1977-84; editorial adv. bd. Accounts of Chem. Rsch., 1977-85; cons. editor Encyclopedia of Science and Technology, 1982-92; contbr. articles to profl. jours.; patentee in field. Fellow AEC, 1951, NSF, 1957-59; named Hon. Citizen of Castrolibero, Italy, 1997; recipient Pietro Bucci prize U. Calabria/Italian Chem. Soc., 1997. Fellow AAAS, Am. Inst. Chemists (Student award 1950), N.Y. Acad. Scis. (chmn. chem. scis. sect. 1969-70, Halpern award in photochemistry 1980), Inter-Am. Photochemical Soc.; mem. AAUP, Am. Chem. Soc. (Disting. Svc. award St. Joseph Valley sect. 1979, Tex. lectr. 1975, Pacific Coast lectr. 1981, Coronado lectr. 1980, 93, 98, N.Y. state lectr. 1993, Hoosier lectr. 1995, Ozark lectr. 1995, Rocky Mountain lectr. 1996, Tex. Coast lectr. 1996, Osage lectr. 1998), Sigma Xi. Roman Catholic. Home: 1329 E Washington St South Bend IN 46617-3340 Office: U Notre Dame Dept Chemistry-Biochemistry Notre Dame IN 46556-5670

TRPIS, MILAN, vector biologist, scientist, educator; b. Mojsova Lucka, Slovakia, Dec. 20, 1930; came to U.S., 1971, naturalized, 1977; s. Gaspar and Anna (Sevcikova) T.; m. Ludmila Tonkovic, Dec. 15, 1956; children: Martin, Peter, Katarina. MS, Comenius U., Bratislava, 1956; PhD, Charles U., Prague, 1960. Research asst. Slovak Acad. Sci., Bratislava, 1953-56, sci. asst., 1956-60, scientist, 1960-62, ind. scientist, 1962-69; ecologist-entomologist East Africa-Aedes Rsch. Unit WHO, Dar es Salaam, Tanzania, 1969-71; asst. faculty fellow dept. biology U. Notre Dame, 1971-73, assoc. faculty fellow, 1973-74; assoc. prof. med. entomology Johns Hopkins U. Sch. Hygiene and Pub. Health, 1974-78, prof., 1978—, dir. labs. med. entomology. Med. entomology; rsch. assoc. U. Ill., Urbana, 1966-67, Can. Dept. Agr., Lethbridge, Alta., 1967-68; dir. Biol. Rsch. Inst. Am., 1971-79; external dir. rsch. Liberian Inst. Biomed. Rsch., 1981-89; dir. AID project on transmission of river blindness in areas of Liberia, Sierra Leone, and Cote d'Ivoire; dir. WHO rsch. grant; tech. adv. com. AID Vector Biology and Control Project, 1986-91; dir. Johns Hopkins U./Fed. U. Tech. Akure Onchocerciasis Project in Nigeria, 1991-94, Johns Hopkins U./Organisation de Coordination et de Cooperation pour la Lutte les Grandes Endemies-Pierre Richet Inst. Onchocerciasis Project, Bouakè, Ivory Coast, 1993-96; dir. Johns Hopkins U./Pierre Richet Inst./ORSTOM onchocerciasis project in Ivory Coast, 1993-96; prof.-advisor doctoral students, Africa, Asia, Cen. Am., 1979—. Editor: Jour. Biologia, 1956-71, Jour. Entomol. Problems, 1960-72; zool. sect.: Jour. Biol. Works, 1960-71; Contbr. articles to profl. jours. Dir. WHO project on prophylactic drugs for river blindness, Liberia, 1985-87. Recipient Slovak Acad. Sci., 1st prize for research project. Mem. AAUP, AAAS, Am. Inst. Biol. Sci., Am. Mosquito Control Assn., Am. Soc. Parasitologists, Helminthol. Soc. Washington, Am. Soc. Tropical Medicine and Hygiene, Entomol. Soc. Am., Am. Genetic Assn., Soc. of Vector Ecology, N.Y. Acad. Scis., Johns Hopkins U. Tropical Medicine Club, Smithsonian Assocs., Royal Soc. Tropical Medicine and Hygiene, Royal Entomol. Soc. of London, Sigma Xi, Delta Omega (Alpha chpt.). Home: 1504 Ivy Hill Rd Cockeysville MD 21030-1418 Office: Johns Hopkins U 615 N Wolfe St Baltimore MD 21205-2103 E-mail: mtrpis@jhsph.edu.

TRUANT, ALLAN L. medical educator, research scientist, health science association administrator; b. July 6, 1950; BS, U. Mich., 1971; PhD, U. Oreg., 1977. Fellow Ctrs. for Disease Control, Atlanta, 1977-79; assoc. prof., assoc. dir. Univ. Tex. Med. Br., Galveston, 1979-85; prof., dir. clin. microbiology, immunology and virology lab. Temple U. Hosp. and Sch. Medicine, Phila., 1985—. Inspector Coll. Am. Pathologists, Chgo., 1983—; mem. exam. bd. Am. Bd. Bioanalysis, St. Louis, 1996—. Editor: Manual of Commercial Methods in Clinical Microbiology, 2002. Recipient Rorer award for manuscript excellence Am. Coll. Gastroenterology, 1983. Office: Temple U Hosp and Sch Medicine Broad Ontario Sts Philadelphia PA 19140 E-mail: truantal@tuhs.temple.edu.

TRUAX, DENNIS DALE, civil engineer, educator, consultant; b. Hagerstown, Md., July 25, 1953; s. Bernard James and Dorothy Hilda Truax; m. Jeanie Ann Knable, Aug. 20, 1977. BS in Civil Engring., Va. Poly. Inst. and State U., 1976; MS, Miss. State U., 1978, PhD, 1986. Registered profl. engr., Miss.; diplomate Environ. Engring. Asst. dep. constrn. mgr. Fairfax County, Va., 1972-74; design engr. Washington County, Md., 1976; instr. Miss. State U., Starkville, 1980-86, asst. prof. civil engring., 1986-91, assoc. prof., 1991-96, prof., 1996—. Prin. corp. pres. ASD, LLC, 1997-2000; prin., v.p. engring. ATi, Inc., 2000—; environ. engring. cons. Assoc. editor ASCE/NSPE Profl. Issues Jour., 1999—. Lay leader Aldersgate United Meth. Ch., Starkville, 1982-85, chmn. pastor/parish rels., 1985-86, chmn. coun. on ministries, 1986-90, chmn. adminstrv. bd., 1990-92, chmn. fin. com., 1992-94, 2001-2003, chmn. bd. trustees, 1996-97; adviser Triangle Fraternity, Starkville, Alumni Bd. Dirs. treas., 1989-96; bd. dirs. Meth. Student Ctr., Miss. State U., 1983-90, chmn. pastor/parish rels., 1984-86, v.p. bd., 1986, pres., 1987-89, treas., 1990-91; del. to ann. conf. Miss. Conf. United Meth. Ch., also vice chmn. com. on higher edn.; active Starkville dist. lay coun. Miss. State Herrin-Hess Prof., 1993-94, 94-95, 95-96. Recipient Golden Key Outstanding Faculty award Golden Key Nat. Honor Soc., 1994, Miss. Outstanding Civil Engr. of Yr., ASCE Miss. sect., 1995; named Outstanding Young Man Am., U.S. Jaycees, 1983. Fellow ASCE (chair student svcs. com. 1995-96, vice chair 1996-97, adv. Miss. State student chpt. 1981—, chair career guidance com. 1991-92, sec. 1990-91, Miss. sect. pres.-elect 1990-91, pres. 1991-92, chmn. student svc. com. 1995-96, scholarship com. 1998—, chair scholarship com. 2000-01, No. Miss. br. pres. 2000-2001, dist. 14 dir. 2001--, fin. com., com. on diversity and women in civil engring.); mem. NSPE, Am. Water Works Assn. (Ala.-Miss. 41 chpt. scholarship bd. dirs. 1994—, bd. sec.-treas. 1998—), Miss. Engring. Soc. (pres., pres.-elect region 3 v.p., bd. dirs., Tombigbee chpt. pres., chpt. pres.-elect, Engring. educator 1995, Educator of the Yr. award 1995), Water Environ. Fedn. (rsch. com.), Sigma Xi (sec., pres.-elect, pres. Miss. State chpt.), Tau Beta Pi, Chi Epsilon. Democrat. Home: 1054 Southgate Dr Starkville MS 39759-8810 Office: Miss State U PO Box 9546 Mississippi State MS 39762-9546

TRUBETSKOY, VLADIMIR SERGEEVICH, polymer chemist; b. Moscow, Oct. 13, 1957; s. Sergey V. and Nina V. Trubetskoy; m. Olga V. Merzlikine, Feb. 9, 1984; children: Sergey, Vassily, Ivan. M in Chemistry summa cum laude, Moscow State U., 1974, MS, 1979; PhD in Biochemistry, USSR Acad. Med. Scis., Moscow, 1984. Sr. rsch. fellow Inst. Exptl. Cardiology, Moscow, 1984-90; postdoctoral fellow dept. biochemistry U. Tenn., Knoxville, 1990-91; asst. in chemistry Ctr. Imaging and Pharm. Rsch., Mass. Gen. Hosp., Boston, 1991-93; assoc. chemist dept. radiology Med. Sch. Harvard U., Ctr. Imaging and Pharm. Rsch., Mass. Gen. Hosp., 1993-96; sr. chemist Mirus Corp., Madison, Wis., 1996—. Co-contbr. articles, contbr. rev. to profl. jours. Radiol. Soc. N.Am. Seed grantee, 1996; Small Bus. Innovation rsch. grantee NIH, 1998, 2000; recipient Outstanding Pharm. Paper award Controlled Release Soc., 1993. Mem. Am. Chem. Soc., Am. Soc. for Gene Therapy, Controlled Release Soc. Eastern Orthodox. Office: Mirus Corp 505 S Rosa Rd Madison WI 53719-1262 Fax: 608-441-2849. E-mail: vladimirt@genetransfer.com.

TRUBKO, SERGEY VLADIMIR, optical designer, scientist; b. St. Petersburg, Russia, Sept. 26, 1948; came to U.S., 1994; s. Vladimir F. Trubko and Polina L. Chornaya; m. Liza Trubko, Oct. 31, 1987; children: Raisa, Tim. BS, U. Fine Mechanics and Optics, St. Petersburg, 1971, MS with honors, 1973, PhD, 1977. From scientist to sr. scientist Metrology Inst., State Optical Inst., St. Petersburg, 1977-94; cons. Bklyn., 1995; sr. optical engr. Symbol Tech., Inc., Holtsville, N.Y., 1996-98; sr. scientist CycloVision Tech., Inc., N.Y.C., 1998-2000; v.p., chief scientist RemoteReality Corp., Westborough, Mass., 2000—. Author: Design of Cemented Doublets, 1984; contbr. articles to profl. jours. Mem. Internat. Soc. Optical Engring. Achievements include invention of three-mirror off-axis system and catadioptric panoramic imaging system; holds 7 patents. Office: RemoteReality Corp 4 Technology Dr Westborough MA 01581-1727 E-mail: strubko@remotereality.com., trubko@hotmail.com.

TRUBO, RICHARD M. writer; b. L.A., Apr. 2, 1946; s. William Trubo, Ida Trubo; m. Donna R. Grodin; children: Melissa, Michael. BA, UCLA, 1967, MS, 1968. Co-host ("Confrontation"), writer KOST-FM, L.A., 1968—71; bur. chief / contbg. editor HEI Pub. / Miller Freeman Pub. (Med. World News), Houston and San Francisco, 1983—88; med. editor, writer, cons. Feeling Fine Co., L.A., 1989—2000. Author: (book) An Act of Mercy, 1975, From Victim to Victor, 1987, The H.A.R.T. Program, 1992, Flying Through Hollywood by the Seat of My Pants, 1992, The Mental Edge, 1999, Tapping the Healer Within, 2001, Courage, 2001, Stairway to Heaven , 2002, (books) 12 books in addition to those listed above (1977-2001), (articles (published 1979-2002)) (New York Times, Los Angeles Times, Harvard Medical School Health Publications Group, CBS HealthWatch, MSNBC, Reader's Digest, Mayo Clinic website, World Book Publishing, The Lancet, others); prodr.: (documentary film) Children of the State, 1977. Recipient Journalism award of Excellence, Am. Acad. Facial Plastic and Reconstructive Surgery, 1990, Blakeslee award, Am. Heart Assn., 1991. Mem.: Am. Soc. Journalists & Authors, Nat. Assn. Med. Communicators, Am. Med. Writers Assn., Nat. Assn. Sci. Writers.

TRUBOW, MARSHALL DAVID, obstetrician-gynecologist; b. Detroit, July 31, 1943; BS, Wayne State U., 1967, MD, 1969. Intern Sinai Hosp., Detroit, 1969-70; resident in ob.-gyn. Beth Israel Hosp., Boston, 1970-71, 74-77, mem. staff, 1978—, Mt. Auburn Hosp., Cambridge, Mass., 1980—; with Harvard Cmty. Health Plan, 1978-97; mem. staff Brigham and Women's Hosp., Boston, Beth Israel Deaconess Hosp., Boston; pvt. practice, Wellesley, Mass., 1997—. Clin. instr. ob.-gyn. Harvard U. Mem. ACOG, Am. Assn. Gynecol. Laparoscopists, Am. Soc. Laser Medicine & Surgeons. Office: Harvard Vanguard Med Assocs 230 Worcester St Wellesley MA 02481-5420 Fax: (781) 431-5548. E-mail: marshall_trubow@VMED.org.

TRUCANO, MICHAEL, lawyer; b. Washington, May 28, 1945; s. Peter Joseph and Fern Margaret (Bauer) T.; m. Doreen E. Struck, 1969; children: Michael, David. BA, Carleton Coll., 1967; JD, NYU, 1970. Assoc. Dorsey & Whitney, Mpls., 1970-75, ptnr., 1976—, head of office, 2000—. Office: Dorsey & Whitney LLP Ste 1500 50 S 6th St Minneapolis MN 55402-1498 E-mail: trucano.mike@dorseylaw.com.

TRUCE, WILLIAM EVERETT, chemist, educator; b. Chgo., Sept. 30, 1917; s. Stanley C. and Frances (Novak) T.; m. Eloise Joyce McBroom, June 16, 1940; children: Nancy Jane, Roger William. BS, U. Ill., 1939; PhD, Northwestern U., 1943. Mem. faculty Purdue U., 1946-88, prof. chemistry, 1956-88, prof. chemistry emeritus, 1988—, asst. dean Grad. Sch., 1963-66. Mem. numerous univ. dept. and profl. coms.; chmn. various profl. meetings; exec. officer Nat. Organic Symposium, 1961; chmn. Gordon Rsch. Conf. on Organic Reactions and Processes; cons. in field. Co-author book; contbr. articles to profl. jours., chpts. to books. Guggenheim fellow Oxford U., 1957 Mem. Am. Chem. Soc., Phi Beta Kappa (sec. Purdue chpt.), Sigma Xi (pres. Purdue chpt.). Achievements include research in new methods of synthesis, devel. new kinds of compounds and reactions. Home: 220 Hopi Pl Boulder CO 80303-3533 Office: Purdue U Dept Chemistry West Lafayette IN 47907 E-mail: etruce@bouldernews.infi.net.

TRUCHAN, THOMAS G. materials engineer; b. Chicago, Ill., Nov. 9, 1972; s. Gerald L. Truchan, Patricia Helen Malloy. Degree in ceramic engring., Iowa State U., 1996; degree in material sci. and engring., Ill. Inst. Tech., 2000. Grad. rschr. Argonne (Ill.) Nat. Lab., 1996—2000; thin film process engr. Spectra Physics Semiconductor Lasers, Tucson, 2000—. (discovery) of improved metallic substrates for high temperature superconductors. Office: Spectra Physics Semiconductor Lasers 3321 E Global Loop Tucson AZ 85706 Personal E-mail: ttruchan@splasers.com. Business E-Mail: ttruchan@splasers.com.

TRUCK, FREDERICK JOHN, artist; b. Mt. Pleasant, Iowa, Sept. 6, 1946; s. Orville William and Odetta Gertrude Allender; m. Lorna Ruth Young, Sept. 30, 1972; 1 child, Benjamin Isaac. BA, Iowa Wesleyan Coll., 1969; student, Am. U., 1969-70; diploma, Des Moines Area C.C., 1975. Freelance artist, Des Moines, 1972—; graphic artist various cos., 1975-85; tech. advisor Art Com., San Francisco, 1985-95. Artist Ars Electronica, Linz, Austria, 1989, Machine Culture SIGGRAPH, Anaheim, Calif., 1993, Vail Geisler, Des Moines, 1998, Des Moines Art Ctr., Steven Vail Gallery, 2001; art resident Banff Ctr. Arts, Alberta, Canada, 1991, Second Look Alternative Traditions in Contemporary Arts, Iowa City, 1995; cons. New Eng. Found. Arts, Boston, 1994; adv. bd. Des Moines Art Ctr., 1999—. Artist: Camping Out B & C, 1975; artist, pub. Electric Bank, 1982. Playwriting grantee Schubert Found. Am. U., 1969, Individual Artists grantee Iowa Arts Coun., 1995. Home: 4225 University Ave Des Moines IA 50311-3421 E-mail: fred@fredtruck.com.

TRUCKENBRODT, YOLANDA BERNABE, retired air force officer, consultant; b. Manila, June 17, 1952; d. Nestor Leynes and Zenaida Bernabe Javier; m. Edmund Phillip Truckenbrodt, July 27, 1972. BA, Far Ea. U., Manila, 1971; AAS, C.C. of the Air Force, 1980; MBA, Angelo State U., 1980; MPA, U. West Fla., 1987; D of Pub. Adminstrn., Nova Southeastern U., 2000; diploma, Air Command and Staff Coll., 1995. Cert. Dept. of Def.'s Acquisition Profl. in Program Mgmt., USAF Software Quality Assurance. Enlisted USAF, 1974, advanced through grades to maj., 1998, ret., 1998; program mgr. KC-135 Reengine Dep. for Airlift and Trainer Sys., Wright-Patterson AFB, Ohio, 1980-84; electronic warfare program mgr. Tactical Sys. Divsn., Eglin AFB, Fla., 1985-88; program mgr. Airborne Warning and Control Sys. Elec. Sys. Ctr., Hanscom AFB, Mass., 1989-91; program analyst ballistic missile def. hdqs. Air Force Material Command, Wright-Patterson AFB, 1992-94; congl. liaison staff officer Plans and Programs Divsn., 1995-98. Flight comdr. detachment 847 Res. Officers Tng. Corps, San Angelo, Tex., 1978-80; chairperson Asian-Am. Pacific Islander Heritage Com., Eglin AFB, 1986-87; officer-in-charge Air Force Assn. Nat. Acquisition Symposium, Wright-Patterson AFB, 1993-94; student in-resident Def. Sys. Mgmt. Coll., Ft. Belvoir, Va., 1994; staff officer Directorate of Plans and Programs, Wright-Patterson AFB, 1995-98; jr. officer the Quarter, Airlift and Trainer Sys., Wright-Patterson AFB, 1983. Contbr. articles to profl. jours. Guest spkr. Nat. Bus. and Profl. Assn., San Angelo, 1993; pres. Filipino-Am. Assn., 1987; bd. dirs. Filipino-Am. Assn., Ft. Walton Beach, Fla., 1987; bd. dirs. Filipino-Am. Coun. N.W. Fla.; vol. Air Force Mus., Dayton, Ohio, 1995-96; vol. income tax preparer Ret. Officers Assn., Wright-Patterson AFB, 1999—; vol. social worker United Way, Dayton, 1982-84. Decorated Meritorious Svc. medal USAF, 1989, 93, 98, Commendation medal USAF, 1984; named Airman of the Quarter, Air Weather Svc. Comms. Squadron, 1975, Career Woman of Yr., Gayfers Career Club of Okaloosa County, Fla., 1987; recipient Appreciation and Recognition award Dyess AFB Human Rels. Coun., 1976, 77, Air Force Res. Tng. Corps (ROTC) Leadership award, 1979, Arnold Air Soc. Outstanding Pledge award, 1979, Drill Commandant of Yr. award, 1978; 2d Pl. Overall winner for half-marathon 4th Internat. Marathon on Great Wall, China, 1999, winner numerous race awards in track and field and Summer Biathlons; Robert G. Carr scholar Detachment 847 ROTC, Angelo State U., 1978, 80; named one of Outstanding Young Women of Am., 1983. Mem. Women in Mil. Svc. for Am. (charter), Air Force Women Officers Assoc., Angelo State U. Alumni Assn. (Disting. ROTC Alumnae of Yr. 2002), Ohio River Rd. Runners Club, Sigma Beta Delta (life). Avocations: travel, arts and music, summer biathlons, marathons, photography.

TRUCKSIS, THERESA A. retired library director; b. Hubbard, Ohio, Sept. 1, 1924; d. Peter and Carmella (DiSilverio) Pagliasotti; m. Robert C. Trucksis, May 29, 1948 (dec. May 1980); children: M. Laura, Anne, Michele, Patricia, David, Robert, Claire, Peter; m. Philip P. Hickey, Oct. 19, 1985 (dec. May 1993). BS in Edn., Youngstown Coll., 1945; postgrad., Youngstown State U., 1968-71; MLS, Kent State U., 1972. Psychometrist Youngstown (Ohio) Coll., 1946-49; instr. ltd. svc. Youngstown State U., 1968-71; libr. Pub. Libr. Youngstown & Mahoning County, Youngstown, 1972-73, asst. dept. head, 1973-74, asst. dir., 1985-89, dir., 1989-97, NOLA Regional Libr. System, Youngstown, 1974-85. Contbr. articles to profl. jours. Mem. bd. Hubbard Sch. Dist., 1980-85. Mem. ALA, Ohio Libr. Assn. (bd. dirs. 1979-81), Pub. Libr. Assn. Address: 133 Viola Ave Hubbard OH 44425-2062

TRUDEL, MARC J. botanist, educator; PhD, Cornell U. Prof. plant physiology and horticulture Laval U., 1969—, former dean sch. agrl. and food scis., 1983-91, former dir. gen. continuing edn., 1992-97, v.p. devel., 1997—. Office: Univ Laval Alphonse-Desjardins Bldg 3555 Quebec QC Canada G1K 7P4 E-mail: marc.trudel@vrd.ulaval.ca.

TRUDNAK, STEPHEN JOSEPH, landscape architect; b. Nanticoke, Pa., Feb. 25, 1947; s. Stephen Adam and Marcella (Levulis) T.; m. Arden Batchelder Weill, Sept. 6, 1980. BS in Landscape Arch., Pa. State U., 1970. Jr. landscape arch. Kling Partnership, Phila., 1970-72; mem. landscape arch. firm Keith French Assocs., Washington, 1972-73; head dept. landscape arch. Linganore Ctr. Design, Frederick, Md., 1973-74, Toups and Loiederman, Rockville, 1974-76; project landscape arch. Kaiser Transit Group, So. Calif. Rapid Transit Dist., Dade County Transit Improvement Program, Metro Rail Transit Cons.; v.p. Harry Weese & Assocs., Ltd., Miami, Fla., 1976-84; v.p. landscape arch. Canin Assocs., Orlando, 1984-87; dir. planning and design Bonita Bay Properties, Inc., Bonita Springs, 1987-91; prin. Stephen J. Trudnak, P.A. Landscape Arch. and Land Planning, 1991—. Bd. dirs., v.p. Koreshan State Hist. Site, 1989-94; mem. 'not for profit' com. Bonita Springs Cmty. Redevel. Agy., 1994-97; v.p. Bonita Springs Mainstreet Program, 1996, 2000, pres., 1997-98; del. for Congressman Porter Goss, Congl. Small Bus. Summit, 1998, 2000, del. representing Fla. state rep. Carol Green Fla. Small Bus. Summit, 1999; bd. dirs. Bonita Springs YMCA, 1999—, mem. exec. com., 2000—, chair facilities design task force, 2000—; bd. dirs. Bot. Gardens of Bonita Springs, 2001—02, mem. exec. com., 2000—02, chair facilities design task force, 2000—02. Fellow Am. Soc. Landscape Archs. (pres. Fla. chpt. 1983, chpt. adv. bd. 1984-85, elections task force 1986, publs. task force 1987, trustee 1987-89, membership task force, chmn. 1989-90, nat. v.p. chpt. and mem. svcs. 1992-94, non-dues revenue task force 1994-95, ASLA On-Line com. 1997—, chair 1999, specifications task force 1998-99), Nat. Xeriscape Coun. (Fla. steering com.), Nat. Speleol. Soc. SCARAB; mem. Bonita Springs C. of C. (chair beautification com. 1991-92, 94-95, chair awards task force 2000, bd. dirs. 1995—, v.p. edn. divsn. 1996-98, vice chmn. cmty. devel. divsn. 1998-99, Affiliate of Yr. 1997, Citizen of Yr. 1999, Charter Class Leadership Bonita Grad. 2000). Home: 2432 Ravenna Blvd # 202 Naples FL 34109 Office: 3876 Bonita Beach Rd Bonita Springs FL 34134 E-mail: stevieland@comcast.net., strudnak@trudnak.com.

TRUE, EDWARD KEENE, architectural engineer; b. Boston, July 12, 1915; s. Edward Payson and Laura Keene (Darling) T.; m. Mildred Louise Richenburg, Aug. 31, 1940; children: Edward Bartlett, Robert Payson, Peter Keene, James Duncan. BS, MIT, 1939. Engr. Concrete Steel Co., Boston, 1939-40; instr. architecture U. Oreg., 1940-42; sr. engr. Raytheon Mfg. Co., Waltham, Mass., 1943-45; mem. faculty Grad. Sch. Design, Harvard U., 1945-76, prof. architecture, 1958-76. Trustee, mem. bd. investment Middlesex Savs. Banks, Natick, Mass., 1954-88; cons. engr. and architect, 1947-59; ptnr. Souza and True, engrs., Cambridge, 1959— ; engr. Souza and True Inc., 1970, pres., 1970-86; chmn. bd. Souza, True and Ptnrs. Inc., 1986— Mem. Concord Planning Bd., 1948-58, chmn., 1954-58; mem. Concord Bd. Appeals, 1959-66, chmn., 1959-61; mem. Concord Bd. Selectmen, 1970-76, chmn., 1972-73; mem. exec. com. Mass. League of Cities and Towns, 1974-76, Searsport Yacht Club; pres. Hope (Maine) Hist Soc., 1994-95m 2002--. Home: PO Box 483 11 Shoreside Ln Searsport ME 04974-0483 Office: 653 Mount Auburn St Watertown MA 02472-2017 E-mail: edwtrue@cs.com.

TRUE, JEAN DURLAND, entrepreneur, oil company executive; b. Nov. 27, 1915; d. Clyde Earl and Harriet Louise (Brayton) Durland; m. Henry Alfonso True Jr., Mar. 20, 1938; children: Tamma Jean (Mrs. Donald G. Hatten), Henry Alfonso III, Diemer Durland, David Lanmon. Student, Mont. State U., 1935-36. Ptnr. True Drilling Co., Casper, Wyo., 1951—94, True Oil Co., Casper, 1951-94, Eighty-Eight Oil LLC, 1955-94, True Geothermal Energy Co., 1980—, True Ranches, 1981-94. Officer, dir. White Stallion Ranch, Inc., Tucson, Smokey Oil Co., Casper. Mem. steering com. YMCA, Casper, 1954-55, bd. dirs., 1956-68; mem. bd. dirs. Gottsche Rehab. Ctr., Thermopolis, Wyo., 1966-93, mem. exec. bd., 1966-93, v.p., 1983-90; mem. adv. bd. for adult edn. U. Wyo., 1966-68; mem. Ft. Casper Commn., Casper, 1973-79; bd. dirs. Mus. of Rockies, Bozeman, Mont., 1983-87, mem. Nat. Adv. Bd., 1997-2000; bd. dirs. Nicolaysen Art Mus., 1988-93, Nat. Cowboy Hall of Fame and Western Heritage Ctr., 1997—, Nat. Cowboy and We. Heritage Mus., 1997-2002, dir. emeritus, 2002--; mem. Nat. Fedn. Rep. Women's Clubs; dep. Rep. nat. conv., 1972; trustee Trooper Found., 1995—. Mem. Casper Area C. of C., Alpha Gamma Delta, Casper Country Club, Petroleum Club. Episcopalian. Office: PO Box 2360 Casper WY 82602-2360

TRUE, LELAND BEYER, civil engineer, consultant; b. Cheyenne, Wyo., Aug. 20, 1921; s. James Beaman and Mary Laura (Beyer) T.; m. Janet R. Hill (dec. Aug. 1976); 1 child, Patricia Ann; m. Alef Collins, May 8, 1977. BSCE, U. Wyo., 1943. Hydrographic field asst. U.S. Geol. Survey, Cheyenne and Laramie, Wyo., 1942-43; engr. P.I Boysen Dam U.S. Bur. Reclamation, Thermopolis, 1946-52; with Morrison-Knudsen Co., Inc., 1952-70, 77-86, project mgr. Greer's Ferry Dam Ark., 1961-63, project mgr. Blue Ridge Dam Payson, Ariz., 1963-65, project mgr., estimator home office Boise, Idaho, 1965-69, project mgr. Toa Vaca Dam Villalba, P.R., 1969-70; resident area engr. metro subway A.A. Mathews, Inc., Washington, 1970-77; asst. chief engr. Morrison-Knudsen Co., Inc., Boise, 1977-86; pvt. practice constrn. cons., 1986—. Staff sgt. U.S. Army Corps Engrs., 1943-46. Mem. ASCE (life). Avocations: fishing, hunting, golf, rocks, RV travel. Home and Office: 6055 N Crewe Ave Boise ID 83703-2066

TRUE, RAYMOND STEPHEN, writer, editor, analyst, consultant; b. Lowell, Mass., June 29, 1934; s. Sylvester Raymond and Madeline Rose (Farrell) T.; m. Doreen Therese Jambrosek BA, U. Chgo., 1961, MBA, 1968, postgrad., 1968-69. Commd. 2nd lt. USAF, 1953, advanced through grades to col., 1980; master navigator U.S. Air Force Reserve, Chgo., 1957-77; regional cons. U.S. Bur. Census, 1970-71; dir. operations U.S. Air Force Reserve, Milw., 1977-80, base civil engr., 1980-87, chief planning analyst, 1987-89; owner Classic Comics Libr., 1990—. Fire marshall Milw. County, 1980-87, chmn. membership Reserve Officers Assn., Wash. 1975-78. Editor Classics Newsletter, 1971-75. Precinct committeeman, Libertyville, Ill., 2000—; pres. ROA chpt. 61, 2000-02; chmn. Rep. Assembly Lake County, 2001-. Mem. Air Force Assn., Grad. Sch. Bus. Exec. Council U. Chgo. Roman Catholic. Avocations: philately, antique books, videophile. Address: 839 Terre Dr Libertyville IL 60048-1649 E-mail: raymon8844@aol.com.

TRUE, ROY JOE, lawyer; b. Shreveport, La., Feb. 20, 1938; s. Collins B. and Lula Mae (Cady) T.; m. Patsy Jean Hudsmith, Aug. 29, 1959; children: Andrea Alane, Alyssa Anne, Ashley Alisbeth. Student, Centenary Coll., 1957; BS, Tex. Christian U., 1961; LLB, So. Meth. U., 1963, postgrad., 1968-69. Bar: Tex. 1963. Pvt. practice, Dallas, 1963—; pres. Invesco Internat. Corp., 1969-70, True & Shackelford and predecessors, 1975—2002; of counsel Shackelford, Melton & McKinley, 2002. Bus. adviser, counselor Mickey Mantle, 1969-95; dir. The Mickey Mantle Found., 1995-98. Mem. editl. bd. Southwestern Law Jour, 1962-63. Served with AUS, 1956. Mem. ABA, Dallas Bar Assn., Tex. Assn. Bank Counsel, Phi Alpha Delta. Home: 5601 Ursula Ln Dallas TX 75229-6429 Office: 10100 N Central Expy 6th Fl Dallas TX 75231

TRUEBLOOD, ALAN STUBBS, former modern language educator; b. Haverford, Pa., May 3, 1917; s. Howard M. and Louise (Nyitray) T. BA, Harvard U., 1938, MA, 1941, PhD, 1951; MA (hon.), Brown U., 1957. Ednl. dir. Chile-U.S. Cultural Inst., Santiago, 1942-43; mem. faculty Brown U., 1947—, prof. Spanish, 1963-82, prof. comparative lit., 1972-82, adj. prof., 1982-87, prof. emeritus, 1987—, chmn. dept. Hispanic and Italian studies, 1967-72, chmn. dept. comparative lit., 1973-77. Fulbright lectr. Am. studies, Colombia, 1972; Sr. Resident scholar Merton Coll., Oxford (Eng.) U., 1973 Author: Experience and Artistic Expression in Lope de Vega, 1974, Antonio Machado, Selected Poems, 1982, (with E. Honig) Lope de Vega, La Dorotea, 1985, Letter and Spirit in Hispanic Writers: Selected Essays, 1986, A Sor Juana Anthology, 1988; transl. Gongora (Picasso), 1985, Garcia Lorca, Complete Poems, 1991, Selected Poems, 1995, Songs, Lament for Ignacio Sanchez Mejias, Villegas, Colombia from the Air, 1993, Villegas, The Route of Humboldt: Colombia and Venezuela, 2 vols., 1994, Borges Selected Poems, 1999. Served to lt. USNR, 1943-46. Fulbright research scholar Chile, 1958; Guggenheim fellow, 1965-66; Nat. Endowment for Humanities grantee, 1977-81; recipient Spanish Govt. award Order of Isabel la Catolica, 1990. Home: 54 Willow Ave Little Compton RI 02837-1532 Office: Brown U PO Box 1961 Providence RI 02912-1961

TRUEBLOOD, HARRY ALBERT, JR. oil company executive; b. Wichita Falls, Tex., Aug. 28, 1925; s. Harry A. and Marguerite (Barnhart) T.; m. Lucile Bernard, Jan. 22, 1953; children: Katherine T. Astin, John B. Student, Tex. A&M Coll., 1942-43; BS in Petroleum Engring., U. Tex., 1948. Petroleum engr. Cal. Co., 1948-51; chief engr. McDermott & Barnhart Co., Colo., Tex., 1951-52; cons. petroleum and geol. engr. Denver, 1952-55; pres. Colo. Western Exploration Inc., 1955-58, Consol. Oil and Gas., Inc., 1958-88, chmn. bd., chief exec. officer, 1969-88, Princeville Devel. Corp., 1979-87, pres., 1984-86; chmn. bd., chief exec. officer Columbus Energy Corp., 1983-2000; pres., mng. mem. HAT Resources LLC, 2001—. Chmn. bd., CEO, Princeville Airways, Inc., 1979-87; chmn. bd. dirs., pres. CEC Resources, Ltd., 1984-99; bd. dirs. Carbon Energy Corp., 2000—. With USNR, 1944-46, ensign, 1949-55. Mem. Soc. Petroleum Engrs., Am. Petroleum Inst., World Pres. Orgn., Chief Execs. Orgn. (bd. dirs.), Ind. Petroleum Assn. Am. (exec. com.), Natural Gas Supply Assn. (exec. com.), Denver Petroleum Club, Cherry Hills Country Club, Univ. Club, One Hundred Club. Roman Catholic. Home: 2800 S University Blvd Apt 82 Denver CO 80210-6056 Office: 1720 S Bellaire St Ste 908 Denver CO 80222-4334

TRUEHEART, HARRY PARKER, III, lawyer; b. Rochester, N.Y., Mar. 27, 1944; s. Harry Parker and Bertha (Hendryx) T.; m. Karen Ellingson, June 26, 1965; children: Eric Parker, Kathryn Marie. BA, JD, Harvard U. Bar: N.Y. 1970, Fla. 1975. Assoc. Nixon, Hargrave, Devans & Doyle LLP (now Nixon Peabody LLP), Rochester, 1969-77, ptnr., 1977—, spkr. fed. ct. practice, 1979-83, mng. ptnr., 1995—. Arbitrator, mediator Ctr. Pub. Resources, Inst. Dispute Resolution, Am. Arbitration Assn. Co-author: Federal Civil Practice; contbr. chpt. to book; contbr. articles on fed. ct. litigation, microfilm records, profl. liability in connection with use of computers to profl. jours. Bd. chair WXXI Broadcasting, The Greater Rochester Metro C. of C.; bd. dirs. High Tech. of Rochester, Inc. Fellow N.Y. Bar Found., The Chartered Inst. Arbitrators, The Coll. Law Practice Mgmt.; mem. ABA, N.Y. State Bar Assn. (chair comml. and fed. litig. sect. 1992-93, house of del.), Monroe County Bar Assn., Fed. Bar Coun. (v.p.), Am. Arbitration Assn. Office: Nixon Peabody LLP Clinton Sq Rochester NY 14604 also: Nixon Peabody LLP 437 Madison Ave New York NY 10022-7001 E-mail: htrueheart@nixonpeabody.com.

TRUELL, GEORGE FOSTER, management consultant; b. N.Y.C., Oct. 17, 1929; s. George Foster and Elaine (Shattuck) T.; m. Patricia Stitt, June 28, 1952; children: Deborah, Nancy, George. BS in Indsl. and Labor Rels., Cornell U., 1951. Cert. mgmt. cons. Inst. Mgmt. Cons. Pers. asst. DuPont Co., Wilmington, Del., 1951-53; pers. supr. Welch Foods, Inc., Westfield, N.Y., 1953-59; v.p. indsl. rels. Graphic Controls Corp., Buffalo, 1959-71; pres. George Truell Assocs., 1971—. Author: How to Manage For More Profitable Results, 1974, Building and Maintaining Your Non-Union Organization, 1980, Performance Appraisal-Current Issues and New Directions, 1980, Coaching and Counseling-Key Skills for Managers, 1981, Building and Managing Productive Work Teams, 1984, How To Obtain Cooperation and Agreement From Others, 1987, Helping Employees Cope With Change-A Manager's Guidebook, 1988, Employee Involvement-A Guidebook for Managers, 1991, Coaching and Counseling in Team-Based Organizations, 1996; contbr. articles to profl. jours. Mem. Am. Mgmt. Assn., Assn. Mfg. Excellence. Republican. Office: George Truell Assocs 495 N Forest Rd Williamsville NY 14221-5036

TRUEMAN, BRETT MICHAEL, finance educator; b. N.Y.C., Mar. 4, 1955; BS, Columbia U., N.Y.C., 1975; MS, Columbia U., 1976, MBA, 1977, PhD, 1981. Asst. prof. UCLA, 1981—88; assoc. prof. U. Calif., Berkeley, 1988—96, prof., 1996—. Contbr. articles. Named Donald and Ruth Seiler Prof. Pub. Acctg., U. Calif.-Berkeley, 1999—; recipient Earl Cheit award for tchg. excellence, Haas Sch. of Bus., 1995. Mem.: Am. Acctg. Assn., Am. Fin. Assn., Am. Econ. Assn. Office: Haas School of Business Univ of California Berkeley CA 94720 Business E-Mail: trueman@haas.berkeley.edu.

TRUEMAN, WILLIAM PETER MAIN, broadcaster, newspaper columnist; b. Sackville, N.B., Can., Dec. 25, 1934; s. Albert William and Jean Alberta (Miller) T.; m. Eleanor Joy Wark, Dec. 22, 1956; children: Anne, Mark, Victoria. Student, U. N.B., 1951-54. UN corr. Montreal Star, 1957-62, Washington corr., 1962-65; parliamentary corr. Toronto Star, Ottawa, Ont., 1965-67; nat. dir. UN Assn. in Can., 1967-68; nat. news writer CBC, Toronto, 1968-69, exec. producer news, head network news, 1969-72; freelance reporter, 1972-73; anchorman Global TV News, Don Mills, Ont., 1974-88; free lance broadcaster, 1988-2000; media critic Toronto Star's Starweek mag., 1988-96; Kingston Whig-Std., 1989-96. Host, mng.editor Canadian Discovery Channel TV series Great Canadian Parks, 1995-2000. Decorated officer Order of Can.; recipient Bowater award for journalism, 1962, Sam Ross award, 1983. E-mail: peter.trueman@sympatico.ca.

TRUEMPER, JOHN JAMES, JR. retired architect; b. Helena, Ark., June 18, 1924; s. John James and Mary Ann (Jacob) T.; m. Julia Clare Wood, Nov. 21, 1956; children: Zachary Wood, John James III, Ann Truemper Penick. BS in Arch., U. Ill., 1950; DHL (hon.), Lyon Coll., 1995. With archtl. firm Cromwell, Truemper, Levy, Thompson, Woodsmall Inc. (and predecessors), Little Rock, 1950-94, v.p., 1972-74, pres., 1974-81, chmn. bd., 1980-89; ret., 1994. Mem. Ark. Bd. Architects, 1974-82. Prin. works include Ark. system for edn. and tng. mentally retarded, 1956-78, Winrock Farm, Morrilton, Ark., 1953-58, Ark. State Parks, 1955-75, Ark. Power & Light Co., 1961-89, Lyon Coll., Batesville, 1983-94; author: A Century of Service, 1885-1985, 1985. Pres. Ark. Arts Ctr., 1979, chmn. bd., 1980; mem. Little Rock Bldg. Code Bd. Appeals, 1961-86, chmn., 1971-86; mem. Ark. Hist. Preservtion Rev. Bd., 1987-99; bd. dirs. Little Rock Met. YMCA, 1975-84; mem. Friends of Libr. Bd., U. Ark., Little Rock, 1989-99, pres. 1995-97; bd. dirs. Greater Little Rock C. of C., 1986-88. With USAAF, 1943-46. Recipient Winthrop Rockefeller Meml. award Ark. Arts Center, 1980 Fellow AIA. Roman Catholic. Home: 5216 Crestwood Dr Little Rock AR 72207-5404

TRUESDALE, JOHN CUSHMAN, government executive; b. Grand Rapids, Mich., July 17, 1921; s. John Cushman and Hazel (Christianson) T.; m. Karin A. Nelson, Feb. 10, 1957; children— John Cushman, Charles N., Margaret E., Andrew C. AB, Grinnell Coll., 1942; MS, Cornell U., 1948; JD, Georgetown U., 1972. Bar: Md. bar 1972, D.C. bar 1973. Field examiner NLRB, Buffalo and New Orleans, 1948-52, adminstrv. analyst Washington, 1952-57, assoc. exec. sec., 1963-68, dep. exec. sec., 1968-72, exec. sec., 1972-77, 81-94, mem., 1977-81, 94, 95, chmn., 1998-2001, labor arbitrator, 1996—98,

2001—; mem. Fgn. Svc. Grievance Bd., 1997—. Dir. info., dir. World Data Center/Rockets and Satellites, IGY, Nat. Acad. Scis., Washington, 1957-63 Editor-in-chief: How to Take a Case Before the NLRB, 1997-98, 2002--. Served with USCG, 1942-46. Recipient Presdl. award Pres. of U.S., 1988. Mem. ABA, D.C. Bar Assn., Assn. Labor Rels. Agys. (pres. 1992-93), Indsl. Rels. Rsch. Assn. (internat. exec. bd. 2002--). Democrat. Congregationalist.

TRUESDELL, STEPHANIE, development officer, university official; b. Princeton, N.J., Oct. 13, 1970; d. Miles Wakeman Jr. and Judith (Roulston) Truesdell; m. Andrew Charles Schmidt, Oct. 7, 1995. AB, Brown U., 1992; MEd, Harvard U., 2002. Officer Brown U. Annual Fund, Providence, 1992-93, asst. dir., 1993-94, asst. dir. spl. gifts, 1994-97; assoc. dir. Harvard Law Sch. Fund, Cambridge, Mass., 1997-99, dir., 1999-2000; assoc. dir. leadership gifts, 2000—. Explorer's Club grantee, 1990. Mem. Women in Devel., Brown Club of Boston (bd. dirs. 1999-2001), Harvard Faculty Club, Kappa Alpha Theta (pres. facility corp. Alpha Epsilon chpt. 1993-99, Lambert award 1997). Presbyterian. Home: 52 Buckingham Rd Milton MA 02186-4418 Office: Harvard Law Sch 125 Mt Auburn St Cambridge MA 02138-2801 E-mail: slt@law.harvard.edu.

TRUESDELL, TIMOTHY LEE, private investor; b. Niles, Mich., Oct. 8, 1951; s. Patrick Daniel and LaVonne Marie (Fries) T. BA, U. Notre Dame, 1974. Asst. to exec. dir. Notre Dame U. Alumni Assn., 1974-77, asst. dir., 1977-79; alumni editor Notre Dame mag., 1979-83; v.p. Truesdell Real Estate Investment, Sacramento, 1983-85; dir. devel. rsch. U. Notre Dame, 1985-99; portfolio mgr. Kamm Partnership, South Bend, Ind., 1999—. Devel. cons. Am. Acad. Neurology, 1991-92, Harvest Devel., Ponte Vedra, Fla., 1999—, Hospice of St. Joseph County, South Bend, Ind., 1992-93, U. St. Thomas, Mpls., Xavier U., Cin., 1993-94, Niles Comty. Libr., 1993-97, St. Joseph Mishawaka (Ind.) Health Svcs., 1995-96, Berrien County ARC, 1996, Advancement Ptnrs., Inc., Columbus, 1996—, Little Flower Cath. Ch., South Bend, Ind., 1997-98, No. Ind. Ctr. for History, South Bend, 1998-2000; bd. dirs. Women's Care Ctr., Mishawaka, Ind., 1999-2000. Councilman City of Niles, 1983-91; pres. St. Mary's Sch Bd. Edn., Niles, 1981-82; chmn. S.W. Mich. Comty. Ambulance, Niles, 1985-89; mem. Berrien County (Mich.) Reps.; pres. Fernwood Bot. Garden, Niles, 1997-98. Mem. Am. Assn. Individual Investors, Assn. Profl. Rschrs. for Advancement, Am. Assn. Individual Investors, Optimists (sec. 1983-84), Knights of Malta, Notre Dame Club of St. Joseph Valley. Republican. Roman Catholic. Avocations: golf, antique collecting, fishing. Office: 11185 Elizabeth Dr Three Rivers MI 49093 E-mail: tim@datacruz.com.

TRUESDELL, WALTER GEORGE, minister, librarian; b. N.Y.C., Oct. 22, 1919; s. George Anson and Hattie (Evans) T.; m. Mary Schurok, June 10, 1944; children: Walter George, Susan Hattie. AB, Columbia U. Columbia Coll., 1941; MA, Columbia U. Tchrs. Coll., 1975; MDiv, Theol. Sem. of the Ref. Episcopal Ch., Phila., 1944; BLS, Pratt Inst., 1950. Ordained to ministry Ref. Episcopal Ch., 1944. Asst. min. First Ref. Episcopal Ch., N.Y.C., 1944-54, sr. assoc. min., 1989—; rector Ch. of the Redemption, Bklyn., 1956—; lectr. apologetics and English Bible Theol. Sem. Ref. Episcopal Ch., Phila., 1945-48, libr. Phila. (relocated to Blue Bell, Pa., Sept. 2000), 1964-93, Shelton Coll., 1951-69; libr. Cummins Meml. Theol. Sem. Reformed Episcopal, Summerville, S.C., 1996—. Chmn. com. on state of ch. Ref. Episcopal Ch., 1960-87, mem., 1987-96, mem. gen. com. 1978-96; real estate broker, 1979—. Editor Episcopal Recorder, 1980-90. Mem. ALA (life), Pa. Libr. Assn., Assn. Statisticians Am. Religious Bodies. Home and Office: 306 E 90th St New York NY 10128-5121 Office: Cummins Meml Theol Sem 705 S Main St Summerville SC 29483-5911 *Out of the privilege of a broad educational background and living in the astonishing technology of the 20th century, and yet to be, in the turbulence of war, crime, starvation, and distress of mind and spirit, I am convicted anew of the need to know Christ, who said, "I am the way, the truth, and the life." Therefore, I labor in Christian education to the strengthening of mind, body, and spirit.*

TRUETT, DALE BRIAN, economics/finance educator, consultant; b. Gary, Ind., July 25, 1940; s. Louis Theodore and Flora (Toma) T.; m. Lila Jean Matile, Apr. 4, 1977; children: Katherine, Patrick. BA, Purdue U., 1962; MA, U. Tex., 1964, PhD, 1967. Asst. prof. U. Fla., Gainesville, 1967-71; assoc. prof., chmn. econ. Fla. Internat. U., Miami, 1971-73; prof., dir. econ./fin. U. Tex., San Antonio, 1973-75, prof., 1976—, Ashbel Smith prof. econs., 1997—. Cons. City Pub. Svc. of San Antonio, 2000—, Southwestern Bell Publs., St. Louis, 1990-99, Ctrl. de Servicios de Carga, Mex., 1994-95, Continental Floral Greens, San Antonio, 1987-88, AHMSA Steel Internat., Mex., 1981. Author: Managerial Economics, 7th edit., 2001; contbr. articles to profl. jours. Rsch. grantee U. Tex., San Antonio, 1993, 94, 95, 96, 2001, U.S. Dept. Edn., 1991-92; recipient Rsch. award U. Tex., San Antonio, 1994, 97. Mem. Am. Econ. Assn., So. Econ. Assn., Western Econ. Assn., Congress of Polit. Economists, Internat. Avocations: international travel, photography. Home: 16402 NW Military Hwy San Antonio TX 78231-1224 Office: Univ Tex Div Econ and Fin 6900 N Loop 1604 W San Antonio TX 78249-1130 E-mail: dtruett@utsa.edu.

TRUETT, HAROLD JOSEPH, III (TIM TRUETT), lawyer; b. Alameda, Calif., Feb. 13, 1946; s. Harold Joseph and Lois Lucille (Mellin) T.; 1 child, Harold Joseph IV; m. Anna V. Billante, Oct. 1, 1983 (dec. June 2000); 1 child, James S. Carstensen; m. Patricia Maynord, Mar. 5, 2002. BA, U. San Francisco, 1968, JD, 1975. Bar: Calif. 1975, Hawaii 1987, U.S. Dist. Ct. (ea., so., no., and cen. dists.) Calif. 1976, Hawaii 1987, U.S. Ct. Appeals (9th cir.) 1980, U.S. Supreme Ct. 1988, U.S. Ct. Fed. Claims, 1995. Assoc. Hoberg, Finger et al, San Francisco, 1975-78, Bledsoe, Smith et al, San Francisco, 1979-80, Abramson & Bianco, San Francisco, 1980-83; mem. Ingram & Truett, San Rafael, 1983-90; prin. Law Office of H.J. Tim Truett, San Francisco, 1991-93, Winchell & Truett, San Francisco, 1994—. Lectr. trial practice Am. Coll. Legal Medicine, 1989-90, Calif. Continuing Edn. of the Bar. Bd. dirs. Shining Star Found. 1991—, pres., 2001—, Marin County, Calif.; mem. Marin Dem. Coun., San Rafael, 1983-90. Lt., aviator USN, 1967-74. Mem. ABA, Hawaii Bar Assn., Calif. Bar Assn. (com. for adminstrn. of justice, conf. of dels.), San Francisco Bar Assn., San Francisco Trial Lawyers Assn., Lawyers Pilots Assn. Roman Catholic. Home: 48 Valley Rd San Anselmo CA 94960 E-mail: hjtimtruett@home.com.

TRUETT, LILA FLORY, economics educator; b. Emporia, Kans., June 30, 1947; d. Ulysses Earl and Ursula Mabel (Schwindt) Matile; m. Donald Gene Flory, May 26, 1967 (div. 1973); m. Dale Brian Truett, Apr. 4, 1977; stepchildren: Katherine, Patrick. BA in Math., Kans. State U., 1968; MA in Econs., U. Iowa, 1971, PhD in Econs., 1972. Teaching asst., then part-time instr. U. Iowa, Iowa City, 1969-71; asst. prof. Iowa Wesleyan Coll., Mt. Pleasant, 1971-73, Appalachian State U., Boone, N.C., 1973-75, U. Tex., San Antonio, 1975-78, assoc. prof., 1978-80, prof., dir. econs. and fin., 1981—. Outside reviewer dept. econs., Colo. State U., Colorado Springs, 1988. Co-author: Intermediate Microeconomics, 1984, Economics, 1987, Managerial Economics, 5th edit., 1995; contbr. numerous articles to profl. jours. Mem. Fin. Execs. Inst., Fin. Mgmt. Assn., Am. Econ. Assn., So. Econ. Assn., Ea. Fin. Assn., Midwest Fin. Assn., Western Econs. Assn., Ea. Econs. Assn., Omicron Delta Epsilon, Beta Gamma Sigma. Brethren. Avocations: reading, music, travel, gardening. Home: 16402 NW Military Hwy San Antonio TX 78231-1224 Office: U Tex at San Antonio Divsn Econs and Fin San Antonio TX 78249-0633

TRUEX, DOROTHY ADINE, retired university administrator; b. Sedalia, Mo., Oct. 6, 1915; d. Chester Morrison and Madge (Nicholson) T. AB, William Jewell Coll., 1936; MA, U. Mo., 1937; EdD, Columbia U., 1956. Asst. dean women N.W. Mo. State U., Maryville, 1939-43, dean women, 1943-45, Mercer U., Macon, Ga., 1945-47, U. Okla., Norman, 1947-69, assoc. prof., 1969-72, dir. rsch. and program devel., 1969-74, prof. edn., 1972-74, dir. grad. program in student pers. svcs., 1969-74; vice chancellor for student affairs U. Ark., Little Rock, 1974-83, alumni specialist, 1983-84, acad. adviser, 1984-87. Exec. bd. N. Cen. Assn. Schs. and Colls., 1977-83. Mem. Nat. Assn. Women Deans, Adminstrs. and Counselors (pres. 1973-74), So. Coll. Pers. Assn. (pres. 1970), Okla. Coll. Pers. Assn. (pres. 1972-73), William Jewell Coll. Alumni Assn. (pres. 1970-73), Pi Beta Phi, Alpha Lambda Delta, Mortar Bd., Sigma Tau Delta, Cardinal Key, Gamma Alpha Chi, Kappa Delta Pi, Pi Lambda Theta, Alpha Psi Omega, Pi Gamma Mu, Delta Kappa Gamma, Phi Delta Kappa, Phi Kappa Phi. (nat. v.p. 1986-89) Avocation: novelist. Home: 14300 Chenal Pkwy Apt 7422 Little Rock AR 72211-5819

TRUEX, SHELLEY ANNE, lawyer; b. Johnson City, N.Y., Sept. 22, 1968; d. Gordon Elbert and Diane Marie Truex; m. Mark Ambrose Quarantillo, Aug. 1, 1998. BA, SUNY, Binghamton, 1989; JD, Union U., 1992. Bar: N.Y. 1993. Staff atty. Niagara County Legal Aid, Inc., Niagara Falls, N.Y., 1993-94; assoc. Gregory A. Pope & Assocs., Lockport, 1994-97; owner, ptnr. Quarantillo & Truex, Niagara Falls, 1997—. Mem. N.Y. State Bar Assn., Erie County Bar Assn., Niagara Falls Bar Assn., Lockport Bar Assn. Office: Quarantillo & Truex 625 6th St Niagara Falls NY 14301-1752

TRUHLAR, DONALD GENE, chemist, educator; b. Chgo. , Feb. 27, 1944; s. John Joseph and Lucille Marie (Vancura) T.; m. Jane Teresa Gust, Aug. 28, 1965; children: Sara Elizabeth, Stephanie Marie. BA in Chemistry summa cum laude, St. Mary's Coll., Winona, Minn., 1965; PhD in Chemistry, Calif. Inst. Tech., 1970. Asst. prof. chemistry and chem. physics U. Minn., Mpls., 1969—72, assoc. prof., 1972—76, prof., 1976—93, Inst. of Tech. prof., 1993—98, Inst. of Tech. disting. prof., 1998—, Lloyd H. Reyerson prof., 2002—. Cons. Los Alamos Sci. Lab.; vis. fellow Joint Inst. for Lab. Astrophysics, 1975-76; sci. dir. Minn. Supercomputer Inst., 1987-88, dir., 1988—. Editor Theoretical Chemistry Accounts (Theoretica Chemica Acta, 1985—98, Computer Physics Comms., 1986—, Topics Phys. Chemistry, 1992—99, Understanding Chem. Reactivity, 1990—92, editl. bd. Jour. Chem. Physics, 1978—80, Chem. Physics Letters, 1982—, Jour. Phys. Chemistry, 1985—87, Understanding Chem. Reactivity, 1993—, Advances in Chem. Physics, 1993—, Internat. Jour. Modern Pphysics C., 1994—, IEEE Computational Sci. and Engring., 1994—98, Internat. Jour. Quantum Chemistry, 1996—2000, Computing in Sci. and Engring., 1999—2001, assoc. editor Theoretical Chemistry Accounts, 1998—2001, chief adv. editor, 2002—. Fellow, John Stauffer fellow, 1965—66, NDEA fellow, 1966—68, Alfred P. Sloan Found. fellow, 1973—77; grantee, NSF, 1971—, NASA, 1987—95, U.S. Dept. Energy, 1979—, NIST, 1995—98, Dept. of Def., 2001—; scholar, Ruhland Walzer Meml. scholar, 1961—62. Fellow AAAS, Am. Phys. Soc.; mem. Am. Chem. Soc. (sec.-treas. theoretical chemistry subdivsn. 1980-89, councilor 1985-87, assoc. editor jour. 1984—, Award for computers in chem. and pharm. rsch. 2000). Achievements include research, numerous publications in field. Home: 5033 Thomas Ave S Minneapolis MN 55410-2240 Office: U Minn 207 Pleasant St SE Minneapolis MN 55455-0431 E-mail: truhlar@umn.edu.

TRUHLAR, DORIS BROADDUS, lawyer; b. Oklahoma City, Sept. 18, 1946; d. Elbridge Sidney and Doris Mary (Prock) Broaddus; m. Robert John Truhlar, June 24, 1978; children: Ivy, Holly;children from previous marriage: Samara Taryle, Brett Taryle(dec.). B in journalism, U. Mo., 1967; MA, U. Denver, 1976, JD with honors, 1980. Bar: Colo. 1981, U.S. Dist. Ct. Colo. 1981, U.S. Ct. Appeals (10th cir.) 1981, U.S. Supreme Ct., 1996. Law clk. to Hon. Robert H. McWilliams, Jr. U.S. Ct. Appeals (10th cir.), Denver, 1980-81; corp. sec., gen. counsel Hart Exploration and Prodn. Co., Englewood, Colo.; ptnr. Truhlar and Truhlar, LLP, Littleton, 1985—. Adj. prof. U. Denver Coll. Law, 1986—92; mem. Thursday Night Bar Adv. Bd., 1995—2001, chair, 1996—98. Active various vol. programs; mem. adv. com. Metro Parenting and Divorce Ctr., 1995—98; transition team Gov. Bill Owens Judiciary com., Colo., 1998; chair pro se com. Gov.'s Task Force on Civil Justice, 1999—2000; vestry bd. Good Shepherd Episcopal Ch., 1992—95. Recipient Woman of Achievement, Entrepreneur of Yr. award, Met. YWCA of Denver, 1993, Denver Gridiron award, 1st pl. Editl. Writing award Nat. Edn. Writers Assn., Charles B. Dillion award for outstanding pub. svc., 1997, honoree for outstanding svc. in providing legal svcs. to the poor, Barristers' Ball, 1998. Mem.: Arapahoe County Bar Assn. (treas. 2000—02, pres. 2002—, Pro Bono Atty. 1992), Colo. Women's Bar Assn. (pres. 2002—, co-chair jud. com., bd. dirs., historian, sec.), Colo. Bar Assn. Office: 1901 W Littleton Blvd Littleton CO 80120-2087

TRUHLSEN, STANLEY MARSHALL, retired physician, educator; b. Herman, Nebr., Nov. 13, 1920; s. Henry and Lola Mollie (Marshall) T.; m. Ruth Haney, June 2, 1943 (dec. Dec. 1976); children: William, Nancy, Stanley M., Barbara; m. Dorothy D. Johnson, Jan 10, 1981. AB, U. Nebr., 1941, MD, 1944. Diplomate Am. Bd. Ophthalmology. Intern Albany (N.Y.) Hosp., 1944-45; resident Barnes Hosp., St. Louis, 1948-51; practice medicine specializing in ophthalmology Omaha, 1951—93; mem. staff U. Nebr., Clarkson, Immanuel; pres. med. staff Immanuel Hosp., 1961, Clarkson Hosp., 1972-73; prof. ophthalmology U. Nebr. Coll. Medicine, 1974-81, clin. prof., 1981-93, interim chmn. dept. ophthalmology, 1989-90; dir. Nebr. Blue Cross and Blue Shield, 1971-95, vice chmn. bd., 1986-96; dir. Health Planning Council Midlands, 1972-75, Clarkson Hosp., 1974-76, Nebr. Soc. Prevention Blindness., Lions Eye Bank of Nebr., 1983-91. Trustee Omaha Home of Boys, 1966—, Brownell Talbot Sch., 1966-69, Omaha Citizens Assembly, 1972-99, U. Nebr. Found., 1985—, Action Internat., Inc., 1994-96; mem. exec. bd. Durham Western Heritage Mus., 1999. With AUS, 1946-48. Recipient Alumni Achievement award U. Nebr., 1986, Disting. Alumnus Achievement award U. Nebr. Med. Ctr., 1989, Ann. Hon. awards for civic and community contbns.; named Omaha Health Citizen of Yr., 1989; named King Aksarben XCI for outstanding contbns. to Nebr. community, 1985. Fellow ACS (bd. govs. 1985-91); mem. Am. Ophthal. Soc. (asst. editor transactions 1973-79, editor 1979-84, coun. 1987-92, v.p. 1994, pres. 1995, Howe medal 2001), Am. Acad. Ophthalmology and Otolaryngology (assoc. editor transactions 1968-75, editor 1975-80), Am. Acad. Ophthamology (1st v.p. 1981, pres. 1983, vice chmn. AAO Found. 1992-98), Nebr. Acad. Ophthalmology (pres. 1975), Am. Eye Study Club (pres. 1962), Omaha Med. Soc. (pres. 1973), Omaha Country Club (pres. 1977-78), U. Nebr. Med. Ctr. Alumni Assn. (pres. 1958), Masons, Rotary (pres. local club 1981-82), Sigma Xi, Alpha Omega Alpha, Sigma Nu, Phi Rho Sigma. Republican. Home: 412 N 97th Ct Omaha NE 68114-2395 E-mail: stantruhl@aol.com.

TRUITT, ANNE DEAN, artist; b. Balt., Mar. 16, 1921; d. Duncan Witt and Louisa Folsom (Williams) Dean; m. James McConnell Truitt, Sept. 19, 1947 (div.); children— Alexandra, Mary McConnell, Samuel Rogers. BA, Bryn Mawr Coll., 1943; postgrad., Inst. Contemporary Art, Washington, 1948-50. Exhibited in one woman shows at Andre Emmerich Gallery, N.Y.C., 1963, 65, 69, 75, 80, 86, 91, Danese Gallery, N.Y.C., 1998, 2001, Minami Gallery, Tokyo, 1964, 67, Balt. Mus. Art, 1969, 75, 92, Pyramid Galleries, Washington, 1971, 73, 75, 77, Whitney Mus. Am. Art, N.Y.C., 1973-74, Corcoran Gallery, Washington, 1974, Osuna Gallery, Washington, 1979, 81, 86, 89, 91-92, Neuberger Mus., Purchase N.Y., 1986, Georgia O'Keefe Mus., Santa Fe, 2000; exhibited in group shows at Balt. Mus. Art, 1970, 72-73, 82, Whitney Mus. Am. Art, 1970-71, 72, 77, Phillips Collection, Washington, 1971-72, Pyramid Galleries, 1972, 73, Mus. Contemporary Art, Chgo., 1974, 77, Indpls. Mus. Art, 1974, Nat. Gallery Art, Washington, 1974, Corcoran Gallery Art, Washington, 1975, numerous others; translator: (with C.J. Hill) Marcel Proust and Deliverance from Time (Germaine Brée), 1955; author: Daybook: The Journal of an Artist, 1982, Turn: The Journal of an Artist, 1986, Prospect: The Journal of an Artist, 1996. Guggenheim fellow, 1970; Nat. Endowment for Arts fellow, 1971, 77; Australia Council for Arts fellow, 1981 Home: 3506 35th St NW Washington DC 20016-3114

TRUITT, CHARLOTTE FRANCES, clergywoman; b. Newark, Feb. 8, 1922; d. Frank Wilson and Charlotte (Hook) T.; m. Robert Kennedy Carter, Mar. 17, 1946 (div. 1972); children: Mary Elizabeth Carter O'Brien, Robert Truitt Carter; m. Robert Harold Bonthius Sr., Apr. 29, 1977. Student, Ohio State U., 1941-46; MA in Christian Edn., Meth. Theol. Sch., Delaware, Ohio, 1976, MDiv, 1977. Ordained to ministry United Ch. of Christ, 1979. Asst. dir. youth program YWCA, Columbus, Ohio, 1965-68, dir. youth program, 1968-70, dir. family life and racial justice programs, 1970-72; mission coord. and youth minister First Cmty. Ch., 1972-75; min. Christian edn. Broad St. United Meth. Ch., 1975-76; cons., trainer Action Tng. Network, Ohio and Maine, 1976-90. Pres. bd. Family Life and Sex Edn. Coun., Columbus, 1971-72; bd. dirs. Ohio Coun. Chs., Columbus, 1973-74; del. United Ch. of Christ, Nicaragua, 1983, and co-founder Nat. Witness for Peace, 1983. Contbr. articles to religious jours. and publs. Pres. bd. dirs. North Ctrl. Mental Health Ctr., Columbus, 1973-74; mem. Columbus Urban League Edn. Commn., 1965-67, Hancock Comprehensive Plan Commn., Hancock, Maine, 1990; chair scholarship bd. Thorsen Scholarship Fund, Hancock, 1988-89; bd. dirs., fin. chair The Next Step Domestic Violence Project, Ellsworth, Maine, 1993-94; bd. dirs. Witness for Peace, pers. chair, 1983-85, chair, 1994-95. Recipient Martin Luther King Jr. award NAACP, Portland, Maine, 1989, Disting. Svc. award The Next Step Domestic Violence Project, Ellsworth, 1994. Mem. Hancock-Waldo Clergy Assn., Friends Taunton Bay, Natural Resources Coun. of Maine, Peace Action, Religious Coalition for Reproductive Choice, United Ch. of Christ Christians for Justice Action, Witness for Peace, Ctr. for Sci. in Pub. Interest, Americans United for Separation Ch. and State, Frenchman Bay Conservancy, Friends of Blue Hill Bay, Blue Hill Heritage Trust. Mem. United Ch. of Christ. Avocations: flower gardening, bird watching, reading, nature walks, drawing. Home and Office: 39 Parker Ridge Ln Blue Hill ME 04614-9608

TRUITT, KENNETH RAY, owner; b. Greensboro, N.C., Feb. 21, 1945; s. Marvin Lee Truitt and Edna Lindsey (Sheffield) Brower; m. Linda Alice Morrison, 1965 (div. 1973); children: Maria Paige, Lisa Christine; m. Victoria Ruth Mize, Aug. 23, 1975. BS in Math., U. N.C., 1970; MS in Indsl. Engring., U. Mo., 1972. Lab. technician Pitts. Testing Lab., Greensboro, 1963-65; indsl. insulation estimator Starr-Davis Co., 1965-66; cons. indsl. engring. dept. Cone Mills Corp., 1968-70; grad. teaching asst. U. Mo., Columbia, 1970-71; dir. mgmt. engring. Med. Ctr., 1971-74; dir. mgmt. svcs. Med. Coll. Va., Richmond, 1974-75; dir. mgmt. engring. Bethany Med. Ctr., Kansas City, 1975-78, v.p. mgmt. svcs., 1978-86, v.p. planning, mktg., 1986-94; asst. dir. Coop. Physicians Svcs., Overland Park, Kans., 1994-95; pres., owner Truitt Supply Co., Kansas City, Mo., 1996—. Planning commr. City of Lake Quivira (Kans.). Mendenhall scholar U. N.C., 1970. Mem. Med. Group Mgmt. Assn., Soc. Hosp. Planning and Mktg., Hosp. Info. Mgmt. Sys. Soc., Inst. Indsl. Engrs. (assoc. dir. confs. 1979-80, pres. health svcs. div. 1981-82), Quivira Lake Country Club, Phi Beta Kappa, Pi Mu Epsilon, Alpha Pi Mu. Avocations: golf, pocket billiards, book collecting. Office: Truitt Supply Co 8224 E Bannister Rd Kansas City MO 64134-1838

TRUITT, MARTIN RONALD, accountant; b. Carmel, Calif., 1962; s. J.L. and Virgie Lucille Truitt. BS, U. So. Calif., 1984, MBT, 1994. CPA, CMA, CIA, CFE, CCP, CDP, CFP, CLU, ChFC, CFS. Staff acct. Apodaca & Finocchiaro & Co., Pasadena, Calif., 1984-86, sr. acct., 1986-88; mgr. Apodaca & Co., 1988-93, ptnr., 1993—. Mem. AICPA (voting com. mem. tax divsn. 1993-95), Inst. Mgmt. Accts., Inst. Internal Auditors, Inst. Cert. Fin. Planners, Assn. Cert. Fraud Examiners, Am. Soc. CLU and ChFC, Calif. Soc. CPAs. Office: Apodaca & Co 301 E Colorado Blvd Ste 800 Pasadena CA 91101-1917

TRUITT, RICHARD BYRON, landscape architect; b. El Paso, Tex., Dec. 25, 1937; s. Charles Lee and Elenia May Truitt; m. Doris Iva House, Feb. 23, 1963; 1 child, Bonnie Leona. Cert. in Hort. and Landscape, Dayton Beach (Fla.) C.C., 1956. Cert. law and ornamental pest control; registered landscape architect, Fla. Pvt. practice, Ormond Beach, Fla., 1956—. Contbr. articles to profl. jours. Pres. Civitan Club, Ormond Beach; vice chair Devel. Rev. Bd., Ormond Beach, 1995-98; chair Beautification Bd., Ormond Beach, 1978-95; bd. dirs., trustee Louitte Manor retirement Ctr., Daytona Beach, 1984-97; charter mem. Bot. Gardens of Volusia County; bd. dirs. Episc. Ch., Diocese of Ctrl. Fla., Orlando, 1979-81; Eucharistic minister Episc. Ch. With Army N.G., 1956-66. Recipient Spl. award City of Ormond Beach for outstanding svcs. as chair and mem. of beautification Bd., 1995. Mem. Ormond Beach C. of C. (pres. 1990, Spl. Award for contbn. and dedication to beautification 1989), Holly Hill C. o C. (pres. 1989), Fla. Nurseryman and growers Assn. (pres. Ctrl. East Coast chpt. 1977). Republican. Episcopalian. Home and Office: 115 Country Club Dr Ormond Beach FL 32176-5415

TRUITT, ROBERT RALPH, JR. lawyer; b. Lincoln-Chaves Counties, N.Mex., Jan. 21, 1948; s. Robert Ralph and Dorothy (Butler) T.; m. Susan Donovan, Nov. 28, 1981; children: Patrick Lynn, Maureen Elizabeth. BA, BBA, Southwestern U., 1970; JD, U. Tex., 1973. Bar: Tex. 1973, U.S. Ct. Appeals (5th cir.) 1976, U.S. Dist. Ct. (we. dist.) Tex. 1977, U.S. Dist. Ct. (no. dist.) Tex. 1981. Assoc. Turpin, Smith & Dyer, Midland, Tex., 1973-77; pvt. practice, 1977—. Chmn. planning and zoning com., City of Midland, 1979-80; chmn., dir. and treas. Midland Downtown Lions Fire Prevention and Hist. Found., 1980—; dir. and sec.-treas. Midland Downtown Lions Youth Found., 1992-98, Midland Masonic Hist. Mus. and Libr. Found., 1996—; dir. Presdl. Mus., 1998-99; sec. El Paso Scottish Rite Libr. and Historical Mus. Found., 1999—. Mem. Tex. Bar Assn., Midland County Bar Assn. Office: 901 W Texas Ave Midland TX 79701-6167

TRUJILLO, ANGELINA, endocrinologist; b. Long Beach, Calif. BA in Psychology, Chapman Coll., 1974; postgrad., U. Colo., 1974-75, MD, 1979. Resident in internal medicine Kern Med. Ctr., Bakersfield, Calif., 1979-82; fellow in endocrinology UCLA, Sepulveda, 1982-84, chief resident dept. internal medicine, 1985-86; chief diabetes clinic Sepulveda (Calif.) VA Med. Ctr., 1986-89; physician specialist Olive View Med. Ctr., Sylmar, Calif., 1989; chief divsn. endocrinology U. S.D. Sch. Medicine, Sioux Falls, 1990—2001; ACOS R&D Royal C. Johnson VA Med. Ctr., 1998—2001. Adj. instr. UCLA, 1982-84, adj. asst. prof. medicine, 1985-89, clin. asst. prof. family medicine, 1994-2001; asst. prof. U. S.D. Sch. Medicine, 1990-94, assoc. prof., 1994—, assoc. dir. internal medicine residency program, 1992-95; spkr. in field. Pub. spkr. in diabetes, women and heart disease. Grantee NIH, 1986-89, Am. Diabetes Assn., 1985-87, Pfizer, Inc., 1990-91, Nat. Heart, Lung, and Blood Inst., 1994—, Bristol-Myers Squibb, 1994-2001 Mem. ACP, Am. Fedn. Clin. Rsch. (med. sch. rep., endo/metabolism subspecialty coun.), Am. Soc. Hypertension, Am. Diabetes Assn., Assn. Program Dirs. in Internal Medicine, Assn. Clerkship Dirs. in Internal Medicine, S.D. State Med. Assn., Seventh Dist. Med. Soc., Wilderness Med. Soc. (mem. environ. coun.). Office: U SD Sch Med 1400 W 22nd St Sioux Falls SD 57105-1505

TRUJILLO, ANNA, food company administrator, city official; b. Brownsville, Tex., Mar. 5, 1945; d. Santos S. and Minerva C. Saldivar; m. Jose Antonio Trujillo, June 5, 1964 (div. 1971); children: Michael A., Joeanna K., David A., Sandra A. Student, Tex. Southmost coll., Brownsville. Notary pub., State of N.Mex., 1990-94. Office mgr., osner La Poblanita Foods, Lovington, N.Mex., 1964-96; officer mgr. N.Mex. Trujillo Foods, 1995—; city commr. City of Lovington, 1988—. Bd. dirs. Lea County Extraterritorial, Lovington, 1992—, Lea County Registration, Lovington, 1985-87. Vice chair Lovington Dem. Party, Hobbs, N.Mex., 1983; mem. com. N.Mex. State Ctrl. Com., 1984. Named Outstanding Lea County Woman, 1991, Lea County Pioneer, 1994; recipient Leadership award Dem. Com. N.Mex., 1996. Mem. Lovington Women's Club (sec. 1981-82), Altar Soc., Rebecca Lodge. Democrat. Roman Catholic. Avocations: reading, oil painting, bike riding, gardening. Home: 400 N East St Lovington NM 88260-3628 Office: Trujillo Foods 721 N Main Ave Lovington NM 88260-3417

TRUJILLO, LORENZO A. lawyer, educator; b. Denver, Aug. 10, 1951; s. Filbert G. and Marie O. Trujillo; m. Ellen Alires; children: Javier Antonio, Lorenzo Feliciano, Kristina Alires. BA, U. Colo., 1972, MA, 1974, postgrad.; EdD, U. San Francisco, 1979; JD, U. Colo., 1993. Bar: Colo. 1994, U.S. Dist. Ct. Colo. 1994, U.S. Ct. Appeals (10th cir.) 1994, U.S. Supreme Ct. 1999; cert. edn. tchr., prin., supt., Colo. Exec. assoc. Inter-Am. Rsch. Assocs., Rosslyn, Va., 1980-82; exec. dir. humanities Jefferson County Pub. Schs., Golden, Colo., 1982-89; pvt. practice edn. cons. Lakewood, 1989-93; gen. corp. counsel Am. Achievement Schs., Inc., 1994-96; atty. Frie, Arndt & Trujillo Law Firm, Arvada, 1994-96, ptnr., 1995-97; dist. hearing officer, dir. of instrn. Adams County Sch. Dist. 14, 1999—, dir. human resources, 1998-99, dist. attendance officer/legal counsel, prin. H.S., 1999—. Co-chair Mellon fellowships The Coll. Bd., N.Y.C., 1987-93; cons. U.S.I.A. Fulbright Tchr. Exch. Program, Washington, 1987-93; editl. advisor Harcourt, Brace, Jovanovich Pub., Orlando, Fla., 1988-93; mem. Colo. Supreme Ct. Multicultural Commn., 1996-98, 99—; mem. Colo. Supreme Ct. Families in the Cts. Commn., 2001—. Contbr. numerous articles to profl. jours. Mem. panel of arbitrators Am. Arbitration Assn., 1994. Recipient Legal Aid Clinic Acad. award Colo. Bar Assn., 1993, Pro Bono award, 1993, Loyola U. Acad. award, 1993, Gov.'s award for excellence in the arts State of Colo., 1996. Mem. Colo. chpt. Am. Assn. Tchrs. of Spanish and Portuguese (pres. 1985-88), Am. Immigration Lawyers Assn., Nat. Sch. Bds. Coun. Sch. Attys., Nat. Assn. Judiciary Interpreters and Translators, Colo. Bar Assn. (probate and trust sect., grievance policy com. 1995-97, ethics com. 1995-96), U. San Francisco Alumni Assn.

(founder, pres. 1987-90), Phi Delta Kappa (chair internat. edn. com. 1988-89), Phi Alpha Delta. Avocation: violinist. Office: Adams County Sch Dist 14 6500 E 72d Ave Commerce City CO 80022-2380

TRUJILLO, MICHAEL H. administrator; b. Laguna Pueblo, N.Mex., Apr. 11, 1944; MS, U. N.Mex., 1970, MD in Family Practice and Internal Medicine, 1974; MPH, U. Minn., 1984. Fellow in preventive medicine Mayo Clin., Rochester, Minn., 1982-84; dep. area dir., chief med. officer Indian Health Svc., Phoenix Area, 1980-81, Aberdeen Area, 1985-89, Portland Area, 1991-94, dir. Rockville, Md., 1994—2002. Assoc. warden med. and hosp. programs, med. dir. Fed. Med. Ctr. of Bur. of Prisons, Rochester, 1989-91. Mem. APHA, Nat. Rural Health Assn., Am. Coll. Physician Execs., Am. Assn. Indian Physicians, We. Can. Am. Health Coun., Assn. Mil. Surgeons of U.S. Office: Indian Health Svc 5600 Fishers Ln Ste 605 Rockville MD 20857-0001 E-mail: michael.trujillo@mail.ihs.gov.

TRUJILLO, SOLOMON D. telecommunications executive; m. Corine Trujillo; 3 children. BS, MBA, U. Wyo. With US West, Denver, 1974-92, pres., CEO mktg. resources, 1992-95, pres., CEO, 1995-97; CEO Graviton, Inc., San Diego, 1997—. Bd. dirs. Dayton Hudson Corp., Bank of Am., World Econ. Forum; mem. Nat. Security Telecom. Coun.; advisor U.S. govt. on trade policy as appointee Investment and Svcs. Policy Adv. Com., Office of the Pres. Bd. trustees Aspen Inst., chair ann. seminar on Hispanic Ams. and the Bus. Cmty.; bd. dirs. Tomás Rivera Policy Inst.; mem. corp. bd. advisors Nat. Coun. of La Raza; bd. fellows Claremont Grad. U.; chmn. bd. trustees Ctr. for the New West, Denver. Named one of 100 Most Influential Latinos in the Nation by Hispanic Bus. Mag.; recipient Cmty. Svc. award NCCJ, Disting. Svc. award Colo. Civil Rights Commn., Corp. Advocate of the Yr. award U.S. Hispanic C. of C. Office: Graviton Inc Ste 200 11025 N Torrey Pines Rd La Jolla CA 92037*

TRUJILLO-CUTHRELL, LORETTA MARIE, chemical engineer; b. Santa Fe, May 22, 1959; d. Jose E.F. and Irene D. (Fernandez) Trujillo; m. Robert Blair Cuthrell, May 16, 1987. BSChemE, U. N.Mex., 1988. Process engr. Kerr McGee Chem., Trona, Calif., 1989-91; chem. engr. N.Am. Chem. Co., 1991-98, quality coord., 1992-98, IMC Chem., Trona, Calif., 1998-2000; lab. supr. GTC, Albuquerque, 2000—. Mem. AIChE (vice chmn. 1995—), Women in Mining.

TRUJILLO-LITMAN, DELIA M. b. Laredo, Tex., Mar. 21, 1949; d. Filiberto and Maria D. (Ramirez) Trujillo; m. Javier S. Moctezuma, June 26, 1971 (div. May 1990); children: Sarita, Javier Jr., Carles, Roberto; m. Pete Litman, Aug. 7, 1999. BS, Tex. A&I Univ., Kingsville, Tex., 1970. Cert. Yoga Instr. Houston Yoga Inst. Math. tchr. secindary schs. Laredo (Tex.) Pub. Schs., 1970—94; adj. faculty Laredo C.C, 1999—; columnist Wellness Laredo Morning Times, 2000—; founder, dir. White Lotus Wellness Inst., Laredo, 2000—. Author: (Book) for Everything There Is a Season, 2001. Home: 1304 Los Ebanos #214 Laredo TX 78041 Office: White Lotus Wellness Inst. #206 109 Calle del Norte Laredo TX 78041

TRULEAR, HAROLD DEAN, minister, theological educator, social researcher; b. Phila., Oct. 4, 1954; s. Harold Holland and Elizabeth C. (Dean) T.; m. Vickie Lynette Butler, June 27, 1981; children: Harold Butler, Jared Morgan, Frances Elizabeth. BA, Morehouse Coll., 1975; MPhil, Drew U., 1979, PhD, 1983. Club dir. Youth for Christ, Paterson, N.J., 1977-83; assoc. prof. ch. and society Drew U., Madison, 1978-87; dir. black ch. studies Ea. Bapt. Theol. Sem., Phila., 1987-90; dean 1st profl. programs N.Y. Theol. Sem., N.Y.C., 1990-96, prof. ch. and society, 1990-98; v.p. Pub./Pvt. Ventures, Phila., 1998—. Assoc. pastor Cmty. Bapt. Ch., Paterson, 1981-87, 91-97; pastor Mt. Zion Bapt. Ch., Phila., 1987-90; assoc. min. Zion Bapt. Ch., Ardmore, Pa.; clergy assoc. St. Mary's Episcopal Ch., Ardmore; cons. Christian Coll. Consortium, 1990, Vanderbilt U. Div. Sch., Nashville, 1995; mem. adv. bd. Phila. Project for Youth Ministry, 1995-97; bd. dirs. N.Y. Christian Higher Edn. Consortium, N.Y.C. Guest editor The Pastor Scholar, 1997; contbr. chpts. to books. Bd. dirs. Paterson Clergy Assn., 1977-83, Opportunities Industrialization Ctr., Paterson, 1981-87, Inter Varsity Christian Fellowship, Madison, Wis., 1995—, Inndwelling, World Impact, Chester, Pa. Grantee N.J. Hist. Commn., 1984, Assn. Theol. Schs., 1984, Ford Found., 1994-95. Fellow Partnership for Rsch. on Religion and At Risk Youth; mem. Am. Acad. Religion, Soc. for the Study Black Religion, Soc. for Pentecostal Studies, Bapt. Mins. Conf., Am. Bapt. Chs. N.J. (mins. coun.), Phi Beta Kappa. Republican. Achievements include research on youth, young adults, religion and public policy. Avocations: collecting baseball cards, travel, railroading. Home: 912 Church Ln Yeadon PA 19050-3717 Office: Pub Pvt Ventures 2005 Market St Ste 900 Philadelphia PA 19103-7060

TRULL, TIMOTHY LANE, financial services executive; b. Charlotte, NC, Mar. 13, 1967; s. Donald Reece and Sally Jean (Jeffries) Trull; m. Teresa Ann Tyne; children: Mary, Timmy, Grace. AA, Coastal Carolina CC, Jacksonville, NC, 1990; BA, U. NC, Pembroke, 1992; MS, Am. Coll., 1999. Cert. residential mortgage lender Nat. Assn. Mortgage Brokers. Broker Midstate Fin. Svcs., Fayetteville, NC, 1994—97; acct. exec. Advante Nat. Bank, Spring House, Pa., 1997—99; chmn. Brick Mortgage Co., Fayetteville, NC, 1999—; pres. Am. Fin. Svcs., 2001—. Capt. USAR, 1986—2000. Mem.: Masons, Kiwanis (treas. 2000—01). Republican. Baptist. Mailing: PO Box 58442 Fayetteville NC 28305 Fax: 910-484-5063. E-mail: timtrull@hotmail.com.

TRULUCK, JAMES PAUL, JR. dentist, vintner; b. Florence, S.C., Feb. 6, 1933; s. James Paul and Catherine Lydia (Nesmith) TruL.; m. Kay Bowen (dec. Oct. 1981); children: James Paul III, David Bowen, Catherine Ann; m. Amelia Nickels Calhoun, Apr. 26, 1983; 1 child, George Calhoun. BS, Clemson (S.C.) U., 1954; DMD, U. Louisville, 1958. Pvt. practice, Lake City, S.C., 1960—; founder, pres. TruLuck Vineyards & Winery, 1976, Chateau TruLuck Natural Water Co., Lake City, 1990. Member bd. advisors Clemson U., 1978-84; mem. bd. visitors Coker Coll., Hartsville, S.C., 1978-84; pres., bd. dirs. Lions, Lake City, 1960-73; chmn. Greater Lake City Lake Commn., 1967-84. Capt. USAF, 1958-67. Recipient S.C. Bus. and Arts Partnership award S.C. State Arts Commn., 1988. Mem. ADA, Am. Assn. Vinters (bd. dirs. 1982-86), Am. Wine Soc. (nat. judge 1982-88), Am. Soc. Clin. Hypnosis (emeritus), Internat. Acad. Laser Dentistry (chartered), S.C. Dental Assn., Florence County Dental Assn., Soc. First Families of S.C. (exec. sec. 1991—), Descs. Colonial Govs. of Am., Descs. Magna Carta Barons Runnymede, Soc. Gem Cutters Am., Soc. of the Decendants of the Knight of the Garter, Soc. of the St. George, Windsor Castle (Eng.). Episcopalian. Avocations: genealogy, gemealogy, tennis, sailing, writing. Home: 1036 Mccutcheon Rd Lake City SC 29560-1265 Office: 125 Epps St Lake City SC 29560-1656

TRUMAN, DAVID BICKNELL, political scientist, educator; b. Evanston, Ill. s. Malcolm George and Jane Mackintosh Truman; m. Elinor Griffenhagen, Feb. 4, 1939; 1 child, Edwin Malcolm. BA, Amherst Coll., 1935; MA, U. Chgo., 1936, PhD, 1939; LHD, Amherst Coll., 1974; LLD, Mt. Holyoke Coll., 1978. Instr. Bennington (Vt.) Coll., 1939-41, Cornell U., Ithaca, N.Y., 1941-43; lectr. Harvard U., Cambridge, Mass., 1946, 47; assoc. prof. Williams Coll., Williamstown, 1947-59; prof., dean, v.p., provost Columbia U., N.Y.C., 1969-78; prof., pres. emeritus Mt. Holyoke, 69-78. Vis. prof. Yale U., 1957-58. Author books, including The Governmental Process, 1951, 71. Trustee Amherst Coll., 1964-70, 20th Century Fund, N.Y., 1968—; trustee, pres. Russell Sage Found., N.Y., 1967—. Lt. (j.g.) USNR, 1943-47. Guggenheim fellow, 1962-63. Fellow Am. Acad. Arts and Letters; mem. Am. Philosophies Soc., Am. Polit. Sci. Assn. (pres. 1965), Student Loan Mktg. Assn. (dir. 1977-88), Social Sci. Rsch. Coun. (dir. 1951-88) Democrat. Home: Apt N-312 700 John Ringling Blvd Sarasota FL 34236-1501 E-mail: DBEGTruman@cs.com.

TRUMAN, EDWIN MALCOLM, federal official; b. Albany, N.Y., June 6, 1941; m. Tracy P. T.; children: David, Christine. BA, Amherst Coll., 1963; MA, Yale U., 1964, PhD, 1967; LLD (hon.), Amherst Coll., 1988. Dir. Divsn. of Internat. Finance, 1977-87; staff dir., bd. govs. FRS, 1987-98; asst. Sec. of the Treas. Fed. Govt. Internat. Affairs, Washington, 1998—. Contr. articles toprofl. jours. Office: Internat Affairs Dept of the Treasury 15th & Pennsylvania Ave NW Washington DC 20220-0001 E-mail: tnttruman2@aol.com., ted.truman@do.treas.gov.

TRUMAN, MARGARET, author; b. Independence, Mo., Feb. 17, 1924; d. Harry S. (32nd Pres. U.S.) and Bess (Wallace) T.; m. E. Clifton Daniel Jr., Apr. 21, 1956; children: Clifton T., William, Harrison, Thomas. LHD, Wake Forest U., 1972; HHD, Rockhurst Coll., 1976. Concert singer, 1947-54, actess, broadcaster, author, 1954—; author: Souvenir, 1956, White House Pets, 1969, Harry S. Truman, 1973, Women of Courage, 1976, Murder in the White House, 1980, Murder on Capitol Hill, 1981, Letters from Father, 1981, Murder in the Supreme Ct., 1982, Murder in the Smithsonian, 1983, Murder on Embassy Row, 1985, Murder at the FBI, 1985, Murder in Georgetown, 1986, Bess W. Truman, 1986, Murder in the CIA, 1987, Murder at the Kennedy Center, 1989, Murder in the National Cathedral, 1990, Murder at the Pentagon, 1992, Murder on the Potomac, 1994, First Ladies, 1995, Murder in the National Gallery, 1996, Murder in the House, 1997, Murder at the Watergate, 1998, Murder in the Library of Congress, 1999, Murder at Foggy Bottom, 2000, Murder in Havana, 2001; editor: Where the Buck Stops: The Personal and Private Writings of Harry S. Truman, 1989. Trustee and v.p. Harry S. Truman Inst.; sec. bd. trustees Harry S. Truman Found.

TRUMBULL, DAVID LEWIS KITCHEN, trade association executive; b. Highland Park, Mich. s. Ben Gordon and Lois Virginia (Wilson) Kitchen. AB, U. Mich., 1991. Rsch. asst. U. Mass., Boston, 1992-93; programmer Commonwealth of Mass., 1993-94; in charge mem. svcs. No. Textile Assn., 1994—; exec. dir. Am. Flock Assn., 1994—2002. Chmn. Cambridge (Mass.) Rep. City Com., 1994-2002; asst. sec. NAACP, Cambridge, 1994-96, v.p., 1996-98. Mem. Textile Club (exec. com. 1996—, treas. 1998—). Episcopalian. Home: 130 Bowdoin St # 1110 Boston MA 02108 Office: No Textile Assn 6 Beacon St # 1125 Boston MA 02108 E-mail: trumbulld@aol.com.

TRUMBULL, WILLIAM ERNEST, surgeon, educator, retired; b. Portland, Oreg., Mar. 16, 1924; MD, NYU, 1951. Bd. cert. in surgery, 1959. Intern L.A. County-Harbor, Torrance, Calif., 1951-52, surg. resident, 1953-58; staff St. John's Hosp.-Health Ctr., Santa Monica; asst. clin. prof. UCLA. Fellow ACS; mem. Calif. Med. Assn., L.A. Surg. Soc., Pacific Coast Surg. Assn. E-mail: wtrumbull@earthlink.net.

TRUMP, DONALD JOHN, real estate developer; b. N.Y.C., 1946; s. Fred C. and Mary Trump; m. Ivana Zelnicek, 1977 (div. 1991); children: Donald, Jr., Ivanka, Eric; m. Marla Maples, Dec. 30, 1993 (div. 1999); 1 child Tiffany. BA, U. Pa., 1968. Pres. Trump Orgn., N.Y.C.; owner Trump Tower, Trump Parc, Trump Palace, The Trump Bldg. at 40 Wall St., GM Bldg., Trump Internat. Hotel and Tower, N.Y.C., Trump Pla., Trump Marina, Trump Taj Mahal, Atlantic City, Trump Casino Riverboat, Buffington Harbor, Ind., Trump 29 Casino, Palm Springs, Calif., West Side Rail Yards to be devel. as Trump Place, N.Y.C., Seven Springs Mansion, Bedford, N.Y., Mar-a-Lago Club, Palm Beach, Fla.; ptnr.-owner 610 Park Avenue and Trump World Tower, N.Y.C., The Delmonico Hotel, Trumpe Grande Ocean Resort and Residence, Miami Beach, Fla.; chmn., pres. Trump Org., N.Y.C. Owner Trump Internat. Golf Club, Palm Beach, Fla., Trump Nat. Golf Club, Briarcliff Manor, NY, Trump Mgmt. Group Modeling/Talent Agy.; pres. Trump Pageants LP, includes Miss Universe, Miss USA and Miss Teen USA. Author: (novels) The Art of the Deal, 1987, Surviving at the Top, 1990, The Art of the Comeback, 1997, The America We Deserve. Co-chmn. N.Y. Vietnam Vets. Meml. Fund; founding mem. constrn. com. Cathedral of St. John the Divine; mem. N.Y. Citizens Tax Coun., Fifth Ave Assn., Realty Found. of N.Y., Met. Mus. of Art's Real Estate Coun.; mem. adv. bd. Lenox Hill Hosp., United Cerebral Palsy; spl. advisor to Pres.'s Coun. on Phys. Fitness and Sports; mem. N.Y. Sportsplex Commn.; chmn. N.Y. citizens com. 78th Ann. NAACP Conv., 1987; grand marshall Nation's Parade, 1995; bd. dirs. Police Athletic League; bd. overseers Wharton Sch.; mem. adv. bd. Wharton Real Estate Ctr.; bd. dirs. Fred C. Trump Found. Named Developer of Yr., Constrn. Mgmt. Assn. Am., 1999, Hotel and Real Visionary of the Century, UTA Fedn., 2000; named to Wharton Hall of Fame; recipient Entrepreneur of Yr. award, Wharton Entrepreneurial Club, 1984, Ellis Island medal of Honor, 1986. Office Fax: 212-935-0141.

TRUMPENER, KATIE, literature educator; Student, U. Freiburgh, West Germany; BA with honors, U. Alberta, Can.; MA in Eng. and Am. Lit., Harvard U.; PhD in Comparative Lit., Stanford U., 1990. Assoc. prof. germanic studies U. Chgo., 1990—. Author: Bardic Nationalism: The Romantic Novel and the British Empire, 1997 (MLZ prize for a First Book, 1998, British Acad. Rose Mary Crawshay prize, 1998); co-editor: Modern Philology. Office: Univ Chgo Eng Dept Gates-Blake 324 1050 E 59th St Chicago IL 60637 Office Fax: 773-702-2495. E-mail: ktrumpen@midway.uchicago.edu.*

TRUNNELL, THOMAS NEWTON, dermatologist; b. Waterloo, Iowa, May 7, 1942; s. Thomas Lyle and Vivian (Dahl) T.; m. Patricia Rautiala, Aug. 2, 1974; children: Suzanne, Thomas, Sarah. AB cum laude, Princeton U., 1964; MD, U. Iowa, 1968. Diplomate Am. Bd. Dermatology, 1973. Intern U. So. Calif., L.A., 1969; resident NYU, 1972; pvt. practice dermatology Tampa, Fla., 1974—; asst. clin. prof. U. S. Fla., 1975—. Contbr. articles to profl. jours. Maj. USAF, 1972-74. Mem. AMA, Am. Acad. Dermatology, Am. Assn. Dermatol. Surgeons, Fla. Med. Assn., Fla. Soc. for Dermatol. Surgeons (pres. 1993), Fla. Dermatol. Soc., Hillsborough County Med. Assn. Republican. United Methodist. Avocations: fishing, hunting. Office: 13801 Bruce B Downs Blvd Tampa FL 33613-3946

TRUNZO, THOMAS HAROLD, JR. lawyer; b. McKeesport, Pa., Oct. 23, 1948; children: Melissa, Kirsten. BA, Tufts U., 1976; JD, Vt. Law Sch., 1980. Bar: N.H. 1980, Mass. 1981, Vt. 1988. Ptnr. Mullaly & Trunzo Law Offices, West Lebanon, N.H., 1980-87; pvt. practice Lebanon, 1987—. Active Sch. Bd. Orford (H.H.) Sch. Dist., 1980—87; mem. Orford Planning Bd., 1991—93; moderator Rivendale Sch. Dist., Orford, 1998—. Mem. Assn. Trial Lawyers Am., Nat. Lawyers Guild, N.H. Bar Assn. (Pro bono award 1987), Vt. Bar Assn., Grafton County Bar Assn. Democrat. Home: RR 1 Box 42 Orford NH 03777-9707 Office: Citizens Bank Bldg PO Box 825 20 W Park St Ste 415 Lebanon NH 03766-1322 E-mail: ttrunzo@innevi.com.

TRUOG, DEAN-DANIEL WESLEY, educator, consultant; b. Denver, Apr. 1, 1938; s. George Calvin and Zelma Elizabeth (Bennett) T.; m. Dorothy Anne Harding, May 31, 1961; children: David Robert, Denise Dawne. Student, Bethel Coll., 1960-61, L'Abri Fellowship Found., Switzerland, 1967-68; diploma in Bible and Leadership Devel., The Navigators Internat. Tng. Inst., 1968; BA in History, U. Colo., 1971; Diploma in Gen. Univ. Studies in French Civilization, U. Strasbourg, France, 1977; MA in Liberal Edn., St. John's Coll., 1986; M of Liberal Arts in History of Sci., Harvard U., 1987; postgrad., Boston U., 1987-93. Sr. resident adv. U. Colo., Boulder, 1964-65; rep., tutor, lectr. biblical studies and practical christianity The Navigators, 1965-93; rep. for greater Washington area, 1965-67; training asst. The Navigators, Colorado Springs, Colo., 1968, rep. at U. Colo. Boulder, 1968-70, No. Colo. dir., 1970-71, spl. adv. Birmingham, Eng., 1971-72, rep. at large Boulder, Colo., 1979-80; founding dir., pres. Les Navigateurs, France, 1972-84, v.p. France, 1984-85, rep. to U. Strasbourg France, 1973-79, rep. to U. Grenoble France, 1980-85; sr. teaching fellow in non-deptmental studies Harvard U., Cambridge, Mass., 1987-90; founding pres., life mgmt. cons./counselor Cornerstone Inst. for Values and Relationships, 1990—; v.p. U.S.-Bulgaria Inst., Cambridge, 1991—; spl. cons. to mems. U.S. Congress, 1993—. Tutor North House, Harvard U., 1987-91; founding chmn. Harvard Christian Assocs., 1987-92; spkr., tchr. profl. confs.; designer, dir. leadership devel. programs, Boston, Washington, Colo., Austria, France, Switzerland. With USN, 1958-59. Mem. AAAS, History of Sci. Soc., Am. Sci. Affiliation, Soc. Christian Philosophers, Assn. for Religion and Intellectual Llife, Inst. on Religion in Age of Sci., Ctr. for Theology and Natural Scis., Nat. Assn. Scholars, Rotary. Presbyterian. Avocations: cycling, gardening, skiing, tennis, swimming. Home and Office: 15 Sheridan Rd Swampscott MA 01907-2046 E-mail: dtru@post.harvard.edu.

TRUOG, WILLIAM EDWARD, III, pediatrician, educator, researcher; b. Kansas City, Mo., Feb. 5, 1947; s. William E. and Virginia (Sylvester) T.; m. Jill D. Jacobson, July 11, 1992. BA cum laude, Carleton Coll., 1969; MD, U. Chgo., 1973. Intern, resident in pediatrics, chief resident Children's Orthopedic Hosp.-U. Wash., Seattle, 1973-76, research fellow in neonatology, 1976-78; asst. prof. pediatrics U. Wash., 1978-82, assoc. prof., 1982-87, prof., 1987-93; med. dir. infant intensive care unit Children's Orthopedic Hosp., Seattle, 1982-91; prof. pediatrics Sch. Medicine UMKC, 1993—; first physician scientist Children's Mercy Hosp., 1993. Author: Critical Care of the Newborn, 1983, 2d edit., 1988; also articles in med. jours. NIH grantee, 1981, 84, 97. Mem. Am. Thoracic Soc. (grantee 1978), Am. Pediatric Soc., Soc. Pediatric Research, Western Soc. for Pediatric Research, Perinatal Rsch. Soc. Episcopalian. Office: Children's Mercy Hosp 2401 Gillham Rd Kansas City MO 64108-4619

TRUONG, JEFF VAN, software engineer; b. Cholon, Vietnam, July 28, 1959; came to U.S., 1980; s. Dinh Thanh and Anh Truong; m. Myra Truong, 1994; children: James, Bryan. AA, Seminole C.C., Sanford, Fla., 1985; BS in Computer Sci., U. Cen. Fla., 1986. Cook Park Plaza Garden Restaurant, Winter Park, Fla., 1980-83; real estate salesman Don Gallagher Realty, 1983-86; sr. software engr. Siemens Stromberg Carlson, Lake Mary, Fla., 1986-92; lead engr. Harris Comm., Novato, Calif., 1992-94; sr. engr. Nortel Network, Santa Clara, 1994-96; sys. engr. ISR Global Telecom, Maitland, Fla., 1996-97; cons. Siemens Telecom Networks, Lake Mary, 1997-98; sys. engr. Triton Network Sys., Orlando, 1998—2001; sr. engr. Siemens ICN, 2001—. Republican. Home: 5645 Magnolia Bloom Ter Oviedo FL 32765-9396

TRUONG, LONG KHANH, software consultant; b. Nhatrang, South Vietnam, Mar. 1, 1952; s. Nhu Van Truong and Thanh Thi Do; m. Chau Duong Nguyen, Feb. 1, 1961; children: Vy Nguyen-Truong, Christopher, Anthony. BS in Mech. Engring., Pa. State U., 1981; MS in Computer Sci. and Applications, Va. Tech., 1999. Mem. tech. staff Electronic Assocs. Inc., Cherry Hill, N.J., 1981-84; sr. engr.tech. staff McDonnell Douglas, St. Louis, 1984-87; prin. engr. Hughes Aircraft, Herndon, Va., 1987-97; sr. mem. tech. staff MITRE Corp., Reston, 1997-2000, SRA Internat., Inc., Fairfax, 2001—. Lt. Artillery Sch., Duc My, South Vietnam, 1971-75. Home: 12606 Blythewood Dr Fairfax VA 22030 Office: SRA Internat Inc 4300 Fair Lakes Ct Fairfax VA 22033 E-mail: long_truong@sra.com.

TRURAN, JAMES WELLINGTON, JR. astrophysicist, educator; b. Brewster, N.Y., July 12, 1940; s. James Wellington and Suzanne (Foglesong) T.; m. Carol Kay Dell'Acy, June 26, 1965; children— Elaina Michelle, Diana Lee, Anastasia Elizabeth. BA in Physics, Cornell U., 1961; MS in Physics, Yale U., 1963, PhD in Physics, 1966. Postdoctoral rsch. assoc. NAS-NRC Goddard Inst. Space Studies, NASA, N.Y.C., 1965-67; asst. prof. physics Belfer Grad. Sch. Sci., Yeshiva U., 1967-70; rsch. fellow in physics Calif. Inst. Tech., 1968-69; assoc. prof. Belfer Grad. Sch. Sci., Yeshiva U., 1970-72, prof., 1972-73; prof. astronomy U. Ill., Urbana, 1973-91; sr. vis. fellow, Guggenheim Meml. Found. fellow Inst. Astronomy, U. Cambridge, Eng., 1979-80; trustee Aspen Ctr. Physics, 1979-85, 91-93, 96-99, v.p., 1985-88; assoc. U. Ill. Ctr. for Advanced Study, 1979-80, 86-87; prof. astronomy astrophysics U. Chgo., 1991—. Alexander von Humboldt-Stiftung sr. scientist Max-Planck Inst., Munich, Germany, 1986-87, 94; Beatrice Tinsley vis. prof. U. Tex., Austin, 1999. Contbr. articles to profl. jours.; co-editor: Nucleosynthesis, 1968, Nucleosynthesis— Challenges and New Developments, 1985, Nuclear Astrophysics, 1987, Type Ia Supernovae: Theory and Cosmology, 2000, Cosmic Chemical Evolution, 2002; editor: Physics Letters B, 1974-80. Co-recipient Yale Sci. and Engring. Assn. annual award for advancement basic or applied sci., 1980 Fellow AAAS, Am. Phys. Soc.; mem. Am. Astron. Soc., Am. Phys. Soc., Internat. Astron. Union. Home: 210 Wysteria Dr Olympia Fields IL 60461-1202 Office: U Chgo Dept Astronomy Astrophysics 5640 S Ellis Ave Chicago IL 60637-1433

TRURAN, WILLIAM RICHARD, electrical engineer; b. Franklin, N.J., Feb. 14, 1951; s. Wilfred Hardy and Stella Eva (Hall) Truran; m. Virginia Lynn Johnson, Aug. 18, 1979; children: Michael, Wendy. BSEE, U. Tenn., 1972; MBA, Fairleigh Dickinson U., 1981; MS in Indsl. Engring., Columbia U., 1994; PhD in Tech. Mgmt., Stevens Inst. Tech., 2000. Registered prof engr, NJ, NY, Pa, Calif, prof planner, NJ; cert. project mgmt. profl. Design engr. Gordos Corp., Bloomfield, N.J., 1972-73; project engr. Edwards Engring., Pompton Plains, 1973-78; sr. engr. Apollo Tech., Whippany, 1978-81; elec. product mgr. Dodge-Newark, Fairfield, 1981-96; pres. Trupower Engring., Sparta, 1984—. Pres TEC Corp NJ, Sparta, 1988—; adj prof Stevens Inst Technology; adj. prof. Seton Hall U.; consult in field. Contbr. articles to profl jours. Active foster child orgn Christian Children's Fund; bd. mgrs. Columbia Engring. Sch. Alumni; v.p. bd. mgrs. Columbia Engring. Sch. Alumni Assn., v.p. student rels. Mem.: NSPE (legis action network, minuteman), Acad. of Mgmt., Nta. Assn. Environ. Profls., Sierra Club, Nature Conservancy. Episcopalian. Avocations: skiing, water skiing, triathalons, marathons, antique Corvettes. Home and Office: 37 Rainbow Trl Sparta NJ 07871-1724 E-mail: wrtl@columbia.edu.

TRUS, BENES LOUIS, structural chemist; b. Tyler, Tex., May 9, 1946; s. Joseph N. and Ruthie Trus; m. Susan Gale Evans, Apr. 23, 1972; children: Aaron Baram, Anthony Phillip. BS cum laude with honors, Tulane U., 1968; PhD, Calif. Inst. Tech., 1972. Rsch. chemist NIH, Bethesda, Md., 1980-83, chief image processing rsch. sect., 1983—. Mem. steering com. NIH wide image processing group, Bethesda, 1984— (NIH Dirs. award, 1987, 94, Group Merit award 1998). Contbr. articles to profl. jours., chpt. to books. Mem. NIH Marathon Team, 1986-88, 1st pl. Marine Corps Marathon, Govt. Team Competition, 1986, 3d pl., 1987, 88, 2d pl. Masters Team, 1993. Jane Ciffon Childs postdoctoral fellow Calif. Inst. Tech., Pasadena, 1972-75, Rsch. fellow NIH, Bethesda, Md., 1975-77, Sr. Rsch. fellow, 1977-80; Tulane U. scholar and fellow, 1965-68. Mem. Chesapeake Soc. for Microscopy, Microscope Soc. Am., Montgomery County Rd. Runners Club, NIH Health's Angels Running Club, Phi Beta Kappa, Sigma Xi. Avocations: music, running, carpentry. Office: NIH Bldg 12A Rm 2033 Bethesda MD 20892-5624

TRUSCHKE, EDWARD F. retired medical association administrator; Formerly with Xerox Corp; past exec. dir. BankAm. Found.; past sr. v.p. social policy, chmn. social policy com., sec. pub. policy com. to bd. dirs., head social policy dept. BankAm. Corp.; pres. Alzheimer's Assn., Chgo., 1994—2001.*

TRUSCIO, JAMES, JR. banker; b. Bronx, N.Y., June 19, 1942; s. James and Louise Marie (Jones) T.; m. Patricia Ann Stanulla, Oct. 16, 1971 (div. 1977); m. Felicie Dorothy Varin, Sept. 22, 1979; children: Robert Stephen, Christine Marie. Grad. high sch., Bronx, N.Y., 1961. Ops. officer, asst. sec. Mfrs. Hanover Trust Co., N.Y.C., 1961-89; asst. treas., compliance officer The Trust Co. of N.J., Ridgefield, 1989-90; asst. mgr. Natureworks N.Mex. Mus. Natural History, Albuquerque, 1992—. Author books of poetry: Feelings Within, 1978, First, Last and Always, 1978. Vice chmn. cable com. Rio Rancho, N.Mex. Republican. Roman Catholic. Avocations: pen and ink drawings, writing, computer graphics, fishing, photography. Office: JT Enterprises 77 Parkside Rd SE Rio Rancho NM 87124-3984

TRUSCOTT, WILLIAM LLOYD, auditor, consultant; b. Allentown, Pa., June 19, 1963; s. Paul Joseph and Eileen (Delozier) T. BS in Bus. Adminstrn., Bridgewater Coll., 1985. Mgr. Citibank, N.A., N.Y.C., 1988-92; examiner Fed. Res. Bank of Phila., 1992-98; global auditor Dresdner Kleinwort Benson, N.Y.C., N.Y., 1998—. Fgn. advisor Fin. Svc. Vol. Corps., Nation Bank of Ukraine, Kiev, 1998. Treas., bd. dirs. Am. Revolution Patriots Fund; bd. dirs. Phila. divsn. Am. Heart Assn.; bd. govs. English-Speaking Union; mem. Hist. Soc. Phila., Friends of the Phila. Mus. of Art. Mem. World Affairs Coun. of Phila., Fgn. Policy Rsch. Inst., Pa. Soc. of Sons of Revolution (bd. mgrs.), Soc. Colonial Wars in State of N.Y., Vet. Corps of Arty., Baronial Order of Magna Charta (bd. dirs.), Racquet Club, Nassau Club. Republican. Episcopalian. Home: 400 Merion Hill Ln Conshohocken PA 19428 Office: Dresdner Kleinwort Benson Global Audit Divsn 75 Wall St New York NY 10005-2833 E-mail: wlt10@mindspring.com.

TRUSSELL, CHARLES TAIT, columnist; b. Balt., May 9, 1925; s. Charles Prescott and Beatrice (Tait) T.; m. Woodley Grizzard, Dec. 27, 1953 (div. 1990); children: Galen Tait, Thomas Marshall; m. Nancy Rathbun Billington, Dec. 19, 1990. BA in Journalism, Washington and Lee U., 1949. Reporter St. Petersburg (Fla.) Times, also; writer Congl. Quar. News Features, 1951-54; reporter Wall St. Jour., 1954-56, Washington Evening Star, 1956; asso. editor Nation's Business mag., 1956-64, mng. editor, 1964-69; sr. editor Congressional Quar., Inc., 1969-70; dir. pub. relations and advt. Investment Co. Inst., Washington, 1970-72; free-lance writer, real estate investor, 1972-74; v.p. Am. Forest Inst., Washington, 1974-79, sr. v.p., 1980-81; v.p. Am. Enterprise Inst., 1981-86; dir. communications Constitution Bicentennial Commn., 1986-88; freelance writer, columnist, 1988—. Producer: documentary record album The Best of Washington Humor, 1963; author: Beating the Competition, 1992; editor: Successful Management, 1964, (with Paul Hencke) Dear NASA Please Send Me a Rocket, 1964, Timeless Truths for Kids, 2002.. Served with USNR,

1944-46. Recipient Loeb Spl. Achievement award for mags. U. Conn., 1961, Benjamin Fine Journalism award, 1992. Mem. Washington Assembly (exec. com. 1961-65, chmn. 1965), Country Club of Mt. Dora, Beta Theta Pi. Home: 6014 Spring Creek Ct Mount Dora FL 32757-6952

TRUSSELL, CHARLIE WARD, physicist; b. Walterboro, S.C., Jan. 30, 1943; s. Charlie Ward Trussell and Addie Pauline Fuller; m. Sharon Kaye Whittaker, Oct. 4, 1970; children: Beth Leigh, Susan Rebecca. BS in Physics, Clemson U., 1965; PhD in Physics, U. Va., 1969. Physicist U.S. Army Night Vision and Electronic Sensors Directorate, Ft. Belvoir, Va., 1969—. Mem. program com. active sensors Mil. Sensing Symposia; mem. peer rev. panel NASA Langley, Va., 1997, 99; U.S. Army rep. TTCP SEN TP5 Panel, U.S., U.K., Australia and Can., 1991—; presenter in field. Contbr. articles to profl. publs.; 6 patents in field. Mem. Optical Soc. Am. (program com. advanced solid state laser conf.). Avocations: golf, tennis, skiing. Home: 12023 William And Mary Cir Woodbridge VA 22192-1634

TRUSSELL, DONNA LAURA, writer; b. Dallas, Aug. 11, 1953; d. Norman Weldon and Mary (Longino) Read; m. Robert Coleman Trussell, May 14, 1977. BA, U. Mo., Kansas City, 1986. Tchr. Writers Pl., Kansas City, Mo., 1994-00; editor and film critic KC Pitch, New Times, 1982-98. Contbr. short stories and poems to lit. publs. and anthologies. Avocations: film, music, literature, travel, history. Home: 7204 High Dr Prairie Village KS 66208-3355 E-mail: thiswaspompeii@aol.com.

TRUSSELL, JAMES, dean; b. Columbus, Ga., Oct. 17, 1949; BS summa cum laude in Maths., Davidson Coll., 1971; BPhil, Oxford U., 1973; PhD in Econs., Princeton U., 1975. From asst. prof. econs. to prof., dean Princeton (N.J.) U., 1975—. Co-author: The Loving Book, 1972, Contraceptive Technology, 1998; contbr. articles to profl. jours. Mem. Am. Statis. Assn., Am. Pub. Health Assn., Population Assn. Am., Australia Population Assn., Phi Beta Kappa., Assn. Reproductive Health Profls., Internat. Union for the Scientific Study of Population. Office: Princeton U Office of Population Rsch Wallace Hall Princeton NJ 08544-2007 E-mail: trussell@princeton.edu.

TRUTTER, JOHN THOMAS, consulting company executive; b. Springfield, Ill., Apr. 18, 1920; s. Frank Louis and Frances (Mischler) T.; m. Edith English Woods II, June 17, 1950 (dec.); children: Edith English II, Jonathan Woods. BA, U. Ill., 1942; postgrad., Northwestern U., 1947-50, U. Chgo., 1947-50; LHD (hon.), Lincoln Coll., 1986. Various positions Ill. Bell, Chgo., 1946-58, gen. traffic mgr., from asst. v.p. pub. rels. to gen. mgr., 1958-69, v.p. pub. rels., 1969-71, v.p. operator svcs., 1971-80, v.p. community affairs, 1980-85; mem. hdqs. staff AT&T, N.Y.C., 1955-57; pres. John T. Trutter Co., Inc., Chgo., 1985—; pres., CEO Chgo. Conv. and Visitors Bur., 1985-88; pres. Chgo. Tourism Coun., 1988-90; v.p. Profl. Impressions Media Group, Inc., 1998-2000, prof. emeritus, 2001. Mem. adv. bd. The Alford Group, Chgo., 1984—, Bozell-Worldwide, Chgo., 1994-96; chancellor Lincoln Acad. of Ill., 1985-2001. Co-author: Handling Barriers in Communication, 1957, The Governor Takes a Bride, 1977 Past chmn., life trustee Jane Addams Hull House Assn.; chmn. United Cerebral Palsy Assn. Greater Chgo., 1967-95, hon. chmn., 1995—, chmn. Canal Corridor Assn., 1991-99; bd. dirs. Chgo. Crime Commn., Abraham Lincoln Assn., Lyric Opera Chgo.; v.p. English Speaking Union, 1989-91, bd. govs., 1980—; chmn. bd. City Colls. Chgo. Found., 1987-91; past chmn. Children's Home and Aid Soc. Ill.; v.p. City Club Chgo.; treas. Chgo. United, 1970-85; mem. Ill. Econ. Devel. Commn., 1985; past presiding co-chmn. NCCJ; numerous others; bd. govs. Northwestern U. Libr. Coun., 1984—; trustee Lincoln (Ill.) Coll., 1987-90, Mundelein Coll., 1988-91; mem. sch. problems coun. State Ill. Assembly, 1985-91, spl. commn. on adminstrn. of justice in Cook County, 1986-92; founding chmn. adv. coun. Evanston Hist. Soc., 1995-98. Lt. col. U.S. Army, 1945. Decorated Legion of Merit; recipient Laureate award State of Ill., 1980, Outstanding Exec. Leader award Am. Soc. Fundraisers, Humanitarian of Yr. award, Jane Addams award The Hull House Assn., 1991, Nat. Infinitec award for individual leadership in assistive technology for disabled people, 1997, Jack Brickhouse award for outstanding svcs., 2000. Mem. Pub. Rels. Soc. Am., Sangamon County Hist. Soc. (founder, past pres.), Ill. State Hist. Soc. (pres. 1985-87), Coun. on Ill. History (chmn. 1991—), U. Ill. Alumni Assn. (bd. dirs. 1990-94), Tavern Club, Econ. Club, Mid-Am. Club, Alpha Sigma Phi (Nat. Merit Achievement award 1994), Phi Delta Phi. Fax: 847-441-0582.

TRYBAN, ESTHER ELIZABETH, lawyer; b. Chgo., Aug. 14, 1958; d. Chester Joseph and Lottie Elizabeth (Napora) T. AAS with honors, Elgin (Ill.) C.C., 1977, AS with honors, 1982; BS with honors, Roosevelt U., Chgo., 1986; JD, U. Chgo., 1989. Bar: Ill. 1989, U.S. Dist. Ct. (no. dist.) Ill. 1989, U.S. Ct. Appeals (7th cir.) 1990, U.S. Supreme Ct., 1996. Supr. adminstrv. svcs. law dept. Motorola, Inc., Schaumburg, Ill., 1977-86; staff law clk. U.S. Bankruptcy Ct., No. Dist. Ill., Chgo., 1989-90; asst. corp. counsel City of Chgo., 1990—. Mem. ABA, Nat. Lawyers Guild, Assn. Former Bankruptcy Law Clks, Ill. State Bar Assn., Chgo. Bar Assn. (chair govt. svc. com. 1996-97). Roman Catholic. Avocations: reading, football, traveling. Office: City Chgo Dept Law 30 N Lasalle St Ste 900 Chicago IL 60602-2503 E-mail: lw00026@ch.chi.il.us.

TRYBUL, THEODORE NICHOLAS, education educator; b. Chgo., Apr. 12, 1935; s. Theodore and Sophie Trybul; children: Adrienne, Barbie, Cathy, Diane, Elizabeth, Teddy. BS summa cum laude, U. Ill., 1957; MS, U. N.Mex., 1963; DSc, George Washington U., 1976. Registered profl. engr., D.C. Dir. Sr. Exec. Svc., ES-IV Fed. Govt., Washington, 1966-83; prof. George Washington U., 1983-94, Tex. Grad. Sch., Corpus Christi, Tex., 1994—; prof. and dir. Natl. U., Grad. Sch. Bus. and Tech., Sacramento. Cons. NSF, Advanced Rsch. Projects Agy., U.S. Dept. Edn., NIH, Advanced Material Concepts Agy., Surgeon Gen.'s Office, Natl. Acad. Scis., IBM, Intel, Microsoft, GTSI; adv. bd. NSF, NIH, Natl. Acad. Engring., Surgeon Gen.'s Office. Contbr. articles to profl. jours. Officer Corpus Christi C. of C., Neuces Club, Millionaires Club, CC Town Club. Col. U.S. Army, 1957. Fellow ASME, Soc. for Computer Simulation, Health Care Execs., Sir Isaac Walton, Audubonn Soc., Sierra Club; mem. Pi Tau Sigma, Phi Betta Kappa, Kappa Mu Epsilon, Sigma Xi, Am. Assn. U. Prof.'s and Adminstr.'s, Soc. Computer Simulation, Am. Mgmt. Assn. Avocations: golf, tennis, fishing, mountain climbing. Office: Auburn Lake Trails CC 2418 Westville Trail Cool CA 95614 Fax: 916-855-4398. E-mail: ttrybul@hotmail.com.

TRYGESTAD, JOANN CAROL, secondary education educator; b. Mpls., Feb. 11, 1950; d. Harvey Oscar and Frances Anne (Libera) T. BS, U. Minn., 1972, MEd, 1983, PhD, 1997. Cert. tchr. social studies, history, English, Minn. Tchr. Sch. Dist. 742, St. Cloud, Minn., 1973-77, Sch. Dist. 196, Rosemount, 1977—. Grad. asst. U. Minn., Mpls., 1988-90; adj. instr. Hamline U., St. Paul, 1987-90, asst. prof., 1999—; steering com. mem. Alliance for Geography, St. Paul, 1988—; cons. in field. Contbr. articles to profl. jours. Mem. Nat. Coun. for Social Studies, Nat. Coun. for Geog. Edn., Am. Ednl. Rsch. Assn. Home: 4133 Arbor Ln Eagan MN 55122-2895 Office: Rosemount Sch Dist 14445 Diamond Path W Rosemount MN 55068-4143

TRYGGVASON, BJARNI V. astronaut; b. Reykjavik, Iceland, Sept. 21, 1945; 2 children. BSc in Engring. Physics, U. Brit. Columbia, 1972; student in Engring., U. We. Ontario. Meteorologist Atmospheric Environ. Svc. , Toronto, Canada, 1972—73; rsch. assoc. U. We. Ont., Canada, 1974—78, lectr. applied math., 1979—82; with Nat. Rsch. Coun., Ottawa, Canada, 1982—83; astronaut NASA, Houston, 1983—. Guest rsch. assoc. Kyoto U., Japan, 1978, James Cook U., Townsville, Australia, 1978; lectr. U. Ottawa, Canada, 1982—92, Carleton U., 1982—92; rep. NASA microgravity measurement working group Can. Space Agy.; astronaut space shuttle STS-85, 1997. Mem.: Can. Aeronautics & Space Inst. Avocations: scuba diving, skiing, parachuting. Office: Astronaut Office CB NASA Johnson Space Center Houston TX 77058*

TRYGSTAD, LAWRENCE BENSON, lawyer; b. Holton, Mich., Mar. 22, 1937; BA, U. Mich., 1959; JD, U. So. Calif., 1967. Bar: Calif. 1968, U.S. Supreme Ct. 1974. Legal counsel Calif. Tchrs. Assn., United Tchrs. L.A., L.A., 1968-71; ptnr. Trygstad & Odell, 1971-80; pres. Trygstad Law Corp., 1980—. Instr., tchr. negotiation U. Calif.-Northridge; panelist TV shows Law and the Teacher. Bd. dirs. George Washington Carver Found., L.A. Mem. ABA, Calif. Bar Assn., L.A. County Bar Assn., Calif. Trial Lawyers Assn., L.A. Trial Lawyers Assn., Nat. Orgn. Lawyers for Edn. Assns., Am. Trial Lawyers Assn., Phi Alpha Delta. Home: 4209 Aleman Dr Tarzana CA 91356-5405 Office: 1880 Century Park E Ste 404 Los Angeles CA 90067-1609

TRYTEK, DAVID DOUGLAS, insurance company executive; b. Cleve., Jan. 18, 1955; s. Edmund Trytek and Mary Elaine Salzwedel Blech; m. Lorie Ann Stone, Apr. 10, 1982; children: Dane, Douglas. BS in BA, Bowling Green (Ohio) State U., 1977. Claims adjuster Liberty Mus. Ins. Co., Toledo, 1977-80, claims supr. Milw., 1980-85, spl. claims examiner Boston, 1986-89, claims mgr. Green Bay, Wis., 1989-93; tech. svcs. mgr. Liberty Mut. Ins. Co., Milw., 1993-95; regional field investigations mgr. Liberty Mutual Ins. Co., 1996—, Wausau Ins. Co., Milw., 2001—. Arbitrator Inter-Co. Arbitration Com., Milw., 1984-85. Coach Toledo Optimists Youth Hockey Assn., 1979-80, Wauwatosa (Wis.) Recreation Dept., 1980-85, YMCA Youth Baseball, 1994; alt. Worker's Compensation divsn. Ins. Adv. Com., Madison, Wis., 19941 youth football coach, Sussex, Wis., 1994-99, youth baseball coach, 1994-99, 2002; bd. dirs. Wis. Street Rod Assn. Mem. Exptl. Aircraft Assn., Air Force Assn., Warbirds of Am., USA Hockey Inc., Internat. Assn. of Spl. Investigation Units, Wis. Street Rod Assn. (bd. dirs. 1999—). Avocations: camping, ice hockey, golf, military aircraft. Office: Liberty Mut Ins Co 11800 W Park Pl Milwaukee WI 53224-3009

TRYTHALL, HARRY GILBERT, music educator, composer; b. Knoxville, Tenn., Oct. 28, 1930; s. Harry Gilbert and Clara Hannah (Akre) T.; m. Jean Marie Slater, Dec. 28, 1951 (div. 1976); children: Linda Marie, Karen Elizabeth; m. Carol King, Sept. 19, 1985. BA, U. Tenn., 1951; MusM, Northwestern U., 1952; DMA, Cornell U., 1960. Asst. prof. music Knox Coll., Galesburg, Ill., 1960-64; prof. music theory and composition George Peabody Coll. Tchrs., Nashville, 1964-75; dean Creative Arts Ctr., 1975-81; prof. music W.Va. U., Morgantown, 1975-96; ret., 1997; pres. Luxikon Music, Pandora-Synthe Records, Westover, W.Va., 1983—. Vis. prof. U. Federal do Espiritu Santo, Vitoria, Brazil, 1999—. Author: Principles and Practice of Electronic Music, 1974, Eighteenth Century Counterpoint, 1993, Sixteenth Century Counterpoint, 1994; past mem. editorial bd. Music Educators Jour.; composer orchestral music, chamber and electronic music. With USAF, 1953-57. E-mail: htrythal@yahoo.com.

TRZCINKA, SHEILA MARIE, education educator; b. Pittsfield, Mass. BA, Boston U., 1970; MEd, Suffolk U., 1972; MS, Purdue U., 1976; PhD, SUNY, Buffalo, 1996. Cert. supt., spl. edn. tchr., N.Y.; cert. dir. spl. edn., spl. edn. tchr., Ind.; cert. counselor, h.s. English tchr., h.s. social studies tchr., Mass. Counselor Lee (Mass.) Ctrl. Schs., 1972-74; tchr. K-12 various schs., Ind., N.Y., Mass., 1974-82; fed. programs dir. Royalton Hartland, Middleport, N.Y., 1986-87; prof. SUNY, Geneseo, 1990, Daemen Coll., Buffalo, 1991; ednl. cons. U.S. Dept. Edn., Indpls., 1993-96; asst. prof. St. Xavier U., Chgo., 1996—. Adv. bd. Langston Hughes Inst., Buffalo, 1981-83; adv. bd. Learning Disabilities Assn., Buffalo, 1982-84; guest spkr. Dalian (China) Key Sch., 1985. Author: Creative Classroom, 1977, Teacher's Attitudes & Curriculum, 1996; contbr. articles to profl. jours. Mem. ASCD, AAUW, Am. Ednl. Rsch. Assn., Nat. Assn. Multicultural Edn., Nat. Assn. Bilingual Edn., Learning Disabilities Assn., Coun. Exceptional Children, Phi Delta Kappa. Avocations: jazz, dance, wildlife preservation. Office: St Xavier U 3700 W 103rd St Chicago IL 60655-3105 Address: 109 French Creek Dr Rochester NY 14618-5274

TRZIL, LOUIS JOSEPH, priest; b. Cedar Rapids, Iowa, Apr. 10, 1926; s. Louis Joseph Trzil and Georgia Marie Nejdl. BA, Loras Coll., 1946. Ordained priest Cath. U. Am., 1950; permanent profl. tchg. cert. Iowa. Asst. pastor, 1950—60; pastor Czech speaking parishes Archdiocese of Dubuque, Iowa, 1960—91; pastor Allamakee County N.E. Iowa, 1991—. Mem. Archdiocesan Priests's Coun., Dubuque, 2002—; moderator KC, Waukon, Iowa, 1995—, Archdiocesan Coun. Cath. Women, Decorah, Iowa, 2002—. Roman Catholic. Avocations: hunting, fishing, walking. Home and Office: 1416 Great River Rd Lansing IA 52151-7519

TRZYNA, CHRISTINE ANN, physical education educator; b. Chgo. d. Edward J. and Helen J. Trzyna. BS, No. Ill. U., 1976, MS, 1983, C.A.S. in Adminstrn. and Supervision, 1991. Cert. tchr. Ill. Tchr., asst. athletic dir. Libertyville (Ill.) HS, 1976—, girls volleyball coach, 1987—. Mem.: AAHPERD, Ill. Athletic Dirs. Assn., Ill. High Sch. Assn. (soccer adv. com.), Ill. Assn. Health, Phys. Edn. Recreation and Dance, Delta Psi Kappa (v.p. 1975—76). Office: Libertyville High School 708 W Park Ave Libertyville IL 60048-2604 Business E-Mail: trzyna.c@mail.district128.org.

TRZYNADLOWSKI, ANDRZEJ MARIA, electrical engineering educator; b. Lvov, Poland, June 14, 1941; came to U.S., 1983; s. Jan and Izabela Trzynadlowski; m. Elzbieta Bramowicz, May 27, 1967 (div. Mar. 1979); 1 child, Andrzej; m. Dorota Malgorzata Maszewska, July 17, 1979; children: Bart, Nicole. MSEE, Tech. U. Wroclaw, Poland, 1964, MS in Electronics, 1969, PhDEE, 1974. Tchg. asst., lectr. Tech. U. Wroclaw, 1966-79; vis. assoc. prof. U. Salahuddin, Arbil, Iraq, 1980-82; vis. asst. prof. U. Tex., Arlington, 1983-84; asst. prof. U. Wyo., Laramie, 1984-87; assoc. prof., then prof. U. Nev., Reno, 1987—. Danfoss vis. prof. Aalborg (Denmark) U., 1997; rsch. fellow Naval Surface Warfare Ctr., Annapolis, Md., 1998. Author: The Field Orientation Principle in Control of Induction Motors, 1994, Introduction to Modern Power Electronics, 1998, Control of Induction Motors, 2000; also articles; patentee in field. Cell vice chmn. Solidarity trade union, Wroclaw, 1980-81. Fellow IEEE (assoc. editor IEEE Transactions on Indsl. Electronics, IEEE Transactions on Power Electronics 1997—); mem. Industry Applications Soc. of IEEE (mem. indsl. drives com., indsl. power converters com. 1987—, Myron Zucker student-faculty grantee 1992), Eta Kappa Nu. Democrat. Roman Catholic. Avocations: travel, reading, walking. Home: 4075 Twin Falls Dr Reno NV 89511-6067 Office: Univ Nev Elec Engring 260 Reno NV 89507 Address: PO Box 9547 Reno NV 89507 E-mail: chin@ee.unr.edu.

TSAI, CHIH-LING, management educator; b. Taipei, Republic of China, Jan. 7, 1952; came to U.S., 1976; s. Liang-Chih and Chen-Ling (Lu) T.; m. Ching-Ju Liao, July 23, 1970; children: Wen-Lin, Wen-Ting. BS, Tamkang Univ., Taipei, 1974; MS, Univ. Ill., 1978; PhD, Univ. Minn., 1983. Asst. prof. bus. NYU, N.Y.C., 1983-85; lectr. Univ. Tex., Austin, 1985-86; from assoc. prof. to prof. mgmt. Univ. Calif., Davis, 1988-93, prof. mgmt., 1993—. Contbr. articles to profl. jours. Office: Grad Sch Mgmt Univ Calif Davis Davis CA 95616-8609

TSAI, CYNTHIA EKBERG, entertainment executive; b. Coronado, Calif., Jan. 22, 1956; d. Gerald Von Ekberg and Kathleen (Horrell) Culver; m. Gerald Tsai, Oct. 31, 1987 (div. 1995). Student, U. Miami, 1974-75; BA in Psychology, U. Mo., 1978. V.p. Merrill Lynch, San Diego, 1979-82, Kidder Peabody, San Diego, 1982-85; pres. Nugene Tech., N.Y., 1996-97, Health-Expo, N.Y., 1995—. Dir. Nugene Tech., 1993—; gen. ptnr. MassTech Ventures, 1993—. Chmn. Am. Friends London Symphony Orch., Amer. London Symphony Orch. Found. Fellow Fgn. Policy Assn.; mem. World Econ. Forum, 1992-98, N.Y. Econ. Club, Women in Sports and Events. Democrat. Roman Catholic. Avocations: walking, travel. Home: 800 5th Ave New York NY 10021-7216 Office: HealthExpo 18 E 41st St New York NY 10017-6222

TSAI, FU-JYA DANIEL, polymer scientist and engineer; b. Taipei, Taiwan, Aug. 3, 1960; came to U.S., 1985; s. S.T. and Y.Y. (Chen) T.; m. Nina Chung, July 19, 1987; children: Angela, Timothy. BS, Nat. Cheng-Kung U., Tainan, Taiwan, 1982; MS, Northwestern U., 1987, PhD, 1990. Chem. engr. Formosa Plastics, Inc., Taipei, 1984-85; sr. rsch. engr. Air Products & Chems., Inc., Allentown, Pa., 1990-92, prin. rsch. engr., 1992-94; assoc. rsch. fellow Kimberly-Clark Co., Neenah, Wis., 1994—. Contbg. author: Progress in Clinical and Biological Research, 1989; contbr. articles to sci. jours. Avocations: tennis, golf, fishing. Home: 2517 E Gatewood Dr Appleton WI 54915-6649 Office: Kimberly-Clark Co 2100 Winchester Rd Neenah WI 54956-9317 E-mail: dtsai@kcc.com.

TSAI, JAMES H. entomologist, educator; b. Fuzhou, China, June 10, 1934; m. Sue-Cheng Huang, Aug. 1, 1959; children: Cynthia, Julie. BS, Nat. Chung Hsing U., Taiwan, 1957; MS, Mich. State U., 1964, PhD, 1969. Scientist Internat. Inst. Tropical Agriculture, Ibadan, Nigeria, 1969-70, Mich. Dept. Agr., East Lansing, 1970-71; rsch. assoc. Mich. State U., 1971-73; asst. prof. U. Fla., Ft. Lauderdale, 1973-78, assoc. prof., 1978-84, prof., 1984—. Chmn. agrl. com. South Fla. Cmty. Urban Resources Partnership, Ft. Lauderdale, 1998—; bd. dirs. Broward County Farm Bur., 1997—. Mem.: N.Y. Entomol. Soc., Fla. Entomol. Soc., Am. Phytopathol. Soc., Entomol. Soc. Am. Office: U Fla 3205 College Ave Fort Lauderdale FL 33314 E-mail: jhtsai@ulf.edu.

TSAI, JINGPHA (JEFFREY TSAI), computer scientist, educator; b. Cha-I, Taiwan; m. Fuh-Te Tsai; children: Edward, Christina. MS, Northwestern U., 1983, PhD, 1985. Prof. U. Ill., 1997—. Author 5 books; co-editor-in-chief: Artificial Intelligence Tools, 1994; contbr. more than 130 articles to profl. jours. Recipient Univ. scholar award U. Ill., Tech. Achievement award IEEE Computer Soc. Fellow IEEE, AAAS, Soc. for Design and Process Sci. Office: MCI 154 EECS Dept 851 S Morgan St Chicago IL 60607-7042

TSAI, TOM CHUNGHU, chemical engineer; b. Kaohsiung, Taiwan, Oct. 24, 1948; came to U.S., 1971, naturalized, 1984; s. Shu and Kwei (Kao) T.; m. Joyce Chionhwa Pai, Dec. 17, 1974; children: Wayne, Jimmy Payne. BS in Chem. Engring., Nat. Taiwan U., Taipei, 1970; MS in Chem. Engring., Purdue U., 1973, PhD in Chem. Engring., 1975. Registered profl. engr., Tex. Sr. process engr. CE-Lummus Co., Bloomfield, N.J., 1975-80; sr. engr. Bechtel Petroleum Inc., Houston, 1980-83; cons. engr. TDS Assocs., 1983-88; process engrng. assoc. Dow Chem. Co., Freeport, Tex., 1988—. Mem. internat. adv. bd. Ency. Chem. Processing and Design, 1995—. Co-author, contbr.: Ethylene-Keystone to the Petrochemical Industry, 1980, Kirk-Othmer Encyclopedia of Chemical Technology, 1980, Pyrolysis: Theory and Industrial Practice, 1983, Refining & Petrochemical Tech. Yearbook, 1987, Encyclopedia of Chemical Processing and Design, 1990, 94, 95, Unit Operations Handbook, 1992; contbr. articles to profl. jours. Bd. dirs. H.S. for Performing and Visual Arts PTO, Houston, 1993-95. 2d lt. Republic of China Army, 1970-71. Mem. Am. Inst. Chem. Engrs., Assn. Am. Chinese Profls. (divsn. chmn. 1988-89, v.p. 2000-01, pres.-elect 2001). Achievements include patents for liquid removal from natural gas and process for recovery of anhydrous hydrogen chloride from mixtures with non-condensable gases; research in flare system design by microcomputer, yield correlations for AGO cracking, sizing a vertical separator by microcomputer, surface reactions in pyrolysis units, technical improvement in heater design for olefins production, hydrodechlorionation of chlorinated hydrocarbons, liquid removal of fuel gas, inspired polycarbonate polymers and monomers, gasoline additives and amines specialty chemicals by reductive amination, propylene oxide/styrene process development, manufacturing of natural plastics, converted epoxy resin and liquid epoxy resin and bis-phenol A projects, ethylene oxide and ethylene glycol process hazard analysis, propylene oxide derivatives projects. Home: 1503 Ashford Hollow Ln Houston TX 77077-3903 Office: The Dow Chem Co 400 W Sam Houston Pkwy S Houston TX 77042-1299 E-mail: tomctsai@dow.com.

TSAI, TSU-MIN, surgeon; b. Taipei, Taiwan, Dec. 15, 1936; arrived in U.S., 1976; m. Fu-Mei Tsai; children: Yi-Yi, Ring-Ring Tsai Tien, Berlin. MD, Taiwan U., 1961. Diplomate with added qualifications in surgery of the hand Am. Bd. Orthopedic Surgeons. Intern Nat. Taiwan U. Hosp., China, 1961-62, resident in urology, surgery and orthopedics China, 1964-70; intern U. Louisville, 1976-77, resident in orthopedics, 1977-79; Christine Kleinert fellow in hand surgery U. Louisville Affiliated Hosps., 1976; clin. prof. orthopaedic surg., dir. divsn. hand surgery Louisville Sch. Medicine, 1980—. Presenter in field, including Am. Soc. Reconstructive Microsurgery, Boca Raton, Fla., 1997, Bombay Hand Soc., 1997, Am. Soc. Orthop. Surgeons, San Francisco, 1997, Hong Kong Soc. Surgery of the Hand, 1997, Madras Hand Inst., India, 1997, Japanese Soc. Surgery of the Hand, Osaka, 1998, Japanese Orthop. Assn., Yokohama, 1998, Am. Assn. Orthop. Surgeons, New Orleans, 1998, Flap course, Focus on Anatomy course, Christine M. Kleinert Inst., Louisville, 1998, Chang Gung Hosp., Taipei, Taiwan, 2000, 01, Nat. Taiwain U., Taipei, 2000, Japanese Soc. for Surgery of Hand/Am. Soc. for Surgeryof Hand Joint Meeting, Maui, Hawaii, 2000, Innominate Soc., Louisville, 2001, Hand Forum, Paris, 2001, Internat. Fedn. of Socs. for Surgery of Hand, Istanbul, Turkey, 2001, Post Congress Mini-Invasive Conf., Rome, 2001; disting. vis. prof. Divsn. Plastic and Reconstructive Surgery Washington Hosp. Ctr., 1990; vis. prof. Duke U., Durham, NC, 2001; chmn. Dept. Surgery Ho-Ping Hosp., Taipei, 1970—75. Contbr. articles to profl. jours. and publs.; editor: (issue) Hand Clinics, 2001. With Nat. Taiwan Armed Svcs., 1963. Fellow: ACS, Am. Acad. Orthopedic Surgeons; mem.: AMA, SICOT Soc., Japanese Orthopaedic Assn., Clin. Orthopedic Soc., Hand Forum, Am. Soc. Surgery of Hand, We. Pacific Orthopedic Assn., Am. Soc. Reconstructive Microsurgery, Internat. Soc. Reconstructive Microsurgery, Ky. Pediat. Soc., Ky. Orthopaedic Soc., Ky. Med. Soc., Jefferson County Orthopaedic Soc., Jefferson County Med. Soc. Avocations: fishing, golf. Office: Kleinert Kutz & Assocs 225 Abraham Flexner Way Louisville KY 40202-1846

TSAI, WEN-YING, sculptor, painter, engineer; b. Xiamen, Fujian, China, Oct. 13, 1928; came to U.S., 1950, naturalized, 1962; s. Chen-Dak and Ching-Miau (Chen) T.; m. Pei-De Chang, Aug. 7, 1968; children: Lun-Yi and Ming Yi (twins). Student, Ta Tung U., 1947-49; BSME, U. Mich., 1953; postgrad., Art Students League N.Y., 1953-57, Faculty Polit. and Social Sci., New Sch., 1956-58. Cons. engr., 1953-63; project mgr. Cosentini Assocs., 1962-63; project engr. Guy B. Panero, Engrs., 1956-60. Creator cybernetic sculpture based on prin. harmonic motion, stroboscopic effects; one-man shows include, Ruth Sherman Gallery, N.Y.C., 1961, Amel Gallery, N.Y.C., 1964, 65, Howard Wise Gallery, N.Y.C., 1968, Kaiser Wilhelm Mus. Haus Lange, Krefeld, Germany, 1970, Hayden Gallery of MIT, Cambridge, Ont. Sci. Centre, Toronto, Can., 1971, Corcoran Gallery Art, 1972, Denise René Gallery, 1972, 73, Musée d'Art Contemporain, Montreal, 1973, Museo de Arte Contemporáneo, Caracas, 1975, Wildenstein Art Center, Houston, 1978, Museo de Bellas Artes, Caracas, 1978, Hong Kong Mus. Art, 1979, Isetan Mus. Art, Tokyo, 1980, Galerie Denise René, Paris, 1983, Nat. Mus. History, Taipei, Taiwan, 1989, Taiwan Mus. of Art, Taichung, 1990, China Nat. Mus. Fine Arts, Beijing, 1997; one man show: Galerie Denise René, Paris, 2000, Shanghai Art Mus., 2002; represented maj. internat. exhbns., also numerous group exhbns., in permanent collections, Centre Georges Pompidou, Paris; Tate Gallery, London, Albright-Knox Gallery, Buffalo Mus., Addison Gallery Am. Art, Andover, Mass., Museo de Arte Contemporáneo, Caracas, Museo de Bellas Artes, Caracas, Whitney Mus., Chrysler Art Mus., Orlando Sci. Ctr., MIT, Hayden Gallery, Kaiser Wilhelm Mus., Mus. Modern Art, Israel Mus., Jerusalem, Artware, Kunst und Elektronik, Honnover-Messe, Great Exploration-The Hands on Mus., Taiwan Mus. Art, Saibu Gas Mus., Nagoya City Mus., Mus. fü Holographie, Kanagawa Sci. Pk., Hong Kong Sci. Mus., others; commd. works include: fountain at Land Mark, Hong Kong, 1980, , water sculpture at Shell Tower, Singapore, 1982, cybernetic upward falling fountains (2), Paris; creator spatial dynamic hydro-cybernetic systems for 42d Internat. Exhbn. Art-La Biennale di Venezia, 1986, Digital Visions-Computers and Art, Everson Mus. of Art, 1987, Contemporary Arts Ctr. Cin., 1987, IBM Gallery of Sci. and Art, N.Y.C., 1988, Phenomena Art Expo, Fukuoka, Japan, 1989, Wonderland of Sci.-Art Kanagawa Internat. Art Sci. Exhbn., Kawasaki, Japan, 1989, Vienna Messe-Wiener Festwochen, 1989, Kanagawa Internat. Art & Sci. Exhbn., Kawasaki, Japan, 1989, Artec 91, Internat. Biennale in Nagoya, Japan, 1991 (Artec Grand Prix winner), Homage à Denise Reñe-Cybernetic Arts, Musée Nat. d'art Modern Ctr. Georges Pompidon, 2001, Developed concept "5 elements," proposal for new modern sculpture park for Oriental Plz., Beijing, 1996-98; creator first CD-ROM version of cybernetic sculpture, 1995, Info-Art Kwang Ju Internat. Biennale Korea, Osaka Triennale, 1995—, Internet Graphics Gallery, 1995; featured: Art for Tomorrow-The 21st Century, CBS-TV, 1969, Video Variation, WGBH-TV, 1971, Science and Art, Japan TV Man Union, 1982, Art and Sci.-Innovation, Sta. WNET-TV, 1988, The World of Wen-Ying Tsai, Taiwan Pub. TV, 1991. Recipient Soc. Merit award U. Mich., 2001; John Hay Whitney fellow, 1963, MacDowell fellow, 1965, fellow Center Advanced Visual Studies, MIT, 1969, 70. Inventor upward falling fountain, computer mural, multiple light computer array, utilizing environ. feedback control system.

TSALIKHIN, ALEXANDER, sculptor, artist; BFA in Sculpture, Art Coll. Russia, 1980. Recipient Dolls of Distinction award, 1997, 98, Artist Showchase award, 1997, Isaac N.Maynard award, 1998. Exhbns. include Ind. Artists Studios Show, Leningrad, Russia, 1987, Modern Art Leningrad, 1988, Chgo. Art Show, 1995, Ja Internat. Jewelry Show, N.Y.C., 1995, Nat. Sculpture Soc., 1996, Am. Internat. Toy Fair, N.Y.C., 1997, 99, Nat. Acad. Mus. Sch. Fine Arts, N.Y.C., 1998, Pfizer Gallery, Croton, Conn., 1998, Agora

Gallery, N.Y.C., 1998, Art Expo 2001, N.Y.C.. Recipient Artist Showcase award Manhattan Arts Intl., 1999. Home: 137 Bergen Ave Apt D1 Ridgefield Park NJ 07660-1590 E-mail: atsalikhin@yahoo.com.

TSANG, TUNG, physics educator, researcher; b. Shanghai, China, Aug. 17, 1932; s. Ngeu F Tsang and Ying W Liu; m. Dolly M Wong, Oct. 12, 1957; children: Susan M Persons. BS, Ta-Tung U., Shanghai, China, 1949; MS, U. Minn., Minneapolis, MN, 1952; PhD, U. Chgo., Chicago, IL, 1960. Phys. chemist Honeywell Inc, Minneapolis, Minn., 1952—56, Argonne Nat. Lab., Argonne, Ill., 1960—67, Nat. Bur. Standards, Washington, 1967—69; physics prof. Howard U., 1969—. Author: (book) Classical Electrodynamics, Statistical Mechanics. Home: 4403 Faroe Place Rockville MD 20853 Office: Howard University Physics Department 6th St NW Washington DC 20059 Office Fax: 202-806-5830.

TSAO, CHANG YONG, pediatric neurologist; b. Taipei, Taiwan, Apr. 10, 1952; came to U.S., 1980; s. Ah Dai and Yu Lan T.; m. Sue Lee, June 12, 1979; 1 child, Clement Lee. MD, Taipei Med. Coll., Taiwan, 1976. Pediatric neurologist Creighton U., Omaha, 1986-90; pediatric neurologist, assoc. prof. Ohio State U., Columbus, 1990—. Cons. in field. Author: Current Neurology, 1997, Textbook of Motor Disorders, 1999. Fellow Am. Acad. Pediatrics; mem. Am. Acad. Neurology, Am. Epilepsy, Am. Med. EEG Soc., Child Neurology Soc. Avocations: music, jogging, fishing. Office: Childrens Hosp 700 Childrens Dr Columbus OH 43205-2696

TSAU, WILLIAM WEN-SHIUNG, civil engineer, consultant; b. Formosa, Taiwan, July 22, 1946; arrived in U.S., 1973, naturalized, 1982; s. Chun Fu and Yu In (Young) Tsau. B. Engring., Northeastern U., Boston, 1978; MSCE, U. Wyo., 1981. Registered profl. civil and structural engr., Ill., N.Mex. Civil engr. Taiwan Power Co., Taipei, Taiwan, 1970—73; grad., tchg. asst. U. Wyo., 1979—81; project/design/resident engr. Johnson-Fermelia & Crank, Inc., also J.F.C. Enterprises, J.F.C. Internat., Inc., Kemmerer and Rock Springs, Wyo., 1981—85; gen. engr. C.E. U.S. Army, 1985—87, civil/structural engr., 1987—. Cons. served to 2nd lt. ROTC Taiwanese Army Engr. Sch., 1969—70. 2nd lt. Taiwanese Army Res., 1970—73. Named to Nat. Profl. Engring. Hall of Fame. Fellow: ASCE; mem.: SAME, IABSE, ACI, Tau Beta Pi, Sigma Xi (life). Achievements include research in on optimization of stiffened and unstiffened hybrid girders, large scale structural system of conventional sheet pile cofferdam with computer applications; bridge design inspection rating evaluation maintenance repair and rehabilitation, computer aided design and drafting in civil and structural engineering. Home: 3368 E Kimberly Rd Davenport IA 52807 Office: US Army Corps Engrs PO Box 4256 Davenport IA 52808-4256 Address: 1515 9th St Rock Springs WY 82901-6057

TSCHALAER, CHRISTOPH, physicist, researcher; b. Zurich, Switzerland, July 25, 1938; came to U.S., 1989; s. Adolf Arnold and Klara Alina Tschalaer; m. Joan Irene Smith, July 17, 1965; children: Ronald Paul, Elisabeth Ann. Diploma in exptl. physics, Fed. Inst. Tech., Zurich, 1962; PhD in Nuclear Physics, U. So. Calif., L.A., 1967. Sr. sci. officer Rutherford High Energy Lab., Chilton, Eng., 1966-69; target group leader Swiss Inst. Nuclear Rsch., Villigen, Switzerland, 1969-72, exptl. facilities sect. leader Switzerland, 1972-77, engring. and exptl. facilities divsn. leader Switzerland, 1978-87; enring. dept. leader Paul Scherrer Inst., 1987-89; sr. rsch. scientist MIT/Bates, Middleton, Mass., 1989-91, assoc. dir. ops., 1991—. Cons. dist. heating Town Coun. Energy Comm., Endingen, Switzerland, 1980-84; guest scientist Los Alamos (N.Mex.) Nat. Lab./LAMPF Divsn., 1977, 85, reviewer LAMPF ops., 1987, reviewer MLNSC Target upgrade, 1996, reviewer LANSCE upgrade, 1996, mem. LANCSE Divsn. Rev. Com., 1997, 99, reviewer LDRD program, 1999; cons. CEBAF constrn. Jefferson Lab., Newport News, Va., 1992; reviewer accelerator product of tritium MIT, Cambridge, 1994, reviewer accelerator driven transmutation of waste, 1998. Contbr. articles to profl. jours.; inventor proton polarisation analiser, 1970, Beam Extraction System, 1986. Hon. mem. Men's Choir, Endingen, 1978-89. Mem. Am. Phys. Soc., Sandy Bay Yacht Club. Avocations: hiking, sailing, singing. E-Mail: Chris@bates. mit.edu. Office: MIT Bates Linear Accelerat 21 Manning Ave Middleton MA 01949-1526

TSCHERNY, GEORGE, graphic designer; b. Budapest, Hungary, July 12, 1924; s. Mendel and Bella (Heimann) T.; m. Sonia Katz, July 7, 1950; children— Nadia, Carla Student, Pratt Inst., Bklyn., 1947-50. Staff designer Donald Deskey & Assocs., N.Y.C., 1950-53; designer, assoc. George Nelson & Assocs., 1953-55; pres. George Tscherny, Inc., 1955—. Instr. Pratt Inst., Bklyn., 1956, bd. advisors, 1979; instr. Sch. Visual Arts, N.Y.C., 1955-64; curriculum cons. Phila. Coll. Art, 1967; Mellon vis. prof. Cooper Union, N.Y., 1978 Retrospective exhbn. Visual Art Mus., N.Y.C., 1992; exhibited in group shows, Germany, 1962-67, Italy, 1974, U.S., 1975; represented in permanent collections Mus. Modern Art, N.Y.C., Cooper Hewitt Mus., N.Y.C., Libr. of Congress, Washington, Bibliotheque nationale de France, Paris, Kunstgewerbeschule der Stadt Zurich. Contbr. design svcs. to UN Assn., Sta. WNET Pub. TV, Am. Lung Assn., Peace Corps, Cystic Fibrosis Found., L.I. State Park Commn. With U.S. Army, 1943-46, ETO. Recipient numerous awards, Am. Inst. Graphic Arts medal, 1988, Art Dirs. Club N.Y. (hall of fame 1997), N.Y. Type Dirs. Club, Silver medal Warsaw Biennale, 1976; inducted into Art Dirs. Club Hall of Fame, 1997. Mem. Am. Inst. Graphic Arts (pres. 1966-68), Alliance Graphique Internationale. Office: 238 E 72nd St New York NY 10021-4503

TSCHINKEL, ANDREW JOSEPH, JR. law librarian; b. Catskill, N.Y., Aug. 8, 1952; s. Andrew Joseph and Marie Frances (O'Connor) T.; m. Frances K. Quigley, Nov. 4, 1989. BA summa cum laude, St. John's Coll., Jamaica, N.Y., 1975, MLS, 1977; MBA, Fordham U., 1983. Grad. asst. div. libr. sci. St. John's U., Jamaica, 1975-77, asst. law libr., 1977-79, adj. law librarian, 1983-87; head librarian Christ the King High Sch., Middle Village, N.Y., 1979-80; sr. law librarian Bklyn. Supreme Ct., 1980-81; prin. law librarian N.Y. Supreme Ct., Jamaica, 1981—. Recipient Pub. Svc. award Queens Borough Pres. and N.Y. Tel. Co., 1986; named Alumnus of Yr. Grad. Sch. Arts & Scis. Divsn. Libr. & Info. Sci. St. John's U., 1993. Mem. Am. Assn. Law Libr.s., Law Libr. Assn. Greater N.Y., Elks, Beta Phi Mu. Republican. Office: NY Supreme Ct Libr 88-11 Sutphin Blvd Jamaica NY 11435-3716

TSCHUMY, FREDA COFFING, artist, educator; b. Danville, Ill., Mar. 18, 1939; d. Frederick Winfield and Minnie Isabelle (Buck) Coffing; m. William Edward Tschumy, Jr., June 17, 1967; 1 child, William Coffing. BA, Vassar Coll., 1961; postgrad., Art Students' League N.Y., 1961-63, Accademia di Belli Arti, Rome, 1963; MFA, U. Miami, 1990. Instr. art Miami (Fla.) Fine Arts Conservatory, 1968; instr. ceramics Grove House, Coconut Grove, Fla., summer 1970; instr. sculpture Upstairs Gallery, Miami Beach, 1971, Continuum Gallery, Miami Beach, 1972-73; instr. painting Barry Coll., Miami, fall 1974; instr. sculpture Met. Mus. Sch., Coral Gables, Fla., 1980-89, Bass Mus. Sch., Miami Beach, 1989-92; teaching asst. U. Miami, Coral Gables, 1988-90, lectr. sculpture, pres., 1991—, dir. foundry, 1992—. Pres. founding mem. Continuum Gallery, Miami Beach, 1971-75, treas. 1975-83; treas. The Gallery at Mayfair, Coconut Grove, 1982-83, pres., 1983-84; artist in residence Hawaii Sch. for Girls, Honolulu, 1987; founding dir. Foundry Guild, U. Miami, Coral Gables, 1993—. Prin. works include sculptures at Dade Metrorail Univ. Sta., Melbourne (Fla.) Libr.; traveling exhbn. various colls., Miami. Mem. Tropical Audubon Soc., Miami, 1975—, Fla. Conservation Found., 1978—, Fla. Pub. Interest Rsch. Group, 1986—, Fla. Abortion Rights Action League, 1985—. Recipient Excellence award, Sculptors Fla. 1972, Fine Art Achievement award Binney & Smith, 1990, award of Excellence, Art in the Downtown Downtown Devel. Authority, Ft. Lauderdale, Fla.; grantee Posey Found., 1989. Mem. Am. Foundryman's Soc., Womens Caucus Art (1st v.p. local chpt. 1981-86, bd. dirs. 1980-91, nat. bd. dirs. 1982-85), Internat. Sculpture Ctr. Avocations: travel, reading, swimming, cycling. Studio: 3610 Bayview Rd Miami FL 33133-6503

TSE, CHARLES YUNG CHANG, drug company executive; b. Shanghai, China, Mar. 22, 1926; s. Kung Chao and Say Ying (Chen) T.; m. Vivian Chang, Apr. 25, 1955; 1 dau., Roberta. BA in Econs, St. John's U., Shanghai, 1949; MS in Acctg. U. Ill., 1950; JD, N.Y. Law Sch., 1990. Asst. to controller Am. Internat. Group, N.Y.C., 1950-54, asst. mgr. Singapore-Malaysia, 1955-57; with Warner-Lambert Co., Morris Plains, N.J., 1957-86, area mgr. S.E. Asia, 1966-68, regional dir. S.E. Asia, 1968-69, v.p. Australasia, 1970-71, pres. Western Hemisphere Group, 1971-72, pres. Pan Am. Mgmt. Center, 1972-76, pres. European Mgmt. Center, 1976-78, pres. Internat. Group, 1979-86, sr. v.p. corp., 1980-83, exec. v.p. corp., 1984-85, vice chmn., 1985-86. Dir. Foster Wheeler Corp., Livingston, N.J., 1984-98, Superior Telecom., Inc., 1996—, Com. of 100; mem. faculty bus. adminstrn. dept. Fairleigh Dickinson U., 1961-64; pres. Cancer Rsch. Inst., Inc., N.Y.C., 1991-92. Bd. visitors CCNY, 1974-78; trustee Morristown Meml. Hosp. (N.J.), 1982-86; bd. dirs. Bus. Council for Internat. Understanding, 1984-87. Mem. NAM (dir. 1984-86), Assn. of the Bar of the City of N.Y. (mem. Asian affairs com. 1991—). Office: 300 Park Ave Fl 17 New York NY 10022-7402

TSE, EDMUND SZE-WING, insurance company executive; b. Hong Kong, Jan. 2, 1938; s. Kai-Sum and Chao-Sui (Tsui) T.; m. Peggy Pik-Kin Wai, Dec. 18, 1965; children: Ada Koon-Hang, Elaine Koon-Ming. BA, U. Hong Kong, 1960; diploma, Life Ins. Agy. Mgmt. Assn., 1972; diploma grad. mktg. mgmt. program, Stanford U., 1980. Dep. gen. mgr. Nan Shan Life Ins. Co., Ltd., Taipei, Taiwan, 1970-74, pres., mng. dir. Taiwan, 1975-83, chmn. Taiwan, 1990; various positions Am. Internat. Assurance Co., Ltd., Hong Kong, 1961-70, chmn., CEO, 2000—, dir., 1996; sr. vice chmn., life ins. Am. Internat. Assurance Co., Ltd. , 2001—, co-chief operating officer, 2002. Bd. dirs. AIA Fin. (Hong Kong) Ltd. (formerly SPC Credit Ltd.), AIG Investment Corp. (Hong Kong) Ltd., AIG Mktg. Corp. Ltd., Am. Internat. Data Ctr. Ltd., Seacliff Ltd., Am. Life Ins. Co., Wilmington, Del., Am. Internat. Life Assurance Co. N.Y., AIG Life Ins. Co., C.V. Starr & Co., Inc., China Am. Holding Co., Del. Am. Life Ins. Co., Pacific Union Assurance Co., numerous other internat. investment, reins., and holding cos. Founding mem. Asia adv. bd. Project HOPE, U.S.A., 1995—; chmn. Asia Adv. Bd., 1997—; pres., dir. AIA Found. Ltd., 1995—; trustee The Harvard Club Found. Hong Kong, 1995—; mem. 1st exec. com. China Overseas Friendship Assn., 1997—; mem. election com. of The HKSAR legis. coun., election 2000; bd. dirs. Project Hope, Hong Kong Found. Ltd., AIA Found. Mem.: China Overseas Friendship Assn. (first exec. com.), Chinese U. Hong Kong (mem. appointments bd.), Pacific Basin Econ. Coun. (Hong Kong com.), Chief Execs. Orgn. (U.S.), Hong Kong Fedn. Insurers, Bus. and Profls. Fedn. Hong Kong (fin. specialist group 1993—, exec. com.), Pacific Ins. Conf. (nat. area chmn. 1985—), Gen. Ins. Coun. Hong Kong (chmn. legis. subcom. 1988—89, chmn. 1989—90). Home: 10C Headland Rd Repulse Bay Hong Kong Office: Am Internat Assurance Co Ltd No 1 Stubbs Rd POB 444 Hong Kong Hong Kong Fax: 852-2572-4695.

TSE, HARLEY Y. immunologist, educator; b. China, July 17, 1947; s. Ton-Cheuk and Hou-Ying (Choy) T.; m. Kwai-Fong Chui, Jan. 13, 1979; children: Kevin Y., Alan C., Leslie W. BS with honors, Calif. Inst. Tech., 1972; PhD, U. Calif., San Diego, 1977; MBA, Rutgers U., 1986. Fellow Arthritis Found., NIH, Bethesda, Md., 1977-80; sr. rsch. immunologist Merck Sharp & Dohme Rsch. Lab., Rahway, N.J., 1980-83, rsch. fellow, 1983-86; adj. asst. prof. Columbia U., 1981-84; assoc. prof. Wayne State U. Sch. Medicine, Detroit, 1986—. Mem. immunol. sci. study sect. NIH, 1995-99. Contbr. articles to profl. jours. Bd. dirs. Chinese Social Svc. Ctr., San Diego, 1975. Recipient NIH Rsch. Career Devel. award, 1992-97; Calif. Biochem. Rsch. fellow, 1975; Arthritis Found. fellow, 1977-80; NIH grantee; Nat. Multiple Sclerosis Soc. grantee, 1988—. Mem. Am. Assn. Immunologists, Chinese Student Assn. (pres. 1974-76), Soc. Chinese Bioscientists in Am., Detroit Immunol. Soc. (pres. 1989-91). Roman Catholic. Home: 5393 Tequesta Dr West Bloomfield MI 48323-2351 Office: Wayne State U Sch Medicine 540 E Canfield St Detroit MI 48201-1928 E-mail: htse@wayne.edu.

TSE, MAN-CHUN MARINA, educational association administrator; b. Kai-Ping, China, Dec. 14, 1948; came to U.S., 1972; d. Sun-Poo and Su-ling Cheung. BA in English, U. Chinese Culture, Taipei, Taiwan, 1970; MS in Spl. Edn., U. So. Calif., 1974. Cert. tchr., spl. edn. tchr., Calif. Rsch. asst. lit. U. Chinese Culture, 1970-72; English tchr. Tang-Suede Mid. Sch., Taiwan, 1970-72; instr. Willing Workers, Adult Handicapped Program L.A. Sch. Dist., 1976-77; instr. ESL Evans Adult Sch., L.A., 1977-82; instr. ESL, polit. sci. Lincoln Adult Sch., 1986-94; spl. edn. tchr. Duarte (Calif.) Unified Sch. Dist., 1977—; dep. dir. Office of English Lang. Acquisition, Lang. Enhancement and Acad. Achievement U.S. Dept. Edn. Commr., program co-chair Calif. Spl. Edn. Adv. Commn., Sacramento, 1994-96; mem. Calif. State Bd. Edn., 1996-99; mem. Calif. State Summer Sch. for the Arts, 1998-99; coun. mem. L.A. County Children Planning Coun., 1995—; com. mem. L.A. County Sci. & Engring. Fair Com., 1993—; hon. adv. bd. Asian Youth Ctr., San Gabriel City, Calif., 1992—; exec. bd. Pres. Com. on Employment of People with Disabilities (U.S.), 1997—; com. mem. tchr. devel. project Nat. Assn. State Bd. Edn., 1977—; mem. Calif. State Supts. Art Task Force, 1997-98; advisor Calif. Coun. Tech., 1996-99; mem. Calif. Rehab. Coun. Appeared on numerous TV and radio programs. Bd. trustee Bruggemeyer Libr., Monterey Park, Calif., 1993-99; pres. L.A. County Coun. Reps., 1994—; mem. Calif. Statewide Focus Group Diversity, Sacramento, 1995-97; chair Chinese Am. Edn. Assn., 1993—; co-chair, co-founder Multi-Cultural Cmty. Assn., 1992—; bd. dirs. Rosemead-Taipei Sister City, 1993—. San Gabriel Valley Charity Night Com., 1992—; chmn. Los Angeles County-Taipei County Friendship Com., 1996—. Recipient Recognition cert. Duarte Edn. Found., 1990, Calif. Legis. Assembly, 1993, cert. Valley View Sch., 1991, award State Calif., 1991, Appreciation award City Rosemead, 1992, Commendation cert. Alhambra Sch. Dist., 1992-93, Edn. award Asian Youth Ctr., 1992, 1992, Commendation cert. City L.A., 1992, commendation County L.A., 1992, award U.S. Congress, 1993, Proclamation City Alhambra, 1993, Chinese Am. PTA award, 1993, John Anson Ford award L.A. County Human Rels. Com., 1993, Appreciation cert. Chinese Consolidated Benevolent Assn., 1994, City Monterey Park, 1995, Recognition cert. Calif. State Senate, 1994, Spl. Achievement award Calif. Spl. Edn. Adv. Commn., 1997, Duarte United Edn. Ctr., 1997, Outstanding Comm. Svc. award City of Duarte, Calif., 1997, Disting. Woman of Yr. award Calif. 24th Dist. Sen.'s Office, 1997, Svc. award Calif. Fedn. Exceptional Children Coun., 1998, Calif. Sanitorial award, 1999, L.A. County Bd. Suprs. Outstanding Svc. award, 1999, Monterey Park City award, 1999. Mem. Calif. Tchr. Assn., Chinese Edn. Assn., Internat. Platform Assn., Nat. Assn. State Bds. Edn. Office: Duarte Unified Sch Dist 1620 Huntington Dr Duarte CA 91010-2534

TSE, PHILIP KUI, airport engineering maintenance consultant; b. Guangzhou, China, May 15, 1934; arrived in Can., 1994; s. Wai-Woon and Yok-Wun (Leung) T.; m. Helen Chow, Jan. 22, 1960; children: Christina Suyen, Elsie Ba-Sai, Tony Yee-Hin. BSc in Archtl. Engring., Union Coll., 1963; postgrad. cert. in strategic planning and mgmt., Calif. State U., Fresno, 1989; postgrad. cert. in project mgmt., Tongji Univ., Shanghai, 1994. Registered profl. civil engr., Hong Kong. Various positions Public Works Dept., Hong Kong Govt., 1956-71; foreman engring. draughtsman class I, asst. engr.-in-tng., asst. engr. drainage works, roads & drainage office, roads & hwys. new territories region PWD, Hong Kong, 1971-75, asst. engr. develop. and airport divsn., 1975-83, engr. devel. sect., devel. and airport divsn., 1983-88; project engr. airport maintenance, devel. and airport divsn. Engring. Devel. Dept., Civil Engring. Svcs. Dept., 1988-93; sr. airport engr. Hong Kong Internat. Airport Civil Engring. Svcs. Dept., Civil Engring. Dept., 1993-95; airport diagnostic engring., environ. mgmt. cons., 1963-68. Lectr. Hong Kong Tech. Coll. (now Hong Kong Poly. U.), 1968—; hon. constrn. and devel. cons., adv. bd. Shun Shin Chee Kit Yin Koon Charity Orgn., Hong Kong, 1968—. Fellow ASCE (life); mem. Hong Kong Instn. of Engrs., Instn. of Pub. Health Engrs. (U.K.), Chartered Instn. of Water and Environ. Mgmt. (U.K.). Toaist. Avocations: hiking, swimming, English and Chinese, calligraphy, reading and drawing. Home: 913-89 Skymark Dr North York ON Canada M2H 3S6 Fax: 416-499-8592.

TSE, ROSE LOU, physician, educator; b. Shanghai, China; came to U.S., 1949. d. Chak and Winne Lou. BA with honors, St. John U., Shanghai, 1949; MA in Chemistry, Mt. Holyoke Coll., South Hadley, Mass., 1950; PhD in Organic Chemistry with honors, Yale U., New Haven, Conn., 1953; MD magna cum laude, Med. Coll. Pa., 1960. Diplomate Am. Bd. Internal Medicine, Am. Bd. Rheumatology. Asst. attending physician Phila. Gen. Hosp., Med. Coll. Pa., Phila., 1964-68; attending physician Episcopal Hosp., 1966-67, Phila. Gen. Hosp., 1968-70; assoc. in medicine U. Pa., Phila., 1968-70, asst. prof., 1970-75, assoc. prof., 1975—86; sr. attending physician Phila. Gen. Hosp., 1970-77; dir. sect. rheumatology Ford Rd. Campus Thomas Jefferson U. Hosp., Phila., 1977—94; pvt. practice internal medicine and rheumatology Bala Cynwyd, 1977—. Tchg. asst. in Chemistry, Yale U., 1950-52; spl. lectr. in biochemistry Med. Coll. Pa., 1963-64, instr. medicine, 1964-68, chief sect. rheumatology, 1972-77; cons. to chief surgeon City of Phila., 1968-85; assoc. chief spl. ward. Phila. Gen. Hosp., 1968-72, co-chief sect. rheumatology, 1971-72; cons. dept. pathology, 1975-77. Asst. editor Chemical Abstracts, 1953-55; contbr. articles to profl. jours. Rsch. fellow Yale U., 1952-53, Ohio State U., 1953-55, U. Pa., 1955-56, Med. Coll. Pa., 1957-64; Skinner scholar, 1950-51; Mary Lyon scholar Mt. Holyoke Coll., 1951-52. Fellow Am. Coll. Physicians, Am. Inst. Chemists, Am. Coll. Angiology; mem. AMA, AAUP (Margaret Snead scholar 1952-53), Am. Chem. Soc., Am. Heart Assn. (nat. and Southea. Pa. chpts.), Am. Coll. Rheumatology (founding), Internat. League Against Rheumatism, Pan Am. League Against Rheumatic Disease, Arthroscopy Soc. (founding), Phila. County Med. Soc., Pa. Med. Soc., Phila. Rheumatism Soc.. Alpha Omega Alpha, Sigma Xi, Sigma Delta Epsilon. Avocations: swimming, tennis, enameling. Office: 333 City Ave IL-51 Bala Cynwyd PA 19004

TSE, STEPHEN, artist, educator; b. Hong Kong, Oct. 20, 1938; came to U.S., 1959, naturalized; s. Kwan-Yeung Tse and So-Kwan Chu; m. May Kam, Mar. 23, 1973; 1 child, Lisa. B.F.A., Washburn U., 1965; M.F.A., U. Idaho, 1967. Instr. in art U. Idaho, Moscow, 1965-66; chmn. art dept. Big Bend Community Coll., Moses' Lake, Wash., 1967— ; art juror drawing competition exhbn. Spokane Fall Community Coll., 1978, 1st Ann. Environ. Art Exhbn., Seattle, 1979. One-man shows U. Idaho Mus. Art, 1966, U. Oreg. Mus. Art, 1977, Kirsten Gallery, 1977, 78, 80, 82, 85, Wenatchee Valley Coll., 1978, Spokane Falls Community Coll., 1978, Wash. State U., 1983, Prichard Art Gallery U. Idaho, 1986; also group shows; represented in permanent collections U. Oreg. Mus. Art, U. Idaho, Moscow, Seattle 1st Nat. Bank, Yakima Valley Coll. Rainier Nat. Bank, Olympia, Pacific Northwest Bell, Seattle, Battelle Northwest Collection, Richland Wash. Wash. State Arts Commn. artist purchase grantee, 1976. Mem. Big Bend Community Coll. Faculty Assn., Oriental Ceramic Soc., Internat. Acad. Ceramics, Am. Fedn. Tchrs., AAUP. Home: 957 S Grand Dr Moses Lake WA 98837-2232

TSEBELIS, GEORGE, educator; b. Athens; s. Panayotis T. and Persefone Karnalaki; children: Alexander, Emily. MA, Nat. Tech. U., Athens, 1969; D of Engring., U. Paris VI, 1974; PhD, Washington U., St. Louis, 1985. Asst. prof. Duke U., Durham, N.C., 1986-87, UCLA, 1987-89, assoc. prof., 1989-91, prof., 1991—. Vis. asst. prof. Stanford U., Palo Alto, Calif., 1985-86. Author: Nested Games, 1990; co-author: Bicamenalism, 1997, Veto Players, 2002. Hoover Inst. fellow, Palo Alto, 1991-92, Guggenheim fellow, 1995-96; Russell Sage fellow, 2001. Mem. Am. Polit. Sci. Assn. Avocations: tennis, swimming. Home: 14747 Oracle Pl Pacific Palisades CA 90272-2643 Office: UCLA 405 Hilgard Ave Los Angeles CA 90095-9000 E-mail: tsebelis@ucla.edu.

TSENG, AMPERE AN-PEI, mechanical engineer, educator, administrator; b. Kiangsi, China, Jan. 21, 1946; came to U.S., 1971, naturalized, 1982; s. Chi-Kung and Ai-Chung; m. Maggie Shih-Ying Yang, Aug. 9, 1975; children: Claire, Karen, Miles. MS, U. Ill, 1974; PhD, Ga. Inst. Tech., 1978. Mech. engr. Taitan (Taiwan) Industries Pty. Ltd., 1968-71; devel. engr. Westinghouse Electric Corp., Tampa, Fla., 1977-79; staff engr. Martin Marietta Labs., Balt., 1979-84; tech. staff, project leader RCA Labs., Princeton, N.J., 1984-85; assoc. prof. Drexel U., Phila., 1985-91, prof., 1991-96; dir. Ctr. for Automation Mfg., 1990-94; prof., dir. Mfg. Inst., Ariz. State U., Tempe, 1996—. Mem. editl. bd. Adv. Mfg. Processes, 1986-88, Jour. Engring. Materials and Tech., 1987-93, Mfg. Rev., 1991-93, Jour. Materials Processing and Mfg. Sci., 1992—, Advances in Polymer Tech., 1995—, Jour. Chinese Mech. Engring., 1997—. Recipient Cert. of Appreciation, Aluminium Assn., 1984, award for superior performance Martin Marietta Labs., 1979-84; grantee NSF, Nat. Inst. Stds. and Tech., Dept. Energy, Dept. Def., 1979-84; Alcoa Found. award, 1987. Fellow ASME (chair materials divsn.). Home: 4946 E Cheery Lynn Rd Phoenix AZ 85018-6550 Office: Ariz State U Mech Engring PO Box 876106 Tempe AZ 85287-6106

TSENG, CHIA-JENG, computer engineer; b. Hsinchu, Taiwan, Republic of China, Mar. 3, 1949; came to the U.S., 1978; s. Kuo-Bang and Shiow-Taur (Liu) T.; m. Suh-Mei Lu, May 11, 1978; children: Daniel Hsueh-Pu, Albert Hsueh-Li. BS, Nat. Cheng Kung U., 1971; PhD, Carnegie Mellon U., 1984. Rsch. engr. Telecommunication Labs., Chung-Li, Taiwan, 1975-77; instr. Nat. Tsing-Hua U., Hsinchu, 1977-78; mem. tech. staff AT&T Bell Labs., Murray Hill, N.J., 1984-94, Whippany, 1994—. Contbr. articles to IEEE Transactions on Computer-Aided Design and various conf. proceedings. Mem. IEEE (sr.), Sigma Xi. Achievements include research in formal methods for high-level synthesis of digital systems including design capture and optimization techniques for data-path synthesis, control-path synthesis and pipeline synthesis; in technology mapping for field programmable gate arrays; in wireless and mobile communications. Office: AT&T Bell Labs 67 Whippany Rd Whippany NJ 07981-1406

TSENG, CHUNG-LI, engineering educator; s. Min-Lang and Chu-Hsi Tseng; m. Joanne Tsai; 1 child Jonathan. PhD, U.Calif. Berkeley, 1996. Risk mgmt. analyst Edison Enterprises, L.A., Calif., 1997—98; asst. prof. U. Md., College Park, 1998—. Contbr. articles to various internat, profl. journals. Mem.: Inst. For Ops. Rsch. and Mgmt. Scis. Avocation: jogging. Office: Univ Maryland Dept Civil Engring College Park MD 20742 Office Fax: 301-405-2585. E-mail: chungli@eng.umd.edu.

TSENG, ELAINE EVELINA, surgeon; b. Statesboro, Ga., Mar. 31, 1969; d. Howard Shih-Chang and Evelina Mei-chih (Yang) T. BS, MIT, 1989; MD, Harvard U., 1993. Rsch. asst. Dana Farber Cancer Inst., Boston, 1986; cancer rschr. Cancer Rsch. Ctr. MIT, Cambridge, 1987, biomed. rschr. Whitehead Inst., 1988-89; biomed. rschr. Harvard-Ctr. for Blood Rsch., Boston, 1990-91; intern Johns Hopkins Hosp., Balt., 1993-94, resident in gen. surgery, 1994-95, 97-98, rsch. fellow in cardiac surgery, 1995-97, chief gen. surgery, 1998-99, cardiac surgery fellow, 1999—2001, chief cardiac surgery fellow, 2001—02; cardiac surgery fellow Royal Brompton and Harefield Hosp, Harefield, Eng., 2000, thoracic surgery fellow Eng., 2001; asst. prof. cardiac surgery U. Calif.-San Francisco, 2002—. House staff councillor Johns Hopkins Hosp., Balt., 1993-95; 2d yr. med. student advisor Harvard Med. Sch., Boston, 1990-91, HST dinner forum com., 1989-90; gifted student advisor for study of mathematically precocious youth Johns Hopkins U., 1989—. Contbr. articles to profl. jours.; presenter in field. Program dir. MIT Forum, Cambridge, 1986, program coord. women and faculty panel discussion, 1986. Virginia A. Linnane scholar Harvard U. Med. Sch., 1990-93, Nina Braunwald scholar Thoracic Surgery Found. for Rsch. and Edn., 1995-97; grantee NIH, 1990, 95-97; recipient rsch. award cardiac surgery dept. Johns Hopkins Med. Inst., 1997, gen. surgery rsch. award Johns Hopkins Med., Inst., 1998, Resident Rsch. award Southeastern Thoracic Surgery Assn., 1998. Mem. AMA, ACS, Assn. Women in Thoracic Surgery, Mass. Med. Soc., Cardiac/Thoracic Surgery Soc., Harvard-Radcliffe Club, Phi Beta Kappa, Alpha Omega Alpha. Avocations: music, travel, reading, arts, golf. Home: 316 Bethel Dr Salisbury NC 28144-2808 Office: Univ of California-San Francisco San Francisco CA 94143 E-mail: elainetseng@hotmail.com.

TSENG, GEORGE SHIHCHI, anesthesiologist; b. Kaeshung, Taiwan, June 20, 1967; s. Tony and Helen T. BA, Boston U., MD, 1992. Diplomate Am. Bd. Anesthesiology. Resident U. Hosp., Utah Sch. Medicine, Salt Lake City, 1994-97; critical care specialist, anesthesiologist St. Francis Med. Ctr., Honolulu, 1999-2000; chief profl. svcs. 154th MDS, Hickam AFB, Hawaii, 2000—. Maj. Hawaii Air N.G. Pediatric anesthesiology fellow St. Louis Children's Hosp., 1997-98, critical care fellow The Cleve. Clinic Found., 1998-99. Mem. AMA, Am. Soc. Anesthesiology, Soc. Critical Care Medicine, Soc. Pediatric Anesthesia/ Republican. Avocations: martial arts, violin, physical fitness, photography. Home: 55 S Judd St #1710 Honolulu HI 96817 Office: St Francis Med Ctr/CCU 2230 Liliha St Honolulu HI 96817 E-mail: gtseng67@aol.com.

TSENG, HOWARD SHIH CHANG, business and economics educator, investment company executive; b. Tainan, Taiwan, Jan. 14, 1935; came to U.S., 1963; s. Picheng and Chaoliu (Wang) T.; m. Evelina M. Young, Dec. 25, 1965; 1 child, Elaine Evelina. BA, Nat. Taiwan U., Taipei, 1957, MA, 1963; PhD, U. Okla., 1972. Chief economist Cooperative Bank Taiwan, Taipei, 1959-61; dir. tax services Bur. Taxation, Govt. Taiwan, Republic China, 1961-63; instr. U. Okla., Norman, 1968; asst. prof. Ga. So. U., Statsboro, 1968-71; prof. bus. and econs. Catawba Coll., Salisbury, 1971—; adj. prof. San Francisco State U., 2002—. Pres. Am. Prudential Investments, Salisbury, 1981-89; pres. Tsengs Investments, 1990—. Author: Investments, 1982; contbr. articles to profl. jours. Coordinator, supporter study mathematically precocious youth Johns Hopkins U., Balt., 1982—; ptnr. World Vision, Calif., 1986-92. Academic research grantee Academia Sinica, Taipei, 1962; Ford Found. fellow, Taipei, 1963. Mem. AAUP, Ea. Econ. Assn., Am. Econ. Assn., Am. Assn. Individual Investors, Taiwan Investment (organizer 1986—), Taiwanese-Am. Assn. Greater Charlotte (pres. 1994-96), Nat. Travel Club. Avocations: antique collector, traveling, reading. Home: 316 Bethel Dr Salisbury NC 28144-2808 Office: Catawba Coll W Innes St Salisbury NC 28144 Fax: 704-637-5724. E-mail: stseng@catawba.edu., stsengs@hotmail.com.

TSENG, ROSE, academic administrator; PhB, Kansas State U.; M, PhD Nutrition, U. Calif., Berkeley. Registered dietician. Chancellor, CEO West Valley-Mission C.C., Calif., 1993—; dean Coll. Applied Scis. and Arts San Jose State U.; sr. v.p. U. Hawaii; chancellor U. Hawaii-Hilo, 1998—. Office: U Hawaii-Hilo 200 W Kawili Hilo HI 96720-4091*

TSEO, GEORGE KUANG YU, geography educator; b. Utica, N.Y., Sept. 28, 1958; s. Cheng Se and Jane Hwa (Lee) Tseo; m. Hui Fu, May 12, 1992; children: Kaleb Yi-Tong, Jessica Yi-Lan. BS in Meteorology, Pa. State U., 1980; PhD in Geology, U. Adelaide, 1987. Rschr., writer Stanford Project for Internat. and Cross Cultural Edn., Palo Alto, Calif., 1987-88; postdoctoral rsch. fellow Lanzhou Inst. for Desert Rsch. Chinese Acad. Scis., Peoples Republic of China, 1988-89; asst. prof. Pa. State U., Hazleton, 1989—. Cons. China Rsch. Ctr. for Mgmt. Sci., Beijing, 1994; co-organizer Sino-Am. Conf. to Promote Employee Ownership, 1994, 2d Internat. Conf. on Enterprise Reform and Sino-Am. Market Opportunity, 1996. Co-author, chief editor: China Trade Manual, 1995; contbr. articles to profl. jours. Mem. Am. Assn. Geographers, Nat. Bur. Asian Rsch., Indsl. Rels. Rsch. Assn., Nat. Ctr. for Employee Ownership, Phi Beta Kappa, Phi Kappa Phi. Avocations: writing fiction, soccer. Office: Pa State Hazelton Highacres Hazleton PA 18201 E-mail: gkt1@psu.edu.

TSIEN, ROGER YONCHIEN, chemist, cell biologist; b. N.Y.C., Feb. 1, 1952; s. Hsue Chu and Yi Ying (Li) T.; m. Wendy M. Globe, July 30, 1982. AB summa cum laude in Chemistry and Physics, Harvard Coll., 1972; PhD in Physiology, U. Cambridge, 1977; D (hon.), Katholieke U., Leuven, Belgium, 1995. Rsch. asst. U. Cambridge, Eng., 1975-78; asst. prof. Dept. Physiology-Anatomy U. Calif., Berkeley, 1981-85, assoc. prof., 1985-87, prof., 1987-89, prof. pharmacology, chemistry and biochemistry San Diego, 1989—; co-found. Aurora Bioscis. Corp., 1994, Senomyx, Inc., 1998. T.Y. Shen vis. prof. Medicinal Chem., MIT, 1991. Contbr. chpts. to books, articles to profl. jours. Recipient Herbert Sober Lectureship, Am. Soc. Biochemistry and Molecular Biology, 2000, Pearse Prize, Royal Microscopical Soc., 2000, Am. Chem. Soc. award for Creative Invention, 2002, Anfinsen award, Protein Soc., 2002, Dr. H.P. Heineken Prize for Biochemistry and Biophysics, 2002, Lamport prize N.Y. Acad. Scis., 1986, Javits Neurosci. Investigator award Nat. Inst. Neurol. Disorders and Stroke, 1989—, Young Scientist award Passano Found., 1991, W. Alden Spencer Neurobiology award Columbia U., 1991, Bowditch lectureship Am. Physiol. Soc., 1992, Gairdner Found. Internat. award, 1995, Doctorate honoris causa, Katholieke Universiteit Leuven, Belgium, 1995; Artois-Baillet-Latour Health prize (Belgium), 1995, Basic Rsch. prize Am. Heart Assn., 1995, Faculty Rsch. lectureship U. Calif., San Diego, 1997, Faculty Rsch. Lectureship, Univ. Calif., San Diego, Acad. Senate, 1997, EG&G Wallac award for Innovation in High Throughput Screening Soc. for Biomolecular Screening, 1998; Comyns Berkeley Rsch. fellow Gonville & Caius Coll., 1977-81; Marshall scholar British Govt., 1972-75, Searle scholar, 1983-86. Mem. AAAS (Amer. Acad. Arts and Scis.), NAS (Natl. Acad. of Scis.), Inst. Medicine, Phi Beta Kappa. Achievements development and extensive biological application of molecules to measure and/or manipulate intracellular calcium, sodium, and hydrogen ions, cyclic adenosine-3', 5'-monophosphate, nitric oxide, inositol phosphates, membrane potential, protein trafficking, protein-protein interaction, and gene expression; developed biochemistry and redesign of green fluorescent protein; elucidation fo signal transduction mechanisms in calcium oscillations and synaptic plasticity; inventor new methods for microscopic imaging and pharmaceutical high-throughput screening. Office: U Calif San Diego Dept Pharmacology Bldg CM-W 9500 Gilman Dr La Jolla CA 92093-5004 E-mail: rtsien@ucsd.edu.

TSIN, ANDREW TSANG CHEUNG, cell biology and biochemistry researcher/educator; b. Hong Kong, July 19, 1950; came to U.S., 1979; m. Wendy L. Wickstrom, Jan. 20, 1979; 1 child, Cathy Mei. BS in Biology, Dalhousie U., Halifax, N.S., Can., 1973; MS in Zoology, U. Alberta, Edmonton, Alta., Can., 1976, PhD in Zoology, 1979; postgrad., Baylor Coll. Medicine, 1979-81. Prof. biochemistry and cell biology U. Tex., San Antonio, 1990—; prof. ophthalmology U. Tex. Health Sci. Ctr., 1990—, minority biomed. rsch. support program dir., 1991—. Cons. Alcon Lab., Ft. Worth, 1989-90; adminstrv. officer radiation and laser safety U. Tex., San Antonio, 1985-92, dir. divsn. life sci., 1994-95; sci. advisor, cons. NIH, Bethesda, Md., 1987—, NSF, Washington, 1987. Contbr. articles to profl. jours. Named postgrad. scholar Nation Rsch. Coun. of Can., 1977-78, postdoctoral fellow Med. Rsch. Coun. Can., 1979-82, Alta. Heritage Found. Med. Rsch. fellow, 1981-82. Mem. AAAS, Am. Soc. Biochemistry and Molecular Biology, Assn. for Rsch. in Vision and Ophthalmology, Am. Physiol. Soc., Soc. for Neurosci. Achievements include research in cell biology of the retina, biochemistry of membrane proteins, metabolism of retinoids, comparative animal physiology, and environmental and evolutionary biology. Office: U Tex San Antonio Dept Biology San Antonio TX 78249 E-mail: atsin@utsa.edu.

TSIRPANLIS, CONSTANTINE N. theology, philosophy, classics and history educator; b. Kos, Greece, Mar. 18, 1935; came to U.S., 1957; m. Sophia Pappas, July 12, 1975; children: Kalliope-Chrysoula, Nike. BA, STM, lic. in theology magna cum laude, Halke Theol. Sem., Istanbul, Turkey, 1957; ThM, Harvard U., 1962; ThD, Union Theol. Sem., 1963; MA, Columbia U., 1966, PhD, 1970, Fordham U., 1973. Instr., organizer Greek-Am. communities, 1958-63; founder, chmn., prof. modern Greek studies NYU, 1963-70; prof. world history N.Y. Inst. Tech. N.Y.C. and Delaware County Coll., Media, Pa., 1967-75; disting. prof. theology, sociology, history, ecumenism, Greek studies Union Theol. Sem., Barrytown, N.Y., 1976-97; chmn., prof. scriptures, patristics, Greek lang. St. Sophia Ukraine Orthodox Theol. Sem. Am., Somerset, N.J., 1999—. Chmn., prof. classics Collegiate Sch., N.Y.C., 1967-69; prof. modern Greek lang. and lit. New Sch. for Social Rsch., N.Y.C., 1968-70; prof. classical mythology Hunter Coll. CUNY, 1968-70. Author numerous books including A Short History of the Greek Language, 1966, rev. edit., 1970, A Modern Greek Reader for Americans, 1967, rev. edit., 1968, A Modern Greek Idiom and Phrase Book, 1978, Mark Eugenicus, 1979, N. Cabasilas, 1979, Greek Patristic Theology, 9 vols.; founder-editor The Patristic and Byzantine Rev., 1981—; pub., editor-in-chief Hellenism In Am., 1969—; contbr. articles to profl. jours. Decorated Medal of Nat. Rebirth 1821 (Greece), medals of Byzantine nobility, including count, baron, G. chevalier, Gt. Prior of N.Am., medal of Accademia Ferdinandea, medals of Diethnés Hetereia Hellenon Logotechnon, also hon. pres. Mem. Am. Soc. Neohellenic Studies (founder, v.p.), Pan Dodecanisian Fedn. U.S., Am. Hist. Assn., Am. Philog. Assn., Am. Acad. Medieval Studies, Internat. Assn. Byzantine Studies, Am. Philos. Assn., N.Am. Patristic Soc., Hellenic Philog. Assn., Am. Soc. Papyrologists, Am. Inst. Patristic-Byzantine Studies (pres., founder), Justinianum Oikoumenikon R.C. (pres., founder), World Acad. Arts and Culture (hon. mem., hon. DLitt. 1993). Home: 12 Minuet Ln Kingston NY 12401-6955 Office: 353-A Minuet Ln Kingston NY 12401 Fax: 845-331-1002.

TSIVIDIS, YANNIS P. electrical engineering educator; b. Piraeus, Greece, Dec. 22, 1946; came to U.S., 1970; s. Pelopidas I. and Maria (Filippa) T. BS, U. Minn., 1972; MS, U. Calif., Berkeley, 1973, PhD, 1976. Asst. prof. elec. engring. Columbia U., N.Y.C., 1976-81, assoc. prof., 1981-84, prof., 1984—, Nat. Tech. U., Athens, Greece, 1992-95; Charles Batchelor chair prof. Columbia U., N.Y.C., Greece, 1998—. Cons. AT&T Bell Labs., Murray Hill, N.J., 1977-88. Author: Operation and Modeling of the MOS Transistor, 1987, 2d edit., 1999, Mixed Analog-Digital VLSI Devices and Technology, 1996; co-editor: Design of Mos VLSI Circuits for Telecommunications, 1985, Integrated Continuous-Time Filters, 1993, Design of Analog-Digital VLSI Circuits for Telecommunications and Signal Processing, 1994; contbr. over 100 articles to profl. jours.; patentee in field. Recipient best paper award European Solid State Cirs. Conf., 1986, Great Tchr. award Columbia U., 1991, Disting. Faculty Tchg. award Columbia Engring. Sch. Alumni Assn., 1998. Fellow IEEE (Baker best paper award 1984, Darlington award 1987, Guillemin-Cauer award 1998, Circuits and Sys. Golden Jubilee 2000). Office: Columbia Univ Dept Elec Engring New York NY 10027

TSIVINSKY, VLADIMIR GEORGE, systems engineer; b. Kiev, USSR, Jan. 24, 1941; came to U.S., 1989; s. George and Rosa (Fridman) T.; m. Ellen Shulman, Feb. 7, 1976; children: Kirk, Leila. M in Info./Measurement, Kiev Inst. Tech., 1964, PhD in Info./Measurement, 1969. Asst. prof. Kiev Inst. Tech., 1964-69, sr. sys. engr., 1969-75, dir. lab. in computerized sys. rsch., 1975-81, tchg. prof. dept. applied math., 1981-89; assoc. MCR Engring., Norfolk, Mass., 1990-92; sr. sys. engr. Forté Tech., Norwood, 1993-94, prin. sys. engr., 1994-2000; sr. software engr. SpeedLine, Franklin, 2000—. Author: Voltage Measurement at Infrasound Range, 1984, Mini and Microcomputers, 1987; 29 inventions in field of measurement/computing; contbr. over 30 articles to profl. jours. Recipient Bronze medal Com. of All-Union Exhbn., Moscow, 1968, 84. Mem. IEEE. Home: 4 Beaver Brook Rd Sharon MA 02067-1002 Office: Speedline 16 Forge Park Franklin MA 02038 E-mail: tsivinsky@hotmail.com.

TSO, MARK ON-MAN, ophthalmologist; b. Hong Kong, Oct. 19, 1936; m. Petrina Chan, Dec. 19, 1964. MBBS, U. Hong Kong, 1961, DSc, 1995. Diplomate Am. Bd. Ophthalmology. Staff ophthalmologist Armed Forces Inst. of Pathology, Washington, 1969-71, rsch. assoc., 1971-76; prof. of ophthalmology U. Ill., Chgo., 1976-94, dir. of Georgiana Theobald Ophthalmic Path. Lab., 1976-94, med. dir. Lions of Ill. Eye Bank, 1989-94; prof., chmn. dept. ophthalmology and visual scis. Chinese U. of Hong Kong, 1994-99; chair XI Acad. Ophthalmologica Internationalis, 1997—; pres. Coll. of Ophthalmologists of Hong Kong, 1997-99; v.p. Internat. Coun. of Ophthalmology, 1998—; prof. ophthalmology and pathology John Hopkins U., Balt., 1999—. Author: Retinal Diseases, 1988. Sr. univ. scholar U. Ill., 1985-88, De Ocampo lectr. The Asia Pacific Acad. of Ophthalmology, 1995; recipient Friedenwald award and lectr. Assn. for Rsch. in Vision and Ophthalmology, 1989. Fellow Royal Coll. Surgeons (Edinburgh). Office: John Hopkins U 600 N Wolfe St Baltimore MD 21287-9142 E-mail: matso@jhmi.edu.

TS'O, PAUL ON-PONG, biophysical chemist, educator; b. July 17, 1929; BS, Lingnan U., 1949; MS, Mich. State U., 1951; PhD, Calif. Inst. Tech., 1955. Teaching asst. Calif. Inst. Tech., 1952-55, rsch. fellow biology div., 1955-61, sr. rsch. fellow, 1961-62; assoc. prof. biophys. chemistry dept. radiol. scis. Johns Hopkins U., Balt., 1962-67, prof., 1967-73, prof., dir. div. biophysics Sch. Hygiene and Pub. Health, 1973-90, prof. dept. biochemistry, 1973—; chmn., CEO Cell Works, Inc., Balt., 1997—. Cons. Nat. Cancer Inst., 1972-75; mem. study sect. A on biophysics and biophys. chemistry NIH, 1976-80; mem. Clearinghouse on Environ. Carcinogens, Nat. Cancer Inst., 1976-80; mem. European expert com. on biophysics UNESCO; mem. sci. com. of the consortium Internat. Biomed. Inst., Bari, Italy; mem. bd. sci. counselors, div. intramural rsch. NIEHS, 1995—; mem. bd. sci. counselors, external adv. com. NIH, 1995—. Editor: Basic Principles in Nucleic Acid Chemistry, Vol. I and II, 1974, The Molecular Biology of the Mammalian Genetic Apparatus, Vol. I and II, 1977; co-editor: The Nucleohistones, 1964, Chemical Carcinogenesis, Part A and Part B, 1974, Polycyclic Hydrocarbons and Cancer: Environment, Chemistry and Metabolism; and Molecular and Cell Biology, Vol. 1 and 2, 1978, Vol. 3, 1981, Carcinogenesis: Fundamental Mechanisms and Environmental Effects, 1980, Interrelationship Among Aging, Cancer and Differentiation, 1985, Structure and Function of the Genetic Apparatus, 1986; mem. editorial bd. Molecular Pharmacology, 1964-83, Biophys. Jour, 1969-72, Biochimica et Biophysica Acta, 1971-81, Cancer Rev, 1973-84, Jour. Environ. Health Scis, 1976-81; assoc. editor: Cancer Research, 1975-87; mem. editorial adv. bd. Biochemistry, 1966-74, Biopolymers, 1979-85; contbr. over 350 articles and revs. to profl. jours. Named Md. Chemist of Yr., 1981; named One of 1000 Most Cited Scientists, Citation Index, 1965-78 Fellow AAAS; mem. Biophys. Soc. (chmn. pub. sci. policy com. 1972-76, coun. mem. 1975-78, exec. bd. 1975), Am. Soc. Biol. Chemists, Am. Soc. Microbiology, Am. Soc. Cell Biology, Biology Alliance for Pub. Affairs (chmn. organizing com. 1973-76), Am. Assn. Cancer Rsch., Am. Chem. Soc., Acadmia Sinica (1st dir. inst. molecular biology, chmn. adv. com. 1982-94), European Acad. Arts, Scis. and Humanities, Sigma Xi. Office: Cell Works Inc Holabird Business Park 6200 Seaforth St Baltimore MD 21224 E-mail: paul@cell-works.com.

TSO, TIEN CHIOH, federal agency official, plant physiologist; b. Hupeh, China, July 25, 1917; came to U.S., 1947, naturalized, 1961; s. Ya Fu and Suhwa (Wang) T.; m. Margaret Lu, Aug. 28, 1949; children: Elizabeth, Paul. BS, Nanking U., China, 1941, MS, 1944; PhD, Pa. State U., 1950; postgrad., Oak Ridge Inst. Nuclear Studies. Supt. exptl. farm Ministry Social Affairs, China, 1944-46; exec. sec. Tobacco Improvement Bur., 1946-47; rsch. chemist Gen. Cigar Rsch. Lab., 1950-51; with USDA, 1952—; prin. plant physiologist crop research div. Agrl. Rsch. Svc./USDA, Beltsville, Md., 1964-66, leader tobacco quality investigations, tobacco and sugar crops research br., 1966-71, chief tobacco lab., 1972-83, sr. exec. service, 1974-83, collaborator, 1984—; exec. dir. Internat. Devel. and Edn. in Agr. and Life Scis., 1984-96, chmn. bd., 1997-2001, hon. chmn. bd., 2001—. Cons. World Bank, Nat. Cancer Inst., Ky. Tobacco Health Rsch. Inst., China Nat. Tobacco Corp., Philippine Tobacco Rsch. Ctr., Philip Morris Tobacco Corp. Author: Physiology and Biochemistry of Tobacco Plants, 1972, Production, Physiology and Biochemistry of Tobacco Plants, 1991, Agriculture in China: 1949-2030, 1998; contbg. author: Ann. Rev. Plant Physiology, Vol. 9, 1958, The Chemistry of Tobacco and Tobacco Smoke, 1972, Toward Less Harmful Cigarettes, 1968, 71, 75, 80; editor: Structural and Functional Aspects of Phytochemistry, 1972, Recent Advances in Tobacco Science, vol. 1, 1975, Agriculture in China: 1949-2030, 1998, also procs. Fellow AAAS, Am. Soc. Agronomy (chmn. colloquium on agr. and life scis. in China 1983, 84, 85, 86, 87, 88-89), Am. Inst. Chemists; mem. Am. Chem. Soc., Am. Soc. Plant Physiologists, Phytochem. Soc. N.Am. (pres. 1971, life mem.), Tobacco Chemists Rsch. Conf. (symposium chmn. 1965, 79, chmn. 1975, 83), World Conf. Smoking and Health (sect. chmn. 1967, 71, 75), Tobacco Workers Conf., N.Y. Acad. Scis., Interag. Smoking and Health Forum (chmn. 1979-83), Nat. Coordinating Com. on Tobacco-Related Rsch., Sigma Xi, Gamma Sigma Delta. Achievements include research publs. on establishment of loci of alkaloid formation, biosynthetic pathway, interconversion and fate of alkaloids in tobacco plants, chem. composition as affected by macro and micro elements, homogenized leaf curing, health-related factors including mycotoxins and phenolics, potential for agricultural self-sufficiency in China in the next century. Home: 4306 Yates Rd Beltsville MD 20705-2758 Office: Beltsville Agr Rsch Ctr Bldg 005 Beltsville MD 20705 also: Ideals Inc 5010 Sunnyside Ave Beltsville MD 20705-2320 E-mail: tsot@ba.ars.usda.gov. *We are thankful to those fools. They are the only ones who dare to dream of something new and seemingly impossible.*

TSODIKOV, ALEXANDER DAVID, biostatistician, educator; b. St. Petersburg, Russia, Dec. 20, 1964; arrived in Germany, 1994; s. David Isac and Vera Semion (Fidelman) Tsodikov; m. Elena Sergei Serbina, Oct. 7, 1999. MS in Applied Math., St. Petersburg Tech. U., 1988, PhD in Math., 1991; diploma in epidemiology and biostats., Karolinska Inst., Sweden, 1992. Engr. St. Petersburg Tech. U., 1988-90, rsch. fellow, 1990-92, sr. rsch. fellow, 1992-93; postdoctoral fellow Inst. Curie, Paris, 1993-94; rsch. scientist U. Leipzig, Germany, 1995-97; rsch. asst. prof. U. Utah, Salt Lake City, 1997—2002, rsch. assoc. prof., 2002—. Author: Statistical Models, 1996; contbr. more than 50 articles to profl. jours. including Math. Biosci., Biometrics, Proc. U.S. Nat. Acad. Scis., Statis. Med., among others. Grantee Ministry of Sci. (France), 1993, Internat. Union Against Cancer (Switzerland), 1992, German Rsch. Found., 1995. Achievements include rsch. in cancer models, optimal screening schedules, and statis. methods in cancer. Home: 5562 Brookridge Dr Apt 14J Salt Lake City UT 84107-6844 E-mail: atsodiko@hci.utah.edu.

TSOH, JANICE YUSZE, clinical psychologist, researcher; b. Hong Kong, Hong Kong, May 26, 1968; d. Ka Kuk Tsoh and Chung Mei Lee; m. Dave Lee, July 26, 1997. BA, SUNY, Binghamton, 1990; MA, U. R.I., 1993, PhD, 1995. Rsch. asst. Cancer Prevention Rsch. Consortium, U. R.I., Kingston, 1990-94; psychology resident U. Miss., VA Med. Ctrs., Jackson, 1994-95; postdoctoral fellow U. Tex, MD Anderson Cancer Ctr., Houston, 1995-97, U. Calif., San Francisco, 1997-99, asst. rsch. psychologist, 1999-2000, asst. adj. prof., 2000—. Cons. Lifescan Inc., Militas, Calif., 1999-2001, Am. Cancer Soc., 2001, nat. Asian Women's Health Orgn., 2000—; guest lectr. U. Calif., Berkeley, 1999. Mem. rev. bd. Am. Jour. Health Behaviors, 1996—99, reviewer Addiction Jour. Drug and Alcohol Dependence, Jour. Consulting and Clin. Psychology, Health Psychology, CNS Drugs, Jour. Abnormal Psychology, Jour. Substance Abuse Treatment; contbr. articles. Recipient Travel award Nat. Inst. on Drug Abuse, 1998, New Investigator award Tobacco-Related Rsch. Program, 1999—, Pilot Study Fund U. Calif. Treatment Rsch. Ctr., San Francisco, 1999, Career Devel. award Nat. Inst. Drug Abuse, 2000—; fellow Univ. Found. U. Tex. MD Anderson Cancer Ctr., Houston, 1996-97. Mem. APA, Soc. Behavioral Medicine, Soc. for Rsch. on Nicotine and Tobacco, Nat. Asian Women's Health Orgn., Phi Beta Kappa, Psi Chi. Office: U Calif Dept Psychiatry LPP I 401 Parnassus Ave 0984-TRC San Francisco CA 94143-0984

TSOI, EDWARD TZE MING, architect, interior designer, urban planner; b. New Orleans, Aug. 7, 1943; s. Edward Mong Yok and Ruby Liu Wei (Hsia) T.; m. Louise Smoyer, June 15, 1968; children: Laura Li Ling, Alison Li Mei. BArch, MIT, 1966; MArch, M in City Planning, U. Pa., 1968, cert. in urban design, 1969. Registered architect, Mass., La. Assoc. Sert/Jackson & Assocs., Cambridge, Mass., 1969-76; assoc. prin. Skidmore Owings & Merrill, Boston, 1976-83; prin. Tsoi/Kobus & Assocs., Inc., Cambridge, 1983—, pres., 1985-89, 93—. Instr. Sch. Design, Harvard U., Cambridge, 1980-84. Designer Marine Resource Ctr., 1994. Chmn. Arlington (Mass.) Redevel. Bd., 1972—; chmn. 1st parish Unitarian Universalist Ch., Arlington, 1990; pres. bd. dirs. Cambridge Salvation Army, 1990—; mem. Boston Civic Design Commn., 1993—. Recipient Best New Med. Facility award Symposium on Healthcare, 1993, Grand Honor award Assn. Gen. Contractors, 1993, award Lotus Devel. Corp. landscape award Urban Design, 1991, nat. award for renovation Ford Model T plant Urban Land Inst., 1995. Fellow AIA; mem. Boston Soc. Architects (pres. 1993-94). Democrat. Avocations: windsurfing, boating, woodworking, carpentry. Home: 16 Devereaux St Arlington MA 02476-8114 Office: Tsoi/Kobus & Assocs Inc PO Box 9114 Cambridge MA 02238-9114 E-mail: etsoi@tka-architects.com.

TSOODLE-MARCUS, CHARLENE, education educator, school system administrator; b. May 8, 1947; d. Charles and Patrita (Lujan) Tsoodle; m. Joe David Marcus, July 29, 1976; 1 child Keith Eagle Marcus. AA in Police Sci., Monterey Peninsula Coll., 1968; BA in Criminal Justice, N. Mex. State Univ., 1971. Indian justice specialist planner Gov. Coun. on Criminal Justice, Santa Fe, 1972-80; records adminstr. N. Mex. Corrections Dept., 1980-93; govs. asst. Taos Pueblo Govs. Office, 1993-94; coord. Taos County Gov. Planning Dept., 1994-95, Northern Pueblos Inst., Northern N. Mex. C. C., Esponola, 1995—2001; jail adminstrn. Taos County Detention Ctr., 2001—. Chmn., housing commr. No. Pueblos Housing Authority, Santa Fe, 1993—; bd. mem. Rocky Mountain Youth, Taos, 1998—; steering com. mem. Rio Arriba Environ. Health, Espanola, 1999—. Photo feature Nat. Geog., 1994. Vice chair, com. mem. Taos County Tax Adv., 1993—95; vol. Indian Culture Clubs, Santa Fe, 1980—93, Taos Indian Bapt. Ch., Taos, 1980—93. Mem.: Am. Indian Sci. & Engring. Soc. (adv. 1999—), Nat. Congress Am. Indians (life), Phi Theta Kappa, Alpha Iota Sigma. Avocations: jewelry making, Indian pottery, arts and crafts. Office: Taos County Adult Detention Ctr Jail Adminstr 105 Albright St Ste J El Prado NM 87529

TSOUCALAS, NICHOLAS, federal judge; b. N.Y.C., Aug. 24, 1926; s. George Michael and Maria (Monogenis) T.; m. Catherine Aravantinos, Nov. 21, 1954; children: Stephanie, Georgia. BSBA, Kent State U., 1949; LLB, N.Y. Law Sch., 1951. Bar: N.Y. 1953. Sole practice, N.Y.C., 1953-55, 59-68; asst. U.S. atty. So. Dist. N.Y., 1955-59; judge Criminal Ct., City of N.Y., 1968-86; acting supreme ct. judge State of N.Y., N.Y.C., 1975-82; judge U.S. Ct. Internat. Trade, 1986—; now sr. judge. Dist. leader Republican Party N.Y. County, N.Y.C., 1961-68; mem. Rep. Exec. Com., N.Y.C., 1961-68. Served with USN, 1944-46, 51-52. Recipient Proficiency in Constl. Law award N.Y. Law Sch., N.Y.C., 1951, Man of Yr. award St. Paul Soc., N.Y.C., 1971. Mem. ABA, N.Y. County Lawyers Assn., Fed. Bar Assn., Greek Am. Lawyers Assn., Am. Hellenic Ednl. Prog. Assn. Lodges: Parthenon, Masons. Republican. Greek Orthodox. Avocations: basketball, racquetball, stamp collecting, walking, dancing. Office: US Ct Internat Trade 1 Federal Plz New York NY 10278-0001

TSOULFANIDIS, NICHOLAS, nuclear engineering educator, university official; b. Ioannina, Greece, May 6, 1938; came to U.S., 1963; s. Stephen and Aristea (Ganiou) T.; m. Zizeta Koutsombidou, June 21, 1964; children: Stephen, Lena. BS in Physics, U. Athens, Greece, 1960; MS in Nuclear Engring., U. Ill., 1965, PhD in Nuclear Engring., 1968. Registered profl. engr., Mo. Prof. nuclear engring. U. Mo., Rolla, 1968—, vice chancellor acad. affairs, 1985-86, assoc. dean for rsch. Sch. Mines and Metallurgy, 1989—. Sr. engr. Gen. Atomic Co., San Diego, 1974-75; researcher Cadarache France, 1986-87. Author: Measurement and Detection of Radiation, 1984, 2d edit. 1995; co-author: Nuclear Fuel Analysis and Management, 1990; editor: Nuclear Technology, 1997, 2nd edit., 1999. Mem. Am. Nuclear Soc. (chmn. radiation protection shielding div. 1987-88), Health Physics Soc., Nat. Soc. Profl. Engring., Rotary. Office: U of Mo Rolla Dept Nuc Engring 1870 Miner Cir Dept Nuc Rolla MO 65409-0001

TSUBAKI, ANDREW TAKAHISA, theater director, educator; b. Chiyoda-ku, Tokyo, Japan, Nov. 29, 1931; s. Ken and Yasu (Oyama) T.; m. Lilly Yuri, Aug. 3, 1963; children: Arthur Yuichi, Philip Takeshi. BA in English, Tokyo Gakugei U., Tokyo, Japan, 1954; postgrad. in Drama, U. Saskatchewan, Saskatoon, Canada, 1958-59; MFA in Theatre Arts, Tex. Christian U., 1961; PhD in Speech & Drama, U. Ill., 1967. Tchr. Bunkyo-ku 4th Jr. High Sch., Tokyo, 1954—58; instr., scene designer Bowling Green (Ohio) State U., 1964—68; asst. prof. speech & drama U. Kans., Lawrence, 1968—73, assoc. prof., 1973—79; vis. assoc. prof. Carleton Coll., Northfield, Minn., 1974; lectr. Tsuda U., Tokyo, 1975; vis. assoc. prof. theatre Tel-Aviv (Israel) U., 1975—76; vis. prof. theatre Mo. Repertory Theatre, Kansas City, Mo., 1976, Nat. Sch. Drama, New Delhi, 1983; prof. theatre, film, east Asian Languages and Cultures U. Kans., Lawrence, 1979—2000, prof. emeritus, 2000—. Dir. Internat. Theatre Studies Ctr., U. Kans., Lawrence, 1971-2000, Operation Internat. Classical Theatre, 1988—; Benedict disting. vis. prof. Asian studies Carleton Coll., 1993; area editor Asian Theatre Jour., U. Hawaii, Honolulu, 1982-94; chmn. East Asian Langs. and Cultures, U. Kans., Lawrence, 1983-90; mem. editl. bd. Studies in Am. Drama, Oxford, Miss., 1985-88. Dir. plays Kanjincho, 1973, Rashomon, 1976, 96, King Lear, 1985, Fujito and Shimizu, 1985, Hippolytus, 1990, Busu and the Missing Lamb (Japan) 1992, Suehirogari and Sumidagawa, 1992, 93, Tea, 1995; choreographed Antigone (Greece), 1987, Hamlet (Germany), 1989, The Resistible Rise of Arturo Ui, 1991, Man and the Masses (Germany), 1993, The Children of Fate (Hungary), 1994, The Great Theatre of the World (Germany); editor Theatre Companies of the World, 1986; contbg. author to Indian Theatre: Traditions of Performance, 1990; contbr. 7 entries in Japanese Traditional plays to the Internat. Dictionary of Theatre, vol. 1, 1992, vol. 2, 1994. Recipient World Univ. Svc. Scholarship U. Saskatchewan, 1958-59, University fellow U. Ill., 1961-62, Rsch. fellow The Japan Found., 1974-75, 90, Rsch. Fulbright grantee, 1983. Fellow Coll. Am. Theatre (elected 2002); mem. Am. Theatre Assn., Asian Theatre Program (chair 1976-79), Assn. for Asian Studies, Assn. Kans. Theatres., Assn. Kans. Theatres U/C Div. (chmn. 1980-82), Assn. for Theatre in Higher Edn., Assn. for Asian Performance. Democrat. Buddhist. Avocations: Ki-Aikido (4th Dan), photography, travel. Home: 924 Holiday Dr Lawrence KS 66049-3005 E-mail: atsubaki@ku.edu.

TSUBOUCHI, DAVID H. Canadian provincial official; BA in English, York U.; LLB, Osgoode Hall Law Sch. Ward 5 councillor Town of Markham, 1988-94; sr. ptnr. Tsubouchi & Nichols & Assocs., 1994-95; apptd. Min. of Cmty. and Social Svcs. Ont. Progressive Conservative Govt., 1995-99; solicitor gen. Province of Ont., 1999—; also chair health and social svcs. policy com. Chmn. planning and devel. com., econ. alliance com., indsl. and corp. devel. com. Markham Hist. Mus.; apptd. Min. Consumer & Comml. Affairs Can., 1996; Registrar Gen. Ontario, 1996; chair Cabinet Legis. & Regulations Com., 96; re-elected mem. Provincial Parliament for Markham Ont. Legislature, 1999; apptd. chair Mgmt. Bd. of Cabinet by Premier Mike Harris, 2001. Named Optimist of Yr., 1985-86; recipient Air Can. Heart of Gold award, 1988; granted Coat of Arms, Gov. Gen.'s Office, 1993. Office: 77 Wellesley St 12th Fl Toronto ON Canada M7A 1N3

TSUCHIDA, GEORGE, engineering executive; b. Wahiawa, Hawaii, Nov. 15, 1945; s. Robert Toshiyuki and Stella (Chiyoko) Tsuchida; m. Lauren Tsuneko Mukai, July 22, 1967; children: Tammy Noriko, Jodi Lynn Tsuchida

Briggs, Justin Toshiyuki. BSEE, U. Hawaii, 1967; MS in Sys. Mgmt., U. So. Calif., 1977. Material readiness dir. Naval Sea Sys. Command, Bethesda, Md., 1979—82, acting program mgr. Arlington, Va., 1982—85, engring dir., program exec. officer submarines, 1985—92, prin. asst. for ops., program exec. officer submarines, 1992—95, plans and programs dir., program exec. officer submarines, 1995—97, strategic planning mgr., 1997—99, dep. dir. Washington, 2000—. Sys. engring. instr. Naval Sea Sys. Command, Arlington, 1993—2000. Den co-leader Boy Scouts Am., Burke, Va., 1990—91; v.p. edn. Toastmasters, Fairfax, 1992—93. Recipient David Packard Acquisition award, Dept. of the Navy, 1996, Meritorious Svc. award, Fed. Asian Pacific Am. Coun., 1998. Mem.: IEEE. Avocations: fishing, bowling, tennis, reading. Home: 13658 Barren Springs Ct Centreville VA 20121

TSUCHIYA, KEN, computer engineer; b. Iiyama, Japan, Dec. 30, 1947; came to U.S., 1967; s. Junzo and Fumi (Shiozaki) T.; m. Viviane M. Clausset, Oct. 6, 1973; 1 child, Aimee. BSEE, U. Minn., 1972. Registered profl. engr., Minn. Design, develop engr. Avionics Honeywell Co., Mpls., 1973-80; sys. design engr. Gen. Mills Co., 1980; sr. design engr. Def. Honeywell Co., 1980-83; prin. engr., cons. Unisys Co., St. Paul, 1983-97; advisory engr. embedded CPU design IBM, Rochester, Minn., 1997-2000, advisory engr. embedded processordesign Research Triangle Park, N.C., 2000—. Patentee in field. Mem. IEEE, Minn. Profl. Engring. Soc. Avocations: travel, skiing, fishing, bicycling. Home: 401 Burgwin Wright Way Cary NC 27502-3807 E-mail: tsuchiya@us.ibm.com.

TSUDA, ROY TOSHIO, marine biologist, educator; b. Honolulu, Dec. 25, 1939; s. Thomas Yoshio and Setsuko Tsuda; m. Sally Yaeko Tsuda, Apr. 10, 1959; children: Mark Takashi, Craig Hiroshi, Ryan Yoshio. PhD Botany, U. of Wisconsin-Milwaukee, Milwaukee, WI, 1970; MS Botany, U. of Hawaii-Manoa, Honolulu, HI, 1966, BS Botany, 1963. Educator marine biology U. of Guam, Mangilao, Guam, 1989—2002, interim pres. Guam, 2000—01; chief environ. svc. Duenas and Associates, Inc., Tamuning, Guam, 1990—2000; academic v.p. U. of Guam, Mangilao, Guam, 1984—89, dean of grad. sch. and rsch. Guam, 1978—84, dir. of marine biology Guam, 1974—76. Elected chmn. Pacific Sci. Assn., Coral Reef Com., Honolulu, 1975—81, Internat. Assn. of Biol. Oceanography, Coral Reef Com., 1971. Contbr. articles to profl. jour. Recipient 75th Anniversary Rainbow Award, U. of Hawaii, 1982. Mem.: Internat. Soc. for Reef Studies. Avocations: swimming, gardening. Office: Marine Laboratory University of Guam UOG Station Mangilao GU Office Fax: 671-734-6767. E-mail: rtsuda@uog9.uog.edu.

TSUI, DANIEL C. electrical engineer, physicist; b. Henan, China, 1939; PhD in Physics, U. Chgo., 1967. Rsch. assoc. U. Chgo., 1967—68; mem. technical staff Bell Labs., Murray Hill, NJ, 1968—82; Arthur LeGrand Doty prof. dept. elec. engring. Princeton (N.J.) U., 1982—. Contbr. articles to profl. jours. Recipient Buckley prize for Condensed Matter Physics, 1984, Benjamin Franklin medal in Physics, 1998, Nobel prize in Physics, 1998. Fellow: AAAS; mem.: NAS, Materials Research Soc., Am. Physical Soc., IEEE, Acad. Sinica. Office: Princeton U Dept Elec Engring Rm B 426 PO Box 5263 Princeton NJ 08544-0001 Fax: 609-258-6279. E-mail: tsui@ee.princeton.edu.*

TSUI, LAP-CHEE, molecular genetics educator; b. Shanghai, Dec. 21, 1950; arrived in Can., 1981; s. Jing Lue Hsue and Hui Ching Wang; m. Ellen Lan Fong, Feb. 11, 1977; children: Eugene, Felix. BS, Chinese U. Hong Kong, 1972, MPhil, 1974, DSc (hon.), 1991; PhD, U. Pitts., 1979; DCL (hon.), U. King's Coll., Halifax, N.S., Can., 1991; DSc (hon.), U. N.B., Can., 1991; DLL (hon.), U. St. Francis Xavier, Antigonish, N.S., Can., 1994. Postdoctoral investigator Oak Ridge (Tenn.) Nat. Lab., 1979-80; postdoctoral fellow Hosp. for Sick Children, Toronto, Ont., Can., 1981-83, geneticist-in-chief Can., 1996—; asst. prof. depts. genetics and med. genetics U. Toronto, Can., 1983-88, assoc. prof. Can., 1988-90, prof. Can., 1990—, univ. prof. Can., 1994—; H.E. Sellers chair in cystic fibrosis, 1998—; head genetics and genomic biology program, 1998—. Chmn. chromosome 7 subcom. Human Gene Mapping Workshop, 1986-97; mem. mammalian genetics study sect. NIH, Bethesda, Md., 1988-93; dir. Cystic Fibrosis Rsch. Ctr., Hosp. for Sick Children Spl. Rsch. Ctr., 1994—; scientist Med. Rsch. Coun. Can., 1989—; advisor European Jour. Human Genetics, 1992—, Molecular Medicine Today, 1995—. Editor Cytogenetics and Cell Genetics, 1988-92, Internat. Jour. Genome Rsch., 1990—; assoc. editor Am. Jour. Human Genetics, 1990-93, Genomics, 1994—; mem. editl. bd. Mammalian Genome, 1990, Clin. Genetics, 1991—, Human Molecular Genetics, 1991-99; communicating editor Human Mutation, 1995—, Molec. Medicine Today, sr. editor: Physiological Genomics, 2000-01; internat. adv. The Chinese Jour. of Medical Genetics, 2000—; contbr. over 300 articles to sci. jours.; co-discoverer cystic fibrosis gene, 1989. Trustee Edn. Found., Fedn. Chinese Canadian Profls., Toronto, 1987—. Recipient Paul di Sant Agnese Disting. Achievement award Cystic Firbosis Found., 1989, Gold medal of honor Pharm. Mfrs. Assn. Can., 1989, award of excellence Genetics Soc. Can., 1990, Gairdner Internat. award 1990, Cresson medal Franklin Inst., 1992, E. Mead Johnson award, 1992, Disting. Scientist award The Canadian Soc. Clin. Investigators, 1992, Canadian Conf. medal 1992, Sarstedt Rsch. prize, 1993, Sanremo Internat. award for Genetic Rsch., 1993, J.P. Lecocq prize Inst. de France, 1994, Henry Friesen award The Canadian Soc. for Clin. Investigation and the Royal Coll. of Physicians and Surgeons of Can., 1995, Can. Med. Assn. award of honour, 1996, Jonas Salk award Ontario March of Dimes, 1997, Initiative Cmty. Svc. award Toronto Biotech., 1998, Disting. Scientist award Med. Rsch. Coun., 2000; named scholar Can. Cystic Fibrosis Found., 1984-86. Fellow Royal Soc. Can., Royal Soc. London, Academia Sinica; pres. Human Genome Orgn., Am. Soc. Human Genetics. Office: Hosp for Sick Children 555 University Ave Toronto ON Canada M5G 1XG

TSUI, SOO HING, educational research consultant; b. Hong Kong, Aug. 2, 1959; came to U.S., 1985; d. Sik Tin and Yuk Kam (Cheung) T. BSW cum laude, Nat. Taiwan U., 1983; MSW cum laude, Columbia U., 1987, postgrad., 1992—. Cert. social worker, N.Y. Dir. cmty. handicapped ctr., Taipei, Taiwan, 1983-85; dir. youth recreational program N.Y., 1986; social work dept. supr. St. Margaret's House, N.Y.C., 1987-89; chief bilingual sch. social work N.Y.C. Bd. Edn., 1990—, rsch. cons., 1993—; rschr. Columbia U., N.Y.C., 1991-95; chief rsch. cons. N.Y.C. Dept. Transp., 1993-96; cheif rschr. immigrant social svcs. N.Y.C. Bd. Edn., 1996—. Bilingual social worker Nat. Assn. Asian/Am. Edn., 1989—; union social work regional rep. N.Y.C. Bd. Edn., 1990-93, citywide bilingual social work rep., 1991-93, citywide social work budget allocation comms. rep., 1992-93; mem. conf. planning com. bd. Amb. For Christ, Boston, 1991-93; coord. doctoral colloquial com. bd., 1991-93, Scholarships Coun. Social Work Edn., Columbia U., N.Y.C., 1992-94; mem. planning com. social work bd. Asian Am. Comms., N.Y.C., 1991-95; exec. dir. alumni bd. Columbia U. Sch. Social Work, 1995—, exec. dir. bd. Columbia newsletters Columbia U. Sch. Social Work, 1996—; exec. bd. dirs. Chinese for Christ, 1993-95. Recipient Nat. Acad. award, 1979-83; Nat. Acad. scholar, 1987-88; Nat. Rsch. fellow Sch. Coun. on Social Work Edn., 1992-94. Home: 65-38 Booth St Apt 2B Rego Park NY 11374

TSUKAYAMA, DERRICK KAWIKA, police sergeant, consultant; b. Honolulu, Oct. 3, 1954; s. Chomei D. and Elfrieda K. Tsukayama; m. Phyllis K. Chun, Nov. 10, 1988; children: Aran Chun, J.D. BS in Human Svcs., Wayland Bapt. U., 2000. Cert. use of force expert U.S. Dist. Ct. Hawaii; cert. constl. law expert U.S. Dist. Ct. Hawaii; cert. laws of arrest/search and seizure expert U.S. Dist. Ct. Hawaii. Br. mgr. Wackenhut Security Corp. Internat., Maui, Molokai, Hawaii, 1975-77; met. police officer Honolulu Police Dept., 1977-95, met. police sgt., 1995—. Bd. dirs. Honolulu Police Fed. Credit Union, credit com., 1999-2000; cons. Clough/Cameron Cons., Honolulu, 1983-90; instr. Calif. POST Cert., Sacramento, 1992-93. Author: (tng. manual) Constitutional Law for Law Enforcement, 1994, (employee rehab. program) Comprehensive Tactical Intervention Program, 1993 (Unit of the Quarter award 1997). Coord., participant Project Grad., Kailua, Hawaii, 1996-2000. Recipient Disting. Police award MADD, 1993, City and County Officer of Yr., City and County of Honolulu, 1999. Avocations: spending time with family, helping others, outrigger canoe paddling, tennis, deep sea fishing. Office: Honolulu Police Dept Ste 330 715 S King St Honolulu HI 96813 Office Fax: (808) 522-7095.

TSUKIJI, RICHARD ISAO, international marketing and financial services consultant; b. Salt Lake City, Jan. 31, 1946; s. Isamu and Mitsuie (Hayashi) T.; children: Angela Jo, Richard Michael. Grad. Sacramento City Coll., 1966; AA, U. Pacific, McGeorge Sch. Law, 1970-72. Grocery mgr. Food Mart, Inc., Sacramento, 1963-65; agy. supr. Takehara Ins. Agy., Sacramento, 1965-68; sales rep. Kraft Foods Co., Sacramento, 1969-71; sales mgr. Olivetti Corp., Sacramento, 1972-73; co-founder Mktg. Devel. and Mgmt. Coll., Sacramento, 1973, pres., 1973-74; pres. Richard Tsukiji Corp., Sacramento, 1974-77; CEO, chmn. bd. Assocs. Investment Group, Sacramento, 1978-82 ; chmn. bd. RichColor Corp. Sacramento, 1978-83, E.J. Sub Factories, Inc., Elk Grove, Calif., 1978-81; gen. agt. Comml. Bankers Life Ins. Co., 1974-82; chmn. bd. Phoenix Industries, Inc., Carson City, Nev., 1981-84, Databank, Inc., Roseburg, Oreg., 1982-83; pres. Computers, Etc. Corp., Carson City, 1982-84; regional v.p. U.S. BankCard Group, Salem, Oreg., 1993-95; pres. Richard Tsukiji Comm., Inc., Sacramento, 1993—; CEO RTC Wireless,Inc., 1994—, Bonaventure Group, Inc., Wilmington, Del., 1995—; bd. dirs. Michton, Inc., Pontiac, Mich., Hunt & Johnson, Inc., Phoenix Group, Melbourne, A.N.D. Corp., New Orleans, ET World Travel, Salt Lake City, Utah, Bonaventure Group, Inc., Wilmington, Del., Royal Am. Bank, Cayman Islands; exec. v.p. Edco Corp., Glide, Oreg., 1982-94; chmn. bd. Computer Edn. Resource Ctr., 1983-90, Bonaventure, Inc., Roseburg, 1984-91, RTC Wireless Group, Inc., Oakland, Calif., 1995—, RTC Wireless Group, Inc., San Jose, Calif.; editor ST World, Melrose, Oreg., 1985-88, publisher, 1988-91; editor ST World Reseller, 1988-91. Mem. Yolo County Oral Rev. Bd., 1975-76; bd. dirs. Valley Area Constrn. Opportunity Program, 1972-76, chmn., 1976-77; bd. dirs. Douglas County Citizens Community Involvement, 1980-82; bd. dirs. Computer Edn. Found., Sacramento, 1983-93, Access Sacramento Cable Television, 1993, Heart to Heart Found., 1993; chmn. pub. rels. Sacramento Asian Pacific C. of C., 1993—; bd. dirs. Chinese Am. Coun. Sacramento, 1994—; mem. Asian Cmty. Ctr., 1994—, Sacramento Chinese Cmty. Svc. Ctr., 1994—; bd. dirs. ARC Sacramento-Sierra chpt., 1995—, ARC Nat. Disaster Team, 1996—, Commr. Sacramento City Coun., Human Rels. and Fair Housing Commn., 1996—, No. Calif. Asian Peace Officers Assn., 1995—, Sacramento Chinese Cmty. Svc. Ctr., 1995—, Japanese Am. Citizens League, 1995—; democratic precinct committeeman, Melrose, Oreg., 1982-86; appt. mem. adv. coun. Sacramento City Minority/Women Bus. Enterprise, 1995; bd. dirs., v.p. Orgn. Chinese Ams., Inc., 1996; commr. Sacramento City/County Human Rights Commn., 1996—. Served with U.S. Army, 1962-63. Recipient Commendation, Calif. Senate, 1978. Mem. Internat. Assn. Fin. Planners, Associated Gen. Contractors, VIC-20 Users Group (pres. Roseburg 1983-84), Atari Computer Enthusiasts (pres. Sacramento 1983-85), U.S. Commodore Council (pres. Natl. 1984-85), Sacramento Jaycees (dir. 1977-78), Orgn. Chinese Ams. (v.p. Sacramento chpt. 1995—), Asian Alliance, Japanese Am. Citizens League, Sacramento Urban League. Democrat. Roman Catholic. Address: 905 K St Sacramento CA 95814-3511

TSUNEOKA, YUTAKA, molecular geneticist; b. Nabari, Mie, Japan, Apr. 15, 1959; s. Tadao and Shuu (Higuchi) T.; m. Yumi Teraoka, Mar. 9, 1986; children: Yu, Ei. BA, Tokyo U. Fgn. Studies, 1984; MD, Kagawa Med. U., 1990, PhD, 1994. Lic. physician, Japan. Rsch. assoc. Nat. Def. Med. Coll., Tokorozawa, Japan, 1994-96, Japan, 1998; postdoctoral fellow U. Cin., 1996-98; staff physician Onaga Hosp., Tokorozawa, 1998-99, Kaishindoh Hosp., Tokyo, 1999; postdoctoral fellow U. Cin., 2000—. Mem. AAAS. Avocations: tennis, skiing, baseball, cycling, basketball. Home: 8115 Village Dr Cincinnati OH 45242-4317 Office: U Cincinnati Dept Environ Health PO Box 670056 Cincinnati OH 45267-0056 E-mail: yutaka.tsuneoka@uc.edu.

TSUNG, CHRISTINE CHAI-YI, financial executive; b. Nanking, China, Mar. 23, 1948; came to U.S., 1970; d. Chi-Huang Tsung and Siao-Tuan Huang. BBA, Nat. Taiwan U., Taipei, 1970; postgrad., Washington U., St. Louis, 1970-71; MBA, U. Mo., 1973. Acct. Capital Land Co., St. Louis, 1972-74; chief acct. Servis Equipment Co., Inc., Dallas, 1974-75; acctg. supr. Calif. Microwave, Sunnyale, 1975-76; budget and sales mgr. Columbia Pictures TV Internat., Burbank, Calif., 1976-77; acctg. mgr. Husquarna, San Diego, 1977-82; sr. acct. City of Poway, Calif., 1982-88, fin. mgr., 1988-95; pres., CEO China Airlines, 2000—. Pres., treas. Jade Poly Investment, Beverly Hills, Calif., 1989—; cons. assoc. Metro Properties, San Diego, 1989—; cons. Kaohsiung City, Taiwan, 2000—. Tchr. San Diego North County Chinese Sch., 1985-86; v.p. San Diego Chinese Culture Assn., 1982-86, bd. dirs., 1988-90, 93-94. Mem. Assn. Asian Pacific Airlines, Pacific Asia Travel Assn. (exec. bd.), Govt. Fin. Officers Assn. (Cert. of Achievement 1988-94), Calif. Soc. Mcpl. Fin. Officers (standing com. membership devel., Cert. of Award 1988-94), Mcpl. Treas. Assn. U.S. and Can., Taiwanese C. of C. of N.Am. (bd. dirs. 1994-95). Avocations: traveling, swimming, tennis, golf, reading. Office: China Airlines 2F 131 Sec 3 Nanking E Rd Taipei Taiwan Fax: 886-2-2514-5889. E-mail: c_tsung@china.airlines.com.

TSUO, ANNE LI, database specialist; b. Taipei, Taiwan, Republic of China, June 5, 1950; d. Bing-Ching Benn and Chong-Jye (Liang) Lee; m. Yuan-Huai Simon Tsuo, Apr. 7, 1974; children: Lee Kirjohn, Leo Kirtie. M in Computer Info. Sci., U. Denver, 1989; postgrad., NYU. Therapeutic dietitian Coney Island Hosp., Bklyn., 1974-75; dietitian Carlton Nursing Home, 1975-76; therapeutic dietitian Flatbush Gen. Hosp., 1976-78; clin. dietitian Johnston-Willis Hosp., Richmond, Va., 1978, Mercy Med. Ctr., Denver, 1982-87; cons. nutritionist Nutrition Cons. Svc., Golden, Colo., 1982—; data analyst Colo. Found. for Med. Care, Denver, 1989-90, tech. program coord., 1990-92; database specialist Nat. Renewable Energy Lab., Golden, 1992-96; mem. tech. staff application software engr., technical lead info. tech. U.S. West Com., Denver, 1996—. Speaker for health and nutrition subjects The Rocky Mountain Engring. and Sci. Coun., Denver, 1989-92. Contbr. articles to profl. jours. Bd. dirs. The Colo. Chinese Club, Denver, 1991-93; record custodian The Boy Scout of Am., Troop 166, Lakewood, Colo., 1992—. Fellow The Am. Dietetic Assn.; mem. The Colo. Dietetic Assn., The Denver Dietetic Assn., The Data Processing Mgmt. Assn., Rocky Mountain Oracle User Group, Oracle Devel. Tools User Group. Democrat. Roman Catholic. Avocations: reading, music, tennis, swimming, photography. Home: 2850 Joyce St Golden CO 80401-1323

TSUTAKAWA, EDWARD MASAO, management consultant; b. Seattle, May 15, 1921; s. Jin and Michiko (Oka) T.; m. Hide Kunugi, Aug. 11, 1949; children: Nancy Joyce, Margaret Ann Langston, Mark Edward. Student, U. Wash., 1941, Wash. State U., 1949. Free-lance comml. artist, Spokane, 1943-47; artist Maag & Porter Comml. Printers, 1947-54; organizer Litho Art Printers, Inc., 1954—, gen. mgr., pres., 1965-80. Charter organizer, dir. Am. Comml. Bank, 1965-80; prin. E.M. Tsutakawa Co., bus. cons. U.S., Japan Trade Negotiator, 1980-89; v.p., operation officer, dir. Mukogawa Ft. Wright Inst.; exec. in residence Whitworth Coll. Grad. Sch., 1999; hon. prof. edn. dept. Wash. State U., 2000. Pres. emeritus Spokane-Nishinomiya Sister City Soc., Sister Cities Assn. of Spokane; mem. Eastern Wash. State Hist. Soc.; bd. dirs. Spokane Regional Internat. Trade Alliance, Leadership Spokane. Recipient Disting. Svc. medal Boy Scouts of Japan, 1967, Cultural medal in Edn., Japan, 1985, Disting. Svc. award City of Nishinomiya, 1971, Disting. Svc. to Expo '74 State of Wash., 1974, Book of Golden Deeds award Exch. Club, 1978, Disting. Cmty. Svc. award UN Assn., 1979, Whitworth Coll., 1987, Svc. to Youth award Spokane YMCA, 1988, Silver Hawk medal Boy Scouts Japan, 1997, Internat. Rels. and Trade Pioneer Recognition, Spokane Area C. of C., 1998; decorated Order of Sacred Treasure medal Govt. of Japan, 1984. Mem. Japanese Am. Citizens League, Japan Am. Soc. Wash. State (pres.'s award 1991), Kiwanis (Spokane). Methodist. Home: 4116 S Madelia St Spokane WA 99203-4229 E-mail: etsutakawa@mfwi.spokanecc-wa.us., edtsu@ipeg.com., etsutakawa@mfwi.org.

TSYBAKOV, BORIS SOLOMON, information theory and communication networks researcher, educator; b. Moscow, May 14, 1934; s. Solomon Mark and Evdokia Tikhon (Tsybakova) Pinsker; m. Lidia Sergey Tsybakova, Oct. 14, 1956; 1 child, Alexander. D of Sci. in Engring., Moscow Inst. of Physics/Tech. Jr. rschr. Inst. for Radio and Electronic Engring., Moscow, 1958-63, sr. rschr., 1963-77; head of lab. Inst. for Info. Transmission Problems, 1977-2000; prin. engr. Qualcomm, Inc., San Diego, 1999—. Prof. Moscow Inst. of Physics and Tech., 1965-93. Mem. editl. bd. Problems of Info. Transmission Jour., 1965—; editor Wireless Personal Comms., An Internat. Jour., 1992—, Jour. Comms. and Networks, 1999—; contbr. articles to profl. publs. Recipient Prominent Comm. Profl. of Russia award Pres. of Russia, 1996, Paper award INFOCOM'95, 1995. Mem. IEEE (Info. Theory Soc. paper award 1981), Russian Acad. Sci. Club. Avocation: lawn tennis. Office: Qualcomm Inc 5775 Morehouse Dr Rm L5Z3H San Diego CA 92121-1714 E-mail: borist@qualcomm.com.

TSYGANOV, EDWARD N. physicist, educator; b. Moscow, Sept. 12, 1933; came to the U.S., 1992; s. Nicolai I. and Elizaveta I. Tsyganova; m. Nina A. Filatova, Feb. 19, 1956; children: Elena, Elizaveta. MS, Moscow State U., 1955; PHD, Joint Inst. for Nuc. Rsch., Dubna, Russia, 1962, DSc, 1975; prof. physics, High Attest Com. of the USSR, Moscow, 1982. Jr. rsch. scientist, dep. dir. Joint Inst. for Nuc. Rsch., Dubna, 1956-92; guest scientist Superconducting Super Collider Lab., Waxahachie, Tex., 1992-95; asst. prof. U. Tex. Southwestern Med. Ctr., Dallas, 1995—. Guest scientist Fermi Nat. Accelerator Lab., Batavia, Ill., 1975-77; sci. coun. Joint Inst. for Nuc. Rsch., 1982-92. Contbr. articles to profl. jours. Recipient Highest Russia award in basic scis. Pres. Russia Fedn., Moscow, 1996. Mem. IEEE, Am. Phys. Soc. Office: U Tex SW Med Ctr 5323 Harry Hines Blvd Dallas TX 75390-9071 E-mail: Edward.Tsyganov@utsouthwestern.edu.

TSZTOO, DAVID FONG, civil engineer; b. Hollister, Calif., Oct. 13, 1952; s. John and Jean (Woo) T.; m. Evelyn Yang, July 31, 1982; children: Michaela Gabrielle, Shawn Michael. BS, Calif. Poly. State U., 1974; MS in Engring., U. Calif., 1976. Registered profl. civil engr., Calif. Engr., dispatcher Conlec Corp., Hollister, Calif., 1972-73; rsch. asst. U. Calif. Engring. Dept., Berkeley, 1975-76; jr. civil engr. Contra Costa County Pub. Works, Martinez, Calif., 1977-78, asst. civil engr., 1978-81, civil engr. III, 1981-83; assoc. civil engr. East Bay Mucpl. Util. Dist., Oakland, 1983-88; sr. civil engr. East Bay Mucpl. Util. Distbr., 1988—. Chpt. chmn. We. Coun. Engrs., Martinez, Calif., 1977-82; mem. Nat. Soc. Profl. Engrs., Martinez, Calif., 1977-82. Co-author: Energy Absorbing Devices in Structures, 1977, EQ Testing of Stepping Frame with Devices, 1977, Development of Energy-Absorbing Devices, 1978. Sponsor Sing & Bring Children's Club, Oakland, San Lorenzo, Calif., 1982-90; v.p. Sun Country Homeowners, Martinez, Calif., 1977-82. Recipient Presdl. Design Achievement award Nat. Endowment for the Arts, Washington, 1984, Mgmt. Achievement award, 1999. Mem. Am. Soc. Civil Engrs., Tau Beta Pi, Phi Kappa Phi. Republican. Baptist. Achievements include patent for application work, Conlec Corp., Hollister, Calif., 1973. Office: E Bay Mcpl Util Dist 375 11th St Oakland CA 94607-4246 E-mail: dtsztoo@ebmud.com.

TU, CHING-I, humanities educator, researcher; b. Nanking, China, May 13, 1935; s. Show-mei and I-fang Tu; m. Sabrina S. Wang, June 14, 1970; children: Stephen Shih-chung, Sylvia Shih-yun. PhD, U. Wash., Seattle, 1967; BA, Nat. Taiwan U., 1958. Prof., chair Rutgers U., New Brunswick, NJ, 1975—, asst. and assoc. prof., 1966—75. Chair, adv. bd. Asian Studies Rutgers U., New Brunswick, NJ, 1998—; vis. prof. Nat. Taiwan U., Taipei, 1974—75; vis. assoc. prof. U. Hawaii, Honolulu, 1971—72. Author: Poetic Remarks in the Human World, 1970, Readings in Chinese Classical Literature, 1981; editor: Tradition and Creativity: Essays on East Asian Civilizations, 1986, Classics and Interpretations: The Hermeneutic Traditions in Chinese Culture, 2000, Anthology of Chinese Literature, 1972. Grantee Grant for Developing Chinese Studies at Rutgers U., Chiang Ching-kuo Found. for Internat. Scholarly Exch., 1993-1996, Grant for Developing Korean Studies at Rutgers U., The Korea Found., 1995-1998, Grant for Developing Japanese Studies at Rutgers U., The Japan Found., 1992-1995, Grant for Developing Korean Studies at Rutgers U., The Korea Found., 2001-2004. Mem.: Assn. Asian Studies, Am. Assn. for Chinese Studies, Assn. for Fgn. Lang. Dept. Chairs. Avocations: travel, reading, exercise. Office: Asian Studies Rutgers University College Ave New Brunswick NJ 08903

TU, SUSAN, b. Taipei, Taiwan, June 10, 1923; arrived in U.S., 1961, naturalized, 1976; d. Tsungming Tu and Sonsui Lin; children: Helene Lin, Andy Lin, Jean Lin, Charlyn Lin. Student, Surugadai Girl's Jr. Coll., Tokyo, 1942, Taihoku Imperial U., Taiwan, 1944, U. Calif., Berkeley, 1961; BA, Utah State U., 1965; MA, U. Utah, 1971; MSLS, La. State U., 1973, cert. of med. librarianship, 1975, MEd, 1977, postgrad., 1976-77. Tchr. Taipei (Taiwan) Mcpl. Girls' High Sch., 1958-61; chief libr. Saints Coll., Lexington, Miss., 1974-76; hosp. libr. U.S. Army, Ft. Polk, La., 1977-79; dist. libr. Rock Island (Ill.) dist. U.S. Army Corps Engrs., 1979-83, div. libr. North Atlantic div., 1984-88; dist. libr. N.Y. Dist., 1988-90. Co-producer various videos, slide prodns., TV program. Mem. adv. bd. The Formosa Chamber Music Soc., Inc. Mem. Spl. Librs. Assn., Chinese-Am. Librs. Assn., Photographic Soc. Am. Avocations: photography, travel, beauty appreciation, literature, music.

TU, WEI-MING, historian, philosopher, writer; b. Kunming, Yunnan, China, Feb. 26, 1940; came to U.S., 1962, naturalized, 1976; s. Shou-tsin (Wellington) and Shu-li (Sonia Ou-yang) T.; m. Helen I-yu Hsiao, Aug. 24, 1963 (div.); 1 son, Eugene L.; m. Rosanne V. Hall, Mar. 17, 1982; children: A. Yalun, Mariana Mei-ling B., Rosa Wen-yun. BA, Tunghai U., 1961; MA, Harvard U., 1963, PhD, 1968. Vis lectr. humanities Tunghai (Taiwan) U., 1966-67; vis. lectr. East Asian studies Princeton U., 1967-68, asst. prof., 1968-71; asst. prof. history U. Calif., Berkeley, 1971-73, assoc. prof., 1973-77, prof., from 1977; vis. prof. Chinese history and philosophy Harvard U., 1981-82, prof. Chinese history and philosophy, 1982—, chmn. com. on study of religion, 1984-87, chmn. dept. East Asian langs. and civilizations, 1991-92, coord. Dialogue of Civilizations, 1990-93. Dir. Inst. Culture and Communication, East-West Ctr., Honolulu, 1990-91; vis. prof. dept. philosophy Peking U., 1985; disting. vis. prof. depts. philosophy and history Taiwan U., 1988; 10th Ch'ien Mu lectr. New Asia Coll., The Chinese U. of Hong Kong, 1989; 1st Henry Chai lectr. Hong Kong U., 1989; vis. prof. Ecole Pratique des Hautes Etudes, U. Paris, 1991; bd. dirs. Inst. Advanced Rsch. in Asian Sci. and Medicine, 1993—; trustee Adironack Work-Study Project, Inc., 1990—; chmn. adv. bd. Inst. Literature and Philosophy, Academia Sinica, 1993—; gov. Inst. East Asian Philosophies, Singapore, 1983-93; pres. Contemporary Mag., Taiwan, 1986-96; acad. adviser Chinese Culture Acad., Beijing; vice-chmn. Internat. Confician Assn., Beijing, 1994, Annual Freeman Lectr. Wesleyan U., 1982; assembly speaker Grinnell Coll., 1983; commencement speaker Grad. Theol. Union at Berkeley, 1990; keynote speaker alumni conf. East-West Ctr., Bangkok, 1990; GET lectr. Bal State U., 1991; panelist 1st World Chinese Enterprises Conv., Singapore, 1991; Paul Desjardins Meml. lectr. Haverford Coll., 1992; baccalaureate speaker Swarthmore Coll., 1993; co-moderator seminar, the Chineses in the Global Community, Aspen Inst., 1994—; nat. lectr. Indian Coun. Philosophy, 1995; guest prof. Wuhan U., Peking U., 1996—, Nanjing U., 1997—, Shandong U., 1998—; Foester lectr. U. Calif. Berkeley, 1996; Green lectr. U. B.C., 1997; Burke lectr. U. Calif. San Diego, 1997; dir. Harvard Yenchnig Inst., 1996—; plenary panelist XXth World Congress Philosophy, Boston, 1998. Author: Neo-Confucian Thought in Action— Wang Yang-ming's Youth, 1976, Centrality and Commonality— An Essay on Chung-Yung, 1976, Humanity and Self-Cultivation— Essays in Confucian Thought, 1980, Confucian Ethics Today: The Singapore Challenge, 1984, Confucian Thought: Selfhood as Creative Transformation, 1985, The Way, Learning, and Politics: Perspective on the Confucian Intellectual, 1988, Toward the "Third Epoch" of Confucian Humanism: Problems and Prospects (in Chinese), 1989, A Reflection on Confucian Self-Consciousness (in Chinese), 1990, The Modern Spirit and the Confucian Tradition (in Chinese), 1993; editor: The Triadic Tension: Confucian Ethics, Max Weber and Industrial East Asia, 1991, The Confucian World Observed, 1992, The Living Tree: Changing Meaning of Being Chinese, 1993, China in Transformation, 1994, Confucian Traditions in East Asian Modernity, 1996; co-editor: Confucianism and Human Rights, 1998; mem. editl. bd. Asian Thought and Soc., 1976—, Harvard Jour. Asiatic Studies, 1983, Philosophy East and West, 1984—, The Twenty-First Century (Chinese); contbr. articles Philosophy East and West, Jour. Asian Studies, Daedalus, The Monist, Chinese lang. jours. and newspapers. Am. Council Learned Socs. fellow, 1968-69; research grantee Center East Asian Studies, Harvard U., 1968-69; research grantee Humanities Council Princeton U., 1970-71; research grantee U. Calif., 1973-74; sr. scholar Com. on Scholarly Communication with People's Republic of China Nat. Acad. Scis., 1980-81; Fulbright-Hays research scholar Peking U., 1985; interviewed by Bill Moyer in World of Ideas, 1991. Fellow Am. Acad. Arts and Scis. (exec com. fundamentalism project 1988-96), Soc. for Study of Value in Higher Edn.; mem. Am. Soc. for the Study Religion, Assn. Asian Studies (dir. 1971-75), Am. Hist. Assn., Soc. Asian and Comparative Philosophy, Am. Acad. Religion, AAAS, Asia Soc. N.Y. Office: Harvard U Dept East Asian Langs and Civilizations Cambridge MA 02138 *As an all-embracing humanist tradition, Confucianism seeks to find integrated and holistic solutions to socio-political problems. One of its core ideas is self-cultivation, signifying that the way to universal peace takes personal knowledge as the point of departure. Learning to be human, in the Confucian perspective, entails an unceasing spiritual transformation. This quest for self-realization involves an* *ever-expanding circle of human-relatedness. It is not simply a search for one's own inner spirituality but a concern for the establishment of a fiduciary community for humankind as a whole.*

TUAN, CHRISTOPHER YOUNG-BEE, structural engineer, researcher; b. Taipei, Taiwan, Republic of China, Apr. 15, 1954; came to U.S., 1977; s. Chang-Yi and Hsiao-I (Chang) T.; m. Deborah Lynn Tollander, Nov. 25, 1989; children: Christopher Brandon, Sean Robert, Benjamin Alexander. BS, Nat. Taiwan U., Taipei City, 1977; MS, U. Wis., 1979, PhD, 1983. Registered profl. engr., Nebr., Tex. Assoc. prof. U. Nebr., Lincoln, 1983-89; sr. engr. Wilfred Baker Engring., Inc., San Antonio, 1989-91, Applied Rsch. Assocs., Inc., Panama City, Fla., 1991-96; assoc. prof. U. Nebr., Lincoln, 1996—. Mem. solar dish rev. panel Sandia Nat. Lab., Albuquerque, 1987; cons. TELTECH, Inc., Mpls., 1990—. Contbr. articles to profl. jours. Mem. ASCE (mem. loading guide group 1985-88), Soc. Am. Mil. Engrs., Prestressed Concrete Inst. (seismic com. 1988), Sigma Xi, Chi Epsilon, Phi Kappa Phi. Achievements include designing of a passive airblast attenuator under sponsorship of U.S. Army Corps of Engineers. Avocations: basketball, volleyball, table tennis, camping. Home: 3314 N 152d Ave Omaha NE 68116-7198

TUAN, DEBBIE FU-TAI, chemistry educator; b. Kiangsu, China, Feb. 2, 1930; came to U.S., 1958; d. Shiau-gien and Chen (Lee) T.; m. John W. Reed, Aug. 15, 1987. BS in Chemistry, Nat. Taiwan U., Taipei, 1954, MS in Chemistry, 1958, Yale U., 1960, PhD in Chemistry, 1961. Rsch. fellow Yale U., New Haven, 1961-64; rsch. assoc. U. Wis., Madison, 1964-65; asst. prof. Kent (Ohio) State U., 1965-70, assoc. prof., 1970-73, prof., 1973—; vis. scientist Yeshiva U., N.Y.C., summer 1966; rsch. fellow Harvard U., Cambridge, 1969-70; vis. scientist SRI Internat., Menlo Park, Calif., 1981; rsch. assoc. Cornell U., Ithica, N.Y., 1983. Vis. prof. Acad. Sinica of China, Nat. Taiwan U. and Nat. Tsing-Hwa U., summer 1967, Ohio State U., 1993, 95. Contbr. articles to profl. jours. Recipient NSF Career Advanced award, 1994—; U. Grad. fellow Nat. Taiwan U., 1955-58, F.W. Heyl-Anon F fellow Yale U., 1960-61, U. Faculty Rsch. fellow Kent State U., 1966, 68, 71, 85; Pres. Chiang's scholar Chinese Women Assn., 1954, 58, Grad. scholar in humanity and scis. China Found., 1955. Mem. Am. Chem. Soc., Am. Phys. Soc., Sigma Xi. Office: Kent State U Chemistry Dept Williams Hl Kent OH 44242-0001

TUBB, JAMES CLARENCE, lawyer; b. Corsicana, Tex. s. Cullen Louis and Sarah Elmore (Chapman) T.; m. Suzanne Alice Smith, Nov. 22, 1954; children: James Richard, Sara Elizabeth, Daniel Chapman. BA, So. Meth. U., 1951, JD, 1954. Bar: Tex. 1954, U.S. Dist. Ct. (no. dist.) Tex. 1955, U.S. Ct. Appeals (5th cir.) 1959, U.S. Supreme Ct. 1978; cert. comml. real estate specialist, 1983; lic. Tex. real estate broker; cert. mediator Dallas Bar Assn. With legal dept. Schlumberger Well Surveying Corp., Houston, 1954-55; claims atty. Franklin Am. Ins. Co., Dallas, 1957-58; ptnr. Vial, Hamilton, Koch, Tubb & Knox and predecessor firm Akin, Vial, Hamilton, Koch & Tubb, 1958-84; dir., ptnr. Winstead, McGuire, Sechrest & Minick, 1984-90; pvt. practice, 1990—. Guest lectr. on real estate broker liability Real Estate Ctr., Tex. A&M U., 1987. Mem. bd. deacons Highland Park Presbyn. Ch., Dallas, 1972—78, ruling elder, 1978—84, 1988—91; mem. permanent jud. commn. Grace Presbytery, 1984—90; bd. dirs. Christian Concern Found., 1965—71, Dallas County affiliate Am. Diabetes Assn., 1991—95. With Tex. Air N.G., 1949—51, 1st lt. JAGC, SAC USAF, 1955—57, 1st lt. USAF, ret. Recipient Outstanding Student award Student Bar Assn., 1954. Fellow Tex. Bar Found.; mem. ABA (chmn. comml. law com. gen. practice sect. 1982-84, real estate probate and trust law sect.), Tex. Bus. Law Found., Tex. Bar Assn., Am. Arbitration Assn. (comml. arbitration panelist), Dallas Country Club, Dallas County Rep. Men's Club (sec. 1978-79). Home and Office: 3407 Haynie Ave Dallas TX 75205-1842

TUBBS, CHARLES ALLAN, protective services official; b. Beloit, Wis., Oct. 21, 1953; s. Charlie C. and Effie M. (Porter) T.; m. Cynthia L. Olstead, May 1, 1982; children: Chelsey, Charles Jr., Collin, Casey. Student, U. Wis., Rock County, 1972-74, U. Wis., Madison, 1995—, U. Wis., Oshkosh, 1987, Blackhawk Tech. Coll., 1974, U. Wis., Oshkosh, 1987; grad. Sch. Police Staff and Command, Northwestern U., 1995; BS in Criminal Justice Adminstrn., Mt. Senario Coll., 1997; grad. Sr. Police Exec. Inst., U. Wis., Madison, 1995. Jr. police officer Beloit Police Dept., 1968-69, patrol officer, recruiting officer, 1974-79, police sch. liaison officer, 1979-80, sgt. patrol, 1980-83, lt., capt., adminstrv. patrol, 1983-87, capt. records dept., 1987-89, capt. profl. stds. and tng., 1990-91, capt. people and pub. issues, 1995-98, cape. patrol east side, 1996—, dep. chief of police, 1998—. Reviewing editor Nat. Gangs Crime Rsch. Ctr., Chgo.; apptd. vice chmn. Wis. Tng. and Stds. Bd., Madison; mem. adv. bd. Wis. Coun. Commn. on Sch. Violence, Madison, Wis. Coun. on Juvenile Justice, Madison; spkr., presenter in field. Commr. Midnight Basketball, 1990-96; former mem. Beloit Pub. Sch. Dist. Bd. Edn., 1991-92; apptd. to Atty. Gen. Law Enforcement Adv. Coun. on Juvenile Justice, State of Wis. Gov.'s Task Force on Correction; vol. coach youth sports. Named Most Popular Police Officer and Pub. Official, Most Respected and Influential Beloiter Beloit Daily News 1991 Reader's Choice, Top Cop Honorable Mention, Nat. Assn. Police Orgn., 1994, Disting. Officer of Yr., Nat. United Law Enforcement Officers Assn. Inc, 1993, Top Black in Law Enforcement-Disting. Officer of Yr. in the USA, Nat. United Law Enforcement Officer Assn. Inc.; named to Top 100 Police Ofcls. Hero Wis., Pres. Bill Clinton, 1994; recipient Spl. Congl. Recognition award, 104th Congress, 1994, Law Enforcement Commendation medal, Nat. Soc. SAR, 1994, Ofcl. of Yr. award, Wis. Fraternal Order of Eagles, 1994, Caleb Blodgett award for outstanding svc. for youth and adults, 1995, Disting. Svc. award, Brother Dutton Parochial Sch., 1996, Cmty. Builders award, Neighborhood Housing Svcs. Beloit/Merrill Revitalization Com., 1997, Leadership Appreciation Cert., Louis Porter Club, 1998, Thrasher award, at. Gang Crime Rsch. Ctr., 1998, Capt. Charles Tubbs Day named in his honor, Cunningham elem. Sch., 1994, four awards from, Gov. Thompson of Wisconsin. Mem. NAACP (Outstanding Leadership award 1993), Nat. Orgn. Black Law Enforcement Execs. (vice chmn. Wis. chpt.), Nat. Assn. Sch. Safety and Law Enforcement Officers (Pres.'s Plaque 1998), Internat. Chiefs of Police Assn., Wis. Profl. Police Assn. (Cert. of Merit for proper technique in the interest of police svcs. 1996), Wis. Law Enforcement Officer Assn., Wis. Women of Police Assn., Internat. Assn. Women Police, Wis. Assn. for Chiefs of Police, Nat. Orgn. Black Law Enforcement Execs., Optimists. Baptist. Avocations: faith, family, working with youth, sports. Home: 2690 Chatsworth Dr Beloit WI 53511-2306 Office: Beloit Police Dept 100 State St Beloit WI 53511-6234

TUBBS, DAVID EUGENE, mechanical engineer, marketing professional; b. Springfield, Ill., Jan. 12, 1948; s. Eugene Lewellyn and Jacqueline Flo (Jones) T.; m. Linda Alyson Smith, Aug. 2, 1970; children: Corbin David, Cavan Scott. BSME, Ill. Inst. Tech., 1970; postgrad., Okla. State U., 1992. Registered profl. engr., Ill., Okla. Project engr. Sargent & Lundy, Chgo., 1970-82, bus. devel. mgr., 1982-83; mgr. power sales Yuba Heat Transfer Corp., Tulsa, 1983-85; with press products mktg. Nordam, 1985-86; dir. mktg. Brooks Aero. Svc. div. Nordam, 1986-91; mech. dept. mgr. The Benham Group, 1991-93; chief mech. engr. EDECO Engrs./Cons., 1993-94; mktg. support mgr. AGC Tech. Svcs. Inc., 1994-97; lead piping engr. Black & Veatch Pritchard, Overland Park, Kans., 1998—. Mem. ASME, Am. Welding Soc., Ill. Inst. Tech. Alumni Assn. (bd. dirs. 1977-80), Delta Tau Delta, Pi Tau Sigma. Clubs: Toastmasters. Republican. Avocations: bridge, racquetball, USSF soccer referee. Home: 9801 W 118th St Apt 10 Overland Park KS 66210-3167 Office: Black & Veatch Pritchard inc 10905 Grandview St Overland Park KS 66210-1504

TUBBS, EDWARD LANE, banker; b. Delmar, Iowa, Apr. 17, 1920; s. Clifton Marvin and Mary Ellen (Lane) T.; m. Grace Barbara Dyer, Nov. 27, 1941; children: Steven, Alan, William. BS, Iowa State U., 1941; postgrad., U. Wis. Grad. Sch. Banking. With Iowa State U. Agrl. Ext. Svc., Newton, 1942; instr. vets. on-farm DeWitt (Iowa) Schs., 1957-58; v.p., dir. Jackson State Bank, Maquoketa State Bank, 1959-66. Pres., dir. Onward Bancshares, Inc.; chmn., dir. 1st Ctrl. State Bank, DeWitt; dir. Tri-County Bank & Trust; pres., dir. Mabsco Agrl. Svcs., Inc., 1982-87; supt. banking State of Iowa, 1987-89; bd. dirs. Iowa Bus. Growth Corp.; lectr. banking schs.; exeh. del. USSR, 1959, 85; banking indsutry del. Baltic Countries, 1993; state dir. Conf. State Bank Supts., 1988-89. Contbr. articles in field. Pres. Elwood (Iowa) Sch. Bd., 1956-62; treas. City of Maquoketa, 1975-81; mem. People to People; trustee Sharar Found., Clinton Coll., 1983-86; v.p., bd. dirs. Timber City Indsl. Devel. Corp.; treas. Maquoketa Cmty. Svcs., 1967-80; trustee Iowa 4-H Found., 1987-91, Hoover Presdl. Libr. Assn. Inc., truatee, 1987—; gov. Iowa State U. Found., 1989—; trustee CCFA Found., 1990-94; elder, moderator United Ch. of Christ. With AUS, 1942-43. Recipient 4-H Club Alumni award, 1962, 2001, Century Farm award Iowa Dept. Agr., 1976, Disting. Pub. Svcs. award Jackson County, 1990, Gold Clover award Iowa 4-H Club, Heart of Gold award, 1996, Iowa Agrl. Ext. Assn. award, 1982, Floyd Andre award, 1985, Cmty. Svc. award Mt. St. Clare Coll., 2002; named Jaycee Boss of Yr., 1970; named to Iowa Agrl. Hall of Fame, 1985, Clinton Fair Hall of Fame, 1999. Mem. Bank Adminstrn. Inst., Am. Bankers Assn. (dir., coun. 1984-86, Ag Banker award 2000, award for lifetime contbn. to agrl. banking 2000, Leach award 2002), Iowa Bankers Assn. (treas. 1978-79, pres. 1980-81), Am. Legion, Isaac Walton League, Iowa State U. Alumni Assn. (dir. 1980-86), Maquoketa C. of C. (dir. 1966-69), Order of Knoll (founders club Iowa State U.), Iowa Friends of Agr. (exec. com. 1987—), Rotary (Paul Harris fellow), Gamma Sigma Delta (Alumni Achievement award 1989), Alpha Zeta. Home: 1605 Blair Ct Maquoketa IA 52060-3301 Office: 203 N Main St Maquoketa IA 52060-2204 E-mail: edtubbs@caves.net.

TUBBS, JOAN ROSE, accountant; b. Brownwood, Tex., May 25, 1943; d. Carl Russell and Alva Mae (Rose) Stanley; m. Thomas Milton Cole, June 1, 1963 (div. Feb. 1965); 1 child, Stanley Milton; m. James Arthur Tubbs, Mar. 22, 1979. Student, Howard Payne U., 1974-82, BBA cum laude, 1992; student, U. Tex. Permian Basin, Odessa, 1985-92. CPA. Sec., bookkeeper J.W. Fisher, P.A., Brownwood, 1962-68; cashier, bookkeeper Weakley-Watson Hardware, 1968-76; acct.'s asst. Leanco Corp., 1976-81; accounts payable clk. FMC Corp., 1981-82; chief acct. asst. Williamson Petroleum, Midland, Tex., 1982-84; full-charge bookkeeper Baytech, Inc., 1984-86; staff acct. EnClean, Inc., Odessa, 1986-93; controller Permian Petroleum Corp., Midland, Tex., 1994-96; v.p. fin., dir. fin. Planned Parenthood of West Tex., Inc., 1996—. Scholar Petroleum Accts. Soc., 1990. Mem. U. Tex. Permian Basin Acctg. ASsn., Am. Bus. Women's Assn. (pres. 1982, Bluebonnet award 1981). Avocations: reading, movies. Home: 6747 N Dixie Blvd Odessa TX 79762-2928 Office: Planned Parenthood of West Tex Inc VP Fin 910 S Grant Ave Ste B Odessa TX 79761-6316

TUBBS, ROBIN LEE, secondary education educator; BA, No. Ky. U., 1993; MEd, Xavier U., 1999. Cert. secondary tchr., Ohio. Tchr. English Norwood (Ohio) H.S., 1993—. Mem. Nat. Tchrs. English (chair English dept.). Republican. Baptist. Avocations: reading, writing, sports, camping, hiking. Office: Norwood High Sch 2020 Sherman Ave Norwood OH 45212-2616

TUBBS, WILLIAM REID, JR. public service administrator; b. Johnson Air Base, Japan, June 1, 1950; s. William Reid and Roberta Daisy (Krenkel) T.; 1 child, Catlin Alyse. BA, Calif. State U., Sacramento, 1973, MPA, 1981. Assoc. analyst adminstrn. and fin. agy. County of Sacramento, 1975-84, program coordinator emergency ops., 1984-85; adminstrv. dir. Sacramento County Mental Health Treatment Ctr., 1985—. Editor: Dept. of Calif. ROA Sentinel. Chmn. Cable TV Adv. Commn., West Sacramento, Calif., 1987-90; mem. City of Sacramento Pipe Band. Lt. comdr. USCGR; sgt. U.S. Army Res. Mem. NRA, Res. Officers Assn., U.S. Naval Inst., Am. Radio Relay League, Scottish-Am. Mil. Soc., St. Andrews Soc. Republican. Avocations: amateur radio, motorcycle touring, history. Office: Sacramento Co Mental Health 2150 Stockton Blvd Sacramento CA 95817-1337

TUBESING, RICHARD LEE, library director; b. Kansas City, Mo., Nov. 25, 1937; s. Clarence and Letha (Thacker) T. BA, Yale U., 1959; MA, U. Chgo., 1969; MSL, Western Mich. U., 1972. Asst. to dir. U. Louisville, 1972-73; reference libr. Ga. Tech. Libr., Atlanta, 1973-76; head bus. and sci. Atlanta Pub. Libr., 1976-79; libr. dir. Lewis U., Romeoville, Ill., 1979-81; collection devel. coord. U. Toledo Libr., 1981-86; libr. dir. Coll. of the Southwest, Hobbs, N.Mex., 1986-89; libr. dir., dir. libr. sci. program Glenville (W.Va.) State Coll., 1989-99; retired, 1999. Author: Architectural Preservation, 1978, Architectural Preservation and Urban Renovation, 1982. Program coord. Lea County Archaeol. Soc., Hobbs, 1987-89. Lt. j.g. USNR, 1960-63. Mem. W.Va. Libr. Assn., Lea County Libr. Assn. (v.p. 1987-88, pres. 1988-89). Avocation: collecting primitive and peasant art. Home: 143 E Valley Dr Glenville WV 26351-9416 Fax: 304-462-5671. E-mail: ricktubesing@lycos.com.

TUBMAN, WILLIAM CHARLES, lawyer; b. N.Y.C., Mar. 16, 1932; s. William Thomas and Ellen Veronica (Griffin) T.; m. Dorothy Rita Krug, Aug. 15, 1964; children: William Charles Jr., Thomas Davison, Matthew Griffin. BS, Fordham U., 1953, JD, 1960; postdoctoral, NYU Sch. Law, 1960-61. Bar: N.Y. 1960, U.S. Ct. Appeals (2d cir.) 1966, U.S. Supreme Ct. 1967, U.S. Ct. Customs and Patent Appeals 1971. Auditor Peat, Marwick Mitchell & Co., N.Y.C., 1956-60; sr. counsel Kennecott Corp., 1960-82, Phelps Dodge Corp., N.Y.C., 1982-85, sec., 1985-95, v.p., 1987-95; pres. Phelps Dodge Found., Phoenix, 1988-95. Author: Legal Status of Minerals Beyond the Continental Shelf, 1966. Mem. scholarship adv. coun. U. Ariz., 1990-92; active Big Bros., Inc., N.Y.C., 1963-73; trustee Phoenix Art Mus., 1989-94; bd. dirs. St. Joseph Hosp. Found., 1994—, chmn., 1994-95; bd. dirs. The Phoenix Symphony, 1994-95. Recipient Disting. Svc. cert. Big Brothers Inc., 1968. Mem.: ABA, N.Y. State Bar Assn. Democrat. Roman Catholic. E-mail: DOT2DOT1@att.net.

TUCCERI, CLIVE KNOWLES, science writer and educator, consultant; b. Bryn Mawr, Pa., Apr. 20, 1953; d. William Henry and Clive Ellis (Knowles) Hulick; m. Eugene Angelo Tucceri, Sept. 1, 1984 (div. Nov. 1991); 1 child, Clive Edna. BA in Geology, Williams Coll., 1975; MS in Coastal Geology, Boston Coll., 1982. Head sci. dept. Stuart Hall Sch., Staunton, Va., 1975-77; mem. sci. faculty William Penn Charter Sch., Phila., 1977-79, Tower Sch., Marblehead, Mass., 1982-86, Bentley Coll., Waltham, 1986-88; adminstrv. dir., co-founder Stout Aquatic Libr. Nat. Marine and Aquatic Edn. Resource Ctr., Wakefield, R.I., 1982-89; mem. sci. faculty Mabelle B. Avery Sch., Somers, Conn., 1989-90; mem. faculty, head sci. dept. MacDuffie Sch., Springfield, Mass., 1992-93; mem. sci. faculty East Hampton (Conn.) Middle Sch., 1993—, sci. team leader, 1994-95, sci. chairperson grades K-12, 1995—, 8th grade advisor, 2000—01. Cons. Longmeadow (Mass.) Pub. Schs., 1989-94, Addison-Wesley Pub. Co., Menlo Prk, Calif., 1986-94; cons., freelance writer Prentice-Hall Inc., Needham, Mass., 1991. Co-head class agt. Williams Coll. Alumni Fund, 2000—; admissions rep. Williams Coll., 2001—; mem. search com. Christ Ch., Middle Haddam, Conn., 2000—01, mem. vestry, 2002—; bd. dirs. People Against Rape, Staunton, 1976—77. Mem. NSTA, NEA, AAUW (bd. dirs., br. pres.-elect 1975-77, v.p. 1985-86, sec. 1986-87), Nat. Marine Edn. Assn. (sec. 1986-87, chpt. rep. 1987-89), Nat. Mid. Level Sci. Tchrs. Assn., Southeastern New Eng. Marine Educators (publs. chair Nat. Conf. com.), Mass. Marine Educators (pres. 1987-89, bd. dirs. 1983-91, editor Flotsam and Jetsam MA Marine Educators newsletter 1991-97), Mass. Environ. Edn. Soc. (bd. dirs. 1985-88), Conn. Sci. Suprs. Assn., Conn. Sci. Tchrs. Assn., Nat. Middle Level Sci. Tchrs. Assn., Conn. Edn. Assn., Cousteau Soc., Sigma Xi. Episcopalian. Avocations: renovating old homes, sailing, gardening, reading. Home: 12 Birchwood Dr East Hampton CT 06424-1312

TUCCERI, ELLEN LEE, retail executive; b. Boston, Feb. 7, 1945; d. Martin and Natalie (Green) Weiner; m. Anthony Tucceri, June 17, 1988 (dec. Mar. 1993). Student, Boston U. Sch. Edn., 1967-68; BS in Bus. Edn., U. Mich., 1969; postgrad. in edn., NYU, 1973-74; MBA in Mktg., Fordham U., 1983. Circulation mgr. McGraw Hill Publs. Co., N.Y.C., 1973-76; mgr. distbn. rsch. McGraw Hill Info. Sys. Co., 1976-80, distbn. mgr., 1980-85, mgr. market adminstrn., 1985-87, dir. mkt. adminstrn., 1987-88; owner, operator The Golden Pearl, Ogunquit, Maine, 1989-2001. Cons. Arts and Bus. Coun., N.Y.C., 1979-80, 84-88; mem. adv. bd. York County Tech. Coll., 1996-2001; bd. dirs. Fairmont Tenants Corp., 1986-88; bd. dirs. Vis. Nurse Assn. So. Maine and Seacoast N.H., 1997—, treas., 1999-2000, v.p., 2000—; bd. dirs. Dunelawn Condominium Assn., 1990-97, pres., 1994-97; mem. bd. selectman Town of Ogunquit, 1990-97, chmn. bd. selectman, 1991; chmn. budget com. Town of Ogunquit, 1989; alternate mem. Appeals Bd. Town of York, 1998-2000, mem. Appeals Bd. Town of York, 2000-01. Mem. Ogunquit Women's Club (v.p. 1991-92), Rotary (Town of York).

TUCCI, ALBERT WILLIAM, retired human resources executive, consultant; b. Canastota, N.Y., Nov. 14, 1938; s. Samuel and Anna (Penna) T.; m. Mary Katherine Moseley, Mar. 25, 1961; children: Anne Elizabeth, Katherine Lynn. BS, St. Lawrence U., 1960; MS, Western Conn. U., 1971; PhD, U. Md., 1984. Advanced profl. certificate in math., pers. adminstrn. and supervision. Math. tchr. Long Beach, Huntington Beach (Calif.) Pub. Schs., 1960-63; supr. pers. Columbia Broadcasting System, N.Y.C., 1963-65; math. tchr. Chappaqua (N.Y.) Pub. Schs., 1965-71; from pers. asst. to mgr. human resources Howard County Pub. Schs., Ellicott City, Md., 1971-96; pvt. practice human resources cons. Speaker colls. and univs., 1973—; assessor Md. Ctr. Progressive Assessments, Balt., 1974—. Author: Teacher Satisfaction, 1984, (manual) The Supervisor Interview, 1991; contbr. numerous articles to profl. publs. Mem. adv. bd. Johns Hopkins U., Balt., U. Md., College Park, 1985-96; fundraiser Am. Heart Assn., 1985, 86, United Way, 1980-83; coach, dir. Howard County Youth Program, Ellicott City, 1976-82; bd. dirs. Md. Youth Symphony Orch., 1997, St. John's Day Sch., 2000. NDEA grantee, 1969; recipient rsch. award U. Md., 1985, award of excellence Nat. Assn. Secondary Sch. Prins., 1987. Mem. SAG, Middle Atlantic Assn. Schs., Colls. and Univs. (emeritus 1996), Mensa, Phi Delta Kappa. Roman Catholic. Avocations: music, theatre, skiing, golf, writing. Home: 10124 Bell Inn Ln Ellicott City MD 21042-5651 E-mail: atucci@home.com.

TUCCI, GERALD FRANK, manufacturing company executive; b. N.Y.C., Sept. 9, 1926; s. Frank and Mary (Fattizzi) T.; m. Eva G. Gyllander, May 14, 1968; children: Francis Henrik, Michael Fredrik, Amy Christina. Student, Dartmouth Coll., 1944; BSc in Naval Sci., Brown U., 1946, BSME, 1948; MBA with distinction, Harvard U., 1950. Mfg. trainee Am. Can Co., Jersey City, 1950-51; asst. v.p., plant mgr. Artcraft Hosiery Mills, Inc., Darby, Pa., 1951-53; v.p. Leach & Garner, Co., Attleboro, Mass., 1953-63, Gen. Findings, Inc., Attleboro, 1953-63; chmn. Micro Contacts, Inc., Hicksville, 1963—, 2001; pres. Micro Pneumatic Logic, Inc., Ft. Lauderdale, Fla., 1973—. Lt. (s.g.) USNR, 1944-47. Mem. ASME, Am. Soc. Mfrs., North Hempstead Country Club, Met. Club (N.Y.), Harvard Bus. Sch. Club N.Y., Frenchman's Creek Country Club, Beta Theta Pi. Republican. Roman Catholic. Office: 62 Alpha Plz Hicksville NY 11801-2618 E-mail: gerrytucci@aol.com.

TUCCI, JANIS A(NN), health unit administrator; b. Columbus, Ohio, Nov. 20, 1947; d. John Anthony and Mildred Frances (Frazier) Tucci; m. William Allen Law, May 18, 1974 (div.); 1 child, Jennifer Erin. Diploma, Mt. Carmel Sch. Nursing, 1968; student, Ohio State U., Columbus, 1969-72, 80; MA in Health Care Adminstrn., Norwich U., 1993. RN, Ohio, Fla., Mich. Asst. clin. instr. Mt. Carmel Sch. Nursing, Columbus, 1969-70; staff educator Mt. Carmel Med. Ctr., 1974-75; head nurse orthopedics unit Ohio State U. Hosps., 1977-79; evening asst. clin. mgr. Humana Women's Hosp., Tampa, Fla., 1986-90; head nurse med. unit Centurion Hosp. Carrollwood, 1990-92, dir. epidemiology, pers. health and nursing edn., 1992-93; infection control practitioner Univ. Community Hosp.-Carrollwood, Tampa, Fla., 1993-95; dir. of nursing Correctional Med. Svcs. Hillsborough County Jails, 1995-97; health unit adminstr. Macomb County Jail, Mt. Clemens, Mich., 1997-2000; health svcs. adminstr. Duval County Jail, Jacksonville, 2000—01; mgr. ambulatory care Tampa Gen. Hosp. , 2001—.

TUCCI, JOSEPH M. computer software and services executive; b. 1947; BA, Manhattan Coll.; MBA, Columbia U. With Sperry Corp., 1970-86; pres. U.S. ops. Unisys Corp., 1986-90; exec. v.p. ops. Wang Labs., Inc., 1990-93, chmn. bd., CEO Mass., 1993—. Office: Wang Labs Inc 600 Technology Park Dr Billerica MA 01821-4130*

TUCCI, MARK A. state agency administrator; b. Trenton, N.J., Dec. 14, 1950; s. William F. and Theresa M. (Miccio) T.; m. Carolyn J. Bilecki, July 10, 1971; children: Nicholas A., Anthony M., Vincent J. BS, Trenton State Coll., 1972, MEd, 1978; cert. pub. mgr., Rutgers U. Cert. N.J. chief sch. adminstr., prin., supr., tchr. of deaf, tchr. of handicapped, N.J.; cert. quality mgr. Am. Soc. Quality. Tchr. Katzenbach Sch. for the Deaf, West Trenton, N.J., 1972-82, spl. asst. to supt., 1982-85; exec. asst. to asst. commr. edn. N.J. Dept. Edn., Trenton, 1985-87; chief of enterprise license bur. N.J. Casino Control Commn., Atlantic City, 1987-91, dir. organizational devel., 1991-99, dir. adminstrn., 1992-93; orgn. devel. leader Dept. Environ. Protection, N.J., 1999—. Adj. faculty Human Resource Devel. Inst., Princeton, N.J., 1996-98; examiner N.J. Quality Achievement Award Program, 1993-94, 96, sr. examiner, 1994, judge, 1997-98; judge N.J. Exemplary State and Local Awards Program, 1994-96, N.J. Quality Achievement Award, 1997—; chmn. N.J. Quality Achievement Award Focus Group, 1994-96; adj. faculty, Ocean Co. Coll., 1999—. Mem. editorial bd. periodical for Trenton chpt. Phi Delta Kappa, 1986-88; columnist Total Quality Management, 1994; contbr. articles to profl. pubs. Chmn. bd. trustees AIDS Support Found., Inc., 1995; cub scout leader Trenton chpt. Boy Scouts Am., 1981-84, dist. com. Jersey Shore Coun., 1995-96; pres. Katzenbach chpt. N.J. State Employees' Assn., 1979; co-chmn. adv. coun. Mercer County Spl. Edn. Assn., 1984; mem. bus. adv. coun. Atlantic C.C., 1990-99; lead judge Gov.'s Award for Performance Excellence, 1998-2000. Leader of team that won Nat. Pub. Svc. Excellence award for state govt. and Gov.'s award for performance excellence, 2000. Mem. Am. Soc. for Quality Control (sr., cert. quality mgr.), Cert. Pub. Mgrs. Soc. N.J. (fellow trustee), Phi Delta Kappa, Kappa Delta Pi. Roman Catholic. Avocations: reading, journalism, martial arts, photography, songwriting. Home: 273 Neptune Dr Manahawkin NJ 08050-5026 Office: NJ Dept Environ Protection PO Box 420 Trenton NJ 08625-0420 E-mail: mtucci@dep.state.nj.us.

TUCCI, STEVEN MICHAEL, health facility administrator, physician, recording industry executive; b. N.Y.C., Oct. 5, 1949; s. Louis Alexander and Nina Ida (Cerone) T.; m. Mari E. Koerner, Nov., 1974; children: Alexander, Michael, Lara. BS, Manhattan Coll., 1971; MS, SUNY, Brockport, 1977; PhD, Albany Med. Coll., 1978, MD, 1981. Diplomate Am. Coll. Phys. Medicine and Rehab., Am. Coll. Pain Mgmt.; cert. Nat. Bd. Med. Examiners. Rsch. fellow Birth Defects Inst. N.Y. State Dept. Health, 1976-81; instr. anatomy Albany (N.Y) Med. Coll., 1977-78, rsch. assoc. divns. endocrinology, 1978-81, asst. prof. anatomy, 1978-79, rsch. assoc. dept. anatomy, 1979-81; commd. officer student trainee, extern Nat. Inst. Neurol. and Communicative Disorders and Stroke/NIH, 1981; from intern to resident divsn. phys. medicine and rehabilitation George Washington Univ., 1981-84; staff fellowclin. ctr. dept. phys. medicine and rehabilitation NIH, 1983-84; mem. staff dept. medicine Commonwealth Hosp., Fairfax, Va., 1983-84; mem. med. staff Doctor's Hosp., Sarastota, Fla., 1984, med. dir. phys. medicine and rehab., 1989, med. dir., 1994—; founding med. dir. The Ctr. at Manatee Springs, Bradenton, 1985-86, The Rehab. Inst. Sarasota, 1986-88; med. dir. Fawcett Meml. Hosp., Port Charlotte, 1988—; med. dir. phys. medicine and rehab. Charlotte Community Rehab. Ctr., 1988; co-founder Sports, Pain and Rehab. Medicine Assocs., Sarasota and Port Charlotte, 1992; med. dir. Manatee Meml. Hosp., Bradenton, 1993—; pres., CEO Groove Tone Records, Sarasota, 1994-96. Writer: (music) Take Me Down to the Ballgame, 1994, Spell on Me, 1994, On the Road to Nowhere, 1994; contbr. articles, papers to profl. jours. Mem. AMA, USTA, Am. Acad. Phys. Medicine and Rehab., Am. Coll. Sprots Medicine, Am. Congress Rehabilitative Medicine, Am. Soc. Pain Mgmt., Fla. Med. Assn., Fla. Soc. Phys. Medicine and Rehab., Major League Baseball Players Alumni Assn., Rep. Presdl. Task Force, Rep. Senatorial Inner Circle. Republican. Roman Catholic. Avocations: musician, tennis, fishing. Office: Sports and Rehab Medicine 7147 Curtiss Ave Sarasota FL 34231-1207

TUCHMAN, AVRAHAM, physicist, researcher; b. N.Y.C., July 1, 1935; s. Max and Rebecca (Brick) T.; m. Sylvia Crystal, Dec. 26, 1957; children: Davida, Ari, Sima, Pnina. BA, Yeshiva U., 1956; PhD, MIT, 1963. Scientist, group leader to sect. chief Avco Rsch. and Advanced Devel., Wilmington, Mass., 1963; prin. scientist, staff scientist to prin. staff scientist Avco Systems Div.; chief scientist Textron Def. Systems, 1988-93; owner, pres., CEO Added Value Innovations (AVI), Brookline, Mass., 1994—. Vis. prof. Weizmann Inst. Sci., Rehovot, Israel, 1974, 78, 82. Contbr. numerous articles to profl. jours. Founder, pres. Kehilla Day Camp of Jewish Community Ctrs., Westwood, Mass., 1975-86; chmn. Brookline (Mass.) Traffic Commn., 1975-81; pres. Mikvah Rescue Svc., Brighton, Mass., 1969-77; pres. Temple Beth Avraham, Brookline, 1969—. Recipient award for outstanding cantorial artistry Am. Soc. Forktwangers, Detroit, 1970. Fellow AIAA (sr.). Avocations: computers, gardening, homecraft, downhill skiing. Office: AVI 138 Tappan St Brookline MA 02445-5818

TUCHMAN, GARY ROBERT, television news correspondent; b. Chgo., Oct. 2, 1960; s. Ronald E. and Louise R. (Lyon) T.; m. Kathy M. Stark, Dec. 1, 1990; children: Lindsay, Daniel, Samantha. BS in Broadcast Journalism, Boston U., 1982. News anchor, reporter Sta. WBOC-TV, Salisbury, Md., 1982-85, Sta. WPEC-TV, West Palm Beach, Fla., 1985-90; nat. corr. CNN,

Atlanta, 1990—. Emmy nominee series on West Bank and Gaza Strip, 1990. Host United Cerebral Palsy TV Telethons. Recipient Emmy award and ACE award for coverage Okla. City bombing, 1995. Avocations: sports, rollerblading, public speaking, traveling. Office: 1 Cnn Ctr NW Atlanta GA 30303-2762

TUCHMAN, MAURICE SIMON, library director; b. Bklyn., Sept. 14, 1936; s. William and Rose (Luria) T.; m. Helene Lillian Bodner, Aug. 30, 1959; children: Joel Aron, Miriam Auri. BA, CUNY, 1958; MLS, Columbia U., 1959; B Hebrew Lit., Jewish Theol. Sem., N.Y.C., 1964; D of Arts in LS, Simmons Coll., 1979. Cataloger. svcs. Buffalo and Erie County, 1959-60; asst. libr. N.Y. State Maritime Coll., Ft. Schuyler, 1962-64; libr. cons. Mid-Hudson Librs., Poughkeepsie, N.Y., 1964-66; 01libr. dir. Hebrew Coll., Brookline, Mass., 1966. Book appraiser, Auburndale, Mass., 1980—; book reviewer Libr. Jour., 1970—. With U.S. Army, 1960-62. N.Y. Regents scholar, 1959. Mem. ALA, Assn. Jewish Librs., Coun. Archives and Rsch. Librs. Jewish Studies, Ch. and Synagogue Libr. Assn. (pres. 1974-75), Fenway Libr. Consortium (coord. 1980-82, treas. 1990-2001). Home: 16 Duffield Rd Auburndale MA 02466-1004 E-mail: mtuchman@lynx.dac.neu.edu. *It is our most difficult task and our greatest accomplishment to reach our potential as a thinking and ethical human being.*

TUCHMAN, NANCY CRANDALL, biology educator, aquatic ecology researcher; b. Ann Arbor, Mich., Jan. 17, 1958; d. Franz Peter and Susan Westing Helm; m. Marc Lawrence Tuchman, Aug. 23, 1987; children: Alexander Avery, Emily Somers. BS, Ctrl. Mich. U., 1980, MS in Biology, 1983; PhD in Aquatic Ecology, U. Louisville, 1988. Instr. biology Loyola U., Chgo., 1987-88, asst. prof. biology, 1988-94, assoc. prof. biology, 1994—2001, prof. biology, 2002—. Adj. prof. aquatic ecology U. Mich. Biol. Sta., Pellston, Mich., 1992—, summers; vis. scientist (grades K-5) Braeside Elem. Sch., Highland Park, Ill., 1995—; aquatic ecology awards coord. Internat. Sci. and Engring. Fair, 1997—. Author: (with others) Freshwater Benthic Ecosystems, 1996; contbr. articles to profl. publs. Mem. Nat. Abortion Rights League, Chgo., 1996—, U. Mich. Land Protection Fund, Ann Arbor, 1998—; adv. bd. Chgo. Jr. Sci. and Humanities Symposium, 1991-95 Rsch. grant NSF, 1993-95, 99—, Nat. Oceanic and Atmospheric Adminstn., 1990-96. Mem. N.Am. Diatomists (symposium organizer), Phycological Soc. of Am., Soc. of Limnology and Oceanography, N.Am. Benthological Soc. (exec. bd.), The Sierra Club. Democrat. Avocations: playing piano, dancing, canoeing, pottery, ice skating. Office: Loyola U Chgo Dept Biology 6525 N Sheridan Rd Chicago IL 60626-5344 E-mail: ntuchma@luc.edu.

TUCHMAN, PHYLLIS, critic; b. Passaic, N.J., Jan. 4, 1947; d. Jack and Evelyn (Sugarman) T. BA, Boston U., 1968; MA, NYU, 1973. Ind. critic, N.Y.C., 1968—. Adj. lectr. Hunter Coll., CUNY, N.Y.C., 1976-79; vis. prof. Williams Coll., Williamstown, Mass., 1981-83; curator Six in Bronze, Williams Coll. Mus. Art and tour, 1985, Big Little Sculpture, Williams Coll. Mus. Art and tour, 1988, Drawing Redux, San Jose Mus. Art and tour, 1992; contbr. N.Y. Newsday, 1985-94, Town & Country, 1995—, Smithsonian Mag., 1998—. Author: George Segal, 1983; contbr. articles to profl. jours. Art Critics grantee NEA, 1978-79; vis. fellow Princeton U., NEH, 1980. Mem. Internat. Assn. Art Critics (Am. sect. pres. 1986-89), Art Table (bd. dirs. 1984-87, v.p. 1986-87). Home: 340 E 80th St New York NY 10021-0927

TUCHMAN, STEVEN LESLIE, lawyer, theatre critic; b. Indpls., Sept. 3, 1946; s. Frederick and Lillian (Alper) T. BA, Ind. U., 1968, JD, 1971; cert. internat. law, City Coll. London, 1970. Bar: Ind. 1971. Advisor Den Danske Bank, Copenhagen, Denmark, 1971-73; assoc. Melvin Simon and Assoc., Inc., Indpls., 1973-81; pvt. practice, 1981-90; critic Sta. WFYI-FM, 1981-90, Sta. WTHR-TV, Indpls., 1987-95; ptnr. Lewis & Kappes, 1990-2001, pres., 2001—. Commr., Ind. Arts Commn., 2000—; adj. prof. real estate law Ind. U. Sch. Bus., 1983-84; mediator Marion County Mcpl. and Superior Ct. mediation program, 1987—. Columnist The New Ties, Indpls., 1989; contbr. articles to profl. jours. V.p. Dance Kaleidoscope, Indpls., 1980-81; pres. Festival Dance Theatre, Indpls. and N.Y.C., 1983-84; chmn. task force subcom. Indpls. Pub. Schs. Referendum, 1985; subcom. chmn. exec. com. Internat. Violin Competition Indpls., 1986-89; chmn. real estate com. community adv. coun. Jr. League Indpls., 1987-90; chmn. Indpls. Com. Fgn. Rels., 1990—; bd. dirs. Planned Parenthood Ctrl. Ind., 1987-92, v.p. 1989-91, pres. 1991-92; steering com., affiliate pres.' coun. nat. com. Planned Parenthood Fedn. Am.; mem. Jewish Community Rels., 1988-90; bd. dirs. Am. Cabaret Theater, 1999—. Mem. Ind. State Bar Assn. (ho. dels. 1986—), Indpls. Bar Assn. (com. long range plans 1987-88, Disting. award), ABA, Am. Immigration Lawyers Assn. (chmn. Ind. chpt., 1994-96, mem. bd. govs., 1994-96), Ind. Supreme Ct. Disciplinary Commn. (grievance com.), Indpls. Bar Found., Am. Theatre Critics Assn. Office: 1700 One American Sq PO Box 82053 Indianapolis IN 46282-2053

TUCHMANN, ROBERT, lawyer; b. N.Y.C., July 7, 1946; s. Frederick C. and Hildegard (Jung) T.; m. Naomi R. Walfish, June 1, 1969; children: David, Paul. AB, Oberlin Coll., 1967; JD, Harvard U., 1971. Bar: Mass. 1971, U.S. Dist. Ct. Mass. 1971. Assoc. Hale and Dorr, Boston, 1971-76, jr. ptnr., 1976-80, sr. ptnr., 1980—. Lectr. Mass. Continuing Legal Edn., 1976—. Pres. Project Bread-The Walk for Hunger, Boston, 1990—98; mem. com. Oberlin Coll., 1990; chair Ctrl. Artery Environ. Oversight Com., 1992—; mem. New Fed. Courthouse Task Force, 1993—99, Mayor's Ctrl. Artery Completion Task Force, 1998—; bd. overseers Rogerson Cmtys., 1995—; co-chair Mayor's Ctrl. Artery Completion Task Force, 2001—. Mem.: Island Alliance (trustee 1997—2000), Downtown Boston Transp. Mgmt. Assn. (chmn. 1996—), Mass. Conveyancers Assn. (com. chmn. 1984—89), Boston Bar Assn. (com. chmn. 1977—81), Abstract Club. Office: Hale and Dorr LLP 60 State St Boston MA 02109-1816 E-mail: robert.tuchmann@haledorr.com.

TUCHSCHERER, MARSHA SMITH, visual artist, university official; b. Pittsfield, Mass., Oct. 27, 1945; d. Henry Crosby and Johanna Stejskal (Kasson) Smith; m. Daniel R. Tuchscherer Jr., Aug. 29, 1979 (dec. 1998); children: Tara Joanna, Jed Crosby. BS, Skidmore Coll., 1967; MA, U. Rochester, 1969. Dir. publs. Salisbury (Conn.) Sch., 1986-88; dir. pub. rels. Simon's Rock Coll., Great Barrington, Mass., 1988-91; graphic designer U. Wis., Oshkosh, 1991-96; art dir., pub. affairs office Lawrence U., Appleton, Wis., 1996—. Mem. art faculty Peninsula Art Sch., Fish Creek, Wis., 1993—; U.S. Nat. Parks artist-in-residence Pictured Rocks Nat. Lakeshore, 2002; featured artist Edgewood Orchard Galleries, Fish Creek, 1998, 2002. Legal advocate vol. Family Violence Ctr., Green Bay, Wis., 1994-96. Visual arts resident Ragdale Found., 1995, 97; recipient Silver award for design Coun. for Advancement and Support of Edn., 1996. Mem. Wis. Painters and Sculptors, Univ. and Coll. Designer Assn. E-mail: marsha.tuchscherer@lawrence.edu.

TUCK, AMY, lieutenant governor, lawyer; b. Starkville, Miss., July 8, 1963; d. Grady William and Mary (Boykin) Tuck. BA in Polit. Sci., Miss. State U., Starkville, 1985; postgrad., Miss. State U., Starkville, 1992—; JD, Miss. Coll., 1989. Legal asst. Ben. F. Hilburn Jr., Atty. at Law, Starkville, Miss., 1984-85; grad. asst. dept. polit. sci. Miss. State U., 1986-87; law clk. Minor Buchanan, Jackson, Miss., 1987-88, Deposit Guaranty Nat. Bank, Jackson, 1988-89; state senator dist. 15 State of Miss., 1990-99, lt. gov., 2000—. Adj. prof. Wood Jr. Coll., Mathiston, Miss., 1990—. Mem. Oktibbeha County Voter Re-Registration Com., Oktibbeha County Fedn. Dem. Women; bd. dirs. Oktibbeha County Am. Cancer Soc., 1991-92; mem. local rels. com. Children and Family Svcs.; assoc. mem. Nat. Mus. Women in the Arts, 1992-93. Mem. NAFE, Am. Legis. Exch. Com., Am. Soc. Pub. Adminstrs., Nat. Conf. State Legislature, Nat. Order Women Legislators, Miss. State U. Alumni Assn., Starkville Area Bus. and Profl. Women's Club, Oktibbeha County C. of C., Gamma Beta Phi, Pi Sigma Alpha, Omicron Delta Kappa, Phi Delta Phi (vice-magister 1988, historian 1988-89). Methodist. Home: 3262 Highway 82 W Maben MS 39750-8674 Office: Miss Lt Governor PO Box 1018 Jackson MS 39215-1018*

TUCK, EDWARD FENTON, venture capitalist; b. Memphis, July 5, 1931; s. Edward Fenton and Jane Florence (Lewis) T.; m. Janet Allene Barber, July 6, 1957; children: Jean, Ann. BSEE, Mo. Sch. Mines, 1953; elec. engr. (hon.), U. Mo., 1980, D Engring. (hon.), 1997. Registered profl. engr., Calif. Various engring. and mfg. mgmt. positions Lenkurt Elec. Co. divsn. GTE, San Carlos, Calif., 1957-62; v.p., co-founder Kebby Microwave Corp., 1962-64; asst. tech. dir. ITT, 1964-67, v.p., tech. dir. N.Am. Telecomms. Group, 1967-72; gen. mgr., pres. Tel-Tone Corp., Kirkland, Wash., 1972-74; v.p. mktg. and engring. Am. Telecomm. Corp., El Monte, Calif., 1975-79; pres. Edward Tuck & Co. Inc., West Covina, 1979-86; gen. ptnr. The Boundary Fund, 1986-95, Kinship Ptnrs. II, 1990—. Prin. Falcon Fund, 1982—, TriQuint Semiconductors, Beaverton, Oreg.; chmn. High Tower Software, Irvine, Calif.; mem. adv. coun. Mann Inst. Contbr. articles to profl. jours. Trustee U. Mo., Rolla; mem. jet propulsion lab. comml. adv. com. Named mem. Acad. Elec. Engring. U. Mo. Fellow Instn. Radio, Elec. and Electronic Engrs. Australia; mem. IEEE (sr., 1st prize for article 1962), AAAS, Assn. Profl. Cons. (pres., bd. dirs. 1979-86). Democrat. Office: Kinship Partners II 100 N Barranca St Ste 920 West Covina CA 91791 E-mail: ed@falconfund.com.

TUCK, EDWARD HALLAM, lawyer; b. Brussels, June 27, 1927; s. William Hallam and Hilda (Bunge) T.; m. Liliane Solmsen, June 8, 1978; children by previous marriage— Edward, Jessica, Matthew BA, Princeton U., 1950; LL.B., Harvard Law Sch., 1953. Bar: N.Y. Assoc. Shearman & Sterling, N.Y.C., 1953-62, ptnr., 1962-86, of counsel, 1986—. Bd. dirs. The French-Am. Found.; bd. dirs. Comml. Bank. Bd. dirs. Belgian Am. Ednl. Found., The Drawing Ctr.; trustee French Inst. Alliance Francaise; chmn. bd. North County Sch., Inc., 1974-78, The Drawing Ctr., Gateway Citizens Com., 1972-74; pres. The Parks Council, 1970-74; chmn. N.Y. State Parks and Recreation Commn., City of N.Y., 1971-76. Served with USN, 1945-46 Mem. Assn. Bar City N.Y., Coun. on Fgn. Rels., Racquet and Tennis Club, The Brook Club, The Ivy Club, Pilgrims, Soc. of the Cin. Episcopalian. Office: Shearman & Sterling 599 Lexington Ave Fl C2 New York NY 10022-6069

TUCK, GRAYSON EDWIN, real estate agent, former natural gas transmission executive; b. Richmond, Va., May 11, 1927; s. Bernard Okly and Erma (Wiltshire) T.; m. Rosalie Scroggs, June 6, 1947; children— Janice Lorrain, Kenneth Edwin, Carol Lynn. BS, U. Richmond, 1950. Payroll clk., cost clk. Gen. Baking Co., Richmond, 1948-51; jr. accountant Commonwealth Natural Gas Corp., 1951-55, sr. accountant, 1956-57, accounting supr., 1957-58, asst. treas., 1959-62, asst. sec., asst. treas., 1963-64, treas., asst. sec., 1965-77; treas. Commonwealth Natural Resources, Inc., 1977-81, CNG Transmission Co. subs., 1977-79; sec.-treas. Air Pollution Control Products, Inc., Richmond, 1970-73; asst. treas., asst. sec. Commonwealth Gas Distbn. Corp., 1969-79; mgr. taxes and cash mgmt. Commonwealth Gas Pipeline Corp., subs. Columbia Gas System Inc., 1981-86; investor, realtor Bill Eudailey & Co., 1986—. Active Boy Scouts Am., 1965—69; bd. dirs. Henrico Area Mental Health Retardation Svcs., 1983—85; active Elpis Christian Ch., 2001—; deacon Presbyn. Ch., 1958—86, elder, 1986—2001, treas., 1968—70. With USNR, 1945—46. Mem. Nat. Assn. Accts. (assoc. dir. 1963-64) Home: 2923 Oakland Ave Richmond VA 23228-5827 Office: 6401 Mallory Dr Richmond VA 23226-2911

TUCK, JOHN CHATFIELD, former federal agency administrator, public policy advisor; b. Dayton, Ohio, May 28, 1945; m. Jane McDonough; 3 children. BS, Georgetown U., 1967. Various positions as asst. to Rep. leaders Ho. of Reps., Washington, 1974-77, chief Rep. floor ops., 1977-81; asst. sec. to majority U.S. Senate, 1981-86, spl. asst. then dep. asst. to pres. for legis. affairs, 1986-87; dep. asst. to Pres. of U.S. and exec. asst. to chief of staff Office Chief of Staff, The White Ho., 1987-88; asst. to Pres. and dir. Office Chief of Staff, 1988-89; under sec. Dept. Energy, Washington, 1989-92; sr. pub. policy advisor Baker, Donelson, Bearman & Caldwell, 1992—. With USN, 1968-73, ret. capt. USNR, 1973-94. Office: Baker Donelson Bearman & Caldwell 801 Pennsylvania Ave NW Ste 800 Washington DC 20004-2616

TUCK, MARY BETH, nutritionist, retired educator; b. Point, Tex., Dec. 9, 1930; d. Basil Barney and Daisy (Morris) Rabb; children: Karen, Kenny (dec.). BS, East Tex. State U., 1952, MEd, 1966; PhD, Tex. Woman's U., 1970. Lic. dietitian, Tex. Tchr. Longview (Tex.) Pub. Schs., 1952-64; instr. nutrition Stephen F. Austin U., Nacogdoches, Tex., 1966-69; assoc. prof. East Tex. State U., Commerce, 1970-96; ret., 1996. Cons. Women, Infants and Children Program, Hunt County, Tex., 1989, East Tex. State U. Wellness Program, Commerce, 1989-93, nutritionist Selvaggi Med. Clinic, Commerce, 1989-93; nutrition del. People to People Citizen Amb. Program, USSR, 1990; lectr. in field. Reviewer, editor textbooks; contbr. articles to profl. jours. Mem. Commerce Leadership Inst., 1997; mem. Commerce Symphony League, 1998—; mem., supporter plan/devel. amphitheater So. Sulphyr River Devel. Assn., 1998—; mem. Bluebonnet Chorale, 2001—, Meth. Mission Work/Study Team, Palestine, 1996, Palestine, 1998, Bolivia, 2001; mem. missions com. 1st United Meth. Ch., mem. SPRC com., 1996—99, choir, chmn. assoc. pastor personage com., 1996—, leader sr. adult ministries, 1997—; bd. dir. commerce divsn. Am. Heart Assn., 1994—97; bd. dir. NorthEast Tex. Symphony Assn., 1998—2001, sec., 1997—. Mem.: NE Tex. Ret. Tchrs. Assn. (v.p. 1996—97, pres. 1999—2001, 3d v.p. 2001—02, dist. 1st v.p. 2002—), Commerce Area Alumni Assn. (1st v.p. 1993—94), Tex. A&M U. Commerce Alumni Assn. (Founder's Circle 1998—, Gold Blazer award 1995), Louise Drake Garden Club (v.p. 1991—92, pres. 1992—93, 1997—98), Afflatus Culture Club (pres. 1988—91, 1st v.p. 2002—), Delta Kappa Gamma (sec. 1988—92, 1994—96).

TUCK, RUSSELL R., JR. former college president; b. June 9, 1934; m. Marjorie Gay Tuck; children: Russell R. III, Catherine Elizabeth. BS in Chemistry, Union U., 1956; MS in Biology, George Peabody Coll. Vanderbilt U., 1957; PhD in Curriculum and Instrn., Vanderbilt U., 1971; study, Wash. U., 1960-61. Instr. biology, asst. coordinator Korean Tchr. Edn. Program George Peabody Coll. Vanderbilt U., Nashville, 1957-59; tchr. biology, chmn. sci. dept. University City (Mo.) Sr. High Sch., 1960-63, from asst. prin. to prin., 1963-70; prin. Parkway North Sr. High Sch., St. Louis County, Mo., 1971-78; asst. supt. Parkway Sch. Dist., 1979-81, assoc. supt., 1981-84; pres. Calif. Bapt. Coll., Riverside, 1984-94, pres. emeritus, 1994—. Contbr. articles to profl. jours. Bd. dirs. Opera Assn.; pres. Riverside County chpt. ARC, 1989-90; active Bapt. Ch., local hosp. assn. bd., local edn. com.; World Affairs Coun. Mem. Calif. Bapt. Hist. Soc. (bd. dirs.), Calif. Bapt. Devel. Found. (bd. dirs.), Am. Assn. Sch. Adminstrs., Inland Empire Higher Edn. Coun. (pres. 1987-88), Rotary, Kappa Delta Pi, Phi Delta Kappa. Lodges: Rotary. Home: 14000 Chelmsford Dr. Gainesville VA 20155

TUCKER, ALAN CURTISS, mathematics educator; b. Princeton, N.J., July 6, 1943; s. Albert William and Alice Judson (Curtiss) W.; m. Amanda Almira Zeisler, Aug. 31, 1968 (div. 1997); children: Lisa, Kathryn, Edward; m. Ann K. Hong, Feb. 16, 1997. BA, Harvard U., 1965; MS, Stanford U., 1967, PhD, 1969. Asst. prof. applied math. SUNY, Stony Brook, 1970-73, assoc. prof. applied math., 1973-78, prof. applied math., chmn., 1978-89, SUNY Disting. Teaching prof., 1989—. Vis. asst. prof. math. U. Wis., Madison, 1969-70; vis. assoc. prof. computer sci. U. Calif., San Diego, 1976-77; vis. prof. ops. research Stanford U., 1983-84; cons. Sloan Found., 1981-85; acad. cons. 40 colls. and univs. Author: Applied Combinatorics, 1980, Unified Introduction to Linear Algebra, 1987, Linear Algebra, 1993; assoc. editor Math. Monthly, 1996—, Applied Maths. Letters, 1986—; contbr. 45 rsch. articles to profl. jours. Ga. U. Consortium Disting. Visitor, 1982; NSF grantee, 1972-86. Mem. Math. Assn. Am. (chmn. publs. 1982-86, editor Studies in Math. series 1979-86, v.p. 1988-90, chmn. ednl. coun. 1990-96, Disting. Tchr. award 1994, Trevor Evans award 1996), U.S. Commn. Math. Instrn., Am. Math. Soc., Ops. Rsch. Soc. Am., Soc. Indsl. Applied Maths., Sigma Xi (chpt. pres. 1987—). Home: 19 Crosby Place Cold Spring Harbor NY 11724-2404 Office: SUNY At Stony Brook Dept Of Applied Math Stony Brook NY 11794-3600 E-mail: atucker@notes.sunysb.edu.

TUCKER, ALAN DAVID, publisher; b. Erie, Pa., Mar. 9, 1936; s. Meredith LaDue and Monica (Klocko) T.; m. Kiyoko Iizuka, Feb. 8, 1963; 1 child, Kumi Tucker. AB, Princeton U., 1957. Lic. real estate salesperson, N.Y. Assoc. editor Hawthorn Books, N.Y.C., 1964-66; editor John Day Co., Inc., 1966-72; mng. editor David McKay Co., Inc., 1972-75, v.p., 1975-78, exec. v.p., editorial dir., 1978-84; editorial dir. Fodor's Travel Guides, Inc., 1978-84; producer, Penguin Travel Guides and other publs., 1984-91; gen. editor Berlitz Travellers Guides, 1991-95; consulting sr. analyst Genesis Group Assocs., Montclair, NJ, 1995—2001; v.p. mktg. strategy Oxygen Advt., Inc. (formerly The Benjamin Group), N.Y.C., 1996—. Real estate sales assoc. The Halstead Property Co., N.Y.C., 1999—. Author: Capitation and Risk Sharing, 1995, Integrated Health Information Systems, 1997, Provider-Sponsored Managed Care, 1998, Convergence in Coordinated Care, 1998; co-author: The Electronic Superhighway 1997-2010: Opportunities for the Healthcare Industry, 1996, Diabetes Disease Management, 1995, 2d edit., 1998, Asthma Disease Management, 1997, 2d edit., 1999, Hypertension Management, 1999, Management of Congestive Heart Failure, 1999, Intelligence Report: Depression, 1999, Intelligence Report: Lung Cancer, 2000, Strategic Audit: Alzheimer's and Parkinson's Diesease, 2000, Strategic Audit: Stroke and Multiple Sclerosis, 2000, Asthma Forum, 2001, Osteoporosis Forum, 2001, Psoriasis Forum, 2001, Congestive Heart Failure Forum, 2001, Obesity Forum, 2002. With USNR, 1957-60. Mem.: Real Estate Bd. N.Y. (Regent's Adv. Coun. N.Y.C. region), Am. Coll. Healthcare Execs., N.Y. Travel Writers Assn. (past pres.), Soc. Am. Travel Writers. Office: 186 Riverside Dr New York NY 10024-1007 also: 34 Still Meadow Rd Sharon CT 06069-2133

TUCKER, ALLAN MARC, mastering engineer; b. Bklyn., May 26, 1949; BA, CUNY, 1971. Rec. engr. Bell Sound Studios, N.Y.C., 1971-73, Platinum/Chess Records, Englewood, N.J., 1975-77, Vanguard Records, N.Y.C., 1977-80, Foothill Sound, N.Y.C., 1971-88; pres., chief mastering engr. Foothill Digital, 1988—. Rec. engr. Malcolm Addey Recorders, N.Y.C., 1972-87; ops. mgr. Nat. Video and Rec. Studios, N.Y.C., 1979-83; freelance studio engr., 1971-88. Mastering engr. over 2,000 albums/CDs. Recipient 2 Visionary awards 3M Corp.; selected Beta/Co-developer by Sonic Solutions, 1988-91; winner Emmy, TEC and Grammy awards. Mem. Nat. Acad. Rec. Arts and Scis., Audio Engring. Soc., Sonic Solutions DVD-Audio Developers Group, Audio Engring. Soc. (vice-chmn. N.Y. chpt.). Office: Foothill Digital Inc 215 W 91st St New York NY 10024-1321 E-mail: tucker@foothilldigital.com.

TUCKER, ALLEN BROWN, JR. computer science educator; b. Worcester, Mass., Feb. 19, 1942; s. Allen Brown and Louise (Woodberry) T.; m. Maida Somerville, Dec. 18, 1965; children: Jennifer, Brian. BA, Wesleyan U., Middletown, Conn., 1963; MS, Northwestern U., 1969, PhD, 1970. Asst. prof. computer sci. U. Mo., Rolla, 1970-71, Georgetown U., Washington, 1971-76, assoc. prof., chmn., 1976-83; MacArthur prof., chmn. Colgate U., Hamilton, N.Y., 1983-88, assoc. dean faculty, 1986-88; Bass prof. Bowdoin Coll., Brunswick, Maine, 1988—. Dir. acad. computing Georgetown U., 1976-83; cons. in field, 1976—. Author: Programming Languages, 1977, 2d rev. edit., 1986, 3d rev. edit., 2001, Text Processing, 1979, Computer Science: A Second Course, 1988, Fundamentals of Computing I, 1992, Fundamentals of Computing II, 1993; assoc. editor Jour. of Computer Langs., 1979—, Jour. of Machine Translation, 1986—; contbr. articles to profl. jours.; : 2d edit., 1995; editor-in-chief: Handbook of COmputer Science and Engineering, 1997. Recipient Fulbright lectureship, 1986, 1992, 2001, Erskine lecureship, U. Canterbury, 1999; fellow, NSF, 1984—86, ACM, 1994—. Fellow: Assn. for Computing Machinery (Outstanding Contbn. award 1991, Outstanding Computer Sci. Educator award 2001); mem.: N.Y. Acad. Scis., Computer Soc. of IEEE, Sigma Xi. Democrat. Episcopalian. Avocations: squash, golf, jogging, music, travel. Home: 1 Boody St Brunswick ME 04011-3005 Office: Bowdoin Coll Dept of Computer Sci Brunswick ME 04011 E-mail: allen@bowdoin.edu.

TUCKER, ALVIN LEROY, retired government official; b. Bklyn., Sept. 7, 1938; s. Alvin Leroy Jr. and Alveria (Klune) T.; m. Jacqueline Twiggs, Aug. 27, 1966; children: Hazel, Pluma, Jacqueline, Alvin. BS, U. Md., 1965. CPA, Md.; cert. internal auditor; cert. govt. fin. mgr.; cert. def. fin. mgr. Auditor Dept. Army, Washington, 1965-67; dep. insp. gen. HUD, 1986-89; auditor Dept. Def., 1967-72, budget analyst, 1972-79, dir. tng. and edn., 1979-83, dep. asst. insp. gen., 1983-86, dep. comptr., 1989-94, dep. CFO, 1991-97, chmn. concessions com., 1989-97; sr. mgr. Grant Thornton, Vienna, 1997—. Mem. steering com. Joint Fin. Mgmt. Improvement Program, 1990-93; mem. CFO's Coun., 1989-97, chmn. fin. sys. com., 1989-97; mem. Fed. Acctg. Stds. Adv. Bd., 1991-97. With U.S. Army, 1958-61. Recipient Defense medal for disting. civilian svc. with Bronze Palm, meritorious sr. exec. medal. Mem. AICPA, Am. Soc. Mil. Comptrs., Assn. Govt. Accts. (nat. exec. com. 1993-94), Kiwanis (club pres. 1981-82, 86-87). Avocation: genealogy. Office: Grant Thornton 333 John Carlyle St Ste 500 Alexandria VA 22314

TUCKER, BERRY KENNETH, lawyer; b. Chgo., Sept. 23, 1946; s. Sheldon K. and Regina E. (Winter) T.; m. Sherry L. Soref, Nov. 20, 1970; children: Jami Leigh, David William BS in Mgmt., No. Ill. U., 1969; JD, Loyola U., Chgo., 1972. Bar: Ill. 1972, U.S. Dist. Ct. (no. dist.) Ill. 1972, U.S. Ct. Appeals (fed. cir.) 1983. Asst. counsel Ill. Dept. Mental Health, Chgo., 1972-74; asst. chief counsel Ill. Dept. Transp., 1974-78; div. chmn. Nat. R.R. Adjustment Bd., 1978-80; sr. ptnr. Berry K. Tucker & Assoc. Ltd., 1980—. Chief counsel Aunt Marthas Youth Svc. Ctr., Wake Forest, Ill., 1974—. Mem. water com. Village of Flossmoor (Ill.), 1987-88. Mem. Ill. Bar Assn. (mem. sect. counsel adminstrv. law com. 1973-76), Chgo. Bar Assn. (mem. environ. law com. 1975-78). Avocations: auto restoration, raquetball, golf. Office: Berry K Tucker & Assocs Ltd 5210 W 95th St Ste 100 Oak Lawn IL 60453-2460

TUCKER, BEVERLY SOWERS, information specialist; b. Trenton, N.J., Dec. 1, 1936; d. Eldon Jones and Verbeda Eleanor (Roberts) Sowers; m. Harvey Richard Tucker, Dec. 27, 1958 (div. Nov. 1983); children: Randall Richard, Brian Alan. BS in Chemistry with distinction, Purdue U., 1958; MS in Geology, No. Ill. U., 1985; MA in Library and Info. Sci., Rosary Coll., 1989. Asst. rsch. librarian CPC Internat., Argo, Ill., 1958-62; chem. patent searcher Chgo., 1962-66; info. specialist C. Berger & Co., Wheaton, Ill., 1986, Amoco Corp., Naperville, 1987-99, Baxter Healthcare, Round Lake, 1999—; faculty Coll. Du Page, Glen Ellyn, 1989—; with Baxter Healthcare, Round Lake, 1999—. Mem. Spl. Libraries Assn., Ill. Fedn. Women's Club (treas. 5th dist. 1979-81, Outstanding Jr. Clubwoman award 1979-80), Garden Club Council Wheaton (pres. 1981-82), Wheaton Jr. Woman's Club (pres. 1977-78, Single Parent scholar 1984), Gardens Etc. Club (pres. 1978-79), Alpha Lambda Delta, Delta Rho Kappa, Theta Sigma Phi, Alpha Chi Omega (grantee 1985). Republican. Presbyterian. Avocations: bridge, needlework, gourmet cooking. Home: 1507 Paula Ave Wheaton IL 60187-6135

TUCKER, BOWEN HAYWARD, lawyer; b. Providence, Apr. 13, 1938; s. Stuart Hayward and Ardelle Chase (Drabble) T.; m. Jan Louise Brown, Aug. 26, 1961; children: Stefan Kendric Slade, Catherine Kendra Gordon. AB in Math., Brown U., 1959; JD, U. Mich., 1962. Bar: R.I. 1963, Ill. 1967, U.S. Supreme Ct. 1970. Assoc. Hinckley & Allen, Providence, 1962-66; sr. atty. Caterpillar, Inc., Peoria, Ill., 1966-72; counsel FMC Corp., Chgo., 1972-82, sr. litigation counsel, 1982-95, assoc. gen. counsel, 1995-2000; v.p. eLaw Forum, 2000—01. Chmn. legal process task force Chgo. Residential Sch. Study Com., 1973-74, mem. Commn. on Children, 1983-85, Ill. Com. on Rights of Minors, 1974-77, Com. on Youth and the Law, 1977-79; mem. White House Conf. on Children, ednl. svcs. subcom., 1979-80; chairperson Youth Employment Task Force, 1982-83; mem. citizens com. on Juvenile Ct. (Cook County), 1978-94, chmn. detention subcom., 1982-92; mem. econ. effects adv. com. Rand Inst. Civil Justice, 1990-92; bd. dirs. Voices Ill. Children, 1998—. 1st lt. U.S. Army, 1962-69. Mem. ABA, Am. Law Inst., Ill. State Bar Assn., R.I. Bar Assn., Chgo. (chmn. com. on juvenile law, 1976-77), Chgo. Lincoln Inn of Ct. (sec., treas. 1996-98), Constrn. Industry Mfrs. Assn. (exec. com. of Lawyers' Coun. 1972, 75-79, vice chmn. 1977, chmn. 1978-79), Mfrs. Alliance (products liability coun. 1974-95, vice chmn. 1981-83, chmn. 1983-85), Product Liability Adv. Coun. (bd. dirs. 1986-2000, exec. com. 1990-97, vice chmn. 1991-93, chmn. 1993-95), ALCU (bd. dirs. Ill. divsn. 1970-79, exec. com. 1973-79, sec. 1975-77), Am. Arbitration Assn. (mem. panel of arbitrators 1985-96), Phi Alpha Delta, Brown Univ. of Chgo. Club (nat. alumni schs. program 1973-85, v.p. 1980-81, pres. 1981-86), Lawyers Club of Chgo. Home: 107 W Noyes St Arlington Heights IL 60005-3747 Office: 200 E Randolph St Ste 6700 Chicago IL 60601-6436 E-mail: bhtu@att.net.

TUCKER, CONSTANCE A. critical care nurse; b. Glens Falls, N.Y., Feb. 25, 1950; d. Anthony F. and Marie H. (Daire) Mitrione; m. William H. Tucker, Mar. 26, 1971; children: Kimberly, Kelly, Jayme. AAS, Adirondack C.C., Glens Falls, 1982. CEN.; cert. trauma nurse, ACLS instr., BLS instr., PALS instr. Pediat. and rehab. staff nurse Glens Falls Hosp., 1982-85, emergency RN, 2001—; staff nurse Great Meadow Correctional Facility, Comstock, N.Y., 1986-88; emergency rm. nurse, sexual assault nurse examiner Saratoga Hosp., Saratoga Springs, 1988-2001, emergency medicine svcs. liaison coord. Nurse instr. N.Y. State EMT Course; paramedic Bay Ridge Rescue Squad, pres. Pres, CEO Bay Ridge Rescue Squad. Capt. U.S. Army Nurse Corp. E-mail: cptcat@yahoo.com., tuckerco@uhpcc.medserv.net.

TUCKER, CYNTHIA DELORES NOTTAGE (MRS. WILLIAM M. TUCKER), political party official, former state official; b. Phila., Oct. 4, 1927; d. Whitfield and Captilda (Gardiner) Nottage; m. William M. Tucker, July 21,

1951. Student, Temple U., Pa. State U., U. Pa.; student hon. degrees, Villa Maria Coll., Erie, Pa., 1972, Morris Coll., Sumter, S.C., 1976; DHL (hon.), U. D.C. Sec. of state Commonwealth of Pa., Harrisburg, 1971-77; nat. pres. Fedn. Democratic Women, 1979-81; v.p. Pa. chpt. NAACP, nat. v.p. bd. trustees; mem. nat. adv. bd. Nat. Women's Polit. Caucus; now chair Black Caucus Nat. Dem. Com. Mem., vice chair Pa. Black Dem. Com., 1966—; chair Women for Dem. Action, 1967—; nat. chair Nat. Polit. Congress of Black Women, Inc., 1992—; sec., mem. Phila. Zoning Bd. Adjustment, 1968-70; vice chair Pa. Dem. State Com., 1970-76; mem. exec. com. Dem. Nat. Com., 1972-76; Dem. candidate lt. gov., Pa., 1978; v.p. Phila. Tribune Newspaper. Del. to White Ho. Conf. on Civil Rights; bd. dirs. Phila. YWCA, New Sch. Music, Martin Luther King Ctr. for Social Change; pres., founder Phila. Martin Luther King Assn.; mem. Commonwealth bd. Med. Coll. Pa.; bd. assocs. Messiah Coll.; founder, pres. Bethune-DuBois Fund; bd. mem. Del. Valley Coll.; mem. adv. bd. Parents TV Coun.; spl. contbn. fund trustee NAACP. Recipient Svc. and Achievement award NAACP, 1964, Phila. Tribune Charities Ann. award, Cmty. Svc. award Opportunities Industrialization Ctr., Emma V. Kelley Achievement award Nat. Elks, 1971, Lincoln U. Nat. Leadership award, 1993, Cmty. Svc. award Quaker City chpt. B'nai B'rith; named Best Dressed Woman of Yr., Ebony mag., One of 100 Most Influential Black Ams., 1973-77; included in 1996 People mag.'s list of Twenty-Five Most Intriguing People; George Gallup Inst. fellow. Mem. Nat. Assn. Secs. State (v.p.), Bus. and Profl. Women's Club, Links (dir.), Alpha Kappa Alpha (hon.) Home: 6700 Lincoln Dr Philadelphia PA 19119-3155

TUCKER, DANA LEHMAN, medical psychologist; b. St. Louis, Mar. 3, 1970; s. Robin Clair and Nora Lynne (Lehman) T.; m.Christine Lina Brunner, Aug. 21, 1993; children: Nathan, Elise. BS in Psychology, Brigham Young U., 1994; MS in Med. Psychology, Uniformed Svcs. U. Health Sci., 1999. Behavioral medicine technician Utah Valley Regional Med. Ctr., Provo, 1994-95; rsch. asst. Washington VA Med. Ctr., 1995—2000; grad. fellow Uniformed Svcs. U. Health Scis., Bethesda, Md., 1995—, tchg. asst., 1996—2000. Adj. faculty dept. social scis. Montgomery Coll., Takoma Park, Md., 1999—; prof. divsn. applied psychology & quantitative methods U. Balt., 2001—. Elders Quorum pres. Ch. of Jesus Christ of Latter-Day Saints, Gaithersburg, Md., 1997-2000. 1st lt. U.S. Army Res., 1997-2001, capt., 2001—, co. comdr. Mil. Police, 1999—. Theresa Thomas scholar, 1996, 97. Mem. APA (student affiliate), Am. Psychol. Soc. (student affiliate). Home: 13 Shuttle Ct Gaithersburg MD 20878 E-mail: dtucker@usuhs.mil.

TUCKER, DARRYL KLEIN, interior designer; b. Suffern, N.Y.; d. Mitchel M. and Judith (Wohlberg) Klein; BS in Interior Design, Drexel U.; 1 child, Nanci Denise. Trainee, B. Altman & Co., N.Y.C., 1958-59; interior designer Contract Sales & Interiors, Canoga Park, Calif., 1964-67, Joseph Paul White, Manhattan Beach, Calif., 1967-68; sr. interior designer Greenbaum Bros., Paterson, N.J., 1968-72; owner Helicon Hall, Ft. Lee. N.J., 1972—; tchr. interior design, Adult Sch., Englewood, N.J., 1970-71; lectr. in field high schs., community orgns. Adv. bd. interior design Dept. Berkeley Schs, N.Y., N.J., tchr. lighting design, 1989—. Mem. Am. Soc. Interior Designers (sec., 1973-74, dir. 1975-78, 84-87, 89—, chmn. various coms.), N.Y. Lighting Designers, Art Deco Soc. N.Y. Address: 2100 Linwood Ave Fort Lee NJ 07024-3186

TUCKER, DON EUGENE, retired lawyer; b. Rockbridge, Ohio, Feb. 3, 1928; s. Beryl Hollis and Ruth (Primmer) T.; m. Elizabeth Jane Parke, Aug. 2, 1950; children: Janet Elizabeth, Kerry Jane, Richard Parke. BA, Aurora Coll., 1951; LL.B., Yale, 1956. Bar: Ohio 1956. Since practiced in, Youngstown, Ohio; asso. Manchester, Bennett, Powers & Ullman, 1956-62, ptnr., 1962-73, of counsel, 1973-87; gen. counsel Comml. Intertech Corp., Youngstown, 1973-75, v.p., gen. counsel, 1975-83, also dir., sr. v.p., gen. counsel, 1983-87, sr. v.p., 1987-93; ret., 1993. Solicitor Village of Poland, Ohio, 1961-63; former chmn. bd., pres., trustee United Cerebral Palsy Assn., Youngstown and Mahoning County; trustee Mahoning County Tb and Health Assn.; former trustee, pres. Indsl. Info. Inst.; former pres., trustee Ea. Ohio Lung Assn.; trustee, former chmn. Cmty. Corp.; trustee, former pres. Butler Inst. Am. Art. With USMCR, 1946-48, 51-53. Mem. Ohio Bar Assn., Mahoning County Bar Assn. (pres. 1972, trustee 1970-73), Youngstown Area C. of C. (chmn. bd. dirs. 1979). Methodist. Home: 6005 Martins Point Rd Kitty Hawk NC 27949-3819

TUCKER, EDWIN WALLACE, law educator; b. N.Y.C., Feb. 25, 1927; s. Benjamin and May Tucker; m. Gladys Lipschutz, Sept. 14, 1952; children: Sherwin M., Pamela A. BA, NYU, 1948; LLB, Harvard U., 1951; LLM, N.Y. Law Sch., 1963, JSD, 1964; MA, Trinity Coll., Hartford, Conn., 1967. Bar: N.Y. 1955, U.S. Dist. Ct. (ea. and so. dists.) N.Y. 1958, U.S. Ct. Appeals (2d cir.) 1958, U.S. Supreme Ct. 1960. Pvt. practice, N.Y.C., 1955-63; Disting. Alumni prof. and prof. bus. law U. Conn., Storrs, 1963—, mem. bd. editors occasional paper and monograph series, 1966-70. Author: Adjudication of Social Issues, 1971, 2d edit., 1977, Legal Regulation of the Environment, 1972, Administrative Agencies, Regulation of Enterprise, and Individual Liberties, 1975, CPA Law Review, 1985; co-author: The Legal and Ethical Environment of Business, 1992; book rev. editor Am. Bus. Law Jour., 1964-65, adv. editor, 1974—; co-editor Am. Bus. Jour., 1965-73; mem. editl. bd. Am. Jour. Small Bus., 1979-86; editor Jour. Legal Studies Edn., 1983-85, editor-in-chief, 1985-87, adv. editor, 1987—; mem. bd. editors North Atlantic Regional Bus. Law Rev., 1984—. With USAF, 1951-55. Recipient medal of excellence Am. Bus. Law Assn., 1979. Mem. Acad. Legal Studies in Bus., North Atlantic Regional Bus. Law Assn. Home: 11 Eastwood Rd Storrs Mansfield CT 06268-2401

TUCKER, FRANK HAMMOND, history educator; b. Millville, N.J., Dec. 29, 1923; s. Frank Edmund and Evalyn Godfrey Tucker; m. Kathryn Churchill Libby (dec. Dec. 1994), Aug. 23, 1947; children: Elizabeth T. Gould, Sarah T. Owens, Margaret T. Mitchell. *Daughter, Elizabeth T. Gould, BA, Mt. Holyoke 1970. MA, University College, Buffalo, 1972 PhD Indiana U.1977. Binghamton U.NY, Folklore professor,1977 to present. Master, Dickinson College of Binghamton U. 1991-1999. Chancellor's Award for Excellence in teaching, 1993.M.Dr. Geoffrey D. Gould, Son, Peter C. Daughter Sarah T. Owens, BA Colo. College 1972. Tax specialist, Seattle, WA. Daughter Margaret T. Mitchell (Mrs. William C.) BA, Mt. Holyoke 1976. MBA, Vanderbilt U. 1978. Communications consultant, Nashville, TN. Children Andrew R., Susan Ann, Brian T.* BS, Johns Hopkins U., 1948; MA, Georgetown U., 1950, PhD, 1954. Bassoonist Balt. Symphony Orch., 1941—43; commd. ensign USN, 1943, advanced through grades to lt. comdr., 1954, ret., 1963; lectr. history extension divsn. U. Md., Yokohama, Japan, 1956-57, lectr. history College Park, 1959-63; prof. history Colo. Coll., Colorado Springs, 1963-89, prof. emeritus, 1989—. *Member, Committee for Content of Katharine Lee Bates America the Beautiful Memorial, Pikes Peak Summit.In charge of producing a history book, 100 years of hiking in the Pikes Peak Region, 1903-2003, Little London Press.* Author: The White Conscience, 1969, The Frontier Spirit and Progress, 1979; contbr. over 35 articles, 40 revs., to profl. jours. Bassoonist Balt. Symphony Orch., 1941-43; bd. mem., Charter Assn., Colorado Springs, 1964-67; pres. Landmarks Preservation Coun., Pikes Peak Region, 1969-73, mem. exec. bd. ARC, 1965-71, head Pike's Peak region Westerners Internat., 1991-92. Fellow Am. Coun. Learned Socs.; mem. Am. Hist. Assn., Rocky Mountain Social Sci. Assn. (bd. mem. 1966-69), Maine Hist. Soc., Gloucester County Hist. Soc., Cumberland County Hist. Soc., Rotary (exec. bd. 1971-73). Episcopalian. Avocation: hiking. Home and Office: 1525 Alamo Ave Colorado Springs CO 80907

TUCKER, GAIL SUSAN, biology science educator; b. N.Y.C., Aug. 30, 1945; d. Albert Eugene and Frances Anna (Kennedy) T.; m. Robert Philip Griffith, Aug. 1, 1987; 1 stepchild, Julie Ellen. BA, Mercy Coll., 1967; PhD, U. Kans., 1973; postdoctoral, Columbia U. Coll. Physicians, 1973-76, Harvard U., 1980. Lic. tchr., Fla.; nat. bd. cert. tchr. adult young adult sci. Head asst. U. Mich. Oceanography Practicum Woods Hole Ocean Inst., 1973; rsch. assoc. U. Miami Sch. of Medicine, 1976-81, rsch. asst. prof., 1981-87; cons. Dade County Pub. Schs. Gifted in Sci. Program, Miami, 1977-86; tchr. Dade County Pub. Schs. New World Sch. of Arts H.S., 1987—. Vis. instr. Mercy Coll., Dobbs Ferry, N.Y., 1974-75, Miami (Fla.)-Dade C.C., 1990—; mail reviewer NSF, Washington, 1980's; grant reviewer NIH; reviewer scientific jours.; project coord. SciTalk, Internet Sci. Discussion Bd. Contbr. articles to profl. jours. Pres. Zonta Club, Miami, 1983-94; pres. Women in Eye Rsch., 1982-84. Fellow Access Excellence, Genentech, 1994, 96; grantee NIH, 1977, 81, United Way, 1979, Fla. Lions Eye Bank, 1977, U. Kans., 1971; Tandy Technology scholar, 1997. Mem. AAAS, Soc. for Neurosci., Nat. Assn. Biology Tchrs. Achievements include identification of degenerative bodies in the cones of the human retina; rsch. analysis of retinal changes in the postnatal cat eye with age. Home: 2121 N Bayshore Dr Apt 1410 Miami FL 33137-5139 Office: New World Sch of the Arts 25 NE 2nd St Miami FL 33132-2103 E-mail: drt@vintageworksinc.com.

TUCKER, GARLAND SCOTT, III, investment banker; b. Raleigh, N.C., June 17, 1947; s. Garland Scott Jr. and Jean Smith (Barnes) T.; m. Greyson Conrad Shuff, Jan. 15, 1972; children— Greyson Carrington, Elizabeth Bradford. B.S. magna cum laude, Washington and Lee U., 1969; M.B.A., Harvard U., 1972. V.p. Tucker Furniture Co., Wilson, N.C., 1972-76; corp. fin. assoc. Investment Corp. of Va., Norfolk, 1976-78; v.p., to pres., chief exec. officer Carolina Securities Corp., Raleigh, N.C., 1978-88; v.p. corp. banking and fin. Chem. Bank, N.Y.C., 1988-90; pres. First Travelcorp., Inc., Raleigh, 1990-2000; ptnr. Chatham Ptnrs., Inc., 1996—; mng. dir., ptnr. Triangle Securities, LLC, 2000—. Mem. N.Y. Stock Exchange, 1983-88; mem. regional firms adv. com. N.Y. Stock Exchange, 1984-87. Dir. Raleigh Rescue Mission, 1980-83; vestry Christ Episcopal Ch., Raleigh, 1981-84; bd. advisors NCO Investors, N.Y.C, 1991-96; trustee N.C. Mus. Art Found., 1990—, Chatham Hall Sch., 1990-96, Penick Episcopal Home for Aging, 1992-94, Trinity Episc. Sem., Pitts., 1991—. FOCUS, N.Y.C., 1995—. Mem. Carolina Securities Corp. (bd. dirs. 1979-88), Securities Industry Assn. (bd. dirs. Mid-Atlantic region 1981-82, 84-88, regional firms com. 1983-86), Raleigh C. of C. (bd. dirs. 1984-86), Phi Beta Kappa. Republican. Clubs: Capital City, Carolina Country (Raleigh); Harvard of N.Y.C., Roaring Gap Club, The Fifty Group. Home: 2327 Lake Dr Raleigh NC 27609-7667 Office: Triangle Securities LLC 1301 Annapolis Dr Raleigh NC 27608-2129

TUCKER, GARY WILSON, nursing educator; b. Oct. 2, 1956; s. Clayton Wilson Jr. and Jewell (Shelton) T. AAS, Cleveland (Tenn.) State Community Coll., 1980; BSW, Lamar U., Beaumont, Tex., 1991; MPH, U. Tex. Sch. Pub. Health, 1996; BSN, Lamar U., 1999. Nurse, relief shift supr. Moccasin Bend Mental Health Inst., Chattanooga, 1980-81; staff nurse pediat. ICU Thompson Childrens', 1981-83; nurse, cons. King Fahad Hosp., Riyadh, Saudi Arabia, 1983; staff nurse ICU/ CCU Beaumont (Tex.) Med.-Surg. Hosp., 1984-88; charge nurse CCU, hemodialysis Bapt. Hosp., Beaumont, 1988-93, cardiovascular nurse educator, 1993-96, dept. head, staff devel. and continuing edn. nurse, 1996-99; rsch. technican U. Tex., Houston Health Sci. Ctr., 1998-99; nursing instr. Lamar U., Beaumont, Tex., 1999—. Mem.: ANA, Tex. Assn. Coll. Tchrs., Am. Assembly Men in Nursing, Tex. Nurses Assn., Sigma Theta Tau. Home: 601 22nd St Beaumont TX 77706-4915 Office: Lamar U Dept Nursing PO Box 10081 Beaumont TX 77710-0081 E-mail: tuckergw@hal.lamar.edu.

TUCKER, GARY EDWARD, botanist, wetland scientist, ecologist; b. Michigan Valley, Kans., Aug. 17, 1941; s. Frank Tucker and Opal Walker; m. Sharon Louise Thompson, Aug. 19, 1960; children: Carrie Elizabeth, Melanie Ann. BA in Biology, Emporia State Tchrs. Coll., 1964; MA in Botany, U. N.C., 1967; PhD in Botany/Ecology, U. Ark., 1976. Prof. biology Ark. Tech. U., Russelville, 1966-89; rsch. botanist U.S. Army Corps Engrs., Waterways Experiment Sta., Vicksburg, Miss., 1978-79; forest botanist, threatened and endangered species coord. U.S. Forest Svc., Russellville, Ark., 1989-91; wetland scientist FTN Assocs., Ltd., Little Rock, 1991—. Mem. commn. Ark. Natural Heritage Commn., Little Rock, 1980-86; mem. tech. adv. com. Nature Conservancy of Ark., Little Rock, 1986—; mem. exec. com. Flora of Ark. Project, 1999—. Tech. editor: Field Guide to Wildflowers, Wildflowers of Arkansas, 1984; contbr. numerous papers to profl. jours. Mem. Soc. Wetland Scientists (cert. profl. wetland scientist), Ark. Native Plant Soc. (organizer, charter mem., chmn. comms./publicity 1997—), Ark. Acad. Sci. (pres. 1986). Democrat. Roman Catholic. Avocations: gardening with native plants, cooking, genealogical research. Home: 2606 W D St Russellville AR 72801-2402 Office: FTN Assocs Ltd 3 Innwood Cir Ste 220 Little Rock AR 72211-2449 Fax: (501) 225-6738. E-mail: get@ftn-assoc.com.

TUCKER, GARY JAY, physician, educator; b. Cleve., Mar. 6, 1934; s. Isadore Martin and Blanche Hanna (Luftig) T.; m. Sharon Ruth Pobby, June 10, 1956; children: Adam, Clare. AB, Oberlin Coll., 1956; MD, Case Western Res. U., 1960; postdoctoral fellow, Yale U., 1961-64; MA (hon.), Dartmouth Coll., 1977. Diplomate Am. Bd. Psychiatry and Neurology. Asst. prof. psychiatry Sch. Medicine Yale U., New Haven, 1967-70, assoc. prof. psychiatry, 1970-71; with Dartmouth Med. Sch., Hanover, N.H., 1971-85, prof. psychiatry, 1974-85, chmn. dept., 1978-85; chmn. psychiatry and behavioral scis. Sch. Med. U. Wash., Seattle, 1985-98; prof. psychiatry U. Wash., 1985—. Bd. dirs. Am. Bd. Psychiatry and Neurology. Co-author: Rational Hospital Psychiatry, 1974, Behavioral Neurology, 1985; contbr. articles to profl. jours. Lt. Commdr. USN, 1964-67. Fellow Am. Psychiat. Assn.; mem. W. Coast Coll. Biol. Psychiatry, Sigma Xi, Alpha Omega Alpha. Democrat. Jewish. Avocations: photography, motorcycles. Office: U Washington Dept Psychiatry PO Box 356560 Seattle WA 98195-6560

TUCKER, GINA LOUISE, women's health nurse; b. Waynesburg, Pa., June 8, 1964; d. Ervin Asa and Loretta Kay (Tennant) Fordyce; m. Thomas L. Tucker II, Sept. 29, 1984; children: Joshua Ervin, Andrew Thomas, Nicholas Aaron, Sarah Marie. AS, Ohio Valley Coll., 1984; AS in Nursing, W.Va. No. Community Coll., 1987; student, Wheeling Jesuit Coll., 1991—. Staff nurse Reynolds Meml. Hosp., Glen Dale, W.Va., 1987-96; staff nurse, labor and delivery Wheeling (W.Va.) Med. Park, 1996—. Mem. Ch. of Christ. Office: Wheeling Hospital 1 Medical Park Wheeling WV 26003-6300

TUCKER, H. RICHARD, oil company executive; b. Streator, Ill., Oct. 2, 1936; s. H.L. and Dorothy A. (Miller) T.; children by previous marriage: Randall R., Brian A.; m. Cheryl L. Kirk, Jan. 14, 1984. BS in Chem. Engring., Purdue U., 1958; MBA, Northwestern U., 1962. Project engr. crude oil supply Amoco Corp., Chgo., 1958-64, specialist product supply, 1965-66, coord. fgn. crude oil supply, 1967-68; coord. orgn. planning Amoco Internat. Corp., 1969-70, Amoco Corp., Chgo., 1970-72, mgr. adminstrv. svcs., 1972-84, mgr. real estate svcs., 1984-86, coord. spl. studies, 1986-89, dir. quality mgmt., 1989-92; mgr. cost mgmt., 1992-94. V.p. Amoco Realty Co., 1984-91, Amoco Devel. Co., 1984-91. Mem. adv. com. Sch. Bd. Wheaton, Ill., 1966; mem. Citizen's Nominating Com., Wheaton, 1972; leader Boy Scouts Am., Wheaton, 1979-82; dir. Oak Brook Colony Condominium Assn., 1992-94. Mem. Westhaven Home Owners Assn. (pres. 1965-67), Phi Eta Sigma, Omega Chi Epsilon, Beta Gamma Sigma, Tau Beta Pi. Avocations: tennis, bridge, hiking.

TUCKER, HILLARY ALBERT, retired intelligence officer, writer; b. Houston, Jan. 18, 1928; s. Hillary Acum and Lola Gladys (Barrow) T.; m. Carolyn Annette Stover (dec., 1988), April 18, 1960; children: Doris Laverne. BS, New York State Univ., 1976. Cert. Meteorologist, USAF. Author: Hillary Acum Tucker and Aloysia Lola Gladys Barrow, 1993, creates genealogical charts in field, 1993, 94, 96, 99. Lt. Col., USAF, 1946-82. Mem. Sons of the Amer. Revolution, 1992—, Veterans of Foreign Wars, 1997—, Magna Carta Barons, 1997—, Mensa, 1989-95, Sons of Confederate Vets. Republican. Roman Catholic. Avocations: genealogy, meteorology. Home: 110 Alton St Houston TX 77012-1410

TUCKER, HOWARD MCKELDIN, investment banker, consultant; b. Washington, Apr. 1, 1930; s. Howard Newell and Bessie Draper (McKeldin) T.; m. Julia Spencer Merrell, Feb. 1, 1952 (div. 1975); children: Deborah, Mark, Alexander, H. David; m. Megan Evans, Aug. 17, 1979. BA, U. Va., 1954; MBA, NYU, 1956. CFA. With pension investment dept. J.P. Morgan & Co., 1954-61; reg. rep.-analyst Mackall & Coe, Washington, 1962-69; dir. internat. dept., analyst Legg Mason Wood Walker & Co., 1969-79; with Govt. Rsch. Corp./Nat. Jour., 1979-82, Potomac Asset Mgmt., 1982-91; ptnr., mng. dir. Capital Insights Group, Washington, 1992-2001. Mem. task force balance-of-payments U.S. Dept. Treasury, 1967-70; cons. County Natwest (Washinton Analysis Corp.), 1985-90; bd. dirs. Monarch Enterprises, Inc., Uniflight, Inc., Sci. Mgmt. Assocs., Inc., Jeffrey Bigelow Assocs. Author: Literature in Medicine, In Memoriam, Michael Halberstam, M.D., 1984; book reviewer Washington Post; contbr. articles to profl. jours. Dir. Washington Area Coun. Chs., 1962-65; vestryman Christ Episcopal Ch., Georgetown, 1962-65; mem. chpt. Washington Nat. Cathedral, 1966-72; del. Va. Republican Conv., 1968; trustee Nat. Cathedral Sch. for Girls, 1972-78; chmn. Missionary Devel. Fund Episcopal Diocese D.C., 1974; co-dir. Andover-Exeter Washington Intern Program, 1976-86; co-organizer U.S.-Ger. Parliamentary Exchange, 1980-82; observer OECD, 1980-82; spl. overseas visitor Australian Govt., 1982; patron West Europe program Woodrow Wilson Ctr., 1985-86. With USNR, 1950-56. Mem.: Fin. Analysts Fedn., Washington Soc. Investment Analysts, Nat. Economists Club, Am. Hort. Soc., Cogswell Soc., Hist. Alexandria Found., Alexandria Seaport Found., Dumplings Yacht Club, Naval and Mil. Club London, Nat. Press Club, Saints and Sinners Club, Georgetown Visitation Tennis Club, Beta Theta Pi. Home: 4 Potomac Ct Alexandria VA 22314-3821

TUCKER, JACK WILLIAM ANDREW, writer, film editor, producer, lecturer; b. Portland, Oreg., May 1, 1944; s. Admyrl Foster and Aileen Eloise (McDaniels) T. BA in English, Portland State U., 1964. Film editor MGM TV, Culver City, Calif., 1984-86, Cannon Film Group, Beverly Hills, 1988, Columbia TV, Burbank, 1988, Paramount Pictures, Hollywood, 1990—. Editor: (TV) Winds of War, 1982 (Emmy award nominee 1983), The Fifth Missile, 1986, 240-Robert, 1979, Flatbed Annie and Sweetpie, 1979, (films) Shogun, 1980, Salsa, 1988, They're Playing With Fire, 1983, Viper, 1988, Nightmare on Elm Street IV, 1988, Distortions, 1987, Diplomatic Immunity, 1991, Illusions, 1992, Double-O-Kid, 1993, A Million to Juan, 1994, To the Ends of Time, 1996, Cotton Mary, 1999; prodr.: The Magazine, 1997, Earth Minus Zero, 1998. Sgt. USAF, 1964-68, Vietnam. Mem. NATAS, Am. Cinema Editors (treas. 1993—, editor CINEMEDITOR mag. 1994—).

TUCKER, JESSIE L., III, health facility administrator, educator; b. Ft. Hood, Tex., Oct. 16, 1967; s. J.L. and G.J. Tucker; m. P.E.K., Dec. 9, 1989. BSBA, U. S.C., 1989; MBA, Troy State U., 1995; PhD, U. Ala., 1998. Diplomate Am. Coll. Health Care Execs. Clin. adminstr. Small Hosp., Ft. Meade, Md., 1989-91; dir. emergency svcs. Amb. Co., 1991-93; COO Multi-Clinic Dental Practice, Ft. Rucker, Ala., 1993-95; cons. Army Ctr. Health Edn., Ft. Sam Houston, Tex., 1998—; prof. Army-Baylor Grad. Program, 1998—. Fellow Am. Coll. Health Care Execs.; mem. Assn. U.S. Army, Inst. Mgmt. Accts., Assn. Mil. Surgeons, Acad. Mgmt., Phi Kappa Phi, Omicron Delta Epsilon, Delta Mu Delta. Office: PO Box 7377 Augusta GA 30905-0377 E-mail: drjt@tucknet.com.

TUCKER, JOHN MARK, librarian, educator; s. Paul Marlin and Edith T.; m. Barbara Ann Wilson, Mar. 22, 1968. BA, David Lipscomb Coll., 1967; MLS, George Peabody Coll. Tchrs., 1968, specialist in edn., 1972; PhD, U. Ill., 1983. Head libr. Freed-Hardeman Coll., Henderson, Tenn., 1968-71; reference libr. Wabash Coll., Crawfordsville, Ind., 1973-79, Purdue U., West Lafayette, 1979-82, asst. prof. libr. sci., 1979-85, assoc. prof. libr. sci., 1985-89, sr. reference libr. Humanities, Social Sci. and Edn. Libr., 1982-90, prof. libr. sci., 1989—, libr. Humanities, Social Sci. and Edn. Libr., 1990—. Grantee com. on instnl. coop. NEH, 1991-94. Co-editor: Reference Services and Library Education, 1983, User Instruction in Academic Libraries, 1986, American Library History, 1989; editor: Untold Stories: Civil Rights, Libraries and Black Librarianship, 1998; editl. bd.: Dictionary of American Library Biography, 2002; contbr. articles to profl. publs. Thomas S. Wilmeth grantee for innovative excellence, 1988, Frederick B. Artz rsch. grantee Oberlin Coll. Archives, 1991; Coun. on Libr. Resources rsch. fellow, 1990. Mem. ALA (chair Libr. History Round Table 1993-94), SCV, Assn. for Bibliography of History, Assn. Coll. and Rsch. Librs., Disciples of Christ Hist. Soc., Soc. for Historians of the Gilded Age and Prog. Era, So. Hist. Assn., Friends of Univ. Ill. Libr., Phi Kappa Phi, Beta Phi Mu. Democrat. Mem. Chs. of Christ. Home: 1055 Southernview Dr S Lafayette IN 47909-3797 Office: Purdue U Humanities Social Sci & Edn Libr 1530 Stewart Ctr West Lafayette IN 47907-1530 E-mail: jmark@purdue.edu.

TUCKER, JOHN ANDREWS, association executive; b. Atlanta, Aug. 3, 1941; s. William Dawsie and Opie (Andrews) T.; m. Allene Smith, June 9, 1963; children: John A. Jr., Laura E., Matthew W. BA, Mercer U., 1963; MA, Mich. State U., 1976. Cert. social worker, Mich. Athletic dir. Boys' Club Macon, Ga., 1962-64, program dir., 1964-66; unit dir. Boys' Club of Lansing, Mich., 1970-76, exec. dir., 1976-79, Youth Devel. Corp., Lansing, 1979—. Pres. Agy. Dirs. Coun., Lansing, 1999-2000. Mem. Mayor's Youth Adv. Coun., Lansing, 1986-97; bd. dirs. Advent House Ministries, Lansing, 1987-97; bd. dirs. Clinton County Coun. for Youth, St. Johns, Mich., 1998—, v.p., 2000-2002; active Capitol Area United Way, Lansing; elder Westminister Presbyn., Lansing, 1997-2000. Lt. USN, 1966-70. Mem. Mich. Assn. Youth Serving Programs (treas. 1980—), Optimist Club Lansing (pres. 1984, 94). Avocations: reading, attending cultural events, sports, Civil War history. Office: Youth Devel Corp 806 N Capitol Ave Lansing MI 48906-5114

TUCKER, JOHN AVERY, academic administrator, electrical engineer; b. Milton, Mass., Jan. 28, 1924; s. Seth Davenport and Ruth Lincoln (Avery) T. BSEE cum laude, Northeastern U., 1949; M. of Engring., Yale U., 1950. Registered profl. engr., Mass. Mem. tech. staff Bell Telephone Labs., Inc., N.Y.C., 1950; engr. New Eng. Tel & Tel. Co., Boston, 1951-56; instr. elec. engring., Lincoln Inst. Northeastern U., 1955; with dept. elec. engring. and computer sci. MIT, Cambridge, 1956—, 1st adminstrv. officer, 1963, dir. VI-A internship program in elec. engring./computer sci., 1969-87, spl. asst. to dept. head, 1987-89, emeritus dir. VI-A program, lectr., 1989—. Deacon emeritus Wellesley Hills Congl. Ch., mem., 1936—; bd. dirs. Wellesley chpt. ARC, 1978; chief of staff Wellesley Vets. Parade, 1996. Sgt. U.S. Army Signal Corps, 1943-46, PTO. Recipient Outstanding Alumnus in Edn. award Northeastern U., 1994, G. Y Billard award MIT, 1981. Mem.: AARP (bd. dirs. MIT/Cambridge chpt. 1990—97), IEEE (life), IEEE (sr.), Am. Soc. Engring. Edn. (life), Wellesley Hist. Soc. (bd. dirs. 1993—, 1st v.p. 1995—98, 2000), MIT Alumni Assn. (hon.), Appalachian Mountain Club, Tau Beta Pi Assn. (v.p. NU chpt. 1949, chief advisor 1971—, Nat. Outstanding Advisor award 1998), Eta Kappa Nu (founder Northeastern U. chpt. 1950, faculty advisor MIT 1956—74, nat. bd. dirs. 1959—61, faculty advisor MIT 1989—). Avocation: photography. Home: 153 Brook St Wellesley MA 02482-6641 Office: MIT 77 Massachusetts Ave Rm 38-473 Cambridge MA 02139-4307

TUCKER, JOSEPH, clergyman, former dean; b. Columbus, Ga., Mar. 5, 1920; s. John Joseph and Irene (Blakely) T.; m. Vivian Theodosia Hampton, Feb. 8, 1948; 1 child, Joy Celeste. BA, Fisk U., 1950; MDiv, Union Theol. Sem., 1953; MS in Libr. Svc., Columbia U., 1970; postgrad., Colgate Rochester Divinity Sch., 1987; DD (hon.), Va. Sem. and Coll., 1988. Asst. dean of men, basic coll. dir. Fisk U., Nashville, 1953-54; periodicals libr. Union Theol. Sem. Libr., N.Y.C., 1959-70; pastoral counselor Harlem Interfaith Counseling Svc., 1967-68; reference libr. Hofstra U. Libr., Hempstead, N.Y., 1970-74; tchr. N.Y. Theol. Sem., N.Y.C., 1977; dean, tchr. Va. Sem. and Coll. N.Y. Extension, Queens Village, N.Y., 1988-91; founder, pres. Lamplighter's Sch. Religious Studies, Hempstead, 1992; founder, pastor Joyful Heart Bapt. Ch., 1969—. Radio bible tchr., 1996—; co-chmn. L.I. Men of Integrity Task Force, 1997—. Mem. Bapt. Ministers' Conf. N.Y. and Vicinity (com. chmn. 1990—), Bapt. Ministers' Conf. Greater N.Y. and Vicinity. Home: 76 E Marshall St Hempstead NY 11550-7406 Office: Joyful Heart Bapt Ch 101 Greenwich St Hempstead NY 11550-5626

TUCKER, JO-VON, marketing executive, writer; b. Dallas, Feb. 7, 1937; d. Worley Charles and Julia Allene (Mayo) Jones; m. George Richard Tucker, Mar. 1, 1958 (div. July 1977); 1 child, Tracy Lynn Tucker Rolsten. Student, Tex. U., 1955-58. Art asst. Bud Biggs Studio, Dallas, 1958-59; illustrator Ed Bearden Art Studio, 1959-62; art dir. The Bloom Agy., 1962-63, Glenn Advt., Dallas, 1963-66; pres. Unltd. Concepts, 1966-73; v.p., creative dir. The Horchow Collection, 1973-75; pres. JVT Direct Mktg., 1975—; owner, chair Clambake Celebrations, Chatham, Mass., 1990—. Cons. P.J. Carroll & Co., Dublin, Ireland, 1988-90; direct mktg. cons. Walt Disney Co., Anaheim, Calif., 1986-87, Neiman-Marcus, Dallas, 1965-71; trustee Direct Mktg. Edni. Found., N.Y.C., 1986-93. Author, photographer: Perspectives, 1981; contbg. author: Successful Direct Marketing Methods, 1985, 87, 89, Ed Nash on Direct Marketing, 1987, 91; co-author: Courage and Information for Life with Chronic Obstructive Pulmonary Disease, 1999; contbr. articles to profl. jours. Active Orleans Selectmen's Com. on Disabilities, 1992-94; bd. dirs. Southeastern Mass. Am. Lung Assn., Nat. Home Oxygen Patients Assn., 2000; founder, coord. Cod Chronic Obstructive Pulmonary Disease Support Group; chair publs. leadership coun. Am. Inst.'s Nat. COPD/Emphysema Assn., 2001. Named Advt. Woman of Yr., Women in Communications, Dallas, 1978, Direct Marketer of Yr., Direct Mktg. Assn. North Tex., 1985, Direct Mktg. Woman of Yr., Women's Direct Response Group, N.Y.C., 1988; recipient graphic awards nat. and internat. groups, Silver Apple award Direct Mktg. Club N.Y., 1999.

Mem. Direct Mktg. Assn. (bd. mem. 1979-85, bd. sec., exec. com. 1984, Echo award 1973, 75, 80, 83, 85), Direct Mktg. Ednl. Found. (trustee 1986-93), Direct Mktg. Idea Exch. (bd. mem. 1980-90), Creative Guild. Republican. Avocations: photography, writing poetry, needlepoint. Office: Clambake Celebrations 1223 Main St Chatham MA 02633-2726

TUCKER, KATHRYN LOUISE, lawyer, educator; b. N.Y.C., July 29, 1959; d. Robert J. and Kathryn Louise (Norton) Sisk; m. Scott L. Tucker, July 1, 1989; children: Torin Norton, Montana Taiga. BA, Hampshire Coll., Amherst, Mass., 1981; JD, Georgetown U., 1985. Bar: Wash. 1985, U.S. Dist. Ct. (we. dist.) Wash., U.S. Dist. Ct. (ea. dist.) Wash., U.S. Ct. Appeals (9th cir.), U.S. Ct. Appeals (2d cir.) 1995, U.S. Supreme Ct. Assoc. Perkins Coie, Seattle, 1988-96; of counsel Perkins Cole, 1996—; dir. legal affairs Compassion in Dying, 1997—; affiliate prof. law U. Wash. Law Sch., 1996—. Author articles on patient rights at the end of life and end-of-life decision making; subject of articles; appeared on network news programs. Mem. ABA. Democrat. Avocations: whitewater kayaking, cross-country skiing. Office: Perkins Coie 1201 3d Ave Seattle WA 98101

TUCKER, KENNETH DANIEL, music educator; b. Honolulu, Jan. 3, 1971; s. Kenneth Daniel Tucker, Sr. and Patricia Ann Tucker; m. Jill Erin McKinney, June 8, 2001. BS, Soutwest Mo. State Univ., Springfield, MO; MM, So. Ill. Univ., Edwardsville, IL. Educator, choir Meramec Valley Schools, Pacific, Mo. Recipient Prelude Award, Mo. Choral Directors, 1999. Mem.: Music Educators Nat. Conf., Am. Choral Directors Assn. R-Liberal. Baptist. Home: 455 Grandview Oaks Drive Union MO 63084-4486

TUCKER, LAKENIA ANDREA, special education educator; b. Americus, Ga., Sept. 11, 1975; d. Alphonzo Colwell, Sr. and Lee Gail Tucker. BS in Spl. Edn., Albany State U., 1998. Cert. spl. edn. tchr. grades K-12. Tchr. DeKalb County Schs., Decatur, Ga., 1998—99, Sumter Co. Schs., Americus, 2000—. Mem. pub. rels. com. Sarah Cobb Elem., Americus, 2001—. Author: (poetry collection) A Daughters Journey to Her Father, 2002. Local coord. Spl. Olympics Area 11, Americus, 2000—01. Home: 308 Alan Dr Americus GA 31709 Office: Sarah Cobb Elem 1901 Valley Dr Americus GA 31709

TUCKER, LAUREY DAN, lawyer; b. El Dorado, Ark., Oct. 23, 1936; s. Floyd A. and Harriet Kathleen (Graves) T.; m. Katherine Washburn, June 21, 1958; children: Laurie Tucker Diaz, Dana Tucker Kleine. BS in Chem. Engring., U. Okla., 1959, LLB, 1962. Bar: Okla. 1962, Tex. 1972. Patent atty. Phillps Petroleum Co., Bartlesville, Okla., 1964-67, Monsanto Co., St. Louis, 1967-70, patent mgr. Texas City, Tex., 1970-74; ptnr. Hubbard, Tucker & Harris, Dallas, 1974-94, Harris, Tucker & Hardin, Dallas, 1994-97, Locke Purnell Rain Harrell, Dallas, 1997-98, Locke Liddell & Sapp LLP, 1999—. 1st lt. U.S. Army, 1962-64. Republican. Episcopalian. Avocations: fishing, hunting, traveling. Office: Locke Liddell & Sapp LLP 2200 Ross Ave Ste 2200 Dallas TX 75201-6776

TUCKER, LOUIS LEONARD, retired historical society administrator; b. Rockville, Conn., Dec. 6, 1927; s. Joseph and Dora (Conn) T.; m. Beverley Jones, Mar. 27, 1953; children: Mark T., Lance K.; m. Carolyn woollen, Sept. 14, 1996. BA, U. Wash., 1952, MA, 1954, PhD, 1957. Instr. history U. Calif., Davis, 1958; fellow Inst. Early Am. History and Culture, Williamsburg, Va., 1958-60; instr. history Coll. William and Mary, 1958-60; dir. Cin. Hist. Soc., 1960-66; asst. commr., state historian of N.Y., N.Y State Edn. Dept., 1966-76; also dir. N.Y. State Bicentennial Commn., 1969-76; dir. Mass. Hist. Soc., Boston, 1977-97. Author: Puritan Protagonist, 1962, Cincinnati During Civil War, 1962, Cincinnati's Citizen Crusaders, 1967, Our Travels, 1968, Cincinnati: Students Guide to Local History, 1969, James Allen, Jr.: From Elkins to Washington, 1969, Connecticut's Seminary of Sedition, Yale College, 1974, Clio's Consort: Jeremy Belknap and the Founding of the Massachusetts Historical Society, 1990, The Massachusetts Historical Society: A Bicentennial History, 1791-1991, 1996, Worthington Chauncey Ford: Scholar and Adventurer, 2001. Dir. Shaker Mus., 1967-74; Am. Heritage Co., 1973-75, Ft. Ticonderoga Assn., 1990-97. Served with AUS, 1946-47. Winston Churchill fellow, 1969 Mem. Am. Assn. State and Local History (pres. 1972-74) Home: 328 Harvard St Cambridge MA 02139-2002

TUCKER, MARC STEPHEN, education policy analyst, author; b. Boston, Nov. 15, 1939; s. David Jones and Natalie (Croman) T.; m. Linda Beth Hepler, Sept 27, 1964 (div. 1973); children: Matthew, Joshua; foster child, Julie Beers. AB, Brown U., 1961; MSS, George Washington U., 1982. Lighting dir., camera Sta. WGBH-TV, Boston, 1962-64, asst. dir. edn. div., 1964-66; asst. to pres. Edn. Devel. Ctr., Newton, Mass., 1966-71; asst. dir. NWREL, Portland, Oreg., 1971-72; assoc. dir. Nat. Inst. Edn., Washington, 1972-81; dir. Project on Info. Tech. and Edn., 1981-84; exec. dir. Carnegie Forum on Edn. and the Econ., 1985-87; pres. Nat. Ctr. on Edn. and the Economy, Rochester, N.Y., 1988—; prof. edn. U. Rochester, 1988—. Staff dir., prin. author Carnegie report-A Nation Prepared: Teachers forthe 21st Century, 1986. Chmn., pres. Brass Chamber Music Soc., Annapolis, Md., 1980-81; mem. bd. advisors Apple Edn. Found., 1984-85, bd. visitors Wake Forest U., 1987—, bd. visitors U. Pitts. Sch. of Edn., 1987—, bd. advisors Bank St. Coll. Edn. Ctr. for Children and Tech., 1987—. Democrat. Office: Nat Ctr on Edn and the Economy Ste 700 1 Thomas Cir NW Washington DC 20005-5802

TUCKER, MARCUS OTHELLO, judge; b. Santa Monica, Calif., Nov. 12, 1934; s. Marcus Othello Sr. and Essie Louvonia (McLendon) T.; m. Indira Hale, May 29, 1965; 1 child, Angelique. BA, U. So. Calif., 1956; JD, Howard U., 1960; MA in Criminal Justice, Chapman U., 1997; BS in Liberal Arts, Regents Coll., SUNY, 1999. Bar: Calif. 1962, U.S. Dist. Ct. (cen. dist.) Calif. 1962, U.S. Ct. Appeals (9th cir.) 1965, U.S. Ct. Internat. Trade 1970, U.S. Supreme Ct. 1971. Pvt. practice, Santa Monica, 1962-63, 67-74; dep. atty. City of Santa Monica, 1963-65; asst. atty. U.S. Dist. Ct. (Cen. Dist.) Calif., 1965-67; commr. L.A. Superior Ct., 1974-76; judge mcpl. ct. Long Beach (Calif.) Jud. Dist., 1976-85; judge superior ct. L.A. Jud. Dist., 1985—; supervising judge L.A. County Dependency Ct. L.A. Superior Ct., 1991-92, presiding judge Juvenile divsn., 1993-94. Asst. prof. law Pacific U., Long Beach, 1984, 86; justice pro tem Calif. State Ct. Appeals (2nd cir.), 1981; mem. exec. com. Superior Ct. of L.A. County, 1995-96. Mem. editl. staff Howard U. Law Sch. Jour., 1959-60. Pres. Community Rehab. Industries Found., Long Beach, 1983-86, Legal Aid Found., L.A., 1976-77; bd. dirs. Long Beach coun. Boy Scouts Am., 1978-92. With U.S. Army, 1960-66. Named Judge of Yr. Juvenile Cts. Bar Assn., 1986, Disting. Jurist Long Beach Trial Trauma Coun., 1987, Honoree in Law Handy Community Ctr., L.A., 1987, Bernard S. Jefferson Jurist of Yr. John M. Langston Bar Assn. Black Lawyers, 1990, Judge of Yr. Long Beach Bar Assn., 1993, Judge of Yr., First Ann. Adoption Cong., 1997, Jurist of Yr., Juvenile Cts. Bar Assn., 1997, Daniel O'Connell award Irish-Am. Bar Assn., 1999; recipient award for Law-Related Edn. Constl. Rights Found./L.A. County Bar Assn., 1992, commendation L.A. County Bd. Suprs., 1994. Fellow Internat. Acad. Trial Judges; mem. ABA, Calif. Judges Assn. (chmn. juvenile law com. 1986-87), Langston Bar Assn. (pres. bd. dirs. 1972, 73), Calif. Assn. Black Lawyers, Santa Monica Bay Dist. Bar Assn. (treas. 1969-71), Am. Inns of Ct., Selden Soc. Avocations: comparative law, traveling. Office: 415 W Ocean Blvd Dept 245 Long Beach CA 90802-4512

TUCKER, MARY MARGARET, county government official; b. Freedom, Ind., Nov. 22, 1934; d. James Edward and Gladys (McAuley) Taylor; m. Odus Lee Tucker, Oct. 3, 1954; children: Craig Allan, Odus Lee Jr. Grad. high sch., Freedom, 1952. Sec. Owen County State Bank, Spencer, Ind., 1952-63; clk. Owen County Cir. Ct., 1971-78; auditor County of Owen, 1979-88, treas., 1989-98, recorder, 1999—. Mem. adminstrv. bd. bd. trustees United Meth. Ch., Spencer, 1980's; pres. Assn. Ind. Counties; bd. dirs. Owen County Cmty. Found., 1988—; Ind. del. Nat. Assn. Counties. Mem. Ind. Recorders' Assn. Home: RR 5 Box 118 Spencer IN 47460-9444 Office: Owen County Recorder Courthouse Spencer IN 47460 Office: Owen County Recorder Courthouse Spencer IN 47460

TUCKER, N(IMROD) H(OLT), III, physician; b. Columbus, Ga., Nov. 22, 1947; s. Nimrod Holt Jr. and Sarah Elizabeth (King) T.; m. Kathryn Gail Waddle, June 6, 1976; children: Jennifer Leigh, Nimrod Holt IV. BS, Auburn (Ala.) U., 1969; MD, U. Ala., 1973. Diplomate Am. Bd. Internal Medicine. Intern and resident ednl. program Jacksonville Hosp. U. Fla., 1973-76; pvt. practice Jacksonville, Fla., 1976—; mem. med. staff St. Vincent's Hosp., 1976—. Bd. dirs. Profl. Found. for Health Care, Tampa, Fla. Bd. dirs. Fla. C.C. Found., Jacksonville, 1986—, St. Vincent's Hosp. Heart and Lung Inst., 1989—, Fla.-Ga. Blood Alliance, 1999—. Fellow ACP (bd. dirs. Fla. chpt. 1988—); mem. Fla. Soc. Internal Medicine (bd. dirs. 1988-, v.p. 1998), AMA, Fla. Med. Assn. (del. 1987, 89), Duval County Med. Soc. (pres. 1999), Jacksonville C. of C. (bd. dirs. 1999), Timuquana Country Club, Fla. Yacht Club, River Club. Methodist. Avocations: racquetball, tennis, golf, poker, bridge. Office: 2149 St Johns Ave Jacksonville FL 32204-4418

TUCKER, PHEBE MARY, psychiatrist, educator; b. Berkeley, Calif., Oct. 1, 1949; d. Daniel Francis and Phebe Dorothy (Gould) O'Shea; m. Leslie Ray Tucker, May 20, 1973; children: Nathan Eugene, Rachel Elizabeth. BA in English Lit., U. Calif., Berkeley, 1971; tchg. cert., Calif. State U., Hayward, 1973; MD, U. Okla., 1985. Diplomate Am. Bd. Psychiatry and Neurology, 1991. Tchr. TEFL U.S. Peace Corps, Divo, Ivory Coast, 1971-72; lead instr. OICW, Union City, Calif., 1975-79; secondary tchr. Pt. Gellibrand H.S., Williamstown, Australia, 1973-75, Barnard White Mid. Sch., Union City, Calif., 1979-81; from resident in psychiatry to prof. U. Okla., Oklahoma City, 1985—2001, prof. psychiatry, 2001—. Contbr. articles to profl. jours. V.p. Parent's Org. U. Okla., Norman, 1996-2000; host mother Am. Field Svc., Edmond, Okla., 1999-2000. Recipient Benjamin Rush award, Coll. of Medicine, Oklahoma City, 1985, C.A. Roeske Cert., Disting. Friend of NAMI award, 2000, Golden Deckert award for sustained excellence in tchg., Dept. Psychiatry, Okla. U. Health Sci. Ctr., 1999. Fellow: Am. Psychiat. Assn. (Cert. of Recognition in Med. Student Edn. 2001); mem.: AMA, Okla. Med. Assn., Ctrl. Okla. Psychiat. Soc. (pres. 1998—99), Okla. Psychiat. Assn. (pres. 1999—2000, mem. exec. coun.), Internat. Soc. Traumatic Stress Studies, Am. Coll. Psychiatrists. Avocations: traveling, reading, sewing. Home: 15509 Claremont Blvd Edmond OK 73013 Office: PO Box 26901 Oklahoma City OK 73126-0901

TUCKER, PHYLLIS ANITA, sales representative, guidance counselor; b. Arkadelphia, Ark., July 26, 1952; d. Charles Wilson and Mary Katherine (Carter) T.; divorced. BS in Edn., Henderson State Coll., 1974, MEd, 1976. Teaching cert. for secondary social studies and guidance counseling. Social studies tchr. Monroe Acad., Wheatley, Ark., 1974-75; peer tutor Henderson State U., Arkadelphia, 1975-76; career orientation tchr. Heber Springs (Ark.) Mid. Sch., 1976-77; counselor Augusta (Ark.) Mid. Sch., 1977-78, Augusta H.S., 1978-86; vocat. special needs counselor White River Vocat.-Tech., Newport, Ark., 1986-87; guidance supr. Ark. Dept. Edn., Little Rock, 1987-89, ednl. supr., 1989-90; sales rep. Holt, Rinehart & Winston, Irving, Tex., 1990—. Chmn. Augusta Heart Fund Drive, 1979; bd. dirs. Saline County Chpt. Am. Cancer Soc., 1991. Named Young Career Woman of Yr. Augusta Bus. and Profl. Women, 1979. Mem. NAFE, Phi Delta Kappa. Republican. Methodist. Avocations: needlework, reading. Office: Holt Rinehart & Winston/HB 1175 N Stemmons Fwy Lewisville TX 75067-2516 E-mail: ptucker@hrw.com.

TUCKER, RICHARD LEE, financial executive; b. Boston, Jan. 16, 1940; s. Frank Lee and Dorothy (Mansell) T.; m. Melinda Nichols, 1970 (div. 1987); children: Anne P., John M.; m. Elizabeth M. Lyne, 1988; children: Christopher B., William M. AB, Harvard U., 1962. CFA. Portfolio mgr. Scudder Stevens & Clark, Boston, 1963-72, v.p. investments, 1972-80; sr. v.p., mgr. trust div. The Boston Co., 1980-86; supervising portfolio mgr., v.p. Trinity Investment Mgmt. Corp., Boston, 1986—, mng. dir., 1992—, CEO, 1999—. Dir. Data Gen. Corp., 1994-99. Trustee Phillips Exeter (N.H.) Acad., 1975-86. Served with U.S. Army, 1962-63. Mem. Inst. Chartered Fin. Analysts, Somerset Club, The Country Club (Brookline). Home: 23 Woodman Rd Chestnut Hill MA 02467-1221 Office: Trinity Investment Mgmt 10 St James Ave Boston MA 02116

TUCKER, ROBERT DENNARD, health care products executive; b. Tifton, Ga., July 18, 1933; s. Robert Buck and Ethel Margaret (Dennard) T.; m. Peggy Angelyn Smith, June 23, 1957; children: Robert Barron, Jennifer Lee. BBA, Ga. State U., 1958. With sales and sales mgmt. Johnson & Johnson Inc., New Brunswick, N.J., 1958-68; v.p., gen. mgr. ASR Med. Industries, N.Y.C., 1968-72, Howmedica Suture div. Pfizer Inc., N.Y.C., 1972-75; exec. v.p., chief operating officer R. P. Scherer Corp., Detroit, 1976-79; pres., chief operating officer Scherer Sci. Inc., Atlanta, 1980-95, also bd. dirs; chmn., chief exec. officer Scherer Health Care Inc., 1980-95, also bd. dirs. Bd. dirs., pres., CEO Splty. Surgictrs., Inc., Atlanta, 1997—2002; bd. dirs., chmn., CEO Maximum Benefits Co., Atlanta; chmn., CEO Throwleigh Techs., LLC, 1995—; bd. dirs. Healthwatch, Inc.; bd. dirs., mem. exec. com. Horizon Med. Products, 2002—. Pub: Tuckers of Devon, 1983; author, pub.: Descendants of William Tucker of Throwleigh, Devon. Chmn. bd. Health Industries Mfrs. Assn. polit. action com., Washington, 1983-85; trustee, past pres. Ga. Horse Found., Atlanta; trustee Brenau Coll., Gainesville, Ga., 1985—. Served with USN, 1951-54, Korea. Decorated Knight of Malta, Imperial Russian Order of St. John; recipient Disting. Service award Brenau Coll., 1987. Mem. Nat. Assn. Mfrs., Health Industries Mfrs. Assn. (bd. dirs. 1979-86, disting. service recognition 1981, 86), Pharm. Mfrs. Assn., Thoroughbred Owners and Breeders Assn. Ky. and Ga. (Man of Yr. 1984). Clubs: Cherokee (Atlanta); Big Canoe (Ga.). Republican. Methodist. Avocations: scuba diving, tennis, genealogical research. Home: 405 Townsend Pl NW Atlanta GA 30327-3037 Office: Throwleigh Techs PO Box 220 Ball Ground GA 30107

TUCKER, ROBERT PAUL, landscape architect, city planner; b. Little Rock, July 1, 1958; s. Jack Arthur and Dorothy Jean Tucker. Student, Tex. A&M U., 1981; B in Landscape Arch., U. Ark., 1983; M in Landscape Arch., Ohio State U., 1989. Registered landscape arch., Ill. Landscape arch. Enplanar, Inc., New Orleans, 1983-85, Laubmann-Reed & Assoc., Atlanta, 1986-87; grad. rsch. assoc. Knowlton Sch. Arch. Ohio State U., Columbus, 1987-89, tutor, 1987-89; planner, landscape arch., urban designer Skidmore, Owings & Merrill, Chgo., 1989-91; urban designer, redevel. specialist Dept. Streets and Sanitation, 1991-99; greening coord. for program mgmt. of renovations to L.A. Unified Sch. Dist. 3d/Internat., Inc., 2000—. Prin. works include Pritzker Park, 1992, Mich. Ave. Streetscape, State St. Renovation, Chgo., Gross Park, McCormick Pl. Conv. Ctr. Expansion Project, among others. Mem. Bright New Cities: A Forum, Chgo., 1993-96; mem. Friends of Downtown, Chgo., 1996-97. Recipient numerous awards. Mem. Am. Inst. Cert. Planners (cert.), Am. Soc. Landscape Archs., Am. Planning Assn. Avocations: landscape photography, hiking, canoeing, urban studies, travel. Office: 3d/Internat Inc 12100 Wilshire Blvd Los Angeles CA 90025-7120 Home: 637 Maze Gln Escondido CA 92025-7917 E-mail: rpt1@pacbell.net.

TUCKER, SHIRLEY LOIS COTTER, botany educator, researcher; b. St. Paul, Apr. 4, 1927; d. Ralph U. and Myra C. (Knutson) Cotter; m. Kenneth W. Tucker, Aug. 22, 1953. BA, U. Minn., 1949, MS, 1951; PhD, U. Calif., Davis, 1956. Asst. prof. botany La. State U., Baton Rouge, 1967-71, assoc. prof., 1971-76, prof., 1976-82, Boyd prof., 1982-95, prof. emerita, 1995—. Adj. prof. dept. biology U. Calif., Santa Barbara, 1995—. Co-editor: Aspects of Floral Development, 1988, Advances in Legume Systematics, Vol. 6, 1994; contbr. numerous articles on plant devel. to profl. jours. Recipient, Outstanding Alumni Achievement award U. Minn., 1999; fellow Linnean Soc., London, 1975—, Fulbright fellow Eng., 1952-53. Mem. Bot. Soc. Am. (v.p. 1979, program chmn. 1975-78, pres.-elect 1986-87, pres. 1987-88, Merit award 1989), Am. Bryological and Lichenological Soc., Brit. Lichenological Soc., Am. Inst. Biol. Scis., Am. Soc. Plant Taxonomists (pres.-elect 1994-95, pres. 1995-96), Phi Beta Kappa, Sigma Xi. Home: 3987 Primavera Rd Santa Barbara CA 93110-1467 Office: U Calif Dept Biology EEMB Santa Barbara CA 93106 E-mail: tucker@lifesci.ucsb.edu.

TUCKER, STEPHEN LAWRENCE, health administration consultant; b. Cin., Oct. 18, 1940; s. Lawrence Henry and Blanche Virginia (Greenwood) T.; m. Lucille Frances Dinda, June 15, 1968; children: Gregory Lawrence, David John. BA, Dartmouth Coll., 1962; MBA, Xavier U., Cin., 1966; D Bus. Adminstrn., George Washington U., 1970. Adminstrv. asst. Presbyn.-U. Pa. Med. Ctr., Phila., 1966-67; assoc. adminstr. Harrisburg (Pa.) Hosp., 1970-73; assoc. prof. Xavier U., 1973-76; dept. chmn. Trinity U., San Antonio, 1976-81, prof. healthcare adminstrn., 1981—87, 1994—2002, dean, 1987-94. Cons. on healthcare adminstrn., San Antonio, 1976—. Co-author: Analysis Manual for Hospital Information Systems, 1980; contbr. articles to profl. jours., chpts. to books. Bd. dirs. Bexar County Mental Health and Mental Retardation Ctr., San Antonio, 1979-85; bd. dirs., chmn. S.W. Neuropsychiat. Inst., San Antonio, 1986-92, Meth. Healthcare Ministries, 1999—, Mission Road Ministries, 2000—. 1st lt. U.S. Army, 1962-64. Recipient Disting. Alumni Svc. award Xavier U., 1984; fellow Accrediting Commn. Grad. Edn. in Hosp. Adminstrn., 1974, WHO, Eng., 1975. Fellow Am. Coll. Healthcare Execs. (various coms. 1966—); mem. Soc. for Healthcare Planning and Mktg. (bd. dirs. 1983-86). Home: 347 Tophill Rd San Antonio TX 78209-3445

TUCKER, STEPHEN RAY, educator, historian; b. Tyler, Tex., May 17, 1951; s. Max Ray and Nelwyn Arlene (Sherman) T.; m. Pamela Kay Bennett, Aug. 17, 1974; children: Jill Kathleen, Mary Claire. BA, Baylor U., 1973; MA, So. Meth. U., 1976; PhD, Tulane U., New Orleans, 1995. Vis. instr. Tulane U., New Orleans, 1984-85; instr., chair dept. social studies C.L. Ganus Sch., 1985-96; instr. Brother Martin H.S., 1996—; freelance historian, lectr., writer, cons., 1979—. Rsch. fellow Hogan Jazz Archive, Tulane U., 1984-85; hist. cons. State of La. Author ency. entries and essays. Recipient George Washington Honor medal Freedoms Found. Valley Forge, 1985, Cominos award Tulane U., 1985, Hogan award Tulane U., 1985; Coe fellow Stanford U., 1992. Republican. Mem. Ch. of Christ. Avocations: trivia, collecting popular music and sports memorabilia. Home: 1701 Pressburg St New Orleans LA 70122-2755

TUCKER, THOMAS EDWARD, music educator; b. Lorain, Ohio, Feb. 16, 1956; m. Diane Tucker, July 2, 1978. BM, Bowling Green State U., Bowling Green, OH, 1978; Masters Edn., ME, Ashland U., Ashland, OH, 1991. Band and choir dir. Minster Local Sch., Minster, Ohio, 1978—79; band dir. Clearview Local Schools, Lorain, 1979—80; band and orch. dir. Lorain City Schools, 1980—. Mem.: Lorain Edn. Assn. (v.p. 1998—2002). Office: Lorain Admiral King 2600 Ashland Lorain OH 44052 Personal E-mail: ttnea@centurytel.net.

TUCKER, THOMAS JAMES, investment manager; b. Atlanta, Sept. 5, 1929; s. Thomas Tudor and Carol (Govan) T.; m. Margaret Guerard. BA, U. of the South, 1952. With CIT Corp, N.Y.C., 1957-72; pres., chief exec. officer AmSouth Fin. Corp., Birmingham, Ala., 1972-82, chmn. bd., 1982, also dir., 1972-93; exec. v.p. AmSouth Bank N.A., Birmingham, 1982-93, chief credit officer, 1992; ret. Tucker Investments, 1993, prin., 1994—. Exec. v.p. AmSouth Bancorp, Birmingham, 1982-93; bd. dirs. Alabanc Properties Corp., Birmingham, chmn., 1991-93; bd. dirs. Birmingham Broadway Series Inc., treas., 1996-97, pres., 1997-99, chmn., 1999-2001. Contbr. articles on credit and leasing to trade jours.; photographer gen. interest mags., 1970—. Bd. dirs. Birmingham Community Devel. Corp.; chmn. bd., 1990-93. 1st lt. USAF, 1952-56. Mem. Vulcan Trail Assn., Birmingham Art Mus. Assn., Birmingham Bot. Soc., Birmingham Canoe Club (bd. dirs. 1990-96), Photography Guild, Shades Valley Camera Club, Cahaba River Soc. (adv. bd. 1991-92, bd. dirs. 1993-98, v.p. orgnl. devel. 1995-98), Ala. Growth Strategies Task Force, Regional Open Space and Trails Alliance, The Club, Jefferson Club. Episcopalian. Avocations: photography, high altitude hiking, white water canoeing. Home and Office: Tucker Investments 4132 Old Leeds Rd Birmingham AL 35213-3210

TUCKER, THOMAS RANDALL, public relations executive; b. Indpls., Aug. 6, 1931; s. Ovie Allen and Oris Aleen (Robertson) T.; m. Evelyn Marie Armuth, Aug. 9, 1953; children: Grant, Roger, Richard. AB, Franklin Coll., 1953. Grad. asst. U. Minn., 1953-54; dir. admissions registrar Franklin Coll., 1954-57; with Cummins Engine Co., Inc., Columbus, Ind., 1957, dir. pub. rels., 1968-88; pub. rels. cons. Mem. sch. bd. trustees Bartholomew County, Ind., 1966-72, pres., 1968-69; mem. Ind. State Bd. Edn., 1977-89; treas. Bartholomew County Rep. Ctrl. Com., 1960-80; sec. Columbus Learning Ctr. Mgmt. Corp.; hon. trustee Franklin Coll.; trustee Ind. State Mus. Mem. Pub. Rels. Soc. Am., Columbus (Ind.) C. of C. (Cmty. Svc. award 1986), Rotary, Sagamore of the Wabash, Kappa Tau Alpha, Phi Delta Theta, Sigma Delta Chi. Lutheran. Home: 4380 N Riverside Dr Columbus IN 47203-1123 Office: PO Box 3005 Columbus IN 47202-3005

TUCKER, THOMAS WILLIAM, mathematics professor; b. Princeton, N.J., July 15, 1945; s. Albert William Tucker and Alice Judson (Curtiss) Beckenbach; m. Mollie Dalton; children: Thomas John, Emily McDonnell. AB magna cum laude, Harvard U., 1967; PhD, Dartmouth Coll., 1971. Instr. Princeton U., 1971-73; from asst. prof. to prof. math. Colgate U., Hamilton, N.Y., 1973-83, prof., 1983—, Charles G. Hetherington prof. math., 1994—, chmn. math. dept., 1982-86, acting dean coll., 1991-92, dir. divsn. nat. sci., 1993-96. Vis. assoc. prof. Dartmouth Coll., Hanover, N.H., 1978-79; cons. Ednl. Testing Svc., 1973—, Inst. for Def. Analyses, Princeton, (summers) 1974, 75, 78, 79, 84, 85; chmn. advanced placement calculus com. Coll. Bd., N.Y.C., 1983-87; pres. Calculus Consortium for Higher Edn., Inc., 1998—. Co-author: Topological Graph Theory, 1987; editor: Priming the Calculus Pump, 1990; contbr. numerous articles to profl. jours. NSF grantee, 1976-77, 80-82, 86-88, 89, 90-97. Mem. Math. Assn. Am. (mem., chmn. many coms., v.p. 1990-92), Am. Math. Soc. Home: 21 Hamilton St Hamilton NY 13346-1329 Office: Colgate U Dept Math Hamilton NY 13346 E-mail: ttucker@mail.colgate.edu.

TUCKER, WATSON BILLOPP, lawyer; b. Dobbs Ferry, N.Y., Nov. 16, 1940; s. Watson Billopp and Mary (Prema) T.; children: Robin, Craig, Christopher, Alexander, John. BS, Northwestern U., Evanston, Ill., 1962; JD magna cum laude, Northwestern U., 1965. Bar: Ill. 1965, U.S. Dist. Ct. (no. dist.) Ill. 1966, U.S. Supreme Ct. 1971, U.S. Dist. Ct. (no. dist.) N.Y. 1976, U.S. Ct. Appeals (2d, 3d, 5th, 6th, 7th, and 9th cirs.). Ptnr. Mayer, Brown & Platt, Chgo., 1972-99, Smith Tucker & Brown, DeKalb, Ill., 1999—. Fellow Am. Coll. Trial Lawyers. Office: Smith Tucker & Brown 115 N 1st St Dekalb IL 60115-3201 E-mail: wbtucker@smithtuckerbrown.com.

TUCKER, WILLIAM DANIEL, English educator; b. N.Y.C., May 29, 1948; s. William Harding and Frances Winifred Tucker; m. Kathryn Jane Hessert, Feb. 16, 1974. BA, Hamilton Coll., Clinton, N.Y., 1970; MAT, Harvard U., 1971; PhD, Boston Coll., 1994. Cert. in secondary English, supervision, Mass. Tchr. English Brockton (Mass.) H.S., 1973-93; supr. student tchrs. Boston Coll., Chestnut Hill, Mass., 1989-90; prof. English Ea. Mich. U., Ypsilanti, 1993—. Dir. Ea. Mich. Writing Project, Ypsilanti, 1997-98, 2002—; test reviewer Mich. Test for Tchr. Cert., Lansing, 1994-95, 99-2000. Contbr. articles to profl. jours. NEH/Coun. for Basic Edn. fellow, 1989, Hemingway Inst. fellow NEH/Boston Writing Project, 1990-91; Ea. Mich. U. Spring-summer Rsch. award, 1996. Mem. Nat. Writing Project (co-dir. 1995-97, dir. 2000—), Nat. Coun. Tchrs. English, Conf. on English Edn. Home: 310 Maple St Ypsilanti MI 48198 Office: Eastern Mich Univ 603F Pray-Harrold Ypsilanti MI 48197 E-mail: eng_tucker@online.emich.edu.

TUCKER, WILLIAM EDWARD, academic administrator, minister; b. Charlotte, N.C., June 22, 1932; s. Cecil Edward and Ethel Elizabeth (Godley) T.; m. Ruby Jean Jones, Apr. 8, 1955; children: Janet Sue, William Edward, Gordon Vance. BA, Barton Coll., Wilson, N.C., 1953, LLD (hon.), 1978; BD, Tex. Christian U., 1956; MA, Yale U., 1958, PhD, 1960; LHD (hon.), Chapman Univ., 1981; DH (hon.), Bethany Coll., 1982; DD (hon.), Austin Coll., 1985; LHD (hon.), Kentucky Wesleyan Coll., 1989. Ordained to ministry Disciples of Christ Ch., 1956; prof. Barton Coll., 1959-66, chmn. dept. religion and philosophy, 1961-66; mem. faculty Brite Div. Sch., Tex. Christian U., 1966-76, prof. ch. history, 1969-76, dean, 1971-76, chancellor, 1979-98, chancellor emeritus, 1998—. Pres. Bethany (W.Va.) Coll., 1976-79; dir. RadioShack Corp., Brown and Lupton Found.; mem. gen. bd. Christian Ch. (Disciples of Christ), 1971-74, 75-87, adminstrv. com., 1975-81, chmn. theol. edn. commn., 1972-73, mem. exec. com., chmn. bd. higher edn., 1975-77; dir. Christian Ch. Found., 1980-83; moderator Christian Ch. (Disciples of Christ), 1983-85 Author: J.H. Garrison and Disciples of Christ, 1964, (with others) Journey in Faith: A History of the Christian Church (Disciples of Christ), 1975; also articles. Bd. dirs. Van Cliburn Found., 1981—, Amon Carter Mus. Mem. Exch. Club, Phi Beta Kappa. Home: 2337 Colonial Pky Fort Worth TX 76109-1030 Office: 100 Throckmorton St Ste 416 Fort Worth TX 76102-2870 E-mail: w.tucker@tcu.edu.

TUCKER, WILLIAM P. lawyer, writer; b. Kingston, N.Y., Jan. 26, 1932; s. Philip and Mary (McGowan) T.; m. Dolores F. Beaudoin, June 10, 1961; children: Andrew M., Thomas B., Mary A. BA with honors, Hunter Coll., 1958; JD with honors, St. John's U., 1962. Bar: N.Y. 1962, U.S. Dist. Ct. (ea. dist.) N.Y. 1963, Fla. 1980. Assoc. Mendes & Mount, N.Y.C., 1962-63; ptnr. Cullen and Dykman, Bklyn. and Garden City, N.Y., 1963-98, Golden, Wexler & Sarnese, Garden City/Purchase/S.I., 1998-2001; pvt. practice, 2001—. Former gen. counsel Broadway Nat. Bank, Wartburg Luth. Svcs., Luth. Ctr. for the Aging, Martin Luther Ter. Apts., Inc., Interfaith Med. Ctr., Roosevelt Savs. Bank, Olympian Bank, GreenPoint Bank, Ridgewood Savs. Bank, Atlantic Liberty Savs., F.A., Bethpage Fed. Credit Union, Mcpl. Credit Union, Lincoln Savs. Bank, Bklyn. Savs. Bank, Met. Savs. Bank, Crossland Savs. Bank, Bushwick Savs. Bank, Anchor Savs. Bank; former spl. counsel OCI Mortgage Corp., Bklyn C. of C., Downtown Bklyn. Bus. Assn., Bank of N.Y., Chase Manhattan Bank, Fleet Bank, Kraft Credit Union, Apple Bank for Savs., Barclays Bank of N.Y.; chmn. bd. dirs. Broadway Nat. Bank. Author: DP-or Billy and Jerry in the Promised Land, 1996, Moving Home Plate, 1999, Excalibur, 2001. Past mem. Selective Svc. Bd.; past pres. St. Vincent Ferrer Home Sch. Assn.; del. Diocesan Union Holy Name Socs.; mem. coun. St. John's U.; mem. coun. of regents St. Francis Coll., Bklyn.; bd. dirs. Faith Home Found., St. Josephs Coll. Mem. Am. Coll. Real Estate Lawyers, N.Y. State Bar Assn., Fla. Bar Assn., Savs. Banks Lawyers Assn. Bklyn., N.Y. Land Title Assn., Suffolk County Bar Assn., Savs. Bank Assn. N.Y. State (law com.), Bklyn. Mcpl. Club (pres.), Knight of Malta. Avocations: co-owner Salem Keizer Volcanoes N.W. League baseball team, Norwich Navigators Ea. League baseball team; v.p. N.W. Profl. Baseball League; bd. dirs. Bklyn. Sportsplex Inc. Home: 23 Bunker Hill Dr Huntington NY 11743-5705 Office: 202 East Main St Ste 303 Huntington NY 11743 E-mail: wptucker@worldnet.att.net.

TUCKMAN, BRUCE WAYNE, educational psychologist, educator, researcher; b. N.Y.C., Nov. 24, 1938; s. Jack Stanley and Sophie Sylvia (Goldberg) T.; children: Blair Z., Bret A. BS, Rensselaer Poly. Inst., 1960; MA, Princeton U., 1962, PhD, 1963. Rsch. assoc. Princeton (N.J.) U., 1963; rsch. psychologist Naval Med. Rsch. Inst., Bethesda, Md., 1963-65; assoc. prof. edn. Rutgers U., New Brunswick, N.J., 1965-70; prof., 1970-78; dir. Bur. Rsch. and Devel.-Rutgers U., New Brunswick, 1975-78; dean Coll. Edn. Baruch Coll., CUNY, 1978-82; sr. rsch. fellow CUNY, 1982-83; dean Coll. Edn. Fla. State U., Tallahassee, 1983-86, prof., 1983—98; prof. dir. acad. learning lab. Ohio State U., Columbus, 1998—. Author: Preparing to Teach the Disadvantaged, 1969 (N.J. Assn. Tchrs. of English Author's award 1969), Conducting Educational Research, 1972, 5th rev. edit., 1999 (Phi Delta Kappa Rsch. award 1973), Evaluating Instructional Programs, 1979, 2d rev. edit., 1985, Analyzing and Designing Educational Research, 1979, Effective College Management, 1987, Testing for Teachers, 1988; (novel) Long Road to Boston, 1988, Educational Psychology: From Theory to Application, 1992, 96, 98, 2002, Learning and Motivation Strategies: Your Guide to Success, 2002. Rsch. dir. Task Force on Competency Stds. Trenton, N.J., 1976. N.Y. State Regents scholar, 1956; Kappa Nu grad. scholar, 1960; NIMH predoctoral fellow, 1961, 62; Rutgers U. faculty study fellow, 1974-75 Fellow APA, Am. Psychol. Soc.; mem. Am. Ednl. Rsch. Assn. Office: 250B Younkin Success Ctr 1640 Neil Ave Columbus OH 43201-2333

TUCK-RICHMOND, DOLETTA SUE, prosecutor; b. Hugo, Okla., June 18, 1966; d. Benny Doyle and Tommie Marie (Cousins) T.; m. Lyle Richmond, Sept. 30, 1995; 1 child, Rachelle Jay Marie. AS, Murray State Coll., Tishomingo, Okla., 1986; BS magna cum laude, S.E. Okla. State U., 1988; JD with highest honors, U. Okla., 1991. Bar: Okla. 1991, U.S. Dist. Ct. (we., ea., and no. dists.), U.S. Ct. Appeals (10th cir.). Summer assoc. Andrews Davis, Oklahoma City, 1989-90; instr. in legal rsch, writing and oral advocacy U. Okla., Norman, 1989-91; assoc. Crowe & Dunlevy, Oklahoma City, 1991-93, Tulsa, Okla., 1993-94; pvt. practice Antlers, 1994; exempt orgn. specialist IRS, Oklahoma City, 1994-95; asst. atty. gen. State of Okla., 1995—; asst. U.S. atty. U.S. Atty's. Office (we. dist.) Okla., 1999—. Author: Joint Defense Agreements Can It Help Your Client, 1998, King For a Day: An Overview of Federal and State Qui Jam Provisions, 1999; contbg. author, editor: Oklahoma Environmental Law Practitioner's Handbook, 1992. Firm com. mem., participant Harvest Food Dr., Oklahoma City, 1991; chairperson Okla. Young Lawyers Rape Victims Assistance Com., 1992-94; bd. dirs. Okla. County Young Lawyers Divsn., 1993; participant, vol. Legal Aide of Western Okla., 1991. Named Miss Murray State Coll., Student Senate Pres., Tishomingo, Okla., 1986-86, Order of Coif U. Okla., Norman, Okla., 1991, Okla. Law Review U. Okla., Norman, 1991. Mem. FBA, Okla. Bar Assn. (bd. dirs., young lawyers divsn. 1993-95, mock trial com. 1994-95), liaison mental health com. 1994-95), Am. Agrl. Law Assn., Phi Delta Phi, Phi Kappa Phi (Spl. Act award for U.S. Atty. 1996, 97). Democrat. Baptist. Avocations: tennis, reading, writing, knitting, sports events. Home: 1624 SW 128th Pl Oklahoma City OK 73170-5018 Office: US Atty's Office Western Dist of Okla 210 Park Ave Ste 400 Oklahoma City OK 73102-5628

TUDOR, BYNUM ELLSWORTH, III, lawyer; b. Winston-Salem, N.C., Mar. 19, 1960; BSBA, U. N.C., 1981; MBA, JD, Wake Forest U., 1986. Bar: Tenn. 1986. Assoc. Dearborn & Ewing, Nashville, 1986-92, Baker, Worthington, Crossley & Stansberry, Nashville, 1993-94; shareholder Tudor Law Firm, P.C., 1994—. Mem. ABA, Tenn. Bar Assn., Nashville Bar Assn., Middle Tenn. Employee Benefits Coun., Tenn. Valley Employee Benefits Coun., Phi Delta Phi. Democrat. Home: 716 Clematis Dr Nashville TN 37205-1030 Office: Tudor Law Firm PC PO Box 198258 221 4th Ave N 5th Fl Nashville TN 37219 E-mail: TudorLawFirm@aol.com.

TUDOR, JOHN MARTIN, lawyer, educator; b. Kenton, Ohio; s. Arthur Davis and Marjorie Maxie (Martin) T.; m. Anda Maija Vilums, Aug. 26, 1961; children: Mara Y. Tudor Ward, Andrew Roland. BA, Ohio State U., 1959; JD, Duke U., 1962. Bar: Ohio 1962, U.S. Dist. Ct. (no. dist.) Ohio 1963, U.S. Supreme Ct. 1973, U.S. Ct. Appeals (6th cir.) 1987, U.S. Dist. Ct. (ctrl. dist.) Ill. 1995. Assoc. Squire, Sanders & Dempsey, Cleve., 1962-65; ptnr. Mahon, Tudor & Van Dyne, Kenton, 1965-88, Tudor, Blue & Cloud, Columbus, Ohio, 1969-88, Tudor, Cloud & Cesner, Kenton, 1988-90; mng. mem. Tudor Law, LLC, 1990—. Gen. counsel Am. BanCorp., Columbus, 1974-80; pres., dir. Village BancShares, Inc., Kenton, 1980-90, mng. mem. Latvian-Am. Trading Co., Ltd., 1997—. Author: We The People, 1987; contbr. articles to profl. jours. Founder Hardin County Hist. Soc., Kenton, 1966. Mem. ATLA, Am. Inns of Ct., Hardin County Bar Assn. (pres.), Eagle Scouts Assn. Republican. Presbyterian. Avocations: snow skiing, sail boating. Home: 411 Cecelia St Kenton OH 43326-1451 Office: 22 N Main St Kenton OH 43326-1552 Fax: (419) 675-2145. E-mail: tudorlaw@kenton.com.

TUDOR, MARY LOUISE DRUMMOND, elementary school educator; b. Long Beach, Calif., Nov. 9, 1937; d. Wesley Carlton and Dora Elizabeth (Blankenbeckler) Drummond; m. Gary Albert Tudor, June 18, 1960 (div. May 1980); children: Tamara Lynn Tudor, Michelle Denise Tudor Chapman. BS in Edn., U. So. Calif., 1959, MS in Edn., 1964; MS in Counseling & Psychology, Calif. State U., Long Beach, 1984. Cert. elem. adminstr., pupil pers. in counseling; cert. lang. devel. specialist, Calif. Tchr. Los Angeles Unified Sch. Dist., 1959-68, Long Beach Unified Sch. Dist., 1968-95; ret., 1995; substitute tchr. Lake Havasu Unified Sch. Dist., 1998—. Mem. Lake Havasu Cmty. Choir, Lake Havasu City Charter Com., 1998. Boyd Found. scholar, Long Beach, 1955, Nat. Meth. Bd. scholar, 1955. Mem. NEA, AAUW (pres.-elect Lake Havasu chpt.), DAR (Lake Havasu chpt.), Route 66 Assn. Ariz., Internat. Soc. Poets, U. So. Calif. Alumni, Long Beach City Coll. Found. Friends of Langs., Order of Ea. Star, Saddleback Valley Alumnae of Delta Delta Delta (past pres. 1973-75, founder), Phi Delta Kappa, Kappa Delta Pi, Phi Delta Gamma, Psi Chi, Delta Delta Delta (pres. Colo. River alumnae 1996-2002, founder), Lake Havasu Elkettes (2d v.p.), Women's Bowling Assn. (1st v.p.). London Bridge Republican Women. Methodist. Avocations: geneology, bowling, reading, travel, line dancing. E-mail: mlthavasu@redrivernet.com.

TUDOR, THOMAS RAE, electric power industry executive; b. Albany, Ga., Jan. 20, 1958; s. Willian Winston and Adelaide Agnes Tudor; m. Deborah Ann Hawks, Aug. 1, 1998; children: Jeffrey Alan Hawks Jr., Steven Michael Hawks, Sean Tare Hawks. AS, SUNY, 1988, BS, 1995. Field engr. Tracor, Inc., California, Md., 1982-87; systems engring. br. mgr. CACI, Inc., Great Mills, 1987-88; contract adminstr. So. Md. Elec. Coop., Inc., Hughesville, 1988—. Mem. Md. Photovoltaics Utilities Working Group, Annapolis, 1993—, Utilities Photovoltaic Group, Washington, 1994—. Bd. dirs. So. Md. Resource Conservation & Devel., Inc., Waldorf, 1995—. With USCG, 1977-81. Recipient Solar Park Power award Md. Energy Adminstr. & Interstate Renewable Energy Coun. St. Clements Island State Park, Md., 1997. Independent. Episcopalian. Avocations: American history, foreign coin collecting, photovoltaics. Office: So Md Elec Coop Inc 15035 Burnt Store Rd Hughesville MD 20637-1937

TUDOSE, STEFANIA DANIELLA, holistic practitioner; b. Romania, Aug. 9, 1953; m. Marin Tudose, Mar. 24, 1973; children: Viorel, Mihai, Alexandra--Marina. PhD in Metaphisics, Am. Inst. of Holistic Theology, Youngstown, Ohio, 1997. Cert. clin. hypnotherapist. Rsch. cons. Estee Lauder Co., Melville, N.Y., 1994—; holistic practitioner Open Mind Ever, Inc., Maspeth, 1997—. Cons. various hosps. Mem. Internat. Assn. Counselors and Therapists, N.Y. Acad. Scis., Noetic Scis. Inst. Achievements include the repair of chronic conditions or crisis situation in human health, visualising cause and initiating healing process, energizing water by hand power. Avocations: biology, chemistry rsch., psychology, painting, writing poems. Office: 200 W 57th St New York NY 10019

TUDRYN, JOYCE MARIE, professional society administrator; b. Holyoke, Mass., July 27, 1959; d. Edward William and Frances Katherine (Bajor) T.; m. William Wallace Friberger III, Sept. 18, 1982; 1 child, Kristen. BS in Comm., Syracuse U., 1981. Asst. editor Nat. Assn. Broadcasters, Washington, 1981-83; dir. programs Internat. Radio and TV Soc. Found., N.Y.C., 1983-87, assoc. exec. dir., 1988-94; exec. dir. Internat. Radio and TV Soc., 1994-97, pres., 1997—. Spkr. in field; nat. adv. bd. Alpha Epsilon Rho Broadcasting Soc., 1988-91, 93-94, hon. trustee, 1994-98, officer, 1999—; v.p. Corp. for Ednl. Radio and TV, 1988-94; adv. bd. Marist Coll. Sch. Comm., 1999—, Syracuse U. Newhouse Sch. Pub. Comm., 1999—; vice chmn. edn. iEmmy Festival, 1999; guest prof. U. Scranton, 2000. Editor-in-chief IRTS News, 1983—; columnist TV Facts, Figures and Film mag., 1983-88; one-woman photography exhbn. Synchronicity Space, N.Y.C., 1998. Recipient Mass. Kodak Photography award, 1977; S.I. Newhouse scholar Syracuse U., 1980-81. Mem. N.Y. Media Roundtable, Gamma Phi Beta. Avocations: photography. Home: 602 Bennington Dr Union NJ 07083-9104 Office: Internat Radio and TV Soc Found Ste 1714 420 Lexington Ave New York NY 10170-1799

TUELL, JACK MARVIN, retired bishop; b. Tacoma, Nov. 14, 1923; s. Frank Harry and Anne Helen (Bertelson) T.; m. Marjorie Ida Beadles, June 17, 1946; children— Jacqueline, Cynthia, James. BS, U. Wash., 1947, LL.B., 1948; S.T.B., Boston U., 1955; MA, U. Puget Sound, 1961, DHS, 1990; D.D., Pacific Sch. Religion, 1966; LLD, Alaska Pacific U., 1980. Bar: Wash. 1948; ordained to ministry Meth. Ch., 1955. Practice law with firm Holte & Tuell, Edmonds, Wash., 1948-50; pastor Grace Meth. Ch., Everett, Wash., 1950-52, South Tewksbury Meth. Ch., Tewksbury, Mass., 1952-55, Lakewood Meth. Ch., Tacoma, 1955-61; dist. supt. Puget Sound dist. Meth. Ch., Everett, 1961-67; pastor 1st United Meth. Ch., Vancouver, Wash., 1967-72; bishop United Meth. Ch., Portland, Oreg., 1972-80, Calif.-Pacific Conf., United Meth. Ch., L.A., 1980-92; interim sr. pastor First United Meth. Ch., Boise, Idaho, 1995. Mem. gen. conf. United Meth. Ch., 1964, 66, 68, 70, 72; pres. coun. of Bishops United Meth. Ch., 1989-90. Author: The Organization of the United Methodist Church, 1970, 9th edit. 2002. Pres. Tacoma U.S.O., 1959-61, Vancouver YMCA, 1968; v.p. Ft. Vancouver Seamens Cnt., 1969-72; vice chmn. Vancouver Human Rels. Commn., 1970-72; pres. Oreg. Coun. Alcohol Problems, 1972-76; trustee U. Puget Sound, 1961-73, Vancouver Meml. Hosp., 1967-72, Alaska Meth. U., Anchorage, 1972-80, Willamette U., Salem, Oreg., 1972-80, Willamette View Manor, Portland, 1972-80, Rogue Valley Manor, Medford, Oreg., 1972-76, Sch. Theology at Claremont, Calif., 1980-92, Methodist Hosp., Arcadia, Calif., 1983-92; pres. nat. div. bd. global ministries United Meth. Ch., 1972-76, pres. ecumenical and interreligious concerns div., 1976-80, Commn. on Christian Unity and interreligious concerns, 1980-84, Gen. Bd. of Pensions,1984-92, Calif. Coun. Alcohol Problems, 1985-88. Jacob Sleeper fellow, 1955 Home and Office: 816 S 216th St # 637 Des Moines WA 98198-6331

TUER, DAVID A. petroleum industry executive; BSME, U. Calgary. Asst. dep. min. energy Govt. of Alta.; mgr. spl. projects PanCanadian Petroleum, Calgary, Alta., 1988, v.p. spl. projects, v.p. mktg., 1989-94, sr. v.p. mktg., info. sys. and downstream bus. devel., 1989-94, pres., CEO. Mem. Bus. Coun. Nat. Issues; co-chair Climate Change Ctrl.; chmn. bd. govs. Mt. Royal Coll., Calgary.

TUFARO, RICHARD CHASE, lawyer; b. N.Y.C., July 9, 1944; s. Frank P. and Stephania A. (Maida) T.; m. Helen M. Tufaro, June 25, 1977; children: Mary C., Edward F., Paul R., Cynthia M. AB magna cum laude, Dartmouth Coll., 1965; LLB cum laude, Harvard U., 1968. Bar: N.Y. 1969, D.C. 1992, Md. 1994; U.S. Dist. Ct. (so. dist.) N.Y. 1973, U.S. Dist. Ct. (ea. dist.) N.Y. 1978, U.S. Dist Ct. (D.C. dist.), 1994; U.S. Dist. Ct. (Md. dist.), 1996, U.S. Ct. Apls. (2d cir.) 1973, (5th cir.) 1976, (9th cir.) 1979, (6th cir.) 1980, (4th cir.), 1995; U.S. Ct. Claims, 1985, U.S. Ct. Appeals (3d cir.) 1990, U.S. Ct. Appeals (D.C. cir.) 1992; U.S. Sup. Ct., 1975. Law clk. Appellate-Div. N.Y. State, N.Y.C., 1970-71, assoc. Milbank, Tweed, Hadley & McCloy, N.Y.C., 1971-72, adminstrv. asst. White House Domestic Coun., Washington, 1972-73, assoc. Milbank, Tweed, Hadley & McCloy, N.Y.C., 1973-77, ptnr. 1978—. Served to capt. U.S. Army, 1968-70. Decorated Bronze Star with oak leaf cluster. Mem. ABA, Am. Mgmt. Assn., Phi Beta Kappa. Home: 7109 Heathwood Ct Bethesda MD 20817-2915 Office: 1825 I St NW Ste 1100 Washington DC 20006-5417

TUFT, MARY ANN, executive search firm executive; b. Easton, Pa., Oct. 11, 1934; d. Ben and Elizabeth (Reibman) T. BS, West Chester (Pa.) State Coll., 1956; MA, Lehigh U., 1960. Cert. assn. exec. Nat. trainer Girl Scouts U.S.A., N.Y.C., 1965-68; cons. Nat. League for Nursing, 1968-69; exec. dir. Nat. Student Nurses Assn., 1970-85; mem. Commn. on Dietetic Registration, Am. Dietetic Assn., 1981-85; pres. Specialized Cons. Ltd., 1983-85; exec. dir. Radiol. Soc. N.Am., Oak Brook, Ill., 1985-88; pres. Tuft & Assocs., Inc., 1989—. Trustee, Found. of the Nat. Student Nurses Assn., 2001—; adv. bd. Cognitive Neurology and Alzheimer's Disease Ctr. of Northwestern Univ./Feinberg Sch. of Medicine. Bd. dirs. Nurses House, Inc., 1981-85, Am. Friends of Hebrew U., Midwest Region, 2000—; bd. dirs. Chgo. Sinai Cong., 1987-91, v.p., 1988. Recipient Disting. Alumnus award West Chester State Coll., 1979; Mary Ann Tuft Scholarship Fund named in her honor Found. Nat. Student Nurses Assn.; Kepner-Tregoe scholar, 1966. Mem. ALA (pub. mem. com. on accreditation 1993-95), Am. Soc. AAssn. Execs. (bd. dirs. 1980-83, trustee for cert. 1980-83, vice chmn. 1983-84), N.Y. Soc. Assn. Execs. (pres. 1978-79, bd. dirs. 1975-78, 1st Outstanding Exec. award 1982), Continuing Care Accreditation Assn. (bd. dirs. 1983-85), Specialized Cons. in Nursing (faculty).

TUFTE, BRIAN NELSON, lawyer; b. Mpls., Dec. 9, 1961; s. Obert N. and Doris H. T.; m. Julie S. Tufte, July 22, 1993; children: Jessica, Brianna. BA in Physics/Math., St. Olaf Coll., 1984; JD magna cum laude, William Mitchell Coll. Law, 1994. Bar: Minn. 1994, U.S. Dist. Ct. Minn. 1994, U.S. Ct. Appeals (8th and fed. cirs.) 1994, U.S. Patent and Trademark Office. Sr. integrated cir. design engr. Honeywell Inc., Solid State Elecs. Ctr., Plymouth, Minn., 1985-93; assoc. atty. Nawrocki, Rooney & Siverston, P.A., Mpls., 1993-98; founding ptnr. Crompton, Seager & Tufte, LLC, 1998—. Mem. Am. Intellectual Property Law Assn., Minn. Intellectual Property Law Assn., Minn. Bar Assn., Hennepin County Bar Assn. Office: Crompton Seager & Tufte LLC 331 2nd Ave S Ste 895 Minneapolis MN 55401-2260 E-mail: tufte@cstlaw.com.

TUFTE, EDWARD ROLF, writer, publisher, statistics educator; b. Kansas City, Mo., Mar. 14, 1942; s. Edward E. and Virginia (James) T.; m. Inge Druckrey BS, Stanford U., 1963, MS, 1964; PhD, Yale U., 1968; HHD (hon.), Cooper Union, 1992, Conn. Coll., 1995, St. Joseph's Coll., 1997, Md. Art Inst., 1999, Mpls. Coll. Art, 2000, Williams Coll., 2000. Asst. prof. pub. policy Princeton U., 1967-71, assoc. prof., 1971-74, prof., 1974-77; prof. polit. sci., stats., computer sci. and graphic design Yale U., New Haven, 1977-99; pres. Graphics Press, Cheshire, 1983—. Author: Quantitative Analysis of Social Problems, 1970, Size and Democracy, 1973, Data Analysis, 1974, Political Control of the Economy, 1978 (Kammerer award 1979, Citation Classic 1989), The Visual Display of Quantitative Information, 1983 (Citation Classic 1992), Envisioning Information, 1990, Visual Explanations, 1997. Pres. Cheshire Neighborhood Assn., 1984-87. Recipient Best Graphic Design award Internat. Design, 1990, Wittenborn award, 1991, Best Book Design award Assn. Ind. Publs., Computer Press Assn. award, 1991, Sci. award Phi Beta Kappa, 1991, AIGA book show, 1998, book award AIA, 1998, book award STC, 1998, book award Internat. Design, 1998, book award Am. Ctr. for Design, 1998; Ctr. for Advanced Study in Behavioral Scis. fellow, 1973-74; Guggenheim fellow, 1977. Fellow Am. Acad. Arts and Scis., Am. Statis. Assn. Office: Graphics Press PO Box 430 Cheshire CT 06410

TUFTE, OBERT NORMAN, retired research executive; b. Northfield, Minn., May 30, 1932; s. Ole Nels and Stella Josephine (Lundene) T.; m. Doris Helen Wisbroecker, Dec. 29, 1956; children, Keith, Brian, Stephen, Jon. BA in Physics, St. Olaf Coll., 1954; PhD in Physics, Northwestern U., 1960. Rsch. scientist Honeywell Inc., Hopkins, Minn., 1960-69, rsch. mgr. Bloomington, 1969-84, rsch. fellow, 1984-87, chief scientist, 1987-93; ret., 1994; pvt. cons. in field, 1994—. Contbr. articles to profl. jours., 1960-88; inventor 7 U.S. patents, 1962-89. Mem. IEEE (sr.), Am. Phys. Soc., Sigma Xi. Home: 14937 Manitou Rd NE Prior Lake MN 55372-1114

TUFTON, JANIE LEE (JANE TUFTON), dental hygienist, animal rights lobbyist, activist; b. Allentown, Pa., Jan. 6, 1949; d. Robert Harry and Jean Lorraine (Seng) T. BS in Edn., Indiana U. Pa., 1979; postgrad. in English, 1979-82. Registered dental hygienist, Pa., N.J., Calif.; cert. tchr., Pa. Dental hygienist pvt. dental practices, Pa., N.J., Calif., 1976-90. Author bd. game for dental health edn., 1974. Lobbyist, activist for animal rights; bd. dirs. and pub. rels. Lehigh Valley Animal Rights Coalition, 1984-93; active civil rights movement, cultural events, literacy programs, detoxification units for drug and alcohol abuse, venereal disease clinics, practical-life workshops for the cognitively impaired, suicide hotlines, YWCA, Girl Scouts U.S. Recipient recognition Pa. Dental Hygienists Assn., 1974 Mem. Am. Anti-Vivisect. Soc., Nat. Humane Edn. Soc., The Fund for Animals, The Humane Soc. of the U.S., Nat. Alliance for Animals, Internat. Soc. for Animal Rights, Physicians Com. for Responsible Medicine, Culture and Animals Found., Animal Legal Def. Fund, People for the Ethical Treatment of Animals, Farm Animal Reform Movement, Farm Sanctuary, Com. to Abolish Sport Hunting, Animal Rights Mobilization, In Def. of Animals, United Animal Nations, Internat. Platform Assn., Internat. Network for Religion and Animals, Humane Religion, Performing Animal Welfare Socs., Disabled and Incurably Ill for Alternatives to Animal Rsch., United Poultry Concerns, Am. Soc. for Prevention of Cruelty to Animals. Avocations: photography, tennis, reading, environmental issues, women's studies. Home: 2102 S Lehigh Ave Whitehall PA 18052-5532

TUFTS, ROBERT B. academic administrator; b. Cleve., Nov. 5, 1940; s. Robert L. and Dora Mae (Yingling) T.; m. Nancy Intihar, June 22, 1968 (div. Feb. 1990); children: Therese, Kevin R.; m. Ellen Sanders, May 29, 1998. BA cum laude, Cleve. State U., 1967; MA, Case Western Res. U., 1972; postgrad., U. Akron, 1973-76. Admissions counselor Cleve. State U., 1967-69, asst. registrar, 1969-70, Youngstown (Ohio) State U., 1970-73, U. Akron (Ohio), 1973-75, assoc. registrar, 1975-78; registrar Portland (Oreg.) State U., 1978-2000, The Art Inst. of Portland, 2000—. Com. mem. Park Recreation Adv. Bd., W. Linn., Oreg., 1981-84; presenter on fraudulent credentials, 1987—. Contbr. articles to profl. jours. With U.S. Army, 1959-62, Korea. Mem. Oreg. Assn. Registrars and Admissions Officers (sec.-treas. 1988-90), Pacific Assn. Collegiate Registrars and Admissions Officers (mem. program com. 1986-87, exec. bd., chair local arrangement 64th Ann. Mtg., Portland 1990, chair facilities com. 73d annual mtg., 1999), Am. Assn. Collegiate Registrars and Admissions Officers (local arrangements com., chair pub. com. 82nd Ann. Mtg., Reno, 1996, mem. facilities planning mgmt. com. 1975-78, chmn. of com. 1977-78), Nat. Assn. Coll. and Univ. Bus. Officers, Theta Rho. Democrat. Mem. Unitarian Ch. Avocations: mountaineering, camping, home projects. Home: 4981 Prospect St West Linn OR 97068-3116 Office: The Art Inst of Portland 2000 SW Fifth Ave Portland OR 97201-4972 E-mail: tuftsr@aii.edu.

TUGCU, NEJAT, investment consultant, information systems expert; b. Antalya, Turkey, Mar. 27, 1945; s. Cavit Fikri and Ayse (Sapci) T.; m. Seyhan Kozanoğlu, May 26, 1976. BS in CE magna cum laude, Robert Coll., Istanbul, Turkey, 1967; MS in Structures, Cornell U., 1969, PhD in Structures and Theoretical and Applied Mechanics, 1970. Data processing and sr. systems analyst Geiger-Berger Assocs., N.Y.C., 1970-72; dep. gen. mgr. info. systems computer ctr. Boğazici U., Istanbul, 1972-75, asst. prof. computer sci., 1975-80; dep. gen. mgr. info. systems Hisarbank, 1980-83; sr. comml. project mgr. Intes Constrn. and Contracting, Inc., 1983-86; exec., shareholder of Yeditepe Beynelmilel Otelcilik Turizm ve Ticaret A.S. Conrad Istanbul Hotel, 1986-94; cons. tourism investment, 1994—. Ptnr., prin. Infotek Enformasyon Sistem A.S., Istanbul, 1980-87. Co-editor Master Plan for Istanbul and Marmara Ports, 1974. Fellow Cornell U., 1967-68. Mem. Rotary. (sec. Istanbul-Findikli chpt. 1982-83, v.p. 1983-84, pres. 1984-85). Moslem. Avocations: playing electronic organ, photography, figure skating, calligraphy. Home and Office: Emirgan Cad 67 Park Apt Emirgan Istanbul 80850 Turkey E-mail: njttgc@yahoo.com.

TUGEND, THOMAS JOSEPH, communications executive; b. Berlin, June 30, 1925; came to U.S., 1939; s. Gustav and Irene Frederika (Fontheim) Tugendreich; m. Rachel Spitzer, Oct. 7, 1956; children: Orlee, Alina, Ronit. BA, U. Calif., Berkeley, 1950; Bachelor's Cert., U. Madrid, 1954; MA, UCLA, 1957. Reporter San Francisco Chronicle, 1951-54; pub. info. officer UCLA, 1957-84, dir. communications Sch. Engring. and Architecture, 1984-89; west coast corr. Jerusalem Post, Israel, 1974—. West coast corr. Jewish Chronicle, U.K., Jewish Telegraphic Agy., N.Y.; pub. relations cons. Weizmann Inst. Sci., Rehovot, Israel, 1963-91. Contbg. editor Jewish Jour., L.A. Bd. dirs. So. Calif. Jewish Hist. Soc., Los Angeles; Machal West (Am. Vet. of Israel), L.A. Served as sgt. U.S. Army, 1944-46, ETO, 1950-51; Israel Def. Forces, 1948-49. Recipient Journalism award for Excellence, Greater Los Angeles Press Club, 1984, 86, Simon Rockower award, 1987. Mem. Nat. Assn. Sci. Writers, Am. Jewish Press Assn. Jewish. Avocations: tennis, swimming, motion picture history.

TUGGLE, FRANCIS DOUGLAS, information technology educator, consultant; b. Portsmouth, Va., Jan. 19, 1943; s. Francis Joyner and Florence Eleanor (Dahlgren) T.; m. Mary Ann Tredway, June 3, 1967; children: Wendy Elizabeth, Laura Michelle. SB, MIT, 1964; MS, Carnegie-Mellon U., 1967, PhD, 1971. Prof. bus. adminstrn. and computer sci. U. Kans., Lawrence, 1968-78; Jesse H. Jones prof. mgmt. Rice U., Houston, 1978-90; dean Kogod Coll. Bus. Adminstrn., Am. U., Washington, 1990-96, prof. info. systems and strategic planning, 1996—. Bd. dirs. Equus II, Inc., Houston, Internat. Expert Sys. Inc., Houston, v.p. mktg. devel.; dir.-at-large Inst. for Ops. Rsch. and Mgmt. Scis., 1995; sr. cons. RWD Techs., Inc.; v.p. Timegate.com. Author: How to Program a Computer, 1975, Organizational Processes, 1978. Com. chmn. United Way Tex. Gulf Coast, Houston, 1985-88. Ford Found. fellowship, 1966. Mem. Inst. for Ops. Rsch. and Mgmt. Scis. (bd. dirs. 1995, v.p. 1992-94), Am. Assn. Artificial Intelligence, Assn. for Computing Machinery, Acad. of Mgmt., Sigma Xi, Beta Gamma Sigma, Alpha Kappa Psi. Episcopalian. Avocations: golf, bicycling, jogging. Home: 4709 Ft Sumner Dr Bethesda MD 20816-2466 Office: Am U Kogod Coll Bus Adminstrn 4400 Massachusetts Ave NW Washington DC 20016-8044 E-mail: Ftuggle@american.edu.

TUGGLE, GLORIA HARRIS, school system administrator; b. Kerrville, Tenn., May 23, 1933; d. Isaiah and Lillian (Gary) Harris; m. Owens E. Tuggle, Nov. 18, 1955; 1 child, Kenneth Tyrone. BS, LeMoyne-Owen Coll., Memphis, 1955; MA, Memphis State U., 1965, postgrad., 1973. Cert. math. tchr., adminstr., supr. Math. instr. spl. programs LeMoyne-Owen Coll., 1968-69, Memphis State U., 1972-74; part-time math. instr. State Tech. Inst., Memphis, 1975-76, Shelby State Coll., Memphis, 1976-79; math. tchr., guidance counselor Memphis City Schs., 1955-79, math. supr., 1979-92, dir. secondary programs, 1992-94, coord. office of accountability, 1994-99. Adv. bd. educator's channel Whittle Ednl. Network, 1990—; site visitor, rev. panelist, super panelist U.S. Dept. Edn. Blue Ribbon Schs. Program, 1986-2002; vis. com. So. Assn. Colls. and Schs., 1981, 82, 88; cons. Nat. Assessment Edn. Progress, 1985-86; reviewer Math. Sci. Edn. Bd., 1987. Bd. dirs. Nat. Civil Rights Mus., Memphis, 1990—, Jessie Mahan Day Care Ctr., Memphis, 1985—, Southeastern Consortium Minorities in Engring., 1994-2000, Curve Optimist Club, 1998-2000; chair Silver Star News Cmty. Adv. Bd., 1993; min. of music Macedonia Bapt. Ch., 1967-95; mem. Leadership Memphis Class of '91, YWCA. Recipient Outstanding Educator award Memphis City Coun., 1987, Outstanding Cmty. Contbns. award Shelby County Govt., 1993, 96, 99, Meritorious Svc. award City of Memphis, 1993, 99, Cert. of Appreciation award U.S. Dept. Edn., Blue Ribbon Schs. Program, 1987-99, Hero Among Homefolk/Global Mentor for Youth and Inspirational Role Model award Macedonia Bapt. Ch., 1990-92, Exemplary Svc. award Southeastern Consortium Minorities in Engring., Inc., 1995, Disting. Role Model award Memphis Alliance Black Sch. Educators, 1995, Woman of Wisdom award Nat. Coalition of 100 Black Women, 1999, Extra Mile award Memphis City Schs., 1999; named Greek of Yr., Memphis Pan Hellenic Coun., 1990, Exemplary Educator, Tenn. Dept. Edn., 2001. Mem. ASCD, NAACP, Nat. Coun. Suprs. Maths. (nomination com. 1987-89), Nat. Coun. Tchrs. Math. (co-chair Memphis meeting 1984, chair miniconf. for ednl. leaders 1990), Tenn. Math. Tchrs. Assn., Benjamin Banneker Assn., Memphis Area Coun. Tchrs. Math. (v.p. 1982-84), Memphis City Schs. Adminstrs. Assn., Phi Delta Kappa, Alpha Kappa Alpha (pres. Memphis chpt. 1990-91, chairperson Southeastern Regional Conf. 1992, Woman of Distinction 1990, Soror of Yr. 1991, Pres. of Yr. Southeastern Region 1992). Democrat. Avocations: organ, piano, reading, travel. Home: 4870 Ortie Dr Memphis TN 38109-6529

TUHRIM, STANLEY, physician, neurologist; b. N.Y.C., Jan. 26, 1954; m. Betty Jane Mintz, Feb. 8, 1981; 1 child, Richard J. BA in Psychology, Haverford Coll., 1975; MD, Mt. Sinai Sch. Medicine, 1979. Intern U. Pa. Hosp., Phila., 1979-80; resident in neurology Mt. Sinai Hosp., N.Y.C., 1980-83; stroke fellow U. Md. Hosp., 1983-84; asst. prof. dept. neurology U. Md., Balt., 1985-87, Mt. Sinai Hosp., N.Y.C., 1987-90, assoc. prof. dept. neurology, 1991—2001, prof. dept. neurology, 2002—; assoc. prof. dept. geriatrics and adult devel. Mt. Sinai Med. Ctr., 1994—. Contbr. articles to profl. jours. Recipient Tchr.-Investigator award NINCDS, 1984, Bressler Rsch. award U. Md., 1985; NINDS clin. investigator, 1988. Fellow: Am. Heart Assn. (stroke coun.); mem.: Am. Acad. Neurology, Nat. Stroke Assn., Am. Med. Informatics Assn., Soc. Critical Care Medicine. Office: Mt Sinai Med Ctr One Gustave Levy Pl PO Box 1137 New York NY 10029-0312

TUKE, ROBERT DUDLEY, lawyer, educator; b. Rochester, N.Y., Dec. 5, 1947; s. Theodore Robert and Doris Jean (Smith) T.; m. Susan Devereux Cummins, June 21, 1969; children: Andrew, Sarah. BA with distinction, U. Va., 1969; JD, Vanderbilt U., 1976. Bar: Tenn. 1976, U.S. Dist. Ct. (mid. dist.) Tenn. 1976, U.S. Ct. Appeals (6th cir.) 1976, U.S. Ct. Appeals (4th cir.) 1978, U.S. Ct. Appeals (fed. cir.) 1993, U.S. Supreme Ct. 1986, U.S. Ct. Internat. Trade 1993. Assoc. Farris, Warfield & Kanaday, Nashville, 1976—79, ptnr., 1980—94, Tuke Yopp & Sweeney, Nashville, 1994—99, Trauger, Ney & Tuke, Nashville, 2000—. Adj. prof. law Vanderbilt U. Law Sch., Nashville; faculty PLI, 1995—; mem. AMA Drs.' Adv. Network. Author: (with others) Tennessee Practice, 1992—; editor-in-chief Vanderbilt Law Rev.; contbr. articles to profl. jours. Mem. Tenn. Adoption Law Study Commn., 1993-96, Metro CATV Com. Capt. USMC, 1969-73. Decorated Cross of Gallantry; Patrick Wilson Merit scholar. Mem. ABA, Am. Health Law Assn., Nat. Assn. Bond Lawyers, Am. Acad. Adoption Attys. (pres.), Tenn. Bar Assn., Nashville Bar Assn., Order of Coif. Democrat. Episcopalian. Avocations: rowing, running, cycling, hiking, travel. Office: 222 4th Ave N Nashville TN 37219-2115 E-mail: rtuke@tntlaw.net.

TUKEY, HAROLD BRADFORD, JR. horticulture educator; b. Geneva, May 29, 1934; s. Harold Bradford and Ruth (Schweigert) T.; m. Helen Dunbar Parker, June 25, 1955; children: Ruth Thurbon, Carol Tukey Schwartz, Harold Bradford. BS, Mich. State U., 1955, MS, 1956, PhD, 1958. Research asst. South Haven Expt. Sta., Mich., 1955; AEC grad. research asst. Mich. State U., 1955-58; NSF fellow Calif. Inst. Tech, 1958-59; asst. prof. dept. floriculture and ornamental horticulture Cornell U., Ithaca, N.Y., 1959-64, assoc. prof., 1964-70, prof., 1970-80; prof. urban horticulture U. Wash., Seattle, 1980-97, prof. emeritus, 1997—, dir. Arboreta, 1980-92, dir. Ctr. Urban Horticulture, 1980-92. Cons. Internat. Bonsai mag., Electric Power Rsch. Inst., P.R. Nuclear Ctr., 1965-66; mem. adv. com. Seattle-U. Wash. Arboretum and Bot. Garden, 1980-92, vice chmn., 1982, chmn., 1986-87; vis. scholar U. Nebr., 1982, 98; vis. prof. U. Calif., Davis, 1973; lectr. U. Western Sydney-Hawkesburg U. Melbourne, Victoria Coll. Agrl. and Horticulture, 1995, Massey U., 1996; Hill prof. U. Minn., 1996; mem. various coms. Nat. Acad. Scis.-NRC; bd. dirs. Arbor Fund Bloedel Res., 1980-92, pres., 1983-84. Mem. editorial bd. Jour. Environ. Horticulture, Arboretum Bull. Mem. nat. adv. com. USDA, 1990—; pres. Ithaca PTA; troop advisor Boy Scouts Am., Ithaca. Lt. U.S. Army, 1958. Recipient B.Y. Morrison award USDA, 1987; NSF fellow, 1958-59; named to Lansing (Mich.) Sports Hall of Fame, 1987; grantee NSF, 1962, 75, Bot. Soc. Am., 1964; hon. dr. Portuguese Soc. Hort., 1985. Fellow Am. Soc. Hort. Sci. (dir. 1970-71); mem. Internat. Soc. Hort. Sci. (U.S. del. to coun. 1971-90, chmn. commn. for amateur horiticulture 1974-83, exec. com. 1974-90, v.p. 1978-82, pres. 1982-86, past pres. 1986-90, chmn. comm. Urban Horticulture 1990-94, hon. mem. 1994), Wash. State Nursery and Landscape Assn. (hon. mem. 1995), Internat. Plant Propagators Soc. (hon., ea. region dir. 1969-71, v.p. 1972, pres. 1973, internat. pres. 1976), Am. Hort. Soc. (dir. 1972-81, exec. com. 1974-81, v.p. 1978-80, citation of merit 1981), Royal Hort. Soc. (London) (v.p. hon. 1993—), Bot. Soc. Am., N.W. Horticulture Soc. (dir. 1980-92), Arboretum Found. (dir. 1980-92), Rotary, Sigma Xi, Alpha Zeta, Phi Kappa Phi, Pi Alpha Xi, Xi Sigma Pi. Presbyterian. Home: 3300 E St Andrews Way Seattle WA 98112-3750 Office: U Wash Ctr Urban Horticulture PO Box 354115 Seattle WA 98195-4115 E-mail: tukeyhb@email.msn.com.

TULAFONO, TOGIOLA T.A. lieutenant governor; b. Aunu'u Island, American Samoa, Feb. 28, 1947; s. Aitu and Silika (Vaatu'itu'i) T.; m. Maryann Taufaasau Mauga, Sept. 17, 1984; children: Puataunofo, Olita, Cherianne, Emema, Timoteo, Rosie. Grad., Honolulu Police Acad., 1967; BA, Chadron State Coll., 1970; JD, Washburn U., 1975. Bar: Kans., Am. Samoa. Police instr. Am. Samoa Police Dept., Pago Pago, 1967; adminstrv. asst. Sec. of Samoan Affairs, 1970-71; legal asst. Atty. Gen., 1971-72; assoc. Law Offices of George A. Wray, 1975-77; v.p. South Pacific Island Airways, 1977-79; judge Dist. Ct. of Am. Samoa, 1979-80; chmn. bd. dirs. Am. Samoa Power Authority, 1978-80; mem. Am. Samoa Senate, 1981-85, 89—; pres. Nayram Samoa, Ltd., 1985-88; lt. gov. Am. Samoa, 1997—. Chmn. Senate Investigation Com., 1993—. Chmn. Bd. Higher Edn., Am. Samoa, 1993—; bd. dirs. Am. Samoa Jr. Golfers' Assn.; deacon Sailele Congrl. Ch. Mem. ATLA, Am. Samoa Bar Assn., Kans. Bar Assn., Samoa Profl. Golfer's Assn. (pres. 1985-87), Am. Samoa Golf Assn. (pres.). Democrat. Congregationalist. Office: Office of the Lt Gov Ter of American Samoa Pago Pago AS 96799*

TULCHIN, DAVID BRUCE, lawyer; b. N.Y.C., Dec. 2, 1947; s. Philip Tulchin and Mary (Weiner) Black; m. Nora Barrett, Aug. 20, 1972; children: Rachel, Daniel, Laura. BA, U. Rochester, 1970; JD, Harvard U., 1973. Bar: N.Y. 1974, U.S. Dist. Ct. (so. & ea. dists.) N.Y. 1975, U.S. Ct. Appeals (2d cir.) 1975, U.S. Supreme Ct. 1977, U.S. Ct. Appeals (5th cir.) 1978, U.S. Ct. Appeals (1st & 6th cirs.) 1984, U.S. Dist. Ct. (no. dist.) Ohio 1984, U.S. Ct. Appeals (3d, 4th & Fed. cirs.) 1988, U.S. Ct. Appeals (7th cir.) 1991, U.S. Dist. Ct. (we. dist.) N.Y., 1996. Law clk. to Judge Frederick V.P. Bryan U.S. Dist. Ct. So. Dist. N.Y., N.Y.C., 1973-75; assoc. Sullivan & Cromwell, 1975-82, ptnr., 1982—. Mem. ABA, Assn. Bar of City of N.Y., Fed. Bar Coun., N.Y. State Bar Assn., Fed. Cir. Bar Assn. Office: Sullivan & Cromwell 125 Broad St Fl 28 New York NY 10004-2489

TULCHIN, STANLEY, banker, lecturer, author, business reorganization consultant; Founder, chmn. bd. Stanley Tulchin Assocs., Westbury, N.Y., 1955-95. Bd. dirs. N.Y. Inst. Credit, Topps Corp.; founder, chmn. Reprise Capital Corp. Recipient Leadership in Credit Edn. award N.Y. Inst. Credit, 1990. Mem. Comml. Law League Am. (Pres'. Cup award 1975, past bd. govs., vice-chmn. bd. editors Comml. Law Jour., bd. dirs. Fund for Pub. Edn.), Nat. Assn. Credit Mgmt. Office: Sta Internat 400 Post Ave PO Box 185 Westbury NY 11590-0185

TULENKO, JAMES STANLEY, nuclear engineer, educator; b. Holyoke, Mass., June 1, 1936; s. John Truman and Anna (Bagdus) T.; m. Lois Anne Wagner, May 1, 1966; children: Mark, Christina, Katherine. BA, Harvard U., 1958, MA, 1960; MS, MIT, 1963; MEA, George Washington U., 1980. Mgr. nuclear dept. United Nuclear Corp., White Plains, N.Y., 1963-70; mgr. physics Nuclear Materials Corp., Pitts., 1970-71; mgr. fuel Babcock and Wilcox, Lynchburg, Va., 1971-80; mgr. engring. automation McDermott Corp., 1980-86; prof., chmn. nuclear engring. scis. dept. U. Fla., Gainesville, 1986—. Oversite rev. bd. Nuclear Assurance Corp., Atlanta, 1987-90; nuclear fellowship rev. bd. Oak Ridge (Tenn.) Associated Univs., 1987-90. Patentee innovative fuel design. Recipient Outstanding Researcher award U. Fla., 1990, 91, 92, 93, 94. Fellow Am. Nuclear Soc. (Silver Anniversary award for Outstanding Contbns. to Nuclear Fuel Cycle 1982, chmn. nuclear engring. accreditation com. 1984-88, chmn. pres. spl. com. on waste mgmt. 1988-90, chmn. fuel cycle and waste mgmt. divsn. 1975-76, chmn. robotics and remote sys. divsn. 1998-99, chmn. material sci. and tech. divsn. 1998-99, bd. dirs. 1999—, Mishma award for outstanding nuc. material rsch. 1997); mem. Am. Soc. for Engring. Edn. (Glenn Murphy award, chmn. nuclear divsn. 1990-91, prof. internat. coun. 1993-95, v.p. 1994-95, bd. dirs. 1993-95, exec. bd. dirs. 1994-95), Nuclear Dept. Heads Orgn. (vice chmn. 1991-92, chmn. 1992-93, commr. engring accreditation com. 1995—, bd. dirs nat. nuclear accreditation 1998—). Home: 10226 SW 49th Ln Gainesville FL 32608-7161 Office: U Fla 202 Nuclear Science Ctr Gainesville FL 32611 E-mail: jimtulenko@mail.com.

TULIN, MARNA, psychotherapist; b. N.Y.C., Feb. 23, 1930; d. Irving Bernsohn and Gloria Bernsohn Turner; m. Harold Klingbeil, Feb. 14, 1948 (dec. May 1952); 1 child, Deborah Klingbeil Tulin-Donnell; m. Stephen Wise Tulin, Jan. 31, 1959; children: Douglas Wise, Andrea Wise, Houlihan. BA, NYU, 1960; MSW, Columbia U., 1962; PhD in Psychology, Tulane-Pacific Western U., 1988. LCSW N.Y., Vt., diplomate social work. Caseworker Cmty. Svc. Soc., N.Y.C., 1962-63, Jewish Child Care Assn., N.Y.C., 1964-67; psychotherapist Jewish Child Care Psychiat. Clinic, 1967-70; cons. pre-K, spl. needs program, home learning Mamaroneck (N.Y.) Sch. Sys., 1976-80; pvt. practice psychotherapist N.Y.C., Westchester, N.Y., 1980-92, North Ferrisburg, Vt., 1993—; cons. parents place Mamaroneck (N.Y.) Sch. Sys., 1980-81; cons. Stamford (Conn.) Sch. Sys., 1981, Bank St. Coll. Edn., N.Y.C., 1987. Chmn. bd. Louise Wise Svc., N.Y.C., 1991—93, dir. emeritus; trustee Howard Ctr. for Human Svcs., Burlington, Vt., 1997—; mem. profl. adv. com. Mental Health Assn. N.Y., 1993—2000. Mem. AAUW, Internat. Conf. for Advancement Pvt. Practice Social Workers, Pi Sigma Alpha. Democrat. Jewish. Avocation: antique dealing. Home and Office: 100 Champlin Hill Rd North Ferrisburg VT 05473-4076 Fax: 802-425-3384.

TULL, C. THOMAS, investment advisor; b. Dayton, Ohio, Sept. 5, 1946; s. James Theron and Emma Louise (Geppinger) T.; m. Carole Lynn Thoryk, June 20, 1970; children: Christopher James, Matthew Thomas. BS, Ohio State U., 1971; MBA, Xavier U., 1975. Chartered fin. analyst. Asst. trust investment officer Nat. City Bank, Cleve., 1973-75; dir. investments Cleve.-Cliffs Iron Co., 1975-83; v.p. Western Res. Capital Mgmt., Inc., Cleve., 1983-87, Dallas, 1987-90, 1984-87; dir. employee benefit fund investments LTV Corp., 1987-90; pres. Tull, Doud, Marsh & Triltsch, Inc., 1990—; founding ptnr., mng. dir. Gulfstream Global Investors, Ltd., 1990-2001. Vis. lectr. Cleve. State U., 1980-83. Sgt. U.S. Army, 1964-67. Mem. Assn. for Investment Mgmt. and Rsch., Dallas Assn. Investment Analysts, Inst. Chartered Fin. Analysts, Internat. Soc. Security Analysts. Avocations: reading, travel, investing.

TULL, THERESA ANNE, retired ambassador; b. Runnemede, N.J., Oct. 2, 1936; d. John James and Anna Cecelia (Paull) T. BA, U. Md., 1972; MA, U. Mich., 1973; postgrad., Nat. War Coll., Washington, 1980. Fgn. svc. officer Dept. State, Washington, 1963, Brussels, 1965-67, Saigon, 1968-70; dep. prin. officer Am. Consulate General, Danang, Vietnam, 1973-75; prin. officer Cebu, Philippines, 1977-79; dir. office human rights, 1980-83; charge d'affaires Am. Embassy, Vientiane, Laos, 1983-86; Dept. State Senior Seminar, 1986-87; ambassador to Guyana, 1987-90; diplomat-in-residence Lincoln U., Pa., 1990-91; dir. office regional affairs, bur. East Asian & Pacific affairs Dept. State, Washington, 1991-93; amb. to Brunei Bandar Seri Begawan, 1993-96. Recipient Civilian Service award Dept. of State, 1970, Superior Honor award, 1977 Mem. Am. Fgn. Svc. Assn., Women's Civic Club (Sea Isle City chpt. pres.). Address: #204 4400 Pleasure Ave Sea Isle City NJ 08243

TULL, WILLIS CLAYTON, JR. librarian; b. Crisfield, Md., Feb. 22, 1931; s. Willis Clayton and Agnes Virginia (Milbourne) T.; m. Taeko Itoi, Dec. 18, 1952. Student, U. Balt., 1948, Johns Hopkins U., 1956; BS, Towson (Md.) State Coll., 1957; MLS, Rutgers U., 1962; postgrad., Miami U., Oxford, Ohio, 1979. Editl. clk. 500th Mil. Intelligence Svc. Group, 1952-53; tchr. Hereford Jr.-Sr. H.S., Parkton, Md., 1957-59; aide Enoch Pratt Free Libr., Balt., 1959-61, profl. asst., 1962-64; coord. adult svcs. Washington County Free Libr., Hagerstown, Md., 1964-67; asst. regional libr. Eastern Shore Regional Libr., Salisbury, 1967; br. libr. Balt. County Pub. Libr., Pikesville, 1968-71, asst. area br. libr. Essex, 1971-72, sr. info. specialist Catonsville, 1972-87, on-line supr. Towson, 1988-89, sr. info. specialist Reisterstown, 1989-90; exec. dir. Milbourne and Tull Rsch. Ctr., 1991—. Contbr. to profl. and geneal. jours. Mem. Rep. Ctrl. Com. Baltimore County, 1971-72. With U.S. Army, 1949-52. Fellow Nat. Congress Patriotic Orgns.; mem. Freedom To Read Found., Md. Libr. Assn. (chmn. intellectual freedom com. 1969-70), Friends Johns Hopkins U. Librs., Md. Assn. for Adult Edn. (coord. Western Md. region 1965-67), Am. Coun. Trustees and Alumni, Am. Acad. Religion, Ctr. for Theology and the Natural Scis., Metaphys. Soc. Am., Nat. Assn. Scholars, Woodrow Wilson Internat. Ctr. for Scholars, Assn. for Asian Studies, World Future Soc., Freedom House, Internat. Rescue Com., Nature Conservancy, Unitarian and Universalist Geneal. Soc. (founder, bd. dirs. 1971-87), Md. Geneal. Soc., Royal Soc. St. George, Sons and Daus. Pilgrims, Descs. Early Quakers, SAR, Soc. War of 1812, Ancient and Hon. Mech. Co. Balt., Rutgers Club, Kappa Delta Pi. Home and Office: 10605 Lakespring Way Hunt Valley MD 21030-2818 E-mail: tullito1@msn.com.

TULLER, HARRY LOUIS, materials science and engineering educator; BS, Columbia U., 1966, MS, 1967, DSc in Engring., 1973. Rsch. assoc. physics Technion, Haifa, Israel, 1974-75; from asst. to assoc. prof. materials sci. and engring. MIT, Cambridge, 1975-81, prof. materials sci. and engring., 1981—; dir. Crystal Physics and Electroceramics Lab., 1985—. Vis. prof. U. Pierre et Marie Curie, Paris, 1990; faculty chair Sumitomo Electric Industries, 1992-98. Co-editor: High Temperature Superconductors, 1988, Electroceramics and Solid State Ionics, 1988, Science and Technology of Fast Ion Conductors, 1989, Sold State Ionics, 1992, Interfacially Controlled Functional Materials: Electrical and Chemical Properties, 2000, Oxygen Ion and Mixed Conductors and Their Technological Applications, 2000; series editor: Electronic Materials: Science and Technology; editor-in-chief Jour. Electroceramics. Fulbright travel grantee, 1990, Alexander von Humboldt fellow, 1997. Fellow Am. Ceramic Soc. (N.E. chair 1983); mem. IEEE, Electrochem. Soc. (co-organizer 1st, 2d and 3d internat. symposium ionic and mixed conducting ceramics 1991, 94, 97, co-organizer 1997 NATO/ASI Oxygen Ion & Mixed Conductors Summer Sch.), Materials Rsch. Soc. Jewish. Avocations: photography, gardening. Office: MIT 77 Massachusetts Ave Rm 13-3126 Cambridge MA 02139-4307

TULLIER, MICHAEL JOSEPH, nonprofit blood center administrator; b. Ruston, La., May 18, 1972; s. Joseph Parker and Patricia Lynn (Hollis) T.; m. Dianna Lynn Davis, Mar. 11, 1995; 1 child, Davis Michael. BA in Mass Comm., La. State U., 1994; MPA, Auburn U., Montgomery, Ala., 1998. Cert. nonprofit mgmt. and leadership. Rsch. asst. Office of Mental Health, State of La., Baton Rouge, 1993-94; resource devel. coord. Greater Baton Rouge Food Bank, 1994-95; cmty. rels. coord. East Ala. Cmty. Blood Bank/Life South, Auburn, 1995-97; br. dir. East Ala. Cmty. Blood Bank, 1997—. Bd. dirs. East Ala. Food Bank, Auburn, 1997—, sec., 1998—; chair pub. rels. com. Saugahatchee Dist. Boy Scouts Am., Auburn, 1996—; chair Leadership Lee County, Ala., 1999—. Recipient Lantern award So. Pub. Rels. Fedn., 1995. Mem. Pub. Rels. Coun. Ala. (state v.p. ethics/projects 1998—, East Ala. chpt. v.p. membership 1998—), Rotary, Opelika C. of C. (amb. 1998—, Above and Beyond award 1998), Omicron Delta Kappa, Pi Kappa Alpha. Home: 543 Owens Rd Auburn AL 36830-2513 Office: Auburn U AUDFS 201 Ross Hall Auburn AL 36849-5341 Office Fax: 334-844-3400. Business E-Mail: mtullier@eng.auburn.edu.

TULLIS, BILL, broadcasting company executive, sound engineer, music producer; b. Valdosta, Ga., Feb. 3, 1953; s. Vennis (Avery) T. BA, Valdosta State Coll., 1974, Ga. State U., 1976. Audio and music dir. Turner Broadcasting System, Inc., Atlanta, 1975—2001; CEO Creative Svcs. Co. & Trollsound Studios, 2001—; mgr., CEO Creative Svcs. Co., 2001—. Recipient Emmy award, 1980, 81, 84, 88, Clio award, 1987, 88, Aurora award (2). 2000, 01. Mem. IEEE, NARAS, Audio Engring. Soc., Nat. Assn. Broadcasters. Avocations: architectural design, music collecting and appreciation. Home: PO Box 49567 Atlanta GA 30359-1567 Office: Creative Svcs Co PO Box 49266 Atlanta GA 30359 E-mail: btullis497@aol.com.

TULLIS, CHAILLÉ HANDY, interior designer, volunteer; b. Evanston, Ill., June 16, 1913; d. Jamison Handy and Ethel (Tremaine) Gray; m. Richard Barclay Tullis, Aug. 17, 1935; children: Sarah Gilmore Tullis deBarcza, Barclay Jamison, Garner Handy. BA, Principia Coll., Elsah, Ill., 1935; MA, Case Western Res. U., 1964. Pres., sole owner Chaillé Interiors, 1983—. Trustee Cleve. Inst. Art (hon.), 1984—, Garden Ctr. Greater Cleve., 1975-78, 83-86, Vero Beach (Fla.) Ctr. for the Arts, 1994-2000. Pres. Country Garden Club, 1961-63; pres. women's com. Cleve. Orch., 1975-77. Mem. Twenty-First Century Club (Ohio), Oak Harbor Club, Bent Pine Golf Club (Vero Beach, Fla.) Kirtland Golf Club (Ohio). Avocations: travel, golf, tennis. Home: 4690 Hamilton Terr Vero Beach FL 32967

TULLIS, EDWARD LEWIS, retired bishop; b. Cin., Mar. 9, 1917; s. Ashar Spence and Priscilla (Daugherty) T.; m. Mary Jane Talley, Sept. 25, 1937; children: Frank Loyd, Jane Allen (Mrs. William Nelson Offutt IV); m. Katharine Crum Irwin, Sept. 4, 1997. AB, Ky. Wesleyan Coll., 1939, LHD, 1975; BD, Louisville Presbyn. Theol. Sem., 1947; DD, Union Coll., Barbourville, Ky., 1954, Wofford Coll., 1976; LHD, Claflin Coll., 1976, Lambuth Coll., 1984. Ordained to ministry Methodist Ch., 1941; service in chs. Frenchburg, Ky., 1937-39, Lawrenceburg, 1939-44; asso. pastor 4th Ave. Meth. Ch., Louisville, 1944-47, Irvine, Ky., 1947-49; asso. sec. ch. extension sect. Bd. Missions, Meth. Ch., Louisville, 1949-52; pastor First Meth. Ch., Frankfort, Ky., 1952-61, Ashland, 1961-72; resident bishop United Meth. Ch., Columbia, S.C., 1972-80, Nashville area, 1980-84, ret., 1984. Instr. Bible Ky. Wesleyan Coll., 1947-48; instr. Louisville Presbyn. Theol. Sem., 1949-52; mem. Meth. Gen. Conf., 1956, 60, 64, 66, 68, 70, 72, Southeastern Jurisdictional Conf., 1952, 56, 60, 64, 68, 72, bd. mgrs. Bd. Missions, 1962-72, mem. bd. discipleship, 1972-80, v.p. Gen. Council on Fin. and Adminstrn., 1980-84; Chaplain Ky. Gen. Assembly, 1952-61; chmn. Frankfort Com. Human Rights, 1956-61, Mayor's Advisory Com. Human Relations, Ashland, 1968-72. Author: Shaping the Church from the Mind of Christ, 1984, The Birth of the Book: A Study in the Origin and Growth of the Bible, 1998. Contbr. articles to religious jours. Sec., bd. dirs. Magee Christian Edn. Found.; trustee Emory U., 1973-80, Alaska Meth. U., 1965-70, Ky. Wesleyan Coll., Martin Coll., Lambuth Coll., McKendree Manor, Meth. Hosps., Memphis, Lake Junaluska Assembly, 1966-88; chair adv. bd. Found. for Evangelism, United Meth. Ch., 1991—. Recipient Outstanding Citizen award Frankfort VFW, 1961, Mayor's award for outstanding svc. Ashland, 1971, Heroes, Sts. and Legends award, Wesley Meth. Village Ky., 1997, Chief Junaluska award Lake Junaluska Assembly, 1998, Outstanding Alumnus award Ky. Wesleyan Coll., 2000, Disting. Alumnus award Louisville Presbyn. Sem., 2002. Mem.: Kiwanis. Home: PO Box 754 Lake Junaluska NC 28745-0754 E-mail: etullis@iopener.net.

TULLIS, THOMAS STUART, human factors specialist; b. Memphis, Apr. 16, 1952; s. Isaac Frank and Selma Virginia (Samuels) T.; m. Susan Cheryl Richardson, May 25, 1973; children: Cheryl Marie, Virginia Susanne. BA, Rice U., Houston, 1974; MA, N.Mex. State U., Las Cruces, 1976; PhD, Rice U., 1984. Mem. tech. staff Bell Labs., Whippany and Piscataway, N.J., 1974-79, 82-83; prin. software designer Burroughs Corp., Mission Viejo, Calif., 1983-85; prin. human factors engr. McDonnell-Douglas Astronautics, Huntington Beach, 1985-88; dir. U.I. technologies Ashton-Tate Corp., Torrance, 1988-91; user interface architect Canon Info. Systems, Costa Mesa, 1991-93; sr. v.p. human interface design Fidelity Investments., Boston, 1993—. Program chair Human Factors Soc. Computer Systems Tech. Group, 1991, bulletin editor, 1992-93, chair, 2001-2002.. Author: (with others) Handbook of Human-Computer Interaction, 1997; contbr. articles to jours. in field. Mem. ACM SIGCHI, Human Factors & Ergonomics Soc., Assn. for Computing Machinery. Avocations: photography, genealogy, astronomy, collecting rare books. Home: 68 Meetinghouse Ln South Easton MA 02375-1001 Office: Fidelity Investments 82 Devonshire St Boston MA 02109-3605 E-mail: tomtullis@aol.com.

TÜLLNER, HORST-ULRICH, research scientist, science administrator; b. Burgstall, Altmark, Germany, Apr. 17, 1945; s. Horst Bruno and Ursula (Wecker) T.; m. Loretta Schinck, July 17, 1970; children: Claudia, Stephan. Diploma in biology, U. Cologne, Germany, 1973, PhD in Natural Sci., 1975. R & D coord. mgmt., project leader MADAUS AG, Cologne, 1975-99, lic. mgr., 1999—. Presenter in field of biology, zoology, electrophysiology, project mgmt. Author: Thieme-Verlag, 1988; contbr. articles to scientific publs. 1st lt. German Air Force, 1971-73. Mem. Internat. Soc. Neurochemistry, German Sailing Assn. Avocations: sailing, hiking, motor biking. Home: Am Dreieck 3 51107 Cologne Germany Office: MADAUS AG Ostmerheimerstr 198 51109 Cologne Germany E-mail: h.tuellner@madaus.de.

TULLOCH, BRIAN ROBERT, endocrinologist; b. Chunya, Tanzania, May 30, 1938; came to U.S., 1977; s. Robert Graeme and Audrey Madelein (Bremner) T.; m. Elizabeth Watkins Rogg, Jan. 26, 1980; children: Nathaniel, Genevieve. BSc, Natal U., S. Africa, 1959, MSc, 1961; BM, BCh, Oxford (Eng.) U., 1966. Lic. small boat cpt. Coast Guard. House physician to specialists in gen., plastic, thoracic surgery, Univ. Coll. Hosp., London, 1965-66; house physician to specialist in gen. and renal medicine Radcliffe Infirmary, Oxford, Eng., 1966-67; house physician to cardiologist Hammersmith Hosp., London, 1967; house physician Brompton Chest Hosp., 1967-68; med. registrar Nat. Heart Hosp., 1968-69; clin. rsch. fellow, sr. registrar, clin. tutor, cons. Med. Rsch. Coun. endocrine unit Royal Postgrad. Med. Sch., 1969-72; Wellcome sr. rsch. fellow dept. medicine Royal Postgrad. Med. Sch., 1972-74; sessional cons. in endocrinology and diabetes St. Charles Hosp., 1973-74; hon. lectr. in medicine Hammersmith Hosp., 1972-74; sr. lectr. in medicine, hon. cons. physician Manchester (Eng. Royal Infirmary), 1974-77; endocrinologist Diagnostic Clinic, Houston, 1977—; clin. assoc. prof. internal medicine and ophthalmology U. Tex. Med. Sch., 1977—, M.D. Anderson Hosp. and Tumor Inst., Houston, 1977—. Attending physician, Diagnostic Ctr. Hosp., Houston, Hermann Hosp., Houston, Park Plaza Hosp., Houston; mem. student promotions com. U. Tex.. tissue com. Hermann Hosp.; NIH site visitor, Diabetes Rsch and Tng. Ctr., NIH advisor Diabetes Epidemiology in Egypt; invited participant NIH Conf. on flushing, markers for Type II Diabetes Mellitus, 1980, Conf. on Lipoprotein Physiology, San Diego, 1981, Lipid Metabolism, N.Y., 1985; reviewer Diabetologia, Hormone and Metabolic Rsch., Clin. Sci., Cardiovascular Rsch., Biochem. Pharmacology, Artery, Metabolism: Clin. and Exptl.; advisor Ministry of Health, Kuwait, 1976-78, ICI Internat., 1976-78; for rev. lectures given to Univs. Cairo, Ain Shams, Assyut, Mansoura and Alexandria in Egypt; invited disting. guest lectr. Sudan Assn. Physicians, Khartoum, 1978. Contbr. numerous articles and abstracts to profl. jours.; speaker to nat. and internat. sci. confs. as well as lay groups on diabetes and related health care topics. Recipient Caltex scholarship, 1955-59, Coun. for Sci. and Indsl. Rsch. scholarship, 1960-61, Charelick Salemon scholarship, 1960-61, Rhodes scholarship, St. Johns Coll. Oxford U., 1961-64, Croxon fellowship, 1964-65, Convenators Trust, 1964-65, Preventive Cardiology Acad. award; grantee: MRC (heavy equipment grant), Manchester Regional Rsch. Fund, 1975, U. Tex., 1977, Am. Diabetes Assn., Warner Lambert-Parke Davis, 1979-81, CO-PI, 1979-82, 1983-86. Fellow ACP, Am. Endocrine Soc., Am. Diabetes Assn. (pres. Houston chpt. 1982-83, pres. Tex. affiliate 1984-86), Royal Coll. Physicians; mem. Brain-Pituitary Soc. (treas. 1981-86), Houston-Galveston Endocrine Assn., Am. Heart Assn., The Endocrine Soc., Harris County Med. Soc., Harveian Soc. London, Manchester Med. Soc., Med. Rsch. Soc., Soc. for Endocrinology, European Assn. for Study of Diabetes, Brit. Diabetic Soc., Royal Soc. Medicine London (com. mem. endocrine sect.), Royal Ocean Racing Club London, Hellenic Travelers Club London, Egypt Exploration Soc. London, Houston Yacht Club (fleet surgeon 1983-84, 97-98), Tex. Offshore Racing Club, Galveston Bay Cruising Assn. (Coast Guard smallboat capt.'s license 2000). Republican. Episcopalian. Avocations: sailboat racing, scuba diving, duck hunting, bird watching, fishing. Office: Diagnostic Clinic 6448 Fannin St Houston TX 77030-1592 E-mail: drtulloch@diagnosticclinic.com.

TULLOCH-REID, ELMA DEEN, nurse, consultant; b. Erie, Pa., June 27, 1938; d. Theodore and Roberta (Hicks) Carlisle; children: Robynne and Stacey (twins). BS, N.C. Agrl. and Tech. State U., 1960; MA, Calif. State U., 1977; Ed.D., Nova U., 1981. Staff nurse Michael Reese Hosp., Chgo., 1960-62; instr. Cook County Sch. Nursing, 1962-64; tchr. St. Joseph Convent, Trinidad, West Indies, 1964-66; med./surg. coordinator St. Vincent Coll. Nursing, L.A., 1966-68, med./surg. coord., 1968-69; charge nurse Century City Hosp., 1971-72; tchr. L.A. Unified Schs., 1972-75; dir. edn. and tng. Imperial Hosp., Inglewood, Calif., 1977-79; pres. Elma Tulloch-Reid Assocs., L.A., 1981—. Asst. prof. dept. continuing edn. Calif. State U., Long Beach, 1977—81, assoc. prof., 1982—; instr. Pilot Program in Health Occupations, Culver City Unified Sch. Dist., 1985—; mem. Citizen Amb. Program to Republic of China, 1995, Citizen Amb. Program to Singapore (World Conf. on Domestic Violence , 1998; DON edn. and rsch. King Drew Med. Ctr., L.A., 1991—95; dir. edn.

Daniel Freeman Hosps., Inc., Inglewood, Calif., 1996—2001; dir. edn. svcs. Queen of Angels/Hollywood Presbyn. Med. Ctr., 2001—; clin. performance examiner Regents Coll. NYU. Cmty. instr. certified basic life support L.A. Cardio-Pulmonary Resuscitation Consortium, 1981-82. Recipient commendation City of Los Angeles XXIII Olympiad, 1984. Mem. Nat. Orgn. Mothers of Twins, NAFE, Am. Nurses Found., Am. Coll. Healthcare Execs., N.C. Agrl. and Tech. State U. Alumni Assn., AAUW, Assn. for Psychological Type, Orgn. Healthcare Educators (sec. 1998—). Phi Kappa Phi. Club: Westside Mothers Twins (pres. 1971-73) (Los Angeles). Home: 1056 S Cochran Ave Los Angeles CA 90019-2857 Office: 5350 Wilshire Blvd Los Angeles CA 90036-4212

TULLOCK, GORDON, economics educator; b. Rockford, Ill., Feb. 13, 1922; s. George and Helen T. JD, U. Chgo., 1947. Fgn. svc. officer, China, 1947-56; postdoctoral fellow U. Va., 1958-59; asst. prof. U. S.C., 1959-60, assoc. prof., 1960-62, U. Va., Charlottesville, 1962-67; prof. econs. and polit. sci. Rice U., Houston, 1967-68; prof. econs. and pub. choice Va. Poly. Inst. and State U., Blacksburg, 1968-72, univ. disting. prof. econs. and pub. choice, 1972-83, George Mason U., Fairfax, Va., 1983-87; prof. U. Ariz., Tucson, 1987-99; prof. law and econ. George Mason U., Arlington, Va., 1999—. Editl. dir. Center for Study of Pub. Choice, 1968-90; vis. disting. scholar Baruch U., N.Y.C., spring 1987; dir. DHC, Eldora, Iowa. Author: (with J.M. Buchanan) The Calculus of Consent, 1962, The Politics of Bureaucracy, 1965, The Organization of Inquiry, 1966, Toward a Mathematics of Politics, 1967, Private Wants, Public Means, 1970, The Logic of the Law, 1971, (with others) The Social Dilemma, 1974, (with Richard B. McKenzie) The New World of Economics, 1975, (with Richard B. McKenzie) Modern Political Economy, 1978, Trials on Trial, 1979, Toward a Theory of the Rent-Seeking Society, 1980, Economics of Income Redistribution, 1983, The Economics of Wealth and Poverty, 1986, Autocracy, 1987, The Economics of Special Privilege and Rent Seeking, 1989. Fellow Am. Econ. Assn.; mem. So. Econ. Assn. (past pres.), Western Econ. Assn. (pres.), Am. Polit. Sci. Assn., Pub. Choice Soc. (sec. 1965—), Assn. for Asian Studies. Home: 3800 Fairfax Dr Apt 213 Arlington VA 22203-1759 Office: George Mason U James Buchanan Ctr 1D3 Carow Hall Fairfax VA 22030 E-mail: gtulloc1@gmu.edu.

TULLY, BERNARD MICHAEL, lawyer; b. Pitts., Aug. 28, 1952; s. Joseph J. and Mary Lorraine T.; m. Feb. 15, 1991; children: Elizabeth, Kevin, Michael, Jessica, Katie. BA, Duquesne, Pitts., 1974; JD, Ohio No. U., 1979. Asst. dist. atty., Pitts., 1979-85; assoc. Stokes, Lurie & Cole, 1985-87; pvt. practice, 1987—. Solicitor Allegheny County Treas., Pitts., 1994-98. Office: Grant Bldg 310 Grant St Ste 716 Pittsburgh PA 15219-2200

TULLY, CAROL THORPE, social work educator, administrator; b. Portsmouth, N.H., Sept. 16, 1946; d. Francis William and Laura Alice (Thorpe) T. BA, U. Ariz., 1968; MSW, Va. Commonwealth U., 1977, PhD, 1983. Licensed social worker. Indexer Nat. Geog. Soc., Washington, 1968-69; social worker Richmond (Va.) City Pub. Welfare, 1971-77; tng. specialist Va. Dept. Welfare, Richmond, 1977-79; asst. prof. W. Va. U. Sch. Social Work, Charleston, W.Va., 1983-86; exec. dir. Ga. Council on Aging, Atlanta, 1986-90; asst. prof. Sch. Social Work U. Ga., Athens, 1990-93; assoc. prof. Sch. Social Work Tulane U., New Orleans, 1993—2000; assoc. dean, prof. Kent sch. social work U. Louisville, Louisville, 2000—. Cons. in field; mem. adv. coun. Coun. on Elder Abuse and Neglect, Atlanta, 1986-87, Ctr. for Hearing Impaired, Atlanta, 1989-93; mem. ho. of dels. Coun. on Social Work Edn., Washington, 1987-89. Contbr. several articles to profl. jours. Bd. dirs. NASW, Atlanta, 1988-90, Atlanta Women's Network, Black Diamond Girl Scout Coun., Charleston, 1985-86; house of dels. Coun. on Social Work Edn., Washington, 1987-89. Recipient Presdl. Recognition award Kanawha Valley United Way, 1985. Mem. Am. Assn. Higher Edn., AAUP, So. Gerontol. Soc., NASW, Coun. on Social Work Edn. Avocations: tennis, writing, walking, bird watching. Home: 618 Floral Ter Louisville KY 40208-2236 Fax: 502-852-0422. E-mail: carol.tully@louisville.edu.

TULLY, DARROW, newspaper publisher; b. Charleston, W.Va., Feb. 27, 1932; s. William Albert and Dora (McCann) T.; m. Victoria Lynn Werner; children: Bonnie Tully Paul, Michael Andrew. Student, Purdue U., 1951; BA in Journalism, St. Joseph's Coll., 1972; PhD in Journalism (hon.), Calumet (Ind.) Coll., 1975. V.p., gen. mgr. Stas. WDSM-AM-FM and WDSM-TV, Duluth, Minn., 1956-59; bus. mgr. Duluth Herald & News Tribune, 1960-62; gen. mgr. St. Paul Dispatch & Pioneer Press, 1962-66; pub. Gary (Ind.) Post-Tribune, 1966-73; v.p., pub. Wichita (Kans.) Eagle & Beacon, 1973-75; pres. San Francisco Newspaper Agy., 1975-78; exec. v.p., pub. Ariz. Republic & Phoenix Gazette, 1978-85; editor., pub., chief exec. officer Ojai (Calif.) Valley News, 1987-90; pres., pub., CEO Beacon Comms., Acton, Mass., 1990-92; asst. to pres. newspaper divsn. Chronicle Pub. Co., 1992-94. Author: Minority Representation in the Media, 1968. Trustee Calumet Coll. Recipient Disting. Achievement award Ariz. State U., 1982, Disting. Journalist award No. Ariz. U./AP, 1983, 1st Pl. Editorial Writing award Ariz. Planned Parenthood, 1983. Mem. Am. Soc. Newspaper Editors, Soc. Profl. Journalists. Office: 9862 Bridgeton Dr Tampa FL 33626-1802

TULLY, HUGH MICHAEL, music educator; b. N.Y.C., Sept. 21, 1947; s. Hugh Joseph and Grace Esther (Glynn) T.; m. Leslie Carol Holmes, June 23, 1972; children: Andrea Clare, Alexander Clayton. BS, Western Conn. State U., 1969; MS, U. N.H., 1980; EdD, Boston U., 1989. Dir. music Ashford (Conn.) Elem. Sch., 1969-72, Berlin (N.H.) Regional Cath. Sch., 1972-77; band dir. Somersworth (N.H.) H.S., 1977—. Founder, liaison Somersworth Music Boosters, 1980—; spokesperson Consortium Chamber Singers, Brookfield, N.H., 1989-91. Mem. Mensa. Avocation: writing children's stories. Home: 204 Wentworth Rd Brookfield NH 03872-7104 Office: Somersworth HS Memorial Dr Somersworth NH 03878 E-mail: geopah@worldpath.net.

TULLY, JOHN CHARLES, research chemical physicist; b. N.Y.C., May 17, 1942; s. Harry V. and Pauline (Fischer) T.; m. Mary Ellen Thomsen, Jan. 23, 1971; children: John Thomsen, Elizabeth Anne, Stephen Thomsen. BS, Yale U., 1964; PhD, U. Chgo., 1968. NSF postdoctoral fellow U. Colo. and Yale U., 1968-70; mem. tech. staff AT&T Bell Labs., Murray Hill, N.J., 1970-82, disting. mem. tech. staff, 1982-85, head phys. chemistry rsch. dept., 1985-90, head materials chem. rsch. dept., 1990-96; Kemp prof. dept. chemistry, physics and applied physics Yale U., New Haven, 1996—. Vis. prof. Princeton (N.J.) U., 1981-82, Harvard U., Cambridge, Mass., 1991. Contbr. articles to sci. jours.; author, prodr. movie Dynamics of Gas-Surface Interactions, 1979. NSF predoctoral fellow, 1965-68. Fellow AAAS, Am. Phys. Soc. (chem. physics exec. com. 1983-86), Am. Acad. Arts & Scis.; mem. Am. Chem. Soc. (chmn. theoretical chemistry subdiv. 1991-92, phys. chemistry div. 1993-94, Peter Debye award 1995, Madison Marshall award 1999), Nat. Acad. Sci., Conn. Acad. Sci. and Engring., Sigma Xi. Achievements include patent on Method and Apparatus for Surface Characterization Utilizing Radiation from Desorbed Particles; fundamental theoretical contributions towards atomic level understanding of chemical reaction dynamics. Office: Yale Univ Dept Chemistry PO Box 208107 New Haven CT 06520-8107

TULLY, SUSAN BALSLEY, pediatrician, educator; b. San Francisco, July 12, 1941; d. Gerard E. Balsley Sr. and Norma Lilla (Hand) Carey; m. William P. Tully, June 19, 1965; children: Michael William, Stephen Gerard. BA in Premed. Studies, UCLA, 1963, MD, 1966. Diplomate Am. Bd. Pediatrics, Am. Bd. Pediatric Emergency Medicine. Intern L.A. County-U. So. Calif. Med. Ctr., 1966-67, jr. resident pediatrics, 1967-68; staff pediatrician, part-time Permanente Med. Group, Oakland, Calif., 1968; sr. resident pediatrics Kaiser Found. Hosp., 1968-69, Bernalillo County Med. Ctr., Albuquerque, 1969-70, chief resident pediatric outpatient dept., 1970; instr. pediatrics, asst. dir. outpatient dept. U. N.Mex. Sch. Medicine, 1971-72; asst. prof. pediatrics, dir. (ambulatory pediatrics) U. Calif., Irvine, 1972-76, asst. prof. clin. pediatrics, vice chair med. edn., 1977-79; staff pediatrician Ross-Loos Med. Group, Buena Park, Calif., 1976-77; assoc. prof. clin. pediatrics and emergency medicine U. So. Calif. Sch. Medicine, 1979-86; dir. pediatric emergency dept. L.A. County/U. So. Calif. Med. Ctr., 1979-87; prof. clin. pediatrics and emergency medicine U. So. Calif. Sch. Medicine, 1986-89; dir. ambulatory pediatrics L.A. County/U. So. Calif. Med. Ctr., 1987-89, L.A. County-Olive View/UCLA Med. Ctr., 1989—; clin. prof. pediatrics UCLA, 1989-93, prof. clin. pediats., 1993-97; prof. emeritus, 1997—; dir. ambulatory pediatrics Olive View-UCLA Med. Ctr., 1989-96, chief pediatrics, 1996-97; vice chair pediat. UCLA, 1996-97; cons. pediatrician Olive View-UCLA Med. Ctr., 1997—. Mem. survey team pediatric emergency svcs. L.A. Pediatric Soc., 1984—86; mem. adv. bd. preventive health project univ. affiliated program Children's Hosp. L.A., 1981—83; lectr. nursing pediat. nurse practitioner program Calif. State U., L.A., 1997—; pediat. toxicology cons. L.A. County Regional Poison Control Ctr. Med. Adv. Bd., 1981—97; clin. faculty rep. UCLA Sch. Medicine, 1992—93; pediatric liaison dept. emergency medicine Olive View/UCLA Med. Ctr., 1989—96, dir. lead poisoning clinic, 1993—99; mem. quality assurance com. Los Angeles County Cmty. Health Plan, 1986—89. Author: (with K.E. Zenk) Pediatric Nurse Practitioner Formulary, 1979; (book chpt. with W.A. Wingert) Pediatric Emergency Medicine: Concepts and Clinical Practice, 1992, 2d edit., 1997; (with others) Educational Guidelines for Ambulatory/General Pediatrics Fellowship Training, 1992, Physician's Resource Guide for Water Safety Education, 1994; reviewer Pediatrics, 1985-89; editl. cons. Advanced Pediatric Life Support Course and Manual, 1988-89, Archives of Pediatrics and Adolescent Medicine, 1996—; dept. editor Pediatric Pearls Jour. Am. Acad. Physician Assts., 1989-94; tech. cons., reviewer Healthlink TV Am. Acad. Pediatrics, 1991; reviewer Pediatric Emergency Care, 1992—; question writer sub-bd. pediatric emergency medicine Am. Bd. Pediatrics, 1993-98; assoc. editor: Curriculum for the Training of General Pediatricians, 1996; cons. to lay media NBC Nightly News, Woman's Day, Sesame Street Parents, Parenting, Los Angeles Times; author numerous abstracts; contbr. articles to profl. jours. Cons. spl. edn. programs Orange County Bd. Edn., 1972-79; mem. Orange County Health Planning Coun., 1973-79; co-chairperson Orange County Child Health and Disability Prevention Program Bd., 1975-76; mem. Orange County Child Abuse Consultation Team, 1977-79; mem. project adv. bd. Family Focussed "Buckle Up" Project, Safety Belt Safe, U.S.A., 1989— Fellow Am. Acad. Pediatrics (life, active numerous sects. and coms., active Calif. chpt.); mem. APHA, Ambulatory Pediatric Assn., L.A. Pediatric Soc. (life). Democrat. Avocations: art needlework, reading. Office: Olive View UCLA Med Ctr Pediatrics 3A108 14445 Olive View Dr Sylmar CA 91342-1495

TULLY, THOMAS ALOIS, building materials executive, consultant, educator; b. Dubuque, Iowa, Nov. 11, 1940; s. Thomas Aloysius and Marjorie Mae (Fosselman) T.; m. Joan Vonnetta Dubay, Nov. 30, 1963; children: Thomas Paul, Maureen Elizabeth. BA, Loras Coll., 1962; postgrad., Georgetown U., 1963-66; MPA, Harvard U., 1968. Mgmt. trainee Office of Sec. Def., Washington, 1962-63, fgn. affairs officer, 1963-70; v.p. Dubuque Lumber Co., 1970-84, pres., 1984-91, Tully's, 1991-92, LBM Mktg. Assocs., Inc., 1992—. Adj. instr. Divine Word Coll., 1971, Loras Coll., 1972; adj. instr. Clarke Coll., 1987-89, instr., 1989-91, asst. prof., 1992-97, chmn. dept. acctg. and bus., 1993-97, dir. small bus. inst., 1994-97; dir. MBA program U. Dubuque, 1997-2000; founder, exec. dir. Dubuque Area Com. on Fgn. Rels., 2001--; pres. Hills and Dales Child Devel. Ctr., Inc., 1992-96; trustee Alverno Apts., 1995-2001, pres., 1999-2001. Mem. Dubuque Human Rights Commn., 1974-75, chmn., 1975, Iowa State Com. for Employer Support of Guard and Res. Forces, 1988—, area chmn., 2000—; city councilman, Dubuque, 1975-79; bd. dirs. League Iowa Municipalites, 1977-79; mayor City of Dubuque, 1978; vice chmn. Iowa Temporary State Land Pres. Policy Com., 1978-79; pres. N.E. Iowa Regional Coordinating Coun.l, 1985-93, East Cen. Intergovtl. Assn. Bus. Growth, Inc., 1987-2002, chmn., 1993-2002; bd. dirs. Pvt. Industry Council of Dubuque and Delaware Counties, Inc., 1983-86; trustee Divine Word Coll., 1989-97; pres. Barn Community Theatre, 1988-89; chmn. bd. trustees United Way Svcs. of Dubuque, 1990, campaign chmn., 1991, bd. mem., 1980-94. Recipient Meritorious Civilian Svc. award Sec. of Def., 1970, Gov.'s Vol. award, 1989. Mem. Nat. Lumber and Bldg. Material Dealers Assn. (exec. com. 1988-90), Iowa Lumbermen's Assn. (pres. 1984, chmn. legis. com. 1985-90), Northwestern Lumbermen Assn. (bd. dirs. 1984-87, 2d v.p. 1988, 1st v.p. 1989-90, pres. 1990-91). Democrat. Roman Catholic. Home: 838 Stone Ridge Pl Dubuque IA 52001-1362 Office: LBM Mktg Assocs 838 Stone Ridge Pl Dubuque IA 52001-6565 E-mail: tully.thomas@alumni.ksg.harvard.edu.

TULSKY, JAMES AARON, physician, researcher; b. Chgo., June 13, 1959; s. Alex Sol and Klara (Glottman) Tulsky; m. Ilana Ruth Saraf, June 16, 1991; children: Noah Saraf, Ezekiel Saraf. AB, Cornell U., 1981; MD, U. Ill., Chgo., 1987. Diplomate Am. Bd. Internal Medicine, Nat. Bd. Med. Examiners. Resident in medicine U. Calif., San Francisco, 1987-90, chief resident in medicine, 1990-91, Robert Wood Johnson clin. scholar, 1991-93; asst. prof. medicine Duke U., Durham, N.C., 1993-99, assoc. prof. medicine, 1999—. Contbr. articles to profl. jours. Bd. dirs. The Greenwall Found., N.Y.C., 1999—. Recipient awards and grants. Fellow: ACP, Am. Acad. Hospice and Palliative Medicine, Am. Soc. Bioethics and the Humanities, Am. Acad. on Physician and Patient, Soc. Gen. Internal Medicine, Alpha Omega Alpha. Office: VA Med Ctr (11-C) 508 Fulton St Durham NC 27705-3875 E-mail: jtulsky@duke.edu.

TULUMELLO, ANDREW SANTO, lawyer; b. Phila., June 22, 1970; s. Theodore Nelson and Madeline Anne (Delahan) Tulumello. AB cum laude, Harvard U., Cambridge, Mass., 1991; JD magna cum laude, Harvard U., 1996. Bar: Calif. 1998, D.C. 2001. Law clk. U.S. Ct. Appeals, Pasadena, Calif., 1996—97; lectr. in law Harvard Law Sch., Cambridge, Mass., 1997—98; law clk. Office of Prosecutor, Internat. Tribunal for former Yugoslavia, The Hague, Netherlands, 1998—99; assoc. Gibson, Dunn & Crutcher, Washington, 1999—. Co-author: (book) Beyond Winning, 2000 (CPR Inst. for Dispute Resolution Book prize, 2001); contbr. articles to legal jours. Fellow (sr.) in law and negotiation, Harvard Negotiation Rsch. Project, Cambridge, Mass., 1997—98. Mem.: Am. Soc. Internat. Law. Avocations: tennis, mil. history. Office: Gibson Dunn & Crutcher LLP 1050 Connecticut Ave NW Washington DC 20036 Office Fax: 202-467-0539. E-mail: atulumello@gibsondunn.com.

TULVING, ENDEL, psychologist, educator; b. Estonia, May 26, 1927; s. Johannes and Linda T.; m. Ruth Mikkelsaar, June 24, 1950; children: Elo Ann, Linda. BA, U. Toronto, Ont., Can., 1953, MA, 1954; PhD, Harvard U., 1957; MA (hon.), Yale U., 1969; FD (hon.), U. Umea (Sweden), 1982; DLitt (hon.), U. Waterloo, 1987, Laurentian U., 1988; D Psychology (hon.), U. Tartu, Estonia, 1991; ScD (hon.), Queen's U., Kingston, Can., 1996. Lectr. U. Toronto, 1956-59, asst. prof., 1959-62, assoc. prof., 1962-65; prof., 1965-70; prof. psychology Yale U., New Haven, 1970-75, U. Toronto, 1972-85, chmn. dept., 1974-80, univ. prof., 1985-92, Univ. prof. emeritus psychology, 1992—. Vis. scholar U. Calif., Berkeley, 1964-65; fellow Ctr. Advanced Study in Behavioral Scis., Stanford, Calif., 1972-73; Commonwealth vis. prof. Oxford (Eng.) U., 1977-78; Tanenbaum chair in cognitive neurosci. Rotman Rsch. Inst. of Baycrest Ctr., Can., 1992—; disting. prof. neurosci., disting. prof. psychology U. Calif., Davis, 1993-98; Clark Way Harrison disting. vis. prof. psychology and neurosci. Washington U., St. Louis, 1996—. Author: Elements of Episodic Memory, 1983; editor Jour. Verbal Leaning and Verbal Behavior, 1969-72, Psychol. Rsch., 1976-88, Memory, Consciousness and the Brain: The Tallinn Conference, 1999, The Oxford Handbook of Memory, 2000; co-editor: Organization of Memory, 1972, Memory Sys. 1994, 1994; mem. editl. bd. Oxford Psychology Series, 1979-95; contbr. numerous articles on memory to sci. jours. Recipient Izaak Walton Killam Meml. prize Can. Coun., 1994, John P. McGovern award AAAS; Meml. scholar, 1976-77, Gold medal award for life achievemnt in psychol. sci. Am. Psychol. Found., 1994; Guggenheim fellow, 1987-88. Fellow NAS (fgn. assoc.), Can. Psychol. Assn. (disting. sci. contbn. award 1983), Am. Psychol. Soc. (disting. sci. contbn. award 1983, William James fellow), Royal Soc. Can., Am. Acad. Arts and Scis. (fgn. hon.), Soc. Exptl. Psychologists (Warren medal 1982), Royal Soc. London; mem. Am. Psychol. Soc., Soc. for Neuroscis., Psychonomic Soc. (governing bd. 1974-80), Royal Swedish Acad. Scis. (fgn.), Cognitive Neurosci. Soc., Academia Europaea (fgn.). Home: 45 Baby Point Crescent Toronto ON Canada M6S 2B7 Office: Rotman Rsch Inst, Baycrest Ctr, Bathurst St Toronto ON Canada M6A 2E1 E-mail: tulving@psych.utoronto.ca.

TUMA, ELIAS H. economist, educator; b. Kafr-Yasif, Palestine, Nov. 12, 1928; s. Hanna Khalis and Bahji Shibli (Kalouche) T.; m. Dorothy M. Tuma, 1959; children: John, Mary, Rubiya. Student, British Inst., Haifa, 1947; BA cum laude, U. Redlands, 1957; PhD in Econs., U. Calif., Berkeley, 1962. Clerical positions Govt. of Palestine, Haifa, 1943-44; clk., asst. storekeeper Eastman Kodak Co., 1944-47; acctg. clk. Iraq Petroleum Co., 1947-48; tchr. Ministry of Edn., Govt. of Israel, 1949-50; probation officer Ministry of Social Welfare, Govt. of Israel, Haifa, 1951-55; asst. prof. econs. San Fernando (Calif.) State Coll., 1962-63, U. Sask., Saskatoon, Can., 1963-65, U. Calif., Davis, 1965-67, assoc. prof., assoc. dean, 1968-71, prof., 1971-94, prof. emeritus. Cons. UN, Israel, Iran, Italy, Egypt, Harvard U. Author: Twenty-six Centuries of Agrarian Reform, 1965, Peacemaking and the Immoral, 1971, Economic and Political Change the Middle East, 1987, The Persistence of Economic Discrimination, 1995, others; contbr. numerous articles to sci. and profl. jours. Fulbright fellow, U.S. Dept. Edn., 1978. Mem. ACLU, Am. Econ. Assn., Mid. East Econ. Assn., Calif. Farm Bur., Phi Beta Kappa. Democrat. Avocations: woodwork, sculpture, carving, photography, swimming, tree farming. Home: 3845 Buffalo Rd Auburn CA 95602-7901 Office: U Calif Dept Econs One Shields Ave Davis CA 95616 E-mail: tuma@ufr.net.

TUMAKOV, VLADIMIR LEONIDOVICH, physicist, researcher; b. Rustavi, Georgia, USSR, Feb. 16, 1957; arrived in Russia, 1974; s. Leonid Grigorievich and Galina Prokofievna (Karpenko) T.; m. Tatiana Pavlovna Gordeeva, June 2, 1977; children: Katerina, Pavel. PhD in Physics and Math., Inst. High Energy Physics, Protvino, Russia, 1996. Lab. asst. Inst. High Energy Physics, 1980-81, jr. rschr., 1981-87, rschr., 1987-97, sr. rschr., 1997-98; rschr. U. Calif., Irvine, 1999—. Fellow high energy rsch. orgn. KEK, Japan, 1997-98. Internat. Sci. Found. grantee, 1994. Office: U Calif Dept Physics And Astronomy Irvine CA 92697-0001 Home: 92 Stanford Irvine CA 92612 E-mail: tumakov@uci.edu.

TUMAN, KENNETH JAMES, anesthesiologist, educator; b. Chgo., May 8, 1955; MD, U. Chgo., 1980. Diplomate Am. Bd. Anesthesiology (dir. 1997—), Am. Bd. Critical Care Medicine. Intern U. Ill., Chgo., 1980-81, resident in gen. surgery, 1981-82; resident in anesthesiology Northwestern Meml. Hosp., 1982-84; fellow in cardiovasc. anesthesiology Rush Presbyn.-St. Lukes Hosp., 1984-85, with, 1985—; prof. anesthesiology, vice chmn. dept. anesthesiology Rush Med. Coll. Fellow Coll. Critical Care Medicine; mem. AMA, Am. Soc. Anesthesiologists, Soc. Cardiovasc. Anesthesiologists, Soc. Critical Care Medicine. Office: Rush Presbyn St Lukes Hosp 1753 W Congress Pkwy Chicago IL 60612-3809

TUMAN, WALTER VLADIMIR, Russian language educator, researcher; b. Heidelberg, Germany, Jan. 21, 1946; came to U.S., 1949; s. Val Alexander Tuman and Valida (Zedins) Grasis; m. Helena Eugenia Makarowsky, June 6, 1970; children: Gregory Vladimir, Larissa Alexandra. BA, Fordham U., 1967; MS in Russian, Linguistics, Georgetown U., 1970, PhD in Russian, 1975. Supr. Russian dept. Def. Lang. Inst., Washington, 1972-75, developer course-curriculum Monterey, Calif., 1975-78; asst. prof. Russian Hollins (Va.) Coll., 1978-84; dir. fgn. lang. lab. La. State U., Baton Rouge, 1984-90; assoc. prof., coord. Russian program Thunderbird Campus Am. Grad. Sch. Internat. Mgmt., Glendale, Ariz., 1990-95, prof., 1995—2001; prof. emeritus, 2001. Cons. various univs.; grant participant, cons. US AID Consortia Am. Buss., NIS, 1993—, U.S. Commerce Dept., Nizhny Novgorod, Volgograd, Am. Bus. Ctrs., 1994—. Author: Think Russian: Level I, 1993; editor: A Bibliography of Computer-Aided Language Learning, 1986; contbg. editor Jour. Ednl. Techniques and Techs., 1987-91; mem. editl. bd.: Jour. Lang. in Internat. Bus.; author book revs., computer programs, conf. presentations; contbr. articles to profl. jours. Georgetown U. fellow, 1969; recipient Prof.'s Exch. award Internat. Rsch. and Exchs. Bd. (USSR), 1979; Mednick Meml. Fund grantee Va. Found. for Ind. Colls. (Australia), 1983, Apple Computer grantee, 1989, U.S. Dept. Edn. grantee Ctr. Internat. Bus. Edn. and Rsch., 1993—. Mem. Am. Assn. Tchrs. Slavic and East European Langs. (v.p. 1981-84, founder Monterey, Calif. chpt.), Am. Coun. on the Teaching Fgn. Langs., Am. Coun. Tchrs. Russian (bd. dirs. 1992-98), Internat. Assn. Learning Lab. Dirs., Assn. Internat. Linguistique Appliquée. Russian Orthodox. Office: Am Grad Sch Internat Mgmt 15249 N 59th Ave Glendale AZ 85306-3236 E-mail: tumanw@t-bird.edu.

TUMAY, MEHMET TANER, geotechnical consultant, educator, research administrator; b. Feb. 2, 1937; came to U.S., 1959; s. Bedrettin and Muhterem (Uybadin) T.; m. Karen Nuttycombe, June 15, 1962; children: Peri, Suna. BSCE, Robert Coll. Sch. Engring., Istanbul, Turkey, 1959; MSCE, U. Va., 1961; postgrad., UCLA, 1963-64; PhD, Tech. U. Istanbul, 1971. Lic. civil engr., La., Ga., S.C., Turkish Chamber of Civil Engring. Instr. civil engring. U. Va., Charlottesville, 1961-62; asst. prof. civil engring. U. Louisville, 1962-63; tchg. fellow UCLA, 1963-64; asst. prof. civil engring. Robert Coll. Sch. Engring., Istanbul, 1966-71; assoc. prof. dept. civil engring. Bogazici U., 1971-75; Ga. Gulf disting. prof. La. State U., Baton Rouge, 1976—; Fugro-Cesco postdoctoral rsch. fellow U. Fla., Gainesville, 1975-76. Adv. prof. U. Vicosa, Minas Gerais, Brazil, 1991—, Tongji U., Shanghai, 1991—; dir. geomechanics program NSF, Washington, 1990-94; dir. rsch. La. Transp. Rsch. Ctr., Baton Rouge, 1994-97; assoc. dean rsch. and grad. studies Coll. Engring., La. State U., 1997—; maitre de conferences Ecole Nationale des Ponts et Chaussees, Paris, 1980-94; geotech. cons. Sauti, Spa, Cons. Engrs., Italy, 1969-72, SOFRETU-RATP, Paris, 1972-73, D.E.A., Cons. Engrs., Istanbul, 1974-75, BOTEK, Ltd., Istanbul, 1975—, Senler-Campbell Assocs., Louisville, 1979-90, Fugro Gulf-Geogulf, Houston, 1980-83; cons. UN Devel. Program, 1982-84, 87; cons. in field. Contbr. articles to profl. jours. AID scholar, 1975-76, French Ministry External Rels. scholar, 1982. Fellow ASCE; mem. ASTM, Am. Soc. Engring. Edn., La. Engring. Soc., Turkish Soil Mechanics Group (charter), Turkish Chamber Civil Engrs., Internat. Soc. Soil Mechanics and Found. Engring., Transp. Rsch. Bd. of the Nat. Acads., Sigma Xi, Chi Epsilon, Tau Beta Pi. Home: 2217 Dove Hollow Dr Baton Rouge LA 70809-1275 Office: La State U Coll Engring Baton Rouge LA 70803-0001 E-mail: mtumay@eng.lsu.edu.

TUMBLESON, ARTHUR LOUIS, civil engineer, contractor; b. Cin., Oct. 9, 1934; s. Albert Newton and Clara Mae T.; m. Shirley Richardson, Oct. 4, 1953 (div. June 1974); children: Michael L., Steven A.; m. Nancy C. Palmer, Feb., 1983 (div. Oct. 1987); m. Janice K. Sligh, Apr. 1989. BCE, U. Cin., 1957. With C.E., U.S. Army; with engring dept. City of Cin., 1953-63; dir. pub. works, bldg. and zoning ofcl. City of Temple Terrace, Fla., 1963-73; gen. contractor Temple Terrace, 1974-76; civil engr., project and constrn. mgr. Tomasino and Assocs., 1976—.

TUMBLESON, RAYMOND DANA, English educator; b. N.Y.C., June 24, 1958; s. John Raymond and Treva Rose Tumbleson; m. Lisa Jeanne Tumbleson, May 25, 1996; children: Elizabeth Grace, Mary Margaret. AB, Harvard U., 1980; MA, Boston U., 1988; PhD, U. Wash., 1993. Asst. prof. Kutztown (Pa.) U., 1994—. Author: Catholicism in the English Protestant Imagination: Nationalism, Religion and Literature, 1660-1745, 1998. Mem. MLA, Am. Soc. for Eighteenth-Century Studies. Home: 316 E Walnut St Kutztown PA 19530 Office: Kutztown U English Dept Main St Kutztown PA 19530

TUMPSON, JOAN BERNA, artist; BA with highest distinction, Northwestern U., 1969; JD, Yale U., 1973. Bar: N.Y. 1974, U.S. Dist. Ct. (so. and ea. dists.) N.Y. 1974, U.S. Ct. Appeals (2d cir.) 1975, U.S. Dist. Ct. (no. dist.) Ohio 1977,. U.S. Supreme Ct., 1977, Ohio 1980, Fla. 1980, U.S. Dist. Ct. (so. dist.) Fla. 1981. Gen. assignment reporter, rewriteman AP, N.Y. Bur., A.P. Stringer, Yale U., 1970-72; assoc. Debevoise Plimpton Lyons & Gates (now Debevoise & Plimpton), N.Y.C., 1973-77; staff atty., lectr. law Cleve. Marshall Law Sch., Cleve. State U., 1977-78; vis. asst. prof. law Case Western Res. U., Cleve., 1978-79; assoc. Sage Gray Todd & Sims, Miami, Fla., 1980-82; ptnr. Tumpson & Astbury, 1982-92, Tumpson & Charchat, Miami, 1993-98; artist, 1998—. Class of 73 sec. Yale Law Sch.; bd. dirs. Greater Miami Jewish Fedn. Cable TV, Inc., 1988-92, long term planning com.; trustee Dade County Art in Pub. Places Trust, 1989-93; host south Fla. talk show One to One Sta. WAXY-AM, 1994-98; active Dem. Bus. Coun., 1996-97. Mem. Fla. Bar, Yale Club Miami Studio: 1555 SW 8th St Miami FL 33135-5218 E-mail: Tumpson@aol.com.

TUNER, JEFF NEAL, minister; b. Birmingham, Ala., 1974; s. Rev. James Alvin and Lucinda Phillips Turner; m. Tanya Cornelius Yurner; children: Logan James Turner, Leah Kay Turner. AS, Wallace State, Hanceville, AL, 1994; BS (of music ed.), Jacksonville State, Jacksonville, AL, 1998. Tchr. /band dir. Cleve. H.S., Cleveland, Ala., 1999—2002. Asst. condr./artistic dir. Muscle Shoals Symphony, Muscle, Ala., 1994—95. Mem.: Ala. edn. assn. (assoc.), NEA (assoc.), Music Educators Nat. Conf. (assoc.). Home: 13 Grandview Drive Oneonta AL 35121 Personal E-mail: jeff@corrwireless.net.

TUNG, KO-YUNG, lawyer; b. Peking, Peoples Republic China, Feb. 20, 1947; came to U.S., 1964; s. Tien-chung and Hung-Fang (Wong) T.; m. Alison Heydt, Feb. 2, 1975; children: Vanessa, Adrian, Cameron, Gregory. BA, Harvard U., 1969; JD, U. Tokyo, 1971. Bar: N.Y., 1973. Assoc. Debevoise &

Plimpton, N.Y.C., 1973-76; ptnr. Tung, Drabkin & Boynton, 1976-84, O'Melveny & Myers, N.Y.C., 1985-99; v.p., gen. counsel The World Bank, Washington, 1999—. Adj. assoc. prof. sch. law NYU, 1974-88. Mem. Coun. on Fgn. Rels., N.Y.C., 1986—, The Brookings Inst., 1990, Overseas Devel. Coun., Washington, 1990-99, The Japan Soc., 1990, Asia Soc., 1994—, Presl. Commn. U.S. Pacific Trade Investment Policy, 1996-97, Trilateral Commn., N.Y.C., 1990-97; chmn., bd. govs. East West Ctr., Honolulu, 1990-99; U.S. Nat. Commn. for Pacific Econ. Cooperation, 1991—; bd. dirs. Asian Am. Legal Def. and Edn. Fund, 1990—; vice chmn. adv. coun. Human Rights Watch/Asia, 1997-99, Am. Law Inst., 1997—. Law Faculty fellow Harvard U., 1993. Mem. Am. Law Inst., Am. Arbitration Assn., Internat. Panel Arbitrators, Phi Beta Kappa. Office: The World Bank 1818 H St NW Washington DC 20433-0001 E-mail: Ktung@worldbank.org.

TUNG, ROSALIE LAM, business educator, consultant; b. Shanghai, China, Dec. 2, 1948; came to U.S., 1975; d. Andrew Yan-Fu and Pauline Wai-Kam (Cheung) Lam; m. Byron Poon-Yang Tung, June 17, 1972; 1 chlid, Michele Christine. BA, York U., 1972; MBA, U. B.C., 1974, PhD in Bus. Adminstrn., 1977. Lectr. diploma divsn. U. B.C., 1975, lectr. exec. devel. program, 1975; asst. prof. mgmt. Grad. Sch. Mgmt., U. Oreg., Eugene, 1977-80; assoc. prof. U. Pa., Phila., 1981-86; prof., dir. internat. bus. ctr. U. Wis., Milw., 1986-90; endowed chaired prof. Simon Fraser U., 1991—. Fgn. expert Fgn. Investment Commn., China; vis. scholar U. Manchester (Eng.) Sci. and Tech., 1980; vis. prof. UCLA, 1981, Harvard U., 1988, Copenhagen Bus. Sch., 1995, 97, Chinese U. Hong Kong, 1997, Peking U., 2001; Wis. disting. prof. U. Wis. Sys., 1988-90, Ming and Stella Wong chair in internat. bus., 1991-; bd. govs. Acad. Mgmt. Author: Management Practices in China, 1980, U.S.-China Trade Negotiations, 1982, Chinese Industrial Society After Mao, 1982, Business Negotiations with the Japanese, 1984, Key to Japan's Economic Strength: Human Power, 1984, The New Expatriates: Managing Human Resources Abroad, 1988; editor: Strategic Management in the U.S. and Japan, 1987, International Management in International Library of Business and Management Series, 1994, Internat. Ency. Bus. and Mgmt., 1996, IEBM Handbook of International Business, 1998, Learning from World Class Companies, 2001. Recipient Leonore Rowe Williams award U. Pa., 1990, U. B.C. Alumni 75th Anniversary award, 1990, Advanced Global Competitiveness Rsch. award, 1997, Woman of Distinction in the Professions, Mgmt. and Trades award YWCA, Vancouver, 1998; York U. scholar, 1972; Univ. fellow, Seagram Bus. fellow, H.R. MacMillan Family fellow; Oppenheimer Bros. Found. fellow, 1973-74, U. B.C. fellow, 1974-75, H.R. Macmillan Found. fellow, 1975-77. Fellow Royal Soc. Can., Acad. Mgmt. (bd. govs. 1987-89, v.p. 2001-02, pres. 2002—), Internat. Acad. Cultural Rsch. (founding); mem. Acad. Internat. Bus. (mem. exec. bd., treas. 1985-86), Internat. Assn. Applied Psychology, Am. Arbitration Assn. (comml. panel arbitrators). Roman Catholic. Avocation: creative writing. Office: Simon Fraser U Faculty Bus Adminstrn Burnaby BC Canada V5A 1S6

TUNG, YEISHIN, research scientist; b. Taipei, Taiwan, Aug. 27, 1962; came to U.S., 1987; s. Wei and Kuoing (Wu) T. BSChemE, Chung Yuan U., Chun Li, Taiwan, 1984; MS in Materials Sci., Rutgers U., 1989, PhD in Materials Sci., 1993. Rsch. asst. Rutgers U., New Brunswick, N.J., 1989-93; rsch. assoc. Fisk U., Nashville, 1994-97, rsch. asst. prof., 1997-98; staff analyst accelerator techiques group Charles Evans & Assocs., Redwood City, Calif., 1998—. Author: (book chpt.) Hyphenated Techniques in Polymer Characterization, 1994. 2d lt. Taiwan infantry, 1984-86. Recipient Coblentz Soc. award Coblentz Soc., 1993. Mem. Am. Phys. Soc., Am. Vacuum Soc., Materials Rsch. Soc., Am. Chem. Soc. Achievements include observation of surface phonon mode of semiconductor quantum dots; measurement of sublimation rates of high explosives.

TUNHEIM, JERALD ARDEN, academic administrator, physics educator; b. Claremont, S.D., Sept. 3, 1940; s. Johannes and Annie Tunheim; children: Jon, Angie, Alec. BS in Engring. Physics, S.D. State U., 1962, MS in Physics, 1964; PhD in Physics, Okla. State U., 1968. Vis. scientist Sandia Corp., Albuquerque, 1970-71, Ames (Iowa) AEC Labs., 1972; asst. prof. S.D. State U., Brookings, 1968-73, assoc. prof., 1973-78, prof., 1978-80, prof., head physics dept., 1980-85; dean Ea. Wash. U., Cheney, 1985-87; pres. Dakota State U., Madison, S.D., 1987—. Bd. dirs. NSF Systemic Initiative, Nat. Skill Stds. Bd., 1998—. Co-author: Elementary Particles and Unitary Symmetry, 1966, Quantum Field Theory, 1966; contbr. articles to profl.jours. Bd. dirs. Lake Area Improvement Corp. Grantee USDA, 1987-88, S.D. Govt. Office Edn. Devel., 1988-89, U.S. Dept. Edn., Eisenhower Program, 1985-86, 87-90, 92-93, 95-96, U.S. Dept. Edn. Math. and Sci. Program, 1989-92; named Tchr. of Yr. S.D. State U., 1972. Mem. NSPE, Am. Phys. Soc., Am. Assn. Physics Tchrs., Madison C. of C. (bd. dirs. 1990—), Rotary. Republican. Lutheran. Office: Dakota State U Office of President 820 N Washington Ave Madison SD 57042-1799 E-mail: Jerald.Tunheim@dsu.edu.

TUNICK, LARAINE DONISI, publishing executive; b. Oyster Bay, N.Y., Jan. 18, 1958; m. Lee M. Tunick, May 18, 1991; children: Benjamin, Allison. BS, N.C. State U., 1980. Advtg. coord. CMP Publications, Inc., Manhasset, N.Y., 1982-85, rsch. analyst, 1985-87, sr. rsch. mgr., 1991-95, rsch. dir., 1995-97, sr. rsch. mgr., 1998—; mkt. rsch. mgr. Cahners Pub. Co., N.Y.C., 1987-89; sr. rsch. mgr. Ziff-Davis Pub. Co., 1989-91. Home: 7 Wainer Ct Centerport NY 11721-1557

TUNIEWICZ, MARK ANTHONY, political activist, corporate credit executive; b. Dover, N.H., Dec. 2, 1961; s. A. Richard and Pauline Juliette T. BS in Fin. & Internat. cum laude, Northeastern U., 1984. U.S. credit mgr. Konica Corp., Portland, Maine, 1990-93; internat. credit mgt. Starter Corp., New Haven, 1993-95; chmn. Libertarian Party N.H., Manchester, 1995-97; dir. corp. credit Maska U.S., Inc., Peterborough, N.H., 1995-97; region 6 rep. Libertarian Party, Washington, 1996-98; dir. Libertarian Party Mass., Boston, 1997-2001; gen. credit mgr. Swank, Inc., Attleboro, Mass., 1998—; treas. Libertarian Party, Washington, 1998-2001. Bd. dirs. NACM-New Eng., Inc., Boston, NACM-R.I., Inc. Dir. comm. Libertarian Party Conn., Hartford, 1993-95; dir. Libertarian Party Mich., Detroit, 1997-98; cmty. leader AOL, Va., 1998-2001; conservation commr. Town of Milford, N.H., 1995-97; commr. Am. and Can. French Cultural Exch. Commn., 2000—; mem. fin. com. Town of Easton, Mass., 2000-, mem. sch. planning com., 2001-. Mem. Nat. Assn. Credit Mgmt. (Conn. sec. 1994-95, east regional dir. 1997-2001, sr. vice chmn. 2001—), Maine Assn. Comml. Creditors, Coalition for Free and Open Elections, Assn. Town Fin. Coms. (bd. dirs., treas. 2002-). Roman Catholic. Home: 3 Indian Cove Way South Easton MA 02375-1760 Office: Swank Inc 6 Hazel St Attleboro MA 02703-3910 E-mail: marktun@bigfoot.com.

TUNINSKAYA, GALINA M. chemist, consultant; b. Lutsk, Volinskiy, Ukraine; came to U.S., 1993; d. Michael and Faina (Metushanska) T.; m. Mark Rokhfeld, Dec. 30, 1979; children: Marianna, Dmitriy. BS, Leningrad Inst. Chem. Engring., Russia, 1975, MS, 1977. Engr., chemist Linen Mfg., Zhitomir, Ukraine, 1977-80; from. prof. to rsch. chemist Pedagogical Inst., Ukraine, 1980-93; from rsch. chemist to chief chemist Applied Consumer Svcs., Miami, 1993-97, tech. dir., 1997—. Active Russian Outreach Program, Miami, 1995—. Mem. AAAS, Am. Chem. Soc., Am. Soc. for Quality. Office: Applied Consumers Svcs 11890 NW 87th Ct Unit 8 Hialeah Gardens FL 33018 E-mail: acsgalina@aol.com.

TUNISON, ELIZABETH LAMB, education educator; b. Portadown, Northern Ireland, Jan. 7, 1922; came to U.S., 1923; d. Richard Ernest and Ruby (Hill) Lamb; m. Ralph W. Tunison, Jan. 24, 1947 (dec. Apr. 1984); children: Eric Arthur, Christine Wait, Dana Paul. BA, Whittier Coll., 1943, MEd, 1963. Tchr. East Whittier (Calif.) Schs., 1943-59; tchr. T.V. TV Channels 13 and 28, So. Calif. Counties, 1960-75; dir. curriculum Bassett (Calif.) Schs., 1962-65; elem. sch. prin. Rowland Unified Schs., Rowland Heights, Calif., 1965-68; assoc. prof. edn. Calif. State Poly. U., Pomona, 1968-71; prof. Whittier Coll., 1968-88, prof. emerita, 1988—. Bd. dirs. Restless Legs Syndrome Found., facilitator for So. Calif. Orgn. Bd. dirs. Presbyn. Intercmty. Hosp. Found.; founder Restless Legs Support Group (chmn. 1995—). Recipient Whittier Coll. Alumni Achievement award 1975; Helen Hefernan scholar 1963. Mem. AAUP, Assn. Calif. Sch. Adminstrs. (state bd., chmn. higher edn. com. 1983-86, region pres. 1981-83, Wilson Grace award 1983), PEO (pres. 1990-92), Assistance League of Whittier (v.p. 1994-96), Delta Kappa Gamma (v.p. 1996-97). Home: 900 E Harrison Ave F-10 Pomona CA 91767 E-mail: tuni22@aol.com.

TUNLEY, NAOMI LOUISE, retired nurse administrator; b. Henryretta, Okla., Jan. 10, 1936; d. Alexander and Ludia Bell (Franklin) T. BSN, Dillard U., 1958; MA, U. Mo., Kansas City, 1974. RN, Okla. Staff nurse, assoc. chief nursing svc. Oklahoma City VA Med. Ctr., 1958-65; instr. Iowa Luth. Hosp. Sch. Nursing, Des Moines, 1965-66; charge nurse emergency rm. Mercy Hosp., Iowa City, 1966-67; charge nurse, assoc. chief nursing svc. Kansas City (Mo.) VA Med. Ctr., 1967-76, charge nurse neurol. unit, 1976-79, nurse mgr. orthopedic unit, 1979-80, nurse mgr. substance abuse unit, 1980-94; ret., 1994. Equal employment opportunity counselor Kansas City (Mo.) VA Med. Ctr., 1976-86; trustee Nat. Coun. Alcohol and Other Drugs, Kansas City, 1986-90. Vol. Am. Cancer Soc., Kansas City, 1971-79, March of Dimes, Kansas City, 1971-79; big sister Big Bros.-Sisters Am., Kansas City, 1974-84. Mem. ARC, Sigma Theta Tau. Avocations: fishing, golf, tennis. Home: 3120 Poplar Ave Kansas City MO 64128-1803

TUNNELL, CLIDA DIANE, air transportation specialist; b. Durham, N.C., Nov. 20, 1946; d. Kermit Wilbur and Roberta (Brantley) T.; m. Michael A. Murphy, May 24, 1997. BS cum laude, Atlantic Christian Coll., 1968; pvt. pilot rating, instr. rating, Air Care, Inc., 1971, 83. Cert. tchr. Tchr. Colegio Karl C. Parrish, Barranquilla, Colombia, 1968-69, Nash County Schs., Nashville, 1969-86; ground sch. instr. Nash. Tech. Coll., 1984-85; specialist Am. Airlines, Dallas-Ft. Worth Airport, Tex., 1987—, A300 lead developer in flight tng. program devel., 1988-89, with flight ops. procedures flight ops. tech., 1990—, F100-fleet splst. flight ops. tech., 1992-98, 737 fleet splst., 1998—. Ednl. cons., Euless, Tex., 1989—; profl. artist. State Tchrs. Scholar N.C., 1964-68, Bus. and Profl. Women Scholar, 1980-81. Mem. 99, Internat. Orgn. Women Pilots (various offices), AMR Mgmt. Club. Avocations: flying, painting, writing, traveling. Home: PO Box 234 Euless TX 76039-0234

TUNNER, WILLIAM SAMS, urological surgeon; b. San Antonio, Nov. 14, 1933; s. William Henry and Sarah Margaret (Sams) T.; m. Sallie Berry Woodul, Dec. 4, 1965; children: William Woodul, Jonathan Sams. Student, Washington and Lee U., 1952-55; MD, U. Va., 1960. Diplomate Am. Bd. Urology. Intern in surgery, then asst. surg. resident Duke Hosp., 1960-62; fellow cancer surgery Cancer Inst. NIH, Bethesda, Md., 1962-64; resident in urol. surgery Cornell-N.Y. Hosp., 1964-68, fellow transplantation, dialysis and biochemistry, instr., 1968-70; asst. prof. urol. surgery U. Tex. Med. Sch., San Antonio, 1970-72; pvt. practice Richmond, Va., 1972—. Mem. staff Henrico County St. Marys Hosp., Chippenham, Johnston-Willis hosps.; asst. clin. prof. urology Med. Coll. Va., 1972—. Contbr. articles to med. jours., films. Fellow: ACS (past pres. Va. chpt., past gov. at large), Am. Acad. Pediatrics (affiliate); mem.: SR (pres. for State of Va. 2001—), AMA, Am. Nephrology Assn., Am. Urol. Assn., Soc. Pediatric Urology, Transplantation Soc., Soc. Internat. Irologie, Va. Soc. Sons of Revolution (pres.), Country Club Va., Beta Theta Pi, Alpha Epsilon Delta. Episcopalian. Avocation: equestrian activities. Home: Braedon Farm 1240 Shallow Well Rd Manakin Sabot VA 23103-2300 Office: St Mary's Hosp Profl Bldg 5855 Bremo Rd Richmond VA 23226-1926

TUNNICLIFF, DAVID GEORGE, civil engineer; b. Ord, Nebr., Sept. 18, 1931; s. George Thomas and Ada Ellen (Ward) T.; m. Elaine Jean Interrante, Oct. 17, 1959 (div.); children: Martha Allison Tunnicliff Loeb, Vivian Jean Tunnicliff; m. Joan Elizabeth Duchesneau, Oct. 25, 1975. BS, U. Nebr., 1954; MS, Cornell U., 1958; PhD, U. Mich., 1972. Registered profl. engr., Nebr., Mass. Engr. Nebr. Dept. Rds., Lincoln, 1954-60; asst. prof., then assoc. prof. Wayne State U., Detroit, 1960-67; chief tech. svcs. Warren Bros. Co., Cambridge, Mass., 1967-79; prin., cons. engr. D.G. Tunnicliff, Cons. Engr., Omaha, 1979—. Contbr. to profl. publs. Rep. precinct del., Detroit, 1965-66. With U.S. Army, 1955-56. Mem. ASTM (chair subcom. 1973-94), ASCE, Assn. Asphalt Paving Tech. (bd. dirs. 1976-78), Transp. Rsch. Bd. (com. chair 1983-89). Mem. Evangel. Covenant Ch. Home and Office: DG Tunnicliff Cons Engr 9624 Larimore Ave Omaha NE 68134-3038

TUNSTALL, DOROTHY FIEBRICH, early childhood educator; b. Elizabeth City, Va., Sept. 18, 1939; d. Louie Ludwig and Nancy Julia (Drafts) Fiebrich; m. Frank S. Clark Jr., June 11, 1961 (div. 1970); children: Sherri Ann D'Alessio, Debra Sue Pate, Frank S. Clark III; m. Jim Tunstall, June 1995 (div.). BA in Elem. Edn., Stetson U., 1961, MA in Edn., 1963; Ed. Spec. in Edn. Adminstrn., U. S.C., 1991, PhD in Early Childhood, 1993. Cert. tchr. Fla., S.C. Substitute tchr. Broward County Schs., Ft. Lauderdale, Fla., 1963-70, EABE tchr., 1972-80; title I, tchr. for fed. govt. South Fla. State Hosp., Pembroke Pines, 1970-72; tchr. spl. edn. Richland Sch. Dist. #2, Columbia, S.C., 1980-81; COBOL programmer Comptr. Gen.'s Office, 1982-85; tchr. spl. edn. Calhoun County Schs., St. Matthews, S.C., 1985-88; tchr. kindergarten Fairfield County Schs., Winnsboro, 1989-92; dir. St. Paul's Child Care Ministry, Columbia, SC, 1997—2000, Good Shepherd Day Sch., 2001—. Adj. prof. U. S.C., Columbia, 1994—. Mem. Lexington County Adolescent Pregnancy Prevention Bd., 1999—, Lexington County First Steps Bd., 2001—. Mem.: AAUW (pres. 1998—2002), Mental Health Assn. in Mid-Carolina (v.p. 1992—93, bd. dirs., Pres. award 1993), Lexington County Arts Assn. (pres. 1992—93, Newcomer's award 1981), Wildlife Action Inc. (pres. 1991—93), Beta Sigma Phi (Girl of Yr. 1967). Avocations: reading, gardening. Home: 159 Corley Mill Rd Lexington SC 29072-7600 Office: Good Shepherd Day Sch 3909 Forest Dr Columbia SC 29204

TUNSTEL, EDWARD WELDON, JR. robotics engineer; b. N.Y.C., Nov. 29, 1963; s. Edward Weldon Sr. and Agnes Luvenia (Solomon) T.; m. Jan Leslie Foster, June 4, 1993; children: Ashlan D., Janaye Elise, Evan Jarell. BS in Mech. Engring., Howard U., Washington, 1986, M Engring., 1989; PhD in Elec. Engring., U. N.Mex., 1996. Info. analyst Engring. Info. Inc., N.Y.C., 1986-89; rsch. asst. Howard U., Washington, 1986-89; robotics engr. NASA Jet Propulsion Lab.-Calif. Inst. Tech., Pasadena, Calif., 1989—. Assoc. editor Intelligent Automation and Soft Computing, an Internat. Jour., 1994—; contbr. articles to profl. jours. Vol. United Way, Greater L.A., 1991-92. Recipient Minority Fellowship NASA Jet Propulsion Lab., Pasadena, 1992. Mem. IEEE, Am. Assn. Artificial Intelligence, Nat. Soc. Black Engrs., Sigma Xi (assoc.). Avocations: music (jazz), sports, science fiction and fact.

TUOHEY, MARK HENRY, III, lawyer; b. Rochester, N.Y., Sept. 27, 1946; s. Mark Henry Tuohey; m. Martha Tuohey; children: Brendan, Sean, Devin. BA in History, St. Bonaventure U., 1968; JD, Fordham U., 1973. Bar: D.C. 1973, U.S. Supreme Ct. 1980, U.S. Ct. Appeals (D.C. cir.) 1974, U.S. Dist. Ct. D.C. 1974, N.Y. 1984. Asst. U.S. atty. U.S. Atty.'s Office, Washington, 1973-77; spl. trial counsel U.S. Dept. Justice, 1977-79; spl. counsel to U.S. Atty. Gen., 1979; co-adminstrv. ptnr. Vinson & Elkins; dep. ind. counsel Whitewater Investigation, 1994-95; spl. counsel D.C. City Coun. Investigation of Met. Police Dept., 1998. Served to 1st lt. U.S. Army, 1970—71. Master: Wm. Bryant Inn. of Ct.; fellow: Am. Bar Found. (bd. dirs. 1980—85), Am. Law Inst., Am. Coll. Trial Lawyers; mem.: ABA (litig. sect. coun. 1980—90, chair standing com. on continuing edn. bar 1980—85, chair Am. Law Inst./ABA com. continuing profl. edn. 1983—), Bar Assn. D.C. (Lawyer of the Yr. 2001), Jud. Conf. U.S. Ct. Appeals (D.C. cir.), D.C. Bar Found. (chair 1998—), D.C. Bar (pres. 1993—94, bd. govs. 1988—94). Home: 1655 Kalmia Rd NW Washington DC 20012-1125 Office: Vinson & Elkins The Willard Office Bldg 1455 Pennsylvania Ave NW Fl 7 Washington DC 20004-1013 E-mail: mtouhey@velaw.com.

TUOMI, TAPANI MIKA, research scientist; b. Loimaa, Finland, July 19, 1966; s. Mikko Paavali and Synnove Eva (Ahlgren) T.; m. Maarit Elisabeth Piirainen, May 21, 1994. MSc, Helsinki (Finland) U. Tech., 1992, Licentiate in Tech., 1994, D in Chem. Engring., 1995. Rsch. scientist Helsinki U. Tech., 1991-95, sr. asst., 1995-97, lectr., 1998—, docent in environ. microbiology and chemistry, 2002; rsch. scientist Finnish Inst. Occupl. Health, Helsinki, 1997-98, sr. rsch. scientist, 1999-2000, head of lab., 2001—. Lectr. Turku (Finland) Poly. U., 1997-98. Contbr. articles to profl. jours., including Applied Biochemistry and Biotech., Clin. Chemistry, Applied and Environ. Microbiology, others; mem. editl. bd. Applied and Environ. Microbiology. Guardsman, Finnish Army, 1989-90, Helsinki. Mem. Internat. Soc. Indoor Air Quality and Climate. Avocations: weight training, motorcycles. Office: Finnish Inst Occupl Health Arinatie 3A FIN00370 Helsinki Finland

TUPPER, RON, public health, policy, and management educator; b. Natick, Mass., Aug. 25, 1945; s. Ralph and Madeline (Boyde) Moore-Tupper; m. Malinda McGilvray, July 28, 1987; children: Michelle, Melissa, Madeline Marie. BA in Psychology, U. Nebr., 1969; MSc in Health Mgmt./Health Edn., S.W. Tex. State U., 1975. Asst. dir.-unit mgmt. Bexar County Hosp., San Antonio, 1971-72; assoc. dir. adminstrv. svcs. Robert B. Green Hosp., 1972-74; hosp. adminstr. Maverick County (Tex.) Hosp., 1975-78, Hosp. Affiliates, Internat., Nashville, 1978-82; divsn. mgr. Mgmt. Recruiters Internat., Irving, Tex., 1983-88; v.p. adminstrn. Stores, Inc., McAllen, 1990—; exec. dir. Area Health Edn. Ctr., Weslaco, 1995-99; dir. South Tex. Ctr. for Rural Pub. Health Tex. A&M U. Sys. Health Sci. Ctr., McAllen, 1999—; prof., dir. Sch. Rural Pub. Health Tex. A&M U. System Health Sci. Ctr., College Station, 2001—; faculty prof., dir. McAllen br. campus Tex. A&M U. Sys. Health Sci. Ctr. Sch. Rural Pub. Health. Founder, bd. chair Cmty. Health Mgmt. Corp.-El Milagro Indigent Clinic, McAllen, 1996—, U. Tex. Med. Br. at Galveston Indigent Cancer Clinic. Chair, health and health edn. adv. com. State of Tex. Senator Appt., Tex./Mex., 1996, mem. South Tex. health adv. com., Lower Rio Grande Valley, 1996; mem. steering com. Tex. A&M U. Sch. of Rural Public Health, Rio Grande Valley rep., 1997—; mem. Tex. Dept. of Health U. Tex. Mobile Health Van com., 1996—. Staff sgt. USAF, 1964-70. Decorated Vietnam Svc. medal, Air Force conduct medal. Mem. Tex./Mex. Border Assn., Midwest Migrant Health Com. Avocations: writing, carpentry, community development. Office: South Tex Ctr for Rural Pub Health Tex A&M Uni Sys Hlth Sci 3700 N 10th St Ste 210 Mcallen TX 78501-1775 E-mail: Tupper@medicine.tamu.edu.

TURANO, DAVID A. lawyer; b. Ashtabula, Ohio, Sept. 9, 1946; s. Egidio A. and Mary Agnes (Bartko) T.; m. Karen J. Emmel, Aug. 29, 1970; children: Aaron, Thad, Bethen, Kyle. BS, Kent State U., 1968; JD, Ohio State U., 1971. Bar: Ohio 1971. Staff atty. The Pub. Utilities Commn. Ohio, Columbus, 1971-72; assoc., then ptnr. George, Greek, King, McMahon and Mcconnaughey, 1972-79; ptnr. Baker & Hostetler, 1979-96, Harris, Carter, Mahota, Turano & Mazza, Columbus, 1996-97, Harris, Turano & Mazza, Columbus, 1997—. Mem. ABA, Ohio State Bar Assn., Columbus Bar Assn., Transp. Lawyers Assn. Roman Catholic. Office: Harris Turano & Mazza 941 Chatham Ln Ste 201 Columbus OH 43221-2416

TURBIDY, JOHN BERRY, investor, management consultant; b. Rome, Oct. 18, 1928; s. Joseph Leo and Louyse (Berry) T.; m. Joan Marsales, Dec. 19, 1958 (dec.); children: John Berry, Trevor Martin; m. Jaquelin Lamond Schulter, June 8, 1995. Grad., Darlington Sch., 1945; BA, Duke U., 1950; postgrad., NYU, 1952, Emory U., 1954-56. Various positions Lockheed Aircraft, Marietta, Ga., 1951-56; gen. mgmt. cons. McKinsey & Co., N.Y.C. and London, 1956-63; v.p. adminstrn. ITT Europe, Inc., Brussels, 1963, v.p., group exec. European consumer products, 1964-65, v.p., group exec. for No. Europe, 1965-67; corp. v.p. adminstrn. Celanese Corp., N.Y.C., 1967-68; pres., mng. dir. SIACE, SP.A. subs., Milan, Italy, 1968-69; chmn. bd., pres. Vecta Group, Kalamazoo, 1970-74; sr. v.p. corp. devel. IU Internat. Corp., Phila., 1974-78, exec. v.p., 1978-83; pres., chief exec. officer Pitcairn Fin. Mgmt. Group, Jenkintown, Pa., 1984-90; chmn. Office John Turbidy, 1990-95; mng. dir. Friedman, Turbidy & Co., Inc., N.Y.C., 1995—. Bd. dirs. Statute of Liberty Ellis Island Found. Served with USNR, 1952. Mem. Sea Bright Lawn and Cricket Club, Sea Bright Beach Club, Rumson Country Club. Address: PO Box 338 Little Silver NJ 07739-0338

TURBIN, RICHARD, lawyer; b. N.Y.C., Dec. 25, 1944; s. William and Ruth (Fiedler) T.; m. Rai Saint Chu-Turbin, June 12, 1976; children: Laurel Mei, Derek Andrew. BA magna cum laude, Cornell U., 1966; JD, Harvard U., 1969. Bar: Hawaii 1971, U.S. Dist. Ct. Hawaii 1971. Asst. atty. gen., Western Samoa, Apia, 1969-70; dep. pub. defender Pub. Defender's Office, Honolulu, 1970-74; dir. Legal Aid Soc. Hawaii, Kaneohe, 1974-75; sr. atty., pres. Law Offices Richard Turbin, Honolulu, 1975—. Legal counsel Hawaii Crime Commn., 1980-81. Co-author: Pacific; author: Medical Malpractice, Handling Emergency Medical Cases, 1991; editor Harvard Civil Rights-Civil Liberties Law Rev., 1969. Legal counsel Dem. Party, Honolulu County, 1981-82; elected Neighborhood Bd., 1985, elected chair, 1990-97; bd. dirs. Hawaii chpt. ACLU, 1974-78, East-West Ctr. grantee, 1971, 72. Mem. ATLA, ABA (chair internat. torts and ins. law and practice com., mem. governing coun., chair tort and ins. practice sect. 1999-2000, chair-elect 1998-99), Hawaii Bar Assn., Hawaii Trial Lawyers Assn. (bd. govs.), Hawaii Jaycees (legal counsel 1981-82), Chinese Jaycees Honolulu (legal counsel 1980-81), Honolulu Tennis League (undefeated player 1983), Hawaii Harlequin Rugby Club (sec., legal counsel 1978-82), Pacific Club, Outrigger Canoe Club. Jewish. Home: 4817 Kahala Ave Honolulu HI 96816-5231

TURCHI, PETER JOHN, aerospace and electrical engineer, physicist, educator; b. N.Y.C., Dec. 30, 1946; s. Charles Orlando and Fay Florence Turchi; m. Judith Ann Radogna, June 13, 1967; children: Janita Nicole, Rebecca Lenore. BSE in Aerospace and Mech. Sci./Physics, Princeton U., 1967, MA, 1969, PhD, 1970. Rsch. assoc. Plasma Propulsion Lab., Princeton (N.J.) U., 1963—70; plasma physicist Air Force Weapons Lab., Kirtland AFB, N.Mex., 1970—72; rsch. physicist Naval Rsch. Lab., Washington, 1972—77, chief Plasma Tech. br., 1977—80; scientist R&D Assocs., Arlington, Va., 1980—81; dir. RDA Washington Rsch. Lab., Alexandria, 1981—89; prof. aerospace engring. Ohio State U., Columbus, 1989—99; leader hydrodynamics and pulsed power sci. Los Alamos (N.Mex.) Nat. Lab., 1999—2002; sr. scientist for high power microwaves and pulsed power Air Force Rsch. Lab., Kirtland AFB, N.Mex., 2002—. Chmn. Megagauss Inst., Inc., Alexandria, 1979—89, bd. dirs.; chmn. mech. and aero. engring. adv. coun. Princeton U., 1988—92, mem. engring. sch. adv. coun., 1988—92, dean's leadership coun., 1992—93; resident/collateral faculty Ohio Aerospace Inst., 1989—95; lab. cons. Los Alamos (N.Mex.) Nat. Lab., 1989—99; intergovtl. sr. rsch. scientist USAF Phillips Lab. and Air Force Rsch. Lab., Kirtland AFB, 1990—2002; vis. chief scientist Advanced Weapons and Survivability, 1996—97; lectr. George Washington U., 1987—89, Air Forced Pulsed Power Lecture Program, 1979—81, Internat. Space U., 1998; cons. on pulsed power tech.; chmn. 2d Internat. Conf. on Megagauss Fields, Arlington, 1979, Spl. Conf. on Prime-Power for High Energy Space Systems, Norfolk, Va., 1982; co-chmn. NASA Conf. on Fusion Space Propulsion, 2000; mem. internat. organizing com. Megagauss Magnetic Field Confs., 1979—; adj. prof. aerospace engring. Ohio State U., Columbus, 1988, 1999—. Editor: Space Propulsion, Propulsion Techniques: Action and Reaction, 1998, Megagauss Physics and Tech., 1980; assoc. editor Jour. Propulsion and Power, 1990-93; guest editor IEEE Transactions on Plasma Sci., 1997-98; contbr. chpts. to books and articles to profl. jours.; patentee in field. Pres. Collingwood (Va.) Civic Assn., 1980-81; rep. Mt. Vernon (Va.) Coun., Mt. Vernon Dist., Fairfax County; pres. Pulsed Power Conf. Inc., Albuquerque, 1985-87, bd. dirs., 1983—. 1st lt. USAF, 1970-72. NSF Grad. fellow, 1967-70; recipient Invention award USAF, 1972, Rsch. Publ. award Naval Rsch. Lab., 1976, USN and Air Force Invention awards, 1978-83. Fellow: IEEE (tech. program chmn. 5th and gen. chmn. 6th pulsed power confs. 1985—87, plasma sci. and applications exec. com. 1987—89, pulsed power sci. and tech. standing com. 1995—, chmn. 2000—02, Erwin Marx award for pulsed power tech. 1999), AIAA (assoc.; mem. tech. com. plasmadynamics and lasers 1983—86, internat. chmn. 18th, 19th, 21st and 22d elec. propulsion confs. 1985—91, mem. elec. propulsion tech. com. 1987—93, chmn. 1991—93, mem. elec. propulsion com. 1997—, mem. standing com. acad. affairs 1997—, mem. editl. adv. bd. 1998—, Nat. Student award 1967); mem.: Planetary Soc., Elec. Rocket Propulsion Soc. (pres. 1994—), Am. Phys. Soc., Albuquerque Aikido Soc., Va. Ki Soc., Princeton Campus, Tau Beta Pi, Sigma Xi. Achievements include research in electromagnetic implosion soft x-ray source, high energy x-ray generation by ultrahigh speed plasma flows, plasma flow switch for magnetic energy delivery above 10 megamperes; stabilized liner implosion system for controlled thermonuclear fusion. E-mail: Peter.Turchi@kirtland.af.mil.

TURCO, LEWIS PUTNAM, English educator; b. Buffalo, May 2, 1934; s. Luigi and May Laura (Putnam) T.; m. Jean Cate Houdlette, May 29, 1934; children: Melora Ann, Christopher Cameron. BA, U. Conn., 1959; MA, U. Iowa, 1962; LHD (hon.), Ashland U., 2000. Instr. Cleve. State U., 1960-64; asst. prof. Hillsdale (Mich.) Coll., 1964-65; asst. prof. to full prof. SUNY, Oswego, 1965-96, poet-in-residence, 1995, prof. emeritus, 1996. Grad. asst. English, U. Conn., 1959; editorial asst. Writer's Workshop, U. Iowa, 1959-60; vis. prof. SUNY, Potsdam, 1968-69; Bingham Poet in Residence, U. Louisville, 1982; Writer in Residence, Ashland U., 1991; founding dir. Cleve. State

U. Poetry Ctr., 1962, program in writing arts, SUNY Oswego, 1968. Author: First Poems, 1960, Awaken, Bells Falling: Poems 1959-67, 1968, The Inhabitant, 1970, Pocoangelini: A Fantography and Other Poems, 1971, American Still Lifes, 1981, numerous other poetry books including The Shifting Web: New and Selected Poems, 1989, The Green Notes of Autumn, Voices in an Old Maine House, 2002; author numerous non-fiction books including The Book of Forms: A Handbook of Poetics, 1968, 3d edit., 2000, Visions and Revisions of American Poetry, 1986, Dialogue, 1989, Emily Dickinson, Woman of Letters, 1993, The Book of Literary Terms, 1999, others; editor: The Life and Poetry of Manoah Bodman, 1999; contbr. articles to profl. jours. Sec. City of Oswego Charter Revision Commn., 1990-91; active Oswego Opera Theater Chorus, Oswego Festival Chorus, 1986—. With USN, 1952-56. Recipient scholarship Meriden Record-Jour. Pub. Co., U. Conn., 1957-58, 58-59, Disting. Alumnus award, 1992, Melville Cane award Poetry Soc. Am., 1986, Bordighera Bilingual Poetry prize Sonia Raiziss-Giop Charitable Found., 1997, John Ciardi award for lifetime achievement in poetry Italian-Am., Found. Am., 1999, others; resident fellowships Yaddo Found., 1959, 77, Faculty fellowships Rsch. Found. of SUNY, 1966-67, 69, 71, 73, 78; grant-in-aid, 1969; inducted into Meriden Hall of Fame, 1993. Home: PO Box 161 Dresden ME 04342-0161 E-mail: mathom@gwi.net.

TURCOT, MARGUERITE HOGAN, innkeeper, medical researcher; b. White Plains, N.Y., May 19, 1934; d. Joseph William (dec.) and Marguerite Alice (dec.) Barrett) Hogan; children: Michael J., Susan A. Turcot, William R. Student, Syracuse U., 1951-54; BSN, U. Bridgeport, 1968. RN, Conn., N.C. Nurse Park City Hosp., Bridgeport, Conn., 1968-69, Meml. Mission Hosp., Asheville, N.C., 1969-70; instr. St. Joseph's Hosp., 1970-71, oper. rm. nurse, 1973-77, charge nurse urology-cystoscopy, 1977-85; tchr. Asheville-Buncombe Tech. Coll., Asheville, 1971-72, Buncombe County Child Devel., Asheville, 1972-73; rschr. VA Med. Ctr., 1988—; owner Reed House Bed & Breakfast, 1985—2001. Bd. dirs. RiverLink, Quality Foreward. Charter mem. French Broad River Planning Com., Asheville, 1987—, Biltmore Village Hist. Mus.; mem. Asheville Bicentennial Commn., 1990-93. Recipient Griffin award, 1994, Friend of the River award, Land of Sky Regional Coun., 1995, Sondley award, Hist. Resources Commn. Asheville and Buncombe County, 1996, Vol. of Yr. award, RiverLink, 2001; grantee U. Bridgeport, 1967—68; scholar Syracuse U. Faculty, 1941—54. Mem. Am. Urology Assn. (presenter VA urology workshop Asheville chpt. 1981, nat. meeting allied), Am. Bd. Urologic Allied Health Profls., Nat. Trust for Hist. Preservation, Preservation Found. N.C., Blue Ridge Pkwy. Assn., Preservation Soc. Asheville and Buncombe County (bd. dirs., past pres.), Asheville Newcomers Club (founder, 1st pres.), Earthwatch, Friends of Blue Ridge Pkwy. Inc. Republican. Roman Catholic. Avocations: preservation, history, architecture, sewing, hiking. Home: 130 School Rd Asheville NC 28806-1532 Office: VA Med Ctr Tunnel Rd Asheville NC 28805-1233

TURCOTTE, DONALD LAWSON, geophysical sciences educator; b. Bellingham, Wash., Apr. 22, 1932; s. Lawson Phillip and Eva (Pearson) T.; m. Joan Meredith Luecke, May 17, 1957; children: Phillip Lawson, Stephen Bradford. BS, Calif. Inst. Tech., 1954, PhD, 1958; M in Aero. Engring., Cornell U., 1955. Asst. prof. aero. engring. U.S. Naval Postgrad. Sch., Monterey, Calif., 1958-59; asst. prof. aero. engring. Cornell U., Ithaca, N.Y., 1959-63, assoc. prof., 1963-67, prof., 1967-73, prof. geol. scis., 1973-85, Maxwell Upson prof., 1985—, chmn., 1981-90. Author: (with others) Statistical Thermodynamics, 1963, Space Propulsion, 1965, Geodynamics, 1982, Fractals and Chaos in Geology and Geophysics, 1992. Trustee U. Space Research Assn., 1975-79. NSF sr. postdoctoral research fellow, 1965-66; Guggenheim fellow, 1972-73; recipient Wegener medal European Union of Geosci, 1991, Disting. Alumni award Calif. Inst. Tech., 1999. Mem. Am. Geophys. Union (Charles A. Whitten Medal, 1995), Geol. Soc. Am. (Day medal 1982), Seismol. Soc. Am., Nat. Acad. Scis., Am. Acad. Arts and Scis. Clubs: Ithaca Country. Home: 703 Cayuga Heights Rd Ithaca NY 14850-1463 Office: Cornell U Snee Hall Ithaca NY 14853 E-mail: turcotte@geology.cornell.edu.

TURCOTTE, MARGARET JANE, retired nurse; b. Stow, Ohio, May 17, 1927; d. Edward Carlton and Florence Margaret (Hanson) McCauley; m. Rene George Joseph, Nov. 24, 1961 (div. June 1967); 1 child, Michael Lawrence. RN, Ohio. Nurse St. Thomas Hosp., 1949-50; pvt. duty nurse, 1950-57; polio nurse Akron Children's Hosp., 1953-54; mem. nursing staff Robinson Meml. Hosp., Ravenna, Ohio, 1958-67, head ctrl. svc., 1963-67; supr. ctrl. svc. Brentwood Hosp., Warrensville Heights, 1967-93, infections control nurse, 1982-91; emergency med. technician. Mem. aux. Robinson Meml. Hosp.; vol. Portage County Vis. Nurse Svc. and Hospice; active RSVP. Mem. St. Thomas Hosp. Alumni Assn. Democrat. Mem. Christian Ch. (Disciples Of Christ). Home: 714 Woodgate Blvd Apt 201 Ravenna OH 44266-2548

TURCU, ION CRISTIAN EDMOND, physicist; b. Bucharest, Romania, Oct. 15, 1951; arrived in Eng., 1984, naturalized, 1993; s. Ionel and Maria (Crivat) T.; m. Monica Luminita Ivan, Apr. 17, 1976; 1 child, Jacqueline Sandra Maria. BSc, London U., 1974, PhD, 1997. Tchr. physics C.A. Rossetti Lyceum, Bucharest, 1974-79; asst. prof. physics Bucharest Tech. U., 1979-84; sr. rsch. assoc. Rutherford Appleton Lab., Oxfordshire, Eng., 1985-88, higher sci. officer Oxford, England, 1988-93, sr. sci. officer, and mgr. of the laser-plasma X-Ray source facility England, 1993-98; dir. Ed Tex Ltd., England, 1994—; chief scientist JMAR Rsch., Inc., San Diego, 1998—. Vis. lectr. King's Coll., U. London, 1992-95; vis. scientist plasma rsch. Inst. Atomic Physics, Bucharest, 1974-84; founding chmn. Harwell Bicycle User Group, Eng., 1995-98. Author: Energia, Incotro?, 1978, X-Rays from Laser-Plasmas: Generation and Applications, 1998; contbr. more than 80 articles to profl. jours. Mem. Wantage (Eng.) Town Coun., 1995-98. Recipient rsch. award EUREKA, 1988, U.S. Advanced Rsch. Project Agy., 1994; Brit. Coun. and Romanian Govt. scholar, 1971-74. Mem. IEEE, Inst. Physics London, Soc. Photo-Optical Instrumentation Engring., Optical Soc. Am., Royal Coll. Sci. Assn., Royal Instn., Brit. Assn. for the Advancement Sci. Achievements include patents and inventions in field; research and development of first high average power plasma source of x-ray radiation at 1 nm wavelength; many world firsts in new field of applications of 1 nm x-rays. Avocations: history, politics, travel, swimming, basketball. Office: JMAR Rsch Inc 3956 Sorrento Valley Blvd San Diego CA 92121-1427 E-mail: eturcu@jmar.com., mturcu@pacbell.net.

TURECEK, FRANTISEK, chemistry educator; b. Prague, Czechoslovakia, Apr. 14, 1950; came to U.S., 1988; s. Frantisek and Marketa (Bilkova) T.; m. Olga Turecek, Dec. 19, 1975; children: Jan, Vaclav, Josef. RNDr, Charles U., 1973, PhD, 1977. Rsch. fellow Heyrovsky Inst., Prague, 1977-83, sr. rsch. fellow, 1983-87; lectr. Cornell U., Ithaca, N.Y., 1988-89; assoc. prof. U. Wash., Seattle, 1990-95, prof., 1995—. Cons. 21st Century Rsch. Corp., Poulsbo, Wash., 1996-99, Zymogenetics, Seatle, 1997-98. Author: Synthesis of Natural Products, 1986, Interpretation of Mass Spectra, 1993; editor: Applications of Mass Spectrometry to Organic Spectrochemistry, 1994; editor Jour. of Mass Spectrometry, 1992—. Recipient 1981 Prize Czech Lit. Fund, 1981; hon. plaque Czech Acad. of Scis., 1983; named to Hall of Fame of Czech Chemists Czech Chem. Soc., 1997. Mem. Am. Chem. Soc., Am. Soc. for Mass Spectrometry. Office: U Wash Bagley Hall PO Box 351700 Seattle WA 98195-1700

TUREK, CHARLES SAUL, bookkeeper; b. N.Y.C., Feb. 16, 1936; s. Benjamin and Minnie (Pearl) T. BA in Philosophy, CCNY, 1965. Clk., bookkeeper Fairway, N.Y.C., from 1995. Author: Some Actual Solutions in the Humanities, 1993, revised and expanded, 1998. Avocations: reading, TV, movies. Home: New York, NY. Died June 29, 2001.

TUREK, DOUGLAS D. lawyer; b. Woodville, Tex., June 6, 1970; s. David E. and Linda M. Turek. BA in History, U. Tex., 1991; JD, U. Houston, 1994. Bar: Tex., 1995, U.S. Dist. Ct. (so. dist.) Tex., 1996, U.S. Ct. Appeals (5th cir.), 1996, U.S. Dist. Ct. (we. dist.) Tex. 2000. Assoc. atty. Glickman & Hughes LLP, Houston, 1995—2001; founding mem. The Turek Law Firm PLLC, 2001—. Mem. editl. adv. bd. Tex. Employment law, 1998; contbr. articles to profl. jours./seminars. Dir. Neartown Youth Baseball League, Houston, 1996-97, coach, 1997-98. Mem. ABA, State Bar Tex., Coll. of State Bar of Tex., Houston Bar Assn. (dir. law practice mgmt. 1998—), Houston Young Lawyer's Assn., Phi Delta Phi. Avocations: golf, hunting, fishing, backpacking, camping. Office: The Turek Law Firm PLLC 25231 Grogan's Mill Rd Ste 110 The Woodlands TX 77380 E-mail: dturek@tureklawfirm.com.

TUREK, PAUL JACOB, urological surgeon; b. Manchester, Conn., July 8, 1960; s. Jacob and Shirley Arlene T. BS, Yale Coll., 1982; MD, Stanford U., 1987. Intern U. Pa. Hosp., Phila., 1987-88, resident, 1988-89, resident, instr., 1989-93; instr. dept. urology Baylor Coll. Medicine, Houston, 1993-94; asst. prof. dept. urology U. Calif., San Francisco, 1994-95, asst. prof. in residence dept. urology, 1995-99; acting chief divsn. urology VA Med. Ctr., 1999—; clin. asst. prof. dept. urology Stanford U., 1996—. Lectr. in field. Contbr. articles to profl. jours. Fellow Baylor Coll. Medicine, 1993-94. Fellow Am. Coll. Surgeons; mem. Am. Urological Assn., Am. Assn. Clin. Urologists, Am. Soc. Andrology (membership com. 1996—), Am. Soc. Reproductive Medicine (abstract com. 1996-98, urology rep. 1997—), Calif. Urological Soc., No. Calif. Urologic Soc., Soc. Study of Male Reproduction (mem.-at-large 1997-98, chmn. adult com. 1997-98), Soc. Male Reproduction & Urology (bd. dirs. 1996, nominating com. 1997—), Pacific Coast Fertility Soc., Golden Gate Fly Fishing Club, Assn. Yale Alumni. Avocations: fly fishing, old cars, surfing. Office: U Calif Dept Urology 2330 Post St Fl 6 San Francisco CA 94115-3465 E-mail: mrvas@itsa.ucsf.edu.

TUREK, PAUL JOHN, III, construction executive; b. Columbia, S.C., Feb. 10, 1964; s. Paul John Jr. and Patricia Veronica (Saluta) T.; m. Emma Lactao, Dec. 24, 1995; children: Samantha Claire, Paul John, Isabella. BS in Civil Engring., Northwestern U., 1986. Registered civil engr., Calif. Constrn. mgr. Brown & Root Inc., Houston, 1990-94; sr. project mgr. Shorenstein Co., San Francisco, 1994-98; v.p. Thompson Brooks, Inc., 1998-2000; mng. ptnr. Summa III, Inc., 2000—. Active Walnut Creek Masters Swim Team. 1st lt. USMC, 1986-90. Mem. NSPE. Republican. Roman Catholic. Avocations: biking, theater. Home: 2121 Carrol Rd Walnut Creek CA 94596-5714 Office: Summa III Inc 235 Montgomery St #716 San Francisco CA 94104 E-mail: turekp@msn.com.

TUREK, ROMAN, hockey player; b. Pisek, Czech Republic, May 21, 1970; Profl. hockey player Dallas Stars, 1996—99, St. Louis Blues, 1999—2001, Calgary Flames, 2001—. Played in NHL All-Star game, 2000. Recipient William M. Jennings Trophy, 1998—99, 1999—2000. Office: Calgary Flames Canadien Airlines Saddledome PO Box 1540 Station M Calgary AB Canada T2P 3B9*

TUREKIAN, KARL KAREKIN, geochemistry educator; b. N.Y.C., Oct. 25, 1927; s. Vaughan Thomas and Victoria (Guleserian) T.; m. Arax Roxanne Hagopian, Apr. 22, 1962; children: Karla Ann, Vaughan Charles. AB, Wheaton (Ill.) Coll., 1949; MA, Columbia U., 1951, PhD, 1955; DSc (hon.), SUNY, Stony Brook, 1989. Lectr. geology Columbia U., 1953-54, rsch. assoc. Lamont-Doherty Earth Obs., 1954-56; faculty, asst. prof. Yale U., 1956-61, assoc. prof., 1961-65, prof. geology and geophysics, 1965-72, Henry Barnard Davis prof. geology and geophysics, 1972-85, Benjamin Silliman prof., 1985—, chmn. dept., 1982-88, curator meteorites, archaeology coun., dir. Ctr. for the Study of Global Change; chmn. studies in the environment, 1992-93; dir. Yale Inst. for Biospheric Studies, 1999—. Cons. Pres.'s Commn. Marine Sci. Engring. and Resources, 1967-68; oceanography panel NSF, 1968-70; NASA exobiology panel Am. Inst. Biol. Scientists, 1966-69; mem. NAS-NRC climate rsch. bd., 1977-80, ocean sci. bd., 1979-82, ocean studies bd., 1989-92, 98-2000, bd. on global change, 1992-95, Commn. Phys. Scis., Math. Resources, 1986-90, Commn. Geoscis., Environment, Resources, 1990-92, Com. Global Change Rsch., 1994-98; mem. com. on techs. for cleanup of subsurface contamination DOE Weapons Complex, 1997-98; mem. group experts sci. aspects Marine Pollution UN, 1971-73. Author: Oceans, 1968, 2d edit., 1976, Chemistry of the Earth, 1972, (with B.J. Skinner) Man and the Ocean, 1973, (with C.K. Drake, J. Imbrie and J.A. Knauss) Oceanography, 1978, Global Environmental Change, 1996; editor: Jour. Geophys. Resource, 1969-75, Earth and Planetary Sci. Letters, 1975-89, Global Biogeochemical Cycles, 1990-95, Geochim. Cosmochim. Acta, 1997-99. Served with USNR, 1945-46. Guggenheim fellow Cambridge U., 1962-63; Fairchild Disting. scholar Calif. Inst. Tech., 1988; recipient Wollaston medal, The Geol. Soc. London, 1998. Fellow AAAS, Geol. Soc. Am., Meteoritical Soc., Am. Geophys. Union (Maurice Ewing medal 1997), Am. Acad. Arts and Scis.; mem. NAS, Am. Chem. Soc., Geochem. Soc. (pres. 1975-76, V.M. Goldschmidt medal 1989), Sigma Xi (pres. Yale chpt. 1961-62). Home: 555 Skiff St North Haven CT 06473-3013 Office: Yale U Dept Geology and Geophysics PO Box 208109 New Haven CT 06520-8109 E-mail: karl.turekian@yale.edu.

TUREL, JOAN MARIE, religious program director; b. Kingston, Pa. d. John Alexander and Anna (Kornova) T. MusB, Marywood Coll., 1964; MA, NYU, 1970, Notre Dame U., 1994. Cert. in music edn., Pa., N.Y. Chairperson music dept. St. Patrick's H.S., Scranton, Pa., 1967-69; music cons. Immaculata, St. Alphonsus, St. Stephen's High Schs., N.Y.C., 1969-72; chairperson music dept. Bishop Hoban High Sch., Wilkes-Barre, Pa., 1971-76; choral dir. Kings Coll., 1978-86; dir. music St. Aloysius Parish, 1983—; dir. worship Roman Cath. Diocese Scranton, Pa., 1986—. Guest condr. Pa. Music Educators Assn., 1978, Nat. Shrine Immaculate Conception, Washington, 1982, Disneyworld, Orlando, Fla., 1983, 84. Editor: (jour.) The Assembly Celebrates, 1987—. State rep. Pa. Music Educators Assn., 1977; founder/condr. Annual Children's Charities Concerts, Wilkes-Barre, 1981-86; mem. Pastoral Formation Inst. Bd., 1988—; mem. Permanent Diaconate Bd., 1992—; mem. Homelitics Bd.; condr. 650 voice Millennium Choir. Recipient Senatorial commendation Pa. Legis., 1973. Mem.: Pastoral Formation Inst. (bd. dirs.), N.Am. Forum (chair two nat insts. 1989, 1991), Fedn. Diocesan Liturgical Com. (nat. bd. dirs. 1991—, chair Eucharist and liturgical yr. com. 2001—, chair nat. task force on sem. liturgical edn., nat. task force on Sunday Celebrations in the Absence of a Priest 2002—), Nat. Assn. Pastoral Musicians (program dir. 1986—, chair nat. conv. 1987, dir. music divsn. 1988—, chair ministry com. 1996—2001). Roman Catholic. Avocations: composing, painting, computers. Office: Diocese of Scranton 300 Wyoming Ave Scranton PA 18503-1243 E-mail: JoanTurel@aol.com.

TURELI, UFUK M. engineering educator; b. Istanbul, Turkey, June 2, 1972; parent Alptan and Gulhan Tureli; m. Didem Tureli. PhD , U. Va., 2000. Rsch. engr. U. Wash., Seattle; asst. prof. Stevens Inst. Tech., Hoboken, NJ, 1997—. Author: (thesis) Multicarrier Communications: Enabling Algorithms, 2000. Office: Stevens Inst Tech Castlepoint on Hudson Hoboken NJ 07030 Home Fax: 201-216-8246; Office Fax: 201-216-8246. Business E-Mail: tureli@ieee.org.

TUREN, BARBARA ELLEN, lawyer; b. Newark, Nov. 4, 1951; d. Samuel and Elaine (Goldfarb) T.; m. Leonard Paul Caplan, May 22, 1982 (div. June 1987); 1 child, Andrew. BA with distinction, George Washington U., Washington, 1973; MA with honors, London U., 1974; JD magna cum laude, Seton Hall U., 1990. Bar: N.J. 1990, U.S. Dist. Ct. N.J. 1990, U.S. Ct. Appeals (3d cir.) 1991, U.S. Supreme Ct. 1995. Fundraiser Am. Pl. Theatre, N.Y.C., 1978-79; lit. scout Warner Theatre Prodns., 1979-80; lit. cons. Theatre Now, Inc., 1980-82; lit. and talent agt. Don Buchwald & Assocs., 1982-85; assoc. Hannoch Weisman, Roseland, N.J., 1990-92, Vogel, Chait, Schwartz and Collins, Morristown, 1992-93; dep. atty. gen. Divsn. Law and Pub. Safety, State of N.J., Newark, 1994—. Adj. prof. law Seton Hall U. Sch. Law, Newark, 1994—. Pre-sch. vol. Head Start, Washington, 1970-73; lit. vol. N.Y.C. Sch. System, 1978-85. Recipient Cert. of Membership Seton Hall Constl. Law Jour., Newark, 1989-90. Mem. ABA, N.J. Bar Assn. Jewish. Avocations: travel, theatre, reading, collecting rare books.

TURER, GARY EVAN, ophthalmologist; b. Bronx, N.Y., June 28, 1959; s. Gerald Alan and Allene (Vogel) T.; m. Nancy Rosman, July 5, 1982; children: Jason Aaron, Carly Melissa, David Ethan. BS, Union Coll., 1981; MD, NY Med. Coll., 1985. Diplomate Am. Bd. Ophthalmology. Pvt. practice medicine, White Plains, N.Y., 1989—. Mem. Am. Acad. Ophthalmology, N.Y. State Med. Soc., Westchester County Med. Soc. Avocations: tennis, piano, swimming, traveling, running. Office: 303 North St White Plains NY 10605-2237

TURETSKY, AARON, lawyer; b. Bklyn., Mar. 23, 1951; s. Victor and Edith (Levine) T.; m. Edna M. Real, July 21, 1990; children: Persephone Fatima, Aaron Jr. BA summa cum laude, Hunter Coll., N.Y.C., 1979; JD magna cum laude, N.Y. Law Sch., 1986. Bar: N.Y. 1986, U.S. Dist. Ct. N.J. 1986, N.Y. 1987, U.S. Dist. Ct. (so. and ea. dist.) N.Y. 1987, U.S. Dist. Ct. (no. dist.) N.Y. 1988. Appellate law rsch. asst. appellate div. 2d dept. Supreme Ct. State of N.Y., 1986-87; atty. North Country Legal Svcs., Inc., Plattsburgh, N.Y., 1987-89; assoc. Holcombe & Bruno, 1989-90; pvt. practice, Keeseville, N.Y., 1990—. Law guardian Essex County Family Ct., 1990—; impartial hearing officer for children with disabilites, 1996—. Chmn. Essex County, N.Y. Conservative Com., 1990—; N.Y. St. Conservative Party N.E. regional vice. chmn., 1992—; eucharistic min. Cath. Community, Keeseville, N.Y. Mem. N.Y. State Bar Assn., Clinton County Bar Assn., Essex County Bar Assn., Elks, KC, Phi Beta Kappa. Roman Catholic. Office: PO Box 367 Keeseville NY 12944-0367

TURETSKY, JUDITH, librarian, researcher; b. Bklyn., Jan. 19, 1944; d. Samuel and Ruth (Moskowitz) Turetsky. BS, Boston U., 1965; MS, Long Island U., 1969. Tchr. Trumbull (Conn.) Bd. Edn., 1965-66; libr. Darien (Conn.) Bd. Edn., 1968-69, Albert Einstein Coll., Bronx, 1969-74; researcher Koskoff, Koskoff & Bieder, Bridgeport, Conn., 1977-86. Author:(book and micro film), The History and Development of the D. Samuel Gottesman Library of Albert Einstein College of Medicine. Mem.: AMIT (life), Med. Libr. Assn., Yeshiva U. Women's Orgn. (life), Hadassah U. Women's Orgn. (life). Democrat. Avocations: reading, classical music, crocheting, doll collecting. Home and Office: 62 Gate Ridge Rd Fairfield CT 06825-

TURGEON, PAUL R. computer engineer; b. Lewiston, Maine, June 18, 1957; s. Roger Marcel and Jeannine Turgeon; m. Louise Turgeon, May 3, 1986. BSEE, Rensselaer Poly. Inst., 1979; M, George Washington U., 1996. Project mgmt. profl. Design engr. IBM, Kingston, N.Y., 1979-87, engring. mgr., mainframe developer, 1987-90, Poughkeepsie, N.Y., 1990-93, sr. engring. mgr., CMOS server developer, 1993-99, sr. engring. mgr., S390 connectivity and I/O design engr., 1999-2001, mgr. e-server I/O hardware devel., 2001—. Contbr. articles to profl. jours.; patentee in field. Mem. Project Mgmt. Inst. (founder Mid-Hudson Valley chpt. 1996—). Avocations: hiking, camping, bass fishing, high end audio, record collecting. Home: 52 Laura Ln Woodstock NY 12498 Office: IBM 2455 South Rd Poughkeepsie NY 12601 E-mail: turgeon@us.ibm.com.

TURGEON, PIERRE, professional hockey player; b. Rouyn, Quebec, Aug. 29, 1969; With N.Y. Islanders, 1992-95, Montreal Canadiens NHL, 1995-97, St. Louis Blues NHL, 1997—2001, Dallas Stars , 2001—. Played in NHL All-Star Game, 1990, 93, 94. Recipient Michel Bergeron Trophy, 1985-86, Michael Bossy Trophy, 1986-87, Lady Byng Meml. Trophy, 1992-93. Mailing: c/o Dallas Stars Reunion Arena 777 Sports St. Dallas TX 75207*

TURI, LOUIS, publishing executive; b. Pont Saint Esprit, French Riviera, France (incl. Monaco), Feb. 26, 1950; s. Marie Angela Di-Rollo, Joseph DiCaprio Turi; life ptnr. Brigitte Marie Turi, Jan. 7, 1986. CEP - FPA, College de Pont St Esprit, Pont Saint Esprit, 1956—73. Cert. FPA -ASME section 9 welding 1973. Recording artist Phillips -Phonogram, Paris, 1975—83; pres. Startheme Pubs. LTD, Phoenix, 1991—. Cons. Servant Corp., Cin., 1994—98; lectr. in field. Author: Astropsychologist -Futuristic Stock Market, 2002. Recipient Distinction Cup Musicianship, Royal Sch. of Music, 1976, Writer's Digest award for 3 books, 2001. Mem.: Am. Assn. of Astrologers (Phoenix 1998—2002, AFA Conv. Fla. 1998). Republican. Christian. Avocation: travel. Home and Office: Startheme Pub LTD 4644 22nd St #2029 Phoenix AZ 85016 Home Fax: 602-957-1678; Office Fax: 602-957-1678. E-mail: dr.turi@cox.net.

TURILLO, MICHAEL JOSEPH, JR. management consultant; b. Hartford, Conn., Aug. 22, 1947; s. Michael Joseph and Alice (Vargas) T.; m. Deborah Sherburne; children: Stephanie, Christopher. BS, Providence Coll., 1969; MBA, Syracuse U., 1972; MS, U. Mass., 1973. Cons. Peat, Marwick, Mitchell & Co. (now KPMG LLP), Boston, 1974-77, mgr., 1977-82, ptnr., 1982—, nat. cons. practice dir. for fin. svc. cos., 1985-91. Chmn. Internat. . Mgmt. Cons. Practice Com. on Banking and Fin., 1986—98; nat. ptnr.-in-charge Fin. Svcs.-Specialized Cons., 1990—93, Capital Strategies, 1995—97; nat. lead ptnr. in charge Global Capital Group, 1993—94; nat. ptnr. in charge fin. svcs. Knowledge Mgmt., 1997—98, global chief officer, 1998—2001; with IBM Practice Exec. Collaborative Commerce, 2001—. Com. mem. United Way, Boston, 1981-83; trustee Elliot Montessori, South Natick, Mass., 1984-85; dir. Greater Boston coun. Boy Scouts Am., 1988—; adv. bd. Lesley Coll. Capt. U.S. Army, 1969-71, Vietnam. Decorated Bronze Star Mem. Bank Mktg. Assn., Assn. Planning Execs., Assn. Corp. Planners, Beta Gamma Sigma. Roman Catholic. Avocations: tennis, photography, travel, golf. Home: 47 South St Natick MA 01760-5526 Office: IBM Global Svcs 404 Wyman St Waltham MA 02454 E-mail: mturillo@us.ibm.com.

TURINO, GERARD MICHAEL, physician, medical scientist, educator; b. N.Y.C., May 16, 1924; s. Michael and Lucy (Arciero) T.; m. Dorothy Estes, Aug. 25, 1951; children: Peter, Phillip, James. AB, Princeton U., 1945; MD, Columbia U., 1948. Diplomate: Am. Bd. Internal Medicine. Intern Columbia U., Bellevue Hosp., 1948-49, asst. resident in medicine, 1949-50; resident in medicine New Haven Hosp., 1950-51; chief resident in medicine Columbia U. div. Bellevue Hosp., 1953-54; sr. fellow N.Y. Heart Assn., 1956-60; career investigator Health Research Council City of N.Y., 1961-71; asst. prof. medicine Columbia U., 1960-67, assoc. prof., 1967-72, prof. medicine, 1973-83, John H. Keating prof. medicine, 1983—; mem. staff Presbyn. Hosp., N.Y.C., 1960—, attending physician, 1983—; dir. med. svcs. St. Lukes-Roosevelt Hosp., N.Y.C., 1983-92; dir. St. Lukes-Roosevelt Hosp. James P. Mara Ctr, 1997. Cons. on sci. affairs Am. Thoracic Soc., 1992—; mem. sci. adv. com. Nat. Heart, Lung, and Blood Inst., Am. Lung Assn., Am. Heart Assn., N.Y. Lung Assn., N.Y. Heart Assn.; mem. staff divsn. med. sci. Nat. Rsch. Coun., Washington; cons. VA Hosp., East Orange, N.J., 1962-67; cons. in medicine Englewood (N.J.) Hosp., Hackensack (N.J.) Hosp., pres.-elect Am. Bur. Med. Advancement in China, 1994, pres., 1994-2001, chmn., 2001-. Contbr. articles to med. jours. Mem. Bd. Edn., Alpine, N.J., 1960-67. Served to capt. USAF, 1951-53. Recipient Joseph Mather Smith prize Columbia U., 1965, Alumni medal, 1983; Silver medal Alumni Assn. Coll. Physicians and Surgeons Columbia U., 1979, gold medal, 1986. Fellow AAAS; mem. Assn. Am. Physicians, Am. Soc. Clin. Investigation, Harvey Soc., Am. Thoracic Soc. (pres. 1987-88), Am. Fedn. Clin. Rsch., Am. Physiol. Soc. (chmn. steering com. respiration sect.), Am. Heart Assn. (award of merit 1980, Disting. Achievement award 1989, bd. dirs.), Am. Bur. for Med. Advancement in China (pres. 1994—), N.Y. Heart Assn. (pres. 1981-83, dir.), N.Y. Lung Assn. (dir.), N.Y. Med.-Surg. Soc. (pres. 1995), N.Y. Clin. Soc., Princeton Club (N.Y.C.), Maidstone Club, Devon Yacht Club, Century Assn. Club. Home: 66 E 79th St New York NY 10021-0244 Office: St Lukes Roosevelt Hosp 1000 10th Ave New York NY 10019-1192 E-mail: GMT1@Columbia.edu.

TURINSKY, PAUL JOSEF, nuclear engineer, educator; b. Hoboken, N.J., Oct. 20, 1944; s. Paul J. and Wilma A. (Budig) T.; m. Karen Ann DeLuca, Aug. 29, 1966; children: Grant Dean, Beth Noelle. BS, U. R.I., 1966; MSE, U. Mich., 1967, PhD, 1970; MBA, U. Pitts., 1979. Asst. prof. Rensselaer Poly. Inst., Troy, N.Y., 1971-73; engr., mgr. nuclear design Westinghouse Elec. Corp., Pitts., 1973-78, mgr. core devel., 1978-80; head dept. nuclear engring. N.C. State U., Raleigh, 1980-88, 99—, prof., 1980—, dir. Electric Power Rsch. Ctr., 1989—; pres. Nuclear Fuel Mgmt. Assocs., 1994—. Bd. dirs. Quantum Rsch. Svcs.; cons. Electric Power Rsch. Inst., Palo Alto, Calif., 1980-98, Sci. Applications Internat. Corp., 1990-92, U.S. Dept. of Energy, 1993; tech. specialist Internat. Atomic Energy Agy., Vienna, Austria, 1982—; mem. nuclear safety rev. bd. Duke Power Co., Charlotte, N.C., 1986-2001; cons. Can. Nuc. Safety Commn., 2000-. Author: (with others) CRC Handbook of Nuclear Reactor Calculations, 1986; contbr. more than 100 articles to tech. jours. Recipient Outstanding Tchr. award, N.C. State U., 1985, Supercomputer award, IBM, 1991, Alcoa Disting. Rschr. award, 1993, E.O. Lawrence award in nuc. tech., U.S. Dept. Energy, 2002. Fellow Am. Nuc. Soc. (chmn. reactor physics divsn. 1987-88, chmn. math. and computer divsn. 1995-96, Mark Mills award 1971, bd. dirs. 1990-93); mem. AAAS (mem. math. com.), IEEE Computer Soc., Am. Soc. Engring. Educators (chmn. nuc. engring. divsn. 1984-85, Glenn Murphy award 1990), Edison Electric Inst. (Power Engring. Educator award 1992), Soc. Indsl. and Applied Math. Office: NC State U Dept Nuclear Engring PO Box 7909 Raleigh NC 27695-7909 E-mail: turinsky@eos.ncsu.edu.

TURK, AUSTIN THEODORE, sociology educator; b. Gainesville, Ga., May 28, 1934; s. Hollis Theodore and Ruth (Vandiver) T.; m. Janet Stuart Irving, Oct. 4, 1957 (div. 1977); children: Catherine, Jennifer; m. Ruth-Ellen Marie

Grimes, July 27, 1985. BA cum laude, U. Ga., 1956; MA, U. Ky., 1959; PhD, U. Wis., 1962. Acting instr. sociology U. Wis., Madison, 1961-62; from instr. to prof. sociology Ind. U., Bloomington, 1962-74; prof. U. Toronto, Can., 1974-88, U. Calif., Riverside, 1988—, chmn. dept. sociology, 1989-94; interim dir. Robert B. Presley Ctr. for Crime and Justice Studies, 1994-95. Author: Criminality and Legal Order, 1969, Political Criminality, 1982; gen. editor crime and justice series SUNY Press, Albany, 1990—; contbr. articles to jours. in field. Mem. Calif. Mus. Photography, 1988—, Citizens Univ. Com., 1990—. Recipient Paul Tappan award Western Soc. Criminology, 1989. Fellow Am. Soc. Criminology (pres. 1984-85); mem. Am. Sociol. Assn. (chair criminology sect. 1975-76), Law and Soc. Assn. (trustee 1982-85), Acad. Criminal Justice Scis. Democrat. Avocations: gardening, reading, swimming, tennis. Office: Dept Sociology U Calif Riverside Riverside CA 92521-0001 E-mail: austin.turk@ucr.edu.

TURK, JAMES CLINTON, federal judge; b. Roanoke, Va., May 3, 1923; s. James Alexander and Geneva (Richardson) T.; m. Barbara Duncan, Aug. 21, 1954; children— Ramona Leah, James Clinton, Robert Malcolm Duncan, Mary Elizabeth, David Michael. AB, Roanoke Coll., 1949; L.L.B., Washington and Lee U., 1952. Bar: Va. bar 1952. Assoc. Dalton & Poff, Radford, Va., 1952-53; ptnr. Dalton, Poff & Turk, 1953-72; U.S. senator from Va., 1959-72; judge U.S. Dist. Ct. (we. dist.) Va., Roanoke, 1972-73, chief judge, 1973—. Dir. 1st & Mchts. Nat. Bank of Radford Mem. Va. Senate, from 1959, minority leader.; Trustee Radford Community Hosp., 1959— . Served with AUS, 1943-46. Mem. Order of Coif, Phi Beta Kappa, Omicron Delta Kappa. Baptist (deacon). Home: 1002 Walker Dr Radford VA 24141-3018 Office: US Dist Ct 246 Franklin Rd SW # 220 Roanoke VA 24011-2214 Fax: (540) 857-5123.

TURK, JAMES CLINTON, JR. lawyer; b. Radford, Va., Oct. 27, 1956; s. James Clinton and Barbara (Duncan) T.; m. Allison Blanding, Oct. 16, 1993; children: Lindsey Leigh, Katherine Alexandra, Alana Rae. BA in Econs., Roanoke Coll., 1979; JD, Samford U., 1984. Bar: Va. 1984, U.S. Dist. Ct. (ea. and we. dists.) Va. 1984, U.S. Bankruptcy Ct. 1985, U.S. Ct. Appeals (4th cir.) 1985, U.S. Supreme Ct. 1988; cert. specialist in civil and criminal trial advocacy Nat. Bd. Trial Advocacy. Ptnr. Stone, Harrison & Turk, Radford, 1985—. Adj. prof. criminal justice dept. Radford U. Sec. Radford Rep. Com., 1984—; fundraising chmn. Am. Heart Assn., Radford, 1986—; bd. dirs. New River Valley Workshop, Inc., v.p., 1990-92, pres., 1992-93; bd. dirs. new River C.C. Ednl. Found.; apptd. chmn. and dir. Va. Student Assistance Authorities by Gov. George Allen, 1994—; escheator City of Radford and Pulaski County; rep. western dist. CJA Panel Attys., Va.; mem. 4th Cir. Jud. Conf. Mem. ATLA (sustaining, fellow Coll. of Advocacy), ABA, Am. Bd. Trial Advs., Am. Coll. Barristers, Va. Bar Assn. (civil litigation sect. coun. 1991—, criminal litigation sect. coun. 1994—), Nat. Assn. Criminal Def. Lawyers (life; death penalty com. and indigent def. com.), Va. Trial Lawyers Assn., Jaycees, Rotary. Republican. Roman Catholic. Avocations: weightlifting, skiing, travel, flying, scuba diving. Home: 460 Quailwood Dr Blacksburg VA 24060-6724 Office: Stone Harrison Turk PC PO Box 2968 Radford VA 24143-2968

TURK, JANIS CAROLYN, literature educator; b. Gary, Ind., Jan. 25, 1962; d. James Turk, Dorothy Carolyn (Beckner) Turk; m. H. A. Daniels II, Aug. 9, 1995; children: Carrie Reid Turk Daniels, H.A. James Daniels III. BA, Tex. Luth. Coll., 1984; MA, SW Tex. State U., 1993. Prof. English Colegio Americano Durango, Durango, Mexico, 1986—87; instr. English Austin C.C., Austin, Tex., 1989—94; dir. ESL program, inst. English Tex. Luth U., Seguin, 1994—. Prof. English Univ. Juarez del Estado de Durango, Durango, 1986—87; sponsor Pirate's Alley Faulkner Soc., New Orleans, 1994—; co-owner Seguin Theatres, Inc., Turk-Daniels Ltd. Author: Trouble I've Seen, 1993. Mem.: ACTFL, TESOL, NAFSA, Modern Lang. Assn., Zonta Internat., Sequin Shakespeare Club, Alpha Phi Omega. Democrat. Lutheran. Home: PO Box 608 102 E Live Oak St Seguin TX 78156-0608 Office: Tex Luth Univ 1000 W Court St Seguin TX 78155

TURK, JOHN COBB, architect, educator; b. Buffalo, Oct. 16, 1930; s. Roswell Lester and Alice Knoche (Cobb) T.; m. Joanna D. Paulat, June, 1959 (dec. Apr. 1966); m. Sandra Miriam Baruch, Mar. 18, 1967 (dec. June 1986); 1 stepchild, Christine Paulat; m. Mary Jean Raftery, June 25, 1988. BA in Fine Arts, Colgate U., 1952. Registered architect, S.C. Apprentice Frank Lloyd Wright's Taliesin Fellowship, Spring Green, Wis., also Scottsdale, Ariz., 1955-57; archtl. draftsman various architects, Buffalo, 1959-72; instr. archtl. engring. tech. Midlands Tech. Coll., Columbia, SC, 1972-77, head dept. archtl. engring. tech., 1977-79, head constrn. tech. dept., 1979-84; arch. Carlisle Assocs., 1984-87; arch., dir. engring. and housing Ft. Jackson, 1987-88; arch., head design and estimating dept. U. S.C. Facilities Mgmt. Office, 1988-2000, arch., 2001—02. Dir. Lake Murray Assn., 2001-02. With C.E., U.S. Army, 1953-55. Mem. AIA, Constrn. Specifications Inst. (bd. dirs. Columbia chpt. 1996-98, v.p. 1998-99, pres.-elect 1999-2000, pres. 2000-01, bd. dirs. 2002, dir. 2001-, constrn. documents technician), Mensa (v.p. Columbia chpt. 1978, sec. 1998-2001, 02--), Intertel. Republican. Unitarian Universalist. Avocation: boating. Home: 112 Schooner Ln Columbia SC 29212-8032 Office: U SC Office of Facilities Mgmt 743 Greene St Columbia SC 29201-3615 E-mail: jct@fmc.sc.edu.

TURK, RICHARD ERRINGTON, retired psychiatrist; b. Staten Island, N.Y., Oct. 6, 1925; s. Richard Jason and Marian (Errington) T.; m. Dec. 30, 1948 (widowed Dec. 23, 1978); children: Stephanie, Jeffrey, Alan. BS, Dartmouth Coll., 1945; MD, Johns Hopkins Med. Sch., 1948. Diplomate Am. Bd. Psychiatry. Intern Highland-Alameda County Hosp., Oakland, Calif., 1948-49; resident Herrick Meml. Hosp., Berkeley, 1949-50; fellow psychiatry Harvard Med. Sch., Boston, 1950-51, 53-54; clin. instr. UCLA Med. Sch., 1954-70; pvt. practice psychiatry Berkeley, 1954-85. Pvt. practice, Walnut Creek, Calif., 1972-88; staff Herrick Meml. Hosp., 1954-85, Walnut Creek Hosp., 1972-88, John Muir Meml. Hosp., Walnut Creek, 1980-88. Capt. USAF Res., 1951—53, Korea. Mem. AMA, Am. Psychiat. Assn., No. Calif. Psychiat. Assn., Calif. Med. Assn., Alameda-Contra Costa County Med. Assn. Avocations: travel, bicycling, boating, car camping.

TURK, ROBERT LOUIS, radiologist; b. Lima, Ohio, Oct. 30, 1940; s. Herman Matthew and Daphne Carol (Stout) T.; m. Penelope Bryant, Mar. 25, 1964 (dec.); children: Marjorie Carol Turk Desmond, Susan Elizabeth Turk Charles. BA, Stanford U., 1962; MD, UCLA, 1966. Diplomate Am. Bd. Radiology, Am. Bd. Nuclear Medicine. Rotating intern U. Iowa, Iowa City, 1966-67; resident in radiology Harbor Gen.-UCLA Hosp., Torrance, Calif., 1967-70; radiologist, chief staff, vice chief, head radiology El Cajon (Calif.) Valley Hosp., 1972-83; pvt. practice, El Cajon, 1983—. Elder Presbyn. Ch., 1966—. Maj. M.C., USAR, 1970-72, Vietnam. Mem.: San Diego Radiol. Soc. (pres. 1990—91, past treas., rep.), Radiol. Soc. N.Am. Democrat. Avocations: tennis, sailing. Home: 1760 Key Ln El Cajon CA 92021-1507 Office: El Cajon X-Ray Imaging 1663 Greenfield Dr El Cajon CA 92021-3599

TURK, THOMAS LIEBIG, cultural organization administrator; b. Indpls., July 4, 1936; s. Laurel Herbert and Esther Lucille (Liebig) T.; m. Judith Ann Prochnow, July 26, 1969; children: Martisha Emily, Benjamin Edward. AB, DePauw U., 1958; MA, Mich. State U., 1960; cert., Harvard U., 1973. Promotion and publicity dir. Sta. WMSB-TV Mich. State U., East Lansing, 1961, asst. editor news bur., 1962-63, fine arts assoc. producer Sta. WKAR-TV, 1963-68, fine arts producer Sta. WKAR-TV, 1969-81; acting dir. publicity DePauw U., Greencastle, Ind., 1961-62; exec. dir. Cultural Activities Ctr., Temple, Tex., 1981-91; mng. dir. Texarkana (Tex.) Regional Arts & Humanities Coun., 1991-93; exec. dir. Met. Nashville (Tenn.) Arts Commn., 1993—. Pres. Met. Lansing (Mich.) Fine Arts Coun., 1975-77, Mich. Assn. Comm. Arts Agys., East Lansing, 1979-81; Gov. apptd. mem. Mich. Coun. for Arts, 1979-81; chmn. Mich. Arts Forum, 1980-81; pres. U.S. Urban Arts Fedn., 1999-2000. Producer, co-producer: 400 programs for local, nat. and internat. distbn. on pub. TV, 1963-81. With USAF, 1960. Mem. Nat. Assembly Local Arts Agys. (bd. dirs. 1979-85), Tennesseans for the Arts (bd. dirs. 2000--), Sigma Chi. Lodges: Rotary. Episcopalian. Home: 105 Harpeth Trace Ct Nashville TN 37221-3105 Office: Nashville Arts Commn 209 10th Ave S Ste 416 Nashville TN 37203-0772 E-mail: tom_turk@metro.nashville.org.

TURKEL, BRUCE, advertising executive; Prin., creative dir. Turkel Advt., Coconut Grove, Fla., 1983-95, Turkel Advt. (merged with Schwartz & Kaplan Advt.), Coconut Grove, 1995; exec. creative dir. Turkel, Schwartz & Ptnrs., 1995—. Office: Turkel Schwartz & Ptnrs 2871 Oak Ave Coconut Grove FL 33133-5207*

TURKEL, STANLEY, hotel consultant, management executive; b. N.Y.C., Sept. 2, 1925; s. Nathan and Mollie (Kurtzman) Turkeltaub; m. Barbara Bell, June 12, 1955 (div. Apr. 1971); children: Marc Alexander, Allison Lee; m. Rima Sokoloff, Apr. 26, 1971; stepchildren: Joshua Bernard Forrest, Benay Debra Forrest. BS, NYU, 1947; MBA, St. Johns U., Jamaica, N.Y., 1980. Laundry cons. Victor Kramer Co. Inc., N.Y.C., 1952-59; v.p., space planner Michael Saphier Assocs., 1959-62; with spl. hotel svcs. Loews Hotel Corp., 1962-63; res. mgr. Americana Hotel, 1963-64; gen. mgr. Drake Hotel, 1964-66; mng. dir. Summit Hotel, 1966-67; product line mgr. hotels ITT, 1968—75; pres. Stanley Turkel Co., Hotel Cons., 1976—. Mem. faculty NYU Ctr. Hospitality, Tourism and Travel Adminstrn. Contbr. articles to N.Y. Times, Wall St. Jour., N.Y. NEwsday, Washington Post, Crain's N.Y. Bus., N.Y. Observer, Smithsonian Mag., N.Y. Mag., N.Y. Post, N.Y. Daily News, Hotel and Motel Mgmt., Cornell Quar., Lodging Hospitality, Lodging Mag., The Bottomline, FIU Hospitality Rev., Nat. Real Estate Investor. Mem. ACLU. With USAAF, 1943-45. Mem.: Civic Affairs Forum (chmn. 1987—93), Internat. Soc. Hospitality Cons. (IHS cert.), Am. Hotel and Lodging Assn. (MHS cert.), City Club NY (trustee 1964—97, pres. 1966—68, chmn. 1977—88, chmn. exec. com. 1988—91). Avocations: Reconstruction period of Am. history, civic affairs, autograph collecting, tennis. Office: 770 Lexington Ave Fl 6 New York NY 10021-8165 E-mail: stanturkel@aol.com. *As a lifelong civic activist, I have learned to cherish the first amendment which provides protection for unpopular speech. We should not carve out exceptions to the first amendment because we are disgusted by vile language or racist epithets.*

TURKO, ALEXANDER ANTHONY, biology educator, hypnotherapist; b. Bridgeport, Conn., Aug. 19, 1943; s. Alexander I. and Elizabeth K. (Kulcsar) T.; m. Nancy Bally Hoinacky, Dec. 30, 1967; children: Michelle Lynn, Mark A. BA, So. Conn. State U., 1965, MS, 1967, postgrad., 1976. Cert. hypnotherapist, cert. master hypnotherapist. Assoc. prof. So. Conn. State U., New Haven, 1965—. Mem. AAUP. Home: 634 Popes Island Rd Milford CT 06460-1742

TURKOVÁ, HELGA, library director; b. Prague, Czech, Apr. 20, 1942; d. Johann Turek and Anna (Kusbachová) Turková. Grad., Charles U., Prague, Czech, 1964, PhD, 1969. Diploma in librarianship. Libr. Czechoslovak Acad. of Scis., Prague, Czech, 1964-65, Prague Info. Svc., Prague, Czech, 1965-67; ind. spez. libr. Dept. of Hist. Castles Libr. Nat. Mus. Libr., Czech, 1967-90, dir. Czech. 1990—. Co-author: (book) Rilke and Kraus and Vrchotovy J., 1985, (catalogue) Catlog incuabula in Castles Libraries, 1992, 2001; editor: Sborník Národního muzea-rada C-literární historie, 1990—. Mem coun Friends Old Prague, 1963—, Soc R M Rilke, 1992—. Mem.: Literary Sci Soc Sci Acad Czech Republic, Spolecnost Národního muzea, Asn Librarians. Roman Catholic. Avocations: history of Prague, history, art. Office: Knihovna Národni muzeum Václavské náměstí 68 115 79 Prague 1 Czech Republic E-mail: helga.turkova@nm.cz.

TURKS, HILDEGARD MARIA (HILDEGARD MARIA CHRONIS), retired security investigator, writer; b. Bruckander Mur, Austria, Nov. 10, 1949; arrived in U.S., 1962; d. Karl Franz Ignaz Popetschnigg and Margarete Galfuss; m. Ray Turks Jr., Apr. 16, 1970 (div. Apr. 20, 1971); 1 child Joana Margarete Lee ; m. James Chronis, Dec. 6, 1975 (dec. Aug. 6, 1994). Various civilian duties USAF, Baumholder and Zweibrucken, Germany, 1964—71; restaurant mgr. Jackson Heights, NY, 1976—84; bartender N.Y.C., 1976—84; undercover investigator, security pers., 1978—85. Author: Little Snapple, 1992. Recipient Golden Globe, World of Poetry, 1989, Editor's Choice award, Internat. Libr. Poetry, 2001. Avocations: art, writing, walking, travel, helping others.

TURKUS-WORKMAN, CAROL ANN, educator; b. Balt., Nov. 12, 1946; d. Stanley Phillip and Catherine Anna (Koppleman) Turkus; m. William Thomas Workman, Apr. 23, 1973 (div. 1983); children: Devin Thomas, Timothy Michael. BA in History, Calif. State U., Long Beach, 1969; spl. cert. classroom mgmt., Centralia Sch. Dist., 1980; M in Adminstrn. Mgmt., U. La Verne, 1997. Cert. crosscultural lang. and acad. devel.; cert. adminstrv. credential. Educator Centralia Sch. Dist., Buena Park, Calif., 1970—, ednl. tech., 1986—. Cons. U. Sch.-Space Sci. Acad., Cleve., 1991. Unit commr. Boy Scouts Am., Orange County Coun., 1989-96; co. systems officer Starfleet Bulletin Bd. System, Long Beach, 1990-94; life mem. PTA, Buena Park. Recipient Gold Leaf, PTA Nat., 1991, Woodbadge Beads, Boy Scouts Am., 1991. Mem. AAUW, Computer Using Educators, Order of Arrow, Kappa Delta Pi. Republican. Roman Catholic. Avocations: sailing, camping, reading, writing. Office: Centralia Sch Dist 6215 San Rolando Way Buena Park CA 90620-3635 Address: 11762 Argyle Dr Los Alamitos CA 90720-4226 E-mail: homego@earthlink.net.

TURLEY, MARIANNE C, statistician; d. Emmet E and Hazel B Turley; m. Brian L Moore, Sept. 3, 2000; children: Elliot Moore. BS, U. Mass., Amherst, 1989; MS, U. Wash., Seattle, 1997, PhD, 1997—2001. Analyst Syscon, New London, Conn., 1990—91; bellringer organizer Salvation Army, Northampton, Mass., 1991—92; analyst Bur. Environ. Svcs., Portland, Oreg., 1992—93; tchg. asst. Ctr. for Quantitative Sciences, U. Wash., Seattle, 1995—97; rsch. asst. Nat. Ctr. for Stats. and the Environ.U. Wash., 1997—2001; math. statistician Bur. Land Mgmt., Portland, 2002—. Mem.: The Internat. Biometric Soc., Am. Statis. Assn. Roman Catholic. Avocations: drawing, hiking, music, photography, sailing. Office: Burf Land Mgmt 333 SW First Ave Portland OR 97208 E-mail: mturley@fs.fed.us.

TURLEY, MICHAEL ROY, lawyer; b. St. Louis, Mar. 7, 1945; s. W. Richard and Mary Jeanne (Ogle) T.; m. Patricia Ederle, Aug. 21, 1968; children: James, Alisyn. AB, Princeton U., 1967; JD, Mo. U., 1970. Bar: Mo. 1970, U.S. Dist. Ct. (ea. dist.) Mo. 1975. Assoc. Lewis, Rice & Fingersh (formerly Lewis & Rice), St. Louis, 1970-71, 74-80, ptnr., 1980—. Mem. Jefferson County Planning and Zoning Commn., 1987—2000; bd. dirs., sec.-treas. Ctr. for Emerging Techs. Mem. ABA, Mo. Bar Assn., St. Louis Met. Bar Assn., Princeton Club. Episcopalian. Office: Lewis Rice & Fingersh 500 N Broadway Ste 2000 Saint Louis MO 63102-2147 E-mail: mturley@lewisrice.com.

TURLEY, ROBERT JOE, lawyer; b. Mt. Sterling, Ky., Dec. 6, 1926; s. R. Joe and Mavis Clare (Sternberg) T.; m. Mary Lynn Sanders, Dec. 17, 1948 (dv.); children: Leighton Turley Isaacs, Lynn Turley McComas, R. Joe, Mavis Lee Turley Scully. Student, Berea Coll., 1944-45, St. Mary's Coll., Calif., 1945-46; LLB, U. Ky., 1949. Bar: Ky. 1949, U.S. Dist. Ct. (ea. dist.) Ky. 1950, U.S. Supreme Ct. 1959. Ptnr. Mooney & Turley and successor firms, Lexington, Ky., 1949-84, Turley & Moore, Lexington, 1984-89, of counsel, 1989-93. Chmn. Fed. Jud. Selection Commn. Ky., 1985-89; gen counsel Shriners Hosps. for Children, 1976-77, trustee, 1981-90, emeritus trustee, 1990—. Author: The Choices Are Yours, 1997, The Bridge of Faith, 2000; contbr. articles to legal jours. With USNR, 1944-46. Diplomate Nat. Bd. Trial Advocacy, 1980. Fellow Am. Coll. Trial Lawyers, Ky. Bar Found. (life); mem. Ky. Bar Assn. (sr. counselor, Outstanding Lawyer award 2001), St. Ives Jour. Club, Champions Trace Golf Club. Masons, Shriners. Home: 111 Woodland Ave Lexington KY 40502-6415

TURLEY, STEWART, retired retail company executive; b. Mt. Sterling, Ky., July 20, 1934; s. R. Joe and Mavis S. Turley; children from previous marriage: Carol Cohen, Karen Shockley; m. Linda A. Mulholland; stepchildren: Kathleen Smiley, Kristine Johnson. Student, Rollins Coll., 1952-53, U. Ky., 1953-55. Plant mgr. Crown Cork & Seal Co., Orlando (Fla.), Phila., 1955-66; mgr. non-drug ops., dir. corporate employee rels. and spl. svcs. Eckerd Corp. (formerly Jack Eckerd Corp.), Clearwater, Fla., 1966-68; v.p. Eckerd Corp., 1968-71, sr. v.p., 1971-74, dir., 1971-97, pres., chief exec. officer, 1974-96, chmn. bd., 1975-97. Bd. dirs. Sprint Corp., Marine Max, Inc., WCI Cmtys., Inc. Past chmn. U.S. Ski Team Found.; trustee emeritus Eckerd Coll., St. Petersburg; bd. dirs. Vilar Ctr. Found., Vail Valley Found. Mem. Nat. Assn. Chain Drug Stores (bd. dirs., chmn. bd. 1978-79, 88-89), Fla. Coun. 100 (past chmn.), World Pres.'s Orgn., Chief Execs. Orgn., Carlouel Yacht Club, Belleair Country Club, Eagle Springs Golf Club, Kappa Alpha. Office: 1465 S Fort Harrison Ave Clearwater FL 33756-2505

TURLIK, IWONA, communication executive; b. Poznan, Poland, May 18, 1951; d. Mieczyslaw and Anna (Rymaszewska) Lemanczyk; m. Marian Turlik, Aug. 25, 1973; 1 child, Daniel. MSEE, Tech. U. Wroclaw, 1973, PhD, 1977. Faculty Tech. U. Wroclaw, Poland, 1977-81; from tech. staff to program mgr. Bell No. Rsch., Research Triangle Park, N.C., 1981-89; prof. U. N.C., Charlotte, 1990-94; v.p., dir. Motorola Advanced Technology Ctr., Tech. Acquisition Office, Schaumburg, Ill., 1994—. Author: Multichip Module Handbook, 1997, Multichip Module Technology Handbook, 1997. Fellow IEEE. Office: Motorola Advanced Technology Ctr 1301 E Algonquin Rd Schaumburg IL 60196-1078

TURLINGTON, BARBARA, educational association administrator; b. Washington, Dec. 8, 1931; d. Edgar and Catherine (Hackett) T. BA, Am. U. Beirut, 1955; postgrad., Columbia U., 1960. Instr. govt. Conn. Coll., New London, Conn.; instr. polit. sci. Mt. Holyoke Coll., South Hadley, Mass., 1963-68; asst., then assoc. dean Hampshire Coll., Amherst, 1969-76; dean, 1976-78; exec. asst. to pres. Assn. Am. Univs., Washington; dir. internat. edn. Am. Coun. Edn., 1984—. Bd. dirs. Alliance Internat. Ednl. and clutural Exch., Washington, 1986—, CAPE: A Cmty. Agile Ptnrs. in Edn., Bethlehem, Pa.; mem. Nat. Coun. Evaln. Fgn. Ednl. Credentials. Co-author: Internationalizing the Curriculum: A Handbook for Campus Leaders, 1992, Spreading the Word II: Promising developments for Undergraduate Forigh Language Instruction, 1996; ; co-author, editor: Spreading the Word: Improving the Way We Teach Foreign Languages, 1994; co-editor: Next Steps for Languages Across the Curriculum: Prospects, Problems, Promis, 1998. Recipient James W. Dodge Meml. Fgn. Lang. Advocate award, N.E. Conf. on the Tchg. of Fgn. Langs., 2002. Democrat. Avocations: travel, gardening. Office: Am Coun Edn One Dupont Cir NW Washington DC 20036-1193 Fax: (202) 785-8056. E-mail: barbara_turlington@ace.nche.edu.

TURLO, GEORGE JERZY, architect, city planner, artist; b. Wilno, Poland, Mar. 13, 1934; came to U.S., 1966; s. Michael and Olga Turlo; m. Stephanie W. Turlo, 1957 (div. 1980); children: Peter A., Ralph C.; m. Christine B. Turlo, Feb. 14, 1981. M.Engring. and Arch., Gdansk (Poland) Poly. Inst., 1958; postgrad., Brown U., 1967, Providence Coll., 1967-69. Sr. city planner Dept. Arch. and Bldg. Inspection, Koszalin, Poland, 1958-60; architect Miastoprojekt Kosalin, 1960-61; dir. dept. City of Kotobrzeg, Poland, 1961-62; planning dir. City of Stupsk, Poland, 1962-66; supr. current planning Dept. Planning City of Providence, 1966-2000. One-man show Turlo Art Gallery, Providence, 1997-2000; exhibited in group shows R.I. Watercolor Soc., Providence Art Club, Wickford Art Assn.; represented in permanent collection Providence Biltmore Hotel, Providence Washington Ins., Mayor's Office, Providence City Hall, Coastal Credit Union, also numerous pvt. collections. Recipient Providence Art Club award, 1998. Mem. R.I. Watercolor Soc., Wickford Art Assn. Avocations: fine art, writing, skiing, bicycling, swimming. Home: 8718 28th Ave E Palmetto FL 34221 E-mail: turlo@msn.com.

TURMAN, MARTIN ALLAN, pediatric nephrologist, educator; b. Akron, Ohio, Aug. 27, 1957; m. Pamela Marie Turman; children: Elizabeth, Alexandra. BA, U. Colo., 1979; MD, PhD, U. Colo., Denver, 1985. Diplomate Am. Bd. Pediatrics. Intern U. Colo. Health Scis. Ctr., Denver, 1985—88; fellow in pediatric nephrology U. Minn., Mpls., 1988-91; assoc. prof. pediat. Ohio State U., Columbus, 1991-2001, Okla. U. Health Scis. Ctr., Oklahoma City, 2001—02, prof. pediat., 2002—. Office: Okla Univ Health Scis Ctr Rm 2B2309 940 NE 13th St Oklahoma City OK 73104

TURMEL, JEAN BERNARD, banker; b. Lac Etchemin, Que., Can., Dec. 17, 1944; s. Joseph N. and Rose Marie (Chabot) T.; m. Lorraine Louise Langevin, June 4, 1966; children— Andree, Elaine, Johanne. B.Commerce, Laval U., Quebec, Can., 1966, M.C.S., 1967. Salesman Macmillan Bloedel, Montreal and Vancouver, Can., 1967-68; money market trader Dominion Securities, Montreal, Que., 1968-78, Merrill Lynch Can., Montreal and Toronto, Can., 1978-81; v.p. treasury Nat. Bank Can., Montreal, 1981-83, sr. v.p. treasury and exchange, 1983-86, exec. v.p. treasury, 1986-89, sr. exec. v.p., 1989—, pres. fin. mkts., treasury and investment bank, 1998—. Chmn. bd. Inst. Fin. Mathématique de Montréal, Natcan Investment Mgmt., Inc.; outside advisor investment com. Assn. Bienfaisance et Retraite de communauté urbaine de Montreal, Nat. Bank Can., Maple Ptnrs.; bd. dirs., chmn. exec. com. Nat. Bank Fin.; mem. Bus. Coun. on Nat. Issues; outside advisor investment.com Found. Lucie and Andre Chagnon & Sogroci. Liberal. Roman Catholic. Avocations: music, golf, fishing. Office: Nat Bank Can 1155 Metcalfe Montreal QC Canada H3B 5G2

TURNAGE, FRED DOUGLAS, lawyer; b. Ayden, N.C., Sept. 24, 1920; s. Fred C. and Lou (Johnson) T.; m. Margaret Futrell, Aug. 21, 1943 (div. Nov. 1980); children: Betty Lou Griffith, Douglas C.; m. Elizabeth Louisa Turnage, Jan. 23, 1981. Grad. Naval Sch. on Far Eastern Civil Affairs, Princeton U., 1945; LLB, Wake Forest U., 1948, LLD, 1970. Bar: N.C. 1948, U.S. Supreme Ct. 1953, U.S. Dist. Ct. D.C. 1965, U.S. Ct. Appeals (D.C. cir.) 1967, U.S. Ct. Appeals (4th and 7th cirs.) 1979. Trial atty. antitrust div. U.S. Dept. Justice, Kansas City, Mo., 1948-51, sr. trial atty. antitrust div. Washington, 1951-65, spl. asst. to atty. gen., 1965; sr. ptnr. Cleary, Gottlieb, Steen & Hamilton, 1968—, counsel, 1990—. Lectr. continuing legal edn. courses, 1973-77. Contbr. articles to profl. jours. Bd. Visitors Wake Forest U. Sch. Law, Winston-Salem, N.C., 1980—. Served to 1st lt. AUS, 1942-46. Recipient Disting. Service in Law citation Wake Forest U., 1979. Mem. ABA (antitrust and litigation sects.), Fed. Bar Assn., Adv. Bd. Antitrust Bulletin, Wake Forest U. Alumni Assn. (pres. 1977), Nat. Lawyers Clubs. Methodist. Avocations: fishing, golf, writing. Home: 02 Fifth Ave Kitty Hawk NC 27949 Office: 2000 Pennsylvania Ave NW Washington DC 20006-1812

TURNAGE, JEAN ALLEN, retired state supreme court chief justice; b. St. Ignatius, Mont., Mar. 10, 1926; JD, Mont. State U., 1951; D Laws and Letters (non.), U. Mont., 1995. Bar: Mont. 1951, U.S. Supreme Ct. 1963. Formerly ptnr. Turnage, McNeil & Mercer, Polson, Mont.; formerly Mont. State senator from 13th Dist.; pres. Mont. State Senate, 1981—85; chief justice Supreme Ct. Mont., 1985-2001. Mem. Mont. State Bar Assn., Nat. Conf. Chief Justices (past pres.), Nat. Ctr. State Courts (past chair). Office: Turnage O'Neill & Mercer PO Box 460 Polson MT 59860

TURNBAUGH, DOUGLAS BLAIR, arts administration executive, author; b. Lewiston, Idaho, May 17, 1934; s. Orville Wendelle and Geneva Violet (Blair) T. BA, U. Wash., 1956. Exec. dir. Fine Arts Workshop, Inc., 1963-73, Brandon Films, Inc., 1966, Dance Notation Bur., Inc., 1967, Dance Theatre Found., Inc., for Alvin Ailey Dance Theatre, 1970; pres. Am. Inst. Choreology, Inc., N.Y.C., 1970—; exec. dir., treas. Ludwig Vogelstein Found., Inc., 1973-83; pres. Direct From Broadway, 1983-86; exec. dir. Poetry Soc. Am., Inc., Manhattan Festival Ballet, 1984; former dir. Inst. Choreology, London, Four Winds Theatre of Cooper Hewitt Mus. of Smithsonian Instn., Dance Theatre Workshop, Inc., Alt. Center for Internat. Arts, Inc., Alternative Mus.; exec. dir. Musica Reservata, Inc., 1979-81. Del. to the U.S.A., mem. conseiller UNESCO's Coun. Internat. de la Danse, 1994—; former dir. Actors Enclave, N.Y.C., 1982; past faculty mem. NYU, N.Y.C.; guest lectr. York U., Toronto; former chmn. bd. Vertices, Inc./D.J. McDonald & Dancers. Author: The Use of Notation in the Dance Theatre, 1970, Notating Asian Dance, 1975, Beat It, 1983, Duncan Grant and the Bloomsbury Group, 1987, Private: The Erotic Art of Duncan Grant (1885-1978), 1989, Le Rôle D'Otto Kahn Dans la Libération de Nijinsky et sa Tournée a Travers les États-Unis, 1992, Strip Show: The Paintings of Patrick Angus, 1992, Grand Pas de Trois: Diaghilev-Kochno-Lifar, 1999; curator: The Private World of Duncan Grant (exhibit held The Nat. Arts Club 1987), Duncan Grant, Paintings and Drawings: 1922-60 (exhibit held 303 Gallery, N.Y.C., 1989); curator exhbns. Ralph Parks Gallery, N.Y.C., 1992, Leslie-Lohman Gallery, N.Y.C., 1992; contbr. articles to various publs. including N.Y. Mag., Atlantic, Playbill, Asia Mag., Poetry Soc. Am. Bull., Appearances mag., Performing Arts Jour., others. Chmn. CID/UNESCO's Ballets Russes Celebration, New Orleans, 2000; ex. dir. Seasoned Citizens Theatre Co., 2000-01. Recipient Vaslav Nijinsky medal, Poland, 1994, Sergei Diaghilev medal Diaghilev House Found., Perm, Russia, 1994; Nat. Endowment for the Arts grantee, 1968. Mem. Assn. Internat. des Amis de Waslaw Nijinsky, Nat. Arts Club (sec. dance com., chmn. Hommage a Nijinsky, 1993). Address: The Rockefeller Apartments 4-A 24 W 55th St New York NY 10019-5320

TURNBAUGH, ROY CARROLL, archivist; b. Peoria, Ill., Oct. 16, 1945; s. Roy Carroll and Zora (Alexander) T.; m. Donna Marie Chase, Mar. 28, 1970; children: Andrew, Peter. BA, Aurora Coll., 1969; AM, U. Ill., 1973, PhD, 1977. Asst. prof. U. Ill., Urbana, 1977-78; archivist Ill. State Archives, Springfield, 1978-85; dir. Oreg. State Archives, Salem, 1985—. Mem. Nat. Hist. Publs. and Records Commn., 2000—. Mem. Nat. Assn. Govt. Archives

Records Adminstrs. (pres. 1998-2000), Soc. Am. Archivists (C.F.W. Coker prize 1984, Fellows Posner prize 1999). Office: Oreg State Archives 800 Summer St NE Salem OR 97310-1347 E-mail: roy.c.turnbaugh@state.or.us.

TURNBAUGH, WILLIAM ARTHUR, archaeologist, educator; b. Williamsport, Pa., June 1, 1948; s. William Hugh and Louise Elizabeth (Muller) Turnbaugh; m. Sarah Ropes Peabody, Oct. 12, 1974. BA in History summa cum laude, Lycoming Coll., 1970; PhD in Anthropology, Harvard U., 1973. Accredited mem. Register Profl. Archaeologists. Curator of archaeology Lycoming County Mus., Williamsport, Pa., 1968-70; tching. fellow, dept. anthropology Harvard U., Cambridge, Mass., 1971-72, asst. to dir. Peabody Mus., 1973-74; asst. prof. anthropology U. R.I., Kingston, 1974-78, assoc. prof. anthropology, 1978-83, prof. anthropology, 1983—. Ind. contracting archaeologist ea. U.S. and Can., 1968—74; dir. U. R.I. Mus., 1975—77; adv. bd. Inst. Conservation Archaeology, Cambridge, 1976—83. Assoc. editor: Historical Archaeology, 1986—; author: (book) Man, Land and Time, 1975, Material Culture of RI-1000, 1984; co-author: Indian Baskets, 1986, R.F.D. Country!, 1988, Indian Jewelry of the American Southwest, 1988, Indian Jewelry of the American Southwest, rev. edit., 1996, Understanding Physical Anthropology & Archaeology, 8th edit., 2002, Basket Tales of the Grandmothers, 1999; contbr. articles and revs. to profl. jours., chapters to books. V.p., acting pres. Lycoming County Hist. Soc., Williamsport, 1968—70; designed offical flag Lycoming County, Pa., 1970. Recipient Archie award, Soc. Pa. Archaeology, 1967, Disting. Alumni citation, Lycoming Coll., 1987, J. Alden Mason award, Soc. Pa. Archaeology, 1988; fellow NSF, 1970—73, Woodrow Wilson Found., 1970—71. Fellow: Explorers Club; mem.: Soc. Hist. Archaeology, Soc. Am. Archaeology, Sigma Xi, Phi Alpha Theta, Phi Kappa Phi. Unitarian Universalist. Avocations: travel, geology, American history. Office: Univ RI Dept Sociol and Anthropol Kingston RI 02881 E-mail: wtu4496u@postoffice.uri.edu.

TURNBULL, ADAM MICHAEL GORDON, financial executive, consultant; b. Dumfries, Scotland, Dec. 29, 1935; emigrated to Canada, 1977; s. Robert Wilson and Catherine Russell (Strang) T.; m. Karen Margaret Walker, June 12, 1965; children: Candida Louise, Andrew Robert. MA, Edinburgh U., 1956, LL.B., 1958. Chartered acct., Scotland, 1960. With Price Waterhouse, Paris, 1960-62, U.S. Time Corp., France and U.S., 1962-64; group chief acct. Formica Internat. Ltd., London, 1965-70; group fin. dir. Donald Macpherson Group Ltd., 1970-77; controller, asst. treas. Indal Ltd., Weston, Ont., Can., 1978-81; controller Indal Inc., 1978-81; v.p., treas. Indal Ltd., Ont., Can., 1981-90; v.p. fin., CFO, Hawker Siddeley Can. Inc., Mississauga, Can., 1990-94, sr. v.p. fin., CFO Can., 1994-99; fin. cons., 1999—. Mem. Inst. Chartered Accts. Scotland Office: 2610 Hammond Rd Mississauga ON Canada L5K 2M3

TURNBULL, ANN PATTERSON, special educator, consultant, research director; b. Tuscaloosa, Ala., Oct. 19, 1947; d. H. F. and Mary (Boone) Patterson; m. H. Rutherford Turnbull III, Mar. 23, 1974; children: Jay, Amy, Kate. BS in Edn., U. Ga., 1968; MEd, Auburn U., 1971; EdD, U. Ala., 1972. Asst. prof. U. N.C., Chapel Hill, 1972-80; prof., co-dir. Beach Ctr. U. Kans., Lawrence, 1980—. Cons. Dept. Edn., Washington, 1987—, Australian Soc. for Study of Intellectual Disability, Adelaide and Washington, 1990. Author: Free Appropriate Public Education, 2000, Exceptional Lives: Special Education in Today's Schools, 2001, Families, Professionals and Exceptionality, 2001. Recipient Rose Kennedy Internat. Leadership award, Kennedy Found., 1990, 20th Century award in Mental Retardation, 1999; Joseph P. Kennedy Jr. Found. fellow, 1987-88. Mem.: Internat. League Socs. for Persons with Mental Handicaps (com. chair 1986—90), The Arc-U.S. (named Educator of Yr. 1982), Am. Assn. on Mental Retardation (bd. dirs. 1986—88, v.p. 2001, pres.-elect 2002). Democrat. Avocations: travel, exercise. Home: 1636 Alvamar Dr Lawrence KS 66047-1714 Office: Univ Kans Beach Ctr 3136 1200 Sunnyside Dr Lawrence KS 66045-7534 E-mail: aturnbull@ku.edu.

TURNBULL, CHARLES VINCENT, retired real estate broker; b. Mpls., May 13, 1933; s. Charles Vivien and Lucille Frances (Dallas) T.; m. Gloria Marlene Tilley, July 21, 1956; children— Charlene Kay, Charles Vincent II, Terry Lucille, Mary Marlene. BA, U. Minn., 1960, MSW., 1962. Unit dir. Mental Health Treatment Service, Cambridge (Minn.) State Hosp., 1962-67, dir. rehab. therapies, 1967-68, program dir., 1973-74, Minn. Valley Social Adaptation Center, St. Peter, Minn., 1968-73; chief exec. officer Faribault (Minn.) State Hosp., 1974-84; owner Turnbull's Shady Acres Resort, 1979-85; adminstr. Minn. Vets. Homes, Mpls. and Hastings, 1984-85; owner, broker Turnbull Realty, Faribault, Minn., 1986-96; realtor Turnbull Bedker Real Estate Co., 1997-98. Program cons. Rochester (Minn.) Social Adaptation Center, 1970-71; cons. St. Louis State Sch. and Hosp., 1973-74 Chmn. United Fund Drive, St. Peter, 1971; scoutmaster Twin Valley council Boy Scouts Am., 1973-75; co-chmn. Faribault Bi-Centennial Horizons Subcom., 1975-76; pres. River Bend Nature Center, 1981-84, bd. dirs. 1976-87; mem. Minn. Developmental Disabilities Planning Council, 1975-79, Chmn. comprehensive plan subcom., 1977-78; mem. Cannon River Adv. Council, 1978-79; Mayor, Village of Lexington, Minn., 1962-64; candidate for U.S. rep. 2d Dist. Minn., 1972, 74. Served with USMC, 1953-56. Mem. Democratic Farmer Labor party. Lutheran. Home: RR 3 Box 38 Saint Peter MN 56082-9514

TURNBULL, CHARLES W. governor; b. St. Thomas, V.I., Feb. 5, 1935; BS, Hampton U., 1958, MS, 1959; PhD, U. Minn., 1976. Elem., sec. sch. tchr., asst. prin. various pub. schs.; prin. Charlotte Amalie H.S.; asst. commr. to commr. Dept. Edn.; prof. history U. V.I.; gov. U.S. V.I., St. Thomas. Chair V.I. Bd. Edn.; bd. dirs. U. V.I., Roy Lester Schneider Hosp. Democrat. Methodist. Office: Office of the Governor Government House 21-22 Kongens Gade Saint Thomas VI 00802 E-mail: rcanton@govhouse.gov.vi.

TURNBULL, DAVID JOHN (CHIEF PIERCING EYES-PENN), cultural association executive; b. Hornell, N.Y., May 18, 1930; s. Gerald and Dorothy Esther (Badgley) T.; m. Martha Lillian Crouse, Aug. 12, 1949 (div. 1960); children: Garry David, Mary Jane Stuhr, Dorothy Grace Houde; m. Frances Early Spring Vickery, May 4, 1985; adopted children: Donna, Ashley, Jessica. Degree in ministry, Elim Bible Coll., 1964. Dir. pub. rels. Elim Bible Inst., Lima, N.Y., 1960-61; pastor Eagle Harbor (N.Y.) Ch., 1962-65, South Lima (N.Y.) Gospel Ch., 1962-66; ind. ins. agent, 1965-82; chief, counselor, performer weddings and funerals Pan-Am. Indian Assn., Nocatee, Fla., 1980—, pub. Pan.-Am. Indian Assn. News, 1984—. Mem. Ministerial Assn. Mem. Nocatee Ch. of God. Avocation: investigative reporter on children's issues. Home and Office: 2902 Airport Rd SE PO Box 244 Nocatee FL 34268-0244

TURNBULL, E. R. (NED TURNBULL), transportation executive; b. Lexington, Ky., Feb. 13, 1961; s. E.R. Turnbull and Nancy (McBryde) Unger; m. Leslee Allison King, July 22, 1988; children: Rand, King, Sid. BA, So. Meth. U., 1984; JD, U. Tulsa, 1990. Bar: Okla. 1990. Asst. dist. atty. major crimes divsn. Tulsa County Dist. Atty.'s Office, Tulsa, 1990-94; state dist. judge Dist. Ct. of State of Okla., 1995—98, chief judge criminal divsn., 1998; pres., LLC mgr. Go Transp., 1998—; CEO, Bull Market Restaurant Group, 2000—. Revised Okla. criminal felony murder statute and Tulsa County criinal ct. rules; mem. rules com. Okla. Ct. Criminal Appeals, 1996, mem. emergency appellate divsn., 1996. Bd. dirs. Youth Svcs. Tulsa, 1992-98, Tri-County Coun. for Aging, Tulsa, 1994-97. Named Outstanding Young Oklahoman, Okla. Jr. C. of C., 1996, gov.'s commendation and exec. dept. proclamation State of Okla., 1996. Mem. Okla. Bar Assn., Tulsa County Bar Assn., Rotary. Presbyterian. Avocations: exercise, reading, child rearing, coaching youth sports.

TURNBULL, H. RUTHERFORD, III, law educator, lawyer; b. N.Y.C., Sept. 22, 1937; s. Henry R. and Ruth (White) T.; m. Mary M. Slingluff, Apr. 4, 1964 (div. 1972); m. Ann Patterson, Mar. 23, 1974; children: Jay, Amy, Katherine. Grad., The Kent (Conn.) Sch., 1955; BA, Johns Hopkins U., 1959; LLB with hon., U. Md., 1964; LLM, Harvard U., 1969. Bar: Md., N.C. Law clerk to Hon. Emory H. Niles Supreme Bench Balt. City, 1959-60; law clerk to Hon. Roszel C. Thomsen U.S. Dist. Ct. Md., 1962-63; assoc. Piper & Marbury, Balt., 1964-67; prof. Inst. Govt. U. N.C., Chapel Hill, 1969-80, U. Kans., Lawrence, 1980—. Prof. spl. edn., courtesy prof. law U. Kans. Editor-in-chief Md. Law Review. Cons., author, lectr., co-dir. Beach Ctr. on Disability, U. Kans.; pres. Full Citizenship Inc., Lawrence, 1987-93; spl. staff-fellow U.S. Senate subcom. on disability policy, Washington, 1987-88; bd. dirs. Camphill Assn. N.Am., Inc., 1985-87; trustee Judge David L. Bazelon Ctr. Mental Health Law, 1993-2000, chmn., 1999—. With U.S. Army, 1960-65. Recipient Nat. Leadership award Nat. Assn. Pvt. Residential Resources, 1988, Nat. Leadership award Internat. Coun. for Exceptional Children, 1996, Nat. Leadership award Am. Assn. on Mental Retardation, 1997, Century award Nat. Trust for Hist. Preservation in Mental Retardation, 1999; named Nat. Educator of Yr., ARC, 1982; Public Policy fellow Joseph P. Kennedy, Jr. Found., 1987-88. Fellow Am. Assn. on Mental Retardation (pres. 1985-86, bd. dirs. 1980-86); mem. ABA (chmn. disability law commn. 1991-95), U.S.A. as sn. for Retarded Citizens (sec. and dir. 1981-83), Assn. for Persons with Severe Handicaps (treas. 1988, bd. dirs. 1987-90), Nat. Assn. Rehab. Rsch. and Tng. Ctrs. (chair govt. affairs com. 1990-93), Internat. Assn. Scientific Study of Mental Deficiency, Internat. League of Assns. for Persons with Mental Handicaps, Johns Hopkins U. Alumni Assn. (prs. N.C. chpt. 1977-79). Democrat. Episcopalian. Home: 1636 Alvamar Dr Lawrence KS 66047-1714 Office: U Kans 3111 Haworth Hall 1200 Sunnyside Ave Lawrence KS 66045-7534 E-mail: Rud@ku.edu.

TURNBULL, JOHN CAMERON, pharmacist, consultant; b. Regina, Sask., Can., Sept. 5, 1923; s. Cameron Joseph and Lillian Irene (Pentz) T.; m. Hazel Evelyn Rockwell, July 31, 1948; children— Lillian Elizabeth, John Rockwell, Jocelyn Hazel. BS in Pharmacy, U. Sask., 1949. Pharmacist with village and city pharmacies, 1945-50; supr. pharm. services Dept. Pub. Health, Province of Sask., Regina, 1950-52; ops. mgr. Nat. Drugs, Ltd., Winnipeg, and Saskatoon, 1953; exec. dir. Can. Pharm. Assn., Toronto, Ont., 1953-78. Sec.-treas., mng. dir. Canadian Pharm. Realty Co. Ltd.; mem. provisional bd. Pharmacare Ltd.; registrar-treas. Pharmacy Examining Bd. of Can., 1963-68, mem. bd., 1963-78; pharmacy cons., dir. drug service Ministry of Health, Barbados, 1979-84; staff assoc. Mgmt. Scis. for Health, Boston, 1984-85; cons. logistics and pharms. USAID, East Caribbean, PanAm. Health Orgn./WHO (Belize, Cen. Am.), 1985—. Chmn. Govt.'s Spl. Com. on Acetylsalicylic Poisonings, 1967; mem. Emergency Health Svcs. Adv. Com.; gen. chmn. Allied Air Forces Reunion, 1995, 96. Served to squadron leader RCAF, 1941-45. Decorated D.F.C., Order of Can., 1975; recipient Can. Centennial medal, 1967, Queen's Jubilee medal, 1977, Can. 125th Anniversary medal, 1992, John C. Turnbull rsch. ann. award in socio-econs. pharmacy established in his honor Can. Pharm. Assn., 1990. Mem. Fedn. Internationale Pharmaceutique (v.p.), Inst. of Assn. Execs. (hon. life), Conf. of Pharmacy Registrars of Can. (sec.), Commonwealth Pharm. Assn. (coun. 1969-78); hon. mem. Am., Canadian, Saskatchewan, B.C., Alta., Ont., Man., N.S. Pharm. Assns., Sask. Pharm. Assn., Ont. Pharmacists Assn., Canadian Soc. Hosp. Pharmacists, Rho Pi Phi. Mem. United Ch. of Canada. Club: Bayview Country (past dir.). Home: 40 Banstock Dr North York Toronto ON Canada M2K 2H6 E-mail: jc.turnbull@sympatico.ca.

TURNBULL, LAWRENCE F. retired anesthesiologist; b. Seattle, Jan. 6, 1921; MD, Northwestern U., 1946. Diplomate Am. Bd. Anesthesiology. Intern King County Hosp., Seattle, 1945-46, resident in anesthesiology, 1948-50; hon. staff Children's Hosp. and Med. Ctr. Fellow Am. Coll. Anesthesiologists; mem. AMA, Am. Bd. Anesthesiologists. Home: 10901 176th Cir NE # 2508 Redmond WA 98052-7248

TURNBULL, MARJORIE REITZ, foundation executive, former state legislator; b. Madison, Wis., July 4, 1940; d. J. Wayne anf Frances H. (Millikan) R.; m. Augustus Bacon Turnbull, Nov. 26, 1965 (dec. Nov. 1991). Student, Agnes Scott Coll., 1958-60; BA, U. Fla., 1962; MA, U. Ga., 1968. Legis. analyst Fla. Ho. of Reps., Tallahassee, 1973-85, staff dir. com. on health and rehab. svcs., 1975-78, exec. asst. to speaker, 1978-80; asst. dir. Devel. Svc. Program Office, 1980-82; dep. asst. sec. Health Planning State Fla., 1982-84; ind. cons. legis. mgmt. and planning, Tallahassee, 1984-95, state rep., 1994-2000; exec. dir. Tallahassee C.C. Found., 1995—. County commr. Leon County, Tallahassee, 1988-94; bd. dirs. Fla. Assn. Counties, Tallahassee, 1993-94, Tallahassee Symphony Orch., 1992—, Apalachee coun. Girl Scouts U.S., Tallahassee, 1988—. Recipient Outstanding Svc. in Govt. award Delta Kappa Omega, Tallahassee, 1996; named Woman of Yr., AAUW, Tallahassee, 1991, County Champion in the Legislature, Fla. Assn. Counties, 1995, Legislator of Yr., Fla. Assn. Sch. Supts., 1999; recipient Girl Scout Woman of Distinction award, 1999, Disting. Svc. award Fla. Student Assn., 2000, Disting. Citizens award Boy Scout Coun., 2000, Meritorious Achievement award Fla. A&M U., 2000, Legis. Advocacy award Fla. Coalition Against Domestic Violence, 2000, Freedom from Violence Leadership awrd, 2000, Model of Achievement award Tallahassee C.C., 2001. Mem. Rotary (program com. 1992—), Zonta Internat., Fla. Blue Key. Democrat. Presbyterian. Avocations: scuba diving, travel, cultural activities. Home: 3221 E Lakeshore Dr Tallahassee FL 32312-2062 Office: Tallahassee C C 444 Appleyard Dr Tallahassee FL 32304 E-mail: turnbulm@tcc.cc.fl.us.

TURNBULL, REGINALD HARRISON, lawyer; b. Springfield, Mo., Nov. 3, 1946; s. John Howard and Margaret Maurine Turnbull; m. Anita K. Propst, Dec. 18, 1972; children: Bryce C., Kyle D., Ryan H. BA, N.W. Mo. State U., 1972; JD, U. Mo., Kansas City, 1976. Bar: Mo. 1976, U.S. Dist. Ct. (we dist.) Mo. 1976. Law clk. Jackson County Cir. Ct., Kansas City, Mo., 1976-77; asst. atty. gen. Mo. Atty. Gen., Jefferson City, 1977-81; dep. dir. for human resources Mo. Dept. of Mental Health, 1981-91; assoc. atty. Waltz & Jordan, Mo., 1991-96; shareholder, atty. Riner Turnbull and Walker P.C., 1996-99, Turnbull Law Office, P.C., Jefferson City. Pres. Jefferson City Parks and Recreation Commn., 1984-90, Jefferson City Parents and Tchrs. Orgn., 1994-96; scoutmaster Troop 1, Jefferson City, 1991-94. Mem. Jefferson City Breakfast Rotary Club, Nat. Acad. of Elder Law Attys. (chmn. trusts spl. interest group, bd. dirs. Mo. chpt.), Mo. Bar Assn. (probate trust, elder law), Nat. Orgn. of Social Security Claimants Reps., Mo. End of Life Coalition. Home: 135 Forest Hill Ave Jefferson City MO 65109-0963 Office: Turnbull Law Office PC 200 E High St Jefferson City MO 65101-3207 Fax: 573-634-7418. E-mail: ribull@aol.com.

TURNBULL, ROBERT GEORGE, philosopher, educator; b. Scotland, S.D., July 1, 1918; s. John Vincent and Mary Fern (Hird) T.; m. Marguerite Hilton, Sept. 1, 1939; 1 child, Bruce Hilton. BA, U. Minn., 1939, PhD, 1952; BD, Oberlin (Ohio) Coll., 1943; DHL, Denison U., Granville, Ohio, 1990. Instr. U. Minn., Mpls., 1957-60; asst. prof. U. Iowa, Iowa City, 1950-54, chair dept. philosophy, 1953-64, assoc. to full prof., 1954-64; vis. prof. Oberlin Coll., 1964-65; prof. and chair dept. philosophy Ohio State U., Columbus, 1966-80, prof. emeritus, 1984—. Author: The Parmenides and Plato's Late Philosophy, 1998; co-author: Motion and Time, Space and Matter, 1976, Studies in Perception, 1978. Capt. U.S. Army, 1943. Ohio Philos. Assn. Disting. scholar, 1980. Mem. Am. Philos. Assn. (sec.-treas. Ctrl. divsn. 1966-69, pres. 1977-78, chair bd. officers 1989-92). Home: 1810-8 Riverside Dr Columbus OH 43212 Office: Ohio State Univ Dept Philosophy 230 N Oval Mall Columbus OH 43210 E-mail: turnbull.3@osu.edu.

TURNBULL, ROBERT SCOTT, manufacturing company executive; b. North Dumfries, Ont., Can., Dec. 19, 1929; s. Leslie William and Marjorie Clara (Scott) T.; m. Dawna Rose Sinclair, Feb. 17, 1956 Sr. Matriculation, Galt U., Ont., 1950; M.T.C., U. Western Ont., 1975. Cert. mgmt. acct. Credit mgr Can. Gen. Tower, Cambridge, Ont., 1951-53, gen. acct., 1953-62, comptroller, 1962-68, v.p. mktg., 1968-78, v.p., gen. mgr., 1978-96, pres., 1996-99, dir., sr. officer. Mem. Chem. Fabrics and Films Assn. (bd. dirs.), Soc. Plastics Industry (mem. Automotive Coun.), Japan Soc. (bd. dirs.), Soc. Mgmt. Accts. Home: 26 Lansdowne Rd S Cambridge ON Canada N1S 2T3

TURNBULL, VERNONA HARMSEN, retired residence counselor, education educator; b. Teeds Grove, Iowa, Dec. 6, 1916; d. Henry Ferdinand and Ida Amelia (Dohrmann) Harmsen; m. Alexander Turnbull, Oct. 12, 1961. *Father, Henry Harmsen, a nominee for Master Farmer, came to the U.S. from Germany in 1892. Later, he and brother, Leo, excelled as cattle feeders for the Chicago market. For many years they won numerous awards at the Annual Live Stock Exposition, including the Grand Championship in the carlot division in 1935. Husband, Alexander Turnbull, served for many years as Director of Safety for the Navy Department and later, for the Department of Defense, from which he retired in 1975. His work took him to many service installations throughout the world.* BA, Cornell Coll., Mt. Vernon, Iowa, 1939; MEd, U. Colo., Boulder, 1947, profl. cert. edn., 1955. Cert. secondary and h.s. tchr. Tchr. English, Latin and phys. edn. Winslow (Ill.) H.S., 1939-45; dir. women's activities, instr. Trinidad (Colo.) State Jr. Coll., 1947-53; counselor women, assoc. prof. edn. Western State Coll., Gunnison, Colo., 1953-54; instr., residence counselor Stephens Coll., Columbia, Mo., 1955-61; ret., 1961. Active Salvation Army Aux. Mem. AAUW, Am. Assn. Ret. Persons (corr. sec. 1986-87), Kena Kampers Camping Club. Avocations: photography, camping, art, dancing, baking.

TURNDORF, HERMAN, anesthesiologist, educator; b. Paterson, N.J., Dec. 22, 1930; s. Charles R. and Ruth (Blumberg) T.; m. Sietske Huisman, Nov. 24, 1957; children: David, Michael Pieter. AB, Oberlin Coll., 1952; MD, U. Pa., 1956. Diplomate Am. Bd. Anesthesiology. Instr. anesthesiology U. Pa. Hosp., 1957-59; asst. anesthetist med. sch. Harvard U., Mass. Gen. Hosp., Boston, 1961-63; assoc. attending anesthesiologist, asst. dir. dept. anesthesiology Mt. Sinai Hosp., N.Y.C., 1963-70, clin. prof. anesthesiology, 1966-70; prof., chmn. dept. anesthesiology W.Va. U. Sch. Medicine and Med. Ctr., Morgantown, 1970-74, NYU Sch. Medicine, 1974—2000; dir. anesthesiology NYU Tisch Hosp., Bellevue Hosp. Ctr., 1974—2000; pres. med. bd., med. dir. Bellevue Hosp. Med. Ctr., 1990—91, 1997; ret., 2000. Co-author: Anesthesia and Neurosurgery, 2nd edit., 1986, Trauma, Anesthesia and Intensive Care, 1990; contbr. over 200 articles to profl. jours. Lt. M.C., USNR, 1959-61. Fellow Am. Coll. Chest Physicians, Am. Coll. Anesthesiologists (mem. bd. govs. 1977-85, chmn. bd. govs. 1984), N.Y. Acad. Medicine; mem. AMA, Am. Soc. Anesthesiologists, Assn. Univ. Anesthetists, Internat. Soc. Study of Pain, Soc. Acad. Anesthesia Chairmen, Soc. Critical Care Medicine, Soc. Neurosurg. Anesthesia and Neurologic Supportive Care, N.Y. Acad. Scis., N.Y. State Soc. Anesthesiologists. Fax: (212) 263-7254.

TURNDORF, JAMIE, psychotherapist; b. Boston, July 12, 1958; d. Gary Owen and Sharon (Sandow) T.; m. Emile Jean Pin, Jan. 2, 1988. AB in Am. Culture, Vassar Coll., 1980; MSW, Adelphi U., 1983; PhD, Calif. Coast U., 1994. Lic. social worker, N.Y. Pvt. practice psychotherapy, N.Y.C. and Millbrook, NY, 1981—. Lead creative movement and psychodrama program Lincoln Farms Work Camp, Roscoe, N.Y., 1976; with Astor Child Guidance Clinic, Poughkeepsie, N.Y., 1982-83; leader various groups Craig House Hosp., Beacon, N.Y., 1982-87, developer, dir. eating disorders program, 1984-86; founder, dir. INC.TIMACY, 1990—, J.T. Developers, Inc., Poughkeepsie, 1983-91; dir. Hudson Valley br. Ctr. for Advancement Group Studies, Ctr. for Emotional Comm., Millbrook, 1990—. Author: Till Death Do Us Part (Unless I Kill You First): A Step-by-Step Guide for Resolving Marital Conflict, 2000, (with Emile Jean Pin) The Pleasure of Your Company: A Socio-Psychological Analysis of Modern Sociability, 1985; columnist Dr. Love various newspapers and World Wide Web (award); love and relationship advice on internet; host Ask Dr. Love, Sta. WEVD, N.Y.C., 1992; creator, inventor LoveQuest: The Game of Finding Mr. Right, 1990 (one of best new games award Fun and Games mag. 1991). Mem.: NASW. Avocations: house restoration, opera singing, antiques. Home and Office: PO Box 475 Millbrook NY 12545-0475 E-mail: drlove@askdrlove.com.

TURNER, ALBERTA, poet, educator emerita; b. N.Y.C., Oct. 22, 1919; d. Albert Tucker; widowed; children: Prue, Brent. BA, Hunter Coll., 1940; MA, Wellesley Coll., 1941; PhD, Ohio State U., 1946. Lectr. Oberlin (Ohio) Coll., 1946-69; from lectr. to prof. Cleve. State U., 1964-90, prof. emerita, 1990—; assoc. editor Field: Contemporary Poetry and Poetics, 1970—. Author (poetry): Need, 1971, Learning to Count, 1974, Lid and Spoon, 1977, A Belfrey of Knees, 1983, Beginning with And: New and Selected Poems, 1994, Tomorrow is a Tight Fist, 2001; editor (anthologies): 50 Contemporary Poets, 1977, Poets Teaching, 1981, 45 Contemporary Poems, 1988; author: To Make A Poem, 1982, Responses to Poetry, 1990; contbr. poems to numerous mags. Address: 482 Caskey Ct Oberlin OH 44074

TURNER, ALMON RICHARD, retired art historian, educator; b. New Bedford, Mass., July 28, 1932; s. Louis Alexander and Margaret (Mather) T.; m. Jane Beebe; children: Louis Hamilton, David Alexander. AB, Princeton U., 1955, MFA, 1958, PhD, 1959. Instr. in fine arts U. Mich., Ann Arbor, 1959-60; from instr. to prof. art and archaeology Princeton (N.J.) U., 1960-68; prof. fine arts Middlebury (Vt.) Coll., 1968-74, dean faculty, 1970-74; prof. fine arts, pres. Grinnell (Iowa) Coll., 1975-79; prof., dir. Inst. Fine Arts NYU, N.Y.C., 1979-82, dean faculty arts and scis., 1982-85, prof. dept. fine arts, 1985-2000, dir. N.Y. Inst. Humanities, 1986-93, Paulette Goddard prof. emeritus in arts and humanities, 1994-2000, prof. emeritus, 2000—. Author: Vision of Landscape in Renaissance Italy, 1966, 73, (With G. Andres and J. Hunisak) Art of Florence (L'Art de Florence), 1988 (prix 1989), Inventing Leonardo, 1993, Renaissance Florence: The Invention of a New Art, 1997, La Pietra: Florence, a Family, and a Villa, 2002 Mem. Coll. Art Assn., Century Assn., N.J. Aubudon Soc. (1st v.p. 1990-93, pres. 1993-96), Phi Beta Kappa. Democrat. Unitarian Universalist. Avocations: birding, photography. Home: PO Box 2322 Cape May NJ 08204-7322

TURNER, ANDREW L. healthcare management company executive; BA, Ohio State Univ. Adminstr skilled nursing facility, Springfield, Ohio, 1970-75; mgr. regional nursing home chain; sr. v.p. ops. Hillhaven Corp.; co-founder Horizon Healthcare Corp., 1986-89; founder, chmn.,CEO Sun Healthcare Group, Albuquerque, 1989—2000; chmn. Ballantrae Healthcare , 2000—; founder, chmn. Endura Care, 2000—, Code Blue Staffing Solutions, 2001—; mem. bd. of directors Sports Clubs/L.A., Watson Pharmaceuticals. Office: Ballantrae Healthcare 1128 Pennsylvania St. NE Albuquerque NM*

TURNER, ARTHUR EDWARD, college administrator; b. Hemlock, Mich., Jan. 31, 1931; s. Alvin S. and Grace E. (Champlain) T.; m. Johann M. Jordan, May 10, 1953; children: Steven Arthur, Michael Scott, Kathryn Jo. BS, Alma (Mich.) Coll., 1952; MEd, Wayne State U., 1954; postgrad., Cen. Mich. U., U. Mich.; LLD, Ashland Coll., 1968; HUD, Colegio Americano de Quito, Ecuador, 1968; LLD, Northwood U., Cedar Hill, Tex., 1984. Admissions counselor Alma Coll., 1952-53, dir. admissions, alumni relations, 1953-59; co-founder Northwood U., Midland, Mich., 1959, 1st pres., 1959-74, chmn. bd., chief exec. officer, trustee, 1974-78, chmn. bd. trustees, 1978-82. Founder, lay minister Presbyn. Ch., Alma, 1956-59; trustee Epilepsy Found., Palm Beach, Fla., 1982; bd. dirs. Margaret Chase Smith Libr., Skowhegan, Maine, 1978, Salvation Army, 1989, Alden B. Dow Creativity Ctr. Northwood U. Recipient People of Peru award, 1966, Horatio Alger award Horatio Alger Assn., 1981, Great Ams. award Internat. City of Care Fund, 1989, Internat. Freedom of Mobility award Nat. Automobile Dealers Assn., 1986, George P. Rutland Gold Medal of Honor, Palm Beach, 1999; named one of Outstanding Young Americans, U.S. Jaycees, 1965. Mem. Palm Beach Round Table (chmn. bd.), Midland Country Club, Beach Club, Gov.'s Club (Palm Beach), Masons (33 deg.), Shriners, Rotary, Alpha Psi Omega, Phi Phi Alpha. Home: 340 S Ocean Blvd Palm Beach FL 33480-4212 Office: Northwood U Office of Trustee West Palm Beach FL 33409

TURNER, B. RUSSELL, tax accountant, real estate broker; b. Fresno, Calif., Nov. 19, 1948; s. Frank Robert T. and Dorothy Elaine Smith; m. LoRayne A. Haye, Aug. 15, 1984 (div. Aug., 1987); 1 child, Tyler Cayden Turner-Haye (dec.); m. Linda Marie Vanderbeke, Sept. 9, 1990; 1 child, R. Vanderbeke Turner. AA, Fresno (Calif.) City Coll., 1971; BS in Psychology, Calif. State U., Fresno, 1973; postgrad., Heald Coll., 1982. Counseling cert. Santa Cruz Suicide Prevention Svc.; neurolinguistics profl. Robbins Rsch. Inst.; Enrolled Agent. Constrn. asst. Barry R. Turner Constrn., Corralitos, Calif., 1973-75; substitute tchr. Pajaro Unified Schs., Watsonville, 1975-77; counselor Suicide Prevention Svc., Santa Cruz, 1977-79; psychoanalyst HELP Youth Tng. Program, 1976-81; property mgr., exec. asst. Juno Fin. Group, San Diego, 1982-91; tax acct., real estate broker Turner Fin. Svcs., 1992—. Software analyst Intuit, Inc., San Diego, 1996-98. Mem. Nat. Assn. Enrolled Agents, Calif. Soc. Enrolled Agents, San Diego Soc. Enrolled Agents (dir. membership 1992), Inland Soc. Tax Accts. Democrat. Avocations: holds Rokkyu in Kenpo Kung Fu, scuba diving, vegetable gardening. Office: Turner Fin Svcs PO Box 86674 San Diego CA 92138-6674

TURNER, BARBARA A. former dance company executive; b. Louisville; BA, U. Ky.; MA, U. Louisville. Dir. devel. Ballet Internat., Indpls., now mng. dir. Office: Ballet Internat 502 N Capitol Ave Ste B Indianapolis IN 46204-1204*

TURNER, BARBARA PRESS, executive; b. Chgo., Mar. 24, 1943; d. John Elmer and Betty (Grace) Press; m. William Stephen Turner; m. June 26, 1965; children: Lisa Turner Laing, Christopher, Melissa, Sarah & Kelly (twins). BS, Cornell U., 1965; MA, U. Chgo., 1966. Rsch. asst., London, 1966-67; cons. Centro de Perfeccionamiento Pedagogico, Santiago, Chile, 1967-70; editor, edn. mag. U. Chgo., 1970-72; exec. v.p. Edu Systems, Walworth, Wis., 1970—. Pres. sch. bd. Big Foot H.S., Walworth, 1988-99; ch. bd., tchr., choir Fontana (Wis.) Cmty. Ch., 1978—; leader Girl Scouts U.S.A., Fontana, 1985. Avocations: choral singing, tennis, golf, swimming. Office: Edu Systems PO Box 1030 Walworth WI 53184-1030

TURNER, BERNICE COOPER, social worker; b. Chgo., Jan. 19, 1924; d. Jasper Lorenzo and Jessie (Jones) Cooper; m. Miles W. Turner, Jr., Aug. 4, 1957; 1 child, Miles W., IV. BA, BS, Wilberforce U., 1946; MSW, Loyola U., 1952. Cert. social worker, Ill. Functional supr. social svc. area Dept. Human Svcs., Chgo., 1979-81, citywide coord., 1980-86; project dir. child abuse Woodlawn Orgn., 1987-92; home health social worker Osteo. Hosp., 1992-96, Columbia-Michael Reese Hosp., Chgo., 1996-99; home health social worker, adv. bd. Alpha-Omega Home, 1997—. Adv. bd. Columbia Home Health, Chgo., 1996-99. Author: Blizzard, 1979. Bd. dirs. Wilberforce U., 1996-98, Woodlawn Maternal Child Health Ctr., Chgo., 1987-97; chair ednl. com. Coppin AME Ch. Coston Missionary Soc. Recipient Gov.'s award State Ill., 1984; named Outstanding Alumnus, Wilberforce U., 1999, Disting. Svc. award, 1999. Mem. NASW (reg., del. 1979-84, minority affairs com., chair affirmative action com. chgo. dist.), Acad. Cert. Social Worker (chair 1994—), Nat. Coun. Social Work Edn., Internat. Assn. Social Work (leader), Assn. Res. U.S. Pub. Health Officers, Ill. Welfare Assn. (sec. 1980-82), Ill. Caucus Teenage Pregnancy, Afro Am. Family Cmty. Svc. Assn. (founder, past bd. dirs., 1986), Delta Sigma Theta (co-chair summit II). African Methodist. Home and Office: 6232 S Saint Lawrence Ave Chicago IL 60637-3333

TURNER, BERNICE HILBURN, recording industry executive; b. Black Rock, Ark., Jan. 13, 1937; d. Floyd W. and Clementime (Higgins) Hilburn; m. Doyle Turner, Feb. 28, 1957 (div. Jan. 1980); children: Johnny, P.J., Danny, Jill, Robby. PhD in Applied Psychology, 1974. Musician Hank Williams Sr., Nashville and Montgomery, Ala., 1950-52, 1952-76; owner Onyx Recording Studio, Memphis, 1985—, Turner Limousine Svc., Memphis, 1988—. Named Pioneer in Country Music, United Music Heritage of Tenn., 1989. Mem. Unity Ch. Home: 1646 Bonnie Dr Memphis TN 38116-5732

TURNER, BILLIE LEE, II, geography educator; b. Texas City, Tex., Dec. 22, 1945; s. Billie Lee and Virginia Ruth (Mathis) T.; m. Linda Lee Van Zandt, June 6, 1968; children: Billie Lee III, Victoria Kelly. BA in Geography, U. Tex., 1968, MA in Geography, 1969; PhD, U. Wis., Madison, 1974. Asst. prof. geography U. Md., Catonsville, 1974-76, U. Okla., Norman, 1976-79, Clark U., Worcester, Mass., 1980-81, assoc. prof., 1981-85, prof., 1985—, dir. grad. sch. geography, 1983-88, 97-98; dir. George Perkins Marsh Inst., 1991-97. The Higgins prof. environment and soc., 1996—. Author: Once Beneath the Forest, 1983, (with T.M. Whitmore) Cultivated Landscapes of Native Middle America on the Eve of Conquest, 2001; editor Pre-Hispanic Maya Agriculture, 1978, Pulltrouser Swamp, 1983, Comparative Farming Systems, 1987, The Earth as Transformed By Human Action, 1990, Population Growth and Agriculture of Change in Africa, 1993, Changes in Land Use and Land Cover: A Global Perspective, 1994, Global Land-Use Change: A Perspective From the Columbian Encounter, 1995, Regions at Risk: Comparisons of Threatened Environments, 1995; contbr. articles to profl. publs. Served with U.S. Army, 1969-71. Rsch. grantee NSF, 1978-82, 84-85, 89-90, 93-96, Nat. Geog. Soc., 1984-85, NEH, 1987-89, A.W. Mellon, 1987-90, Rockefeller Bros., 1988, NASA, 1992-94, 97—, SSRC, 1993, Centenary medal Royal Scottish Geog. Soc., 1996; Guggenheim fellow, 1981-82; sr. fellow Green Ctr. for Sci. and Soc., 1994; fellow Ctr. for Advanced Studies in the Behavioral Scis., 1994-95. Mem. NAS, AAAS, Am. Acad. Arts & Scis., Assn. Am. Geographers (rsch. honors 1995), Soc. Am. Archeology. Home: 19 Farnum St Worcester MA 01602-2101 Office: Grad Sch Geography Clark U Worcester MA 01610 E-mail: bturner@clarku.edu.

TURNER, BONESE COLLINS, artist, educator; b. Abilene, Kans. d. Paul Edwin and Ruby (Seybold) Collins; m. Glenn E. Turner; 1 child, Craig Collins. BS in Edn., MEd, U. Idaho; MA, Calif. State U., Northridge, 1974. Instr. art L.A. Pierce Coll., Woodland Hills, Calif., 1964—. Prof. art Calif. State U., Northridge, 1986-89; art instr. L.A. Valley Coll., Van Nuys, 1987-89, Moorpark (Calif.) Coll., 1988-98, Arrowmont Coll. Arts & Crafts, Gatlinburg, Tenn., 1995-96; advisor Coll. Art and Arch. U. Idaho, 1988—; juror for art exhbns. including Nat. Watercolor Soc., 1980, 91, San Diego Art Inst., Brand Nat. Watermedia Exhbn., 1980, 96-97, prin. gallery Orlando Gallery, Tarzana, Calif. Represented in permanent collections Smithsonian Inst., Olympic Arts Festival, L.A.; one-woman shows include Angel's Gate Gallery, San Pedro, Calif., 1989, Art Store Gallery, Studio City, Calif., 1988, L.A. Pierce Coll. Gallery, 1988, Brand Art Gallery, Glendale, Calif., 1988, 93, 2000, Coos (Oreg.) Art Mus., 1988, U. Nev., 1987, Orlando Gallery, Sherman Oaks, Calif., 1993, 98, 2002, Brand Libr., Glendale, Calif., 2000, Burbank (Calif.) Creative Arts Ctr., 2000; prin. works in pub. collections The Smithsonian Inst., Hartung Performing Arts Ctr., Moscow, Idaho, Robert V. Fulton Mus. Art, Calif. State U., San Bernardino, Calif., Home Savs. and Loan, San Bernardino Sun Telegram Newspapers, Oreg. Coun. for the Arts, Newport, Oreg. Pub. Librs., Brand Libr., Glendale, Lincoln (Nebr.) Indsl. Tile Corp. Recipient Springfield (Mo.) Art Mus. award, 1989, 2002, 1st prize Brand XXVIII, 1998, Glendale, Calif., 1998, Butler Art Inst. award, 1989, Nat. award Acrylic Painters Assn. Eng. and U.S.A., 1996. Mem. Nat. Acrylic Painters Assn. of Eng. (award 1996), Nat. Mortar Bd. Soc., Nat. Watercolor Soc. (life, past pres., Purchase prize 1979), Watercolor U.S.A. Honor Soc. (award), Watercolor West. Avocations: bicycling, music, singing.

TURNER, BRACHA, Naive Landscape painter; b. Jerusalem; Exhbns. include 55 solo exhbns. and numerous juried exhbns.: J.F. Kennedy Art Gallery, Montreal, New Eng. Fine Arts Inst., Boston, Internat. Women in the Arts Conf., Beijing; permanent display of paintings include Hadassah Hdqtrs., N.Y., ZOA House, Tel-Aviv, Nat. Coun. of Jewish Women, N.Y., Ichilov Hosp., Tel-Aviv, Office of the Mayor of Jerusalem, Israel, The Bible Mus. Tel Aviv, Office of the Mayor N.Y.C., Rambam Hosp., Haifa, Israel, others; painting reproduced on cards by Hadassah; contbr. drawings to Sara's Daughters Sing, 1989.

TURNER, BRUCE EDWARD, lawyer; b. Wichita Falls, Tex., Oct. 31, 1947; s. Charles William and Marie Jeanne (Masson) T.; m. Barbara Lu Oakes, Oct. 8, 1982; children: Gradie, Anna Marie, Kelly. BA, Tex. Tech U., 1970, JD, 1973; LLM, NYU, 1974. Bar: Tex. 1974, U.S. Dist. Ct. (so. dist.) Tex. 1975, U.S. Tax Ct. 1975, U.S. Ct. Appeals (8th cir.) 1979, U.S. Dist. Ct. (no. dist.) Tex. 1988; bd. cert. comml. real estate. Assoc. Dillingham, Schleider & Marquelette, Houston, 1974-76, Johnston & Feather, Dallas, 1976-80; tax counsel Atlantic Richfield Co., 1980-81; corp. counsel Lehndorff, 1981—; owner Turner & Assocs., 1983—. Spkr., contbg. writer Advanced Real Estate Seminar, 1994. Mem. Tex. Bar Assn., Dallas Bar Assn., ICC Practitioners. Clubs: Downtown Mens (Dallas). Republican. Methodist. Home: 3708 Southwestern Blvd Dallas TX 75225-7220 Office: Ste 1150 4120 International Pkwy Carrollton TX 75007-1959

TURNER, CARL JEANE, international business consultant, electronics engineer; b. Sevierville, Tenn., July 27, 1933; s. Kenneth Albert and Lenna Faye (Christopher) T.; m. Flossie Pearl Ingram, Dec. 11, 1954; children: Marcia, Kenneth, Theresa, Christopher, Robin. BEd, BSEE, MBA, Columbia Pacific U., PhD, 1983. With Civil Air Patrol, Fla. Wing., 1947-50, Fla. Air Nat. Guard, 1948-50, USAF, 1950-72, aviator, electronics engring., AEW & C, tactical reconnaissance, electronic warfare, spl. ops., Korea and Vietnam, advanced through grades to chief master sgt., ret. 1972; field engring., internat. mktg. Itek Corp., 1972-77, 78-81, sr. engr./analyst, chief instr. E-Systems, Inc., Greenville, Tex., 1977-78; gen. mgr. Optical Systems div. Itek Internat. Corp., Athens, Greece, 1978-79, gen. mgr. German programs joint venture Itek Internat. Corp./AEG Telefunken AG, Ulm, Germany, 1979-81, mgr. program planning and control, internat. ops. Applied Tech. div., Sunnyvale, Calif., 1981; mgr. export mktg. GTE Corp., Govt. Systems Group, Western Div., Mountain View, Calif., 1981-83; internat. sales mgr. Probe Systems, Inc., Sunnyvale, Calif., 1983-84; dir. internat. mktg. Gen. Instrument Corp., Def. Systems Group, Hicksville, N.Y., 1984-90; founder, pres., chief exec. officer Intermanagement Tech. Co., Longview, Tex., 1990—; bd. dirs. Am. Air Mus. in Britain, div. Imperial War Mus. Author, editor electronic warfare mgmt. courses and internat. bus. books. Named to Order of Seasoned Weasels; recipient George Washington Honor medal Freedoms Found., 1965, Presdl. Achievement award, 1982, Pres.'s Medal of Merit, 1982. Mem. IEEE, Assn. Old Crows, Nat. Assn. Profls. Office: 400 W Terrace Dr Longview TX 75601-3823

TURNER, CHARLES ROBERT, JR. music educator; b. Maysville, Ky. s. Charles Robert Sr. and Margaret Katherine Davison Turner; m. Jenny Conley, Mar. 11, 1971 (div. June 1987); children: Bethany Leigh, Ashley Lauren; m. Jean Elaine Price, Jan. 20, 1989; children: Doris Margaret, Erin Rebecca. MusB in Edn., Morehead State U., 1974, MusM, 1978, Ind. U., 1983; D of Mus. Arts, U. N.C.-Greensboro, 2000. Asst. condr. Morehead (Ky.) State U., 1976-78; performer, adminstr. Detroit Concert Band, Grosse Pointe Woods, Mich., 1978-85; condr. Pikeville (Ky.) Coll., 1979-80; assoc. instr. Ind. U., Bloomington, 1980-83; adminstrv. asst. Harvey Phillips Found., Ind., 1980-83; asst. prof. S.W. Tex. State U., San Marcos, 1984-87; faculty N.C. Gov.'s Sch., Winston-Salem, N.C., 1986—; dir. music edn., condr. Berea (Ky.) Coll., 2001—. Dir. instrumental music Myers Park Magnet H.S., Charlotte, N.C., 1989-94; condr. N.C. State U., Raleigh, 1995-96; dir. mus. edn., condr. Wilkes U., Wilkes-Barre, Pa., 1998-2001; advisor Encore Music Camp, Wilkes-Barre, 1999. Editor: (performance edit. music) Six Trios by H. Schiltz, 2000; contbr.: (book) Strategies for Teaching, 1998. Regional coord. Tuba Christmas, Wilkes-Barre, 1998-2000; mem. Lexington Brass Band, 2002—. Mem. Ky. Music Educators Nat. Conf. (regional chair 1979-80, regional festivals mgr. 1979-80), Ky. Music Educators Assn., Music Educators Nat. Conf., Condr.'s Guild, Coll. Music Soc., Tubists Universal Brotherhood Assn., Pi Kappa Lambda. Avocations: jogging, tennis. Home: 204 Jessie Ct Berea KY 40403 E-mail: charles_turner@berea.edu.

TURNER, DANIEL LYNN, music educator, department chairman; b. Manchester, Iowa, Apr. 26, 1950; s. Altyn James and Iva Patterson Turner; m. Jamie Langston Turner; 1 child Jess Langston. BS, Bob Jones U., 1972; MS, U. Ill., Urbana-Champaign, 1979, EdD, 1988. Dir. pre-coll. bands Bob Jones Acad., Greenville, SC, 1972—84, dir. bands, 1983—, chair dept. music edn., 1990—. Author: (book) Conductor's Choice, 1989, Standing Without Apology: the History of Bob Jones University, 1997, Reflecting God's Light, 2002; composer: (band transcription) Toward a New Life (Joseph Suk), 2002. Bd. mem. Greenville County Youth Orch., 1999—2001. Mem.: Coll. Band Dirs. Nat. Assn., S.C. Band Dirs. Assn., Music Educator's Nat. Conf. Baptist. Avocations: tennis, golf, gardening. Home: 15 Tranquil Ave Greenville SC 29615 Office: Bob Jones Univ 1700 Wade Hampton Blvd Greenville SC 29614 Personal E-mail: dturner@bju.edu. Business E-Mail: dturner@bju.edu.

TURNER, DANIEL SHELTON, civil engineering educator; b. Montgomery, Ala., Dec. 9, 1945; s. Daniel H. and Emma Augusta (Nelson) T.; m. Peggy Joyce Eads McDaniel, Nov. 12, 1965 (div. 1976); children: Daniel Johnathan, David Jerome; m. Linda C. Sharpe, Dec. 30, 1978. BCE, U. Ala., 1968, MCE, 1970; PhD in Civil Engring., Tex. A&M U., 1980. Registered profl. engr. and land surveyor. Asst. prof. civil engring. tech. Ga. So. Coll., Statesboro, 1973-76, U. Ala., Tuscaloosa, 1976-81; asst. rsch. engr. Tex. Transp. Inst., College Station, 1980; acting dir. engring. tech. program dept. civil engring. U. Ala., Tuscaloosa, 1981-84, prof., head dept. civil and environ. engring., 1984—. Cons. legal proc., Tuscaloosa, 1983—. Contbr. over 260 articles to profl. jours., books. Bd. dirs. Am. Cancer Soc., Bulloch County, Ga., 1976; mem. oversight com. Bapt. Student Union, U. Ala., 1985-89; dir. Bapt. High Sch. Bapt. Young Men., Tuscaloosa County, 1987-91; mem. exec. subcom. Gov.'s Task Force Against Drunk Driving, Ala., 1983-85. Capt. USAF, 1969-73. Mem. ASCE (state pres. 1988-89, nat. bd. dirs. 1992-95, chair tech. activities 1995-96, nat. treas. 1996-97, nat. pres. 1998-99), Inst. Transp. Engrs. (state pres. 1987-88, dist. pres. 1994, pres. internat. edn. coun. 1991-92, chair legis. com. 1996, Hensley award as Outstanding Transp. Engr. in So. U.S. 1991), Nat. Safety Coun. (traffic records com., roadway environ. com.), Capstone Engring. Soc. Office: U Ala Civil Engring Dept PO Box 870205 Tuscaloosa AL 35487-0154

TURNER, DAVID ELDRIDGE, lawyer; b. Washington, Jan. 16, 1947; s. Olan Eldridge and Bernice Adele (Bothwell) T.; m. Lauren Turner-Hudson; children: Matthew David, Elizabeth Kristine, Jacob Michael. BS, Pa. State U., 1969; JD cum laude, Temple U., 1974. Bar: Pa. 1974, U.S. Dist. Ct. (ea. and mid. dists.) Pa. 1974, U.S. Ct. Appeals (3d cir.) 1983, U.S. Supreme Ct. 1985. With Liberty Mut. Ins. Co., Allentown, Pa., 1969-71; ptnr. Rhoda, Stoudt & Bradley, Reading, 1974-80, Kozloff, Diener, Turner & Payne P.C., Wyomissing, 1980-84; pres. Bingaman, Hess, Coblentz & Bell, P.C., Reading, 1985—. Instr. Pa. State U., Berks County, 1974-80; jud. appointee Berks County Ct. of Common Pleas, Reading, 1982-83. Supr. Robeson Twp. Bd. Suprs., Berks County, Pa., 1980-82. Mem. ABA, Pa. Bar Assn., Berks County Bar Assn., Pa. Trial Lawyers Assn., Pa. Def. Inst., Endlich Law Club, Mensa. Avocations: sculpture, rock climbing. Office: Bingaman Hess Coblentz & Bell Treeview Corp Ctr Ste 100 2 Meridian Dr Wyomissing PA 19610 E-mail: deturner@bhcb.com.

TURNER, DAVID G. information technology executive; married; 1 child. B in Computer Sci. and Math., Del. State U., 1986; MS, Fairleigh Dickinson U.; exec. MBA program, Dartmouth Coll. Various sales and mktg. positions AT&T, 1986—2000; sr. v.p. sales and mktg. Gateway, Poway, Calif., 2000—. Named Small Bus. Adv. of Yr., U.S. Dept. Commerce Small Bus. Adminstrn., 1996; recipient Nat. Salute to Achievers in Industry award, YMCA, 1999, Cmty. Svc. award, Inst. for Student Achievement, 2000. Office: Gateway 14303 Gateway Pl Poway CA 92064 Office Fax: 585-848-3407.*

TURNER, DAVID LOWERY, system safety engineer; b. Atlanta, Feb. 2, 1936; s. Albert Olson and Ella May (Waldrop) Turner; m. Jeanette Smith, Mar. 25, 1962 (div. 1968); m. Sharon Kay Brewer, May 26, 1972 (div. 1978); m. Rita M. Robertson, Aug. 25, 1993 (div. 2001); children: Angela Kay, Jacqueline Kay. Student, Samford U., 1958-60, U. Ala., 1960-62, U. Houston, 1977-79; BS in Safety Engring., Kennedy-Western U., 1991. Registered profl. safety engr.; lic. claims adjuster, Tex., real estate agt., Tex. Safety engr. USF&G, Birmingham, Ala., 1963-69, Parker Bros. Co. Inc., Houston, 1969-80; safety dir. MGF Oil Corp./MGF Drilling Co., 1980-84; safety mgr. Creole Prodn. Svcs. Inc., 1985-86; safety div. mgr. Mason Chamberlain Inc., Stennis Space Center, Miss., 1986-91; sys. safety engr. Raytheon Engrs. and Constructors, A Raytheon Co., Johnston Island, 1991—2001, Washington Group Internat., 2001—. Cons. Fullbright and Jaworski Law Firm, Houston, 1980-81. Vol. West Meml. Vol. Fire Dept., Katy, Tex., 1979-80. With USAF, 1954-58. Mem. Am. Soc. Safety Engrs. (profl.), Nat. Safety Coun., Sys. Safety Soc., Tex. Safety Assn., Nat. Ready Mix Concrete Assn., Internat. Assn. Drilling Contractors, NASA Safety Coun., Gulf Coast Safety Coun., MCI Exec. Safety Coun. (co-chmn. 1986-91). Republican. Baptist. Avocations: hunting, fishing, golf, tennis, bowling. Home: PO Box 098 APO AP 96558 Office: Washington Group Internat Johnston Island APO AP 96558 E-mail: dTurner@jacads.com.

TURNER, DAVID R. social worker, educator; b. Newark, Sept. 24, 1952; s. James R. and Bonnie M. Turner. BA in Psychology, Rutgers U., MSW, 1990. Sch. social worker N.J. Dept. Edn., 90, supr. N.J. Dept. Edn., 01. From in-patient mental health asst. to juvenile counselor Hunterdon Med. Ctr., Flemington, NJ, 1974—80; dir. counseling Hunterdon Learning Ctr., Califon, 1980—. Avocations: guitar, fishing, boating, harmonica, padaling. Office: Hunterdon Learning Ctr 32 Hoffmans Crossing Rd Califon NJ 07830

TURNER, DAVID REUBEN, publisher, author; b. N.Y.C., Dec. 9, 1915; s. Charles and Eva (Turner) Moskowitz; m. Ann Louise Perkins, Apr. 29, 1946 (div. 1976); children— Eve (Mrs. William Watters), Ruth. BS, Coll. City N.Y., 1936, MS in Edn, 1937. Co-founder Arco Pub. Co., N.Y.C., 1937, pub., dir., 1937-78; v.p. parent co. Prentice-Hall, Inc., 1979-80; pres. Turner Pub., 1980-92. Pub. cons. under Ford Found. contract Burma Translation Soc., Rangoon, 1959-60 Author: more than 300 books on tests and testing, including High School Equivalency Diploma Tests, 1951, 75, How to Win a Scholarship, 1955, Scoring High On College Entrance Tests, 1969, 71, Food Service Supervisor, 1968, Bank Examiner, 1968, Accountant-Auditor, 1960, 77, Officer Candidate Tests, 1978, Professional-Administrative Career Exams, 1979, English Grammar and Usage for Test-Takers, 1976, College Level Examination Program, 1979. Adviser bd. publs. Union Am. Hebrew Congregations. Home and Office: 13 Glengary Rd Croton On Hudson NY 10520-2139

TURNER, DOUGLAS LAIRD, writer, editor, columnist; b. Buffalo, Jan. 5, 1932; s. Henry Albert and Effie Donna (McIndoo) T.; m. Mary Joan Hassett, July 7, 1962; children: Christopher Henry, Mary Julia, Albert William. BA, Brown U., 1954; postgrad., Stanford U., 1968. Reporter Buffalo (N.Y.) Courier-Express, 1957-60, state capital corr., 1960-64, fin. editor, 1964, city editor, 1964-70, exec. editor, 1971-80, Washington bur. chief, 1981-82; Washington corr. Buffalo (N.Y.) Evening News, 1982, Washington columnist, 1983, Washington bur. chief, 1989—. Adj. assoc. prof. faculty social scis. State Univ. at Buffalo, 1995, N.Y. State Commn. on Pub. Access to Records, 1976-81; founder, pres. Friends of Williamsburg Rowing Inc., 1993—. Mem. U.S. Olympic Rowing Team, 1956. With U.S. Army Counter Intelligence Corps, 1956-57. Nation champion four-oared shell with cox, 1956; winner Hanlan Trophy, Royal Can. Henley Regatta, 1956; recipient numerous awards Am. Newspaper Guild, N.Y. State Associated Press Assn., personal citations Erie County Legislature, N.Y. State Assembly, Buffalo Common Coun. Mem. Nat. Press Club (former gov. 1988), Potomac Boat Club, Gridiron Club (Wash.). Roman Catholic. Home: 7923 Saint George Ct Springfield VA 22153-2741 Office: Buffalo News Washington Bur 1141 National Press Building Washington DC 20045-2101

TURNER, DUNCAN CALVERT, lawyer; b. Gulfport, Miss., Jan. 28, 1953; s. Francis McRae and Elizabeth Calvert T.; m. Rebecca Reuter, Dec. 29, 1977; children: Aaron, Laura, Samuel. BS, U.S. Mil. Acad., 1974; MBA, JD, U. Miss., 1980. Bar: Miss. 1990, U.S. Dist. Ct. 1990, Wash. 1991, U.S. Ct. Fed. Claims 1995. Commd. 2d. lt. U.S. Army, 1974, advanced through grades to maj., 1986; atty. Bogle & Gates, Seattle, 1990-96, Badgley Mullins Law Group, Seattle, 1996—. Avocations: music, golf, hiking. Office: Badgley Mullins Law Group 5100 Wash Mutual Tower 1201 3rd Ave Seattle WA 98101-3029

TURNER, DWAYNE CURTIS, lawyer; b. Atlanta, Sept. 13, 1960; s. George Aiken Turner and Mary Inez (Rowe) Holley. BA in Anthropology, Calif. State U., Long Beach, 1989; MA in Anthropology, UCLA, 1991, MPH, 1992, PhD in Anthropology, 1994; JD, Benjamin M. Cardozo Sch. Law, 1999. Bar: N.Y. First Dept. Assoc. dir. planning AIDS Project of L.A., 1992-94; adj. faculty anthropology Calif. State U., L.A., 1994-96; rsch. assoc. UCLA Sch. Medicine, Dept. Health Svcs., 1994-96; asst. prof. health scis. CUNY, 1996-99; asst. corp. coun. lead paint unit N.Y.C. Law Dept., 1999—2001; adjunct prof. health law CUNY, 1999—; exec. dir. N.Y. State Task Force on Life and the Law, 2001—. Evaluation ocns. Teen Canteen/Travelers AID, L.A., 1993-94; adj. prof. health scis. CUNY, 1999—. Author: Risky Sex: Gay Men and HIV Prevention, 1997; contbr. articles to profl. jours. Bd. dirs. UCLA Ctr. for clin. AIDS Rsch. and Edn., 1994, AVANCE Humana Svcs., L.A., 1994; organizer Com. for Ann. Women and HIV Conf., L.A., 1992-94; vol. Being Alive, Long Beach. Calif., 1987-89; mem. AIDS Coalition to Unleash Power, L.A., 1990-92. Mem. APHA, Am. Anthropol. Assn., Soc. for Med. Anthropology, Soc. for Applied Anthropology (adv. bd. AIDS task force 1994), N.Y. State Bar Assn., City Bar Assn. of N.Y., N.Y. Acad. Scis. Avocation: music. Home: 150 W 56th St Apt 3811 New York NY 10019 Office: 5 Penn Plaza 3d Fl New York NY 10001 E-mail: dct01@health.state.ny.us.

TURNER, E. DEANE, lawyer; b. Auburn, N.Y., Aug. 4, 1928; s. Alfred Edward and Bertha (Deane) T. AB summa cum laude, Princeton U., 1950; LLB cum laude, Harvard U., 1953. Bar: N.Y. 1953. Assoc. Dewey Ballantine LLP and predecessor firms, N.Y.C., 1953-63, ptnr., 1963—, of counsel, 1991—. Treas. Harvard Law Sch. Assn., N.Y.C., 1964-83; elder, trustee Brick Presbyn. Ch., N.Y.C., 1976—, pres. bd. trustees, 1988-90; trustee Presbytery N.Y.C., 1993-98, pres. bd. trustees, 1995-98; com. to adminstr. James N. Jarvie Endowment, 1993-2000. Fellow Am. Coll. Investment Counsel (emeritus); mem. Union Club, John's Island Club, Phi Beta Kappa. Republican. Home: 1120 5th Ave New York NY 10128-0144 also: 381 Llwyds Ln Johns Island Vero Beach FL 32963 Office: Dewey Ballantine LLP 1301 Avenue Of The Americas New York NY 10019-6022

TURNER, ELAINE S. allergist, immunologist; b. Glen Cove, N.Y., 1947; MD, Med. Coll. Pa., 1974. Diplomate Am. Bd. Allergy & Immunology, Am. Bd. Internal Medicine. Intern Michael Reese Hosp., Chgo., 1974-75; resident in internal medicine Cleve. Clinic, 1976-78; fellow in allergy & immunology Northwestern U., Chgo., 1978-80; with St. Mary's Hosp., Va., Henrico Drs. Hosp. Mem. ACP, Am. Acad. Allergy, Asthma and Immunology, Va. Allergy Soc., Richmond Acad. Medicine. Office: Va Adult & Pediat Allergy & Allergy Ste 103 7605 Forest Ave Richmond VA 23229-4936

TURNER, ELIZABETH ADAMS NOBLE (BETTY TURNER), real estate company executive; b. Yonkers, N.Y., May 18, 1931; d. James Kendrick and Orrel (Baldwin) Noble; m. Jack Rice Turner, July 11, 1953; children: Jay Kendrick, Randall Ray. BA, Vassar Coll., 1953; MA, Tex. A&I U., 1964. Ednl. cons., Tex. sales mgr. Noble & Noble Pub. Co., N.Y.C., 1956-67; psychometrist Corpus Christi Guidance Ctr., 1967-70; psychologist Corpus Christi State Sch., 1970-72, dir. programs, asst. supt., 1972, dir. devel. and vol. svc., 1972-76, dir. rsch. and tng., 1977-79; psychologist Tex. Mental Health and Mental Retardation, 1970-79, program cons., 1979-85; pres. Turner Co., 1975-82; mayor pro tem Corpus Christi, 1981-85; mayor, 1987-91; CEO, pres. Corpus Christi C. of C., 1991-94; pres. Betty Turner Real Estate, 1999—. V.p. bus. and govt. rels. ctrl. and south Tex. divsns. Columbia Healthcare Corp., 1994—99. Dir. alumni Corpus Christi State U., 1976-77; coord. vols. Summer Head Start Program, Corpus Christi, 1967; chmn. spl. gifts com. United Way, Corpus Christi, 1970; mem. Corpus Christi City Coun., 1979-91; family co-founded Barnes and Noble, N.Y.C.; founder Com. of 100 and Goals for Corpus Christi; pres. USO; bd. dirs. Coastal Bend Coun. Govts., Corpus Christi Mus., Harbor Playhouse, Cmtys. in Schs., YWCA, Y-Teen Sponsor, Del Mar Coll. Found., Tex. A&M at Corpus Christi Pres.' Coun., Food Bank, Hispanic C. of C., TAMACC Corp. Ptnrs., Salvation Army, Jr. League, Coun. Deaf Silent Found.; bd. Southside Cmty. Hosp., 1987-93, Gulfway Nat. Bank, 1985-92; strategic planning com. Meml. Hosp., 1992, Tex. Capital Network Bd., 1992-95, Humana Hosp., Physician Relocation and Condo Sales, Rehab. Hosp., dir. of vols., South Tex., Admiral Tex. Navy; bd. dirs. Pacific Southwest Bank, 1997-2000, St. David's/Austin and Medth. Healthcare Sys., San Antonio, 1997-99; apptd. Gov.'s Commn. for Women, 1984-85, Leadership Tex. Class I, Corpus Christi, Class II; founder Goals for Corpus Christi, Bay Area Sports Assn., Assn. Coastal Bend Mayor's Alliance; founder Mayor's Commn. on the Disabled, Mayor's Task Force on the Homeless; active Port Aransas Cmty. Ch., U. Tex. Sch. Nursing Adv. Coun., 1998-99; bd. dirs. Del Mar Coll. Found., 1998—, Am. Heart Assn., 1999-2000, Bethune Day Care Nursery, 1999—, Jr. League Cmty. Adv. Coun., 1999-2000, Strategic Planning Com., 2000-, Silent Found., 2001—, 21st Century Charter Sch., 2001-2002, Boys and Girls Club of Corpus Christi, 2002--, Food Bank, 2002--, Nat. AARP, 2002-. Named Corpus Christi Newsmaker of Yr., 1987; recipient Love award, YWCA, 1970, Y's Women and Men in Careers award, 1988, Recognition award, Rotary, 1991, Comdr.'s award for pub. svc., U.S. Army, Scroll of Honor award, Navy League, award, Tex. Hwy Dept., Road Hand award, Tex. Hwy. Commn., Women of Distinction award, Girl Scouts Tex. Mem. NAACP (life), Tex. Psychol. Assn. (pres., mem. exec. bd.), Psychol. Assn. (pres., founder), Tex. Mcpl. League (bd. dirs.), Jr. League Corpus Christi, Tex. Bookman's Assn., Tex. Assn. Realtors, Corpus Christi Town Club, Corpus Christi Yacht Club, Jr. Cotillion Club, Ch. Good Shepherd, Kappa Kappa Gamma. Home: 403 Blue Heron Dr Port Aransas TX 78373

TURNER, ELVIN L. retired educational administrator; b. Springfield, Ohio, Jan. 9, 1938; s. Willie and Jinada (Lawson) T.; m. Betty Jo Breckinridge, June 11, 1966 (div. Jan. 1972); 1 child, Anthony; m. Carrie Johnson, Aug. 3, 1972; 1 child, Brenetta Bell. BS in Biology and Chemistry, Knoxville (Tenn.) Coll., 1962; MEd, U. Cin., 1968; postgrad., Nova U., Ft. Lauderdale, Fla., 1973, Kensington U., Glendale, Calif., 1993—. Cert. secondary prin., tchr., Ohio. Spl. edn. tchr. Cin. Pub. Schs., 1965-69, coord. spl. edn., 1969-72, asst. prin., 1972-78, prin., 1978-90, asst. prin., 1990-93. Part-time adj. prof. Mt. St. Joseph (Ohio) Coll., 1987—88; mem. adv. com. Millcreek Psychiat. Ctr. for Children, Cin., 1988—89; bus driver Bristol Village Retirement Cmty., 1997—99; ombudsman Pro-Srs. , Cin., 1993—96, Waverly , Ohio, 1997—; vol. ombudsman rep. Area Agy. on Aging Dist. Seven, Inc., Portsmouth, Ohio; sec. Bristol Village Residents Assn., 1997. Vol. Ohio Dept Aging, Columbus; elected sec. exec. adv. coun. Bristol Village Nat. Ch. Residencies, Waverly, 1997; mem. bd. deacons New Hope Bapt. Ch., Hamilton, 1993; Sunday sch. tchr. Bethel AME Ch., Lebanon, 1996, Pilgrim Missionary Bapt. Ch.,

Columbus, 2000—; Bible study course instr. Asbury North United Meth. Ch., 2000—01, instr. Vacation Bible Sch., 2000; bd. dirs. Big Bros./Big Sisters, Cin., 1973. Recipient plaques and grants, including plaque for statewide outstanding sr. vol. radio, TV and newspaper coverage, Independence, Ohio, 2001. Mem. Nat. Assn. for Secondary Sch. Prins., Prins. Assn. Secondary Sch. Adminstrs., Knoxville Coll. Alumni Assn., Phi Delta Kappa, Alpha Phi Alpha. Avocations: bowling, golf, reading, travel. Home: PO Box 13617 Columbus OH 43213-0617 Office: 923 Findlay St Portsmouth OH 45662 Fax: 740-354-6015.

TURNER, EUGENE ANDREW, manufacturing executive; b. Bridgeton, N.J., Aug. 7, 1928; s. Benjamin Homer and Pearl Irene (Wolbert) T.; m. Paula Ann Webb, 1987; children: Mary Ann, John-Reed. BA, Rutgers U., 1966; student, Columbia U., 1980. With Owens Ill., 1950-73, regional mgr. West Coast, 1970-73; v.p. adminstrn. Midland Glass Co., Cliffwood, N.J., 1973-76, pres., chief operating officer, 1981-82, also bd. dirs.; v.p., gen. mgr. Anchor Hocking Corp., Lancaster, Ohio, 1976-81; dir. ops. Theo Chem. Labs., Tampa, Fla., 1988-90, Profit Counselors Inc, Sarasota, 1990-94; pres. Profit Sys. Inc., Oklahoma City, 1994—. Mng. cons. 1987-88. Mem. Harbor Island Club, Seaview Country Club, Navesink Country Club. Home: 1103 Tedford Way Oklahoma City OK 73116-6006 E-mail: gene227@hotmail.com. *Take time to learn the chosen business then develop credibility by doing what you say you will do.*

TURNER, EVAN HOPKINS, retired art museum director; b. Orono, Maine, Nov. 8, 1927; s. Albert Morton and Percie Trowbridge (Hopkins) T.; m. Brenda Winthrop Bowman, May 12, 1956; children: John, Jennifer. AB cum laude, Harvard U., 1949, MA, 1950, PhD, 1954; hon. degree, Swarthmore Coll., Sir George Williams U., Cleve. State U.; Case Western Res. U., 2001. Head docent svc. Fogg Mus., Cambridge, Mass., 1950-51; curator Robbins Art Collection of Prints, Arlington, 1951; teaching fellow fine arts Harvard U., 1951-52; lectr., research asst. Frick Collection, N.Y.C., 1953-56; gen. curator, asst. dir. Wadsworth Atheneum, Hartford, Conn., 1956-59; dir. Montreal Mus. Fine Arts, Que., Can., 1959-64, Phila. Mus. Art, 1964-77, Ackland Art Mus., 1978-83, Cleve. Mus. Art, 1983-93. Adj. prof. art history U. Pa., U. N.C., Chapel Hill, 1978-83; disting. vis. prof. Oberlin Coll., 1993-95. Author: Ray K. Metzker: Photographs, 2001. Recipient Chevalier L'Ordre Arts Lettres. Mem. Assn. Art Mus. Dirs., Coll. Art Assn. Am., Am. Mus. Assn., Century Assn. Club. Home: 2125 Cypress St Philadelphia PA 19103-6507

TURNER, FLORENCE FRANCES, ceramist; b. Detroit, Mar. 9, 1926; d. Paul Pokrywka and Catherine Gagal; m. Dwight Robert Turner, Oct. 23, 1948; children: Thomas Michael, Nancy Louise, Richard Scott, Garry Robert. Student, Oakland C.C., Royal Oak, Mich., 1975-85, U. Ariz., Yuma, 1985, U. Las Vegas, 1989—. Pres., founder Nev. Clay Guild, Henderson, 1990-94, mem. adv. bd., 1994-2000, v.p., 2000—. Workshop leader Greenfield Village, Dearborn, Mich., 1977-78, Plymouth (Mich.) Hist. Soc., 1979, Las Vegas Sch. System, 1989-90, Detroit Met. area, 1977-85. Bd. dirs. Las Vegas Art Mus., 1987-91; corr. sec. So. Nev. Creative Art Ctr., Las Vegas, 1990-94. Mem.: Nev. Camera Club, Las Vegas Gem Club, So. Nev. Rock Art Enthusiasts, Phi Kappa Phi. Avocations: photography, collecting gems, travel. Office: Nev Clay Guild PO Box 50004 Henderson NV 89016-0004

TURNER, FRED L. fast food company executive; b. 1933; married. BS, Drake U., 1954. With McDonald's Corp., Oak Brook, Ill., 1956—, exec. v.p., 1967—68, pres., chief adminstrv. officer, 1968—73, CEO, 1973—87, chmn., 1977—90, now sr. chmn., 1990, also bd. dirs., 1968—. Bd. dirs. Baxter Internat. Inc., W.W. Grainger, Inc. US Army, 1954-56. Office: McDonald's Corp One Kroc Dr Oak Brook IL 60523

TURNER, FRED LAMAR, accountant, lawyer; b. LaGrange, Ga., Oct. 8, 1949; s. John Cletus and Dean (Norris) T.; m. Mary Katherine Daws, Sept. 27, 1969; children: Jessica, Jennifer, Judson. AA in Electronics, Troup Tech. Sch., LaGrange, 1969; BA, Columbus (Ga.) Coll., 1973; M in Taxation, Ga. State U., 1979, JD, 1986. Bar: Ga. Elec. installer N. Electric Co., Orlando, Fla., 1969-70; instr. La Grange (Ga.) Coll., 1979-81; prin., owner J.K. Boatwright & Co., PC, La Grange, 1973—; pres., bd. dirs. J.K. Boatwright & Co. Bd. dirs. Troup County Local Devel. Corp., Troup County Planning Commn.; trustee LaGrange Coll., Callaway Found. Inc., Clark Holder Clinic Ednl. Found.; treas., bd. dirs. Chattahoochee Valley Art Assn., LaGrange; chmn. bd. LaGrange Indsl. Devel. Authority. Named Acct. Advocate of Yr. for Ga. SBA, Atlanta, 1986. Mem. AICPA (tax div.), Ga. Soc. CPAs, LaGrange C. of C. (bd. dirs., treas., pres. 1988), Troup County C. of C. (pres.), Rotary (bd. dirs., treas. LaGrange chpt. 1984-85, pres. 1984-85). Baptist. Avocations: boating, fishing. Home: 867 Whitaker Rd Lagrange GA 30240-3768 Office: J K Boatwright Co PC 17 1/2 N Lafayette Sq Lagrange GA 30240-3210

TURNER, GEORGE MASON, lawyer; b. Butte, Mont., Sept. 2, 1935; s. William Dale and Bernice (Ownby) T.; m. Angela Gloria Aparicio, Oct. 14, 1995; children: Esther, Lesley, Allyson, Aarin, Alexander. BS in Polit. Sci., Brigham Young U., 1959, MS in Polit. Sci., 1960; JD, UCLA, 1968. Bar: Calif. 1969, U.S. Dist. Ct. Calif. 1969, U.S. Supreme Ct. 1976, U.S. Ct. Claims 1981, U.S. Tax Ct. 1981. Assoc. Munns & Kofford, Pasadena, Calif., 1969-72; ptnr. Turner & Smart, 1972-85, The Law Offices of George M. Turner, Pasadena, 1985—; pvt. practice, 1972—. Instr. estate tax law Am. Coll. Bryn Mawr, Pa., 1976; monitor Continuing Edn. of Bar, Calif., 1985. Author: Revocable Trusts, 1983, 4th edit., 1998, Irrevocable Trusts, 1985, 3d edit., 1997, Trust Administration and Fiduciary Responsibility, 2d edit., 2000, Revocable Trusts-The Centerpiece of Estate Planning, 1998. V.p. San Gabriel Valley Boy Scouts Am., Pasadena, 1976-78; pres. San Gabriel Valley Estate Planning Co., Pasadena, 1979-80; bd. dirs., chmn. bd. Calif. Family Study Ctr., North Hollywood, 1975-92, Ettie Lee Homes, Los Angeles, 1984-90. Recipient Silver Beaver award Boy Scout Am., 1979. Mem. ABA, Calif. Bar Assn., Los Angeles Bar Assn., Pi Sigma Alpha. Republican. Mem. Lds Ch. Avocation: photography.

TURNER, GEORGE PEARCE, consulting company executive; b. Dallas, Aug. 22, 1915; s. Fred Horatio and Florence (Phillips) T.; m. June Lori Haney, Feb. 4, 1943 (div. 1976); children: Bruce Haney, Brian Phillips, Mark Richardson; m. Kathryn Blank Hauf, June 1976. Student, U. Tex., 1932-33, 35-36, 40-41, So. Methodist U., 1934; BA in Internat. Rels. cum laude, U. So. Calif., 1962, MS in Internat. Pub. Adminstrn. summa cum laude, 1966; PhD in Econs. and Internat. Rels., Columbia Pacific U., 1982, PhD in Pub. Adminstrn. and Internat. Rels., 1985. Archtl. designer, L.A., 1946-48; prin. Lieburg & Turner (cons. engrs.), Pasadena, Calif., 1947-48; pres. Radiant Heat Engring., Inc., 1948-53; exec. asst. to dir. fgn. subsidiaries S.Am. Fluor Corp. Ltd., L.A., 1953-54; mem. exec. staff Coast Fed. Savs. & Loan Assn., 1954-55; exec. staff Holmes & Narver, Inc., L.A., 1955-61; mgr. project devel. S.Am. ops. Southwestern Engring. Co., 1962; pres. Haney Devel. Corp., 1964-90, Fomento e Inversiones Quisqueyanos C. por A., Santo Domingo de Guzman, Dominican Republic, 1967-98; gen. mgr. for Venezuelan ops. Hale Internat. Inc., Caracas, 1970-71; dir., mgr. Consortium Lomas de La Lagunita, 1970, Consortium Desarrollos Urbanos, Valencia, Venezuela, 1970; pres. Haney Investment Corp. (HANCO), 1974-90, Casa FOMIQ, 1978-98, Caribbean Vagabond Ltd., Grand Cayman Island, B.W.I., 1981-90, Kay Pearce & Turner, Ltd., Newtown Square, Pa., 1981-98; sec. Integrated Industries of Atlantic County, N.J.; gen. ptnr. N.Y. Ave. Parking Assocs., Atlantic City, 1980-91. Adviser, provisional pres., Dominican Republic, 1965-66, constl. pres. of republic, 1966-68; projects programmer Nat. Planning Inst. Peru Tri-Partite Mission, 1962-65; ofcl. OAS adviser Nat. Office Tourism Dominican Republic, 1966-67, Nat. Office Cultural Patrimony, Liga Mcpl. Dominicana, 1967-68; cons., dir. projects, programming, tech. matters Mission Recovery and Rehab., Dominican Republic, 1965-67; dep. dir. Tech. Assistance Mission Dominican Republic, 1967-68; cons. assignments for program assistance Inter-Am. Tng. Ctr., Fed. U. Ceara, Brazil; OAS adviser on tech. assistance to Chile, Argentina, Uruguay, Peru, Brazil, 1962-68; cons. Wildwood Ocean Towers, N.J., 1969-70, Capital Investment Devel. Corp., Downing Ctr., Downingtown, Pa., 1971-77; dir. for Project Monitor and owners agt., hosp. tower Hahnemann Med. U. and Hosp., Phila., 1975-78; pres. Urban Planning and Devel. Corp., Exton, Pa., 1978-79; cons., corp. sec., v.p. Constrn. Devel. and Properties Mgmt. Group, Integrated Industries Inc., Exton, 1978-80; ltd. ptnr. Marsh Creek Assocs. Two, 1985-98; apptd. to faculty Columbia Pacific U., 1987; cons. internat. consortium for multi-billion dollar econ. devel. program with projects in countries of Pacific Rim and Ea. Europe, 1993-95; established Casa FOMIQ awards program, 1995. Author: An Analysis of the Economy of El Salvador, 1961, The Alliance for Progress: Concept Versus Structure, 1966, Some Observations on the Decade of the 1960s - U.S. vis-a-vis Latin America, 1982, Latin American Odyssey, 1985, Third Generation, 1990, Growing Up Male in America: With the Prince Charming Mystique, 1993; pub., editor Fountain of Age, The Jour. of Casa FOMIQ, 1995; contbr. articles to profl. publs., including Archtl. Record, S.W. Builder and Contractor, House & Garden, Wood, Artistic Homes, Perfect Home mag., Ranch and Modern Homes. With USAF, 1941-45. Decorated OAS Medal of Honor; recipient Citation for Valiant Svc. in Dominican Republic, 1965-66, Ofcl. OAS Commendation for Program Contbns., Peru, Dominican Republic, Brazil, Venezuela, 1969. Mem. Delta Phi Epsilon, Alpha Sigma Lambda. Home and Office: 8 Fox Run Ln Newtown Square PA 19073-1004

TURNER, GLORIA TOWNSEND BURKE, social services association executive; b. Lumberton, N.C., Nov. 16, 1938; d. John B. and Alice (Haite) Townsend; m. James Rae Burke, June 3, 1957 (dec. 1974); children: William H., Sonya Kyle; m. Robert R. Turner,June 23, 1977 (dec. May, 2002). Student, U. S.C., 1974; degree in nursing, York Tech. Coll./U. S.C., 1976. RN, S.C. Staff nurse, head nurse York Gen. Hosp., Rock Hill, S.C., 1976-78; head med. dept., indsl. nursing J.P. Stevens Plant, 1976-78; hsop., nursing home auditor S.C. Med. Found., Columbia, 1978-79; exec. dir. Kershaw County Coun. on Aging, Camden, S.C., 1979-93; dir. med.-surg. units Conway (S.C.) Hosp., 1993-98; house supervisor Scotland Meml. Hosp., Laurinburg, N.C., 1998—; adminstr. Active Nursing Svc., Myrtle Beach, S.C., 2000—. Bd. dirs. S.C. Fedn. Older Ams., 1988-95; mem. state adv. com. on Alzheimers, Columbia, 1984—; trustee Kershaw County Meml. Hosp., Camden, 1989-93. Congl. nurse Belin Meth. Ch., Murrells Inlet, SC. Mem. Camden C. of C., Rotary. Methodist. Avocations: reading, watching football and basketball, travel. Home: 147 Dusty Trail Ln Surfside Beach SC 29575-8852

TURNER, GWENDOLYN YVONNE, education educator; b. Little Rock, Sept. 17, 1951; d. Thomas Edward and Pearl Ellen (Hamilton) T. BA, Ark. State U., Jonesboro, 1973; MEd, U. Ark., Fayetteville, 1978, EdD, 1983. Cert. reading specialist, adult edn. and social studies tchr., Ark. Tchr. Ft. Smith (Ark.) Public Schs., 1978-79; reading specialist U. Central Ark., 1979-80; instr. U. Ark., Fayetteville, 1980-83, asst. prof., 1983-86, Okla. State U., Stillwater, 1986-89; assoc. prof. U. Mo., St. Louis, 1989—. Cons. Okla. Pub. Schs., Oklahoma City, Edmond, Tulsa, 1986-89, Augusta (Ark.) Pub. Schs., 1988; family literacy cons.; mem. profl. devel. schs. collaborative Regional Ednl. Partnership, 1993, Commn. on Tchrs. in Diverse Settings, 1991—; literacy place adv. bd. Scholastic Pub. Co., 1993-95. Reviewer: Free Inquiry in Creative Sociology, 1989—, Reading Rsch. and Instruction, 1993; co-author: Making Schools a Place of Peace; contbr. articles to profl. jours. Bd. dirs. St. Louis Literacy Coun., 1990—, LWV, Fayetteville, Ark., 1986; mem. State Evaluation Team for Certification of Colls. of Edn. Inst. on Writing, Reading and Civic Education grantee, Harvard U., 1990; recipient Achafoa Apple for Teacher award Mortar Board, Okla. State U., 1989-90, Cert. of Appreciation Laubach Literacy Internat., 1990, Wilson award Ark. Bus. & Profl. Women's Club, Mo. NEA Spl. Svc. award, 1991, Cert. of Honor Ctr. for Community Edn. Okla. State U., 1989; Gerald Howard Read Internat. Seminar Scholar People's Republic China, 1985; Modern Curriculum Acad. Rsch. Scholarship. Mem. ASCD, Am. Assn. Colls. for Tchr. Edn. (instl. rep.), Internat. Reading Assn. (sch. rev. team 1990), Coll. Reading Assn. (monography rev. bd. 1989, adult learning divsn. 1990-92), Assn. Tchr. Educators (monograph rev. bd. 1989, com. mem. 1989-92, cert. of appreciation 1990), Am. Ednl. Rsch. Assn., Phi Kappa Phi. Avocations: reading, traveling, collecting ethnic art. Office: U Mo 8001 Natural Bridge Rd Saint Louis MO 63121-4401

TURNER, HAROLD EDWARD, education educator; b. Hamilton, Ill., Nov. 22, 1921; s. Edward Jesse and Beulah May (White) T.; m. Catherine Skeeters, Apr. 5, 1946; children: Michele Turner Nimerick, Thomas, Barbara Turner McMahon, Krista Turner Landgraf. AB, Carthage Coll., 1950; MS, U. Ill. - Urbana, 1951, Ed.D. (George Peabody fellow), 1956. Tchr. Taylorville (Ill.) Jr. H.S., 1951-52, Moline (Ill.) Jr. H.S., 1952-54; dir. elem. edn. Jefferson County, Colo., 1955-57; prin. Jefferson County H.S., 1957-60; asst. prof. edn. North Tex. State U., Denton, 1960-63; asst. supt. curriculum Sacramento City Schs., 1963-66; assoc. prof., chmn. dept. curriculum and instrn. U. Mo., St. Louis, 1966-69, prof., 1971-85, prof. emeritus, 1985—, chmn. dept. adminstrn., founds., secondary edn., 1977-78, dept. chmn., 1983-85. Vis. prof. Adams State Coll., Alamosa, Colo., 1959, U. Ga., Athens, 1981-82; adj. prof. NYU, 1965, U. Ill., 1980; cons. various sch. dists., Tex., Mo.; spl. cons. Mo. State Dept. Edn., 1973. Author: (with Adolph Unruh) Supervision for Change and Innovation, 1970; contbr. articles to profl. jours. Served with USNR, 1942-46. Mem. Profs. Supervision. Presbyterian (elder). Home: 685 S La Posada Cir # 1202 Green Valley AZ 85614 E-mail: gazvk@aol.com.

TURNER, HARRY EDWARD, lawyer; b. Mt. Vernon, Ohio, Dec. 25, 1927; s. Paul Hamilton and Harriett (Krafft) T.; m. Shirley Marilyn Eggert, July 8, 1950; children: Harry Edward, Thomas Frederick (dec. Mar. 1995). BA, Baldwin Wallace Coll., 1951; JD, Ohio No. U., 1954. Bar: Ohio 1954, U.S. Supreme Ct. 1966. Practice in Mt. Vernon, 1954—; state rep. Ohio Gen. Assembly, 1973-85; solicitor Mt. Vernon, 1958-62. Prosecutor Mt. Vernon Municipal Ct., 1955-58 Mem. Mt. Vernon City Sch. Bd., 1964-70, pres., 1965-70; trustee Ohio Sch. Bd. Assn., 1968-70, Hannah Browning Home, 1987—, Sta. Break/Commn. on Planning Svcs., 1989-95; mem. Knox County Pub. Defender Commn., 1987-91. With USN, 1946-47. Mem. Ohio State Bar Assn., Knox County Bar Assn. (pres. 1970), Alpha Sigma Phi, Sigma Delta Kappa. Republican. Lutheran. Home: 1575 Yauger Rd Apt 15 Mount Vernon OH 43050-8299 Office: 118 E High St Mount Vernon OH 43050-3443

TURNER, H(ARRY) SPENCER, preventive medicine physician, educator; b. Dayton, Ohio, July 25, 1938; s. Eli and Daphne (Cunagin) T.; children: Michael, Mary, Daniel. BA, Manchester Coll., North Manchester, Ind., 1960; MD summa cum laude, Ohio State U., 1963, MS in Preventive Medicine, 1968. Diplomate Am. Bd. Preventive Medicine. Resident in preventive (aerospace) medicine Ohio State U., Columbus, 1966-69, chief resident, 1968-69, clin. asst. prof. dept. preventive medicine, 1969-80, dir. Univ. Health Svc., 1970-80; pvt. practice Dayton, 1980-90; dir. Univ. Health Svc., head team physician U. Ky., Lexington, 1991—, prof. preventive medicine and environ. health, 1991—. Editor: (textbook) History and Practice of College Health; contbr. articles and papers to profl. jours. and meetings. Bd. dirs. Blue Shield, 1981-86; mem. Cin. Internat. Chorale, 1989-94; mem. Lexington Singers, 1992—. Capt. U.S. Army, 1964-66. Fellow Am. Coll. Preventive Medicine, Am. Coll. Health Assn. (pres. 1980, Ruth Boynton award 1982, Edw. Hitchcock award 1996), Alpha Omega Alpha. Lutheran. Avocation: music. E-mail: jturner@pop.ky.edu.

TURNER, HARRY WOODRUFF, lawyer; b. Blairsville, Pa., May 2, 1939; s. James McKinnie and Dorothy Elizabeth (Tittle) T.; m. Mary Elizabeth Phelan, Dec. 30, 1972; children: James William, David Woodruff. AB, U. Pitts., 1961; JD, Harvard U., 1964. Bar: Pa., 1965, U.S. Supreme Ct., 1979. Assoc. Kirkpatrick & Lockhart, Pitts., 1964-71, ptnr., 1971—. Mem. Fed. Jud. Selection Commn. Pa., 1995—, chair, 1997—. Trustee Hist. Soc. Western Pa. 1996—, vice-chmn., 1999—; trustee U. Pitts., 1995—, Wilson Coll., Chambersburg, Pa., 1978-89; trustee, sec. Pitts. Opera, 1993—; pres. U. Pitts. Nat. Alumni Assn., 2001—; alt. del. Rep. Nat. Conv., Miami, 1968, Houston, 1992, Phila., 2000, Rep. State Com., 1996—; trustee, v.p. Torrance (Pa.) State Hosp., 1969-73; trustee ann. giving fund U. Pitts. 1982-95; chair distbn. com. William L. Benz Found., 1985—; bd. dirs. Pitts. divsn. Am. Heart Assn., 1993—; bd. vis. U. Pitts. Med. Sch., 1995—, U. Pitts. Coll. Arts & Scis., 1988—, chair bd. vis. Sch. Info. Scis. Mem. ABA, Pa. Bar Assn., Am. Law Inst., Internat. Acad. Trial Lawyers, Allegheny County Bar Assn., Allegheny County Acad. Trial Lawyers, SAR (pres. 1995-96), Fox Chapel Golf Club, Duquesne Club, Allegheny Club. Presbyterian. Office: Kirkpatrick & Lockhart 1500 Oliver Building Pittsburgh PA 15222-2312 E-mail: wturner@KL.com.

TURNER, HENRY BROWN, finance executive; b. N.Y.C., Sept. 3, 1936; s. Henry Brown III and Gertrude (Adams) T.; m. Sarah Jean Thomas, June 7, 1958 (div.); children: Laura Eleanor, Steven Bristow, Nancy Carolyn. AB, Duke U., 1958; MBA, Harvard U., 1962. Controller Fin. Corp. of Ariz., Phoenix, 1962-64; treas., dir. corporate planning Star-Kist Foods, Terminal Island, Calif., 1964-67; dir., 1st v.p. Mitchum, Jones & Templeton, Los Angeles, 1967-73; asst. sec. Dept. Commerce, Washington, 1973-74; v.p. fin. N-Ren Corp., Cin., 1975-76; v.p. Oppenheimer & Co., N.Y.C., 1976-78; exec. v.p., mng. dir. corporate fin. Shearson Hayden Stone Inc., 1978-79; sr. mng. dir. Ardshiel Inc., 1980-81, pres., 1981-93, chmn. emeritus, 1994—. Vis. lectr. U. Va. Sch. of Bus.; bd. dirs. MacDonald & Co., Pembrook Mgmt., Inc., Golden State Vitners, Inc., Cellu-Tissue Corp., Wrangler Stewart Ranch, Cave Creek, Ariz. Sponsor Jr. Achievement, 1964-67. Served to lt. USNR, 1958-60. Coll. Men's Club scholar Westfield, N.J., 1954-55 Mem. Fed. Govt. Accountants Assn. (hon.), Duke Washington Club, Omicron Delta Kappa.

TURNER, HUGH JOSEPH, JR. lawyer; b. Paterson, N.J., Oct. 5, 1945; s. Hugh Joseph and Louise (Sullivan) T.; m. Charlene Chiappetta, Feb. 11, 1983. BS, Boston U., 1967; JD, U. Miami, Coral Gables, Fla., 1975. Bar: Fla. 1975, U.S. Dist. Ct. (so., no. and mid. dists.) Fla. 1975, U.S. Ct. Appeals (11th cir.) 1981, U.S. Supreme Ct. 1984. Tchr. Browne & Nichols, Cambridge, Mass., 1968-72; ptnr. Smathers & Thompson, Miami, Fla., 1981-87, Kelley Drye & Warren, Miami, 1987-93, English, McCaughan & O'Bryan, Ft. Lauderdale, 1993—2001, Redgrave & Turner LLP, Boca Raton, Fla., 2001—. Chmn. Fla. Bar internat. law sect., 1988-89. Contbg. author book on internat. dispute resolution Fla. Bar, 1989; contbr. articles to profl. jours. Bd. dirs. Japan Soc. South Fla., Miami, 1989-97; mem. Sea Ranch Lakes Village Coun., 1997-2000; mayor Sea Ranch Lakes, 2000-02. Mem. ABA, Def. Rsch. Inst. Avocation: running. Office: Redgrave & Turner LLP Ste 450 120 E Palmetto Park Rd Boca Raton FL 33432

TURNER, JAMES, congressman; b. Feb. 6, 1946; m. Ginny; 2 children. BBA, U. Tex., 1968, MBA, JD, U. Tex., 1971. Lawyer; state govt. official; mem. 105-106th Congresses from 2nd Tex. dist., 1997—; mem. govt. oversight com.; mem. nat. security com. Mem. Econ. Growth, Natural Resources, and Regulatory Affairs subcom., Nat. Security, Internat. Affairs, and Criminal Justice subcom. House Govt. Reform and Oversight Com., Mil. Rsch. and Devel. subcom., Mil. Procurement subcom. House Nat. Security Com. Democrat. Baptist. Office: Ho of Reps 208 Cannon Hob Washington DC 20515-4302 also: Rm 201 701 N 1st St Ste 201 Lufkin TX 75901-2804 Fax: 409-632-8588; 202-225-2401. E-mail: tx02wyr@mail.house.gov.*

TURNER, JAMES DANIEL, computer company executive; b. Chevely, Md., Dec. 16, 1950; s. Allen Ephrem and Mary Lynn (Thompson) T.; m. Hari Kertonadi, Nov. 20, 1978; children: Melinda Lee, Imelda Rose. BS in Physics, George Mason U., Fairfax, Va., 1974; ME in Engring. Physics, U. Va., 1976; PhD in Engring. Sci. and Mechanics, Va. Poly. Inst. and State U., Blacksburg, 1980. Dynamics sect. chief Charles Stark Draper Lab., Cambridge, Mass., 1979-84; dynamics and control group leader Photon Rsch. Assocs., 1984-92, divsn. mgr., 1992; v.p. Moldyn (PRA Subs.), 1991-92; pres. Amdyen Systems, 1992—; assoc. dir. NSF Industry & Univ. Coop. Rsch. Ctr. Virtual Proving Ground, Nat. Advanced Driving Simulation, U. Iowa, Iowa City, 1996-2001; adj. prof. mech. engring. U. Iowa, 2001—. Exec. bd. Electricore, Indpls., 1996—; adj. assoc. prof. U. Iowa, 2001; cons. in field. Author: Optimal Spacecraft Rotational Maneuvers, 1986; contbr. chpts. to books. Recipient Rsch. award Sigma Xi, 1981, grants from govt. and industry. Mem. AIAA, Assn. Astronautical Sci., Am. Chem. Soc. Republican. Methodist. Achievements include patents for molecular dynamics simulation method and apparatus, demonstration of applications of advanced multibody dynamics modelling techniques for atomic systems for drug design. Office: NADS Simulation Ctr 2401 Oakdale Blvd Iowa City IA 52242-5003 E-mail: jturner@nads-sc.uiowa.edu.

TURNER, JAMES REGINALD, lawyer; b. Wilmington, N.C., Sept. 4, 1934; s. Reginald and Sarah Marie (Terrell) T.; m. Carolyn Frances Simpkins, Feb. 4, 1967; children: Susannah Lynn, William Joel. AB, U. N.C., 1956; JD, Yale U., 1962. Bar: N.C., 1963. Assoc. Smith & Moore, Greensboro, 1962-69; founder, sr. ptnr. Turner, Enochs & Lloyd, P.A., 1969—. Senator State Legislature, N.C., 1979-80; lectr. on affordable housing Carolinas Coun., Nat. Assn. Housing and Redevelopment Ofcls., N.C., S.C., 1972-01, chmn. Guilford Co. Bd. of Elections, 2001—. Reviewer architecture Triad Bus. News. Mem. ecclesiastical ct. of the Episcopal Diocese of N.C., Greensboro, 1996. Capt., USN, 1956-59, Persian Gulf. Democrat. Episcopalian. Office: Turner Enochs & Lloyd PA 717 Green Valley Rd Greensboro NC 27408-7019 Home: 505 Willoughby Blvd Greensboro NC 27408

TURNER, JAMES THOMAS, judge; b. Clifton Forge, Va., Mar. 12, 1938; s. James Thomas and Ruth (Greene) T.; m. Patricia Sue Renfrow, July 8, 1962; 1 child, James Thomas. BA, Wake Forest Coll., 1960; JD, U. Va., 1965. Bar: Va. 1965, U.S. Ct. Appeals (4th and fed. cirs.), U.S. Supreme Ct. Assoc. Williams, Worrell, Kelly & Greer, Norfolk, Va., 1965, ptrn., 1971-79; U.S. magistrate U.S. Dist. Ct. (ea. dist.) Va., 1979-87; judge U.S. Ct. Fed. Claims, 1987—. Mem. ABA, Fed. Bar Assn., Va. Bar Assn., Norfolk and Portsmouth Bar Assn. (sec. 1975-79). Office: 717 Madison Pl NW Washington DC 20439-0002

TURNER, JANET SULLIVAN, painter, sculptor; b. Gardiner, Maine, Nov. 15, 1935; d. Clayton Jefferson and Frances (Leighton) Sullivan; m. Terry Turner, Oct. 6, 1956; children: Lisa Turner Reid, Michael Ross, Jonathan Brett. BA cum laude, Mich. State U., 1956. Rep. Am. Women in Art, UN World Conf. on Women, Nairobi, Kenya, 1985. One-woman shows include San Diego Art Inst., 1971, St. Joseph U., Phila., 1981, Villanova (Pa.) U. Gallery, 1982, Pa. State U., Middletown (Pa.), 1985, Temple U. (Pa.), 1986, Widener U. Art Mus., Chester, Pa., 1987, 94, Rosemont Coll., Pa., 1995, Sande Webster Gallery, Phila., 1998, 2000; exhibited in group shows at Del. Art Mus., Wilmington, 1978, Woodmere Art Mus., Phila., 1980, Port of History Mus., Phila., 1984, Allentown Art Mus., 1984, Trenton (N.J.) City Mus. Ellarslie Open VIII, 1989, Ammo Gallery, Bklyn., 1989, Pa. State Mus., Harrisburg, 1990-94, Galeria Mesa, Ariz., 1991, Del. Ctr. for Contemporary Arts, Wilmington, 1992, Holter Mus., Helena, Mont., 1992, S.W. Tex. State U., San Marcos, 1993, Fla. State U. Mus., Tallahassee, 1993, Newark Mus., 1993, U. Del., 1994, 1st St. Gallery, N.Y.C., 1994, Noyes Mus., N.J., 1995, Sande Webster Gallery, Phila. 1995-2000, Phil. Art Mus., 1997, Krasdale Gallery, White Plains, N.Y., Noyes Mus., Oceanville, N.J.; represented in permanent collections Nat. Mus. Women in Arts, Washington, Kresge Art Mus., East Lansing, Mich, ARA Svcs. Inc., Phila., Blue Cross/Blue Shield, Phila., Am. Nat. Bank and Trust co., Rockford, Ill., Burroughs Corp., Lisle, Ill., State Mus. Pa., Harrisburg, Bryn Mawr (Pa.) Coll., Rosemont Coll., Villanova (Pa.) Coll., LaSalle U. Art Mus., Phila., Noyes Mus., N.J., Nat. Liberty Mus., Phil. Bd. dirs. Fine Arts Ann., Phila., 1984—86. Recipient 2d pl. award San Diego Art Inst. 19th Ann. Exhbn., 1971, award of merit Pavilion Gallery, Mt. Holly, N.J., 1991, 3d pl. Katonah Mus. of Art, N.Y., 1992, purchase award State Mus. of Pa., Harrisburg, 1992. Mem. Artists Equity (pres. 1987-88), Phila. Watercolor Club, Delta Phi Delta. Republican. Roman Catholic. Home: 88 Cambridge Dr Glen Mills PA 19342-1545

TURNER, JERROLD ALAN, medical director; b. Cedars Falls, Iowa, June 15, 1931; m. Ellen Woolfson. MD, UCLA, 1958; Diploma in Tropical Medicine and Hygiene, Royal Coll. Phys. and Surg. Diplomate Am. Bd. Internal Medicine. Internal medicine intern UCLA Med. Ctr., 1958-59; resident in internal medicine Harbor-UCLA Med. Ctr., 1964-66, chief resident in internal medicine, 1966-67, dir. med. edn. Calif., 1968—, dir. parasitology sect., 1968—, assoc. med. dir., 1983—; prof. medicine UCLA Sch. of Medicine, 1979—, asst. dean, student affairs, 1976—. Dir. Turner Parasitology Lab., Carson, Calif. Co-author: Medical Microbiology: A Short Course, 1994. Mem. Alpha Omega Alpha. Office: Harbor-UCLA Med Ctr 1000 W Carson St # 2 Torrance CA 90502-2004

TURNER, JOAN GLORIA MCELROY, columnist; b. Union City, N.J., Aug. 4, 1926; d. Peter Joseph McElroy, Grayce Clausen Taylor; m. James Aloysius Turner; children: Taylor, Peter. Student, CCNY. Social writer Hudson Dispatch, Union City, NJ; reporter, feature writer Daily Register, Middletown; reporter The Courier, feature writer, columnist. Contbr. ; author: poems in anthology pubs. Vol. Dem. Club., Keansburg Libr., NJ; pres. West Side Girls, 1972—74; v.p. Kinlin Women's Assn., 2001—02. Recipient Citation, N.J. State Assembly, Cert. of Appreciation, Keansburg Police Dept. Mem.: Drama Soc. Democrat. Avocations: reading, swimming, writing. Office: The Courier PO Box 399 Middletown NJ 07748

TURNER, JOHN SIDNEY, JR. retired otolaryngologist, educator; b. Bainbridge, Ga., July 25, 1930; s. John Sidney and Rose Lee (Rogers) T.; m. Betty Jane Tigner, June 5, 1955 (dec.); children: Elizabeth, Rebecca, Jan Marie; m. Nina Jones, June 16, 1999. BS, Emory U., 1952, MD, 1955. Diplomate Am. Bd. Otolaryngology. Intern U. Va. Hosp., 1955-56; resident in otolaryngology Duke U. Med. Ctr., 1958-61; prof. otolaryngology Emory U., Atlanta, 1961-95, chmn. divsn., 1961—95, prof., 1995; ret. Ear specialist, chief otolaryngology Emory Clinic, 1961-95; area cons. in field U.S. 3d Army, 1962-69; assoc. dir. heart disease control program Fla. Bd. Health, 1956-58; Ga. state chmn. Deafness Rsch. Found., 1968-95; v.p. Clifton Casualty Ins. Co., Atlanta, 1975-95. Mem. internat. editl. bd. Drugs Jour., 1982—, Ethicals in Med. Progress, 1982—, Dialogue Jour., 1988-95; mem. editl. bd. Otolaryngolog—Head and Neck Surgery, 1991; contbr. chpts. to books, articles to profl. jours. With USPHS, 1956-58. Recipient Appreciation award Children of Fulton County and Fulton County Health Dept., 1975, Citation for Disting. Svc., Fla. divsn. Am. Cancer Soc., 1957, Lester A. Brown award Ga. Soc. Otolaryngology*Head and Neck Surgery, 1995. Mem. AMA, So. Med. Assn. (chmn. otolaryngology sect. 1974, cert. of appreciation 1974), Am. Acad. Otolaryngology--Head and Neck Surgery (Honor award 1994), Triological Soc. (v.p., chmn. so. sect. 1991—), Am. Acad. Otolaryngic Allergy, Ga. Soc. Otolaryngology (pres. 1973), Med. Assn. Ga., Med. Assn. Atlanta, Assn. Acad. Depts. Otolaryngology, Optimists (pres. Atlanta 1975), Alpha Omega Alpha. Democrat. Methodist. Home: 3451 Marina Crest Dr Gainesville GA 30506-1061

TURNER, JOHN ANDREW, economist; b. Chgo., July 9, 1949; s. Henry Andrew and Mary Margaret (Tilton) T.; m. Kathleen King Peery, June 21, 1975; 1 child, Sarah. BA, Pomona Coll., Claremont, Calif., 1971; MA, Stanford U., 1972; PhD, U. Chgo., 1977. Rsch. econ. SSA, Washington, 1976-80, U.S. Dept. Labor, Washington, 1980-96, ILO, Geneva, 1996-98; rsch. econ. Office of Sec. U.S. Dept. Labor, 1999-2000, Pub. Policy Inst., 2000—, AARP, 2000—. Cons. OECD, Paris, 1989, IMF, 1995, AFL-CIO, 1996; chmn. Internat. Pension Conf., U.S. Dept. Labor, Washington, 1990; adj. prof. George Washington U., 1994-96. Author: Pension Policy for a Mobile Labor Force, 1993; editor: Trends in Pensions, 1989 (transl. into Japanese 1991), Pension Policy: An International Perspective, 1991, Trends in Health Benefits, 1993, Private Pension Policies in Industrialized Countries, 1995, Securing Employer-Based Pensions, 1996, Social Security: Development and Reform, 2000. Fulbright scholar Institut de Recherches Economiques et Sociales, France, 1994. Mem. Am. Econ. Assn. Methodist. Avocation: tennis. Home and Office: 3713 Chesapeake St NW Washington DC 20016-1813 Office: AARP 601 E St NW Washington DC 20049

TURNER, JOHN AUGUSTUS, chemist; b. Boise, Idaho, July 16, 1948; s. John Augustus and Judy Ann Turner; m. Dixie Oldham; 1 child Rebecca Grant 1 child Christian. BS in Chemistry, Idaho State U., 1971; PhD, Colo. State U., 1977. Postdoctoral fellow Calif. Inst. Tech., Pasadena, 1977—79; prin. scientist Nat. Renewable Energy Lab., Golden, Colo., 1979—. Contbr. articles to profl. jours. Bd. trustees Colo. Christian U., Lakewood, 1998—2002. With Colo. N.G., 1972—78. Mem.: Electrochem. Soc., Am. Chem. Soc. Avocation: bicycling. Office: Nat Renewable Energy Lab 1617 Cole Blvd Golden CO 80401-3393 Office Fax: 303-275-4271. Personal E-mail: John.Dixie@att.net. Business E-Mail: jturner@nrel.gov.

TURNER, JOHN CHARLES, retired language educator; b. Montgomery, Ala., Nov. 19, 1946; s. Lucian Claude and Frances Elizabeth Turner; m. Deborah Lee Hyden; children: John Ashley, Jonathan Ian, Ross Camp. AA, Reinhardt Coll., 1971; BA, Jacksonville State U., 1974. Enlgish, art and drama tchr. Chattooga County Bd. Edn., Summerville, Ga., 1974—2002, ret., 2002. Founder Global Village Internat., 1992, Global Best Quest, 1992—2002, The World Frinedship Flag, 1995—96. Inventor (game) Shooting Stars, 1990, Battle Royale, 1990, Hookball, 1992. Advisor Inter-Act Club, Summerville and Trion, Ga., 1992—97; chmn. Indsl. Devel. Authority, Summerville, 1990—93; founder The Howard Finster Art Festival. With USAF, 1967—69. Named Tchr. of Yr., Optimist Club, 1993; recipient Pres.'s award, Chattooga County C. of C., 1993. Mem.: Mil. Order of the Star and Bars, Sons of Am. Revolution, Internat. Soc. Descs. of Charlemagne. Methodist. Avocations: writing, art, inventor. Home: 20 Greenmeadow Dr Trion GA 30753

TURNER, JOHN FREELAND, federal agency administrator; b. Jackson, Wyo., Mar. 3, 1942; s. John Charles and Mary Louise (Mapes) T.; m. Mary Kay Brady, 1969; children: John Francis, Kathy Mapes, Mark Freeland. BS in Biology, U. Notre Dame, 1964; postgrad., U. Innsbruck, 1964-65, U. Utah, 1965-66; MS in Ecology, U. Mich., 1968. Rancher, outfitter Triangle X Ranch, Moose, Wyo.; chmn. bd. dirs. Bank of Jackson Hole, 1985-89; photojournalist; mem. Wyo. Ho. of Reps., 1970-74, Wyo. Senate, 1974-89, pres., 1987-89; dir. Fish and Wildlife Svc. Dept. Interior, Washington, 1989-93; pres. Conservation Fund, Arlington, Va., 1993—2001; asst. sec. for oceans, int. environ., and scientific affairs U.S. Dept. State , Washington, 2001—. Chmn. bd. dirs. Inst. Environ. and Natural Resources, U. Wyo., Laramie; exec. adv. Hancock Timber Resource Group, 1993—2001; chmn. rev. com. Argonne Nat. Lab.-West, U. Chgo., 1999—2001; bd. dirs. Land Trust Alliance, 1994—2000, vice-chmn.; bd. dirs. N.E. Utilities, 1995—2001; mem. Nat. Coal Coun., 1995—, Teton Sci. Sch. Bd., Nat. Wetland Forum, 1983, 87; mem. exec. com. Coun. of State Govts.; chmn. Pride in Jackson Hole Campaign, 1986; chmn. steering com. UN Conv. on Wetlands of Internat. Importance, 1990—93; head U.S. delegation Conv. on Internat. Trade Endangered Species. Author: The Magnificent Bald Eagle: Our National Bird, 1971. Named Citizen of Yr. County of Teton, 1984; recipient Nat. Conservation Achievement award Nat. Wildlife Fedn., 1984, Sheldon Coleman Great Outdoors award, 1990, Pres.'s Pub. Svc. award The Nature Conservatory, 1990, Stewardship award Audubon Soc., 1992, Nat. Wetland Achievement award Ducks Unlimited, 1993, Chevron/Times-Mirror Nat. Conservation Leadership award, 1995. Mem. Nat. Wildlife Refuge Assn. (bd. dirs.), Boone and Crocket Club (profl. mem.). Republican. Roman Catholic. Office: US Dept State Oceans, Int Environ & Scientific Affairs 2201 C St NW Washington DC 20520*

TURNER, JOHN NAPIER, former prime minister of Canada, legislator; b. Richmond, Eng., June 7, 1929; s. Leonard and Phyllis (Gregory) T.; m. Geills McCrae Kilgour, May 11, 1963; children: Elizabeth, Michael, David, Andrew. BA with honors in Polit. Sci., U. B.C., Can., 1949; BA, Oxford U., Eng., 1951, BCL, 1952; MA, Oxford U., 1957; postgrad., U. Paris, 1952-53; LLD, U. N.B., 1968, York U., Toronto, 1969, U. B.C., 1994, U. Toronto, 1996; D. of Civil Law (hon.), Mt. Allison U., N.B., 1980. Bar: Eng. 1953, Que. 1954, Ont. 1968, B.C. 1969, Y.T. 1969, N.W.T. 1969, Barbados 1969, Trinidad 1969. With Stikeman, Elliot, Tamaki, Mercier and Turner, Montreal, Que., 1953-65, McMillan Binch, Toronto, 1976-84; M.P. for St. Lawrence-St. George Montreal, 1962-68, Ottawa-Carleton, 1968-76; parliamentary sec. to Minister of Northern Affairs and Nat. Resources, 1963-65; minister without portfolio, 1965-67; registrar-gen. Govt. of Can., 1967-68, minister of consumer and corp. affairs, 1968, solicitor-gen., 1968, minister of justice and atty.-gen. of Can., 1968-72, minister of fin., 1972-75, prime minister of Can., 1984; leader Liberal Party Can., 1984-90; mem. parliament Vancouver Quadra, 1984-93; with Miller Thomson, Toronto, 1990—. Created Queen's Counsel, Ontario and Quebec, 1968. Author: Senate of Canada, 1961, Politics of Purpose, 1968. Can. Track Field Champion, 1948; mem. English Track and Field Team, 1950-51. Appointed Companion of Order of Can., 1995. Mem. Eng. Bar Assn., Grey's Inn London, Bar. Assns. of Ont., Que., B.C., Barbados, Trinidad, Mt. Royal Club, Montreal Racquet Club, Queen's Club, Badminton and Racquet Club, York Club, The Vancouver Club, Nat. Club. Liberal. Roman Catholic. Avocations: tennis, canoeing, skiing. Home: 59 Oriole Rd Toronto ON Canada M4V 2E9 Office: Miller Thomson LLP 2500 20 Queen St W Toronto ON Canada M5H 3S1 E-mail: jturner@millerthomson.ca.

TURNER, KELLEY BAILEY, non-profit consultant, volunteer program administrator; b. Houston, Mar. 17, 1962; d. Myron Edgar Bailey and Georgia Numsen (Reynolds) White; m. Mark Edward Turner, May 21, 1994. BA in Art History and Comms. cum laude, U. St. Thomas, 1993. Lic. FCC. Coord. sch. svcs., asst dir. vis. svcs. Houston Mus. Natural Sci., Edn. Sch. Svcs., Houston, 1991-94; coord. vol. svcs. and comty. partnerships Hermann Hosp., 1996-98; adminstr. Vols. in Pub. Schs. Cmty. Partnerships Houston Ind. Sch. Dist., 1998-2001; prin. Cmty. Devel. Resources, 2001—01; dir. vol. svcs. and cmty. outreach Bering Omega Cmty. Svcs., 2002—. Presenter Internat. Conf. on Vol. Adminstrn., Chgo., 1999—; instr. Vol. Mgmt. Acad., Houston C.C. Cen. Mem. Jr. League of Houston, Inc., 1990-94; floor presenter Mus. Natural Sci., 1991-94; vol. Houston SPCA; mem. adv. bd. Houston Internat. Festival, 1992-93, chmn. curriculum guide, 1992-93, chmn. curriculum guide com.; bd. dirs. country selection com. Chrysalis Repertory Dance Co., 1995-97; bd. dirs., membership chair Houston Assn. Vol. Adminstrs., 1998-2000; mem. adv. coun. Ret. Srs. vol. Program, Interfaith Ministries of Greater Houston, 1999-2000; vol. team capt. Houston Mayor's Summit on Women, 1999; mem. com. Internat. Yr. of Vols., 2000—; mem. bd. advocates Planned Parenthood Houston and Southeast Tex., 2000—. Named Vol. of Yr. Jr. League Houston, 1991. Home and Office: 1923 Vassar St Houston TX 77098-5429 Fax: 713-526-9256 *9.

TURNER, LAURENCE H. lawyer, engineer; b. N.Y.C., Nov. 29, 1949; s. Sidney and Sylvia Turner. B in Mech. Engring., Pratt Inst., N.Y., 1973; MBA, Baruch Coll., 1977; JD, Bklyn. Law Sch., 1996. Bar: N.Y. 1997; lic. profl. engr., N.Y., N.J. Adminstrv. engr. N.Y.C. Dept. Environ. Protection, Elmhurst, N.Y., 1984—. Avocations: water skiing, travel. Home: 99-72 66 Rd #5V Rego Park NY 11374-4442

TURNER, LELAND S., JR. (LEE TURNER), civil engineer, consultant, former utilities executive; b. Dallas, Nov. 5, 1926; s. James A. and Fay Sims; m. Donetta Mae Johnson, Jan. 17, 1947. BCE, Tex. A&M U., 1948; JD, So. Meth. U., 1957. Engr. Dallas Power & Light Co., 1948, various exec. positions, pres., chief exec., 1967-76; dir. Tex. Utilities Co., 1967-82, exec. v.p., 1976-84; cons., 1984—96. Trustee Com. for Econ. Devel., Southwestern Med. Found.; past pres., bd. dirs. Dallas Citizens Coun.; bd. dirs. So. Meth. U. Found. for Sci. and Engring.; past chmn. Children's Med. Ctr.; past chmn. United Way, YMCA, Community Coun. of Greater Dallas; past pres. Greater Dallas Ahead, Inc., Dallas Assembly. With U.S. Army, 1945-46. Mem. ABA, Am. Arbitration Assn. Presbyterian.

TURNER, LESTER NATHAN, lawyer, international trade consultant; b. Colmar, Ky., July 11, 1933; s. Clifford G. and Minnie G. (Ensor) T.; m. Sandra B. Ward, July 3, 1976; children: Kimberly L., Michele M., Renee S., Mark L., Jeffrey S., Derek Kyle. BS, Lincoln Meml. U., 1955; JD, U. Mich., 1959. Bar: Mich. 1960, U.S. Dist. Ct. (ea. and we. dist.) Mich., U.S. Ct. Appeals (6th cir.), U.S. Supreme Ct. 1982. Law clk. to presiding justice, research atty. Mich. Supreme Ct., Lansing, 1960-62; ptnr. Sinas, Dramis, Brake & Turner, 1960-78; sole law practice, bus. law, internat. cons. primarily in Mid. East Countries with emphasis on Palestine Nat. Authority, Lansing, Harbor Springs, Mich., 1978—; prin., CEO Palestinian Tourism Co. Ltd., Palestinian Co. Transp. Ltd., North Bay Ltd. Mem. std. jury instrn. com. Mich. Supreme Ct., Lansing, 1963-73; cons. higher commn. investment and fin. Palestinian Pres., 1997—. Mem. Mich. State Bar Assn., Mich. Trial Lawyers Assn. (bd. dirs. 1963-74, vice pres. 1974). Methodist. Office: PO Box 499 Harbor Springs MI 49740-0499 E-mail: intlaw@chartermi.net.

TURNER, LETITIA RHODES, artist; b. Media, Pa., Aug. 17, 1923; d. Samuel Noblit and Letitia (Eves) Rhodes; m. Ellwood Jackson Turner Jr., Aug. 1, 1942; children: Rue Baronsky, Letitia Mayo, Elizabeth Rorke. Sec., treas. Rose Tree Realty Inc., Media, Pa., 1961-81. Dance tchr., 1939, 40, 41. Portrait painter (Portrait of Mary 3d pl. 1990, Portrait of Brett 2d pl. 1987) Pres. Am. Legion Aux., Media, 1991-2002, photographer, 1992, sec., 1993—; 1st v.p. Woman's Aux. Media Presbyn. Ch., Media, 1963; mem. D.A.R.E., Media, 1983-91, 92, 93—. Mem. Artist Guild Del. County, Art League Del. County. Republican. Avocations: needlepoint, holiday spa, art design for ch. bulletin covers. Home and Office: 302 Lexington Media PA 19063-6021

TURNER, LILLIAN ERNA, retired nurse; b. Coalmont, Colo., Apr. 22, 1918; d. Harvey Oliver and Erna Lena (Wackwitz) T. BS, Colo. State U., 1940, Columbia U., 1945; cert. physician asst., U. Utah, 1978. Commd. 2d lt. Nurse Corps, U.S. Army, 1945; advanced through grades to lt. comdr. USPHS, 1964; 1st lt. U.S. Army, 1945-46; U.S. Pub. Health Svc., 1964-69; dean of women U. Alaska, Fairbanks, 1948-50; head nurse Group Health Hosp., Seattle, 1950-53; adviser to chief nurse Hosp. Am. Samoa, Pago Pago, 1954-60; head nurse Meml. Hosp., Twin Falls, Idaho, 1960-61; shift supr. Hosp. Lago Oil and Transport, Siero Colorado, Aruba, 1961-63; nurse adv. Province Hosp., Danang, South Vietnam, 1964-69, Cho Quan Hosp., South Vietnam, 1970-72; chief nurse, advisor Truk Hosp., Moen, Ea. Caroline Islands, 1972-74; nurse advisor Children's Med. Relief Internat., South Vietnam, 1975; physician's asst. U. Utah, 1976-78, Wagon Circle Med. Clinic, Rawlins, Wyo., 1978-89, Energy Basin Clinic Carbon County Meml. Hosp., Hanna, 1989-96; ret., 1996. Named Nat. Humanitarian Physician Asst. of Yr., 1993, Wyo. Physician Asst. of Yr., 1992, Disting. Alumnus of Yr., Columbia U.-Presbyn. Hosp., N.Y.C., 1997. Mem. VFW (life), Wyo. Acad. Physician Assts. (bd. dirs. 1982-83), Am. Acad. Physician Assts., Nat. Assn. Physician Assts., Wyo. Physician Assts., Am. Legion (life). Avocations: reading, wood carving, sewing, hiking, beach combing, watching Denver Bronco football. Home: PO Box 337 Hanna WY 82327-0337 *Personal philosophy: You only go this way once so get as much out of it and put as much in as possible in the time allotted.*

TURNER, LISA HILL, county official; b. Rexburg, Idaho, Sept. 11, 1959; d. Dale A. and Betty Jean (Owens) Hill; m. Rick I. Turner, June 10, 1979; 1 child, Keith D. Staff mem. Fremont County Herald-Chronicle, St. Anthony, Idaho, 1977-93, editor, 1985-93; chief dep. treas. Fremont County, 1994-95, info. sys. adminstr., 1995—. Bd. dirs. Foster Grandparents, Fremont Gen. Hosp. Found.,; sec. fisherman's breakfast com., v.p. pub. affairs Pioneer Days Com., St. Anthony, Idaho. Named Most Respected Citizen, Free Fisherman's Breakfast, 1991, Hon. Chef, 1987; recipient Cert. of Appreciation, Idaho Gov. Cecil Andrus, 1990. Mem. So. Fremont C. of C. (sec. 1985-88, dir. 1986-89). Mem. Lds Ch. Avocations: golf, horseback riding, camping, snowmobiling.

TURNER, LISA PHILLIPS, human resources executive; b. Waltham, Mass., Apr. 10, 1951; d. James Sinclair and Virginia Turner. BA in Edn. and Philosophy magna cum laude, Washington Coll., Chestertown, Md., 1974; AS in Electronics Tech., AA in Engring., Palm Beach Jr. Coll., 1982; MBA, Nova U., 1986, DSc, 1989; PhD, Kennedy Western U., 1990. Cert. Sr. Profl. in Human Resources, quality engr.; lic. USCG capt.; lic. pvt. pilot FAA. Founder, pres. Turner's Bicycle Svc., Inc., Delray Beach, Fla., 1975-80; electronics engr., quality engr. Audio Engring. and Video Arts, Boca Raton, 1980-81; tech. writing instr. Palm Beach Jr. Coll., Lake Worth, Fla., 1981-82; adminstr. tng. and devel. Mitel Inc., Boca Raton, 1982-88; mgr. communications and employee rels. Modular Computer Systems, Inc., Ft. Lauderdale, Fla., 1988-89; U.S. mktg. project mgr. Mitel, Inc., Boca Raton, 1990-91; v.p. human resources Connectronics, Inc., Ft. Lauderdale, 1991-93; sr. mgr. human resources Sensormatic Electronics Corp., Boca Raton, 1993-98, dir. human resources, 1998—2001; chief tng. officer Tyco Fire and Security Svcs., Inc., 2001—. Contbg. author Kitplanes Mag. With USCG Aux. Recipient Human Resources Profl. Excellence award Soc. Human Resource Mgmt., 1999. Mem. Soc. for Human Resource Mgmt., Internat. Assn. Quality Cirs., Am. Soc. Quality Control, Fla. Employment Mgmt. Assn., Am. Acad. Mgmt., Employment Assn. Fla., Am. Capts. Assn., Citizens Police Acad., Aircraft Owners and Pilot's Assn., Exptl. Aircraft Assn., Fla. Aero. Club. Achievements include being the first female to construct, complete and fly a pulsar XP aircraft. Home: 1358 Fairfax Cir E Boynton Beach FL 33436-8612 Office: Tyco 6600 Congress Ave Boca Raton FL 33487 E-mail: llsaturner@prodigy.net., lisaturnerl@tycoint.com.

TURNER, LLOYD DANIEL, musician; b. Hollywood, Calif., May 11, 1951; s. Lloyd Gardner and Mary Lorrina Turner. Student, Golden West Coll. With Electronic Factory, Culver City, Calif.; jazz musician Rodger Williams, Dottie Town Pipers, Lake Tahoe. Home: 19610 Sitzman Way Reseda CA 91335

TURNER, LOYD LEONARD, advertising executive, public relations executive; b. Grady, N.Mex., Nov. 5, 1917; s. James R. and Maude (Brown) T.; m. Lee Madeleine Barr, Apr. 13, 1944; children: Terry Lee, Loyd Lee. Student, Tex. Tech. U., 1935-36, Okla. Bapt. U., 1936-37; BA, Baylor U., 1939, MA, 1940; postgrad., U. Pa., 1940-42. Instr. dept. English U. Pa., Phila., 1940-42; pub. relations coordinator Consol. Vultee Aircraft Corp., San Diego, 1946-48, dir. pub. relations Fort Worth, 1948-53; asst. to pres. Fort Worth div. Gen. Dynamics Corp., 1953-72; exec. asst. to pres. and chmn. bd. Tandy Corp., Fort Worth, 1972-76, v.p., 1976-85; sr. v.p. Witherspoon and Assocs., Inc., Fort Worth, 1986-97, cons., bd. dirs., 1998—. Mem. Gov.'s Com. on Public Sch. Edn., Tex., 1966-69; pres. Tex. Council Major Sch. Dists., 1968-69 Author: The ABC of Clear Writing, 1954. Bd. dirs. Tarrant County chpt. ARC, 1956-59; bd. dirs. Pub. Communication Found. for North Tex., 1970-76, Tex. Com. Pub. Edn., 1961-69; bd. dirs. Ft. Worth Child Study Ctr., 1974-81, 85-88, v.p., 1986-88; bd. dirs. Parenting Guidance Ctr., 1976-78, Longhorn coun. Boy Scouts Am., 1976-91, One Broadway Plaza, 1978-88; planning and research coun. United Way, Tarrant County, 1976-80; bd. dirs. Casa Manana Musicals, 1978—, pres., 1978-80; bd. dirs. Fort Worth Citizens Organized Against Crime, 1976-90, vice chmn., 1978-89; bd. dirs. Jr. Achievement Tarrant County, 1982-87, North Central chpt. March of Dimes, 1983-84; mem. Christian edn. coordinating bd. Bapt. Gen. Conv., Tex., 1976-80; trustee Ft. Worth Pub. Libr. Bd., 1953-63, pres., 1958-63; trustee Ft. Worth Bd. Edn., 1959-71, pres., 1965-71; trustee Baylor U., Waco, Tex., 1980-89. Served with USAAF, 1942-46. Named Library Trustee of Yr. Tex. Library Assn., 1961; Paul Harris fellow Rotary Internat., 1983; recipient Silver Beaver award Boy Scouts Am., 1986. Mem. Pub. Relations Soc. Am. (pres. N.Tex. chpt. 1977), Pub. Rel. Soc. Am. (Paul M. Lund Pub. Service award 1980), Nat. Mgmt. Assn., Tex. Congress of Parents and Tchrs. (hon. life mem.), West Tex. C. of C. (bd. dirs. 1982-87, v.p. 1985-87, Leadership award 1966, 69), NEA (pres. Best Bd. of Large Sch. Systems in U.S. 1968), Tex. Assn. of Sch. Bds. (bd. dirs. 1966-71, Outstanding Service award 1971), Advt. Club of Fort Worth (pres. 1977-78), Air Force Assn. (Spl. citation 1962), Assn. for Higher Edn. of N. Tex. (vice chmn. 1979-82), Fort Worth C. of C. (bd. dirs. 1974-76, 78-81, 83-87, vice chmn. 1985-87), Arts Council of Fort Worth (dir. 1973-75, 80-89), Tex. Assn. Bus. (bd. dirs. 1977-82, 83-86), Tex. Research League (bd. dirs. 1979-87), Baylor U. Devel. Council (pres. 1975-77), Baylor U. Alumni Assn. (bd. dirs. 1958-61), Fort Worth Safety Council (bd. dirs. 1980-83), Am. Advt. Fedn. (Silver Medal award 1981), Soc. Profl. Journalists (pres. Fort Worth chpt. 1961-62), Am. Airlines Admirals Club, Baylor Bear Found., TCU Frog Club, Rotary (pres. 1974-75, William B. Todd Svc. Above Self award 1987). Baptist. Home: 3717 Echo Trl Fort Worth TX 76109-3432 Office: Witherspoon and Assocs Inc 1000 W Weatherford St Fort Worth TX 76102-1842

TURNER, MABEL CROUGHAN, retired microbiologist; b. Macomb, Ill., Jan. 13, 1920; d. Walter Wilson and Mary Frances (Miner) Wilson-Johnson; m. Claire Malloy Croughan, July 18, 1940 (dec.); children: Jack, Caitlin, Shelley Booth, Timothy, Mary Minihane-Croughan, Matthew; m. Hubert Edwards Turner, Jan. 16, 1996. AA, UCLA, 1939; B Arts and Sci., U. Calif., Berkeley, 1940. Cert. pub. health lab. technician, pub. health bacteriologist, clin. lab. technician, clin. lab. technologist, Dept. Health, State Calif.; cert. approval dairy bacteriology Dept. Agr., State Calif. Lab. dir. Santa Cruz (Calif.) County Hosp., 1945-46, Campbells Clin. Lab., Santa Cruz, 1946-50; clin. technologist Marin Med. Lab., San Rafael, Calif., 1954-55, 1961-66; lab. dir. Ross Gen. Hosp. Lab., Kentfield, Calif., 1955-56, Ross Valley Doctors Lab., Kentfield, 1956-57, Doctors Clin. Lab., El Dorado, Kans., 1958-61, Pub. Health Lab. Marin County, San Rafael, 1966-88; ret. Trustee Novato Unified Sch. Dist., 1973-90; cook, hostess, supr. Homeless Shelter, Presbyn. Ch., Novato, 1980; state com. on tchr. credentials State of Calif., Sacramento, 1987-89; elder, mem. nominating com. for pastor Novato Presbyn. Ch., 1992-95; liason com. Cmty. Buck Ctr. on Aging, Novato, 1994—; active Commn. on Aging, County of Marin, San Rafael, 1995-96. Named Life Member PTA and Outstanding Parent, 1954, 65, Woman of the Yr. and Woman of Distinction, Soroptimist Club, 1983, 95, Sr. Citizen of Yr., Calif. State Senate and Assembly, 1993. Achievements include co-discovery of new virus "Marin Agent" which causes diarrhea and vomiting in patients. Avocations: family activities, traveling by trailer. Home: 8 Haverhill Ct Novato CA 94947-2037

TURNER, MALCOLM ELIJAH, biomathematician, educator; b. Atlanta, May 27, 1929; s. Malcolm Elijah and Margaret (Parker) T.; m. Ann Clay Bowers, Sept. 16, 1948; children: Malcolm Elijah IV, Allison Ann, Clay Shumate, Margaret Jean; m. Rachel Patricia Farmer, Feb. 1, 1968; children: Aleta van Riper, Leila Samantha, Alexis St. John, Walter McCamy. Student, Emory U., 1947-48; BA, Duke U., 1952; M.Exptl. Stats., N.C. State U., 1955, PhD, 1959. Analytical statistician Communicable Disease Center, USPHS, Atlanta, 1953; rsch. assoc. U. Cin., 1955, asst. prof., 1955-58; asst. statistician N.C. State U., Raleigh, 1957-58; assoc. prof. Med. Coll. Va., Richmond, 1958-63, chmn. div. biometry, 1959-63; prof., chmn. dept. statistics and biometry Emory U., Atlanta, 1963-69; chmn. dept. biomath., prof. biostats. and biomath. U. Ala., Birmingham, 1970-82, prof. biostats. and biomath., 1982—, prof. emeritus biostats., 1998—. Instr. summers Yale U., 1966, U. Calif. at Berkeley, 1971, Vanderbilt U., 1975; prof. U. Kans., 1968-69; vis. prof. Atlanta U., 1969; cons. to industry. Mem. editorial bd. So. Med. Jour., 1990—; contbr. articles to profl. jours. Fellow Ala. Acad. Sci., Am. Statis. Assn. (hon.), AAAS (hon.); mem. AAUP, AMA (affiliate), Biometrics Soc. (mng. editor Biometrics 1962-69), Soc. for Indsl. and Applied Math., Mensa, Sigma Xi, Phi Kappa Phi, Phi Delta Theta, Phi Sigma. Home: 1734 Tecumseh Trl Pelham AL 35124-1012 E-mail: malcolmt@scientist.com. *The logic of induction is the quest.*

TURNER, MARGUERITE ROSE COWLES, library administrator; b. June 21, 1941; d. John Clinton and Marquerite Eileen (Slaybaugh) Cowles; 1 son, Jeffrey Jason. BA, U. New Orleans, 1963; MLS, La. State U., 1966; MA in History, U. So. Miss., 1970. Reference libr. Pascagoula (Miss.) Jr. H.S., 1970-71, Irwin County H.S., Ocilla, Ga., 1971-72; dir. Fitzgerald (Ga.) Carnegie Libr., 1974-80; adminstrv. librarian Assumption Parish Libr., Napoleonville, La., 1980-83; dir. Jacob S. Mauney meml. Libr., Kings Mountain, N.C., 1983—. Author poems, short stories; writer weekly column Kings Mountain Herald, Shelby Star; contbr. articles to profl. jours. Sunday sch. tchr., First Baptist Ch., librarian, 1975—, Fitzgerald, 1978-80, Napoleonville, 1980-83. Mem. ALA, N.C. Libr. Assn., Broad River Libr. Assn. Democrat. Republican. Office: 100 S Piedmont Ave Kings Mountain NC 28086-3414

TURNER, MARVIN WENTZ, insurance company executive; b. Lower Marion, Pa., Oct. 17, 1959; s. Gilbert Jr. and Frances (McAlister) T.; m. Julia (Davis) Turner. BBA, Howard U., 1981; postgrad., Temple U., 1984-86; MBA, George Washington U., 1988; JD, Georgetown U., 1998. Registered investment advisor; cert. fund specialist. Claim advisor Prudential Ins., Fort Washington, Pa., 1982-84; ptnr. Mgmt. Enterprise, Phila., 1984-86; analyst CNA Fin. Group, Washington, 1986-88; fin. analyst Bell Atlantic, Arlington, Va., 1988-93; CFO Local Govt. Ins. Trust, Columbia, Md., 1993—; mng. dir. Hopkins Turner Wharton, Inc., Bethesda, 1995—. Adv. bd. mem. Access Washington; ptnr. Target Group Investors, Upper Marlsboro, Md., 1990—; fin. advisor Turner Mgmt. Group, Watkins Park, Md., 1991. Ptnr. The Tucker Group, Cheverly, Md., 1990. Recipient Elizabeth B. Adams Meml. award George Washington U., 1988, minority fellowship, 1987. Mem. Nat. Black MBA Assn. (exec. bd. D.C. chpt., treas. 1988-90, v.p. 1992-94), Fin. Exec. Inst. Home: 13300 Burleigh St Uppr Marlboro MD 20774-1960 Office: Fin Assets Capital LLC 1201 Pennsylvania Ave NW Washington DC 20004-2401

TURNER, MARY JANE, educational administrator; b. Colorado Springs, Colo., June 1, 1923; d. David Edward and Ina Mabel (Campbell) Nickelson; m. Harold Adair Turner, Feb. 15, 1945 (dec.); children: Mary Ann, Harold Adair III. BA in Polit. Sci., U. Colo., 1947, MPA in Pub. Adminstrn., 1968, PhD in Polit. Sci., 1978. Secondary tchr. Canon City (Colo.) Sch. Dist., 1950-53; tchr. assoc. in polit. sci. U. Colo., Denver, 1968-70, Boulder, 1970-71; rsch. asst. Social Sci. Edn. Consortium, 1971, staff assoc., 1972-77; dir. Colo. Legal Edn. Program, 1977-84; assoc. dir. Ctr. for Civic Edn., Calabasas, Calif., 1984-88; dir. Close Up Found., Alexandria, Va., 1988-92, sr. edn. advisor Arlington, 1992—. Author: Political Science in the New Social Studies, 1972; co-author: American Government: Principles and Practices, 1983, 4th edit., 1996, Law in the Classroom, 1984, Civics: Citizens in Action, 1986, 2d edit., 1991, U.S. Government Resource Book, 1989; contbg. author: Internat. Ency. Dictionary of Edn., 2000. Chair curriculum com. Idaho State Bar Found., 2000—. Recipient Isadore Starr award for spl. achievement in law-related edn. ABA, 1997. Mem. Nat. Coun. for Social Studies (chair nominations 1983-84, chair bicentennial com. 1986), Social Sci. Edn. Consortium (pres. 1986-87, bd. dirs. 1984-87, 99—), Pi Lambda Theta, Pi Sigma Alpha. Democrat. Presbyterian. Office: Close Up Found 44 Canal Center Plz Alexandria VA 22314-1592 E-mail: turnermj@dmi.net.

TURNER, MAX ALLEN, career officer, chemical engineer; b. Cordell, Okla., Sept. 7, 1918; s. Jacob Allen and Rosa Cordelia (Anderson) T.; m. Grace Ava Dinsmore (dec. 1947); children: Brenda Sue Lamkins, Donna Rose Ahrens; m. Ethel Beatrice Danyeur Sexton, July 30, 1995. BSChemE, U. Okla., 1944; MSChemE, Georgia Tech., 1949; MBA, U. Houston, 1980. Reg.

profl. engr., Tex. From 2d lt. to lt. col. (ret.) U.S. Air Force, 1943-71; weather officer Army Air Corps., 1943-48; chem. engr. Naval Ordinance Test Sta., Calif., 1951-52; engr. Oak Ridge (Tenn.) Nat. Lab., 1952-55, Boeing Airplane, Wichita, Kans., 1955-57; nuclear engr. Babcock & Wilcox Co., Lynchburg, Va., 1957-60; aerospace engr. GE, Houston, King of Prussia, Pa., 1960-71; engr. Brown & Root, Houston, 1971-72, Todd Rsch. Tech., Galveston, Tex., 1973-75; asst. prof. U. Houston, 1975-92; engr. Tex. Nat. Resource Conservation Com., Austin, 1992-98. Mem. AIChE, AIAA, Instrument Soc. Am. Democrat. Avocation: internet. Home and Office: 5151 Buffalo Speedway #4123 Houston TX 77005 E-mail: max.turner@sbcglobal.net.

TURNER, MEGAN WHALEN, author; b. Fort Sill, Okla., Nov. 21, 1965; d. Donald Peyton and Nora Courtenay (Green) Whalen; m. Mark Bernard Turner, June 20, 1987; children: John Whalen, Donald Peyton. BA in English Lang. and Lit. with honors, U. Chgo., 1987. Buyer children's books Harper Court Bookstore, Chgo., 1988-89, Bick's Books, Washington, 1991-92. Author: Instead of Three Wishes, 1995, The Thief, 1996 (Newbery Honor award 1997), The Queen of Attolia, 2000. Mem. Authors' Guild. Address: care Greenwillow Books 1350 Ave of the Ams New York NY 10019

TURNER, MICHAEL STANLEY, astrophysics educator; b. L.A., July 29, 1949; s. Paul Joseph and Janet Mary (Lindholm) T.; m. Terri Lee Shields, Aug. 1978 (div. Sept. 1980); m. Barbara Lynn Ahlberg, Sept. 10, 1988; children: Rachel Mary, Joseph Lucien. BS in Physics, Calif. Inst. Tech., 1971; MS in Physics, Stanford U., 1973, PhD in Physics, 1978. Enrico Fermi fellow U. Chgo., 1978-80, from asst. to assoc. prof. physics and astronomy and strophysics, 1980-85, prof., 1985—, chmn. dept. astronomy and astrophysics, 1997—, Bruce V. and Diana M. Rauner Disting. Svc. prof., 1998—; scientist Fermi Nat. Accelerator Lab., Batavia, Ill., 1983—. Trustee Aspen (Colo.) Ctr. Physics, 1984—97, pres., 1989—93; Halley lectr. Oxford U., 1994; Klopsteg lectr. Am. Assn. Physics Tchrs., 1999; Neils Bohr lectr. Copenhagen U., 2001. Author: (with E.W. Kolb) The Early Universe, 1990; contbr. over 200 articles to profl. jours. Bd. trustees Ill. Math. Sci. Acad., 1998—. Sloan fellow A.P. Sloan Found., 1983-88, W. Paul fellow Bonn U., 2000. Fellow Am. Acad. Arts and Scis., Am. Phys. Soc. (mem. exec. bd. 1992-94, chmn. publ. oversight com. 1993-94, chmn. nominating com. 1999-2000, Lilienfeld prize 1997); mem. NAS (NRC astronomy astrophysics survey com. 1998-2000, chair NRC com. Physics of Universe, 2000-02), Am. Astron. Soc. (Helen B. Warner prize 1984), Internat. Astron. Union, Sigma Xi. Office: U Chgo Astron & Astrophysics Ctr 5640 S Ellis Ave Chicago IL 60637-1433 E-mail: mturner@oddjob.uchicago.edu.

TURNER, MICHAEL D. chemical engineer; b. Cleve., July 17, 1967; s. Thomas J Turner, Carol J Jespersen; m. Jean L Smith; children: Dane, Liam, Rebecca. BS in Physics, U. Wis. - Parkside, Kenosha, 1988. Chemist Abbott Labs., Abbott Park, Ill., 1995—2000; engr. Becton Dickinson and Co., Franklin, Wis., 2000—. Home: 7410 - 14th Ave Kenosha WI 53143 Office Fax: 414-423-6960. Personal E-mail: turnermd@nomad.net. Business E-Mail: Mike_Turner@BD.com.

TURNER, NANCY DELANE, nutritionist, educator, researcher; b. Atlanta, Nov. 8, 1956; d. Pheron Oclesia and Dicie Ethel (Kent) T. Student, Emory U., 1974-75; BS, Tex. A&M U., 1978, MS, 1984, PhD, 1995. Cert. nutrition specialist. Student tech. Tex. A&M U., College Station, 1980-84, rsch. assoc., 1984-95, asst. rsch. scientist, 1996-98, rsch. asst. prof., 1998—. Freelance cons., manuscript editor, College Station, 1986—; ptnr. O.O.C. Cons.; assoc. mem. Interdisciplinary Fac. Nutrition, 1996—, exec. coun., 2001—, assoc. head, 2002--, Interdisciplinary Fac. Toxicology, 2001—. Contbr. chpts. to books, abstracts and articles to refereed publs.; mem. editl. bd. Jour. Animal Sci., 1999-2002; ad hoc reviewer Bioresource Tech., 1995-2002, Jour. Nutrition, 1997—, Jour. Animal Sci., 1998-99, Am. Jour. Clin. Nutrition, 2000—, Nutrition and Cancer, 2000—, Alcohol, 2002—, Biochinica et Biophysica Acta, 2002—; assoc. editor Am. Soc. Nutrition Scis. Nutrition Notes. Judge Brazos Valley Sci. Fair, 1998—; mem. pub. rels. com. Bryan/College Sta. chpt. Habitat for Humanity, 1998—2002. Recipient Ethel Ashworth-Tsutsui Meml. award for mentoring, 1998; Dan. F. Jones Meml. scholar Tex. A&M U., 1990. Mem. AAAS, Am. Soc. Animal Sci., Am. Assn. Cereal Chemists, N.Y. Acad. Scis., Soc. Exptl. Biology and Medicine, Am. Soc. Nutritional Scis., Am. Physiol. Soc., Microscopy Soc. Am., Sigma Xi, Gamma Sigma Delta. Achievements include definition of phys. mechanism whereby structure modifications in response to new ammonia treatment increases digestibility of fibrous material and grain for ruminants; rsch. in defining physiol. mechanisms of altered tissue and bone growth patterns in transgenic mice; the role of fiber, fat and phytochemicals in colon cancer etiology. Office: Tex A&M U Dept Animal Sci Human Nutrition Sect 218 Kleberg 2471 Tamu College Station TX 77843-2471 E-mail: nancy-turner@ansc.tamu.edu.

TURNER, NANCY ELAINE, writer; b. Dallas, Nov. 20, 1953; d. Stanley Edward and Wahnemia Jo (Belcher) Groves; m. John Charles Turner; children: April E. Bracht, John Sterling. BFA, U. Ariz., 1999. Instr. fiction writing Pima C.C., Tucson, 2001. Author: These Is My Words, 1998 (Ariz. Adult Author of Yr., Ariz. Libr. Assn., 1999, nominated Pulitzer prize, 1998), The Water and the Blood, 2001. Avocations: piano, ceramics, painting. Office: PO Box 685 Sanders AZ 86512

TURNER, PAMELA, psychologist; b. Glen Ridge, N.J., Aug. 29, 1952; d. Warren H. and Lucille M. Turner. BS in Math., Bucknell U., 1974; MS in Computer Sci., Rutgers U., 1978; MA in Psychology, Columbia U., 1986, EdD in Psychology, 1992. Lic. psychologist, N.J. Sr. tech. assoc. Bell Labs., Holmdel-West Long Branch, N.J., 1974-80, mem. tech. staff West Long Branch, 1981-83, Bell Comm. Rsch., Piscataway and Red Bank, N.J., 1984-88, orgnl. devel. specialist Morristown, 1989-90; intern U. Ga. Counseling and Testing Ctr., Athens, 1990-91; psychotherapist Advanced Psychol. Svcs., Freehold, NJ, 1993-96; staff psychologist Kimball Med. Ctr.-St. Barnabas Behavioral Health, Toms River, 1997—; psychologist in pvt. practice Jackson, 1996—. Adj. asst. prof. Columbia U. Tchrs. Coll., N.Y.C., 1994-95 Singer: Monmouth Civic Chorus, 1975—97; soloist: Brookdale C.C. Opera, 1986, soloist: Athens (Ga.) Choral Soc., 1990—91; singer: Met. Singers/Greek Choral Soc., 1989—97, Jackson Summer Theater, 2000, Jackson Civic Chorus, 1999—, Jackson Civic Chamber Ensemble, 2000—. Cmty. lectr. Monmouth and Ocean Counties, NJ, 1993—; mem. drug and alcohol abuse adv. com. Jackson Twp. Bd. Edn., 1997; mem. Jackson Twp. Mcpl. Alliance for Prevention of Alcohol and Drug Abuse, 1996—98; mem. Jackson Twp. Youth Adv. Bd., 1997—98; mem. founding bd. Jackson (NJ) Coun. for Arts, 1998—, chair, 2002—. Mem.: APA, N.J. Psychol. Assn., East Coast Regional Dressage Assn. (newsletter editor 1997—). Avocations: singing, horses, desktop publishing. Office: Jackson Psychology and Wellness Ctr PO Box 752 Jackson NJ 08527 E-mail: jpwc@monmouth.com.

TURNER, PATRICIA, retired librarian; b. Indpls., June 17, 1928; d. Clarence and W. Marie (Jarrett) T. BA, Butler U., 1950; MA, Ind. U., 1960; cert. of specialist, U. Minn., 1977. Librarian Indpls. Pub. Libr., 1956-60, N.Y. Pub. Libr., N.Y.C., 1960-63; humanities librarian U. Ariz., Tucson, 1963-66, 68-70; reference libr., bibliographer U. Minn., Mpls., 1967-69, 74-94, ret., 1994. Author: Afro-American Singers: An Index and Preliminary Discography of Opera, Choral Music and Song, 1977, Dictionary of Afro-American Performers: 78 RPM and Cylinder Recordings of Opera, Choral Music, and Songs c. 1900-1949, 1990; contbr. articles to profl. jours. Bd. dirs. Schubert Club. Grantee U.S. Dept. of Edn., 1966. Mem. Assn. of Recorded Sound Collections, Nat. Assn. of Negro Musicians (Disting. Contbn. award 1992), Beta Phi Mu. Episcopalian. Avocations: discographer, book collector. Home: 325 E 10th St Indianapolis IN 46202-3315

TURNER, PATRICK NOEL WADDINGTON, fund manager; b. Burnham, Eng., Mar. 31, 1960; came to U.S., 1981; s. Noel Walter and Shirley (Vaughn) T.; m. Hilary Jennifer Cosell, Sept. 18, 1982 (div. Dec. 1989); 1 child, Payton; m. Amber Lea Bohmfalk, Feb. 2, 1991; children: Benton, Lily. BA with honours, Oxford (Eng.) U., 1981, MA with honours, 1982; MBA in Fin., NYU, 1988. Asst. treas. Bankers Trust Co., N.Y.C., 1981-84; v.p. Marine Midland Bank, 1984-89; dir. Barclays Bank PLL, 1989-95; mng. ptnr. Canterbury Mezzanine Capital LP, 1985—. Bd. dirs. LV Environ., N.Y., True Temper Sports, Tenn. Treas., trustee Manhattan Sch. Music, N.Y.C., 1998—. Mem. Racquet and Tennis Club, Creek Club, Tuxedo Club. Episcopalian. Avocations: cello, golf, skiing, tennis, charities. Office: Canterbury Mezzanine Capital 600 Fifth Ave 23d Fl New York NY 10020

TURNER, PEGGY ANN, graphic designer, visual artist, educator; b. Memphis, Jan. 17, 1951; d. James Patrick and Margaret Helen (Brastock) T. BFA, U. Tenn., 1974, MFA summa cum laude, 1992. Art dir. Turner Design, Knoxville, 1972-84; designer, illustrator Creative Displays, 1974-75; designer alumni affairs U. Tenn., 1975-81; sr. art dir. Whittle Comm., 1982-85; creative dir. Sullivan-St. Clair Advt., Mobile, Ala., 1985-89; grad. teaching asst. dept. art U. Tenn., Knoxville, 1989-91; prof. graphic design Savannah (Ga.) Coll. Art and Design, 1991-92; asst. prof. graphic design Va. Polytechnic Inst. and State U., 1992-96; owner True G.R.I.T. Graphics Inc., Paper Whites Custom Invitations, 1996-99; assoc. prof. Tusculum Coll., Greeneville, Tenn., 1999-2000; adj. prof. Pellissippi State Tech. C.C., Knoxville, 1999-2000. Assoc. faculty Tusculum Coll., Knoxville and Greeneville, Tenn.; adj. faculty Pellissippi St. Tech. C.C.; sr. lectr. Wanganui Sch. of Design, Wanganui, New Zealand, 2000—. Solo exhbns. include S. Morris Gallery, Savannah, 1992, Ewing Gallery, Knoxville, 1992, Armory Art Gallery, Va. Poly. Inst. and State U., 1993, Gallery 303, Ga. So. U., 1994, Littman-White Gallery, Portland (Oreg.) State U., 1996, Allison Gallery, Tusculum Coll., Greeneville, Tenn., 1999; group shows include Women's Art Works III, Rochester, N.Y. (jury prize), Nat. Expos II, Chgo., 1993, Current Works '93, Kansas City, Mo., U. West Fla., 1994, Paper Stars, San Francisco, 1994, Nat. Exposures, Winston-Salem, N.C. Recipient nat. citation Coun. for Advancement Edn., 1981, award Warren Paper Co., 1984; Fred M. Roddy scholar, 1970, Blinn scholar for fgn. study, 1991; grantee Va. Poly. Inst. and State U., 1992, 93, Women's Rsch. Inst., 1993, 95. Mem. Alpha Lambda Delta. Democrat. Episcopalian. Avocations: world hunger, women's rights, art censorship. Office: Wanganui Sch Design Pvt Bag 3020 Wanganui New Zealand E-mail: peg@mail.cgd.whanganui.ac.nz.

TURNER, PETER MERRICK, retired manufacturing company executive; b. Toronto, Ont., Can., July 4, 1931; s. William Ian MacKenzie and Marjorie (Merrick) T.; m. Beverley Brophey, Sept. 13, 1958 (dec.); children: Peter Merrick, Christopher Harold, David MacKenzie; m. Alix Johanna Houston, Aug. 17, 1991 (div. 1999). BASc, U. Toronto, 1954; MBA, Harvard U., 1956. Staff asst. controllers dept. Bridgeport Brass Co., Conn., 1956-57; sec. treas. Perkins Paper Products Co., Montreal, Que., Can., 1957-58; with Texaco Can. Ltd., 1958-68, treas., 1966-68; dir. budgeting and planning, corp. devel. Molson Breweries Ltd., 1968—; v.p. planning Molson Breweries Can. Ltd., 1968-70; v.p. corp. devel. Molson Industries Ltd., Toronto, 1970-72; exec. v.p. Bennett Pump Inc., Muskegon, Mich., 1972-73, pres., chief exec. officer, 1973-78; v.p. corp. planning and devel. Sealed Power Corp., 1978-83, group v.p. internat., 1981-83, group v.p. Gen. Products Group, 1984-89; v.p. bus. devel. SPX Corp., 1989-91, v.p. ops., 1991-92, v.p. corp. planning and devel., 1992-94; ret., 1994; vice chmn. Bennett Pump Co., 1998—. Lectr. extension dept. McGill U., 1960-67, Grand Valley State Coll., 1979 Gen. chmn. red shield appeal Montreal Salvation Army, 1969-70; chmn. McGill Assocs., Montreal, 1969-70; bd. dirs. Hackley Hosp., 1975-94, West Shore Symphony Orch., 1976-94; bd. dirs. Muskegon C.C. Found., 1976-94. Mem. Mount Royal Club, Granite Club, Lake O'Hara Trail Club, Zeta Psi. Episcopalian. Home: 4292 E Glen Ct Muskegon MI 49441-4587

TURNER, PHILIP MICHAEL, university official and dean, author; b. West Acton, Mass., Nov. 26, 1948; s. William Albert and Evelyn Olena (Peterson) T.; m. Lis Jane VanderBeke, Aug. 16, 1969; children: Gabrielle, Adrienne. BS in Edn., Boston State Coll., 1970; MS, U. Wis. at La Crosse, 1972; MSLS, EdD, East Tex. State U., 1977. Tchr. math. Edgewood Jr. High Sch., Merritt Island, Fla., 1969-71; ptnr. Video Guide Prodn. Co., Denver, 1973; libr. media specialist Edison Jr. High Sch., Green Bay, Wis., 1973-76; prof. libr. sci. U. Ala., Tuscaloosa, 1977-88; dean Sch. Libr. and Info. Studies U. North Tex., Denton, 1996—; asst. vice chancellor acad. affairs U. Ala. System, 1991-96; assoc. v.p. for acad. affairs for distance edn. U. North Tex., Denton, 1996—. Author: Handbook for In-School Media Personnel, 1980, Helping Teachers Teach, 1985, 2d edit., 1993. Vol. Meals on Wheels, Tuscaloosa, 1987-96. Recipient Outstanding Commitment To Teaching award U. Ala. Alumni Assn., 1979, Outstanding Svc. award Ala. Libr. and Media Prodrs., 1987, publ. award Div. Sch. Libr. Media Specialist, 1987, award for mng. info. tech., 1994, Ala. Libr. Assn. Disting. Svc. award, 1996; named Libr. of Yr., Beta Phi Mu, 1991. Mem. ALA, Assn. Sch. Librs. (chair rsch. com. 1987-90, bd. dirs. 1990-94), Assn. for Ednl. Comm. and Tech. (chair evaluation com. 1979). Unitarian Universalist. Office: U North Tex Sch Libr and Info Scis PO Box 311068 Denton TX 76203-1068 E-mail: pturner@unt.edu.

TURNER, RALPH HERBERT, sociologist, educator; b. Effingham, Ill., Dec. 15, 1919; s. Herbert Turner and Hilda Pearl (Bohn) T.; m. Christine Elizabeth Hanks, Nov. 2, 1943; children: Lowell Ralph, Cheryl Christine. BA, U So. Calif., 1941, MA, 1942; postgrad., U. Wis., 1942-43; PhD, U. Chgo., 1948. Rsch. assoc. Am. Coun. Race Relations, 1947-48; faculty UCLA, 1948—, prof. sociology and anthropology, 1959-90, prof. emeritus, 1990—, chmn. dept. sociology, 1963-68; chmn. Acad. Senate U. Calif. System, 1983-84. Vis. summer prof. U. Wash., 1960 , U. Hawaii, 1962; vis. scholar Australian Nat. U., 1972; vis. prof. U. Ga., 1975, Ben Gurion U., Israel, 1983; vis. fellow Nuffield Coll. Oxford U., 1980; disting. vis. prof. Am. U., Cairo, Egypt, 1983; adj. prof. China Acad. Social Scis., Beijing, People's Republic China, 1986. Author: (with L. Killian) Collective Behavior, 1957, 2d edit., 1972, 3d edit., 1987, The Social Context of Ambition, 1964, Robert Park on Social Control and Collective Behavior, 1967, Family Interaction, 1970, Earthquake Prediction and Public Policy, 1975, (with J. Nigg, D. Paz, B. Young) Community Response to Earthquake Threat in So. Calif., 1980, (with J. Nigg and D. Paz) Waiting for Disaster, 1986; editl. cons., 1959-62; editor: Sociometry, 1962-64; acting editor: Ann. Rev. of Sociology, 1977-78; assoc. editor, 1978-79, editor, 1980-86; adv. editor: Am. Jour. Sociology, 1954-56, Sociology and Social Rsch., 1961-74; editl. staff: Am. Sociol. Rev., 1955-56; assoc. editor: Social Problems, 1959-62, 67-69; cons. editor: Sociol. Inquiry, 1968-73, Western Sociol. Rev., 1975-79; mem. editl. bd. Mass Emergencies, 1975-79, Internat. Jour. Crit. Sociology, 1974-76, Symbolic Interaction, 1977-90, 95—, Mobilization, 1996—. Mem. behavioral scis. study sect. NIH, 1961-66, chmn., 1963-64; dir.-at-large Social Sci. Rsch. Coun., 1965-66; chmn. panel on pub. policy implications of earthquake predictions Nat. Acad. Scis., 1974-75, also mem. earthquake study del. to Peoples Republic of China, 1976; mem. policy adv. bd. So. Calif. Earthquake Preparedness program, 1987-92, mem. com. social edn. and action L.A. Presbytery, 1954-56. Served to lt. (j.g.) USNR, 1943-46. Recipient Faculty prize Coll. Letters and Scis. UCLA, 1985; Faculty Rsch. fellow Social Sci. Rsch. Coun., 1953-56; Sr. Fulbright scholar U.K., 1956-57; Guggenheim fellow, U.K., 1964-65; Faculty Rsch. lectr. UCLA, 1987, UCLA Emeritus of Yr., 1997. Mem. AAAS (exch. del. to China 1988), AAUP, Am. Sociol. Assn. (coun. 1959-64, chmn. social psychology sect. 1960-61, pres. 1968-69, chmn. sect. theoretical sociology 1973-74, chmn. collective behavior and social movements sect. 1983-84, Cooley-Mead award 1987), Pacific Sociol. Assn. (pres. 1957), Internat. Sociol. Assn. (coun. 1974-82, v.p. 1978-82), Soc. Study Social Problems (exec. com. 1962-63), Soc. for Study Symbolic Interaction (pres. 1982-83, Charles Horton Cooley award 1978, George Herbert Mead award 1990), Sociol. Rsch. Assn. (pres. 1989-90), Am. Coun. of Learned Soc. (exec. com. of coun. 1990-93), UCLA Emeriti Assn. (coun. , pres. 1992-93), U. of Calif. Emeriti Assns. (chair-elect 1996-97, chair 1997-98, Panunzio award 2002). Home: 1126 Chautauqua Blvd Pacific Palisades CA 90272-3808 Office: UCLA 405 Hilgard Ave Los Angeles CA 90095-9000

TURNER, RALPH JAMES, obstetrician, gynecologist; b. Waco, Tex., 1952; BS, McMurry U., 1974, BA, 1976; MD, U. Tex. Southwestern, Dallas, 1978. Cert. in med. mgmt. Am. Coll. Physician Exec., Tulane U., 1996, diplomate Am. Coll. Physician Execs.; diplomate Am. Bd. Ob-Gyn. Intern Tripler Army Med. Ctr., Honolulu, 1978-79, resident ob-gyn., 1979-82; ob-gyn. Darnall U.S. Army Cmty. Hosp., Ft. Hood, Tex., 1982-86, Presbyn. Hosp., Dallas, 1986—. Trustee Genesis Physicians Group, 1992—, chmn. 1997—; ob-gyn. Columbia Med. Ctr., Plano, Tex., 1994—, Presbyn. Hosp., Plano, 1994—; med. adminstr., interim med. dir. Sys. Health Providers Inc., 1995-97, 99—; bd. dirs. Found. Am. Assn. Gynecol. Laparoscopists, Santa Fe Springs, Calif., 1996-2001; presenter in field. Contbr. articles to profl. jours. Exec. dir. Found. of Am. Assn. Gynecol. Laparoscopists, 2001—. Mem. ACOG, Am. Assn. Gynecol. Laparoscopists (bd. trustees 2001—), Am. Coll. Physician Execs., Am. Inst. Ultrasound in Medicine, Am. Soc. for Reproductive Medicine. Methodist. Office: 8160 Walnut Hill Ln Ste 324 Dallas TX 75231-4391 also: Ste 101 1600 Colt Rd Plano TX 75075

TURNER, RAYMOND EDWARD, science educator, researcher, administrator; b. Portsmouth, Va., Dec. 13, 1948; s. Vernon and Kate Alicia (Ely) T.; m. Merlene Jeanette Blackett, Aug. 12, 1972 (div. June 1982); 1 child, Ebony Elysia; m. Margaret Elizabeth Alleyne, May 25, 1985. BS in Chemistry, Bklyn. Coll., 1974; MS, Fordham U., 1982; MS, PhD, Poly. U., Bklyn., 1986; postgrad., Harvard U., 1997. Rsch. technician Cornell U. Med. Sch., 1974-79; rsch. worker Columbia U. Med. Sch., 1979-81; postdoctoral fellow Sch. of Pub. Health Harvard U., Boston, 1987-88; prof. math. and chemistry Roxbury C.C., 1987-94, assoc. dean math., sci. and tech., 1995-98, exec. dean of sci., media and info. technology, 1999—. Author: (textbook) Developing Concepts in Science, 1991, rev. 2d edit., 1994. Major MSC, USAR, Vietnam. Vis. scholar Harvard U., 1997—. Mem. Am. Chem. Soc., Sigma Xi. Methodist. Achievements include research on the solution properties of hyaluronic acid oligosaccharides. Office: Roxbury Cmty Coll 1234 Columbus Ave Boston MA 02120-3423

TURNER, RICHARD L. retired computer software engineer; b. Kniman, Ind., Jan. 2, 1938; s. Lewis Lee and Amy T.; m. Judith A. Turner, Dec. 14, 1963; children: John, Nora. BS, Purdue U., 1960; MBA, U. Chgo., 1965. Industl. engr. U.S. Steel, Gary, Ind., 1960-63, computer system analyst Pitts., 1963-68; compute software engr. Goodyear T. & R., Akron, Ohio, 1968-87, engr. mgr. Luxembourg, 1987-88, info. tech. regional engr. N.Am., 1988-00; retired, 2000. Contbr. articles to profl. jours. Member MENSA (editor 1995—, recipient 6 publication awards), Intertel. Avocation: RV travel, reading. Home: 889 Martindale Dr Tallmadge OH 44278-2974

TURNER, ROBERT ALEXANDER, JR. rheumatologist, consultant; b. Englewood, N.J. s. Robert Alexander and Marie Antoinette (Fensterer) T.; m. Florence McGowan, June 25, 1960; children: John, Kathryn, Andrew. AB in English, U. N.C., 1959; MD, Med. Coll. Ala., 1966. Intern and resident in internal mediicne N.C. Bapt. Hosp., Winston-Salem, N.C., 1966-69; fellow in rheumatology U. Pa. Hosp., Phila., 1969-71; from asst. prof. to prof. medicine and rheumatology Bowman Gray Sch. Medicine, Winston-Salem, 1971-89; med. dir. The Arthritis Ctr., West Palm Beach, Fla., 1990—; clin. prof. medicine, divsn. rheumatology U. South Fla., Dept. Internal Medicine, Tampa, 1990-97; pres. Turner Arthritis Assocs., West Palm Beach, 1990—; clin. prof. medicine and rheumatology Nova Southeastern U., Ft. Lauderdale, Fla., 1998—. Co-editor: Textbook of Rheumatology, 1986; contbr. articles to profl. jours. Fellow ACP, Am. Coll. Rheumatology (founding, pres. southeast region 1989); mem. Soc. Exptl. Biology and Medicine, So. Soc. Clin. Investigation, Am. Soc. Internal Medicine, Fla. Soc. Internal Medicine, Palm Beach County Med. Soc. (com. of editors 1990-94). Avocations: opera, windsurfing, teaching, medical writing, clinical research. Office: The Arthritis Ctr 2151 45th St Ste 203 West Palm Beach FL 33407-2009

TURNER, ROBERT COMRIE, composer; b. Montreal, Que., Can., June 6, 1920; s. William Thomson and Myrtle Wellsteed (Snowdon) T.; m. Sara Nan Scott, June 30, 1949; children: Alden, Martin, Carolyn. BM, McGill U., 1943, MusD, 1953; postgrad., Royal Coll. Music, 1947-48; MusM, George Peabody Coll. Tchrs., 1950. Sr. music producer Canadian Broadcasting Corp., Vancouver, B.C., 1952-68; lectr. music U. B.C., 1955-57; asst. prof. music Acadia U., Wolfville, N.S., Can., 1968-69; prof. composition U. Manitoba, Winnipeg, 1969-85, prof. emeritus, 1985—. Composer-in-residence MacDowell Colony, Peterborough, N.H., 1987. Over 70 compositions including Opening Night: A Theatre Overture, 1955, The Third Day (Easter Cantata), 1962, Symphony for Strings, 1960, Capriccio Concertante, 1975, Third String Quartet, 1975, opera The Brideship, 1967, Trio (transition) for Violin Cello and Piano, 1969, The Phoenix and the Turtle, 1964, Concerto for Two Pianos and Orchestra, 1971, Johann's Gift to Christmas, 1972, Eidolons, 1972, Variations on The Prairie Settler's Song, 1974, From a Different Country, 1976, Lament for Linos, 1978, Amoroso Canto, 1978, Shadow Pieces (after Joseph Cornell), 1981, opera Vile Shadows, 1983, Symphony in One Movement, 1983, Encounters I-IX, 1984, Time for Three, 1985, Playhouse Music, 1986, Concerto for Viola and Orchestra, 1987, Shades of Autumn, 1987, Manitoba Memoir, 1989, Third Symphony, 1990, a Group of Seven, 1991, The River of Time, 1994, House of Shadows, 1994, Four "Last Songs", 1995, Festival Dance, 1997, Diverti-Memento for Chamber Orch., 1997; All-Turner concert, 1989, Canada House, London; com. mem. Vancouver Internat. Festival; adjudicator Met. and San Francisco Opera auditions; Bramwell Tovey and The Winnipeg Symphony Orch. premiered The River of Time for SATB chorus and orch. in celebration of Robert Turner's 75th yr., 1996. Served with Royal Can. Air Force, 1943-45. Recipient Commemorative medal for 125th Anniversary of Confedn. of Can., 1993; overseas scholar Royal Coll. Music, 1947-48; fellow Can. Coun., 1966-67; grantee Man. Arts Coun., 1982-83, 85, Can. Coun. Artists, 1990-92. Mem. Soc. Composers, Authors and Music Pubrs. of Can., Can. League Composers, Can. Music Ctr., MacDowell Colony. Home: 1725 Beach Dr Victoria BC Canada V8R 6H9

TURNER, ROBERT EDWARD, psychiatrist, educator; b. Hamilton, Ont., Can., June 8, 1926; s. Robert William and Alice May (Johnson) T.; m. Gene Anne Stewart, Sept. 27, 1952; children: Margaret, John, Robert, Richard. BA with honors in Zoology and Chemistry, McMaster U., 1948; MD, U. Toronto, 1952. Intern Hamilton Gen. Hosp., 1952-53; resident Bristol (Eng.) Mental Hosps. Group, 1953-55; practice medicine specializing in psychiatry Toronto, Ont.; dir. Forensic Clinic Toronto Psychiat. Hosp., 1958-66; sr. psychiatrist forensic service Clarke Inst. Psychiatry, Toronto, 1966, chief forensic service, 1967-69, med. dir., 1969-76; asst. prof. dept. psychiatry U. Toronto, 1964-68, prof., 1973-77, prof. forensic psychiatry, 1977-91, prof. emeritus, 1991—. Cons. in psychiatry Law Reform Commn. Can., 1972-85; staff psychiatrist, 1977—; dir. Met. Toronto Forensic Service, 1977-87; hon. cons. Clarke Inst. Psychiatry, 1991—. Author: Pedophilia and Exhibitionism, 1964; contbr. articles on psychiatry and law to profl. jours. Pres. Kenneth G. Gray Found., 1971—; mem. legal task force Com. on Mental Health Svcs. for Ont., Ont. Coun. Health, 1978-79; dep. warden Cathedral Ch. of St. James, Toronto, 1978-79, 92-94, rector's warden, 1994-96; bd. dirs. Clin. Inst. Addiction Rsch. foun. Ont., 1973-86, chmn., 1985-86; bd. dirs. Addiction Rsch. Found., 1982-86. Fellow Royal Coll. Physicians and Surgeons Can., Am. Psychiat. Assn. (life), Can. Psychiat. Assn. (life, bd. dirs. 1974-77), Ont. Psychiat. Assn. (life, pres. 1975-76), Can. Med. Assn., Ont. Med. Assn., Med.-Legal Soc. Toronto (coun. 1979-82). Home: 301 1387 Bayview Ave Toronto ON Canada M4G 3A5 Office: U Toronto Dept Psychiatry 250 College St Toronto ON Canada M5T 1R8 E-mail: dr_turner@rogers.com.

TURNER, ROBERT FOSTER, law educator, former government official, writer; b. Atlanta, Feb. 14, 1944; s. Edwin Witcher and Martha Frances (Williams) T. AB, Ind. U., Bloomington, 1968; postgrad., Stanford U., 1972-73; JD, U. Va., 1981, SJD, 1996. Bar: Va. 1982, U.S. Supreme Ct. 1986. Rsch. assoc., pub. affairs fellow Hoover Instn. on War, Revolution and Peace, Stanford U., 1971-74; spl. asst., legis. asst. U.S. Sen. Robert P. Griffin, 1974-79; assoc. dir. Ctr. for Nat. Security Law U. Va., Charlottesville, 1981, 87—; sr. fellow, 1985-86; spl. asst. undersec. for policy Dept. Def., 1981-82; counsel Pres.'s Intelligence Oversight Bd., White House, 1982-84; prin. dep. asst. sec. for legis. and intergovtl. affairs Dept. State, 1984-85; pres. U.S. Inst. Peace, Washington, 1986-87; lectr. in law and in govt. and fgn. affairs U. Va., Charlottesville, 1988-93, assoc. prof., 1993-97, prof., 1997—; Charles H. Stockton prof. internat. law Naval War Coll., 1994-95. Disting. lectr. U.S. Mil. Acad., West Point, 1995. Author: Myths of the Vietnam War: The Pentagon Papers Reconsidered, 1972, Vietnamese Communism: Its Origins and Development, 1975, The War Powers Resolution: Its Implementation in Theory and Practice, 1983, Nicaragua v. United States: A Look at the Facts, 1987, Repealing the War Powers Resolution: Restoring the Rule of Law in U.S. Foreign Policy, 1991, The ABM Treaty and the Senate: Issues of International and Constitutional Law, 1999, The Real Lessons of the Vietnam War, 2002, The Jefferson-Hemings Controversy, 2002, (with John Norton Moore) The Legal Structure of Defense Organization, 1986, International Law and the Brezhnev Doctrine, 1987, Readings on International Law, 1995, (with John Norton Moore and Frederick Tipson) National Security Law, 1990, (with John Norton Moore and Guy B. Roberts) National Security Law Documents, 1995; contbr. articles to profl. jours. and newspapers. Pres. Endowment of U.S. Inst. Peace, 1986-87; trustee Intercollegiate Studies Inst., 1986-92; bd. dirs.

Thomas Jefferson Inst. for Pub. Policy, 1997—; chmn. scholars commn. on Jefferson-Hemings matter Thomas Jefferson Heritage Soc., 2000-01 Grantee Hoover Press, 1972, Earhart Found., 1980, 1989-90, Inst. Ednl. Affairs, 1980, Carthage Found., 1980. Mem. ABA (chmn. com. on exec.-congl. rels., sec. internat. law and practice 1983-86, adv. com. on law and nat. security 1984-86, standing com. on law and nat. security 1986-92, chmn. 1989-92, editor ABA Nat. Security Law Report 1992-99), Federalist Soc. (chmn. subcom. on nat. security law 1998—), Bd. Rsch. Cons., Inst. Fgn. Policy Analysis, Mensa, Am. Soc. Internat. Law, Nat. Eagle Scout Assn., Coun. on Fgn. Rels., Acad. of Polit. Sci. Office: Univ Va Sch of Law Ctr for Nat Security Law 580 Massie Rd Charlottesville VA 22903-1738 E-mail: rturner@law5.law.virginia.edu.

TURNER, ROBERT GERALD, university president; b. Atlanta, Nov. 25, 1945; s. Robert B. and Oreta Lois (Porter) T.; m. Gail Oliver, Dec. 21, 1968; children: Angela Jan, Jessica Diane AA, Lubbock Christian Coll., 1966, LLD (hon.), 1985, Pepperdine U., 1989; BS, Abilene Christian U., 1968; MA, U. Tex., 1970, PhD, 1975. Tchr. Weatherford High Sch., Tex., 1968-69; tchr. Lanier High Sch., Austin, 1969-70; instr. psychology San Antonio Coll., 1970-72; instr. Prairie View A & M U., Tex., 1973-75; asst. prof. psychology Pepperdine U., Malibu, Calif., 1975-78, assoc. prof. psychology, 1978-79, dir. testing, 1975-76, chmn. social sci. div., 1976-78, assoc. v.p. univ. affairs, 1979; assoc. prof. psychology U. Okla., Norman, 1979-84, exec. asst. to pres., 1979-81, acting provost, 1982, v.p. exec. affairs, 1981-84; chancellor U. Miss., University, 1984-95; pres. So. Meth. U., Dallas, 1995—. Pres. Southeastern Conf., 1985-87; rsch. asst. Tex. Adoption Study, 1973-75; mem. Pepperdine U., 1994-95; mem. Commn. on Telecomm., Nat. Assn. State Univs. and Land-Grant Colls., 1985-86, chmn. Commn. on Edn. for Tchg. Profession, 1990-91; mem. Pres.'s Commn., NCAA, 1989-92, chmn., 1991-92; mem. Knight Commn. on Intercollegiate Athletics, 1991-95; chmn. pres. coun. Miss. Assn. Colls., 1985-86; mem. def. adv. com. Svc. Acad. Athletic Programs, 1992—; bd. dirs. ChemFirst, J.C. Penney, Am. Advantage Funds. Author: (with L. Willerman) Readings About Individual and Group Differences, 1979. Contbr. articles to profl. jours. Recipient Outstanding Alumni award Abilene Christian U., 1989; inducted New Boston H.S. Athletic Hall of Fame, 1993. Mem. Young Pres. Orgn., Coun. on Competitiveness, Am. Inst. Pub. Svc. (bd. nominators 1989), Sigma Xi, Beta Alpha Psi, Phi Theta Kappa, Alpha Chi, Phi Kappa Phi. Mem. Ch. of Christ. Avocations: tennis; golf; reading; traveling. Office: So Meth Univ Office Of The Pres Dallas TX 75275-0001

TURNER, ROBERT LLOYD, state legislator; b. Columbus, Miss., Sept. 14, 1947; s. Roosevelt and Beatrice (Hargrove) T.; m. Gloria Harrell; children: Roosevelt, Robert, Ryan. BS, U. Wis., Racine, 1976. Mgr. French Quarter Restaurant, Racine, 1989; legislator Wis. State Assembly, Madison, 1990—, mem. transp. com. bldg. commn., mem. ways and means com., labor com., fin. institutions com.; minority vice chmn. caucus, highway com. Br. sales mgr. ETG Temporaries, Inc., Racine, 1989—; pub. Communicator News, Racine, 1989—; v.p. Racine Raider Football Team. State chmn. Dem. Black Polit. Caucus, Madison; pres. Bd. Health, Racine; chmn. Wis. State Elections Bd., Madison, 1990; alderman Racine City Coun., 1976—; chair Econ. Devel. Com., Racine; regional dir. Badger State Games, Racine; active Pvt. Industry Coun. Southeastern Wis., 1988-89, bd. dirs. Racine County Youth Sports Assn.; active Racine Juneteenth Day Com., bd. advisors Big Bros./Big Sisters. Sgt. USAF, 1967-71, Vietnam. Decorated Commendation medal; named Man of Yr. 2d Missionary Bapt. Ch., 1983. Mem. Urban League (pres. bd. dirs.), NAACP (2d v.p.), VFW, Vietnam Vets. Am. (life mem.), Am. Legion, Masons (supreme coun. 33rd degree), Shriners. Home: 36 Mckinley Ave Racine WI 53404-3414 Office: Wis Assembly PO Box 8953 Madison WI 53708-8953

TURNER, ROBERT STANLEY, orthopaedic surgeon, bioethicist; b. Waterloo, Iowa, Nov. 24, 1928; s. Henry George Turner and Ruby Lydia McMillin; m. Dorothy Lavonne Burgess, Sept. 5, 1953 (dec.); children: Bruce, Ann, Kent; m. Karen Lou Howard, May 19, 1990; children: Rebecca, Geoffrey, Strom. BA, State u. Iowa, 1952, MD, 1954. Diplomate Am. Bd. Orthopaedic Surgery. Intern Meml. and Maricopa County Hosps., Phoenix, 1954-55; med. officer USPHS Hosp., Tahlequah, Okla., 1955-57, orthopaedic res. San Francisco, 1957-60, Shriner's Hosp. Crippled Children, Phila., 1960-61; orthopaedic surgeon Lovelace Clinic Med. Ctr., Albuquerque, 1961-95, chmn. orthopaedic surgery dept., 1966-93; clin. assoc. prof. to clin. prof. orthopaedic surgery U. N.Mex., 1965—; contract orthopaedic surgeon Lovelace Clinic Med. Ctr., 1995—. Founder Dorothy Turner Meml. Ecumenical Seminars, 1987—; bd. govs. Lovelace Clinic Med. Ctr., 1968-81; trustee Lovelace Med. Found., 1972-93; mem. adv. bd. Carrie Tingley Hosp. for Children, Albuquerque, 1989-95; mem. bd. N.Mex. Mus. Natural History Found., Albuquerque, 1989-95, Black River Ctr. for Learning, Carlsbad, N.Mex., 2000—; mem. coun. trustees Lovelace Respiratory Rsch. Inst., 1997—; moderator ch. bd. Monte Vista Christian Ch., Albuquerque, 1996-97, bd. mem. Tres Rios Area Christian Chs., Carlsbad, N.Mex., 1998-2000. Sr. surgeon, USPHS, 1961-95. Recipient Ecumenical Svc. award Tres Rios Area Christian Ch., 1987, Svc. award Carrie Tingley Hosp. for Children, 1995, Meritorious Svc. award N.Mex. Orthopaedic Assn., 1994. Fellow ACS, Am. Acad. Ortho. Surgeons; mem. Clin. Orthopaedic Soc., We. Orthopaedic Assn., Gtr. Albuquerque Med. Assn., N.Mex. Med. Soc., Hibbs Soc. (co-pres. 1984-85). Disciple of Christ. Republican. Avocations: bio-ethical events, family, world travel, gardening, investments. Home: 560 Black Bear Pl NE Albuquerque NM 87122-1821 E-mail: rst560NM@aol.com.

TURNER, ROSS JAMES, investment corporation executive; b. Winnipeg, Man., Can., May 1, 1930; permanent U.S. resident, 1980; s. James Valentine and Gretta H. (Ross) T.; children: Ralph, Rick, Tracy. , U. Man. Extension, 1951, Banff Sch. Advanced Mgmt., 1956. Chmn./pres., CEO Genstar Corp., San Francisco, 1976-86, also bd. dirs.; chmn. Genstar Investment Corp., 1987—. Bd. dirs. Rio Algom Ltd., U. Man. Found. USA. Fellow Soc. Mgmt. Accts. Can.; mem. Pacific Union Club, Rancho Santa Fe Golf Club, Peninsula Golf and Country Club. Office: Genstar Investment Corp 555 California St Ste 4850 San Francisco CA 94104-1700 E-mail: dcordell@gencap.com.

TURNER, ROY M. computer science educator; b. Bardstown, Ky., Mar. 24, 1959; s. Marvin and Jo Anna Turner; m. Elise H. Turner; 1 child Kathrina. BS in Computer Sci., U. Louisville, 1980; MS in Computer Sci., Ga. Inst. Tech., 1987, PhD in Computer Sci., 1989. Rsch. asst. prof. U. N.H., Durham, 1989—95; vis. sr. rsch. scientist Marine Sci. Ctr. Northeastern U., Nahant, Mass., 1995; asst. prof. dept. computer sci. U. Maine, Orono, 1995—99, assoc. prof., 1999—. Mem.: IEEE, Cognitive Sci. Soc., Assn. Computing Machinery, Am. Assn. Artificial Intelligence, Golden Key (hon.). Congregationalist. Achievements include research in artificial intelligence (context-sensitive reasoning, control of autonomous underwater vehicles and other real-world agents, multiagent systems, medical diagnosis); modeling complex biological systems. Office: Univ Maine Dept Computer Sci Orono ME 04469

TURNER, SANDRA GOODSPEED, psychotherapist, educator; b. Louisville, Dec. 29, 1943; d. James A. Turner and Alice Hayes Hill; 1 child Kelly. BA, Northwestern U., 1966; MSW, Fordham U., 1975; PhD, Rutgers U., 1986. Asst. chief St. Vincents Hosp., N.Y.C., 1975—89; assoc. prof. Fordham U., 1989—. Contbr. chapters to books, articles to profl. jours. Avocation: photography. Home: 75 Bank St 6G New York NY 10014 Office: Fordham Univ Graduat Sch Social Sci 113 W 60 St New York NY 10023 E-mail: sturner@forham.edu.

TURNER, STEVEN CORNELL, agricultural economics educator; b. Atlanta, Dec. 4, 1953; s. Arthur Cleaborn and Charlotte Elizabeth (Cornell) T.; m. Virginia Louise Bond, Aug. 27, 1988. BA, Mercer U., 1975; MS, U. Ga., 1981; PhD, Va. Tech., 1986. Asst. prof. U. Ga., Athens, 1986-92, assoc. prof., 1993—. Mem. Am. Econ. Assn., Am. Agrl. Econ. Assn., So. Agrl. Econ. Assn., Western Agrl. Econ. Assn. Mem. Ch. of Christ. Home: 234 Greystone Ter Athens GA 30606-4461 Office: U Ga Conner Hall Athens GA 30602

TURNER, TED (ROBERT EDWARD TURNER), former television executive, philanthropist; b. Cin., Nov. 19, 1938; s. Robert Edward and Florence (Rooney) T.; m. Judy Nye (div.), m. Jane Shirley Smith, June 1965 (div. 1988); children: Beau, Rhett, Jennie; children by previous marriage: Laura Lee, Robert Edward IV; m. Jane Fonda, Dec. 21, 1991, (div. 2001). Grad. in classics, Brown U.; DSc in Commerce (hon.), Drexel U., 1982; LLD (hon.), Samford U., 1982, Atlanta U., 1984; D Entrepreneurial Sci. (hon.), Cen. New Eng. Coll. Tech., 1983; D in Pub. Adminstrn. (hon.), Mass. Maritime Acad., 1984; D in Bus. Adminstrn. (hon.), U. Charleston, 1985. Account exec. Turner Advt. Co., Atlanta, 1961-63, pres., chief oper. officer, 1963-70; pres., chmn. bd. Turner Broadcasting System, Inc., 1970-96; vice chmn. Time Warner Inc. (merger Turner Broadcasting System), 1996—2000; bd. dirs. Atlanta Hawks; owner Atlanta Braves. Bd. dirs. Martin Luther King Ctr., Atlanta. Won America's Cup in his yacht Courageous, 1977; named Yachtsman of Yr. 4 times.Recipient Outstanding Entrepreneur of Yr. award Sales Mktg. and Mgmt. Mag., 1979, Salesman of Yr. award Sales and Mktg. Execs., 1980, Pvt. Enterprise Exemplar medal, Freedoms Found. at Valley Forge, 1980, Communicator of Yr. award Pub. Rels. Soc. Am., 1981, Communicator of Yr. award N.Y. Broadcasters, 1981, Internat. Communicator of Yr. award Sales and Mktg. Execs., 1981, Nat. News Media award VFW, 1981, Disting. Svc. in Telecommunications award Ohio U. Coll. Communication, 1982, Carr Van Anda award Ohio U. Sch. Journalism, 1982, Spl. award Edinburgh Internat. TV Festival, Scotland, 1982, Media Awareness award United Vietnam Vets. Orgn., 1983, Bd. Govs. award Atlanta chpt. NATAS, 1982, Spl. Olympics award Spl. Olympics Com., 1983, Dinner of Champions award Ga. chpt., Multiple Sclerosis Soc., 1983, Praca Spl. Merit award N.Y. Puerto Rican Assn. for Community Affairs, 1983, World Telecommunications Pioneer award, N.Y. State Broadcasters Assn., 1984, Golden Plate award Am. Acad. Achievement, 1984, Outstanding Supporter Boy Scouting award Nat. Boy Scout Coun., 1984, Silver Satellite award Am. Women in Radio and TV, Lifetime Achievement award N.Y. Internat. Film and TV Festival, 1984, Corp. Star of Yr. award Nat. Leukemia Soc., 1985, Disting. Achievement award U. Georgia, 1985, Tree of Life award Jewish Nat. Fund, 1985, Bus. Exec. of Yr. award Ga. Security Dealers Assn., 1985, Life Achievement award Popular Culture Assn., 1986, George Washington Disting. Patriot award S.R., 1986, Mo. Honor medal Sch. Journalism, U. Mo., 1987, Golden Ace award Nat. Cable TV Acad., 1987 Sol Taishoff award Nat. Press Found., 1988, Citizen Diplomat award Ctr. for Soviet-Am. Dialogue, 1988, Chmn.'s award Cable Advt. Bur., 1988, Directorate award NATAS, 1989, Paul White award Radio and TV News Dirs. Assn., 1989 Bus. Marketer of Yr. Am. Mktg. Assn., 1989, Disting. Svc. award Simon Wiesenthal Ctr., 1990, Glasnost award Vols. Am. and Soviet Life mag., 1990, numerous others; inducted into Hall of Fame, Promotion and Mktg. Assn., 1980, Dubuque (Iowa) Bus. Hall of Fame, 1983, Nat. Assn. for Sport and Phys. Edn. Hall of Fame, 1986. Mem. Nat. Cable TV Assn. (Pres.'s award 1979, 89, Ace Spl. Recognition award 1980), NAACP (life, bd. dirs. Atlanta chpt., Regional Employer of Yr. award 1976), Nat. Audubon Soc., Cousteau Soc., Bay Area Cable Club (hon.) Avocations: sailing, fishing.*

TURNER, THOMAS MARSHALL, telecommunications executive, consultant; b. Cumberland, Md., Aug. 17, 1951; s. James Richard and Laura Roselie (Durst) T. BS in Indsl. Tech. and Mgmt., U. Md., 1973, MA in Indsl. Tech. and Mgmt., 1980. Grad. asst U. Md., College Park, 1975-76; sales assoc., gen. mgr. Equity Trades Reality, Riverdale, Md., 1976-83; account exec. RCA Corp., Greenbelt, 1983; sr. telecomm. cons. CMC, Inc., Washington, 1984-86, ORS Assoc., McLean, Va., 1986-87; owner, pres. T-1 Comm., Boca Raton, Fla., 1987—, Optimum Reconciliation Svc., Inc., Pompano Beach, 1996—. Cons. Marriott Corp., Bethesda, Md., 1990-99, Group Health, Inc., N.Y.C., 1991-92, Colgate-Palmolive Co., 1993-94, State of Md., 1993, Trump Corp., 1993, Martin-Marietta, 1994, Matsushita, 1994, Montgomery Wards, 1994, Nabisco Foods, 1994, Harris Corp., 1995-99, Urban League, 1995-99, EDS, 1995-99, Chem. Bank, 1996-99, Chase Manhattan Bank, 1997-99, Arnold & Porter, 2001, Bechtel, 2001—, Booz, Allen & Hamilton, 2002, Comsat, 2001—, Fairchild, 2001—, GEICO, 2001—, Howard Hughes Med. Inst., 2001—, IBM, 2001—, State Farm Ins., 2001—, Swales Aerospace, 2002—, Wells Fargo, 2001—; grad. asst. instr. Dale Carnegie Inst., 1992. Contbr. articles to profl. jours. Vol. ARC, Riverdale, Md., 1977-80; instr. Jr. Achievement Bus. Co-op, Rockville, Md., 1979-82. Recipient Highest Achievment award Dale Carnegie Inst., 1989. Mem. ASTD, Telecomm. Mgrs. Assn. of Capital Area, Toastmasters, Sigma Alpha Epsilon Alumni Assn.

TURNER, TINA (ANNA MAE BULLOCK), singer; b. Brownsville, Tenn., Nov. 26, 1939; m. Ike Turner, 1956 (div. 1978); children: Craig, Ike Jr., Michael, Ronald. Singer with Ike Turner Kings of Rhythm, and Ike and Tina Turner Revue; appeared in films: Gimme Shelter, 1970, Soul to Soul, 1971, Tommy, 1975, Sgt. Pepper's lonely Hearts Club Band, 1978, Mad Max Beyond Thunderdome, 1985, Break Every Rule, 1986, Last Action Hero, 1993; concert tours of Europe, 1966, Japan and Africa, 1971; Showtime TV concert of Wildest Dreams; albums with Ike Turner include Hunter, 1970, Ike and Tina Show II, Ike and Tina Show, 1966, Ike and Tina Turner, Bad Dreams, 1973, Ike and Tina Turner Greatest Hits, vol. 1,2 and 3, 1989, Greatest Hits, 1990, Proud Mary, 1991, The Ike and Tina Turner Collection, 1993; solo albums include Let Me Touch Your Mind, 1972, Tina Turns the Country On, 1974, Acid Queen, 1975, Love Explosion, 1977, Rough, 1978, Airwaves, 1979, Private Dancer, 1984, Break Every Rule, 1986, Tina Live In Europe, 1988, Foreign Affair, 1989, Simply the Best, 1991, What's Love Got to Do With It? (soundtrack), 1993, The Collected Recordings: Sixties to Nineties, with others, 1994, Wildest Dreams, 1996, Twenty Four Seven, 2000; performed with USA for Africa on song We are The World, 1985; author (autobiography) I, Tina, 1985 (filmed as What's Love Got To Do With It?, 1993). Recipient Grammy award, 1972, 85 (three), 86, Grammy nomination (Best Pop Female Vocal) for "I Don't Wanna Fight", 1994; inducted into Rock and Roll Hall of Fame, 1991.*

TURNER, WALLACE L. reporter; b. Titusville, Fla., Mar. 15, 1921; s. Clyde H. and Ina B. (Wallace) T.; m. Pearl Burk, June 12, 1943; chldren: Kathleen Turner, Elizabeth Turner Everett. B.J., U. Mo., 1943; postgrad. (Nieman fellow), Harvard U., 1958-59. Reporter Springfield (Mo.) Daily News, 1943, Portland Oregonian, 1943-59; news dir. Sta. KPTV, Portland, 1959-61; asst. sec. HEW, Washington, 1961-62; reporter N.Y. Times, San Francisco, 1962—, bur. chief, 1970-85, Seattle bur. chief, 1985-88. Author: Gamblers Money, 1965, The Morman Establishment, 1967. Recipient Heywood Broun award for reporting, 1952, 56; Pulitzer Prize for reporting, 1957 Office: Box 99269 Magnolia Sta Seattle WA 98199-4260

TURNER, WARREN AUSTIN, state legislator; b. Berkeley, Calif., Dec. 21, 1926; s. Warren Mortimer and Rebecca Oline (Noer) T.; m. Beverly Daune Mackay, Mar. 29, 1952; children: Daune Scott, Warren Adair, Alan Corey. BA, U. Calif., Berkeley, 1950, BS, 1952, MPH, 1958. Pub. acct. Price Waterhouse, San Francisco, 1951-52, AW Blackman, Las Vegas, Nev., 1952-56; asst. adminstr. Marin Gen. Hosp., San Rafael, Calif., 1958-60; assoc. dir. UCLA Hosp., 1960-68; founding adminstr. Walter O. Boswell Meml. Hosp., Sun City, Ariz., 1968-81; pres. Sun Health Corp., 1981-89; mem. Ariz. Senate, Phoenix, 1993-97, chmn. rules com., vice chair health com., mem. appropriations, family svcs. and transp. com., 1995-97. Chmn. appropriation subcom. K-12, C.C.'s and natural resources. With USN, 1944-46. Mem. Ariz. Acad. Republican. Avocations: breeding and showing Siamese cats, fishing, mining. Home: 18432 W Glendale Ave Waddell AZ 85355-9737

TURNER, WELD W(INSTON), industrial psychologist; b. St. Paul, July 25, 1931; s. Frank and Hazel Thirza (Weld) Prevratil; m. Helen Theo Kralicek, June 12, 1953 (div. 1969); children; Jean Ann, Alan Weld. BS in Commerce, Okla. A&M Coll. (now Okla. State U.), 1954; MS, Purdue U., 1955, PhD in Indsl. Psychology, 1959. Pers. evaluation assoc. GM Inst., Flint., 1955-60; supr. pers. rsch. B.F. goodrich Co., Akron, 1960-67; sr. manpower adv. Mobil Oil Corp., N.Y.C., 1967—. Lectr. adult edn. divsn. U. Akron, part-time. With U.S. Army, 1951-52. Mem. APA, Am. Psychol. Soc., Sigma Xi, Phi Kappa Phi, Pi Gamma Mu. Home: 601 Rosery Rd NE Apt 3905 Largo FL 33770-3829 Office: Western Regional Rsch Ctr USDA 800 Buchanan St Berkeley CA 94710-1105

TURNER, WESLEY R. publishing executive; m. Shirley; children: Sara, Leslie. Grad., U. Tex. With Ft. Worth Press, 1973-75; from advtsg. sales rep. to v.p. advtsg. Ft. Worth Star-Telegram, 1975-86, pres., publ., 1997—; exec. v.p., gen. mgr. Kansas City Star, 1990-97; pres. Sutton Industries, 1987-90. Office: Knight Ridder Inc 400 W 7th St Fort Worth TX 76102-4701*

TURNER, WILLIAM COCHRANE, international management consultant; b. Red Oak, Iowa, May 27, 1929; s. James Lyman and Josephine (Cochrane) T.; m. Cynthia Dunbar, July 16, 1955; children: Scott Christopher, Craig Dunbar, Douglas Gordon. BS, Northwestern U., 1952; LLD (hon.), Am. Grad. Sch. Internat. Mgmt., 1993. Pres., chmn. bd. dirs. Western Mgmt. Cons., Inc., Phoenix, 1955-74, Western Mgmt. Cons. Europe, S.A., Brussels, 1968-74; U.S. amb., permanent rep. OECD, Paris, 1974-77, vice chmn. exec. com., 1976-77, U.S. rep. Energy Policy Com., 1976-77, mem. U.S. dels. internat. meetings, 1974-77; chmn., CEO Argyle Atlantic Corp., Phoenix, 1977—. Mem. western internat. trade group U.S. Dept. Commerce, 1972-74; U.S. Rep. Consultative Group parent orgn. Coord. Com. (COCOM) Multilateral Export Controls Communist Nations, Paris, 1974-77; chmn. European adv. coun., 1981-88, Asia Pacific adv. coun. AT&T Internat., 1981-88; mem. U.S.-Japan Bus. Coun., Washington, 1987-93, European adv. coun. IBM World Trade Europe/Mid. East/Africa Corp., 1977-80; mem. Asia Pacific adv. coun. Am. Can Co., Greenwich, Conn., 1981-85, GE of Brazil adv. coun. GE Co., Coral Gables, Fla., 1979-81, Caterpillar of Brazil adv. coun. Caterpillar Tractor Co., Peoria, Ill., 1979-84, Caterpillar Asia Pacific Adv. Coun., 1984-90, U.S. adv. com. Trade Negotiations, 1982-84; bd. dirs. Rural/Metro Corp., Microtest, Inc., Phoenix; chmn., dir. WorldWideTalk, Inc., Melbourne, Fla., 1999--; founding mem. Pacific Coun. Internat. Policy, L.A., 1995—; chmn. internat. adv. coun. Avon Products, Inc., N.Y.C., 1985-98; mem. Spencer Stuart adv. coun. Spencer Stuart and Assocs., N.Y.C., 1984-90; chmn., mem. internat. adv. coun. Advanced Semiconductor Materials Internat. NV, Bilthoven, The Netherlands, 1985-88; bd. dirs. The Atlantic Coun. of U.S., Washington, 1977-92; co-chmn. internat. adv. bd. Univ. of Nations, Lausanne, Switzerland and Kona, Hawaii, 1985—; bd. dirs. World Wildlife Fund/U.S., 1983-85, World Wildlife Fund/The Conservation Found., 1985-89, Nat. Coun., 1989-95, 96—; bd. govs. Joseph H. Lauder Inst. Mgmt. and Internat. Studies, U. Pa., 1983-01; trustee Heard Mus., Phoenix, 1983-86, mem. nat. adv. bd., 1986-93. Mem. vestry Am. Cathedral, Paris, 1976—77; nat. trustee Phoenix Country Day Sch., 1971—74; bd. govs. Atlantic Inst. Internat. Affairs, Paris, 1977—88; dir. AT&T Internat., Inc., Basking Ridge, NJ, 1980—84, Atlantic Inst. Found., Inc., N.Y.C., 1984—90; mem. European Cmty.-U.S. Businessmen's Coun., 1978—79; nat. trustee Nat. Symphony Orch. Assn., Washington, 1973—83, Am. Sch., Paris, 1976—77, Orme Sch., Mayer, Ariz., 1970—74; mem. nat. coun. Salk Inst., 1978—82; mem. U.S. Adv. Com. Internat. Edn. and Cultural Affairs, 1969—74; nat. rev. bd. Ctr. Cultural and Tech. Interchange Between East and West, 1970—74; mem. trade and environ. com. Nat. Adv. Coun. for Environ. Policy and Tech.-U.S. EPA, Washington, 1991—95; chmn. Internat. Adv. Coun. Plasma Tech., Inc., Santa Fe, 1992—97; trustee Thunderbird Am. Grad Sch. Internat. Mgmt., 1972—, chmn. bd. trustees, 1987—89; adv. bd. Ctr. Strategic and Internat. Studies, Georgetown U., 1977—81; dir. Pullman, Inc., Chgo., 1977—80, Nabisco Brands, Inc., Parsippany, NJ, 1977—85, Salomon, Inc., N.Y.C., 1980—93; bd. govs. Am. Hosp. of Paris, 1974—77; pres., bd. dirs. Phoenix Symphony Assn., 1969—70; chmn. Ariz. Joint Econ. Devel. Com., 1967—68; exec. com., bd. dirs. Ariz. Dept. Econ. Planning and Devel., 1968—70; chmn. bd. Ariz. Crippled Children's Svcs., 1964—65; treas. Ariz. Rep. Com., 1956—57; chmn. Ariz. Young Rep. League, 1955—56; dir. and founding chmn. bd. Mercy Ships Internat., Inc., A Ministry of Youth With a Mission, Lindale, Tex., 1985—2000; dir. exec. com., chmn. internat. com. Ariz. Econ. Coun., Phoenix, 1989—93; dir. exec. com. Orgn. for Free Trade and Devel., 1991—93. Recipient East-West Ctr. Disting. Svc. award, 1977. Mem. U.S. Coun. Internat. Bus. (trustee, exec. com.), Coun. Fgn. Rels., Coun. Am. Ambs. (vice chmn. bd.), Nat. Adv. Coun. on Bus. Edn., Met. Club, Paradise Valley (Ariz.) Country Club, Bohemian Club (San Francisco). Episcopalian. Fax: 480-948-4674. E-mail: wct-aac@mindspring.com.

TURNER, WILLIAM IAN MACKENZIE, JR. investment company executive; b. Sharon, Pa., Jan. 17, 1929; BSc in Mech. Engrng. with Honors, U. Toronto, 1951; MBA, Harvard U., 1953; LLD (hon.), Mount Allison U., 1984; DCL (hon.), Bishop's U., 1987; LLD (hon.), Concordia U., 1989. Registered profl. engr., Ont., Que. Pres. Power Corp. of Can., 1966-70; chmn., CEO Consolidated-Bathurst, Inc., 1970-88, Exsultate, Inc., Montreal, 1988—. Chmn. compensation com. Bombardier Inc.; chmn. exec. com. Celanese Can.; chmn. exec. and fin. coms. Newmont Mining, Denver; chmn. audit com. Schroders PLC, London; chmn. bd. Can. Marconi Co., Proudfoot PLC, London; bd. dirs. Axel Johnson, Stamford, Conn., Power Corp. of Can., Montreal, Remington Energy Ltd., Calgary, SNC-Lavalin, Inc., Montreal; adv. com. Ingersoll Rand Can., Montreal. Vice chmn. and chmn. exec. com. Carnegie Instn. of Washington; vice chmn. World Econ. Coun., Geneva, Switzerland. Mem. Hillside Tennis, Montreal Racket, Mount Royal, Toronto, Brook (N.Y.C.), Knickerbocker (N.Y.C.), Order of Can. Home: 4294 Montrose Ave Westmount QC Canada H3Y 2A5 Office: Ste 575 1981 McGill College Ave Montreal QC Canada H3A 2X1 Fax: 514-982-0190.

TURNER, WILLIAM WEYAND, writer; b. Buffalo, Apr. 14, 1927; s. William Peter and Magdalen (Weyand) T.; m. Margaret Peiffer, Sept. 12, 1964; children: Mark Peter, Lori Ann. BS, Canisius Coll., 1949. Spl. agt. in various field offices FBI, 1951-61; free-lance writer Calif., 1963—; sr. editor Ramparts Mag., San Francisco, 1967—. Investigator and cons. Nat. Wiretap Commn., 1975; U.S. del. J.F.K. Internat. Seminar, Rio de Janeiro, 1995. Author: The Police Establishment, 1968, Invisible Witness: The Use and Abuse of the New Technology of Crime Investigation, 1968, Hoover's F.B.I.: The Men and the Myth, 1970, Power on the Right, 1971, (with Warren Hinckle and Eliot Asinof) The Ten Second Jailbreak, 1973, (with John Christian) The Assassination of Robert F. Kennedy, 1978, (with Warren Hinckle) The Fish is Red: The Story of the Secret War Against Castro, 1981, updated, expanded, retitled as Deadly Secrets: The CIA-Mafia War Against Castro and the Assassination of JFK, 1992, Rearview Mirror: Looking Back at the FBI, the CIA and Other Tails, 2001; contbg. author: Investigating the FBI, 1973; contbr. articles to popular mags.; book reviewer L.A. Times. Dem. candidate for U.S. Congress, 1968. Served with USN, 1945-46. Mem. Authors Guild, Internat. Platform Assn., Press Club of San Francisco. Roman Catholic. Avocation: tennis. Home and Office: 163 Mark Twain Ave San Rafael CA 94903-2820

TURNER-SILVIA, JOANN, writer, vocalist, actress, music producer; b. Berkeley, Calif., July 6, 1952; d. Willie Turner and Bessie Lee Allen-Turner; m. William Louis Silvia, Apr. 16, 1996 (div. Apr. 17, 2000); 1 child Anthon Julien Smith. Cert., Burbank (Calif.) Film Workshop, 1970; AA, Modesto (Calif.) Jr. Coll., 2001. Singer, prodr. JoAnn Turner Inc., Las Vegas, 1970—, CEO, 1974—75; peace officer Dept. of Corrections, San Rafael, Calif., 1983—86; entertainment promoter Turner Prodns., Alameda, 1986—90; actress Q Casting, San Francisco, 1990—; writer Jats Visions, Modesto, 1999—. Author: (screenplays) Mahogany, 1973, (plays) Just Another Day in Oakland, 1999, others; actor: (plays) Boundary Line, 1994. Mem. adv. bd. Mandela Ho., Oakland, Calif., 1985—; co-founder Nat. Coalition of Oppression, Seattle, 1970. Named Miss Congeniality, Beauty Pageant of Am., San Francisco, 1977. Mem.: NAACP. Avocations: walking, movies, reading, golf. Home: 3001 Hahn Dr # 244 Modesto CA 95350 Fax: 209-572-5002.

TURNEY, DENISE, portfolio manager, writer; b. Dayton, Ohio, Sept. 4, 1962; d. Richard E. Turney, Doris Jean Turney; m. Gregory E. Campbell. Student, U. Tenn. Adminstrv. asst. Coll. N.J., Trenton, 1989—91; mgr. portfolio Merrill Lynch, Princeton, NJ, 1991—. Adminstr. No Longer Bound, Bristol, Pa. Author: Portin, 1998, Love Has Many Faces, 2000, Spiral, 2002. With USN, 1984—88. Recipient Navy Achievement medal, 1985, 1987.

TURNEY, JAMES EDWARD, computer scientist; b. Greensburg, Pa., May 14, 1933; s. James Edward and Mary Elizabeth (Koch) T.; m. Joan Lois Sweeney, Sept. 1, 1957 (dec. Jan. 1982); m. Audra Varnagy, Mar. 27, 1982; children: Audrey, Jennifer, Jill, Joy. BS in Indsl. Engrng., Northeastern U., 1961; MS in Indsl. Mgmt., MIT, 1964; PhD in Mgmt., Calif. Coast U., 1993. Sr. cons. Peat Marwick Mitchell Co., L.A., 1965-68; gen. mgr. Technicolor, Inc., Hollywood, Calif., 1968-70; dir. Intercontinental Computing, Inc., Kansas City, Mo., 1970-72; v.p. Insight Systems, Ltd., Des Moines, 1972-76; pres. Pro Data Sys., Inc., Austin, Tex., 1976—. Prof. computer sci. Park U., Austin, 1997—; online instr. Park U., Austin, 2001—, U. Phoenix, Austin, 2002—. Bd. dirs. Luth. Ch., Wayland, Mass., 1964-66, Palos Verdes, Calif., 1967-71, Overland Pk., Kans., 1973-76, San Jose, Calif., 1991-92, Corpus Christi, Tex., 1993-95. Sgt. U.S. Army, 1953-56. Mem. ASTD (v.p. fin. 1998—), Am. Inst. Indsl. Engrs. (pres. 1966-67), Mensa (local sec. 1994-97), Tex. Jazz Festival Soc. (pres. 1995-97), Autin Runners Club (mem. coord. 1999), Project Mgmt. Inst. Republican. Avocations: sailing, music, photography, writing, running. Home and Office: Pro Data Systems Inc 6508 Convict Hill Rd Austin TX 78749-1770 E-mail: drjet@onr.com.

TURNHEIM, JOY KAREN, lawyer; b. Jersey City, Apr. 21, 1965; d. Palmer and Gloria Grace (Freer) T. AB, Dartmouth Coll., 1985; JD, Northwestern U., 1988; MBA with distinction, DePaul U., 1993; MPhil, NYU, 1997. Bar: Ill. 1988, U.S. Dist. Ct. (no. dist.) Ill. 1988. Law clk. to Hon. Sophia H. Hall Ill.

Circuit Ct., Chgo., 1988-89; assoc. Nathanson & Wray, 1989-90, Horvath & Wigoda, Chgo., 1990; pvt. practice Law Offices Joy K. Turnheim, 1991—; exec. dir. Chenny Troupe, Chgo., 1993. Adj. prof. Columbia Coll., 1992-94; chpt. atty. Assn. Women in Metals Industry, 1989-91. Treas. Presbyn. Women in 4th Ch., Chgo., 1989-94; chmn. Silver Apple Ball, Chgo., 1990; moderator Kairos Fellowship, Chgo., 1990-92; deacon 4th Presbyn. Ch., 1992-95; mem. Jr. League Chgo., 1992—; chair Project CON!CERN, 1995—; founding mem., women's bd. Community Support Svcs., 1992-95; mem. Friends of Red Cross, 1990-94. Mem. ABA, Ill. State Bar Assn., Chgo. Bar Assn., Chgo. Soc. Clubs, Am. Inns of Ct. (Wigmore chpt.). Avocations: tennis, skiing, golf.

TURNIPSEED, BARNWELL RHETT, III, journalist, public relations consultant; b. Apr. 6, 1929; s. Barnwell Rhett and L. (Rogers) T.; m. Jane Whitley, June 12, 1982. BA in Journalism, U. Ga., 1950, MA in Journalism, 1960. With Sta. WGGA, Gainesville, Ga., 1943-46; prodn. mgr.. Sta WGGA, 1958-60; with Sta. WRFC, Athens, 1947-50; program dir. Sta. WKYW, Louisville, 1953, Sta. WGBA, Columbus, Ga., 1953-55; sr. corr., sci. editor Voice of Am. Worldwide English, 1960-72; coord. radio-TV pub. affairs HEW, 1972-73; mem. staff Ga. Congressman Phil Landrum, 1974-75; dir. solar energy tech. info. Dept. Energy, Washington, 1975-77, spl. asst., 1977-81; pvt. practice, 1981-88, 94—; instr. West Ga. Coll., Carrollton, 1988-89, 90-94; asst. prof. Brenau Coll., Gainesville, Ga., 1989-90; mgr. WWGC-FM, Carrollton, 1990-94. Dir. Ga. Broadcasters Annual Awards, 1998—. Author: History of Georgia Broadcasting, 1972; prin. corr. Voice of Am. (Peabody award winning space exploration broadcasts, 1969). Symphony Guild rep. Louisville, Columbus, Ga. Jaycees; active symphony and arts devel. Sgt. U.S. Army, 1950-52. Recipient 2 Meritorious Svc. awards USIA. Mem. Nat. Assn. Sci. Writers (life), Aircraft Owners and Pilots Assn., Sigma Delta Chi. Democrat. Methodist. Home and Office: 295 Greenfield Cir Fayetteville GA 30215-2622

TURNIPSEED, VICTORIA LEE, foundation administrator, public relations executive; b. Yakima, Wash., Jan. 13, 1951; d. Kenneth Ray and Shirley Ann (Dexter) T. BA, Okla. State U., 1973; MSW, U. Okla., 1975. Dir. med. social svcs. Espanola (N.Mex.) Hosp./S.W. Community Health Svcs., 1975-82; assoc. dir. devel. S.W. Community Health Svcs., Albuquerque, 1982-83; exec. dir. found. and pub. rels. Swedish Health Systems, Englewood, Colo., 1983-86; assoc. dir. resource devel. Scripps Meml. Hosp. Found., La Jolla, Calif., 1986-90; v.p. major gifts/found. rels. Sharp Hosps. Found., San Diego, 1990—. Devel. cons. Child Abuse Prevention Found., San Diego, 1990, Internat. Aerospace Hall of Fame, San Diego, 1990, Assn. Western Hosps., San Francisco, 1983; program devel. cons. El Centro de Vida Nueva, Espanola, N.Mex. Contbr. articles to profl. jours. Mem. mktg. and spl. events com. LEAD San Diego, Inc., 1990—; vol. Planned Parenthood. Recipient Golden Leaflet award Colo. Hosp. Assn., 1985; named one of Outstanding Young Women of Am., 1983. Mem. Assn. for Healthcare Philanthropy (cert., nat. nominating com. 1990, sec. Region 9/regional conf. 1982-83, pub. rels. com. 1983, pub. rels. chmn. Regions 10 and 11/regional confs. 1988), Women's Inst. for Fin. Edn. (pub. rels. coord. 1988-90), Jr. League of San Diego (nominating com. 1991-92, project and com. chmn. 1987-90, endowment com. 1991-93), City Club of San Diego. Avocations: dance aerobics, snow skiing, theatre, contemporary southwestern art. Home: 1075 Klish Way Del Mar CA 92014-2647 Office: Sharp Health Care Found 8525 Gibbs Dr Ste 302 San Diego CA 92123-1700

TURNLUND, JUDITH RAE, nutritionist; b. St. Paul, Sept. 28, 1936; d. Victor Emanuel and Vida Mae (Priddy) Hanson; m. Richard Wayne Turnlund, Nov. 9, 1957; children: Michael Wayne, Mark Richard, Todd Hanson. BS in Chemistry and Psychology, Gustavus Adolphus Coll., 1958; PhD in Nutrition, U. Calif., Berkeley, 1978. Registered dietitian. Postdoctoral fellow U. Calif., Berkeley, 1978-80, lectr., 1984-92, adj. assoc. prof., 1989-97; rsch. nutrition scientist Western Regional Rsch. Ctr./Western Human Nutrition Ctr., USDA, San Francisco, Albany, and Davis, Calif., 1980—; rsch. leader Western Human Nutrition Ctr. USDA, San Francisco, 1993-96; prof. nutrition Grad. Nutrition Group, U. Calif., Davis, 2000—. Vis. asst. prof. Am. U. Beirut, Lebanon, 1979, 80. Editor: Stable Isotopes in Nutrition, 1984; contbr. articles to profl. jours. Recipient Cert. of Merit, USDA/ARS, 1984, 93, 98, Disting. Alumni citation Gustavus Adolphus Coll., 1988, Am. Inst. Nutrition's Lederle award in Human Nutrition, 1996; USDA grantee, Nat. Dairy Coun. grantee. Mem. Am. Soc. Nutritional Scis., Am. Soc. Clin. Nutrition, Am. Dietetic Assn. Home: 2276 Great Hwy San Francisco CA 94116-1555 Office: U Calif USDA/ARS Western Human Nutrition Rsch One Shields Ave Davis CA 95616 E-mail: jturnlun@whnrc.usda.gov.

TURNOVSKY, STEPHEN JOHN, economics educator; b. Wellington, New Zealand, Apr. 5, 1941; came to U.S., 1981; s. Frederick and Liselotte Felicitas (Wodak) T.; m. Michelle Henriette Louise Roos, Jan. 21, 1967; children: Geoffrey George, Jacqueline Liselotte. BA, Victoria U., Wellington, 1962, MA with honors, 1963; PhD, Harvard U., 1968. Asst. prof. econs. U. Pa., Phila., 1968-71; assoc. prof. U. Toronto, Ont., Can., 1971-72; prof. Australian Nat. U., Canberra, 1972-82; IBE disting. prof. econs. U. Ill., Champaign, 1982-87; prof. econs. U. Wash., Seattle, 1987—, chmn. dept., 1990-95; Castor prof., 1993—. Rsch. assoc. Nat. Bur. Econ. Rsch., Cambridge, Mass., 1983-93. Author: Macroeconomic Analysis and Stabilization Policy, 1977, International Macroeconomic Stabilization Policy, 1990, Methods of Macroeconomic Dynamics, 1995, 2d edit., 2000, International Macroeconomic Dynamics, 1997; mem. editl. bd. several jours.; contbr. articles to profl. jours. Fellow Econometric Soc., Acad. Social Scis. in Australia; mem. Soc. Econ. Dynamics and Control (pres. 1982-84, editor Jour. Econ. Dynamics and Control 1981-87, 95-2001). Avocations: skiing, hiking, music. Home: 6053 NE Kelden Pl Seattle WA 98105-2045 Office: Dept Econs U Wash Box 353330 Seattle WA 98195-3330 E-mail: sturn@u.washington.edu.

TURNQUIST, GARY EDWARD, systems consultant, educator; b. Detroit, Apr. 1, 1943; s. Carl Edward and Jeanne Gloria (Hansen) T.; m. Kathleen Ann Mark, Aug. 12, 1966; children: Shon Edward, Eric A., Mark Anthony. BA, Ea. Mich. U., 1967, MA, 1972. Programmer Burroughs, Detroit, 1969-71, Whittaker, Detroit, 1971-74; network analyst Burroughs/Unisys, 1974-89; network cons. Sun Micro Systems, Southfield, Mich., 1989—. Prof. Ea. Mich. U., Ypsilanti, 1980—; presenter seminar, 1990. Mem. Soc. Mfg. Engring., Bldg. Industry Cons. Svc. Internat., Civitans (dir. Plymouth/Canton chpt. 1980—). Avocations: golf, computers, reading, basketball. Office: Sun Micro Systems 1000 Town Ctr Ste 1700 Southfield MI 48075-1233

TURNQUIST, JERRY L. teacher, journalist; b. Elgin, Ill., Mar. 5, 1949; s. Ralph C. and Frances B. T.; m. Kathleen A. Turnquist, Dec. 29, 1984; adopted children: Dennis, Eric. AA, Elgin C.C., 1969; BS, No. Ill. U., 1971, MS, 1979. Tchr. history and sci. Sch. Dist. U. - 46, Elgin, Ill., 1972—; tax preparer H&R Block Premium, 1977—. Columnist Daily Herald, Elgin, 1995—; co-host: (local radio show) Elgin 100 Years Ago, Sta. WRMN, 1995—. Trustee Gail Borden Pub. Libr., Elgin, 1995—; bd. dirs. Ill. State Hist. Soc., Elgin, Springfield, 1998-2000; chmn. Elgin Heritage Commn., 1986-91, others. Named Disting. Alumnus Elgin C.C., 1989, Keyman of the Yr., Elgin Jaycees, 1981; recipient Outstanding Svc. award Elgin Heritage Commn., 1995. Mem. Elgin Area Hist. Soc. (bd. dirs. 1986-98). Home: 1021 W Highland Ave Elgin IL 60123-5219 E-mail: ibemrt@aol.com.

TURNQUIST, PAUL KENNETH, agricultural engineer, educator; b. Lindsborg, Kans., Jan. 3, 1935; s. Leonard Otto and Myrtle Edith (Ryding) T.; m. Peggy Ann James, Dec. 22, 1962; children: Todd, Scott, Greg. BS Agrl. Engring., Kans. State U., 1957; MS in agrl. engring., Okla. State U., 1961, PhD agrl. engring., 1965. Registered profl. engr., Okla. Rsch. engr. Caterpillar Tractor Co., Peoria, Ill., 1957; instr., asst. prof. Okla. State U., Stillwater, 1958-62; assoc. prof., prof. S.D. State U., Brookings, 1964-76; prof., dept. head Auburn (Ala.) U., 1977-98, prof. and head emeritus, 1998. Mem. ABET Engring. Accreditation Commn., 1992-97. Co-author: Tractors & Their Power Units, 1989; contbr. articles to profl. jours. Fellow Am. Soc. Agrl. Engrs. (life, trustee found. 1990-93, bd. dirs. edn. com. 1992-94). Methodist. Home: 1216 Nixon Ave Auburn AL 36830-6350

TURO, JOANN K. psychoanalyst, psychotherapist, consultant; b. Westerly, R.I., Feb. 13, 1938; d. Angelo and Anna Josephine (Drew) T. BS in Biology and Chemistry, U. R.I., 1959; MA in Human Rels. and Psychology, Ohio U., 1964; postgrad., NYU, 1966-71, N.Y. Freudian Inst., N.Y.C., 1977-85, Mental Health Inst., 1977-80. Rsch. asst. biochemistry studies on schizophrenia Harvard U. Med. Sch., Boston, 1959-60; indsl. psychology asst. studies on managerial success N.Y. Telephone Co., N.Y.C., 1964-66; staff psychologist Testing and Advisement Ctr. NYU, 1966-70; psychology intern Kings County Hosp., Bklyn., 1970-71; staff psychologist M.D.C. Psychol. Svcs., N.Y.C., 1971-72; clin. dir. Greenwich House Substance Abuse Clinic, 1973-76; cons. psychotherapist Mental Health Consultation Ctr., 1977-82; pvt. practice, 1981—. Mental health cons. Bklyn. Ctr. for Psychotherapy, 1976-78; with Psychoanalytic Consultation Svcs., 1994—; presenter in field. Mem. Itnernat. Psychoanalytic Assn. (cert.), Soc. for Personality Assessment (cert.), N.Y. Freudian Soc. (cert., co-chmn. grad. com. 1985-86, mem. continuing edn. com. 1986—, pub. rels. com. 1992-93, psychoanalytic consult svc. 1994—, tng. and supr. psychoanalyst 1995—, ethics com. 1999—, tng. analyst panel 2000—), N.Y. Coun. Psychoanalytic Psychotherapists (cert.), Met. Assn. for Coll. Mental Health Practitoners (cert.). Office: 175 W 12th St Apt 15A New York NY 10011-8211

TURO, RON, lawyer; b. Fort Wayne, Ind., Apr. 2, 1955; s. John B. and Joan L. (Gluntz) T.; m. Claire Teresa Fetterman T., May 24, 1980; children: Andrew Jacob, Patricia Erin, Dominic Earl. BA in History with honors, Pa. State U., 1978; JD, Dickinson Sch. Law, 1981. Bar: Pa. 1981, U.S. Dist. (mid. dist.) Pa. 1982, U.S. Supreme Ct. 1987, U.S. Ct. Appeals (3d cir.) 1989. Ast. pub. defender Cumberland County, Carlisle, Pa., 1981-84; ptnr. Griffie & Turo, 1984-89; pvt. practice, 1989—. Lectr. Dickinson Sch. Law, 1996—, Weidener U. Sch. Law, 2000, adj. prof., 2001—. Founder Cumberland County Police Recognition Dinner, Carlisle, Pa., 1985—; mem. Nat. Cath. Com. on Scouting, 1988—; chmn. Region III, Pa., N.J., 1993-95, parliamentarian and legal coun., 1991—, advisor religious act, 1998-2000; bd. dirs. AHEDD, Inc., 1993-94, vice chmn. 1994-95, chmn., 1995—; trustee David E. Baker Scholarship Trust, 1997—; bd. dirs. Pa. Assn. for the Blind, 1998—, exec. search com., 1999-2000. Recipient St. George Emblem Boy Scouts Am., 1983, Eagle Scout 1969, Golden AAD Emblem, 1989. Mem. Nat. Lawyer's Assn., Nat. Assn. Criminal Def. Lawyers, Pa. Bar Assn., Pa. Assn. Criminal Def. Lawyers, Solicitor's Assn., Pa. Boroughs, Pa. Twp. Assns., Cumberland County Bar Assn. (social chmn. 1985-98, pub. rels. com. 1998—, bench-bar com. 1998—, membership chmn. 2000—), St. Thomas More Soc. (v.p. 1996-98, treas. 1998—), Mensa (local sec. 1990-92, editor 1992-95, ombudsman 2000—), KC (pres. Capital area chpt. 1989, Knight of Yr. 1981, grand knight 1985-87, 93-95, fin. sec. 1996—, dist. dep. 1998—). Republican. Roman Catholic. Avocations: scuba diving, travel. Office: 28 S Pitt St Carlisle PA 17013-3211 E-mail: RonTuro@TuroLaw.com.

TUROCK, BETTY JANE, library and information science educator; b. Scranton, Pa., June 12; d. David and Ruth Carolyn (Sweetser) Argust; m. Frank M. Turock, June 16, 1956; children: David L., B. Drew. BA magna cum laude (Charles Weston scholar), Syracuse U., 1955; postgrad. (scholar), U. Pa., 1956; MLS, Rutgers U., 1970, PhD, 1981. Library and materials coordinator Holmdel (N.J.) Public Schs., 1963-65; story-teller Wheaton (Ill.) Public Library, 1965-67; ednl. media specialist Alhambra Public Sch., Phoenix, 1967-70; br. librarian, area librarian, head extension service Forsyth County Public Library System, Winston-Salem, NC, 1970—73; asst. dir., dir. Montclair (N.J.) Public Library, 1973—76; asst. dir. Monroe County Library System, Rochester, N.Y., 1978-81; asst. prof. Rutgers U. Sch. Comms., Info. and Libr. Studies, 1981-87; assoc. prof. Rutgers U. Sch. Comm. Info and Libr. Studies, 1987-93, prof., 1994—, dept. chair, 1989-95, dir. MLS program, 1990-95, assoc. dean, 2002—. Vis. prof. Rutgers U. Grad. Sch. Library and Info. Studies, 1980-81; adviser U.S. Dept. Edn. Office of Libr. Programs, 1988-89. Author: Serving Older Adults, 1983, Creating a Financial Plan, 1992; editor: The Bottom Line, 1984-90; contbr. articles to profl. jours. Trustee Raritan Twp. (N.J.) Pub. Libr., 1961—62, Keystone Coll., 1991—, Freedom to Read Found., 1994—97, Librs. for the Future, 1994—97, Fund for Am.'s Librs., 1995, Trejo Found., 1995—; trustee Bd. Am. Libr., Paris, 1999—; mem. Bd. Edn. Raritan Twp., 1962—66; ALA coord. Task Force on Women, 1978—80; mem. action coun.; treas. Social Responsibilities Round Table, 1978—82. Charles Weston scholar Syracuse U., 1955; recipient N.J. Libr. Leadership award, 1994; named Woman of Yr. Raritan-Holmdel Woman's Club, 1975. Mem. AAUP, Am. Soc. Info. Sci., Assn. Libr. and Info. Sci Edn., Am. Libr. Assn. (pres. 1995-96, pres.-elect 1994-95, exec. bd. 1991-97, coun. 1988-97, equality award 1998), Rutgers U. Grad. Sch. Library and Info. Studies Alumni Assn. (pres. 1977-78, Disting. Alumni award 1994, Extraordinary Libr. Advocate of 20th Century award 2000), Phi Theta Kappa, Psi Chi, Beta Phi Mu, Pi Beta Phi. Unitarian Universalist. Home: 39 Highwood Rd Somerset NJ 08873-1834 Office: Rutgers U 4 Huntington St New Brunswick NJ 08901-1071 E-mail: bturock@scils.rutgers.edu.

TUROCK, JANE PARSICK, nutritionist; b. Peckville, Pa., Apr. 15, 1947; d. Paul Charles and Elizabeth Dorothy (Mistysyn) Parsick; m. Michael John, July 12, 1968; children: Eric Matthew, Nathan Andrew, J. Seth, Melanie Kay. BS, Marywood Coll., Scranton, 1969; MS, Marywood Coll., 1982. Registered dietitian; cert. nutrition specialist. Registered dietitian Jane P. Turock, Scranton, Pa., 1985—; founder and chief dietitian Gastric Bubble, 1986—; prof. Penn State Coll., 1987—; dietitian & presenter WNEP TV Healthwatch, Avoca, 1988—; dir. & chief dietitian Vascular Inst. of Northeast Pa., 1989—; owner, mgr. Nutrition...Plus/Fitness Unlimited, Scranton, 1991—. Cons. Home Health Care Assn., Clarks Summit, 1985—; dietitian Clarks Summit, 1985—; founder Nat. Nutrition Month Bakeoff; dir. Camp Jane. Treas. Lackawanna County Med. Soc. Aux., 1974-76, pres., 1979-80, bd. dirs., 1980-81; allocations com. United Way Lackawanna County, 1990—; mem. bd. dirs. Lupus Found., 1995, St. Francis of Assissi Kitchen, 1995. Mem. Am. Dietic Assn., Northeast Dist. Pa. Dietic Diet Therapy, Consulting Nutritionists in Pvt. Practice, Am. Diabetic Assn., Northeast Womens Network, Allied Wedding Firm. Republican. Roman Catholic. Avocations: skiing, tennis, gourmet cooking, jogging, swimming. Office: Nutrition Plus/Lady Jane Fitness 375 N 9th Ave Scranton PA 18504-2005 also: Abington Family Svcs 211 N State St Clarks Summit PA 18411-1087 also: Lady Jane Inc dba The Ski Habit Union Dale PA 18470 also: Nate's Outdoor Sports Ctr 611 State St Clarks Summit PA 18411 also: Tand A Assocs A Comml Devel Co 397 N 9th Ave Scranton PA 18504-2005

TUROCY, CATHERINE, performing company executive; BFA magna cum laude, Ohio State U., 1974. Tchr. Baroque dance STEPS Dance Studio, N.Y.C., 1991—95; tchr. The Baroque Ballet Workshop , Calif., 1995—, Baroque Dance Workshops, 1996—; dancer Cleve. Ballet Co., 1967—70, Modern Dance Troupe, Ohio State U., 1971—74, The Baroque Dance Ensemble, 1972—80, The Auk Mime and Dance Troupe, 1974—75, The Max Co., 1976—77, The Mitchell Rose Dance Co., 1977—78, Court Dance Co. N.Y., 1977—79; dancer, artistic dir. The N.Y. Baroque Dance Co., 1976—. Guest choreographer; vis. lectr.; vis. artist. Creator (video) The Art of Dancing: An Introduction to Baroque Dance, 1979 (Dance Film award, 1979); author: Moving History/Dancing Cultures: A Dance History Reader, 2001, Dance Masters: Roseman, Janet Lynn, 2001; dancer numerous videos, TV, plays, stage, choreographer numerous musicals, modern dance, stage. Named Chevalier in Order of Arts and Letters, French Govt., 1995; recipient N.Y. Dance and Performance award, 2001, Jerome Found. award for choreographic creation, 1985; fellow, Nat. Endowment for Arts, 1980—81, 1987, N.Y. Found. for Arts, 1990, Nat. Endowment for Arts Choreography, 1980, 83, 84, 86-88, 90, 94-96, 96-97; grantee, Nat. Endowment for Arts Heritage and Preservation, 1997—98; scholar, Getty, 1997. Mem.: Alpha Lambda Delta. Home: 6901 Gaston Ave Dallas TX 75214*

TUROCZY, D. ANN, counseling administrator, educator; b. Allentown, Pa., Mar. 11, 1968; d. Charles C. and Patricia Perna; m. Istvan Z. Turoczy; children: Michael, Nicholas. BA in Sociology/Criminal Justice, Bloomsburg (Pa.) U., 1990; cert., Am. Inst. Paralegal Studies, 1993; MEd in Secondary Sch. Counseling, Kutztown (Pa.) U., 2001. Youth care worker Northampton County Juvenile Detention Ctr., Easton, Pa., 1993—95; tutor coord. Kutztown U., 1999—2000; lectr. Lehigh Carbon C.C., Schnecksville, 1999—; intern Eyer Mid. Sch., Macungie, 2000—01. Cons., group leader Beth's Group Lehigh Valley Multiple Sclerosis Ctr., Bethlehem, Pa., 2000—; adj. prof. Northampton C.C., 2002—. Author, editor: Kutztown Counselor, 1998. Vol. Lower Macungie Elem. Sch., Wescosville, Pa., 2001—. Scholar, Hungarian Evang. Reform Ch., 2000—01. Mem.: ACA, Lehigh Carbon Sch. Counselor Assn., Pa. Sch. Counselor Assn. (scholar 1999), Am. Sch. Counselor Assn., Grad. Student Assn. (pres. 2000—01), Alpha Epsilon Lambda (pres., v.p., sec. 1998—2001), Phi Kappa Phi. Avocations: genealogy, reading.

TUROFSKY, CHARLES SHELDON, landscape architect; b. Chgo., Oct. 1, 1942; s. Joseph and Lillian R. (Brownstein) T.; m. Diane Adrienne Haber, Aug. 22, 1971; children: Benjamin, Alexi, Nicole. BFA, U. Ill., 1964; M Landscape Architecture, U. Mich., 1966; student, Harvard Grad. Sch. Design, 1971. Registered landscape architect, N.Y., Conn., N.J., Mass., N.C. Assoc. landscape architect Sasaki Office, Watertown, Mass., 1966-71; prin. landscape architect Charles Turofsky, P.C., Great Neck, N.Y., 1971—; pres. Turlab Constrn. Corp., 1984—. Prof. Rutgers U., 1975-76, Westchester Community Coll., Valhalla, N.Y., 1971-75, N.Y. Bot. Garden, Bronx, N.Y., 1975-81; tchr. Yonkers (N.Y.) Pub. Schs., 1973-85; teaching fellow U. Mich., Ann Arbor, 1965. Prin. works include Tarry Town Corp. Ctr., GE World Hdqrs., Fairfield, Conn., Rosecliff Condominiums, Briarcliff, N.Y., Tarry Elm Bus. Ctr., Elmsford, N.Y., Woodmere (N.Y.) Country Club, Hampshire Country Club, Mamaroneck, N.Y., adult handicapped playground Young Adult Inst., Tarrytown, N.Y., Hebrew Hosp., Valhalla, N.Y., Mita Copy Star, Fairfield, N.J., AT&T Switching Ctr., Rego Park, Horizon Ho., Great Neck, N.Y., 104 Corporate Dr., Purchase, N.Y., Ophir Farms, Purchase, N.Y., Eastchester Glen, Eastchester N.Y., 1998, Hammer Libr., Columbia U., Ind. Plaza, N.Y.C., 1990, Seward Park, N.Y.C., 2000, Temple Emanuel Playground, Great Neck, N.Y., landscape for new Police Athletic League Bldg, Great Neck, 2000. Recipient award Garden Clubs of Am., 1982, award N.Y. State Nurserymen Assn., 1987, 88. Mem. Am. Soc. Landscape Architects, N.Y. State United Tchrs. (rep. 1983-85), Westchester-Putnam Builders Inst. (Excellence in Landscaping award 1986). Jewish. Avocations: painting, fishing, gardening, travel, theatre, museums. Office: 6 Bly Ct Great Neck NY 11023-1706 Fax: 516-482-2423. E-mail: ctpc@clandscapearchitecture.com.

TUROK, PAUL HARRIS, composer, music reviewer; b. N.Y.C., Dec. 3, 1929; s. Joseph and Esther (Pashman) T.; m. Susan Kay Frucht, Mar. 24, 1967. BA, Queens Coll., N.Y.C., 1950; MA, U. Calif., Berkeley, 1951; MS, Baruch Coll., 1986. Music dir. Sta. KPFA, Berkeley, 1955-56; lectr. CCNY, 1959-63; vis. prof. Williams Coll., Williamstown, Mass., 1963-64; music critic New York Herald-Tribune, 1964-65; critic, columnist Music Jour., New York, 1964-79, Ovation mag., New York, 1980—; critic, contbr. New York Times, 1984—, Sta. WQXR, First Hearing, New York, 1985—. Pub. Turok's Choice, 1990—. Composer musical compositions, premiered Indpls. Symphony, 1971, Louisville Orch., 1973, Cleve. Orch., 1973, Phila Orch., 1976; opera Richard III, 1975, Sousa Overture, 1976, Lanier Songs, 1978, English Horn Quintet, 1982, Cello Sonata, 1984, Organ Toccata, 1984, Tourist Music, 1985, String Quartet No. 4, 1986, Rhapsody for Band, 1987, Piano Dance, 1988, Violin Sonata, 1989, From Sholem Aleichem, 1990, Abac for trumpet and organ, 1990, Partita for three winds, 1991, Concerto for two violins and orchestra, 1991, Piano Trio, 1992, C.C. 6 for bassoon and orchestra, 1992, Fantasy for 4 flutes and piano, 4 hands, 1994, Clap, Cluck, Count: Three Interactive Proverbs for Children and Orchestra, 1995, Sonata No. 2 for Cello and Piano, 1996, Concerto for Piano and Orch., 1997, Canzone Concertante No. 7 for viola, percussion and strings, 1998, Reeling in the Y2K, 1999, Flute Sonata, 2000, Behold, Thou Art Fair, 2001, Sextet for piano and winds, Partita No.3 for English horn, 2002. Served with U.S. Army, 1953-55. Hertz travelling scholar, U. Calif., 1956-58; Grammy nominee 1992, 93. Jewish. Avocations: world travel, computing.

TUROV, DANIEL, financial writer, investment executive; b. Bklyn., Jan. 15, 1947; s. Bernard and Mildred (Stevelman) T.; m. Rosalyn B. Kalishock, Aug. 25, 1968 (dec.); children: Joshua Nathaniel, Steven Russell. Registered investment advisor. Account exec. Walston & Co., 1969-72, Thomson McKinnon Securities, 1972-75; sr. v.p. Faulkner Dawkins & Sullivan, 1975-77, Cowen & Co., N.Y.C., 1977-80; dir. Turov Investment Group divsn. Moore & Schley, Cameron & Co., 1980-82; v.p. Dean Witter Reynolds, Inc., 1982-83, sr. v.p., 1983-84; pres. Just Right Comm., 1992—. Chmn. Philtrum Advt. Corp., 1982-84; mem. faculty N.Y. Inst. Fin., New Sch. Social Rsch.; mem. panel The Wall St. Transcript's Option Roundtable; interviewer toCNN, 2000; spkr. in field. Author: (monthly) Turov on Investments and Hedging, 1972-80; monthly investment column Best Buys Mag., 1982-83; editor New Innovations Pub. Corp., 1979-86, Turov on Timing, 1993—; contbr. articles to profl. jours. and newspapers; interviewd on CNN, 2000. Recipient Supertrader of Yr. award Stock Traders Almanac, 2001. Mem. Nat. Futures Assn. (registered commodity trading advisor). Office: Just Right Comm 154 Whippoorwill Ln Oak Ridge TN 37830-8645

TURPIN, CALVIN COOLIDGE, retired university administrator, educator; b. Granite City, Ill., Nov. 8, 1924; s. Golden and Gertrude (West) T.; m. Eudell Coody, June 29, 1944; children: Susan Turpin Jones, John Thomas. BA, Baylor U., 1949, MA, 1952; BD, So. Bapt. Theol. Sem., 1955, M of Religious Edn., 1958; MA, Vanderbilt U., 1962; MDiv, So. Bapt. Theol. Sem., 1973; DSc in Theology, Golden Gate Bapt. Theol. Sem., 1967. Prof. history and Greek Jacksonville Coll., Tex., 1950-52; prof. religion Belmont Coll., Nashville, 1955-56, Austin-Peay State U., Clarksville, Tenn., 1956-57; assoc. libr. Inst. of Old Testament Golden Gate Bapt. Theol. Sem., Mill Valley, Calif., 1961-66; dir. librs., prof. libr. sci. Minot (N.D.) State Coll., 1966-67; dir. librs., prof. religion Judson Coll., Marion, Ala., 1967-70; prof. religion, dir. librs. Hardin-Simmons U., Abilene, Tex., 1970-77. Vis. prof. Tex. Woman's U., Denton, 1974-75. Author: Beyond My Dreams: Memories and Interpretations, 1992, Writings and a Selected Bibliography of Calvin C. Turpin, 1995, 50 Years of Ministry: Challenges and Changes, 1997; co-author: Rupert N. Richardson: The Man and His Works, 1971, History of the First Baptist Church, Gilroy, California, 1995; contbr. numerous articles to profl. publs. Nat. dep. chief chaplains CAP-USAF Aux., 1990-92; Calif. dept. chaplain Am. Legion, San Francisco, 1990-92, 94-95; nat. chaplain, Am. Legion, Indpls., 2000-01; vets. pk. commr. San Benito County, Hollister, Calif., 1990-92; rent control commr. City of Hollister, 1993-95. Brigadier gen. USSC, 1992—. Lilly Endowment scholar Lilly Found., 1962. Mem. Rotary Club, Lions Club, Beta Phi Mu, Phi Delta Kappa, Gamma Iota. Republican. Baptist. Avocations: volunteer chaplaincy, writing, authentic cowboy cooking. Home: 188 Elm Dr Hollister CA 95023-3430

TURPIN, DAVID HOWARD, biologist, educator; b. Duncan, B.C., Can., July 14, 1956; s. George Howard and Marilyn Elizabeth (Jones) T.; m. S. Laurene Clark, Oct. 4, 1985; children: Chantal, Joshua. BSc in Biology, U. B.C., 1977, PhD in Botany, Oceanography, 1980. Post-doctoral rsch. fellow Natural Sci. & Engring. Coun., 1980-81; rsch. assoc. Simon Fraser U., 1980; v.p. Sigma Resource Cons., Vancouver, B.C., 1980-81; from asst. prof. to assoc. prof. Queen's U., Kingston, Ont., Can., 1981-90, prof. biology, 1990-91, dean arts & sci., 1993-95, vice prin. acad., 1995-2000; prof., head botany U. B.C., 1991-93; pres., vice-chancellor U. Victoria, B.C., 2000—. Invited speaker profl. meetings univs. worldwide. Co-editor: Plant Physiology, Biochemistry and Molecular Biology, 1990, 2d edit., 1996; mem. editl. bd. Jour. Phycology, 1992-96, Plant Physiology, 1988-92, Plant Cell and Environ., 1994—, Jour. Exptl. Botany, 1995—; contbr. chpts. to books; author numerous articles, conf. procs. V.p. Great Lakes Tomorrow, 1986-90; mem. program com. Great Lakes Course-Ont. Sci. Ctr., 1988; Kingston City rep. Cataraqui Regional Conservation Authority, 1984-86. Recipient Excellence in Teaching Alumni award Queen's U., 1989, Outstanding Alumni award U. B.C., 1990, Darbaker prize in phycology Am. Bot. Assn., 1991; Natural Sci. and Engring. Rsch. Can. E.W.R. Stacie Meml. fellow, 1989-90; Capt. T.S. Byrne Meml. scholar U. B.C., 1980; postgrad. scholar Natural Scis. and Engring. Rsch. Coun., 1979-81, Edith Ashton Meml. scholar U. B.C., 1979, Nat. Rsch. Coun. scholar, 1978-79; Natural Scis. and Engring. Rsch. Coun. grantee, 1982—. Fellow Royal Soc. Can.; mem. Phycological Soc. Am., Am. Soc. Limnology and Oceanography, Can. Soc. Plant Physiologists (C.D. Nelson award 1989), Am. Soc. Plant Physiologists (cert. recognition 1992) Office: Off of the Pres - U Victoria Business & Economic Bldg Rm 454 Victoria BC Canada V8W 2Y2

TURPIN, ELIZABETH LOUISE, music educator; b. Cohoes, N.Y., July 29, 1936; d. Omer Frederick and Marie Anne (Chouinard) Marcil; m. Eugene E. Turpin, Sept. 8, 1956 (div.); children: David, Lynn, Mark, Steven, Lisa, Eric, Jill. AA, Regents External Degree, 1973; BS, Empire State Coll., 1973; postgrad., SUNY, 1974-82. Sales assoc. Macys Colonie, Albany, 1986-91; chiropractic asst. Dr. Joseph S. Gulyas, Clifton Park, N.Y., 1993-95; tchr. piano pvt. practice, 1991—. Mem. adv. bd. Rehab. Support Svcs., Albany, 1985-91; active Pub. Employees Fedn., 1994, trustee membership benefit fund 1991-93; ind. distbr. Neways Internat., 2001. Mem. Music. Tchrs. Nat. Assn., Northeast Region Assn. Rsch. & Enlightenment (treas. 1996), N.Y. State

Music Tchrs. Assn., Nat. Music Tchrs. Assn., N.Y. State Music Tchrs. Assn. Avocations: knitting, crocheting, sewing, reading. Home and Office: 24 Madrid Ct Clifton Park NY 12065-4917

TURPIN, JOSEPH OVILA, counselor, educator; b. Rockford, Ill., July 11, 1943; s. D. John and Mona Belle (Albright) T.; m. Hester R. Thompson, June 26, 1969; children: Matthew, Michael. AB in Sociology, Ind. U., 1965, MS in Mental Retardation, 1966, postgrad., 1966-67; PhD in Rehab. Psychology, U. Wis., 1986. Rsch. assoc. Ind. U., Bloomington, 1966-67; instr. U. Wis. Parkside Extension, Kenosha, 1967-71; tchr. Kenosha Unified Sch. Dist., 1967-71; coord. Racine area Gov.'s Com. on Spl. Learning State of Wis. Dept. Adminstrn., 1971-73; dir. Racine County Comprehensive Mental Health, Mental Retardation, Alcohol and Other Drug Abuse Svcs. Bd, 1973-78; vocat. cons., counselor supr. Industrial Injury Clinic, Neenah, Wis., 1978-83; owner, vocat. expert Vocat. Counseling Svc., Inc., Madison, 1983-88; teaching intern, counseling supr., student tchr. supr. U. Wis., 1983-86; asst. prof. rehab. counselor edn. Ohio U., Athens, 1986-89; assoc. prof. rehab. counseling program Calif. State U., San Bernardino, 1989-94, prof. rehab. counseling program, 1994—, coord. rehab. counseling program, 1990-94, 2000—. Mem. sch. psychologist exam. com. Dept. Edn. State of Ohio, 1989; rschr., presenter, cons. in field. Contbr. articles to profl. publs. Bd. dirs. United Cerebral Palsy of Racine County, 1969-73, Children's House, Inc., Racine, 1971-73, Ctrl. Ohio Regional Coun. on Alcoholism, 1987-89, Ctr. for Cmty. Counseling and Edn., 1993-99, pres., 1998; bd. dirs. Inland Caregivers Resource Ctr., 1993-99, Health and Hosp. Planning Com. of Racine County, 1976; treas. Cub Scout Pack # 68, Boy Scouts Am., Neenah, 1981-83, Whitcomb Village Assn., Inc., 1984; bd. dirs. Aquinas H.S., 1992-94, pres. 1994; H.S. liaison West Point Parents Club of Inland Empire, 1992-94; budget rev. com. United Fund Racine County, 1975. Grantee Rehab. Svcs. Adminstrn., 1985-88, Ohio U., 1987-88, Ohio U. Coll. Osteo. Medicine and Coll. Edn., 1989, Office Spl. Edn. and Rehab., 1989-92, Inland Reg. Ctr., 1999. Mem. ACA (pub. policy and legis. com. 1992-94, various subcoms.), APA, Assn. Counselor Educators and Suprs. (we. region legis. chair 1996-98), Am. Rehab. Counseling Assn. (exec. coun. 1992-94, ethics com. 1990-91, chair coun. on profl. preparation and stds. 1992-94), Nat. Rehab. Counseling Assn. (bd. dirs. 1993-94, chmn. grievance com., pres. 1997), Nat. Rehab. Assn. (bd. dirs. 1998), Alliance Rehab. Counseling (bd. dirs. 1996-98, co-chair 1998). Office: Calif State U 5500 University Pkwy San Bernardino CA 92407-2318 Business E-Mail: jturpin@csusb.edu. E-mail: rx300xx@aol.com.

TURPIN, RICHARD BEN, civil engineer; b. Bedford, Va., Jan. 1, 1935; s. Charles W. and Francis (Wilson) T.; m. Patty Boggess, May 29, 1958; children: Barbara Phillips, Tracy Patterson, Steven. BSCE, Va. Poly. Inst., 1962. Registered profl. engr., W.Va., Va., N.C., Fla.; profl. surveyor, W.Va., Va., N. C., Fla. Engr., surveyor Va. Iron, Coal and Coke Co., Roanoke, Va., 1962-64; project design engr. Hayes, Seay, Mattern and Mattern, 1964; city engr. City of Radford, Va., 1964-65; pvt. practice Bedford, 1965-66; project engr. U.S. Forest Svc., Roanoke, and Tallahassee, Fla., 1966-68, cadastral surveyor Asheville, N.C., 1968-69; asst. dir. pub. works City of Danville, Va., 1969, supt. gas & water, 1969-73; pub. works dir. City of Roanoke, 1973-76; dir. engrng. CSX Hotels, Inc.-The Greenbrier, White Sulphur Springs, W.Va., 1976-96. Owner Richard B. Turpin & Assocs., P.C. Land Surveying and Consulting Engrng., Bedford, Va. With U.S. Army, 1953-55. Fellow ASCE (pres. Lynchburg chpt. 1997-98); mem. Va. Soc. Profl. Engrs. (pres. Lynchburg chpt. 1997-98), W.Va. Soc. Profl. Engrs. (pres. 1992-93). Republican. Southern Baptist. Home and Office: 1737 Patterson Mill Rd Bedford VA 24523-3896

TURPIN, RICHARD E. sales executive; b. Hamilton, Ohio, Aug. 10, 1950; 1 child, Vincent Paul Huntington Turpin. Degree, UCLA, 1972. Dir. sales Pepsico, Hamilton; dir. mktg. Tri-State, Inc., Columbus, Ohio; dir. sales CMR, Inc., 1985-96; self-employed cons. Turpin Assocs., Cin., 1996—; former v.p. U.S. Plywood/Champion Papers; sr. exec. Arch Wireless, 1996—. Vol. Children's Svcs., Columbus, 1994—. Recipient Citizenship award Chgo., 1970. Mem. Columbus C. of C. (com. chmn. 1993-94), Columbus Exec. Sales Assn., Dayton Realtors, Dayton C. of C., Pres.'s Club. Roman Catholic. Home: 4535 Bonita Dr Unit 180 Middletown OH 45044-6788 E-mail: 2615860@archwireless.net.

TURQUETTE, ATWELL RUFUS, logician; b. Texarkana, Tex., July 14, 1914; s. Rufus Watson and Dale Cook (Warmack) Turquette; m. Lucille Case Le Roy, June 2, 1937 (dec. Feb. 1956); m. Maxine Harriot Kennedy, Apr. 2, 1958 (dec. Aug. 1992); m. Frances D. Bond, Dec. 27, 1998. BA, U. Ark., 1936; MA, Duke U., 1937; PhD, Cornell U., 1943. Asst. prof. Fla. So. Coll., Lakeland, 1937-38; fellow U. Chgo., 1938-39; assoc. prof. Fla. So. Coll., Lakeland, 1939-40; assistantship, fellow Cornell U., Ithaca, N.Y., 1940-43, instr., 1943-45; asst. prof. U. Ill., Champaign-Urbana, 1945-48, assoc. prof., 1948-52, prof., 1952-75, prof. emeritus, 1975—. Co-author: Many-valued Logics, 1952; contbg. author: Les 265 communications, Congrès International des Mathématiciens, Nice, 1970; editor: Jour. of Symbolic Logic, 1950-68; patentee in field. Duke U. scholar, 1936; U. Chgo. fellow, 1938; grantee NSF, 1968-70, Rockefeller Gen. Edn. Bd., 1954. Mem. Am. Math. Soc., Soc. Indsl. and Appl. Math., Symbolic Logic Assn., London Math. Soc., Calcutta Math. Soc., AAAS, N.Y. Acad. Scis., Am Phil. Assn. Achievements include design for multi-valued circuits, functional completeness and incompleteness results for many-valued logics; minimal axiomatizations for many-valued logics; relating Pascal triangles to Post sets; deciphering Peirce's triadic logic. Avocations: travel, physical exercise. Home: 914 W Clark St Champaign IL 61821-3328 E-mail: aturquette1@iopener.net.

TURQUETTE, FRANCES BOND, editor; b. Atlanta, Sept. 25, 1931; d. Sewell Hinton and Lavonia DeLay Dixon; m. Charles Eugene Bond, Sept. 12, 1952 (div. Jan. 1969); children: Turner D., Laura S., L. Irene, Cynthia D., Nelson K.; m. Atwell Rufus Turquette, Dec. 27, 1998 Student, Wesleyan Coll., 1948-50; BA in Journalism, U. Ga., 1952; MA in Art History, U. Ill., 1971. Editl. asst. Meth. Pub. Ho., Nashville, 1952-53, Rsch. Press, Champaign, Ill., 1972-73; editing supr. McGraw-Hill Book Co., N.Y.C., 1974-80; publs. editor pub. affairs U. Ill., Urbana, 1974, 80-88; editor Nat. Ctr. for Supercomputing Applications, Champaign, 1988-96. Vis. faculty, editor Coll. of Commerce, U. Ill. Urbana, 1972-74; ref. com., Editorial and Composition Standards McGraw Hill Book Co., N.Y.C., 1975-77; editor, writer access, 1988-96. Mem. program chair, liaison, bd. govts. Channing Murray Found., Urbana, 1982-92; mem. adv. bd. to freeze nuclear weapons 15th Congrl. Dist., 1982-87; co-pres. SANE/Freeze, Champaign County, 1992-94. Mem. Nat. Assn. Sci. Writers, Art Inst. Chgo. (nat. assoc.), Lyric Opera Chgo., Theta Sigma Phi. Unitarian Universalist. Avocations: travel, writing, gardening, photography. Home: 914 W Clark St Champaign IL 61821-3328 E-mail: aturquette1@iopener.net.

TURRELL, RICHARD HORTON, SR. retired banker; b. Kingston, Pa., Apr. 9, 1925; s. George Henry and Margaret (Clark) T.; m. Sally Wolfe, May 28, 1955; children: Richard H. Jr., David C., Douglas W. (dec.). Student, Cornell U., 1943; BS in Commerce, Washington and Lee U., 1949. Rep. sales Del. Lackawanna and Western Coal Co., Phila., 1949-51; asst. to pres. N.Y.C., 1951-58; broker Auchincloss Parker & Redpath, 1958-61; mgr. investments Fiduciary Trust Co. Internat., 1961-94, v.p., 1965-94, sr. v.p., 1968-94, sec., 1971-84. Asst. sec. Blue Coal Corp., N.Y.C., 1953-58; v.p., bd. dirs. Pine Raleigh (N.C.) Corp., 1966-93. Trustee, overseer Simon's Rock of Bard Coll., Gt. Barrington, Mass., 1968-93; trustee Monmouth Univ., West Long Branch, N.J., 1980—, chmn. bd. trustees, 1989-92; chmn. Millburn-Short Hills (N.J.) Rep. Com., 1973-78; trustee Children's Specialized Hosp. Found., Mountainside, N.J., 1989-95; bd. dirs. ARC Martin County, Fla., 2000. With Signal Corps, U.S. Army, 1943-46, PTO. Named Disting. Alumnus, Washington and Lee U., 1986. Mem. Baltusrol Golf Club (Springfield, N.J., gov. 1977), Capitol Hill Club (Washington), Turtle Creek Club (Tequesta, Fla.), Masons, Irem Temple Aaonms, Phi Beta Kappa, Phi Eta Sigma, Alpha Kappa Psi, Omicron Delta Kappa (hon.), Beta Gamma Sigma, Phi Delta Theta. Presbyterian. Avocations: golf, history, education. Home: 114 Turtle Creek Dr Tequesta FL 33469-1547

TURRENTINE, HOWARD BOYD, federal judge; b. Escondido, Calif., Jan. 22, 1914; s. Howard and Veda Lillian (Maxfield) T.; m. Virginia Jacobsen, May 13, 1965 (dec.); children: Howard Robert, Terry Beverly; m. Marlene Lipsey, Nov. 1, 1991. AB, San Diego State Coll., 1936; LLB, U. So. Calif., 1939. Bar: Calif. 1939. Practiced in, San Diego, 1939-68; judge Superior Ct. County of San Diego, 1968-70, U.S. Dist. Ct. (so. dist.) Calif., Calif., sr. judge, 1970—. Served with USNR, 1941-45. Mem. ABA, Fed. Bar Assn., Am. Judicature Soc. Office: US Dist Ct 940 Front St San Diego CA 92101-8994

TURRI, JOSEPH A. lawyer; b. Seneca Falls, N.Y., July 24, 1943; s. Louis Arthur and Assunta (Faiola) T.; m. Susan Ruth Testa, Dec. 29, 1975; 1 child, Michael James. BA, SUNY, Buffalo, 1965; JD, Cornell U., 1970. Bar: N.Y. 1971, U.S. Dist Ct. (we. dist.) N.Y. 1971, U.S. Supreme Ct. 1974, U.S. Dist. Ct. (so. dist.) N.Y. 1996, U.S. Ct. Appeals (2d cir.) 1996. Ptnr. Harris Beach LLP, Rochester, N.Y., 1970—, mgmt. ptnrs. com., 1991-97, chmn. constrn. law dept., 1992-98, chmn. litigation dept., 1994-96, pres., 1999—. Bd. dirs. Thousand Island Park Corp., N.Y.; v.p. Castle Bay Ltd., Rochester, N.Y.; arbitrator Am. Arbitration Assn., Syracuse, 1985—. Bd. dirs. Rochester Downtown Devel. Corp., 1992-97. Mem. N.Y. State Bar Assn., Monroe County Bar Assn., Assn. Gen. Contractors, Met. Forum (trustee). Avocations: horseback riding, antique wooden boats. Home: 21 Evergreen Ln Rochester NY 14618-4719 Office: Harris Beach LLP 99 Garnsey Rd Pittsford NY 14534

TURRILL, FRED LOVEJOY, surgeon; b. Redlands, Calif., Sept. 14, 1922; s. Gardner Stilson and Virginia Marie (Johnson) T.; m. Edith Mae Brown, Mar. 17, 1951; children: Brian Casey, Kevin Michael, Ann Louise, Mark. AS, Glendale Coll., 1942; BSE, U. Mich., 1944; MD, U. So. Calif., 1950. Diplomate Am. Bd. Surgery. Intern L.A. County/U. So. Calif. Med. Ctr., 1950-52, resident surgery, 1952-56; surgeon Turrill, Shader & Myles, Glendale, Calif., 1956—. Prof. surgery U. So. Calif., L.A., 1974—. Contbr. articles to profl. jours. With U.S. Army, 1942-46. Grantee USPS, 1956-57. Mem. ACS (gov. 1977-84), Collegium Internat. Chirurgiae, Pacific Coast Surg. Assn. (councillor 1980-83), We. Surg. Assn., Soc. Grad. Surgeons (life hon., pres. 1970-71), L.A. Surg. Soc. (pres. 1975). Republican. Avocations: fishing, boating, hunting, travel.

TURRISI, BRIAN CHARLES, pulmonologist; b. Orange, N.J., June 18, 1952; s. Andrew and Marjorie (Carney) T.; m. Elaine Frances Glenn, July 3, 1997. BA, Coll. Holy Cross, 1974; MD, Georgetown U., 1978. Diplomate Am. Bd. Internal Medicine. Intern Georgetown U., Washington, 1978-79, resident in internal medicine, 1979-81; chief med. resident VA Hosp., 1981-82; fellow in pulmonary diseases George Washington U., 1982-84; pvt. practice, 1984—. Fellow Am. Coll. Chest Physicians. Avocation: flying. E-mail: bcturrisi@cs.com.

TURRO, NICHOLAS JOHN, chemistry educator; b. Middletown, Conn., May 18, 1938; s. Nicholas John and Philomena (Russo) T.; m. Sandra Jean Misenti, Aug. 6, 1960; children: Cynthia Suzanne, Claire Melinda. BA, Wesleyan U., 1960, DSc (hon.), 1984; PhD, Calif. Inst. Tech., 1963. Instr. chemistry Columbia U., N.Y.C., 1964-65, asst. prof., 1965-67, assoc. prof., 1967-69, prof. chemistry, 1969—. William P. Schweitzer prof. chemistry, 1982—, chmn. chemistry dept., 1981-84, co-chmn. dept. chem. engrng. and applied chemistry, 1997-2000, prof. earth and environ. engrng., 1998—. Author: Molecular Photochemistry, 1965; author: (with A.A. Lamola) Energy Transfer and Organic Photochemistry, 1971; author: Modern Molecular Photochemistry, 1978; mem. editl. bd.: Jour. Reactive Intermediates. Recipient Eastman Kodak award for excellence in grad. rsch. pure chemistry, 1973, award, E.O. Lawrence U.S. Dept. Energy, 1983, Porter medal, European Photochem. Soc., Inter-Am. Photochem. Soc., 1994, Havinga medal, Leiden, The Netherlands, 1994, Disting. Alumnus award, Calif. Inst. Tech., 1996, Strahlenchemie preis, Max-Planck-Inst., Mülheim, Germany, 1998; fellow NSF, Alfred P. Sloan Found., Guggenheim fellow, Oxford U., 1985. Mem.: AAAS, NAS, European Photo-Chem. Assn. (Porter medal), Inter-Am. Photochemistry Soc. (award 1991, 1994), N.Y. Acad. Scis. (Freda and Gregory Halpern award in photochemistry 1977), Am. Chem. Soc. (mem. editl. bd. jour. 1984—87, Fresenius award 1973, award for pure chemistry 1974, Harrison Howe award Rochester, N.Y. sect. 1986, Arthur C. Cope award 1986, James Flack Norris award 1987, award in colloid and surface chemistry 1999, Gibbs medal award Chgo. sect. 2000), Sigma Xi, Phi Beta Kappa. Office: Columbia U 3000 Broadway New York NY 10027-6941

TURSCHMAN, KYLE ANDREW, civil engineer; b. Holyoke, Mass., Oct. 6, 1958; s. Kenneth Richard and Marjorie Helene (Martel) T.; m. Joanne Tarza, Sept. 10, 1988; 1 child, John Andrew. BSCE, U. Lowell, 1984; MBA, Rensselaer Polytech., Hartford, Conn., 1997. Registered profl. engr., Conn. Engr. 1 C.E. Maguire, New Britain, Conn., 1984-86; project engr. Close, Jensen & Miller, Wethersfield, 1986-94; sr. project engr., project mgr. WMC Consulting Engrs., West Hartford, 1994-96; sr. engr. Purcell Assocs., Glastonbury, 1996—. Mem. ASCE, Nat. Soc. Profl. Engrs., Project Mgmt. Inst. Office: Purcell Assocs 90 National Dr Glastonbury CT 06033-1247 Home: 57 Nathaniel Dr Wethersfield CT 06109-2540

TURSO, FRANK JOSEPH, music educator; b. Port Jefferson, Ny, Dec. 5, 1948; s. Rucco and Camille Turso; m. Marya Shepherd-Turso, July 13, 1984. MA Music, SUNY, Fredonia, New York, 1977, BA, 1970. New York State Permanent Teaching Certificate NY State Edn. Dept., 1977. Band dir. William Floyd Sch. Dist., Mastic Beach, NY, 1976—, Maryvale Sch. Dist., Checktovega, 1970—76. H.s. all-county band chair Suffolk County Music Educator's Assn., Suffolk County, NY, 1999—; county band libr. Suffolk County Music Educators Assn., Suffolk County, NY, 1995—. Pres. Bellport Beach Property Owner's Assn., East Patchogue, NY, 1993—97. Specialist 5 NY Army N.G., 1970—76, New York. Mem.: NY State Band Director's Assn., NY State Sch. Music Assn. Avocations: golf, jogging, bicycling. Home: 67 Otis Road East Patchogue NY 11772 Office: William Floyd High School 240 Mastic Beach Road Mastic Beach NY 11951

TURSO, VITO ANTHONY, public relations executive; b. N.Y.C., Jan. 3, 1948; s. Vito Anthony and Helen (Smanko) T.; m. MaryAnn Ponzo, July 12, 1980; children: Lisa Lynn, Laura Mae, Nicole Vita. Student, Queens Coll., Flushing, N.Y., 1965-69. Reporter L.I. Press, Jamaica, N.Y., 1966-77; asst. Metro editor The Trib, N.Y.C., 1977-78; dir. pub. affairs N.Y.C. Dept. Sanitation, 1978-90; dep. commr. for pub. affairs N.Y.C. Dept. Correction, 1990-94; dep. commr. for pub. affairs and community svcs. N.Y.C. Dept. of Environ. Protection, 1994-95; sr. v.p. Dan Klores Assoc. Pub. Rels., 1995—. Guest lectr. N.Y.U., 1998, New Sch. for Social Rsch., N.Y.C., 1988, Pace U., 1990. Host pub. affairs shows on TV and radio, 1981, 88; contbr. articles to pop. mags. Bd. dirs. Ozone Tudor Civic Assn., Ozone Park, N.Y., 1982-90. Recipient Bronze medal Internat. Film and TV Festival N.Y., 1985, Page One award N.Y. Newspaper Guild, 1976. Mem. Pub. Rels. Officers Soc. N.Y. (pres. 1983-85), Pub. Rels. Soc. Am. (bd. dirs. 1987-88), Am. Diabetes Assn. (bd. dirs. N.Y. chpt. 1989-91), Bklyn. Tech. H.S. Alumni Assn. (bd. dirs. 1984—), N.Y. Press Club, Inc. (bd. dirs. 1978), Old Pucks Old Timers Ice Hockey Club, KC. Roman Catholic. Avocations: ice hockey, softball, music. Home: 13333 84th St Ozone Park NY 11417-1919 Office: 386 Park Ave S New York NY 10016-8804

TURTELL, NEAL TIMOTHY, librarian; b. N.Y.C., Nov. 1, 1949; s. Richard Roland and Ann Grace (Glover) T. AB, Fordham U., 1971; MLS, Pratt Inst., 1975. Cataloger-libr. Ford Found., N.Y.C., 1972-75, U.S. Dept. Transp., Washington, 1975-77; spl. projects libr. Smithsonian Instn., 1977-81, chief catalogue records, 1981-82; asst. dir. tech. svcs. U. Wis., Oshkosh, 1982-83, asst. prof. libr. sci., 1982-83; asst. chief libr. Nat. Gallery of Art, Washington, 1983-87, exec. libr., 1987—. Contbr. to book revs. Libr. Jour., 1972-75, exhbn. catalogue. Bd. trustees Pyramid Atlantic Ctr. for Printmaking and the Art of the Book, Riverdale, Md., 1988—, v.p. bd. trustees, 1991—. Mem. Art Librs. Soc. N.Am., Rsch. Librs. Group (steering com. for art and architecture 1988-89), Grolier Club. Home: 1631-B S Hayes St Arlington VA 22202-2713 Office: Nat Gallery of Art 4th & Constitution Ave NW Washington DC 20565-0001

TURTURRO, JOHN, actor; b. Brooklyn, Feb. 28, 1957; s. Nicholas and Katherine Turturro; m. Katherine Borowitz; children: Amedeo, Diego. Grad., SUNY (New Paltz), 1978; student, Yale Drama Sch. (Worked in regional theater and off-Broadway prodns.): Danny and the Deep Blue Sea; Men Without Dates; Tooth of the Crime; La Puta Vida; Chaos and Hard Times; The Bald Soprano; Of Mice and Men; The Resistable Rise of Arturo Ui, 1991; Waiting for Godot; (appeared in Broadway prodn.): Death of a Salesman, 1984; (appeared in films): Raging Bull, 1980; The Flamingo Kid, 1984; To Live and Die in L.A., 1985; Desperately Seeking Susan, 1985; Hannah and Her Sisters, 1986; Gung Ho, 1986; Offbeat, 1986; The Color of Money, 1986; The Sicilian, 1987; Five Corners, 1988; Do the Right Thing, 1989; Miller's Crossing, 1990; Men of Respect; Mo Better Blues, 1990; Jungle Fever, 1991; Barton Fink, 1991; Backtrack, 1991; Brain Donors, 1992; Fearless, 1993; Festival, 1991; Being Human, 1994; Quiz Show, 1994; Grace of My Heart, 1994; Search and Destroy, 1995; Unstrung Heroes, 1995; Clockers, 1995; Box of Moonlight, 1996; Girl 6, 1996; The Big Lebowski, 1997; Animals, 1997; The Truce, 1998; Lesser Prophets, 1998; Rounders, 1998; He Got Game, 1998; The Source, 1999; The Cradle Will Rock, 1999; Company Man, 1999; Two Thousand and None, 1999; Oh Brother, Where Art Thou?, 1999; The Man Who Cried, 1999; The Luzhin Defense, 1999; dir.: (films, debut) Mac; (films) Illuminata, 1998, Thirteen Conversations About One Thing, 2000, Collateral Damage, 2000, Monday Night Mayhem, Deeds, Secret Passage, 2001. Office: care ICM 40 W 57th St New York NY 10019-4001 also: 16 N Oak St 2 A Ventura CA 93001-5620

TUSCHER, VINCENT JAMES, author; b. Newton, Mass., Aug. 25, 1917; s. Jacob Francis and Honor Veronica (Oldfield) T.; m. Mary Alys Allen, Oct. 18, 1952. Reporter Boston Herald, 1937-46, News Tribune, Waltham, Mass., 1946-49; dir. pub. rels. IBEW Local # 1505, 1949-53; freelance pub. rels. practitioner Newton, 1953-55, 64-67; v.p. Newsome & Co., Inc., Boston, 1955-64; command speech writer Air Force Sys. Command, Lexington, Mass., 1967-71; dir. pub. affairs Fed. Emergency Mgmt. Agy., Boston, 1971-81; freelance writer Newton, 1981—. Author: (novels) For Every Man — For Every Woman, 1983, Boston Marathon Caper, 1992, (ednl. film) Survival in Winter Storm, 1975 (Cannes 1976). Dir. pub. rels. VFW, Kansas City, Kans., 1956. Served in U.S. Army, 1942-45, Europe. Mem. Nat. Def. Exec. Res. (pub. affairs dir. 1985—). Democrat. Roman Catholic. Avocations: jazz record collecting, salt water fishing, photography. Home: 19 Craigie Ter Newton MA 02460-2106

TUSCHMAN, JAMES MARSHALL, lawyer; b. Nov. 28, 1941; s. Chester and Harriet (Harris) T.; m. Ina S. Cheloff, Sept. 2, 1967; children: Chad Michael, Jon Stephen, Sari Anne. BS in Bus., Miami U., Oxford, Ohio, 1963; JD, Ohio State U., 1966. Bar: Ohio 1966, U.S. Ct. Appeals (6th and 7th cirs.), U.S. Supreme Ct. Assoc. Shumaker, Loop & Kendrick, Toledo, 1966—84, ptnr., 1970—84; co-founder, chmn. ops. com. Jacobson Maynard Tuschman & Kalur, 1985—97; COO Ohio Ferrous Group Omnisource Corp., 1998—99; dir. bus. devel. Northern Ohio Group, 1999—2001; counsel Berkan & Robon Ltd., Maumee, Ohio, 2002—. Chmn. bd., sec. Tuschman Steel Co., Toledo, 1969-76, Toledo Steel Supply Co., 1969-86; vice-chmn. bd. Kripke Tuschman Industries, Inc., 1977-85; ptnr. Starr Ave. Co., Toledo, 1969-86. Chmn. bd. trustees U. Toledo; past trustee, chmn. fin. com., past treas. Maumee Valley Country Day Sch.; past trustee, v.p., treas. Temple B'nai Israel, 1984-88. Fellow Internat. Soc. Barristers; mem. Am. Bd. Trial Advocates, Ohio Bar Assn., Toledo Bar Assn., Toledo Club, Inverness Country Club, Zeta Beta Tau, Phi Delta Phi. Home: 2579 Olde Brookside Rd Toledo OH 43615-2233 Office: Barkan & Robon Ltd 1701 Woodland Dr Maumee OH 43537-4092

TUSEO, NORBERT JOSEPH JOHN, marketing executive, consultant; b. N.Y.C., Apr. 9, 1950; s. Joseph R. and Lorraine (Babcock) T.; 1 child, Christine. AAS in Hotel and Restaurant Mgmt., N.Y. C.C., 1969, AA in Real Estate Mgmt., 1978. Lic. real estate broker, Fla.; lic. mortgage broker; lic. securities series 63, 22; cert. radon measurement technician, Fla. Mgr. Steak & Brew, N.Y.C., 1971-75; pres. Howard Beach (N.Y.) Racquet Club, 1978-80; dir. sales mktg. and tng. Vacation Interval Mktg., Ponta Gorda, Fla., 1980-83; v.p. sales mktg. and tng. Treco/Sunstate, Jacksonville, 1984-86; pres. Sunstate Mktg., Inc., St. Augustine and Jacksonville, 1986—. Pres. Sunstate Radon Cons., 1986—; mortgage broker Sunstate Fin. Svcs.; real estate broker Interval Sunstate Mktg. and Sunstate Realty & Devel., Inc.; mgr. Sunstate Travel Agy.; developer Frank B. Butler Cert. 1906 Historic Bldg.; developer and marketer Sand and Surf Resort, Daytona Beach, Fla.; pub., founder St. John's County edit. The Real Estate Book, Jacksonville edit. The Real Estate Book. Appeared in TV commls.; pub. (periodicals) Real Estate Books; contbr. numerous articles to profl. jours. Leader Boy Scouts Am., Queens, N.Y., 1963-70, vol. campaign to elect Neil Perry sheriff St. John's County, Robert Vogal sheriff Volusia County. Recipient Capitol award Nat. Leadership Coun., 1991, Silver award for mktg., sales Am. Resort Devel. Assn., 1991, trng., 1991-93, Capitol award NAt. Leadership Coun., 1991, Gold Record of Achievement award, Lifetime Achievement award Am. Biog. Inst., 1994, Platinum Record for Exceptional Performance award, 1998, Presidential Seal of Honor, 1998; named Am. Biog. Inst. Man of Yr., 1992, Am. Biog. Inst. Personality of Yr., 1995, 5000 Personalities of the World, 1994-96, 98, Internat. Directory of Dist. Leadership, 1994, Bachelor of Mo., Women's Digest, 1995, Men of Achievement, 1996, 500 Leaders of Influence, Internat. Directory Dist. Leadership, 1997, Internat. Leaders in Achievement, 1997, Internat. Book of Honor, 1998, ABI Man of Yr., 1998, others. Fellow World Literary Acad. (Cambridge, Eng.); mem. Am. Resort and Residential Devel. Assn. (registered resort profl., Nat. Silver award Mktg., 1991, Silver award Sales, 1991, Silver award Tng., 1991, 92, 93, Capitol award 1992), Kiwanis (pub. rels. com. 1980). Avocation: bicycling, investments, economics, bible study, walking. Home: 101 La Quinta Pl Saint Augustine FL 32084-4318 Office: Sunstate Mktg 101 La Quinta Pl Saint Augustine FL 32084-4318

TUSHINGHAM, A. DOUGLAS, museum administrator; b. Toronto, Ont., Can., Jan. 19, 1914; s. Arthur Douglas and Lottie Elizabeth (Betts) T.; m. Margaret McAndrew Thomson, Apr. 9, 1948; children: Margaret Elizabeth, Ian Douglas. BA, U. Toronto, 1936; B.D., U. Chgo., 1941, PhD, 1948, LL.D., 1982. Instr. U. Chgo., 1948-51; ann. prof. Am. Sch. Oriental Research, Jerusalem, 1951-52, dir., 1952-53; assoc. prof. Queen's U., 1953-55; head art and archaeology div. Royal Ont. Mus., Toronto, 1955-64, chief archaeologist, 1964-79, head Jerusalem project, 1979—, trustee, 1984-90; prof. emeritus dept. Nr. Eastern studies U. Toronto, Ont., 1955-79. Assoc. dir. Jericho Excavations, 1952, 53, 56; dir. Dhiban Excavations, 1952-53; assoc. dir. Jerusalem Excavations, 1962-67; mem. Toronto Hist. Bd., 1960— , chmn., 1967-73 Author: (with V.B. Meen) Crown Jewels of Iran, 1968, (with Denis Baly) Atlas of the Biblical World, 1971, The Excavations at Dibon (Dhîbân) in Moab, 1952-53, 1972, Gold for the Gods, 1976, Ancient Peruvian Metalworking, 1979, Excavations in Jerusalem, I, 1985. Served as lt. Royal Canadian Navy, 1942-45. Fellow Soc. Antiquaries of London, Royal Soc. Can., Canadian Museums Assn. (pres. 1964, 65), Archaeol. Inst. Am. Home: Richmond Hill, Canada. Died Feb. 28, 2002; Richmond Hill, Ont., Can..

TUSHNET, MARK VICTOR, law educator; b. Newark, Nov. 18, 1945; s. Leonard and Fannie (Brandchaft) T.; m. Elizabeth Alexander, Aug. 23, 1969; children: Rebecca, Laura. BA magna cum laude, Harvard U., 1967; JD, MA in History, Yale U., 1971. Law clk. Judge George Edwards, Detroit, 1971-72, Justice Thurgood Marshall, Washington, 1972-73; prof. U. Wis. Law Sch., 1973-81, Georgetown U. Law Ctr., Washington, 1981—, assoc. dean rsch. and scholarship, 1992-96, Carmack Waterhouse prof. constl. law, 1996—. Vis. prof. U. Tex., 1977-78, U. So. Calif., 1989, U. Chgo., 1994, Columbia U., 1999-2000. Author: (with Stone, Seidman and Sunstein) Constitutional Law, 1986, 3d edit., 1996, (with Fink) Federal Jurisdiction: Policy and Practice, 1984, 2d edit., 1987, (with Fink, Mullenix and Rowe) Federal Courts in the 21st Century, 1996, The American Law of Slavery, 1981, The NAACP's Legal Strategy Against Segregated Education 1925-1950, 1987 (Littleton-Griswold prize Am. Hist. Assn.), Red, White, and Blue: A Critical Analysis of Constitutional Law, 1988, (with Jackson) Comparitive Constitutional Law, 1999; editor: Comparative Constitutional Federalism: Europe and America, 1990, Making Civil Rights Law: Thurgood Marshall and the Supreme Court, 1936-61, 1994, (with Seidman) Remnants of Beliefs: Contemporary Constitutional Issues, 1996, Making Constitutional Law: Thurgood Marshall and the Supreme Court, 1961-1991, 1997, Taking the Constitution Away from the Courts, 1999; contbr. articles to profl. jours. Fellow: Am. Acad. Arts and Sci. Jewish. Office: Georgetown U Law Ctr 600 New Jersey Ave NW Washington DC 20001-2022 E-mail: tushnet@law.georgetown.edu.

TUSIANI, JOSEPH, foreign language educator, author; b. Foggia, Italy, Jan. 14, 1924; came to U.S., 1947, naturalized, 1956; s. Michael and Maria (Pisone) T. Dottore in Lettere summa cum laude, U. Naples, 1947, Litt.D., 1971. Lectr. in Italian lit. Hunter Coll., 1950-62; chmn. Italian dept. Coll. Mt. St. Vincent, 1948-71. Vis. assoc. prof. NYU, 1956-64, CUNY, 1971-83; prof. Herbert H. Lehman Coll., 1971-83; NDEA vis. prof. Italian Conn. State Coll., 1962. Author: Dante in Licenza, 1952, Two Critical Essays on Emily Dickinson, 1952, Poesia Missionaria in Inghilterra Ed America, 1953, Sonettisti Americani, 1954, Melos Cordis; poems in Latin, 1955, Lo Speco Celeste, 1956, Odi Sacre; poems, 1958, The Complete Poems of Michelangelo, 1960, Rind and All, 1962, Lust and Liberty (The Poems of Michiavelli), 1963, The Fifth Season, 1963, Dante's Inferno (Introduced to Young People), 1964, Envoy from Heaven, 1965, Dante's Purgatorio (Introduced to Young People), 1969, Dante's Paradise (Introduced to Young People), 1970, Tasso's Jerusalem Delivered; verse transl., 1970, Boccaccio's Nymphs of Fiesole, 1971, Italian Poets of the Renaissance, 1971, From Marino to Marinetti, 1973, The Age of Dante, 1973, America the Free, 1976, Tireca Tàreca, 1978, Tasso's Creation of the World, 1982, Rosa Rosarum, poems in Latin, 1984, In Exilio Rerum, poems in Latin, 1985; poems, 1978, Gente Mia and Other Poems, 1978; (autobiography) La Parola Difficile, vol. I, 1988, (poems in Latin) Confinia Lucis et Umbrae; La Parola Nuova, vol. II, 1991, La parola antica, vol. III, 1992, (poems in Italian) Il Ritorno, 1992, Bronx America, 1992, Annemale Parlante, 1994, Carmina Latina, 1994, Le Poesie Inglesi di G.A. Borgese, 1995, La Poceide, 1996, (poems in Apulian dialect) Na Vota é impise cola, 1997, (1st English translation) Luigi Pulci's Morgante, 1998, Carmina Latina, vol. 11, 1998, Li Quatte Staggione, 1998, Lu Deddù, 1999, Maste Peppe Cantarine, 2000, Lu Ponte de SÒla, 2001, In Quattro Lingue, 2001, Dante's Divine Comedy (As told for young people), 2001, L'ore de Gesu Bambine (a Christmas play in verse), 2001. Recipient Greenwood prize for poetry in England, 1956, outstanding tchr. award, 1969, cavaliere ufficiale Italian Republic, 1973, Leonardo Covello's educator award, 1980, Leone di San Marco award, 1982, Avis award, 1983, Joseph Tusiani scholarship fund established in his honor at Lehman Coll., 1983, Congl. medal merit, 1984, Progresso medal liberty, 1986, gold plaque City Hall San Marco, 1986, outstanding tchr. award Am. Assn. Tchrs. Italian, 1986, Renoir literary award, 1988; Joseph Tusiani, Poet, Translator, Humanist (An Internat. Homage), 1995, Enrico Fermi award, 1995, Fiorello La Guardia award, 1998; Melvin Jones fellow, 1995; Joseph Tusiani Found. established at U. Lecce, 1998, Nat. Endowment for the Humanities, 1998; recipient Gov.'s award for excellence, 1999, Apulia prize Regione Puglia, 1999. Mem. Poetry Soc. Am. (v.p.), Cath. Poetry Soc. Am. (dir. 1958, Spirit gold medal 1968) Home: 308 E 72nd St New York NY 10021-4727 *Strange how this continually re-edited Who's Who forces one to work and achieve.*

TUSKA, JON, author, publisher; b. South Milwaukee, Wis., Apr. 30, 1942; s. Andrew and Florence Catherine (Tommet) T.; m. Vicki Piekarski, May 24, 1980; 1 child, Jennifer Lee. BA, Marquette U., 1965. Owner Pers. Cons., Milw., 1969-74; editor, pub. Views & Revs. mag., 1969-75; freelance writer, 1975--91; co-owner, agt. Golden West Literary Agy., Portland, Oreg., 1992—. Mem. adj. faculty MA and tchg. program and undergrads. Lewis and Clark Coll., 1979-88' staff music critic Ovation mag., 1987-89, Fanfare mag., 1989-95; spl. film. cons. Images of Indians, PBS, 1980, Images of Appalachia, PBS, 1984, Mommy, Who's Winning Now? The Cold War in America, Turner, 1986, Say It with Music: Irving Berlin's America, PBS, 1986, Broadway's Eternal Romantics: Lerner and Loewe, PBS, 1988, John Wayne: Standing Tall, PBS, 1989, Big Guns Talk, Turner, 1997; prodr. classical music programs, art and news features and interviews with musicians and motion picture personalities, and film revs. for radio stas. Oreg. Pub. Broadcasting. Author: Philo Vance: The Life and Times of S.S. Van Dine, 1973, The Films of Mae West, 1973, The Filming of the West, 1976, The Detective in Hollywood, 1978, The Vanishing Legion: A History of Mascot Pictures 1927-35, 1982, 2d edit., 1986, Billy the Kid: A Bio/Bibliography, 1983, Dark Cinema: American Film Noir in Cultural Perspective, 1984, The American West in Film: Critical Approaches to the Western, 1985, In Manors and Alleys: A Case-Book on the American Detective Film, 1988, A Variable Harvest: Essays and Reviews in Literature and Film, 1989, Encounters with Filmmakers: Eight Career Studies, 1991, The Complete Films of Mae West, 1992, Billy the Kid: His Life and Legend, 1994, (with Vicki Piekarski) The Frontier Experience: A Reader's Guide to the Life and Literature of the American West, 1984; editor-in-chief (with Piekarski) Ency. of Frontier and Western Fiction, 1983; editor: The Western Story: A Chronological Treasury 1894-1994, 1994, Shadow of the Lariat, 1995, Star Western: Twenty-Two Western Stories from the Golden Age, 1995, The Big Book of Western Action Stories, 1995, (with Piekarski) The Morrow Anthology of Great Western Short Stories, 1997, The First Five Star Western Corral, 2000, Five Star Westerns. Avocations: reading, classical music, film history, book collecting. Home and Office: 2327 SE Salmon St Portland OR 97214-3943 E-mail: jtuska@qwest.net.

TUSZYNSKI, DANIEL J., JR. sales, management and marketing consultant; b. Erie, Pa., Aug. 22, 1947; s. Daniel and Dorothy (Tlyman) T. Grad., Iroquois Trade Sch., 1968; AA, L.A. City Coll., 1971; BS, Calif. State U., 1975; MBA, Gannon U., 1979; postgrad., The Cons. Inst., 1989. Cert. profl cons. Indsl. engr. Gen. Electric Co., Erie, Pa., 1965-75; sales mgr. Burroughs Corp., Culver City, Calif., 1975-76; regional sales mgr. Gen. Electric Co., Erie, 1976-81; dir. sales, mktg. Peerless Mfg. Co., Inc, Dallas, 1981-85; v.p. sales, mktg. Consumat Systems, Inc., Richmond, Va., 1985-88; v.p. mktg. Sutton Holding Co., 1988-89; pres., chief exec. officer Tech. Mktg. Inc., 1989—; v.p. sales and mktg. Hobart Tafa Technologies, Inc., Concord, N.H., 1990-91; pres. Music Treasures Co., Richmond, 1991—. Author: (manual) Peerless Air Inlet Systems, 1984. 1st lt. USNG, 1968-75. Mem. Am. Mktg. Assn., Am. Cons. League, Porsche Club Am. Roman Catholic. Avocations: sailing, carpentry, skiing, flying. Home: 11227 Linderwood Dr Mechanicsville VA 23116-3137 Office: Music Treasures Co PO Box 9138 Richmond VA 23227-0138 E-mail: musict@musictreasures.com.

TUTASHINDA, KWELI (BRIAN P. ALTHEIMER), chiropractic physician, educator; b. Wynne, Ark., May 14, 1956; s. Joe Porché and Lura Ella (Darden) Altheimer; divorced; 1 child, Chinyere R.; m. Leonor Quiñonez, June 13, 1987; children Xihuanel, Rukiya, Jomoké. BA in Philosophy summa cum laude, U. Ark., 1978; D of Chiropractic cum laude, Life Chiropractic Coll. West, San Lorenzo, Calif., 1989. Tchr. English Oakland (Calif.) Pub. Schs., 1984-86; tchr. spl. programs U. Calif., Berkeley, 1984-92, 94-95, 98-00; instr. phys. diagnosis and chiropractic tech. Life Chiropractic Coll. West, Haywood, Calif., 1989—99; pvt. practice Berkeley, 1989—; owner Imhotep Chiropractic & Wellness Clinic; dir. Imhotep Wellness Workshops & Seminars. Developer rehab. tng. Editor, pub. Foresight Mag., 1982-84; author, pub. Toward a Holistic Worldview, 1985, Therapeutic Exercises for the Spine, 1999; contbr. articles to Chiropractic History. Recipient 1st degree Black Belt Tae Kwon Do, 1976. Mem. Assn. Chiropractic History, Somatics Soc. Mem. Sufi Order of the West, Naqshbandi Sufi Order. Islam. Avocations: yoga, martial arts, writing, reading, jogging. Office: 3358 Adeline St Berkeley CA 94703-2737 E-mail: tutateam@awol.

TUTHILL, JAY DEAN, II, investment executive; b. Wilmington, Del., Dec. 10, 1953; s. Jay Dean Tuthill and Annabelle (Carney) Kressman; m. Laura Ann Behr, Nov. 23, 1972 (div. May 1981); 1 child, Elizabeth; m. Assunta Sera, Oct. 10, 1991; children: Lori, Michael, Mark. BSChemE, U. Del., 1981; MBA with honors, U. Mich., 1988. Engr. Exxon, Detroit, 1981-86; mgr. bus. planning Am. Cyanamid, Wayne, NJ, 1988-94; portfolio mgr. Am. Express, Paramus, 1994-95; pres. Buckingham Fin., Ridgewood, 1995—; CFO Prismatic Corp. , Newburgh, NY, 1997—; mng. dir. Tuthill & Merker LLC, Ridgewood, NJ, 1999—. Mem. Assn. Investment Mgmt. and Rsch., N.Y. Soc. Security Analysts (vice chair comms. and mktg. com. 1994—, Vol. of Yr. award 1995), Inst. Chartered Fin. Analysts (chartered CFA), Ridgewood C. of C. (profl. com. 1996), Beta Gamma Sigma, Tau Beta Pi. Republican. Roman Catholic. Avocations: golf, piano. Home: 530 Valley Rd Apt 1M Montclair NJ 07043-2714 Office: Tuthill & Merker LLC 1250 E Ridgewood Ave Ste 18 Ridgewood NJ 07450-3930

TUTHILL, WALTER WARREN, financial executive, international business consultant; b. Madison, N.J., Nov. 28, 1941; s. Walter Warren and Elizabeth Emma (Kniskern) T.; m. Barbara Ann Stephens, Apr. 22, 1967. BSBA, U. N.C., 1964. CPA, Calif., N.Y., N.J., N.C.; cert. info systems auditor, cert. internal auditor. Sr. mgr. Price Waterhouse, N.Y.C., 1964-77; dir. internal audit Carter Hawley Hale Stores Inc., L.A., 1977-82, gen. auditor, 1982-85, v.p., 1985-93; sr. v.p. retail control Broadway Stores, Inc., 1993-96; v.p. retail control Federated Dept. Stores, Inc., 1996-97; COO, Gelfand, Rennert & Feldman divsn. PricewaterhouseCoopers LLP, 1997-2001; dir. cons. Wong-Holland LLP, CPAs, Woodland Hills, Calif., 2001—. Lectr. in field. Contbr. articles to profl. jours. Pres. Twin W Rescue Squad, Princeton Junction, N.J., 1976-77. Mem. AICPA, N.Y. Soc. CPAs, Am. Acctg. Assn., Nat. Retail Mchts. Assn. (chmn. bd. internal audit group 1982-84, bd. dirs.), Info. Sys. Audit and Control Assn. Avocations: international travel, computers, classical music, photography. Office: Wong Holland LLP CPA 4919 Topanga Canyon Blvd Woodland Hills CA 91364-3113 E-mail: wwtuthill@earthlink.net. *Life is what happens when we're planning something else.*

TUTINS, ANTONS, electronics and audio engineer; b. Ludza, Latvia, May 2, 1933; s. Francis and Veronika (Seipulniks) Tutins; came to U.S., 1950, naturalized, 1963; student U. Minn., 1951-55; BS in Elec. Engring., Ill. Inst. Tech., 1970; MBA, U. Chgo., 1974; m. Raita Snebergs, July 8, 1961; 1 child, Robert. With Motorola Communications div., Chgo., 1964-73; product engring. mgr. Knowles Electronics, Inc., Franklin Park, Ill., 1973-81; dir. quality assurance and mfg. engring. Perma Power Electronics Inc., Chgo., 1982-95; pres. AT Systems, Des Plaines, Ill., 1995—; tech. cons. Accord, Inc., Westchester, Ill., 1995—. Bd. dirs. Spl. Interest Group of Object Oriented Tech., 1995—. With USN, 1955-57. Mem. IEEE, Acoustical Soc. Am., Chgo. Acoustical and Audio Group (pres. 1977-78), Audio Engring. Soc, Midwest Acoustics Conf. (exec. com., pres. 1980), Latvian Cath. Student Assn. Dzintars (pres. 1979-81), Am. Latvian Cath. Assn. (registered agt. 1978— , v.p. 1985), Baltic Info. Exch. (v.p. 1991—), Motorola Engring. Club (pres. 1970-71). Roman Catholic. Home: 1338 Briar Ct Des Plaines IL 60018-2146 Office: 10301 W Roosevelt Rd Westchester IL 60154-2575

TUTKO, ROBERT JOSEPH, law enforcement officer, radiology administrator; b. Buffalo, Nov. 18, 1955; s. Robert Edward and Agatha (Pagliaccio) T.; m. Susan Joy Biddle, Oct. 29, 1976; children: Suzan Denise, Nicola Marie. Student, SUNY, Brockport, 1973-74; AAS, Trocaire Coll., 1982; BS, Pacific Western U., 1992, MS, 1995, PhD, 1998; postgrad. in nursing, SUNY, 1997. Dir. X-ray svcs. Fla. Ctr. for Knee Surgery, Clearwater, 1985-86; surgery X-ray technologist St. Joseph's Hosp., Tampa, Fla., 1986-90; dir. radiology Met. Gen. Hosp., Pinellas Park, 1990-91; dir. med. imaging Univ. Gen. Hosp. and Women's Med. Ctr., Seminole, 1991-92; program dir. Sch. Radiology St. Joseph Hosp., Memphis, 1992-94; physician asst. DeSoto Family Practice, Olive Branch, Miss., 1995-96; mem. med. staff Klein Internal Medicine, Germantown, Tenn., 1996-98; police officer Memphis Police Dept., Memphis, 1998—. Founder, dir. continuing edn. TCB Med. Edn., Palm Harbor, Fla., 1985-91, pres., CEO, Germantown, Tenn., 1992—; tchr. Hillsborough County Schs., Tampa, 1989-92; lectr. profl. confs.; nat. radiology specialist Concorde Career Colls., Inc., Kansas City, Mo., 1994-95; advisor U. Memphis Rsch. Project, 1997-98. Author: (curriculum) Limited X-Ray, 1995, Limited Basic Medical Assistant, 1996, Occupational Burnout in Healthcare Workers, 1996; contbr. articles to profl. jours. County chmn. radiology group Pinellas County Non-Profit Hosp. Venture Group, 1990-91; lectr. Pinellas County Sch. System, 1984-91; vol. Shelby County Sheriff's Dept. Tng. Acad., 1997; mem. MPD Crisis Intervention Team. Sgt. U.S. Army, 1974-75. Recipient commendation letter Pinellas Park Police Dept., 1991. Mem. Am. Legion, Am. Educators Radiol. Scis., Am. Soc. Radiol. Technologists, Tenn. Soc. Radiol. Technologists, Fla. Soc. Radiol. Technologists, Ga. Soc. Radiol. Technologists, Colo. Soc. Radiol. Technologists, Am. Healthcare Radiology Adminstrs., Fraternal Order of Police, Tenn. Law Enforcement Assn., KC (treas. 1989-91, Knight of Month Dec. 1989). Democrat. Roman Catholic. Avocations: cooking, sports, cars, golf, music. Home: 3265 Foxbriar Dr Memphis TN 38115-3107 Office: Memphis Police Dept N Precinct 545 S Main St Memphis TN 38103 E-mail: mpdphd29@midsouth.rr.com.

TUTT, LOUISE THOMPSON, lawyer; b. Centerville, Iowa, Nov. 10, 1937; d. Lawrence Eugene and Alice Helen (Thompson) T. B.A., U. Ariz., 1963, J.D., 1969. Bar: Calif. 1972, U.S. Dist. Ct. (so. dist.) Calif. 1972, Mo. 1976. Practice law, San Diego and LaJolla, Calif., 1972-75; appeals referee Div. Employment Security, Jefferson City, Mo., 1977-79; counsel Labor and Indsl. Rels. Commn., Jefferson City, Mo., 1979-80; legal adviser Div. Workers Compensation, Jefferson City, 1980-94, St. Louis, 1994—. Bd. dirs. LaJolla Sinfonia, 1975. Democrat. Office: 11 N 7th St Rm 250 Saint Louis MO 63101-1607

TUTTLE, ARTHUR NORMAN, JR. architect, university administrator, educational facilities planner; b. Balt., May 14, 1929; s. Arthur Norman and Georgia Pauline (Roberts) T.; m. Betty Gray Finney, Aug. 9, 1952 (dec. 1979); children: Arthur Norman III, George Gray; m. Barbara Jean Hassler, Apr. 15, 1983; 1 child, Katherine Elizabeth James Olsen. BS, Va. Poly. Inst. and State U., 1952; MFA, Princeton U., 1956; M in Regional Planning, U. N.C., Chapel Hill, 1962. Registered architect, N.C., Va., S.C., Okla.; cert. urban planner. Urban planner City of Charlestown, S.C., 1957; rsch. fellow U. N.C., Chapel Hill, 1958, dir. planning, 1959-70; architect-planner U. Okla. Health Scis. Ctr., Oklahoma City, 1970-73; univ. architect U. Okla., Norman, 1973-95, spl. asst. to v.p., 1995; cons. architect, 1996—. Hosp. planning cons. U. N.C., 1962-66, lectr. in planning, 1965-69; assoc. prof. health U. Okla., Oklahoma City, 1970-95, prof. architecture U. Okla., Norman, 1970-95. Sec. Capitol-Med. Ctr. Planning Commn., Oklahoma City, 1974—81; chmn. Town Planning Bd., Chapel Hill, NC, 1964—69. 1st lt. U.S. Army, 1952—54, lt. col. USAR, 1954—80. Fellow Assn. Univ. Architects (pres. 1990-91); mem. AIA, Am. Planning Assn., Am. Inst. Cert. Planners, AIA Acad. Architecture for Health (v.p. 1993-97), Am. Coll. Healthcare Architects. Presbyterian. Avocations: travel, historic preservation, archtl. history, photography. Home and Office: 1813 Cedar Hill Rd Norman OK 73072-3161 E-mail: tuttlearch@aol.com.

TUTTLE, ASHLEY, dancer; b. Columbia, SC; Student, Sch. Am. Ballet. Mem. Am. Ballet Theatre, N.Y.C., 1987—, soloist, 1992—, prin. ballerina, 1997—. Roles include Mathilda Kchessinska in Anastasia, Callipe and Polyhymnia in Apollo, Nikiya in La Bayadere, mother/sweathear in Billy the Kid, Cinderella and the Spring Fairy in Cinderella, Prayer in Copellia, Gulnare and the pas de deux in Le Cosaire, the Queen of the Driads, Amour and flower girl in Don Quixote, others, featured roles in Ballet Imperial, Cruel World, Drink to Me Only With Thine Eyes, The Leaves are Falling, leading roles in Brahms-Haydn Variations, The Elements, Jump Start, Piece D'Occasion. Office: Am Ballet Theatre 890 Broadway New York NY 10003

TUTTLE, BYNUM R., JR. brokerage house executive; b. Burlington, N.C., Jan. 7, 1950; s. Bynum R. Sr. and Ruby B. T.; m. (div.); children: Andrew Scott, Anna Katherine. MS, Mars Hill Coll., 1973; MEd, U. N.C., 1978. Tchr. Greensboro (N.C.) City Schs., 1973-78; group sales Pilot Life Ins. Co., Greensboro, 1978-84; sales mgr. The Ins. Ctr. N.C., 1984-87; pres., cons. Employee Benefit Designs, Denton, 1987—; mng. ptnr. Triune Tech., LLC, N.C., 1998—. Agt. adv. com. Ptnrs. Nat. Health Plan, Winston-Salem, N.C., 1999—, N.C. Dept. Ins., Raleigh, N.C., 1997-98, Lincoln Nat. Life, Ft. Wayne, Ind., 1986; com. mem. Citizens for Bus. & Industry, Raleigh, 1992. Adv. com. Energy United Electric Membership, Lexington, N.C., 1996—; bd. dirs. Family Affair Care Group, Gibsonville, N.C., 1992—, J.E. Rogers Meml. Scholarship Fund, Denton, 1995—, Greensboro Jaycees, 1980; coun. mem. Summerville Bapt. Ch. Recipient Ten Key Men award Jaycees, 1979. Mem. Nat. Assn. Health Underwriters (v.p. 1999, nat. legis. chmn. 1997), N.C. Assn. Health Underwriters (pres. 1996-97, Frederick W. Joyner Disting. Svc. award 1998, Honor Coun. award 1993, 95-99), Triad Assn. Health Underwriters (pres. 1994-95). Avocations: water sports, golf, reading, travel. Home: 706 Mountain Shore Dr Denton NC 27239 Office: Employee Benefit Designs Inc PO Box 1110 Denton NC 27239-1110

TUTTLE, DAVID BAUMAN, electrical engineer; b. N.Y.C., Oct. 25, 1948; s. John Bauman and Charlotte (Root) T.; m. Mildred Suzanne Lamb, May 5, 1973 (div. May 1978); m. Nancy Viola Caraber, Mar. 14, 1981; children: Jason David, John Paul. Student, MIT, 1966-69. Assoc., sr. assoc. programer IBM Cambridge (Mass.) Sci. Ctr., 1968-71; staff programmer IBM VM/370 Devel., Burlington, Mass., 1971-76; sr. prin. S/W engr. Digital Equipment Corp., Maynard, 1976-78; mgr. Cambridge Telecom/GTE Telenet, Burlington, 1978-81; sr. scientist GTE Telenet, 1981-84, chief scientist, 1984-85; sr. tech. cons. Prime Computer, Inc., Framingham, Mass., 1985-86, prin. tech. cons., 1986-89; sr. rsch. engr. Ungermann-Bass Inc., Andover, Mass., 1990-91; chief engr. Ungermann-Bass, Inc., 1991-93; cons. engr. Augment Sys., Inc., Bedford, 1993-95; chief tech. officer Augment Systems Inc., Westford, 1995-97; cons. engr. VideoServer Connections, Inc., Marlborough, 1997-99; chief engr. NorthStar Internetworking, Waltham, 1999-2000; project engr. Hammer Techs. Inc., Wilmington, 2000; prin. engr. Vividon, Inc., Sudbury, 2000—. Strategy forum del. Corp. for Open Systems, McLean, Va., 1986-89, architecture com. mem., 1989, strategy forum nominating com., 1986-87; patent rev. com. Prime Computer, Inc., 1985-89; sole proprietor Viewpoint Cons., Reading, Mass., 1994—. Co-author and editor: 3270 Display System Protocol, 1981, 83, Hotline BSC Access Method, 1970. Donor mem. Smithsonian Inst., Washington, 1980—. Mem. IEEE, IEEE Computer Soc., Nat. Space Soc. (life mem.), The Cousteau Soc., USS Constitution Mus. Assn., Assn. for Computing Machinery, Black and Blues of Killington (treas. 1986-89), Mandala Folk Dance Ensemble (dancer 1970-73). Republican. Presbyterian. Avocations: Duplicate Bridge (life master, Am. Contract Bridge League, 1983), alpine skiing. Home: 27 Heather Dr Reading MA 01867-3961 Office: Vividon Inc 142 North Rd Sudbury MA 01776-1142 E-mail: dtuttle@acm.org.

TUTTLE, JEREMY BALLOU, neurobiologist; b. N.Y.C., Oct. 9, 1947; s. John Bauman and Charlotte Marion (Root) T.; m. Sara Jane Stasko, Mar. 23, 1971. AB, U. Rochester, 1969; PhD, Johns Hopkins U., 1977. Postdoctoral fellow U. Conn., Storrs, 1976-79, vis. asst. prof., 1980, asst. prof. in residence, 1981-84; asst. prof. physiology U. Va., Charlottesville, 1984-87, asst. prof. neuroscience, 1987-90, rsch. asst. prof., 1990-93, assoc. prof. urology neuroscience, 1993-98, prof., 1998—. Contbr. articles to Devel. Biology, Science, Jour. Neuroscience, others. Chmn. mem. Common Area Planning Commn., 1984-87; pres. bd. Earlysville Forest Homeowner's Assn., 1986-89, Earlysville, Va.; chmn. urology spl. emphasis panel NIH, 1996-2001; chmn. spl. emphasis panel on female pelvic floor disorders Nat. Inst. Child Health and Human Devel., 1999. U. Rochester Hon. scholar, 1965-69, Regent's scholar for Medicine, 1969, NIH predoctoral fellow, 1971-75, Nat. Rsch. Svc. fellow, 1976-79, Nat. Spinal Cord Injury Found. rsch. fellow, 1979-80; recipient Rsch. Career Devel. award Nat. Inst. Neurol. Disease/NIH, Muscular Dystrophy Assn. Rsch. award, 1990—; Am. Heart Assn. grantee, 1987-89, 90—, fellowship, Fogarty Internat. Ctr. for Rsch. NIH, Japan, 1997. Achievements include research on NGF dynamics in hypertrophic disease, carbon dioxide transport and chemosensitivity, molecular mechanisms of quantal synaptic transmission, nerve growth factor synthesis by vascular smooth muscle, trophic regulation of motor neurons, neurodegenerative diseases. Office: U Va Med Sch PO Box 801392 Charlottesville VA 22908-1392 E-mail: tuttle@virginia.edu.

TUTTLE, JERRY OWEN, retired naval officer, business executive; b. Hatfield, Ind., Dec. 18, 1934; s. Charles Merritt and Wenonah Hathaway (Parker) T.; m. Barbara Ann Bonifay, Dec. 31, 1956; children: Michael Charles, Vicky Ann, Mark Jerreld, Stephen Scott, Monique Therese. Grad., Devry Tech. Inst., 1954; BS, Naval Postgrad. Sch., 1962; MA in Internat. Relations, George Washington U., 1969; postgrad., Naval War Coll., 1968-69. Enlisted U.S. Navy, 1955, commd. ensign, 1956, advanced through grades to vice adm., 1987; aide and flag lt. to comdr-in-chief Pacific Fleet, 1969-70; exec. officer Attack Squadron 174, 1970-71, Attack Squadron 81, comdg. officer, 1971-73; mem. staff comdr. U.S. Naval Air Forces, Atlantic Fleet, 1973-74; comdr. Attack Carrier Air Win 3, 1974-75; comdg. officer USS Kalamazoo, 1975-76, comnavairlant, 1976-77; comdg. officer USS John F. Kennedy, 1977-78, 78-79; spl. asst. to chief of naval ops. Def. Intelligence Agy., Washington, 1979, dir. for plans and policy div., 1979-81; comdr. Carrier Group 8, Norfolk, Va., 1981-83, Carrier Group 2/Battle Force 6th Fleet, Naples, Italy, 1983-84; naval insp. gen. Washington, 1984-85; dep., chief of staff U.S. Atlantic Fleet/Chief of Staff, U.S. Atlantic Command, 1985-86; dir. for command, control, communication systems Office of Joint Chiefs of Staff, 1987-89, dir. space & electronic warfare, 1989-93; ret. USN, 1993; v.p. bus. devel. Oracle Corp., 1994-96; pres. ManTech Sys. Engring. Corp. (formerly Savantage Govt. Svcs.), 1996-2000, SAVANTAGE (formerly Reltek Sys. and Design, Inc.), 2000—02; pres., CEO J.O.T. Enterprises, LLC, 2002—. Decorated Def. Superior Svc. medal, Legion of Merit (4), Meritorious Svc. medal (2), D.F.C. (3), Air medal (23), Def. Disting. Svc. medal, Disting. Svc. medal; comdr. Nat. Order of Merit (France); recipient John Paul Jones awd for inspirational leadership Navy League, 1978; listed in Fed. Computer Week's 1991, 92 Federal 100 for his impact on govt. computer systems. Mem. AIAA (Control, Com. and Intelligence award for contbn. to overall effectiveness of C3I Systems 1991), AFCEA (contbn. award 1989, Jon Boyce award 1992), Assn. Naval Aviators (Gold Eagle). Fax: 703-241-8806. E-mail: jerryotuttle@aol.com., jt@sseusa.com. *Drive yourself to lead others; to think only of the best; to work only for the best and expect only the best; to be just as enthusiastic about the success of others as you are about your own.*

TUTTLE, KENNETH LEWIS, engineering educator, consultant; b. Toledo, Apr. 4, 1944; s. Martin Lewis and Norma Corinne (Nichols) T.; m. Susanna Anna Maria Woodworth, June 24, 1967; children: Stephanie, Meghan, Lewis. BS, U.S. Naval Acad., 1967; MS, Oreg. State U., 1974, PhD, 1978. Registered profl. engr., Oreg. (environ. branch added in 1995). Commd. ensign USN, 1967, advanced through grades to lt., 1971, line officer Va., 1967-69, intelligence officer Tan An, Vietnam, 1970-71; grad. asst. Oreg. State U., Corvallis, 1972-76; rsch. engr. Weyerhaeuser Co., Tacoma, 1977-81; pvt. practice Federal Way, Wash., 1982-83; assoc. prof. mech. engring. U.S. Naval Acad., Annapolis, Md., 1983—, dir. marine propulsion labs., 1984-90. Dir. Ocean and Marine Engring. Divsn., Am. Soc. for Engring. Edn., Washington , 1989-91; mem. com. on shipboard pollution control, Nat. Rsch. Coun., Washington, 1994-96; chmn. environ. panel Soc. Naval Arch. and Marine Engrs., Jersey City, 1993-2000; prin. cons. Solid Fuel Rsch., Annapolis, 1984—. Author: Combustion Mechanisms in Wood Fired Boilers, 1978, Review of Biomass Gasification in Progress in Biomass Conversion, 1984, Thermodynamics: A Computer-Based Approach; contbr. articles to profl. jours. Mem. Combustion Inst., George C. Marshall Inst., N.Y. Acad. Scis. Achievements include patent for the method of regulating the amount of under fire air for combustion of wood fuels in spreader-stoker boilers; aided in development of pulverized wood burner and fixed-bed wood gasifier. Home: 1098 Broadview Dr Annapolis MD 21401-4824 Office: U.S. Naval Acad 590 Holloway Rd Annapolis MD 21402-1314 E-mail: tuttle@unsa.edu.

TUTTLE, MARSHALL, musician, educator; b. Berkeley, Calif., Nov. 19, 1950; s. Alan Tuttle and Norma Jean de Preter; m. Natalia Nikolaevna Degtayreva. D of Musical Arts, Stanford U., 1986. Cert. tchr. music K-12. Head of music Vienna (Austria) Internat. Sch., 1988—89, Pingree Sch., South Hamilton, Mass., 1989—93; lectr. Okla. City U., 1993—95; lectr. in music Langston (Okla.) U., 1994—2000; music dir. Peace Luth. Ch., Edmond, 1995—99, Episcopal Ch. of the Resurrection, Oklahoma City, 1999—2000; orch. dir. Cobb County Sch. Dist., Marietta, Ga., 2000—. Founder and dir. The Furstenau Quartet, Berkeley, 1969—76; co-founder, asst. condr. Berkeley Symphony Orch., Berkeley, Calif., 1971—72; founder and music dir. Pingree Philharm. Soc., South Hamilton, 1990—93; music dir. 4 Peace, Edmond, 1995—99; dir. Latino Cmty. Devel. Agy. Summer Music Camp and Youth Orch., Oklahoma City, 1997. Author: Musical Structures in Wagnerian Opera, 2000; composer: (opera) Kiyoyori, 1985 (Hubbel prize in composition, 1985). Named alt., Fulbright Meml. Fund, 2002; grantee, Kellogg's, 1997—98. Green Party. Avocations: sailing, wilderness activities. Office: Orch Dir 4500 Due West Rd Kennesaw GA 30152 Fax: 770-528-6643. Personal E-mail: inotmark@aol.com. Business E-Mail: inotmark@aol.com.

TUTTLE, MARTHA BENEDICT, artist; b. Cin., Feb. 4, 1916; d. Harris Miller and Florence Stevens (McCrea) Benedict; m. Richard Salway Tuttle, June 3, 1939; children: Richard, Jr., McCrea Benedict (dec.), Martha (dec.), Elisabeth Hall. Grad. high sch., Cin.; student, Art Acad. Cin., 1934-38. V.p. Barg Bottling Co., Cin., 1948-80. One-woman shows include KKAE Gallery, 1963, Univ. Club, 1967, Miller Gallery, 1971, St. Clements, N.Y., 1973, Livingston Lodge, 1974, Holly Hill Antiques, 1979, Peterson Gallery, 1983, Art Acad. Cin., 1984, Closson Gallery, 1986, Camargo Gallery, 1992; represented in permanent collection Cin. Art Mus. Tchr. Sunday sch. Grace Episcopal Ch. and Indian Hill Ch., Cin., 1953-75; shareholder Cin. Art Mus.; founder partnership to save the William and Phebe Betts House; donor with partnership to The Nat. Soc. Colonial Dames of Am. the William and Phebe Betts House for establishing a Rsch. Ctr. Mem. Soc. Colonial Dames Am. (bd. dirs. 1976-89), Camargo Club, Univ. Club. Republican. Home: # 3C 2401 Ingleside Ave Cincinnati OH 45206-2118

TUTTLE, MARY CELIA PUTNAM, social worker, retired; b. Brookings, S.D., Jan. 7, 1927; d. Henry Oakes and Hazel Una (Bacon) Putnam; m. Lewis Potter Tuttle, May 9, 1953; children: Amy Lucinda, Brian Paul, Rebecca Susan. Student, Cottey Coll., 1944-45; BA, U. Minn., 1948; MSW, Mich. State U., 1984. Cert. social worker, Mich., ACSW. Dir. YWCA Teen-Age Program, Santa Monica, Calif., 1948-50, Lansing, Mich., 1950-53; vol. coord.

CPCAN Family Growth Ctr., 1980-81; drug educator project parent Tri-County Cmty. Mental Health Bd., 1981, 82-83; med. social worker Sparrow Hosp., 1984, nephrology social worker dialysis unit, 1984-95, ret., 1995. Active Edgewood United Ch. of Christ. Mem. NASW, LWV (v.p. Dearborn 1966-67, pres. 1967-69, Mich. bd. dirs. 1971-73), Physicians for Nat. Health Program, Universal Health Care Action Network, Mich. Universal Health Care Access Network, P.E.O. (pres. Mich. chpt. CJ 1969-71, chpt. AG 1974-76, 97-99), Acad. Cert. Social Workers, Phi Alpha. Democrat. Avocation: advocacy for universal health care system, travel, photography. Home: 4322 Oakwood Rd Okemos MI 48864-2949

TUTTLE, ROGER LEWIS, lawyer, educator; b. Wyandotte County, Kans., Nov. 9, 1930; s. Emmett Joseph and Freda Alberta (Lewis) T.; m. Beverly Jean Campbell, Aug. 3, 1957; children— Pamela Anne, Deborah Jean Tuttle Edwards. B.A., U. Kans., 1952; J.D., U. Miss., 1958. Bar: Miss. 1958, U.S. Dist. Ct. (so. dist.) Miss. 1958, U.S. Dist. Ct. (no. dist.) Miss. 1959, U.S. Dist. Ct. (ea. dist.) La. 1963, U.S. Ct. Appeals (4th cir.) 1964, Va. 1965, U.S. Dist. Ct. (ea. dist.) Va. 1971, U.S. Supreme Ct. 1971, U.S. Dist. Ct. (we. dist.) Va. 1976, Okla. 1982, U.S. Dist. Ct. (no. dist.) Okla. 1983, U.S. Ct. Appeals (10th cir.) 1983. Assoc. Neill, Clark & Townsend, Indianola, Miss., 1958-61, Heidelberg, Woodliff & Franks, Jackson, Miss., 1961-62; area atty. Exxon, New Orleans and Charlotte, N.C., 1962-65; asst. counsel Lawyers Title Ins. Corp., Richmond, Va., 1965-71; gen. atty. A.H. Robins Co., Richmond, 1971-76; asst. gen. counsel Dan River Inc., 1976-82; prof. law Oral Roberts U., Tulsa, 1982-85, dean, 1985-87, clin. prof. med. jurisprudence, 1987-88; chief legal officer, corp. sec. Oral Roberts Ministries, 1986-88; of counsel Freed & Haskins, Richmond, 1988-89, Conner & Edwards, Richmond, 1989, Davis & Tuttle, 1989-90, pvt. practice, 1990—. Mem. Spl. Adv. Counsel to Mayor, Richmond, 1971-76; mem. Richmond Air Pollution Control Bd., 1972-73; bd. dirs. Richmond Met. Authority, 1973-76. Served to lt. col. M.I., USAR, 1952-73. Decorated Mil. Cross (Belgium), Bronze Star, Army Commendation Medal with oak leaf cluster; named Prof. of Yr., Oral Roberts U., 1984-85. Mem. Va. Bar Assn., Miss. Bar Assn., Okla. Bar Assn. (civil procedure com., mem. continuing legal edn. com.), Assn. Trial Lawyers Am., Am. Coll. Legal Medicine, Assn. Former Intelligence Officers, Army CIC Vets. Assn., Phi Alpha Delta, Pi Kappa Alpha. Republican. Presbyn. Clubs: Masons, Scottish Rite, Shriners. Contbr. articles to legal publs. Office: 13624 Northwich Dr Midlothian VA 23112-4932

TUTTLE, WILLIAM G(ILBERT) T(OWNSEND), JR. research executive; b. Portsmouth, Va., Nov. 26, 1935; s. William Gilbert and Edith Inez (Ritter) T.; m. Helen Lynn Warren, Dec. 27, 1959; children: Lynn, Robert, Jonathan. BS, U.S. Mil. Acad., 1958; MBA, Harvard U., 1963. Commd. 2d lt. U.S. Army, 1958, advanced through grades to gen., 1989; dir. combat service support (Office Combat Devels., Hdqrs. Tng. and Doctrine Command), Ft. Monroe, Va., 1976-77; comdr. 3d Armored Div. Support Command Frankfurt, Germany, 1977-79; comdr. Mil. Traffic Mgmt. Command Eastern Area Bayonne, N.J., 1979-81; dir. force mgmt. Hdqrs. Dept. Army, Washington, 1981-82; chief policy and programs br. Supreme Hdqrs. Allied Powers Europe, 1982-84; comdr. U.S. Army Operational Test and Evaluation Agy., 1984-86; dep. comdg. gen. Logistics, Tng. and Doctrine Command and comdg. gen. U.S. Army Logistics Ctr., Ft. Lee, Va., 1986-89; comdg. gen. U.S. Army Materiel Command, Alexandria, 1989-92; ret., 1992; pres., CEO, trustee Logistics Mgmt. Inst., McLean, Va., 1993—2001, ret., 2002—. U.S. Army Kermit Roosevelt lectr., 1991; bd. dirs. Procurement Round Table; mem. bd. advisors Nat. Contract Mgmt. Assn.; cons. to Def. Sci. Bd., 1994-98, NRC, 2000-01. Prin., Coun. on Excellence in Govt.; nat. councillor Atlantic Coun. Recipient DSM (5). Mem. Nat. Def. Transp. Assn., Nat. Def. Indsl. Assn. (Logistician Emeritus award 1998), Assn. U.S. Army (Pres.'s award 1992). Lutheran. Office: Logistics Mgmt Inst 2000 Corporate Rdg Mc Lean VA 22102-7805 E-mail: btuttle@lmi.org.

TUTTLE, WILLIAM MCCULLOUGH, JR. history educator; b. Detroit, Oct. 7, 1937; s. William McCullough and Geneva (Duvall) T.; m. Linda Lee Stumpp, Dec. 12, 1959 (div.); children: William McCullough III, Catharine D., Andrew S.; m. Kathryn Nemeth, May 6, 1995. BA, Denison U., 1959; MA, U. Wis., 1964, PhD, 1967. Faculty mem. U. Kans., Lawrence, 1967—, prof. history, 1975-2000, intra-univ. prof., 1982-83; sr. fellow in So. and Negro history Johns Hopkins U., 1969-70; Charles Warren fellow Harvard U., Cambridge, Mass., 1972-73; vis. prof. U. Sc., Columbia, 1980; assoc. fellow Stanford Humanities Ctr., 1983-84; rsch. assoc. U. Calif., Berkeley, 1986-88; prof. Am. Studies U. Kans., Lawrence, 2000—. Vis. scholar Radcliffe Coll., 1993-94. Author: Race Riot: Chicago in the Red Summer of 1919, 1970, 2d edit., 1996, W.E.B. Du Bois, 1973, (with David M. Katzman) Plain Folk, 1982, (with others) A People and A Nation, 1982, 6th edit., 2001, "Daddy's Gone to War": The Second World War in the Lives of America's Children, 1993; contbr. chpts. to books, numerous articles to profl. jours. Dem. precinct committeeman, Lawrence, 1980-90. Lt. USAF, 1959-62 Recipient Merit award Am. Assn. for State and Local History, 1972; Younger Humanist fellow NEH, 1972-73, Guggenheim fellow, 1975-76, NEH fellow, 1983-84, rsch. fellow Hall Ctr., 1990, Kemper fellow for tchg. excellence, 1998; grantee Evans, 1975-76, Beveridge, 1982, NEH, 1986-89. Mem. Soc. Am. Historians (elected), Am. Hist. Assn., Orgn. Am. Historians, Am. Studies Assn., Assn. for Study of African Am. Life and History, Lawrence Trout Club, Golden Key (hon.), Omicron Delta Kappa, Phi Beta Delta, Phi Gamma Delta. Home: 713 Louisiana St Lawrence KS 66044-2339 Office: U Kans Dept Am Studies Lawrence KS 66045-0001 E-mail: tuttle@ku.edu.

TUTTLE, WILLIAM ROGER, lawyer, financial advisor; m. Meredith Anne Weatherbee, July 23, 1960; children: William Stetson, Samuel Alexander, Andrew Roger. Banking cert., Brown U., 1971; BS in Acctg., Bentley Coll., 1973, MS in Fin., 1980; cert. exec. devel. program, U. Mass., 1974; JD, Suffolk U., 1977; cert. in fin. studies, Fairfield U., 1981; LLM, Boston U., 1987. Bar: Mass. 1977, U.S. Dist. Ct. Mass. 1978, U.S. Supreme Ct. 1982; lic. real estate broker. With South Shore Nat. Bank, Mass., 1957-59, Home Savs. Bank, Boston, 1959-85; lawyer, pres. Abington (Mass.) Legal Ctr., 1985—; pres. William R. Tuttle, Esquire, P.C., Abington, 1985—. Publ. (weekly bank report) New England Bank and Thrift Stock Report, 1985-93. Mem. judicial nominating coun. S.E. dist. Commonwealth of Mass., 1991-2000; mem. Mass. Rep. State Com., former dep. chmn., asst. treas.; mem. Abington Rep. Town Com.; coach Abington Sr. Little League Baseball, Abington Youth Soccer League; trustee Massasoit C.C., Brockton, Mass., 1997—. Mem. Boston Econ. Club. Home: 101 Highfields Rd Abington MA 02351-2449 Office: 79 Bedford St PO Box 2091 Abington MA 02351-0591 E-mail: tuttleesq@aol.com.

TUUL, JOHANNES, physics educator, researcher; b. Tarvastu, Viljandi, Estonia, May 23, 1922; came to U.S., 1956, naturalized, 1962; s. Johan and Emilie (Tulf) T.; m. Marjatta Murtoniemi, July 14, 1957 (div. Aug. 1971); children: Melinda, Melissa; m. Sonia Esmeralda Manosalva, Sept. 15, 1976; 1 child, Johannes. Elem. Tchg. Credential, Tartu Normal Sch., Estonia, 1941; diploma in Elec. Engring., Stockholm Tech. Inst., 1947; BS, U. Stockholm, 1955, MA, 1956; ScM, Brown U., 1957, PhD, 1960. Tchr. Valuste Elem. Sch., 1941-43; escaped to Finland December, 1943; after Finland surrendered to Russia escaped to Sweden, 1944; instr. Stockholm Tech. Inst., 1947-49; lab. engr. Electrical Prospecting Co., Stockholm, 1949-53; elec. engr. LM Ericsson Telephone Co., 1954-55; rsch. physicist Am. Cyanamid Co., Stamford, Conn., 1960-62; sr. rsch. physicist Bell & Howell Rsch. Ctr., Pasadena, Calif., 1962-65; from asst. to assoc. prof. Calif. State Poly. U., Pomona, 1965-68, chmn. physics and earth scis. dept., 1971-75, prof. physics, 1975-91; prof. emeritus, 1992—. Vis. prof. Pahlavi U., Shiraz, Iran, 1968-70; cons. Bell & Howell Rsch. Ctr., Pasadena, Calif., 1965, Teledyne Co., Pasadena, Calif., 1968; guest researcher Naval Weapons Ctr., China Lake, Calif., 1967, 72; resident dir. Calif. State U. Internat. Programs in Sweden and Denmark, 1977-78. Author: Physics Made Easy, 1974; contbr. articles to profl. jours. Pres. Group Against Smoking Pollution, Pomona Valley, Calif., 1976; foster parent Foster Parents Plan, Inc., Warwick, R.I., 1964—; block capt. Neighborhood Watch, West Covina, Calif., 1982-84; citizen amb. People to People Internat., 1990—; mem. Physics Edn. Del. to Peoples Rep. China, 1990; mem. Baltic Assist Delegation, 1992; mem. Industry and Sci. Initiative 1 Delegation to Cuba, 2000. Fellow Brown U., 1957-58; rsch. grantee U. Namur (Belgium), 1978, Ctr. Nat. Recherche Scientifique, France, 1979; recipient Humanitarian Fellowship award Save the Children Fedn., 1968, spl. award Travelers' Century Club, 1998. Mem. AAAS (life), N.Y. Acad. Scis., Am. Phys. Soc. Republican. Roman Catholic. Achievements include research in energy conservation and new energy technologies.

TUZCU, EMIN MURAT, physician, researcher; b. Isparta, Turkey, July 5, 1953; came to U.S., 1985; s. Omer Lufti and Guzide T.; m. Füsun Tuzcu, Apr. 26, 1982; children: Omer C., Hande N. MD, Istanbul Med. Faculty, 1977. Diplomate Am. Bd. Internal Medicine. Intern, resident Istanbul U. Sch. Medicine, 1971—81; fellow in cardiology Cleve. Clinic, 1985—89, staff physician, 1992—, prof. medicine, 1992—; fellow Mass. Gen. Hosp., 1989—91. Contbr. articles to profl. jours. Office: Cleveland Clinic 9500 Euclid Ave Cleveland OH 44195-0002

TUZIL, TERESA JORDAN, clinical social worker, psychotherapist; b. N.Y.C., May 13, 1948; d. Lester Francis and Kathleen Geraldine (Brady) Jordan; m. Joseph Stephen Tuzil, Jan. 15, 1972; children— Joseph IV, Brian Joseph; BA, St. John's U., 1970; MSW, Hunter Coll., 1973. Cert. in gerontology; credentialed alcoholism counselor, alcoholism and substance abuse counselor. Social worker Salvation Army Foster Care and Adoption Services, N.Y.C., 1971-72; sr. caseworker Jewish Assn. for Services to the Aged, N.Y.C., 1973-78; program cons. Community Council of Greater N.Y., N.Y.C., 1978-79; pvt. practice individual and family psychotherapy, Seaford, N.Y., 1976— ; caseworker Nassau County Dept. Social Services Children's Protective Service, 1983-90, Pennsula Counseling Ctr. Outpatient Alcoholism Treatment Ctr.; adj. clin. instr. Hunter Grad. Sch. Social Work, 1975-78; field instr. Grad. Sch. Social Work, Rutgers U., 1975-77; program cons. Assn. for Services to Aged, Bklyn., 1981— . Certified, registered clin. social worker, N.Y. Mem. Nat. Assn. Social Workers, Acad. Certified Social Workers. Editor: Jour. of Gerontological Social Work, 1977— ; contbr. articles to profl. publs. in field. Home and Office: 3859 Tiana St Seaford NY 11783-3508

TUZLA, KEMAL, mechanical engineer, scientist; b. Adapazari, Sakarya, Turkey, Feb. 23, 1943; came to U.S., 1974; s. Hayrettin and Muberra (Horozlu) T.; m. Asuman Fatma Cokmez. MME, Istanbul (Turkey) Tech. U., 1966, PhD in Mech. Engring., 1972. Instr. Istanbul Tech. U., 1966-72, asst. prof., 1974, assoc. prof., 1978-81; instr. Air Force Coll., Istanbul, 1973-74; rsch. asst. prof. U. Wash., Seattle, 1974-78; sr. rsch. scientist Lehigh U., Bethlehem, Pa., 1981—. Mem. organizing com. 2d Thermal Sci. Conf., Istanbul; 1979, 3d Conf., Trabzon, Turkey, 1981; cons. Goodyear Tire & Rubber Co., Akron, Ohio, 1984-86, Exxon Nuclear, Richland, Wash., 1985-88. Editor Proc. 2d Thermal Sci. Conf., 1979; contbr. articles in area of thermal scis. to profl. jours. Co-founder Turkish Am. Cultural Assn., Seattle, 1977. Rsch. grantee Goodyear Tire & Rubber Co., 1985-86, Los Alamos (N.Mex.) Nat. Lab., 1989-91, Ben Franklin Tech. Ctr., Bethlehem, 1989-99, Gas Rsch. Inst., 1987-91, Elec. Power Rsch. Inst., 1991-94. Mem. ASHRAE, AIChE, Sigma Xi. Achievements include research in heat transfer in two-phase flows, boiling, fluidized beds, electronic components and nuclear safety. Avocations: skiing, tennis, chess, bridge. Home: 96 Valley Park S Bethlehem PA 18018-1335 Office: Lehigh U Chem Engring Iacocca Hall 111 Research Dr Bethlehem PA 18015-4732

TVERSKOY, ALEXANDER, physician; b. Poltava, Ukraine, Sept. 2, 1938; came to U.S., 1994; s. Leonid Tverskoy and Judith Kaganovskaya; m. Margarita Rodovskaya, July 16, 1963; 1 child, Mark. MD, 1st Moscow Med. Sch., 1961. Cert. Am. Bd. Internal Medicine.

TWACHTMAN-CULLEN, DIANE, communication disorders and autism specialist; b. Hartford, Conn. d. Peter and Olga Margaret (DeSarro) DeMaio; m. Walter A. Twachtman, Jr.; children: Jennifer Leigh, Erich Todd; m. James T. Cullen. BA, MA in Speech-Lang. Pathology, U. Conn., diploma in early chilhood spl. edn., 1002, PhD, 1994. Lic. speech lang. pathologist, Conn. Pvt. practice autism cons.; exec. dir. Autism and Devel. Disabilities Consultation Ctr., Higganum, Conn., 1991—. Former instr., clin. supr. U. Conn.; adj. faculty mem. Ctrl. Conn. State U.; mem. profl. adv. bd. Boston Higashi Sch. Author: A Passion to Believe, Trevor Trevor, How to Be A Para Pro: A Comprehensive Traiing Manual for Paraprofessionals. Mem. Am. Speech-Lang.-Hearing Assn., Conn. Speech-Lang.-Hearing Assn., Autism Soc. Am. (bd. profl. advisors), Autism Soc. Ohio, Autism Soc. Conn. (past pres. 2 terms, mem. profl. adv. bd.), Asperger's Assn. New Eng., Greater Hartford Autism Soc. (founding). Address: 61 Landing Rd Higganum CT 06441-4140

TWADDELL, SOPHIA HANTZES, communications executive; b. Washington, Apr. 12, 1952; d. Harry Nicholas and Mary (Protos) Hantzes; m. Jeffery Alan Maass, June 21, 1975 (div. Feb. 1994); children: Alexander Reilly, Edward Andrew, William Whittaker; m. Michael Edwards Twaddell, Dec. 27, 1997. BA, Conn. Coll., 1974; MA, Northwestern U., 1978. Researcher ABA, Washington, 1974-75; with Northwestern U., Evanston, Ill., 1975-78; analyst Am. Hosp. Supply Corp., 1978-82; product mgr. Am. Heyer-Schulte Corp., Goleta, Calif., 1980-82; project dir., account supr. Sieber & McIntyre, Chgo., 1982-86; group mgr. mktg. communications Baxter Healthcare Corp., Deerfield, 1986-91; dir. communications Boots Pharms., Inc., Lincolnshire, 1991-92; acct. mgr. Jack Morton Prodns., Chgo., 1992-94; v.p. Bozell PR, 1994; freelancer, 1995-97; v.p. Vector Securities Internat., Inc., Deerfield, Ill., 1997-99; sr. v.p., ptnr., nat. biotech. practice leader Fleishman-Hillard, Inc., 1999—. Producer documentary film: Make A Splash! Volunteer!, 1988 (Emmy 1988); co-editor cookbook: Connecticut College Cookbook, 1982. Bd. dirs. Jr. League of Chgo., 1981-88. Mem. Nat. Investor Rels. Inst. Home: 2444 Ridgeway Ave Evanston IL 60201-1858 Office: 875 N Michigan Ave Ste 3300 Chicago IL 60611 E-mail: twaddels@fleishman.com.

TWAIN, SHANIA, country musician; b. Windsor, Can. Recs. include Shania Twain, The Woman in Me (Album of Yr. Canadian Country Music Awards, 1995, Female Video Artist of Yr. ABC Radio Networks Country Music Awards, 1995, Album of Yr. Acad. Country Music Awards, 1996, Grammy award for Best Country Album 1996). Recipient Rising Star award Country Music TV/Europe, 1993, Favorite New Country Artist Am. Music Awards, 1995, Female Vocalist award Canadian Country Music Awards, 1995, Outstanding New Artist award RPM's Big Country Awards, 1995, Top New Female Vocalist award Acad. of Country Music Awards, 1996, Favorite New Country Artist award Blockbuster Entertainment Awards, 1996, Female Artist of Yr. Country Music TV/Europe, 1996, Internat. Rising Star award Gt. British Country Music Awards, 1996, Country Female Vocalist award Juno, 1996, Entertainer of Yr. award Juno, 1996, Songwriter of Yr. Juno, 2000, Best Country Female Artist Juno, 2000, others. Office: Mercury Nashville 54 Music Sq E Nashville TN 37203-4315 also: Fan Club PO Box 1150 Timmins ON Canada P4N 7H9 Address: Shore Fire Media c/o Georgette Pascale 32 Court St Fl 16 Brooklyn NY 11201-4404*

TWALE, DARLA JEAN, education educator; b. McKeesport, Pa., Sept. 23, 1951; d. Franklin Louis and LaVerne (Morgenstern) T. BA, Geneva Coll., 1973; MA, DuQuesne U., 1976, U. Pitts., 1980, PhD, 1985. H.S. tchr. Elizabeth (Pa.)-Forward H.S., 1973-74; sociology instr. C.C. of Allegheny County, West Mifflin, Pa., 1976-77, Pa. State U., McKeesport, 1979-80, Geneva Coll., Beaver Falls, Pa., 1982; vis. prof. edn. U. Pitts., 1986-87; edn. prof. Auburn (Ala.) U., 1987-98; prof. edn. U. Dayton, Ohio, 1998—. Contbr. articles to profl. jours. Mem. Am. Sociol. Assn., Mon-Yough Trail Coun., Am. Ednl. Rsch. Assn., Ea. Ednl. Rsch. Assn., Nat. Assn. of Student Pers. Adminstrs., Assn. for the Study of Higher Edn., Aircraft Owners and Pilots Assn. Methodist. Avocations: trail biking, gardening, flying. Office: Univ Dayton 300 College Park Dayton OH 45469-0002 E-mail: darla.twale@notes.udayton.edu.

TWANMOH, VALERIE HURLEY, lawyer, mediator, arbitrator; b. Englewood, N.J., May 27, 1957; d. Orval Franklin Jr. and Judith Ann (Kaplan) Hurley; m. Joseph Richard Twanmoh, June 21, 1981; children: Kai Hurley, Darren Hurley, Ross Hurley. BA, Hamilton Coll., 1979; JD, U. Conn., 1982. Bar: N.J. 1982, U.S. Dist. Ct. N.J. 1982, Mich. 1984, U.S. Dist. Ct. (we. dist.) Mich. 1984, U.S. Dist. Ct. (ea. dist.) Mich. 1986, Md. 1995; cert. civil and divorce mediator, N.J., 1996—. Intern Congressman James J. Howard, Washington, 1977; assoc. Cholette, Perkins & Buchanan, Grand Rapids, Mich., 1983-86, Conlin, Conlin, McKenney & Philbrick, Ann Arbor, 1986-87; ptnr. Rogers & Twanmoh, P.C., 1988-93, Valerie Hurley Twanmoh, P.C., Ann Arbor, 1993-94; mediator, arbitrator Fallston, Md., 1994—; intern Civil Mediation Inst., Seton Hall Law Sch., 1995; comml. arbitrator Am. Arbitration Assn., Southfield, Mich., 1994—. Bd. dirs. Ctr. for Occupational and Personalized Edn.-O'Brien Ctr., 1992-94, Nat. Assn. Mothers' Ctrs., 1995—, FACETS, 1995—; mem. com. Planned Parenthood Mid-MIch., Ann Arbor, 1987-90; vice-chair for orgn. Dukakis for Pres. campaign, Ann Arbor, 1988; campaign dir. Rebecca McGowan for U. Mich. Regent, 1992. Mem. ABA, Mich. State Bar Assn., Washtenaw County Bar Assn., Women Lawyers' Assn. (Washtenaw region v.p. program 1989, v.p.-pres. elect 1990-92, pres. 1992-93), Women Lawyers' Assn. Mich. (dir. at large 1993—), Lions (treas. 1989). Democrat. Avocations: tennis, piano, reading.

TWARDOWICZ, STANLEY JAN, artist, photographer; b. Detroit, July 8, 1917; s. Joseph and Anna Ligenski; m. Lillian Dodson, Mar. 15, 1971. Student, Meinzinger Art Sch., Detroit, 1940-44, Skowhegan (Maine) Sch. Painting and Sculpture, summer 1946. Instr. Ohio State U., 1946-51; prof. Hofstra U., 1965-87. Exhibited paintings Mus. Modern Art, Guggenheim Mus., Whitney Mus., Art Inst. Chgo., Carnegie Internat., Pa. Acad. Fine Arts, Am. Acad. Arts and Letters, Houston Mus., Milw. Art Ctr., Peridot Gallery, N.Y.C., others; retrospective exhbns. Hecksher Mus., Huntington, N.Y., 1974, Emily Lowe Gallery, Hempstead, N.Y., 1979, 40 Yr. Retrospective of Paintings Firehouse Gallery, Garden City, N.Y.; exhibited photographs Images Gallery, N.Y.C., one man show: Odeon Gallery, Sag Harbor, N.Y., 1993, Ursala Lanning Gallery, Columbus, Ohio, 1995, Mitchell Algus Gallery, N.Y.C., 1996-2000, Phoenix Art Mus., 2001-02; represented in permanent collections Mus. Modern Art, L.A. County Mus., Newark Mus., Milw. Art Ctr., Ball State Tchrs. Coll., Harvard U., Vassar Coll., Hirshhorn Mus. and Sculpture Garden, others. Guggenheim fellow, 1956 Home: 133 Crooked Hill Rd Huntington NY 11743-3811

TWARDY, STANLEY ALBERT, JR. lawyer; b. Trenton, N.J., Sept. 13, 1951; s. Stanley Albert Twardy and Dorothy M. Stonaker. BS with honors, Trinity Coll., 1973; JD, U. Va., 1976; LLM, Georgetown U., 1980. Bar: Conn. 1976, D.C. 1978, U.S. Supreme Ct. 1979, U.S. Ct. Appeals (2d cir.) 1984. Assoc. Whitman & Ransom, Greenwich, Conn., 1976-77; counsel com. on small bus. U.S. Senate, 1977-79, counsel to Senator Lowell Weicker Jr., 1979-80; ptnr. Silver, Golub & Sandak, Stamford, Conn., 1980-85; U.S. atty. Dist. of Conn., 1985-91; chief of staff Office of Gov. Lowell Weicker, Conn., 1991-93; ptnr. Day, Berry & Howard, Stamford, 1993—. Mem. nat. alumni exec. com. Trinity Coll., 1985—90, mem. athletic adv. com., 1992—; bd. dirs. Spl. Olympics World Summer Games Organizing Com., Inc., 1993—95; chmn. City of Stamford Police Chief Selection Panel, 1993—94; mem. area adv. com. U. Conn. at Stamford, 1993—96; mem. strategic planning mgmt. com. U. Conn., 1993—95; bd. dirs. Drugs Don't Work!, 1989—93, 1994—2000, chmn. program com., 1989—91; bd. trustees Trinity Coll., 1996—2002; bd. dirs. Rehab. Ctr., Stamford Health Found.; trustee Trinity Coll., 1996—2002; Mem. vestry St. John's Episc. Ch., Stamford, 1983—86; vestry mem. St. John's Episcopal Ch., 1983—86; bd. dirs. Spl. Olympics World Summer Games Organizing Com., Inc., 1993—95, Stamford Health Found., 1995—. Mem.: ABA, Conn. Trial Lawyers Assn., Assn. Trial Lawyers Am., Conn. Bar Assn., Phi Beta Kappa. E-mail: satwardy@dbh.com.

TWARJAN, COLLEEN ANN, dental hygienist; b. Manchester, N.H., Jan. 1, 1956; d. Robert Francis and Josephine Margaret (O'Brien) H.; m. John Paul Twarjan Jr., Oct. 9, 1982; children; Jesse, Max, Sam. AA, N.H. Tech. Inst., Concord, 1977. Dental hygienist Dr. Steven Christenson, Concord, N.H., 1977-78, Dr. Joseph Maroun, Salem, 1978-83, Dr. Christos Giotopoulos, Manchester, 1978-84, Lindner Dental Assocs., Bedford, 1997—. Mem. Smyth Rd. PTO, Manchester, N.H., 1988—, treas. 1989-96, v.p., 1996, pres., 1997-99; v.p. Hillside PTO, 1999-2000, pres. 1997-98. Roman Catholic. Avocations: gardening. Office: Lindner Dental Assocs Bedford NH 03110

TWAROG, SOPHIA NORA, economist, international civil servant; b. Columbus, Ohio, Nov. 29, 1964; d. Leon I. and Katherine (Foster) T.; m. Alberto Klaas, July 2, 1993; children: Kevin Leon Twarog Klaas, Christina Joy Katherine Klaas. BA in Econs. magna cum laude, U. Notre Dame, Ind., 1987; MA in Economics, Ohio State U., 1989, PhD in Economics, 1993. Intern Ctr. of Concern, Washington; vol. in Ctr. America Sisters of the Assumption, Phila., 1987-88; vol. in India Christian Found. for Children & Aging, Kansas City, Mo., 1988; rsch. cons. Nat. Bur. Econ. Rsch., Cambridge, Mass., 1990; grad. teaching assoc. Ohio State U., Columbus, 1989-91; econ. affairs officer UN Conf. on Trade and Devel., Geneva, 1993-96, Spl. Programme for Trade Efficiency, 1993-96; economist Office of Dep. Sec.-Gen. of UNCTAD, 1997-98; economist Trade, Environment and Devel. sect. Divsn. Internat. Trade in Goods and Svcs. and Commodities, 1999—. Contbd. to preparation of UN Internat. Symposium on Trade Efficiency, Columbus, 1994. Contbr. articles to books and popular mags. Founder, pres. Overseas Devel. Network-U. Notre Dame, 1986-87; chmn. First Ann. Great Hunger Clean-up, South Bend, Ind., 1987; chmn., co-chmn. Third World Awareness Week, U. Notre Dame, 1986-87. Glenna R. Joyce scholar Joyce Found., 1983-87; recipient John W. Gardner Leadership award U. Notre Dame, 1987; U. Multi-Yr. fellow Ohio State U., 1988, 92, Rsch. fellow Rheinische Friedrich-Wilhelms U., Bonn, 1990-91, Dice fellow Ohio State U., 1993. Mem. Phi Beta Kappa, Phi Kappa Phi. Avocations: travel, hiking, salsa dancing. Home: 182 Oakland Park Ave Columbus OH 43214-4122 Office: UN Conf on Trade & Devel Palais Des Nations Ch 1211 Geneva 10 Switzerland E-mail: sophia.twarog@unctad.org.

TWEED, JOHN LOUIS, consultant, association executive, lecturer, small business owner; b. Neptune, N.J., Sept. 27, 1947; s. Harry Scullion and Mary Jane (Manniello) T.; m. Joan Marie Parente, Sept. 12, 1970 (div. Apr. 1989); children: Jennifer F., Christin A., Jonathan M.; m. Carolyn G. Joos, June 21, 1992; stepchildren: Jennifer G. Joos, Kimberly K. Joos, Edward S. Joos. AA in Bus. Adminstrn., Ocean County Coll., Toms River, N.J., 1978. Notary pub.; registered legis. agt. Br. mgr. Retail Delivery Service, Paterson, N.J., 1969-75; pres., chief exec. officer Ambicab, Inc., Toms River, 1975-85; owner Tony's Texaco, Pt. Pleasant, N.J., 1977-79; proprietor Bob's Auto Wax Shop, Asbury Park, 1985-87; mng. ptnr. Investment Enterprises, Toms River, 1984-86; founder John L. Tweed & Assocs., 1984—; v.p. strategic planning Multi-Care Emergency Med. Service, Matawan, 1986-89; founder Formal Limousine Service Inc., Toms River, 1988-90; ptnr. Ultimate Achievement, 1994—. V.p. On the Double Messenger Svc., Inc., Aberdeen, N.J., 1988-91; chmn. bd. Performax Inc., Toms River, 1995—; neutral chmn. labor-mgmt. com. N.J. Dept. Labor, 1991. Sec. Toms River Soccer Assn., 1987-89; coach divsn. I girls and divsn. III boys N.J. Youth Soccer Assn., 1981-89; coach Toms River Basketball Assn., 1989-97; pres. Dover Twp. Dem. Club, 1990-91; committeeman Dover Twp., 1990; mem. Cities in Schs. Pre-Implementation Com.; mem. adv. coun. Ocean County Human Svcs.; mem. adv. bd. Toms River Alt. Learning Ctr., 1989-96, Family Life Bur., Diocese of Trenton, 1989-94; mem. Ocean County Planning Bd., 1990-94; usher St. Joseph's Ch., 1993-98; transp./access com. Bldg. a Healthier Ocean County; govt. rels. dir. Coalition for Responsible Day Care, 1998-99; exec. dir. Livery Ops. Coalition, 1998-2000; mem. parish coun. St. Catharine of Siena, Seaside Park, N.J., 2000—, v.p., 2001-2002, pres. 2002. Sgt. USAF, 1965-69; mem. N.G., 1976-77. Mem. Am. Ambulance Assn. (dir.-at-large 1982-87), Nat. Med. Transp. Assn. (bd. dirs. 1995-98), N.J. Assn. Execs., Med. Transp. Assn. N.J. (pres. 1978-84, exec. dir. 1985—), Assn. Residential Care Homes (exec. dir. 1995—), Am. Entrepreneur's Assn., Am. Soc. Assn. Execs., Partial Care Ctrs. Assn. N.J. (exec. dir. 1999—), 200 Club Ocean County, Kiwanis Daybreak (bd. dirs. Toms River club 1982-83), Optimist Club (pres. 1992-93, v.p. 1991), Facilitator Divorced and Separated Groups, St. Joseph's Holy Name Soc. (pres. 1996-98), Ocean County Coll. Alumni Assn. (sec. 1996-97, v.p. 1997-2000, pres. 2001—), Ocean County Coll. Found. Roman Catholic. Home and Office: 19 8th Ave Seaside Park NJ 08752-1811

TWEEDY, ROBERT HUGH, equipment company executive; b. Mt. Pleasant, Iowa, Mar. 24, 1928; s. Robert and Olatha (Miller) T.; B.S. in Agrl. Engring., Iowa State U., 1952; m. Genevieve Strauss, Aug. 15, 1969; children— Bruce, Mark; 1 stepdau., Mary Ellen Francis. Sr. engr. John Deere Waterloo Tractor Works, Waterloo, Iowa, 1953-64; mktg. rep. U.S. Steel Corp., Pitts., 1964-68; mgr. product planning agrl. equipment div. Allis-Chalmers Corp., Milw., 1969-76, mgr. strategic bus. planning Agrl. Equipment Co., 1976-85; mgr. strategic bus. planning Deutz-Allis Corp., 1985-89; project mgr. AGCO Corp., Batavia, Ill., 1989-94; retired, 1994; chmn. agrl. research com. Farm and Indsl. Equipment Inst., Chgo., 1974-76, mem. safety policy adv. com., 1972-89; mem. farm conf. Nat. Safety Council, Chgo., 1973-89; mem. industry sector adv. com. No. 16, U.S. Dept. Commerce, 1982-85; bd.

dirs. C.V. Riley Meml. Found. Recipient citation in engring. Iowa State U., 1983. Fellow Am. Soc. Agrl. Engrs. (v.p. 1974-78, pres. 1981-82, gen. chmn. hdqrs. bldg. project 1968-70; chmn. Found. Trustees 1983-88, Wis. Engr. of Year award 1980, McCormick-Case Gold medal 1989), Masons. Patentee in field. Home: 3301 Alt 19 Lot 172 Dunedin FL 34698-1524

TWEEL, DONNA SHANK, lawyer; b. Huntington, W.Va., Jan. 3, 1960; BA, Marshall U., 1982; JD cum laude, U. Dayton, 1990. Bar: Ohio 1990. Jud. staff atty. State of Ohio Ct. Appeals, 2d dist., Dayton, 1990-94; assoc. Turner & McNamee Co., LPA, 1994-96; ptnr. Chernesky, Heyman & Kress, PLL, 1996—. Mem. U. Dayton Law Rev. Coun. mem. Village of Waynesville, Ohio, 1993-96. Mem. ABA, Ohio State Bar Assn., Dayton Bar Assn., Dayton Women's Bar Assn. Office: Chernesky Heyman & Kress PLL 1100 Courthouse Plz SW Dayton OH 45402 E-mail: dst@chklaw.com.

TWERSKY, JONATHAN, lawyer; b. Kiev, Ukraine, July 31, 1961; came to U.S., 1976; s. David and Polina Twersky; m. Ninah Beliavsky, Mar. 27, 1988; children: Michaella S., Delilah L. AA in Hebrew Lit., BA in Polit. Sci., Yeshiva U., 1982; JD, Benjamin Cardozo Sch. Law, 1985. Bar: N.Y., U.S. Dist. Ct. (ea. and so. dist.) N.Y. Staff atty., svcs. staff atty. Bklyn. br. Legal Svcs. for N.Y.C., 1985-92, dir. housing law unit, 1992—. Bd. dirs. Shorefront Jewish Cmty. Counsel, Bklyn., 1997—. Mem. Phi Delta Phi. Office: Legal Svcs for NYC Bklyn Br 186 Joralemon St Ste 703 Brooklyn NY 11201-4326 E-mail: jtwersky@lsnybb.org.

TWICHELL, CHASE, poet; b. New Haven, Aug. 20, 1950; d. Charles P. and Ann (Chase) T. BA, Trinity Coll., Hartford, 1973; MFA, U. Iowa, 1976. Editor Pennyroyal Pr., W. Hatfield, Mass., 1976-84; assoc. prof. English U. Ala., 1984-88; mem. MFA Program in Creative Writing, Warren Wilson Coll., 1999—; editor Ausable Press, 1999—. Asst. prof. Hampshire Coll., 1983-84; co-editor Alabama Poetry Series, 1984-88; lectr. Princeton U., 1990-98; faculty MFA program in creative writing Goddard Coll., 1997-99. Author: (poetry) Northern Spy, 1981, The Odds, 1986, Perdido, 1991, The Ghost of Eden, 1995; editor: The Practice of Poetry, 1992, The Snow Watcher, 1998. Recipient Acad. award in lit. Am. Acad. Arts and Letters, 1994; Nat. Endowment for Arts fellow, 1987, 93, Guggenheim fellow, 1990.

TWICHELL, FREDERICK C. fund raiser; b. New Britain, Conn., June 21, 1937; s. Edward Stow and Gertrude Shaffer Twichell; m. Marion Cunningham, Sept. 22, 1962; children: Jonathan E., Marion F., Catherine S. BA, Middlebury Coll., 1959; MBA, Cornell U., 1961; MALS, Wesleyan U., 1970. Platform asst. Mfrs.-Hammer Trust, N.Y.C., 1962-63; math. tchr. Berkshire Sch., Sheffield, Mass., 1963-69; chmn. math. dept. Thacher Sch., Ojai, Calif., 1969-83, fund raiser, 1983—2002. Spkr. in field. Chmn. bldg. campaign Ojai Valley Mus. and Hist. Soc., 1984-96; chmn. bd. edn. Monica Ros Sch., 1985-92, 94-2000; reader First Ch. of Christ, Ojai, 1989-92, 2001—, also bd. dirs.; chmn. bd., nat. bd. dirs. Asher Found. With USNG, 1961-62. Mem. Rotary Club. Republican. Christian Scientist. Avocations: hiking, collecting coins and old tools, golf. Office: Thacher Sch 5025 Thacher Sch Ojai CA 93023 E-mail: TTwichell@thacher.org.

TWIETMEYER, DON HENRY, lawyer; b. Rochester, N.Y., June 4, 1954; s. Frederick Herman and Norma Frances (Porter) T.; m. Victoria Lynne Engleman, July 1, 1989; children: Laura Elizabeth, Jill Ann Cafarelli, Anthony R. Cafarelli. BA in Polit. Sci., Econs. with honors, SUNY, Buffalo, 1976; JD, Union U., 1979; LLM in Taxation, U. Miami, 1980; MBA in Acctg., Rochester Inst. Tech., 1983. Bar: N.Y. 1980, Fla. 1980, U.S. Dist. Ct. (we. dist.) N.Y. 1980, U.S. Dist. Ct. (so. dist.) Fla. 1980, U.S. Tax Ct. 1980, U.S. Ct. Appeals (5th and 11th cirs.) 1981, U.S. Supreme Ct. 1994, U.S. Bankruptcy Ct. 1994; CPA, N.Y. Tax acct. Davie, Kaplan & Braverman, Rochester, 1980-82; assoc. DeHond-Stowe Law Office, 1982-84, Lacy, Katzen, Ryen & Mittleman, Rochester, 1984-87; mng. atty. DeHond Law Office, 1987-91, prin., 1991-92; assoc. Fix, Spindelman, Brovitz, Turk, Himelein & Shukoff, 1992-98; of counsel Hiscock Barclay Saperston & Day, 1998—. Lectr. estate and gift taxes Found. Acctg. Edn., 1987-96. Author: Review and Update for Experienced Practitioners: Fiduciary, Estate and Gift Taxation, 1987-96. V.p. coun. Hope Luth. Ch., 1989-91, active meml. fund com., 1990-91, chmn. bldg. use com., 1990-91; chmn. missions and social concerns com. Bethlehem Luth. Ch., 1992-2000, mem. ch. coun., 1993-95, pres. ch. coun., 1994-95, deacon, 1994-95; mem. orgn. com. Luth. Charities Rochester Region, 1993-95, pres., dir., 1995-2000, adv. bd. dirs., 2000—; dir. Prevention Ptnrs., Inc., 1997—, pres., 2000—, fin. com., 1997—; mem. planned and deferred giving com. The Genesee Hosp. Found., 1998-2000; mem. planned giving com. Rochester Gen. Hosp. Found., 2001—. Mem. ABA (tax sect., entertainment and sports industries forum) Fla. Bar Assn. (tax sect., out of state practitioners divsn., real property, probate and trust sect.), N.Y. State Bar Assn. (tax sect., entertainment and sports law sect, trusts and estates sect.), Monroe County Bar Assn. (tax sect. and trusts and estates sect., exec. coun. 1996—, sec. 2000-01, chair 2001-02, elder law com., intellectual property law com.), N.Y. State Soc. CPAs, Am. Assn. Atty.-CPAs, Estate Planning Coun. Rochester (exec. coun. 2000—), Rotary (internat. svc. com. 1994—, Rotary Internat. Found. com. 1994-2002, chairperson com. 1996-2002, Rochester Rotary Golf Tournament com. 1995-2000, planned giving com. 1997—, world cmty. svc. com. 2002—), Phi Beta Kappa, Phi Alpha Delta, Omicron Delta Epsilon, Phi Eta Sima. Republican. Lutheran. Avocations: golf, tennis, skiing, philately. Office: 2000 HSBC Plz Rochester NY 14604 Fax: 585-325-5458. E-mail: dtwietmeyer@hiscockbarclay.com.

TWIFORD, ALICE KATE, lawyer; b. York, Pa., Mar. 16, 1956; d. James R., Sr. and Helen M. (McTague) Markle; m. Lester D. Twiford, Nov. 14, 1981. BS, York Coll. of Pa., 1976; JD, Coll. of William and Mary, 1991, LLM, 1992. Bar: Va. Commd. 2d lt. U.S. Army, 1976, advanced through grades to capt., 1980, resigned, 1988; pvt. practice Williamsburg, Va., 1992—. Chmn. Social Svcs. Adv. Bd., James City County, Va., 1992- 96; treas. bd. dirs. Olde Towne Med. Ctr., 2000—. Mem. ABA, Va. State Bar (bd. govs. gen. practice sect., 1993-2000, bd. govs. mil. law sect. 1999—), Williamsburg Area Trial Lawyers Assn. (pres. 1993-94), Greater Peninsula Women's Bar Assn. (bd. dirs. 2001—), Soroptimist of Williamsburg (rec. sec. 2002—). Office: PO Box 5068 Williamsburg VA 23188-5068 Fax: (757) 253-0937. E-mail: aktwiford@widomaker.com.

TWIFORD, JIM, former state legislator; b. Wheaton, Wy., Nov. 17, 1942; m. Jenne Lee Twiford. Pres. senate Wy. Ho. of Reps., 1999—2000; dir. of transp. and physical plant Converse County School District #1, Douglas, Wyo., 2001. Roman Catholic. Office: 615 Hamilton Street Douglas WY 82633 Fax: 307-358-3515. E-mail: jim@twiford.org.*

TWIGGS, DENNIS GLENN, psychologist, writer; b. Marion, N.C., Feb. 5, 1946; s. James Glenn and Velra Ledford Twiggs; m. Tamara Jean Hatley, July 13, 1969; 1 child Jason Scott. BS, Appalachian State U., 1965—69, Masters, 1972—73; PhD, Tulane U., 1973—77. Lic. psychologist NC, 1979, Tex., 1978. Counselor US Army Green Beret, Fort Bragg, NC, 1972; therapist Mt. Vernon Clinic, Wilmington, 1972; tchg. asst. Tulane U., New Orleans, 1974—77; staff psychologist Mexia State Sch., Mexia, Tex., 1978; dir. adjunctive therapy San Antonio State Sch., 1978; lic. psychologist pvt. practice, Winston Salem, NC, 1979—. Cons. Cardiac Rehab. , NC, 1980—85; bd. psychologists Vocat. Rehab., NC, 1980—2000; adj. faculty High Pt. U., High Point, NC, 1983—90. Author: (book) Psychological and Spiritual Evolution, 1995, Integrational Psychology, 1996, Psyche, Soul, and Spirit, 1998. Co-founder Soc. Reform Mental Health, 2002, bd., 2002, Assn. Mentally Handicapped, Winston Salem, 1981, pres., 1982; bd. Piedmont Handicapped Assn., 1983. 1st lt. Army Green Beret USAR, 1969—72, various. Recipient Nat. Hon. Rsch. Soc., Sigma Xi, 1978, Disting. Svc. Award, NC Rehab. Assn., 1982; grantee Grant for Delayed Stress, Veterans Admin., 1982. Achievements include discovery of Integrational Psychology; In media: Science, 1979, Age and Environ. Interaction in Recovery of loss of Brain Function; Journ. Am. Phys. Assn., 1981, Use of biofeedback in tng. Mentally Handicapped; In press: Sci. Found. Neurotic and Psychotic Reactions. Avocations: book reviewer lib. journ and others, classical guitar, reading, study of physics and cosmology, hiking. Home: 3664 Heathrow Dr Winston Salem NC 27127 Office: Pvt Practice PO Box 25881 Winston Salem NC 27114

TWIGG-SMITH, THURSTON, newspaper publisher; b. Honolulu, Aug. 17, 1921; s. William and Margaret Carter (Thurston) Twigg-S.; m. Bessie Bell, June 9, 1942 (div. Feb. 1983); children: Elizabeth, Thurston, William, Margaret, Evelyn; m. Laila Roster, Feb. 22, 1983 (div. Dec. 1994); m. Sharon Smith, Feb. 28, 1996. B.Engring., Yale U., 1942. With Honolulu Advertiser, 1946-2000, mng. editor, 1954-60, asst. bus. mgr., 1960-61, pub., 1961-86; pres., dir., chief exec. officer Honolulu Advertiser, Inc., 1962-93, chmn., 1993-2000. Chmn., dir., CEO Persis Corp., 1962-2002, chmn. Twigg-Smith Group LLC, 2002—; bd. dirs. Atalanta/Sosnoff Capital Corp., N.Y. Trustee Honolulu Acad. Arts, The Contemporary Mus., Hawaii, The Skowhegan Sch., Maine, Yale Art Gallery, New Haven. Maj. AUS, 1942-46. Mem. Waialae Country Club, Pacific Club, Oahu Country Club, Outrigger Canoe Club. Office: Twigg-Smith Group LLC 2447 Makiki Heights Dr Honolulu HI 96822-2547 E-mail: ttwiggsmith@aol.com.

TWILLEY, JOSHUA MARION, lawyer; b. Dover, Del., Mar. 23, 1928; s. Joshua Marion and Alice Hunn (Dunn) T.; m. Rebecca Jane Buchanan, Dec. 27, 1952; children: Stephanie, Jeffrey, Linda Edgar, Joshua; m. Rosemary Miller, Dec. 1, 1972. BA cum laude, Harvard U., 1950, JD, 1953. Bar: Del. 1953, U.S. Dist. Ct. Del. 1960, U.S. Supreme Ct. 1976. Pvt. practice, Dover, 1955-72; sr. ptnr. Twilley, Jones & Feliceangeli, 1972-88, Twilley, Street & Brayerman, Dover, 1988-95, Twilley & Street, Dover, 1995—. Pres. Del. Indsl. Enterprises, Inc.; chmn. Incorporating Svcs. Ltd., Del. Incorporating Svcs. Ltd.; bd. dirs. 1st Nat. Bank Wyo.; sec. Sunshine Builders, Inc. mem. Del. Pub. Svc. Commn., 1975—, vice chmn. 1995—; pres. Kent County Levy Ct., 1970-75. Mem. exec. com. Del. Dem. Com., 1970-93; pres. Elizabeth Murphey Sch., 1957—. With U.S. Army, 1953-55. Mem ABA, Del. Bar Assn., Kent County Bar Assn. Democrat. Lutheran. Avocations: gardening, landscape architecture. Home: 124 Meadow Glen Dr Dover DE 19901-5544 Office: 426 S State St Dover DE 19901-6724 E-mail: rtwilley@erols.com.

TWILLMAN, ROBERT KEITH, psychologist; b. Boonville, Mo. s. Ralph W. and Doris L. T.; m. Nancy A. Thompson, July 23, 1983; 1 child, Talia. AB, U. Chgo., 1983; PhD, UCLA, 1989. Lic. psychologist. Staff psychologist Pitts. Cancer Inst., 1990-92; clin. asst. prof. psychiatry U. Kans., Kansas City, 1992-2001; dir. psychosocial svcs. U. Kans. Cancer Ctr., 1992—2001; clin. assoc. prof. psychiatry U. Kans., 2001—; pain mgmt. program dir. U. Kans. Hosp., 2001—. Mem. Am. Soc. Psychosocial Behavioral Oncology/AIDS (dir. 1995—), Am. Alliance Cancer Pain Initiatives (dir. 1996—), Kans. Cancer Pain Initiative (pres. 1997—). Office: U Kans Cancer Ctr 3901 Rainbow Blvd Kansas City KS 66160-0001 Fax: 913-588-4720. E-mail: rtwillma@kumc.edu.

TWINAME, JOHN DEAN, minister, human services administrator; b. Mt. Kisco, N.Y., Dec. 27, 1931; s. C. G. and Constance Jean (Ulmer) Twiname; m. Carolyn Anderson, Aug. 6, 1955; children: Karen, Jeanne, Julia. AB, Cornell U., 1953; MBA, Harvard U., 1957; MDiv, Union Theol. Sem., 1983. Ordained to ministry Presbyn. Ch., 1983. Sales rep. Am. Hosp. Supply Corp., Evanston, Ill., 1957-60, dir. product research, 1961, sales mgr., 1962, asst. to div. pres., 1963, product mgr., 1964, mktg. mgr., 1965-67, mktg. v.p., 1968-69; dep. adminstr. Social and Rehab. Svc., HEW, Washington, 1969-70, adminstr., 1970-73; adminstr. Office Health Office Health, Cost of Living Coun., 1973-74; pvt. cons. Mott-McDonald Assocs., Inc., Washington, 1974-76, pres., 1976-78; exec. v.p. Am. Health Found., N.Y.C., 1978-81; co-pres. HealthCare Chaplaincy, Inc., 1983-93, co-chair exec. com., 1993-94, life trustee, 1995—. Cons. exec. Coll. Chaplains, 1997; acting sr. min. Green's Farms Ch., Westport, Conn., 2001—. Treas. U.S. com. Internat. Coun. Social Welfare, 1977—80; mem. pres. coun. United Hosp. Fund, 1991—; voting mem. Empire Blue Cross/Blue Shield, 1994; chmn. bd. dirs. Bauman Bible Telecasts, Inc., 1976—80; sec. bd. dirs. U.S. Coun. Internat. Yr. of Disabled Persons, 1979—81; founding bd. dirs. Am. Paralysis Assn. (formerly Paralysis Cure Rsch.), 1976—83; bd. dirs. Epilepsy Found. Am., 1978—85; chmn. bd. dirs. Chgo. Bus.-Indsl. Project, 1967—68, People to People Com. for Handicapped, 1976—78; bd. dirs. N.Y. Regional Transplant Program, 1988—92, Beck Mack & Oliver Ptnrs. Fund, 2000—. 1st lt. AUS, 1953—55. Recipient Disting. Svc. award, Coll. Chaplains, 1992; scholar Baker, Harvard U. Home: 163 Harbor Rd Southport CT 06490-1378 Office: HealthCare Chaplaincy Inc 307 E 60th St New York NY 10022-1505 E-mail: JTwiname@healthcarechaplaincy.org.

TWISDALE, HAROLD WINFRED, dentist; b. Roanoke Rapids, N.C., Apr. 28, 1933; s. James Robert and Elma (Smith) T.; m. Barbara Ann Edmonds, Aug. 2, 1958 (div. Apr. 1974); children: Harold Winfred, Leigh Ann.; m. Frances Jean Winstead, July 1983. BS in Dentistry, U. N.C., 1955, D.D.S., 1958. Individual practice dentistry, Charlotte, N.C., 1961—; head, dept. dental prosthetics Meml. Hosp., 1964-66; lectr. dental subjects.; pres., gen. mgr. WCTU-TV, Charlotte Telecasters, Inc., 1967-69, WATU-TV, Augusta, Ga., Augusta Telecasters, Inc., 1968-69, Television Presentations, Inc., Charlotte, 1967-69; partner Twisdale and Steel Assos., 1965-70; propr. Twisdale Enterprises, 1965-70. Pres. Memphis Telecasters, Inc., 1966-76, Va. Telecasters, Inc., Richmond, 1966— , Durham-Raleigh Telecasters, Inc., Durham, N.C., 1966-70, Gentil Elite, Inc., 1979— Transp. chmn. Miss N.C. Pageant, 1965; v.p. N.C. Jaycees, 1963-64; Trustee Boys Home, Lake Waccomaw, N.C., 1966-67. Served to capt. USAF, 1958-60. Recipient various awards Charlotte Jaycees, 1962-66. Fellow Acad. Dentistry Internat.; mem. ADA, N.C. Dental Found., N.C. Dental Soc., Charlotte Dental Soc. (chmn. various coms. 1961—), Am. Analgesia Soc., Internat. Analgesic Soc. (dir. 1980-85), N.C. Dental Soc. Anesthesiology (v.p. 1983-84), Charlotte Analgesia Study Club (co-founder 1970), N.C. 2d Dist. Dental Soc., Metrolina Dental Soc. (founder 1994, pres. 1994-95), U. N.C. Dental Alumni Assn., Southeastern Analgesia Soc. (founder 1972, pres. 1972-74), Lambda Chi Alpha, Delta Sigma Delta. Republican. Methodist. Home: 2221 Streatley Ln Matthews NC 28105-6648 Office: 6623 Executive Circle #110 PO Box 25528 Charlotte NC 28229-5528 *I must give the full credit for any achievement I might have accomplished in life to my mother and father. They not only provided me the means and direction one needs to make even the slightest accomplishment in our mortal life, but most of all, they gave me love, understanding, and a sense of values. These values have never deserted me, nor have they been compromised, even in the darkest hours of depression or during the brightest times of accomplishment. They have been my steady companions.*

TWISS, ROBERT MANNING, prosecutor; b. Worcester, Mass., Aug. 2, 1948; s. Robert Sullivan Jr. and Marion (Manning) T.; m. Joan Marie Callahan, Aug. 4, 1979. BA, U. Mass., 1970; JD, U. San Francisco, 1975; MA in Criminal Justice, Wichita State U., 1979; LLM, Georgetown U., 1981. Bar: Mass. 1976, Calif., 1988, U.S. Ct. Appeals Armed Forces 1976, U.S. Dist. Ct. Mass. 1976, U.S. Ct. Appeals (1st cir.) 1976, U.S. Ct. Appeals (5th cir.) 1986, U.S. Ct. Appeals (9th cir.) 1988, U.S. Dist. Ct. (ea. and cen. dist.) Calif. 1989. Atty. office chief counsel IRS, Washington, 1980-86; trial atty. criminal div. U.S. Dept. Justice, 1986-87, asst. U.S. atty. Sacramento, 1987-93, 94—, chief organized crime and narcotics, 1991-92, 1st asst. U.S. atty., 1992-93, U.S. atty., 1993, exec. assst. U.S. atty., 1994. Contbr. articles to profl. jours. Capt. JAGC, U.S. Army, 1976-80 Named to McAuliffe Honor Soc. U. San Francisco, 1975; recipient Markham award Office Chief Counsel IRS, Washington, 1985. Avocation: athletics. Office: Office US Atty 501 I St 10th Fl Sacramento CA 95814-7306

TWISS, WANDA MAY, interior designer; b. Marengo, Ind., Oct. 28, 1934; d. Gamford Ingle and Anjie Pearl (Beld) Tate; m. Eugene Clyo Twiss, Nov. 27, 1952; children: Sheryll Lynn, Carol Ann. Student pub. schs., Newcastle, Ind. Decorator Decorating Den, Leesburg, Fla., 1970-85, franchise owner, 1983—, regional coordinator, instr., 1984—, designer, 1985—. Mem. Am. Soc. Interior Designers (allied mem.). Mem. Ch. of Nazarene. Home: 41640 County Road 25 Weirsdale FL 32195-5172 Office: Decorating Den 1031 W Main St Leesburg FL 34748-4965

TWIST, PAUL FRANCIS, JR. neonatologist; b. Buffalo, Nov. 6, 1946; s. Paul Francis and Hazel Mary (Schoetz) T.; m. Angela Margaret McNerney, Aug. 7, 1970; children: Patrick, Michael, Brendan. BS in Pharmacy, St. John's U., Jamaica, N.Y., 1969; DO, U. Osteo. Medicine, Des Moines, 1973. Lic. physician Ohio, Ill., N.Y.; lic. pharmacist, Iowa. Resident in pediatrics Good Samaritan Hosp., Cin., 1973-75, fellow in neonatology, 1975-76, Loyola Med. Ctr., Maywood, Ill., 1976-77; dir. neonatology and newborn medicine Winthrop-Univ. Hosp., Mineola, N.Y., 1977—, attending physician dept. pediatrics and obstetrics, 1978—; assoc. clin. prof. sch. nursing Adelphi U., Garden City, 1985—; asst. prof. pediatrics N.Y. Coll. Osteo. Medicine, Westbury, 1980-85, assoc. prof. pediatrics, 1985—. Attending physician Mercy Hosp., Rockville Centre, N.Y., 1978—, Nassau County Med. Ctr., East Meadow, N.Y., 1980—; cons. Glen Cove (N.Y.) Community Hosp., 1980—, St. Francis Hosp., Roslyn, N.Y., 1983—; lectr. in field. Contbr. articles to profl. jours. Bd. dirs. Little Village Sch., Garden City, 1980—; mem. internal rev. bd. St. John's U., Jamaica, 1981—; pres. St. Pius X Sch. Bd., Plainview, N.Y.; treas. Sch. of the Holy Child Fathers Club, Old Westbury, N.Y. Mem. Am. Pharm. Assn., N.Y. State Med. Soc., Nassau County Pediatric Soc. (rep. dist. II 1987-90), Am. Osteo. Assn., N.Y. State Osteo. Soc., Am. Acad. Pediatrics, Nat. Perinatal Assn. (com. on fetus and newborn 1979, chpt. 2 dist. II, N.Y.), N.Y. State Perinatal Soc., Assn. of N.Y. State Regional Perinatal Ctr., Am. Soc. for Parenteral and Enteral Nutrition. Roman Catholic. Home: 1 Equestrian Ct Huntington NY 11743-6637 Office: Winthrop-Univ Hosp 259 1st St Mineola NY 11501-3987

TWITCHELL, E(RVIN) EUGENE, lawyer; b. Salt Lake City, Mar. 4, 1932; s. Irvin A. and E. Alberta (Davis) T.; m. Joyce A. Newey, Aug. 9, 1957 (div. May 1989); children: Robert R., Lauren E., David J., Michael S.; m. Linda Sue Wilson, 1991; children: Bonnie Wilson, Jimmy Wilson, Benjamin Wilson, Stefanie Wilson. Student, Brigham Young U., 1954-55; BA, Calif. State U., Long Beach, 1959; JD, UCLA, 1966. Bar: Mich. 1977, U.S. Dist. Ct. (ea. dist.) Mich., U.S. Supreme Ct. 1987. Contract adminstr. Rockwell No. Am. Aviation, Seal Beach, Calif., 1966-68; sr. contracts adminstr. McDonnell Douglas Corp., Long Beach, 1968-73; in-house counsel Albert C. Martin & Assocs., L.A., 1973-77; instr. bus. law Golden West Coll., Huntington Beach, 1973-74; corp. counsel, corp. sec. Barton Malow Co., Southfield, Mich., 1977-97, ret., 1997. Mem. Detroit EEO Forum, 1983-87; arbitrating and cons., 1997—. Editl. cartoonist Eufaula Tribune, 2001—; host (local TV show) Who's Who in Eufaula, 2002—. Pres. Corona (Calif.) Musical Theater, 1975-76; dist. chmn. Boy Scouts of Am.-North Trails, Oakland County, Mich., 1978-80; treas. Barton Malow PAC, Southfield, 1983-97. Sgt. USAF, 1950-52. Mem. ABA, Mich. Bar Assn., Am. Arbitration Assn. (arbitrator Detroit, Ala., Ga., and Fla. areas 1985-97, arbitrator Ala.-Ga. area 1997—), Am. Corp. Counsel Assn. (v.p., dir. 1983-97). Republican. Mem. Lds Ch. Avocations: cartooning, painting, karate, music, theatre, writing. Home and Office: PO Box 747 Eufaula AL 36072-0747 E-mail: twitchell@mindspring.com.

TWITCHELL, KENT, artist; b. Lansing, Mich., Aug. 17, 1942; s. Robert E. and Wilma Doris (Berry) T.; m. Susan Catherine Fessler, Dec. 27, 1975 (div. 1986); m. Pandora Seaton, Feb. 23, 1990; children: Rory, Artie. AA, East L.A. Coll., 1969; BA, Calif. State U., 1972; MFA, Otis Art Inst., 1977; DA (hon.), Biola U., 1989; DFA (hon.), Otis Coll. Art and Design, 1996. Illustrator USAF, 1960-65; display artist J.C. Penney Co., Atlanta, 1965-66; abstract artist, painter L.A., 1968-70; mural artist, 1971—. Instr. L.A. County High Sch. for the Arts, L.A., 1987-90, Otis/Parsons Art Inst., L.A., 1980-83; cons. Olympic Murals Program, L.A., 1983-84. Executed exterior murals at Union at 12th St. (Steve McQueen monument), L.A., 1971, Hollywood Fwy. (The Freeway Lady), L.A., 1974, Hill St. at Olympic (Edward Ruscha monument), 1987, 405 Fwy. (La Marathon mural), Inglewood, Calif., 1988, 1234 Ridge Ave. (Dr J monument), Phila., 1989, Harbor Fwy. (La Chamber Orch.), L.A., 1991-93, (Will Rogers Monument), Calif. Theater, San Bernardino, Calif., 1998-99, Hillside Meml. Park murals, 2001-02; one-man shows include: L.A. Mcpl. Art Gallery, 1980, Loyola Marymount U., L.A., 1985, Thinking Eye Gallery, L.A., 1986, Valparaiso (Ind.) U. Art Mus., 1987, Westmont Coll. Art Gallery, Santa Barbara, Calif., 1987, Biola U. Art Gallery, La Mirada, Calif., 1987, Vincent Price Gallery-East L.A. Coll., 1990, Lizardi-Harp Gallery, Pasadena, Calif., 1991, U. Redlands Art Gallery, 1997, Koplin Gallery, L.A., 1998; exhibited in group shows at L.A. Mcpl. Art Gallery, 1977, 81, 94, 96, Calif. Polytech. U., Pomona, 1978, Santa Monica Coll., 1978, L.A.C.E. Gallery, L.A., 1981, Otis/Parsons Art Inst., L.A., 1987, Mayer Schwarz Gallery, Beverly Hills, 1988, 90, Principia Coll., Elsah, Ill., 1989, Koplin Gallery, Santa Monica, 1992, 95, 98, L.A. County Mus. Art, 1992, Robert Berman Gallery, Santa Monica, 1995, Art Ctr./Coll. Design, Pasadena, 1996, Riverside (Calif.) Art Mus., 1996. Mem. adv. bd. Artists Equity Assn., 1980-88, Mural Conservancy of L.A., 1988—. Grantee Calif. Arts Coun., 1978, Nat. Endowment for Arts, 1986. Avocation: theology. Home: 9505 Main St PO Box 145 Upper Lake CA 95485-0145 E-mail: artkent@saber.net.

TWITCHELL, THOMAS EVANS, neurologist, educator; b. Springfield, Ohio, Sept. 4, 1923; s. Ernst Albert and Charlotte Marie (Schelling) T.; m. Patricia Ann O'Brien, Nov. 18, 1956; children: Carol, Susan, Mauyra, Evelyn. MD, U. Mich., 1946. Rsch. fellow in neurophysiology Yale U., New Haven, 1947; intern in neurology Boston City Hosp., 1947-48, rsch. fellow in neurology, 1948-49; USPHS rsch. fellow in neurophysiology Yale U., 1949-51; asst. resident in medicine New Eng. Med. Ctr., Boston, 1954, chief resident in neurology, 1954-55, neurologist, 1955-88; instr. neurology Tufts U. Sch. Medicine, 1955-56, asst. prof. neurology, 1956-62, assoc. prof. neurology, 1963-83, prof., 1983-88, prof. neurology, 1983-88, prof. emeritus, 1988—. Rsch. assoc. in psychology MIT, Cambridge, 1963-77. Served to capt. USAF, 1952-54. Mem. Am. Acad. Neurology, Am. Neurol. Assn. (sr.), Mass. Med. Soc. Avocations: music, philosophy, physics, literature. Home: 54 Longfellow Rd Wellesley MA 02481-5221

TWITCHIN, JOHN GORDON, management consultant, independent producer; b. Cleethorpes, England, Feb. 21, 1941; s. Gordon T. and Eileen (Lowrence) Keane; divorced; 1 child, Mischa. BA with honors, Oxford (England) U. Producer BBC World Svc., England, 1963-64; news journalist BBC Radio News, England, 1964-68; sr. producer BBC TV, England, 1974-92; ind.producer JTL Prodns., London, 1992—; co-dir. Ctr. Inter-Cultural Devel., 1993—. Tutor Marylebone Inst., London, 1968-89; dir. Diversity Works, London. Author: Multicultural Education, 1981, 2d edit., 1985, The Black and White Media Book, 1988, 3d edit., 1992. Fellow Inst. Personnel and Devel. Home and Office: Ctr Inter-Cultural Devel 27 Langland Gardens London NW3 6QE England

TWITTY, H.R. hospital official; b. Columbia, S.C., May 9, 1941; s. Archie Hazel Twitty and Sara (Murphy) Avritt; m. Marlene Faye Wingate, June 9, 1961; children: William Thomas, Michael David. BA, Tenn. Temple Coll., 1964. Cert. profl. for hosp. material mgmt. Mgr. store room Erlanger Hosp., Chattanooga, 1961-69; purchasing agt. Meml. Hosp., 1969-71, dir. facility svcs., 1999—2001, dir. material, 1972-99, bd. dirs. credit union, 1986-92, CSR coord., 2002—, exec. to United Way, 2001. United Way Loaned Exec., 2001; deacon Duncan Park Bapt. Ch., Chattanooga, 1986—88, 1991—92, 1995—96, 1997—2000, chmn. bd. deacons, 1983, 1988, mem. leadership com., 1995—96, chmn. bd. deacons, 0998—2000. Mem. Am. Hosp. Assn. Purchasing Mgrs. (cert. sr.), Internat. Hosp. Soc. Material Mgrs. (Disting. Profl.), Tenn. Hosp. Soc. Material Mgrs. (bd. dirs. region III 1979-82, pres. 1983-84, 89-92, Mgr. of Yr. award 1991, bd. dirs. 1994—), Chattanooga Area Purchasing Soc. (pres. 1985-87), Optimist. Home: 369 Prater Rd Rossville GA 30741-4692 Office: Meml Hosp 2525 Desales Ave Chattanooga TN 37404-1102 E-mail: hrtwitty@memorial.org.

TWO FEATHERS, MORWEN, event coordinating company executive; b. Hartford, Conn., Aug. 1, 1956; d. Gerald I. and Estelle F. (Prant) Swilling; m. Paul W. Ingle, Jr., June 7, 1985 (div. July 1991); m. Jimi Two Feathers, Aug. 10, 1991; 1 child, Kaylin Kewanee. BA in Psychology, Trinity Coll., Hartford, 1978; MA in Sociology, Boston U., 1984. Edn. dir. Conn. Women's Edn. and Legal Fund, Hartford, 1978-79; dir. Rape Crisis Svcs. of Greater Lowell, Mass., 1984-86; co-dir. Boston Fuel Consortium, 1986-88; assoc. dir., exec. dir. Support Ctr. of Mass., Boston, 1988-94; co-dir. Earth Drum Coun., Concord, Mass., 1990—; prin. Idea Facilitation Svcs., 1995—. Adj. faculty Clark U., Worcester, 1989-93, Tufts U., Medford, Mass., 1997—. Contbr. articles to profl. jours.; prodr.: (dance theatre) A Fool's Fable, 1989. Bd. dirs. Mass. Coalition Rape Crisis Svcs., 1984-86; conf. coord. Harvest Gathering, Mt. Washington, Mass., 1997; fundraising event coord. Mass. Coalition for Homeless, Boston, 1986-87; tchr. Concord Carlisle Adult Edn., 1997, Boston Ctr. for Adult Edn., 1996-97. Mem. Phi Beta Kappa. Avocations: music, dance, travel, camping. Office: Earth Drum Coun PO Box 1284 Concord MA 01742-1284

TWOHY, CYNTHIA HOWARD, research scientist; b. Long Beach, Calif., Jan. 5, 1960; d. Richardson James Twohy and Virginia Lee Hall; m. James E. Ragni, Dec. 30, 1989. BS summa cum laude, U. Calif., Davis, 1981; MS, U. Wash., 1988, PhD, 1992. Sr. food technologist Case-Swayne Co., Inc., Santa Ana, Calif., 1981-85; grad. rsch./tchg. asst. U. Wash., Seattle, 1985-88; atmospheric scientist Nat. Ctr. for Atmospheric Rsch., Boulder, Colo., 1988-99; asst. prof., sr. rsch. Oreg. State U., Corvallis, 1997—. Rev. of jour. publs., 1990—. Contbr. articles to profl. jours. Math. tutor United Way, Lafayette, Colo., 1992; sci. fair judge Kohl Elem. Sch., Broomfield, Colo., 1996-98; pet visitation for srs. Elm's Haven Care Ctr., Thornton, Colo., 1995-97; master gardener Colo. State U. Cooperative Ext., Adams County, Colo., 1997. Postdoctoral fellow Nat. Ctr. for Atmospheric Rsch., Boulder, 1992-94; rsch. grant In-Situ Measurement of Cirrus Cloud Properties, NASA, 1995-96; rsch. grantee NSF, 1999-2002, others. Mem. Am. Assn. Aerosol Rsch. (chair atmospheric aerosols 2001-02), Prytanean Women's Honor Soc., Am. Geophys. Union, Phi Kappa Phi. Avocations: horseback riding, gardening, genealogy, mosaic. Office: Oreg State Univ Oceanography Admin 104 Corvallis OR 97331 E-mail: twohy@coas.oregonstate.edu.

TWOMBLY, JEAN SAWYER, musician, educator; b. Bethlehem, Pa., Feb. 12, 1946; d. Edwin A. and Elizabeth (Stempel) Sawyer; m. Stephen Doane Twombly, Dec. 29, 1979. BS in Music Edn. magna cum laude, Susquehanna U., 1968; MMus in Early Music Performance, Longy Sch. Music, Cambridge, Mass., 1994. Artistic dir. Ensemble Soleil, N.H., 1995—. Adj. asst. prof. Colby-Sawyer Coll., New London, N.H., 1986—; pvt. music tchr., New London, 1983—. Grantee N.H. Humanities Coun., 1997-99, N.H. State Coun. on Arts, 1998, 99. Mem. Boston Musician's Assn., Early Music Am., Viola da Gamba Soc. New Eng. (bd. dirs. 1999—). Avocations: stained glass, poetry, skiing, sailing. Office: Ensemble Soleil PO Box 933 New London NH 03257-0933

TWOMBLY, STEPHEN DOANE, magazine publisher; b. Summit, N.J., July 26, 1953; s. Doane and Betty (Bowers) T.; m. Jean Sawyer. BA summa cum laude, Drew U., 1976. Dist. mgr. McGraw-Hill Publs. Co., N.Y.C., 1978-83; dir. advt. IDG Communications, Peterborough, N.H., 1983-84, pub. RUN, 1984-87, pub. AmigaWorld, 1985—; group pub. Consumer/Home Mag., Special Products, 1987-88; v.p. IDG Communications/Peterborough, 1988-89, exec. v.p., 1989—; pub. dir. PC Resource, 1988; exec. v.p., pub. dir. PCResource IDG Communications/Peterborough, 1989—. Mem. Sigma Phi. Avocations: composing, painting, outdoor sports. Home: PO Box 1365 New London NH 03257-1365 Office: IDG Communications 86 Elm St Peterborough NH 03458-1052

TWOMEY, THOMAS A., JR. lawyer, educator; b. N.Y.C., Dec. 8, 1945; s. Thomas A. and Mary (Maloney) T.; m. Judith Hope Twomey, Dec. 15, 1979; stepchildren: Erling Hope, Nisse Hope. *Great-great-grandfather, Michael Twomey, was born in Macroom, County Cork, Ireland, and immigrated to Boston in 1841 during the Great Famine. The family, thereafter, settled in Sheepshead Bay, Brooklyn, where father, Thomas Twomey, was born in 1915. Grandmother Grace Ketchcham's ancestry is traced to Englishman, Edward Ketcham, and his son, John, who helped found Southold and Huntington Towns on Long Island in mid-17th Century. Other ancestors helped found Southampton, Islip, Hempstead, Jamaica, and New Utrecht, serving as legislators, Town officials, and an occasional pirate.* BA, Manhattan Coll., 1967; postgrad., U.Va., 1967-68; JD, Columbia U., 1970. Bar: N.Y. 1972, U.S. Tax Ct. 1974. Asst. town atty. Town of Southampton N.Y., 1973-74; spl. asst. dist. atty. Suffolk County, N.Y., 1973-74; pvt. practice law Riverhead, 1974-75; ptnr. Hubbard & Twomey, 1976-79, Twomey, Latham, Shea & Kelley, Riverhead, 1980—. Chair N.Y. State East End Econ. and Environ. Task Force, 1993; mem. deans coun. Stonybrook Sch. Medicine, 1991—; adj. prof. environ. law Southampton Coll., 1977-78. *Over the last 25 years, Mr. Twomey helped build his law firm into one of the largest in Suffolk County, with 45 attorneys and staff. Martindale-Hubbell has given its highest rating to the firm for legal competence and reliability. All of its attorneys are involved in community organizations, including Mr. Twomey who recently raised $3.6 million to expand and restore the East Hampton Library, of which he is now the President. As Chair of the Lecture Series of The East Hampton 350th Anniversary, he recently edited Awakening the Past, a history of the Town, and served in 1999 as Town historian.* Bd. dirs. East End Arts Coun., Riverhead, 1983, Guild Hall East Hampton, 1993—; bd. dirs. East Hampton Libr., 1994—, pres., 1998—; trustee L.I. Power Authority, 1989-94; town historian, Town of East Hampton, 1999, vice chair East Hampton Town 350th Anniversary com., 1998, editor East Hampton Histor. Collection; historian N.Y. State Dem. Com., 2000-01; chair East Hampton 350th lecture series, 1998. Recipient Environ. award, U.S. EPA, 1980, Citizen of Yr. award L.I. FArm Bur., 2002. Mem. ABA, Suffolk County Bar Assn., State Energy Coun., N.Y. State Fresh Water Wetlands Appeals Bd. Democrat. Home: #9 Two Holes of Water Rd East Hampton NY 11937

TWOMLEY, BRUCE CLARKE, commissioner, lawyer; b. Selma, Ala., Jan. 23, 1945; s. Robert Clarke and Eleanor Jane (Wood) Anderson T.; m. Sara Jane Minton, June 13, 1979; children: Christopher Mario, Jonathan Marion. BA in Philosophy, Northwestern U., 1967; JD, U. Calif., San Francisco, 1970; postgrad., Nat. Jud. Coll., Reno, Nev., 1983, 88. Bar: Calif. 1972, Alaska 1973, U.S. Dist. Ct. Alaska 1973, U.S. Ct. Appeals (9th cir.) 1982. VISTA vol., Anchorage, 1972-73; lawyer Alaska Legal Services Corp., 1973-82; commr. Alaska Comml. Fisheries Entry Commn., Juneau, 1982-83, chmn., 1983—; mem. Gov.'s Fisheries Cabinet, 1983—, Child Support Enforcement Divsn. Rural Task Force, 1985—. Mem. Alaska Fedn. of Natives Task Force on IRS and Alaska Native Fishermen, 1994; cons. IRS, Sta. WNED-TV, Buffalo, 1988; mem. Bristol Bay Native Assn. Blue Ribbon Commn. on Ltd. Entry, 1994—. Contbr.: Limited Access Management: A Guidebook to Conservation, 1993. Recipient Alaska Legal Services Disting. Service award, 1983, 92. Mem. Juneau Racquet Club (adv. bd. 1989—), Kappa Sigma (pres. interfraternity council 1966-67). Home: PO Box 20972 Juneau AK 99802-0972 Office: Alaska Comml Fisheries Entry Commn 8800 Glacier Hwy Ste 109 Juneau AK 99801-8079

TWOTREES, KAYLYNN, artist; b. Des Moines, June 14, 1955; d. Art and Lacie Mae (Johnson) Jones; m. Michael J. Sullivan, Dec. 3, 1968 (div. June 1983); 3 children. Studied with, K. Kia Bunseki Fu Kiau, Wallace Black Elk; Dell Wihongi. Pres. KLS Mgmt., N.Y.C., 1977-80; prodn. dir. Schaubuhne, Berlin, 1980-82; Acad. Challenge scholar Miami U., Oxford, Ohio, 1990-92, Markley lectr., 1993-96, scholar in residence, 1994-96; founding dir. Earthtime, Flagstaff, Ariz., 1995—; scholar in residence Cleve. Inst. Art, 1997—. Vis. artist/lectr. U.S. colls. and univs., 1982-90; bd. dirs. Media Working Group, Covington, Ky., 1992—; Seven Directions cons. Earthtime, 1995—. Art work includes installation Leave No Footprints, 1990, performance of Sipiwi on Ky. Pub. TV, 1992, earth sculpture Trail of Hope, 1994; author: Somebody Always Singing You, 1997. Invited mem. Pu Hau Rango Trust, Auckland, New Zealand, 1993-96; chair Indigenous People's Conf. Com., 1996-98. Recipient Internat. Artist award Lila Wallace/Readers Digest Found., 1993, Documentary Prodn. Flow Fund, 1994; Performance grantee N.Y. State Coun. on the ARts, 1984, Franklin Furnace/Jerome Found., 1986. Mem. Aoteroa Maonanui A Kiwa Weavers, Iyeska (founder). Home: PO Box 31086 Flagstaff AZ 86003-1086

TWYMAN, NITA (VENITA TWYMAN), music educator; b. Beloit, Wis., July 14, 1948; d. W.R. and Geneva L. (Goodman) Corvin; m. Dennis D. Twyman, Aug. 16, 1969; children: Christopher Grant, Kevin Scott. AA with honors, Southwestern Coll., Oklahoma City, 1968; B Music Edn. cum laude, So. Nazarene U., 1971; postgrad., U. Okla., 1970-71, 91-94; MMus, Oklahoma City U., 1975. Piano instr. Oklahoma City Southwestern Coll., 1968-70; pvt. music instr. Twyman Piano Studio, Oklahoma City, 1968—. Adj. faculty mem. Redlands C.C., El Reno, Okla., 1995—; creative cons. Great Start in Music edn1. music video; choir dir. Ctrl. Ch., Oklahoma City, 1989; staff accompanist Oklahoma City First Pentecostal Holiness Ch., 1966-68. Solo performances at local churches. Mem. Nat. Guild Piano Tchrs. (nat. tchr. cert., nat. adjudicator), Music Tchrs. Nat. Assn. (nat. cert. in piano and music theory, Piano Technicians Guild grantee 1991), Okla. Music Tchrs. Assn. (adjudicator), Ctrl. Okla. Music Tchrs. Assn. (sec., parliamentarian, treas., mem. various coms.), Okla. Fedn. Music Clubs (adjudicator), Oklahoma City Pianists Club (performer), Phi Kappa Lambda. Avocations: scuba diving, bicycling, water skiing, snow skiing. Office: Nita Twyman Piano Studio 5915 NW 23rd St Ste 107 Oklahoma City OK 73127-1254

TYACK, THOMAS MICHAEL, lawyer; b. Columbus, Ohio, June 20, 1940; s. George E. and E. Naomi (Ballard) T.; m. Patricia J. Clark, Sept. 7, 1969; children: Jonathan, Jeffrey, James, Justin. BA cum laude, Ohio State U., Columbus, 1962, Jd, 1965. Bar: Ohio 1965, U.S. Ct. Appeals (6th cir.) 1970, U.S. Supreme Ct. 1970, U.S. Dist. Ct. (so. dist.) Ohio 1972. Ptnr. Tyack, Scott & Colley, Columbus, 1965-79, Tyack Scott & Wiseman, Columbus, 1979-81; prin. Thomas M. Tyack Assocs. Co., L.P.A., 1981-90; ptnr. Tyack & Blackmore Co., L.P.A., 1991-94; pres. Tyack, Blackmore & Liston Co. LPA, 1994—. Bar examiner Ohio supreme Ct., 1975-80; lectr., legal asst. program Capital U., Ohio, 1977-90. Fellow Am. Coll. Trial Lawyers; mem. ABA, Ohio Bar Assn., Columbus Bar Assn., Franklin Ct. and Trial Lawyers, Assn. Trial Lawyers Am., Ohio Acad. Trial Lawyers, Ohio Acad. Trial Lawyers, Ohio Acad. Criminal Def. Lawyers, NDCDL. Republican. Methodist. Office: 536 S High St Columbus OH 43215-5605

TYBOUT, RICHARD ALTON, economics educator; b. Phila., Sept. 28, 1920; s. Richard Raymond and Lillian (Alton) T.; m. Rita Holloway, Sept. 7, 1946; children: Alice Marie, James Richard, Robert Maxwell. BChemE, U. Del., 1943; MSChemE, U. Mich., 1946, MA in Econs., 1947, PhD in Econs., 1952. Instr. U. Mich., Ann Arbor, 1952-54; asst. prof. Ohio State U., Columbus, 1954-57, assoc. prof., 1957-62, prof., 1962-88, prof. emeritus, 1988—. Editor: Economics of Research and Development, 1965, Environmental Quality and Society, 1975; author: Government Contracting in Atomic Energy, 1956, The Reactor Supply Industry, 1960, Atomic Power and Energy Resource Planning, 1958; co-author: The Columbus Area Economy, 1966. Named Ford Faculty Study Fellow, Ford Foun., 1959-60, Phoenix Predoctoral Fellow, U. Mich., 1949-51. Mem. Am. Econ. Assn., Sierra Club (chmn. econs. com. 1975-85), Tau Beta Pi, Phi Kappa Phi, Beta Gamma Sigma. Avocations: construction, swimming, sailing. Home: 324 Pingree Dr Columbus OH 43085-3158 Office: Ohio State U Dept Econs 1945 N High St Columbus OH 43210-1120

TYCHOWSKI, CHRISTOPHER ROMAN, engineer; b. Chorzow, Poland, Sept. 20, 1937; came to U.S., 1973; s. Feliks and Maria Jadwiga (Napierala) T.; m. Slavomira Maria Zbierska, Sept. 16, 1975 (div. Mar. 1979). Bachelors Degree, Poznan (Poland) Tech. Coll., 1958; Masters Degree, Poznan Politechnik, 1965; PhD, Warsaw (Poland) Inst. Tech., 1972. Sr. project engr. Warsaw Inst. Tech., 1969-73; project engr. Arthur G. McKee, San Mateo, Calif., 1974-76; pvt. practice cons. Phoenix, 1976-78; civil engr. W.B.C. Cons., 1978-79; project engr. Peter A. Lendrum Architects, 1979-80; sr. structural engr. Sullivan-Mason, Inc. Architects-Engrs., 1981-83; plans rev. engr. City of Phoenix Bldg. Safety Dept., 1981-83; sr. project engr. Magadini Alagia Assoc., Phoenix, 1983-84; pres. C.R.T. Corp., Tempe, Ariz., 1984—. Realtor Realty Experts, Inc., Phoenix, 1987—; pres. Alliance Bldg. Corp., Phoenix, 1988—, Acorn Bldg. Corp.; exec. v.p. Gemcraft Constrn. Co., Inc., Phoenix, 1988—. Patentee in field. Recipient Recognition awards, Polish Assn. of Architects, 1968, 70, Tech. Excellence award Polish Normalization Com., 1971, Best Sports Pub. of Yr. award Polish Nat. Olympic Com., 1972. Mem. Am. Inst. Steel Constrn., Structural Engrs. Assn., Phoenix Bd. Realtors. Republican. Roman Catholic. Avocations: stamp collecting, tennis, classical music. Office: CRT Corp 1370 E 8th St Ste 2 Tempe AZ 85281-4383

TYE-MURRAY, NANCY, research scientist; b. Bittburgh, Germany, Feb. 11, 1955; parents U.S. citizens; d. Joe B. and Janelle (Bowen) Tye; m. David John Murray, May 15, 1983; children: Ellen, Aubrey. BS, Tex. Christian U., 1977; MA, U. Iowa, 1979, PhD, 1984. Cert. clin. competency-audiology. Rsch. asst. dept. psychology U. Iowa, Iowa City, 1983-85; asst. rsch. scientist U. Iowa Hosps., 1985-90, assoc. rsch. scientist, 1990—. Author, editor: Cochlear Implants and Children: A Handbook, 1992; author: Communications Training for Children and Teenagers, 1992; contbr. articles to Jour. of the Acoustical Soc. Am., Jour. Speech and Hearing Rsch., Ear and Hearing. Prin. investigator Easter Seal Rsch. Found., 1986-89, Deafness Rsch. Found., 1987-89, Children's Miracle Network, 1989-90; investigator NIH/NINCDS Program Project, 1990—. Recipient editors award Volta Rev., 1992. Mem. Am. Speech-Lang.-Hearing Assn. (rev. bd. 1989-92, com. on noise exposure 1990-92), Acoustical Soc. Am., Acad. Rehab. Audiology (monograph editor 1992—), Alexander Graham Bell Assn. (rev. bd. 1992—). Achievements include rsch. in speech sci., aural rehab. and cochlear implants; developed four laser videodisc speech reading tng. programs which are used by cochlear implant recipients. Office: Dept Otolaryngology Univ Iowa Hosps Iowa City IA 52242

TYER, TRAVIS EARL, library consultant; b. Lorenzo, Tex., Oct. 23, 1930; s. Charlie Earl and Juanita (Travis) T.; m. Alma Lois Davis, Nov. 6, 1951; children: Alan Ross, Juanita Linn. BS, Abilene Christian U., 1952; BLS, U. North Tex., 1959; AdM in LS, Fla. State U., 1969, postgrad., 1969-71. Librarian, tchr. pub. schs., Gail, Lubbock, and Seminole, Tex., 1952-61; with Dallas Pub. Library, 1961-66, coordinator young adult services, 1962-66; library dir. Lubbock Pub. Library, 1966, Lubbock City-County Libraries, 1967-68; grad. library sch. faculty-state personnel coordinator Emporia (Kans.) State U., 1971-72; sr. cons. profl. devel. Ill. State Library, Springfield, 1972-80; exec. dir. Great River Libr. Sys., Quincy, Ill., 1980-94; cons. pub. rels. and comm. Alliance Libr. Sys., 1994-97; ind. libr. cons., 1997—. Lectr. summer workshops Tex. Woman's U., U. Okla., U. Utah, Fla. State U., U. North Tex.; adj. faculty U. Mo., 1986-89; cons. in field; mem. adv. com. Ill. State Libr., 1984-87, 93-96; pres. Resource Sharing Alliance West Ctrl. Ill., Inc., 1981-94, sec., 1994-97; pres. Ill. Libr. System Dirs. Orgn., 1992-94. Contbr. articles to library jours. Inductee U. North Tex. Libr. and Info. Sci. Hall of Fame, 1990. Mem. ALA, Ill. Libr. Assn., Ill. Ctr. for the Book, Friends of Librs. U.S.A., U. North Tex. Sch. Libr. and Info. Sci. (life), Friends Lubbock City-County Librs. (life), Ill. Sch. Libr. MEdia Assn. Democrat. Mem. Ch. of Christ. Home and Office: 2008 S Arrowood Ct Quincy IL 62305-8961

TYGRETT, HOWARD VOLNEY, JR. lawyer; b. Lake Charles, La., Jan. 12, 1940; s. Howard Volney and Hazel (Wheeler) T.; m. Linda Lee; children: Carroll Diane, Howard V. III. BA, Williams Coll., 1961; LLB, So. Methodist U., 1964. Bar: Tex. 1964. Gen. atty. SEC, 1964-65; law clk. to chief judge U.S. Dist. Ct. No. Dist. Tex., 1965-67; ptnr. Tygrett & Walker and predecessors, Dallas, 1968-98. Bd. dirs. Routh St. Center, 1976-83, Theatre Three, 1974-75, Shakespeare Festival, 1978-81, Suicide and Crisis Ctr., 1983-8; chmn. Terrell Hist. Preservation Commn., 2000—. Mem. Tex. Bar Assn., Civitan (lt. gov. Tex. dist. 1976-77, gov. 1979-80), Terrell Heritage Soc. (v.p. 1999—), Delta Phi, Delta Theta Phi. Episcopalian. Home: 505 Pacific Ave Terrell TX 75160-2073 Office: 505 Pacific Ave Terrell TX 75160-2073

TYHACH, RICHARD JOSEPH, medical products executive, researcher; b. N.Y.C., Aug. 14, 1949; s. Joseph and Pauline Tyhach; m. Elaine Barbara Goral, Nov. 11, 1973; children: Jeffrey, Matthew. BA, CUNY, 1970, MA, 1973, PhD, 1976. Postdoctoral fellow Med. Sch. Harvard U., Cambridge, Mass., 1976-78; rsch. scientist diagnostics div. Miles Inc., Elkhart, Ind., 1978-81, staff scientist diagnostics div., 1981-85, supr. R & D diagnostics div., 1985-87, mgr. R & D diagnostics div., 1987-89, dir. urine chemistry products R & D diagnostics div., 1989-92, dir. reagt. devel./instrument engring., urine chemistry unit, 1992-95; dir. new products Bayer Corp. Bus. Group Diagnostics, 1995-97; dir., v.p. rsch. and devel. GDS Tech., 1998—2002, dir. clin. and regulatory affairs, 2001—02; clin. project mgmt. cons. Eli Lilly and Co., 2002—. Inventee in field. Damon Runyon-Walter Winchell Cancer Fund fellow, 1976. Mem. Am. Assn. for Clin. Chemistry, Am. Chem. Soc., Phi Beta Kappa, Sigma Xi.

TYKESON, DONALD ERWIN, broadcast executive; b. Portland, Oreg., Apr. 11, 1927; s. O. Ansel and Hillie Martha (Haveman) T.; m. Rilda Margaret Steigleder, July 1, 1950; children: Ellen, Amy, Eric. BS, U. Oreg., 1951. V.p., dir. Liberty Comm., Inc., Eugene, Oreg., 1963-67, pres., CEO, dir., 1967-83; mng. ptnr. Tykeson/Assocs. Enterprises, 1983—; chmn. bd. Bend Cable Comm., LLC, 1983—2002, vice chmn., 2002—; chmn. bd. Acacia Internat., 1988—, Ctrl. Oreg. Cable Advt., LLC, 1992—, Bend Cable Data Svcs. LLC, 1998—. Mem. coun. pub. reps. NIH, 2002—; pres. Tykeson Found., 1995—. Bd. dirs. Nat. Multiple Sclerosis Soc., 1987—, Nat. Coalition Rsch. in Neurol. and Communicative Disorders, 1984-89, Sacred Heart Med. Ctr. Found., 1995—; chmn. Nat. Coalition in Rsch. pub. and govt. info. com., 1986-89, C-SPAN, 1980-89; mem. bus. adv. coun. U. Oreg. Coll. Bus. Adminstrn., 1973—, steering com. 1997—, dean search com., 1998-99; trustee U. Oreg. Found., 1996—; vice-chmn. we. area Nat. Multiple Sclerosis Soc., 1983—, dir., mem. rsch. and med. programs com., 1986-99; trustee Eugene Art Found., 1980-85, Oreg. Health Scis. U. Found., 1988-91, investment com., 1992-95, neurosci. com., 1999—; mem. Oreg. Investment Coun. State of Oreg., vice-chmn., 1988-92. Mem. Nat. Assn. Broadcasters, Nat. Cable TV Assn. (dir. 1976-83), Chief Execs. Orgn., Vintage Club (bd. dirs. 1996-99, chmn. fin. com., treas. 1996-99, pres. Custom Lot Assn. 1992-97), Country Club Eugene (dir. 1975-77, sec. 1976, v.p. 1977), Multnomah Athletic Club, Arlington Club, Rotary, Alexis de Tocquevill Soc. Home: 447 Spyglass Dr Eugene OR 97401-2091 Office: Tykeson Assocs Enterprises PO Box 70006 Eugene OR 97401-0101

TYKOT, ROBERT HOWARD, social sciences educator, archaeologist; b. N.Y.C., June 30, 1961; s. Howard Benson Tykot and Joan Florence Spitaleri; m. Cynthia Armstrong Grant, Apr. 29, 1989; children: Jeffrey Nathan, Matthew William. BS in Chemistry & Archaeology, Tufts U., 1983, MA in Classical Archaeology, 1984; PhD in Anthropology, Harvard U., 1995. Tchg. and rsch. asst. Tufts U., 1982-84; tchg. fellow Harvard U., 1987-94, mgr. Archaeometry Lab., 1990-96; lectr. anthropology U. Mass., Boston, 1995-96; asst. prof. U. South Fla., Tampa, 1996-2001, assoc. prof., 2001—. Field dir., asst. project dir. Excavations at Santa Barbara, Sardinia, Italy, 1987-91; prin. investigator Field Survey of Monte Arci, Sardinia, 1987-90, Lipari, Palmarola and Pantelleria, 2000—. Editor: Sardinia in the Mediterranean: A Footprint in the Sea, 1992, Sardinian and Aegean Chronology, 1998, Social Dynamics of the Central Mediterranean, 1999; contbr. articles to profl. jours. Rsch. grantee Sigma Xi, 1991, Nat. Sci. Found., 2000—, grantee Wenner-Gren Found., 1995; travel grantee Am. Coun. Learned Socs., Italy, 1996, S.H. Kress Found., France, 1995, Italy, 2000; recipient Presdl. Young Faculty award USF, 1998. Mem. Soc. Archaeol. Scis. (bull. editor 1997—), Archaeol. Inst. Am. (pres. Boston chpt. 1993-96, v.p. Tampa chpt. 1998—), Harvard Archaeol. Soc. (pres. 1987-90), Soc. Am. Archaeology. Avocations: photography, golf, model rocketry. Office: U South Fla Dept Anthropol 4202 E Fowler Ave Stop Soc107 Tampa FL 33620-8100 E-mail: rtykot@chuma1.cas.usf.edu.

TYKSINSKI, EUGENE KORY, broadcast executive; b. Rome, Jan. 14, 1935; s. Kostyn Stanley and Mary Jenny (Farraggio) T.; m. Ann Elizabeth Percival, June 21, 1965 (div. Sept. 1981); children: Cory, Stephen, Mary Beth; m. Elizabeth Salter Roetter, Aug. 15, 1987; 1 child, Matthew. Student, Utica Coll., 1952-54; BS, Lemoyne Coll., 1959. Budget analyst N.Y. State Divsn. Budget, Albany, 1963-67; prin. analyst N.Y. Senate Fin. Com., 1967-83, sec., 1983-93; exec.dir. Assn. Pub. Broadcasting Stas. N.Y., 1993—. Co-author: Criminal Justice Process of New York, 1965. Capt. USMC, 1959-63. Recipient Pub. Svc. award Rockefeller Inst. Pub. Adminstrn., Albany, 1992. Fellow State Acad. Pub. Adminstrn. (bd. dirs. 1995—); mem. Am. Soc. Pub. Adminstrn. (past pres.), Fort ORange Club. Avocations: sailing, golf, reading. Home: 830 Creek Ct Slingerlands NY 12159-3007 Office: Assn Pub Broadcasting Stas 120 Washington Ave Albany NY 12210-2283

TYL, NOEL JAN, baritone, astrologer, writer; b. West Chester, Pa., Dec. 31, 1936; BA, Harvard U., 1958. Bus. mgr. Houston Grand Opera Assn., 1958-60; account exec. Ruder and Finn Pub. Rels., N.Y.C., 1960-62; profl. astrologer, 1970—; editor Astrology Now mag., 1974-79. Pres. Tyl Assocs., Inc. pub. rels. and advt., 1980-89; media spokesman; internat. lectr., locations including U.S., Moscow, London, Oslo, Copenhagen, Berlin, Amsterdam, The Netherlands, Toronto, Ont., Tel Aviv, Bologna. Winner Am. Opera Auditions, 1964; opera singer U.S. and Europe, 1964-80; Wagner specialist; appearances include Vienna State Opera, Düsseldorf, Rome, Milan, Barcelona, N.Y.C. Opera, also throughout U.S.; author: Principles and Practice of Astrology, 12 vols., 1973-75, Teaching and Study Guide, 1976, The Horoscope as Identity, 1974, Holistic Astrology, 1980, Prediction in Astrology, 1991, Synthesis and Counseling in Astrology, 1994, Astrology of the Famed, 1995, Predictions for a New Millennium, 1996, Astrological Timing of Critical Illness, 1998, Creative Astrologer, 1999, Solar Arcs, 2001, Intimacy, Sexuality, and Relationship, 2001. Mem. Astrology's World Orgn./AFAN (presiding officer 1982-98). Home: 17005 E Player Ct Fountain Hills AZ 85268-5721

TYLENDA, JOSEPH N. library director; b. Dickson City, Pa., June 26, 1928; s. William Vincent and Josephine Elizabeth (Mruk) T.. AB, U. Scranton, 1948; STL, Weston Coll., 1961; STD, Gregorian U., 1964. Prof. theology Woodstock (Md.) Coll., 1964—70, Gregorian U., Rome, 1970—73; mng./book rev. editor Theol. Studies, Washington, 1974—85; fellow Jesuit Hist. Inst., Rome, 1985—94; dir. Woodstock Theol. Libr., Washington, 1994—. Author: (book) Jesuit Saints and Martyrs, 1984, Pilgrim's Guide to Rome's Principal Churches, 1993; translator: Imitation of Christ, 1984. Roman Catholic. Avocations: Jesuit history, Reformation, theology of John Calvin, haliography. Office: Woodstock Theol Libr Georgetown U 37 and O Sts NW Washington DC 20057

TYLER, ANNE (MRS. TAGHI M. MODARRESSI), author; b. Mpls., Oct. 25, 1941; d. Lloyd Parry and Phyllis (Mahon) T.; m. Taghi M. Modarressi, May 3, 1963 (dec. Apr. 1997); children: Tezh, Mitra. BA, Duke U., 1961; postgrad., Columbia U., 1962. Author: If Morning Ever Comes, 1964, The Tin Can Tree, 1965, A Slipping-Down Life, 1970, The Clock Winder, 1972, Celestial Navigation, 1974, Searching for Caleb, 1976, Earthly Possessions, 1977, Morgan's Passing, 1980, Dinner at the Homesick Restaurant, 1982, The Accidental Tourist, 1985, Breathing Lessons, 1988 (Pulitzer Prize for fiction 1989), Saint Maybe, 1991, (juvenile) Tumble Tower, 1993, Ladder of Years, 1995, A Patchwork Planet, 1998, Back When We Were Grownups, 2001; contbr. short stories to nat. mags. Home: 222 Tunbridge Rd Baltimore MD 21212-3422 E-mail: atmBaltimore@aol.com.

TYLER, CARL WALTER, JR. physician, health research administrator, retired; b. Washington, Aug. 22, 1933; s. Carl Walter and Elva Louise (Harlan) T.; m. Elma Hermione Matthias, June 23, 1956 (dec. Dec. 1991); children: Virginia Louise, Laureen, Jeffrey Alan, Cynthia T. Crenshaw. AB, Oberlin Coll., 1955; MD, Case-Western Res. U., 1959. Diplomate Am. Bd. Ob-Gyn. Rotating intern Univ. Hosps. of Cleve., 1959-60, resident in ob-gyn, 1960-64; med. officer USPHS, 1964; obstetrician-gynecologist USPHS Indian Health Service, Tahlequah, Okla., 1964-66; epidemic intelligence service officer Bur. Epidemiology, Ctrs. for Disease Control, Atlanta, 1966-67, dir. family planning evaluation div., 1967-80, asst. dir. for sci., 1980-82, acting dir. Ctr. for Health Promotion and Edn., 1982, dir. epidemiology program office, 1982-88, med. epidemiologist Office of Dir., 1988-90, asst. dir. for acad. programs, pub. health practice program office, 1990-97; clin. assoc. prof. ob.-gyn. Emory U. Sch. Medicine, Atlanta, 1997-98. Clin. asst. prof. ob-gyn Emory U. Sch. Medicine, Atlanta, 1966-80, clin. assoc. prof., 1980— , also clin. assoc. prof. preventive medicine and community health, adj. assoc. prof. sociology Coll. Arts and Scis., 1977-90; adj. assoc. prof. pub. health Sch. Pub. Health, 1990—; clin. prof. pub. health and community medicine Morehouse Sch. Medicine, Atlanta, 1990—; mem. Nat. Sleep Disorders Rsch. Commn., 1990—; mem. adv. com. on oral contraception WHO, Geneva, 1974-77, mem. adv. com. maternal and child health, 1982-88; lectr. in field Editor: (monograph) Venereal Infections; assoc. editor: Maxcy-Rosenau Textbook of Public Health and Preventive Medicine, 13th edit., 1992; contbr. articles to profl. jours. Chmn. Dekalb County Schs. com. on instruction programs, subcom. on health, phys. edn. and safety, (Ga.), 1967-68; active Ga. State Soccer Coaches Assn., Atlanta, 1973-79, DeKalb County YMCA Josiah Macy Found. fellow, 1956-58; NIH grantee, 1961-64; recipient Superior Service award, 1974, Meritorious Service medal USPHS, 1984, Disting. Service medal, 1988; Carl S. Shultz Population award APHA, 1976, medal of Excellence Ctrs. for Disease Control, 1984. Fellow Am. Coll. Ob-Gyn (chmn. community health com. 1974-77), Am. Coll. Preventive Medicine, Am. Coll. Epidemiol.; mem. Am. Epidemiologic Soc., Internat. Epidemiologic Assn., Assn. Tchrs, Preventive Medicine (bd. dirs. 1988-89), Am. Pub. Health Assn. (governing council 1976-78), Assn. Planned Parenthood Profls., Population Assn. Am., Sierra Club Avocations: photography; camping.

TYLER, CECILIA KAY, career officer; b. McCall, Idaho, May 18, 1956; d. Cecil Edward and Ruby Ilene (Wine) Oatney; m. Nelvin Eugene (Gene) Tyler Jr., Dec. 24, 1991. BBA in Acctg., Idaho State U., 1978; MS in Econs. and

Ops. Research, Colo. Sch. Mines, 1987; MS in Nat. Resourcing Strategy, Nat. Def. U., 2000; student, Command and Gen. Staff Coll., Leavenworth, Kans., 1989—90, Indsl. Coll. Armed Forces Nat. Def. U., Ft. McNair, Washington, 1999—2000. Commd. 2d lt. U.S. Army, 1978, advanced through grades to col., 2000, platoon leader A, B and C Cos. 8th Signal Battalion Fed. Republic of Germany, 1978-81, logistics officer Fed. Republic of Germany, 1981; promoted to capt., 1982; divsn. radio officer 2AD U.S. Army, Ft. Hood, Tex., 1982—83, comdr. C co. 142d Signal Battalion, 1983—85, chief market analysis 6th Recruiting Brigade Ft. Baker, Calif., 1987-89; promoted to maj., 1990; chief strategic systems plans br. 5th Signal Command U.S. Army, Fed. Republc of Germany, 1990-91, chief plans & programs div. Fed. Republc of Germany, 1991, exec. officer 509th Signal Battalion Italy, 1991-92, exec. officer office dep. chief staff, info. mgmt. Germany, 1992-94, promoted to lt. col., 1994; dep. brigade comdr. 2d Sig BDE, Germany, 1994—96; comdr. 504th Signal Battalion, Fort Huachuca, Ariz., 1996-98; chief current ops. divsn. Army Signal Command, Fort Huachua, 1998-99; dep. dir. Coalition Warfare, Internat. Cooper. Office of Under Sec. of Def. Acquisition, Tech. & Logistics, Pentagon/Washington, Va., 2000—; promoted to col., 2000. Pres. 4-H Club, Valley County, Idaho, 1973-74. Mem. Armed Forces Communication-Electronics Assn., Assn. U.S. Army. Avocations: skiing, sewing, reading, fishing. E-mail: (home) (office). Home: 8661 Pohick Forest Ct Springfield VA 22153 Office: OUSD (AT&L)/IC 3070 Defense Pentagon Rm 2E173A Washington DC 20301 E-mail: tylercg@worldnet.att.net., cecilia.tyler@osd.mil.

TYLER, DARLENE JASMER, retired dietitian; b. Watford City, N.D., Jan. 26, 1939; d. Edwin Arthur and Leola Irene (Walker) Jasmer; m. Richard G. Tyler, Aut. 26, 1977 (dec.); children: Ronald, Eric, Scott. BS, Oreg. State U., 1961. Registered dietitian. Clin. dietitian Salem (Oreg.) Hosp., 1965-73; sales supr. Sysco Northwest, Tigard, Oreg., 1975-77; clin. dietitian Physicians & Surgeons Hosp., Portland, 1977-79; food svc. dir. Meridian Park Hosp., Tualatin, 1979-2000; ret., 2000. Mem. Am. Soc. Hosp. Food Svc. Adminstrs., Am. Dietetic Assn., Oreg. Dietetic Assn., Portland Dietetic Assn. Episcopalian. Home: 4314 Botticelli Lake Oswego OR 97035 E-mail: darlenejtyler@aol.com.

TYLER, DAVID EARL, veterinary medical educator; b. Carlisle, Iowa, July 12, 1928; s. Guy Earl and Beatrice Virginia (Slack) T.; m. Alice LaVon Smith, Sept. 6, 1952; children: John William, Anne Elizabeth. BS, Iowa State U., 1953, D.V.M., 1957, PhD, 1963; MS, Purdue U., 1960. Instr. dept. vet. sci. Purdue U., 1957-60; asst. prof. dept. pathology Coll. Vet. Medicine, Iowa State U., 1960-63, asso. prof., 1963-66; prof., head dept. pathology and parasitology Coll. Vet. Medicine, U. Ga., 1966-71, head dept. pathology, 1971-79, prof., 1971-91, prof. emeritus, 1991—, ret., 1991. Co-founder internat. vet. pathology slide bank, 1984, co-dir., 1984-98; apptd. discussant Charles L. Davis Found. for Advancement Vet. Pathology, 1977-91. Cub Scout master, 1967-69, scout com. chmn., 1970-72; elder Disciples of Christ Ch., 1968—, chmn. ch. bd., 1973-74, 92-94; mem. citizens com. to County Bd. Edn., 1968-70; bd. dirs. Christian Coll., Ga., 1974-77. With AUS, 1946-48. Recipient Borden award Gail Borden Co., 1956, Norden Disting. Teaching award Norden Labs., 1964, 69, 81, 85, 91, Prof. of Yr. award Coll. Vet. Medicine, Iowa State U., 1965, Outstanding Prof. award Coll. Vet. Medicine, U. Ga., 1970, 76, 80-81, 83, 86, 87-88, 90, Joshia Meigs Teaching award, 1985, Stange award Coll. Vet. Med., Iowa State U., 1987, Phi Zeta Teaching award, 1985, N.Am. Outstanding Tchr. award, 1991, Omicron Delta Kappa Outstanding Prof. award U. Ga., 1981, Harold W. Casey award C.L. Davis Found., 1995. Mem. AVMA, Farm House, Am. Coll. Vet. Pathologists (mem. council 1975-77, exam. com. 1982-85), Am. Assn. Vet. Med. Colls. (chmn. com. teaching-learning materials 1975-77), Nat. Program for Instructional Devel. in Vet. Pathology (adv. com. 1976-77), Aghon, Sigma Xi, Phi Eta Sigma, Alpha Zeta, Gamma Sigma Delta, Phi Kappa Phi, Phi Zeta (chpt. sec.-treas. 1982-84), Omega Tau Sigma. Home: 160 Sunny Brook Dr Athens GA 30605-3348

TYLER, DONALD CHARLES, anesthesiologist; b. Phila., June 19, 1944; s. Charles Orlan and Pauline Trexler T.; m. Ingrid Elisabeth Johnson, Aug. 18, 1973; children: Scott, Andrew. AB, Brown U., 1966; MD, U. Pa., 1970; MBA, U. Wash., 1997. Diplomate Am. Bd. Anesthesiology, Am. Bd. Pediatrics. Intern, then resident in pediatrics Children's Hosp., Seattle, 1970-72; resident in anesthesiology U. Wash., 1974-77; anesthesiologist Children's Hosp., 1977-98. Editor: Pediatric Pain, 1990. Lt. cmdr. U.S. Navy, 1972-74. Avocations: sailing, boat building. Office: Children's Hosp Phila. 34th St & Civic Ctr Blvd Philadelphia PA 19104 E-mail: tyler@email.chop.edu.

TYLER, DONALD EARL, urologist; b. Ontario, Oreg., Oct. 3, 1926; s. Charles Maurice and Iva (Hess) T.; 1 child, Paul Donald. MD, U. Oreg., 1950; JD, U. Denver, 1967. Diplomate Am. Bd. Urology, Am. Coll. Legal Medicine. Fellow in gen. surgery, urology The Mayo Found., Rochester, Minn., 1952, 55-58; clin. instr. in urology U. Utah Med. Sch., Salt Lake City, 1959-64. Author: A New and Simple Theory of Gravity, 1970, Originations of Life from Volcanoes and Petroleum, 1983, Earliest Man of America in Oregon, USA: With Photographs of Paleolithic Artifacts, 1986, The Other Guy's Sperm: The Cause of Cancer and Other Diseases, 1994, Homo Americanus: an Original American Species, 1998, American Paleolithic: Boat Building Eight Million Years Ago, 1999. Lt. USNR, 1944-45, 52-54, WWII, Korea. Mem. Alpha Omega Alpha, Phi Eta Sigma. Avocations: archaeology, anthropology, geology, skiing, swimming. Home: 1092 SW 2d Ave Ontario OR 97914-2121

TYLER, ELIZABETH COWLEY, writer; b. Dec. 3, 1942; BA, Elmira Coll., 1964; MA, Middlebury Coll., 1989. Ofcl. ct. reporter trial ct. Dept. Superior Ct. Mass., 1979—; writer Cambridge, Mass., 1995—. Home: 9 Washington Ave # B Cambridge MA 02140-2836

TYLER, ERIC OWEN, pediatrician; b. Columbia, Tenn., Oct. 18, 1955; s. Harry Everett and Elizabeth (Lawrence) T.; m. Fran Till Tyler, July 29, 1978; children: Emily, Mallory, Mollie. BS, Harding U., 1977; MD, U. Tenn., 1981. Intern, resident U. Ala., Birmingham, 1984; pediatrician Pediat. Assocs. Alexander City, Ala., 1985—. Bd. dirs. ARC, Tallapoosa County, 1998—. Fellow: Am. Acad. Pediats., Am. Coll. Pediats.; mem.: Am. Coll. Physician Execs. Avocations: reading, gardening. Office: Pediat Assocs of Alex City PO Box 1269 1962 Cherokee Rd Alexander City AL 35010-3437

TYLER, GAIL MADELEINE, nurse; b. Dhahran, Saudi Arabia, Nov. 21, 1953; (parents Am. citizens); d. Louis Rogers and Nona Jean (Henderson) T.; m. Alan J. Moore, Sept. 29, 1990; 1 child, Sean James. AS, Front Range C.C., Westminster, Colo., 1979; BSN, U. Wyo., 1989. RN, Colo. Ward sec. Valley View Hosp., Thornton, Colo., 1975-79; nurse Scott and White Hosp., Temple, Tex., 1979-83, Meml. Hosp. Laramie County, Cheyenne, Who., 1983-89; dir. DePaul Home Health, 1989-91; field staff nurse Poudre Valley Hosp. Home Care/Poudre Care Connection, 1991-98, Rehab. and Vis. Nurses Assn., Fort Collins, Colo., 1999—. Mem., parish nurse Rocky Mountain Health Ministry. Avocations: collecting internat. dolls, sewing, reading, travel.

TYLER, H. RICHARD, physician, educator; b. Bklyn., Oct. 16, 1927; s. Max M. and Beatrice F. T.; m. Joyce Colby, June 17, 1951; children—Kenneth, Karen, Douglas, Lori. AB, Syracuse U., 1947; BS in Medicine, MD, Washington U., 1951; MA (hon.), Harvard U., 1989. Diplomate Am. Bd. Neurology and Psychiatry. Intern Peter Bent Brigham Hosp., Boston, 1951-52; resident in neurology Boston City Hosp., 1952-54; public health fellow Neurol. Inst., Queen's Sq., London, Salpêtriére, Paris, 1954-55; asst. in pediatrics and neurology Johns Hopkins Hosp., Balt., 1955-56; neurologist Peter Bent Brigham Hosp., Boston, 1956-74; asst. in neurology Harvard Med. Sch., 1956-59, assoc. in neurology, 1959-61, instr., 1961-64, asst. prof., 1964-68, assoc. prof., 1968-73, prof., 1974-98, prof. emeritus, 1999—. Sr. physician Brigham and Women's Hosp., Boston, 1974—, dir. neurol. svc., 1979-88. Co-editor: Current Neurology I and II, 1979, 80; mem. editorial bd.: Jour. Neurology, 1979-84, Classics on Neurology and Neurosurgery Libr., 1983—; contbr. articles in field to profl. jours. Trustee Brookline Pub. Libr., 1970-2001, chmn. bd. trustees, 1985-86, 90-91. Served with U.S. Army, 1946-47. Mem. Am. Neurol. Assn., Am. Acad. Neurology, Mass. Med. Soc. Office: 1 Brookline Pl Ste 503 Brookline MA 02445-7224 E-mail: HTyler1798@aol.com.

TYLER, JOHN EDWARD, III, lawyer; b. Kansas City, Mo. BA, U. Notre Dame, 1986, JD, 1989. From assoc. to ptnr. Lathrop & Gage L.C., Kansas City, 1989-99; sr. v.p., gen. counsel, sec. Ewing Marion Kauffman Found., 1999—. Adj. prof. Rockhurst U., Kansas City, 2000—. Contbr. articles to profl. jours. Pres. Genesis Sch., Kansas City, 1995-96, 96-97; pres. Archbishop O'Hara H.S., Kansas City, 1994-95, 95-96, 96-97, bd. dirs.; chair tax increment fin. commn. city of Raytown, Mo., 1997-99; bd. dirs. Ctr. for Mgmt. Assistance, Kansas City, pres., 1999-01. Named Man of Yr. Leukemia Soc., Kansas City, 1998, Bernie Hoffman award for cmty. svc. Cmty. Svc. Awards Found., 1997. Mem. ABA, Mo. Bar Assn. (Thomas D. Cochran award for cmty. svc. 1995), Kans. Bar Assn., Kansas City Metro. Bar Assn. (young lawyer of yr. 1998). Home: 2420 SW Wintercreek Ct Lees Summit MO 64081-4085 Office: Ewing Marion Kauffman Found 4801 Rockhill Rd Kansas City MO 64110-2046

TYLER, JOHN W. private secondary school educator, editor; b. Wilmington, Del., May 21, 1951; s. James Blaine and Virginia Elizabeth (Pepper) Tyler II. BA with honors, Trinity Coll., 1973; MA, Princeton U., 1975, PhD, 1980. Chmn. history dept. Groton (Mass.) Sch., 1978—; editor of pubs. Colonial Soc. of Mass., Boston, 1984—. Chmn. focus group Nat. U.S. History Standards Project, 1993; mem. selection com. James Madison Meml. Fellowships, Washington, 1992, 94; v.p., mem. founding bd. Orgn. of History Tchrs., 1987-93; adv. bd. Concord Review, Concord, Mass., 1987—. Author: Smugglers and Patriots, 1986, Connecticut Loyalists, 1977. Chmn. Hist. Dists. Commn., Groton, Mass., 1984-94; mem. Groton town bldg. com., 1990-93. Recipient Kidger award for disting. tchg., writing and svc. to the hist. profession New Eng. History Tchrs.' Assn., 1998. Mem. Am. Hist. Assn., Orgn. Am. Historians, Orgn. of History Tchrs., Club of Odd Volumes, Mass. Hist. Soc. (pubs. com. 1992—), Boston Athenaeum, Phi Beta Kappa. Episcopalian. Avocations: sailing, tennis, cross-country skiing. Office: Colonial Society of Mass 87 Mount Vernon St Boston MA 02108-1330

TYLER, KENNETH LAURENCE, neurologist, researcher; b. Boston, May 6, 1953; s. H. Richard and Joyce (Colby) T.; m. Lisa Johnson, Oct. 27, 1979; children: Maxwell Johnson, Eric Johnson. AB magna cum laude, Harvard U., 1974; MD, Johns Hopkin's U., 1978. Diplomate Am. Bd. Internal Medicine, Am. Bd. Psychiatry and Neurology. Resident in medicine Brigham S. Women's Hosp., Boston, 1978-80; resident in neurology Mass. Gen. Hosp., 1980-83; rsch. fellow Med. Sch. Harvard U., 1983-84, instr. Med. Sch., 1984-86, asst. prof. Med. Sch., 1986-91; assoc. prof. med. sch. U. Colo., Denver, 1991-95, prof. med. sch., 1995—, vice-chmn. neurology dept. med. sch., 1998-2000, Revler-Lewin Family prof. neurology, 2001—. Chief neurology svc. Denver VA Med. Ctr., 1994—. Mem. editorial bd. Microbial Pathogenesis, 1990—, Jour. Neurol. Scis., 1990-97, Jour. Virology, 1991-98, Jour. Hist. Neurosci., 1993-96, Archives of Neurology, 1997—, Jour. Neurovirology, 1995—; editor: Infections in the Central Nervous Systems; contbr. articles to profl. jours. Alfred P. Sloan Found. fellow, 1988-90. Fellow ACP, Am. Acad. Neurology (past pres. history sect. program com., S. Weir Mitchell award, Lawrence McHenry award 2000); mem. Am. Soc. Neurol. Investigation (past pres., sec., treas.), Am. Soc. Clin. Investigation, Am. Soc. Virology, Soc. for Exptl. Neuropathology (coun.), Am. Neurol. Assn., Soc. Neurosci. Home: 788 Milwaukee St Denver CO 80206-3902 Office: U Colo Hlth Sci Ctr 4200 E 9th Ave B-182 Neurology Denver CO 80262-0001 E-mail: ken.tyler@uchsc.edu.

TYLER, PEGGY LYNNE BAILEY, lawyer; b. Seattle, Oct. 15, 1948; d. John Thomas and Doris Mae (Lindgren) Bailey; m. Tom Kenneth Newton, May 25, 1975 (div. 1980); m. Allan Gregory Lambert, Aug. 3, 1980 (div. May 1996); m. Charles Kevin Tyler, Sept. 12, 1997; children: Eli Raven, Joshua Alec. BA in Psychology, Beloit Coll., 1970; MS in Counseling Psychology, Ill. Inst. Tech., 1973; JD, Syracuse (N.Y.) U., 1978. Bar: D.C. 1983. Mental health specialist Ill. Dept. Mental Health, Chgo., 1971-72; mem. rsch. faculty Cornell U., Ithaca, N.Y., 1973-75; assoc. O'Connor, Sovocool, Pfann and Greenburg, 1978, Dacy, Richin & Meyers, Silver Springs, Md., 1979-81; ins. adminstr. Nat. Assn. Broadcasters, Washington, 1981-86, dir. ins. programs, 1986-90; assoc. Architect of the Capitol, 1990—. Co-author, editor: Broadcaster's Property and Liability Insurance Buying Guide, 1989. Bd. dirs. Hartford-Thayer Condominium Assn., 1994—, pres., 1995-96, sec., 1996-2000, treas., 2000—. Mem. D.C. Bar Assn. (mem. steering com. of arts entertainment, sports law sect. 1989-90, sect. editor newsletter 1989-90). Independent. Jewish. Avocations: antiques, gourmet cooking, ballet. Office: Architect of the Capitol Office of Employment Counsel Rm H2-202 Ford House Office Bldg Washington DC 20515-0001 E-mail: ptyler@aoc.gov.

TYLER, PRISCILLA, retired English language and education educator; b. Cleve., Oct. 23, 1908; d. Ralph Sargent and Alice Lorraine (Campbell) T. BA in Latin and Greek, Radcliffe Coll., 1932; MA in Edn., Case Western Res. U., 1934, PhD in English, 1953; LLD (hon.), Carleton U., Ottawa, Ont., Can., 1993. Parole officer, case worker Cleve. Sch. for Girls, 1934-35; tchr. English, Latin and French Cleveland Heights (Ohio) Pub. Schs., 1935-45; instr. to asst. prof. English Flora Stone Mather Coll., Cleve., 1945-59; asst. dean Flora Stone Mather Coll. Western Reserve U., 1957-59; asst. prof. edn., head dept. English Sch. of Edn. Harvard U., Cambridge, Mass., 1959-63; assoc. prof. English, U. Ill., Champaign-Urbana, 1963-67, dir. freshman rhetoric, 1966-67; prof. English and edn. U. Mo., Kansas City, 1967-78, prof. emeritus, 1978—. Instr. N.S. (Can.) Dept. Edn., Halifax, summers 1972-73; condr. numerous seminars; former lectr. U. Calif., Berkeley, U. Chgo., Purdue U., U. Mo., Columbia, U. Nebr., Emory U., Fresno State U., Calif. State U., Hayward, San Jose State Coll., Mills Coll., Ala., Tift Coll., Ga., Va. Poly. Inst. and Midwestern U., Tex. Editor: Harpers Modern Classics, 19 vols., 1963, Writers the Other Side of the Horizon, 1964; co-author, co-editor: (with Maree Brooks) Inupiat Paitot, 1974, Sevukakmet, Ways of Life on St. Lawrence Island (Helen Slwooko Carius), 1979, The Epic of Qayaq (Lela Kiana Oman), 1995, World Literature Written in English, 1965-69; interviewed authors, Jan Carew, Wilson Harris, Guyana, George Lamming, Barbados, Christopher Okigbo and Chinua Achebe, Nigeria, Derek Wolcott, St. Lucia, Andrew Salkey, Jamaica; also articles. Mem. Ohio Gov.'s Com. on Employment of Physically Handicapped, 1957; mem. Friends of Art of Carleton U., Nelson Atkins Mus. Art, Kansas City, Ottawa (Kans.) Art Gallery, Friends of Libr., Ottawa, Kansas. Recipient Outstanding Achievement and Contbns. in Field of Edn. award Western Res. U., 1962, Disting. Alumna award Laurel Sch., Cleve., 1994; Priscilla Tyler Endowment Fund named in her honor Case Western Res. U., 1980. Mem. MLA, NEA, Archaeol. Inst. Am., Nat. Coun. Tchrs. English (v.p. 1963, mem. com. on history of the profession 1965-68, Commn. on Composition 1968-71, trustee Rsch. Found. 1970-78, Disting. Svc. award 1978), Conf. on Coll. Composition and Comm. (pres. 1963), Arctic Inst. N.Am., Inuit Art Found., Franklin County (Kansas) Hist. Assn., Calif. Assn. Tchrs. English (hon., Curriculum Commn. Ctrl. Calif.), Delta Kappa Gamma (pres. Upsilon chpt. 1950-52). Democrat. Presbyterian. Avocations: collecting rare books of American and English grammar, Inuit art, history and culture, travel. Home: 4213 Kentucky Ter Ottawa KS 66067-8715

TYLER, RICHARD FREDERIC, hospital management consultant, educator; b. Cin., Apr. 18, 1940; s. Richard Smith and Torre Decarol (Atkinson) T.; m. Jacqueline Anne Steinke, Aug. 10, 1974; children: Torri Anne, Jacqueline Atkinson. BA, U. Cin., 1963; MBA, Am. U., 1970, PhD, 1987. Diplomate Am. Coll. Healthcare Execs. Adminstrv. resident Good Samaritan Hosp., Cin., 1964-65; adminstrv. asst. Balt. City Hosp., 1965-69; asst. hosp. adminstr. Georgetown Univ. Hosp., Washington, 1970-74; CEO R.F.T. Assocs., P.A., Annapolis, Md., 1974—; prof. bus. and hosp. adminstrn. Anne Arundel Coll., Arnold, 1974—. Adj. assoc. prof. Georgetown Univ. Sch. Medicine, Washington, 1974—; editor, mem. editl. rev. bd. Allyn & Bacon Pubs., Boston, 1980—, Roxbury Press, Pasadena, Calif., 1984—. Grad. fellow Cornell Univ., Ithaca, N.Y., 1963-64. Mem. Am. Hosp. Assn., Assn. Tchrs. Preventive Medicine, Assn. Computing Machinery, Acad. Mgmt., Hist. Annapolis Inc., Annapolis Yacht Club, Leland (Mich.) Yacht Club (fleet capt. 1961-62), Leland (Mich.) Country Club, N.Am. Yacht Racing Assn. Republican. Episcopalian. Avocations: off shore sailing/racing, tennis. Home: 114 Duke Of Gloucester St Annapolis MD 21401-2516 Office: RFT Assocs PA 101 College Pkwy Arnold MD 21012-1857

TYLER, RICHARD JAMES, personal and professional development educator; b. Warwick, R.I., June 16, 1957; s. Virginia (Campanella) Tyler. Gen. mgr. Gem Exch., Charlotte, N.C., 1977; nat. sales mgr. So. Merchandising, 1978; pres. Direct Import Distributing, New Orleans, 1981; nat. territorty dir. TV Fanfare Pub., 1982; v.p. ARC Pub., New Orleans, 1983; exec. v.p., gen. mgr. Superior Bedrooms, Inc., 1984; CEO Richard Tyler Internat., Inc., Houston, Internat. Bus. Inst., Inc., Houston, Tyler Internat. Rsch. Inst., Inc., Houston, Shopportunities, Houston, Richard Tyler Investments Ltd., 2000. Mem. adv. bd. Sales and Mktg. Mag., N.Y.C., 1991—; founder Leadership of Tomorrow program; profl. speaker, cons. in field. Author: Creating Excellence in Quality and Service, 1991, The Science and Art of Excellent Selling, 1993, Richard Tyler's Guide to Entrepreneurial Excellence, 1993, Richard Tyler's Smart Business Strategies: The Guide to Small Business Marketing Excellence, 1996, The Power of Professional Selling Program, 2002; pub. newsletter Richard Tyler's Excellence Edge, 1992, Entrepreneur Cover Story, 1999; contbr. articles to profl. publs. Mem. Rep.-Senatorial Inner Cir., Washington, 1991; mem. presdl. victory team Rep. Nat. Com., 2002, Tex. rep. pres. club, 2002; bd. dirs. Be An Angel Fund Charity, 2002. Mem. ASTD, Soc. Human Resource Mgmt., Nat. Speakers Assn., Internat. Platform Assn., Internat. Assn. Entrepreneurs. Avocations: sports, theater, deep sea fishing, amateur wrestling. E-mail: richardtyler@richardtyler.com.

TYLER, RONNIE CURTIS, historian; b. Temple, Tex., Dec. 29, 1941; s. Jasper J. and Melba Curtis (James) T.; m. Paula Eyrich, Aug. 24, 1974. BSE, Abilene (Tex.) Christian Coll., 1964; MA, Tex. Christian U., 1966, PhD (Univ. fellow), 1968; DHL, Austin Coll., 1986. Instr. history Austin Coll., Sherman, Tex., 1967-68, asst. prof., 1968-69; asst. dir. collections and programs Amon Carter Mus., Ft. Worth, 1969-86; dir. Tex. State Hist. Assn., 1986—; prof. history U. Tex., Austin, 1986—. Adj. prof. history Tex. Christian U., 1971-72; cons. visual materials Western. Am. art. Author: Santiago Vidaurri and the Confederacy, 1973, The Big Bend: The Last Texas Frontier, 1975, The Image of America in Caricature and Cartoon, 1975, The Cowboy, 1975, The Mexican War: A Lithographic Record, 1974, The Rodeo Photographs of John Addison Stryker, 1978, Visions of America: Pioneer Artists in a New Land, 1983, Views of Texas: The Watercolors of Sarah Ann Hardinge, 1852-56, 1988, Nature's Classics: John James Audubon's Birds and Animals, 1992, Audubon's Great National Work: The Royal Octavo Edition of the Birds of America, 1993, Prints of the West, 1994, Alfred Jacob Miller: Artist as Explorer, 1999; (with Paula Eyrich Tyler) Texas Museums: A Guidebook, 1983; editor: (with Lawrence R. Murphy) The Slave Narratives of Texas, 1974, Posada's Mexico, 1979, Alfred Jacob Miller: Artist on the Oregon, 1982, Wanderings in the Southwest in 1855 (J.D.B. Stillman), 1990, Prints and Printmakers of Texas, 1997. Pres. Tarrant County (Tex.) Hist. Soc., 1975-77. Good Neighbor Commn. scholar Instituto Tecnologico Monterrey, Mex., 1967; Am. Philos. Soc. grantee, 1970-71; recipient H. Bailey Carroll award, 1974; Coral H. Tullis award, 1976 Mem. Am. Antiquarian Soc., Tex. Inst. Letters (Friends of Dallas Pub. Libr. award), Philos. Soc. Tex. (sec. 1990—), Phi Beta Kappa. Home: 4400 Balcones Dr Austin TX 78731-5710 Office: Ctr Studies Tex Hist 2/306 Richardson Hall University Tex Austin TX 78712 E-mail: rtyler@mail.utexas.edu.

TYLER, THOMAS EDWARD, principal; b. Shreveport, La., Feb. 27, 1958; s. Edward Artie Tyler, Virginia Pearl Tyler; m. Kimberly Jeanne Ellis; children: Zachary. AS, Chattanooga State Tech. C.C., 1985; BA, U. Tenn., 1987, BS, 1989, MEd, 1995; EdS, Mid. Tenn. U., 1998. Cert. tchr. Ga., 1999. Tchr. Ringgold High Sch., Ringgold, Ga., 1989—95, asst. prin., 1995—99, Boynton Elem. Sch., 1999—. Fellow Econ. Teaching fellow, U. Tenn. Ctr. Econ. Edn., Chattanooga, 1993. Mem.: Nat. Assn. Educators, Phi Kappa Phi, Kappa Delta Phi. Home: 508 Sharondale Rd Chattanooga TN 37412 Office: Boynton Elem Sch 3938 Boynton Dr Ringgold GA 30736 Office Fax: 706-861-6641. Personal E-mail: ttyler@catoosa.k12.ga.us. Business E-Mail: ttyler@catoosa.k12.ga.us.

TYLER, W(ILLIAM) ED, finance company executive; b. Cleve., Nov. 3, 1952; s. Ralph Tyler and Edith (Green) Kauer; m. Vickie Sue Boggs, Feb. 7, 1976; children: Stacia Leigh, Adam William. BS in Elec. Engring., Ind. Inst. Tech., 1974; MBA, Ind. U., 1977; postgrad., Harvard U., 1981; postgrad. in bus., Baruch U., 1988. From electronic engr. to exec. v.p. R.R. Donnelley & Sons Co., Warsaw, 1974—95, exec. v.p. & chief tech. officer, 1995—2001; CEO, pres. Moore Corp. Ltd., 2001—, Willoughby Capitol, Lake Forest, Ill., 2001—. E-mail: edtyler1@aol.com.

TYLER, WILLIAM HOWARD, JR. advertising executive, educator; b. Elizabethton, Tenn., May 21, 1932; s. William Howard and Ethel Margaret (Schueler) T.; m. Margery Moss, Aug. 31, 1957; children: William James, Daniel Moss. Student, Iowa State U., 1950-52, U. Iowa, 1952; AB in Lit., BJ in Advt., U. Mo., 1958, MA in Journalism, 1966. Advt. mgr. Rolla (Mo.) Daily News, 1958-59; instr. sch. journalism U. Mo., Columbia, 1959-61; copy writer, then v.p. copy dir. D'Arcy Advt. Agy., St. Louis, 1961-67; writer, producer, creative supr. Gardner Advt. Co., 1967-69; sr. v.p., creative dir. D'Arcy, McManus, Masius, 1969-77; exec. v.p., creative dir. Larson Bateman Advt. Agy., Santa Barbara, Calif., 1977-80; v.p. advt. Pizza Hut, Inc., Wichita, Kans., 1980-82; v.p., creative dir. Frye-Sills/Y&R, Denver, 1980; exec. v.p., creative dir. Gardner Advt. Co., St. Louis, 1982-88; exec. v.p., ptnr., creative dir. Parker Group, 1988-91; pres. Tylertoo Prodns., 1991—. Assoc. prof. St. Louis U., 1993—. Mng. editor St. Louis Advt. Mag., 1992-95. Trustee Blackburn Coll., Carlinville, Ill., 1983—84; bd. advisors U. Mo. Journalism Sch., 1986—91. Named AAF 9th Dist. Educator of Yr., 1998. Mem. U. Mo. Alumni Assn. (bd. dirs. 1969-70), Advt. Club Greater St. Louis, Golden Key (hon.), Mensa, Kappa Tau Alpha (hon.). Episcopalian. Office: Saint Louis U Dept Comm 3733 W Pine Blvd Saint Louis MO 63108-3305 E-mail: tylerwh@slu.edu.

TYLEVICH, ALEXANDER V. sculptor, architect, educator; b. Minsk, Belarus, Sept. 12, 1947; came to U.S., 1989; s. Wulf Tylevich and Asia Klebanova; m. Poline M. Dvorkin, Jan. 22, 1981; children: Alexei, Katherine. BA in Arch., Minsk Archtl. Inst., 1965; MA in Arch., Byelorussian Poly. Inst., Minsk, 1971. Prin., sr. arch. Minskprojekt, 1971-84; artist, arch. Fine Arts Found., Minsk, 1984-89; sculptor-arch. Tylevich Arts, St. Paul, 1989—. Prin. works include Vincentian Letter sculpture, DePaul U., Chgo., Blue Springs-.Net, Blue Springs, Mo., Letters of Creation, Wayzata, Minn., Montessori's Vision: Through the Eyes of a Child, Lake Country Sch., Mpls., Tree of Life, U. Minn., Mpls., Sculpture Anoka Ramsey C.C., Coon Rapids, Minn. (suspended recognition), Resurrection, Ch. of St. Stephen, Anoka, Minn., Madonna and Child, The Ch. of St. Mary, Alexandria, Minn., Gateway to Belief/Point of Belief, St. Mary's U., Winona, Minn., Thomas Becket, The Cath. Cmty. of Thomas Becket, Eagan, Minn., Tribute to Erich Mendelsohn, FORECAST Pub. Artwork, St. Paul, Zenon Possis, North Meml. Hosp., Mpls., Winona Tech. Coll. Aviation Facility (Minn. Percent for Art in Pub. Pls. program), North Shore Synagogue, Syosset, N.Y., Mt. Zion Temple, St. Paul, St. Paul Sem., St. Joseph Abbey, St. Benedict, La., Mepkin Abbey, S.C., master plan for Ctr. of Minsk, Minsk City Govt. Bldg., Subway Sta., Minsk, pvt. collections, exhibited in group shows at Monumental Art of Byelorussia, Minsk, 1989, Sacred Image, Sacred Text, Nat. Jewish Mus., Washington, 1993, Harvard U. Grad. Sch. Design New Eng., 1993, St. John's U., Collegeville, Minn. Grantee Minn. Met. Regional Arts Coun., 1991, Howard B. Brin Arts Endowment, 1991, FORECAST Pub. Artworks, 1993. Fellow Archtl. Assn. USSR. Home: 1937 Highland Pkwy Saint Paul MN 55116-1350 E-mail: tyleart@aol.com.

TYLLIA, FRANK MICHAEL, university official, educator; b. Rossland, B.C., Can., Dec. 1, 1942; came to U.S., 1942; s. Alex J. and Lenora M. (Janni) T.; m. Kathryn A. McWalter, Mar. 21, 1970. BBA, Gonzaga U., 1965, BA in Edn., 1967; MA in Edn., Seattle U., 1972. Tchr. pub. schs., Seattle, 1967-72, prin., 1972-78, Edmonds Sch. Dist., Lynnwood, Wash., 1978-97; field supr. M Tchg. City U., Bellevue, 1997—. Adj. prof. Seattle Pacific U., 1990—. Active alumni mentoring program Gonzaga U., Seattle, 1993—; mem. Kirkland Cmty. Accountability Bd.; active King County Juvenile Justice, 1997—; mem. King County Diversion Adv. Bd., 1998—. Mem. ASCD, Assn. Wash. Sch. Prins. (various coms.), Washington Athletic Club, Phi Delta Kappa. Home and Office: 4527 103d Ln NE Kirkland WA 98033-7639

TYNAN, GEORGE, engineer, educator; BS in Aerospace Engring., Calif. Polytech., Pomona, 1983; MS in Engring., UCLA, 1987, PhD in Engring., 1991. Rsch. engr. UCLA, 1991—99; asst. prof. U Calif. San Diego, San Diego, 1999—2001, assoc. prof., 2001—. Office: Univ Calif San Diego 9500 Gilman Dr La Jolla CA 92093-5004

TYNDALL, DAVID GORDON, business educator; b. Bangalore, India, Nov. 19, 1919; s. Joseph and Annie E. (Parsons) T.; m. Margaret Patricia Davies, Apr. 4, 1942; children: Caroline Lee, David Gordon, Benjamin. BComm, U.

Toronto, 1940, MA, 1941; PhD, U. Calif., 1948. Asst. prof. bus. adminstrn. Cornell U., Ithaca, N.Y., 1947-49; assoc. prof. Carnegie-Mellon U., Pitts., 1949-53; assoc. prof., dir. analytical studies U. Calif., Berkeley, 1955-67, lectr., 1979-82. V.p. fin. and adminstrn., investment officer U. Alta., Edmonton, 1967-74; prof. fin., 1974-79; investment adv. Berkeley, 1979-96. Served with Royal Can. Air Force, 1942-45. Fulbright fellow, 1952 Unitarian-Buddhist. Home: 88 Clarewood Ln Oakland CA 94618-2243 E-mail: gtyndall@pacbell.net.

TYNDALL, JAY MARK, lawyer; b. Indpls., Feb. 29, 1964; s. William Mark and Jewetta Corine (Main) T.; m. Yuko Shigetomi, Feb. 14, 1991; children: Saige Mark, Hanna. BA, Earlham Coll., 1986; JD, U. Dayton, 1991. Bar: Wash. 1992, D.C. 2002. Fgn. law advisor Kitahama Law Office, Osaka, 1994-96; fgn. assoc. Adachi, Henderson, Miyatake & Fujita, Tokyo, 1996-98; contract atty. Puget Sound Area, 1999—. Presenter profl. seminars. Mem.: ABA, D.C. Bar Assn., Wash. State Bar Assn. (mem. rules on profl. conduct com. 2000—02). Office: 10020 Main St Ste A/288 Bellevue WA 98004

TYNDALL, RICHARD LAWRENCE, microbiologist, researcher; b. Mt. Joy, Pa., Mar. 29, 1933; s. William Leroy and Reba May (Ream) T.; m. Thelma Mae Sherk, June 19, 1955; children: Sharon Tyndall Headley, Michael L., Sandra Tyndall Holland. BS in Microbiology, Pa. State U., 1955, MS in Microbiology, 1959, PhD in Microbiology, 1961. Rsch. staff biology div. Oak Ridge (Tenn.) Nat. Lab., 1961-73; rsch. staff med. div. Oak Ridge Assoc. Univs., 1973-76; assoc. prof. rsch. zoology dept. U. Tenn., Knoxville, 1976-87; adj. rsch. assoc. Biology and Environ. Scis. div. Oak Ridge Nat. Lab., 1976-87; rsch. staff mem. Health and Safety Rsch. div. Oak Ridge Nat. Lab., 1988—; founder, CEO Microbial Monitoring, Clinton, Tenn., 1985—; co-founder Reprotech Inc., Knoxville, 1981. Cons. in field. Contbr. numerous articles to profl. jours.; patentee in field. Mem. com. for control of Legionella, State of Wis. With U.S. Army, 1955-57. AEC postdoctoral fellow. Fellow Am. Acad. Microbiology; mem. AAAS, ASHRAE (subcom. on Legionella), Am. Soc. Microbiology, Phi Sigma, Gamma Sigma Delta (awards). Methodist. Avocations: travel, humor, jazz, the Arts. Home: 209 Woodland View Rd Clinton TN 37716-5923

TYNER, HOWARD A. publishing executive, newspaper editor, journalist; b. Milw., May 30, 1943; s. Howard Arthur and Katharine Elizabeth Tyner; m. Elizabeth Jane Adams, May 3, 1969; children: Sophie Elizabeth, Ian Adams. BA, Carleton Coll., 1965; MSJ, Northwestern U., 1967. Sports editor Chippewa Herald-Telegram, Chippewa Falls, Wis., 1965-66; fgn. corr. UPI, Europe, 1967-77; with Chgo. Tribune, 1977—, fgn. corr., 1982-85, fgn. editor Chgo., 1985-88, asst. mng. editor, 1988-90, dep. mng. editor, 1990-92, assoc. editor, 1992-93, v.p., editor, 1993—. Mem. adv. bd. Alfred Friendly Press Fellowships, Washington, 1988—; mem. exec. bd. World Press Inst., 1994—. Mem. Am. Soc. of Newspaper Editors (mem. found. bd. 1994—), Am. Press Inst. (bd. dirs. 1997—), Found. for Am. Comms. (adv. bd. 1997—). Home: 2700 Park Pl Evanston IL 60201-1337 Office: Chgo Tribune Co 435 N Michigan Ave Chicago IL 60611-4066*

TYNER, LEE REICHELDERFER, lawyer; b. Annapolis, Md., Mar. 12, 1946; d. Thomas Elmer and Eleanor Frances (Leland) Reichelderfer; m. Carl Frederick Tyner, Aug. 31, 1968; children: Michael Frederick, Rachel Christine, Elizabeth Frances. BA, St. John's Coll., 1968; MS, U. Wash., 1970; JD, George Washington U., 1975. Bar: Wash., D.C., U.S. Dist. Ct. (D.C.), U.S. Ct. Appeals (4th cir., 1st cir., 9th cir., D.C. cir., 5th cir., 8th cir., 11th cir., 10th cir.), U.S. Ct. Claims, U.S. Supreme Ct. Profl. staff U.S. Senate Commerce Com., Washington, 1970-72; trial atty. Land and Natural Resources div. U.S. Dept. Justice, 1975-85; atty. Office of Gen. Counsel U.S. EPA, 1985—. Bd. dirs. Grace Episcopal Day Sch., Silver Spring, Md., 1987-89, vestry Grace Episcopal Ch., 1997—; den leader, cubmaster Boy Scouts Am., Silver Spring, 1987-91. Recipient Bronze medals, U.S. EPA, 1988, 92. Mem. Order of the Coif. Episcopalian. Home: 1416 Geranium St NW Washington DC 20012-1518 Office: US EPA 2366A 1200 Pennsylvania Ave NW Washington DC 20460 E-mail: skildpadde@aol.com., tyner.lee@epa.gov.

TYNER, NEAL EDWARD, retired insurance company executive; b. Grand Island, Nebr., Jan. 30, 1930; s. Edward Raymond and Lydia Dorothea (Kruse) T.; children: Karen Tyner Redrow, Morgan. BBA, U. Nebr., 1956. Jr. analyst Bankers Life Nebr., Lincoln, 1956-62, asst. v.p. securities, 1962-67, v.p. securities, treas., 1967-69, fin. v.p., treas., 1970-72, sr. v.p. fin., treas., 1972-83, pres., chief exec. officer, 1983-87, chmn., pres., chief exec. officer, 1987-88, chmn., CEO, 1988-95; pres. Net Cons., Paradise Valley, Ariz., 1995—. Bd. dir. Union Bank & Trust Co. Trustee U. Nebr. Found., Lincoln Found.; bd. govs. Nebr. Wesleyan U. Capt. USMC, 1950-54, Korea. Fellow: CFAs; mem.: Omaha/Lincoln Soc. Fin. Analysts, Mountain Shadows Golf Club. Lutheran. Avocations: tennis, computers. Office: 8225 N Golf Dr Scottsdale AZ 85253-2716

TYNER, WALLACE EDWARD, economics educator; b. Orange, Tex., Mar. 21, 1945; s. Richard D. and Jeanne (Gullahorn) T.; m. Jean M. Young, May 2, 1970; children: Davis, Jeffrey. BS in Chemistry, Tex. Christian U., 1966; MA in Econs., U. Md., 1972, PhD in Econs., 1977. Vol. Peace Corps., India, 1966-68, math, sci., ednl. skill desk chief, 1968-70; grad. teacher asst. U. Md., Balt., 1971-73; assoc. scientist Earth Satellite Corp., Washington, 1973-74; rsch. assoc. Cornell U., Ithaca, N.Y., 1974-77; asst. prof., assoc. prof. natural resource econs. and policy Purdue U., West Lafayette, Ind., 1977-84, prof., asst. dept. head, 1983-88, dept. head, 1989—. Cons. UN Food and Agrl. Orgn., Rome, Office Tech. Assessment, Washington, U.S. Dept. Interior, Washington, OECD, Paris, World Bank, Washington, USDA, Washington. Author: Energy Resources and Economic Development in India, 1978, A Perspective on U.S. Farm Problems and Agricultural Policy, 1987. Mem. Am. Assn. Agrl. Economists, Am. Econs. Assn., Internat. Assn. Agrl. Economist, Sigma Xi, Gamma Sigma Delta. Home: 116 Arrowhead Dr West Lafayette IN 47906-2105 Office: Purdue U Krannert Bldg West Lafayette IN 47907-1145 E-mail: wtyner@purdue.edu.

TYNG, ANNE GRISWOLD, architect; b. Kuling, Kiangsi, China, July 14, 1920; d. Walworth and Ethel Atkinson (Arens) T. (parents Am. citizens); 1 child, Alexandra Stevens. AB, Radcliffe Coll., 1942; M of Architecture, Harvard U., 1944; PhD, U. Pa., 1975. Assoc. Stonorov & Kahn, Architects, 1945-47; assoc. Louis I. Kahn Architect, 1947-73; pvt. practice architecture Phila., 1973—; adj. assoc. prof. architecture U. Pa. Grad. Sch. Fine Arts, 1968-96. Assoc. cons. architect Phila. Planning Commn. and Phila. Redevel. Plan, 1954; vis. disting. prof. Pratt Inst., 1979-81, vis. critic architecture, 1969; vis. critic architecture Rensselaer Poly. Inst., 1969, 78, Carnegie Mellon U., 1970, Drexel U., 1972-73, Cooper Union, 1974-75, U. Tex., Austin, 1976; lectr. Archtl. Assn., London, Xian U., China, Bath U., Eng., Mexico City, Hong Kong U., 1989, Baltic Summer Sch., Architecture and Planning, Tallinn, Estonia, Parnu, Estonia, 1993, Alicante U., Spain, 1997, Barcelona U., Spain, 1997; panel spkr. Nat. Conv. Am. Inst. Architects, N.Y.C., 1988, also numerous univs., throughout U.S. and Can.; asst. leader People to People Archtl. del. to China, 1983; vis. artist Am. Acad., Rome, 1995. Subject of films Anne G. Tyng at Parsons Sch. of Design, 1972, Anne G. Tyng at U. of Minn., 1974, Connecting, 1976, Forming the Future, 1977; work included in Smithsonian Travelling Exhbn., 1979-81, 82, Louis I. Kahn: In the Realm of Architecture, 1990-94, Mus. Contemporary Art Travelling Exhbn., L.A., 1998—; author, editor: Louis Kahn to Anne Tyng, The Rome Letters 1953-1954, 1997; contbr. articles to profl. publs.; prin. works include Walworth Tyng Farmhouse (Hon. mention award Phila. chpt. AIA 1953); builder (with G. Yanchenko) Probability Pyramid, 1984. Fellow Graham Found. for Advanced Study in Fine Arts, 1965, 79-81. Fellow AIA (Brunner grantee N.Y. chpt. 1964, 83, dir., mem. exec. bd. dirs. Phila. chpt. 1976-78, John Harbeson Disting. Svc. award Phila. chpt. 1991); mem. Nat. Acad. Design (nat. academician), C.G. Jung Ctr. Phila. (planning com. 1979-97), Form Forum (co-founder, planning com. 1978-85). Democrat. Episcopalian. Home and Office: 2511 Waverly St Philadelphia PA 19146-1049 E-mail: agtyng@aol.com.

TYREE, ALAN DEAN, clergyman; b. Kansas City, Mo., Dec. 14, 1929; s. Clarence Tillman and Avis Ora (Gross) T.; m. Gladys Louise Omohundro, Nov. 23, 1951; children: Lawrence Wayne, Jonathan Tama, Sharon Avis. BA, U. Iowa, 1950; postgrad., U. Mo.-Columbia, 1956-58, U. Mo.-Kansas City, 1961-62. Ordained to ministry Cmty. of Christ, 1947. Appointee min., Lawrence, Kans., 1950-52; mission adminstr. (Mission Sanito), French Polynesia, 1953-64; regional adminstr. Denver, 1964-66; mem. Council Twelve Apostles, Independence, Mo., 1966-82, sec., 1980-82, mem. First Presidency, 1982-92; ret. First Presidency, 1992; pastor East 39th Street Congregation Cmty. of Christ, Independence, 2000—02. Mem. Joint Coun. and Bd. Appropriations, 1966-92; originator music appreciation broadcasts Radio Tahiti, 1962-64, Mission Sanito Radio Ministry, 1960-64; instr. Music/Arts Inst., 1992—, Met. C.C.'s, 1994—. Editor: Cantiques des Saints French-Tahitian hymnal, 1965, Exploring the Faith: A Study of Basic Christian Beliefs, 1987; mem. editing com.: Hymns of the Saints, 1981; author: The Gospel Graced by a People: A Biography of Persons in Tahiti, 1993, Evan Fry: Proclaimer of Good News, 1995, Priesthood: For Other's Sake, 1996, God: Getting to Know the Unknown, 1998. Bd. dirs. Outreach Internat. Found., 1979-82, mem. corp. body, 1982-92; mem. corp. body Independence Regional Health Ctr., 1982-92, v.p., 1983-92, bd. dirs., 1984-93; mem. bd. publs. Herald House, 1984-92; mem. corp. body Restoration Trail Found., 1982-92; chmn. Temple Art Com., 1988-94; bd. dirs. Independence Symphony Orch., 1992-96, pres., 1995-96; mem. human rels. commn. city of Independence, 1995-97, chmn., 1996-97. Recipient Elbert A. Smith Meml. award for publ. articles, 1968, 72 Mem. Phi Beta Kappa, Phi Eta Sigma. Home and Office: 3408 S Trail Ridge Dr Independence MO 64055 E-mail: tyree@mail.com.

TYREE, DONALD ANDREW, financial educator; b. St. Louis, Nov. 19, 1930; s. Wesley F. and Dena (Krieter) T.; m. Sherry Johnson, Nov. 18, 1978; 1 son, Paul H. (dec.); children by previous marriage: Wesley G., Thomas A. BS, BA, Washington U., St. Louis, 1953, MBA, 1956; PhD in Finance, U. Tex. at Austin, 1959. Research asso. Washington U., 1953; lectr. U. Tex., 1956-59; mem. faculty St. Louis U., 1959—2000, prof. finance, 1969—2000, chmn. dept., 1968—80, 1983—95, assoc. dean Sch. Bus. Adminstrn., 1973-74. Cons. in field. Mem. St. Louis County Ins. Com., 1962-68 Author: Small Loan Industry in Texas, 1960, School Insurance Administration, 1975, Urban Residential Mortgage Financing: Lending Practices in St. Louis, 1979. Served with AUS, 1953-55. Wienhiemer fellow, 1955-56; Tex. Savs. and Loan Assn. fellow, 1956-59 Home: 14 Huntleigh Woods Saint Louis MO 63131-4818

TYREE, LEWIS, JR. retired compressed gas company executive, inventor, technical consultant; b. Lexington, Va., July 25, 1922; s. Lewis Sr. and Winifred (West) T.; m. Dorothy A. Hinchcliff, Aug. 21, 1948; children: Elizabeth Hinchcliff, Lewis III, Dorothy Scott. Student, Washington & Lee U., 1939-40; BS, MIT, 1947. Cryogenic engr. Joy Mfg. Co., Michigan City, Ind., 1947-49; v.p. Hinchcliff Motor Service, Chgo., 1949-53; cons. engr. Cryogenic Products, 1953-76, Liquid Carbonic Corp., Chgo., 1960-76; exec. v.p. Liquid Carbonic Industries, 1976-87. Bd. dirs. Liquid Carbonic Industries, Chgo., Worldwide Cryogenics (MVE), New Prague, Minn. Patentee in cryogenics. Served to 1st lt. U.S. Army, 1943-46, PTO. Mem. Soc. Cin., ASME, Am. Soc. Heating, Refrigeration, and Air Conditioning Engring., Hinsdale Golf Club, Lexington Golf and Country Club. Republican. Episcopalian. Home: Mulberry Hill 115 Liberty Hall Rd Lexington VA 24450-1703

TYREE, TRACEY JORDAN, elementary school educator; b. East Point, Ga., June 4, 1970; d. Roger Stephen and Joan Zehms Jordan; m. Troy Wiles Tyree; children: Jordan, Sidney. EdS in Early Childhood Edn., U. West Ga., 1996. Cert. T-6 tchr. Ga. Tchr. 1st grade Lee St. Elem., Jonesboro, Ga., 1992—99, Hawthorne Elem., Hampton, 1999—2001; co-owner My Sight Word Box Inc., Fayetteville, 2001—. Home: 100 Chitwood Ct Fayetteville GA 30215 Office: My Sight Word Box Inc PO Box 1900 Fayetteville GA 30214 Home Fax: 770-461-6363; Office Fax: 866-WOR-DBOX. Personal E-mail: TraceyJTyree@msn.com. Business E-Mail: mysightwordbox@aol.com.

TYRER-FERRARO, POLLY ANN, music instructor, software developer; b. St. Louis, Aug. 25, 1964; d. Jack Harold and Elizabeth (Neff) Tyrer; m. Joseph Scott Ferraro, Aug. 12, 1994; 1 child Maria Ann Ferraro. BM, Cen. Meth. Coll., 1986; MM, Southern Meth. Univ., 1988. Ind. piano tchr., Dallas, 1988—; ptnr., owner Concert Master, 1993—; owner Keynote Studio. Adv. bd. Dallas Southwest MTA, De Soto, Tex., 1990-97, Jr. Pianist Guild, Dallas, 1996-97, Dallas Music Tchr., 1990-92; mem. tchr.'s evaluation panel Hal Leonard, Milw., 1996; presenter Tex. Music Tchr. Conv., 1994. Author: Technique TIme, 1997; composer (music): Various Ensembles, 1995-97; arranger various Technique Disks, 1994-97; contbr. articles to profl. jours. Active Downwinders, Dallas, 1996—, Planned Parenthood, Dallas, 1992—. Recipient Nat. Honor Roll award Nat. Guild Music Tchrs., 1994. Mem. Dallas Southwest Music Tchrs. (pres. 1991-92, treas. 1997-98), Jr. Pianist Guild (v.p. 1996-98), World of Music Com. Avocations: cats, music, doll houses. Home: 1308 Carriage Creek De Soto TX 75115-3637 Office: The Keynote Studio 1308 Carriage Creek Dr De Soto TX 75115-3637

TYRITY, KATHY MILICA, reporter, editor; b. Akron, Ohio, Dec. 19, 1953; d. Zirovko Chirich and Ada Fay Tyrity; m. Robert Laird Brockruoy, Oct. 12, 1974 (div. Dec. 19, 1977); children: Sara Bays. BS, Butler U., Indianapolis, IN; Diploma (hon.) , Silva. Asst. tchr. Akron Pub. Schools, Akron, Ohio, 2002—02; corr. reporter Sun Newspaper, Medina, 2002—02; sec. Estate of Don Quist, Hudson, 2002—02; city editor Coshocton Tribune, Coshocton, 2002—02; corr. reporter Akron Beacon Jour., Akron, 2002—02; reporter Sarasota herald Tribune, Sarasota, Fla., 2002—; city editor Sarasota Times, 2002—. Active Republicans of Sarasota Club, Sarasota, Fla., 1977—89; psychic Akron Psychic Fairs, Cleveland, Akron, Canton, Ohio; healer Akron Theosophy Soc., Akron. Recipient Second Pl., Nat. Associated Collegiate Press, 1976, Mark Distinciton as Photo Editor, 1976, Most Coop., Journalism Award, Kenmore H.S., 1971. Mem.: Grand Cross, Rainbow Order (advisor 1970—74), Internat. Theosophy Club, Sigma Delta Chi (hon.; journalist 2002—02). Protestant. Achievements include research in Notable findings in medical research on psychics. Avocations: drawing, sketching, sketching, giving readings, giving readings. Office: Baltic Sea Mystic Entertainment PO Box 3984 Akron OH 44314

TYRL, PAUL, mathematics educator, researcher, consultant; b. Prague, Czech Rep., Dec. 24, 1951; came to U.S., 1970, naturalized, 1978; s. Vladimir Tyrl and Marta Kocian. BA with honors, N.J. City U., 1977, MA, 1980; EdD, Rutgers U., 1987. Cert. tchr. secondary edn., higher edn. N.J. quality controller Agfa-Perutz, Munich, 1969-70; technician AT&T, Kearny, N.J., 1970-73; acquisition librarian N.J. City U., 1973-74, post office supr., 1974-76, dir. math. lab., instr. math., 1976-80; instr. math. Hudson County C.C., N.J., 1980-82, assoc. prof., coord. math., 1982-84; prof., chmn. math., acad. coord., curriculum dir. Sch. New Resources-New Rochelle Coll., N.Y.C., 1984—. Rschr. Rutgers U., New Brunswick, N.J., 1980—; cons. Jersey City Bd. Edn., N.J., 1982—. Contbr. articles to profl. jours. Recipient Commemorative medal of honor, 1986. Mem. AAAS, ASCD, Nat. Coun. Tchrs. Math. (reviewer and referee), N.Y. Acad. Scis., Am. Ednl. Rsch. Assn., Math. Assn. Am., Am. Math. Assn. 2-Yr. Colls., Am. Math. Soc., Am. Mus. Natural History, Nat. Geog. Soc., Nat. Wildlife Fedn., Smithsonian Instn. Roman Catholic. Achievements include research in mathematics anxiety and mathematics problem solving.

TYRONE, GREG L. secondary school educator; b. Las Vegas, N.Mex., Feb. 19, 1948; s. Champ B. Tyrone and Ava L. McClintock; m. Diane C. Stewart, Sept. 1, 1971; children: Lisa N. Tyrone Stewart, Nicholas. BA, N.Mex. Highlands U., 1970, MA, 1971; pvt. student, Roger Bobo, L.A. Philharmonic, 1979. Music tchr. Las Vegas (N.Mex.) City Schs., 1971—; staff, choir camp Ea. N.Mex. U., Portales, 1990—; staff tubaist N.Mex. Music Festival at Taos, 1979—82. Composer: numerous compositions and arrangements, 1966—. Mem.: N.Mex. Music Educators' Assn. (dist. pres. 1978—79). Office: Las Vegas City Schs 901 Douglas Ave Las Vegas NM 87701

TYRRELL, GERALD GETTYS, banker; b. Canton, China, Dec. 27, 1938; came to U.S., 1940. s. Gerald Fraser and Virginia Lee (Gettys) T.; m. Jane Haldeman, June 1961 (div. Aug. 1975); children: Gerald F., Jane N., Robert M.; m. Elizabeth Ann Drautman, Mar. 31, 1978. BA, Yale U., 1960; MA, Rutgers U., 1971. Cert. real estate financier. With 1st Nat. Bank of Louisville, 1961—89, sr. v.p., 1975—81, exec. v.p., 1981—89; pres., chmn. Churchill Mortgage Corp., 1975—77; chief fin. cons. City of Louisville Office of Downtown Devel., 1989—2000; exec. v.p. Univ. Group, Consultants for Bus., Prospect, 2000—. Vice chmn. bd. dirs. Porcelain Metals Corp., 2001—, bd. dirs. Author: A Positive Approach to Financing Black Business, 1972 Trustee, treas. Patton Mus., Ft. Knox, Ky., 1970—96; treas. Soc. Colonial Wars in Commonwealth of Ky., 1970—89, sec., 1996—99, gov., 2000—; mem. exec. bd. Boy Scouts Am., 1983—; bd. dirs. The Louisville Orch., 1984—90, Crane Ho., The Asia Inst., 1988—, pres., 1995—97; bd. dirs., chmn. fin. com. Glassworks Found., Inc., 2001—. Served to capt. U.S. Army, 1960—68. Recipient Disting. Service Ribbon Ky. Nat. Guard, 1966 Mem. Robert Morris Assocs., Nat. Soc. Real Estate Fin. (bd. govs) Clubs: Louisville Country, Pendennis. Democrat. Avocations: fine wines, tennis. E-mail: betsyandgerald@aol.com.

TYRRELL, ROBERT EMMETT, JR. periodical editor, writer; b. Chgo., Dec. 14, 1943; s. R. Emmett and Patricia (Rogers) T.; m. Judy Mathews Tyrrell, Feb. 12, 1972 (div. Dec. 1989); children: Patrick, Kathryn, Anne; m. Jeanne Hauch Tyrrell, May 23, 1998. BA, Ind. U., 1965, MA, 1967. Founder, editor-in-chief The Am. Spectator, Arlington, Va., 1967—. Chmn. Am. Alternative Found., Inc., Arlington, Va., 1967—. Author: Public Nuisances, 1979, The Liberal Crack-Up, 1984, The Conservative Crack-up, 1992, Boy Clinton: The Political Biography, 1996, (with anonymous author) The Impeachment of William Jefferson Clinton, 1997; editor: Network News Treatment of the 1972 Democratic Presidential Candidates, 1972, The Future That Doesn't Work, 1977, Orthodoxy, 1987; writer nationally syndicated polit. column; contbg. editor: The New York Sun. Recipient Am. Eagle award Invest in Am. Coun., 1977; named Greatest Pub. Svc. Performed by an American 35 Years or Under award Am. Inst. for Pub. Svc., 1977, Ten Most Outstanding Young Men in Am., Jaycees, 1978. Roman Catholic. Avocations: handball, fishing, listening to classical music, reading. Office: The American Spectator 2020 14th St N Ste 750 Arlington VA 22201-2515

TYSON, CHARLOTTE ROSE, software development manager; b. San Mateo, Calif., Aug. 14, 1954; d. Herbert Parry and Rose (Goldner) T.; m. Edward Phillip Sejud, Aug. 11, 1979; children: Laura Rose, Elizabeth Ann. AA in Physics, DeAnza Coll., 1974; BS in Elec. Engring., U. Calif.-Berkeley, 1976; MS in Computer Info. Systems, U. Denver, 1992. From engr. to engr. to mgr. software mfg. ops. IBM, Boulder, Colo., 1976—93; systems devel. and program mgr. Storage Tek, Louisville, 1993—, mgr. software solutions integrated svcs., 1996-97, mgr. multiplatform solns devel., 1997-98, mgr. client server tape software, 1999-2000, dir. storage solutions integration ctr., 2000—02, dir. storage solutions ops., 2002—. V.p. corp. adv. bd. women in engring. program U. Colo., 2000—; women in tech. com. 2001 Women's Summit, 2001—; corp. rep. to bd. dirs. Colo. Software and Internet Assocs. , 2002—. Leader Mountain Prairie Coun. Girl Scouts U.S., 1992-94; fund raiser Longmont Symphony Guild, 1994; team mgr., treas. girls competitive soccer St. Vrain Express, 1995-96; dir. Longmont Lightning Girls Competitive Basketball League, 1997-99; host gardener Longmont Garden Tour, 1999; gen. mgr. girls basketball Longmont H.S., 2000— Mem.: IEEE (chmn. Denver sect. 1982—83, Debt of Gratitude award 1981, 1982, 1983), AAUW, Electromagnetic Compatability Soc. (chmn. Boulder chpt. 1979—91, registration chmn. EMC internat. symposium 1981, bd. dirs. 1985—90, awards and membership chmn. 1986—90, treas. 1998, EMC symposium 1996—99), Soc. Women Engrs. (sr.; life), St. Vrain Hist. Soc. Office: Storage Tek One StorageTek Dr Louisville CO 80028-0001 E-mail: charlotte_tyson@storagetek.com.

TYSON, CYNTHIA HALDENBY, academic administrator; b. Scunthorpe, Lincolnshire, Eng., July 2, 1937; came to U.S., 1959; d. Frederick and Florence Edna (Stacey) Haldenby; children: Marcus James, Alexandra Elizabeth. BA, U. Leeds, Eng., 1958, MA, 1959, PhD, 1971. Lectr. Brit. Council, Leeds, 1959; faculty U. Tenn., Knoxville, 1959-60, Seton Hall U., South Orange, N.J., 1963-69; faculty, v.p. Queens Coll., Charlotte, N.C., 1969-85; pres. Mary Baldwin Coll., Staunton, Va., 1985—. Contbr. articles to profl. jours. Mem. Va. Internat. Trade Commn., Richmond, 1987; trustee Am. Frontier Culture Mus., Va.; mem. Va. Lottery Bd., 1987-94; chair selection com. State of Va. Rhodes Scholarship Competition, 1993-97; bd. dirs. Cmty. Found. Staunton, Augusta County and Waynesboro, 1993-98. Fulbright scholar, 1959; Ford Found. grantee Harvard U., 1981; Shell Oil scholar Harvard U., 1982. Mem.: Assn. Presbyn. Colls. and Univs. (bd. dirs. 1998), So. Assn. Colls. and Schs. (vice chair 1998, pres.-elect 2001, pres. 2002), Assn. Va. Colls. and Univs. (pres. 1997—98), So. Assn. Colls. for Women (pres. 1980—81). Republican. Office: Mary Baldwin Coll Office of the President Staunton VA 24401 E-mail: chtyson@mbc.edu.

TYSON, DAVID RICHARD, former lawyer, political party official; BA in Polit. Sci., W.Va. U., 1975, MA, 1976; JD, Calif. Western Sch. Law, 1980. Bar: W.Va. 1980, U.S. Dist. Ct. (so. dist.) W.Va. 1980. Mng. ptnr. Tyson & Tyson, Huntington, W.Va., 1980-95; pvt. practice, 1980—. Counsel W.Va. Dept. Agr., 1987-93; mcpl. judge Village of Barboursville, W.Va., 1987-88; hearing examienr Workers Compensation Commn., 1987-91; spl. dep. atty. gen. State of W.Va., 1987-88; acting mcpl. judge City of Huntington, 1981-82; ex-officio mem. W.Va. Bd. Regents, 1978-80; adj. prof. law Marshall U., Huntington, 1981-89, adj. prof. dept. polit. sci., 1986-87, 92-94. Dir. paralegal program Cabell County Jail, Huntington, 1984—; dep. mental hygiene commr., Wayne County, W.Va.; mem. Republican State Exec. Com. of W.Va., 1980—, state chmn., 1997-2001; del./alt. Rep. Nat. Conv., 1976, 84, 88, 92, 96; sate sec. W.Va. Legal Svcs., 1982-84; mem. St. Joseph H.S. Bd., 1986—, v.p., 1989—; mem. Cabell County Com. on Crime and Delinquency, 1982; bd. dirs. YMCA, 1984—, sec., 1996; bd. dirs. Guyandotte Med. Ctr., 1982-84. Mem. ABA (vice chair profl. competency com. 1986), W.Va. State Bar, W.Va. Bar Assn., Cabell County Bar Assn., Rotary Club of Huntington (bd. dirs. 1994—, pres. 1997-98). Office: 418 11th St Huntington WV 25701-2209*

TYSON, DAVID T. academic administrator; b. Gary, Ind., 1948; Postgrad in sociology & theology, U. Notre Dame; EdD, Ind. U., 1980. Prof. mgmt. U. Notre Dame, v.p. student affairs; pres. U. Portland, Oreg., 1990—. Trustee St. Mary's Coll., Ind.; bd. mem. Assn. Catholic Colls. & Univs. (ACCU); trustee U. Notre Dame; bd. mem. USAF's Air U. Office: U Portland Office Pres 5000 N Willamette Blvd Portland OR 97203-5743*

TYSON, EDITH SLOSSON, retired librarian, writer; b. Richmond, Va., Apr. 11, 1935; d. Preston William Slosson and Lucy Chase (Denny) Wright; m. Ivan Maurice Aron, Mar. 24, 1967 (dec. May 1968); m. Dean Eyster Tyson, July 23, 1976 (dec. Dec. 1995); stepchildren: David Dean, Mary Jane Tyson Strickler. BA with distinction, U. Mich., 1966, MA in Comparative Lit., 1967; MLS, Clarion U. of Pa., 1984. Tchr. asst. in English U. N.Mex., Albuquerque, 1966-67; post-H.S. tchr. Milan (Mich.) Fed. Prison, 1967-68; tchr. program in religious studies U. Mich., Ann Arbor, 1972-79; cmty. resource tchr. Cmty. H.S., 1976-79; religious edn. dir. Knox (Pa.) Parish, 1979-84; librarian ref. and young adult svcs. Warren (Ohio)/Trumbull County Pub. Libr., 1985-99; ret., 1999. Author: Books for Teens: Stressing the Higher Values, 1993; contbr. articles to to profl. jours. Mem. Ch. and Synagogue Libr. Assn. (lectr., workshop leader 1987—). Democrat. Presbyterian. Avocation: family. Home: Apt 430 1216 Fifth Ave Youngstown OH 44504 E-mail: edithtyson@hotmail.com.

TYSON, GAIL L. health federation administrator; b. Havre de Grace, Md., Dec. 28, 1954; d. William Alva Way and Virginia Lorena Tyson; m. Joseph Matthew Pease, May 17, 1986; 1 child, Loren Juliette Tyson Pease. BA, Dickinson Coll., 1976. Dir. edn. Harrisburg (Pa.) Area Rape Crisis Ctr., 1976-77; cmty. info. specialist CONTACT Harrisburg, 1978-81, asst. dir., 1981-85; pub. info. coord. Dauphin County Human Svcs., Harrisburg, 1985-87; unit exec. dir. Am. Cancer Soc., 1988-92; exec. dir. Nat. Voluntary Health Agys. Pa. Com., 1992-99; pres., CEO Cmty. Health Charities of Pa., 2000—. V.p. Human Svcs. Program, 1987; chmn. Nat. Voluntary Health Agys. Coun. State Affiliates, 1997, 98. Mem. adv. com. Harrisburg Area C.C., 1985-87; mem. adv. bd. Ret. Sr. Vol. Program, Harrisburg, 1986-88, sec., 1987; lifetime mem. Girl Scouts U.S., bd. dirs. Hemlock coun., 1977-91, v.p., 1982-88, pres., 1988-91, chmn. diversity task force, 1992. Recipient Thanks badge Hemlock coun. Girl Scouts U.S., 1991. Mem. Wheel and Chain Hon. Soc. Methodist. Office: Community Health Charites of Pa 2213 Forest Hills Dr Ste 3 Harrisburg PA 17112-1090

TYSON, H. MICHAEL, retired bank executive; b. Houston, Aug. 16, 1938; s. Howard Ellis and Myrle (Daunoy) T.; m. Judith O. Gilbert, June 24, 1960; children: H. Michael II, Michelle Lee. BBA cum laude, U. Tex., 1962; postgrad., Stonier Grad Sch. Banking, Rutgers U., 1974. Personnel mgr. Foods div. Anderson Clayton Co., Dallas, 1962-70; exec. v.p. adminstrn. Tex. Commerce Bancshares, Houston, 1970-79; v.p. fin. and adminstrn., chief fin. officer, dir. Houston Chronicle Pub. Co., 1979-87; vice chmn., dir. Tex.

Commerce Bank-Houston; exec. v.p., exec. trust officer Tex. Commerce Bancshares, 1987-95. Dir. Paranet Inc., Assoc. Bldg. Svcs., MCG/Dulworth Inc. Bd. dirs. Sam Houston coun. Boy Scouts Am., Houston Livestock Show & Rodeo, Houston Festival Found.; trustee McCullough Found., W.A. Smith Found.; chmn. The Houston Parks Bd. Served with USMCR, 1961-67. Mem. Houston C. of C. (com. chmn.), Pers. Round Table, Am. Newspaper Pub. Assn., Houston Indsl. Rels. Group, Fin. Execs. Inst. (bd. dirs.), Internat. Newspaper Fin. Execs., Houston Club (dir., pres.), River Oaks Country Club (dir.), Houston Yacht Club (dir.). Methodist. E-mail: hmtyson@prodigy.net.

TYSON, HELEN FLYNN, civic leader; b. Wilmington, N.C.; d. Walter Thomas and Fannie Elizabeth (Smith) Flynn; Student Guilford Coll., Am. U., Washington; m. James Franklin Tyson, Dec. 25, 1940 (dec.). U.S. Civil Svc. auditor, Disbursing Office, AUS, Ft. Bragg, N.C., 1935-46, chief clerical asst. Disbursing Office, Pope AFB, N.C., 1946-49, asst. budget and acctg. officer, 1949-55, supervisory budget officer hdqrs. Mil. Transport Command, USAF, 1955-57, budget analyst Hdqrs. USAF, Washington, 1957-74, ret. Active Arlington Com. 100, Ft. Belvoir, Salvation Army Women's Aux., Inter-Svc. Club Coun. of Arlington. Recipient awards U.S. Treasury, 1945, 46, U.S. State Dept., 1970, Good Neighbor award Ft. Belvoir Civilian-Mil. Adv. Coun., 1978; awards U.S. First Army, 1973, ARC, 1977; named Arlington Woman of Yr., 1975; recipient Cert. of Recognition, 1981, Vol. Activists award Greater Washington Met. Area, 1981. Mem. NAFE, Nat. Fedn. Bus. and Profl. Women's Clubs, Am. Assn. Ret. Fed. Employees (hon.), Am. Soc. Mil. Comptrs. (hon., Outstanding Mem. award Washington chpt. 1988), Am. Inst. Parliamentarians, Guilford Coll. Alumni Assn., N.C. Soc. Washington, Altrusa Internat. Home: PO Box 6611 Falls Church VA 22040-6611

TYSON, JOHN H. food products executive; b. Springdale, Ark., Sept. 5, 1953; s. Don and Jean Tyson; m. Kimberly McCoy; children: John Randal, Olivia Laine. BBA, So. Meth. U., 1975. Complex mgr. N.C. area Tyson Foods, Inc., Springdale, v.p. mktg. corp. accounts, purchasing mgr., retail sales mgr. N.E. states, pres. beef and pork divsn.; pres. & chmn. Tyson Foods Inc., 1998-00, pres., chmn. & CEO, 2000—01, chmn., CEO. Polit. liaison to Washington and Little Rock, Tyson Foods, Inc. Bd. dirs. area United Way; supporter Farm Aid; vol. activities for well-being and edn. of Ark. children. Named Man of Yr., Ark. Poultry Industry, 1994. Mem. Nat. Assn. Mfrs., Am. Meat Inst., Ark. Poultry Fedn. (past pres.). Avocations: golf, deep sea fishing, music. Office: Tyson Foods Inc 2210 W Oaklawn Dr Springdale AR 72762-6999*

TYSON, JON EDWARD, pediatrician, neonatologist, epidemiologist, educator; b. Mobile, Ala., July 3, 1943; s. John Edward and Martha (Haralson) T.; m. Blanche Newton; children: Jon Jr., Julia, Laura, Kate. Student, Rice U., 1961-63, Tulane U., 1963-64, MD, 1968; MPH, U. Tex., Houston, 1994. Diplomate Am. Bd. Pediatrics. Prof. pediatrics and ob-gyn. U. Tex. Southwestern Med. Ctr., Dallas, 1990-98; prof. pediatrics, obstets., medicine and epidemiology U. Tex. Med. Sch., Houston, 1998—, dir. Ctr. Clin. Rsch. and Evidence-based Medicine, 1998—. Mem. editl. bd. Cochrane Collaboration, Oxford, Eng., 1987—. Contbr. over 130 articles to profl. jours. Maj. U.S. Army, 1971-72. Fellow Am. Acad. Pediatrics; mem. Soc. Pediat. Rsch., Am. Pediat. Soc. Episcopalian. Avocation: swimming. Office: U Tex Med Sch 6431 Fannin St MSB 2.106 Houston TX 77030

TYSON, KIRK W. M. management consultant; b. Jackson, Mich., July 2, 1952; s. George Carlton and Wilma Marion (Barnes) T.; m. Terri Lynn Long, Mar. 25, 2000. BBA, Western Mich. U., 1974; MBA, DePaul U., Chgo., 1982. CPA, Ill.; cert. mgmt. cons. Bus. cons. Arthur Andersen & Co., Chgo., 1974-84; v.p. cons. First Chgo. Corp., 1984; chmn. Kirk Tyson Internat., 1984-2000; pres. Corp. Growth Assocs., Chgo., 2001—. Author: Business Planning, 1982, Business Intelligence: Putting It All Together, 1986, Competitor Intelligence: Manual and Guide, 1990, Competition in the 21st Century, 1996, The Complete Guide to Competitive Intelligence, 1998 2d rev. edit. 2002. Pres., Chgo. Jr. Assn. Commerce and Industry Found., 1977-79; active Easter Seals Soc., 1977, Am. Blind Skiing Found., 1977-78, Jr. Achievement, 1976-77, United Way Met. Chgo., 1979-80, Urban Gateways, 1975; Rep. precinct committeeman Downers Grove Twp., 1985-88; treas. St. Charles H.S. Football Booster club, 1994-95. Fellow Soc. Competitive Intelligence Profls.; mem. Rotary Club of Chgo., Alpha Kappa Psi (Disting. Alumni Svc. award 1974-86). Office: Corporate Growth Assocs 30 South Wacker Dr Ste 2200 Chicago IL 60606-7456 E-mail: kirk.tyson@kirktyson.com.

TYSON, NEIL DEGRASSE, museum director; BA in Physics, Harvard U., 1980; MA in Astronomy, U. Tex., Austin, 1983; PhD in Astrophysics, Columbia U., 1991; DS (hon.), CUNY, 1997, Ramapo Coll., 2000, Dominican Coll., 2000, U. Richmond, 2001, Bloomfield Coll., 2002. Postdoctoral rsch. assoc. dept. astrophysics Princeton U., 1991—94; staff scientist Am. Mus.-Hayden Planetarium, N.Y.C., 1994—95, acting dir., 1995—96; chair dept. astrophysics Am. Mus. Natural History, 1997—99, Frederick P. Rose dir. Hayden Planetarium, 1999—. Contbr. articles to profl. jours. Named Sexiest Astrophysicist Alive, People Mag., 2000; named one of 40 under 40, Crains Mag., 1996; recipient Medal of Honor, Columbia U., 2001. Fellow: N.Y. Acad. Scis.; mem.: Nat. Soc. Black Physicists, Internat. Planetarium Soc., Astron. Soc. Pacific, Am. Phys. Soc., Am. Astron. Soc. Office: Dept Astrophysics Am Mus Natural History Central Park W at 79th St New York NY 10024*

TYSON, TERRI LYNN, television programming producer, consultant; b. Dayton, Ohio, May 11, 1962; d. Charles Albert Long and Patsy Arlene Fox; m. Kirk W.M. Tyson, Mar. 25, 2000. AA, Miami-Dade C.C., 1983; BA in Theater, Fla. State U., 1985. Singer, actress, 1985-91; dir. devel. Chgo. Christian Indsl. League, Chgo., 1993-95; dir. comm. Greater Chgo. Food Depository, 1995-97; ptnr. Horizons Comms. Group, 1997-99; pres. Piper Prodns., Inc., 1999-2001, Tyson Chgo., 2001—. Prodr.: (TV documentaries) The Corner Pub, 1997 (Emmy nomination 1997, Telly award 2000), The Long Way Home, 1998 (Emmy nomination 1998, Telly award 2000), The Hunger Heroes, 2000 (Emmy nomination 2000, Gracie Allen award 2000). Mem. Am. Women in Radio and TV, Rotary One Chgo. Democrat. Presbyterian. Office: Tyson Chgo 980 N Michigan Ave Ste 1400 Chicago IL 60611 E-mail: piperpro@aol.com.

TYSZKOWSKI, ROBERT, business executive; b. Boston, May 25, 1961; s. Walter and Nora Francis (Lange) T.; m. Patricia Anne McArdle, Dec. 30, 1995. Sci. diploma, Riverside Mil. Acad., 1979; grad., U.S. Army ROTC Program, 1979; BA, U. Mass., 1983; BS, U. N.H., 1985; postgrad., Harvard U., 1985-87, 90-93. Lic. cons. Mass. Dept. Pub. Health; cert. instr. Mass. State Police. Rsch. asst. Ritzman Rsch. Lab., Durham, N.H., 1984-85; clin. pathology intern Brigham & Women's Hosp., Harvard Med. Sch., Boston, 1985-87; clin. rschr., cell biologist Mass. Gen. Hosp., Harvard Med. Sch., 1987—; CEO Lange Internat., 1987—; dir. ops. Renal Rsch. Unit, 1989—, radiation safety officer, 1990-96; exec. dir. Radiation Safety Svcs., Inc., 1996—; sr. ptnr. P.M.T. Assoc., Inc., 1996—; sr. v.p. Evidaunt Investigations, Inc., N.Y.C., 1997-99, CFO, 1999—; sr. ptnr. Back Bay Assocs., Boston, 2001—. Vice-chmn. bd. Evidaunt Investigations, Inc., Boston, 1997—; chmn. bd. Ea. Equine Assocs., Inc., Hamilton, Mass., 1985—, Lange Internat., Boston, 1987—, Radiation Safety Svcs., Inc., Boston, 1996—, Armser Corp., 1999—; mem. adv. com. U.S. Combined Tng. Assn., 1986-90, Ptnrs. Healthcare Sys., 1997—; mem. adv. bd. P.M.T. Assocs. Inc., Boston, 1996—, Middlesex County Dep. Sheriff's Assn., 2000—, Mass. Assn. Italian-Am. Police Officers, 2000—. Author: Why Children Fail, 1982, Battle in the North Georgia Hills, 1983, The Judges, Part I and II, 1987, Brief History of the Union Club of Boston, 1997, Biography of Pastor G.B. Dangers, 2000; editor, contbg. author The Centurion, 2000—, The Guardian, 2000—; contbr. numerous articles to profl. jours. Co-chmn. organizing com. Harvard-Yale Benefit Polo, Hamilton, 1990, U. N.H. Fund Raising Event, Boston, 1991; mem. organizing com. U. N.H. Equestrian Events, 1983-85, Ledyard Three-day Event, Wenham, Mass., 1987-88, 90, U. Mass. Fund Raising Drive, Amherst, 1980-81. Dana fellow, 1981-82, fellow Harvard U., 1987-89. Mem. AAAS, Am. Coll. Forensic Examiners, Am. Nuc. Soc., Admiral Nimitz Found., N.Y. Acad. Scis., Am. Soc. Notaries, Assn. of Offcl. Analytical Chemists Internat., Boston Athenaeum (life), Health Physics Soc., Inst. of Early Am. History and Culture (inst. assoc.), New Eng. Hist. Geneal. Soc., Nat. Assn. Investigative Specialists, Mus. Fine Arts/Boston, Redwood Libr. and Athenaeum, Nimitz Mus. Pacific War, Tex. State Archives, Manhattan C. of C., U.S. Ct. Tennis Assn., U.S. Golf Assn., U.S. Polo Assn., Faculty Club, Nat. Tennis Club (Newport, R.I.), Myopia Polo Club, Tennis and Racquet Club, Union Club, Univ. Club. Republican. Episcopalian. Avocation: equestrian sports, royal tennis. Office: Lange Internat PO Box 5669 Boston MA 02114-0011 also: Armser Corp 100 Park Ave Fl 16 New York NY 10017 also: Evidaunt Investigations Inc 60 State St Ste 700 Boston MA 02109-1803 E-mail: armser@aol.com.

TYTELL, JOHN, humanities educator, writer; b. Antwerp, Belgium, May 17, 1939; came to U.S., 1941; s. Charles and Lena (Gano) T.; m. Mellon Gregori, May 28, 1967. BA, CCNY, 1961; MA, NYU, 1963, PhD, 1968. Grad. reader NYU, 1963-67; lectr. Queens Coll., N.Y.C., 1963-68, assoc. prof., 1968-73, 1973-76, prof. English, 1977—; exec. editor Am. Book Rev., 1979—; vis. prof. Rutgers U., 1980, U. Paris, 1983; cons. Nat. Humanities Faculty, Ga., 1978—. Author: The American Experience, 1970, Naked Angels, 1976, Ezra Pound: The Solitary Volcano, 1987, Passionate Lives, 1991, The Living Theatre: Art, Exile and Outrage, 1995, Paradise Outlaws: Remembering the Beats, 1999; contbr. articles to mags. including Am. Scholar, Partisan Rev., Vanity Fair, Fame. NEH fellow, 1974 Home: 69 Perry St New York NY 10014-3297 Office: Queens Coll Flushing NY 11367

TYTLA, PETER T. artist; b. Hollywood, Calif., Feb. 21, 1939; s. William Tytla and Adrienne LeClerc. Student, Mitchell Coll. Film editor Preferred Film Svcs., N.Y.C., 1961-62; film dir., 1963-83; photographic collage artist, 1984—. Citations: Creative Collage Techniques, 1994, Gas Station Memories, 1994, Collage Techniques, 1994; featured artist Positively Connecticut, 1998. Recipient Best in Show 47th Ann. Art Exhbn. Slater Mus., 1990, 1st place Profl. Divsn. CRT Nat. Arts Program, 1991, Best of Show/1st prize Shoreline Alliance Arts, 1992, 1st place Mystic Photo 14 Show, 1992, EAF Shearer Meml. award 46th Ann. Rossi Corp. Award, 1993, New Eng. Found. Arts award, 1994, 1st place Arts Atlantica '97 Art Show, 1st place 35th Ann. Faifield Festival Arts, 1997, 1st place/1st honors Choices '97 Statewide Juried Exhbn., award Spectra 97, 1st place Mystic Art Assn., 1998, 1st place Image in Memory award Mystic Art Assn. Art Show, 1st place 38th Annual Niantic Art and Craft Show, 1st place Gould Chalker award 52nd Annual Exxex Art Show, Joyce and Michael Schiavone prize 98th Ann. New Haven Paint and Clay Club, 1999, 2000, 01, numerous internat. and nat. CLIO awards; winner art contest Art Expo, N.Y.C., 1999, Nat. Cover Artist*Making a Living as An Artist award Art Calendar Mag., 1998, 1st place Niantic Ann. Arts and Crafts Show, award Nat. Juried Competition of the Camera Club of N.Y., Marie Wood Cash award 53rd Ann. Essex Art Show, 1st place Mystic Art Assn. Ann. Photo Show XXI, 2000, Ann. New Haven Paint & Clay Club cash prize, 1999, The Photo Rev. Mag., 2000, Acad. Fine Arts Exhbn., 2000, Niantic Art & Craft Show, 2001, Best in Show awards Mystic Art Assn., 2001, Artworks Gallery, Hartford, Conn., 2002, numerous other awards; one of 4 finalists chosen for one-man show Viridian Artists, N.Y.C., 2000. Avocations: physical fitness, jogging, photography.

TYTLER, LINDA JEAN, communications and public affairs executive, retired state legislator; b. Rochester, N.Y., Aug. 31, 1947; d. Frederick Easton and Marian Elizabeth (Allen) T.; m. George Stephen Dragnich, May 2, 1970 (div. July 1976); m. James Douglas Fisher, Oct. 7, 1994. AS, So. Va. Coll., Buena Vista, Va., 1967. Spl. asst. to Congressman John Buchanan, Washington, 1971-75; legis. analyst U.S. Senator Robert Griffin, 1975-77; ops. supr. Pres. Ford Com., 1976; office mgr. U.S. Senator Pete Domenici Re-election, Albuquerque, 1977; pub. info. officer S.W. Cmty. Health Svc., 1978-83; cons. pub. rels. and mktg., 1983-84; account exec. Rick Johnson & Co., Inc., 1983-84; dir. mktg. and comm. St. Joseph Healthcare Corp., 1984-88; mktg. and bus. devel. cons., 1987-90; dir. comm. and pub. affairs Def. Avionics Systems, Honeywell Inc., 1990-2000, dir. comms., 2000—02; dep. dir. pub. affairs Los Alamos Nat. Lab., 2002—. Capt. N.Mex. Mounted Patrol, 1998-2002; bd. dirs. Jobs for N.Mex.; mem. N.Mex. Ho. of Reps., Santa Fe, 1983-95, ret. 1995, vice chmn. appropriations and fin. com., 1985-86, chmn. Rep. Caucus, 1985-88; chmn. legis. campaign com. Rep. Com.; co-chair del. to Republic of China, Am. Coun. Young Polit. Leaders, 1988. Bd. dirs. N.Mex. chpt. ARC, Albuquerqu, 1984. Recipient award N.Mex. Advt. Fedn., Aluquerque, 1981, 82, 85, 86, 87, Honeywell Cmty. Svc. award, 1997. Mem. Am. Soc. Hosp. Pub. Rels. (cert.), Nat. Advt. Fedn., Soc. Hosp. Planning and Mktg., Am. Mktg. Assn., N.Mex. Assn. Commerce and Industry (bd. dirs., exec. com. 1996—). Republican.

TYUNAITIS, PATRICIA ANN, elementary school educator; b. Kenosha, Wis., Feb. 15, 1942; d. John Anton and Antoinette (Tunkieicz) T. BS, Alverno U., 1966; MAT, Webster U., 1982; postgrad., Walden U., 1994—. Cert. elem., secondary tchr., Wis. Tchr. St. John the Bapt. Sch., Johnsburg, Wis., 1964-67, St. Matthew's Sch., Campbellsport, 1967-68, St. Monica's Sch., Whitefish Bay, 1968-71; math. tchr. New Holstein (Wis.) Elem. Sch., 1971—, mem. sch. restructuring com., 1994; owner Miss T's Learning Ctr., Pipe Village, 2000—. Adj. prof. Silver Lake Coll., Manitowoc, Wis., 1993—, Marian Coll., Fond du Lac, Wis., 1993-98; tchr. U. Wis., Oshkosh, 1995—, St. Mary's U., 1995—. Mem. performance assessment tng. team Dept. Pub. Instrn., Madison, Wis., 1992—. Recipient Herb Kohl award for excellence in teaching State of Wis., 1996, Wis. Presdl. award for excellence in tchg. math., Wisc. Disting. Math. Tchr. Yr., 1999. Mem. ASCD, Nat. Coun. Tchrs. Math., Math. Assn. Am., Nat. Assn. Tchrs. Am., New Holstein Edn. Assn., Wis. Math. Coun., Optimist Club (coord. local forensic contest 1991—, sch. coach Odyssey of the Mind 1986—, sch. coord. Odyssey of the Mind 1992, regional dir. Stevens Point chpt. 1992—). Home: N10335 Hwy 151 Malone WI 53049-1225 E-mail: tyunaitis@cs.com.

TZAGOURNIS, MANUEL, physician, educator, university administrator; b. Youngstown, Ohio, Oct. 20, 1934; s. Adam and Argiro T.; m. Madeline Jean Kalos, Aug. 30, 1958; children: Adam, Alice, Ellen, Jack, George. BS, Ohio State U., 1956, MD, 1960, MS, 1967. Intern Phila. Gen. Hosp., 1960-61; resident Ohio State U., Columbus, 1961-63, chief med. resident, 1966-67, instr., 1967-68, asst. prof., 1968-70, assoc. prof., 1970-74, prof., 1974—, asst. dean Coll. Medicine, 1973-75, assoc. dean, med. dirs. hosps., 1975-80, v.p. health svcs., dean of medicine, 1981-95, v.p. health scis., 1995-99; pvt. practice endocrinology, 1967—; mem. staff Ohio State U. Hosps./James Cancer Hosp. & Rsch. Ctr. Mem. Coalition for Cost Effective Health Services Edn. and Research Group State of Ohio, 1983 Contbg. author: textbook Endocrinology, 1974, Clinical Diabetes: Modern Management, 1980; co-author: Diabetes Mellitus, 1983, 88; contbr. chpts. to books. Citation Ohio State Senate Resolution No. 984, 1989. Capt. U.S. Army, 1962-64; bd. trustees Hellenic Coll./Holy Cross. Recipient Homeric Order of Ahepa Cleve. chpt., 1976, Phys. of Yr. award Hellenic Med. Soc. N.Y., 1989; citations Ohio State Senate and Ho. of Reps., 1975, 83 Mem. AMA, Am. Red Cross (past chair, bd. dirs. ctrl. Ohio 1996—), Assn. Am. Med. Colls., Columbus Med. Assn., Deans' Coun. Mem. Greek Orthodox Ch. Home: 4335 Sawmill Rd Columbus OH 43220-2243 Office: Ohio State U Coll Medicine 1024 Cramblett Hall 456 W 10th Ave Columbus OH 43210-1238

TZAKIS, ANDREAS GERASIMOS, surgeon, educator; MD, U. Athens, Greece, 1974; PhD, Nat. U. Athens, 1999. Intern Mt. Sinai Hosp., N.Y.C., 1977—78, resident surgery, 1978—79, SUNY at Stony Brook, Long Island, 1979—82, chief resident surgery, 1982—83; fellow in transplantation surgery U. Pitts., 1983—85; asst. prof. surgery U. Pitts. Sch. Medicine, 1985—89, assoc. prof. surgery, 1989—94, prof. surgery, 1994, U. Miami (Fla.) Sch. Medicine, 1994. Mem. adv. bd. Archives of Gastroenterohepatology, 1997; presenter, panelist, lectr. in field. Mem. editl. bd.: Clin. Tranplantation, 1993; author: Tranplantation Procs., 1993, Transplantation, 1994, Pediat. Transplantation, 1997, Jour. Investigative Surgery, 1997, Graft, 1998, Annals Gastroenterology, 1999, Liver Transplantation, 1999; contbr. numerous articles to profl. jours. 2nd lt. Med. Corp Greek Air Force, 1974—77. Mem.: ACS, AMA, Internat. Pediat. Transplant Assn., Inc., Xenotransplantation Assn., Am. Surg. Assn., Am. Assn. for the Study of Liver Diseases, Internat. Coll. Surgeons, Am. Coll. Angiology, Internat. Pancreas and Islet Transplant Assn., Hellenic Tranplantation Soc., Soc. Internat. Surgery, Soc. U. Surgeons, Assn. for Acad. Surgery, Acad. Surg. Rsch., The Transplantation Soc., Am. Soc. Transplant Surgeons. Office: Univ Miami Sch Medicine Miami FL 33101

TZEKOV, TZEKOV CHRISTO, neurosurgeon, educator, consultant; b. Vratza, Bulgaria, Oct. 22, 1950; s. Tzeko Christov Tzekov and Vatza Mihaylova Vekova; m. Valentina Radkova Tomova, Mar. 6, 1983; children: Vanya, Asen. Diploma, Med. Acad., Sofia, Bulgaria, 1974, qualification, 1979, qualification, 1983. Surgeon Dist. Hosp., Vratza, 1974-79; neurosurgeon Higher Med. Inst., Sofia, 1979-2001; asst. prof. Cons. Nat. Emergency Ctr., Sofia, 1989-2001. Co-author: Tumors of CNS in Childhood, 1987, Pediatric Neurosurgery, 1989; contbr. articles to profl. jours.; inventor in field. Mem. European Assn. Neurosurgery, European Assn. Pediat. Neurosurgery, Nat. Geog. Soc. Avocations: philately, hiking. Home: Mladost 2 Block 250 Floor 8 ap 35 1799 Sofia Bulgaria Office: Higher Med Sch Neurosurgery 1 G Sofiiski St 1431 Sofia Bulgaria E-mail: neurosurg-alex_hosp@hotmail.com.

TZIMAS, NICHOLAS ACHILLES, orthopedic surgeon, educator; b. Greece, Apr. 18, 1928; came to U.S., 1955, naturalized, 1960; s. Archilles Nicholas and Evanthia B. (Exarchou) T.; m. Helen J. Papastylopoulos, Apr. 22, 1958; children: Yvonne, Christina. MD, U. Athens, Greece, 1952. Intern St. Mary's Hosp., Hoboken, N.J., 1955-56; resident in gen. surgery Misericordia Hosp., N.Y.C.; resident in orthopedic surgery Bellevue Hosp., 1957-60; instr. orthopedic surgery N.Y. U. Sch. Medicine, 1961-63, asst. clin. prof., 1963-65, asso. clin. prof., 1965-71; clin. prof., 1971—. Mem. staff Univ. and Bellevue Hosps.; chief children's orthopedics, 1966— ; orthopedic cons. Inst. Rehab. Medicine, N.Y. U., 1966— , St. Agnes Hosp., White Plains, N.Y., 1972— ; advisory com. Bur. Handicapped Children, N.Y.C., 1975— ; spl. invitations for teaching, Osaka, Japan, 1970, Jerusalem, 1974, São Paolo, Brazil, 1976, Taranto, Italy, 1977, Bari, Italy, 1978, Barquisimeto, Venezuela, 1979, Bogotá, Colombia, 1983, Buenos Aires, Argentina, 1983 Author articles on spina bifida child mgmt. Served with M.C. Greek Army, 1952-55. Named ofcl. Knight of Italian Republic, 1979 Fellow Am., Internat. colls. surgeons; mem. N.Y. Acad. Medicine, N.Y. State, N.Y. County med. socs., Am. Acad. Orthopedic Surgeons, Am. Congress Rehab. Medicine, Am. Acad. Cerebral Palsy. Mem. Greek Orthodox Ch., Archon of the Ecumenical Patriarchate of Constantinople. Home: 33 Edgewood St Tenafly NJ 07670-2909 Office: 530 1st Ave New York NY 10016-6402

TZIMOPOULOS, NICHOLAS D. educational administrator; b. Eptachorion, Greece, Feb. 19, 1941; came to U.S., 1956; s. Demetrius and Soultana (Davos) T. BA in Chemistry and Math., U. N.H., 1965; MS in Analytical Chemistry, Boston Coll., 1967, PhD in Phys. Chemistry, 1971. Dir. rsch. So. N.H. Services, Manchester, 1978-80; prof. phys. chemistry U. Northern Fla., Jacksonville, 1981-82; chmn. math and sci. The Bartram Sch., Fla., 1980-83; prof. chemistry Valencia C.C., Orlando, 1983-84; dir. sci. edn. Schs. of the Tarrytowns, North Tarrytown, N.Y., 1984-91; dir. sci., math. and tech. Lexington (Mass.) Pub. Schs., 1989—. Adj. prof. sci. edn. Boston U., 1993—; nat. acad. advisor The Tesseract Group, Inc., 1997—. Author: Modified Null-Point Potentiometry, 1967, Irreversible Processes, 1971, mathematics-Science Curricula, 1982, Modern Chemistry, 1990, 93, Life, Earth, Physical Sciences, 1987, 90, General Sciences Books 1 and 2, 1987, 90, The Next Generation: Teachers Resources Curriculum Guide, 1993, The Stuff of Dreams: Teachers Resource Curriculum Guide, 1993. N.H. rep. N.E. Metric Action Council, 1978-80; Tufts U. del. New Eng. Energy Congress, 1978; liaison Kiwanis Regional Sci. and Engring. Fair, Jacksonville, 1983; founder N.H. Legis. Acad. Sci. and Tech., Concord, 1980; mem. operating com. Mass. Sci. Fair, 1990—. Recipient Outstanding commendations in sci. achievement Internat. Sci. and Engring. Fair, 1986, CMA Catalyst award, 1987, N.Y. State Presdl. award for excellence in sci. and math., 1989. Fellow: Signa Xi (exec. bd. Harvard U. chpt. 1998); mem.: NSTA (coordination and superision sci. edn. com. 2001—), ASCD, AAAS, Nat. Sci. Tchrs. Assn., Fla. Acad. Sci., N.Y. Acad. Sci., Am. Chem. Soc. (Fla. congl. del. 1984, treas. Fla. sect. 1983, 1984, chmn. Jacksonville sect. 1982—83, dir. Westchester County, N.Y. sub-sect. 1986—, high sch. esams. com. 1982—86, Outstanding Chem. Tchr. Fla. 1982, S F U S. 1983, Nichols award 1986), Greek Orthodox Youth Assn. (pres. Manchester, N.H. 1963—65), Rotary Internat. Democrat. Avocations: photography, classical music, guitar, travel, soccer.

TZOU, ROBERT DA, engineering educator; b. Koashong, Taiwan, Sept. 3, 1955; s. Tze-Shing and Moo-Lang T.; m. Na Li Tzou; children: Patricia, Andy. BSME, Nat. Cheng-Kung U., Taiwan, 1979; PhD in Applied Mechanics, Lehigh U., Bethlehem, Pa., 1987. Asst. prof. dept. mech. engring. U. N.Mex., Albuquerque, 1988-92, assoc. prof. dept. mech. engring., 1992-96; prof. dept. mech. and aerospace engring. U. Mo., Columbia, 1996-97, prof., chmn. dept. mech. and aerospace engring., 1997—. Keynote lectr. 1997 Brazilian Congress of Mech. Engring., Macro-to Microscale Heat Transfer: The Lagging Behavior; invited spkr. SPIE 44th Annual Meeting and Exhbn., Ultrafast Heat Transport: The Lagging Behavior, 1999. Author: Annual Review of Heat Transfer, Vol. IV, 1992, Macro-to Microscale Heat Transfer: The Lagging Behavior, 1997. Recipient Rsch. Excellence award U. N.Mex., Albuquerque, 1994, Teaching Excellence award U. N.Mex., Albuquerque, 1991. Fellow ASME; mem. Sigma Xi Soc. Scientific Rsch., Tau Beta Pi Nat. Soc. Engring. Sci., Pi Tau Sigma Nat. Soc. Mech. Engring. Office: Dept Mech & Aerospace Engr University Of Missouri Columbia MO 65211-0001 Fax: 573-884-5090. E-mail: TzouR@missouri.edu.

UBALDI, MICHAEL VINCENT, lawyer; b. Stockton, Calif., May 2, 1948; s. Ben Raymond and Audrey Grace (Smalley) U.; m. Terryanne Ubaldi (div. Apr. 1990); children: Jennifer N., Justin M.; m. Linda A. Ubaldi, Feb. 14, 1991. BA, Calif. State U., Sacramento, 1971; JD, U. Calif., San Francisco, 1974. Bar: Calif. 1974. Assoc. Bullen, McKone & McKinley, Sacramento, 1974-81; ptnr. Duncan, Ball, Evans & Ubaldi, 1981—. Bd. dirs. Sutter Hosps. Found., Sacramento, 1985-92, Make-A-Wish Found., Sacramento, 1990-98, Mercy Hosps. Found., Sacramento, 1993—; mem. bus. adv. bd. Sch. Bus. Calif. State U., Sacramento, 1999—. Mem. No. Calif. Assn. Def. Counsel (bd. dirs. 1998—). Avocations: golf, art, travel. Office: Duncan Ball Evans & Ubaldi 641 Fulton Ave Fl 2D Sacramento CA 95825-4800

UBELL, EARL, magazine health editor, consultant; b. Bklyn., June 21, 1926; s. Charles and Hilda (Kramer) U.; m. Shirley Leitman, Feb. 12, 1949; children— Lori Ellen, Michael Charles. BS, CCNY, 1948; DSc (hon.), N.Y. Tech., 2001. With N.Y. Herald Tribune, 1943-66, successively messenger, asst. sec. to mng. editor, reporter, 1943-53, sci. editor, 1953-66, syndicated columnist, 1956-66; sci. commentator MBS, 1958-59; spl. sci. editor WNEW, N.Y., 1962; health and sci. editor WCBS-TV, N.Y.C., 1966-72, 78-95; health editor PARADE mag., 1983-97, contbg. editor, 1997—. Dir. TV news NBC News, N.Y.C., 1972-76; producer spl. broadcasts TV news, 1976-78; producer documentaries Medicine in America, 1977, Escape from Madness, 1977; author: The World of Push and Pull, 1964, The World of The Living, 1965, The World of Candle and Color, 1969, How to Save Your Life, 1972, (with Carol C. Flax) Mother/Father/You, 1980, (with Randi Londer) Parade Family Health Companion, 1996. Pres. Council Advancement Sci. Writing, Inc., 1960-66, bd. dirs., 1960-96, founder, 1996—; chmn. Center Modern Dance Edn., Inc., 1962-82; pres. North Jersey Cultural Coun., 1966-72; bd. dirs. Dance Notation Bur., 1968— , chmn. bd., 1975-94; bd. dirs. Sex Info. and Edn. Council U.S., 1967-69, YMHA, Bergen County, 1968-73, Nat. Center Health Edn., 1977. Served as aviation radioman USNR, 1944-46 . Recipient Mental Health Bell award N.Y. State Soc. Mental Health, 1957, Albert Lasker med. journalism award, 1958, Nat. Assn. Mental Health award for radio program, 1962, Sci. Writers award Am. Psychol. Found., 1965, Westinghouse award AAAS, 1960, Empire State award, 1963, TV Reporting award N.Y. Assoc. Press, 1969, 71, N.Y. Emmy award, 1971, Samuelson award N.Y. League for Hard of Hearing, Legal-Med. award Milton Helpern Library of Legal Medicine, Spl. Achievement award Deadline Club, 1982, Disting. Contbn. award, 1983, Nat. Media award Am. Diabetes Assn., 1985, N.Y. State Mental Health Council award, 1987, Ann. Svc. award Dance Notation Bur., 1990. Mem. Nat. Assn. Sci. Writers (pres. 1960-61), Nuclear Energy Writers Assn. (pres. 1965-66), Phi Beta Kappa (pres. Gamma chpt. 1976-77). *I learn something new, in depth, every 5 years—x-ray crystallography, French, statistics, polling, stock market—I am refreshed.*

UBELL, ROBERT NEIL, editor, publisher, educator, consultant; b. Bklyn., Sept. 14, 1938; s. Charles and Hilda (Kramer) U.; m. Rosalyn Deutsche, Sept. 24, 1976; children: Jennifer Hayslett-Ubell, Elizabeth Miller. BA, Bklyn. Coll., 1961; postgrad., Acad. Fine Arts, Rome, Italy, 1959-60, CUNY, 1961-62, Pratt Graphic Arts Workshop, N.Y.C., 1972-73. Assoc. editor Nuclear Industry, Atomic Indsl. Forum, 1962-64; from editor to sr. editor Plenum Pub. Corp., N.Y.C., 1965-70, v.p., editor in chief, 1970-76; editor The Sciences, N.Y. Acad. Scis., N.Y.C., 1976-79; Am. pub. Nature, 1979-83; founding pub. Nature Biotechnology, 1983; pres. Robert Ubell Assocs., N.Y.C., 1983-97, BioMedNet, Ltd., 1996-97; exec. v.p. Marcel Dekker, Inc.,

N.Y.C., 1997-99; dir. web-based distance learning Stevens Inst. Tech., 1999-2001, dean online learning, 2001—. Instr. MIT, 1987, Columbia U. Coll. Physicians and Surgeons, 1987; mem. editl. com. The Scientist, 1987-90; mem. Book Industry Study Group, Inc., 1992; vis. com. Nat. Acad. Press, NRC, NAS, 1986; mem. books subcom. Am. Inst. Physics, 1985-91; mem. awards com. Am. Inst. Physics-U.S. Steel Sci. Writing Awards, 1982-83; mem. publs. com. Am. Inst. Biol. Scis., 1994, N.Y. Acad. Scis., 1976-97; cons. Lotus Devel. Corp., 1987-89, Coalition for Networked Info., 1995-98; mem. pub. info. com. Nat. Acad. Engring., 1989—; mem. program com. Soc. Scholarly Pub., 1989-91; mem. rev. panel NSF, Nat. Sci., Math. and Tech. Edn. Digital Libr., 2000; distance learning observer Middle States Commn. on Higher Edn., 2000—; cons. BankStreetBook.com, 2000; cons. Peterson's Guides, 2000; cons. media group Bank St. Coll. Edn., 2000-01; chair Sloan Foundn., ALN Conf., N.Y.C., 2002; mem. plannig com. Sloan Foundn.Conf., Breakthrough Thinking in Online Bus. Edn., 2002—; mem. adv. panel, Nanwae Rsch Inst. on wireless and Industry, 2002—; Co-host, Casltle point Radio, WCPR, 2002—; mem adv. bd, comm., tech. coun. Industry Newtork, NJ, 2002— Author: (with Marvin Leiner) Children Are the Revolution, 1974; (with Mark Tesoriero) Negotiating Networked Licensing Agreements, 1995, Cost Centers and Measures in the Networked Information Value Chain, 1997, The R&D Economics in the Digital Environment, 1998; editor Nature Directory of Biologicals, 1981, Physics Today Buyer's Guide, 1984-89; exec. editor: Linguistics: The Cambridge Survey, 1987-88, Pre-Med Handbook, 1986, International Encyclopedia of the Social Sciences, Vol. 19, 1991, Encyclopedia of Astronomy and Astrophysics, 1991, Sci. Am. Triumph of Discovery, 1995, Oxford Encyclopedia of Climate and Weather, 1996; cons. editor ISI Press, 1985-87, Am. Inst. of Physics Book Program, 1986-96; Am. Chem. Soc. Book Program, 1989; cons. pub. Computers in Physics, 1987-91; series editor Masters of Modern Physics, 1991-96, Creators of Modern Chemistry, 1994-95, Sci. Am. Focus, 1995-96; mem. editl. bd. ISI Press, 1986-90, Grants Mag., 1981—, Nonprofit Mgmt. and Fin., 1980—; editl. dir. Nutrition Advisor, 1998-99, Innovations in End of Life Care, 1999—; editl. advisor Cancer Practice, Am. Cancer Soc., 1997-98; contbr. articles to profl. jours. Chmn. bd. The Woodword Sch., 1971-74; mem. adv. com. Children's TV Workshop, 1980; bd. dirs. Parkinson's Walk Found., 2001—. Mem. AAAS, N.Y. Acad. Scis. (mem. publs. com. 1976-97), Nat. Assn. Sci. Writers. Office: Stevens Inst Tech Grad Sch Castle Point on Hudson Hoboken NJ 07030

UBERALL, HERBERT MICHAEL STEFAN, physicist, educator; b. Neunkirchen, Austria, Oct. 14, 1931; came to U.S., 1953, naturalized, 1963; s. Michael and Stefanie (Hacker) U.; m. Reyna Tosta, 1981; children by previous marriage: Bernadette Chauvallon, Bertrand. PhD, U. Vienna, Austria, 1953, Cornell U., 1956; PhD (honoris causa), U. Le Havre, France, 1987. Staff mem. Signal Corps Labs., Ft. Monmouth, N.J., 1953-54; research asst. Cornell U., 1954-56; research fellow Nuclear Physics Research Lab., U. Liverpool, Eng., 1956-57; Ford Found. fellow CERN, Geneva, Switzerland, 1957-58; research physicist Carnegie Inst. Tech., Pitts., 1958-60; asst. prof. U. Mich., Ann Arbor, 1960-64; assoc. prof. Cath. U. Am., Washington, 1964-65, prof. physics, 1965-94, prof. emeritus, 1994—. Vis. prof. U. Paris VII Jussieu, 1984-85, U. Le Havre, 1990, 92, 94, 96, U. Bordeaux, 1993, 95, U. Aix-Marseille II and Lab. Mech. Acoustics, 1995, Ecole Centrale de Lille, 1997, Tech. U. Denmark, 1998; cons. Naval Rsch. Lab., Washington, 1966-96. Author: Electron Scattering from Complex Nuclei, 1971; co-author: Giant Resonance Phenomena, 1980, Nuclear Pion Photoproduction, 1991; editor: Acoustic Resonance Scattering, 1992; co-editor: Long Distance Neutrino Detection, 1979, Classical and Quantum Dynamics, 1991, Coherent Radiation Sources, 1985, Coherent Radiation Processes in Strong Fields, 1991, Radar Target Imaging, 1994; contbr. 300 articles to profl. jours. Recipient Fgn. medal French Soc. Acoustics, 1996. Fellow IEEE, Am. Phys. Soc., Acoustical Soc. Am., Washington Acad. Scis. (Achievement award 1984); mem. AAUP, Am. Acad. Mech., Electromagnetics Acad., Internat. Union Radio Sci. Home: 5101 River Rd Apt 1417 Bethesda MD 20816-1571 Office: Catholic U Dept Physics Washington DC 20064-0001 E-mail: huberall@aol.com.

UBEROI, MAHINDER SINGH, aerospace engineering educator; b. Delhi, India, Mar. 13, 1924; came to U.S., 1945, naturalized, 1960; s. Kirpal Singh and Sulaksha (Kochar) U. BS, Punjab U., Lahore, India, 1944; MS, Calif. Inst. Tech., 1946; D.Eng., Johns Hopkins U., 1952. Registered profl. engr. Mem. faculty U. Mich., Ann Arbor, 1953-63, prof. aeros., 1959-63, vis. prof., 1963-64; prof. aerospace engring. U. Colo., Boulder, 1963—, chmn. dept. aerospace engring., 1963-75; fellow F. Joint Inst. for Lab. Astrophysics, 1963-74. Hon. rsch. fellow Harvard U., 1975-76; invited prof. U. Que., Can., 1972-74; vis. scientist Max Planck Inst. for Astrophysics, Munich, 1974. Author numerous rsch. publs. on dynamics of ionized and neutral gases and liquids with and without chem. reactions, gravity and electromagnetic fields; editor Cosmic Gas Dynamics, 1974. Council mem. Ednl. TV Channel 6, Inc., Denver, 1963-66. Guggenheim fellow Royal Inst. Tech., Stockholm, Sweden, 1958; exchange scientist U.S. Nat. Acad. Scis.; exchange scientist Soviet Acad. Scis., 1966 Mem. Am. Phys. Soc., Tau Beta Pi. Home: 819 6th St Boulder CO 80302-7418

UBOVICH, BEN A. music educator; b. Pasadena, Calif., Aug. 8, 1952; s. Lourdes Ubovich. BA, San Diego State U., 1975; MM, Calif. State U., 2002. Music dir. La Serna H.S., Whittier, Calif., 1986—87, San Marino H.S., 1988—2002. Music dir. Covina Concert Band, 2001—02. Recipient Meritorious Svc. Award, So. Calif. Sch. Band and Orch. Assn., 1995. Mem.: Calif. Sch. Band and Orch. Assn. Conservative. Home: 2275 Huntington Dr #224 San Marino CA 91108 Office: San Marino HS 2701 Huntington Dr Pasadena CA 91108 Business E-Mail: bubovich@san-marino.k12.ca.us.

UBUKA, TOSHIHIKO, biochemistry educator, dean; b. Kagaminocho, Okayama, Japan, Jan. 31, 1934; s. Yoshio and Shigeko (Hashimoto) U.; m. Satoko Iwamiya, Oct. 18, 1960; children: Takayoshi, Hiromi, Atsue. MD, Okayama U., 1959, PhD, 1964. With Okayama U., 1964-73, asst. prof., 1973-80, assoc. prof. Med. Sch., 1980-81, prof. Med. Sch., 1981-99, dean Med. Sch., 1997-99, prof. emeritus, 1999—; prof., dean Kawasaki U of Med. Welfare, 1999-2001; rsch. assoc. Med. Coll. Cornell U., N.Y.C., 1968—71. Co-author: Methods in Enzymology, vol. 143, 1987; editor Acta Med Okayama, 1980-99, Physiol Chem Phys and Med NMR, 1982—, Amino Acids, 1991—; chief editor Acta Med Okayama, 1987-90. Fellow Japanese Biochem. Soc., Japanese Soc. Nutrition and Food Sci.; mem. AAAS, N.Y. Acad. Scis., Internat. Soc. Amino Acid Rsch., Soc. Study Inborn Errors Metabolism, The Protein Soc. Achievements include research in in sulfur biochemistry, sulfur nutrition, cysteine metabolism in mammals, protein modification with mixed disulfides; inborn errors of cysteine metabolism, analysis of sulfur compounds. Home: 527-1 Nishikarakawa Okayama 701-1213 Japan Office: Kawasaki U Med Welfare De Clin Nutrition 288 Matsushima Kurashiki Okayama 701-0193 Japan

UCCELLO, VINCENZA AGATHA, artist, director, educator emerita; b. Hartford, Conn., May 11, 1921; d. Salvatore and Josephine (Bordonaro) U. BS, St. Joseph Coll., West Hartford, Conn., 1956; DHL, St. Joseph Coll., 2000; MA in Liberal Studies, Wesleyan U., 1961; MFA, Villa Schifanoia, Florence, Italy, 1963. Tchr. art Glastonbury High Sch., Conn., 1957-61, East Hartford Pub. Schs., 1963-64; prof. fine arts St. Joseph Coll., 1964—, chmn. dept. fine arts, 1967-85, acting curator, dir. coll. art collections, 1978—. One-woman shows Villa Schifanoia, Florence, 1963, St. Joseph Coll., 1965, 81, Pump House Gallery, Hartford, Conn., 1986; group shows Am. Painters in Paris Exhbn., Nat. Print and Drawing Exhbn., Ohio U., Athens, Ball State U., Muncie, Ind., Austin Art Ctr., Trinity Coll., Hartford, Munson Gallery, New Haven; represented in permanent collections St. Joseph Coll., N.Y. Pub. Libr., Ctr. for Book Arts, Conn. Nat. Bank, Hartford; pvt. collections. Trustee West Hartford Art League. Recipient Harper Meml. award in painting, 1969; fellow Venice Artists Workshop, 1965; Yale U. fellow Andrew U. Mellon Found., 1980; second prize Atria Gallery Blues Show, Disting. Alumnae award St. Joseph Coll. Mem. Coll. Art Assn. Am. Conn. Women Artists (pres. 1974-76), Canton Artists Guild, Am. Assn. Mus., Assn. Colls. and Univ. Mus. and Galleries. Home: 51 Hilltop Dr West Hartford CT 06107-1434

UCCI, DONALD RICHARD, electrical engineering educator, consultant; b. Apr. 1, 1948; s. Gaetano Richard and Rose Marie (Girardi) U.; m. Frances Jean Di Maiuta, Apr. 1, 1979; children: April Beth, Matthew Lucas, Russell James. BS, CCNY, 1970; MS, 1972, PhD, 1979. Asst. prof. dept. elec. engring. SUNY-Stony Brook, 1979-81, 82-87; interim chmn., assoc. prof. dept. elec. and computer engring Ill. Inst. Tech., Chgo., 1987—2002; pres., assoc. dean Armour Coll. Engring. and Scis., Ill. Inst. Tech., 2002—. Sr. staff engr. Hazeltine Corp., Greenlawn, N.Y., 1981-82; pres. DR Cons. Services, Stony Brook; cons. S. Cons. Svc., SCS Telecom, Inc., Sands Point, N.Y., Grumman Aerospace, Bethpage, N.Y. Contbr.a rticles to profl. jours. and books. Mem. IEEE (sr., dir. edn. com.), Am. Soc. Engring. Edn., N.Y. Acad. Sci., Sigma Xi, Eta Kappa Nu, Tau Beta Pi. Avocations: home computing, swimming, touring, hiking.

UCCIARDO, FRANK JOSEPH, television journalist, reporter; b. N.Y.C. s. Joseph J. and Jeanne Barraca Ucciardo. BFA in Comms., MA in Comms., N.Y. Inst. Tech. UN corr. Mut. Radio Network, N.Y.C.; corr. Newsday, Melville, N.Y., CNN Cable News Network, N.Y.C.; anchorman Fin. News Network; corr. NBC Radio Network; bur. chief UPI Radio; reporter NEWS 12, L.I., N.Y.; TV journalist, investigative reporter Sta. WPIX-TV, N.Y.C.; film cameraman, editor Channel 67, Action News, Long Island, N.Y.; dir., prodr. All Points Broadcasting, N.Y.C.; reporter Sta. WOR-Radio 710; corr., anchorman Sta. WLIW-TV PBS, Garden City, N.Y.; anchor, reporter Sta. WATR-TV, Channel 20, Waterbury, Conn.; reporter Sta. WNEW Radio, N.Y.C.; TV journalist, investigative reporter UPN 9 News, Secaucus, N.J., 2000—. Writer, dir., prodr.: (documentary) The Berlin Candy Bomber, 1998 (Deadline Club News Feature award Soc. Profl. Journalists 1999). Folio award for investigative reporting L.I. Coalition for Fair Broadcasting, 1996, (2), 2000, award for investigative journalism Silaurian Soc. N.Y.; RIAS fellow in econs. and politics. Mem. UN Corrs. Assn. (broadcasting chmn. UN hdqs. 1996), Soc. Profl. Journalists (treas. Deadline club, Deadline Club News Feature award 1999), Am. Fedn. Radio & T.V. Artists, NATAS (N.Y. chpt., Emmy award N.Y. chpt. 1997), N.Y. Press Club (emeritus mem.), Drama Desk of N.Y., Press Club L.I. Avocations: travel, cinema, dance, boating, theater. E-mail: unca42@usa.net.

UCHIDA, JANICE YUKIKO, plant pathologist/mycologist, researcher; b. Kealakekua, Hawaii, Jan. 17, 1949; d. Tamotsu Tom and Misao (Oshima) Kadooka; m. Raymond Sueyoshi Uchida; children: Duane, Janelle. BA in Botany, U. Hawaii, 1970, MS in Bot. Sci., 1972, D in Bot. Sci. in Plant Pathology, 1984. Instr. dept. gen. sci. U. Hawaii, Honolulu, 1972-76, rsch. assoc. dept. plant pathology, 1976-87, asst. plant pathologist dept. plant pathology, 1987-94, assoc. plant pathologist dept. plant pathologist, 1994—. Contbr. rsch. articles and papers to sci. jours. Coord. Urata Music, Honolulu, 1995—. Ednl. Challenge grantee USDA, 1997-99, grantee State of Hawaii, 1980-95, 96—, USDA, 1999—; NSF scholar, 1995-96. Mem. Am. Phytopathol. Soc., Mycol. Soc. Am., Phi Kappa Phi, Gamma Sigma Delta. Office: U Hawaii Dept Plant Pathology and Environ Protect 3190 Maile Way Honolulu HI 96822-2232 Fax: 808-956-2832. E-mail: juchida@hawaii.edu.

UCHIDA, MITSUKO, pianist; b. Dec. 20, 1948; d. Fujio and Yasuko Uchida. Student, Hochschule für Musik, Vienna, Austria. Performer: performs regularly with Berlin Philharm., Vienna Philharm., Cleve. Orch., others, recs. include complete piano sonatas and concertos of Mozart, Beethoven's piano concertos, Debussy's Etudes, Schumann's Carnaval, Schoenberg Piano Concerto. Recipient 1st prize, Beethoven Competition, Vienna, 1968, Gramophone award, 2001. Achievements include First recital at age 14 in Vienna; performed complete Mozart sonatas in London, 1982, Tokyo, 1983, N.Y.C., 1991. Avocation: music. Address: Van Walsum Mgmt Ltd 4 Addison Bridge Pl London W14 8XP England E-mail: mail@vanwalsum.co.uk.

UCHIDA, PRENTISS SUSUMU, entrepreneur, management executive; b. Nov. 30, 1940; s. Fred Toshio and Elise Chiyoye (Kurasaki) U.; m. Patrica Ann White, Oct. 17, 1981; children: S. Akemi, Toshio C., K. Kansai P. BA, San Jose State U., 1963; postgrad., Santa Clara U. Bus. Sch., 1965, Stanford U. Exec. Inst., 1975. Programmer Lockheed Missiles & Space Co., Sunnyvale, Calif., 1963-66, Adage Inc., L.A., 1966-69; founder, pres., chmn. Vector Gen. Inc., Woodland Hills, Calif., 1969-79; pres. InnerGame Corp., L.A., 1979-83; chmn. bd., CEO Secom Gen. Corp., Calabasas, Calif., 1984-86; pres. Rice Sys. Co., 1981-89. Bd. dirs. Instar Informatique, Paris; chmn. bd. dirs. Potter Electronics, Inc., Yanceyville, N.C., 1984-86, Secom Communications Co., Southfield, Mich., 1984-86, Nickel Equipment Co., Grand Rapids, Mich., 1985-86; mgmt. cons., Agoura, Calif., 1986-87; real estate developer, Palm Beach County, Fla., 1987-91, Futurestrader, Jupiter, Fla., 1989-91, nat. mktg. dir. and ind. distbr. Nat. Safety Assocs., Memphis, 1990-97, pres. VanderBolt Co., 1995-98, Getbetter, Inc., Agoura Hills, Calif., 1998—, InKahootz, Inc., San Francisco, 2001--. Mem. adv. com. Stanford U. Exec. Inst., 1975—76; bd. dirs. United Crusade/United Way, 1977—79. Mem. Assn. Computer Machinery, Am. Mgmt. Assn., Aircraft Owners and Pilots Assn., Jupiter C. of C., Thousand Lakes/Westlake Village C. of C., Calabasas C. of C.

UCHINO, KENJI, electrical engineer; b. Tokyo, Apr. 3, 1950; came to U.S., 1991; s. Yutaka and Akie (Hamazaki) U.; m. Michiko Uchino. BSc, Tokyo Inst. Tech., 1973, MS, 1975, PhD, 1981. Rsch. assoc. Tokyo Inst. Tech., 1976-85; assoc. prof. Sophia U., Tokyo, 1985-93; prof. Pa. State U., University Park, 1991—. Dir. Internat. Ctr. for Actuators & Transducers, Pa. State U., 1992—; v.p. NF Elec. Instruments, Inc., 1992-94; exec. assoc. editor Kluwer Academic, Boston, 1994—; profl. com. mem. Space Shuttle Utilizing Com., Tokyo, 1986-88; standing auditor Tokyo Savor Elec. Co., Ltd., 1986-91. Author: Piezoelectric/Electrostrictive Actuators, 1986, Piezoelectric Actuators — Problem Solving, 1991, Piezoelectric Actuators and Ultrasonic Motors, 1997; editor (video) Piezoelectric Actuators, 1991. Recipient Best Paper award Japan Soc. Oil/Air Pressure Control, 1987, Best Movie Meml. award Japan Sci. Movie Fesitval, 1989. Fellow Am. Ceramics Soc.; mem. IEEE, Japanese Soc. Applied Physics, Smart Actuators/Sensors Soc. (chmn.), Japan Tech. Transfer Assn. Achievements include patents for multiple ceramic actuator designs. Office: Pa State U 134 Materials Research Lab University Park PA 16802-4800

UCHITELLE, LOUIS, journalist; b. N.Y.C., Mar. 21, 1932; s. Abraham and Alice Lee (Cronbach) U.; m. Joan Eva Shapiro, Oct. 7, 1966; children: Isabel Anne, Jennifer Emily. BA, U. Mich., 1954. Reporter Mt. Vernon (N.Y.) Daily Argus, 1955-57; with AP, 1957-80, fgn. corr. and bur. chief P.R., 1964-67, Buenos Aires, 1967-73; supervising editor AP Newsfeatures, N.Y.C., 1974-76; bus. news editor AP, 1977-80; asst. bus. and fin. editor N.Y. Times, 1980-87, econ. writer, 1987—. Instr. journalism Sch. Gen. Studies, Columbia U., 1976-89. Home: 11 Ridgecrest W Scarsdale NY 10583-2046 Office: NY Times 229 W 43rd St New York NY 10036-3959

UCHRIN, CHRISTOPHER GEORGE, environmental engineer and scientist; b. South Amboy, N.J., Oct. 27, 1950; s. George Christopher and Annette Rose Marie (Skokan) U.; m. Lisa C. Ferguson, July 31, 1998; 1 child, George Henry. B in Civil Engring., Manhattan Coll., 1972, M. in Environ. Engring., 1974; PhD in Environ. Engring., U. Mich., 1980. Registered profl. engring. N.Y. Environ. engr. U.S. EPA, N.Y.C., 1972-77; Rackham fellow U. Mich., Ann Arbor, Mich., 1977-78, rsch. asst., 1978-80; asst. prof. Rutgers U., New Brunswick, N.J., 1980-86, assoc. prof., 1986-90, prof. environ. sci., 1990—. Chair dept. environ. sci. Rutgers U., New Brunswick, 1991-94, dir. grad. program in environ. sci., 1986-91; co-dir. Joint PhD Program in Exposure Assessment, Rutgers U. & UMDNJ/Robert Wood Johnson Med. Sch., 1991—, coord. undergrad. curriculum in bioresource engring., 1999—. Mem. ASCE, Am. Chem. Soc., Water Environment Fedn., Am. Soc. for Materials, Soc. Environ. Toxicology and Chemistry, N.J. Acad. Sci. (pres. 1991-92). Office: Rutgers U Dept Environ Sci PO Box 231 New Brunswick NJ 08903-0231

UCHUPI, ELAZAR, geologist, researcher; b. N.Y.C., Oct. 31, 1928; parents Alfonso and Carmen (Urbizu) U. BS, CCNY, 1952; MS, U. So. Calif., 1954, PhD, 1962. Rsch. asst. U. So. Calif., L.A., 1955-62, Woods Hole (Mass.) Oceanographic Inst., 1962-64, assoc. scientist, 1964-79; sr. scientist Woods Hole (Mass.) Oceanog. Inst., 1979-93, sr. scientist emeritus, 1993—, J. Seward Johnson chmn. oceanography, 1989-93. Mem. Gulf of Mexico panel Joint Oceanog. Instns. Deep Earth Sampling, 1972-74; mem. Sci. Com. for Oceanic Rsch. Working Group 41, 1973-74; mem. steering com. U.S. Oceanog. Office Relief Map Worlds' Oceans; mem. site survey panel Joint Oceanog. Instns., 1978-85; compiler geol. maps on ocean margin drilling; adj. rschr. Inst. Exploration, Mystic, Conn., 1997—. Mem. editl. staff Offshore Mag., 1972-74, Marine Geology, 1971-75; co-author 4 books North Atlantic, geology of Atlantic Ocean, and morphology of rocky mems. of Solar Sys. Recipient cert. of recognition Nat. Assn. Geology Tchrs., Inc., and its Crustal evolution Edn. project, 1979, medal editl. adv. bd. Offshore Mag., 1974, Frances P. Shepard award, 1991. Mem. Am. Geophys. Union, Archeol. Inst. Am., Sociedad Geologica de España. Achievements include research in seismic reflection, magnetic and gravity profiles of the eastern Atlantic continental margin and adjacent deep seafloor, Caribbean, Bahamas, Iberian Margins, New England margin, Branefield Trough, South Scotia Ridge, Canary Islands, Red Sea, Persian Gulf, Gulf of Oman, Black Sea, Egyptian Margin, Western Mediterranean, East Pacific Rise, Mohns Ridge, suspended matter and other properities of surface waters of the northeastern Atlantic Ocean, the continental margin off western Africa: Angola to Sierra Leone, Senegal to Portugal, sediments of 3 bays of Baja, Calif.: Sebastian Viscaino, San Cristobal and Todos Santos, characteristics of sediments of the mainland shelf of southern Calif., submarine geology of the Santa Rosa-Cortes Ridge, sediments on the continental margin off eastern U.S., the continental slope between San Francisco and Cedrow Island, Mex., sediments of the Palos Verdes shelf, sediments and topography of Kane Basin, statistical parameters of Cape Cod Beach and eolian sands, basins of Gulf of Mex., structure of Georges Bank, and the continental margin of the Atlantic coast of the U.S. and off west Africa, topography and structure of Northeast Channel, Gulf of Mex., and Cashes Ledge, Gulf of Maine, distribution and geologic structure of Triassic rocks in the Bay of Fundy and the northeastern part of the Gulf of Maine, microrelief of the continental margin south of Cape Lookout, N.C., shallow structure of the Straits of Fla., sub-surface morphology of L.I., Block Island, Rhode Island sounds, and Buzzards Bay, bathymetry of the Gulf of Mex., slumping on the continental margin southeast of L.I., N.Y., woody debris on the mainland shelf off Ventura, southern Calif., the continental margin south of Cape Hatteras, N.C., the Atlantic continental shelf and slope of the U.S., geological structure of the continental margin off Gulf Coast of the U.S., and more. Office: Woods Hole Oceanographic Inst Dept Geology Geophysic Woods Hole MA 02543

UCKO, DAVID ALAN, museum consultant; b. N.Y.C., July 9, 1948; s. Lawrence L. and Helen H. Ucko; m. Barbara Alice Clark, Aug. 13, 1977; 1 child Aaron. BA, Columbia Coll., N.Y.C., 1969; PhD, MIT, 1972. Asst. prof. chemistry Hostos C.C., CUNY, Bronx, 1972-76, Antioch Coll., Yellow Springs, Ohio, 1976-79, assoc. prof. chemistry, 1979; rsch. coord. Mus. Sci. and Industry, Chgo., 1979-80, dir. sci., 1981-87, v.p., 1986-87; dep. dir. Calif. Mus. Sci. and Industry, L.A., 1987-90; pres. Kansas City (Mo.) Mus., 1990-2000, Sci. City at Union Sta., 1999-2000; exec. dir. Koshland Sci. Mus. and Sci. Outreach, NAS, Washington, 2001—02; pres. Mus. + More LLC, 2002—; guest faculty mus. mgmt. program U. Colo., Boulder, Colo., 2001—. Rsch. assoc., assoc. prof. dept. edn. U. Chgo., 1982—87; adj. staff scientist C. F. Kettering Rsch. Lab., Yellow Springs, 1977—79. Author: (book) Basics for Chemistry, 1982, Living Chemistry, 2d edit.; contbr. articles to profl. jours.; host, prodr. (radio program) Science Alive!, 1983—87, developer numerous mus. exhibits. Apptd. Nat. Mus. Svcs. Bd., 1996; v.p., bd. dirs. Heritage League, Greater Kansas City, 1991—92; mem. Mid. Am. Regional Coun. Regional Amenities Task Force, Kansas City, 1990—96; trustee Mus. Without Walls, 1996—2000, Sci. Pioneers, 2000; bd. dirs. Cultural Alliance Greater Kansas City, 1995—98. Recipient Up and Comers award, Jr. Achievement Mid.-Am., 1992; fellow Woodrow Wilson, 1969, NIH postdoctoral, 1972; grantee, NSF, NEH, U.S. Dept. Edn., Ill. Humanities Coun., 1976—88. Fellow: AAAS (at large sect. Y 1987—93); mem.: Greater Kansas City C. of C. (edn. com. 1993—96), Assn. Sci. Tech. Ctrs. (publs. com. 1984—94, chmn. 1988—94, ethics com. 1994—95, legis. com., chmn. 1996—2000), Phi Lambda Upsilon, Sigma Xi, Alpha Sigma Nu (hon.). Home: 2528 Queen Anne's Ln NW Washington DC 20037

UCKO, FRANZ, research scientist, consultant, writer; b. Kattowitz, Silesia, Germany, Sept. 28, 1919; naturalized, 1946; s. Arthur and Else Ucko; m. Betty Jean Eshelman, Mar. 20, 1948 (div. Feb. 1993); children: John Arthur (dec.), Marianne Elizabeth; m. Ruth Helene Holmes, July 1, 1997. Degree in mech. engring., Technische Hochschule, Berlin, Germany, 1939. Dir. R&D Buckbee-Mears Co., St. Paul, 1949-59; mgr. microlithography Motorola Semiconductors, Phoenix, 1960-63; sr. rsch. scientist Control Data Corp., Mpls., 1964-86. Rsch. cons. Cross Tech., Mpls., 1987-90. Author: A New Beginning, 1993; patentee in field; contbr. articles to profl. jours. Chair citizens adv coun. Hubbs Ctr. for Continuing Learning, St. Paul, 1999. With U.S. Army, 1945-47, lt., 1947-48, PTO. Recipient Outstanding Svc. award St. Paul Cmty. Edn. Adv. Coun., 2001. Presbyterian. Avocations: writing, lithographic jewelry making. Home: 664 Sextant Ave W Roseville MN 55113-3425

UDAGAWA, TAKESHI, physicist, educator; b. Tokyo, May 3, 1932; came to U.S., 1970; s. Saheiji Udagawa and Teruko (Yamazaki) Urayama; m. Yukiko Amano, Mar. 20, 1960 (dec. Oct. 1989); children: Yoichi, Taturo; m. Mami Eto, Apr. 15, 1991. BS, Tokyo Inst. Sci., 1957; MS, Tokyo U. of Edn., 1959, PhD, 1962. Instr. Tokyo Inst. Tech., 1962-64; rsch. assoc. Fla. State U., Tallahassee, 1964-66; rsch. fellow Niels Bohn Inst., Copenhagen, 1966-68; assoc. prof. Kyoto (Japan) U., 1968-70; prof. dept. physics U. Tex., Austin, 1970—. Rsch. fellow Kernforschungsanlage, Juelich, Germany, 1981-95. Contbr. articles to profl. jours. Rsch. grantee Dept. Energy, Washington, 1970-96. Mem. Am. Phys. Soc., Japanese Phys. Soc. Achievements include contbns. to various aspects of nuclear reaction theories. Home: 4018 Amy Cir Austin TX 78759-8146 Office: U Tex Dept Physics Austin TX 78712 E-mail: udagawa@physics.utexas.edu.

UDALL, CALVIN HUNT, lawyer; b. St. Johns, Ariz., Oct. 23, 1923; s. Grover C. and Dora (Sherwood) U.; m. Doris Fuss, Dec. 11, 1943; children: Fredric, Margaret Udall Moses, Julie (Mrs. Blair M. Nash), Lucinda Udall Romney, Tina Udall Rodriguez. LL.B., U. Ariz., 1948. Bar: Ariz. 1948. Ptnr. Fennemore Craig, 1953—. Ariz. spl. counsel Arizona v. California, 1954-62; mem. Coun. on Legal Edn. Opportunity, 1983-93. Mem. cast, Phoenix Mus. Theatre, 1959-65. Fellow Am. Coll. Trial Lawyers, Am. Bar Found. (bd. dirs. 1986-89, fellows chmn. 1988-89), Ariz. Bar Found. (Disting. Svc. award 1993); mem. ABA (ho. dels. 1962-92, bd. govs. 1981-84, exec. com. 1983-84, chmn. task force on minorities 1984-86), Maricopa County Bar Assn. (pres. 1957, Disting. Pub. Svc. award 1986), State Bar Ariz. (bd. govs. 1960-65), Ariz. Law Coll. Assn. (bd. dirs. 1967-80, pres. 1978-79, U. Ariz. Disting. Citizen award 1984, bd. visitors 1991—). Office: Fennemore Craig 3003 N Central Ave Ste 2600 Phoenix AZ 85012-2913

UDALL, JOHN NICHOLAS, JR. pediatric gastroenterologist; b. Washington, Dec. 30, 1940; BS, Brigham Young U., 1965; MD, Temple U., 1969; PhD, MIT, 1980. Diplomate Nat. Bd. Med. Examiners, Am. Bd. Pediatrics, Sub-bd. Pediatric Gastroenterology, Am. Bd. Nutrition; lic. physician Calif., Mass., Ariz., La. Rotating intern L.A. County/U. So. Calif. Med. Ctr., L.A., 1969-70, resident in pediatrics, 1972-74; postdoctoral rsch. fellow in pediatric gastroenterology Baylor Coll. Medicine, Houston, 1974-76; postdoctoral rsch. fellow pediatric pharmacology neonatology U. Ariz. Health Scis. Ctr., Tucson, 1976-77; postdoctoral rsch. fellow in clin. nutrition Children's Hosp., Harvard Med. Sch., Boston, 1977-79; instr. pediatrics, asst. prof. pediatrics Harvard Med. Sch., 1979-81, 81-86; lectr. dept. nutrition/food sci., asst. dir. clin. rsch. ctr MIT, Cambridge, Mass., 1980-85; sci. staff, dir. pediatric rsch. Shriners Burn Inst., Boston, 1981-86, 85-86; assoc. prof. pediatrics U. Ariz. Coll. Medicine, Tucson, 1986-92; prof. pediatrics La. State U., New Orleans, 1992—; chief sect. pediatric gastroenterology and nutrition New Orleans Children's Hosp., 1992—; clin. prof. pediatrics Sch. Medicine Tulane U., New Orleans, 1992—. Resident physician Clin. Rsch. Ctr., MIT, 1977-80, prin. investigator, 1980-85; assoc. staff physician Mass. Rehab. Hosp., Boston, 1978-85; asst. in pediatrics Mass. Gen. Hosp., Boston, 1979-86; dir. nutrition support svc. Children's Hosp., Boston, 1983-85, assoc. in medicine/gastroenterology, 1983-86; dir. sect. pediatric gastroenterology U. Ariz. Health Scis. Ctr., Tucson, 1986-92. Contbr. numerous articles to profl. jours., chpts. to books; editorial bd. Mass. Gen. Hosp. Dietary Manual, 1982, Seminars in Pediatric Gastroenterology and Nutrition, 1990—, Healthy Kids: The Magazine for Parents, 1990—, Jour. Pediatric Gastroenterology and Nutrition, 1991—, Nutrition: The Internat. Jour. of Applied and Basic Nutrition Scis., 1993—; editorial adv. bd. Snyder Comms., Rockville, Md., 1990-92; book rev. editor Jour. Pediatric Gastroenterology and Nutrition, 1983-90. With USPHS, 1970-72. Grantee NIH, 1978-80, 81-83, 83-86, 84-89, 86-89, 1993, Shriners Hosp., 1986-89, Ariz. Disease Control Rsch. Commn., 1988-90, U. Ariz. Small Grants Project, 1988-89, Joseph and Mary Cacioppo Found., 1988-89. Fellow Am. Acad. Pediatrics; mem. Internat. Soc. Supramolecular Biology, N.Am. Soc. for Pediatric Gastroenterology, Soc. for Pediatric Rsch., Am. Burn Assn., AAAS, Am. Soc. Clin. Nutrition (nomination com.

1993), Am. Inst. Nutrition, Western Soc. Pediatric Rsch., Am. Gastroenterol. Assn., Nat. Ileitis and Colitis Found., Am. Soc. Parenteral and Enteral Nutrition, Pima County Pediatric Soc. (sec. 1988), Ariz. Pediatric Soc., Am. Pediatric Soc., Tucson Area Soc. Parenteral and Enteral Nutrition Office: Children's Hosp Pediatric Gastroenterology 200 Henry Clay Ave New Orleans LA 70118-5720

UDALL, MARK, congressman; b. Tucson, July 18, 1950; m. Maggie Fox; children: Jed, Tess. B.Am. Civilization, Williams Coll., 1972. Course dir., educator Colo. Outward Bound Sch., 1975-85, exec. dir., 1985-95; mem. dist. 13 Colo. Ho. of Reps., 1997-99; mem. U.S. Congress from 2d Colo. dist., Washington, 1999—; Dem. dep. regional whip for western U.S.; mem. resources com., small bus. com., sci. com. Democrat. Avocation: mountain climbing. also: 1333 W 120th Ave Ste 210 Westminster CO 80234-2710 Office: US House of Representitives 115 Cannon HOuse Office Building Washington DC 20515*

UDALL, THOMAS (TOM UDALL), congressman; b. Tucson, May 18, 1948; s. Stewart and Lee Udall; m. Jill Z. Cooper; 1 child, Amanda Cooper. BA, Prescott Coll., 1970; LLB, Cambridge U., Eng., 1975; JD, U. N.Mex., 1977. Law clk. to Hon. Oliver Seth U.S. Ct. Appeals (10th cir.), Santa Fe, 1977-78; asst. U.S. atty. U.S. Atty.'s Office, 1978-81; pvt. practice Santa Fe, 1981-83; chief counsel N.Mex. Health & Environ. Dept., 1983-84; ptnr. Miller, Stratvert, Togerson & Schlenker, P.A., Albuquerque, 1985-90; atty. gen. State of N.Mex., 1991-98; mem. 106th Congress from NM 3rd dist., 1999—, mem. small bus. com., mem. resources com., mem. vets.' affairs com. Past pres. Rio Chama Preservation Trust; mem. N.Mex. Environ. Improvement Bd., 1986—87; bd. dirs. La Compania de Teatro de Albuquerque, Santa Fe Chamber Music Festival, Law Fund. Mem. Nat. Assn. Attys. Gen. (pres. 1996), Kiwanis. Democrat. Office: US Ho Reps 502 Cannon HOB Washington DC 20515-0001 E-mail: tom.udall@mail.house.gov.*

UDASHEN, ROBERT NATHAN, lawyer; b. Amarillo, Tex., June 10, 1953; s. Leo Joe and Esther K. (Klugsberg) U.; m. Dale Lynn Sandgarten, Aug. 15, 1976. BA with high honors, U. Tex., 1974, JD, 1977. Bar: Tex. 1977, U.S. Ct. Appeals (5th cir.) 1978, U.S. Dist. Ct. (no. and so. dists.) Tex. 1978, U.S. Ct. Appeals (11th cir.) 1981, U.S. Supreme Ct. 1981, U.S. Dist. Ct. (ea. dist.) Tex. 1989, U.S. Dist. Ct. (we. dist.) Tex. 1991, U.S. Dist. Ct. (ea. and we. dists.) Ark. 2000, U.S. Ct. Appeals (8th cir.) 2002. Staff atty. Staff Counsel for Inmates, Huntsville, Tex., 1977-79; assoc., ptnr. Crowder, Mattox & Udashen, Dallas, 1979-85; ptnr. Udashen & Goldstucker, 1985-87; pvt. practice, 1987-94; ptnr. Milner, Lobel, Goranson, Sorrels, Udashen & Wells, Dallas, 1995-2000, Milner, Goranson, Sorrels, Udashen & Wells, Dallas, 2000—02, Sorrels & Udashen, Dallas, 2002—. Bd. dirs. Open, Inc., Dallas; instr. trial advocacy Sch. Law So. Meth. U., 1993-95; adj. prof. criminal procedure Sch. Law So. Meth. U., 1998-99, 2001-02. Contbr. articles to profl. jours. Adv. bd. Coalition for Safer Dallas, 1994. Mem. State Bar Tex. (penal code com. 1992-93), Nat. Assn. Criminal Def. Lawyers, Tex. Criminal Def. Lawyers Assn., Dallas Criminal Def. Lawyers Assn. Office: Sorrels & Udashen 2301 Cedar Springs Rd Ste 400 Dallas TX 75201 E-mail: rnu@surrelsudashen.com.

UDDIN, NASIM, civil engineer, educator; b. Chittagong, Bangladesh, Jan. 3, 1963; came to U.S., 1988; s. Jalal Ahmed and Jainab Begam; m. Jamina Jabeen, Mar. 20, 1994. BSCE, Bangladesh U. Engring. and Tech., Bangladesh, 1986; MSCE, U. Okla., 1989; PhD, SUNY, Buffalo, 1992. Registered profl. engr., Ind., N.Y. Lectr. civil engring. Bangladesh U. Engring. and Tech., Bangladesh, 1986-88; staff engr. Acres Internat., Buffalo, 1992-97; asst. prof. U. Evansville, Ind., 1997—; assoc. prof. U. Ala., Birmingham, 2001—; assoc. scientist Ctr. Disaster Preparedness, 2001—. Contbr. articles to profl. jours. Coord. HAZUS Program, Evansville, 1997—; exec. com. Disaster Resistant Cmty., Evansville, 1997—. Mem.: ABET (assessment coord. 2001—), Internat. Com. Large Dams, Internat. Soc. Computational Engring., Am. Soc. Engring. Edn., ASCE (mem. nat. com. engring. mgmt. and bus. practices 2001—), Islamic Soc. Evansville (gen. sec. 1998—). Avocations: jogging, weight lifting, gardening. Home: 3747 Rolling Rock Ave Evansville IN 47711 Office: U Ala Dept Civil and Environ Engring Birmingham AL 35294-4440 E-mail: nuddin@uab.edu.

UDEBIUWA, OPARAUGO IHENTUGE, psychiatrist; b. Lagos, Nigeria, July 5, 1959; came to the U.S., 1988; s. Moses Ezebunwa and Florinda Nnenna Udebiuwa; m. Angela Chinyere Udebiuwa, Nov. 18, 1995; children: Victoria, Amanze, Anagamelcchi. Student, U. Nigeria, Nsukka, 1977-80; MD, U. Nigeria, Enugu, 1984. Intern Howard U., Washington, 1990-91, resident, 1991-94, chief resident dept. psychiatry, 1993; attending psychiatrist Walter P. Carter Ctr., Dept. Health and Mental Hygiene, Balt., 1994—; staff psychiatrist Health Svcs. Dept. Corrections Washington, Lorton, Va., 1993—2001. Diplomate Am. Bd. Psychiatrists and Neurologists; mem. AMA, Nat. Med. Assn., Am. Psychiat. Assn., U. Nigeria Alumni Assn. (pres. Washington chpt. 1993—). Avocations: table tennis, reading, dancing. Office: Walter P Carter Ctr 630 W Fayette St Baltimore MD 21201-1585 E-mail: oudebiuwa@yahoo.com.

UDEN, DAVID ELLIOTT, cardiologist, educator; b. Montreal, Sept. 7, 1936; s. Reginald and Elsie Ada (Elliott) U.; children: Thomas Elliott, Linda Ann, Christopher Elliott. BSc, McGill U., 1958; MD, McGill U., Quebec, Can., 1962. Diplomate Am. Bd. Internal Medicine; cert. cardiovascular disease, cert. interventional cardiology. Attending cardiologist Toronto Western Hosp., 1972-93, The Wellesley Hosp., Toronto, 1990-93; asst. prof. medicine U. Toronto, 1975-93; chief of cardiology Oconee Meml. Hosp., Seneca, S.C., 1993-97, chief of medicine, 1994-96, 2000—; elected mem. S.C. Med. Discipline Commn., 1996-98, 2000—; apptd. Discipline Commn., 2000—. Contbr. articles to sci. and profl. jours. With RCAF, 1963-66. Fellow Am. Coll. Cardiology, Am. Heart Assn. Coun. on Clin. Cardiology. Avocations: travel, photography. Office: Oconee Cardiology Assocs 109 A Omni Dr Seneca SC 29672

UDEVITZ, NORMAN, publishing executive; b. Cheyenne, Wyo., Jan. 22, 1929; s. Jay and Edith (Stienberg) U.; m. Marsha Rae Dinner, Dec. 17, 1960; children: Jane, Kathryn, Andrew. Student, U. Colo., 1946-49. With Cheyenne Newspapers Inc. Cheyenne, 1949-54; editor-pub. Wyo. Buffalo, Cheyenne, 1954-63; account supr. Tilds & Cantz Advt. Agy., L.A., 1963-66; exec. v.p. Fitzgerald, Maahs & Miller, 1966-71; staff writer The Denver Post, 1971-88; dir. pubs. Am. Water Works Assn., Denver, 1988-97; ret., 1997. Sgt. USNG, 1950-53. Named Colo.'s Outstanding Journalist, U. Colo., 1977; recipient Pulitzer Prize Gold medal Columbia U., 1986. Mem. Investigative Reporters and Editors Inc., (bd. dirs. 1978-80, 81-83), The Newspaper Guild (McWilliams award 1976, 77). Jewish. Home: 4677 E Euclid Ave Littleton CO 80121-3224

UDLER, RUBIN YAKOVLEVITCH, linguist; b. Braila, Muntenia, Romania, Sept. 27, 1925; came to U.S., 1992; s. Yakov Aronovitch and Dina Vladimirovna (Gleizer) U.; m. Malka Il'initchna Alexenberg, July 8, 1956; children: Arthur, Angela. B in Philol. Sci., U. Chernovtsy, Ukraine, 1951; M in Philol. Sci., USSR Acad. Scis., Moscow, 1961; D in Philol. Sci., USSR Acad. Scis., Leningrad, 1974. Dep. chmn. fgn. langs. dept. Chernovtsy State Pedagogical Inst., 1951-56; jr. sci. rschr. dialectology sect. Moldavian br. USSR Acad. Scis., Kishinev, Moldova, 1956-61; chief dialectology and exptl. phonetics sect. Moldavian Acad. Scis., 1961-80, chief dialectology and history of lang. sect., 1980-86, chief dialectology and linguistic geography dept., 1986-92, dep. of academician-sec. of social studies dept., 1989-92; ctr. assoc. U. Ctr. for Internat. Studies U. Pitts., 1994—. Translator Soviet Bucovina newspaper, Chernovtsy, 1951-52; mem. editl. bd. Moldavian Lang. and Lit., 1961-91, Jour. Linguistics and Study of Lit., 1991-92; sr. sci. rschr. All-Union Cert. Com., Moscow, 1963; presentor at cong., confs., and symposiums. Author: Moldavian Dialects of the Chernovtsy Area Consonantism, 1964, Dialectological Division of the Moldavian Language, Parts 1 and 2, 1976; co-author: The Moldavian Linguistic Atlas, 4 parts, 1968-73, Dialectological Dictionary, 5 vols., 1985-86, Dialectological Texts, 6 parts, 1969-87, The Historical Grammar of the Moldavian Language, 1964, Notes on Modern Moldavian Literary Language, 1967, Moldavian Dialectology, 1976, The Carpathian Dialectological Atlas, 6 vols., 1987-98; author more than 235 pub. works with total volume of more than 430 editl. sheets; mng. editor, co-editor approximately 60 monographs, dictionaries, atlases, collection of dialectological texts, collections of articles, theses, brochures with total volume of more than 1275 editl. sheets. Corr. mem. Moldavian Acad. Scis. Presidium of Moldavian Acad. Scis.; mem. Holocaust Ctr. United Jewish Fedn. Greater Pitts. Jewish. Avocations: collecting old books, coins, travel. Home: 1535 Shady Ave Pittsburgh PA 15217-1455 Office: Univ Ctr Internat Studies U Pitts 41 G40 Forbes Quadrangle Pittsburgh PA 15260

UDOFF, ERIC JOEL, diagnostic radiologist; b. Balt., Oct. 8, 1948; s. Melvin Jerome and Esther (Fisher) U.; m. Ronni Ann Chapin, June 7, 1980; children: Brian Evan, Jonathan Andrew. AB, Washington U., 1969; MD, U. Rochester, 1973. Intern, resident in diagnostic radiology U. Chgo., 1973-77; instr. in cardiovasc. radiology Johns Hopkins U., Balt., 1977-79; radiologist Sinai Hosp., 1979-86, Mt. Sinai Med. Ctr., Milw., 1986-88, Sinai Hosp., Balt., 1988-90; asst. prof. radiology Johns Hopkins U. Hosp., 1990-91; radiologist North Fulton Regional Hosp., Roswell, Ga., 1991-97; instr. thoracoabdominal imaging U. Va., 1997-98, Radiologist, Diagnostic Imaging Specialists, Atlanta, 1998—. Mem. AMA, Am. Roentgen Ray Soc., Am. Coll. Radiology, Radiol. Soc. N.Am., Ga. Radiol. Soc., Phi Beta Kappa. Avocation: reading, tennis. Office: 340 West Ponce de Leon Ave PO Box 1007 Decatur GA 30031-1007 E-mail: esurad@aol.com.

UDOWITZ, ROBERT HOWARD, public relations executive; b. Bklyn., Oct. 21, 1963; s. Stanley and Jane Ruth (Pearl) U.; m. Kristen Karczewski, Nov. 9, 1996. BA, SUNY, Buffalo, 1985. Intern Burson-Marsteller, N.Y.C., 1984; account exec. Howard J. Rubenstein Assocs., 1986-90; pub. rels. mgr. Devel. Corp. for Israel, 1991-94; corp. comm. assoc. Connie Lee Ins. Corp., Washington, 1994-95; sr. counsellor Powell-Tate, 1995-98; mng. supr. Fleishman-Hillard, 1998—2001; corp. comm. mgr. Am. Mgmt. Systems, Fairfax, Va., 2001—. Mem. Pub. Rels. Soc. Am., Soc. Coll. Journalists (treas. 1982-85, Best News Story 1984), Publicity Club N.Y. Avocations: photography, music. Office: Am Mgmt Systems 4050 Legato Rd Fairfax VA 22033 E-mail: udowitz@usa.net.

UDVARHELYI, GEORGE BELA, neurosurgery educator emeritus, cultural affairs administrator; b. Budapest, Hungary, May 14, 1920; came to U.S., 1955; s. Bela and Margaret (Bakacs) U.; m. Elspeth Mary Campbell, July 24, 1956; children: Ian Steven, Susan Margaret, Jane Elizabeth. BS, St. Stephen Coll., 1938; MD, U. Budapest, 1944, U. Buenos Aires, 1952; D honoris causa, Semmelweis Med. Sch., Budapest, 1988, Western Md. Coll., 1997. Diplomate Am. Bd. Neurol. Surgery. Intern resident in surgery Red Cross Hosp./11th Mil. Hosp., Budapest, 1942-44; asst. resident Neurol. Univ. Clinic, 1944-46; postdoctoral fellow U. Vienna, Austria, 1946-47; fgn. asst. Psychiat. Clinic, U. Berne, Switzerland, 1947-48; asst. resident in neurosurgery Hosp. Espanol, Cordoba, Argentina, 1948-50; resident neurosurgeon Inst. Neurosurgery, U. Buenos Aires, 1950-53; asst. Neurolsurgical Clinic, U. Cologne, Fed. Republic Germany, 1953-54; registrar Royal Infirmary, Edinburgh, Scotland, 1954-55; from fellow to full prof. Johns Hopkins U., Balt., 1955-84, prof. emeritus, dir. cultural affairs, 1984-92, assoc. prof. radiology, 1963-84, Phi Beta Kappa lectr., 1980. Neurosurg. cons. Social Security Adminstrn., Balt., 1962-89, Disability Determination Svc., Balt., 1991-93; vis. prof., guest lectr. U. Va., Charlottesville, 1977, Children's Hosp. Ea. Ont., Ottawa, Can., 1977, U. Salzburg, Austria, 1981, U. Vienna, Austria, 1983, Mayo Clinic, Rochester, Minn., 1983, U. Cape Town, Republic of South Africa, 1984, U. Porto, Portugal, 1985; vis. prof. Temple U., Phila., 1979, U. Vt., Burlington, 1980, Aukland (New Zealand) Gen. Hosp., 1989, George Washington U., 1991, U. Mainz, Fed. Republic Germany, 1991, numerous others; lectr. in field. Contbr. numerous articles to profl. jours., book chpts. Mem. program com. Balt. Symphony Orch., 1972-80, edn. com. Walters Art Gallery, Balt., 1985-88. Recipient Lincoln award Am. Hungarian Found., 1980, Eisenberg award Humanities, 1996; Humanities grantee NEH, 1984-91. Fellow ACS; mem. AAUP, Am. Assn. Neurol. Surgeons (life, Humanitarian award 1991), Congress Neurol. Surgeons (sr.), Am. Assn. Neuropathologists, Pan-Am. Med. Assn., Soc. Brit. Neurol. Surgeons (corr.), Pavlovian Soc. N.Am., German Neurol. Soc. (corr.), Internat. Soc. Pediatric Neurosurgery (founding), Hungarian Neurosurg. Soc. (corr.), Argentine Acad. Sci. (corr.), Am. Soc. for Laser Medicine and Surgery (charter), Johns Hopkins Med. Assn., Johns Hopkins Faculty Club, 14 West Hamilton Club (chair steering com. 1977-83), Cosmos Club (chair program subcom. 1991—), Landsdowne Club (London), Alpha Omega Alpha. Roman Catholic. Avocations: music, literature, travel, chess. Home and Office: 111 Hamlet Hill Rd Apt 1414 Baltimore MD 21210-1518

UDWADIA, FIRDAUS ERACH, engineering educator, consultant; b. Bombay, Aug. 28, 1947; came to U.S., 1968. s. Erach Rustam and Perin P. (Lentin) U.; m. Farida Gagrat, Jan. 6, 1977; children: Shanaira, Zubin. BS, Indian Inst. Tech., Bombay, 1968; MS, Calif. Inst. Tech., 1969, PhD, 1972; MBA, U. So. Calif., 1985. Mem. faculty Calif. Inst. Tech., Pasadena, 1972-74; asst. prof. engring. U. So. Calif., Los Angeles, 1974-77, assoc. prof. mech., civil, and aerospace engring. and bus. adminstrn., 1977-83, prof. mech. engring., civil engring. and bus. adminstrn., 1983-86, prof. engring, bus. adminstrn., maths., 1986—, prof. engring., bus. adminstrn., math., 1999—; also bd. dirs. Structural Identification Computing Facility, U. So. Calif. Cons. Jet Propulsion Lab., Pasadena, 1978—, Argonne Nat. Lab., 1982-83, Air Force Rocket Lab., Edwards AFB, Calif., 1984—; vis. prof. applied mechanics and mech. engring. Calif. Inst. Tech., Pasadena, 1993. Editor (assoc.): (jour.) Applied Math. and Computation, Jour. Optimization Theory and Applications, Jour. Franklin Inst., Jour. Differential Equations and Dynamical Sys., Nonlinear Studies, Jour. Math. Analysis and Applications, Jour. Math. Problems in Engring.; editor: Jour. of Aerospace Engring.; author: (book) Analytical Dynamics, A New Approach, 1996; mem. adv. bd.: jour. Jour. Tech. Forecasting and Social Change; editor: Advances in Dynamics and Control, 2000; contbr. articles to profl. jours. Bd. dirs. Crisis Mgmt. Ctr., U. So. Calif. NSF grantee, 1976—; recipient Golden Poet award, 1990. Mem. AIAA, ASCE, Am. Acad. Mechanics, Soc. Indsl. and Applied Math., Seismological Soc. Am., Sigma Xi (Earthquake Engring. Research Inst., 1971, 74, 84). Achievements include patents for in field. Avocations: writing poetry, piano, chess. Home: 2100 S Santa Anita Ave Arcadia CA 91006-4611 Office: U So Calif 430K Olin Hall University Park Los Angeles CA 90007 E-mail: fudwadia@usc.edu.

UECKER, BOB, actor, radio announcer, former baseball player, TV personality; b. Milw., Jan. 26, 1935; m. Judy Uecker, 1976 (div. 2001); 4 children. Major league baseball player Milw. Braves, Nat. League, 1962, 63; major league baseball player St. Louis Cardinals, 1964, 65, Phila. Phillies, 1966-67, Atlanta Braves, 1967; radio-TV announcer Milw. Brewers, 1971—; commentator ABC Monday Night Baseball, 1976-82; commentator playoff and world series NBC Baseball, 1994-98. Host War of the Start, Bob Ueckers Wacky World of Sports, Saturday Night Live; guest Tim Conway show, Who's the Boss, Peter Marshall Show; appeared in Fatal Instinct. Co-star TV series Mr. Belvedere, ABC-TV, 1985-1990; guest TV appearances include Late Night with David Letterman, The Tonight Show, Midnight Special, LateLine, 1998; also numerous commls.; author: Catcher in the Wry, 1985; films include: Major League, 1989, Major League 2, 1994, (voice over) Homeward Bound II: Lost in San Francisco, 1996, Major League: Back to the Minors, 1998, Andre the Giant: Larger Than Life, 1999. Recipient Big B.A.T. award Baseball Assistance Team, 1995; inducted Wis. Performing Artists Hall of Fame, 1993, Wis. Broadcasters Assn. Hall of Fame, 1994, Wis. Sports Hall of Fame, 1998. Office: Milw Brewers Baseball Club Milw County Stadium 1 Brewers Way Milwaukee WI 53214-3651*

UEDA, PEGGY, physician; b. L.A., Oct. 9, 1949; m. Reed Ueda, 1970; children: Katya, Alyona. BA, UCLA, 1970; MA, U. Ill., 1972; MD, Tufts, 1987. Resident in internal medicine New England Deaconess, Boston, 1987-90; physician MGH, 1990; instr. Harvard Med. Sch., 1990; co-investigator Harvard-BCH ACTU, 1990. Med. dir. New England Eye & Tissue Transplant Bank , 1995—2001. Mem. ACP, Mass. Med. Soc. Office: Infectious Disease Assocs M6H-FND 8 Boston MA 02114

UEDA, REED TAKASHI, historian, educator; b. Honolulu, Sept. 14, 1949; s. Goro and Mildred (Yoshimoto) U.; m. Peggy Lynn Rubin, Aug. 9, 1970; children: Katya, Alyona. BA, UCLA, 1970; MA, U. Chgo., 1973, Harvard U., 1976, PhD, 1981. Rsch. editor Harvard Encyclopedia of Am. Ethnic Grups, Cambridge, Mass., 1977-79; instr. Harvard U., 1980-81; prof. Tufts U., Medford, 1981—; assoc. Ctr. for Am. Polit. Studies, Harvard U. Vis. prof. Brandeis U., Waltham, Mass., 1986, Harvard U., 1987—89, 1996, assoc. Ctr. Am. Polit. Studies; mem. steering group com. on internat. migration MIT; mem. Boston History Collaborative, 1998—; staff historian Dreams of Freedom Immigration Mus., Boston, 1999—; mem. planning com. immigration and urban history sem. Mass. Hist. Soc., 1999—. Author: Avenues to Adulthood, 1987, Postwar Immigrant America, 1994; assoc.-editor: Jour. of Interdisciplinary History, 1996—; mem. editl. bd. Harvard Educational Review, 1977-78, Am. Quar., 1993, Mass. Hist. Rev., 2000. Mem. Gov.'s Edn. Reform Rev. Commn., Commonwealth of Mass. Fellow Am. Coun. Learned Soc., Woodrow Wilson Internat. Ctr., NEH, Charles Warren Ctr. Fellow: Mass. Hist. Soc.; mem.: St. Botolph Club. Office: Tufts U Dept History Medford MA 02155

UEHLEIN, E(DWARD) CARL, JR. lawyer; b. Boston, May 7, 1941; s. Edward Carl and Elizabeth (Thatcher) U.; m. Judith Taylor, June 16, 1962; children: Christine, Sara. Student, Bowdoin Coll., Brunswick, Maine, 1958-59; BA, Swarthmore Coll., 1962; LLB, Boston Coll., 1965. Bar: Mass. 1965, D.C. 1968. Atty. Nat. Labor Relations Bd., Atlanta, 1965-68; assoc. Morgan, Lewis & Bockius, Washington, 1968-71; exec. asst. to sec. U.S. Dept. Labor, 1971-73; ptnr. Morgan Lewis & Bockius, 1973—2001, of counsel, 2001—. Sec.-treas. Carlou Corp., Wilmington, Del., 1969-71. Fellow Ford Found., 1961. Mem. ABA, FBA, D.C. Bar Assn., Belle Haven Country Club, Ballybunion Golf Club, Royal Dornoch Golf Club. Republican. Avocations: travel, golf, reading. Office: Morgan Lewis & Bockius 1111 Pennsylvania Ave Washington DC 20004 E-mail: ecuehlein@morganlewis.com.

UEHLING, BARBARA STANER, educational administrator; b. Wichita, Kans., June 12, 1932; d. Roy W. and Mary Elizabeth (Hilt) Staner; children: Jeffrey Steven, David Edward. BA, U. Wichita, 1954; MA, Northwestern U., 1956, PhD, 1958; hon. degree, Drury Coll., 1978; LLD (hon.), Ohio State U., 1980. Mem. psychology faculty Oglethorpe U., Atlanta, 1959-64, Emory U., Atlanta, 1966-69; adj. prof. U. R.I., Kingston, 1970-72; dean Roger Williams Coll., Bristol, R.I., 1972-74; dean arts scis. Ill. State U., Normal, 1974-76; provost U. Okla., Norman, 1976-78; chancellor U. Mo.-Columbia, 1978-86, U. Calif., Santa Barbara, 1987-94; sr. vis. fellow Am. Council Edn., 1987; mem. Pacific Rim Pub. U. Pres. Conf., 1990-92; exec. dir. Bus. and Higher Edn. Forum, Washington, 1995-97. Cons. North Ctr. Accreditation Assn., 1974-86; mem. nat. educator adv. com. to Compt. Gen. of U.S., 1978-79; mem. Commn. on Mil.-Higher Edn. Rels., 1978-79, Am.Coun. on Edn., bd. dirs. 1979-83, treas., 1982-83, mem. Bus.-Higher Edn. Forum, 1980-94, exec. com. 1991-94; Commn. on Internat. Edn., 1992-94, vice chair 1993; bd. dirs. Coun. of Postsecondary Edn., 1986-87, 90-93, Meredith Corp., 1980-99; mem. Transatlantic Dialogue, PEW Found., 1991-93. Author: Women in Academe: Steps to Greater Equality, 1979; editorial bd. Jour. Higher Edn. Mgmt., 1986-95; contbr. articles to profl. jours. Bd. dirs., chmn. Nat. Ctr. Higher Edn. Mgmt. Sys., 1977-80; trustee Carnegie Found. for Advancement of Teaching, 1980-86, Santa Barbara Med. Found. Clinic, 1989-94; bd. dirs. Resources for the Future, 1985-94; mem. select com. on athletics NCAA, 1983-84, also mem. presdl. commn.; mem. Nat. Coun. on Edn. Rsch., 1980-82. Social Sci. Research Council fellow, 1954-55; NSF fellow, 1956-57; NIMH postdoctoral research fellow, 1964-67; named one of 100 Young Leaders of Acad. Change Mag. and ACE, 1978; recipient Alumni Achievement award Wichita State U., 1978, Alumnae award Northwestern U., 1985, Excellence in Edn. award Pi Lambda Theta, 1989. Mem. Am. Assn. Higher Edn. (bd. dirs. 1974-77, pres. 1977-78), Western Coll. Assn. (pres.-elect 1988-89,k pres. 1990-92), Golden Key, Sigma Xi. E-mail: bcharlton3@hotmail.com.

UEHLING, GORDON ALEXANDER, JR. investment company executive; b. Providence, Sept. 1, 1939; s. Gordon Alexander and Alice Bishop (Tomb) U.; m. Victoria M. Eckert, Dec. 30, 1967 (div. Oct. 1975); 1 child, Gordon A. III; m. Mary Elizabeth Shields, Sept. 15, 2002. BS, U.S. Naval Acad., 1961; postgrad., Columbia U., 1968. Mktg. mgr. Communitype Corp., N.Y.C., 1968-70; asst. treas. Mfrs. Hanover Trust Co., 1970-73; v.p. The Manhattan Savs. Bank, 1973-87; pres. Turnstone, Inc., Cresskill, NJ, 1988—2000; gen. ptnr. Palisades Ptnrs., L.P., 1988—. Lt. USN, 1961-67, Vietnam. Recipient Air medal (14 awards), USN, 1967. Mem. Naval Inst., Naval Acad. Alumni Assn., Army Navy County Club, Gipsy Trail Club. Republican. Avocations: flying, playing tennis, skiing. Home: 222 Ruckman Rd Closter NJ 07624 Office: Palisades Ptnrs LP 100 Union Ave Cresskill NJ 07626-2137 E-mail: duehling@alpineassocs.com.

UEHLING, KAREN SCHENDEL, English educator; b. Manhattan, Kans., Oct. 11, 1950; d. James Walter and Jane Elizabeth (Cary) Schendel; m. Kasman E. Thomas, Sept. 1, 1973 (div. Aug. 1983); m. Jon R. Uehling, Dec. 28, 1985; children: Jessie K., Mycah R. BA in English cum laude, U. Calif. Irvine, 1972; Std. Tchg. Credential, Calif. State U., Sacramento, 1974; MA in English, U. Calif. Davis, 1976. Standard Secondary Teaching Credential, Calif. Instr. English, Mars Hill (N.C.) Coll., 1976-80; asst. prof. English, Boise (Idaho) State U., 1981-94, assoc. prof., 1994—. Chair, 1983-86, exec. bd., 1992—, Conf. on Basic Writing; edtl. bd. Jour. Basic Writing, N.Y.C., 1996—. Author: Starting Out or Starting Over, 1993, Vision and Revision, 1994; contbr. articles to profl. jours. NEH fellow U. So. Calif., 1980-81; grantee Boise State U., 1995. Mem. Conf. on Coll. Composition and Comm., Conf. on Basic Writing. Avocation: outdoor activities. Office: English Dept Boise State U 1910 University Dr Boise ID 83725 E-mail: kuehling@boisestate.edu.

UELAND, ELIZABETH PRITCHARD, English language educator; b. Mpls., Dec. 28, 1937; d. Manion John and Elizabeth (McCann) Pritchard; m. Mark Ueland, Aug. 26, 1960; children: Mara Humphreys, Anne Bailey, Michael. BA, Manhattanville Coll., 1959; MEd, Temple U., 1983. English cert., Pa. Tchr. Girard Coll., Phila., 1983-84, Chestnut Hill Acad., Phila., 1985-86, Country Day Sch. of the Sacred Heart, Bryn Mawr, Pa., 1988-91, Merion Mercy Acad., Merion Station, 1991—, dept. chair English, 1996—. Mem. Nat. Coun. Tchrs. English. Roman Catholic. Avocation: reading. Home: 560 W Mermaid Ln Philadelphia PA 19118-4206 Office: Merion Mercy Acad 511 Montgomery Ave Merion Station PA 19066-1295 E-mail: elizueland@comcast.net.

UELAND, ERIC MATTHEW, legislative staff executive; b. Portland, Oreg., July 12, 1965; s. Robert Milo and Jane Celeste Ueland; m. Cathleen Delia O'Donnell, Feb. 20, 1967; children: Stephen, Brigid, Charlotte. BA, U. San Francisco, 1988. Editl. intern Am. Spectator, Washington, 1988-89; asst. editor Senate Rep. Policy Com., 1989-90, editor, 1990-91, rsch. dir., 1991-93, press sec., 1992-95, economist, 1993-95, policy and comm. dir., 1995-96; asst. majority leader, dep. chief, then chief of staff U.S. Senate, 1996—. Candidate issue briefer Nat. Rep. Senatorial Com., 1994, 96; mem. platform staff Rep. Nat. Com., San Diego, 1996; parliamentarian, asst. editor Platform, Rep. Nat. Com., Phila., 2000; editor Pachyderm Press, Arlington County Reps., Arlington, Va., 1993-95. Asst. to campaign mgr. Inhofe for Senate, Oklahoma City, Okla., 1994. Mem. KC. Roman Catholic. Office: US Senate Asst Majority Leader The Capitol S-321 Washington DC 20510

UELAND, SIGURD, JR. retired lawyer; b. Mpls., June 1, 1937; s. Sigurd and Harriet (Scofield) U.; m. Harriet Moulton, Dec. 27, 1963; children: Scott, Leif, Tora, Sigurd III. BA, Yale U., 1959; LL.B., U. Minn., 1962. Bar: Minn. 1963. Asso. firm Neville, Johnson & Thompson, Mpls., 1963-67; corp. atty. Whirlpool Corp., Benton Harbor, Mich., 1968-69, Honeywell Inc., Mpls., 1969-97, sec., 1977-97, asst. gen. counsel, 1980-93, v.p., 1983-97. Mem. Am. Soc. Corp. Secs. (chmn. 1996-97). Congregationalist. Home: 12998N E Bay Dr Hayward WI 54843

UELLENDAHL, GAIL ELIZABETH, psychologist; b. Freeport, N.Y., Dec. 3, 1952; d. Edwin W. and Claire E. (Stryker) U. AAS in Child Care, Nassau Community Coll., Garden City, N.Y., 1973; BA in Edn., Queens Coll., 1974; MS in Spl. Edn., Hofstra U., 1977; PhD in Counseling Psychology, NYU, 1990. Diplomate Am. Bd. Profl. Disability Cons. Substitute tchr. Uniondale (N.Y.) pub. schs., 1974-75; counselor Queens Coll., Flushing, N.Y., 1975-79, dir. spl. svcs., 1979-91; supervising psychologist Orange County (Calif.) Cmty. Hosp., 1991-94; assoc. prof. Calif. Luth. U., Thousand Oaks, 1992—, dir. counseling and guidance program, 1999—. Clin. psychology intern L.I. Jewish Med. Ctr., Glen Oaks, N.Y., 1987-88; 504 cons. CUNY Law Sch., 1989—, Performance Prosthetic-Orthotic Ctr., Santa Monica, Calif., 1991. Contbr. articles to profl. jours. Bd. dirs. Queens Ind. Living Ctr., Jamaica, N.Y., 1985-87. U.S. Dept. Edn. grantee, 1979-91; recipient Profl. Recognition award Assn. on Handicapped Student Svc. Programs in Postsecondary Edn., 1984. Mem. APA, ACA, CACD, CACES, CUNY Com. for the Disabled (exec. bd. 1984-91), Metro Assn. on Handicapped Student Svc. Programs in

Postsecondary Edn. (treas. 1988—), Calif. Assn. for Counseling and Devel., Ventura County Sch. Counselors Assn. Avocations: dancing, jazz, sailing, hiking, skiing. Office: Calif Luth U 60 W Olsen Rd Thousand Oaks CA 91360-2787

UEMURA, TERUKI, child brain developmentalist; b. Tokyo, Mar. 25, 1944; came to U.S., 1973; s. Kiichi and Teru (Koizumi) U. BA, Keio U., Tokyo, 1967, diploma in bus. adminstr., 1972; M Mgmt., Northwestern U., 1975; postgrad., U. Pa., 1976-81. Mem. staff Aichi Steel Works, Ltd., Nagoya, Japan, 1967-81; coord. Insts. for Achievement Human Potential, Phila., 1984—; vice dir. intellectual growth at The Children's Ctr. The Children's Ctr., 1984-91; vice dir. The Children's Ctr. Insts. for Achievement Human Potential, 2001; vice dir. Insts. Achievement of Intellectual Excellence, 1994—. Rsch. asst. Harvard U., Cambridge, Mass., 1972-74, U. Pa., Phila., 1979-81; translator U.S. State Dept., Washington, 1980—. Program coordinator Coun. Internat. Visitors, Phila., 1978-81. Recipient Brazilian Gold medal of Humanities, World Orgn. for Human Potential, 1984, 88, Sakura Koro Sho award, 1986, Leonardo da Vinci award, 1993, Founder's award Internat. Acad. Child Brain Devel., 1998. Fellow Internat. Acad. Child Brain Devel., Japan Group II; mem. Friends of Japanese House and Garden, Japan Am. Soc. Greater Phila. Avocations: reading, tennis, travel, history, science. E-mail: teruki_u@iahp.org.

UENG, CHARLES EN-SHIUH, engineering educator, consultant; b. Kiangtu, Kiangsu, China, Sept. 8, 1930; s. San Yu and Shu Chi (Hsu) U.; m. Shirley Wen-Hwa Chen, Oct. 20, 1962; children: Vivian, Grace. BS, Nat. Cheng-Kung U., Tainan, Taiwan, 1953; MS, Kans. State U., 1960, PhD, 1963. Registered profl. engr., China. Asst. structural engr. Tawan Power Co., 1954-58; asst. prof. engring. Kans. State U., 1963-64, Ga. inst. Tech., Atlanta, 1964-67; assoc. prof. Ga. Inst. Tech., 1967-77, prof., 1977—97, dir. Composites Edn. and Rsch. Ctr., 1994—97, prof. emeritus, 1997—. Cons. to industry. Contbr. articles to profl. jours. NSF grantee, 1964, 74, NASA grantee, 1967, 68, Soc. Mfg. Engring. grantee, 1981, FHWA grantee, 1992. Mem. ASCE (award 1983), Soc. Engring. Sci., Am. Soc. Engring. Edn., Am. Acad. Mechanics. Republican. Baptist. Home: 2037 Chesterfield Dr NE Atlanta GA 30345-3703 E-mail: Charles.ueng@gte.net.

UFBERG, MURRAY, lawyer; b. Danville, Pa., July 30, 1943; s. Alfred Eugene and Leah (Abrams) U.; m. Margery Ann Fishman, June 29, 1969; children: Aaron, Joshua, Rachel. BA, Bucknell U., 1964; JD, Duquesne U., 1968. Bar: Pa. 1969, U.s. Dist. Ct. (mid. dist.) Pa. Assoc. Rosenn, Jenkins & Greenwald, Wilkes-Barre, Pa., 1969-74; ptnr. Rosenn, Jenkins & Greenwald, L.L.P., 1974—. Chair Greater Wilkes-Barre Partnership, Inc., bd. dirs., 2000—, WVIA TV/FM/HDTV. Chmn. United Way Wyoming Valley Gen. Campaign , Wilkes-Barre, 1990, bd. dirs., 1992—99; mem. Luzerne County adv. com. Pa. Economy League; mem. pres. adv. coun. Keystone Coll.; past pres. Ohav Zedek Synagogue, Wilkes-Barre, 1986—88, Jewish Cmty. Ctr. Wyoming Valley, 1982—83, Seligman J. Strauss lodge B'nai B'rith, Wilkes-Barre , 1970—74; chmn. Jewish Cmty. Bd. of Wyoming Valley, 1997—; pres. Jewish Fedn. Greater Wilkes-Barre; trustee United Hebrew Inst.; bd. dirs., chmn. cmty. rels. coun. Jewish Cmty. Bd., 1993—97, 2000; trustee Coll. of Misericordia. Recipient Disting. Svc. award Wilkes-Barre Jaycees, 1979. Mem. ABA, Pa. Bar Assn., Luzerne County Bar Assn. (chmn. cmty. rels. com. 1997—), Wilkes-Barre Law and Libr. Assn., Duquesne U. Law Alumni Assn. (bd. govs.). Jewish. Avocations: sports, recreational reading. Home: 644 Charles Ave Kingston PA 18704 Office: Rosenn Jenkins & Greenwald LLP 15 S Franklin St Wilkes Barre PA 18711-0075 also: 120 E Broad St Hazleton PA 18201 also: 120 Wyoming Ave Scranton PA 18503 E-mail: mufberg@rjglaw.com.

UFFELMAN, MALCOLM RUCJ, electronics company executive, electrical engineer; b. Clarksville, Tenn., Oct. 22, 1935; s. Malcolm C. and Margaret Lillian (Davidson) U.; m. Sarah White Barksdale, June 11, 1957; children: Malcolm Rucj Jr., Katharina White, Davidson Barksdale, Jefferson Churchill. BS, Vanderbilt U., 1957; MS, George Washington U., 1963. Engr. Melpar, Inc., Falls Church, Va., 1957-60; v.p. Scope, Inc., Reston, 1960-73; sr. cons. MRI, Inc., McLean, 1973-78; v.p. Racal Communications Inc., Rockville, Md., 1978-80; sr. cons. MRJ, Inc., Fairfax, Va., 1980-82; v.p., gen. mgr., Ctr. Advanced Planning and Analysis E-Systems Inc., 1982-96; v.p. Constellation Comm., Inc., 1996-99; patent agent, cons., 1999—2000; exec. v.p. Contact Corp., 2000—. Pvt. practice patent agt., Vienna, Va., 1999—. Contbr. numerous articles to profl. jours.; holder 7 patents in field. Scoutmaster Troop 183 Boy Scouts Am., Oakton, Va., 1973-79. Capt. USAR, 1957-69. Fellow IEEE; mem. Cosmos Club (Washington), Internat. Brotherhood Magicians. Republican. Episcopalian. Avocations: sailing, reading, travel, magic, fly fishing.

UFFNER, MICHAEL S. retail automotive executive; b. Phila., July 18, 1945; s. Ray and Shirley A. (Block) U.; m. Marilyn A. Ursomarso; 1 child, Lauren R. BA, MA, U. Pa., 1971. V.p. Union Park Pontiac, BMW, Honda, Wilmington, Del., 1972-82; pres. Del. Motor Sales Inc., 1982—. Mem. manpower tng. adv. com. Gen. Motors Corp., pres. dealer adv. coun., 1985; mem. Gen. Motors Dealer policy bd., 1990-91. Mem. New Castle County Small Bus. Commn., 1993—, Wilmington Police Bus. Adv. Coun., 1991—; bd. dirs., mem. exec. com. BBB Del., 1992—, chmn., 1998-2000; bd. dirs. Del. chpt. Am. Heart Assn., 1981-98, pres., 1985-86, chmn., 1986-87. Recipient numerous awards, including Time Mag. Quality Dealer award, 1997, Gold Heart award Am. Heart Assn., 1989. Mem. Cadillac Motor Car Divsn. Nat. Dealers Coun. (vice chmn. 1989-90, chmn. 1990-91, chmn. DeVille brand com. 1995-97), Am. Heart Assn. (v.p., bd. dirs. Nat. Ctr. 1987-90), Am. Econ. Assn., Del. Automobile and Truck Dealers Assn. (bd. dirs., v.p. 1992-93, pres. 1994-95), U. Pa. Alumni Assn. (v.p. Del. chpt. 1978-80, pres. 1980-81), Del. C. of C. (chmn. small bus. com. 1991-95, vice chmn. bd. dirs. 1996-99, bd. dirs. 1993—, mem. exec. com. 1995—, chmn. small bus. alliance 1995-96, chmn. bd. dirs. 2000-02), U.S. C. of C. (bd. dirs. 1998—, chmn. pub. affairs com. 2001—), Fieldstone Golf Club, Delaware Nat. Country Club, Ocean City Yacht Club, Univ. Whist Club, Tavistock Civic Assn. (pres. 1976-77). Office: 1606 Pennsylvania Ave Wilmington DE 19806-4018 E-mail: cadillac@conectiv.net.

UFFORD, CHARLES WILBUR, JR. lawyer; b. Princeton, N.J., July 8, 1931; m. Isabel Letitia Wheeler, May 20, 1961; children: Eleanor Morris Ufford Léger, Catherine Latourette Ufford-Chase, Alison Wistar Ufford Salem. BA cum laude (Francis H. Burr scholar), Harvard U., 1953, LLB, 1959; postgrad. (Lionel de Jersey Harvard studentship), Cambridge U., Eng., 1953-54. Bar: N.Y. 1961, U.S. Tax Ct. 1963. Assoc. Riggs, Ferris & Geer, N.Y.C., 1959-61; from assoc. to ptnr. Jackson, Nash, Brophy, Barringer & Brooks, 1961-78; ptnr. Skadden, Arps, Slate, Meagher & Flom, N.Y.C., 1978-92, of counsel, 1993-96. Bd. dirs. Friends Fiduciary Corp., 2000—, Friends Fiduciary Corp. Contbr. articles to legal jours. Trustee Nat. Squash Racquets Ednl. Found., N.Y.C., 1972-81; mem. Princeton monthly Meeting, Soc. of Friends, clk., 1986-88, 99; mem. exec. com. Friends Com. on Nat. Legislation, 1997-98; dir. Pennswood Village, 1998—. Nat. Intercollegiate Squash Racquets champion, 1952-53; mem. NCAA All-Am. Soccer 1st team, 1952. Fellow Am. Coll. Trust and Estate Counsel (transfer tax study com. 1990-93); mem. ABA, N.Y. Bar Assn. (chmn. trusts and estates law sect. 1984), Assn. Bar City N.Y., N.Y. State Office of Ct. Adminstrn. (Surrogates Ct. Adv. Com., 1994-96), U.S. Squash Racquets Assn. (hon. life; trustee endowment fund 1984-96), Internat. Lawn Tennis Club U.S.A. (dir. 1982—). Office: 150 Mercer St Princeton NJ 08540-6827 E-mail: cuffordl@aol.com. *Integrity, perseverance, compassion and humor are all very well--but the key is to be blessed by a Divine Improvidence.*

UFIMTSEV, PYOTR YAKOVLEVICH, physicist, electrical engineer, educator; b. Ust'-Charyshskaya Pristan', Altai Region, Russia, July 8, 1931; s. Yakov Fedorovich and Vasilisa Vasil'evna (Toropchina) U.; m. Tatiana Vladimirovna Sinelschikova; children: Galina, Ivan, Vladimir. Grad., Odessa State U., USSR, 1954; PhD, Cen. Rsch. Inst. of Radio Industry, Moscow, 1959; DSc, St. Petersburg State U., Russia, 1970. Engr., sr. engr., sr. scientist Cen. Rsch. Inst. of Radio Industry, Moscow, Russia, 1954-73; sr. scientist Inst. Radio Engring. & Electronics Acad. Scis., Russia, 1973-90; vis. prof., adj. prof. UCLA, 1990—; prin. engr. Northrop Grumman Corp., 1995—2001. Mem. Sci. Bd. of Radio Waves, Acad. Scis., Moscow, 1960-90. Author: Method of Edge Waves in the Physical Theory of Diffraction, 1962; contbr. articles to profl. jours. Recipient USSR State Prize, Moscow, 1990, Leroy Randle Grumman medal for outstanding sci. achievement, N.Y.C., 1991, 20th Century Achievement medal, Cambridge, 1996, Hall of Fame medal, Cambridge, 1996. Fellow IEEE; assoc. fellow AIAA; mem. Electromagnetics Acad. (U.S.), A.S. Popov Sci. Tech. Soc. Radio Engring., Electronics & Telecommunication (Russia). Achievements include origination of the Physical Theory of Diffraction, used for design of American stealth aircrafts and ships; for radar-cross-section calculation, and antenna design. Office: UCLA Dept Elec Engring 420 Westwood Plz Los Angeles CA 90095-1594

UGGAMS, LESLIE, entertainer; b. N.Y.C., May 25, 1943; d. Harolde Coyden and Juanita Ernestine (Smith) U.; m. Grahame John Kelvin-Pratt, Oct. 16, 1965; children: Danielle Nicole Pratt, Justice Harolde John Kelvin-Pratt. Student, Juillard Sch. Music, 1961-63; degree (hon.), Jarvis Coll., Tyler, Tex., Wilberforce (Ohio) U. Appeared on TV show Beulah, 1949; featured on Sing Along with Mitch, 1961-64; starred in Broadway play Hallelujah Baby, 1967 (Tony award 1968), Her First Roman Broadway Musical, 1968; star of weekly TV variety show The Leslie Uggams Show, 1969; appearances in nightclubs, top TV mus. variety shows; appeared in films, including Two Weeks in Another Town, Black Girl, 1962, Skyjacked, 1972, Poor Pretty Eddie, 1973, (ABC-TV film mini-series) Roots, 1977 (Critics Choice award as best supporting actress 1977), (TV) Sizzle, 1981, Harlem, 1993; star Broadway musicals Blues in the Night, 1982, Jerry's Girls, 1985, Anything Goes, 1987, (off-Broadway) The Old Settler, 1999 (Audelco award as best actress), (dramatic play) The Old Settler, 1999; star (TV mini-series) Backstairs at the White House, 1979; co-host Fantasy TV, 1982-83 (Emmy award 1983); author: The Leslie Uggams Beauty Book, 1966. Founding mem. BRAVO chpt. City of Hope, Los Angeles, 1969, treas. 1969-79. Chosen best singer on TV, 1962, 63; recipient Drama Critics award Newspaper and TV critics, 1968, Tony award 1968, Emmy award 1983. Mem. AFTRA, NARAS, SAG, Actors' Equity Assn. Democrat. Presbyterian. Avocations: needlepoint, knitting, tennis, squash, exercising. Office: The Gage Group Inc care Phillip Adelman 315 W 57th St Frnt 4H New York NY 10019-3158 E-mail: leslie@leslieuggams.com.

UGGEN, CHRISTOPHER, sociologist, criminologist; b. St. Paul, May 29, 1964; s. Kermit Stanley and Nancy Lee Uggen; m. Rhonda Marie Breakfield, Aug. 2, 1986; children: Tor Stanley, Hope Kathryn. BA, U. Wis., 1986, MS, 1990, PhD, 1995. Assoc. prof. and McKnight Presdl. fellow U. Minn., Mpls., 1995—. Editl. adv. bd. Jour. Criminal Law and Criminology, Am. Jour. Sociology; contbr. articles to profl. jours. Grantee Nat. Inst. Justice, 1998, NSF, 1999, Soros Found., 2000; scholar Internat. Soc. Criminology, 1998. Mem. Am. Soc. Criminology (nat. policy com. 1998-99, Cavan award for outstanding scholarly contbns. 2000), Am. Sociol. Assn. Avocations: running, playing guitar, reading fiction. E-mail: uggen@atlas.socsci.umn.edu.

UGHETTA, WILLIAM CASPER, lawyer, manufacturing company executive; b. N.Y.C., Feb. 8, 1933; s. Casper and Frieda (Bohland) U.; m. Mary L. Lusk, Aug. 10, 1957; children: William C., Robert L., Edward F., Mark R. AB, Princeton U, 1954; LLB, Harvard U., 1959. Bar: N.Y. 1959. Assoc. Shearman & Sterling, N.Y.C., 1959-67; asst. sec. Corning Glass Works, N.Y., 1968-70, sec., counsel, 1971-72, v.p., gen. counsel, 1972-82, sr. v.p., gen. counsel, 1983-98. Bd. dirs. Chemung Canal Trust Co., Covance Inc. Bd. dirs. Steuben Area coun. Boy Scouts Am.; trustee Corning C.C. Lt. (j.g.) USN, 1954-56. Mem. Assn. of Bar of City of N.Y., ABA, N.Y. State Bar Assn., Am. Corp. Counsel Assn. (trustee 1982-85), Princeton Club (N.Y.C.), Univ. Club (N.Y.C.), Corning Country Club. Home: 10519 North Rd Corning NY 14830-3235

UH, DAVID KEUN, civil engineer; b. Korea, Jan. 28, 1935; s. Kwang Sun and Hyo Sook (Lee) Uh; came to U.S., 1956, naturalized, 1968; student Barclay Coll., 1956, So. Nazarene U., 1956-57; B.S. in Engring., U. Mich., 1961; M.S., Columbia U., 1968; m. Meong Jae Kim, June 4, 1966; children—Benjamin, Steven. Design engr. Allied Chem. Corp., 1963-66; sr. design engr. Frederick Snare Corp., 1966-68; project engr. Edwards & Hjorth, 1968-70; sr. engr. Soros Assocs., Inc., 1970-73; assoc. cons. engr., corp. engring. and cons. engring. dept. Ebasco Services Inc., 1973-92 (all N.Y.C.); cons. on offshore nuclear power plant, highrise comml. bldgs., offshore coal handling, and new ch. constrn.; David K. Uh cons. engr., 1980—. Mem. governing bd. dirs., sec. Korean Cultural Ctr., 1969-72, 74-80, editor News Bull., 1970-72, chmn. edn. com., 1986; chmn. bd. trustees L.I. Central Korean Ch., 1981-82, pres. Korean Inst., 1981-87; mem. L.I. Presbyn. Ch., chmn., sec. edn. com., 1990, chmn. fin. com., treas., 1991-92, governing elder, 1991—. Registered profl. engr., N.Y., N.J., Guam. Mem. ASCE, Kyunggi Alumni Assn. Am. (exec. dir. 1971-91), Kyunggi Alumni Assn. N.Y. (pres. 1969-72), Korean Student Assn. N.Y. (pres. 1962-63), U. Mich. Alumni Assn. (life), Columbia U. Engring. Alumni Assn. Republican. Club: The U. Mich. L.I. (bd. govs. 1986-88) Home: 24 Woodbine St Coram NY 11727-1138 Office: 307 Fashion Ave Rm 706 New York NY 10001-6007

UHDE, LARRY JACKSON, joint apprentice administrator; b. Marshalltown, Iowa, June 2, 1939; s. Harold Clarence and Rexine Elizabeth (Clemens) U.; m. Linda-Lee Betty Best, Nov. 19, 1960; children: Mark Harold, Brian Raymon. Student, Sacramento City Coll., 1966, Am. River Coll., Sacramento, 1975. Equipment supr. Granite Constrn., Sacramento, 1962-69; truck driver Iowa Wholesale, Marshalltown, Iowa, 1969-70; mgr. Reedy & Essex, Inc., Sacramento, 1970-71; dispatcher Operating Engrs. Local Union 3, 1971-73; tng. coord. Operating Engrs. Joint Apprenticeship Com., 1973-83, apprenticeship div. mgr., 1983-87, adminstr., 1987-95; ret., 1995; instr. asst. advanced transp. tech. Sacremento City Coll., 1996—. Chmn. First Women in Apprenticeship Seminar, 1972, Calif. Apprentice Coun., 1992, chair Blue Ribbon com.; com. mem. Sacramento Gen. Joint Apprenticeship Com., 1973-74; rep. Sacramento Sierra's Bldg. and Constrn. Trades Coun., 1973-75; com. mem. Valley Area Constrn. Opportunity Program, 1974-77; commr. State of Calif. Dept. Indsl. Rels., Calif. Apprenticeship Coun., chmn. 1992; mem. Apprenticeship Adv. Com. Internat. Union Oper. Engrs. Contr: Options; contbr. articles to trade papers. Mgr., v.p. Little League, 1971-75; co-chmn. Fall Festival St. Roberts Ch., 1973-75; v.p. Navy League Youth Program, 1978-81; instr. ARC, 1978-87; counselor United Way 1980—; bd. mem. County CETA Bd., 1981-82; coun. mem. Calif. Balance of State Pvt. Industry Coun., 1982-83, Sacramento Pvt. Industry Coun., 1982-83; coord. Alcholic Recovery Program, 1984-87. With USN, 1956-60. Inducted into Calif. Apprenticeship Hall of Fame, 1996. Mem. Western Apprenticeship Coords. Assn. (statewide dir. 1987—), U.S. Aprenticeship Assn., Sacramento Valley Apprenticeship Tng. Coords. Assn. (rep.), Rancho Murieta County, U.S. Golf Assn., Bing Maloney Golf Club. Democrat. Roman Catholic. Avocations: golf, archery, bowling, hunting, camping, dancing.

UHL, CHRISTOPHER MARTIN, lawyer; b. Balt., Feb. 21, 1958; s. Robert Henry and Marie Antoinette (Carosella) U.; m. Gael Anna Evangelista, Feb. 16, 1991; children: Christopher Martin Uhl, Grace Molinari Uhl. BS in Acctg., Northeastern U., 1989, MBA, 1991; JD, New Eng. Sch. Law, 1992. Bar: Mass. 1993, N.Y. 1993, U.S. Dist. Ct. Mass. 1993, D.C. 1994, Maine 1994, U.S. Dist. Ct. D.C. 1994, U.S. Dist. Maine 1994, Conn. 1995, U.S. Supreme Ct., 1998, U.S. Dist. Ct. (ea. and so. dists.) N.Y. 1999, U.S. Dist. Ct. Conn. 1999, U.S. Ct. Appeals (1st cir.) 2000. Fingerprint technician FBI, Washington, 1976-79; project mgr. various constrn. cos., Balt., 1979-87, Admiral Constrn. Co., Boston, 1987-91; asst. dist. atty. Worcester (Mass.) Dist. Atty.'s Office, 1992-96; prin. Christopher Uhl, Attorney at Law, Worcester, 1997—. Prof. Becker Coll., Worcester, 1993-97. Bd. dirs. Am. Cancer Soc., Boston, 1990-96; ward coord. Reelect Dist. Atty. Campaign, Worcester, 1994; elected mem. Southborough Rep. Town Com., Southborough Housing Authority, Northborough/Southborough Regional Sch. Com. Named Hon. Mem. Rep. State Com. Republican. Roman Catholic. Roman Catholic. Office: 5 State St Worcester MA 01609-2893 Fax: (508) 797-4210. E-mail: attorney@uhllaw.com.

UHL, PHILIP EDWARD, artist, photographer, cinematographer; b. Toledo, Aug. 19, 1949; s. Philip Edward and Betty Jean U. Student, Dayton Art Inst., 1967-68, Art Students League, 1974. Creative dir. Ctr. for Civic Initiative, Milw., 1969-71; VISTA vol. Office Econ. Opportunity, 1969-71; artist, photographer Assn. Honolulu Artists, 1974-77; pres. Uhl Enterprises div. Makai Photography, Honolulu, 1977—, Videoscapes div. Channel Sea TV, Honolulu, 1977—. Cons. Pan Am. Airways, N.Y.C., Honolulu, 1979-84, ITTC Travel Ctr., Honolulu, 1982-83, Royal Hawaiian Ocean Racing Club, Honolulu, 1984—, Sail Am.-Am's Cup Challenge, Honolulu, 1985-86, Am. 3 Found., Am. Cup Def., San Diego, 1991-92, Am. 3 Found. Womens Team, 1994-95, UHL Studios, Hawaii, 2000—. Co-prodr. video documentary White on Water, 1984 (Emmy 1984), Racing the Winds of Paradise (Golden Monitor award Internat. TV Assn. 1989); prodr.: Joy of Life (Golden Monitor award Internat. TV Assn. 1988), Sailors on the Sea, 1990, Teamwork, Talent, Technology (Tele award 1993); cameraman, prodr.: Pan Am. Clipper Cup 1980, 82, 84, Kenwood Cup, 1986, 88, 90, 92, 94, 96, 98, 2000 (2 Tele awards 1994), ESPN Kenwood Cup, 1990, 92, 94, ESPN Am.'s Cup, 1991-92, 94-95, Transpac, 1991, 93, 95, 97, 99 (video documentary) Rocking the Boat, 1994-95, Dateline NBC Setting Sail 1994-95, numerous spls., reports on ABC-TV, NBC-TV, CBS-TV, PBS, NHK, BBC, TFI, F1, TVNZ and numerous other major worldwide broadcast networks; prodr. At the Helm, America' Cup 2000 TVNZ; photographer, dir. graphic design/photography (video documentary) Transpac 100 years across the Pacific, 2001: (book) Nautical Quar. (Soc. Pub. Designer award 1984); contbr. numerous articles, photos to yachting publs., numerous exhbns. fine/digital art; exhibited in group shows in Honolulu, Tokyo, Hong Kong, Syndey, Isle of Wight, Las Vegas, N.V., San Diego, San Francisco, L.A., N.Y.C., Osterville, Mass.; represented in permanent collections City & County of Honolulu, Hawaii Maritime Mus., UCLA Med. Ctr., others. Mem. Soc. Internat. Nautical Scribes, Internat. Yacht Restoration Sch., Honolulu Printmakers, Digital Art Soc. Hawaii, Assn. Hawaii Artists, U.S. Sailing Assn., Royal Hawaiian Ocean Racing Club, Tutukaka S. Pacific Yacht Club, Waikiki Yacht Club. Office: UHL Enterprises 1750 Kalakaua Ave Ste 3-757 Honolulu HI 96826-3766 E-mail: hiseaart@aol.com.

UHL, SCOTT MARK, state agency administrator; b. Balt., July 6, 1950; s. Edward George and Maurine Barbara (Keleher) Uhl; m. Charlene Hughins, Feb. 29, 1988. BA, Lehigh U., 1972. Cmty. systems developer Md. Mental Hygiene Adminstrn., Balt., 1979-82, chief, housing and cmty. support, 1982-89; adminstr., cmty. programs, dep. secretariat pub. health Md. Health and Mental Hygiene, 1989-95; dep. dir. Md. Devel. Disabilities Adminstrn., 1995—. Consult in field; pres Waterfields Press, Inc, 1994—; mem adv bd CARE Md Dept Human Resources, Baltimore, 1987—94; prin staff Md Gov's Task Force Long Term Fin Planning Individuals with Diasabilities, 1991—92. Gov's appointee State Adv Coun Admin Hearings, 1993—97. Recipient Gov's Citation, 1992. Republican. Home: 2004 Sleepy Hollow Dr Woodbine MD 21797 Office: Md Health & Mental Hygiene 201 W Preston St Baltimore MD 21201-2323

UHLENHUTH, EBERHARD HENRY, psychiatrist, educator; b. Balt., Sept. 15, 1927; s. Eduard Carl Adolph and Elisabeth (Baier) Uhlenhuth; m. Helen Virginia Lyman, June 20, 1952; children: Kim Lyman, Karen Jane, Eric Rolf. BS in Chemistry, Yale U., 1947; MD, Johns Hopkins U., 1951. Intern Harborview Hosp., Seattle, 1951-52; resident in psychiatry Johns Hopkins Hosp., Balt., 1952-56, asst. psychiatrist in charge outpatient dept., 1956-61, psychiatrist in charge, 1961-62; chief adult psychiatry clinic U. Chgo. Hosps. Clinics, 1968-76; instr. psychiatry Johns Hopkins U., 1956-59, asst. prof., 1959-67, assoc. prof., 1967-68, U. Chgo., 1968-73, prof., 1973-85, acting chmn., 1983-85; prof. psychiatry U. N.Mex., Albuquerque, 1985-97, prof. emeritus, 1997—, vice chmn. for edn., 1991-94. Cons. in field; mem. clin. psychopharmacology rsch. rev. com. NIMH, 1968-72, treatment devel. and assessment rev. com., 1987; mem. psychopharmacology adv. com. FDA, 1974-78; mem. adv. group to Treatment of Depression Collaborative Rsch. Program, NIMH, 1978-92; study rev. com. Xanax Discontinuation Program, The UpJohn Co., 1988-92, Nat. Adv. Coun. on Drug Abuse, NIDA, 1989-92, Coop. Studies Evaluation Com., VA, 1989-92. Mem. editl. bd. Jour. Affective Disorders, 1978—, Psychiatry Rsch., 1979-96, Behavioral Medicine, 1982—, Neuropsychopharmacology, 1992-94, Exptl. and Clin. Psychopharmacology, 1992-99, Anxiety, 1993—; contbr. articles to profl. jours. Recipient Research Career Devel. award USPHS, 1962-68, Research Scientist award, 1976-81 Fellow Am. Coll. Neuropsychopharmacology (pres. 1986), Am. Psychiat. Assn., Am. Psychopath. Assn.; mem. Balt.-Washington Soc. for Psychoanalysis, Collegium Internat. Neuro-Psychopharmacologicum, Psychiat. Rsch. Soc. Office: U NMex Dept Psychiatry 2400 Tucker NE Albuquerque NM 87131-5326 E-mail: uhli@unm.edu.

UHLER, WALTER CHARLES, government official, writer, reviewer; b. Lebanon, Pa., Feb. 23, 1948; s. Victor Cornelius and Barbara Jean (Martin) U.; m. Judy Ann Sherk, Aug. 7, 1967 (div. 1984); children: Terry Allen, Matthew David. Life partner: Carol A. DePrisco. BA in Polit. Sci. cum laude, BA in Russian cum laude, cert. Russian area, Pa. State U., 1973, MPA, 1992. Tchg. asst. Pa. State U., University Park, 1975-76; procurement agt. Naval Aviation Supply Office, Phila., 1976-80; contracts adminstr. GSA, 1980-81; contracting officer Def. Logistics Agy., 1981-86, corp. contracting officer, 1986-94; chief fin. svcs., 1993—; chief of ops. Def. Contract Mgmt. Agy., Lockhead Martin, Del. Valley, 2001—, Def. Contract Mgmt. Agy., Lockheed Martin Delaware Valley, 2001—; regional cons. Def. Logistics Agy., L.A., 1985-86, nat. cons. Cameron Station, Va., 1989-90, leader Testing Labs. Privatization Assessment Team Ft. Belvoir, 1997-98. Participant Air Force Intelligence Conf. on Soviet Affairs, Arlington, Va., 1988, Venona Conf., Washington, 1996, Ballistic Missile Def. Conf., Washington, 1998, AP/Harriman Inst. Conf., N.Y.C., 1999, State of the World Forum, N.Y.C., 2000; testified against nat. missile def., Vt. Ho. of Reps., 2002; gave radio interviews on nat. missile def., Vt., Calif., Wis., Radio Free Europe/Radio Liberty, 2002; presenter, 11th ann. Russia-Am. Conf., St. Petersburg, Russia, 2002; spkr. on contracts DOD Conf., Cleve., 1988, on restructuring costs, Memphis, 1994; chmn. Ann. Nat. Conf. Contracting Officers and Auditors, 1987-93; mem. Citizen Amb. Archivists' Del. to Russia and Poland, 1995, Citizen Amb. Del. to China, 1996, Russia and Finland, 1998; prodr., interviewer (with George Enteen) Sergei Vasilievich Utechin's Oral Reminiscences, 1997—. Contbr. articles to profl. jours. Baseball coach Valley Athletic Assn., Bensalem, Pa., 1979-88, basketball coach, 1980-85, coord., 1981; tutor Ctr. for Literacy, Phila., 1991-93, Project GIVE, Phila., 1995-98. Recipient Comdrs. Excellence award Defense Contract Mgmt. Area Ops., 1993. Mem. Am. Assn. for Advancement Slavic Studies, Soc. for Mil. History, Acad. Polit. Sci., Nat. Book Critics Cir., Am. Acad. of Polit. and Social Scis., Friends of the Free Libr. of Phila., Am. Hist. Assn. Democrat. Avocations: history, literature, Pa. State U. football. Office: DCMA LMDV L-3 Bldg 1 Federal St Camden NJ 08102 E-mail: waltuhler@aol.com.

UHLER, WILLIAM GRANT, IV, transportation executive; b. Darby, Pa., Nov. 22, 1942; s. William Grant III and Elizabeth Ellen (Johnson) U.; m. Jennie Lou Iliff, Apr. 15, 1963; children: William Grant V, David Michael. BS, Friends U., Wichita, Kans., 1996. Computer operator USAF, Offutt AFB, Nebr., 1963-67; field rep. A.C. Nielsen, Detroit, 1967-69; ins. agt. Coll. Life Ins. Co., Manhattan, Kans., 1969-71; br. mgr. ITT Continental Baking, Topeka, 1971-81; weight and rsch. rerate specialist Yellow Transp., 1981—2001; revenue specialist III Yellow Freight, 2001—. Treas. Prairie Trace Cmty., Topeka, 1986-88. Sgt. USAF, 1963-67. Mem. Mensa, Alpha Psi Omega. Republican. Methodist. Avocation: carpentry/cabinet making. Home: 3312 SW Belle Ave Topeka KS 66614-4547

UHLIG, FRANK, JR. editor, writer; b. N.Y.C., June 15, 1927; s. Franklin R. Uhlig and Elisabeth (Lazenby) Sutherland; m. Inna Winocour, 1957; children: Valerie, Melissa. BA in History, Kenyon Coll., 1951. Head book dept. U.S. Naval Inst., Annapolis, Md., 1960-62, editor Naval Rev., 1962-81, sr. editor U.S. Naval Inst., 1969-81; editor Naval War Coll. Rev. Naval War Coll., Newport, R.I., 1981-93, wargame commentator, 1982-99, head advanced rsch., 1984-88, emeritus, sponsored rsch. scholar, 1993—. Writer, spkr., tchr. Naval War Coll., and other orgns., 1970—; spkr. on naval matters, WWII, Vietnam, 1970—. Author: How Navies Fight, 1994; editor: Vietnam: The Naval Story, 1986; contbr. more than 50 articles to profl. publs. Mem. Mystic Seaport Mus. With USN, 1945-47. Recipient A.T. Mahan award for lit. achievement Navy League of U.S., 1970. Mem. N.Am. Soc. Oceanic History, U.S. Naval Inst., Soc. for Mil. History, Naval War Coll. Found. Episcopalian. Avocations: politicial issues, military, maritime and technological developments. Home: 60 Boulevard Ter Middletown RI 02842-4908 Office: Naval War Coll Code 3 686 Cushing Rd Newport RI 02841-1213

UHLIR, ARTHUR, JR. electrical engineer, university administrator; b. Chgo., Feb. 2, 1926; s. Arthur and Helene (Houghteling) U.; m. Ingeborg Williams, July 24, 1954; children: Steven, Donald, David. BS, Ill. Inst. Tech., 1945, MSChemE, 1948; SM in Physics, U. Chgo., 1950, PhD in Physics, 1952. Process analyst Douglas Aircraft, Chgo., 1945; asst. engr. Armour Rsch. Found., 1945-48; tech. staff Bell Telephone Labs., Murray Hill, N.J., 1951-58; dir. semi- condr. research and devel., mgr. semicondr. div., group v.p. engring. Microwave Assos., Inc., Burlington, Mass., 1958-69; dir. rsch. Computer Metrics, Rochelle Park, N.J., 1969-73; prof. elec. engring. Tufts U., Medford, Mass., 1970-94, chmn. dept. elec. engring., 1970-75, dean of engring., 1973-80. AEC fellow, 1949-51 Fellow IEEE, AAAS; mem. Am. Phys. Soc., Sigma Xi. Home: 45 Kendal Common Rd Weston MA 02493-2159 Office: Tufts Univ Dept Elec Engring & Computer Sci Medford MA 02155 E-mail: auhlir@mailaps.org.

UHLIR, FRANK ALLEN, counselor, consultant; b. Berwyn, Ill., Nov. 20, 1952; m. Rebecca C. Uhlir, Nov. 18, 1978; children: Laura, Frank, Eric. BA, Ea. Ill. U., Charleston, 1974; MA in Edn., Concordia U., River Forest, Ill., 1978; postgrad., U. Fla., 1986-87. Cert. tchr., Fla. Wilson sporting goods merchandiser Pepsi-Cola Corp., River Grove, Ill., 1975-79; social svcs. counselor Fla. Human Resource Svcs., New Port Richey, 1980-82, group treatment leader Lacoochee, 1982-84; counselor Citrus County Schs., Inverness, Fla., 1984-88, Hernando County Sch., Brooksville, 1988—. Cons. runaway alternatives program, Port Richey, Fla., 1982. Organizer, coord. living history program Ft. Clinch State Park, Fla., 1986, 88, 89. Recipient vol. award State of Fla., 1986, 88, 89, V.I.P. award U.S. Dept. Interior, 1989. Mem. AACD, Am. Sch. Counselor Assn. Republican. Lutheran. Avocations: Civil War era living history, tennis, skiing, collecting antique photographs. Home: PO Box 23235 Tampa FL 33623

UHLMANN, ELENORE ARLENE, interior designer, writer; b. Ada., Mich., July 18, 1922; d. Arthur Benjamin and Arla Mary (Kriedler) Hale; m. Robert Carl Uhlmann, Jan. 14, 1939 (dec. Jan. 5, 1995); children: J. Louise Uhlmann Zielke, Nancy Jean Uhlmann Gill. Student, U. Mich., 1939, 68, Kendall Sch. Design, 1940, Heaneys Bus. Coll., 1941. Designer, sales rep. Mfr.'s Showroom, Grand Rapids, Mich., 1966-71; designer, decorator Regent Interiors, Clearwater, Fla., 1971, Chandlers, Dunedin, 1972-76, Square Yard, Dunedin, 1976-80; instr. Palm Harbor (Fla.) Libr., 1997-98. Presentor at numerous workshops and clubs. Contbr. articles and essays to mags. Mem. Jr. League, 1972-89. Avocations: writing, painting, travel.

UHLMANN, FREDERICK GODFREY, commodity and securities broker; b. Chgo., Dec. 31, 1929; s. Richard F. and Rosamond G. (Goldman) U.; m. Virginia Lee Strauss, July 24, 1951; children: Richard, Thomas, Virginia, Karen, Elizabeth. BA, Washington and Lee U., 1951. Ptnr. Uhlmann Grain Co., Chgo., 1951-61; v.p. Uhlmann & Co., Inc., 1961-65; sr. v.p. H. Hentz & Co., 1965-73, Drexel Burnham Lambert Inc., Chgo., 1973-84; exec. v.p., dir. bus. futures Dean Witter Reynolds Inc., 1984-85; sr. v.p., mgr. commodity dept. Bear, Stearns & Co., Inc., 1985-88; exec. v.p. Rodman & Renshaw, Inc., 1988-95; sr. v.p. LIT-Divsn. of First Options Inc., Chgo., 1995-98; chmn. Chgo Bd. Trade, 1973-74; sr. v.p., exec. dir. MAN Internat., 1998—. Ptnr. Uhlmann Investments, LLC. Trustee Highland Park Hosp., Ill.; bd. dirs. Dist. 113 H.S. Found., 1990—, Mt. Sanai Hosp. Inst., Chgo., 1999—. Mem. Nat. Futures Assn. (dir. 1981—, vice chair 1998—), Futures Industry Assn. (bd. dirs., chmn. 1975-76), Futures Industry Inst. (bd. dirs.). Home: 783 Whiteoaks Ln Highland Park IL 60035-3656 E-mail: fgu73@aol.com.

UHLRICH, MARJORIE ANN, civic worker; b. Ft. Benton, Mont., Apr. 18, 1920; D. Albert E. and Anna C. (Holzer) Sternhagen; m. Herman F. Uhlrich, May 25, 1973; children: Carol, Barbara, Gerald, Daniel. BS, Mont. State U., 1941. Med. ctr. chmn. Gen. Fedn. Women's Clubs Internat., Bridger, Mont., 1958-60; chmn. Braille Trail, Gt. Falls, 1968-70. Conservation confs. chmn., Mont., 1968-70, state pres., 1978-80, environ. chmn., 1980-82, policy devel. staff, 1982-84; pres. Conservation Dists. Aux.-Mont., 1970-72. Editor-in-chief Mont. Woman, 1978-80; watercolorist. Mem. devel. com. Coll. Great Falls Ctr., 1982-84; co-chmn. Art Train, Mont. Arts Council, 1973. Editor-in-chief Mont. Woman, 1978-80; watercolorist. Mem. devel. com. Coll. Gt. Falls Ctr., 1982-84; co-chmn. Art Train Mont. Arts Coun., 1973. Named Woman of Yr. Soroptimists Ctrl. Mont., 1980, Jaycees Ctrl. Mont., 1982; recipient Mont. Artist award GFCW Internat., 1978. Mem. AAUW (bd. dirs. 1974-80), Mont. Watercolor Soc. (signature, v.p. 1982-84), Miniature Art Soc. Fla., Mont. Miniature Art Soc. Roman Catholic. Home: 1000 Fountain Terrace Dr # 303 Lewistown MT 59457-1973

UHR, JONATHAN WILLIAM, immunologist, educator, researcher; b. N.Y.C., Sept. 8, 1927; s. Jacques Stanley Uhr and Mary Wetsman; m. Roberta Joy Klibanoff (div.); children: Jacqueline, Sarita. AB, Cornell U., 1948; MD, NYU, 1952. Diplomate Am. Bd. Internal Medicine. Dazian fellow dept. microbiology NYU Med. Ctr., 1955-56; chief resident in medicine Mt. Sinai Hosp., N.Y.C., 1956-57; instr. dept. microbiology NYU Sch. Medicine, 1957-58, asst. prof. medicine, 1958-62, assoc. prof., 1962-68, prof., 1968-72; prof. dept. microbiology and internal medicine U. Tex. Southwestern Med. Ctr. & Cancer Immunobiology Ctr., Dallas, 1972—; chair dept. microbiology U. Tex. Southwestern Med. Ctr., 1972-97. Dir. Irvington House Inst. for Rheumatic Fever and Allied Diseases, N.Y.C., 1962-72; vis. prof. microbiology Yale U., 1970-72; assoc. attending physician Univ. Hosp., N.Y.C., 1963-72; assoc. vis. physician Bellevue Hosp., N.Y.C., 1959-72; cons. internal medicine Manhattan Vet.'s Hosp., 1964-74. Contbr. articles to profl. publs. With USN, 1945-46. Recipient Newcomb Cleveland prize AAAS, 1963, Squibb award Infectious Diseases Soc. Am., 1971, NAS award, 1984, Faculty medal Med. Sch. Montpellier, France, 1984, Abbott-ASM Lifetime Achievement award, 1999; Commonwealth fellow Walter and Eliza Hall Inst. Med. Rsch., 1961-62. Mem. Am. Assn. Immunologists (pres. 1989—), Am. Assn. Pathologists, Am. Soc. Clin. Investigation, Transplantation Soc., Assn. Am. Physicians. Office: U Tex Southwestern Med Ctr Dept Cancer Immunobiology 5323 Harry Hines Blvd Dallas TX 75390-8576 E-mail: Jonathan.Uhr@southwesternmed.edu.

UHRIG, ROBERT EUGENE, nuclear engineer, educator; b. Raymond, Ill., Aug. 6, 1928; s. John Matthew and Anna LaDonna (Fireman) U.; m. Paula Margaret Schnepf, Nov. 27, 1954; children: Robert John, Joseph Charles, Mary Catherine, Charles William, Jean Marie, Thomas Paul, Fredrick James. BS with honors, U. Ill., 1948; MS Iowa State U, 1950, PhD, 1954; grad. Advanced Mgmt. Program, Harvard U., 1976. Registered profl. engr., Iowa, Fla. Instr. engring. mechanics Iowa State U., 1948-51; assoc. engr., research asst. Inst. Atomic Research (at univ.), 1951-54, assoc. prof. engring. mechanics and nuclear engring., also group leader, 1956-60; prof. nuclear engring., chmn. dept. U. Fla., Gainesville, 1960-68, on leave, 1967-68, dean Coll. Engring., 1968-73; dean emeritus, 1989—; dep. asst. dir. research Dept. Def., Washington, 1967-68; dir. nuclear affairs Fla. Power & Light Co., Miami, 1973-74, v.p. for nuclear affairs, 1974-75, v.p. nuclear and gen. engring., 1976-78, v.p. advanced systems and tech., 1978-86; disting. prof. engring. U. Tenn., Knoxville, 1986-98, 1986—; disting. scientist Oak Ridge Nat. Lab., 1986—. Rep. Dept. Def. to com. on acad. sci. and engring. Fed. Council Sci. and Tech., 1967; chmn. engring. adv. com. NSF, 1972-73; bd. dirs. Engring. Council Profl. Devel., 1968-72; mem. commn. edn. for engring. profession Nat. Assn. State Univs. and Land Grant Colls., 1969-72; apptd. mem. adv. com. on reactor safeguards U.S. Nuc. Regulatory Commn., 1997-2001. Author: Random Noise Techniques in Nuclear Reactor Systems, 1970, trans. into Russian, 1974; co-author: (with Lefteri H. Tsoukalas) Fuzzy and Neural Approaches in Engineering, 1997—. Served to 1st lt. USAF; instr. engring. mechanics U.S. Mil. Acad. 1954-56. Recipient Sec. of Def. Civilian Service award, 1968, Outstanding Alumni award U. Ill. Coll. Engring., 1970, Alumni Profl. Achievement award Iowa State U., 1972, President's medallion U. Fla., 1973; Disting. Achievement citation Iowa State U. Alumni Assn., 1980, Glenn Murphy awd., Am. Soc. for Engineering Education, 1992. Fellow ASME (life, Richards Meml. award 1969), AAAS, Am. Nuclear Soc. (chmn. edn. com. 1962-64, chmn. tech. group for edn. 1964-66, bd. dirs. 1965-68, exec. com. bd. 1966-68); mem. Am. Soc. Engring. Edn. (pres. S.E. sect. 1972-73, chmn. nuclear engring. divsn. 1966-67, 88-89, rsch. award S.E. sect. 1962, Glenn Murphy award as Outstanding Educator 1992), John Henry Newman Honor Soc., Sigma Xi, Tau Beta Pi, Phi Mu Epsilon, Pi Tau Sigma, Phi Kappa Phi (Disting. Mem. award 1997). Home: 5221 NW 44th Pl Gainesville FL 32606-4328 Office: U Tenn Pasqua Nuclear Engring Bldg Knoxville TN 37996-2300 E-mail: ruhrig@utk.edu.

UHRIK, CARL THOMAS, computer scientist, educator; b. Cedar Rapids, Iowa, Dec. 9, 1957; s. Richard Lee and Shirley Marie Uhrik; m. Michael W. Burkart, Sept. 1, 1999. BSEE, Tex. A&M U., 1980, MS in Computer Sci., 1981; MS, U. Ill., 1985, PhD, 1991. Asst. lab. mgr. Lab. for Informatic Engring. U. Trento, Italy, 1990-95; speech recognition engr. Berdy Med. Sys., Boulder, Colo., 1996-99; prof. U. Phoenix, Denver, 1996—; internationalization engr. Intl.com/Lionbridge, Boulder, 1999—. Fulbright scholar, 1986-87. Roman Catholic. Avocations: vegan vegetarian cooking, reading, films, outdoors, biking. Home: 3725 Birchwood Dr Apt 23 Boulder CO 80304-1421 E-mail: uhrik@hotmail.com.

UHT, AUGUSTUS KINZEL, computer engineering researcher; b. N.Y.C., July 19, 1955; s. Charles Frederick and Carol (Kinzel) U. BS, Cornell U., 1977, MEE, 1978; PhD, Carnegie-Mellon U., 1985. Registered profl. engr., N.Y., Pa. Assoc. engr. IBM, Hopewell Junction, N.Y., 1978-80, sr. assoc. engr., 1980-82; teaching intern dept. elec. and computer engring. Carnegie-Mellon U., Pitts., 1983, grad. asst., then vis. asst. prof., 1983-86; asst. prof. dept. computer sci. and engring. U. Calif.-San Diego, La Jolla, 1986-92; asst. prof. U. R.I., 1992-98, assoc. prof., 1998-2001, rsch. prof., 2001—. Mem. sci. adv. bd. Parallax Co., San Diego, 1988-90; adj. assoc. prof. Northeastern U., 2001; rschr. and cons. in field. Contbr. to profl. publs.; inventor in computer concurrency field. Mem. IEEE, NSPE, Assn. Computing Machinery, Pitts. Cornell Alumni (head secondary schs. com. 1984-85), Sigma Xi, Eta Kappa Nu. Avocations: computer, sailing. E-mial. E-mail: uht@ele.uri.edu.

UICKER, JOHN JOSEPH, JR. mechanical engineer, consultant; b. Derry, N.H., July 11, 1938; s. John Joseph and Elizabeth Josephine (Flint) U.; m. Ann Marie Schumacher, Aug. 12, 1961 (div. May 1986); children: Theresa Ann, John Joseph III, Joseph Michael, Dorothy Jean, Barbara Ann, Joan Elizabeth. BME, U. Detroit, 1961; MS, Northwestern U., Evanston, Ill., 1963, PhD, 1965. Registered profl. engr., Wis. From asst. prof. to assoc. prof. mech. engring. U. Wis., Madison, 1967-75, prof. mech. engring., 1975—. Co-author: Theory of Machines & Mechanisms, 2d edit., 1995. Capt. U.S. Army, 1965-67. Recipient Resident in Engring. Practice award Am. Soc. Engring. Edn., 1972-73, Best Paper award Am. Foundrymens Soc., 1987, Historic Paper award ASME, 1986; Fulbright-Hayes sr. lectr. award, 1978-79. Achievements include development of computer software systems. Office: Univ Wisc 1513 University Ave Madison WI 53706-1539

UICKER, JOSEPH BERNARD, retired engineering company executive; b. Mar. 29, 1940; s. John Joseph and Elizabeth Josephine (Flint) U.; m. Mary Catherine Howze, June 5, 1965 (div. Oct. 1971); children: Patricia, Suzzane; m. Janet Ann Ballman, Sept. 22, 1973. BSME, U. Detroit, 1963, MS, 1965. Registered profl. engr., Mich. Engr. Smith Hinchman & Grylls, Detroit, 1964-72, chief mech. engr. health facilities, 1972-73, asst. dir. health facilities, 1973-75, v.p., dir. mech. engring., 1975-82, v.p., dir. profl. staff, 1983-2000; also bd. dirs.; ret., 2000. Dir. Smith Group, Detroit, 1984-2000. Capt. U.S. Army, 1966—67. Mem. NSPE, ASME, ASHRAE, Soc. Am. Mil. Engrs., Engring. Soc., Athletic Club. Avocations: golf, photography, gardening. Home: 15250 Knolson St Livonia MI 48154-4736 E-mail: juicker@ameritech.net.

UJIFUSA, GRANT MASASHI, editor; b. Worland, Wyo., Jan. 4, 1944; s. Tom Mamoru and Mary Takayo (Okugawa) U.; m. Katherine Adams Glover, June 23, 1969 (div. June 1974); m. Amy Jane Brooks, Sept. 9, 1978; children: Steven, Andrew. BA, Harvard U., 1965; MA, Brandeis U., Waltham, Mass., 1967; postgrad., Brown U., Providence, 1969. Book editor Houghton Mifflin, Boston, 1974-77, Random House, N.Y.C., 1977-84, Macmillan, N.Y.C., 1984-88; mag. editor Reader's Digest, Pleasantville, N.Y., 1988-98; founder, CEO Best Am. Minds, Pubs., 2000—. Founding editor, co-author: The Almanac of American Politics, 1972—. Chief strategist Japanese-Am. Redress Effort, Japanese Am. Citizen's League, 1982-92; hon. mem. Co. K, 442d Regtl. Combat Team; bd. dirs. Japanese Am. Nat. Mus., Nat. Japanese Am. Meml. Found. Recipient Spl. award Japanese Am. Citizens League, San Francisco, 1988, Excellence 2000 award Outstanding Asian Am., 1992. Mem. U.S. Pan Asian C. of C. Home: 9 Greenridge Dr Chappaqua NY 10514-1303 E-mail: Captain129@aol.com.

UJIOKA, TAKESHI, endocrinologist; b. Kumamoto, Japan, Apr. 21, 1963; s. Irei and Fumiko U.; m. Akiko Sakata, Nov. 16, 1996; 1 child, Hirotaka. MD, Miyazaki Med. Coll., 1991; PhD, Kumamoto U., 1998. Cert. physician, Japan. Resident Kumamoto Univ. Hosp., Japan, 1991-94; rsch. scientist Trinity U., San Antonio, 1998—. Contbr. articles to profl. jours. Grantee The Lalor Found., Providence, R.I., 1999. Mem. Japan Soc. Ob/Gyn, Japan Endocrine Soc., Japan Soc. Fertility and Sterility. Avocations: polit. sci., Asian history. Office: Trinity Univ/Dept Biology 715 Stadium Dr San Antonio TX 78212-3104 E-mail: tujioka@trinity.edu.

UKAEGBU, DAVID OKWUKANMANIHU, accountant, management consultant; b. Umuahia, Abia, Nigeria, Jan. 28, 1939; s. Amos Ukaegbu Iweha and Sussanah Ihejiaba Anyim-Ukaegbu; divorced. Attended, Kings Coll., Lagos, 1957-58; A level, U. Ibadan, Lagos, Nigeria, 1959; Cert.O/A level, Wolsey Hall Coll., Oxford (Eng.) U., 1960; attended, Inst. Taxation, London, 1961-64, H. Houlks Lynch London Tax. & Accountancy, 1961-68; Article of Clerkship, Inst. of Chartered Accts., 1967-70; attended, Inst. Chartered Accts. in England & Wales, 1967-70; postgrad., Calif. Coast U., 1982. Cert. fin. mgmt. cons.; chartered adminstr. Chief clk. Stewart & Co., Lagos, 1956-60; asst. mgr. audits Banner Mounsey Chartered Accts., 1960-64, B Harmood & Co. Chartered Accts., Lagos, 1964-66; articled clk. Morris Gregory Chartered Acct., Eng., 1967-68, Harmood, Banner, Midgeley, Snelling & Barnes Chartered Accts., Lagos, 1969-70; acct., auditor Charter House Auditors, 1971-74; reporting acct. Silver Shoes Mfg. Co. Ltd., 1974-85, chief acct., cons., 1976—. Titular rschr. dept. applied econs. U. Cambridge, 1975-79; edn. com. Inst. Adminstrv. Accts., Lagos, 1981; mgmt. cons. Lagos State Consultancy Bd., 1987—. Program convener YMCA, Lagos, 1965-66. Recipient Men of Achievement, 1995, Internat. Leadership Achievement, 1995, Am. medal of Hoor, 2002. Fellow Inst. Fin. Accts. (launching com. 1990-93), Assn. Cost and Exec. Acctg.; mem. AAAS, Am. Mgmt. Assn., Brit. Inst. Mgmt., Brit. Inst. Securities Laws, Inst. Inc. Pub. Accts. (Dublin), Inst. Chartered Accts. (articled clk.), Inst. of Chartered Secs. and Adminstrs., Nigeria Employers Cons. Assn. (treas. Eal Frin 1990-93), Planetary Soc., N.Y. Acad. Scis. Avocations: reading, table tennis, lawn tennis. Office: Charter House PO Box 998 Umuahia Abia State Nigeria

UKE, ALAN KURT, company executive; b. L.A., Nov. 24, 1952; s. Mustafa Tugrul Uke and Gladys Jean Hunnicott; m. Lisa Joyce Katter, 1975 (div.); 1 child, Gregory; m. Diane Christiansen, Jan. 12, 1985; children: Leslie, John. Student, Dartmouth Coll., 1971; degree, Univ. Calif., San Diego, 1975. Prin., owner Underwater Kinetics, Powag, Calif., 1971—; pres. UK Corp., Del Mar, 1980—. Patentee, inventor in field. Pres. San Diego Aircraft Carrier Mus., 1993—. San Diego Taxpayers Assn. Found., 1996-98, North County Coun. Aging, Vista, Calif., 1998-2000; chmn. learning for life divsn. Boy Scouts Am., 1999-2000. Recipient Entrepreneur of Yr. award San Diego County, 1997, Headliner of Yr. award San Diego Press Club, 1997. Mem. The Exec. Com., San Diego State Pres. Assn., Young Pres. Orgn. (spl. events chmn. 1996-97), Lincoln Club (events chmn. 1989—), Adam Smith Inst. Republican. Lutheran. Avocations: travel, reading, astronomy. Office: Underwater Kinetics 13400 Danielson St Poway CA 92064 E-mail: auke@uwkinetics.com.

UKEN, MARCILE RENA, music educator; b. Avon, S.D., Sept. 16, 1931; d. Martin Andrew and Helen (Janssen) Bertus; m. Emil Jaden Uken, Dec. 8, 1953 (dec. 1990). BS, Southern State Coll., 1952. Cert. secondary sch. tchr., Nebr. Tchr. pub. sch., Delmont, S.D., 1952-53, Carroll (Nebr.) Pub. Sch., 1954-56; spl. edn. tchr. State of Nebr., Wayne, 1953-60; piano tchr. pvt. studio, 1955. Co-chairperson Am. Cancer Soc., Wayne, 1964-76; mem. Federated Women's Club, Wayne. Fellow Nat. Fedn. Music Clubs, Music Tchrs. Nat. Assn., Nebr. Music Tchrs., Siouxland Music Tchrs.; mem. Bus. and Profl. Women. Avocations: exercise group, bible studies, music concerts, Nebr. Huskers football, working with youth groups.

UKROPINA, JAMES R. lawyer; b. Fresno, Calif., Sept. 10, 1937; s. Robert J. and Persida (Angelich) Ukropina. AB, Stanford U., 1959, MBA, 1961; LL.B., U. So. Calif., 1965. Bar: Calif. 1966. Assoc. firm O'Melveny & Myers, Los Angeles, 1965-72, ptnr., 1972—80, 1992—2000, of counsel, 2001—; exec. v.p., gen. counsel Santa Fe Internat. Corp., Alhambra, Calif., 1980-84, dir., 1981-86; exec. v.p., gen. counsel Pacific Enterprises, Los Angeles, 1984-86, pres. and dir., 1986-89, chmn. bd. and chief exec. officer, 1989-91. Bd. dirs. Lockheed Martin Corp., Pacific Life Ins. Co., Trust Co. of the West, Ctrl. Natural Resources., Indymac Bancorp, Keck Found. Editor in chief So. Calif. Law Rev, 1964-65. Trustee Stanford U., 1991-2000 Mem. ABA, Calif. Bar Assn., Los Angeles County Bar Assn., Annandale Golf Club, Calif. Club, Beta Theta Pi. Office: O'Melveny & Myers 400 S Hope St Los Angeles CA 90071-2899

ULAKOVICH, RONALD STEPHEN, real estate developer; b. Youngstown, Ohio, Nov. 17, 1942; s. Stephen G. and Anne (Petretich) U. B.S., Indsl. Engring. Coll., 1967; M.S., Method Engring., Ill. Inst. Tech., 1969. Methods engr. Supreme Products, Chgo., 1964-66; pres. Contract Chair, 1966-70; v.p. sales Amrep Corp., Rosemont, Ill., 1970-73; pres. Condo Assoc., Ltd., Arlington Heights, Ill., 1973— , Am. Resorts Internat. Ltd., 1983. Named Employee of Yr., 1965; recipient Nat. Home Builders Grand award, 1977, Million Dollar Circle award Chgo. Tribune, 1978, Cert. of Recognition award Congressional Com., 1982, Cert. of Merit award Pres. Reagan's Task Force, 1984; named to Ky. Col., State of Ky., 1982. Mem. Am. Assn. Investors, Apt. Owners Assn., Real Estate Soc. of Syndicators and Investors, Am. Resort and Resdl. Devel. Assn. Roman Catholic. Avocations: auto racing, golf. Home: 510 Van Buren Dundee IL 60118

ULANOFF, STANLEY M. communications executive; b. Bklyn., May 30, 1922; s. Samuel H. and Minnie (Druss) U.; m. Bernice Mayer, June 15, 1947; children: Roger, Amy Ulanoff Christie, Lisa M. Ulanoff, Dory Ulanoff Kennedy. BA in Journalism, U. Iowa, 1943; MBA in Mktg., Hofstra U., 1955; PhD in Comm., NYU, 1968. Copywriter promotions dept. N.Y. Times, 1946—49; asst. to pres. SUNY, Stony Brook, 1962-64; prof. mktg., head advt., sales promotion & pub. rels. divsn. Baruch Coll. (CUNY), NY, 1964—86; pres. Viewmark Prodns. Inc. d.b.a. Advisions, 1986—. Cons. U.S. Dept. Def., Grosset & Dunlap pubs., Siebel/Mohr, U.S. Postal Svc.; cons, asst. to pres. Compton Advt.; arbitrator N.Y. Stock Exch., Nat. Assn. Securities Dealers; cons. Hasbro Toys. Author or editor 32 books including Handbook of Sales Promotion, also mags., newspaper articles, rsch. papers; prodr. over 200 video documentaries. 2nd lt. U.S. Army, 1945; Brig. gen. USAR, Mil. Svc., 1942-84. Decorated Chevalier dans l'Ordre des Palmes Academique, Republic of France, Legion of Merit, Meritorious Svc. medal, Army Commendation medal, Army Achievement medal, U.S. Army, Silver Conspicuous Svc. Cross, medal for merit, State of N.Y., 1st prize award Am. Assn. Advt. Agys.; named VIP (Very Important Prof.) Splty. Adv. Assn. Internat. (2); Am. Assn. Advt. Agys. fellow, Eastman-Kodak fellow in film prodn.; Lewis Kleid Direct Mail Advt. scholar. Mem. Mil. Intelligence Res. Soc. (pres.), Res. Officers Assn. (pres.); disting. alumnus, Hofstra Univ. Office: 17 The Serpentine Roslyn NY 11576-1736 Fax: 516-484-2930.

ULANOV, ALEXANDER, consultant, former literature educator; b. N.Y.C., Sept. 6, 1970; s. Barry and Ann (Belford) U. AB summa cum laude, Princeton (N.J.) U., 1992; PhD, Yale U., 1999. Rsch. asst. dept. history Princeton U., summmer 1991; rsch. asst. dept. Slavic langs. and lit. Columbia U., fall 1992; tchg. fellow Yale U., 1994-96, prize tchg. fellow, 1997-98, lectr., 1998-99; co-founder diversity practice interest group, co-dir. Latino recruiting Boston Cons. Group, N.Y.C., 1999—. Vis. instr. Wesleyan U., 1998. Contbr. articles to profl. jours. Co-dir. Young Profls. Ferrer Mayoral Campaign, N.Y.C., 1999—2001. Richard J. Franke Interdisciplinary Founding fellow, 1994-97, A. Bartlett Gianatti Grad. fellow, 1992-94, Yale U. fellow, 1992-94, dissertation fellow, 1996-97, Marion C. Sheridan Traveling fellow, 1996-97; rsch. grantee Richard J. Franke interdisciplinary Fellowship, 1994; Berkeley Travel scholar, 1994, Fulbright Fgn. scholar, 1992, Rotary Ambassadorial scholar, 1996-97; recipient Alice Derby Lang prize, 1994. Home: 379 Pleasant AVe Apt 4 New York NY 10035 Office: Boston Cons Group 135 E 57th St Fl 22D New York NY 10022-2050 E-mail: uptown125@aol.com., ulanov.alex@bcg.com.

ULBRECHT, JAROMIR JOSEF, chemical engineer; b. Ostrava, Czechoslovakia, Dec. 16, 1928; s. Josef and Leopolda U.; m. Vera Krafneter, July 10, 1952; children: Jan Stanislav, Magdalena Vera. Ing., Czech Inst. Tech., Prague, 1952, PhD, 1958. Dept. head rsch. divsn. synthetic rubber co., Zlin, Czechoslovakia, 1958-63; head lab. engring. rheology Czechoslovak Acad. Scis., Prague, 1963-68; prof. chem. engring. U. Salford, Eng., 1968-78; prof., chmn. dept. chem. engring. SUNY, Buffalo, 1978-83; chief div. chem. process metrology Nat. Bur. Standards, Washington, 1984-88; dep. dir. office tech. evaluation and assessment Nat. Inst. Standards and Tech. (formerly Nat. Bur. Standards), 1989-90, dir. tech. programs, tech. svcs., 1991-94; pres. OFI Tech Svcs., Rockville, Md., 1994—. Author: Non-Newtonian Liquids, 1967, Mixing of Liquids by Mechanical Agitation, 1985, Process Sensing and Diagnostics, 1989, Competitiveness of the U.S. Chemical Industry in International Markets, 1990; editor: Chemical Engineering Communications, 1976-86; contbr. numerous articles to profl. jours. Recipient Outstanding Scholarship award Czech Acad. Scis., 1965, 67; Alexander von Humboldt fellow, 1967 Fellow Am. Inst. Chem. Engrs.; mem. Soc. Rheology, Am. Chem. Soc., Czech Acad. Engring. (hon. fgn.), Sigma Xi. Office: OFI Tech Svcs Inc 311 High Gables Dr #308 Gaithersburg MD 20878 E-mail: ofiserve@aol.com.

ULC, OTTO, political science educator; b. Pilsen, Czech Republic, Mar. 16, 1930; came to U.S., 1960. s. Frantisek and Marie (Skrabkova) Ulc; married, Oct. 9, 1964; 1 child, Ota. JD, Charles U., 1953; MA, Columbia U., 1961, PhD, 1964. Dist. judge Czechoslovak judiciary, Pilsen, 1956-59; asst. prof. SUNY, Binghamton, N.Y., 1964-68, assoc. prof., 1968-75, prof., 1975—. Advisor Premier of the Cook Islands, South Pacific, 1978. Author: The Judge in A Communist State, 1972, Politics in Czechoslovavia, 1974, numerous other. Mem. P.E.N. Club, Czech Writers Union. Avocations: foreign travel, writing. Home: 124 Martha Rd Vestal NY 13850-3511 E-mail: ulc@binghamton.edu.

ULE, GUY MAXWELL, JR. stockbroker; b. Chgo., Jan. 2, 1940; s. Guy Maxwell and Margaret (Karahuta) U.; m. Angela Joanne Genelli, Nov. 17, 1975. BA, Harvard U., 1961, MBA, 1967. Analyst, phys. distbn. specialist TWA, N.Y.C. and Phila., 1967-69, supr. comml. passenger sales N.Y.C., 1969-71; pvt. practice cons., 1971-72; mgr. sales mktg. Source Equities, 1972; ptnr., N.Y.C. office mgr. Daley, Coolidge & Co., 1972-77; v.p., divsn. mgr. Rosenkrantz, Ehrenkrantz, Lyon & Ross Inc., 1977-85, Ingham Becker & Co., Inc., 1985-87; v.p., asst. sec. Meyers, Pollock, Robbins Inc., 1987-89; v.p., Max Ule divsn. Herzog Heine Geduld Inc., 1989-2000; v.p. investments Shields & Co., Inc., 2000—. Pres. Max Ule & Co., Inc., N.Y.C., 1977—, Max Ule Advt. & Mktg., Inc., N.Y.C., 1980—; brokerage info. cons. Internet World Wide Web, 1995. Creator first discount brokerage system on computer, 1980. Chmn., pres. Assn. in Manhattan for Autistic Children, 1985-86. Lt. USN, 1962-65. Mem.: Racquet Club Phila., Knickerbocker Club, Racquet and Tennis Club. Republican. Episcopalian. Avocations: photography, court tennis, overseas travel. Home: 8 Gramercy Park S Apt 5B New York NY 10003-1721 Office: Shields and Co 140 Broadway 44th Fl New York NY 10005

ULEN, EISA NEFERTARI, writer, educator; b. Phil., Dec. 22, 1968; d. Clive Antony Ulen and Cheryl Theresa Duguid. BA, Sarah Lawrence Coll., 1990; MA, Columbia U., 1995. Mem. staff Hunter Coll., N.Y.C., 1996—. Instr. Hunter Coll., 2002—. Author (with others): Am I the Last Virgin?, 1997, Letters of Intent: Women Cross the Generations to Talk about Family, Work, Sex, Love and the Future of Feminism, 1999, Sacred Fire: The QBR 100 Essential Black Books, 1999, Living Free Within Ourselves: Lessons for Black Writers, 1999, Step into a World: A Global Anthology of the New Black Literature, 2000, The African American Guide to Writing and Publishing Nonfiction, 2002; contbr. to anthologies, profl. jours. and mags. Jr. com. mem. Boy's Harbor Inc., N.Y.C., 1992-95. Frederick Douglass Creative Arts Ctr. fellow 1995, Fine Arts Work Ctr. scholar Provincetown, 1999; nominated Nat. Assn. Black Journalists award Essence Mag., 2002. Democrat. Moslem. E-mail: eisaulen@aol.com.

ULEN, GENE ELDRIDGE, elementary school educator; b. Detroit, June 13, 1939; d. James Swan and Dorothy Benson Eldridge; m. Ian Paul Ulen, Aug. 10, 1933; children: Heather Jean, Lori Dorothy. BA in Edn., Mich. State U.,

1960, MA in Edn., 1961; adminstrv. credential, Point Loma U., 1987. 2nd grade tchr. San Diego Unified Schs., San Diego, 1962—70; 6th grade tchr. Crown Pointe Elem. Sch., 1971—86; 4th-5th gifted class tchr. Cadman Elem. Sch., 1987—2000; substitute tchr. All Saints Sch., 2000—. Active San Diego Nat. Women Polit. Group, 1995—2000; sec. LaJolla (Calif.) Dem. Club, 2000—02. Mem.: LWV, LaJolla Book Club, Phi Delta Kappa (bd. mem. 1986—2000). Episcopalian. Avocations: roses, sailing, bridge, tennis. Home: 5840 Cozzens St San Diego CA 92122

ULETT, GEORGE ANDREW, psychiatrist; b. Needham, Mass., Jan. 10, 1918; s. George Andrew and Mabel Elizabeth (Caswell) U.; m. Pearl Carolyn Lawrence; children: Richard Carlton, Judith Anne, Carol Lynn. BA in Psychology, Stanford U., 1940; MS in Anatomy, U. Oreg., 1943, PhD in Anatomy, MD, U. Oreg., 1944. Diplomate Am. Bd. Psychiatry and Neurology. Asst. psychiatrist Barnes Hosp., St. Louis, 1950-64; med. dir. Malcolm Bliss Hosp., 1951-61; dir. Mo. Dept. Mental Health, Jefferson City, Mo., 1962-72; prof., chair Mo. Inst. Psychiatry, St. Louis, 1964-73; dir. psychiatry Deaconess Hosp., 1973-94; interim dir. Mo. Inst. of Mental Health, 1990-91, assoc. dir. for policy and ethics, 1991-94; clin. prof. dept. family and cmty. medicine St. Louis U. Sch. Medicine, 1995-98. Mem. adv. coun. Mental Health Assn. St. Louis, 1965-66, 69-70, mem. profl. adv. com., 1965; chair health and hosp. com. Health & Welfare Coun. St. Louis, 1960; mem. alcohol rev. com., psychopharmacology study sect., alcoholism study sect., 1993, grants rev. com. for alternative medicine NIMH, Rockville, Md.; prof. psychiatry Washington U. Sch. Medicine, St. Louis, 1956-61; clin. prof. psychiatry St. Louis U. Sch. Medicine, 1981-89, U. Mo. Sch. Medicine, 1990—. Author 10 books, including The Biology of Acupuncture, 2001; contbr. over 270 articles to profl jours. Capt. U.S. Air Force, 1946-47. Recipient Ann. award Mo. Assn. for Mental Health, 1966, Recognition award, 1970, AMA Honorable Mention award Foster Com. Exhibit, 1974, Pax Mundi Fellowship award for profl. excellence, 1989; named hon. mem. Turkish Coll. Neuropharmacology, 1969. Fellow Am. Psychiat. Assn.; mem. Am. Soc. Acupuncture (past pres.), Am. Soc. of Med. Psychiatry (past pres.), Mo. Acad. Psychiatry (past pres.). Office: Mo Inst Mental Health 5400 Arsenal St Saint Louis MO 63139-1400 E-mail: gulett@earthlink.net.

ULEVICH, NEAL HIRSH, photojournalist; b. Milw., June 18, 1946; s. Ben and Lea Jean (Klitsner) U.; m. Maureen Ann Vaughan, Sept. 25, 1974; children: Jacob Vaughan, Sarah Beatrice. BA in Journalism, U. Wis., 1968. Reporter A.P., 1968-69, photographer, photo editor, 1971-78, Asia photo editor, 1978-83. Freelance writer, Vietnam, Hong Kong, 1969-71; fellow in journalism U. Wis.-Madison, 1971-72 Recipient Pulitzer prize for news photography, 1977. Jewish. Home: 2841 Perry St Denver CO 80212-1442 E-mail: nulevich@qwest.net.

ULIANO, ANTHONY, JR. industrial hygienist, educator; b. Mt. Vernon, N.Y., Apr. 29, 1949; s. Anthony and Angelina-Rose (DeBellis) U.; m. Andrea Joan Norinsky, Sept. 22, 1984; children: Megan Emily, Caitlin Elizabeth. BS in Environ. Scis., U. New Haven, 1975; MS in Environ. Health Scis., CUNY, 1989. Cert. indsl. hygienist, Am. Bd. Indsl. Hygiene; cert. hazardous materials mgr., Inst. Hazardous Materials Mgmt. Indsl. hygienist Dept. Labor/OSHA, Washington, 1976-78, Bklyn., 1978-82, Westbury, N.Y., 1982-86; regional indsl. hygienist VA, Castle Point, 1986-90, indsl. hygienist mgr. Portland, Oreg., 1990-99; mgr. environ. health and safety Oreg. Health Scis. U., 1999—. Instr. environ. health and safety Clark Coll., Vancouver, Was,. 1991—, Portland State U., 1997—, Portland C.C., 1995—; instr. pollution and toxicology Marylhurst U., 1999—; spkr. Pacific N.W. Indsl. Hygiene Conf., 1996, Seattle, 1998, N.W. Hazardous Waste Mgmt. Conf., Portland, 1997, Acad. Cert. Hazardous Material Mgrs. Conf., 2000, Oreg. Gov.'s Conf., 2001; mem., pub. rels. rep. Oreg. Indsl. Hygiene Coun., 1997—; pvt. cons. EH&S. Contbg. author: Guidelines for the Assessment of Bio-Aerosols in the Indoor Environment, 1996, New Asbestos Standards/Awareness Guide, 1996, Hazardous Materials Management Desk Reference, 2000. Mem. spkrs. bur. Oreg. Assn. Environ. Profls., Portland, 1997-98. With U.S. Army, 1969-71, Vietnam. Mem. Am. Biol. Safety Assn., Nat. Environ. Health Assn., Am. Indsl. Hygiene Assn., Internat. Occupl. Health Assn., Am. Conf. Govt. Indsl. Hygienists, Am. Acad. Hazardous Materials Mgrs., Oreg. Indsl. Hygiene Coun., Parkrose Bus. Assn. Avocations: naturalist, hiking, archery. Office: Oreg Health Scis U 3181 SW Sam Jackson Park Rd Portland OR 97239 E-mail: ulianot@ohsu.edu.

ULIN, SAMUEL ALEXANDER, computer systems developer; b. Nov. 8, 1955; s. Webster Beattie Ulin and Ann (Fletcher) Rainier; m. Lida Ohan, May 30, 1992. Student, U. Del., 1973-78. Systems design cons. Alpha Ro Inc., Wilmington, Del., 1982-83, Command Computer Svcs., N.Y.C., 1983-84; systems designer DBS Films, Inc., Malvern, Pa., 1984-86; dir. engring. Flight Safety Inc., ISD, 1986-87, Irving, Tex., 1987-89; sr. system designer Litigation Scis., Culver City, Calif., 1989-96; v.p. engring. IDEA, Inc., Seattle, 1996—. Designer software for interactive tng. on aircraft sys., 1983, one of first interactive ct. evidence presentation systems used in fed. ct., 1987. Avocations: electronics, stamp and coin collecting, winter sports. Home: 12500 Lithuania Dr Granada Hills CA 91344 Office: Luminent Inc 20550 Nordhoff St Chatsworth CA 91311 E-mail: sulin@trialpro.com.

ULITIN, VLADIMIR GREGOR, retired Russian language and literature educator; b. Kamensk, Russia, Sept. 29, 1908; came to U.S., 1949; s. Gregory Anton and Taisiya Alexandra (Dubovskaya); m. Helen Sawa, Nov. 20, 1958 (div. 1968); m. Sophia Gregor Kishkovsky, Fev. 2, 1969; 1 child, Leonid. Student, Robert Coll., Istanbul, Turkey, 1924-28; BS, U. Belgrade, Yugoslavia, 1932; BA, Pomona Coll., 1968. Civil engr. Austrian firm, Yugoslavia, Austria, Poland, Italy, 1932-45; social worker, dir. refugee children UNRRA, Austria, 1945-49; dir. refugee pr. Am. Friends Svc. Com., Pasadena, Calif., 1950-57; instr. Russian, Calif. Inst. Tech., 1957-61, Pasadena City Coll., 1957-61, U. Calif., Riverside, 1960-61; asst. prof. Russian lang. and lit. Pomona Coll., Claremont, Calif., 1960-64, assoc. prof., 1964-74, disting. prof. Calif., 1968-74, prof. emeritus, 1974—. Editor Vestnik jour., 1961-70; contbr. articles to mags. Mem. Congress Russian-Ams. (So. Calif. rep.), Claremont Univ. Club (hon.). Russian Orthodox. Avocations: gardening, roses, sports. Home: 841 Miami Ct Claremont CA 91711-2531

ULKU, ALPAY KILICARSLAN, poet; b. Ankara, Turkey, Apr. 1, 1964; came to the U.S., 1982; s. Alparslan and Ilknur Ulku; m. Anne-Marie Gallagher, July 7, 1989. BA, U. Redlands, 1986; MFA, U. Iowa, 1988. Coll. instr. various orgns. Portland, Pitts., Iowa City, 1989-98; freelance writer various orgns., Pitts., Chgo., 1996—. Author: Meteorology, 1999; author of poems. Fellow Millay Colony for the Arts, Auterlitz, N.Y., 1989, Fine Arts Work Ctr., Provinceton, Mass., 1994-96; grantee Iowa Arts Coun., 1992; Notable Debut Acad. Am. Poets, 1999. Islamic. Avocation: camping. E-mail: alpayulku@ziplip.com.

ULLAS, YVONNE LEE, primary school educator; AA, Yakima Valley C.C., 1979; BA in Edn., Ctrl. Wash. U., 1981, postgrad., 1991, Antioch U., 1992; MEd, Heritage Coll., 1995. Parent educator Yakima Sch. Dist., 1975-79; camp dir. Yakima Parks and Recreation, 1979-86; tchr. St. Joseph's Grade Sch., Yakima, 1981-86, Naches Primary Sch., 1988—. Commr. Gov.'s commn. on Early Learning, 1998-2000; bd. dirs. Gov.'s Profl. Educator Standards bd. Named Tchr. of Month, KAPP TV, 1993, US West Washington State Outstanding Tchr., 1994, Wash. State Tchr. of Yr., 1998; recipient Christa McAuliffe Excellence in Edn. award, 2000; grantee Share 105 Tech., 1997. Mem. NEA, Wash. Edn. Assn., Naches Edn. Assn. (dist. del.), Naches Edn. Assn. (bldg. rep.), Yakima Valley C.C. Alumni Assn., Ctrl. Washington U. Alumni Assn., Heritage Coll. Alumni Assn., Retired Tchrs. Assn., N.W. Regional Ednl. Lab., Nat. State Tchr. of Yr. Assn., Parent, Tchr., Student Assn. Office: Naches Valley Primary Sch 2700 Old Naches Hwy Yakima WA 98908-8900 Home: 1615 S 13th Ave Yakima WA 98902

ULLBERG, KENT JEAN, sculptor; b. Gothenburg, Sweden, July 15, 1945; came to U.S., 1974; s. Jean Wilgot and Kerstin Aina (Axelson) U.; m. Veerle Rufina Vermeir, May 5, 1978; children: Robert, Gerald. Diploma in sculpture, Swedish State Sch. Art, 1966. Cert. conservator German Assn. Museology. Curator Nat. Mus. and Art Gallery, Botswana, Africa, 1971-74; curator III Mus. Natural History, Denver, 1974-75. Sculptor: works include Lincoln Ctr. Eagle, Dallas, 1981, Wind in the Sails, Corpus Christi, Tex., 1983, Genesee Eagle, Mumford, N.Y., 1984, Deinonychus Dinosaurs, Phila., 1987, Whooping Cranes Fountain, Washington, 1989, Swordfish Monument, IGFA Hdqs., Dania, Fla., 1999, Broward Conv. Ctr., Fountain, Ft. Lauderdale, Fla., Rudor Monument, Stockholm, 1991, Monumental Triptych Art Mus. South Tex., 1993, Bird Mountain Telecom. Hdqs., Stockholm, 1994, Christ Monument, Corpus Christi, 1995, Grizzly Bear Monument, Nat. Mus. Wildlife Art, Jackson, Wyo., 1994, King Penguin Monument, Mystic Marine Life Aquarium, Conn., 1997, R.T. Peterson Meml., Mystic Sealife Aquarium, Conn., 1997, Cougar Monument San Antonio Zoo, 1998, Otters Monument St. Louis Zoo, 1998, Tex. State Aquarium, 1998, Swordfish Monument, Dania Beach, Fla., 1998, Spanish Bull Monument, Johnson C. Smith U., Charlotte, N.C., 1999, Ram Monum, U. N.C., Chapel Hill, 2001, First Nat. Bank Omaha Can. Geese Monument, 2002. Recipient Gold medal Tex. Rangers Hall of Fame, 1980, Rungius award Nat. Mus. Wildlife Art, 1996, Prix de West award Nat. Cowboy Hall of Fame, 1998; named Master Wildlife Artist, 1987. Fellow: NAD (academician 1990, Barnett prize 1995, Speyer prize 1995), Am. Soc. Marine Artists, Nat. Acad. Western Art (gold medal 1981, 1982, 1988, 1995, 1999), Nat. Sculpture Soc. (Percival Dietsch award 1979, gold medal 1983, Hering award 1993, Silver medal and John Cavanaugh Meml. prize 2002); mem.: Soc. for Wildlife Art of Nations, Allied Artists of Am. (N.Y. Silver medal 1989), Soc. Animal Artists (medal merit 1979, 1980, 1982, 1987, 1996, 2001, E. Haller award 2001, Sponsor award 2002), Explorers Club N.Y.C. Home: 14337 Aquarius St Corpus Christi TX 78418-6003

ULLESTAD, MERWIN ALLAN, tax services executive; b. Hampton, Iowa, June 29, 1949; s. Allan L. and Georgia E. (Simms) U.; m. Crystal R. (Kleppinger), Sept. 17, 1977. BS, Iowa State U., 1971. CPA, PFS, Iowa, Tenn.; lic. capt. inland waters USCG. Ptnr. Coopers and Lybrand, Des Moines, 1971-83; ptnr. in charge, tax svcs. Touche Ross and Co., Nashville, 1983-89; ptnr. tax svcs. Deloitte & Touche, LLP, 1989—. Adj. tax prof. Simpson Coll., 1981-82; spkr. prof. acct. seminar Lipscomb U., 1990-2001. Editor: Abingdon Clergy Income Tax Guide, 1989-98. Sustaining membership capt. Mid. Tenn. coun. Boy Scouts Am., 1985—88; mem. Econ. Devel. Com., 1988—90; mem. ednl. adv. com. Nashville Health Care Coun., 1998—; bd. dirs., mem. exec. com., treas. United Way Mid. Tenn., 1990—96, mem. allocations panel, 1983—89; bd. dirs., mem. exec. com. Am. Cancer Soc., Des Moines, 1977—83, Nashville City Ballet, 1983—85; bd. dirs., chmn. fin. com. Watkins Coll. Art and Design, 1996—2001; bd. dirs. Gilda's Club, Nashville, treas., 1996—; trustee Tenn. Fed. Tax Inst., 2001—. Mem. AICPA (cert. Pers. Fin. Specialist), Tenn. Soc. CPAs, Iowa Soc. CPAs, Internat. Assn. for Fin. Planning (pres., bd. dirs. Nashville chpt. 1987-90), Nashville Estate Planning Coun. (pres. 1996-97, dir.), Nashville Songwriters Assn. Internat. (fin. cons. to bd. dirs. 1990-97), Nashville C. of C. (employment coun. 1999—, editor HR notes 2000—), Seven Seas Cruising Assn., Old Hickory Country Club, Nashville City Club, Commonwealth Yacht Club, Niue Yacht Club. Avocations: sailing, hiking, music. Office: Deloitte and Touche LLP 424 Church St Ste 2400 Nashville TN 37219-2396 E-mail: mullestad@deloitte.com.

ULLIAN, JOSEPH SILBERT, philosophy educator; b. Ann Arbor, Mich., Nov. 9, 1930; s. Hyman Benjamin and Frieda G. (Silbert) U. AB, Harvard U., 1952, AM, 1953, PhD, 1957. Instr. philosophy Stanford U., Calif., 1957-58; asst. prof. philosophy Johns Hopkins U., Balt., 1958-60; vis. asst. prof. philosophy U. Pa., Phila., 1959-60, rsch. assoc. in linguistics, 1961-62; vis. asst. prof. philosophy U. Chgo., 1962-63; asst. prof. U. Calif., Santa Barbara, 1964-66; assoc. prof. Washington U., St. Louis, 1965-70, prof., 1970—. Lectr. U. Calif., Berkeley, 1961; cons. Rsch. Directorate System Devel. Corp., Santa Monica, Calif., 1962-70. Co-author: The Web of Belief, 1970, 2d edit., 1978; contbr. articles to profl. jours. Mem. Am. Philos. Assn., Assn. for Symbolic Logic (exec. com. 1974-77), Am. Soc. for Aesthetics, Phi Beta Kappa. Democrat. Avocations: sports, theatre, music. Home: 984 Tornoe Rd Santa Barbara CA 93105-2229 Office: Washington U Dept Philosophy 1 Brookings Dr Saint Louis MO 63130-4899

ULLMAN, EDWIN FISHER, biotechnology consultant; b. Chgo., July 19, 1930; s. Harold P. and Jane F. Ullman; m. Elizabeth J. Finlay, June 26, 1954; children: Becky L., Linda J. BA, Reed Coll., 1952; MA, Harvard U., 1954, PhD, 1956. Research chemist Lederle Labs., Am. Cyanamid, Pearl River, N.Y., 1955-60; group leader central research div. Am. Cyanamid, Stamford, Conn., 1960-66; sci. dir. Synvar Research Inst., Palo Alto, Calif., 1966-70; v.p., dir. research Syva Co., 1970-95; v.p., dir. rsch. Behring Diagnostics Inc., San Jose, Calif., 1995-97; scientific cons., 1997—. Mem. various sci. adv. bds.; mem. adv. bd. San Francisco State U. Coll. of Sci. and Engring., 1994-96. Mem. editl. bd. Jour. Organic Chemistry, 1969-74, Jour. Immunoassay, 1979—, Jour. Clin. Lab., Analysis, 1986-87, Jour. Clin. Ligand Assay Soc., 1999—; contbr. articles to sci. jours.; patentee in field. NSF predoctoral fellow, 1952-53; U.S. Rubber Co. fellow, 1954-55. Recipient Clin. Ligand Assay Soc. Mallinckrodt award, 1981, Can. Soc. Clin. Chemists Health Group award, 1982, Inventor of Yr. award Peninsula Patent Law Assn., 1987. Fellow AAAS; mem. Am. Chem. Soc., Am. Assn. Clin. Chemistry (Van Slyke award N.Y. sect. 1984, No. Calif. sect. award 1991, Outstanding Contbns. to Clin. Chemistry in Selected Area of Rsch. award 1997, Ann. Edwin F. Ullman award established 1998), Phi Beta Kappa.

ULLMAN, JEFFREY DAVID, computer scientist, educator; b. N.Y.C., Nov. 22, 1942; s. Seymour and Nedra L. (Hart) Ullman; m. Holly E. Ullman, Nov. 19, 1967; children: Peter, Scott, Jonathan. BS, Columbia U., 1963; PhD, Princeton U., 1966, U. Brussels, 1975, U. Paris-Dauphine, 1992. Mem. tech. staff Bell Labs., Murray Hill, NJ, 1966-69, cons., 1969-89; prof. elec. engring., computer sci. Princeton (N.J.) U., 1969-79; prof. computer sci. Stanford (Calif.) U., 1979—, chmn. dep., 1990-94, Stanford W. Ascherman prof. computer sci., 1994—. Mem. computer sci. adv. panel NSF, 1974—77, mem. info., robotics and intelligent sys. adv. panel, 1986—88; mem. exam. com. computer sci. grad. record exam. Endl. Testing Svc., 1978—86; chmn. doctoral rating com. computer sci. N.Y. State Regents, 1989—93, 1998—99; mem. tech. adv. bd. Google.com, 1998—, Viquity, 1999—2002, Surromed, 1999—, Whizbang Labs, 1999—2002, Quiq, 1999—2002; bd. dirs. Kirusa; adv. bd. World Wide Web Consortium, 1998—99. Author: (book) Principles of Database and Knowledge-Base Systems, 1988, 1989; author: (with A. V. Aho and J. E. Hopcroft) Data Structures and Algorithms, 1983; author: (with A. V. Aho and R. Sethi) Compilers: Principles, Techniques and Tools, 1986; author: (with A. Va. Aho) Foundations of Computer Science, 1992, Elements of ML Programming, 1994, 1998; author: (with J. Widom) A First Course in Database Systems, 1997; author: (with J. E. Hopcroft and R. Motwani) Introduction to Automation, Languages, and Computation, 2001; author: (with H. Garcia-Molina and J. Widom) The Complete Book of Database Systems, 2002. Fellow Guggenheim, 1989. Fellow: Assn. Computing Machinery (coun. 1978—80, Spl. Interest Group Mgmt. Data Contbns. award 1996); mem.: NAE, Spl. Interest Group Mgmt. Data (vice chmn. 1983—95), Computing Rsch. Assn. (bd. dirs. 1994—2001), Spl. Interest Group Automata and Computability Theory (sec.-treas. 1973—75). Home: 1023 Cathcart Way Palo Alto CA 94305-1048 Office: Stanford U Dept Computer Sci 411 Gates Hall 4A-Wing Stanford CA 94305-9040 E-mail: Ullman@cs.stamford.edu.

ULLMAN, JOEL CLARKE, obstetrician/gynecologist; b. N.Y.C., 1937; s. Daniel and Sylvia (Miller) U.; m. Evelyn Janet Faust, June 11, 1961; children: Carin, Steven, Randie. BA, U. Vt., 1969; MD, NYU, 1963. Diplomate Am. Bd. Ob/gyn. Intern Beth Israel Hosp., N.Y.C., 1963-64, resident, 1964-66, 68-69; staff New Rochelle (N.Y.) Hosp. Medicine, Beth Israel Med. Ctr., N.Y.C.; asst. clin. prof. ob/gyn. Albert Einstein Med. Coll.; dir. gynecol. endoscopic surgery Sound Shore Med. Ctr. Bd. dirs. Planned Parenthood, Westchester, N.Y. Fellow Am. Coll. Obstetricians/Gynecologists; mem. AMA, Am. Fertility Soc.

ULLMAN, LEO SOLOMON, lawyer; b. Amsterdam, The Netherlands, July 14, 1939; s. Frank Leo and Emily (Konijn) U.; m. Katharine Laura Marbut, Aug. 27, 1960; chldren: Laura, Susan, Valerie, Frank. AB, Harvard U., 1961; JD, MBA, Columbia U., 1964. Bar: N.Y. 1966, U.S. Ct. Claims 1966, U.S. Tax Ct. 1969, U.S. Customs Ct. 1970. Assoc. Sullivan & Cromwell, N.Y.C., 1965-68; pres., mem. Ullman, Miller & Wrubel and predecessors, 1970-81; mem. Reid & Priest, 1984-91, of counsel, 1991-92, Schnader, Harrison, Segal & Lewis, N.Y.C., 1993-99. Adj. prof. internat. bus. NYU, 1972-77; lectr., panelist profl. organs. programs; chmn. Cedar Income Fund, Ltd., Cedar Bay Realty Advisors, Inc., SKR Mgmt., Inc., Brentway Mgmt., Inc. Co-author: Investeringen in Onroerend Goed in de Verenigde Staten, 1982; editor: European Taxation, Internat. Bur. Documentation, Amsterdan, 1964-65; founding editor: Taxation of Private Investment Income in Europe; contbr. articles to profl. publs. Mem. Port Washington (N.Y.) Bd. Edn., 1970-73, pres., 1972-73; bd. dirs. Found. for Jewish Hist. Mus. in Amsterdam, Inc.; bd. dirs. Anne Frank Ctr., U.S.A., chmn., 1994-2000. Served with USMCR, 1959-65. Co-recipient Cmty. Svc. award, Port Washington, 1981; Harlan Fiske Stone scholar Columbia Law Sch., 1963. Mem. ABA (tax sect. com. U.S. taxation of fgn. persons), N.Y. State Bar Assn. (tax sect. com. internat. trade and investment), Harvard Club, Netherlands Club. Home: Seacoast Ln Sands Point NY 11050-1230 Office: 44 S Boyles Ave Port Washington NY 11050 E-mail: leoullman@aol.com.

ULLMAN, MYRON EDWARD, III, retail executive; b. Youngstown, Ohio, Nov. 26, 1946; s. Myron Edward Jr. and June (Cunningham) U.; m. Cathy Emmons, June 20, 1969; children: Myron Cayce, Denver Tryan, Peter Brynt, Benjamin Kyrk, Kathryn Kwynn, Madylin Ming Yan. BS in Indsl. Mgmt., U. Cin., 1969; postgrad. Inst. Ednl. Mgmt., Harvard U., 1977. Internat. account mgr. IBM Corp., Cin., 1969-76; v.p. bus. affairs U. Cin., 1976-81; White House fellow The White House, Washington, 1981-82; exec. v.p. Sanger Harris div. Federated Stores, Dallas, 1982-86; mgr. dir., chief oper. officer Wharf Holdings Ltd., Hong Kong, 1986-88; chmn., CEO, dir. R.H. Macy & Co. Inc., N.Y.C., 1988-95; dir., deputy chmn. Federated Dept. Stores, Inc.; chmn., CEO DFS Group Ltd., San Francisco, 1995-98, group chmn., 1999-2000; also bd. dirs.; dir. gen., group mng. dir. LVMH, Louis Vuitton Moet Hennessy, Paris, 1999—2002. Mng. dir. Lane Crawford Ltd., Hong Kong, 1986-88; bd. advisors Gt. Traditions Corp., Cin.; chmn. Omni Hotels, Hampton, N.H., 1988; chmn. bd. dirs. Mercy Ships Internat., 1992-; bd. dirs. Asia Global Crossing, Kendall Jackson, DFS Group Ltd., Miami Cruiseline Svcs., Lucille Packard Found. for Children's Health, Stamford U. Internat. v.p. U. Cin. Alumni Assn., 1980—; bd. dirs. Nat. Multiple Sclerosis Soc., N.Y.C.; bd. dirs. Brunswick Sch., Greenwich, Conn., U. Cin. Found., Lincoln Ctr. Devel., Deafness Rsch. Found., 1997-2001, U. Calif. Med. Ctr. Found., San Francisco, 1998—. Mem. White House Fellow Alumni Assn., Econ. Club N.Y.C. (bd. dirs., exec. com.), Nat. Retail Fedn. (vice chmn., bd. dirs., exec. com. 1993—), Delta Tau Delta (treas. 1967-68). Republican. Office: Jackson Hale Group Ste 935 100 Spear St San Francisco CA 94105 E-mail: mike@meallman.com.

ULLMAN, NELLY SZABO, statistician, educator; b. Vienna, Austria, Aug. 11, 1925; came to U.S., 1939; d. Viktor and Elizabeth (Rosenberg) Szabo; m. Robert Ullman, Mar. 20, 1947 (dec.); children: Buddy, Wiliiam John, Martha Ann, Daniel Howard. BA, Hunter Coll., 1945; MA, Columbia U., 1948; PhD, U. Mich., 1969. Rsch. assoc. MIT Radiation Lab, Cambridge, Mass., 1945; instr. Polytechnic Inst. of Bklyn., 1945-63; from asst. prof. to prof. Ea. Mich. U., Ypsilanti, 1963—2002, prof., 2002—. Author: Study Guide To Actuarial Exam, 1978; contbr. articles to profl. jours. Mem. Am. Math. Assn., Am. Assn. Univ. Profs. Office: Ea Mich Univ Dept Math Ypsilanti MI 48197 E-mail: mth_ullman@online.emich.edu.

ULLMAN, PIERRE LIONI, retired Spanish educator; b. Nice, France, Oct. 31, 1929; came to U.S., 1940; s. Eugene Paul and Suzanne (Lioni) U.; m. Mary Meade McDowell, June 9, 1956; children: Katherine Meade Turner, Susan Randolph Johnson. BA, Yale U., 1952; AM, Columbia U., 1956; PhD, Princeton (N.J.) U., 1962. Instr. Rutgers U., New Brunswick, N.J., 1961-63; asst. prof. U. Calif., Davis, 1963-65; assoc. prof. U. Wis., Milw., 1965-69, prof., 1969-94, prof. emeritus, 1994—. Vis. prof. U. Minn., Mpls., 1970-71, U. Mich., Ann Arbor, 1975. Author: Mariano Jose de Larra and Spanish Political Rhetoric, 1971, A Contrapuntal Method for Analyzing Spanish Literature, 1988; contbr. articles to profl. jours. Pres. U. Wis. Milw. Retired Faculty Assn., 2000-2002. With U.S. Army, 1952-54. Fellow U. Wis. Mem. MLA (emeritus), U. Esperanto Assn. (2d prize for drama 1981), Esperanto League for N.Am., Sigma Delta Pi. Office: U Wis Milw PO Box 413 Milwaukee WI 53201

ULLMAN, ROGER ROLAND, lawyer, realtor; b. Darby, Pa., Nov. 16, 1948; s. David Ulrich and Carolyn Elizabeth (Wensink) U.; m. Minnie Lean Zanzinger, May 26, 1968; children: Roger II, Craig, David. BA, W.Va. Wesleyan Coll., 1970; MBA, Pepperdine U., 1976; JD, Del. Law Sch., Wilmington, 1980. Officer USMC, 1970-77; realtor Pa., 1977—. Solo practice law, Swarthmore, Pa., 1981—. Vol. Boy Scouts Am., 1977—. With USAR, 1989—. Mem. Rotary. Home: 199 Harvard Ave Swarthmore PA 19081-1625 Fax: (610) 543-8789. E-mail: rrullmansr@aol.com.

ULLMAN, SARAH ELIZABETH, educator; BA, Hamilton Coll., 1985; PhD, Brandeis U., 1990. Postdoctoral fellow UCLA, 1991-93; asst. prof. U. Ill., Chgo., 1993-99, assoc. prof., 1999—. Postdoctoral fellow UCLA, L.A., 1991-93. Mem. APA, Internat. Soc. Traumatic Stress Studies. Office: U Ill 1007 W Harrison St Chicago IL 60607-7140

ULLMAN, SUSAN JOYCE FELDMAN, social worker; b. N.Y.C., May 22, 1953; d. Irving and Helen (Manus) Feldman; m. Alan Howard Ullman, May 26, 1974; children: Ian Michael, Joni Michelle. BA cum laude, CUNY, Bklyn., 1974; MSW, U. Pa., Phila., 1976. Lic. ind social worker, Ohio. Social worker N.E. Fla. State Hosp., Macclenny, 1976-78; clin. social worker U. Cin. Med. Ctr., 1978-80; pvt. practice social work Montgomery, Ohio, 1984-89; contract therapist Clermont Counseling Ctr., Milford, 1988—95. Cons., group therapist Princeton Jr. High Sch., Cin., 1989—. Mem. NASW. Avocations: running, flower gardening. Office: Clermont Counseling Ctr 43 E Main St Amelia OH 45102-1993

ULLMANN, BARBARA, maternal/child health and community health nurse; b. Wichita, Sept. 7, 1945; Diploma, Welsey Med. Ctr., Wichita, 1966; BSN, Wichita State U., 1983; MSN, Ariz. State U., 1990. Cert. family nurse practitioner. Coord. maternal-child health Rapid City (S.D.) Regional Hosp., 1981-87; nursing cons. Ariz. Dept. Health Svcs., Phoenix, 1990-91; nurse practitioner in ob-gyn. Mesa, Ariz., 1991-94; clin. coord. nurse practitioner program U. Phoenix, 1993-98, asst. dean nurse practitioner program, 1998-99, dir. nurse practitioner program, 1999—. Mem. Am. Acad. Nurse Practitioners (pub. rels. com. 1990-99), Nat. Orgn. Nurse Practioner Faculty (rsch. com. 1994-99), Sigma theta Tau (sec., bd. dirs., elibigility chairperson).

ULLMANN, OWEN, journalist; b. Neptune, NJ, Nov. 16, 1947; s. Marcel Andre Ullmann and Jane Horowitz; m. Lois M. Kietur, Aug. 6, 1977; children: Cara L., Daniel E. BA, Rutgers U., 1969; MA, U. Wis., 1973. Reporter Daily Jour., Elizabeth, NJ, 1969—71, State Jour., Madison, Wis., 1972; automotive reporter AP, Detroit, 1973—77, labor, econs. reporter Washington, 1977—83; econs., White House, State Dept. reporter Knight-Ridder Newspapers, 1983—93; econs. corr., news editor Bus. Week, 1993—99; reporter, editor USA Today, 1999—. Author: (biography) Stockman: The Man, The Myth, The Future, 1986; editor: Internat. Economy, 2000—; contbg. editor: Washingtonian, 1987—. Recipient Merriman Smith award, White House Corrs. Assn., 1988, Aldo Beckman award, 1989, Disting. Journalist award, U. Wis. Journalism Sch., Madison, 1999. Office: USA Today 1100 NY Ave Washington DC 20005

ULLRICH, CHRISTOPHER GEORGE, neuroradiologist; b. Rochester, N.Y., Dec. 31, 1950; s. George Anthony and Marion Saeli U.; m. Betsy Coleman, May 26, 1973. BS, St. John Fisher Coll., 1972; MD, SUNY, Syracuse, 1976. Diplomate Am. Bd. Radiology. Resident SUNY, Syracuse, 1976-80; fellow in neuroradiology Johns Hopkins Hosp., Balt., 1980-82; neuroradiologist Charlotte (N.C.) Radiology PA, 1982—; chief of radiology Carolinas Med. Ctr., Charlotte, 2001—. Clin. faculty Johns Hopkins Sch. Medicine, 1982-88, Mallinkrodt Inst. Radiology, St. Louis, 1988-99. Fellow Am. Coll. Radiology (pres. N.C. chpt. 1998-2000); mem. Am. Soc. Neuroradiology, Am. Soc. Spinal Radiology (exec. com. 1998-99), Am. Roentgen Ray Soc. (bronze medal 1979), Cervical Spine Rsch. Soc. (pres. 2000), Southeastern Neuroradiology Soc. (pres. 2000), N.C. Med. Soc. Avocations: photography, travel, politics. Office: Charlotee Radiology PA 3030 Latrobe Dr Charlotte NC 28211-4866

ULLRICH, LINDA J. medical technologist; b. Rockford, Ill., May 10, 1944; d. Glenn H. and R. Catherine (Mathews) Person; m. John R. Brody, June 11, 1966 (div. July 1978); children: Kevin R. Brody, Keith A. Brody; m. Sterling O. Ullrich Sr., Mar. 10, 1979 (dec. Oct. 1999); stepchildren: Sterling O. Jr., Eugene, Lee Anna, Michelle. BA, Thiel Coll., 1966; MPA, Kent State U., 1993, postgrad., 1996—. Cert. med. tech. Am. Soc. Clin. Pathologists, specialist in hematology. Staff med. tech. Sharon (Pa.) Gen. Hosp., 1966-76; supr. hematology, coagulation, urinalysis sects. Sharon Regional Health Sys. (formerly Sharon Gen. Hosp.), 1976-96, lab. mgr., 1996—. Edn. coord. Beaver

County C.C., Pa., 1976-80; tech. supr. lab. Cancer Care Ctr., Hermitage, Pa., 1993—; adj. prof. Thiel Coll., Greenville, Pa., 1994-95, 97-99; com. mem. Sharon Regional Health Sys., 1990—. Merit badge counselor, com. mem. Troop 67 Boy Scouts Am., Newton Falls, Ohio, 1982-95. Lutheran. Avocations: bicycling, hiking, knitting, reading. Home: 775 Lynita Dr NE Brookfield OH 44403-9605 Office: Sharon Regional Health Sys 740 E State St Sharon PA 16146-3328 E-mail: lullrich@srhs-pa.org., ljullrich@aol.com.

ULLRICH, ROXIE ANN, special education educator; b. Ft. Dodge, Iowa, Nov. 10, 1951; d. Rocco William and Mary Veronica (Casady) Jackowell; m. Thomas Earl Ullrich, Aug. 10, 1974; children: Holly Ann, Anthony Joseph. BA, Creighton U., 1973; MA in Teaching, Morningside Coll., 1991. Cert. tchr. Iowa, cons. in spl. edn. Iowa. Tchr. Corpus Christi Sch., Ft. Dodge, Iowa, 1973-74, Westwood Community Schs., Sloan, 1974-80, Sioux City Community Schs., 1987—. Cert. judge Iowa High Sch. Speech Assn., Des Moines, 1975—; supt. Woodbury County Fair; leader 4H Club. Mem. Am. Paint Horse Assn., Am. Quarter Horse Assn., Sioux City Hist. Assn., Sioux City Art Ctr., M.I. Hummel Club, Phi Delta Kappa. Avocations: doll collector, plate collector, horse-back riding. Home: PO Box W 819 Brown St Sloan IA 51055

ULMAN, LLOYD, retired social sciences educator; b. N.Y.C., Apr. 22, 1920; s. Harry Richmond Ulman and Ruth Joanna Langer; m. Lassie Agoos Finck, July 4, 1948. AB, Columbia Coll., 1940; AM, U. Wis., 1941; PhD, Harvard U., 1950. Asst. prof. econs. U. Minn., Mpls., 1950—52, assoc. prof. econs., 1952—56, prof. econs., 1956—58; prof. econs. and indsl. rels. U. Calif., Berkeley, 1958—90, dir. Inst. Indsl. Rels., 1963—81. Sr. labor economist Coun. Econ. Advisors, Washington, 1961—62; cons. Fed. Res. Bd., Washington, 1966—67; mem. Pres. Pay Adv. Com., Washington, 1979—80. Author: (novels) The Rise of the National Trade Union, 1955; co-author Unionism, Economic Stabilization and Incomes Policies, 1983, Work and Pay in the United States and Japan, 1997. Active City of Berkeley Personnel Bd., 1980. Lt. USN, 1942—46, PTO, Africa. Named to Order of the Northern Star, King of Sweden, 1979; fellow vis. fellow, All Souls Coll. Oxford U., 1973—74. Mem.: Am. Econ. Assn., Indsl. Rels. Rsch. Assn. (pres. 1985—86). Achievements include work in areas in development of labor institutions and their impact on economic stabilization policies. Avocations: tennis, gardening. Home: 776 Creston Rd Berkeley CA 94708-1254 Office: Dept Econs U Calif Berkeley Berkeley CA 94720

ULMAN, LOUIS JAY, lawyer; b. Balt., Mar. 24, 1946; s. Erwin Ira And Rose (Clayman) U.; m. Diana Lynn Milford, Aug. 17, 1969; children: Kenneth, Douglas. BA, Dickinson Coll., 1967; JD, Am. U., 1970. Bar: Md. 1970. Assoc. Ulman & Cohan, Balt., 1970-75; ptnr. Ulman & Ulman, 1975-80, Weinberg & Green, Columbia, Md., 1980-92; prin. Hodes, Ulman, Pessin & Katz, 1992—. Adj. prof. law Washington Coll. of Law, Am. U., 1997-98; vice chmn. Md. Pub. Broadcasting Commn.; chmn. Md. Racing Commn. Pres. Santa Claus Anonymous, Balt., 1975; mem. Howard County Bd. Social Svc., Ellicott City, Md., 1990. Mem. Md. State Bar Assn. (com. on rels. with fin. profls. 1985-92), Howard County Bar Assn., Internat. Assn. for Fin. Planning. Democrat. Jewish. Office: 10500 Little Patuxent Pkwy Columbia MD 21044-3585

ULMEN, KATHRYN T. neuroscience clinical nurse specialist; b. Green Bay, Wis., Dec. 23, 1952; d. Joseph H. and Dorothy M. (Gavronski) Ulmen. RN, Holy Family Hosp. Sch. Nursing, Manitowoc, Wis., 1976; BSN, U. Wis., 1980; MS, Tex. Woman's U., Dallas, 1981. CNRN. Staff nurse U. Wis. Hosp., Madison; neurosci. clin. nurse specialist St. Vincent Hosp., Green Bay. Mem.: ANA, Am. Heart/Stroke Assn., Nat. Stroke Assn., Am. Assn. Neurosci. Nurses, Am. Brain Tumor Assn., Am. Assn. Neurol. Surgeons, Sigma Theta Tau.

ULMER, FRANCES ANN, lieutenant governor; b. Madison, Wis., Feb. 1, 1947; m. Bill Council; children: Amy, Louis. BA in Econs. and Polit. Sci., U. Wis.; JD with honors, Wis. Sch. Law. Polit. advisor Gov. Jay Hammond, Alaska, 1975-81; former mayor City of Juneau; mem. Alaska Ho. of Reps., 1986-94, minority leader, 1992-94; lt. gov. State of Alaska, 1995—. Home: 1700 Angus Way Juneau AK 99801-1411 Office: Office Lt Gov PO Box 110015 Juneau AK 99811-0015 E-mail: lt_governor@gov.state.ak.us.

ULMER, JAMES HOWARD, potter; b. Carrington, N.D., Oct. 12, 1945; s. James Francis and Lois Adelle (Wolf) U.; m. Ann Cecile Gerlach, May 28, 1977; children: Jesse Gerlach, Matthew James. BSBA, N.D. State U., 1969; MS, U. N.D., 1973. Geologist UND Engring. Sta., Grand Forks, N.D., 1974-76; potter Stoneware by Jim Ulmer, Frazee, Minn., 1972—. Dir. Lake Region Arts Coun., Fergus Falls, Minn., 1990-92; dir. intern program U.N.D., Grand Forks, 1976-93, Moorhead (Minn.) State U., 1976-93. Author of poems. Mem. Mich. Guild Artists, Minn. Craft Coun. Home and Office: 15158 330th Ave Frazee MN 56544-8810 E-mail: ulmerstoneware@yahoo.com.

ULMER, JEFFERY TODD, sociology educator; b. Harrisburg, Pa., Mar. 2, 1966; s. Charles Alvin and Louise T. Ulmer; m. Gail Johnston, Dec. 29, 1994; children: Jacob, Kathryn. BA in Sociology, Susquehanna U., 1988; MA in Sociology, Pa. State U., 1994, PhD in Sociology, 1993. Rsch. assoc. Pa. Commn. on Sentencing, State College, 1992-94; asst. prof. sociology Purdue U., West Lafayette, Ind., 1994-2000; assoc. prof. sociology and crime, law and justice Pa. State U., University Park, 2000—. Author: Social Worlds of Sentencing: Court Communities Under Sentencing Guidelines, 1997; contbr. articles to profl. jours. Mem. Am. Sociol. Assn., Am. Soc. Criminology, Soc. for Study of Symbolic Interaction, Soc. for Study of Social Problems. Home: 624 Wayland Pl State College PA 16803 Office: Pa State Univ Dept Sociology 211 Oswald Tower University Park PA 16802 E-mail: jtu100@psu.edu., ulmerg@penn.com.

ULMER, MELVILLE JACK, economist, educator; b. N.Y.C., May 17, 1911; s. Saul and Lillian (Ulmer) U.; m. Naomi Zinken, June 1, 1937; children: Melville Paul, Stephanie Marie. BS, NYU, 1937, MA, 1938; PhD, Columbia, 1948. Writer N.Y. Am., 1930-37; chief, price research sect. Bur. Labor Statistics, 1940-45; sr. economist Smaller War Plants Corp., 1945; chief financial analysis sect. Dept. Commerce, 1946-48; editor Survey of Current Bus., 1948-50; asso. prof. econs. Am. U., 1950-52, prof., 1952-61, chmn. dept., 1953-61; prof. econs. U. Md., 1961-86, emeritus prof., from 1986. Vis. prof. econs. Netherlands Sch. Econ., Rotterdam, 1958-59, 65-66; research asso. Nat. Bur. Econ. Research, 1950-60; cons. OAS, 1954, Dept. Commerce, 1955, Gen. Services Adminstrn., 1957, Dept. State, 1962, Bur. Budget, 1967-69 Author: numerous books including The Economic Theory of Cost of Living Index Numbers, 1949, Trends and Cycles in Capital Formation by U.S. Railroads, 1870-1950, 1954, Economics: Theory and Practice, 2d edit., 1965, Capital in Transportation, Communications and Pub. Utilities, 1960, The Welfare State: U.S.A. 1969, The Theory and Measurement of International Price Competitiveness, 1969; co-author: (with John M. Blair) Wartime Prices, 1944, (with C. Wright Mills) Small Business and Civic Welfare, 1946; contbg. editor: The New Republic, 1970-80; contbr. articles in Am. Econ. Rev., Jour. Am. Statis. Assn., Commentary, Atlantic Monthly, Challenge, Am. Spectator, Pub. Interest, Jour. of Econ. Issues, also others. Recipient Sr. Fulbright award, 1958, 65, Medal of Honor Free U. of Brussels, 1986; Merrill Found. fellow, 1957; Wilton Park fellow Gt. Britain, 1966; Peoples Coll. fellow Denmark, 1966; Nuffield fellow Can., 1971; Nat. Endowment for Humanities sr. fellow, 1973; NSF grantee, 1973; State Dept. econ. specialist grantee, 1977, 78. Fellow AAAS; mem. Am. Econ. Assn., Am. Statis. Assn., Econometric Soc., Assn. Evolutionary Econs. (exec. bd.), Atlantic Econ. Soc. (disting assoc.), Artus Soc., Pi Gamma Mu. Clubs: Cosmos (Washington). Home: Potomac, Md. *Failure must be taken as an instructive experience that aids in exposing the pitfalls to achievement.* Died Feb. 9, 2001.

ULMER, WALTER FRANCIS, JR. consultant, former army officer; b. Bangor, Maine, Apr. 2, 1929; married; 3 children BS in Engring., U.S. Mil. Acad., 1952; M of Regional Planning, Pa. State U., 1973. Commd. 2d lt. U.S. Army, 1952, advanced through grades to lt. gen., 1982; dep. comdr. U.S. Army Armor Ctr., Ft. Knox, Ky., 1974-75; commandant-of cadets U.S. Mil. Acad., West Point, N.Y., 1975-77; dir. human resources devel. U.S. Army, Washington, 1978-79; comdr. 3d Armored Div., Frankfurt, Germany, 1979-82; comdg. gen. III Corps and Ft. Hood, Tex., 1982-85, ret., 1985; pres., CEO Ctr. for Creative Leadership, Greensboro, N.C., 1985-94; ind. cons., 1995—. Lectr. in field Contbr. articles to profl. jours. Home: 250 Riverbay Dr Moneta VA 24121-3138 E-mail: riverbay6@aol.com.

ULOSEVICH, STEVEN NILS, social scientist, consultant, educator, trainer; b. Tampa, Fla., Nov. 19, 1947; s. Steven Anthony and Coragene (Paulson) U.; m. Pamela Elmeda Locke, June 27, 1970; children: Christina, Garrett. BA, U. N.C., Greensboro, 1969; MBA, Webster U., 1981; EdD, U. So. Calif., 1990. Commd. 2d lt. USAF, 1970, advanced through grades to maj., 1992, ret., 1992; sr. assoc. JWK Internat., Inc., Universal City, Tex., 1992-93; owner, prin. cons. Ulosevich & Assocs., China Grove, 1993—; sr. scientist, program mgr. Veridian Corp., San Antonio, 1995-98; dir. cons. and tng. svcs. Holt Cons. Svcs., Inc., 1998-99; dir. tng. and orgnl. devel. So. Steel Co., 2000—. Asst. prof. Embry-Riddle Aero U., Honolulu, 1988-91, San Antonio, 1992—; prof. Troy State U. Sch. Edn., Honolulu, 1990-91, Webster U., San Antonio, 1992—, U. of Incarnate Word, San Antonio, 1996-97; with San Antonio New Schs. Devel. Found., 1991-95, San Antonio 2000; bd. dirs. Alumni Assn. U. N.C., Greensboro, 1998-2001, Alamo Tech Prep Consotrium; bd. govs. Character Edn. Inst., 1996-99. Contbr. articles to profl. jours. Educare scholar U. So. Calif., 1989. Mem. ASTD, Survival and Flight Equipment Assn. (chpt. pres. 1986-88), Human Factors and Ergonomics Soc., Air Force Assn., Order of Daedalians, Phi Delta Kappa, Delta Epsilon. Avocations: gardening, golf, music, photography, reading.

ULREY, PRESCOTT DAVID, lawyer; b. Atlanta, Apr. 1, 1966; s. David Michael Ulrey and Barbara Ann (Johnson) Middendorf. AB, U. Calif., Berkeley, 1988; MALD, Fletcher Sch. Law & Diplomacy, 1991; JD, Columbia U., 1994. Bar: N.Y. 1995. Atty. Brown & Wood, N.Y.C., 1994-97, N.Y.C. Office Mgmt. & Budget, N.Y.C., 1997—. Gen. counsel N.Y.C. Transitional Fin. Authority. Mem.: Assn Bar City of N.Y. Office: NYC Office Mgmt & Budget 75 Park Pl New York NY 10007-2146 E-mail: ulreys@omb.nyc.gov.

ULRICH, JERRY, music educator; b. Lawrenceville, Ill., Oct. 7, 1955; s. Omer and Josephine Ulrich; m. Deborah Davis Ulrich, Aug. 2, 1980; children: Anna, Kathryn, Davis. BA, Ea. Ill. U., Charleston, IL, 1974—77; MA, So. Meth. U., Dalks, TX, 1977—78; Ph. D, Cin. Conservatory, Cincinnati, OH, 1981—86. Teaching Ill., NY. Educator Fulton County Pub. Schools, Atlanta, 1978—82; music educator Ashland U., Ashland, Ohio, 1984—96, Hofstra U., Hempstead, NY, 1996—2001, NYC Pub. Schools, New York, 2001—. Guest condr. various events throughout the US; assoc. dir. Manhattan Concert Prodn., New York, NY. Contbr. articles to profl. jour. Mem.: Music Educators Nat. Conf., Coll. Music Soc., Am. Choral Directors Assn. (life). Home: PO Box 702 Northport NY 11768 Personal E-mail: jerryaulrich@aol.com.

ULRICH, JODY L. accountant; b. Marshfield, Wis., Mar. 18, 1969; d. Robert Harold and Donetta Marie (Oertel) U.; m. Harley Hastings Thomas IV, July 23, 1994 (div. Aug. 1998). BS, Marquette U., 1991. Cost acct. Schwarz Pharm., Mequon, Wis., 1992-93, Wis. Dairies Coop., Baraboo, 1993-94, Acme Die Casting, Inc., Racine, Wis., 1994-97; sr. cost acct. Bosch Automation Tech., 1997-2001; gen. acctg. supr. Bosch Rexroth Corp., Sturtevant, 2001; budget analysis mgr. Unifund , Cin., 2001—02; v.p. budget and fin. analysis Unifund , 2002—. Mem. Inst. Mgmt. Accts., Kiwanis (bd. dirs. 1999, nominating com. 1999). Republican. Avocations: volleyball, golf, skiing, piano/music, gardening. Home: 3754 Mt Vernon Ave Cincinnati OH 45209 Office: Unifund 11802 Conrey Rd Cincinnati OH 45249

ULRICH, LAUREL THATCHER, historian, educator; b. Sugar City, Idaho, July 11, 1938; d. John Kenneth and Alice (Siddoway) Thatcher; m. Gael Dennis Ulrich, Sept. 22, 1958; children: Karl, Melinda, Nathan, Thatcher, Amy. BA in English, U. Utah, 1960; MA in English, Simmons Coll., 1971; PhD in History, U. N.H., 1980. Asst. prof. humanities U. N.H., Durham, 1980-84, asst. prof. history, 1985-88, assoc. prof., 1988-91, prof., 1991-95; prof. history and women's studies Harvard U., Cambridge, Mass., 1995—, James Duncan Phillips prof. early Am. history, 1997—, dir. Charles Warren Ctr., 1997—. Audiocourse cons. Annenberg Found.; cons., participating humanist numerous exhibits, pub. programs, other projects; project humanist Warner (N.H.) Women's Oral History Project; bd. editors William & Mary Quar., 1989-91, Winterthur Portfolio, 1991—. Author: Good Wives: Image and Reality in the Lives of Women in Northern New England, 1650-1750, 1982, A Midwife's Tale: The Life of Martha Ballard Based on Her Diary, 1785-1812, 1990 (Pulitzer Prize for history 1991); contbr. articles, abstracts, essays and revs. to profl. publs. Coun. mem. Inst. Early Am. History and Culture, 1989-91; trustee Strawberry Banke Mus., 1987-93. John Simon Guggenheim fellow, 1991-92, NEH fellow, 1982, 84-85; women's studies rsch. grantee Woodrow Wilson Fellowship Found., 1979; co-recipient Best Book award Berkshire Conf. Women's Historians, 1990; recipient Best Book award Soc. for History of Early Republic, 1990, John S. Dunning prize and Joan Kelly Meml. prize Am. Hist. Assn., 1990, Bancroft Prize for Am. History, 1991. Mem. Orgn. Am. Historians (nominating com. 1992—, ABC-Clio award com. 1989), Am. Hist. Assn. (rsch. coun. 1993-96). Office: Harvard U Charles Warren Ctr Emerson Hall 4th Fl Cambridge MA 02138*

ULRICH, LUCINDA DYKES, librarian; b. New London, Conn., Nov. 1, 1949; d. Kenneth Raymond and Alma Jane (McVeigh) Dykes; m. Glenn F. Ulrich, Aug. 11, 1990. BA, U. Pitts., 1971, MLS, 1974. Cert. libr., Pa. Children's libr. Carnegie Libr. Pitts., 1975-85, divsn. head Woods Run br. libr., 1986—. Book reviewer Pitts. Post-Gazette, 1993—. Mem. Brighton Heights Citizens Fedn., Pitts., 1990—; chair book sale Fall Festival of Children's Books. Mem. Pa. Libr. Assn. (conf. com. 1990, 92), Carnegie DRA Users Commn., Electronic Info. Network Users Group. Republican. Methodist. Avocations: cross-stitching, reading, car racing fan, singing. Home: 71 Frankfort Ave Pittsburgh PA 15229-2015 Office: Woods Run Libr 1201 Woods Run Ave Pittsburgh PA 15212-2335

ULRICH, MAX MARSH, retired executive search consultant; b. Kokomo, Ind., Mar. 21, 1925; s. Max Dan and Esther Stone (Marsh) U.; m. Mary Ellen Fisher, Sept. 12, 1950; children— Max Dwight, Jeanne Nanette; m. Geraldine A. Kidd, Jan. 25, 1973; 1 child, Amanda Marsh BS, U.S. Mil. Acad., 1946; MS in Civil Engring, Mass. Inst. Tech., 1951. Comd. 2d lt. C.E. U.S. Army, 1946, advanced through grades to capt., 1950; resigned, 1954; asst. to mng. dir. Edison Electric Inst., 1954-58; with Consol. Edison Co., N.Y.C., 1958-71, asst. v.p., 1962-63, v.p. charge advt. and pub. relations, 1963-67, v.p. customer service, 1968-69, v.p. Bklyn. div., 1969-71; prin., dir. Ward Howell Internat. Inc., N.Y.C., 1971-74, pres., chief exec. officer, 1974-84, chmn., chief exec. officer, 1984-88; pres. Ward Howell Internat. Group, Inc., 1988-92; ret., 1992; cons. Ward Howell Internat. Group, Inc., 1992-98. Mem. Sigma Xi. Home: 2 Kingswood Dr Orangeburg NY 10962-1806 E-mail: maxmul@aol.com.

ULRICH, PAUL GRAHAM, lawyer, writer, editor; b. Spokane, Wash., Nov. 29, 1938; s. Donald Gunn and Kathryn (Vandercook) U.; m. Kathleen Nelson Smith, July 30, 1982; children: Kathleen Elizabeth Pennington, Marilee Rae McCracken, Michael Graham Ulrich. BA with high honors, U. Mont., 1961; JD, Stanford U., 1964. Bar: Calif. 1965, Ariz. 1966, U.S. Supreme Ct. 1969, U.S. Ct. Appeals (9th cir.) 1965. Law clk. judge U.S. Ct. Appeals, 9th Circuit, San Francisco, 1964-65; assoc. Lewis and Roca, Phoenix, 1965-70, ptnr., 1970-85; pres. Paul G. Ulrich P.C., 1985-92, Ulrich, Thompson & Kessler, P.C., Phoenix, 1992-94, Ulrich & Kessler, P.C., Phoenix, 1994-95, Ulrich, Kessler & Anger, P.C., Phoenix, 1995-2000, Ulrich & Anger, P.C., Phoenix, 2000—; owner Pathway Enterprises, 1985-91. Judge pro tem divsn. 1, Ariz. Ct. Appeals, Phoenix, 1986; instr. Thunderbird Grad. Sch. Internat. Mgmt., 1968-69, Ariz. State U. Coll. Law, 1970-73, 78, Scottsdale C.C., 1975-77, also continuing legal edn. seminars. Author and pub.: Applying Management and Motivation Concepts to Law Offices, 1985; editor: Arizona Appellate Handbook, 1978-2000, Working With Legal Assistants, 1980, 81, Future Directions for Law Office Management, 1982, People in the Law Office, 1985-86; co-author, pub.: Arizona Healthcare Professional Liability Handbook, 1992, supplement, 1994, Arizona Healthcare Professional Liability Defense Manual, 1995, Arizona Healthcare Professional Liability Update Newsletter, 1992-99; co-author, editor: Federal Appellate Practice: Ninth Circuit, 1994, 2d edit., 1999, supp. 2002; contbg. editor Law Office Econs. and Mgmt., 1984-97, Life, Law and the Pursuit of Balance, 1996, 2d edit., 1997. Mem. Ariz. Supreme Ct. Task Force on Ct. Orgn. and Adminstrn., 1988-89; mem. com. on appellate cts. Ariz. Supreme Ct., 1990-91; bd. visitors Stanford U. Law Sch., 1974-77; adv. com. legal assisting program Phoenix Coll., 1985-95; atty. rep. 9th Cir. Jud. Conf., 1997-2000. With U.S. Army, 1956. Recipient continuing legal edn. award State Bar Ariz., 1978, 86, 90, Harrison Tweed spl. merit award Am. Law Inst./ABA, 1987. Fellow Ariz. Bar Found. (founding 1985—); mem. ABA (chmn. selection and utilization of staff pers. com., econs. of law sect. 1979-81, mem. standing com. legal assts. 1982-86, co-chmn. joint project on appellate handbooks 1983-85, co-chmn. fed. appellate handbook project 1985-88, chmn. com. on liaison with non-lawyers orgns. Econs. of Law Practice sect. 1985-86), Am. Acad. Appellate Lawyers, Am. Law Inst. (life), Am. Judicature Soc. (Spl. Merit citation 1987), Ariz. Bar Assn. (chmn. econs. of law practice com. 1980-81, co-chmn. lower ct. improvement com. 1982-85, co-chmn. Ariz. appellate handbook project 1976-2000), Coll. Law Practice Mgmt., Maricopa County Bar Assn. (bd. dirs. 1994-96), Calif. Bar Assn., Phi Kappa Phi, Phi Alpha Delta, Sigma Phi Epsilon. Democrat. Home: 2529 E Lupine Ave Phoenix AZ 85028-1823 Office: Ste 250 3707 N 7th St Phoenix AZ 85014-5057 E-mail: ulanpc@aol.com.

ULRICH, PETER HENRY, banker; b. Munich, Germany, Nov. 24, 1922; s. Hans George and Hella (Muschweck) U.; m. Carol A. Peek, Oct. 21, 1944; children: Carol Jean Hewes, Patricia Diane (Mrs. Damon Eberhart), Peter James. Student, Northwestern U., 1941-42, U. Iowa, 1943, Sch. Mortgage Banking, 1954-56. Lic. real estate broker, cert. mortgage banker; cert. rev. appraiser; cert. mortgage underwriter. Escrow officer Security Title Ins. Co., Riverside, Calif., 1946-53; asst. cashier Citizens Nat. Trust & Savs., 1953-57; v.p. Security First Nat. Bank, 1957-63; sr. v.p. Bank of Calif. (N.A.), Los Angeles, 1963-72; pres. Ban Cal Mortgage Co., 1972-74, Ban Cal Tri-State Mortgage Co., 1974-75; cons., 1975-76; pres., dir. Beneficial Standard Mortgage Co., 1976-88; real estate cons., 1988—. Instr. real estate and bus. San Bernardino Valley Coll., Riverside City Coll., Pasadena City Coll. Pres. Residential Rsch. Com. So. Calif., 1965, Riverside Opera Assn., 1956—59, Riverside Symphony Soc., 1959—61; trustee Idyllwild Arts Found., 1957—, pres., 1970—73, sec., 1986—87; mem. adv. bd. Salvation Army, 1959—, vice chmn., 1971—74, chmn., 1975, Harbor Light Com., 1965—68; convocator Calif. Luth. U., 1976—80, 1981—83, regent, 1981—90; v.p. Guild Opera Co., 1991—99; pres. Lark Ellen Lions Charities, 1987—90, 1994—; treas. Opera Buffs, 1983—; mem. Arcadia Beautiful Commn., 1989—95, vice chair, 1991—92, chmn., 1992—93; trustee Calif. Luth. Edn. Found., 1989—2001; v.p. Arcadia Tournament Roses Assn., 1997; mem. Arcadia City Coun., 1995—96; trustee Arcadia Pub. Libr., 1997—, chair, 1999; v.p. South Pasadena-Arcadia Adult Reading Ctrs., 2000, pres., 2002; bd. dirs. Guild Opera Co., Lark Ellen Lions Charities, Arcadia Tournament Roses Assn., Am. Heart Assn. Foothill divsn. chair, 1997—99, South Pasadena-Arcadia Adult Reading Ctrs., 1998—, pres., 2002; bd. dirs. Arcadia Coordinating Coun. With AUS USAR, 1943—46. Recipient Resolution of Commendation Riverside City Council, 1963; Resolution of Appreciation Los Angeles City Council, 1968, 1973, Arcadia Vol. of Yr., 1997. Mem. Nat. Mortgage Bankers Assn. (chmn. Life Ins. Co. com. 1986-87), Calif. Mortgage Bankers Assn. (sec. 1965, dir. 1972-75, Disting. Svc. award 1997), So. Calif. Mortgage Bankers Assn. (dir. 1975, 80-81, v.p. 1982, pres. 1983), Indland Empire Mortgage Bankers Assn. (pres. 1962, hon. dir.), Assn. Corp. Real Estate Execs. (sec. 1967-71, pres. 1974-75), Lambda Alpha. Lutheran. Office: 37 E Huntington Dr Arcadia CA 91006-3210 Home: Apt 232 618 Fairview Ave Arcadia CA 91007-6784 E-mail: pulrich@sprintmail.com. *Being of foreign birth, I particularly appreciate and cherish the American way of life. I am grateful for the opportunities which it has afforded me. I also feel strongly that we who have had the benefit of these opportunities owe something in return to our communities and to our country. I have tried to the best of my abilities to conduct myself and my business affairs in an honorable and forthright manner, thus helping to preserve what I feel is still the best life style in the world.*

ULRICH, ROBERT GENE, judge; b. St. Louis, Nov. 23, 1941; s. Henry George Ulrich and Wanda Ruth (Engram) Webb; m. JoAnn Demark, July 3, 1965; children— Jill Elizabeth, Jane Ashley BA, William Jewell Coll., 1963; JD, U. Mo., Kansas City, 1969, LLM, 1972, U. Va., 2001. Bar: Mo. 1969. Assoc. Von Erdmannsdorff, Voigts & Kuhlman, North Kansas City, Mo., 1969—72; pvt. practice Raytown, 1972; asst. U.S. atty. Dept. Justice, Kansas City and Springfield, 1973-76, 78-81; ptnr. Pine & Ulrich, Warrensburg, 1976-77; litigation atty. Shifran, Treiman, et al., Clayton, 1977-78; U.S. atty. We. Dist. Mo., Kansas City, 1981-89; judge Mo. Ct. Appeals (we. dist.), 1989—, chief judge, 1996-98. Mem. U.S. Atty. Gen.'s Econ. Crime Council, 1983-89 , Atty. Gen.'s Adv. Com. of U.S. Attys., 1983-89, chmn. 1986-89, adv. com. U.S. Ct. Appeals (8th cir.), 1983-86. Appointed mem. steering com. Protect our Children Campaign, Gov. of Mo., chmn. legis. subcom., 1985; mem. resource bd., personnel mgmt. bd. Dept. Justice, 1985-89; trustee Liberty Meml. Assn., 1989—; vice chmn. Orgn. Crime Drug Enforcement Task Force Nat. Program, Dept. Justice, 1987-89. Col. USMCR, 1963-66. Mem.: U. Mo.-Kansas City Alumni Assn. (v.p. 1997—98, pres. 1998—2001), U. Mo.-Kansas City Law Found., U. Mo.-Kansas City Law Sch. Alumni Assn. (v.p. 1994—95, pres. 1995—96), Marine Corps Res. Officers' Assn. (exec. councillor 1986—87), Kansas City Met. Bar Assn., Mo. Bar Assn., Inst. Jud. Adminstrn., Am. Judicature Soc. Office: Missouri Ct Appeals 1300 Oak St Kansas City MO 64106-2904

ULRICH, ROBERT J. retail executive; b. 1944; Grad., U. Minn., 1967, Stanford U., 1978. Chmn., chief exec. officer, dir. Dayton Hudson Corp.; with Dayton Hudson Corp. (now Target Corp.), Mpls., 1967—, exec. v.p. dept. stores divsn., 1981-84, pres. dept. stores divsn., 1984-87, chmn., CEO Target stores divsn., 1987-93, dir., 1993—; chmn, CEO Target Corp. (formerly Dayton Hudson Corp.), 1994—. Office: Target Corp 1000 Nicollet Mall Minneapolis MN 55403-2467*

ULRICH, SUSAN KATHERINE, community health specialist; b. Balt., Aug. 10, 1953; d. William Smith and Gertrude Edith (Eccles) U. Diploma in nursing, York (Pa.) Hosp. Sch. Nursing, 1979; BA, U. Md., 1979, BSN, 1987; MS, U. Calif., San Francisco, 1991. RN, Ariz., Md.; cert. pub. health nursing, Calif.; cert. emergency nurse; cert. ACLS, PALS. Clin. nurse US DPH Indian Health Svc., Ft. Defiance, Ariz., 1980-82, Gallup, N.Mex., 1983, St. Joseph's Hosp., Tucson, 1984-88; sr. pub. health nurse Pima County Health Dept. Home Health Div., 1987-88; clin. nurse emergency dept. U. Calif. Med. Ctr., San Francisco, 1988-91; clin. nurse St. Francis Meml. Hosp. Home Health, 1989-95; clin. rsch. coord. U. Calif. San Francisco Gen. Hosp., 1991-95; asst. clin. prof. dept. physiol. nursing U. Calif. Sch. of Nursing, 1993-95; nurse sr. health promotion clinics for srs. U. Ariz. Coll. Nursing, Tucson, 1995-97; utilization rev./case mgmt. nurse Carondelet Health Network, 1997-99; clin. nurse emergency dept. St. Joseph's Hosp., 1995—. Assoc. rech. emergency dept. triage study U. Calif. San Francisco, 1992; presenter in field. Contbr. articles to profl. jours. CPR instr. Am. Heart Assn., 1983-88; vol. Tucson Rape Crisis Ctr., 1984-86; bd. dirs. com. chair Mary Elizabeth Inn, San Francisco, 1989-95; no. Calif. telephone tree coord. Nat. Space Soc., Washington, 1989-94. Scholar Nat. Student Nurses Assn., 1978, York Hosp. Sch. Nursing Alumni, 1987; recipient Indian Health Svc. award, 1982, Fed. Nurse Traineeship, 1989-90. Mem.: Emergency Nurses Assn., Soc. Rogerian Scholars, Soc. Space Nursing, Newfoundland Club Ariz., Newfoundland Club Am., Newfoundland Rescue Mesquite, Sigma Theta Tau (newsletter editor Beta Mu chap. 2001—), Phi Kappa Phi. Avocations: reading, hiking, travel, dog carting and training. Home: 4313 E Montecito St Tucson AZ 85711-4857

ULRICH, THEODORE ALBERT, lawyer; b. Spokane, Wash., Jan. 1, 1943; s. Herbert Roy and Martha (Hoffman) Ulrich; m. Nancy Allison, May 30, 1966; children: Donald Wayne, Frederick Albert. BS cum laude, U.S. Mcht. Marine Acad., 1965; JD cum laude, Fordham U., 1970; LLM, NYU, 1974. Bar: N.Y. 1971, U.S. Ct. Appeals (2nd cir.) 1971, U.S. Supreme Ct. 1974, U.S. Ct. Claims 1977, U.S. Customs Ct. 1978, U.S. Ct. Internat. Trade 1981, U.S. Ct. Appeals (5th cir.) 1988, U.S. Ct. Appeals (D.C. cir.) 1992, Colo. 1993, U.S. Ct. Appeals (10 cir.) 1994. Mng. clk. U.S. Dept. Justice, N.Y.C., 1968-69, law clk. to federal dist. judge, 1969-70; assoc. Cadwalader, Wickersham & Taft, 1970-80, ptnr., 1980-94, Popham, Haik, Schnobrich & Kaufman, Ltd., Denver, 1994-96; sole practice law, 1996—. Co-author: Encyclopedia of International Commercial Litigation, 1991, Arbitration of Construction Contracts, V, 1991; contbg. author: Marine Engineering Economics and Cost Analysis, 1995; author, editor Fordham Law Rev., 1969. Leader Boy Scouts Am., Nassau County, N.Y., 1984-94, Denver, 1994—. Capt. USCGR, 1965-86. Mem. ABA, Colo. Bar, Denver Bar, Maritime Law Assn., Am. Soc. Internat. Law, Soc. Naval Architects and Marine Engrs., U.S. Naval Inst., Am. Arbitration Assn. Home and Office: 4300 E 6th Ave Denver CO 80220-4940 E-mail: tnulrich@gte.net.

ULRICH, WERNER, patent lawyer; b. Munich, Germany, Mar. 12, 1931; came to U.S., 1940, naturalized, 1945; s. Karl Justus and Grete (Rosenthal) U.; m. Ursula Wolff, June 28, 1959; children— Greta, Kenneth. BS, Columbia U., 1952, MS (NSF fellow 1952-53), 1953, Dr.Engring. Sci., 1957; MBA, U. Chgo., 1975; JD, Loyola U., Chgo, 1985. Bar: Ill., 1985. With AT&T Bell Labs, Naperville, Ill., 1953-95; head electronic switching dept. AT&T Bell Labs., 1964-68; dir. Advanced Switching Tech., 1968-77, head maintenance architecture dept., 1977-81; sr. atty. Intellectual Property Law Orgn., 1981-95. Vis. lectr. U. Calif., Berkeley, 1966-67 Inventor of over 20 telecommunications inventions; patentee electronic switching systems. Fellow IEEE; mem. ABA, Ill. State Bar Assn., Am. Intellectual Property Law Assn., Tau Beta Pi, Beta Gamma Sigma. Office: 434 Maple St Glen Ellyn IL 60137-3826

ULRICH, WERNER RICHARD, union education administrator; b. N.Y.C., Sept. 26, 1941; s. Werner and Erna (Schreiner) U.; m. Marie Sciacca, July 18, 1965; children: Kenneth, Clifford, Richard. AAS, Voorhees Tech. Inst., 1969; BA, SUNY, Old Westbury, 1985; MS, N.Y. Inst. Tech., 1990. Mechanic "A" Con Edison of N.Y., N.Y.C., 1963-68; apprentice steamfitter Steamfitters', Local Union # 638, Long Island City, N.Y., 1968-73, journeyman steamfitter, 1973-85; dir. edn. Steamfitters' Edn. Fund, N.Y.C., 1985—. Blood dr. coord. Steamfitters', Local Union # 638, Long Island City, 1987—; usher, capt. Holy Name of Mary Roman Cath. Ch., 1984—; mem. steering coun. L.I. Women's Coun., 1992—; skilled worker emeritus N.Y. State Tng. Partnership Coun., 1993—; mem. S.I. Job Svc. Employer Com., 1993—. With U.S. Army, 1959-62. Recipient John J. Theobald award N.Y. Inst. Tech., 1989, Commr.'s award N.Y. State Dept. Labor, 1991, L.I. Women's award L.I. Women's Coun., 1991, N.Y. State Gov.'s cert. of Appreciation, 1994, Donald Grabowski Outstanding Apprenticeship Program award, N.Y. State Commnr. Labor, 2001. Mem. ASME, Nat. Fire Protection Assn., U.S. Apprenticeship Assn., Am. Legion, KC. Avocation: horticulture.

ULSTROM, ROBERT A. pediatrician, educator; b. Mpls., Feb. 23, 1923; m. Mary Janet McGrath, 1946 (dec. 1981); 3 children; m. Betty Bernard, 1982 (div. 1985). BS, U. Minn., 1944, MD, 1946; postgrad., Strong Meml. Hosp. Lic. physician, Minn., Calif.; diplomate Am. Bd. Pediatrics with subspecialty in endocrinology (bd. dirs. 1980-86, v.p. 1985, chmn. rsch. and devel. com. 1980-86, tech. adv. com. for devel. of computerized examinations 1983-86), Am. Bd. Emergency Medicine (bd. dirs. 1982-86). Intern, resident in pediats. U. Rochester, 1946-48; instr., asst. prof. U. Minn., Mpls., 1950-53, assoc. prof., 1956-61, prof. pediatrics, 1961-64, 66-90, prof. emeritus, 1990—, acting head dept. pediatrics, 1961-62, 67-76, assoc. dean Coll. Med. Scis., 1967-70; asst. prof. UCLA, 1953-56, prof., 1964-67, chmn. dept. pediatrics, 1964-67; vis. prof. medicine U. So. Calif., 1982-83. Chief pediats. 97th Gen. Hosp., 1949-50; cons. in pediats. Harbor Gen. Hosp., L.A., 1953-56, 64-67, Mpls. Gen. Hosp., 1956-64, Hennepin County Gen. Hosp., 1967-90, hon. staff, 1990—; Well Child Clinic cons. City of L.A., 1953-56; track physician Donneybrooke Racetrack, Brainerd, Minn., 1968-73; dir. Reg. Ctr. for Metabolic Defects, 1975-79; cons. Ellwood & Assocs., 1986-87; med. legal cons. various plantiffs, 1985-95; mem. med. adv. bd. Group Health, Inc., 1967-90, Diabetes Detection and Edn. Ctr., 1969-71; mem. grants review com. Human Growth Inc., 1974-78; mem. tech. adv. com. on human genetics Minn. State Bd. Health, 1976-90; mem. pers. selection com. NIH, 1979, mem. gen. medicine study sect. NIH, 1964-68; mem. divsn. med. scis. NRC, 1961-64; oral examiner Am. Bd. Pediats., 1970-89; expert witness for prosecution U.S. Fed. Dist. Ct., Mpls., 1994-95; instr. computer course for beginners Elder Learning Inst., Coll. Continuing Edn., U. Minn., 1995—, bd. dirs., 1996—, webmaster, author, 1997—, v.p., 1998-99. Mem. editl. bd. Jour. Pediats., 1962-65; contbr. articles to profl. jours. Sec.-treas. Minn. Med. Found., 1967-68. With M.C., U.S. Army, 1948-50. Markle scholar in med. scis., 1954-59; Pew Found. fellow, 1985-86; recipient Wyeth award for med. rsch., 1963. Mem. AAAS, Am. Pediat. Soc., Am. Soc. Clin. Investigation, Ctrl. Soc. for Clin. Rsch., Endocrine Soc., Lawson-Wilkins Pediat. Endocrine Soc. (founding mem., membership com. 1971-75, chmn. 1975), Midwestern Pediat. rsch. Soc. (coun. 1961-64), Soc. for Pediat. Rsch. (NRC rep. 1961-64), Western Soc. for Clin. rsch., Western Soc. for Pediat. Rsch., Alpha Omega Alpha, Phi Rho Sigma. Home: 4616 Sunset Rdg Minneapolis MN 55416-3335 E-mail: ulstr001@maroon.tc.umn.edu.

ULTAN, LLOYD, historian, educator; b. Bronx, N.Y., Feb. 16, 1938; s. Louis and Sophie U. BA cum laude, Hunter Coll., 1959; MA, Columbia U., 1960. Assoc. Edward Williams Coll., Fairleigh Dickinson U., Hackensack, N.J., 1964-74, asst. prof. history, 1974-75, assoc. prof., 1975-83, prof., 1983—. Cons. in field. Editor Bronx County Hist. Soc. Jour., 1964—, Bronx County Hist. Soc. Press, 1981—; author: The Beautiful Bronx, 1920-50, 1979, Legacy of the Revolution: The Valentine-Varian House, 1983, The Bronx in the Innocent Years, 1890-1925, 1985, The Presidents of the United States, 1989, The Bronx in the Frontier Era: From the Beginning to 1696, 1993, The Bronx: It Was Only Yesterday, 1935-65, 1993, Roots of the Republic, Vol. VI, 1996, The Bronx Cookbook, 1997, Bronx Accent; A Literary and Pictorial History of the Borough, 2000, The Birth of The Bronx, 1609-1900, 2000; contbr. Ency. N.Y. City, 1995. Gen. sec. Bronx Civic League, 1964-67; v.p. bd. trustees Bronx County Hist. Soc., 1965-67, 77-84, curator, 1968-71, pres., 1971-76, historian, 1986—; founding mem., bd. dir. Bronx Coun. on Arts, 1968-71; chmn. Bronx County Bicentennial Commn., 1973-76, Bronx Borough Pres.'s Bicentennial Adv. Com., 1974-76; vice chmn. Commn. Celebrating 350 Yr. of the Bronx, 1989; program guidelines com. N.Y.C. Dept. Cultural Affairs, 1976-77; bd. dirs. Nat. Shrine Bill of Rights, Mt. Vernon, N.Y., 1983—; mem. N.Y.C. Com. on Cultural Concerns, 1982-88; bd. sponsors Historic Preservation com. St. Ann's Ch. Morrisania, 1987—; bd. dirs. 91 Van Cortlandt Owners Corp., 1986—; official historian Bronx Borough, N.Y., 1996—. Recipient Fairleigh Dickinson U. 15-Yr. award, 1979, 20-Yr. award, 1984, 25-Yr. award, 1989, 30-Yr. award, 1994, 35-Yr. award, 1999, Outstanding Tchr. of Yr. award, 1994; named N.Y.C. Centennial Historian, 1999, N.Y.C. Book award for borough history N.Y. Soc. Libr., 2001; named to Hunter Coll. Alumni Hall of Fame, 1974; N.Y. State Regents Coll. tchg. fellow, 1959. Mem. AAUP (v.p. Teaneck chpt. 1992-93, sec. coun. of FDU chpts. 1992-93), Am. Hist. Assn., N.Y. Hist. Soc., Phi Alpha Theta, Alpha Chi Alpha, Sigma Lambda, N.Y.C. Task Force on Spontaneous Memls., 2002. Home and Office: 91 Van Cortlandt Ave W Bronx NY 10463-2712 *Transmitting the heritage of the past to the youth and to the mature adult, either through the spoken or written word, not only ensures that the civilization we inherited will be passed on, it will also warn people about earlier mistakes that should now be shunned and will, hopefully, inspire them to add their own positive contribution. I believe I am continuing to perform this service.*

ULVEN, MARK EDWARD, lawyer; b. Sioux City, Iowa, Mar. 23, 1954; s. Marvin Edward and Bonnie Mae Ulven; m. Kathleen Lynn Lanini, Jan. 9, 1982 (div. June 1993); m. Debra Anne Cappellino, Sept. 3, 1993; children: Alexandra, Allison, Nicholas. BS, U. S.D., 1976; MA, U. Mo., 1982; JD, Georgetown U., 1994. Bar: Pa. 1994, DC 1994. Instr. U. Mo., Columbia, 1981-82; asst. editor Texarkana (Tex.) Gazette, 1982-83; legis. asst. U.S. Ho. of Reps., Washington, 1983-86, U.S. Senate, Washington, 1986-92; legis. analyst Dorsey & Whitney, 1992-94; assoc. Jones Day Reavis & Pogue, 1994-98, Klett Rooney Lieber & Schorling, Pitts., 1998-2001, Buchanan Ingersoll, Pitts., 2001—. Adj. instr. Duquesne U., 1999—2002. Contbr. articles to profl. jours. Recipient Am. Jurisprudence award, 1994, award for editl. cartooning/illustration Va. Press Assn., 1989. Mem.: Allegheny County Bar Assn. Republican. Episcopalian. Avocations: drawing and painting. Home: 2006 White Oak Ct Moon Township PA 15108-9050 Office: Buchanan Ingersoll One Oxford Centre Pittsburgh PA 15219 E-mail: ulvenme@bipc.com.

ULVEN, MATTHEW ERIC, family practice physician, educator; b. Cherokee, Iowa, May 11, 1963; s. Marvin E. and Bonnie M. Ulven. BS, Morningside Coll., 1985; MD, U. Iowa, 1989. Diplomate Am. Bd. Family Practice. Commd. 2d. lt. USAF, 1989, advanced through grades to maj., 1997, intern Md., 1989-90, resident, 1989-92; staff physician Rhein-Main AB, Frankfurt, Germany, 1992-95; staff faculty physician Scott AFB, Ill., 1995-97; staff physician Franciscan-Skemp Healthcare, Tomah, Wis., 1997-99; asst. prof. medicine St. Louis U., 1999—. Mem. La Crosse (Wis.) Chamber Chorale, 1998-99, Masterworks Chorale, Belleville, Ill., 1999—. Mem. Am. Acad. Family Practice, Uniformed Svcs. Acad. Famkly Practice, Ctr. for Bioethics and Human Dignity, Christian Med. and Dental Assn. (co-chair singles commn. 1999—, chmn. St. Louis area local coun. 2001). Republican. Mem. Evangelical Free Ch. Avocations: bicycling, hiking, music, piano. Home: 221 Bourdelais Dr Swansea IL 62226-1074 Office: St Louis U Family Practice Residency Program 180 S 3d St Ste 400 Belleville IL 62222 Fax: (618) 222-4792. E-mail: mulven@earthlink.net.

ULVILA, JACOB WALTER, management consultant; b. Chgo., May 13, 1950; s. Toivo Einor and Belle Evelyn (Vanderbilt) U.; m. LouAnna Notargiacomo, Aug. 7, 1976; 1 child, Alexander Michael. BSEE, U. Ill., 1972; MBA, U. Mich., 1974; DBA, Harvard U., Boston, 1979. Decision analyst Decisions & Designs, Inc., McLean, Va., 1974-77, 79-80; vis. assoc. prof bus. adminstrn. U. Va., Colgate Darden Grad. Sch. Bus. Adminstrn., Charlottesville, 1982-83; exec. v.p., also dir. Decision Sci. Consortium, Inc., Reston, 1980-91; founder, prin. Decision Sci. Assocs., Inc., Vienna, 1991—. Contbr. articles to profl. jours., chpts. to books. Recipient Franz Edelman award for mgmt. sci. achievemednt, Inst. Mgmt. Sci., 1987. Mem. Inst. Ops. Rsch. Mgmt. Sci., Maserati Club Am., Lamborghini Owners Club, Lamborghini Club Am., Maserati Club Internat. Avocation: exotic Italian automobiles. Office: Decision Sci Assocs Inc PO Box 969 Vienna VA 22183

UMAKANTHAN, JEREMIAH, geriatrician; b. Jaffna, Sri Lanka, Feb. 3, 1940; came to U.S., 1971; s. Arasarkone and Nagalaskshmi (Pirasoody) Jeremiah; m. Padminidevi Canagaratnam, Oct. 26, 1968; children: Ramanan, Branavan, Janani. B of Medicine & Surgery, U. Sri Lanka, Peradeniya, 1967. Diplomate Am. Bd. Psychitry and Gen. Nuerology; cert. in geriatric and addiction psychiatry. Intern St. Francis Hosp., Poughkeepsie, N.Y., 1971-72; resident in psychiatry Hudson River Psychiat. Ctr., 1972-75, psychiatrist II, 1975-81, psychiatrist, mobile crisis team, 1977-88, chief adolescent unit, 1981-84, dep. dir. psychogeriatric unit, 1984-93, dep. dir. geriatric rehab. svc., 1992-96; cons. psychiatrist Dutchess County Mental Health Ctr., 1976-80, cons. Methadone Clinic, 1979-86; psychiatrist Desert Valley Med. Group, Appple Valley, Calif., 1996—2002; staff psychiatrist Victor Valley Behavioral Health Clinic, Victorville. Attg. clin. dir. Hudson River Psychiat. Ctr., Poughkeepsie, 1992-93; cons. psychiatrist Nathan Kline Inst., Orangeburg, N.Y., 1993-94. Hindu. Office: Desert Valley Med Group 18419 Hwy 18 Apple Valley CA 92307

UMAN, MARTIN ALLAN, electrical engineering educator, researcher, consultant; b. Tampa, Fla., July 3, 1936; s. Morrice S. and Edith G. (Brown) U.; m. Dorit Brigitta Kalbas, Mar. 6, 1962; children: Jon, Mara, Derek. BS in Engring., Princeton U., 1957, MA, 1959, PhD, 1961. Assoc. prof. elec. engring. U. Ariz., Tucson, 1961-65; fellow physicist Westinghouse Rsch. Labs., Pitts., 1965-71; prof. dept. elec. and computer engring. U. Fla., Gainesville, 1971-91, prof., chmn. dept., 1991—; pres. Lightning Location & Protection, Inc., Tucson, 1975-83. Mem. Internat. Commn. on Atmospheric Electricity, 1975-92; cons. Boeing Aircraft, Patrick AFB, Mobil Oil Corp., McDonnell Douglas, United Techs., IBM, Flamex Corp., NOAA, NASA, No. Telecom Can., Tampa Cable TV, Bonneville Power Adminstrn., Martin Marietta, Sandia Nat. Labs., Walt Disney World, SRI, other cos. Author: Introduction to Plasma Physics, 1964, Lightning, 1969, rev. edit., 1984, Understanding Lightning, 1971, All About Lightning, 1986, The Lightning Discharge, 1987, rev. edit., 2001; mem. editl. bd. Jour. Geophys. Rsch., 1980-83; contbr. articles to profl. jours.; patentee in field. Mem. senate U. Fla., 1988-90, 93—, bd. dirs. div. sponsored rsch., 1989-91. Recipient Editor's Citation, Jour. Geophys. Rsch., 1989, Outstanding Fla. Scientist award Fla. Acad. Scis., 1991, Group Achievement award for Galileo Spacecraft NASA, 1992, 96; rsch. grantee various orgns. Fellow IEEE (com. mem. working group on lightning performance distbn. ins. 1979—, working group on estimating performance transmission ins. 1985—, Heinrich Hertz medal 1996), Am. Geophys. Union (John Adam Fleming medal 2001), Am. Meteorol. Soc. E-mail: uman@ece.ufl.edu.

UMAN, SARAH DUNGEY, editor; b. Dayton, Ohio, July 22, 1942; d. Arthur Bertram and Lucretia M. (Nash) Dungey; children: Michael Uman, Sebastian Rosset. Student, New Sch. for Social Rsch., 1962-64. Editl. assoc., publicity dir. Grove Press, Inc., N.Y.C., 1970-79; sr. editor Playboy Paperbacks 1979-81, Berkley Pub., N.Y.C., 1982-85; exec. editor Consumer Reports Books, Yonkers, N.Y., 1985-94; dir. Red Bear Editl. Svcs., N.Y.C., 1996—.

UMANS, ALVIN ROBERT, manufacturing company executive; b. N.Y.C., Mar. 11, 1927; s. Louis and Ethel (Banner) U.; m. Nancy Jo Zadek, June 28, 1953 (div.); children: Kathi Lee Umans Lind, Craig Joseph; m. Madeleine Sayer, Sept. 21, 1985; 1 child, Valentine Brett. Student, U. Rochester, 1945. Sales mgr. Textile Mills Co., Chgo., 1954-56; regional sales mgr. Reflector Hardware Corp., Melrose Park, Ill., 1956-58, nat. sales mgr., 1959-62, v.p., 1962-65, pres., treas., dir., 1965-92; pres., CEO RHC/Spacemaster Corp., 1992-97, chmn., CEO, 1997—. Chmn., bd. dirs. Goer Mfg. Co., Inc., Charleston, S.C.; chmn., dir. Discovery Plastics, Oreg., Morgan Marshall Industries, Inc., Ill., Capitol Hardware, Inc., Ill.; chmn., dir. Spartan Showcase Inc., Mo.; v.p., dir. Adams Comm., Chgo.; bd. dirs. Monroe Comm., Chgo.; chmn., treas., dir. Spacemaster Corp., Del. Trustee Mt. Sinai Hosp. Med. Ctr., Chgo., 1970—, chmn. bd., 1987-89; trustee Schwab Rehab. Hosp., Chgo., 1987—, chmn. bd., 1987-89; trustee Sinai Health Sys., Chgo., 1993—, chmn., 1995-97; mem. Cook County Bur. Adv. Com., 1994—; trustee Driehaus Mutual Funds, 1996—; bd. dirs. Milton & Rose Zadek Fund, 1965-78; governing bd. mem. Cinema/Chgo., 1988-89. Served with AUS, 1945-46. Mem. Nat. Assn. Store Fixture Mfrs. (dir. 1969-70), World Pres.'s Orgn., Chgo. Pres.'s Orgn. Clubs: Standard (Chgo.). Home: 132 E Delaware Pl Chicago IL 60611-1445 Office: RHC/Spacemaster Corp 1400 N 25th Ave Melrose Park IL 60160-3001 E-mail: arumans@rhcspacemaster.com.

UMBAYEMAKE, LINDA, librarian, rehabilitation counselor; b. Cleve., Feb. 19, 1953; d. Charles Morgan and Helen Loretta (Ballard) McDonald; m. Bari S. Zaka, Dec. 17, 1972 (div. Jan. 1979); children: Manu, Kumar, Bari; m. Nola UmBayemakeJoachim, Dec. 20, 1984 (div. June 1989); children: Mayi, Thurayya; divorced; 1 child, GlennChinua. AA, Cuyahoga C.C., Cleve., 1980; BA, Kent State U., 1984; MLS, Tex. Woman's U., 1989; MRC, U. Ky., 1998. Dir. African Am. Ctr. Toledo (Ohio)-Lucas County Pub. Libr., 1989; libr. young adult, correctional and homebound Cuyahoga County Pub. Libr., Warrensville, Ohio, 1989-90; libr. supr. Western N.Mex. Correctional Facility, Grants, 1990; instr., libr. supr. Santa Fe C.C., 1990; libr. supr. Ga. Dept. Corrections, Buford, 1991; instr. head circulation Ky. State U., Frankfort, 1992-93, instr./ILL reference libr., 1993-96; pub. svcs. asst. libr. Owensboro (Ky.) C.C., 1996; substitute tchr. Franklin County Pub. Schs., Frankfort, Ky., 1997-99; offender rehab counselor, substance abuse program Luther Luckett Correctional Ctr., 1999; collection devel. specialist Book Wholesalers Inc., 1999-2000; STAR program coord. U. Akron, 2001—; br. mgr. East Cleve. Pub. Libr. Caledonia Br., 2001—. Founder Learning Upgrades Behavior Around You, 1997—. Apptd. to Ky. Foster Care Rev. Bd., 1999—2000; child support/visitation com. Franklin County Family Ct., 1999—2000; mem. Bd. Elections Franklin County. Mem.: NAMI, Nat. Rehab. Assn., Black Caucus of ALA (chair new mem. orientation com. 1994—96, membership com. 1989—96, ALA Shirley Olofson com. 1993—96, mem. minority recruitment com. 1993—96), Chi Sigma Iota. E-mail: lumbay2000@yahoo.com.

UMBEHOCKER, KENNETH SHELDON, priest; b. Mpls., Sept. 23, 1934; s. Kenneth and Mildred Adeline (Johnson) U. BA, Vanderbilt U., 1956; MDiv, Seabury-Western, Evanston, Ill., 1959, 2000; M Mgmt., U. Ga., 1974. Ordained to ministry Episcopal Ch., 1959. Priest-in-charge St. John's Ch., Hallock, Minn., 1959-62; rector St. Paul's Ch., Virginia, 1962-67; priest-in-charge Emmanuel Ch., Rushford, 1968-74; asst. to dean Gethsemane Cathedral, Fargo, N.D., 1974-86; priest-in-charge St. Peter's Ch., Warroad, Minn., 1986-90; rector Ch. of the Good Shepherd, Windom, 1990-94, St. John's by the Lake, Worthington, 1990-94, Holy Trinity, Luverne, 1990-94, Episcopal Parish of St. Mark and St. John, Jim Thorpe, Pa., 1995—. Community developer, 1968-86; trustee Episcopal Diocese of Minn., Mpls., 1987-90, coun. mem., 1980-94; mem. standing com. Diocese of Bethlehem, 1998—. Field rep. Am. Cancer Soc., Mpls., 1965-67; dept. mgr. Rochester (Minn.) Area C. of C., 1967-74; exec. dir. Fargo Parking Authority and Downtown Assn., 1974-86. Seabury fellow Seabury-Western Sem., 1980; named Young Man of Yr. Rochester Jaycees, 1970; recipient Order of Purple Cross, York Rite Coll. North Am., 1988; Canterbury scholar Canterbury Cathedral of Canterbury, Eng., 1996. Mem. Am. Acad. Parish Clergy, Am. C. of C. Execs., Nat. Parking Assn. (v.p. 1983-86, Disting. Svc. award 1985), Union League Phila., Knights Templar (grand comdr. N.D. club 1985-86), Masons (grand chaplain Minn. club 1994), Seven Continents Club, Rotary Internat. Home: 32 Race St Jim Thorpe PA 18229-2004 E-mail: markjohn@ptd.net. *Working in the secular world as well as in the sacred makes a person more attuned to the needs and wants of the people in the pew and I find that that has enhanced my life tremendously.*

UMBREIT, WAYNE WILLIAM, bacteriologist, educator; b. Markesan, Wis., May 1, 1913; s. William Traugott and Augusta (Abendroth) U.; m. Doris McQuade, July 31, 1937; children: Dorayne Loreda, Jay Nicholas, Thomas Hayden. BA, U. Wis., 1934, MS, 1936, PhD, 1939. Instr. soil microbiology Rutgers U., 1937-38; faculty U. Wis., Madison, 1938-44, asst. prof. bacteriology and chemistry, 1941-44; faculty Cornell U., 1944-47, prof. bacteriology, 1946-47; head dept. enzyme chemistry Merck Inst., Rahway, N.J., 1947-58; asso. dir., 1958; chmn. dept. bacteriology Rutgers U., New Brunswick, N.J., 1958-75, prof. microbiology, dir. grad. programs, 1969-83, prof. emeritus microbiology, 1983—; dir. labs. So. Br. Watershed Assn., 1983-89. Author: (with Burris, Stauffer) Manometric Techniques, 1945, 5th edit., 1972, (with Oginsky) An Introduction to Bacterial Physiology, 1954, Metabolic Maps, 1960, Modern Microbiology, 1962, Essentials of Bacterial Physiology, 1976; Editor: Advances in Applied Microbiology, vols. 1-10, 1959-68; Contbr. articles to profl. jours. Recipient Biochem. Congress Symposium medal Paris, France, 1952 Fellow Am. Acad. Microbiology, N.Y. Acad. Sci., A.A.A.S.; mem. Am. Soc. for Microbiology (Eli Lilly award in bacteriology 1947, Carski Found. award for distinguished teaching 1968), Soc. Biol. Chemists, Am. Chem. Soc., Theobald Smith Soc. (Waksman award in microbiology 1957, past pres.), AAUP, Sigma Xi. Home: 812 Covered Bridge Rd Holland PA 18966 E-mail: wumbreit@aol.com.

UMBS, MATTHEW LEE, accountant; b. St. Paul, May 7, 1973; s. Rudolph Michael and Jannis Ann Umbs. BS in Acctg., U. Wis.-Parkside, Kenosha, 1996; MBA, U. San Diego, 1998. CPA, Calif.; cert. mgmt. acct., fin. mgmt.; cert. internal auditor; cert. fraud examiner. Claims analyst Nat. Steel and Shipbldg. Co., San Diego, 1996-97; bus. assurance and adv. cons. Arthur Andersen, Washington, 1998-99, San Diego, 1999—. Mem. AICPA, Inst. Mgmt. Accts., Inst. Internal Auditors, Assn. Cert. Cert. Fraud Examiners.

UMEADI, ALBERT NKUNI, civil engineer, consultant; b. Lagos, Nigeria, Sept. 26, 1955; came to U.S., 1978; s. Michael Okoye and Mercy (Udezue) U.; m. Frances Chinwe Iloemezue, Apr. 1, 1995. BSc, U. Md., 1984. Registered profl. engr., Tex. Asst. project engr. IBM, Austin, Tex., 1985-94; project engr., cons. Profl. Svcs. Industries Inc., 1994-96, Raba-Kistner Cons. Inc., Austin, 1996—. Mem. ASCE (assoc.), Am. Concrete Inst. Avocations: tennis, traveling, dancing. Home: # 146 1901 E Anderson Ln Apt 148 Austin TX 78752-1908 E-mail: aumeadi@yahoo.com.

UMEBAYASHI, CLYDE SATORU, lawyer; b. Honolulu, Sept. 2, 1947; s. Robert S. and Dorothy C. Umebayashi; m. Cheryl J. Much, June 27, 1975. BBA in Travel Industry Mgmt., U. Hawaii, 1969, JD, 1980. Spl. dept. atty. gen. Labor and Indsl. Rels. Appeals Bd., Honolulu, 1980-81; atty., dir., shareholder Kessner, Duca, Umebayashi, Bain & Matsunaga, 1981—. Commr. Hawaii Criminal Justice Commn. Bd. dirs. Wesley Found., Honolulu, 1993-97. Mem. Hawaii State Bar Assn. Office: Kessner Duca Umebayashi Bain & Matsunaga 220 S King St Fl 19 Honolulu HI 96813-4526

UMEH, MARIE ARLENE, English language educator; b. Bklyn., Aug. 29, 1947; d. Rudolph Vasper and Erma Eunice (Hinds) Linton; m. Davidson C. Umeh, Jan. 7, 1976; children: Ikechukwu, Uchenna, Chizoba, Ugochukwu. BA, St. John's U., Jamaica, N.Y., 1970; MS, Syracuse U., 1972; MPS, Cornell U., 1977; MA, U. Wis., 1980, PhD, 1981. Instr. SUNY, Brockport, 1972-74, Oneonta, 1974-75; asst. instr. Cornell U., Ithaca, N.Y., 1976-77; prin. lectr. Anambra State Coll., Awka, Nigeria, 1982-89; substitute assoc. prof. Medgar Evers Coll., CUNY, Bklyn., 1989; adj. prof. Hostos C.C., CUNY, Bronx, 1990, Queens Coll., CUNY, Flushing, N.Y., 1990; assoc. prof. English John Jay Coll., CUNY, 1990—, faculty advisor, 1989—. Adj. prof. SUNY, Stony Brook, 2000—. Editor: Flora Nwapa, 1998, Buchi Emecheta, 1996; editor Rsch. in African Lit., 1995, Who's Who Among American Teachers, 1998; contbg. editor: Who's Who in Contemporary Women's Writing, 2001. Recipient Africademic award, John Jay Coll. African Students Assn., 1996, Dominican Students award, 1993, PSC-CUNY award, 1998, 1999, Gender Studies award, John Jay Coll.,CUNY, 2001; fellow NEH, 1991. Mem.: AAUW, MLA (African Lit. Divsn. exec. 1999—2001), Virginia Woolf Soc., N.Y. African Studies Assn., African Lit. Assn. Avocations: reading, writing, aerobics, jazz. Office: CUNY John Jay CollCriminal Justice Dept English 445 W 59th St New York NY 10019-1104 E-mail: msumeh@aol.com.

UMEMOTO, TERUO, chemist, researcher, chemicals executive; b. Hikari, Yamaguchi, Japan, Jan. 11, 1949; s. Katsuichi Ikeda and Masa (Nakahara) U.; m. Toshiko Kanamori, Mar. 26, 1978; children: Yukio, Makiko. BS, Okayama (Japan) U., 1971; MS, Osaka (Japan) U., 1973, DSc, 1976. Rschr. Sagami Chem. Rsch. Ctr., Sagamihara, Japan, 1976-81, sub-chief rschr., 1981-88, chief rschr., 1988-90; sr. rschr. MEC Lab., Daikin Industries, Ltd., Tsukuba, Japan, 1990-93, mgr., 1993-98; chief rschr. Fuji Chem. Industry Co. Ltd., Toyama, Japan, 1998; pres. IM&T Rsch., Inc., Denver, 1999—. Lectr. Sci. U. Tokyo, 1992-93, Kyushu U., Fukuoka, Japan, 1993, Chiba (Japan) U., 1993, Gifu U., Japan, 1998; vis. rschr. Nagoya Indsl. Inst. Japanese Govt., 1995. Inventor Jour. Am. Chem. Soc., 1990, 93, Jour. Organic Chemistry, 1994. Mem. Am. Chem. Soc., Chem. Soc. Japan (Progress award 1983), The Soc. of Synthetic Organic Chemistry (Japan), Japanese Assn. Fluorine Chemists.

UMHOLTZ, CLYDE ALLAN, financial analyst; b. Du Quoin, Ill., Dec. 20, 1947; s. Frederick Louis and Opal Kathleen (Beard) U. BS, U. Ill., 1969; MS, U. Miss., 1972; MBA, Memphis State U., 1983, PhD, 1986; Dr of Higher Learning (hon.) , London Sch. Econs., 2002. CFA; cert. systems profl., tax practitioner; registered profl. engr.; cert. data processor. Supr. quality control Champion Internat. Corp., Oxford, Miss., 1971-72; mgr. divsn. quality control Cook Industries, Memphis, 1973; engring. planner Northwest Industries and subsidiaries, 1974-75; long range planning and analysis W.R. Grace and Co. and subsidiaries, 1975-78; mgr. planning and analysis Ctr. Nuclear Studies, Memphis State U., 1979-83; data processing mgr. Shelby County (Tenn.) Govt., 1983-87, dep. adminstr., 1987—, spl. asst. to county exec., 1989—. Adj. prof. U. Tenn., Memphis, 1985—; ptnr. Custom Data Systems Inc., Memphis, 1987—, Western Techs. Inc., Memphis, 1988—; bd. dirs. Am. Tech. Inst., Memphis, Am. Info. Cons., Atlanta, Eastgate Corp., Anaheim, Calif.; bd. underwriters Lloyd's of London; diplomate editl. adv. bd. Brent's Peerage, London, Memphis-Amsterdam Gateway Com., Holland, 1997; Goodwill Amb. Am. Ukrainian Trade Alliance, Kiev, 1997—, Asian Econ. Recovery Coun., Tokyo, 1998—; elected to U.S. China Bd. of Trade, 2002; mem. adv. bd. Fed. Res. Bank, Memphis br., 1998—; mem. Am./Japanese Tire Safety Adv. Bd., 2000, Tenn. Commn. on Homeland Security, 2002—; cons. in field. Author: Prototyping of Computerized Financial Systems, 3rd edit., 1997, Context Analysis in System Design, 2nd edit., 1999, The Family Partnership-An Estate Planning Model, 3rd edit., 2000, The Use of Chemical Molecules as Computer Switches, 2002; contbr. articles to profl. jours.; inventor angle trisector. Active presdl. election campaigns, 1968, 72, 80, 84, 88, 92, 96, 2000; del. Rep. Nat. Conv., 1996, 2000; active mayoral campaign, Memphis, 1975, 83, 87, 91, Shelby County, 1990, 94, sheriff's campaign Shelby County, 1990, 94, Mid-South Billy Graham Crusade, 1978; del. So. Govs.' Conf., 1992-93; gov. staff State of Tenn., 1993-94; mem. Mayor's Adv. Com., Memphis, 1991; mem. steering com. Future Memphis, 1992, Arena Football League, Memphis, 1994; mem. Houston Oilers Relocation Com., 1996; mem. adv. coun. Kordes' Gardens, Hamburg, Germany; study com. Nat. Electoral Coll., 2001; mem. oversight com. Fin. Acctg. Standards Bd., 2002--. Recipient Oratorical award Optimist Club, 1963, Leadership and Human Rels. award Dale Carnegie Inst., 1977, Disting. Svc. award State of Tenn., 1991; NSF fellow, 1970-72. Fellow NAS, Australian Acad. Scis., N.Y. Acad. Scis., Am. Acad. Info. Tech.; mem. AAAS, AIChE, Am. Mgmt. Assn., Fin. Execs. Inst., Am. Chem. Soc., Assn. MBA Execs., Data Processing Mgmt. Assn., Planning Execs. Inst., U. Ill. Alumni Assn., U. Miss. Alumni Assn., Memphis State U. Alumni Assn., Am. Rose Soc. (accredited life rose judge 1990), Am. Iris Soc., Am. Hemerocallis Soc., Elvis Presley Meml. Soc., Am. Horticultural Soc., Internat. Platform Assn., Gt. Am. Pyramid Boosters Memphis, Mensa,

Adams Club, Oxford Club, London Club, Exec. Club Memphis, Petroleum Club Memphis, Olympic Soc. Atlanta, Order of De Molay. Baptist. Home: 3580 Hanna Dr Memphis TN 38128-3451 E-mail: Cau@HannaMem.gov., CAU@memphis.gov.

UMLING, DAVID ARTHUR, urban planner; b. Portsmouth, N.H., Feb. 14, 1962; s. John Frederick and Wilma (Woodman) Umling; m. Barbara Anne Hitchcock, May 11, 1991; 1 child Michael David. BA in Sociology, cert. in applied social rsch., U. Hartford, 1984; M in City Planning, U. Calif., Berkeley, 1986. Regional planner Lakes Region Planning Commn., Meredith, N.H., 1987-89; planner Addison County Regional Planning Commn., Middlebury, Vt., 1989-91; planning dir. Mid. Ga. Regional Devel. Ctr., Macon, 1991-94, City of La Grange, Ga., 1995-96, E. Ala. Regional Planning Devel. Commn., Anniston, 1996-99, 2000—, Upper Valley Lake Sunapee Regional Planning Commn., Lebanon, N.H., 1999-2000. Pres., co-founder Innovative Planning Concepts, Inc., Macon, 1993-94; bd. dirs. Design Ala., Inc. Bd. dirs. Middlebury Cmty. TV, 1990-91; treas. Lake Wildwood Assn., Macon, 1993-94. Mem. Small Towns Inst., Am. Planning Assn., Ala. Chpt. Am. Planning Assn., Alliance Transylvania Saxons, Design Ala., Moose. Avocations: hiking, canoeing, astronomy. Home: 825 Timothy Dr Oxford AL 36203-1435 Office: East Ala Regional Planning Devel Commn PO Box 2186 Anniston AL 36202-2186 E-mail: daumling@adss.state.al.us.

UMMINGER, BRUCE LYNN, government official, scientist, educator; b. Dayton, Ohio, Apr. 10, 1941; s. Frederick William and Elnora Mae (Waltemathe) U.; m. Judith Lackey Bryant, Dec. 17, 1966; children: Alison Grace, April Lynn BS magna cum laude with honors in biology, Yale U., 1963, MS, 1966, MPhil, 1968, PhD, 1969; postgrad., U. Calif., Berkeley, 1963-64; cert. univ. adminstrv./mgmt. tng. program, U. Cin., 1975; cert., Fed. Exec. Inst., 1984. Asst. prof. dept. biol. scis. U. Cin., 1969-73, assoc. prof. dept. biol. scis., 1973-75, acting head dept. biol. scis., 1973-75, prof. dept. biol. scis., 1975-81, dir. grad. affairs, 1978-79; program dir. regulatory biology program NSF, Washington, 1979-84, dept. dir. cellular bioscis. divsn., 1984-89, mem. sr. exec. svc., 1984—, acting divsn. dir., 1985-87, 88-89, divsn. dir. cellular bioscis. divsn., 1989-91, divsn. dir. integrative biology and neurosci. divsn., 1991-99, sr. scientist office integrative activities, office of dir., 1999—; sr. advisor on health policy Office of Internat. Health Policy Dept. State, 1988; sr. advisor on biodiversity Smithsonian Instn., 1993-94. Exec. sec. Nat. Sci. Bd. Com. on Ctrs. and Individual Investigator Awards, 1986-88; mem. NSF rev. panel Exptl. Program to Stimulate Competitive Rsch., 1989, Rsch. Improvement in Minority Instns., 1986, 87, U.S.-India Coop. Rsch. Program, 1981-82, U.S.-India Exchange of Scholars Program, 1979-81; vice chmn. biotech. rsch. subcom. Fed. Coord. Coun. on Sci. Engring. and Tech., Office Sci. and Tech. Policy, 1991-94; exec. sec. subcom. biodiversity and ecosystem dynamics, com. on environment and natural resources Nat. Sci. and Tech. Coun., 1994; mem. group nat. experts on safety in biotech., OECD, 1988-89; mem. sr. exec. panel Exec. Potential Program, Office Pers. Mgmt., 1988-89; mem. space shuttle proposal rev. panel in life scis. NASA, 1978, rsch. assocs. in space biology award com., 1985-91, chmn. cell and devel. biology discipline working group, space biology program, 1990-91, chmn. gravitational biology panel, NASA Specialized Ctrs. Rsch. and Tng., 1990, chmn. NASA specialized ctrs. rsch. and tng. peer rev. panel, 1995, mem. exec. steering com. in life scis., 1991, mem. gravitational biology facility sci. working group, 1992-95, mem. space sta. biol. rsch. project sci. working group, 1995-96, mem. NASA neurolab. steering com., 1993; mem. panel study biol. diversity, Bd. Sci. and Tech. Internat. Devel. NRC, 1989; exec. sec. adv. planning bd. Nat. Biodiversity Info. Ctr., Smithsonian Instn., 1993-94; mem. adv. screening com. in life scis. Coun. for Internat. Exchange of Scholars, 1978-81; liaison rep. nat. heart, lung and blood adv. coun. NIH, 1979-87, nat. adv. child health and human devel. coun., 1990-99; recombinant DNA adv. com., 1988; liaison representative agrl. biotechnology Rsrch. Adv. com., USDA, 1989-94; mem. Interagency Rsch. animal com., 1984-88; Interagency working group on Internat. Biotechnology, 1988-94. Author book chpts. and contbr. articles to profl. jours.; assoc. editor Jour. Exptl. Zoology, 1977-79; editorial adv. bd. Gen. and Comparative Endocrinology, 1982 Mem. world mission com. Ch. of the Redeemer, New Haven, 1967-68; Sunday Sch. steering com. Calvary Episcopal Ch., Cin., 1972-73, sr. acolyte, 1972-77, adult edn. com., 1975-76; deacon Faith Presbyn. Ch., Springfield, Va., 1996-99; adv. com. mem. Wakefield H.S., 1991-92, PTA exec. bd., 1991-92; sci. adv. com. Arlington Pub. Schs., 1987-92, adv. coun. on instrn., 1991-92; adv. bd. mem. Campbell Comml. Coll., Cin., 1977-79. Recipient George Rieveschl, Jr. Rsch. award U. Cin., 1973, Presdl. Rank Meritorious Exec. award NSF, 1992; U. Cin. Grad. Sch. fellow 1977—. NSF fellow 1964; rsch. grantee NSF 1971-79. Fellow AAAS (coun. 1980-83, 89-90, mem. program com. for 1989 ann. meeting 1988, chairperson-elect sect. G-Biol. Scis. 1987-88, chairperson 1988-89, ret. 1989-90), N.Y. Acad. Scis.; mem. Am. Soc. Zoologists (sec., mem. exec. com. 1979-81, chmn. nominating com. 1981, sec. divsn. of comparative physiology and biochemistry 1976-77, chmn. Congl. Sci. Fellow Program com. 1986-89, mem. 1991-93), Soc. for Integrative and Comparative Biology, Am. Physiol. Soc. (program adv. com. 1978-81, program exec. com., 1983-86, mem. steering com., comparative physiology sect. 1978-81, sec. Am. Physiol. Soc.-Am. Soc. Zoologists Task Force on Comparative Physiology 1977-78), Am. Inst. Biol. Scis. (chmn. selection com., congl. sci. fellow zool. scis. 1987, mem. congl. fellow liaisons com. 1991), Sr. Execs. Assn., Assn. of Yale Alumni (del. 1990-93), Mory's Assn., Yale Club (Washington), Masons (32 degree), Shriners, Sigma Xi (Disting. Rsch. award U. Cin. chpt. 1973, pres. U. Cin. chpt. 1977-79), Mensa. Episcopalian. Achievements include development of science policy in biodiversity, space biology, integrative biology, neuroscience, and biotechnology; research in low temperature biology, in comparative physiology, endocrinology and biochemistry of fish, and in visual orientation of crustacea. Home: 4087B S Four Mile Run Dr Arlington VA 22204-5604 Office: NSF Ofc Integrative Activities 4201 Wilson Blvd Rm 1270 Arlington VA 22230-0001 E-mail: bumminge@nsf.gov.

UMPIERRE, LUZ MARIA, women studies educator, foreign language educator; b. Santurce, P.R., Oct. 15, 1947; d. Eduardo Umpierre-Pulzoni and Providencia (Herrera) Umpierre. BA, Sagrado Corazón, Santurce, 1970; MA, Bryn Mawr Coll., 1976, PhD, 1978; postgrad., U. Kans., 1981-82, New Sch. for Social Rsch., 1995-96. Asst. prof. Rutgers U., New Brunswick, N.J., 1978-84, assoc. prof., 1984-89; prof., head dept. Western Ky. U., Bowling Green, 1989-91; prof., chair dept. SUNY, Brockport, 1991-94, sr. lectr. Cortland, 1996-97. Vis. asst. prof. Ithaca (N.Y.) Coll., 1997-98; assoc. prof. Bates Coll., Maine, 1998-2000. Author: (poems) In Wonderland, 1982, ...And Other Misfortunes, 1985, The Margarita Poems, 1987, For Christine, 1995; mem. editl. bd. Third Woman Press, 1990—, The Américas Rev., 1989-94. Guest spkr. AIDS Mass., Boston, 1990; sec. N.J. Voters for Civil Liberty, 1984. Named Woman of Yr. Western Ky. U., 1990; recipient Lifetime Achievement award Coalition of Gay & Lesbian Orgn. in N.J., 1990; Ford Found. fellow, 1981. Mem. MLA (del. 1978), Melus, Feministas Unidas. Avocations: writing, reading, lobbying. Home: PO Box 568 Auburn ME 04212-0568 E-mail: LUmpierre@aol.com.

UMPLEBY, STUART ANSPACH, management consultant, educator; b. Tulsa, Mar. 5, 1944; s. Joseph Gray and Mary Carolyn (Woerheide) U.; m. Gertraud Maria Zangl, Mar. 7, 1986; children: Oliver Gray, Nicholas Anspach. BS in Engring., BA in Polit. Sci., U. Ill., 1967, MA in Polit. Sci., 1969, PhD in Comm., 1975. Engr. Westinghouse Electric Corp., Pitts., 1966, Machinen Fabrik Froriep, Dusseldorf, Germany, 1967; instr. U. Ill., Urbana, 1968—70; prof. George Washington U., Washington, 1975—, dir. rsch. prog. in social and orgnl. learning, 1993—. Cons. U.S. AID, Washington, 1979, IBM Intertrade, Vienna, 1990, Bled, Yugoslavia, 1990, World Bank, 2000; lectr. Hitachi Ltd., Tokyo, 1970, Inst. for Systems Studies, Soviet Acad. of Scis., Moscow, 1983, 87, 91, Union of Scientists, Sofia, Bulgaria, 1988; guest scholar U. Pa., Phila., 1983, Internat. Inst. for Applied Systems Analysis, Vienna, 1984, U. Maribor, Slovenia, 1998; guest prof. U. Vienna, 1990, Inst. for Adv. Studies, Vienna, summer 1997; faculty facilitator Quality and Innovation Initiative GW Sch. of Bus. and Pub. Mgmt., 1994-97. Author: (with others) Adequate Modeling of Systems, 1983, Power, Autonomy, Utopia: New Approaches toward Complex Systems, 1986, Managers and National Culture, 1993, A Science of Goal Formulation: American and Soviet Discussions of Cybernetics and Systems Theory, 1991, also editor (with Vadim N. Sadovsky), Cybernetics of National Development, 1991, also editor (with Robert Trappl); contbr. articles to Cybernetics and Systems, Futures, Population and Environ., Systems Practice, Telecommunications Policy, Soc., Bus. and Soc. Rev., Ekistics, Policy Scis., Jour. Aesthetic Edn., others. Vol. human devel. projects Inst. of Cultural Affairs, Washington, 1976-82. Rsch. grantee NSF, U. Ill., 1972-73, George Washington U., 1977-80, C.F. Kettering Found., U. Ill., 1973, Charles Stewart Mott Found., George Washington U., 1995, Nathan Cummings Found., George Washington U., 1999, U.S. Dept. State Bur. Ednl. and Cultural Affairs, George Washington U., 1994–. Mem. Am. Soc. for Cybernetics (pres. 1980-82), Austrian Soc. for Cybernetic Studies (assoc. editor jour. 1990—). Office: George Washington U Dept Mgmt Sci Washington DC 20052-0001

UMSTADTER, DONALD PHILLIP, engineering educator, plasma physicist; b. N.Y.C., Oct. 7, 1954; s. Gerald and Renee (Flynn) U.; m. Rachel A. Simpson. BS in Physics, U.C.L.A., 1981, MS in Physics, 1983, PhD in Physics, 1989. Postdoc. candidate AT&T Bell Labs, Murray Hill, N.J., 1987-89; rsch. scientist U. Mich., Ann Arbor, 1989-97, adjunct prof., 1994-97, assoc. prof., 1997—. Author, inventor: Method and apparatus for generating x-rays, 1996, method and apparatus for generating a plasma wave to accelerate electrons, 1996, method and apparatus for generating and accelerating ultrashort electron pulses; contbr. 45 scientific publs. Named Outstanding Rsch. Scientist U. Mich., Ann Arbor, 1996; recipient Outstanding Achievement award Coll. Engring., 1997, 99. Mem. Optical Soc. Am., Am. Phys. Soc. Achievements include development of an all-optical electron accelerator, which can produce the shortest duration electron pulses and first self-guided laser wakefield acceleration of electrons. Home: 405 Potter Ave Ann Arbor MI 48103-5540 E-mail: dpu@umich.edu.

UNAKAR, NALIN JAYANTILAL, biological sciences educator; b. Karachi, Sindh, Pakistan, Mar. 26, 1935; came to U.S., 1961; s. Jayantilal Virshankar and Malati Jaswantrai (Buch) U.; m. Nita Shantilal Mankad; children: Rita, Rupa. BS, Gujerat U., Bhavnagar, India, 1955; MSc, Bombay U., 1961; PhD, Brown U., 1965. Research asst. Indian Cancer Research Ctr., Bombay, 1955-61; USPHS trainee in biology Brown U., Providence, 1961-65; research assoc. in pathology U. Toronto, Ont., Can., 1965-66; asst. prof. biology Oakland U., Rochester, Mich., 1966-69, assoc. prof., 1969-74, prof., chmn. biology dept., 1974-87, prof., 1974-2000, prof. emeritus, 2000—, adj. prof. biomed. scis., 1984—. Mem. coop. cataract research group Nat. Eye Inst., Bethesda, Md., 1977—; mem. visual scis. study sect. NIH, Bethesda, 1982-86, mem. cataract panel, 1980—. Mem. vis. bd. Lehigh U., Bethlehem, Pa., 1986-89. Grantee Nat. Cancer Inst., NIH, 1967-70, Nat. Eye Inst., NIH, 1976-97. Mem. AAAS, Am. Soc. Cell Biology, Assn. Rsch. in Vision and Ophthalmology, Sigma Xi. Home: 2822 Rhineberry Rd Rochester Hills MI 48309-1912 Office: Oakland U Dept Of Biol Scis Rochester MI 48309

UNAL, GOZDE, computer engineer; b. Iskenderun, Hatay, Turkey, May 4, 1974; d. Guner and Zerrin Bozkurt; m. Alper Unal. MSc, Bilkent U., Ankara, Turkey, 1998; PhD, N.C. State U., 2002. Cert. elec. and electronics engr., Turkey. Rsch. asst. Bilkent U., Ankara, Turkey, 1996—98, N.C. State U., Raleigh, 1998—. Summer rsch. intern Xerox Corp., Webster, NY, 2001. Contbr. articles to profl. jours. Mem.: IEEE, Eta Kappa Nu. Avocation: technical and nontechnical reading.

UNANGST, GREGORY JOHN, communications engineer, administrator; b. Detroit, June 8, 1946; s. Russell Samuel and Florence Unangst; m. Catherine Lee Howell, Dec. 28, 1968 (div. June 1989); children: Stephanie Ann, Geoffrey John; m. Pamela RoAnn Baird, Aug. 13, 1993. BS, U.S. Mil. Acad., 1968; MBA, MS in Engring., U. Pa., 1974; MPhil, NYU, 1985; grad., U.S. Army Command-Gen. Staff Coll., Ft. Leavenworth, Kans., 1987, U.S. Air War Coll., Maxwell AFB, Ala., 1992. Commd. 2d lt. U.S. Army, 1968, advanced through grades to capt., 1970; assigned to Ft. Benning, Ga., 1968, Ft. Wainwright, Alaska, 1969, Vietnam, 1970, Ft. Monmouth, N.J., 1974; resigned, 1978; lt. col. USAR, 1978-96; chief program analyst Ford Motor Co., Dearborn, Mich., 1978-80; mgr. sys. design Ford Aerospace Corp., Palo Alto, Calif., 1980-83, mgr. bus. devel. Colorado Springs, Colo., 1983-88; mgr. advanced programs Loral Space and Range Sys., Sunnyvale, Calif., 1988-95; mgr. advanced satellite comm. Western Devel. Labs., Lockheed Martin, San Jose, 1995—. Decorated Bronze Star, Purple Heart, Defense Meritorious Svc. medal. Mem. IEEE (chmn. live entity integration working group std. 1278, 1992-95), Coyote Point Yacht Club. Home: 2476 W Middlefield Rd Apt B Mountain View CA 94043-2748 E-mail: gunangst@compuserve.com.

UNANUE, ENRIQUE J. architect; b. Havana, Cuba, Sept. 23, 1947; came to U.S., 1961; Grad., U. Ill., 1972. Arch. Solomon-Cardwell Buenz, Chgo., Harry Weese Assoc., Chgo., Perkins & Will, Chgo., Enrique J. Unanue, Arch., Springfield, Ill., Ill. Dept. Pub. Health, Springfield, divsn. chief. Past chmn. City of Springfield, Hist. Sites Commn., Sangamon Valley Youth Symphony, Springfield, Downtown Landscape Design Group, Springfield. Fellow U. Ill. Pub. Health Inst. Mem. AIA, Nat. Coll. Health Care Archs. (founding mem.), Acad. Arch. Health (leadership coun.). Home: 1331 S Dial Ct Springfield IL 62704 Office: Ill Dept Pub Health 525 W Jefferson Springfield IL 62761

UNCAPHER, MARK ELSON, lawyer, trade association administrator; b. Buffalo, Aug. 4, 1953; s. Mark Elson Uncapher Jr. and Joan (Willard) Gruen; m. Robin Nixon, Aug. 27, 1977; children: Peter McLane, Elizabeth Cameron. BA, George Washington U., 1975; JD, N.Y. Law Sch., 1978. Bar: N.Y., 1979, D.C. 1998. Asst. counsel Comptr. State of N.Y., N.Y.C., 1978-83; sales exec. Sta. WZFM-FM, Pleasantville, N.Y., 1983-86; sales exec. Sta. WPAT Park Comm., Inc., N.Y.C., 1986-94; nat. pres. The Ripon Soc., Washington, 1987-90; co-owner Sta. WWCO, Waterbury, Conn., 1994-97; dir. audit svcs. N.Y.C. Dept. Homeless Svcs., 1994-95; counsel House Subcom. on Govt. Mgmt., Info. and Tech., 1995-98; v.p. and counsel divsn. internet commerce and comm. Info. Tech. Assn. Am., Arlington, Va., 1998—. Chmn. Ripon Ednl. Fund, 1982-89, bd. dirs., 1982-97; mng. dir. Signal Properties, Brooklyn Heights, N.Y., 1987-95; ptnr. McLane Farms, LaPorte, Inc., 1980-95; U.S. chmn. 5th Transatlantic Conf., London and Cambridge, Eng., 1988. Contbr. articles to profl. jours. including Broadcast Fin. Jour., Ripon Forum. Chmn. Mark O. Hatfield Scholarship Com., Washington, 1985-97; del. candidate for George Bush 14th Congl. Dist., Bklyn., 1980; fin. chmn. Kings County Rep. Com., 1993-94, Montgomery County (Md.) Rep. Com., 2000. Mem. ABA, Fed. Comm. Bar Assn., Computer Law Assn., Capitol Hill Club (Washington). Republican. Congregationalist. Home: 6210 Greentree Rd Bethesda MD 20817-3362 Office: Info Tech Assn Am 1401 Wilson Blvd Ste 1100 Arlington VA 22209-3101 E-mail: muncapher@ITAA.Org.

UNDAR, AKIF, b. Istanbul, Uskudar, Turkey, Aug. 3, 1963; s. Fikret and H. Neriman Undar; m. F. Pinar Albayrak; children: Damla. BS, Yildiz U., Istanbul, Turkey, 1986; MS, S.W. Tex. State U., 1992; MSE., U. Tex., 1994, PhD, 1996. Asst. prof. surgery Baylor Coll. Medicine, Houston, 1999—2002; dir. rsch. Tex. Children's Hosp., 2001—02; instr. Baylor Coll. Medicine, 1997—99; asst. instr. UTHSC, San Antonio, 1996—97, dir. surg. rsch., 1996—97. Dir. perfusion rsch. Texas Children's Hosp., Houston, 1997—2001; tchg. asst. U. Tex., Austin, 1994—96; presenter, lectr. in field. Contbr. 135 sci. articles. Grantee Rsch., NIH, 2000, Tanox, Inc., Houston, TX, 1999-2001, AHA, Tex. affiliate, 1998-2000. Mem.: ASAIO, AHA (cert. 2000), Internat. Soc. Rotary Blood Pumps, Biomedical Engring. Soc., Internat. Soc. Artificial Organs. Office: Baylor Coll Medicine 6621 Fannin St WT 19-345-H Houston TX 77030-2399 Office Fax: 832-825-1904. Personal E-mail: aundar@bcm.tmc.edu. Business E-mail: aundar@bcm.tmc.edu.

UNDERBERG, MARK ALAN, lawyer; b. Niagara Falls, N.Y., July 9, 1955; s. Alan Jack and Joyce Love (Wisbaum) U.; m. Diane Englander, Mar. 22, 1986; children: Andrew Englander, James Englander. BA, Cornell U., 1977, JD, 1981. Bar: N.Y. 1981. Law clk. to chief judge U.S. Ct. Appeals (3d cir.), Wilmington, Del., 1981-82; assoc. Debevoise & Plimpton, N.Y.C., 1982-87; mng. dir., dep. gen. counsel Henley Group, Inc., 1987-90, mng. dir., gen. counsel, 1990-92; v.p., gen. counsel Abex Inc., Hampton, N.H., 1992-95. V.p., gen. counsel Fisher Sci. Internat. Inc., Hampton, N.H., 1991-97, cons. 1997-98; counsel Paul, Weiss, Rifkind, Wharton & Garrison, N.Y.C., 1998-99, ptnr., 2000—. Editor-in-chief Cornell Law Rev., 1980-81. Mem. ABA, Assn. of Bar of City of N.Y., Genesee Valley Club, University Club. Office: Paul Weiss Rifkind Wharton & Garrison Rm 200 1285 Avenue Of The Americas New York NY 10019-6065

UNDERDOWN, DAVID EDWARD, historian, educator; b. Wells, Eng., Aug. 19, 1925; s. John Percival and Ethel Mary (Gell) U. BA, U. Oxford, 1950, MA, 1951, Yale U., 1952; B.Litt., U. Oxford, 1953; D.Litt. hon., U. of South, 1981. Asst. prof. U. of South, Sewanee, Tenn., 1953-58, assoc. prof., 1958-62; then assoc. prof. U. Va., Charlottesville, 1962-68; prof. Brown U., Providence, 1968-85, Munro-Goodwin Wilkinson prof., 1978-85; vis. prof. Yale U., New Haven, 1979, prof., 1986-94, George Burton Adams prof., 1994-96, emeritus, 1996—. Dir. Yale Ctr. Parliamentary History, 1985-96; vis. Mellon prof. Inst. for Advanced Study, 1988-89; vis. fellow All Souls Coll., Oxford, 1992; Ford's lectr. Oxford U., 1992. Author: Royalist Conspiracy in England, 1960, Pride's Purge, 1971, Somerset in the Civil War and Interregnum, 1973, Revel, Riot and Rebellion, 1985, Fire from Heaven, 1992, A Freeborn People, 1996, Start of Play, 2000. Guggenheim fellow, 1964-65, 91-92, fellow Am. Coun. Learned Socs., 1973-74, NEH fellow, 1980-81. Fellow Royal Hist. Soc., Brit. Acad. (corrs.); mem. Am. Hist. Assn., Conf. Brit. Studies. Office: Yale U Dept History New Haven CT 06520 E-mail: dunderd@attglobal.net.

UNDERDUE, LUCINDA JUANITA, poetess; b. East Orange, N.J., Dec. 11, 1957; d. Herbert Hughes and Sandra Ann Underdue. AA, Bloomfield (N.J.) Coll., 1978. Security patrol guard Bloomfield Coll., 1981-83, security officer guard, 1983-84; with Liss Ctr. Pharmacy, Livingston, N.J., 1984-86; postal carrier USPS, Glen Ridge, 1987-88; with Burns Internat. Security. Author: (book of poetry) Did I Touch You Somewhere?, 1997. With Nat. Guard U.S. Army, 1991—92. Avocations: house painting, writing, music, decorating. Home: 913-228 Virginia Beach Blvd Virginia Beach VA 23451-5622

UNDERHILL, JACOB BERRY, III, retired insurance company executive; b. N.Y.C., Oct. 25, 1926; s. Jacob Berry, Jr. and Dorothy Louise (Quinn) U.; m. Cynthia Jane Lovejoy, Sept. 9, 1950 (div. Sept. 1962); children: David Lovejoy, Kate Howell Underhill Kerwin, Benedict Quinn; m. Lois Beachy, Nov. 2, 1963 (div. July 1987); m. Betsy F. Ashton, Oct. 17, 1987. Grad., Phillips Exeter Acad., 1944; AB, Princeton U., 1950. Editor Courier & Freeman, Potsdam, N.Y., 1950-53; reporter Democrat & Chronicle, Rochester, 1953-56; chief editorial writer St. Petersburg (Fla.) Times, 1956-59; asso. editor McGraw Hill Publ. Co., N.Y.C., 1959-61, Newsweek, N.Y.C., 1961-63; asst. press sec. to Gov. N.Y., 1963-67; dep. supt., 1st dep. supt. State N.Y. Ins. Dept., 1967-72; v.p., sr. v.p., exec. v.p., dir., vice chmn. bd., pres. N.Y. Life Ins. Co., N.Y.C., 1972-86. Hon. chmn. bd. dirs. Manhattan Eye, Ear and Throat Hosp.; trustee emeritus Nat. Trust for Hist. Preservation. With USNR, 1944-46. Mem. Players Club, Links Club, Piping Rock Club (Locust Valley, N.Y.). Home: 410 E 57th St New York NY 10022-3059

UNDERHILL, ROBERT ALAN, consumer products company executive; b. Columbus, Ohio, June 9, 1944; s. Robert Alan and Grace Ruth (Smith) U.; m. Lynn Louise Stentz, Oct. 18, 1963 (dec. Dec. 1997); children: Robert Alan III, Richard Louis; m. Lynn Carol Riviere, July 4, 1998. Student, Case Western Res. U., 1962-64, Ohio State U., 1965. With tech. svc. dept. Gen. Tire & Rubber Co., Akron, Ohio, 1966-69; quality control engr. Edmont-Wilson Co., Canton, 1969-70; mgr. quality assurance Pharmaseal Labs., Massillon, 1970-72; mgr. R&D Internat. Playtex Corp., Paramus, N.J., 1972-78; from mgr. to dir. R&D Kimberly-Clark Corp., Neenah, Wis., 1978-83, v.p. R&D, 1983-93, sr. v.p. R&D, sr. tech. officer, 1994-99; trustee United Health Group, 1994-99, exec. com., vice-chmn., 1997-99, chmn. compensation com., 1994-99; pres. Tech. Solutions, Inc., Appleton, Wis., 1999—. Trustee Novus Health Group, 1993—94; bd. dirs. Appleton (Wis.) Med. Ctr., 1993—96; trustee Thedacare, 1999—, chmn., 2000—01. Patentee (U.S. and fgn.) med. device; mem. editl. bd. Revs. in Process Chemistry and Engring. jour. Mem. exec. bd. Bay Lakes Coun. Boy Scouts Am., 1988-92; bd. dirs. Outagamie County (Wis.) chpt. ARC, 1993-99, chmn. nominations com., 1993-99, mem. exec. com., 1994-99, sec., 1994-99; bd. dirs. Cmty. Blood Ctr., Appleton, Wis., 1996-2001, chmn., 1999-2000; bd. dirs. Cmty. Found. Fox Valley Region, 1997—, vice-chmn. 1998—; bd. dirs. Silver Lake Coll., Manitowoc, Wis., 1998-2000; corp. bd. dirs. U. Wis. Med. Sch. Fox Valley Family Practice Residency Program, 1998—; mem. rsch. adv. com. Inst. Paper Sci. and Tech., 1998-99; trustee Lawrence U., 1998-2001; bd. dirs. Appleton Med. Ctr. Found., 1999—, United Way Fox Cities, 2000—. Goodwill of North Ctrl. Wis., Inc., 2000—, Vis. Nurse Assn. Cmty. Hospice Found., 2001—; active 1st Congl. Ch., Appleton; mem. dean's adv. coun. U. Mo. Coll. Engring., Columbia, 1999-2001. Mem. AAAS, N.Y. Acad. Scis., Am. Assn. Blood Banks (stds. com. 1997-99), Svc. Corps. Ret. Execs., Rotary Internat., Riverview Country Club, Appleton Rotary Club, Butte des Morts Country Club, Pi Delta Epsilon. Republican. Avocations: stock market investment analysis, travel. Home and Office: 2525 W Prospect Ave Appleton WI 54914-8718 E-mail: rau@athenet.net.

UNDERNEHR, LAURA LEE, elementary education educator; b. Tulsa, Apr. 22, 1947; d. James Marion and Opal Lee (Bradford) Garman; m. Donnie Ray Undernehr, Aug. 12, 1971. BS, Northeastern State U., 1969, MEd, 1973; postgrad., Okla. State U., 1973-85, cert., 1988. Cert. elem. edn. and reading tchr., Okla. Tchr., team leader Tulsa Pub. Schs., 1969-88, tchr., 1988—, dean of students, 1998—, asst. prin., 1998-99, prin., 1999—. Treas. Tulsa Daniel Webster Alumni Found., 1991—. Mem. NEA, Okla. Edn. Assn., Tulsa Classroom Tchrs. Assn., Tulsa County Reading Coun., Civitans (v.p. 1997—, pres.-elect Tulsa 1987-88, pres. 1989-90), Delta Zeta (pres. Tulsa chpt. 1989—). Home: 8125 S 40th West Ave Tulsa OK 74132-3042 Office: Clinton Mid Sch 2224 W 41st St Tulsa OK 74107-6706 E-mail: underla@tulsaschools.org.

UNDERWEISER, IRWIN PHILIP, mining company executive, lawyer; b. N.Y.C., Jan. 3, 1929; s. Harry and Edith (Gladstein) U.; m. Beatrice J. Kortchmar, Aug. 17, 1959; children: Rosanne, Marian, Jeffrey. BA, CCNY, 1950; LL.D., Fordham U., 1954; LL.M., NYU, 1961. Bar: N.Y. 1954. With firm Scribner & Miller, N.Y.C., 1951-54, 56-62; partner firm Feuerstein & Underweiser, 1962-73, Underweiser & Fuchs, 1973-77, Underweiser & Underweiser, 1977—. V.p., sec. Sunshine Mining Co., Kellogg, Idaho, 1965-70, chmn. bd., 1970-78, pres., 1971-74, 77, v.p., 1977-83; vice chmn., dir. Underwriters Bank and Trust Co., N.Y.C., 1969-73; sec., dir. Bus. Consortium Fund, 1994—, Triad Capital Corp. N.Y., 1994—; dir. Anchor Post Products, Inc. Bd. dirs. Silver Inst. Inc., vice chmn., 1998-2001; bd. dirs. Bronx Mus. of the Arts, 1993-2001, Sheltering the Homeless is Our Responsibility, 19932001; gen. counsel, mem. bus. council Friends City Center Music and Drama, N.Y.C., 1966-67; pres. W. Quaker Ridge Assn., 1969-70; treas. Scarsdale Neighborhood Assn. Presidents, 1970-71. Served with AUS, 1954-56. Mem. Am., N.Y. State bar assns., Bar Assn. City N.Y., Phi Beta Kappa, Phi Alpha Theta. Home: 7 Rural Dr Scarsdale NY 10583-7701 Office: 405 Park Ave New York NY 10022-4405

UNDERWOOD, BENJAMIN ISAAC, graphics designer, illustrator; b. Zanesville, Ohio, Oct. 30, 1971; s. Christina S. and Alan R. Underwood; m. Lori M. Christen, May 29, 1993; children: Isaac. AAS, Art Ctr., Tucson, 1996. Computer cons. Kinko's, Tucson, 1995—98; graphic artist QwestDex, Portland, Oreg., 1998—2001. Mem. Diversity Team, Portland, 2000—01. Avocations: movies, television, stories.

UNDERWOOD, CECIL H. governor, company executive; b. Josephs Mills, W.Va., Nov. 5, 1922; s. Silas and Della (Forrester) U.; m. Hovah Hall, July 25, 1948; children: Cecilia A., Craig Hall, Sharon. AB, Salem (W.Va.) Coll., 1943; AM, W.Va. U., 1952; rsch. fellow, Amelia Earhart Found., Ann Arbor, Mich., 1954-56; LLD, Marietta (Ohio) Coll., 1957, Bethany (W.Va.) Coll., 1957, W.Va. U., 1957, W.Va. Inst. Tech., 1957, W.Va. State Coll., 1961, Concord Coll., 1960; D of Humanics, Salem Coll., 1957; Dr. Pub. Adminstrn., W.Va. Wesleyan Coll., 1958; LHD (hon.), Shepherd Coll., 1964; LittD, Western New Eng. Coll., 1969; LHD, Marshall U., 1997; D in Pub. Svc., Alderson Broaddus Coll., 1997; DSc (hon.), W. Va. Sch. Osteopathic Med., 1998; hon. degree, Davis and Elkins Coll., 1998, Fairmont State Coll., 1999. Tchr. high sch., 1943-46; staff Marietta Coll., 1946-50; v.p. Salem Coll., 1950-56; gov. State of W.Va., 1957-61, 97—; v.p. Island Creek Coal Co., 1961-64; dir. civic affairs Monsanto Co., 1965-67, v.p., 1967; pres. Cecil H. Underwood Assocs., 1965-80, Franswood Corp., 1968-75, Bethany (W.Va.) Coll., 1972-75, Princess Coals, Inc., Huntington, 1978-81, Morgantown (W.Va.) Indsl. Park, Inc., 1983-96, Software Valley, 1989-92, Mon View Heights of W.Va., 1993-96; field underwriter N.Y. Life Ins. Co., 1976-78; chmn. bd. Princess Coals, Inc., Huntington, 1981-83. Sec. bd. dirs. Huntington Fed. Savs. and Loan Assn., 1961-96; pres. Huntington Found. Mem. W.Va. Ho. Dels., 1944-56, minority floor leader, 1949, 51, 53, 55; Mem. exec. com. Gov.'s Conf., 1959; chmn. So. Regional Edn. Bd., 1959-60, 1999-2000; Pres. Young Republican League of W.Va., 1946-50; parliamentarian Young Rep. Nat. Conv., Boston, 1951;

del.-at-large Rep. Nat. Conv., 1960, 64, 72, 76, 80, 84, 88, 2000, temporary chmn., 1960; Chmn. bd. dirs. W.Va. Found. Ind. Colls., Appalachian Regional Hosps.; chmn. bd. dirs. W.Va. div. Am. Cancer Soc., nat. bd. dirs., chmn. nat. crusade com., 1976-77, chmn. com. on legacies and planned giving, 1979; chmn. bd. dirs. Salem Coll., 1978-89, Salem Internat. U., 1989—; bd. dirs. Higher Edn. Loan Program of W.Va., 1980-94; chair W.Va. Coun. on Vocat. Edn., 1982-96, W.Va. State Coll. System, 1991, Nat. Edn. Goals Panel, 1998-99; regional vice chmn. Boy Scouts Am., 1961-67. Mem. Nat. Assn. State Coun. Vocat. Edn. (pres. 1994-96), Masons, Shriners, Elks, Rotary, Sigma Phi Epsilon, Pi Kappa Delta. Methodist. Home: 1578 Kanawha Blvd E 1-C Charleston WV 25311

UNDERWOOD, DEANNA KAY, librarian; b. Medicine Lodge, Kans., Oct. 2, 1962; d. Kenneth Edward and Janet Sue (Hammond) Winters; m. Roger Alan Underwood, Aug. 2, 1986; children: Lane Alan, Lindsey Kay. BS in Elem. Edn., Sterling (Kans.) Coll., 1984. Tchr. 4th grade White Rock Elem. Sch., Burr Oak, Kans., 1984-86, tchr. kindergarten Esbon, 1986-87; libr. aide mid. and high schs. White Rock Schs., Esbon and Burr Oak, 1987-91, K-12 libr. Kans., 1992—. Mem. site-based coun., chmn. reading com., mem. ELT com. Unified Sch. Dist. 104, Esbon and Burr Oak, 1993—. Chmn. adminstrv. coun. United Meth. Ch., Esbon, 1989—, trustee coun., 1993—. Mem. KASL. Republican. Avocations: reading, cooking, cross-stitch. Home: RR 1 Box 14 Esbon KS 66941-9703 Office: White Rock HS PO Box 345 633 Main St Burr Oak KS 66936-9738

UNDERWOOD, EVELYN B. elementary and secondary educator, consultant, counselor; b. Hernando, Miss., Jan. 6, 1943; d. Herbert Miller and Sallie Bell Campbell; children from previous marriage: James Lee, Theodore, Timothy, Angela Renee, Herbert Dwayne; m. King James Underwood, May 28, 1977. BA BOG, Ea. Ill. U., 1983, MS in Edn., 1988, EdS, 1993; JD, Ind. U., 1987; PhD, U. Ill., 2000; DHL (hon.), Faith Grant Coll., Birmingham, Ala., 1995. Cert. tchr. h.s. and upper elem. guidance, Ill.; cert. in adminstrn., Ill.; ordained elder (minister) Free Will Bapt. Ch. Asst. to mgr. Shelton Laundry, Urbana, Ill., 1961-63; sec. U. Ill., 1964-68, asst. to exec. dir. Afro Am. Studies Commn., 1969-71, asst. to dir. minority student affairs, 1971-84, 87-89; educator, counselor Urbana Sch. Dist. 116, 1983-93, counselor, 1993—. Elected. mem., sec. Urbana Bd. Edn., 1968-80; cert. legal intern to fed. judge, legal svcs., atty. gen., Indpls., Bloomington, Ind., Champaign, Ill., 1986-87; founder Evelyn Burnett Underwood Instrumental Music Student Assistance Program, Urbana Sch. Dist. 116, 1994—. Contbr. articles and papers to profl. publs. Mem. exec. com. Concerned Citizens Com., Champaign, 1963-85; overseer U. Ill. YWCA Endowment Com., Champaign, 1994—; v.p. Mnisterial Alliance of Champaign-Urbana and Vicinity, 1999—. Recipient Outstanding Achievement to Nat. Sch. Bd. Assn. Black Caucus, 1976; fellow U. Ill., 1990. Mem. AAUW, Ill. Assn. Multicultural Counseling (pres.-elect 2000), Ill. Edn. Assn. (region 9 rep. 1999—), Ill. Counseling Assn., Urbana Edn. Assn. of NEA/Ill. Edn. Assn. (v.p. 1994-98), Ill. Career Devel. Assn., Ill. Sch. Counselors Assn., Optimist Club Internat. Democrat. Avocations: missionary work, tutoring and counseling youth.

UNDERWOOD, JANE HAINLINE HAMMONS, anthropologist, educator; b. Ft. Bliss, Tex., Oct. 30, 1931; d. Frank and Lydia (Williams) Hammons; m. Van K. Hainline, Oct. 20, 1947 (div. 1966); children: Michael K., Susan J.; m. John W. Underwood, July 4, 1968; 1 dau., Anne K. AA, Imperial Valley Coll., 1957; BA, U. Calif., Riverside, 1960; MA, UCLA, 1962, PhD, 1964. Asst. prof. U. Calif., Riverside, 1963-68; research anthropology Yap Islands, 1964, 65-66; prof. anthropology U. Ariz., Tucson, 1968-99, prof. emeritus, 1999—, assoc. dean Grad. Coll., 1979-80, asst. provost for grad. studies, 1980-82, acting dir. Sch. Health Related Professions, 1980-82, asst. v.p. research, assoc. dean Grad. Coll., 1982-87; assoc. Micronesian Area Rsch. Ctr., 1987—. Contbr. articles to profl. jours. Woodrow Wilson fellow, 1960-61; UCR Jr. Faculty fellow, 1968 Fellow AAAS; mem. Am. Assn. Phys. Anthropologists (v.p. 1980-82), Assn. Study Human Biology, Pacific Sci. Assn. (life), Assn. for Study Social Biology (bd. dirs. 1996-99), Sigma Xi (pres. U. Ariz. chpt. 1991-92). Home: 2228 E 4th St Tucson - AZ 85719-5118 E-mail: kammagar@prodigy.net.

UNDERWOOD, JOHN H. research engineer; b. Swampscott, Mass., Jan. 25, 1941; s. John Harvie Underwood and Esther F. (Butterfield) Charron; m. Margaret L. Paine, Dec. 26, 1964; children: Kristen Lee, John Harvie, Brian Thomas. BSME, U. Mass., 1962; MS in Metallurgy, NYU, 1965. Project engr. Bendix Corp., Teterboro, N.J., 1962-65; rsch. engr. Army Armament Rsch., Devel. and Engring. Ctr., Watervliet, N.Y., 1965—. Vis. scientist Materials Rsch. Labs., Melbourne, Australia, 1987. Author, editor: Application of Fracture Mechanics for Selection of Metallic Structural Materials, 1982; editor: Chevon-Notched Specimens: Testing and Stress Analysis, 1984, Fracture Mechanics: Seventeenth Volume, 1986, Fatigue and Fracture Mechanics: 28th Vol., 1997; co-editor: Surface Crack Growth: Models, Experiments and Structures, 1990, Fracture Mechanics: 26th Edition, 1995. Chmn., bd. dirs. Cambridge (N.Y.) United Fund, 1967-69; pres. bd. edn. Cambridge Cen. Sch., 1973-74, 78-79. Recipient Outstanding Engring. Alumni award U. Mass., 1991. Fellow ASTM (mem. exec. com. E8 on fatigue and fracture 1980-95, chmn. symposium on fatigue and fracture mechanics 1996, chmn. symposium on fracture mechanics 1984, Irwin medal 1990, Wessel award 1999); mem. Soc. Exptl. Mechanics. Achievements include development of new methods for measurement and modeling of fracture and fatigue behavior of metals and composites. Avocations: hiking, house construction, photography, forest management. Home: 193 Middle Rd Salem NY 12865-4517 Office: Army Armament Rsch Devel and Engring Ctr Bldg 115 Watervliet NY 12189 E-mail: junder@pica.army.mil.

UNDERWOOD, JOHN THOMAS, IV, trade association executive, lobbyist; b. Louisville; s. John Thomas III and Agnes Duvall Underwood; m. Mary Angela Underwood, Apr. 25, 1994; children: Ryan, Alexander. BBA, U. Ky., 1983, MBA, 1984. Pres. Assn. Profls. Inc., Frankfort, Ky., 1986—. Contbr. to Bus. First, Ky. Gazette. Mem. Am. Soc. Assn. Execs., Assn. Osteopathic State Exec. Dirs., Assn. State Podiat. Execs., Internt. Coun. Lib. Exec. Dirs., U. Ky. Alumni Assn. Avocations: restoration of British sports cars. Office: Assn Profls Inc 1501 Twilight Trail Frankfort KY 40601

UNDERWOOD, LUCINDA JEAN, poet, playwright, small business owner, researcher; b. Troy, Mich., Aug. 1, 1964; d. Harold L. and Betty Jo (Arms) U. Grad. high sch., Livingston, Tenn., 1982. With Dawn Wells, Nashville, 1976-80; owner, mgr. Cindy's Critter Care, Cookeville, 1986—. Author: (poetry) The Mystic, 1996; songwriter. Mem. Nat. Pony Express Assn. Office: Cindy's Critter Care 836 Bray St Apt B Cookeville TN 38501-3733

UNDERWOOD, PAUL BENJAMIN, gynecologist, educator; b. Greer, S.C., Aug. 8, 1934; s. Paul Benjamin and Gladys (Guest) U.; m. Peggy Joyce Outen, July 7, 1957; children: Paul Benjamin III, Mary Barton. MD, Med. U. S.C., 1959. Diplomate Am. Bd. Ob-Gyn, Am. Bd. Gynecol. Oncology. Intern Med. U. S.C., Charleston, 1959-60, resident, 1960-64; fellow M.D. Anderson Hosp. and Tumor Inst., Houston, 1966-67; asst. prof. U. S.C., 1967-70, assoc. prof., 1970-74, prof., 1974-79; chmn. dept. ob-gyn U. Va. Sch. Medicine, Charlottesville, 1979-99; staff Med. U. S.C., Charleston, 1999—. Contbr. numerous articles to med. jours. With USN, 1964-66. Recipient Alumni of Yr. award Med. U. S.C., 1989. Mem. Am. Coll. Ob-Gyn., Soc. Gynecol. Oncologists (coun. 1972-75, v.p. 1977-78, pres. 1983), Am. Assn. Ob-Gyn. (sec. 1992-95, pres. 1999—), Felix Rutledge Soc. (pres. 1977), Am. Gynecol. Club (pres. 1996), So. Med. Soc., Charlottesville Med. Soc., S.C. Ob-Gyn. Soc., Thegos Soc., Alpha Omega Alpha. Office: 171 Ashley Ave Charleston SC 29425-0001

UNDERWOOD, RALPH EDWARD, computer systems engineer; b. Houston, Sept. 26, 1947; s. Harry Anson and Ethel Jackson Underwood; m. Linda Sue Merkel, Apr. 10, 1976. BS in Biology, Baker U., 1969; JD, Washburn U., 1973; MS in Computer Sci., Kans. U., 1984. Bar: Kans, 1973. Free-lance stock and options trader, Prairie Village, Kans., 1974-79; mem. staff BDM Corp., Leavenworth, 1982-84; sr. research and devel. engr. Ford Aerospace and Communications Corp., Colorado Springs, Colo., 1984-87, subcontract adminstr., 1987-89; sr. engr., program mgr. CTA Inc., 1989-93; sr. staff system engring. MCI Telecomms. Corp., 1993-95; cons. in computer security and risk mgmt. Englewood, Colo., 1995-99; sr. engr. Computer Tech. Assocs., Colorado Springs, 1999—. Patentee in field. Mem. Kans. Bar Assn., Upsilon Pi Epsilon, Sigma Phi Epsilon (social chmn. 1968, asst. house mgr. 1968, sec./treas. sr. coun. 1969), Phi Alpha Delta. Avocations: hunting, fishing, tennis, skiing. *Personal philosophy: Treat every person with equal respect and dignity, without regard to their position or personal achievements.*

UNDERWOOD, RICHARD ALLAN, English language educator; b. Plymouth, Mich., Mar. 28, 1933; s. Harold Raymond and Yvonne Clara (Foster) U.; m. Sandra Jane Hayes, Nov. 17, 1962; 1 child, Eric Michael. BA, U. Mich., 1955, MA, 1967, PhD, 1970. Asst. prof. Clemson (S.C.) U., 1970-77, assoc. prof., 1977-84, prof. English, 1984—. Author: A Little Bit of Love, 1963, Shakespeare's "The Phoenix and Turtle": A Survey of Scholarship, 1974, Shakespeare on Love: The Poems and the Plays, 1985, The Two Noble Kinsmen and Its Beginnings, 1993; translator: En Smula Karlek, 1969, 81; editor: Phoenix with a Bayonet: A Journalist's Interim Report on the Greek Revolution (by Bayard Stockton), 1971. 1st lt. U.S. Army, 1955-57. Fellow Bread Loaf Writers Conf., 1963; vis. scholar Rackham Sch. Grad. Studies, U. Mich., 1983-85, 90-91, 91-92, 92-93, 93-94. Avocation: piano music. Home: 111 Lakeview Cir Clemson SC 29631-1019 Office: Clemson U 809 Strode Clemson SC 29631-1436

UNDERWOOD, ROBERT LEIGH, venture capitalist; b. Paducah, Ky., Dec. 31, 1944; s. Robert Humphreys and Nancy Wells (Jessup) Underwood; m. Susan Lynn Doscher, May 22, 1976; children: Elizabeth Leigh, Dana Whitney, George Gregory. BS with gt. distinction, Stanford U., 1965, MS, 1966, PhD, 1968; MBA, Santa Clara U., 1970. Rsch. scientist, project leader Lockheed Missiles & Space Co., Sunnyside, Calif., 1967—71; spl. asst. for engring. scis. Office Sec., Dept. Transp., Washington, 1971—73; sr. mgmt. assoc. Office Mgmt. and Budget, Exec. OFfice Pres., 1973; with TRW Inc., L.A., 1973—79, dir. retail nat. accts., 1977—78, dir. product planning and devel., 1978—79; pres., CEO OMEX, Santa Clara, 1980—82; v.p. Heizer Corp., Chgo., 1979—85, No. Trust; pres. No. Capital Corp., Chgo., 1985—86; mng. ptnr. ISSS Ventures, 1986—88; founding ptnr. N.Am. Bus. Devel. Co., Chgo., 1988—. Trustee Burridge Mut. Funds, 1996—98; NSF adv. com. Indsl. Innovation. Contbr. articles to profl. jours. Mem. sch. bd. Avoca Dist. 37, 1990—99, v.p., 1996—99; mem. adv. bd. Leavy Sch. Bus. and Adminstrn. Santa Clara U., 1995—; elder Presbyn. Ch., 1978—79. Fellow, NASA, NSF; scholar, Alcoa. Mem.: IEEE, Indian Hill Club (Winnetka, Ill.), Chgo. Club, Union League Chgo., Beta Gamma Sigma, Tau Beta Pi, Phi Beta Kappa, Sigma Xi. Home: 59 Woodley Rd Winnetka IL 60093-3748 Office: 135 S La Salle St Chicago IL 60603-4159

UNDERWOOD, ROBERT MILTON, JR. real estate broker; b. Dallas, 1959; s. Robert Milton Underwood and Charlsie Ruth Edwards; m. Deborah Lynn Underwood. BS, U. Tex., 1981, BA, 1983; MBA, S.W. Tex. State U., 1994; MS, City U., 2002. Cert. residential specialist, Tex. Tax examiner IRS, Austin, 1984-85; broker Underwood Investments, 1986—. Instr. informal classes U. Tex., Austin, 1998—. Eagle Scout, 1973. Mem. Nat. Assn. Realtors, Residential Sales Coun., Tex. Assn. Realtors, Am. Assn. Individual Investors, Austin Bd. Realtors. Avocations: computer systems, martial arts (Black Belt in Karate). Home: 11502 Juniper Ridge Dr Austin TX 78759-3845 E-mail: robertunderwood@bigfoot.com.

UNDERWOOD, STEVEN CLARK, publishing executive; b. Arlington Heights, Ill., Dec. 1, 1960; s. Donald William and Mary Frances (Clark) U. BBA, U. Tex., 1982, MBA, 1987; JD, So. Meth. U., 1985. Bar: Tex. 1985. Sr. fin. analyst CBS, Inc., N.Y.C., 1987-89; assoc. bus. mgr. Supplementary Edn. Group Simon & Schuster, Englewood Cliffs, N.J., 1989-90, bus. mgr. Fearon/Janus/Quercus divsn. Belmont, Calif., 1990-92, pres. Fearon/Janus/Quercus divsn., 1992-93, pres. Globe Fearon divsn. Upper Saddle River, NJ, 1993-96; v.p., dir. of bus. devel. Secondary Edn. Group, Simon and Schuster, 1996-97; v.p. bus. devel. Simon and Schuster, 1997-98; v.p. sch. markets Troll Comms., Mahwah, 1998—2001; v.p., contr. Current Med. Directions divsn, MediMedia USA, Inc., N.Y.C., 2002—. Mem. ABA, Am. Mgmt. Assn. (pres.'s assn.), Assn. Am. Pubs., Nat. Eagle Scout Assn., Coll. Bus. Adminstrn. Found., Tex. Bar Assn., Tex. Alumni Assn., U. Tex. Century Club, Alpha Phi Omega, Beta Gamma Sigma, Phi Kappa Phi, Phi Eta Sigma, Golden Key. Republican. Methodist. Avocations: sailing, scuba diving, karate, camping, rafting. Home: 902 Somerset Ct Ramsey NJ 07446-2919

UNDERWOOD, THOMAS WOODBROOK, communications company executive; b. Royal Oak, Mich., Nov. 29, 1930; s. Elmer and Della Marie (Zimmer) U.; m. Louise Virginia, May 24, 1953 (dec. Feb. 1979); children: Ann Marie Underwood Shuman, Dan and Dave (twins). BAS in Elec. Engring., Milw. Sch. Engring., 1957, MS in Comms., 1995, PhD in Comms., 1998. Service analyst, writer ITT Gillfillan, Los Angeles, 1958-60; sr. tech. editor, writer Smithkline Beckman, Fullerton, Calif., 1960-78, tech. com. mgr. Brea, 1978-85; pres. Tranwood Communications, Santa Ana, 1985—. Tech. editor, writer manuals for manned space flights to Mars and the moon. Served to staff sgt. USAF, 1950-54, Korea. Fellow Soc. Tech. Comms. (Orange County chpt., assoc., pres. 1992, 93, treas. 1966, 88), Am. Med. Writers Assn, U.S. C. of C., Santa Ana C. of C. Democrat. Home and Office: Tranwood Comm PO Box 1852 Palm Springs CA 92263-1852

UNDLIN, CHARLES THOMAS, banker; b. Madison, Minn., Mar. 4, 1928; s. Jennings C. and Alice M. (Berg) U.; m. Lois M. Anderson, June 23, 1953; children: Sarah, Mary Lee, Margaret, Thomas. BA, St. Olaf Coll., 1950. Asst. cashier Northwestern State Bank, Osseo, Minn., 1950-55, N.W. Bancorp., Mpls., 1955-57, Security Bank & Trust Co., Owatonna, Minn., 1957-59, Norwest Bank Black Hills, Rapid City, S.D., 1959-67; pres. and chief exec. officer Norwest Bank S.D., 1967-84, vice-chmn., 1984-85; pres. Norwest Bank Nebr., Omaha, 1985-88, also bd. dirs.; dir. Rushmore State Bank, Rapid City, 1988—. Past bd. dirs. Children's Hosp., Omaha, 1986. Sgt. U.S. Army, 1951-52. Mem. S.D. Bankers Assn. (past pres.), Arrowhead Country Club. Republican. Lutheran. Avocations: golf, skiing, fishing.

UNGAR, ERIC EDWARD, mechanical engineer; b. Vienna, Austria, Nov. 12, 1926; came to U.S. 1939; s. Irwin Isidor and Sabina (Schlesinger) U.; m. Goldie Edna Becker, July 1, 1951; children: Judith Fishman, Susan Green, Ellen Borgenicht, Sharon Ungar Lane. BSME, Washington U., St. Louis, 1951; MS, U. N.Mex., 1954; Eng.Sc.D., NYU, 1957. Aero-ordnance engr. Sandia Corp., Albuquerque, 1951-53; rsch. scientist, asst. prof. NYU, 1953-58; chief cons. engr. Bolt Beranek & Newman, Inc., Cambridge, Mass., 1958-96. Chief engring. scientist Acentech Inc., Cambridge, 1993—. Co-author: Structure-Borne Sound, 1973, 2nd edit. 1988; contbr. articles to profl. jours., chpts. to books. 1st lt. U.S. Army, 1945-48; ETO. Recipient Per Bruel Gold Medal for Noise Control and Acoustics, Am. Soc. of Mechanicl Engineers, 1994. Fellow ASME (life; chmn. design engring. divsn. 1978-80, Centennial medallion 1981, AIAA (assoc.), Acoustical Soc. Am. (pres. 1991-92, Trent-Crede Silver medal 1983); mem. Inst. for Noise Control and Engring. (bd. cert., pres. 1985). Home: 15 Considine Rd Newton MA 02459-3603 Office: Acentech Inc 33 Moulton St Cambridge MA 02138-1118 E-mail: eungar@acentech.com.

UNGAR, IRWIN ALLAN, botany educator; b. N.Y.C., Jan. 21, 1934; s. Isidore and Gertrude (Fageles) U.; m. Ana Celia Del Cid, Aug. 10, 1959; children: Steven, Sandra, Sharon. BS, CCNY, 1955; MA, U. Kans., Lawrence, 1957, PhD, 1961. Instr. U. R.I., Kingston, 1961-62; asst. prof. Quincy Coll., Ill., 1961-66, Ohio U., Athens, 1966-69, assoc. prof., 1969-74, prof. botany, 1974—, chmn. dept. botany, 1984-89. Dir. Dysart Woods Lab., 1985—99, Environ. Studies Program, 1991—95; vis. prof. dept. plant scis. and vis. fellow Wolfson Coll., Oxford (Eng.) U., 1990—91; panelist Nat. Sea Grant Program, 1984; grant proposal reviewer NSF, 1980—2002. Contbr. articles to profl. jours.; manuscript reviewer Am. Jour. Botany, Internat. Jour. Plant Scis. NSF grantee, 1974-76, 76-78, 80-83, 94-95, 98-2001; rsch. grantee Petroleum Environ. Rsch. Forum, 1992-96. Fellow Ohio Acad. Sci.; mem. AAAS, Am. Inst. Biol. Scis., Bot. Soc. Am., Ecol. Soc. Am., Sigma Xi. Home: 44 Walker St Athens OH 45701-2252 Office: Ohio Univ Dept Of Botany Athens OH 45701 E-mail: ungar@ohio.edu.

UNGAR, MANYA SHAYON, volunteer, education consultant; b. N.Y.C., May 30, 1928; d. Samuel and Ethel M. (Liese) Shayon; m. Harry Fireman Ungar, June 25, 1950; children: Paul Benedict, Michael Shayon. BA, Mills Coll., 1950. Cert. tutor LVA/UC adult learners2001. Actress TV and radio NBC, CBS, N.Y.C., 1950-58; founder, pres., bd. dirs. chpt. AFS, Scotch Plains-Fanwood, N.J., 1963-70; vol. project dir. handicapped cub scouts Boy Scouts Am., Plainfield, 1958-61; founder, co-dir. Summer Theater Workshop, Scotch Plains, 1967-78; legis. v.p. N.J. State PTA, 1977-79, pres., 1979-81; legis. v.p. Nat. PTA, Chgo., 1981-85, 1st v.p., 1985-87, pres., 1987-89. Mem. arts edn. adv. panel Nat. Endowment Arts, Washington, 1988-91, panel Nat. Inst. Work and Learning, 1988-91; adv. coun. Nat. Panel Drug Free Schs., Washington, 1989-91, edn. adv. bd. NBC, 1988-91, PBS, 1988-91, Scholastic, Inc., 1990-94; bd. dirs. Math. Sci. Edn. Bd., 1988-92. Trustee N.J. Children's Specialized Hosp., 1990—99, N.J. Pub. Edn. Inst., 1987—; mem. adv. coun. Natural Resources Def. Coun., Mothers and Others, 1999—99; mem. geography assessment adv. coun. Nat. Assessment Edn. Progress, 1991—92, mem. nat. oversite commn. on geog. stds., 1992—94; mem. N.J. Basic Skills Coun., 1990—94; chmn. N.J. Math. Coalition, 1994—; mem. accreditation com. APA, 1992—98; mem. tchr. programs adv. panel Ednl. Testing Svc., 1990—94; mem. external rev. com. CDC Preventing Rsik Behaviors in Adolescents, 1993; chmn. scholarship com. Fanwood-Scotch Plains Coll. Club, 1997—; mem. N.J. United for HIgher Stds., 2000—; mem. stds. rev. com. N.J. Dept. Edn., 2001—; bd. dirs. Washington Rock Girl Scout Coun., 1995—98, Literacy Vols. of Am., Union County, 2001—. Manya Shayon Ungar Scholarship and Scotch Plains H.S. Auditorium named in her honor, 1989; named Outstanding Citizen N.J. Jaycees, 1979, Scotch Plains Twp., 1989, 92, State of N.J., 1987, Bd. of Freeholders, 1987; named life mem. nat. PTA, 45 state PTAs. Mem.: LWV (chmn. votes svc. Westfield area 1991—95, N.J. fiscal policy and edn. coms. 1998—). Avocations: piano, acting, singing, recording talking books. Home: 10 Brandywine Ct Scotch Plains NJ 07076-2550 E-mail: mpsu530@aol.com.

UNGAR, ROBERT ARTHUR, lawyer, lobbyist; b. N.Y.C., Oct. 31, 1955; s. Albert Joseph and Elayne Lee (Fruhling) U.; m. Eileen P. Doherty, June 11, 1988. BS summa cum laude, Mercy Coll., 1983; JD, St. John's U., 1987. Bar: Conn. 1987, N.Y. 1988. Pres. Alton Cons., Inc., Great Neck, N.Y., 1975-81; mgr. met. zone N.Y. Motorola Inc., Queens, 1981-85; br. mgr. Wang Info. Svcs. Corp., N.Y.C., 1985-86; asst. to dean sch. law St. John's U., Queens, 1986-87; counsel to insp. gen. Fire Dept. N.Y.C. Dept. Investigation, Bklyn., 1987-88; atty. Sullivan & Liapakis, P.C., N.Y.C., 1988-90; first asst. commr. N.Y.C. Fire Dept., Bklyn., 1990; sr. ptnr. Ungar, Gerstman & Pomerance, Garden City, N.Y., 1990-92; pvt. practice Robert A. Ungar, P.C., 1993—; pres. Robert A. Ungar Assocs., Inc., 1995—. Adj. prof. law Mercy Coll., 1990-92. Chmn. drug task force Cmty. Planning Bd. #7, Queens, 1988-89; legis. counsel N.Y.C. Fire Marshals Devevolent Assn., N.Y.C., Fire Alarm Dispatchers Benevolent Assn., Met. Buglar and Fire Alarm Assn., N.Y.C. EMS and Paramedics Union; gen. counsel N.Y.C. Fire Dept. Ner Tamid Soc. Recipient outstanding community svc. award Community Planning Bd. Queens #1, 1981; named Hon. Battalion Chief N.Y.C. Fire Dept., 1989. Mem. ABA, N.Y. State Bar Assn., Queens County Bar Assn., Assn. of Bar of City of N.Y., Assn. Trial Lawyers Am., N.Y. State Trial Lawyers Assn. (bd. dirs.), Nassau County Bar Assn., Capitol Hill Club (Washington), Fire Bell Club, N.Y. Press Club. Avocations: electronics, radio communications. Home: 150-16 17 Ave Whitestone NY 11357-3121 Office: 595 Stewart Ave Ste 410 Garden City NY 11530-4736

UNGAR, ROSELVA MAY, primary and elementary educator; b. Detroit, Oct. 31, 1926; d. John and Elva Rushton; m. Kenneth Sawyer Goodman, Dec. 26, 1946 (div. 1950); m. Fred Ungar, June 22, 1952 (div. 1977); children: Daniel Brian, Carol Leslie, Lisa Maya. Student, U. Mich., 1946-48; BA, UCLA; MA, Pacific Oaks Coll. Cert. elem. tchr., early childhood tchr., bilingual cert. of competency in Spanish. Recreation dir. Detroit City Parks and Recreation, 1946-50, L.A. Unified Sch. Dist., 1950-52, tchr., 1984—2001, mentor tchr. elem. edn., 1988-94, ret., 2001; tchr. head start Found. Early Childhood Edn., L.A., 1965-73; staff organizer Early Childhood Fedn. Local 1475 AFT, 1973-79; staff rep. Calif. Fedn. Tchrs., 1979-83. Contbr. articles to profl. jours. Mem. Gov.'s Adv. Com. Child Care, L.A., 1980-83; mem. Sierra Club, 1978—; mem. So. Calif. Libr. Social Studies, L.A., 1989—; charter mem. Mus. Am. Indian Smithsonian Inst., 1994—; Nat. Ctr. Early Childhood Workforce, Children's Def. Fund, Womens Internat. League for Peace and Freedom, ACLU, So. Poverty Law Ctr., Food First, Meiklejohn Civil Liberties Inst.; bd. dirs., pres. Found. for Early Childhood Edn., 1997—, Coalition Progressive L.A. Mem. Nat. Assn. Multicultural Edn. Adv. Bd. (teach L.A., UCLA Ctr.), Calif. Assn. Bilingual Edn., So. Calif. Assn., Edn. Young Children, Early Childhood Fedn. (pres. emeritus 1979—), United Tchrs. L.A. (chpt. chair 1984-96, east area dir. and UTLA bd. dirs. 1996-99), Coalition Labor Union Women (bd. mem. 1980-86). Avocations: guitar, folk songs, hiking. Home: 20349 Jay Carroll Dr Santa Clarita CA 91350-1959 E-mail: r_ungar@hotmail.com.

UNGARETTI, RICHARD ANTHONY, lawyer; b. Chgo., May 25, 1942; s. Dino Carl and Antoinette (Calvetti) U.; children: Joy A., Paul R. BS, DePaul U., 1964, JD, 1970. Bar: Ill. 1970, U.S. Dist. Ct. (no. dist.) Ill. 1970, U.S. Supreme Ct. 1980. Assoc. Kirkland & Ellis, Chgo., 1970-74; ptnr. Ungaretti & Harris, 1974—. Mem. adv. coun. DePaul Coll. Law, Chgo., 1988. Mem. ABA, Chgo. Bar Assn., Ill. State Bar Assn., Internat. Coun. Shopping Ctrs., Am. Coll. Real Estate Lawyers, Justinian Soc., Urban Land Inst. (assoc.), Lamda Alpha Avocations: golf, fishing, hunting. Office: Ungaretti & Harris 3500 Three First Nat Plz Chicago IL 60602 E-mail: raungaretti@uhlaw.com.

UNGARO, EMANUEL MATTEOTTI, fashion designer; b. Aix-en-Provence, France, Feb. 13, 1933; s. Cosimo and Concetta (Casalino) U.; m. Laura; 1 dau. Student, Lycée, Aix-en-Provence, 1943-50. Worked with father as tailor, Aix-en-Provence, 1951-54; then for Camps Paris, 1955-57. With Cristobal Balenciaga, Paris, 1957-64, dir. Balenciaga br., Madrid, 1958-60; worked for André Courréges, Paris, 1964; ind. couturier, Paris, 1965. Designer of both couture and ready-to-wear men's and women's fashions; also fragrance designer since 1977. Office: 2 Ave Montaigne F 75008 Paris France

UNGARO, JOSEPH MICHAEL, newspaper publishing executive, consultant; b. Providence, Nov. 4, 1930; s. Rocco and Lucy (Mott) U.; m. Evelyn Short, Apr. 15, 1961; children: Elizabeth Anne, Joseph Michael, Ellen Lucia. BA, Providence Coll., 1952; MS in Journalism, Columbia, 1953. With Providence Jour.-Bull., 1951-73, mng. editor Evening Bull., 1967-72; mng. editor Eve. Bull., also dir. planning and devel. Providence Jour. and Bull., 1972-73; mng. editor Westchester-Rockland Newspapers, White Plains, N.Y., 1974-75, v.p., exec. editor, 1975-84, pres., gen. mgr., 1984-86, pres., publisher, 1986-90; pres., chief exec. officer Detroit Newspaper Agy., 1990-91; cons., 1991—. Mem. Am. Newspaper Pubs. Assn. (past chmn. research inst., conv. program com.), Am. Soc. Newspaper Editors, AP Mng. Editors Assn. (past pres.) Home: 379 Pond Shore Dr Charlestown RI 02813-2007 E-mail: jungaro@aol.com.

UNGARO, MARIO, pathologist, educator; s. Fabricio Ungaro and Enriquetta Zevallos. MB, Nat. U. San Marcos, Peru, 1954, MD. Diplomate in pathology. Intern Marymount Hosp., Cleve., 1954-55; resident St. Vincent Charity Hosp., 1955-57; resident in pathology New Britain Gen. Hosp., 1958-59, Roswell Park Meml. Inst., Buffalo, 1959-60; fellow forensic pathology Frank E. Bunts Ed. Inst., Cleve., 1957-58; asst. pathologist Mercy Hosp., Buffalo, 1960-61; prof. pathology Nat. U. Trujillo, Peru, 1961—87; chmn. pathology Hosp. Regional Tchg. Hosp., Trujillo, Peru, 1980—87; prof. emeritus Nat. U. Trujillo, 1992. Mem. Peruvian Assn. Pathology, Peruvian Med. Assn., Nat. Club, Golf Country Club. Avocation: swimming. Office: Hosp Regional Tchg Hosp Trujillo Peru

UNGER, ARLENE KLEIN, medical company executive, counselor, consultant; b. Bklyn., May 12, 1952; d. Eli and Harriet Barbara (Shapiro) Klein; m. Stefan Howard Unger, Aug. 19, 1979; children: Max Elias, Elana Rose. BS with distinction, Emerson Coll., 1974; MS, So. Conn. State U., 1976, Calif. State U., Hayward, 1981; PhD, Western Grad. Sch. Psychology, Palo Alto, Calif., 1991. Site adminstr., teaching specialist Severely Delayed Langs. Program Santa Clara (Calif.) County, 1976-81; language-movement counselor Peninsula Children's Ctr., Palo Alto, 1981-83; marriage, family and child counselor Woodside (Calif.) Psychol. Services, 1983-84; dir. tng. and sales Human Resource Services Employee Assistance Program, Sunnyvale, Calif., 1984-86; pvt. practice psychol. counseling Palo Alto, 1984-86; regional Employee Assistance mgr. Occupational Health Services, Sunnyvale, 1986-91; pvt. practice Counseling and Cons. Resources, Palo Alto, 1991—; founder, CEO Allied Health Svcs., A Med. Corp., 1992—. Mental health counselor, instr. Foothill Coll., Los Altos, Calif., 1984-85; exec. dir. Sunnyvale Children's Arts and Movement Program, 1979-81, Cafe Motek, 1976-81; vol. instr.

in music and movement Ohlone Sch., Palo Alto, 1986—; founder, pres. Boutique Supply, Palo Alto, 1985; founder Let's Talk Program, Western Athletic Clubs, 1991—; speaker to various groups and orgns. Active Palo Alto Docent. Mem. ACA, Assn. Labor Mgmt. Adminstrs. and Cons. on Alcoholism (conf. chair Santa Clara chpt. 1987—), Calif. Assn. Marriage and Family Counselors, Calif. Psychol. Assn., Assn. Tng. and Devel., Am. Dance Therapy Assn., Palo Alto Run, Santa Clara Decathlon. Avocations: swimming, running, bicycling. Home: 2250 Webster St Palo Alto CA 94301-4053

UNGER, GARY ALLEN, recording industry executive, singer, lyricist, composer, music publisher; b. Clinton, Iowa, Aug. 14, 1947; s. Charles Elmer Unger and Lois Grace Haack. Grad. high sch., Ill., 1967. Internat. import-export mgr. G & U Enterprises, Clinton, 1968—; mgr., pres. Groove Song Music, 1968—, Narrowroad Music, Clinton, 1968—; mgr., v.p. ACI, 1978-79; mgr., pres. ECI Internat. Records, 1980-96, GTM, Clinton, 1973, Aci Am. Comm. Ind. Corp., Nashville, 1976—; pres. Sugarvine Music (BMI). On Art Bell Radio Talk Show, Radio Network, 1996-97. Lyricist: songs Home, I Will Always Love You Part I and II, Lyricist: songs I Like It, I Love It, Lyricist: songs Thinkin About You, Lyricist: songs Give Them All to Jesus, Lyricist: songs My White Rabbi6, 1995, Lyricist: songs My Coloring Book, 1955, Lyricist: songs In My Life, 0158, Lyricist: songs I Knew You When, 1958, Lyricist: songs A Stranger In My House, 1959, Lyricist: songs Birthday, 1959, Lyricist: songs God Bless the Service, Lyricist: songs Please! Don't Tell Me No More Lies, Lyricist: songs The Wink, Lyricist: songs Lord I Lift Your Name on High, 1961, Lyricist: songs Jesus Oh! Jesus, Oh!, Lyricist: songs The Shake, 1961, Lyricist: songs You and Me, 1961, Lyricist: songs The Closer You Get, 1961, Lyricist: songs Home, 1961, Lyricist: songs You Light Up My Life, 1968, Lyricist: songs Don't Tell Me No Lies, 1963, Lyricist: songs Check Yes or No, Lyricist: songs Country Sunshine, 1965, Lyricist: songs Tennessee River, 1965, Lyricist: songs Blue, 1965, Lyricist: songs One Day At a Time, 1965, Lyricist: songs Dancin Shaggin on the Boulevard, 1965, Lyricist: songs Carving Your Love With Me, 1965, Lyricist: songs If Your Not In It for Love I'm Out of Here, 1966, Lyricist (with G. Russen): songs The Love in Her Soul, Lyricist: songs Heart to Heart, 1968, Lyricist: songs Fool for Your Love, Lyricist: songs God Bless You Jesus, 1967, Lyricist: songs God Bless the Service, Lyricist: songs Born in This U.S.A., 1967, Lyricist: songs No Doubt, Parts I, II, and III, Lyricist: songs I've Never Been to England, Lyricist: songs Real Love, Lyricist: songs, Lyricist: songs Hey June and Darline, Lyricist: songs I Got Jesus on My Mind, Lyricist: songs God Bless the Service, Parts I and II, Lyricist: songs Heaven O Sweet Angel, Lyricist: songs Please Remember Me, Lyricist: songs Oh! Country Doll, Lyricist: songs Oh! Baby Doll, Lyricist: songs You Win My Love, Lyricist (with G.A. Unger and J. Ward): songs Oh! Sweet Honey, 1997, Lyricist: songs Girl, I Love You, Lyricist: songs Love is Like a Butterfly, Lyricist: songs Let Us Pray Together, Lyricist: songs Lost in the 50's Tonight, Lyricist: songs Kentucky Rain , Lyricist: songs Blue I'm So Blue, Lyricist: songs All I Want is a Life with You Jesus, Lyricist: songs On the 4th of July, Lyricist: songs Boot Scootin Boogie, Lyricist: songs Love Is, Lyricist (with Joan Brothers): songs Almost Like a Song, Lyricist : songs Why Can't Every Day Be Like Christmas, Lyricist : songs Moody Blues, Lyricist : songs Third Rock From the Sun, Lyricist : songs God Bless Texas Too, Lyricist : songs Maybe You Can Drive My Car, Lyricist : songs Oh, My, My, Lyricist : songs Those Rock N Years, Lyricist : songs My Achin Breakin Heart, Lyricist : songs Born to Love You, Lyricist : songs We Were Meant for Each Other, Lyricist : songs Jesus OH! Jesus I Love You, Lyricist : songs Don't Worry Be Happy Like Happy, Lyricist): songs Please Don't Bump the Jukebox, Lyricist : songs Hey It's a Small Town, Lyricist : songs God Bless the U.S.A. (Born in the USA), Lyricist : songs The Happiest Guy in the Whole USA, Lyricist : songs God Writes the Songs, Lyricist : songs When You Walked In, Lyricist : songs You Better Think Twice Again, Lyricist : songs My Coloring Book, Lyricist : songs Independence Day, Lyricist : songs Together With Our Heartfelt Love, Lyricist : songs She's Gone Country, Lyricist : songs You Light Up My Life, Lyricist : songs Give Them All to Jesus, Lyricist : songs Chasing That Neon Rainbow, 1963, Lyricist : songs Touched By a Holy Angel?, Lyricist : songs Almost Everywhere, Lyricist : songs No One Else on Earth, Lyricist : songs Praise the Lord, Lyricist : songs On American Bandstand, Lyricist : songs Love Is, Lyricist : songs If Tomorrow Never Comes, Lyricist : songs In My Life, Lyricist : songs The Long and Winding Roads, Lyricist : songs Please! Remember Me, Lyricist : songs Hello-Good-Buy, Lyricist : songs Oh! Country Doll, Lyricist : songs Creator of the Stars, Lyricist : songs Our Heart Felt Love, 1997, Lyricist (with Joan Brothers): songs Sweet Country Girl, 2001, Lyricist (with G.A. Unger and W. Cochran): songs God Bless the American Veterans, 2001, Lyricist : songs Tennessee Love In America, lyricist: songs The Power of His Love, lyricist: songs God Bless the U.S.A. and Those Who Were Born in the U.S.A. Mem. RIAA, GNACMAI, Nat. Assn. Songwriters Internat., Nat. Music Found. Home and Office: 1001 Briarcliff Ln Clinton IA 52732-6272 Fax: 563-243-1334.

UNGER, GERE NATHAN, physician, lawyer; b. Monticello, N.Y., May 15, 1949; s. Jessie Aaron and Shirley (Rosenstein) U.; m. Alicen J. McGowan, July 21, 1990; children: Elijah, Breena, Ari, Sasha, Arlen. JD, Bernadean U., 1979; MD, Inst. Polytecnico, Mexico City, 1986; D Phys. Medicine, Met. U., Mexico City, 1987; postgrad., Boston U., 1993, Harvard Law Sch., 1994-96; LLM in Med. Law, U. Glasgow, 2001. Dipomate Am. Bd. Forensic Examiners, Am. Bd. Med. Legal Analysis in Medicine and Surgery, Am. Bd. Forensic Medicine, Am. Bd. Risk Mgmt. Med. dir. Vietnam Vets. Post-Traumatic Stress Disorder Program, 1988-90; emergency rm. physician, cons. in medicaid fraud Bronx (N.Y.)-Lebanon Hosp., 1990—; clin. legal medicine Paladin Profl. Group, P.A., Palm Beach, Fla., 1992-98; pres. Albany Law Jour. Co., Inc., 1998—; jurisconsult Office of Gere Unger, M.D., J.D., 1999—. Mediator, arbitrator World Bank, 2000—; mediator, arbitrator, negotiator World Intellectual Property Orgn., 1994; mem. peer rev. com. Nat. Inst. on Disability and Rehab. Rsch., Office Spl. Edn., U.S. Dept. Edn., 1993; mem. clin. ethics com. Inst. Medecine Legale et de Medecine Sociale, Strasbourg, France, 1994; mem. surg. critical care com. Am. Soc. Critical Care Medicine, 1992; N.Y. state capt. Am. Trial Lawyers Exch., 1992. Mem. editl. bd. Am. Bd. Forensic Examiners, 1993, Jour. Neurol. and Orthopaedic Medicine and Surgery, 1993. Commandant Broward County Marine Corps League, 1995—. With USMC, 1968—72. Diplomate Am. Bd. Disability Analysts; fellow Internat. Coll. Surgeons (mem. ethics com. 1994, mem. emergency response program Ea. region 1994), Am. Acad. Neurol. and Orthopaedic Surgeons, Am. Coll. Legal Medicine, Am. Coll. Forensic Examiners, Exec. Practice Mgmt.; mem. ABA, ATLA, FBA (health com., rep. ABA 1994, chmn. med. malpractice/tort com. and FBA liaison to AMA), Nat. Coll. Advocacy, Internat. Bar Assn., Am. Coll. Physician Execs. (chair forum on law and med. mgmt. 1995), Kennedy Inst. Ethics, Am. Soc. of Laser Medicine and Surgery, Nat. Assn. of Forensic Econs., Am. Bd. Disability Analysts, Internat. Royal Soc. of Medicine (London). Avocations: flying, boating. Office: 100 State St Ste 910 Albany NY 12207 E-mail: jurismed@justicemail.com.

UNGER, HOWARD ALBERT, artist, photographer, educator; b. Mt. Vernon, N.Y., Oct. 13, 1944; s. Howard Albert and Florence A. (Peterson) U.; m. Anrita Abelow, Aug. 25, 1972; 1 son, Christopher Howard. Student, Art Students League, N.Y.C., 1960-61, Sch. Visual Arts, 1975-76, N.Y. Inst. Holography, 1976; BFA, Kent State U., 1966, MA, 1968; MEd, Columbia U., 1972, EdD, 1975; MA, N.Y. Inst. Tech., 1994. Cert. open water diver, 1988, advanced scuba diver, 1989. Grad. tchg. fellow in photo-journalism Kent State U., 1966-67, instr. in art, 1966-67, grad. teaching fellow in art, 1967-68; head program in art, tchr. art Kew-Forest Prep. Sch., Kew Gardens, N.Y., 1968-69; technician TV sta. Tchrs. Coll., Columbia U., 1971-72, instr. art and edn., 1972-75, instr. curriculum and tchg., 1976-82, instr. dept. comm., computing and tech. in edn., 1982—; asst. prof. visual comm. tech. dept. humanities Ocean County Coll., 1972-78, assoc. prof., 1979-82, prof., 1982—, gallery coord. Fine Arts Ctr., 1972—. Part-time grad. instr. comm. arts N.Y. Inst. Tech., N.Y.C., 1994-95; instr. comm. and edn. Sch. Edn. NYU, 1973-74; design and photograph coord. RCA Records, N.Y.C., 1969-70; freelance designer, 1965— Exhibitor photography in one-man shows, Photographis Societas Photographis, Columbia U., 1971, Ziegfeld Gallery, N.Y.C., 1972; group shows, Kent State U., 1965-68, Ocean County Coll., 1973-83, 14 Sculptor Gallery, N.Y.C., 1995; permanent collections, Internat. Ctr. Photography, N.Y.C., Mus. Holography, N.Y.C., Kent State U., Ocean County Coll., Tchrs. Coll., Columbia U., pvt. collections; lectr. in photography; co-author: (with William Maxwell) photog. illustrator Printmaking: A Beginner's Handbook, 1977; photog. illustrator: The Fourth R. Stewart Kranz, 1971; contbg. author: A Tour Through The Realm of Science Plus Art, 1974; photography critic: Village Voice, 1976-77; photography columnist Soho Weekly News, 1977-78. Recipient 1st place award Am. Greeting Card Competition, 1966; recipient honorarium dept. curriculum and teaching Tchrs. Coll., Columbia U., 1973 Mem. Soc. Photography Educators, NEA, Mus. Modern Art, N.J. Edn. Assn., Met. Mus. Art, Am. Mus. Natural History, Profl. Assn. Diving Instrs. (lic. advanced scuba diver), Nat. Assn. Underwater Instrs. (lic. advanced scuba diver). Republican. Home: 515 E 79th St New York NY 10021-0705 Office: Ocean County Coll College Dr Toms River NJ 08754-2001

UNGER, IRWIN, historian, educator; b. Bklyn., May 2, 1927; s. Elias C. and Mary (Roth) U.; m. Bernate Myra Spaet, Feb. 1956 (div.); children— Brooke David, Miles Jeremy, Paul Joshua; m. Debi Irene Weisstein, May 11, 1970; stepchildren— Anthony Allen, Elizabeth Sarah. B.Social Scis., City Coll. N.Y., 1948; MA, Columbia, 1949, PhD, 1958; student, U. Wash., 1949-51. Instr. Columbia, 1956-58; vis. lectr. U. P.R., 1958-59; asst. prof. Long Beach (Calif.) State Coll., 1959-62; assoc. prof. U. Calif., Davis, 1962-66; prof. history NYU, NYC, 1966—. Author: The Greenback Era: A Social and Political History of American Finance: 1865-1879, 1964, The Movement: A History of the American New Left, 1974, (with Debi Unger) The Vulnerable Years: The United States, 1896-1917, Turning Point: 1968, 1988, The Best of Intentions: The Rise and Fall of the Great Society Programs, 1996, (with Debi Unger) LBJ: A Life, 1999. Served with AUS, 1952-54. Recipient Pulitzer prize for history, 1965; Guggenheim fellow, 1972-73, Rockefeller humanities fellow, 1980-81, Harry Frank Guggenheim fellow, 1987-88. Home: 473 W End Ave New York NY 10024-4934

UNGER, J. MARSHALL, linguist, foreign language educator; b. Cleve., May 28, 1947; s. Roy Brown and Grace Lillian (Friedman) U.; m. Mutsuyo Okumura, Oct. 18, 1976. AB, U. Chgo., 1969, AM, 1971; MA, Yale U., 1972, PhD, 1975. Sr. lectr. U. Canterbury, Christchurch, New Zealand, 1975-76; asst. prof. U. Hawaii, Honolulu, 1977-82, assoc. prof., 1982-87, prof., 1987-92, U. Md., College Park, 1992-96, Ohio State U., 1996—. Chmn. curriculum framework task force, Japanese lang. initiative for U.S. high-schools (Nat. Fgn. Lang. Ctr., Coll. Bd., NEH), 1991-92. Author: The Fifth Generation Fallacy, 1987, Studies in Early Japanese Morphophonemics, 1977, 2d edit., 1993, Literacy and Script Reform in Occupation Japan, 1996. Recipient grants Control Data Corp., 1980-82, Japan Found., 1985, NSF, 1990; Japan Ministry of Edn. fellow, 1991. Mem. Linguistic Soc. Am., Am. Oriental Soc., Assn. for Asian Studies, Assn. Tchrs. of Japanese. Avocations: piano, go, magic. Office: Ohio State U Dept East Asian Langs 204 Cunz Hall Columbus OH 43210-1229 E-mail: unger.26@osu.edu.

UNGER, KEN R. writer; b. Cleve., Jan. 8, 1949; s. Roy V. Unger and Lucille M. Lehmann, Ken Lehmann (Stepfather); children: Christian , Seth, Kelly, Heather. MDiv, Ashland (Ohio) Theol. Sem., 1977; BS, Ashland U., 1971. Clergy 1977. Pres. Genesis Creative Group, L.A., 1999—; exec. dir. One Life Ministries, Ala., 1982—. Agt. Kimble Unger Literary Group, L.A., 2002—. Author: (book) True Sexuality, 1987, The 13th Step, 2001, All the King's Horses, (workbooks) Scriptural Discipleship, 1989, (novels) Ritual, 1996, (novel) Eye of the Pyramid, 1998. Gov.'s appointee White House Conf. on Families, Cleve., 1979—80. Named Scholar of Yr., Sigma Nu, 1971; fellow study abroad fellow, Rotary Internat., 1971. Avocations: skiing, sailing, tennis, rollerblading, films. Home: Ste 104 28126 Peacock Ridge Palos Verdes Peninsula CA 90275 Personal E-mail: KENRUNGER@AOL.COM.

UNGER, MICHAEL, physician, researcher, educator; b. Haifa, Israel, Feb. 11, 1944; m. Sue Ann Unger; children: Darian, Noam. MD, U. Bordeaux, France, 1971. Diplomate Am. Bd. Internal Medicine, Am. Bd. Pulmonary Disease. Intern Wayne State U., Detroit, 1971—72; internal medicine resident Mount Sinai, NY, 1972—74; pulmonary fellow Cornell Med. Coll., 1974—76; dir. pulmonary endoscopy Pa. Hosp., Phila., 1985; dir. pulmonary endoscopy high risk lung cancer program Fox Chase Cancer Ctr., dir. pulmonary cancer detection and prevention program, 1997—; clin. prof. medicine Jefferson Med. Coll., 1995. Editor: Chest Clinic North America, 1985; contbr. articles to profl. jours. Office: Fox Chase Cancer Ctr 7701 Burholme Ave Ste 201 Philadelphia PA 19111-2497 E-mail: m_unger@fccc.edu.

UNGER, PAUL A. international packaging specialist; b. San Diego, Sept. 10, 1914; s. Louis A. and Ray (Seidman) U.; m. Sonja Franz, Jan. 2, 1947; children: Alan, Gerald, Tamara Unger-Hyman. AB, Harvard U., 1936. With pub. rels. dept. Works Progress Adminstrn., Washington, 1936-39; with community rels. Dept. U.S. Housing Authority, 1939-44; relief adminstr. UN Relief and Rehab. Adminstrn., Egypt and Yugoslavia, 1944-47; deputy asst. sec. U.S. Dept. of Interior, Washington, 1947-50, internat. specialist, 1950-53; devel. mgr. The Unger Co., Cleve., 1953-57, pres., 1957-62, 64-88, chmn., 1988-93; sr. advisor, 1994—, The Unger Co., Cleve., 1994—; dep. adminstr. U.S. Dept. Commerce, Washington, 1962-63. Mem. U.S. com. Internat.Coun. on Social Welfare; organizer, leader tours to Yugoslavia, Hungary, Austria, Czechoslovakia, East Germany, Poland, USSR, China; leader trade mission to Australia and New Zealand U.S. Dept. of Commerce; mem. U.S. Trade Agreements Com.; U.S. del. GATT Trade Negotiations Confs. Pres. Coun. Internat. Programs; chmn. Cleve. adv. subcom. U.S. Commn. on Civil Rights; chmn. Mayor's Urban Renewal Task Force, Presdl. Campaign Cmns. for No. Ohio, Gov.'s Internat. Trade Coun.; chmn. Unger Croatia Inst. Pub. Adminstrn. Kennedy Sch. Govt., Harvard U., The Urban Ctr., Cleve. State U. Recipient Recognition award Rotary, 1974, Neighborhood Ctrs. Assn., 1978, Internat. Exch. award Coun. Internat. Programs, 1985; inductee Hall of Fame City Club of Cleve., 1995, Cleveland Heights H.S. Hall of Fame, 1997. Mem. City Club (trustee 1972-75, v.p. 1975), Forum Found. (pres. 1988-91), Cleve. Coun. on World Affairs (program chmn., v.p., mem. exec. com.), English Speaking Union (past pres. Cleve. br., nat. v.p.), Cleve. Skating Club, Cleve. Playhouse Club, Cleve. Blue Book. Home: 13515 Shaker Blvd Apt 2 A Cleveland OH 44120-1506 Office: 13110 Shaker Sq Cleveland OH 44120-2313 E-mail: paunger@executiveconeeptsinc.com.

UNGER, PAUL WALTER, retired soil scientist; b. Winchester, Tex., Sept. 10, 1931; s. Edwin Herman and Elsie Anna (Schmidt) U.; m. Barbara Charlene Dutton, Sept. 13, 1960; children: Gary Robert, Paula Dianne. BS, Tex. A&M U., 1961; MS, Colo. State U., 1963, PhD, 1966. Soil scientist USDA Agrl. Rsch. Svc., Bushland, Tex., 1965-81, soil scientist/rsch. leader, 1981-87, supervisory soil scientist/rsch. leader, 1987-93, soil scientist, 1993-2000; ret., 2000. Cons. Food and Agrl. Orgn. UN, Rome, 1986. Author or co-author bulls. and articles; co-editor conf. proc.; editor book. With U.S. Army, 1952-55. Recipient Disting. Svc. award Great Plains Agrl. Coun., 1984; named Scientist of Yr., USDA-Agrl. Rsch. Svc., So. Plains Area, 1987. Fellow Am. Soc. Agronomy (selection com. 1988-89), Soil Sci. Soc. Am. (assoc. editor 1977-82, divsn. chmn. 1986, mem. selection com. 1994-95, Applied Rsch. award 1991), Soil and Water Conservation Soc. (various local and state offices, photography awards 1990-92); mem. Internat. Soil Tillage Rsch. Orgn., Internat. Union Soil Scis., World Assn. Soil and Water Conservation. Lutheran. Avocations: photography, gardening, woodworking. Office: USDA Agrl Rsch Svc PO Box 10 Bushland TX 79012-0010 Personal E-mail: pwunger@tcac.net. Business E-Mail: pwunger@cprl.ars.usda.gov.

UNGER, PETER KENNETH, philosophy educator; b. N.Y.C., Apr. 25, 1942; s. Sidney and Naomi (Fein) U.; m. Susan Gill, June 2, 1977; 1 child, Andrew. BA, Swarthmore Coll., 1962 DPhil, Oxford U., Eng., 1966. Instr. U. Wis., Madison, 1965-66, asst. prof., 1966-70, assoc. prof., 1970-72; assoc. prof. NYU, N.Y.C., 1972-75, prof., 1975—. Author: Ignorance, 1975, Philosophical Relativity, 1984, Identity, Consciousness and Value, 1990, Living High and Letting Die, 1996; contbr. articles to profl. jours. Guggenheim fellow, 1974, NEH fellow, 1993. Mem. Am. Philos. Assn. Democrat. Home: 100 Bleecker St New York NY 10012-2202 Office: Dept Philosophy NYU 503 Main Bldg Washington Sq New York NY 10003

UNGER, PETER VAN BUREN, lawyer; b. Cin., Nov. 15, 1957; s. Sherman Edward and Polly Van Buren (Taylor) U.; m. Laura Meth Simone, June 29, 1991; children: Simone Taylor, Natalie Van Buren. BA in History, Polit. Sci., Miami U., Oxford, Ohio, 1980; JD, U. Cin., 1983; LLM in Securities, Georgetown U., 1987. Bar: Ohio 1984, D.C. 1985, U.S. Supreme Ct. 1991. Law clk. chief judge U.S. Dist. Ct. (so. dist.) Fla., Ft. Lauderdale, 1983-85; atty. enforcement divsn. SEC, N.Y.C., 1986-88; assoc. Fulbright & Jaworski, Washington, 1988-89, participating assoc., 1990-94, ptnr., 1995—. Mem. ABA (bus. law sect., com. fed. regulation of securities, sub-com. on civil litigation and SEC enforcement matters 1989—, litigation sect. com. on securities litigation sub-com. on SEC enforcement practice 1990—), Securities Industry Assn. (compliance and legal divsn.), D.C. Bar Assn. (corp., fin. and securities law sect. steering com.). Home: 3308 N St NW Washington DC 20007-2807 Office: Fulbright & Jaworski LLP 801 Pennsylvania Ave NW Washington DC 20004-2615 E-mail: punger@fulbright.com.

UNGER, RHODA KESLER, psychology educator; b. Bklyn., Feb. 22, 1939; d. Gustav and Ellen (Samuels) Kesler; m. Burton M. Unger, Apr. 11, 1966; children: Laurel, Rachel. BS, Bklyn. Coll., 1960; AM, Radcliffe Coll., 1964; PhD, Harvard U., 1966. Asst. prof. Hofstra U., Hempstead, N.Y., 1966-72; asst. prof., assoc. prof. psychology Montclair State Coll., Upper Montclair, N.J., 1972-81, prof., 1981-96, prof. emeritus, 1999—, dir. honors, 1985-96. Vis. prof. U. Haifa, Israel, 1988-89; editor Analyses of Social Issues and Public Policy, 1998—. Author: Female and Male, 1979, Resisting Gender, 1998; co-author: Women and Gender, 1992, 96, 2000; editor: Representations, 1989, Handbook of the Psychology of Women and Gender, 2001; co-editor: Women, Gender and Social Psychology, 1985, In our own Words, 1997, 2000. Fulbright sr. prof., 1988-89; resident scholar women's studies rsch. ctr. Brandeis U., 1998—. Fellow APA (pres. div. psychology of women 1980-81, mem. disting. leadership award com. for women in psychcology 1991, 1st Carolyn Wood Sherif Meml. award 1985), Am. Psychol. Soc., Soc. for Psychol. Study Social Issues (exec. com. 1980-86, pres. 1998-99); mem. Assn. Women in Psychology (Disting. Publ. award 1984, 86, Disting. Career award 1990). Jewish. Avocations: travel, cooking, reading, speculative fiction. Home: 3 Newport Rd Apt 4 Cambridge MA 02140-1587 Office: Brandeis U Womens Studies Rsch Ctr Waltham MA 02454-9110

UNGER, RICHARD WATSON, history educator; b. Huntington, W.Va., Dec. 23, 1942; s. Abraham I. and Marion Patterson U.; 1 child, Emily Patterson. BA, Haverford Coll., Pa., 1963; AM, U. Chgo., 1965; MA, Yale U., 1967, MPhil, 1969, PhD, 1971. Prof. dept. history U. B.C., Vancouver, Can., 1969—. Author: Dutch Shipbuilding Before 1800, 1978; The Ship in the Medieval Economy, 600-1600, 1980; The Art of Medieval Technology: The Image of Noah the Shipbuilder, 1991, Ships and Shipping in the North Sea and Atlantic, 1400-1600, 1997, A History of Brewing in Holland, 900-1900, Economy, Technology and the State, 2001; editor: Cogs, Caravels and Galleons, 1994; co-editor Studies in Medieval and Renaissance History, 1978-95; contbr. articles to profl. jours. Trustee Vancouver Maritime Mus., 1979-83, 97-98. Mem. Medieval Assn. Pacific (pres. 1994-96), Econ. History Soc., Soc. Nautical Rsch., Soc. Hist. Tech. Office: U BC Dept History 1297-1873 East Mall Vancouver BC Canada V6T 1Z1 E-mail: richard.unger@ubc.ca.

UNGER, ROGER HAROLD, physician, scientist; b. N.Y.C., Mar. 7, 1924; s. Lester and Beatrice (Raphael) Unger; m. Barbara Latz, June 28, 1946; children: Christine, Craig, Jimmy; m. Marlise Mantel, Dec. 16, 1981; 1 child Romy-Michelle. BS, Yale U., 1944; MD, Columbia U., 1947; MD (hon.), U. Geneva, 1976, U. Liège, Belgium, 1980. Diplomate Am. Bd. Internal Medicine. Asst. prof. internal medicine U. Tex. Med. Sch., Dallas, 1959—64, assoc. prof., 1964—69, prof., 1969—; dir. Ctr. for Diabetes Rsch., U. Tex. Health Sci. Ctr., 1985—, Touchstone/West Disting. chair diabetes rsch., 1989—. Sr. med. investigator VA Med. Ctr., Dallas, 1979—99; mem. Nat. Diabetes Adv. Bd., Bethesda, Md., 1985—; mem. adv. coun. Nat. Inst. Diabetes, Digestive and Kidney Diseases, 1990—94. Editor: Glucagon, 1972, Glucagon Physiology etc., 1981; assoc. editor (jour.) Diabetes, 1979—84, mem. editl. bd., 1975—79, Endocrinology, 1976—81; author: 50 chpts. in textbooks; contbr. With U.S. Army, 1946—48, with USPHS, 1950—52. Recipient Lilly award, Am. Diabetes Assn., 1964, Banting medal, 1975, David Rumbough award, Juvenile Diabetes Assn., 1975, Joslin medal, Harvard U., 1979, Claude Bernard award, European Assn. for Study of Diabetes, 1979, Fred Conrad Koch award, Endocrine Soc., 1983. Mem.: Am. Soc. for Clin. Investigation (emeritus), Assn. Am. Physicians, Am. Acad. Arts and Scis., NAS. Office: Ctr for Diabetes Research 5323 Harry Hines Blvd Dallas TX 75390-7208

UNGER, RUTH, clinical social worker, consultant; b. Bklyn., Jan. 19, 1922; widow; children: Ellen Ross-Monarch, Susan Hansen. MSW, Ariz. State U., 1974. Diplomate Am. Bd. Examiners in Clin. Social Work; cert. ind. social worker Ariz.; interactive guided imagery, eye movement desensitization and reprocessing, bd. cert. expert in traumatic stress. Child protective svc. worker Ariz. Dept. Econ. Security, Tucson, 1966-70, supr. child protective svc., 1970-89; pvt. practice therapy, 1976—. Mem. allied staff Tucson Psychiat. Inst., 1989—, Sonora Desert Hosp., Tucson, 1989—; cons. on child sexual abuse. Mem. Pima County Coalition Against Abuse Now, Tucson, 1980—. Recipient award Parents United, Inc., Tucson, 1978, Indian Child and Family Svc., 1981, Ariz. Group Psychotherapy Soc., 1987, Open Inn, Inc., 1978, 23-Yr. Svc. award Ariz. Dept. Econ. Security, 1989, Outstanding Dedication award Roots and Wings, Inc., 1986. Mem. NASW (Outstanding Social Worker of Yr. award 1980), Acad. Cert. Social Workers. Home and Office: 5930 E Grant Rd Tucson AZ 85712-2305

UNGER, STEPHEN ALLAN, publishing executive, editor; b. Rochester, N.Y., Jan. 24, 1953; s. Raymond Frederick Jr. and Marjorie June (Pitizids) U.; m. Sherry Thurston; 1 child, Amanda Clare. BA in Polit. Sci., Kalamazoo Coll., 1976; MA in Mgmt., Nazareth Coll., 1986. Dir. pub. rels. Detroit Express Soccer Team, Pontiac, Mich., 1977-79; various positions in profl. soccer, 1979-81; dir. residences life, athletics Nazareth Coll., Kalamazoo, 1982-86; tchr., athletic dir. Cape Fear Acad., Wilmington, N.C., 1986-87; mng. editor The Coastal Carolinian Newspaper, 1987-88; editor, pub. Pender Sounds Mag., Hampstead, N.C., 1988-93, Sounds Mag., Hampstead, 1993—, Topsail Voice Newspaper, Hampstead, 1991—; ptnr. Thurston Art Gallery, 2001—02. Mng. ptnr. Unger, Crandall, Johnson, Hampstead, 1990-91; profl. soccer referee, 1997-2001. Editor: Treasure Coast Phone Book, 1994-97; contbr. Cape Fear Arts Alive, 2000-01. Named Man of Yr., Hampstead Lions, 1997. Mem. ACLU, N.C. Press Assn. (1st pl. serious columns award 1995, 99, 2d pl. investigative reporting award 1995, 3rd pl. feature writing, 1997, 1st pl. editl. page 2001), Triangle Intercollegiate Soccer Ofcls. Assn. (assignment com. 1996-97), Greater Topsail C. of C., Greater Hampstead C. of C. (dir. 1993-95) Democrat. Avocations: soccer, writing, photography, art. Home: 106 Sanderling Ct Hampstead NC 28443-7129 Office: Topsail Voice Newspaper PO Box 880 Hampstead Crossing Hampstead NC 28443 E-mail: HMvoice@aol.com.

UNGERER, HORST, international economist, lecturer, writer; b. Stuttgart, Germany, Dec. 14, 1930; came to U.S., 1970; s. Max and Elisabeth Ungerer; m. Rajka Ungerer, Sept. 26, 1970; 1 stepchild, Daniel Kolak. Diploma in Econs., U. Tuebingen, Germany, 1956, D in Econs., 1959. Tchg. asst. U. Tuebingen, 1956-59; sect. chief Deutsche Bundesbank, Frankfurt, Germany, 1959-65; alt. exec. dir. Internat. Monetary Fund, Washington, 1965-68; dept. head Deutsche Bundesbank, 1968-70; divsn. chief Internat. Monetary Fund, 1970-73, advisor, 1973-80, asst. dir., 1980-91. Dep. mem. monetary com. European Cmty., Brussels, 1968—70; guest prof. Bundeswehr U., Hamburg, Germany, 1992, Duke U., Durham, NC, 1993, U. Saarbruecken, Germany, 1994, Am. U., Washington, 2002; lectr. in field, 1991—98. Author: A Concise History of European Monetary Integration, 1997; contbr. numerous articles to profl. jours. Avocations: piano and harpsichord, classical music and jazz, history of art, travelling, photography. Home: PO Box 1779 Edgartown MA 02539-1779 E-mail: horstungerer@aol.com.

UNGERER, WALTER JOHN, minister; b. Bklyn., Nov. 11, 1936; s. Walter and Alice Elizabeth (Fleischmann) U.; m. Janet M. Hagmann, Aug. 25, 1962; children: Cheryl Lyn, Walter J., Brian Alan. Cert., Northeastern Bible Coll., 1959; BS, Nyack Coll., 1961; DivB, New Brunswick Theol. Sem., 1964; M of Theology, Princeton Theol. Sem., 1965, D of Ministry, 1983. Ordained to ministry, Presbyn. Ch., 1965. Student pastor Olivet Presbyn. Ch., Bklyn., 1958-62; student supply Fairfield (N.J.) Presbyn. Ch., 1964-65; asst. pastor Webster (N.Y.) Presbyn. Ch., 1965-66, assoc. pastor, 1967-71; sr. pastor Northfield (Ohio) Presbyn. Ch., 1972-77, 1st Presbyn. Ch., Kokomo, Ind., 1977-2001. Co-founder, chmn. bd. dirs. Man to Man Internat.; moderator Presbytery Wabash Valley, Ind., 1983; mem. gen. assembly coun. Presbyn. Ch., Louisville, 1991-97; pres. bd. dirs. Synod Lincoln Trails, Indpls., 1989-91; bd. dirs. Kokomo Rescue Mission, 1992—, v.p. 1995-99, pres.,

1999—, chmn. new facility task force, 1997-98; bd. dirs. Peabody Retirement Home, North Manchester, Ind., 1997—; candidate for moderator 211th Gen. Assembly Presbyn. Ch. (USA), 1999; bd. advisors Waterford Pl., Kokomo, Ind., 1999—. Author: Habakkuk, The Man with Honest Questions, 1976, A Look Up, 1992; co-author: Miltenberg Germany to Brooklyn, 1988. Pres. Presbyns. United for Biblical Concerns, 1986-88. Recipient Leadership award Man to Man Assn. Ohio, Columbus, 1977; named Alumnus of Yr., Northeastern Bible Coll., 2000. Mem. Rotary. Democrat. Avocations: 18th and 19th century antiques, antique tools, fly fishing, golf, geneaology. Home: 2808 Locust Ct E Kokomo IN 46902-2952 Office: 1st Presbyn Ch 2000 W Jefferson St Kokomo IN 46901-4126 E-mail: drwjungerer@prodigy.net.

UNGERLEIDER, LESLIE G. neuroscientist; b. N.Y.C., Apr. 17, 1946; d. Albert and Frieda (Mandel) Cohen; m. Robert Desimone, Sept. 6, 1982; 1 child, Matthew David. BA magna cum laude, SUNY, Binghamton, 1966; PhD, NYU, 1970. Asst. prof. psychology Okla. State U., Oklahoma City, 1970-72; postdoctoral fellow Dept. Psychology Stanford (Calif.) U., 1972-75, Neuropsychology Lab. NIMH, Bethesda, Md., 1975-78, staff fellow, 1978-80, sr. staff fellow, 1980-85, rsch. psychologist, 1985-91, chief sect. neurocircuitry, 1992—. Mem. editorial bd. Neuropsychologia, 1990—, Visual Neurosci., 1990-93, Human Brain Mapping, 1993—; contbr. articles to profl. jours. Fellow Am. Psychol. Assn., Am. Psychol. Soc.; mem. Soc. Neurosci. (program com. 1990-93), AAAS, Inst. Medicine. Achievements include basic research on nonhuman primates revealing neural mechanisms and cortical circuitry underlying visual perception and memory. Office: NIH Bldg. 10 / Room 4C104 10 Center Dr Bethesda MD 20892-0001*

UNGLESBY, LEWIS O. lawyer; b. New Orleans, July 6, 1949; s. Lewis Huber and Mary Jane (Holloway) U.; m. Gail Hoy, Aug. 15, 1970; children: Lewis, Lance, Blake. BS, U. Miss., 1971; JD, La. State U., 1974. Bar: La. 1974, U.S. Dist. Ct. (ea., mid., and we dists.) La. 1974, U.S. Ct. Appeals (5th cir.) 1974, U.S. Supreme Ct. 1980; bd. cert. criminal and civil trial adv. Nat. Bd. Trial Advocacy. With Unglesby Law Firm; mem. judge's benchbook com. La. Supreme Ct., 1982—. Spl. counsel La. State Senate, 1991-98, Gov. La., 1996-98; lectr. La. Assn. Criminal Def. Lawyers, 1987-91. Editor criminal law sect. La. Trial Lawyers Brief, 1988—. Fellow Am. Bd. Criminal Lawyers; mem. ABA, La. Bar Assn. (ho. of dels. 1979-87, lectr.), NACDL, ATLA (criminal law com. 1989-90), La. Trial Lawyers Assn. (chmn. criminal law sect. 1983-85, bd. govs. 1983-94, exec. com. 1991-2000, lectr.). Home: 14415 Highland Rd Baton Rouge LA 70810-5312 Office: 246 Napoleon St Baton Rouge LA 70802-5937

UNGVARI, TAMAS, writer, university educator; b. Budapest, Hungary, Sept. 25, 1930; s. Sandor Ungar and Szerena Weisz; m. Katalin Szekrenyesy; children: David, Benjamin. PhD, Eotvos Lorand U., Budapest , 1955; Doctoral Mem. Acad., Hungarian Acad. Scis., 1986. Full prof. Hungarian U. Drama and Film, Budapest, Hungary, 1975—99; guest prof. UCLA XLS, L.A., 1997—. Sec. gen. P.E.N. Club Hungarian Chpt., Budapest, 1995—2000; lectr. Calif. State U., Northridge. Author: (novels) Das Gestaendniss, 1989, (monography) The 'Jewish Question' in Europe - The Case of Hungary, 2000. Recipient Fulbright Tchg. award, Fulbright Commn., 1985—89, Attila Jozsef prize for creative writing, Hungarian Govt., 1985, Cross of Honor, The Pres. Hungary, 1995. Mem.: MLA. Office: Calif State U Northridge 18111 Nordhoff St Northridge CA 91330 Office Fax: 818-677-3614. Personal E-mail: tungvari@ucla.edu. Business E-Mail: tamas.ungvari@csun.edu.

UNHOLZ, STEFAN PAUL, lawyer; b. London, June 13, 1953; s. Werner Albert and Lilly Emma (Denzler) U.; m. Brigitte Rutishauser, Nov. 22, 1990. Lic., Zurich U., 1979. Bar: Zurich, 1983. Legal probationer Dist. Ct. Bulach, Bulach-Zurich, Switzerland, 1979-80, clk. ct. Switzerland, 1981; lawyer Winterthur, Switzerland, 1983—. Contr. numerous articles and photographs on ry. transport to mags. and books in field. Mem. Swiss Bar Assn., Zurich Bar Assn., Zurich U. Soc., Cantonal High Sch. Soc. Winterthur, Tramway Mus. Zurich. Avocations: collecting records, photography. Office: Stadthausstrasse 39 CH-8402 Winterthur Switzerland

UNIKEL, EVA TAYLOR, interior designer; b. Hungary; arrived in Can., 1956; came to U.S., 1967; d. Istvan Domolky and Lea Maria (Koszegi) Coan; m. Alan L. Unikel; 1 child, Renee Christine; m. June 26, 1993. BS, So. Ill. U., 1972. Dir. mktg. Lococo Design, St. Louis, 1982-83; project mgr., nat. dir. mktg. hosp. div. Hotel Restaurant Planners div. Profl. Interiors, 1983-87; founder Interior Solutions Inc., Hinsdale, Ill., 1987—. Mem. AIA (assoc.), Nat. Assn. Women Bus. Owners, Am. Soc. Interior Design (chairperson 1984-86), Nat. Assn. Indsl. Office Pks., Bldg. Owners and Mgrs. Assn., Internat. Interior Design Assn. Roman Catholic. Office: 500 E Ravine Rd Hinsdale IL 60521-2449

UNIS, RICHARD L. judge; b. Portland, Oreg., June 11, 1928; BS, JD, U. Oreg. Bar: Oreg. 1954, U.S. Dist. Ct. Oreg. 1957, U.S. Ct. Appeals (9th cir.) 1960, U.S. Supreme Ct. 1965. Judge Portland Mcpl. Ct., 1968-71, Multnomah County Dist. Ct., 1972-76, presiding judge, 1972-74; former judge Oreg. Cir. Ct. 4th Judicial Dist., 1977-90; former sr. dep. city atty. City of Portland; assoc. justice Oreg. Supreme Ct., Portland, 1990-96; spl. master U.S. Dist. Ct. House, 1996—. Adj. prof. of local govt. law and evidence Lewis & Clark Coll. Northwestern Sch. Law, 1969-76, 77-96; spl. master supr. La.-Pacific Inner-Seal Siding nationwide class action litig.; faculty mem. The Nat. Judicial Coll., 1971-2000; former faculty mem. Am. Acad. Judicial Edn. Author: Procedure and Instructions in Traffic Court Cases, 1970, 101 Questions and Answers on Preliminary Hearings, 1974. Bd. dirs. Oreg. Free from Drug Abuse; mem. Oreg. Adv. Com. on Evidence Law Revision, chmn. subcom., 1974-79. Maj. USAFR, JAGC, ret. Recipient Meritorius Svc. award U. Oregon sch. Law, 1988; named Legal Citizen of Yr. Oreg. Law Related Edn., 1987; inducted into The Nat. Judicial Coll. Hall of Honor, 1988. Mem. Am. Judicature Soc. (bd. dirs. 1975, Herbert Harley Nat. award 1999), Am. Judges Assn., Multnomah Bar Found., Oregon Judicial Conf. (chmn. Oreg. Judicial Coll. 1973-80, legis. com. 1976—, exec. com. of judicial edn. com., judicial conduct com.), N.Am. Judges Assn. (tenure, selection and compensation judges com.), Dist. Ct. Judges of Oreg. (v.p., chmn. edn. com.), Nat. Conf. Spl. Ct. Judges (exec. com.), Oreg. State Bar (judicial adminstrn. com., sec. local govt. com., com. on continuing certification, uniform jury instrn. com., exec. com. criminal law sect., trial practice sect. standards and certification com., past chmn., among others), Oreg. Trial Lawyers Assn. (named Judge of Yr. 1984). Office: US Dist Ct House 1000 SW 3rd Ave Portland OR 97204-2930

UNISON-PACE, WENDY JANE, emergency trauma nurse, quality coordinator; b. Mar. 20, 1964; d. Harvey Charles and Bette Adele (Aimone) U. BS, No. Ill. U., 1988; BSN, Concordia U. and West Suburban Coll. Nursing, 1995; MSN in Nursing Adminstrn., Va. Commonwealth U., 2002. Cert. Trauma Nurse Core Course, Emergency Nurse Pediats., PALS, ACLS. Residential supr., instr. in sign lang. Mental Health & Deafness Resources Inc., Ctr. on Deafness, Des Plaines, Ill., 1989-95; RN oncology unit West Suburban Hosp. Med. Ctr., Oak Park, 1995; RN cardiac care unit and level 2 ER Raliegh Gen. Hosp., Beckley, W.Va., 1995-97; faculty mem. Coll. at W.Va., 1996-97; RN level 1 trauma ctr./ER, clin. nurse 3 Charleston Area Med. Ctr., Charleston, W.Va., 1997-98; RN level 1 trauma ctr./ER, EDNet clin. coord., quality coord., clin. nurse III, quality coord., reward/recognition facilitator, newsletter editor Med. Coll. Va. Hosps./Va. Commonwealth U. Health Sys., Richmond, Va., 1998—; asst. Office of Health Policy, Va. Commonwealth U. Health Sys., 2001—02. Educator, instr., ARC, Lombard, Ill., 1986-98. Recipient award of Hon. 1st Place Addison Cultural Arts Devel. Commn., 1982, Vol. Educator Excellence awards ARC, 1987-91, Cmty. Health Edn. & Safety Svcs. award, ARC, 1988, Cert. Appreciation, 1992, Dr. Alma J. Labuski Leadership award Student Nurses Assn. Ill., 1994, Pres. Svc. award West Suburban Coll. of Nursing, 1995. Mem.: AACN, ANA, Nat. Assn. for Healthcare Quality, Va. Assn. for Healthcare Quality, Va. Nurses Assn., W.Va. Emergency Nurses Assn. (co-chair com. on bylaws 1997—98), Ill. Nurses Assn., Emergency Nurses Assn. Va., Emergency Nurses Assn., Nat. League Nursing, Student Nurse's Assn. Ill. (hon.; v.p. 1994—95, programs com. chair 1994—95), Sigma Lambda Sigma (v.p. 1985—86, pres. 1986—87). E-mail: WJaneU@aol.com.

UNITHAN, DOLLY, visual artist; b. Kelantan, Malaysia; came to U.S., 1976; BFA, Hornsey Coll. Art, 1975; MFA, Pratt Inst., 1978; postgrad., Brit. Coun. Fine Arts Exch., 1974, Ecole Nationale des Beaux Arts de Nancy, France, 1974. Summer intern Guggenheim Mus., N.Y.C., 1976; panelist, artist in residence Asian Am. Arts Ctr., N.Y.C., 1993; lectr. in field. One-person shows include Internat. Art Ctr., London, 1975, Am. Assn. State Colls. and Univs., Orlando, Fla., 1977, Sloan Gallery, Lock Haven State Coll., Pa., 1978, Permanent Mission of Malaysia to UN, N.Y.C., 1987, Kerr Gallery, N.Y.C., 1987, Lyman Allyn Art Mus., New London, Conn., 1990, U.N. Secretariat, N.Y.C., 1991, Gracie Mansion, N.Y.C., 1994, Angel Orensanz Found., N.Y.C., 1995, Cathedral of St. John the Divine, N.Y.C. St. Boniface Chapel Gallery, 1996; exhibited in group shows including Palace of Westminster, Hos. of Parliament, London, 1978, City Mus. and Art Gallery, Gloucester, Eng., 1978, Mus. Art, Hove, Eng., 1978, Contemporary Gallery, Warsaw, Poland, 1978, BWA Gallery, Wroclaw and Szczecin, Poland, 1978, Arts Coun. Gallery, Belfast, No. Ireland, 1978, Parrish Art Mus., Southampton, N.Y., 1979, Modern Art Ctr., Guadalajara, Mex., 1979, Alternative Mus., N.Y.C., 1981, Nat. Mus. Fine Arts, Havana, Cuba, 1986, Hillwood Art Mus., Brookville, N.Y., 1988, PS 1 Mus., N.Y.C., 1990, Nat. Art Gallery, Kuala Lumpur, 1991-92, League of Nations Archives, Palais des Nations, Geneva, 1993, Jewish Mus., Vienna, Austria, 1993, Peace Mus., Remagen, Germany, Westbeth Galleries, N.Y.C., Tweed Courthouse Gallery, N.Y.C., 1994, China Art Mus., Beijing, 1995, Raiffeisenkasse, Ulrich bei Steyr, Peace parish, Austria, 1996, Ctrl. Children's and Youth Arts Palace, Samarkand, Uzbekistan, 1997; Palais des Nations, United Nations Office, Geneva, 1998, represented in permanent collections including Lock Haven State Coll., Pa., Alternative Mus., N.Y.C., Am. Assn. State Colls. and Univs., Washington, Permanent Mission of Malaysia to UN, Wilfredo Lam Ctr., Havana, Malaysian Embassy, Washington, Spirit Found., N.Y.C., Asian Am. Arts Ctr., N.Y.C., World Bank, Washington; artwork included in (jours.) Multicultural Edn., 1994, Artspiral, 1994, (book) Sculpture, Technique, Form, Content, Imagine Strawberry Fields. Recipient Artist award Rainbow Art Found., N.Y.C., 1985, Art award ArtQuest '88 Internat. Art Competition, Calif., 1988; named to Archives of Contemporary Arts Venice Biennale, 1990; grantee Lee Found., Singapore, 1972, 76, Pollock-Krasner Found., 1991-92; grad. scholar Mara, Malaysia, 1976-78. Avocation: collecting antiques.

UNKELBACH, L. CARY, lawyer; b. New York, July 25, 1950; d. Kurt and Evelyn (Haskell) U.; m. David W. Olmstead, Sept. 11, 1993. BA, William Smith Coll., Geneva, N.Y., 1972; JD, U. Denver, 1979. Bar: Colo. 1979, U.S. Dist. Ct. Colo. 1979, U.S. Ct. Appeals (10th cir.) 1987. Dep. dist. atty. Jefferson County Dist. Attys. Office, Golden, Colo., 1979-84; asst. atty. gen. Atty. Gen.'s Office, Denver, 1984-86; assoc. John Faught PC, Englewood, Colo., 1986-90; asst. county atty. Arapahoe County, Littleton, 1990—. V.p., bd. mem. 2nd Appletree West Condo Assn., Denver, 1985-92. Mem.: Colo. County Attys. Assn. (bd. dirs. 1997—2000). Avocations: hiking, snowshoeing, travel, photography, animals. Home: PO Box 532 Franktown CO 80116-0532 Office: Acapahoe County Atty Office 5334 S Prince St Littleton CO 80120-1136

UNNI, CHANDRA SHEILA, psychiatrist; b. India, July 28, 1940; came to U.S., 1972; d. Deshraj and Satyawati (Arora) Deshraj; m. K. Krishnan Unni, June 16, 1968; children: Akhil, Aditya, Adosh. Premed. Edn., Delhi U., India, 1958; MB, BS, All India Inst. Medical Scis., New Delhi, India, 1963. Diplomate Am. Bd. Psychiatry and Neurology. Intern All Indian Inst. Med. Scis., New Delhi, 1964; resident Irwin Hosp., 1964-65; pvt. practice, 1967-68, 70-72, Rochester, Minn., 1983—; staff physican Rochester State Hosp., 1968-70, sr. staff physician and psychiatrist, 1973, 78-81; pres., exec. dir. Aiimsonion Clinic, Rochester, 1984—. Acting med. dir. mental health unit Health Cen. Owatonna, Minn., 1987-88; cons. psychiatris The Gables, Rochester, 1984-88, psychiatric dir., 1988-89; cons. psychiatrist Rice County Family Svcs., Faribault, Minn., 1980-81, 83—; Hiawatha Valley Mental Health Ctr., Winona, Minn., 1984—; asst. clin. prof. U. Minn., St. Paul, 1990—. Office: Aiimsonion Clinic 300 3rd Ave SE Ste 206 Rochester MN 55904-4632

UNRUH, ERIC W. music educator, academic administrator; s. Cecil A. and Maurine Unruh; m. Gayle A. Christenson, Aug. 23, 1980; children: D. Alexander, Michael, Christopher. BA, Bethany Coll., 1979; MusM, Northwestern U., Evanston, Ill., 1981, Mus D, 1989. Chmn. dept. music Casper Coll., Casper, Wyo., 1991—. Commr. cmty./jr. coll. accreditation Nat. Assn. Schs. Music, Reston, Va., 1998—. Composer: (music composition) Magnificat, 2000 (Rosenthal Outstanding Educator award, 1998). Grantee, Wyo. Cmty. Found., 1999. Mem.: Music Educator's Nat. Conf. Home: 4440 S David Casper WY 82601 Office: Casper Coll 125 College Dr Casper WY 82601 Home Fax: 307-268-3023; Office Fax: 307-268-3023. E-mail: unruh@caspercollege.edu.

UNRUH, HOWARD K., JR. military officer, university administrator; b. Balt. m. Diane R. Caslow; three children: Meredith, Allison, H. Kirk III. Diploma, Princeton U., 1970; MEd, Harvard U.; MA in Am. Studies, U. Hawaii. Commd. ensign USN, 1970, advanced through ranks to rear adm.; various assignments to Dep. Comdr. Naval Sintack Fonck, U.S. Atlantic Fleet, Newport, RI, 1995—; comdr. Readiness Command Midwest. Dir. campaign rels. Princeton U.; trustee or bd. dirs. several civic orgns. Decorated Legion of Merit, Meritorious Svc. medal (2 times), Navy Commendation medal (4 times), Nat. Def. medal with Bronze Star, Republic of Vietnam Svc. medal with Bronze Star, Armed Forces Res. medal with hourglass, Republic of Vietnam Campaign medal, others. Mem. Naval Res. Assn., Surface Navy Assn., Univ. Cottage Club, Princeton Club N.Y.C. Office: Princeton Univ Dir of Devel Rels 330 Alexander St Princeton NJ 08540-7123

UNRUH, JAMES ARLEN, banking executive; b. Goodrich, N.D., Mar. 22, 1941; m. Candice Leigh Voight, Apr. 28, 1984. BSBA, Jamestown Coll., 1963; MBA, U. Denver, 1964. Dir. corp. planning and analysis Fairchild Camera & Instrument, Calif., 1974-76, v.p. treasury and corp. devel., 1976-79, v.p. fin., 1979-80, Memorex Corp., Santa Clara, 1980-82, Burroughs Corp. (now known as Unisys Corp.), Detroit, 1982-84, sr. v.p. fin., 1984-86, exec. v.p. fin., 1986, exec. v.p., 1986-89, pres., COO, 1989-90, pres., CEO, 1990-91, chmn. bd. dirs., CEO, 1991-97; founding prin. Alerion Capital Group L.L.C., Scottsdale, Ariz., 1998—. Bd. dirs. Prudential Fin. Corp., Apex Microtech. Corp. Trustee Jamestown Coll., N.D. Home: 5426 E Morrison Ln Paradise Valley AZ 85253 E-mail: jimunruh@alerion.com.

UNRUH, RICHARD GREENWOOD, III, artist; b. Bryn Mawr, Pa., May 29, 1964; s. Richard Greenwood Jr. and Deborah Crittenden Unruh; m. Hollis McLellan Unruh; 1 child, Campbell James. BA, Conn. Coll., 1986. Investment trainee Kidder Peabody & Co., Paris, 1986; internat. equities position trader Jefferies & Co., N.Y.C., 1987-88; equity sales trader Lazard Freres & Co., LLC, 1988-95; fine artist, 1995-97; comml. artist, 1997—. Illustrator: Blinker, The Little Star That Learned To Shine, 2000; solo exhbns. New London Art Soc. Gallery, New London, Conn., 1999, Bruce Hurley Gallery, SoHo, N.Y., 1998; nat. group exhbns. Old Slave Mart Mus., Charleston, S.C., 1999, Art Ctr. of Northern N.J., Milford, 1997 (2d prize High Achievement award), Silvermine Arts Guild Ctr., New Canaan, Conn., 1996, Mystic (Conn.) Art Assn., 1995; featured in American Showcase, 2000, 2001, Illustrators and Designers, Vols. 23, 24. Home: 17 Elm St Stonington CT 06378-1272 Office: 395 Broadway Apt 3A New York NY 10013-3540

UNSAL, CEM, electrical engineer, educator; b. Ankara, Turkey, 1967; arrived in U.S., 1991, permanent resident; m. Berrak Pinar Basim, 1997. BSEE, Bogazici (Bosphorus) U., Istanbul, Turkey, 1991—91; M.Sc. in EE, Va. Tech, Blacksburg, VA, USA, 1991—93; PhD in EE, Va. Tech, Blacksburg, 1997. Postdoctoral fellow Carnegie Mellon U., Robotics Inst., Pitts., 1997—2000; project scientist Carnegie Mellon U., ICES, 2000—01; software engr. Atoga Systems, Inc., Fremont, Calif., 2001—. Adj. faculty San Jose (Calif.) State U., 2002—. Mem.: IEEE, Am. Assn. for Artificial Intelligence. Office: Atoga Systems Inc 49026 Milmont Dr Fremont CA 94538 Business E-Mail: unsal@ieee.org.

UNSAL-TUNAY, NURAN, geological engineer, researcher; b. Igdir, Turkey, Dec. 26, 1956; came to U.S., 1995; d. Kamil and Feride (Gunay) Tunay; m. Ilhan Unsal, Oct. 28, 1979; 1 child, Volkan. Diploma in Geol. Engring., Earth Sci. Geol. Engring., Turkey, 1982; cert. in Civil Engring., Min. of Pub. Works, Ankara, Turkey, 1985. Geol. engr. Gen. Directorate of Bank of Provinces, Konya-Ankara, Turkey, 1982-84, Gen. Directorate of Hwy., Kayseri-Ankara, Turkey, 1984-89, Adminstrn. Pub. Works, Manisa, Turkey, 1989-95. Cons. Pub. Works, Manisa, Turkey, 1989-95; adv. bds. Pub. Works, Municipality, Civil Cts., Manisa, Turkey, 1992-94. Inventor: Adaptation of Stabilized Hydrated Lime, Publication of the Chamber of Geol. Engring. of Turkey, 1993. Recipient of presentations 46th Congress of Geology of Turkey, Ankara, 1993. Fellow Geol. Assn. Can.; mem. Geol. Soc. Am., Chamber of Geol. Engrs. of Turkey. Achievements include the soil improvement with hydrated lime stabilization; applied in the area of Manisa Teachers House Buildings, was one of the first applications in Turkey. Home: 30-69 Hobart St Apt 1N Flushing NY 11377

UNSELL, LLOYD NEAL, energy organization executive, former journalist; b. Henryetta, Okla., May 12, 1922; s. John William and Rhoda Elizabeth (Martinez) U.; m. Nettie Marie Rogers, Sept. 24, 1944 (dec.); children: Lloyd Neal, Jonna Kay Unsell Wilhelm, James Allan (dec.). Student, U. Ill., Kalamazoo Coll., 1942-43. Mem. editorial staff Tulsa Daily World, 1947-48; successively staff writer, dir. communications, v.p. pub. affairs, exec. v.p., pres. and chief exec. officer Ind. Petroleum Assn. Am., Washington, 1948-87. Chmn. selection com. for Milburn Petty award Am. Petroleum Inst.-Assn. Petroleum Writers, 1972-86 Author reports and articles in field. Co-chmn. corp. adv. com. Vietnam Vets. Meml., 1981-82. Served with U.S. Army, 1942-46, ETO, PTO. Recipient Spl. award as outstanding petroleum industry communicator Assn. Petroleum Writers, 1960, Russell B. Brown Meml. award, 1981, Robert J. Enright award Am. Petroleum Inst./Assn. Petroleum Writers, 1986, Disting. Service award Nat. Energy Resources Orgn., 1987, Lloyd N. Unsell award established in his honor Ind. Petroleum Assn. Am., 1993; named Hon. Chief Roughneck U.S. petroleum industry, 1986. Mem. Nat. Press Club, Rocky Mountain Oil and Gas Assn. (hon. life), The Jefferson Energy Found. (co-founder 1987). Clubs: Washington Golf and Country. Republican. Baptist. Home: 38335 Point Breeze Rd Coltons Point MD 20626 Office: Ste 300 1201 15th St NW Washington DC 20005 E-mail: lunsell@erols.com.

UNSELL, LLOYD NEAL, JR. association executive; b. Shawnee, Okla., May 6, 1947; s. Lloyd Neal and Nettie Marie (Rogers) Unsell; m. Marie Louise Ames, May 3, 1969; children: Jennifer Marie Seay, Erin Elizabeth Schaefer, Timothy Scott. Student, Northern Va. C.C., 1965-67. Life/health sales specialist Sentry Ins., Steven's Point, Wis., 1980-85; nat. ins. specialist Nat. Assn. Home Builders, Washington, 1985-90; sr. corp. account exec. Home Owner's Warranty Corp., Arlington, Va., 1990-93; exec. dir. Potomac Valley chpt. AIA, College Park, 1993—. Prin., owner wedsights.com, pvwebdesign.com. Mem. Am. Soc. Assn. Execs., Coun. Archtl. Component Execs. (chmn. site selection com.), Toastmasters. Republican. Roman Catholic. Avocations: computers, internet, photography, videography. Office: AIA Potomac Valley Chpt 3907 Metzerott Rd College Park MD 20740-2078 Fax: 240-465-0253. E-mail: lloyd@aiapvc.org.

UNSWORTH, RICHARD PRESTON, minister, educator, school administrator; b. Vineland, N.J., Feb. 7, 1927; s. Joseph Lewis and Laura (MacMillan) U.; m. Joy Merritt, Aug. 20, 1949; children: Sarah, John, Mary, Lucy. BA, Princeton U., 1948; BD, Yale U., 1954; ThM, Harvard U., 1963; STD, Dickinson Coll., 1971; LHD, Washington and Jefferson Coll., 1971; LLD, Smith Coll., 1992. Ordained to ministry Presbyn. Ch., 1953. Tchr. Bible and English Mt. Hermon Sch., 1948-50; asst. chaplain Yale U., New Haven, 1950-54; chaplain, assoc. prof. Smith Coll., Northampton, Mass., 1954-64, chaplain, prof. religion, 1967-80; dean William Jewett Tucker Found. and prof. religion Dartmouth (N.H.) Coll., 1963-67; headmaster Northfield (Mass.) Mt. Hermon Sch., 1980-88, pres., 1989-91, headmaster emeritus, 1991—; headmaster Berkshire Sch., Sheffield, Mass., 1991-96; dean of the chapel Smith Coll., 1996-98, lectr. religion, 1996—99, sr. fellow Kahn Inst., 1998—. Pres. Critical Langs. and Area Studies Consortium, 1987-97; cons. Ednl. Assocs., Inc., 1967-69, U.S. Office Edn., 1969-77. Author: Sexuality and the Human Community, 1970, Dignity and Exploitation: Christian Reflections on Images of Sex in the 1970s, 1974, A Century of Religion at Smith College, 1975; (with Arnold Kenseth) Prayers for Worship Leaders, 1978; contbg. author; Sex Edn. and the Schs., 1967. Leader Operation Crossroads Africa unit, Nigeria, 1961, mem. adv. bd., 1961-66; mem. adminstrv. com. Student Christian Movement New Eng., 1964; mem. Mass. unit So. Christian Leadership conf., 1968; trustee Conf. on Religion in Ind. Schs., 1961-63; pres. Am. Friends of Coll. Cevenol, France, 1957-63, 90-94, Am. rep., 1958-82; trustee Mt. Holyoke Coll., 1982-89, chair, 1984-89, chmn. emeritus, 1989—, Am. Sch. Tangier, Morocco, 1982-87, Eaglebrook Sch., 1992-98, Acad. Music, Northampton, 1998-99, Mus. Sci., Boston, 1993-95; bd. dirs. Family Planning Coun. Western Mass., 1972-81; bd. dirs. Ind. Schs. Assn. Mass., 1992-96. Mem. AAUP, Nat. Assn. Coll. and Univ. Chaplains, Am. Acad. Religion, Assn. Ind. Schs. New Eng. (pres. 1993-96), Headmasters Assn., Nat. Commn. on Asia in Schs., Asia Soc. N.Y.C., U. Club. Home: Apt 2603 500 Crestwood Dr Charlottesville VA 22903-4884

UNTERBECK, AXEL JOACHIM, research director, pharmaceutical executive; b. Leipzig, Germany, Nov. 10, 1953; came to U.S., 1986; s. Joachim and Brigitte (Noack) U.; m. Anett Maria Sartor-Unterbeck, Aug. 29, 1987. Abitur, Gymnasium, Bergneustadt, Germany, 1973; MS in molecular biology, U. Bonn., Germany, 1982; PhD, U. Cologne, Germany, 1986. Rsch. assoc. U. Cologne, 1982-86; sr. rsch. scientist Bayer AG, West Haven, Conn., 1986-89, assoc. dir. Wuppertal, Germany, 1989-92; dir. Bayer Corp., West Haven, 1992—. Cons. Software House, Cologne, 1978-86; adv. bd. Dahlem Confs., Berlin, 1990-91; rev. com. mem. NIH, Bethesda, Md., 1988-92. Author: Molecular Biology of Aging, 1989; inventor in field. Mem., trainer Life Rescue, Germany, 1973-75; trainer German Air Force, 1973-75. Sgt. German Air Force, 1973-75. Mem. N.Y. Acad. Scis., Swimming Club, Yacht Club. Avocations: photography, sailing, travel, swimming, music. Office: Bayer Corp 400 Morgan Ln West Haven CT 06516-4175

UNTERBERGER, BETTY MILLER, history educator, writer; b. Glasgow, Scotland, Dec. 27, 1923; d. Joseph C. and Leah Miller; m. Robert Ruppe, July 29, 1944; children: Glen, Gail, Gregg. BA, Syracuse U., N.Y., 1943; MA, Harvard U., 1946; PhD, Duke U., 1950. Asst. prof. E. Carolina U., Greenville, 1948-50; assoc. prof., dir. liberal arts ctr. Whittier Coll., Calif., 1954-61; assoc. prof. Calif. State U.-Fullerton, 1961-65, prof., chmn. grad. studies, 1965-68; prof. history Tex. A&M U., College Station, 1968—. Vis. prof. U. Hawaii, Honolulu, summer 1967, Peking U., Beijing, 1988; vis. disting. prof. U. Calif., Irvine, 1987—, Patricia and Bookman Peters prof. history, 1991—; vis. prof. Charles U., Prague, Czechoslovakia, summer 1992, Regents prof., 2000—; mem. adv. com. fgn. rels. U.S. Dept. State, 1977-81, chair, 1981; mem. hist. adv. com. U.S. Dept. Army, 1980-82, USN, 1991—; mem. Nat. Hist. Publs. and Records Commn., 1980-84; mem. history rev. panel to Dir. of CIA, 1999—. Author: America's Siberian Expedition 1918-1920: A Study of National Policy, 1956, 69 (Pacific Coast award Am. Hist. Assn. 1956); editor: American Intervention in the Russian Civil War, 1969, Intervention Against Communism: Did the U.S. Try to Overthrow the Soviet Government, 1918-20, 1986, The United States, Revolutionary Russia and the Rise of Czechoslovakia, 1989, paperback edit. with a 2000 yr. perspective, 2000; contbr.: Woodrow Wilson and Revolutionary World, 1982, The Liberal Persuasion, 1997, The United States and the Russian Civil War, microfilm edit., 25 reels, 2001; mem. editl. adv. bd. The Papers of Woodrow Wilson, Princeton U., 1982-92, Internt. History, 1999—; bd. editors: Diplomatic History, 1981-84, Red River Valley Hist. Rev., 1975-84. Trustee Am. Inst. Pakistan Studies, Villanova U., Pa., 1981—, sec., 1989-92; mem. League of Women Voters. Woodrow Wilson Found. fellow, 1979; recipient Disting. Univ. Tchr. award State of Calif. Legislature, 1966. Mem. LWV, NOW, AAUW, Am. Hist. Assn. (chair 1982-83, nominating com. 1980-83), Orgn. Am. Historians (govt. relations com.), Soc. Historians of Am. Fgn. Relations (exec. council 1978-81, 86-89, govt. relations com. 1982-84, v.p. 1985, pres. 1986, co-winner Myrna F. Bernath prize 1991), Am. Soc. for Advancement Slavic Studies, Coordinating Com. on Women in Hist. Profession, Rocky Mountain Assn. Slavic Studies (program chair 1973, v.p. 1973-74), So. Hist. Assn., Asian Studies Assn., Assn. Third World Studies, Czechoslovak Soc. Arts and Scis., Czechoslovak History Conf., Women in Nat. Security, Women's Fgn. Policy Coun., Beyond War, Peace History Soc., Sierra Club, Phi Beta Kappa, Phi Beta Delta. Office: Tex A&M U Dept History College Station TX 77843-0001 E-mail: bettymu@tamu.edu.

UNTERMAN, THOMAS, venture capitalist, lawyer; b. Newport, R.I., Oct. 23, 1944; s. Martin D. and Ruth (Marcus) U.; m. Janet M. Mead, Sept. 27, 1980; children: Rebecca, Amy. AB, Princeton U., 1966; JD, U. Chgo., 1969. Bar: Calif. 1970. Assoc. Orrick, Herrington & Sutcliffe, San Francisco,

1969-75, ptnr., 1975-86, Morrison & Foerster, San Francisco, 1986-92; sr. v.p., gen. counsel The Times Mirror Co., L.A., 1992-95, sr. v.p., CFO, 1995—, exec. v.p., CFO, 1998-99; mng. ptnr. Rustic Canyon Ventures, Santa Monica, Calif., 2000—. Democrat. Jewish. Office: Rustic Canyon Ventures 2425 Olympic Blvd Ste 6050W Santa Monica CA 90404-4030

UNTERMEYER, CHARLES GRAVES (CHASE UNTERMEYER), academic administrator; b. Long Branch, N.J., Mar. 7, 1946; s. Dewitt Edward and Marguerite Alonza (Graves) U.; m. Diana Cumming Kendrick, Oct. 6, 1990; 1 child, Ellyson Chase. AB, Harvard Coll., 1968. Polit. reporter Houston Chronicle, 1971-74; exec. asst. County Judge of Harris County, Houston, 1974-76; state rep. Tex. Ho. of Reps., Austin, 1977-81; exec. asst. V.P. U.S., Washington, 1981-83; from dep. asst. sec. to asst. sec. Navy Dept., 1983-88; asst. to the pres. White House, 1989-91; dir. Voice of Am., 1991-93; dir. govt. affairs Compaq Computer Corp., Houston, 1993—2002; exec. v.p., prof. pub. policy U. Tex. Health Sci. Ctr., 2002—. Bd. visitors U.S. Naval Acad., Annapolis, Md., 1993-96, chmn., 1995; mem. Tex. State Bd. Edn., 1999-, chmn., 1999-2001. Author: Houston Survival Handbook, 1980. Commnr. Port of Houston, 1995-98; bd. dirs. Nat. Pub. Radio, 1996-98. Lt. USNR, 1968-70. Inst. Politics fellow Harvard U., 1980; recipient George Washington Honor medal Freedoms Found., 1969. Republican. Episcopalian. Home: 3608 Locke Ln Houston TX 77027-4004 Office: Univ Tex Health Sci Ctr 7000 Fannin 17th Fl Houston TX 77030

UNTRACHT, STEVEN HARRIS, surgeon; b. Bklyn., Jan. 30, 1955; s. Harry and Lillian (Barshatzky) U. BA summa cum laude, Boston U., 1975; PhD in Biophysics & Theoretical Biology, U. Chgo., 1980, MD, 1981. Diplomate Am. Bd. Surgery, Nat. Bd. Med. Examiners, Am. Bd. Forensic Examiners. Resident in surgery Mass. Gen. Hosp., Boston, 1981-86, clin. and rsch. fellow, 1986; hon. sr. registrar in thoracic surgery Wessex Cardiothoracic Ctr., Southampton, Eng., 1987; clin. fellow in surgery Harvard Med. Sch., Boston, 1981-87; asst. attending physician Morristown (N.J.) Meml. Hosp., 1987-88; active staff dept. of surgery West Jersey Health Sys., Camden, N.J., 1988-92; assoc. in gen. surgery Guthrie Med. Group, P.A., Corning, N.Y., 1992-94; attending surgeon U. Pitts. Med. Ctr.-Lee Regional & Conemaugh Meml. Med. Ctr., Johnstown, Pa., 1994—. Tchg. attending, surg. residency Conemaugh Meml. Med. Ctr., Johnstown, 1994—; mem. profl. adv. bd. Lee Regional Hospice, Johnstown, 1995—; mem. Drs. Without Borders, 1996—, med. missionary Batticaloa, Sri Lanka, 1996, Vavuniya, Sri Lanka, 1997; clin. asst. prof. surgery Temple U., Phila., 1997—. Contbr. articles to profl. jours. Mem. Amnesty Internat. Recipient Med. Alumni award U. Chgo., 1981; joint recipient Nobel Peace prize, 1999. Fellow ACS (liaison physician commn. on cancer U. Pitts. Med. Ctr.-Lee Regional 1997—), Am. Coll. Forensic Examiners; mem. Soc. Critical Care Medicine, Phi Beta Kappa. Office: 321 Main St Ste 5J Johnstown PA 15901-1632 E-mail: shuntracht@pol.net.

UNVERFERTH, BARBARA PATTEN, small business owner; b. Hartford, Conn., Sept. 27, 1945; d. Leslie A. and Mildred B. (Owen) Patten; m. Robert L. Gerbig, June 1968 (div. 1977); children: Patricia G. Toohey, R. Braden Gerbig, Jo Ann Gerbig; m. Donald Unverferth, Dec. 29, 1978 (deceased); children: Katherine J. Unverferth, Megan M. Unverferth. BA cum laude, Ohio Wesleyan U., 1967; MS in Zoology, Ohio U., 1969; MS in Pathology, Ohio State U., 1980. Rsch. asst. Scripts Inst., LaJolla, Calif., 1969-70; tchr. biology Mariemont H.S., Cin., 1970-71; rschr. dept. cardiology Ohio State U., Columbus, 1980-84; gen. ptnr. Art Access, 1993—. Founder, pres. Unverferth House Inc., Columbus, 1988—; mem. dirs. cir. Wexner Ctr., Columbus, 1995—. Author (book chpt.) Dilated Cardiomyopathy, 1985. Corr. sec. Jr. League, Columbus, 1974; corr. sec., mem. exec. bd. Childhood League, Columbus, 1980-85; sec. womens bd. Mus. of Art, Columbus, 1992-93; mem. Columbus AIDS Task Force, 1998. NSF grantee, 1966, NSF fellow, 1968; named Woman of Yr. Rotary Club Upper Arlington, Ohio, 1993. Mem. Kappa Alpha Theta (pres. alumni club 1976). Avocations: tennis, skiing. Office: Art Access 540 S Drexel Ave Bexley OH 43209 E-mail: unvi@aol.com.

UOTILA, URHO ANTTI KALEVI, geodesist, educator; b. Pöytyä, Finland, Feb. 22, 1923; came to U.S., 1951, naturalized, 1957; s. Antti Samuli and Vera Justina (Kyto) U.; m. Helena Vanhakartano, Aug. 6, 1949; children: Heidi, Kirsi, Elizabeth, Julie, Trina, Caroline. BS, Finland's Inst. Tech., 1946, MS, 1949; PhD, Ohio State U., 1959. Surveyor, geodesist Finnish Govt., 1944-46, 46-51; geodesist Swedish Govt., 1946; research asst. Ohio State U., 1952-53, research assoc., 1953-58, research supr., 1959-88, lectr. in geodesy, 1955-57, asst. prof., 1959-62, assoc. prof., 1962-65, chmn. dept. geodetic sci., 1964-84, prof., 1965-89, chmn., prof. emeritus, 1989—. Mem. Solar Eclipse Expdn. to Greenland, 1954; Mem. adv. panel on geodesy U.S. Coast and Geodetic Survey, Nat. Acad. Sci., 1964-66; mem. geodesy and cartography working group, space sci. steering com. NASA, 1965-67, mem. geodesy/cartography working group, summer conf. lunar exploration and sci., 1965, mem. geodesy and cartography adv. subcom., 1967-72; mem. ad hoc com. on N.Am. datum div. earth scis. Nat. Acad. Scis.-N.A.E., 1968-70; bd. dirs. Internat. Gravity Bur., France, 1975-83; mem. com. on geodesy Nat. Acad. Scis., 1975-78 Mem. editorial adv. com.: Advances in Geophysics, 1968-77; Contbr. articles to profl. jours., encys. Served with Finnish Army, 1942-44. Recipient Kaarina and W.A. Heiskanen award, 1962, Apollo Achievement award NASA, 1969, Disting. Svc. award Surveyor's Inst. Sri Lanka, Earle J. Fennell award Am. Congress on Surveying and Mapping, 1989. Fellow Am. Geophys. Union (v.p. geodesy sect. 1964-68, pres. 1968-70), Am. Congress Surveying and Mapping (nat. dir. 1970-73, 2d v.p. 1977-78, pres.-elect 1978-79, pres. 1979-80), Internat. Assn. Geodesy (pres. spl. study group 5.30 1967-71, pres. sect. V 1971-75, exec. com. 1971-79); mem. Am. Assn. Geodetic Surveying (pres. 1984-86), Am. Soc. Photogrammetry, Can. Inst. Surveying, Univs. Space Research Assn. (trustee 1973-75), Finnish Nat. Acad. Scis. (fgn.), Profl. Land Surveyors Ohio (hon.), Ala. Soc. Profl. Land Surveyors (hon.), Tenn. Assn. Profl. Surveyors (hon.) Achievements include: research in geometric geodesy, phys. geodesy and statis. analysis of data. Home: 4329 Shelbourne Ln Columbus OH 43220-4243 Office: Ohio State U 2070 Neil Ave Columbus OH 43210-1226

UPADHIAYA, UMESH CHANDRA, engineer; b. Dabha, India, July 11, 1927; came to U.S. 1977; s. Bhagwati Prashad and Shri Devi U.; m. Susila Devi, Nov. 7, 1954; children— Anita, Amit. Diploma in Elec. and Mech. Engring., Tech. Coll., Dayalbagh, India, 1948; MSME Fla. Inst. U., Miami, 1990. Registered profl. engr., Fla. Asst. engr. Hindusthan Sugar, Gola, India, 1954-60; mech. engr. Bagpat Sugar, (India), 1060-61; erection engr. Dhampur Sugar (India), 1961-62; cons. Mehta Group Uganda, 1962-73; project mgr. KCP Ltd., Madras, India, 1973-74; design engr. joint sugar project unit, Surabaya, Indonesia, 1974-77; cons. engr. Tate & Lyle Enterprises Inc., Miami, Fla., 1977-85. Contbr. articles to profl. publs. Home: 6510 Sedgewyck Cir W Davie FL 33331-3455

UPADHYAY, YOGENDRA NATH, physician, educator; b. Gorakhpur, India, Dec. 21, 1938; arrived in U.S., 1963; s. Murlidhar and Vansraji (Pande) U.; m. Cecile R. Yonish; children: Asha, Sameer, Sanjay. MB, BS, All India Inst. Med. Scis., New Delhi, 1962. Diplomate Am. Bd. Psychiatry and Neurology, Am. Bd. Pediatrics. Instr. in pediatrics Johns Hopkins U. Sch. Medicine, Balt., 1969-71; fellow in child psychiatry Johns Hopkins Hosp./Johns Hopkins U., 1971-72; resident, then sr. resident in psychiatry Albert Einstein Coll. Medicine/Bronx Mcpl. Hosp. Ctr., 1972-74, fellow in child psychiatry, 1974-75; chief, partial hosp. program for children, dept. psychiatry Brookdale Hosp., Bklyn., 1976-77; med. dir. West Nassau Mental Health Ctr., Franklin Sq., N.Y., 1977-80; asst. prof. clin. psychiatry SUNY, Stony Brook, 1978-92; dir. child and adolescent psychiatry Nassau County Med. Ctr., East Meadow, N.Y., 1980-92; sr. psychiatrist South Oaks Hosp., Amityville, 1992—, pres. med. staff, 1995-97, svc. med. dir. child and adolescent psychiatry, 1995-97, med. dir., 1997—; sr. v.p., Medical Affairs South Oak Hosp. and Broadlawn Nursing Home, 2001—. Sr. v.p. med. affairs LI Home, Amityville, NY, 2001—. Fellow Am. Psychiat. Assn. (cons. task force treatments psychiat. disorders 1989—), Am. Acad. Child and Adolescent Psychiatry, Allmsonians of Am. (founding pres. 1982-86). Office: S Oaks Hosp 400 Sunrise Hwy Amityville NY 11701-2508

UPATNIEKS, JURIS, retired optical engineer; b. Riga, Latvia, May 7, 1936; arrived in U.S., 1951; s. Karlis and Eleonora (Jegers) Upatnieks; m. Ilze Induss, July 13, 1968; children: Ivars, Ansis. BSEE, U. Akron, Ohio, 1960; MSEE, U. Mich., 1965. Rsch. asst., then rsch. assoc. Willow Run Labs. U. Mich., Ann Arbor, 1960-69; rsch. engr. Inst. Sci. and Tech., U. Mich., 1969-72, Environ. Rsch. Inst. Mich., Ann Arbor, 1973-93; sr. engr. Applied Optics, 1993—2001; ret., 2001. Lectr. elec. engring. dept. U. Mich., 1971—73, adj. assoc. prof. elec. engring. and computer sci. dept., 1974—2001, adj. rsch. scientist dept. mech. engring. and applied mechanics, 1996—2001. Contbr. articles to profl. jours. 2d lt. U.S. Army, 1961—62. Recipient Holley medal, ASME, 1976, Inventor of the Yr. award, Assn. Advancement Invention and Innovation, 1976. Fellow: Latvian Acad. Sci. (Grand medal 1999), Acad. Soc. Austrums, Soc. Photographic Instrumentation Engrs. (Robert Gordon award 1965), Optical Soc. Am. (R. W. Wood prize 1975), Am. Latvian Assn. Achievements include patents in field. Avocations: camping, gardening, hiking. Office: Applied Optics 2662 Valley Dr Ann Arbor MI 48103-2748 E-mail: upatnks@ic.net.

UPBIN, HAL JAY, consumer products executive; b. Bronx, N.Y., Jan. 15, 1939; s. David and Evelyn (Sloan) U.; m. Shari Kiesler, May 29, 1960; children: Edward, Elyse, Danielle. BBA, Pace Coll., 1961. CPA, N.Y. Tax sr. Peat, Marwick, Mitchell & Co., N.Y.C., 1961-65; tax mgr. Price Waterhouse & Co., 1965-71; dir. taxes Wheelabrator-Frye Inc., 1971-72, treas., 1972-74; pres. Wheelabrator Fin. Corp., 1974-75; v.p., chief fin. officer Chase Manhattan Mortgage and Realty Trust (became Triton Group Ltd. 1980), 1975-76, pres., 1976-78, pres., chmn., 1978-83, also dir.; chmn., pres., dir. Isomedics, 1983-85; chmn., pres. Fifth Ave. Cards, Inc., Fifth Retail Corp., Ashley's Stores, Ashley's Outlet Stores, 1984-88; bd. dirs. Stacy Industries, 1984-88; vice chmn. Am. Recreation Products, St. Louis, 1985-88, vice chmn., pres., 1988—, chmn., 1992—; v.p. corp. devel., chmn. acquistion com. Kellwood Co., Chesterfield, 1990—, exec. v.p. corp. devel., chmn. acquisition com., 1992—, pres., COO, 1994—, pres., COO, dir., 1995-97, pres., CEO, 1997—, also bd. dirs., chmn. Alumni advisor to bd. trustees Pace U.; past pres. Jewish Temple. Mem. AICPA, N.Y. State Soc. CPA's, Franklin Jaycees (v.p.). Home: 625 S Skinker Blvd Saint Louis MO 63105-2301 Office: Kellwood Co PO Box 14374 Saint Louis MO 63178-4374 E-mail: HJU@kellwood.com.

UPBIN, SHARI, theatrical producer, director, agent, educator; b. N.Y.C. children: Edward, Elyse, Danielle. Master tap instr. Talent mgr. Goldstar Talent Mgmt., Inc., N.Y.C., 1989-91. Faculty Nat. Shakespeare Conservatory, N.Y. Dir.(asst.): (plays, 1st Black-Hispanic Shakespeare prodn.) Julius Caesar, 1979, (choreographer); (plays) Matter of Opinion, 1980, Side by Side, 1981; prodr.(dir.): Vincent, The Passions of Can Gogh, 1981, : (Broadway plays) Bojangles, TheLife of Bill Robinson, 1984; dir.: Captain America, 1996; (plays) Fiddler of the Roof, Cabaret, Life with Father, Roar of the Grease Paint, 1979—82, Feminist Movements, 1997; co-prodr.: One Mo' Time; prodr.(dir): Flypaper, 1991—92, Women on Their Own, Things My Mother Never Told Me, How Could Cupid Be So Stupid!, 1999, 20th Ann. One Mo' Time, 2000, Vintage 2001. Founder Queens Playhouse, N.Y., Children's Theatre, Flushing, N.Y.; mem. Willy Mays' Found. Drug Abused Children. Recipient Jaycees Svc. award Jr. Miss Pageants Franklin Twp., N.J., 1976. Mem. League Profl. Theatre Women (past pres.), Soc. Stage Dirs. and Choreographers, Coalition of Women in Arts & Media (bd. dirs.), Actors Equity Assn., Villagers Barn Theatre (1st woman pres.), N.Y. Womens Agenda (bd. dirs.). E-mail: shariupbin@earthlink.net.

UPCHURCH, MICHAEL V. critic, writer; b. Rahway, N.J., Feb. 5, 1954; s. Edward F. and Patricia A. Upchurch. BA, U. Exeter, Devon, Eng., 1975. Book critic Seattle Times, 1998—. Author: (novel) Passive Intruder, 1995, The Flame Forest, 1989, Air, 1986. Mem.: Nat. Book Critics Cir. Office: Seattle Times 1120 John St Seattle WA 98109 E-mail: michaelupchurch@msn.com.

UPDIKE, HELEN HILL, investment manager, financial adviser; b. N.Y.C., Mar. 27, 1941; d. Benjamin Harvey and Helen (Gray) Hill; m. Charles Bruce Updike, Sept. 7, 1963 (div. 1989); children: Edith Hill, Nancy Lamar; m. Asa Rountree, Oct. 10, 1998. BA, Hood Coll., 1962; PhD, SUNY, Stony Brook, 1978; postgrad., Harvard U., 1986. Asst. prof. Suffolk U., Boston, 1965-67; lectr. SUNY, Stony Brook, 1969-75, vis. asst. prof., 1977-78; asst. prof. U. Mass., Boston, 1975-77, Hofstra U., Hempstead, N.Y., 1978-85, assoc. prof., 1985-90, chmn. dept. econs. and geography, 1981-84, assoc. dean Hofstra Coll., 1984-87; prin. Bridgewater Advisors, N.Y.C. Bd. dirs. Faberge, McCrory Corp.; cons. on econ. policy, 1973—; commentator WNYC Radio, 1997—. Author: The National Banks and American Economic Development, 1870-1900, 1985. Trustee, v.p. L.I. Forum for Tech., 1979-85; trustee Madeira Sch., Greenway, Va., 1984-88, N.Y. Outward Bound, 1988-97, Literacy, Inc., 1997—; mem. nat. adv. bd. Outward Bound USA, 1986-92. Mem. AAAS, Cosmopolitan Club. Home: 10 Mitchell Pl New York NY 10017-1801 Office: Bridgewater Advisors 452 Fifth Ave New York NY 10018

UPDIKE, JOHN HOYER, writer; b. Shillington, Pa., Mar. 18, 1932; s. Wesley R. and Linda G. (Hoyer) U.; m. Mary E. Pennington, June 26, 1953 (div. 1976); children: Elizabeth, David, Michael, Miranda; m. Martha Bernhard, Sept. 30, 1977. AB, Harvard U., 1954; student, Ruskin Sch. Drawing and Fine Art, 1954-55. With New Yorker mag., N.Y.C., 1955-57. Author: (fiction) The Poorhouse Fair, 1959 (Richard and Hinda Rosenthal Found. award Am. Acad. and Nat. Inst. Arts and Letters 1960), The Same Door, 1959, Rabbit, Run, 1960, Pigeon Feathers, 1962, The Centaur, 1963 (Nat. Book award 1963, Prix Medicis Etranger 1966), Olinger Stories, 1964, Of the Farm, 1965, The Music School, 1966, Couples, 1968, Bech: A Book, 1970, Rabbit Redux, 1971, Museums and Women, 1972, Warm Wine, 1973, A Month of Sundays, 1975, Marry Me, 1976, Couples, 1976, The Coup, 1978, From the Journal of a Leper, 1978, Problems, 1979, Too Far to Go: The Maples Stories, 1979 (Am. Book award nomination 1980), Three Illuminations in the Life of an American Author, 1979, Your Lover Just Called: Stories of Joan and Richard Maple, 1980, The Chaste Planet, 1980, Rabbit Is Rich, 1981 (Pulitzer prize for fiction 1982, Nat. Book Critics Circle award 1982, Am. Book award 1982), Invasion of the Book Envelopes, 1981, Bech Is Back, 1982, The Beloved, 1982, The Witches of Eastwick, 1984, Confessions of a Wild Bore, 1984, Roger's Version, 1986 (Nat. Book Critics Circle award nomination 1986), Trust Me, 1987, More Stately Mansions, 1987, S., 1988, Rabbit at Rest, 1990 (Pulitzer prize for fiction 1991, Nat. Book Critics Circle award 1991), Memories of the Ford Administration, 1992, Brazil, 1994, The Afterlife, 1994, In the Beauty of the Lilies, 1996, Toward the End of Time, 1997, Bech at Bay, 1998, Gertrude and Claudius, 2000, Licks of Love, 2000, , Seek My Face, 2002, (poetry) The Carpentered Hen and Other Tame Creatures, 1958, Telephone Poles, 1963, A Child's Calendar, 1965, The Angels, 1968, Bath after Sailing, 1968, Midpoint, 1969, Seventy Poems, 1972, Six Poems, 1973, Tossing and Turning, 1977, Sixteen Sonnets, 1979, Five Poems, 1980, Spring Trio, 1982, Jester's Dozen, 1984, Facing Nature, 1985, Collected Poems 1953-1993, 1993, A Helpful Alphabet of Friendly Objects, 1995, In the Cemetery High Above Shillington, 1996, Americana, 2001, (plays) Three Texts from Early Ipswich, 1968, Buchanan Dying, 1974, (non-fiction) Assorted Prose, 1965, On Meeting Authors, 1968, A Good Place, 1973, Picked-Up Pieces, 1975, Hub Fans Bid Kid Adieu, 1977, Talk from the Fifties, 1979, Ego and Art in Walt Whitman, 1980, Hawthorne's Creed, 1981, Hugging the Shore, 1983 (Nat. Book Critics Circle award 1984), Emersonianism, 1984, Just Looking, 1989, Self-Consciousness, 1989, Odd Jobs, 1991, Golf Dreams, 1996, More Matter, 1999; adapter: (librettos) The Magic Flute, 1962, The Ring, 1964, (plays) Bottom's Dream, 1969; author words and music: (with Gunther Schuller) The Fisherman and His Wife, 1970; editor: Pens and Needles, 1970, (with S. Ravenel) The Best American Short Stories 1984, 1984, A Century of Arts and Letters, 1998 (with K. Kenison) The Best Am. Short Stories of the Century, 1999. Recipient O. Henry First Short Story award, 1966, 91, MacDowell medal for literature, 1981, Medal of Honor for literature Nat. Arts Club, 1984, PEN/Malamud Meml. prize PEN/Faulker award Found., 1988, Nat. Medal of Arts, 1989, Harvard Arts medal, 1998, Nat. Book Found. award Lifetime Achievement, 1998; Guggenheim fellow, 1959. Mem. AAAL, Am. Acad. Arts. and Scis. Democrat. Episcopalian.

UPDIKE, JOHN R. municipal administrator; b. Neenah, Wis., Dec. 29, 1961; s. Edward C. and Daureen Updike; m. Katherine E. Updike, Apr. 21, 1985; 1 child, Christina C. Miller. BA in Regional Devel., U. Ariz., 1985. Negotiations coord. City of Tucson, 1991-97, project mgr., 1997—. Bd. dirs. Tucson Downtown Alliance, 1999-2001. Mem. Project Mgmt. Inst. (pres. Tucson chpt. 1997-99, v.p. corp. svcs. 1999-2001), Ariz. Mcpl. Mgmt. Assts. Assn. Office: City of Tucson 255 W Alameda 10th fl Tucson AZ 85701 E-mail: jupdike1@CI.Tucson.AZ.US.

UPDIKE, LINDA S. personnel placement firm executive; b. Detroit, May 22, 1956; d. Arthur E. Nowak and Loraine J. (Zalewski) Jacks; m. Keith N. Updike, June 19, 1981; children: Elizabeth A., Jason J. AS in Bus. Mgmt., Macomb Cmty. coll., 1983. Adminstrn. clk. Graham Mortgage, Southfield, Mich., 1974-78; sec. Conveyor Engring., Detroit, 1978; sec. product sales dept.l Haden Uniking, Troy, Mich., 1978-83; mem. sales dept. Rapid Installations, Louisville, 1983, Harcon Engring., Madison Heights, Mich., 1984-86; adminstrv. asst. Design Systems Inc., Farmington Hills, 1987-94; gen. mgr. Staff Resources Inc., 1994; pres. GBL Resources Inc., Troy, 1994—. Mem. NAFE. Avocations: golf, travel. Office: GBL Resources Inc 6966 Crooks Rd Ste 20 Troy MI 48098-1798

UPGREN, ARTHUR REINHOLD, JR. astronomer, educator, writer; b. Mpls., Feb. 21, 1933; s. Arthur Reinhold and Marion (Andrews) U.; m. Joan Koswoski, Jan. 7, 1967; 1 child, Amy Joan. BA, U. Minn., 1955; MS, U. Mich., 1958; PhD, Case Western Res. U., 1961. Research assoc. Swarthmore Coll., Pa., 1961-63; astronomer U.S. Naval Obs., Washington, 1963-66; asst. prof. Wesleyan U., Middletown, Conn., 1966-73, assoc. prof., 1973-81, dir. Van Vleck Obs., 1973-93, John Monroe Van Vleck prof., 1981—, chmn. dept. astronomy, 1968-86, 90-93; v.p. Fund Astrophys. Research, N.Y.C., 1973—, chmn. grants com., 1985—. Vis. lectr. U. Md., 1964-66, George Washington U., 1965-66, Thames Sci. Ctr., New London, Conn., 1990, 92; vis. prof. Yale U., 1979-80, sr. rsch. scientist, 1997—; adj. prof. U. Fla., 1984-99; outdoor lighting cons. Wesleyan U., 1991—, Vt. State Agy. Natural Resources, 1993-94; dir. Internat. Dark-Sky Assn., 1997—; reviewer books in astronomy, meteorology, classical music and urban demographics. Author: Night Has a Thousand Eyes: A Naked-Eye Guide to the Sky, its Science and Lore, 1998; co-author (with Jurgen Stock): Weather: How it Works and Why It Matters, 2000, The Turtle and The Stars: Observations of an Earthbound Astronomer, 2002; editor: The Nearby Stars and the Stellar Luminosity Function, 1983, Mapping the Sky-Past Heritage and Future Directions, 1988, Star Catalogues: A Centennial Tribute to A.N. Vyssotsky, 1989, Fundamentals of Astronomy, 1990, Precision Photometry: Astrophysics of the Galaxy, 1991, Objective Prism and Other Surveys, 1991, Databases for Galactic Structure, 1993, Hot Stars in the Halo, 1994, New Developments in Array Technology and Applications, 1995, Anni Mirables: A Symposium Celebrating the 90th Birthday of Dorrit Hoffleit, 1997. Conn. state chair New Eng. Light Pollution Adv. Group, 1994—. Grantee NSF, 1967-99; fellow Wesleyan Ctr. for Humanities, 1996. Fellow Royal Astron. Soc.; mem. Internat. Astron. Union (commn. v.p. 1982-85, pres. commn. 24 1985-88), Am. Astron. Soc. (Harlow Shapley lectr. 1977—, vice-chmn. dynamical astronomy div. 1988-89, chmn. 1989-90, chmn. AAS com. on light pollution 2000—), Astron. Soc. Pacific, Illuminating Engring. Soc. N.Am., Internat. Dark Sky Assn. Office: PO Box 208101 Yale U New Haven CT 06520

UPHAM, STEADMAN, anthropology educator, university dean, academic administrator; b. Denver, Apr. 4, 1949; s. Albert Tyler and Jane Catherine (Steadman) U; m. Margaret Anne Cooper, Aug. 21, 1971; children: Erin Cooper, Nathan Steadman. BA, U. Redlands, 1971; MA, Ariz. State U., 1977, PhD, 1980. Dist. sales mgr. Ind. News Co. Inc., Los Angeles, 1971-72; regional sales mgr. Petersen Pub. Co, 1972-74; archeologist, researcher Bur. Land Mgmt., Phoenix, 1979; research asst. Ariz. State U., Tempe, 1979-80; chief archeologist Soil Sytems Inc., Phoenix, 1980-81, N.Mex. State U., Las Cruces, N.Mex., 1981-85, asst. prof. to assoc. prof., 1982-87, assoc. dean, 1987-90; prof. anthropology, vice provost for rsch., grad. dean U. Oreg., Eugene, 1990—. Inerim dir. Cultural Resources Mgmt. divsn. N.Mex. State U., Las Cruces, 1988; mem. exec. com. Assn. Grad. Schs., 1994—; bd. dirs. Coun. Grad. Schs., 1995—. Author: Polities and Power, 1982, A Hopi Social History, 1992; editor: Computer Graphics in Archaeology, 1979, Mogollon Variability, 1986, The Sociopolitical Structure of Prehistoric Southwest Societies, 1989, The Evolution of Political Systems, 1990; also articles. Advanced seminar grantee Sch. of Am. Research, 1987, research grantee NSF, 1979, 1984-85, Hist. Preservation grantee State of N.Mex., 1982-84, 1991, 92, Ford Found. 1991-92, U.S. Dept. Edn. 1991-93. Fellow Am. Anthropol. Assn.; mem. Nat. Phys. Sci. Consortium (pres. 1992-95), We. Assn. Grad. Schs. (pres. 1994-95), Assn. Grad. Schs. (exec. com. 1995—), Coun. Grad. Schs. (bd. dirs. 1995—). Office: U Oreg Office Acad Affairs 207 Johnson Hall Eugene OR 97403

UPHOFF, JAMES KENT, education educator; b. Hebron, Nebr., Sept. 1, 1937; s. Ernest John and Alice Marie (Dutcher) U.; m. Harriet Lucille Martin, Aug. 6, 1962; 1 child, Nicholas James. BA, Hastings Coll., 1959; MEd, U. Nebr., 1962, EdD, 1967. Tchr. Walnut Jr. H.S., Grand Island, Nebr., 1959-65, dept. chmn., 1962-65; instr. dept. edn. U. Nebr., Lincoln, 1965-66; curriculum intern Bellevue (Nebr.) Pub. Schs., 1966-67; asst. prof. edn. Wright State U., Dayton, Ohio, 1967-70, assoc. prof., 1970-75, prof. edn., 1975—, co-dir. pub. edn. religion studies ctr., 1972-75, dean br. campuses, 1974-79, dir. lab. experiences, 1982-91, chmn. dept. tchr. edn., 1994-97, dir. coll. student svcs., 1994-97, dir. profl. field experiences, prof. emeritus, 1997—, assoc. dir. Ctr. for Tchg. and Learning, 1999—. Vis. prof. U. Dayton, 1968-69, 98, 99. Author: (with others) Summer Children: Ready or Not for School, 4th edit., 1986, School Readiness and Transition Programs: Real Facts from Real Schools, 1990, 2d edit., 1995; editor: Dialogues on Development Curriculum K and I, 1987, Changing to a Developmentally Appropriate Curriculum-Successfully: 4 Case Studies, 1989; bi-weekly columnist Oakwood Register newspapers, the Kettering-Oakwood Times andthe Centerville-Bellbrook Times; weekly commentator on edn. WYSO-FM Pub. Radio. Bd. dirs. pub. edn. fund Dayton Found., 1985-97; mem. Luth. Ch. coun., 1987-90, chair, 1988-90; mem. Oakwood City Schs. Bd. Edn., 1989—, v.p., 1994-95, pres., 1996, 97, 99—. Phi Delta Kappa scholar, 1969; Malone fellow in Arab Islamic studies, 1989; U. Nebr. Alumni award, 2002. Mem. ASCD (dir. 1974-79, editor early childhood network 1989-98, editor and facilitator pub. edn. and religion network 1992—), Western Ohio Edn. Assn. (pres. 1974-75, exec. com. 1979-85), Assn. Tchr. Educators, Assn. Childhood Edn. Internat., Ohio Assn. Supervision and Curriculum Devel. (v.p. 1972-73), Nat. Coun. Social Studies, Ohio Coun. Social Studies, Ohio Sch. Bds. Assn. (chair rules com. 1993-94, mem. policy and legislation com. 1994—, Achievement award 1995, 96, 98, bd. trustees 1996—, exec. com. 1998-99, pres.-elect 2000, pres. 2001), Nat. Assn. Edn. Young Children, Dayton Area Coun. Social Studies (pres. 1970-71, 85-87), Ohio Assn. Edn. Young Children (com. chair 1992-95), Dayton Assn. for Young Children (exec. bd. 1988-94), LWV Greater Dayton (edn. dir. 1981-85), Ohio Coun. Chs. (edn. com. 1973-75), Optimists Club (pres. 1983-85, sec.-treas. 1988-99), Phi Delta Kappa (chpt. pres. 1983-84, 98—, chpt. advisor 1988-94, area 5-i coord. 2001—), Kappa Delta Pi. Republican. Home: 150 Spirea Dr Dayton OH 45419-3409 Office: Wright State U CTL 023 Library Dayton OH 45435 E-mail: james.uphoff@wright.edu.

UPPMAN, THEODOR, concert and opera singer, voice educator; b. San Jose, Calif., Jan. 12, 1920; s. John August and Hulda Maria (Thörnström) U.; m. Jean Seward, Jan. 31, 1943; children: Margot, Michael. Student, Coll. of Pacific, 1938-39, Curtis Inst. Music, 1939-41, Stanford U., 1941-42, U. So. Calif., 1948-50. Mem. profl. com. regional auditions Met. Opera; voice faculty Mannes Coll. Music, 1977—, Manhattan Sch. Music, 1988—; tchr. master classes Britten-Pears Sch. Advanced Mus. Studies, 1985—, Glimmerglass Opera, Cooperstown, N.Y., 1990, 93, Opera Theatre of St. Louis, 1993, Steans Inst. at Ravinia Festival, 1995; dir. vocal dept. Music Acad. of the West, Santa Barbara, Calif., 1988. Profl. debut as baritone, No. Calif. Symphony, 1941, appeared in Pelléas with Mélisande, San Francisco Symphony, 1947; performed in: Pelleas et Melisande, City Ctr. Opera Co., N.Y., 1948; debut, San Francisco Opera Co., 1948, N.Y. recital, Times Hall, 1950; appeared: title role Billy Budd opera premiere, Royal Opera House, London, Eng., 1951, Theatre des Champs Elysees, Paris, France, 1952; performed in: Billy Budd, NBC-TV Opera Theatre, 1952; Met. Opera Co. prodsn. including Pelleas et Melisande, 1953-62, Magic Flute, 1956-77, La Perichole, 1956-71, Don Giovanni, 1957-73, Madam Butterfly, 1961-78, Cosi fan Tutte, 1962-71, L'Italiana in Algeri, 1973-75; Britten's Gloriana, Cin. May Festival, 1956 (U.S. premiere); world premieres of Floyd's The Passion of Jonathan Wade, N.Y.C. Opera, 1962, Villa Lobos' Yerma, Santa Fe Opera, 1971, Pasatieri's Black Widow, Seattle Opera, 1972, Barab's Philip Marshall, Chautauqua, 1974; Aix en Provence Festival, summer 1964, Aldeburgh Festival, summer 1975, Chgo. Lyric Opera debut, 1964, War Requiem by Britten, Dallas, Cleve., Cin. orchs., 1965, Damnation of Faust, N.Y. Philharmonic, 1966; Am. premiere: Billy

Budd, Chgo. Lyric Opera, 1970, Death in Venice (Britten), Geneva Opera, 1983; World premiere: A Quiet Place (Bernstein), Houston Opera, 1983, A Quiet Place, LaScala, 1984, A Quiet Place, Vienna Staatsoper, 1986; recordings include world premiere broadcast Billy Budd, 1951, Fauré Requiem, 1951, The Art of Theodor Uppman, 1954-57; concert opera symphony appearances throughout, U.S., also radio, TV. Hon. dir. Britten-Pears Sch. for Advanced Mus. Studies, 1987—. With U.S. Army, 1943-46, World War II. Recipient 1st prize Atwater Kent Found. Auditions, Gainsborough Found. award, 1947. Address: 201 W 86th St New York NY 10024-3328

UPPOOR, RAJENDRA, pharmaceutical scientist, pharmacist, educator, researcher, private pilot; b. Ripponpete, Karnataka, India, Feb. 11, 1960; came to U.S., 1989; s. Vittal Kamath and Suvarna (Vittal) U.; m. VenKata Ramana K. Sista, Oct. 31, 1995; 1 child, Vivek Vittal. B in Pharmacy, Govt. Coll. of Pharmacy, Bangalore, India, 1981, M in Pharmacy, 1984; diploma in pharmaceutical tech., State U. Ghent, Belgium, 1986; PhD, Med. U. of S.C., Charleston, 1995. Registered pharmacist Karnataka State Pharmacy Coun., India; lic. pharmacist, Md.; cert. pvt. pilot. Co-founder, prodn. mgr. Gururaj Micropulverizers, Bangalore, India, 1979-85; student trainee Burroughs Wellcome, Bombay, 1981; trainee supr. Eskaylab India, Bangalore, 1982; asst. prof. St. John's Pharmacy Coll., 1984-85; mktg. officer Associated Capsules, Bombay, 1985-87; devel. officer Sci. Tech. Ctr., 1986-87; pharmacist Ministry of Health, Riyadh, Saudi Arabia, 1987-88; tchg. asst. Duquesne U. Sch. Pharmacy, Pitts., 1989; rsch. asst. Med. U. of S.C., Charleston, 1989-94; cons. Ohmeda PPD, Inc., Murray Hill, N.J., 1994, sr. scientist, 1994-96, lead scientist, 1996. Review chemist Office New Drug Chemistry-Ctr. for Drug Evaluation and Rsch.-FDA, Rockville, Md., 1996—, anti-inflammatory, analgesic and ophthalmic drug products team, 1996-98, ophthalmic drug products team, 1998-2000, oncology drug products team, 2000—; cardio-renal drug products team, 2001—; pharmacist CVS/Pharmacy, Montgomery County, Md., 1997—, Prince George's County, 1997—; mem. drug products tech. com. CDER/FDA, 1998—2002 drug product tech. com. Product Quality Rsch. Inst., Inc., Arlington, Va., 2000—; process analytical tech. rev. and inspection team Office of Pharm. Sci. CDER-ORA, 2002—. Pres. Internat. Student Orgn. Med. Univ. S.C., Charleston, 1991-92; gen. sec. Pharm. Soc. The Govt. Coll. of Pharmacy, Bangalore, India. 1983-84; student rep. in Indian schs. and colls., 1966-84. Recipient Spl. Recognition award ONDC, 1999, Team Excellence award CDER, 1999, Excellence in Comm. award, 2000, 01, 02, Spl. Citation award, 2000; Nat. Merit scholar Govt. of India, 1975-81, U. Grants Commn. scholar, 1982-84; Internat. fellow WHO, Geneva, State U. Ghent, Belgium, 1986. Mem. Am. Assn. Pharm. Scientists, Vivekananda Kendra Yoga Therapy and Rsch. Ctr.(instr. 1981-82, life), Pharmacy Hon. Soc., Nat. Cadet Corps (Naval Wing 1972-77), Aircraft Owners and Pilots Assn., TSS Flying Club, Montgomery County Airpark Assn., Rho Chi. Achievements include rsch. in concentric coating technique/application for sustained release of drugs, application of glucose oxidase-catalase as an antioxidant system in pharmaceutical solutions, formulation, product development, scale-up and manufacturing of lipid emulsions for intravenous use, freeze drying of pharmaceuticals. Avocations: flying, philately, travel, history, photography. Home: 6 Beauvoir Ct Rockville MD 20855-1250 Office: HFD-810/150 Divsn New Drug Chemistry I/Oncology Team Woodmont Office Complex 2 1451 Rockville Pike Rockville MD 20852-1420 E-mail: uppoorra@cder.fda.gov.

UPRIGHT, DIANE WARNER, art dealer; b. Cleve. d. Rodney Upright and Shirley (Warner) Lavine. Student, Wellesley Coll., 1965-67; BA, U. Pitts., 1969; MA, U. Mich., 1973, PhD, 1976. Asst. prof. U. Va., Charlottesville, 1976-78; assoc. prof. Harvard U., Cambridge, Mass., 1978-83; sr. curator Ft. Worth Art Mus., 1984-86; dir. Jan Krugier Gallery, N.Y.C., 1986-90; sr. v.p., head contemporary art dept. Christie's, 1990-95; pres. Diane Upright Fine Arts, 1995—. Author: Morris Louis: The Complete Paintings, 1979, Ellsworth Kelly: Works on Paper, 1987, various exhbn. catalogues; contbr. articles to art jours. Mem. Art Table, Inc. Office: Diane Upright Fine Arts 188 E 76th St New York NY 10021-2826

UPSHAW, HARRY STEPHAN, psychology educator; b. Birmingham, Ala., July 10, 1926; s. N.H. and Florence (Arnold) U.; m. Paula Binyon, June 18, 1950; children: Alan Binyon, Phyllis, David Arnold, Stephan Lipner. Student, U. Ala., 1946-47; AB, U. Chgo., 1949; MA, Northwestern U., 1951; PhD, U. N.C., 1956. Asst prof. psychology U. Ala., 1954-57; spl. instr. psychology Simmons Coll., Boston, 1957-58; research assoc. Ednl. Research Corp., Cambridge, Mass., 1957-58; asst. prof., then assoc. prof. pub. health U. N.C., 1958-61, lectr., assoc. prof. psychology, 1958-64, rsch. prof. psychology, 1991-97; assoc. prof. Bryn Mawr (Pa.) Coll., 1964-65; assoc. prof., then prof. emeritus psychology U. Ill., Chgo., 1965-91, prof. emeritus, 1991—, dept. head, 1968-72; assoc. dir. Office of Social Sci. Rsch., 1981-87. Guest prof. U. Mannheim, Germany, 1975, Fulbright scholar Technische Universitaet Berlin, 1978-79; vis. scholar Inst. for Rsch. in Social Sci., U. N.C., 1991-92. Editorial cons., Jour. Exptl. Social Psychology, Research in Personality, Jour. Applied Social Psychology, Jour. Personality Social Psychology; Contbr. articles to profl. jours. Served with AUS, 1944-46. Fellow Am. Psychol. Assn., Soc. Exptl. Social Psychol. Home: 155 N Harbor Dr Apt 1303 Chicago IL 60601-7397 E-mail: hupshaw@uic.edu.

UPSHAW, LISA GAYE, business computer systems analyst; b. Alamogordo, N.Mex., June 27, 1959; d. James Leroy Upshaw and Margaret (Shackelford) Carrell; m. Michael J. Zamora, Nov. 3, 1976 (div. July 1983); 1 child, Jeremy Brandon; m. Eddie Gonzalez, Mar. 19, 1984 (div. 1989). BS in Bus. Computer Systems, U. N.Mex., 1983. Govt. and large account system analyst Office Systems, Alburquerque, 1982-84; sr. system analyst, nat. accounts mgr. Bell Atlantic/CompuShop, Houston, 1984-89; nat. account mgr. CompuCom Systems, Inc., 1988—, mem. president's coun., 1988-89, br. mgr. Atlanta, 1990-93, nat. sales mgt., 1993—. Cons. Bell Atlantic President's Club, Dallas, 1986-87, 88, Bell Atlantic Leaders Club, 1986-89. Chmn. publicity Ronald McDonald House, Alburquerque, 1982, chairwoman spl. events, 1983; chairwoman Rep. Vol. Community, Houston, 1986; sponsor Houston Ballet, Theatre of Arts, Fundraising Heart Assn. Mem. NAFE (network dir. 1987-88), Assn. Info. System Profls., Houston Area League Personal Computer Specialists, NOW, VFW, CompuCom Leaders Club. Avocations: tennis, golf, traveling, ballet. Office: CompuCom Systems 2580 Cumberland Pky NW Ste 400 Atlanta GA 30339-3909

UPSHUR, CAROLE CHRISTOFK, psychologist, educator; b. Des Moines, Oct. 18, 1948; d. Robert Richard and Margaret (Davis) Chistofk; 1 child, Emily. AB, U. So. Calif., 1969; EdM, Harvard U., 1970, EdD, 1975. Lic. psychologist, Mass. Planner Mass. Com. on Criminal Justice, Boston, 1970-73; licensing specialist, planner, policy specialist Mass. Office for Children, 1973-76; asst. prof. Coll. Pub. and Cmty. Svc. U. Mass., 1976-81, assoc. prof., 1982-93, prof., 1993-2001, chmn. Ctr. for Cmty. Planning, 1979—81, 1984—86, 1995—96. Sr. rsch. fellow Maurice Gaston Inst. Latino Pub. Policy, 1993—, Ctr. Social Devel. & Edn., 1991-2001, Gerontology Inst., 1996-2001, McCormack Inst. for Pub. Affairs, dir. PhD in Pub. Policy program, 1995-2001; cons. to govt. and cmty. agencies; assoc. in pediatrics, sr. rsch. assoc. U. Mass. Med. Sch., 1983-94; adj. prof. Heller Sch. Social Welfare, Brandeis U., 1985-98; vis. prof. family medicine and cmty. health U. Mass. Med. Sch. and Meml. Health Care, 2001—. Contbr. articles to profl. jours. Mem. Brookline Human Rels.-Youth Resources Commn., 1988-91, Gov.'s Commn. on Facility Consolidation, 1991-92, Mass. Healthcare Adv. Com., 1993—. Fellow Mass. Psychol. Assn.; mem. APA, APHA, Am. Assn. Mental Retardation (cons. editor Jour. Mental Retardation 1981—, Pub. Health Reports 1998—), Assn. for Pub. Policy Analysis and Mgmt. Office: U Mass Med Sch Dept Family Med 55 Lake Ave N Worcester MA 01655

UPSHUR, DORIS NASH, interior designer, consultant, researcher; b. Charlotte, N.C., Oct. 21, 1921; d. John Clayton and Jessie (Bound) Nash; m. Robert Irving Upshur, May 30, 1918; children: David Nash, John Irving. BA, U. S.C., 1944. Interior designer Dora Gray Studios, Columbia, S.C., 1944-65, Columbia Office Supply Co., 1964-65; owner Doris Upshur Interiors, Columbia, 1965—. Pres. Carolinas chpt. Am. Inst. Decorators, 1950-70, accredited mem., 1970; nat. dir., charter mem. Carolinas chpt. Nat. Home Fashions League, 1967; design coord. Women's Symphony Showhouse, 1980-81, 85-86. Bd. dirs. Columbia Lyric Opera, 1979-89; mem. Trinity Housing Corp., Trinity Environ. Task Force; pres. Episc. Ch. Women, 1971; pres. Opera Guild Greater Columbia, 1990; chmn. Wednesdays at Trinity. Fellow Am. Soc. Interior Designers (life, nat. v.p. southeastern region 1969-71, Dora Gray award Carolinas chpt. 1984); mem. Nat. Trust for Hist. Preservation (bd. mem. 1989-90) Republican. Home: 1631 Tanglewood Rd Columbia SC 29204-3305

UPSON, DONALD V. financial executive, retired; b. Hutchinson, Kans., Feb. 8, 1934; s. William Ernest and Luella Beatrice (Hutchison) U.; m. Janis Carol Anderson, Sept. 16, 1956; children: Mark Steven, Brent William. BS, Kans. State U., 1956. C.P.A. With Peat, Marwick, Mitchell & Co., 1956, 60-81, ptnr., 1974-81; exec. v.p., dir. internal audit Del E. Webb Corp., Phoenix, 1981-85; mgr. info. systems Tiernay Turbines Inc., 1986; chief fin. officer Schomac Corp., Tucson, 1986-88; adminstr. U. Ariz., 1988-90; pres., chief exec. officer Ariz. Commerce Bank, 1990-91; chief fin. officer O'Connor, Cavanagh, Anderson, Westover, Killingsworth & Beshears, P.A., Phoenix, 1991-94; fin. cons., 1995-97; ret., 1997. Pres. Community Orgn. for Drug Abuse, Alcohol and Mental Health Services, Inc., 1977-78; bd. dis. Phoenix council Boy Scouts Am., elder Presbyterian Ch. Served to lt. USAF, 1956-59. Mem. Am. Inst. C.P.A.s, Ariz. Soc. C.P.A.s, Beta Theta Pi (pres. 1955-56) Republican. Home and Office: 1313 E Sheena Dr Phoenix AZ 85022-4485 E-mail: DVUPSON@aol.com.

UPSON, HELEN RENA, retired history educator; b. Southington, Conn., Aug. 18, 1912; BA, Grinnell (Iowa) Coll., 1958; MA, U. Iowa, 1960, PhD, 1969. Commd. USN, 1943, advanced through grades to lt. comdr., ret., 1958; adminstv. officer math., scis. divsn. Office of Naval Rsch., Washington, 1949-50; instr. Armed Forces Info. Sch., Carlysle, Pa., Ft. Slocum, N.Y., 1950-53; tng. officer Naval Air Sta., Hutchinson, Kans., 1953-55; pub. info. officer 17th Naval Dist., Kodiak, Alaska, 1955-57, Office of Chief of Info., Office of Sec. Navy, Washington, 1957-58; grad. asst. instr. U. Iowa, 1958-65; assoc. prof. Am. and European history Calif. Western U./U.S. Internat. U., San Diego, 1965-76, adj. prof. Am. econ. history and internat. European problems, 1976-81. Author: Order and System: Charles Frances Adams Jr. and the Railroad Problem, 1970, The western Odyssey of Nin Connecticut Brothers: An Intimate History of American Enterprise, 1989. Mem. Tierrasanta Cmty. Coun., San Diego and chmn. lit. com., 1982-83. Mem. AAUW, Nat. Ind. Scholars, Am. Hist. Soc. Unitarian Universalist. Avocations: swimming, hiking, skiing, photography, travel. Home: 183 3rd Ave Apt 310 Chula Vista CA 91910-1822

UPSON, STUART BARNARD, advertising agency executive; b. Cin., Apr. 14, 1925; s. Mark and Alice (Barnard) U.; m. Barbara Jussen, Nov. 2, 1946; children: Marguerite Nichols, Anne Marcus, Stuart Barnard. BS, Yale U., 1945. With Dancer, Fitzgerald, Sample, Inc., N.Y.C., 1946-86, sr. v.p., 1963-66, exec. v.p., 1966-67, pres., 1967-74, chmn., 1974-86, DFS-Dorland, N.Y.C., 1986-87; dir. Saatchi & Saatchi Inc., 1987—. Bd. dirs. Fresh Air Fund, N.Y., Advt. Coun. With USNR, 1943-46. Mem. St. Elmo Soc. Clubs: Wee Burn Country (Darien); Sky (N.Y.C.); Blind Brook, Pine Valley Golf, Ocean Forest Golf. Home: 16 Wrenfield Ln Darien CT 06820-2201 Office: Saatchi & Saatchi Inc 375 Hudson St New York NY 10014-3658

UPSON, THOMAS FISHER, judge, former state senator, lawyer; b. Waterbury, Conn., Sept. 30, 1941; s. J. Warren and Grace (Fisher) U.; m. Barbara Secor (div. Jan. 1979); children: Secor, Chauncey Julius; m. Katherine Wolff, June 1, 1996. BA in History, Washington and Jefferson Coll., 1963; LLB, U. Conn., 1968; postgrad., Trinity Coll., 1969-72, Georgetown U., 1971-72. Bar: Conn., 1969, U.S. Dist. Ct. (2d dist.), 1969, U.S. Supreme Ct. 1973. Lawyer Upson & Secor, Waterbury, 1969-70, 74-76; lawyer, spl. asst. U.S. Dept. Commerce, Washington, 1970-72; lawyer, spl. asst. to adminstr. GSA, 1973-74; dir. admissions St. Margaret's McTernan Sch., Waterbury, 1977-78; with div. spl. revenue State of Conn., Hartford, 1978-82; assoc. Moynahan & Ruskin, Waterbury, 1979-81; ptnr. Upson & Daly, 1981-2001; mem. Conn. Senate, Hartford, 1985-2001, chmn. gen. law com., vice-chmn. jud. com., majority whip, 1985-86, asst. minority leader, 1987-88, 89-90, minority leader protempore, 1991-92, dep. minority leader, 1993-94, dep. majority leader, chmn. jud. com., 1995-96, dep., then asst. minority leader, ranking mem. jud. com., 1997-2000; judge Superior Ct. State of Conn., 2001—. Moderator 1st Congl. Ch., Waterbury, 1986-91; bd. dirs. Easter Seals-United Way, Waterbury, 1984-88; Rep. candidate for Congress, 6th Dist. Conn., 1976; mem. Conn. Rep. Ctrl. com., 1983-91; mem. Waterbury Rep. Town Com., 1980-85; dir. Mattatuck Mus., 1993—; former dir. Waterbury Symphony Orch.; former sec. and dir. First Ch. Housing, Inc.; pres. Naugatuck Valley Devel. Corp., 1975-76. Mem. ABA, Conn. Bar Assn., Waterbury Bar Assn., SAR, Soc. Colonial Wars, Soc. of the Founders of the Hartford, Phi Gamma Delta, Univ. Club (Waterbury). Lodges: Kiwanis (former pres., lt. gov. SW New Eng. dist.), Elks. Republican. Congregationalist. Avocations; hiking, music, history. Home: 210 Southwest Rd Waterbury CT 06708-3214

UPTIGROVE, KENNETH R. library administrator; b. Flint, Mich., Oct. 6, 1943; s. Kenneth R. and Ilah L. (Horton) U.; m. Suzanne C. Glass, Apr. 6, 1968; children: Chad K., Kathy S. BA, U. Mich., 1967, MLS, 1969. Br. rsch. libr. Genesee County Libr., Flint, 1963-69; sch. libr. Kearsley Community Schs., 1969-70; dir. Owosso (Mich.) Pub. Libr., 1970—94, Shiawassee Dist. Libr., Owosso, 1994—. Contbr. articles to mags. Mem. ALA, Mich. Library Assn. (Pub. library div. sec.-treas. 1981-82, chmn. coop. caucus 1986-87, mgmt. and adminstrn. caucus, sec.-treas. 1988-89), Flint Area Library Assn. (pres. 1970), Ruffed Grouse Soc. (pres. Lansing chpt. 1979-81, treas. Mich. coun. 1983-89, pres. 1989—), Owosso Circulators (pres. 1987-88), Kiwanis (Chmn. coms. 1980—, pres. 1999-2000, sec. 2001-02). Congregationalist. Office: Shiawassee Dist Libr 502 W Main St Owosso MI 48867-2687

UPTON, ARTHUR CANFIELD, experimental pathologist, educator; b. Ann Arbor, Mich., Feb. 27, 1923; s. Herbert Hawkes and Ellen (Canfield) Upton; m. Elizabeth Bache Perry, Mar. 1, 1946; children: Rebecca A., Melissa P., Bradley C. Grad., Phillips Acad., Andover, Mass., 1941; BA, U. Mich., 1944, MD, 1946. Intern Univ. Hosp., Ann Arbor, 1947, resident, 1948—49; instr. pathology U. Mich. Med. Sch., 1950—51; pathologist Oak Ridge (Tenn.) Nat. Lab., 1951—54, chief pathology-physiology sect., 1954—69; prof. pathology SUNY Med. Sch. at Stony Brook, 1969—77, chmn. dept. pathology, 1969—70, dean Sch. Basic Health Scis., 1970—75; dir. Nat. Cancer Inst., Bethesda, Md., 1977—79; prof., chmn. dept. environ. medicine NYU Med. Sch., N.Y.C., 1980—92, prof. emeritus, 1993—95; clin. prof. radiology U. N.Mex. Sch. Medicine, 1993—95, clin. prof. pathology, 1992—95; clin. prof. environ. and cmty. medicine U. Medicine and Dentistry N.J.-Robert Wood Johnson Med. Sch., 1995—. Attending pathologist Brookhaven Nat. Lab., 1969—77; dir. Inst. Environ. Medicine, Med. Sch., NYU, 1980—92; mem. various coms. nat. and internat. orgns.; lectr. in field. Assoc. editor Cancer Rsch., mem. editl. bd. Internat. Union Against Cancer. Served with U.S. Army, 1943—46. Named nat. lectr., Sigma Xi, 1989—91; recipient Ernest Orlando Lawrence award for atomic field, 1965, Comfort-Crookshank award for cancer rsch., Inst. Medicine, NAS, 1979, Claude M. Fuess award, 1980, Sarah L. Poilley award for pub. health, 1983, CHUMS Physician of Yr. award, 1985, Basic Cell Rsch. in Cytology Lectureship award, 1985, Fred W. Stewart award, 1986, Ramazzini award, 1986, Lovelace Med. Found. award, 1993. Fellow: N.Y. Acad. Sci., Soc. Risk Analysis (Outstanding Achievement award 1997); mem.: Ramazzini Inst. (pres. 1992—), Assn. Univ. Environ. Health Sci. Ctrs. (pres. 1982—90), Internat. Assn. Radiation Rsch., N.Y. State Health Rsch. Coun. (chmn. 1982—90), Soc. Exptl. Biology and Medicine, Sci. Rsch. Soc. Am., Gerontol. Soc., AAAS, Peruvian Oncology Soc. (hon.), Japan Cancer Assn. (hon.), Am. Soc. Exptl. Pathology (pres. 1967—68), Am. Assn. Cancer Rsch. (pres. 1963—64), Internat. Assn. Radiation Rsch. (pres. 1983—87, 1983—87), Radiation Rsch. Soc. (councilor 1963—64, pres. 1965—66), Inst. Medicine of NAS, Internat. Acad. Pathology, Am. Assn. Pathologists and Bacteriologists, Sigma Xi, Nu Sigma Nu, Alpha Omega Alpha, Phi Gamma Delta, Phi Beta Kappa. Achievements include research on pathology of radiation injury and endocrine glands, on cancer, on carcinogenesis, on experimental leukemia on aging. Office: 317 George St Ste 202 New Brunswick NJ 08901-2008 Home: 7743 S Galileo Ln Tucson AZ 85747-9605 E-mail: acupton@eohsi.rutgers.edu.

UPTON, FREDERICK STEPHEN, congressman; b. St. Joseph, Mich., Apr. 23, 1953; s. Stephen E. and Elizabeth Brooks (Vial) U.; m. Amey Richmond Rulon-Miller, Nov. 5, 1983; 2 children. BA in Journalism, U. Mich., 1975. Staff asst. to Congressman David A. Stockman, Washington, 1976-81; legis. asst. Office Mgmt. and Budget, 1981-83, dep. dir. legis. affairs, 1983-84, dir. legis. affairs, 1984-85; mem. U.S. Congress from 6th Mich. dist., 1987—; mem. edn. and the workforce com., energy and commerce com. Field mgr. Stockman for Congress, St. Joseph, 1975; campaign mgr. Globensky for Congress, St. Joseph, 1981. Republican. Office: US House of Reps 2333 Rayburn HOB Washington DC 20515-2206 also: 157 S Kalamazoo Mall Ste 180 Kalamazoo MI 49006*

UPTON, HOWARD B., JR. management writer, lawyer; b. Tahlequah, Okla., May 17, 1922; s. Howard B. and Marjorie (Ross) U.; m. Jean Devereaux, June 14, 1945; children— Pamela, Barbara, Martha, Brian BA, U. Okla., 1943, LLB, 1948. Cert. assn. exec. Dir. indsl. relations Western Petroleum Refiners Assn., Tulsa, 1948-51; exec. v.p. Petroleum Equipment Inst., 1951-87; dir. Telex Corp., 1972-88; mgmt. columnist Inflight Mag. of Southwest Airlines, 1988-93. Lectr. dept. engring. profl. devel. U. Wis., 1988-97, U. Alaska, Fairbanks, 1991-93. Frequent contbr. to Wall St. Jour.; columnist Petroleum Equipment and Tech. Mag. Dir. Tulsa Zoo Friends, Inc., 1993-97. Mem. Am. Soc. Assn. Execs. (bd. dirs. 1964-68, Gold Circle award 1977, 82), Okla. Bar Assn., Mens Forum of Tulsa. Republican. Home: 5133 E 25th Ct Tulsa OK 74114-3749 Office: Upton Comm 5133 E 25th Ct Tulsa OK 74114-3749 E-mail: uptoncomm@mindspring.com.

UPTON, RICHARD THOMAS, artist; b. Hartford, Conn., May 26, 1931; s. Ray Granville and Helen Marie (Colla) U.; 1 son, Richard Thomas, II. BFA, U. Conn., 1960; MFA, Ind. U., 1963. Artist-in-residence Artists for the Environ., Del. Water Gap, 1972, UGA Program Abroad, Cortona, Italy, 1982-85. Exhibitions include E'stampe Contemporaine, Galerie Mansart, Bibliot Nat., France, 1969, 1974, L'estampe aujourd'hui, 1973—78, Sala Internat., Palacio de Bellas Artes, Mexico City, 1969, Sept. Graveures un Sculpteur de Medailles, Mus. Deonon, Chalon-Sur Saone, France, 1973, Brit. Internat. Print Biennale, U.S. sect. touring Eng., 1973, Del. Water Gap, Corcoran Gallery Art, Washington, 1975, Everson Mus. Art, Syracuse, N.Y., 1975, Nat. Collection Prints and Poetry, Libr. of Congress, 1976—77, U. Ga., Palazzo Vignoti, Cortona, Italy, retrospective prints from Atelier 17, Paris, 1977, Okla. Art Ctr., Oklahoma City, 1977, Tweed Mus. Art, Duluth, Minn., 1977, Weatherspoon Art Gallery, Greensboro, N.C., 1977, Chiesadi San Stae, Venice, Italy, 1989, Grey Gallery, N.Y.C., 1990, Everson Mus. of Art, Krannert Mus. Art, 1990—, Paysage Demoralise: Landscape at the End of the Century, Grey Art Gallery and Study Ctr., N.Y.C., 1990—, Tuscany Rediscovered: Richard Upton at Cortona, Everson Mus. Art, Syracuse, 1991, Richard Upton: Italian Landscapes, Krannert Art Mus., Champaign, Ill., 1992, The Italian Landscapes: Richard Upton at Cortona, Mus. Am. Art, New Britain, Conn., 1992, Richard Upton: Ten Years of Italian Landscapes, James Michener Art Mus., Pa., 1994, Phila. Art Alliance, 1994, Condeso/Lawler Gallery, N.Y.C., 1995, Nat. Acad. of Design, 1996, The Language of Landscape, 1997, Sordoni Art Gallery, 1997, The Drawings of Richard Upton: Ireland & Italy, List Art Gallery, Swarthmore, Ben Shahn Art Galleries, 1998, Landscape and Memory: The Paintings and Drawings of Richard Upton, 1982-1999, Houghton Gallery, The Cooper Union for the Advancement of Sci. and Art, N.Y.C., 1999, Represented in permanent collections Zimmerli Art Mus., Nat. Mus. of Am. Art, Smithsonian Instn., Mus. Modern Art, N.Y.C., Victoria and Albert Mus., London, Bibliot Nat., Paris, Montreal Mus. Fine Arts, Rose Art Mus. Brandeis, Mus. Fine Art, Houston, Nat. Acad. Design, N.Y.C., Met. Mus. Art, commns. include, . With USNR, 1950-54. Recipient designer award Interlaken Corp., 1967; subject of monographs: Richard Upton and the Rhetoric of Landscape, Paul Hayes Tucker, U. Mass., U. Wash. Press, 1991, The Tuscan Landscapes of Richard Upton, Stanley C. Grand, Sordoni Art Gallery & Fred Licht, curator, Collezione Peggy Guggenheim, Venice, Wilkes U., 1997, The Drawings of Richard Upton, David Shapiro, Salmagundi, Skidmore Coll., 1997, Landscape & Memory: The Paintings & Drawings of Richard Upton, 1982-98, The Irwin S. Chanin Sch. Architecture of Cooper Union, 1999, A Table of Green Fields: Richard Upton's Corona Landscapes, Richard Howard, 1999, List Gallery, Ben Shahn Galleries; fellow Fulbright Found., 1964, Ballinglen Arts Found., Ireland, 1994; grantee Nat. Endowment for Arts/Artists for Environ., 1972, Richard Florsheim Fund, 1992; elected to Nat. Acad. of Design, 1995. Home: 1 North Ln Saratoga Springs NY 12866-4369

UPTON, THOMAS VERNON, medical educator; b. Antigo, Wis., Apr. 27, 1948; s. Laverne Leo and Mildred Helen (Burmeister) U.; m. Teresa Anne Ugis, June 11, 1977; children: Mark, Paul, Catherine, Marie. BA, Cath. U. Am., MA, 1972, PhD, 1977. Assoc. prof Gannon U., Erie, Pa., 1977-83, 84—. Vis. prof. Cath. U. Am., Washington, 1983-84; cons. in field. Contbr. articles to profl. jours. Basselin Found. scholar, 1968-71; J.K. Ryan Found. fellow, 1974-77, NEH fellow, 1980, 83, 86, 88. Mem. Am. Philos. Assn., Cath. Philos. Assn. (bd. dirs. 1984-86), Soc. Ancien. Republican. Roman Catholic. Avocations: jogging, fishing, reading, exercising, golf. Office: Gannon U PO Box 3098 Erie PA 16508-0098 E-mail: Upton001@Gannon.edu.

URAL, OKTAY, civil engineering educator; BA in Math., Trinity U., 1956; BS in Civil Engring., Tex. A&M U.; MSCE, U. Tenn., 1959; PhD in Civil Engring., N.C. State U., 1964; BSCE, 1958. Asst. prof. U. Mo., Rolla, 1967-69, assoc. prof., 1969-73, prof., 1973, founding dir. Inst. for Interdisciplinary Housing Studies; prof. Fla. Internat. U., Miami, 1973—, founding dir. constrn. div. Coll. Engring. and Applied Scis., dir. Inst. Housing and Bldg. Lectr. various univs.; chmn., dir., 30 nat. and internat. confs.; bd. dirs. Internat. Found. Earth Constrn., Internat. Coun. Bldg. Rsch. Studies and Documentation, Rotterdam, The Netherlands, 1978-80; mem. sci. adv. panel UN Disaster Relief Orgn.; pres. Turkish Housing Authorit, advisor to prime min. Turkish Republic, 1990-92. Author: Matrix Operations and Use of Computers in Structural Engineering, 1971, Finite Element Method: Basic Concepts and Applications, 1973, A Systematic Approach to Basic Utilities in Developing Countries, 1974, Construction of Lower-Cost Housing, 1980; editor-in-chief Internat. Jour. Housing Sci. and Its Applications, 1977—; editor 22 vols. of sci. congress procs.; contbr. articles to profl. jours. Grantee HUD, Washington, Com. on Banking and Currency, U.S. Ho. of Reps., NSF, Fla. Power and Light Co., Fla. Internat. U. Found., Inc., Dept. Edn., State Fla.; recipient Medail de Vermeil for Experts, Govt. France. Fellow ASCE (chmn. structures com. on electronic computation edn. com., urban planning and devel. div. housing com., control group, Harland Bartholomew award); mem. Internat. Assn. Housing Sci. (pres.), Am. Soc. Engring. Edn. (internat. com.), Sigma Xi, Tau Beta Pi, Phi Kappa Phi, Chi Epsilon. Home: 3608 Anderson Rd Coral Gables FL 33134 Office: Fla Internat U Inst Housing & Bldg Dept Civil Engring Miami FL 33199-0001 E-mail: ural@itu.edu.tr.

URAM, GERALD ROBERT, lawyer; b. Newark, July 11, 1941; s. Arthur George and Mildred (Stein) U.; m. Melissa Gordon, May 27, 1995; children: Michael, Alison, Carolyn Gordon Lewis. BA, Dartmouth Coll., 1963; LLB, Yale U., 1967. Bar: N.Y. 1967. Assoc. Paul, Weiss, Rifkind, Wharton & Garrison, N.Y.C., 1967-74; v.p., corp. counsel Prudential Bldg. Maintenance Corp., 1974; ptnr. Davis & Gilbert, 1974—. Lectr. N.Y. Law Sch. Contbr. to profl. publs. Bd. dirs. St. Francis Friends of Poor, Inc., Jerusalem Coll. Tech. Mem. ABA, N.Y. State Bar Assn., Assn. Bar City of N.Y. Office: 1740 Broadway Fl 3 New York NY 10019-4315

URATO, BARBRA CASALE, entrepreneur; b. Newark, Oct. 10, 1941; d. Dominick Anthony and Concetta (Castrichini) Casale; m. John Joseph Urato, June 20, 1965; children: Concetta U. Graves, Gina E., Joseph D. Student, Seton Hall U., 1961-63. File clk. Martin Gelber Esquire, Newark, 1956-58; policy typist Aetna Casualty Ins., 1959-61; sec. to dean Seton Hall U., South Orange, N.J., 1961-63; paralegal sec. Judge Robert A. McKinley, Newark, 1963-65, Joseph Garrubbo, Esquire, Newark, 1965-66; office mgr. Valiant I.M.C., Hackensack, N.J., 1971-73; asst. pers. mgr. Degussa Inc., Teterboro, 1975-78; night mgr. The Ferryboat Restaurant, River Edge, 1976-78; mgr. Fratello's and Ventilini's, Hilton Head, S.C., 1978-80; day mgr. Ramada Inn Restaurant, Paramus, N.J., 1980-81; mgr. Gottlieb's Bakery, Hilton Head, 1982-83; asst. mgr. closing dept. Hilton Head Mortgage Co., 1983-84; owner, mgr. All Cleaning Svc., Hilton Head, 1984—; owner Hilton Head Investigations, 1990-93, Hilton Head Island, 1990-92, Aaction Investigators, 1992-94. Mem. NAFE, Profl. Women of Hilton Head, Assn. for Rsch. and Enlightenment, Rosicrucian Order. Roman Catholic. Avocations: metaphysics, music, gardening, learning.

URBACH, ANDREW HARLEY, pediatrician; b. Staten Island, N.Y., Sept. 18, 1954; s. Mac and Janet Irene (Sitzman) U.; m. Cindy Patrice Horowitz; children: Alexa Jordan, Brook Alexandra. BA in Biology with distinction, U. Rochester, 1975; MD, SUNY, Buffalo, 1979. Diplomate Am. Bd. Pediatrics,

Am. Bd. Pediatric Critical Care; lic. physician, Pa. Resident in pediatrics Children's Hosp. Pitts., 1979-82, chief resident in pediatrics, 1982-83; asst. prof. pediatrics U. Pediatric Diagnostic Referral Svc./Childrens Hosp. Pitts., 1983-89, assoc. prof. pediatrics, 1989-97, prof. pediatrics, 1997—; staff mem. Transitional Infant Care, 1985—, U. Ctr. Pediatrics, 1995—96; dir. clin. svc. Children's Hosp. Pitts., 1998—; asst. prof. pediats. U. Pitts. Sch. Medicine, 1983—89, assoc. prof. pediats., 1989—97, prof. pediats., 1997—. Human rights com. mem. Childrens Hosp. Pitts., 1982-83, ICU com. mem., 1982-83, libr. com. mem., 1982-83, intern selection com., 1982-83, pediatric continuity clinic preceptor, 1983—, art com. mem., 1987—, satellite com. mem., 1988, literacy com. mem., 1990, computer com. mem., 1992-93; mem. subboard to establish bds. in pediatric critical care medicine Am. Bd. Pediatrics, 1985-89; instr. pediatric history and physical diagnosis course U. Pitts., 1983—, instr. patient-physician relationship course, 1992—. instr. patient interviewing course, 1993; cons. Pitts. Press, Pitts. Post Gazette, KDKA, WTAE, WPXI, WDVQ, CBS, CNN, AP, UPI, USA Today, Life mag., Reuters News Svc., Washington Post, Picture Weekly, Parenting and Parents Mag. on AIDS, Liver Transplantation, Kawasaki Disease and Choosing a Pediatrician, 1983—, cons. AIDS policy Transitional Infant Care Pitts., 1988, Cath. Charities Diocese Pitts., Inc. 1987; mem. accreditation coun. Grad. Med. Edn., 1989; reviewer Pediatric Critical Care Medicine Program Accreditation, 1989; cons. Am. Internat. Health Alliance, 1993; presenter and lectr. in field. Reviewer Pediatrics, 1987; contbr. articles to profl. jours. Vol. KDKA Children's Hosp. Pitts. Telethon, 1982—; mem. steering com. March of Dimes Fusical, 1992. N.Y. State Regents scholar, 1971; Rsch. grantee Am. Found. for AIDS Rsch., 1989-91; recipient Pediatric Radiology award, 1983; named Tchr. of Yr. Childrens Hosp. Pitts., 1987. Fellow Am. Acad. Pediatrics; mem. Am. Bd. Pediatrics (question writer pediatric critical care sub-bd. 1990—, program for renewal cert. in pediatrics 1992—), Pa. Med. Soc. (adv. subcom. on AIDS 1991—), Pitts. Pediatric Soc. Avocations: squash, running, art, architecture. Home: 130 W Lyndhurst Dr Pittsburgh PA 15206-4541 Office: Childrens Hosp Pittsburgh 1 Children's Pl 3705 5th Ave Pittsburgh PA 15213-2524

URBACH, FREDERICK, physician, educator; b. Vienna, Austria, Sept. 6, 1922; s. Erich and Josepha (Kronstein) U.; m. Nancy Ann Phillips, Dec. 20, 1952; children: Erich J., Gregory M., Andrew D. AB cum laude, U. Pa., 1943; MD, Jefferson Med. Coll., 1946; MD (hon.), U. Göttingen, Fed. Republic Germany, 1987. Diplomate: Am. Bd. Dermatology. Intern Jefferson Hosp., 1946-47; fellow in dermatology U. Pa. Hosp., 1949-52; fellow pediatric dermatology Children's Hosp., Phila., 1950-52; asst. vis. physician Phila. Gen. Hosp., Skin and Cancer Hosp., U. Pa. Hosp., 1952-54; assoc. chief cancer research (dermatology) Roswell Park Meml. Inst., Buffalo, 1954-55, chief cancer research (dermatology), 1955-58; asst. med. dir. Skin and Cancer Hosp. Phila., 1958-67, med. dir., 1967-88; research prof. physiology U. Buffalo Grad. Sch., 1955-58; assoc. prof. dermatology Temple U. Sch. Medicine, 1958-60, prof. research dermatology, 1960-67, chmn. dept. dermatology, 1967-88; dir. Ctr. for Photobiology, 1977-89, prof. dermatology emeritus, 1989—; dep. dir. Health Rsch. Inc., Buffalo, 1954-58. Mem. U.S. nat. com. photo-biology Nat. Acad. Sci., 1973-80 Author: The Biology of Cutaneous Cancer, 1963, The Biologic Effects of Ultraviolet Radiation, 1969, (with Parrish, Anderson and Pitts) UVA, 1978; (with Gange) Biologic Effects of UVA Radiation, 1985, Responses to UVA Radiation, 1992; contbr. articles to profl. jours. Served with AUS, 1943-46; with USAAF, 1947-49. Recipient Ritter Meml. medal German Dermatology Soc., 1980 Fellow AAAS, N.Y. Acad. Sci.; mem. AMA, ACP, FACP, Am. Soc. Photobiology (councilor 1973-76, pres. 1977), Am. Assn. Cancer Rsch. Soc. Exptl. Biology and Medicine, Internat. Assn. Photobiology (v.p. 1976-79, pres. 1980-84, Finsen medal 1992); hon. mem. Danish Soc. Dermatology, Swedish Soc. Dermatology (Hellerstoöm medal 1977), Polish Soc. Dermatology, Austrian Soc. Dermatology, German Soc. Dermatology, Philippine Soc. Dermatology. Achievements include research on epidemiology of cancer, photobiology, phototherapy. Home: 438 Clairemont Rd Villanova PA 19085-1706 E-mail: drfredu@aol.com.

URBAITIS, ELENA, artist; b. Kaunas, Lithuania, June 4, 1922; came to U.S., 1950; d. Ignas and Elena (Brazionyte) U. Student, Akademie der Bildenden Künste, Munich, 1946-48; Diploma in Fine Arts, Ecole des Arts et Metiers, Freiburg, Germany, 1950; BA in Fine Arts, Montevallo U., 1951; MA, Tchrs. Coll., Columbia U., 1960. One-woman show includes Space Flight/stainless steel sculpture, Press Ctr., Vilnius, Lithuania, 1992, Reflectorizes stainless steel sculpture, Vilnius, Lithuania, 1995, Libr. Tech., Vilnius, 1996, others; groups shows include Outdoor Sculpture Now, Islip Art Mus., East Islip N.Y., 1989, Lights: Recent Issues in Illuminating Sculpture, Morris Mus. of Arts and Sci., Morristown, N.J., 1982, 83, Works on Paper -- Women Artists, The Bklyn. Mus., N.Y., 1976, Elena Urbaitis Kaunas State Mus. Art, Kaunas, Lithuania, 2000, numerous others; author: Elena Urbaitis Works on Paper, 2000; contbr. articles/interviews to profl. jours. French Ministry Cultural Affairs Arts fellow Paris, 1950; recipient award of Excellence L.I. Artists League, Heckscher Mus., L.I., N.Y., 1975, Gold medal Lithuanian Cultural Ctr., N.Y.C., 1977, 1st prize Lituanian-Am. Cultural Coun., Chgo., 1993. Mem. Am. Soc. Contemporary Artists (award in sculpture 1988), Artists Equity. Home: 2292 Willow St Wantagh NY 11793-4227

URBAN, CARRIE, computer specialist; b. Summit, N.J., Nov. 30, 1969; BS in Fin., U. Colo., Colorado Springs, 1994, MBA in Info. Systems, 1996; grad. child psychology, Stratford Career Inst., Washington, 1999, grad. sewing and dressmaking, 2000. Sys. operator Celestial Light BBS, Colorado Springs, 1984-98, Country Estate BBS, Casa Grande, Ariz., 1999; freelance computer cons., 1998—. Intern Interactive Mgmt. Systems, Colorado Springs, 1997; tech. support profl. Gateway Computers, Colorado Springs, 1998; computer tutor Judith Crawford, Colorado Springs, 1998-99; computer troubleshooter Summit Home Health Care, Colorado Springs, 1999, Millie Forbush, Casa Grande, 2000. Writer newsletter column Transgender Connection, 1996-97, Transgender Jour., 1998-99; writer Ground Zero, Colorado Springs, 1996-97. Mem. adv. coun. Equality Colo., Colorado Springs, 1998-99. Mem. Nat. Rifle Assn. (cert. personal protection course), Christian Broadcasting Network, Concerned Women of Am., Humane Soc. U.S. Republican. Baptist. Avocations: reading, bowling, singing, writing. Home: 1728 E Catalina Ave Casa Grande AZ 85222-5716 E-mail: carrieu@cybertrails.com.

URBAN, CATHLEEN ANDREA, graphic designer; b. Elizabeth, N.J., June 7, 1947; d. Emil Martin and Susan (Rahoche) Cupec; m. Walter Robert Urban, Nov. 5, 1966; children: Karen Louise, Kimberly Ann. Student, Rutgers U., 1965-66, 91-94; AS in Bus. Adminstrn., AAS in Computer Programming, Raritan Valley C.C., North Branch, N.J., 1990. Office mgr. K-Mart Corp., Somerville, N.J., 1987-90; software developer Bellcore, Piscataway, 1990-93, sys. tech. support cons., 1993-94, software developer, 1994-96, software quality assurance tester, 1996-97, project mgr., 1997—; graphic designer, owner CathiCards, Inc., Neshanic Station, N.J., 1995—. Leader Somerset County 4-H Program, Bridgewater, 1978-87. Mem. NAFE, AAUW, Nat. Space Soc., Internat. Platform Assn., Project Mgmt. Inst., Internat. Guild Candle Artisans, Golden Key Honor Soc., Mensa, Phi Theta Kappa. Roman Catholic. Avocations: science fiction, reading, dog shows, candle making. Office: Bell Comm Rsch 444 Hoes Ln Piscataway NJ 08854-4104 Home: 570 Amwell Rd Hillsborough NJ 08844-3404

URBAN, DONALD WAYNE, lawyer; b. Belleville, Ill., Oct. 9, 1953; s. Andrew Anthony and Eileen Marie (Tibbitt) U.; m. Mary Beth Evans, June 9, 1979 (div. Oct. 1994); m. Georgianna Dowling, Feb. 2, 1995; 1 child, Andrew Jared. BA, So. Ill. U., 1976; JD, Washington U., 1979. Assoc. Sprague & Sprague, Belleville, 1979-96; ptnr. Sprague & Urban, 1996—. Author, lectr. Ill. Inst. for CLE, Springfield. Author: Blasting & Subsidence Illinois Institute for Continuing Legal Education Handbook, 1983, vol. 2, 1986, vol. 3, 1989. Pres. Looking Glass Playhouse, Lebanon, Ill., 1988-90, 95-97, 99-01; spokesman St. Clair County Bicentennial, Belleville, 1989. Mem. Gamma Theta Upsilon. Democrat. Avocation: community theatre. Home: 815 Belleville St Lebanon IL 62254-1312 Office: Sprague & Urban 26 E Washington St Belleville IL 62220-2101

URBAN, GARY ROSS, computer and information processing consultant; b. Corpus Christi, Tex., May 17, 1947; s. Ross. O. and Nell (Hall) U.; m. Jeanette Corbitt, Dec. 14, 1968 (div. 1979); children: Kimberly, Bryan, Sheryl. Pvt. practice computer and info. processing cons. GRU Enterprises, Houston, 1972—. Recipient Achievement cert. U.S. Army, 1971. Mem. Mensa. Office: GRU Enterprises PO Box 4333 Thousand Oaks CA 91359-1333

URBAN, HENRY ZELLER, newspaperman; b. Buffalo, July 11, 1920; s. George Pennock and Florence Lenhard (Zeller) U.; m. Ruth deMoss Wickwire, Apr. 28, 1948; children: Ruth Robinson Urban Smith, Florence de Moss Urban Hunn, Henry Zeller, Ward Wickwire. Grad., Hotchkiss Sch., 1939; BS, Yale U., 1943. Treas. George Urban Milling Co., 1946-53; with Buffalo Eve. News, 1953—, asst. bus. mgr., 1957-62, bus. mgr., 1962-71, treas., dir., 1971-74, pres., pub., 1974-83. Dir. G. F. Zellers Sons, Inc., 1948-53 Bd. dirs. Travelers Aid Soc., 1953-59, Buffalo Fine Arts Acad., 1960-63, 73-76, 82-85, 86-89, YMCA, 1955-68; trustee Elmwood-Franklin Sch., 1967-70; trustee Canisius Coll., 1977-83, bd. regents, 1972-78; adv. bd. Medaille Coll., 1968-83; chmn. parents council Hamilton Coll., 1977. Served to lt. USNR, 1942-46. Mem. Buffalo C. of C., N.Y. State Pubs. Assn. (dir. 1970-73, 76-79) Clubs: Mid-day (Buffalo), Tennis and Squash (Buffalo), Buffalo (Buffalo), Buffalo Country (Buffalo), Saturn (Buffalo), Pack (Buffalo); Sankaty Head (Nantucket); Nantucket Yacht. Home: 57 Tudor Pl Buffalo NY 14222-1615 Office: 1 News Plz Buffalo NY 14203-2930

URBAN, JOSEPH JAROSLAV, engineer, consultant; b. Chocen, Czechoslovakia, Mar. 11, 1922; came to U.S., 1955; s. Josef and Ludmila (Moravcova) U.; children: H.U. Heinicke, R. Bruce. Diploma in engring., U. Prague, Czechoslovakia, 1948; postgrad., U. Toronto, 1952-55. Registered profl. engr. Mgr. Urban Mfg., Chocen, 1942-48; prof. Masaryk U., Nuernberg, Fed. Republic Germany, 1950; designer C.A. Meadows Cons. Engrs., Toronto, 1952-55, Rondo Devel. Corp., Stamford, Conn., 1955-58; designer, chief engr., v.p. Huck Co. Inc. Engrs., Montvale, N.J., 1958-72, also bd. dirs.; pvt. practice cons. engr. Pleasantville, N.Y., 1972—. Exec. cons. Crown Cork and Seal Co. Inc., Phila., 1972=94. Designer various types of machines for U.S. govt. and U.S. industries-printing presses, book binding and can mfg. equipment, pinsetter, computers, glass machines; writer tech. books; patentee in field. Recipient World War II decoration Field Marshall Alexander, 1945. Mem. Acad. Art and Sci., Moose, Sir Knight Columbus. Roman Catholic. Avocations: protection of wildlife, naturalist, painting, classical music, fine art collector. Home and Office: 71 Bacon Hill Rd Pleasantville NY 10570-3501

URBAN, MAREK W. chemistry and polymers educator; b. Oct. 3, 1953; came to U.S., 1979; s. Ludwig and Wieslawa (Domon) U.; m. Kasia Bernecka, Apr. 21, 1979; 1 child, Anna. MS in Phys. Inorganic Chemistry, Marquette U., 1981; PhD in Phys. Polymer Chemistry, Mich. Technol. U., 1984. Tchg. rsch. asst. Marquette U. Milw./Mich. Technol. U., Houston, 1979-84; rsch. assoc. dept. macromolecular sci. Case Western Res. U., Cleve., 1984-86; asst. prof. polymers and coatings N.D. State U., Fargo, 1986-89, assoc. prof., 1989-94, prof., 1994-99, chmn. dept., 1994-99; prof. polymer sci. U. So. Miss., Hattiesburg, 1999—. Dir. NSF Industry/Univ. Rsch. Ctr., 1995—; lectr., cons., expert witness in field. Author: Vibrational Spectroscopy of Molecules and Macromolecules on Surfaces, 1993, ATR Spectroscopy of Polymers, 1996, Laboratory Handbook of Organic Chemistry. Recipient Faculty award 3M Co., 1986-91, William Megger award Fedn. of Analytical Chemistry and Spectroscopy Socs., 1990, Alcoa Rsch. Found. award, 1996, award Roon Found., 1999, Disting. Alumni award Mich. Technol. U., 1999. Mem. AAAS, Am. Chem. Soc. (book editor, polymer chemistry and polymeric materials, sci. and engring. divns.), Am. Phys. Soc., So. Soc. for Coatings Tech., Soc. for Applied Spectroscopy (chmn. Minn. chpt. 1988-89, tech. focus spkr. 1999, recipient Merit Achievement award 2000). Office: U So Miss Sch Polymers and High Performance Materials PO Box 10076 Hattiesburg MS 39406 E-mail: marek.urban@usm.edu.

URBAN, PATRICIA A. former elementary school educator; b. Chgo., Oct. 15, 1932; d. Clifford and Caroline (Viegi) Brocken; m. Francis C. Urban, Oct. 20, 1956; children: Jim, David, Anthony, Mary Joan, Barbara, Margaret, Judy, Sharon, Jennifer. BA, Rosary Coll., River Forest, Ill., 1954; MS in Edn., Chgo. State U., 1979; MEd, Loyola U., Chgo., 1986. Cert. tchr., reading tchr., Ill. Tchr. St. Joseph Ch. Sch., Summit, Ill., 1954-56; profl. reading tutor Loyola U., 1987-90; tchr. social studies and reading Dist. 104 Schs., Summit, 1974-94; ret., 1994. Named. Dist. 104 Tchr. of Yr., 1987. Home: 1019 Walter St Lemont IL 60439-3920

URBAN, PETER, priest, social worker; b. Wallace, Kans., Aug. 31, 1929; s. Adam Urban and Rosa Bittel. Degree in theology, St. Thomas Sem., Denver, 1958. Social worker St. Alfonso Mission, Juarez, Mexico, 1990—. Guitar tchr.; tchr. ESL, Greeley, Colo., 1960—90. Avocations: singing, guitar, bicycling. Home: Montebello Cath Parish Ch Ascension 110 W Simpson St Lafayette CO 80026

URBAN, PETER ANTHONY, consulting company executive; b. Prague, Czechoslavakia, Sept. 29, 1934; arrived in Can. 1968; came to U.S. 1989; s. Frantisek and Jirina (Vopalkova) U.; m. Jana Vojtechova, June 9, 1962; children: Andrea G., Michelle H. MS in Engring. and Econs., Prague U., 1959. Engring. researcher Skoda A.S., Pilsen, Czechoslovakia, 1959-64; project mgr. Heavy Engring. Corp., Ranchi, India, 1964-68; mktg. mgr. Westinghouse Inc., Pitts. and Hamilton, Ont., 1968-73; ops. mgr. Hendrickson Inc., Chgo., 1973-76; gen. mgr., v.p. McInnis Equipment Ltd., Windsor, Ont., 1976-82; pres. Camex Inc., Hamilton, 1982-89; sr. indsl. splst. World Bank Group, Washington, 1989-97. Editor: (mag.) Automation Products & Technology, 1982; contbr. numerous articles to profl. jours. Pres. CIM/McMaster U., Hamilton, Ont., 1984-86; dir. Can. Inst. Internat. Affairs, Toronto, 1982-89; vice chmn. adv. bd. Mohawk Coll., Hamilton, 1982-89. Mem. Assn. Profl. Engrs. Ont., Soc. Mfg. Engrs., Acad. Sci./Quality (hon., life). Avocations: art collecting, skiing, reading. Office: IFC/ World Bank Group 2121 Pennsylvania Ave NW Washington DC 20433-0001

URBANAS, ALBAN WILLIAM, estate planner; b. Balt., Jan. 5, 1952; s. William Peter and Anna Mary (Danaitis) U.; m. Elizabeth Iza Davis, Nov. 18, 1995. BA, U. Paris-Sorbonne, 1976, PhD, 1982; MBA, George Mason U., 1994. Instr. ESL The Paris-Am. Acad., Paris, 1977-78; coord. French & English programs Marubeni-France, 1978-81; adj. asst. prof. English U. Paris, 1978-81; coord. French and English programs CACI Lang. Ctr., Arlington, Va., 1983-85; adj. asst. prof. philosophy Georgetown U., Washington, 1983-84; vis. asst. prof. French George Washington U., 1985, adj. asst. prof. philosophy, 1985-86; asst. prof. philosophy & French Franklin Coll., Lugano, Switzerland, 1986-89; vis. asst. prof. philosophy Colby Coll., Waterville, Maine, 1989-90; vis. asst. prof. French NYU, Paris, 1990; assoc. prof. philosophy and French Wesley Coll., Dover, Del., 1990-97; vis. assoc. prof. philosophy Washington Coll., Chestertown, Md., 1997-98; estate planner, 1998—. Moderator Aspen Inst., 1997—. Author: La notion d'accident chez Aristote, 1988; contbr. articles to profl. jours. Bd. dirs. Dover Arts Coun., 1993-96, Del. Ballet, 1994-95; bd. dirs., v.p. Alliance Française of Wilmington, Del., 1993-96. Recipient Lithuanian Lang. Inst. Title grant USSR Ministry Culture, 1986; NEH grantee U. Ill., 1991; French Cultural Svcs. scholar, Strasbourg, 1992; Jesse Ball duPont Found. fellow, 1992, 96. Mem. Am. Philos. Assn., Am. Mgmt. Assn., Internat. Assn. Mgmt., Balt. Coun. Fgn. Rels. Avocations: marathon running, investment theory, international travel, hiking, skiing. Office: Sagemark Cons Inc 2070 Chain Bridge Rd Ste 300 Vienna VA 22182-2596

URBANETTI, JOHN SUTHERLAND, internist, consultant; b. Mineola, N.Y., Aug. 14, 1943; s. Anthony Joseph and Mildred S. U.; children: Andrew, Alexis. AB, Johns Hopkins U., 1964, MD, 1967. Diplomate Am. Bd. Internal Medicine and Pulmonary Diseases. Internal medicine intern Johns Hopkins Hosp., Balt., 1967-68, internal medicine resident, 1968-69; fellow in pulmonary cardiology McGill U., Montreal, Can., 1971-74; asst. prof. medicine and dir. pulmonary lab. Tufts New Eng. Med. Ctr. Hosp., Boston, 1974-80; asst. prof. clin. medicine and pulmonary diseases Yale U., New Haven, 1980—. Cons. toxic inhalation US Surgeon Gen., U.S. Army, USN, USAF, 1974—; cons. biochem. terrorism Dept. of Def., Dept. Justice, 1974—, Dept. State, 1999—. Author: Carbon Monoxide Poisoning, 1980, Pulmonary Management of Surgical Patients, 1982, Battlefield Chemical Inhalation, 1988, Chemical and Biological Warfare, 1997; contbr. articles to profl. jours. Capt. USAF, 1969-71. Recipient Commdr's award for pub. svc. U.S. Army, 1990. Fellow Royal Coll. Physicians and Surgeons (Can.), Am. Coll. Physicians, Am. Coll. Chest Physicians; mem. Am. Thoracic Soc., Aerospace Medicine Soc. Avocation: swimming. Office: Southeastern Pulmonary Assocs 155 Montauk Ave New London CT 06320-4842

URBANI, LORI A. registrar; b. McKees Rocks, Pa., Jan. 9, 1969; d. Paul Joseph Jr. and Mary Ann Urbani. BA, Duquesne U., 1990, MA, 1997. Adminstrv. asst. Duquesne U., Pitts., 1993-94, asst. registrar, 1994-2000; registrar Ga. Southwestern State U., Americus, 2000—. Mem. NAIA, AAC-RAO. Office: Ga Southwestern State Univ 800 Wheatley St Americus GA 31709 E-mail: lurbani@canes.gsw.edu.

URBANI, ROBERT S. music educator; b. Uniontown, Pa., Sept. 19, 1950; s. Paul J. and Mary A. Urbani; m. Kathy L. Kennedy, Oct. 22, 1977; children: Heather, Jennifer, Lindsay. BA, Salem Coll., 1975; MA, Ind. U., 1979. Cert. tchr. Ind. Band dir. Peru (Ind.) HS, 1974—85; high band/choir dir. Peru Jr. High, 1985—. Staff mem. Gt. Lakes Music Camps, Indpls., 1992—. Orch. dir. Ole Olson Meml. Theater, Peru, 1985—2000, Logansport (Ind.) Civic Players, 1990—94, Wabash (Ind.) City Players, 1997—2002; guest dir., soloist Culver (Ind.) Mil. Summer Sch., 1997; choir dir. First Presbyn. Ch., Peru, 1985—2002. Avocations: arranging, swimming, weekend ensembles, computer software, pianics. Office: Peru Junior HS 30 E Daniel St Peru IN 46970 Office Fax: 765-473-4007. E-mail: burbani@peru.k12.in.us.

URBANIK, THOMAS, II, research civil engineer; b. Oceanside, N.Y., Feb. 15, 1946; s. John George and Helen Rita (Waterhouse) U.; m. Cynthia Ellen Myers, Feb. 23, 1948; children: Michael T., Steven J. BS, N.Y. State Coll. Forestry, 1968; BSCE, Syracuse U., 1969; MSCE, Purdue U., 1971; PhD, Tex. A&M U., 1982. Registered profl. engr., Mich., Tex., Tenn. Traffic engr. City of Ann Arbor (Mich.), 1971-76; rsch. engr. Tex. A&M U., College Station, 1977-2001; prof., Goodrich chair of excellence in transp. U. Tenn., Knoxville, 2001—. Cons. Battelle Pacific N.W. Labs., Richland, Wash., 1987—, Fed. Hwy. Adminstrn., Washington, Kittelson and Assocs., Portland, Oreg., Entergy, Buchanan, NY; mem. com. on advanced traffic mgmt. sys. Intelligent Transp. Soc. Am. Mem. ASCE, Inst. Transp. Engrs., Transp. Rsch. Bd. (assoc.). Republican. Lutheran. E-mail: turbanik@utk.edu.

URBANOWSKI, FRANK, publishing company executive; b. Balt., Mar. 5, 1936; s. Frank and Tofilla (Jakubik) U.; m. Julia Blocksma; children: Alexandra, Tasha. BS in Ceramic Engring., Va. Poly. Inst.; postgrad., Columbia U. Rep. Ronald Press, 1960-61; editor coll. dept. Macmillan Co., 1961-66; editorial dir. Glencoe Press, 1966-68, v.p., 1968-72, pub., 1972-73; dir. market devel. Ednl. Testing Service, 1973-75; dir. Mass. Inst. Tech. Press, Cambridge, 1975—. Chmn. exec. coun. Profl. Scholarly Publs. divsn., 1979-81; bd. dirs. Cambridge Insight Meditation Ctr., 1985—; bd. dirs. Wisdom Press, U. Calif. Press. Mem. Am. Assn. Pubs. (dir. 1979-81), Assn. Am. Univ. Press (dir. 1979-81, pres. 1990-91), Cambridge Boat Club. Home: 915 Snake Mountain Rd Middlebury VT 05753-9220 also: 129 Franklin St Cambridge MA 02139-4160 Office: MIT Press 5 Cambridge Ctr Cambridge MA 02142-1407 E-mail: furb@mit.edu.

URBANOWSKI, JOHN RICHARD, lighting systems company official; b. Jamaica, N.Y., May 31, 1947; s. John Casimir and Alfreda (Dabrowski) U.; m. Linda Holmes, Dec. 17, 1967 (div. June 1973); 1 child, Richard. BA, U. South Fla., 1968. Cert. lighting profl. Nat. Coun. Qualifications for Lighting Professions. Ptnr. Freeman Assocs., Ft. Lauderdale, Fla., 1972-76; sales engr. Holophane Lighting Co., Portland, Oreg., 1977—. Author computer program Microlux, 1984. With USN, 1969-72. Mem. Illuminating Engring. Soc. (bd. dirs. 1981-86, 96-98, pres. 1983-84, Cert. Tech. Knowledge 1996, lighting cert. 1998), Holophane Lighting Co. Dir.'s Club, Founder's Club. Unitarian Universalist. Avocations: writing, aviation. Office: Holophane Lighting Co 3015 NE Couch St Portland OR 97232 E-mail: jurbanowski@attbi.com.

URBANSKI, MARIUSZ, finance educator; b. Lubichowo, Gdansk, Poland, Nov. 17, 1958; s. Henryk Urbanski and Anna Urbanska; m. Irena Czulado; children: Joanna, Dariusz. Habilitation, Polish Acad. of Sci., Warsaw, Poland, 1991. Assoc. prof. U. No. Tex., Denton, Tex., 1994—99, prof., 1999—. Rsch. vis. prof. SFB 170, Goettingen, Niedersachsen, Germany, 1990—91. Office: Univ of No Tex PO Box 311430 Denton TX 76203-1430

URBERO, BRUNO, information scientist; b. Maisons-Alfort, France, Sept. 4, 1965; s. Marc Urbero and Annette Chene; life partner: Laurence Vidal; 1 child, Jean. PhD, U. Orsay, 1993. Editl. asst. Genome Database, Balt., 1994-95; head informatics Orphanet/INSERM, Villejuif, France, 1996—. Office: Orphanet/INSERM 102 rue Didot Paris 75014 France

URBIK, JEROME ANTHONY, financial consultant; b. Chgo., Oct. 30, 1929; s. Anthony Frank and Sophie Elizabeth Urbik; m. Barbara Jean Chamernik, Sept. 1956; children: Laura M. Kern, Michael A., Anthony J., Mary L. King, John T., Maria M. BA in Philosophy, St. Mary's Coll., Techny, Ill., 1953; CLU degree, Am. Coll., 1970, ChFC degree, 1979. Chartered fin. cons. Field underwriter MONY Fin. Svcs., Chgo., 1955-59; merchandising specialist Mut. of N.Y., N.Y.C., 1959; pvt. practice brokerage cons. Northfield, Ill., 1960-64; CEO Hinsdale (Ill.) Assocs. Fin. Svcs. Corp., 1964-90, CEO emeritus, 1990—. V.p. Interstate Coll. Personology, San Diego, 1982-87; pres. Gen. Agts. Mgrs. Conf., 1967-68. Mem. publ. com. Crisis mag., Washington, 1989—; contbr. articles on industry to profl. jours.; mem. editl. bd. Leaders mag., 1981-90. Mem. adv. coun. Congressman Henry Hyde, Nat. Rep. Com., Washington; mem. Small Bus. Devel. Ctr. exec. bd. advisors Lewis U., Lockport, Ill., 1987-90; exec. coord. Legatus of Chgo., 1990-91 (Cath. CEO); bd. dirs. United Rep. Fund, 1987-92; bd. advisors Am. Life League, Washington, 1990-98, Cath. Citizens Ill., 1997—; bd. dirs. Nat. Rep. Coalition for Life. Named Small Bus. Acct. of Yr. for State of Ill. SBA, 1987. Mem. Am. Soc. CLUs, Chgo. Orchestral Assn., Chgo. Lyric Opera, Latin Liturgy Assn. (v.p. Chgo. chpt. 1997—). Roman Catholic. Avocations: reading, writing, power boating, classical music. Home: 474 South St Elmhurst IL 60126-4120 Office: Hinsdale Assoc Fin Svc Corp 15 Spinning Wheel Rd Ste 414 Hinsdale IL 60521-2987 E-mail: jurbik@ameritech.net.

URBINA, FEBE GLORIA, elementary school principal; b. Nuevo Laredo, Tamaulipas, Mexico, Aug. 25, 1942; came to U.S., 1947; d. Manuel Urbina and Irene Salce de Urbina. BA, Howard Payne Coll., 1965; MEd, U. Houston, 1975. Cert. tchr., adminstr., biling. educator, spcl. edn., mid mgmt., ednl. diagnostician, Tex. Cashier Weingarten Grocery, Houston, 1960-64; social worker Neighborhood Ctrs. Assn., 1965-68; elem. sch. tchr. Houston Ind. Sch. Dist., 1968-70, curriculum coord., 1970-2000, prin., 1973—. Adj. instr. Adult Edn. Houston C.C., 1965-71; mem. Legal United L.Am. Citizens Ednl. Adv. Bd., Houston, 1975-76; adj. English tchr. Harris County C.C., Pasadena, Tex., 1986-88; mem. supt.'s adv. bd. Houston Ind. Sch. Dist., 1990-97; presenter Conv. of Excellence, 1988, 90, 95, 98, Conv. Sch. External Funds, 1998, Lightspan Conv., 1998. Co-author: (book) Strategies for Bilingual/ESL Teachers, 1968. Sunday Sch. Tchr. Southmain Bapt. Ch., Houston, 1970-76; ch. pianist Heights Bapt. Temple, Houston, 1976-86; mem. Meadowbrook Civic Club, Houston, 1987-98. Recipient Mary Hill Davis award Home Mission Bd., Atlanta, 1961; named Hispanic Principal of Yr., Houston Ind. Sch. Dist. 1975, Principal of Yr. 1994. Mem. ASCD, Houston Assn. for Sch. Adminstrs. Avocations: travel, music, mission trips, translating, reading. Home: 899 Old Genoa Red Bluff Rd Houston TX 77034-4010 Office: Bonner Elem Sch 8100 Elrod St Houston TX 77017-5216

URBINA, MANUEL, II, legal research historian, history educator; b. Rodriguez, Nuevo Leon, Mex., Sept. 23, 1939; came to U.S., 1947; s. Manuel and Irene (Salce) de Urbina. BA, Howard Payne Coll., 1962; postgrad., Nat. Autonoma U. Mex., Mexico City, 1963-64; MA, U. Tex., 1967, PhD, 1976; postgrad., Cambridge (Eng.) U., 1982; JD, U. Houston, 1983. Prof. Latin Am. history Coll. of the Mainland, Texas City, 1967—. Founder, curator Urbina Mus. History of Mex., Houston, 1990—; chmn., legal counsel Urbina Found., Houston, 1985—; chmn., CEO Urbina Pub. Co. Inc., Houston and Mexico City, 1985—. Author: (TV Series) The Mexican Side of the Texas Revolution, 1985, The Mexican Side of the Mexican War, 1985, The Battle of San Jacinto-A Mexican Viewpoint, 1985, The Battle of the Alamo-A Mexican Viewpoint, 1986, Relations Between the United States and Mexico, 1987, General Emiliano Zapata in North American Historiography, 1989, The Mexican War in International Law, 1995, The Mexican War in United States Constitutional Law, 1996, Efectos De La Independencia De Texas Sobre El

Gobierno, La Política, Y La Sociedad De México, 1996, Bilingual Dollars of the Bank of Texas (1835) in the Context of the Separation of Texas From Mexico, 1998, General Pancho Villa in International Law, 1999; editor, interviewer history videos, oral history interviews with participants in the Mexican Revolution; contbr. articles to newspapers and mags. including Houston Chronicle, Mexico City Novedades, San Antonio Light, Boletin Del Archivo General Del Estado de Nuevo León, Boletin de la Sociedad Numismatica de Mexico. Founder Cinco de Mayo Assn., Galveston County, Tex., 1976; founder, faculty sponsor Mex. Am. Student Assn., Coll. of Mainlan, 1974—. Named Hispanic of Yr. Galveston County League of United Latin Am. Citizens, 1982; NEH grantee, 1971-72; U.S. Dept. State scholar diplomat, 1979. Mem. League of United Latin Am. Citizens, Tex. State Hist. Assn., Howard Payne U. Alumni Assn., U. Houston Law Alumni Assn., U. Tex. Alumni Assn., Interam. C. of C., Soc. Numismatica Mex. Democrat. Baptist. Avocations: reading, research, travel, trumpet playing, volunteer work. Home: 889 Old Genoa Red Bluff Rd Houston TX 77034-4010

URBINA, SUSANA PATRICIA, psychology educator, consultant; came to U.S., 1962; d. Fernando Alfredo and PatriciaU. BA magna cum laude, Mary Manse Coll., Toledo, 1966; MA, Fordham U., 1968, PhD, 1972. Lic psychologist, Fla. Asst. prof. psychology Marywood Coll., Scranton, Pa., 1972-73, Mary Manse Coll., Toledo, 1973-75; dir. YWCA Women's Ctr., 1975; lectr. in psychology U. Md. European Divsn., Germany, 1975-76; adviser, asst. prof. psychology U. North Fla., Jacksonville, 1976-80, assoc. prof., 1980-98, prof., 1998—. Field supr. Psychol. Corp., N.Y.C., 1979; pvt. practice psychol. assessment, 1978-92. Author books, reports and jour. articles in field. Bd. dirs. Hubbard House, Jacksonville, 1983-86. Mem. Am. Psychol. Assn. (vol. abstractor 1977-81, com. profl. practice and standards 1992-94, chair 1994, com. psychol. tests and assessment 1998-2000, chair 1999), Southeastern Psychol. Assn. Soc. for Personality Assessment, Jacksonville Women's Network, Sigma Xi, Kappa Gamma Pi. Democrat. Avocations: bicycling, swimming, reading, movies. Office: U North Fla Dept Psychology 4567 Saint Johns Bluff Rd S Jacksonville FL 32224-2646

URBOM, WARREN KEITH, federal judge; b. Atlanta, Dec. 17, 1925; s. Clarence Andrew and Anna Myrl (Irelan) U.; m. Joyce Marie Crawford, Aug. 19, 1951; children: Kim Marie, Randall Crawford, Allison Lee, Joy Renee. AB with highest distinction, Nebr. Wesleyan U., 1950, LLD (hon.), 1984; JD with distinction, U. Mich., 1953. Bar: Nebr. 1953. Mem. firm Baylor, Evnen, Baylor, Urbom, & Curtiss, Lincoln, Nebr., 1953-70; judge U.S. Dist. Ct. Nebr., 1970—; chief judge U.S. Dist. Ct. Dist. Nebr., 1972-86, sr. judge, 1991—. Mem. com. on practice and procedure Nebr. Supreme Ct., 1965-95; mem. subcom. on fed. jurisdiction Jud. Conf. U.S., 1975-83; adj. instr. trial advocacy U. Nebr. Coll. Law, 1979-90; bd. dirs. Fed. Jud. Ctr., 1982-86; chmn. com. on orientation newly apptd. dist. judges Fed. Jud. Ctr., 1986-89; mem. 8th Cir. Com. on Model Criminal and Civil Jury Instrns., 1983—; mem. adv. com. on alternative sentences U.S. Sentencing Com., 1989-91. Contbr. articles to profl. jours. Trustee St. Paul Sch. Theology, Kansas City, Mo., 1986-89; active United Methodist Ch. (bd. mgrs., bd. global ministries 1972-76, gen. com. on status and role of women, 1988-96, gen. conf. 1972, 76, 80, 88, 92, 96, 2000); pres. Lincoln YMCA, 1965-67; bd. govs. Nebr. Wesleyan U., chmn. 1975-80. With AUS, 1944-46. Recipient Medal of Honor, Nebr. Wesleyan U. Alumni Assn., 1983. Fellow Am. Coll. Trial Lawyers; mem. ABA, Nebr. Bar Assn. (ho. of dels. 1966-70, Outstanding Legal Educator award 1990), Lincoln Bar Assn. (Liberty Bell award 1993, pres. 1968-69), Kiwanis (Disting. Svc. award 1993), Masons (33 deg.), Am. Inns of Ct. (Lewis F. Powell Jr. award for Professionalism and Ethics 1995). Methodist. Home: 4421 Ridgeview Dr Lincoln NE 68516-1516 Office: US Dist Ct 586 Fed Bldg 100 Centennial Mall N Lincoln NE 68508-3859 E-mail: urbom1@aol.com.

URCH, DIANE SHERMAN, librarian; b. Woodbury, N.J., Nov. 17, 1936; d. Arthur T. and Elizabeth V. (Haines) Sherman; m. Juergen K. Schoeler, Mar. 20, 1959 (div. June 1975); children: Jodi L. Schoeler Hecht, Susan E. Schoeler Anderson, Ellen Nell Schoeler; m. Wesley V. Urch, Apr. 18, 1991. BA in History, U. Del., 1958; MA in Librarianship, U. Denver, 1970. Circulation and acquisitions libr. Emporia (Kans.) State U., 1970-79; acquisitions libr. U. Tex., El Paso, 1979-84; asst. dir. libr. U. Wis., Oshkosh, 1984—. Mgr. adminstrv. programming unit U. Wis., Oshkosh, 1996-97. Mem., mem. Oshkosh adv. bd. Children's Svcs. Soc. Wis., 1991—. Mem. ALA, AAUW (pres. Oshkosh br. 1996-98), Wis. Libr. Assn. Office: U Wis Librs and Learning Resource 800 Algoma Blvd Oshkosh WI 54901-3551

URCIOLO, JOHN RAPHAEL, II, real estate developer, real estate and finance educator; b. Washington, June 29, 1947; s. Joseph John and Phillie Marie (Petrone) U.; m. Jean Marie Manning, Jan. 2, 1972 (dec. Jan. 1990); m. Andrea Zedalis Stevenson, Mar. 9, 2002. BBA, Am. U., 1969, MS in real estate, 1971. Cert. real estate broker, appraiser. Rschr. Homer Hoyt Inst., Washington, 1967-69; econ. Nat. Assn. Home Builders, 1971-75; lectr., assoc. prof. Montgomery Coll., Rockville, Md., 1971-72; assoc. prof. U. Md., College Park, 1972-79; property mgr. Urciolo Realty Co., Washington, 1976-79; comml. broker Urciolo & Urciolo, 1980-82, real estate developer Takoma Park, Md., 1982—. Cons. Nat. Ski Area Assn., Hartford, 1978-79, Montgomery County Govt., Rockville, 1980-81; adj. prof. Am. U., Washington, 1980-91; court expert Superior Ct. for D.C., Civil and Criminal divsns.; lectr. to various orgns. Author: Real Estate Manual, 1976; co-author: The White Book of Ski Areas (U.S. and Can.), 1977-79, Industry Edition-The White Book, 1978, The Housing Fact Book, 1976, Housing Component Costs, 1975, 2d edit., 1976, Material Usage in Housing, 1970; co-editor: Labor Wage Rate Bulletin, 1976. Co-chair bd. dirs. Liz Lerman Dance Exch., Takoma Park, Md., 1997—; chmn. Econ. Devel. Com., City of Takoma Park; pres. Lido Civic Club of Washington. Fellow Urban Mass Transp. Assn., 1969, Am. U., 1970; Soc. Real Estate Appraisers scholar, 1968. Mem. Cert. Real Estate Appraisers, Am. Planning Assn., Am. Univ. Real Estate Assn. (charter, v.p. edn., v.p. award 1983), Rho Epsilon (editor newsletter 1969). Republican. Roman Catholic. Avocations: skiing, golf. Office: Urciolo & Urciolo 6935 Laurel Ave Ste 100 Takoma Park MD 20912-4413

URCIUOLI, J. ARTHUR, investment executive; b. Syracuse, N.Y., Nov. 13, 1937; s. Joseph R. and Nicoletta Anne (Phillips) U.; m. Margaret Jane Forelli, Aug. 13, 1966; children: Caryn Sloan Jacoby, Christian J.A. BS, St. Lawrence U., 1959; JD, Georgetown U., 1966; grad. Advanced Mgmt. Program, Harvard Bus. Sch., 1982. Bar: N.Y. 1966. Atty. Brown, Wood, Fuller, Caldwell & Ivey, N.Y.C., 1966-69; internat. investment banker, dir. internat. fin. Merrill Lynch, N.Y.C., Paris, 1970-78; pres. Merrill Lynch Internat., 1978-82; chmn. Merrill Lynch Internat. Bank, London; dir. banking div. Merrill Lynch Capital Markets, 1980-84; dir. Merrill Lynch Bus. Fin. Services, Merrill Lynch Co., 1984-93; dir. mktg. group Merrill Lynch Pvt. Client, 1993-97, chmn. Internat. Pvt. Client Group, 1997-99, ret., 1999; chmn. Archer Group, 1999—. Bd. dirs. Kroll Inc., DeVisscher Olson & Allen. Contbr. articles to profl. jours. Trustee St. Lawrence U., 1976-89, Bruce Mus., Greenwich, Conn., 1990-94; bd. dirs. United Way, Greenwich, 1978-81. Capt. USMC, 1959-63. Mem. Securities Assn. (chmn. sales and mktg. com. 1987-89), Forum for Investor Advice (chmn. 1996-98), River Club (N.Y.C.), N.Y. Yacht Club, Riverside (Conn.) Yacht Club, The Oaks Club (Sarasota, Fla.). Republican. Congregationalist. E-mail: archie22@comcast.net., archercorp@home.com.

URDANG, ALEXANDRA, book publishing executive; b. N.Y.C., June 29, 1956; d. Laurence Urdang and Irena (Ehrlich) Urdang de Tour. BA in English Lit., U. Conn., 1977. Customer svc. and fulfillment mgr. Universe Books, N.Y.C., 1978-79, sales mgr., assoc. mktg. mgr., 1980-82; asst. v.p., dir. spl. sales Macmillan Pub. Co., 1982-88; v.p. new markets Warner Books, Inc., 1988-97. Avocations: architecture, art, antiques. Office: Apt 2A 201 E 69th St New York NY 10021-5472

URDANG, LAURENCE, lexicographer, publisher; b. N.Y.C., Mar. 21, 1927; s. Harry Rudman and Annabel (Schafran) U.; m. Irena B. Ehrlich vel Sluszny, May 23, 1952 (div.); children: Nicole Severyn, Alexandra Stefanie. BS, Columbia U., 1954, postgrad., 1954-58. Lectr. gen. linguistics NYU, 1956-61; assoc. editor dictionary dept. Funk & Wagnalls, Inc., N.Y.C., 1957; reference editor Random House, Inc., 1957-61, dir. reference dept., 1962-69; pres. Laurence Urdang, Inc., Old Lyme, Conn. and Aylesbury, Eng., 1969—; chmn. bd. Laurence Urdang Assocs., Ltd., Aylesbury, 1969-78; editor Verbatim Books, Old Lyme and Aylesbury, 1974—. Compiler, editor, author numerous books; mng. editor: Random House Unabridged Dictionary, 1966; editor in chief: Random House College Dictionary, 1968, Random House Dictionary of Synonyms and Antonyms, 1960, N.Y. Times Everyday Reader's Dictionary of Misunderstood, Misused, Mispronounced Words, 1972, 2d edit., 1985, Editor, Verbatim, The Language Quar., 1974-97, Dictionary of Advertising Terms, 1977, Official Associated Press Almanac, 1976, Hammond Almanac, 1977, Picturesque Expressions, 1980, 2d edit., 1985, Illustrated Children's Dictionary, 1979, Basic Dictionary of Synonyms and Antonyms, 1979, 2d edit., 1986, The Synonym Finder, 1979, Collins English Dictionary, 1979, Verbatim: Vols. I, II, 1978, Vols. III, IV, V, VI and Index, 1981, -Ologies & -Isms, 1978, 81, 86, Twentieth Century American Nicknames, 1979, A Treasury of Biblical Quotations, 1980, The Timetables of American History, 1981, 3d edit., 2001, Mosby's Medical and Nursing Dictionary, 1983, Allusions, 1982, 86, Modifiers, 1982, Suffixes, 1982, Prefixes, 1984, Holidays and Anniversaries, 1985, Slogans, 1985, Mottoes, 1986, Numerical Allusions, 1986, Names and Nicknames of Places and Things, 1987, Loanwords Dictionary, 1987, The Whole Ball of Wax, 1988, The Dictionary of Confusable Words, 1988, A Fine Kettle of Fish, 1990, The Oxford Thesaurus, 1992, 2nd edit., 1997, The Oxford Desk Dictionary, 1995, The Oxford Desk Thesaurus, 1995, The New Century Dictionary, 1996, The New Century Thesaurus, 1996, The Compact Oxford Thesaurus, 1997. Served with USNR, 1944-45. Mem. Linguistic Soc. Am., Am. Name Soc., Am. Dialect Soc., Dictionary Soc. N.Am., Soc. Indexers, Euralex, Naval Club (London).

URE DUNAGAN, HEATHER EILEEN, writer; b. Columbia, S.C., Aug. 11, 1973; d. Lincoln Richard Ure III and Jeanne Maureen O'Hara Ure; m. John David Dunagan II, July 10, 1999; children: Lavinia Kate Dunagan and Owen Patrick Dunagan (twins). BA, Wellesley Coll., 1995; BA, MA, Oxford (Eng.) U., 1997; MA, Boston U., 1998. Intern Mike Zuhl for Mayor, Salt Lake City, 1991; rsch. asst. Office for Resources Wellesley (Mass.) Coll., 1991-97, tutor English and Italian, 1992-95; intern Karen Shepherd for Congress, Salt Lake City, 1992, The Hon. Karen Shepherd, Washington, 1994; tchg. fellow Boston U., 1997-98; tchr. English The Roxbury Latin Sch., West Roxbury, Mass., 1998-2000; class of 1995 asst., class rep. Wellesley (Mass.) Coll., 2000—. Mem. Mass. selection com. for Rhodes Scholarship, Boston, 1998—2001, RI. selection com. for Rhodes Scholarship , Providence, 1997. Author: (poetry collection) Bird Without a Gun, 1998, Great Salt Lake, 2002. Mem. steering com. Wellesley Coll. Friends of the Libr., 2000—02; vol. study hall proctor Mother Caroline Acad., Dorchester, Mass., 2000—01; stewardship vol., conv. del. position on vestry Ch. of Our Saviour, Brookline, 2000—01. Rhodes scholar, 1995. Episcopalian. Avocations: Nordic skiing, dance. Home: 502 224th Pl NE Sammamish WA 98074 E-mail: huredunagan@yahoo.com.

URELIUS, SHAWN RENEA, lawyer; b. Ft. Dodge, Iowa, Feb. 13, 1963; d. Norman Dean and Ruby Lee Urelius. BA summa cum laude, BS summa cum laude, N.E. Mo. State U., Kirksville, 1985; JD, U. Va., 1988. Bar: Tex. 1988, D.C. 1990, Va. 1991. Assoc. Haynes and Boone, Dallas, 1988-91, McSweeney, Burtch & Crump, Richmond, Va., 1991-97; asst. gen. counsel Hamilton Beach/Proctor Silex, Inc., 1997—. Mem. ABA, Tex. State Bar Assn., D.C. Bar Assn., Va. Bar Assn. Office: Hamilton Beach Proctor-Silex Inc 4421 Waterfront Dr Glen Allen VA 23060-3375 E-mail: shawn.urelius@hamiltonbeach.com.

URENA-ALEXIADES, JOSE LUIS, electrical engineer; b. Madrid, Spain, Sept. 5, 1949; s. Jose L. and Maria (Alexiades Christodulakis) Urena y Pon. MSEE, U. Madrid, Spain, 1976; MS in Computer Science, UCLA, 1978. Rsch. asst. UCLA, 1978; systems analyst Honeywell Info. Systems, L.A., 1978-80; mem. tech. staff Jet Propulsion Lab., Pasadena, Calif., 1980-91; exec. dir. Empresa Nacional de Innovacion S.A., L.A., 1991-96; sr. technologist Boeing Satellite Sys., 1996—. Contbr. various articles to profl. jours. Two times recipient NASA Group Achievement award. Mem. IEEE, IEEE Computer Soc., IEEE Communications Soc., Assn. for Computer Machinery, World Federalist Assn., Spanish Profl. Am. Inc. Roman Catholic. Avocations: active photographer, Master's swimming. Home: 904 Dickson St Marina Del Rey CA 90292-5513 Office: Hughes Space & Comm Mail Stop S50 x366 1700 E Imperial Hwy Los Angeles CA 90059-2559

URETZ, MICHAEL ALBERT, health and fitness executive; b. Chgo., Oct. 19, 1942; s. George and Frances (King) U. JD, DePaul U., 1966. Asst. states atty. Ill. States Atty., Chgo., 1967-70; atty. pvt. practice, L.A., 1972-88; pres. World Gym Lic. Ltd., Santa Monica, Calif., 1983—. Mem. Eldorado Polo Club, Empire Polo Club, Sigma Chi (life). Independent. Avocation: polo. Office: World Gym Lic Ltd 2210 Main St Santa Monica CA 90405-2275

URGO, JOSEPH ROCCO, English language and humanities educator; b. Hartford, Conn., Jan. 29, 1956; s. Joseph S. and Rose (Zito) U.; m. Lesley Dretar, July 30, 1983; 1 child, George Dretar Urgo. BA, Haverford Coll., 1978; MALS, Wesleyan U., Middletown, Conn., 1982; PhD, Brown U., 1985. Asst. prof. Am. civilization Syracuse (N.Y.) U., 1985-86; asst. prof. English, Andrew W. Mellow fellow in Am. studies Vanderbilt U., Nashville, 1986-89; asst. prof. English and humanities Bryant Coll., Smithfield, R.I., 1989-91, assoc. prof., 1991-95, prof. English, chmn. dept., 1995-2000, U. Miss., Oxford, 2000—. Andrew W. Mellon fellow in Am. studies Vanderbilt U., 1986-89. Author: Faulkner's Apocrypha: A Fable, Snopes, and the Spirit of Human Rebellion, 1989, Novel Frames: Literature as Guide to Race, Sex, and History in American Culture, 1991, Willa Cather and the Myth of American Migration, 1995, In the Age of Distraction, 2000; book rev. editor: College Literature; contbr. numerous articles and revs. to profl. jours. Recipient George Whatley prize for best article, 1987; Fulbright lectr., Spain, 1992; Kenan-Venture grantee, 1987. Mem. MLA, Am. Lit. Assn., Am. Studies Assn., William Faulkner Soc., Willa Cather Soc., Fulbright Assn. Home: 804 Brentwood Cove Oxford MS 38655 Office: PO Box 1848 Oxford MS 38655-1848 E-mail: jurgo@olemiss.edu.

URHAUSEN, JAMES NICHOLAS, real estate developer, construction executive; b. Berwyn, Ill., Oct. 6, 1943; s. Jack Nicholas and Florence Frances (Stalzer) U.; m. Philomena Anne Malizia, July 16, 1966 (div. 1980); children: Kristen Anne, James Nicholas III; m. Anne Siegert, July 22, 1983; children: Bradley James, Samantha Elise. BA, St. Procopius Coll., Lisle, Ill., 1965. High sch. tchr. Nazareth Acad., LaGrange Park, Ill., 1965-66; asst. village mgr. Village of Hinsdale, 1966-69; village mgr. Village of Oak Brook, 1969-73; v.p., sec.-treas. Collins Devel. Corp., St. Charles, 1973-80; exec. v.p. Westway Constrn. Corp., 1980-84, pres., chief exec. officer, 1984—. Guest lectr. No. Ill. U., Dekalb, 1976—; expert witness Ill. Dept. of Transp., Chgo., 1976—; dir. Harris Bank/St. Charles, Ill., 1992—. Chmn. Hotel Baker Bd. Gov.'s St. Charles, 1982-84, Bd. of Fire and Police Commmrs., St. Charles, 1986—; mem. 708 Comty. Mental Health Bd., St. Charles, 1986—, Kane County Selective Svc. Sys. Bd., St. Charles, 1981—, Kane County Solid Waste Adv. Com., Geneva, 1990—, Metra Citizen's Adv. Bd., 1993—; bd. dirs. Neighborhood Improvement Assn., St. Charles Twp., 1992—, pres., 1996—; bd. dirs. Delnor Cmty. Health Sys., 1993—, Glenwood Sch. for Boys, 1996—; chair tech. adv. com. Kane County Stormwater Mgmt. Com., 1996—. Mem. Home Bldrs. Assn. Greater Chgo. (dir. 1989—), Nat. Assn. Home Bldrs., No. Ill. Home Bldrs. Assn., Fox Valley Polit. Action Group, St. Charles C. of C. (amb. 1988, Community Devel. award 1989, Charlemagne award 1993, Sam Walton Bus. Leadership award 1996). Republican. Roman Catholic. Avocations: golf, rail photography, power boating, model trains. Home: 3103 Greenwood Ln Saint Charles IL 60175-5627 Office: Westway Constrn Corp 440 S 3rd St Saint Charles IL 60174-2854

URI, GEORGE WOLFSOHN, accountant; b. San Francisco, Dec. 8, 1920; s. George Washington and Ruby Uri; m. Pamela O'Keefe, May 15, 1961. AB, Stanford U., 1941, IA, 1943, MBA, 1946; postgrad., U. Leeds, Eng., 1945. CPA, Calif.; CFP. CMA, ChFC; Accredited Estate Planner. Mem. acctg., econs. and stats. depts. Shell Oil Co., Inc., San Francisco, 1946-48; ptnr., ret. Irelan, Uri, Mayer & Sheppie; pres. F. Uri & Co., Inc. Instr. acctg. and econs. Golden Gate Univ., 1949-50. Contbr. articles to profl. jours. Chmn. San Rafael Redevel. Adv. Com., 1977-78, mem., 1978-91, mem. emeritus, 1991— ; bd. dirs. San Francisco Planning and Urban Renewal Assn., 1958-60. Served with AUS, 1942-46, to col. Aus. (ret.). Recipient Key Man award San Francisco Jr. C. of C.; Meritorious Service medal Sec. of Army, 1978 Mem. AICPA (hon., cert. personal fin. specialist), Calif. Soc. CPAs (hon.; sec.-treas. San Francisco chpt. 1956-57, d ir. 1961-63, state dir. 1964-66, mem. Forbes medal com. 1968-69, chmn. 1969-71), Am. Econs. Assn., San Francisco Estate Planning Coun. (dir. 1965-68, Am. Soc. Mil. Comptrollers, Execs. Assn. San Francisco (pres. 1965-66), Inst. Cert. Mgmt. Accts. (Disting. Performance cert. 1978), Soc. Fin. Profls., World Trade Club (San Francisco), Commonwealth Club (quar. chmn. 1971), Stanford (San Francisco; dir. 1990-99), Army and Navy (Washington). Office: 1209 Tennessee St San Francisco CA 94107

URIAS, JOHN M. military officer, government agency administrator; b. Vandenberg AFB, Calif. BS, U. Calif., Davis; MS in Elec. Engring., Naval Postgrad. Sch.; MA in Nat. Security and Strategic Studies, Naval War Coll.; grad., Air War Coll., Def. Systems Mgmt. Coll., Coll. of Naval Command and Staff. Commd. 2d lt. U.S. Army, 1975, advanced through grades to brig. gen.; dep. for systems acquisition U.S. Army Tank-Automotive and Armaments Command, 1998—99; project mgr. Warfighter Info. Network-Terrestrial U.S. Army Space and Missile Def. Command; platoon leader, exec. officer Battery C, 2nd Battalion,1st Air Def. Artillery, Germany; adj. 4th Supply and Transport Battalion, Ft. Carson, Colo.; battery comdr., ops. officer and exec. officer 4th Battalion, 61st Air Def. Artillery; comdr. 2nd Battalion, 44th Air Def. Artillery, 101st Airborne Divsn., Ft. Campbell, Ky.; R&D coord. U.S. Army Missile and Space Intelligence Ctr., Redstone Arsenal, Ala.; exec. asst. to the sci. and tech. advisor comdr.-in-chief USCINCPAC, chief R&D br. strategic planning and policy directorate; asst. project mgr. for command, control, comm. and intelligence Army Tactical Missile System; asst. project mgr. for army airspace command and control Air Def. Command and Control Systems; program exec. officer for air and missile def. and dep. commdg. gen. for rsch., devel. and acquisition U.S. Army Space and Missile Def. Command, Huntsville, Ala., 1999—. Office: USArmy Space and Missile Defense Command PO Box 1500 Huntsville AL 35807-3801*

URIBE, JAVIER MIGUEL, investment executive; b. Baranquilla, Colombia, Sept. 4, 1941; s. Jose and Ofelia (Diaz-Granados) U.; m. Dena Rue Whitaker, Apr. 1, 1963 (div. Sept. 1987); children: Sandra J., Joseph J., Cristina; m. Diana L. Anglada, Dec. 4, 1987. BS in Indsl. Mgmt., Purdue U., 1967. With Citibank, N.A., 1967, resident v.p. Colombia, 1975-76, v.p. Port of Spain, Trinidad, 1976-78, N.Y.C., 1978-80, San Juan, P.R., 1980-85; pres. Citicorp Fin. Svcs. Corp., P.R., 1980-85; chmn., chief exec. officer Merrill Lynch Govt. Securities, 1985-88; pres. San Juan Capital Corp., 1988—. Advisor exec. program Ind. U., Bloomington, 1978-80; chmn. Trinfinance Leasing, Port of Spain, Trinidad, 1976-78, Met. Mortgage Co., San Juan, 1989—; trustee Ashford Presbyn. Community Hosp., San Juan, 1990-96. Bd. dirs. Maracaibo (Venezuela) Botanical Gardens Found., 1974-75. Mem. Securities Industry Assn. of P.R. (founder, treas. 1985-86), N.Am. Assn. (bd. dirs. Caracas, Venezuela chpt. 1973-74), Dorado Beach Golf Club, Centro Ecuestre de P.R. (pres. 1989-91), Equestrian Fedn. (v.p. 1989-91), Ingenio Polo Club. Roman Catholic. Avocation: golf. Home: PO Box 9023462 San Juan PR 00902-3462 Office: San Juan Capital Corp Tetuan 103 Ste One San Juan PR 00901 E-mail: sjcc-jmu@worldnet.att.net.

URIE, JOHN JAMES, lawyer, retired Canadian federal judge; b. Guelph, Ont., Can., Jan. 2, 1920; s. G. Norman and Jane A. U.; m. Dorothy Elizabeth James.; children: David, Janet, Alison. B.Commerce, Queen's U.; LL.B., Osgoode Hall Law Sch. Bar: Ont. 1948. Ptnr. firm Burke-Robertson, Urie, Weller & Chadwick, Ottawa, Ont., 1948-73; judge Fed. Ct. Can., 1973-90; counsel Scott and Aylen, 1991-2000, Borden, Ladner, Gervais, Ottawa, 2000—. Gen. counsel to Joint Com. of Senate and House of Commons on Consumer Credit; chmn. planning com. First Nat. Conf. on Law, Ottawa, 1972; judge Ct. Martial Appeal Ct., 1973-90. Past pres. County of Carleton Law Assn.; past v.p. Children's Aid Soc.; past pres. Eastern Profl. Hockey League. Served with Cameron Highlanders of Ottawa Can. Army, 1942-45. Mem. Royal Can. Mil. Inst., Phi Delta Phi. Mem. United Ch. of Canada. Clubs: Cameron Highlanders of Ottawa Assoc. (Ottawa), Ottawa Hunt and Golf (Ottawa), Rideau (Ottawa). Office: Borden Ladiver Gervais 60 Queen St Ottawa ON Canada K1P 5Y7

URION, DAVID KIMBALL, pediatric neurologist, researcher, educator; b. Cin., Aug. 4, 1954; s. Phillip Allen and Lenore (Barrow) U.; m. Kerrie Eileen Flynn, Mar. 6, 1982 (div. Oct. 1986); 1 child, Kara Flynn; m. Deborah Choate, Sept. 27, 1987; 1 child, Rufus Walker Choate. AB, Dartmouth Coll., 1976; MD, Stanford U., 1980. Diplomate Am. Bd. Psychiatry and Neurology. Intern Peter Bent Brigham Hosp., Boston, 1980-81; resident, neurology Longwood Area Neurology Program, 1981-82; resident, pediatrics Children's Hosp., 1982-83; resident, child neurology Longwood Area Neurology Program, 1983-84, chief resident, child neurology, 1984-85; instr. neurology Med. Sch., Harvard U., 1985-87, asst. prof., 1987-2000; assoc. prof., 2000—; mem. faculty Sch. Edn. Harvard U., Cambridge, Mass., 1985—; asst. in neurology Children's Hosp., Boston, 1985-88; assoc. in neurology, 2000—; dir. learning disabilities-behavioral neurology program Children's Hosp., Boston, 1985—, dir. neurology clinics, 1987-91. Treas. Children's Hosp. Neurology Found., 1986—, v.p., 1992—99, clerk, 1999—. Author: Pediatric Neurology for the House Officer, 1988; translator: The Brain Machine (Jeannerod), 1985; contbr. articles to med. jours., chpts. to books. Mem.: Internat. Child Neurology Assn., Child Neurology Soc., Am. Acad. Neurology. Democratic Socialist. Episcopalian. Office: Children's Hosp Neurology 300 Longwood Ave Boston MA 02115-5724 E-mail: david.urion@tch.harvard.edu.

URIS, ALAN M. lawyer; b. N.Y.C., Apr. 4, 1934; m. Sheila Jones, June 24, 1970; 1 child, Genevieve Uris. BA, Dartmouth Coll., 1955; LLB, NYU, 1958. Bar: Vt. 1970, N.Y. 1959. Atty. Uris & Lisa, N.Y.C., 1965-70, Uris & Hutton, Westfield, Vt., 1970-84; asst. dist. atty. Dist. Atty.'s Office Queens County, 1984-87; sole practice N.Y.C., 1987-94; of counsel DeVagno, Borchert, Levine & LaSpina, Whitestone, N.Y., 1994—. Town atty. Warren, Vt. Mem. Queens County Bar Assn., Queens County Asst. Dist. Attys. Assn. Democrat. Jewish. Office: DeVagno Borchert Levine & LaSpina 19-02 Whitestone Expy Whitestone NY 11357-3099 Home: 1329 Michael Pl Bayside NY 11360-1169

URISTA, DIANE JEAN, music educator, researcher; b. Mpls., Mar. 28, 1957; d. Joseph and Jean Helen (Sanzenbach) U.; m. Peter John Quehl, June 1, 1985 (div. Sept. 1994); m. Jonathan Jaye Niefeld, July 6, 1996. MusB, Concordia Coll., Moorhead, Minn., 1979; MusM, Northwestern U., 1990; MPhil, Columbia U., 1996. Coord. Children's Music Program Am. Conservatory Music, Chgo., 1986-90; instr. music humanities Columbia U., N.Y.C., 1993—; instr. music theory NYU, 1997—. Foster parent, Plan Internat., Honduras, 1985— Mellon fellow Columbia U., 1993-97. Mem. AAUW (Am. Dissertation fellow 1997), Coll. Music Soc., Soc. Music Theory, Mu Phi Epsilon. Avocations: reading, poetry, ice skating, movies.

URKA, MARTIN C. soil scientist, retired; b. Brethren, Mich., Nov. 11, 1924; s. Tony and Ann U.; m. Peggy Jean Crane; four children. Cert., Mich. State U., 1948. From conservation aide to soil scientist USDA Soil Conservation Svc., Jackson, Mich., 1948-79; from soil scientist to natural resource specialist USDI Bur. Indian Affairs, Cedar City, Utah, 1979-88, ret., 1988. Freelance writer in field. Vol. master gardener Coop. Ext. Svc., Fla. Mem. Soil Conservation Soc., Soc. Range Mgmt., Assn. Retired SCS Employees. Home: 1322 Corner Oaks Brandon FL 33510

URKOWITZ, MICHAEL, banker; b. Bronx, N.Y., June 18, 1943; s. David and Esther (Levy) U.; m. Eleanor Naomi Dreazen, July 2, 1966; children—Brian, Denise. B.Engring., CCNY, 1965, M.M.E., 1967. Project engr. Lunar Module program Grumman Corp., Bethpage, N.Y., 1964-72; asst. to dep. commr. for housing code compliance, project mgr. City of N.Y., 1972-74; 2d v.p. Chase Manhattan Bank, N.Y.C., 1974-77, v.p. group exec. ops. dept., 1977-80, sr. v.p., 1980-85, exec. v.p., corp. ops. and sys. exec., 1985-87; sector exec. Chase InfoServ Internat., 1987-95, exec. consumer products integration and tech., 1995-96, Chase credit card bus. exec., 1996-2000, ret. N.Y.C. , 2000; sr. adv. Deloitte Cons., N.Y.C. Bd. dirs. CEDEL, Luxembourg, Master Card U.S., Depository Trust Co., N.Y.C., 1992-95, Bank Leumi, U.S.; lectr. CCNY, 1967-68. Contbg. author: Thermal Control and Radiation, 1972. Mem. adv. bd. N.Y. C. chpt. Salvation Army, 1989—2001. Mem. Tau Beta Pi, Pi Tau Sigma. Office: Deloitte Cons 2 World Fin Ctr New York NY 10281-1414 *Working against my own standards as opposed to the standards set by others, provides the greater challenge but yields greater satisfaction.*

URMAN, JEFFREY DAVID, physician, educator; b. N.Y.C., May 23, 1944; s. Julius and Rose Claire Urman; m. Marian K. Kleinfeld, June 28, 1970; children: Jamie David, Daniel Jay. BS, U. Conn., 1967; MD, Cornell U., 1972. Diplomate Am. Bd. Internal Medicine and Rheumatology. Int. Wash. Hosp. Ctr., Wash., D.C., 1972-73, res., 1973-75; fellshp. in rheumatology Univ.

Conn. Health Ctr., Farmington, CT, 1975-77; physician Redwood Med. Clinic, Redwood City, Calif., 1977-90; clin. prof. medicine Stanford (Calif.) U. Med. Ctr., 1977—; physician Permanente Med. Group, Mountain View, Calif., 1990—, physician-in-charge, 1995—. Contbr. articles to profl. jours. Fellow: ACP, Am. Coll. Rheumatology. Office: 555 Castro St Mountain View CA 94041-2060

URMAN, RHODA M. social worker, psychotherapist; b. Newark, Sept. 9, 1946; d. George M. and Jean (Schlein) U.; m. Cristos Gianakos, Nov. 21, 1982; 1 child, Maia. BA cum laude, U. Pa., 1964-68; MSW, Yeshiva U., 1992; postgrad., Postgrad. Ctr. Mental Health, N.Y.C., 1999. Pvt. practice psychotherapy, N.Y.C., 1992—; coord. Inst. Performing & Creative Artists Postgrad. Ctr., 2000—. Recipient scholarship Jewish Found. for the Edn. of Women, N.Y.C., 1991. Mem.: Eastern Group Psychotherapy Soc., N.Y. State Soc. for Clin. Social Work. Avocations: travel, art. Office: 156 5th Ave Ste 612 New York NY 10010-7002

URMER, DIANE HEDDA, management firm executive, financial officer; b. Bklyn., Dec. 15, 1934; d. Leo and Helen Sarah (Perlman) Leverant; m. Albert Heinz Urmer, Sept. 2, 1952; children: Michelle, Cynthia, Carl. Student, U. Tex., 1951-52, Washington U., St. Louis, 1962-63; BA in Psychology, Calif. State U., Northridge, 1969. Asst. auditor Tex. State Bank, Austin, 1952-55; v.p., contr. Enki Corp., Sepulveda, Calif., 1966-70, aos. bd. dirs., 1971—; v.p. fin. Cambia Way Hosp., Walnut Creek, 1973-78; v.p., contr. Enki Health & Rsch. Sys., Inc., Reseda, 1978-93, sr. v.p., 1993—, also bd. dirs. Contbr. articles to profl. jours. Pres. Northridge PTA, 1971; chmn. Northridge Citizens Adv. Coun., 1972=73. Mem. Women in Mgmt., Tex. Execs. Club. Avocations: bowling, sailing, handcrafts, golf. Office: Enki Health and Rsch Systems Inc 21601 Devonshire St Chatsworth CA 91311-2946

URMY, NORMAN B. hospital administrator; b. Ft. Smith, Ark., June 26, 1944; married. BA, Williams Coll., 1966; MA, U. Chgo., 1969. Various positions Mass. Gen. Hosp., Boston, 1966-67; adminstrv. resident NYU Med. Ctr., 1968, adminstrv. asst., 1969-70, asst. adminstr., 1970-76, assoc. adminstr., 1976-79, adminstr., v.p. ops., 1979-82; exec. dir. Vanderbilt Univ. Hosp. & Clinic, Nashville, 1985-98; exec. v.p. clin. affairs Vanderbilt Univ. Med. Ctr., 1998—; exec. dir. and CEO Vanderbilt U. Hosp. and Clinic, 2002—. Mem. ACHE. Office: D-3300 MCN Vanderbilt U 1161 21st Ave Nashville TN 37232-2104*

URNESS, DAVID JOHN, secondary school educator; b. Winana, Minn., Sept. 28, 1952; s. Edward Ole and Ruth Louise (Schultze) Urness; children: Alison Marie, Mason Edward. BS in Music, Winona State U., 1976. Orch. tchr. Mankato (Minn.) East H.S., 1978—. Musician (prin. bassist): Mankato Symphony, 1978—84, 1986—. Orch. dir. St. Pauls Luth. Ch., North Mankato, Minn., 1998—; bd. dirs. Mankato Symphony, 1986—90. Mem.: NEA. Lutheran. Avocations: model railroading, music. Office: Mankato East HS 2600 Hoffman Rd Mankato MN 56001

UROWSKY, RICHARD J. lawyer; b. N.Y.C., June 28, 1946; s. Jacob and Anne (Granick) Urowsky. BA, Yale U., 1967, JD, 1972; BPhil, Oxford U., Eng., 1970. Bar: N.Y. 1973, U.S. Dist. Ct. (so. dist.) N.Y. 1973, U.S. Ct. Appeals (2d cir.) 1973, U.S. Supreme Ct. 1977. Law clk. to Justice Reed U.S. Supreme Ct., Washington, 1972-73; assoc. Sullivan & Cromwell, N.Y.C., 1973-80, ptnr., 1980—. Mem. ABA, Assn. of the Bar of the City of N.Y., Fed. Bar Coun., N.Y. County Lawyers Assn., Yale Club, Links, Lyford Cay Club. Office: Sullivan & Cromwell 125 Broad St New York NY 10004-2489 E-mail: urowskyr@sullcrom.com.

URQUHART, JOHN, medical researcher, educator; b. Pitts., Apr. 24, 1934; s. John and Wilma Nelda (Martin) U.; m. Joan Cooley, Dec. 28, 1957; children: Elizabeth Urquhart Vdovjak, John Christopher (dec. 1965), Robert Malcolm, Thomas Jubal. BA with honors, Rice U., 1955; MD with honors, Harvard U., 1959; D (honoris causa), U. Utrecht, 1997. Lic. physician, Calif. Walter B. Cannon fellow in physiology Harvard Med. Sch., Boston, 1956; Josiah Macy, Jr. fellow, 1956-58, 59-61; intern in surgery Mass. Gen. Hosp., 1959-60; asst. resident, 1960-61; investigator Nat. Heart Inst., NIH, Bethesda, Md., 1961-63; asst. prof. physiology U. Pitts. Sch. Medicine, 1963-66; assoc. prof., 1966-68; prof., 1968-70; prof. biomed. engring. U. So. Calif., L.A., 1970-71; prin. scientist ALZA Corp., Palo Alto, Calif., 1970-86; dir. biol. scis., 1971-74; pres. rsch. divsn., 1974-78; dir., 1976-78; chief scientist, 1978-82; sr. v.p., 1978-85. Co-founder APREX Corp., Fremont, Calif., pres., 1986-88, dir., 1986-95, chmn., 1988-91, chief scientist, 1988-95; co-founder, chief scientist AARDEX Ltd., Zug, Switzerland, 1995—; vis. prof. pharmacology U. Limburg Sch. Medicine (now Maastricht U.), Maastricht, The Netherlands, 1984-85, vis. prof. pharmaco-epidemiology, 1986-91; prof. pharmaco-epidemiology, 1992—; adj. prof. biopharm. scis. U. Calif.-San Francisco, 1984—; mem. dir.'s adv. com. NIH, 1986-88; Boerhaave lectr. U. Leiden, The Netherlands, 1991, 94, 95, 97. Co-author: Risk Watch, 1984; contbr. numerous articles to sci. jours.; patentee therapeutic systems for controlled drug delivery and regimen compliance monitoring (43). Trustee Kettering U. (formerly GMI Engring. and Mgmt. Inst.), Flint, Mich., 1983—; bd. dirs. Inveresk Rsch. Group, Ltd., Cary, NC, vice-chmn. 2002—. Served with USPHS, 1961-63. NIH grantee, 1963-70; Bowditch lectr. Am. Physiol. Soc., 1969; recipient Disting. Alumni award, Rice U., 2002. Fellow Royal Coll. Physicians of Edinburgh, AAAS; mem. Biomed. Engring. Soc. (pres. 1976), Boyleston Med. Soc., Internat. Soc. Pharmaco-epidemiology, Am. Soc. Clinical Pharmacology and Therapeutics, Soc. for Clinical Trials, Endocrine Soc., Saturday Morning Club Palo Alto, Am. Physiol. Soc., Soc. Risk Analysis, Calif. Acad. Medicine. Home and Office: 975 Hamilton Ave Palo Alto CA 94301-2213 E-mail: urquhart@ix.netcom.com.

URQUHART, KARIN MAY, foundation administrator, environmentalist; b. Oakland, Calif., Feb. 2, 1935; d. Charlotte Muriel Hively and Alfred Jonathon Alstrom; m. G. Donald Urquhart, Oct. 6, 1956; children: Gaylene Urquhart, Steve Hart, Cindy McDonell, Shelly Urquhart, Laurie Swisher, Scott Urquhart, James Urquhart. Exec. dir. Marin Conservation League, San Rafael, Calif., 1980-95; trustee Marin Cmty. Found., Larkspur, 1995—; exec. dir. Digital Village Found., Novato, 1996-97. Founding chair Marin Conservation Corps, San Rafael, 1982-87; mem. citizens adv. com. Citizen's Energy Impact Program, San Rafael, 1979-83; pres. Environ. Forum Marin, Kentfield, Calif., 1974-76, Marconi Conf. Ctr., Marshall, Calif., 1995—; mem. adv. com. Marin Resource Recovery Com., San Rafael, 1974-76; com. mem. Marin County Visitor Svcs. Com., San Rafael, 1995-96; mem. Marin County Waste Mgmt. Adv. Com., San Rafael, 1987-92; commr., pres. Marin County Parks Recreation and Open Space Commn., San Rafael, 1975-95; bd. dirs. Marin Agrl. Land Trust, Point Reyes, Calif.; spkr. in field. Illustrator (children's book) Mr. Buckeye Nut, 1970; contbr. numerous articles to newspapers and mags. Active steering com. Marin Women's Hall of Fame, San Rafael, 1994-96; mem. Marin County Trails Com., San Rafael, 1975-95; pesticide safety instr. U. Calif. Statewide Integrated Pest Mgmt. Project, Davis, 1994; mem. environ. sci. adv. bd. Dominican Coll., San Rafael, 1994-96; chair com. to appoint Marin Cmty. Found. trustees Marin Coun. Agencies, San Rafael, 1994; trustee Marin Cmty. Found., 1995, mem. cmty. partnership com., 1995, mem. earth day every day com., 1996; mem. Wed. Morning Dialogue, San Rafael, 1994-99; mem. adv. coun. Calif. Dept. Transp., Dist. IV, San Francisco, 1991-92; founding chair, bd. dirs. Marin Environ. Alliance, San Rafael, 1988-96; dir. Marin County Fair, San Rafael, 1985-2000; chair Marin County Open Space Com., San Rafael, 1973-95; bd. dirs. Marin Agrl. Land Trust, 1995; bd. dirs., pres. Marconi Conf. Ctr., 1995; vice-chair Lake Almanor Cmty. Found. Recipient Women Making History 11 annual award Senator Barbara Boxer, 1983, First Women of Achievement award AAUW, 1987, Exec. Dir. of Yr. award for excellence in developing cmty. partnerships Marin Coun. Agencies, 1989, Vol. award Environ. Fedn. Calif., 1989, Cert. of Recognition for recycling leadership Californians Against Waste, 1989, Conservation award DAR, 1995, inclusion award Congrl. Record of U.S., 1995; named Marin County's Outstanding Cmty. Vol., Calif. Dept. Parks and Recreation, 1995; named to Marin Women's Hall of Fame, 1993. Mem.: Marin County C. of C. (mem. govtl. affairs com. 1989—90), Marin Soc. Artists. Avocations: traveling, gardening, painting, swimming, cooking. Home: 383 Cascade Dr Fairfax CA 94930 Fax: 415-460-0260. E-mail: Karinur@aol.com.

URQUHART, TONY, artist, educator; b. Niagara Falls, Ont., Can., Apr. 9, 1934; s. Archer Marsh and Maryon Louise (Morse) U.; m. Madeline Mary Jennings, July 1958 (div. 1976); children: Allyson, Robin, Marsh, Aidan; m. Mary Jane Carter Keele, May 1976; 1 dau., Emily. B.F.A., U. Buffalo, 1958. Artist-in-residence U. Western Ont., London, 1960-63; 64-65, asst. prof. fine arts, 1967-70, assoc. prof., 1970-72; prof. fine art U. Waterloo, Ont., 1972-99, chmn. dept., 1977-79, 82-85, 94-96, ret., 1999; lectr. McMaster U., Hamilton, 1966-67. One-man shows Winnipeg Art Gallery, 1959, Walker Art Gallery, Mpls., 1960, Richard Demarco Gallery, Edinburgh, Scotland, 1975, group shows, Pitts. Biennial, 1958, Guggenheim Internat., N.Y.C., 1958, Art of the Ams. and Spain, Madrid, Barcelona, Rome, Paris, 1964, Nat. Gallery Can., Toronto, 1972, Mus. Modern Art, Paris, 1976; represented permanent collections, Nat. Gallery Can., Art Gallery, Ont., Fed. Art Bank of Ottawa, Montreal Mus., Vancouver Art Gallery, Mus. Modern Art, Victoria and Albert Mus., London, Museo Civico, Lugano, Switzerland, Hirshhorn Mus., Washington, Bibliotec Nat., Paris; chmn., Jack Chambers Meml. Found., 1978-85; resident artist, Kitchener-Waterloo Art Gallery, Kitchener, Ont., 1981-83; illustrator: The Broken Ark: A Book of Beasts, 1969, I Am Walking in the Garden of His Imaginary Palace by Jane Urquhart, 1982, False Shuffles by Jane Urquhart, 1982, (50 drawings) Cells of Ourselves (text G.M. Dault), 1989, Memories of a Governor General's Daughter, 1990, Warbrain: poems by Stuart MacKinnon, 1994, Walking to the Saints, by Anne McPherson, 2000. Decorated Order of Can.; recipient Edits, I Arts Coun., Ont., 1974, Kilchener Waterloo Visual Arts award, 1994; winner Nat. Outdoor Sculpture Competition MacDonald Stewart Art Ctr., 1987, Outdoor Sculpture competition, Rim Park, Waterloo, 2002; grantee Can. Coun. award, 1963, 79, travel grantee, 1967, 69, 70, 74, 75, 76, 88, 91, project cost grantee, 1981, 82, short-term grantee, 1991, All Can. Coun. Mem. Can. Artists Representation (1 of 3 founding mem.'s, sec. 1968-71, life 1999), Nat. Gallery of Can. (life), Art Gallery of Ont. (life), London Regional Art Gallery (life), MacDonald Stewart Art Centre Gallery Stratford (life). Office: Dept Fine Arts U Waterloo Waterloo ON Canada N2L 3G1

URROZ-RAPOLD, PATRICIA JULIA S. retired diplomat, writer; b. Key West, Fla., Feb. 16, 1949; children: Jean Sebastien Bodin Rapold , Nicolas Richard Rapold. BA in Polit. Sci., Boston U., 1971. Consul ad-honorem Nicaragua Boston Ministerio de Relaciones Exteriores, Managua, Nicaragua, 1969—74; social security disability examimer Mass. Rehab. Commn., Boston, 1971—72. Author, pub., poet: Seasonal Living In The Catskills Windham High Peak And Trails, 1994 (Internat. Poet Of Merit award, 1996). Hospitality coord. for fgn. visitors Internat. Ctr., N.Y.C., 1991—93. Recipient Appreciation award for vols., Internat. Ctr., N.Y.C., 1993. Mem.: AAUW (member). Roman Catholic. Avocations: hiking, swimming, reading, collecting. Home: Meadow Winds Rt 52 211 Sara Ln Newburgh NY 12550 Office: Worldstar Corp 245 E 93d St Apt 29 C New York NY Home Fax: 845-566-8266; Office Fax: 212-410-5417. Personal E-mail: Rapold@aol.com. Business E-Mail: LordSeb@aol.com.

URRUTIA, VICTORIA, psychiatrist; b. N.Y.C., Aug. 3, 1958; d. Manuel Urrutia-Lleo and Esperanza (Llaguno) U.; m. Kevin J. Wilson May, 25, 1991; children: Michael Alexander, Caroline Victoria. MD, U. Zaragoza, Spain, 1987. Diplomate Am. Bd. Psychiatry and Neurology, Am. Bd. Child and Adolescent Psychiatry; bd. cert. in psychiatry, child and adolescent psychiatry, forensic psychiatry. Resident in psychiatry Met. Hosp. Ctr., N.Y.C., 1988-91; fellow in child and adolescent psychiatry L.I. Jewish Med. Ctr., New Hyde Park, 1991-93, Schneider Children's Hosp., New Hyde Park, 1991-93; attending psychiatrist Mental Hygiene Clinic, VA Med. Ctr., Miami, Fla., 1994—2001; asst. prof. psychiatry U. Miami, 1994—; psychiatrist Mental Hygiene Clinic, 2001—. Mem. Am. Acad. Child and Adolescent Psychiatry, Nat. Assn. VA Physicians and Dentists, Am. Acad. Psychiatry and the Law. Avocations: reading, music, bicycling. Office: Miami VA Med Ctr Dept Psych Mental Hygiene Clinic 1201 NW 16th St Miami FL 33125-1624 E-mail: Victoria.Urrutia@med.va.gov.

URRUTY, KATHERINE JEAN, secondary school educator; b. Buffalo, Apr. 3, 1948; d. Sauveur and Stella (Washut) Inchauspe; m. John M. Urruty, Dec. 10, 1969; 1 child, Terry John. BA in English, Gonzaga U., Spokane, Wash., 1970; MA in Curriculum and Instrn., U. Wyo., 1978, postgrad., Ea. Mont. State U., Seattle Pacific U., U. Wyo. Cert. tchr., Wyo. Tchr. lang. arts, head dept. chair NCA accreditation Clear Creek Mid. Sch., Buffalo; secondary tchr. Johnson County Sch. Dist., 1970; pvt. tchr. kindergarten, 1971-74; mid. sch. tchr. lang. arts Johnson County Sch. Dist., 1974—. Mem. Instrnl. and Profl. Devel. Commn., Profl. Standards and Practices Commn., Spl. Svcs. and Membership Commn.; tchr. trainer Six-trait Analytical Scoring Model for Student Writing; mentor tchr. coach Essential Elements of Edn. Mem. ASCD, Nat. Coun. Tchrs. English, Wyo. Assn. Tchrs. English (pres. 1988-89), Wyo. Edn. Assn. (assembly del., edn. com., chpt. pres., sec., bldg. rep., treas.), Rocky Mountain Mid. Schs. Assn. (pres. 1987-88), Wyo. ASCD, Delta Kappa Gamma (treas. 1987-90), Phi Delta Kappa. Office: 58 N Adams Ave Buffalo WY 82834-1809

URRY, GRANT WAYNE, retired chemistry educator; b. Salt Lake City, Mar. 12, 1926; s. Herbert William and Emma (Swanner) U.; m. Lillian Alibertini, Sept. 4, 1946; children— Lisa, Claudia, Serena, Anthony. SB, U. Chgo., 1947, PhD, 1953. Research asst., then research assoc. U. Chgo., 1949-53, research assoc., asst. prof., 1954-55; asst. prof. Washington U., St. Louis, 1955-58; assoc. prof. Purdue U., Lafayette, Ind., 1958-64, prof., 1964-68; prof. chemistry Tufts U., Medford, Mass., 1968-92, Robinson prof. chemistry, 1970-92, chmn. dept., 1968-73, Robinson prof. emeritus chemistry, 1992—. Alfred P. Sloan fellow, 1956-58 Fellow N.Y. Acad. Scis., Am. Inst. Chemists, AAAS; mem. Am. Chem. Soc., Am. Soc. Sci. Glassblowers, Fedn. Am. Scientists, Sigma Xi, Phi Lambda Upsilon. E-mail: gurry@erols.com.

URSANO, ROBERT JOSEPH, psychiatrist; b. Heidelberg, Ger., May 26, 1947; s. James Joseph and Neoma Faye (Summers) U.; m. Diane T. Ursano; children: Amy, Anna. BS magna cum laude, U. Notre Dame, 1969; MD, Yale U., 1973; grad., Washington Psychoanalystic Ins, 1986. Diplomate Nat. Bd. Med. Examiners, Am. Bd. Psychiatry and Neurology; lic. physician N.Y., Tex., Md. Resident in psychiatry Wilford Hall USAF Med. Ctr., 1973-75; postdoctoral fellow in psychiatry Yale U./Yale Psychiat. Inst., 1975-77; staff psychiatrist USAF Sch. Aerospace Medicine, Brooks AFB, Tex., 1977-79; clin. asst. prof. U. Tex. Health Sci. Ctr., San Antonio, 1977-79; asst. prof. and dir. third yr. clerkships Dept. psychiatry, Uniformed Svcs. U. Health Scis., Bethesda, Md., 1979-81, assoc prof. and dir. 3rd yr. clerkships, 1981-83, assoc. prof. and assoc. chmn. dept. psychiatry, 1983-86, prof. and assoc. chmn. dept. psychiatry, 1987-92; prof., chair dept. psychiatry Uniformed Svcs. U. Health Scis., Bethesda, Md., 1992—. Examiner Am. Bd. Psychiatry and Neurology, 1984—; asst. prof. Nat. Naval Med. Ctr Dept. Psychiatry, Georgetown U. Sch. Medicine, Washington, 1980-84, assoc. prof., 1984-88, prof., 1988—. Author: Concise Guide to Psychodynamic Psychotherapy, 1990, Concise Guide to Principles and Practice of Psychodynamic Psychotherapy in the Era of Managed Care, 1998; editor: Individual and Community Responses to Trauma and Disaster: The Structure of Human Chaos, 1994, Emotional Aftermath of The Persian Gulf War: Veterans, Families, Communities and Nations, 1996, Acute and Chronic PTSD, 1997; reviewer Am. Jour. Psychiatry, Jour. Nervous and Mental Disease, Psychosomatics, Psychiatry, Jour. Applied Social Psychology, Archives of Gen. Psychiatry, Hosp. and Community Psychiatry, all 1986—, Jour. Neuropsychiatry and Clin. Neurosci., 1988—, Jour. Traumatic Stress, 1989—; editor-in-chief Psychiatry, 1999—; mem. editl. bd. Mil. Medicine; contbr. numerous articles to profl. jours., chpts. to books. Decorated Air Force Commendation medal; recipient Dept. Def. Humanitarian Svc. medal, Dept. Def. Superior Svc. award, William C. Porter award Assn. Mil. Surgeons of U.S.; recipient Disting. Tchg. award Am. Soc. Psychoanalysts Physicians, Life Time Achievement award Internat. Soc. Traumatic Stress Studies. Fellow Am. Psychiat. Assn., Am. Coll. Psychiatrists, Am. Coll. Psychoanalysts; mem. Am. Psychoanalytic Assn., Internat. Psychoanalytic Assn., Am. Psychosomatic Soc., Washington Psychiat. Soc., Washington Psychoanalytic Soc., Soc. of USAF Psychiatrists (v.p. 1981-82), Assn. for Acad. Psychiatry, Alpha Epsilon Delta, Phi Beta Kappa. Home: 3900 Cleveland St Kensington MD 20895-3804 Office: Uniformed Svcs U Health Sci 4301 Jones Bridge Rd Bethesda MD 20814-4712

URSHAN, NATHANIEL ANDREW, minister, church administrator; b. St. Paul, Aug. 29, 1920; s. Andrew David and Mildred (Hammergren) U.; m. Jean Louise Habig, Oct. 1, 1941; children: Sharon, Annette, Nathaniel, Andrew. Student, Columbia U., 1936-39; DTh (hon.), Gateway Coll. Evangelism, 1976. Ordained to ministry United Pentecostal Ch. Internat. Evangelist, 1941-44; assoc. pastor Royal Oak, Mich., 1944-46, N.Y.C., 1947-48, Indpls., 1948-49; pastor Calvary Tabernacle, 1949-78; presbyter Ind. Dist. United Pentecostal Chs., 1950-77; asst. gen. supt. United Pentecostal Ch. Internat., 1971-77, gen. supt. Mo., 1978—; chancellor Urshan Grad. Sch. of Theology, Florissant, 2002. Host radio show Harvestime, 1961-78, 81—; chaplain Ind. Ho. of Reps., 1972. Author: Consider Him, 1962, These Men Are Not Drunk, 1964, Book of Sermons of the Baptism of the Holy Spirit, 1968, Major Bible Prophecy, 1971. Mem. internat. com. YMCA, 1958-79, bd. dirs. Indpls. chpt. 1961-79, world service chmn. Region L., 1969-71; chmn. Heart Fund Campaign, 1968-69; mem. screening com. Marion County Reps., Ind., 1973-74; chmn. Ministerial Com. of Richard Lugar for May of Indpls., 1968, William Hudnut for Mayor, 1975; bd. dirs. Little Red Door, Cancer Soc. Indpls., 1974-77. Recipient gold and brass medallion Heart Fund., Indpls., 1968-69; Nathaniel A. Urshan Day named in his honor, Nov. 3, 1979, Mayor Hudnut, Indpls. Mem. Indpls. Ministerial Assn. Office: United Pentecostal Ch Internat 8855 Dunn Rd Hazelwood MO 63042-2212

URSIAK, DAVID ALLEN, operations executive, consultant; b. Ford City, Pa., Mar. 25, 1952; s. Nicholas and Josephine Sophia (Recny) U.; m. Judy M. Thiry, Aug. 18, 1973 (div. June 1989); children: Jennifer M., David A. Jr.; m. Roberta F. Mattioli, June 16, 1990. BS in Math., Indiana U. Pa., 1974, MS in Bus., 1977, MBA in Fin., 1979, PhD in Bus. Adminstrn., Fin. and Mgmt., 1997. Indsl. engr. McCreary Tire and Rubber CO., Indiana, Pa., 1975-80; mfg. engr. Fisher Scientific Co., 1980-86; program mgr. Liberty Mirror Co., Brackenridge, 1986-93, mgmt. ops., computer cons., 1993-98; sr. program mgr. Alstom Drives & Controls Inc., Pitts., 1998—. Instr. Ind. U. Pa., 1986-89. Mem. Am. Inst. Indsl. Engrs. Home: 1031 Terrace Ave Ford City PA 16226-9729

URSTADT, CHARLES DEANE, real estate executive; b. N.Y.C., June 13, 1959; s. Charles Jordan and Elinor McClure Urstadt. BA cum laude, NYU, 1982. Mng. agt. Sulzberger-Rolfe, Inc., 1982-83; v.p., mem. exec. com., dir. residential sales Urstadt Property Co. (was Pearce, Urstadt, Mayer & Greer), Bronxville, N.Y., 1984-86, exec. v.p., 1986-97, pres., 1997—; pub., editor-in-chief N.Y. Constrn. News, N.Y.C., 1984-92; assoc. broker Brown Harris Stevens Inc., 1992-96, exec. dir., 1996-97, sr. v.p., sales dir., 1997—. Bd. dirs. 61 E 86th St Owners Corp., 1987-89, 90-95, sec., 1990-95; bd. dirs. 18 East 81st St Tenants Corp., 1996-2001. Bd. dirs. The Ensemble Studio Theater, 1988-91, The Friends of 13 Inc., 1992—, East Side Assn., 1988-97, v.p., 1990-95, pres., 1995-97; mem. bd. dirs. Urstadt Biddle Properties, Inc. (formerly HRE Properties), 1991—, Preservation League N.Y., 2001—; mem. N.Y. State Bd. Hist. Preservation, 1996—. Mem. N.Y. Bldg. Congress (bd. dirs. 1988-91), treas. 1989-91). Office: 2112 Broadway New York NY 10023-2142 also: 2 Park Pl Ofc 3 Bronxville NY 10708-4107

URSTADT, CHARLES J. real estate executive; b. Oct. 27, 1928; s. Charles G. and Claire C. (Jordan) U.; m. Elinor McClure Funk, Mar. 23, 1957; children: Charles Deane, Catherine Urstadt Biddle. BA, Dartmouth Coll., 1949, MBA, 1951; LLB, Cornell U., 1953; LLD with honors, Pace U., 1990. Bar: N.Y. Assoc. Nevius Brett & Kellogg, N.Y.C., 1953-58; asst. sec. Webb & Knapp, Inc., 1958-63; v.p., sec., counsel Alcoa Residences, Inc., 1963-67; commr. N.Y. State Divsn. Housing and comty. Renewal, 1967-73; chmn. Battery Park City Authority, 1968-78, Urstadt Property Co. Inc., 1979—. Chmn. Urstadt Biddle Properties, 1986—; trustee Tchrs. Ins. and Annuity Corp., 1985-97; N.Y. Trustee Pace U., 1973— Hist. Hudson Valley, 1997—; mem. fin. com. N.Y. Rep. State Com., 1981—, del. Rep. Nat. Conv., 1988; mem. Gov.'s Task Force on N.Y. Housing, 1988-90; bd. dirs. N.Y.C. Partnership, Inc., 1984-93; chmn. Realty Found. of N.Y., 1989—, N.Y. State Statue of Liberty Celebration Found., 1983-84, N.Y. State Housing Fin. Agy., 1969, Tri-State Regional Planning Commn., 1969-70; vice-chmn. Battery Park City Authority, 1997—; mem. Pres.'s Commn. on Housing, 1981-82, others. Lt. USNR, 1954-56. Office: Urstadt Biddle Properties 321 Railroad Ave Greenwich CT 06830-6306

URSU, ANNE ELIZABETH, writer; b. Mpls., June 6, 1973; d. John Joseph and Mary Willis U.; m. John Eric Broich, Dec. 31, 1998. BA with honors, Brown U., 1996. Theatre critic City Pages, Mpls., 1997-98, Portland Phoenix, 1999-2000. Author: (book) Spilling Clarence, 2002, 2002. Named Best Portland Writer Casco Bay Weekly, 2000.

URSU, JOHN JOSEPH, lawyer; b. 1939; BA, U. Mich., 1962, JD, 1965. Bar: Mich. 1966, Ky. 1970, Minn. 1972. Trial atty. FTC, 1965-67; staff mem. Pres.'s Commn. on Civil Disorders, 1967; advisor to commr. FTC, 1968-69; legal counsel GE, 1969-72; divsn. atty. 3M, 1972-74, sr. atty., 1974-76, assoc. counsel, 1976-81, asst. gen. counsel, 1981-86, assoc. gen. counsel, 1986-90, dep. gen. counsel, 1990-92, gen. counsel, 1992-93, v.p. legal affairs & gen. counsel, 1993-96, sr. v.p. legal affairs and gen. counsel, 1997—. Adj. faculty William Mitchell Coll. Law, 1978-82. Office: 3M Gen Offices 3M Ctr Bldg 220-14W-07 Saint Paul MN 55144-1000

URSYN, ANNA, computer graphics artist, educator; b. Warsaw, Poland, Feb. 11, 1955; came to U.S., 1986; MFA, Fine Arts U., Warsaw, 1982, U. Wyo., 1988, PhD, 1994. Asst. prof. U. No. Colo., Greeley, 1993-95, assoc. prof., 1995-2000, prof., 2000—. Presenter in field; liaison for symposium & gallery of Digital Art of IEEE Internat. conf on Info. Visualization, London, 1998—. Exhibited in group shows at SIGGRAPH-Assn. Computing Machinery Spl. Interest Group on Computer Graphics, Internat. Computer Art Shows, Boston, 1989, Dallas, 1990, Chgo., 1992, Orlando, Fla., 1994, 98, L.A., 1995, 98, 99, 2001, San Antonio, 2002, Der Prix Ars Electronica Internat. Computer Graphics Contests, Linz, Austria, 1988-2002, Eurographics Internat. Computer Graphics Contest, Slide, Video and WWW Competitions, Vienna, Austria, 1991, Poitiers, France, 1996 (award), Lisboa, Portugal, 1998 (award), Milano, Italy, 1999, Internat. Symposia on Electronic Art, Groningen, The Netherlands, 1990, Sydney, Australia, 1992, Helsinki, 1994, Rotterdam, The Netherlands, 1996, Chgo., 1997, Small Computers in the Arts Symposia, Phila., 1990, 92-93, ArCADE Internat. Exhbn. Computer in Art and Design, Brighton, Eng., 1995, 97, 98, 2001, Ann. N.Y. Digital Salon Visual Arts Mus., N.Y.C., 1995, 96, 98, 99, 20th Century Matrix, Tokyo, 1997—, Computerkunst, Gladbeck, Germany, 1996, 98, Digital Visions Etruria, Grosetto, Italy, 1997— (Honorable mention); contbr. art to numerous publs. including Internat. Jour. Computer Graphics, Jour European Assn. Rsch. on Learning and Instrn., Leonardo Visual Computer, Computer Artist, Computer Graphics World, others. Faculty Senate mem. U. No. Colo., 1998—. Recipient Best of Show award U. Wyo. Art Mus., Laramie, 1989, Fine Art Achievement award Binney & Smith Inc. Liquitex, 1991, Scholar of Yr., U. No. Colo. Coll. Performing & Visual Arts, 1995-96, 99—, Grand prize Internat. Competition Dream Centenary, Japan, 1999; grantee U. No. Colo. Found., Greeley, 1996, 99, Ednl. Tech. Improvement Project grantee U. No. Colo., 1997. Mem. Assn. Computing Machinery (Spl. Interest Group on Computer Graphics grantee 1990), Artist Using Sci. and Tech./YLEM, Internat. Soc. for Arts, Scis. and Tech. (assoc.), Inter-Soc. for Electronic Arts, Am. Ednl. Rsch. Assn., Nat. Art Edn. Assn. (conf. 2000, 01), Colo. Art Edn. Assn., Kappa Delta Pi (hon.), Phi Delta Phi (hon.). Avocations: music, skiing, sailing. Office: U No Colo Dept Visual Arts Greeley CO 80639-0001 E-mail: ursyn@unco.edu.

URVAL, KRISHNA RAJ, health facility administrator, educator; b. Mangalore, India, July 3, 1955; came to U.S., 1984; s. Rajgopal Rao and Bhoomi Devi (Kanemar) U.; m. Purnima K. Hebbar, May 23, 1985; children: Nikita, Nikhil. MBBS, MD, Govt. Med. Coll., Mysore City, India, 1979; DCH, U. West Indies, Kingston, Jamaica, 1985. Bd. cert. pediatrics, allergy/immunology. Resident pediats. U. West Indies, Jamaica, 1980—85, Interfaith Med. Ctr., Bklyn., 1985—88, chief resident, 1987—88; fellow immunology U. South Fla., St. Petersburg, 1988—90; assoc. Wyo. Chest and Allergy Clinic, Casper, 1990—91; med. dir. Ohio Valley Allergy Inst., Wheeling, W.Va., 1991—; clin. assoc. prof. W.Va. U., Morgantown, 1991—. Bd. dirs. W.Va. Am. Lung Assn., Charleston. Bd. dirs. Child Care Resource Ctr., Wheeling, 1992—; med. dir. Asthma Support Group, Wheeling, 1992—. Fellow Am. Acad. Pediatrics; mem. AMA, Am. Coll. Allergy/Immunology, Am. Acad. Allergy/Immunology. Democrat. Hindu. Avocations: tennis, ping pong, shuttle badmitton. Office: Ohio Valley Allergy Inst 2101 Jacob St Ste 601 Wheeling WV 26003-3844

URY, CLAUDE MAX, educational consultant, book reviewer; b. Paris, May 5, 1937; Came to U.S., 1941. s. George Lewis and Genia Ury. AB in Econs., San Francisco State U., 1962, MA in Counseling, 1966; MA in Social Sci., U.

Colo., 1981; PhD in History of Edn., U. Santa Barbara, 1993. Tchr. San Francisco Schs., 1973-79; ednl. cons. San Francisco, 1980—; rschr., 1980—. Book reviewer for 22 maj. pub. firms in U.S.; contbr. articles to profl. jours. Mem. Ednl. Rsch. Assn., Am. Econ. Assn., Am. Hist. Assn. Democrat. Jewish. Avocations: travel, bowling, reading, writing. Home: 906 Lake St San Francisco CA 94118-1121 E-mail: Claudem@earthlink.net.

USACHEVA, MARINA NIKOLAEVNA, photochemist, researcher; b. Kiev, Ukraine, Apr. 22, 1941; came to U.S., 1995; d. Nicholas K. and Irina A. (Piskunova) U.; m. Mikhail A. Ayzenberg, Jan. 6, 1963; 1 child, Yuriy. MS in Chemistry, Kiev Poly. U., 1963; PhD in Phys. Chemistry/Photochemistry, Acad. Scis./Kiev Phys. Chem. I, 1970. Postdoctoral rsch. scientist The Phys. Chemistry Inst., Kiev, 1971-76, sr. rsch. scientist, 1976-91; lead sr. rsch. scientist R & D Ctr. of Biotech. Systems "Sonar", 1991-95; rsch. assoc. Minn. Ear, Nose and Throat Rsch. Found., Mpls., 1996—. Contbr. articles to profl. jours. Mem. Am. Soc. Photobiology, European Photochemistry Assn., Russian Mendeleev Chem. Assn. Avocations: jogging, swimming, tennis. Home: 1333 7th St SW New Brighton MN 55112-7653 Office: Advanced Photodynamics Techs Inc 2715 4th St SE Ste 70 Minneapolis MN 55414 E-mail: amaumn@email.msn.com.

USALIS, GEORGE JEROME, metal processing executive; b. Cleve., Aug. 26, 1948; s. George and Amelia (Bugala) U.; children: Mary Beth, Edward. BA, John Carroll U., 1970. Tchr. Gesu Sch., Cleve., 1970-71; asst. dir. admissions John Carroll U., 1971-72; gen. supr. materials dept. White Motor Corp., 1972-75, materials mgr., 1978-81; materials mgr. indoor lighting div. ITT Corp., Vermillion, 1975-78; group mgr. materials and contracts SIFCO Industries Forge Group, Cleve., 1981-94; ptnr., gen. mgr. Accurate Electronics, Inc., Elyria, 1994-96; mgr. materials and finishing ops. Park Drop Forge, Park Ohio Industries, Cleve., 1996; v.p. ops. Cleve. City Forge, Park Ohio Industries, Wellington, 1996-97, pres., gen. mgr., 1997-99; pres. Park Ohio Structural Hardware Co., OH, 1999—; pres. and officer Cleve. City Forge, Inc., 2000—. Assoc. credit com. St. Charles Borromeo Credit Union, Parma, Ohio, 1982-86. Mem. Greater Cleve. Growth Assn., 1981—; cons. Jr. Achievement, Cleve., 1986-94; vol. St. John West Shore Hosp., 1986-95, Cleve. Foodbank, 1991. Mem. Purchasing Assn. Cleve., Nat. Assn. Pruchasing Mgmt., Am. Prodn. and Inventory Control Soc., Am. Mgmt. Assn., John Carroll Alumni Assn. (trustee S.W. Cleve. chpt. 1991—), First Friday Club Cleve., Am. Soc. of Metals. Republican. Roman Catholic. Avocations: fishing, golf, personal computers, travel. Home: 6606 Rockledge Dr Brecksville OH 44141-1743

USCHEEK, DAVID PETROVICH, retired chemist; b. University Heights, Ohio, July 9, 1937; s. Peter Ivanovich and Marie (Ocasek) U. BS, Case Western Res. U., 1959; PhD in Chem. Engring., LaSalle U., 1998. Chemist The Glidden Co., Cleve., 1963-67, Mobil Chem. Co., Cleve., 1967-71, Limbacher Coatings, Cleve., 1971-72; tech. dir. Continental Products, Euclid, Ohio, 1972-80; chemist Body Bros. Paint Corp., Bedford, 1980-83, Harrison Paint Corp., Canton, 1983-88, Akron (Ohio) Paint and Varnish, 1988-95, Ritrama Duramark, 1995-98, Mahoning Paint Corp., 1999-2000; ret., 2000—. Cons. The Analyst, Chardon, Ohio, 1991—. Mem. Am. Chem. Soc., Internat. Union of Pure and Applied Chemists, N.Y. Acad. Scis. Home: 8602 Auburn Rd Chardon OH 44024-8711 Fax: 440-392-9728.

USCHUK, PAMELA MARIE, writer, educator; b. Lansing, Mich., June 10, 1948; d. George and Ella Marie Uschuk; m. Jerome W. Gates, June 7, 1973 (div. Sept. 1981); m. William Pitt Root, Nov. 6, 1987. BA in English, Ctrl. Mich. U.; MFA in Poetry and Fiction, U. Mont., 1986. Poet in-schs. Mont. Arts Coun., Helena, Mont., 1983-87; writer in-residence Poets in Pub. Svc., N.Y.C., 1987-91, Pacific Luth U., Tacoma, 1990; instr. Marist Coll., Poughkeepsie, N.Y., 1987-92; writer-instr. Arts Reach, Tucson, 1994—; instr. U. Ariz. Writing Works Ctr., 1995—. Bd. dirs. Arts Reach, program dir. 1998-99; mem. faculty Ft. Lewis Coll., Durango, Colo., vis. poet, 2001; Tucson/Pima Arts fellow in writing, 2001; dir. Ctr. for Women Writers, Salem Coll., Winston-Salem, N.C., 2002. Author: Finding Peaches in the Desert, 2000, Without Birds, Without Flowers, 1991 (Flume Press award 1990), One-legged Dancer, 2002; editor-in-chief CutBank, 1984-86; guest editor (intro-series) AWP, 1986; contbr. poetry to publs. Recipient Kings English award Ellipses mag., 1990, Iris Poetry award Iris mag., 1991, Ronald H. Bayes Poetry award The Sandhills Rev., 1996, Internat. Poetry award Struga Poetry Evenings, Poetry award Tucson Pima Arts Coun., 2001; Bertha Morton fellowship U. Mont., 1986. Mem. Acad. of Am. Poets, Poets and Writers, Poetry Soc. of Am., Associated Writing Program, Amnesty Internat., World Wildlife Fund, Defenders of Wildlife. Avocations: photography, hiking, stained glass creations, snorkeling, traveling. Home: 2022 E 5th St Tucson AZ 85719-5203 also: 3282 Valley Rd Winston Salem NC 27106-2504

USDIN, GENE LEONARD, physician, psychiatrist; b. N.Y.C., Jan. 31, 1922; s. I. L. and Eva (Miller) U.; m. Cecile Weil, Nov. 8, 1947; children: Cecile Catherine Burka, Linda Ann, Steven William, Thomas Michael. Student, U. N.C., 1939-40, U. Fla., 1940-41; BS, Tulane U., 1943; MD, 1946. Diplomate: Am. Bd. Psychiatry and Neurology (asst. examiner, 1956-80), Am. Bd. Legal Medicine. Intern Touro Infirmary, New Orleans, 1946—47; resident psychiatry Cin. Gen. Hosp., 1949—51; fellow psychiatry Tulane Sch. Medicine, 1951—52; pvt. practice psychiatry New Orleans, 1952—86; pvt practice psychiatry, 1996—; asst. prof. clin. psychiatry Tulane U., 1959—62, assoc. clin. prof., 1962—67, La. State U., 1967—71, clin. prof., 1971—96, clin. prof. emeritus, 1996—; sr. psychiatrist Ochsner Clinic, 1986-96, sr. psychiatrist emeritus, 1996—; prof. Notre Dame Sem., 1969-75; chief divsn. neurology and psychiatry Touro Infirmary, New Orleans, 1962—66, dir. psychiat. svcs., 1966—71. McLaughlin-Gallie vis. prof. Royal Coll. Physicians and Surgeons of Can., 1983; Robert O. Jones lectr. Atlantic Maritime Provinces Psychiat. Assn. (Can.), 1976; sr. psychiatrist DePaul and Charity Hosps.; sr. psychiat. cons. Oshsner Med. Found., New Orleans, 1980-85, Timberlawn Psychiat. Hosp., Dallas, 1979-93; chmn. psychiat. cons. com. Am. Bar Found., 1970-73; mem. nat. psychiatric adv. bd. Achievement and Guidance Ctrs. Am., Inc., 1991-92. Editor in chief Psychiatry Digest, 1964-71, 75-79, Psychiatry Digest (Europe), 1981-92, ACP-Psychiatric Update, 1980-94, 2000-, co-editor, 1994-95, editor 1995-96, 2000-; editor Medilex Digest of Psychiatry, 1980—; mem. editorial bd. Academic Psychiatry, 1989-92, Mental Hygiene, 1969-76, Clin. Medicine, 1965-71, 75-88, Med. Digest, 1965-71, Jour. Hosp. and Community Psychiatry, 1975, chmn., 1980-81, Jour. Psychiat. Edn., 1975-89, Am. Jour. Family Therapy, 1978—, Am. Jour. Social Psychiatry, 1981-87, Swiss Med. Digest, Psychiatry, 1981—, Extracta Medica Practica Psychiatrie, 1981— , Behavioral Scis. and the Law, 1982-92, Dynamic Psychotherapy, 1982-90, Psychiat. Medicine, 1982-88, Advances in Therapy, 1983-96, Clin. Psychiatry News, 1983-92, Contemporary Psychiatry, 1984-93, Health Disease, 1986—, The Psychiat. Times, 1985— (book rev. editor 1988—), Clinical Advances in the Treatment of Psychiatric Disorders, 1987—, Jour. Ottawa Med. Sch, 1976-90, Psychiatry Bookshelf, 1976-78, Women's Psychiat. Health, 1992—; mem. internat. adv. bd. Jour. Psicopatologia, Madrid, 1989-94; editor: Psychoneurosis and Schizophrenia, 1966, Practical Lectures in Psychiatry for the Medical Practitioner, 1966, Adolescence: Care and Counseling, 1967, Perspectives on Violence, 1972, (with Peter A. Martin and A.W. Swipe) A Physician in the General Practice of Psychiatry, 1970, The Psychiatric Forum, 1973, Sleep Research and Clinical Practice, 1973, Psychiatry: Education and Image, 1973, Overview of the Psychotherapies, 1975, Schizophrenia: Biological and Psychological Perspective, 1976, Depression: Clinical, Biological and Psychological Perspectives, 1977, Psychiatric Medicine, 1977, (with Charles K. Hofling) Aging: The Process and the People, 1978, (with Jerry M. Lewis, II) Psychiatry in General Medical Practice, 1979, (with David R. Hawkins) The Office Guide to Sleep Disorders, 1980, (with Jerry M. Lewis) Treatment Planning in Psychiatry, 1982; Contbr. articles to profl. jours. Bd. trustees United Fund Greater New Orleans, 1966-70. Served to lt. (j.g.) USNR, 1947-49. Recipient Physician of Yr. award Orleans Parish Med. Soc., 1984, Outstanding Alumni Lectr. award Tulane U. Sch. Medicine, 1986, Seymour Pollack Disting. Svc. award Am. Acad. Psychiatry and the Law, 1988, Outstanding Contbrn. to Social Psychiatry award Am. Assn. for Social Psychiatry, 1993, Lifetime Achievement awards Tulane Med. Alumni Assn., 1996, Fla. Hosp. Ctr. for Psychiatry, 1996, La. State U. Sch. Medicine Dept. Psychiatry Chmn.'s award, 1998-99, Champion of Pub. Health award Tulane U. Sch. Pub. Health and Tropical Medicine, 2001; named Psychiatrist of Yr., La. Psychiat. Med. Assn., 1994, Psychiat. Times, 1997. Fellow Am. Psychiat. Assn. (chmn. com. on psychiatry and law 1964-68, mem. com. on ethics 1970-74, com. on membership 1970-74, com. on evaluation svcs. bd. 1974-77, com. on pub. affairs 1976-78, chmn. ad hoc com. on election procedures, 1980-81, trustee at large 1978-81, coun. on internat. affairs 1986-91, sec. gen. Interamerican Coun. of Psychiatric Orgns. 1988-91, recipient 3d ann. Certificate of Recognition for Excellence in Med. Student Edn. 1993, Warren Williams award, 1995, Spl. Presdl. commendation 1998), So. Psychiat. Assn. (bd. regents 1969-72, chmn. 1971-72, pres. 1973-74), La. Psychiat. Assn. (past pres.), Am. Coll. Psychiatrists (bd. regents 1967-70, pres. 1978-79, E.B. Bowis award for Outstanding Contbns. 1973, Disting. Service award for Oustanding Contbns. in Am. Psychiatry 1980), Acad. Psychosomatic Medicine (mem. exec. council 1974-76), New Orleans Soc. Psychiatry and Neurology (past pres.), Group Advancement Psychiatry (bd. dirs. 1970-77, treas. 1973-77), Am. Assn. Social Psychiatry (pres. 1986-88), World Assn. for Social Psychiatry (exec. coun. 1988-90); mem. La. Med. Soc. (chmn. com. on mental health 1966-70), Orleans Parish Med. Soc., Nat. Assn. Mental Health (mem. profl. advisory counc. 1968-75), Inst. of Mental Hygiene (pres. 1978-79). Home and Office: 3 Newcomb Blvd New Orleans LA 70118-5527

USEEM, RUTH HILL, sociology educator; b. Hamilton, Ohio, May 31, 1915; d. William E. and Anna E. (Starlin) Hill; m. John Hearld Useem, June 6, 1940; children: Michael, Howard Sheldon, Bert. BA, Miami U., Oxford, Ohio, 1936; PhD, U. Wis., 1947. Asst. prof. Queens Coll., N.Y.C., 1942-43, 1944-45; rsch. cons. Mich. State U., East Lansing, 1951-52, instr., 1952-58, asst. prof., 1958-60, assoc. prof., 1960-70, prof. sociology and edn., 1970-85, prof. emerita, 1985—. Sr. fellow East-West Center, 1970 Author: (with J. Useem) The Western-Educated Man in India, 1955, (with F. Kempf) Psychology: Dynamics of Behavior in Nursing; contbr. articles to profl. jours. Disting. scholar Internat. Soc. Ednl., Cultural and Sci. Interchanges, 1979; recipient Excellence award Mich. State U. Faculty Women's Assn., 1979, award for Research in Internat. Ednl. Exchange, Council Internat. Ednl. Exchange, 1986; Edward W. Hazen Found. grantee India, 1952-53, 58; Edward W. Hazen Found. grantee Philippines, 1968-75; recipient Lee Founders' award for disting. career Soc. for Study of Social Problems, 1987, Pioneering Rsch. on Third Culture Kids award Global Nomads Internat., 1988. Mem. Am. Sociol. Assn. (council 1973-75, com. on coms. 1975-76, com. world sociology 1975-77, com. nominations 1979-81, liaison AAAS com. 1986-87), North Cen. Sociol. Assn. (council 1976-77, v.p./program chmn. 1977-78, pres. 1979-80, Disting. Profl. Service award 1984), Sociologists for Women in Soc., Soc. Internat. Edn., Tng. and Research (council 1978-81), Internat. Soc. Ednl., Cultural and Sci. Interchanges, Sociol. Research Assn., Mortar Bd.; fellow Am. Anthrop. Assn. Home: 227 Chesterfield Pkwy East Lansing MI 48823-4110

USELMANN, CATHERINE ROSE (KIT USELMANN), small business owner, network marketer, behavioral researcher, financial independence consultant; b. Madison, Wis., Sept. 17, 1960; d. Richard Lewis and Evelyn Mae (Parr) U. AA, Madison Area Tech. Coll., 1982; BA in Sociology, U. Wis., 1984, MA in Rsch. and Analysis, 1985; DD (hon.), Charter Ecumenical Ministries Internat., 1994. Pub. utility rate analyst Pub. Svc. Commn. Wis., Madison, 1986-89; rsch. mgr. Wis. Lottery, 1989-90; energy cons., tech. analyst II HBRS, Inc., 1990-91; sr. cons., project mgr. XENERGY, Inc., Burlington, Mass., 1991-93; pres. CRU Prodns., Madison, 1993-97; exec. Nutrition For Life Internat., Houston, 1995—, Trudeau Mktg. Group, Chgo., 1995-98; team coord. I-Team, Cyberspace, 1996-98. Speaker Nat. Assn. Regulatory Utility Commrs., 1987-89; contbg. mem., speaker Assn. for Demand-Side Mgmt. Profls., 1991-93. Univ. rep. operating com. Mall/Concourse, Madison, 1982-84; lobbyist Inst. for Rsch. Poverty, Madison, 1984; activist, mem. People for Ethical Treatment Animals, Washington, 1989—. Mem. Fin. Independence Assn., U. Wis. Alumni Assn., Badger Quarter Horse Assn. (life) Lutheran. Avocations: gourmet cooking, health, wealth. Home and Office: 3753 Robin Hood Way Madison WI 53718-6243

USELTON, BILL W. secondary education educator; b. Oklahoma City, Dec. 14, 1959; s. Jerry Max and Minnie Jewel Uselton; m. Cathy Sue Uselton, Oct. 16, 1982; children: Kelly Irene, Jennifer Elaine. A in Fine Arts, Oscar Rose Jr. Coll., Midwest City, Okla., 1980; BFA, Ctrl. State U., Edmund, Okla., 1982. Cert. secondary sch. tchr. Constract substitute Choctaw (Okla.) Pub. Schs., 1982-84; tchr. Choctaw Jr. H.S., 1984-86, Choctaw H.S., 1986—. Author: Triad of Evil, 1993. Mem. World Jewish Congress; tour guide S.W. Radio Ch., Oklahoma City, 1982; chmn. Confederate Meml., Choctaw, 1996—. Republican. Baptist. Home: 1024 S Anderson Rd Choctaw OK 73020 E-mail: buselton@mmcable.com.

USELTON, DARRELL BRENT, social sciences educator; b. Union City, Tenn., Mar. 17, 1954; s. James Edward Uselton and Nancy Eleanor Sawyer; m. Rebecca Gail Barnett, Mar. 9, 1974 (div.); m. Mary Beth Doty, May 8, 1982. BA, U. Memphis, 1995; grad., Mil. Police Sch., Ft. Gordon, Ga., 1973, Tenn. Law Enforcement Tng. Acad., Nashville, 1977; MA, U. Memphis, 1997. Legal investigator, bus. mgr. Gerber & Gerber law firm, Memphis, 1979—83; exec. adminstr. Fogelman Properties, Inc., 1983—84; sales adminstr., asst. v.p. Union Planters Investment Ganking Group, 1984—88; regoinal mgr., asst. v.p. Storage USA, Inc., 1988—89; asst. mgr. ednl. coord. Mississippi River Mus., 1995; history instr. U. Memphis, 1998—; social scis. instr. Mid-South C.C., West Memphis, Ark., 1998—. Bd. dirs. Sales and Mktg. Execs. of Memphis, Inc., 1989; faculty advisor Phi Theta Kappa Nat. Honors Soc., 1999—. Contbr. articles to profl. jours. Coord. Citizens for Better Govt. PAC, Memphis, 1983—84. Mem.: Phi Alpha Theta.

USHAKOV, YURI VIKTOROVICH, diplomat; b. Moscow, Mar. 13, 1947; married; 1 daughter. Grad., Moscow State Inst. Internat. Relations, 1970; PhD in History, Diplomatic Acad. With Soviet Embassy in Denmark Ministry Fgn. Affairs of the USSR, 1970-75, with, 1975-86; dep. chief mission, min.-counsellor Embassy of the USSR/Russian Fedn., Denmark, 1986-92; dir. Directorate of All-European Coop. Ministry Fgn. Affairs Russian Fedn., 1982-96; amb., permanent rep. Russian Fedn. to the Orgn. Security and Coop. Europe, Vienna, Austria, 1996-98; dep. min. fgn. affairs Govt. Russian Fedn., 1998-99, amb. to the U.S., 1999—. Office: Embassy of the Russian Fedn 2650 Wisconsin Ave NW Washington DC 20007-4600 Fax: 202-298-5749.

USHER, BETHANY MCKAY, biologist; b. Richmond, Va., July 11, 1970; d. Cecil H. and Elizabeth Mowray Usher; m. Jaimin David Weets. PhD, Pa.State U., 2000. Archaeologist, graphics mgr. R. Christopher Goodwin & Assoc., Inc., Frederick, Md., 1991—93; tchg. and rsch. asst. Ariz. State U., Tempe, 1993—95; asst. prof. anthropology Shippensburg (Pa.) U., 1999—2000; asst. prof. biol. anthropology SUNY, Potsdam, NY, 2000—02. Scholar Fulbright Fgn. scholar, Fulbright Assn., 1997—98. Mem.: Am. Assn. Phys. Anthropologists. Office: SUNY Coll at Potsdam 118A MacVicar Hall Potsdam NY 13676 Office Fax: 315-267-3176. Personal E-mail: usherbm@potsdam.edu. Business E-Mail: usherbm@potsdam.edu.

USHER, CHARLES LINDSEY, social work educator, public policy analyst; b. Portsmouth, Va., Aug. 12, 1949; s. Henry George and Lottie Frances (Dickens) U.; m. Janan Bailey, Aug. 14, 1971; children: Lindsay Erin, Ellen Ashley. BA in Polit. Sci., Old Dominion U., 1971, M in Urban Studies, 1974; postgrad., U. Mich., 1975; PhD in Polit. Sci., Emory U., 1976. Planning and evaluation specialist Dept. Social Svcs., Portsmouth, 1972-73; asst. prof. polit. sci. Miami U. of Ohio, Oxford, 1976-78, U. N.C., Charlotte, 1978-80; policy analyst, sr. policy analyst Rsch. Triangle Inst., Rsch. Triangle Park, N.C., 1980-84, dir. Ctr. for Policy Studies, 1985-92; exec. dir. Northeastern N.C. Tomorrow, Inc., Elizabeth City, 1984-85; Wallace H. Kuralt Sr. prof. pub. welfare policy/adminstrn. U. N.C., Chapel Hill, 1993—. Presenter in field. Assoc. editor Evaluation Rev., 1987-89; contbr. articles to profl. jours. Bd. dirs. Arc of Durham County, 1992-98. Grantee Ctr. for Study of Social Policy, 1990-93, Annie E. Casey Found., 1992—, Edna McConnel Clark Found., 1995-96. Mem. ASPA, Am. Evaluation Assn., Am. Pub. Human Svcs. Home: 4215 Swarthmore Rd Durham NC 27707-5389 Office: U NC Sch Social Work 301 Pittsboro St Chapel Hill NC 27516-2911

USHER, MARY MARGARET, special education educator; b. Chgo., July 5, 1949; d. Earl Raymond and Rebecca Patricia (McElroy) Asher; m. James Lee Usher; children: Sherri, Michael, Lori. BS in Edn., U. North Tex., 1971; cert. in behaviorally disorder, Harris Stowe State Coll., 1991. Cert. tchr., Mo.; cert. tchr. learning disabled, mentally handicapped. Substitute tchr. Fox Sch. Dist., Arnold, Mo., 1986-87, 89—, Windsor Sch. Dist., Imperial, 1985-87, 89—, Spl. Svcs. Co-op., Imperial, 1987, 89—; paraprofessional physically impaired class Pevely Elem., 1992—; juvenile detention ctr. tchr. Jefferson County Children's Home, Mo., 1993-96; spl. edn. tchr. Mo. Eastern Correctional Ctr., Pacific, 1997-2000, Windsor H.S., Imperial, Mo., 2000-01; substitute tchr. Spl. Sch. Dist. St. Louis County, St. Louis, 2001—02, Mehlville Sch. Dist., St. Louis, 2001—02; spl. edn. tchr. Hawthorne Children's Psychiatric Hosp., 2002—. V.p. bd. dirs. Imperial Khoury League, 1987—89, chmn. ways and means com., 1989—90; dist. sec. United Meth. Women, 1993—96; pres. New Hope United Meth. Ch., 1990—91, sec., 1998—99, coord. for interpretation of edn. in mission, nominating com., pres., 2002; pres. New Hope United Meth. Women, 2001—. Mem. Coun. for Exceptional Children (pres. 1991, v.p. Jefferson County chpt. 1994-95, pres. Jefferson County chpt. 1995-96), St. Louis Zoo Friends Assn., Friends of Jefferson County Libr., Kappa Delta. Avocations: reading, crossword puzzles, travel, country western dancing. Home: 5125 Darkmoor Ln Imperial MO 63052-3032 E-mail: mmu1949@hotmail.com.

USHER, NANCY SPEAR, retired language arts educator; b. Malden, Mass., Mar. 13, 1938; d. George Alonzo and Mary Elizabeth (York) Spear; m. Walter Lansley Whitlock, June 13, 1959 (div. Oct. 1961); m. Frederic Laurence Usher, Apr. 19, 1970 (dec. April 1998). BS in Edn., U. So. Maine, 1960; postgrad., Boston U., Salem State Coll., 1964-68. 5th grade tchr. Melrose (Mass.) Sch. Dept., 1961-63, 7th grade English tchr., 1963-65, 71-97, 7th grade spl. needs tchr., 1965-70; ret., 1997. Freshman girls' basketball coach Melrose High Athletic Dept., 1973-77. Mem. U. So. Maine Alumni Assn. Avocations: golf, boating, reading. E-mail: nusher38@aol.com.

USHER, PHYLLIS LAND, state official; b. Winona, Miss., Aug. 29, 1944; d. Sandy Kenneth and Ruth (Cottingham) Land; m. William A. Usher (dec. Dec. 1993). BS, U. So. Miss., 1967; MS, U. Tenn., 1969; postgrad., Purdue U., Ind. U., Utah State U. Libr. Natchez (Miss.) - Adams County Schs., 1967-68; materials specialist Fulton County Bd. Edn., Atlanta, 1969-71; cons. divsn. instructional media Ind. Dept. Pub. Instrn., Indpls., 1971-74, dir. divsn., 1974-82, dir. fed. resources and sch. improvement, 1982-85; acting assoc. supt. Ind. Dept. Edn., 1985, sr. officer Ctr. Sch. Improvement, 1985-96, asst. supt., 1996—. Pres. bd. dirs. INCOLSA, mcpl. corp., 1980-82; pres., owner Usher Funeral Home, Inc.; pres. NU Realty Corp.; mem. task force sch. Libraries Nat. Commn. Libraries and Info. Sci.; cons. in field. Bd. dirs. Hawthorne Cmty. Ctr.; mem. Gov. Inst. Conf. Children and Youth Task Force. Recipient citation Internat. Reading Assn., 1975; Title II-B fellow, U. Tenn., 1968-69. Mem. ALA, Nat. Assn. State Ednl. Media Profls., West Deanery Bd. Edn., Indpls. Archdiocese, Delta Kappa Gamma. Office: State House Rm 229 Indianapolis IN 46204-2728

USHIJIMA, JOHN TAKEJI, state legislator, lawyer; b. Hilo, Hawaii, Mar. 13, 1924; s. Buhachi and Sano (Nitahara) U.; m. Margaret Kunishige, June 6, 1954. BA, Grinnell Coll., 1950; JD, George Washington U., 1952. Bar: Hawaii, 1953. Ptnr. Pence & Ushijima, Hilo, 1953-61, Ushijima & Nakamoto, Hilo, 1961-69; mem. Hawaii Senate, 1959—, pres. pro tem, 1974—. Bd. dirs. Cyanotech Corp., Woodinville, Wash. Bd. dirs. Waiakea Settlement YMCA. With AUS, 1943-46, ETO. Mem. Am. Bar Assn., Phi Delta Phi. Democrat. Home: 114 Melani St Hilo HI 96720-2766 Office: 192 Kapiolani St Hilo HI 96720-2687

USINGER, MARTHA PUTNAM, counselor, educator; b. Pitts., Dec. 10, 1912; d. Milo Boone and Christiana (Haberstroh) Putnam; m. Robert Leslie Usinger, June 24, 1938 (dec Oct. 1968); children: Roberta Christine (dec.), Richard Putnam. AB cum laude, U. Calif., Berkeley, 1934, postgrad., 1935—36, Oreg. State U., 1935—37, U. Ghana, 1970, Coll. Nairobi, 1970. Tchr. Oakland (Calif.) Pub. Schs., 1936-38, Berkeley (Calif.) Pub. Schs., 1954-57, dean West Campus, counselor, 1957-78. Lectr., photographer in field. Author: Ration Books and Christmas Crackers, 1989; contbg. author Robert Leslie Usinger, Autobiography of an Entomologist, 1972. Mem. DAR, Berkeley Ret. Tchrs., U. Calif. Emeriti Assn., U. Calif. Alumnae Assn., Prytanean Alumnae Assn. (alumnae pres. 1952-54), Berkeley Camera Club, Mortar Bd., Am. Friends of Puttenham, P.E.O., Delta Kappa Gamma. Avocations: photography, slide shows and lectures, ethnic textiles, travel, geneology.

USKI, TORE KALEVI, neurosurgeon, researcher; b. Kumla, Sweden, May 12, 1954; s. Toivo and Maire (Räsänen) U. Grad. in Medicine, Lund U., Sweden, 1975; MD, Lund U., 1979, PhD, 1984. House surgeon dept. neurosurgery Univ. Hosp., Lund, 1981-83, registrar, 1983-87, sr. registrar, 1987-89, sr. registrar, assoc. prof., 1989-94, cons., assoc. prof., 1994—, acting prof., chmn. acad. dept. neurosurgery, 1994-95. Rsch. scientist, acad. dept. neurosurgery, 1987-91. Contbr. articles, revs. to profl. jours. Fellow Swedish Soc. Medicine; mem. Soc. Cerebral Blood Flow and Metabolism (founding). Avocations: gliding, computers. Office: Dept Neurosurgery Univ Hosp Lund S 221 85 Sweden E-mail: tore.uski@neurokir.lu.se.

USSERY, ALBERT TRAVIS, lawyer, investment company executive; b. Gulfport, Miss., Mar. 12, 1928; s. Walter Travis and Rosamond (Sears) U.; m. Margaret Grosvenor Paine, Nov. 22, 1950; children: Margaret Rosamond, John Travis, Marilyn Ann, Meredith Lee. AB, Washington U., St. Louis, 1950; LLB, U. N.Mex., 1951, JD, 1968; LLM, Georgetown U., 1955. Bar: N.Mex. 1951. Ptnr. Gallagher and Ussery, Albuquerque, 1951-53, Threet, Ussery & Threet, Albuquerque, 1957-60; assoc. with Alfred H. McRae, Albuquerque, 1961-63; ptnr. McRae, Ussery, Mims, Ortega & Kitts, Albuquerque, 1964-65; chmn. Am. Bank Commerce, 1966-70, pres., 1967-70; ptnr. Ussery, Burciaga & Parrish, Albuquerque, 1969-79; pres. Ussery & Parrish, P.A., Albuquerque, 1980—; spl. counsel to Albuquerque on water law, 1956-66; chmn. Rio Grande Valley Bank, Albuquerque, 1972-83, Bank of S.W., 1980-83; lectr. mil. law U. N.Mex., 1956, instr. corp. fin., 1956-57, lectr. bus. law, 1960-61; bd. dirs. 1st City Investment Brokers, Inc., 1983-85, Lovelace Med. Systems and Techs., Inc., 1983-84. Chmn. water adv. com. Albuquerque Indsl. Devel. Svc., 1960-66; vice chmn. N.Mex. Coun. on Econ. Edn., 1969-74; mem. N.Mex. Regional Export Expansion Council, 1969-74, mem. Albuquerque Armed Forces Adv. Assn., 1977—. Trustee Village Los Ranchos de Albuquerque, 1970-72; chmn. adv. bd. Lovelace-Bataan Med. Ctr., 1976-78; trustee Lovelace Med. Found., 1978-96, vice chmn., 1988-96; trustee Lovelace Respiratory Rsch. Inst., 1996—, chmn., 1966—; bd. dirs. Goodwill Industries N.Mex., 1957-65, Albuquerque Travelers Assistance, 1956-66, Family Consultation Svc., 1961-64, Albuquerque Symphony Assn., 1964-68, Hispanic Culture Found., 1983-92, Lovelace Health Plan Inc., 1985-89; bd. dirs. N.Mex. Arthritis Found., 1969-74, pres., 1971. Mem. Am., Fed., Albuquerque (treas. 1957-60) bar assns., State Bar N.Mex., Estate Planning Coun. Albuquerque (pres. 1962), N.Mex. Zool. Soc. (dir., pres. 1977-78), Am. Legion (comdr. 1962-63), Lawyers Club. (pres. 1983-84). Lodge: Kiwanis (dir. 1957-60). Home: 37 Chaco Loop Sandia Park NM 87047-8505 Office: Ussery & Parrish PA 200 Rio Grande Valley Bldg 501 Tijeras Ave NW Albuquerque NM 87102-3109

USUI, LESLIE RAYMOND, retired clothing executive; b. Wahiawa, Hawaii, Feb. 2, 1946; s. Raymond Isao and Joyce Mitsuyo (Muramoto) U.; m. Annie On Nor Hom, Oct. 23, 1980; 1 child, Atisha. BA in Zool., U. Hawaii, 1969, MA in Edn., 1972. Cert. tchr., Hawaii. Flight steward United Airlines, Honolulu, 1970; spl. tutor Dept. Edn., 1971-73; v.p. Satyuga, Inc., Honolulu, 1974-80, pres., 1980-97; also bd. dirs.; ret., 1997. Cons. Hawaii Fashion Guild, 1978-79. Composer: Song to Chenrayzee, Song to Karmapa. Co-founder, bd. dirs. Kagyu Thegchen Ling Meditation Ctr., 1974—, pres., 1997-99; bd. dirs. Maitreya Inst., 1983-86, Palpung Found., 1984—; mem. U.S. Senatorial Bus. Adv. Bd., Washington, 1988; charter mem. Citizens Against Govt. Waste, 1988—, Citizens for Sound Economy, 1987-91, Nat. Tax Limitation Com., 1988-89. Mem. Am. Biog. Inst. (life, bd. govs. 1990), Internat. Biog. Centre (life), World Inst. Achievement (life), Cousteau Soc., Nature Conservancy, Waikiki Aquarium. Republican. Buddhist. Avocations: oriental gardening, music. Home: PO Box 161257 Honolulu HI 96816-0926 Office: Satyuga Inc PO Box 161257 Honolulu HI 96816-0926

UTELL, MARK JEFFREY, medical educator; b. N.Y.C., July 25, 1946; m. Lois Brooks; 1 child, Michael Jon. BA cum laude, Dartmouth Coll., 1968; MD, Tufts U., 1972. Diplomate Am. Bd. Internal Medicine. Intern St. Elizabeth's Hosp., Boston, 1972-73, resident in internal medicine, 1973-75; from instr. to prof. sch. medicine U. Rochester, N.Y., 1975-92, prof. Sch. Medicine, 1992—, prof. medicine and environ. medicine Sch. Medicine. Dir. respiratory and med. ICUs Strong Meml. Hosp., Rochester, 1977-89, mem.

intensive care com., 1977-87; co-dir. pulmonary and critical care sch. medicine U. Rochester, 1984-91, dir. pulmonary and critical care, 1991—; occupl. medicine program, 1988—, assoc. chmn. clin. affairs dept. environ. medicine, 1992—, dir. occupl. and environ. medicine divsn., 1992—, acting chair dept. medicine, 1998-99; cons. VA, 1977—, EPA, 1980—, mem. clean air sci. adv. com., 1988-94; chmn. Environ. health Com., 1998—; mem. exec. com. EPA Sci. adv. bd.; reviewer site visit com. NIH, 1982, outside reviewer respiratory and applied physiology sect. NHLBI, 1982; mem. rev. study sect. Nat. Inst. Environ. Health Scis., 1990-94, mem. task force for rsch. planning; mem. health rsch. com. Health Effects Inst., 1985-94, chair, 2000—; mem. N.Y. State Commr.'s Panel on Tuberculosis, Syracuse, 1988; mem. commn. life scis. NRC, NAS, 1989; mem. panel airborne particulate matter in spacecraft NASA, 1987, mem. environ. health scis. working group, 1993-94. Co-author: Inhalation Toxicology of Air Pollution: Clinical Research Considerations, 1985, Susceptibility to Inhaled Pollutants, 1989; co-editor: Advances in Controlled Clinical Inhalation Studies, 1993; mem. editl. bd. Jour. Aerosol Medicine, Annals of Internal Medicine, 1997-99, Inhalation Tech., Environ. Health Perspectives, Inhalation Toxicology, 1989-2001; guest reviewer various jours.; contbr. over 100 articles to profl. jours. Bd. dirs. Am. Lung Assn. N.Y. State, 1986-88. Grantee Nat. Inst. Environ. Health Scis., Nat. Heart Lung and Blood Inst., EPA, Elec. Power Rsch. Inst., Dow Corning Corp. Fellow AAAS, ACP, Am. Coll. Chest Physicians (mem. steering com. sect. environ. occupl. health 1983-87, assessment asthma in workplace com. 1994); mem. Am. Physiol. Soc., Am. Thoracic Soc. (chmn. scientific assembly on environ. and occupl. health 1987, mem. planning com., 1992-94, respiratory protective guidelines com., 1993-95, other coms.), Am. Coll. Occupl. Environ. Medicine, N.Y. Trudeau Soc. (pres. 1986). Home: 16 Framingham Ln Pittsford NY 14534-1048 Office: U Rochester Sch Medicine Dept Medicine Pulmonary 601 Elmwood Ave Dept Medicine Rochester NY 14642-0001

UTER, CARMENLITA, secondary school educator, genealogist; b. Sea Islands Coast; d. Charles and Helena (Uter) Cook; m. Gottfried Lehmann, Apr. 10, 1968; children: Michael Lehmann, Sharon Lehmann. BA, Hunter Coll., 1974, MA, 1979; postgrad., Coll. New Rochelle, N.Y., 1994. Cert. tchr. Spanish and English, N.Y. Tchr. fgn. langs. N.Y.C. Bd. Edn., 1974—; founder, dir. Creole/Crioulo-Am. Geneal. Soc., Inc., N.Y.C., 1983—. Propr. Creole Collection, Ltd., art, artifacts and memorabilia. Author: (book of poetry, under pen name of Miss Utera) The Malada's Lament, 1989, (book) The Creole-Americans, 1999. Mem. Assn. Am. Tchrs. Spanish and Portuguese, Archivist Round Table of Met. N.Y., Assn. Profl. Genealogists. Roman Catholic. Avocations: translation, genealogy, writing. Home: PO Box 740501 Flushing NY 11374-0501

UTERMOHLEN, HERBERT GEORG, dermatologist; b. Göttingen, Germany, Nov. 27, 1948; came to U.S., 1990, permanent resident; s. Paul Ernst and Gertrud (Quentin) U.; 1 child, Christian. MD, U. Göttingen, 1976. Specialist in dermatology and allergy U. Hosps. Göttingen, 1980-84; pvt. practice Hamburg, Germany, 1986-89, Scarsdale, N.Y., 1990—. With German Armed Forces, 1977-79. Mem. AMA, AAAS, N.Y. Acad. Scis., Deutsche Gesellschaft Für Psychiat. and Nervenheilkunde, Deutsche Dermatology Gesellschaft. Home: 923 Saw Mill River Rd Ste 263 Ardsley NY 10502-1106

UTHEZA, HERVE JEAN LOUIS, communications executive; b. Toulouse, France, Mar. 26, 1967; s. Guy and Jacqueline (Couget) U. BA, Lycee Pierre de Fermat, Toulouse, France, 1989; MBA, Hautes Etudes Commerciales, Paris. Pres., CEO HEC Jr. Conseil, Paris, 1989-90; U.S. rep. Thomson CSF Ventures, Palo Alto, Calif., 1991-93; fin. analyst Thomson Multimedia, 1993-94; contracts and licensing mgr. Thomson Sun Interactive, Mountainview, 1994-96; bus. devel. mgr. Navio Comm., Sunnyvale, 1997-98; bus. devel. mgr. Europe Network Computer, Redwood Shores, 1998—. Author: Valeur Ajoutée et Taxe Professionelle, 1989, (poetry) Silences Murmurés, 1993; author mkt. studies Investing in Florida, 1990, Venture Capital in Silicon Valley, 1992; dir. Pay TV Europe. Mem. French-Am. C. of C. Avocations: philosophy, writing, painting, photography, cooking. Home: 27 Levant St San Francisco CA 94114-1409 Office: Network Computer 1000 Bridge Pkwy Redwood City CA 94065-1157

UTHMAN, BASIM MOHAMMAD, neurologist, epileptologist, consultant; b. Tripoli, Lebanon, Sept. 25, 1958; came to the U.S., 1984; s. Mohammad Assa'ad and Mariam Mohammad (Moukalled) U. BSc, Am. U. Beirut, 1978, MD, 1984. Diplomate Am. Bd. Clin. Neurophysiology, Am. Bd. Psychiatry and Neurology (adult neurology), Am. Bd. Psychiatry and Neurology with spl. qualifications in clin. neurophysiology. Intern Am. Univ. Beirut Med Ctr., Lebanon, 1983-84; resident in neurologyDept. Neurology U. Cin., 1984-87, clin. fellow in neurophysiology, epilepsy, preceptor, 1987-88; clin. rsch. fellow in epilepsy, neurophysiology and neuropharmacology U. Fla., Gainesville, 1988-90, clin. instr., 1990-91, vis. asst. prof. dept. neurology, 1991—92, asst. prof. dept. neurology, 1992—96, assoc. prof. dept. neurology, 1996—; assoc. prof. dept. neurosci. U. Fla. Brain Inst., 1997—; staff neurologist VA Med. Ctr., Gainesville, 1990—, asst. chief neurology svc., 1992—, dir. status epilepticus team, 1990-95, contracting officers tech. rep., 1990-92, acting chief neurology svc., 1993, dir. clin. neurophysiology lab. EEG/EP, 1991—, dir. vagus nerve stimulation therapy, 1991—; champion dementia clin. practice guidelines Southeast Dept. Vets. Affairs Med. Ctrs., 1997—99. Chmn. med. record rev. com. VA, 1995-99; chmn. adminstrv. bd. investigation VA Med. Ctr., Gainesville, 1993; attending epileptologist Shands Hosp., 1993-98; mem. instnl. rev. bd. U. Fla. Health Sci. Ctr., 1994-96; mem. subcom. for clin. investigations Malcom Randall VA Med. Ctr., 1996-2002; mem. pharmacy benefit mgmt./med. adv. panel VA Med. Ctrs. Sys., 1998—. Ad hoc referee U.S. Pharmacopeial Conv., 1988-89, Drug Evaluations, 1990, Epilepsia, 1990, Jour. Neuroimaging, 1990, Drugs, 1993-2001; contbr. articles to profl. jours., chpts. to books. Active emergency blood donation campaign, Beirut, 1982-83, worker war disaster plan, 1982-83; vol. Lebanese Red Cross, Beirut, 1982-83; organizer children's med. ednl. presentations, 1984; profl. adv. bd. Epilspsy Found. Fla., 1992-93, chmn., 1993. A.S. Khalidi scholar Am. U. Beirut, 1978, Azeez B. Ajloini scholar, 1979, Tamari-Saab scholar, 1979, Dr. Haddad, 1980; fellow Bowman Gray Med. Sch., Winston-Salem, N.C., 1987; grantee Epilepsy Rsch. Found. Fla., 1988-90, Cyberonics, 1989-98, Marion Merryl Dow and Hoechot, Marion, Roussel, Inc., 1994-98, VA Coop. Studies Program Coordinating Ctr., 1990-95, 97—, VA Affairs Med. Ctr. Allotment, 1991-92, Abbott Labs., 1991--, U. Fla., 1991-92, Ceiba-Geigy, 1991-94, U. Fla. Brain Inst., 1992, Parke-Davis 1993-2000, Novartis, 1998—, Pfizer, 2000--, Elan, 2000-01, Schwarz, 2001--, Ivax, 2001--, Nat. Brain Injury Fund for Treatment and Tchg., 2001--; recipient J. Kiffin Penry Eagle award, 1998. Mem. AMA, Am. Acad. Neurology, Am. Epilepsy Soc., Am. Sleep Disorders Assn., Am. Electroencephalographic Soc., Am. Soc. Neurophysiological Monitoring, Am. Coll. Internat. Physicians, Nat. Stroke Assn., So. Clin. Neurol. Soc., So. Electroencephalographic Soc., Fla. Med. Assn., Alachua County Med. Soc., Nat. and Internat. Spkrs. Bur. (Parke-Davis, Marion Merryl Dow, Burroughs Wellcome, Abbott Labs., Ciba-Geigy, Cyberonics 1993—), Internat. Neuromodulation Soc. (bd. dirs. 1996—). Moslem. Avocations: tennis, cooking, traveling, jogging, music. Office: VA Med Ctr-Neurology Svc 127 1601 SW Archer Rd Gainesville FL 32608-1135

UTIAN, WULF HESSEL, gynecologist, endocrinologist; b. Johannesburg, South Africa, Sept. 28, 1939; came to U.S., 1976; s. Harry and Ethel Utian; m. Moira Mervis, Oct. 4, 1964; children: Brett David, Lara Peta. MBBCh, Witwatersrand U., Johannesburg, S.Africa, 1962; PhD, U. Cape Town, S. Africa, 1970. Cons. ob-gyn Groote Schuur Hosp., Cape Town, 1967-76; dir. reprodn. endocrinology Univ. Hosps., Cleve., 1976-80; dir. ob-gyn Mt. Sinai Med. Ctr., 1980-89; pres. U. Ob-Gyn. Specialties, Inc., 1980-99; dir. Cleve. Menopause Clinic, 1986-2000; prof., chmn. dept. reproductive biology Case Western Reserve U., Cleve., 1989-99; dir. ob-gyn. U. Hosps. of Cleve., 1989-99. Cons. Internat. Health Found., Geneva, 1976-92; cons. women's health Cleve. Clinic Found., 2000—; cons. women's midlife health to nat. media, pharm. industry and health providers; assoc. prof. Case Western Res. U., Cleve., 1976-89, prof. reproductive biology, 1989-99, prof. emeritus reproductive biology and ob-gyn., 2000—; pres. Rapid Med. Rsch., 1996—. Author: Menopause in Modern Perspective, 1980, Your Middle Years, 1980, The Menopause and Hormonal Rplacement Therapy--Facts and Controversies, 1991, Managing Your Menopause, 1992; editor: Maturitas, 1980-93, Premenstrual Syndrome, 1981, Menopause Management, 1988—, Menopause, 1993—. Fellow ACOG, Royal Coll. Ob-Gyn. (Am. rep. to com. 1994-2000), Internat. Coll. Surgeons (v.p. 1983-89); mem. Internat. Menopause Soc. (exec. com. 1981-96, pres. 1993-96, sec. Coun. Affiliated Menopause Socs. 1996-99, chmn. 1999—), N.Am. Menopause Soc. (exec. dir., hon. founding pres. 1989—). Avocations: sailing, hiking. Home: Point East P-7 27500 Cedar Rd Beachwood OH 44122-8105 Office: RMR Inc 29001 Cedar Rd Ste 202 Cleveland OH 44124-4041 E-mail: utian@menopause.org.

UTIGARD, PHILIP RICHARD, real estate executive; b. Indpls., July 18, 1952; s. Richard Charles and Maedell (Hazen) U.; m. Becki A. Elliott, Sept. 27, 1975; children: Emilie, Benjamin, Kevin. BS, Miami U., Oxford, Ohio, 1974. Mktg. rep. IBM Corp., West Lafayette, Ind., 1974-80, regional mktg. rep. Detroit, 1981, mktg. mgr. Ft. Wayne, Ind., 1981-85, adminstr. asst. to chmn. Armonk, N.Y., 1985-86, br. mgr. N.Y.C., 1986-89; v.p. LaSalle Ptnrs. Ltd., Chgo., 1989-93, John Buck Co., Chgo., 1993, mng. dir., 1994, prin., 1995—; mng. dir. Mesinow Stein Real Estate Co., 1996. Bd. dirs. Heartland Alliance for Human Rights and Needs. Fellow Leadership Greater Chgo. Mem. Internat. Devel. Rsch. Coun., Met. Club. Avocations: family, skiing, travel, boating. Home: 6235 S Grant St Burr Ridge IL 60527-5134 Office: Mesinow Stein Real Estate Co 350 N Clark St Chicago IL 60610-4712

UTKE, ROBERT AHRENS, minister; b. Milw., Mar. 15, 1933; s. Gustave Peter and Beth E. (Ahrens) U.; m. Doris Lucille Gissenaas, Sept. 17, 1960; children: Robert John, William Gissenaas, Richard David. BA, Elmhurst Coll., 1955; BD, Eden Theol. Sem., 1959. Ordained to ministry United Ch. of Christ, 1959. Min. Zion-St. John United Ch. of Christ, Waterloo and Fults, Ill., 1957-59, Immanuel United Ch. of Christ, Milw., 1959-64; min., initiator, adminstr. Fellowship Community Ch., 1965-67; initiator, coord. Milw. Assocs. In Urban Ministries, 1967-69; adminstr., property mgr. Lenore St. Garden Homes, Robert's Park Apts., Nashville, 1969-90; min. St. John's United Ch. Christ, Johannesburg, Ill., 1982—2002, St. Peter's United Ch. of Christ, Store Ch., 1982—. V.p., treas. United Campus Christian Fellowship, Milw., 1959-64; dir. lab. sch. Wis. Conf. United Ch. of Christ, Green Lake, 1962, Urban Seminar for Wis. Coun. Chs., 1964-67 Editor, contbr.: A Guide to Prayer, 1965; columnist Living Your Life, 1965-67; contbr. articles to profl. jours. Chaplain Cosmopolitan Internat. convs. in U.S., Mex., Can., 1955-67; mem. steering com. Am. Friends Svc. Com. Weekend Workcamp, Milw., 1959-64; chmn. Milw. Planned Parenthood Clergy Com., Milw., 1963-64; pres. Met. Milw. Civic Alliance, 1966; sec. Ill. South Pastors Fellowship, 1995—; bd. dirs. Uni-Pres Kindercottage Child Care Ctr., East St. Louis, Ill., 1994-2001; chair Bldg. Fund Raising for Uni-Pres. for Ill. South Conf., United Ch. of Christ, 1994-97. Recipient Presdl. citation Cosmopolitan Internat., 1965, citation for youth work Senate of State of Wis., 1965; named Mr. Cosmopolitan Internat. Editor Cosmo Topics mag., 1963, Clergyman of Yr. Milw. Sentinal newspaper, 1966. Mem. Washington County Ministerial Alliance, Uni-Pres. Kindercottage Chilc Care Ctr. Home and Office: St Peter's Ch 4272 Stone Church Rd Addieville IL 62214-1527 *Accomplishments fade. Life's meaning comes from being a worthy servant of Christ, reaching out to those in need, remembering that I am simply a servant among servants. Life for all and all of life is to minister.*

UTKU, SENOL, civil engineer, computer science educator; b. Suruc, Turkey, Nov. 23, 1931; s. Sukru and Sukufe (Gumus) U.; m. Bisulay Bereket, May 9, 1964; children: Ayda, Sinan. Diploma in engring., Istanbul Tech. U., 1954; MS, MIT, 1959, ScD, 1960. Civil engr., Istanbul, Turkey. Rsch. engr. IBM, 1959-60; asst. prof. structural engring MIT, 1960-62; assoc. prof. Middle East Tech U., Ankara, Turkey, 1962-63; exec. dir. Computation Ctr., Istanbul Tech. U., 1963-65; tech. staff Jet Propulsion Lab., Pasadena, Calif., 1965-70; assoc. prof. civil engring Duke U., Durham, N.C., 1970-72, prof. NC, 1972-79, prof. civil engring., prof. computer sci., 1979—2001, dir. undergrad. studies, 1980-87, dir. grad. studies, 1987-89, prof. emeritus civil engring. and computer sci., 2002—; prof. emetirus engring. scis. Istanbul Tech. U., 1994—. Sr. Fulbright lectr., Turkey, 1998. Author: ELAS Software, 1968, Elementary Structural Analysis, 4th edit., 1991, Linear Analysis of Discrete Structures, 1991, Theory of Adaptive Structures, 1998; co-author: Dynamics of Offshore Structures, 1984, Finite Element Handbook, 1987, Parallel Processing in Computational Mechanics, 1992, Intelligent Structural Systems, 1992; contbr. articles to profl. jours. Fulbright scholar, Turkey, 1957; recipient Pres.'s Fund award Calif. Inst. Tech., 1981, NASA award, 1969, 71, 77, 84, 86-87, Internat. Joint Rsch. award NSF, 1991-92. Fellow ASCE; mem. AAUP, Am. Acad. Mechanics, Fulbright Assn., Am. Soc. for Engring. Edn., Structural Engring. Inst. (charter), Chi Epsilon. Office: Duke U 121 Hudson Hall Durham NC 27708-0287 Home: care Ayda Utku 2701 Homestead Rd # 816 Chapel Hill NC 27514 E-mail: senol.utku@duke.edu.

UTLEY, F. KNOWLTON, library director, educator; b. Northampton, Mass., May 4, 1935; s. Frederick K. and Florence E. (Moore) U.; m. Faith E. Green, July 2, 1960; children: Richard F., Stephen R., David E. BS, Castleton State Coll., 1960; MA, U. Conn., 1967; EdD, Boston U., 1979; MLS, U. Ala., 1993. Tchr. indsl. arts Montpelier (Vt.) High Sch., 1960-61, Southwick (Mass.) High Sch., 1961-63; tchr., drafting instr. Putnam (Conn.) High Sch., 1963-68; media specialist Cen. Conn. State U., New Britain, 1968-69, dir. media svcs., 1969-72; doctoral teaching fellow Boston U., 1972-73; dir. libr., media svcs. Manchester (Mass.) Pub. Schs., 1973-79; assoc. prof. libr. scis. U. Maine, Farmington, 1979-80; dir. grad. program libr. media Livingston (Ala.) U., 1980-83; dir. libr. media svcs. Am. Internat. Coll., Springfield, Mass., 1983—. Pres. C/W Mars-Cen. and Western Mass. Auto Res., 1987-88; chmn. bd. dirs. Cooperating Librs. of Great Springfield, 1988-89, Western Mass. Media Coun., 1991-93; founder, headmaster Hampshire Christian Acad., South Hadley, Mass., 1996-2002. Mem. Belchertown Housing Authority, 2000—. Mem. ALA, Am. Christian Schs. Internat., Assn./Edn. Comm. and Tech. New Eng. Edn. Media Assn., New Eng. Libr. Assn., Mass. Sch. Libr. Media Assn., Mass. Libr. Assn., Phi Delta Kappa. Home: 11 Canal Dr Belchertown MA 01007-9224 Office: Am Internat Coll 1000 State St Springfield MA 01109-3151 E-mail: kutley@cwmars.org.

UTLEY, JANE BESON, poet; b. Houston, Dec. 14, 1954; d. John Mark and Frances Ester (Rupert) Beson; m. Ronald Gene Utley, June 29, 1985. Asst. mgr. McCoy Devel. Corp., Houston, 1978-81; with accounts receivable dept. Arpco Office Supply, 1981; payroll analyst Toshiba Internat., 1981-86. Songwriter Jeff Roberts Pub., 1996-97. Contbr. poems to Best Poems of the 90's, 1996, American Poetry Annual, 1997, Word Weaver, 1997, Treasure the Moment, vol. X, 1997, A Celebration of Poets, 1997, (audio tape) Internat. Libr.'s The Sound of Poetry, anthologies; pub. comml. song Majestic Records and Countrywine Pubs. Mem. Top RecordsSongwriters Assn. Avocations: writing, fishing, gardening, reading. Office: Flooring Cons PO Box 1610 Brookshire TX 77423-1610 E-mail: jutley3169@aol.com.

UTLEY, JON BASIL, think tank director, journalist; b. Moscow, Mar. 10, 1934; came to U.S., 1939, naturalized, 1952; s. Arcadi and Freda (Utley) Berdichevsky; m. Ana Maria Hijar, 1968. BS, Georgetown U., 1956; student, U. Munich, 1952, Alliance Française, Paris, 1956. Mgr. Am. Internat. Underwriters, Cali, Colombia, 1959-60; editor, pub. Bogotá Bull., 1960-61; v.p. Universal Investors Svcs., Nassau, 1962-67; real estate developer Washington, 1968—; mng. gen. ptnr. Kimwill Oil Assocs., Warren, Pa., 1978-86; pres. Ocean McLean Corp., 1989-97, Needle in a Haystack, Washington, 1990-98, Needle Express, 1993-98; fgn. corr. Jour. Commerce, Internat. Reports, S. Am., 1969-74; columnist Times of the Ams., 1974-92, assoc. editor, 1981-92; columnist Washington Inquirer, 1981-90, Washington Times, 1981-82; contbg. editor Conservative Digest, 1984-89; mem. editl. adv. bd. Internat. Reports, 1981-91. Lectr. Accuracy in Media, treas., Ukraine, 1997, Cyprus, 99, Freedoms Found. Valley Forge; commentator Voice of Am., 1985—2002; Jamestown Found. observer Russian elections, 2000; dir. Russian think tank project Atlas Found., 2000—. Contbr. articles to Washington Post, Harvard Bus. Rev., Nat. Rev., Human Events, Miami Herald, Lincoln Rev., N.Y.C. Tribune, Am. Legion mag., El Salvador Gazette, Lima Times, others. Observer Guatemalan elections Georgetown U. Ctr. Strategic Studies, 1985, Romanian elections, 1990; trustee Ctr. Internat. Rels., adv. com. Solidarity Endowment; co-founder Com. to Avert a Mideast Holocaust, 1990-94; Russia porjects dir. ATlas Found., 2000--. Assoc. scholar Competitive Enterprise Inst., 1995-98; Robert A. Taft fellow Ludwig Von Mises Inst., 1998—. Mem.: Atlas Econ. Rsch. Found. (dir. Russian projects 2001—), Coun. Nat. Policy, Ams. Against Bombing/Ams. Against World Empire (chmn. 1998—), Hispanic Am. Ctr. Econ. Rsch. (bd. dirs. 1997—), World English Lang. Newspaper Assn. (pres. 1996), United Srs. Assn. (bd. dirs. 1993—2001), Coun. Inter-Am. Security (bd. dirs. 1988—93), Phila. Soc., Nat. Press Club. Office: 910 17th St NW Ste 422 Washington DC 20006-2605 E-mail: Jutly@aol.com.

UTRATA, CARL IGNATIUS, corporate counsel, corporate executive; b. Trnava, Slovak Republic, Sept. 23, 1940; came to U.S., 1949, naturalized, 1955; s. Joseph and Irma Mary Utrata; m. Mary Ann M. Nypaver, June 17, 1972; children: Edward Joseph, Stephanie Ann. BS in Fgn. Service, Georgetown U., 1963; JD, Case Western Res. U., 1971. Bar: Ohio 1972, U.S. Dist. Ct. (no. dist.) Ohio 1983, U.S. Ct. Appeals (6th cir.) 1987. Indsl. rels. staff asst. Republic Steel Corp., Buffalo, 1967-68, safety-labor supr. Cleve., 1969-84, coord., mgr. equal employment opportunity, 1972-79, corp. dir. equal employment opportunity, 1979-84; pvt. practice, 1985-91; corp. counsel ISK Bioscis. Corp., Mentor, Ohio, 1991-98; pvt. practice Cleve., 1998—. Dean legal studies, instr. Acad. Ct. Reporting, Cleve.; lectr. in field; tng. media producer. Pres. Lakewood Neighbors Assn., Ohio, 1974, libr. levy chmn., 1975, mem. zoning initiative com., 1976-78; trustee Coun. on Human Rels., Cleve., 1982-88, pres., 1985-88; assoc. v.p. United Way Svcs., Cleve., 1984-85; trustee legal Aid Soc. Cleve., 1986-88; co-founder, pres. bus., industry and edn. con. Urban League Cleve., 1978-79. With U.S. Army, 1963-65, ETO. Mem. ABA (pesticide subcom. 1995-98), Am. Crop Protection Assn. (law com. 1995-98), Cleve. Employers Equal Opportunity Assn. (co-founder, chmn. 1982, pres.' cup 1983). Home and Office: 1506 Arthur Ave Cleveland OH 44107-3804 E-mail: ciutrata@hotmail.com.

UTRECHT, PAUL F. lawyer; b. The Hague, The Netherlands, Aug. 31, 1960; s. Robert Packard and Arnolda (Cohen) U. BA, Claremont McKenna Coll., 1980; student, Sorbonne, Paris, 1980; JD, U. Calif., Berkeley, 1983. Bar: Calif. 1985, U.S. Ct. Appeals (9th cir.) 1986, U.S. Supreme Ct. 1990. Law clk. to Judge M. Joseph Blumenfeld U.S. Dist. Ct., Hartford, Conn., 1983-84; assoc. Pillsbury Madison & Sutro, San Francisco, 1984-87, Law Offices of S.G. Archibald, Paris, 1987; pvt. practice San Francisco, 1987—. Contbr.: Rule 11 and Other Sanctions, 1986. Office: 235 Montgomery St Ste 600 San Francisco CA 94104-2909

UTSCHIG, STEVEN MARK, educator; b. Appleton, Wis., Oct. 3, 1949; s. Reno Albert and Jeannette U.; m. Patricia Jean Dinauer, Aug. 30, 1975; children: Jillian, Andrew. BS, U. Wis., Oshkosh, 1973. Lead supr. Crystal Print, Inc., Little Chute, Wis., 1980-89; instr. flexographic printing Fox Valley Tech. Coll., Appleton, 1990—. Tech. editor Converting mag., 1996—. Recipient NISOD Tchg. Excellence award, 2001. Mem. Flexographic Tech. Assn. Independent. Office: Fox Valley Tech Coll 5 Systems Dr Appleton WI 54914

UTT, GLENN S., JR. motel investor, former biotech and pharmaceutical industry company executive; b. Neodesha, Kans., Aug. 7, 1926; s. Glenn S. and Reba Pauline (White) U.; m. Mary Lou Ford, Aug. 8, 1948; 1 child, Jan A. BSEE, BSBA, Kans. State U., 1949; MBA, Harvard U., 1951. Salesman Drexel Furniture Co., N.C., 1951-55; v.p. Booz Allen & Hamilton, Chgo. and Zurich, Switzerland, 1955-62; exec. v.p. Abbott Labs., North Chicago, Ill., 1962-83, also dir., ret., 1983. Chmn. bd. Janmar Enterprises, Minocqua, Wis., Marjan Inc., Houghton, Mich., U.P. Hotel Group Inc., Houghton. Co-author: Lalique Perfume Bottles, 1990. Alderman City of Lake Forest, Ill., 1972-76, chmn. recreational bd., 1975-78; mem. exec. com. Lake County Republican Fedn., Waukegan, Ill., 1974-83. With USN, 1944-46, USAF (res.), 1949-53. Mem.: Beta Theta Pi. Avocations: antiques, objects of art. Home: PO Box 810 Houghton MI 49931

UTTAL, WILLIAM R(EICHENSTEIN), psychology and engineering educator, research scientist; b. Mineola, N.Y., Mar. 24, 1931; s. Joseph and Claire (Reichenstein) U.; m. Michiye Nishimura, Dec. 20, 1954; children: Taneil, Lynet, Lisa. Student, Miami U. Oxford, Ohio, 1947-48; BS in Physics, U. Cin., 1951; PhD in Exptl. Psychology and Biophysics, Ohio State U., 1957. Staff Psychologist, mgr. behavioral sci. group IBM Research Center, Yorktown Heights, N.Y., 1957-63; assoc. prof. U. Mich., Ann Arbor, 1963-68, prof. psychology, 1968-86, research scientist, 1963-86, prof. emeritus, 1986—; grad. affiliate faculty dept. psychology U. Hawaii, 1986-88; research scientist Naval Ocean Systems Ctr.-Hawaii Lab., Kailua, 1985-88; prof., chmn. dept. psychology Ariz. State U., Tempe, 1988-92, prof. dept. indsl. engring., 1992—99, affiliated prof., Dept. of Computer Sci. and Engring., 1993-98, prof. emeritus, 1999—. Vis. prof. Kyoto (Japan) Prefectural Med. U., 1965-66, Sensory Sci. Lab., U. Hawaii, 1968, 73, U. Western Australia, 1970-71, U. Hawaii, 1978-79, 80-81, U. Auckland, 1996, U. Freiburg, 1997, U. Sydney, 1999; pres. Nat. Conf. on On-Line Uses Computers in Psychology, 1974. Author: Real Time Computers: Techniques and Applications in the Psychological Sciences, 1968, Generative Computer Assisted Instruction in Analytic Geometry, 1972, The Psychobiology of Sensory Coding, 1973, Cellular Neurophysiology and Integration: An Interpretive Introductin, 1975, An Autocorrelation Theory of Visual Form Detection, 1975, The Psychobiology of Mind, 1978, A Taxonomy of Visual Processes, 1981, Visual Form Detection in Three Dimensional Space, 1983, Principles of Psychobiology, 1983, The Detection of Nonplanar Surfaces in Visual Space, 1985, The Perception of Dotted Forms, 1987, On Seeing Forms, 1988, The Swimmer: A Computational Model of a Perceptual Motor System, 1992, Toward a New Behaviorism: The Case Against Perceptual Reductionism, 1998, A Computational Model of Vision: The Role of Combination, 1999, The War Between Mentalism and Behaviorism, 2000, The New Phrenology: Limits on the Localization of Cognitive Processes in the Brain, 2001, A Behaviorist Looks at Form Recognition, 2002; also numerous articles; editor: Readings in Sensory Coding, 1972; assoc. editor Behavioral Research Method and Instrn., 1968-90, Computing: Archives for Electronic Computing, 1963-75, Jour. Exptl. Psychology; Perception and Performance, 1974-79; cons. editor Jour. Exptl. Psychology: Applied, 1994—. Patentee in field. Served to 2d lt. USAF, 1951-53. USPHS spl. postdoctoral fellow, 1965-66; NIMH research scientist award, 1971-76 Fellow AAAS, Am. Psychol. Assn., Am. Psychol. Soc. (charter), Soc. Exptl. Psychologists (chmn. 1994-95); mem. Psychonomics Soc. Office: Ariz State U Dept Indsl Engring Tempe AZ 85287-1104 E-mail: aowru@asu.edu.

UTTER, DONALD L. music educator; b. Poughkeepsie, N.Y., Apr. 18, 1951; s. Clarence and Marion (Cobb) U. BS, Susquehanna U., 1974; MusM, Ind. U., 1979. Music educator Webutuck Ctrl. Sch., Anenia, N.Y., 1979-84, Pawling (N.Y.) High Sch., 1984—. Rep. N.Y. State Sch. Music, Pawling, 1995-98; solo festival judge N.Y., 1990—; past v.p. Tchrs. Assn., 1993-94. Bd. dirs. Pawling (N.Y.) Concert Series, 1988—, County Farm Bur., Millbrook, N.Y., 1991-95, Rep. Party, Pawling, 1993—. Named Coach of the Yr., Pawling High Sch., 1994. Mem. Dutchess County Music Educators (chmn. All-County Music Festival 1993-95), Music Educators Nat. Conf., Am. Fedn. Musicians Local 85. Republican. Methodist. Avocations: golf, coach high sch. golf team, snow skiing, reading. Home: 93 Harmony Rd Pawling NY 12564-0089 Office: Pawling Jr/Sr HS Reservoir Rd Pawling NY 12564

UTTER, FRED M, science educator, researcher; b. Seattle; s. John Madison and Besse Alden Utter; m. Nancy Gene Darrow, Sept. 5, 1958; children: Jennifer, Jeffrey, Judy. BA, Coll. of Puget Sound, Tacoma, WA, 1950—54; MS, U. Wash., Seattle, WA, 1958—64; PhD, U. Calif. (Davis), Davis, CA, 1966—69; Dr Honoris Causa (hon.) , U. Girona, Girona, Spain, 1997. Chemist US Bur. Comm Fisheries, Seattle, 1959—68; rsch. geneticist US Nat Mar Fish Svc, 1969—88; affiliate prof. U. Wash., 1970—; editor Am Fish Soc, 1993—. Vis. prof. U of Girona, Girona, Spain, 1988—99, U Oviedo, Oviedo, Spain, 1989—98; cons. Don Chapman Assocs, Boise, Idaho, 1991—96. Author: (book) Population Genetics and Fishery Management, Salmon Aquaculture. Trustee Northhaven Retirement Res, Seattle, 1968. Sp-3 US Army, 1954—57, Europe. Recipient Award of Excellence, Am Fish Soc (West Div), 1996, Disting. Svc., Am Fish Soc, 2001, Outstanding Achievement, Am Inst Fish Res Biologists, 2002. Independent. Protestant. Avocation: cellist. Home: 19424 10th NE Shorline WA 98155 Office: U Wash Sch Aquat and Fish Sciences Box 355020 Seattle WA 98195 Office Fax: 206-685-7471. E-mail: fmutter@u.washington.edu.

UTTER, ROBERT FRENCH, retired judge; b. Seattle, June 19, 1930; s. John and Besse (French) Utter; m. Elizabeth J. Stevenson, Dec. 28, 1953; children: Kimberly, Kirk, John. BS, U. Wash., 1952; LLB, 1954. Bar: Wash. 1954. Pros. atty., King County, Wash., 1955-57; individual practice law

Seattle, 1957-59; ct. commr. King County Superior Ct., 1959-64, judge, 1964-69, Wash. State Ct. Appeals, 1969-71, Wash. State Supreme Ct., 1971-95, chief justice, 1979-81; ret., 1995; lectr. Ctrl. and Eastern European Legal Inst., Prague, Czech Republic, 2000, 01, Czech Republic, 2002, dean faculty Czech Republic, 2001—. Lectr. in field; leader comparative law tour, China, 1986, China, 87, China, 88, China, 91, Russia, 89, South Africa, 97, Ukraine, 98, Hungary, 98, Czech Republic, 98; adj. prof. constl. law U. Puget Sound, 1987—94; cons. CEELI, 1991, 1993—, USIA, 1992; visitor to Kyrgystan Judiciary, Kazakhstan, 1993—96, Mongolia, 1997; lectr. Albanian Judiciary, 1994, 95, 2000, Georgian Judiciary, 1999, Servian Judiciary, 2001. Editor: books on real property and appellate practice; author: books on state consl. law. Pres., founder Big Brother Assn., Seattle, 1955—67, Job Therapy Inc., 1963—71; mem. exec. com. Conf. Chief Justices, 1979—80, 1981—86; pres. Thurston County Big Bros./Big Sisters, 1984; lectr Soviet Acad. Moscow, 1991; USIA visitor to comment on jud. sys. Latvia, 1992, Kazakhstan, 1993—94; trustee Linfield Coll. Named Alumnus of the Yr., Linfield Coll., 1973, Judge of the Yr., Wash. State Trial Lawyers, 1989, Outstanding Judge, Wash. State Bar Assn., 1990, Seattle-King County Bar Assn., 1992, Conder-Faulkner lectr., U. Wash. Sch. Law, 1995, Disting. Alumnus, Sch. Law U. Wash., 1995; recipient Henry Jackson Disting. Pub. Svc. award, Nat. Wash. Sch. Law, 2000; scholar Disting. Jud., U. Ind., 1987. Fellow: Chartered Inst. Arbitrators; mem.: ABA (commentator on proposed constns. of Albania, Bulgaria, Romania, Russia, Lithuania, Azerbaijan, Uzbekistan, Byelarus, Kazakhstan, and Ukraine), Am. Judicature Soc. (sec. 1987—, chmn. bd. dirs., mem. exec. com., Herbert Harley award 1983, Justice award 1998), Order of Coif. Baptist.

UTTERBACK, WILL HAY, JR. labor union administrator; b. Amarillo, Tex., Mar. 10, 1947; s. Will Hay and Marie (Willey) U.; m. Margaret Jane Smith, July 31, 1982. JD (hon.), Pacific Northwestern U., 1980. Cert. Genealogical Record Splist. Pres. BillCo Enterprises, Amarillo, Tex., 1974-86, Communications Workers Am. Local 6128, Amarillo, 1988—. Audiovisual cons. Franklin D. Roosevelt Libr., Hyde Park, N.Y., 1971—; cons. Smithsonian Instn., Washington, 1983; lectr. Ind. Scholar Network, Amarillo, 1982—; spl. cons. Ednl. Video Group, Greenwood, Ind., 1989—. Contbr. articles to profl. publs.; reconstructor newsreel film, 1974—. Bd. dirs. Panhandle Tech-Prep Consortium; mem. citizens budget com. United Way. Mem. Am. Hist. Assn., Nat. Hist. Soc., Ctr. for Study of Presidency. Mem. Ch. of Christ. Avocations: genealogy, fishing. Home: PO Box 150 Amarillo TX 79105-0150

UVENA, FRANK JOHN, retired printing company executive, lawyer; b. Ernest, Pa., Feb. 2, 1934; AB, Ohio U., Athens, 1959; LLB, Ohio State U., Columbus, 1963. Bar: Ill. 1963. Assoc. firm McDermott, Will & Emery, Chgo., 1963-68; atty. R.R. Donnelley & Sons, 1968-75, v.p., gen. counsel, 1975-84, sr. v.p. law and corp. staffs, 1984-95. Bd. dirs. Am. Liver Found., Chgo., 1996, Parents/Friends Elizabeth Ludeman Devel. Ctr., 1986. With AUS, 1954-56. Mem. ABA, Ill. Bar Assn., Chgo. Bar Assn.

UVERSKY, VLADIMIR NIKOLAEVICH, biophysicist, researcher; b. Borovichi, Novgorod, USSR, Apr. 20, 1963; s. Nikolay Valentinovich and Galina Alexeevna (Ivanova) U.; m. Elena Borisovna Shubina, Apr. 11, 1987; children: Alexey, Sergey. Bachelor's degree, Leningrad State U., USSR, 1986; Candidate of Scis., Inst. Protein Rsch., Pushchino, Russia, 1991. Cert. physicist. Probationer Inst. Protein Rsch., Pushchino, 1986-88, jr. scientist, 1991-93, scientist, 1993—; tchr. Moscow State U., 1991-93; asst. prof. Pushchino State U., 1994—. Contbr. to sci. jours. Mem. trade-union com. Inst. Protein Rsch., Pushchino, 1987-93. Recipient premium for Young Russian Scientists, European Acad., 1992; grantee Human Frontier Sci. Program, 1993-96, Russian Found. for Fundamental Rschs., 1993-96. Fellow Biochem. Soc.; mem. Russian Biochem. Soc. Avocations: books, wood and natural materials crafts, fishing, cooking. Office: Inst Protein Rsch Russian Acad Scis 142292 Pushchino Russia

UWUJAREN, GILBERT PATRICK, economist, consultant, realtor; b. Oza Agbor, Bendel, Nigeria, May 6, 1945; came to U.S., 1985; s. Jacob Aghahowa and Victoria (Lasila) Uwujaren; m. Ngozi Buzugbe, Aug. 25, 1973; children: Jane, Janice, Jacob, Jo-Anne, Joseph, Jarune. BSc, U. Ibadan, Nigeria, 1971; MA, Columbia U., 1975, MPhil, PhD, Columbia U., 1977. Asst. lectr. U. Ife, Ibadan, 1972-73, sr. lectr. Ile-Ife, Nigeria, 1977-85; economist World Bank, Washington, 1985-89, cons., 1989-95; pres. Econ. Devel. Assocs., Burke, Va., 1993—; realtor Weichert Realtors, Springfield, 1993-95, Fairfax Realty, Inc., Falls Church, 1995-98; cons. African Devel. Bank, Abidjan, Ivory Coast, 1998—. Contbr. articles to profl. jours. Recipient German Acad. award Govt. Fed. Republic Germany, Ibadan, 1970-71, Rockefeller award Rockefeller Found., Ibadan, 1971-73. Mem. Am. Econ. Assn. Office: 5801 Shana Pl Burke VA 22015-3663

UYEDA, SEIYA, geophysics educator; b. Tokyo, Nov. 28, 1929; s. Seiichi and Hatsuo (Okino) U.; m. Mutsuko Kosaka, July 6, 1952; children: Taro, Makiko, Naoko. BS, U. Tokyo, 1952, DSc, 1958; DSc (hon.), U. Athens, Greece, 1996. Rsch. assoc. Earthquake Rsch. Inst. U. Tokyo, 1957-64, assoc. prof. Geophys. Inst., 1964-69, prof. Earthquake Rsch. Inst., 1969-90; prof. dept. marine sci. and tech. Tokai U., Shimizu, Japan, 1990-94, dir. earthquake prediction rsch. ctr. Japan, 1995-96; prof. Tex. A&M U., College Station, 1990-95. Dir. Internat. Frontier Program on Earthquake Rsch. Riken, 1996—. Author: Debate About the Earth, 1966, Island Arcs, 1973, The New View of the Earth, 1978. Recipient Tanakadate prize Soc. Terrestrial Magnetism and Electricity, 1955, G.P. Woollard award Geol. Soc. Am., 1989, Matsumae Prize for Academic Accomplishment, Tokai Univ., 1992. Fellow AAAS (hon.), Nat. Acad. Sci. (fgn. assoc., A Agassiz medal 1972), Russian Acad. Scis. (fgn.), Geol. Soc. London (hon.), European Union Geoscis. (hon.), Am. Geophys. Union (Walter Bucher medal 1991); mem. Am. Acad. Arts and Scis. (fgn.), Soc. Geology France (assoc.), Japan Acad. (Acad. prize 1987). Home: 2-39-6 Daizawa Setagaya-ku Tokyo 155-0032 Japan Office: Tokai U 3-20-1 Orido Shimizu 424 Japan E-mail: suyeda@st.rim.or.jp.

UYEHARA, CATHERINE FAY TAKAKO (CATHERINE YAMAUCHI), physiologist, educator, pharmacologist; b. Honolulu, Dec. 20, 1959; d. Thomas Takashi and Eiko (Haraguchi) Uyehara; m. Alan Hisao Yamauchi, Feb. 17, 1990. BS, Yale U., 1981; PhD in Physiology, U. Hawaii, Honolulu, 1987. Postdoctoral fellow SmithKline Beecham Pharms., King of Prussia, Pa., 1987-89; mem. grad. faculty in pediatrics U. Hawaii John Burns Sch. Medicine, Honolulu, 1991—; rsch. pharmacologist Kapiolani Med. Ctr. for Women and Children, 1990-91. Statis. cons. Tripler Army Med. Ctr., Honolulu, 1984-87, 89—, chief rsch. pharmacology , 1991—, dir. collaborative rsch. program, 1995—; mem. grad. faculty in pharmacology U. Hawaii John A. Burns Sch. Medicine, 1993—; grad. faculty Interdisciplinary Biomed. Sci. program, 1995-98, Cell and Molecular Biology program, 1998—, mem. grad. faculty in physiology, 1999—. Contbr. articles to profl. jours. Mem. Am. Fedn. for Med. Rsch., Am. Physiol. Soc., Soc. Uniformed Endocrinologists, Endocrine Soc., We. Soc. Pediatric Rsch., N.Y. Acad. Scis., Hawaii Acad. Sci., Sigma Xi. Democrat. Mem. Christian Ch. Avocations: swimming, diving, crafts, horticulture, music. Office: Dept Clin Investigation 1 Jarrett White Rd Bldg 40 Tripler Army Medical Center HI 96859

UYEHARA, HARRY YOSHIMI, library educator; b. Honolulu, Jan. 6, 1934; s. Saburo and Uto (Yamashiro) U. BEd, U. Hawaii, 1958; AMLS, U. Mich., 1965; MA, Columbia U., 1970, EdD, 1978. Cert. sch. libr., media specialist. Tchr., libr. Waiakea-Kai Elem. & Intermediate Sch., Hilo, Hawaii, 1960-61; libr. Wahiawa (Hawaii) Intermediate Sch., 1961-66; program specialist Hawaii State Dept. of Edn., Honolulu, 1966-76; asst. prof. library studies U. Hawaii, 1976-83; dean learning resources U. Guam, Mangilao, 1983-89; assoc. prof. libr. and info. studies U. Hawaii, Honolulu, 1989-91; assoc. prof. Edn. U. Guam, Mangilao, 1991-93; prof. libr. faculty Guam C.C., 1994-96, ret., 1997; ednl. and libr. cons., 1998—. Mem. in-svc. adv. coun. Hawaii State Dept. of Edn., Honolulu, 1977-80, adv. coun. of librs. Guam Pub. Libr., Agana, 1983-89. Editor (jours.) HLA Jour., 1978, The Golden Key, 1981, 82. With U.S. Army, 1958-60. Mem. Hawaii Libr. Assn. (pres. 1977-78), Hawaii Assn. Sch. Librs. (pres. 1982-83), Guam Libr. Assn. (pres. 1984-85), Phi Delta Kappa, Kappa Delta Pi. Home: 99-723 Aiea Heights Dr Aiea HI 96701-3502

UYEHARA, OTTO ARTHUR, mechanical engineering educator emeritus, consultant; b. Hanford, Calif., Sept. 9, 1916; s. Rikichi and Umi (Nakayama) U.; m. Chisako Suda, Aug. 12, 1945; children: Otto Kenneth, Susan Joy Uyehara Schultheiss, Emi Ryu Uyehara-Stewart. BS, U. Wis., 1942, MS, 1943, PhD, 1946. Postdoctoral fellow U. Wis., Madison, 1945-46, rsch. assoc., 1946-47, asst. prof., then assoc. prof., 1949-57, prof., 1957-82, prof. emeritus, 1982—; pvt. practice cons. Anaheim, Calif., 1985—. Mem. sci. adv. com. Echlin Corp., Branford, Conn., 1980—. Recipient Sci. Achievement award Japan Soc. Automotive Engrs, Internal Combustion Engine award ASME, 1994. FEllow Soc. Automotive Engrs.; mem. ASME (internal combustion divsn., Internal Combustion award 1994), Japan Soc. Mech. Engrs. (hon.). Home: Apt 303 380 S Anaheim Hills Rd Anaheim CA 92807-4062

UYGUR, MUSTAFA ETI, materials and mechanical engineering educator; b. Kayseri, Turkey, Jan. 22, 1941; s. Ali and Mumine (Oktay) U.; m. Selime Kobakci, Dec. 16, 1971; children: Ayse, Esra, Zeynep, Ali. BSME, Mid. East Tech. U., Ankara, Turkey, 1963, MSc in Mech. Engring., 1964; MSc in Engring., Purdue U., 1967; PhD in Materials Sci. and Engring., Mid. East Tech. U., Ankara, Turkey, 1971. Rsch. assoc. Am. Oil Co. Rsch. Labs., Whiting, Ind., 1967; instr. Mid. East Tech. U., Ankara, Turkey, 1967-71, asst. prof. Turkey, 1971-77, assoc. prof. Turkey, 1977-84; prof. Gazi U., Turkey, 1984-90; prof. mech. engring. dept. King Saud U., Riyadh, Saudi Arabia, 1990—. Asst. chmn. materials sci. and engring. dept. Mid. East Tech. U., Ankara, 1977-80; dep. dean faculty tech. edn. Gazi U., Ankara, 1984-86, mem. coll. coun., grad. coll. coun., univ. senate, 1984-90; tech. & sci. advisor to dep. Min. of Nat. Def., Def. Industries Devel. Adminstrn., Ankara, 1987-90. Author: Dynamic NDT of Materials, 1976, 83, Glossary of Powder Metallurgy Terms, 1982, X-Ray Crystallography, 1983, Materials Science and Engineering, 1997, 2d edit., 2002, Laboratory Manual for Materials Science and Engineering, 1997, 2d edit., 2002, CD-Materials Sci & Engring., 1997, 4th edit., 2002, CD-Laboratory for Materials Science and Engineering, 1998, 3d edit., 2002; editor-in-chief: Science-Research-Technology Five-Year Main Plan, 1988; contbr. over 100 articles to profl. jours.; supr. for devel. of many ednl. computer programs. Specialization com. on nonferrous materials State Planning Orgn., Ankara, 1982, chmn. specialization com. on transfer of high tech. and employment, 1987-88, specialization com. on sci. rsch., tech., 1987-88, chmn. editl. com. on sci., rsch., tech., 1988. Lt. (engr.) Turkish Army Tech. Svc.-Weapons Dept., 1973-74. Scholar Turkish Iron-Steel Works, 1963-64; rsch. grantee Turkish Sci. Rsch. Coun., 1971-73. Mem. Internat. Plansee Soc. Powder Metallurgy, Internat. Soc. Crystallographers, Am. Powder Metallurgy Inst. Internat., Am. Soc. for Metals Internat., Am. Soc. for Metals Internat.-Metall. Soc., Materials Rsch. Soc., Turkish Assn. for Powder Metallurgy (founder). Avocations: reading, music, computers, swimming, bowling. E-mail: mustafauygur@hotmail.com.

UYS, JURGEN PETER BRINKER, securities analyst; b. South Africa, Dec. 22, 1952; came to U.S., 1955; s. Johannes Marthinus and Reinette McKay (Weidemann) U. BS, U. Pa., 1974; MBA, Columbia U., 1977. CFA. Securities analyst Equibank, N.A., Pitts., 1974-76; fin. analyst Amax Inc., Greenwich, Conn., 1978-80; v.p. Equitable Investment Mgmt., N.Y.C., 1980-85; securities analyst Swiss Am. Securities, 1986-91; gen. ptnr. Peter Uys Partnership, Ltd., 1991—. Mem. Huguenot Soc. Am. (treas. 1991-92), Assn. for Investment Mgmt. and Rsch., Psi Upsilon. Episcopalian.

UZMAN, BETTY BEN GEREN, pathologist, retired educator; b. Fort Smith, Ark., Nov. 17, 1922; d. Benton Asbury and Myra Estelle (Petty) Geren; m. L. Lahut Uzman, Dec. 17, 1955 (dec.); 1 dau., Betty Tuba. Student, Fort Smith Jr. Coll., 1939-40; BS, U. Ark., 1942; MD, Washington U., 1945; postgrad., M.I.T., 1948-50; MA (hon.), Harvard U., 1967. Intern Childrens Hosp., Boston, 1945-46; resident in pathology Barnes Hosp., St. Louis, 1946-48; Am. Cancer Soc. research fellow MIT, Cambridge, Mass., 1948-50; chief biol. ultrastructure and exptl. pathology Children's Cancer Research Found., Boston, 1950-71; instr. Harvard Med. Sch., 1949-53, assoc., 1953-56, research assoc., 1956-67, assoc. prof., 1967-71, prof., 1971-72; head research dept. Sparks Regional Med. Center, Fort Smith, 1972-74; prof. pathology La. State U., Shreveport, 1974-77, U. Tenn., Memphis, 1978-89. Assoc. chief staff rsch. VA, Shreveport, 1974-77; staff pathologist VA, Memphis, 1978-89, chief lab. svc., 1986-87; chief field ops., spl. asst. to dir. VA Central Office, Washington, 1978-79, dir. med. rsch. svcs., 1979-80; chmn. pathology A Study sect. NIH, 1973-76; cons. to sci. dir. Children's Cancer Rsch. Found., Boston, 1971-73; mem. adv. com. on prevention, diagnosis and treatment Am. Cancer Soc., 1970-73, 77-80; mem. adv. bd. Office Regeneration Rsch., VA, 1985-89; disting. vis. investigator Inst. Venezolano Investigation Cientificas, Caracas, 1972-74 Decorated Order of Andres Bello 1st class Venezuela; recipient Weinstein award United Cerebral Palsy, 1964; Am. Cancer Soc. research fellow, 1948-50 Mem. AAAS (emerita), Am. Soc. Cell Biology, Soc. Devel. Biology, Am. Acad. Neurology (assoc.), Am. Soc. Neurochemistry, Microscopy Soc. Am. (Diatome poster award 1985), Internat. Acad. Pathology, Am. Assn. Neuropathology (assoc.), Soc. Neurosci., Am. Assn. Cancer Rsch. Home and Office: Geren Farm 16048 E State Highway 197 Scranton AR 72863-0048 E-mail: bguzman@aol.com.

UZZELL-BAGGETT, KARON LYNETTE, career officer; b. Goldsboro, N.C., Apr. 28, 1964; d. Jesse Lee and Ernestine Smith Uzzell; m. Ronald Walter Baggett, July 26, 1990; 1 child, Kathleen; stepchildren: Christina, Brian, Adam. BS, U. N.C., 1986; postgrad., U. Md., 1993-96. Commd. 2nd lt. USAF, 1986, advanced through grades to lt. col., 1990, exec. officer 6ACCS Va., 1986-88, ops. tng. officer 7393MUNSS Murted AFD, Turkey, 1988-89, command and control officer 52FW Spangdahlem AB, Germany, 1989-92, SENEX mission dir. 89AW Andrews AFB, Md., 1992-95, dep. chief classified control Office Sec. Def., 1995-97, chief classified control Office Sec. Def., 1998-99, flight comdr., dir. ops. 82TRSS Sheppard AFB, Tex., 1999-2001; detachment comdr. USAFE MSS, Vicenza, Italy, 2001—02; comdr. 78HSS, Robins AFB, Ga., 2002—. Emergency med. technician Orange County Rescue Squad, Hillsborough, N.C., 1985-86; treas. Melwood PTA, Upper Marlboro, Md., 1994-97; meml. vol. Women in Mil. Svc., Washington, 1993—; entitlements vol. Whitman Walker Clinic, Washington, 1993-98. Mem. Women in Mil. Svc. for Am., So. Poverty Law Ctr. Democrat. Baptist. Avocations: running, weightlifting, sewing, cross stitching, gardening. Home: 121 Spring Chase Cir Kathleen GA 31047

UZZI, JAMES CHRISTOPHER, music educator, conductor; b. Flushing, Ny, Jan. 20, 1965; s. Gerard Joseph and Justine Inez Uzzi; m. Bernadette Felczak, June 30, 1990; children: Sarah, Vincent. BM, State U Coll. at Potsdam, Potsdam, NY, 1987; MA, SUNY at Stony Brook, Stony Brook, NY, 1990. Music Teacher Certification K-12 NY, 1987, Certified All State Adjudicator NYSSMA. Orch. dir. Bellport Mid. Sch., Bellport, NY, 1987—, Bellport H.S., Brookhaven, 1992—. Condr. Gemini Youth Orch., Melville, NY, 1997—. Mem.: NY State Sch. Music Assn, Music Educators Nat. Conf. Achievements include guest orchestra conductor for Suffolk County Music Educators Assn and Nassau County Music Educators Assn. Avocations: golf, fishing, camping.

VABLE, MADHUKAR, mechanical engineer, educator, mechanical engineer, researcher; b. Ajmer, Rajasthan, India, Aug. 1951; s. Krishna Rao and Saudamini Gautam Vable; m. Pushpa Murthy; children: Anusha, Adhiraj. B in Tech., Indian Inst. Tech., Kanpur, India, 1973, M in Tech., 1976; PhD, U. Mich., 1980. Asst. prof. Mich. Technol. U., Houghton, Mich., 1984—90, assoc. prof., 1990—. Author: (Book) Mechanics of Materials, 2002, (Software) BEAMUP (Boundary Element Analysis from Michigan's Upper Peninsula; mem. editl. bd.: Internat. Jour. Boundary Element Methods Comm., 1994—. Recipient Disting. Faculty Mem. award, Mich. Assn. of Governing Bds. State Univs., 1999, Most valuable research project award, Mich. Materials and Processing Inst., 1994—95. Mem.: ASME, Internat. Soc. Boundary Elements, Am. Soc. Engring. Edn. Independent. Hindu. Avocations: bridge, swimming. Office: Mich Technol Univ ME-EM Dept Houghton MI 49931 Office Fax: 906-487-2822. Business E-Mail: mavable@mtu.edu.

VACANTI, JOSEPH PHILIP, pediatric surgeon, transplant surgeon; b. Omaha, Oct. 31, 1948; BS summa cum laude, Creighton U., 1970; MD with high distinction, U. Nebr., 1974. Diplomate in gen. surgery and pediatric surgery Am. Bd. Surgery. Clin. fellow in surgery Harvard Med. Sch., Boston, 1979-83; asst. in surgery Children's Hosp., 1983-90, sr. assoc. in surgery, 1990-98, dir. organ transplant, 1990-98, dir. lab. for transplant and tissue engring., 1990—; asst. prof. surgery Harvard Med. Sch., 1983-90, assoc. prof., 1990-97, prof., 1997—; John Homans prof. surgery Harvard Med. Sch./Mass. Gen. Hosp., 1998—. Rsch. affiliate MIT, Cambridge, 1988—. Author some 30 book chpts. and more than 150 sci. articles; co-founder, sr. editor Tissue Engrng.; mem. editl. bd. Cell Transplantation; mem. editl. adv. bd. Tissue Engrng. Intelligence Unit, R.G. Landes. Recipient Sidney Farber award Children's Hosp., 1983, Spl. Recognition award Am. Liver Found., 1987. Fellow ACS; mem. Tissue Engrng. Soc. (co-founder, pres.), Am. Soc. Transplant Surgeons, Transplantation Soc., Am. Pediat. Surg. Assn., Soc. Univ. Surgeons, Inst. Medicine. Office: Mass Gen Hosp 55 Fruit St Boston MA 02114-2696*

VACAR, RICHARD M. airport executive; BS, MBA, Calif. State U.; JD, Loyola Marymount U. Dir. Dept. Aviation Houston Airport Sys.; also dir. aviation Ellington Field, Bush Intercontinental Airport (Houston), William P. Hobby Airport. Office: Houston Airport Sys 16930 JFK Blvd Houston TX 77032*

VACCA, JOHN JOSEPH, JR. television executive; b. Chgo., Apr. 7, 1922; s. John Joseph and Caroline (Bain) V.; m. Alice Isabel Ure, May 2, 1944; children: John Joseph, Dawn Susan, Kim Frances. Student, Northwestern U., 1940-42, Internat. Corr. Schs., 1950-54, Harvard U., 1966. Editor, Midwest Times, Chgo., 1940-41; with prodn. dept. NBC Radio, 1946-47; news dir. sta. KECK, Odessa, Tex., 1947-49, chief announcer, 1948-49; program mgr. KOSA-Radio, Odessa, 1949-55; sta. mgr. KOSA-TV, 1955-61, gen. mgr., 1962-72; v.p., dir. Trigg Vaughn Stas., Inc., Odessa, 1962-67; sec. Odessa Broadcasting Co., 1950-72; asst. sec. Doubleday Broadcasting Co., 1967-77, v.p., 1967-75, sr. v.p., 1975-77; gen. mgr. KDTV, Dallas, 1972-73; TV cons., 1978—; v.p., dir., gen. mgr. Heart O'Texas Broadcasting, Waco, Tex., 1978-83; v.p. Dunn Prodns., Inc., Dallas, 1984-88, pres., 1989-92; ind. TV producer, 1992—. Author: Seven Keys to Success, 1981. Bd. dirs. Odessa Community Chest, 1964-72, Better Bus. Bur., 1956-72; campaign maj. ARC, 1951-72; publicity adviser Ector County chpt. Nat. Found. for Infantile Paralysis, 1949-72; campaign coordinator Civic Music Assn., 1950-72; sponsor, adviser Permian Playhouse, 1959-72, v.p., bd. dirs., 1971-72, City councilman, Odessa, 1962-64; Bd. dirs. Am. Cancer Soc. Served with USAAF, 1942-46. Recipient Zeus award Epsilon Sigma Alpha, 1971 Mem. Nat., Tex. assns. broadcasters, Tex. AP Broadcasters Assn., Advt. Club Odessa (pres. 1960-61, dir. 1960-63), C. of C. (publicity adviser 1950-72), Holy Name Soc. Clubs: K.C. (sec. Odessa 1950-51). Roman Catholic. Home and Office: 646 Harvest Hill Ln Lewisville TX 75067-3588 *A philosophy of service, personal and through broadcasting, coupled with a sincere approach to excellent Human Relations have formed the keystone of my career. Consistent honesty and a constant effort to give and produce much more than required have always been guiding principles. My goals have been set with flexible policies to implement them, ever mindful that 'change' is an integral part of life and progress.*

VACCARO, JEROME VINCENT, psychiatrist, educator, healthcare executive; b. Bklyn., Apr. 17, 1955; s. Louis Sylvio and Margaret Gertrude (Miller) V.; m. Andra M. Penbrook, Apr. 20, 1991; children: Alexandra, Hunter. BS, CUNY, 1977; MD, Albert Einstein U., 1981. Diplomate Am. Bd. Psychiatry. Chief resident Albert Einstein U., Bronx, N.Y., 1984-85; assoc. prof. U. Hawaii, Honolulu, 1985-89, UCLA, 1989—. Med. dir. PacifiCare Behavioral Health, 1996-2001, pres., CEO, 2001--; pres., CEO PacifiCare Dental/Vision, 2001- Editor: Community Psychiatry, 1995; contbr. articles to med. jours. including Hosp. and Comty. Psychiatry, Comty. Mental Health Jour. Mem. Am. Psychiat. Assn., Am. Assn. Comty. Psychiatrists (editor jour. 1984-93).. Office: Pacificare Behavioral Health 23046 dela Carlota Laguna Hills CA 92653

VACCARO, JOSEPH PASCAL, retired marketing educator, marketing consultant; b. Cambridge, Mass., Feb. 7, 1935; s. Orazio E. and Margaret G. (Grosso) V.; m. Patricia A. Murphy, June 29, 1963; children: Paul J., Anne M., Theresa M., Rose P. BSBA, Boston Coll., 1957; MBA, Suffolk U., 1969, JD, 1976. Exec. trainee J. M. Fields, Natick, Mass., 1957; mgr. Prince Leaning Tower of Pizza, West Yarmouth, 1959-60; owner, mgr. Vaccaro's Iron Rail Restaurant, Waltham, 1961-66; instr. mktg. and mgmt. Burdett Coll., Boston, 1966-71; prof. mktg. Sawyer Sch. Mgmt., Suffolk U., 1971—2001; prof. emeritus, 2001—. Cons. Blanchard, Inc., Boston, 1968-88; dir. mktg./advt. plans Am. Advt. Fedn.; reviewer Prentice-Hall, Harper/Collins, Winthrop Pub., Allyn and Bacon, Inc., West Pub., Kent Pub. Co., The Rev.of Bus. Studies, Jour. Promotion Mgmt., Internat. Jour. of Bus., Jour. of Retailing and Consumer Svcs., Jour. of Customer Svc. in Mktg. & Mgmt.; mem. editoral adv. com., jour. reviewer Jour. Profl. Svcs., Mktg., Svc. Mktg. Quar., Health Mktg. Quar., Jour. Hosp. Mktg.; conv. speaker. Author: Decision Making with Cases in Marketing, 1971, Consumer Behavior Cases: A Marketing Management Approach, 1977, Instructor's Manual Sales Management: Text, Readings and Cases, 1987, Sales Management: Text, Readings and Cases, 1987, Managing Sales Professionals: The Reality of Profitability, 1995; contbr. numerous articles to profl. jours. Past chair Ward Com.; past pres. Corpus Christi Holy Name Soc., Newton Jr. C. of C.; active PTA, Auburndale Community Assn., Newton High Sch. Alumni Assn., Boston Coll. Alumni Assn., Suffolk U. Alumni Assn. Named Outstanding Young Man of Newton, Four Outstanding Young Men of Mass.; recipient Disting. Svc. and Outstanding Leadership award Newton Jr. C. of C. Mem. Assn. Mktg. Educators, Am. Acad. Advt., Am. Advt. Fedn. (mem. acad. com., Cert. of Commendation, nat. student competition judge), Am. Assn. Advt. Agy., Am. Mktg. Assn. (Boston chpt. collegiate v.p., bd. dirs., Hugh G. Wales Faculty Advisor of the Yr. award, Cert. of Recognition), Delta Sigma Pi. Democrat. Roman Catholic. Home: 36 Oakwood Rd Auburndale MA 02466-2248 E-mail: juaccaro@suffolk.edu.

VACCARO, RALPH FRANCIS, marine biologist; b. West Somerville, Mass., Apr. 30, 1919; s. Angelo Ralph and Adelaide (Alberlini) V.; m. Martha Ann Walsh, Apr. 19, 1955; children: Christopher Ralph, Adelaide Marie, John Michael, Mark Joseph, Thomas James (dec.), Peter Anthony. BS, Tufts U., 1941; M.P.H., MIT, 1943. Sanitary engring. aide Commonwealth of Mass., Boston, 1946-47; pub. health bacteriologist Assn. Am. Railroads, Balt., 1947-48; sr. rsch. scientist Woods Hole Oceanographic Inst. (Mass.), 1948-86, chmn. dept. biol., 1984-85; cons. environ. quality; assoc. math.-sci. staff Falmouth (Mass.) High Sch., 1989—. Patentee in field. Served with USPHS, 1956— ; served with U.S. Army, 1943-46. Mem. Am. Soc. Limnology and Oceanography, AAAS Republican. Roman Catholic. Home: PO Box 245 West Falmouth MA 02574-0245

VACCHIANO, JULIE CATHERINE, special education educator; b. Neptune, N.J., Oct. 16, 1948; d. James and Rose (Infanto) V. BS in Edn., Trenton State Coll., 1972; MS in Edn., Monmouth Coll., 1979, MS in Edn. in Spl. Edn., 1988. Remedial asst. Holmdel (N.J.) Bd. Edn., 1972-73; classroom tchr. St. Benedict Sch., Holmdel, 1973-85; founder/dir. acad. support svcs. students with learning disabilites Monmouth Coll., West Long Branch, NJ, 1981-94, reading coord., 1980—90; learning disabilities tchr., cons. Jackson (N.J.) Bd. Edn., 1995—. Adj. prof. Brookdale C.C., Lincroft, N.J., 1975-85; adj. prof. ednl. dept. Monmouth Coll., West Long Branch, 1988-94. Contbr. articles to manuals; presenter ednl. issues statewide, 1988—. Mem. N.J. Learning Cons. Assn., Kappa Delta Pi. Office: Jackson Bd Edn 101 Don Donnor Blvd Jackson NJ 08527-5019

VACHER, CLIVE GRAHAM, aerospace executive; b. Oxford, Eng., Mar. 25, 1970; s. Peter John and Polly Mary Anne (King) V. BA with honors, London Sch. Econs., 1992; MBA, MIT, 1998. Sgt. Lancashire Police, Preston, Eng., 1992-96; gen. mgr. Conn. airfoil repair ops. United Techs. Pratt and Whitney Aircraft Engines, East Hartford, Conn., 1998—. Home: 465 Buckland Hills Dr Apt 29111 Manchester CT 06040-9122 Office: Pratt & Whitney Aircraft 400 Main St East Hartford CT 06108-0968

VACHHER, PREHLAD SINGH, psychiatrist; b. Rawalpindi, Punjab, Pakistan, Nov. 30, 1933; came to U.S., 1960; s. Thakar Singh and Harbans Kaur (Ghai) V.; m. Margaret Mary Begley, Oct. 9, 1963; children: Paul, Sheila, Mary Ann, Eileen, Mark. Grad., Khalsa Coll., India, 1950; MD, Panjab U., Amritsar, India, 1956. Diplomate Am. Bd. Psychiatry. Staff N.J. State Hosp., Trenton, 1965-66, Wayne County Gen. Hosp., Eloise, Mich., 1966-68; pvt. practice Livonia, 1966-75, Woodstock, Va., 1991-96; pres. Vachher Psychiat. Ctr., P.C., Livonia, 1975-91. Dir. community psychiatry Northville (Mich.) State Hosp., 1968-71; cons. staff Kingswood Hosp., Ferndale, Mich., 1967-72, Annapolis Hosp., Wayne, 1967-88, St. Joseph Mercy Hosp., Ann Arbor, 1970-89; westland staff Margaret Montgomery Hosp., 1988-91; bd. dirs.

Oakland Rental Housing Assn., 1990-91; med. dir. mental health unit Shenandoan County Meml. Hosp., Woodstock, Va., 1991-94. Mem. Am. Psychiat. Assn., Va. Psychiat. Soc., Sikh Physicians in Mich. (bd. dirs. 1987), Canton C. of C. (pres. 1975), Sikh Bus. Profl. Coun. (pres. 1988—), Rotary (Canton and Plymouth, Mich., Woodstock).

VACHON, LOUIS, psychiatrist, educator; b. Montreal, June 15, 1932; m. Monique Blain, June 25, 1960. BA, U. Montreal, 1952, MD, 1958. Diplomate Am. Bd. Psychiatry and Neurology. Intern Hotel Dieu de Montreal, Que., 1957-58, resident in psychiatry, 1958-61; psychiat. resident Instiut Albert Prevost, Montreal, 1958-61; sr. physician Medfield (Mass.) State Hosp., 1961-62; rsch. assoc., then instr. Boston U. Med. Sch., 1962-68, asst. prof., then assoc. prof., 1968-87, interim chmn. div. psychiatry, 1985-87, prof., chmn. div. psychiatry, 1987-96. Dir. psychiatry outpatient svc. Univ. Hosp., Boston, 1978-85, interim psychiatrist-in-chief, 1985-87, psychiatrist-in-chief, 1987-96, vis. physician in psychiatry, 1987—. Contbg. author: Comprehensive Textbook of Psychiatry, 1989. Fellow Am. Psychiat. Assn.; mem. Boston Psychoanalytic Soc. Inst., Am. Psychoanalytic Assn., Internat. Psychoanalytic Assn., Mass. Psychiat. Soc., Am. Psychosomatic Soc., Mass. Med. Soc., Boston. Office: Boston U Sch Medicine 85 E Newton St # M957 Boston MA 02118-2340

VACHON, LOUIS, bank executive; With Bankers Trust, 1990—96; sr. v.p. treasury and fin. markets Nat. Bank Can., Montreal, 1997—. Office: Nat Bank Canada Nat Bank Tower 600 de la Gauchetière West Montreal QU Canada H3B 4L2*

VACHON, MARILYN ANN, retired insurance company executive; b. Fort Wayne, Ind., Dec. 12, 1924; d. Robert J. and Maude (Shaffer) V. Asst. treas Lincoln Nat. Life Ins. Co., Fort Wayne, Ind., 1961-87, asst. v.p., 1973-87, sec., 1980-87; asst. sec. Lincoln Nat. Corp., 1977-80, asst. treas., 1977-87, sec., 1980-87. Home: 1825 Cortland Ave Fort Wayne IN 46808-2446

VACHON, REGINALD IRENEE, mechanical engineer; b. Norfolk, Va., Jan. 29, 1937; s. Rene Albert Vachon and Regina (Galvin) Radcliffe; m. Mary Eleanor Grigg, Jan. 16, 1960; children: Reginald Irenee, Eleanor Marie. Student, U.S. Naval Acad., 1954-55; BME, Auburn U., 1958, MS, 1960; PhD, Okla. State U., 1963; LLB, Jones Law Sch., 1969. Bar: Ala. 1971; registered profl. engr., Ala., Ga., Miss., La., Wis., Tex. Engr. Hayes Internat., 1958; instr., rsch. asst. Auburn U., 1958-60, rsch. assoc., 1961, assoc., prof., 1963-78; R&D engr. E.I. DuPont, 1960; aerospace engr., technologist NASA Marshall Space Flight Ctr., summers, 1964, 65; pres. Vachon Nix & Assocs., 1977—, VNA Sys. Inc., 1982—. Chmn. bd. Optimal Systems Internat., Inc., 1969-95; COO Thacker Constrn. Co., Thacker Orgn. Inc., 1981-90; pres., CEO Compris Techs., Inc., 1991-92; chmn., Global Risk Managers, Inc., 1992—; prin. Gipco Holdings Internat., Ltd., 1994—; COO United Info. Techs., Inc., Global Interated Techs. Inc. Contbr. articles to profl. jours.; patentee in field. With U.S. Army, 1960-61. Fellow AIAA (assoc.); mem. ABA, NSPE, ASME (hon. mem.), Ala. Bar Assn., The Phoenix Soc. of Atlanta, Cosmos Club, N.Y. Yacht Club, Peachtree Racket Club. Roman Catholic. Home: 1414 Epping Forest Dr NE Atlanta GA 30319-2539 Office: PO Box 190093 Atlanta GA 31119-0093 E-mail: vachonr@asme.org.

VACHRIS, MICHELLE ALBERT, economist; b. Norfolk, Va., June 1, 1962; d. Walter John and Irene Jeanette (Piché) Albert; m. Scott Charles Vachris, Oct. 3, 1987. BA in Econs., Coll. William and Mary, 1984; MA in Econs., George Mason U., 1988, PhD in Econs., 1992. Economist divsn. internat. prices Bur. Labor Stats., Washington, 1984-91, chief sect. info. and analysis, 1991—. Cons. Orgn. Econ. Cooperation and Devel., Paris, 1986; adj. asst. prof. dept. econs., Loyola Coll. Md., 1993—. Contbr. articles to profl. jours. Mem. Am. Econs. Assn., Soc. Govt. Economists. Roman Catholic. Home: # 542 4312 Lookout Rd Virginia Beach VA 23455-1521 Office: Bur Labor Stats 2 Massachusetts Ave NE Washington DC 20212-0022

VACHSS, ANDREW HENRY, lawyer, author, juvenile justice and child abuse consultant; b. N.Y.C., Oct. 19, 1942; s. Bernard and Geraldine (Mattus) V. BA, Case Western Res. U., 1965; JD magna cum laude, New Engl. Sch. Law, 1975. Bar: N.Y. 1976, U.S. Dist. Ct. (so. and ea. dists.) N.Y. 1976. Program rep. USPHS, Ohio, 1965-66; unit supr N.Y.C. Dept. Social Svcs., 1966-69; urban coord. Community Devel. Found., Norwalk, Conn., 1969-70; dir. Uptown Community Orgn., Chgo., 1970-71; dep. dir. Medfield (Mass.)-Norfolk Prison Project, 1971-72; dir. intensive treatment unit ANDROS II, Roslindale, Mass., 1972-73; project dir. Mass. Dept. Youth Svcs., Boston, 1972-73; dir. Juvenile Justice Planning Project, N.Y.C., 1975-85; pvt. practice, 1976—. Organizer, coord. Calumet (Ind.) Community Congress, 1970; bd. dirs. Libra Inc., Cambridge, Mass., Advocacy Assocs., N.Y. and N.J.; adj. prof. Coll. New Resources, N.Y.C., 1980-81; lectr. trainer, speaker to numerous orgns.; cons. on juvenile justice and child abuse to numerous orgns., 1971—. Author: The Life-Style Violent Juvenile: The Secure Treatment Approach, 1979, (novels) Flood, 1985, Strega, 1987, Blue Belle, 1988, Hard Candy, 1989, Blossom, 1990, Sacrifice, 1991, Shella, 1993, Another Chance to Get it Right, 1995, Down in the Zero, 1994, Footsteps of the Hawk, 1995, Batman: The Ultimate Evil, 1995, False Allegations, 1996, Safe House, 1998, Choice of Evil, 1999, Dead and Gone, 2000, Pain Management, 2001, Only Child, 2002, (graphic novels) Predator: Race War, 1995, (audiobook) Proving It, 2001, short stories; editor-in-chief: New Eng. Law Rev., 1974—75; contbg. editor: Parade; contbr. articles. Bd. of counselors Childtrauma Acad., Baylor Coll. of Medicine; mem. expert adv. panel on catastrophic child abuse N.Y. State Office of Mental Health. Recipient Grand Prix de Lit. Policiére, 1988, Falcon award Maltese Falcon Soc. Japan, 1988, Deutschen Krimi Preis, Die Jury des Bochumer Krimi Archivs, 1989, Raymond Chandler award Giuria a Noir Festival, 2000; Indsl. Area Found. Tng. Inst. fellow, 1970-71, John Hay Whitney Found. fellow, 1976-77. Mem. PEN, Writers Guild of Am. Office: Ste 2805 420 Lexington Ave New York NY 10170-2899

VACKETTA, CARL LEE, lawyer, educator; b. Danville, Ill., Aug. 3, 1941; s. Peter G. and Julia M. (Columbus) V. BS, U. Ill., 1963, JD, 1965. Bar: Ill. 1965, D.C. 1968, U.S.Dist. Ct. D.C. 1968, U.S. Ct. Fed. Claims 1968, U.S. Supreme Ct. 1970. Tax lawyer GM, Detroit, 1965-66; ptnr. Sellers, Conner & Cuneo, Washington, 1968-74, Pettit & Martin, 1974-95, Piper & Marbury, 1995-99, Piper Marbury Rudnick & Wolfe LLP, 1999—2002, Piper Rudnick LLP, 2002—. Adj. prof. law Georgetown U., 1971—. Co-author: Government Contract Default Termination, 1991, 93, 95, 97, 99; co-editor Extraordinary Contractual Relief Reporter, 1974—. Capt. U.S. Army, 1966-68. Fellow ABA (sec. pub. contract law sect. 1978-79, coun. 1979-82, pub. contract law sect., editor in chief Pub. Contract Law Jour. 1994—), Nat. Contract Mgmt. Assn.; mem. Fed. Bar Assn., D.C. Bar Assn., Nat. Assn. Purchasing Mgrs., University Club (Washington). Roman Catholic. Office: Piper & Rudnick LLP 1200 19th St NW Fl 7 Washington DC 20036-2430 also: Piper & Rudnick LLP 6225 Smith Ave Baltimore MD 21209-3600 E-mail: carl.vacketta@piperrudnick.com.

VACKO, ROBERT J., JR. real estate development executive; b. Winfield, Ill., Oct. 20, 1967; s. Robert J. Sr. and Jo-Ann M. Vacko; m. Laura J. Pirtle, Aug. 31, 1991; children: Kylie, Katharine, Colynn. MBA, Emory U., 1995. Contr. Portman Holdings, L.P., Atlanta, 1991-98; CFO Colony Homes, LLC, Woodstock, Ga., 1998—. Office: Colony Home LLC 110 Londonderry Ct Ste 136 Woodstock GA 30188

VADUS, GLORIA A. scientific document examiner; b. Forrestville, Pa. Diploma, Cole Sch. Graphology, Calif., 1978; BA in Psychology Counseling, Columbia Pacific U., 1981, MA in Psychology, 1982; diploma handwriting expert, Edith Eisenberg, Bethesda, Md., 1991. Cert. Am. Acad. Graphology, Washington, 1978, ct. qualified document examiner, registered graphologist 1978, cert. behavioral profiling and cert. questioned documents Am. Bd. Forensic Examiners. Pres., owner Graphinc, Inc., 1985—. Accredited instr. graphology Montgomery County Schs., Md., 1978—79; instr. Psychogram Centre, 1978—85, Coun. Graphol. Socs., 1980; testifier superior and probate cts.; pub. forum panelist, lectr., rschr., script therapist pers. selection specialist; writer in field; cons. graphologist; developed Trilogy base for rsch. Am. Handwriting Analysis Found. Author: numerous studies and papers in field, also environ. papers. Chmn. Letter of Hope for POWs; vol. Montgomery County, 1987—88; bd. dirs., cmty. affairs chair East Gate I Civic Assn., Potomac, 1985—87. Named one of 500 Leaders World Influence; named to Hall of Fame: Leading Intellectuals of the World, ABI, 2002; recipient Gold Nib Analyst of Yr. award, Am. Handwriting Analysis Fedn., 1982, Dancing Fan award, Marine Tech. Soc., Tokyo chpt., 1991, Spl. award, U.S./Japan Marine Facilities Panel Valuable Contbns. Japanese Panel UJNR/MFP, 1978—94, Profound Contbns. to Soc. to the Yr., 2000, Bronze Am. Honor medal, ABI, 2001. Fellow: Am. Bd. Forensic Examiners (life; awards chair 1993—94, diplomate, Meritorious award 1994, Outstanding Contbn. cert.); mem.: Coun. Graphical Socs. (bd. dirs. 1982—84), Soc. Francaise de Graphologie for Am. Handwriting Analysis Found., Nat. Assn Document Examiners (bd. dirs. 1985—92, ethics hearing bd. 1986, chmn. nominations com. 1987—88, elections chmn. 1988, parliamentarian 1988—92), Nat. Forensic Ctr., Am. Handwriting Analysis Found. (life; chmn. rsch. com., chmn. adv. bd. 1981—87, bd. dirs. 1981—91, pres. 1982—84, chmn. nominations com. 1985—86, officiator 1986, policy planning and ethics com. 1986—91, ethics chmn. 1989—91, chmn., past pres. adv. bd. 1989—91, hon. profl. women's adv. bd. 1999, cert.), Nature Conservancy, Charles F. Menninger Soc., IEEE-Distaff (internat. chmn. bd. dirs. 1969—72, fashion show chair 1969—72), Internat. Platform Assn., Nat. Wildlife Fedn., Nat. Capitol Jaguar Owners Club (judge 1975—78), Sierra Club, Henry Hicks Garden Club of the Westburys, N.Y. (v.p., pres. elect, judge, chair flower shows, bd. dirs. 1967—71), Soroptimist Internat. (internat. chair, v.p., Bethesda chpt. Montgomery County, bd. dirs. 1987—92), Nat. Writers Club. Home: 8500 Timber Hill Ln Potomac MD 20854-4237 E-mail: fvadus@erols.com.

VADZEMNIEKS, MICHAEL LESTER, plastics company executive; b. Buffalo, Oct. 31, 1955; s. Olgerts and Linda Lou (Evans) V. Assoc. Archtl. Tech., Williamsport (Pa.) Cmty. Coll., 1975. Plant mgr. Engineered Plastics, Inc., Lake City, Pa., 1977-83; prodn. supr. Hoover Universal, Erie, 1983-84; engring. mgr. OEM/Erie, Inc., 1984-88; plant mgr. PHB-Molding Divsn., Fairview, Pa., 1988-93; gen. mgr. Springfield Plastics, Inc., East Springfield, 1993-2000, v.p. ops., 2000—. Founding trustee Old Lake Rd. Summer, East Springfield, Pa., 1986; pres., trustee City Trust, 1987-89, 95-2000, treas., 2000-01; dir. Lake Erie Cmty. Fed. Credit Union, pres. 1989-99; organist, pianist Federated Ch., 1988—. Mem. Northwestern Sportsmen's Club (treas. 1990-95). Republican. Avocations: music performance-piano, downhill skiing, gourmet cooking, carpentry, gardening. Home: 13478 Old Lake Rd East Springfield PA 16411-9765 Office: Springfield Plastics Inc 3247 Route 215 East Springfield PA 16411-9707

VAETH, AGATHA MIN-CHUN FANG, clinical nurse, nursing administrator, consultant; b. Beijing, Feb. 19, 1935; d. Yung-Cheng and Wen-Pu (Cheng) Fang; m. Randy H. Vaeth, July 20, 1971; children: David Sun, Elizabeth Cheng, Philip Cheng. Diploma, Maryview Hosp. Sch. Nursing, Portsmouth, Va., 1959; student, Okla. State U., 1969-73; BS, St. Joseph's Coll., North Windham, Maine, 1986, postgrad., 1989-93, La. State U., 1986. Staff nurse, charge nurse Stillwater (Okla.) Mcpl. Hosp., 1969-74; clin. nurse USINH Hosp., Pawnee, Okla., 1974-75; clin. nurse, relief supr. Gillis W. Long Hansen's Disease Ctr., Carville, La., 1975-91, supervisory clin. nurse, 1991-99, project officer, 1995-99, nursing quality assurance coord., 1990-95, nursing MIS coord., 1991-99; ret., 1999. Wellness cons.; part-time home health nurse, 1993-97. Translator video cassettes on Hansens Disease; illustrator herpetology lab manuel; art exhbns. at Barton Rouge Art & Artist Guild, 1976-77. Recipient Outstanding Performance award GWLHD, PHS, DHHS, 1991, 1993, High Quality Performance award, 1978, 92, 94, 98, Dedicated Svc. to Clin. Br. award, 1981, Outstanding Nurses award Baton Rouge Dist. Nurses' Assn., 1994. Fellow Internat. Biog. Assn. (life); mem. ANA, AAUW, La. Nurses Assn. (nominating com. 1990-94), Baton Rouge Nurses Assn., Chinese Culture Assn. of Baton Rouge (officer-sec. 1993—). Avocations: ballroom dancing, swimming, travel, painting, writing. Home: 1274 Marilyn Dr Baton Rouge LA 70815-4928 E-mail: afmcv@msn.com.

VAGELOS, PINDAROS ROY, pharmaceutical company executive; b. Westfield, N.J., Oct. 8, 1929; s. Roy John and Marianthi (Lambrinides) V.; m. Diana Touliatos, July 10, 1955; children: Randall, Cynthia, Andrew, Ellen. AB, U. Pa., 1950; MD, Columbia U., 1954; DSc (hon.), Washington U., 1980, Brown U., 1982, U. Medicine and Dentistry of N.J., 1984, NYU, 1989, Columbia U., 1990; LLD (hon.), Princeton U., 1990; LHD (hon.), Rutgers U., 1991; DSc (hon.), N.J. Inst. Tech., 1992, SUNY, 1994, Mt. Sinai Med. Sch., 1997, U. B.C., 1998, U. Pa., 1999. Intern medicine Mass. Gen. Hosp., 1954-55, asst. resident medicine, 1955-56; surgeon Lab. Cellular Physiology, NIH, 1956-59, Lab. Biochemistry, 1959-64, head sect. comparative biochemistry, 1964-66; prof. biochemistry, chmn. dept. biol. chemistry Washington U. Sch. Medicine, St. Louis, 1966-75, dir. divsn. biology and biomed. scis., 1973-75; sr. v.p. research Merck, Sharp & Dohme Research Labs., Rahway, N.J., 1975-76, pres., 1976-84; corp. sr. v.p. Merck & Co., Inc., 1982-84, exec. v.p., 1984-85, CEO, 1985-86, chmn., CEO, 1986-94, ret. chmn., CEO, 1994; chmn. Regeneron Pharms., Inc., Tarrytown, N.Y., 1995—. Mem. Inst. Medicine, NAS, 1974—; chmn. sci. adv. bd. Ctr. for Advanced Biotech. and Medicine, 1985-94; bd. dirs. Prudential Ins. Co., 1989-2001. Trustee U. Pa., 1988-99, chmn. bd., 1994-99; trustee Rockefeller U., 1976-94, Danforth Found., 1978—; mem. President's Commn. on Environ. Quality, 1991-93, Adv. Com. Trade Policy and Negotiations, 1992-94, Bus. Coun., 1987-95; bd. mng. dirs. Met. Opera Assn., Inc., 1989-95; bd. dirs. N.J. Performing Arts Ctr., 1989-99, co-chmn , 1992. Recipient award for chemistry in svc. to soc., NAS, 1995, Pupin medal, 1995. Mem. Am. Chem. Soc. (Enzyme Chemistry award 1967), Am. Soc. Biol. Chemists, Nat. Acad. Scis., Am. Acad. Arts and Scis., Am. Philosophical Soc., Bus. Roundtable (policy com. 1987-94). Avocations: jogging, tennis. Discoverer of acyl-carrier protein. Office: Merck & Co Inc 1 Crossroads Dr Bldg A Bedminster NJ 07921-2688

VAGLEY, RICHARD THOMAS, plastic surgeon; b. Charleroi, Pa., Dec. 11, 1945; Children: Sarah E., Adam S., Andrew C., Christian C. BS, Pa. State U., 1966; MD, Jefferson Med. Coll., Phila., 1968. Diplomate Am. Bd. Plastic Surgery. Pvt. practice, Pitts., 1976—. Lt. USN, 1969-71. Fellow ACS. Office: Pitts Inst Plastic Surgery 5989 Penn Circle South Pittsburgh PA 15206-3828

VAGLIANO, ALEXANDER MARINO, banker; b. Paris, France, Mar. 15, 1927; came to U.S., 1940, naturalized, 1945; s. Andre M. and Barbara (Allen) V.; children: Barbara A., Andre M., Justin C. Grad., St. Paul's Sch., Concord, N.H., 1944; BA, Harvard, 1949, LL.B. cum laude, 1952. Bar: N.Y. bar 1952. Asso. firm White & Case, N.Y.C., 1952-58; asst. treas. J.P. Morgan & Co., Inc., 1959; v.p. Morgan Guaranty Trust Co., 1959-62, 65-66, sr. v.p., 1968-76, exec. v.p., 1976-81; chief exec. officer Banca Vonwiller, Milan, Italy, 1967-68; chmn. Morgan Guaranty Internat. Finance Corp., 1976-81, J.P. Morgan Overseas Capital Corp., 1976-81; ptnr. Price Waterhouse and Ptnrs., 1983-85; chmn. Sunset Ridge Farm, Inc., 1983—, Michelin Fin. Corp., Greenville, S.C., 1985-98; chmn. bd. advisors Equity Linked Investors, N.Y.C., 1985—; pres. The N.Y. Farmers, 1992-94. Bd. dirs. Holographics, Inc., N.Y.; dir. office of capital devel. and fin. Near East and South Asia, AID, 1963-65; adviser Yale Econ. Growth Ctr., 1973-80, NYU Inst. French Studies, 1979-86; trustee Coun. for Excellence in Govt., 1990-93. Pres. Parks Council N.Y.C., 1971-73; bd. dirs. French Am. Found. , N.Y.C., 1986-93; gov. The Atlantic Inst. Internt. Affairs, 1986-90; active Norfolk Ct. Zoning and Planning Commn. Served with AUS, 1945-47. Mem. Coun. Fgn. Rels. Clubs: Brook (N.Y.C.); Travellers (Paris). Home and Office: Sunset Ridge Farm Inc Norfolk CT 06058 E-mail: vagliano@earthlink.net.

VAGN-HANSEN, CARSTEN PETER MATHIAS, health consultant, physician; b. Copenhagen, Apr. 5, 1938; s. Christian Ebbe Theodor and Annie Margaretha Vagn-Hansen; m. Joan Poula Kruse, June 30, 1962; children: Christian Aksel, Mette Marie, Lotte Marie, Rikke Marie. MD, U. Copenhagen, 1965. Jr. dr. Aabenraa Hosp., Denmark, 1965-67; registrar Naestved County (Denmark) Hosp., 1967-68, sr. registrar, 1968-70; gen. practitioner Aabenraa, Denmark, 1970-88; health cons. Denmark, 1988—. Pres. Internat. Soc. Gen. Practioners, 1979-82; temp. advisor WHO, 1983. Author: Type 2 Diabetes, 1980, 86, Politike, 1984, 93, 96, Health and Well-Being, 1986, Live Your Life, 1993, When It Hurts, 1996, The Good Life, 1999, Ask About Your Health, 1999; med. editor HELSE mag., 1988—; editor, host Denmark's radio and TV, 1985—. Recipient Hippocrates medal Soc. Internat. Med. Gen., Klagenfurt, Austria, 1988, Pharmacia prize Danish Coll Gen. Practice, 1988, Dandy prize, Denmark, 1991, Health for All prize Denmark Com. on Health Info., 1992, Internat. Nature Medicine Honorary prize, 2002. Mem. Danish Med. Assn., Danish Coll. Gen. Practitioners (bd. dirs. 1975-82). Avocations: singing, studies on early Christianity. Home and Office: Knabberupvej 40 DK 7100 Vejle Denmark E-mail: cavaha@posthus.ddk.dk.

VAGNINI, LIVIO LEE, chemist, forensic consultant; b. North Bergen, N.J., Apr. 26, 1917; s. Frank S. and Margaret (Avondo) V.; m. Daniele Hogge, Sept. 29, 1949; children: Frank, Stephen, Eric. BS in Chemistry, Fordham U., 1938; postgrad., U. Md. Med. Sch., 1938-39. Diplomate Am. Bd. Forensic Examiners. Chemist H.A. Wilson Co. div. Englehard Industries, Inc., 1940-42; chief chemist U.S. Army Graves Registration, Liege, Belgium, 1946-48; chief forensic chemist U.S. Army Criminal Investigation Lab., Frankfurt, Fed. Republic Germany, 1948-60; sr. chemist FDA, Washington, 1960-62, CIA, Washington, 1963-73; project engr. Mitre Corp., McLean, Va., 1973-75; staff scientist Planning Research Corp., 1975-77; program dir. L. Miranda Assocs., Washington, 1978-81; forensic cons. Carmel, Calif., 1981—. Contbr. articles to profl. publs. Mem. Ft. Ord (Calif.) Retiree Coun., 1988, 89—; treas. Alliance Francaise Monterey Peninsula; adv. commn. Monterey County Commn. Vets. Svcs., 1990, 91, 92; Assn. Former Intelligence Officers, 1973—. Served with U.S. Army, 1942-46, lt. col. ret., 1975. Decorated Bronze Star; named Vet. of Yr. in Monterey County, 2000. Fellow Am. Inst. Chemists, Am. Acad. Forensic Scis., Am. Chem. Soc.; mem. Nat. Assn. for Uniformd Svcs. (Monterey chpt.)Internat. Soc. Blood Transfusion, Internat. Soc. Forensic Toxicology, Ret. Officers Assn. (pres. Monterey County chpt. 1985), Sons in Retirement (pres. Pebble Beach br. 1986), Am.-Scandinavian Soc. (1st v.p., program dir. Monterey County 1989), Internat. Assn. of Forensic Sci., Am. Coll. of Forensic Examiners (diplomate). Roman Catholic. Home: 26069 Mesa Dr Carmel CA 93923-8952 E-mail: liviaki@aol.com.

VAGO, ANTHONY SCOTT, investment representative; b. Albuquerque, Jan. 4, 1975; s. Robert Nicholas and Rita V.; m. Kelly Erica Florence, Aug. 26, 2000; children: Austin, Alexander. B of Liberal Studies, So. Ill. U., 1999, MPA, 2000; postgrad., Webster U., 2000—. Respiratory care practitioner II St. Elizabeth's Hosp., Belleville, Ill., 1995-2000; sr. bus. analyst The Boeing Co., St. Louis, 2000—01; investment rep. Edward Jones Co., 2001—. Mem. Sigma Phi Epsilon. Avocations: travel, exercising, boating.

VAGTS, DETLEV FREDERICK, lawyer, educator; b. Washington, Feb. 13, 1929; s. Alfred and Miriam (Beard) V.; m. Dorothy Larkin, Dec. 11, 1954; children: Karen, Lydia. Grad., Taft Sch., 1945; AB, Harvard U., 1948, LLB, 1951. Bar: Mass. 1961. Assoc. Cahill, Gordon, Reindel & Ohl, N.Y.C., 1951-53, 56-59; asst. prof. law Harvard Law Sch., 1959-62, prof., 1962—, Eli Goldston prof., 1981-84, Bemis prof., 1984—, dir. internat. tax program, 1998-2000. Counselor internat. law Dept. State, 1976-77 Author: (with others) Transnational Legal Problems, 1968, 4th edit., 1994, Basic Corporation Law, 1973, 3d edit., 1989, Transnational Business Problems, 2d edit., 1998; editor: (with others) Secured Transactions Under the Uniform Commercial Code, 1963-64; assoc. reporter: (with others) Restatement of Foreign Relations Law; book rev. editor Am. Jour. Internat. Law, 1986-93, co-editor-in-chief, 1993-98. 1st lt. USAF, 1953-56. Recipient Max Planck Rsch. award, 1991. Mem. ABA, Am. Soc. Internat. Law, Coun. Fgn. Rels., Phi Beta Kappa. Home: 29 Follen St Cambridge MA 02138-3502 Office: Sch Law Harvard U Cambridge MA 02138 E-mail: vagts@law.harvard.edu.

VAHAVIOLOS, SOTIRIOS JOHN, electrical engineer, researcher, engineering executive; b. Mistra, Greece, Apr. 16, 1946; s. John Apostolos and Athanasia (Pavlakos) Vahaviolos; m. Aspasia Felice Nessas, June 1, 1969; children: Athanasia, Athena, Kristy. BSEE, Fairleigh Dickinson U., 1970; MSEE, Columbia U., 1972, M in Philosophy, 1975, PhDEE, 1976. Mem. tech. staff Bell Tel. Labs., Princeton, NJ, 1970-75, supr., 1975-76, dept. head, 1976-78; founder, pres., CEO Phys. Acoustics Corp., 1978—, MISTRAS Holdings Corp., Princeton, 1984-94, chmn. quality svcs. labs., 2000—. Adviser Greece Ministry Def., Athens, 1986—88; bd. dirs. Orthosonics, Inc., N.Y.C.; chmn. policy com. Internat. Com. Nondestructive Testing. Contbr. scientific papers to profl. pubs. Chmn. Princeton sect. United Fund, 1976—78; adv. bd. Trenton State Coll., 1983—; chmn. Greek Independence Parade, N.Y.C., 2002; v.p. Fedn. Greek Soc. in Greater N.Y.; bd. dirs. Holy Cross Greek Orthodox Sch. Theology, Boston, 1989—; pres. bd. trustees St. George Greek Orthodox Cmty., Trenton, NJ. Recipient Spartan Merit award, Spartan World Soc., 1987, Entrepreneur of the Yr. award, Arthur Young/Inc. Mag., 1989. Fellow: IEEE (Centennial Medal award 1984, Mittlemen Achievement award 1993), Acoustic Emission Working Group, Am. Soc. Nondestructive Testing (bus. and fin. com. 1984—87, 1988—, bd. dirs. 1985, sec. 1989, treas. 1990, v.p. 1991, pres. 1992, chmn. bd. 1993, chmn. internat. com. nondestructive testing 1994—, editor handbook on acoustic emission 1988, Lester Honor award 1998, Gold medal 2001); mem.: ASTM, Internat. Fund Advancement Nondestructive Testing (v.p.), N.Y. Acad. Scis., IEEE Indsl. Electronics Soc. (sr. mem. adminstv. com. 1988, founder, v.p. conf. 1974—78, editor Trans. on Indsl. Electronics 1976—82, 2d prize Student Paper Contest 1970, Outstanding Young Engr. award 1984). Greek Orthodox. Achievements include 13 U.S. patents; 7 fgn. patents. Avocations: bird hunting, soccer, technical writing, gardening. Home: 7 Ridgeview Rd Princeton NJ 08540-7601 Office: Phys Acoustics Corp PO Box 3135 Princeton NJ 08543-3135 E-mail: sotirios@pacndt.com.

VAHRADIAN, MELINDA, fine artist; b. Ridgecrest, Calif., Nov. 20, 1956; d. Judson Calkins and Susan Frances (Huffaker) Smith; m. Scott Kendall Vahradian, July 11, 1987; children: Daniel Judson, Michael Joseph, Dylan Robert. BS in Social Ecology, U. Calif., Irvine, 1978. Cert. tchr. multiple subjects, cert. learning handicapped specialist, Calif. Learning handicapped specialist San Lorenzo Valley Unified Sch. Dist., Felton, Calif., 1984-91; artist, owner Naptime Prodns., Santa Cruz, 1996—. Bd. dirs., leader Nursing Mothers Coun., Santa Cruz, 1990-99; leader Diabetes Support Group, Santa Cruz, 1999; participant Open Studios Cultural Coun., 1999-2002. Democrat. Office: Naptime Prodns 121 Pacheco Ave Santa Cruz CA 95062-1534

VAICYS, CESLOVAS, neurosurgeon; b. Kaunas, Lithuania, Dec. 31, 1959; came to U.S., 1993; s. Mecislovas Vaicys and Elena Vaiciene; m. Nerija Vaiciene, Aug. 3, 1984; children: Vytautas Vaicys, Zygimantas Vaicys. MD, Kaunas Medical Inst., Kaunas, Lithuania, 1983; PhD, N.N. Burdenko Inst. Neurosurgery, Moscow, Russia, 1988. Diplomate Am. Bd. Neurol. Surgery. Neurosurgery resident N.N. Burdenko Inst. Neurosurgery, Moscow, Russia, 1983-89; staff neurosurgeon, neurosci. rschr. Kaunas (Lithuania) Med. Acad., 1990-91; gen. surgery resident Luth. Gen. Hosp. U. Chgo., 1993-94; stereotactic and functional neurosurgery fellow Wayne State U., Detroit, 1994-95; neurosurgery resident UMDNJ Neurol. Inst. N.J., Newark, 1995-2000; neurosurgeon Meml. Healthcare System, Hollywood, Fla., 2000—. Contbr. articles, chapters to profl. jours. Mem. AMA, Am. Assn. Neurol. Surgeons, Cong. of Neurol. Surgeons, Lithuanian Medical Assn., Moscow Neurosurgery Soc. Roman Catholic. Achievements include successful separation of Siamese twins, Moscow, 1989. Avocations: collecting art, music, water sports. Office: 1150 N 35th Ave Ste 300 Hollywood FL 33021 E-mail: vaicysc@hotmail.com.

VAIDYA, KIRIT RAMESHCHANDRA, anesthesiologist, educator; b. Sihor, India, Feb. 20, 1937; came to U.S., 1971; s. Rameshchandra Harilal Vaidya and Kanta Bachubhai Mulani; m. Rashmi Kirit Vaidya; children: Kaushal, Sujal. BSc, Gujrat U., India, 1959; MB BS, Karnatak U., India, 1965. Intern St. Joseph Hosp., Providence, 1971-72; resident in anesthesiology R.I. Hosp., 1973, Boston City Hosp., 1974-76; clin. instr. anesthesiology Boston U. Sch. Medicine, 1977-79; staff anesthesiologist Bridgeport (Conn.) Hosp., 1979—; asst. clin. prof. anesthesiology U. Conn. Med. Ctr., Farmington, 1987—. Mem. Am. Assn. Physicians from India, Conn. Assn. Physicians from India (pres. 2000-2002), Fairfield County Med. Assn., Conn. State Soc. Medicine, Conn. State Soc. Anesthesiologists, Am. Soc. Anesthesiologists, Internat. Anesthesiology Assn. Hindu. Home: 54 Quail Trl Trumbull CT 06611-5259 Office: Bridgeport Anesthesia Assocs 965 White Plains Rd Ste 301 Trumbull CT 06611-4566 E-mail: kvaidya@pol.net.

VAIL, CHARLES DANIEL, veterinarian, consultant; b. Denver, June 11, 1936; s. Allan Paden and Katherine Marie (Phillips) V.; m. Jean Williams Ebsen, June 15, 1963; children: Ellen Marie, David Elston. BS, Colorado A&M, 1958; DVM, Colo. State U., 1960. Asst. veterinarian Colo. Racing Commn., Littleton, 1958-60; equine practitioner Littleton Large Animal Clinic, 1960—; track veterinarian Centennial Race Track, Littleton, 1962-63. Editor in chief Equine Practice, 1986-2000; contbr. articles to profl. jours. Mem. selection com. Outstanding Biology Tchr. award Colo., 1978-80, 88—, Arapahoe Fair Assn., Littleton, 1965-84, gallery disting. grads. Colo. State U. Coll. Vet. Medicine, 1989; chmn. Littleton Rotary Western Heritage Art Fair; bd. dirs. Animal Assistance Found. Denver, 1991—, v.p., 1995-96, pres.,

1996-97; bd. dirs. Western Vet. Conf., 1997-2000, v.p., 2001; bd. dirs. Friends Littleton Pub. Libr./Mus., 2000—, Rocky Mountain Stroke Assn. Recipient Honor Alumni award Coll. Vet. Medicine, Colo. State U., 1991. Mem. AVMA (publs. com. 1981-87), Am. Assn. Equine Practitioners (pres. 1985), Colo. Vet. Medicine Assn. (pres. 1980, Veterinarian of Yr. award 1987), Denver Area Vet. Medicine Soc. (pres. 1975), Arapahoe Town and Gown Soc. (v.p. 1999, pres. 2000), Colo. State U. Alumni Assn. (pres. 2001-02), Nottingham Club, Rotary (pres. Littleton 1992-93), Sigma Alpha Epsilon, Omicron Delta Kappa. Home: 5921 S Cherrywood Cir Littleton CO 80121-2465 Office: Littleton Large Animal Clinic PC 8025 S Santa Fe Dr Littleton CO 80120-4305 Office Fax: 303-794-9466.

VAIL, IRIS JENNINGS, civic worker; b. N.Y.C., July 2, 1928; d. Lawrence K. and Beatrice (Black) Jennings; grad. Miss Porters Sch., Farmington, Conn.; m. Thomas V.H. Vail, Sept. 15, 1951; children: Siri J., Thomas V.H. Jr., Lawrence J.W. Mem. exec. com. Garden Club Cleve., 1962—83; mem. women's coun. Western Res. Hist. Soc., 1960—, Cleve. Mus. Art. 1953—. Chmn. Childrens Garden Fair, 1966-75, Public Square Dinner, 1975; bd. dirs. Garden Center Greater Cleve., 1963-77; trustee Cleve. Zool. Soc., 1971-98, life trustee 1998—; mem. Ohio Arts Coun., 1974-76, pub. sq. com. Greater Cleve. Growth Assn., 1976-93, pub. sq. preservation and maintenance com. Cleve. Found., 1989-93, chmn. pub. sq. planting com., 1993. Hon. trustee Cleve. Bot. Garden, 2001. Recipient Amy Angell Collier Montague medal Garden Club Am., 1976, Ohio Gov.'s award, 1977. Mem. Chagrin Valley Hunt Club, Cypress Point Club, Kirtland Country Club, Colony Club, Women's City of Cleve. Club (Margaret A. Ireland award). Home: 14950 County Line Rd Chagrin Falls OH 44022-6800

VAIL, MARY BARBARA, publicist; b. Kingsville, Tex., Apr. 24, 1956; d. Fred G. and Nora J. (Smith) Leon; m. David L. Vail, Mar. 30, 1980; children: Sean Kristofer, Ashley Noel. Student, Tex. A&I U.; BS, U. Hawaii, 1982; postgrad., Hawaii Pacific U., 1991-92. Display specialist Linda's, Kingsville, 1986-87; mktg./membership dir. Malibu (Calif.) Riding and Tennis Club, 1990-91; mktg. dir. Pacific Aerospace Mus., Honolulu, 1991-93; pres. Vail Media, Inc. (Scarlett Mktg. & Promotions), Aiea, Hawaii, 1993-95; owner, sole propr. Mary B. Vail Publicist. Vol. fundraiser AOWC, Point Mugu, Calif., 1990-91; vol. Laguna Vista Elem. Sch., Camarillo, Calif., 1990, Barbers Point (Hawaii) Elem. Sch., 1992—; vol., mil. liaison 1st Night Honolulu, 1991; co-chmn. Aloha Family Festival, Pearl Harbor, Hawaii, 1991, Fly Thru Time, 1992, 93, 94, Mugu Air Show, Chinese C. of C. Fashion Show, 1994, Narcissus Festival;, Ho'Okipa Aloha, HIA Hospitality Tng. Coun.; vol. numerous orgns. including Salvation Army, Spl. Olympics, Honolulu C. of C., Am. Diabetes Assn., Am. Diabetes Found., Japanese C. of C., Muscular Dystrophy Assn., Juvenile Diabetes Assn., Make-A-Wish Metro N.Y., Children's Miracle Network, Susan G. Komen Breast Cancer Found., Las Vegas C. of C., Profl. Black Women's Alliance, Hadassah Jewish Women's Orgn., Maddux Found., Candlelighters for Childhood Cancer, USA mag. Make A Difference Day, Shade Tree, women and children's shelter, Sunrise Children's Hosp. Make A Wish Found., Leukemia an Lymphomia Soc., Leukemia Soc., Andre Agassi Grand Slam for Children, Andre Agassi Holiday Party for At-Risk Youths, Fox-5, Children's Miracle Network Telethon, Cystic Fibrosis, , St. Jude Children's Hosp., Clark County Heritage Mus., Girl Scouts Am. Decorated knight Dynastic Mil. Constantinian Order St. George; recipient Nev. Womens Role Model award Nev. State Atty. Gen., 2001; named Female Humanitarian, Las Vegas C. of C., 2000, Nev. Womens Role Model Nev. Atty. Gen., 2001. Mem. NAFE, Pub. Rels. Soc. Am., Pub. Rels. Soc. Hawaii, U. Hawaii Alumni Assn., Food Science and Numan Nutrition Alumni Assn., So. Nev. Homebuilders Assn. Avocations: jogging, crafts, sewing, landscaping, decorating. E-mail: davidvail@earthlink.net.

VAIL, VAN HORN, German language educator; b. Buffalo, Dec. 23, 1934; s. Curtis Churchill and Faith Newbrook (Ely) V.; m. Michele Juliette Edelstein, May 5, 1969; 1 son, Mark Curtis. BA, U. Wash., 1956; MA, Princeton U., 1961, PhD, 1964. Instr. Princeton U., 1962-65, asst. prof., 1965-66; asst. prof. German Middlebury (Vt.) Coll., 1966-69, assoc. prof., 1969-75, prof., 1975—; chmn. dept. Middlebury Coll., Vt., 1970-73, 87-88, dir. studies Middlebury Sch. in Germany, 1967-68, 70-71, 74-75, 85-86, 88-89, 92-93, 95-96. Mem. nat. screening com. Fulbright Scholarships, 1979-81 Author: German in Review, 1967, 2d edit., 1986, 3d edit., 2000, Der Weg zum Lesen, 1967, 2d edit., 1974, 3d edit., 1986, Modern German, 1971, 2d edit., 1978, 3d edit., 1992, Tonio Kröger als Weg zur Literatur, 1974, Workbook for Modern German, 1992, Student Manual for 3d Edit. of German in Review, 2000. Served to 1st lt. M.I., U.S. Army, 1956-58. Fulbright scholar U. Heidelberg, 1958-59 Mem. MLA Home: 352 Cider Mill Rd Middlebury VT 05753-9407 Office: Middlebury Coll Middlebury VT 05753 E-mail: vail@middlebury.edu.

VAILIONIS, ARTURAS, physicist; b. Zarasai, Lithuania, Jan. 19, 1964; s. Juozas and Sabina V.; m. Inga Juskaite, June 7, 1997; 1 child, Eva. PhD, Royal Inst. Technology, Stockholm, 1997. Rsch. assoc. U. Ill., Urbana, 1997-2000; sr. rsch. assoc. Stanford (Calif.) U., 2000—. Mem. AAAS, Am. Vacuum Soc., Materials Rsch. Soc. Office: Stanford U McCullough Bldg 476 Lomita Mall Stanford CA 94305-4045

VAILLANCOURT, JEAN-GUY, sociology educator; b. Chelmsford, Ont., Can., May 24, 1937; s. Royal A. and Marie (Lavallée) V.; m. Pauline Hansen, June 6, 1966 (div. 1983); 1 child, Véronique. BA magna cum laude, Laurentian U., Sudbury, Ont., 1957; licenciate in philosophy, Faculté des Jésuites, Montreal, Que., Can., 1961; licentiate in sociology, Gregorian U., Rome, 1964; PhD in Sociology, U. Calif., Berkeley, 1975. Lectr. St. Boniface (Man.) Coll., Can., 1964-65; asst. prof. U. de Montréal, Que., Can., 1969-76, assoc. prof. Can., 1976-83, prof. sociology Can., 1983—, chmn. dept. Can., 1984-87. Adminstr., 1998; mem. consultative com. Can. ambassador for disarmament, Ottawa, Ont., 1984-91, consultative com. on environ. Hydro-Que., 1984-90. Author: Papal Power, 1980, Essais d'écosociologie, 1982; co-editor: Le processus électoral au Québec, 1976, Roots of Peace, 1986, Environnement et développement Problèmes socio-politiques, 1991, Gestion de l'environnement, éthique et société, 1992, Instituer le développement durable, 1994, Aspects sociaux des prècipitations acides au Québec, 1994, La recherche sociale en environnement Nouveaux paradigmes, 1996, L'énergie au Québec Quels sont nos choix? Montréal Ecosociété, 1998, Les sciences sociales de l'environnement, 1999, La gestion écologique des déchets, 2000; editor-in-chief Sociologie et Sociologie et Sociétés, 1978-87. Mem. coun. City of Dunham, Que., 1976-80; bd. dirs. Oxfam-Que., 1976-79, Can. Inst. Internat. Peace and Security, Ottawa, Ont., 1986-89, European Univ. Ctr. for Peace Studies, Burg Schlaining, Burgenland, Austria, 1989-93, Groupement forestier du Haut-Yamaska, 1993—, Club 2/3, 1995—. Grantee Conseil de Recherche en science sociale du Quebec, 1982, FCAR, 1989-95, 96—, Social Sci. Rsch. Coun., 1983-86, 90—, Can. Inst. Internat. Peace and Security, 1985, 91; fellow Can. Coun., 1965-68. Mem. Internat. Sociol. Assn., Assn. Can. des sociologues et anthropologues de langue française, Sci. for Peace, Pugwash, Group 78. Roman Catholic. Avocations: tree farming, travelling. Home: 953 Cherrier Apt 2 Montréal QC Canada H2L 1J2 Office: U Montréal Dept Sociology Montreal QC Canada H3C 3J7

VAIOS, CHRISTOS IOANNIS, systems engineer; b. Grevena, Macedonia, Greece, Feb. 14, 1961; s. Ioannis and Eugenia (Tzialla) V.; m. Nilda Collazo, Aug. 12, 1986; 1 child, Eugene. AS in Engring., No. Essex Coll., Haverhill, Mass., 1982; BSEE, U. Mass., 1985, MS in Systems Engring., 1987; MBA, U. Phoenix, 1995. Rsch. engr. Ctr. for Atmospheric Rsch., Lowell, Mass., 1984-87; systems engr. AT&T Bell Labs., Holmdel, N.J., 1987-96; MTS design supr. Lucent Technologies, 1996-97; mng. dir. advanced techs. Bus. Consulting Lucent Technologies, 1997-98; dir. strategic mktg. and bus. devel. GlobeSpan, Inc., Red Bank, N.J., 1998—. Sr. mem. tech. staff AT&T Labs. Holmdel, N.J., 1995-96, mem. tech. staff, 1989-95, mem. tech. staff I, 1987-89; rsch. asst. Ctr. for Atmospheric Rsch., Lowell, 1984-87. Patentee in field. Mem. Aliockmon Soc. of Macedonians, N.Y.C., 1993, Homeless Soup Kitchen, Red Ban, N.J., 1992, The Concord Coalition, Washington, 1992. Mem. IEEE, N.Y. Acad. Scis., Delta Mu Delta, Zeta Iota, Eta Kappa Nu. Avocations: tennis, carpentry, classic luxury cars, mountain hiking. Home: 84 Garden Rd Shrewsbury NJ 07702-4474 Office: Netblind Inc 125 Half Mile Rd Red Bank NJ 07701

VAIRA, PETER FRANCIS, lawyer; b. McKeesport, Pa., Mar. 5, 1937; s. Peter Francis and Mary Louise (Bedogne) V.; m. Mary Hohler, 1981. BA, Duquesne U., 1959, JD, 1962. Bar: Pa. 1963, D.C. 1968, Ill. 1984, U.S. Ct. Appeals (D.C. cir.) 1964, Ill. Supreme Ct. Ill. 1984, U.S. Dist. Ct. (no. dist.) Ill., U.S. Dist. Ct. (ea. dist.) Pa. Atty. Chgo. Strike Force, Justice Dept., 1968-72; atty. in charge Phila. Strike Force, 1972-73, Chgo. Strike Force on Organized Crime, 1973-78; U.S. atty. Phila., 1978-83; ptnr. Lord Bissel & Brook, Chgo., 1983-86, Fox, Rothschild, O'Brien & Frankel, Phila., 1986-90, Buchanan Ingersoll, Phila., 1990-92, Vaira & Assocs., Phila., 1992-93, Vaira & Riley, Phila., 1993—. Exec. dir. Pres.'s Commn. on Organized Crime, 1983; ind. hearing officer Laborers Internat. Union N.Am., 1995—; panelist, seminar, controlling internat. organized crime, Rome, Sorrento, Italy, June 1994; panelist, Internat. Conf. on Trial by Jury, Buenos Aires, Oct. 1996. Author: Corporate Responses to Grand Jury Investigations, 1984, Eastern District Practice Rules Annotated, 1996; contbr. articles to profl. jours. Mem. Mayor's Search Com. for Police Commr., Phila., 1992; corruption task force Phila. Police, 1997. Lt. USNR, 1963-68. Recipient Spl. Commendation award Justice Dept., 1976 Fellow Am. Coll. Trial Lawyers (chmn. criminal procedure com. 1995-98, mem. comms. com.); mem. ABA (mem. criminal justice coun. 1986), Am. Law Inst., Union League (Chgo.), Phila. Country Club. Office: Vaira & Riley 1600 Market St Ste 2650 Philadelphia PA 19103-7226 E-mail: variley@aol.com.

VAIRAVAN, KASIVISVANATHAN, mathematician, educator; b. Kandanur, India, July 9, 1939; BE, U. Madras, India, 1962; MS, George Washington U., 1965; PhD, U. Notre Dame, 1968. Asst. prof. to prof. U. Wis., Milw., 1968—, chmn. computer sci. dept., 1987—. Cons. in field. Mem.: IEEE Computer Soc. (pres. Milw. chpt. 1970, Milw. sect. Meml. award 1984). Avocation: photography, reading, biography and history, travel. Office: Univ Wis Computer Sci Dept Milwaukee WI 53217

VAIRO, ROBERT JOHN, insurance company executive; b. Bklyn., Sept. 27, 1930; s. John and Antonietta (DeRose) V.; m. Carol P. Andross, Apr. 8, 1951 (div. Feb. 1979); children: Robert J., Gregory J.; m. Inge R. Buhlbecker, Feb. 20, 1979. Student, Coll. Ins., N.Y.C., 1953-62; Exec. Program in Bus. Adminstrn., Columbia U., 1973. CPCU. Under asst. mgr. Atlantic Cos., N.Y.C., 1952-62; underwriter mgr., v.p. Fireman's Fund Ins. Co., 1962-75; v.p., sr. v.p. underwriting C & F Ins. Cos., Morristown, N.J., 1975-79; exec. v.p., pres. U.S. Ins. Group, 1979-82; chmn., chief exec. officer C & F Underwriters Group and The North River Ins. Co., 1982-86; pres., chief oper. officer Crum and Forster, Inc., 1987-88, pres., chief exec. officer, 1988-90, chmn., pres., chief exec. officer, 1990-92, also bd. dirs. Chmn. Ins. Services Office, N.Y.C., 1983, Am. Ins. Assn., Washington, 1990. Pres. Lincoln Park City Council, N.J., 1971-76. Served with USMC, 1951-53. Mem. Soc. CPCUs, Am. Inst. for Chartered Property Casualty Underwriters (dir., chmn. 1991-92), Desert Highlands Golf Club (pres. 1997-99). Roman Catholic. Home: # 451 10040 E Happy Valley Rd Scottsdale AZ 85255-2388 E-mail: sonoran@aol.com.

VAISEY, DAVID GEORGE, librarian, archivist; b. Tetbury, Eng., Mar. 15, 1935; s. William Thomas and Minnie (Payne) V.; m. Maureen Anne Mansell, Aug. 7, 1965; children: Katharine, Elizabeth. BA, Oxford U., Eng., 1959, MA, 1962. Archivist Staffordshire County Council, Stafford, Eng., 1960-63; from asst. librarian to sr. asst. librarian Bodleian Library, Oxford, Eng., 1963-75, keeper of western manuscripts Eng., 1975-86, Bodley's librarian Eng., 1986-96, Bodley's librarian emeritus Eng., 1997—. Dep. keeper Oxford U. Archives, 1966-75, keeper, 1995-2000; vis. prof. dept. library studies UCLA, 1985; commr. Royal Commn. Hist. Manuscripts, 1987-98; founding chmn. Nat. Coun. Archives, 1988-91. Served to 2d lt. Brit. Army, 1954-56. Decorated encomienda Order of Isabel la Catolica (Spain), comdr. Order Brit. Empire; fellow Exeter Coll., Oxford, 1975, emeritus fellow, 2000; hon. rsch. fellow, Univ. Coll., London, 1987, hon. fellow Kellogg Coll., Oxford, 1996. Fellow: Soc. Antiquaries, Royal Hist. Soc.; mem.: Soc. Archivists (pres. 1999—2002), Brit. Records Assn. (v.p. 1998—). Office: Bodleian Libr Broad St Oxford OX1 3BG England E-mail: david.vaisey@bodley.ox.ac.uk.

VAITKUS, STEVEN ANTHONY, sociologist, researcher, educator; b. Dayton, Ohio, July 11, 1955; arrived in Germany, 1987; s. Stanley Joseph and Helen Louise (Avizynis) V.; m. Sibyl Ute Ahlert, Aug. 9, 1989; children: Juliana Roswita, Justin Anthony. BA in Philosophy, BA in Sociology, Purdue U., 1977; MA in Sociology, U. Toronto, Ontario, Can., 1978, PhD in Sociology, 1986. Assoc. prof. Adam Mickiewicz U., Poznan, Poland, 1989-90; guest lectr. U. Toronto, 1990; lectr. U. Bielefeld, Germany, 1991-92, sr. lectr. Germany, 1995-99; scientific dir. Marianne Weber Inst., Germany, 1999—. Dir. Florian Znaniecki Archive, Bielefeld, Germany, Poznan, Poland, 1987—; guest assoc. prof. U. Constance, Germany, 1992; mem. fgn. editl. bd. Critique and Humanism, Sofia, Bulgaria, 1991—; editl. advisor Internat. Sociology, 1990-96; acad. adminstrv. officer devel. sociology in Russia (tempus: Trans-European Coop. Scheme for Higher Edn.), Bielefeld-Moscow, 1994-97; fgn. advisory mem. governing coun. Russian Ctr. for Humanitarian Edn. U., Moscow, Russia, 1994-98. Author: (book) How Is Society Possible?, 1991 translated into Japanese, 1995; contbr. chpts. to books, articles to Internat. Sociology and other profl. publs. Mem. Am. Sociol. Assn., Internat. Sociol. Assn., German Soc. for Phenomenolog. Rsch., Phi Beta Kappa, Phi Beta Phi. Home: Zillertaler str 9 42349 Wuppertal Germany Office: Marianne Weber Inst Postfach 100111 42001 Wuppertal Germany

VAJK, HUGO, manufacturing executive; b. Ljubljana, Slovenia, Mar. 26, 1928; emigrated to Can., 1947, naturalized, 1953; s. Hugo and Magda (Slatnar) V.; m. Barbara Lois Hallin, June 13, 1953; children: Tanja Astrid, Hugo Anthony, Madeleine Louise, Anita Marie, Nicolette Cecile, Moira Suzanne. Student, Inst. Poly., Grenoble, France, 1947; B.Eng. with honors, McGill U., Montreal, Que., Can., 1951; MS, Carnegie Mellon U., 1953. Product mgr. Joy Mfg. Co., Buffalo, 1957-59, dir. gen. Paris, 1960-63; with Massey-Ferguson, Ltd., 1964-78; pres. Moteurs Perkins S.A., Paris, 1964-65, Massey-Ferguson Ltd., Paris, 1966-69, v.p. logistics parent co. Toronto, 1970-72, exec. v.p., 1973-78; dir. GEC Inc., subs. Gen. Electric Co., Eng., 1979; chmn. English Electric Corp., Elmsford, N.Y., 1979; with Garret Corp. div. Signal Cos., 1980-84; v.p. Garrett Automotive Products; pres. Garrett Automotive Group, Allied-Signal, Inc., 1985-87; chmn. Inovatek Advisors, Inc., New Port Richey, Fla., 1988—; pres. ATM Communications Internat., Inc., Wilmington, Del., 1991—. Mem.: ASME, Nat. Assn. Corp. Dirs., Inst. Mgmt. Cons., Inst. Mgmt. Sci. Inst. Dirs, Assn. Profls. Engrs. Ont., Soc. Automotive Engrs., Yacht Club de France (Paris), Union Interaliée (Paris), Royal Can. Yacht Club (Toronto), Univ. Club of Toronto. Office: ATM Comm Internat Inc 103 Foulk Rd Ste 200 Wilmington DE 19803-3742 E-mail: direct@cardpay.com.

VAJTAY, STEPHEN MICHAEL, JR. lawyer; b. New Brunswick, N.J., Mar. 18, 1958; s. Stephen Michael and Veronica Gizella (Fehèr) V.; m. Gabriella Katherine Soltèsz, Aug. 5, 1989; children: Stephen, Andrew, Gregory, Daniel. BA, Rutgers U., 1980; JD, Georgetown U., 1983; LLM, NYU, 1989. Bar: N.J. 1984, U.S. Tax Ct. 1985. Assoc. McCarter and English LLP, Newark, 1983-91, ptnr., 1991—. Trustee Hungarian Scout Assn. in Exteris, Garfield, N.J., 1985—; trustee Partnership for a Drug-Free N.J., Inc., Montclair, 1993—; adj. prof. law Seton Hall U. Sch. Law, Newark, 1995—; spkr. at lectrs. and seminars, 1992—. Contbr. articles to profl. jours. Mem. Bd. of Adjustment, New Brunswick, N.J., 1993-98. Mem. ABA, N.J. Bar Assn. (chmn. tax sect. 2001-02), Essex County Bar Assn., Phi Beta Kappa. Roman Catholic. Office: McCarter and English LLP Four Gateway Ctr 100 Mulberry St Newark NJ 07102 E-mail: SVAJTAY@MCCARTER.com.

VAKERICS, THOMAS VINCENT, lawyer; b. Lorain, Ohio, Mar. 26, 1944; s. Paul Peter and Margaret Theresa (Dobos) V.; m. Kathryn Ida Rogers, Aug. 7,1965; children: Meredith Vakerics Ehler, Mitchell Thomas. BA, Bowling Green State U., 1965; JD with honors, George Washington U., 1968. Bar: U.S. Dist. Ct. D.C. 1968, U.S. Ct. Appeals (D.C. cir.) 1969, U.S. Supreme Ct. 1974, U.S. Ct. Internat. Trade 1982, U.S. Ct. Appeals (Fed. cir.) 1982. Antitrust trial atty. FTC, Washington, 1969-73; assoc. Gore, Cladouhos & Brashares, 1973-75; ptnr. O'Connor & Hannan, 1975-84, Bayh, Tabbert & Capehart, Washington, 1984-86, Morgan, Lewis & Bockius, Washington, 1986-88, Winthrop, Stimson, Putnam & Roberts, Washington, 1988-94, Perkins Coie, 1994—. Vis. prof. Nihon U., Tokyo, 1981-88. Author: Antitrust Basics, 1985, Antidumping, Countervailing Duty and Other Trade Actions, 1987; contbr. articles to profl. jours. Mem. ABA (vice chmn. internat. antitrust law com. sect. internat. law and practice 1992-95), Internat. Bar Assn., D.C. Bar Assn., Solar Energy Rsch. Inst. (editl. adv. bd. Solar Energy Law Reporter 1979-82), Order of Coif, Phi Delta Phi, Pi Sigma Alpha, Phi Alpha Delta, Sigma Chi. Democrat. Roman Catholic. Home: 12820 Tewksbury Dr Herndon VA 20171-2427 Office: Perkins Coie 607 14th St NW Ste 800 Washington DC 20005-2003 E-mail: vaket@perkinscoie.com.

VAKHARIYA, VINOD R. physician; b. Nipani, India, 1936; MB BS, U. Bombay, India, 1961. Intern Lawrence Gen. Hosp., 1965-66; resident Crittenton Hosp., Detroit, 1966-68, Sinai Hosp., Detroit, 1968-69; chmn. ob-gyn. dept. Wyandotte Gen. Hosp., Mich., 1985-88, mem. med. staff, 1990-94, Henry Ford bd. trustees, 1994-97. Chief med. staff Henry Ford Wyandotte Hosp., 1993-95, trustee, 1997—. Mem.: ACOG, Mich. State Med. Soc. Office: 1650 Fort St Trenton MI 48183-2041

VAKILI-MIRZAMANI, JALALEDDIN, civil engineer, researcher; b. Tehran, Iran, Sept. 19, 1943; came to U.S., 1979; s. Moussa and Farkhondeh V.; m. Parvin Mojarrab, Aug. 27, 1971; children: Mojgan, Kamran. BS, Tabriz (Iran) U., 1965; MS, PhD in Engring., Sorbonne U., Paris, 1969. Registered profl. engr., Calif., Alaska, Idaho. Rsch. assoc. U. Utah, Salt Lake City, 1971-72; chmn. CE dept Tabriz U., Iran, 1972-75, Arya-Mehr U., Iran, 1975-79; vis. prof. U. Calif., Berkeley, 1979-80; sr. engr. Morrison-Knudsen Co, Boise, Idaho, 1980-85; prin. engr. Battelle Meml. Inst., Columbus, Ohio, 1985-88, Leighton and Assocs., Inc., Irvine, Calif., 1988-93; chief engr. Ninyo & Moore, Inc., 1993—. Author: Linear Viscoelasticity, 1973, Soil Mechanics, 1973; contbr. articles to Jour. Res. Mechanica, Jour. Rheology, Jour. Exptl. Mechanics, Trans. SME-AIME. Mem. transportation com. Indsl. League Orange County, Calif., 1990—. Recipient Fulbright Hays award, U.S. Govt., 1971, 79; Rsch. grant, French Govt., 1965. Mem. ASCE (constn. com. 1987-88), French Soc. Dr.-Engrs., Internat. Soc. Soil Mechanics and Found. Engring. Achievements include development and implementation of equipment and procedures for in situ determination of dynamic properties pavement and subgrades; determination of viscoelastic material model for asphalt concrete; co-development of a material model for rock salt as a host medium for a nuclear waste repository. Office: 9272 Jeronimo Rd Ste 123A Irvine CA 92618-1914

VAKOCH, DOUGLAS ALLEN, psychologist, researcher; b. Ada, Minn., June 16, 1961; s. Alvin Harris and Stella Mae Vakoch; m. Julie Gnarl Bayless, Sept. 2, 2000. BA in Religion, Carleton Coll., 1983; MA in History and Philosophy of Sci., U. Notre Dame, 1991; MA, SUNY, Stony Brook, 1994, PhD in Clin. Psychology, 1996. Clin. intern U. Wis.-Madison Hosp. and Clinics, 1995-96; postdoctoral fellow Vanderbilt U., Nashville, 1996-98; rsch. assoc. dept. psychology U. Calif., Davis, 1999—; columnist SPACE.com, 2000—; social scientist Search for Extraterrestrial Intelligence (SETI) Inst., Mountain View, Calif., 1999—, interstellar message group leader, 2001—. Co-chair Internat. Astron. Congress Search for Extraterrestrial Intelligence Rev. Meeting, Melbourne 1998, Toulouse 2001, Houston, 2002; mem. conf. com. internat. conf. on optical search for extraterrestrial intelligence Internat. Soc. for Optical Engring., San Jose, Calif., 1999-01; chair internat. workshop on interstellar message constrn., Toulouse, 2001; chair internat. workshop on Art and Sci. of Interstellar Message Composition, Paris, 2002. Contbr. articles to profl. jours. V.p. Minn. Jr. Acad. Sci., St. Paul, 1978. Recipient Grant-in-Aid of Rsch., Sigma Xi, Excellence in Rsch. award, 1993, 94, John Templeton Found. grant, 2001; Nat. Merit scholar Carleton Coll., 1979-83, fellow Am. Psychoanalytic Assn., 1997-98. Mem. Internat. Soc. for Arts, Scis. and Tech. (mem. space and arts adv. com. 2001-), Internat. Acad. Astronautics (search for extraterrestrial intelligence com., subcom. on issues of policy concerning comms. with extraterrestrial intelligence, subcom. on media and edn., subcom. on arts and lit., subcom. on post-detection sci. and tech.). Avocations: astronomy, 3-D animation. Office: Search for Extraterrestrial Intelligence (SETI) Inst 2035 Landings Dr Mountain View CA 94043-0818 Fax: 650-968-5830. E-mail: vakoch@seti.org.

VALADE, ALAN MICHAEL, lawyer; b. Berwyn, Ill., Jan. 26, 1952; s. Merle F. and Vera M. Valade; m. June 17, 1978. Student, Oakland C.C., 1970—72; BA, U. Mich., 1974; JD, Wayne State U., 1977; LLM in Taxation, NYU, 1978. Bar: Mich. 1978, Fla. 1987. Assoc. Kemp, Klein, Endelman & Beer, Southfield, Mich., 1978-79; shareholder Valade, MacKinnon & Higgins, P.C., Detroit, 1979-84, Schwendener & Valade, P.C., Mason, 1985-91; ptnr. Honigman Miller Schwartz and Cohn LLP, Lansing, 1991—. Co-author: The Michigan Single Business Tax, 1991; contbr. articles to profl. jours. Fellow Mich. State Bar Found.; mem. ABA, State Bar Mich. (chmn. state and local tax com. 1991, tax. coun. 1989-92), State Bar Fla. Office: Honigman Miller Schwartz and Cohn LLP 222 N Washington Sq Ste 400 Lansing MI 48933-1800

VALADEZ, JOSEPH JAMES, epidemiologist, researcher; b. San Diego, Mar. 12, 1949; s. Frank Lopez and Helen Marie (Farmakis) V. BA, Northwestern U., 1971; PhD, Lancaster (Eng.) U., 1978; MPH, Harvard U., 1983, DSc, 1988; diploma in infectious disease epidemiol., Ctr. Ministry Health Mex. Asst. prof. U. Md., College Park, 1979-85; assoc. Harvard Inst. for Internat. Devel., Cambridge, Mass., 1986-90; dir. African Med. Rsch. Found., Nairobi, Kenya, 1991-94; sr. health officer UNICEF, Kigali, Rwanda, 1994; sr. assoc. Johns Hopkins U., Balt., 1994—; health coord. Plan Internat., Arlington, Va., 1996—, sr. monitoring evaluation advisor Non Govtl. Orgn. Networks, 1998—, chmn. bd. dirs., founder, 1998-01. Cons. World Bank, Washington, 1981-94, U.S. AID, Nairobi, 1994, CARE Internat., Nairobi, 1992. Author: Simulated International Processes: Theories and Research on Global Modeling, 1981, Assessing Child Survival Programs in Developing Countries, 1991, Monitoring and Evaluating Social Programs in Developing Countries, 1994; actor in motion picture The Ascent, 1994. Recipient Thayer Merit award Harvard U., 1987-88, Merit Rsch. award and Spl. award Am. Soc. Landscape Architects, 1981; Sr. Ford Minority fellow Ford Found., Washington, 1985—. Mem. Nat. Coun. for Internat. Health, Am. Pub. Health Assn. Avocations: running, acting, mountain climbing, international travel, deep sea diving. Office: NGO Networks for Health Plan Internat 2000 M St NW Ste 500 Washington DC 20036 E-mail: JosephValadez@compuserve.com.

VALADEZ, ROBERT ALLEN, lawyer; b. McAllen, Tex., May 27, 1960; s. Ventura S. and Maria G. (De los Santos) V.; m. Kelly Curll Valadez; 1 child, Ashley Marie. BBA, U. Tex., 1982, JD, 1985. Bar: Tex. 1985, U.S. Dist. Ct. (so., we., ea. & no. dists.) Tex. Briefing atty. Tex. Supreme Ct., Austin, 1985-86; assoc. Fulbright & Jaworski, San Antonio, 1986-89, participating assoc., 1989-92; assoc. Wright & Greenhill, 1992-93; shareholder Shelton & Valadez, 1993—. Home: 15 Camden Oaks San Antonio TX 78248-1606 Office: Shelton & Valadez 112 E Pecan 2600 Weston Centre San Antonio TX 78205-1517 E-mail: rvaladez@shelton-valadez.com.

VALADEZ, RUDOLPH ANTONIO, security firm executive, consultant, writer, artist; b. Elmertownship, Mich., July 30, 1942; s. Aldofo Valadez and Catalina Gamez; m. Jo Ann Gomez; children: John L. children: Rudolph A., Monique M., Emilio Alejandro. BS, Am. U., 1971; postgrad., St. Thomas U., 1990, Pacific West Coll., 1995. Spl. agt.-mgr., chief Soviet CounterIntelligence, Chief of Counter Internat. Terrorism FBI, Washington, 1967—92; adminstr.-commr. Western Regional U.S. Immigration & Naturalization Svc., Laguna Niguel, Calif., 1992—93; TV and radio commentator Spanish Channel 52, KTNQ, L.A., 1993—95; security cons. Valadez Assocs. Internat., Inc., 1994—. Author: (Book) Uncommon Common Sense: The Anatomy of Peril, 2001, Instant Philosopher, 2002, Emilio Kosterlitzky, 2002;exhibitions include Global Art Gallery, Seattle, 2002, Cambria (Calif.) Art Gallery, 2002. Bd. dirs. Basic Adult Spanish Edn. for Spanish Illiteracy, L.A., 1986—90. Recipient Pub. Svc. Recognition, Calif. State Senate, 1992, Outstanding Pub. Svc. award, L.A. County Bd. Suprs., 1992, Cold War Svc. Recognition award, U.S. Dept. Def., 2001. Mem.: Am. Soc. Indsl. Security. Roman Catholic. Achievements include patents for handcuff holster; self recharging battery; automobile third rear light to indicate driver activity and pending action. Avocations: painting, flying, woodworking, travel. Home: 4353 Teesdale Ave Studio City CA 91604 Office: Valadez Assocs Internat Inc. Ste 2 4353 Teesdade Ave Studio City CA 91604 Home Fax: 818-505-9211; Office Fax: 818-505-9211. Personal E-mail: r.valadez@attworldnet.com. Business E-Mail: r.valadez@mai_assoc.com.

VALAINIS, GREGORY THOMAS, physician; b. Richmond, Va., Dec. 26, 1952; s. Joseph and Yvonne Valainis; m. Phyllis Kae Vess, Jan. 24, 1981; children: Lauren M., Gregory T., Harrison J., William J. BS, Va. Tech., 1976; MD, Med. Coll. of Va., 1980. Cert. Nat. Bd. Med. Examiners, 1981, Am. Bd. Internal Medicine (internal medicine), 1983, Am. Bd. Internal Medicine (infectious disease), 1986. Intern, resident U. Fla. Health Sci. Ctr., Jacksonville, 1980-83, chief resident dept. internal medicine, 1983-84; clin. instr. U. Fla., 1983-84; fellow sect. on infectious disease Alton Ochsner Med. Found., New Orleans, 1984-86; asst. prof. of medicine, dept. of medicine, infectious diseases sect. Tulane U. Sch. of Medicine, 1986-89; asst. prof. medicine, dept. medicine Med. U. S.C., 1989-91; assoc. prof. of medicine Med. U. of S.C., Spartanburg, 1991—. Asst. physician Tulane U. Hosp., 1986-89; asst. vis. physician Charity Hosp. of New Orleans, 1986-89; dir. Tulane Infectious Diseases Clin., 1986-89; intermittent staff VA Med. Ctr., New Orleans, 1986-89; dir. clin. evaluations for AIDS Clin. Trials Unit, 1987-89; active staff dept. of internal medicine Spartanburg Regional Med. Ctr., 1990—, cons. infection control 1992—; cons. Mary Black Hosp., Spartanburg, 1989-97, 98—, Doctor's Meml. Hosp., 1990-94. Presenter in field; contbr. articles to profl. jours., chpts. to books. Mem. ACP, Am. Soc. Microbiology, Southwestern Assn. Clin. Microbiology, Infectious Diseases Soc. Am., S.C. Infectious Diseases Soc., Internat. AIDS Soc., Spartanburg County Med. Soc. Roman Catholic. Avocations: tennis, wine collecting. Office: Spartanburg Regional Med Ctr Divsn Med Edn 101 E Wood St Spartanburg SC 29303-3072 Fax: 864-560-6063. E-mail: gvalainis@srhs.com.

VALANCE, MARSHA JEANNE, library director, story teller; b. Evanston, Ill., Aug. 2, 1946; Children's libr. trainee N.Y. Pub. Libr., N.Y.C., 1968-69; ref. libr. Acton (Mass.) Meml. Pub. Libr., 1969-70; mgr. The Footnote, Cedar Rapids, Iowa, 1976-78; assoc. editor William C. Brown, Dubuque, 1978-79; dir. Dubuque County Libr., 1979-81, G.B. Dedrick Pub. Libr., Geneseo, Ill., 1981-84, Grand Rapids (Minn.) pub. Libr., 1984-89; mgmt. libr. Wis. Regional Libr. for Blind and Physically Handicapped, 1989—. Workshop coord., participant, sect. chmn. profl. confs.; LSCA grant reviewer Dept. Edn., 1989-95. Author: (with others) Mystery, Value and Awareness, 1979, Pluralism, Similarities and Contrast, 1979; contbr. articles and book revs. to pubis. Troop leader Miss. Valley Coun. Girl Scouts USA, Cedar Rapids, 1976-78; mem. liturgy com. St. Malachy's Roman Cath. Ch., Geneseo, 1983; com. judging clinic 4-H, Moline, Ill., 1984; trustee KAXE No. Cmty. Radio, 1986-89, ICTV, 1988-90; sec. Grand Rapids Cmty. Svcs. Coun., 1986; coach Itasca County 4-H Horse Bowl Team, 1987; dir. Grand Rapids Storyfest, 1987-89; program chmn. Spotlight on Books Conf., 1989; bd. dirs., trustee Vols. in Svc. to the Visually Handicapped, 1989—; audio describer Artreach, Milw., 1991-98. Nat. merit scholar, 1964-68; recipient Weavers award Telephone Pioneers, 1992, outstanding svc. award Badger Assn., 1999; grantee Iowa Humanities Bd. 1981, Minn. Libr. Found., 1985, 86, 87, Blandin Found., 1986, Arrowhead Regional Arts Coun., 1987, 89, Ms. Soc., 1989, Sunrise Found., 2000. Mem. ALA, Wis. Libr. Assn., Iowa Librs. Medium Size (sec. 1981), Northlands Storytelling Network (bd. dirs. 1988-94, v.p. 1989, pres. 1990, editor Grapevine 1991-94), Nat. Storytelling Assn., Alliance Info. and Referral Svcs., DAR (constn. chmn. 1983-84), Miss. Valley Morgan Horse Club, Wis. Morgan Horse Club (newsletter editor 1994-95, sec. 1995), Am. Morgan Horse Assn., Geneseo Jr. Women's Club (internat. chmn. 1983-84), UCLA Club Wis. (pres. 1990-91), Alpha Gamma Delta. org. Home: 343 N 62d St Milwaukee WI 53213-4130 Office: Wis Regional Libr Blind & Physically Handicapped 813 W Wells St Milwaukee WI 53233-1436 E-mail: mvalan@mpl.org.

VALAND, THEODORE LLOYD, media company executive; b. Bklyn., Nov. 9, 1943; s. Theodore and Ruth (Johansen) V.; m. Ann Reed, May 22, 1999; children: Theodore L. II, Meghan K. BS, NYU, Bronx, 1964; MA, NYU, N.Y.C., 1971; postgrad., U. Cin., 1969—. Sr. rsch. analyst NBC Owned TV Stas. Divsn., N.Y.C., 1976-77; dir. computer ops. and rsch. planning Group W TV Sales/Radio Sales, 1977-82; mgr. info. systems Group W TV Sta. Group, 1982-86; v.p., gen. mgr. Basys, Inc., Mountainview, Calif., 1986-88; pres., CEO The VBS Group, Inc., N.Y.C., 1988—; co-founder, co-dir. The Media Devel. Project Inc., 1989-93; v.p. rsch. and tech. New World Sales & Mktg., 1994-97, Petry Interactive, N.Y.C., 1997-98; prin. The Web Selling Zone, 1998—; pres. Myers Custom Studies, Myers Reports, Inc., 2000. Taft fellow dept. history U. Cin., 1971-72. 1st lt. U.S. Army, 1966-68. Mem. NATAS, Data Processing Mgmt. Assn./Assn. Info. Tech. Profls. (bd. dirs. N.Y. chpt. 1987-92, pres. 1998—), Radio and TV News Dirs. Assn., Nat. Assn. TV Program Execs., Radio and TV Rsch. Coun., N.Y. New Media Assn., Cable and Telecom. Assn. for Mktg. Home: 140 Cadman Plz W Brooklyn NY 11201-1852 Office: VBS Group Inc Rockefeller Ctr Sta Box 5576 New York NY 10185 Fax: 718 858-5221. E-mail: tvaland@vbsgroup.com.

VALANIS, KIRK CHRISTIAN, theoretical mechanics researcher, educator; b. Lefkara, Larnaca, Cyprus, Mar. 6, 1930; came to U.S., 1961; s. Christakis and Panayota Valanis; m. Lilian E. Salisbury, Sept. 10, 1955 (div.); children: Christina, Paul, Catherine; m. Barbara G. Geesey, Sept. 11, 1978. BS with honors, Imperial Coll., London, 1955, MSc, 1957; PhD, Purdue U., 1963. Prof. Iowa State U., Ames, 1964-68; prof., head U. Iowa, Iowa City, 1968-78; dean engring. U. Cin., 1978-83, prof., 1983-86; rsch. prof. U. Portland, Oreg., 1998—; pres. Endochronics Inc., Vancouver, Wash., 1986-96; owner Endochronics Co., 1996—. Cons. S-Cubed, La Jolla, 1976-92, Jet Propulsion Lab., Pasadena, Calif., 1966-92; bd. dirs. U. Crete, 1978-86. Author: Irreversible Thermodynamics, 1977; editor, author: Constitutive Equations, 1976; contbr. articles to profl. jours. Rsch. grantee NSF, 1978, Amy Rsch. Office, 1984, AF Office of Scientific Rsch., 1969, Waterways Experiment Sta., 1992. Fellow ASME; mem. Soc. of Engring. Sci., Math. Assn. of Am., Acad. of Mechanics. Greek Orthodox. Avocations: bridge, chess, tennis, hiking, stamp collecting. Home: 8605 NW Lakecrest Ct Vancouver WA 98665-6520 Office: Endochronics Co 8605 NW Lakecrest Ct Vancouver WA 98665-6520

VALASQUEZ, JOSEPH LOUIS, industrial engineer; b. Balt., Apr. 15, 1955; s. Jose Louis and Edith Rosabel (Saunders) V.; m. Nicole Diane Feldser, Sept. 4, 1983; children: Alexandra Nicole, Joseph Jr. AA, Essex Coll., 1977; BS in Indsl. Engring., U. Ariz., 1982; MBA in Fin., So. Ill. U., 1985. Registered profl. engr., Fla.; cert. quality engr.; cert. quality auditor; cert. quality mgr.; cert. project mgmt. profl.; cert. integrated resource mgmt.; pvt. pilots license. Machinist Bausch & Lomb, Balt., 1974-77; indsl. engr. IBM Corp., Tucson, 1980-81; sr. indsl. engr. Gen. Dynamics, San Diego, 1981-83; supr. engring. Avco Corp., Nashville, 1983-84; mgr. engring. Burroughs Corp., Coral Springs, Fla., 1984-85; dir. total quality mgmt. Lambda Novatronics, Inc., Pompano Beach, 1984-94; championt of continuous improvement Allied Signal, 1994-97, Sensormatic Corp., 1997-98; v.p. corp. quality Sunbeam Corp., Delray Beach, Fla., 1998-2001; quality/productivity exec. Bank Am., Charlotte, N.C., 2001—. Computer cons., Margate, Fla., 1987; founder, owner E.P.I. Cons., Pompano Beach. Mem. Am. Inst. Indsl. Engrs., Fla. Engring. Soc. Republican. Roman Catholic. Avocations: real estate management, computer programming, mountain climbing, canoeing, private pilot. Home: PO Box 49616 Charlotte NC 28277-0082 E-mail: joe.l.valasquez@bankofamerica.com.

VALCHEVA-TRAYKOVA, MARIA LOZANOVA, chemist, scientist; b. Sofia, Bulgaria, Aug. 16, 1952; d. Lozan and Milka Kostova (Petrova) Valchev; m. Trayko Todorov Traykov, Dec. 21, 1982; 1 child, Lozan Traykov Todorov. MS in Chemistry, U. Sofia, 1977; PhD in Chemistry, Bulgarian Acad. Scis., Sofia, 1993. Rsch. fellow Inst. Organic Chemistry, Sofia, 1977-85, Inst. Kinetics and Catalysis, Sofia, 1985-97; sr. rsch. assoc. CAAMP, NU, Boston, 1997-98. Contbr. articles to profl. jours. Mem. Bulgarian Catalysis Soc., Bulgarian Zeolite Soc., European Zeolite Assn. Avocations: travel, computers, books. Home: 5 San-Stefano Str 1504 Sofia Bulgaria Office: Northeastern U CAMMP Dept Chem Engring 342 Snell Engrg Ctr 360 Huntington Ave Boston MA 02115

VALDES, JACQUELINE CHEHEBAR, psychologist, consultant, researcher; b. Bklyn., Sept. 17, 1962; d. Gabriel and Rosy (Mosseri) Chehebar; m. Manuel Valdes, June 3, 1990; children: Raquel Elena Valdes, Michael Aaron Valdes. BA, U. Conn., 1983; cert. in substance abuse studies, Nova U., 1987, MS, 1988; PhD, Nova U., Ft. Lauderdale, 1992. Diplomate Am. Coll. Forensic Examiners, Am. Coll. Psychol. Specialties in Neuropsychology. Children's outpatient coord. Jewish Family Svc., Miami Beach, Fla., 1988-89; neuropsychology apprentice Robert A. Levitt, Ph.D., PA, 1989-90; intern Columbia Presbyn. Med. Ctr., N.Y.C., 1990-91; fellow and resident Robert A. Levitt, PhD, PA, Ft. Lauderdale, 1991-93; pvt. practice, Hollywood, Fla., 1993—; dir. neuropsychology svcs. Meml. Regional Hosp., 1995-99; cons. neuropsychology Devel. and Early Intervention Clinic Joe DiMaggio Children's Hosp., 2000—. Psychology supr., educator Sunrise (Fla.) Rehab. Hosp., 1992-93; rschr. North Broward Med. Ctr., 1992-93, asst. dir. internship, 1993-94, Memory Disorders Ctr. Neurolog. Inst., Pompano, Fla., 1992-98, dir., 1994-98; neuropsychologist Neurologic Cons., Fort Lauderdale, Fla., 1992-98, Neurol. Cons., Hollywood, Fla., 1992-97; neuropsychology cons. Sunrise (Fla.) Rehab. Hosp., 1992-94; chairperson minority affairs Broward County Psych. Assn., 1997-98. Contbr. articles to profl. jours. Sec. Spanish Speaking Neuropsychology Interest Group, L.A., 1993-94; apptd. Child Sexual Abuse Svc. Provider Task Force, 1989. Mem. APA, Internat. Neuropsychol. Soc., Nat. Acad. Neuropsychologists, Am. Acad. Neurology, Brain Injury Assn., Fla. Psychol. Assn. Democrat. Jewish. Home: 520 E Mt Vernon Dr Plantation FL 33325-3600 Office: 2214 Hollywood Blvd Hollywood FL 33020-6605

VALDES, JUAN CARLOS, marketing executive; b. Santiago de las Vegas, Habana, Cuba; came to U.S., 1966; s. Hidalgo Valdes and Angela Teresa Valdes Montes de Oca. AA, Miami Dade C.C., Miami, Fla., 1976; student, Fla. Internat. U., 1977-78, Internat. Coll. Naples, Fla., 1988-89. Purchasing coord. Barnett Bank, Miami, 1975-76; internat. purchasing v.p. Mid-East Caribbean Trading Co., Miami and London, 1976-80; internat. mktg. devel. Mid-East Caribbean Petroleum Co., London, 1978-80; exec. v.p. internat., COO Rysell Internat., various locations, 1980—. Cons. Rysell Internat. Mktg. Devel. Group, St. Domingo, Dominican Republic, 1984—, Forest Internat. Group, Manaus, Brazil, 1988—; comptr. Rancho Santa Barbara, Clemiston, Fla., 1986-90; COO Juan Valdes & Son Cigar Co., Dominican Republic and Miami, 1988—; exec. v.p., COO, Amazon Trade Devel. Corp., Miami and Manaus, 1988—; bd. dirs. A Place Called Hope. Roman Catholic. Avocation: traveling. Office: ATDC 13876 SW 56th St Miami FL 33175-6021 E-mail: jcv1357@aol.com.

VALDES, ROLANDO HECTOR, library director, law librarian; b. Havana, Cuba, Jan. 13, 1939; came to U.S., 1966; s. Juan Manuel Valdes-Anciano and Sylvia (Nunez) Marasco. BA, Sancti-Spiritus Coll., Las Villas, Cuba, 1961; MLS, Havana (Cuba) U., 1963, postgrad. in tchr. edn., 1963-65. Libr. asst. The Newberry Libr., Chgo., 1966-68; reference libr. Sandard and Poor's Corp., N.Y.C., 1968-72; evening supr. Hunter Coll. Libr., 1970-72; med. social worker Flower and Fifth Ave. Hosps., 1973-76; social worker Mt. Carmel Guild, Union City, N.J., 1976-79, Queensborough Soc. for Prevention of Cruelty to Children, 1979-82, State of Fla. Dept. Health and Rehab. Svcs., 1982-84; libr. specialist, law libr., libr. dir. Dade Correction Instn. Librs., Florida City, Fla., 1984—. Contbr. articles to profl. jours. Direct opera co. of incarcerated prisoners. Mem. Dade County Libr. Assn., Reforma. Avocations: opera studies, audio-visual collector, chess, baseball, art films. Home: 38277 SW 192nd Ave Lot 28 Florida City FL 33034-6606 Office: Dade Correctional Libr 19000 SW 377th St Florida City FL 33034-6409

VALDEZ, ARNOLD, dentist, lawyer; b. Mojave, Calif., June 27, 1954; s. Stephen Monarez Jr. and Mary Lou (Esparza) V.; m. Brandy Radovich, Dec. 31, 1994; children: Bayleigh, Briton, Barrington. BS in Biol. Sci., Calif. State U., Hayward, 1976; BS in Dental Sci. and DDS, U. Calif., San Francisco, 1982; MBA, Calif. State Poly. U., 1985; BS and JD cum laude, Pacific West Coll. Law, 1995. Bar: Mex., 1996; diplomate Am. Bd. Forensic Medicine, Am. Bd. Forensic Dentistry; cert. ind. med. examiner, qualified med. examiner, Calif. Pvt. practice specializing in temporomandibular joint and Myofascial Pain Dysfunction Disorders, Pomona, Calif., 1982, Claremont, 1982—; CEO, Valcom, 1994—; assoc. Marin, O'Connell & Meché, 1996. CEO, Valcom-A Telecom. Corp.; network adminstr. Amiga and IBM compatibles; mem. adv. com. dental assisting program Chaffey Coll., Rancho Cucamonga, Calif., 1982—; mem. staff Pomona Valley Hosp. Med. Ctr.; ptnr. Marin, O'Connell & Meché; mem. digital adv. group Soradex, 2000. Vol. dentist San Antonio Hosp. Dental Clinic, Rancho Cucamonga, 1984—, Pomona Valley Assistance League Dental Clinic, 1986—; bd. dirs. Pacific West Coll. Law, 1993—, v.p. fgn. devel., 1996—, v.p. curriculum, 1998—, Fellow Am. Coll. Forensic Examiners, Acad. Gen. Dentistry (mastership 1994); mem. ADA, Am. Equilibration Soc., The Cranial Acad., Newport Harbor Acad. Dentistry, Calif. Dental Assn. (table clinic judge 1998—), Tri-County Dental Soc. (co-chmn. mktg. 1986, chmn. sch. screening 1987, Golden Grin award), Acad. Gen. Dentistry, Acad. Osseo Integratiion, Acad. Computerized Dentistry, U. Calif.-San Francisco Alumni Assn., U. So. Calif. Sch. Dentistry Golden Century Club, Toastmasters, Psi Omega, Delta Theta Phi. Democrat. Roman Catholic. Avocations: skiing, gymnastics, kenpo karate (2d degree black belt), racquet sports, dancing. Home: 515 Seaward Rd Corona Del Mar CA 92625-2600 Office: 410 W Baseline Rd Claremont CA 91711-1607 E-mail: dentski@home.com. *Personal philosophy: Life is a journey, not a destination!.*

VALDMAN, ALBERT, language and linguistics educator; b. Paris, France, Feb. 15, 1931; came to U.S., 1944, naturalized, 1953; s. Jacques and Rose (Standman) V.; m. Hilde Wieners, Aug. 19, 1960; 1 child, Bertrand André. AB, U. Pa., 1953; AM, Cornell U., 1955, PhD, 1960; PhD (hon.), U. Neuchâtel, 1991; Doctorate honoris causa, U. Neuschâtel, 1991. Linguistic scientist Fgn. Service Inst., 1957-59; asst. prof. Romance langs. Pa. State U., 1959-60; mem. faculty Ind. U., Bloomington, 1960—, prof. French, Italian and linguistics, 1966—, chmn. dept. linguistics, 1963-68, Rudy prof., 1986—; vis. prof. Harvard, summer 1965. Vis. lectr. U. West Indies, 1965-66; Fulbright lectr. U. Nice, France, 1971-72, 75-76, 83-85, 86, 87, 89; cons. in field, 1959— Author: Applied Linguistics-French, 1960, Drillbook of French Pronunciation, 1964, 70, Trends in Language Teaching, 1966, College French in the New Key, 1965, Saint-Lucian Creole Basic Course, 1969, Basic Course in Haitian Creole, 1970, First and Second Level High School French, 1972, 2d edit., 1977, Langue et Culture, 1975, Introduction to French Phonology and Morphology, 1976, Le Creole: Structure, Statut et Origine, 1978, Haitian Creole-French English Dictionary, 1982; co-author: En Route—Introduction au français et au monde francophone, 1986; editor: Pidgin and Creole Linguistics, 1977, Le Francais hors de France, 1979; co-editor: Theoretical Orientations in Creole Studies, 1980, Historicity and Variation in Creole Studies, 1981, Issues in International Bilingual Education, 1982, Haiti Today and Tomorrow: An Interdisciplinary Study, 1984, The Evaluation of Foreign Language Proficiency, 1987, Ann pale KreyÒl: Learning Haitian Creole, 1987, Dis-Moi!, Viens Voir!, C'est Ça!, 1989, Bien Entendu! Introduction a la prononciation francaise, 1993, Learners' Dictionary of Haitian Creole, 1996, French and Creole in Louisiana, 1997, Chez Nous, 1997, Dictionary of Louisiana Creole, 1998. Decorated comdr. and officer de l'Ordre des Palmes Academiques; recipient Florence Steiner prize, Am. Coun. Tchg. Fgn. Langs., 1998; fellow, guggenheim, 1968, Fulbright, 1985. Mem. Internat. Assn. Applied Linguistics (sec.-gen. 1984-87, pres. 1987-94), Am. Assn. Tchrs. of French (v.p. 1990-94, pres. 1995-98), Comité Internat. des Créolistes (v.p. 1996—), Phi Beta Kappa. Office: Ind U CREDLI BH 604 Bloomington IN 47405 E-mail: valdman@indiana.edu.

VALE, WYLIE W. biochemist; BS, Rice U., 1964; PhD in Physiology & Biochemistry, Baylor U., 1968. Biochemist The Salk Inst., La Jolla, Calif., 1970-78, Clayton Found. Lab. Peptide Biology br. The Salk Inst., La Jolla, 1978—. Elected mem. Inst. of Medicine, 2000. Recipient Fred Conrad Koch award Endocrine Soc., 1997. Office: Clayton Found Lab Peptide Biology The Salk Inst 10010 N Torrey Pines Rd La Jolla CA 92037-1002*

VALEK, BERNARD MICHAEL, accounting executive; b. Joliet, Ill., Nov. 19, 1945; s. Peter Anthony and Ann Monica (Hertko) V.; m. Myonghui Kim, July 2, 1999; 3 children. BS, No. Ill. U., 1968, MBA, 1969. CPA, Calif., Ill. Asst. prof. Ferris State U., Big Rapids, Mich., 1969-72; staff mgr. Arthur Andersen & Co., Chgo., 1972-78; dir. Calif. CPA Fedn., Palo Alto, 1979-84; pres. Alliance of Practicing CPAs, Long Beach, Calif., 1985—99, bd. dirs. 1985—; CFO Pilgrim Pl., Claremont, 1999—. Cons. ANA, L.A., 1984-86. Author: ANA Practice Management Manuals, 1985; pub. (newsletter) The CPAdvocate, 1990—. Bd. dirs. Am. Heart Assn., Long Beach, 1993-94; bd. dirs., treas. Cities in Schs. Long Beach, 1988-99, Long Beach Phone Friend, 1988-93. Named One of 100 Most Influential People in Acctg., Acctg. Today newspaper, 1996. Mem. AICPA (bd. dirs. 1982-84), Calif. CPA Soc. (bd. dirs. 1979-84). Roman Catholic. Avocations: exercising, hiking, travel, health. Address: 12149 Fremont St Yucaipa CA 92399-4025 Office: 12149 Fremont St Yucaipa CA 92399-4025

VALENCIA, JOSEPH NORBERT, engineer; b. Oxnard, Calif., Sept. 15, 1958; s. Joe Hernandez and Rachel Tafoya Valencia; m. Tracey Lorraine Rouda, July 9, 1994; children: Ryan, Nicholas stepchildren: Daniel, Sara. AA, Allan Hancock Coll., Santa Maria, Calif., 1980. Sr. logistics engr. Author: The Fire Season, 1996. Mem.: Vandenberg Surfing Assn. Avocations: coaching soccer and baseball, surfing, hiking. Home: 327 N Lupine Lompoc CA 93436

VALENCIA, MARGARITA, Spanish language educator; b. Bogotá, Colombia, Nov. 28, 1952; came to U.S., 1973; BA, MA in Polit. Sci., U. Calif., Santa Barbara. Profl. clear single subject tchg. credential in Spanish; cert. eligibility for Calif. prelim. adminstrv. svcs. credential. Tchr. Spanish Manual Arts H.S. L.A. Unified Sch. Dist., 1994—. Mem. L.A. World Affairs Coun., Acad. Polit. Sci. N.Y., Sierra Club.

VALENCIA, ROGELIO PASCO, electronics engineer; b. Paombong, Bulacan, The Philippines, Mar. 18, 1939; came to U.S., 1959; s. Silvino Carlos and Basilia Galang (Pasco) V.; m. Amelia Almendarez Gomez, May 31, 1965; children: Zenaida Leticia, Lucinda Amelia, Rogelio Pasco II. Student mech. engring., Mapua Inst. Tech., Manila, 1955-59; student English and math., Coll. William and Mary, 1963-64, numerous USCG tng. schs. Enlisted man USCG, 1959, advanced through grades to chief warrant officer; with USCG cutter Rush, Vietnam, 1970-71; sr. tech. officer USCG Loran Sta., Hokkaido, Japan, 1977-78, exec. officer Dana, Ind., 1978-79; ret., 1979; computer analyst Wyman & Gordon Co., Danville, Ill., 1979-80; precision measurement electronics lab. technician USAF, Rantoul, 1980-88, digital computer engr., 1988—. Achievements include designing synchronous Loran clock, field telephone monitor. Home: 1303 Bradford Cir Saint Joseph IL 61873-9625

VALENCIANO, RANDAL GRANT BOLOSAN, lawyer; b. Waimea, Hawaii, Nov. 17, 1958; s. Placido Dias and Maria (Bolosan) V.; m. Debbie F.I.; children: Marisa Claire Ihara, Dreana Rae Ihara, Randon Grant Ihara. BS, U. Oreg., 1980; JD, U. Wash., 1983. Bar: Hawaii 1983. Dep. pub. def. State of Hawaii, 1983-84; dep. prosecutor County of Kauai, 1984-87; ptnr. Valenciano & Zenger, Lihue, 1989-91; pvt. practice, 1996—. Arbitrator 5th Jud. Cir. State of Hawaii, 1988-91; mem. Defender Coun. State of Hawaii, 1989-91. Lawyer, coach Waimea High Sch. Mock Trial Team, 1986-88; bd. dirs. Hawaii United Meth. Union, Honolulu, 1987-91. Mem. Hawaii State Bar Assn., Kauai Bar Assn. (v.p. 1988-89), Kauai County Coun. (vice chair 1990—). Democrat. Avocation: sports card collecting, bonsai plants. Home: Pua Nani St Lihue HI 96766 Office: 3016 Umi St Ste 211A Lihue HI 96766-1346

VALENTA, JANET ANNE, substance abuse professional; b. Cleve., Sept. 22, 1948; d. Frank A. and Ann (Kogoy) Shenk; m. Mario Valenta, May 22, 1971. BA, Cleve. State U., 1970; postgrad., Rutgers U., 1973, U. Cin., 1976-84. Cert. prevention cons., Ohio, 1989—. Purchasing clk./typist Restaurant div. Stouffer Foods Corp., Cleve., 1967-71; cmty. info. specialist Trumbull Warren Office of Econ. Opportunity, Warren, Ohio, 1972; edn. dir. Trumbull County Coun. on Alcoholism, 1973-78; rehab. counselor Trumbull County Bur. Vocat. Rehab., Niles, Ohio, 1979-80; owner, operator Ironsmith, 1978-79; cons., trainer Ohio Network Tng. and Assistance to Schs. and Cmty., Youngstown, Ohio, 1987—; prevention edn. coord. Cmty. Recovery Resource Ctr., 1979-94; prevention coord. Neil Kennedy Recovery Clinic, 1994—. Ohio tng. coord. Babesworld Home, Inc., Detroit, 1986-99; nat. chair pub. health caucus Nat. Assn. Prevention Profls., Chgo., 1976-77. Publicity chair Trumbull Art Guild, Warren, 1974—76; mem. policy coun. Youngstown Cmty. Action, Headstart, 1988—90; mem. Summer Arts Butler Art Mus., 1997—; active Ohio Violence Prevention Process, 2002; bd. dirs. Ebony Life Support Group, Inc., Youngstown, 1992. Named Woman of Yr., Warren Bus. and Profl. Women's Assn., 1978. Mem. Alcohol and Drug Abuse Prevention Assn. Ohio. Office: Neil Kennedy Recovery Clinic 2151 Rush Blvd Youngstown OH 44507-1535

VALENTE, JOHN FREDERICK, transplant surgeon; b. San Francisco, June 23, 1960; s. Joseph Louis and Sonja Fredericka (Zobel) V. BS in Biology, U. San Francisco, 1983; MD, U. Calif., San Francisco, 1987. Resident gen. surgery U. Ariz., Tucson, 1987-92; fellow trauma/critical care U. Cin., 1992-93, fellow transplantation surgery, 1993-95, asst. prof. surgery, 1996—; fellow rsch. Shriners Burns Inst., Cin., 1995-96; surg. dir. kidney transplant program Univ. Hosps. of Cleve., 2001—. V.p. NovaCell Biotechs. Inc., Cin., 1996—. Contbr. articles to profl. jours., chpts. to books. ARCS scholar ARCS Found., 1981. Mem. AMA, ACS (candidate), Shock Soc., Surg. Infection Soc., Am. Soc. Transplant Surgeons (mem. edn. com. 1998-2001, Pharmacia-Upjohn award 1996), Alpha Sigma Nu. Republican. Roman Catholic. Achievements include patent on co-culturing bone marrow cells for immunomodulation; patent on enhancement of transplant graft survival through nutritional immunomodulation. Office: 1100 Euclid Ave Cleveland OH 44115-1603

VALENTE, LOUIS PATRICK (DAN VALENTE), business and financial executive; b. Somerville, Mass., July 26, 1930; s. Luigi and Mary Constance (Fedele) V.; m. Jeanne Barbara Peters, Oct. 3, 1992; children: Louis, Marianne, Steven, Diane, Richard, Carol, Susan. CPA, Bentley Coll., Boston, 1955. Cost acct. Cambridge Corp., Lowell, Mass., 1953-55; sr. acct. Flaherty, Bliss & Co., CPAs, Boston, 1956-61; fin. analyst Sanders Assocs., Nashua, N.H., 1961-62; contract audit adminstr. Dept. Def. Audit Agy., Boston, 1962-66, DOE, Las Vegas, 1966-68; asst. controller EG&G, Inc., Wellesley, Mass., 1968-71, asst. v.p., treas., 1971-74, dir. fin., 1974-79, officer, corp. treas., 1979-83, v.p. bus. devel., 1985-91, sr. v.p. mergers, acquisitons and investments, 1991-95; bus. and fin. cons., 1995-97; chmn., CEO Palomar Med. Tech., Inc., Burlington, Mass., 1997—. Bd. dirs. Meditech Inc., Westwood, Mass., Patient Care Tech., Atlanta, MKS Instruments, Inc., Andover, Mass., Palomar Med. Tech. Inc., Burlington, SurgiLight, Inc., Orlando, Fla. Selectman Town of Burlington, 1970-73, 76-79, chmn., 1972-79; trustee, mem. fin. com. Choate-Symmes Hosp., Woburn, Mass., 1972-80; pres.'s adv. coun. Bentley Coll. With USAF, 1951-53. Mem. AICPA, Fin. Execs. Inst., Mass. Soc. CPAs, Bentley Coll. Alumni Assn., New Eng. Coun., KC Lodge. Roman Catholic. Home: 44 Concord Rd Weston MA 02493-1223

VALENTI, FREDERICK ALAN, actor, screenwriter; b. Wiesbaden, Fed. Republic Germany, Feb. 24, 1967; s. Fred and Arietta Maxinne (Deline) V.; m. Melissa Ann Valenti. BA in Theater Arts, San Francisco State U., 1988; MA in Film History & Criticism, UCLA. Model Kim Dawson Agy., Dallas, 1982-84; actor, screenwriter I.C.M., San Francisco, 1992—. Play dir. Children's Theater Workshop, San Francisco, 1987—. Actor: (films) This is Spinal Tap, 1984, Home Alone, 1990, Presumed Innocent, 1990, Silence of the Lambs, 1991, Groundhog Day, 1993, Clueless, 1995, The English Patient, 1997, The Sixth Sense, 1999, (play) Breaking New Ground, 1986 (Critics award 1986); screenwriter The Hip Guys, 1988; prodr. (stage) The Magic of D.R. Gibson, 1997, Chef Ken Takes the Cake, 1999; dir., playwright Pokie Cobb is Returning Home, 1998. Organizer San Francisco Youth for a Better Day rally, 1987; spokesman Just Say No to Drugs campaign, San Francisco, 1987, 88; chmn. Dallas Area Labor Day Telethon, 1990; chmn. Dallas chpt. AMFAR, 1992-95; founder Melissa Ann Valenti Found. for Benefit of Korean Adoptees, 1999. Recipient Youth in Film award Acad. Motion Picture Arts and Scis., 1984, Cauldron award Dallas Ctr. of Performing Arts, 1990, Emmy for The Longest Day, 1993; Cable Ace award for Dennis Miller Live, 1995, Emmy for writing Seinfeld, 1997. Fellow Screen Actors Guild, Actors Equity Assn.; mem. Internat. Brotherhood of Magicians. Democrat. Roman Catholic. Avocations: flying, auto racing, surfing, culinary arts, cycling. Home: 3704 Julienne Dr Plano TX 75023-7073 Office: Valenti Prodns 1708 Timberway Dr Richardson TX 75082-4530 E-mail: hawaii73@aol.com.

VALENTI, MICHAEL A. lawyer; b. Cleve., Jan. 26, 1960; s. Richard A. and Josephine A. Valenti; m. Kelly Jeane Vance, Jan. 26, 1990; children: Alexander P., Nicholas R., Dylan V. BA in French, Coll. of Holy Cross, 1982; JD, Am. U., 1986. Bar: Ky. 1987, U.S. Dist. Ct. (we. and ea. dists.) Ky. 1987, U.S. Ct. Appeals (fed. cir.) 1988, U.S. Ct. Appeals (6th cir.) 1989, U.S. Dist. Ct. (so. dist.) Ind. 1996, Colo. 1998; cert. NFLPA contract advisor. Assoc. Greenbaum, Doll & McDonald, Louisville, 1986-87, Hirn, Reed & Harper, Louisville, 1987-95; ptnr. Hirn, Reed, Dohery & Harper, 1997, VAlenti Hanley & Crooks

PLLC, Louisville, 1997—99. Chmn. bd. dirs. RMD Corp. Pro bono svc. work Legal Aid Soc., Louisville. Mem. Ky. Bar Assn. (continuing legal edn. awarad 1996). Office: Valenti Hanley & Crooks PLLC 2121 PNC Plaza Louisville KY 40202-2823 E-mail: mav@vhclaw.com.

VALENTI, PAULA ANNE (PELAK), art educator, supervisor; b. Danville, Pa., Feb. 2, 1956; d. Daniel Timothy and Marie Vincenzia (Folger) Pelak. BA, Kean U., 1978, MA, 1983; supr. cert., Montclair U., 1998; postgrad., Seton Hall U., 2001—. Cert. supr. art, art educator grades K-12, elem. educator with specialty in gifted and talented. Art tchr. Montclair (N.J.) Pub. Schs., 1978-84, Dumont (N.J.) H.S., 1984-86, Ridgewood (N.J.) Pub. Schs., 1986-99; supr. art Newark Pub. Schs., 1999—2001. Founding mem. Hands and Minds Inst./Art Edn. N.J., 1991—; curriculum cons. Yavneh Acad., Paramus, N.J., 1998-99. Exhibited in group shows Kean Coll., 1977, 78, Faculty Show, Ridgewood, N.J., 1987, 92, Priory, Newark, 2000, 2001, Univ. Coun. for Art Edn., Bklyn., 2001; juried shows include St. John's, Newark, 2000. Recipient Govs. award State N.J., State Museum, 1993, 96; grantee N.J. State Coun. Arts, Trenton, 1989. Mem. Nat. Art Edn. Assn. (ea. region rep. 1994-96, profl. materials com. 1998—, Ea. Region Elem. Art Educator of Yr. 1993), Art Educators N.J. (pres. 1991-92, Disting. Achievement award 1995), Phi Delta Kappa. Democrat. Roman Catholic. Home: 80 Lincoln Pl Waldwick NJ 07463-2115 Office: Newark Pub Schs Office Visual Arts 15 State St Newark NJ 07104 E-mail: pells@verizon.net.

VALENTINE, ALAN DARRELL, symphony orchestra executive; b. San Antonio, July 18, 1958; s. Lonnie Darrell Jr. and Marjorie (Childs) V.; m. Jari Ann Ruhl, Aug. 10, 1979 (div. 1987); children: Brandon Darrell, Chelsea Michelle; m. Karen Kay Bingham, Oct. 21, 1989 (div. 2001); 1 child, Nathan Lee; m. Connie Linsler, July 21, 2002. MusB, U. Houston, 1981. Orch. mgr. U. Houston Symphony, 1977-81; gen. mgr. Mid-Columbia Symphony Soc., Richland, Wash., 1981-83, Greensboro (N.C.) Symphony Soc., 1983-85; orch. mgr. Symphony Soc. San Antonio, 1985-87; mng. dir. Chattanooga Symphony and Opera, 1987-88; exec. dir. Okla. Philharm. Soc., Oklahoma City, 1988-98, Nashville Symphony, 1998—. Mem. adj. faculty Arts Administrn., Oklahoma City U., 1992— Recs. include Best of Greensboro Symphony Orchestra Silver Season, 1983, A Christmas Festival-San Antonio Symphony, 1986, A Time of Healing-Oklahoma City Philharmonic, 1995; (CD) Howard Hanson The Nashville Symphony, 2000, Charles Ives The Nashville Symphony, 2000, George Whitefield Chadwick-Nashville Symphony, 2002; TV prodns. include Music of the Americas-Placido Domingo with San Antonio Symphony, 1986, Perry Como Christmas Special-San Antonio Symphony, 1986, Sagebrush Symphony-Oklahoma City Philharmonic with Michael Martin Murphey, 1996, Kathie Lee: Just In Time for Christmas-Okla. City Philharmonic & Guests, 1996, Martina McBride Christmas Special Nashville, Symphony and Guests, 1998. Bd. dirs. Classen Sch. for Artistically and Academically Gifted, 1995-98, Arts Festival Okla., 1991-. Mem. NARAS (bd. dirs. 2002-), Am. Symphony Orch. League (bd. dirs. Cmty. and Urban Symphony Orch. divsn. 1981-83, policy com. A 1995-98, chmn. group III mgrs. 1996-98), Rotary, Phi Mu Alpha. Presbyterian. Avocations: computers, racquetball, reading. Office: Nashville Symphony 2000 Glen Echo Ste 204 Nashville TN 37215 E-mail: alandv@aol.com.

VALENTINE, BRIAN, information technology executive; BS in Computer Sci., Ea. Washington U. Software engr. Intel Corp.; from engring. mgr. to sr. v.p. Microsoft, Redmond, Wash., 1987—98, sr. v.p. windows divsn., 1998—. Office: One Microsoft Way Redmond WA 98052-6399*

VALENTINE, CONSTANCE, health service program analyst, researcher; b. Phila., June 19, 1943; 2 children. BA, Smith Coll., 1965; MS, Calif. State U., San Francisco, 1976. Accredited tchr. cmty. coll., Calif. Determinations interviewer Employment Devel. Dept., San Francisco, 1968-76; rehab. counselor Dept. Rehab., 1976-92, asoc. govt. program analyst, 1992—. Coord. eight child abuse confs.; frequent spkr. and educator. Contbr. articles to profl. publs. Hotline coord. Violence Prevention, Davis, 1989—. Named Vol. of Yr. Mental Health Assn,. 1998, Recognition award Yolo Cty. Care Continuum Davis, 1990. Mem. Incest Survivors Spkrs. Bur. of Yolo County (founding mem.), Calif. Protective Parents Assn. (pres.). Democrat. Lutheran. Avocations: reading, crocheting. E-mail: CPPA001@aol.com.

VALENTINE, DEBRA A. attorney; b. Cleve., Apr. 16, 1953; AB magna cum laude in History, Princeton U., 1976; JD, Yale U. Law School, 1980. Bar: D.C., U.S. Dist. Ct. D.C., U.S. Ct. Appeals (D.C. Cir., 3d Cir., 11th Cir.), U.S. Supreme Ct. Law clk. Judge Arlin M. Adams, U.S. Ct. Appeals, 3d Cir., Phila., 1980-81; atty./advisor Office of Legal Counsel, Dept. of Justice, Washington, 1981-85; assoc. O'Melveny & Myers, 1985-91, ptnr., 1991-95; dep. dir. policy planning FTC, 1995-96, asst. dir. for internat. antitrust, 1996-97, gen. counsel, 1997-2001; ptnr. O'Melveny & Myers, 2001—. Cons. Sec. of State's Adv. Com. South Africa. Contbr. articles to profl. jours. Adv. mem. bd. dirs. The Washington Ballet. Fulbright scholar, 1976-77. Mem. ABA, Am. Law Inst., D.C. Bar, Coun. on Fgn. Rels., Phi Beta Kappa. Home: 2853 Ontario Rd NW Apt 605 Washington DC 20009-2246 Office: O'Melveny and Myers Ste 500 555 Thirteenth St NW Washington DC 20004 E-mail: dvalentine@omm.com.

VALENTINE, FOY DAN, clergyman; b. Edgewood, Tex., July 3, 1923; s. John Hardy and Josie (Johnson) V.; m. Mary Louise Valentine, May 6, 1947; children: Mary Jean, Carol Elizabeth, Susan Foy. BA, Baylor U., 1944, LLD (hon.), 1979; ThM, Southwestern Baptist Theol. Sem., 1947, ThD, 1949; DD, William Jewell Coll., 1966, Louisiana Coll., 1989. Ordained to ministry Bapt. Ch., 1942. Dir. Bapt. student activities colls. in Houston, 1949-50; pastor First Bapt. Ch., Gonzales, Tex., 1950-53; dir. Christian life commn. Bapt. Gen. Conv. Tex., 1953-60; exec. dir., treas. Christian life commn. So. Bapt. Conv., 1960-87, exec. officer for devel., 1987-88; chmn. So. Bapt. inter-agy. council, 1965-67. Willson lectr. applied Christianity Wayland Bapt. Coll., 1963; Christian ethics lectr. Bapt. Theol. Sem., Ruschlikon-Zurich, Switzerland, 1966; Layne lectr. New Orleans Bapt. Theol. Sem., 1974; Jones lectr. Union U., 1976; Staley Disting. Christian scholar/lectr. La. Coll., 1981; Simpson lectr. Acadia Divinity Coll., Nova Scotia, 1982; H.I. Hester lectr. on preaching Midwestern Bapt. Theol. Sem., 1984; Belote lectr. Christian ethics Hong Kong Bapt. Theol. Sem., 1990; co-chmn. commn. religious liberty and human rights Bapt. World Alliance, 1966-75, chmn. commn. Christian ethics, 1976-80, mem. gen. coun., 1976-80; mem. Nashville Met. Human Rels. Commn., 1966-78, Pres.'s Commn. for Nat. Agenda for the Eighties, 1980; guest columnist USA Today; lectr. on Christian ethics Bible Inst. for Evangelism and Missions, St. Petersburg, USSR, 1991. Author: Believe and Behave, 1964, Citizenship for Christians, 1965, The Cross in the Marketplace, 1966, Where the Action Is, 1969, A Historical Study of Southern Baptists and Race Relations 1917-1947, 1980, What Do You Do After You Say Amen?, 1980, Hebrews, James, 1 and 2 Peter: Layman's Bible Book Commentary, 1981; editor: Christian Faith in Action, 1956, Peace, Peace, 1967, Christian Ethics Today, 1995-2000; contbr. to numerous anthologies, articles to profl. jours. Pres. Ctr. for Christian Ethics, 1990-2000; trustee Interfaith Alliance, 1994—, Ams. United for Separation of Ch. and State, 1960-93, pres., 1989-93; bd. dirs. Bapt. Joint Com. Pub. Affairs, 1960-87, Chs. Ctr. Theology and Pub. Policy, 1976-87, T.B. Maston Found., Texans Against Gambling; mem. bd. fellows Interpreter's House, 1967-78, Ctr. for Dialogue and Devel., 1987-96. Recipient Disting. Alumnus award Southwestern Bapt. Theol. Sem., 1970, Brooks Hays Meml. Christian Citizenship award, 1983, Disting. Alumni award Baylor U., 1987. Mem. Am. Soc. Christian Ethics. Democrat. Home and Office: 12527 Matisse Ln Dallas TX 75230-1741

VALENTINE, GENE C. securities dealer; b. Washington, June 19, 1950; s. John N. and Jane S. Valentine. BS in Psychology, Bethany Coll., 1972; student, U. Vienna, Austria, 1971-72. Commd. ensign USN, 1972, advanced through grades to lt., 1987, hon. discharged, 1978; owner Horizon Realty, San Francisco, 1978-82; dir. land acquisitions Windfarms Ltd. subs. Chevron, U.S.A., 1980-82; v.p. mktg. Christopher Weil & Co., Sherman Oaks, Calif., 1982-85; chmn., CEO Pacific Asset Group Inc. (name now Fin. West Group, Inc.), Westlake Village, 1985—. Bd. dirs. Fin. West Group, Inc., Paradox Holdings; founder, chmn., dir. Second Byte Found.; founder, chmn. Peace Point Farms Equestrian Facility, LLC and Found., Bethany, W.Va. Trustee Bethany Coll., W.Va., 1998—; mem. Rep. Party, L.A. Mem. NASD, Internat. Assn. Fin. Planning (bd. dirs. L.A. chpt. 1982-87). Episcopalian. Avocations: equestrian, sailing, tennis, golf, running. Office: Fin West Group Inc 2663 Townsgate Rd Westlake Village CA 91361-2702 Fax: 805-495-9935. E-mail: gturner@fwg.com.

VALENTINE, GEORGE EDWARD, dentist; b. Medford, Mass., Oct. 17, 1942; s. James Harold and Eleanor Alice (Newton) V.; 1 child, Adam Newton; m. Nilda Tavares. BA in Microbiology, U. Mass., Boston, 1969; DDS, Georgetown U., 1973; MS in Health Care Mgmt., Hartford Grad. Ctr., 1980, MS in Corp. Mgmt., 1987. Lic. dentist, Conn. Sr. ptnr. Higganum/Middlesex Dental Assocs., Middletown, Conn., 1976-90; sr. attending surgery dept. Middlesex Meml. Hosp., 1976-90, 98—; dir. ops. N.E., Cigna Employee Benefits Cos., 1989-93; pres. Sigma Mgmt. Group, 1993-94; v.p. Jardine Group Svcs., Latham, N.Y., 1994-97; prin. Valentine & Assocs., Dental Cons., 1998—. Pres., founder Biohazardous Environ. Cons., Middletown, 1988-89. With USAF, 1960-64. Mem. ADA, Conn. Dental Assn., Hartford Dental Soc., Am. Mgmt. Assn., Acad. Gen. Dentistry, Chgo. Dental Soc., Am. Assn. Dental Cons. Office: Physician's Office Bldg 80 S Main St Middletown CT 06457-3648 E-mail: george.valentine@snet.net.

VALENTINE, H. JEFFREY, legal association executive; b. Phila., Sept. 28, 1945; s. Joshua Morton and Olga W. (Wilson) V.; 1 child, Karyn. BS, St. Louis U., 1964, postgrad., 1966-68. Programmer, systems analyst Honeywell Electronic Data Processing, Wellesley Hills, Mass., 1964-66; account exec. Semiconductor div. Tex. Instruments, New Eng., 1966-68; New Eng. sales exec., Mid-Atlantic regional mgr. Electronic Instrumentation Co., 1968-70; pres. Nat. Free Lance Photographers Assn., Doylestown, Pa., 1970-89; pres., dir. Towne Print & Copy Ctrs. Inc.; v.p., exec. dir. Nat. Paralegal Assn., 1982—; pres. Paralegal Assocs., Inc., 1982—; chief operating officer Doylestown Parking Corp., 1977-88. Bd. dirs. Law Enforcement Supply Co., Solebury, Valtronics Supply Co., Towne Print & Copy Centers Inc., Solebury, Doylestown Stationery and Office Supply, Energy Mktg. Assocs., Inc., Solebury, Paralegal Placement Network; pres. Paralegal Pub. Corp., 1983-90; pub. Paralegal Jour.; pres. Valco Enterprises Inc., 1986—, Paralegal Employment Sys., Inc., 1988, Solebury Press, Inc., 1989—; ptnr. J&S Gen. Contractors, 1993—, J&S Landscaping Tree Svc., 1993—; owner Specialized Computer Consulting, 1992—. Author: Photographers Bookkeeping System, 1973, rev. edit., 1978, Photographers Pricing Guides, 1971, 72, 74, 75, Available Markets Director's - 4 Vols., 1973-77, National Model Sources Directory, Nat. Paralegal Salary and Employment Survey, 1985-86, 88, 90-92, 93-94; also articles, bulls. and pamphlets. Exec. sec. Doylestown Bus. Assn., 1972-78, pres., 1979, 83, v.p., 1981. Recipient Internat. Men of Achievement award, 1988; named Personalities of the Am., 1988. Mem. London Coll. Applied Scis., Nat. Fedn. Paralegal Assns., Photog. Industry Coun., Nat. Assn. Legal Assts., Am. Soc Assn. Execs., Soc. Assn. Mgrs., Nat. Fedn. Ind. Business (mem. action coun. com.), Nat. Parking Assn., Nat. Office Products Assn., Graphic Arts Assn. Delaware Valley, Nat. Assn. Federally Licensed Firearms Dealers, Nat. Compostition Assn., Internat. Platform Assn. Office: PO Box 406 Solebury PA 18963-0406

VALENTINE, JAMES WILLIAM, paleobiology educator, writer; b. Los Angeles, Nov. 10, 1926; s. Adelbert Cuthbert and Isabel (Davis) V.; m. Grace Evelyn Whysner, Dec. 21, 1957 (div. 1972); children— Anita, Ian; m. Cathryn Alice Campbell, Sept. 10, 1978 (div. 1986); 1 child, Geoffrey; m. Diane Mondragon, Mar. 16, 1987. BA, Phillips U., 1951; MA, UCLA, 1954, PhD, 1958. From asst. prof. to assoc. prof. U. Mo., Columbia, 1958-64; from assoc. prof. to prof. U. Calif., Davis, 1964-77, prof. geol. scis. Santa Barbara, 1977-90, prof. integrative biology Berkeley, 1990-93, emeritus, 1993—. Author: Evolutionary Paleoecology of the Marine Biosphere, 1973; editor: Phanerozoic Diversity, 1985; co-author: Evolution, 1977, Evolving, 1979; also numerous articles, 1954— Served with USNR, 1944-46; PTO Fulbright research scholar, Australia, 1962-63; Guggenheim fellow Yale U., Oxford U., Eng., 1968-69; Rockefeller Found. scholar in residence, Bellagio, Italy, summer 1974; grantee NSF, NASA Fellow Am. Acad. Arts and Scis., Geol. Soc. Am.; mem. NAS, AAAS, Paleontol. Soc. (pres. 1974-75, medal 1996). Avocation: collecting works of Charles Darwin. Home: 1351 Glendale Ave Berkeley CA 94708-2025 Office: U Calif Dept Integrative Biology Berkeley CA 94720-0001 E-mail: jwvsossi@socrates.berkeley.edu.

VALENTINE, JOHN LESTER, state legislator, lawyer; b. Fullerton, Calif., Apr. 26, 1949; s. Robert Lester and Pauline C. (Glood) V.; m. Karen Marie Thorpe, June 1, 1972; children: John Robert, Jeremy Reid, Staci Marie, Jeffrey Mark., David Emerson, Patricia Ann. BS in Acctg. and Econs., Brigham Young U., 1973, JD, 1976. Bar: Utah 1976, U.S. Dist. Ct. Utah, U.S. Ct. Appeals (10th cir.), U.S. Tax Ct., U.S. Supreme Ct. 2002; CPA. Atty. Howard, Lewis & Petersen, Provo, Utah, 1976—; mem. Utah Ho. Reps., 1988-98, Utah Senate, Dist. 14, Salt Lake City, 1999—. Instr. probate and estates Utah Valley State Coll.; instr. fin. planning., adj. prof. law Brigham Young U.; chmn. revenue and taxation com. Utah Senate, 1999-2000, vice chmn. exec. appropriations com., judiciary com., pub. edn. subcom.; mem. exec offices, cts., corrections and legis. appropriations subcom., Utah Ho. of Reps., 1988-90, capital facilities subcom., 1988-90, retirement com., 1988-90, judiciary com., 1988-92, strategic planning steering com., 1988-90, interim appropriations com., 1988-94, tax. review commn., 1989-98, ethics com., 1990-92, human svcs. and health appropriations subcom., 1990-92, revenue and taxation com., 1988-98, vice chmn. 1990-92; vice chmn. exec. appropriations., 1990-92; chmn. exec. appropriations com., 1992-94, chmn. rules com., 1994-96, higher edn. appropriations com. 1994-96, asst. majority whip, 1996-98; apptd. to state senate, 1998, elected, 2000, majority whip, 2000—. Mem. adv. bd. Internat. Sr. Games, 1988—; active Blue Ribbon Task Force on Local Govt. Funding, Utah League Cities and Towns, 1990-94, Criminal Sentencing Guidelines Task Force, Utah Judicial Coun., 1990-92, Access to Health Care Task Force, 1990-92, Utah County Sheriff Search and Rescue, Orem Met. Water Bd., Alpine Sch. Dist. Boundary Line Com., 1986-90, Boy Scouts Am.; bd. regents Legis. Adv. Com. UVCC.; mem. exec. bd. Utah Nat. Parks Coun.; mem. adv. coun. Orchard Elem. Sch., Mountainlands Com. an Aging; bd. trustees Utah Opera Co.; judge nat. and local competitions Moot Ct.; voting dist. chmn.; state, county del.; lt. incident command sys. Utah County Sheriff. Recipient Silver Beaver award Boy Scouts Am., Taxpayer Advocate award Utah Taxpayer Assn. Mem. ABA (tax sect.), Utah State Bar, CPA Com., Tax Sect. Specialization Com., Bicentennial Com. Republican. Mem. Lds Ch. Avocation: mountain climbing. Office: Howard Lewis & Petersen 120 E 300 N Provo UT 84606-2907

VALENTINE, MARK CONRAD, dermatologist; b. Parkersburg, W.Va., Sept. 26, 1948; s. Sestel and Margaret Elaine (Sabolo) V.; m. Elizabeth Michelle Monezis, Apr. 21, 1975; children: Perry Martin, Owen Mark. BA, W.Va. U., 1970; MD, Johns Hopkins U., 1974. Intern, resident U. Hosps. Cleve., 1974-76, resident, 1976-79; dermatologist pvt. practice, Everett, Wash., 1979—. Clin. assoc. prof. U. Wash., Seattle, 1979—; active med. staff Providence Gen. Med. Ctr., Everett, 1979—. Editl. bd. Jour. of Am. Acad. Dermatology, 1998—. Bd. dirs., sec. City Libr. Bd., Mukilteo, Wash., 1994-99; bd. dirs., v.p. Everett Symphony Bd., 1982-85, 2001—; bd. dirs. Book Arts Guild, Seattle, 1988-90. Nat. Merit scholar, 1966. Mem. AMA, Am. Acad. Dermatology (adv. coun. 1983-86), Wash. State Dermatological Assn. (pres.-elect 1996, pres. 1996-97), Seattle Dermatology Soc. (pres. 1985-86), Rotary (Everett), Phi Beta Kappa. Avocations: book collecting, book binding, guitar, piano. Office: 3327 Colby Ave Everett WA 98201-6403 E-mail: mark1105@aol.com.

VALENTINE, RALPH SCHUYLER, chemical engineer, research director; b. Seattle, Nov. 3, 1932; s. John Campbell and Elizabeth Florence (Patterson) V.; m. Jeanne Marie Belanger, June 15, 1957; children: Susan Diana, Jacqueline Leigh, John Campbell. BSChemE, U. Wash., 1955, PhDChemE, 1963; MSChemE, U. Ill., 1956. Registered profl. engr., Calif., Va., Wash. Rsch. engr. Chevron Rsch. Corp., Richmond, Calif., 1956-61; instr. U. Wash., Seattle, 1961-63; mgr. fluid dynamics Aerojet-Gen., Sacramento, 1963-69; mgr. chem. tech. Atlantic Rsch. Corp., Alexandria, Va., 1969-79; mgr. rsch. United Techs. Chem. Systems, San Jose, Calif., 1979-91. Lectr. U.S. Naval Postgrad. Sch., Monterey, Calif., 1968, UCLA Modern Devels. in Propulsion, L.A., 1967-68, USAF Astronautics Labs., Lancaster, Calif., 1967, U.S. Army R & D Unit, Sacramento, 1966. Contbr. 23 tech. articles to profl. jours.; patentee in field. Recipient NASA commendation for Apollo work, Houston, 1969, 1st prize Ceramographic Exhbn. Am. Ceramics Soc., 1974. Mem. Am. Inst. Chem. Engrs. (life). Republican. Avocations. Home: 1515 Satterfield Dr Pocatello ID 83201-8002 E-mail: ralph_s_valentine@yahoo.com.

VALENTINE, ROBERT JOHN (BOBBY VALENTINE), former professional baseball manager; b. Stamford, CT, May 13, 1950; m. Mary Branca, Jan. 8, 1977; 1 child, Robert John Jr. Student, U. Southern California, Arizona State U. Player Pioneer League, Ogdon, 1968, Pacific Coast League, Spokane, WA, 1969-71, Los Angeles Dodgers, Los Angeles, CA, 1971-72, California Angels, 1973-75, International League, Charleston, WV, 1975, Pacific Coast League, Salt Lake City, 1975, Hawaii, HI, 1976, San Diego Padres, San Diego, 1975-77, New York Mets, NY, 1977-78, Seattle Mariners, Seattle, 1979; scout, infield instr. San Diego Padres, San Diego, 1981; minor league infield instr. New York Mets, 1982, third base coach, 1983-85; mgr. Texas Rangers, Arlington, TX, 1985-96, N.Y. Mets, 1996—2002. Owner Bobby Valentine's Sports Gallery Cafe, Conn., Tex., and R.I. Named Am. League Mgr. of Yr. UPI, 1986; recipient William A. Shea Disting. Little League Grad. award, 1987; inductee Italian Am. Sports Hall Fame, 1990.*

VALENTINE, RUTHANN, counseling company executive; b. Washington; d. David and Carolyn Stevens. BSN, U. Pitts., 1965, M in Nursing Edn., 1968; MS in Edn., Duquesne U., 1988; D of Ministry, Grad. Theol. Found., 1992. RN, Pa.; cert. adult psychiatric clin. specialist. Med. surg. nurse Washington (Pa.) Hosp., 1961-62, Presbytn. U. Hosp., Pitts., 1962-63; instr. Presbytn. U. Sch. Nursing, 1963-66; psychiatric staff nurse, clin. specialist Forbes Regional Health Ctr., Monroeville, Pa., 1977-88; program dir. psychiatry Horizon Health Mgmt., Oak Brook, Ill., 1988-89; dir. community edn. Pitts. Pastoral Inst., 1989-92; pres. Harvest House Cons. & Counseling Svcs., Monroeville, 1992—. Psychiat. instr. Westmoreland (Pa.) Commun. Coll., 1985-86; lectr. Seton Hill Coll., Greensburg, Pa., 1991, Pitts. Theol. Sem., 1991; cons. Conflict Resolution Internat., Pitts., 1991; founder adult psychiat. program Forbes Regional Health Ctr., 1986; seminar and workshop leader in field, 1991. Dir. religious edn. St. John Fisher Ch., Pitts., 1985-90; adv. bd. C.C. Allegheny County, Monroeville, 1987; task force geriatric care Forbes Regional Health Ctr., Monroeville, 1986; com. mem. Eldercare Sisters of Mercy, Pitts., 1992. Sisters of Mercy grantee, Pitts., 1991. Fellow Geriatric Edn. Ctr. Pa. (Achievement of Excellence award 1988), Grad. Theol. Found.; mem. ANA, Am. Assn. Pastoral Counselors, Sisters of Mercy, Sigma Theta Tau. Roman Catholic. Avocations: sewing, reading, hiking. Office: Harvest House Cons & Counseling Svcs 1212 Harvest Dr Monroeville PA 15146-4804

VALENTINE, STEVEN RICHARDS, lawyer; b. Memphis, Jan. 30, 1956; s. William Robert and Lenita Joanne (Nelms) V.; m. Susan Marie Burke, Jan. 14, 1984; children: Christina Michele, William Robert II, Steven Richards Jr., Thomas Burke, Diana Elizabeth. Grad., Capitol Page Sch., Washington, 1974; student, Earlham Coll., 1974-77; B of Gen. Studies with distinction, Ind. U., 1979, JD, 1982. Bar: Ill. 1983, D.C. 1985, U.S. Ct. Appeals (D.C. cir.) 1986, U.S. Supreme Ct. 1986, U.S. Ct. Appeals (9th cir.) 1989. Chief investigator consumer protection divsn. Office Atty. Gen., State of Ind., 1980-82; exec. dir. Ams. United for Life Legal Def. Fund, Chgo., 1982-83; chief counsel subcom. on separation of powers U.S. Senate, Washington, 1983-85, chief counsel subcom. on cts., 1985; adminstrv. asst. U.S. Senator John P. East, 1985-86; dir. Office of Policy Devel. and Comm. Legal Svcs. Corp., 1986-87; counselor to asst. atty. gen. civil divsn. U.S. Dept. Justice, 1987-88; dep. asst. atty. gen. civil divsn. U.S. Justice Dept., 1988-93, gen. counsel to U.S. Senator Robert C. Smith, 1993-99; legis. dir. to U.S. Senator Robert C. Smith, 1996-99; of counsel Preston Gates Ellis & Rouvelas Meeds LLP, Washington, 1999—2002; ptnr. Preston Gates Ellis & Roubelas Meeds LLP, 2002—. Mem. exec. com., bd. dirs. Deluxe West, Inc.; vice chmn. bd. dirs. D. Elton Trueblood Yokefellow Acad. Endowment, Inc.; mem. bd. visitors Earlham Coll.; bd. dirs. The Preston Project, Inc.; sr. fellow John C. Stennis Ctr. for Pub. Svc. Author: Each Time A Man, 1978, All Shall Live, 1980, (with others) Abortion and the Constitution, 1987; contbr. articles to profl. jours. Recipient spl. commendation U.S. Atty. Gen., 1993; John C. Stennis Congl. staff fellow, 1995-96. Mem.: SAR, ABA, Rep. Nat. Lawyers Assn., John Carroll Soc., Federalist Soc., Capitol Hill Club. Republican. Roman Catholic. Avocations: history, baseball. Home: 6487 Warwick Cir Alexandria VA 22315-5045 Office: 1735 New York Ave NW Ste 500 Washington DC 20006-5209 E-mail: rickv@prestongates.com., rsv1984@aol.com.

VALENTINE, TIMOTHY EUGENE, nuclear engineer, researcher; b. Knoxville, Tenn., Sept. 26, 1969; s. Dennie G. and Anita L. Valentine; m. Jennifer Suzanne Mash. BS, U. Tenn., 1991, MS, 1992, PhD, 1995. Sr. rsch. engr. Oak Ridge (Tenn.) Nat. Lab., 1993—. Adj. asst. prof. U. Tenn., Knoxville, 1995—. Contbr. chapters to books, articles to profl. jours. Mem.: Am. Nuc. Soc. (program com. reactor physics divsn. 1999—2002, pub. policy com. 2001—, exec. com. reactor physics divsn. 2001—, Young Members Engring. Achievement award 1998). Avocations: hiking, running, weightlifting, travel. Office: Oak Ridge Nat Lab Bethel Valley Rd Oak Ridge TN 37831 Office Fax: 865-574-6182. Business E-Mail: valentinete@ornl.gov.

VALENTINE, VALERIE, volunteer; b. Chgo., Dec. 12, 1942; d. John Henry and Muriel Joan (Bennett) V. Student, Gregg Coll. Investment banker Cruttenden Podesta, Chgo., 1960-67; v.p. Greek Heritage Found., 1960-83; vol. coord. Dept. Aging City of Chgo., 1983—. Circulation dir. Greek Heritage, 1963-68. Sec., bd. dirs. Friends of Chgo. Pub. Libr., 1989-92; pres. Backgammon Club Chgo., 1973-89. Avocation: backgammon. Home: 5008 N Mozart St Chicago IL 60625-3616

VALENTINE, WILLIAM NEWTON, physician, educator; b. Kansas City, Mo., Sept. 29, 1917; s. Herbert S. and Mabel W. Valentine; m. Martha Hickman Winfree; children: William, James, Edward. Student, U. Mich., Ann Arbor, 1934—36, U. Mo., Columbia, 1936—37; MD, Tulane U., New Orleans, 1942. Diplomate Am. Bd. Internal Medicine. Intern Strong Meml. Hosp., Rochester, NY, 1942—43, asst. resident in medicine, 1943, chief resident in medicine, 1943—44; specialist, attending physician in internal medicine Wadsworth Hosp., L.A., 1949—88, VA Ctr., L.A., 1949—88; specialist, attending physician in internal medicine Ctr. Health Scis. UCLA, 1949—, prof. medicine, 1957—88, chmn. dept., 1963—71, prof. emeritus medicine, 1988—. Contbr. articles to profl. jours. Capt. MC AUS, 1944—47. Recipient Mayo Soley award for excellence in rsch., Western Soc. Clin. Rsch., 1978, 53d Annual UCLA faculty rsch. lectr., 1978. Master: ACP (John Phillips Meml. award for disting. achievements in internal medicine 1979); fellow: Am. Soc. Hematology (Henry Stratton lectr. 1978), Internat. Soc. Hematology (v.p. U.S. 1976—80); mem.: NAS, Am. Acad. Arts and Scis., Western Soc. Clin. Rsch., Western Assn. Physicians (pres. 1969—70), Assn. Am. Physicians, Am. Soc. Clin. Investigation (v.p. 1962), Am. Bd. Internal Medicine. Republican.

VALENTINE-BRIEL, PATRICIA JEAN, personnel director; b. Mt. Vernon, N.Y., June 4, 1951; d. Nelson David and Joan Ann (Fischer) Valentine; m. Francis P. Briel, Jr., May 26, 1973 (div. Oct. 1985); children: Holly J. Briel, Travis. P. Briel. BA in Sociology, Lycoming Coll., 1973; MPA, Marywood U., 1994. Adminstrv. asst. Blast Intermediate Unit # 17, Williamsport, Pa., 1973-79, office mgr., 1980-87; asst. dir. personnel Williamsport Area Sch. Dist., 1987-93, dir. personnel, 1993-94, Bucks County Intermediate Unit # 22, Doylestown, Pa., 1994—. Pres. bd. dirs. Lycoming County Mental Health, Williamsport, 1990-91; mem. Lycoming County United Way Bd., 1989-92, Lycoming County Assn. for Retarded Citizens, 1987-96. Mem. Am. Assn. Sch. Personnel Dirs. (membership com. 1995-96), Pa. Assn. Sch. Personnel Dirs. (sec. 1993-96, membership com. 1994-96), Soc. Human Resource Mgrs. Democrat. Methodist. Avocations: hot air ballooning, softball coach. Home: 124 Krista Ct Chalfont PA 18914-3903 Office: Bucks County Intermediate 705 N Shady Retreat Rd Unit 22 Doylestown PA 18901-2507

VALENTINO, NICHOLAS ANTHONY, university educator; b. Riverside, CA, July 10, 1968; s. Dominic Anthony Valentino, Catherine Andrea Valentino; m. Beatrice Anne Zuniga; children: Dominic, Tobias. AB, Brown U., 1990; PhD, UCLA, 1997. Asst. prof. U. Mich., Ann Arbor, 1997—. Grantee, NSF, 2002—. Mem.: Am. Polit. Sci. Assn. Office: 4244 Inst for Social Rsch PO Box 1248 426 Thompson St Ann Arbor MI 48106 Personal E-mail: nvalenti@umich.edu.

VALENTINO, SPYDER, musician; b. Grosse Point, Mich., Sept. 1, 1965; s. Clark Huston and Shirley Ann (Molinaro) Stokes. Asst. rec. engr. Images Surreal Prodns., San Diego, 1986-87, exec. rec. engr., 1987-88, exec. v.p., 1988—; lead vocalist Rogue, 1987; lead vocalist, asst. engr., producer Crystal Visions, 1988—; ind. vocalist, guitarist, 1988—. Novelist: Dunhurst, 1987. Mem. Nat. Acad. Songwriters, Nat. Assn. Record Merchandisers, Nat. Assn. Rec. Arts and Scis., Am. Fedn. Musicans, Los Angeles Songwriters Showcase. Roman Catholic. Avocation: scriptwriting. Home and Office: 2927 Talbot St San Diego CA 92106-3026

VALENZUELA, JULIO SAMUEL, sociologist, educator; b. Concepción, Chile, Mar. 30, 1948; came to U.S., 1970; s. Raimundo Arms and Dorothy Dueul (Bowie) V.; m. Erika Fresia Maza, Mar. 22, 1969. Licenciatura, Universidad de Concepcion, 1970; PhD, Columbia U., 1979. Asst. prof. Yale U., New Haven, 1977-80, Harvard U., Cambridge, Mass., 1980-85, assoc. prof., 1986, U. Notre Dame, Ind., 1987-89, prof., dept. chairperson, 1989-92, fellow Kellogg Inst., 1987—. Sr. assoc. fellow St. Antony's Coll., Oxford U., 1992-93, 96—. Author: Democratizacion via Reforma, 1986; co-editor: Chile: Politics And Society, 1976, Military Rule In Chile, 1986, Issues In Democratic Consolidation, 1992; contbr. chpts. to books, articles to profl. jours. Fellow NEH ind. scholarship rsch. 1983-84, conf. grant 1987; John Simon Guggenheim fellow, 1996. Mem. Am. Sociol. Assn., Internat. Sociol. Assn. (v.p. rsch. com. #44 1990—), Latin Am. Studies Assn. (nominating com. 1987-88); New Eng. Coun. Latin Am. Studies (pres. 1984-85). Methodist. Office: U Notre Dame Dept Sociology Notre Dame IN 46556

VALENZUELA, MANUEL ANTHONY, JR. lawyer; b. L.A., Dec. 4, 1955; s. Manuel and Artimesa B. (Ruiz) V.; m. Guadalupe Roa, Nov. 8, 1980; children: Manuel Anthony III, Nancy Christine. BA in Polit. Sci., UCLA, 1978; MPA, U. So. Calif., 1982; JD, Southwestern U., L.A., 1987. Bar: Calif. 1987, U.S. Dist. Ct. (cen. dist.) Calif. 1987, U.S. Ct. Appeals (9th cir.) 1988, U.S. Supreme Ct. 1991. Legis. analyst L.A. City Coun., 1981-88; legal extern ACLU, L.A., 1985; assoc. county counsel County of Los Angeles, 1988-89, sr. assoc county counsel, 1989-90, dep. county counsel, 1990-94, sr. dep. county counsel, 1994-98, prin. dep. county counsel, 1998—. Mem.: Constnl. Rights Found. (mock trial competition 1997—99, 2001), UCLA Latino Alumni Assn. (founder, bd. dirs. 1989—90, scholarship com. 1995—99), L.A. County Counsel Assn. (bd. dirs. 1989—99), Mexican Am. Bar Assn. (bd. dirs. 1990, 1991), L.A. County Bar Assn. (exec. com. govtl. law sect. 1990—91, sec. govtl. law sect. 1991—92, 2d vice chair govtl. law sect. 1992—93, 1st vice chair govtl. law sect. 1993—94, chair govtl. law sect. 1994—95, exec. com. govtl. law sect. 1995—96, bd. trustees 1995—96, exec. com. govtl. law sect. 1996—). Democrat. Roman Catholic. Avocations: tennis, backpacking, photography, reading. Home: 9647 Val St Temple City CA 91780-1438 Office: Office of County Counsel 648 Hall of Adminstrn 500 W Temple St Los Angeles CA 90012-2713 E-mail: MValenzuela@counsel.co.la.ca.us.

VALERIANI, RICHARD GERARD, news broadcaster; b. Camden, N.J., Aug. 29, 1932; s. Nicholas and Christine (Camerota) V.; m. Kathie Berlin, Apr. 20, 1980; 1 child, Kimberly. BA, Yale U., 1953; postgrad., U. Pavia, Italy, 1953-54, U. Barcelona, Spain, 1954. Reporter The Trentonian, Trenton, 1957; with AP, 1957-61, corr. Cuba, 1959-61; with NBC-TV News, 1961—, corr., 1964-83, nat. corr. N.Y.C., 1983-88; free-lance journalist and media cons., 1988—. Participant 2d Carter-Ford debate, 1976. Author: Travels With Henry, 1979; actor: (feature film) Crimson Tide, 1995. With AUS, 1955-56. Recipient Overseas Press Club award for best radio reporting, 1965 Mem. Elihu Soc. Home: 23 Island View Dr Sherman CT 06784-2036 E-mail: rvaleriani@aol.com.

VALERIO, JOSEPH MASTRO, architectural firm executive, educator; b. Dec. 26, 1947; m. Linda A. Searl; children: Joseph Jr., Anthony. BArch, U. Mich., 1970; MArch, UCLA, 1972. Registered architect, Wis., Ill., Ind., Mo., Calif., Tex., Ariz., Minn., Ala., Iowa, Ind., Md., Mich., Okla., Ga., Mass., N.Y., Va., Utah; cert. Nat. Coun. Archtl. Registration Bds. Pres. Chrysalis Corp. Architects, 1970-85; assoc. prof. U. Wis., 1973-86; design dir. Swanke Hayden Connell Architects, 1985-86; v.p. architecture A. Epstein and Sons, Inc., 1986-88; pres. Valerio-Assocs. Inc., 1988-94; prin. Valerio Dewalt Train Assocs., Inc., Chgo., 1994—. Speaker Ariz. State U., UCLA, U. Ariz., U. Cin., others; cons. USG Interiors, Formica Corp., AAAS, NAS, NEA: vis. critic and lectr. in field. Prin. works include corp., high-tech. indsl., retail, health and residential bldgs.; author: Movie Palaces, 1983; (monograph) Joe Valerio, 1999; editor: Architectural Fabric Structures, 1985; featured in Inside Architecture, Domestic Interiors, 1997, New Am. Apt., 1997, Internat. Interiors, 1997, Lofts/Living and Working Spaces, 1999. Mem. exec. bd. men's coun. Mus. Contemporary Art, 1989-91; mem. exec. bd. Contemporary Arts Coun., 1994-96 (pres. 1999). Recipient Honor awards Wis. Soc. Architects, 1975, 81, 84, 85, Gov.'s Award for Design Excellence, State of Mich., 1979, Gold medal Inst. Bus. Designers, 1988, Design award Progressive Architecture, 1991, Architectural Record Interiors award 1993, 95, 96, Disting. Interior award Inst. Bus. Designers, Chgo., 1993; honored by Emerging Voices series Archtl. League N.Y., 1984, Met. Home mag., Interiors mag. Fellow AIA (programs chmn. design com. Chgo. chpt. 1990, mem. long range planning com. 1992, chair nat. com. on design 1997, Nat. Honor award 1981, 93, Interiors award Chgo. chpt. 1988, 90, 92, 95-97, 99, 2000, 01, Disting. Bldg. award 1991, 93, Nat. Interior Honor award 1993, 96, Divine Detail award 1999, 2001), Chgo. Architecture Club (pres. 1994). Office: Valerio Dewalt Train Assocs 500 N Dearborn St Fl 9 Chicago IL 60610-4900

VALERIO, MICHAEL ANTHONY, financial executive; b. Detroit, Sept. 20, 1953; s. Anthony Rudolph and Victoria (Popoff) V.; m. Barbara Ann Nabozny, Oct. 8, 1983. BA, U. Mich., Dearborn, 1975. CPA, Mich. Jr. acct. Carabell, Bocknek CPA's, Southfield, Mich., 1975-76; sr. acct. Purdy, Donovan & Beal, CPA's, Detroit, 1976-77; mgr. Buctynck & Co., CPA's, Southfield, 1978-79; controller Transcontinental Travel, Harper Woods, Mich., 1979-80; exec. v.p. Holland Cons., Inc., Detroit, 1980-85; controller, CFO SLC Recycling Industries, Inc., Warren, Mich., 1985-98; owner Pinnacle Fin. Consulting, PLLC, Livonia, 1994—. Owner Pinnacle Profl. Planning, LLC, 2002—. Mem. AICPA, Mich. Soc. CPAs, Acctg. Rsch. Found. Roman Catholic. Office: Pinnacle Fin Consulting PLLC 33300 Five Mile Rd Ste 102 Livonia MI 48154-3074

VALERO, RENÉ ARNOLD, clergyman; b. N.Y.C., Aug. 15, 1930; s. Caesar J. and Maria Luisa (Cordova) Valero; B.A. in Liberal Arts, Immaculate Conception-Cathedral Coll., 1952; M.S.W., Fordham U., 1962. Ordained to ministry Roman Cath. Ch., 1956; asso. pastor St. Michael-St. Edward, Bklyn., 1956-57, St. Agatha, Bklyn., 1957-60; dir. Bklyn. Cath. Charities Family Service, 1960-69; dir. Bklyn. Diocesan Office for Aging, 1969-74; coordinator Bklyn. Diocesan Hispanic Apostolate, 1974-79; pastor Blessed Sacrament, Jackson Heights, N.Y., 1979-82; aux. bishop Diocese of Bklyn., 1980— ; vicar for immigrants and refugees Diocese of Bklyn., 1983-90; regional bishop Queens, 1990-94, Queens North, 1994—. Home: 34-43 93rd St Jackson Heights NY 11372-3743 Office: Immaculate Conception Ctr 7200 Douglaston Pky Douglaston NY 11362-1941

VALESKIE-HAMNER, GAIL YVONNE, information systems specialist; b. San Francisco, May 16, 1953; d. John Benjamin and Vera Caroline (Granstrand) Valeskie; m. David Bryan Hamner, May 21, 1983. Student, Music Conservatory, Valencia, Spain, 1973, U. Valencia, 1973; BA magna cum laude, Lone Mountain Coll., 1973, MA, 1976. Fgn. exchange broker trainee Fgn. Exchange Ltd., San Francisco, 1978-79; fgn. exchange remittance supr. Security Pacific Nat. Bank, 1979-81; exec. sec. Bank of Am., 1981-83, fgn. exchange ops. supr, 1983-84; word processing specialist Wolborg-Michelson, 1984-86; office mgr. U.S. Leasing Corp., 1986-88; cons. Valeskie Data/Word Processing, 1987-89, pres., 1989—. Soc. chmn., mem. mission edn. com. Luth. Women's Missionary League, Vallejo, Calif., 1986-94; vol. Luth. Braille Workers, Vallejo, 1987; organist Shepherd of Hills Luth. Ch., San Francisco, 1988—. Mem. NAFE, Profl. Assn. Secretarial Svcs. (pres. 1993—), Am. Guild Organists, Am. Choral Dirs. Assn. Avocations: singing, ceramics, piano, needlework, writing.

VALETTE, JEAN PAUL, writer; b. Paris, Oct. 21, 1937; s. Jean and Monique (Lavie) V.; m. Rebecca M. Valette, Aug. 6, 1959; children: Jean-Michel, Nathalie, Pierre. Baccalaureat, U. Poitiers, France, 1954; Diplome, Hautes Etudes Commls. de Paris, 1959; PhD, U. Colo., 1962. Acct. Arthur Andersen, 1964-66; rsch. economist Charles River Assocs., 1966-69. Author: Lisons, 1968, The Role of Transportation in Regional Economic Development, 1971, France, A Cultural Review Grammar, 1973, C'est comme ca, 1978, 86, Spanish for Mastery, 1980, 84, 88, 96, French for Mastery, 1975, 81, 86, 89, 90, Contacts: langue et culture francaises, 1976, 82, 85, 89, 94, 97, 2001, French for Fluency, 1985, Rencontres, 1985, Situaciones, 1988, 94, Discovering French, 1993, 94, 95, 97, 2000, Discovering French Interactive, 1994, A votre tour, 1995, Ventanas, 1998, Europak, 2000, Weaving the Dance, Navajo Yeibicei Textiles (1910-1950), 2000. Decorated Palmes Académiques (France). Mem. Am. Assn. Tchrs. French, Am. Coun. on Tchg. of Langs. Address: 16 Mount Alvernia Rd Chestnut Hill MA 02467-1019

VALETTE, REBECCA MARIANNE, Romance languages educator; b. N.Y.C., Dec. 21, 1938; d. Gerhard and Ruth Adelgunde (Bischoff) Loose; m. Jean-Paul Valette, Aug. 6, 1959; children: Jean-Michel, Nathalie, Pierre. BA, Mt. Holyoke Coll., 1959, LHD (hon.), 1974; PhD, U. Colo., 1963. Instr., examiner in French and German U. So. Fla., 1961-63; instr. NATO Def. Coll., Paris, 1963-64, Wellesley Coll., 1964-65; asst. prof. Romance Langs. Boston Coll., 1965-68, assoc., 1968-73, prof., 1973—. Lectr., cons. fgn. lang. pedagogy; Fulbright sr. lectr., Germany, 1974; Am. Council on Edn. fellow in acad. adminstrn., 1976-77 Author: Modern Language Testing, 1967, rev. edit., 1977, French for Mastery, 1975, rev. edit., 1988, Contacts, 1976, rev. edit., 1993, 97, 2001, C'est Comme Ça, 1978, rev. edit., 1986, Spanish for Mastery, 1980, rev. edit., 1989, 94, Album: Cuentos del Mundo Hispanico, 1984, rev. edit., 1992, French for Fluency, 1985, Situations, 1988, rev. edit., 1994, Discovering French, 1994, 97, 2001, A votre tour, 1995, Ventanas Uno, 1998, Images 1, 2, 3, 1999, Reflections on the Connolly Book of Hours, 1999, Weaving the Dance, 2000; contbr. articles to fgn. lang. pedagogy and Native Am. art publs. Decorated officer Palmes Académiques, chevalier Ordre Nat. du Mérite (France). Mem. MLA (chmn. div. on tchg. of lang. 1980-81), Am. Coun. on Tchg. Fgn. Langs., Am. Assn. Tchrs. French (v.p. 1980-86, pres. 1992-94), Phi Beta Kappa, Alpha Sigma Nu, Pi Delta Phi. Home: 16 Mount Alvernia Rd Chestnut Hill MA 02467-1019 Office: Boston Coll Lyons 311 Chestnut Hill MA 02467-3804 E-mail: valette@bc.edu.

VALFRE, MICHELLE WILLIAMS, nursing educator, administrator, writer; b. Reno, Feb. 12, 1947; d. Robert James and Dolores Jane (Barnard) Williams; m. Adolph A. Valfre, Nov. 7, 1998. BSN, U. Nev., Reno, 1973; M Health Svc., U. Calif., Davis, 1977. RN, Oreg., Ariz. Staff nurse VA Hosp., Reno, 1973-77; family nurse practitioner Tri-County Indian Health Svc., Bishop, Calif., 1977-81; instr. nursing Roque C.C., Grants Pass, Oreg., 1981-82; psychiat. nurse VA Hosp., Roseburg, 1982; dir. edn. Josephine Meml. Hosp., Grants Pass, 1983-84; geriat. nurse practitioner Hearthstone Manor, Medford, Oreg., 1984-86; chmn. nursing dept. Roque C.C., Grants Pass, 1986-89, instr. social scis., 1997-98; prin. Health and Ednl. Cons. Inc., Tucson, 1989—; DON Highland House Nursing Ctr., Grants Pass, 1990. Bd. dirs. Tri-County Indian Health Svc.; cons. for nursing svcs. in long-term care facilities. Author: Professional Skills for Leadership, Foundations of Mental Health Care, 2000, 2d edit., 2001; contbr.: Fundamental Health Care: Concepts and Skills. Mem. Josephine County Coalition for AIDS, Grants Pass, 1990. With USN, 1965-69. Mem. NAFE, Nat. League Nursing, Oreg. Ednl. Assn., Oreg. State Bd. Nursing (mem. re-entry nursing com. 1992-93). E-mail: avalfre@mindspring.com.

VALGEMAE, MARDI, English educator; b. Viljandi, Estonia, Nov. 10, 1935; came to U.S., 1949; s. Parfeni and Ella (Peterson) V.; m. Mare M. Kivijarv, Dec. 28, 1957; children: Monika L., Sven M. BA, Rutgers U., 1957; PhD, UCLA, 1964. Asst. prof. English UCLA, L.A., 1964-68; assoc. prof. English Lehman Coll., CUNY, Bronx, 1968-74; prof. English Lehman Coll. CUNY, 1975—; dir. city and humanities program Lehman Coll., CUNY, 1984-88, chmn. English dept., 1988-97. Vis. asst. profl. lectr., George Washington U., Washington, 1968. Author: Accelerated Grimace, 1972, Ikka Teatrist Moteldes, 1990, Linn ja Teater, 1995, Kaugekone, 1999; co-editor: Baltic Literature and Linguistics, 1973. 1st lt. U.S. Army. 1958-60. ACLS European Travel grantee, 1970, 81; Woodrow Wilson fellow, 1960. Mem. Modern Lang. Assn. Am., Assn. Advancement Baltic Studies, PEN. Office: CUNY Lehman Coll Dept English Bronx NY 10468 E-mail: mardival@mindspring.com.

VALIA, HARDARSHAN S. research scientist; b. Khurda, Orisa, India, June 15, 1945; arrived in U.S., 1969; s. Santokh Singh and Harbans Kaur; m. Bhupinder Kaur Valia, Jan. 10, 1982; children: Vikram Singh, Anu Kaur. MS, Nagpur (India) U., 1968; MA, Bryn Mawr Coll., 1971; PhD, Boston U., 1976. Asst. prof. Case Western U., Cleve., 1978, Oberlin (Ohio) Coll., 1978—79; staff scientist Inland Steel, East Chicago, Ind., 1979—. Mem. tech. com. Am. Iron and Steel Inst., Washington, 1995—2001. Contbg. author Kirk-Othmer Encyclopedia, 1993, Making, Shaping, and Treating of Steel, 1999, (website) Am. Iron and Steel Inst. Recipient J.B.T. gold medal, Nagpur U., 1965, medal, Am. Iron and Steel Inst., 1989. Mem.: Soc. for Organic Petrology, Iron and Steel Soc. (program com. 1995—, chmn. J. Becker award 2001—, Joseph Becker award 1999). Home: 2116-44th St Highland IN 46322 Office: Ispat Inland Steel 3001 E Columbus Dr East Chicago IN 46312

VALIANT, LESLIE GABRIEL, computer scientist, educator; b. Mar. 28, 1949; s. Leslie and Eva Julia (Ujlaki) V.; m. Gayle Lynne Dyckoff, 1977; children: Paul A., Gregory J. BA, Kings Coll., Cambridge, U.K., 1970; DIC, Imperial Coll., London, 1973; PhD, U. Warwick, U.K., 1974. Vis. asst. prof. Carnegie-Mellon U., Pitts., 1973-74; lectr. U. Leeds, Eng., 1974-76; lectr., reader U. Edinburgh, Scotland, 1977-82; vis. prof. Harvard U., 1982, Gordon McKay prof. computer sci. and applied math., 1982-2001, T. Jefferson Coolidge prof. computer sci. and applied math., 2001—. Guggenheim fellow, 1985-86; recipient Nevanlinna prize Internat. Math. Union, 1986, Knuth prize, 1997. Fellow Royal Soc., Am. Assn. for Artificial Intelligence; mem. NAS. Office: Harvard U 33 Oxford St Cambridge MA 02138-1903

VALIANTI, DEBORAH L. playwright; b. Marlboro, Mass., May 10, 1952; d. Frank J. and Kathlyn V. Valianti; m. Henry J. Klim; children: Genevieve Marie Klim, Delia Goodness Klim. MAET, Lesley Coll., Cambridge, MA, 1992; MA, Boston U., Boston, MA, 1987; BA, Goddard Coll., Plainfield, VT, 1977. Dir. Mission-in-Action Players, Mission Hill, Mass., 2000—, All-bad Teen Theater Co., Brighton, 1993—98; educator expressive therapies Lesley Coll., Cambridge, 1992—98; dir. City Hall Smoking Cessation Project, Boston Against Drugs, Boston, 1995; dir. and co-founder Uppity Productions, Boston Playwright Theater, 1985—90; tchg. fellow Creative Writing Program, Boston U., 1985—87. Democrat-Npl. Roman Catholic. Avocations: singing, tap dance, liturgical dance, liturgical dance, liturgical dance. Home: 8 Oak Square Avenue Brighton MA 02135-2517

VALINE, DELMAR EDMOND, SR. corporate executive; b. Edwardsville, Ill., May 2, 1919; s. Edward and Clara Louise (Schon) V.; m. Geraldine Goley, Aug. 26, 1939; children: Jayne M. Valine Klein, Linda L. Valine Hay, Delmar E. Jr. Student, Summer Bus. Coll., 1939. Purchasing agt. Swift and Co., Nat. Stockyards., Ill., 1937-58; asst. to pres. St. Louis Nat. Stock Yards Co., Nat. Stockyards, 1958-60; exec. v.p. St. Louis Livestock Mkt. Found., 1960-64; exec. sec. Nat. Museum of Transport, St. Louis; v.p. First Ill. Bank, East St. Louis, Ill., 1967-81; bd. chairman Southwest Regional Port Dist., 1961—. Bd. dirs. First Ill. Bank, East St. Louis, 1982—, Target 2000, East St. Louis, 1977—, Inland Rivers Port and Terminals 1987—, Port of Metropolitan St. Louis, 1975—, sec., treas. Gateway Ctr. Metropolitan St. Louis, 1976—; exec. v.p. East Side Associated Industries, East St. Louis, 1990—. Mayor village of Dupo, Ill., 1945-49, mem. sch. bd. dist. 193, Dupo, 1955-56, Selective Service bd., East St. Louis, 1950-55; mem. Fed. Agy. Adv. Com., 1964-70; commr. Southwestern Ill. Planning Comm., 1976—. Recipient Medallion award, Boys Club Am., 1969. Mem. U.S. C. of C., Rotary (past pres.), Boys Club, Mo. Athletic Club, Royal Order of Jesters. Republican.

VALIS, NOËL MAUREEN, language educator; b. Lakewood, N.J., Dec. 24, 1945; d. Lee Ritter, Katherine Rafferty; 1 child Maura Katherine. BA summa cum laude, Douglass Coll., New Brunswick, N.J., 1968; MA, Bryn Mawr Coll., Pa., 1970; PhD, Bryn Mawr Coll., 1975. Lectr. Spanish Rosemont Coll., Pa., 1971—72, 1976—77; asst. prof. Spanish U. Ga., Athens, 1977—81, assoc. prof. Spanish, 1981—85, prof. Spanish, 1985—86, U. Mich., Ann Arbor, 1986—91, Johns Hopkins U., Balt., 1991—99, Yale U., New Haven, 1999—. Vis. prof. NYU, 1995, Bryn Mawr Coll., Pa., 1993, U. Pa., 1989; rsch. libr. and asst. Privacy Protection Study Commn., Washington, 1975—76; rsch. specialist Office of Econ. Opportunity, Washington, 1973. Author: The Decadent Vision in Leopoldo Alas, 1981, The Novels of Jacinto Octavio Picón, 1986, Leopoldo Alas (Clarin): An Annotated Bibliography, 1986, 2d edit., 2002, Mi casa me recuerda/My House Remembers Me, 2002, The Culture of Cursilerta: Bad Taste, Kitsch and Class in Modern Spain, 2002; co-editor (with Carol Maier): In The Feminine Mode. Essays on Hispanic Women Writers, 1990; editor: Malevolent Insemination and Other Essays on Clartin, 1990; translator: Las conjuradoras. Antologita bilingüe de seis poetas estadounidenses, 1993, Prelude to Pleasure, 1993, The Poetry of Julia Uceda, 1995; contbr. articles to profl. jours. Fellow Hon. Woodrow Wilson fellow, 1968, Grad. fellow, NDEA, 1968—71, Summer fellow, NEH, 1981, Rsch. fellow, Treaty of Friendship between U.S. and Spain, 1986. Mem.: MLA, Assn. Internacional de Galdosistas, Nat. Assn. Scholars, Phi Beta Kappa. Avocations: antiques, piano, travel. Home: 248 Bradley St New Haven CT 06510 Office: Yale Univ Dept Spanish/Portuguese 82-90 Wall St New Haven CT 06520

VALK, HENRY SNOWDEN, physicist, educator; b. Washington, Jan. 26, 1929; s. Henry Snowden and Dorothy (Blencowe) V.; m. Gillian Wedderburn, June 20, 1968; children— Alison, Diana, Robert, Richard. BS, George Washington U., 1953, MS (Agnes and Eugene Meyer scholar), 1954; postgrad., Johns Hopkins, 1953-54; PhD (Shell fellow), Washington U., St. Louis, 1957. Profl. asst. NSF, 1957, asst. program dir. physics, 1959-60; asst. prof. physics U. Oreg., 1957-59; mem. faculty U. Nebr., 1960-70, prof. physics, 1964-70, chmn. dept., 1966-70; prof. physics Coll. Scis. and Liberal Studies, Ga. Inst. Tech., Atlanta, 1970—, acting dir. physics, 1991-96, dean, 1970-82. Cons. physics sect. NSF, 1961-62, program dir. theoretical physics, 1965-66; chmn. Gordon Rsch. Conf. Photonuclear Reactions, 1969; vis. prof. U. Frankfurt/Main, Germany, 1970, Rensselaer Poly. Inst., 1982, 88, Cath. U. Am., 1982-83, 88-89; chmn. SE regional Marshall scholarship com., 1974-92. Author: (with M. Alonso) Quantum Mechanics: Principles and Applications, 1973; contbr. articles to profl. jours. Decorated Most Excellent Order Brit. Empire. Fellow Am. Phys. Soc.; mem. Am. Math. Soc., Am. Assn. Physics Tchrs., Math. Assn. Am., Cosmos Club (Washington), Phi Beta Kappa, Sigma Xi. Office: Sch Physics Ga Inst Tech Atlanta GA 30332-0001 E-mail: henry.valk@physics.gatech.edu.

VALK, ROBERT EARL, corporate executive; b. Muskegon, Mich., Aug. 21, 1914; s. Allen and Lulu (Schuler) V.; m. Ann Parker, August 9, 1941 (div. July 1959); children: James A., Sara C.; m. Alice Melick, Dec. 29, 1960 (dec. 1999); children: Marie, Susan. BS in Mech. Engring, U. Mich., 1938. With Nat. Supply Co., 1938-55, plant mgr., 1945-48, works mgr. Toledo, Houston and Gainesville, Tex., 1949-55; asst. v.p. prodn. Electric Auto-Lite Co., Toledo, 1956, v.p., group exec. gen. products, 1956-60; gen. mgr. mfg. automotive div. Essex Internat., Inc., 1960-66, v.p. corp., gen. mgr. automotive div., 1966-74; pres. ITT Automotive Elec. Products Div., 1974-80; v.p. ITT N.Am. Automotive Ops. Worldwide, 1980-86; chmn. Chamberlin, Davis, Rutan & Valk, 1986—. Trustee Henry Ford Health Care Sys., Detroit. Bd. dirs. Ecumenical Theological Ctr. Mem. Am. Soc. Naval Engrs., Soc. Automotive Engrs., Am. Ordnance Assn., Am. Mgmt. Assn., Air Force Assn., Am. Mfrs. Assn., Wire Assn., Nat. Elec. Mfrs. Assn., Engring. Soc. Detroit. Clubs: Country (Detroit), Renaissance Club, Yondotega, Economics (Detroit); Grosse Pointe, Bay View Yacht; Little Harbor (Harbor Springs, Mich., Question Club. Republican. Episcopalian. Home: 80 Renaud Rd Grosse Pointe Shores MI 48236-1742 Office: 21 Kercheval Ave Ste 270 Grosse Pointe Farms MI 48236-3633

VALLADO, DAVID ANTHONY, aerospace engineer; b. Winchester, Mass., May 14, 1958; s. Anthony C. and Rebecca B. V.; m. Laura Ann Vallado, March 18, 1984; children: Simone, Kathleen, Samuel. BS in Astrodynamic Engring., USAF Acad., 1980; MS in Sys. Mgmt., U. So. Calif., 1982; MS in Astrodynamic Engring., AF Inst. Tech., Wright-Patterson AFB, Ohio, 1984. Commd. 2d lt. USAF, Norton AFB, Calif., 1980; advanced through grades to lt. col., 1997; MX stage I project officer Ballistic Missile Office, Norton AFB, Calif., 1980-83; trajectory applications engr. 544th Strategic Intelligence Wing, Offutt AFB, Nebr., 1985-88; asst. prof. USAF Acad., Colo., 1988-92; dep. chief astrodynamics AF Rsch. Lab., Kirtland AFB, N.Mex., 1992-98; orbital analyst U.S. Space Command, Peterson AFB, Colo., 1998-2000; prin. engr. Raytheon, Aurora, 2000—. Mem. adj. faculty Colo. Tech. U., Colorado Springs, 1990-92. Co-author: Systems Engineering Design, 1993; author Fundamentals of Astrodynamics and Applications, 1997; contbr. articles to profl. jours. Recipient Outstanding Young Men of Am., 1998. Mem. Am. Astronautical Soc. (mem. space flight mech. com.), Am. Inst. Aeronautics and Astronautics (com. on standards). Lutheran. Avocations: classical piano, woodworking, stained glass, hiking, biking. Office: Raytheon C3I Sys MS A3601 Bldg S75 16800 E Centertech Pky Aurora CO 80011 E-mail: valladodl@worldnet.att.net., davallado@west.raytheon.com.

VALLARTA, JOSEFINA M. retired child neurologist; b. Manila, Philippines, June 23, 1935; came to U.S., 1966; d. Salvador Del Mundo and Josefa Gotauco; m. Leopoldo Vallarta, May 28, 1959; children: Jocelyn Devita, Vivien Temperani, Maria Vallarta, Paula Jurion. AA, U. Santo Tomas, Manila, 1953, MD magna cum laude, 1958; MSc in Neurology, McGill U., Montreal, Can., 1963. Diplomate Am. Bd. Pediatrics, Am. Bd. Psychiatry and Neurology. Resident, fellow Montreal Children's Hosp., 1959-62; fellow in neuropathology Montreal Neurol. Inst., 1962-63; child neurologist Rainier Sch., buckey, Wash., 1967-75, Children's Orthopedic Hosp., Seattle, 1967-75, Marybridge Children's Hosp., Tacoma, 1974-93, Neurology and Neurosurgery Assoc., Tacoma, 1975-90, Child Devel. and Mental Retardation Ctr., U. Wash., Seattle, 1976-89; pres. med. staff Marybridge Children's Hosp., Tacoma, 1980, med. dir. neurodevel. program, 1979-93; clin. instr., assoc. prof. pediatrics and neurology U. Wash., 1967—; ret., 1994. Examiner Am. Bd. Neurology, San Diego, L.A. and Seattle, 1982, 85, 90, 91; bd. dirs. Am. Bd. Neurology; presenter in field; mem. pediat. ICU Marybridge Children's Hosp., 1976-90; mem. med. bd. Wash. Elks therapy Program, 1981-93. Author: Caring for Our Special Children Early: Intervention Services, 1996; contbr. articles to med. jours. Winthrop scholar, 1957-58. Mem. Wash. State Med. Assn., Child Neurology Soc., S.W. Wash. Pediatric Soc., N.w. Pacific Soc. Neurology and Psychiatry, Soc. Devel. and Behavioral Pediatrics, Med. Soc. Pierce County (pub. sch. health com. 1981-83, ethics com. 1980-93). Avocations: travel, jazzercise, hiking, dancing, quilting. Home: 10408 SW 268th St Vashon WA 98070-8424 also: 22607 N Via De La Caballa Sun City West AZ 85375-2215

VALLBONA, CARLOS, physician; b. Granollers, Barcelona, Spain, July 29, 1927; came to U.S., 1953, naturalized, 1967; s. José and Dolores (Calbó) V.; m. Rima Gretel Rothe, Dec. 26, 1956; children— Rima Nuria, Carlos Fernando, María Teresa, Marisa. BA, BS, U. de Barcelona, 1944, MD, 1950. Diplomate Am. Bd. Pediatrics. Child health physician Escuela de Puericultura, Barcelona, 1952, Stagier Etranger Hôpital des Enfants Malades, Paris, 1952-53; intern, resident U. Louisville, 1953-55; resident Baylor Coll. Medicine, Houston, 1955-56, prof. rehab. medicine, 1967—, assoc. prof. physiology and pediatrics, 1962-69, prof., chmn. dept. community medicine, 1969-95, prof. family medicine, 1980-95, Disting. Svc. prof. family and cmty. medicine, 1995—. Adj. prof. U. Tex. Sch. Pub. Health, U. Tex. Health Sci. Ctr., Houston; chief community medicine service Harris County Hosp. Dist.; staff gen. med. service Tex. Children's Hosp.; staff The Inst. Rehab. and Research; staff St. Luke's Episcopal Hosp., con. staff VA Med. Ctr., Houston; Fulbright vis. prof., 1967; cons. WHO, NIH, Nat. Center Health Stats. Pan Am. Health Orgn., Nat. Center Health Service Research; advisor Conseller Sanitat, Catalunya. Author numerous articles in field; editorial bd. several Sci. jours. French Ministry of Edn. fellow, 1952; Children's Internat. Center fellow, 1953; co-recipient Gold medal 6th Internat. Congress Phys. Medicine, 1972; Public Citizen of Yr. San Jacinto chpt. Nat. Assn. Social Workers, 1974; Outstanding Tchr. award Baylor Coll. Medicine Class of 1980, 83, 85, 87, 88; decorated officer Order of Civil Merit (Spain), Medalla Narcis Monturiol (Catalunya). Mem. Am. Acad. Family Physicians, Am. Coll. Med. Informatics (founding mem. 1984), Nat. Acad. Practice (disting. practitioner 1984), Soc. Pediatric Research (emeritus), AMA, Tex. Med. Assn., Am. Coll. Chest Physicians, Am. Pub. Health Assn. (chmn. elect med. care sect. 1989-90), Am. Coll. Preventive Medicine, U.S.-Mex. Border Health Assn., AAAS, Am. Congress Rehab. Medicine, Catalan Soc. Pediatrics (hon.), Argentinian Soc. Internal Medicine (hon. 1986), Argentinian Med. Soc. (hon. 1986), Spanish Acad. Pediatrics (ambulatory pediatrics sect. hon. 1987), Assn. Tchrs. Preventive Medicine, Spanish Profls. Am. (pres. 1988), Soc. Catalana Hipertensio (hon. pres.), Sigma Xi, Alpha Omega Alpha. Roman Catholic. Home: 2001 Holcombe Blvd Houston TX 77030-4222 Office: Baylor Coll Medicine One Baylor Plz Rm 650E Houston TX 77030-3404

VALLBONA, RIMA-GRETEL ROTHE, foreign language educator, writer; b. San Jose, Costa Rica, Mar. 15, 1931; d. Ferdinand Hermann and Emilia (Strassburger) Rothe; m. Carlos Vallbona, Dec. 26, 1956; children: Rima-Nuri, Carlos-Fernando, Maria-Teresa, Maria-Luisa. BA/BS, Colegio Superior de Senoritas, San Jose, Costa Rica, 1948; diploma, U. Paris, 1953; diploma in Spanish Philology, U. Salamanca, Spain, 1954; MA, U. Costa Rica, 1962; D in Modern Langs., Middlebury Coll., 1981. Tchr. Liceo J.J. Vargas Calvo, Costa Rica, 1955-56; faculty U. St. Thomas, Houston, 1964-95, prof. Spanish, 1978-95, Cullen Found. prof. Spanish, 1989, head Spanish dept., 1966-71, chmn. dept. modern fgn. lang. 5, 1978-80, prof. emeritus, 1995—. Vis. prof. U. Houston, 1975-76, Rice U., 1974, 80-83, 95, U. St. Thomas, Argentina, 1972; vis. prof. U. St. Thomas, Merida program, 1987-95. Author: Noche en Vela, 1968, Yolanda Oreamuno, 1972, La Obra en Prosa de Eunice Odio , 1981, Baraja de Soledades , Las Sombras que Perseguimos , 1983, Polvo del Camino , 1972, La Salamandra Rosada , 1979, Mujeres y Agonias, 1982, Cosecha de Pecadores, 1988, El arcangel del perdon , 1990, Mundo, demonio y mujer, 1991, Los infiernos de la mujer y algo mas, 1992, (crit. edit.) Vida i sucesos de la Monja Alferez , 1992, Flowering Inferno-Tales of Sinking Hearts, 1994, La narrativa de Yolanda Oreamuno, 1996, Tormy, la Prodigiosa Gata de Donaldito, 1997; mem. (editl. bd.) Letras Femeninas, 1984—98, Alba de America, U.S. , sec. (culture) Inst. Literario y Cultural Hispanico ; co-dir.: Foro Literario, 1987—89; contbg. editor: The Americas Rev., 1989—95; contbr. numerous articles and short stories to lit. mags. Mem. scholarship com. Inst. Hispanic Culture, 1978, 79, 88, 91, chmn., 1979, bd. dirs., 1974-76, 88-89, 91-92, chmn. cultural activities, 1979, 80, 85, 88-89; bd. dirs. Houstoh Pub. Libr., 1984-86; bd. dirs. Cultural Arts Coun. Houston, 1991-92. Recipient Aquileo J. Echeverria Novel prize, 1968, Agripina Montes del Valle Novel prize, 1978, Jorge Luis Borges Short Story prize, Argentina, 1977, Lit. award, S.W. Conf. Latin Am. Studies, 1982, Constantin Found. grant for rsch., U. St. Thomas, 1981, Ancora Lit. award, Costa Rica, 1984, Civil Merit award, King Juan Carlos I of Spain, 1989. Mem.: Nat. Writers Assn., Inst. Lit. y Cultural Hispanico, Casa Argentina de Houston, Inst. Hispanic Culture Houston, Latin Am. Writers Assn. Costa Rica, Inst. Internat. de Lit. Iberoam., Latin Am. Studies Assn., Academia Norteamericana de la Lengua Espanola (elected), S.W. Conf. Orgn. Latin Am Studies, South Ctrl. MLA, Houston Area Tchrs. Fgn. Lang., Houston Area Tchrs. Spanish and Portuguese, Am. Assn. Tchrs. Spanish and Portuguese, Sigma Delta Pi, Phi Sigma Iota. Roman Catholic. Home: 3706 Lake St Houston TX 77098-5522 E-mail: rvallbona@aol.com.

VALLBONA-FREEMAN, MARISA FREEMAN, public relations counselor; b. Houston, Jan. 2, 1964; d. Carlos and Rima (Rothe) Vallbona; m. Don R. Rayner Jr., July 12, 1986 (div.); children: Donald R. Rayner III, Timothy Carlos Rayner; m. Roger A. Freeman, Dec. 1, 2000. Student, U. Colo., U. de Dijon, France; BS in Journalism, U. Tex. Account exec. Jae Stefan & Assocs., Austin, Tex., 1987-88; media rels. asst. America's Cup XXVII, 1988; sr. account exec. pub. rels. Berkman & Daniels, 1988-90; prin. Rayner & Vallbona Inc. Advt. & Pub. Rels., San Diego, 1990-97; pres. CIM, Inc., 1997—. Editor: Flowering Inferno, 1994, Soldiers Cry By Night, 1994, Assumed Name, 1994, People on the Prowl, 1995; contbr. articles to profl. jours. Mem. pub. affairs disaster task force ARC, 1993—97; pub. rels. chair Sunkist Am. Cancer Soc. Cup Regatta, 1989; mem. elections mktg. task force City of San Diego, 1989; pub. rels. chair, bd. dirs. Women of St. James Episc. Ch., 1994, 1st v.p. Mem.: Health Care Communicators San Diego (v.p., bd. dirs. 1994, sec. 1993, numerous awards), Am. Soc. Health Care Mktg. and Pub. Rels., Pub. Rels. Soc. Am. (San Diego chpt. chair accreditation com. 1994, dir.-at-large 1995, bd. dirs. 1996—2000, sec. 1997, assembly del. 1999—2000, bd. universal accreditation and western dirs. bd. dirs. 2001—, accredited), United Cerebral Palsy Assn., Jr. League San Diego (sustainer mem.), Pub. Rels. Club San Diego (exec. bd. dirs. 1991—92, various awards). Avocations: snow skiing, tennis, sailing, marathon running. Office: CIM Inc 8459 Sugarman Dr La Jolla CA 92037

VALLE, PABLO F. civil engineer, traffic engineer; b. Ambato, Ecuador, June 1, 1972; came to U.S., 1979; s. Luis Alberto and Nancy (Manobanda) V.; m. Tanya Nirlene Castro, Dec. 17, 1994; children: Justin Paul, Jeremy Timothy. B in Civil Engring., CCNY, 1997. Rsch. asst. CUNY Inst. for Transp. Systems, N.Y.C., 1993-96; coll. intern Met. Transit Authority N.Y. City Transit, Bklyn., 1995; instr. Transp. Rsch. Activities Ctr., N.Y.C., 1993-97; field engr. Testwell Craig Labs., 1997-98; asst. traffic engr. Urbitran Assocs., N.Y.C., 1998—. Grantee: Rsch. Careers for Minority Scholars, Rsch. Found., CCNY. 1995. CUNY Hispanic Serving Insts., Rsch. Found., 1996; recipient Advanced Inst. for Transp. Scholarship U. Transp. Rsch. Ctr., CCNY, 1997. Mem. ASCE (assoc., student chpt. CCNY sec. 1995-96, pres., 96-97). Democrat. Avocations: soccer, skiing, computers, reading. Home: 13737 94th St Ozone Park NY 11417-2813 Office: Urbitran Assocs Inc 71 W 23d St New York NY 10010

VALLE, RAFAEL F. obstetrician-gynecologist; b. Mendoza, VE, Mex., Sept. 6, 1935; came to U.S., 1966; MD, Madrid U., 1965. Diplomate Am. Bd. Ob-Gyn. Intern Mt. Sinai Hosp., Mpls., 1966-67, resident in surgery, 1967-69; resident in ob-gyn. U. Minn., 1969-72; attending physician Hennepin County Med. Ctr. and U. Minn. Hosps., 1972—75, Northwestern U. Hosp., Chgo., 1975—, practice in ob-gyn., 1975—. Prof. OB-GYN Northwestern U. Med. Sch. Mem. ACOG, Assn. Prof. Obs. Gynecol., Am. Assn. Gynecol. Laparoscopists, Am. Fertility Soc., Chgo. Gynecol. Soc., Internat. Soc. Gynecol. Endoscopy, European Soc. Human Reprodn. and Embryology. Office: Northwestern U Med Sch Prentice Womens Hosp 333 E Superior St Ste 1552 Chicago IL 60611-3015 E-mail: rvalle@nmff.org.

VALLEE, JUDITH DELANEY, environmentalist, writer, fundraiser; b. N.Y.C., Mar. 14, 1948; d. Victor and Sally Hammer; m. John Delaney, Apr. 9, 1974 (div. 1978); m. Henry Richard Vallee, May 15, 1987. BA, CUNY, 1976. Exec. dir. Save the Manatee Club, Maitland, Fla., 1985—. Apptd. U.S. Manatee Recovery Plan Team, Jacksonville, Fla., 1988-97, Fla. Manatee Tech. Adv. Coun., Tallahassee, 1989—, Save the Manatee Com., Orlando, Fla., 1985-92, World Conservation Union/Sirenia Specialist Group, Switzerland, 1996; advisor Save the Wildlife Inc., Chuluota, Fla., 1992-93; bd. dirs. Environ. Fund for Fla. Lobbyist Save the Manatee Club, 1989; vol. Broward County Audubon Soc., Ft. Lauderdale, 1983-84, Wild Bird Care Ctr., Ft. Lauderdale, 1984. Recipient Refuge Support award Chassahowitzka Nat. Wildlife Refuge, 1989. Democrat. Avocations: creative writing, antiques, wildlife observation, canoeing. Office: Save the Manatee Club Inc 500 N Maitland Ave Ste 210 Maitland FL 32751-4458 E-mail: jvallee@savethemanatee.org.

VALLEE, ROY, electronics company executive; Field salesman, sys. bus. mgr., gen. sales mgr. Avnet, Inc., Great Neck, N.Y., from 1977, regional dir., v.p., until 1989, pres. Hamilton/Avnet Computer, 1989-90, sr. v.p., dir. worldwide electronics ops., 1990-91, vice chmn., pres., COO, 1991-98, chmn., CEO Phoenix, 1998—, also mem. bd. dirs. Office: Avnet Inc 2211 S 47th St Phoenix AZ 85034-6403*

VALLENTYNE, PETER LLOYD, philosophy educator; b. New Haven, Mar. 25, 1952; s. John Ruben and Ann Vera (Tracy) V.; m. Marie Helene Pastides, June 26, 1981. BA, McGill U., Montreal, Que., Can., 1978; MA, U. Pitts., 1981, PhD, 1984. Actuarial supr. Great West Life Assurance Co., Winnipeg, Man., Can., 1973-75; asst. prof. U. Western Ont., London, 1984-88, Va. Commonwealth U., Richmond, 1988-90, assoc. prof. philosophy, 1990-2000, prof. philosophy, 2000—. Editor: Contractarianism and Rational Choice: Essays on Gauthier, 1991, The Origin of Left-Libertarianism, 2000, Left-Libertarianism and Its Critics, 2000; assoc. editor: Politics, Philosophy and Economics, 2000, Desert and Justice, 6 vols., 2003; bd. editors Utilitas, 1994—, Econs. and Philosophy, 1998—. Mem. Am. Philos. Assn., Can. Philos. Assn., So. Soc. Philosophy and Psychology, Va. PHilos. Assn. (pres. 1994-95). Avocations: piano, ballroom dance, art films. Office: Va Commonwealth U Dept Philosophy 915 W Franklin St Richmond VA 23284-2025 E-mail: Peter.vallentyne@vcu.edu.

VALLERAND, PHILIPPE GEORGES, sales executive; b. Montreal, Que., Can., June 12, 1954; came to U.S., 1982; s. Louis Philippe and Beatrice (Goupil) V.; m. Laura Jean Frombach, Sept. 25, 1979; children: Harmonie May, Jeremy Thomas, Emilie Rose. Student, U. Montreal, 1974, U. Sherbrooke, 1975, U. Que., 1976, White Mgmt. Sch., London, 1981. Cert. mktg. and sales Internat. Orgn. for Standardization 150, ISO 9002. Dir. resort Club Mediterranee Inc., Bahamas, Switzerland, Africa, Guadelupe, West Indies, 1978-80; v.p. Franglo/Sunsaver Inc., London and Hyeres, France, 1980-82; v.p. sales Source Northwest, Inc., Woodinville, Wash., 1982-93; pres., CEO Prime Resource Group. Sr. comdr. Royal Rangers Boys Club, Monroe, Wash., 1988-96; bd. dirs. Christian Faith Ctr., Monroe, 1988-94; mem. Rep. Nat. Com.; co-chmn. Rep. Bus. Adv. Coun. Recipient Disting. Sales & Mktg. Exec. award Internat. Orgn. Sales & Mktg. Execs., 1993, 96; named Republican of Yr., Wash. State, 2000-02; named to 500 Inc. Mag., 1983, 89. Mem. Am. Mktg. Assn. (adv. bd.), Sales and Mktg. Execs. Internat. Avocations: skiing, world travel.

VALLERGA, BERNARD A. engineering administrator; BS, U. Calif. Berkeley, 1943, MS, 1948. Materials testing engr. Hershey Inspection Bur., Oakland, Calif., 1946-48; asst. prof. civil engring. U. Calif. Berkeley, 1948-53; mng. engr. Pacific Coast Divsn. Asphalt Inst., San Francisco, 1953-60; v.p. prodn. devel. & mktg. GBO Divsn. Witco Chem. Co., L.A., 1960-64; pres. & CEO Material Rsch. & Devel., Inc., Oakland, 1964-72; v.p., mng. prin. Woodward-Clyde Consults, San Francisco-Oakland, 1968-76; pres. B.A. Vallerga, Inc. Consulting Civil Engring., Oakland, 1977—. Chmn. Triaxial Inst. Structural Design Pavements, 1950-52; bd. dirs. Woodward-Clyde Consultants, 1980-82; mem. bd. dirs., v.p. Asphalt Inst., 1962-64; v.p. Design Divsn., Am. Road Builders Assn., 1968-70; chmn. bd. dirs. Woodward Envicon, 1969-72. Subcom. Asphalt Durability, Transp. Rsch. Bd., 1980—; gen. cons. Off Energy Related Inventions, Bur. Stds., Dept. Com., 1980—. Fellow ASCE (mem. Airfield Pavement Com. 1972-79); mem. ASTM (Provost Hubbard award 1989), Internat. Soc. Asphalt Pavements, Assn. Asphalt Paving Technologists (mem. bd. dirs. 1960-62, Recognition award 1988), Nat. Acad. Engring., Sigma Xi. Office: 5881 Balmoral Dr Oakland CA 94619-2438

VALLES, JUDITH, mayor, former academic administrator; b. San Bernardino, Calif., Dec. 14, 1933; d. Gonzalo and Jovita (Lopez-Torices) V.; m. Chad Bradbury, Sept. 30, 1956 (dec. Sept. 1969); children: Edith Renella, Nohemi Renella, Chad; m. Harry Carl Smith, Oct. 13, 1985. BA in English, Redlands (Calif.) U., 1956; MA in Spanish Lit., U. Calif., Riverside, 1966; doctorate (hon.), U. Redlands, 2000. Instr. Spanish San Bernardino (Calif.) Valley Coll., 1963-84, head dept. fgn. lang., 1971-76, chair div. humanities, 1976-81, dean extended day, 1981-83, adminstrv. dean acad. affairs, 1983-87, exec. v.p. acad. and student affairs, 1987-88; pres. Golden West Coll., Huntington Beach, Calif., 1988—; mayor San Bernardino, 1998—. Mem. adv. com. Police Officers Standards and Tng. Commn., Sacramento, 1991—. Author fgn. lang. annals and sociol. abstracts. Speaker statewide edn. and community orgns., 1988—; bd. dirs. exec. coun. and chief exec. officers Calif. Community Colls., 1990—. Named One of Outstanding Women Orange County YWCA, 1990, Citizen of Achievement LWV, 1989, Woman of Distinction Bus. Press, 1998, Influential Latina of the Yr. Hispanic Lifestyle, 1998, State of Calif. Woman of the Yr., 1999, Humanitarian Yr. Cath. charities, 1999, Citizen Yr. Boy Scouts Am., 1999, Empire Woman Yr. State Assembly, 1999; inducted into Hall of Fame, San Bernardino Valley Coll. Mem. Women's Roundtable Orange County, Conf. and Visitors Bur., C. of C. (Vanguard), Kiwanis, Charter 100. Avocations: opera, theater, reading, running. Office: Conf Mayors 300 N D St San Bernardino CA 92418-0001

VALLIANOS, CAROLE WAGNER, lawyer; b. Phila., Aug. 19, 1946; d. F. Leonard Wagner and Helen Rose Pikunas; m. Peter Denis Vallianos, June 22, 1963; children: Kelly, Denis, Jamie Vallianos-Healy. BA, Calif. State U., Fullerton, 1981; JD, Southwestern U., 1995. Bar: Calif. 1997. Nonprofit cons., Manhattan Beach, Calif., 1982—; atty. in pvt. practice, 1997—. Non-profit cons. USIA, Turkey, 1997, Cyprus, 1997, Bosnia, 1998, India, 1999; bd. dirs. Rsch. and Edn. Inst., Harbor-UCLA Med. Ctr. Pres. LWV Calif., 1989—91; mem. com. on pvt. judging Calif. Jud. Coun., 1989—91, mem. com. on race and ethic bias in the cts., 1991—96, mem. com. on access and fairness in the cts., 1994—97, mem. task force on jury sys. improvements, 1998—; mem. Women Lawyers L.A. Jail Project; mem. adv. bd. U. Fla. Marion Brechner Citizen Access Project; bd. dirs. LWV U.S., 1992—98, LWV Edn. Fund U.S., 1992—98. Mem. LWV Beach Cities (former pres.), Am. Judicature Soc. (bd. dirs. 1996—, exec. com. 2001-), First Amendment Coalition Calif. (bd. dirs. 1995—), Coalition for Justice (v.p. 1993—), Benjamin Aranda Inn of Ct. Avocations: travel, political memorabilia, literature.

VALLIANT, JAMES STEVENS, lawyer; b. Glendale, Calif., Sept. 29, 1963; s. William Warren and Carol Dee (Heath) V.; m. Holly Lynne White. BA, NYU, 1984; JD, U. San Diego, 1989. Bar: Calif. 1989. Law instr. U. San Diego, 1988-89; dep. dist. atty. Dist. Atty.'s Office, San Diego, 1989—. Host talk show WJM Prodns., Hollywood, Calif., 1996. Contbr. articles in objectivism and early Christianity. Recipient Citation of Appreciation, MADD, 1993. Office: Dist Attys Office 330 W Broadway San Diego CA 92101-3825

VALLICELLA, WILLIAM F. b. Monterey Park, Calif., Jan. 1, 1950; married. PhD, Boston Coll., 1978. Assoc. prof. U. of Dayton (Ohio), 1978—89; vis. assoc. prof. Case Western Res. U., Cleve., 1989—91. Author: A Paradigm Theory of Existence, 2002. Scholar, Nat. Endowment for the Humanities, 1981, 1984, 1986, 1995. Mem.: Am. Philos. Assn. Independent. Avocations: chess, running, hiking, backpacking. Personal E-mail: BillVallicella@compuserve.com.

VALLIERE, FLORA LEE, law firm official; b. Neptune, N.J., Dec. 4, 1950; d. Joseph Sidney and Anna (Warar) Rosenthal; m. Lewis Ira Weinstein (div. 1976); m. Robrt John Valliere (div. 1986); children: Stuart Glenn, Gillian Melissa. AA, Miami-Dade Jr. Coll., 1972; student, Fla. Internat. U., 1973-74; grad. in cosmetology, Norwood Beauty Sch., North Miamia, Fla., 1975; student, Nova Southeastern U., Davie, Fla., 1996. Notary pub., Fla. Waitress Windmill Restuarant, West End, N.J., 1966-72; artist, antique dealer, 1972-75; hairdresser Century Plaza Salon, Deerfield Beach, Fla., 1976-80; saleswoman Fedco Drugs, Ft. Lauderdale, 1986-93; cashier, pharmacy technician Winn-Dixie Supermarkets, 1994-96; receptionist, sec. Law Firm Lonergan, Murawski, Vizcarrondo & Usan, 1996-99. Vol. Coop. Feeding Program, Ft. Lauderdale, 1996, 99, Arnold Abbot's Love Thy Neighbor Feeding Program for Homeless, 1999. Democrat. Jewish. Avocations: frequenting art shows, beach, collecting antiques, music, reading. Address: 3047 Perry Ave Greenacres FL 33463-2060

VALLIERE, ROLAND EDWARD, performing company executive; b. Pawtucket, R.I., Oct. 3, 1954; s. Roland Edgar and Anita Alice (Dubois) V.; m. Stacey Lyn Rein, June 3, 1984 (separated). MusB, New England Conservatory, 1978; MFA, Brandeis U., 1984. Regional mgr. Syracuse (N.Y.) Symphony, 1984-86; gen. mgr. N.H. Symphony, Manchester, 1986-89; exec. dir. Hudson Valley Philharmonic, Poughkeepsie, N.Y., 1989-92, Omaha Symphony, Nebr., 1992-95, Kansas City Symphony, Mo., 1995—2002, dir. tech, 2002—. Presenter Am. Symphony Orchestra League, Washington, 1987, 90. Office: PO Box 22534 Kansas City MO 64113-0534*

VALLO, VICTOR WILLIAM, JR. military officer, music educator; b. New York, Ny, Mar. 1955; s. Victor William and Vincie Phyllis Vallo; m. Eileen B. Vallo, Dec. 28, 1991; children: Lisa Kula, Vincent; m. Rowena Manriquez, Aug. 14, 1982 (div. Feb. 23, 1987); m. Rowena Manriquez, Aug. 14, 1982 (div. Feb. 23, 1987). MusB Edn., Syracuse U., Syracuse, NY, 1977; Masters of Music, George Wash. U., Washington, DC, 1981; PhD music edn., U. of Fla., Gainesville, FL, 1991. Asst. educator So. Ark. U., Magnolia, Ark., 1991—93; assoc. educator Jacksonville State U., Jacksonville, Ala., 1993—99; music educator Anderson Coll., Anderson, SC, 1999—. Vice-president Ala. Music Edn. Assn., Tuscaloosa, Ala., 1998—99, Ark. Music Edn. Assn., Little Rock, 1991—93. Author: (article) Phi Mu Alpha (music), Southeastern Journal of Music Education, Research Perspectives in Music Education. Lt. col. US Army, 1977—2002, Georgia. Recipient Hon. Mem., Phi Mu Alpha (music), 1995-2002, Rsch. Awards, Jacksonville State U., 1995-1999, Wilmot Award, U. of Fla., 1989. Mem.: SC Music Educator Assn., Coll. Music Soc., Internationsl Trumpet Guild. Roman Catholic. Avocations: tennis, raquetball, foreign cars, foreign cars. Office: Division of Fine Arts (Music) 316 Boulevard Street Anderson SC 29621 Home Fax: 864-231-2083; Office Fax: 864-231-2083. Personal E-mail: vvallo@earthlink.net. E-mail: vvallo@earthlink.net.

VALLONE, JOHN CHARLES, motion picture production designer; b. Phila., June 23, 1953; s. Louis Phillip and Laura Anne (Gagilone) Vallone; divorced; children: Gabriella, Lilli. BFA, NYU, 1975. Pres., owner Archtl. Dreams, Park City, Utah, 1997—, Against the Wind Prodns. Ltd., Park City, Vallone Design Group, Park City, VDG Aircraft Co. Ltd., Park City. Prodn. designer: (feature films) Southern Comfort, 1981, 48 Hours, 1982, Brainstorm, 1983, Streets of Fire, 1984, Brewster's Millions, 1985, Commando, 1985, Predator, 1987, Red Heat, 1988, The Adventures of Ford Fairlane, 1990, Die Hard 2, 1990, Rambling Rose, 1991, Cliffhanger, 1993, Bad Boys, 1995, 3 Wishes, 1995, (TV pilots) Private Eye, 1987, Sweet Justice, 1994, (TV movies) Shannon's Deal, 1989, Angel City, 1990, (TV series) Cover Me, 1999-2000; art dir.: (film) Star Trek: The Motion Picture, 1979 (Academy award nomination best art direction 1979), (TV miniseries) Firestarter, 2002, Everwood, 2002—. Mem. AOPA, SMPTVAD, Acad. Motion Picture Arts and Scis. (Best Art Direction award nomination 1981). Republican. Avocations: restoration of wooden yacht, pilot, sailing, woodworking, skiing.

VALLUNAS, ALGIS, writer, bass-baritone; b. N.Y.C., N.Y., Jan. 3, 1954; s. Jonas Algirdas and Adele Danute Valiunas. AB, Dartmouth Coll., 1975; BA, MA, Trinity Coll., Cambridge, 1977; PhD, U. Chgo., 1998. Opera singer various companies, Chgo., 1986—90, Palm Beach, Fla., 2001—. Author: Churchill's Military Histories, 2002; contbr. articles to mags. Fellow, Danforth Found., 1978—82, Bradley-Bellow fellow, Bradley Found., 1988—90; grantee, Harper-Wood Travelling Studentship, St. John's Coll., Cambridge, 1977—78.

VALOIS, ROBERT ARTHUR, lawyer; b. N.Y.C., May 13, 1938; s. Frank Jacob and Harriet Frances (LaCroix) V.; m. Ruth Emilie Skacil, Dec. 23, 1961; children: Marguerite Jeannette, Robert Arthur Jr. BBA, U. Miami, 1962; JD, Wake Forest U., 1972. Bar: N.C. 1972, Fla. 1972, U.S. Ct. Appeals (4th cir.) 1973, U.S. Dist. Ct. (ea. and mid. dists.) 1974, U.S. Supreme Ct. 1975, U.S. Ct. Appeals (6th cir.) 1986. Field examiner NLRB, Winston-Salem, N.C., 1962-70; from assoc. to ptnr. Maupin, Taylor, Ellis & Adams, P.A., Raleigh, 1972—; chmn. labor and employment sect. Maupin, Taylor & Ellis, P.A., 1972-97, chmn. bd. dirs., pres., 1997—2002. Vice chmn. Legal Svcs. Corp., Washington, 1984-90, bd. dirs. Served with USN, 1956-59. Mem. Greater Raleigh C. of C. (chmn. fed. govt. com. 1991—). Democrat. Presbyterian. E-mail: rvalois@maupintaylor.com.

VALONE, JAMES AUSTIN, JR. retired surgeon; b. Winston-Salem, N.C., Aug. 1, 1948; s. James A. Valone and Ethel M. Fielder; m. Christiane Ellis Valone, Sept. 6, 1975. BS, Yale Coll., 1970; MD, Yale U., 1974. Diplomate Am. Bd. Ophthalmology. Intern in medicine U. Va., Charlottesville, 1974—75; resident in ophthalmology Mass. Eye and Ear/Harvard, Boston, 1976—78, fellow in retinal diseases, 1978—80; retinal surgeon Norfolk, Va., 1980—97; chief ophthalmology Med. Ctr. Hosps., 1983—84; dir. residency tng. Ea. Va. Med. Sch., 1984—90, prof. clin. ophthalmology, 1995. Trustee The Ballentine Home, Norfolk, 1995—; mem. devel. com. The Chrysler Mus. Art, 2001—; vestry St. Andrews Episcopal Ch., 1993—96, 2002—. Mem.: The Retina Soc., Norfolk Acad. Medicine, Am. Acad. Ophthalmology, Norfolk Yacht and Country Club. Home: 1423 Runnymede Rd Norfolk VA 23505

VALSARAJ, KALLIAT THAZHATHUVEETIL, chemical engineering educator; b. Tellichery, Kerala, India, Oct. 2, 1957; came to U.S., 1980; s. Mundayat B. Nambiar and Kalliat T. Bhanumathy; m. Nisha Valsaraj, Dec. 24, 1990; children: Viveca, Vinay. MS, Indian Inst. Tech., Madras, India, 1980; PhD, Vanderbilt U., 1983. Affiliate faculty U. Ark., Fayetteville, 1983-86; sr. rsch. assoc. Hazardous Waste Rsch. Ctr. La. State U., Baton Rouge, 1986-90, asst. prof., 1990-93, assoc. prof., 1994-99, Ike East prof. chem. engring., 1999—, dept. chem. engring. Mem. panel directions in separations NSF, 1989-90; cons. Balsam Engr. Cons., Salem, N.H., 1990-91, Vicksburg (Miss.) Chems., Borden Chems. and Plastics, La.; presenter in field. Author: Elements of Environmental Engineering: Thermodynamics and Kinetics, 1995, 2nd edit., 2000; contbr. numerous articles to profl. jours. Grantee Dept. Def., 1986-89, NSF, 1989, 92-95, 2001—, EPA, 1989-92, 93-97, 97-98, U.S. Army, 1998—. Mem. Am. Chem. Soc., Am. Inst. Chem. Engrs., Nat. Geographic Soc., Air and Waste Mgmt. Assn. Achievements include patent for innovative groundwater treatment. Home: 6348 Hope Estates Dr Baton Rouge LA 70820 Office: La State U Dept Chem Engring Baton Rouge LA 70803-0001 E-mail: valsaraj@che.lsu.edu.

VALVASSORI, GALDINO E. physician; b. Milan, Italy, 1926; MD, U. Milan, 1950. Diplomate Am. Bd. Radiology. Intern Columbus Hosp., Chgo., 1957; resident Meml. Ctr.-Cornell, 1954-56; fellow Columbus Hosp., Chgo., 1958-59; mem. staff U. Ill. Hosp., 1966—; prof. radiology and otolaryngology U. Ill., 1966—; prof. U. Chgo., 1960-65; cons. dept. radiology St. Francis Hosp., Evanston, Ill., 2001—. Mem. AMA, Am. Coll. Radiology, Am. Roentgen Ray Soc., Roentgen Soc. N.Am., Am. Soc. Neuroradiology, Am. Soc. Head and Neck Radiology. Office: St Francis Hosp Dept Radiology 355 Ridge Ave Evanston IL 60202

VALVO, BARBARA-ANN, lawyer, surgeon; b. Elizabeth, N.J., June 7, 1949; d. Robert Richad and Vera (Kovach) V. BA in Biology, Hofsta U., 1971; MD, Pa. State U., 1975; JD, Loyola Sch. Law, 1993. Diplomate Am. Bd. Surgery; Bar: La. 1993. Surg. intern Nassau County Med. Ctr., East Meadow, N.Y., 1975-76; resident gen. surgery Allentown-Sacred Heart Med. Ctr., Allentown, Pa., 1976-80; asst. chief surgery USPHS, New Orleans, 1980-81; pvt. practice gen. surgery, 1981-89; pvt. practice med. malpractice law, 1995—. Upjohn scholar, 1975. Fellow ACS; mem. ABA, FBA, La. Bar Assn., La. Trial Lawyers Assn. Republican. Avocations: computers, raising animals. Office: 4130 Loire Dr Ste A Kenner LA 70065 Fax: 504-467-8762. E-mail: bavalvo@att.net.

VALYO, JUDY ANN, dean; b. N.Y.C., Mar. 25, 1945; d. John Andrew and Josephine Theresa (Hricko) V. BA, Molloy Coll. for Women, 1967; MA, NYU, 1969; EdD, Columbia U., 1985. Cert. secondary edn. educator, social studies, N.Y. state. Residence hall dir. Hofstra U., Hempstead, N.Y., 1969-71, area coord., 1971-72; asst. dir. student activities Ramapo Coll., Mahwah, N.J., 1972-74, dir. student activities, 1974-76, Rockland C.C., Suffern, N.Y., 1976-81; assoc. dean students N.J. Inst. Tech., Newark, 1981-87, 88-89, acting dean of students, 1987-88, 89-90, dean freshman studies, 1990—. Peer reviewer NSF, Washington, 1991, 93. Literacy vol. LVA-Englewood (N.J.) Pub. Libr., 1988-93; bd. dirs. YWCA of Hackensack, 1989-90. Grantee NSF, 1991-92, 92-94, 94-97. Mem. Bus. & Profl. Women (v.p. 1983-84, 94-95, pres. 1995-97), Am. Soc. Engring. Edn., Am. Assn. Higher Edn., Women Engrs. Program Advocates Network. Avocations: travel, walking, reading. Office: NJ Inst Tech University Heights Newark NJ 07102 E-mail: valyo@njit.edu.

VAMOS, FLORENCE M. lawyer; b. N.Y.C., Apr. 09; d. Joseph Calabro and Louise Marie Horvath; m. Joseph S. Vamos. BA magna cum laude, U.Minn., 1974; JD, William Mitchell Coll. Law, St. Paul, 1978. Bar: Ind. 1978, Mich. 1982, U.S. Dist. Ct. (so. dist.) Ind. 1978, U.S. Dist. Ct. (no. dist.) Ind. 1979, U.S. Dist. Ct. (so. dist.) Mich. 1981, U.S. Dist. Ct (ea. dist.) Mich. 1982. Pvt. practice, South Bend, Ind., 1978-90, Mishawaka, 1990-2000, Edwardsburg, Mich., 2001—. Mem. Ind. State Bar Assn., Mich. State Bar Assn., Cass County (Mich.) Bar Assn., St. Joseph County (Ind.) Bar Assn., Nat. Inst. Trial Advocacy.

VAMVAKETIS, CAROLE, health services administrator; b. Bklyn., Mar. 1, 1943; d. William and Helen (Calacanis) Vamvaketis; 1 child, William. AA, Packer Collegiate Inst., Bklyn., 1962; BS, Columbia U., 1964; MA, Columbia Tchrs. Coll., 1969; AAS in Nursing, Rockland C.C., Suffern, N.Y., 1981; BSN, Dominican Coll., 1991. Tchr. elem. sch. A. Fantis Parochial Sch., 1964-67; tchr. Adelphi Acad., 1967-72, girls dean, 1968-72; nurse Nyack (N.Y.) Hosp., 1981-91; nurse mgr. Kings Harbor Care Ctr., 1991-93; assoc. dir. nursing Port Chester Nursing Home, 1993-94; CQI/edn. coord. Highbridge Woodycrest Ctr., 1994-95; profl. svcs. cons. Multicare Cos., Inc., Nanuet, N.Y., 1995-96, personal svcs. cons., 1995-96, divsn. dir. clin. svcs., 1996—; asst. dir., dir. staff devel. Beth Abraham Health Svcs., Bronx, 1996-97; dir. of nursing Ridgewood Nursing and Rehab. Ctr., Multicare Cos., Inc., 1997; insvc. coord. Del. Valley Hosp., Walton, N.Y., 1997-99; nurse aide evaluator NACES, 1997-99; instr. Del., Chenango, Madison and Otsego counties Bd. of Cooperative Ednl. Svcs., 1998-99; coord. health svcs. Monticello, N.Y., 1999-2000; home care and assisted living nurse Hilltop Retirement Cmty., Johnson City, NY, 2000—01; dir. inservice and infection control St. Teresa's Nursing Home,

Middletown, 2001—; asst. dir. nursing, QI coord. Binghamton, 2001—; dir. Insvc. Infection Control, Middletown, 2002—. Home: 90 Downs Rd Monticello NY 12701 Office: Home Care Svcs Hilltop Retirement Comty Johnson City NY 13790

VAN, PETER, lawyer; b. Boston, Sept. 7, 1936; s. Frank Lewis and Ruth (Spevack) V.; m. Faye Anne Zitock, 1991; children: Jami Lynne, Robert Charles. BA, Dartmouth, 1958; LLD, Boston Coll., 1961. Bar: Mass. 1962. Assoc. Brown, Rudnick, Freed and Gesmer, Boston, 1961-63; assoc. Fine and Ambrogne, 1963-65, ptnr., 1966-73, sr. ptnr., 1973—, mng. ptnr., chmn. exec. com., 1988-90; ptnr., mem. exec. com. Mintz, Levin, Cohn, Ferris, Glovsky and Popeo, P.C., 1990-97; ptnr. Bingham, Dana LLP, 1997—. Mem. fin. com., overseer Beth Israel Hosp. Boston. Mem. Masons. Office: Bingham Dana LLP 150 Federal St Boston MA 02110-1713 E-mail: pvan@bingham.com.

VANAGAS, RIMANTAS ANDRIUS (RAY VANAGAS), entrepreneur; b. Chgo., Jan. 10, 1958; s. Liudas and Birute A. (Bielskis) Vanagas. Student, Northwestern U., 1980-81; BA in Physics, Econs. and Polit. Sci., Lake Forest (Ill.) Coll., 1982. Prof. basketball player European divsn., Munich, 1982; ski instr., capt. race team Breckenridge (Colo.) Ski Sch., 1979-80; chmn. bd. dirs. Vancher Corp., Wheeling, Ill., 1980-84; sales exec. Chgo. HMO, 1984-85; exec. dir. Physique, Inc., Highland Park, 1985; pres., CEO Sports Life, Inc., 1985-88; sr. v.p. JPC Consulting, Chgo., 1988-91; pres., CEO Printing Advisors, Inc., Naperville, 1990-94; sr. exec. George S. May Internat. Consulting Co., Park Ridge, 1994-95; pres., CEO Cafe Alexander, Naperville, 1995—2002. Cons. Nautilus Exercise Ctrs., Inc., Wheeling, 1979—83, G. Ross Comm., Lake Bluff, Ill., 1986; mng. dir. Ford Model Mgmt., Chgo., 2000—; pres., CEO Alexander Talent Mgmt., 2001—. Actor: , 1981—; prodr.: , 1981—; actor: (films) Shut-Eye, 2001; prodr.: music videos. Leader Lithuanian Air Scouts, 1976—80; campaign asst. Ronald Reagan Re-Election Campaign, Ill., 1983; active Baltic Nations Athletic Olympiad; vol. coach basketball, baseball, 1984—87. Roman Catholic. Avocations: collecting coins and stamps, travel, skiing, golf, tennis. Home: 1680 Greene Ridge Dr Naperville IL 60565-6753 Fax: 630-305-9328.

VAN AKEN, JOHN HENRY, retired marine surveyor, engineer, consultant; b. Haarlem, The Netherlands, Sept. 26, 1922; came to U.S., 1952; s. Antony and Maria Petronella (Renzen) van Aken; m. Hendrika A. Bonneur, Sept. 25, 1947 (div. Feb. 1960); 1 child Antony Laurens ; m. Helen Jemison, July 17, 1962 (dec. Feb. 1978); m. Marilyn McDaniel, July 13, 1980 (dec. Sept. 2001). Marine Engr., Acad. Tech. Sci. and Arts, of Design, Rotterdam, 1940. Asst. mgr. repair dept. Wilton-Feyenoord Dockyards, Schiedam, The Netherlands, 1945-52; supt. machinery Ala. Dry Dock & Shipbldg. Co., Mobile, 1958-60; project mgr. Kerr-McGee Oil Industries, Oklahoma City, 1954-58, 60-63; insp. George Sharp Co., Naval Architects, Newport News, Va., 1960; pres. John H. van Aken Co. Inc., Marine Surveyors and Cons. Inc., Mobile, 1963-99; ret., 2002—. Non-exclusive surveyor Panama Bur. Shipping, Internat. Cargo Gear Bur., Registr. Italiano Navale, Lloyd's Register of Shipping. Named hon. consul gen. Republic of South Africa; decorated comdr. Order Good Hope, South Africa; Paul Harris fellow Rotary. Mem. Soc. Naval Architects and Marine Engrs., Nat. Assn. Marine Surveyors, Netherlands Soc. Marine Technologists, Athelstan Club, Fairhope Yacht Club, Mobile Rotary. Home: 500 Spanish Ft Blvd #52 Spanish Fort AL 36527-5004 E-mail: jhvanaken@aol.com.

VAN AKKEREN, LORRAINE SUE, research assistant; b. Balt., July 22, 1943; d. Gordon David and Ida (Rackoff) Goldstein; children: Adrienne Dawn Mandeville, Joel Rackoff. BA, Monmouth Coll., 1965. Chief art and photography depts. Nat. Biomed. Rsch. Found., Washington, 1965-74; prodn. control asst. Optimum Sys., Inc., Rockville, Md., 1974-76; sr. assoc. Computer Documentation & Tng., Kensington, 1976-91; mem. svcs. rep., survey asst. Group Health Assn., Washington, 1989; sr. rsch. asst. Am. Assn. of Colls. of Osteo. Medicine, Chevy Chase, 1989—; chair osteo. medicine Ed. Leadership Task Force, AACOM, 2000—. Vice-chair Rockville mem. adv. coun. Group Health Assn., 1992-94, vice-chair cen. mem. adv. com., Washington, 1992-94, mem. claims appeals com., Washington, 1993-94, mem. complaints com., Washington, 1992-94, mem. benefits com., 1989-92, mem. mental health task force, 1988-90. Artist: (book covers) Atlas of Protein Sequence and Structure, 1966-74 (1st prize Comml. Illustration Silver Spring Showcase of Md. 1968), Engineering Analysis of Dental Forces: Theory and Application, 1970, (jour. cover) Pattern Recognition, 1969. Carpool chair Charles E. Smith Jewish Day Sch., Rockville, 1982-96, gift cert. fundraiser, 1991-94, chair subcom. on arts, 1983-85; Sunday sch. and faculty records Luth. Ch. St. Andrew Sunday Sch., Wheaton, Md., 1983-94; mem. Bethesda Jewish Congregation Choir; advisor Montgomery County 1st Aid unit Boy Scout Explorer Post 521 (formerly Montgomery County ARC 1st Aid unit), 1995—; rep. ctrl. mem. adv. panel Humana Group Health Plan, Inc., mem. Rockville, chair Montgomery County, mem. adv. panel, 1994-97; mem. New Beginnings, Inc., 1996—; active mobile adoption unit Montgomery County Humane Soc. foster dog program, 2000—. Avocations: crossword puzzles, swimming, needlework, volunteer work, cooking. Home: 3814 Delano St Wheaton MD 20902-1031 Office: Am Assn Colls Osteo Med 5550 Friendship Blvd #310 Chevy Chase MD 20815-7231 E-mail: dachsielover@mindspring.com., lorrie@aacom.org.

VAN ALLEN, BARBARA MARTZ, marketing professional; b. Frederick, Md., Mar. 9, 1954; d. Walter Atlee and Barbara Jean (Winebrenner) Martz; m. Peter Cushing Van Allen, Sept. 3, 1983; children: Caroline Kent, Peter Cushing Jr. BA with honors, U. N.C., 1976; MA, George Washington U., 1983; MBA, NYU, 1993. Legis. asst. U.S. Ho. of Reps., Washington, 1976-81, legis. dir., 1981-83; dir. ITT Corp., N.Y.C., 1984-90; pres. Van Allen Assocs., 1990-93, 2000—; mng. dir. Cushman & Wakefield, Inc., 1994-2000. Bd. dirs. Washington Nat. Cathedral Coll. Preachers, 2000—. Mem. N.Y.C. Jr. League, 1986—; mem. econ. devel. task force N.Y.C. Mayoral Campaign and Transition Team, 1994—95; bd. dirs. 801 West End Avenue Corp., N.Y.C., 1995—99. Recipient Star awards for print campaign and internal comm. Bus. Mktg. Assn., 1996, nat. pro-comm. profl. excellence award for radio, 1996, Pro Com. award, 1997, Impact award, 1998. Mem. NAFE, Internat. Assn. Bus. Communicators (Iris Merit award 1996, Ace Merit award 1996, Ace award of excellence for pub. 1997, Ace award of merit for Reporter's Handguide 1997, N.Y. Fest. award, BMA Pro Comm. award for Direct Mail: Soup to Nuts, 1998, APEX award for Real Estatements publ., 1998), Bus. and Profl. Women's Club, YWCA Acad. Women Achievers. Home: 4407 Hadfield Ln NW Washington DC 20007-2034

VAN ALLEN, KATRINA (FRANCES SHERRILL) (KATRINA FRANCES), painter; b. Phoenix, Feb. 18, 1933; d. Benjamin Cecile Sherrill and Magdalen Mary (Thomas) Adams; m. Ray C. Bennett II, Dec. 31, 1950 (div. 1955); m. William Allen Van Allen, Mar. 15, 1963 (dec. Mar. 1971); m. Donovan Wyatt Jacobs, Apr. 22, 1972; children: Ray Crawford Bennett III, Sherri Lou Bennett Maraney. Student, Stanford U., 1950, 51, 52, Torrance C.C., 1962, 63; MA, U. Tabriz, Iran, 1978; studied with Martin Lubner, Jerold, Burchman, John Leeper, L.A.; student, Otis Art Inst., Immaculate Heart Coll.; studied with the late Russa Graeme, 1968, 69, 70. Office mgr. H.P. Adams Constrn. Co., Yuma, Ariz., 1952-59; nurse Moss-Hathaway Med. Clin., Torrance, Calif., 1962-63; interviewer for various assns. N.Y.C., 1964-70. Solo shows include: Zella 9 Gallery, London, 1972, Hambleton Gallery, Maiden Newton, Eng., 1974, Intercontinental Gallery, Teheran, Iran, 1976, USIA Gallery, Teheran, 1977, 78, Tabriz, 1977, Mashad, 1978, Esfahan, 1978, Shiraz, 1978, Coos Art Mus., Coos Bay, Oreg., 1993; exhibited in group shows at La Cienega Gallery, L.A., 1970, 79, 80, 81, 82, Design Ctr. Gallery, Tucson, 1985, Coos Art Mus., 1992-97, 98, 99, 2000, 01, 02, Expressions West, 2000, 01; represented in permanent collections at Bankers Trust Bd. Room, London, Mfrs. Hanover Bank, London, U. Iowa Med. Sch., Iowa City, Bank of Am., Leonard E. Blakesley Internat. Law Offices, Marina del Rey, Calif., and numerous pvt. collections. Bd. dirs. Inst. for Cancer and Leukemia Rsch., 1966-67, 68. Recipient Five City Tour and Honorarium, Iran Am. Soc., 1977. Mem. Nat. Women in the Arts, L.A. Art Assn., Bay Area Art Assn., Lower Umpqa Flycasters, Coos Country Club. Avocations: fly-fishing, hiking, bridge, golf, the arts. Home: 91513 Cape Arago Hwy Coos Bay OR 97420-9604 Fax: 541-888-5861. E-mail: vanallen33@earthlink.net.

VAN ALLEN, VERONICA ELAINE, marketing and public relations professional; b. Jamaica, N.Y., May 6, 1936; d. William James and Florence Veronica (Lester) Van Allen; children: Veronica E. Davis, Valerie E. Boyd; m. Ian Helsby, July 4, 1998. BEd, U. Miami, 1963; cert., U.S. Chamber Inst. Orgn. Mgmt., Boulder, Colo., 1984-88. Cert. tchr., Fla. English, phys. edn. tchr. Dade County Sch. Sys., Miami, Fla., 1963-67; founder, coach girls' track team Acad. of the Holy Names, Tampa, 1971—74; exec. dir. Royal Palm Festival Inc., West Palm Beach, 1978-82; exec. v.p. No. Palm Beaches C. of C., Palm Beach Gardens, 1982-88; dir. mktg., pub. rels. Operation Explore, 1993—. Exec. dir. World Trade Coun., 1983-86. Editor (newspaper supplement) Royal Palm Festival, 1978-82 (Advt. Club aw ard 1980), video pub., 1981 (Internat. Festival Assn. award 1981); editor (ann. chamber mag.) Guide to No. Palm Beaches, 1984-88, Air Show mag., 1987. Vice chmn. Tourist Devel. Coun. Palm Beach County, 1987, mem., 1983—88; vice chmn. Leadership Palm Beach County, 1985—86, bd. dirs., 1984—89; mem. mil. acad. screening com. Congressman Tom Lewis, Palm Beach Gardens, 1986—94; bd. dirs. Sun Fest, 1982—84; mem. Internat. Coun. Air Shows, 1981—86, Alumni Assn.LPBC, 1987—; coord. religious instrn. St. Paul of the Cross, North Palm Beach, Fla., 1977—80. Mem. U. Miami Alumni Assn., Internat. Festival Assn., Am. C. of C. Execs. Republican. Roman Catholic. Avocations: reading, snow skiing, theater, tennis, aerobics. Home: 192 Hampton Cir Jupiter FL 33458-8124 E-mail: Ronnieandian@aol.com.

VAN ALLEN, WILLIAM KENT, lawyer; b. Albion, N.Y., July 30, 1914; s. Everett Kent and Georgia (Roberts) Van A.; m. Sally Schall, Nov. 11, 1944; children: William Kent, Jr., George Humphrey, Peter Cushing. AB, Hamilton Coll., 1935; LL.B., Harvard U., 1938. Bar: N.Y. 1938, D.C. 1939, N.C. 1951, U.S. Dist. Ct. (we. dist.) N.C. 1951, U.S. Dist. Ct. (mid. dist.) N.C. 1953, U.S. Ct. Appeals (4th cir.) 1951, U.S. Ct. Claims 1946, U.S. Tax Ct. 1940, FCC 1939, ICC 1940, U.S. Supreme Ct. 1946. With Hanson, Lovett & Dale, Washington, 1938-41, 46-50; ptnr. Lassiter, Moore and Van Allen and Moore and Van Allen, Charlotte, N.C., 1951-87; of counsel Moore & Van Allen, 1988—. Permanent mem. Jud. Conf. 4th Jud. Circuit. Vestryman Episc. Ch., 1957-60, 66-69; mem. Mecklenburg County Bd. Public Welfare, 1954-59, chmn. 1957-59; bd. dirs. N.C. Found. Commerce and Industry, 1965-73, Found. U. N.C. at Charlotte, 1979-89, Charlotte Symphony Orch., 1981-82, Mercy Health Svcs., 1983-88; chmn. Charlotte Area adv. coun. Am. Arbitration Assn., 1967-76; bd. dirs. United Community Svcs., 1972-77, v.p., 1972; bd. mgrs. Charlotte Country Day Sch., 1956-61, chmn., 1959-61, bd. visitors, 1978—, chmn., 1987-88; bd. advisers U. N.C.-Charlotte, 1983-84; trustee Spastics Hosp., 1951-60, Mint Mus. Art, 1976-79, Surtman Found., 1955-90, Mercy Hosp. Found., 1979-84; bd. visitors Johnson C. Smith U., 1978-89; pres. Charlotte Symphony League, 1980-81, Friends of U. N.C. at Charlotte, 1990-91. Served with USNR, 1941-45, commdg. officer destroyer escort ATO and PTO; released to inactive duty as lt. comdr. Mem. ABA, Charlotte C. of C. (bd. dirs. 1971-75, v.p. 1972-75). Mil. Order of Carabao, Holland Soc. N.Y., Charlotte Country Club, Charlotte City Club, Chevy Chase Club (Md.), Mullett Lake Country Club (Mich.), Mill Reef Club, Phi Beta Kappa, Chi Psi. Office: Moore & Van Allen 4700 NationsBank Corp Ctr Charlotte NC 28202-4003 E-mail: billvanallen@mvalaw.com.

VAN ALMEN, KAREN, art educator; b. Cleve., Oct. 13, 1940; d. Richard Earl and Arla Marie (Northam) Van Al.; m. Ken Connell 1963 (div. 1981); children: Korby Matthew, Kathren Diane, Kevin Andrew; m. Ronald Sackett, Feb. 14, 1985. BA, Baldwin-Wallace Coll., 1962; MA, Ohio State U., 1977. Cert. tchr. art edn., social studies, K-12, Mich. Art tchr. jr. high Bay Village (Ohio) City Schs., 1962-63; art tchr. H.S. Westchester County Schs., Hamilton, Ohio, 1963-64; art tchr. elem. Whitehall City Schs., Columbus, 1964-66; tchr. Pennfield City Schs., Battle Creek, Mich., 1984-95. Med. art work purchased by Mich. State U. Med. Sch., East Lansing, 1990; participant Summer Tchr. Inst. on Latino Art and Culture in U.S., at Nat. Mus. Am. Art-Smithsonian Instn., 1995; tchr. art sr. citizens. Exhibited in group shows at Traverse City (Mich.) Resort, 1987, Stouffer's Battle Creek MAEA Exhibit, 1988, Tecumseh (Mich.) Radison Resort, 1989, Downtown Gallery, Grand Rapids, 1990, Noble Schuler's Gallery, Albion, Mich., 1990, Internat. Art and Galleries, Grand Rapids, 1990, Western Mich. U. Adminstrn. Bldg., Med. Art Exhbt., Kalamazoo, 1991, MAEA Exhibit, Battle Creek, 1991, Access Vision, Battle Creek, 1992, Fife Lake (Mich.) Gallery, 1994, Kalamazoo Area Shows, 1996, 98, Pub. Tea Ceremony, 1996, 98, Kalamazoo Art Inst. Area Show, 1996-98, S.W. Mich. Watercolors Artist Assn. Show, Sturgis, 1998, others; pub. Teen Tour...Chicago's Sculptures, 1995, The Gallery, Battle Creek, Mich., 1999-2000, Art Ctr. Gallery at Commerce Point, Battle Creek, 2000-01, Art Works, Big Rapids, Mich., 2001; exhbt. med. art Bronson Hosp., Kalamazoo, Mich., 2001-2002, Med. Art on Tour Med. Hosps., 2002-. Amb. to Japan-Tchr. Exch., 1991. Recipient Outstanding Educator award W.K. Kellogg Found., Battle Creek, 1992. Mem. NEA, Nat. Art Edn. Assn., Mich. Art Edn. Assn. (coun. mem. liaison 1995-96), Mich. Edn. Assn., Pennfield Edn. Assn., S.W. Mich. Watercolor Soc. Avocations: canoeing to remote areas for photography and painting of wild life, creating art surrounding history of old towns in Mich. Home: Westlake Woods Studio 55 Hickory Nut Ln Battle Creek MI 49015-1325 Studio: Little Manatee Springs Studio 3012 N Lemon Lime Dr Wimauma FL 33598 E-mail: kvanalmen@hotmail.com.

VAN ALSTINE, RUTH LOUISE, medical language specialist, writer; b. Oneonta, N.Y., Sept. 12, 1953; d. Charles Henry and Katherine L. (Hickein) Van A.; m. Frank Vincent Rock, Sept. 19, 1970 (div. Apr. 1974); 1 child, Walter Scott; m. Richard Gobin, June 4, 2000. AS, Ctrl. Fla. C.C., Ocala, 1978. Cert. tutor Literacy Vols. Am. Med. lang. specialist Monroe Regional Med. Ctr., Ocala, 1977-88; med. sec. Miami (Fla.) Heart Inst., 1988-91; med. lang. specialist Lanier Profl. Svcs., Miami, 1991-2000; asst. mgr. dept. transp. Palo Alto (Calif.) Med. Found., 2000—. Editor Path of Light, 1996; contbr. poetry to publs. Den mother Cub Scouts Am., Ocala, 1980. Mem. Poetry Soc. Am., Poets House, Acad. Am. Poets (assoc.), Ocala Jaycettes (v.p. fundraising 1982, Jaycette of Yr. 1982), Phi Theta Kappa (hon.). Avocations: music, theater, gardening, crafts.

VAN ALSTYNE, JUDITH STURGES, English language educator, writer; b. Columbus, Ohio, June 9, 1934; d. Rexford Leland and Wilma Irene (Styan) Van A.; m. Dan C. Duckham (div. 1964); children: Kenton Leland, Jeffrey Clarke. BA, Miami U., Oxford, Ohio, 1956; MEd, Fla. Atlantic U., 1967. Sr. prof. Broward C.C., Ft. Lauderdale, Fla., 1967-88; ret., 1988. Spl. asst. for women's affairs Broward C.C., 1972-88, dir. cmty. svcs., 1973-74, dir. cultural affairs, 1974-75; spkr., cons. Malaysian Coll., 1984; ednl. travel group tour guide, 1984-88; v.p., ptnr. Downtown Travel Ctr., Ft. Lauderdale, Fla., 1993—. Author: Write It Right, 1980, Professional and Technical Writing Strategies, 5th edit., 2002; freelance writer travel articles; contbr. articles and poetry to profl. jours. Bd. dirs. Broward C.C. Found., Inc., 1973—, Broward Friends of the Libr., 1994-98, Broward Friends of Miami City Ballet, 1994-99 active Sister Cities/People to People, Ft. Lauderdale, 1988-99; docent Ft. Lauderdale Mus. Art, 1988—, docent coun., 1999-2002, docent pres., 2001—; officer, mem. Friends of Mus., Ft. Lauderdale, 1992—, Broward Pub. Libr. Found., 1998. Recipient award of achievement Soc. for Tech. Comm., 1986, award of distinction Fla. Soc. for Tech. Comm., 1986. Mem. English-Speaking Union (bd. dirs. 1984-89). Democrat. Episcopalian. Home and Office: # 265 1688 S Ocean Ln Fort Lauderdale FL 33316-3346 E-mail: ladyvanj@aol.com., judithvanalstyne@aol.com.

VAN ALSTYNE, VANCE BROWNELL, arbitration management consultant; b. Rochester, N.Y., Feb. 3, 1924; s. Guy and Jessie Van Alstyne; m. Jane Van Alstyne, Aug. 12, 1950; children: Cary B., Stacey E. BA, U. Rochester, 1948; LLB, Blackstone Coll. Law, 1964. Rsch. asst. Gilbert Assocs., Inc., N.Y.C., 1950-56; corp. sec., v.p., dir. R.C. Simpson & Staff Inc., Newark and Ridgewood, N.J., 1956-74; pres., dir. R.C. Simpson, Inc., Charlotte, N.C., 1975—. Mem.: Indsl. Rels. Rsch. Assn., Am. Arbitration Assn., Atlantic Salmon Fedn. Office: RC Simpson Inc South Trust Plaza 5950 Fairview Rd Ste 604 Charlotte NC 28210-3178 E-mail: van.fsh@att.net.

VAN ALSTYNE, W. SCOTT, JR. lawyer, educator; b. East Syracuse, N.Y., Sept. 21, 1922; s. Walter Scott and Cecil Edna (Folmsbee) Van A.; m. Margaret Reed Hudson, June 23, 1949 (div.); children: Gretchen Anne, Hunter Scott; m. Marion Graham Walker, May 3, 1980. BA, U. Buffalo, 1948; MA, U. Wis., 1950, LL.B., 1953, S.J.D, 1954. Bar: Wis. 1953. Assoc. Shea & Hoyt, Milw., 1954-56; asst. prof. law U. Nebr., 1956-58; pvt. practice Madison, Wis., 1958-72; prof. law U. Fla., 1973-90, prof. emeritus, 1990—; lectr. law U. Wis., 1958-72; lectr. Cambridge-Warsaw Trade Program Cambridge U. (Eng.), 1976. Vis. prof. law Cornell U., 1977, U. Leiden, The Netherlands, 1988, 91; spl. lectr. U. Utrecht, The Netherlands, 1991; vis. prof. Wake Forest U., 1997; spl. counsel Gov. of Wis., 1966-70; bd. dirs. non-resident divsn. State Bar Wis., 1981-96, pres., 1988-90, bd. govs. 1988-90. Prin. author: Goals and Missions of Law Schools, 1990; contbr. articles to profl. jours. Mem. Gov.'s Commn. on Edn., Wis., 1969-71; cons. Wis. Commn. on Legal Edn., 1995-96. Served with AUS, 1942-45, 61-62; col. Res., ret. Decorated Legion of Merit. Fellow: Wis. Bar Found. (life); mem.: Holland Soc. (NY), SR (NY), Netherland Club (N.Y.C.), Madison (Wis.) Club, Ft. Rensselaer (NY) Club, Phi Beta Kappa, Order of Coif, Phi Delta Phi, Omicron Delta Kappa. Republican. Presbyterian. Office: U Fla Holland Law Ctr Gainesville FL 32611

VAN ANTWERPEN, FRANKLIN STUART, federal judge; b. Passaic, N.J., Oct. 23, 1941; s. Franklin John and Dorothy (Hoedemaker) Van A.; m. Kathleen Veronica O'Brien, Sept. 12, 1970; children: Joy, Franklin W., Virginia. BS in Engring. Physics, U. Maine, 1964; JD, Temple U., 1967; postgrad., Nat. Jud. Coll., 1980. Bar: Pa. 1969, U.S. Dist. Ct. (ea. dist.) Pa. 1971, U.S. Ct. Appeals (3d cir.) 1971, U.S. Supreme Ct. 1972. Corp. counsel Hazeltine, Corp., N.Y.C., 1967-70; chief counsel Northampton County Legal Aid Soc., Easton, Pa., 1970-71; assoc. Hemstreet & Smith, 1971-73; ptnr. Hemstreet & VanAntwerpen, 1973-79; judge Ct. Common Pleas of Northampton County, Pa., 1979-87, U.S. Dist. Ct. (ea. dist.) Pa., Phila., 1987—. Appointed to U.S. Sentencing Commn. Jud. Working Group, 1992-93; appointed to U.S. Jud. Conf. Com. on Defender Svcs., 1997, chmn. subcom. on fed. defender funding, 2000-01; trial judge U.S. vs. Scarfo, 1988-89; adj. prof. Northampton County Area C.C., 1976-81; solicitor Palmer Twp., 1971-79; gen. counsel Fairview Savs. and Loan Assn., Easton, 1973-79. Contbr. articles to Cardozo Law Rev. Recipient Booster award Bus. Indsl. and Profl. Assn., 1979, George Palmer award Palmer Twp., 1980, Citizen of Yr. award, 1981, Law Enforcement Commendation medal Nat. Soc. SAR, 1990, Disting. Alumni Achievement award Newark Acad., 2001; named an Alumnus Who Has Made a Difference in the World, U. Maine, 1991. Mem. ABA (com. on jud. edn.), Fed. Bar Assn. (hon.), Fed. Cir. Bar Assn., Pa. Bar Assn., Northampton County Bar Assn., Am. Judicature Soc., Fed. Judges Assn., Pomfret Club, Nat. Lawyers Club Washington, Union League Club, Pa. Soc. Club, Sigma Pi Sigma. Office: US Dist Ct Holmes Bldg 2nd and Ferry St Easton PA 18042

VAN ANTWERPEN, REGINA LANE, underwriter, insurance company executive; b. Milw., Aug. 16, 1939; d. Joseph F. Gagliano and Sophia B. (Johannik) Wolfe; widowed; children: Thomas II, Victoria. Student, U. Wis., Milw., 1954-57. Office mgr. Gardner Bender Inc., Milw., 1972-80; mfg. rep. Rosenbloom & Co., Chgo., 1980-81; spl. agt. Northwestern Mut. Life Equities Inc., Milw., 1981-88, registered rep., 1985-88; account rep. Fin. Instn. Mktg. Co., 1988-93; investment specialist Fimco Securities Group, Inc., 1993—; pres. Anvers Ltd., 1990—, 1990—. Author: (poetry) One More Its Christmas, 1978, True Friendship, 1979, Beautiful Brown Eyes, 1990 (award 1992). Mgr. Sch. Bd. Elections, Fox Point, 1969; v.p. Suburban Rep. Women's CLub, Milw., 1968-72; vol. tchr. St. Eugene Sch., Milw., 1968-72. Mem. AAUW, Milw. Life Underwriters, Women's Life Underwriters (v.p. 1982-83), Legis. Orgn. Life Underwriters, Nat. Assn. Securities Dealers (lic.), Investment Club (sec. 1989-90, pres. 1990—). Republican. Roman Catholic. Avocations: writing, service work, gardening. Office: Fin Instn Mktg Co 3900 W Brown Deer Rd Milwaukee WI 53209-1220 E-mail: gina.vanantwerpen@fimcoinc.com.

VAN APPLEDORN, MARY JEANNE, composer, music educator, pianist; b. Holland, Mich., Oct. 2, 1927; d. John and Elizabeth (Rinck) van A. MusB with distinction, Eastman Sch. Music, 1948, MusM, 1950, PhD in Music, 1966; postgrad., MIT, 1982. Chmn. music theory and music composition Tex. Tech. Univ., Lubbock, 1950—, chmn., founder symposium of contemporary music, 1951-82, chmn. grad. studies in music, 1970-81, Paul Whitfield Horn prof., 1989—. Mem. Ann. ASCAP Std. Panel Awards, 1980—2002. Author: (novels) Keyboard Singing and Dictation Manual, 1968; composer: Suite for Carillon (1st prize World Carillon Fedn. 1980), 1980, Cacophony for Band (Va. Coll. Band Dirs. Nat. Assn. award 1981), Legend of Sankta Lucia for Band, 1982, Liquid Gold for Saxophone and Tape (Premio Ancona award 1986), 1986, Four Duos for Viola and Cello (1st prize Tex. Composers Guild), 1987, Set of Seven (N.Y.C. Ballet) , 1988, Sonatine for Clarinet and Piano, Weill Recital Hall, N.Y.C., 1988, 7th World Congress Women in Music, 1991, Concerto for Trumpet and Band, 1990, Festival a Kerkrade, Cantata: Rising Night After Night, 1990; music recorded by Vienna Modern Masters, Slovak Radio Orch. and Chorus, Bratislava, Czechoslovakia; composer: Terrestrial Music, a double concerto for violin and piano with string orch., 1997, (songs) Cycles of Moons and Tides for concert band, 1995, Rhapsody for violin and orch. recorded by Polish Radio Orch., 1997, Les hommes vides (T.S. Eliot's "The Hollow Men" in French translation by Pierre Leyris) for unaccompanied SATB choir, 1996, (Rhapsody violin, orchestra) Symphony for percussion orchestra, 2000, (songs) Opus One CD177: Cycles of Moons and Tides for Symphonic Band, 1995, Passages (Brit. Trombone Assn. award 1996), Music of Enchantment for Native Am. flute, strings and percussion, 1997, Gestures for clarinet quartet, Miniatures for Trombone Quartet, 2000, Songs without Words for 2 coloratura sopranos and piano, 2000, Meliora, fanfare for orchestra, 2000. Commd. for carillon work Skybells Crystal Cath. Carillon, 1991. Recipient Internat. Trumpet Guild Brass Trio Competition award for Trio Italiano, 1996, Rhapsody for Violin and Orch., 1996, Incantations for Oboe and Piano, 1998, Five Psalms for Trumpet, Tenor Voice and Piano, 1998, Galilean Galaxies for Flute, Bassoon and Piano, 1998, Symphony for Percussion Orch., 2000, Festive Fanfare and Postlude for Trumpets, Snare Drums and Cymbals, 2000; faculty rsch. grantee Tex. Tech. U ., 1982, MIT, 1982. Mem. ASCAP, Soc. Composers Inc., Internat. League Women Composers, Delta Kappa Gamma (internat. scholar 1959-60), Mu Phi Epsilon, Alpha Chi Omega, Kappa Kappa Psi, Tau Beta Sigma. Home: 1629 16th St Apt 216 Lubbock TX 79401-4703 Office: Tex Tech U PO Box 42033 Lubbock TX 79409-2033 E-mail: mvanappl@ttacs.ttu.edu.

VAN ARENDONK, SUSAN CAROLE, elementary school educator; b. Marshalltown, Iowa, Feb. 16, 1954; d. Ernest Jerome and Alice Marjorie (Harmon) Groff; m. Wayne Alan Van Arendonk, Aug. 14, 1994. BS, Iowa State U., 1976; MS in Edn., U. Kans., 1981; EdS, U. Iowa, 2001. Professionally recognized spl. educator Coun. for Exception Children, 1999; nat. bd. cert. tchr. exceptional needs. Resource rm. aide Pinckney Elem., Lawrence, Kans., 1976-77; tchr. spl. edn. Booth Elem. Sch., Wichita, 1977-78; tchr. resource rm. Clinton (Iowa) Cmty. Schs., 1978-80; tchr. spl. edn. Henry Sabin Elem. Sch., Clinton, 1980-83; edn. specialist U. Iowa, 1984; cons. No. Trails Area Edn. Agy., Clear Lake, Iowa, 1984-86; tchr. resource rm. Tomiyasu Elem. Sch., Las Vegas, 1986-88, 90-92, tchr. 3d grade, 1988-90, 92-94; tchr. lang. arts, spl. edn. Haysville (Kans.) Mid. Sch., 1996-97; tchr. behavior disorders Heartspring, Wichita, Kans., 1997-98; tchr. spl. edn. Gammon Elem., 1998-2000, Curtis Mid. Sch., Wichita, 2000—. Edn. specialist, student tchr. supr. U. Iowa, 1983, grad. asst. 1984; cons. Heartland Area Edn. Agy., Johnston, Iowa, 1994-96. Treas. State Rep. Campaign, Iowa, 1974, publicity chmn., 1974. Mem. Coun. Exceptional Children, Iowa State Alumni Assn. (life), U. Iowa Alumni Assn. (life), Humane Soc. Am., U. Kans. Alumni Assn. Democrat. Jewish. Home: 2359 N Parkridge Ct Wichita KS 67205-2002 Office: Curtis Mid Sch 1031 S Edgemoor Wichita KS 67218 E-mail: wvonarendonk@cox.net.

VAN ARK, JOAN, actress; d. Carroll and Dorothy Jean (Hemenway) Van A.; m. John Marshall, Feb. 1, 1966; 1 child, Vanessa Jeanne. Student, Yale Sch. Drama. Appeared at Tyrone Guthrie Theatre, Washington Arena Stage, in London, on Broadway; performances include: (stage) Barefoot in the Park, 1965, School for Wives, 1971, Rules of the Game, 1974, Cyrano de Bergerac, Ring Round the Moon, A Little Night Music, 1994, Three Tall Women, 1995; (TV series) Temperatures Rising, 1972-73, We've Got Each Other, 1977-78, Dallas, 1978-81, Knots Landing, 1979-92 (also dir. episodes Letting Go, Hints and Evasions), (voice) Santa Bogito, 1995; (TV movies) The Judge and Jake Wyler, 1972, Big Rose, 1974, Shell Game, 1975, The Last Dinosaur, 1977, Red Flag, 1981, Shakedown on the Sunset Strip, 1988, My First Love, 1989, Murder at the PTA, 1990, To Cast a Shadow, 1990, Always Remember I Love You, 1990, Grand Central Murders, 1992, Tainted Blood, 1992, Someone's Watching, 1993, When the Darkman Calls, 1994, Loyal Opposition: Terror in the White House, 1998, Intimate Portrait: Michele Lee, 1999, Tornado Warning, 2002; (TV miniseries) Testimony of Two Men, 1978, Knots Landing: Back to the Cul-de-Sac, 1997; dir., star ABC-TV Afterschool Spl.

Boys Will Be Boys, 1993; films, Held for Ransom, 2000, UP Michigan, 2001. Recipient Theatre World award, 1970-71, L.A. Drama Critics Circle award, 1973, Outstanding Actress award Soap Opera Digest, 1986, 89. Mem. AFTRA, SAG, Actors Equity Assn., San Fernando Valley Track Club. Address: care William Morris Agy Inc c/o Marc Schwartz 151 S El Camino Dr Beverly Hills CA 90212-2704*

VAN ARNAM, MARK STEPHEN, manufacturing executive; b. Erie, Pa., Oct. 27, 1949; s. George Mark and Patricia Anne (Dunne) Van Arnam; m. Lisa Osborne; children: Emerald Scout, Mark Stephen Jr. Student, Geneseo State U., 1967-68, Daytona Beach Community Coll., 1971-73. EMT, Fla. Dir. ops. Emergency Med. Svcs., Daytona Beach, Fla., 1972-81; v.p. Wheeled Coach Industries, Orlando, 1982-91; pres. and CEO Am. Emergency Vehicles, Jefferson, N.C., 1991—, Am. Emergency VEH, 1991—, INTERFLEET, 1995—; exec. v.p. Halcore Group, 1998—. Bd. dirs. Vann Data Systems, Daytona Beach; mem. risk adv. bd. Azstar Casualty Co., Scottsdale, Ariz., 1989-92. With USN, 1967-71, Vietnam. Mem. Nat. Ambulance Mfrs. Assn. (pres. 1987-90), Am. Ambulance Assn., Calif. Ambulance Assn. Methodist. Avocation: travel. Office: Am Emergency Vehicles 165 American Way Jefferson NC 28640

VANARSDALE, DIANA CORT, social worker; b. N.Y.C., Oct. 27, 1934; d. Arthur and Augusta Deutsch; m. Leonard VanArsdale, Sept. 17, 1978; children by previous marriage: Hayley, Daniel. BS, NYU, 1955; MSW, Colmbia U., 1957. Clinician Payne Whitney Clinic, N.Y. Hosp., N.Y.C., 1957-59; clinician psychiat. clinic Jewish Bd. Guardians, 1959-61; founder, pres. Bix Six Towers Nursery Sch., 1962-67; dir. intake and social svc. L.I. Consultation Ctr., Forest Hills, N.Y., 1966-84, clin. dir., coord. clin. svcs., 1984-86; supr. faculty mem. L.I. Inst. Mental Health, 1981-87; dir. Srs. Option Svc., Allendale, NJ, 1980—90. Author: Transitions: A Woman's Guide To successful Retirement, 1991. Mem. NASW, N.Y. Soc. Clin. Social Workers. Home: 47-30 61st St 18C Woodside NY 11377-5763

VAN ARSDALE, KATHY, music educator; b. Boulder, Colo., June 10, 1947; d. Eldon Ellesworth and Ruth Law O'Neal; m. Peter W. Van Arsdale, June 7, 1969; children: Sarah, Amy, Mark. B in Music Edn., U. Colo., 1969; MA, U. Denver, 1980. Pace piano cert. levels I-V. Music tchr. Howard County Md. Schs., Columbia, 1969-72; gen. music tchr. Jefferson County Colo. Schs., Arvada, 1972-76; humanities tchr. Cherry Creek County Schs., Englewood, Colo., 1993-94; choral dir. Denver Christian H.S., 1994—. Cons. Internat. Piano Tchg. Found., N.Y.C., 1984—; pres. Pacesetter Music Tchrs., Denver, 1985-86, 90-91; adj. instr. U. Colo., Denver, 1990—; v.p. Colo. State Music Tchrs. Assn., 1991-94; founder Cherry Creek Schs., 1993; dir. Metro League Choral Festival, Denver, 1998—; bd. dirs. Colo. All State Choir, Denver Metro Gov. Colo. All State Choir. Author: Music of the Asmat of New Guinea, 1982; contbr. Encyclopedia of World Cultures, 1991, Encyclopedia of World Music, 1998. Mem. State of Colo. Child Health Coun., Denver, 1980-87; lay leader Univ. Park United Meth. Ch., Denver, 1981-84; fundraiser Hospice Metro Denver, 1983-84; sec. Ctr. for Cultural Dynamics, Denver, 1986—. Mem. Am. Choral Dirs. Assn., Nat. Guild Piano Tchrs. (judge 1987—, chair 1993—), Music Educators Nat. Assn., South Suburban Music Tchrs. Assn. (pres. 1988-90, Outstanding Local Assn. award 1990), Colo. State Music Tchrs. Assn. (v.p. 1991-94), Colo. Music Educator's Assn. (bd. dirs. dist. vocal coun. rep. 2001), Pi Kappa Lambda. Republican. Avocations: travel, skiing, hiking. Home: 7321 E Long Ave Englewood CO 80112-2664 Office: Denver Christian HS 2135 S Pearl St Denver CO 80210-4431

VAN ARSDALE, MARIE DELVECHIO, artist; b. New Orleans, May 25, 1943; d. James and Mavis (Willoughby) Delvechio; m. Walton Starkes, Apr. 13, 1965; 1 child, James Walton Van Arsdale. BFA, U. N. Tex., 1991. Exhibited in group shows at Lost and Found: Nat. Open Exhbn., 1997, 5th annual Govs. Exhbn., 1997, Tex. Visual Arts Assn. Membership Exhbn., 1998, Diverse Works Art By Women, Dallas City Hall, 1999, Sixteenth Annual Nat. Juried Art Exhbn., 1999, Dallas Visual Art Ctr. Membership Exhbn., 1997, New Tex. Talent, 2000, Visions Reflected, Agora Gallery, Soho, N.Y., 2001, one-woman shows include The Right Combination, U. Arlington, 1993, Golden Acres , Dallas, 1993, Kathleen's Art Cafe, 1997, Natural Magic, Northlake C.C. Trainer Boy Scouts Am., Richardson, Tex., 1978—. Recipient Silver Beaver, Circle Ten Coun., Dallas, 1992, disting. commr. award of merit, Boy Scouts, Richardson, Tex., 1983; recipient scholarship S.W. Watercolor Soc., 1985, Cecil Wallace Fordham award, 1989. Mem.: Tex. Photographic Soc., Dallas Ctr. for Contemporary Arts, Tex. Visual Arts Assn. (signature chmn.). Home: 6 Harolds Cir Richardson TX 75081-3822

VAN ARSDALE, STEPHANIE KAY LORENZ, cardiovascular clinical specialist, nursing educator, researcher; b. Butte, Mont., June 20, 1952; d. Hubert Nelson and Pauline Anna (Tebo) Lorenz; m. Roy Burbank Van Arsdale, June 18, 1978; children: Christopher, Erica. Diploma, St. Johns McNamara, Sch. Nursing, 1975; BSN cum laude, U. Utah, 1978, MSN, 1979; EdD, U. Ark., 1993. RN, Tenn.; cert. ACLS instr., Am. Heart Assn.; cert. BLS instr.-trainer, Am. Heart Assn. Staff nurse cardiovascular surg. ICU Presbyn. Hosp. Ctr., Albuquerque, 1975-76; staff nurse surg. ICU and CCU U. Utah Med. Ctr., Salt Lake City, 1976-78; clin. specialist residency LDS Hosp., 1979; asst. prof. dept. Baccalaureate Nursing Ea. Ky. U., Richmond, 1980-84; staff nurse critical care unit Pattie A. Clay Hosp., 1981-83; med. clinician Washington Regional Med. Ctr., Fayetteville, Ark., 1985; cardiovascular clin. specialist VA Med. Ctr., 1985-93; assoc. prof. U. Memphis, 1993-96; asst. prof. U. Ark. for Med. Scis., Little Rock, 1996-98; prof. Bapt. Coll. Health Scis., Memphis, 1998—. CPR instr. in cmty., Fayetteville and Richmond, 1980-93; mem. adj. faculty div. nursing Northeastern State U., Tahlequah, Okla., 1986-93, U. Ark., Fayetteville, 1989-93; mem. adj. clin. faculty U. Ark. for Med. Scis. Coll. Nursing, Little Rock, 1988-93; charter mem., spkr. N.W. Ark. Critical Care Consortium, Area Health Edn. Ctr., Fayetteville, 1989-93; presenter in field. Contbr. articles to profl. jours. Coord., vol. Home Meals Delivery Program, Richmond, Ky., 1981-84; adminstrv. bd., Sunday sch. tchr., sec. adult forum Ctrl. United Meth. Ch., Fayetteville, 1986-87; troop leader Girl Scouts Am. NOARK Coun., Fayetteville, 1987-90; sound sys. operator Christ United Meth. Ch., 1993-96, choir mem. Recipient Nurse of Yr. award for excellence in nursing practice, Dist. 9, Ark. State Nurses Assn., 1987, Loewenberg Sch. of Nursing Uotstanding Faculty award, U. Memphis, 1995; grantee, Ctrl. U.S. Earthquake Consortium, 1993, U.S. Geologic Survey, 1994, Miss. Emergency Mgmt. Agy., 1996, Ill. Emergency Mgmt. Agy., 1998, Ind. Emergency Mgmt. Agy., 1998, USGS, 1996, 1999. Mem.: AACN (CCRN, bd. dirs., chpt. sec. program com. 1994—96, pres.-elect 1998, pres. 1998—2000), ANA (v.p. Dist. 9 1985—86, pres. 1987—88, mem. image com. 1990—93, chmn. program com. 1986—87, state 2d v.p. 1988—90, clin. nurse specialist coun. 1991—93), Nat. League for Nursing (mem. nominating com. Ky. 1984—85), Sigma Theta Tau. Methodist. Avocations: skiing, tennis, ceramics. Home: 8872 Farmoor Rd Germantown TN 38139 Office: Bapt Coll of Health Scis 1003 Monroe Ave Memphis TN 38104

VAN ARSDALEN, KEITH NORMAN, urologist; b. Plainfield, N.J., Sept. 26, 1951; s. Norman Charles and Thelma Marie Svendsen Van Arsdalen; children: Bryce, Leigh, Jill, Kyle. BS, Muhlenberg Coll., 1973; MMS, CMDNJ, 1975; MD, Med. Coll. Va., 1977. Intern, resident U.Md., Balt., 1977-79; resident Med. Coll. Va., Richmond, 1979-82; asst. prof. surgery, urology U. Pa., Phila., 1983-89, asst. prof. surgery, urology, radiology, 1989-97, prof. surgery, urology, radiology, 1997—. Dir. male fertility sect. U. Pa. Sch. Medicine Divsn. Urology, 1983—, dir. shock wave lithotripsy svcs., 1985—; attending urologist Children's Hosp. Phila., 1989—; chief urology sect. Phila. V.A. Med. Ctr., 1990—2001; expert adv. panel U.S. Pharm. Conv., Rockville, Md., 1990—95; mem. scientific bd. Nat. Kidney Found., N.Y.C., 1992—98. Asst. editor Jour. Endourology, 1987—; contbr. articles to profl. jours., chpts. to books. Recipient Paul Rodin Leberman Teaching award Urology Residents, Phila, 1993, 98, Alumni Star award Va. Commonwealth U., 1993, John Morgan award, 1998; U. Pa. NKF-AUA rsch. fellow, 1982-83. Fellow: ACS (program com. 1992); mem.: AAAS, Urodynamics Soc., Soc. Univ. Urologists, Soc. Study Male Reproduction, Soc. Study Impotence, Soc. Reproductive Surgeons, Soc. Minimally Invasive Therapy, Soc. Laparoendoscopic Surgeons, Soc. Basic Urologic Rsch., Internat. Soc. Urology, Phila. Urol. Soc. (sec.-treas. 1992—98, pres.-elect 1998—99, pres. 1999—2000), Urol. Assn. Pa., Assn. Acad. Surgery, Am. Soc. Reproductive Medicine, Am. Soc. Andrology, Am. Assn. Clin. Urologists, Am. Urol. Assn., Coll. Physicians Phila. (mid-Atlantic sect. edn. com. 1989—90, rsch. com. rep. 1990—94, local arrangements com. 1991—94, chmn. 1992—93, program com. 1996—97, rsch. com. rep. 1999—2002). Avocations: fishing, skiing, swimming, reading, house restoration. Office: Urology 1 Rhoads 3400 Spruce St Philadelphia PA 19104-4206

VAN ARSDALL, ROBERT ARMES, engineer, retired air force officer; b. Omaha, Oct. 5, 1925; s. Samuel Peter and Althea (Armes) Van A.; m. Margaret Cooper Kiersted, June 9, 1948; children— Robert Armes, Janet Althea, Susan DeBaun, Kathryn Ann. BS, U.S. Mil. Acad., 1948; postgrad., U. Colo., spring 1961; MS, George Washington U., 1968. Commd. 2d lt. USAF, 1948, advanced through grades to col., 1968; grad. Randolph AFB, Tex., 1949; assigned 5th Air Rescue Group, Westover AFB, Mass., 1949-51; student USAF Squadron Officer Sch., Maxwell AFB, Ala., 1950; pilot, ops. officer 9th Air Rescue Group, Burton-Wood, Manston and Bushy Park, Eng., 1951-55; ops. officer Hdqrs. Air Rescue Service, Orlando AFB, Fla., 1955-57; plans officer Hdqrs. Air R & D Command, Balt., also Andrews AFB, Md., 1957-60; grad. USAF jet qualification course, Randolph AFB, 1959; tng.-with-industry Air Force Inst. Tech., Martin Co., Denver, 1960-61; chief plans div. Hdqrs. Space Systems Div., L.A., 1961-63; exec. officer Office Space Systems, Office Sec. Air Force, 1963-67; assoc. Air War Coll. program, Washington, 1964-66; student Naval War Coll., 1967-68; dep. dir. Dept. Def. Manned Space Flight Support Office, Patrick AFB, Fla., 1968-69; dir. range engrng., 1969-70; dir. range ops. Air Force Eastern Test Range, 1970-72; comdr. USAF Satellite Test Ctr., Sunnyvale, Calif., 1972-73; vice comdr. USAF Satellite Control Facility, L.A., 1973-74, comdr., 1974-76; staff engr. Pan Am. World Airways, Cocoa Beach, Fla., 1976-78, project dir., 1978-79, program mgr., 1980-85, dir. internat. projects, 1985-88; program dir. Diego Garcia, 1989, ret., 1989. Decorated Air Force Commendation medal with two oak leaf clusters, Legion of Merit with oak leaf cluster. Life mem. Assn. Grads. U.S. Mil. Acad.; charter mem. Nat. Soujourners, USAF Acad. Athletic Assn. Clubs: Mason, Burtonwood Air Force (gov.), Bushy Park Air Force (gov.), Orlando Air Force (gov.), Andrews Air Force (gov.), Space Systems Division Air Force (gov.). Republican. Methodist. Home: 660 Cinnamon Ct Melbourne FL 32937-4301 E-mail: bobvan@peoplepc.com.

VANARSDALL, ROBERT LEE, JR. orthodontist, educator; b. Crewe, Va., Feb. 7, 1940; s. Robert Lee Sr. and Margie Mae (Jenkins) V.; m. Sandra E. Hoffman, Aug. 11, 1962; children: Robert Lee III, Lesley, Ashley. BA in Econs., Coll. William and Mary, 1962; DDS, Med. Coll. Va., 1970; cert. Orthodontics and Periodontics, U. Pa., 1973. Diplomate Am. Acad. Periodontology, Am. Bd. Orthodontics. Staff Children's Hosp., Phila., 1973—; prof. orthodontics, chmn. dept. orthodontics U. Pa., 1981—; prof. dentistry, chmn. Med. Coll. Pa., 1989—. K.G. prof. orthodontics U. Sydney, Australia, 2001; bd. dir. Nat. Dental Ins. Co., Denver. Editor: Internat. Jour. Adult Orthodontics and Orthognathic Surgery, 1986—. Orthodontics: Current Principles and Techniques, 2d edit., 1994, 3rd edit., 2000; editorial bd. profl. jours.; contbr. articles to profl. jours. Bd. dirs. Phila. Soc. William and Mary Alumni Assn. Lt. USNR, 1962-65. Fellow Coll. Physicians of Phila. 1978, Am. Coll. Dentistry 1980. Mem. ADA, Am. Assn. Orthodontists, Stomatological Club Phila., Angle Soc. Orthodontists, Phila. Soc. Orthodontists (pres. 1989, chmn. sci. affairs coun. 1990—), Internat. Coll. of Dentists. Roman Catholic. Avocations: antiques, architecture. Home: 208 Ashwood Rd Villanova PA 19085-1504 Office: Penn Dental Curtis Ctr 625 Walnut St Philadelphia PA 19106 Office Fax: 215-625-2430.

VAN ARSDEL, EUGENE PARR, tree pathologist, meteorologist; b. Emaus, Pa., Dec. 4, 1925; s. William Campbell and Mabel Elizabeth (Hedde) Van A.; m. Rose Price, Aug. 23, 1948 (div. Aug. 1991); children: Jonathan Eugene, Elizabeth Rose. BS in Forestry, Purdue U., 1947; MS, U. Wis., 1952, PhD, 1954. Plant pathologist Lake States Forest Expt. Sta. U. Wis., Madison, 1956-62; prin. plant pathologist, project leader No. Conifer Disease Rsch., No. Ctrl. Forest Expt. Sta. U. Minn., St. Paul, 1962-68, prof. plant pathology, 1967-68; assoc. prof. plant sci. Tex. A&M U., College Station, 1968-80; plant pathologist, forester Profl. Tree Svc., Inc., Bryan, Tex., 1981-96, Van Arsdel Tree Svc., Inc., 1996—2001; vol. U.S. Forest Svc., 1994—. Prin. plant pathologist (ret. vol.), USDA Forest Svc., Rocky Mountain Rsch. Sta.; vis. prof. Yale U., New Haven, 1965-66. Assoc. editor Ecol. Soc. Am. Jour., 1968-71; contbr. chpts. to books, articles to Am. Meteorol. Soc., Am. Soc. Foresters, Am. Phytopath. Soc., others. Organizer, mem. Barzos Valley Chorale, Bryan, Tex., 1970—97; wndower rsch. on white pine blister rust site hazard predictions and epidemiology U.S. Forest Svc. Rsch., U. Wis.; endower rsch. on phytophthora root rot Clemson U., 1996; endower professorship in forest pathology U. Wis., 1998—, Clemson U., 1996—. Grantee NSF, 1962-63, Tex. Peanut Producers Bd., 1972, USDA Forest Svc., 1973-77, Mrs. Lyndon B. Johnson, 1977-82, I.S.A. Rsch. Trust, 1986. Fellow AAAS; mem. Soc. Am. Foresters, Internat. Soc. Arboriculture, Am. Phytopath Soc. (emeritus). Achievements include development of effective treatment for wilt diseases in oaks of Texas; study of climatic.microclimatic relationship of the spread of white pine blister rust; research in long-distance transport of fungous spores. E-mail: epvan@highfiber.com.

VANARSDEL, ROSEMARY THORSTENSON, English studies educator; b. Seattle, Sept. 1, 1926; d. Odin and Helen Catherine (McGregor) Thorstenson; m. Paul P. VanArsdel Jr., July 7, 1950 (dec. Jan. 1994); children: Mary M., Andrew P. BA, U. Wash., 1947, MA, 1948; PhD, Columbia U., 1961. Grad. tchg. asst. Columbia U., N.Y.C., 1948-50; acting instr. U. Wash., Seattle, 1961-63; asst. prof. U. Puget Sound, Tacoma, 1967-69, assoc. prof., 1970-77, prof. English, 1977-87, disting. prof. emeritus, 1987—, dir. Writing Inst., 1976-86, dir. semester abroad, 1977, dir. Legal English program Sch. Law, 1973-77. Vis. prof. Gonzaga U., Pacific Luth. U., Whitman Coll., Willamette U., 1977. Author: Victorian Periodicals: A Guide to Research, Vol. I, 1978, Vol. II, 1989, George Eliot: A Centenary Tribute, 1982, Victorian Periodicals and Victorian Society, 1994, Periodicals of Queen Victoria's Empire, An Exploration, 1996, Florence Fenwick Miller: Victorian Feminist, Journalist, Educator, 2001; mem. editl. bd. Wellesley Index to Victorian Periodicals, 1824-1900, 1968-88; contbr. articles to profl. jours. Recipient Doris Bronson Morrill award Kappa Kappa Gamma, 1982, Disting. Alumnae award Broadway H.S., Seattle, 1991. Fellow Royal Soc. Lit.; mem. MLA, Oxford Bibliog. Soc., Nat. Coun. Tchrs. English (Achievement awards, dir. 1974-77), Rsch. Soc. for Victorian Periodicals (pres. 1981-83). Home: 5051 50th Ave NE Apt 48 Seattle WA 98105-2863

VANARSDEL, THOMAS PAUL, architect, engineering consultant; b. Phila., July 7, 1923; s. William Campbell and Mabel Elizabeth V.; m. Carolyn Jean Beall; children: Thomas II, Peter Roland, Carolyn Sue, Richard, Kathryn Jean (dec.). BS in Sci., Purdue U., 1943; degree in Elec. Engring., U.S. Army, 1944; JD cum laude, Bernadean U., 1983. Registered profl. engr., Ind., Ohio, Miss.; registered architect, Ohio. Chief structural engr. Fanning and Howey, Celina, Ohio, 1968-74; dir. pipeline safety divsn. Pub. Svc. Commn. State of Ind., Indpls., 1976-87; engr. Rundell-Ernstberger, Muncie, Ind., 1987-97; arch. City of Fortville, 1997; pvt. practice architect, engr. Fortville, 1997—. Patentee in field; expert witness in Mich., Ohio, Ind., 1987-99. World record holder Sr. Masters Divsn. 220# class bench press competition Mem. AAAS, AIA, Nat. Soc. Profl. Engrs., Bldg. Officials Code Adminstrs. Internat., Indpls. Scientific and Engring. Found. (chmn. of ops. com.), N.Y. Acad. Scis., Indpls. Scientech. Club, Scottish Rite Mason, Murat Shrine. Home and Office: PO Box 4 Fortville IN 46040-0004

VANASKIE, THOMAS IGNATIUS, judge; b. Shamokin, Pa., Nov. 11, 1953; s. John Anthony and Delores (Wesoloski) V.; m. Dorothy Grace Williams, Aug. 12, 1978; children: Diane, Laura, Thomas. BA magna cum laude, Lycoming Coll., 1975; JD cum laude, Dickinson U., Carlisle, Pa., 1978. Bar: Pa. 1978, U.S. Dist. (mid. dist.) Pa. 1980, U.S. Ct. Appeals (3rd cir.) 1982, U.S. Supreme Ct. 1983. Law clk. to chief judge U.S. Dist. Ct. (mid. dist.) Pa., Scranton, 1978-80; assoc. Dilworth, Paxson, Kalish & Kauffman, 1980-85, ptnr., 1986-92; prin. mem. Elliott, Vanaskie & Riley, 1992-94; chief judge U.S. Dist. Ct. (mid. dist.) Pa., Scranton. Counsel Gov. Robert P. Casey Com., Harrisburg, Pa., 1987-92; mem. Jud. Conf. Com. Info. Tech.; mem. Third Cir. Jud. Coun.; mem. automation and tech. com. U.S. Cir. Ct. 3d cir., 1998, co-chair 3d cir. task force on info. resources, 1998—; lectr. in field. Contbr. articles to profl. jours. Mem. Scranton Waste Mgmt. Com., 1989; trustee Scranton Prep. Sch., 1997—. Recipient James A. Finnegan award Finnegan Found. Mem. Judicature, Pa. Bar Assn., Fed. Judges Assn. (bd. dirs. 1998). Democrat. Avocations: golf, reading. Office: William J Nealon Fed Bldg & US Courthouse PO Box 913 235 N Washington Ave Scranton PA 18501

VAN ASSENDELFT, ONNO WILLEM, hematologist; b. Brummen, The Netherlands, Aug. 23, 1932; came to U.S. 1976; s. Frederik and Anna Maria (Veenbaas) Van A.; m. Theodora Henriette Teunissen, July 15, 1960; children: Anne C.E., Frederik H.B., Albert H.P., Diederik A.A., Catharina E.E. MD, U. Groningen, 1959, PhD, 1970. Rsch. scientist, assoc. prof. Lab. Regulatory Physiology, Groningen, 1961-76; sec., dean Groningen Med. Sch., 1973-75; supervisory med. rsch. officer Ctrs. for Disease Control and Prevention, Atlanta, 1976—. Cons. FDA, 1979—; bd. secretariat Internat. Coun. Standardization in Hematology, 1978—, chmn. secretariat, 1994—; bd., exec. com. Nat. Comm. Clin. Lab. Stds., Wayne, Pa., 1982-94, pres., 1990-92; chmn. U.S. delegation to ISO/TC 212 on clin. lab. testing and in vitro diagnostic test sys., 1995—; dir. regulated diagnostic labs. Nat. Ctr. Infectious Diseases, 1993—. Author: Spectrophotometry of Hemoglobin Derivatives, 1970; editl. bd. ECRI Healthcare Product Comparison System, Lab. Hematology; contbr. articles to profl. jours., chpts. to books. Capt. Royal Netherlands Army, 1959-61. Recipient Sec. Group award USPHS, 1986, Bronze plaque Ministry of Health, Chile, 1983, Russel J. Eilers award Nat. Com. for Clin. Lab. Stds., Wayne, 1988, Spl. award Nat. Hemophilia Found., 1992. Mem. AAAS, Am. Soc. Hematology, Internat. Soc. Lab. Hematology, N.Y. Acad. Scis. Achievements include research on hematology and clinical laboratory testing. Office: Ctrs Disease Control Prevention 1600 Clifton Rd NE Atlanta GA 30329-4018 E-mail: owv1@cdc.gov.

VANASUPA, PRABHUNDHA, retired neurological surgeon; b. Dhonburi, Thailand, Sept. 18, 1928; came to U.S., 1953; s. Lung and Rew Vanasupa; m. Verna-lee Antonia, June 17, 1960; children: Ted K., Linda S., Diane M. Grad., Chulalongkorn U., Bangkok, 1948; MD, U. Med. Scis., Bangkok, 1952. Lic. physician, Thailand, Pa., N.Y., and Mich.; diplomate Am. Bd. Neurol. Surgery. Intern Chulalongkorn Hosp. Med. Sch., Bangkok, 1952-53, attending neurosurgeon, clin. instr. neurol. surgery, 1962-64; intern Jewish Hosp. St. Louis, 1953-54, asst. resident gen. surgery, 1954-55, 56-57, Ellis Fischell State Cancer Hosp., Columbia, Mo., 1955-56; research fellow neurology and neurophysiology Washington U., St. Louis, 1957-59; asst. resident clin. neurology Barnes Hosp. Med. Ctr., 1959; asst. resident neurol. surgery SUNY Upstate Med. Ctr., Syracuse, 1959-60, sr. resident neurol. surgery, 1960-61, chief resident neurol. surgery, 1961-62; practice medicine specializing in neurol. surgery, Bay City, Mich., 1965-83, Saginaw, 1983-96. Author: A Guide Book for Thai Medical Students In Neurological Examination (Thai lang.), 1963; contbr. articles to profl. jours. Mem. ACS, Thai Med. Assn., Mich. Med. Soc., Saginaw Med. Soc., Mich. Assn. Neurol. Surgeons, Congress of Neurol. Surgeons N.Am., Am. Assn. Neurol. Surgeons, Saginaw Med. Soc., Saginaw Surg. Soc. Fax: 989-671-0045.

VANATTA, BOB, athletic administrator; b. Columbia, Mo., July 7, 1918; s. Claude W. and Viola (Toler) V.; m. Lois A. Williams; children: Robert, Thomas, Timothy. BA, Ctrl. Meth. Coll., 1942; MEd, U. Mo., 1949. Tchr., coach Boonville (Mo.) High Sch., 1942-43, Kemper Mil. Sch., Boonville, 1943-44, Springfield (Mo.) High Sch., 1944-47; tchr., dir. athletics, coach Ctrl. Meth. Coll., Fayette, Mo., 1947-50, S.W. Mo. State U., Springfield, 1950-53; coach U.S. Mil. Acad., West Point, N.Y., 1953-54; dir. athletics, coach Bardley U., Peoria, Ill., 1954-56; tchr., coach Memphis State U., 1956-62, U. Mo., Columbia, 1962-68; bank mktg. officer Empire Bank, Springfield, 1968-71; profl. basketball exec. dir. Memphis Pros, 1971-72; tchr., coach Delta State U., Cleve., 1972-73; dir. athletics Oral Roberts U., Tulsa, 1973-77; commr. Ohio Valley Athletic Conf., Nashville, 1977-80, Trans Am. Athletic Conf., Shreveport, La., 1980-83; dir. athletics La. Tech. U., Rustin, 1983-86; commr. Sunshine State Athletic Conf., Jupiter, Fla., 1986-94; dir. athletics Oral Roberts U., Tulsa, 1973-77. Assoc. dir athletics Fla. Atlantic U. Author: Coaching Pattern Play Basketball, 1959; contbr. articles to profl. jours. Chpt. mem. Nat. Football Found. Hall of Fame. Named to Ctrl. Meth. Coll. Hall of Fame, S.W. Mo. State U. Hall of Fame, Nat. Athletic Intercollegiate Assn. Hall of Fame, Greater Springfield Hall of Fame, John Q. Hammons Mo. Sports Hall of Fame, U. Memphis Hall of Fame, Nat. Assn. Collegiate Dir. of Athletics, Nat. Assn. Collegiate Dir. of Athletics Hall of Fame, 1997; recipient Lifetime Achievement award in football All-Am. Football Found., 1997, NCAA Divsn. II Commrs. award Merit, 1999. Mem. Nat. Assn. Basketball Coaches, Am. Football Coaches Assn., Nat. Assn. Collegiate Dirs. Athletics, All Am. Football Found. (Bud Dudley Outstanding Exec. award in Football, 2000, Asa Bushnell Commr. award 2001).

VAN ATTA, CHERI MARIE, equine instructor; b. Ft. Lauderdale, Fla., June 2, 1972; d. Bobby Allen and Patricia Louise (Starn) Wetherington; m. Richard Carl Van Atta, Jan. 16, 1993. Cert. in Horse Farm Mgmt., Delaware Valley Coll., Doylestown, Pa., 1990. Cert. Lic. massage therapist Nat. Certification Bd. Therapeutic Massage and Body Work, 2000; Cert. riding instr. hunt seat ARICP/N.J., Cert. riding instr. English and Western CHA/Tex., registered optometric asst. Optometric asst. Vision 21, Tallahassee, 1989-90; riding instr., 1991-95; contact lens mgr. Drs. Stephens & Orsillo, 1993-95; ophthalmic asst. Newberry Eye Clinic, Panama City, Fla., 1996-97; riding instr. Pensacola (Fla.) Riding Sch., 1997—. Riding dir. Camp Merrie-Woode, Sapphire, N.C., 1995, Camp Laurel, Readfield, Maine, 1998, 99. Recipient Grand Champion Open Working Hunter award Seminole Hunter-Jumper Assn., Tallahassee, 1987, Grand Champion Pony Pleasure award, 1987, Reserve Grand Champion Pony Hunter, 1988. Mem. Am. Optometric Assn., Am. Massage Therapy Assn., Am. Horse Shows Assn., Am. Riding Instrs. Assn., Am. Assn. for Horsemanship, Safety and Edn., Seminole Hunter-Jumper Assn. (jrs. pres. 1988). Avocations: tennis, working out. Office: 1495-B Creighton Rd Pensacola FL 32504

VANATTA, CHESTER B. retired business executive, educator; b. Bartlesville, Okla., Sept. 3, 1935; s. Benjamin Franklin and Iona Ruth (Hayes) V.; m. Patsy Lou Straub, May 29, 1958; children— Tracy Ann, Christopher B., John Scott BS in Mktg., U. Kans., Lawrence, 1959, MS in Acctg., 1962; Advanced Mgmt. Program, Harvard U., Cambridge, 1972. Mem. staff Arthur Young & Co., Kansas City, Mo., 1962-69, regional dir, Dallas, 1969-72, ptnr., 1969-85, mng. ptnr. Chgo., 1972-76, dir., 1973-85, mng. ptnr., vice chmn. ops. N.Y.C., 1976-81, mng. ptnr., vice chmn. S.W. Region Dallas, 1981-85; pres. Exec. Cons. Group, Lawrence, Kans., 1985-96; exec. in residence, Paul J. Adam Disting. lectr. U. Kans. Sch. Bus., 1985-90. Bd. dirs. Atlantis Plastics, Inc., Miami, Fla. Trustee Kans. U. Endowment Fund, 1983—; bd. dirs. Kans. Alumni Assn., 1984-91, pres., 1986-87. Mem. AICPA, Kans. Soc. CPAs (Gold Key 1962), Skyline Country Club, Forest Highlands Gulf Club. Republican. Avocations: golf, travel, auctioneering, photography. Home: 5140 E Mission Hill Dr Tucson AZ 85718-2612 Personal E-mail: chet@aboutvanatta.com.

VAN ATTA, DAVID MURRAY, lawyer; b. Berkeley, Calif., Oct. 20, 1944; s. Chester Murray and Rosalind (Eisenstein) Van A.; m. Jo Ann Masaoka; 1 child, Lauren Rachel. BA, U. Calif., Berkeley, 1966; JD, U. Calif., Hastings, 1969. Bar: Calif. 1970. Asst. gen. counsel Boise Cascade Corp., Palo Alto, Calif., 1970-73; ptnr. Miller, Starr & Regalia, San Francisco, 1973-87, Graham & James, San Francisco, 1987-93, Hanna & Van Atta, Palo Alto, 1993—. Instr. Golden Gate U., San Francisco, 1984-85; U. Calif., Berkeley, 1976-84. Author: (with Hanna) California Common Interest Developments Law and Practice, 1999. Mem. ABA, Am. Coll. Real Estate Lawyers (bd. govs.), Calif. Bar Assn. (vice chmn. exec. com. real property law sect. 1982-85, chmn. condominium and subdivsn. com. real property law sect. 1981-83), Cmty. Assn. Inst., Urban Land Inst., Anglo-Am. Real Property Inst., Rotary Club Palo Alto, Lambda Alpha Internat. Soc. Avocations: skiing, tennis, painting. Office: Hanna & Van Atta 525 University Ave Ste 705 Palo Alto CA 94301-1921

VANAUKEN, ALAN BRADLEY, management consultant; b. Rochester, N.Y., June 13, 1957; s. Richard Arnold and Roberta May (Ketchell) V. BS, Rensselaer Poly. Inst., 1979; MBA, Harvard U., 1984. Asst. product mgr. Hallmark Cards, Inc., Kansas City, Mo., 1984-86, project mgr., 1986-87, product devel. mgr., 1987-88, sr. new bus. strategist, 1988-90, bus. devel. mgr., 1990-92, mktg. mgr., food team, 1992-95, dir. brand mgmt. and mktg., 1995-98; pres. Brand Forward Inc., 1999—. Ptnr., co-founder Nadler Assocs., Troy, N.Y., 1978-79; staff cons. Arthur Andersen & Co., N.Y.C., 1979-81, sr.

cons., 1981-82; adv. coun. Keller Grad. Sch. Mgmt., Kansas City, 1988-96. Product champion (new products) The Birthday Times, 1986, The Anniversay Times, 1987, The Brand Management Checklist. Mem. adv. com. Arts Ptnrs., Kansas City, 1987-88; mem. exec. com., bd. dirs. Young Audiences, Inc., Kansas City, 1987-90; chmn. RPI Alumni Admissions com., Kansas City, 1984—, alumni admissions steering com., 1988-94, 98-99, vice-chmn. 1990-92, chmn. 1992-94, 98-99; dist. activities chmn. Boy Scouts of Am., 1995-96, coun. exec. bd. 1997—, coun. membership chmn. 1996—; mem. United Way Chmn.'s Club, 1992—. Recipient James E. West Fellowship award 1994, various awards Boy Scouts Am.; named to Top 25 (Kansas City) Up and Comers, 1997. Mem. Renesselaer Alumni Assn. (bd. dirs. 1990-99, v.p. 1994-98, Dir.'s award 1989, Alumni Key award 1994, Alumni Admissions Recognition of Excellence award 1994), Harvard Club, Lake Stockton Yacht Club, Johnson County Philosophy Club, Cellarmasters. Mem. Christian Ch. Avocations: skiing, sailing, swimming, music, reading. Home and Office: 145 Pond Rd Honeoye Falls NY 14472-9352

VANAUKER, LANA, recreational therapist, educator; b. Youngstown, Ohio, Sept. 19, 1949; d. William Marshall and Joanne Norma (Kimmel) Speece; m. Dwight Edward VanAuker, Mar. 16, 1969 (div. 1976); 1 child, Heidi. BS in Edn. cum laude, Kent (Ohio) State U., 1974; MS in Edn., Youngstown (Ohio) U., 1989. Cert. tchr., Ohio; nat. cert. activity cons. Phys. edn. instr. St. Joseph Sch., Campbell, Ohio, 1973-75; program dir. YWCA, Youngstown, 1975-85; exercise technician Youngstown State U., 1985-86, 1985-86; health educator Park Vista Retirement Ctr., Youngstown, 1986-87; sch. tchr. Salem (Ohio) City Sch., 1987-88; recreational therapist Trumbull Meml. Hosp., Warren, Ohio, 1988—. Activity cons. Mahoning/Trumbull Nursing Homes, Warren, 1990-92; adv. bd. rep. Ohio State Bur. Health Promotion Phys. Fitness, 1996—; mem. adv. bd. Ohio State Executive Physical Fitness Dept. Health, 1996; tchr. Mohican Youth Ctr., Loudonville, Ohio, 1998-99. Producer chair exercise sr. video Excercise is the Fountain of Youth, 1993; photographer, choreographer; cover photography feature Mahoning County Med. Soc. Bull., 2000; exhibited in group show Forum Health, 1999. Vol. Am. Cancer Soc., 1980—, Am. Heart Assn., 1986—, Dance for Heart, 1980-86; mem. State of Ohio Phys. Fitness Adv. Bd., 1996-97. Youngstown State U. scholar, 1986-89; recipient 1st pl. Kodak Internat. Newspaper Snapshot award, 1998-99, 1st Place Internat. Libr. Photography, 2000. Mem.: AAHPERD, U.S. Amateur Ballroom Dance Assn. (v.p. 2002), Pa. Activity Profl. Assn. (pres., spkr. 2001), Resident Activity Profl. Assn. (pres. 1994—96, 2001—02), Youngstown Camera Club (social chair 1989—90, pres. 1993—95), Kappa Delta Pi. Democrat. Presbyterian. Avocations: photography, international dance, volleyball, aerobics, travel. Home: 5764 S Turner Rd Canfield OH 44406-8737 Office: 4N Unit Forum Health 1350 E Market St Warren OH 44483-6608

VAN BAALEN, DONNA GALE, artist, retired pharmacist; b. Sterling, Colo., Jan. 29, 1930; d. Felix Thomas and Edna (Burgess) Ems; m. Chase Van Baalen, June 20, 1954 (dec. Jan., 1986); children: Patricia, Aaron, Julie. Mem. Miniature Artists Am., Miniature Art Soc. Fla., Hilliard Soc. Miniaturists, World Fedn. Miniaturists, Art Ctr. Corpus Christi, Corpus Christi Art Guild. Home: 116 N 11 PO Box 417 Port Aransas TX 78373 E-mail: dvanbd@netscape.net.

VANBEBBER, GEORGE THOMAS, federal judge; b. Troy, Kans., Oct. 21, 1931; s. Roy Vest and Anne (Wenner) V.; m. Alleen Sara Castellani. AB, U. Kans., 1953, LLB, 1955. Bar: Kans. 1955, U.S. Dist. Ct. Kans. 1955, U.S. Ct. Appeals (10th cir.) 1961. Pvt. practice, Troy, 1955-58, 1961-82; asst. U.S. atty. Topeka, Kansas City, Kans., 1958-61; county atty. Doniphan County, Troy, 1963-69; mem. Kans. House of Reps., 1973-75; chmn. Kans. Corp. Commn., Topeka, 1975-79; U.S. magistrate, 1982-89; judge U.S. Dist. Ct., Kansas City, Kans., 1989-95, chief judge, 1995-2001. Mem. ABA, Kas. Bar Assn. Episcopalian. Office: US Dist Ct 529 US Courthouse 500 State Ave Kansas City KS 66101-2403

VAN BERKEL, JACK, information technology executive; b. May 6, 1960; BSBA, San Diego State U., 1982. V.p. human resources Walker Interactive Sys., Bank of Am., Western Digital, Irvine, Calif., 1995—99; sr. v.p. human resources Netigy Corp., San Jose, 1999—2001, Gateway, Poway, 2001—. Office: Gateway 14303 Gateway Pl Poway CA 92064 Office Fax: 858-848-3402.*

VAN BLARCOM KUROWSKI, ANNE, artist, educator; b. Glen Ridge, N.J., Jan. 22, 1940; d. Gerald and Thelma Aurora (Lawless) Van Blarcom; m. Robert John Kurowski, Sept. 8, 1962; children: Robin Anne, Evan Jon, Jaime Lara. BA, Montclair State Coll., 1962, MA, 1971. Art tchr., New Brunswick, N.J., 1967-68, Matawan, 1969-71, Woodbridge (N.J.) Twp., 1987—, substitute tchr., 1989—; ind. artist Edison, N.J., 1987—. Dir. life classes Barron Arts Ctr., Woodbridge, 1983-98. Author, designer, illustrator (book) Have Fun; contbr. The Best of Portrait Painting, 1998, The Best of Oil Painting, 1998, The Best of Watercolor III, 1999. Recipient Beth Born Meml. Portrait award N.J. Ctr. Visual Arts, 1989, Gold medal Barron Arts Ctr., 1990, Degas Pastel award Pastel Soc. Am., 1994, Ida Wells and Clara Stroud award Am. Artists Profl. League; grantee Artistworks-Middlesex County Cultural and Heritage Commn., 1997, 99. Mem. N.J. Watercolor Soc. (membership chair, Henry Gasser Meml. award 1993), N.J. Ctr. Visual Arts, Garden State Watercolor Soc. (award 1998, 99), Phila. Water Color Soc. Unitarian Universalist. Avocations: country dancing, roller skating, miniatures. Home: 3929 Appleton Way Wilmington NC 28412-7305 E-mail: annevank@a0l.com.

VAN BLERKOM, DIANNA L. education educator; b. Altoona, Pa., Nov. 25, 1946; d. Simon and Rachel Adelman; m. Malcolm L. Van Blerkom, Sept. 10, 1967; 1 child, Sharon Eileen Van Blerkom Smith. BS, Pa. State U., 1968, MEd, 1981. Cert. secondary sch. English tchr., reading specialist, Pa. Instr. Pa. State U., Altoona, 1980-81, Sharon, 1982-83; English tchr. Hickory H.S., Hermitage, 1985-86; dir. Learning Ctr. Thiel Coll., Greenville, Pa., 1985-89, U. Pitts., Johnstown, 1989-98, asst. prof. edn., 1998—. Author: Orientation to College Learning, 3d edit., 2001; musician: College Study Skills, 4th edit., 2002; mem. editl. adv. bd.: Jour. Coll. Reading and Learning, 1998—. Mem. Coll. Reading and Learning Assn., Nat. Assn. Devel. Educators, Internat. Reading Assn., Pi Lambda Theta. Avocations: reading, sewing, cooking, cross-stitch. Office: U Pitts at Johnstown 148 Biddle Hall Johnstown PA 15904

VANBRODE, DERRICK BRENT, IV, trade association administrator; b. Elgin, Ill., Sept. 3, 1940; Grad., N.Y. Inst. Criminology, 1963. Sr. v.p. Am. Fraternal Programmers, Inc., North Miami, Fla., 1977—. Mgmt. cons. Am. Fedn. Police, Am. Law Enforcement Officers Assn., Nat. Assn. Chiefs of Police, Am. Police Acad. Editor: Who's Who in American Law Enforcement, 1976-93, Crime Watch mag, 1981—, Police Times/Command, 1975—. Pres. Greater Miami Assn. Licensed Beverage Owners, 1973— . Decorated Grand Cross Knights of St. Michael; comdr. Royal Knights of Justice. Mem. Greater North Port Fla. C. of C. (founder, pres.) Clubs: Miami Millionaires (founder, past pres.), Millionaires Internat. (pres. 1983—), Miami Shores Country, Racquet. Office: 3801 Biscayne Blvd Miami FL 33137-3732

VAN BROEKHOVEN, ROLLIN ADRIAN, federal judge; b. Dallas, June 3, 1940; s. Harold and Loraine (Chafer) Van B.; m. Diana Gullett, Oct. 6, 1962; children: Gretchen, Heidi. BS, Wheaton Coll., 1962; JD cum laude, Baylor U., 1968; LLM, George Washington U., 1975; DPhil, Oxford U., 1991, DLitt, 1993; DPS (hon.), Gordon Coll., 1997. Bar: Tex. 1968, U.S. Ct. Mil. Appeals 1970, U.S. Ct. Claims 1970, U.S. Supreme Ct. 1975. Commd. 2nd lt. U.S. Army, 1962, advanced through grades to maj., 1969; trial atty. Ft. Hood, Tex., 1968-70, Heidelberg, West Germany, 1970-71; gen. counsel U.S. Army Procurement Agy., Frankfurt, West Germany, 1971-74; asst. gen. counsel Dept. Army, Washington, 1975-77, resigned, 1977; dep. counsel NAVSUP, Dept. Navy, Washington, 1977-80; judge Armed Svcs. Bd. Contract Appeals, 1980—. Editor-in-chief Baylor Law Rev., 1968; contbg. author textbooks; contbr. articles to legal jours. Pres. PTA, Frankfurt, 1972-74; mem. Frankfurt Cmty. Adv. Coun., 1972-74; mem. Child Abuse Coun., Killeen, Tex., 1968-69; elder, chmn. Evang. Free Ch., Manassas, Va., 1980-84; bd. dirs. Trinity Sem., Deerfield, Ill., 1982-88; trustee Outreach, Inc., Grand Rapids, Mich., 1977-95; mem. gen. bd. Evang. Free Ch. of Am., 1982-88, mem. stds. com. Evans Coun. for Fin. Accountability, 1982—; bd. regents, bd. incorp mems Dallas Theol. Seminary, 1988—; chmn. stds. com., bd. dirs. Evang. Coun. Fin. Accountability, 1982—. Recipient Spl. Recognition award Mariano Galvez U., Guatemala, 1984; decorated in svc. Mem. ABA, FBA, Tex. Bar Assn., Contract Appeals Judges Assn. (bd. dirs.), Oxford Soc. Scholars (chmn.). Republican. Home: 8026 Whitting Dr Manassas VA 20112-4705

VAN BRUGGEN, COOSJE, artist; b. Groningen, The Netherlands, June 6, 1942; came to U.S., 1978, naturalized, 1993; f. J.A.R. Van Bruggen and A.M. Andriessen; m. Claes Oldenburg, July 22, 1977. MS in Art History, Rijks U. of Groningen, 1967; DFA (hon.), Calif. Coll. Art and Craft, 1996; DLitt (hon.), U. Teesside, Middlesbrough, Eng., 1999. Asst. curator Stedelijk Mus., Amsterdam, The Netherlands, 1967-71; prof. Acad. Fine Arts, Enschede, The Netherlands, 1971-76; sr. critic dept. sculpture Yale U., New Haven, 1996-97. Editor Catalogue Sonsbeek, 1971; mem. selection com. Documenta 7, Kassel, Germany, 1982; curator (with Dieter Koepplin) Bruce Nauman: Drawings, 1965-1986, Basel, Switzerland, 1986-88. Co-author (with Claes Oldenburg): Claes Oldenburg: Sketches and Blottings Toward the European Desk Top, 1990, Large-Scale Projects, 1994, Claes Oldenburg Coosje van Bruggen, 1999, Down Liquidlumbar Lane: Sculpture in the Park, 2001;Exhibited in group shows at No. Ctr. Contemporary Art, Sunderland, 1988, Leeds City Art Gallery, 1988, Palais des Beaux-Arts, Brussels, 1988, IVAM Ctr. Julio González, Valencia, 1988, Galleria Christian Stein, Milan, 1990, Leo Castelli Gallery, N.Y.C., 1990, Pace Gallery, 1994, Venice Biennale, 1997, Museo Correr, Venice, 1999, Museu Serralves, Porto, 2001, Metropolitan Mus. Art, N.Y.C., 2002, PaceWildenstein, 2002, Frederik Meijer Gardens and Sculpture Park, Grand Rapids, Mich., 2002, Guggenheim Mus., N.Y.C., 1993, Nat. Gallery, London, 2000; sculptor numerous public sculptures. Mem. exec. dir.'s leadership coun. Artist's Call Against U.S. Intervention, Amnesty Internat. Recipient Distinction in Sculpture, Sculpture Ctr., N.Y.C., 1984, Nathaniel S. Saltonstall award, ICA, Boston, 1996. E-mail: studio@oldenburgvanbruggen.com.

VAN BRUMMELEN, HARRO WALTER, education educator; b. The Hague, The Netherlands, Jan. 7, 1942; arrived in Can., 1953; s. Henry William and Nancy (Ryksen) Van B.; m. Wilma P. Demoor, Oct. 24, 1942; children: Glen, Timothy, Yolanda. BSc, McGill U., Montreal, Que., Can., 1963; MEd, U. Toronto, Ont., Can., 1972; EdD, U. B.C., Vancouver, 1984. Tchr. math. King City (Ont.) Secondary Sch., 1963-65, Toronto Dist. Christian H.S., Woodbridge, 1965-69; tchr., prin. Edmonton (Alta., Can.) Christian H.S., 1969-77; edn. coord. Soc. Christian Schs. B.C., Surrey, 1977-86; chair edn. dept. Trinity Western U., Langley, B.C., Can., 1986-94, dean faculty social scis. and edn. Can., 1991-97, dean undergrad. studies, 1997—. Author: Telling the Next Generation, 1986, Walking With God in the Classroom, 1988, 2d edit., 1998, Steppingstones to Curriculum, 1995; co-author: Vision With a Task, 1993; editor: Nurting Christians as Reflective Educators, 1997. Bd. mem. Inst. Christian Studies, Toronto, 1989-92; chair ch. coun. Christian Reformed Ch., Langley, B.C., Can., 1992-95; mem. adv. bd. Tchrs. Christian Fellowship, Montreal, Que., 1992-95; mem. task force on edn. Evang. Fellowship Can., Markham, Ont., 1994-98; pres., Derby Reach Regional Park Assn., 1996-99. Recipient award of recognition Min. Edn., Govt. B.C., Victoria, 1992, Award for Exceptional Contbns., Christian Schs. Internat., 1995. Mem. ASCD, Can. Soc. Study Edn., Can. History of Edn. Soc., Can. Assn. Curriculum Studies, Christian Tchrs. Assn. B.C. (hon.). Office: Trinity Western U 7600 Glover Rd Langley BC Canada V2Y 1Y1 E-mail: vanbrumm@twu.ca.

VAN BRUNT, ALBERT DANIEL, advertising agency executive; b. N.Y.C., Nov. 13, 1920; s. Ernest Robert and Helen (Rothschild) Isaacs. BS in Mktg., NYU, 1942. Dir. advt. Air France, N.Y.C., 1947-50; v.p. Buchanan Advt. Agy., 1951-57; pres. Van Brunt & Co., Advt.-Mktg., Inc., 1958-88, chmn. bd., 1989-90; pres. IMAA, Inc., 1965-70, sr. v.p., 1970-89; exec. v.p. Van Brunt & Co., Chgo., Inc., 1969-76, Van Brunt/Schaeffer, 1979-89; v.p. HBC/Van Brunt, Chgo., 1976-77; pres., chief exec. officer WDB Advt., Inc., N.Y.C., 1990—. Trustee N.Y. chpt. Leukemia Soc. Am., 1979-80; bd. dirs. Leukemia program Coll. Physicians and Surgeons, Columbia U. Served to lt. USNR, 1942-46. Mem. Am. Assn. Advt. Agys. (dir. N.Y. council 1969-74), Internat. Advt. Assn., SAR. Clubs: Wings (N.Y.C.), Lotos (N.Y.C.) (dir. 1966-72, 76-87, dir. emeritus 1987—, sec. 1972-75, treas. 1975-76). Home: 419 E 57th St New York NY 10022-3060 Office: WDB Prodns Inc 419 E 57th St New York NY 10022-3060

VAN BRUNT, ARTHUR HOFFMAN, economist, educator; b. Orange, Nj, May 27, 1942; s. Arthur Hoffman Van Brunt, Jr. and Mary Emily Van Brunt; m. Debi Sue Stec, Oct. 10, 1999; m. Priscilla Davis Scott, May 10, 1986; children: Justin, Kristina Elena. BA, Economics, Tufts Univ., Medford, MA, 1965; MBA, Wharton Sch., Univ. PA, Philadelphia, PA, 1967. Coop. vol. Peace Corps, Barquisimito, Venezuela, 1967—69; tng. ctr. dir. BASICO, Inc., San Jose, Costa Rica, 1970—75; asst. v.p. Manufacturer's Hanover Trust Co., New York, NY, 1976—80; dir., strategic planning Save the Children Fedn., Westport, 1980—84; regional manager-latin am. CARE, Inc., New York, 1984—89; assoc. prof. SUNY Delhi, Delhi, 1990—. Cons. CARE, Inc., New York, NY, 1991, Save the Children Fedn., Westport, Conn., 1992—93, Lawyers in Del. County, Delaware County, NY, 1991—. Contbr. articles to profl. jours. Treas., v.p., pres., & adv. bd. mem. Habitat for Humanity, Delaware County, NY, 1990; treas., v.p., exec. bd. United U. Professors of Delhi, Delhi, 2000. Mem.: Nat. Bus. Edn. Assn., Teachers of Acctg. at Two Yr. Colleges. Avocations: reading, bicycling, playing chess, playing tennis. Home: 752 Tanglewood Lake Road De Lancey NY 13752 Office: State Univ New York at Delhi Sanford Hall Delhi NY 13753 E-mail: vanbruap@delhi.edu.

VAN BRUNT, EDMUND EWING, physician; b. Oakland, Calif., Apr. 28, 1926; s. Adrian W. and Kathryn Anne (Shattuck) Van B.; m. Claire Monod, Feb. 28, 1949; children: Karin, Deryk, Jahn. BA in Biophysics, U. Calif., Berkeley, 1952; MD, U. Calif., San Francisco, 1959; ScD (hon.), U. Toulouse, France, 1978. Postdoctoral fellow NIH, 1961-63; rsch. assoc. U. Calif., San Francisco, 1963-67; staff physician Kaiser Permanente Med. Ctr., 1964-91; dir. div. rsch. Kaiser Permanente Med. Program, Oakland, Calif., 1979-91; assoc. dir. Kaiser Found. Rsch. Inst., 1985-91, sr. cons., 1991—; Kaiser Permanente Med. Program No. Calif. region. Adj. prof. U. Calif., San Francisco, 1975-92; chmn. instnl. rev. bd. Kaiser Permanente No. Calif. region, 1986—; pres. bd. trustees French Found. Med. Rsch. and Edn., San Francisco, 1994-98. Contbr. articles to profl. books and jours. With U.S. Army, 1944-46. Fellow ACP, Am. Coll. Med. Informatics; mem. AAAS, Calif. Med. Assn., U. Calif. Emeritus Faculty Assn. Avocations: flying, photography, swimming. E-mail: vanbrunt@pacbell.net.

VAN BRUNT, MARCIA ADELE, social worker; b. Chgo., Oct. 21, 1937; d. Dean Frederick and Faye Lila (Greim) Slauson; m. Orris E. Bartholomew; children: Suzanne, Christine, David. Student, Moline (Ill.) Pub. Hosp. Sch. Nursing, 1955—57; BA with disting. scholastic record, U. Wis., Madison, 1972, MSW (Fed. tng. grantee), 1973. Social worker divsn. cmty. svcs. Wis. Dept. Health Social Svcs., Rheinlander, 1973, regional adoption coord., 1973—79, chief adoption and permanent planning no. region, 1979—83, asst. chief direct svcs. and regulation no. region, 1983—84; adminstr., clin. social worker No. Family Svcs., Inc., 1984—. Counselor, psychotherapist, pub. spkr., cons. in field of clin. social work. Home: 5264 Forest Ln Rhinelander WI 54501-7900 Office: Northern Family Services Inc 5 W Frederick St PO Box 237 Rhinelander WI 54501-0237 E-mail: barmar@newnorth.net. *The greatest and most immediate resource a person has to use is herself. Learning how to be a resource to yourself and others is a constant process. When there are setbacks in life, allow time to react and regroup. Then find a way to change the setback into a move forward by using it as an impetus to make a positive change in life.*

VANBRUNT-KRAMER, KAREN, business administration educator; b. Milw., May 1, 1934; D. Roy Charles and Viola Marguerita (Yerges) VanBrunt; m. Allen Lloyd Weitermann (div. 1963); 1 child, Tera Lee Johnson; m. Keith Kramer (div. 1979); children: Holden Jon, Stafford James. BS, U. Wis., 1956; MA, NYU, 1976; PhD, Ohio State U., 1992. Owner Design By Karen Lee, Larchmont, N.Y., 1975-82; interior designer Maurice Valency Design, N.Y.C., 1976-79; grad. rsch. assoc. Ctr. on Edn. and Tng. for Employment, Columbus, Ohio, 1987-92; assoc. prof. bus. adminstrn. St. Joseph Coll., West Hartford, Conn., 1992-99. Lectr. and curriculum developer entrepreneurship state vocat. schs., high schs., colls., and univs. throughout U.S. and Ea. Europe, 1987-92; instr. Berkeley Sch., White Plains, N.Y., 1968-82; adj. prof. N.Y.C. C.C., 1979-83, Milw. Area Tech. Coll., 1983-85, Columbus (Ohio) State C.C., 1986-90, Capital U., Columbus, 1998, U. Wis. Milw., Mt. Mary Coll., Milw.; participant Women in Soc. Citizen Amb. Program to China, 1997, leader Women in Exec. Mgmt. Bus., 1998; mem. Inst. World Affairs, U. Wis., Milw., 1999—. Mem. Wadsworth Atheneum, Hartford, 1992—99, West Hartford Art League, 1993—99; vol. U. Conn. Health Ctr., Farmington, Little Sisters of the Poor, St. Joseph Residence, Enfield, Conn., 1989—92, Milw. Art Mus.; docent Columbus Symphony Orch., 1986—92; mem. women's guild First Cmty. Ch., Columbus, 1985—92. Mem. AAUP (membership chair 1993-97), AAUW (past social chair Wis. br.), NAFE, World Affairs Coun., Am. Vocat. Assn., Ohio Vocat. Assn., Coalition for Effective Orgns., Am. Mktg. Assn., Am. Mgmt. Assn., Nat. Edn. Ctr. for Women in Bus., World Federalist Assn. (Milw. sec./treas. 2001—), Phi Beta Kappa, Phi Kappa Phi, Phi Lambda Theta, Phi Delta Kappa, Delta Pi Epsilon, Omicron Tau Theta. Avocations: theatre, art, music, photography, ice dancing. Home: 125 N University Dr Unit 322S West Bend WI 53095-2954

VAN BULCK, HENDRIKUS EUGENIUS, accountant; b. Beek en Donk, The Netherlands, Dec. 13, 1950; came to U.S., 1972; s. Marcellus Maria and Josephina Theodora (Koelman) Van B.; m. Margaret West, Aug. 7, 1976; children: Marcel Allen, Sydney Josette. Grad., Nijenrode, The Netherlands, 1972; MBA, U. Ga., 1974, PhD in Bus. Adminstrn., 1979. CPA, S.C. Instr. U. S.C., Sumter, 1975-77; asst. prof. Clemson (S.C.) U., 1977-80; chmn. dept., assoc. prof. St. Andrew's Presbyn. Coll., Laurinburg, N.C., 1980-83; staff acct. L. Allen West, CPA, Sumter, 1983-84; ptnr. West & Van Bulck, CPAs, 1984-88, Van Bulck & Co., Sumter, 1989—. Part time instr. U. S.C., Sumter, 1983-85; cons. med. practice mgmt./bus. valuations. Contbr. articles to profl. jours. Chmn. Make-a-Wish Found., Midlands, S.C., 1983-90. Recipient Mktg. award Netherlands Ctr. of Dirs., 1972. Mem. AICPA (accredited in bus. valuation 1999), S.C. Assn. CPAs, Ga. Soc. CPAs, Physicians Viewpoint Network, Habitat for Humanity, Kiwanis (pres. Sumter chpt. 1996-97), Med. Group Mgmt. Assn., Beta Gamma Sigma. Presbyterian. Avocations: sailing, photography. Home: 234 Haynsworth PO Box 1327 Sumter SC 29151-1327 Office: Van Bulck & Co CPAs 15 Broad St Sumter SC 29150-4224

VAN BULCK, MARGARET WEST, accountant, financial planner, educator; b. Chgo., Nov. 25, 1955; d. Lee Allen and Margaret Ellen (Sauls) West; m. Hendrikus E.J.M.L. van Bulck, Aug. 7, 1976; children: Marcel Allen, Sydney Josette. BS in Mktg., U. S.C., 1978; MA in Econs., Clemson U., 1981. CPA, S.C. Econs. instr. St. Andrews Presbyn. Coll., Laurinburg, N.C., 1980-82; staff acct. L. Allen West, CPA, Sumter, S.C., 1982-84; ptnr. West & Van Bulck, CPAs, 1984-88, Van Bulck & Co., CPA's, Sumter, 1989—. Part time instr. U. S.C., Sumter, 1985-87, mem. full time faculty, 1989-92. Contbr. articles to profl. jours. Treas. Make-A-Wish Found., Sumter, 1985-87, wish granting chmn. 1987-88; edn. found. chmn. Laurinburg/Scotland County chpt. AAUW, 1981-83; treas. Friends Sumter County Library, 1986-88, Sumter Gallery of Art, 1989-91; mem. Jr. Welfare League, Sumter; Circle Bible leader, Sunday Sch. tchr., hospice vol., 1990-92; deacon First Presbyn. Ch., 1994-97; den leader pack 86 Boy Scouts of Am., 1992-95, troop com. mem., advancement chair, 1998-2001, troop com. treas., 2000-. Recipient Sirrine Found. award, Clemson U., 1978, 79; grantee U.S. Dept. Labor, 1979-80. Mem. AICPA, S.C. Assn. CPAs, Internat. Assn. Fin. Planning, Sumter Estate Planning Coun. (past treas.), Trian Club (treas. 1998—), Carolinian Club, Omicron Delta Epsilon. Presbyterian. Home: 234 Haynsworth St PO Box 1327 Sumter SC 29151-1327 Office: Van Bulck & Co CPAs PO Box 1327 Sumter SC 29151-1327 E-mail: margaretvb@sc.rr.com., margaret@vanbulckCPAs.com.

VAN BUREN, ABIGAIL (JEANNE PHILLIPS), columnist, lecturer; b. Mpls., Apr. 10, 1942; d. Morton and Pauline (Friedman) Phillips, (the founder of the Dear Abby advice column in 1956). Student, U. Colo., 1960—62. Writer Dear Abby Radio Show, CBS, 1965—71; columnist Dear Abby, 1987—. Bd. mem. Planned Parenthood of L.A., 1989—90; lifetime cons. Group for Advancement of Psychiatry, 1995—; bd. advisors Alzheimer's Assn. of L.A., 1996—; bd. mem. Rose and Jay Phillips Found., 1991—, ACLU of So. Calif. Found., 1998—; adv. bd. L.A. Internat. Women's Media Found. Courage in Journalism, 2000—; bd. advisors UCLA Med. Ctr., Ctr. for Rsch. and Tng. in Humane and Ethical Care (CHEC), 2000—. Recipient Generations of Choice award, Planned Parenthood of L.A., 1999, Minority Organ/Tissue Transplant Edn. Program (MOTTEP) Key of Life award, Howard U., Wash. D.C., 2000, Award of Appreciation, U.S. Gen. Svcs. Adminstrn. Fed. Consumer Info. Ctr., 2000, Star on Hollywood Walk of Fame for Dear Abby Radio Show, 2001, Recognition by the Office of Nat. Drug Control Policy (ONDCP), award from the White House and Substance Abuse and Mental Health Svcs. Adminstrn. for help in launching Nat. Inhalants and Poisons Awareness Week, 2001, Erasing the Stigma Leadership award, Didi Hirsch Mental Health Ctr., 2001, MOTTEP Award of Excellence, 2001, Commendation for Operation Dear Abby and OperationDearAbby.net, Dept. Navy and USMC, 2002, Appreciation for support of the military svc. mems. of the U.S. for Operation Dear Abby and OperationDearAbby.net, Space and Naval Warfare Sys. Ctr. (SPAWAR), 2002. Syndicated in the U.S., Brazil, Mex., Japan, Philippines, Fed. Republic Germany, India, Holland, Denmark, Can., Korea, Thailand, Italy, Hong Kong, Taiwan, Ireland, Saudi Arabia, Greece, France, Dominican Republic, P.R., Costa Rica, U.S. Virgin Islands, Bermuda, and Guam; published on the Internet at DearAbby.com and OperationDearAbby.net for messages to the military. Office: Universal Press Syndicate 4520 Main St Ste 700 Kansas City MO 64111-7701

VANBUREN, DENISE DORING, corporate communications executive; b. Troy, N.Y., May 15, 1961; d. James L. and Eunice A. (Myers) Doring; m. Steven Paul VanBuren, Apr. 1, 1989; children: Schuyler Paul, Troy James Doring, Brett Steven VanBuren. BA in Mass Comm. magna cum laude, St. Bonaventure U., 1983; MBA, Mount St. Mary Coll., 1997. Reporter, news anchor Sta. WGNY-AM-FM, Newburgh, N.Y., 1984; news dir., anchor NewsCtr. 6, Dutchess County, 1985-90; dir. media rels. Ctrl. Hudson Gas & Electric, Poughkeepsie, 1993—, mgr. corp. comms., 1998-99, asst. v.p. corp. comm., 1999-2000, v.p. corp. comm. and cmty. rels., 2000—. Adj. prof. Marist Coll., Poughkeepsie, N.Y. Co-author: Historic Beacon. Councilwoman City of Beacon, 1992-93, chmn. 85th anniversary celebration; pres. Beacon Hist. Soc., 1989-94; bd. dirs. Craig House Hosp., Beacon, chmn. bd.; bd. dirs. Putnam Hosp. Inc. Recipient Salute to Women in Bus. & Industry award D.C. YWCA, 1990, 97, Outstanding Chpt. Regent award N.Y. State orgn. DAR, 1999; named Vol. of Yr. award, City of Beacon, 1999. Mem.: DAR (vice regent Melzingah chpt. 1990—98, regent 1998—2001, nat. chmn. PR 1999—, chmn. pub. rels. com. NY state), Orgn. Nat. Soc. Daughters of Union Vets. of the Civil War. Republican. Roman Catholic. Avocations: genealogy, needlework. Office: CH Energy Group Inc 284 South Ave Poughkeepsie NY 12601-4838

VAN BUREN, WILLIAM BENJAMIN, III, retired pharmaceutical company executive; b. Bklyn., Mar. 25, 1922; s. William Benjamin and Dorothy Marjorie (Way) Van B.; m. Joan Cottrell Whitford, Sept. 11, 1948 (dec. June 1997); children— Susan (dec.), Patricia, William S., Richard W.; m. Norma A. Sutton, Mar. 6, 1999. BA, Washington and Lee U., 1944; LLB, Yale U., 1949. Bar: N.Y. 1950. V.p., sec. Merck & Co., Inc., 1976-86; pres. Merck & Co. Found., 1982-86. Served with USNR, 1943-46. Mem. Phi Beta Kappa. Home: 600 Furlong Dr Austin TX 78746-4126

VAN BURKLEO, BILL BEN, osteopath, emergency physician; b. Tulsa, Nov. 21, 1942; s. Walter Russell and Joan Vera (Brimm) Van B.; m. Paula Mae Brinkley, Mar. 5, 1965 (div. Feb. 1974); children: Baron, Kristy and Kelly (twins). BS, U. Tulsa, 1965; DO, Okla. State U., 1981. Diplomate Nat. Bd. Osteo. Examiners. Defensive back, quarterback, punter Can. Football League, Ottawa, Calgary, 1966-73; dir. sports and spl. events Tulsa Cable TV, 1974-78; rotating intern Corpus Christi (Tex.) Osteo. Hosp., 1981-82; family physician Antlers (Okla.) Med. Clinic, 1982-90, Colbert (Okla.) Med. Clinic, 1989-90; dir. dept. emergency Valley View Regional Hosp., Ada, Okla., 1990-97; regional med. dir. Okla., N.Mex., Ariz., Calif. Okla. Spectrum Emergency Care, Inc., 1994-97; dir. emergency dept. Carl Albert Hosp., AOA, Ada, Okla., 1997—. Mem. clin. faculty Coll. Osteo. Medicine, Okla. State U.; dir. emergency svcs. Chickasaw Indian Nation, 1997-99; v.p. med. affairs Annashne Corp., 1999—; lectr. U. Hefei MEd. Sch., China. Author newspaper column, several computer programs. Mem. Rep. Senatorial Inner Ctr., Washington, 1990-99 (medal of Freedom 1994, 99); affiliate faculty Am. Heart Assn. Named to Alltime Greats of Okla., Jim Thorpe Award Com., 1975. Fellow Assn. Emergency Physicians; mem. Am. Assn. Physician Specialists,

Am. Osteo. Assn., Am. Coll. Family Practice, Okla. Osteo. Assn., S.W. Okla. Osteo. Assn. (pres. 1990-91). Avocations: tennis, flying, sailing. Home: PO Box 181199 Corpus Christi TX 78480-1199 E-mail: vanb@brightok.net.

VANBUTSEL, MICHAEL R. real estate broker, builder and developer; b. Alma, Nebr., Dec. 7, 1952; s. Julius and Margaret (McCorkle) VanB.; m. Jené Hendley; children: Vanessa, Stephanie, Jamie. BArch, U. Nebr., 1975. Lic. real estate broker, Fla. Asst. to v.p. constrn. cen. adminstrn. U. Nebr., Lincoln, 1975-76; architect Consol. Architects Engrs., Omaha, 1976-77; archtl. project mgr. Dana, Larson, Roubal Architects, Phoenix, 1977-79; mktg. dir. Dick, Fritsche Architects, 1979-81; mktg. mgr. Lendrum Design Group, Phoenix, San Diego, 1982-85; owner Developers Mgmt. Group, Phoenix, 1985-86; contracts mgr. Turner Constrn., 1986-87; v.p. devel. The Bay Plaza Co., C.J.C. Nichols Co., St. Petersburg, Fla., 1987-96; COO, exec. v.p. Internat. Care Mgmt., Inc., 1996-98; pres. North Star Devel., 1998—; real estate mgr., v.p., designated broker Mida Group, Danka, Corp. Real Estate Svcs., 1998-99; v.p., group environ. dir. Skanska USA Bldg. Co., Tampa, Fla., 1999—. Dir. Am. Invitational Championship Amateur Kickboxing, Battle of Tampa Bay, 1998—; bd. dirs. Jenés Tropicals Garden Ctr., 1996—; pres. Spicegrower-.com., 2000—; vice-chair environ. devel. commn., St. Petersburg, 2002—; chair adv. bd. St. Petersburg campus, U. So. Fla., 1998—. Commr. Housing Commn., City of Phoenix; mem. Paradise Valley Planning Com.; bd. dirs. Am. Stage Theater, Cmty. Water Leadership Program; chair campus adv. bd. U. South Fla., St. Petersburg, 1998—, chmn. facilities and strategic planning com., 1999—2002, chmn. acad. planning com.; bd. dirs. Pinellas Econ. Devel. Coun.; vice-chair environ. adv. com. S.W. Fla. Water Mgmt. Dist., 2002—; Pinellas adv. bd. ARC; allocations com. United Way, 1998—2000; mem. Real Estate Investment Coun., St. Petersburg USA and Russia Birthday Commemoration, 2002—03; pres. Mariners for Sen. John McCain, Ariz.; surrogate spkr. for Congressman Eldon Rudd; mem. Senate roundtable Sen. Connie Mack, Fla.; Westside campaign chair Rick Baker for Mayor, 2001; mem. Ivory Club Pinellas County Rep. Party, 2001—; bd. dirs. Gran Prix St. Petersburg 2003 Found.; mem. Gulf Coast Museum of Art. Mem. Fla. Gulfcoast Comml. Assn. Realtors, Pinellas Leadership (Pinellas County FL) 2001, Leadership Tampa Bay, St. Petersburg C. of C. (chair environ. com., chair transp. com.), Valley Leadership (Phoenix)., Nat. Assn. Office and Indsl. Parks. Republican. Avocations: gourmet cooking, geo-political books, tai chi, kung fu chen tou karate. Office: Skanska USA 4950 W Kennedy Blvd Ste 600 Tampa FL 33609 Business E-Mail: michael.vanbutsel@beers.skanska.com.

VAN CAMP, BRIAN RALPH, judge; b. Halstead, Kans., Aug. 23, 1940; s. Ralph A. and Mary Margaret (Bragg) Van C.; m. Diane D. Miller, 1992; children: Megan M., Laurie E. AB, U. Calif., Berkeley, 1962, LLB, 1965. Bar: Calif. 1966. Dep. atty. gen., State Calif., 1965-67; agy. atty. Redevel. Agy., City of Sacramento, 1967-70; asst./acting sec. Bus. and Trans. Agy., State of Calif., 1970-71; commr. of corps. State of Calif., Sacramento, 1971-74; partner firm Diepenbrock, Wulff, Plant & Hannegan, 1975-77, Van Camp & Johnson, Sacramento, 1978-90; sr. ptnr. Downey, Brand, Seymour & Rohwer, 1990-97; judge Superior Ct., Sacramento County, 1997—. Lectr. Continuing Edn. Bar, Practicing Law Inst., Calif. CPA Soc. Contbr. articles to profl. jours. Mem. Rep. State Ctrl. Com. Calif., 1974-78; pres. Sacramento Area Commerce and Trade Orgn., 1986-87; mem. electoral coll. Presdl. Elector for State of Calif., 1976; mem. Calif. Health Facilities Fin. Authority, 1985-89; mem. Capital Area Devel. Authority, 1989-97, chmn., 1990-97; mem. Calif. Jud. Coun. Task Force on Quality of Justice, 1998-99; bd. dirs. Sacramento Symphony Assn., 1973-85, 92-94, Sacramento Symphony Found., 1993—, Sacramento Valley Venture Capital Forum, 1986-90, League to Save Lake Tahoe, 1988-95, Valley Vision, Inc., 1993-97; elder Fremont Presbyn. Ch., 1967—. Recipient Sumner-Mering Meml. award Sacramento U. of Calif. Alumni Assn., 1962, Thos. Jefferson award Am. Inst. Pub. Svc., 1994, Excellence in Achievement award Calif. Alumni Assn., 1997; named Outstanding Young Man of Yr., Sacramento Jaycees, 1970, Internat. Young Man of Yr., Active 20-30 Club Internat., 1973. Mem. Boalt Hall Alumni Assn. (bd. dirs. 1991-94), Lincoln Club Sacramento Valley (bd. dirs. 1975-90, pres. 1984-86), U. Calif Men's Club (pres. 1968), Sutter Club, Kanadhar Ski Club, Rotary Club Sacramento (pres. 1993-94, Paul Harris Fellow award 1995), Comstock Club (pres. 1976-77). Republican. Presbyterian. Office: 720 9th St Sacramento CA 95814-1302 E-mail: Vancamp@saccourt.com.

VAN CAMPEN, STEPHEN BERNARD, executive recruiter, consultant; b. East Stroudsburg, Pa., Oct. 1, 1941; s. Bernard Allen and Marion (Van Whye) Van C.; m. Ellen Baars, July 22, 1989; children: Brendon, Regan, Meghan, Taylor, Hannah. BS in Sci. and Pre-Veterinary Med., Pa. State U., 1959-64; postgrad. in indsl. rels., George Washington U. Grad. Sch, 1965-68; law student, U. Balt., 1966-68. With FDA, Balt., Washington, 1964-66; indsl. rels. officer Joseph E. Seagrams & Sons, Balt., N.Y.C., San Francisco, 1966-72; worldwide dir. exec. staffing RCA/Hertz Corp., N.Y.C., 1972-74; dir. internat. indsl. rels. Revlon Internat., 1974; pres./owner/cons. Gilbert & Van Campen Exec. Search, Internat. (subs.: J.B. Gilbert Assocs., Inc., Amtrade Assocs., Internat., GVC Fin. Svcs.), 1974—; owner, pres. Lillagaard Hotel Corp., Ocean Grove, N.J., 1992—; owner N.J. Profl. Meeting Planners Group, No. Shore Region Convention and Vis. Bur., Gilbert & Van Campen Internat., 1988—, Encore Svcs., Hackettstown, N.J., 1999—. Appointed to N.J. Gov.'s Commn. on Internat. Trade, 1992; Bush White House nominee to Nat. Parks Adv. Commn., Dept. Interior; chmn. internat. trade subcom. ad hoc N.J. Assembly Small Bus. Adv. Coun.; bd. dirs. N.J. SBDC, N.J. Shore Region Tourism Coun.; named to Commerce and Econ. Devel. Transition Team for Gov.-elect Christine Todd Whitman; chmn. Econ. Devel. Task Force, Warren County, N.J., 1994; participant 1st U.S.-Cuba Bus. Summit, Havanna, 1998. Rep. fundraiser; active N.J. Rep. Gov.'s Club, N.J. State Fin. Com.; appointed to Congressman Zimmer's Warren County N.J. Fed. Adv. Com., Warren County Econ. Adv. Coun., N.J. Gov.'s appointee 1988— and chmn. fed. enacted Del. Water Gap Nat. Recreation Area citizens adv. com., Gov.-elect Christie Todd Whitman Transition Team-Commerce and Econ. Devel.; elected to Warren County Rep. Com.; chmn. adv. bd. Warren Presdl. Correctional Facility; chmn. Calno Cemetery Assn.; chmn. Warner County Econ. Devel. Blue Ribbon Task Force; vice chmn. bd. trustees Warren County C.C., 1983—, chmn. found. bd.; exec. bd. Tri-County Washington coun. and George Washington coun. Boy Scouts Am.; bd. dirs. N.J. Shore Regional Tourism Coun., N.Y. SBDC, N.J. Juvenile Justice Adv. Bd.; mem. 1st N.J. Trade Del. Soviet Union; mem. commerce and econ. devel. transition team Gov.-elect Christie Whitman, N.J., 1994; chmn. N.J. assembly bus. retention Com. of Task Force for Bus. Rentention, Attraction, Expansion and Internat. Trade; chmn. N.J. Gov.'s Conf. Travel and Tourism, Atlantic City, 1994; chmn. N.J. No. Shore Region CUB Allaire Airport Conv. Ctr.; pres.-elect Warren County Econ. Partnership. Recipient Medal of Honor, Ellis Island, 1994, Disting. Citizen award Boy Scouts Am., 1992. Mem. ASTD, Am. Mgmt. Assns., Am. Coun. on Germany, U.S. C. of C., Nat. Fgn. Trade Coun., World Trade Inst., U.S.-USSR Trade and Econ. Coun., N.Y. C. of C. and Industry, N.J. C. of C., Commerce and Industry Assn. N.J., Am. C. of C.s and U.S. Bus. Couns. Abroad, Soc. Human Resource Mgmt., Nat. Assn. Corp. and Profl. Recruiters, Employment Mgmt. Assn., N.J. Hotel/Motel Assn. (bd. dirs., mem. exec. bd.), N.J. Travel Industry Assn. (bd. dirs., v.p. exec. bd.), N.Y. Pers. Mgmt. Assn., Soc. Plastics Engrs., Soc. Cosmetic Chemists, Small Bus. Adv. Coun., Ocean Grove C. of C. (vice chmn.). Republican. Methodist. Home: 37 Petersburg Rd Hackettstown NJ 07840-4903 Office: Gilbert & Van Campen Intl 420 Lexington Ave New York NY 10170-0002 also: Gilbert & Van Campen Intl Conference Ctr 99 Lake Dr Belvidere NJ 07823

VAN CASPEL, VENITA WALKER, retired financial planner; b. Sweetwater, Okla. d. Leonard Rankin and Ella Belle (Jarnagin) Walker; m. Lyttleton T. Harris IV, Dec. 26, 1987. Student, Duke, 1944-46; BA, U. Colo., 1948, postgrad., 1949-51, N.Y. Inst. Fin., 1962. CFP. Stockbroker Rauscher Pierce & Co., Houston, 1962-65, A.G. Edwards & Sons, Houston, 1965-68; founder, pres., owner Van Caspel & Co., Inc., 1968—, Van Caspel Wealth Mgmt.; owner, mgr. Van Caspel Planning Svc., Van Caspel Advt. Agy.; sr. v.p. investments Raymond James and Assocs., 1987-95; ret., 1995. Moderator PBS TV show The Money Makers and Profiles of Success, 1980; 1st women mem. Pacific Stock Exchange. Author: Money Dynamics, 1978, Money Dynamics of the 1980's, 1980, The Power of Money Dynamics, Money Dynamics for the 1990's, 1988; editor: Money Dynamics Letter. Bd. dirs. Horatio Alger Assn., Robert Schuller Ministries; trustee Northwood U.; founding mem. Com. of 200. Recipient Matrix award Theta Sigma Phi, 1969, Horatio Alger award for Disting. Americans, 1982, Disting. Woman's medal, Northwood Univ., 1988, George Norlin award U. Colo. Alumni Assn., 1987. Mem. Internat. Assn. Fin. Planners, Inst. Cert. Fin. Planners, Phi Gamma Mu, Phi Beta Kappa. Methodist. Home: 4 Saddlewood Estates Dr Houston TX 77024-6841 Office: 6524 San Felipe St Ste 102 Houston TX 77057-2611

VANCE, CARMEN LEE, retired university official; b. St. Louis, May 19, 1942; d. Ira E. and Helen Carlene (Milner) V. BS in Edn., U. Mo., 1964; MEd, Pa. State U., 1968; EdD, Ind. U., 1978. Life cert. tchr., Mo. Tchr. math. George Mason Jr.-Sr. H.S., Falls Church, Va., 1964-67; asst. dean students Pa. State U. Capitol Campus, Middletown, 1968-71; dir. housing Frostburg (Md.) State Coll., 1971-75; assoc. dir. residential life U. Conn., Storrs, 1978-81, dir. residential life, 1981-83, asst. v.p. student affairs/dir. residential life, 1983-93, assoc. v.p. student affairs, 1993-97, interim vice chancellor student affairs, 1997-98, assoc. v.p. student affairs/dir. residential life emeritus, 1998—. Cons. various coll. housing programs in U.S.; chair Columbia Bd. of Edn. Contbr. articles to profl. jours. Treas. Columbia (Conn.) Lakes Assn., 1995-96; pres. Columbia Lake Assn., 2001-03. Mem. Assn. Coll. and Univ. Housing Officers Internat. (treas. 1981-84, pres. 1987-88, monthly columnist Talking Stick 1987-88, pres. rsch. and ednl. found. 1989-90, Leadership and Svc. award 1991), Nat. Assn. Women Educators, N.E. Assn. Coll. and Univ. Housing Officers (Lifetime Svc. award 1992). Avocations: golf, boating. Home: 1 Beach Rd Columbia CT 06237-1301

VANCE, CAROL STONER, lawyer; b. Beaumont, Tex., July 26, 1933; s. Carol Stoner and Fanelle (Philp) V.; m. Carolyn Ruth Kongabel, Dec. 6, 1954; children: Lynnell, Carroll III, Karen, Harold, Cheryl. BBA, U. Tex., 1955, LLB, 1958. Bar: Tex. 1957, U.S. Dist. Ct. (so. dist.) Tex. 1960, U.S. Dist. Ct. (no. dist.) Tex. 1964, U.S. Ct. Appeals (5th cir.) 1964, U.S. Supreme Ct. 1964. Dist. atty. Harris County , Houston, 1966-79; sr. ptnr. Bracewell & Patterson, 1979—2001; ret., 2001. Adj. prof. law U. Houston Sch. Law, 1972-79; chmn. Tex. Dept. Criminal Justice, 1992-95. Recipient Outstanding Young Man of Houston award Houston Jr. C. of C., 1967. Mem. ABA (spl. com. on criminal justice standards 1975-77, coun. sect. criminal justice 1972-79), Am. Coll. Trial Lawyers, Tex. Bar Assn. (chmn. criminal law sect. 1969-70), Houston Bar Assn. (appellate judiciary com.), Houston Bar Found., Nat. Coll. Dist. Attys. (founder, past chmn.), Tex. Bar Found. (life), Tex. Assn. Def. Counsel, Tex. Young Lawyers Assn. (bd. dirs. 1963-66, Outstanding Young Lawyer of Tex. award 1970), Tex. Dist. Atty.'s Assn. (pres. 1969-70), Nat. Dist. Atty.'s Assn. (pres. 1972-73, Outstanding Dist. Atty. award 1972), Houston Young Lawyers' Assn. (pres. 1964), Nat. Coll. Dist. Attys. (chmn. bd. regents 1979-80, mem. bd. 1973—), Phi Alpha Delta. Avocations: tennis, golf. Office: Bracewell & Patterson South Tower Pennzoil Pl 711 Louisiana St Ste 2900 Houston TX 77002-2781

VANCE, CYNTHIA LYNN, psychology educator; b. Norwalk, Calif., Mar. 31, 1960; d. Dennis Keith and Donna Kay (Harryman) V. BS, U. Oreg., 1982; MS, U. Wis., Milw., 1987, PhD, 1991. Tchg. asst. U. Wis., Milw., 1983-89; computer graphics mgr. Montgomery Media, Inc., 1987-92; asst. prof. Cardinal Stritch Coll., 1992-93, Piedmont Coll., Demorest, Ga., 1993-99, assoc. prof., 1999—. Contbr. articles to profl. jours. Mem. bd. advisors North Ga. Tech. Inst., 1997-99; vol. Dunwoody (Ga.)-DeKalb Kiwanis Club, 1993—. Ga. Gov.'s Tchr. fellow, 2000-01. Mem. AAUP, APA, Assn. Women in Psychology, S.E. Psychol. Assn., Am. Psychol. Soc., Am. Assn. Higher Edn. Office: Piedmont Coll PO Box 10 Demorest GA 30535-0010

VANCE, DAVID A. information systems educator; b. Anchorage, 1948; s. Alvin V. and Mary Vance; m. Nancy Niemann; children: John, Emily, Ryan. AA, Grossmont Coll., 1976; BBA, Nat. U., 1982, MBA, 1984, postgrad., 1985; PhD, So. Ill. U., 2000. Tech. supr. USN, San Diego, 1970-74; engr., project mgr. Wavetek Data Communications, 1975-79; v.p. ops. Specialized Systems, Inc., 1979-81; prin. Sunhill R&D, 1981-84; exec. dir. Brunswick Inst. Tech., 1985; tech. staff mem. Veda, Inc., Orlando, Fla. and San Diego, 1985-88; tng. analyst Eagle Tech., Inc., Winter Park, Fla., 1988-89; prof. mgmt. Fla. So. Coll., Orlando, 1988-94; tchr., student mgmt. doctoral program So. Ill. U., Carbondale, 1994-99; asst. prof. Miss. State U., 1999—. Prin. DA Vance & Assocs., Winter Park, 1986-94; adj. prof. mgmt. Webster U., 1991-94; vis. asst. prof. So. Ill. U., 1991-94. Author, lectr. on mgmt. and tech. Rep. precinct committeeman, Orange County, Fla., 1988, del. state conv., 1988; chmn. svc. com. CSO, Inc., 1991. Recipient Achievement award ACCESS, San Diego, 1980; Worthy scholar Woodrow Wilson Found., 1966, Leadership scholar Nat. U., San Diego, 1984. Mem. Am. MENSA, Ltd., Internat. Platform Assn., Acad. of Mgmt., Info. Resources Mgmt. Assn., Computer Profls. for Social Responsibility. Avocations: outdoor sports, music. Office: Miss State U Dept Mgmt and IS PO Box 9581 Mississippi State MS 39762-9581

VANCE, ELBRIDGE PUTNAM, mathematics educator; b. Cin., Feb. 7, 1915; s. Selby Frame and Jeannie (Putnam) V.; m. Margaret Gertrude Stoffel, Aug. 5, 1939 (div. 1975); children: Susan (Mrs. Timothy Griffin), Peter Selby, Douglas Putnam, Emily (Mrs. Charles Harold Beynon III); m. Jean Haigh, Jan. 1975. Student, Haverford Coll., 1932-33; AB, Coll. Wooster, 1936; MA, U. Mich., 1937, PhD, 1939. Asst. U. Mich., 1937-39; instr. U. Nev., 1939-41, asst. prof., 1941-43; vis. lectr. Oberlin (Ohio) Coll., 1943-46, asst. prof., 1946-50, asso. prof., 1950-54, prof., 1954-83, prof. emeritus, 1983—, chmn. dept., 1948-77, acting dean Coll. Arts and Scis., 2d semester, 1965-66, 1st semester, 1970-71. Chmn. advanced placement com. Coll. Entrance Exam. Bd., 1961-65, chief reader, 1956-61; chmn. com. examiners math. Comprehensive Coll. Tests, Ednl. Testing Service, 1965-67 Author: Trigonometry, 2d edit, 1969, Unified Algebra and Trigonometry, 1955, Fundamentals of Mathematics, 1960, Modern College Algebra, 3d edit, 1973, Modern Algebra and Trigonometry, 3d edit, 1973, An Introduction to Modern Mathematics, 2d edit, 1968, Mathematics 12, 1968, Solution Manual for Mathematics 12, 1968; Book review editor: Am. Math. Monthly, 1949-57; asso. editor, 1964-67. Mem. Oberlin Sch. Bd., 1952-60, pres., 1957-60. NSF Faculty fellow, 1960-61 Mem. Math. Assn. Am., Nat. Council Tchrs. of Math., Am. Math. Soc., Phi Beta Kappa, Sigma Xi, Phi Kappa Phi. Home: 315 Yorktown Pl Apt D4 Vermilion OH 44089-2104

VANCE, ELIZABETH ANN, retired elementary school educator; b. Macon, Ga., Aug. 30, 1947; d. William Poole and Frances Irene (Cooner) V. AB in English, Mercer U., 1969, MEd in Elem. Edn., 1972, EdS in Early Childhood Edn., 1991. Cert. tchr., Ga. Tchr. 1st grade Eugenia Hamilton Sch.-Bibb County, Macon, 1969-70; tchr. Danforth Primary-Bibb County, 1970—2000; intervention program tchr. Florence Bernd Sch.-Bibb County, 2001—02. Mem. Macon Jr. Woman's Club, 1984-96, sec. 1986, 88, 92; MJW Club rep. to the Mus. of Arts Scis. Bd. Dirs.; mem. Prof. Aux. of Mus. of Arts and Scis., Macon, 1979-91; chmn., 1985-87. Mem. ASCD, Profl. Assn. Ga. Educators, Internat. Reading Assn., Macon Symphony Guild, Mus. Guild Inc. of Mus. Arts and Scis. (sec. 1993—), Macon 2000 Ptnrship, Middle Ga. Hist. Soc., Phi Delta Kappa, Delta Kappa Gamma (sec. 1992-96, pres. 1996-98), Alpha Delta Kappa (sec. 1984-86, v.p. 1992-94, pres. 1994-96). Presbyterian. Avocations: gardening, vol. mus. work. Home: 797 Boulevard Macon GA 31211-1404 Office: Danforth Primary Sch Bibb County 1301 Shurling Dr Macon GA 31211-2194

VANCE, JIMIE A. dentist; b. Lansing, Mich., Feb. 9, 1921; s. Arby Franklin and Grace Emma (Scott) V.; divorced, 1979; children: Jimie A., Fred Arthur, Anita Jean Kadzierski. BS, Concord Coll., Athens, W.Va., 1947; DMD, U. Louisville, 1954; PhD, Wheeling Coll., 1980. Dentist, Kent, Ohio, 1955-64, Miami, 1964-95, Melbourne, Fla., 1995—. Pres., dir., officer Dade County Dental Rsch. Clinic, Miami and Melbourne, 1964—; lectr., various profl. meetings, Clin. Hypnosis, Acad. Therapists and Councillors. Contbr. articles to profl. jours. Mem. bd., Kent Meth. Ch., 1955-64, Kuedall Meth. Ch. (Miami), 1964-72, Olympia Heights Meth. Ch. (Miami), 1987-85, deacon Assemblies of God Ch. (Miami, liturgist, mem. bldg. com., 1972-87, mem. choir Bowe Gardens Bapt. Ch, Melbourne, 1995—. With USN, 1941-46, PTO, USAFR, 1952-54. Named top dentist in Am. 2001, Consumers Rsch. Coun. Am. Mem. ADA, Fla. Dental Assn., Ctrl. Dist. Dental Soc., Brevard County Dental Soc., Acad. Gen. Dentistry (officer), Fla. Acad. Gen. Dentistry (officer, editor newsletter 1962-65), Southeast Fla. Acad. Gen. Dentistry (founder 1952), Dental Study Club (Melbourne), Am. Legion (post 163), Moose Lodge (Melbourne), Masons, Shriners, Delta Sigma Delta. Methodist. Republican. Avocations: travel, photography. Office: 1121 S Wickham Rd West Melbourne FL 32904

VANCE, LESLIE EDWIN, artist, photographer, video producer; b. Richland Center, Wis., Sept. 28, 1949; s. Leslie William Vance and Beata Ann (Harris) Elliott. BA, U. Wis., 1979, MA, 1981; PhD, Pa. State U., 1986. Announcer Sta. WRCO, Richland Center, Wis., 1966—68, Sta. WCOW, Sparta, 1968—69; news dir. Sta. WRJC, Mauston, 1969—72; photographer Richland Center, 1972—76; rsch. asst. Ctr. for Comm. Rsch., Madison, Wis., 1979—81; mgr. instrnl. support ctr. Pa. State U., State College, 1981—86; ednl. technologist Princeton (N.J.) Ctr. Edn., 1986—87; tech. architect Accenture (formerly Andersen Cons.), St. Charles, Ill., 1987—2001; info. tech. coord. S.W. Wis. Tech. Coll., Fennimore, 2001—02; artist, photographer, video prodr. Richland Center, Wis., 2002—. Cons. Rite Aid Corp., Camp Hill, Pa., Electronic Pub. Task Force, Motorola U., Schaumberg, Ill., U. Wis., Madison, Learning and Evaluation Assocs. Inc., State College, Pa.; exec. adv. bd., The Journal of Management Executive. Contbr. chpts. to books, articles to profl. jours.; presenter in field; prodr. (ednl. video) The Wisconsin Sesquicentennial Coach Run, Dressage Schooling for the Horse and Rider; designer (courses) Object Technology Starter Kit, 1995, Spreadsheets for Educators, 1984; designer, co-designer computer programs on instrnl. devel. Mem.: Assn. for Career and Tech. Edn. Avocations: carriage driving, equine photography. Home: PO Box 265 Richland Center WI 53581

VANCE, ROBERT PATRICK, lawyer; b. Feb. 12, 1948; s. James Robert and Lucy Juanita (McMath) V.; m. Sarah Elizabeth Savoia, June 11, 1971; 1 child, Robert Patrick, Jr. BA with honors, La. State U., 1970, JD, 1975. Bar: La. 1975, U.S. Dist. Ct. (ea. dist.) La. 1975, U.S. Dist. Ct. (mid. dist.) La. 1978, U.S. Dist. Ct. (we. dist.) La. 1979, U.S. Ct. Appeals (5th cir.) 1975, U.S. Ct. Appeals (11th cir.) 1981, U.S. Supreme Ct. 1981. Assoc. Jones, Walker, Waechter, Poitevent, Carrere & Denegre, New Orleans, 1975-80, ptnr., 1980—, exec. com., 1991-95, 97—, mng. ptnr., 1994-95,99-2000. Contbr. articles to profl. jours. Fellow Am. Coll. Bankruptcy, Nat. Bankruptcy Conf.; mem. ABA (past chair bankruptcy litigation com.), Am. Law Inst., La. State Bar Assn. (past chair consumer and bankruptcy law sect., chmn. continuing legal edn. com.), New Orleans Bar Assn., La. Bankers Assn. (chmn. bank counsel com. 1992-93), Pi Sigma Alpha, Phi Beta Kappa (Faculty Group award), Phi Kappa Phi. Democrat. Roman Catholic. Home: 1821 State St New Orleans LA 70118-6219 Office: Jones Walker Waechter Poitevent Carrere & Denegre 201 Saint Charles Ave Ste 5200 New Orleans LA 70170-5100 E-mail: pvance@joneswalker.com.

VANCE, SANDRA JOHNSON, secondary school educator; b. Parkersburg, W.Va., Oct. 23, 1945; d. Maurice Aubrey and Louise Mindwell (Price) Johnson; m. Larry Wayne Vance, June 24, 1970; children: Edward Maurice, James Allen. BS in Phys. Edn., W.Va. U., 1969; MEd, Ga. State U., 1972, EdS, 1985. Cert. mental retardation, career, phys. edn. and health, gen. sci., vocat. edn., instrnl. supervision. Tchr. interrelated resource Birney Elem. Sch., Cobb, Ga., 1969-80; tchr. MIMH Tapp Mid. Schs., 1980-85; related vocat. instruction specialist Pebblebrook H.S., 1980-83; related vocat. instrn. specialist Douglas County H.S., Douglasville, 1983—, advisor for related vocat. instrn., head dept. spl. edn., 1999—. Treas. Related Vocat. Instrn. Enrichment Camp, 1985-93; advisor related vocat. instrn. Douglas County H.S. Club, Douglas County Student Coun. for Exceptional Children, 1988-95; instr. for staff devel. on computers, 1995—; mem. spl. edn. adv. panel Ga. Dept. Edn., 1997-99. Mem. Tech. Com.; instr. ARC; com. treas. Troop 749 Boy Scouts Am., Mableton, 1993-95. Mem. NEA, ASCD, Ga. Assn. Career and Tech. Ed., Coun. for Exceptional Children, Ga. Fedn. Coun. for Exceptional Children (treas. 1989-91), Ga. Edn. Assn., Douglas County Assn. Educators, Douglas County Coun. for Exceptional Children (pres. 1986), Metro Atlanta Coun. for Exceptional Children (pres. 1987), Kappa Delta Pi. Home: 4636 Rodney Pl Austell GA 30106-1938 Office: Douglas County High Sch 8705 Campbellton St Douglasville GA 30134-2299

VANCE, STEPHANIE, consultant; b. Rochester, N.Y., Oct. 9, 1966; d. Dennis William Vance and Constance Davenport; m. Timothy William Silva, Oct. 19, 1996. BA in Polit. Sci., Chapman U., 1988; MA in Legis. Affairs, George Washington U., 1991. Telecom. policy analyst Preston & Rouvelas Meeds, Washington, 1988-92; legis. asst. Rep. Mike Kreidler, 1993-94; nat. affairs assoc. Nat. Pub. Radio, 1995-96; legis. dir. Rep. Anna Eshoo, 1996; staff dir. Rep. Blumenauer, 1997-99. Author: Government by the People: How to Communicate with Congress, 1999. German Marshall fellow, 1999. Mem. George Washington Univ. Club. Democrat. Avocations: flute performance, jewelry design, Tae Kwon Do (black belt). Office: Advanced Consulting 4000 Albemarle St NW Ste 302 Washington DC 20016 E-mail: vance@advocacyguru.com.

VANCE, TERRY, interior designer; b. Cleve., Sept. 22, 1929; d. Toby and Edith (Zulli) Gesualdo; m. Edward Francis Vance, May 26, 1951; children—Victoria, Deborah, David, Rebecca, Sarah, Barbara. B.A., Case Western Res. U., 1951. Interior designer Bonhard Interiors, Cleve., 1968-80; pres., interior designer Terry Vance, Inc., Shaker Hts., Ohio, 1980— . Mem. Am. Soc. Interior Designers. Office: 9906 Fairmount Rd Newbury OH 44065-9530

VANCE, THOMAS RAY, engineer executive; b. Charleston, W.Va., Sept. 24, 1938; s. Bethel Raymond and Madolyn Elizabeth (Fisher) V.; m. Janice Lee Jordan, Dec. 23, 1958; children: Barbara Vance, Jeffrey Ross, Deborah. BSME, W.Va. U., 1960, MSTAM, 1966, PhD, 1968. Registered profl. engr., W.Va., Ohio. Devel. engr. The Babcock and Wilcox Co., Alliance, Ohio, 1960-63; staff engr. Los Alamos (N.Mex.) Scientific Lab., 1964-66; program mgr. Tech. divsn. IBM Corp., Hopewell Junction, N.Y., 1968-92; dir. W.Va. State Farm Mus., Point Pleasant, 1994-97; prin. Vance & Assocs., 1992—. Instr. coll. engrng. W.Va. U., Morgantown, 1966-68; instr. evening divsn. Dutchess C.C., Poughkeepsie, N.Y., 1962-68; chmn. adv. com. Dept. Engrng. Ohio State U., 1988-91; mem. Stevens Inst. of Tech., Alliance for Tech. Mgmt., Hoboken, N.J.. Contbr. articles to profl. jours. Vice chmn. Point Pleasant River Mus. Com., 1993-94; mem. Point Pleasant Hist. Dist. Com., 1993-94. Scholarship NASA. Mem. W.Va. Assn. of Profl. Engrs., Nat. Assn. of Profl. Engrs. Republican. Lutheran. Achievements include patent in repair of thin film lines. Home and Office: 4 Main St Point Pleasant WV 25550

VANCE, VERNE WIDNEY, JR. retired lawyer; b. Omaha, Mar. 10, 1932; s. Verne Widney and June Caroline (Henckler) V.; m. Anita Paine, June 27, 1970; children: Lisa J. Castleton, Charles Hebard Paine, Virginia Caroline. AB, Harvard U., 1954, JD, 1957. Bar: D.C. 1957, Mass. 1964. Law clk. U.S. Dist. Judge, Mass., 1957-58; assoc. Covington & Burling, Washington, 1958-60; atty. adv. Devel. Loan Fund, 1960-61; legal counsel US AID, 1961-63; assoc. Foley, Hoag & Eliot LLP, Boston, 1963-67, ptnr., 1967-2000; ret., 2000. Lectr. law Boston U., 1964-66; corp. clk. S.S. Pierce Co., 1971-72. Pres. UN Assn. Greater Boston, 1964-66, 77-78, treas., 1974-77; mem. Mass. Adv. Council on Edn., 1969-75, chmn., 1975; mem. Dem. City Com., Newton, Mass., 1972—, Gov.'s Local Govt. Adv. Commn., 1986-90; alderman City of Newton, 1982-91; pres. Newton Bd. of Aldermen, 1988-91; mem. Newton Sch. Com., 1994-2001, chair 2000-01; trustee Judge Baker Children's Ctr., 1994—, clk., 2002—; trustee Mass. Bay C.C., 1987-98, vice chmn., 1989-91, chmn. 1991-97; pres. Mass. C.C. Assn., 1996-97. Mem. Boston Bar Assn. (bd. editors bar jour. 1986-90), Longwood Cricket Club. Home: 101 Old Orchard Rd Chestnut Hill MA 02467-1202 Office: Foley Hoag & Eliot LLP 1 Post Office Sq Boston MA 02109-2106 E-mail: vvance@fhe.com.

VANCE SIEBRASSE, KATHY ANN, legislative staff member; b. Kansas City, Kans., Oct. 28, 1954; d. Donald Herbert Vance and Barbara June (Boris) Vance-Young; m. Charles Richard Siebrasse, Mar. 8, 1980; 1 stepson, Michael (dec.); 1 son, Bradley. BS in Journalism, No. Ill. U., 1976. Reporter Des Plaines (Ill.) Suburban Times and Park Ridge Herald, 1974-75, DeKalb (Ill.) Daily Chronicle, 1976-78; stringer Rockford (Ill.) Register Star, 1978; editor The MidWeek Newspaper, DeKalb, 1978-81, owner and pub., 1982—2001; legis. aide Ill. State Senator J. Bradley Burzynski, Sycamore, 2001—. Active No. Ill. U. Found., 1992-99, mem. exec. bd., 1994-99, chair bus. and industry for No. Ill. U. campaign, 1993-94; pres. DeKalb Athletic Barb Boosters, 1995-97; chair Kishwaukee Hosp. Health Coun., Comm. Com., 1984-92, DeKalb County Partnership for a Substance Abuse Free Environment, 1990—; bd. dirs. DeKalb Edn. Found., sec., 1987-89, pres., 1989-93, active, 1987-94;

sponsor Big Bros./Big Sisters Bowl-a-Thon, food drive Salvation Army, 1990-2002; bd. mem. Am. Heart Assn., 2000—; active Relay for Life, Am. Cancer Soc., 1999-2001, Heart Walk, Am. Heart Assn., 2000—; chair capital campaign Tails Humane Soc., 2002; publicity chair Joseph F. Glidden Homestead Found.; bd. mem. fundraising campaign Suicide Prevention Svcs., Batavia, 2002. Recipient Comty. Svc. award Nat. Assn. of Advt. Pubs., 1980, Athena award Oldsmobile, DeKalb C. of C., 1990, Bus. of Yr., 1994. Mem. Soc. Profl. Journalists, Ill. Press Assn., No. Ill. Newspaper Assn., Ind. Free Papers Am. (Cmty. Svc. award 1992-93, 2nd pl. nat. gen. excellence award 1996), DeKalb County Farm Bur., DeKalb and Sycamore C. of C. (editor Sycamore newsletter 1994-96, mem. DeKalb Athena award com., bd. dirs., v.p. DeKalb 1996, chair 1997, Sam Walton Bus. Leader of Yr. De Kalb chamber 1999). Avocations: photography, reading, swimming, skiing, sailing. Office: State Sen J Bradley Burzynski 505 DeKalb Ave Sycamore IL 60178

VAN CLEAVE, KIRSTIN DEAN (KIT VAN CLEAVE), martial arts educator, writer, educator, publishing executive; b. Ft. Worth, Jan. 9, 1940; d. Henry Shibley and Lola Kathryn (Wimberly) van C. BA in Journalism, North Tex. State U., 1961; MA in English, U. Houston, 1972; DLitt in English, London Inst., 1973. Cert. self-defense instr. Tex. Commn. Law Enforcement Officer Stds. and Edn., 1992, Nat. Women's Martial Arts Fedn., 1994. Reporter Associated Gen. Contractors News Svc., Houston, 1961-62; dir. pub. rels. Diboll Advt. Agy., 1963-64; writer Goodwin, Dannenbaum, Littman and Wingfield Advt. Agy., 1964-65; reporter Houston Tribune, 1965-68; copywriter sales promotion dept. Gulf Pub. Co., Houston, 1968-70; Houston editor, then mng. editor Metrobeat, Dallas, 1970; editor publs., dir. pub. rels., press rep. Baroid divsn. NL Industries, Inc., Houston, 1973-74; presdl. speechwriter Gulf Oil Co., 1974-76; CEO Inner-View Pub. Co., 1980-92. Instr. self-def. Houston Area Women's Ctr., 1989-94, Harris County Sheriff's Dept., 1991-94; guest lectr. U. Coll., Cork, Ireland, 1994-95; chief instr. Kingwood Karate Chayon-Ryu, 1995—; instr. Houston C.C., 1996—; past mem. faculty U. Houston, Coll. of Mainland, Texas City, Tex., St. Agnes Acad., Houston; trainer Nat. Women's Martial Arts Fedn., 1994, 97, 2000. Author: They Still Do, 1973, Folklore of Texas Cultures, 1975, (poetry) Day of Love (set into a song cycle which was nominated for Pulitzer prize in Mus. Composition), 1978, Amourette, 1979, Laurels, 1980; librettist: Four Songs (composer Thomas Pasatieri), 1980; editor Inner-View mag., Houston; columnist Houston Home and Garden, Houston Guide, Scene mag., In Houston, Billboard; contbr. articles to mags. Regional coord. South and S.W. region, leader Houston chpt. Guardian Angels, 1986-90. Recipient Excellence in Journalism award Houston Exec. Adv. Coun., 1986, 1st Pl. award Harris County Med. Soc., 1986, Clean Houston Pub. Svc. award, 1986-87, Mayor's Vol. award City of Houston, 1988, Presdl. Sports award, 1994, 4th degree Black Belt Chayon-Ryu; named one of fifty Most Interesting Houstonians, City Mag., 1985, Goodwill Amb., City of Houston, 1994. Mem.: AAUP, Houston C. of C., Music Critics Assn., Am. Soc. Authors and Journalists, Internat. Asn. Bus. Communicators, Am.-Ireland Martial Arts Assn. (pres. 1992—), Pacific Assn.Women Martial Artists, Nat. Women's Martial Arts Fedn., Cha Yon Ryu Black Belt Assn. Home and Office: PO Box 66127 Houston TX 77266-6127 E-mail: kvc2@hotmail.com.

VAN CLEAVE, WILLIAM ROBERT, international relations educator; b. Kansas City, Mo., Aug. 27, 1935; s. Earl Jr. and Georgiana (Offutt) Van C.; children: William Robert II, Cynthia Kay. BA in Polit. Sci. summa cum laude, Calif. State U., Long Beach, 1962; MA in Govt. and Internat. Rels., Claremont (Calif.) Grad. Sch., 1964, PhD, 1966. Political scientist Stanford U., 1964-67; mem. faculty U. So. Calif., 1967-87, prof. internat. rels., 1974-87, dir. def. and strategic studies ctr., 1971-87; prof., dept. head, dir. Ctr. for Def. and Strategic Studies Southwest Mo. State U., 1987—; sr. rsch. fellow Hoover Instn. Stanford U., 1981-97. Chmn. Strategic Alternatives Team, 1977-90; acting chmn. Pres.'s Gen. Adv. Com. on Arms Control, 1981-82; spl. asst. Office Sec. Def., mem. Strategic Arms Limitation Talks (SALT) delegation, 1969-71; mem. B team on Nat. Intelligence Estimates, 1976; mem. exec. panel, bd. dirs. Com. Present Danger, 1980-93; dir. transition team Dept. Def., 1980-81; sr. nat. security advisor to Ronald Reagan, 1979-80; mem. nat. security affairs adv. council Republican Nat. Com., 1979-89; research council Fgn. Policy Research Inst., Inst. Fgn. Policy Analysis; co-dir. Ann. Internat. Security Summer Seminar, Fed. Republic Germany, 1981-98; trustee Am. com. Internat. Inst. Strategic Studies, 1980—; vis. prof. U.S. Army Advanced Russian Inst., Garmisch, Fed. Republic Germany, 1978-79; chmn. adv. bd. Internat. Security Coun., 1991-96; cons. in field, mem. numerous govt. adv. coms. Co-author: Strategic Options for the Early Eighties: What Can Be Done?, 1979, Tactical Nuclear Weapons, 1978, Nuclear Weapons, Policies, and the Test Ban Issue, 1987, Strategy and International Politics, 2000; author: Fortress USSR, 1986; mem. bd. editors Global Affairs. Co-chmn. Scholars for Reagan, 1984; mem. exec. coun., dir. NCAA rels. Haka Bowl, NCAA Postseason Football Bowl. With USMC, 1953-61. Recipient Freedom Found. award, 1976, Outstanding Contbn. award Air War Coll., 1979, award teaching excellence U. So. Calif., 1980, 86; named Outstanding Prof. U. So. Calif., 1977, Disting. Alumnus Claremont Colls., 1978; Woodrow Wilson fellow, 1962, NDEA fellow, 1963-65. Mem. Internat. Inst. Strategic Studies (U.S. com., bd. trustees). Home: 8226 E Panther Hollow Ln Rogersville MO 65742-8386 Office: Dept Def and Strategic Studies Southwest Mo State U Southwest Mo State U Springfield MO 65804-0095

VAN CLEEF, JABEZ LINDSAY, marketing professional; b. Cooperstown, N.Y., Nov. 19, 1948; s. John Henry and Persis (Hathaway) V. BA, Cornell U., 1970. Mgr. Willard Gallery, N.Y.C., 1976-78; mgr., prin. Writing Specialists, Atlanta, 1979-82; account exec. A.B. Isacson Assocs., N.Y.C., 1982-85; account supr. Gilbert, Whitney & Johns, Whippany, N.J., 1985-86; from mktg. mgr. to dir. mktg. Hosokawa Micron Internat., N.Y.C., Summit, 1986-93; mgr., prin. Van Cleef Assocs., Madison, 1993-97; dir. mktg. Komline-Sanderson, Peapack, 1997-99; mgr., prin. Jabez VanCleef Indusl. Mktg., Madison, 2000—. Sec. editl. bd. KONA, 1989—93; co-author: Fundamentals of Powder Technology, 1991; contbr. articles; author: (musical composition) Animalium Cantata (text with music by Elliot Z. Levine), 1996, Gospels in Verse, A Text Resource for Musicians and Composers, 1999, Gospels in Verse, Vol. II, 2002. Mem. N.Y. Acad. Scis., Harmonium Classical Choral Soc. Episcopalian. Home: 20 Pine Ave Madison NJ 07940-1119 E-mail: jabez.vancleef@verizon.net.

VAN CLEVE, ROBERT BALDWIN, cardiologist; b. St. Louis, Dec. 1, 1931; s. William T. and Catherine Cornelia (Moore) Van C.; m. Sarah Agnes Towers, July 9, 1955; children: Sarah Elizabeth Weldon, Catherine Moore Bauman, Mary Agnes Miller, Robert B. Jr. AB, Princeton U., 1954; MD, Columbia U., 1958. Diplomate Am. Bd. Internal Medicine, Am. Bd. Cardiovascular Disease. Intern, resident U. of Va. Hosp., Charlottesville, 1958-61; ward resident Barnes Hosp., St. Louis, 1962; Harvard fellow Mass. Gen. Hosp., 1965; cardiologist Riverside Clinic, Jacksonville, Fla., 1965-98, Jacksonville Cardiology Clinic, 1998—. Cardiology cons. USN Hosp., Jacksonville, 1965-72; clin. prof. medicine U. Fla., 1977-88; chief of staff Riverside Hosp., Jacksonville, 1983-84, chief cardiology, 1985-90; chmn. hosp. authority U. Hosp.; v.p. attending staff Found. Duval County Interns and Residents. Contbr. articles to profl. jours., including Circulation, Jour. Am. Med Assn., Jour. Fla. Med. Assn. Chmn. recreation adv. bd. City of Jacksonville; bd. dirs. Salvation Army, Jacksonville; elder 1st Presbyn. Ch. Lt. comdr. USN, 1962-64. Harvard Med. Sch. fellow, 1965. Fellow ACP, Am. Coll. Cardiology. Republican. Avocations: tennis, scuba diving, golf, gardening. Home: 3500 Richmond St Jacksonville FL 32205-9422 Office: 3900 University Blvd S Jacksonville FL 32216-4313 Fax: 904-82805508.

VAN CLEVE, RUTH GILL, retired lawyer, government official; b. Mpls., July 28, 1925; d. Raymond S. and Ruth (Sevon) Gill; m. Harry R. Van Cleve, Jr., May 16, 1952 (dec. Oct. 2001); children: John Gill, Elizabeth Webster, David Hamilton Livingston. Student, U. Minn., 1943; AB magna cum laude, Mt. Holyoke Coll., 1946, LL.D., 1976; LL.B., Yale, 1950. Bar: D.C. 1950, Minn. 1950. Intern Nat. Inst. Pub. Affairs, 1946-47; atty. Dept. Interior, 1950-54, asst. solicitor, 1954-64; dir. Office Territorial Affairs, 1964-69, 1977-80, dep. asst. sec., 1980-81, acting asst. sec., 1993; atty. Solicitor's Office, 1981-93, FPC, 1969-75, asst. gen. counsel, 1975-77. Author: The Office of Territorial Affairs, 1974, The Application of Federal Laws to the Territories, 1993. Recipient Fed. Woman's award, 1966, Disting. Service award Dept. Interior, 1968, Presdl. Rank award, Pres. U.S., 1989. Mem. Phi Beta Kappa. Unitarian Universalist. Home: 4400 Emory St Alexandria VA 22312-1321

VAN CLEVE, SANDRA ROSE, retired nursing educator; b. Olney, Ill., Aug. 31, 1938; d. Muriel William and Marjorie May (Houchin) Cutshall; m. Charles Chadwick, June 14, 1958 (dec. Mar. 1988); children: Rosemarie Finley, Gilbert, Kent. Diploma, Union Hosp. Sch. Nursing, 1960; BA, Ea. Ill. U., 1974; MS in Edn., So. Ill. U., 1980. RN, Ill. Med./surg. staff nurse Good Samaritan Hosp., Mt. Vernon, Ill., 1960-61; staff nurse obstetrics Meml. Hosp., Carbondale, 1961-62; surg. staff nurse St. Mary's Hosp., Centraila, 1963-64, staff nurse obstetrics Centralia, 1969-70; nursing asst. instr. Centralia Jr. Coll., 1964-65; practical nursing instr. Mt. Vernon C.C., 1965-69, Rend Lake Coll., Ina, Ill., 1970-94, ret., 1994. Textbook reviewer W. B. Saunders Co., Orlando, Fla., 1990. Pres. Centralia Bus. and Profl. Woman's Club, 1990-91; mem. Centralia Little Theater Players, Centralia Choral Soc. Recipient Outstanding Faculty award Rend Lake Coll. Found., 1986, Outstanding Community Coll. Faculty Mem. award Ill. Community Coll. Trustees Assn., 1986. Mem. ANA, AAUW (pres. 1997-98), Ill. Nurses Assn. (bd. dirs. 10th dist. 1975-84), Delta Kappa Gamma. Democrat. Methodist. Avocations: collecting crystal miniature animals, reading. Home: PO Box 309 Irvington IL 62848-0309 E-mail: srvc2000@yahoo.com.

VAN CLEVE, WILLIAM MOORE, lawyer; b. Mar. 17, 1929; s. William T Van Cleve and Catherine (Baldwin) Moore Van Cleve; m. Georgia Hess Dunbar, June 27, 1953; children: Peter Dunbar, Robert Baldwin, Sarah Van Cleve Van Doren, Emory Basford. Grad., Phillips Acad., 1946; AB in Econs., Princeton U., 1950; JD, Washington U., St. Louis, 1953, LLD (hon.), 2001. Bar: Mo. 1953. Assoc. Dunbar and Gaddy, St. Louis, 1955-58; ptnr. Bryan Cave LLP (and predecessor firm), 1958-2000, chmn., 1973-94, sr. counsel., 2001—. Bd. dirs. Emerson Electric Co. Trustee Washington U., 1983—, vice chmn. bd. trustees, 1988-93, 95-2000, chmn., 1993-95, mem. exec. com., 1985—; pres. Eliot Soc., 1982-86; chmn. Law Sch. Nat. Coun., 1986-93; commr. St. Louis Sci. Ctr., 1993-2000, bd. trustees, 2001—; bd. dirs., Parents As Tchrs. Nat. Ctr., 1991—, pres., 1997-2000. Mem. ABA, Bar Assn. Met. St. Louis, Mound City Bar Assn., St. Louis County Bar Assn., Order of Coif (hon.). Clubs: Princeton (pres. 1974-75), Noonday (pres. 1985), St. Louis Country, Bogey (pres. 1990-91), Round Table (St. Louis). Democrat. Episcopalian. Home: 8 Dromara Rd Saint Louis MO 63124-1816 Office: Bryan Cave LLP 211 N Broadway Fl 36 Saint Louis MO 63102-2750 E-mail: wmvancleve@bryancave.com.

VANCLIEF, LYLE, federal official; b. Prince Edward County, Can. m. Sharon Hall; children: Kurt, Vanessa. Student, Belleville Coll. Inst.; BS in Agr., U. Guelph, 1966. Mem. family-owned bus. Willowlee Farms Ltd., Prince Edward County; mem. parliament House of Commons, Prince Edward-Hastings, 1988-97, min. agrl. and agri-food, 1997—. Parliamentary sec. to Minister of Agr. and Agri-food, 1993; mem. standing com. on Agr.; co-critic for agr., assoc. critic for pub. works, House of Commons, 1988-93; mem. Ont. Task Force Health and Safety in Agr., 1983-85; mem., chmn. several coms. for Minister of Agr.; speaker in field of agrl. econs. and politics. Past twp. councillor, chmn. planning bd. Prince Edward Hastings; mem. bd. edn. Prince Edward County, chmn. bd. dirs., chmn. salary negotiating com.; active United Ch., past chmn. bd. dirs. Rednersville Pastoral Charge. Mem. Ont. Inst. Agrologists, Agrl. Inst. of Can. Office: House of Commons 207 Confederation Bldg Ottawa ON Canada K1A 0A6*

VANCO, JOHN L. art museum director; b. Erie, Pa., Aug. 21, 1945; s. John Jr. and Alice (Crozier) V.; m. Kathleen Merski, 1971; children: John H., Jesse L. BA, Allegheny Coll., 1967. Dir. Erie (Pa.) Art Mus., 1968—. Mem. adv. panels Pa. Coun. on the Arts, Harrisburg, 1974—, Mid Atlantic Arts Found., Balt., 1992, 2002, Nat. Endowment for Arts, 2000; curator Contemporary Music Series, 1982—, Erie Art Mus. Blues and Jazz Festival, 1992—. Photographer miscellaneous exhbns.; curator miscellaneous exhbns. including A Peculiar Vision: The Work of George Ohr, The Mad Potter of Biloxi, From Mickey to the Grinch: Art of the Animated Film, Poems in Clay: Arthur Osborne's Plastic Sketches for the Low Art Tile Works, Teco: Art Pottery of the Prairie Sch., In Harmony with the Earth; author: A Roycroft Desktop: Musings on Elbert Hubbard and the Roycroft Shops, 1994, Loud & Clear: Resonator Guitars and the Dopyera Brothers' Legacy to American Music, 1998. Chief adminstrv. officer Discovery Square, Erie, 1991-92. Office: Erie Art Mus 411 State St Erie PA 16501-1106

VAN COTT, HAROLD PORTER, human factors professional; b. Schenectady, Nov. 16, 1925; s. Harrison Horton and Edith (Porter) Van C.; m. Madeleine P. Bouvier, Oct. 8, 1953; children: Laurent, Jeanne Marie, Anne. BA in Psychology, U. Rochester, 1948; MA in Psychology, U. N.C., 1952, PhD in Psychology, 1954. Dir. rsch. Am. Insts. Rsch., Washington, 1964-69; mng. editor APA, 1969-75; div. chief Nat. Bur. Stds., Rockville, Md., 1975-80; chief scientist Biotech. Inc., Arlington, Va., 1980-81; v.p. Essex Corp., Alexandria, 1982-85; prin. staff officer NRC, Washington, 1985-92; cons. Van Cott Assocs., Bethesda, Md., 1992—. Cons. Idaho Nat. Engring. Lab., Idaho Falls, 1992—, Planning Rsch. Corp., Reston, Va., 1992—, NRC, Washington, 1992—, Interscience Am., Leesburg, Va., 1993—, Comcast Cellular, Waynesboro, Pa., 1994—, Nat. Rsch. Coun., Washington, 1994—, U. Tex. Med. Ctr., Dallas, 1997—. Editor: Human Engineering Guide to Equipment Design, 1972; assoc. editor Jour. Human Factors Soc. With U.S. Army, 1945-46. Fellow AAAS, APA (pres. div. 21 1983-84), Human Factors Soc., Washington Acad. Sci. Presbyterian. Home and Office: Van Cott Assocs 8300 Still Spring Ct Bethesda MD 20817-2728 E-mail: vancottdoc@aol.com.

VAN CURA, JOYCE BENNETT, librarian; b. Madison, Wis., Mar. 25, 1944; d. Ralph Eugene and Florence Marie (Cramer) Bennett; m. E. Jay Van Cura, July 5, 1986. BA in Liberal Arts (scholar), Bradley U., 1966; MLS, U. Ill., 1971. Libr. asst. Rsch. Libr. Caterpillar Tractor Co., Peoria, Ill., 1966-67; ref. libr., instr. libr. tech. Ill. Ctrl. Coll., East Peoria, 1967-73; asst. prof. Sangamon State U. (U. Ill.-Springfield), Springfield, 1973-80, assoc. prof., 1980-86; head libr. ref. and info. svcs. dept. Ill. Inst. Tech., 1987-90; dir. Learning Resources Ctr. Morton Coll., 1990—. Reviewer Libr. Jour., Am. Ref. Books Ann.; convenor Coun. II, Ill. Clearinghouse for Acad. Libr. Instrn., 1978; presentor 7th Ann. Conf. Acad. Libr. Instrn., 1977, Nat. Women's Studies Assn., 1983, others; participant Gt. Lakes Women's Studies Summer Inst., 1981, Nat. Inst. Leadership Devel. seminar, 1995. Contbr. articles to profl. jours. Pres. Springfield chpt. NOW, 1978—79; invited Susan B. Anthony luncheon, 1978, 1979; mem. adv. bd. Suburban Libr. Sys., 1992—94, Nat. Commn. Learning Resources; v.p. membership Riverside chpt. Lyric Opera Chgo., 1994—96, 1999—; active Riverside Arts Ctr.; Dem. precinct Committeewoman, 1982—85; vice-moderator Fourth Presbyn. Women, 1989—90; elder Riverside (Ill.) Presbyn. Ch., 1992—. mem. session, 1993—96, 2000—, mem. adminstrn. com., 1993—, chmn. adminstrn. com., 1993—96, 1999, 2000—, mem. endowment com., 1996—98; bd. dirs. Berwyn-Cicero Coun. on Aging. Ill. state scholar, 1962-66; recipient Citizenship award Am. Legion, 1962, Cert. of Recognition Ill. Bicentennial Commn., 1974. Mem.: AAUW (chmn. standing com. on women Springfield br., com. on women Ill. state divsn., bd. dirs. Riverside br. 1992—94, 1997—99), ALA, Ill. Libr. Assn. (presenter 1984), Nat. Assn. Women in C.C., Springfield Art Assn., No. Ill. Learning Resources Coop. (del. 1990—, steering com. West Suburban postsecondary consortium 1996—), Nat. Women's Studies Assn. (presenter 1983, 1984, 1995), Women in Mgmt., Am. Mgmt. Assn., No. Ill. Learning Resources Consortium Bd., Spl. Librs. Assn., Ill. Assn. Coll. and Rsch. Librs. (bibliog. instrn. com.), Libr. Info. and Tech. Assn., Libr. Adminstr. and Mgmt. Assn. (ref. and adult svcs. divsn.), Assn. Coll. and Rsch. Librs., Am. Opera Soc. of Chgo., Nat. Trust Hist. Preservation, Beta Phi Mu. Home: 181 Scottswood Rd Riverside IL 60546-2221 Office: Morton Coll Learning Resources Ctr 1151 S Wood St Chicago IL 60612-4329

VANCURA, STEPHEN JOSEPH, radiologist; b. Norton, Kans., June 26, 1951; s. Cyril William J. and Clara Mae (Ruthstrom) V.; BA in Chemistry magna cum laude, Kans. State U., 1972; MD, Kans. U., 1976; m. Lydia Acker, Dec. 10, 1976. Intern in medicine Letterman Army Med. Center, San Francisco, 1976-77, resident in radiology, 1977-80; practice medicine specializing in radiology, 1980—; chief dept. radiology Darnall Army Hosp., Ft. Hood, Tex., 1980-82; pvt. practice diagnostic radiology, 1982—; chief of staff Metroplex Hosp., 1985-86, 88-90. Served to maj. M.C., U.S. Army, 1976-82 Recipient Ollie O. Mustala award in clin. pharmacology Kans. U. Med. Center, 1974; A. Morris Ginsberg award in phys. diagnosis Kans. U. Med. Center, 1975; Resident Tchr. of Yr. award Letterman Army Med. Center, 1979; Staff Tchr. of Yr. award Darnall Army Hosp., 1982. Trembly Meml. scholar, 1972. Diplomate Am. Bd. Radiology. Mem. Am. Coll. Radiology, Radiologic Soc. N. Am., AMA, Tex. Med. Assn., Tex. Radiol. Soc., Ind. Med. Practitioners Assn. Ctrl. Tex. (pres.), Clinical Magnetic Resonance Soc., Sigma Xi, Alpha Chi Sigma, Alpha Omega Alpha. Home: 3302 Walnut Cir Harker Heights TX 76548-8715 Office: Metroplex Hosp Dept Radiology 2201 Clear Creek Rd Killeen TX 76549-4110

VANDAHM, THOMAS EDWARD, economist, educator; b. Chgo., Feb. 20, 1924; s. Thomas and Sarah (Toren) VanDahm; m. Lois I. Stanton; 1 child Ruth E. AB, Hope Coll., 1948; MA, U. Mich., 1949, PhD, 1959. Asst. prof. econs. bus. Ctrl. Coll., Pella, Iowa, 1950—53, Augustana Coll., Rock Island, Ill., 1954—55, Hope Coll., Holland, Mich., 1955—60, So. Ill. U., Edwardsville, 1960—64; prof. econs. Carthage Coll., Kenosha, Wis., 1964—91; ret., 1991. Author: Money and Banking, 1975; contbr. articles to profl. jours. Served to cpl. U.S. Army, 1943—46. Fellow Ford Found., 1969. Mem.: Midwest Econs. Assn., Recorders of Merrywoode (founder, dir. 1995—), Kiwanis (pres. 1985—86). Home: 8065 43rd Ave Kenosha WI 53142-4588

VAN DALEN, GORDON JOHN, physicist, educator; b. Tokyo, Sept. 19, 1951; came to the U.S., 1952; s. John and Ruth Margaret (Payne) Van D.; m. Carolyn Margaret Boutin, Apr. 8, 1978; children: John Edward, Stephen Michael. BS, U. Calif., Riverside, 1973, MS, 1975, PhD, 1978. From rsch. asst. to assoc. prof. U. Calif., Riverside, 1975-89, prof., 1990—. Assoc. dean U. Calif., Riverside, 1990-93, dept. chmn., 1994-95. Contbr. articles to profl. jours. Fellow AAAS; mem. Am. Phys. Soc., Am. Assn. Physics Tchrs., Phi Beta Kappa. Achievements include rsch. in experimental particles. Office: Univ Calif Dept Physics Riverside CA 92521-0413 E-mail: gordon.vandalen@ucr.edu.

VAN DAM, HEIMAN, psychoanalyst; b. Leiden, The Netherlands; s. Machiel and Rika (Knorringa) van D.; m. Barbara C. Strona, Oct. 6, 1945; children: Machiel, Claire Ilena, Rika Rosemary. AB, U. So. Calif., 1942, MD, 1945. Fellowship child psychiatry Pasadena (Calif.) Child Guidance Clinic, 1950; gen. practice psychiatry and psychoanalysis L.A., 1951—; instr. L.A. Psychoanalytic Inst., 1959—, co-chmn. com. on child psychoanalysis, 1960-67, tng. and supervising psychoanalyst, 1972—; supr. child and adolescent psychoanalysis So. Calif. Psychoanalytic Inst., 1986—. Cons. Reiss Davis Child Study Center, 1955-76, Neighborhood Youth Assn., Los Angeles, 1964-69; asso. clin. prof. psychiatry and pediats. UCLA Sch. Medicine, 1960-96, clin. prof. psychiatry and pediats., 1996—; vis. supr. child psychoanalysis San Francisco Psychoanalytic Inst., 1969-79, Denver Psychoanalytic Inst., 1972-74; mem. adv. bd. Western State U. Coll. Law, Fullerton, Calif., 1965-83. Corr. editor Arbeits Hefte Kinderanalyse, 1985— ; contbr. articles to profl. jours. Trustee, mem. edn. com. Center for Early Edn., 1964-92, v.p., 1978-79; bd. dirs. Child Devel. and Psychotherapy Tng. Program, Los Angeles, 1975-80, pres., 1975-77; bd. dirs. Los Angeles Child Devel. Center, 1977-86, treas., 1978-80; mem. cult clinic Jewish Family Service, Los Angeles, 1978-86; bd. dirs. Lake Arrowhead Crest Estates, 1990-99. Served to capt. M.C. AUS, 1946-48. Mem. Am. Psychoanalytic Assn. (com. on ethics 1977-80), Assn. Child Psychoanalysis (councillor 1966-69, sec. 1972-74, mem. nominating com. 1978-84, membership com. 1988—, Marianne Kris lectr. 1995), Internat. Assn. Infant Psychiatry (co-chmn. program com. 1980-83), Internat. Soc. Adolescent Psychiatry (sci. adv. com. 1988—), Phi Beta Kappa. Office: 10436 Santa Monica Blvd Los Angeles CA 90025-5079

VANDAME, JEAN-MARIE RICHARD, professional services company executive; b. Gien, France, Oct. 30, 1960; s. Marc and Antoinette (Dumouchel de Premare) V.; m. Chantal Geraldine de Blocquel de Croix de Wismes, Sept. 3, 1983; children: Thomas, Camille, Clemence, Alix. Engring. Degree, Inst. Super. Electronique, Paris, 1982; MBA, Inst. Adminstrn. Entreprises, Paris, 1984. Product mktg. engr. Tex Instruments, Paris, 1983-84, field sales engr. Rennes, France, 1984-86; sr. mgr. Ernst & Young, Paris, 1986-92, assoc. dir., 1995-96, internat. ptnr., 1996—; pres. KnowledgeWare, Brussels, 1992-95. Home: 3725 N Magnolia Ave Chicago IL 60613 Office: CG Ernst & Young Sears Tower 233 S Wacker Dr Chicago IL 60606 E-mail: jean-marie.vandame@cgeyc.com.

VANDAMENT, WILLIAM EUGENE, retired academic administrator; b. Hannibal, Mo., Sept. 6, 1931; s. Alva E. and Ruth Alice (Mahood) V.; m. Margery Vandament, Feb. 2, 1952; children: Jane Louise, Lisa Ann. BA, Quincy Coll., 1952; MS, So. Ill. U., 1953; MS in Psychology, U. Mass., 1963, PhD, 1964; LittD, No. Mich. U., 1997. Psychologist Bacon Clinic, Racine, Wis., 1954-61; NDEA fellow U. Mass., Amherst, 1961-64; asst. prof. SUNY, Binghamton, 1964-69, univ. examiner and dir. instl. research, 1969-73, asst. v.p. planning, instl. research, 1972-76; exec. asst. to pres., dir. budget and resources Ohio State U., Columbus, 1976-79, v.p. fin. and planning, 1979-81; sr. v.p. adminstrn. NYU, N.Y.C., 1981-83; provost, vice chancellor acad. affairs Calif. State U. System, Long Beach, 1983-87; Trustees prof. Calif. State U., Fullerton, 1987-92; pres. No. Mich. U., 1991-97, ret., 1997. Contbr. articles to psychol. jours. and books on higher edn. Office: 2662 E 20th St Apt 310 Signal Hill CA 90804-5616 E-mail: vandament@aol.com.

VANDEBURGT, HENDRIK JOZEF, designer; b. Arnhem, The Netherlands, Sept. 18, 1913; s. Hendrik L.S. and Emerentiana A.C. (Boelens) V.; m. Pauline H. Boonstra, Aug. 21, 1945; children: Ancilla Fr., Veritas M. (dec.), Rensje, Frances. Diploma cum laude, Art Coll. Kunstoefening, Arnhem, Netherlands, 1936. Chief designer J&R Lamb Studios Inc., Clifton, NJ, 1952—, Wilmark Studios, Pearl River, N.Y., 1980—, Michael & Son Studios, S.I., 1958—, Holyland Art Comp., Westwood, N.J., 1982—. Designed stained glass and murals in over 400 places of worship. Democrat. Roman Catholic. Home: 157 Prospect Ave Westwood NJ 07675-2113

VAN DECKER, WILLIAM ARTHUR, cardiologist; b. Passaic, N.J., May 27, 1957; s. William and Louise Adelaide (Meli) Van D.; m. Generosa Grana; children: Stephanie, William, Christopher. BS in Biology summa cum laude, Fairfield (Conn.) U., 1979; MD, Georgetown U., 1983. Diplomate Am. Bd. Internal Medicine, Cert. Coun. Nuclear Cardiology. Am. Bd. Cardiovascular Diseases; Am. Soc. Echocardiography spl. competency testing. Intern Temple U. Hosp., Phila., 1983—84, resident internal medicine, 1984—86, cardiology fellow, 1986—88, non-invasive cardiology imaging tng./rsch. fellow, 1988—89; assoc. dir. Non-Invasive Imaging, dir. Cardiology Clinic Med. Coll. Pa. Hosp.-Drexel U. Coll. Medicine, 1989—95, asst. prof. medicine and cardiology, 1989—, dir. Heart Sta., 1990—. Mem. com. on radiation safety, 1990—, chmn. 1993—, mem. pharmacy and therapeutics com., 1992—, chmn. pharmacy and therapeutics com. 1993—, mem. continuing med. edn. com., 1992-96, vice-chmn. quality assurance com., 1993—, group leader freshman bioethics, 1992-95, med. student advisor, 1992—; presenter in field, bd. dir. Cert. Bd. Nuclear Cardiology, 2002-, bd. dir. Philadelphia Cnty. Med. Soc., 2002-2003. Manuscript Peer reviewer Annals of Internal Medicine, 1993—; contbr. articles to profl. jours. Fellow Am. Heart Assn., Am. Coll. Cardiology, Am. Coll. Chest Physicians; mem. AMA, ACP, Am. Soc. Echocardiography, Am. Fedn. Med. Rsch.(ea. sect. chair 2001-2002), Pa. Med. Soc., Soc. Nuc. Medicine, Am. Assn. Nuc. Cardiology (founder), Am. Soc. Nuc. Cardiology (founder, bd. dirs., chmn. membership com. 2000—, bd. dirs. cert. bd. 2002—), Soc. Cardiovasc. Magnetic Resonance (founding mem.), Philadelphia County Med. Soc. (ho. of dels. 1996—, bd. dirs. 2002—), Alpha Epsilon Delta, Alpha Omega Alpha. Office: MCP 3300 Henry Ave Philadelphia PA 19129-1191 E-mail: william.vandecker@drexel.edu.

VANDE HEY, JAMES MICHAEL, corporate executive, former air force officer; b. Maribel, Wis., Mar. 15, 1916; s. William Henry and Anna (Zimmerman) VandeH.; m. Jean Margretta Schilleman, June 23, 1944; children: James Todd, Dale Michael, Dean Clark. Student, U. Wis., 1947-49; BA, U. Philippines, 1955; postgrad., Air War Coll., Maxwell AFB, Montgomery, Ala., 1956-57. Commd. 2d lt. USAAF, 1941; advanced through grades to brig. gen. USAF, 1967; fighter pilot PTO, 1941-45; including Hawaii, Dec. 7, 1941; duty in command and USAF level including duty in Europe (NATO) and Philippines, 1945-69; dep. chief of staff Hdqrs. USMACV, Saigon, Vietnam, 1969-71; assigned Hdqrs. Tactical Air Command, 1971—; mem. faculty Air War Coll., 1957-59, dep. for acads., dean of faculty, 1959-61; ret.,

1971; pres. Vanson Inc., 1971—, Vande Hey Inc., 1976—. Decorated D.S.M., Legion of Merit with two oak leaf cluster, D.F.C. with two oak leaf cluster, Bronze Star, Air medal with 7 oak leaf clusters, decorations from Philippine, Vietnamese and Korean govts. Mem. USAF Hist. Found., Air Force Assn., Pearl Harbor Survivors Assn., Iwo Jima Survivors Assn. Roman Catholic. Home: 3374 S El Dorado Austin TX 78734-5232

VANDEHEY, KELLY MATTHEW, priest; b. Hillsboro, Oreg., May 16, 1963; s. Antone George Vandehey, Shirley Marie Hoffman. BA, Mount Angel Sem., St. Benedict, Oreg., 1990; MA, Mount Angel Seminary, St. Benedict, Oreg., 1993, MDiv, 1995; Licentiate in Canon Law, JCL, The Cath.U.Am., Washington, D.C., 1999. Ordained priest. John Deere partsman Hillsboro Implement Co., Hillsboro, Oreg., 1981—86; transitional deacon St. James Cath. Ch., McMinnville, 1995—96; parochial vicar Sacred Heart Cath. Ch., Medford, 1996—98, Cathedral of the Immaculate Conception, Portland, 1999—2000; marriage tribunal judge Archdiocese of Portland in Oreg., 1999—; pastor St. Charles Borromeo Cath. Ch., 2000—. Presbyn. coun. Archdiocese of Portland in Oreg., Portland, 1996—, clergy remuneration com., 2000—01, sacramental practices com., 2000—, annual Cath. appeal steering com., 2001—; adj. prof. canon law Mount Angel Sem., St. Benedict, 2000—. Mem.: Canon Law Soc. Am. (resolutions com. mem. 2000—). Roman Catholic. Avocations: movies, travel, music. Home and Office: St. Charles Borromeo Parish 5310 N.E. 42nd Avenue Portland OR 97218

VAN DE KAMP, ALEXANDRA P. writer, educator, poet, editor; b. Portchester, N.Y., Apr. 23, 1965; d. Theodore John van de Kamp and Patricia Ann Bruno; m. William Daniel Glenn, June 28, 1997. BA in English, Johns Hopkins U., 1987; MFA in Poetry, U. Wash., 1991. Office mgr. Kaplan Ednl. Ctr., Seattle, 1992-93; instr. ESL Linguacenter, Madrid, 1993-94; instr. Linford Acad., 1994-95, 96-98, dir. studies, 1995-96; instr. Tng. Express, 1999-2000; adj. prof. English L.I. U., Bklyn., 2000—. Author: (poetry vol.) The Rainiest May in the Twentieth Century, 2002; editor, co-founder: Bilingual Lit. Jour., 1998—, editor, co-founder: Terra Incognita; contbr. poems to periodicals, Mag. Avocations: exercise, film, travel, cultural exploration. Home: 469 47th St Brooklyn NY 11220 E-mail: avandekamp@earthlink.net.

VAN DE KAMP, JOHN KALAR, lawyer; b. Pasadena, Calif., Feb. 7, 1936; s. Harry and Georgie (Kalar) Van de K.; m. Andrea Fisher, Mar. 11, 1978; 1 child, Diana. BA, Dartmouth Coll., 1956; JD, Stanford U., 1959. Bar: Calif. 1960. Asst. U.S. atty., L.A., 1960-66; U.S. atty., 1966-67; dep. dir. Exec. Office for U.S. Attys., Washington, 1967-68, dir., 1968-69; spl. asst. Pres.'s Commn. on Campus Unrest, 1970; fed. pub. defender L.A., 1971-75; dist. atty. Los Angeles County, 1975-83; atty. gen. State of Calif., 1983-91; ptnr. Dewey Ballantine, L.A., 1991-96, of counsel, 1996—; pres. Thoroughbred Owners, Calif., 1996—. Bd. dirs. United Airlines. Mem. Calif. Dist. Attys. Assn. (pres. 1975-83), Nat. Dist. Attys. Assn. (v.p. 1975-83), Peace Officers Assn. L.A. County (past pres.), Nat. Assn. Attys. Gen. (exec. com. 1983-91), Conf. Western Attys. Gen. (pres. 1986). Office: Dewey Ballantine LLP 333 So Grand Ave Ste 2600 Los Angeles CA 90071-1530

VANDEL, DIANA GEIS, performance consultant; b. San Antonio, Apr. 2, 1947; d. John George and Elma Ruth (Triplett) Geis; m. Jerry Dean Vandel, Apr. 17, 1976; 1 child, Jeremy Kyle. MusB, U. Tex., 1969. Cert. tchr., Tex. Tchr. music Zilker Elem. Pub. Sch., Austin, Tex., 1969-70, Isely Sch., Austin, 1986; asst. adminstr. Hillside Manor Nursing Home, Inc., San Antonio, 1970-76, 78-79, mgmt. cons., 1979-89, adminstr., 1988; mgmt. cons. Promoting Excellence Consultation, Austin, 1991-95, Winning Solutions, Austin, 1995—; owner Your Biggest Fan, 1999—. Owner, facilitator creative music and relaxation in motion classes, workshops and retreats, San Antonio, 1982-84; fine arts facilitator Cedar Creek Elem. Sch., Austin, 1988-91; seminar leader Movement Spiritual Inner Awareness, Austin, 1986—, min., 1989—. Austin rep. Peace Theol. Sem., L.A., 1988-93; exec. bd. Cedar Creek Booster Club, 1989-91. Avocations: photography, yoga, meditation, gardening, reading. Home: 916 Terrace Mountain Dr Austin TX 78746-2732 Office: Winning Solutions and Your Biggest Fan 916 Calithea Rd Austin TX 78746-2716 E-mail: dvandel@earthlink.net.

VANDELL, KERRY DEAN, real estate and urban economics educator; b. Biloxi, Miss., Jan. 8, 1947; s. Benedict Sandy and Eleanor Ruby (Lenhart) V.; m. Deborah Ann Lowe, May 16, 1970; children: Colin Buckner, Ashley Elizabeth. BA, BMME, Rice U., 1970; M City Planning, Harvard U., 1973; PhD, MIT, 1977. Assoc. engr. Exxon Co., USA, Houston, 1970-71; asst. prof. So. Meth. U., Dallas, 1976-80, assoc. prof., 1980-86, prof., chmn. dept., 1986-89; prof. real estate and urban land econs., chm. dept. U. Wis., Madison, 1989-93, dir. Ctr. for Urban Land Econs. rsch., 1989—, Tiefenthaler chairholder, 1996—; exec. dir. Bolz Ctr. Arts Adminstrn., 2000—. Vis. assoc. prof. Harvard U., Cambridge, Mass., 1985-86; vis. prof. U. Calif., Berkeley, 1988-89, U. Hong Kong, 1997; bd. dirs. Park Bank, Madison, U. Rsch. Pk., Chrisken Realty Trust. Mem. editl. bd. Jour. Real Estate Fin. and Econs., 1989—, Land Econs., 1989—, Jour. Property Rsch., 1989-94; contbr. numerous articles on mortgage default risk, neighborhood dynamics, econs. of architecture, and appraisal theory to profl. jours. Fellow Homer Hoyt Advanced Studies Inst. (faculty 1989—, bd. dirs.); mem. Urban Land Inst., Am. Real Estate and Urban Econs. Assn. (2nd v.p. 1989, 1st v.p. 1990, pres. 1991, co-editor jour. 1991-96). Episcopalian. Home: 3301 Topping Rd Madison WI 53705-1436 Office: U Wis Sch Bus 975 University Ave Madison WI 53706-1324 E-mail: kvandell@bus.wisc.edu.

VAN DE MARK, BRIAN, historian, educator; b. Houston, July 12, 1960; s. John Stevens and Lucy Ellen (Ferguson) Van De M.; m. Dian Owen, July 16, 1983; 1 child, Grey. BA, U. Tex., Austin, 1981, MA, 1983; PhD, UCLA, 1988. Teaching assoc. UCLA, 1986-87; rsch. asst. Clark Clifford, Washington, 1987-90; asst. prof. U.S. Naval Acad., Annapolis, Md., 1990-93, 95-98; assoc. Robert McNamara, Washington, 1993-95; Freeman prof. Hopkins-Nanjing Ctr., China, 1999-2000; assoc. prof. U.S. Naval Acad., 1998—. Author: Into the Quagmire, 1991; co-author: In Retrospect, 1995. Participant study groups Coun. Fgn. Rels., Washington, 1996-99. Mem. Am. Hist. Assn., Orgn. Am. Historians, Soc. Historians Am.-Fgn. Rels., Authors Guild Democrat. Avocations: art collecting, birdwatching, reading, travel. Home: 12 Franklin St Annapolis MD 21401 Office: US Naval Acad Dept History Annapolis MD 21402 E-mail: brianvandemark@yahoo.com.

VANDEMARK, MICHELLE VOLIN, critical care, neuroscience nurse; b. Sioux Falls, S.D., Feb. 14, 1962; d. Verlynne V. and Suzanne (Cronin) Volin; m. Richard E. VanDemark, June 5, 1982; children: Andrew Porter, Hannah Elizabeth. BA in Biology, Lake Forest (Ill.) Coll., 1984; BSN, Northwestern U., Chgo., 1986; MS in Nursing, Loyola U., Chgo., 1990. RN, Ill., S.D.; cert. neurosci. nursing, CNRN, ACLS. Staff nurse neurosci. unit Evanston Hosp., Ill., 1986-90, staff nurse intensive care unit, 1990-93; neurosci. clin. nurse specialist Sioux Valley Hosp., Sioux Falls, S.D., 1995—. Mem. Am. Assn. Neurosci. Nurses (pres. Gt. Plains chpt. 1995-96, bd. dirs. 2000—), Sigma Theta Tau, Alpha Sigma Nu. Home: 321 E 27th St Sioux Falls SD 57105-3032

VAN DE MARK, RICHARD J. retired writer, artist; b. Seattle, June 24, 1933; m. Diane Van de Mark, Sept. 5, 1959; 1 child Jennifer. Student, Western Wash. U., 1951—53, student, 1956—58, student, 1967—68. Self-employed fishing boat operator, Bellingham, Wash., 1951—56; office exempt-ops. rsch. The Boeing Co., Seattle, 1959—67; lab. microbiologist Western Wash. U., Bellingham, 1970—93. Author: Steelhead Fly Fishing in Low Water, 1996. Environ. activist various orgns. With U.S. Army, 1953—55. Mem.: Environ. Def., Earth Justice, Union Concerned Scientists, Sons of Norway. Democrat. Avocations: astronomy, fly fishing, birdwatching, poetry, hiking. Home and Studio: 1434 Humboldt St Bellingham WA 98225

VANDEMARK, ROBERT GOODYEAR, retired retail company executive; b. Youngstown, Ohio, Sept. 1, 1921; s. Arthur Glenn and Lola (Goodyear) V.; m. Jean Chapman, Sept. 19, 1943; children: Ann (Mrs. William K. Butler), Peggy Lynn (Mrs. Michael Murray). BSc, Ohio U., 1943. Dept. mgr. F. & R. Lazarus, Columbus, Ohio, 1947-54; asst. controller Boston Store, Milw., 1954-57; v.p., treas. Cleland Simpson Co., Scranton, Pa., 1957-65; asst. to exec. v.p. Bergdorf Goodman, N.Y.C., 1965-68; treas. Garfinckel, Brooks Bros., Miller & Rhoads, Inc., Washington, 1968-69, v.p., 1969-73, exec. v.p., 1973-79, vice chmn., 1979-83; chmn., chief exec. officer Garfinckel's, 1983-87. Head dept. and specialty stores div. United Fund, Scranton, Pa., 1960-65; bd. dirs. Goodwill Industries, 1964-65; treas. Washington Nat. Cathedral. Served to 1st lt. AUS, 1943-46; col. Res. Decorated Bronze Star with V and cluster, Mil. Order of Wilheim. Mem. Fin. Execs. Inst., Nat. Retail Mchts. Assn. (sec., treas., 1st v.p., pres., dir., mem. exec. com. fin. exec. divsn.), Delta Tau Delta, City Club Washington, Washington Golf and Country Club, Army-Navy Club, Burning Tree Golf Club, Laurel Oak Country Club (Fla.), Masons (32d degree), Kiwanis (Fla.). Home: 933 Woburn Ct Mc Lean VA 22102-2132 also: 3362 Charles MacDonald Dr Sarasota FL 34240

VAN DEMARK, RUTH ELAINE, lawyer; b. Santa Fe, May 16, 1944; d. Robert Eugene and Bertha Marie (Thompson) Van D.; m. Leland Wilkinson, June 23, 1967; children: Anne Marie, Caroline Cook. AB, Vassar Coll., 1966; MTS, Harvard U., 1969; JD with honors, U. Conn., 1976; MDiv, Luth Sch. Theology, Chgo., 1999. Bar: Conn. 1976, Ill. 1977, U.S. Dist. Ct. Conn. 1976, U.S. Dist. Ct. (no. dist.) Ill., U.S. Ct. Appeals (7th cir.) 1984, U.S. Supreme Ct. 1983; ordained to ministry, Luth Ch., 1999. Instr. legal rsch. and writing Loyola U. Sch. Law, Chgo., 1976-79; assoc. Wildman, Harrold, Allen & Dixon, 1977-84, ptnr., 1985-94; prin. Law Offices of Ruth E. Van Demark, 1995—; pastor Wicker Park Luth. Ch., 1999—. Mem. rules com. Ill. Supreme Ct., 1999—, chair appellate rules subcom., 1996—; mem. dist. ct. fund adv. com. U.S. Dist. Ct. (no. dist.) Ill., 1997—. Assoc. editor Conn. Law Rev., 1975-76. Bd. dirs. Lutheran Soc. Svcs. Ill., 1998—, sec., 2000—02, chmn., 2002-; mem. adv. bd. Horizon Hospice, Chgo., 1978—, YWCA Battered Women's Shelter, Evanston, Ill., 1982-86; del.-at-large White House Conf. on Families, L.A., 1980; mem. alumni coun. Harvard Divinity Sch., 1988-91; vol. atty. Pro Bono Advocates Chgo., 1982-92, bd. dirs., 1993-99, chair devel. com., 1993; bd. dirs. Friends of Pro Bono Advocates Orgn., 1987-89, New Voice Prodns., 1984-86, Byrne Piven Theater Workshop, 1987-90, Luth. Social Svcs. Ill. (sec., 2000—), 1998—; founder, bd. dirs. Friends of Battered Women and Their Children, 1986-87; chair 175th Reunion Fund Harvard U. Div. Sch., 1992. Mem. ABA, Ill. Bar Assn., Conn. Bar Assn., Chgo. Bar Assn., Appellate Lawyers Assn. Ill. (bd. dirs. 1985-87, treas. 1989-90, sec. 1990-91, v.p. 1991-92, pres. 1992-93), Women's Bar Assn. Ill., Jr. League Evanston (chair State Pub. Affairs Com. 1987-88, Vol. of Yr. 1983-84), Chgo. Vassar Club (pres. 1979-81), Cosmopolitan Club (N.Y.C.). Home: 2046 W Pierce Ave Chicago IL 60622-1946 Office: 225 W Washington St Ste 2200 Chicago IL 60606-3408 E-mail: revlaw@msn.com.

VANDEN, HARRY EDWIN, political science educator; b. Wilmington, Del., Sept. 29, 1943; s. Harry Edwin Sr. and Rena Baker (Van Zandt) V.; m. Vera Esther Ballin, Sept. 3, 1967 (div. Feb. 1995); children: David Jeffrey, Jonathan Harry. Diploma, U. Madrid, 1965; BA, Albright Coll., 1966; MA, Cert. in L.Am. Studies, Syracuse U., 1969; PhD, New Sch. Social Rsch., 1976. Field rsch. coord. Nat. Opinion Rsch. Ctr., N.Y.C., 1969-70; adj. asst. prof. Richmond Coll., CUNY, 1971; Fulbright scholar U.S. Govt., Lima, Peru, 1973-74; tech. expert Inst. Nacional Administración Pública, 1974-75; from asst. prof. to prof. U. South Fla., Tampa, 1975—, dir. Caribbean and L.Am. Ctr., 1993-97. Author: Mariátegui: influencias en su formación ideológica, 1975, National Marxism in Latin America, 1986, A Bibliography of Latin American Marxism, 1991; co-author: Democracy and Socialism in Sandinista Nicaragua, 1993, Latin America: The Power Game, 2002; co-editor: The Undermining of the Sandinista Revolution, 1997; contbr. articles to profl. jours., chpts. to books. V.p. bd. dirs. WMNF Cmty. Radio, Tampa, 1990-96; bd. dirs. Hispanic Svcs. Coun., Tampa, 1996—. NEH grantee, 1980. Mem. Soc. for Iberian and L.Am. Thought (pres. 1983-85), Southeastern Coun. on L.Am. Studies (pres. 1988-89), L.Am. Studies Assn. (co-chair Ctrl. Am. sect. 1997-2000), Am. Polit. Sci. Assn., Am. Soc. Internat Law. Democrat. Avocations: judo, swimming, auto repair and restoration. Office: U South Fla Dept Govt 4202 E Fowler Ave Tampa FL 33620-8100 E-mail: vanden@chuma1.cas.usf.edu.

VANDENBERG, BYRON F. cardiologist; b. Sacramento, Aug. 15, 1953; s. John Byron and Jeannette Vandenberg; m. Anne Carroll. BA, Occidental Coll., 1975; MD, Georgetown U., 1980. Intern, resident Parkland Hosp., Dallas, 1980-83; mem. faculty U. Iowa Coll. Medicine, Iowa City, 1985-97; cardiologist Prairie Cardiovascular Cons., Springfield, Ill., 1997—. Med. dir. adult echocardiography lab. Prairie Heart Inst., Springfield, 1997—; mem. editl. bd. Am. Jour. Cardiology, Dallas, 1997—. Contbr. articles to profl. jours. Named Best Drs. in Am., Woodward/White, 1998, 99, 2000. Fellow ACP, Am. Coll. Cardiology, Am. Heart Assn. Office: Prairie Cardiovascular Cons Ltd PO Box 19420 Springfield IL 62794-9420

VANDENBERG, DAVID DUANE, acupuncturist; b. Knob Noster, Mo., May 1959; s. Duane Evert Vandenberg and Peggy Joyce Ward; m. Victoria Dessoff, May 10, 1990 (div. Mar. 1994); m. Janet Rounds, July 7, 1997; 1 child, Emelie Adeline. BA, U. Tex., 1983; PhD, U. N.C., 1994; M of Acupuncture, Traditional Acupuncture Inst., 1998. Lic. acupuncturist, Washington. Screenwriter BBC, Glasgow, Scotland, 1993-94; asst. prof. Emory and Henry Coll., Va., 1994-95; acupuncturist in pvt. practice Washington, 1996—. Acupuncturist Carl Vogel Found., Washington, 2002—. Author (screenplay) Trees Off Cape Kanin Nos, 1994, (short story) The Man Who Knew..., 1994; transl. (short story) The Star of Unhappiness, 1992. Fulbright Commn. grantee, 1983; fellow Edward Albee Found., 1993, Ragsdale Found., 1993. Mem. Nat. Certifying Commn. (diplomate), Holland Soc. N.Y., DC Acupuncture Soc. (founder, pres. 2002-). Office: 1840 18th St NW Washington DC 20009

VANDENBERG, DONALD, retired education educator, philosopher; b. Milw., Aug. 4, 1931; arrived in Australia, 1976; s. Richard Albert and Elsie Eleanor Dorothy (Sheamann) V.; m. Erma Jean Pinkston, May 19, 1955; children: Marta, Donald Jr., Sara Ellen. BA cum laude, Maryville Coll., 1958; MA, U. Wis., 1961; PhD, U. Ill., 1966. Cert. high school English tchr., philosopher of edn. at tertiary level. English tchr. Whitehall (Mich.) Sr. H.S., 1960-62; philosopher of edn. U. Calgary, Alta., Can., 1965-68, 72-73, Pa. State U., State College, 1968-72, UCLA, 1973-76; reader in edn. U. Queensland, Brisbane, Australia, 1976-96, ret. Australia, 1996. Author: Being and Education, 1971, Human Rights in Education, 1983, Education as a Human Right, 1990; editor : Phenomenology and Educational Discourse, 1997; contbr. articles to profl. jours. With USN, 1949-53. Coe fellow in Am. studies, U. Wyoming, Laramie, 1958-59; recipient GTA award U. Ill., Urbana, 1962-65. Fellow Philosophy of Edn. Soc. (program com. 1971-72). Avocations: running, swimming, gardening, housekeeping. Home: 737 W Broad St Eufaula AL 36027-1913 E-mail: dranden1@earthlink.net.

VANDENBERG, EDWIN JAMES, chemist, educator; b. Hawthorne, N.J., Sept. 13, 1918; s. Albert J. Alida C. (Westerhoff) V.; m. Mildred Elizabeth Wright, Sept. 9, 1950; children: David James, Jean Elizabeth. ME with distinction, Stevens Inst. Tech., 1939, Dr.Engring. (hon.), 1965. Rsch. chemist Hercules Inc. Rsch. Ctr., Wilmington, Del., 1939-44; asst. shift supr. Sunflower Ordnance Works, Kans., 1944-45; rsch. chemist Rsch. Ctr., Wilmington, 1945-57, sr. rsch. chemist, 1958-64, rsch. assoc., 1965-77, sr. rsch. assoc., 1978-82. Adj. prof. chemistry Ariz. State U., Tempe, 1983-91, rsch. prof. chemistry, 1992—; chmn. Gordon Rsch. Conf. on Polymers, 1978. Author: Polyethers, 1975; Coordination Polymerization, 1983; Contemporary Topics in Polymer Science V, 1984, Catalysis in Polymer Synthesis, 1992; patentee in field; adv. bd. Jour. Polymer Sci. 1967-93, Macromolecules, 1979-81. Recipient Indsl. Rsch. 100 award, 1965, Internat. award Soc. Plastics Engrs., 1994. Mem. Am. Chem. Soc. (councillor Del. sect. 1974-81, chmn. 1976, chmn. divsn. polychemistry 1979, coord. indsl. sponsors 1982—, Del. sect. award 1965, 79, Polymer Chemistry award 1981, Exceptional Svc. award 1983, 95, Applied Polymer Sci. award 1991, Charles Goodyear medal 1991, Herman F. Mark award 1992). Home: 16223 E Inca Ave Fountain Hills AZ 85268-4518 Office: Ariz State U Dept Chemistry and Biochemistry Tempe AZ 85287-1604

VAN DEN BERG, EGERTON, airport executive; m. Caroline Merritt; 7 children. Legal counsel Orlando Exec., Orlando Internat. Airport , 1967—76, 1980—95; exec. dir. Orlando Internat. Airport, Orlando, Fla., 1997—. Office: Orlando Internat Airport One Airport Blvd Orlando FL 32827*

VANDENBERG, JOKA MARIA, physicist, researcher; b. Heemstede, The Netherlands, Jan. 24, 1938; came to the U.S., 1968; d. Antonius Vandenberg and Maria Elisabeth Van Amerongen; m. Rudolf Johannes Voorhoeve, May 11, 1968 (div. Aug. 1975); children: Lucy, Niels; m. James Charles Phillips, Mar. 1, 1996. B in Physics, State U., Leiden, The Netherlands, 1959, M in Phys. Chemistry, 1962, PhD in Solid State Physics, 1964. Tchg. asst. Lab. Inorganic Chemistry, Leiden, 1959-60; rsch. asst. Lab. Crystallography, Amsterdam, 1962-64; rschr. Royal Dutch Shell Lab., The Netherlands, 1964-68; postdoctoral staff Bell Labs., Murray Hill, N.J., 1968-69, cons., 1972; mem. tech. staff Lucent Techs., 1973-2001. Mem. affirmative action com. Bell Labs., Murray Hill, 1990-91. Mem. IEEE, Am. Phys. Soc., Royal Dutch Acad. Scis. (corr.). Achievements include patent for super conducting films. Avocations: yoga, hiking, cross country skiing, reading, swimming. Home: 204 Springfield Ave Summit NJ 07901 E-mail: joka_berg@comcast.net.

VANDENBERG, PETER RAY, magazine publisher; b. Geneva, Sept. 8, 1939; s. Don George and Isabel (Frank) V.; m. Kathryn Stock, June 1973 (div. Apr. 1977). BBA, Miami U., 1962. Creative adminstr. E.F. McDonald Incentive Co., Dayton, Ohio, 1966-73; mfrs.' rep. Denver, 1974-75; mgr. Homestake Condominiums, Vail, Colo., 1975-76; desk clk. Vail Run Resort, 1976-77; sales rep. Colo. West Advt., Vail, 1977-79, pres., 1980-83, Colo. West Publ., Vail, 1983—, casa-sol.com Mexican Vacation Rentals, Puerto Vallarta, Mexico, 1999—. With U.S. Army, 1963-66. Mem. Sigma Chi. Avocations: sports, music, reading.

VAN DEN BERG, SARA JANE, English educator; b. St. Paul, May 19, 1942; d. Henry John and Edith Ann (Hutchins) Streich; m. Kent Talbot van den Berg, June 12, 1976; 1 child, David Talbot. BA summa cum laude, U. Minn., 1964; MA, Yale U., 1965, PhD, 1969. Instr. Fordham U., N.Y.C., 1968-70; asst. prof. Fairfield (Conn.) U., 1970-73, Occidental Coll., L.A., 1973-76, Ohio State U., Columbus, 1976-80, U. Wash., Seattle, 1980-87, assoc. prof. English, 1987—, chmn. curricular policy bd., 1996-98. Mem. editl. bd. Modern Lang. Quar., 1995—, The Ben Jonson Jour., 1995—, Psyart: The Jour., 1997—; author: The Action of Ben Jonson's Poetry, 1987. Huntington Libr. fellow, 1987, NEH fellow, summer 1987. Mem. MLA (chmn. divsn. lit. and psychology 1990-94), Renaissance Soc. Am., Milton Soc. Am., Pacific Ancient and Modern Lang. Assn. (exec. com. 1997—). Office: Univ of Washington Dept English PO Box 354330 Seattle WA 98195-4330

VAN DEN BERGH, SIDNEY, astronomer; b. Wassenaar, Netherlands, May 20, 1929; emigrated to U.S., 1948; s. Sidney J. and Mieke (van den Berg) vandenB.; m. Paulette Brown; children by previous marriage: Peter, Mieke, Sabine. Student, Leiden (The Netherlands) U., 1947-48; AB, Princeton U., 1950; M.Sc., Ohio State U., 1952; Dr. rer. nat., Goettingen U., 1956, DSc (honoris causa), 1995, DSc (honoris causa), 2001. Asst. prof. Perkins Obs., Ohio State U., Columbus, 1956-58; research assoc. Mt. Wilson Obs., Palomar Obs., Pasadena, Calif., 1968-69; prof. astronomy David Dunlap Obs., U. Toronto, Ont., Can., 1958-77; dir. Dominion Astrophys. Obs., Victoria, B.C., 1977-86; prin. rsch. officer NRC Can., 1977-98. Adj. prof. U. Victoria, 1977—. Decorated officer Order of Can. Fellow Royal Soc. London; mem. Am., Royal Astron. Soc. (assoc.), Canadian Astronomy Soc. (sr. v.p. 1988-90, pres. 1990-92). Home: 418 Lands End Rd Sidney BC Canada V8L 5L9 E-mail: sidney.vandenbergh@nrc.ca.

VAN DEN BERGHE, PIERRE LOUIS, sociologist, anthropologist; b. Lubumbashi, Congo, Jan. 30, 1933; s. Louis and Denise (Caullery) van den B.; m. Irmgard C. Niehuis, Jan. 21, 1956; children— Eric, Oliver, Marc. BA, Stanford U., 1952, MA, 1953; PhD, Harvard U., 1960. Asst. prof. sociology Wesleyan U., Middletown, Conn., 1962-63; asso. prof. sociology SUNY, Buffalo, 1963-65; prof. sociology and anthropology U. Wash., Seattle, 1965-98, prof. emeritus, 1998—. Vis. prof. U. Natal, South Africa, 1960-61, Sorbonne, Paris, 1962, U. Nairobi, Kenya, 1967-68, U. Ibadan, Nigeria, 1968-69, U. Haifa, Israel, 1976, U. New South Wales, Australia, 1982, U. Strasbourg, France, 1985, U. Tuebingen, Fed. Republic Germany, 1986, Tel Aviv U., 1988, U. Cape Town, South Africa, 1989; fellow Advanced Study in Behavioral Scis., Stanford, Calif., 1984-85 Author: 22 books including South Africa, A Study in Conflict, 1965, Race and Racism, 1967, Academic Gamesmanship, 1970, Man in Society, 1978, Human Family Systems, 1979, The Ethnic Phenomenon, 1981, Stranger in Their Midst, 1989, State Violence and Ethnicity, 1990, The Quest for the Other, 1994. Served with M.C. U.S. Army, 1954-56. Mem. Am. Sociol. Assn., Am. Anthrop. Assn., Sociol. Research Assn., Human Behavior and Evolution Soc. Home: 2006 19th Ave E Seattle WA 98112-2902 Office: U Wash Dept Sociology 353340 Seattle WA 98195-3340 E-mail: plvdb@u.washington.edu.

VAN DEN BOGERT, ANTONIE JOHANNES, biomechanics researcher, consultant; b. Hedel, The Netherlands, Apr. 15, 1959; s. Cornelis A. and Celia H. (Lenselink) Van den B.; m. Elizabeth C. Hardin, June 8, 1997; children: Celia V., William A. PhD, U. Utrecht (The Netherlands), 1989. Rsch. assoc. U. Utrecht, 1988-91; postdoct. fellow U. Calgary (Can.), Alta., 1991-92; asst. prof., 1993-98; staff scientist Cleve. Clinic Found., Cleve., 1998—. Cons. Motion Analysis Corp., Santa Rosa, Calif., 1996—; moderator BIOMCH-L Internet Discussion Forum. Mem. AAAS, Internat. Soc. Biomechanics (exec. coun. 1995-2001), Soc. Indsl. and Applied Maths. Office: Cleve Clinic Found 9500 Euclid Ave Cleveland OH 44195 Fax: (216) 444-9198. E-mail: bogert@bme.ri.ccf.org.

VANDEN BOUT, PAUL ADRIAN, astronomer, physicist, educator; b. Grand Rapids, Mich., June 16, 1939; s. Adrian and Cornelia (Peterson) Vanden B.; m. Rachel Ann Eggebeen, Sept. 1, 1961; children: Thomas Adrian, David Anton AB, Calvin Coll., 1961; PhD, U. Calif.-Berkeley, 1966. Postdoctoral fellow U. Calif., Berkeley, 1966-67; postdoctoral fellow Columbia U., N.Y.C., 1967-68, instr., 1968-69, asst. prof., 1969-70, U. Tex., Austin, 1970-74, assoc. prof., 1974-79, prof., 1979-84; dir. Nat. Radio Astronomy Obs., Charlottesville, Va., 1985—. Cons. NSF, NASA Fellow Fulbright Found., Heidelberg, Fed. Republic Germany, 1961-62, Leiden, Netherlands, 1977 Fellow AAAS, Am. Phys. Soc.; mem. Am. Astron. Soc., Internat. Astron. Union, Internat. Radio Sci. Union. Office: Nat Radio Astronomy Obs 520 Edgemont Rd Charlottesville VA 22903-2454 E-mail: pvandenb@nrao.edu.

VAN DEN BRANDE, RENE ALBERT, retired accountant; b. Antwerp, Belgium, Aug. 14, 1916; arrived in Can., 1925; s. Henry Van den Brande and Maria Josephine Christ; m. Lily Perrson, July 7, 1947 (dec.). Cert. in pub. adminstrn., Queen's U., Ont., Can., 1963. Chartered acct., Can. Instr. Leamington Bus. Coll., 1938—40; asst. dept. head Dept. Nat. Revenue, Toronto, 1948—51; pvt. practice acct. Oakville, 1951—54; office mgr. Erb Lumber Co., Royal Oak, Mich., 1954—57; mgr. Sullivan Homes Inc., Dunedin, Fla., 1957—80; county adminstr. County of Essex, 1980—81; cons. Fed. Bank Can., Windsor, 1981—83; town adminstr. Town of South Palm Beach, Fla., 1983—88; ret. Flying officer Royal Can. Air Force, 1940—45, Camp Borden. Avocations: woodworking, reading. Home: 700 Via Lugano Cir Apt 101 Boynton Beach FL 33436 Home Fax: 561-738-6671. Personal E-mail: van814@email.com.

VANDENBROUCKE, RUSSELL JAMES, theatre director, writer, educator; b. Chgo., Aug. 16, 1948; s. Arthur C. Sr. and Ardelle (Barker) V.; m. Mary Allison Dilg, Sept. 7, 1974; children: Aynsley Louise, Justin Arthur. BA, U. Ill., 1970; MA, U. Warwick, Coventry, Eng., 1975; MFA in Drama, Yale U., 1977, DFA in Drama, 1978. Asst. literary mgr. Yale Repertory Theatre, New Haven, 1977-78; lit. mgr., dramaturg Mark Taper Forum, Los Angeles, 1978-85; assoc. producing dir. Repertory Theatre St. Louis, 1985-87; artistic dir. Northlight Theatre, Evanston, Ill., 1987-98. Vis. prof. Yale U., 1978, La. State U., 1981, U. Calif.-San Diego, 1983, Middlebury Coll., 1985, Washington U., 1986; adj. assoc. prof. Northwestern U., 1987-2001; prof., chair theater arts U. Louisville, 2001—. Author: Truths the Hand Can Tough: The Theatre of Athol Fugard, 1985, The Theatre Quotation Book: A Treasury of Insights and Insults, 2001; editor: Contemporary Australian Plays; play adapted for radio and stage: Los Alamos Revisited, 1984, play adapted for radio and stage: , 1987, play adapted for tv: Eleanor: In Her Own Words, 1985, play adapted from Truman Capote: Holiday Memories, 1991, adapted play: Feiffer's America, 1988, adapted play: An Enemy of the People, 1991, adapted play: Atomic Bombers, 1997; dir.: (plays) Feiffer's America, 1988, Eleanor: In Her Own Words, 1990, Lucky Lindy, Love Letters on Blue Paper, 84 Charing Cross Rd, Three Women Talking, Smoke on the Mountain, The White Rose, Betrayal, My Other Heart, Later Life, Hedda Gabler, Bubbe Meises, Valley Song, Fires in the Mirror, The Glass House, Philoctetes, Blood Knot, Atomic Bombers, Proof, Humana Festival, Snapshot, (play for radio): Three Women Talking; contbr. articles. Recipient L.A. Drama Critics Cir. award, 1984, Spl. Actors Equity Assn. award, 1990; Fulbright sr. scholar, Australia, 1996. Avocation: basketball. E-mail: russ.van@aya.yale.edu.

VAN DEN BULTE, CHRISTOPHE, finance educator; b. Elsene (Brussels), Belgium, Mar. 24, 1966; s. Victor Van den Bulte. PhD, Pa. State U., 1997. Lectr. Wharton Sch., U. Pa., Phila., 1997—98, asst. prof. mktg., 1998—. Fellow: Belgian Am. Ednl. Found. Office: U Pa Wharton Sch 3730 Walnut St Philadelphia PA 19104

VANDENBURG, KATHY HELEN, small business owner, career coach, resume writer; b. Clifton, N.J., Feb. 6, 1969; d. Milan and Helen (Derco) Suchanek; m. James Joseph Vandenburg III, Aug. 31, 1996. BA in Psychology, Montclair State U., 1991; MA in Edn., Seton Hall U., 1995; postgrad., Rider U., 1997-98. Cert. job and career transition coach Career Planning and Adult Devel. Network. Admissions counselor William Paterson U., Wayne, N.J., 1995-96; career counselor New Brunswick (N.J.) Pub. Schs., 1996-2000, Cornerstone Relocation Group, Warren, NJ, 2000-01; career tng. advisor Transitions Ctr. for Women, Warren County C.C. , Washington, 2001—02, Transitions Ctr. for Women, Washington, 2002—. Career tng. advisor Transitions Ctr. for Women Warren County C.C., 2001—. Mem.: Warren County C.C. Transitions Ctr. Women, Profl. Assn. Resume Writers and Career Coaches, Career Masters Inst., Nat. Resume Writers Assn., Hunterdon County C. of C. Avocations: swimming, travel, classical music, theatre, cooking.

VANDEN EYNDEN, CHARLES LAWRENCE, mathematician, educator; b. Cin., June 25, 1936; s. Lawrence Norbert George and Sophia (Koester) Vanden Eynden; m. Joan Brody, Aug. 3, 1967; children: Lisa, Jennifer. BS, U. Cin., 1958; MA, U. Oreg., 1960, PhD, 1962. NSF fellow U. Mich., Ann Arbor, 1962-63; asst. prof. U. Ariz., Tucson, 1963-65, Miami U., Oxford, Ohio, 1965-67; vis. asst. prof. Pa. State U., State College, 1967-68; asst. prof. Ohio U., Athens, 1968-69; from assoc. prof. to prof. math. Ill. State U., Normal, 1969—. Author: Elementary Number Theory, 1987; co-author: Discrete Mathematics, 1987, 93, 97, Elementary Abstract Algebra, 1993. Office: Ill State U Dept Math Normal IL 61761

VAN DEN HENDE, FRED J(OSEPH), human resources executive; b. Chgo., Sept. 28, 1953; s. Maurice Everett and Alice Helen (Davey) Van Den H.; m. Sharon Joyce Kucharski, Oct. 4, 1975; children: John Michael, Karen Michelle. BA, DePaul U., 1975; grad., U. Wash. Sch. Exec. Dev., 1981; MS, Nat. Louis U., 1998. Cert. sr. profl. human resources. Asst. v.p. human resources Land of Lincoln Savs. and Loan, Berwyn, Ill., 1977-84; v.p. human resources Uptown Fed. Bank FSB, Niles, 1984-88; dir. human resources Archdiocese of Chgo., 1988—; adj. faculty Grad. Sch. Mgmt. and Bus. Nat. Louis U., 1998—. Mem. Savs. Assn. Pers. Adminstrn., Berwyn, 1977-84; part-time instr. Inst. Fin. Edn., Chgo., 1984-90, Moraine Valley C.C., Palos Hills, Ill., 1984-90. Sch. bd. treas. St. Rene Sch., Chgo., 1981; sch. bd. mem. St. Daniel the Prophet Sch., Chgo., 1986-88, 93-95, sch. bd. chmn., 1988-89; boy scout leader St. Daniel Parish, Chgo., 1987-94. Recipient Oustanding Achievement in the Field of Athletics award St. Rita H.S. Alumni Assn., Chgo., 1991; Athletic scholar DePaul U., Chgo., 1971-75. Mem. Nat. Assn. Ch. Pers. Adminstrs., Soc. for Human Resource Mgmt. (mem. sch.-to-work com. 1998—), Ill. State C. of C. (human resources com. 1979—, healthcare com. 1998—), Inst. Internat. Human Resources, Am. Mgmt. Assn. (Chicago Area Tng. Coun. 2001—). Roman Catholic. Avocations: camping, fishing, coaching youth sports teams, horseback riding. Home: 5130 S Mulligan Ave Chicago IL 60638-1316 Office: Archdiocese of Chgo 155 E Superior St Chicago IL 60611-2911 E-mail: fvandenhende@archdiocese-chgo.org.

VAN-DEN-NOORT, STANLEY, neurologist, educator; b. Lynn, Mass., Sept. 8, 1930; s. Judokus and Hazel G. (Van Blarcom) van den N.; m. June Le Clere, Apr. 17, 1954; children: Susanne, Eric, Peter, Katherine, Elizabeth. AB, Dartmouth, 1951; MD, Harvard, 1954. Intern then resident Boston City Hosp., 1954-56, resident neurology, 1958-60; rsch. fellow neurochemistry Harvard U., 1960—62; instr. medicine Case Western Res. U., Cleve., 1962-66, asst. prof., 1966-69, assoc. prof., 1969-70; prof. neurology U. Calif., Irvine, 1970—, chief dept. neurology, 1970—72, chair dept. neurology, 1986—98, assoc. dean Coll. Medicine, 1972-73, dean, 1973-85. Mem. cons. staff U. Calif., Irvine Med. Center; mem. Long Beach (Calif.) Meml. Hosp., Long Beach VA Hosp.; mem. com. of revision U.S. Pharmacopoeial Conv., 1990-95. Mem. med. adv. bds., Nat. Multiple Sclerosis Soc./Myasthenia Gravis, 1971—, Orange County chpt. Nat. Multiple Sclerosis Soc., 1971—, Orange County Health Planning Coun., 1971-85, Nat. Com. Rsch. in Neurol. Disease, 1982-87. Lt. M.C. USNR, 1956-58. Fellow ACP, Am. Acad. Neurol.; mem. AAUP, AMA, Am. Neurol. Assn., Nat. Multiple Sclerosis Soc. (chief med. officer 1997-2002), Orange County Med. Assn., Calif. Med. Assn., Am. Heart Assn. Home: 17592 Orange Tree Ln Tustin CA 92780-2353 Office: U Calif Dept Neurology 100 Irvine Hall Irvine CA 92697-4275 E-mail: svandenn@uci.edu.

VANDEN WEGHE, KRISTOF NICO, medical device company executive; b. Korbtryk, Belgium, Dec. 29, 1960; s. Teroom Victor Vanden Weghe and Maria Josephe Couckuyt. MD, Kul, Leuven, Belgium, 1988, degree in biomed. engring., 1994, MBA, 1995. Intern H. Hart Hosp., Belgium, 1988-90; chief resident Hosp., Belgium, 1990-93; project mgr. ESAT/KUL, Belgium, 1993-95; clin. rsch. mgr. Zeneca, England, 1995-98; sales-mktg. engring. mgr. Cardiac Pathways, Mountain View, Calif., 1998—; CEO Rupain Holdings, Belgium, 2000—. Prin. investigator Kul Dept. Medicine Econs., Belgium, 1992-93; rsch. assoc. Kul-Thrombovascular Rsch. Ctr., Belgium, 1986-87; cons. in field. Mem. BPCR, N.Y. Acad. Scis., Deutsche Mgmt. Orgn., European Soc. Medicine & Engring. Avocations: tennis, golf. Home: 545 8th Ave Ste 401 New York NY 10018 Fax: 212-714-1453. E-mail: knvd@phphost.funet.be.

VANDEPITTE, DANIËL CAMILLE CORNELIS, civil engineering educator; b. Poperinge, Belgium, May 29, 1922; s. Henry C. and Maria M. (Lemahieu) V.; m. Hilda S. L. Loos, Aug. 24, 1959; children: Dirk V.H., Frank K.T., Jan W. Degree in civil engring., Ghent (Belgium) U., 1944, degree in higher edn., 1953; M Engring., Yale U., New Haven, 1949. Design engr. Stabilis, Ghent, 1945-46; mem. staff Ministry Pub. Works, 1946-56; lectr. Ghent U., 1950-56, assoc. prof. civil engring., 1956-60, prof., 1960-87, pres., 1969-73, hon. pres., 1973—, prof. emeritus, 1987—. Mem. tech. coun., Bureau SECO, Brussels, 1956-80, chmn., 1980-98; com. chmn., Standardization Inst., Brussels, 1982-95; pres. Nat. Fund Sci. Rsch., Brussels, 1970-71; initiator engring. edn., Nat. U. Rwanda, Butare, 1973. Author: Structural Analysis (3 vols.), 1979; editor: Stability of Plates and Shells, 1987; contbr. numerous articles to profl. publs. Recipient Fernand De Waele prize, Nat. Fund for Sci. Rsch., 1983. Mem. Royal Acad. Belgium, Royal Flemish Soc. Engrs. (pres. 1963-65), Soc. Study Materials (pres. 1981-85), European Conv. Constrnl. Steelwork (com. chmn. 1974-93), Order of the Prince. Roman Catholic. Avocation: reading. Home: Sint Denijslaan 433 B 9000 Ghent Belgium

VANDER AARDE, STANLEY BERNARD, retired otolaryngologist; b. Orange City, Iowa, Sept. 26, 1931; s. Bernard John and Christina (Luchtenberg) Vander A.; m. Agnes Darlene De Beer, June 19, 1956; children: Paul, David, Debra, Mary. BA, Hope Coll., 1953; MD, Northwestern U., 1957. Diplomate Am. Bd. Otolaryngology. Intern Cook County Hosp., Chgo., 1957-59; resident in otolaryngology Northwestern U. Hosp., 1966-70; mem. staff Mary Lott Lyles Hosp., Madanapalle, India, 1961-66, 71-87, Affiliated Med. Clinic, Willmar, Minn., 1987-95, ret., 1995. Served to capt., USAF, 1959-60. Fellow ACS, Am. Bd. Otolaryngology, Am. Acad. Otolaryngology. Republican. Mem. Reformed Church in America. Home: 708 2nd St SE Apt 112 Orange City IA 51041-2165 Office: Affiliated Med Clinic 101 Willmar Ave SW Willmar MN 56201-3556

VAN DER BEEK, JAMES, actor; b. Chesire, Conn., Mar. 8, 1977; s. Jim and Melinda. Appeared in films Angus, 1995, I Love You, I Love You Not, 1996, Varsity Blues, 1999, Harvest, 1999, Scary Movie, 1999, Jay and Silent Bob Strike Back, 2001, Texas Rangers, 2001, The Rules of Attraction, 2002; Dawson's Creek (TV series), 1998. Office: J Michael Bloom & Assocs 9255 W Sunset Blvd Fl 7 Los Angeles CA 90069-3309*

VANDERBEKE, PATRICIA K. architect; b. Detroit, Apr. 3, 1963; d. B. H. and Dolores I. VanderBeke. BS in Architecture, U. Mich., 1985, MArch, 1987. Registered arch., Ill. Archtl. intern Hobbs & Black, Assocs., Ann Arbor, Mich., 1984-86, Fry Assocs., Ann Arbor, 1988; arch. Decker & Kemp Architecture/Urban Design, Chgo., 1989-92; prin., founder P. K. VanderBeke, Arch., 1992—. Mem. adv. com. dept. arch., Triton Coll. Contbr. photographs and articles to Inland Arch. mag.; contbr. photographs to AIA calendar. Chair recycling com. Lake Point Tower Condo. Assn., Chgo., 1990—, chair. ops. com., 1993; mem. benefit com. The Renaissance Soc., U. Chgo., Redmoon Theater, Chgo. George S. Booth travelling fellow, 1992. Mem. AIA (participant 1st ann. leadership inst. 1997, 1st place nat. photog. contest award 1992, hon. mention 1994, membership com. Chgo. chpt.), Chgo. Archl. Club, hon. mention 2000 Burnham Prize Competition, The Cliff Dwellers (mem. arts com.). Office: 155 W Burton Pl Apt 16 Chicago IL 60610-1326

VANDERBILT, ARTHUR T., II, lawyer; b. Summit, N.J., Feb. 20, 1950; s. William Runyon and Jean (White) V. BA, Wesleyan U., Middletown, Conn., 1972; JD, U. Va., 1975. Bar: N.J. 1975, U.S. Dist. Ct. N.J. 1975, U.S. Supreme Ct. 1978. Jud. clk. to presiding justice N.J. Superior Ct., 1975-76, dep. atty. gen., 1976-78, asst. counsel to gov., 1978-79; ptnr. Carella, Byrne, Bain & Gilfillan, Roseland, N.J., 1979—. Chmn. Supreme Ct. Ethics Com.; mem. Supreme Ct. Adv. Com. Profl. Ethics. Author: Changing Law 1976, Jersey Justice, 1978, Law School, 1981, Treasure Wreck, 1986, Fortune's Children, 1989 (Book of the Month Club, Readers Digest and fgn. edits.), New Jersey's Judicial Revolution, 1997, Golden Days, 1998 (fgn. edits.), Jersey Jurists, 1998, The Making of a Bestseller, 1999. Trustee Elizabeth (N.J.) Presbytery. Named to N.J. Literary Hall of Fame. Fellow: ABA Found.; mem.: ABA (Scribes award 1976), Nat. Writers Union, The Authors Guild, Inc., Nat. Assn. Bond Lawyers, Am. Judicature Soc., N.J. Bar Assn., Capitol Hill Club, Hyannis Yacht Club, N.J. Lit. Hall of Fame. Republican. Presbyterian. Avocation: writing. Office: Carella Byrne Bain & Gilfillan 6 Becker Farm Rd Roseland NJ 07068-1735

VANDERBILT, KERMIT, English language educator; b. Decorah, Iowa, Sept. 1, 1925; s. Lester and Ella (Qualley) V.; m. Vivian Osmundson, Nov. 15, 1947; 1 dau., Karen Paige. BA, Luther Coll., Decorah, 1947, Litt. D. (hon.), 1977; MA, U. Minn., 1949, PhD, 1956. Instr. English U. Minn., 1954-57; instr. U. Wash., 1958-60, asst. prof. English, 1960-62; asst. prof. San Diego State U., 1962-65, assoc. prof., 1965-68, prof., 1968-90, prof. emeritus, 1990—. Vis. prof. Am. lit. U. B.C., Can., Vancouver, summer 1963; vis. prof. U. Oreg., summer 1968 Author: Charles Eliot Norton: Apostle of Culture in a Democracy, 1959, The Achievement of William Dean Howells: A Reinterpretation, 1968, American Literature and the Academy: The Roots, Growth and Maturity of a Profession, 1986 (Choice award for outstanding acad. books), Theodore Roethke in A Literary History of the American West, 1987; editor: (with others) American Social Thought, 1972, April Hopes (W.D. Howells), 1975, The Rise of Silas Lapham, 1983, spl. issue Am. Literary Realism, winter 1989, La Litterature Americaine, 1991, 3d edit., 1997, The Beautiful and Damned (F. Scott Fitzgerald), 1998; mem. edit. bd. U. Wash. Press, 1960-62, Twentieth Century Lit., 1969—; contbr. numerous articles to profl. jours. Served with USNR, 1943-46. Outstanding Prof. San Diego State U., 1976; Guggenheim fellow, 1978-79; Huntington Library fellow, 1980; Am. Philos. Soc. grantee, 1964, Am. Council Learned Socs. grantee, 1972, Nat. Endowment for Humanities grantee, 1986. Mem. Am. Studies Assn. (exec. council 1968-69), So. Calif. Am. Studies Assn. (pres. 1968-69), Philol. Assn. Pacific Coast (chmn. sect. Am. lit. 1968), MLA, Internat. Mark Twain Soc. (hon.), United Profs. of Calif. (Disting. prof. 1978) Home: 6937 Coleshill Dr San Diego CA 92119-1920

VAN DER BOSCH, SUSAN HARTNETT, real estate broker; b. St. Louis, Mar. 19, 1935; d. Leo Joseph and Mary Julia (O'Neill) Hartnett; m. George Arthur Van Der Bosch, Sept. 10, 1955; children: Mary Jo Van Der Bosch Schauer, Anne, Leo, Ellen, George Jr. Student, Barat Coll., 1953-55. Lic. real estate salesman, real estate broker, Grad Realtor's Inst.; cert. residential specialist. Assoc. broker Covered Bridge Realty, Long Grove, Ill., 1980-83, McKee Real Estate, Long Grove, 1983—. Office mgr. McKee br. office Fields of Long Grove, 1986. Trustee Vernon Pub. Libr., Prairie View, Ill., 1978-84; pres. Villagers, Long Grove, 1986-87; bd. dirs. Citizens' Transp. Coalition, 1988-98; dir. Long Grove Open Space Found., 1994—; Long Grove Village rep. Ela Area YMCA Steering Com., 1996-98; commr. Long Grove Park Dist., 2001—, v.p., 2002—. Mem. N.W. Suburban Bd. Realtors, Barrington Bd. Realtors, North Shore Bd. Realtors, Realtors Inst., Realtors Mktg. Inst., Biohome (bd. dirs. 1989-98). Avocations: golf, environment, bridge, travel. Home: Box 3253 RFD Long Grove IL 60047 Office: McKee Real Estate 145 N Old Mchenry Rd Long Grove IL 60047-8860 E-mail: shvdb@aol.com., mckee@techinter.com., SHVDB@AOL.COM.

VANDERBURG, PAUL STACEY, insurance executive, consultant; b. Detroit, Apr. 13, 1941; s. Harold Stacey and Alice Bertha (Lyle) V. Cert. in plastics tech., Oakland U., 1966; AS in Bus., C.S. Mott C.C., 1971; Casualty Claims Law Assoc., Am. Ednl. Inst., 1986; BA in Bus. Adminstrn. and Mgmt., Columbia Pacific U., 1990; cert. in human resource devel., U. South Fla., 1992; fraud claims law assoc., Am. Ednl. Inst., 1995. Lic. ins. adjuster Mich., Fla.; cert. cir. civil mediator U. South Fla. Mediation Inst., 2001, county mediator State Fla. Supreme Ct., 2002. Ins. field claims adjuster Underwriters Adjusting Co., Pontiac, Mich., 1972-76; pres., CEO Sun Cycle, Inc., Drayton Plains, 1975-77; sr. ins. claims adjuster Kemper Ins. Group, Tampa, Fla., 1979-80; ins. field claims adjuster Auto-Owners Ins. Co., Lakeland, 1981-82; sr. recovery specialist CIGNA Corp., Tampa, 1984-85; ins. field claims adjuster Seaboard Adjustment Bur., Lakeland, 1985-87; sr. field claims ins. adjuster Hallmark Ins. Adjusters, Clearwater, Fla., 1987-88; pvt. practice Tampa, 1988—. Author: Insurance Subrogation Management, 1991. Apptd. law enforcement rep. Hillsborough County (Fla.) Human Rels. Bd., 1999—. Staff sgt. U.S. Army, 1963-69. Mem.: Soc. of Claims Law Assocs., Assn. of Workers' Compensation Claims Profls., Fla. Acad. Profl. Mediators, Ctr. for Internat. Security Studies, Fla. Sheriffs Assn., Am. Security Coun. (nat. adv. bd.), Am. Legion. Republican. Avocations: boating, fishing, photography. Home and Office: 5448 Circle Dr (WWG) Spring Hill FL 34607-1407 Fax: (352) 592-2191.

VANDERCOOK, KEITH D. investment company executive; b. Grand Rapids, Mich., Aug. 19, 1932; s. Wayne Lewis Vandercook, Mildred Georgeanne Botts; children: Susan N., Lisa L., Daniel J. B in Psychology, We. Mich. U., 1955; computers degree, Jordan Coll., 1982. CLU Mich.; registered rep. NYSE, 1958, cert. real estate Mich., lic. pvt. pilot Mich. Rep. NYSE, Chgo., 1958—63; officer trust investment Old Kent Barik & Trust, Grand Rapids, Mich., 1964—66; rep. bus. and legal Prentice-Hall Inc., 1967—77; ptnr. Ind. Door Co., 1977—87; rschr. Harvard U., Cambridge, Mass., 1987—90; agt. real estate Greenridge Realty, Grand Rapids, 1990—99; vol. Sr. Neighbors and Area Agy. on Aging, 2000—. Bd. dirs. chmn. Oak Ridge & Bailey Grove Realty, Grand Rapids; bd. dirs. Sr. Neighbors; mem. adv. bd. Area Agy. on Aging, 2002—; bd. dirs. South High Alumni Scholarship. SP4 U.S. Army, 1955—57. Recipient Cook Valley Wet Lands award, State of Mich., 2001. Mem.: World Affairs Group, Amvets, Early Risers Breakfast Club. Republican. Avocations: reading, music. Home: 3781 Giddings SE Apt 114 Grand Rapids MI 49508-5556

VAN DER ELST, DIRK HENDRIK, cultural anthropologist, educator; b. Dordrecht, South Holland, June 15, 1933; arrived in U.S., 1948; s. Dingeman (Dick) and Clasina V.; m. JoAnne L. Kipps, June 20, 1981; children: Darren Paul, Bram Adam. BA, U. Utah, 1960, MA, 1961, Northwestern U., 1962, PhD, 1970. Rsch. asst., lectr. U. Nev., Reno, 1964-65; lectr. Marietta (Ohio) Coll., 1965-69; asst. prof. anthropology Calif. State U., Fresno, 1969, assoc. prof. anthropology, 1972, prof. anthropology, 1975, chmn. anthropology, 1980-90, prof. emeritus, 1993—. Fieldwork among the Kwinti of Suriname, 1972, 73, 75. Co-author: Asking and Listening, 1999; author: Culture As Given, Culture As Choice, 2000. Cpl. U.S. Army, 1952-55. Home: 42604 Snow Rd Auberry CA 93602 Office: Anthropology Dept California State Univ Fresno CA 93640

VANDERGINST, DENNIS ALLEN, lawyer; b. Moline, Ill., July 16, 1962; s. Kenneth James and Barbara Ann (Garard) V.; m. Jean Elizabeth Pauwels, July 10, 1992. BA, Ill. U., 1985; JD, DePaul U., 1989. Bar: Ill. 1989, U.S. Dist. Ct. (no. dist.) Ill. 1989, U.S. Ct. Appeals (7th cir.) 1990, U.S. Dist. Ct. (ctrl. dist.) Ill. 1992, Iowa 1994, Wis. 1996. Law clk., atty. Law Offices Elliott Samuels, Chgo., 1987-90; atty. pvt. practice, 1990-91, Wylie, Mulherin, Rehfeldt & Varchetto, Wheaton, 1991-92; ptnr. Braud/Westensee, Rock Island, Wheaton and Chgo., 1992-99, VanDerGinst, Roche & Westensee, Rock Island, Wheaton and Chgo., 1999—. Adj. prof. Black Hawk Coll., Moline, Ill., 1993—. Mem. ABA (medicine and law com., products, gen. liability and consumer law com., automobile law com., litigation sect., tort law and ins. sect.), ATLA (interstate trucking litigation group, motor vehicle collision hwy. and premises liability sect., ins. sect. 1994—), Ill. State Bar Assn., Ill. Trial Lawyers Assn. (procedural rules com. 1994—, membership com., legis. com. 1994—, med. negligence com., ins. law com., product liability com. 1994—), Iowa State Bar Assn. (law panels com. 1994—, svcs. to the elderly com.), Iowa Trial Lawyers Assn., Rock Island County Bar Assn., Jaycees, KC, Winnebago County Bar Assn. (profl. responsibility com., legal/med. com., editl. bd., profl. responsibility com.), Chgo. Bar Assn. (class litigation com. 1998—, ins. law com., tort litigation com. 1998—). Office: VanDerGinst Riche & Westensee 1705 2nd Ave Fl 6 Rock Island IL 61201-8718

VANDERGRAFF, DONNA JEAN, dietitian; b. Milw., Oct. 24, 1956; d. Wayne Eugene and Geraldine Louise (Brever) Zabler; m. Jess Lee Vandergraff, Oct. 11, 1980; children: Daniel Joseph, Joshua David. BS in Dietetics with distinction, Purdue U., 1978, MS in Nutrition, 1990. Registered dietitian. Clin. dietitian Logansport (Ind.) State Hosp., 1979-81, Ind. Vets.' Home, Lafayette, Ind., 1981-84; pvt. practice dietitian West Lafayette, 1984-90; rsch. asst. foods and nutrition Purdue U., 1988-90, ext. foods and nutrition asst., 1990-93; acting coord. Expanded Food and Nutrition Edn. Program Purdue U.Food and Nutrition Edn. Program, 1993-94, coord. Expanded Food and Nutrition Edn. Program, 1994—. Cons. dietitian Woodland Manor Nursing Ctr., Attica, Ind., 1985-88; presenter in field. Author: (brochures) Food, Dietary Fiber and You, 1989, Diabetes, Food and You, 1990; co-author: Have a Healthy Baby, 1991, Money Management, 1993, Exploring Food Pyramid With Professor Popcorn's Hooked on Health, Rev. , 1996, Ten Un Bebe Sano, 1999, EFNEP Curriculum, 2000; editor: Safe Food and You, 2001. Mem. com. bd. western region Am. Heart Assn., Lafayette, 1985-88; youth advisor Covenant Presbyn. Ch., West Lafayette, 1980-89; active Interagy. Coun. Community Health Edn., Lafayette, 1984-88; mem. Concerned Women for Am., 1985—; pub. rels. com. Greater Lafayette and Tippecanoe County Interagy. Coun. for Community Health Edn., 1984-85, mem. health at worksite com., 1985; weight reduction group leader West Lafayette Parks and Recreation Dept., 1985, YWCA, 1985. Named Outstanding Young Woman of Am., 1984, 86; Lute Troutt fellow Ind. Dietetic Assn., 1989; recipient Mary Hebenstreit Meml. award Ind. Dietetic Assn., 1988; named Recognized Young Dietitian of Yr., Ind. Dietetic Assn., 1987, Epsilon Sigma Phi team award 1996. Mem.: Ind. Nutrition Coun. (mem. 5 Star Task Force for Child Nutrition 1996), Ind. Interagy. Nutrition Edn. Network, Western Ind. Dist. Dietetic Assn. (pres. 1983—84, spkrs. bur. chmn. 1985—87, cmty. dietetics chmn. 1987—92, career guidance 1994—95, ch-chmn. cmty. dietetics, chmn. pub. rels.), Ind. Dietetic Assn. (chmn. coun. on practice 1987, nominating chmn. 1987—88, continuing edn. chmn. 1988—91, sec. 1991—93), Soc. for Nutrition Edn., Am. Dietetic Assn., Nat. Perinatal Assn., APHA, Healty Mothers, Healty Babies Coalition (bd. dirs., breastfeeding task force), Epsilon Sigma Phi, Kappa Omicron Nu, Gamma Sigma Delta, Gamma Phi Beta, Purdue Alumni Assn. Republican. Presbyterian. Avocations: swimming, reading, family activities. Home: 2937 Wilshire Ave West Lafayette IN 47906-1562 Office: Purdue Univ Dept Foods and Nutrition 1264 Stone Hall West Lafayette IN 47907-1264

VANDERGRIFF, KENNETH LYNN, minister; b. Knoxville, Tenn., Nov. 12, 1954; s. Kenneth Charles and Dorothy Jean Vandergriff; m. Beth Foster, Aug. 6, 1976; children: Kenny, Jeananne. BS in English Edn., Fla. State U., 1976; MDiv, Southwestern Bapt. Seminary, Ft. Worth, 1981, PhD in Old Testament, 1988. Teaching fellow Southwestern Bapt. Theol. Seminary, 1984-87, adj. instr., 1989; min. of edn. Northwest Hills Bapt. Ch., San Antonio, 1989-95. Instr Inst Christian Studies, Ft Worth, Tex., 1983, Ft Worth, 86, Wayland Bapt Univ, San Antonio, 1988—95, Campbell Univ, NC, 1996—. Recipient Stella Rossa Award, Southwestern Bapt Theological Sem, 1981. Mem.: Christians Biblical Equality, Am Acad Religion, Soc Biblical Literature. Democrat. Home: 212 Forest Brook Dr Apex NC 27502-5836 E-mail: kenv2@mindspring.com. *Integrity in relationships and the pursuit of excellence in endeavors—these I have found yield a life of satisfaction and joy.*

VANDER HEIDE, RICHARD STUART, pathologist, educator, research scientist; b. Grand Rapids, Mich., Apr. 30, 1959; s. John Sjeord and Patricia Jane (King) Vander H.; children: Benjamin Richard, Samuel Sjeord. BS, Calvin Coll., 1981; PhD, Northwestern U., 1986, MD, 1989. Diplomate Am. Bd. Pathology. Intern, resident Duke U. Med. Ctr., Durham, N.C., 1989-93; asst. prof. Wayne State U., Detroit, 1994-2000, assoc. prof., 2000—. Chief of pathology John D. Dingell VA Med. Ctr., Detroit, 1999—. Contbr. articles to profl. jours. NIH grantee 1999-02. Mem. Internat. Soc. Heart Rsch., Am. Heart Assn. (grant in aid 1994-99). Avocations: amateur radio, history, golf, travel, art. Office: John D Dingell VAMC 4646 John Rd Detroit MI 48201-2018 E-mail: rvanderh@med.wayne.edu.

VANDERHEYDEN, MARC A. academic administrator; b. Belgium; m. Diana. M, D, Cath. U. V.p. acad. affairs Cedar Crest Coll., dean faculty; pres. St. Michael's Coll., 1993—. Office: St Michael's Coll 1 Winooski Park Colchester VT 05439-0001*

VANDER HEYDEN, MARSHA ANN, business owner; b. Milw., Sept. 15, 1942; d. Bernard Aloysius and Leona Adeline (Zimpel) Vander H. BA, Alverno Coll., 1964; postgrad., Layton Sch. Art, 1966; MFA, Cornell U., 1969; diploma in carpentry and cabinetmaking, Manhattan Trade Sch., 1975. Rschr. The Nigerian Mus., Lagos, 1970; tchr. The Cloisters/The Met. Mus. Art, N.Y.C., 1973-74; woodshop instr. The New Lincoln Sch., 1973-75; tchr. Grand Street Settlement, 1974-76; mgr., head tchr. The Woodsmith's Studio, 1976-77; founder, pres. Trade Links, Inc. (runs Me Too Kids program); owner, operator Vander Heyden Woodworking, Inc., 1977—, Tapestries etc. dba Vander Heyden Woordworking Inc., N.Y.C. Designer pet products under name Doggone Purrrty; patentee frame assembly. Mem. Urban-rural Coalition. Recipient award of excellence The Archtl. Woodwork Inst., Washington, 1989. Mem. Women's Dem. Club N.Y., Miniatures Industry Assn. Am. Avocations: gardening, her dog and cats, hiking, animal and human rights issues, reading. Home and Office: 151 W 25th St 8th Fl New York NY 10001-7204 E-mail: marsha@tapestries.com.

VANDERHEYDEN, MIRNA-MAR, retired resort management and services executive; b. Freeport, Ill., Oct. 8, 1932; d. Orville Ray and Frances Elmira (Miller) Van Brocklin; m. Roger Eugene Vanderheyden, Dec. 23, 1950 (div. 1983); children: Romayne Lee, Adana Dawn, Grayling Dwayne, Willow B., Tiffany LaMarr. Cert., Brown's Bus. Coll., Freeport, Ill., 1949; BA, Milliken U., 1953. Paralegal, various locations, 1953-93; pres. Carlin Bay Corp., Coeur d'Alene, Idaho, 1981-97; retired, 1997. Lobbyist PTA, Springfield, Ill., 1972. Avocations: painting, water sports, reading, gardening, skiing. Home and Office: 609 W Apple Dr Delta CO 81416-3062

VANDERHOEF, LARRY NEIL, academic administrator; b. Perham, Minn., Mar. 20, 1941; s. Wilmar James and Ida Lucille (Wothe) Vanderhoef; m. Rosalie Suzanne Slifka, Aug. 31, 1963; children: Susan Marie, Jonathan Lee. BS, U. Wis., Milw., 1964, MS, 1965; PhD, Purdue U., 1969. Postdoctorate U. Wis., Madison, 1969—70; asst. prof. biology U. Ill., Urbana, 1970-74, assoc. prof., 1974—77, prof., 1977—80, head dept. plant biology, 1977—80; provost Agrl. and Life Scis., U. Md., College Park, 1980—84; exec. vice chancellor U. Calif., Davis, 1984—91, exec. vice chancellor, provost, 1991—94; chancellor, 1994—. Rsch. assoc. U. Wis., 1970—72; vis. investigator Carnegie Inst., 1976—77, Edinburgh (Scotland) U., 1978; cons. in field. Fellow, NRC, 1969—70, Eisenhower fellow, 1987; grantee Dimond Travel grantee, 1975, NSF, 1972, 1974, 1976—79, NATO, 1980. Mem.: AAAS, Nat. Assn. State Univ. and Land Grant Colls. (exec. com. 2000—), Am. Soc. Plant Physiology (bd. editors 1977—82, trustee, exec. com., treas. 1982—88, chmn. bd. trustees 1994—97). Home: 16 College Park Davis CA 95616-3607 Office: U Calif Davis Office Chancellor Davis CA 95616

VANDERHOEK, SHERRY A. counselor; b. Chgo., July 20, 1956; d. John Albert and Stella Rose Troike; m. Herman Vanderhoek (dec.); stepchildren: Michiel, Martin. AAS, Prairie State Coll., 1992; BA, Govs. State U., 1994, MA, 1997. Lic. prof. counselor, Ill.; cert. counselor Nat. Bd. Cert. Counselors. Counselor South Suburban Coun. on Alcoholism, East Hazel Crest, Ill., 1990-93, South Suburban Family Shelter, Hazel Crest, 1996-97; facilitator Aunt Martha's Youth Svcs. Ctr., Inc., Park Forest, 1991-92; grad. asst. Govs. State U., University Park, 1995-97; pvt. practice counselor Matteson, 1998—. Mem. ACA, Ill. Counseling Assn. (founder Govs. State chpt., pres. 1996, regional gov. 1997-2000), Ill. Alcohol and Other Drug Profl. Cert. Assn., Ill. Counselor Educators and Suprs. (Outstanding Grad. Student award 1996), Internat. Assn. Addiction and Offender Counselors, Assn. for Counselor Edn. and Supervision (Outstanding Grad. Student Scholarship award 1997), Psi Chi (chpt. founder, pres. 1997), Chi Sigma Iota (chpt. sec. 1995). Avocations: stained glass, cross-stitch, cooking. Home and Office: 3761 W 216th Pl Matteson IL 60443

VANDERHOOFT, ROB, investment company executive; b. Winnipeg; Grad., U. Manitoba, Can., 1987. Equity analyst Great West Life Assurance Co.; with Greystone Managed Investments Inc., Regina, Canada, 1991—, pres., chief investment officer Canada, 1995—. Office: Greystone Managed Investments 300 Park Ctr 1230 Blackfoot Dr Regina SK Canada

VANDER HORST, KATHLEEN PURCELL, nonprofit association administrator; b. Glen Rock, N.J., Jan. 15, 1945; d. Thomas Ralph and Elizabeth Jeanne (Burnett) Purcell; m. John Vander Horst Jr., Feb. 12, 1972 (div. Oct. 1993). Dir. devel. svcs. Johns Hopkins U., Balt., 1968-71; dir. devel. Union of Colls. of Art, Kansas City, Mo., 1971-72; dir. pub. rels. Md. Ballet and Ctr. Stage, Balt., 1973-76; dir. program devel. Joint Ctr. for Polit. and Econ. Studies, Washington, 1976-90, v.p. for program devel., 1990—. Dir., Roland Park Community Found., Balt., 1990—, vice chmn., 1998—; dir., chair program com. Centro de la Comunidad, Balt., 1997—.

VANDERKOLK, MARY DEDECKER, nursing educator; b. Highland Park, Mich., Feb. 7, 1951; d. Frank Joseph and Jean Marie (Halmich) DeDecker; m. Michael Homer VanderKolk, June 18, 1977; children: Lauren, Christopher, Nicole, Allison. BS in Psychology, Mich. State U., 1972, BSN, 1975; MSN, Wayne State U., 1980, postgrad., 1989—; MBA, Lake Superior State U., 1993. Nurse externe E.W. Sparrow Hosp., Lansing, Mich., 1974-75, charge nurse gen. surgery unit, 1975-76, staff nurse ICU, 1976-77; staff nurse SICU Catherine McCauley Health Ctr., Ann Arbor, 1977-81, summer 1982; asst. prof. Ea. Mich. U., Ypsilanti, 1981-84; mem. contingency staff ICU Munson Med. Ctr., Traverse City, Mich., 1984-85; lead instr. advanced med./surg. nursing Northwestern Mich. Coll., 1985-87, dept. head nursing, 1987-98, nursing prof., 1998—. Defendant nurse expert witness, 1989-94, 96, 97-98; mem. adj. fculty MSN program Grand Valley State U., Grand Rapids, Mich., 1991; com. mem. devel. coun. Munson Med. Ctr., 1992-93; sec./treas. Rural Emergency Med. Edn. Consortium, Traverse City, 1993-95, bd. dirs., 1993-99; bd. dirs., sec. Twin Bays Skating Club, 2000—. Co-author: Adoption Without Fear, 1989; co-author, co-prodr. (video) Tracheostomy Care and Suctioning Techniques, 1984. Coord. health edn. team Immaculate Conception Ch., Traverse City, 1994-95, mem. adv. com. health ministry, 1994—; mem. course devel. team Nursing Virtual C.C. Collaborative of Mich., 2000-01. Recipient Excellence in Teaching award Nat. Inst. Staff & Orgnl. Devel., 1993. Mem. ANA, Nat. League Nursing, Mich. Nurses Assn. (mem. cabinet adminstrn. and edn., rep. at large bd. dirs. 1987-89, 89-91, rec. sec. 1988-89), Mich. Coun. Nursing Edn. Adminstrs. (corr. sec. bd. dirs. 1988-89, 89-90, v.p./pres. elect 1990-91, pres. 1991-92, immediate past pres. 1992-93), Mich. League Nursing (dir. area V 1994-96), King. Internat. Nursing Soc. (founding mem. 1996—), County Med. Soc. Aux., Sigma Theta Tau. Avocations: travel, water sports, downhill skiing, figure skating. Office: Northwestern Mich Coll 1701 E Front St Traverse City MI 49686-3016

VAN DER KROEF, JUSTUS MARIA, political science educator; b. Djakarta, Indonesia, Oct. 30, 1925; came to U.S., 1942, naturalized, 1952; s. Hendrikus Leonardus and Maria Wilhelmina (van Lokven) van der K.; m. Orell Joan Ellison, Mar. 25, 1955 (dec.); children: Adrian Hendrick, Sri Orell. BA, Millsaps Coll., 1944; MA, U. N.C., 1947; PhD, Columbia U., 1953. Asst. prof. fgn. studies Mich. State U., 1948-55; Charles Dana prof., chair dept. polit. sci. and sociology U. Bridgeport, Conn., 1956-92, prof. emeritus, 1992—, mem. faculty Internat. Coll., 1999—. Vis. prof. Nanyang U., Singapore, U. Philippines, Quezon City, Vidyodaya U., Sri Lanka, Colombo, U. B.C., Vancouver, Can.; dir. Am.-Asian Ednl. Exchange, 1969-80; chmn. editl. bd. Comms. Rsch. Svcs., Inc., Greenwich, Conn., 1971-80; mem. internat. adv. bd. Union Trust Bank, Stamford, Conn., 1974-88, adv. bd., 1988-94; mem. nat. acad. adv. council Charles Edison Meml. Youth Fund; bd. dirs. WUBC-TV, Bridgeport, Conn., 1978-80. Author: Indonesia in the Modern World, 2 vols., 1954-56, Indonesian Social Evolution. Some Psychological Considerations, 1958, The Communist Party of Indonesia: Its History, Program and Tactics, 1965, Communism in Malaysia and Singapore, 1967, Indonesia Since Sukarno, 1971, The Lives of SEATO, 1976, Communism in Southeast Asia, 1980, Kampuchea: The Endless Tug of War, 1982, Aquino's Philippines. The Deepening Security Crisis, 1988, Territorial Claims in the South China Sea, 1992, The South China Sea Problem: Some Alternative Scenarios, 1994; mem. editorial bd. World Affairs, 1975—, Jour. Asian Affairs, 1975—, Asian Affairs, 1980—, Asian Profile, 1983—, Jour. of Govt. and Adminstrn., 1985—, Jour. of Econ. and Internat. Relations, 1987—, Asian Affairs Jour. (Karachi), 1992—; mng. editor: Asian Thought and Society, 1986-96; book rev. editor: Asian Thought and Soc, 1976-85; contbr. more than 200 articles to profl. jours. Mem. City Charter Revision Com. City of Bridgeport, 1983-86, 90-92. Served with Royal Netherlands Marine Corps, 1944-45. Sr. fellow Research Inst. Communist Affairs, Columbia U., 1965-66, Rockefeller Found.; fellow U. Queensland, Brisbane, Australia, 1968-69; research fellow Inst. Strategic Studies, Islamabad, Pakistan, 1982—; research fellow Mellon Research Found., 1983, 90; research fellow Internat. Ctr. Asian Studies, Hong Kong, 1983—. Mem. Univ. Profs. Acad. Order (nat. pres. 1970-71), Pi Gamma Mu, Phi Alpha Theta, Lambda Chi Alpha, Alpha Sigma Lambda Phi Sigma Iota. Home: 165 Linden Ave Bridgeport CT 06604-5730

VANDER LAAN, MARK ALAN, lawyer; b. Akron, Ohio, Sept. 14, 1948; s. Robert H. and Isabel R. (Bishop) Vander L.; m. Barbara Ann Ryzenga, Aug. 25, 1970; children: Aaron, Matthew. AB, Hope Coll., 1970; JD, U. Mich., 1972. Bar: Ohio 1973, U.S. Dist. Ct. (so. dist.) Ohio 1973, U.S. Ct. Appeals (6th cir.) 1978, U.S. Supreme Ct. 1981. Assoc. Dinsmore, Shohl, Coates & Deupree, Cin., 1972-79; ptnr. Dinsmore & Shohl, 1979—. Chair litig. dept., 2001—, spl. counsel Ohio Atty. Gen.'s Office, 1983—; spl. prosecutor State of Ohio, 1985-94; city solicitor City of Blue Ash, Ohio, 1987—, City of Silverton, Ohio, 1999—; trustee Cin. So. Railway, 1994—, pres., 1999—; trustee, chair Grassroots Leadership Acad., 1997—. Mem. Cin. Human Rels. Commn., 1980-86; mem. Leadership Cin. Class XIII, 1989-90; trustee Legal Aid Soc. of Cin., 1981-94, pres., 1988-90. Mem. ABA, Ohio Bar Assn., Cin. Bar Assn. (ethics com. 1983—), Sixth Cir. Jud. Conf. (life), Potter Stewart Inn of Ct. (master), Queen City Club. Office: Dinsmore & Shohl 1900 Chemed Ct 255 E 5th St Cincinnati OH 45202-4700

VANDERLINDEN, CAMILLA DENICE DUNN, telecommunications industry manager; b. Dayton, July 21, 1950; d. Joseph Stanley and Virginia Danley (Martin) Dunn; m. David Henry VanderLinden; Oct. 10, 1980; 1 child, Michael Christopher. Student, U. de Valencia, Spain, 1969; BA in Spanish and Secondary Edn. cum laude, U. Utah, 1972, MS in Human Resource Econs., 1985. Asst. dir. Davis County Community Action Program, Farmington, Utah, 1973-76; dir. South County Community Action, Midvale, 1976-79; supr. customer service Ideal Nat. Life Ins. Co., Salt Lake City, 1979-80; mgr. customer service Utah Farm Bur. Mutual Ins., 1980-82; quality assurance analyst Am. Express Co., 1983-86, quality assurance and human resource specialist, 1986-88, mgr. quality assurance and engring. Denver, 1988-91; mgr. customer svc. Tel. Express Co., Colorado Springs, Colo., 1991-97; dir. Call Ctr. United Membership Mktg. Group, Lakewood, 1997-98; telesvcs. industry mgr. Piton Found., Denver, 1998—; customer care and tng. dir. SafeRent, 2000—; pvt. call ctr. cons., 2000—; dir. quality assurance Tele-Servicing Innovations, 2000—. Mem. adj. faculty Westminster Coll., Salt Lake City, 1987-88. mem. adj. faculty, mem. quality adv. bd. Red Rocks C.C., 1990-91. Vol. translator Latin Am. community; vol. naturalist Roxborough State Park; internat. exch. coord. EF Fgn. Exch. Program. Mem. Internat. Customer Svc. Orgn. (officer call ctr. chpt.), Colo. Springs Customer Svc. Assn. (officer). Christian. Avocations: swimming, hosting foreign exchange students. Home: 10857 Snow Cloud Trail Littleton CO 80125-9211 E-mail: camillavan@usa.net.

VAN DER LINDEN, FRANK MORRIS, historian; b. Hendersonville, N.C., Mar. 8, 1919; s. William Harrison and Floride Bowden (Morris) van der L.; m. Georgia Kathlyn Huddle, Feb. 11, 1951; children: Frank Robert, Margaret Lyn, Anne Morris. AB, Lenoir-Rhyne Coll., 1939. Reporter, editl. writer Hickory N.C. Daily Record, 1939-42; mng. editor Hickory Daily Record, 1942-45; reporter Cottrell News Bur., Washington, 1945-52; Washington bur. chief Nashville Tenn. Banner, 1952-86; White House corr. Sacramento Calif. Union, 1979-89; columnist United Feature Syndicate, N.Y., 1971-76. Guest panelist NBC-TV Meet the Press, 1956-75. *Frank van der Linden's book, Lincoln: The Road to War, has been praised by reviewers as a "lively and provocative book" with "the sizzle of a gripping suspense thriller." It contends that the Civil War, with its bloody toll of six hundred thousand dead, was a terrible mistake; that President Lincoln could have avoided it by using conciliation, instead of force, in regard to the seceding states. He is continuing his research into original sources to discover why so many northern people opposed the war.* Author: Dark Horse, 1944, The Turning Point: Jefferson's Battle for the Presidency, 1962, Nixon's Quest for Peace, 1972, The Real Reagan, 1981, Lincoln: The Road to War, 1998. Mem. The Lincoln Commn., Washington, 1989-98. Mem. U.S. Capitol Hist. Soc. (oral history program dir. 1976-94), The Cosmos Club (editl. bd. 1988—). Presbyterian. Avocations: historical research. Home and Office: 5301 Westbard Cir Apt 247 Bethesda MD 20816-1430

VAN DER LINDEN, JOHN EDWARD, newspaper broker, consultant; b. Des Moines, Aug. 8, 1917; s. John and Kathleen Pomeroy (Gaylord) van der L.; m. Marjorie Rose Wetherbee, Nov. 27, 1948; children: Peter J., Dirk J., Thomas J. BS, Iowa State U., Ames, 1940. Mgr. van der Linden Advt., Ames, 1935-36; farm editor Scott County Tribune, Walcott, Iowa, 1937; reporter Mason City (Iowa) Globe-Gazette, 1940-41; dir. expansion Am. Legion Iowa, Des Moines, 1946-47; editor Marshall (Minn.) Messenger, 1947-48, Northwood (Iowa) Anchor, 1948-60; editor, pub. Sibley (Iowa) Gazette-Tribune, 1960-77; pres. N.W. Pub., Inc., Spirit Lake, Iowa, 1977—. Sec. N.W. Iowa Peach, Inc., Sibley, 1966-87. Editor: (book) Iowa Legion Handbook, 1947, (mag.) Dairymen's Digest, 1970-91. Bd. dirs. Spirit Lake Kiwanis Club, 1984—; lt. gov. Kiwanis Nebr.-Iowa Dist., Spirit Lake, 1980-81; Dem. cand. for Iowa State Senate, 1980; county chmn. Osceola County Dem. Com., Sibley, 1978-80; county ctrl. com. Dickinson County Dem. Com., Spirit Lake, 1980-96; pres. Iowa Sch. Bd. Assn., Des Moines, 1965-66. Lt. col. U.S. Army, 1941-46, PTO. Apptd. to State Ednl. TV Bd. by Gov. of Iowa, Des Moines, 1967-76, State Bd. Pub. Instrn. by Gov. of Iowa, Des Moines, 1970-82; named Disting. Lt. Gov. by Nebr.-Iowa Kiwanis, Spirit Lake, 1981. Mem. Iowa Newspaper Assn. (Master Editor-Pub. award 1975), Minn. Newspaper Assn., Res. Officers Assn. (50 yr. mem.), Kiwanis, Shriners, Masons, Am. Legion, VFW, Sierra Club. Methodist. Avocations: travel, art, photography, choir singing, community service. Office: Northwest Pub Inc PO Box 275 Spirit Lake IA 51360-0275 Fax: 712-336-0611. E-mail: johnvan@rconnect.com.

VAN DER MARCK, JAN, art historian; b. Roermond, The Netherlands, Aug. 19, 1929; arrived in U.S., 1957; s. Everard and Anny (Finken) van der Marck; m. Ingeborg Lachmann, Apr. 27, 1961 (dec. 1988); m. Sheila Stamell, May 24, 1990. BA, U. Nijmegen, The Netherlands, 1952, MA, 1954, PhD in Art History, 1956; postgrad., U. Utrecht, The Netherlands, 1956-57, Columbia U., 1957-59. Curator Gemeentemuseum, Arnhem, Netherlands, 1959-61; asst. dir. fine arts Seattle World's Fair, 1961-62; curator Walker Art Center, Mpls., 1963-67; dir. Mus. Contemporary Art, Chgo., 1967-70; assoc. prof. art history U. Wash., 1972-74; dir. Dartmouth Coll. Mus. and Galleries, 1974-80, Center for Fine Arts, Miami, 1980-85; curator 20th century art, chief curator Detroit Inst. Arts, 1986-95, consultative curator, 1998—. Author: (book) Romantische Boekillustratie in Belgie, 1956, George Segal, 1975, Arman, 1984, Bernar Venet, 1988, The Art of Contemporary Bookbinding, 1997, Art and the American Experience, 1998, Lucio Pozzi, 2001; contbr. articles to art jours., essays to catalogues. Fellow Pierpont Morgan Libr. Decorated officer Order Arts and Letters, knight Order of Orange Nassau; fellow Netherlands Orgn. Pure Rsch., 1954—55, Rockefeller Found., 1957—59, Aspen Inst., 1974, 1994, Vis. Sr., Ctr. Advanced Study in Visual Arts, 1986. Mem.: Les Amis de la Reliure Originale, Assn. Internat. Bibliophilie, Internat. Art Critics Assn., Grolier Club.

VAN DER MEER, SIMON, physicist; b. The Hague, The Netherlands, Nov. 24, 1925; s. Pieter and Jetske (Groeneveld) van der M.; m. Catharina M. Koopman, Apr. 26, 1966; children: Esther, Mathijs. Engring. degree in physics, Poly. U., Delft, The Netherlands, 1952; Dr. (hon.), U. Geneva, 1983, U. Amsterdam, The Netherlands, 1984, U. Genoa, Italy, 1985. Research engr. Philips Physics Lab., Eihdhoven, The Netherlands, 1952-55; sr. engr. CERN European Orgn. Nuclear Research, Geneva, 1956-90; ret., 1990. Co-recipient Nobel prize for physics, 1984. Mem. AAAS (fgn., hon.), Royal Netherlands Acad. Scis. (corr.). E-mail: vdmeer@freesurf.ch.

VAN DER MEULEN, JOSEPH PIERRE, neurologist; b. Boston, Aug. 22, 1929; s. Edward Lawrence and Sarah Jane (Robertson) VanDer M.; m. Ann Irene Yadeno, June 18, 1960; children: Elisabeth, Suzanne, Janet. AB, Boston Coll., 1950; MD, Boston U., 1954. Diplomate: Am. Bd. Psychiatry and Neurology. Intern Cornell Med. div. Bellevue Hosp., N.Y.C., 1954-55, resident, 1955-56, Harvard U., Boston City Hosp., 1958-60, instr., fellow, 1962-66; assoc. Case Western Res. U., Cleve., 1966-67, asst. prof., 1967-69, assoc. prof. neurology and biomed. engring., 1969-71; prof. neurology U. So. Calif., L.A., 1971—; also dir. dept. neurology Los Angeles County/U. So. Calif. Med. Center; chmn. dept. U. So. Calif., 1971-78, v.p. for health affairs, 1977—, dean Sch. Medicine, 1985-86, 95-97, vice dean med. affairs, 1995-97; dir. Ind. Health Professions, L.A., 1991—. Vis. prof. Autonomous U. Guadalajara, Mex., 1974; pres. Norris Cancer Hosp. and Research Inst., 1983-98. Contbr. articles to profl. jours. Mem. med. adv. bd. Calif. chpt. Myasthenia Gravis Found., 1971-75, chmn., 1974-75, 77-78; med. adv. bd. Amyotrophic Lateral Sclerosis Found., Calif., 1973-75, chmn., 1974-75; mem. Com. to Combat Huntington's Disease, 1973—; bd. dirs. Calif. Hosp. Med. Ctr., Good Hope Med. Found., Doheny Eye Hosp., House Ear Inst., L.A. Hosp. Good Samaritan, Children's Hosp. of L.A., Phila. Health Edn. Corp., Barlow Respiratory Hosp., USC U. Hosp., chmn., 1991—; bd. govs. Thomas Aquinas Coll.; bd. dirs. Assn. Acad. Health Ctrs., chmn., 1991-92; pres. Scott Newman Ctr., 1987-89. Served to lt. M.C. USNR, 1956-58. Nobel Inst. fellow Karolinska Inst., Stockholm, 1960-62; NIH grantee, 1968-71 Mem. AMA, Am. Neurol. Assn., Am. Acad. Neurology, L.A. Soc. Neurology and Psychiatry (pres. 1977-78), L.A. Med. Assn., Mass. Med. Soc., Ohio Med. Soc., Calif. Med. Soc., L.A. Acad. Medicine, Alpha Omega Alpha (councillor 1992—), Phi Kappa Phi. Home: 39 Club View Ln Palos Verdes Peninsula CA 90274-4208 Office: U So Calif 1540 Alcazar St Los Angeles CA 90089-9001

VANDERMOLEN, ROBERT L. construction executive; b. Grand Rapids, Mich., Apr. 23, 1947; s. Robert L. and Marjorie Molo VanderMolen; m. Deborah Stenman, Dec. 16, 1980; children: Seaon, Colin. BA, Mich. State U., 1971; MFA, U. Oreg., 1973. Painting contractor VanderMolen Painting, Grand Rapids, Mich., 1980—. Author: (poetry) Of Pines, 1989, Peaches, 1998, Breeeath, 2000. Fellow, Nat. Endowment for Arts, 1995. Avocation: fishing. Home: 2771 Glencairn Dr Grand Rapids MI 49504

VANDER MOLEN, THOMAS DALE, lawyer; b. Ann Arbor, Mich., Oct. 30, 1950; s. John and Eleanor Ruth (Driesens) Vander M.; m. Judith P. Wrahlstad, June 16, 2001; children from previous marriage: Laura, David, Eric. BA, Calvin Coll., 1972; JD magna cum laude, Harvard U., 1975. Bar: Minn. 1976, U.S. Dist. Ct. Minn. 1981, U.S. Claims Ct. 1983, U.S. Tax Ct. 1977, U.S. Ct. Appeals 1988. Law clk. to judge U.S. Ct. Appeals-First Cir., Boston, 1975-76; assoc. Dorsey & Whitney, Mpls., 1976-81; ptnr. Dorsey & Whitney LLP, 1982—, gen. counsel, 1993—2001. Mem. editorial bd. Harvard Law Rev., 1973-75. Presbyterian. Office: Dorsey & Whitney LLP 50 South 6th St Minneapolis MN 55402

VANDER MYDE, PHILIP LOUIS, architectural design firm executive; b. Whiteside County, Ill., Apr. 4, 1931; s. Louis John and Ann Marie (Pals) Vander; m. Martha T. Grier, Mar. 15, 1969; children: Jane Gray, John Philip, Martha Maslin. Studnet, Cen. Coll., 1949-50; BA in Arch., U. Minn., 1958. Registered architect, Va., Md., D.C., N.C., Tenn., Pa., Mich., N.J., Ill., W.Va., Del. Architect Vosbeck-Ward & Assocs., Alexandria, Va., 1962-64; assoc. ptnr. Vosbeck Vosbeck & Assocs., 1966; ptnr. VVKR Partnership, 1967-70, mng. ptnr., 1967-70, mng. ptnr. Md. office University Park, 1970-80; prin. VVKR, Inc., Alexandria, 1980-83; mng. ptnr. for architecture Dewberry & Davis, Fairfax, Va., 1983-87; mng. ptnr. Senseman/VanderMyde, Alexandria, 1987-89; prin. ADD, Inc., Washington, 1989-92; pres., CEO Additions, Inc., Va., 1992—. Prin. works include Prince Georges Hosp. Ctr., 1977, U. Md. LawLibr., 1978, Frederick County Courthouse, 1979, Md. Dept. Agr. Hdqrs., 1980, Belle Haven Country Club, 1988, First Am. Bank Va., North Tower, 1989, Naval Res. Assn., Hdqrs., 1998, Fine Arts Ctr. & Theatre, St. Mary's Ryken H.S., 1999. Capt. USNR, 1959-61. Recipient Honor award Bicentennial Design awards, AIA; 17 design awards, 1970-86; Paul Harris fellow, 1992. Mem. AIA (pres. Potomac Valley chpt. 1977-78, fed. Liaison Task Force 1991-93), Vauxlceuse Citizens Assn. (past pres.), Minn. Alumni Assn., Belle Haven Country Club, Potomac Soc., Rotary (pres. 1994-95, Disting. Rotarian award 1998), The Priory St. King Charles the Martyr, Soveriegn Mil. Order of Temple of Jerusalem, Knight of Order (Grand Cross), Sigma Alpha Epsilon (past pres.). Republican. Presbyterian. Avocations: golf, fishing, boating, photography. Home: 261 N Dogwood Trail Southern Shores NC 27949-3138 E-mail: additions@mindspring.com.

VANDER NAALD EGENES, JOAN ELIZABETH, business owner, educator; b. Des Moines, Feb. 13, 1936; d. Bert and Cathryn Alice (Bunger) Vander Naald; m. David Iddings Grant, July 25, 1959 (div. Oct. 1984); children: Jeffrey, Pamela, Elizabeth, Jennifer. BA, U. Iowa, 1958. Cert. profl. in edn., Iowa, Colo.; cert. travel agt., Iowa. Instr. St. Katherine's Sch., Davenport, Iowa, 1958-59, Iowa Ctrl. C.C., Fort Dodge, 1959-61; city councilwoman Boone, 1980-86; instr. Des Moines Area C.C., Boone Campus, 1983; founder, owner, importer Global Ednl. Svcs., Des Moines, 1992-97; receptionist, sec. Automobile Club of So. Calif., West Los Angeles, 1997-2001. Bd. mem. Iowa Psychology Bd. Examiners, Des Moines, 1984-93; rsch. interviewer Iowa State U., Ames, 1984; resource tchr., workshop presenter about Russia, 1988-94; freelance photographer, 1988—. Lifetime mem. Rep. Senatorial Inner Circle, Washington, 1987—; pres. Iowa 4th Dist. Rep. Women, 1990-91, Polk County (Iowa) Rep. Women, 1994; precinct chair 12, ward 01, Des Moines, 1995-97; pres. Des Moines Metro Opera Guild, 1996-97, coun. sec., 1995-97; extensive vol. activities, including various fundraising chairs. Recipient 1st prize Youth Projects, Iowa Devel. Commn., 1983, Women Helping Women award for volunteerism, Boone, 1983; named Entrepreneur of Yr. in Iowa award GE, 1995. Republican. Avocation: swimming. Home: 36047 Palomino Way Palm Desert CA 92211 E-mail: joanevan@aol.com.

VANDERPAL, GEOFFREY ALAN, financial planner; BS in Fin., Mktg., Mgmt., Columbia Coll., 1995; MBA, Webster U., 1997; cert. fin. planning, U. Calif., Berkeley, 2000. Cert. fin. planner, fund specialist, registered fin. cons. Asst. v.p., sr. fin. exec. Citicorp Investment Svcs., Danville, Calif., 1992—2000; v.p., fin. advisor First Union Securities, Inc., Balt., 2000—. Arbitrator NASD and NYSE, NY, 1999. Actor: (films) Getting Hal, 2001. Trustee Village of Cary, Ill., 1995—97. Mem.: Fin. Planning Assn. Avocations: world travel, reading, politics. Office: First Union Securities Inc 3rd Fl D 2414 7 St Paul St Baltimore MD 21202

VANDERPLOEG, JAMES M. preventive medicine physician; b. Upland, Calif., Nov. 22, 1950; BA, U. Iowa, 1975. Intern U. Hosp./U. Calif., San Diego, 1975-76; resident in otolaryngoloty U. Iowa Hosps., Iowa City, 1978-79; resident in occupational medicine U. Tex. Sch. Pub. Health, Houston, 1980-82, assoc. prof. occupational health; mem. staff St. John Hosp., Nassau Bay, Tex.; pvt. practice, ptnr. group practice Ctr. Aerospace & Occupl. Medicine; exec. dir. Am. Bd. Preventive Medicine, Schiller Park, Il. Part-time med. adminstr. Mem. Am. Coll. Occupational Medicine, ACPrM-AerosMA. Office: Ctr for Aerospace & Occupl Medicine 700 Gemini St Ste 110 Houston TX 77058-2735*

VANDER PLOEG, SCOTT DAVID, literature educator, writer; b. Kokomo, Ky., July 3, 1957; s. John Edwin and Virginia Lee Vander Ploeg; m. Sandal May King; children: Nicholas, Susannah. BA in English, Purdue U., 1979, MA in English, 1982; PhD, U. Ky., 1988, postgrad., 1994. Prof. humanities Madisonville (Ky.) Coll., 1988—. Contbr. essays and commentaries to PBS radio affiliate, articles to profl. jours. Chair steering com. Watershed Watch-Tradewater and Lower Green River Basin, Madisonville, 2000—02; bd. dirs. Ky. Humanities Coun., Lexington, 2001—. Mem.: John Donne Soc., Modern Language Assn., Ky. Philol. Assn. (exec. dir. 2002—), Ky. Cols. Taoist. Avocations: tai chi, science fiction/fantasy, local politics. Office: Madisonville Coll 2000 College Dr Madisonville KY 42431 Office Fax: 270-821-1555. Business E-Mail: scott.vanderploeg@kctcs.edu.

VAN DER PLUIJM, BERNARDUS ADRIANUS (BEN VAN DER PLUIJM), geologist, educator; b. Enschede, The Netherlands, Sept. 30, 1955; came to the U.S., 1985; m. Elisabeth H. Quint; children: Wouter, Robert. MS, U. Leiden, 1981; PhD, U. New Brunswick, 1984. Asst. prof. U. Mich., Ann Arbor, 1985-91, assoc. prof., 1991-96, prof., 1996—, dir. global change program, 2000—. Office: U Mich Dept Geological Sciences Ann Arbor MI 48109 E-mail: vdpluijm@umich.edu.

VANDERPOEL, JAMES ROBERT, lawyer; b. Harvey, Ill., Sept. 27, 1955; s. Waid Richard and Ruth (Silberman) V.; m. Deanne Czabaranek, May 1987; children: Jacqueline, Robert, Jennifer. BS in Fin., Ind. U., 1978; JD, Santa Clara U., 1982. Bar: Calif. 1982, U.S. Dist. Ct. (no. dist.) Calif. 1982. Sr. dir. contracts Motorola Personal Telematics Group, Tempe, Ariz., 1984—. Avocations: basketball, hiking, golf, snorkeling, gardening. Office: Motorola Personal Telematics Group 2900 S Diablo Way Tempe AZ 85282

VANDERPOOL, WARD MELVIN, management and marketing consultant; b. Oakland, Mo., Jan. 20, 1918; s. Oscar B. and Clara (McGuire) V.; m. Lee Kendall, July 7, 1939. MEE, Tulane U. V.p. charge sales Van Lang Brokerage, Los Angeles, 1934-38; mgr. agrl. div. Dayton Rubber Co., Chgo., 1939-48; pres., gen. mgr. Vee Mac Co., Rockford, Ill., 1948—; pres., dir. Zipout, Inc., 1951—, Wife Saver Products, Inc., 1959—. Chmn. bd. Zipout Internat., Kenvan Inc., 1952—, Shevan Corp., 1951—, Atlas Internat. Corp.; pres. Global Enterprises Ltd., Global Assos. Ltd.; chmn. bd. dirs. Am. Atlas Corp., Atlas Chem. Corp., Merzat Industries Ltd.; trustee Ice Crafter Trust, 1949—; bd. dirs. Atlas Chem. Internat. Ltd., Kenlee Internat., Ltd., Shrimp Tool Internat. Ltd.; mem. Toronto Bd. Trade; chmn. bd. dirs. Am. Atlas Corp., Am. Packaging Corp. Mem. adv. bd. Nat. Security Council, congl. adv. com. Heritage Found.; mem. Rep. Nat. Com., Presdl. Task Force, Congrl. Adv. Com. Hon. mem. Internat. Swimming Hall of Fame. Mem. Nat. (dir. at large), Rock River (past pres.), sales execs., Sales and Mktg. Execs. Internat. (dir.), Am. Mgmt. Assn., Rockford Engring. Soc., Am. Tool Engrs., Internat. Acad. Aquatic Art (dir.), Am. Inst. Mgmt. (pres. council), Am. Ordnance Assn., Internat. Platform Assn., Heritage Found., Ill. C. of C., Jesters Club, IAA Swim Club, Elmcrest Country Club, Pyramid Club, Dolphin Club, Marlin Club, Univ. Club, Athletic Club, Oxford Club, Masons (consistory), Shriners, Elks. Home: 374 Parkland Dr SE Cedar Rapids IA 52403-2031 also: 40 Richview Rd # 308 Toronto ON Canada M9A 5C1 also: 704 Park Center Dr Santa Ana CA 92705-3563 Office: PO Box 1972 Cedar Rapids IA 52406-1972 also: 111 Richmond St W Ste 318 Toronto ON Canada M5H 1T1

VANDERRYN, JACK, philanthropic foundation administrator; b. Groningen, The Netherlands, Apr. 14, 1930; came to U.S., 1939; s. Herman Gabriel and Henrietta S.E. (Hartog) V.; m. Margrit Wolfes, Mar. 18, 1956; children: Judith, Amy, Daniel. BA, Lehigh U., 1951, MS, 1952, PhD, 1955. Rsch. and grad. teaching asst. Lehigh U., Bethlehem, Pa., 1952-55; asst. prof. chemistry Va. Poly. Inst., Blacksburg, 1955-58; rsch. participant Oak Ridge (Tenn.) Nat. Lab., 1957; chemist AEC, Oak Ridge, 1958-62, tech. adviser to asst. gen. mgr. R & D, Washington, 1962-67, asst. to gen. mgr., 1971-72, tech. asst. to dir. div. applied tech., 1972-73, chief energy tech. br., div. applied tech., 1973-75; acting dir. div. energy storage Energy Rsch. and Devel. Adminstrn., Washington, 1975, dir. Office Internat. R & D Programs, 1975-77; dir. Office Internat. Programs Dept. Energy, 1977-82; dir. energy and natural resources AID, 1982-91; program dir. environment Moriah Fund, 1991—. Sr. sci. adviser U.S. Mission to Internat. Atomic Energy Agy., Dept. State, Vienna, Austria, 1967-71; lectr. Brookings Instn., 1965-66. Mem., dep. pres., exec. bd. Am. Internat. Sch., Vienna, 1968-71; v.p. Oak Ridge Civic Music Assn., 1959-60; pres. Washington Print Club, 1986-91; pres. Consultative Group on Biodiversity, 1997-2000. Home: 8112 Whittier Blvd Bethesda MD 20817-3123 Office: Moriah Fund Ste 1000 1634 I St NW Washington DC 20006-4003 E-mail: jvanderryn@moriahfund.org.

VANDERSLICE, RONNA JEAN, education educator; b. Woodward, Okla., Apr. 22, 1965; d. Ronnie Leroy and Norma Jean (Semmel) V. BA, Southwestern Okla. State U., 1986; MEd, Tex. Tech U., 1990, EdD, 1995. Cert. tchr., reading specialist, counselor spl. edn., learning disabilities, psychometry, early childhood, Tex.; mid-mgmt. cert., gifted and talented endorsement. Tchr. Highland Elem. Sch., Plainview, Tex., 1986-91; counselor 6th grade learning ctr. Ash Sch., 1991-93; assoc. prof., chair sch. svc. programs Southwestern Okla. State U., Weatherford, 1993—. Mem. Higher Edn. Alumni Coun. Okla., Weatherford Kiwanis, Phi Delta Kappa, Delta Kappa Gamma, Kappa Kappa Iota. Lutheran. Avocations: sports, reading, crafts. Home: 416 Texas St Weatherford OK 73096-5632 Office: SW Okla State U 100 Campus Dr Weatherford OK 73096-3098

VANDERSLICE, STEPHANIE M. humanities educator; b. Queens, N.Y., Feb. 4, 1967; d. William Muller and Maureen Pettei; m. John Vanderslice, July 2, 1993; children: Jackson H., Wilson A. MFA, George Mason U., 1992; PhD, U. La., 1997. Asst. prof. writing U. Ctrl. Ark., Conway, 1997—. Dir. Ctrl. Ark. Writing Project, Conway, 1999—; mem. vis. writers program Ark. Arts Coun., 1999. Contbr. articles to profl. jours. Grantee Deep South Writing Conf. Program grantee, La. Arts Coun., 1995,1996. Mem.: MLA, Conf. on Coll. Composition and Comm., Nat. Coun. Tchrs. of English. Avocations: travel, walking, collecting children's books. Office: Univ Ctrl Arkansas 201 Donaghey Ave, Irby 105F Conway AR 72035 Office Fax: 501-450-3343. Business E-Mail: stephv@mail.uca.edu.

VANDERSLICE, THOMAS AQUINAS, electronics executive; b. Phila., Jan. 8, 1932; s. Joseph R. and Mae (Daly) V.; m. Margaret Hurley, June 9, 1956; children: Thomas Aquinas, Paul Thomas Aquinas, John Thomas Aquinas, Peter Thomas Aquinas. BS in Chemistry and Philosophy, Boston Coll., 1953; PhD in Chemistry and Physics, Cath. U. Am., 1956. With GE, Fairfield, Conn., from 1956, gen. mgr. electronic components bus. div., 1970-72, v.p., 1970, group exec. spl. systems and products group, 1972-77, sr. v.p., sector exec. Power System Sector, 1977-79, exec. v.p., sector exec. Power System Sector, 1979-84; pres., chief oper. officer, dir. Gen. Tel. & Electronics Corp., Stamford, 1979-83; chmn., CEO, Apollo Computer, Inc., Chelmsford, Mass., 1984-89, M/A COM, Inc., Lowell, 1989-95. Bd. dirs. Texaco, Inc. Patentee low pressure gas measurements and analysis, gas surface interactions and elec. discharges; co-author: Ultra High Vacuum and Its Applications, 1963; reviser: Scientific Foundations of Vacuum Technique, 1960; contbr. to profl. jours. Trustee Boston Coll., past chmn., past trustee Comm. Econ. Devel. Recipient Bicentennial medal Boston Coll., 1976; Fulbright scholar, 1953-56. Mem. NAE, ASTM, Am. Vacuum Soc., Am. Chem. Soc., Am. Inst. Physics, Royal Poinciana Golf Club (Naples, Fla.), Oyster Harbors Club, Sigma Xi, Tau Beta Pi, Alpha Sigma Nu, Sigma Pi Sigma. Office: LeRivage Unit 10N 4351 Gulf Shore Blvd N Naples FL 34103-2697

VANDERSPEK, PETER GEORGE, management consultant, writer; b. The Hague, Netherlands, Dec. 15, 1925; came to U.S., 1945; s. Pieter and Catherine Johanna (Rolf) V.; m. Charlotte Louise Branch, Aug. 18, 1957. Student, Tilburg (Netherlands) U., 1944; MA in Econs., Fordham U., 1950, PhD in Econs., 1954; postgrad., George Washington U., 1967-68. Internat. economist Mobil Oil Corp., N.Y.C., 1956-59; mgr. internat. market rsch. Celanese Corp., 1959-63; internat. economist Bethlehem (Pa.) Steel Corp., 1964-65; sr. tech. adviser Battelle Meml. Inst., Washington, 1965-66; indsl. adviser Inter-Am. Devel. Bank, 1967-69; economist Fed. Res. Bank, N.Y.C., 1970-72; mgr. internat. market rsch. Brunswick Corp., Skokie, Ill., 1973-76; mgr. advanced planning Sverdrup Corp., St. Louis, 1979-87, cons., 1988-90; pres. OBEX, Inc., San Luis Obispo, Calif., 1988—. Author: Planning for Factory Automation, 1993; contbr. to profl. jours. Thomas J. Watson fellow, IBM-Fordham U., 1945-49. Mem. Nat. Assn. Bus. Economists, Mensa. Avocations: travel, writing. Home and Office: 1039 Vista Brisa San Luis Obispo CA 93405

VAN DER SPIEGEL, JAN, engineering educator; b. Aalst, Belgium, Apr. 12, 1951; came to U.S., 1980; s. Robert and Celestine Van der Spiegel. BSEE, U. Leuven, 1971, MSEE, 1974, PhD in Elec. Engring., 1979; M of Arts and Sci., U. Pa., 1988. 2d lt. Belgian Air Force, 1979-90; asst. prof. elec. engring. U. Pa., Phila., 1981-87, assoc. prof., 1987-95, prof. elec. engring., 1995—, dir. Ctr. Sensor Tech., 1989-98, chmn. dep. elec. engring., 1998—. Patentee integ. ambient sensing, radiation sens. retina sens., gen prupost neural comp., novel ferroelectric sensors; editor Sensors and Actuators, 1986—. Postdoctoral fellow U. Pa., 1980-81; named Presdl. Young Investigator The White House, 1984. Fellow IEEE (sr.); mem. Neural Network Soc., Tau Beta Pi. Office: U Pa Ctr Sensor Techs Moore Sch Elec Engring 200 S 33d St Rm 203 Philadelphia PA 19104-6314

VANDERSTAPPEN, HARRIE ALBERT, Far Eastern art educator; b. Heesch, The Netherlands, Jan. 21, 1921; came to U.S., 1959; s. Johannes and Johanna (van de Poel) V. Student, Theol. Sch., Helvoirt and Teteringen, The Netherlands, 1939-45, Chinese Lang. Sch., Peking, People's Republic of China, 1946-48; PhD in Far Eastern Art, U. Chgo., 1955. Ordained priest Roman Catholic Ch., 1945. Student lang., also tchr., writer, Tokyo, 1955-57; tchr. Nansan U., Nagoya, Japan, 1957-59; prof. Far Eastern art U. Chgo., 1959-92, chmn. dept. art, 1964-69, prof. emeritus dept. art, 1991—. Author: The T.L. Yuan Bibliography of Chinese Art and Archaeology, 1975; author, editor: Ritual and Reverence, 1989; assoc. editor Monumenta Serica, 1955—; contbr. articles to profl. jours. Recipient Teaching of Art History award Nat. Coll. Art Assn. Am., 1985; Harrie A. Vanderstappen Disting. Chair established at U. Chgo., 1995. Mem. Asia Soc., Assn. Asian Arts Home: 1901 Waukegan Rd Techny IL 60082-6000

VANDERSTEEL, WILLIAM, transportation executive; b. Hilversum, The Netherlands, Mar. 21, 1919; s. Dionijs VanderSteel Schonegevel and Marion Scott Hamilton Martin; m. Betsey Stoddard, June 21, 1946 (div. Oct. 1963); children: Stoddard, Marion, William; m. Lee Benfield, Mar. 19, 1966; children: Ann, Tina. BS, MIT, 1940. Engr. Gen. Motors Corp., Detroit, 1941-42; chief engr. Cox and Stevens Aircraft Corp., Mineola, N.Y., 1945-48; pres., chief exec. officer Ampower Corp., Alpine, N.J., 1948—, Tubexpress Systems Inc., North Bergen, NJ, 1982—98. Bd dirs Natural Pack Sys, Inc. Mem planning bd, Alpine, NJ, 1982—90; bd dirs Citizens for a Sound Econ, Washington, Nat Alliance Const Money, Washington. Capt, test pilot USAF, 1942—45. Mem.: Royal Scottish Automobile Soc, Experimental Aircraft Asn, Phi Beta Epsilon. Achievements include patents for ship stabilizer, underground freight pipeline. Home: Highwood Pl Alpine NJ 07620 Fax: 201-768-1653. E-mail: ampower@att.net.

VANDERSYPEN, LIEVEN MARK KOENRAAD, researcher; b. Leuven, , Belgium, Sept. 19, 1972; BSEE, MSEE, Cath. U. Leuven, 1996; MS and PhD in Elec. Engring., Stanford U., 2001. Rsch. assoc. IBM Almaden Rsch. Ctr., San Jose, Calif., 1998—2001; postdoctoral rschr. Delft (Netherlands) U. Tech. , 2001—. Fellow Francqui fellow, Belgian-Am. Ednl. Found., 1996—97, Yansouni Family Stanford grad. fellow, 1997—2001.

VANDERSYPEN, RITA DEBONA, guidance counselor, academic administrator; b. Alexandria, La., Sept. 13, 1953; d. Sam S. and Myrtle (Genova) DeBona; m. Robert Louis Vandersypen, Aug. 17, 1974; children: Regina Marie, Ryan Matthew. BA summa cum laude, La. Coll., 1975; MEd, La. State U., 1980, postgrad., 1982; EdS, Northwestern State U., Natchitoches, La., 1993. Eligibility worker Rapides Parish Office Family Svcs., Alexandria, 1975-78; welfare social worker Rapides Parish Foster Care Svcs., 1978-79; tchr. A. Wettermark High Sch., Boyce, La., 1979-84; tchr. English English Alexandria Sr. High Sch., 1984-92, guidance counselor, 1992-2000; asst. prin., curriculum coord. Brame Jr. H.S., Alexandria, La., 2000—. Contbr. to handbook and curriculum guide. Sponsor Future Voters Am. Club, 1984-89, 4-H Club, 1988-97. Mem. Rapides Assn. Principals, Rapides Fedn. Tchrs., La. Assn. Principals, La. Vocat. Assn., La. Mid. Sch. Assn., Rapides Livestock Club, Belgian-Am. Club, Am. Quarter Horse Assn., Phi Kappa Phi, Kappa Delta Pi. Roman Catholic. Office: Brame Jr HS 4800 Dawn St Alexandria LA 71301-3301

VAN DER TUIN, MARY BRAMSON, headmistress; b. Tiquisate, Guatemala, Dec. 28, 1939; came to U.S., 1957; d. George Peabody Jr. and Edelgard (Kohkemper-Meza) Hamlin; (div.); children: Rachel Bramson, Ruth Bramson. BA, Wellesley Coll., 1961; cert. tchr., Swarthmore Coll., 1981; MA in Ednl. Adminstrn., Mich. State U., 1992. Tchr.'s aide Wellesley (Mass.) Coll. Nursery Sch., 1960; recreation aide Judge Baker Guidance Clinic, Boston, 1961; tchr. English and history St. Dunstan's Episcopal Sch., Christiansted, U.S.V.I., 1964-65; tchr. history Marple-Newtown (Pa.) Sr. H.S., 1967-74, Springside Sch., Chestnut Hill, Pa., 1976-84, dir. upper sch., 1975-80; headmistress Kingswood Sch. Cranbrook, Bloomfield Hills, Mich., 1980-85, Eton Acad., Birmingham, 1986—. Evaluator Ind. Schs. Assn. of Ctrl. States, Downers Grove, Ill., 1984—, North Ctrl. Assn. Colls. and Schs., Ann Arbor, Mich., 1990—. Pres. Assn. Ind. Mich. Schs., 1982-85, 2001—; bd. dirs. Overseas Edn. Fund, Washington, 1978-80, Ind. Ednl. Svcs., Princeton, N.J., 1982-85, Henry Ford Med. Ctr., West Bloomfield, 1990-96, Arts Found. of Mich., Detroit, 1992-96, Reading to Reduce Recidivism, 1994-99, The Friends' Sch., Detroit, 1997-2000; mem. sch. bd. Wallingford-Swarthmore (Pa.) Sch. Dist., 1975-78; pres. Birmingham Cmty. Coalition, 2000—. Mary Bramson Faculty Devel. Fund created in her honor, Cranbrook Schs., Kingswood Sch. Alumnae, 1985; Klingenstein Vis. fellow Tchrs.' Coll., Columbia U., N.Y.C., 1997; recipient Athena award Birmingham C. of C., 2002. Mem. ASCD, Nat. Coun. Tchrs. of Math., Nat. Coun. Tchrs. for Social Studies, Mich. Assn. Learning Disabilities Educators. Avocations: learning, reading in Spanish and English, volunteering for Latino agendas, arts, gardening. Office: Eton Academy 1755 E Melton Rd Birmingham MI 48009-7277 E-mail: mvandertuin@etonacademy.org.

VANDERVEEN, JOHN E. federal agency administrator, emeritus scientist; b. Prospect Park, N.J., May 13, 1934; m. Ernestine Neuhardt, June 3, 1967; children: Keith Bradley, Kimetha Leigh. BS, Rutgers U., 1956; PhD, U. N.H., 1961. Nutritionist USAF, 1961-75; dir. divsn. nutrition FDA, Washington, 1975-92, dir. office plant & dairy foods and beverages, 1992-98. Served to 1st lt. USAF, 1961-64. Office: FDA Ctr Food Safety and Applied Nutrition 200 C St SW Washington DC 20204-0001 E-mail: jvanderv@cfsan.fda.gov.

VANDERVEEN, JOSEPH RICHARD, special education administrator; b. Muskegon, Mich., June 12, 1937; s. J. Barnie and M. Gertrude (Dwyer) V.; m. Hollee Beadle, Feb. 1962 (div. Feb. 1989); children: Joseph, Heather, Patrick. BA, Western Mich. U., 1960, MA, 1965, EdS, 1971. Cert. secondary sch. tchr., sch. psychologist, adminstr., Mich. Tchr., coach Ravenna (Mich.) Schs., 1960-63, Springfield (Mich.) Pub. Schs., 1963-65; sch. psychologist St. Joseph Intermediate Sch. Dist., Centreville, Mich., 1965-67; dir. psychol. svcs. Kent Intermediate Sch. Dist., Grand Rapids, 1967-76, regional dir. spl. edn., 1984-90; dir. spl. edn. Forest Hills Pub. Schs., 1976-84; regional dir. spl. edn. Kentwood (Mich.) Pub. Schs., 1990-96; ret., 1996. Clin. psychologist Psychiat. Cons. Svcs., Grand Rapids, 1976-85; adj. prof. Mich. State U., Lansing, 1975-77, Grand Valley State U., Allendale, Mich., 1978-90. Author: Handbook for School Psychologists, 1974, also curriculum materials. Mem. exec. bd. Kent County Spl. Olympics, Grand Rapids, 1971-76; advisor Kent County Community Mental Health Bd., Grand Rapids, 1974-76. Mem. Coun. for Exceptional Children (pres. Grand Rapids chpt. 1990-93), West Mich. Pers. and Guidance Assn. (pres. 1980-81), Grand Rapids Area Psychol. Assn. (sec. 1973-79), Mich. Assn. Sch. Psychologists (pres. 1976), Nat. Assn. Sch. Psychologists (del. 1978-81), Mich. Assn. Soc. Spl. Edn. Adminstrs., KC, Phi Delta Kappa (sec. 1991-96). Roman Catholic. Avocations: tennis, basketball, softball, furniture refinishing, golf. Home: 1559 E Westchester Dr Chandler AZ 85249

VANDER VEER, SUZANNE, aupair business executive; b. Phila., Sept. 21, 1936; d. Joseph Bedford Vander Veer and Ethel K. Short; m. James Robb Ledwith, Nov. 29, 1958 (div. Sept. 1978); children: Cheryl Day, James Robb Jr., Scott Wiley; m. Herbert Keyser Zearfoss, Nov. 14, 1992. AA, Colby Sawyer Coll., 1957; postgrad., State U. Iowa, 1957-58. Tchr. Booth Sch., Bryn Mawr, Pa., 1958; profl. tour guide Cities of Phila., N.Y.C. and Washington, D.C., 1976-89; regional dir. Transdesigns, Woodstock, Ga., 1979-87; area rep. Welcome Wagon Internat., Tenn., 1987-93, mem. local bd., 1987-93; condo. complex mgr. St. Davids, Pa., 1990-93; area dir. E.F. Aupair, Cambridge, Mass., 1993—. Art cons., 1979—. Chair host family program Internat. House of Phila., 1966-74; mem. women's com. Pa. Hosp., 1966-71; mem. com. Phila. Antique Show, 1995—; docent Phila. Mus. of Art, 1974-80; bd. dirs. Plays for Living, Phila., 1966-84, Kynett Found., 2002—; chair congl. care coun. Office of Deacon Bryn Mawr Presbyn. Ch., 1997-2002. Mem. PEO (past pres.), Jr. League of Phila. (bd. dirs., sustainer chair 1993-95, Pres.' Cup 1995, sustainer bd. 1985—, Sustainer of the Yr. award 2001), Kynett Found., Merion Cricket Club. Home: 532 Candace Ln Villanova PA 19085-1702

VANDERVELD, JOHN, JR. international business development specialist; b. Chgo., Oct. 24, 1926; s. John J. and Rose (Renkema) V. Pres. Nat. Disposal Contractors, Barrington, Ill., 1952-71; sr. v.p., dir. Browning Ferris Industries, Houston, 1971-78; pres. Pioneer Equities, Inc., 1975-90, C.J.V. Corp., Dallas, 1990-92; sr. corp. advisor Vector Environmental Techs., Inc., 1993-96. Dir. Am. Far East, Inc., Dallas and Tokyo; adv. bd. Southwestern Legal Found. Bd. dirs. Internat. Bible Soc., 1972-98, mem. exec.com., 1982-98. Mem. Nat. Solid Waste Mgmt. Assn. (former chmn. govt. industry coordinating council, mem. environ. research com.) Home: 7031 Brookshire Dr Dallas TX 75230-4248 E-mail: aquilajv@aol.com.

VANDER VELDE, WALLACE EARL, aeronautical and astronautical educator; b. Jamestown, Mich., June 4, 1929; s. Peter Nelson and Janet (Keizer) Vander V.; m. Winifred Helen Bunai, Aug. 29, 1954; children: Susan Jane, Peter Russell. BS in Aero Engring, Purdue U., 1951; Sc.D., Mass. Inst. Tech., 1956. Dir. applications engring. GPS Instrument Co., Inc., Newton, Mass., 1956-57; mem. faculty Mass. Inst. Tech., 1957—, prof. aero. and astronautics, 1965—. Cons. to industry, 1958— Author: Flight Vehicle Control Systems, Part VII of Space Navigation, Guidance and Control, 1966, (with Arthur Gelb) Multiple-Input Describing Functions, 1968; also papers. Served to 1st lt. USAF, 1951-53. Recipient Edn. award Am. Automatic Control Coun., 1988. Fellow AIAA; mem. IEEE. Home: 50 High St Winchester MA 01890-3314 Office: MIT Rm 9-467 Dept Aero and Astronautics Cambridge MA 02139

VANDERVER, TIMOTHY ARTHUR, JR. lawyer; b. Birmingham, Ala., Jan. 25, 1944; s. Timothy Arthur and Jeanette (Grimes) V.; m. Virginia Cassandra Nye, Oct. 1, 1966 (dec. July 2001); children: Timothy A. III, Glenn Bruce, Benjamin Richard. BA, Washington and Lee U., 1965; BA in Law, Oxford (Eng.) U., 1967, MA, 1983; JD, Harvard U., 1969. Bar: D.C., U.S. Ct. Appeals (D.C. cir.) 1969, U.S. Ct. Appeals (5th cir.) 1984, U.S. Ct. Appeals (3d and 11th cirs.) 1989, U.S. Supreme Ct. 1978. Assoc. Covington & Burling, Washington, 1969-72, Dept. of Interior, Washington, 1972-76; ptnr. Patton Boggs L.L.P., 1976—. Editor: Clean Air Law and Regulation, 1992, Environmental Law Handbook, 1994. Capt. U.S. Army, 1970-71. Presbyterian. Home: 9000 Congressional Ct Potomac MD 20854-4608 Office: Patton Boggs LLP 2550 M St NW Ste 500 Washington DC 20037-1350

VANDERVERT, LARRY RAYMOND, psychologist, educator, writer; b. Spokane, Wash., Dec. 28, 1938; s. Curtis Clark and Edythe Marie (Peachey) V.; m. Betty Jean McKinney, Jan. 21, 1967; children: Kimberly Jean Balocco, Bryce Raymond. BA in Psychology, Ea. Wash. U., 1966, MSc in Psychology, 1967; PhD, Wash. State U., 1977. Coll. faculty Spokane (Wash.) Falls C.C., 1969-2000. Author: Introductory Psychology, 1992; editor: (nat. newsletter) Network, 1987-91; editor (jours.) Jour. Mind and Behavior, 1997, New Ideas in Psychology, 1999, (book) Cyber Education, 2001; contbr. articles to Neurological Positivism. Author: Introductory Psychology, 1992; contbr. articles to Neurological Positivism. Fellow APA (editor newsletter Network 1987-91, named tchr. of yr. in two yr. coll. 1989); mem. Soc. for Chaos Theory in Psychology (pres. 1991, co-founder), Am. Nonlinear Systems (founder, pres. 1993). Achievements include developed brain based epistemology termed Neurological Positivism. Address: 1529 W Courtland Ave Spokane WA 99205-2608 E-mail: lvandervert@cs.com.

VAN DER VEUR, PAUL W. humanities educator; b. Medan, Indonesia, Aug. 28, 1921; came to U.S., 1947; s. Wilhelmus Marius and Johanna (Guldemond) van der Veur; m. Karol Anne Kaiser, July 21, 1951 (div. Aug. 1971); children: Julia, Paul Roscoe; m. Barbara Walker, Sept., 1973; children: Anne, Mark. BA, Swarthmore Coll., 1949; MA, U. Minn., 1950; PhD, Cornell U., 1955. Instr. Yale U., New Haven, 1954-56; asst. prof. U. Hawaii, Honolulu, 1956-59, assoc. prof., 1959-61; sr. rsch. fellow Australian Nat. U., Canberra, 1961-66; prof. No. Ill. U., DeKalb, 1966-67, Ohio U., Athens, 1967-91, prof. emeritus, 1991—, dir. S.E. Asia studies, 1967-73, 77, 1981-85, 88-90. Cons. Veriation Films, Menlo Park, Calif., 1984-85. Co-editor, author: Papua-New Guinea Elections, 1965, Toward a Glorious Indonesia, 1987; author: New Guinea Boundaries, 2 vols., 1966. Mem. Athens County Soil and Conservation Agy., 1967-91. With Royal Netherlands Indies Army, 1941-47 (POW, Japan, 1942-45). Fulbright fellow U.S. Fulbright Assn., 1980-81. Mem. Assn. for Asian Studies. Democrat. Avocations: tree planting and management. Home: 209 Valley Rd Toccoa GA 30577-3139

VANDER VLIET, VALERIE JEANNE, biology educator; b. Chgo., June 6, 1951; d. Ralph Robert and Virginia Rose Marie Ruppert; m. Steven Jay Vander Vliet, Sept. 29, 1979; children: Erin, Jackie, Steven Jr. BA, Blackburn Coll., 1973; MS, So. Ill. U., 1974; BS, U. Mich., 1979. Adj. instr. biology Mundelein Coll., Chgo., 1979-80; instr. Coll. St. Francis, Joliet, Ill., 1980-81, adj. asst. prof., 1981-90, Trinity Christian Coll., Palos Heights, 1984-90, Wheaton (Ill.) Coll., 1987-89; assoc. prof. Lewis U., Romeoville, Ill., 1991—. Presenter Am. Forum for Global Edn. and UN Assn. U.S., N.Y.C., 1995, Ill. State Bd. Higher Edn., Chgo., 1999-2000; mem. Women in Sci. del. to Cairo, People to People Amb. Program, Seattle, 2000. Active area sch. bd., Tinley Park, Ill., 1994-98, chair curriculum and assessment task force, 1992-94, mem. sch. bd., 1994-98, v.p. sch. bd., 1997-98; mem. steering com. Edn. 2000 Task Force, Tinley Park, 1990-97. Recipient Those Who Excel Parent Vol. award Ill. State Bd. Edn., 1992-93. Mem. Am. Edn. Rsch. Assn., Nat. Sci. Tchrs. Assn., Nat. Assn. Rsch. in Sci. Tchg., Assn. Coll. and Univ. Biology Educators, Nat. Assn. Biology Tchrs., Am. Soc. Microbiology, Ill. State Acad. Sci. Office: Lewis Univ 1 University Pky Romeoville IL 60446 Fax: 815-836-5955. E-mail: vanderva@lewisu.edu.

VAN DER VOO, ROB, geophysicist; b. Zeist, The Netherlands, Aug. 4, 1940; arrived in U.S., 1970; s. Maximiliaan and Johanna Hendrika (Baggerman) Van der V.; m. Tatiana M. C. Graafland, Mar. 26, 1966; children— Serge Nicholas, Bjorn Alexander. BS, U. Utrecht, Netherlands, 1961, MS, 1965, PhD, 1969. Rsch. asst. U. Utrecht, 1964-65, rsch. assoc., 1965-69, sr. rsch. assoc., 1969-70; vis. asst. prof. U. Mich., Ann Arbor, 1970-72, asst. prof., 1972-75, assoc. prof., 1975-79, prof. geophysics, 1979—, chmn., 1981-88, 91-95, Arthur F. Thurnau prof., 1994-97, dir. honors program, Coll. Lit., Sci. & the Arts, 1998—2003. Guest prof. ETH, Zurich, Switzerland, 1978, Kuwait U., 1979, Utrecht U. and Delft U. Tech., 1997-98. Author: Paleomagnetism of the Atlantic, Tethys and Iapetus Oceans, 1993; contbr. articles to profl. jours. Recipient Russell award, U. Mich., 1976, Disting. Faculty Achievement award, 1990, Benjamin Franklin medal in Earth Scis., 2001. Mem. Geol. Soc. Am., Am. Geophys. Union, Geologische Vereinigung (W.Ger.), Royal Acad. Scis. (Netherlands), Royal Norwegian Soc. Scis. and Letters, Sigma Xi, Phi Kappa Phi. Home: 2305 Devonshire Rd Ann Arbor MI 48104-2703 Office: U Mich 4534 CC Little Bldg Ann Arbor MI 48109-1063 E-mail: voo@umich.edu.

VANDER VOORT, DALE GILBERT, textile company executive; b. Paterson, N.J., Feb. 7, 1924; s. Gilbert H. and Lillian (Hatton) Vander V.; m. Florine E. Storey, Aug. 6, 1944; children: Lydia Ann, Dale Gilbert, Roy Lee. B.M.E., Clemson U., 1944. Gen. mgr., dir. Stevens Linen Assos., Webster, Mass., 1954-56; gen. mgr. Montreal Cottons Ltd., Valleyfield, Que., Can., 1951-54; supt. Mill 4 Dan River Mills, Danville, Va., 1946-51; sr. v.p. United Merchants & Mfrs. Inc., N.Y.C., 1972-77; chmn. bd. Asso. Textiles Can. Ltd., 1969-77; pres., chief exec. officer Arnold Print Works, Inc., Adams, Mass., 1977-83, Alton Fabrics, Allentown, Pa., 1983-85; pres. Asheville Dye & Finishing, Swannanoa, N.C., 1985-87; pres., chief exec. officer River Dyeing and Finishing Co., Asheville, 1988—. Dir. Northwestern Bank, Asheville, N.C., Western Carolina Industries Inc., Brit. Silk Dyeing Co., Valchem Australia, Profile Sports Corp., West Lebanon, N.H. Mem. coun. Luth. Ch., 1962—. Lt. AUS, 1943-46. Decorated Bronze Star, Purple Heart. Mem. ASME, Am. Assn. Textile Chemists and Colorists, Can. Textile Inst. (dir.), Soc. Advancement of Mgmt. (nat. gov. 1961-62), Can. Club (N.Y.), Asheville Country Club. Home: 214 Stratford Rd Asheville NC 28804-1440 also: 131 Riverside Dr Asheville NC 28801-3136 E-mail: riverdyle@aol.com., vv@aol.com.

VANDERVOORT, DEBRA JEAN, counseling psychology educator, psychologist; b. St. Paul, Nov. 16, 1953; d. Charles Floyd and Marjorie Elaine VanderVoort. BA in Philosophy, St. Olaf Coll., 1975; MA in Philosophy, U. Calif., Santa Barbara, 1979; MA in Ednl. Psychology, San Francisco State U., 1985; PhD in Ednl. Psychology, U. Utah, 1990; postgrad., U. Calif., Berkeley, 1990-92. Lic. psychologist. Intern Shasta County Mental Health Ctr., Redding, Calif., 1989-90; postdoctoral fellow U. Calif., Berkeley, 1990-92; lectr. San Francisco State U., 1991-92; prof. U. Hawaii, Hilo, 1992—. Faculty advisor U. Hawaii, 1992—, mem. search and screening com., 1994, 95, 97, vice chair faculty senate curriculum rev. com., 1994—95, senator Coll. Arts and Scis. Faculty Senate, 1995—96, mem. acad. affairs com., 1996—, mem. MA in Counseling Psychology com., 1998—99, chair psychology dept., 2001—; presenter in field. Editor: Encyclopedia of Human Behavior, 1993; contbr. articles to profl. jours. Recipient rsch. grants, 1993—. Mem. Western Psychol. Assn. (adv. bd. 1993—, review com. 1993—, session chair 1994, 97, coun. of reps. 1994—), Phi Kappa Phi. Avocations: hiking, camping, dancing, skiing, gardening. Home: PO Box 983 Pepeekeo HI 96783-0983 Office: Univ Hawaii Coll Arts and Scis 200 W Kawili St Hilo HI 96720-4075 E-mail: dvanderv@hawaii.edu.

VANDER VOORT, GEORGE FREDERIC, metallurgist; b. Phila., Sept. 1, 1944; s. Frederic Clarendon and Frances Catherine (Hosenfeld) Vander V.; m. Brenda Louise Schlaner, June 20, 1970; children: Robert, Juliana. BS Metall. Engring., Drexel U., 1967; MS Metall. and Materials Sci., Lehigh U., 1974. Tech. asst. Bethlehem (Pa.) Plant/Bethlehem Steel, 1967-68, investigator, 1968-69, explt. engr., 1969-72, asst. metallographer, 1972-73, rsch. engr. Homer Rsch. Lab., 1973-83; supr. metal physics Carpenter Tech. Corp., Reading, Pa., 1983-92, supr. materials characterization, 1992-94, specialist materials characterization, 1994-96; dir. rsch. & tech. Buehler Ltd., Lake Bluff, Ill., 1996—. Author: Metallography: Principles and Practice, 1984; editor: Applied Metallography, 1984, Atlas of Time, Temperature Diagram I, II, 1991; (video course) Priciples of Metallography, 1988; assoc. editor Materials Characterization; mem. editl. adv. bd. Praktische Metallographie; patentee in field. Fellow ASTM (chmn. com. E-4 1990-93), ASM Internat. (trustee 2001—); mem. Internat. Metallographic Soc. (pres. 1981-83), Internat. Soc. Stereology, The Metall. Soc., Royal Microscopical Soc., Microscopy Soc. Am., Deutsche Gesellschaft für Materialkunde, Microscopy Soc. Southern Africa, State Microscopical Soc. Ill. Roman Catholic. Avocations: photography, wine, hiking, travel. Office: Buehler Ltd 41 Waukegan Rd Lake Bluff IL 60044-1699 E-mail: george.vandervoort@buehler.com.

VAN DERVORT, SHARYN L. secondary education educator; b. Warren, Ohio, Apr. 6, 1958; d. Leonard Scott and Betty Arlene (Barber) Van D. BS in Edn., Ohio U., 1980; MS in Edn., U. Dayton, 1995. Tchr. English, Zanesville (Ohio) City Schs., 1980-84, Newark (Ohio) City Schs., 1984—, coord. phase II, 1995. Mem. NEA, Nat. Coun. Tchrs. English, Ohio Edn. Assn., Newark Tchrs. Assn. Avocations: travel, reading, golf. Office: Newark City Schs 314 Granville St Newark OH 43055-4483

VANDERWALKER, DIANE MARY, materials scientist; b. Springfield, Mass., Nov. 1, 1955; BS, Boston Coll., 1977; PhD, MIT, 1981. NATO fellow U. Oxford, Eng., 1981-82; asst. prof. SUNY, Stony Brook, 1983-85; materials rsch. engr. Army Rsch. Lab. (formerly U.S. Army Materials Tech. Lab.), Watertown, Mass., 1986-94. Cons. IBM, Yorktown Heights, N.Y. Contbr. articles to profl. publs. Mem. N.Y. Acad. Scis. Roman Catholic.

VAN DER WATEREN, JAN FLORIS, librarian, psychotherapist, consultant; b. Pretoria, South Africa, May 14, 1940; arrived in Eng., 1965; s. Jacob and Wilhelmina D. (Labuschagne) van der W. BA, Potchefstroom U., 1962, BA, 1963, MA, 1966; postgrad. diploma in librarianship, Univ. Coll., London, 1969. Registered U.K. Coun. Psychotherapy. Dep. libr. Royal Inst. Brit. Archs., London, 1971-78; mng. libr. Brit. Archtl. Libr., 1978-83, dir., Sir Banister Fletcher libr., 1983-88; keeper, chief libr. Nat. Art Libr., 1988-2000. Pvt. practice psychotherapy, 1983—; cons. for libr. bldgs. Contbr. numerous articles on art librarianship to profl. jours. Fellow Libr. Assn., Royal Soc. Art, Royal Inst. Brit. Archs. (hon.). Avocation: 20th Century Japanese literature. Home: 52 Blenheim Crescent London W11 1NY England E-mail: jan.vanderwateren@ukgateway.net.

VANDERWERF, MARY ANN, elementary school educator, consultant; b. Buffalo, Aug. 18, 1938; d. Richard and Petronella Gertruida (Hell) V.; m. Malcolm Donald Brutman, Apr. 30, 1989; 1 child, Susan Still. BS in Edn., SUNY, Buffalo, 1970, MA in English, 1971, PhD in Rsch. and Evaluation in Edn., 1981. Cert. tchr., N.Y. Legal sec. Hetzelt & Watson, Buffalo, 1957-64;

exec. sec. Bell Aerospace Corp., Wheatfield, N.Y., 1964-69; tchr. Amherst (N.Y.) Ctrl. Schs., 1972-94; instr. SUNY, Buffalo, 1979, 85-86, children's lit. cons., 1980-92; pres., cons., facilitator The Synergy Advantage, Inc., Amherst, 1994-99; collaborator U.S. Space and Rocket Ctr./U.S. Space Acad., Huntsville, Ala., 1995-97. Presenter Williamsville Ctrl. Schs., Internat. Reading Assn., Ireland, 1982, Anaheim, Calif., 1983, New Orleans, 1985, 89, Toronto, Ont., Can., 1988, N.Y. State English Coun., Amherst, 1984, St. Bonaventure U., 1984, Amherst Ctrl. Sch. Dist., 1986, 92, 94, Creative Problem Solving Inst., Buffalo, 1986—, Early Childhood Edn. Conf., 1988, Early Childhood Edn. Coun. Western N.Y., Buffalo, 1990, U. Nev., Las Vegas, 1991; book reviewer Harper Collins Children's Books, 1991; adj. prof. tchg. strategies Canisius Coll., Buffalo, 1997-99. Author: (with others) Science and Technology in Fact and Fiction/Children's, 1989, Science and Technology in Fact and Fiction: Young Adult, 1990, Teacher to Teacher: Strategies for the Elementary Classroom, 1993; contbr. articles to profl. jours. Advisor child life dept. Children's Hosp., Buffalo, 1984-85. Mem. Am. Fedn. Tchrs., Internat. Reading Assn. (cons. Niagara Frontier Reading Coun.), Creative Edn. Found., N.Y. State Coun. Tchrs. English (presenter), Children's Lit. Assn., Hans Christian Andersen Soc., Pi Lambda Theta (Alpha Nu chpt.). Avocations: sailing, reading, grandparenting, traveling. Home: 1860 N Forest Rd Williamsville NY 14221-1321 also: 3933 Cape Cole Blvd Punta Gorda FL 33955-3818

VANDER WILT, CARL EUGENE, banker; b. Ottumwa, Iowa, Aug. 17, 1942; s. John Adrian and Wilma (Hulsbos) V W.; m. Carol Anne Szymanski, Jan. 29, 1977; children— Dirk Francis, Neal Adrian BS, Iowa State U., 1964, PhD, 1968; grad. Advanced Mgmt. Program, Harvard U., 1986. Research economist Fed. Res. Bank, Chgo., 1970-73, asst. v.p., 1973-74, v.p., 1974-79, sr. v.p., 1979-84, sr. v.p., chief fin. officer, 1984—. Mem., bd. dirs. Goodwill Industries of Southeastern Wis., Met. Chgo., Chgo. Bd. Roosevelt U. Served to capt. U.S. Army, 1968-70. Mem. Chgo. Coun. Fgn. Rels., Execs. Club Chgo. (dir., chmn. reception com.), Banker's Club Chgo., Econ. Club Chgo. Home: 656 Locust St Winnetka IL 60093-2012 Office: Fed Res Bank 230 S La Salle St Chicago IL 60604-1496

VAN DER WYST, GEON, dancer; b. Melbourne, Australia; Student, Australian Ballet Sch. Mem. Australian Ballet, 1991—95, soloist, 1995—96, sr. artist, 1996—2001; prin. dancer Nat. Ballet Can., Toronto, Canada, 2001—. Dancer (ballets) The Sleeping Beauty, Romeo and Juliet, Cinderella, Onegin, Manon, Apollo, The Competition, Madam Butterfly, Anna Karenina, The Merry Widow, Don Quixote, Songs of a Wayfarer, Theme and Variations, The Taming of the Shrew, Etudes, In the Night, Divergence, Jardi Tancat, Gemini, Three of Us, Fall River Legend, Por vos Muero, Rites, Equus. Office: Walter Carsen Ctr Nat Ballet Can 470 Queens Quay West Toronto ON Canada M5V 3K4

VAN DE STEEG, GARET EDWARD, chemical consultant, environmental consultant; b. Mpls., Feb. 8, 1940; s. Clarence Henry and Dolorous Estell Van De Steeg; m. Dorothy Joan Henry, Sept. 5, 1965; children: Garet Erik, Leigh Bryan. BS in Chemistry, Marquette U., 1962; PhD, U. N.Mex., 1968. Sr. rsch. chemist Kerr-McGee Corp., Oklahoma City, 1968-76, sr. group leader, 1976-84, mgr. analytical chemistry, 1984-89, sr. project mgr., 1989-99; owner, CEO LED Van De Steeg, Inc., 2000—, 4-V Farms, Oklahoma City, 1980—. Adj. prof. U. Okla., Norman, 1985—. Contbr. articles to profl. jours.; patentee n field. Troup leader Boy Scouts Am., Oklahoma City, 1975-95; coach Frontier Soccer Assn., Oklahoma City, 1973-79. AEC grad fellow U. N.Mex., 1963-68. Mem. Am. Chem. Soc. (sec. Okla. sect. 1982-84, chmn. Okla. sect. 1984-85), Sigma Xi. Avocations: golf, hunting, fishing, flying. Home: 2312 NW 113th Pl Oklahoma City OK 73120-7305 Office: 2312 NW 113th Pl Oklahoma City OK 73120-7305 Fax: (405) 751-0146. E-mail: gvandesteeg@msn.com.

VANDEUSEN, BRUCE DUDLEY, company executive; b. Lorain, Ohio, Aug. 20, 1931; s. Clarence Elmer and Margaret (Richards) VanD.; m. Ann Marie Groves, Aug. 17, 1957; children: David Bruce, Elizabeth Ann. Janet Marie. BA, Ohio Wesleyan U., 1952; MS, U. Mich., 1958, PhD, 1971; MAE., Chrysler Inst. Engring., Highland Park, Mich., 1958. Registered profl. engr., Mich. Fellow Ohio State U., Columbus, 1953-54; student engr. Chrysler Corp., Highland Park, 1956-58, sr. research scientist, 1958-67; chief engr. Chrysler Def., Inc., Center Line, Mich., 1967-79, mgr. advanced devel., 1979-82; dir. advanced devel. Gen. Dynamics, Warren, 1982-87, program dir., 1987-93; pres. Edn. Svcs., Birmingham, 1994—. Contbr. numerous articles to profl. publs.; patentee electronic cirs. Trustee Birmingham Bd. Edn., Mich., 1976-88, pres., 1979-84, 87-88; trustee Birmingham Community House, 1981-87. Mem. Soc. Automotive Engrs. (chmn. sci. engring. activity 1967-69, Arch T. Colwell award 1968). Republican. Methodist. Home: 4173 Chatfield Ln Troy MI 48098-4327 Office: Edn Svcs PO Box 170 Birmingham MI 48012-0170 E-mail: BVD@EducationServicesInc.com., Vandeus@yahoo.com. *Accept, embrace and instigate change, not for the sake of change but for the sake of improvement.*

VAN DEUSEN, CHERYL A. business educator, consultant; b. Sarasota, Fla. BS, Va. Tech. U., 1979; MBA, Appalachian State U., 1989; PhD, U. S.C., 1993. Cert. hotel adminstr., hotel educator. Vis. asst. prof. Hawaii Pacific U., Honolulu, 1997—98; assoc. prof. U. North Fla., Jacksonville, 1998—. Internat. cons. Cultural Assets Mgmt., 1992—. Contbr. articles to refereed jours. Cmty. svc. coord. Jr. Achievement, Jacksonville, 1998—2002; vol. leader Coronado of Silver Sands 4-H, Daytona and New Smyrna Beach, 1996—2002; faculty advisor Soc. for Human Resource Mgmt., Jacksonville, 1999—2002. Grantee Rsch. and Tchg. grantee, U.S. Dept. of Edn., 2000—02. Fellow: UNF Ctr. for Internat. Bus. Studies (rsch. assoc. 1999—2002); mem.: Acad. of Mgmt., Internat. Assn. for Bus. and Soc., Acad. of Internat. Business-S.E. USA (vice-chair 1999—2002). Office: U North Fla COBA 4567 St Johns Bluff Rd Jacksonville FL 32224 Office Fax: 904-620-2782.

VANDEVENDER, DEBORAH ANN, critical care nurse; b. Syracuse, N.Y., Nov. 24, 1954; d. Charles Arthur and Patricia Ann (McGreevy) Kieffer; m. Robert Vandevender II, Sept. 26, 1992. BA in Biology, U. Toledo, 1980, BS in Nursing, 1983; MSN, DePaul U., 2002. RN, Ohio, N.Y., Pa., Ill., Calif., Iowa; cert. CCRN. Critical care nurse elinician III Toledo Hosp., 1977-89, St. Joseph Hosp., Syracuse, N.Y., 1989-91; critical care nurse II Brandywine Hosp., Coatsville, Pa., 1991; critical care nurse St. Therese Med. Ctr., Waukegan, Ill., 1991-93; sr. clinician Rush Northshore Med. Ctr., Skokie, 1993-94; critical care nurse St. Lukes Hosp., Davenport, Iowa, 1994; nurse practitioner critical care surg. svcs. Rush North Shore Med. Ctr., Skokie, Ill., 1994—. With USN, 1972-77; lt. USNR, 1977-2001. Mem. AACN, Fractional Currency Collectors Bd., Smithsonian Inst. (assoc.), Nat. Trust for Hist. Preservation, Am. Legion, VFW, Sigma Theta Tau, Zeta Sigma. Avocations: amateur radio, numismatics, arts, crafts. Home and Office: PO Box 1010 Plainfield IL 60544-1010

VANDEVENDER, ROBERT LEE, II, nuclear engineering consultant; b. Muncie, Ind., Nov. 16, 1958; s. Robert Lee and Evelyn June (Matthews) V.; m. Laura Jo Longfellow, June 11, 1977 (div. July 1990); children: Holly Suzanne, Robert Lee III, Bryan Matthew; m. Deborah Ann Kieffer, Sept. 26, 1992. Grad., Naval Nuclear Power Sch., Orlando, Fla., Nuclear Power Tng. Unit, West Milton, N.Y., 1979, Naval Engring. Lab. Technician Sch., West Milton, 1979; AS, Mohegan C.C., Norwich, Conn., 1983; grad., GE Thermodynamics, Heat Transfer and Fluid Flow Sch., 1986; cert. achievement, Joliet Jr. Coll., 1986; grad., GE Sr. Reactor Operator Sch., 1986. Lead engring. lab. technician, staff instr. Knolls Atomic Power Lab. U.S. Dept. Def., West Milton, 1979-81; sr. reactor operator, simulator instr. GE Nuclear Tng. Svcs., Morris, Ill., 1985-87; sr. lead engr., nuclear engring. cons. ABB Impell Corp., Melville, N.Y., 1991-93; nuclear engring. cons. Megan Corp., Allentown, Pa., 1993-94, Primera Engrs., Inc., Chgo., 1994-95, Estes Corp., Joliet, Ill., 1995-2001; co-founder V-Team, Inc., Channahon, 1997-98; co-founder, co-owner, pres. Am. Paper Connection, Inc., Joliet, 1998—, GDS Assocs., Downers Grove, Ill., 1999; nuclear engring. cons. Ferg & Assocs., 2001—. Adminstrv. coord., cons. Davis Besse Nuc. Power Sta. Toledo Edison, 1987—88; adminstrv. cons., supr. ops. support Nine Mile Pt. Nuc. Sta. Niagara Mohawk Power Corp., Oswego, NY, 1988—90; lead engring. cons. design baseline compilation Phila. Electric Co., King of Prussia, Pa., 1991; engring. cons. final safety analysis Zion (Ill.) Nuc. Sta. Commonwealth Edison Co., 1991, lead engr. dual unit outage fire protection sentry procedure devel., 93; engring. cons. Quad Cities Nuc. Power Sta., Cordova, Ill., 1994, Dresden Nuc. Power Sta., Morris, Ill., 1994—96; project mgr. Dresden Sta. Dept. Nuc. Safety, 1997; engring. cons. tech. specification upgrade project Zion Sta., 1996, supr. ops. procedures group, 1997—98; lead writer, condensate prfilter mod. project LaSalla (Ill.) Nuc. Sta., 2000; tech. cons., ops. supr. fuel transfer project Yankee Rowe (Mass.) Nuc. Power Sta., 2001—. Author: The Vandevender, Wilson, McAshlan, Silvers and Kimmel Families, 1990, (with Robert Friedberg) Paper Money of the United States, 13th and 14th edits., (with John Schwartz) Standard Guide to Small Size U.S. Paper Money, 1994, (with Gene Hessler) Comprehensive Catalog of U.S. Paper Money, 1997. Vol. examiner FCC, Gettysburg, 1985—; merit badge counselor Boy Scouts Am., Muncie, 1983. With USN, 1977-85, Ind. Guard Res., 1975-76, USNR, 1976-77, 85-87. Recipient radiosport diploma for operating achievement Internat. Amateur Radio Union, 1984, 85. Mem. Am. Legion (life), Am. Nuclear Soc. (life), Am. Radio Relay League (life, asst. tech. coord. 1985-87), Internat. Platform Assn., Am. Numismatic Assn. (life), VFW (life), Masons (life), Scottish Rite (life), Odd Fellows (grand ruler Ind. 1975-76, pres. region X 1975-76, rep. to UN Pilgrimage for Youth 1976), NRA (life), Soc. Paper Money Collectors (life), Profl. Currency Dealers Assn. Republican. Avocations: genealogy, amateur radio, numismatics. Home: PO Box 1010 Plainfield IL 60544-1010 Office: Am Paper Connection Inc PO Box 2816 Joliet IL 60434-2816

VANDEVER, JUDITH ANN, county official; b. Hemstead, N.Y., Aug. 6, 1941; d. John Anthony Klym and Kathryn M. (Lane) Trexler; children: Garret, Kimberlee Vandever Johnson. Dep. recorder Clark County Recorder, Las Vegas, Nev., 1979-91, chief dep. recorder, 1991-93, asst. recorder, 1993-94, county recorder, 1995—. State chair Nev. Young Woman of the Yr., 1991; mem. S.M.A.R.T. Team Clark County Sch. Dist., 1994—95; mem. ctrl. com. State/County Dem. Ctrl. Com., 1988—; state dir. Women Ofcls. Nat. Assn. Counties, 1997—. Recipient Leadership Dedication award Amigos De HIP, 1996, Women Elected Ofcls. Spotlight award Women's Dem. Club, 1996. Mem. ASPA, Nat. Assn. County Recorders and Clks. (bd. dirs. 1999—), Nat. Assn. County Recorders, Election Ofcls. and Clks. (bd. dirs. 1999-02), Assn. of Profl. Mortage Women,Assn. of Recorders Mgrs. and Adminstrs., U. Nev.-Las Vegas Jean Nidetch Women's Ctr. (original founder), Leadership Las Vegas Alumni Assoc., Las Vegas C. of C. (bd. of trustees, cmty. coun. 1995-98). Office: Clark County Recorder 500 S Grand Central Pkwy Las Vegas NV 89106-4506

VANDEVER, WILLIAM DIRK, lawyer; b. Chgo., Aug. 1, 1949; s. Lester J. and Elizabeth J. V.; m. Kathi J. Zellmer, Aug. 26, 1983; children: Barton Dirk, Brooke Shelby. BS, U. Mo., Kansas City, 1971, JD with distinction, 1974. Bar: Mo. 1975, U.S. Dist. Ct. (we. dist.) Mo. 1975. Dir. Popham Law Firm, Kansas City, Mo., 1975—. Lectr. in field, Kansas City Mo., 1979—. Issue editor U. Mo.-Kansas City Law Rev., 1974. Fellow Am. Bd. Trial Advs. (Best Lawyers in Am.-tort law); mem. ABA, ATLA, Mo. Assn. Trial Attys., Kansas City Met. Bar Assn. (treas., sec., pres., elected to 16th Jud. Commn. 1988-94), Kansas City Bar Found. (treas. 1992, sec. 1994, pres. 1996-98, pres. award domestic violence 1999), Interest on Lawyer Trust Accts. of Mo. (bd. govs.), Kansas City Mem. Svcs. (pres. 1988—, commr. 16th jud. cir. selection com.), U. Mo. Kansas City Found. (fin. com. 1998), Phi Delta Phi, Beta Theta Pi. Avocations: tennis, skiing, running, reading. Home: 11380 W 121st Ter Shawnee Mission KS 66213-1978 Office: Popham Law Firm 1300 Commerce Trust Bldg Kansas City MO 64106

VANDEWALKER, DAVID W. music educator; s. Linda K. Vandewalker; m. Pamela D. Clampitt, June 17, 1996. MusB in Edn., Baylor U., 1989; MA in Edn., Ctrl. Mich. U., 2002. Cert. music edn. K-12. Band dir. Belton (Tex.) Ind. Sch. Dist., 1989—91, Kleb Intermediate/Klein (Tex.) Ind. Sch. Dist., 1991—96, Harrison HS, Kennesaw, Ga., 1996—. Pres., sr. editor Vision Publs., Marietta, Ga., 1991—. Associate condr.: Harrison HS Wind Ensemble; editor: Made for Praise, Volume 4, 1998. Deacon, music & drama specialist Johnson Ferry Bapt. ch., Marietta, 1996—2002. Mem.: Ga. Music Educators Assn., Music Educators Nat. Conf., World Assn. Symphonic Bands & Ensembles, Nat. Band Assn., Kappa Kappa Psi. Office: Harrison HS 4500 Due West Rd Kennesaw GA 30152 Personal E-mail: dvandewalker@earthlink.net. E-mail: davidwvandewalker@cobbk12.org.

VAN DE WALLE, ETIENNE, demographer; b. Namur, Belgium, Apr. 29, 1932; came to U.S., 1961; s. Arnould and Yolande (Blommaert) Van De W.; m. Francine Robyns de Schneidauer, Aug. 24, 1955; children: Dominique, Nicolas, Jean-Francois, Patrice. Dr. in Law, U. Louvain, Belgium, 1956, MA in Econs., 1957, PhD in Demography, 1973. Researcher Irsac, Rwanda, Burundi, 1957-61; rsch. assoc. Princeton (N.J.) U., 1962-64, rsch. staff, 1964-67, rsch. demographer, 1967-72; vis. lectr. U. Calif., Berkeley, 1971-72; prof. U. Pa., Phila., 1972—. Dir. Population Studies Ctr., U. Pa., 1976-82; sr. assoc. The Population Coun., Bamako, Mali, 1982. Author: The Female Population of France, 1974; co-author: The Demography of Tropical Africa, 1968. Fellowship Woodrow Wilson Ctr. for Scholars, 1976. Mem. Internat. Union for Scientific Study of Population, Population Assn. of Am. (pres. 1992). Home: 261 Sycamore Ave Merion Station PA 19066-1545 Office: Population Studies Ctr 3718 Locust Walk Philadelphia PA 19104-6209 E-mail: etienne@pop.upenn.edu.

VANDEWALLE, GERALD WAYNE, state supreme court chief justice; b. Noonan, N.D., Aug. 15, 1933; s. Jules C. and Blanche Marie (Gits) VandeW. BSc, U. N.D., 1955, JD, 1958. Bar: N.D., U.S. Dist. Ct. N.D. 1959. Spl. asst. atty. gen. State of N.D., Bismarck, 1958-75, 1st asst. atty. gen., 1975-78; justice N.D. Supreme Ct., 1978-92, chief justice, 1993—. Mem. faculty Bismarck Jr. Coll., 1972-76; mem. Nat. Ctr. for State Cts. Rsch. adv. coun.; mem. fed.-state jurisdiction com. Jud. Conf. of the U.S. Editor-in-chief N.D. Law Rev., 1957-58. Active Bismarck Meals on Wheels Recipient Sioux award U. N.D., 1992, Ednl. Law award N.D. Coun. Sch. Attys., 1987, Love Without Fear award Abused Adult Resource Ctr., 1995, N. Dakota State Bar Assoc. Dist. Service Award, 1998. Mem. ABA (co-chmn. bar admissions com. 1991-99, mem. coun. sect. legal edn. and admissions, chmn. coun. sect. legal edn. and admissions), State Bar Assn. N.D., Burleigh County Bar Assn., Conf. of Chief Justices (past pres., bd. dirs. 1996-98, chmn. fed.-state tribal rels. com.), Am. Contract Bridge League, Order of Coif, N.D. Jud. Conf. (exec. com.), Elks, KC, Phi Eta Sigma, Beta Alpha Psi (Outstanding Alumnus award Zeta chpt. 1995), Beta Gamma Sigma, Phi Alpha Delta. Roman Catholic. Office: ND Supreme Ct State Capitol 600 E Boulevard Ave Bismarck ND 58505-0530 E-mail: gvandewalle@ndcourts.com.

VAN DE WATER, READ, federal agency administrator; Degree, U. South, 1986; M, George Washington U.; JD, Georgetown U. Appropriations assoc., legis. asst. Congressman Tom DeLay, Tex., 1987—91; legis. coun., dir. govt. affairs Northwest Airlines, 1991—97; legis. coun. internat. trade and investment Bus. Roundtable, 1997—99; founder Carson King Cons., 2000; asst. sec. aviation & internat. affairs U.S. Dept. Transp., Washington, 2001—. Office: US Dept Transp Aviation and Internat Affairs 400 7th St SW Washington DC 20590 Office Fax: 202-493-2005.

VAN DE WIJGERT, JANNEKE, clinical epidemiologist; b. Veghel, The Netherlands, Sept. 13, 1966; came to U.S., 1990; d. Johannes van de Wijgert and Wilhelmina van den Oetelaar. Drs. Med. Biology, U. Utrecht, 1990; MPH, U. Calif., Berkeley, 1993, PhD in Epidemiology, 1997; postgrad., U. Calif., San Francisco, 1997-99. Program assoc. Population Coun., N.Y.C., 1999—. Spkr. in field; founding mem. Internat. Health Focus Group U. Calif., 1991-94. Contbr. chpts. to books and articles to profl. jours.; peer reviewer various jours., 1999—. Fellowship U. Calif., Berkeley, 1993; recipient Award Internat. chpt. PEO Sisterhood, 1991-93. Mem. Internat. Working Group on Microbicides, Alliance for Microbicide Devel., Internat. Epidemiol. Assn., Internat. AIDS Soc., Vereniging voor Epidemiologie, Am. Pub. Health Assn., Post Hoc Ergo Propter Hoc. Office: Population Coun One Dag Hammarskjold New York NY 10017 E-mail: jvandewijgert@popcouncil.org.

VANDE WOUDE, GEORGE FRANKLIN, molecular biologist, cancer researcher; b. Brooklyn, N.Y., Dec. 25, 1935; s. George Franklin Sr. and Alice Beatrice (Leudesdorff) V.W.; m. Dorothy Helen Stapel, Apr. 5, 1959; children: Susan Joan, Gail Louise, Cynthia Irene, Alice Helene. Student, Hope Coll., 1953-54; BA, Hofstra U., 1959; MS, Rutgers U., 1962, PhD, 1964. Postdoctoral rsch. assoc. USDA Plum Island, Greenport, N.Y., 1964-65, rsch. scientist, 1965-72; chief virus tumor biochemistry Nat. Cancer Inst. NIH, Bethesda, Md., 1972-81, chief lab. molecular oncology, 1981-83; dir. basic rsch. program Nat. Cancer Inst.-Frederick (Md.) Cancer R & D Ctr., 1983—98; dir. Van Andel Rsch. Inst., Grand Rapids, Mich., 1999—. Contbr. over 100 articles and sci. papers to profl. publs., 35 book chpts. Recipient Robert J. and Claire Pasarow Found. award, 1989. Mem. AAAS, Am. Soc. for Microbiology, Am. Assn. for Cancer Rsch. Achievements include research in fields of biology and cancer. Office: Van Andel Inst 333 Bostwick NE Grand Rapids MI 49503*

VAN DE ZILVER, PETER A.L. economist, business executive; b. June 26, 1949; MA in Econs., U. So. Calif., 1979. CFA, Calif. MIS mgr. Sunnyglen Corp., Newport Beach, Calif., 1984-92; v.p., quantitative analyst PIMCO, 1992—. E-mail: zilver@pimco.com.

VAN DINE, ALAN CHARLES, advertising agency executive, writer; b. Ford City, Pa., Jan. 12, 1933; s. Albert and Helen (Remaley) Van D.; m. Joan Anne Hodges, Jan. 29, 1955 (div. Jan. 1971); children: Lynn, Mark, Barbara, Michael; m. Holly Long Shefler, Apr. 23, 1977. BA, Duquesne U., 1955; postgrad., U. Pitts., 1968-71. Editor Mt. Lebanon News, Pa., 1956-58; editorial dir. Pitts. Suburban Newspapers, 1958-61; writer and assoc. creative dir. Batten, Barton, Durstine & Osborne, Pitts., 1961-70; pres., creative dir. Van Dine, Horton, McNamara, Manges, Inc., 1970-89; chmn. Van Dine, Humphrey, Inc., 1989-95; cons. in field, 1996—. Mem. adv. coun. Internat. Poetry Forum, Pitts., 1969-80. Author: Can You Imagine?, 1967, Unconventional Builders, 1977, revised edit., 2001, (humor) The Encyclopedia of Advertising, 1987, Clyde Hare's Pittsburgh, 1994, Light Verse for a Heavy Universe, 2002; columnist Pitts. mag., 1977-78, Pa. Illustrated, 1979-81; contbr. articles, essays, short stories, and poems to mags. 1st lt. USAF, 1956. Recipient numerous awards Art Dirs. Club N.Y., 1964—, Bus. and Profl. Advt. Assn., 1964—, Am. Advt. Fedn., 1999. Mem. Chartiers Country Club. Avocations: golf, tennis, darkroom photography, cartooning, computer programming. E-mail: AVDZZZ@bellatlantic.net.

VAN DINE, HAROLD FORSTER, JR. architect, artist; b. New Haven, Aug. 28, 1930; s. Harold Forster and Marguerite Anna (Eichstedt) Van D.; m. Maureen Kallick, Mar. 1, 1983; children by previous marriage: Rebecca Van Dine, Stephanie Van Dine Natale, Gretchen Van Dine Natale. BA, Yale Coll., 1952; MArch, Yale Sch. Arch., 1958. Registered architect. Designer Minoru Yamasaki & Assocs., Detroit, 1958-60; chief designer Gunnar Birkerts & Assocs., 1960-67; prin. Straub, Van Dine & Assocs., Troy, Mich., 1967-80; chief architecture and design officer Harley Ellington Design, Southfield, 1980-95; archtl. cons. Birmingham, 1995—. V.p. Fields, Devereaux, HEPY, L.A., 1984-95. Prin. works include Mcpl. Libr., Troy, Mich., campuses for Oakland (Mich.) Community Coll., North Hills Ch., Troy, First Ctr. Office Plaza, chemistry bldgs at U. Mich. and Ind. U., G.M.F. Robotics Hdqrs., Flint Ink Rsch. and Devel. Ctr., Comerica Bank Ops. Ctr., Christ the King Mausoleum, Chgo., Resurrection Mausoleum, Staten Island, Mich. Biotech Inst., Ford Sci. Rsch. Labs, Fetzer Inst. Hdqrs. and Retreat Ctr., Cen. Mich. U. Music Sch., Oakland U. Sci. Techs. Bldg., Corning (N.Y.) Credit Union. Bd. dirs. Cultural Coun. Birmingham/Bloomfield, 1990-99. Served to lt. (j.g.) USN, 1952-55 Recipient Book award AIA, 1958, Excellence in Architecture Silver medal AIA, 1958, Gold medal Detroit chpt. AIA, 1987, Mich. Soc. of Architects gold medal, 1991, over 50 major design awards; William Wirt Winchester travelling fellowship Yale U. Sch. Architecture, 1958; elect. to AIA Coll. Fellows, 1979. Mem. Pewabic Soc. (bd. dirs. 1983—) Home: 1000 Stratford Ln Bloomfield Hills MI 48304-2930 E-mail: harryv@mediaone.net., jmrandhv@got.com.

VAN DINE, VANCE, investment banker; b. San Francisco, July 2, 1925; s. Melvin Everett and Grace Winifred (Harris) Van D.; m. Isabel Erskine Brewster, Sept. 8, 1956; 1 dau., Rose M. (dec.). BA, Yale U., 1949; LLB, NYU, 1955. Assoc. Morgan Stanley & Co., N.Y.C., 1953-59, 61-63, ptnr., 1963-75; mng. dir. Morgan Stanley & Co., Inc., N.Y.C., 1970-83; adv. dir. Morgan Stanley & Co., 1983—. Cons. Internat. Bank for Reconstn. and Devel., 1959-61; chmn. Doane Western Co. Author: The Role of the Investment Banker in International Transactions, 1970, The U.S. Market After Controls, 1974. Bd. dirs. Yale U. Alumni Fund, Combined Health Appeal of Greater N.Y., Rec. for Blind, Inc., N.Y.C., 1979-89; trustee Cancer Rsch. Inst., N.Y.C., Nassau County Art Mus., L.I. U., 1979-91; gov. dir. Fgn. Policy Assn., 1980-89. With USN, 1943-46. Recipient Yale Class of 1949 Disting. Service award, 1983. Mem. The Pilgrims of the U.S., Union Club, Piping Rock Club, N.Y. Yacht Club, Seawanhaka Corinthian Yacht Club, Church Club, Yale Club (N.Y.C.), Met. Opera Club. Republican. Episcopalian. Office: Morgan Stanley & Co Ste C2E 1221 Avenue Of The Americas New York NY 10020-1008 E-mail: vancevandine@msdw.com.

VANDIVER, DONNA, public relations executive; BJ, MBA in Mgmt. Pres. Vandiver Group, St. Louis, 1993—. Bd. dirs. Am. Heart Assn.; mem. adv. bd. Pky. Edn. Found. Named Small Bus. Person of the Yr. SBA, 1998; recipient Quest award Nat. Fedn. Press Women, 1999. Mem. Nat. Assn. Women Bus. Owners (Bd. dirs. St. Louis chpt., Disting Women Bus. Owner of the Yr. award 1999), Assn. Corp. Growth, St. Louis Press Club, Downtown St. Louis Partnership, St. Louis Regional Commerce and Growth Assn., Media Club. Office: Vandiver Group 10411 Clayton Rd Saint Louis MO 63131-2928*

VANDIVER, FRANK EVERSON, institute administrator, former university president, author, educator; b. Austin, Tex., Dec. 9, 1925; s. Harry Shultz and Maude Folmsbee (Everson) V.; m. Carol Sue Smith, Apr. 19, 1952 (dec. 1979); children: Nita, Nancy, Frank Alexander; m. Renée Aubry, Mar. 21, 1980. Rockefeller fellow in humanities, U. Tex., 1946-47, Rockefeller fellow in Am. Studies, 1947-48, MA, 1949; PhD, Tulane U., 1951; MA (by decree), Oxford (Eng.) U., 1963; HHD (hon.), Austin Coll., 1977; DHL (hon.), Lincoln Coll., 1989, BA (hon.), 1994. Apptd. historian Army Service Forces Depot, Civil Service, San Antonio, 1944-45, Air U., 1951; prof. history La. State U., summers 1953-57; asst. prof. history Washington U., St. Louis, 1952-55, Rice U., Houston, 1955-56, assoc. prof., 1956-58, prof., 1958-65, Harris Masterson Jr. prof. history, 1965-79, chmn. dept. history and polit. sci., 1962-63, dept. history, 1968-69, acting pres., 1969-70, provost, 1970-79, v.p., 1975-79; pres., chancellor N. Tex. State U., Denton and Tex. Coll. Osteo. Medicine, 1979-81; pres. Tex. A&M U., College Station, 1981-88, pres. emeritus, disting. U. prof., 1988—; founding pres. Acad. Marshall Plan, 1992; Sara and John Lindsey chair in humanities, 1988. Harmsworth prof. Am. history Oxford U., 1963-64; vis. prof. history U. Ariz., summer 1961; master Margarett Root Brown Coll., Rice U., 1964-66; Harmon lectr. Air Force Acad., 1963; Keese lectr. U. Chattanooga, 1967; Fortenbaugh lectr. Gettysburg Coll., 1974; Phi Beta Kappa assoc. lectr., 1970— ; vis. prof. mil. history U.S. Mil. Acad., 1973-74; hon. pres. Occidental U., St. Louis, 1975-80; chmn. bd. Am. U. Cairo, 1992-97, acting pres., 1997-98. Editor: The Civil War Diary of General Josiah Gorgas, 1947, Confederate Blockade Running Through Bermuda, 1981-65: Letters and Cargo Manifests, 1947, Proceedings of First Confederate Congress, 4th Session, 1953, Proceedings of Second Confederate Congress, 1959, A Collection of Louisiana Confederate Letters; new edit., J.E. Johnston's Narrative of Military Operations; new edit., J.A. Early's Civil War Memoirs, The Idea of the South, 1964, Battlefields and Landmarks of the Civil War, 1996; author: Ploughshares Into Swords: Josiah Gorgas and Confederate Ordnance, 1952, Rebel Brass: the Confederate Command System, 1956, Mighty Stonewall, 1957, Fields of Glory, (with W.H. Nelson), 1960, Jubal's Raid, 1960, Basic History of the Confederacy, 1962, Jefferson Davis and the Confederate State, 1964, Their Tattered Flags: The Epic of the Confederacy, 1970, The Southwest: South or West?, 1975, Black Jack: The Life and Times of John J. Pershing, 1977 (Nat. Book Award finalist 1978), (address) The Long Loom of Lincoln, 1986, Blood Brothers: A Short History of the Civil War, 1992, Shadows of Vietnam: Lyndon Johnson's Wars, 1997, 1001 Things Everyone Should Know About the Civil War, 1999, 1001 Things Everyone Should Know About World War II, 2002; also hist. articles, mem. bd. editors: U.S. Grant Papers, 1973—. Mem. bd. trustees Am. U. in Cairo, 1988, chmn., 1992-97. Recipient Laureate Lincoln Acad., Ill., 1973, Carr P. Collins prize Tex. Inst. Letters, 1958, Harry S. Truman award Kansas City Civil War Round Table, Jefferson Davis award Confederate Meml. Lit. Soc., 1970, Fletcher Pratt award N.Y. Civil War Round Table, 1970, Outstanding Civilian Svc. medal Dept. Army, 1974, Nevins-Freeman award Chgo. Civil War Round Table, 1982, T. Harry Williams Meml. award, 1985, Pres. medal Am. U. in Cairo, 1999; named Hon. Knight San Jacinto, 1993, Hon. Mem. Sons of Republic of Tex., 1986; rsch. grantee Am. Philos. Soc., 1953, 54, 60, Huntington Libr. rsch. grantee, 1961; Guggenheim fellow, 1955-56. Fellow Tex. Hist. Assn.; mem. Am. Hist. Assn., So. Hist. Assn. (assoc. editor jour. 1959-62, pres. 1975-76), Tex. Inst. Letters (past pres.), Jefferson Davis Assn.

(pres., chmn. adv. bd. editors of papers), Soc. Am. Historians (councillor), Tex. Philos. Soc. (pres. 1978), Civil War Round Table (Houston), Orgn. Am. Historians, Phi Beta Kappa, SAR of Tex. (hon., Knight San Jacinto 1993). Clubs: Cosmos, Army and Navy (Washington); Briarcrest Country (College Station). Achievements include originating idea of Coll. space grant program. Office: The Mosher Inst for Internat Policy Studies Texas A&M U 2400 TAMU College Station TX 77843-2400 E-mail: smaxwell@tamu.edu.

VANDIVER, MICHAEL PATRICK, retail executive; b. St. Augustine, Fla., Apr. 22, 1968; s. Alton Lynn and Suzzanne Marie Vandiver. MusB Edn., Fla. State U., Tallahassee, 1992. Cert. Tchr. Fla., 1993. Tchr. Cape Coral (Fla.)H.S., 1993—2000, Murray Ctr. for the Arts , St. Augustine, Fla., 2000—02; store mgr. Am. Music, Inc., Jacksonville, 2002—. Mem.: Fla. Bandmasters Assn. Roman Catholic. Avocation: music. Home: 8787 Southside Blvd #2604 Jacksonville FL 32256 Office: American Music Jacksonville FL Personal E-mail: mvandiver@attbi.com.

VANDIVER, PAMELA BOWREN, research scientist; b. Santa Monica, Calif., Jan. 12, 1946; d. Roy King and Patricia (Woolard) Evans; m. J. Kim Vandiver, Aug., 1968 (div. 1984); 1 child, Amy. BA in Humanities and Asian Studies, Scripps Coll., 1967; postgrad., U. Calif., Berkeley, 1968; MA in Art, Pacific Luth. U., 1971; MS in Ceramic Sci., MIT, 1983, PhD in Materials Sci. and Near Eastern Archeology, 1985. Instr. in glass and ceramics Mass. Coll. of Art, Boston, 1972; lectr. MIT, Cambridge, 1973-78, rsch. assoc., 1978-85; rsch. phys. scientist Conservation Analytical Lab., Smithsonian Instn., Washington, 1985-89; sr. scientist in ceramics Smithsonian, Ctr. for Materials Rsch. and Edn., 1989—. Instr. semester-at-sea U. Pitts., spring 1995; vis. prof. Northwest Inst. Light Industry, Xianyang, China, 1996; bd. dirs. Rolatape Corp., Spokane, Wash.; guest rschr. Nat. Inst. Stds. and Tech., Gaithersburg, Md., 1989-91. Co-author: Ceramic Masterpieces, 1986; co-editor: Materials Issues in Art and Archaeology, vol 1 1988, vol. 5, 1997; bd. editors Archeomaterials, 1986-93; contbr. over 100 numerous articles to profl. jours. Sponsor mentorship program Thomas Jefferson H.S. of Sci. and Tech., Alexandria, 1992. Recipient Disting. Alumna Achievement award Scripps Coll., 1993. Fellow Am. Anthrop. Assn.; mem. AAAS, Am. Inst. Archeology, Soc. Am. Archeology, Internat. Inst. of Conservation, Soc. for History of Tech., Am. Ceramics Soc. (ancient ceramics com. 1978—), Materials Rsch. Soc. (guest editor bull. 1992, 2001), Am. Chem. Soc., Annapolis Yacht Club, Cosmos Club, Sigma Xi. Avocations: sailing, diving, photography. Office: Smithsonian Inst Ctr For Materials Rsch Edn Washington DC 20560-0001 E-mail: vandiverp@scmre.si.edu.

VANDIVER, RENEE LILLIAN AUBRY, interior designer, architectural preservator; b. New Iberia, La., Nov. 7, 1929; d. Harold George and Josephine Fortier (Brown) Aubry; m. Arthur Roderick Carmody, Jr., Jan. 1952 (div. 1979); children: Helen Bragg Carmody Stroud, Renee Josephine Carmody Mathews, Arthur Roderick III, Patrick Gerard, Timothy H.A., Mary Joellyn, Virginia Caroline, Joseph Barry; m. Frank Everson Vandiver, Mar. 21, 1980. BFA, Sophie Newcomb Coll. Tulane U., 1951; postgrad., U. Paris, 1951-52, Centinary Coll., 1966-68, La. State U., Shreveport, 1978. Designer, supt. art New Iberia Parish Elementary Schs., 1951; archtl. drafter and designer Perry L. Brown, Inc., Baton Rouge, 1950-52; tchr. art St. Joseph's Elem. Sch., Shreveport, 1960-69; designer, illustrator, saleswoman Stierwalt Interiors, 1974-78; design cons. for president's homes and gardens North Tex. State U., Tex. A&M U., Denton, College Station, 1980-88; design cons., planner, saleswoman, pres. Renee Aubry Vandiver Interiors, College Station, Tex., 1980—; design cons. Am. U. in Cairo, 1997—; proofreader, editor, rschr., asst. Office of Frank E. Vandiver, College Station, 1998—. Interior design and house constrn. cons. Heritage Antiques and Interiors, New Iberia, 1972—; interior design cons., Tenn., La., S.C., 1980—; invited student Middle Eastern master painter Sabri Raghab. Editl. and illustrations collaborator works on gen. mil. history with Frank E. Vandiver, 1990—. Mem. NAFE, DAR, Constrn. Specifications Inst., Dallas Market Ctr., Houston Market Ctcr., Jr. League, Textile Mus., Mus. Women in Arts, Tex. A&M U. Women's Club (hon. pres. 1981—), Fedn. Tex. A&M U. Mother's Club. Avocations: painting, playing piano, gardening, travel, reading. Home: PO Box 10600 College Station TX 77842-0600

VANDIVIER, BLAIR ROBERT, lawyer; b. Rapid City, S.D., Dec. 24, 1955; s. Robert Eugene and Barbara Jean (Kidd) V.; m. Elizabeth Louise Watson, July 26, 1980; children: Jessica Elizabeth, Jennifer Louise. BS magna cum laude, Butler U., 1978; JD cum laude, Ind. U., 1981. Bar: Ind. 1981, U.S. Dist. Ct. (so. dist.) Ind. 1981, U.S. Tax Ct. 1985. Assoc. Henderson, Daily, Withrow, Johnson & Gross, Indpls., 1981-83; assoc., ptnr. Johnson, Gross, Densborn & Wright, 1983-85, of counsel, 1985-87; v.p., sec. Benchmark Products, Inc. (formerly Benchmark Chem. Corp.), 1985-91, pres., 1991—, also bd. dirs.; ptnr. Gross & Vandivier, 1987-89; of counsel Riley, Bennett & Egloff, 1990—; mgmt. rep. Pro Com, L.L.C., 1991—. V.p. Seleco Inc., Indpls., 1988-93, pres., 1993—. Mem. com. Conner Prairie Settlement Fund Dr., Indpls., 1983-85, Riley Run, 1987—; mem. regulatory study com. City of Indpls., 1993-98. Mem. ABA, Ind. Bar Assn., Indpls. Bar Assn (bd. dirs. young lawyers divsn. 1982-85), Am. Electroplaters and Surface Finisher's Soc. (chmn. nat. law com. 1986-97, pres. Indpls. br. 1989, bd. mgrs. 1997—, tech. conf. bd. 1991-97, chmn. surface finishers ann. tech. conf. and exhbn. 1994, chmn. surface finishers focus group 1994—, Tech. Conf. Bd. Recognition award 1996), Nat. Assn. Metal Finishers (bd. dirs. 1998—, exec. com. 1998—, sec./treas. 2000-2001, v.p. 2001, pres. 2001—), Metal Finishing Suppliers Assn. (spl. projects svcs. com., 1988-93, chmn. 1993—, chmn. hazardous materials br. 1991-93, trustee 1992-95, v.p. 1995-97, pres. 1997-99, past pres. 1999—, Award of Merit 1997, August P. Munning Commenorator award of merit 2001), Crooked Stick Golf Club, Highland Country Club (chmn. ins. com. 1989-94, golf. com. 1992-94, bd. dirs. 1995-97, chmn. fin. com. 1996-97) Surface Finishing Industry Coun. (bd. dirs., sec. 1997-98, pres. 1999), Econ. Club Indpls., Metal Finishing Found. (pres. 1999), Delta Tau Delta (chmn. 1987-97, bd. dirs. Beta Zeta Found. 1986, Outstanding Alumnus Beta Zeta chpt. 1986). Republican. Episcopalian. Avocations: reading, golf, aviation. Home: 8927 Woodacre Ln Indianapolis IN 46234-2848 Office: Benchmark Products Inc PO Box 68809 Indianapolis IN 46268-0809

VANDIVIERE, H. MAC, medical educator; b. Ga., Mar. 26, 1921; s. Augustus Vandiviere and Luna Castlebury; m. Margaret Reynolds, (dec. Feb. 1967); children: Christopher, Martin; m. Irene G. Melvin, March 23, 1968. AB, Mercer Coll., 1943, MS, 1944; MD, U. N.C., 1960. Intern St. Antoine's Hosp., Jeremie, Haiti, 1961-66; dir. spl. svc. unit Ga. Dept. Health, Rome, 1948-51; rsch. bacteriologist N.C. Sanatorium Sys., McCain, 1951-53, dir. clin. lab., 1953-67; from asst. prof. to prof. emeritus U. Ky., Lexington, 1967-91, prof. emeritus, 1991—; pvt. practice Lancaster, Ky., 1991—. Dir. TB control and remedial svcs. Ky. Dept. Health, Frankfort, 1971-76; cons. Southeastern Consortium for Internat. Devel., Lexington, Ky., Chapel Hill, N.C., 1988-89. Contbr. articles to profl. jours. Pres. com. Hospice of Lexington, 1980-81; chmn. program planning and evaluation Bluegrass Mental Health, Mental Retardation Bd., Lexington, 1983-85, 90-99; pres., co-chmn. Am. Lung Assn. of Ky., Louisville, 1971-97. Fellow Am. Soc. Geriatrics, Am. Pub. Health Soc.; mem. Am. Ky. Med. Soc., So. Assn. Geriatric Medicine, So. Assn. Family Practice, So. Med. Assn. (Disting. Svc. award 1999). Republican. Episcopalian. Home: 8 Deer Path Lancaster KY 40444-9006 Office: 405 Danville St Lancaster KY 40444-1032

VAN DOESBURG, HANS, chemical engineer, management consultant; b. Rotterdam, Netherlands, Mar. 10, 1948; s. Jan and Leida (Helbich) Van D.; m. Joette Sanchez, July 21, 1979; children: Steffen, Evin, Eric. BSc cum laude, U. Tech., Delft, Netherlands, 1970, MSc cum laude, 1971, PhD cum laude, 1974. Asst. prof. U. Tech., Delft, 1971-75; rsch. engr. Shell Devel. Co., Houston, 1975-78; sr. econ. specialist Shell Oil Co., 1978-80; mgmt. cons. Kinsey & Co., Amsterdam, Houston, Düsseldorf, 1980-86; ptnr. Booz Allen & Hamilton, The Hague, Netherlands, 1986-94; mng. ptnr. Andersen Cons., Houston, 1994—. Bd. dirs. Think Tank Found., Amsterdam, 1990-92. Contbr. articles to profl. jours. Avocations: music, sailing, travel, scuba diving, jogging, golf.

VAN DOMELEN, JOHN EMORY, retired English studies educator, gemstone dealer; b. Macon, Ga., Dec. 5, 1935; s. John Bouwens and Margaret Lucinda Van Domelen; m. Paula Joyce Van Domelen, Aug. 25, 1962; children: John Paul, Elizabeth Dawn, Clifford Bruce. BA, Calvin Coll., 1957; MA, U. Mich., 1960; PhD, Mich. State U., 1964. Asst. prof. English Wis. State U., Platteville, 1963-67; assoc. prof. English U. No. Iowa, Cedar Falls, 1967-70; prof. English Tex. A&M U, College Station, 1970-96. Propr. The Carat Patch, College Station, 1990-2002. Author: Tarzan of Athens, 1987, Bibliography: John Heath-Stubbs, 1987, The Haunted Heart, 1993. Bd. dirs. Mus. Natural History, Bryan, Tex., 1974-75. Fulbright scholar, 1990-91. Republican. Methodist. Avocations: reading, travel, gardening. Home: 310 Lee Ave College Station TX 77840-3149 E-mail: carat310@juno.com.

VAN DOMELEN, JOHN FRANCIS, academic administrator; b. Havana, Cuba, Oct. 19, 1942; s. Floyd and Sara (Molina) Van D.; m. Naomi Ruth Kittlesen. BS in Applied Physics, Mich. Tech. U., 1964; MS in Water Res. Mgmt., U. Wis., Madison, 1972; PhD in Civil Engring., U. Wis., 1974. Commd. 2nd lt. USAF, 1964, advanced through grades to col., 1988; mgr. engring. Charmin Paper Products Co., Green Bay, Wis., 1969-70; asst. prof. Norwich U., Northfield, Vt., 1974-79, head engring. and tech. dept., 1979-83, head engring. and tech. div., 1983-85, v.p. acad. affairs, dean of faculty, 1985-90; pres. Wentworth Inst. Tech., Boston, 1990—. Mem. Engring. Workforce Commn. Contbr. articles to profl. jours. Mem. MassPep, Boston, 1990—. Decorated Cross of Gallantry (Vietnam); recipient Centennial medal IEEE, 1984. Mem. ASCE, Am. Soc. Engring. Edn., Sci. Rsch. Soc. N.Am. Avocations: golf, science fiction. Office: Wentworth Inst Tech 550 Huntington Ave Boston MA 02115-5998 E-mail: vandomelenj@wit.edu.

VAN DONGEN, HANS PHILEMON ANNA, research scientist, educator; b. Bergen op Zoom, The Netherlands, June 21, 1969; came to U.S., 1998; s. Marinus Elvire Johannes and Agnes Catharina Maria (Van Willegen) Van D.; m. Judith Catharina Van Peppen, Aug. 20, 1999. MSc in Astrophysics, Leiden U., The Netherlands, 1993, PhD in Chronobiology, 1998. Post doctoral fellow U. Pa., Phila., 1998-99, rsch. asst. prof. sleep and chronobiology, 1999—, mem. instnl. rev. bd., 2000-2001, chmn. instnl. rev. bd. for sociobehavioral scis., 2001—. Pres. rsch. group physiol. systems analysis Leiden U., 1994-98; invited lectr. in field, 1995—; sci. reviewer jour. manuscripts for Sleep, Sleep Medicine Revs., Jour. Sleep Rsch., Clin. Neurophysiology, Biol. Rhythm Rsch., Jour. Biol. Rhythms, Neoro-psychopharmacology and Giol. Psychiatry, Behavioral Neurosci.; mem. Ctr. for Neurobiology and Behavior, U. Pa., Ctr. for Sleep and Respiratory Neurogiology, U. Pa. Contbr. articles to profl. jours. Recipient Trainee Rsch. Merit award Associated Profl. Sleep Socs., 1999, Microsoft Corp. award, Internat. Soc. Chronobiology, Congress, 1999. Mem. Am. Psychol. Soc., Internat. Soc. Chronobiology, Soc. for Rsch. Biol. Rhythms, European Sleep Rsch. Soc., Sleep Rsch. Soc., Dutch Soc. for Sleep-Wake Rsch., David Mahoney Inst. Neurol. Scis. Avocations: tenor vocalist, open water diving, skiing. Office: U Pa Sch Medicine 423 Guardian Dr 1019 Blockley Hall Philadelphia PA 19104-6021 E-mail: vdongen@mail.med.upenn.edu.

VAN DOREN, EMERSON BARCLAY, mediator; b. Rahway, N.J., Dec. 30, 1940; s. Emerson Maynard and Jaqueline Pendleton (Hicks) Van D.; m. Janet Elisabeth Bumbarger, Dec. 28, 1963; children: Pendleton Barclay, Virginia Cary. BA, Harvard U., 1962; JD, U. Mich., 1965; postgrad. degree (hon.), Air War Coll., Maxwell AF Base, Ala., 1985. Bar: Ky. 1965, N.H. 1971, U.S. Dist. Ct. (we. dist.) Ky. 1966, U.S. Dist. Ct. N.H. 1972. Assoc. Brown, Ardery, Todd & Dudley, Louisville, 1965-66; judge adv. USAF, 1966-71, 72-76; pvt. practice N. Conway, N.H., 1971-72; sr. procurement atty. U.S. Dept. Energy, Washington, 1976-81, dep. asst. gen. counsel for procurement, 1981-85; adminstrv. judge, mediator U.S. Energy Bd. Contract Appeals, Arlington, Va., 1985, chmn., chief adminstrv. judge, 1985—2001. Chmn. U.S. Energy Fin. Assistance Appeals Bd., U.S. Energy Invention Licensing Appeals Bd., U.S. Energy Patent Compensation Bd.; mediator. Capt. USAF, 1966-76, col. USAFR, command mobilization asst. to staff judge adv., 1988-90, ret., 1990. Decorated Meritorious Svc. medal with one oak leaf cluster, Commendation medal with one oak leaf cluster, Legion of Merit award; Leckie fellow, Resident fellow U. Mich.; named Outstanding Young Judge Adv., AF Systems Command, 1975. Mem. ABA, FBA, Sr. Execs. Assn. (chpt. pres. 1993-96), Bd. Contract Appeals Bar Assn. (co-chair practices and policy com.), N.H. Bar Assn., Ky. Bar Assn. Avocations: surf and fly fishing, mountain hiking. Home and Office: 92 Pronghorn Trail # 30 Cameron MT 59720

VAN DOREN, HENRIETTA LAMBERT, nurse, anesthetist; b. Birmingham, Ala., Sept. 21, 1946; d. Martin Lee and Maude Elizabeth (Land) Lambert; m. Terry Lee Van Doren, Oct. 14, 1969; children: Terry Lee Jr., Timothy Wayne. AA in Nursing, Meridian (Miss.) Jr. Coll., 1968; cert., Charity Hosp. Sch. Anesthesia, New Orleans, 1971; PhD in Health Svcs./Nursing Adminstrn., Columbia Pacific U., 1982. RN; cert. nurse anesthetist. Chief nurse anesthetist Riley Meml. Hosp. HMA, Meridian, Miss., 1972-00; self-employed. Mem. Am. Assn. Nurse Anesthetists, Miss. Assn. Nurse Anesthetists, Sierra Club. Republican. Baptist. Avocation: piano. Home: 2551 Campground Rd Lauderdale MS 39335-9621

VAN DOVER, KAREN, middle and elementary school educator, curriculum consultant, language arts specialist, lecturer; b. Astoria, N.Y. d. Frederick A. and Frances L. (Thomas) Van D. BA, CUNY; MALS, SUNY, Stony Brook; postgrad., St. John's U., Jamaica, N.Y. Cert. permanent N-6 tchr., art tchr. K-12, sch. adminstr., supr., N.Y. Tchr., sch. dist. adminstr. St. James (N.Y.) Elem. Sch.; tchr. Nesaquake Intermediate Sch., St. James, lead tchr. English, 1984-92, Smithtown Mid Sch., St. James, 1992-93, curriculum specialist, 1993—. Leader staff devel. and curriculum devel. workshops Smithtown Sch. Dist., 1984—, mem. supt.'s adv. com. for gifted and talented, mem. supt. adv. com. for lang. arts assessment, mem. textbook selection coms. site-based mgmt. team, 1994—, chair 1996-99, master tchr. bd. Prentice Hall, Englewood Cliffs, N.J., 1990—, chair ELA com. for curriculum and the stds., 2000. Contbg. author: Prentice Hall Literature Copper, 1991, 94. Corr. sec. Yaphank Taxpayers and Civic Assn., 1984-86, Nesaquake Sch. PTA, 1990-91, mem., 1977-92; mem. Smithtown Mid. Sch. PTA, 1992—. Mem. ASCD, Am. Ednl. Rsch. Assn., Nat. Assn. Secondary Sch. Prins., Nat. Coun. Tchrs. English, Internat. Reading Assn., Nat. Middle Schs. Assn., N.Y. State English Coun., Nat. Assn. of Elem. Sch. Prins., Internat. Platform Assn., Phi Delta Kappa. Home: 8 Penn Commons Yaphank NY 11980-2025 Office: Smithtown Middle Sch 10 School St Saint James NY 11780-1800 E-mail: kvandover@smithtown.kiz.ny.us.

VAN DRESER, MERTON LAWRENCE, ceramic engineer; b. Des Moines, June 5, 1929; s. Joseph Jerome and Victoria (Love) Van D.; m. Evelyn Lenore Manny, July 12, 1952; children: Peter, Jennifer Sue. BS in Ceramic Engring., Iowa State U., 1951. Tech. supt. Owens-Corning Fiberglas Corp., Kansas City, Mo., 1954-57; rsch. engr. Kaiser Aluminum & Chem. Corp., Milpitas, Calif., 1957-60, rsch. sect. head, 1960-63, lab. mgr., 1963-65, assoc. dir. rsch., 1965-69, dir. refractories rsch. Pleasanton, 1969-72, dir. non-metallic materials rsch., 1972-83, v.p., dir. rsch. Indsl. Chem. div. and Harshaw/Filtrol Partnership, 1983-85, dir. bus. devel. Pleasanton, 1985-88, cons., 1988—. Mem. adv. bd. dept. ceramic engring. U. Ill., 1974-78; chmn. tech. adv. com. Refractories Inst., 1980-84; mem. nat. materials adv. bd. Nat. Acad. Sci.; mem. Indsl. Rsch. Inst. Contbr. articles to sci. jours.; patentee in field. Sustaining membership chmn. local dist. Boy Scouts Am., 1980; pres. PTA, 1967-68; vol. exec. Pakistan Internat. Exec. Svc. Corps, 1990-91. Aviator C.E., U.S. Army, 1951-54. Recipient Profl. Achievement citation Iowa State U., 1978; named to Lambda Chi Alpha hall of fame, 1996. Fellow: Am. Ceramic Soc. (v.p. 1973—74); mem.: AIME, ASTM (hon.), Metall. Soc., Nat. Inst. Ceramic Engrs., Brit. Ceramic Soc., Masons, Rotary (pres. Pleasanton Club 2002—, Paul Harris fellow), Keramos (pres. 1976—78, herald 1980—84, Greaves Walker Roll of Honor award). Avocation: comml. pilot. E-mail: m_evandreser@msn.com.

VAN DUSEN, ALBERT CLARENCE, university official; b. Tampa, Fla., Aug. 30, 1915; s. Charles H. and Maude E. (Green) Van D.; m. Margaret Davis, Jan. 3, 1943; children: Margaret Van Dusen Pysh, Jane Katherine, Sara Elizabeth (Mrs. Frank J. Matyskiela). BS, U. Fla., 1937, AM, 1938; PhD, Northwestern, 1942; LittD, U. Tampa, 1959; L.H.D., Duquesne U., 1967. Instr., asst. prof. dept. psychology U. Fla., 1938-41; asso. prof. psychology Northwestern U., 1946, dir. summer session, 1948-52, v.p. pub. relations, 1952-56; prof. psychology, bus. adminstrn. and edn. U. Pitts., 1956-85, asst. chancellor for planning and devel., 1956-59, vice chancellor the professions, 1959-67, vice chancellor program devel. and pub. affairs, 1967-71, vice chancellor, sec. univ., 1971-80, vice chancellor emeritus, spl. asst. for pub. affairs, 1980-85, vice chancellor emeritus, prof. emeritus psychology, bus. adminstrn. and edn., 1985—, ctr. assoc. univ. ctr. for internat. studies, 1986—. Bd. dirs. Dollar Bank, Pitts. Editor: Proc. Am. Coll. Personnel Assn; contbr. articles to profl. jours. Bd. govs. Pinchot Inst. Conservation Studies; vice chmn., bd. dirs. The Buhl Found., World Affairs Coun. Pitts., vice chmn. bd. dirs. Duquesne U., acting chmn., 1987-88; bd. dirs. Pitts. YMCA, ACTION Housing, Inc., Assn. Am.'s Pub. TV Stas., QED Communications Inc., chmn. 1981-88; bd. dirs. Japan-Am. Soc. Pa.; mem. Pa. Pub. TV Network Commn.; chmn., bd. trustees Pitts. History and Landmarks Found.; pres. bd. trustees H.C. Frick Ednl. Commn., United Way Pa.; dir. South Hills Child Guidance Ctr.; chmn. selfcare study Health Edn. Ctr., Pitts., 1979-80; mem. Walter Reed Hovey Fellowship com. Pitts. Found. Lt. USNR, 1942-46. Fulbright sr. scholar Australian-Am. Ednl. Found., 1980 Fellow Am. Psychol. Assn., Am. Psychol. Soc., Pa. Psychol. Assn., Internat. Found. Social Econ. Deve.; mem. Internat. Assn. Schs. Insts. Adminstrn., C. of C. (dir. 1953-55), Am. Coll. Pub. Rels. Assn. (v.p. 1956-58), Assn. Deans and Dirs. Summer Sessions (sec. 1950-51), Profl. Schs. and World Affairs Com. (chmn. edn. and world affairs 1965-67), Am. Pers. and Guidance Assn., Midwest Psychol. Assn., Ea. Psychol. Assn., Pitts. Psychol. Assn., Internat. Assn. Applied Psychology, Western Pa. Coun. Econ. Edn., Internat. Assn. Schs. and Insts. Adminstrn., Friends of Art for Pitts. Schs. (charter mem.), Phi Beta Kappa, Sigma Xi, Beta Theta Pi, Beta Gamma Sigma. Clubs: Univ. (Pitts.), Duquesne (Pitts.), St. Clair Country (Pitts.). Home: 108 Blue Spruce Cir Pittsburgh PA 15243-1026

VAN DUSEN, BLANCHE BAKER, actress, sculptor; b. N.Y.C., Dec. 20, 1956; d. Jack and Carroll (Baker) Garfein; m. R. Bruce Vandusen; children: Zane, Dara, Wynn. Student, Wellesley Coll. Sculpture rep. by River Gallery, Irvington, N.Y., Sculpture Showcase, New Hope, Pa. Appeared in films The Handmaid's Tale, Shakedown, Raw Deal, Sixteen Candles, Cold Feet, The Seduction of Joe Tynan, TV program Holocaust (Emmy award for Best Supporting Actress); sculpture exhibited in shows at Nat. Arts Club, N.Y.C., Pen and Brush Club, N.Y.C., Salmagundi Club, N.Y.C. , Cropsey-Newington Found., N.Y., Perry House Galleries, Alexandria, Va., Balch Inst., Phila., Alexandria Mus. Art, La., Coos Art Mus., Coos Bay, Oreg., Pound Ridge (N.Y.) Mus., Farmington Mus., N.Mex., Nat. Sculpture Soc., N.Y.C.; solo show Grants Pass Mus. Art, Eugene, Oreg., 2000. Named Anti-defamation League Woman of Achievement, 1979; recipient Philip Isenberg award Pen and Brush Club, 1995, Leonard Meiselman award Salmagundi Club, 1998, Agop Agopoff Meml. award Salmagundi Club, 1998, 2000, Leonard Meiselman award The Pen and Brush Club, 1999, Agop Agopoff Meml. award Newington Cropsey Found., 1998, H.A. Fahdli award Salmagundi Club, 1996, Pietro Montana award HVAA Newington Cropsey Found., 1997, 98, Helen Beling award Coos Art Mus., 1998; winner Manhattan Artists Showcase Manhattan Arts Internat., 1996-98; named Best in Show Pound Ridge Mus., 1998.

VAN DUSEN, DONNA BAYNE, communications consultant, educator, researcher; b. Phila., Apr. 21, 1949; d. John Culbertson and Evelyn Gertrude (Godfrey) Bayne; m. David William Van Dusen, Nov. 30, 1968 (div. Dec. 1989); children: Heather, James; m. L. John Maki, Dec. 27, 1996. BA, Temple U., 1984, MA, 1986, PhD, 1993. Instr. Kutztown (Pa.) U., 1986-87, Ursinus Coll., Collegeville, Pa., 1987-96; cons., rschr. Comm. Rsch. Assoc., Valley Forge, 1993-96; asst. prof. MS in Mgmt. program Regis U., Denver, 1998—. Rschr. Fox Chase Cancer Ctr., Phila., 1985-86; adj. faculty Temple U. Law Sch., 1994-97, LaSalle U., 1994-96, Wharton Sch., U. Pa., 1994-95; asst. prof. Beaver Coll., Glenside, Pa., 1995-96; faculty Internat. U., 1996-99, Metro State U., Denver, 1997-99; cons. Human Comm. Resources and Solutions, 1997—. Writer Mountain Connection, 1998—. Vol. Friends in Transition; vol. mediator Victim Offender Reconciliation Program. Mem.: Nat. Comm. Assn. Avocations: oil painting, creative writing, sailing, gardening, reading. Home: 2589 Alkire St Golden CO 80401 E-mail: dvanduse@regis.edu.

VAN DUSEN, GLENN T. controller, secretary, treasurer; b. Houston, Dec. 25, 1944; s. Glenn Thornton Van Dusen and Barbara L. (Folse) Hanna; m. Jeanette Bearden Nosky, Feb. 14, 1976; children: Cheryl C., Kimberly D. BBA in Acctg., U. Tex., 1972. Store controller Montgomery Ward, Brownsville, Tex., 1972-78; acctg. mgr. Norton Co., 1978-83; owner Photo Finish, Missouri City, Tex., 1984-85; corp. controller Basic Sys., Inc., Houston, 1985-87, Backlog Group, Houston, 1988-95, Staff Force, Inc., Houston, 1995—. Treas. PTA, Katy, Tex., 1987-89, Homeowner's Assn., Katy, 1994-96. With U.S. Army, 1967-71, Germany. Mem. Inst. Mgmt. Accts., Tex. Assn. Staffing. Republican. Avocations: golfing, geneaology, traveling, coins. Office: Staff Force Inc 15915 Katy Fwy Ste 160 Houston TX 77094-1707 E-mail: gvanduson@staff-force.com.

VAN DUSEN, MARGARET DAVIS, community volunteer, consultant; b. Mangum, Okla., Oct. 13, 1918; d. Bunyan Hoyt and Lonie Lee (Jeter) Davis; m. Albert Clarence Van Dusen, Jan. 3, 1943; children: Margaret V.D. Pysh, Jane Van Dusen, Sara V.D. Matyskiela. BS, U. Okla., 1940; MA, Northwestern U., 1942; postgrad., U. London, 1971, U. Pitts., 1991—. Counselor Office of Dean of Students Northwestern U., Evanston, Ill., 1940-42; asst. to dir. pers. Continental Ill. Nat. Bank, Chgo., 1942-43; community vol. Pitts., 1956—. Mem. adv. coun. Presdl. Task Force-Rep. Party, Washington, 1990—92; officer, founding bd. dirs. Music for Mt. Lebanon Keynotes, Pitts., 1959—63; co-founder Ten O'Clock Scholars Program, Mt. Lebanon; founding mem. Southminster Presbyn. Ch. Scholarship Com.; bd. dirs. Presbyn. Univ. Hosp. Vols., Pitts., 1965—, pres., 1986—; bd. dirs. South Hills Coll. Club Pitts., 1959—, lecture com., chmn. antiques study group, officer investment study group; bd. dirs. Mt. Lebanon Nature Conservancy, 1987—98, Children's Festival Pitts., Pitts., 1987—90, Twentieth Century Club Pitts., Pitts., 1958—, YWCA, 1960—64; bd. dirs., officer Pitts. Coun. for Internat. Visitors, 1965—90. Recipient Hon. Life membership Pa. Congress of Parents and Tchrs. Mem. AAUW, Nat. Early Am. Glass Club, Twentieth Century Investment Club (bd. dirs.), UN Assn. Pitts. (bd. dirs.), Women's Fortnightly Rev. (bd. dirs. 1975-85, pres. 1983-84), Northwestern U. Alumni Assn. Pitts. (bd. dirs. 1987-90), Asian Women Inst., Women's Assn. U. Pitts., South Hills Garden Club, Mortar Board, Phi Beta Kappa, Alpha Lambda Delta, Omicron Nu. Avocations: writing, travel, reading, participatory sports, gourmet cooking. Home: 108 Blue Spruce Cir Pittsburgh PA 15243-1026

VAN DUYN, MONA JANE, poet, educator; b. Waterloo, Iowa, May 9, 1921; d. Earl George and Lora G. (Kramer) Van D.; m. Jarvis A. Thurston, Aug. 31, 1943. BA, U. No. Iowa, 1942; MA, U. Iowa, 1943; D.Litt. (hon.), Washington U., St. Louis, 1971, Cornell Coll., Iowa, 1972, U. No. Iowa, 1991, U. of the South, Sewanee, Tenn., 1993, George Wash. U., 1993; LHD, Georgetown U., 1993. Instr. in English U. Iowa, Iowa City, 1943-46; instr. in English U. Louisville, 1946-50; lectr. English Univ. Coll., Washington U., 1950-67; poetry editor, co-pub. Perspective, A Quar. of Lit., 1947-67. Lectr. Salzburg (Austria) Seminar Am. Studies, 1973; adj. prof. poetry workshop Washington U., Spring 1983; vis. Hurst prof., 1987; poet-in-residence Sewanee Writers Conf., 1990, Breadloaf Writing Conf., Mass., 1974. Author: Valentines to the Wide World, 1959, A Time of Bees, 1964, To See, To Take, 1970, Bedtime Stories, 1972, Merciful Disguises, 1973, Letters from a Father and Other Poems, 1983, Near Changes, 1990 (Pulitzer Prize for poetry 1991), Firefall, 1993, If It Be Not I, 1993, Selected Poems, 2002. Recipient Eunice Tietjens award, 1956, Helen Bullis prize, 1964, 76, Harriet Monroe award, 1968, Hart Crane Meml. award, 1968, Borestone Mountains 1st prize, 1968, Bollingen prize, 1970, Nat. Book award, 1971, Sandburg prize Cornell Coll., 1982, Shelley Meml. prize Poetry Soc. Am., 1987, Lilly prize for poetry, 1989, Mo. Arts award, 1990, Golden Plate award Am. Acad. Achievement, 1992, Arts and Edn. Coun. St. Louis award, 1994; named U.S. Poet Laureate, 1992-93; grantee Nat. Coun. Arts, 1967, NEA, 1985; Guggenheim fellow, 1972. Fellow Acad. Am. Poets (chancellor 1985-99); mem. NAAS, Nat. Acad. Arts and Letters (Loines prize 1976), Acad. Arts Scis.

VAN DUYSE, FRANCIS DONALD, retired publisher; b. Sturgeon Bay, Wis., May 2, 1926; s. Francis Lewis and Gertrude (Simon) Van D.; m. Dorothy Marie Walden, May 15, 1953 (div. Feb. 1978); children: Susan, Rebecca, Francis Roy, Sarah. BBA, Spencerian Coll., 1949. Baseball announcer Albany (Ga.) Cardinals, 1953-54, Waycross (Ga.) Bears, 1955, Valdosta (Ga.) Tigers, 1956; pub., editor Wis. All-Sports, Green Bay, 1958-68, Wis. Playground, Green Bay, 1958—68, Pro Football Exclusive, 1969—72; sports dir. WLUK-TV, Channel 11, Green Bay, 1962-63; CEO, announcer Gemini Broadcasting Co., Appleton, Wis., 1980-82; pres., CEO MegaPrint Internat., Sturgeon Bay,

1986—2000. Author: History of the Green Bay Packers, 1965; editor, pub. (yearbooks) Salute to the Packers 1961-1968. With USN, 1944-46. Avocations: chess, fitness, marathons, writing. Home: 1811 Michigan St Apt 1E Sturgeon Bay WI 54235-3704

VAN DYCK, NICHOLAS BOORAEM, minister, foundation official; b. Pasadena, Calif., Aug. 10, 1933; s. David Bevier and Anna Booraem (Richardson) van D.; m. Marcia Perera, June 14, 1958; children: Karen Rhoads, Jennifer Bevier, Sarah Paxson, Rebecca Booraem. BA, Rutgers U., 1959; BD, Union Theol. Sem., N.Y.C., 1962; PhD, U. St. Andrews, 1965. Ordained to ministry Presbyn. Ch., 1962. Pastor Palisades (N.Y.) Presbyn. Ch., 1964-68; tchr., adminstr. Princeton (N.J.) Theol. Sem., 1968-76; exec. dir. Action Research Corp., Princeton, 1976-77; exec. dir., founder Nat. Council for Children & TV, Princeton, N.Y.C. and Los Angeles, 1977-82; pres. Nat. Council for Families and TV, 1982-87; pres., chief exec. officer Religion In Am. Life, Princeton, Phila, N.Y.C., 1988-2000. Chmn. bd. Action Research Corp., Princeton, 1987—; chmn. Assn. for Theol. Field Edn., U.S. and Can., 1975-76. Pub., editor TV and Families, 1982-87; contbr. articles to profl. jours. Bd. dirs. ARC, Princeton, 1984-89, Princeton Youth Fund, 1983-89, YMCA, Princeton, 1986-89, George H. Gallup Internat. Inst., 1990-2000. Lt. USNR, 1954-58. Scholar-in-residence Aspen (Colo.) Inst. for Humanistic Studies, 1985. Mem. Soc. for Psychol. Study Social Issues, Ind. Sector, Princeton Club, Nassau Club, Rotary (pres. Princeton club 1981-82, bd. dirs. found. 1985-95). Avocation: collecting antique autos.

VAN DYCK, WENDY, dancer; b. Tokyo; Student, San Francisco Ballet Sch. With San Francisco Ballet, 1979—96, prin. dancer, 1987—96, instr., tchr., 1996; co-dir. Lawrence Pech Dance, 1996—. Performances include Forgotten Land, The Sons of Horus, The Wanderer Fantasy, Romeo and Juliet, The Sleeping Beauty, Swan Lake, Concerto in d: Poulenc, Handel-a Celebration, Menuetto, Intimate Voices, Hamlet and Ophelia pas de deux, Connotations, Sunset, Rodin, In the Night, The Dream: pas de deux, La Sylphide, Beauty and the Beast, Variations de Ballet, Nutcracker, The Comfort Zone, Dreams of Harmony, Rodeo, Duo Concertant, Who Cares; performed at Reykjavik Arts Festival, Iceland, 1990, The 88th Conf. of the Internat. Olympic Com., L.A., 1984, with Kozlov and Co. Concord Pavilion; guest artist performing role Swan Lake (Act II), San Antonio Ballet, 1985, Giselle, Shreveport Met. Ballet, 1994; featured in the TV broadcast of Suite by Smuin. Mailing: PO Box 1 Littleriver CA 95456

VAN DYK, FREDERICK THEODORE, political scientist, researcher; b. Bellingham, Wash., Oct. 6, 1934; s. Ted and June Ellen (Williams) Van D.; m. Julia Jean Covacevich, Nov. 22, 1957(dec. 1996); children: Theodore, Robert, Terry Jean, Sue Ellen. BA, U. Wash., 1955; MS, Columbia U., 1956. Reporter, editor Seattle Times, 1956-57; advt. public relations exec. Boston and N.Y.C., 1958-62; acting dir. European Community Info. Service, Washington, 1962-64; asst. to Hubert Humphrey, Vice Pres. of U.S., 1964-68; v.p. Columbia U., N.Y.C., 1968-69; pres. Van Dyk Assocs., Washington, 1969-76; asst. adminstr. AID, 1977; v.p. Weyerhaeuser Co., Tacoma, 1978-80; pres. Center for Nat. Policy, Washington, 1981-85, Van Dyk Assocs., 1985-98; exec. v.p. Milken Inst., Santa Monica, Calif., 1998-99; vis. scholar Claremont (Calif.) Grad. U., 1999-2000; sr. fellow UCLA Sch. Pub. Policy and Social Rsch., 1999-2000; columnist Seattle Post-Intelligencer, 2001—; vis. scholar Inst. for Internat. Policy, U. Wash., Seattle. Contbr. essays on govt. and politics to gen. publs. including L.A. Times, N.Y. Times, Wall St. Jour., Washington Post. Bd. dirs. Com. for Study of Am. Electorate, Franklin and Eleanor Roosevelt Inst., Jean Monnet Coun., Humphrey Inst., Wash. News Coun.; mem. Coun. on Fgn. Rels., Presdl. Commn. on Fgn. Assistance, Pacific Coun. on Internat. Policy. Served with M.I. AUS, 1957, 61-62. Mem. Rainier Club (Seattle), Delta Upsilon. E-mail: t_van_dyk@hotmail.com.

VAN DYKE, CATHERINE CLAIRE, retired school social worker; b. Buffalo, Jan. 7, 1924; d. Herman and Sadie (Reinstra) Van D. Student, State Tchrs. Coll., Buffalo, 1941-43; BA in Sociology, D'Youville Coll., 1945; MSW, U. Buffalo, 1949. Cert. sch. social worker, guidance counselor, N.Y. Foster care worker Cath. Charities, Buffalo, 1945-46; child protection worker Children's Aid and Soc. Prevention of Cruelty to Children, 1946-49; caseworker Ingleside Home, 1949-55; adoption worker Children's Aid Soc., 1955-66; social worker Williamsville (N.Y.) Cen. Sch., 1967-85; ret., 1985. Founding bd. dirs. Hamburg (N.Y.) Counseling Svc., 1970-71; presenter at profl. confs. Mem. Erie County Rep. Com., Hamburg, 1968—; vol. Theodore Roosevelt Inaugural Site, Buffalo; vol. ARC, Hamburg, 1988—. Mem. NASW (charter mem., treas. Western N.Y. chpt. 1959-61), N.Y. State Sch. Social Workers (conf. chmn. 1974). Roman Catholic. Avocations: gardening, knitting, travel. Home: 3289 Lakeview Rd Hamburg NY 14075-6114

VAN DYKE, CLIFFORD CRAIG, retired banker; b. Ft. Madison, Iowa, June 23, 1929; s. Charles Clifford and Frances Mary (Butterwick) Van D.; m. Edith Ellicott Powers, Aug. 4, 1951 (dec. Oct. 1980); children: Carol Elizabeth, Deborah Ellicott, Jill Anne, Lisa Ellicott. BA, Knox Coll., 1951; MBA, Harvard U., 1955. Asst. v.p. Nat. Bank of Detroit, 1962-65, v.p., 1965-76; pres. Peoples Nat. Bank & Trust Co. of Bay City, Mich., 1976-78, chmn. bd., pres., 1979-86; chmn. bd., pres., chief exec. officer New Ctr. Bank Corp., Bay City, 1986; chmn. First of Am. Bank-Bay City, N.A., 1987-89; sr. v.p. First of Am. Bank-Mid Mich. N.A., 1990-94; ret., 1994. Trustee Kantzler Found., Bay City, 1979—; bd. dirs., pres. Bay County Growth Alliance, 1987—. 1st lt. U.S. Army, 1951-53, Korea. Mem. Bay City Country Club, Saginaw Valley Torch Club, Rotary. Republican. Unitarian Universalist. Office: Bay County Growth Alliance PO Box 369 Bay City MI 48707-0369 E-mail: bcga@concentric.net.

VAN DYKE, DICK, actor, comedian; b. West Plains, Mo., Dec. 13, 1925; m. Marjorie Willett, Feb. 12, 1948; children: Christian, Barry, Stacey, Carrie Beth. Ed. high sch. With Wayne Williams, founded advt. agy., Danville, Ill., 1946. Chmn. Nick at Nite, 1992—. Appeared school plays, civic theatre prodns.; appeared with Philip Erickson in pantomine act The Merry Mutes, Eric and Van, 1947-53; TV master ceremonies The Music Shop, Atlanta, Morning Show, CBS, 1955, Cartoon Show, 1956; TV variety show Dick Van Dyke Show, New Orleans; guest appearances TV shows, 1958; TV host Flair, ABC, 1960; Broadway debut in The Girls Against the Boys, 1959, Van Dyke and Company, 1976, The Van Dyke Show, CBS, 1988; performed in Broadway musical Bye Bye Birdie, 1960-61 (also motion picture version); (TV) Dick Van Dyke Show, CBS, 1961-66, New Dick Van Dyke Show, 1971-74; performer weekly comedy program Carol Burnett Show; (TV series) Diagnosis Murder, 1993-2002; (TV movies) Daughters of Privilege, 1991, The House on Sycamore Street, 1992, Diagnosis of Murder, 1992, A Twist of the Knife, 1993, The Dick Van Dyke Show Remembered, 1994; performed in motion pictures including What a Way To Go, 1964, Mary Poppins, 1965, Divorce American Style, 1967, Chitty, Chitty, Bang, Bang, 1968, The Comic, 1969, Some Kind of Nut, 1969, Cold Turkey, 1971, The Morning After, 1974, The Runner Stumbles, 1979, Drop-Out Father, 1982, Found Money, 1983, Dick Tracy, 1990; Author: Faith, Hope, and Hilarity, 1970. With USAAC, World War II. Recipient Theater World award 1960, Antoinette Perry award for best mus. comedy actor 1961, Emmy award for comedy Nat. Acad. TV Arts and Scis. 1962, 64, 65 Office: William Morris Agy Inc care Sol Leon 151 S El Camino Dr Beverly Hills CA 90212-2775

VAN DYKE, DONALD LEE, systems engineer, consultant; b. Portsmouth, Ohio, Oct. 2, 1947; arrived in South Africa, 1973; s. Donald Kenneth and Marion (Grimmer) Benk; m. Karin Frylinck, May 18, 1983; 1 child, Bradley. BS in Aeronautical Engring., Embry-Riddle Aero. U., 1995. Cert. aero. engr., airline transport pilot, flight instr., South Africa. Project engr. Sierra Rsch. Corp., 1970-73; mng. dir. Dynamic Tech., South Africa, 1973-82; cons./pilot Magnum Airlines, South Africa, 1982-84; chief exec. Advanced Mgmt. Concepts, Bonaero Park, South Africa, 1984—. Radar cons. South Africa Coun. for Sci. and Indsl. Rsch., 1973—74; sr. cons. Sun Air, South Africa, 1996; dir. ops. Internat. Air Transport Assn., Montreal, 1998, dir. tech. ops., 2000; mem. ops. panel Internat. Civil Aviation Orgn. Inventor radar range normalization unit; patentee in field of light detection; developer (software) Flitebase Airline Info. Mgmt. Sys. Mem. AIAA, IEEE Computer Soc., N.Y. Acad. Scis. Republican. Roman Catholic. Home: 429 Concord Dr Beaconsfield QC Canada H9W 5T1 Office: Internat Air Transport Assn 800 Pl Victoria, PO Box 113 Montreal QC Canada H4Z 1M1

VAN DYKE, GENE, oil company executive; b. Normal, Ill., Nov. 5, 1926; s. Harold and Ruby (Gibson) Van D.; children: Karen, Scott, Janice, Mary Katherine, Tor, Staffan. BS in Geol. Engring., U. Okla., 1950. Geologist Kerr-McGee, Oklahoma City, 1950; chief geologist S.D. Johnson Co., Wichita Falls, Tex., 1950-51; ind. geologist, oil operator, 1951-58; ptnr. Van Dyke and Mejlaender, Houston, 1958-62; owner, pres. Van Dyke Oil Co. (now Vanco Energy Co.), 1962—; also bd. dirs. Bd. dirs. Van Dyke Netherlands, Inc.; chmn. operating com. Vanco Gabon Group. Compiler index of geol. articles to South La. With AC U.S. Army, 1945. Named Living Legend in Wildcatting, Houston Geol. Soc., 2000; named to Hall of Fame, Dutch Am. Heritage Soc., 2001. Mem. Am. Petroleum Inst., Ind. Petroleum Assn., Am. Assn. Petroleum Geologists, Houston Club, Houston Petroleum Club, Houstonian Club, Univ. Club. Republican. Episcopalian. Office: Vanco Energy Co 3 Greenway Plz 12th Fl Houston TX 77046 E-mail: info@vancoenergy.com.

VAN DYKE, HENRY LEWIS, retired educator, writer; b. Allegan, Mich., Oct. 3, 1928; s. Henry Lewis and Bessie Charlotte V. BA, U. Mich., Ann Arbor, 1953, MA, 1955. Prof. Kent (Ohio) State U., 1969-94, ret., 1994. Author: Ladies of the Rachmaninoff Eyes, 1965, Blood of Strawberries, 1968, Dead Piano, 1971, Lunacy and Caprice, 1986. Corp. U.S. Army, 1948-50. Recipient Guggenheim award, 1970, Literature award Am. Acad. Letters, 1972.

VAN DYKE, JOSEPH GARY OWEN, computer consulting executive; b. N.Y.C., Dec. 21, 1939; s. Donald Wood and Gladys Ann (Tague) Van D.; m. Lynne Diane Lammers; June 25, 1966; children: Alison Baird, Jeremy Wood, Matthew Kerr. BA, Rutgers U., 1961; postgrad., R.I. Sch. of Design, 1962, Am. U., 1964-67. Computer programmer System Devel. Corp., Paramus, N.J., 1962-64, sect. head computer tech. div. Falls Church, Va., 1964-67; project mgr. Informatics Inc., Bethesda, Md., 1967-70, dept. dir. Rockville, 1970-74, v.p., gen. mgr., 1974-78; owner, pres. J G Van Dyke and Assoc., Inc., Bethesda, 1978—. Chmn. bd., chief exec. officer The Outreach Group, Inc., 1987—. Bd. dirs. Westbrook Sch., Bethesda, 1981-82, St. Columba's Ch., Washington, 1980-84; founder Computer Edn. Workshop, Bethesda, 1981; coach MSI soccer, Bethesda, 1979-89. Mem. Inst. Elec. Engring. Democrat. Episcopalian. Avocations: coaching soccer, sailing, graphic designing. Home: 5117 Dalecarlia Dr Bethesda MD 20816-1807 Office: JG Van Dyke & Assocs Inc 7900 Westpark Dr # T100 Mc Lean VA 22102-4242

VAN DYKE, LARRY DAVID, consultant; b. Healdsburg, Calif., Sept. 9, 1947; s. Lester Myers and Marjorie E. Van D.; m. Candise Maureen Ellwood, Dec. 19, 1970; children: David, Shawn, Todd. BA, U. Wash., 1978; MAR, Emmanuel Sch. Religion, 1982. Dir. pub. rels. Emmanuel Sch. Religion, Johnson City, Tenn., 1978-85, exec. dir. devel., 1985-88; pres. CMA Resource Devel., Inc., 1988-96; sr. cons. Goettler Assocs., Columbus, Ohio, 1997-99, Nat. Cmty. Devel. Svcs., Atlanta, 1999—. Instr. NSFRE, Alexandria, Va. With USN, 1969-73. Decorated Navy Achievement medal. Mem. Nat. Soc. Fund Raising Execs. (cert.). Republican. Avocations: fly fishing, canoeing, skiing, wood working. Home: 811 Corday Dr #103 Naperville IL 60540 Office: World Vision-Chicago 5001 W Harrison St Chicago IL 60644 Fax: 423-926-5154. E-mail: Larryvan47@aol.com.

VAN DYKE, MILTON DENMAN, aeronautical engineering educator; b. Chgo., Aug. 1, 1922; s. James Richard and Ruth (Barr) Van D.; m. Sylvia Jean Agard Adams, June 16, 1962; children: Russell B., Eric J., Nina A., Brooke A. and Byron J. and Christopher M. (triplets). BS, Harvard U., 1943; MS, Calif. Inst. Tech., 1947, PhD, 1949. Research engr. NACA, 1943-46, 50-54, 55-58; vis. prof. U. Paris, France, 1958- 59; prof. aero. Stanford, 1959—; prof. emeritus, 1992—. Pres. Parabolic Press. Author: Perturbation Methods in Fluid Mechanics, 1964, An Album of Fluid Motion, 1982; editor: Ann. Rev. Fluid Mechanics, 1969-99. Trustee Soc. For Promotion of Sci. and Scholarship, Inc. Served with USNR, 1944-46. Guggenheim and Fulbright fellow, 1954-55 Mem. Am. Acad. Arts and Scis., Nat. Acad. Engring., Am. Phys. Soc., Phi Beta Kappa, Sigma Xi, Sierra Club. Office: Stanford U Div Mechs & Computation Stanford CA 94305-4040

VAN DYKE, THOMAS WESLEY, lawyer; b. Kansas City, Mo., May 12, 1938; s. Harold Thomas and Elizabeth Louise (Barritt) Van D.; m. Sharon Edgar, Jan. 30, 1960; children: Jennifer Van Dyke Winters, Jeffrey. BA, U. Kans., 1960; JD, U. Mich., 1963. Bar: Mo. 1963, Kans. 1983. Atty. SEC, Washington, 1963-64; legal asst. to commr. Hamer E. Budge, 1964-65; from assoc. to ptnr. Linde Thomson Langworthy Kohn & Van Dyke, P.C., Overland Park, Kans., 1965-91. Co-chmn. ALI-ABA Tax and Bus. Planning Seminar, 1987-96; mem. securities adv. panel Sec. of State of Mo., 1984-89. Mem. ABA (fed. regulation securities com. bus. law sect. 1982-2002, negotatiated acquisitions com. 1989-2002), Kans. Bar Assn., Mo. Bar Assn. (corp. banking and bus. law com., chmn. full com. 1983-84, past chmn. securities law subcom.), Carriage Club (bd. dirs. 1986-89). Republican. Avocations: tennis, golf, reading. Office: Bryan Cave LLP 7500 College Blvd Ste 1100 Overland Park KS 66210-4097

VAN DYKE, WILLIAM GRANT, manufacturing company executive; b. Mpls., June 30, 1945; s. Russell Lawrence and Carolyn (Grant) Van D.; m. Karin Van Dyke; children: Carolyn Julie, Colin Grant, Alexander Grant, Stephanie Joyce. BA in Econs., U. Minn., 1967, MBA, 1972. V.p., CFO Northland Aluminum Co., Mpls., 1977-78; controller Donaldson Co., Inc., 1978-80, v.p. controller, 1980-82, v.p., CFO, 1982-84, v.p., gen. mgr. indsl. group, 1984-94, pres., COO, 1994-96, chmn., pres., CEO, 1996—, also bd. dirs. Bd. dirs. Graco Inc., Alliant Techsystems. Served to lt. U.S. Army, 1968-70, Vietnam. Mem. Kappa Sigma Alumni Assn. Avocations: running; bicycling. Office: Donaldson Co Inc 1400 W 94th St Minneapolis MN 55431-2370

VAN DYKE-COOPER, ANNY MARION, retired financial company executive; b. Howard, Ont., Can., Sept. 30, 1928; d. Anthony and Anna (Koolen) Van D.; m. John Arnold Cooper, Apr. 9, 1983. BA, Concordia U., 1959. CFA. Tchr. Lanoraie Sch. Bd., 1946-47; sec. Can. Nat. Rys., Montreal, Que., 1947-51; sec. Sorel (Que.) Industries Ltd., 1952-53; with Bell Investment Mgmt. Corp. and BIMCOR, Inc. subs. Bell Can., Montreal, 1953-83; portfolio mgr. U.S. Equities, 1971-83; chmn., dir. Cooper, Van Dyke Assocs. Inc., Bloomfield Hills, Mich., 1983-96; ret. Mem. Inst. Chartered Fin. Analysts (trustee 1979-80), Assn. Investment Mgmt. and Rsch. (treas. 1977-78, vice-chmn. 1978-79, chmn. 1979-80), Fin. Analysts Soc. Detroit, Montreal Soc. Fin. Analysts (program chmn., pres. 1974-75), Can. Coun. Fin. Analysts (vice-chmn. 1976-77). Home: 2425 Gulf of Mexico Dr Unit 13B Longboat Key FL 34228-3215 E-mail: marionvdc@hotmail.com.

VAN DYNE, MICHELE MILEY, information engineer; b. Harrisburg, Pa., Sept. 8, 1959; d. Joseph Lawrence Miley and Tina Theresa (Dudash) Smollack; m. David Franklin Buck, Aug. 8, 1981 (div. July 1984); m. David George Van Dyne, Sept. 9, 1989. BA in Psychology, U. Mont., 1981, MS in Computer Sci., 1985; postgrad., U. Kans., 1992—. Div. sr. tech. programmer, analyst Allied-Signal Aerospace, Kansas City, Mo., 1985-89; knowledge engr. United Data Svcs., Inc., United Telecom, Overland Park, Kans., 1989-90; pres. IntelliDyne, Inc., Kansas City, Mo., 1990—. Cons. Comprehensive Devel. Ctr., Missoula, Mont., 1984; speaker Sigart, Kansas City, 1988; chmn. Expert-Systems-Kans. and Mo. (ESKaMo), 1990-92. Vol. Planned Parenthood Greater Kansas City, 1986. United Bldg. Ctrs. scholar, 1976. Mem. IEEE Computer Soc., Am. Assn. for Artificial Intelligence, Internat. Neural Network Soc., Instrnl. Tech. Network (steering com. 1990-92), Women in Tech. Network (steering com. 1990-91, chmn. pub. rels. com. 1991-92), Alpha Lambda Delta. Democrat. Episcopalian. Avocations: reading, skiing, softball, decorating. Home and Office: 6040 Wornall Rd Kansas City MO 64113-1418 E-mail: mvandyne@worldnet.att.net.

VANE, JOHN ROBERT, pharmacologist; b. Worcestershire, Eng., Mar. 29, 1927; s. Maurice and Frances Florence Vane; m. Elizabeth Daphne Page, Apr. 4, 1948; children: Nicola, Miranda. BSc in Chemistry, U. Birmingham, 1946; MSc in Pharmacology, Oxford U., 1949, D Phil., 1953, DSc, 1970; MD (hon.), U. Cracow, Poland, 1977, Copernicus Acad. Medicine, Cracow; doctorate (hon.), Rene Descartes U., Paris, 1978; DSc (hon.), CUNY, 1980, Aberdeen U., 1983, N.Y. Med. Coll., Birmingham U., U. Surrey, 1984, Camerino U., Italy, 1984, Louvain, 1986, Buenos Aires, 1986; DHC in Medicine and Surgery (hon.), U. Florence; DSc (hon.), U. London, 1995, U. Verona, 1997. Fellow Therapeutic Rsch. Coun., Oxford U., 1946—48; rsch. worker Sheffield U., 1948-49; rschr. worker Nuffield Inst. Med. Rsch., Oxford U., 1949—51; Stothert rsch. fellow Royal Soc., 1951—53; instr., then asst. prof. pharmacology Yale U. Med. Sch., 1953—55; mem. faculty Inst. Basic Med. Scis., Royal Coll. Surgeons Eng., 1955—73, prof. exptl. pharmacology, 1966—73; group R & D dir. Wellcome Found. Ltd., Beckenham, 1973—85; dir.-gen. William Harvey Rsch. Inst. St. Bartholomew's/Royal London Sch. of Medicine/Dentistry, Queen Mary/Westfield Coll., U. London, 1986—97, hon. life pres. William Harvey Rsch. Inst., 1997—. Bd. dirs. De Code Genetics Inc., Iceland, MetaPhone Pharms. U.S.A. Co-editor: Adrenergic Mechanisms, 1960, Prostaglandin Synthetase Inhibitors, 1974, Metabolic Functions of the Lung, 1977, Handbook of Experimental Pharmacology, 1978, Prostacyclin, 1979, Interaction Between Platelets and Vessel Walls, 1981, Endothelin, 1989, 1991, 1993, 1995, 1998, New Targets in Inflammation, 1996, Therapeutic Roles of Selective Cox-2 Inhibitors, 1998, Selective Cox-2 Inhibitors, 2001; contbr. numerous articles to profl. jours. Freeman City of Scranton (Pa.), 1988, City of Taipei (Taiwan), 1989, City of New Orleans, 1995; hon. life pres. William Harvey Rsch. Found., 2000—. Decorated knight bachelor; recipient Baly medal, Royal Coll. physicians, Albert Lasker Basic Med. Rsch. award, Peter Debye prize, Nuffield Gold medal, Ciba Geigy Drew medal, Soc. Endocrinology, 1981, Nobel prize in Physiology or Medicine, 1982, Galen medal, Worshipful Soc. Apothecaries, 1983, Louis Pasteur Found. prize, Santa Monica, Calif., 1984, Nat. Headache Found. award, 1988, Hamburg Gold medal, Royal Pharm. Soc. Gt. Britain, 1996. Fellow: ACP (hon.), Royal Soc. (Royal medal 1989), Inst. Biology, Royal Coll. Physicians London (hon.), Royal Coll. Pathologists (hon.), Royal Coll. Surgeons of Eng. (hon.), Brit. Pharm. Soc. (hon.), Royal Nat. Acad. Medicine (hon.); mem.: NAS (fgn. assoc.), Soc. Drug Rsch., Am. Acad. Arts and Scis. (fgn. hon.), Physiol. Soc. (hon.), Polish Pharm. Soc. (hon.), Polish Acad. Scis. (fgn.), Royal Netherlands Acad. Arts and Scis., Royal Acad. Medicine Belgium, Alpha Omega Alpha (hon.). Office: William Harvey Research Inst 1826 R St, NW Washington DC 20009 E-mail: clmeasures@mds.qmw.ac.uk.*

VANE, SYLVIA BRAKKE, anthropologist, publisher, cultural resource management company executive, writer; b. Fillmore County, Minn., Feb. 28, 1918; d. John T. and Hulda Christina (Marburger) B.; m. Arthur Bayard Vane, May 17, 1942; children: Ronald Arthur, Linda, Laura Vane Ames. AA, Rochester Jr. Coll., 1937; BS with distinction, U. Minn., 1939; postgrad, Radcliffe Coll., 1944; MA, Calif. State U., Hayward, 1975. Med. technologist Dr. Frost and Hodapp, Willmar, Minn., 1939-41; head labs. Corvallis (Oreg.) Gen. Hosp., 1941-42; dir. lab. Cambridge (Mass.) Gen. Hosp., 1942-43; staff Peninsula Clinic, Redwood City, Calif., 1947-49; vice pres. Cultural Systems Rsch. Inc., Menlo Park, 1978—; pres. Ballena Press, 1981—. Cons. resource mgmt. So. Calif. Edison Co., Rosemead, 1978-81, San Diego Gas and Elec. Co., 1980-83, Pacific Gas and Elec. Co., San Francisco, 1982-83, Wender, Murase & White, Washington, 1983-87, Yosemite Indians, Mariposa, Calif., 1982-91, San Luis Rey Band of Mission Indians, Escondido, Calif., 1986-89, U.S. Ecology, Newport Beach, Calif., 1986-89, Riverside County Flood Control and Water Conservation Dist., 1985-95, Infotec, Inc., 1989-91, Alexander & Karshmer, Berkeley, Calif., 1989-92, Desert Water Agy., Palm Springs, Calif., 1989-90, Met. Water Dist., 1992-2001, Nat. Park Svc., 1992-, 2001, Applied Earthworks, Inc., 1997-99. Author: (with L.J. Bean), California Indians, Primary Resources, 1977, rev. edit., 1990, The Cahuilla and the Santa Rosa Mountains, 1981, The Cahuilla Landscape, 1991, Ethnology of the Alta California Indians, vol. I Pre Contact, vol. II POst Contact, 1992, Spanish Borderlands Sourcebooks, vols. 3, 4; contbr. chpts. to several books. Bd. dirs. Sequoia Area coun. Girl Scouts U.S., 1954-61; bd. dirs., v.p., pres. LWV, South San Mateo County, Calif., 1960-65. Fellow Soc. Applied Anthropology, Am. Anthropology Assn.; mem. Southwestern Anthropology Assn. (prog. chmn. 1976-78, newsletter editor 1976-79), Soc. for Am. Archaeology, Soc. Calif. Archaeology (Martin A. Baumhoff Spl. Achievement award 1998). Mem. United Ch. of Christ. Office: Ballena Press 823 Valparaiso Ave Menlo Park CA 94025-4206

VANE, TERENCE G., JR. financial services company executive, lawyer; b. Elgin, Ill., Jan. 17, 1942; s. Terence Gregory and Velma Mary (Mersman) V.; m. Patricia Bryant, Aug. 29, 1964; children: Terence Gregory III, Lourdene DeLynne, Christopher Theodore. BA, Ind. U., 1964, JD, 1967. Bar: Ind. 1967, Tex. 1977, N.C. 1992; cert. house counsel Fla. 1996, 2002. Staff atty. Assocs. Discount Corp., South Bend, Ind., 1967-69; asst. gen. counsel Assocs. Mgmt. Corp., 1969-74, Assocs. Comml. Corp., South Bend, 1974-76, Assocs. Ins. Group, Inc., Dallas, 1976-77; gen. counsel, v.p. ins. ops. Assocs. Corp. N.Am., 1977-80, gen. counsel, sr. v.p. ins. ops., 1981-82, gen. counsel, sr. v.p. consumer fin. and ins. ops., 1982-86, gen. counsel, sr. v.p. diversified consumer fin. services and credit card ops., 1986-88; exec. v.p., gen. counsel, sec., dir. Barclays Am. Corp., Charlotte, N.C., 1988-91; pres. Vector Fin. Svcs., Inc., 1991-95, bd. dirs.; sr. v.p., assoc. gen. counsel EquiCredit Corp., Jacksonville, Fla., 1996-97; sr. v.p., gen. counsel, sec. First Street Mortgage Corp., 1997-98, Home Alliance Mortgage Co., Jacksonville, 1998-2000, Alliance Capital Ptnrs. Group, Jacksonville, 2000—02, Slott & Barker, Jacksonville, 2002—. Chmn. bd. dirs., sec. Youth Concert Found. for Promotion Creative Arts, 1981—; bd. dirs. N.C. Bus. Com. Edn., 1988-91. Mem. ABA (com. on consumer fin. svcs. law), Fla. Bar Assn., Ind. Bar Assn., Tex. Bar Assn., N.C. Bar Assn., Nat. Assn. Ind. Insurers (laws com. 1978-86), Consumer Credit Ins. Assn. (chmn. property ins. legis. com. 1979-85), Am. Fin. Svcs. Assn. (law com., chmn. environ. law subcom.), Conf. Consumer Fin. Law (governing com.), Nat. Home Equity Mortgage Assn., Lawyers Round Table. Home: 13802 Fiddlers Point Dr Jacksonville FL 32225-5427 Office: 334 East Duval Street Jacksonville FL 32202-2718

VAN EECKHOUDT, MARC VICTOR CELESTIN, purchasing manager; b. Pamel, Belgium, July 24, 1950; s. Alfons and Alma (Staels) Van E.; m. Beatrix J.F. Ruttens, Dec. 21, 1973; children: Karlien, Bastiaan, Pepijn, Stoffel. Lic., Vlekho, Brussels, 1972; grad., Cath. U. Leuven, Belgium, 1972, MBA, 1978, PhD, 1980. Analyst Essochem Belgium, Brussels, 1977-79, acctg. mgr., 1982-84; acctg. supr. Essochem Plastics, Meerhout, Belgium, 1980-81; coord. Exxon Chem. Co., Darien, Conn., 1984-87; contr. Esso Benelux, Breda, The Netherlands, 1988-92, Exxon Chem. Europe, Brussels, 1992-95; mgr. purchasing and contracting Esso Internat., 1995-99; dep. mgr. procurement Exxon Mobil, Fairfax, Va., 2000—. Home: 9809 Kirktree Ct Fairfax VA 22032 Office: Exxon Mobil Procurement 3225 Gallows Rd Fairfax VA 22037 E-mail: vaneeckhoudt@yahoo.com.

VANEK, EUGENIA POPORAD, medical educator, consultant; b. Cleve., June 23, 1949; d. George and Anna P. (Dumitru) Poporad; m. John Albert Vanek, Aug. 28, 1971; children: Matthew Dumitru, Jessica Petera. BS, Case Western Res. U., 1970; MA (fellow), Boston U., 1972; EdD, U. Rochester, 1974. Tchr. Cleveland Heights (Ohio) H.S., 1970; instr. Monroe C.C., 1972-74, Rochester (N.Y.) Inst. Tech., 1972-74; asst. prof. med. edn. rsch. Case Western Res. U., Cleve., 1974-80, asst. prof. family medicine, 1979-80, asst. cíln. prof. cmty. dentistry, 1978-87; adj. prof. Goddard Coll., Plainfield, Vt., 1980-81, ednl. cons., 1980—. With Cleve. Clinic Ednl. Found., Case Western Res. U. Med. Sch., Lorain County (Ohio) Access to Higher Edn. Program, Elyria (Ohio) Pub. Schs., Kent State U.; rsch. dir. R.W. Johnson Program, Office of Med. Edn., Case Western Res. U., 1986-89, ednl. coord. primary care Sch. Medicine, 1986-89, program coord. health scis. edn. program, 1975-79. Author: In Piagetian Research: Compilation and Commentary, Vol. 4, 1976; contbr. numerous articles to publs. Chmn. Northeastern Ohio alumni scholarship admissions com. U. Rochester, 1974—76, 1979—80; active N.E. Ohio affiliate Am. Heart Assn., 1977; mem. Task Force on Heart Disease in Young; trustee Oberlin Friends of Pub. Libr., 1982—84; active Lorain County Bd. Health, 1986—88; mem. med. edn. evaluation commn. Ohio State Med. Bd., 1987—88; appointee design rev. bd. Oberlin City Coun., 1995—99; mem. resident rights com. Kendal at Oberlin; trustee Oberlin (Ohio) Early Childhood Ctr., 1980—83; bd. dirs. No. Ohio Youth Orch., 1993—95, Oberlin (Ohio) Srs., Inc. , 1993—99, Neighborhood House Assn. Lorain County, Inc., 1995—2000. Mem. ASCD. Home and Office: 46 Stewart Ct Oberlin OH 44074-1334

VAN ENGELSDORP, DENNIS, apiculturist, university official; b. Rotterdam, The Netherlands, Aug. 10, 1969; s. Bernardus and Marleen van Engelsdorp; m. Rosemary Elizabeth Magee, Oct. 8, 1964. BSc in Agr., U. Guelph, Ont., Can., 1993, MSc, 1995. Cons. CUSO, Willikies Village, Antigua and Barbuda, 1995-98; apiculture extension support specialist Cornell U., Ithaca, Can., 1998—. Contbr. articles to profl. jours. Office: Cornell U Dept Entomology Comstock Hall Ithaca NY 14850 Fax: 607-255-0939. E-mail: dv23@cornell.edu.

VAN ENGEN, THOMAS LEE, state legislator; b. Sioux Center, Iowa, Mar. 28, 1953; s. Leo Herman and Dolores (Nelma) Van E.; m. Rosalyn Faye Vander Plaats, 1979; children: Matthew Thomas, David James, Jeremy Lee. BA, Dordt Coll., Sioux Center, 1979. Chair dist. 15 Minn. Ho. of Reps., St. Paul, 1992-94, mem., 1994-98; life and health ins. agt. Am. United Life Ins. Co. and Blue Cross Blue Shield Minn., 1997-98; devel. cons. Terwisscha Construction, Willmar, 1998—. Del. Rep. dist. and state convs., 1984-2000, Minn. Rep. Ctrl. Com., 1989-2000; chmn. Pipestone County Com., Minn., 1988-89, Kandiyohi County Com., 1991-93; co-chmn. dist. 15 Minn. Senate, 1990-92, chmn., 1992-94; candidate for Minn. Ho. of Reps., 1992, 2002; chmn. edn. com. Cmty. Christian Sch. Bd., 1990-94; elder Christian Reformed Ch., 1985-88, 96-99, 2001—, handicapped children and adults, 1978-82, chem. dependency counselor, 1982-94. With U.S. Army, 1972-74. Mem. CAP (mission pilot 1996—, moral leadership officer 2000—, squadron comdr. 2000—), Am. Legion, Kiwanis. E-mail: tve@tds.net.

VAN ERON, KEVIN JOSEPH, organizational development consultant, psychologist; b. Hutchinson, Kans., Apr. 9, 1957; s. Kenneth J. and Meriam J. (Buller) Van Eron; m. Ann M. Schwartz, Jan. 1, 1984. B in Gen Studies, U. Md., 1980; MA, Ill. Sch. Profl. Psychology, 2000. Chartered life underwriter. Dist. rep. Aid Assn. for Luths., Appleton, Wis., 1980-83, dist. mgr., 1983-84, gen. agt., 1984-87, gen. mgr., 1987-91, v.p., mem. field svcs., 1992, sr. v.p., mem. field svcs., 1993-95, sr. v.p. creating mem. relationships, 1996-97; prin. Potentials, Chgo., 1997—. Mem. APA, Jungian Inst. Democrat. Avocations: traveling, reading, hiking. Home and Office: 195 N Harbor Dr Apt 3706 Chicago IL 60601-7534 E-mail: kjvaneron@aol.com.

VAN ETTEN, ELWYN ROBERT, retired marketing specialist; b. Corning, N.Y., Apr. 13, 1925; s. Clyde Abram and Ellen Marian (Reynolds) V.E.; m. Virgina Church Conant, Jan. 10, 1945; children: Peter Clyde. BBA, Syracuse U., 1947; M in Sci. Edn., Elmira (N.Y.) Coll., 1975. Sales and budget mgr. Firestone Tire, Elmira, 1947-49; budget mgr. Barrys U.S. Tire Co., 1950-52; supply officer USN, Shumaker, Ark., 1952-54; internal auditor Nat. Fireworks Co., 1954-56; acct. and planner Corning (N.Y.) Glass Works, 1956-62, Corning Glass Works, 1962-72, mktg. specialist, 1972-84. Organizer, pres. Nat. Assn. Accts., Lexington, Ky., 1957-62. Author: Van Etten Beginnings and Endings, 1993; contbr. periodicals. Parks commr. town of Big Flats, N.Y., 1976-83, town historian, 1993—; vol. Steele Meml. Libr., Elmira, N.Y. Named Disting. Citizen of Yr., 1996. Mem. Elks, Lions Club (pres. 1997-98). Republican. Avocations: golf, gardening, reading, travel, genealogy. Home: PO Box 95 Big Flats NY 14814-0095

VAN ETTEN, PETER WALBRIDGE, foundation executive; b. Boston, May 10, 1946; s. Royal Cornelius Van Etten and Peggy June (Walbridge) Hutchins; m. Mary Peters French, Sept. 5, 1968; children: Molly, Clarissa, Ellen. BA, Columbia U., 1968; MBA, Harvard U., 1973. Br. mgr. BayBanks, Brookline, Mass., 1968-71; loan officer Bank of Boston, 1973-76; CFO Univ. Hosp., Boston, 1976-79; exec. v.p., CFO New Eng. Med. Ctr., 1979-89; pres., CEO Transition Systems, 1986-89; dep. chancellor U. Mass. Med. Ctr., Worcester, 1989-91; CFO Stanford (Calif.) U., 1991-94; pres., CEO Stanford Univ. Hosp., 1994-97; CEO UCSF Stanford Health Care, 1997-99; exec. com. U. Healthsystem Consortium, 1997-99, vice chmn., 1998-99; dir. Calif. Healthcare Assn., 1998-99, IDX Sys., Inc., 1999-2001; pres., CEO Juvenile Diabetes Found. Internat., N.Y.C., 2000—. Dir. Transition Sys., Inc., 1996-98. Chair campaign United Way San Francisco, 1998. Office: Juvenile Diabetes Found 120 Wall St New York NY 10005-3904 E-mail: pvanetten@jdf.org.

VANEVERY, C(YNTHIA) DARLENE, counselor, educator; b. Grove City, Pa., Apr. 10, 1951; d. Roy Milton and Dorothy Grace (O'Conner) Uber; m. James Robert Robotham, Nov. 15, 1972 (div. July 1980); m. Harry Paul VanEvery, Apr. 17, 1981; 1 child, Christopher Paul. BA, Park Coll., 1979; MA, Cath. U. Am., 1984; DA, George Mason U., 1999. Enlisted USAF, 1975, advanced through grades to maj., 1993, ret., 1995; program devel. specialist George Mason U., Fairfax, Va., 1997-99; adj. prof. psychology No. Va. C.C., Alexandria, 1997—; workforce sr. program mgr. Info. Tech. Assn. Am., 1999—. Decorated Air Force Commendation medal with 2 oak leaf clusters, Meritorious Svc. medal. Mem. Am. Counseling Assn., Am. Coll. Counseling Assn., Assn. for Specialists in Group Work, Va. C.C. Assn., Assn. C.C. Educators (pres. 1998-99). Avocations: reading, watercolor painting, beads, homeopathy. Home: 6504 Lakeview Dr Falls Church VA 22041-1102

VAN EYS, JAN, retired pediatrician, educator, administrator; b. Hilversum, The Netherlands, Jan. 25, 1929; came to U.S., 1951; s. Jan and Geertruida (Floor) van E.; m. Catherine Travis; children: Jan Peter, D. Catherine. PhD in Biochemistry, Vanderbilt U., 1955; MD, U. Wash., 1966. Diplomate Nat. Bd. Med. Examiners, Am. Bd. Pediatrics, Am. Bd. Pediatric Hematology/Oncology. Postdoctoral fellow McCollum Pratt Inst., Johns Hopkins U., Balt., 1955-57; asst. prof. biochemistry Vanderbilt U., Nashville, 1957-62, assoc. prof., 1962-71, prof., 1971-73; intern, resident in pediatrics Vanderbilt U. Hosps., 1966-69; pediatrician M.D. Anderson Hosp. U. Tex., Houston, 1973-94, prof. pediatrics, 1973-94, Mosbacher prof. pediatrics, 1979-87, Mosbacher chair, 1988-90, chmn. dept., 1983-88, head div., 1983-90, chmn. dept. exptl. pediatrics, 1983-90; David R. Park prof. pediatrics U. Tex. Med. Sch., 1990-94, chmn. dept., 1987-94; clin. prof. pediat. Sch. Medicine, Vanderbilt U., Nashville, 1994—. Cons. Cancer Info. Svcs. for Code Ethics and Pediatric Cancers, 1986-89. Author: (with T.S. Carter and C. Jordan) The Howell Kindred, 1979, Humanity and Personhood: Personal Reactions to a World in Which Children Can Die, 1981, (with M. Weiner) Nicotinic Acid, Drug, Nutrient and Cofactor, 1983; contbr. numerous articles, abstracts, papers, book chpts., and revs. to profl. publs.; editor: (with J.T. Truman and C. Pochedly) Human Values in Pediatric Hematology/Oncology, 1986, (with R.A. Dowell and D. Copeland) The Child With Cancer in the Community, 1988, Cancer in the Very Young, 1989; chief editor pediatric sect. Year Book of Cancer, 1978-87, cons. editor, 1974-78; assoc. editor Nutrition and Cancer, 1978—, Jour. Pediatric Hematology/Oncology, 1982-92, Houston Med. Jour., 1986-93, Cancer Prevention Internat., 1993—, The Pharos, 1994—; also editor/co-editor proc. of workshops, clin. and mental health confs., ann. symposiums, etc. Pres. bd. trustees Inst. Religion, Houston, 1989-94; mem. adminstrv. bd. Westbury United Meth. Ch., Houston, 1989-94; bd. dirs. McKendree Sr. Care Corp., Nashville, 1996—, Alive Hospice, Nashville, 1998—, Nat. Hemophilia Found.; chmn. Health and Welfare TN Ann. Conf. United Methodist Ch., 1996. Fellow Am. Acad. Pediatrics, Am. Coll. Nutrition; mem. Am. Pediatric Soc., Am. Soc. Hematology, Am. Soc. Clin. Oncology, Am. Med. Writers Assn., Am. Soc. for Parental and Enteral Nutrition, So. Med. Assn., World Fedn. for Hemophilia, Tex. Pediatric Soc., Houston Pediatric Soc. (pres. 1981-82), Houston Acad. Medicine, Harris County Med. Assn., U. Tex. M.D. Anderson Cancer Ctr. Assocs., Sigma Xi, Alpha Omega Alpha. Home and Office: 3504 Ruland Pl Nashville TN 37215-1812 E-mail: jan.van-eys@mcmail.vanderbilt.edu., janvaneys@cs.com.

VAN FLEET, DAVID DOMINIC, finance educator; b. Binghamton, N.Y., Nov. 27, 1940; s. Walter Anthony Van Fleet, Sr. and Katherine Elizabeth Van Fleet; m. Ella Webb Webb, Aug. 27, 1966; children: Marijke, Dirk. BS, U. Tenn., 1962, PhD, 1969. Instr. U. Tenn., Knoxville, 1963—67, Kingsport Grad. Study Program, Kingsport, 1967—70; asst. prof. U. Akron, Akron, 1970—73; from asst. prof. to prof. Tex. A&M U., College Station, 1973—89; prof. Ariz. State U. W., Phoenix, 1989—, MBA dir., 1999—2003. Prin. lectr. A. Frank Smith Jr. Lectureship series Southwestern U., 2000. Author: (book) Military Leadership: An Organizational Behavior Perspective, 1986, Organizational Behavior: A Managerial Viewpoint, 1983, Contemporary Management (3rd. edition), 1994, Contemporary Management (2nd edition), 1991, Contemporary Management (1st edition), 1991, Behavior in Organizations, 1991; contbr. ; editor: N-File Newsletter, 1976—0978, Jour. of Mgmt., 1987—89, Acad. of Mgmt. Newsletter, 1979—82. Recipient Faculty Achievement Award in Rsch., Scholarship, and Creative Activity, Ariz. State U. W., 2001, Outstanding Svc. award, Coll. Bus. Adminstrn., Tex. A&M U., 1985. Fellow: Acad. Mgmt.; mem.: Southwestern Fedn. of Adminstrv. Disciplines (bd. dirs. 1985—87), Allied So. Bus. Assn. (pres. 1995), S.W. Acad. of Mgmt. (pres. 1986—87), So. Mgmt. Assn. (pres. 1995), Acad. of Mgmt. Mgmt. History Divsn. (chmn. 1980—81, bd. govs. 1983—85, sec. 1996—99). Home: 4849 E Altadena Ave Scottsdale AZ 85254 Office: Arizona State University West PO Box 37100 Phoenix AZ 85069-7100 Office Fax: 602-543-6249. Personal E-mail: ddvf@asu.edu. Business E-Mail: MBA@asuwest-online-west.asu.edu.

VAN FLEET, GEORGE ALLAN, lawyer; b. Monterey, Calif., Jan. 20, 1953; s. George Lawson and Wilma Ruth (Williams) Van F.; m. Laurie Elise Koch, July 20, 1975; children: Katia Elaine, Alexander Lawson. BA summa cum laude, Rice U., 1976; JD, Columbia U., 1977. Bar: Tex. 1978, U.S. Dist. Ct. (so. dist.) Tex. 1978, U.S. Dist. Ct. (we. dist.) Tex. 1987, U.S. Dist. Ct. (no. dist.) Tex, 1988, U.S. Dist. Ct. (ea. dist.) Tex. 1991, U.S. Tax Ct., 1984, U.S. Ct. Appeals (5th cir.) 1978, U.S. Ct. Appeals (11th cir.) 1981, U.S. Ct. Appeals (D.C. cir.) 1982, U.S. Ct. Appeals (fed. cir.) 1993, U.S. Supreme Ct. 1981. Law clk. U.S. Ct. Appeals (2d cir.), N.Y.C., 1977; assoc. Vinson & Elkins, Houston, 1977-84, ptnr., 1984—. Co-chmn. Antitrust Practice Group. Editor: Annual Review of Antitrust Law Developments, 2000; co-author: Federal Civil Procedure Before Trial--Firth Circuit, 1997, supplement, 1999, The Competition Laws of NAFTA, Canada, Mexico and the United States , 1997, Business and Commercial Litigation in Federal Courts, 1998, American Legal Ethics Library, 1998, State Antitrust Practice and Statutes, 1999, Doing Business in Texas, 2002; contbr. articles to profl. jours. Mem. bd. visitors Columbia U., 1992—; mem. City of Houston Ethics Com., 1992—98, chmn., 1995—98; bd. dirs. Nat. Appleseed Found., 2002—, Tex. Appleseed Ctr., 1998—, vice chmn., 1999—2002, chmn., 2002—. Recipient Ordroneaux prize Columbia U., 1977, W. Frank Newton award for outstandign contbns. in provision of access to legal svcs. to the poor State Bar Tex., 2002; James Kent scholar Columbia U., 1974-77. Fellow Tex. Bar Found.; mem. ABA (com. chmn. 1987-95, mem. coun. 1996-99, com. chmn. 2000—, mem. ho. dels. 2002—, sect. officer 2002—), Houston Bar Assn. (sect. chair 1991-93), Tex.-Mex. Bar Assn. (pres. 1998-2000), Phi Beta Kappa. Democrat. Jewish. Home: 3430 S Parkwood Dr Houston TX 77021-1238 Office: Vinson & Elkins LLP 1001 Fannin St Ste 2300 Houston TX 77002-6760 E-mail: avanfleet@velaw.com.

VAN FLEET, SHARON KAY, psychiatric clinical nurse specialist; BS cum laude, U. Colo.; MS in Psychiat.-Mental Health Nursing, U. Mich. Cert. clin. nurse specialist. Staff nurse U. Chgo. Hosps.; clin. nurse specialist psychiat. sect. U. Tex. M.D. Anderson Cancer Ctr., Houston; psychiatric clin. nurse specialist H. Lee Moffitt Cancer Ctr., Tampa, Fla., 2001—. Recipient Edith Galt Morgan Meml. award for outstanding grad. rsch. U. Mich.; dean's fellowship. Mem. ANA, Fla. Nurses Assn., Am. Psychiat. Nurses Assn., Internat. Soc. Psychiat. Mental Health Nurses, Oncology Nursing Soc., Alpha Omicron Pi, Sigma Theata Tau. Office: H Lee Moffitt Cancer Ctr MCC Nursing Adminstrn 12902 Magnolia Dr Tampa FL 33612 E-mail: vanflesk@moffitt.usf.edu.

VANG, TIMOTHY TENG, religious organization administrator; b. Xieng Khouang, Laos, May 10, 1956; came to U.S., 1976; s. Nao Chai and Mai (Yang) V.; m. Chee Yang, Jan. 1, 1974 (dec. June 1975); m. Lydia Joua Xiong, July 7, 1979; children: Jennifer P., Nathan K., Victor C., Richard M., Tiffany P., Jasmine M. BS in Missions, Cin. Bible Coll., 1984; MDiv in Ch. Ministries, Can. Theol. Sem., Regina, Sask., 1991; DMin in Ch. Leadership, Fuller Theol. Sem., Pasadena, Calif., 1999. Ordained to ministry Ch. of Christ, 1984, Christian and Missionary Alliance, 1986. Machine operator Pellet Co., Green Bay, Wis., 1977-78; mental health worker Inst. Human Design, Oshkosh, 1978-80; ch. planter Ch. of Christ, Eau Claire, 1984-86; pastor Boulder (Colo.) Hmong Alliance Ch., 1986-87; dir. Christian edn. Hmong dist. Christian and Missionary Alliance, Brighton, Colo., 1986-87, dist. supt., 1991-96; sr. pastor Sacramento Hmong Alliance, 1997—. Mem. bd. mgrs. Christian and Missionary Alliance, 1994-97; trustee Crown Coll., 1992-96. Organizer Fox Valley Lao/Hmong Assn., Appleton, Wis., 1979. Lt. U.S./Hmong Allied Army, 1971-75. Avocations: reading, writing, walking. Office: Sacramento Hmong Alliance Ch 9131 Locust St Elk Grove CA 95624-2017 E-mail: tmtvang@aol.com.

VAN GELDER, MARC CHRISTIAAN, retail executive; b. Amsterdam, The Netherlands, May 21, 1961; s. Bob Frits and Maria Johanna (Van Teeseling) Van G.; m. Karah L. Henry, July 7, 1990; children: Alexander F., Robert H. M of Econs., Erasmus U., Rottendam, The Netherlands, 1986; MBA, U. Pa., 1990. Asst. v.p. Drexel-Burnham Lambert, N.Y.C., 1986-88; sr. mgr. McKinsey & Co., Amsterdam, 1990-96; dir. bus. devel. Ahold, Netherlands, 1996—98; v.p. supply chain mgnt. The Stop & Shop Supermarket Company, 1998—99, sr. v.p., logistics & supply chain mgnt., 1999-2000; pres. & CEO Peapod Inc., Skokie, IL, 2000—. Author: Venture Capital Market , 1985. Mem. Wharton Alumni Club The Netherlands (pres. 1991-98), Netherlands Am. C. of C. (bd. dirs.). Avocations: skiing, horseback riding, arts. Office: Peapod Inc 9933 Woods Dr Ste 375 Skokie IL 60077-1057

VAN GELDEREN, ELLY, linguistics educator, researcher; b. Geertruidenberg, The Netherlands, Sept. 20, 1958; came to U.S., 1995; d. Antonij Johannes and Elsje (Schuttevaar) van G.; m. Harry M. Bracken, June 19, 1985. BA, Utrecht U., The Netherlands, 1979, MA, 1981; PhD, McGill U., Montreal, Can., 1986. Assoc. prof. Ariz. State U., Tempe, 1995—2002, prof., 2002—, dir. programs in linguistics and TESL, 2001—. Author: The Rise of Functional Categories, 1993, Verbal Agreement, 1997, A History of English Reflexive Pronouns, 2000, An Introduction to the Grammar of English, 2002. Chair Amnesty Internat. Can., Ottawa, 1984-85. Mem. Soc. Germanic Linguistics (pres. 2000—). Office: Ariz State Univ PO Box 870302 Tempe AZ 85287-0302 E-mail: ellyvangelderen@asu.edu.

VANGELISTI, PAUL LOUIS, poet; b. San Francisco, Sept. 17, 1945; s. Nicholas Thomas V. and Josephine Marie Zangani; m. Margaret G. Dryden, Dec. 31, 1966 (div. July 1980); children: John Tristan, Simone. BA in English, U. San Francisco, 1967; MA in Am. Lit., U. So. Calif., 1970. City editor Hollywood Reporter, L.A., 1972-74; cultural affairs dir. Sta. KPFK FM Radio, 1974-83; dir. Casa Italiana UCLA, 1992-97; chair graduate writing Otis Coll. Art, L.A., 1984—. Author: Portfolio, 1978, Another You, 1981, Villa, 1991, Nemo, 1995, Alphabets, 1999, Embarrassment of Survival: Selected Poems, 2000. Avocation: fly fishing. Office: Otis Coll Art & Design 9045 Lincoln Blvd Los Angeles CA 90045-3505

VANGER, MILTON ISADORE, history educator; b. N.Y.C., Apr. 11, 1925; s. Max Manuel and Rose (Rothstein) V.; m. Elsa M. Oribe, Sept. 10, 1956; children: John, Mark, Rachel. AB, Princeton U., 1948; MA, Harvard U., 1950, PhD, 1958. Teaching fellow history Harvard U., 1952-56; instr. Okla. State U., 1956-58; asst. prof. history Sacramento State Coll., 1958-62; mem. faculty Brandeis U., Waltham, Mass., 1962—, prof. history, 1973-84, prof. emeritus, 1984—. Chmn. com. Latin Am. studies, 1971-81; invited lectr. 50th anniversary conf. commemorating death of Batlle y Ordoñez of Uruguay, 1979; invitee to inauguration of pres. Sanguinetti, Uruguay, 1985; Barnette Miller vis. prof. history, Wellesley Coll., 1990. Author: José Batlle y Ordoñez of Uruguay: The Creator of His Times, 1902-1907, 1963, 2d edit., 1980, Spanish transl., 1968, 2d edit., 1992, The Model Country: José Batlle y Ordoñez of Uruguay, 1907-1915, 1980, Spanish transl., 1983, 2d edit., 1991, Reforma o Revolución La Polémica Batlle-Mibelli, 1917, 1989; outside reviewer NEH, Radcliffe Inst.; contbr. articles to profl. jours. Juror for Lindahl Prize, Inst. Latin Am. Studies, Stockholm. With AUS, 1943-45. Doherty Found. fellow, 1950-52; grantee Am. Philos. Soc., 1966; recipient Hermes prize for best history pub. in Uruguay, 1983. Mem. New Eng. Council Latin Am. Studies (sec.-treas. 1970-72), Am. Hist. Assn., Conf. on Latin Am. History, Amnesty Internat., Phi Beta Kappa. Democrat. Jewish. Address: 931 Massachusetts Ave Ste 503 Cambridge MA 02139

VAN GESTEL, ALLAN, judge; b. Boston, Dec. 3, 1935; BA, Colby Coll., 1957; LLB, Boston U., 1961; MA (hon.), Colby Coll., 1999. Bar: Mass. 1961, U.S. Dist. Ct. Mass. 1963, U.S. Ct. Appeals (1st cir.) 1969, U.S. Supreme Ct. 1972, U.S. Ct. Claims 1979, U.S. Ct. Appeals (2d cir.) 1980, U.S. Dist. Ct. (no. dist.) N.Y. 1980, U.S. Dist. Ct. (we. dist.) N.Y. 1993, U.S. Ct. Appeals (3d cir.) 1993, U.S. Ct. Appeals (5th cir.) 1995. Assoc. firm Goodwin, Procter & Hoar, Boston, 1961-70, ptnr., 1970-96; assoc. justice Superior Ct. Mass., 1996—; presiding justice Suffolk County Bus. Litigation Session, 2000—. Spl. counsel Boston Fin. Commn., 1974; spl. counsel to Mass. Commn. on Jud. Conduct, 1986; mem. Scituate (Mass.) Bd. Zoning Appeals, 1970, Scituate Planning Bd., 1972; spl. counsel Gov. of N.Y. on Indian Land Claims, 1985-96; spl. counsel to Gov. and Atty. Gen. of Vt. on Indian Claims, 1987-90; chmn. standing adv. com. Mass. Rules Civil Procedure, 1986-93 ; overseer Colby Coll., 1990-99, trustee, 1999—. Contbr. numerous articles on Eastern Indian land claims, ct. administrn., capital punishment to profl. jours. Fellow Am. Coll. Trial Lawyers; mem. ABA, Mass. Bar Assn., Boston Bar Assn. (chmn., task force on drugs and the cts.), Supreme Jud. Ct. Hist. Soc. (chmn. bd. overseers 1993-96), Mass. Hist. Soc.

VAN GILDER, JOHN CORLEY, neurosurgeon, educator; b. Huntington, W.Va., Aug. 14, 1935; s. John Ray and Sarah Pool (Corley) Van G.; m. Kerstin Margarita Olesson, Mar., 1965; children: Sarah, John, Rachel, David. BA, W.Va. U., 1957, BS, 1959; MD, U. Pitts., 1961. Diplomate Am. Bd. Neurol. Surgery. (examiner 1976, 79, 84). Intern Pa. Hosp., Phila., 1961, asst. resident in surgery, 1964-65, Wilkes-Barre (Pa.) Hosp., 1962; asst. resident neurosurgery Barnes Hosp., St. Louis, 1966-68, sr. resident, 1968-69; instr. neurosurgery Yale U. Sch. Medicine, New Haven, 1970, asst. prof., 1970-73, assoc. prof., 1973-76; prof. neurosurgery U. Iowa, Iowa City, 1976—, chmn. div. neurosurgery, 1976—, exec. com. dept. surgery, 1978-81. Fellow neurosurgery Wash. U. Sch. Medicine, St. Louis, 1965 -66, instr., 1966; attending neurosurgeon VA Hosp., New Haven, 1970-73, cons. 1973-76; assoc. to attending neurosurgeon Yale-New Haven Med. Ctr., 1970-76; cons. VA Hosp., Iowa City, 1976—; neurol. surg. cons. Vets. Affairs Hdqrs., Washington; mem. clin. coordinating com. U. Iowa Cancer Ctr., 1979—; presenter numerous papers at profl. meetings., confs., symposia; vis. prof. U. Tenn., 1984, Tufts U. Med. Ctr., Boston, 1986, U. Tex., San Antonio, 1987, U. Mich., Ann Arbor, 1988, People's Republic China at Hunan Med. Coll., Beijing Neurol. Inst., Tianjin Med. Coll. Hosp., Tiantan Xili, Xian Gen. Hosp., 2d Mil. Coll., Shanghai, Suzhou Med. Coll. Shanghai, 1985, USSR at Burdenk Inst., Kiev Neurol. Inst., Leningrad Neurol. Soc., 1989, Western Reserve U., Cleve., 1993, Yale U., New Haven, Conn., 1994, U. Wash., Seattle, 1997, Mayo Clinic, 1998, U. Calif., San Francisco, 1998, Ind. U., 1999. Author: (with others): Principles of Surgery, 2d edit., 1973, Brief Textbook of Surgery, 1976, Aneurysmal Subarachnoid Hemorrhage, 1981, Operative Neurosurgical Techniques, Indications, Methods, and Results, 1982, Sports Medicine, 1982, Neurosurgery, 1982, Clinical Neurosurgery, 1982, Operative Neurosurgical Technique, Vol. II, 1982, 88, Vol. III, 1995, Current Therapy in Neurosurgical Surgery, 1985, 2d edit. , 1987, Craniovertebral Junction Abnormalities, 1987, Decision Making in Neurological Surgery, 1987, Neurological Surgery, 3d edit., 1988, Anterior Cervical Spine Surgery, 1993, Brain Surgery: Complication Avoidance and Management, 1993, Neurosurgical Emergencies, 1994, Techniques of Spinal Fusion and Instrumation, 1995, Somatic Gene Therapy, 1995, Infections in Neurological Surgery, 1999; contbr. numerous articles and abstracts to profl. jours.; co-author teaching films; mem. editorial bd. Neurosurgery jour., 1978-84. Capt. USAF, 1962-64. Grantee NIH, 1973-78, Nat. Cancer Inst., 1980-88. Fellow: ACS (membership com. Iowa dist. #1 1983—); mem.: AMA, Am. Bd. Neurol. Surgery (dir. 1992—98, chmn. 1997—98, residency rev. com.-neurol. surgery 1995—2001, neurosurgery chmn. 1999—2001), Am. Acad. Neurol. Surgery (v.p. 1995—), Midwest Surg. Assn., Soc. Neurol. Surgeons (chmn. membership com. 1986—87, treas. 1991—, pres 1997—98, treas. 1991—96, pres. 1997), Iowa-Midwest Neurosurg. Soc. (pres. 1978—79), Johnson County Med. Soc. (program com. 1984—88, chmn. 1985—86), Iowa Med. Soc., Neurol. Soc. Am. (long range planning com. 1984—, v.p. 1985, pres. 1998—99), Rsch. Soc. Neurol. Surgeons, Am. Assn. Neurol. Surgeons (awards com. 1986—87, bd. dirs. 1986—90, chmn. 1987—88), Congress Neurol. Surgeons (resident placement com. 1970), Am. Physiol. Soc., Ga. Neurosurg. Soc. (hon.), Sigma Xi. Home: 330 S Summit St Iowa City IA 52240-3220 Office: U Iowa Hosps & Clinics Dept Neurosurgery 200 Hawkins Dr Iowa City IA 52242-1009

VAN GINKEL, BLANCHE LEMCO, architect, educator; b. London, Dec. 14, 1923; d. Myer and Claire Lemco; m. H. P. Daniel van Ginkel, 1956; children: Brenda Renee, Marc Ian. B.Arch., McGill U., 1945; M.C.P., Harvard U., 1950. Tech. asst. Nat. Film Bd. Can., 1943-44; mgr. City Planning Office, Regina, Sask., Can., 1946; architect Atelier Le Corbusier, Paris, 1948; asst. prof. architecture U. Pa., 1951-57; ptnr. van Ginkel Assocs., Montreal, Que., Can., also Toronto, Ont., Can., 1957—; prof. architecture U. Toronto, 1977—, dir. Sch. Architecture, 1977-80, dean faculty architecture and landscape architecture, 1980-82. Vis. critic Harvard U., 1958, 70; adj. prof. U. Montreal, McGill U., others; curator exhbns. RCA, U. Toronto, others. Contbr. articles to profl. jours. Mem. adv. com. Nat. Capital Planning Com., Ottawa; mem. adv. com. Nat. Mus.'s Corp.; mem. Que. Provincial Planning Commn.; founder, v.p. Corp. of Urbanists of Que., 1963-65; bd. dirs. Montreal Internat. Film Festival, 1961-66. Decorated Order of Can.; recipient Internat. Fedn. Housing and Planning Grand Prix award, 1956, Massey medal for arch., 1962, Mademoiselle Mag. award, 1957, Queen's Silver Jubilee medal, 1977, Citizenship citation Can. Govt., 1991. Fellow AIA (hon.), Royal Archtl. Inst. Can. (exec. com. 1971-74), Toronto Soc. Arch.; mem. Can. Inst. Planners (bd. dirs. 1961-64), Assn. Collegiate Schs. Architecture (bd. dirs. 1981-84, v.p. 1985-86, pres. 1986-87, Disting. Prof. award 1989), Assn. Royal Inst. Brit. Archs. (assoc.), Royal Can. Acad. Art (bd. dirs. 1992—), Internat. Archive of Women Architects (bd. dirs. 1985-2001), Ont. Assn. Arch. (life), Order of Can. Office: 38 Summerhill Gardens Toronto ON Canada M4T 1B4

VAN GORDER, CHRIS, medical executive; MS in Health Adminstrn., U. So. Calif., 1984, MS in Pub. Adminstrn., 1986. Chief of health care opers., exec. v.p. Scripps Health System, 1999—; pres., CEO Scripps Health, 2000—. Office: 4275 Campus Point Ct San Diego CA 92121-1513

VAN GORDER, JOHN FREDERIC, lawyer; b. Jacksonville, Fla., Mar. 22, 1943; s. Harold Burton and Charlotte Louise Van G.; m. Sandra Joan Hagen, June 4, 1977 (div. June 1995); children: Alyssa Jane, Kathryn Ann; m. Ann Michele Brancato, Oct. 7, 1995. Grad., Dover (Eng.) Coll., 1961; AB, Dartmouth Coll., 1965; postgrad., Air Force Inst. Tech., 1967-68; MS in Adminstrn., George Washington U., 1973; postgrad., U. Va., Coll. William and Mary, Cath. U. Am., Northeastern U., Babson Coll., U. South; JD, Fordham U., 1981. Bar: N.J. 1981, U.S. Dist. Ct. N.J. 1981, N.Y. 1983, U.S. Supreme Ct. 1989. Commd. 2d lt. USAF, 1965, advanced through grades to capt., 1968; weapons contr. Aerospace Def. Commd., Ft. Lee, Va., 1965-67; buyer electronics sys. divsn. Air Force Sys. Commd., Bedford, Mass., 1968-69; project mgr. rsch. and devel. Hdqrs. USAF, Washington, 1969-73, br. chief pers., 1973-74; presdl. social aide The White House, 1971-74; assoc. Louis C. Kramp & Assocs., 1975; program officer J.M. Found., N.Y.C., 1975-81; assoc. Winne, Banta & Rizzi Esqs., Hackensack, N.J., 1981-83; asst. sec., program adminstr. Glenmede Truste Co., Phila., 1983-86; exec. dir., asst. sec. Leon Lowenstein Found., 1986—. Atty. Rent Leveling Bd., Borough of Bergenfield, N.J., 1983; pres. Vanguard Corp., Massapequa, N.Y., 1996-2001; adj. prof. Grad. Sch. Edn., Fordham U., N.Y.C., 1997—. Chmn. N.Y.C. steering com. Nat. Congress on Volunteerism and Citizenship, 1976; mem. exec. com. Mayor's Vol. Action Coun., 1977-78; bd. govs. N.Y. Jaycees Found., 1978-79; bd. govs., 4th v.p. First Assembly Dist. Rep. Club, 1977-82; vestryman All Saints Episc. Ch., Bergenfeld, 1982-83; mem. Tabernacle Twp. Planning Bd., 1985-88, Tabernacle Bd. Edn., 1988-91, Tabernacle Rep. Club, 1983-93; jr. warden, 1987-88, sr. warden, 1989-90, vestryman, lay reader St. Peter's Episc. Ch., Medford, N.J., 1985-93; program adv. com. Toshiba Am. Found., 1993-99; trustee, dir. Support Ctr. of N.Y., N.Y.C., 1995-97, Robert A. Taft Inst. Govt., N.Y.C., 1994-97; bd. dirs. N.Y. C. Pub./Pvt. Initiatives, Inc., 1996-2000, bd. dirs. NY Regional Assn. Grantmakers, 1998—. Col. USAFR, ret. Named Outstanding Young Man of Am., 1975, USAF Res. Officer of Yr., 1985. Mem. Internat. (senator; v.p. 1975; rep. to UN 1976), U.S. (nat. v.p. 1973-74), D.C. (pres. 1972-73), N.Y.C. (bd. govs. 1978-79) Jaycees, SAR, Soc. Mayflower Descs., ABA, N.Y. Bar Assn., Student Bar Assn. (class pres. 1978-81), Toastmasters (local pres. 1969-70, area gov. 1970-71), Lions (pres. Medford Twp. club 1985-86, co-chmn. Charity Ball 1987), Masons, Alpha Delta Phi. Republican. Episcopalian. Address: 7 E Bayview St Massapequa NY 11758-7602

VAN GORP, GARY WAYNE, clergyman; b. Reasnor, Iowa, July 16, 1953; s. Laverne Leroy Sr. and Emma Jean (Meyers) Van G.; m. Marietta Louise Burns, Dec. 29, 1972; children: Caleb Aaron, Kari Beth, Micah Alan, Faith Elise, Melinda Amy, Joy Annette, Kristina Nicole. Diploma in Pastoral Studies, Bible and Doctrine, Berean Coll., 1975; BS in Pastoral Studies, Religious Edn., North Cen. Bible Coll., Mpls., 1978; Diploma in profl. office mgmt., Alexandria (Minn.) Tech. Sch., 1984; various positions, ADIA

Employment, 1993. Ordained to ministry Assembly of God Ch., 1981. Pastor Verndale (Minn.) Assembly of God Ch., 1979—82; asst. mgr., caretaker Lake Geneva Bible Camp, Alexandria, 1982—83; Christian edn. and outreach pastor Alexandria Assembly of God Ch., 1983—84; pastor, adminstrv. asst. Allison Park (Pa.) Assembly God Ch., 1984—90; interim pastor Assembly God Ch., Bklyn. Ctr. and Winona, Minn., 1991; mem. maintenance pers. staff South Ridge Mall, 1991—92; farmhand J&V Van Gorp, Inc., 1992; developer ministry program Berean Assembly of God Ch., Des Moines, 1992; founder, owner GW Enterprize, 1993—; with ADIA The Employment People, Temp. Svc., 1992—94; pastor Lighthouse Assembly of God, Glencoe, Minn., 1994—99; security officer Roland Security, 1995—99; office mgr. Spruce Ridge Resource Mgmt., 1999—2000; adminstrv. asst. Koobi LLC, 2000—; sr. pastor Two Rivers Fellowship, Greeley, Colo., 2001—. Chmn. Glencoe Ministerium, 1995-96; vice prin. Faith Acad. Christian Sch., 1980-82; mgr. book store Gospel Supply Ctr., Minn., 1981-82; pastor Elbow Lake (Minn.) Assembly of God, 1983-84. Bd. dirs., treas., mem. adv. bd. The DoorWay, Inc., Pitts., 1988-92; mem. adv. bd. Glory Home Sch. Corp., Des Moines, 1994; coord. West League Jr. Bible Oyuiz for State of Minn., 1995-2001. Mem. Nat. Assn. Ch. Bus. Adminstrs. (pres. Pitts. chpt. 1987-90). Home and Office: 3915 W 21st St Greeley CO 80634

VAN GRAAFEILAND, ELLSWORTH ALFRED, federal judge; b. Rochester, N.Y., May 11, 1915; s. Ivan and (Gohr) Van Graafeiland; m. Rosemary Vaeth, May 26, 1945; children: Gary, Suzanne, Joan, John, Anne. AB, U. Rochester, 1937; LLB, Cornell U., 1940. Bar: N.Y. 1940. Practiced in, Rochester; now sr. judge U.S. Ct. Appeals (2d cir.). Fellow: N.Y. Bar Found., Am. Bar Found.; mem.: ABA (ho. dels. 1973—75), Am. Coll. Trial Lawyers., Monroe County Bar Assn. (past pres.), N.Y. State Bar Assn. (v.p. 1972—73, pres. 1973—74, chmn. negligence compensation and ins. sect. 1968—69), Oak Hill Country Club, Kent Club, Masons. Home: 1 Tiffany Ct Pittsford NY 14534-1067 Office: Fed Bldg 100 State St Ste 423 Rochester NY 14614-1309

VAN GRACK, STEVEN, lawyer; b. Memphis, Oct. 6, 1948; s. Irving and Edna (Schwartz) Van Grack; m. Gail Beverly Lang, Nov. 18, 1972 (div.); children: Adam, Ryan, Brandon; m. Susan M Freeland, May 21, 1993. BA, U. Md., 1970, JD, 1974. Bar: 1974 (Md), DC 1976, US Dist Ct Md 1976, US Dist Ct DC 1976, US Ct Appeals (4th cir) 1977, US Supreme Ct 1978. Law clk. to presiding justice Montgomery County Cir. Ct., Rockville, Md., 1974-75; assoc. Joseph Roesser Law Offices, Silver Springs, 1975-78; ptnr. Ebert & Bowytz, Washington, 1978-80; mng. ptnr. Van Grack, Axelson & Williamowsky, Rockville, 1980—. Instr, lectr Montgomery Col, Germantown, Md., 1983—85. Cubmaster packs 1343 and 1449 Boy Scouts Am; coach Rockville Baseball Asn; trustee Shady Grove Adventist Hosp Found; co-chmn Montgomery County March of Dimes WalkAmerica Comt, 1998—2000; campaign mgr Comt to Elect the Sitting Judges, Rockville, 1982; mayor City of Rockville, 1985—87; gen counsel Montgomery County Dem Cent Comt, Kensington, Md., 1978—82; Dem cand 8th Congl Dist Md, 1994; chmn Md Real Estate Comn, 2001—; bd dirs Washington Met Coun Govts. With USAR, 1970—71. Named one of Oustanding Young Men Am, Jaycees, 1978, 1981; recipient Fifth Ann Pro Bono Serv Award, Montgomery County Bar Found, 1998, Extraordinary Commitment to the Delivery of Legal Servs Award, 1999, Nancy Dworkin Award, Montgomery County Comn Children and Youth, 2001. Fellow: Md Bar Found (Profl. Legal Excellence award 2002); mem.: ATLA, ABA, Rockville CofC (bd dirs), Montgomery County Bar Asn (Outstanding Comt Chair of the Yr Award 2001), Md Trial Lawyers Asn, Md Bar Asn. Jewish. Avocations: running, swimming, exercising, coin collecting, political button collecting. Home: 808 Fordham St Rockville MD 20850-1018 Office: Van Grack Axelson & Williamowsky 110 N Washington St Fl 5 Rockville MD 20850-2223 E-mail: sug@vawlaw.com.

VAN GRUNSVEN, PAUL ROBERT, lawyer; b. Green Bay, Wis., Mar. 11, 1961; s. David Edward and Carol Ann (Janssen) Van G. BS, Marquette U., 1983, JD, 1986; LLM in Health Law, De Paul U., 1995. Bar: Wis. 1986, U.S. Dist. Ct. (ea. dist.) Wis. 1986. Mem. Techmeier & Van Grunsven, S.C., Milw., 1986-89, shareholder, 1989-2001; chair health law dept. Kasdorf, Lewis & Swietlik, S.C., 2001—. Adj. prof. Marquette U. Law Sch., Milw., 1995—. Recipient Am. Jurisprudence award Lawyer's Coop. Pub. Co., 1986. Mem. ATLA, Wis. Trial Lawyers for Public Justice, Wis. Acad. Trial Lawyers (bd. dirs., co-editor The Verdict), Wis. Bar Assn., Milw. Bar Assn. (co-chair health law sect.). Roman Catholic. Avocations: golf, football, baseball, basketball. Office: Kasdorf Lewis & Swietlik SC 11270 W Park Pl Ste 500 Milwaukee WI 53224-

VAN GUNDY, GREGORY FRANK, lawyer; b. Columbus, Ohio, Oct. 24, 1945; s. Paul Arden and Edna Marie (Sanders) Van G.; m. Lisa Tamara Langer. BA, Ohio State U., Columbus, 1966, JD, 1969. Bar: N.Y. bar 1971. Asso. atty. firm Willkie Farr & Gallagher, N.Y.C., 1970-74; v.p. legal, sec. Marsh & McLennan Cos., Inc., 1974-79, v.p., sec., gen. counsel, 1979-2000, sec., 2000—. Mem. ABA, Phi Beta Kappa. Clubs: University (N.Y.C.). Roman Catholic. Home: 232 Fox Meadow Rd Scarsdale NY 10583-1640 Office: Marsh & McLennan Cos Inc 1166 Avenue Of The Americas New York NY 10036-2728

VAN GUNDY, SEYMOUR DEAN, nematologist, plant pathologist, educator; b. Feb. 24, 1931; s. Robert C. and Margaret (Holloway) Van G.; m. Wilma C. Fanning, June 12, 1954; children: Sue Ann, Richard L. BA, Bowling Green State U., 1953; PhD, U. Wis., 1957. Asst. nematologist U. Calif., Riverside, 1957-63, assoc. prof., 1963-68, prof. nematology and plant pathology, 1968-73, assoc. dean rsch., 1968-70, vice chancellor rsch., 1970-72, chmn. dept. nematology, 1972-84; prof. nematology and plant pathology, assoc. dean rsch. Coll. Natural and Agrl. Scis., 1985-88, acting dean, 1986, interim dean, 1988-90, dean, 1990-93, emeritus dean, prof., 1993—. Former mem. editl. bd. Rev. de Nematologie, Jour. Nematology and Plant Disease; contbr. numerous articles to profl. jours. NSF fellow, Australia, 1965-66; grantee Rockefeller Found., Cancer Rsch., NSF, USDA. Fellow AAAS, Am. Phytopathol. Soc., Soc. Nematologists (editor-in-chief 1968-72, v.p. 1972-73, pres. 1973-74, hon. mem. 1997). Home: 1188 Pastern Rd Riverside CA 92506-5619 Office: U Calif Dept Nenatology Riverside CA 92521-0001 E-mail: seymour.vangundy@ucr.edu.

VAN HAMEL, MANETTE C. artist, writer; b. Deventer, The Netherlands, Aug. 4, 1913; d. Hendrik Cramer and Maria Christina Heyligers; m. Diederik A. van Hamel, Feb. 6, 1940; children: Alfred, Jan Willem, Martine. Student, Conservatory Music, Holland; studied art with Rolph Scarlett. Profl. violinist. One-woman shows of sculpture to wear include Stedelijk Mus., Amsterdam, 1971, Rosenthal Studio Haus, N.Y.C., 1968; exhibited in group show at Cooper Hewitt Mus., N.Y.C., 1978, Jewelry Mus., Phorzheim, Germany, 1973; represented in permanent collections including Metropolitan Mus. Art, Stedelyk Mus.; author: The Flamboyent Tree, numerous short stories. Recipient 1st prize CNE Toronto, 1965, 1st prize Craftsmen N.Y., 1970. Avocations: chamber music. Home: 10 Lower Byrdcliffe Rd Woodstock NY 12498-1214 E-mail: manettev@ureach.com.

VANHANDEL, RALPH ANTHONY, retired librarian; b. Appleton, Wis., Jan. 17, 1919; s. Frank Henry and Gertrude Mary (Schmidt) Van H.; m. Alice Catherine Hogan, Oct. 27, 1945; children: William Patrick, Karen Jean, Mary Jo. BA, U. Wis., 1946; AB in Libr. Sci., U. Mich., 1947. Head libr. Lawrence (Kans.) Free Pub. Libr., 1947-51, Hibbing (Minn.) Pub. Libr., 1951-54; libr. dir. Gary (Ind.) Pub. Libr., 1954-74, Wells Meml. Pub. Libr., Lafayette, Ind. (name now Tippecanoe County Pub. Libr.), 1974-84, libr. cons., 1963—. Mem. Ind. Library Cert. Bd., 1969-84, Ind. State Library and Hist. Bldg. Expansion Commn., 1973-81. Named Ind. Librarian of Year, 1971, Sagamore of Wabash, 1984 Mem. ALA, KC, Anselm Forum (sec. 1964, v.p. 1965), Ind. Libr. Assn. (pres. 1963-64), Kans. Libr. Assn. (v.p. 1951). Home: 3624 Winter St Lafayette IN 47909-3838

VAN HAREN, W(ILLIAM) MICHAEL, lawyer; b. Grand Rapids, Mich., Feb. 15, 1948; s. Adrian William and Donna Bell (Burkett) Van H.; m. Kathryn Mary Desmet, Aug. 7, 1971; children: Ryan C., Amy K., Andrew M., Megan E. BS, U. Mich., 1970; JD magna cum laude, U. Detroit, 1975. Bar: Mich. 1975, U.S. Dist. Ct. (we. dist.) Mich. 1975. Assoc. Warner, Norcross & Judd, Grand Rapids, 1975-81, ptnr., 1981—. Adj. prof. taxation Seidman Sch. Bus., Grand Valley State U., Grand Rapids, 1983-85. Assoc. editor U. Detroit Sch. Law Jour. Urban Law, 1974-75; co-editor (handbook) Probate Practice in Decedents Estates, 1985. Co-chmn. profl. divsn. Kent County United Way, Grand Rapids, 1983, 84; pres. Garfield Pk. Nature Ctr., Grand Rapids, 1977, Garfield Pk. Neighborhhod Assn., Grand Rapids, 1979; bd. dirs. Western Mich. Estate Planning Coun., 1986-89, Cath. Social Svcs., 1997—; mem. fin. com. St. Robert's Ch., Grand Rapids, 1997—. Fellow Am. Coll. Trust and Estate Coun.; mem. Mich. Bar Assn. (probate and estate planning coun. 1981-93, treas. 1987-88, sec. 1989-90, vice chmn. 1990-91, chair 1992-93, exec. officer 1993—), Mich. Bar Found., Univ. Club. Republican. Roman Catholic. Avocations: squash, golf, hunting. Home: 9007 Conservation St NE Ada MI 49301-9797 Office: Warner Norcross & Judd 900 Old Kent Bldg 111 Lyon St NW Ste 900 Grand Rapids MI 49503-2487

VAN HEMMEN, HENDRIK FOKKO, vehicle engineer; b. Dordrecht, The Netherlands, Jan. 8, 1960; came to U.S., 1976; s. Henk and Geertruida Sabiena (Teffer) Van H.; m. Anne Crosley Forsyth, Apr. 5, 1986; children: Hendrik James, Hannah Gretchen, Abigail Ruth. BS in Aerospace & Ocean Engring., Va. Polytech Inst. and State U, 1982. Registered profl. engr. N.Y. Engr. MAR Inc., Rockville, Md., 1980-81; engr., surveyor Am. Bur. Shipping, N.Y.C., 1982-84; chief engr. Johan Valentjn Inc., Newport, R.I., 1984-88; cons. Francis A. Martin & Ottaway Inc., N.Y.C., 1988-92; ptnr. Martin, Ottaway & Van Hemmen, Inc., 1992—. Cons. to underwriters, fin. institutions, attys., shipping cos. and vehicle mgrs. Designer various sail and power yachts, 1975—. Mem. AIAA (sr., student engrs. coun. rep. 1981-82, Design Competition award 1982), NSPE, Nat. Acad. Forensic Engrs., Nat. Fire Protection Assn., Soc. Naval Architects and Marine Engrs. (vice chmn. student chpt. 1981-82, N.Y. State papers chmn. 1992, Nat. Student Paper award 1982), U.S. Naval Inst. (life). Office: Martin Ottaway & Van Hemmen Inc 172 Monmouth St Red Bank NJ 07701-1164

VAN HENGEL, MAARTEN, banker; b. Amsterdam, The Netherlands, Mar. 29, 1927; came to U.S., 1950, naturalized, 1957; s. Adrianus J. and Helena (Gips) van H.; m. Drusilla Drake Riley, Dec. 1, 1951; children: Maarten, Virginia, Hugh, Drusilla. Student, Kennemer Lyceum, Bloemendaal, Holland, 1939-45. With tng. programs of Amsterdamsche Bank, N.V., Amsterdam, Lazard Bros. & Co. Ltd., London and Canadian Bank of Commerce, Montreal, Que., Can., 1945-49; with Brown Bros. Harriman & Co., 1950—, ptnr., 1968—. Bd. dirs. Netherlands-Am. Found. Served with AUS, 1951-53. Mem.: India House, Netherland (N.Y.C.); Fishers Island Country, Hay Harbor (Fishers Island); Sleepy Hollow Country (Scarborough, N.Y.). Home: 350 River Rd Briarcliff Manor NY 10510-2418 Office: Brown Bros Harriman & Co 59 Wall St New York NY 10005-2808

VAN HENGEL, MAARTEN R. financial executive; b. Montreal, Que., Can., Jan. 3, 1953; s. Maarten and Drusilla van H.; m. Claudia Bressan, May 13, 1979; children: Peter, Christina. BA, Wagner Coll., 1977. Formerly v.p. Prometheus Group, N.Y.C., 1972-81; pres. Carret Securities, 1987-90; sr. v.p. Carret & Co., 1981-90; exec. v.p. Clifford/Russell, Inc., 1990-92; v.p. Swiss Bank Corp., 1992-93; prin. Bankers Trust Co., 1993-2000; mng. dir., trainer Wortham & Co., 2000—02; ptnr. Highmount Capital, LLC, 2002—. Dir. Metallized Carbon Corp., Ossining, N.Y. Mem. Assn. Investment Mgmt. Sales Execs., Hay Harbor Club, Sleepy Hollow Country Club, Fishers Island Yacht Club. E-mail: mvanhengel@hmcap.com.

VAN HOFTEN, JAMES DOUGAL ADRIANUS, business executive, former astronaut; b. Fresno, Calif., June 11, 1944; s. Adriaan and Beverly (McCurdy) van H.; m. Vallarie Davis, May 31, 1975; children: Jennifer Lyn, Jamie Juliana, Victoria Jane. BS, U. Calif.-Berkeley, 1966; MS, Colo. State U., 1968, PhD, 1976. Asst. prof. U. Houston, 1976-78; astronaut NASA, Houston, 1978-86; sr. v.p. mgr. advanced systems line Bechtel Nat., Inc., San Francisco, 1986-93; project mgr. Hong Kong New Airport projects, 1993-96; sr. v.p., mgr. N.E. Asia, gen. mgr. Bechtel Civil Co., Hong Kong, 1996-98; sr. v.p., mgr. N.Am. projects Bechtel Infrastructure, San Francisco, 1998-99; program mgr. New Scottish Air Traffic Control Ctr., London, 1999-2000; dir. programmes Nat. Air Traffic Svcs., 2000—02; mng. dir. aviation Bechtel Corp., 2002—. Served with USN, 1969-74; lt. col. Air N.G. 1984-88. Recipient Disting. Service award Colo. State U., 1984; Disting. Citizen award Fresno Council Boy Scouts Am., 1984; Disting. Achievement award Pi Kappa Alpha, 1984 Assoc. fellow AIAA; mem. ASCE (Aerospace Sci. and Tech. Application award 1984) Republican.

VAN HOLDE, KENSAL EDWARD, biochemistry educator; b. Eau Claire, Wis., May 14, 1928; s. Leonard John and Nettie (Hart) Van H.; m. Barbara Jean Watson, Apr. 11, 1950; children: Patricia, Mary, Stephen, David. BS, U. Wis., 1949, PhD, 1952. Research chemist E.I. du Pont de Nemours & Co., 1952-55; research assoc. U. Wis., 1955-56; asst. prof. U. Wis. at Milw., 1956-57; mem. faculty U. Ill., Urbana, 1957-67; prof. dept. biochemistry and biophysics Oreg. State U., Corvallis, 1967; Am. Cancer Soc. rsch. prof., 1977-93; disting. prof., 1988-93; disting. prof. emeritus, 1993—; instr.-in-charge physiology course Marine Biol. Lab., Woods Hole, Mass., 1977-80; mem. research staff Centre des Recherches sur les Macromolecules, Strasbourg, France, 1964-65; mem. study sect. USPHS, 1966-69, 91—; staff Weizmann Inst., Israel, 1981, Lab. Léon Bnillouin, Saclay, France, 1989-90. Author: Physical Biochemistry, 1971, Chromatin, 1988; (with C. Mathews) Biochemistry, 1989, 2nd edit., 1995, 3d edit, 2000, Principles of Physical Biochemistry, 1998; editor: Biochmica Biophysica Acta, 1966-68; mem. editl. bd. jours. Biol. Chemistry, 1968-75, 81-87, 91-92, assoc. editor, 1992—, Biochemistry, 1973-76, 82-89; contbr. profl. jours. Trustee Marine Biol. Lab., Woods Hole, 1979-82, 84-92. NSF sr. postdoctoral fellow, 1964-65; Guggenheim fellow, 1973-74; European Molecular Biology Orgn. fellow, 1975; Humbolt fellow, 2000-01. Fellow AAAS; mem. NAS, Am. Soc. Biochemistry and Molecular Biology, Biophys. Soc., Am. Acad. Arts and Scis. Home: 229 NW 32nd St Corvallis OR 97330-5020 Office: Oreg State U Dept Biochemistry Corvallis OR 97331 E-mail: vanholdk@ucs.orst.edu.

VAN HOOMISSEN, GEORGE ALBERT, state supreme court justice; b. Portland, Oreg., Mar. 7, 1930; s. Fred J. and Helen F. (Flanagan) Van H.; m. Ruth Madeleine Niedermeyer, June 4, 1960; children: Geroge T., Ruth Anne, Madeleine, Matthew. BBA, U. Portland, 1951; JD, Georgetown U., 1955, LLM in Labor Law, 1957; LLM in Jud. Adminstrn., U. Va., 1986. Bar: D.C. 1955, Oreg. 1956, Tex. 1971, U.S. Dist. Ct. Oreg. 1956, U.S. Ct. Mil. Appeals 1955, U.S. Ct. Customs and Patent Appeals 1955, U.S. Ct. Claims 1955, U.S. Ct. Appeals (9th cir.) 1956, U.S. Ct. Appeals (D.C. cir.) 1955, U.S. Supreme Ct. 1960. Law clk. for Chief Justice Harold J. Warner Oreg. Supreme Ct., 1955-56; Keigwin teaching fellow Georgetown Law Sch., 1956-57; dep. dist. atty. Multnomah County, Portland, 1957-59; pvt. practice, 1959-62; dist. atty. Multnomah County, 1962-71; dean nat. coll. dist. attys., prof. law U. Houston, 1971-73; judge Cir. Ct., Portland, 1973-81, Oreg. Ct. Appeals, Salem, 1981-88; justice Oreg. Supreme Ct., 1988—2001. Adj. prof. Northwestern Sch. Law, Portland, Willamette U. Sch. Law, Portland State U.; mem. faculty Am. Acad. Judicial Edn., Nat. Judicial Coll.; Keigwin Teaching fellow Georgetown U. Law Sch. Mem. Oreg. Ho. of Reps., Salem, 1959-62, chmn. house jud. com. With USMC, 1951-53; col. USMCR (ret.). Recipient Disting. Alumnus award U. Portland, 1972. Master Owen M. Panner Am. Inn of Ct.; mem. ABA, Oreg. State Bar, Tex. Bar Assn., Oreg. Law Inst. (bd. dirs.), Arlington Club, Multnomah Athletic Club, Univ. Club. Roman Catholic. E-mial. Office: Oreg Supreme Ct 2105 SW Elm St Portland OR 97201 E-mail: gavanhoomissen@qwest.net.

VAN HORN, HUGH M. physicist, astronomer; b. Williamsport, Pa., Mar. 5, 1938; s. Robert Dix and Virginia Elizabeth (Moody) Van H.; m. Mary Susan Boon, Sept. 17, 1960; children: Kathleen Susan, Mary Margaret, Michael Hugh George. BSc, Case Inst. Tech., 1960; PhD, Cornell U., 1965. NASA predoctoral trainee Cornell U., Ithaca, 1963-65; rsch. assoc. U. Rochester, 1965-67, asst. prof., 1967-73, assoc. prof., 1973-77, prof., 1977-96, chmn. dept. physics and astronomy, 1980-86, acting assoc. dean Coll. Arts and Scis., 1987-89, acting chmn. dept. physics and astronomy, 1992-93; Shapley lectr. Am. Astron. Soc., 1981-95; dir. divsn. astron. sci. NSF, Arlington, Va., 1993-2000, sr. sci. advisor Directorate Math. Phys. Sci., 2000—02, dir. nat. facilities divsn. materialsrch., 2002—. Vis. fellow Joint Inst. Lab. Astrophysics, 1973—74; sr. scientist Lab. Laser Energetics, 1985—96; vis. prof. U. Tex., 1987; vis. investigator dept. terr. magnetism Carnegie Inst. Washington, 2000—02; prin. investigator NASA and NSF grants; adj. prof. U. Rochester, 1996—. Editor: (with V. Weidemann) White Dwarfs and Variable Degenerate Stars, 1979, (with S. Ichimaru) Strongly Coupled Plasma Physics, 1993; contbr. articles on white dwarfs, neutron stars and dense matter to profl. jours. Fellow AAAS; mem. Am. Astron. Soc., Internat. Astron. Union. Office: NSF Divsn Materials Rsch 4201 Wilson Blvd Arlington VA 22230-0001 E-mail: hvanhorn@nsf.gov.

VAN HORN, JOHN HENRY, secondary school educator; b. Mendota, Ill., Dec. 21, 1938; s. John W. and Jane (Van Schoick) Van H.; m. Barbara Ann Tentler, June 26, 1958; children: Michael J., Pamela R. (dec.), Jon C. EdB, Ill. State U., 1960, MS, 1963. Cert. secondary tchr. and adminstr., Ill. Tchr. math. Sch. Dist. 3, Downs, Ill., 1960-63, Sch. Dist. 155, Crystal Lake, 1963-79, coord. coop. edn., 1979-94, coord. computers, 1987-94; ret. Coach Little League Crystal Lake, 1975-78. NSF grantee U. Oreg., Ill. Inst. Tech., Northwestern U. Mem. NEA, Ill. Edn. Assn., Dist. 155 Edn. Assn. (pres. 1976-77), NRA, Isaac Walton League, Bat Conservation Internat., Orgn. for Bat Conservation. Avocations: hunting, fishing, camping. Home: 879 Cayuega Marengo IL 60152

VAN HORN, KEITH, professional basketball player; b. Oct. 23, 1975; m. Amy Van Horn; children: Sabrina, Nicholas. Grad., U. Utah, 1997. Basketball player N.J. Nets, East Rutherford, 1997—2001; player Phila. 76ers, 2002—. Named first team All-Am., U. Utah, 1997 Achievements include being the top scorer U. Utah and Western Athletic Conf. hist.; 3 time Western Athletic Conf. Player of Yr., 1995-97. Office: First Union Center 3601 S Broad St, Ste 4 Philadelphia PA 19148*

VAN HORN, O. FRANK, retired counselor, consultant; b. Grand Junction, Colo., Apr. 16, 1926; s. Oertel F. and Alta Maude (Lynch) Van H.; m. Dixie Jeanne MacGregor, Feb. 1, 1947 (dec. Nov. 1994); m. Evelyn Anne Carroll, Mar. 22,1998; children: Evelyn, Dorothy. AA, Mesa Coll., 1961; BA, Western State Colo., 1963; MEd, Oreg. State U., 1969. Counselor, mgr. State of Oreg.-Employment, Portland and St. Helens, 1964-88; pvt. practice counselor and cons. St. Helens, 1988-96. Chair Task Force on Aging, Columbia County, 1977-79; advisor Western Interstate Commn. on Higher Edn., Portland, 1971, Concentrated Employment and Tng., St. Helens, 1977, County Planning Bd., Columbia County, Oreg., 1977-80, City Planning Bd., St. Helens, 1978, Youth Employment Coun., St. Helens, 1978, Task Force on Disadvantaged Youth, St. Helens, 1980; counselor Career Mgmt. Specialists Internat.; instr. Portland C.C. Mem. ACA, Oreg. Counseling Assn., Internat. Assn. Pers. in Employment Svc. (Outstanding Achievement award 1975), Nat. Employment Counselors Assn. Democrat. Home: 1364 Mesa Ave Grand Junction CO 81501-7632

VAN HORN, REBECCA ANN, presentation specialist; b. Cleve., Feb. 10, 1957; d. Ross Edward and Virginia Mary (Connell) V. BA, Ohio State U., 1979. Dental hygienist Dr. Michael Zimmerman DDS, Columbus, Ohio, 1980-85, St. Mary of Nazareth Hosp. Dental Ctr., Chgo., 1985-87, Dr. Katherine Lauterbach DDS, Chgo., 1985-87; mgr. profl. edn. Oral-B Lab. Pres., Ohio State U. Dental Hygiene Alumni Assn., Columbus, Ohio, 1982-83; adv. bd. Dental Hygiene Program Kalamazoo Cmty. Coll. Mem. Am. Dental Hygienists Assn., Ill. Chgo. Dental Hygienists Assn.

VAN HORNE, JAMES CARTER, economist, educator; b. South Bend, Ind., Aug. 6, 1935; s. Ralph and Helen (McCarter) Van H.; m. Mary A. Roth, Aug. 27, 1960; children: Drew, Stuart, Stephen. AB, De Pauw U., 1957, DSc (hon.), 1986; MBA, Northwestern U., 1961, PhD, 1964. Comml. lending rep. Continental Ill. Nat. Bank, Chgo., 1958-62; prof. fin. Stanford U. Grad. Sch. Bus., 1965-75, A.P. Giannini prof. fin., 1976—, assoc. dean, 1973-75, 76-80; dep. asst. sec. Dept. Treasury, 1975-76. Bd. dirs. BB&K Internat. Fund, BB&K Fund Group, Suntron Corp.; chmn. Montgomery St. Income Securities; commr. workers compensation Rate Making Study Commn., State of Calif., 1990-92. Author: Function and Analysis of Capital Market Rates, 1970, Financial Market Rates and Flows, 2001; co-author: Fundamentals of Financial Management, 2001, Financial Management and Policy, 2002; assoc. editor Jour. fin. and Quantitative Analysis, 1969-85, Jour. Fin., 1971-73, Jour. Fixed Income, 1990—. Mem. bd. trustees DePauw U., 1989-96. With AUS, 1957. Mem. Am. Fin. Assn. (past pres., dir.), Western Fin. Assn. (past pres., dir.), Fin. Mgmt. Assn. Home: 2000 Webster St Palo Alto CA 94301-4049 Office: Stanford U Grad Sch Bus Stanford CA 94305

VAN HORNE, R. RICHARD, oil company executive; b. Milw., June 7, 1931; s. Ralph Rupert and Edna (Benson) Van H.; m. Elizabeth Whitaker Dixon, July 3, 1954; children— Ann Van Horne Arms, R. Ross, Margaret Van Horne Shuya BBA, U. Wis., 1953. Various positions Anaconda Am. Brass Co., Milw. and Kenosha, Wis., 1955-72, pres., chief exec. officer Waterbury, Conn., 1972-74, Anaconda Aluminum Co., Louisville, 1974-82; sr. v.p. pub. affairs Atlantic Richfield Co., Los Angeles, 1982-85. Bd. visitors Sch. Bus., U. Wis., Madison; mem. U. Wis. Found.; trustee Louisville Cmty. Found. 1st lt. U.S. Army, 1953-55 Sr. fellow Bellarmine Coll. Mem. Mchts. and Mfrs. Assn. (bd. dirs. 1983-85), Am. Petroleum Inst., Nat. Planning Assn. (com. on new Am. realities 1982-84), Bascom Hill Soc., Minocqua Country Club, Sara Bay Country Club. Republican. Episcopalian. Avocations: golf; reading; gardening. Home: Unit 261 3040 Grand Bay Blvd Longboat Key FL 34228-4401 Office: Atlantic Richfield Co 515 S Flower St Ste 3700 Los Angeles CA 90071-2201

VAN HORSSEN, CHARLES ARDEN, manufacturing executive; b. Mpls., June 28, 1944; s. Arden Darrel and Margaret E. (Ellingsen) V H.; m. Mary Katherine Van Kempen, Sept. 11, 1967 (div. 1975); children: Lisa, Jackie; m. Mary Ann Pashuta, Aug. 11, 1983; children: Vanessa, Garrett. BSEE, U. Minn., 1966. Design engr. Sperry Univac, Mpls., 1966-68, sr. project engr. Salt Lake City, 1975-80; systems engr. EMR Computer, Mpls., 1968-75; pres. A&B Industries Inc., Phoenix, 1980—, Axian Tech Inc., Phoenix. Patentee in field. Mem. Ariz. Tooling and Machining Assn. (bd. dirs., v.p. 1987-89, pres. 1989-91). Republican. Episcopalian. Office: Axian Tech Inc 21622 N 14th Ave Phoenix AZ 85027-2841 E-mail: van@darkmill.com. *Personal philosophy: The secret of success in business is attention to detail. The attainment of very high levels of quality, which is now a prerequisite for success, is the result of a correspondingly high level of attention to detail. Mistakes are like rabbits... they multiply.*

VAN HOUTEN, ELIZABETH ANN, corporate communications executive, painter; b. Washington, Feb. 22, 1945; d. Raymond R. and Marian Edna (Hovemann) Van H. BA, Mary Washington Coll., 1966. Analyst U.S. Gov., Washington, 1966-68; dep. chief of publs. Found. for Coop. Housing, 1968-72; editor Nat. League of Savs. Inst., 1972-76; dir. pub. relations Fed. Nat. Mortgage Assn., 1976-83; v.p. communications & investor relations Sallie Mae (Student Loan Mktg. Assn.), 1983-93; v.p. corp. and investor rels. Sallie Mae, 1993-95; ret., 1995; curator Monhegan (Maine) Hist. and Cultural Mus., 1995-98; painter. Apptd. by city coun. to Master Plan Task Force, Alexandria, Va., 1987—92; sec. Monhegan Assocs., 1995—97, trustee, 1998—2001, mem. nominating com., 1999—2002; chmn. Watergate of Alexandria, 1993—95; mem. campaing com. for Del Pepper, Alexandria, 1987; bd. dirs. Washington Studio Sch., 1995—99, Watergate of Alexandria, 1985—95, pres, 1988—89; chmn. emeritus Liz Lerman Dance Exch. Mem.: Women Artists of Monhegan Island, Monhegan Artists Open Studio List, Nat. Assn. Real Estate Editors. Avocations: music, visual arts, reading.

VAN HOUTEN, FRANKLYN BOSWORTH, geologist, educator; b. N.Y.C., July 14, 1914; s. Charles Nicholas and Hessie Osborne (Bosworth) Van H.; m. Jean Oliver Sholes, Feb. 18, 1943; children: Jean S., F. Bosworth, David Gordon. BS, Rutgers U., 1936; PhD, Princeton U., 1941. Instr. dept. geology Williams Coll., 1939-42; asst. prof. Princeton U., 1946-51, assoc. prof., 1951-55, prof., 1955-85, prof. emeritus, 1985—; vis. prof. geology UCLA, 1964, State U. N.Y. at Binghamton, 1971; geologist U.S. Geol. Survey, 1948-67. Temporary geologist Geol. Survey Can., 1953, Yukon Expdn., geol. expdns. to Morocco, Tunisia, Libya, Egypt, Madagascar Author reports and articles on geology. Served as lt. USN, 1942-46. Fellow Geol. Soc. Am.; mem. Am. Assn. Petroleum Geologists, Soc. Econ. Paleontologists and Mineralogists (hon. mem., Twenhofel medal), Internat. Assn. Sedimentologists, Colombia Geol. Soc. (hon.), Delta Upsilon. Home: 168 Fitzrandolph Rd Princeton NJ 08540-7224

VAN HOUTEN, JAMES FORESTER, insurance company executive; b. Fullerton, Calif., Jan. 13, 1942; s. James Forester and Lois Evangeline (Trout) V.H.; m. Mary Ann Nelson; children: Kimberly Evangeline, Lori Lynn. BA in

English Lit., St. Mary's U.; MBA, Ill. State U. CPCU, CLU. Sales mgr. for Can. Motors Ins. Corp. divsn. GM, Detroit, 1963-74; v.p. sales Volkswagen Group, St. Louis, 1974-78; v.p. personal lines mktg. Wausau Ins. Cos., 1978-80, v.p., chief mktg. officer life and health, 1980-84; v.p., chief mktg. and strategic planning officer Country Cos., Bloomington, Ill., 1984-89; pres., CEO Mut. Svc. Ins. Cos., St. Paul, 1989—. Prof. strategic mgmt. MBA program U. Minn., 1990—, bd. dirs. Strategic Mgmt. Rsch. Ctr., U. Minn.; prof. strategic mgmt. Metro State U. Program leader Youth Black Achievers, St. Paul; mem. exec. bd. arrowhead coun. Boy Scouts of Am., Minn. Assn. Scholars. Mem. Ins. Fedn. Minn. (past chmn. bd.), Minn. Assn. Mutual Ins. Cos. (pres.), Nat. Coop. Bus. Assn. (bd. dirs. and exec. com., chair fin. com.), Minn. Bus. Partnership (bd. dirs., Minn. K-12 edn. com .), Ctr. Am. Experiment Think Tank (bd. dirs., ex com., chair fin. and audit com., treas.). Office: Mut Svc Ins Cos 2 Pine Tree Dr Arden Hills MN 55112-3715

VAN HOUTTE, RAYMOND A. financial executive; b. Detroit, Aug. 1, 1924; s. Maurice and Gabrielle (Hoorelbeke) Van H.; m. Margaret Graves, June 17, 1950; children— Raymond C., Jonathan P., Nancy J. BBA, U. Mich., 1949; JD, U. Conn., 1955. Bar: N.Y. 1963; CPA, Conn. Sole practice, Hartford, Conn., 1955-58; mem. new product devel. staff Nestle Co., White Plains, N.Y., 1958-60; pres. Ithaca Gun Co., 1960-68; v.p. Tompkins County Trust Co., Ithaca, 1968-73, pres., chief exec. officer, 1973-89, pres. emeritus, counselor, 1990—. Pres. Tompkins County Area Devel., Ithaca, 1985; trustee Mut. Funds for Bank Trust Depts., Boston. Author: Responsibilities of Bank Directors, 1974 Bd. dirs. Ithaca City Sch. Dist., 1965-66, Tompkins Comty. Hosp.; trustee Paleontol. Rsch. Instn., Kendal at Ithaca. With USAF, 1944-45. Mem. AICPA, N.Y. State Bankers Assn. (2d v.p. 1985-86, pres. 1987-88), Chi Phi (treas.). Lodges: Rotary (chmn.). Home: 1 Strawberry Ln Ithaca NY 14850-1413

VAN HOUTUM, DIANA CHANG, real estate executive and developer; b. Shanghai, Republic of China, Jan. 25, 1945; d. Harry and Rebecca Chang; m. Arnold van Houtum, Oct. 6, 1974 (div. June 1981). BS, Wheelock Coll., Boston, 1968. Flight attendant Ea. Airlines, Boston, 1968-86; pres. van Houtum Properties, Cambridge, Mass., 1979—. Mem. Boston Real Estate Bd., Greater Boston C. of C. (Execs. Club). Avocations: archaeology, scuba diving, travel. Home and Office: 28 Foster St Cambridge MA 02138-4825

VAN HOUWELING, DOUGLAS EDWARD, university administrator, educator; b. Kansas City, Mo., Sept. 20, 1943; s. Cornelius Donald and Roberta Irene (Olson) Van H.; m. Andrea Taylor Parks, Aug. 28, 1965; children: Robert Parks, Benjamin Parks BS, Iowa State U., Ames, 1965; PhD, Ind. U., 1974. Asst. prof. Cornell U., Ithaca, N.Y., 1970-81, dir. acad. computing, 1978-81; vice provost Carnegie-Mellon U., Pitts., 1981-84, adj. assoc. prof., 1981-84; vice provost, dean, prof. U. Mich., Ann Arbor, 1984-88, prof., 1984—, pres., CEO univ. corp. for advanced internet devel., 1998—. Mem. research adv. com. Online Coll. Library Consortium, Dublin, Ohio, 1984-87; trustee EDUCOM, vice chmn. bd. dirs., 1987-91; Princeton, vice chmn., 1987, council chmn., 1986-87; co-founder Interuniv. Corsortium for Ednl. Computing, 1984; chmn. bd. MERIT computer network, 1986-90, Advanced Network and Svcs., 1990—; state of Mich. del. Midwest Tech. Inst., 1986-87. Contbr. chpts. in books, articles to profl. publs. NSF fellow, 1968; Indiana U. fellow, 1969; CAUSE nat. leadership award, 1986. Mem. Simulation Symposiums (pres. 1971; grants chmn. 1972-75), N.Am. Simulation and Gaming Assn. Home: 920 Lincoln Ave Ann Arbor MI 48104-3508 Office: Univ Corp for Advanced Internet Devel 3025 Boardwalk St Ann Arbor MI 48108-3230

VAN HOVEN, JAY, retired school system administrator; b. Holland, Mich., Aug. 11, 1944; s. Leonard Jay and Mary Helene (Schaap) Van Hoven; m. Nancy L. Voight, June 27, 1975; children: Joshua, Janna, Lydia. BA, Hope Coll., 1966; student, Wayne State U., 1966-68; MA, No. Mich. U., 1971; postgrad., Mich. State U., 1973-75. Vol. Peace Corps, S.Am., 1968-69; tchr. St. Dunstans Sch., U.S. V.I., 1969-70; community sch. dir. Des Moines Schs., 1970-72; adminstr. Ctr. for Community Edn., Alma, Mich., 1973-75; asst. ombudsman Mich. State U., East Lansing, 1975; fin. mgr. Sch. Nursing U. N.C., Chapel Hill, 1976-78; desegregation specialist Ind. U., Indpls., 1979-82; ptnr. Westlake Profl. Services, 1982-85; asst. supr. fin. Melvindale (Mich.) Schs., 1985-86; supt. Detour (Mich.) Schs., 1986-91, Mendon Schs., 1991-93, Mason Schs., 1993-97; ret., 1997. Pres. Med. Specialty Disability Ins. Corp., Indpls., 1983-86. Rep., Interurban Coll. and Univ. Consortium, Des Moines, 1971-72; adminstr. Urban Cities, Flint, Mich., 1970; mem. Hispanic Edn., Des Moines, 1971-72; mem. Ind. Community Edn. Adv., Indpls., 1979—. Mott fellow, 1970-71, 73-75, 79-85. Mem. Mich. Assn. Sch. Adminstrs., Phi Delta Kappa. Lutheran.

VANIER, JACQUES, physicist; b. Dorion, Que., Can., Jan. 4, 1934; s. Henri and Emma (Boileau) V.; m. Lucie Beaudet, July 8, 1961; children: Lyne, Pierre. BA, U. Montreal, 1955, BSc, 1958; MSc, McGill U., 1960, PhD, 1963. Lectr. U. Montreal, 1961-63, McGill U., 1960-63; physicist Varian Assocs., Beverly, Mass., 1963-67, Hewlett Packard Co., Beverly, 1967; prof. elec. engring. U. Laval, Que., 1967-83; physicist Nat. Rsch. Coun., Ottawa, 1983-94, head elec. and time standards, 1984-86, dir. Lab. Basic Standards, 1986-90, dir. gen. Inst. for Nat. Measurement Standards, 1990-93; prof. physics U. de Montreal, 1995—. Cons. Comm. Components Corp., Costa Mesa, Calif., 1974-76, EGG Co., Salem, Mass., 1979-82, Kernco, Danvers, Mass., 1995—; chmn. com. A URSI, 1990-93; chmn. exec. com. CPEM, 1990-94; mem. Internat. Com. Weights and Measures, 1992-96; guest worker IEN, Torino, Italy, 1996-97. Author: Basic Theory of Lasers and Masers, 1971, (with C. Audoin) The Quantum Physics of Atomic Frequency Standards, 1989; contbr. articles to profl. jours.; patentee (4) in field. Recipient Disting. Precision Time and Time Interval Svc. award Precision Time and Time Interval Svc. Organizing Com., 1998. Fellow IEEE (Centennial medal 1984, I.I. Rabi award 1994, Instrument & Measurement Soc. award 1999), Royal Soc. Can., Am. Phys. Soc. E-mail: jac.vanier@sympatico.ca.

VANIER, JERRE LYNN, art director; b. Phoenix, June 11, 1957; i. Jerry Dale Barber and Betty Jane (Brady) Barber Hughes; m. Kent Douglas Wick, May 4, 1979 (div. June 1994); 1 child, Jared Kent Wick; m. Jay David Vanier, June 6, 1994; 1 child, Jolie Jacqueline. BA in Art History magna cum laude, Ariz. State U., 1978, MA in Humanities. Chmn., vice chmn. Internat. Friends of Art, Scottsdale, Ariz., 1990-96; dir. 19th and 20th century art Joy Tash Gallery, 1996-97; dir. estate art Vanier Fine Art, Ltd., 1997-98, dir., 1998—, Vanier Galleries on Marshall, Scottsdale, 1999—. Mem. pub. art collection adv. bd. Scottsdale Cultural Coun., 1990—, Phoenix Jr. League, Art Renaissance Initiative Faces of Ariz. Mem. DAR (Ariz. page continental congress 1993, Ariz. vice chmn. Jr. Am. Citizen com. 1998, 3d vice regent Camelback chpt. 1993), Colonial Dames Am., Daus. Republic of Tex. (non-resident), Nat. Soc. Arts and Letters (Valley of Sun chpt. bd. dirs. 1988-92, art chmn. 1988-90, membership chmn. 1990-92), Jr. League Phoenix, Alpha Delta Pi, Phi Kappa Phi. Republican. Avocations: genealogy, collecting contemporary art. Office: 7106 E Main St Scottsdale AZ 85251-4316

VAN INWAGEN, PETER JAN, philosophy educator; b. Rochester, N.Y., Sept. 21, 1942; s. George Butler and Mildred Gloria (Knudson) van I; m. Margery Bedford Naylor, Mar. 31, 1967 (div. Apr. 1988); 1 child, Elizabeth Core; m. Elisabeth Marie Bolduc, June 3, 1989. BS, Rensselaer Poly. Inst., 1965; PhD, U. Rochester, 1969. Vis. asst. prof. U. Rochester, N.Y., 1971-72; asst. prof. Syracuse U., 1972-74, assoc. prof., 1974-80, prof. philosophy, 1980-95; John Cardinal O'Hara prof. of philosophy U. Notre Dame, South Bend, Ind., 1995—. Vis. prof. U. Ariz., Tucson, 1981; lectr. Oxford U., 2001, U. London, 1998. Author: An Essay on Free Will, 1983, Material Beings, 1990, Metaphysics, 1993, God, Knowledge and Mystery, 1995, The Possibility of Resurrection, 1997, Ontology, Identity, and Modality, 2001; editor: Time and Cause, 1980, Alvin Plantinga, 1985, Metaphysics: The Big Questions, 1998; mem. editl. bd. Jour. Faith and Philosophy, Philos. Perspectives, Nous, Philos. Studies, Jour. of Ethics, Philosophy and Phenomenological Rsch.; contbr. articles to profl. jours. Served to capt. U.S. Army, 1969-71 NEH grantee, 1983-84, 89-90. Mem. Am. Philos. Assn., Soc. Christian Philosophers. Democrat. Episcopalian. Home: 52145 Farmington Square Rd Granger IN 46530-6403 Office: U Notre Dame Dept Philosophy South Bend IN 46556-4619 E-mail: peter.vaninwagen.1@nd.edu.

VAN ITALLIE, JEAN-CLAUDE, playwright; b. Brussels, May 25, 1936; came to U.S., 1940; s. Hughes Ferdinand and Marthe Mathilde Caroline (Levy) van I. BA, Harvard U., 1958; PhD (hon.), Kent State U., 1977. Tchr. theater, playwriting New Sch. for Social Research, N.Y.C., 1966, Yale U. Sch. Drama, New Haven, 1969, 84, Naropa Inst., Boulder, Colo., 1976-83, 87-88, Princeton U., N.J., 1976-88, NYU, 1982-88, U. Colo., Boulder, 1985, 89, 91, Columbia U., 1986, Am. Repertory Theatre, Cambridge, Mass., 1990. Vis. Mellon prof. Amherst Coll., Mass., fall 1976. Playwright for Open Theatre ensemble, N.Y.C., 1963-68; playwright War, 1963, Almost Like Being, 1965, I'm Really Here, 1965, America Hurrah, 1966 (Drama Desk award, Outer Cir. Critics award 1967), The Serpent, 1968 (Obie award 1969), A Fable, 1975, King of the United States, 1972, Mystery Play, 1973, America Hurrah & Other Plays, 1978, Medea, 1979, Bag Lady, 1979, Tibetan Book of the Dead, 1983, Early Warnings, 1983, The Traveler, 1986, new English versions Chekhov's The Seagull, 1973, Cherry Orchard, 1977, Three Sisters, 1982, Uncle Vanya, 1983, Paradise Ghetto, 1981, Struck Dumb, (with Joseph Chakin), 1987, Ancient Boys, 1989; transl.: Genet's The Balcony, 1986, The Odyssey (mus.), 1991, Bulgakhov's Master & Margarita, 1993, Chekhov, The Major Plays, 1995, Tibetan Book of the Dead (opera libretto), 1996, The Playwright's Workbook, 1997, The Tibetan Book of the Dead for Reading Aloud, 1998, War, Sex and Dreams, an evening with Jean Claude van Itallie, 1998; performer, writer Guys Dreamin, 1996. Grantee Rockefeller Found., 1973, Ford Found., 1979, Creative Artists Pub. Service, 1975; recipient Playwrights award NEA, 1986, Creative Artists Pub. Service award, 1975, Last Frontier Lifetime Achievement award, 1999; Guggenheim fellow, 1963, 83. Buddhist.

VAN KAMPEN, AL, lawyer; b. Detroit; s. Al J. and Laureen Ann Van Kampen; m. Lisa Alice Gonnason, Sept. 1, 1990; children: Kyle, Grant. BA in Econs., U. Mich., 1979, JD, 1983. Bar: Wash. 1983. Ptnr. Bogle & Gates, Seattle, 1983-99. V.p. A.V. Kurt Constrn. Co., Ferndale, Mich., 1980-92. Editor, co-author: Contribution and Claims Reduction in Antitrust Litigation, 1986, Sample Jury Instructions in Civil Antitrust Cases, 1999. Mem. Mayor's Citizen Forecast Com., Seattle, 1987. Mem. ABA, Wash. State Bar Assn. (chair antitrust sect.). Avocations: sailing, skiing. Office: Burkett Burdette & Van Kampen 600 Stewart St Ste 305 Seattle WA 98101-1257

VANKEERBERGEN, BERNADETTE CHANTAL, educator; b. Mechelen, Belgium, Jan. 16, 1968; arrived in U.S., 1991; d. Jean Gabriel and Claude Eva (Schmit) V. BA in Translation, Inst. Libre Marie Haps, 1990; MA in English Lit., U. La., Monroe, 1994; postgrad., U. Tex., 2000-01, Ohio State U., 2001—. Translator Eurologos, Brussels, 1990-91; French tchr. U. La., Monroe, 1992-94, 99-00, Claiborne Elem., West Monroe, La., 1994-95; English/French tchr. Cedar Creek H.S., Ruston, 1995-99; tchg. asst. in English U. Tex., Austin, 2000-01; grad. teaching assoc. English Ohio State U., Columbus, 2001—. Home: 7593 Cortina Ct Worthington OH 43085-1584 E-mail: vankeerbergen.1@osu.edu.

VAN KIRK, DONALD JOHN, forensic specialist, consultant, engineering executive, consultant, writer; b. Detroit, Jan. 6, 1935; s. Kenneth John and Helen Van Kirk; m. Wyva A. Moore, Apr. 28, 1956; 1 child Cheryl Ann. AS, Henry Ford CC, 1961; BSEE, Wayne State U., 1964, MS in Engring. Mechanics, 1969; MBA, U. Mich., 1975. TV technician Sta. WXYZ-TV, Detroit, 1959—60, Sta. WTVS-TV, Detroit, 1960—64; product design engr. Ford Motor Co., Dearborn, 1964—66, rsch. engr., 1969—73, sr. design engr., 1973—84; pres. D. J. Van Kirk P.E. & Assocs., Inc., 1985—98, Creations & Innovations Unlimited, Ihnc., 1998—2002, Van Kirk Enterprises, 2002—. Instr. Henry Ford CC, Ford continuing edn. programs; mgmt. cons. Contbr. articles to profl. jours. Vol. Consumer Product Safety Com., Washington, 1977; chmn. Consumer Affairs Com., Dearborn, 1977—79; vol. traffic safety com. Dearborn Police Dept., 1979; chmn. bldg. and plans com. Dearborn Hills Home Owners Assn., 1973—75. With USN, 1955—59. Recipient Editors award, Internat. Shrine Clown Assn. mag. Fellow: Am. Acad. Forensic Scis.; mem.: ASTM, Mich. Soc. Profl. Engrs. (past pres.), Oakland County Traffic Safety Assn., Soc. Automotive Engrs., Nat. Soc. Profl. Engrs., Am. Coll. Forensic Examiners (diplomate), Am. Bd. Forensic Examiners, Dearborn Exch. Club (Fairlane chpt. past pres., Outstanding Svc. award 1974, Man of the Yr. award 1975), Scottish Rite, Shriners, Masons (grand master 1996—97, 33 degree). Presbyterian. Achievements include patents for cold weather diesel starting aid. Home: 731 Ridgemont Ave Dearborn MI 48124-1220

VAN KIRK, JOHN ELLSWORTH, retired cardiologist; b. Dayton, Ohio, Jan. 13, 1942; s. Herman Corwin and Dorothy Louise (Shafer) Van K.; m. Patricia L. Davis, June 19, 1966 (div. Dec. 1982); 1 child, Linnea Gray. BA cum laude, DePauw U., Greencastle, Ind., 1963; BS, Northwestern U., Chgo., 1964, MD with distinction, 1967. Diplomate Am. Bd. Internal Medicine, Am. Bd. Internal Medicine subspecialty in cardiovasc. disease; cert. Nat. Bd. Med. Examiners. Intern Evanston (Ill.) Hosp., 1967-68; staff assoc. Nat. Inst. of Allergy & Infectious Diseases., Bethesda, Md., 1968-70; resident internal medicine U. Mich. Med. Ctr., Ann Arbor, 1970-72, fellow in cardiology, 1972-74, instr. internal medicine, 1973-74; staff cardiologist Mills Meml. Hosp., San Mateo, Calif., 1974—2001, vice-chief medicine, 1977-78, dir. critical care, 1978-96, critical care utilizaton rev., 1988-99, dir. pacemaker clinic, 1976-99; staff cardiologist Mills-Peninsula Hosp., Burlingame, 1996-99; ret., 1999. Dir. transitional care, 1996—99; mem. courtesy staff Sequoia Hosp., 1984—2001, ret., 1999. Contbr. rsch. articles to profl. jours. Recipient 1st prize in landscaping Residential Estates, State of Calif., 1977. Fellow Am. Coll. Cardiology; mem. AMA (Physician's Recognition award 1968, 72, 75, 77, 80, 82, 85, 87, 89, 93, 97, 2000), Calif. Med. Assn., San Mateo County Med. Soc., Am. Heart Assn., San Mateo County Heart Assn. (bd. dirs. 1975-78, mem. Bay area rsch. com. 1975-76, mem. edn. com. 1975-77, pres.-elect 1976-77, pres. 1977-79), Alpha Omega Alpha. Republican. Mem. United Brethren Ch. Avocations: gardening, computer science, tennis, woodworking, electronics, ham radio. Home: 235 Amherst Ave San Mateo CA 94402-2201 E-mail: John-VanKirk@msn.com.

VAN KIRK, ROBERT JOHN, nursing case manager, educator; b. Jersey City, Sept. 18, 1944; s. Robert and Doris V.; m. Marjorie Ann Carroll, Mar. 23, 1968 (div. Nov. 30, 1993); children: Walter, Michael, Robert Jr., Peggy; m. Nancy A. Fix, Aug. 31, 1996. BA cum laude, U. Conn., 1974; MEd, Kent State U., 1983; D of Nursing, Case Western Reserve U., 1986. RN, Ohio. Sales mgr. Nutmeg Home Protection, Middlebury, Conn., 1972-74; theater mgr. SBC Mgmt. Corp., Boston, 1974; dist. supr. Selected Theatres Mgmt. Corp., Lyndhurst, Ohio, 1974-86; nat. sales mgr. ZBS Video, Inc., 1981-82; staff nurse Cleve. Clinic Found., 1986-87, clin. instr., 1987-88, head nurse, 1988-93, case mgr., 1993—; asst. clin. prof. Case Western Reserve U., Frances Payne Bolton Sch. Nursing, Cleve., 1990—; case mgr. Cleve. Clin. Home Care, 1993—2002; CEO Lifelong Learning, Inc., 2002—. Health officer Lake County (Ohio) Bd. Alcohol, Drug Addiction and Mental Health Svcs., 1991—; co-chmn. United Way, Cleve., 1991-93. Staff sgt. U.S. Army, 1964-71, Vietnam. Recipient Achievement award Greater Cleve. Nurses Assn., 1986. Mem. AACN, Am. Assn. Tchrs. German, Am. Assn. Tchrs. Portuguese and Spanish, Assn. Specialists in Aging, Frances Payne Bolton Sch. Nursing Alumni Assn. (pres. 1992-93), Kappa Delta Pi, Sigma Theta Tau. Avocations: pocket billards, furniture making. Home: 495 Bell St Chagrin Falls OH 44022-3346 Office: Cleve Clinic Found 9555 Rockside Rd Valley View OH 44125-6231 E-mail: drbobvankirk@adelphia.net.

VAN KIRK, THOMAS L. lawyer; b. Pa., June 25, 1945; s. Theodore and Mary Jane (Young) Van K.; children: Thomas Jr., Christopher. BA, Bucknell U., 1967; JD cum laude, Dickinson U., 1970. Bar: Pa., U.S. Dist. Ct. (we. and ea. dists.) Pa. 1971, U.S. Ct. Appeals (3d cir.) 1972, U.S. Supreme Ct. 1976. Clk. Pa. Superior Ct., 1970-71; assoc. Buchanan Ingersoll, Pitts., 1971-77, ptnr., 1978—, chief oper. officer, 1985—. Bd. dirs. Buchanan Ingersoll P.C.; v.p. State Pa. Economy League; bd. dirs. Western Pa. Economy League, chair, 1998. Chmn. Allegheny County Heart Assn. Walk, 1992; chair Pitts. Downtown Partnership, 1995-97; bd. dirs. Capital divsn. Pa. Economy League, sec./treas., 1995; bd. dirs. Pitts. Cultural Trust, 1998, SPIRC bd., PEG bd., U. Pitts. Cancer Inst. bd. Mem.: ABA, Allegheny County Bar Assn., The Club at Nevillewood, Rivers Club, Duquesne Club. Democrat. Lutheran. Home: 1010 Osage Rd Pittsburgh PA 15243-1014 Office: Buchanan Ingersoll PC 301 Grant St Fl 20 Pittsburgh PA 15219-1410

VAN KLAVEREN, NICO, engineer, consultant; Office: Vankay Consulting 57 Rancho Del Sol Camino CA 95709 E-mail: vankay@d-web.com.

VAN KOUWENBERG, MARTHA NESTER, secondary education educator; b. Allentown, Pa., Aug. 29, 1946; d. Franklin George and Jean Elizabeth (Schleicher) Nester; children: Beverly, Matthew. BS, Moravian Coll., Bethlehem, Pa., 1968; postgrad., Lehigh U., 1968-71; MEd, Pa. State U., 1997. Cert. math. tchr., N.J., Pa. Asst. treas. Upper Dublin Twp., Fort Washington, Pa., 1965-68; math. tchr. Salisbury Twp. High Sch., Allentown, 1968-70, New Phila. (Ohio) High Sch., 1970-71; coll. preparatory instr. St. Louis High Sch., Seoul, Korea, 1975; math. instr. Burlington County Community Coll., Ft. Dix, N.J., 1976-79; GED instr. Temple U., Mainz, Germany, 1980-82; math. tchr. Ephrata (Pa.) High Sch., 1984-85, Red Lion (Pa.) Area High Sch., 1985—. Mem. Lancaster Found. for Ednl. Enrichment. Named one of People Who Made a Difference USA Today, 1988; recipient award Pa. Dept. Edn. and Assn. Elem. and Secondary Prins., 1990. Mem. NEA, Assn. for Supervision and Curriculum Devel., Red Lion Area Edn. Assn. (treas. 1991-94, pres. 1995—), Pa. State Edn. Assn. (prof. ethics, chair so. region), Pa. Coun. Tchrs. Math., Nat. Coun. Tchrs. Math., Phi Delta Kappa. Home: 746 E Chestnut St Lancaster PA 17602-3126 Office: Red Lion Area Sch Dist 200 Horace Mann Ave Red Lion PA 17356-2403

VAN LARE, BARRY LEE, social welfare executive; b. Sodus, N.Y., Nov. 21, 1940; s. Roland C. and Bertha E. (Elve) Van L.; m. Phyllis G. Judd, Sept. 25, 1940; children: Sherryl, Ian, Susan. BA, U. Rochester, N.Y., 1962. Assoc. commr. Social Security Adminstrn., Washington, 1976-80; dep. asst. sec. U.S. Dept. Health and Human Svcs., 1979-80; spl. adminstr. for gasoline rationing U.S. Dept. Energy, 1980; dep. exec. dir., dir. state svcs., dir. human resources Nat. Govs.' Assn., 1981-95; sr. mgr. Deloitte & Touche Mgmt. Consulting, Seattle, 1995-99; exec. dir. Welfare Info. Network, Washington, 1996—, The Fin. Project, Washington, 1998—. Asst. sec. to gov. State of N.Y., Albany, 1969-71; exec. dep. commr. N.Y. State Dept. Social Svcs., Albany, 1971-72; dir. cmty. svcs. Wash. State Dep. Social and Health Svcs., Olympia, 1974-76; commr. Erie County Dept. Social Svc., Buffalo, 1976. Mem. Am. Soc. for Pub. Adminstrn., Am. Pub. Human Svcs. Assn. Avocations: hiking, reading, American history. Office: The Finance Projects 1401 New York Ave NW Ste 800 Washington DC 20005

VAN LARE, WENDELL JOHN, lawyer; b. Newark, Mar. 1, 1945; s. Julian J. and Doris Elizabeth (Lacknor) Van L.; m. Sheila Gilbert, Aug. 20, 1967 (div. Apr. 1987); children: Jonathan S., Allison R.; m. L. Karen Stack, May 7, 1987. BS, SUNY, New Paltz, 1967; JD, Union U., 1972. Bar: N.Y. 1973, U.S. Supreme Ct., 1980. Assoc. Harter, Secrest & Emery, Rochester, N.Y., 1972-77; asst. dir. labor rels. Gannett Co., Inc., 1977-80, dir. labor rels. Rochester and Arlington, 1980-93, v.p., labor counsel Arlington, 1993-94, v.p., sr. labor counsel, 1994—. Comments editor Albany Law Rev., 1971-72. Pres. Opera Theatre of Rochester, N.Y., 1983-85. Lt. (j.g.) USNR, 1968-70. Mem. ABA, N.Y. Bar Assn., River Bend Golf and Country Club. Avocation: genealogy. Office: Gannett Co Inc 7950 Jones Branch Dr Mc Lean VA 22102

VAN LEEUWEN, DIRK JACOB, hepatology educator; b. Emmen, The Netherlands, Nov. 9, 1951; s. Hendrik J. and Gerarda C. Creutzberg. MD, U. Amsterdam, 1979, PhD, 1988. Internist, gastroenterologist Dutch Splst. Registration Com. Med. dir. hepatobiliary unit Acad. Med. Ctr. U. Amsterdam, 1987-92; med. dir. hepatology and liver transplantation U. Ala., Birmingham, 1992-95, prof., medicine, pub. health, hepatologist, 1992—. Editor: Imaging in Hepatobiliary and Pancreatic Disease, 2000. Mem. Am. Assn. Study of Liver, Am. Gastroenterology Assn., Internat. Liver Pathology Study Group (Elves), European Assn. Study of Liver. Office: U Ala Liver Ctr 1918 Un Blvd Birmingham AL 35294-0005

VAN LEUVEN, ROBERT JOSEPH, lawyer; b. Detroit, Apr. 17, 1931; s. Joseph Francis and Olive (Stowell) Van Leuven; m. Merri Lee Van Leuven; children: Joseph Michael, Douglas Robert, Julie Margaret. Student, Albion Coll., 1949-51; BA with distinction, Wayne State U., 1953; JD, U. Mich., 1957. Bar: (Mich.) 1957. Since practiced in, Muskegon, Mich.; ptnr. Hathaway, Latimer, Clink & Robb, 1957-68, McCroskey, Libner & Van Leuven, 1968-81, Libner-Van Leuven, 1982—99; ret., 1999. Past mem. coun. negligence law sect. State Bar Mich. Bd. dirs. Muskegon Children's Home, 1965—75. Served with U.S. Army, 1953—55. Fellow: Am. Coll. Trial Lawyers, Mich. Bar Found.; mem.: ATLA, Mich. Trial Lawyers Assn., Muskegon Country Club, Delta Sigma Phi. Home: 410 Ruddiman Dr # 4 Muskegon MI 49445-2795 Office: Libner-Van Leuven 4th Fl Comerica Bank Bldg 801 W Norton Ave Muskegon MI 49441

VAN LIEROP, JOHN HENRY, JR. music educator; b. St. Louis, Oct. 3, 1947; s. John Henry and Mary Frances Van Lierop. BA in Music Edn., Seattle Pacific U., 1969; postgrad., U. Wash., 1976—78. Cert. tchr. Wash. 6th grade tchr. Seattle Christian Sch., Seattle, 1969—74; 3d grade tchr. Clark County Christian Sch., Vancouver, 1974—75; 2d grade tchr. Mountlake Christian Sch., Mountlake Terrace, 1975—76; pvt. piano instr. West Seattle Piano Studio, Seattle, 1976—. Organist, pianist Mount Baker Park Presbyn. Ch., Seattle, 1976—80, Tibbetts United Meth. Ch., Seattle, 1981—; piano adjudicator Am. Coll. Musicians, Austin, Tex., 1987—, Nat. Fedn. Music Clubs, Indpls., 1988—. Contbr. articles to profl. publs. Named Tchr. of Yr., Western Assn. Christian Schs., 1976; named to Hall of Fame, Am. Coll. Musicians, 1992. Mem.: Seattle Music Tchrs. (pres. 1984—86), Nat. Guild Piano Tchrs., Nat. Fedn. Music Clubs (treas. 1988—). Republican. Methodist. Avocations: hiking, trains, cats. Home and Office: 6552 40th Ave SW Seattle WA 98136 E-mail: musicman@nwlink.com.

VAN LINT, VICTOR ANTON JACOBUS, physicist; b. Samarinda, Indonesia, May 10, 1928; came to U.S., 1937; s. Victor J. and Margaret (DeJager) Van L.; m. M. June Woolhouse, June 10, 1950; children: Lawrence, Kenneth, Linda, Karen. BS, Calif. Inst. Tech., Pasadena, 1950, PhD, 1954. Instr. Princeton (N.J.) U., 1954-55; staff mem. Gen. Atomic, San Diego, 1957-74; physics cons., 1974-75; staff mem. Mission Research Corp., 1975-82, 83-91; cons., 1991—; spl. asst. to dep. dir. sci. and tech. Def. Nuclear Agy., Washington, 1982-83. Author, editor: Radiation Effects in Electronic Materials, 1976; contbr. articles to profl. jours. Served with U.S. Army, 1955-57. Recipient Pub. Service award NASA, 1981. Fellow IEEE. Republican. Mem. United Ch. of Christ. Home and Office: 1032 Skylark Dr La Jolla CA 92037-7733

VAN LOKEREN, MARY ANN KREY, beer wholesaler executive; b. St. Louis, June 17, 1947; d. Frederick Curtis and Phyllis M. (Terry) R.; m. John F. Krey III (dec. Nov. 1986); 1 child, Laura Christine; m. Michael Van Lokeren, Apr. 15, 1994. BA, Washington U., St. Louis, 1969, MBA, 1988. Sec. Krey Distbg., St. Charles, Mo., 1978-80, v.p., 1980-86, pres., chief exec. officer, 1986—. Bd. dirs. Laclede Gas Co., St. Louis, Commerce Bancshares, Inc., Kansas City, Mo., Masco Corp. Mem. Mo. Clean Water Commn., Jefferson City, 1988—; bd. dirs. Arts and Edn. Coun. St. Louis, St. Louis Art Mus., Kids Under Twenty-One, World Affairs Coun., Variety Club, SBA Region VII, St. Louis Children's Hosp.; bd. dirs., trustee Washington U. Recipient Leadership award YWCA, 1993; named Mo. Anheuser-Buscher wholesaler, 1989, Woman of Yr. Variety Club, 1994. Mem. Young Pres. Orgn., Regional Commerce and Growth Assn. (bd. dirs. 1990—), Jr. League St. Louis. Office: Krey Distbg 150 Turner Blvd Saint Peters MO 63376-1078

VAN LONE TRIESCHMAN, JANET ANNE, graphic arts educator; b. Huntington, N.Y., Oct. 27, 1963; d. Ross Bowering and Anne Katherine (Feder) Van Lone; m. Daniel Wade Trieschman, Aug. 27, 1994. BS in Comms., Purdue U., 1985; MFA in Graphic Design, Ind. U., 1991; MS in New Media, Ind. U.-Purdue U., Indpls., 2001. Tchg. asst. Ind. U., Bloomington, 1990-91; asst. prof. Art Acad. Cin., 1991-94; from asst. to assoc. prof. Md. Coll. Art, Silver Spring, 1994-96, head dept., 1996; adj. prof. Marian Coll., Indpls., 1997, asst. prof., 1998-2000, assoc. prof., 2000—. Adj. faculty U. Indpls., 1996—97, Herron Sch. Art, Indpls., 1996—97; vis. asst. prof. Purdue U., West Lafayette, Ind., 1997—98; v.p. Laser Artistry, Indpls., 1997—2001. Recipient Potlatch award of excellence N.W. Paper Divsn., 1994; faculty grantee Marian Coll., 1998-99. Mem. Am. Inst. Graphic Arts (bd. dirs. Indpls. chpt. 1999—, co-chair edn. com. 1999—, chmn. membership com. 2000—, exec. com. 2000—), Coll. Art Assn., Found. in Art Theory and Edn., Creative Arts Soc. (faculty liaison 1999—). Office: Marian Coll 3200 Cold Spring Rd Indianapolis IN 46222-1960

VAN LOPIK, JACK RICHARD, geologist, educator; b. Holland, Mich., Feb. 25, 1929; s. Guy M. and Minnie (Grunst) Van L.; 1 son, Charles Robert (dec.). BS, Mich. State U., 1950; MS, La. State U., 1953, PhD, 1955. Geologist, sect. chief, asst. chief, chief geology br. U.S. Army C.E., Waterways Expt. Sta., Vicksburg, Miss., 1954-61; chief engrs. environ. adv. bd. U.S.

Army C.E., 1988-92; chief area evaluation sect., tech. dir., mgr. Space and Environ. Sci. Programs, tech. requirements dir. geosciences ops. Tex. Instruments, Inc., Dallas, 1961-68; chmn. dept. marine sci. La. State U., Baton Rouge, 1968-74; prof. dept. marine sci., dir. sea grant devel., dean Center for Wetland Resources, La. State U., 1968-91; prof. dept. oceanography and coastal scis. La. State U., 1991—; exec. dir. sea grant devel., La. State U., 1991—; chmn. Coastal Resources Directorate of U.S. Nat. Com. for Man and Biosphere, U.S. Nat. Commn. for UNESCO, 1975-82. Dir. Gulf South Rsch. Inst., 1974-89; mem. Nat. Adv. Com. Oceans and Atmosphere, 1978-84; mem. Lower Miss. River Waterway Safety Com. USCG 8th dist., 1983-94; mem. adv. coun. Nat. Coastal Resources Rsch. and Devel. Inst., 1985-98; ofcl. del. XX Congreso Internacional, Mexico City, 1956, XII Gen. Assembly Internat. Union Geodesy and Geophysics, Helsinki, 1960; chmn. panel on geography and land use Nat. Acad. Scis.-NRC, com. on remote sensing programs for earth resources surveys, 1969-77. Fellow Geol. Soc. Am., AAAS; mem. Am. Astronautical Soc. (dir. S.W. sect. 1967-68), Am. Soc. Photogrammetry (dir. 1969-72, chmn. photo interpretation com. 1960, 65, rep. earth scis. divsn. NRC 1968-71), Am. Geophys. Union, Am. Assn. Petroleum Geologists (acad. adv. com. 1973-78), Assn. Am. Geographers, Soc. Econ. Paleontologists and Mineralogists (rsch. com. 1962-65), Am. Mgmt. Assn., Soc. Rsch. Adminstrs., Marine Tech. Soc., Am. Water Resources Assn., Soc. Am. Mil. Engrs., Sea Grant Assn. (exec. bd. dirs. 1972-74, 80-82, 88-91, pres.-elect 1988-89, pres. 1989-90), Nat. Ocean Industries Assn. (adv. coun. 1973-83), Nat. Conf. Advancement Rsch. (exec. com. 1988-92), La. Partnership for Tech. and Innovation (bd. dirs. 1989—), Sigma Xi. Home: 9 Rue Sorbonne Baton Rouge LA 70808-4682 Office: La State U Office Sea Grant Devel Baton Rouge LA 70803-0001 E-mail: jvl@lsu.edu.

VAN LOUCKS, MARK LOUIS, venture capitalist, business advisor; b. Tampa, Fla., June 19, 1946; s. Charles Perry and Lenn (Bragg) Van L.; children: Brandon, Charlie; m. Lee Ann Rose, Oct. 1, 1998. BA in Comm. and Pub. Policy, U. Calif., Berkeley, 1969. Sr. v.p. mktg., programming and corp. devel. United Cable TV Corp., Denver, 1970-81, advisor, 1983-89; sr. v.p., office of chmn. Rockefeller Ctr. TV Corp., N.Y.C., 1981-83; advisor United Artists Commun. Corp., Englewood, 1989-91; investor, business advisor in pvt. practice, 1983—; founder, prin. owner Glory Hole Saloon & Gaming Hall, Central City, Colo., 1990—, The Canyon Casino, Black Hawk, 1990—; chmn., CEO Bask Internat., Englewood, 1990—. Bd. dirs. Wild West Devel. Corp., Denver; sr. v.p., bd. dirs. GSI Cable TV Assocs., Inc., San Francisco, 1984-90; guest lectr. on cable TV bus., 1985-91; cons. Telecommunications, Inc., Denver, 1989-93. Producer HBO spl. Green Chili Showdown, 1985; producer TV spl. 3 Days for Earth, 1987; producer, commd. artist nuclear war armament pieces; contbr. articles to profl. jours. Chmn. Cops in Crisis, Denver, 1990—; bd. dirs. The NOAH Found., Denver, 1976—; founding dir. Project for Responsible Advt., Denver, 1991-92; chmn. mayor's mktg. adv. bd., Central City, Colo. Named hon. capt. Denver Police Dept., 1991—, fin. advisor L. Rose Co., 1995—. Mem. Casino Owners Assn. (founding dir. 1989—), Colo. Gaming Assn. (dir. 1990—), recipient S'nnaeel Evol award, 1995), Glenmoor Country Club, The Village Club. Republican. Jewish. Avocations: music, woodworking, philanthropy, vintage autos. Office: MLVL Inc 333 W Hampden Ave Ste 1005 Englewood CO 80110-2340

VAN LOVEREN, HARRY RONALD, neurosurgeon; b. Hilversum, The Netherlands, Jan. 7, 1953; came to U.S., 1956; BS, U. Cin., 1975, MD, 1979. Intern U. Cin., 1979-80, resident, 1980-85; neurosurgeon Mayfield Clinic and Spine Inst., Cin., 1985—2002; prof. neurosurgery U. S. Fla., Tampa, 2002—. Dir. grad. med. edn. in neurosurgery Good Samaritan Hosp., Cin., 1991—; prof., vice chmn. dept. neurosurgery U. Cin., 1994—; team physician Cin. Reds, 1996—. Author: Atlas of Microsurgery, 1998; contbr. articles to profl. jours. Mem. Frank H. Mayfield Soc. (pres. 1991-92), Am. Assn. of Neurolog. Surgeons (nat. rep. 1995), Soc. of Neurol. Surgeons. Avocations: snow skiing, skydiving, boating, traveling. Office: U S Fla Dept Neurosurgery 4 Columbia Dr Ste 730 Tampa FL 33060 E-mail: hvanloveren@aol.com.

VAN LUVEN, WILLIAM ROBERT, management consultant; b. Toledo, Feb. 15, 1931; s. Harold Calvin and Ruth Frick (Routson) Van L.; m. Lyda Marie Buchanan Jones, Nov. 15, 1956 (div. Sept. 1960); children: Lynn Chase, Michael Frick; m. Barbara Wilson Ehni, Aug. 17, 1968; children: Eric Finley, Jay Palmer. BBA, U. Toledo, 1957; postgrad., U. Va., 1979. Group gen. mgr. Union Camp Corp., Wayne, N.J., 1961-73, 1979-82; pres.container & carton divs. Clevepak Corp., White Plains, N.Y., 1973-79; v.p., gen. mgr. Jefferson Smurfit Corp., Clayton, Mo., 1982-84; pres. Wm. R. Van Luven & Assocs. Inc., St. Louis, 1984—; exec. dir. Exec. Svcs. Corps of St. Louis. Bd. dirs. Smurfit Industries, Alton, Ill., 1982-84, O'Connor Pharm. Corp., Detroit, 1982-84; pres. Mo. Clippers, Inc. (Great Clips for Hair Franchise), 1988—. Cons. United Way of Greater St. Louis, 1987—; chair United Way Mgmt. Assistance Ctr., 1988-90; dir. Combined Health Appeal, Sherwood Forest Camp, Places for People, Inc., Christian Svc. Ctr. With USN, 1951-53. Recipient Keyman award Toledo C. of C., 1956. Mem. Fibre Box Assn., Composite Can & Tube Inst. (pres. 1979), Paperboard Packaging Council, U.S. Brewers Assn., Racquet Club (St. Louis), Aspetuch Country Club (Weston, Conn.), Univ. Club (St. Louis), Shriner, Sigma Nu. Republican. Episcopalian. Avocations: running, skiing, biking. Home: 2 Portland Ct Saint Louis MO 63108-1291 E-mail: wrvl@aol.com.

VAN MAERSSEN, OTTO L. aerospace engineer, consulting firm executive; b. Amsterdam, The Netherlands, Mar. 2, 1919; came to U.S., 1946; s. Adolph L. and Maria Wilhelmina (Edelmann) Van M.; m. Hortensia Maria Velasquez, Jan. 7, 1956; children: Maria, Patricia, Veronica, Otto, Robert. BS in Chem. Engring., U. Mo., Rolla, 1949. Registered profl. engr., Tex., Mo. Petroleum engr. Mobil Oil, Caracas, Venezuela, 1949-51; sr. reservoir engr. Gulf Oil, Ft. Worth and San Tome, Venezuela, 1952-59; acting dept. mgr. Sedco of Argentina, Comodoro Rivadavia, 1960-61; export planning engr. LTV Aerospace and Def., Dallas, 1962-69, R & D adminstr. ground transp. div., 1970-74, engr. specialist new bus. programs, 1975-80; mgr. cost and estimating San Francisco and Alaska, 1981-84; owner OLVM Cons. Engrs., Walnut Creek, Calif., 1984—. Cons. LTV Aerospace and Def., Dallas, 1984—. Served with Brit. Army. Intelligence, 1945, Germany. Mem. Soc. Petroleum Engrs. (Legion of Honor), Toastmasters (sec.-treas. Dallas chpt. 1963-64), Pennywise Club (treas. Dallas chpt. 1964-67). Democrat. Roman Catholic. Avocations: travel, photography. Home and Office: OLVM Cons Engrs 1649 Arbutus Dr Walnut Creek CA 94595-1705 E-mail: ottovm@attbi.com.

VANMARCKE, ERIK HECTOR, civil engineering educator; b. Menen, Belgium, Aug. 6, 1941; arrived in U.S., 1965, naturalized, 1976; m. Louis Eugene and Rachel Louisa (van Hollebeke) V.; m. Margaret Maria Delesie, May 25, 1965 (div. Feb. 22, 1999); children: Lieven, Ann, Kristien; m. Marilyn Durkee, July 14, 2001. BS, U. Leuven, Belgium, 1965; MS, U. Del., 1967; PhD in Civil Engring, MIT, 1970. From instr. to prof. civil engring. MIT, Cambridge, 1969-85, Gilbert W. Winslow Career Devel. prof., 1974-77, dir. civil engring. systems group, 1976-80; prof. civil engring. and ops. rsch. Princeton U., 1985—, dir. grad. studies civil engring. and ops. rsch., 1990—. Cons. Office Sci. and Tech. Policy, 1978-80; vis. scholar in engring. Harvard U., 1984-85; Shimizu Corp. vis. prof. Stanford U., 1991; cons. various govt. agys. and engring. firms; mem. exec. com. Princeton Materials Inst., 1991-93; mem. Princeton Environ. Inst., 1996—; affiliated faculty mem. Princeton U. Bendheim Ctr. Fin., 1998—; mem. com. on vulnerability of critical infrastructure Nat. Res. Coun., 1999-2001. Author: Random Fields: Analysis and Synthesis, 1983, Quantum Origins of Cosmic Structure, 1997; editor: Internat. Jour. Structural Safety, 1981-91. Named Disting. Probabilistic Methods Educator, Soc. Automotive Engrs., 2002; recipient Sr. Scientist award for study in Japan, Japan Soc. for Promotion of Sci., 1991, Disting. Engring. Alumnus award, U. Del., 1994. Mem. ASCE (Raymond C. Reese rsch. award 1975, Walter L. Huber rsch. prize 1984, chair com. on risk assessment and mgmt. of the Geo-Inst. 1996—, chair com. on risk and vulnerability, Coun. Natural Disaster Reduction 1998—), Am. Geophys. Union, Seismol. Soc. Am., Internat. Soc. Soil Mechanics and Geotech. Engring. (chair com. TC32 on risk assessment and mgmt. 1998-2001), Royal Acad. Arts and Scis. of Belgium (fgn.). Home: 578 Province Line Rd Hopewell NJ 08525-3104 E-mail: evm@princeton.edu.

VAN MARTER, LINDA JOANNE, pediatrician, educator, neonatologist, researcher; d. Neal Dahl and Martha Erickson Van Marter. BS, U. Pitts., 1976, MD, 1980; MPH, Harvard U., 1985. Resident in pediatrics Children's Hosp. Med. Ctr., Boston, 1980—83; fellow in neonatal perinatal medicine Joint Program in Neonatology, 1983—86; from instr. pediat. to assoc. ptof. pediat. Harvard Med. Sch., 1986—2002, assoc. prof. pediatrics, 2002—. Reviewer Pediat., Jour. of Pediat., Am. Jour. Pub. Health, New Eng. Jour. Medicine. Recipient Richard L. Day award in pediat. U. Pitts. Sch. Medicine, 1980. Fellow Am. Acad. Pediats. (perinatal sect. exec. com. 1999—, neo-prep working group 1996—, chair 2002-); mem. Ea. Soc. for Pediat. Rsch. (mem. coun. 1998—), Soc. for Pediat. Epidemiol. Rsch. (sec., treas. 1987-91, pres. 1992-93), Soc. for Pediat. Rsch., Alpha Omega Alpha. Office: Children's Hosp Newborn Medicine 300 Longwood Ave Boston MA 02115-5737

VANMEER, MARY ANN, publisher, writer, researcher, webmaster; b. Mt. Clemens, Mich., Nov. 22, 1947; d. Leo Harold and Rose Emma (Gulden) VanM. Student, Micha. State U., 1965-66, 67-68, U. Sorbonne, Paris, summer 1968; BA in Edn., U. Fla., 1968-70. Pres. VanMeer Tutoring and Translating, N.Y.C., 1970-72; freelance writer, 1973-79; pres. VanMeeer Publs., Inc., Clearwater, Fla., 1980-88, VanMeer Media Advt., Inc., Clearwater, 1987-88; exec. dir., founder Nat. Ctrs. for Health and Med. Info., Inc., Palm Beach, Fla., 1990-93; pres., CEO ThriftyTraveling.com, Inc. (formerly Traveling Free Pubs.,), 1993—. Author: Traveling with Your Dog, U.S.A., 1976, How to Set Up a Home Typing Business, 1978, Freelance Photographer's Handbook, 1979, See America Free, 1981, Free Campgrounds, U.S.A., 1982, Free Attractions, U.S.A., 1982, VanMeer's Guide to Free Attractions U.S.A., 1984, VanMeer's Guide to Free Campgrounds, 1984, The How to Get Publicity for Your Business Handbook, 1987, Asthma: The Ultimate Treatment Guide, 1991, Allergies: The Ultimate Treatment Guide, 1992, Thrifty Traveling, 1995, 2d edit., 1996; pub. Nat. Health and Med. Trends Mag., 1986-88, ThriftyTraveling.com Newsletter and website, 1993—, online and hard-copy edits., 1999—, Over 50 Thrifty Traveler Newsletter, 1997-98, Net News for the Thrifty Traveler Newsletter, 1997-98, LuxuryTraveling.com newsletter and website, 2001—; webmaster ThriftyTraveling.com, LuxuryTraveling.com and VanMeer.com websites. Pub. info. chairperson, bd. dirs Pinellas County chpt. Am. Cancer Soc., Clearwater, 1983-84, 86-88; mem. fin. devel. com. ARC, Palm Beach County, 1990-92. Mem. Am. Booksellers Assn., Soc. Am. Travel Writers. Office: ThriftyTraveling.com Inc PO Box 8168 Clearwater FL 33758-8168 E-mail: editor@thriftytraveling.com.

VAN METER, ABRAM DEBOIS, lawyer, retired banker; b. Springfield, Ill., May 16, 1922; s. A.D. and Edith (Graham) Van M.; m. Margaret Schlipf, Dec. 1, 1956; children: Andy, Alice, Ann. BS, Kings Point Coll., 1946; JD, Northwestern U., 1948. Bar: Ill. 1949. Ptnr. Van Meter, Oxtoby & Funk, Springfield, 1949—2001; adminstrv. asst. to treas. State of Ill., 1963; v.p. Ill. Nat. Bank, 1964-65, pres., 1965-88, chmn. bd. dirs., 1988-90, also bd. dirs.; chmn. bd. dirs. First of Am.-Springfield, N.A., 1990-93, dir. emeritus, 1993—. Chmn. bd. dirs. Ill. Housing Devel. Authority, 1977—; chmn. bd. trustees So. Ill. U., 1989—; bd. dirs., mem. exec. com. Meml. Med. Ctr. (emeritus). Mem. ABA, Ill. Bar Assn., Sangamon Bar Assn., Chgo. Club, Chgo. Athletic Club, Sangamo Club, Island Bay Yacht Club. Home: 6 Fair Oaks St Springfield IL 62704-3222 Office: Nat City 1 N Old State Capitol Plz Springfield IL 62701-1323

VANMETER, VANDELIA L. retired director; b. Seibert, Colo., July 17, 1934; d. G.W. and A. Pearl Klockenteger; m. Victor M. VanMeter, Jan. 21, 1954; children: Allison C., Kristopher C. BA, Kansas Wesleyan U., 1957; MLS, Emporia State U., 1970; PhD, Tex. Woman's U., 1986. Cert. libr. media specialist. Tchr. Ottawa County Rural Sch., Kans., 1954-55; social scis. tchr. McClave (Colo.) High Sch., 1957-58, Ellsworth (Kans.) Jr. High Sch., 1959-68; libr., media specialist Ellsworth (Kans.) High Sch., 1968-84; asst. prof. libr. sci. U. So. Miss., Hattiesburg, 1986-90; chair dept. libr./info. sci. Spalding U., Louisville, 1990-96, libr. dir., 1991-99. Cons. to sch., pub. and spl. librs., Kans., Miss., Ky., 1970-99; mem. Ky. NCATE Bd. Examiners. Author: American History for Children and Young Adults, 1990, World History for Children and Young Adults, 1992, America in Historical Fiction, 1997; editor: Mississippi Library Media Specialist Staff Development Modules, 1988, Library Lane Newsletter, 1991-99; contbr. chpts. to books; contbr. articles to profl. jours. Active City Coun., Ellsworth, Kans., 1975-79, Park Bd., Ellsworth, 1975-79; bd. dirs. Robbins Meml. Libr., 1977-79. Grantee Kans. Demonstration Sch. Libr., 1970-72, Miss. Power Found., 1989, Project Technology Enhances Curriculur Instrn., 1996-97; named Women of Yr. Bus. and Profl. Women of Ellsworth, Kans., 1976. Mem. ALA, Assn. Coll. and Rsch. Librs., Ky. Libr. Assn., Assn. for Libr. and Info. Sci. Educators.

VAN METRE, MARGARET CHERYL, artistic director, dance educator; b. Maryville, Tenn., Nov. 24, 1938; d. Robert Fillers and Margaret Elizabeth (Goddard) Raulston; m. Mitchell Robert Van Metre II, Aug. 25, 1956; 1 child, Mitchell Robert. Elem., intermediate and advanced tchg. certs. Dir. Van Metre Sch. of Dance, Maryville, 1958-96; artistic dir. Appalachian Ballet Co., Maryville Coll., 1972-96; founding dir. Appalachian Ballet Co., 1972; dir. Van Metre Arts Mgmt., S.C., 1996—. Chmn. dance panel Tenn. Arts Commn., 1973-74; chmn. Bicentennial Ballet Project, Tenn., 1975-76; mem. Nat. Bd. Regional Dance Am., 1997-2002; owner Van Metre Arts Mgmt., Edisto Island, S.C., 1996—. Choreographer ballets: Delusion, 1965, Hill Heritage Suite, 1972, Dancing Princesses, 1983. Mem. Tenn. Assn. of Dance (pres. 1972), Southeastern Regional Ballet Assn. (pres. 1996, 97, 98, 99). Democrat. Episcopalian. Home: 2103 Myrtle St Edisto Island SC 29438-3437

VAN MIDDLESWORTH, LESTER, physiology, biophysics and medicine educator; b. Washington, Jan. 13, 1919; s. Lester and Hazel Lucile (Brandt) VanM.; m. Nellie Rue Franklin, June 29, 1948; children: Linda V. Anderson, Jane V. Norman, Frank L., Paul E. BS in Chemistry, U. Va., 1940, MS in Chemistry, 1942, MS in Physiology, 1944; PhD in Physiology, U. Calif., Berkeley, 1946; MD, U. Tenn., 1951. Teaching asst. dept. physiology U. Va., 1944, U. Calif., Berkeley, 1944-45; instr. U. Tenn. Med. Units, Memphis, 1946-52, instr. in medicine, 1953-57, asst. prof. physiology, 1952-54, assoc. prof., 1954-59, prof., 1959-89, prof. emeritus physiology and biophysics, 1989—, asst. prof. medicine, 1957-61, assoc. prof., 1961-72, prof. medicine, 1972-89, prof. medicine emeritus, 1989, Disting. prof. physiology and medicine, 1986—. Rotating intern City of Memphis Hosps., 1951-52; cons. chief chemist Piedmont Apple Products Corp., Charlottesville, Va., 1940-46, Crocker Radiation Lab., U. Calif., Berkeley, 1946-47, Oak Ridge Inst. Nuclear Studies, 1950-54; guest co-investigator Endocrine Labs. Tufts Med. Coll., Boston, summers 1954, 55, 56, 59, 61, 64, 66, 69, Scripps Clinic and Rsch. Found., La Jolla, Calif., 1957; guest investigator in endocrinology Harbor Gen. Hosp., UCLA, 1971, Frederick Joliot Hosp., Orsay, France, 1972, Lawrence Livermore Radiation Lab. U. Calif., 1970; staff mem. clinic for med. thyroid disease patients, City of Memphis and U., Tenn., 1951-89. Author 114 publs. in profl. jours., 163 abstracts and oral presentations. Recipient Disting. Svc. award, 1985, Disting. Alumnus award U. Tenn. Coll. Medicine, 1989; USPHS career rsch. grantee, 1962-89. Mem. Am. Chem. Soc., Am. Physiol. Soc., AAAS, Soc. Exptl. Biology and Medicine, Am. Soc. Clin. Investigation, So. Soc. Clin. Investigation, Health Physics Soc., Endocrine Soc., Am. Thyroid Assn. (Disting. Svc. award 1988), Sigma Xi (rsch. award 1944, 86, nat. lectr. 1989-91), Alpha Chi Sigma Research emphasis: thyroid physiology, iodine metabolism, and radioiodine fallout. Home: 1950 Lyndale Ave Memphis TN 38107-5109 Office: U Tenn Health Sci Ctr 894 Union Ave Memphis TN 38103-3514

VAN MILLIGEN, JAMES M. health care administrator; b. Chgo., Feb. 12, 1949; s. Alferd C. and H. Patricia Van M.; m. Jane Standley, May 5, 1971. B of Health Sci., Wichita State U., 1977, M of Health Sci., 1984. Physician asst. Wichita Osteo. Clinic, 1977-84; data mgr. Preferred Health Care, 1984-85; dir. network devel. Equicor, 1986-87; chief oper officer WPAA, Inc., 1987—, WPPA-HMO, Inc., 1995-2000. Mem. Wichita Traffic Commn., 1980-86, pres. 1985; pres. Wichita Ind. Neighborhoods, 1994-95, bd. dirs., 1995-98; pres. Fairmount Neighborhood Assn., Wichita, 1986-95; advisor United Sch. Dist. #249 Bus. & Tech. Com., Wichita, 1993-94, Mayor's Adv. Coun., Wichita, 1989-92; bd. dirs. Cmty. Housing Svcs., 2000—, v.p., 2000-01. With U.S. Army, 1970-73, Vietnam. Mem. Nat. Assn. Health Underwriters (Journalism award 1991), Am. Assn. Health Plans (PPO coun. 1998—), Kans. Assn. Health Underwriters (bd. dirs. 1994-95), Ctrl. Kans. Assn. Health Underwriters (bd. dirs. 1990-95, pres. 1994, Med. Soc. Sedgewick County (assoc. exec. dir. 1987—), Wichita Area C. of C. Avocations: historic restoration, farming. Home: 1717 Fairmount St Wichita KS 67208-1919 Office: WPPA Inc 1102 S Hillside St Wichita KS 67211-4004 E-mail: van@wppainc.com.

VAN MOL, LOUIS JOHN, JR. public relations executive; b. Knoxville, Tenn., Oct. 7, 1943; s. Louis John and Evelyn (Ramsay) Van M.; m. Deborah Ruth Boyd, Nov. 1, 1969; children: Derek, Millicent. BS, U. Tenn., 1966. Staff writer, editor AP, Knoxville and Nashville, 1963-66, 69; account exec. to exec. v.p. Holder, Kennedy & Co., Nashville, 1970-74, exec. v.p., 1978-79; dir. info. TVA, Knoxville, 1974-78; co-founder, ptnr. Dye, Van Mol & Lawrence, Nashville, 1980—. Bd. dirs. East Tenn. Children's Hosp., Knoxville, 1977-78, Martha O'Bryan Ctr., Nashville, 1985-87, United Way Comm. Com., 1987-91, Am. Heart Assn. Mid. Tenn., Nashville, 1991-92, Leadership Nashville, 1992-93, Crime Stoppers Nashville, 1986-92, Alcohol and Drug Coun. Mid. Tenn., Nashville, 1991-93, Martha O'Bryan Found., 1998-2000; chmn. bd. dirs. Nashville Downtown Partnership, 1999-2000; bd. govs., exec. com. Nashville C. of C., 1999-2000; chmn. Goodwill Industries Mid. Tenn., 1996-97. Lt. U.S. Army, 1966-68. Decorated Bronze Star. Mem. Richland Country Club (bd. dirs. 1997-99, pres. 1999), Cumberland Club, Sigma Delta Chi. Presbyterian. Home: 712 Bowling Ave Nashville TN 37215-1049 Office: Dye Van Mol & Lawrence Pub Rels 209 7th Ave N Nashville TN 37219-1802 E-mail: john.van.mol@dvl.com.

VAN MOLS, BRIAN, publishing executive; b. L.A., July 1, 1931; s. Pierre Matthias and Frieda Carthyll (MacArthur) M.; m. Barbara Jane Rose, Oct. 1, 1953 (dec. 1968); children— Cynthia Lee, Matthew Howard, Brian; m. Nancy Joan Martell, June 11, 1977; children— Thomas Bentley, Cynthia Bentley, Kristi AB in English, Miami U., Oxford, Ohio, 1953. Media supr. McCann-Erickson Inc., 1955-58; salesman Kelly Smith Co., 1959; with sales Million Market Newspaper Inc., 1959-63; sales mgr. Autoproducts Mag., 1964; sr. salesman True Mag., 1965-68, Look Mag., 1969-70; regional advt. dir. Petersen Pub. Co., Los Angeles, 1971-74; pub. Motor Trend, 1982-84; nat. automotive mktg. mgr. Playboy Enterprises, Inc., N.Y.C., 1984-85, nat. sales mgr., 1985—; western advt. dir. Playboy mag., 1985-86; assoc. pub., advt. dir. Cycle World CBS, Inc., Newport Beach, Calif., 1974-81, pub., 1981; v.p., advt. dir. Four Wheeler Mag., Canoga Pk., 1986-88; v.p., dir. advt. western div. Gen. Media, Inc., 1988-91; v.p., dir. new bus. devel. Paisano Pub., Inc., Agoura Hills, Calif., 1991-92; dir. mktg. Crown Publs., 1993-94; exec. v.p. Voice Mktg. Inc., Thousand Oaks, Calif., 1994, DMR The Reis Co., Tustin, 1995-96; COO Mesa Exhaust Products, Inc., Costa Mesa, 1996-97. Mktg. dir. McMullen Argus Pub., Inc., Anaheim, Calif., 1998-2001. Served with U.S. Army, 1953-55 Mem. Los Angeles Advt. Club, Adcraft Club Detroit, Advt. Sportsmen of N.Y. Republican. Episcopalian. Home: 57 St Andrews Cir Durango CO 81301 E-mail: bvanmols@frontier.net.

VANN, JOHN DANIEL, III, library consultant, historian; b. Raleigh, N.C., June 14, 1935; s. John Daniel Jr. and Sybil Dean (Wilson) V.; m. Ellen Jane Rogers, June 21, 1969; children: John Daniel IV, Justin Fitz Patrick. BA with honors, U. N.C., 1957; MA, Yale U., 1959, PhD, 1965; M in Librarianship, Emory U., 1971; postgrad., Columbia U., 1962-63, Stanford U., 1977-78. Ordained deacon, elder Presbyn. Ch., commd. temporary supply preacher Northumberland Presbytery. Assoc. prof. history Campbell Coll., Buie's Creek, N.C., 1961-63; bibliographer European history and lit. Newberry Libr., Chgo., 1963-65, asst. reference librarian, 1963-65; prof. history Calif. Bapt. Coll., Riverside, 1965-66; dir. libr., prof. history Bapt. Coll. at Charleston, S.C., 1966-69; libr. Keuka Coll., Keuka Park, N.Y., 1969-71; chief libr., prof. libr., chmn. libr. dept. S.I. Community Coll. CUNY, 1971-76; prof. libr. Coll. S.I. CUNY, 1976-79; head libr. Lockwood Libr./SUNY, Buffalo, 1979-80; asst. dir. for planning, univ. librs. SUNY, 1980-81; exec. dir. librs. and learning resources, prof. U. Wis., Oshkosh, 1981-87; dir. libr. svcs. Bloomsburg U. Pa., 1987-89, dean libr. svcs., 1989-98; spl. asst. to vice chancellor for info. technology Pa. State Sys. Higher Edn., 1999; prin. J. Daniel Vann Consulting, 2000—. Resident planner, cons. on libr. bldgs. and collection devel.; bd. dirs. Coun. Wis. Librs., 1983-86, Susquehanna Libr. Coop., 1987-98, sec./treas., 1993-95. Mem. internat. editl. bd. Libr. Times Internat., 1984—; contbr. chpts. to books, articles to profl. jours. Trustee Maplewood (N.J.) Meml. Libr., 1977-79, v.p., 1979; bd. dirs. Coun. Wis. Librs., 1983-86, Midwest Rotary Multi-Dist. Short Term Internat. Youth Exch., 1987, Oshkosh (Wis.) Symphony Assn., 1986-87, Protestant campus ministry Bloomsburg U., 1999—, United Cerebral Palsy of Winnebagoland, Oshkosh, 1986-87; active coms. Winnebago Presbytery, Presbyn. Ch., 1984-87; com. on min. Northumberland Prsbytery, Presbyn. Ch., 1992-96, com. on preparation for ministry, 1996—, coun., 1999—; commr. Synod of Trinity Presbyn. Ch. (USA), 1999—; bd. dirs. Protestant campus ministry Bloomsburg U., 1999—. Acad. Libr. Mgmt. intern Coun. on Libr. Resources Stanford U., 1977-78. Mem. ALA (com. mem.), Am. Hist. Assn., Archons of Colophon, Assn. for Libr. Collections and Tech. Svcs., Assn. Coll. and Rsch. Librs. (com. chmn., sec. chmn. 1977-78, editl. bd., bd. dirs. 1976-78), Bibliog. Soc. Am., Libr. Adminstrn. and Mgmt. Assn. (com. mem.), Libr. and Info. Tech. Assn., Reference and User Svcs. Assn., Medieval Acad. Am., Pa. Libr. Assn. (coun., sect. dir., mem. coun., Round Table chair), Bloomsburg Rotary Club (Paul Harris fellow), Beta Phi Mu, Phi Alpha Theta. Republican. Home: 810 E 2nd St Bloomsburg PA 17815-2011 also: 1216 Rennie Ave Richmond VA 23227-4723

VAN NATTA, DON, JR. journalist; b. Ridgewood, N.J., July 22, 1964; s. Donald Sr. and Liette Van Natta; m. Lizette Ann Alvarez, Oct. 30, 1964; children: Isabel Emma Natta, Sofia Francisca Natta. BS, Boston U., 1986. Investigative reporter Miami (Fla.) Herald, 1987-95; Washington corr. N.Y. Times, Washington, 1995—. Recipient Silver Gavel award, ABA, 1993, Gold medal, Investigative Reporters and Editors, 1995, Pulitzer prize for Nat. Reporting, 2000, Disting. Alumnus award, Boston U. Coll. Comm., 2000, Pulitzer prize for Explanatory Reporting, 2002. Mem. Soc. Profl. Journalists (Green Eyeshade award Atlanta chpt. 1993, 95). Office: NY Times 1627 Eye St NW Washington DC 20006 E-mail: vannatta@nytimes.com.

VANNATTA, SHANE ANTHONY, lawyer; b. Williston, N.D., May 5, 1968; s. Marlyn Laverne and Karen (Rossland) V. BA in Polit. Sci. with high honors, U. Mont., 1990, JD with honors, 1993. Bar: Mont. 1993, U.S. Dist. Ct. Mont. 1993. Clk./intern Worden Thane & Haines, P.C., Missoula, Mont., 1991-93, assoc., 1993-96, sr. assoc., 1996-2000, shareholder, 2001—. Contbr. articles to profl. jours. In-house campaign exec. United Way of Missoula, 1994—. Mem. Western Mont. Bar Assn. (pres. 2000-01), Mont. State Bar (new lawyers sect., pres. 1996-97, trustee 2002—), Missoula New Lawyers Assn. (pres. 1993-94), Missoula C. of C. (chair Leadership Missoula 1998-99). Roman Catholic. Avocations: Tae Kwon-Do (cert. 2d dan), bicycling. Office: Worden Thane & Haines PC 111 N Higgins Ave Ste 600 Missoula MT 59802-4494 E-mail: svanatta@wthlaw.net.

VAN NESS, JAMES EDWARD, electrical engineering educator; b. Omaha, June 24, 1926; s. Hubert James and Jean (Woodruff) Van N.; m. Mary Ellen Dolvin, Dec. 28, 1948; children: Rebecca Ellen, Barbara Jean, Margaret Ann, Julie Lynn. BS, Iowa State U., 1949; MS, Northwestern U., 1951, PhD, 1954. Faculty elec. engring. dept. Northwestern U., 1952—, prof. emeritus, chmn. dept., 1969-72; dir. Computer Center, 1962-65; vis. assoc. prof. U. Calif., Berkeley, 1958-59. Vis. prof. MIT, 1973-74, Ariz. State U., winter 1984 Contbr. Articles to profl. jours. Served with USNR, 1944-46. Fellow: IEEE; mem.: NAE (elected). Home: 2333 Central St Unit 404 Evanston IL 60201 E-mail: vanness@northwestern.edu.

VAN NESS, JOHN RALPH, university official, educator; b. Columbus, Ohio, Oct. 22, 1939; s. Ralph Taylor and Norma Gertrude (Thorp) Van N.; children: Heather Thorpe, Hilary Clark; m. Sandra M. Martinez, Jan. 1999; 1 stepchild, Alejandro. BA, The Colo. Coll., Colo. Springs, 1965; MA, U. Pa., 1969, PhD, 1979. Instr. West Chester (Pa.) U., 1969-70, Knox Coll., Galesburg, Ill., 1970-73, Fort Lewis Coll., Durango, Colo., 1974-76; cons. fund raising pvt. practice Phila., 1977-79; capital campaign con. John F. Rich Co., 1979-84; v.p. for coll. rels., adj. prof. anthropology Ursinus Coll., Collegeville, Pa., 1984-89; exec. v.p., prof. Moore Coll. Art and Design, Phila., 1989-90, pres., 1990-92, Mus. N.Mex. Found., Santa Fe, 1992-93, N.Mex. State U. Found., 1995-97; asst. v.p. Lehigh U., 1997-98, assoc. v.p., 1998—. Bd. dirs. Ctr. for Land Grant Studies, Santa Fe, 1978-94; editl. bd. Jour. of the West, Manhattan, Kans., 1980-88. Co-author: Cañones: Values, Crisis and Survival in a Northern New Mexico Village, 1981; author: Hispanos in Northern New Mexico, 1991; co-editor: Spanish and Mexican Land Grants in New Mexico and Colorado, 1980, Land, Water and Culture, 1987; editor: New Mexico Land Grant Series, vols. 1-5, 1983, 84, 87, 89, 94. Recipient Teaching Fellowship U. Pa.; grantee Ford Found., Nat. Sci. Found. Mem. Am.

Anthrop. Assn., Am. Assn. Museums, Coun. for Advance and Support Edn., Nat. Soc. Fund Raising Execs., Pi Gamma Mu, Phi Delta Theta. Democrat. Avocations: architecture, art, sports. Fax: 610- 868-6560. E-mail: jrv3@lehigh.edu.

VAN NESS, PATRICIA WOOD, religious studies educator, consultant, author; b. Peterborough, N.H., Sept. 12, 1925; d. Leslie Townsend and Bernice E. (Coburn) Wood; m. John Hasbrouck Van Ness, June 13, 1953; children: Peter Wood, Stephen Hasbrouck, Timothy Coburn. BA, U. Wash., 1947; MA, Inst. Transpersonal Psychology, Palo Alto, Calif., 1993. Leader various workshops and retreats, 1979—; records mgr. dept. pub. rels. Standard Oil Co. (New Jersey) (now Exxon Corp.), N.Y.C., 1948-50; sec. pub. rels. dept. Standard Oil Co., 1951; sec. law dept. Johnson & Johnson, New Brunswick, N.J., 1953-54; reporter Hudson Valley Newspapers, Highland, N.Y., 1972-74; acting assoc. dir. office of pub. rels. SUNY, New Paltz, 1974; ednl. cons. Ulster County Assn. for Mental Health, Kingston, N.Y., 1973-76, Meth. Ch., New Paltz, NY, 1976-78, White Plains (N.Y.) Presbyn. Ch., 1978-81; adminstrv. asst. Ctr. for Cont. Edn. Calif. Economy, Palo Alto, 1983-84; profl. rep. pvt. practice, 1984; adminstrv. asst. Inventory Transfer Systems Inc., 1984-85; ednl. cons. Bedford (N.H.) Presbyn. Ch., 1986-88; coord. pub. rels., adminstrv. asst. Inst. Transpersonal Psychology, Menlo Park, 1981-83. Workshop leader and cons. Author: Transforming Bible Study with Children, 1991; assoc. editor and writer Bible Workbench, 1993—; contbr. numerous articles to profl. jours. Trustee Peterborough (NH) Players, 1998—2001. Mem. Assn. Presbyn. Ch. Educators. Avocations: swimming, reading, contra dancing, theater . Home: 11 Jaquith Rd Jaffrey NH 03452-6406 E-mail: pwvn@monad.net.

VAN NESS, PATRICIA CATHELINE, composer, violinist; b. Seattle, June 25, 1951; d. C. Charles and Marjorie Mae (Dexter) Van N. Student, Wheaton (Ill.) Coll., 1969-70, Gordon Coll., 1972. Composer: ballet score for Beth Soll, 1985, 87, 94, for Monica Levy, 1988, for Boston Ballet, 1988, 90, for Charleston Ballet Theatre, 1994; text and music for voices and early instruments with text translated into Latin for Evensong, 1991, Five Meditations, 1993, Cor Mei Cordis, 1994, Arcanae, 1995, Ego sum Custos Angels, 1995, Tu Risa, 1996, The Nine Orders of the Angels, 1996; various scores, 1985-2000; rec. violinist A&M Records, Private Lightning, 1980, Telarc Internat. Arcanae and Ego sum Custos Angela, 1996, Telarc Internat. Michael and Thronorum, 1999, Telarc Internat. The Fourth River, 1999; composer-in-residence First Church in Cambridge (Mass.), Congregational, 1996—, Coro Allegro, 1998, The Boston Athenaeum, 2002-. Grantee Mass. Cultural Coun., 1993, 96, New Eng. Biolabs. Founds., 1989, Mass. Arts Lottery Coun., 1988, Meet the Composer, 1997, 98; recipient Spl. Recognition award Barlow Internat. Composition for Evensong, 1993, 1st prize His Majestie's Clerkes Choral Competition, 1997. Mem.: ASCAP (Std. award 1996—2001), Alliance Women in Music, Am. Music Ctr., Chamber Music Am. Avocation: major league baseball.

VANNI, ROBERT JOHN, lawyer; b. Richmond, Va. s. Anthony John and Jeanette V. BSBA, Babson Coll., 1966; JD, NYU, 1969; cert., U. Catholique L'Ouest, Angers, France, 1971; MBA, Columbia U., 1977. Bar: N.Y. 1969. Asst. econ. affairs officer UN Secretariat, N.Y.C., 1969-72; assoc. Shearman & Sterling, 1972-79; gen. counsel N.Y.C. Dept. Cultural Affairs, 1979-86; v.p., gen. counsel, asst. sec. N.Y. Pub. Libr., Astor Lenox and Tilden Founds., 1986—. Bd. dirs. Nonprofit Coordinating Com., 2001—; chair, of counsel N.Y.C. cultural instns., 1987—; bd. advisors Nat. Ctr. Philanthropy and the Law, 1997—. Bd. dirs. Afghanistan Relief Com., N.Y.C., 1980-86, Am.-Italy Soc., N.Y.C., 1983-95, Jazz Found. Am., N.Y.C., 1990-95; trustee Louis Armstrong Edn. Found., 1997—. Named one of Outstanding Young Men in Am. Mem. Nat. Assn. Coll. and Univ. Attys. (co-chair com. on museums and libs. 1996-2000), N.Y.C. Bar Assn. (chair com. on internat. trade 1983-87, mem. long range planning com., nonprofit orgn. com., art law com. 2000—). Office: N Y Pub Libr 5th Ave and 42d St New York NY 10018

VANNIASINGHAM, SAMUEL KANAGASABAPATHY, accountant; b. Singapore, Oct. 16, 1950; arrived in U.K., 1974; s. Nathan Kesagar and Mabel Gnanaratnam (Subramaniam) V.; m. Heather Christine Clark, August 5, 1981; children: Daniel James, David Joseph. Diploma in Acctg., Stamford Ctr., Singapore, 1972; degree Profl. Acctg., Chartered Assn. Cert. Accts., London, 1979. Articled clk. Peat, Marwick, Mitchell, Singapore, 1974-75; part-time tchr. Adult Edn. Bd., 1972-75; mgmt. trainee E. Russell Ltd., London, 1977-79, accounts mgr., 1980-85; mgmt. acct. MAT Transport Internat. Ltd., 1985-86, group mgmt. acct., 1986-87, group acct., 1988; group fin. contr. and co. sec. C & S Group, 1989; mgr. fin. acct. Channel Four TV, London, 1989-92; pvt. practice Sam Vann & Co., Chartered Cert. Accts., 1992—. Non-exec. dir. Trans Enterprise Computer Comm., Ltd., 1999—. Staff sgt. in nat. svc. Police dept., Singapore, 1968-75. Recipient Bravery commendation medal Police Force, Singapore, 1974. Fellow Chartered Assn. Cert. Acct., Mem. Brit. Inst. Mgmt., Singapore Cricket Assn. (test cricketer 1971-75), North London Enterprise Club (dir. 1994—), North London C. of C. (co-opted dir. 1999—). Clubs: Hazelwood Squash (North London). Methodist. Avocations: squash, cricket. Home: 17 Hyde Way Edmonton London N9 9RU England Office: Sam Vann & Co DPK House 186 Chase Side London N14 5HN England

VANNICE, M. ALBERT, chemical engineering educator, researcher; b. Broken Bow, Nebr., Jan. 11, 1943; s. Duane M. and Eugenia R. (Farmer) V.; m. Bette Ann Clark, Jan. 2, 1971. BSChemE, Mich. State Univ., 1964; MS, Stanford Univ., 1966, PhD, 1970. Engr. Dow Chemical Co., Midland, Mich., 1966, Sun Oil Co., Marcus Hook, Pa., 1970; sr. rsch. engr. Esso Rsch. & Engr. Co., Linden, N.J., 1971-76; assoc. prof. Pa. State Univ., State Coll., 1976-80, prof., 1980—2000, disting. prof., 1991—; M.R. Fenske prof. chem. engring., 1996—. Cons. Eastman Chem. Co., Kingsport, Tenn., 1980-2000; mem. adv. bd. Adsorption Sci. & Tech., 1982-95. Mem. editl. bd. Jour. of Catalysis, 1988-94, assoc. editor, 1994-2001; contbr. articles to profl. jours. Recipient N.Y. Catalysis Soc. award, 1985, P.H. Emmett award, 1987, Pa.-Cleve. Catalysis Soc., 1988, Humboldt Rsch. award, 1990, Fulbright award, 1996. Mem. AIChE (profl. Progress award 1986), Am. Chem. Soc., N.Am. Catalysis Soc. (pres. 1997-2001). Achievements include 9 patents; effects of strong metal-support interactions on catalytic behavior; studies of CO hydrogenation, NOx reduction, catalyst characterization. Office: Pa State Univ 107 Fenske Lab University Park PA 16802-4400 E-mail: mavche@engr.psu.edu.

VANNICE, SANDRA SUE, elementary education educator; b. Greencastle, Ind., Mar. 16, 1943; d. Paul and Christine (Rhea) Wise; m. William Allen VanNice, Aug. 24, 1968. B, Ind. State U., 1965, M, 1968. Tchr. kindergarten Northwood Elem. Sch., Franklin, Ind., 1965-67; tchr. 1st grade Mill Creek Community Schs., Clayton, 1967-71; tchr. kindergarten Plainfield (Ind.) Van Buren Elem., 1971-90, tchr. Plainfield Kindergarten Ctr., 1990—. Bd. dirs. Christian edn. Clayton Baptist Ch., 1990, clk. 2002-; sec.-treas. Weekday Religious Edn., Amo, Ind., 1990. Recipient Homemaker award Crisco Co., 1961, Citizenship award DAR, 1961, ROSE award, 1995, Outstanding Educator award Optimist Club, 1995; grantee Plainfield Sch. Corp., 1989; scholar State of Ind., 1961. Mem. Profl. Edn. Assn., Ind. Assn. Edn. Young Children, Country Squares. Avocations: square dance, garden, knitting, sewing. Office: RR 6 Box 136 Danville IN 46122-9805

VAN NOORD, DIANE C. artist, educator; b. Muskegon, Mich., Dec. 12, 1950; d. Ernest Raymond and Judith Ann Olsen; m. Calvin G. Van Noord, Sept. 26, 1981; children: Tawn Star, Brian Calvin, Timothy John. BA, Hope Coll., 1991; MA, Western Mich. U., 1994. Artist, Holland, Mich., 1989—; substitute tchr. Holland (Mich.) Christian Schs., 1996—99; pvt. art tchr. Holland, 2000—. Guest lectr. Counterpart Assn., Grand Haven, Mich., 1997, Lakeland Painters, Grand Haven, 1997, Traverse City (Mich.) Art Assn., 1997, Holland Christian Schs., 1998, 99, 2000. Exhbns. include Neville Pub. Mus., Green Bay, Wis., 1994, Carillon Gallery, Ft. Worth, 1995, 97, Sedona (Ariz.) Arts Ctr., 1995, 96, 99, Holland Area Arts Coun., 1995, Pitts. Ctr. for the Arts, 1995, Miss. Mus. Art, Jackson, 1995, Unitarian Universalist Ch., Phoenix, 1996, Lakeland Painters, Grand Haven, Mich., 1996, Sun Cities Mus. Art, Sun City, Ariz., 1997, Art Inst. Phoenix, 1998, Hill Country Arts Found., Ingram, Tex., 1998, Mus. Tex. Tech. U., Lubbock, 1998, Dunton Gallery, Arlington Heights, Ill., 2000, Internat. Mus. Art, El Paso, 2000, among others; one-woman shows include Gallery Upstairs, Grand Haven, 1996, Moynihan Gallery, Holland, 1997, Trinity Presbyn. Ch., Denton, 1997, Show Sabbatical, 1998, 99, Freedom Village, Holland, 2000, Acad. Artists Assn., Spriongfield, Mass., 2001, Hilton Head Art League, 2002, Oil Painters Am., Chgo., 2002, others; permanent collections in Fla., Ariz., Mich., Nebr., Ind.; contbr. articles to profl. jours. Recipient Merchant's award Lakeland Painters, 1996, No. Ariz. Watercolor Soc., Sedona Arts Ctr., 1999, Diane Parssinen Meml. awrd No. Ariz. Watercolor Soc., 2001, 2d prize Internat. Artist Mag., 2002, Hon. Mention, Artists Mag., 2002. Mem. Ariz. Watercolor Assn., No. Ariz. Watercolor Assn., Oil Painters Am. (assoc.), Nat. Watercolor Soc. (assoc.), Allied Artists (assoc.), Am. Women Artists. Republican. Home: 6418 Oakridge Dr Holland MI 49423-8999 E-mail: dvn@dianevannoord.com.

VAN NORDEN, BRYAN WILLIAM, Asian studies educator; b. Latrobe, Pa., Dec. 9, 1962; s. Charles Rutherford and Helen (Kwiecinski) Van N.; m. Sarah Rebecca Thomas, July 7, 1990; children: Charles Rutherford III, Melissa Caroline. BA, U. Pa., 1985; PhD, Stanford U., 1991. Lectr. Stanford (Calif.) U., 1990-91; vis. asst. prof. U. Vt., Burlington, 1991-93, U. No. Iowa, Cedar Falls, 1994-95; asst. prof. Vassar Coll., Poughkeepsie, NY, 1995—2001, assoc. prof., 2001—. Editor: The Ways of Confucianism, 1996; editor, contbr.: Readings in Classical Chinese Philosophy, 2001, editor, contbr.: Confucius and the Analects, 2002; contbr. articles to profl. jours. Fellow Woodrow Wilson found., 1985, Chiang Ching-kuo found., Taiwan, 1993. Mem. Assn. for Asian Studies, Am. Philosophical Assn. (adv. com. on non-western philosophy 2000—), Soc. for the Study of Early China, Internat. Soc. for Chinese Philosophy. Democrat. Office: Vassar Coll 124 Raymond Ave Poughkeepsie NY 12604-0310 E-mail: brvannorden@vassar.edu.

VAN NORMAN, WILLIS ROGER, computer systems researcher; b. Windom, Minn., June 17, 1938; s. Ralph Peter and Thelma Pearl (Bare) Van N.; m. Irene Anna Penner, Sept. 7, 1959; children: Eric Jon, Brian Mathew, Karin Ruth. AA, Worthington Jr. Coll., 1958; BS, Mankato State Coll., 1960; MS, St. Thomas U., 1991. Tchr. chemistry, St. Peter, Minn., 1961, Byron, 1962; tchr. spl. edn. Rochester, 1963-65; instr. Pilots Ground Sch., Rochester Jr. Coll., 1968-69; with Mayo Clin., Rochester, 1962-88; developer biomed. computer sys., 1974—; staff analyst Analyst Internat., 1988—. Instr. Gopher Aviation, 1968-71; founder, mgr. Van Norman's Flying V Ranch, 1972—, Van Norman Airport, St. Charles, 1977—. Woodland advisor, 1995—; founding mem. Zumbro Valley Woodland Coun., 1996; treas. United Meth. Ch. Named Olmstead County Conservation Farmer of Yr., 1992; recipient River Friendly Farmer award, 1997. Mem. NEA, Minn. Edn. Assn., Mankato State Alumni Assn. (dir.), Minn. Flying Farmers (v.p., pres.), Internat. Flying Farmers (dir.), Am. Radio Relay League (mgr. Minn. sec. traffic net), Rochester Amateur Radio Club (pres.). Home: 19230 26th St NE Saint Charles MN 55972-2016 Office: IBM Rochester MN 55901 E-mail: wvannorman@analysts.com.

VAN NOSTRAND, CATHARINE MARIE HERR, writer, gender equity specialist; b. Dubuque, Iowa, June 17, 1937; d. King George and Julia Marie (Hansen) Herr; m. David Michael Van Nostrand, July 16, 1960; children: Laura Susan Van Nostrand Caviani, Catharine Louise, Maren Thyra. Student, Grinnell Coll., 1955-57; BA in Music Edn., U. Iowa, 1959; MA in Human Devel., St. Mary's U. of Minn., Winona, 1989. Music specialist, Bound Brook, N.J. and Brookline, Mass., 1959-62; coord. music and worship First United Meth. Ch., St. Cloud, Minn., 1970-75; founder, prin. cons. Catharine Van Nostrand & Assocs., 1975—. Guest lectr., author-in-residence nat. colls. and univs., regional, statewide, nat. and internat. acad. symposia, 1975—; tng. and devel. cons. numerous bus., govt., health and edn. orgns.; keynote spkr. and workshop facilitator regional and nat. confs. and convs., 1987—; cons./featured spkr. on Equal Opportunity for European Union countries, 1995. Author: Gender-Responsible Leadership: Detecting Bias, Implementing Interventions, 1993; contbr. articles to profl. jours. Capt. prof. div. fundraising for area family YMCA, St. Cloud, 1975; founding bd. dirs. St. Cloud Civic Orch.; vol. radio interviewer Minn. Pub. Radio and WJON Radio, Collegeville/St. Cloud, 1976-77. Mem. AAUW, Forum Exec. Women. Democrat. Methodist. Avocations: bicycle touring, reading, gardening, cultural events. Home: 2854 Winnebago Rd Sartell MN 56377-2373 Office: 14 7th Ave N Saint Cloud MN 56303-4766

VAN NOY, CHRISTINE ANN, restaurateur; b. Oakland, CA, Mar. 25, 1948; d. Julio Ceaser and Bernice Thelma (Rose) Lucchesi; m. David Craik Van Noy, July 10, 1971; children: James Allan, Joseph Julio. Student, U. Calif., Berkeley, 1971-73, U. Phoenix, 1994—. Exec. sec. Kaiser Permanente Med. Care Program, Oakland, 1966-76; owner Secret Closet Boutique, Moraga, Calif., 1972-82; owner, operator The Wordshop, 1976-86; owner, cons. Van Noy & Assocs., 1979—; exec. sec. to sr. v.p., regional mgr. Kaiser Permanente Med. Care Program, 1986-88, chmn., CEO, 1988-92, dir. adminstrv. svcs., 1992-98, v.p. adminstrv. svcs., 1999-2000; owner Giulio's Catering, 1999-2000; pres. Kaiser Permanente Internat.; owner Cafe Dolce, 2000—02; prin. Guillio's Catering, 2002—. Instr. U. Calif., Santa Cruz, 1983-84, Diablo Valley Coll., Concord, Calif., 1984; cons. Nat. Alliance Homebased Businesswomen, San Francisco, 1981-84. Author: Homebased Business Guide, 1982, (with others) Women Working Home, 1982. Mem. bd. Joaquis Moraga Sch. Dist., 1983-84, Calif. Federated Jr. Women's Clubs, 1972-77; bd. dirs. Orinda/Moraga Recreational Swimming Assn., 1984-85, St. Mark's United Methodist Ch., Moraga, 1983-84; pres. bd. Protect Our Nation's Youth Baseball Assn., 1987-90; dir. Ctr. for Living Skills, 1990—. Mem. Women Health Care Execs. Democrat. Roman Catholic. Avocations: graphic design, painting, writing. Home: 181 Paseo Del Rio Moraga CA 94556-1641 Office: Cafe Dolce 100 Pringle Ave #120 Walnut Creek CA 94596 E-mail: cafedolce@hotmail.com.

VAN NOY, TERRY WILLARD, health care executive; b. Alhambra, Calif., Aug. 31, 1947; s. Barney Willard and Cora Ellen (Simms) V.; m. Betsy Helen Pothen, Dec. 27, 1968; children: Bryan, Mark. BS in Bus. Mgmt., Calif. State Poly. U., 1970; MBA, Pepperdine U., 1991. CLU. Group sales rep. Mutual of Omaha, Atlanta, 1970-74, dist. mgr., 1974-77, regional mgr. Dallas, 1977-82, nat. sales mgr. Omaha, 1982-83, v.p. group mktg., 1983-87, div. dir. Orange, Calif., 1987-95; pres., CEO, Amil Internat., Las Vegas, 1995-98; prin. Van Noy Consulting Group, Henderson, Nev., 1998—. Bd. dirs. State Nev. Reinsurance Program. Presenter in field. Vice chmn. Morning Star Luth. Ch., Omaha, 1987; mem. adv. bd. Chapman U. Sch. Bus.; mem. exc. com. ABL Orgn.; chmn. bd. trustees Desert Rsch. Inst. Found.; mem. State of Nev. Reins. Bd. Mem. Am. Soc. CLU, Orange County Employee Benefit Coun., We. Pension and Benefits Conf., Las Vegas Valley Soaring Assn. (v.p.). Republican. Avocations: skiing, scuba diving, soaring. Home and Office: 2312 Prometheus Ct Henderson NV 89074-5324

VANNOZZI, THOMAS, cameraman; b. Apr. 3, 1951; s. Isidor and Mary. Student, U. Nev.-Las Vegas, 1969-71; student, UCLA, 1973. Freelance video camera operator, Las Vegas and Los Angeles, 1971—; video camera operator ABC, HBO, NBC, Fox, Hollywood, Calif. Handheld, pedestal, lighting cameraman, videography. Creator/prodr. The Las Vegas Salute to the Troops Show, 1991; prodr. whole state founding conv. via satellite television teleconf., 1994; created boxing camera shots walk-in and rope drop using early handheld cameras. State coord. Nevadans for Brown Presdl. Campaign, 1992; treas. Nevadans for Carter Presdl. Campaign, 1975. Recipient Emmy award for Outstanding Camera on a Spl., 1993, L.A. Emmy award for Camera on Live Sports Event, 1995; nominated for L.A. Sports Emmy, 1994. Democrat. Roman Catholic. Avocations: running.

VAN NUYS, FRANK, historian, educator; b. Rapid City, SD, July 20, 1961; s. Kelvin and Rena Van Nuys; m. Janet Edwards, June 27, 1986; 1 child Maya. BA, SD State U., Brookings, 1984; MA, Calif. State U., Chico, 1990—93; PhD, U. Wyo., Laramie, 1997. Lectr. U. Wyo., Laramie, Wyo., 1996—99; asst. prof. of history No. Mich. U., Marquette, 2000—02, SD Sch. of Mines & Tech., Rapid City, 2002—. Author: (book) Americanizing the West: Race, Immigrants, and Citizenship, 1890-1930, 2002; contbr. articles and essays in jours. and mags. Recipient John Topham & Susan Redd Butler Faculty Rsch. Award, Charles Redd Ctr. for Western Studies, Brigham Young U., 1999-2000. Mem.: Orgn. of Am. Historians, Immigration and Ethnic History Soc., Wyo. State Hist. Soc. Home: 4020 W Main St Rapid City SD 57702 Office: SD Sch Mines & Tech 501 East St Joseph St Rapid City SD 57701

VAN OEVEREN, EDWARD LANIER, lawyer, biologist, physician; b. Washington, Apr. 12, 1954; BA with high distinction, U. Va., 1976; MD, Med. Coll. Va., 1995; JD, U. Va., 1981; BS with distinction, George Mason U., 1983; MPH, Johns Hopkins U., 1998. Bar: Va. 1981, U.S. Dist. Ct. (ea. dist.) Va. 1988, U.S. Temporary Emergency Ct. Appeals 1989; lic. physician, Va.; bd. cert. pub. health & preventive medicine. Pvt. practice legal cons., Falls Church, Va., 1984-85; pvt. practice law, 1986-89; pvt. practice law and biology, 1989-95; intern Med. Coll. Va., 1996-97; resident in preventive medicine Johns Hopkins U., Balt., 1997-99; pvt. practice law, medicine and biology Falls Church, 1997—. Editor: Federal Special Court Litigation, 1982; contbr. articles to profl. jours. Election officer Fairfax County (Va.) Electoral Bd., 1989-90, 94-2001. Capt. Va. Army NG, 1996-97; 1st lt. USAR, 1995-96, capt., 1997—. Mem.: George Mason U. Alumni Assn. (scholarship, awards, rules and policies coms. 1989—91), Va. State Bar Assn., Alpha Chi. Avocation: photography. Home: 3304 Patrick Henry Dr Falls Church VA 22044-1514 E-mail: EVanOeveren@pol.net.

VANORA, JEROME PATRICK, lawyer; b. Dec. 18, 1941; s. Jerome Anthony and Mary (Fitzpatrick) V.; m. Marianne Elizabeth Hartmann, Oct. 12, 1968; children: Judith, Kimberly. BA, Queens Coll., 1963; JD, St. John's U., 1966. Bar: N.Y. 1967. Atty. N.Y. Dept. of State Corp. Bur., Albany, 1967-70; sr. atty. divsn. human rights N.Y.C., 1970-81; assoc. atty. divsn. housing cmty. renewal, 1981—2002. Dir. hearings unit (chief adminstrv. law judge) office of rent adminstrn., div. housing and community renewal, N.Y.C., 1984-99; asst. counsel Nassau County Rent Guidelines Bd., 1982-86; lectr. (twice yearly) L.I. U., Greenvale, N.Y., 1984-85 . Contbr. articles to profl. jours. Mem.: N.Y. State Bar Assn., Nat. Assn. Adminstrv. Law Judges, Phi Beta Kappa. Republican. Roman Catholic. Home: 1100 Delmar Ave Franklin Square NY 11010-2703

VAN ORDEN, LUCAS S. psychiatrist; b. Nov. 3, 1928; MD, Northwestern U., 1956; PhD in Pharmacology, Yale U., 1966. Med. dir. forensic unit Las Vegas (Nev.) Med. Ctr., 1991-94; pvt. practice psychiatry Santa Fe, 1992-98; psychiat. consultation practice Nashville, 1998—2002; psychiat. cons. onsite workshops Charlotte, 1998—2002; psychiat. cons. Cumberland Heights Treatment Ctr., 1998—2002. Home: 101 Fox Trl Nashville TN 37221-2224

VAN ORDEN, PHYLLIS JEANNE, librarian, educator; b. Adrian, Mich., July 7, 1932; d. Warren Philip and Mabel A. Nancy (Russell) Van O. BS, Ea. Mich. U., 1954; AMLS, U. Mich., 1958; EdD, Wayne State U., 1970. Sch. librarian East Detroit (Mich.) Pub. Schs., 1954-57; librarian San Diego Pub. Library, 1958-60; media specialist Royal Oak (Mich.) Pub. Schs., 1960-64; librarian Oakland U., Rochester, Mich., 1964-66; instr. Wayne State U., Detroit, 1966-70; asst. prof. Rutgers U., New Brunswick, N.J., 1970-76; prof. library science Fla. State U., Tallahassee, 1977-91, assoc. dean for instrn., 1988-91; prof. libr. sci. program Wayne State U., Detroit, 1991-93; dir. Grad. Sch. of Libr. and Info. Sci. U. Wash., Seattle, 1993-96; cons. in field, 1996—. Editor: Elementary School Library Collection, 1974-77; author: Collection Program in Schools, 2001, Library Service to Children, 1992, Selecting Books for the Elementary School Library Media Center, 2000. Fla. State Libr. grantee, 1984, 86, 88; Lillian Bradshaw scholar Tex. Woman's U., 1993. Mem.: ALA (libr. resources and tech. svcs. divsn., Blackwell/N.Am. scholarship award 1983), Assn. for Libr. and Info. Sci. Edn. (pres. 1990, Svc. award 1997), Assn. Libr. Svc. to Children (past pres., Dist. Svc. award 2002), Pi Lambda Theta. Avocations: music, knitting, physical fitness, cooking, travel. E-mail: vanordp@u.washington.edu.

VAN ORMAN, JEANNE, planning consultant; b. N.Y.C., Apr. 9, 1939; d. Wayne and Jean (O'Gara) Van O.; m. Robert F. Brown, 1963 (div. 1975); children: Frank Van Orman Brown, Virginia Corbin Brown. BA, Smith Coll., 1961; M City Planning, Harvard U., 1974. Land use planner Mass. Exec. Office Cmtys. and Devel., Boston, 1975-85, dir. strategic planning grants, 1985-87; prin. Van Orman & Assocs., Arlington, Mass., 1987—. Adj. prof. Bridgewater State Coll., 1997—; instr. Harvard U. Grad. Sch. Design, summer 1999, summer 2000. Contbr. articles to profl. jours. Selectman Town of Easton, Mass.; mem. Trinity Ch., Boston, lay eucharistic min. Grantee NEA, 1981, Mass. Housing Partnership, 1987; recipient Disting. Svc. award Easton Jaycees, 1973. Mem. AICP (cert.), Am. Planning Assn. Avocations: sailing, Reiki (level II) practitioner. Address: PO Box 91 Arlington Heights MA 02475 Office: One School St Arlington MA 02476 E-mail: vanorman@aol.com.

VAN OSDOL, DONOVAN HAROLD, mathematics educator; b. Plymouth, Ind., Sept. 27, 1942; s. Harold Isaac Van Osdol and Freida Marie (Culp) Mangus; m. Marie A. Gaudard, Jan. 2, 1983. AB, Earlham Coll., Richmond, Ind., 1964; AM, U. Ill., 1966, PhD, 1969. Asst. prof. Wilkes Coll., Wilkes-Barre, Pa., 1969-70; from asst. prof. to assoc. prof. U. N.H., Durham, 1970-79, prof., 1979—. Rsch. assoc. U. Oslo, 1972-73; assoc. exec. dir. Am. Math. Soc., Providence, 1989-91; vol. assoc. sec. Math. Assn. Am., Washington, 1994-98. Contbr. rsch. articles to math jours. Lance cpl. USMC, 1962-64. Mem. Am. Legion. Office: U NH Dept Math Durham NH 03824

VAN PATTEN, JAMES JEFFERS, education educator; b. North Rose, N.Y., Sept. 8, 1925; s. Earl F. and Dorothy (Jeffers) Van P.; married. BA, Syracuse U., 1949; ME, Tex. Western Coll., 1959; PhD, U. Tex., Austin, 1962. Asst. prof. philosophy and edn. Central Mo. State U., Warrensburg, 1962-64, assoc. prof., 1964-69; assoc. prof. fis. overseas U. Okla., Norman, 1969-71; prof. edn. U. Ark., Fayetteville, 1971-99, prof. emeritus, 1999—. Visiting scholar, U. Mich., 1981, UCLA, 1987, U. Tex., Austin, 1987; vis. prof./scholar U. Fla., Gainesville, 1994; adj. Fla. Atlantic U., 2001, 2002. Editor: Conflict, Permanency and Change in Education, 1976, Philosophy, Social Science and Education, 1989, College Teaching and Higher Education Leadership, 1990, Social-Cultural Foundations of Educational Policy in the U.S., 1991; author: Academic Profiles in Higher Education, 1992, The Many Faces of the Culture of Higher Education, 1993, 2d edit. 2000, (with John Pulliam) History of Education in America, 7th edit., 1999, The Culture of Higher Education: A Case Study Approach, 1996, What's Really Happening in Education: A Case Study Approach, 1997, Individual and Collective Contributions to Humaneness In Our Time, 1997; editor: Watersheds in Higher Education, 1997, Challenges and Opportunities For a New Millennium, 1998, Challenges and Opportunities for Education in the 21st Century, 1999, Higher Education Culture, Case Studies For A New Century, 2000, A New Century In Retrospect and Prospect, 2000; contbr. articles to profl. jours. including Futures Rsch. Quar.; founder Jour. of Thought, Educational Systems for the 21st Century, Futures Rsch. Quarterly, summer 2000. Served with inf. U.S. Army, 1944-45. Decorated Purple Heart. Mem. Am. Ednl. Studies Assn., Southern Future Soc., World Future Soc., Am. Philosophy Assn., Southwestern Philosophy of Edn. Soc. (pres. 1970), Am. Ednl. Rsch. Assn., Edn. Law Assn., Nat. Assn. Legal Assts., Kiwanis, Phi Delta Kappa (pres. chpt. U. Ark. 1976-77). Home: 434 W Hawthorn St Fayetteville AR 72701-1934 E-mail: jvanpatt@aol.com.

VAN PELT, FRANCES EVELYN, management consultant; b. Oregon, Ill., Aug. 25, 1937; d. Henry Benjamin and Bessie May (Himes) Ulferts; m. R. Richard Van Pelt, Oct. 28, 1953; children: R. Richard Jr., Robin F. Van Pelt Dobbs, Raymond Scott, Ronda Jean. Student, Waubonsee Coll., Sugar Grove, Ill., 1971-75. Adminstrv. asst. Sears, Roebuck & Co., Aurora, Ill., 1960-73; owner, mgr., pres. Outdoor World, Inc., 1973-87; 20 group dir. Spader Mgmt. Groups, Inc., Sioux Falls, S.D., 1988—. Bd. dirs. RV Consumer Care Commn., Fairfax, Va., 1985-88. Contbr. articles to profl. jours. Bd. dirs. Breaking Free, Aurora, 1988-90; cellist Fox Valley Symphony, Aurora, 1961-81. Mem. Aurora C. of C. Recrational Vehicle Dealers Assn. (bd. dirs. 1978-79, exec. bd. 1980-82, pres. 1983, chmn. bd. dirs. 1984), Ill. RV Dealers Assn. (pres., bd. dirs. 1978-79, exec. bd. 1980-82, pres. 1983, chmn. bd. dirs. 1984). Republican. Roman Catholic. Avocations: music, tennis. Home: PO Box 6852 Hilton Head Island SC 29938-6852 Office: PO Box M Sioux Falls SD 57101-1937

VAN PELT, ROBERT IRVING, firefighter; b. Chgo., May 4, 1931; s. Irving Henry and Lillian Christene (Balder) Van P.; m. Donna Arlene Bengtson, Feb. 3, 1962; children: Robert Scott, Barbara Gail, James Arthur. Grad. high sch., Chgo. Fire dept. capt. Chgo. Fire Dept., 1954-89, ret., 1989. Dir. Edgebrook Cmty. Assn., Chgo., 1974-95, U. Ill. Dad's Assn., 1988-92; dist. vice chmn. programs Chgo. Area coun. Boy Scouts Am., 1985-93; scouting coord. Edgebrook Luth. Ch., Chgo., 1971—; mem. PTA Edgebrook Sch., Taft H.S. With U.S. Naval Air Res., 1949-65. Decorated Combat Air Crew Wings, 1951, Armed Svcs. medal, 1961; recipient Award of Merit, Boy Scouts Am., 1982, Silver Beaver award, 1987, Svc. award VFW, 1987, Lamb award Luth. Ch., 2000; inductee Chgo. Sr. Citizen Hall of Fame, 2000; PTA scholar, 1956. Mem. Naval Air Mus. (founding life), Exptl. Aviation Assn., War Birds Am.,

E.A.A. War Bird Squadron 4, Am. Legion, Order of Arrow, Liberator (San Diego), U.S. Navy Meml. Washington (plank). Avocations: photography, woodworking, model making. Home: 6317 N Hiawatha Ave Chicago IL 60646-4219

VAN PRAAG, HERMAN MEIR, psychiatrist, educator, researcher; b. Schiedam, The Netherlands, Oct. 17, 1929; s. Marinus Maurits and Charlotte Frederique (Leverpoll) V.P.; m. Cornelia Eikens; children: Marinus, Gido, Charlotte, Bart. MD, Leiden U., The Netherlands, 1956; PhD in Neurobiology, U. Utrecht, The Netherlands, 1962. Chief of staff dept. psychiatry Dijkzigt Hosp., Rotterdam, The Netherlands, 1963-66; founder, head dept. biol. psychiatry Psychiat. Univ. Clinic State U., Groningen, The Netherlands, 1966-77; prof., head dept. psychiatry Acad. Hosp. State U., Utrecht, 1977-82, Albert Einstein Coll. Medicine, Bronx, N.Y., 1982-92; from prof., chmn. dept. psychiatry and neuropsychology to sci. adv. Acad. Hosp. U. Maastricht, Netherlands, 1992—2002, sci. advisor dept. psychology and neuropsychology, 2002—. Emeritus prof. Albert Einstein Coll. Medicine, 1992—; psychiatrist-in-chief Montefiore Med. Ctr., Bronx, 1982—92; Lady Davis vis. prof. Hebrew U. Hadassah U. Hosp., Jerusalem, 1976—77; head WHO Nat. Ref. Ctr. for Study of Psychotropic Drugs, 1969, Who Collaborating Ctr. for Rsch. and Tng. in Biol. Psychiatry, 1974; founder Found. for Psychiatry and Religion; guest lectr. numerous univs. around the world. Editor: Psychiatria Neurologia Neurochirurgia, 1968-70, Advances in Biological Psychiatry, 1978—; editor-in-chief Psychiatria Neurologia Neurochirurgia, 1971-74, Biology of Behavior, 1975-82, Handbook of Biological Psychiatry, 1975-81, Einstein Monograph Series in Experimental and Clinical Psychiatry, 1988—; European chief-editor Progress in Neuro-Psychopharmacology, 1993—; mem. editl. bd. numerous publs. in field; reviewer Am. Jour. Psychiatry, Archives of Gen. Psychiatry, Jour. Nervous and Mental Disease; mem. internat. scientific commn. Jour. Brazilian Psychiat. Assn. Decorated Knight in the Order of the Dutch Lion, Order Beatrix of The Netherlands, 1988; recipient numerous awards and honors. Fellow Am. Coll. Neuropsychopharmacology; mem. Royal Acad. of Scis. of The Netherlands, Soc. Biol. Psychiatry, Collegium Internationale Neuro-Psychopharmacologicum, Assn. for Advancement of Psychotherapy, Internat. Group for Study of Affective Disorders, Internat. Soc. Psychoneuroendocrinology, European Brain and Behavior Soc., Internat. Assn. for Suicide Prevention, Brit. Pharmacol. Soc., European Soc. for Clin. Investigation, Bataafsch Genootschap der Proefondervindelijke Wijsbegeerte, Am. Coll. Neuropharmacology, Deutsche Gesellschaft fur Psychiatrie und Nervenheilkunde, Israel Med. Assn., Psychiat. Rsch. Soc., N.Y. Acad. Medicine, Am. Psychopathol. Assn., Internat. Coll. Neurobiology, Biol. Psychiatry and Psychopharmacology, Serotonin Club, Internat. Soc. for Rsch. on Emotion, Internat. Soc. Psychoneuroendocrinology, Arbeitsgemeinschaft fur Neuropsychpharmakologie und Pharmakopsychiatrie. Office: Acad Hosp Maastricht PO Box 5800 6202 AZ Maastricht Netherlands E-mail: willeke.beekers@spsy.azm.nl.

VAN PRAAGH, RICHARD, pediatrician, pediatric cardiologist, pathologist; b. London, Can., Apr. 11, 1930; came to U.S., 1956; s. David and Helen (Anderson) Van P.; m. Stella Zacharioudakis, June 16, 1962; children: Andrew, Helen, Alexander. MD, U. Toronto, Ont., Can., 1954; AM, Harvard U., 1989. Diplomate Am. Bd. Pediatrics (Am. Sub-bd. Pediatric Cardiology). Intern Toronto Gen. Hosp., 1954-55; intern in pediatrics Hosp. Sick Children, Toronto, 1955-56; asst. resident in pathology Children's Hosp., Boston, 1956-57, sr. resident, 1957-58; sr. resident in internal medicine Sunnybrook Hosp., Toronto, 1958-59; fellow in pediatric cardiology Johns Hopkins Hosp., Balt., 1959-60; fellow in cardiopulmonary physiology Mayo Clinic, Rochester, Minn., 1960-61; sr. rsch. fellow in pediatric cardiology Hosp. Sick Children, 1961-63; assoc. pathologist Hektoen Inst. Med. Rsch., Chgo., 1963-64, asst. dir., 1964-65; dir. Cardiac Registry Children's Hosp., Harvard Med. Sch., Boston, 1965—. Vis. scientist dept. embryology Carnegie Instn., Balt., 1966; vis. prof. Columbia U., N.Y.C., 1992, U. Mich., Ann Arbor, 1992, Washington U., St. Louis, 1993, Chinese Acad. Med. Scis., Beijing, 1993; invited lectr. Asian Soc. Cardiovascular Surgery, Nagoya, Japan, 1994, Asian-Pacific Congress Pediatric Cardiology, Taipei, Taiwan, 1994, Internat. Symposium Pediatric Cardiology, Punta del Este, Uruguay, 1994, Internat. Heart Sch., Bergamo, Italy, 1995; vis. prof. C.S. Mott Children's Hosp., U. Mich. Med. Ctr., Ann Arbor, 1994, U. Iowa Hosps. and Clinics, Iowa City, 1995, Duke U. Med. Ctr., Durham, N.C., 1995, Izaak Walton Killam Hosp. for Children, Halifax, Can., 1995, Herzzentrum der U. Kütn, Cologne, Germany, 1998; F. Marsico lectr. Nat. Congress Italian Soc. Pediatric Cardiology, Fiuggi, Italy, 1995; Garbose Family lectr. Nat. Children's Med. Ctr., Washington, 1998. Author: Survival, 1985; editor: Etiology and Morphogenesis of Congenital Heart Disease, 1980; mem. editorial bd. Am. Jour. Cardiology, 1970-75, 81-96, Circulation, 1974-78, 86-90, Jour. Am. Coll. Cardiology, 1982-88. Co-recipient Disting. Lifetime Achievement award for 1999, Soc. Cardiovascular Pathology. Fellow Am. Coll. Cardiology; mem. Am. Heart Assn. (Coun. on Disease in the Young). Avocations: reading, writing, public speaking, traveling. Office: Children's Hosp 300 Longwood Ave Boston MA 02115-5737

VAN PUTTEN, MARK, environmentalist; b. Mich. 3 children. Grad. magna cum laude, U. Mich. Founding dir. Great Lakes Natural Resource Ctr., Ann Arbor, Mich., 1982—96; pres., CEO Nat. Wildlife Fedn., Reston, Va., 1996—. Avocation: fishing, hiking.. Office: Nat Wildlife Fedn 11100 Wildlife Ctr Dr Reston VA 20190-6000

VAN PUTTEN, MAURICE H.P.M. applied mathematician; b. Aklmaar, N.H., Aug. 21, 1964; s. Anton F.P. and Maria (Veeken) van P. MSc in Elec. Engring., Delft (Netherlands) U. Tech., 1986; MSc, U. Del., 1988; PhD in Applied Math., Calif. Inst. Tech., 1992. Rschr. U. Calif., Santa Barbara, 1992-94, Cornell U., Ithaca, N.Y., 1994-96; asst. prof. math. MIT, Cambridge, 1996—. Co-founder VP Instruments B.V., The Netherlands. Contbr. articles to profl. jours. Mem. Am. Astron. Soc., Am. Phys. Soc., Am. Math. Soc., Soc. Indsl. and Applied Math. Achievements include patents in field. Office: MIT 77 Massachusetts Ave Rm 2-378 Cambridge MA 02139-4307

VAN PUTTEN, PAUL LAWRENCE, II, communications executive; b. Chgo., May 11, 1964; s. Paul Lawrence, Sr. and Gloria Yvonne (Nebblett) van P. BA in Comm., Oakwood Coll., Huntsville, Ala., 1991; MS in Media Mgmt., U. Wis., Menomonie, 1992; PhD in Communication, LaSalle U., Manderville, La. Cert. profl. audio engr. Prodn. mgr. Van's Litho Svc., Ft. Lauderdale, Fla., 1983-87; v.p. Teruya Media, Sunrise, 1987-88; videographer, prodn. asst. Oak Prodns., Huntsville, 1988-91; prodr., dir. Instrl. TV, Menomonie, 1991-92; asst. dir. mktg. Off-Shore Entertainment, Hollywood, Fla., 1992-93; sr. prodr. WJMK Prodns., Boca Raton, 1993-94; asst. prof. comm. Oakwood Coll., Huntsville, 1994-96; v.p. visual prodn. VLS, Inc., Ft. Lauderdale, 1996—. Bd. dirs. Bionic Web.com; media cons. United Negro Coll. Fund, Huntsville, 1994-96, Atlanta Olympic Broadcast com., 1994-96. Writer, prodr. Jes'Us Prodns., Huntsville, 1993-96; exec. prodr. Young Adventist's With a Message Prodns., Huntsville, 1994-96, (video) The Presidents of Oakwood Coll. 1896-1996, 1995, OUTREACH, 1995-96, 100 Years in 5 Minutes, 1996. Sponsor Men of Distinction, 1994-96. Mem. Internat. TV Assn., So. Soc. Adventist Comm. (bd. dirs. 1994). Avocations: travel, gourmet cooking, in-line skating, music composition, writing. Office: 5256 NW 94th Ter Sunrise FL 33351-7750

VAN RAALTE, BARBARA G. realtor; b. Rochester, N.Y., Apr. 11, 1932; d. Maurice Harry and Estelle Belle (Breman) Goldman; m. John Allen Van Raalte, Sept. 5, 1954 (div. July 1974); children: John Allen Jr., Peter Baird, Thomas Douglas, Skye Van Raalte Herzog. BA in Econs. and Polit. Sci., Wellesley Coll., 1954; postgrad., Harvard Grad. Sch. Design, 1993, 95. Cert. buyer rep., N.C. Dir. devel. Stowe (Vt.) Sch., 1975-77; assoc. dir. devel. NYU Med. Ctr., The Rusk Inst. Rehab. Medicine, N.Y.C., 1977-80; dir. devel. Planned Parenthood of Vt., Burlington, 1980-83; realtor, sr. assoc. Foulsham Farms Real Estate, South Burlington, 1983-95, Trombley Real Estate, Burlington, 1995-97; sr. assoc. CBR Re/Max Preferred Real Estate, South Burlington, 1997-99; sr. assoc. Pall Spera Co. Real Estate, Stowe, Vt., 1999—. Bd. dirs., treas. Hist. Soc., Stowe, 1974-75; bd. dirs. emeritus Katonah (N.Y.) Mus. Art, 1980—; mem. Nat. Spkrs. Bur., United Jewish Appeal, 1982-84; guide Shelburne (Vt.) Farms, 1994—. Mem. Nat. Assn. Realtors, Vt. Assn. Realtors, Hadassah (bd. dirs. Mid. East affairs 1996-98). Jewish. Avocations: architecture, landscape design, photography, travel, cross country skiing. Home: 5 Southwind Dr Burlington VT 05401-5463 Office: Pall Spera Co Real Estate PO Box 539 Mountain Rd Stowe VT 05672 Fax: 802-253-9993.

VAN RAALTE, POLLY ANN, reading and writing specialist, photojournalist; b. N.Y.C., Sept. 22, 1951; d. Byron Emmanuel and Enid (Godnick) Van R. Student, U. London, 1972; BA, Beaver Coll., 1973; MS in Edn., U. Pa., 1974, EdD, 1994, West Chester State Coll., 1977. Title I reading tchr. Oakview Sch., West Deptford Twp. Sch. Dist., Woodbury, N.J., 1974-75, title I reading supr., 1975 summer; lang. arts coord. Main Line Day Sch., Mitchell Sch., Haverford, Pa., 1975-76; reading supr. Salvation Army, Phila., summer 1976; reading Huntingdon Jr. H.S., Abington (Pa.) Sch. Dist., 1976-78; reading specialist No. 2 Sch., Lawrence Pub. Sch., Inwood, N.Y., 1978-87; high sch. reading specialist Cedarhurst, 1988-93, Lawrence (N.Y.) H.S., 1988-93; elem. reading specialist No. 5 Sch., 1992—; reading specialist Hewlett (N.Y.) Elem. Sch., Hewlett-Woodmere Pub. Sch., 1987-88, Lawrence Mid. Sch., 1993-95; instr. reading and spl. edn. dept. Adelphi U., 1979—. Columnist South Shore Record, featured columnist, 1992—; columnist Boulevard Mag., 1995-97; photojournalist Manhattan Reports, 1997—; feature columnist www.TimBoxer.com. Bd. dirs., mem. exec. bd. Five Towns Cmty. Ctr., 1991-93, co-chmn. ednl. youth svcs. edn. com., 1991-93; cons. to sch. dists.; advisor Am. Biog. Inst., Inc.; coord. Five Towns Young Voter Registration, Hewlett, N.Y., summer 1971; chmn. class fund Beaver Coll., also mem. internat. rels. com. U. Pa. scholar, 1977-78; mem. assoc. divsn. Jewish Guild for Blind; mem. N.Y. City Sports Commn.; co-chair youth svcs. com. Mem. Internat. Reading Assn., Wis. Reading Assn., Nat. Coun. Tchrs. English, Nassau Reading Coun., N.Y. Reading Assn., Coun. Exceptional Children, Coun. for a Beautiful Israel, Nat. Assn. Gifted Children, Am. Assn. of the Gifted, Nat./State Leadership Tng. Inst. on the Gifted and Talented, Children's Lit. Assembly, N.Y. State English Coun., Assn. Curriculum Devel., Am. Israel Pub. Affairs Com., New Leadership Com. of Jewish Nat. Fund, State of Israel Bonds New Leadership, Simon Wiesenthal New Leadership Soc., Nat. Polit. Action Com., Am. Friends of Hebrew U. (torch com.), Technion Soc., Am. Friends David Yellin Tchr.'s Coll., Am. Friends Israel Philharm., Am. Friends of Tel Aviv U., Am. Israel Cultural Found., Hadassah, Film Soc. Lincoln Ctr., U.S. Olympic Soc., Friends of N.Y.C. Sports Commn., Cooper-Hewitt Mus., Mus. Modern Art, Met. Mus. Art, Whitney Mus., Phila. Mus. Art, Smithsonian Inst., Friends of Carnegie-Hall, Friends of Am. Ballet Theatre, Friends of Am. Theatre Wing, Women's Am. Orgn. for Rehab. Through Tng. (citi women divsn. N.Y.C.), U. Pa. Alumni Assn. N.Y.C., Dorot Soc., Human Rels. Club (sec.), Actors'Fund, Pi Lambda Theta, Kappa Delta Pi (sec.), Internat. Tennis Hall of Fame). Home: 26 Meadow Ln Lawrence NY 11559-1828 Office: #5 Sch Cedarhurst Ave Cedarhurst NY 11516

VAN RANST, ALFRED F. information technology security consultant; BS, Cornell U., 1974, MBA, 1976. CPA, Mass. Ptnr. KPMG LLP, Boston, 1975—. Office: KPMG LLP 99 High St Boston MA 02110-2320

VAN REES, CORNELIUS S. lawyer; b. N.Y.C., May 29, 1929; s. Cornelius Richard and Beatrice Martin (Shreve) Van R.; m. Virginia Vandewater, Mar. 15, 1953 (div. 1984); children: Pamela Millet Van Rees Lundquist, Claire Katherine; m. Alix McIvor, Jan. 2, 1985. BA, Denison U., 1951; JD, Columbia U., 1954. Bar: N.Y. 1956, U.S. Dist. Ct. (so. dist.) N.Y. 1956, Conn. 1994. Assoc. Thacher Proffitt & Wood, N.Y.C., 1956-62, ptnr., 1963-93, of counsel, 1994—. Mem. exec. com., officer, bd. dirs. Graham Corp.; lectr. in field. Writer in field. Trustee, sec. Williston Northhampton Sch.; mem. senate, honors and prizes com. Columbia U. Harlem Fisk Stone scholar Columbia U., 1954. Mem. ABA (coms. on internat. fin. trans., maritime fin. and devel. in bus. fin.), Alumni Fedn. Columbia U., Inc. (Alumni medal 1984, pres. 1979-81). Avocation: sailing. Home and Office: 35 Cove Side Ln Stonington CT 06378-2902

VAN REMMEN, ROGER, management consultant; b. Los Angeles, Sept. 30, 1950; s. Thomas J. and Elizabeth (Vincent) V.; B.S. in Bus., U. So. Calif., 1972. Account mgr. BBDO, Los Angeles, 1972-78; account mgr. Dailey & Assocs. Advt., L.A., 1978—, v.p., mgmt. supr., 1980-84, sr. v.p., 1985-90; dir. mktg. communications, Teradata, 1990-91, ptnr. Brown, Bernardy, Van Remmen Exec. Search, L.A., 1991—. Bd. dirs. Advt. Emergency Relief Fund., Richstone Family Ctr. Mem. Univ. So. Calif. Alumni Assn., Advt. Club of Los Angeles. Roman Catholic. Home: 509 3rd St Manhattan Beach CA 90266-6414 Office: Brown Bernardy Van Remmen 12100 Wilshire Blvd Ste M40 Los Angeles CA 90025-7122

VAN RENSSELAER, MILES, artist, sculptor; b. Morristown, N.J., Aug. 30, 1973; s. Robert Mickle Miles Van Rensselaer and Hilary Jenkins Prouty. BA, Kenyon Coll., 1996; cert. lang. study and art, Kegervan Inst., Indonesia, 1995. Studio mgr. Tobin Studios, Coopersburg, Pa., 1996—2001; founder, operator Van Rensselaer Studios, 2002—. Exhibited in group shows Heller Gallery, N.Y.C., 1999--, Marta Hewitt Gallery, Cin., 199--, Rachael Collections, Aspen, Colo., 1999. Recipient Art award Boston Globe, 1991, Harlov-Davis award Phillips Mill Art Assn., 1998, Centerfold winner Art Calender Mag., 1999; CGP grantee, 2001. Mem. Am. Craft Coun., Internat. Sculpture Ctr. Democrat. Avocations: photography, travel, S.E. Asia. Home: PO Box 272 Riegelsville PA 18077-0272 E-mail: babirussa8@aol.com.

VAN RHEE, JAMES ALAN, physician assistant, educator; b. Grand Rapids, Mich., Aug. 11, 1960; s. George Edwin and Meryl Jean Van Rhee; m. Tamara Jean Russell, Nov. 16, 1984; children: Christopher, Allison, Alec. BS in Med. Tech., Grand Valley State U., 1982; BS in Medicine, U. Iowa, 1989; MS in Physician Asst. Studies, Finch U., 1998. Cert. physician asst. Nat. Commn. Cert. Physician Assts. Med. technologist CBC Lab., Grand Rapids, 1982-86, U. Iowa Hosps. and Clinics, Iowa City, 1987-89; physician asst. Henry Ford Hosp., Detroit, 1989-90, Spectrum Health, Grand Rapids, 1990-2001; acad. coord. Grand Valley State U., Allendale, Mich., 1996-97; chairperson/program dir. dept. physician asst. Western Mich. U., Kalamazoo, 1997—. Fellow: Am. Acad. Physician Assts. (Packrat test item writer 1997—); mem.: Mich. Acad. Physician Assts. Republican. Avocations: baseball, sports. Office: Western Mich Univ 1903 W Michigan Ave Kalamazoo MI 49008 E-mail: jim.vanrhee@wmich.edu.

VAN RIPER, KENNETH ALAN, nuclear engineer; b. New Brunswick, Nj, Feb. 7, 1949; s. Raymond Walsh and Beulah Mae Van Riper. PhD, U. of Pa, Philadelphia, Pennsylvania, 1976; AB, Cornell U., Ithaca, New York, 1970. Propr. White Rock Sci., Los Alamos, N.Mex., 1995—; tech. staff Los Alamos Nat. Lab., 1981—95; rsch. assoc. U. of Ill., Urbana, Ill., 1978—81, U. of Chgo., Chicago, 1976—78. Editor: (book) Isolated Pulsars; contbr. articles to profl. jours. Mem.: Am. Phys. Soc., Am. Astron. Soc., Am. Nuc. Soc. Avocation: ice hockey. Home: PO Box 4729 Los Alamos NM 87544 Office: White Rock Science PO Box 4729 Los Alamos NM 87544

VAN RIPER, PAUL PRITCHARD, political science educator; b. Laporte, Ind., July 29, 1916; s. Paul and Margaret (Pritchard) Van R.; m. Dorothy Ann Dodd Samuelson, May 11, 1964; 1 child, Michael Scott Samuelson. AB, DePauw U., 1938; PhD, U. Chgo., 1947. Instr. Northwestern U., 1947-49, asst. prof. polit. sci., 1949-51; mgmt. analyst Office Comptroller Dept. Army, 1951-52; mem. faculty Cornell U., 1952-70, prof., 1957-70; chmn. gov. bd., exec. com. Cornell Social Sci. Research Center, 1956-58; prof., head dept. polit. sci. Tex. A&M U., 1970-77, prof., 1977-81, prof. emeritus, 1981—, coordinator M.P.A. program, 1979-81, named prof. Bush Sch. Govt. and Pub. Svc., 1997—. Vis. prof. U. Chgo., 1958, Ind. U., 1961, U. Strathclyde, Scotland, 1964, U. Mich., 1965, U. Okla., 1969-97, U. Utah, 1979. Author: History of the United States Civil Service, 1958, Some Educational and Social Aspects of Fraternity Life, 1961, (with others) The American Federal Executive, 1963, Handbook of Practical Politics, 3d edit., 1967; editor and co-author: the Wilson Influence on Public Administration, 1990. Mem. exec. com. Civil Svc. Reform Assn., N.Y., 1960-64, hist. adv. com. NASA, 1964-66; bd. dirs. Brazos Valley Cmty. Action Agy., 1975-79, Brazos County Hist. Commn., 1976—; charter mem. Brazos Heritage Soc., pres. 1977-79. Maj. AUS, 1942-46; lt. col. USAR ret. Decorated Croix de Guerre (France). Mem. Am. Polit. Sci. Assn., So. Polit. Sci. Assn., S.W. Polit. Sci. Assn. (exec.com. 1975-77), Am. Soc. Pub. Adminstrn. (nat adv. com. 1957-60, Dimock award 1984, Waldo award 1990), Internat. Personnel Mgmt. Assn., Rotary (pres. Bryan club 1991-92), Phi Beta Kappa, Beta Theta Pi (v.p. 1962, gen. sec. 1963-65), Pi Alpha Alpha, Pi Sigma Alpha, Phi Kappa Phi, Sigma Delta Chi. Republican. Baptist. Home: 713 E 30th St Bryan TX 77803-4789 Office: Tex A and M Univ Dept Polit Sci College Station TX 77843-4348

VAN RIPER, ROBERT AUSTIN, writer, retired public relations executive; b. Mt. Vernon, N.Y., June 18, 1921; s. Austin Millard and Gladys Brownell Van R.; m. Barbara Jean Jacobs, Dec. 2, 1944; children: Alexandra, Tracy. BA, Oberlin Coll., 1943. Acct. exec. Edward L. Bernays Pub. Rels., N.Y.C., 1946-50, N.W. Ayer & Son, Inc., N.Y.C., 1950-54, acct. supr. Phila., 1954-61, v.p. N.Y.C., 1961-67, sr. v.p., 1967-73; pub. rels. counsel Fin. Acctg. Standards Bd., Norwalk, Conn., 1973-91, ret., 1991. Author: (novels) A Really Sincere Guy, 1958, The Governor, 1970, (nonfiction) Setting Standards for Financial Reporting: FASB and the Struggle for Control of a Critical Process, 1994, A Life Divided: George Peabody, Pivotal Figure in Anglo-American Finance, Philanthropy and Diplomacy, 2000; contbr. articles to profl. jours. Bd. dirs., exec. com. United Fund, Phila., 1956-61; trustee Lawrence Hosp., Westchester County, 1966-73, v.p., 1971-73. Lt. (j.g.) USN, 1943-46. Mem. Pub. Rels. Soc. Am. (pres. Phila. chpt. 1960-61), Fairfield County Pub. Rels. Assn. (bd. dirs. 1987-89), Holland Soc., Bronxville Field Club (N.Y.). Presbyterian. Avocations: tennis, music. Home: 90 Glen Side Wilton CT 06897

VAN ROSENDAAL, JOHN, journalist; b. Steenbergen, The Netherlands, Nov. 18, 1962; s. Bas and Jo Van R.; m. Kyoko M. Shiotani, June 12, 1994; children: Kai, Maya. MS, Columbia Sch. of Journalism, 1990; Dutch LLM, Utrecht U., 1989. Nat. copyreader Dow Jones & Co., N.Y.C., 1990-91, staff corr. Zurich, 1992-93; U.S. corr. Elsevier, Het Financieele Dagblad, N.Y.C., 1993-98, Teleac/NOT, JvR Media, N.Y.C., 1997—; sr. v.p. PlanSponsor.com, Greenwich, Conn., 1999—. Fulbright grantee The Netherlands, 1989-90. Mem. Fgn. Press Assn. (asst. treas. 1997-99). Avocations: travel, photography. Office: PlanSponsor.com 125 Greenwich Ave Greenwich CT 06830-5527 E-mail: jvr@plansponsor.com.

VAN ROY, BENJAMIN, research scientist, educator; b. Bangkok, Thailand, Sept. 15, 1971; s. Edward and Amporn Van Roy. SB, SM, PhD, MIT. Asst. prof. Stanford U., Stanford, Mass., 1998—. V.p. of r & d Enuvis, Inc., San Francisco, 2000—02; rsch. scientist Unica Corp., Lincoln, Mass., 1993—96; bd. dir. Enuvis, Inc., San Francisco, 2000—. Contbr. chapters to books; author: (book) Solving Data Mining Problems through Pattern Recognition, 1997; contbr. articles to profl. jours. Recipient George C. Newton award, MIT, 1993, Morris J. Levin Meml. award, 1995, George M. Sprowls award, 1998, CAREER award, NSF, 2000; fellow Frederick E. Terman fellow, Stanford U., 1998. Mem.: IEEE, INFORMS. Office: Stanford University Management Science and Eng Terman Bldg Stanford CA 94305

VAN RY, GINGER LEE, school psychologist; b. Alexandria, Va., June 26, 1953; d. Ray Ellsworth Hensley and Bernice Anne (Weidel) Wolter; m. Willem Hendrik Van Ry, Aug 23, 1986; 1 child, Anika Claire. AA, U. Nev., Las Vegas, 1973; BA, U. Wash., 1983, MEd, 1985. Cert. sch. psychologist (nationally). Psychometrist The Mason Clinic, Seattle, 1980-84, supr., psychology lab., 1984-86; sch. psychologist Everett (Wash.) Sch. Dist., 1986—. Mem. profl. ednl. adv. bd. U. Wash. Sch. Psychology, Seattle, 1995—; mem. early childhood devel. del. to China, 2000. Author: (with others) Wash. State Assn. of Sch. Psychologists Best Practice Handbook, 1993. Co-pres. Lake Cavanaugh Hghts. Assn., Seattle, 1994-95, chmn. long-range planning com., 1995—. Mem. AAUW, NEA, NASP (nationally cert. sch. psychologist), Wash. State Assn. Sch. Psychologists (chair profl. devel. com. 1995-2001), Wash. State Edn. Assn., U. Wash. Alumni Assn. Democrat. Avocations: reading, travel, fgn. cultures, woodworking, horticulture. Office: The Everett Sch Dist PO Box 2098 Everett WA 98203-0098

VAN RYZIN, GARY JAMES, lawyer, accountant; b. Appleton, Wis., Apr. 26, 1953; s. Howard John and Roseanne Julie Van Ryzin; m. Pamela Jean Casey, Aug. 23, 1975; children: Kimberly, Andrew, Benjamin. MA, U. Ga., 1976; MBA in Acctg., Rosary Coll., 1979; MS in Bus., U. Wis., 1989, JD, 1994. CPA, Wis.; Bar: Wis., 1996, U.S. Dist. Ct. (we. dist.) Wis. 1996; cert. assn. exec., cert. mgmt. acct. Projects mgr. Nat. Roofing Contractors Assn., Chgo., 1977-80; v.p. fin. Credit Union Nat. Assn., Madison, Wis., 1980-88; CFO Bus. Graphics Group, 1989-94, Full Compass Sys., Ltd., Middleton, Wis., 1994-99; fin. mgr. Famous Footwear, Inc., 1999-2001; v.p. fin., contr. Great Lakes Higher Edn. Corp., Madison, 1999—. Recipient Winners Circle award Am. Soc. Assn. Execs., 1987. Fellow Wis. Inst. CPAs, AICPA; mem. Inst. Cert. Mgmt. Accts., Inst. Mgmt. Accts., ABA (taxation divsn.), Wis. Bar Assn., Constrn. Industry Fin. Mgrs. Assn., Beta Gamma Sigma, Kappa Tau Alpha. Home: 50 Fuller Dr Madison WI 53704-5925 Office: Great Lakes Higher Edn Corp 2401 International Ln Madison WI 53704 E-mail: gvanryzin@glhec.org.

VAN RYZIN, ROBERT RICHARD, magazine editor; b. Appleton, Wis., July 7, 1953; s. Richard Gerald and Adrianna Theodora (Koenen) Van R.; m. Rachel Marie Siler, May 31, 1975 (div. 1987); m. Sharon Ann Huber, Sept. 18, 1993. BA, U. Wis., Oshkosh, 1975, MA, 1986. Edit. staff World Coin News Krause Publs., Iola, Wis., 1986-88, edit. staff Numismatic News, 1988-92, mag. edit. Numismatic News, 1992-94, editor Coins Mag., Coin Prices Mag., 1994—. Spkr. in field. Author: Striking Impressions, 1992, Twisted Tails, 1995, Crime of 1873, 2001; contbg. author Grolier's New Book of Knowledge, 1993—, North American Coins and Prices, 1992—. Mem.: Soc. for U.S. Commemorative Coins (v.p. 2000—), Ctrl. States Numismatic Soc., Civil War Token Soc., Token and Medal Soc., Numismatists of Wis. (mem. bd. govs. 1984—2001, v.p. 1986—88, pres. 1988—90), Numismatic Lit. Guild (bd. dirs. 1998—2001), Am. Numismatic Assn. Democrat. Roman Catholic. Office: Krause Publs 700 E State St Iola WI 54990-0001

VAN SANT, JOANNE FRANCES, academic administrator; b. Morehead, Ky., Dec. 29, 1924; d. Lewis L. and Dorothy (Green) Van S. BA, Denison U., Granville, Ohio; MA, The Ohio State U.; postgrad., U. Colo. and The Ohio State U.; LLD (hon.), Albright Coll., 1975. Tchr., health and phys. edn. Mayfield (Ky). H.S., 1946—47; instr. Denison U., Granville, Ohio, 1948; instr. women's phys. edn. Otterbein Coll., Westerville, 1948-52, assoc. prof., 1955-62, dept. chmn., 1950-62, chmn. div. profl. studies, 1961-65, dean of women, 1952-60, 62-64, dean of students, 1964-93, v.p. student affairs, 1968-93; v.p., dean student affairs emeritus, 1993—; cons. Instnl. Advancement, 1993—. Co-pres. Directions for Youth, 1983-84, pres., 1984-85; bd. dirs. North Area Mental Health, Friendship Village of Columbus, 1996—, pres. bd., 1998—; trustee Westerville Civic Symphony at Otterbein Coll., 1983-88; active numerous other community orgns.; ordained elder Presbyn. Ch., 1967. Named to hon. Order of Ky. Cols., 1957; recipient Focus on Youth award Columbus Dispatch, 1983, Vol. of the Yr. award North Area Mental Health Svcs., 1982, citation Denison U., 1996. Mem. Am. Assn. Counseling and Devel., Ohio Personnel and Guidance Assn., Ohio Assn. Women Deans, Adminstrs., Counselors (treas., exec. bd. 1972-73), Nat. Assn. Student Personnel Adminstrs., Ohio Coll. Personnel Assn., Mortar Bd. (hon.), Zonta Internat. (pres. Columbus, Ohio club 1978-80, dist. gov. 1988-90, internat. svc. chmn. 1996-98, internat. found. bd. 1997-2001), Vocal Arts Resource Network (chair bd. dirs. 1994-96), Cap and Dagger Club, Torch and Key Hon., Order Omega, Alpha Lambda Delta, Theta Alpha Phi, others. Avocations: musical and children's theater production, choreography. Home: 9100 Oakwood Pt Westerville OH 43082-9643 Office: Otterbein Coll Instnl Advancement Westerville OH 43081 E-mail: deanvan@aol.com.

VAN SAVAGE, JOHN G. pediatric urologic and reconstructive surgeon; b. New Brunswick, N.J., Mar. 13, 1963; s. John Fabian and Philomena Mary (Beaton) Van Savage; m. Elizabeth Mary English, Sept. 21, 1996; 1 child Jacqueline A. ; children: Isabella M., John G. II. BA in Biology and French, Johns Hopkins U., 1985; MD, Vanderbilt U., 1989. Resident in surgery and urology U. N.C. Sch. Medicine, Chapel Hill, 1989-94; fellow in pediatric urology U. Toronto/Hosp. for Sick Children, 1994-96; asst. prof. surgery div. urology, dept. surgery U. Louisville Sch. Medicine, 1996—2001, dir. pediatric urology, regional urology, 2001—. Mem. surg. care Kosair Children's Hosp., Louisville, 1996—2001. Contbr. articles to profl. jours. Recipient James M. McLaughlin award in microbiology and immunology Vanderbilt U. Sch. Medicine, 1987, 1st prize Vanderbilt Rsch. Forum, 1987; Prostate Growth fellow NIH, 1992. Mem.: ACS, AMA, Soc.Fetal Urology, Soc. Pediatric Urology, Am. Acad. Pediatrics (urology sect.), N.Y. Acad. Scis., Assn. Acad.

Surgeons, Am. Urol. Assn. Republican. Roman Catholic. Avocations: sailing, windsurfing, skiing, roller blading, surrealism. Office: Regional Urology 255 Bert Kouns Shreveport LA 71106 E-mail: jvansavage@regionalurology.com.

VAN SCHAACK, ERIC, art historian, educator; b. Evanston, Ill., June 10, 1931; s. Cornelius Peter and Sigrid (Schold) Van S.; m. Carol Fryling, June 16, 1965; children— Elizabeth M., Leslie A. AB, Dartmouth Coll., 1953; PhD, Columbia U., 1969. Lectr., rsch. asst. The Frick Collection, N.Y.C., 1960-62; asst. prof. fine arts, then full prof. visual arts Goucher Coll., Balt., 1964-77; prof. and art history Colgate U., Hamilton, N.Y., 1977-96, chmn. dept. art and art history, 1978-83, prof. art and art history emeritus, 1996—; vis. prof. fine arts Md. Inst. Coll. Art Johns Hopkins U., Balt. Author: Master Drawings in Private Collections, 1962, Baroque Art in Italy, 1964; contbr. articles to profl. jours., encys. Served with U.S. Army, 1954-56 Grantee Fulbright/Italian Govt., 1962-63, Ford Found., 1972-73, Colgate U. faculty, 1979-80, 92-93, others. Mem. Coll. Art Assn., Am. Soc. Archtl. Historians, Nat. Trust Hist. Preservation Clubs: Hamilton. Home: 28 W Pleasant St Hamilton NY 13346-1216

VAN SCHILFGAARDE, JAN, retired agricultural engineer, government agricultural research service administrator; b. The Hague, Netherlands, Feb. 7, 1929; came to U.S., 1946, naturalized, 1957; married; 3 children. BS, Iowa State Coll., 1949, MS, 1950, PhD in Agrl. Engring. and Soil Physics, 1954. Instr., assoc. agrl. engr. Iowa State Coll., 1949-54; asst. prof. agrl. engring. N.C. State Coll., 1954-57, assoc. prof., 1957-62, prof., 1962-64; drainage engr. Agrl. Rsch. Svc. USDA, Raleigh, N.C., 1954-64; chief water mgmt. engr. soil/water conservation rsch. div. UDSA, Beltsville, Md., 1964-67, assoc. dir., 1967-71, dir., 1971-72; dir. Salinity Lab. USDA, Riverside, Calif., 1972-84, dir. Mountain States Area Agrl. Rsch. Svc. Ft. Collins, Colo., 1984-86, assoc. dir. no. plains area Agrl. Rsch. Svc., 1986-91, assoc. dep. adminstr. for natural resources Agrl. Rsch. Svc. Beltsville, Md., 1991-96, dir. Pacific West area, 1996-97; ret., 1997. Vis. prof. Ohio State U., 1962 Mem. ASCE, NAE, Am. Soc. Agrl. Engrs., Soil Sci. Soc., Soil Conservation Soc. Am. E-mail: j.-r.vanschlifgaarde@worldnet.att.net.

VAN SCOTTER, RICHARD DALE, education policy executive; b. Elkhorn, Wis., Sept. 2, 1939; s. Henry Irving and Helen Evelyn (MaGill) Van S.; m. Suzanne Starmer, Feb. 29, 1964 (div.); children: Shannon, Philip; m. Pamela Gale Burnett, Aug. 15, 1987; 1 child, Caitlin. BA, Beloit (Wis.) Coll., 1961; MA, U. Wis., 1966; PhD, U. Colo., 1971. Tchr. Homewood Flossmoor H.S., Flossmoor, Ill., 1966-68; adj. prof. U. Colo., Boulder, 1971-77; asst. prof. Grinnell (Iowa) Coll., 1973-77; curriculum dir. Social Issues Resources, Inc., Boca Raton, Fla., 1977-83; project dir., writer IBM Corp., 1983-86; v.p. edn. Jr. Achievement, Inc., Colorado Springs, Colo., 1986—. Adj. prof. U. Colo., Colorado Springs, 1993—; mem. editl. bd. Citizens' Project, Colorado Springs, 1992—; pres. governing bd. The CIVA Sch., a charter h.s., 1997—. Author: Public Schooling in America, 1991, Social Foundations of Education. Mem. advocacy com. Citizens' Goals, 1993; bd. dirs. Citizen's Project, 1995. Lt. USN, 1961-65. Mem. ASCD, Nat. Coun. Social Studies. Avocations: running, bicycling. Office: Jr Achievement Inc One Education Way Colorado Springs CO 80906

VAN SCOY, GARY, social services administrator; b. Williamsport, Pa., Feb. 12, 1950; s. Thomas Van Scoy and Velma Lee (Coats) Valentine; m. Paula Maria Kovach, May 31, 1975; 1 child, Justin. BA in Sociology, King's Coll., 1972; MSW, Marywood Coll., 1974. Lic. social worker. Child abuse specialist Childrens Bur. Lehigh County, Allentown, Pa., 1974-76; program founder Parents Anonymous, Wilkes-Barre, 1976-78; family counselor Cath. Social Svcs., 1976-80, program dir., 1980-86, asst. dir. Scranton, Pa., 1986-91, exec. dir., 1991-93; sr. outpatient therapist Children Svc. Ctr., Wilkes-Barre, Pa., 1993—, dir. managed care, 1994—. Pres. Child Welfare Luzerne County, Wilkes-Barre, 1978-80. Bd. dirs. St. Michael's Sch., Tunkhannock, Pa., 1986-89; alumni mem. Leadership Wilkes-Barre, 1984. Named Outstanding Young Citizen, Scranton Jaycees, 1988; recipient award of harmony Barbershops Singers, 1980, Disting. Svc. award Wilkes-Barre Jaycees, 1980, Benjamin Rush award Luzerne County Med. Soc., 1980, 449th Daily Point of Light award Pres. of U.S., 1991. Mem. NASW (Social Worker of Yr. award 1989), KC (4 degree). Democrat. Roman Catholic. Avocations: swimming, photography. Home: 300 Chapel St Swoyersville PA 18704-1966 Office: Children Svc Ctr 335 S Franklin St Wilkes Barre PA 18702-3808

VANSELOW, NEAL ARTHUR, university administrator, physician; b. Milw., Mar. 18, 1932; s. Arthur Frederick and Mildred (Hoffmann) Vanselow; m. Mary Ellen McKenzie, June 20, 1958; children: Julie Ann, Richard Arthur. AB, U. Mich., 1954, MD, 1958, MS, 1963. Diplomate Am. Bd. Internal Medicine, Am. Bd. Allergy and Immunology. Intern Mpls. Gen. Hosp., 1958—59; resident Univ. Hosp., Ann Arbor, Mich., 1959—63; instr. medicine U. Mich., 1963—64, asst. prof., 1964—68, assoc. prof., 1968—72, prof., chmn. dept. postgrad. medicine and health professions edn., 1972—74; dean Coll. Medicine U. Ariz., Tucson, 1974—77; chancellor med. ctr. U. Nebr., Omaha, 1977—82, v.p., 1977—82; v.p. health scis. U. Minn., 1982—89, prof. internal medicine, 1982—89; chancellor Tulane U. Med. Ctr., New Orleans, 1989—94, chancellor emeritus, 1997—; prof. internal medicine Tulane U., 1989—97, prof. internal medicine emeritus, 1997—. Adj. prof. health sys. mgmt. Tulane U., New Orleans, 1993—99, prof. emeritus, 1999—; chmn. Joint Bd. Osteo. and Med. Examiners Ariz., 1974—77; chmn. coun. on Grad. Med. Edn. Dept. Health and Human Svcs., 1986—91; mem. com. on educating dentists for future Inst. Medicine NAS, 1993—95, chairperson com. on future of primary care, 1994—96, co-chairperson com. on U.S. physician supply, 1995—96, scholar in residence, 1994—95, mem. com. to assess occupl. health and safety tng. needs, 1999—2000; chairperson continuing eval. panel Am. Internat. Health Alliance, 2000—01; mem. adv. com. Medschool.com, 2000—. Panel on interdisciplinary health profl. edn. Nat. League Nursing, 1996—97; exec. com. United Way Midlands, 1980—82, vice-chmn. 1981 campaign; mem. Commn. on Health Professions Pew Charitable Trusts, 1990—92, 1997—99, Commn. on the Future of Med. Edn. U. Calif, 1996—97; mktg. mgmt. governing coun. U. Hosp. Consortium, 1993—95; trustee Meharry Med. Coll., 1996—; pres., chmn. bd. Am. Friends London Sch. Hygiene and Tropical Medicine, 1998—; com. on relationships between medicine and nursing Josiah Macy Jr. Found., 1999—2000; mem. Gov.'s Pan Am. Commn., La., 1991—92; bd. dirs. Devel. Authority for Tucson's Economy, 1975—77, Minn. High Tech. Coun., 1983—86, Minn. Coalition for Health Care Costs, 1983—87, La. Health Care Authority, 1989—90, United Way Greater New Orleans Area, 1992—97; bd. dirs., exec. com. Health Planning Coun. Midlands, Omaha, 1978—82, v.p., 1981—82. Fellow: ACP (workgroup on physician workforce and financing med. edn. 1996), Am. Coll. Physician Execs., Am. Acad. Allergy; mem.: Inst. Med. NAS, Soc. Med. Adminstrs., Assn. Acad. Health Ctrs. (bd. dirs. 1983—89, chmn. bd. dirs. 1988), Rio Verde (Ariz.) Cmty. Assn. (bd. dirs. 2000—), Phi Beta Kappa, Nu Sigma Nu, Beta Theta Pi, Alpha Omega Alpha, Sigma Xi. Office: Tulane U 18942 E Mountainaire Dr Rio Verde AZ 85263-7093

VAN SELST, MARK G(ORDON) A(EGID), psychology educator, researcher; b. Castlegar, B.C., Can., Nov. 3, 1967; came to U.S., 1995; s. Aegid and Anna Van Selst. BA, U. B.C., 1989; MA, U. Waterloo, Ont., Can., 1991, PhD, 1995. NRC postdoctoral rsch. assoc. NASA-Ames Rsch. Ctr., Moffett Field, Calif., 1995-98, rsch. assoc., 1998-2000; asst. prof. Dept. of Psychology, San Jose State U., 1997—. Contbr. articles to profl. jours. Mem. Psychonomic Soc., Cognitive Sci. Soc., Can. Soc. for Brain Behavior and Cognitive Sci., Calif. Faculty Assn., Berkeley Yacht Club (exec. com.). Avocation: yacht racing. Home: 1 Seawall Dr Berkeley CA 94710 Office: Dept of Psychology San Jose State U 1 Washington Sq San Jose CA 95192-0120 E-mail: mvselst@email.sjsu.edu.

VAN SETERS, JOHN, biblical literature educator, retired; b. Hamilton, Ont., Can., May 2, 1935; s. Hugo and Anne (Hubert) Van S.; m. Elizabeth Marie Malmberg, June 11, 1960; children: Peter John, Deborah Elizabeth. BA, U. Toronto, 1958; MA, Yale U., 1959, PhD, 1965; BD, Princeton Theol. Sem., 1962; ThD (hon.), U. Lausanne, Switzerland, 1999. Asst. prof. dept. Near Eastern studies Waterloo Luth. U., 1965-67; assoc. prof. Old Testament Andover Newton Theol. Sch., 1967-70; assoc. prof. dept. Near Eastern studies U. Toronto, 1970-76, prof., 1976-77; James A. Gray prof. Bibl. lit., dept. religion U. N.C., Chapel Hill, 1977-2000, chmn. dept. religious studies, 1980-88, 93-95, prof. emeritus, 2000—. Adj. prof. dept. religion and culture Wilfrid Laurier U., 2000—. Author: The Hyksos: A New Investigation, 1966, Abraham in History and Tradition, 1975, In Search of History, 1983, Der Jahwist als Historiker, 1987, Prologue to History, 1992, The Life of Moses, 1994, The Pentateuch, 1999, A Law Book for the Diaspora, 2002. Recipient James Henry Breasted prize Am. Hist. Assn., 1985, Book award Am. Acad. Religion, 1986; Woodrow Wilson fellow, 1958; J.J. Obermann fellow, 1962-64; Guggenheim fellow, 1979-80; NEH fellow, 1985-86, Am. Coun. Learned Socs. fellow, 1991-92, sr. rsch. fellow Cath. U. Leuven, Belgium, 1998. Mem. Soc. Bibl. Lit., Am. Schs. Oriental Rsch., Soc. Study of Egyptian Antiquities, Am. Oriental Soc., Soc. for Old Testament Study, Cath. Bibl. Assn., Can. Soc. Bibl. Studies (pres. 1999-2000). Home: 600 Maple Forest Pl Waterloo ON Canada N2T 2S8 E-mail: john.seters@sympatico.ca.

VANSICKLE, BARBARA JEAN, computer services coordinator; b. Parkersburg, W.Va., Oct. 18, 1948; d. Robert Syrl and Evelyn June (Anderson) McGraw; m. John Vernon Morrison Jr., Oct. 7, 1968 (dec. June 1981); children: John Vernon III, Deborah Margarette; m. Danny Ray Vansickle, Oct. 1, 1983. AS, Shawnee State Community Coll., 1984; BA, Wilmington Coll., 1990, , 1990. Keypunch operator Columbus (Ohio) Mut. Life Ins. Co., 1966-67, Steele Data Processing, Washington Court House, Ohio, 1971-74; data entry operator F&R Lazarus, Columbus, 1978-79; clk. III Parker Hannifin Corp., Waverly, Ohio, 1979-80; computer programmer Shawnee State U., Portsmouth, 1981-88; coord. computer svcs. Wilmington (Ohio) Coll., 1988-92, Hamilton Clermont Coop. Assn., Mount Healthy, Ohio, 1992—. Instr. part-time Southeastern Bus. Coll., Portsmouth, 1982-83. Mem. Valley High Sch. PTA, Lucasville, Ohio, 1982-85; pres. Valley High Sch. Band Boosters, 1986-87, v.p., 1985-86. Mem. Data Processing Mgmt. Spl. Interest Group for Edn., Data Processing Mgmt. Assn., Digital Equip. Corp. Users Soc. (assoc.). Republican. Avocations: reading, sewing, bowling, racquetball. Office: Hamilton Clermont Coop Assn 7615 Harrison Ave Cincinnati OH 45231-3107

VAN SICKLE, BRUCE MARION, federal judge; b. Minot, N.D., Feb. 13, 1917; s. Guy Robin and Hilda Alice (Rosenquist) Van S.; m. Dorothy Alfreda Hermann, May 26, 1943; children: Susan Van Sickle Cooper, John Allan, Craig Bruce, David Max. BSL, JD, U. Minn., 1941. Bar: Minn. 1941, N.D. 1946. Pvt. practice law, Minot, 1947-71; judge U.S. Dist. Ct. N.D., 1971-85, sr. judge, 1985—. Mem. N.D. Ho. of Reps., 1957, 59. Served with USMCR, 1941-46. Mem. ABA, N.D. Bar Assn., N.W. Bar Assn., Ward County Bar Assn., Am. Trial Lawyers Assn., Am. Coll. Probate Counsel, Am. Judicature Soc., Bruce M. Van Sickle Inns of Ct., Masons, Shriners, Elks, Delta Theta Phi. Office: US Dist Ct US Courthouse Rm 428 PO Box 670 Bismarck ND 58502-0670

VAN SICKLE, FREDERICK L. federal judge; b. 1943; m. Jane Bloomquist. BS, U. Wis., 1965; JD, U. Wash., 1968. Ptnr. Clark & Van Sickle, 1970-75; prosecuting atty. Douglas County, Waterville, Wash., 1971-75; judge State of Wash. Superior Ct., Grant and Douglas counties, 1975-79, Chelan and Douglas Counties, 1979-91, U.S. Dist. Ct. (ea. dist.) Wash., Spokane, 1991—. Co-chair rural ct. com. Nat. Conf. State Trial Judges, 1987-91. 1st lt. U.S. Army, 1968-70. Mem. Am. Adjudicature Soc., Wash. State Bar Assn., Masons (pres. Badger mountain lodge 1982-83), Scottish Rite, Spokane Rotary, Shriners. Office: US Dist Cts US Courthouse PO Box 2209 920 W Riverside Ave Rm 914 Spokane WA 99201-1010

VAN SIHERT, BARBARA, retired education educator, writer; b. Panora, Iowa, Dec. 14, 1935; d. Dean Leonard Culver and Lola Mae Rich; m. Logan Earl Van Sittert, June 9, 1957; 1 child Todd Van Sittert. PhD, Ariz. State U., 1975, MA, 1962; BS, Iowa State U., 1958. Tchr., adminstr. Phoenix Coll., 1962—98. Dir. honors program Phoenix Coll., 1982—98, dir. founder classics program, 1990—98. Contbr. articles. Exec. com. Ariz. Commn. of Arts, Phoenix, 1976—82; chmn. Charter Govt. Commn., 1980—81; pres. Maricopa Coll. Faculty Assn., 1980—82. Mem.: Nat. Soc. Arts & Letters. Home and Office: 7007 N Wilder Rd Phoenix AZ 85021 Fax: 602-997-2049.

VAN SLOOTEN, RONALD HENRY JOSEPH, dentist; b. Paterson, N.J., July 12, 1937; s. Henry and Edythe (De Marco) Van S.; m. Joyce Elenor Mandel, 1962 (div. 1969); children: Ronald Henry Jr., Timothy Jay, Lauren; m. Barbara Rose Durante, July 1, 1979; children: Jonathan Henry, Brian Joseph. DDS, Farleigh Dickinson U., 1962; FAGD, Acad. Gen. Dentistry, 1986. Dentist pvt. practice, Paterson, N.J., 1965-76, Ridgewood, 1969-78, Ho Ho Kus, 1978—; staff mem. Bainert Meml. Hosp., Paterson, 1966-75, Ridgewood Valley Hosp., 1975—; assoc. prof. Fairleigh Dickinson Dental Sch., Hackensack, N.J., 1973-90; pres. Van Slooten Harbour Marina Inc., Port Henry, N.Y., 1989—. Cons. N.J. Mfrs. Ins. Co., Trenton, 1966—. Pres. Fairleigh Dickinson Sch. Dentistry Alumni Assn., 1976-77. Lt. comdr. USN, 1962-65. Fellow Acad. Gen. Dentistry, Acad. Dentistry Internat.; mem. ADA, Internat. Dental Health Found., N.J. Dental Soc., Bergen County Dental Soc. (chmn. Nat. Dental Health Week citation 1970), Moriah C. of C., Ho-Ho-Kus C. of C. Republican. Roman Catholic. Avocations: racquetball, fishing, boating. Office: Ho Ho Kus Profl Bldg 110 Warren Ave Ho Ho Kus NJ 07423-1561

VANSONNENBERG, ERIC, physician; b. Jan. 11, 1947; s. George and Virginia vanS. MD, U. Cin. Cert.: Am. Bd. Internal Med.; Am. Bd. of Radiology. Resident, fellow, jr. faculty Harvard Med. Sch., Boston, 1977-82; from asst. prof. to prof. U. Calif., San Diego, 1983-93; prof., chmn. dept. radiology U. Tex. Med. Br., Galveston, 1993-98; vis. prof. radiology Harvard Med. Sch., 1999—; chief of radiology Dana Farber Cancer Inst. Radiology dir. UTMB Allied Health; Robert Parrish meml. lectr. Toronto Hosp., 1993; Chas. T. Dotter meml. lectr. Oreg. Health Scis. U., 1995, internal radiologist, Brigham and Women's Hosp., Harvard Med. Sch. Author manual; editor Jour. Interventional Radiology; inventor radiologic catheters, med. needles; Editor: Cardiovasc. Interventional Radiology. Mem. Soc. Gastrointestinal Radiology (pres.), Soc. Thoracic Radiology, Soc. Urol. Radiology, Soc. Advancement of Women's Imaging (exec. bd.), Internat. Soc. Hepato-Biliary Radiology (pres. 1995-96), Internat. Soc. Hepato-Biliary Pancreatic Radiology (pres. 1994), Exec. Comm. Dana Faribel Cancer Inst. Mem. Soc. Gastrointestinal Radiology (exec. bd.). Avocations: baseball, basketball, tennis, banjo, church choir, clogging. Office: 44 Bynner St Boston MA 02130-1127 E-mail: evansonn@ofci.harvard.edu.

VAN STAVOREN, WILLIAM DAVID, consultant, retired government official; b. Lunenburg, Va., Mar. 14, 1936; s. James Eugene and Marion Estelle (Boyer) Van S.; m. Rosa Kouyoundijian, Dec. 29, 1962; children: John, Christopher, Diane. BS, Va. Poly. Inst., 1960, MS, 1966. Budget analyst U.S. Treasury Dept., Washington, 1963-68; fin. mgr. AID, 1968-69, U.S. Dept. Justice, Washington, 1969-74, dep. asst. atty. gen., 1977-84, dep. assoc. atty. gen., 1984-85; mgmt. cons., 1985—; pvt. practice cons., 1986—. Mgmt. advisor Va. Commn. on State Govt. Mgmt., Richmond, 1974-76. Served with U.S. Army, 1954-56. Methodist. Office: 2526 E Meredith Dr Vienna VA 22181-4038

VAN STEENWYK, JOHN JOSEPH, health care plan consultant, educator; b. Mpls., July 25, 1931; s. Elmer Arnold and Marion Ione (Thompson) van S.; m. Janice Kevin Sharp, July 11, 1959; children: Jennifer Lee, Edward Arnold, Julie Ann. AB, Oberlin Coll., 1953; MBA, U. Pa., 1955. V.p., cons. The Segal Co., N.Y.C., 1957-81; pres. Health Econs., Inc., Spring House, Pa., 1982—. Clin. asst. prof. cmty. and preventive medicine, N.Y. Med. Coll., Valhalla, N.Y., 1980—. With USN, 1955-57. Mem. APHA, Assn. for Health Svcs. Rsch, Am. Assn. Health Plans. Episcopalian. Avocation: gardening. Home: 921 Tennis Ave PO Box 710 Ambler PA 19002-2312 Office: Health Economics Inc 768 N Bethlehem Pike Spring House PA 19477 E-mail: healtheconomics@compuserve.com.

VAN STONE, WILLIAM WEBB, psychiatrist; b. Denver, Mar. 14, 1929; s. Wilfred Douglas and Cora Coleman (Kampf) Van S.; m. Joan Kay Kinnear, Nov. 27, 1958; children: Lisa Kay, Kathryn Louise, David William. BA, Swarthmore Coll., 1951; MD, Cornell U., 1955. Intern Mary Hitchcock Meml. Hosp., Hanover, N.H., 1955-56; resident Menninger Sch. Psychiatry, Topeka, 1958-61; unit chief Topeka VA Hosp., 1963-67; asst. chief of staff Palo Alto (Calif.) VA Med. Ctr., 1967-89, chief treatment svcs., 1989-2000; assoc. chief for psychiatry VA Central Office, Washington, 2001—. Clin. assoc. prof. psychiatry emeritus Stanford (Calif.) U. Med. Sch., 1968—; mem. faculty Menninger Sch. Psychiatry, 1963-67. Contbr. 30 articles to profl. jours., chpts. to books. Bd. chmn. Miramonte Mental Health Assn., Palo Alto, 1976; pres. Northern Calif. Psychiat. Soc., San Francisco, 1986-87, Sertoma Club, Palo Alto, 1982; bd. dirs. Community Sch. Music & Arts, Mountain View, Calif., 1969-75. Capt. USNR, 1956-79. Postdoctoral fellow C.F. Menninger Meml. Hosp., 1961-63. Fellow Am. Psychiat. Assn. (life); mem. Am. Assn. Geriatric Psychiatrists, Washington Psychiat. Assn., Group Advancement Psychiatry (com chmn.). E-mail: wvsdc@aol.com.

VANSTROM, MARILYN JUNE CHRISTENSEN, retired elementary education educator; b. Mpls., June 10, 1924; d. Harry Clifford and Myrtle Agnes (Hagland) Christensen; m. Reginald Earl Vanstrom, Mar. 20, 1948; children: Gary Alan, Kathryn June Vanstrom Marinello. AA, U. Minn., 1943, BS, 1946. Cert. elem. tchr., N.Y., Ill. Tchr. Pub. Sch., St. Louis Park, Minn., 1946-47, Deephaven, 1947-50, Chicago Heights, Ill., 1950-52, Steger, 1964, substitute tchr. Dobbs Ferry, N.Y., 1965-72, Yonkers, 1965-92. Mem. Ch. Women, Christ Meml. Luth. Ch. Mem. AAUW (life, pres. So. Westchester br. 1988-90, Ednl. Found. award 1990), Morning Book Club, Evening Book Club (Met. West br. Minn., So. Westchester br. N.Y.), Yonkers Fedn. Tchrs. Democrat. Avocations: painting, sketching, choir, piano, travel. Home: 12300 Marion Ln W Apt 2105 Minnetonka MN 55305-1317

VAN STRYLAND, ERIC WILLIAM, physics educator, consultant; b. South Bend, Ind., June 3, 1947; s. Robert Gerritt and Nancy Jean (Coggan) Van S.; m. Barbara Van Strylan, Dec. 31, 1987. BS in Physics, Humboldt State U., 1970; MS in Physics, U. Ariz., 1975, PhD in Physics, 1976. Tchg. asst. in physics U. Ariz., Tucson, 1970-72, rsch. asst. Optical Scis. Ctr., 1972-73, rsch. assoc. Optical Scis. Ctr., 1973-76; rsch. scientist Ctr. for Laser Studies U. So. Calif., 1976-78; asst. prof. physics U. North Tex., 1978-82, assoc. prof. physics, 1982-86, chmn. Ctr. for Applied Quantum Electronics, Physics, 1983-85, prof. physics, 1986-87, disting. rsch. prof., 1987, adj. prof., 1987-92; prof. physics and elec. engring. CREOL U. Ctrl. Fla., Orlando, 1987—. Vis. prof. physics Heriot-Watt U., Edinburgh, Scotland, 1985; hon. prof. Sch. Physics and Astronomy, U. St. Andrews, Scotland, 1995-96; presenter IEEE Conf. Laser Engring. and Applications, San Diego, 1978, Lasers 83, San Francisco, 1983, S.W. Conf. on Optics, Albuquerque, 1985, SPIE 1985 L.A. Tech. Symposium on Optical and Electo-Optical Engring., L.A., 1985, Optical Properties of Liquid Crystals Conf., Naples, Italy, 1986, Cetraro, Italy, 1990, Laser 87, Lake Tahoe, Nev., 1987, Internat. Conf. on Nonlinear Optics, Ashford Castle, Ireland, 1988, Optical Soc. Am., Santa Clara, Calif., 1988, Orlando, Fla., 1989, Kirtland AFB, 1989, Interdisciplinary Laser Sci. conf., Stanford, Calif., 1989, Lasers 89, New Orleans, 1989, Conf. on Nonlinear Optics, Kauai, Hawaii, 1990, Lasers 90, San Diego, 1990, Program on Eye Protection against the Battlefield Laser Threat, Washington, 1990, Nonlinear Optics 1991, Adelaide, Australia, 1991, Workshop on Liquid Cell Power Limiters, Washington, 1991, Am. Ceramic Soc., Crystal City, Va., 1991, 4th Conf. on Crystal Growth, Atlantic City, N.J., 1991, XIV Internat. Conf. on Coherent and Nonlinear Optics, Leningrad, 1991, 22nd Winter Colloquium on Quantum Electronics, Snowbird, Utah, 1992, 23th Winter Colloquium, 1993, Internat. Sch. on Nonlinear Photonics and Optical Physics, Capri, Italy, 1992, IQEC, Vienna, 1992, Gordon Rsch. Conf. on Crystal Growth, Oxnard, Calif., 1993. Author: (with others) Optical Materials, 1994, Nonlinear Optics of Organic Molecular and Polymeric Materials, 1995, Novel Optical Materials and Applications, 1995, among others; assoc. editor: The Handbook of Optics, 1994; topical editor Optics Letters, 1995—; mem. editl. bd. Rev. Sci. Instruments, 1978-81, Nonlinear Optics, 1991—; contbr. more than 100 articles to profl. jours. including IEEE Jour. Quantum Electronics, Phys. Rev., Optics Letters, Molecular Crystal Liquid, Jour. Chem. Physics, among others. Grantee NSF, 1981-83, 83-87, 87-91, 92-95, 94—, Rsch. Corp., 1979, 82-86, Naval Weapons Ctr., 1979-80, Office Naval Rsch., 1981-84, Robert A. Welch Found., 1981-84, Def. Advanced Rsch. Projects Agy., 1983-89, U.S. Army Night Vision Lab., 1984-86, 88-92, Night Vision-Electro-Optics Ctr., 1986-87, Battelle Columbus Labs., 1987-88, 92, Gen. Dynamics, 1987-88, Fla. High Tech. and Indsl. Coun., 1988, 89, 90, 91, McDonnell Douglas, 1988-89, Jet Propulsion Lab., 1988-89, Army Rsch. Office, 1990, SBIR with Schwartz E-O, 1991, Air Force Office Sci. Rsch., 1991—, Hughes Rsch. Labs., 1992, Dept. Sponsored Rsch. UCF, 1991—. Joint Svcs. Program Naval Air Warfare Ctr., 1993-97, NATO, 1994-96, 96-97, Jet Process Corp., 1994-96, DURIP, 1994-95, Rocketdyne Divsn., Rockwell Internat., 1994-95, among others. Fellow Optical Soc. Am. (edn. coun., laser safety stds. com., advisor Fla. student sect., chair nonlinear optics sect. tech. coun. 1993, quantum electronics divsn. tech. coun. 1994—, chair Fla. fundraising for educator's day ann. meeting Orlando, physics judge for 1991 Internat. Sci. and Engring. Fair Orlando); mem. IEEE (sr., ultrafast subcom.), Soc. Photo-Optical Instrumentation Engrs., Materials Rsch. Soc., Am. Phys. Soc., Laser Inst. Am. (bd. govs.), Phi Kappa Phi, Sigma Pi Sigma. Achievements include rsch. in characterization of the nonlinear optical properties of materials (particularly semiconductors), multiphoton absorption and associated nonlinear refraction, laser induced damage, measurement of ultrashort relaxation times, ultrashot pulse prodn., and ultrasensitive detection of nonlinear optical properties. Avocations: windsurfing, jogging. Office: U Ctrl Fla Ctr for Rsch Optics & Lasers 4000 Central Florida Blvd Orlando FL 32816-8005

VAN TASSEL, CHARLES J. physician, urologist; b. Indpls., Apr. 1, 1922; s. Charles J. and Irma (Weyerbacher) Van T.; m. Marjorie LIttle, Aug. 23, 1943; chldren: James W., Cynthia Van Tassel Yeo. AB, Wesleyan U., Middletown, Conn., 1943; MD, Ind. U., 1946. Diplomate Am. Bd. Urology. Resident in urology Ill. Med. Ctr., 1949-51; resident in surgery and pathology St. Vincent Hosp., Indpls., 1947-49, chmn. urology dept., 1960-96, pres., 1971-72; clin. prof. urology Ind. U. Med. Ctr., 1978—. Recipient Otis R. Bowen Disting. Leadership award, 1996, Disting. Physician award St. Vincent Hosp., 1997. Mem. AMA, ACS, Ind. State Med. Soc. (sr.), Marion County Med. Soc. (sr.), Am. Urol. Assn., Am. Assn. Clin. Urologists. Republican. Episcopalian. Avocations: fly fishing, golf. Home: 11607 Williams Creek Dr Carmel IN 46032-9511

VAN TASSEL, DANIEL ELLSWORTH, academic administrator, consultant, educator; b. Mpls., Apr. 28, 1940; s. Prosper Ellsworth and Margaret Theresa (Klanderud) Van T.; m. Rhoda Helen Howie, Sept. 21, 1962; children: Abigail Nell, Nathaniel Barron. BA, St. Olaf Coll., 1962; MA, U. Iowa, 1964, PhD, 1970. Instr. Concordia Coll., Moorhead, Minn., 1964-66, Chapman Coll., Orange, Calif., 1966-67; tchr., rsch. asst. U. Iowa, Iowa City, 1967-70; from asst. prof. to full prof., dean humanities div. Pacific Luth. U., Tacoma, 1970-81; v.p. acad. affairs, prof. English Muskingum Coll., New Concord, Ohio, 1981—. Contbr. articles to profl. jours. Mem., ruling elder Coll. Dr. Presbyn. Ch.; bd. dirs., mem. exec. Southeastern Ohio Symphony Orch. Shell grantee U.K., 1979, NEH grantee U. Va., 1979. Mem. Modern Lang. Assn. Am., North Cen. Assn. Colls. and Schs. (cons., evaluator), Thomas Hardy Soc., Ld.

VAN TASSEL, JAMES HENRY, retired electronics executive; b. LaCrosse, Wis., Feb. 15, 1929; s. John Henry and Agnes Cecilia (Anderson) Van T.; m. Mary Louise Carman, Dec. 23, 1961; children: John, James. BS, U. Wis.-LaCrosse, 1951; MS, Tex. Tech. Coll., 1957, PhD, 1959. Postdoctoral fellow Princeton U., N.J., 1959-60; mem. tech. staff, mgr. Tex. Instruments Co., Dallas, 1960-80; v.p. microelectronics div. NCR Corp., Dayton, Ohio, 1980-91; ret., 1991. Cons. in field; mem. adv. group on electron devices DOD, 1992-97; bd. dirs. Chartered Semiconductor, Singapore, 1994—. Contbr. articles to profl. jours.; patentee in field; co-inventor of hand-held caculator Bd. dirs. Dayton Philharm. Orch., 1983-89, Miamisburg (Ohio) Mound Cmty. Improvement Corp., 1993—. Recipient Florilege d'Or Am Ecia, Paris, 1976, Disting. Alumnus award U. Wis.-LaCrosse, 1979, Holley medal ASME, 1989. Episcopalian.

VAN TASSEL, LOWELL THOMAS, mathematics educator; b. Mpls., Jan. 31, 1932; s. Evan Thomas Van Tassel and Sophia Anna Huebner; m. Diane Laura Diedrich, June 14, 1953; children: Thomas, Laurie, Karin. BS, U. Minn., 1952, MA, 1962. Cert. secondary tchr. Calif. Rsch. asst. U. Minn., Mpls., 1954-56; math. tchr. San Diego Unified Sch. Dist., 1956-65; prof. math. San Diego C.C. Dist., 1965-92, prof. emeritus of math., 1992—. Dept. chmn. math. dept. San Diego City Coll., 1971-72, 74-75; math/physics instr. Naval Tgn. Ctr., San Diego, 1962-66; proctor profl. engring. exams State of Calif. License Bd., Sacramento, 1957-65. Contbr. articles to profl. jours. V.p. Am. Fedn. of Tchrs., San Diego, 1971-72; faculty advisor Ind. Dems. for Action San Diego City Coll., 1967-71; mem. Clairemont Dem. Club, San Diego, 1966-76; juror, criminal trial Superior Ct., San Diego, 1990; elder Holy Cross Luth. Ch., San Diego, 1972-74, 92-94. With USMC, 1951-54; USMCR,

1954-71, maj., 1966-71. Mem. Math. Assn. Am., Calif. Retired Tchrs. Assn., Marine Corps Mus., U. Minn. Alumni Assn. (life.), Nat. Coun. of Tchrs. of Math., Am. Fedn. of Tchrs. (retiree mem.), Phi Delta Kappa, Psi Chi. Lutheran. Avocations: travel, reading, word puzzles, games, bridge. Home: 5550 Lodi St San Diego CA 92117-1138 E-mail: lowellv@webtv.net.

VAN TASSEL, ROBERT ALFRED, cardiologist, consultant; b. Eau Claire, Wis., Dec. 29, 1938; s. Alfred Robert and Doris Myrtle Van Tassel; m. Betty Ilo Strandquist, July 9, 1960; children: Paul, Mary, John. BS, U. Minn., 1960, MD, 1964. Diplomate Am. Bd. Internal Medicine, Am. Bd. Cardiovasc. Disease. Intern Hennepin County Gen. Hosp., Mpls., resident in internal medicine; fellow U. Minn.; cons. cardiologist Mpls. Heart Inst., 1972—, also bd. dirs. Bd. dirs. Abbott Northwestern Hosp., Mpls., AtriTech Inc., Mpls., TriCardia LLC, Mpls., TriCardia Ventures. Fellow Am. Coll. Cardiology, Soc. Angiography and Interventions; mem. AMA, Minn. State Med. Assn. Avocations: travel, boating. Office: Mpls Heart Inst 920 E 28th St Ste 300 Minneapolis MN 55407-1139 E-mail: rvt@mplsheart.com.

VAN'T HOF, WILLIAM KEITH, lawyer; b. N.Y.C., Feb. 18, 1930; s. William and Nell (DeValois) Van't H.; m. Barbara Marie Rogers, Oct. 6, 1961; children: Sarah Lynn, David Edward. BA, Hope Coll., 1951; LLB, U. Mich., 1954. Bar: Mich. 1954, Conn. 1955, U.S. Dist. Ct. (we. dist.) Mich. 1956, U.S. Ct. Appeals (6th cir.) 1956. Assoc. Gumbart, Corbin, Tyler & Cooper, New Haven, 1954-56; ptnr. McCobb, Heaney & Van't Hof, Grand Rapids, Mich., 1959-72, Schmidt, Howlett, Van't Hof, Smell & Vana, Grand Rapids, 1972-82, Varnum, Riddering, Schmidt & Howlett, Grand Rapids, 1983-99. Mem. faculty Inst. Continuing Legal Edn., Ann Arbor, Mich., 1974-99. Chmn. Mich. Heart Assn., 1973-75; pres. United Way Kent County, 1979-80, hon. life mem., 1986—; chmn. Am. Heart Assn., Dallas, 1989-90. Mem. ABA, State Bar Mich. (grievance and arbitration panel 1970-91, 94-, chmn. com. on coops. and condos. 1982-86), Grand Rapids Bar Assn. (trustee 1965-67), West Mich. Hort. Soc. (pres. 1992-93), Cascade Hills Country Club, Univ. Club. Home: 3508 Windshire Dr SE Grand Rapids MI 49546-3698 Office: Varnum Riddering Schmidt & Howlett 333 Bridge St NW Ste 1700 Grand Rapids MI 49504-5356 E-mail: wkvanthof@varnumlaw.com.

VANT-HULL, LORIN L. physics educator, consultant; b. Matlock, Iowa, June 26, 1932; s. John Vant-Hull and Bessie A. Vissar; m. Mary E. Prunty, Feb. 4, 1955; children: Julia, Barry, Brian. BS, U. Minn., 1954; MS, UCLA, 1957; PhD, Calif. Inst. Tech., 1967. Rsch. asst. Calif. Inst. Tech., Pasadena, 1959-66; staff scientist Ford Scientific Lab., Newport Beach, Calif., 1966-69; dir. solar thermal program Energy Lab., U. Houston, 1975-98, assoc. prof., 1969-78, prof. physics, 1978-2001, prof. emeritus, 2001—. Author, editor: Solar Power Plants, 1991. Mem. Am. Solar Energy Soc. (bd. dirs. 1995-2001), Internat. Solar Energy Soc., Phi Beta Kappa, Sigma Xi, Phi Kappa Phi. Avocations: pottery, camping, hiking, water skiing, solar energy. Home: 128 N Red Bud Trail Bastrop TX 78621 Office: U Houston S & RI Dept Physics Houston TX 77004-5005 E-mail: vanthull@uh.edu.

VAN TIL, JON, sociology educator; b. Columbus, Ohio, May 15, 1939; m. Trudy Heller, Jan. 2, 1976; children: Ross, Claire. B.A., Swarthmore Coll., 1961; M.A., U.N.C., 1963; Ph.D., U. Calif.-Berkeley, 1970. Instr. sociology Purdue U., West Lafayette, Ind., 1965-66; instr. Swarthmore (Pa.) Coll., 1966-69, asst. prof., 1969-72; rsch. assoc. Brookings Inst., Washington, 1970-71; exec. dir. Pa. Law and Justice Inst., Phila., 1972-74; prof. dept. urban studies and community devel. Rutgers U., Camden, N.J., 1974—. Author: Mapping the Third Sector, 1988, Critical Issues in American Philanthropy, 1990, Growing Civil Society, 2000; contbr. articles to profl. jours.; editor-in-chief: Nonprofit and Voluntary Sector Quarterly, 1979-92. Mem. Phi Beta Kappa. Office: Rutgers U Coll Arts and Scis Camden NJ 08102

VAN TIL, WILLIAM, education educator, writer; b. Corona, N.Y., Jan. 8, 1911; s. William Joseph and Florence Alberta (MacLean) Van T.; m. Beatrice Barbara Blaha, Aug. 24, 1935; children: Jon, Barbara, Roy. BA, Columbia U., 1933; MA, Tchrs. Coll., 1935; PhD, Ohio State U., 1946. Tchr. N.Y. State Tng. Sch. for Boys, 1933-34; instr. dept. univ. schs. Coll. Edn., Ohio State U., 1934-36, asst. prof., 1936-43, on leave, 1943-45; researchist, writer Consumer Edn. Study NEA, 1943-44; dir. learning materials Bur. Intercultural Edn., 1944-47; prof. edn. U. Ill., 1947-51; prof. edn., chmn. div. curriculum and teaching George Peabody Coll. Tchrs., Nashville, 1951-57; prof. edn., chmn. dept. secondary edn. N.Y. U., 1957-66, head div. secondary and higher edn., 1966-67; Coffman disting. prof. edn. Ind. State U., Terre Haute, 1967-77, prof. emeritus, 1977; dir. univ. workshops Writing for Profl. Publs., 1978—; founder Lake Lure Press, 1983. Author: The Danube Flows Through Fascism, Economic Roads for American Democracy, The Making of a Modern Educator, Modern Education for the Junior High School Years, The Year 2000: Teacher Education, One Way of Looking At It, Education: A Beginning, Another Way of Looking At It, Van Til on Education, Secondary Education: School and Community, Writing for Professinal Publication, rev., 1986; autobiography My Way of Looking At It, 1983, expanded 2d edit., 1996; Sketches, 1989; editor: Forces Affecting American Education, Curriculum: Quest for Relevance, ASCD in Retrospect, 1986, Critique on Work Teaching Education, 1993; author and subject: Teachers and Mentors: Profiles of Distinguished Twentieth Century Professors of Education, 1996; co-editor: Democratic Human Relations, Intercultural Attitudes in the Making, Education in American Life; adv. editor Houghton Mifflin, 1964-70; interviewed in Social Education, 1989, Preface to the Eight Year Study Revisited, 1998; contbr. to numerous other publs. including Saturday Rev., Woman's Day, Parents; author articles, reviews and editorials; columnist: Ednl. Leadership, Contemporary Edn., Kappan; adv. bd. Profl. Educator, 1984-95. Mem. Ill. Interracial Commn., 1949-51; moderator Nashville Sch. desegregation meetings, 1955-57; mem. adv. bd. Jour. Tchr. Edn., 1956-59; co-organizer Nashville Community Rels. Conf., 1956; cons. Phelps-Stokes Fund project, 1958-62; mem. staff P.R. Edn. Survey, 1958-59, Iran Tchr. Edn. Survey, 1962, V.I. Edn. Survey, 1964; lectr. abroad, 1974; mem. staff U. Ind. Phi Delta Kappa Inst., 1984-90; 1st Ann. Van Til lectr. Ind. State U., 1989. Recipient Centennial Achievement award, Ohio State U., 1970; awards N.J. Collegiate Press Assn., 1962; N.J. Assn. Tchrs. English, 1962; inducted into Edn. Hall of Fame, Ohio State U., 1989; Annual Van Til Lectr. Series, Ind. State U., est. 1989, est. Annual Van Til Writing award, 1989, award of recognition Spring conf., 1999. Mem. John Dewey Soc. (v.p. 1957-60, acting pres. 1958-59, pres. 1964-66, award 1977, 86, Outstanding Achievement award 1991), Assn. Supervision and Curriculum Devel. (dir. 1951-54, 57-60, pres. 1961-62, chmn. rev. council 1972-73, resolutions com. 1982-85), United Educators (chmn. bd. educators 1969-77), Nat. Soc. Coll. Tchrs. Edn. (pres. 1967-68), Am. Edn. Studies Assn. (editorial bd. 1970-77), Asso. Orgn. Tchr. Edn. (adv. council 1967-73, chmn. issues tchr. edn. 1972-73), Nat. Soc. Study Edn. (editor Yearbook Issues in Secondary Edn. 1976), Kappa Delta Pi (laureate 1980—, chmn. book-of-yr. com. 1984-86, contbr. Honor in Teaching Reflections 1990). Home: 1120 E Davis Dr Terre Haute IN 47802-4065 *As an educator and writer, I believe that mankind's best hope is education which meets individual needs, illuminates social realities, fosters democratic values and utilizes relevant knowledge.*

VAN TILBURG, JOANNE, archaeologist, educator, foundation administrator; b. Mpls., Apr. 20, 1942; d. Everton George and Ruth (Butler) Becker; m. Johannes Franciscus Pieter Van Tilburg, Aug. 10, 1968; 1 child, Marieka Joanna. BS, U. Minn., 1965; MEd, UCLA, 1976, PhD, 1986. Rsch. assoc. Inst. Archaeology UCLA, 1986—, dir. Rock Art Archive, Cotsen Inst. Archaeology, 1996—; assoc. rschr. Inst. de Estudios U. de Chile, Isla de Pascua, 1986—. Lectr. Archaeol. Inst. Am., 1995—, Brit. Mus., 1990—; instr. UCLA Extension, 1990—. Author: Easter Island Archaeology, Ecology and Culture, 1994, H.M.S. Topaze on Easter Island, 1992; editor: Ancient Images on Stone, 1983; contbr. articles to profl. jours. Pres. Mana Found. Grantee Nat. Geog. Soc., 1989, Calif. Coun. for the Humanities, 1980, 95. Fellow Royal Geog. Soc.; mem. Archaeol. Inst. Am. (Golden Trowel campaign medallion 1999), Soc. for Am. Archaeology, Pacific Arts Assn. Office: UCLA Inst Archaeology Fowler Mus Cultural History 405 Hilgard Ave Los Angeles CA 90095-9000

VAN TINE, KIRK K. federal agency administrator; Grad., U.S. Naval Acad., 1970, cert. in Nuclear Engring., 1971; JD, U. Va., 1978. Bar: D.C. With Baker Botts , 1978—2001, ptnr., 1987—2001; gen. counsel U.S. Dept. Transp., Washington, 2001—. Mem.: D.C. Bar Assn. (co-chair litig. and law practive mgmt. sect., chair election bd.). Office: US Dept Transp Gen Counsel 400 7th St SW Washington DC 20590 Office Fax: 202-366-3388.

VAN TINE, MATTHEW ERIC, lawyer; b. Tomahawk, Wis., June 21, 1958; s. Kenneth G. and Louise (Olson) Van T.; m. Rena Marie David, Apr. 30, 1988; 1 child, Kristen. AB cum laude, Harvard Coll., 1980; JD magna cum laude, Boston U., 1983. Bar: Ill. 1983, Mass. 1983, U.S. Dist. Ct. Mass. 1984, U.S. Dist. Ct. (no. dist.) Ill. 1986, Seventh Cir., 2001. Law clk. to Hon. Raymond J. Pettine U.S. Dist. Ct. R.I., Providence, 1983-84; assoc. Palmer & Dodge, Boston, 1984-85, Schiff, Hardin & Waite, Chgo., 1985-88; asst. corp. counsel City of Chgo., 1988-92; assoc. to ptnr. Saunders & Monroe, Chgo., 1993-99; of counsel Miller Faucher and Cafferty, 2000—. Exec. editor: Boston University Law Rev., 1982-83. Mem. ABA, Chgo. Bar Assn., Inns of Ct. Office: Miller Faucher and Cafferty 30 N Lasalle St Ste 3200 Chicago IL 60602-2506 E-mail: mvantine@millerfaucher.com.

VAN TUYLE, GREGORY JAY, nuclear engineer; b. Chgo., Feb. 19, 1953; s. Willard D. and Mary E. (Kershner) Van T.; m. Frances A. Weinstein, Aug. 16, 1994; 1 child, William Steven. BSE magna cum laude, U. Mich., 1975, MSE, 1976, PhD of Nuclear Engring., 1978. From dep. divsn. head to program mgr. Brookhaven Nat. Lab., Upton, N.Y., 1978-97; program mgr. Los Alamos (N.Mex.) Nat. Lab., 1997—. Contbr. articles to profl. jours. Mem. Am. Nuc. Soc. (Reactor Safety divsn. program com. sec. to vice-chmn. 1991-96, chmn. 1996-97, past pres., v.p., treas. L.I. chpt. 1979-97, founder and chair Accelerator Applications divsn. 1996-98), Brookhaven Nat. Lab. Toastmasters (pres., v.p. 1990-95, awards 91, 92, 94). Achievements include performing computer simulation of Chernobyl-4 accident based on Soviet explanation prior to release of Soviet analyses, subsequently cross-comparing analyses, confirming similarities and evaluating differences. Office: Los Alamos Nat Lab Mail Stop K760 PO Box 1663 Los Alamos NM 87544-0600 E-mail: vantuyle@lanl.gov.

VAN TYNE, ARTHUR MORRIS, geologist; b. Syracuse, N.Y., Aug. 12, 1925; s. Roy Hanford and Isabelle Marguerite (Hoag) Van T.; m. Patricia Wilson Boyd, July 13, 1946; children: Judith, Cynthia, Mark, Peter. AB, Syracuse U., 1951, MS, 1958. Cert. petroleum geologist; lic. geologist, Pa. Field asst. Syracuse U. Rsch. Inst., 1951-53; geologist Shell Oil Co., Rockies, Gulf Coast, 1953-57; sr. geologist-in-charge N.Y. State Geol. Survey-Oil and Gas Rsch. Office, Wellsville and Alfred, N.Y., 1958-81; geol. cons. Van Tyne Cons., Wellsville, N.Y.C., 1981—. Gov. appointee mem. N.Y. State Oil, Gas, and Solution Mining Adv. Bd., 1996. Contbr. articles to profl. jours. Dep. mayor Village of Wellsville, 1992—; mem. Allegany County Econ. Devel. Com.; committeeman Rep. Party, 1962—77, 1998—2000; bd. dirs. Jones Meml. Hosp., Wellsville, 1973—2001, bd. chmn., 1986—95; bd. dirs. Wellsville United Way, 1968—80, pres., 1974—75; Drake Well Found. Recipient Cert. of Appreciation Am. Petroleum Inst., 1975, 80, Award of Merit Internat. Oil Scouts Assn. and Appalachian Sect., 1961, 66, 88. Mem.: Syracuse U. Geol. Devel. Coun., Geol. Soc. Am. (pres. Wellsville 1979—80), No. Appalachian Geol. Soc. (pres. 1966—68), Ind. Oil and gas Assn. NY (pres. 1985—88), NY State Oil Producers Assn. (exec. com. 1980—, dir., Svc. award 1981, Oilman of Yr. award 2001), Russian Assn. Oil and Gas Geologists (Oilman of Yr. 2001, Paul Harris fellow), Am. Assn. Petroleum Geologists (sec., dir. 1989—91, Ho. of Dels. svc. award 2001, nat. and ea. sect. hon. mem., Nat. Disting. Svc. award 1994, John T. Galey Meml. award ea. sect. 1997, House of Dels. long svc. award 2001), NY Acad. Scis., Rotary (pres. Wellsville 1979—80). Achievements include discovery of gas production from Queenston formation in N.Y; Bass Islands thrust structure, a major oil and gas producer in N.Y. and Pa.; contributed for N.Y. State to Appalachian Gas Atlas. Home: 24 Oak St Wellsville NY 14895-1026 Office: Van Tyne Cons PO Box 326 159 1/2 N Main St Wellsville NY 14895-1149

VAN UMMERSEN, CLAIRE A(NN), academic administrator, biologist, educator; b. Chelsea, Mass., July 28, 1935; d. George and Catherine (Courtovich); m. Frank Van Ummersen, June 7, 1958; children: Lynn, Scott. BS, Tufts U., 1957, MS, 1960, PhD, 1963; DSc (hon.), U. Mass., 1988, U. Maine, 1991. Rsch. asst. Tufts U., 1957-60, 60-67, grad. asst. in embryology, 1962, postdoctoral tchg. asst., 1963-66, lectr. in biology, 1967-68; asst. prof. biology U. Mass., Boston, 1968-74, assoc. prof., 1974—76, assoc. dean acad. affairs, 1975-76, assoc. vice chancellor acad. affairs, 1976-78, chancellor, 1978-79, dir. Environ. Sci. Ctr., 1980-82; assoc. vice chancellor acad. affairs Mass. Bd. Regents for Higher Edn., 1982-85, vice chancellor for mgmt. systems and telecommunications, 1985-86; chancellor Univ. System N.H., Durham, 1986-92; sr. fellow New Eng. Bd. Higher Edn., 1992-93; sr. fellow New Eng. Resource Ctr. Higher Edn. U. Mass., 1992-93; pres. Cleve. (Ohio) State U., 1993—2001; v.p., dir. Office of Women Am. Coun. Edn., 2001—. V.p., dir. Women Higher Ed. Am. Coun. Ed.; cons. Mass. Bd. Regents, 1981-82, AGB, 1992—, Kuwait U., 1992-93; asst. Lancaster Course in Ophthalmology, Mass. Eye. and Ear Infirmary, 1962-69, lectr., 1970-93, also coord.; reviewer HEW; mem. rsch. team which established safety stds. for exposure to microwave radiation, 1958-65; participant Leadership Am. program, 1992-93; bd. dirs. Nat. Coun. Sci. Environ., 1998. Active N.H. Ct. Systems Rev. Task Force, 1989-90, Leadership Cleve. Class '95, Gov.'s Coun. on Sci. and Tech., 1996-98, Strategy Coun. Cleve. Pub. Schs., 1996-98, Cleve. Sports Commn., 1999-2001, Cleve. Mcpl. Sch. Dist. Bd., 1999-2001; New Eng. Bd. Higher Edn., 1986-92, exec. com., 1989-92, N.H. adv. coun., 1990-92; chair Rhodes Scholarship Selection Com., 1986-91; bd. dirs. N.H. Bus. and Industry Assn., 1987-93; governing bd. N.H. Math. Coalition, 1991-92; exec. com. 21st Century Learning Cmty., 1992-93; state panelist N.H. Women in Higher Edn., 1986-93; bd. dirs. Urban League Greater Cleve., 1993-2001, strategic planning com., chair edn. com., 1996-99, sec., exec. com., 1997-99; bd. dirs. Great Lakes Sci. and Tech. Ctr., 1993-2001, edn. com., 1995-2001; bd. dirs. Greater Cleve. Growth Assn., 1994-2001, Civic Vision 2000 and Beyond, Cleve., 1997-98; bd. dirs., exec. com. Sci. and Tech. Coun. Cleve. Tomorrow, 1998-99; rep. Northeast Ohio Tech. Coalition, 1999-2001; trustee Ohio Aerospace Inst., 1993-2001, exec. com., 1996-2001; strategic planning com. United Way, 1996-2000, chair environtl. scan subcom. 1996-2001; leadership devel. com. ACE, 1995-98, women's commn., 1999-2001; bd. dirs. United Way, 1995-2001; co-chair Pub. Sector Campaign, 1997-98; bd. dirs. NCAA, divsn. 1, exec. com., 1999-2001; mem. AGB Ctr. for Pub. Higher Edn. Trusteeship and Goverance, 2001-; adv. com. Assn. Liaison Officers Adv. Com., 1998-2001. Recipient Disting. Svc. medal U. Mass., 1979, Woman of the Yr. Achievement award YWCA, 1998; Am. Cancer Soc. grantee Tufts U., 1960. Mem. Am. Coun. on Edn. (com. on self-regulation 1987-91), Nat. Conf. Cmty. & Justice (program com.), State Higher Exec. Officers (fed. rels. com., 1986-92, cost accountability task force, exec. com. 1990-92), ACE (com. leadership devel.), Nat. Assn. Sys. Heads (exec. com. 1990-92), Nat. Ctr. for Edn. Stats. (network adv. com. 1989-92), Am. Assn. State Colls. and Univs. (comn. on urban agenda 1996-2001), New Eng. Assn. Schs. and Colls. (commn. on higher edn. 1990-93), North Ctrl. Assn. Schs. and Colls. (evaluator 1993-2001, chair accreditation teams 1986-90), Greater Cleve. Round Table (bd. dirs. 1993-2001, exec. com. 1995), Cleve. Playhouse (trustee 1994-2001), Nat. Assn. State Univs. and Land Grant Colls. (exec. com. on urban agenda, mem. commn. tech. transfer, state rep. Am. Assn. State Colls. and Univs. (bd. dirs. 1996-99, mem. emerging issues task force 1996-98), Phi Beta Kappa, Sigma Xi. Office: American Coun on Edn One DuPont Cir NW Washington DC 20036-1193 E-mail: claire_van_ummersen@acc.nche.edu.

VAN VALER, JOE NED, lawyer, land developer; b. Gas City, Ind., Mar. 13, 1935; s. Richard Carl and Wilma Amy (Kelly) Van V.; m. Constance Joy Richardson, June 25, 1960; children: Kimberly Joy, Kelli June, Lynn Louise, Joseph Jeffrey. AB, Franklin Coll., 1959; LLB, Ind. U., 1963. Bar: Ind. 1963, U.S. Dist. Ct. (so. dist.) Ind. 1963. Assoc. Van Valer Law Firm and predecessor firms, 1963-65, ptnr., 1965-75, sr. ptnr., 1975—. Pres. Home Owners Warranty Corp. of Central Ind., Indpls., 1984-91, chmn. bd. dirs. 1991-95; cons. bd. Nat. City Bank Greenwood; chmn. adv. group Home Owners Warranty Corp., Washington, 1988-90, 92-94 also bd. dirs.; pros. atty. 8th Jud. Dist., Franklin, Ind., 1967-74; chmn. Johnson County, Ind., Contractors' Listing Bd.; chmn. bd. Bldg. Industry Svc. Corp., 1995-2000. With AUS, 1957-58. Recipient Alumnus Citation award Franklin Coll., 1996. Mem. ABA, Indpls. Bar Assn., 8th Jud. Cir. Bar Assn., Nat. Assn. Home Builders (bd. dirs.), Ind. Home Builders Assn., Builders Assn. Greater Indpls. (dir.), Indpls. Soc. Republican. Methodist. Office: Van Valer Law Firm PO Box 7575 299 W Main St Greenwood IN 46142-3129 E-mail: Joe@vanvalerlaw.com.

VAN VALKENBURG, EDGAR WALTER, lawyer; b. Seattle, Jan. 8, 1953; s. Edgar Walter and Margaret Catherine (McKenna) Van V.; m. Turid L. Owren, Sept. 29, 1990; children: Ingrid Catherine, Andrew Owren. BA, U. Wash., 1975; JD summa cum laude, Willamette Coll. of Law, 1978; LLM, Columbia U., 1984. Bar: Oreg. 1978, U.S. Dist. Ct. Oreg. 1979, U.S. Ct. Appeals (9th cir.) 1980. Law clk. to assoc. justice Oreg. Supreme Ct., Salem, 1978-79; assoc. Stoel, Rives, Boley, Fraser & Wyse, Portland, Oreg., 1979-82, 84-86; ptnr. Stoel Rives LLP, 1986—; instr. Columbia U., N.Y.C., 1982-84. Bd. dirs. Portland Oregon Sports Authority. Editor-in-chief: Williamette Law Jour. 1977-78. Bd. dirs., chmn. Multnomah County Legal Aid, 1997-98; bd. dirs. Oreg. Legal Aid, 1998—. Mem. ACLU (pres. Oreg. chpt. 1991-93), Oreg. State Bar (chmn. antitrust sect. 1989-90, mem. Ho. of Dels. 1996-98). Office: Stoel Rives LLP 900 SW 5th Ave Ste 2300 Portland OR 97204-1229 E-mail: wvanvalkenburg@stoel.com.

VAN VALKENBURGH, HOLLY VIOLA, librarian, consultant; b. N.Y.C., Nov. 22, 1936; d. Horace Bulle III and Viola Frieda (Gerfe) Van V.; children: Leland V. Lammert, Jeni L. Muniz, Gary F. Ohm. BA, U. Colo., 1957; MA, U. Denver, 1965; MEd, Lesley Coll., Cambridge, Mass., 1988. Elem. sch. tchr., Tenn., 1958-60, Colo., 1961-62; sch. librarian, 1962-66, Wyo., 1984-88; coll. librarian Sheridan (Wyo.) Coll., 1966-74, Morrison Coll., Reno, 1989-92; owner, operator Nanny Placement Agy., 1991-96, Word Pro, Carson City, Nev., 1996—. Cons. Nev. State Libr., Carson City, 1993—; adminstr. weatherization assistance project Dept. of Energy, Sheridan, 1975-84. Bd. dirs. Grassroots Lobby, Carson City, 1995—; chair Nev. Women's History Project, Reno, 2000—; treas., mem. Sheridan County Recreation Bd., 1972-78. Josephine Halverson Morris scholar U. Denver, 1965. Mem. AAUW (newsletter editor, pres. local chpts. 1972, 73, 96-97, 97-98), Nat. Assn. Van Valkenburgh Family (newsletter editor, 1991—, bd. dirs. 1998—), Nev. Libr. Assn. (newsletter editor, pres. elect, 2001—, pres. 2002). Avocations: white water rafting, reading. Home: 184 Lake Glen Dr Carson City NV 89703-5215 Office: Nev State Libr and Archives 100 N Stewart St Carson City NV 89701-4285

VAN VLEET, SUSAN ELLEN BASH, management consultant; b. Trenton, N.J., Dec. 10, 1946; d. Albert and Marion Bash; m. John Tyler Van Vleet, Feb. 10, 1979; children: Charles Tyler, Adam Joshua. BA in Sociology, Fairleigh Dickinson U., 1968; MSW, Rutgers U., 1974. Social worker Div. Youth and Family Svcs., Trenton, 1968-76; dir. govt. rels. Effectiveness Tng. Inc., Solano Beach, Calif., 1976-79; pres. Susan Van Vleet Cons., Inc., Castle Rock, Colo., 1979—, V2 Cons., Inc., Castle Rock, 1992—. Mem. Calif. State Com. for Children and Youth, Sacramento, 1978-79; mem. pers. com. Temple Sinai, 1990-92; del. Women's Coalition Denver, 1991-92.. Mem. NASW, Nat. Foster Parent Assn., Nat. Coun. Jewish Women (life, bd. dirs. 1979—). Republican. Jewish. Office: Susan Van Vleet Cons Inc PO Box 520 Castle Rock CO 80104-0520

VAN VLEET, WILLIAM BENJAMIN, retired lawyer, life insurance company executive; b. Milw., Dec. 4, 1924; s. William Benjamin and Irene (Peppey) Van V.; m. Marilyn Nilles, Dec. 26, 1946; children: Terese Van Vleet Svetich, Susan Van Vleet Waldo, William Benjamin III, Monica Van Vleet McCarthy, Mark. Student, Marquette U., 1942-43, Lawrence Coll., Appleton, Wis., 1943-44; LLB, JD, Marquette U., 1948. Bar: Wis. 1948, Ill. 1950. Gen. counsel George Rogers Clark Mut. Casualty Co., Rockford, Ill., 1948-59, Pioneer Life Ins. Co. Ill., Rockford, 1950-68, 81-94, v.p., 1959-91, gen. counsel, 1968-91, exec. v.p., 1981-95, also bd. dirs.; exec. v.p., gen. counsel Pioneer Fin. Svcs., Inc., 1985-95, gen. counsel emeritus, dir., 1995-97; pres. Nat. Group Life Ins. Co., 1992-93, exec. v.p., gen. counsel, 1993-94, also bd. dirs. Pres. Western Life Ins. Co. Am., Rockford, 1981-82, Health & Life Ins. Co. Am., Rockford, 1984-92, exec. v.p., gen. counsel, 1993-94; pres. Manhattan Nat. Life Ins. Co., Cin., 1990-92, exec. v.p., gen. counsel, 1993-94, also bd. dirs.; exec. v.p., gen. counsel Continental Life and Accident Co., Boise, Idano, 1993-94, also bd. dirs.; bd. dirs. Nat. Health Svcs. Milw. Mem. adminstrn. Boylan Ctrl. Cath. H.S., Rockford, 1965-72; pres. Diocesan Bd. Edn., Rockford, 1970-78; v.p., pres. Nat. Assn. Bds. Edn., 1972-78; mem. bd. advisors Marion Coll., 1976-79; mem. adv. bd. St. Anthony's Hosp., Rockford, 1978-91; bd. dirs. Crimestoppers, Rockford, 1982-90; co-chmn. United Cerebral Palsy Telethon, Rockford, 1985-95. Mem. Ill. Bar Assn., Winnebago County Bar Assn.

VAN VLIET, CAROLYNE MARINA, physicist, educator; b. Dordrecht, Netherlands, Dec. 27, 1929; emigrated to U.S., 1960, naturalized, 1967; d. Marinus and Jacoba (de Lange) Van V. BS, Free U. Amsterdam, Netherlands, 1949, MA, 1953, PhD in Physics, 1956. Rsch. fellow Free U. Amsterdam, 1950-54, rsch. assoc., 1954-56, asst. dir., 1958-60; postdoctoral fellow U. Minn., Mpls., 1956-57, faculty, 1957-58, 60-70, prof. elec. engring. and physics, 1965-70; prof. theoretical physics U. Montreal, Que., Can., 1969-95, sr. rschr. math. rsch. ctr., 1969-2000, prof. emerita, 1998—. Vis. prof. U. Fla., 1974, 78-88; prof. elec. and computer engring. Fla. Internat. U., 1992-2000; adj. prof. physics U. Miami, 2001—. Contbg. author: Fluctuation Phenomena in Solids, 1965; contbr. articles to profl. jours. Rsch. grantee NSF, Air Force OSR, Nat. Sci. and Engring. Rsch. Coun., Ottawa. Fellow IEEE (life); mem. Am. Phys. Soc., N.Y. Acad. Scis., Associated Artists, Mid. Ea. Dance. Office: U Miami James L Knight Physics Bldg 1320 Campo Sano Dr Coral Gables FL 33146 E-mail: vanvliet@physics.miami.edu. *The purpose of life is to honor God and to serve mankind.*

VAN VLIET, CLAIRE, artist; b. Ottawa, Ont., Can., Aug. 9, 1933; d. Wilbur Dennison and Audrey Ilene (Wallace) Van V. AB, San Diego State Coll., 1952; MFA, Claremont Grad. Sch., 1954; DFA (hon.) , U. of the Arts, Phila., 1993, San Diego State U., 2002. Instr. printmaking Phila. Coll. Art, 1959-65; owner The Janus Press, 1954—; vis. lectr. printmaking U. Wis.-Madison, 1965-66. Mem. bd. advisors Hand Papermaking. One-man exhbns. include Print Club Phila., 1963, 66, 73, 77, Wiggin Gallery, Boston Pub. Libr., 1977, Rutgers U. Art Gallery, 1978, AAA Gallery, Phila., 1980, Dolan/Maxwell Gallery, Phila., 1984, 91, Mary Ryan Gallery, N.Y.C., 1986, Mills Coll., 1986, U. of the Arts, Phila., 1989, Victoria and Albert Mus., London, 1994, Ottawa Sch. of Art Gallery, Can., 1994, Bates Coll. Mus. of Art, Lewiston, Maine, 1994, 99, N.D. Mus. Art, 1999, Rosenwald Wolf Gallery Univ. Arts.Phila, 2001; group exhbns. include Bklyn. Nat., Phila. Arts Festival, Kunst zu Kafka, Germany, Paper as Medium, Smithsonian Instn., Washington, Paper Now, Cleve. Mus. Art, 1986, Boyle Arts Festival, Ireland, 1993, Libr. Congress, 1997—, N.D. Mus. Art, 1999; represented in permanent collections Nat. Gallery Art, Phila. Mus. Art, Boston Pub. Libr., Libr. of Congress, Cleve. Mus. Art, Montreal Mus. Fine Arts, Victoria and Albert Mus. London, Tate Gallery, London. NEA grantee, 1976-80, Ingram-Merrill Found. grantee, 1989; MacArthur fellow, 1989-94. Mem. NAD, Soc. Printers Boston, Vt. Arts and Scis. Address: 101 Schoolhouse Rd West Burke VT 05871-9773

VAN VOORHIS, NANCY ELLEN, social services administrator; b. Somerville, N.J., May 22, 1950; d. John Millar and Jeanne Elizabeth Van V. BA cum laude, Stanford U., Palo Alto, Calif., 1972; MA, U. Va., Charlottesville, 1975. Rsch. libr. Nat. Pub. Radio, Washington, 1984-87; program officer, cons. Ohio Humanities Coun., Columbus, 1989-91; audio describer for blind and visually impaired A Thousand Words, Upper Arlington, Ohio, 1993—. Mem. Audio Description Internat. Home and Office: 4305 Shelbourne Ln Columbus OH 43220-4243

VAN VOORST, ROBERT E. theology educator, minister; b. Holland, Mich., June 5, 1952; s. Robert Eugene and Donna Mae (Boeve) Van V.; m. Mary Lind Bos, June 15, 1974; children: Richard William, Nicholas John. BA, Hope Coll., 1974; MDiv, Western Sem., 1977; PhD, Union Sem., N.Y., 1988. Ordained to ministry Classis of Holland Reformed Ch. in Am., 1977. Pastor Rochester Reformed Ch., Accord, N.Y., 1977-89; prof. religion Lycoming Coll., Williamsport, Pa., 1989-99, dept. chair, 1997-99; prof. New Testament Western Theol. Sem., Holland, Mich., 1999—. Adj. prof. Susquehanna U., Selinsgrove, Pa., 1991, Bucknell U., Lewisburg, Pa., 1993; vis. prof. Westminster Coll., Oxford, Eng., 1997; N.T. seminar lectr. Oxford U., 2000; interim pastor Lycoming Presbyn. Ch., Williamsport, 1997-99. Author: Ascents of James, 1989, Building New Testament Vocabulary, 1990, 3d edit., 2001, Anthology of World Scriptures, 1994, 4th edit., 2002, Readings in Christianity, 1996, 2d edit., 2000, Jesus Outside the New Testament, 2000, Anthology of Asian Scriptures, 1999; co-author: Death of Jesus in Early Christianity, 1998; editor Reformed Rev., 2000-02; contbr. articles Eerdmans

Dictionary of the Bible, 2001, Ency. of Jesus in History, Culture and Thought, 2002; contbr. numerous articles to profl. jours. Mem. Phi Beta Kappa, Phi Kappa Phi, Eta Sigma Phi, Phi Sigma Iota. Avocations: golf, cooking. Home: 1114 Post Ave Holland MI 49424-2550 Office: Western Theol Sem 101 E 13th St Holland MI 49423-3622 E-mail: bob.vanvoorst@westernsem.org.

VAN WACHEM, LODEWIJK CHRISTIAAN, petroleum company executive; b. Pangkalan Brandan, Indonesia, July 31, 1931; m. Elisabeth G. Cristofoli, June 10, 1958; 3 children. Degree Mech. Engring., Delft U., Delft, The Netherlands., 1953. With Bataafsche Petroleum Maatschappij, The Hague, The Netherlands, 1953; pres. Royal Dutch Petroleum Co., The Netherlands, 1982-92; chmn. com, mng. dir. Royal Dutch/Shell Group, The Netherlands, 1985-92; chmn. supr. bd. Royal Dutch Petroleum Co., Netherlands, 1992—2002. Chmn. bd. dirs. Shell Oil Co. USA, 1982—92, De Nederlandsche Bank N.V., , 1987—92; non. exec. dir. IBM Corp., Armonk, 1992—2002, Credit Suisse Holding, Zurich, 1992—96, Atco Ltd., Calgary, 1993—, AAB Area Brown Boveri Ltd, Zurich, 1996—99; vice chmn. Zurich Fin. Svcs., 2001—02, chmn. bd. dirs., 2002—; supervisory bd. AKZO Nobel n.v., Arnhem, 1992—2002, Philips Electronics n.v, Eindhoven, 1993—, chmn. supervisory bd., 1999; supervisory bd. BMW A.G., Munich, 1994—2002, Bayer A.G., Leverkusen, 1997—2002. Decorated C.B.E. (hon.), Knight Brit. Empire (hon.), Comdr. Order of Oranje Nassau, Knight Order Netherlands Lion, Pub. Svc. Star (Singapore). Office: Royal Dutch Petroleum Co 30 Carel van Bylandtlaan 2596 HR The Hague Netherlands

VAN WAGNER, ALBERT EDWIN, JR. lawyer; b. Bronxville, N.Y., Jan. 28, 1946; s. Albert Edwin and Margaret (Libby) Van W.; m. Marie Teresa; 1 child, Eric. BS, Ariz. State U., 1976, MBA, 1977, JD, 1978. Bar: Ariz. 1979, U.S. Dist. Ct. Ariz. 1979, U.S. Ct. Appeals (9th cir.) 1979. Assoc. Eldridge & Brown, Phoenix, 1979-80; ptnr. Eldridge & Van Wagner, 1981-84; sole practice, 1984-90; ptnr. Van Wagner & Erhart, 1991—. Council mem. City of Litchfield Park (Ariz.), 1992-99, vice mayor, 1996-98. With USMC, 1966-68. Mem.: Maricopa County Bar Assn. Democrat. Avocations: bridge, golf. Office: 649 N 3rd Ave Phoenix AZ 85003-1522

VAN WAY, CHARLES WARD, III, surgery educator; b. Ft. Jay, N.Y., May 1, 1939; s. Charles Ward and Hazel (Shattuck) Van W.; children: Craig Brandon, Brian Ward; m. Gail E. Wilson, Sept. 12, 1987; 1 child, Whitney Elizabeth. BA, Yale U., 1960; MD, Johns Hopkins U., 1964. Diplomate Am. Bd. Surgery-Surg. Critical Care, Am. Bd. Thoracic and Cardiovascular Surgery. Resident in surgery Vanderbilt U., Nashville, 1964-72; prof., dir. surg. nutrition U. Colo. Sch. Medicine, Denver, 1985-88; fellow in clin. pharmacology Vanderbilt U., Nashville, 1967-69; asst. prof. surgery U. Colo. Sch. Medicine, Denver, 1974-78, assoc. prof., 1978-85; chief surgery Denver Gen. Hosp., 1978-85; prof. surgery U. Mo., Kansas City, 1988—, vice-chmn., 1995—2000, chmn., 2000—. Program dir. surgery St. Luke's Hosp., Kansas City, Mo., 1988—95. Author: Surgical Skills in Patient Care, 1978, Pocket Manual of Basic Surgical Skills, 1988; editor: Critical Decisions in Trauma, 1984, Handbook of Surgical Nutrition, 1991, Nutritional Secrets, 1998, Nutrition in Clinical Practice, 2001. Scoutmaster Cub Scouts, Denver, 1974-80; vice chmn. Cherry Creek Village Homeowners Assn., Denver, 1975-78; commr. Greenwood Village Planning and Zoning Commn., Denver, 1981-83. Maj. U.S. Army, 1972-74, col. USAR, 1991—. Fellow ACS (Mo. chpt. pres. 1995-96), Am. Coll. Chest Physicians, Am. Coll. Critical Care Medicine; mem. AMA, Am. Soc. Clin. Nutrition, Am. Soc., Nutritional Scis., H. William Scott Jr. Soc., Colo. Trudeau Soc. (pres. 1980-81), Cen. Surg. Assn., Am. Soc. Parenteral and Enteral Nutrition (bd. dirs. 1987-89), Colo. Soc. Parenteral and Enteral Nutrition (pres. 1986-87), Internat. Cardiovascular Soc., Southwestern Surg. Congress, Am. Med. Info. Assn., Assn. for Computing Machinery, Am. Coll. Physician Execs., Kans. City Surg. Soc., Mo. Med. Assn., Met. Med. Assn. (bd. dirs. 1991—, pres.-elect 1997, pres. 1998), Rocky Mountain Vascular Soc., Colo. Vascular Surg. Soc., Am. Assn. Thoracic Surgery, Soc. Internat. de Chirurgerie, Western Vascular Soc., Western Surg. Assn., Soc. Critical Care Medicine, Assn. Surg. Edn., Assn. Program Dirs. in Surgery Episcopalian. Avocations: photography, skiing, hiking, computer programming. Office: 2301 Holmes St Kansas City MO 64108-2640 E-mail: charles.vanway@tmcmed.org.

VAN WEELDEN, THOMAS H. waste industry company executive; b. 1955; With Waste Mgmt.; co-owner hauling co. and 3 landfills, nr. Chgo.; exec. v.p. Allied Waste Industries, Inc., Houston, 1997-97, pres., COO Phoenix, 1992-97, CEO, pres. Scottsdale, Ariz., 1997—, chmn., 1998—, also bd. dirs. Bd. dirs. Reid Plastics, Inc. Office: Allied Waste Industries Inc Ste 100 15880 N Greenway Hayden Loop Scottsdale AZ 85260-1649*

VAN WESTERING, JAMES FRANCIS, management consultant, educator; b. Bklyn., Dec. 7, 1940; s. Frederick Joseph and Agnes Teresa (Powell) Van W.; m. Karen Lyn Almy, Aug. 27, 1966. BA, Bklyn. Coll., 1963; MBA, Baruch Coll., 1972. Spl. asst. Fed. Res. Bank, N.Y.C., 1967-76; sr. cons. Coopers & Lybrand, 1976-77; 2nd v.p. Chase Manhattan Bank, 1977-78; pres. Internat. Comml. Sys., Inc., Forest Hills, N.Y., 1978—; dir. Nat. Data Corp., Atlanta, 1981-82. Adj. asst. prof. Mgmt. Inst., N.Y.U., 1992—. Bd. dirs. Forest Hills (N.Y.) Gardens Corp., 1987-90; pres. N.Y. Forum on Ea. Europe, N.Y.C., 1991—; mem. exec. bd. Sister City program City of N.Y. and Budapest, Hungary, 1995. Served USMCR, 1959-60. Mem. Am. Econs. Assn., Electronic Banking Econs. Soc., Slovak-Am. C. of C. (mem. adv. bd. 1994—). Avocation: archtl. preservation. Home: 17 Ingram St Forest Hills NY 11375-6828 Office: Internat Comml Sys Inc PO Box 4176 Parkside Sta Forest Hills NY 11375

VAN WESTRUM, ANTHONY, lawyer, arbitrator, mediator; b. Indpls., Apr. 10, 1944; s. Colby S. and Edith Hartsock van Westrum; m. Jennifer Ellis, June 18, 1966; children: Derek, Heather. BS in Mech. Engring., Purdue U., 1966; JD cum laude, U. Mich., 1969. Bar: Colo. 1969. Assoc., ptnr. Davis, Graham & Stubbs, Denver, 1969-90; shareholder Burns, Wall, Smith & Mueller, PC, 1991-94, of counsel, 1994—; pvt. practice Anthony van Westrum LLC, 1994—. Mem. Colo. Sec. of State Adv. Com., 1987--. Mem. Am. Arbitration Assn. (nat. panel comml. arbitrators), Am. Law Inst., Colo. Assn. Corp. Counsel (pres. 1994-95), Colo. Bar Assn. (bus. law sect. chair 1995-97, ethics com., amicus curiae briefs com., legis. policy com., Burch Legis. award 2001). Office: Anthony van Westrum LLC 621 Seventeenth St Ste 1515 Denver CO 80293-1501

VAN WHY, REBECCA RIVERA, retired guidance counselor; b. Casa Blanca, N.Mex., Sept. 14, 1932; d. Charles and Doris (Thompson) Rivera; m. Raymond Richard Van Why, Aug. 27, 1955; children: Raymond R., Ronald R., Randall R. BS, U. N.Mex., 1959. Tchr. Bur. of Indian Affairs, Albuquerque, 1960-62, guidance counselor, 1969-94, tchr., supr., 1973-74, acting dir. student life, 1987, ret., 1994; head tchr. Laguna (N.Mex.) Headstart OEO, 1967-69, acting dir., 1969. Appt. N.Mex. Youth Conservation Corps Commn., 1992-98. Recipient Cert. of Recognition, Sec. of Interior, 1975, Cert. of Appreciation, State of N.Mex., 1986, N.Mex. Commn. on the Status of Women, 1993; named honoree Internat. Women's Day, U. N.Mex., 1987. Republican. Avocations: sewing, travel, boating, fishing, dancing. Home: 14417 Central Ave NW Albuquerque NM 87121-7756

VAN WIE, PAUL DAVID, secondary school educator, historian, educator; b. Manhasset, N.Y., Sept. 29, 1956; s. Joseph Paul and Florence Elizabeth (Wagner) van W.; m. Ellen Mary van Wie, June 25, 1983; children: Mary Ellen, Elisabeth, Paul David, Joseph. BA, C.W. Post Coll., 1978, MA, 1987; PhD, CUNY, 1989. Cert. secondary edn. Tchr. Spackenkill High Sch., Poughkeepsie, N.Y., 1981-82, Schreiber High Sch., Port Washington, 1982-84, Wheatley Sch., Old Westbury, 1984—; adj. prof. N.Y. Inst. Tech., 1987-92, Hofstra U., Hempstead, N.Y., 1992—. Mem. dean's adv. com. L.I. U., Old Brookville, N.Y., 1992-96. Author: The Way it Was, 1994, Image, History and Politics, 1998. Historian Village of Franklin Square, N.Y., 1979—, libr. trustee, 1989—; landmarks commr. Town of Hempstead, 1989—; pres. Franklin Square Hist. Soc.; v.p. Franklin Square Cmty. League, 1990-96. Nat. Humanities fellow U.S. Govt., 1988, Fulbright scholar U.S. Govt., 1990, Coun. Basic Edn. fellow, 1996; recipient Leadership award Nat. Soc. Daughters of Am. Revolution, 1982, N.Y. State Tchr. of Yr. award N.Y. Dept. Edn., 1992. Mem. Am. Hist. Assn., L.I. Coun. Social Studies, Franklin Square Hist. Soc. (pres.). Office: The Wheatley Sch 11 Bacon Rd Old Westbury NY 11568-1502

VAN WINKLE, EDGAR WALLING, retired electrical engineer, computer consultant; b. Rutherford, N.J., Oct. 12, 1913; s. Winant and Jessie Walcott (Mucklow) Van W.; m. Jessie Stetler, Apr. 23, 1938 (dec. 1992); children: Barbara Van Winkle Clifton (dec. Mar. 2000), Catrina Van Winkle Poindexter, Cornelia Van Winkle Schloss; m. Martha Polyé, May 22, 1993. BEE, Rutgers U., 1936; MS in Indsl. Engring., Columbia U., 1943, PE in Indsl. Engring., 1966. Registered profl. engr., N.J. Elec. engr. A.B. Dumont Labs., Passaic, N.J., 1943-48; chief engr. Facsimile Electronics, 1948-52; cons. Bur. Ships, Washington, 1952; asst. sr. staff scientist Bendix Corp., Teterboro, N.J., 1952-67; sr. staff scientist Conrac Corp., West Caldwell, 1967-78; pres. Empac, Inc., Rutherford, 1979-2001; ret., 2001. Contbr. articles to profl. jours.; patentee in field. Ruling elder Presbyterian Ch., Rutherford, 1984-91, chmn. endowment com., 1984—. Mem. IEEE (life, treas. artificial intelligence sect. North N.J. Chpt. 1982-84), Bendix Mgmt. Club (life), North N.J. Automatic Control Group (chmn. 1967-68), Met. Engring. Mgmt. (chmn. 1966-67), Mensa, Holland Soc., Green Pond Yacht Club (past commodore), Upper Montclair Country Club, Delta Phi. Republican. Achievements include work in artificial intelligence, with subspecialty in mathematical software. Address: 154 Lake End Rd Newfoundland NJ 07435-1207 E-mail: empacem@aol.com.

VAN WINKLE, HANS A. military officer; BS, U.S. Mil. Acad., 1971; MS in Pub. Policy, U. Calif., Berkeley, 1976. Registered profl. engr., Va., 1980. Commd. C.E. U.S. Army, 1971, advanced through grades to maj. gen.; comdr. Co. A, 10th Combat Engr. Bn., 3d Inf. Divsn. U.S. Army Europe, Germany, 1977—79, comdr. 10th Combat Engr. Bn., 3d Inf. Divsn. Germany; asst. prof. econs. U.S. Mil. Acad., West Point, NY, 1979—82; exchange officer Royal Sch. Mil. Engring., England, 1983—85; exec. officer 82d Engr. Bn. U.S. Army Europe, Germany, 1985—87, ops. officer 7th Engr. Brigade, 1987—89; comdr. 8th Engr. Bn., 1st Cavalry Divsn. U.S. Army, Ft. Hood, Tex., 1989—91, comdr. Divsn. Engr. Brigade, 4th Inf. Divsn. Ft. Carson, Colo., 1992—94; dir. tng. U.S. Army Engr. Sch., Ft. Leonard Wood, Mo., 1994—95; dep. chief of staff, engr. U.S. Army Europe and 7th Army, Heidelberg, Germany, 1995—97; comdr., divsn. engr. Great Lakes and Ohio River Divsn. U.S. Army C.E., Cin. and Chgo., 1997—99, dep. commanding gen. Washington, 1999—. Decorated Legion of Merit, Bronze Star medal, Army Commendation medal (3), Meritorious Svc. medal (3), many others. Office: US Army Corps of Engineers 441 G St NW Washington DC 20314-1000*

VANWINKLE, JOHN RAGAN, lawyer; b. Ft. Knox, Ky., Dec. 18, 1951; s. John Lloyd and Kate (Morris) VanW.; m. Cathy M. VanWinkle, Dec. 9, 1983; stepchildren: William Gabriel Gammons, Virginia Leigh Gammons. BS, State Coll. Ark., Conway, 1974; JD, U. Ark., 1980. Bar: Ark. 1980, U.S. Ct. Appeals 1981, U.S. Supreme Ct. 1989. Caseworker Mental Retardation Devel. Disabilities Svc., Ft. Smith, Ark., 1974-77; dep. pros. atty. Pros. Atty.-12th Dist., 1980-81; ptnr. Person & VanWinkle, 1982-86, Sexton, Kirkpatrick, Nolan, VanWinkle & Caddell, Ft. Smith, 1986-89, Hewett, Shock & VanWinkle, Ft. Smith, 1989-91; chancery judge 12th Jud. Cir., 1991-92; ptnr. Rose & VanWinkle, Fayetteville, Ark., 1993—, Rose, VanWinkle & Woods, Fayetteville, 1998-2000; pvt. practice, 2000—. Bd. dirs. Family Support Svcs., 1995—, N.W. Ark. Regional Indsl. Devel. Corp., 1996—; v.p. Habitat for Humanity, 1996—; Dem. nominee for Congress 3d Congl. Dist.-Ark., Ft. Smith, 1992; chmn. Sebastian County Dem. Ctr. Com., Ft. Smith, 1989-91; del. Dem. Nat. Conv., 1988. Mem. ATLA, Ark. Trial Lawyers Assn. Methodist. Avocations: golf, reading. also: Law Offices of John R VanWinkle 2101 Green Acres Rd Fayetteville AR 72703 E-mail: john@vanwinkle.com.

VAN WINKLE, WESLEY ANDREW, lawyer, educator; b. Kansas City, Mo., Sept. 22, 1952; s. Willard and Cleone Verlee (O'Dell) Van W.; m. Ruth Kay Shelby, Apr. 10, 1984. JD, San Francisco Law Sch., 1987. Bar: Calif. 1987, U.S. Dist. Ct. (no. dist.) Calif. 1987, U.S. Supreme Ct. 1994. Atty. Bagetelos & Fadem, San Francisco, 1987-91; pvt. practice Berkeley, Calif., 1991—. Prof. law San Francisco Law Sch., 1990—; apptd. mem. Calif. Appellate Indigent Def. Oversight Adv. com., 1997-99. Editor (legal newspaper/rev.) Res Ipsa Loquitur, 1986. Mem. Calif. Attys. for Criminal Justice, Calif. Appellate Def. Counsel (pres. 1998-99), San Francisco Law Sch. Alumni Assn. (bd. dirs.), Delta Theta Phi. Democrat. Office: PO Box 5216 Berkeley CA 94705-0216

VAN WOERT, HOWARD CLARK, JR. chemist, librarian; b. Lewisburg, Pa., Nov. 14, 1950; s. Howard Clark and Gladys (Cooper) Van W. Student, Ohio State U., 1972; BA in Chemistry and English, Capital U., 1973; MS in Organic Chemistry, Tex. A&M U., 1976; postgrad., Ohio U., 1977; PhD in Phys. Chemistry, Okla. State U., 1982; MLS in Libr. and Info. Svc., U. Ky., 1995. Lab. asst., sci. libr. dept. chemistry Capital U., Columbus, Ohio, 1970-73; tchg. asst., rsch. asst. chemistry dept. Tex. A&M U., College Station, 1973-76; tchg. asst. gen. chemistry Ohio U., Athens, 1976-77; tchg. and rsch. asst. biochemistry and chemistry depts. Okla. State U., Stillwater, 1977-82; instr. organic and biochemistry basic sci. dept. Columbus Tech. Inst., 1983; chemist dept. clin. investigation William Beaumont Army Med. Ctr., El Paso, Tex., 1983-84; rsch. scientist NYU, N.Y.C., 1985-86, Tenn. State U., Nashville, 1986-87; rsch. scientist dept. material sci. and engring. U. Ky., Lexington, 1987-88, 89-91, 93-99, instr., 1993, 94, Columbus State C.C., 1989; rsch. chemist Chem. Sensors, Perfect View, Inc., Raleigh, N.C., 1989; rsch. assoc. dept. chemistry and biochemistry U. Del., Newark, 1999-2000; rsch. assoc. Johns Hopkins Applied Physics Lab., 2001—. Instr. S.E. C.C., Cumberland, Ky., 1991-93, Lexington C.C., 1994; spkr. nat. meetings and symposia. Contbr. articles to sci. jours., including Advances in Polymer Tech., Jour. Chem. Edn., Jour. Am. Chem. Soc. Sunday sch. tchr. Our Savior's Luth. Ch., College Station, 1973-75, Luth. Ch., El Paso, 1983-84, 5th Street Presbyn. Ch., N.Y.C., 1985, Gethsemane Luth Ch., Lexington, 1987-88, 90, Meth. Ch., Cumberland, 1991-92. Welch fellow Tex. A&M U., 1974, 76. Mem. AAAS, Am. Chem. Soc., Am. Soc. Metals, Del. Chem. Soc., Sigma Xi. Republican. Lutheran. Achievements include patent applied for in inorganic superdonducting materials in cured polymers. Avocations: swimming, soccer, piano, baritone horn, reading. Home: 3626 A6 Valley Terrace Baltimore MD 21244 E-mail: how@ubmc.edu.

VAN WYCK, GEORGE RICHARD, insurance company executive; b. Wilmington, Vt., Feb. 6, 1928; s. Harold Wait Van Wyck and Ruth Anna Learnard; m. Jeanne Mildred Anderson, Apr. 17, 1948; children: Diana Lee Van Wyck Jenkins, Beryl Jeanne. BS in Math. cum laude, St. Lawrence U., 1953. Actuarial clk. Aetna Life Ins. Co., Hartford, Conn., 1953-55; with Am. Bankers Ins. Group, Miami, Fla., 1955-91, sec., bd. dirs., 1983-89, ret., 1991. Bd. dirs. Jr. Achievement of Greater Miami, 1966-83, pres., 1975-76; bd. dirs. Epworth Village Retirement Complex, Miami, 1966-2000, v.p., 1998-99, chmn. investment com. 1995-99; founding dir., pres. Brickel Children's Ctr., Miami, 1980-82; mem. pers. adv. bd., vice chmn. Dade County, Miami, 1987-89. With USAF, 1946-49. Fellow Life Office Mgmt. Inst.; mem. 1st United Meth. Ch. So. Miami, Phi Beta Kappa. Democrat. Methodist. Avocations: photography, golf, bridge. Home: 8455 SW 44th St Miami FL 33155-4126 E-mail: gvanwyck@cs.com.

VAN WYK, CHRISTOPHER JOHN, computer science educator; b. Fairborn, Ohio, Sept. 5, 1955; s. John Derek and Marie Louise (Riordan) Van W.; m. Claudia Sarro, Aug. 23, 1980; children: Margaret, Abigail. BA in Math. with high honors, Swarthmore Coll., 1977; PhD in Computer Sci., Stanford U., 1980. Mem. tech. staff AT&T Bell Labs., 1980-91; assoc. prof. math. and computer sci. Drew U., Madison, N.J., 1990-92, prof. math. and computer sci., 1992—, assoc. dean, 1999—, dir. instl. rsch. Vis. asst. prof. Stevens Inst. Tech., 1984—85; honors examiner Swarthmore Coll. , 1986, 88; vis. lectr. Princeton U., 1987; instr. (summers) N.J. Govs. Sch. in the Scis., 1984, 89, 92, 93; mem. program com Fourth Ann. Symposium Computation Geometry, 1988; cons. Bell Labs. , Murray Hill, NJ, 1991—2001; faculty cons. Ednl. Testing Svcs. , 1996—2002; cons. Sedgwick, Algorithms C++, Publs. 1-4, 1998, Sedgwick, Algorithms C++, Publ. 5, 2002. Author: Data Structures and C Programs, 1988; guest editor Jour. Computer and Sys. Scis., 1989, assoc. editor, 1990-94. Recipient Fed. Jr. fellowship Nat. Bur. Standards, 1973-76, Spl. Achievement award Nat. Bur. Standards, 1975, 76, grad. fellowship NSF, 1977-80, teaching fellowship Stanford U., 1978, George E. Forsythe Meml. award for excellence in student teaching, 1979. Mem.: Math. Assn. Am., Soc. for Indsl. and Applied Math. (mem. edn. com. 1995—), Assn. Computing Machinery (mem. spl. interest groups automata, computability, theory edn-.graphics), Computer Soc. IEEE, Sigma Xi, Phi Beta Kappa. Episcopalian. Office: Drew U Dept Math and Computer Sci Madison NJ 07940

VAN WYK, JUDSON JOHN, endocrinologist, pediatric educator; b. Maurice, Iowa, June 10, 1921; s. John Cornelius and Amelia Susan (Menning) Van W.; m. Persis Ruth Parker, June 8, 1944; children: Judith Parker, Persis Allen, Peter Menning, Judson John. AB, Hope Coll., 1943, ScD (hon.), 1979; postgrad. in biochemistry, St. Louis U., 1943-44; MD, Johns Hopkins U., 1948. Diplomate Am. Bd. Pediatrics. Intern Johns Hopkins Hosp., 1948-49, resident in pediatrics, 1949-50, fellow in pediatric endocrinology, 1953-55; resident in pediatrics Cin. Children's Hosp., 1951-52; investigator Nat. Heart Inst., 1953-55; asst. prof. pediatrics U. N.C. Sch. Medicine, 1955-59, assoc. prof., 1959-62, prof., 1962-91, prof. biology, 1987—, Kenan prof. pediatrics, 1975-91, prof. emeritus, 1992—, chief div. endocrinology, 1955-89, dir. tng. program in endocrinology and metabolism, 1962-89; mem. staff N.C. Meml. Hosp. Cons. Womack Army Hosp., Ft. Bragg, N.C., 1957-88; vis. scientist Karolinska Institutet, Stockholm, 1968-69; mem. div. cell biology Lineberger Cancer Rsch. Ctr., 1976—; vis. prof. basic med. scis. Mich. State U., 1984; vis. prof. U. NSW, Sydney, Australia, 1992. Editor Progress in Growth Factor Research, 1988-94; mem. editl. bd. Jour. Clin. Endocrinology and Metabolism, 1956-71, editor, 1983-89; mem. editl. bd. Pediatrics, 1969-70; contbr. chpts. to books, articles to profl. jours. Mem. basic sci. adv. com. March Dimes, 1985-88. With USPHS, 1951-53. Recipient numerous fellowships and grants, Lauria honoris causa, U. Genoa, "To commemorate 500th Anniversary of Discovery of N. Am. by Christopher Columbus", 1992, O. Max Gardner award for contbns. to welfare of human race Bd. Govs. U. N.C., 1980. Fellow Am. Acad. Pediatrics; mem. NIH (endocrine study sect. 1968-720, Endocrine Soc. (mem. coun. 1975-79, awards com. 1991-96, publs. com. 1996-99, Fred Conrad Koch medal 1989), Soc. Pediatric Rsch., Am. Pediatric Soc., So. Soc. Clin. Investigation, Am. Fedn. Clin. Rsch., So. Soc. Pediatric Rsch., Lawson Wilkins Pediatric Endocrine Soc. (prs. 1976-77), Internat. Endocrine Soc. (ctrl. com. 1988—), La Sociedad Peruana de Pediatria (hon.), Sociedad Pediatrica de Trujillo (hon.), European Soc. for Pediatric Endocrinology (corr.), Japanese Pediatric Endocrine Soc. (hon.). Presbyterian. Home: 1020 Highland Woods Rd Chapel Hill NC 27517-4410 Office: U NC Sch Medicine Dept Pediatrics CB 7220 509 Burnett Womack Chapel Hill NC 27599-0001 E-mail: judvw@med.unc.edu.

VAN WYK, ROBERT NICHOLAS, philosopher, educator; b. Paterson, NJ, Feb. 26, 1940; s. Adrian and Gertrude Cornelia Van W.; m. Audrey, May 16, 1964; children: Christine Friant, Mark. AB, Coll. Wooster, 1961; MDiv, Pitts. Theol. Sem., 1964; PhD, U. Pitts., 1971. Assoc. prof. philosophy U. Pitts., 1970-99. Author: Introduction to Ethics, 1991, (chpt.) Kindred Matters, 1993, (chpt.) Values and Education, 1998, (chpt.) Groups and Group Rights, 2001, others; contbr. articles to profl. jours. Nat. Endowment Humanities fellow, 1987, 88, Ctr. Philosophy Pub. Policy, 1995. Mem. Internat. Soc. Philosophy Law Social Philosophy, Am. Philos. Assn., N.Am. Soc. Social Philosophy, Soc. Christian Philosophers. Democrat. Presbyterian. Avocations: bike riding, classical music. Home: 1205 Luzerne St Johnstown PA 15905 Office: U Pitts Johnstown PA 15904 E-mail: rnvanwyk@yahoo.com.

VAN WYLEN, GORDON JOHN, former college president; b. Grant, Mich., Feb. 6, 1920; s. John and Effa (Bierema) Van W.; m. Margaret E. DeWitt, Dec. 29, 1951; children— Elizabeth Ann Van Wylen Rudenga, Stephen John, Ruth Margaret Van Wylen Jasperse, David Gordon, Emily Jane Van Wylen Overway. AB, Calvin Coll., 1942; BSE., U. Mich., 1942, MS, 1947; Sc.D., MIT, 1951. Indsl. engr. duPont Co., 1942-43; instr. mech. engring. Pa. State U., 1946-48; asst. prof. mech. engring. U. Mich., 1951-55, assoc. prof., 1955-57, prof., 1957-72, chmn. dept., 1958-65, dean Coll. Engring., 1965-72; pres. Hope Coll., Holland, Mich., 1972-87, pres. emeritus, 1987—. Author: Thermodynamics, 1959, (with R.E. Sonntag) Fundamentals of Classical Thermodynamics, 1965, 5th edit., 1998, Fundamentals of Statistical Thermodynamics, 1966, Introduction to Thermodynamics, 1971, 3d edit., 1991, Encounter at Dea, 1994; contbr. articles to profl. jours. Trustee Van Andel Edn. Inst. Lt. USNR, 1943-46. Fellow ASME, AAAS; mem. Phi Beta Kappa (hon.), Sigma Xi, Tau Beta Pi, Phi Kappa Phi. Mem. Reform Ch. Am. Home: Apt 600 145 Columbia Ave Holland MI 49423-2980

VAN ZANTE, SHIRLEY M(AE), magazine editor; b. Elma, Iowa; d. Vernon E. and Georgene (Woodmansee) Borland; m. Dirk C. Van Zante. AA, Grandview Coll., 1950; BA, Drake U., 1952. Assoc. editor Mchts. Trade Jour., Des Moines, 1952-55; copywriter Meredith Pub. Co., 1955-60, book editor, 1960-67; home furnishings editor Better Homes and Gardens Spl. Interest Publs., Meredith Corp., 1967-74; home furnishing and design editor Better Homes and Gardens mag., 1974-89; writer, editl. cons., 1989-98. Named Advt. Woman of Yr. in Des Moines, 1961; recipient Dorothy Dawe award, 1971, 73, 75, 76, 77, Dallas Market Ctr. award, 1983, So. Furniture Market Writer's award, 1984. Mem. Alpha Xi Delta. Address: 1905 74th St Des Moines IA 50322-5701

VAN ZANTEN, FRANK VELDHUYZEN, retired library system director; b. Heemstede, The Netherlands, Oct. 21, 1932; came to U.S., 1946, naturalized, 1953; s. Adrian V. and Cornelia (Van Eesteren) Van Z.; m. Lois Ruth Holkeboer, June 17, 1961; children— Kiki Maria, Lili Roxanne, Amy Suzanne. AB, Calvin Coll., Mich., 1959; postgrad., U. Wash., 1960; MA in L.S, U. Mich., 1961. Cataloger, extension project asst. Mich. State Library, Lansing, 1961-62; dir. Dickinson County (Mich.) Library, 1962-65, Mid-Peninsula Library Fedn., Iron Mountain, Mich., 1963-65, St. Clair County (Mich.) Library, 1965-68, Tucson Pub. Library, 1968-73; library cons. Ill. State Library, Springfield, 1973-75, assoc. dir. for library devel., 1975-78; dir. Mid-Hudson Library System, Poughkeepsie, N.Y., 1978-95; ret., 1996. Served with AUS, 1953-55. Mem. ALA, N.Y. Libr. Assn. Home: 138 Wilbur Blvd Poughkeepsie NY 12603-4635 E-mail: FVZcolors@aol.com.

VAN ZELST, THEODORE WILLIAM, civil engineer, natural resource exploration company executive; b. Chgo., May 11, 1923; s. Theodore Walter and Wilhelmina (Oomens) Van Z.; m. Louann Hurter, Dec. 29, 1951; children: Anne, Jean, David. BS, U. Calif., Berkeley, 1944; BS in Naval Sci., Northwestern U., 1944, BAS., 1945, MS in Civil Engring., 1948. Registered profl. engr., Ill. Pres., Soil Testing Services, Inc., Chgo., 1948-52; pres. Soiltest, Inc., 1948-78, chmn. bd., 1978-80; sec., dir. Exploration Data Cons., Inc., 1980-82; exec. v.p. Cenco Inc., Chgo., 1962-77, vice chmn., 1975-77, also dir., 1962-77. Bd. dirs. Minann, Inc., Testing Sci., Inc., Van Zelst, Inc., Rsch. Park, Inc., Northwestern U., 1992-95, chmn. bd. dirs. Envirotech Svcs., Inc., 1983-85; sec., bd. dirs. Van Zelst, Inc. Wadsworth, Ill., 1983—; pres., bd. dirs. Geneva-Pacific Corp., 1969-83, Geneva Resources, Inc., 1983-91. Treas. Internat. Road Fedn., 1961-64, sec., 1964-79, dir., 1973-88, vice chmn., 1980-87; pres. Internat. Road Edn. Found., 1978-80, 87-88, hon. life bd. dirs., 1988—; bd. dirs. Chgo. Acad. Scis., 1983-86, v.p., 1985-86, hon. dir., 1986—; bd. dirs. Pres.'s Assn., Chgo., 1985-86; mem. adv. bd. Mitchell Indian Mus., Kendall Coll., 1977-94. Lt. (j.g.) USNR, 1942-45. Lt. j.g. USNR, 1944—46. Recipient Service award Northwestern U., 1970, Merit award, 1974, Alumni medal, 1989, Svc. award U. Wis., 1971, La Sallian award, 1975; named Disting. Engring. Alumnus, U. Calif., Berkeley, 2002. Mem. ASCE (Chgo. Civil Engr. of Yr., 1988), Nat. Soc. Profl. Engrs., Western Soc. Engrs., Evanston C. of C. (v.p. 1969-73), Ovid Esbach Soc. (pres. 1968-80), Northwestern U. Alumni Assn., Tau Beta Pi, Sigma Xi. Clubs: Economic, North Shore. Achievements include invention of engring. testing equipment for soil, rock, concrete and asphalt; co-invention of Swing-wing for supersonic aircraft. Home: 1213 Wagner Rd Glenview IL 60025-3297 Office: PO Box 582 Glenview IL 60025-0582

VAN ZILE, PHILIP TAYLOR, III, lawyer, educator; b. Detroit, Feb. 17, 1945; s. Philip Taylor II and Ruth (Butzel) Van Z.; m. Susan Jones, Sept. 12, 1981; children: Caroline Sage, Philip Taylor IV. BA, Oberlin Coll., 1968; MDiv, Union Theol. Sem., 1971; JD, Mich. State U., 1975. Bar: Mich. 1976, D.C. 1976, U.S. Dist. Ct. (ea. dist.) Mich. 1976, U.S. Ct. Appeals (6th cir.) 1976, U.S. Supreme Ct. 1977, Pa. 1981. Law clk. Mich. Ct. Appeals, Detroit, 1976-78, Mich. Supreme Ct., Detroit and Lansing, Mich., 1978-80; asst. corp. counsel Office of Corp. Counsel, Washington, 1980-87; assoc. Killian & Gephart, Harrisburg, Pa., 1987-89; prin. Law Office of Philip T. Van Zile, 1989-91; assoc. coun. Office Chief Coun. Pa. Dept. Conservation and Natural Resources, 1991—; assoc. realtor M.C. Walker Realty, Mechanicsburg, Pa.,

1997—. Teaching fellow Detroit Coll. Law, 1976-80; teaching asst. Detroit Gen. Hosp., 1978-80; teaching assoc. Acad. Med. Arts and Bus., Harrisburg, 1990-91. Contbr. articles to profl. jours. Ordained elder Mechanicsburg Presbyn. Ch., 1995—, chmn. vol. ministries, 1995, chmn. peacemaking, 1996, chmn. staff, 1997—. Mem. ABA, Kenwood Club (Chevy Chase, Md.). Office: Pa Dept Conservation/Natural Resources Office Chief Counsel 400 Market St Harrisburg PA 17101-2301

VARACALLI, JOSEPH ANTHONY, humanities educator, writer; b. Jersey City, Jan. 14, 1952; s. Joseph and Theresa Marie Varacalli; m. Lillian Elizabeth Varacalli, June 4, 1988; children: Thomas F.X., John Paul, Theresa Elizabeth. PhD Sociology, Rutgers U., New Brunswick, NJ, 1980; MA Sociology, U. of Chgo., Chicago, IL, 1975; BA Sociology, Rutgers Coll., New Brunswick, NJ, 1973. Dir. ncc ctr. for cath. studies Nassau CC, Garden City, NY, 1981—, sociology educator, 1981—; sociology educator asst. Newark Coll. of Arts and Sci., Newark, 1975—78. Bd. mem. Faculty for Life, Long Island, NY, 2001—, American-Italian Hist. Assn., Garden City, NY, 1986—88, Fellowship of Cath. Scholars, Garden City, NY, 1993—95; co-founder Soc. of Cath. Social Scientists, Garden City, NY, 1992—. Contbr. articles to profl. jours. Roman Catholic. Office Fax: 516-572-7257. E-mail: varacaj@sunynassau.edu.

VARADARAJAN, KALATHOOR, educator, researcher; b. Bezwada, India, Apr. 13, 1935; parents Kalathoor Soundara and Parimalavalli (Parimalavalli) Rajan; m. Pattu Varadarajan, June 22, 1961; children: Suchitra, Srinivasan. BA with honors, Loyola Coll., Madras, India, 1955; PhD, Columbia U., 1960. Rsch. fellow Tata Inst. Fundamental Rsch., Bombay, 1960-61, fellow, 1961-67; vis. assoc. prof. U. Ill., Urbana, 1967-69; reader Tata Inst. Fundamental Rsch., Bombay, 1969-71; assoc. prof. U. Calgary, Alta., Can., 1971-73, prof. Can., 1973—. Nat. bd. vis. prof. Nat. Bd. Higher Math, India, 1986, 91; vis. prof. Univ. Sydney, Australia, 1984. Author: The Finiteness Obstruction of C.T.C. Wall, 1989; contbr. more than 100 articles to profl. jours. Home: 5944 Dalridge Hill NW Calgary AB Canada T3A1L9 Office: U Calgary Dept Math 2500 Univ Dr NW Calgary AB Canada T2N1N4 E-mail: varadara@math.ucalgary.ca.

VARALLO, D. VINCENT, educator; b. Paterson, N.J., Mar. 28, 1955; s. D. Vincent and Doris (Mitch) V.; m. Carmen Ivette, Nov. 10, 1984; children: Alexander, Nicole. BA in Am. Studies, Ramapo Coll. N.J., 1977; MA in English, So. Ill. U., 1981. Editl. asst. So. Ill. U., Carbondale, writing instr., 1978-81; dir. First Sch., Union City, N.J., 1981-84; dir.-founder Bergen Lang. Inst., Teaneck, 1984-93; founder-pres. Varallo Internat., Midland Park, 1994—. Mem. ASTD, Soc. Human Resource Mgmt. Office: Varallo Internat PO Box 336 Midland Park NJ 07432-0336 E-mail: varalloint@erols.com.

VARCHETTA, FELIX R. advertising executive; b. Chgo., July 11, 1920; s. Vincent and Anne (Allegretti) V. BS in Mktg., De Paul U., 1949; MBA, Northwestern U., 1952. Advt. and sales promotion mgr. O-Cedar Corp., Chgo., 1951-62, StromBecker Corp., Chgo., 1963-67; product mgr. Helene Curtis Industries, 1962-63; account exec., owner Phil Varchetta & Assocs., 1968—. 1st sgt. U.S. Army, 1942-46. 1st sgt. U.S. Army, 1942—46. Mem. Assn. Profl. Orchestra Leaders (bd. dirs.), Am. Philatelic Soc., Chgo. Fedn. Musicians. Democrat. Roman Catholic. Avocations: reading, philately. Home: 5617 N Knox Ave Chicago IL 60646-6635 Office: Phil Varchetta & Assocs 5901 N Cicero Ave Ste 410 Chicago IL 60646-5716

VARCHMIN, THOMAS EDWARD, environmental health administrator; b. Chgo., Dec. 5, 1947; s. Arthur William and Laurie Eileen (Allen) V.; m. Beth Virginia Plank, Dec. 16, 1972; children: Jeffrey Thomas, Brian Arthur, Jennifer Beth, Matthew James. BA, St. Mary's Coll., Winona, Minn., 1969; MS, Western Ill. U., Macomb, 1977. Registered sanitarian, Wis. Virologist, microbiologist Chgo. Dept. Health, 1974-78; environ. health and safety mgr. Great Atlantic & Pacific Tea Co., Chgo., 1978-79; adminstr. occupational safety and environ. health Nat. Safety Council, 1979-80; mgr. environ. health Lake County Health Dept., Waukegan, Ill., 1980-84, mgr. environ. health and pub. relations, 1984-87; mgr. environ. health Cook County Dept. Pub. Health, Oak Park, 1987-89, asst. dir. environ. health, mgr. intergovtl. rels., 1989-98, dir. environ. health, 1998—. Environ. health cons. Editor: Food and Beverage Newsletter, Hospital and Health Care Newsletter, Trades and Services Newsletter, 1979-80. NSF grantee, 1968-69 Mem. Nat. Environ. Health Assn. (registered environ. health specialist), Ill. Environ. Health Assn. (lic. environ. health practitioner), Nat. Safety Coun., Am. Soc. Microbiology, Anvil Club of Ill., Phi Mu Alpha, Delta Epsilon Sigma. Achievements include research on autumn food habits of game fish, behavioral and phys. devel. of barred owl nestlings in Ill. Office: Cook County Dept Pub Health 1010 Lake St Ste 300 Oak Park IL 60301-1133

VARDAMAN, JOHN WESLEY, lawyer; b. Montgomery, Ala., Apr. 22, 1940; s. John Wesley and Elizabeth (Merrill) V.; m. Marianne Fay, June 14, 1969; children: Thomas, Shannon, John Wesley III, Davis. BA, Washington & Lee U., 1962; JD, Harvard U., 1965. Bar: D.C. 1966, U.S. Dist. Ct. (D.C.) 1967, U.S. Supreme Ct. 1970. Law clk. to justice Hugo Black U.S. Supreme Ct., 1965-66; assoc. Wilmer, Cutler & Pickering, Washington, 1966-70; ptnr. Williams & Connolly, 1970—; gen. counsel U.S. Golf Assn., 1999—. Contbr. articles to profl. jours. Mem. ABA, Am. Coll. Trial Lawyers, Congl. Country Club (Bethesda, Md.). Baptist. Avocation: golf. Office: Williams & Connolly 725 12th St NW Washington DC 20005-5901

VARDAN, SUMAN, medical educator; b. Monghyr, Bihar, India, July 25, 1937; came to U.S., 1970; s. Damodar and Sarojini Prasad; m. Asha Vardan, Feb. 25, 1965; children: Sandeep, Swati. MB BS, Bihar U., Laheraisari, 1959, MD, 1964; diploma in tropicae medicine and hygiene, Bihar U., 1965. Diplomate Am. Bd. Internal Medicine, Am. Bd. Clin. Hypertension, Am. Soc. Hypertension, Am. Bd. Cardiovascular Disease. Med. resident Brown U., Providence, 1972—73, cardiology fellow, 1973—75; asst. prof. medicine SUNY, Syracuse, 1975—83, assoc. prof. medicine, 1983—93, prof. medicine, 1993—; staff physician cardiology and gen. medicine VA Med. Ctr., 1975—2000, dir. hypertension clinic, 1980—, dir. cardiac rehab. program, 2000—; staff cardiologist, 2001. Fellow ACP, ACC; mem. Am. Assn. Physician from India (patron), Am. Soc. Hypertension, Indian Med. Assn. (life). Home: 6292 Danbury Dr Jamesville NY 13078-8737 Office: VA Med Ctr 800 Irving Ave Syracuse NY 13210-2716

VARELA, FERNANDO, anesthesiologist; b. Madrid, Spain, Aug. 8, 1936; MD, Madrid U., 1962. Diplomate Am. Bd. Anesthesiology. Fellow Am. Coll. Anesthesiologist; intern Flower Hosp., Toledo, 1968-69; resident anesthesiologist Phila. Gen. Hosp., 1969-70; resident in anesthesiology U. Chgo. Hosps., 1970-72; asst. prof. anes. Med. Coll. Ga., Augusta, 1972-73; hosp. staff mem. Trinity Med. Ctr., Moline, Ill., 1973—. Mem. AMA, Am. Soc. of Anesthesiologists, Ill. Med. Soc., Ill. Soc. Anesthesiologists, Rock Island County Med. Soc. Office: 550 30th Ave Ste 7 Moline IL 61265-5975 Home: Apt 1810 988 Boulevard Of The Arts Sarasota FL 34236-4849 E-mail: fervalop@aol.com.

VARELAS, PANAYIOTIS, neurologist; b. Athens, Greece, Dec. 8, 1959; came to U.S., 1994; s. Nikolaos and Eleni Varela; m. Marianna Spanaki, Oct. 8, 1995. Med. diploma, U. Athens, 1983. Specialist in neurology Greek Ministry of Health. Neurology resident U. Athens Med. Sch., 1988-91; rsch. fellow Baylor Coll. Medicine, Houston, 1994; intern Meth. Hosp., Memphis, 1994-95; neurology resident Yale U. Sch. Medicine, New Haven, 1995-97, neurology chief resident, 1997-98, neurology instr., 1997-98; neuro-critical care unit sr. fellow Johns Hopkins Hosp., Balt., 1998-00; dir. neur. ICU, asst. prof. neurology and neurosurgery Med. Coll. Wis., Milw., 2000—. Internal medicine resident Athens Med. Sch., 1996, psychiatry resident, 1998; anesthesiology resident 251 Air Forces Hosp., Athens, 1994-95. Lt. Air Force of Greece, 1993-95. Hon. scholar U. Athens Med. Ctr., 1977-83, scholar NATO, 1994-95, Alexander Onassis Found., 1994-95. Mem. Am. Acad. Neurology (scholar for residents 1998), Am. Epilepsy Soc., Greek Neurol. Assn., Athens Med. Assn. Greek Orthodox. Avocation: chess. E-mail: pvarelas@mcw.edu.

VARELLAS, SANDRA MOTTE, judge; b. Anderson, S.C., Oct. 17, 1946; d. James E. and Helen Lucille (Gilliam) Motte; m. James John Varellas, July 3, 1971; children: James John III, David Todd. BA, Winthrop U., 1968; MA, U. Ky., 1970, JD, 1975. Bar: Ky. 1975, Fla. 1976, U.S. Dist. Ct. (ea. dist.) Ky. 1975, U.S. Ct. Appeals (6th cir.) 1975, U.S. Supreme Ct. 1978. Instr. Midway Coll., Ky., 1970-72; adj. prof. U. Ky. Coll. Law, Lexington, 1976-78; instr. dept. bus. adminstrn. U. Ky., 1976-78; ptnr. Varellas, Pratt & Cooley, 1975-93, Varellas & Pratt, Lexington, 1993-97, Varellas & Varellas, Lexington, 1998—. Fayette County judge exec., Ky., 1980—; hearing officer Ky. Natural Resources and Environ. Protection Cabinet, Frankfort, 1984-88. Committeewoman Ky. Young Dems., Frankfort, 1977-80; pres. Fayette County Young Dems., Lexington, 1977; bd. dirs. Ky. Dem. Women's Club, Frankfort, 1980-84, bd. dirs., Bluegrass Estate Planning Coun., 1995-98; grad. Leadership Lexington, 1981; chairwoman Profl. Women's Forum, Lexington, Ky., 1985-86, bd. dirs., 1984-87, Aequum award com., 1989-92; mem. devel. coun. Midway Coll., 1990-92; co-chair Gift Club Com., 1992. Named Outstanding Young Dem. Woman, Ky. Young Dems., Frankfort, 1977, Outstanding Former Young Dem., Ky. Young Dems., 1983. Mem. Ky. Bar Assn. (treas. young lawyers divsn. 1978-79, long range planning com. 1988-89), Fla. Bar, Fayette County Bar Assn. (treas. 1977-78, bd. govs. 1978-80), LWV (nominating com. 1984-85), Greater Lexington C. of C. (legis. affairs com. 1994-95, bd.d irs. coun. smaller enterprises 1992-95). Club: The Lexington Forum (bd. dirs. 1996-99), Lexington Philharm. Guild (bd. dirs. 1979-81, 86—), Nat. Assn. Women Bus. Owners (chmn. cmty. liaison/govtl. affairs com. 1992-93), Lexington Network (bd. dirs. and sec. 1994-98). Office: Varellas & Varellas 167 W Main St Ste 1310 Lexington KY 40507-1398

VARESE, FEDERICO, political science educator; b. Italy, Nov. 12, 1965; m. Galia Kravtchenko. Laurea, Bologna (Italy) U., 1990; PhM, Cambridge (Eng.) U., 1991; PhD, Oxford (Eng.) U., 1997. Rsch. fellow Oxford U., 1996-2000; William H. Orrick asst. vis. prof. Yale U., New Haven, 2000—02; asst. prof. Williams Coll., Williamstown, 2002—. Author: The Russian Mafia, 2001. Cpl. maj. paratrooper Italian armed forces, 1992-93. Grantee Internat. Consortium for Polit. and Social Rsch., 1997; Nuffield Coll. studentship, 1991; Lester B. Pearson scholar Ministry of Fgn. Affairs, 1982; receipient Ed. A. Hewett Book Prize, Am. Assoc. for the Advancement of Slavic Studies, in conj. with Nat. Coun. for Eurasian and East European Rsch., 2002. Mem. Am. Polit. Sci. Assn. Home: 846 Orange St New Haven CT 06511 Office: 406 Stetson Hall Williamstown MA 01267-2133 Fax: 413-597-4305. E-mail: fvarese@williams.edu.

VARET, MICHAEL A. lawyer; b. N.Y.C., Mar. 9, 1942; s. Guster V. and Frances B. (Goldberg) V.; m. Elizabeth R. Varet, June 3, 1973; 3 children. BS in Econs., U. Pa., 1962; LLB, Yale U., 1965. Bar: N.Y. 1966, U.S. Supreme Ct. 1975, U.S. Dist. Ct. (ea. and so. dists.) N.Y. 1975, U.S. Tax Ct. 1975, U.S. Claims Ct. 1975, U.S. Ct. Appeals (2d cir.) 1975. Mem., chmn. Varet & Fink P.C. (formerly Milgrim Thomajan & Lee P.C.), N.Y.C., 1982-95; mem. firm Piper Rudnick LLP, 1995—. Bd dirs., exec. com., audit com. Salisbury Bank and Trust Co., Lakeville, Conn., Salisbury Bancorp, Inc., Lakeville. Trustee Montefiore Med. Ctr., Bronx, N.Y., 1980-92, mem. exec. com., 1985-92; bd. dirs. Sem. Libr. Corp. Jewish Theol. Sem., N.Y.C., 1983-87, United Jewish Appeal-Fedn. Jewish Philanthropies of Greater N.Y., Inc., 1979-86, mem. coun. of overseers, 1986-95; bd. dirs. Mosholu Preservation Corp., Bronx, 1982-88, Yale Law Sch. Fund, 2000—; bd. overseers Jewish Theol. Sem., 1982-90, Jewish Publ. Soc. of Am., 1986-96, exec. com., 1989-94, 95-96; mem. exec. com. Yale Law Sch. Assn., 1990-93; bd. dirs. B. de Rothschild Found. for Advancement Sci. in Israel, 1986—, Piatigorsky Found., 1990—; v.p., sec., bd. dirs. Am. Found. for Basic Rsch. in Israel, 1990—; dir. Plz. Jewish Cmty. Chapel, 2001—; bd. dirs. Am. and Internat. Friends of Victoria and Albert Mus., Inc., 1997-99, treas., 1997-99. Mem. ABA, N.Y. State Bar Assn., Assn. of Bar of City of N.Y. (bd. dirs., exec. com. 1971-75), Internat. Fiscal Assn., Internat. Tax Planning Assn., Yale Club, Lotos Club. Democrat. Office: Piper Rudnick LLP 1251 Ave of Americas New York NY 10020-1104 E-mail: mav@varet.com., michael.varet@piperrudnick.com.

VARGA, DEBORAH TRIGG, music educator, entertainment company owner; b. Dayton, Ohio, Dec. 15, 1955; d. Ernest Cushman and Phyllis Ann (Martz) Trigg; m. Ali M. Abadi, Dec. 30, 1980 (div. July 1987); 1 child, Darren Vincent; m. Richard Charles Varga, June 25, 1994; 1 child, Kathryn Lenore. B of Music Edn. in Violin Performance, Converse Coll., Spartanburg, S.C., 1977. Music educator Seminole County Sch. Bd., Sanford, Fla., 1978-92, Howard County Pub. Schs., Ellicott City, Md., 1993—. Co-founder, co-owner Gold Star Entertainement, Inc., Orlando, Fla., 1984-86, Ctr. Stage Entertainment, Inc., Maitland, Fla., 1986-92; owner Varga Music Entertainement, Highland, Md., 1993—, Composer children's songs, 1990—, Martin Luther King Tribute, Human Rights Commn., Howard County, 1997-00. Mem. Am. Fedn. Musicians, Music Educators Nat. Conf., Am. String. Tchrs. Assn., Nat. Orch. Assn. Avocations: waterskiing, whitewater rafting, tennis, golf, reading. Home: 13464 Allnutt Ln Highland MD 20777-9743

VARGA, NICHOLAS, historian, archivist, retired educator; b. Elizabeth, N.J., Sept. 13, 1925; s. Joseph and Anna (Buchko) V.; m. Margaret Joan Skinner, Sept. 8, 1951; children: Deidre Kayne, Damian Guy, Colin Piere. BS cum laude, Boston Coll., Chestnut Hill, Mass., 1951, MA, 1952; PhD with honors, Fordham U., 1960. Instr. history Loyola Coll., Balt., 1955-59, asst. prof., 1959-62, assoc. prof., 1962-66, prof., 1966-92, chmn. dept., 1964-68, prof. emeritus, 1992—, coll. archivist, 1976—. Author: Baltimore's Loyola, 1990. Advisor Jo Tydings Election Campaign, Balt., 1964, 70; bd. dirs. UN Assn. Md., Balt., 1966-70; pres. Woodbourne Sch. PTA, Balt., 1967-68; mem. Howard County Bicentennial Com., Ellicott City, Md., 1974-77. Publ. grantee Md. Hist. Soc., 1989. Mem. AAUP (founder, pres. Loyola Coll. chpt. 1966-69), Am. Hist. Assn. (interviewer Cate report 1966), Am. Cath. Hist. Assn. (nominating com. 1975-78), Soc. Am. Archivists, Mid-Atlantic Region Archivists Conf., Alpha Sigma Nu (hon.). Democrat. Byzantine Catholic. Office: Loyola Coll 4501 N Charles St Baltimore MD 21210-2601

VARGA, RICHARD STEVEN, mathematics educator; b. Cleve., Oct. 9, 1928; s. Steven and Ella (Krejcs) V.; m. Esther Marie Pfister, Sept. 22, 1951; 1 dau., Gretchen Marie. BS, Case Inst. Tech. (merged with Case Western Res. U.), 1950; AM, Harvard U., 1951, PhD, 1954; hon. doctorate, U. Karlsruhe, 1991, U. Lille, 1993. With Bettis Atomic Power Lab., Westinghouse Electric Co., 1954-60, adv. mathematician, 1959-60; full prof. math. Case Inst. Tech. (now Case We. Res. U.), 1960-69; Univ. Prof. math. Kent (Ohio) State U., 1969—, dir. rsch. Inst. for Computational Math. Cons. to govt. and industry. Author: Matrix Iterative Analysis, 1962, Functional Analysis and Approximation Theory in Numerical Analysis, 1971, Topics in Polynomial and Rational Interpolation and Approximation, 1982, Zeros of Sections of Power Series, 1983, Scientific Computation on Mathematical Problems and Conjectures, 1990, Matrix Iterative Analysis, 2d revised and expanded edit., 2000; editor: Numerical Solution of Field Problems in Continuum Physics, 1970, Padé and Rational Approximations: Theory and Applications, 1977, Rational Approximations and Interpolation, 1984, Computational Methods and Function Theory, 1990, Numerical Linear Algebra, 1993; editor-in-chief. Numerische Math., 1988-2002, Electronic Transactions Numerical Analysis; mem. editl. bd. Linear Algebra and Applications, Constructive Approximation, Computational Mathematics (China), Numerical Algorithms, Analysis, Electronic Jour. Linear Algebra, Comms. in Applied Analysis. Recipient Rsch. award Sigma Xi, 1965, von Humboldt prize, 1982, Pres.' medal Kent State U., 1981; Guggenheim fellow, 1963; Fairchild scholar, 1974. Home: 7065 Arcadia Dr Cleveland OH 44129-6065 Office: Kent State U Inst Computational Mat Kent OH 44242-0001 E-mail: varga@mcs.kent.edu.

VARGA, STEVEN CARL, human resources professional; b. Columbus, Ohio, Jan. 19, 1952; s. Stephen Thomas and Eva Jeney Varga; m. Michelle L. Auld, Nov. 17, 1973; children: Zachary Steven, Joshua Lewis. BA in Psychology and Philosophy magna cum laude, Carthage Coll., 1977; MSA with honors, Ctrl. Mich. U., 1986. Svc. mgr. Chem-Law Corp., Columbus, 1972-75; respiratory therapist St. Catherine's Hosp., Kenosha, Wis., 1975-77; policy analyst Nationwide Ins. Cos., Columbus, 1978-79, asst. mgr. Corp. Tng. Ctr., 1979-86; dir. ednl. tng. Sullivan Payne Co., Seattle, 1986-88, asst. v.p. human resource devel., 1989-93; v.p. Reinsurance Solutions, Inc., 1994-95; sr. v.p. Unltd. Potential, Inc., 1995-99; chief human resources officer Columbus Distbg. Co., 2000—. Mem. civic action program com., 1979-86, Nat. Mental Health Assn., 1972-79; mem. occupl. adv. coun. Bellevue C.C., 1989—; v.p. Kenosha County chpt., 1975-77; mem. Franklin County (Ohio) Mental Health Assn., 1978-86. Rhodes scholar, 1976-77. Mem. APA, ASTD, Soc. Broadcast Engrs., Ins. Inst. Am. (contbg. author Principles of Reinsurance, vol. I and II, nat. adv. com. assoc. in reinsurance program), Brokers and Reinsurers Markets Assn. (edn. and tng. co-chair), Am. Mgmt. Assn., Soc. Ins. Trainers and Educators (chmn. regional area planning com.), Carthage Coll. Alumni Assn., Phi Beta Kappa, Psi Chi. Office: Columbus Distbg Co 4949 Freeway Dr E Columbus OH 43229-5401

VARGAS, ARIONEL P. dancer; b. Cuba; Student, Centro Pro Danza, Havana, Cuba. Mem. Royal Winnipeg Ballet, 1996—2000, prin. dancer, 2000—. Dancer (ballets) Dracula, Royal Winnipeg Ballet, Allegro Brillante, Ballo Della Regina, Nutcracker, La Bayadere, Act II, The Leaves are Fading, A Touch of Strauss, 5 Tangos, Creatureshood, Miroirs, The Rite of Spring, Galina Yordanova, Nutcracker, Butterfly, As Above, So Below. Recipient Gold medal, Brazil's Internat. Ballet Competition, 1995, Bronze medal, N.Y. Internat. Ballet Competition, 1996. Office: Royal Winnipeg Ballet 380 Graham Ave Winnipeg MB Canada R3C 4K2*

VARGAS, JOE FLORES, insurance claims executive; b. Corpus Christi, Tex., Dec. 18, 1940; s. Jose Arispe and Francisca (Flores) V.; m. Anita Munoz, Feb. 16, 1963; children: Joseph Dean, Bernice Ann Vargas Burns. AA, Del Mar Jr. Coll., 1973; BS, Tex. A&M at Corpus Christi, Corpus Christi, 1979. Life ins. underwriter Am. Nat. Ins. Co., 1962—65; ct. interpreter Nueces County, Corpus Christi, 1966-70, dep. sheriff, ct. bailiff, 1970-78; ins. adjuster Greene Claims Svc., 1978; pvt. investigator Equifax, 1978-79; ins. claims rep. Crum & Forster Commercial Ins., 1979-86; owner, pres., ins. claims adjuster South Tex. Claims Svc. Inc., 1986—. Mem. Tex. Claims Assn. Avocations: hunting, camping. Office: South Tex Claims Svc Inc PO Box 270276 Corpus Christi TX 78427-0276

VARGAS, KATHLEEN DIANE, legal administrator; b. Boston, Feb. 22, 1951; d. Joseph Ernest and Barbara Shirley (Dundas) Emge; children: Christian Andrew Fabian, Michelle Diane; m. Howard Vargas, 1995. BA in Anthropology/Archaeology, MA in Anthropology/Archaeology, Pacific Luth. U., 1984; JD, Am. Coll. of Law, 1989. Tchr. English Castillo Escuela, Guadalajara, Mexico, 1972-74; rsch. asst. U. Calif., Irvine, 1978-80; rsch. assoc. Hoko River Archaeol. Project, Pullman, Wash., 1981-84; law clk., investigator Law Offices of Leonard Moen, Tacoma, 1984-86; law clk. Law Offices of Thomas Moga, Upland, Calif., 1986-90; hearing rep. Law Offices of Grant Lynd, Westminster, 1990—. Disc jockey, music dir. Sta. KUCI Radio, Calif., 1978-80, Sta. KPLU Radio, 1981-82. Asst. (film) Battered Women/Convicted Killers, 1981. Recipient Am. Jurisprudence award for appellate advocacy Lawyers Coop/Bancroft Whitney Pub., 1988, Am. Jurisprudence award for uniform comm. code, 1988. Mem. Bus. and Profl. Women's Assn., Nat. Notary Assn. Democrat. Avocations: archaeology, drawing, science fiction, travel. Office: Law Offices of Grant A Lynd 14340 Bolsa Chica Rd Ste B Westminster CA 92683-4868

VARGAS, PILAR, physician, consultant; b. Rio Pedras, P.R., June 5, 1944; d. Pedro Vargas and Pilar Vargas de Bodas; m. Sten H. Vermund, Apr. 8, 1978; children: Julian, Gabriel. BS in Chemistry, U. P.R., Rio Piedras, 1966; PhD in Biology, CUNY, 1975; MD, Albert Einstein Coll. Medicine, 1977. Diplomate Am. Bd. Neurology and Psychiatry. Intern medicine N.Y. Med. Coll., N.Y.C., 1977-78; resident psychiatry Bronx (N.Y.)-Mcpl. Hosp. Ctr., 1978-80, fellow child psychiatry, 1981-83; instr. psychiatry Albert Einstein Coll Medicine Yeshiva U., N.Y.C., 1983-89; cons. State of Ala. Dept. Edn., Birmingham, 1995—. Contbr. articles to profl. jours. Fellow NIMH, Bronx, 1981-82. Mem. Am. Psychiat. Assn., Am. Acad. Child and Adolescent Psychiatry. Office: State Ala Dept Edn 2545 Rocky Ridge Ln Birmingham AL 35216-4836 E-mail: pilarvv@aol.com.

VARGAS LEGASPI, JUAN, manufacturing company executive; b. Aguascalientes, Mex., Feb. 25, 1953; s. Juan Medina and Maria Legaspi De La Luz; m. Martha Perez Carreño; children: Juan, Abrham, Christopher. Bookkeeper, UNAM, Mexico City, 1974-78; diploma in taxes and fin., Inst. of Specialization, Mexico City, 1987; diploma human resources, U. Iberoam., Mexico City, 1979; diploma in fin. analysis, Dun & Bradstreet Inc., 1980; diploma in econs., Inst. Integration Ibero Am., Mexico City; M in Mgmt., Grad. Coll., Mexico City, 1992. Dir. Guantes Vargas, S.Am., 1977—. Chmn. bd. Colegio de Graduados en Alta Direccion, 1995-2000, Centro de Investigaciones sobre la Libre Empresa, A.C., 1990-2000; CEO Grupo Banacci, 1996-2000; fin. cons. in field. Contbr. articles to profl. publs. Cesar Gaviria's bus. assessor Am. States Orgn., 1994-98. Roman Catholic. Avocations: writing, speaking, karate, soccer. Home: Col Indsl Calz de Guadalupe 392 07800 Mexico City Mexico Office: Guantes Vargas SAm, Col Indsl Calz de Guadalupe 392 07800 Mexico City Mexico

VARGAS MONIZ, PAULO RODRIGUES LIMA, education educator; b. Lisboa, Portugal, July 24, 1962; s. Luis Alfredo Campos Vargas Moniz and Ana Maria dos Santos Rodrigues Vargas Moniz; m. Teresa Maria Pinto Ramos Goncalve Pinto Ramos Goncalves, July 29, 1990. Univ. Lic., Univ. Lisbon, 1986; MS, U. Lisbon, 1989, PhD, 1993. Asst. trainee U. Minho, Braga, Portugal, 1986-88, Inst. Superior Tech., Lisboa, 1988-90; postdoctoral fellow U. Cambridge, E. Anglia, Gt. Britain, 1993-98; aux. prof. U. Beira Interior, Covilha, Portugal, 1998-2000, assoc. prof. Portugal, 2000—. Head of rsch. Group Astrophysics and Cosmology, Covilha, 1988—; nat. coord. Portuguese Cosmology Network (Portugal); prin. investigator Sci. and Technology Found., Lisboa, 1998—; referee European Union Rsch. Divsn., Brussels, 1999; referee Classical and Quantum Gravity, Bristol, Gt. Britain, and No. Ireland; lectr./presenter Public Understanding of Sci., Lisboa and Covilha, 2000. Contbr. articles to profl. jours. Mem. Cats Protection League, London, 1996 Postdoctoral fellow European Union, U. Cambridge, 1993-98; ESO rsch. grantee, 1998; grantee Brit. Coun. Rsch., 1999, DAAD, Germany, 1999, CERN, 1999, Pub. Understanding of Sci., 2000, Sapiens Rsch. Program, 2000. Mem. Inst. of Physics. Office: U Beira Interior/Phys Dept Rua Marques d'Avila Bolama Covilha 6200 Portugal Home: Apartado 12022 Lisboa 1069-001 Portugal Fax: 351 275 319 719. E-mail: black_cat@net.sapo.pt.

VARGHESE, GEORGE, physician, educator; b. India, Aug. 11, 1944; came to U.S., 1971; m. Molly Varghese; children: Smitha, Sapna, Martin. MD, St. John's Med. Coll., Bangalore, Ind., 1969. Diplomate Am. Bd. Phys. Medicine and Rehab., Am. Bd. Electrodiagnostic Medicine. Intern Nazareth Hosp., Phila., 1972; resident N.Y. Med. Coll., N.Y.C., 1973-75, rehab. med. instr., 1976-77; asst. prof. rehab. medicine U. Kans. Med. Ctr., Kansas City, 1977-81, assoc. prof. rehab. medicine, 1981-86, asst. dean for student affairs, 1999—, prof. rehab. medicine, 1986—. Vis. prof. Med. Coll. Trivandru, India, 1980, Nat. Spinal Injury Ctr., Stoke Mandeville, London, Eng., 1985; invited examiner Am. Bd. Phys. Medicine and Rehab., 1982-98; presenter in field. Author: (with others) Rehabilitation of Burn Patients, 1984, Orthotics et cetera, 1983, Rehabilitation Management of Amputees, 1983, Traumatic Brain Injury, 1992; contbr. articles to profl. jours. including Jour. Kans. Med. Soc., Orthotics and Prosthetics, Strasibmus, Paraplegia. Recipient Appreciation award Kans. chpt. Nat. Head Injury Assn., 1984; named Miracle Worker Kansas City Mag., 1983; grantee Internat. Latex Corp., Kans. U., Knit-Rite Corp., Norwich-Eaton Labs. Mem. AMA, Am. Spinal Injury Assn., Am. Assn. Electrodiagnostic Medicine, Am. Acad. Phys. Medicine and Rehab., Assn. Acad. Physiatrists, Kans. Med. Soc., Wyandotte/Johnson County Med. Soc. Office: U Kans Med Ctr 3901 Rainbow Blvd Kansas City KS 66160-0001

VARGHESE, SAMUEL, research scientist; b. Kottayam, Kerala, India, June 6, 1952; came to U.S., 1979; s. George and Achamma Varghese; m. Alison Elizabeth Heick, July 7, 1990; children: Daniel, Elizabeth. BSc, U. Kerala, India, 1972; MSc, Gujarat U., India, 1976; PhD, U. Medicine & Dentistry N.J., Newark, 1988. Rsch. fellow in medicine Mass. Gen. Hosp., Boston, 1988-92, Harvard Med. Sch., Boston, 1988-92; rsch. scientist St. Francis Hosp., Hartford, Conn., 1992—; asst. prof. medicine U. Conn., Farmington, 1992—. Contbr. articles to profl. jours. Recipient Nat. Rsch. Scholarship award NIH, 1989-92, Young Investigator award Donaghue Med. Rsch. Found., 1992-95, Child Health Rsch. award Charles H. Hood Found., 1996-97. Mem. AAAS, Am. Soc. for Bone and Mineral Rsch., Endocrine Soc., Sigma Xi. Achievements include research of gene regulation by vitamin D3; cloning of thymosin Beta 4, an actin binding protein gene; hormonal regulation of collagenase in bone cells. Office: St Francis Hosp and Med Ctr 114 Woodland St Hartford CT 06105-1208

VARGHESE, ZUBIN ABRAHAM, computer vision engineer, consultant; b. Alleppey, Kerala, India, Jan. 29, 1962; s. Abraham and Annie (Abraham) V.; m. Rachel George, June 24, 1994; children: Ratan Abraham, Nithin George. B Tech. with honors, Indian Inst. Tech., Kharagpur, 1986; MS, U. Mass., 1989;

PhD, Pa. State U., 1991. Registered profl. engr., New Brunswick, Can. Dir. rsch. and devel. Lizotte Cons. Ltd., Green River, N.B., Can., 1992—. Project leader rsch. and devel. Machine Vison Inspection of Seams of Food Cans, 1997, Computer Vision Inspection and Grading of Herring Roe, 1998. Mem. Soc. Mfg. Engrs., Am. Soc. Agrl. and Biol. Engrs., Internat. Soc. Optical Engring. Avocations: tennis, stock market, politics. Home: 37 Sormany Edmunston NB Canada E3V 1Y3 Office: Lizotte Cons Ltd 4 Montreuil St Green River NB Canada E7C 2M6

VARGISH, THOMAS, English language educator; b. Fair Haven, Vt., Feb. 13, 1939; s. Andrew and Frieda (Baer) V.; m. Linden K-C Foo, 1963 (div. 1976); m. Elizabeth Deeds Ermarth, 1979; children: Nicholas, Andrew, Roland Vargish Ermarth. BA, Columbia U., 1960; BA, MA, Oxford (Eng.) U., 1963, 68; PhD, Princeton U., 1966. From instr. to prof. English Dartmouth Coll., Hanover, N.H., 1965-82; prof. English U. Md., Balt., 1982-99, U. Gothenburg (Sweden), 1994-97. Author Newman: The Contemplation of Mind, 1970, The Providential Aesthetic in Victorian Fiction, 1985, Inside Relativity, 1988, Inside Modernism, 1999. Rhodes scholar, 1960, Guggenheim fellow, 1972. Mem. MLA, Soc. for Lit. and Sci., Phi Delta Phi. Home: 5289 S Joliet Way Englewood CO 80111-3827

VARGO, BETH COPELAND, poet, curator; b. Fukuoka, Japan, Jan. 14, 1951; d. Edwin Luther and Louise Tadlock Copeland; m. Charles Joseph Vargo, Jan. 14, 1978; children: Sarah, Joseph. BA in English, St. Andrews Presbyn. Coll., 1973; MFA in Creative Writing, Bowling Green State U., 1975. Author: (poetry) Traveling Through Glass, 2000 (Bright Hill Press Nat. Poetry Book award, 1999), Obi, 2001 (First Pl. in Poetry - Sixth Ann. Peregrine prize, 2001), (short stories) Painted Angels, 2000 (Sheila K. Smith Short Story award The Nat. League of Am. Pen Women, 2000), poetry. Mem.: Acad. of Am. Poets.

VARIN, ROGER ROBERT, textile executive; b. Bern, Switzerland, Feb. 15, 1925; came to U.S., 1951; s. Robert Francois and Anna (Martz) V.; m. Annemarie Louis, May 24, 1951; children: Roger R.R., Edward C.H., Viviane A.H. BBA, Mcpl. Coll., Bern, 1944; PhD in Chemistry, U. Bern, 1951. Rsch. fellow Harvard U., Cambridge, Mass., 1951-52; rsch. assoc. E.I. DuPont De Nemours, Wilmington, Del., 1952-62; dir. rsch. Riegel Textile Corp., Ware Shoals, S.C., 1962-71; founder, chief exec. officer Varinit Corp., Greenville, 1971—. Founder, chief exec. officer Varinit S.A., Geneva, 1974—. Pres. Greenville Sister City Internat., 1993; bd. dirs. Greenville Symphony Assn., 1997-2000; trustee Brevard Music Ctr., 2000—. Mem. Am. Chem. Soc., Fiber Soc., Soc. Advanced Materials and Process Engring., Rotary (pres. Greenville chpt. 1979-80), Sigma Xi. Office: Varinit Corp PO Box 6602 Greenville SC 29606-6602

VARIO, JOYCE, graphic designer; b. Warwick, R.I., July 28, 1959; d. Ralph Peter and Irene Louise (Beauregard) V. Grad., Art Inst. Boston, 1981. Prodn. artist Fin. Publ. Co., Boston, 1982-84; art dir., prodn. mgr. Kasmar Publs., Inc., Torrance, Calif., 1986-89; asst. mgr. desktop Copy Spot Printing, Santa Monica, 1989-90; graphic designer Crestec L.A., Inc., Gardena, 1990-92, Canter & Assocs., Inc., Santa Monica, 1992-97; owner Joyce Vario Illustration/Graphic Design, Inglewood, 1992—. Recipient Maggie Cert. Best New Publ./Consumer Kitchens by Profl. Designers, 1989, Maggie Cert. Annuals/Consumer Kitchens by Profl. Designers, 2001. Mem. Nat. Corvette Restorers Soc. (bd. dirs. So. Calif. chpt. newsletter editor 1994-98, chmn. 1999-2000), L.A. Macintosh Users Group. Avocations: Corvettes, collecting record albums. Office: Illustration/Graphic Design 1324 Welton Way Inglewood CA 90302-1309

VARKONYI, ANNA, communication company executive, consultant; b. Budapest, Hungary, Dec. 18, 1946; d. Geza and Gézáné (Bozzai) V.; m. Tamas Revesz, Jan. 31, 1970; children: Judit, Andras. MS, Tech. U. Budapest, 1970, PhD in Environ. Economy, 1996. Rsch. worker Hungarian Acad. Scis., Budapest, 1970-78; editor Buvar Mag., 1978-89; exec. Herald Agy., 1991—; pres. Ecovision LLC, Cliffside Park, N.J., 1996—. Cons. Tetra Pak, Budapest, 1994-2000, European Union, Budapest, 1992-96; lectr. Balint Gyorgy Sch. Journalism, Budapest, 1996-98; mem. Hungarian Commn. on Sustainable Devel., Budapest, 1994-98; vis. prof. Fairleigh Dickinson U., Teaneck, NJ, 2001-. Mem Environ. Mgmt. and Law Assn. (bd. dirs. 1994—), Danube Circle (founder), Soc. Environ. Journalists, Assn. of Hungarian Chemists. Jewish. Avocations: cooking, nature hiking. Home: 300 Winston Dr # 1812 Cliffside Park NJ 07010-3222 Office: Herald Pub House Bimbó út 64 1022 Budapest Hungary E-mail: avarkonyi@cs.com.

VARLEY, HERBERT PAUL, Japanese language and cultural history educator; b. Paterson, N.J., Feb. 8, 1931; s. Herbert Paul and Katharine L. (Norcross) V.; m. Betty Jane Geiskopf, Dec. 24, 1960 BS, Lehigh U., 1952; MA, Columbia U., 1961, PhD, 1964; DHL (hon.), Lehigh U., 1988. Asst. prof. U. Hawaii, Honolulu, 1964-65; asst. prof. dept. East Asian Langs. and Cultures Columbia U., N.Y.C., 1965-69, assoc. prof., 1969-75, prof., 1975-94, prof. emeritus Japanese history, 1994—, chmn. dept. East Asian Langs. and Cultures, 1983-89. Sen Soshitsu XV prof. Japanese Cultural History U. Hawaii, spring 1991-93, 94—. Author: The Onin War, 1967, The Samurai, 1970, Imperial Restoration in Medieval Japan, 1971, Japanese Culture, 1973, 4th edit., 2000, A Chronicle of Gods and Sovereigns, 1980, Tea in Japan: Essays on the History of Chanoyu, 1989, Warriors of Japan, As Portrayed in the War Tales, 1994; co-editor Sources of Japanese Tradition, Vol. 1, 2d edit., 2001. Bd. govs. Japanese Cultural Ctr. of Hawaii. Served with U.S. Army, 1952-54, Japan Recipient Imperial Decoration Govt. Japan, Order of Rising Sun, Gold Rays With Rosette Mem. Assn. Asian Studies, Japan Soc., Soc. Am. Magicians (pres. local chpt. 1983-84) Avocations: sleight of hand magic; piano. Home: 38 S Judd St Apt 15B Honolulu HI 96817-2609 Office: U Hawaii History Dept Sakamaki Hall A 203 2530 Dole St Honolulu HI 96822-2303 E-mail: pvarley@hawaii.edu.

VARLOTTA, LAURIE, pediatrician, pediatric pulmonologist; b. Oct. 27, 1959; MD, SUNY Downstate Med., Brooklyn, 1985; BA in chemistry, Emory U., Atlanta, 1981. Fellow pediat. pulmonology Children's Hosp. Phila., 1989-92; attending pulmonologist St. Christopher's Hosp. Children, Phila., 1992—, acting chief pulmonology, 1999-2000, chief sect. pulmonology and allergy, 2000—01, dir. Cystic Fibrosis Ctr., med. dir. respiratory therapy. Contbr. articles to profl. jours. Office: Ped Pulmonology/Children St Christophers Hosp Erie Ave & Front St Philadelphia PA 19134 E-mail: lv24@drexel.edu.

VARMA, AMIY, civil engineer, educator; b. Patna, Bihar, India, Apr. 14, 1963; came to U.S., 1986; s. Devendra Prasad and Bimal (Prasad) V.; m. Jaya Johari, Mar. 2, 1994; children: Ashish, Anurag. BTech. in Civil Engring., Indian Inst. Tech., Bombay, 1985; MSCE, Vanderbilt U., 1987; PhD, Purdue U., 1993. Registered profl. engr., N.D. Planning engr. Tata Electric Cos., Bombay, 1985-86; rsch. asst. Vanderbilt U., Nashville, 1986-87, Purdue U., West Lafayette, Ind., 1987-90; asst. prof. N.D. State U., Fargo, 1990-96, assoc. prof., 1996—. Contbr. articles to Tranp. Rsch., Transport Revs., Trasnp. Rsch. Record, others. S.D. Dept. Transp. rsch. grantee, 1994, 99, N.D. State U. grantee, 1994, 96, NSF, 1995, NSF EPSCOR grantee, 1996, 98. Mem. ASCE, Am. Inst. Cert. Planners, Inst. Transp. Engring. (various couns.), World Conf. Transp. Rsch. Soc., Chi Epsilon. Achievements include expertise in sustainable transportation and transportation financing and economics; research experience in infrastructure management, transportation systems, airport planning and design, traffic engineering and computer-aided design. Avocation: tennis. Home: 1505 N University Dr Apt 4 Fargo ND 58102-2275 Office: ND State U Dept Civil Engring Fargo ND 58105

VARMA, ARVIND, chemical engineering educator, researcher; b. Ferozabad, India, Oct. 13, 1947; s. Hans Raj and Vijay L. (Jhanjhee) V.; m. Karen K. Guse, Aug. 7, 1971; children: Anita, Sophia. BS ChemE, Panjab U., 1966; MS ChemE, U. N.B., Fredericton, Can., 1968; PhD ChemE, U. Minn., 1972. Asst. prof. U. Minn., Mpls., 1972-73; sr. research engr. Union Carbide Corp., Tarrytown, N.Y., 1973-75; asst. prof. chem. engring. U. Notre Dame, Ind., 1975-77, assoc. prof., 1977-80, prof., 1980-88, Arthur J. Schmitt prof., 1988—, chmn. dept., 1983-88; dir. Ctr. for Molecularly Engineered Materials, 2000—. Vis. prof. U. Wis., Madison, 1981; Chevron vis. prof. Calif. Inst. Tech., Pasadena, 1982; vis. prof. Ind. Inst. Tech.-Kanpur, 1989, U. Cagliari, Italy, 1989, 92; vis. fellow Princeton U., 1996. Piercy visiting prof., U. of Minn. 2001,Co-author: Mathematical Methods in Chemical Engineering, 1997, Parametric Sensitivity in Chemical Systems, 1999, Catalyst Design, 2001; editor: (with others) The Mathematical Understanding of Chemical Engineering Systems, 1980, Chemical Reaction and Reactor Engineering, 1987; series editor: Cambridge Series in Chemical Engineering, 1996—; contbr. numerous articles to profl. jours. Recipient Tchr. of Yr. award Coll. Engring. U. Notre Dame, 1991, Spl. Presdl. award 1992, R.H. Wilhelm award AIChE, 1993, Burns Grad. Sch. award 1997, E.W. Thiele award AIChE, 1998, Chemical Engring. Lectureship award, ASEE, 2000, Rsch. Achievement award U. Notre Dame, 2001; Fulbright scholar; Indo-Am. fellow, 1988-89. Home: 52121 N Lakeshore Dr Granger IN 46530-7848 Office: Dept Chem Engring U Notre Dame Notre Dame IN 46556

VARMA, BAIDYA NATH, sociologist, broadcaster, poet; b. India; m. Savitri Devi. PhD, Columbia U., 1958. Radio broadcaster to India UN; Asian News Moderator Nat. Edn. TV Network, N.Y.C.; prof. emeritus sociology CUNY. Prodr. radio dramas Voice of Am.; wrote, narrated over 200 documentary films, News of the Day; lectr. numerous univs. U.S., Can., Eng., India; chair Plenary Sessions World Congress of Sociology, Internat. Congress Anthrop. and Enthnological Scis; cons. Nat. Endowment Humanities, Ctr. Migration Studies, Dept. Energy, Wenner-Gren Found. Anthrop. Rsch. in U.S., Can. Coun., Indian Law Inst.; chair faculty seminars Columbia U.; presided Centenary Celebrations Indian Writers, N.Y.C.; vis. prof. Columbia U., other U.S., Indian Univs.; chair panel on religions and sexuality Parliament of World's Religions, 1993. Author: The Sociology and Politics of Development: A Theoretical Study, 1980, Social Science and Indian Society, 1985, New Directions in Theory and Methodology, 1993, Contemporary India (cert. of merit German Govt.), Love Feast, 1995, Spring of Civilization, 1995, Love and Life, 1999, India from Civilization to Nation, 1999; author, editor others; contbr. articles Ency. Americana, profl. jours.; edit. adv. nat., internat. sociol. jours.; author numerous poems. Assoc. trustee Wordsworth Trust; trustee Taraknath Das Found.; bd. scholars Buddhist Cultural Inst., U.S.; judge Permanent People's Tribunal Indsl. and Environ. Hazards and Human Rights, Rome; established Varma Found.; chmn. Sravi Found.; founding mems. Lincoln Ctr. for Performing Arts, N.Y.C.; chmn. bd. trustees Soc. for Restoration of Ancient Vidyadhams of India; trustee Internat. Found. for Vedic Edn., U.S., U.S. Capitol Hist. Soc.; mem. BC Millenium Time Capsule Commn. Sr. faculty fellow Am. Inst. Indian Studies, 1964-65, 84-85; elected to Am. Film Inst.; guest fellow Oxford U., The Sorbonne, Inst. Advanced Study, Simla, India; named Hon. Citizen, Colonial Williamsburg; recipient Cert. of Merit, City Coun. Pres. Yonkers; named Disting. Poet of 1996, Internat. Soc. Poets; elected patron of Am. Acad. Poetry, 1996; inducted Internat. Poetry Hall of Fame, 1996; named Outstanding Scientists of the 20th Century, 500 Leaders of Influence for the Next Millenium, 100 Founding Mem. Libr. of Congress, U.S. Mem. N.Y. Acad. Scis., South Asian Sociols. (1st pres.), Soc. Indian Acads. in Am. (exec. com.), Global Orgn. People of Indian Origin (life), U.S. Capitol Hist. Soc. (trustee). Home: 62 Belvedere Dr Yonkers NY 10705-2814

VARMA, DATLA G.K. radiologist, researcher; b. Bobbili, Andhra, India, June 2, 1951; came to U.S., 1976; now naturalized; s. Datla V. Raju and Datla Satyavathi; m. Siva Kumari, Dec. 20, 1980; children: Datla Kirti, Datla Vivek. MBBS, Andhra Med. Coll., 1975. Diplomate Am. Bd. Radiology, Am. Bd. Nuclear Medicine. Intern King George Hosp., Visakha Patnam, India, 1974-75; resident in anat. pathology Good Samaritan Hosp., Cin., 1977-78; resident in nuclear medicine Univ. Hosp., 1978-80, resident in radiology, 1980-83; asst. prof. radiology Tulane U., New Orleans, 1983-88, med. dir. diagnostic svcs./radiology dept., 1987-89, assoc. prof. radiology, 1988-89, sect. chief body CT, 1983-89, sect. chief body MRI, 1988-89; assoc. prof. radiology U. Tex./M.D. Anderson Cancer Ctr., Houston, 1989-99, acting sect. chief MRI, 1991-99, prof. radiology, 1999—. Contbr. articles to profl. jours., chpts. to books. Avocations: sports, travel, reading. Home: 3915 Marlowe St Houston TX 77005-2045 Office: Md Anderson Cancer Ctr PO Box 57 Houston TX 77001-0057 E-mail: dvarma@di.mdacc.tmc.edu.

VARMA, MATESH N. materials scientist, director; b. Saugor, Madhya Pradesh, India, Sept. 9, 1943; s. Niranjan Lal and Yashoda Devi Varma; m. Neelima Sinha; children: Namita, Ramit, Samit. PhD, Case Western Res. U., 1971. Sr. scientist Brookhaven Nat. Lab., Upton, NY, 1972—87; program dir. U.S. Dept. of Energy, Germantown, Md., 1987—. Author: (book) Physical and Chemical Mechanisms in Molecular Radiation Biology, 1991, Biophysical Modelling of Radiation Effects, 1992; patentee differential auger spectroscopy, 1976, apparatus and method for monitoring the intensities of charged particle beams, 1981. Pres. Kayasth Parivar, Rockville, 1990—92. Recipient Dist. Svc. to Sci. award, Fla. State U., 1992, Dept. Citation, Coll. Physicians and Surgeons, Columbia U., 1991. Mem.: Health Physics Soc., Radiation Rsch. Soc., Materials Rsch. Soc. Home: 7220 Deer Lake Ln Rockville MD 20855 Office: US Dept of Energy 19901 Germantown Rd Germantown MD 20874 Office Fax: 301-903-9513. Personal E-mail: mateshneelima@yahoo.com. Business E-Mail: matesh.varma@science.doe.gov.

VARMA, RAJENDER SINGH, organic chemist; b. New Delhi, India, July 26, 1951; came to U.S., 1983; s. Raj Mal and Roopvati V.; m. Manju Chandna, Dec. 18, 1977; children: Abhishek, Prashant. BS in Chemistry and Physics, Punjab (India) U., 1970; MS in Organic Chemistry, Kurukshetra (India) U., 1972; PhD in Organic Chemistry, Delhi (India) U., 1976; postgrad. diploma in pulp and paper, Norwegian Inst. Technology, Trondheim, Norway, 1978. Rsch. fellow Coun. Sci. & Indsl. Rsch., New Delhi, India, 1973-75; sr. rsch. fellow Ctr. Advanced Study in Chemistry, 1975-76; rsch. scientist Gwalior Rayon Silk Mfg. Co. Ltd., Calicut, Kerala, India, 1976-77; norad fellow Norwegian Inst. Technology, Trondheim, 1977-79; post-doctoral rsch. fellow The Robert Robinson Lab. The Univ. Liverpool, England, 1979-82; sr. rsch. assoc. U. Tenn., Knoxville, 1983-86; group leader Houston Biotechnology Inc., The Woodlands, Tex., 1986-90; asst. prof. Baylor Coll. Medicine, Ctr. for Biotechnology, 1986-93; rsch. scientist Houston Advanced Rsch. Ctr., 1993—; rsch. prof. dept. chemistry Sam Houston State U., Huntsville, Tex., 1995-99; chemist U.S. Environ. Protection Agy., Cin., 1999—. Patentee in field; contbr. chpts. to books, encys. and over 190 rsch. articles to profl. jours. Norad fellow Govt. of Norway, 1977; grantee Am. Cancer Soc., 1988, 89-92, NIH, 1991—. Mem. Am. Chem. Soc. Avocations: reading, jogging. Home: 8294 Millview Dr Cincinnati OH 45249-2240 E-mail: rajvarma@hotmail.com.

VARMA, RANBIR, economics educator; b. Nov. 29, 1928; BA, Patna U., 1949; MA, Columbia U., 1952; PhD, New Sch. for Social Rsch., 1957. Lectr. Columbia U., 1955-57; asst. prof. L.I. U., 1959-63, assoc. prof., 1963-66, prof. econs., 1966—, chmn. econs. dept., 1963-76, 85—. Bd. dirs. L.I. U.-Chung-and U. Program, 1963-64; chmn. commn. I, Bklyn. Ctr., 1964, chmn. dean's selection com., 1969-70; assoc. Columbia U. Faculty Seminar; cons. USIA, 1953-66; session chairperson devel. funds vs. needs, 8th World Conf., Soc. for Internat. Devel., 1966; session chairperson Montclair State Coll., 1977; conf. chairperson Eastern Econ. Assn., Washington, 1978. Author: (with others) Contemporary India, 1964, Goals Priorities and Dollars-The Next Decade, 1966, The Yearbook of the American Philosophical Society, 1968; contbr. articles to profl. jours; mem. editorial bd. Internat. Jour. of Devel. Planning Literature. Sidney Hillman fellowship, 1953-54; grantee Am. Philos. Soc., 1968. Mem. Am. Econ. Assn., Met. Econ. Assn., Soc. for Internat. Devel. Home: 565 W End Ave New York NY 10024-2705 Office: Long Island U Dept Econs University Pla Brooklyn NY 11201

VARMA, SURENDRA K. pediatrician, educator; b. Lucknow, India, Dec. 10, 1939; arrived in U.S., 1968; s. Raghubir P. and Leela Varma; m. Kamlesh Varma, Feb. 25, 1967; children: Rishi Anand, Ritu. MB, BChir, King George Med. Sch., Lucknow, 1962, MD, 1968. Diplomate Am. Bd. Pediat., Am. Subboard Pediat. Endocrinology. Rsch. assoc. MIT, Cambridge, Mass., 1972—74; asst. prof. Tex. Tech. U. Health Sci. Ctr., Lubbock, 1974—78, assoc. prof., 1978—83, prof., 1983—98, univ. dist. prof., 1998—. Instr. Harvard Med. Sch., Boston, 1973—76; vice chair resident rev. com. pediat. Accreditation Coun. Grad. Med. Edn., Chgo., 1997—; presenter in field. Contbr. articles to profl. jours. Lt. col. U.S. Army, 1990—91. Fellow: Am. Coll. Clin. Endocrinology, Am. Acad. Pediat.; mem.: Alpha Omega Alpha. Home: 4617 5th St Lubbock TX 79416 Office: Tex Tech Univ Health Scis Ctr 3601 4th St Lubbock TX 79430

VARMUS, HAROLD ELIOT, health science administrator, educator, science researcher; b. Oceanside, N.Y., Dec. 18, 1939; s. Frank and Beatrice (Barasch) V.; m. Constance Louise Casey, Oct. 25, 1969; children: Jacob Carey, Christopher Isaac. AB, Amherst Coll., 1961, DSc (hon.), 1984; MA, Literature, Harvard U., 1962; MD, Columbia U. Med. Sch., 1966. Lic. physician, Calif. Intern, resident Presbyn. Hosp., N.Y.C., 1966-68; clin. assoc. NIH, Bethesda, Md., 1968-70; lectr. dept. microbiology U. Calif., San Francisco, 1970-72, asst. prof., depts. microbiology and immunology, biochemistry and biophysics, 1972-74, assoc. prof., 1974-79, prof., 1979—93, Am. Cancer Soc. research prof., 1984—93; dir. NIH, Bethesda, Md., 1993—99; pres., CEO Meml. Sloan-Kettering Cancer Ctr., N.Y.C., 2000—. Chmn. bd. on biology NRC, 1991—93. Editor: Molecular Biology of Tumor Viruses, 1982, 1985, Readings in Tumor Virology, 1983. Co-recipient Lasker Found. award, 1982, Passano Found. award, 1983, Armand Hammer Cancer prize, GM Alfred Sloan award, 1984, Shubitz Cancer prize, 1984; named Calif. Acad. Sci. Scientist of the Yr., 1982; recipient Nobel Prize in Physiology or Medicine, 1989. Mem. AAAS, NAS, Inst. Medicine of NAS, Am. Soc. Virology, Am. Soc. Microbiology, Am. Acad. Arts and Scis. Democrat. Achievements include research (with J. Michael Bishop) on the replication of retroviruses. Office: Meml Sloan-Kettering Cancer Ctr 1275 York Ave New York NY 10021-6094*

VARN, WILFRED CLAUDE, lawyer; b. DeLand, Fla., Mar. 14, 1919; s. Claude Grady and Marjorie Amelia (Boor) Varn; m. Betty Jean Davenport, Nov. 12, 1949; children: Mary Patricia Varn Moore, Wilfred Claude Jr., George Seward. BSBA, U. Fla, 1947, LLB, (reconferred JD 1967), 1948. Bar: Fla. 1948, U.S. Dist. Ct. (no. dist.) Fla. 1948, U.S. Dist. Ct. (mid. dist. and trial bar so. dist.) Fla. 1956, U.S. Ct. Appeals (5th cir.) 1958, U.S. Supreme Ct. 1959, U.S. Ct. Appeals (5th and 11th cirs.), 1981. Ptnr. Spear and Varn, Panama City, Fla., 1948-54; asst. U.S. Atty. Dept. Justice No. Dist. Fla., 1954-58, U.S. Atty., 1958-61; ptnr. Ervin, Varn, Jacobs & Ervin, Tallahassee, 1961—92; of counsel Ervin, Boyd & Allaman, 1992—. Vice chancellor Episcopal Diocese of Fla., Jacksonville, 1994—; Rep. state com. mem. 1961-66. 2d lt. U.S. Army, 1942-46. PTO. Decorated Legion of Merit, U.S. Army, 1972. Fellow Am. Coll. of Trial Lawyers, Am. Bar Found.; mem. Fla. Bar Assn. (50 yr. Membership award 1998), Kiwanis Club (bd. dirs.). Avocations: painting, exercise, travel, hiking, swimming. Home: 705 Kenilworth Rd Tallahassee FL 32312-3045 Office: Ervin Varn & Allaman 223 S Gadsen St Tallahassee FL 32301-1811

VARNEDOE, JOHN KIRK TRAIN, art historian, educator; b. Savannah, Ga., Jan. 18, 1946; s. Samuel Lamartine and Lilla (Train) V.; m. Elyn Zimmerman. BA with honors, Williams Coll., 1967, DFA (hon.), 1994; MA, Stanford U., 1970, PhD, 1972; DFA (hon.), Pratt Inst., 1997. Asst. instr. art history Williams Coll., 1967-68; asst. prof. art history Stanford (Calif.) U., 1973-74; asst. prof. Columbia U., N.Y.C., 1974-80; assoc. prof. Inst. Fine Arts, NYU, 1980-84, prof. fine arts, 1984-88; chief curator dept. painting and sculpture Mus. Modern Art, N.Y.C., 1989—2001; prof. Sch. Hist. Studies Inst. Advanced Study, Princeton, NJ, 2001—. Vis. lectr. in law Columbia U. Law Sch., 1980-81; adj. curator dept. painting and sculpture Mus. Modern Art, 1985-88; mem. adv. bd. J. Paul Getty Program for Art on Film, 1985-87, Ctr. for Advanced Study in Visual Arts, 1990-93; mem. selection panel J. Paul Getty Postdoctoral Fellowships, 1985-88, J. Paul Getty Sr. Fellowships, 1988-90; Slade prof. art history Oxford (Eng.) U., 1992; lectr. in field. Author: The Drawings of Auguste Rodin, 1971, Vienna 1900, 1986, Gustave Caillebotte, 1987, Northern Light, 1988 (Henry Allen Moe prize 1983), A Fine Disregard--What Makes Modern Art Modern, 1990, High and Low: Modern Art and Popular Culture, 1990, Cy Twombly: A Retrospective, 1994, Jasper Johns: A Retrospective, 1996 ed. Jasper Johns: Writings, Sketchbook Notes, Interviews, 1996, Jackson Pollock, 1998; mem. editl. bd. The Art Bull., 1985-90; contbr. articles and revs. to profl. jours. Decorated knight The Royal Order of Donnebroge (Denmark), officer Order of Arts and Letters (France); David E. Finley fellow Nat. Gallery Art, 1970-73, NEH fellow, 1977-78, MacArthur Found. fellow, 1984-89; Rsch. grantee Columbia U., 1975, Travel grantee Am. Coun. Learned Socs. Fellow Am. Acad. Arts & Scis., NYU Soc. Fellows. Office: Inst Advanced Study Einstein Dr Princeton NJ 08540

VARNER, BRUCE H., JR. fire department official, educator; b. Washington, June 21, 1946; s. Bruce H. Varner and Rose A. (Parrish) Lewis; m. Elaine L. Nelson (div. 1974); 1 child, Paul A.; m. Susan A. Nungesser, Oct. 7, 1989 (div. 2000). AA in Fire Protection, Phoenix Coll., 1972; student, Ariz. State U., 1973-77. Firefighter Phoenix Fire Dept., 1967-72, fire engr., 1972-77, fire capt., 1977-83, div. chief, 1983-85, dep. chief, 1985-92; fire chief Carrollton (Tex.) Fire Dept., 1992—. Mem. Nat. Fire Protection Assn. (tech. corr. com. fire svc. protective clothing and equipment), Internat. Assn. Fire Chiefs, Dallas County Fire Chiefs (pres. 2001), S.W. Fire Chiefs, Denton County Fire Chiefs, North Tex. Fire Chiefs Assn. (pres. 1996), Internat. Soc. Fire Svc. Instrn., Hon. Order Ky. Cols., Career Fire Chief of Yr. Fire Chief Mag., 2001; U.S./U.K. Chief Fire Officers Symposium, Wingspread IV Conf., 1996. Avocations: sailing, travel, photography, raquetball. Office: Carrollton Fire Dept 1945 Jackson PO Box 110535 Carrollton TX 75011-0535 E-mail: brucevarner@cityofcarrollton.com.

VARNER, CHARLEEN LAVERNE MCCLANAHAN (MRS. ROBERT B. VARNER), nutritionist, educator, administrator, dietitian; b. Alba, Mo., Aug. 28, 1931; d. Roy Calvin and Lela Ruhama (Smith) McClanahan; student Joplin (Mo.) Jr. Coll., 1949-51; BS in Edn., Kans. State Coll. Pittsburg, 1953; MS, U. Ark., 1958; PhD, Tex. Woman's U. 1966; postgrad. Mich. State U., summer, 1955, U. Mo., summer 1962; m. Robert Bernard Varner, July 4, 1953. Apprentice county home agt. U. Mo., summer 1952; tchr. Ferry Pass Sch., Escambia County, Fla., 1953-54; tchr. biology, home econs. Joplin Sr. H.S., 1954-59; instr. home econs. Kans. State Coll., Pittsburg, 1959-63; lectr. foods, nutrition Coll. Household Arts and Scis., Tex. Woman's U., 1963-64, rsch. asst. NASA grant, 1964-66; assoc. prof. home econs. Central Mo. State U., Warrensburg, 1966-70, adviser to Colhecon, 1966-70, adviser to Alpha Sigma Alpha, 1967-70, 72, mem. bd. advisers Honors Group, 1967-70; prof., head dept. home econs. Kans. State Tchrs. Coll., Emporia, 1970-73; prof., chmn. dept. home econs. Benedictine Coll., Atchison, Kans., 1973-74; prof., chmn. dept. home econs. Baker U., Baldwin City, Kans., 1974-75; owner, operator Diet-Con Dietary Cons. Enterprises, cons. dietitian, 1973—, Home-Con Cons. Enterprises. Mem. Joplin Little Theater, 1956-60. Mem. NEA, Mo., Kans. state tchrs. assns., AAUW, Am., Mo., Kans. dietetics assns., Am., Mo., Kans. home econs. assns., Mo. Acad. Scis., AAUP, U. Ark. Alumni Assn., Alumni Assn. Kans. State Coll. of Pittsburg, Am. Vocat. Assn., Assn. Edn. Young Children, Sigma Xi, Beta Sigma Phi, Beta Beta Beta, Alpha Sigma Alpha, Delta Kappa Gamma, Kappa Kappa Iota, Phi Upsilon Omicron, Theta Alpha Pi, Kappa Phi. Methodist (organist). Home: PO Box 1009 Topeka KS 66601-1009

VARNER, CHILTON DAVIS, lawyer; b. Opelika, Ala., Mar. 12, 1943; d. William Cole and Frances (Thornton) Davis; m. K. Morgan Varner III, June 19, 1965; 1 child, Ashley Elizabeth. AB with distinction, Smith Coll., 1965; JD with distinction, Emory U., 1976. Assoc. King & Spalding, Atlanta, 1976-83, ptnr., 1983—. Trustee Emory U., Atlanta, 1995—; bd. dirs. Wesley Woods Healthcare, 11th Cir. Ct. Appeals Hist. Soc.; bd. trustees Product Liability Adv. Coun. Found., 1996—. Author: Appellate Handbook for Georgia Lawyers, 1995. Mem. Leadership Atlanta, 1984-85; asst. clk., elder, bd. elders Trinity Presbyn. Ch., Atlanta, 1985-88; exec. com. Ate Arts Alliance, Atlanta, 1981-85; mem. Atlanta Symphony Chorus, 1970-74. Recipient Disting. Alumna award Emory U. Law Sch., 1998. Fellow Am. Coll. Trial Lawyers; mem. ABA, Ga. Bar Assn., Atlanta Bar Assn., Order of Coif, Phi Beta Kappa. Office: King & Spalding 191 Peachtree St NE Ste 4900 Atlanta GA 30303-1740

VARNER, DAVID EUGENE, lawyer; b. Dallas, Oct. 9, 1937; s. E.C. and D. Evelyn (Bauguss) V.; m. Joan Paula Oransky, Aug. 13, 1962; children: Michael A., Kevin E., Cheryl L. BA, So. Meth. U., Dallas, 1958, JD, 1961. Bar: Tex. 1961, Fla. 1974, Okla., 1977, U.S. Supreme Ct. 1978. Assoc. Eldridge, Goggans, Davidson & Silverberg, Dallas, 1962-65; atty., asst. sec. Redman Industries, Inc., 1965-66; assoc. gen. atty. Tex. Instruments, Inc., 1966-73; sr. atty., asst. sec. Fla. Gas Co., Winter Park, 1973-76; v.p., gen. counsel, sec. Facet Enterprises, Inc., Tulsa, 1976-78, Summa Corp., Las Vegas, Nev., 1978-82; sr. v.p., gen. counsel, sec. Transco Energy Co., Houston, 1982-95. Mng. editor Southwestern Law Jour., 1960-61 Mem. ABA, Tex. Bar, Okla. Bar, Fla. Bar. Office: PO Box 79571 Houston TX 77279-9571

VARNER, GARY ROBERT, social services administrator, writer; b. Keokuk, Iowa, Oct. 30, 1951; s. Robert O. and Edith L. Varner; m. Susan S. Sapone; children: Timothy, Brenna. AA, Palomar Coll., San Marcos, Calif., 1976. Program analyst State Dept. Health Svcs., Sacramento, 1993—2001, Calif. Dept. Social Svcs., Sacramento, 2001—. Author: (book) Essays in Contemporary Paganism, 2000, Sacred Wells: A Study in the History, Meaning and Mythology of Holy Wells and Waters, 2002; head writer: Pagan Sanctuary Network , 1999. Mem.: United Authors Assn. Avocations: rare books, photography, travel, history. Personal E-mail: paganessays@yahoo.com. Business E-Mail: gary.varner@dss.ca.gov.

VARNER, HELEN, communications educator; b. Biddeford, Maine, Jan. 21, 1946; d. E. Harold Kemper and Darlene Ruth (Marcus) Meeks; m. Foy E. Varner, Jr., May 26, 1977; children: Dawn Hedgpeth, Jennifer Thompson, Foy E. III. B in Applied Arts and Scis., Stephen F. Austin State U., 1981, MA, 1983; EdD, Tex. A&M U., 1990. Reporter Galveston (Tex.) Daily News, 1964-65; acct. exec. John Gilbert Advt. Agy., Miami, Fla., 1965-67; chief Correspondence Sch., U.S. Army Edn. Ctr., Mannhiem, Germany, 1967-70; coord. pub. info. Galveston Coll., 1970-74; pub. rels., advt. dir. Sea-Arama Marineworld, Inc., Galveston, 1974-77; owner, chief exec. officer The Varner Pub. Rels. & Advt. Agy., 1977-81; instr. Stephen F. Austin State U., Nacogdoches, Tex., 1981-88; assoc. prof. journalism N.E. La. U., Monroe, La., 1988-90, Chaminade U. of Honolulu, 1990-91; assoc. prof. comm. Hawaii Pacific U., Honolulu, 1991—, v.p. univ. rels. and dean of comm., 1998. Pres. Galveston Conv. & Vis. Bur., Galveston, 1978-79. Pres. Galveston Press Club, 1977, ARC, Galveston Chpt., 1976, Nacogdoches Chpt., 1980; dir. Girl Scouts Am, Gulf Coast, Galveston, 1976. Named Outstanding Adviser Pub. Rels. Student Soc. Am., 1989, Outstanding Prof. Omicron Delta Kappa, 1989, Favorite Prof. Alpha Lambda Delta, 1988; recipient Mentor award Mortarboard Sr. Leadership Soc., 1990, Outstanding Adviser award Women In Communication, Inc., 1986-87, 85-86. Mem. Assn. for Edn. in Journalism and Mass Communication, Tex. Pub. Rels. Assn. (pres. 1987-88), Pub. Rels. Soc. Am., Pub. Rels. Assn. La. (sec. 1989), So. Pub. Rels. Fedn., Women In Communications (pres. Honolulu Profl. chpt. 1995-96), Orgn. of Women Leaders (Woman Leader of Yr. 1995-96), Pub. Rels. Found. Tex. Avocation: miniatures collection. Home: 46-082 Puulena St Apt 1224 Kaneohe HI 96744-3754 Office: Hawaii Pacific U 1132 Bishop St Ste 504 Honolulu HI 96813-2820 E-mail: hvarner@hpu.edu., communication@hpu.edu.

VARNER, JOYCE EHRHARDT, retired librarian; b. Quincy, Ill., Sept. 13, 1938; d. Wilbur John and Florence Elizabeth (Mast) Ehrhardt; m. Donald Giles Varner, Sept. 12, 1959; children: Amy, Janice, Christian, Matthew, Nadine. BA, Northeastern Okla. State U., 1980; MLS, U. Okla., 1984. Lab. analyst Gardner Denver Co., Quincy, 1956-60; sales rep. Morrisonville, Ill., 1963-69; libr. clk. U. Ill., Urbana, 1973-75; libr. tech. asst. Northeastern Okla. State U., Tahlequah, 1976-86; asst. reference libr. Muskogee (Okla.) Pub. Libr., 1986-90; libr. Jess Dunn Correctional Ctr., Taft, Okla., 1990-98; ret., 1998; field office supr. Census 2000 Dept. of Commerce, Welling, Okla., 1998. Editor Indian Nations Audubon Nature Notes, 1977-81, 96—; contbr. articles to newspaper. Vol. Lake-Wood coun. Girl Scouts U.S.A., 1975-98, bd. dirs. 1992-98, pres., 1995-96; sec.-treas. Cherokee County Rural Water Dist. 7, 1987—; edn. chmn. Indian Nations chpt. Nat. Audubon Soc., 1989-2000, pres., 2000—. Recipient Thanks Badge, Lake-Wood coun. Girl Scouts U.S.A., 1990. Mem. AAUW (chair diversity com. 2000), Okla. Libr. Assn. (nominating com. 1989), Okla. Acad. Sci., Okla. Ornithol. Soc. (chmn. libr. com. 1978-88, Award of Merit 1990, pres.-elect 1994, pres. 1995-96), Alpha Chi, Beta Beta Beta, Phi Delta Kappa (Found. rep. 1984-86, historian 1992—). Avocations: nature study, needlework, square dancing, genealogy. Home: 20582 S Welling Rd Welling OK 74471-2001

VARNER, ROBERT BERNARD, counselor, educator; b. Ellsworth, Kans., May 31, 1930; s. Bernard Lafayette and Leota (Campbell) V.; B.S., Kans. State U., Pittsburg, 1952; M.S., U. Ark., 1959; postgrad. Mich. State U., summer 1955, U. Mo., summer 1962, (grantee) U. Kans., 1972-73; m. Charleen LaVerne McClanahan, July 4, 1953. Athletic coach, social sci. tchr. Joplin (Mo.) Sr. High Sch., 1956-63; head social sci. dept. R.L. Turner High Sch., Carrollton, Tex., 1963-66; asst. athletic coach, jr. high sch. social sci. tchr. Warrensburg, Mo., 1966-70; coach, social sci. tchr., Emporia, Kans., 1970-72; asst. cottage dir., counselor Topeka Youth Ctr., 1973— ; substitute tchr. Topeka Pub. Schs., 1974— . Recreation dir. Carrollton-Farmers Branch (Tex.) Recreation Center, 1964-66; city recreation dir., Warrensburg, Mo., 1966-68. Served with USN, 1953-54. Mem. NEA, Kans. State U.-Pittsburg Alumni Assn., U. Ark. Alumni Assn., Phi Delta Kappa, Sigma Tau Gamma. Democrat. Methodist. Club: Elks. Address: PO Box 1009 Topeka KS 66601-1009

VARNER, STERLING VERL, retired oil company executive; b. Ranger, Tex., Dec. 20, 1919; s. George Virgle and Christina Ellen (Shafer) V.; m. Paula Jean Kennedy, Nov. 17, 1945; children: Jane Ann, Richard Alan. Student, Murray State Sch. Agr., 1940, Wichita State U., 1949. With Kerr-McGee, Inc., 1941-45; with Koch Industries, Inc., Wichita, Kans., 1945-90, pres., chief operating officer, 1974-86, vice chmn., 1987-90, chmn. bd. dirs., 1990, now bd. dirs.; ret. Owner Shadow Valley Ranch; bd. dirs. Koch Industries Inc. Mem. Wichita Country Club, Crestview Country Club. Mem. Ch. of Christ. Home: 1515 N Linden Ct Wichita KS 67206-3312 Office: Koch Industries Inc PO Box 2256 411 E 37th St N Wichita KS 67219

VARNERIN, LAWRENCE JOHN, physicist, retired educator; b. Boston, July 10, 1923; s. Lawrence John and Josephine (Nangeroni) V.; m. Marie Elizabeth Hynes, Apr. 19, 1952; children: Melanie Viscelli, Lawrence, Gregory, Sharon Cenci, Suzanne Dahlinger, Bruce, Carol Levandowski, Jeffrey. SB in Physics, MIT, 1947, PhD in Physics, 1949. Supr. TR/ATR microwave tube, electronics divsn. Sylvania corp., Boston, 1949-52; acting mgr. physics dept. Westinghouse Rsch. Labs., Pitts., 1952-57; head heterojunction IC and materials dept. AT&T Bell Labs., Murray Hill, N.J., 1957-86; Chandler-Weaver prof. elec. engring., chmn. elec. engring. computer sci. dept. Lehigh U., Bethlehem, Pa., 1986-92, Chandler-Weaver prof. emeritus, 1992—. Assoc. editor Jour. Magnetism and Magnetic Materials, 1973-94. Served with U.S. Army, 1943-46. Fellow IEEE, Am. Phys. Soc.; mem. Magnetics Soc. Roman Catholic. Home: PO Box 1107 Wolfeboro NH 03894-1107 E-mail: varnerjn@ieee.org.

VARNES, JILL TUTTON, university official, health educator; b. Rome, Sept. 15, 1947; d. Mather M. and Patti L. (Fricks) Tutton; m. G. Peter Wilson, Dec. 1966 (div. Oct. 1973); children: James G. II, Jennifer Anne; m. Paul R. Varnes, Nov. 24, 1977; 1 child, Julia Rae. AA, Lake Sumter Community Coll., Leesburg, Fla., 1967; BS in Phys. Edn., U. Fla., 1973, MA, 1974; EdD, U. So. Miss., 1978. Cert. tchr., health educator, health edn. specialist, Fla. Tchr., coach Marion County Schs., Dunnellon, Fla., 1974-76; asst. coord. comprehensive health edn. demonstration model Fla. Dept. Edn., Tallahassee, 1977-78; asst. prof. health edn. U. Fla., Gainesville, 1978-83, assoc. prof., 1983-96, dir. living well employee wellness program, 1985-89, asst. dean Coll. Health and Human Performance, 1989-2000, assoc. dir. Ctr. for Health Promotion, Rsch. and Devel., 1989—, prof., 1996—, dir. accreditation/new degree programs Office Acad. Affairs, 2000—. Presenter to numerous internat., nat., state and local orgns. on wellness, sch. health programs, profl. preparation and gerontology; cons. to numerous govt., pub. and pvt. agys. on curriculum devel., health promotion, program and pers. evaluation, and worksite wellness programs. Contbr. articles to profl. jours. Bd. dirs. Am. Lung Assn. Fla., also various coms., also mem. NE br. bd. dirs.; mem. nat. coms. Am. Lung Assn., N.Y.C. Grantee Fla. Dept. Edn., 1987-89, Nat. Cancer Inst., 1989-97, Univ. Fla., Coll. of Health and Human Performance Alumni Recognition Awd., 1997. Fellow Assn. for Fitness in Bus. (pres. region 3, 1988-89); mem. AAHPERD (nominating com. 1986, nominating com. chair 1995, bd. govs., pres. 1998-99, chair, fin. com. 1999-2000, chair awards com. 2001—, Am. Assn. Health Edn. fellow's com. 2001—, bd. dirs. so. dist., 1989-91, v.p. health 1986-89, honor award 1989, 97), Fla. Assn. for Health, Phys Edn., Recreation and Dance (v.p. health div. 1978-80, pres. 1980-83, honor award 1983, pres. citation, 1998), Virginia AHPERD Pres. Citation, 1998, Fla. Assn. Profl. Health Educators (sec., Health Edn. award 1990), Assn. for Advancement of Health Edn. (Profl. Recognition award 1996), Miss. Assn. for HPERD (Ikey Carr Meml. lectr.). Office: U Fla Office of Acad Affairs Tigert 235 Gainesville FL 32611 E-mail: jvarnes@hhp.ufl.edu.

VARNEY, CARLETON BATES, JR. interior designer, columnist, educator; b. Lynn, Mass., Jan. 23, 1937; s. Carleton Bates and Julia (Raczkowskos) V.; divorced; children: Nicholas, Seamus, Sebastian. BA, Oberlin Coll., 1958; student, U. Madrid, 1957; MA, NYU, 1969; LHD (hon.), U. Charleston, 1987. Sch. tchr., 1958-59; asst. to pres. Dorothy Draper & Co., Inc., 1959-63, exec. v.p., 1963-66, pres., 1966—; dean Carleton Varney Sch. of Art & Design, U. Charleston, W.Va. Designer: chairs, decorative fabrics, dinnerware and china, crystal glassware, table and bed linen, ready to wear resort collection Cruzanwear, 1987, mens' wear furnishings for Rawlinson & Marking, London, 1987; Ready to wear resort coll., "A Perfect Day in Paradise", 1998, Colours Resort Collection, 2000, Varney and Sons Furniture Collection for Kindel Furniture Co., 2000, Linen Designs for Thief River Linens, 2000, Lamps and Light Fixtures for Tyndale, a divsn. of Frederick Cooper, 2000, Carleton VArney By-the-Yard Fabric Line, 2000; interior designer: Dromoland Castle, Ireland, 1963, 88, Westbury Hotel, Belgium, 1964, N.Y. World's Fair, 1965, Clare Inn, Ireland, 1968, Greenbrier Hotel, White Sulphur Springs, W.Va., 1968, Westbury Hotel, San Francisco, 1973, Copley Plaza Hotel, Boston, 1976, Amway Grand Plaza Hotel, Grand Rapids, Mich., 1980, The Grand Hotel, Mackinac Island, Mich., 1978, Equinox House, Manchester, Vt., 1984, Brazilian Ct. Hotel, Palm Beach, Fla., 1985, Waldorf Towers, N.Y.C., 1985, Dawn Beach Hotel, St. Maarten, 1985, Christian Broadcasting Conv. Ctr., 1986, Met. Opera House boutique, N.Y.C., 1985, (cruise ship) World Discoverer, 1984, Arrowwood Conv. Ctr., Purchase, N.Y., 1987, Boca Raton Hotel and Club, Fla., 1987, Speedway Club, Charlotte, N.C., 1987, Coccoloba Plantation, Anguilla, Brit. Virgin Islands, 1987, Villa Madeleine, St. Croix, V.I., 1987, Ashford Castle, Ireland, 1988, Adare Manor, Ireland, 1988, The Breakers, Palm Beach, Fla., 1989, Jackson Lake Lodge, Wyo., 1989, V.P.'s Residence, Washington, 1989, Cormorant Cove, St. Croix, V.I., 1990, The Buccaneer Hotel, St. Croix, 1991, Dromoland Castle, Internat. Ctr., Ireland, 1991, West Village Golf Resort, Tokyo, 1993, Half Moon Bay Club, Jamaica, The Copely Plz., Boston, 1997, The Plaza, N.Y., 1997, The Hibiscus Restaurant, Palm Beach, Fla., 1999, numerous others; designer: White House party for celebration Israel-Egypt Peace Treaty, 1979; Palm Beach Cares fashion benefit for Am. Found. for AIDS Research, 1988, log home for Pres. and Mrs. Carter, Ellijay, Ga., 1983; color cons. Carter Presdl. Library, 1986; trustee and curator: former presdl. yacht U.S.S. Sequoia, 1982; retail stores: Carleton Varney By-The Yard Showroom , Sarasota, Fla., Carleton Varney Rose Cottage, Newmarket-on-Fergus, Ireland, 1991; author: numerous books including You and Your Apartment, 1960, The Family Decorates a Home, 1962 Carleton Varney Decorates Windows, 1975, Be Your Own Decorator, 1979, There's No Place Like Home, 1980, Down Home, 1981, Carleton Varney's ABC's of Decorating, 1983, Staying in Shape: An Insider's Guide to the Great Spas, 1983, Room by Room Decorating, 1984, Color Magic, 1985, The Draper Touch, 1988, Kiss the Hibiscus Goodnight, 1992, The Decorator, 1999; syndicated columnist: Your Family Decorator, 1968—; decorating column Familyclick.com, 2000, Inside Design column N.Y. Post, 2001; contbg. editor Good Housekeeping Mag., 1993-95; style editor Men's Style mag.; editor-at-large Hamptons Mag., 2000—. Recipient Shelby Williams award for design achievement, 1967, Tommy design award for Covington's Heraldry collection, 1989, Interior Design Hall of Fame award, 1990. Mem. Indsl. Designers Soc. Am., N.Y. State Bd. for Interior Design. Clubs: N.Y. Athletic; Shannon Rowing (Ireland); Millbrook Golf and Tennis (N.Y.). Office: Dorothy Draper & Co Inc 60 E 56th St New York NY 10022-3204 also: Rose Cottage Newmarket-on-Fergus County Clare Ireland also: Carleton Varney by the Yard 2239 15th St # B&C Sarasota FL 34237-2828 E-mail: dorothydraper1@aol.com. *My success, I believe, is due to an ability to understand and use vibrant color appropriately, and to strive for perfection of detail in all my designs as details separate the excellent from the ordinary.*

VARNEY, GLENN HERBERT, management educator; b. Jefferson, Ohio, Dec. 1, 1926; s. Herbert Henry and Edna (Schwartz) V.; m. Ruth Constance Park, June 30, 1951; children: Janice McKnight, Kenneth. BSc in Bus. Adminstrn., Ohio State U., 1949, MBA, 1951; PhD, Case Western Res. U., 1971. Cert. sr.profl. in human rels. Pers. mgr. Glidden Co., Cleve., 1951-55; mgr. recruitment and mgmt. devel. Diamond Shamrock, Dallas, 1955-65; dir. human resources Harshaw Chems., Cleve., 1965-68; asst. to dean Case Western Res. U., 1968-70; dir. Mgmt. Ctr. Bowling Green (Ohio) State U., 1970-83, prof. mgmt. emeritus, 1970—; pres. Mgmt. Adv. Assocs., Bowling Green, 1968—. Bd. dirs. Self-Directed Resource Ctr., Bowling Green, 1992—, Inst. for Orgnl. Effectiveness, 1979-96; cons. numerous U.S., internat. orgns. Author: Building Productive Teams, 1990, Management by Objectives, 1969, 3 other books; co-author (with Robert Golembiewski) Cases in Organizational Development, 1999; contbr. over 100 articles to profl. jours. Vol. work with non-profit orgns.; mem. various ch. and cmty. related coms. and projects. Mem. ASTD (nat. v.p. 1980-81, award for leadership 1992, award for excellence 1993); Soc. for Human Resources (life accreditation, Disting. Svc. award 2001), Acad. of Mgmt., Beta Gamma Sigma, Omicron Delta Kappa. Republican. Avocations: farm managment, jogging. Home: 546 Hillcrest Dr Bowling Green OH 43402-3616 Fax: (419) 354-8781. E-mail: gvarney@bgnet.bgsu.edu.

VARNEY, RICHARD ALAN, medical center administrator; b. Concord, N.H., July 8, 1950; s. John Berry and Hattie Elizabeth (Harrington) V.; m. Cheryl Suzanne Glaab, Dec. 31, 1983; stepchildren: Alysen Suzanne, Craig Judson. BS in Phys. Edn., U. N.H., 1972; MHA in Healthcare Adminstrn., Baylor U., 1984; diploma, Command and Gen. Staff Coll., 1986. Commd. 2d lt. U.S. Army, 1973, advanced through grades to lt. col., 1991; dep. asst. CEO Cutler Army Hosp., Ft. Devens, Mass., 1973—76; field med. asst. 38th ADA Bde.,, Osan Air Base, Republic of Korea, 1977—78; dep. asst. CEO 15th Med. Battalion, Ft. Hood, Tex., 1979—81; adminstrv. resident Ireland Army Hosp., Ft. Knox, Ky., 1982—83; COO, exec. officer U.S. Army Dental Activity, 1983—86; grad. instr. Army-Baylor Healthcare Program, San Antonio, 1986—90; project mgr. Office of the Army Surgeon Gen., Washington, 1990—93; ret. U.S. Army, 1993; office mgr. Aebi, Ginty, Romaker & Sprouse MD's, Inc., Lancaster, Ohio, 1993—2000; dir. gen. internal medicine program The Ohio State U. Med. Ctr., Columbus, 2000—. Mem. Source Selection Evaluation Bd.-Champus Reform, Arlington, Va., 1987; mem. adv. com. for assoc. degree program in med. assisting Ohio U., Lancaster, 1998-2000. Adult leader Boy Scouts Am., Tex., Va. and Ohio, 1988-97; mem. Lancaster City Bd. of Health, 1996-2001, pres. pro tem, 1999-2001; mem. Fairfield County Combined Gen. Health Dist. Bd., 2002--. Decorated Legion of Merit, Order of Mil. Med. Merit award, Expert Field Med. badge; named to Hon. Order Ky. Cols., 1989, Outstanding Young Man of Am., 1982. Fellow Am. Coll. Healthcare Execs.; mem. Ctrl. Ohio Health Adminstrs. Assn., Ohio Med. Group Mgmt. Assn., Mid-Ohio Med. Mgmt. Assn., Profl. Assn. Med. Mgrs., Am. Assn. Procedural Coders, Lancaster Area Soc. for Human Resource Mrmt. (legis. rep. 1998-99, membership chair 1999—), Am. Hosp. Assn., Nat. Eagle Scout Assn., The Ret. Officers Assn., Am. Legion, Fraternal Order of Eagles, Alpha Phi Omega. Avocations: home improvement, music. Home: 1025 E 5th Ave Lancaster OH 43130-3276 Business E-Mail: varney-1@medctr.osu.edu. E-mail: richvarney@buckeyeinternet.com.

VARNEY, ROBERT NATHAN, retired physicist, researcher; b. San Francisco, Nov. 7, 1910; s. Frank Hastings Sr. and Emily Patricia (Rhine) V.; m. Astrid Margareta Riffolt, June 19, 1948; children: Nils Roberts, Natalie Rhine. AB with highest honors in Physics, U. Calif., Berkeley, 1931, MA, 1932, PhD, 1935; DSc (hon.), Leopold Franzens U., Innsbruck, Austria, 1983. Instr. NYU, 1936-38; asst. prof., assoc. prof., prof. Washington U., St. Louis, 1938-64; mem. rsch. lab. Bell Labs, Murray Hill, N.J., 1951-52; sr. mem. rsch. lab., sr. sci cons. Lockheed Missiles & Space Co., Palo Alto, Calif., 1964-75; guest prof. Leopold Franzens U., Innsbruck, 1977-78. Mem. Mo. Gov.'s Sci. Adv. Com., St. Louis, 1960-64. Author: Engineering Physics, 1948; (with others) Methods of Experimental Physics, 1968, Introduction to ... Atmospheric Pollution, 1972, Brain Injury without Head Injury, 1999; contbg. author textbook; contbr. 82 articles to scholarly and profl. jours. Comdr. USNR, 1931-57. Fulbright fellow Leopold Franzens U., Innsbruck, 1971-72, 76-77, NSF sr. postdoctoral fellow Inst. Tech., Stockholm, 1958-59, NRC sr. postdoctoral fellow U.S. Army Ballistic Rsch. Lab., Aberdeen, Md., 1975-76; recipient Cross of Honor 1st Class Austrian Govt., 1981. Fellow Am. Phys. Soc.; mem. Am. Assn. Physics Tchrs., Phi Beta Kappa, Sigma Xi, Tau Beta Pi, Omicron Delta Kappa. Episcopalian. Achievements include research in electron swarms and atmospheric pollutants; studies of closed head brain injuries. Home: 4156 Maybell Way Palo Alto CA 94306-3820 E-mail: riffolt@batnet.com.

VARNEY, SUZANNE GLAAB, health facility administrator; b. Ft. Meade, Md., Dec. 17, 1951; d. Lawrence Harold and G. Sue (Strain) Glaab; m. Richard Alan Varney, Dec. 31, 1983; children: Alysen Suzanne, Judson Dietrich. Student, Ohio U., Lancaster, 1969. Cert. med. staff coord. Transp. asst. U.S. Army, Seoul, 1979-81; pers. specialist U.S. Army Hosp., Ft. Knox, Ky., 1982-84, credentials specialist, 1984-86; adminstrv. asst. Brooke Army Med. Ctr., Ft. Sam Houston, Tex., 1987, adminstr. credentials program, 1988-90; credentials program adminstr. Walter Reed Army Med. Ctr., Washington, 1990-92; med. staff coord. Fairfield Med. Ctr., Lancaster, Ohio, 1992-97; coord. med. staff Charlotte Regional Med. Ctr., Punta Gorda, Fla., 1997-98; ind. cons., 1998. Seminar leader officer basic course Army Med. Dept., Ft. Sam Houston, 1988-90. Rep. Brookwood Neighborhood Assn., San Antonio, 1987—90; mem. N.E. Ind. Sch. Dist. PTA, 1986—90; den leader Cub Scouts/Boy Scouts Am., 1986—90; bd. dirs. Fairfield County Big Bros./Big Sisters, 2000—01, Fairfield Area Humane Soc., 2001—, Big. Bros./Big Sisterrs Fairfield County, 1999—2001, Fairfield Area Humane Soc., 2001—. Mem. NAFE, Nat. Assn. Med. Staff Svcs., Tex. Hosp. Assn., Tex. Soc. Med. Staff Svcs., Ohio Assn. Med. Staff Svcs., Fla. Assn. Med. Staff Svcs. Avocations: piano, gymnastics, outdoor activities, travel, golf. E-mail: szanvarney@yahoo.com.

VARNUM, JAMES WILLIAM, hospital administrator; b. Grand Rapids, Mich., May 29, 1940; s. Robert Otto and Jeannette (Badger) V.; m. Lucinda Hotchkiss, June 6, 1964; children: Kenneth James, Susan Lucinda. AB, Dartmouth Coll., 1962; M.Hosp. Adminstrn. with honors, U. Mich., 1964. Adminstrv. asst. U. Wis. Hosps., Madison, 1963-64, asst. supt., 1964-68, asso. supt., 1968-69, supt., 1969-73; hosp. adminstr. U. Wash. Hosps., Seattle, 1973-78; pres. Mary Hitchcock Meml. Hosp., Lebanon, N.H., 1978—; prof. Med. Sch., Dartmouth Coll., 1978—. Bd. dirs. Ledyard Nat. Bank, Hanover, N.H.; Chmn. VHA, Inc., Irving, Tex.; pres. Dartmouth-Hitchcock Alliance, 1983—. Mem.: Am. Hosp. Assn. (trustee 1994—97). Office: Mary Hitchcock Meml Hosp 1 Medical Center Dr Lebanon NH 03756-0001

VARNUM, KEITH ADDISON, entrepreneur; b. Titusville, Pa., Apr. 15, 1948; s. Herbert Earle and Maryanne Varnum. BA in Comm., U. Mich., 1970. Lic. acupuncturist, Mass. Dir. East-West Ctr., L.A., 1970-72; v.p. mktg., bd. dirs. Erewhon Natural Foods, Boston, 1973-76; owner-chef Boca Loca Natural Foods Restaurants, 1977-79; dir. Touchstone Wellness Ctr., Cambridge, Mass., 1980-84; profl. acupuncturist Oriental Arts Ctr., Boston, 1984-88; facilitator Avatar course, Phoenix, 1989-94; founder, dir. The Dream Seminars, 1995—. Host radio talk show: Beyond Belief. Author: Living the Dream, 1997. Bd. dirs. Nat. Hypertension Inst., Phoenix, 1986-88. Avocations: hiking, travel, cooking, writing, reading. Home and Office: The Dream 11248 N 11th St Phoenix AZ 85020-5827

VARRIALE, PHILIP, cardiologist; b. N.Y.C., July 30, 1934; s. John J. and Florence (Ferrara) V.; m. Eileen D. Rubencamp, Dec. 28, 1968; children: Donna, Philip, David. BA, NYU, 1955; MD, SUNY, 1959. Attending physician Dept. of Medicine, St. Vincent Hosp., 1963—; chief of cardiology Cabrini Med. Ctr. of N.Y., 1964—. Co-author: Textbook of Vectorcardiography, 1970; author: Cardiac Pacing, A Concise Guide to Clinical Practice, 1979. Lt. col. U.S. Army Med. Corps, 1968-70. Fellow ACP, Am. Coll. of Cardiology, Am. Coll. of Chest Physicians. Avocations: music, trumpet player. Home: 37 North Rd Bronxville NY 10708-1930 Office: 222 E 19th St New York NY 10003-2607

VARRICCHIO, FREDERICK ELIA, pathologist, biochemist; b. N.Y.C., May 18, 1938; s. Elia and Anna M. Varricchio; m. Claudette Goulet, Dec. 29, 1962; children: Nicole, Erika. BS, U. Maine, 1960; MS, U. N.D., 1964; PhD, U. Md., 1966; MD, Univ. Autonoma Ciudad Juarez, Mex., 1986. Assoc. in exptl. pathology Meml. Sloan Kettering Cancer Ctr., N.Y.C., 1972-77; assoc. prof., dir. grad. studies Life Sci. Ctr., Nova U., Ft. Lauderdale, Fla., 1977-79; vis. prof. Max Planck Inst. fuer Ernaehrungsphysiologie, Dortmund, Germany, 1979; prof., chmn. dept. chemistry Nat. Coll., Lombard, Ill., 1980-83; resident assoc. Argonne (Ill.) Nat. Lab., 1980—; faculty rsch. participant Oak Ridge Nat. Lab., 1979-83; adj. instr. chemistry Coll. of Du Page, Ill., 1980-85; clin. prof. biochemistry Loyola U. Dental Sch., 1983-84; resident in pathology Cook County Hosp., Chgo., 1986-90; lt. col., flight surgeon USAFR, 1989—; med. officer FDA, 1990—. Contbr. articles to profl. jours. Am. Cancer Soc. fellow, 1966-68, Deutscher Akademischer Austauschdienst fellow, 1979. Mem. Am. Soc. Biol. Chemists, Am. Assn. Pathologists, Am. Assn. for Cancer Rsch., Am. Chem. Soc., Sigma Xi, Sigma Chi (sec. N.Y.C. alumni chpt. 1977). Home: 6130 Roseland Dr Rockville MD 20852-3649

VARRICCHIO, LOUIS, radio and television producer, science writer, personality, journalist, journalist; b. Allentown, Pa., Apr. 3, 1954; s. Louis and Sarafina (Bigatel) V.; m. Marilyn Gail Davidson, Aug. 19, 1989. AS, Grahm Coll., Boston, 1974; BA, Temple U., 1976. Mng. editor The Free Press, Emmaus, Pa., 1976-80; pub. rels. dir. Exec. Source, Tempe, Ariz., 1980-83; sr. editor Kulicke & Soffa Ind., Willow Grove, Pa., 1984-87; sr. communications mgr. Lutron Electronics, Coopersburg, 1987-89; dir. pub. info., news Champlain Coll., Burlington, Vt., 1989-99; TV prodr., writer U. N.D., 1999; mng. editor Addison Eagle Newspaper, Middlebury, Vt., 2000—; sr. writer NASA Ames Rsch. Ctr., 2000—01. Exec. prodr. Labyrinth Pub. Radio Prodns., 1993—; exec. prodr. various spl. programs Pub. Radio Internat., Mpls., PBS-TV/U. N.D. Author: Lost Worlds, 1982; co-author stage play: The Stranger Wakes, 1977 (Down Center Stage 1977). Mem. Vt. Pub. Rels. Group, Soc. Profl. Journalists, New Eng. Sci. Writers, Theosophical Soc. Avocations: astronomy, geology, hiking, gardening. Home and Office: Labyrinth Pub Radio Prodn 1341 Halladay Rd Middlebury VT 05753-8728 Office: Addison Eagle News Middlebury VT 05753-0670

VARRO, BARBARA JOAN, retired editor; b. East Chicago, Ind., Jan. 25, 1938; d. Alexander R. and Lottie R. (Bess) V. BA, Duquesne U., 1959. Feature reporter, asst. fashion editor Chgo. Sun-Times, 1959-64, fashion editor, 1964-76, feature writer, 1976-84; v.p. pub. rels. Daniel J. Edelman Inc., Chgo., 1984-85; v.p. PRB/Needham Porter Novelli, 1985-86; editor Am. Hosp. Assn. News, 1987-94; editor spl. sects. Chgo. Tribune, 1995-2000; ret. Recipient awards for feature writing Ill. AP, 1978, 79, 80 Mem.: PEO.

VARSHAVSKY, ALEXANDER JACOB, molecular biologist; b. Moscow, Nov. 8, 1946; came to U.S., 1977; s. Jacob M. and Mary B. (Zeitlin) V.; m. Vera Bingham, Aug. 30, 1990; children: Roman, Anna, Victoria. BS in Chemistry, Moscow State U., 1970; PhD in Biochemistry, Inst. of Molecular Biology, Moscow, 1973. Asst. prof. dept. biology MIT, Cambridge, 1977-80, assoc. prof., 1980-86, prof., 1986-92; Smits prof. cell biology Calif. Inst. Tech., Pasadena, 1992—. Author more than 150 articles in the field of genetics and biochemistry; holder 14 patents. Recipient Novartis-Drew award Novartis, 1998, Merit award NIH, 1998, Gairdner Internat. award (Can.), 1999, Shubitz prize U. Chgo., 2000, Hoppe-Seyler award (Germany), 2000, Sloan prize GM Cancer Rsch. Found., 2000, Lasker award, 2000, Merck award Am. Soc. Biochemistry and Molecular Biology, 2001, Pasarow Found. award, 2001, Wolf prize Wolf Found., 2001, Massry prize Massry Found., 2001, Max Planck Rsch. prize, Germany, 2001, Horwitz prize Columbia U., 2001, Wilson medal Am. Soc. Cell Biology, 2002. Mem. AAAS, NAS, Am. Acad. Microbiology, Am. Philos. Soc. Achievements include discoveries in the fields of DNA replication, chromosome structure, ubiquitin system, and intracellular protein turnover. Office: Calif Inst Tech Divsn Biology Pasadena CA 91125-0001

VARSHNEY, PRAMOD KUMAR, engineering educator; b. Allahabad, India, July 1, 1952; came to U.S., 1970; s. Raj Kumar and Narvada Devi Varshney; m. Anju Varshney, Aug. 9, 1978; children: Lav Raj, Kush Raj. BS with highest honors, U. Ill., 1972, MS, 1974, PhD, 1976. From asst. prof. to assoc. prof. Syracuse (N.Y.) U., 1976-86, prof., 1986—. Cons. in field. Contbr. numerous articles to profl. publs. Recipient Dow Outstanding Young Faculty award Am. Soc. Engring. Edn., 1981. Fellow IEEE (3d Millennium medal 2000), Internat. Soc. for Info. Fusion (pres. 2001). Office: Syracuse U 121 Link Hall Syracuse NY 13244 E-mail: varshney@syr.edu.

VARSHNEY, UPKAR, information systems educator; b. Moradabad, India, Sept. 5, 1966; s. Laxman P. and Vimala Varshney; m. Smita Gugale, 1991; children: Juhi, Jaaie. BSEE, U. Roorkee, India, 1988; PhD, U. Mo., Kansas City, 1995. Asst. prof. computer info. scis. Washburn U., Topeka, 1994-98; asst. prof. info. sys. Ga. State U., Atlanta, 1998—. Spkr., participant confs. and workshops. Editor IEEE Computer, 2000; contbr. articles to profl. jours. Mem. IEEE. Office: 35 Broad St Fl 9 Atlanta GA 30303-2302

VARSHNI, YATENDRA PAL, physicist; b. Allahabad, India, May 21, 1932; emigrated to Can., 1960; s. Harpal and Bhagyawati V. BSc, U. Allahabad, 1950, MSc, 1952, PhD, 1956. Asst. prof. U. Allahabad, 1955-60; postdoctoral fellow NRC, Ottawa, Ont., Can., 1960-62; asst. prof. U. Ottawa, 1962-65, assoc. prof., 1965-69, prof., 1969-97, prof. emeritus, 1997—. Contbr. numerous articles to profl. jours. Fellow: Inst. Physics U.K., Royal Astron. Soc. (U.K.), Am. Phys. Soc., Indian Phys. Soc.; mem.: Astron. Soc. India, Can. Astron. Soc., Royal Soc. Chemistry (assoc.; U.K.), Am. Astron. Soc. Office: Dept Physics U Ottawa Ottawa ON Canada K1N 6N5 E-mail: ypv@uottawa.ca.

VARTANIAN, ISABEL SYLVIA, retired dietitian; b. Duquesne, Pa. d. Apel and Mary (Kasparian) V. BS, U. Ala., 1957; MS, Columbia U., 1962. Registered dietitian. Dietetic intern N.Y. Hosp./Cornell Med. Ctr., N.Y.C., 1957-58; therapeutic dietitian Vets. Affairs Med. Ctr., Bronx, N.Y., 1958-60, adminstrv. dietitian, 1960-62, nutrition clinic dietitian, 1962-63, rsch. and nutrition clinic dietitian Coral Gables, Fla., 1963, nutrition clinic dietitian Richmond, Va., 1963-66, chief nutritional therapy edn. and rsch. sect., 1966-83, nutrition support dietitian, 1983-2000; ret. Bd. dirs. Richmond Cmty. Action Program, 1978—83, Hopewell Preservation, Inc.; mem. adv. com. Social Svcs., Hopewell, Va., 1991—2001; mem. Sr. Citizens Adv. Commn., 2000—; bd. trustee Appomattox Regional Libr. Sys., 2000—; mem. Greater Richmond Assn. for Continuity of Care, 2000, Ft. Lee Officers and Civilian Club Adv. Coun., 2000—. Recipient Outstanding awards Vets. Affairs Med. Ctr., Superior Performance awards, Outstanding award. Mem. Richmond Dietetic Assn. (chairwoman diet therapy sect. 1966-67, pres.-elect 1967-68, pres. 1968-70, chairwoman Dial-A-Dietitian 1972-74, chairwoman pub. rels. 1973-74, 78-81, chairwoman Divsn. Cmty. Dietetics 1983-85, chairwoman program planning com. 1985), Va. Dietetic Assn. (chairwoman career guidance com. 1963-65, edn!. exhibits 1967, Dial-A-Dietitian 1972-74, pub. rels. 1982-84, visibility campaign 1984, exhibit com. 1984, program planning com. 1988, divsn. cmty. dietetic 1989-91), Va. Soc. Parenteral and Enteral Nutrition (chairwoman program planning com. 1988-89, membership com. 1990), Am. Dietetic Assn. (life), Va. Dietetic Assn., Richmond Dietetic Assn. Home: 2005 Jackson St Hopewell VA 23860-3633

VARTANIANTS, IVAN ANATOLIEVICH, research crystallographer, physicist, theorist; b. Moscow, May 5, 1956; s. Anatoly Ivanovich Surzhansky and Anna Dmitrievna Vartaniants. Diploma summa cum laude, Moscow Phys. Engring. Inst., 1979, PhD, 1984. Engr. Moscow Phys. Engring. Inst., 1982-84; rsch. scientist/sr. rsch. scientist/leading scientist Inst. Crystallography, Moscow, 1984—. Vis. scientist Inst. Physics, Warsaw, Poland, 1992, 96, Max-Planck-Inst., Stuttgart, Germany, 1995-99, U. Ill., Urbana, 1996-99. Contbr. articles to profl. jours. Avocations: mountain hiking, books, art, swimming, jogging, cycling. Office: Inst Crystallography RAS PO Box 12 111395 Moscow Russia

VARWIG, DAVID LEE, investment banker; b. St. Louis, Jan. 18, 1962; s. Harry Julius and Ruby JoAnn (Womble) V.; m. Deborah Sue Smith, Sept. 14, 1985 (div. Sept. 2000); children: Jeffrey David, Kyle Evan. BA in Chemistry, Northwestern U., 1984. V.p. A.D. Jack & Co., Northfield, Ill., 1984-89; mng. dir. LINC Group, Chgo., 1989-90; sr. mng. dir., CEO Citadel Group, 1990—. Mem. Union League Club Chgo., Wynstone Golf Club, Chi Psi. Home: 4 Hillburn Ct N Barrington IL 60010-6927 Office: Citadel Group 37th Fl 233 E Wacker Dr Chicago IL 60601

VARY, EVA MAROS, retired chemical company executive; b. Kecskemet, Hungary, Apr. 13, 1933; came to U.S., 1958; d. Anthony and Kathleen (Czencz) Maros; m. Eugen Szent-Vary, June 13, 1956 (div. 1958); 1 child, Susan Marie. Chem. engring. diploma, Tech. U. Budapest (Hungary), 1956; PhD in Phys. Chemistry, UCLA, 1966. Chem. engring. area supr. Ujpesti Textile Plant, Budapest, 1956-57; chemist geology dept. UCLA, 1958-65; rsch. chemist, staff chemist Fabrics and Finishes Dept. Dupont, Phila., 1966-71, rsch. supr., 1971-79, tech. area supt. Parlin, N.J., 1979-80, asst. plant mgr. Parlin, Toledo, 1980-85; product supt. mng. Tedlar plant Dupont Fabricated Products, Buffalo, 1985-87, environ. cons. Wilmington, Del., 1987-90; dir. product safety, regulatory affairs pigments div. Ciba-Geigy Corp., Newport, 1990-98; ret., 1998. Inventor, patentee release coatings. Com. chair Zonta Internat., Toledo, 1984, Buffalo, 1987. Mem. Am. Chem. Soc. Roman Catholic. Avocations: tennis, skiing, travel, photography. Home: 1100 Lovering Ave Apt 1508 Wilmington DE 19806-3288 E-mail: varyeva@aol.com.

VARY, PATRICIA SUSAN, biologist, educator, geneticist, researcher; b. Wewoka, Okla., Nov. 20, 1941; d. Clayton Loring and Margaret Elizabeth Potter; m. James C. Vary Sr., Jan. 20, 1967 (div. Dec. 20, 1987); children: Catherine A. Vary , James C. Vary Jr. BS in Microbiology, Tex. Christian U., 1963, MS in Microbiology, 1965; MS in Biochemistry, U. Wis., 1967; PhD, Stanford U., 1969. Asst. prof. No. Ill. U., DeKalb, 1977—83, assoc. prof., 1983—95, full prof. biology, 1990—, chair dept. biol. sci., 1995—99. Cons. Abbott Labs., Chgo., 1988—95. Bd. mem. LWV, Wheaton, Ill., 1969—85, pres., 1976—77; adv. com. Wheaton Sch. Bd., 1980; violinist Cmty. Symphony; mem. Women's Chorus, Dem. Precinct Com., DeKalb, 2000—. Fellow Fogarty internat. fellow, NIH, 1989—90; grantee, NSF, 1979—92, NIH, 1989—. Mem.: AAAS, Soc. Indsl. Microbiology, Genetic Soc. Am., Am. Soc. Microbiology (mem. editl. bd.), Sigma Xi (local pres. 1992—93). Unitarian Universalist. Achievements include patents for plasmidless B.megaterium, lac-B.megaterium. Avocations: travel, bicycling. Office: No Ill Univ Dept Biol Scis Dekalb IL 60115

VARZEGAR, MINOO, English educator, reading specialist; b. Kerman, Iran; d. Abdolrahim and Amjad (Vali) Varzegar; m. Saeid Fatemi, May 8; children: Delaram, Arezou. BA in English, U. Tehran, 1966; MA in Tchg. English, U. Tchr. Edn., 1967; MA in Psychology, U. Tehran, 1969; MA in Tchg. English as a Second Lang., U. Ill., 1971, PhD in Tchg. English as a Second Lang., 1975, postgrad., 1994. Cert. tchr. English, cert. high acad. adminstrn. Asst. prof. U. Tehran, 1979-84, assoc. prof., 1984-94, prof. dept. English, 1984-97, head Dept. English of Evening Classes, 1975-83, dir. Lang. Lab., 1975-80, dir. lang. ctr., 1981-83, head dept. English, 1983-97. Vis. prof. U. Ill., Champaign-Urbana, 1997-99, rsch. scholar, 1997-99; assoc. faculty Columbia U., N.Y.C., 1999-2001; lectr. Eng. dept. Rutgers U., Newark, 1999—, William Paterson U., Wayne, N.J., 1999-2001; dir. Ctr. for testing and Psychometrics, Min. of Culture and Higher Edn., Tehran, 1975-77. Author: Children's English series, 1990-95, Reading Through Reading (Best Acad. Book), 1992, Testing and Measurement (Best Acad. Book), 1993, A Comprehensive Grammar of English, 1996, Testing TEFL, 1997; author/editor: Issues in Teaching English as a Second Language, 1990, English for the Students of Medicine, 1989; co-author: English for Medical Students, 1974; editor: English for the Students of Medicine (II), 1993, Novin English-Persian Dictionary, vols. I and II, 1993; co-editor: Yadvareh Persian-English Dictionary, vols. I, II, III, 1991, Yadvareh English-Persian Dictionary, vols. I and II, 1991, Yadvareh Unabridged English-Persian Dictionary, 1993, others; contbr. numerous articles to profl. jours. Mem. com. Ctr. Studying and Compiling Univ Books in Humanities Min. Culture and Higher Edn., 1984—97, mem. com. curriculum devel., 1984—97, com. for testing, 1977—79; mem. com. lang. testing Lang. Ctr., 1979—81. Recipient Award for creating an Innovative Model of Reading Comprehension, U. Ill., 1975, Cert. of Appreciation for best adminstrn. U. Mich., 1998, award for extraordinary ability INS, 1998, Disting. Prof. award, 2000, Disting. Rschr. award, 2000; U. Ill. grantee, 1975; Fulbright scholar, 1970-75, Profl. Deveol. scholar TESOL, 1999; fellow in rsch. U. Ill., 1973-75. Mem. Tchrs. of English to the Speakers of Other Langs., U. Ill. Alumni Assn., Am. Assn. for Applied Linguistics, Nat. Coun. Tchrs. English, Internat. Reading Assn. Avocations: computers, reading, painting, tennis, swimming. Home: 277 Prospect Ave #10E Hackensack NJ 07601 Office: Rutgers U 232 Smith Hall 101 Warren St Newark NJ 07102-1811 E-mail: varzegar@aol.com.

VASALY, ANN CAROL, classical studies educator; b. Mpls., Mar. 14, 1949; d. Thomas Peter and Carol Margaret Vasaly; m. Richard Allen Young, Mar. 21, 1975. BA, U. Minn., 1972, MA, 1975; PhD, Ind. U., 1983. Asst. prof. classical studies Boston U., 1983-93, assoc. prof. classical studies, 1993—. Mem. adv. bd. Am. Acad. in Rome, mem. exec. coun. 1997—. Author: Representations: Images of the World in Ciceronian Oratory, 1993; contbr. articles to profl. jours. Fulbright fellow, Italy, 1982-83, Von Humboldt fellow, Tübingen, Germany, 1985-86; Rockefeller Found. grantee, Bellagio, Italy, 1997; recipient Rome prize Am. Acad. in Rome, 1982-83. Mem. Am. Philol. Assn., Classical Assn. New England. Democrat. Roman Catholic. Avocations: piano, travel, tennis. Office: Boston U Dept Classical Studies 745 Commonwealth Ave Dept Boston MA 02215-1401

VASANTHAN, NADARAJAH, research scientist, educator; b. Jaffna, Sri Lanka, Oct. 6, 1962; , U.S., 1988; m. Sumathy Vasanthan; children: Jeevan. BSc Chemistry, U. Jaffna, Sri Lanka, 1986; PhD, CUNY, 1993. Staff scientist AlliedSignal, Morristown, 1995—97; sr. scientist TRI/Princeton, NJ, 1997—. Fellow, City U., 1990, 1992. Mem.: Am. Chem. Soc. Home: 94 Joann Ct Monmouth Junction NJ 08852

VASENIUS, LINDA LEA, librarian, consultant; 1 child, Derek Lee Piper. BA, U. No. Colo., 1968, MA, 1971; MLS, U. Denver, 1976. Cert. elem. tchr. and libr. Dir. libr. Aims C.C., Greeley, Colo., 1970-80; head adult svcs. Loveland (Colo.) Pub. Libr., 1983-86, Weld Libr. Dist., Greeley, 1986-89; coord. children's dept. and media dept. Maricopa County Libr., Phoenix, 1989-91; info. svcs. coord. Weld Libr. Dist., Greeley, 1991-98; cons. High Plains Regional Libr. Svc. Sys., 1999—2001, ret., 2001; life coach, 2002—. Mem.: AAUW, Delta Kappa Gamma (v.p. 1991—). Avocations: reading, traveling, gardening.

VASEY, JAMES ANTHONY, psychotherapist, consultant; b. N.Y.C., May 25, 1958; s. Joel Marshal and Joan Blossom (Lewis) V. BA/BS, Kean Coll., Union, N.J., 1978-83; MSW, Columbia U., 1984-86; advanced cert. in Social Work, NYU, 1990-92. Sr. primary therapist Jersey City Med. Ctr., 1987-89; family counselor Fair Oaks Hosp., Paramus, N.J., 1989; coord. day treatment Newark-Beth Israel Med. Ctr, 1989-90; psychotherapist Essex County (N.J.) Guidance Ctr., East Orange, 1990-91, Contemporary Counseling and Psychotherapy Inst., Teaneck, N.J., 1991—, East Orange (N.J.) Gen. Hosp., 1993—. Mem. spkrs. bur. East Orange Gen. Hosp., 1993—. Recipient Golden Poet award World of Poetry, 1992. Mem. NASW (lic. clin. social worker N.J.). Avocations: yoga, poetry, photography, chess. Office: E Orange Gen Hosp 300 Central Ave East Orange NJ 07018-2819 E-mail: vasey@webtv.net.

VASH, CAROLYN L. psychologist, writer; b. Oil City, Pa., Oct. 11, 1934; d. Roberto Carlos and Sib yl Baum Conine; m. Roger Emerson Wetmore, Aug. 8, 1958 (div. July 1969); m. Richard Paul Vash, Nov. 9, 1969. PhD in Psychology, UCLA, 1964. Lic. psychologist Calif. Bd. Psychology. Clin. psychologist Rancho Los Amigos Med. Ctr., Downey, Calif., 1963—67, chief, vocat. svc., 1967—73; chief dep. dir. State Dept. Rehab., Sacramento, 1973—77; v.p. IIS, McLean, Va., 1977—85; sr. rschr. PSI, Fairfax, 1985—86, Conwal, McLean, 1986—99; writer Altadena, Calif., 1979—. Mem. bd. World Rehab. Fund, N.Y.C., 1998—2001; mem. Assistive Tech. Sys. steering com., Sacramento, 1992—98; Coulter lectr. 40th Internat. Exch. Experts in Rehab., Phoenix, 1990, Yugoslavia, 84, New Zealand, 94. Author: The Burnt Out Administrator, 1979, The Psychology of Disability, 1981, Personality and Adversity, 1994. Commr. L.A. County Commn. on Disability, 1978—89. Mem.: APA (com. on disability issues 1998—2000, bd. psychology in the pub. interest 2001—). Avocations: illustration, stationery design, jewelry making. Home: 35 E Las Flores Dr Altadena CA 91001

VASHOLZ, LOTHAR ALFRED, retired insurance company executive; b. Milw., Feb. 20, 1930; s. Alfred and Charlotte Vasholz; m. Marji Cartwright, Dec. 26, 1954; children: Julie, Ann, Eric. BS, U. Colo., 1952; M (hon.), U. Rio Grande. ChFC. Sr. cons. Life Ins. Mktg. & Rsch., Hartford, Conn., 1966-70; v.p. N.Am. Life, Chgo., 1970-73; sr. v.p. Bankers Mut., Freeport, Ill., 1973-75; sales dir. Security Life of Denver, 1975-81; v.p. Union Cen. Life Ins. Co., Cin., 1981-85, sr. v.p., 1985-86, mgr. Columbus, Ohio, 1986-87, sr. v.p., chief mktg. officer Cin., 1987-91, exec. v.p., corp. mktg. officer, 1991-95; chmn. Carillon Investments, 1991-95; cons. on mktg. and sales to life ins. industry, 1995—; co-founder, pres. The Stewardship Co., 2001—. Trustee U. Rio Grande, Ohio. Fellow Life Mgmt. Inst.; mem. Phi Delta Theta (past internat. pres.). Republican. Fax: 760-771-9593.

VASILAKIS, ALEXANDER, cardiothoracic surgeon; b. Sewickley, Pa., Dec. 15, 1958; s. George and Irene (Hronas) V.; m. Marion Lynn Kolokouris, Sept. 29, 1991; children: Georgia Maria, Kristen Harriet. BS, U. Pitts., 1979, MS, 1980; MD, W.Va. U. Sch. Medicine, 1985. From instr. surgery to assoc. prof. surgery W.Va. U. Sch. Medicine, Morgantown, 1992-99; dir. cardiac surgery Heritage Valley Health Sys. Med. Ctr., Beaver, Pa., 1999—. Attending surgeon Monongalia Gen. Hosp., Morgantown, 1992-99, W.Va. U. Hosps., 1992-99. Fellow Am. Coll. Surgeons; mem. Soc. Thoracic Surgery, So. Thoracic Surgery Assn., AMA, Southeastern Surg. Congress. Avocations: gardening, travel, music. Office: Cardiothoracic Surg Assocs The Med Ctr Beaver 1000 Dutch Ridge Rd Beaver PA 15009 E-mail: avasilakis@webtv.net, avasilakis@hvhs.org.

VASILE, GENNARO JAMES, health care executive; b. Auburn, N.Y., Jan. 16, 1946; s. Louis Joseph and Regina Elena (Santaniello) V.; m. Mary Ellen Dwyer, Aug. 10, 1968; children: Kevin, Colleen, Brian. BA, St. John Fisher Coll., 1967; MBA, Xavier U., 1969; PhD, U. Iowa, 1973. Asst. adminstr. St. Elizabeth Hosp., Utica, N.Y., 1971-74; sr. cons. Booz-Allen & Hamilton, Inc., N.Y.C., 1974-75; asst. provost adminstrn. Med. Coll. Va., Va. Commonwealth U., Richmond, 1975-78; dir. hosp. and health services mgmt. consulting Booz-Allen & Hamilton, Inc., Bethesda, Md., 1978-79; exec. dir. Strong Meml. Hosp. of U. Rochester, N.Y., 1979-84; pres. United Health Services Inc., Binghamton, 1984-93; exec. v.p. Johns Hopkins Hosp., Balt., 1993-95; v.p. Gemini Cons. Am's. Healthcare Practice, 1995-98; exec. v.p., COO Bassett Healthcare, 1998—2002; exec. v.p. healthcare affairs Excillus, Rochester, NY, 2002—. Asst. prof. U. Rochester, Med. Coll. Va.; assoc. prof. Johns Hopkins U.; vis. prof. U. Rochester Med. Ctr.; dir., pres. Med. Ctr. Ins. Co.; cons. health-related agencies. Author: Comprehensive Health Planning, 1971, 74. Bd. dirs. Rochester Soc. Prevention of Cruelty to Children, 1980, asst. treas., 1981; bd. dirs. Pittsford Vince Lombardi Youth Football, 1980, v.p., 1981; bd. dirs. St. Ann's Home, Voluntary Hosps. Am. Inc., Broome County C. of C., 1985, United Way, 1985; trustee St. John Fisher Coll. Recipient Dean's award for contbns. to Sch. Medicine Med. Coll. Va., 1978, Outstanding Contbn. to Mankind, 1993, Exec. of Yr., 1985, Preceptor of Yr. Xavier U., 1992. Fellow Am. Coll. Health Care Execs., Am. Acad. Med. Care Adminstrs. (bd. dirs. 1988); mem. Am. Coll. Hosp. Adminstrs., Am. Hosp. Assn., Council Teaching Hosps., Assn. Am. Med. Colls. Roman Catholic. Home: 7644 Linkside Dr Manlius NY 13104-2371 *The approach I have taken to my professional and personal life has been to seek out the world as it is, formulate a vision as to how it can be improved, and strive to bridge the resultant gaps. If I have been successful in bridging any gaps, it is only because of the substantial support I have received along the way.*

VASILIADIS, HARALAMBOS VASILIOS, civil and environmental engineer, educator, consultant; b. Kastoria, Greece, Aug. 10, 1963; came to U.S., 1971; s. Vasilios H. and Arhontia T. (Amanatidis) V. B of Engring., Aristotelian U., Thessaloniki, Greece, 1986; MSc, Poly. U., Bklyn., 1988, PhD, 1991. Registered profl. engr., N.Y. Adj. assoc. prof. Poly. U., Bklyn., 1987—; vis. asst. prof. Pratt Inst., 1991-95; adj. asst. prof. U. New Haven, West Haven, Conn., 1993; asst. prof. Rutgers U., Piscataway, N.J., 1992; cons. engr. Arch Cons. Inc., Rego Park, N.Y., 1991-96; adj. assoc. prof. City Coll., N.Y.C., 1993—, Hofstra U., Hempstead, N.Y., 1996—. Tech. advisor Panagia Soumela, Astoria, N.Y.; mem. adv. bd. Omonoia, N.Y.C. Contbr. articles to profl. jours. Recipient scholarships. Mem. ASCE, N.Y. Acad. Scis., Krikos Inc. Internat. Sci. (pres. 1997—), Sigma Xi. Christian Orthodox. Avocations: telecommunications, psychology, ethnic issues. Home: 24-11 35th St # 2 Astoria NY 11103

VASILIAUSKAS, EDMUND, chemistry educator; b. Lithuania, June 18, 1938; came to the U.S., 1957; s. Vincent and Elena V.; m. Jura B. Gelazius, Jan. 24, 1970 (dec. 1991); children: Eric, Lora, Paul, Thomas; m. Maria Miksiunas, Aug. 4, 1995. BS, Rochester Inst. Tech., 1963; PhD, Loyola U. Chgo., 1970. Chemist Olin Corp., Rochester, N.Y., 1964-65, Witco Corp., Chgo., 1970-71; prof. Moraine Valley Coll., Palos Hills, Ill., 1971—. Mem. Am. Chem. Soc. Avocations: travel, music, gardening. Office: Moraine Valley Coll 10900 S 88th Ave Palos Hills IL 60465-2175 E-mail: vasiliauskas@moraine.cc.il.us.

VASILJEV, ALEXANDER VALERJOVICH, metallurgical engineer, economist; b. Kuragata, Kazahstan, June 21, 1955; s. Valery Alexandrovich and Olga Vladimirovna Vasiljev; m. Marina Genadievna Tuzovskay, Dec. 31, 1985; children: Olga, Nataliya. Diplomate of engring., Metall. Inst., 1977; Candidate Scis., Inst. Engring., Moscow, 1982; postgrad., Inst. Sociology Acad. Scis., Moscow, 1992; PhD in Econs., Acad. Mgmt. Russia, Moscow, 1993. Jr., then sr. scis. employee Inst. Mariupol, Ukraine, 1980-84, mgr. rsch. lab. socioecon. problems. Ukraine, 1985-87; mgr. socially econ. lab. Inst. Labour of Ukraine, Mariupol, 1987-90; mgr. sect. social econ. problems of port's indsl. cities Inst. Econ.-Law Rsch., Nat. Acad. Scis. Ukraine, 1993-98, organizer Mariupol br., 1995-97; chmn. sci. coun. Inst. Econ. and Social/Cultural Rsch., 1989—. Prof. PriAzov State Tech. U., Mariupol, 1993-98; v.p. Azov, Ukrainian Dept., Acad. Econ., Scis. and Entrepreneurship, Mariupol, 1999—; rep. Azov Ukrainian Econ. Dept. Acad. Econ., Sci. and Entrepreneurship in West Europe and Am., Warsaw, 2000—, West Europe Am. Azov Ukrainian Dept. Econ. Scis. and Entrepreneurship, Warsaw, 2000—. Author monographs in field. Scholar Acad. Russia, 1991-92 Probationer Inst. IBMER Poland, 2000-2001; recipient cert. Frederick P. Furth Found., 1990, medal "Met. Gotey & Cafa, St. Ignatia", 1999. Mem. N.Y. Acad. Scis., 1817 Heritage Soc. N.Y. Acad. Scis., Union Econ. Ukraine, Acad. Econ. Scis. and Entrepreneurship (hon.). Avocations: tennis, windsurfing, travel. Home: Fl 41 Zelinsky 1 St 87534 Mariupol Ukraine Office: Inst Econ/Social/Cult Rsch Stroiteley 39 Ave Box N7 87534 Mariupol Ukraine E-mail: 481990@nyas.org.

VASILY, JOHN TIMOTHY, information systems executive, state government official; b. Everett, Mass., Feb. 5, 1961; s. Andrew and Catherine Agnes (Coyne) V. BA, U. Mass., 1983; MBA, Suffolk U., 1992. Data analyst Higher Edn. Coord. Coun., Boston, 1984-92; sr. programmer, analyst Babson Coll., Babson Park, Mass., 1992-96; dir. new sys. devel. Mass. Dept. Youth Svcs., Boston, 1996-2000; chief info. officer Mass. Dept. Mental Retardation, 2000—. Adj. instr. Newbury Coll., Brookline, Mass., 1992—, Suffolk U., Boston, 2001—. Co-author: Massachusetts Integrated Post Secondary Education Data System, 1990; author: 1986-87 Completions Supplement, 1989. Recipient Citation for Outstanding Performance Commonwealth of Mass., 1998. Mem. IEEE, Delta Mu Delta, Omicron Delta Epsilon. vocations: bowling, fishing, hiking, golf, photography. E-mail: John.Vasily@dmr.state.ma.us.

VASKA, LAURI, chemist, retired educator; b. Rakvere, Estonia, May 7, 1925; came to U.S., 1952; s. Jakob and Emilie (Lugenberg) V.; widowed, May 1999; children: Andres, Marcus, Kristina, Matthias, Paul. BS, U. Göttingen, Germany, 1949; PhD, U. Tex., 1956. Postdoctoral fellow Northwestern U., Evanston, Ill., 1956-57; ind. rsch. fellow Mellon Inst., Pitts., 1957-64; assoc. prof. chemistry Clarkson U., Potsdam, N.Y., 1964-67; prof. chemistry, 1990—; prof. emeritus, 1990—. Cons. chem. cos. Mem. editl. bd. varios chem. jours; contbr. over 80 articles to Am. and European profl. publs. AAAS fellow; recipient Boris Pregel award for rsch. in chem. physics N.Y. Acad. Scis., 1971. Mem. Estonian Chem. Soc. (fgn., medal of honor). Achievements include discovery of Vaska complex. Avocations: literature, classical music, gardening. Home: 118 Pleasant Valley Rd Norwood NY 13668 Office: Clarkson Univ Box 5810 Potsdam NY 13699

VASKEVITCH, DAVID, information technology executive; 3 children. BS in Math., Computer Sci., Philosophy, M in Computer Sci., U. Toronto. Owner PlanDesign; with 3Com Corp.; dir. U.S. mktg. Microsoft, 1986, gen. mgr. enterprise computing, chief architect, 1998—99, sr. v.p. Bus. Applications Divsn., sr. v.p., chief tech. officer Bus. Platform. Author: Client/Server Strategies: A Survival Guide for Corporate Re-engineers, 1993. Avocations: photography, horseback riding. Office: Microsoft One Microsoft Way Redmond WA 98052-6399*

VASKO, PETER THEODORE FREDERICK, priest; b. Bklyn., Nov. 28, 1943; s. Theodore Frederick and Catherine (Buday) V. BA in Philosophy, Cath. U. Am., 1966, BD in Theology, 1969; postgrad., Duke U., 1972-73, Franciscan Studium Biblicum, Jerusalem, 1985-86. Ordained priest Roman Cath. Ch., 1987. Pub. rels. asst. Holiday Inn/Oak Grove, Durham, N.C., 1972-74; dir. devel. NAA, Charlotte, 1974-76; dir. CETA, New Orleans, 1976-78; v.p. sales Peachtree Corners Corp. Travel, Atlanta, 1978-81; bd. dirs. Franciscan Custody, Jerusalem, 1992—; pres. The Holy Land Found., 1994—. Editor photo essay See the Holy Land, 1993, The Holy Land and the Milennium, 2000; editor The Holy Land Mag., 1993-95; writer, narrator video On the Road of Christ, 1994; narrator video The Life of Jesus: Scriptural Journey, 1997; guest on Mother Angelica Live, 1996, 97, 98, Pat Robertson 700 Club, 1996, others; co-prodr. documentary Crisis in the Holy Land, 1994. Bd. dirs. St. Ives Soc., Jerusalem, 1992-94; guide White House Via U.S. Embassy, Jerusalem, 1992—; chaplain U.S. Marines/U.S. Consulate, Jerusalem, 1988—. Recipient Achievement in Pub. Rels. award Pub. Rels. Soc., Raleigh, 1975, Marine Security Guard Bn. Co. B Cert. of Appreciation, 1995, 99, U.S. Marine Security Detachment Comdr. Commendation award, 1999; named Jaycee of Yr., N.C. chpt., 1973; decorated mem. Equestrial Order of the Holy Sepulchre, 1992.

VASLEF, STEVEN NICHOLAS, surgeon; b. Colorado Springs, Colo., Aug. 16, 1958; s. Nicholas P. and Irene I. (Koncz) V.; m. Maria E. Vaslef, July 11, 1988. BS, MIT, 1980; MD, U. Va., 1984; PhD, Northwestern U., 1990. Diplomate Am. Bd. Surgery with subspecialty in surg. critical care. Intern U. Ill., Chgo., 1984-85, resident in gen. surgery, 1985-92; mem. staff Evanston/Glenbrook Hosps., 1992-94; asst. prof. surgery, asst. pro. bio-med. engring. Northwestern U. Med. Sch., Chgo., 1992-94; asst. prof. surgery Duke U. Med. Ctr., Durham, N.C., 1994-2000, assoc. prof., 2000—, asst. prof. bio-med. engring., 1994—, asst. prof. anesthesiology, 1996—. Mem. ACS; mem. Soc. Critical Care Medicine, Am. Soc. Artificial Internal Organs, Soc. for Surgery of Alimentary Tract, Am. Assn. Surgery of Trauma, Ea. Assn. for Surgery of Trauma. Office: Duke Univ Med Ctr Dept Surgery PO Box 2601 Durham NC 27715-2601 E-mail: vasle001@mc.duke.edu.

VASQUEZ, ANGELA CHRISTINE, poet, language educator; b. Annapolis, Md., Nov. 21, 1967; d. Gregory Christopher and Cherry Delores Vasquez; m. Jerry Lane Anderson, Sept. 5, 1992 (div. Feb. 13, 1998). BA in English, Drake U., 1996. Various positions Midland Savs. Bank, Des Moines, 1989, fin. counselor, 1990; one call rep. AmerUS Bank, 1991—92, one call supr., 1992—93; one call asst. mgr. AmerUS Group, 1993—97, loan administr. Bellevue, Wash., 1997—98; advt. asst. Seattle Times, 1998; office/ops. mgr. ASS Corp., Seattle, 1999—. ESL tchr., vol. Casa Latina, Seattle, 1998—; spkr. in field. Author: poetry. Avocations: reading, hiking, swimming, rollerblading, journaling. Home: 1723 Sturgus Ave S # 2 Seattle WA 98144 Office: ASS Corp 3817 Woodland Pk Ave N Seattle WA 98103

VASQUEZ, GADDI, federal agency administrator; b. Carrizo Springs, Tex., Jan. 22, 1955; m. Elaine Vasquez; 1 child, Jason. AA in Criminal Justice, Rancho Santiago C.C., 1972; BA in Pub. Svc. Mgmt., U. Redlands, 1980. Police officer City of Orange, Calif., 1975-79; coord. community rels., mgr.'s office City of Riverside, 1979-81; exec. asst. Orange County Bd. Supervisors, 3d Dist., 1981-85; mem. Orange County Bd. Supervisers 3d Dist., 1987—; area mgr. So. Calif. Edison Co., 1985; hispanic liaison Office of Gov. George Deukmejian, Calif., 1985, from dep. appointments sec. to chief dep. appointments sec., 1985-87; dir. Peace Corps, Washington, 2002—. Mem. Transp. Corridor Agys. Bd., 1987—, chmn. 1990-91; local agy. formation commn., 1988-93, chmn. 1990-91; mem. Calif. Film Commn., 1988-91, Calif. Coun. Criminal Justice, 1989—; founder, co-chair, Orange County Health Care Task Force, 1990—; with White House Fellowships Commn., 1990-91; co-chmn. Orange County Congestion Mgmt. Policy Task Force, 1990—; bd. dirs. Orange County Transp. Authority, 1991—, exec. com. 1992—, vice chmn. 1993—; regional advisory and planning coun., 1991—, vice chmn. 1992, chmn. 1993; official observer Armenian Independence elections, 1991. Bd. dirs. Future Leaders Am., Southwest Voter Rsch. Inst., calif. First Amendment Coalition, Orange County Boy Scout Coun., So. Area Foster Care Effort, Orange County Performing Arts Ctr., Opera Pacific; trustee Am. Coun. Young Polit. Leaders; adv. bd. Pediatric Cancer Rsch. Found, Orange County

Juvenile Connection Project, Calif. Office Traffic Safety, The Salvation Army Orange County, Project AERO, Constitutional Rights Found. Orange County; community coun. Prentice Day Sch.; hon. adv. bd. Adam Walsh Ctr.; hon. bd. govs. Bower Mus.; leadership coun. Orange County Points Light. Named Officer of Yr., Am. Legion, 1977. Outstanding Young Man of Am. U.S. C.of C., 1985, One of 100 Most Influential Hispanics in U.S. Hispanic Bus. Mag., 1986-87, 88-89, 91-92, 92-93, Govt. Hispanic Bus. Advocate of Yr. U.S. Hispanic Champer Region I, 1991; recipient Alumni Achievement award, Santa Ana Coll., 1988, Alumni of Yr.award U. Redlands, 1989, Humanitarian award Nat. Conf. Christians and Jews, 1989, award State Child Devel. Adv. Com., 1990, Tree of Life award Jewish Nat. Fund, 1991, Ralph E. Hudson Open Space award Landscape Architects Found., 1992. Office: Peace Corps Off of the Dir 1111 20th St NW Washington DC 20536-0001 Office Fax: 202-692-2101.*

VASQUEZ, MARCIA JOHNSON, management consultant; b. Griffin, Ga., July 2, 1936; d. George Leonard Walker and Gladys Georgiana Duplessis; m. Raymond Marshall Johnson, Dec. 10, 1960 (dec. Oct. 1983); children: Erik Neil Johnson, Kristin Lynn Johnson, Linnea Britt Johnson; m. Jose Domingo Vasquez III, June 23, 1990. BA in Math. magna cum laude, Vanderbilt U., 1957; MS in Computer Sci., Northwestern U., 1966, PhD in Mktg., 1982. Mktg. rsch. mgr. Montgomery Ward, Chgo., 1969-77; asst. prof. U. Calif., Berkeley, 1979-83; product mgr., sr. project mgr. Fair, Isaac & Co., San Rafael, Calif., 1984-93; chmn. undergrad. bus. studies Dominican U., 1998-99; owner, prin. The Profl. Marketer, 1993—. Rsch. engr. Northwestern U., Evanston, Ill., 1966-69; project mgr. Johnson Cons., Evanston, 1963-66; sys. engr. IBM, Chattanooga, 1959-62; mathematician tech. feasibility studies office NASA/Redstone Arsenal, Huntsville, Ala., 1958. Author: (book) Optimal Allocation of Marketing Resources, 1981; contbr. articles to profl. jours. Dir. Marin Suicide Prevention Ctr., 1988-90; ESL tchr. Tiburon (Calif.) Bapt. Ch., 1997-99. Fulbright scholar U.S. Gov., U. Paris, 1957-58; Consortium fellow Am. Mktg. Assn., U. Chgo., 1978. Mem. Am. Mktg. Assn., North Bay Software and Info. Tech. Assn. (bd. dirs., corp. v.p. 1994-00, pres. 2000-2001), Inst. Mgmt. Cons. (dir. 1997-98), Ops. Rsch. Soc. Am. (chmn. Chgo. chpt. 1974-76), San Rafael C. of C. (Vol. of Quar. 1997). Avocations: Web page design, aerobic dancing. Office: The Profl Marketer # 143 454 Las Gallinas Ave San Rafael CA 94903-3618 E-mail: mvasquez@promarketer.com.

VASQUEZ, WILLIAM LEROY, business educator, consultant; b. Austin, Tex., Mar. 9, 1944; s. Eliseo M. and Janie (Garcia) V. BS with distinction, Nova Southeastern U., 1983, MBA, 1985, DBA, 1992. Cert. Inst. Cert. Profl. Mgrs., 1990, Inst. Cert. Computing Profls., 1993. Svc. mgr. Data Gen. Corp., various, Latin Am., 1972-80; product mgr. Gould, Inc., Ft. Lauderdale, Fla., 1980—84, Tektronix Inc., Portland, Oreg., 1984—86, Racal-Milgo, Ft. Lauderdale, 1988—90, Citibank Internat., Ft. Lauderdale, 1991—2001; ret., 2001. Instr. City U., Portland campus, 1987-88; Maryhurst Coll., 1985-88, Nova Southeastern U. (domestic and internat.), 1988—, pres. internat. alumni assn.; instr. St. Thomas U., 1989—, Fla. Atlantic U., 1993—. Mem. VFW, Nat. Bus. Edn. Assn., U.S. Submarine Vets., Inc., Mensa. Republican. Presbyterian. Avocations: guitar, model trains, fine arts. Home: 9788 NW 18th St Coral Springs FL 33071-5824 Office: Fla Met Univ Grad Sch Business 1040 Bayview Dr Fort Lauderdale FL 33304

VASS, JOAN, fashion designer; b. N.Y.C., May 19, 1925; d. Max S. and Rose L.; children: Richard, Sara, Jason. Student, Vassar Coll., 1941; BA, U. Wis., 1946. Pres. Joan Vass, Inc., N.Y.C., 1977—, Vass-Ludacer, N.Y.C., 1993—. Recipient Prize de Cashet, Prince Machiabelli, 1980, Coty award, 1979, Disting. Woman in Fashion award Smithsonian Instn., 1980. Office: Joan Vass Inc 36 E 31st St New York NY 10016-6821 also: 260 W 39th St Fl 11 New York NY 10018-6850 E-mail: joanvass@worldnet.att.net.

VASS, STEVEN T. economist, educator; b. Budapest, Hungary, Dec. 9, 1932; came to U.S., 1957; s. Istvan and Emilia (Mozsar) V.; m. Agnes G. Toth, June 28, 1957; children: Steven, Julius. BS, Kossuth Mil. Sch., Budapest, 1953, Black Hills State U., Spearfish, S.D., 1961; MA, U. Mich., 1965, PhD, 1973. V.p. T.L. Machine Works Ltd., Toronto, 1972-81; prof. Cen. U. Peru, Huancayo, 1963-64, Washtenaw Community Coll., Ann Arbor, Mich., 1967-83, prof., chmn. dept. econs., 1983—. Cons. Bechtel Corp., Ann Arbor, 1972-76; advisor, translator Ford Motor Co., Dearborn, Mich., 1990. Co-chmn. Mich. Econ. Devel. Group, Lansing, 1977-78; bd. dirs. Huron Valley Credit Union, Ann Arbor, 1971-74; state dir. gymnastics YMCA, Mich., 1967-68. With Hungarian Armed Forces, 1953-54. Mem. NEA (founding mem. Nat. Faculty Assn.), Mich. Acad. Scis., Mich. Econ. Soc. (chmn. 1983), Econ. Club Detroit, Am. Econ. Assn., Internat. Econ. Assn. Avocations: travel, numismatics, stamp collecting, classical music. Home: 4904 Bella Terra Dr Venice FL 34293-6074 Office: Washtenaw Community Coll 4800 W Huron River Dr Ann Arbor MI 48103-9418

VASSALLE, MARIO, physiologist; b. Viareggio, Lucca, Italy, May 26, 1928; came to U.S., 1958; s. Giuseppe and Antonietta (Vassalle) V.; m. Anna Maria Petrucci; children: Andrew G., Alessandra A., Massimo B., Roberto M., Francesca A. MD cum laude, U. Pisa, Italy, 1953, specialization in cardiology cum laude, 1955; doctorate honoris causa, U. Ferrara, Italy, 1990. Med. diplomate. Intern Istituto di Medicine and Cardiology U. Pisa, 1953-55, asst. Istituto di Patologia Medica, 1956-58; acting chief resident in medicine French Hosp., N.Y.C., 1958-59; trainee cardiovascular rsch. & tng. program dept. physiology Med. Coll. Ga., Augusta, 1959-60; postdoctoral fellow dept. physiology SUNY-Downstate Med. Ctr., Bklyn., 1960-61, N.Y. Heart Assn. fellow dept. physiology, 1961-62, instr., 1962, vis. asst. prof., 1964-65, asst. prof., 1965-66, assoc. prof., 1966-71, prof., 1971—; NIH fellow Physiologisches Institut U. Bern, Switzerland, 1962-64. Vis. prof. U. Ferrara, 1971, U. Vt., Burlington, 1978, Cath. Univ. Gemelli, Rome, 1984-85, SUNY at Stony Brook, 1994; assoc. editor Am. Jour. Physiology: Heart and Circulatory Physiology, 1976-80; mem. editorial bd. Circulation Rsch., 1974-80, European Jour. Pharmacology, 1985-90, Jour. Electrocardiology, 1985—; mem. editorial bd. New Trends in Arrhythmias, 1985-96, assoc. editor, 1991-96; editorial cons. Am. Jour. Physiology, Circulation, Science, Jour. Molecular Cell Cardiology, Cardiovascular Rsch; cons. NIH; mem. NIH Cardiopulmonary Study Sect., 1981-85, ad hoc mem., 1988; invited participant numerous confs., symposiums and workshops. Author (editor): Research in Phusiology, 1971, Cardiac Physiology for the Clinician, 1976, Excitation and Neural Control of the Heart, 1982; author: Diario di un Fisiologo del Cuore, 1992, Lost Emotions, 1994, the Riddle of the Mind, 1996, The Reality of the Self, 2000; editor: Chanderl McCuskey Brooks: The Scientist and the Man, 1990; author: Dunes, 2001; actor: (numerous papers, revs., chpts. and abstracts). Fulbright travel grantee, 1958-62; recipient A. and A. Sinsheimer Fund award, 1966-71, N.Y. Health Rsch. Coun. award, 1972-75. Mem. AAAS, Am. Physiol. Soc., Am. Heart Assn. (coun. on basic scis. 1969—), N.Y. Heart Assn. (bd. dirs. 1978-84), N.Y. Acad. Scis., Cardiac Muscle Soc., Cardiac Electrophysiol. Group (pres. 1972-73), Internat. Study Group for Rsch. in Cardiac Metabolism, Harvey Soc., Mex. Soc. Cardiology (hon.), Sigma Xi (pres. Downstate Med. Ctr. chpt. 1984), Roman Catholic. E-mail: mvassalle!netmail.hschklyn-.edu. Home: 104 Huntington Rd Port Washington NY 11050-3511 Office: SUNY Health Sci Ctr 450 Clarkson Ave Brooklyn NY 11203-2056

VASSALLO, EDWARD E. lawyer; b. N.Y.C., Aug. 12, 1943; BS, Columbia U., 1965, MS, 1967; JD cum laude, Fordham U., 1973. Bar: N.Y. 1974. Ptnr. Fitzpatrick, Cella, Harper & Scinto, N.Y.C. Mem.: ABA, N.Y.C. Bar Assn., N.Y. Patent, Trademark and Copyright Law Assn. (bd. mem., v.p.), Fed. Cir. Bar Assn., Internat. Trademark Assn., Am. Intellectual Property Law Assn. Office: Fitzpatrick Cella Harper & Scinto 30 Rockefeller Plz Fl 38 New York NY 10112-3800

VASSALLO, JOHN A. lawyer; b. N.Y.C., Aug. 19, 1937; s. John and Gilda (Di Desidero) V.; divorced; children: John C., Elena, Edward F. AB, Columbia U., 1959, LLB, 1962. Bar: N.Y. 1963, U.S. Dist. Ct. (so. and ea. dists.) N.Y. 1964, U.S. Ct. Appeals (2nd cir.) 1965. Assoc. Saxe, Bacon & O'Shea, N.Y.C., 1962-68; ptnr. Barovick & Konecky, 1968-70, Kurtz & Vassallo, N.Y.C., 1970-78, Franklin, Weinrib, Rudell & Vassallo, N.Y.C., 1978—. Fellow Am. Acad. Matrimonial Attys. (bd. govs.); mem. N.Y. State Bar Assn., Am. Coll. Family Trial Laywers (diplomate), Friars Club. Home: 285 Central Park W New York NY 10024-3006 Office: Franklin Weinrib Rudell & Vassallo 488 Madison Ave New York NY 10022-5702

VASSALLO, NICOLO, business consultant; b. Palermo, Sicily, Italy, Jan. 1, 1946; s. Francesco Paolo and Rosa (Mancino) V.; m. Flavia Giarrusso, Feb. 14, 1981; children: Marianna, Daniela. Student, Palermo, Italy. Acct. Crimal, Palermo, 1964-65, Seidita Costruzioni, Palermo, 1965-68; fin. cons. Fundus, Torino, Italy, 1969-70; gen. sales agt. Maeci, Milan, Italy, 1971-72; gen. mgr. Sofirs, Palermo, 1972-86; mgmt. cons. S&I-Servizi & Imprese, Altofonte, Italy, 1986-92. Chmn. Avis-Alfofonie, Unisystem, Palermo; chmn. La Provvidenza Altofonte; bd. dirs. Sinergia, Altofonte. Devel. office mgr. Democrazia Cristiana, Altofonte, 1989; chmn. econ. com. Town of Altafonte, Italy, 1997—. Roman Catholic. Office: S&I Servizi & Imprese Via Vito Virgilio 4 90030 Altofonte Palermo Italy

VASSAR, BARBARA ELLEN, educational consultant; b. Springfield, Mass. d. Albert Leo and Grace Katherine (Duffy) Benhard; m. William Gerald Vassar, June 21, 1952; children: William G. Jr., James P., Richard G., Carol A. Vassar Pettit. BA in Psychology, Ctrl. Conn. State U., 1975, MS in Edn., Guidance and Counseling, 1976. Cert. sch. counselor., intermediate adminstr. and supr., Conn. Ednl. counselor State of Conn. Correctional Instn., Cheshire, 1976-78; guidance counselor Roosevelt Mid. Sch., New Britain, Conn., 1978-81, Rockville H.S., Vernon, 1982-98; ednl. cons. Newington, 1999—. Mem. Conn. Assn. Counseling and Devel., Conn. Sch. Counselors Assn., Phi Delta Kappa. Democrat. Roman Catholic. Home: 47 Dowd St Newington CT 06111-2611

VASSELL, GREGORY S. electric utility consultant; b. Moscow, Dec. 24, 1921; came to U.S., 1951, naturalized, 1957; s. Gregory M. and Eugenia M. Wasiljeff; m. Martha Elizabeth Williams, Apr. 26, 1957; children: Laura Kay, Thomas Gregory. Dipl. Ing. in Elec. Engring, Tech. U. Berlin, 1951; MBA in Corp. Fin., NYU, 1954. With Am. Electric Power Svc. Corp., Columbus, Ohio, 1951-88, v.p. system planning, 1973-76, dir., 1973-88, sr. v.p. system planning, 1976-88; electric utility cons. Upper Arlington, Ohio, 1988—. Bd. dirs. Columbus & Southern Ohio Electric Co., 1981-88, Cardinal Operating Co.; mem. tech. adv. com. transmission FPC, 1968-70, FERC Task Force on Power Pooling, 1980-81; mem. U.S. com. World Energy Coun. Contbr. articles to profl. jours. Fellow IEEE (life); mem. NAE, Internat. Conf. Large High Voltage Electric Systems, Am. Arbitration Assn., Athletic Club of Columbus. Home and Office: 2247 Pinebrook Rd Columbus OH 43220-4327

VASSILAKIS, THEODORE, judge, lawyer; b. Alexandria, Egypt, Sept. 18, 1942; came to U.S., 1970; s. Nicholaos and Maria (Panagiotakis) V.; m. Ellen Kourtides, Apr. 1, 1976. BA in Polit. Sci., Panteios U., Athens, Greece, 1964; LLD in Law, U. Thessaloniki, Greece, 1967; LLM in Corp. Law, NYU, 1979. Bar: Athens, Greece 1994, N.Y. 1985, U.S. Dist. Ct. (so. and ea. dists. 1988), U.S. Supreme Ct. 1996. Adminstrv. officer Greek Ministry of Commerce, Athens, 1967-70; protocol officer Greek Embassy, Osaka, Japan, 1970; comml. attache Consulate Gen. Greece, N.Y.C., 1970-76; legal cons. Seward Rafael & Kourides, 1977-81; field underwriter N.Y. Life Ins. Co., 1981-84; real estate agt. Cooper Hill, 1984-85; atty.-at-law Bonaguidi & Assocs., 1985-90; adminstrv. law judge N.Y. State Office Temporary & Disability Assistance, 1990—; founding ptnr. Corcoran & Vassilakis, Attys. at Law, 1998—. Sub-lt. Greek Mil., 1964-66. Mem. Pan-Macedonian Orgn. (hon. mem.), N.Y. State Adminstrv. Law Judges Assn. (co-pres. 1993—), Alexander the Great Found. (founding mem., gen. counsel 1991—), Hellenic-Am. C. of C. Home: 405 E 56th St New York NY 10022-2412

VASSILIOU, EUSTATHIOS, chemist, consultant; b. Athens, Greece, Aug. 22, 1934; s. Theodore Vassiliou and Evlalia Porfiriou; m. Kleoniki Irene Parri; children: Theodore, Helen Apostolico, Evelyn Gearing. PhD, Chem., Victoria Univ. Manchester, Manchester, England, 1960—64; BS, Chem. Eng., Nat. Tech. Univ., Athens, Greece, 1953—58; Post Doctoral (hon.) , Harvard Univ., Cambridge, MA, 1966—67. Rsch. chemist DuPont, Wilmington, Del., 1968—73, staff chemist Philadelphia, Pa., 1973—78, rsch. assoc., 1978—85, sr. rsch. assoc. Wilmington, Del., 1985—91; fellow Intell. prop. , 1991; pres. WTPA, Inc., Newark, 1991—. Pres. PatCore, Inc., Newark, 1993—96; v.p. Health Style, Inc., Newark, 1993—97, 21st Century Rsch. Corp., Pulsbo, Wash., 1994—98. Author: (book) Physical Chemistry of Glasses. Pvt. Greek Army, 1958—60, Greece. Scholar, Greek Scholarship Found., 1960-1964, NATO, 1964. Mem.: Licensing Executives Soc., Harvard Chemists Assn. Achievements include invention of Sole inventor of DuPont's Silverstone coatings for cookware; Over 120 US patents; co-inventor, Dupont's granite type Corian. Office: WTPA Inc 12 South Townview Lane Newark DE 19711 E-mail: ev@wtpa.biz.

VASTA, EDWARD, humanities educator; b. Forest Park, Ill., Jan. 18, 1928; s. Joseph and Josephine (Mallimaci) V.; m. Geraldine Stocco, Nov. 28, 1953; children: John, Paula, Joseph, Catherine, Barbara, Salvatore. BA in English, U. Notre Dame, 1952; MA in English Lang. and Lit., U. Mich., 1954; PhD in English and Humanities, Stanford U., 1963. Tchg. intern, acting instr. Stanford U., Palo Alto, Calif., 1956-58; instr. U. Notre Dame, Ind., 1958-61, asst. prof., 1961-66, assoc. prof., 1966-69, fellow Medieval Inst., 1993-97, prof., 1969-97, prof. emeritus, 1998—. Author: The Spiritual Basis of Piers Plowman, 1965, Tales from the Hidden Apple, 2002, Novellas Back and Forth, 2002, Mudpie Mysteries, 2002; editor: Middle English Survey, 1965, Interpretations of Piers Plowman, 1968; co-editor: Chaucerian Problems and Perspectives, 1979; co-translator: Dante Alighieri, Vita Nuova, 1995. With USN, 1946-48. Fulbright scholar, 1952-53; Grad. Honors fellow Stanford U., 1958, 59; Danforth grantee, 1961; Creative Writing fellow Nat. Endowment for Arts, 1979. Democrat. Roman Catholic. Home: 52140 Harvest Dr South Bend IN 46637-2923 E-mail: evasta@nd.edu.

VASTA, VINCENT JOSEPH, JR. lawyer; b. N.Y.C., Jan. 15, 1944; s. Vincent Joseph and Frances (Monetta) V. BS in Chem. Engring., Manhattan Coll., 1965; MS in Chem. Engring., N.J. Inst. Tech., 1968; JD, Fordham U., 1972. Bar: N.Y. 1972, Conn. 1988; registered patent atty. Project engr. Exxon Rsch. and Engring. Co., Florham Park, N.J., 1965-68, Hoffman-LaRoche Co., Nutley, 1968-72; assoc. Pennie & Edmonds, N.Y.C., 1972-77; sr. assoc. Morgan, Finnegan, Pine, Foley & Lee, 1977-80; participating sr. assoc. Bryan & Bollo, Stamford, Conn., 1980-81; sole practice N.Y.C., 1981-83; internat. patent counsel Gen. Electric Co., 1983-86; div. patent counsel Union Carbide Corp., Danbury, Conn., 1986-89, UOP, Tarrytown, N.Y., 1989-90; ptnr. Sprung, Horn, Kramer & Woods, N.Y.C. and Tarrytown, 1990-92, Reiss, Walzer, Vasta & Starks, New Canaan, Conn., 1992-95; pvt. practice Law Offices of Vincent J. Vasta Jr., 1995—; spl. counsel Cowan, Liebowitz & Latman, P.C., N.Y.C., 1995—; pres. 47 Pineco Inc., New Canaan, 1993-98. Pres. Black Mountain Risin Enterprises, Inc., New Canaan, 1992-93, Vincent J. Vasta Jr. P.C., N.Y.C., 1981-90; bd. dirs., gen. counsel Calif. Taste, Inc., Santa Monica, 1982-88. Contbr. articles to profl. jours. Bd. dirs. student support com. Manhatten Ctr. High Sch., 1985-86; mentor Manhattan Ctr. High Sch. Mentor Program, 1985-86; bd. dirs., treas. ELFUN, N.Y.C., 1985-86. Mem. ABA, N.Y. Bar Assn., Conn. Bar Assn., Assn. Bar City N.Y., Am. Patent Law Assn., N.Y. Intellectual Property Law Assn. (chmn. ADR com. 1994-96). Avocations: investing, landscape architecture. Office: Law Offices of Vincent J Vasta Jr 65 Locust Ave PO Box 494 New Canaan CT 06840-0494

VASTAGH, GEORGE FREDERICK, physician; b. Budapest, Jan. 11, 1936; s. Alajos Gusztaf and Ilona Kuthan Vastagh; m. Ann Beam Devos, Mar. 12, 1976 (div. Aug. 1987); children: Andrew, Victoria, Joseph, Vincent. MS, U. Budapest, 1954; MD, U. Graz, 1959; DSc (hon.), U. Budapest, 1963; JD (hon.), U. Minn., 1971. Prof. medicine U. Tex., Dallas, 1962-72; assoc. med. dir. Abbott Labs., North Chicago, Ill., 1972-82; med. dir. Schering-Plough Co., Memphis, 1982-87; pres. G.F. Vastagh, 1987—. Legal med. cons. Tenn. Bar Assn., Memphis, 1987-91. Author: Muscle Metabolism, 1971; patentee in field; contbr. articles to profl. jours. Maj. U.S. Army, 1960-62. Fellow Rockefeller Inst.; mem. Pilots Assn., Hungarian Univ. Students in Exile (pres. 1960). Roman Catholic. Avocations: woodworking, flight instructor, gourmet cooking. Home and Office: 2427 Redbud Trail Dr Germantown TN 38139-6427 E-mail: Gvastagh@aol.com.

VASTERLING, PAUL, artistic director; B in Dance and Theater magna cum laude, Loyola U., New Orleans. Profl. dancer Nashville Ballet, Ohio Ballet, Ballet Austin; dancer, faculty mem., ballet master, resident choreographer Nashville Ballet, artistic dir., 1998—. Participant Carlisle Project, Oreg. Ballet Theatre's Am. Choreographers Showcase, Pacifica Choreographic Workshop, New Choreographers on Point program, N.Y.; creator Pub. Libr. Collaboration, Westminster Sch. Program, Oasis Ctr.; lectr. in field. Choreographer Nashville Ballet, Ballet Pacifica, Milw. Ballet, Oreg. Ballet Theatre, Classical Ballet Memphis, Epiphany; prin. works include Firebird, This Heart, Robin Hood, Pop, Nashville Ballet, Saltimbanques, Ballet Pacifica. Recipient Tenn. Individual Artists Fellowship for Choreography, 1995. Office: Nashville Ballet 3630 Redmon Dr Nashville TN 37209-4827*

VASTRUP, CLAUS, economist; b. Copenhagen, Mar. 24, 1942; s. Niels and Inger (Friis) V.; m. Lis Werdelin Petersen, Nov. 26, 1966; children: Jacob, Pernille. Degree in econs., U. Copenhagen, 1966; D of Econs., U. Aarhus, Denmark, 1983. Economist Denmark Nat. Bank, Copenhagen, 1966-69; asst. prof. U. Copenhagen, 1969-72; assoc. prof. econs. U. Aarhus, Denmark, 1972-83, prof., 1983—. Mem. Council Econ. Advisors, Copenhagen, 1986-93, chmn. 1988-93; bd. dirs. Den Danske Bank. Bd. dirs. Danish Inst. Internat. Affairs, 1995—. Office: Inst Econs Universitetsparken 8000 Aarhus C Denmark E-mail: cvastrup@econ.au.dk.

VASULKA, STEINA (STEINUNN BRIEM BJARNADOTTIR), artist, educator; b. Reykjavik, Iceland, 1940; m. Woody Vasulka. Student, Music Conservatory, Prague, Czech Republic. Mem. Icelandic Symphony Orch., 1964; freelance musician N.Y.C., 1965; co-founder The Kitchen media arts theater, 1971; mem. faculty Ctr. for Media Study State U. N.Y., Buffalo, 1974; artist-in-residence Nat. Ctr. for Experiments, KQED-TV, San Francisco, WNET-TV, N.Y.C., U.S./Japan Friendship Com., 1993; artist and Art and Sci. Lab., Santa Fe, 1980—. Instr. Acad. for Applied Arts, Vienna; instr. Inst. for New Media Staedelschule, Frankfurt, Germany; instr. Coll. Arts and Crafts, Reykjavik. Organizer A Special Video Tape Show, Whitney Mus. Modern Art, N.Y.C., (exhibitions) Eigenwelt der Apparate-Welt: Pioneers of Electronic Art, Linz, Austria, 1992. Recipient Maya Deren award, Am. Film Inst., 1992, Siemens Media Art prize, 1995; grantee, NY State Coun. on Arts, Corp. for Pub. Svc., Nat. Endowment Arts, Corp. Pub. Broadcasting, Guggenheim Found., N.Mex. Arts Divsn.; scholar, Czechoslovak Ministry of Culture, 1959. Office: Art and Sci Lab 369 Montezuma Ave Santa Fe NM 87501-2626*

VASULKA, WOODY (BOHUSLAV PETER VASULKA), artist, educator; b. Brno, Czech Republic, 1937; m. Steina Vasulka. Degree in metal tech. and hydraulic mechanics, Shc. Indsl. Engring., Brno, 1956; student, Acad. Performing Arts, Prague, Czech Republic. Co-founder The Kitchen media arts theater, 1971; mem. faculty Ctr. for Media Study State U. N.Y., Buffalo, 1974; artist-in-residence Nat. Ctr. for Experiments in TV, WNET-TV, N.Y.C., KQED-TV, San Francisco; artist and Art and Sci. Lab., Santa Fe, 1980—. Vis. prof. faculty art Poly. Inst., Brno. Organizer (exhibitions) Eigenwelt der Apparate-Welt: Pioneers of Electronic Art, Linz, Austria, 1992. Recipient Maya Deren award, Am. Film Inst., 1992, Siemens Media Art prize, 1995; fellow, Soros Found., 1993; grantee, NY State Coun. on Arts, Corp. Pub. Svc., Nat. Endowment Arts, Corp. Pub. Broadcasting, Guggenheim Found., N.Mex. Arts Divsn. Achievements include development of digital image articulator. Office: Art & Sci Lab 369 Montezuma Ave #812 Santa Fe NM 87501-2626*

VASZILY, BRIAN WILLIAM, writer; b. Chgo., Jan. 30, 1970; s. William Victor and Maryann Michelle (Banas) V.; m. Mireya Edith Renteria, Dec. 1, 1990 (div. Feb. 1998); 1 child, Evihn William; m. Beth Ann Bottini, June 22, 2001; 1 stepchild, Katelynn Michelle Jacob. BA, No. Ill. U., 1994. Mktg. coord. Woodfield Mall, Schaumburg, Ill., 1994-96; mgr. mktg. comm. BTI Americas, Northbrook, 1996-98; mgr. internet strategy Caremark, 1998-99; affiliate implementations mgr. Ourhouse.com., Evanston, Ill., 1999—2001; writer, editor, mktg. prof. www.mercola.com, 2002—. Mktg. comms. cons., Arlington Heights, Ill., 1996-98. Author: (novel) Beyond Stone and Steel: A Memorial to the September 11, 2001 Victims, 2002. Mem. Internat. Assn. Bus. Communicators. Avocations: creative writing, camping, reading, basketball, travel. E-mail: bvaszily@about.com.

VATANDOOST, NOSSI MALEK, art school administrator; b. May 22, 1935; d. Adullah Goodar and Mahtaban (Goodar) Malek; m. Ira Varandoost, May 30, 1964; children: Debbie, Cyrus. BA, Western Ky. U., 1970. Art tchr. Met.-Davidson County Sch. Sys., Nashville, 1970-71; dir., owner Nossi Coll. Art, Goodlettsville, Tenn., 1973—. Dir Tenn. Proprietary Bus. Sch. Assn., Inc., pres. Crimson Corp.; treas. Malek & Assos. Inc., 1976; dir. EXCEL Edn. Corp., 1980-86; vis. lectr., cons. EXCEL Bus. Inst., 1980-86. Active mem. Nat. Trust for Hist. Preservation. Mem.: NAFE, Internat. Coun. Design Schs. (pres. 1997—98), Art Inst. Nashville (founder, CEO), Career Coll. Assn., Art Resources of Tenn. (pres. 2000—01), Nat. Assn. of Schs. of Art and Design, Nat. Mus. Women in the Arts (charter), Hendersonville Art Guild, Hendersonville Art Coun. (com. chmn.). Club: Soroptimists (Upper Cumberland Valley, Tenn.). Home: 104 Whirlaway Ct Hendersonville TN 37075 Office: 907 Two Mile Pky Goodlettsville TN 37072-2324 E-mail: nossi@unidial.com.

VATAVUK, WILLIAM MICHAEL, chemical engineer, author; b. Sharon, Pa., Jan. 30, 1947; s. William James and Amelia Agnes (Lenarcic) V.; m. Betsy Ann Chandler, Oct. 27, 1973; 1 child, William Chandler. B in Engring., Youngstown State U., Ohio, 1969. Registered profl. engr., N.C. Chem. engr. E.I. DuPont de Nemours, Richmond, Va., 1969-70; sr. chem. engr. U.S. EPA, Durham, N.C., 1970-99; pres. Vatavuk Engring., 1999—. Author: Dawn of Peace, 1989 (Pulitzer nomination 1990), Estimating Costs of Air Pollution Control, 1990, Marketing Yourself with Technical Writing, 1992; mem. publs. com. Oilfield Jour.; inventor Vatavuk Air Pollution Control Cost Indexes; contbr. articles to profl. jours. Chmn. bd. dirs. Bennett Pl. Hist. Site Adv. Com., Durham, 1992—; publicity chmn. Hist. Preservation Soc. Durham, 1989-90; bd. dirs. N.C. 4-H Devel. Fund, Raleigh, N.C., 1990-93; tchr., Sunday sch. CCD, 1993; mem. mgmt. com. Durham Youth Coordinating Bd., 1999-2002. Capt. USPHS, 1970-99. Mem. N.C. Farm Bur., Mercer County Hist. Soc. (life mem.), USPHS Commd. Officers Assn. (pres. N.C. br. 1975-76, 84-85), Ret. Officers Assn. (life). Democrat. Roman Catholic. Avocations: reading, writing, jogging, gardening, solving puzzles. Office: 3512 Angus Rd Durham NC 27705-5404 E-mail: williamvatavuk@verizon.net.

VATCHER, JAMES GORDON, retired physician; b. Long Beach, Calif., June 14, 1925; s. Marshall James and Elise Ione (McElhinney) V.; m. Helen Stockwell (div.); children: Michael Gordon, Howard Peter, Donald Alan, Mary Helen, Kimberly Ann; m. Dorothy Caswell, June 1978. BA, Leland Stanford Jr. U., 1950; MD, Stanford U., 1954. Intern in surgery Stanford (Calif.) U. Hosp., 1953-54; resident Stanislaus County Hosp., Calif., 1954-56; physician surgeon Calif. Instn. for Women Dept. Corrections, Frontera, 1982-97; ret. Bsn Mate III USN CB, 1943-46. Democrat. Avocations: complementary medicine, nutrition, anti oxidant molecular/functional medicine, communication. Home: 872 S Cedarwood St Orange CA 92869-5301

VATER, CHARLES J. lawyer; b. Pitts., Feb. 8, 1950; s. Joseph A. and Helen M. (Genellie) V.; m. Diane E. Vater, June 10, 1972; children: Allison D., Elizabeth A. BA, U. Notre Dame, 1971; JD, U. Pitts., 1975. Bar: Pa. 1975, U.S. Dist. Ct. (we. dist.) Pa. 1975, U.S. Ct. Appeals (3d cir.) 1979. Assoc. Tucker Arensberg, P.C., Pitts., 1975-80, ptnr., shareholder, 1980—. Contbr. articles to profl. jours. Mem. Allegheny County Bar Assn. (probate coun. 1988-98, 99-2000, treas. 2001, sec. 2002), Estate Planning Coun. Pitts. (bd. dirs. 1988-90, 95-97, pres. 2001, past pres. 2002), Order of Coif, Phi Beta Kappa. Home: 1615 Trolist Dr Pittsburgh PA 15241-2650 Office: Tucker Arensberg 1 Ppg Pl Ste 1500 Pittsburgh PA 15222-5413 E-mail: cvater@tuckerlaw.com.

VATTER, PAUL AUGUST, business administration educator, dean; b. Boston, Sept. 14, 1924; s. August John and Elizabeth Emelia (Kunstler) V.; m. Josette Roman, July 23, 1966; children: Joel Paul, Katherine Alexandra. BA, Holy Cross Coll., 1944; MA, U. Pa., 1947, PhD, 1953; MA (hon.), Harvard U., 1970. Instr. U. Pa., Phila., 1945-53, asst. prof., 1953-58, vice dean of men, 1953-58; asst. dean Harvard U. Bus. Sch., Boston, 1958-62, assoc. prof. bus. adminstrn., 1962-70, prof., 1970-95, Lawrence E. Fouraker prof. bus. adminstrn., sr. assoc. dean, 1989-91, Lawrence E. Fouraken prof. bus. adminstrn. emeritus, 1995—; assoc. fellow Templeton Coll. Oxford (Eng.) U. Author: Quantitative Methods in Management, 1978, The Structure of Retail Trade by Size of Store, 1979, also video tapes. Home: 244 Clifton St Belmont MA 02478-2647 Office: Harvard U Bus Sch Soldiers Fld Boston MA 02163-1317

VATTILANA, JOSEPH WILLIAM, retired chief state safety inspector; b. Wilmington, Del., Mar. 22, 1928; s. Andrew and Elizabeth (Castiglione) V.; (div. 1974); children: Joseph W., Joy Ann; m. Gladys Mary Spence, Nov. 18, 1978. Student, Del. Tech. Community Coll., 1966-70, 89—, Pa. State U.,

1976-80. Cert. field instr., instr. for radiation control, work zone safety supr., dir. fleet maintenance, flagger instr. Heavy equipment mechanic Dept. Hwys. and Transp., Bear, Del., 1963-70, equipment supt., 1970-79, hwy. safety engr., 1979-84, chief safety inspector, 1984—. Instr. Flagger-Nat. Safety Coun., 1997; safety cons. for pvt. engring. co., 1994—; speaker and instr. in field. Author: Safety Manual Pass the Word, 1987, Equipment Certification Manuel, 1987, Do Something-Traffic Controls for Emergency Personnel, 1999. Dep. chief, asst. chief-chief driver, bd. dirs., capt. of rescue, sec. Talleyville (Del.) Vol. Fire Co., 1946-98; instr. ARC Del. chpt., Wilmington, 1956—; hon. life mem. Wilmington Manor Vol. Fire Co., 1985—. Recipient disting. svc. award State of Del., 1986, Lammot duPont Jr. meml. award Del. chpt. ARC, 1989, nat. safety award Am. Traffic Safety Svcs., 1992, Outstanding Vol. of Yr. award Del. Safety Coun., 1996; named man of yr. 1994 Am. Soc. Hwy. Engrs., hon. staff officer Del. State Police, 1994; recipient spl. recognition safety award Federal Hwy. Adminstrn., 1994. Mem. Am. Soc. Hwy. Engrs. (exec. dir. 1st State chpt. 1997, mem. 1st State Hwy. Hall of Fame 2001), New Castle County Fire Chiefs Assn. (pres. 1985-86), New Castle County Vol. Firemans Assn. (pres. 1986-87), Del. State Fire Chiefs Assn. (pres. 1993-94), Del. Hwy. Engrs. (1st and 2nd v.p. 1987-89), Soc. Hwy Engrs. (pres. 1st state chpt. 1988-90), Del. State Fire Police Assn. (hon. life), Del. Safety Engrs. (pres. 1986-87), Am. Legion (life), VFW (life). Roman Catholic. Avocations: woodworking, gardening, fishing. Home: 3333 Silverside Rd Wilmington DE 19810-4804

VAUCLAIR, MARGUERITE RENÉE, communications and sales promotion executive; b. Englewood, N.J., Jan. 26, 1945; d. Maurice Joseph and Yvonne Jeanne (Reynaud) V.; m. William Augustus Peeples II, (div. 1986). BS in Journalism, Bowling Green State U., 1967. Asst. promotion mgr. Internat. Herald Tribune, Paris, 1967-70; Europe promotion mgr. Vision-The European Bus. Mag., London, 1971; dir. programs and promotion Am. C. of C. in France, Paris, 1973-76; promotion and rsch. mgr. Johnston Internat. Pubs., N.Y.C., 1977-80; prin. Marguerite Vauclair Promotion-Pub. Rels.-Advt., 1981—; promotion mgr. L.A. Times Syndicate, 1985-88; advt. promotions and spl. sects. mgr. Soundings Publs. Inc., Essex, Conn., 1990. Collaborator on books, author: (guide) Guest Houses, Bed-and-Breakfasts, Inns and Hotels in Newport, R.I., 1982; contbr. travel articles and photographs to mags. and newspapers. Mem. Pub. Rels. Soc. Am. (Prisms awards com. L.A. 1988), Women in Comm. (bd. dirs. L.A. 1987-89), French-Am. C. of C. in U.S., Inc. (publs. com. 1993-98), Alliance Francaise de Westchester (bd. dirs. 2002—), Advt. Club of Westchester (bd. dirs. 1994-97), Fairfield County Pub. Rels. Assn., Conn. Press Club (bd. dirs. 2000—), Kappa Delta (bd. dirs. UCLA chpt. 1986-88, U. Conn. 1990-91). Office: 131 Purchase St Rye NY 10580-2139

VAUDRY, J. WILLIAM, JR. lawyer; b. Jacksonsville, Fla., Jan. 18, 1941; BBA, Tulane U., 1962, LLB, 1967. Bar: La. 1967. Mem. Lemle & Kelleher, LLP, New Orleans. Bd. editors Tulane Law Rev., 1965-67. Lt. (j.g.) USN, 1962-64. Mem. ABA, La. State Bar Assn., Order of Coif, Phi Delta Phi. Address: Lemle & Kelleher LLP Pan Am Life Ctr 21st flr 601 Poydras St New Orleans LA 70130-6029

VAUGHAN, ALDEN TRUE, history educator; b. Providence, Jan. 23, 1929; s. Dana Prescott and Muriel Louise (True) V.; m. Lauraine A. Freethy, June 1, 1956 (div. 1981); children: Jeffrey Alden, Lynn Elizabeth; m. Virginia Mason Carr, July 16, 1983. BA, Amherst Coll., 1950; MEd, Columbia U., 1956, MA in History, 1958, PhD, 1964. Tchr. Hackley Sch., Tarrytown, N.Y., 1950-51, A.B. Davis High Sch., Mt. Vernon, 1956-60; From history instr. to prof. Columbia U., N.Y.C., 1961—, prof. emeritus, 1994. Editor Polit. Sci. Quar., N.Y., 1970-71; gen. editor Early Am. Indian Documents, Univ. Pubs. of Am., 1977—; assoc. editor Ency. of the N.Am. Colonies, Scribners, N.Y., 1993; vis. adj. prof. CUNY, Lehman Coll., N.Y.C., 1971; vis. prof. Clark U., Worcester, Mass., 1987. Author: New England Frontier, 1965, rev. edit., 1979, 3d edit., 1995, American Genesis, 1975, Shakespeare's Caliban, 1991, Roots of American Racism, 1995, others; co-editor: Arden Shakespeare's The Tempest, 1999; contbr. articles to Am. Heritage, Am. Hist. Rev., New Eng. Quar., others. Lt. (j.g.) USNR, 1951-55. Recipient fellowship Guggenheim Found., 1973, Sr. fellowship Folger Shakespeare Libr., 1977, 89, Sr. fellowship Am. Antiquarian Soc., 1983. Mem. Am. Antiquarian Soc. (sr. fellowship), Am. Soc. for Ethnohistory, Shakespeare Assn. Am., Soc. Am. Historians (exec. sec., treas. 1965-70), Orgn. Am. Historians (program chmn. 1976), Inst. Early Am. History and Culture (coun. mem. 1985-87), Colonial Soc. Mass., Mass. Hist. Soc. Home: 50 Howland Ter Worcester MA 01602-2631

VAUGHAN, ALICE FELICIE, accountant, real estate executive, tax consultant; b. Laredo, TX, July 14, 1937; d. Wilfred John and Mayme Alice (Mitchell) Peck; m. Sam J. Vaughan, Feb. 27, 1960; children: Nicole Pam, Bonnie Kay, Kimberly Ann, Linda Marie. AS, AA, Del Mar Coll., 1981; BBA, Corpus Christi State U., 1982, MBA, 1983. Staff acct. Robin Perrone, CPA, Corpus Christi, Tex., 1985-86; owner Alice Vaughan Realty, 1982—; mgr. Country Club Estates Parks, Inc., 1986-89; tax acct. Jon Hurt, CPA, Tex., 1989—; v.p., sec., treas. Sa-Gu Corp., 1989—. Bus. tchr. Incarnate Word Acad. High Sch., Corpus Christi, 1988. Aquatic instr. YMCA, Corpus Christi, 1986—88; water safety instr. ARC; chmn. Corpus Christi Housing Improvement Corp./Loan Rev. Com., 2000—02. Recipient 20 Yr. Svc. award, ARC, Corpus Christi, 1991. Mem.: Country Club Civic Assn. Republican. Roman Catholic. Avocations: sailing, swimming, sailboarding. Home and Office: 6410 Coral Gables Dr Corpus Christi TX 78413-2612

VAUGHAN, CLYDE VERNELSON, program director; b. Nashville, Mar. 5, 1941; s. Clearwood Vernelson and Mamie May (Patterson) V.; m. Linda Carol Bean, Dec. 5, 1977; children: Vaudi, Gary, Christopher, Patrick, Cheryl, Pamela. AA in Mgmt., Hawaii Pacific Coll., 1984; BBA in Econs., Campbell U., 1987, MBA, 1990. Printer Palm Beach Post, West Palm Beach, Fla., 1960-64; coord. VA Campbell U., Buies Creek, N.C., 1987-90, dir. Pope AFB, 1990-99, Ft. Bragg, 1999—. Mem. bd. transfer com. Fayetteville (N.C.) Tech. Coll., 1993—. Vice chmn. Cumberland County Bd. Adjustments, Fayetteville, 1991-98. With U.S. Army, 1964-87. Mem. VFW, Am. Vets. Fgn. Wars, Am. Legion, Am. Motorcycle Assn., Kiwanis. Baptist. Avocation: motorcycling. Home: 126 Circle Ct Fayetteville NC 28301-3864 Office: Campbell Univ Campus PO Box 70659 Fort Bragg NC 28307-0659 E-mail: vaughan@mailcenter.campbell.edu., cuau997631@aol.com.

VAUGHAN, DAVID GEORGE, writer; b. London, May 17, 1924; came to U.S., 1950; s. Albert George Vaughan and Rose Stocks Martin. Archivist Cunningham Dance Fedn., N.Y.C., 1959—. Sec. Cunningham Dance Fedn., N.Y.C., 1964—, trustee John Cage trust, N.Y.C., 1992—. Author: Merce Cunningham: 50 Years, 1997, Frederick Ashton and His Ballets, 1977, 2d rev. edit., 1999 (Bueno prize 1977); editl. bd. Internat. Ency. of Dance, 1998. Staff sgt. Royal Army Svc. Corps., 1943-47. Recipient Outstanding Leadership in Dance Rsch. award, Congress on Rsch. in Dance, 2000, N.Y. Dance and Performance award, 2001. Mem. Dance Critics Assn., Soc. of Dance History Scholars. Democrat. Avocation: singing. Office: Cunningham Dance Found 55 Bethune St New York NY 10014-2010 E-mail: vaughan@merce.org.

VAUGHAN, DAVID JOHN, distribution company executive; b. Detroit, July 17, 1924; s. David Evans and Erma Mildred V.; divorced; children: David John, Melissa Ann, Julia Crawford McLaughlin; m. Anne McKeown Miles, Aug. 21, 1975. AB, U. Ill., 1950. Chemist Midland Electric Colleries, Galesburg, Ill., 1950-52; pres. Varrco Distbg. Co., Peoria, 1953—, David Vaughan Investments, Inc., Peoria, 1970—. Advisory bd. Charles Schwab Inc. Trustee Eureka Coll., chmn. bd. trustees; trustee Opera Ill.; Lt. USAAF, 1942-46, USAF, 1951-52, Korea. Mem. Peoria Country Club, Northport Point Club (Mich.), Peoria Skeet Club, Racquet Club, Naples Club (Fla.), Naples Bath & Tennis Club, Royal Poinciana Country Club (Naples), Masons, Shriners, Alpha Tau Omega, Phi Eta Sigma, Phi Alpha Delta. Republican. Presbyterian. Office: 5823 N Forest Park Dr Peoria IL 61614-3559 also: 824 N Birchwood Dr Peoria MI 49670-9761 also: Office Comstock Bldg Winter Park FL 32789 Home: 861 Swallow Pointe Naples FL 33942 also: 4413 Grandview Dr Peoria IL 61614 E-mail: dvaughan@dviequity.com.

VAUGHAN, EDWIN DARRACOTT, JR. urologist, surgeon; b. Richmond, Va., May 13, 1939; s. Edwin Darracott and Blanche V. (Bashaw) V.; m. Virginia Anne Lloyd, June 30, 1962; children: Edwin Darracott III, Barbara Anderson. BS, Washington and Lee U., 1961; MD, U. Va., 1965, MS, 1969; DSc, Washington and Lee U., 1982. Diplomate Am. Bd. Urology (trustee, v.p. 1988, pres. 1989). Intern Vanderbilt U., 1965-66, asst. resident, 1966-67; chief resident in urology U. Va., 1970-71, asst. prof. urology, 1973-75, assoc. prof., 1975-78, prof., 1978; clin. research fellow Columbia U., 1971-72, research assoc. dept. medicine, 1972-73; James J. Colt prof. urology, chmn. dept. urology Cornell U. Med. Coll., N.Y.C. and; attending urologist-in-chief N.Y. Hosp., N.Y.C., 1978—; sr. assoc. dean clin. affairs Cornell U. Med. Coll., 1993-2001, chmn. dept. urology, 1993-2001. Chief med. officer Cornell Physician Orgn., 1997—; mem. sci. adv. bd. Nat. Kidney Found., 1977-81; sec.-treas. Urology Coun., 1977-80, chmn., 1980-81; mem. med. adv. bd. Coun. High Blood Pressure, 1977; acting co-chief exec. officer Columbia-Cornell Care, L.L.C., 1997. Editor: Seminars in Urology, 1983-95; assoc. editor Investigative Urology, 1977-78, mem. editorial bd., 1978-94; editor Campbell's Urology; contbr. articles on obstructive uropathy, renal hemodynamics, hypertension to profl. jours. Recipient Research Career Devel. award NIH, 1976-78, Russell and Mary Hugh Scott award Am. Found. Urol. Disease, 1998, J.K. Latimer award N.Y.-N.J. Kidney Found., 1999, Valentine medal N.Y. Acad. Medicine, 2000; NIH tng. grantee, 1967-68; USPHS grantee, 1971-73, 74-77; Am. Heart Assn. grantee, 1976-79 Mem. ACS, AAAS, Internat. Soc. Urology, N.Y. Acad. Scis., Soc. Univ. Urologists, Am. Urol. Assn. (chmn. rsch. com. 1980-91, treas. N.Y. sect. 1985, v.p. N.Y. sect. 1986, pres. N.Y. sect. 1987, bd. dirs. 1992-97, pres.-elect 2000, pres. 2001, Golden Cystoscope award 1981, Disting. Contbn. award 1992, Hugh Hampton Young award 2000), Urol. Soc. Australasia (hon.), Soc. Exptl. Biology and Medicine, Soc. Univ. Surgeons, Soc. Internat. Urology (chmn. bd. 1997—), Am. Found. Urol. Disease (pres. 1987-92), Nat. Kidney and Urol. Disease Adv. Bd. (dep. chmn.), Intersoc. for Kidney and Urol. Disease Rsch. (chmn. 1987), Am. Assn. Genito-Urinary Surgeons (Barringer medal 1993), Am. Surg. Assn., British Assn. Urol. Surgeons (hon., St. Paul's medal), Japanese Urol. Soc. (hon.), Sigma Chi (Significant Sig award 2000), Alpha Omega Alpha (award 1976), Omicron Delta Kappa (award 1981). Home: 1165 Park Ave Apt 6A New York NY 10128-1210 Office: 525 E 68th St New York NY 10021-4870 E-mail: evaughan@mail.med.cornell.edu.

VAUGHAN, EUGENE H. investment company executive; b. Brownsville, Tenn., Oct. 5, 1933; s. Eugene H. Sr. and Margaret (Musgrave) V.; m. Susan Bolinger Westbrook, May 11, 1963; children: Margaret Corbin, Richard Bolinger. BA, Vanderbilt U., 1955; MBA, Harvard U., 1961. CFA, 1967. Security analyst Putnam Mgmt. Co., Boston, 1961-64; dir., dir. rsch. Underwood, Neuhaus & Co., Inc., Houston, 1964-70; pres., chief exec. officer Vaughan, Nelson & Boston, Inc., 1970-77, Vaughan, Nelson, Scarborough & McCullough, L.P., Houston, 1970—. Chmn. bd. dirs. Dreyfus Founders Asset Mgmt. Co., Denver, 1970—. Chair Fin. Analyst Fedn., N.Y.C., 1973-74, bd. dirs., 1969-76; dir. U. Tex. Health Sci. Ctr., Houston, 2002—; pres. Houston Soc. Fin. Analysts, 1967-68; trustee exec. com. Vanderbilt U., Nashville, 1972—, St. John's Sch., Houston, 1980-85, Goodwill Industries, Houston, 1978—, United Way of Tex. Gulf Coast, 1994—; elder First Presbyn. Ch., 1976—; founding chmn., trustee Presbyn. Sch., Houston, 1986-90. Lt. USN, 1955-58. Recipient Disting. Svc. award Fin. Analyst Fedn., 1978, Humanitarian award Am. Jewish Com., 1993, Bus. Leader of Yr. award U. St. Thomas, 1996. Mem. Inst. Chartered Fin. Analysts (trustee 1986-93, chmn. 1989), Assn. for Investment Mgmt. and Rsch. (founding chmn. 1990-91, gov. 1990-93), Greater Houston Partnership (bd. dirs. 1990—, exec. com. 1993—, chair Ctr. Houston's Future 1999—), Houston Club (pres. 1983-84, bd. dirs. 1979-85, chair centennial celebration, 1992-94), Houston Country Club, Coronado Club (Houston), Houston Forum (pres. 1991-92, chmn. 1992-93), Harvard U. Bus. Sch. Club Houston (pres. 1968-69, bd. dirs. 1966-71, 86-90), Vanderbilt Club Houston (chmn. 1984—, pres. 1966-68, Disting. Svc. award 1994), Conferie des Chevaliers du Tastevin, Belle Meade Country Club (Nashville). Republican. Avocations: traveling, sailing. Home: 3465 Inwood Dr Houston TX 77019-3129 Office: Vaughan Nelson Scarborough & McCullough 600 Travis Ste 6300 Houston TX 77002

VAUGHAN, GARY DAVID, history educator; b. Nashville, July 30, 1950; s. William Clifton and Joyce Marie (marlin) V.; m. Mary Lynn Sharpe, Dec. 7, 1989; 1 child, Kelly Ryan. BA in History, U. Tenn., 1972, MA in History, 1997; MS in Internat. Rels., Troy State U., 1981. Enlisted USAF, 1974, commd. 2d lt., 1984, honorably discharged, 1993, intelligence ops./imagery/reconaissance officer, 1974-93; field ops. supr. U.S. Commerce Dept. Bur. Census, Louisville, 1989-90; rschr., tchg. asst. U. Tenn., Knoxville, 1991-97; field ops. supr. mgr. Census 2000 U.S. Commerce Dept. Bur. Census, 1998-2000; taxpayer edn. customer/compliance rep. IRS, Nashville, 2001; with U.S. Treasury Dept., 2000—01; faculty Nashville State Tech. Cmty. Coll., 2001—. Adj. faculty in history Nashville State Tech. Inst., 2001—; spkr. in field. Rschr./asst.: Lives at Risk: Hostages and Victims of U.S. Foreign Policy, 1995, Major Crises of Contemporary American Foreign Policy: A Documentary History, 1997. Del. Dem. Nat. Conv., 1996; bd. govs. Knox County Dems., Knoxville, 1995-97, 99-2000; mem. Tenn. Dem. Party; mem. GORE Corps. Decorated Air Force Commendation medal with bronze oak leaf cluster, Air Force Achievement medal, others. Mem. So. Poverty Law Ctr., Nat. Geog. Soc. E-mail: vaughanventures@comcast.net.

VAUGHAN, HERBERT WILEY, retired lawyer; b. Brookline, Mass., June 1, 1920; s. David D. and Elzie G. (Wiley) Vaughan; m. Ann Graustein, June 28, 1941 (dec. June 2002). Student, U. Chgo., 1937-38; BS cum laude, Harvard U., 1941, LLB, 1948. Bar: Mass. 1948. Assoc. Hale and Dorr, Boston, 1948-54, jr. ptnr., 1954-56, sr. ptnr., 1956-89, co-mng. ptnr., 1976-80, of counsel, 1990—. Bd. dirs., fin. com. Boston and Maine R.R., 1961—64; vis. fellow New Coll., Oxford U., 1985. Mem. standing com. Trustees of Reservations, 1986—98, chmn., 1988—92, sec., asst. sec., mem. adv. coun., 1998—; mem. bd. trustees Am. Friends New Coll. (Oxford U.); mem. adv. coun. James Madison Program in Am. Ideals and Instns., Princeton U. Fellow: Mass. Hist. Soc., Am. Bar Found. (life); mem.: ABA, Am. Coun. Trustees and Alumni (mem. alumni leadership coun.), Am. Coll. Real Estate Lawyers, Am. Law Inst., Boston Bar Assn., Mass. Bar Assn., Longwood Cricket Club (Brookline), Boston Econ. Club, Union Club (Boston), Badminton and Tennis Club, Bay Club. Office: Hale and Dorr LLP 60 State St Boston MA 02109-1816 E-mail: Herbert.Vaughan@haledorr.com.

VAUGHAN, JERALD DENNY, management consultant, organizational development specialist, educator; b. South Boston, Va., Feb. 7, 1947; s. James Otha Vaughan and Frances Briggs (Lowery) Scott; m. Linda Sue Morris, Apr. 6, 1968; children: Lisa Ann, Leslie Alison, Laura Arlene (dec.). BS cum laude, Franklin U., 1973; MBA, Capital U., 1977. Staff assoc. Ohio Hosp. Mgmt. Svcs., Columbus, 1970-73; staff scheduler, nursing Mt. Carmel Med. Ctr., 1973-74, adminstrv. asst. nursing svc., 1974-79; svc. planning mgr. Xerox Corp., 1979-82, tech. adminstrn. mgr., 1982-83, field mgr. customer svc., 1983-89, dist. quality mgr., 1989-92. Adj. prof. mgmt., mktg. Franklin U., Columbus, 1980-92, vis. prof. bus. mgmt., 1993, prof. orgnl. leadership and mgmt., 1994-98, chair orgnl. leadership and mgmt. program, 1994-97; founder, prin. Discovery Orgnl. Cons., Columbus, Ohio, 1992—. Vol. instr. Project Bus., Jr. Achievement, Columbus, 1984, 85; Xerox dist. coord. ann. campaign dr. United Way, Columbus, 1988, 89. Mem. Acad. Mgmt., Am. Soc. Quality Control, Soc. Bus. Ethics. Republican. Avocations: golf, reading, music. Office: 2460 E Livingston Ave Columbus OH 43209-2912 also: Xerox Corp 15th Fl 471 E Broad St Columbus OH 43215-3842 also:

VAUGHAN, JOAN BERNADINE, library media specialist; b. Derby, Conn., Dec. 1, 1947; d. Harry Emmanuel and Theresa Rosemary (D'Aiuto) Erikson; m. Richard A. Vaughan, Aug. 11, 1973; 1 child, Richard A. Jr. BS in Libr. Sci., So. Conn. State U., 1970, MSLS, 1973. Cert. libr. media specialist, K-12, libr.-tchr., K-12, Conn. Libr. media specialist Stratford (Conn.) Bd. Edn., 1970—. Webelos den leader Cub Scout Pack 803, North Haven, Conn., 1993-95, com. chairperson, 1993-95. Mem. NEA, Conn. Edn. Assn., Stratford Edn. Assn., Conn. Ednl. Media Assn. Avocations: cooking, quilting, ceramics, candy making. Home: 36 Shawmut Ave North Haven CT 06473-2626 Office: Flood Mid Sch 490 Chapel St Stratford CT 06614-1690

VAUGHAN, JOHN CHARLES, III, horticultural products executive; b. N.Y.C., July 30, 1934; s. John Charles II and Lucille Grace (Dixon) V.; m. Ruth Darden MacLeod, Mar. 4, 1962; children: Elizabeth, John IV, George. AB in Econs., Cornell U., 1956; MBA, Northwestern U., 1962. Salesman Hall & Ellis, Chgo., 1959-62; br. mgr. Vaughan's Seed Co., Downers Grove, Ill., 1963-74, exec. v.p., 1974-76, pres., 1976-84, chmn. bd., 1985-93, ret., 1993. Regional v.p. Am. Seed Trade Assn., Washington, 1985-88; pres. Atlantic Seedsmen's Assn., N.Y.C., 1968; dir. McHutchison LLC. Bd. dirs. George Williams Coll., Downers Grove, 1982-92. 1st Lt. USMCR, 1956-59. Mem. Downers Grove C. of C. (chmn. 1989). E-mail: jvaug5668@aol.com.

VAUGHAN, JOSEPH LEE, JR. education educator, consultant; b. Charlottesville, Va., Dec. 31, 1942; s. Joseph Lee and Ann (Doner) V.; m. Linda Marie De Silva; children: Leigh Ann, Kelley, Stephen, Kathleen. BA, U. Va., 1964, MEd, 1968, EdD, 1974. Tchr. Madison (Va.) High Sch., 1965-67, Darlington Sch., Rome, 1967-69, Woodberry Forest (Va.) Sch., 1969-74; asst. prof. edn. U. Ariz., Tucson, 1974-80; prof. Tex. A&M U.-Commerce, Mesquite, 1980—, dir. programs in reading edn., 1980-86, 91-92. Dir. programs in reading edn. East Tex. State U., 1980—86, 1991—92; dir. Tex. Ctr. Learning Styles, 1989—95; exec. dir. Children's Inst. of Learning Devel., Inc., 1995—; dean of faculty St. Alban's Episc. Sch., Arlington, Tex., 2001—. Co-author: Reading and Learning in Content Classrooms, 1978, 2d rev. edit., 1985, Reading and Reasoning Beyond The Primary Grades, 1986. Bd. govs. Sancta Sophia Sem., 1991-98. Mem. ASCD, Nat. Reading Conf., Internat. Reading Assn., Soc. Effective Affective Learning. Unitarian Universalist. Avocations: golf, travel, reading, antiques. Home: 10112 Shadow Way Dallas TX 75243-5049 Office: Tex A&M U-Commerce 2600 Motley Dr Mesquite TX 75150-3840

VAUGHAN, KENNETH EDWARD, systems analyst, programmer; b. Richmond, Va., 1965; s. Lewis Edward and Jalna Vaughan. BA in history, Va. Tech., 1983-87; MS in information mgmt., Marymount U., 1996. Dir. libr. and rcds. mgmt. Cassidy & Assocs., Inc., Washington, 1988-98; developer Fannie Mae, 1998—. Mem. Brotherhood of St. Andrew, Lorton, Va., Operations Friends. Mem. Am. Indian Sci. and Engring. Soc., Delta Mu Delta, Delta Epsilon Sigma. Avocations: fishing, softball, reading, computers, cooking. Home: 12867 Mill House Ct Woodbridge VA 22192-2928 Office: Fannie Mae 3900 Wisconsin Ave NW Washington DC 20016-2892

VAUGHAN, KENNETH HAROLD, psychologist; b. Denville, N.J., Mar. 10, 1964; s. Harold Leroy and Roberta V.; m. Celeste Marie Therese, Aug. 12, 1994. BA, Drew U., 1986; MA, Fairleigh Dickinson U., 1988; PsyD, U. Hartford, 1995. Lic. clin. psychologist. Psychologist New Lisbon (N.J.) Devel. Ctr., 1995-97, Ctr. Family Guidance, Marlton, N.J., 1997—. Mem. APA, N.J. Psychol. Assn. Avocations: physical fitness, mountain biking. Home: 11 Tin House Rd Medford NJ 08055

VAUGHAN, MARK ASHBY, systems analyst; b. St. Ann, Mo., Dec. 18, 1952; BA in Human Resources, Lindenwood U., 1993; M of Info. Mgmt., Washington U., St. Louis, 2000. Team leader Southwestern Bell Corp., St. Louis, 1978—. Home: 7408 Bear Paw Dr Oakville MO 63129

VAUGHAN, MARTHA, biochemist, educator; b. Dodgeville, Wis., Aug. 4, 1926; d. John Anthony and Luciel (Ellingen) V.; m. Jack Orloff, Aug. 4, 1951 (dec. Dec. 1988); children: Jonathan Michael, David Geoffrey, Gregory Joshua. Ph.B., U. Chgo., 1944; MD, Yale U., 1949. Intern New Haven Hosp., Conn., 1950-51; research fellow U. Pa., Phila., 1951-52, Nat. Heart Inst., Bethesda, Md., 1952-54, mem. research staff, 1954-68; head metabolism sect. Nat. Heart and Lung Inst., 1968-74; acting chief molecular disease br. Nat. Heart, Lung and Blood Inst., 1974-76, chief cell metabolism lab., 1974-94; dep. chief pulmonary and critical care medicine br. Nat. Heart, Lung, and Blood Inst., 1994—. Mem. metabolism study sect. NIH, 1965-68; mem. bd. sci. counselors Nat. Inst. Alcohol Abuse and Alcoholism, 1988-91. Mem. editl. bd. Jour. Biol. Chemistry, 1971-76, 80-83, 88-90, assoc. editor, 1992—; editl. adv. bd. Molecular Pharmacology, 1972-80, Biochemistry, 1989-94; editor: Biochemistry and Biophysics Rsch. Comms., 1990-91; contbr. articles to profl. jours., chpts. to books. Bd. dirs. Found. Advanced Edn. in Scis., Inc., Bethesda, 1979-92, exec. com., 1980-92, treas., 1984-86, v.p., 1986-88, pres., 1988-90; mem. Yale U. Coun. com. med. affairs, New Haven, 1974-80. Recipient Meritorious Svc. medal HEW, 1974, Disting. Svc. medal NEW, 1979, Commd. Officer award USPHS, 1982, Superior Svc. award USPHS, 1993. Mem. NAS, Am. Acad. Arts and Scis., Am. Soc. Biol. Chemists (chmn. pub. com. 1984-86), Assn. Am. Physicians, Am. Soc. Clin. Investigation. Home: 11608 W Hill Dr Rockville MD 20852-3751 Office: Nat Heart Lung & Blood Inst Nih Bldg 10 Rm 5N 307 Bethesda MD 20892-0001 E-mail: vaughanm@nih.gov.

VAUGHAN, MARY KATHLEEN, anatomy educator; b. Houston, Sept. 7, 1943; d. William Asa and Ana Maria (Lopez) Cotten; m. George Martin Vaughan, July 2, 1966; children: Thomas Emanuel, Charles Martin, Christopher Nicholas. BA in Biology, U. St. Thomas, Houston, 1965; PhD in Anatomy, U. Tex., Galveston, 1970. Lectr. U. Rochester, N.Y., 1970-71; asst. prof. U. Tex. Health Sci. Ctr., San Antonio, 1975-80, assoc. prof., 1980—. Contbr. numerous chapters to books and articles to profl. jours. Mary Gibbs Jones scholar, 1961-65, USPHS spl. rsch. fellow, 1974-75. Mem. Am. Assn. Anatomists, Endocrine Soc., Soc. for Experimental Biology and Medicine, Neurosci. Soc., Am. Physiol. Soc., Internat. Soc. Neuroendocrinology, Sigma Xi. Democrat. Roman Catholic. Avocations: stamp collecting, computing, reading. Office: U Tex Health Sci Ctr Dept Cellular Structural 7703 Floyd Curl Dr San Antonio TX 78284-6200

VAUGHAN, MICHAEL RICHARD, lawyer; b. Chgo., Aug. 27, 1936; s. Michael Ambrose and Loretta M. (Parks) Vaughan; m. Therese Marie Perri, Aug. 6, 1960; children: Charles Thomas, Susan Enger. Student, U. Ill., 1954-59; LLB, U. Wis., 1962. Bar: Wis. 1962. Chief atty. bill drafting sect. Wis. Legislature, Madison, 1962-68, dir. legis. attys., 1968-72; assoc. Murphy & Desmond, and predecessor, 1972-73, ptnr., 1974—. Mem. Commn. Uniform State Laws, 1966—72; cons. Nat. Commn. Marijuana and Drug Abuse, 1971—73; lectr. CLE seminars. Contbr. articles to profl. jours. Warden, vestryman St. Dunstan's Episcopal Ch., 1973—78, 1980—87; mem. Wis. Episcopal Conf., 1972—76. Mem.: ABA, Dane County Bar Assn., State Bar Wis. (dir. govtl. and adminstrv. law sect. 1971—78, mem. interprofl. and bus. rels. com. 1976—89), Nakoma Golf Club, Madison Club, U. Wis. Law Sch. Bencher Soc., Delta Kappa Epsilon. Home: 4714 Lafayette Dr Madison WI 53705-4865 Office: 2 E Mifflin St Ste 800 Madison WI 53701-2038

VAUGHAN, NADINE, psychologist; b. Tampa, Fla., Aug. 30, 1947; d. Joseph Marcus and Velna Pearl (Jones) Williams; m. E.L. Vaughan III, 1966 (div. Aug. 1976); children: Edward L. Vaughan, Heather Vaughan Oyarzun; m. Dennis Wayne Kroeker, Apr. 9, 1982 (div. July 1997); 1 child, Melanie Sage. BA in Criminal Justice, U. South Fla., 1974, MA with honors in Rehab. Counseling, 1975; PhD in Psychology, Saybrook Inst., 1990. Lic. clin. psychologist, Calif., Wash. Co-founder Women's Resource Ctr., Tampa and Nevada City, Calif., 1973—; cmty. and organizational devel. specialist State of Calif., Berkeley, Sacramento, 1978-82; cons., trainer N. Vaughan, PhD, 1982—; regional trainer APA Hope Program, 1994—. Mem. adj. faculty psychology Sierra Coll., Peninsula Coll., Chapman U., Santa Barbara City Coll., 1998—, Hillsborough C.C., U. Tampa, Fla. Met. U.; owner Living Theatre Co. Mem. APA, Am. Coll. Forensic Examiners (diplomate psychol. spltys., med. psychology). Democrat. Avocations: theatrical directing and performance, scriptwriting.

VAUGHAN, OTHA H., JR. retired aerospace engineer, research scientist; b. Anderson, S.C., July 1, 1929; s. Otha H. and Ethel (Mayfield) V.; m. Betty Frances McCoy; children: Thera Virginia, Leslie, Frances. BS in Mech. Engring, Clemson U., 1951, MS in Mech. Engring., 1959; postgrad., U. Tenn. Space Inst., Tullahoma, 1975-81, U. Ala., Huntsville, 1974-75. Registered profl. engr., Ala. Commd. 2nd lt. USAF, 1951, advanced through grades to lt. col., 1972; mem. Von Braun R&D group Army Ballistic Missile Agy. (ABMA), Redstone Arsenal, Ala., 1956-60; retired USAF, 1979; rsch. engr., charter mem. NASA Marshall Space Flight Ctr., Huntsville, Ala., 1960-99, ret., 1999. Contbr. over 60 articles to profl. jours. Charter Mem. Aviation Hall of Fame, Dayton, Ohio; inductee Thomas Green Clemson Acad. of Engrs. and Scientists, Clemson U., 2001. Fellow: AIAA (assoc. Herman Oberth award Ala.-Miss. sect. 1999 1999); mem.: Res. Officers Assn. (life), Air Force Assn. (life; past v.p. Huntsville chpt.), Exptl. Aircraft Assn., Antique Aircraft Assn. (life), 8th Air Force Hist. Soc. Blackbirds, Minute Man Soc. Ala., Interplanetary Free Floaters (zero-gravity flights in NASA KC-135 aircraft), Nat. Space Club, Shriners, Masons. Achievements include patent in Lunar Communications Receiver and Transmitter for Lunar Surface Missions; participation in design of rocket and space vehicle systems, research and development of Redstone, Jupiter, Jupiter C, Juno, Saturn I, Saturn IB, and Saturn V, Skylab and Apollo program, and the Space Shuttle launch vehicle systems; development of design criteria for lunar surface operations and mobility for Lunar Rover program; research in environmental design criteria for lunar and planetary exploration vehicles, zero-g atmospheric cloud physics, and atmosphere electricity research. Home: 10102 Westleigh Dr SE Huntsville AL 35803-1647 E-mail: skeetv@knology.net.

VAUGHAN, SAMUEL SNELL, editor, author, publisher; b. Phila., Aug. 3, 1928; s. Joseph and Anna Catherine (Alexander) Vaughan; m. Jo LoBiondo Vaughan, Oct. 22, 1949; children: Jeffrey Marc, Leslie Jane, Dana Alexander, David Samuel. BA, Pa. State U., 1951. Deskman King Features Syndicate, N.Y.C., 1951; asst. mgr. Doubleday Syndicate, 1952—54; advt. mgr. Doubleday, N.Y.C., 1954—56; sales mgr., 1956—58; sr. editor, 1958—68; exec. editor Doubleday, 1969—70; pub., pres. pub. div. Doubleday & Co., Inc., 1970—82, v.p. parent co., 1970—86, editor in chief, 1982—86; sr. v.p., editor Random House, Inc., 1986—90, editor-at-large, 1990—2001. Mem. faculty, Columbia U., 1978-88; lectr. Harvard-Radcliffe U., Libr. Congress, U. Denver, Bowker meml. lectr. Author: (juveniles) Whoever Heard of Kangaroo Eggs? 1957, New Shoes, 1961, The Two-Thirty Bird, 1965, (history) The Little Church, 1969, Medium Rare: A Look at the Book and Its People, 1977, (humor) Little Red Hood, 1979, The Accidental Profession, 1979, The Community of the Book, 1983, The State of the Heart, 1985; editor: Buckley: The Right Word, 1996; contbr. to N.Y. Times, Sunday Times of London, Daedalus, Am. Heritage, others. Served with USMC, 1946-48. Named Disting. Alumnus Pa. State U., 1977, Alumni fellow, 1981 Mem. Tenafly Tennis Club, Quantuck Beach Club (Westhampton, N.Y.), Century Assn. Episcopalian. Home: 23 Inness Rd Tenafly NJ 07670-2714 E-mail: samuelsvaughan@aol.com.

VAUGHAN, TED WAYNE, music and communications educator, musician; b. Bloomington, Ind., Dec. 17, 1942; s. Delmas Leon Vaughan and Katheryn Rebecca (Knight) Starks Slade; m. Stephanie Ellen Milford Copeland, June 12, 1966 (div. 1981); children: Kevin Howard, Jennifer Leah V. Scott; m. Susan Ginnette Adams, July 26, 1987. B in Music Edn., Ind. U., 1965, MS, 1967, Edn. Specialist, 1968; EdD, N.Mex. State U., 1974. Cert. in music and instrumental edn., Ind.; cert. comml. pilot; cert. flight instr. Asst. prof., ops. mgr. KENW-TV Ea. N.Mex. U., Portales, 1968-70; instr. U. Wyo., Laramie, 1971-74, asst. prof., 1974-81, assoc. prof., 1981-86; assoc. prof. media arts U. S.C., Columbia, 1986-88; prof. comm. studies, chair dept. comm. studies Gardner-Webb U., Boiling Springs, N.C., 1991—. Contbr. articles to profl. jours.; mem. editl. adv. bd. Instrnl. Innovator, 1979-83; prodr. numerous film and multi-image formats, 1973-86. Bass trombonist S.C. Philharm., Columbia, 1986-98, Western Piedmont Symphony, Hickory, N.C., 1990—. Prodn. grantee Wyo. Dept. Edn., 1984. Mem. Assn. Ednl. Comm. and Tech. (accreditation task force N.C. chpt. 1986-94, chair cert. com. 1986-88, pres. MDPD divsn. 1985-87, mem. coms. 1976), Audio Engring. Soc., Phi Delta Kappa. Avocations: personal computing, pilot, motorcycle touring, antiques. Home: 415 Tanglewood Trl Lake Lure NC 28746-9151 Office: Gardner-Webb U Communication Studies Boiling Springs NC 28017 E-mail: tvaughan@gardner-webb.edu.

VAUGHAN, THERESE MICHELE, insurance commissioner; b. Blair, Nebr., June 12, 1956; d. Emmett John and Lonne Kay (Smith) V.; m. Robert Allen Carber, Aug. 14, 1993; 1 child, Kevin Leo Vaughan-Carber. BBA, U. Iowa, 1979; PhD, U. Pa., 1985. CPCU. Asst. prof. Baruch Coll., CUNY, 1986-87; cons. Tillinghast, N.Y.C., 1987-88; dir. ins. ctr. Drake U., Des Moines, 1988-94; ins. commr. State of Iowa, 1994—, dir. dept. commerce, 1996-98. Dir. EMC Ins. Group, Des Moines, 1992—94; trustee Am. Inst. for CPCU, Malvern, Pa., 1996—2002. Chair Jour. of Ins. Regulation Bd., Kansas City, Mo., 1995-99; co-author: Fundamentals of Risk and Insurance, 1996, 99, 2002, Essentials of Insurance: A Risk Management Approach, 1995, 2d edit., 2000; contbr. articles to profl. jours. Dir. Young Women's Resource Ctr., Des Moines, 1992-96; mem. Iowa Ins. Devel. Bd., Des Moines, 1990-. S.S. Huebner fellow U. Pa., 1979-82; named Outstanding Young Alumnus U. Iowa, 1996. Mem. Nat. Assn. Ins. Commrs. (pres. 2002, v.p. 2001, sec.-treas. 2000, chair Midwest Zone 1996-99), Am. Acad. Actuaries, Soc. Actuaries, Casualty Actuarial Soc., Soc. CPCU, Am. Risk and Ins. Assn., Beta Gamma Sigma, Omicron Delta Epsilon. Avocations: hiking, biking, reading. Home: 4632 Elm St West Des Moines IA 50265-2993 Office: Iowa Ins Divsn 330 Maple St Des Moines IA 50319-0065

VAUGHAN, THOMAS JAMES GREGORY, historian, writer; b. Seattle, Oct. 13, 1924; s. Daniel George and Kathryn Genevieve (Browne) V.; m. Elizabeth Ann Perpetua Crownhart, June 16, 1951; children: Meagan, Margot, Stephen, Cameron. BA, Yale U., 1948; MS, U. Wis., 1950, doctoral residence, 1951-53; LittD, Pacific U., 1969; LLD, Reed Coll., 1975. Exec. dir. Oreg. Hist. Soc., Portland, 1954-90; editor in chief Oreg. Hist. Quar., 1954-89; adj. prof. Portland State U., 1968—. Chmn. bd. Salar Enterprises, Ltd.; bd. dirs. Am. Heritage Pub. Co., 1976-85; film producer, 1958-99; historian laureate State of Oreg., 1989—. Author: A Century of Portland Architecture, 1967, Captain Cook, R.N, The Resolute Mariner: An International Record of Oceanic Discovery, 1974, Portland, A Historical Sketch and Guide, 1976, 2d edit., 1983, Voyage of Enlightenment: Malaspina on the Northwest Coast, 1977; editor: Space, Style and Structure: Building in Northwest America, 2 vols., 1974, The Western Shore, 1975, Ascent of the Athabasca Pass, 1978, Wheels of Fortune, High and Mighty, 1981, Soft Gold, 1982, 2d edit., 1990, To Siberia and Russian America, Vols. I, II and III, also others.; co-editor: Siberica, 1989; mem. adv. bd. Am. Heritage Mag., 1977-90; prodr. film The Crimean War, 1994, Wellington's Last Parade, 1997, George Dewey: The Monarch of the Seas. 1st chmn. Oreg. State Com. for Humanities, NEH, 1969— ; 1st chmn. Gov.'s Adv. Com. on Historic Preservation Oreg., 1970-77; sec. Oreg. Geog. Names Bd., 1958-89; adviser 1000 Friends of Oreg., 1972— ; lay mem. Oreg. State Bar Disciplinary Rev. Bd., 1975-82; vice chmn. adv. panel Nat. Endowment Arts, 1975—; mem. Nat. Hist. Publs. and Records Commn. Matrix, 1975-76; historian laureate State of Oreg., 1989. With USMC, 1942-45. Decorated comdr. Order Brit. Empire; recipient Aubrey Watzek award Lewis and Clark Coll., 1975;, Edith Knight Hill award, 1977, Disting. Svc. award U. Oreg.; grantee English Speaking Union, 1961; Columbia Maritime Mus. 1st rsch. fellow, 1992. Fellow Royal Geog. Soc.; mem. Am. Assn. State and Local History (bd. dirs. 1955-74, pres. 1976-78), Am. Assn. Mus. (coun., exec. com.), Nat. Trust Hist. Preservation (adv. coun.), Ctr. for Study Russian Am., Russian Acad. Scis., City Club (Portland, bd. govs.), Univ. Club (Portland, bd. govs.), The Arts Club (London). Home: 2135 SW Laurel St Portland OR 97201-2367

VAUGHAN, WILLIAM WALTON, atmospheric scientist; b. Clearwater, Fla., Sept. 7, 1930; s. William Walton and Ella Vermelle (Warr) Vaughan; m. Wilma Geraldine Stapleton, Dec. 23, 1951; children: Stephen W., David A., William D., Robert T. BS with honors, U. Fla., 1951; grad. cert., USAF Inst. Tech./Fla. State U., 1952; PhD, U. Tenn., 1976. Sci. asst. Air Force Armament Ctr., Eglin AFB, Fla., 1955-58, Army Ballistic Missile Agy., Huntsville, Ala., 1958-60; chief aerospace environ. div. Marshall Space Flight Center, NASA, 1960-76, chief atmospheric scis. div., 1976-86; rsch. prof. atmospheric sci. U. Ala., 1986—, dir. Rsch. Inst., 1986-94; ret., 1994. Cons. atmospheric sci. and tech. stds.; mem. adv. com. NASA. Reviewer: ; contbr. articles to profl. jours. Served to capt. USAF, 1951—55. Recipient Exceptional Svc. medal, NASA, 1971. Fellow: AIAA (assoc. Losey Atmospheric Scis. award 1980), Am. Meteorol. Soc.; mem.: AAAS, ASME, Am. Geophys. Union, Stds. Engring. Soc., Sigma Xi. Office: Univ Ala Atmospheric Sci Dept Huntsville AL 35899-0001

VAUGHAN, WORTH EDWARD, chemistry educator; b. N.Y.C., Feb. 1, 1936; s. Royal Worth and Sylvia Marie (Fernholz) V.; m. Diane Marilyn Mayer, Aug. 9, 1969; 1 child, Wayne John BA, Oberlin Coll., 1957; MA, Princeton U., 1959, PhD, 1960. Asst. prof. chemistry U. Wis.-Madison, 1961-66, assoc. prof., 1967-76, prof., 1977—. Mem. bd. advisors Am. Exchange Bank West Br., Madison, 1983-87. Author: Dielectric Properties and Molecular Behavior, 1969; editor: Digest of Literature on Dielectrics, 1974; translation editor: Dipole Moments of Organic Compounds, 1970; contbr. articles to profl. jours. Mem. Am. Chem. Soc. (pres. Wis. sect. 1968, sec. 1968, 98), Am. Phys. Soc., AAAS, Phi Beta Kappa, Sigma Xi, Alpha Chi Sigma Avocations: canoeing, contract bridge. Home: 501 Ozark Trl Madison WI 53705-2538 Office: Univ Wis 1101 University Ave Madison WI 53706-1322 E-mail: vaughan@chem.wisc.edu.

VAUGHN, ANN MARIE, art educator, artist; b. Newton, Mass., Jan. 20, 1941; d. James Charles and Eugenia Marie (Gillis) Murphy; m. Kenneth W. Vaughn Jr., 1964 (div. 1989); children: Kenneth W. III, James Duncan, Catherine Ellen; m. Louis Frederick Roensch, 1996. BA, Regis Coll., 1963; MA, Case We. Res., 1989, Cleve. Inst. Art, 1989. Cert. tchr., visual art specialist. Art tchr. Linn Benton C.C., Albany, Oreg., 1984-87, Bainbridge (Ohio) H.S., 1989-90; owner, operator Woodcrest Studio, Aurora, Oreg., 1992-94, art tchr. Richmond, Va., 1994—. Mem. Shokoe Bottom Arts Ctr., Richmond, 1993—97, Womens Caucus Art, Richmond, 1995—99, NOVA, 1991, Cleve. Ctr. Contemporary Art, 1991; represented U.S. in Brussels Belgium World's Fair, 1959. One-woman shows include Albany Libr., 1984, Rocky Neck Art Colony, Gloucester, Mass., 1965, Creative Arts Guild Gallery, Albany, 1985, Albany Gen. Hosp., 1985, Corvallis Country Club, 1986, Wickendon Gallery, 1989, Case Western Res. U., Cleve., 1989, Fairmont Gallery, Novelty, Ohio, 1991, Woodburn Art Assn., Oreg., 1992, Cedarfield Gallery, Richmond, 1997, Henry Clay Inn, Ashland, Va., 1998, St. Mary's Hosp. Gallery, Richmond, 1998, two persons shows. Mem. Rep. Womans Club, Albany, New Virginians, Richmond, Va. Mus. Art. Recipient Judges Choice award, Belgrade Art Show, 1997, others. Mem.: PEO, AAUW (v.p.), Nat. League Am. Pen Women, Richmond, Bon Air Artists Assn. (v.p. 1996—98), Richmond Watercolor Assn., Va. Watercolor Assn., USTA W. Banc Investment Club, Raintree Swim and Racquet Club. Roman Catholic. Avocations: tennis, bridge, cooking, ballet, opera. Home: 213 W Brook Run Dr Richmond VA 23233 Office: Woodcrest Studio PO Box 29121 Richmond VA 23242 E-mail: annartist@attbi.com.

VAUGHN, BETTY JEAN, obstetrician/gynecologist; b. Birmingham, Ala., 1932; MD, U. Ala. Sch. Medicine, 1956. Cert. ob/gyn 1967. Intern Mt. Sinai Hosp., Miami Beach, Fla., 1956-57; resident og/gyn Jackson Meml. Hosp., Miami, 1957-60; instr. ob-gyn. Sch. Medicine U. Miami, 1960-63, clin. asst. prof. ob-gyn., 1964-71; pvt. practice Coral Gables, Fla., 1960-66; project dir. Maternity Care and Family Planning Project Dade County Dept. Health, 1971-80; dep. dir. Orange County Dept. Health, 1980-86, state cons. quality assurance, 1987-90, ret., 1990. Mem. Am. Coll. Ob-Gyn., Orange County Ob-Gyn.

VAUGHN, BILLY ELDRIDGE, psychology educator, publisher; b. Houston, Mar. 2, 1951; s. David Isaac Vaughn and Willie Beatrice (Barzeron) Ward; m. Elizabeth Francis, Aug. 22, 1984 (div. Oct. 1995); 1 child, David Torrey; m. Karin Margareta Ingvarsdotter, Aug. 11, 1996. BS, U. Calif., San Diego, 1978, MS, 1984, PhD, 1986. Faculty Alliant Internat. U. (formerly Calif. Sch. of Profl. Psychology), San Diego, 1987—, Calif. State U., Fullerton, 1989-96; pres. Diversity Tng. U. Internat. LLC, 1999—. Author: Walking on Multicultural Eggs, 1996, Ethnic Diversification of Psychology, 1990; inventor cultural game. Bd. dirs. Elem. Inst. of Sci., San Diego, 1993—. Mem.: APA, Nat. Assn. for Multicultural Edn. (pres. 1996—99), Soc. for Psychol. Studies of Social Issues, Nat. Coun. Profl. Schs. of Psychology. Avocations: fly fishing, travel, writing, horse racing. Office: PO Box 720207 San Diego CA 92172-0207 Home: 15551 Andorra Way San Diego CA 92129 E-mail: billy@diversityuintl.com.

VAUGHN, GREGORY LAMONT, professional baseball player; b. Sacramento, July 3, 1965; Student, Sacramento City Coll., Miami Coll. Player Milw. Brewers, 1989—96, San Diego Padres, 1996-98; outfielder Cincinnati Reds, 1999, Tampa Bay Devil Rays, St. Petersburg, 2000—. Mem. Am. League All-Star Team, 1993, 96. Named Midwest co-MVP, 1987, Am. Assn. MVP, 1989. Office: Tampa Bay Devil Rays One Tropicana Dr Saint Petersburg FL 33705*

VAUGHN, IMA JEAN, minister, educator; b. Checotah, Okla., Sept. 7, 1931; d. John Harry and Anna Mae (Barber) Ford; m. Eldon Dewey Vaughn, June 18, 1949; children: Candace Lynn, Linda Jean. BS, Kans. State Coll., 1961, MS, 1967; EdS, Wichita State U., 1975; Edn. for Ministry, U. of the South, 1985. Nat. cert. counselor. Tchr. Chanute (Kans.) Pub. Schs., 1954-69; counselor, psychologist, adminstr. Wichita (Kans.) Pub. Schs., 1969-91; min. Christian Ch. Kans., Wichita, 1985-91, counselor, tchr., min. Chanute, 1991—, coord. Disciples Women Topeka, 1997—. Advocate Kans. Christian Home, 1996. Author: A Setting of Silver, 1996. Chaplain Neosho Meml. Regional Med. Ctr., Chanute, 1991-97; elder, tchr. First Christian Ch.; pres. Kans. Christian Women's Fellowship, 1996-00. Recipient travel award to Israel Delta Kappa Gamma, 1984. Mem. Chanute Area Retired Tchrs. Assn., MENSA. Democrat. Avocation: writing. Home: RR 2 Box 108 Chanute KS 66720-9403 Office: Christian Ch in Kans 2914 SW Macvicar Ave Topeka KS 66611-1710

VAUGHN, JAMES ENGLISH, JR. neurobiologist; b. Kansas City, Mo., Sept. 17, 1939; s. James English and Sue Katherine (Vaughn); m. Christine Singleton, June 18, 1961; children: Stephanie, Stacey. BA, Westminster Coll., 1961; PhD, UCLA, 1965. Postdoctoral rsch. fellow in brain rsch. U. Edinburgh, Scotland, 1965-66; asst. prof. Boston U. Sch. Medicine, 1966-70; head sect. molecular neuromorphology Beckman Rsch. Inst., City of Hope, Duarte, Calif., 1970—, pres. rsch. staff, 1986, chmn. divsn. neurosci., 1987—2001. Editor (assoc. editor): (Jour.) Jour. Neurocytology, 1978—86; contbr. articles to profl. jours.; mem. editl. bd. (Jour.) Synapse, 1986—, reviewer for Jour. Comparative Neurology, 1974—, Brain Research, 1976—. Fellow Neurosci. Rsch. Program, 1969; grantee rsch. grantee, NIH, 1969—, NSF, 1983—87. Mem.: AAAS, N.Y. Acad. Scis., Internat. Brain Rsch. Orgn., Soc. for Neurosci. (chmn. short course 1977), Am. Assn. Anatomists, Am. Soc. Cell Biology, Sigma Xi. Office: City of Hope Beckman Rsch Inst 1450 Duarte Rd Duarte CA 91010-3011

VAUGHN, JAMES T. former state police officer, state senator; b. Cheswold, Del., Apr. 12, 1925; s. Charles Townsend and Ada (Van Pelt) V.; m. Sylvia Harris, Nov. 12, 1947; children: James T., Robert G., Judith A. Student schs. Smyrna, Del. Policeman, Del. State Police, 1946-66; with Vaughn Law Office, Dover, Del., 1966-76; commr. Dept. Corrections, Del., 1976-79; chief police dept. Smyrna, 1980; mem. Del. Senate, 1980—. Mgr., coach Smyrna-Clayton Little League, 1957-98; mem. Bd. Edn., Smyrna, 1966-81. Served with USMC, 1943-46. Mem. F.B.I. Nat. Acad., Del. Assn. Chiefs of Police, Am. Legion, VFW. Democrat. Methodist. Lodge: Masons. Office: Del State Senate Legis Hall Dover DE 19901

VAUGHN, JOANN WOLFE, family nurse practitioner; b. Knoxville, Tenn., Mar. 4, 1947; d. Paul Albert and Elizabeth (Umburger) Wolfe; m. Neville Dewayne VAughn, Nov. 8, 1985. Diploma, Johnston Meml. Hosp., Abingdon, Va., 1968; BSN, East Tenn. State U., Johnson City, 1981, MSN, 1996. Cert. family nurse practitioner, ACLS. Staff nurse Bristol (Tenn.) Meml. Hosp., 1968-70, Med. Coll. Va., Richmond, 1970-72; staff nurse ICU/CCU Chippenham Hosp., 1972-73; staff nurse Bristol Regional Med. Ctr., 1973-92, asst. nurse mgr. emergency dept., 1992-96; family nurse practitioner Johnston Meml. Hosp., Abingdon, Va., 1996-98, Holston Med. Svcs., Damascus, 1998-99; family nurse practitioner emergency dept. Bristol Regional Med. Ctr., 1999, employee health nurse practitioner, 1999-2001; family nurse practitioner Blountville Internal Medicine, 2001—02, Bluff City Med. Ctr., 2002—. Mem. ANA, Northeast Tenn. Nurse Practitioners Assn., Nurse Practitioner/Physician Asst. Assn., Emergency Nurses Assn. (pres. Appalachian chpt. 1983-84), Sigma Theta Tau, Phi Kappa Phi. Republican. Methodist. Avocations: swimming, reading, walking. Home: PO Box 201 Bristol VA 24203-0201 Office: Bluff City Med Ctr 229 Highway 19E Bluff City TN 37618 E-mail: joann_w_vaughn@wellmont.org.

VAUGHN, JOHN CARROLL, minister, educator; b. Louisville, Sept. 22, 1948; s. Harold D. and Morel (Johnson) V.; m. Brenda Joyce Lyttle, June 17, 1968; children: Deborah, John, Rebecca, Daniel, Joseph. BA, Bob Jones U., 1977, MMin, 1991, DD, 1989. Ordained to ministry Bapt. Ch., 1978. Sr. pastor Faith Baptist Ch., Greenville, S.C., 1977—; founder/adminstr. Hidden Treasure Christian Sch., 1980-84; founder Iglesia Bautista de la Fe, 1981-93. Founder/dir. Hidden Treasure Ministries, Greenville, 1985—; exec. bd. Associated Gospel Chs., Hopewell, Va., 1987-93; chaplain Greenville Police Dept., 1987—. Editor: (instrnl. video) Sufficient Grace, 1987, Frontline Mag., 1997—; author: (textbook) Special Education: A Biblical Approach, 1991, (biography) More Precious Than Gold, 1994. Chmn. Greenville County Human Rels. Commn., 1986-89; counselor Greenville County Crisis Response Team, 1987-91; co-chmn. Greenville County Sex Edn. Adv. Com., 1988-91; mem. exec. bd. dirs. Fundamental Bapt. Fellowship, 1988-98, exec. dir., 1997-98, exec. v.p. 1998—; mem. exec. bd. dirs. The Wilds, 1992—, Internat. Bapt. Missions, 1993—, Christians for Religious Freedom, 1993-98. Mem. SAR, Internat. Conf. Police Chaplains, Am. Assn. Christian Schs. (exec. bd. dirs. 1992-98), ACFT Owners and Pilots Assn., Am. Legion, S.C. Assn. Christian Schs. (pres. 1988—). Republican. Avocations: flying, golf, gardening, reading, history, writing. Home: 117 Frontline Dr Taylors SC 29687-2675 Office: Faith Bapt Ch 500 W Lee Rd Taylors SC 29687-2513

VAUGHN, JOHN ROLLAND, auditor; b. Iola, Kans., Aug. 4, 1938; s. Ralph H. and Alice (Dille) V.; m. Doris K. Black, Sept. 4, 1960; children: Lisa Ann, Brian Douglas. BS in Bus, Emporia State U., 1960. Sr. auditor Arthur Andersen & Co., Kansas City, Mo., 1961-66; gen. auditor First Nat. Bank Kansas City, 1966-69, Commerce Bancshares, Inc., 1969-73; sr. v.p. Adminstrv. Services div. Peoples Trust Bank, Ft. Wayne, Ind., 1973-77; dep. gen. auditor, v.p. Crocker Nat. Bank, San Francisco, 1978-79; v.p., gen. auditor S.W. Bancshares, Houston, 1980-83; sr. v.p., gen. auditor MCorp., 1984-87, mng. dir., 1988-89; audit dir. Banc One Corp., Dallas, 1990-92; v.p., gen. auditor St. Paul Cos., St. Paul, 1992-97; dir. internal audit Conseco Fin., 1998—2001; v.p., chief audit officer Calif. State Automobile Assn., 2001—. Treas. Overland Park (Kans.) Jr. C. of C., 1965—66; outside dir. Overland Park Credit Union; contr. Ft. Wayne Bicentennial Commn., 1974—77; mem. chmns. cabinet Indianhead coun. Boy Scouts Am., 2000—01. Mem. Inst. Internal Auditors (1st v.p. Kansas City 1969-70, pres. 1970-71, midwest regional v.p. 1971-72, Twin Cities chpt. gov. 1993-97, pres. 1994-95, internat. profl. conf. com. 1995-98, internat. ednl. products com. 1999-2002), Fin. Execs. Inst. (dir. Ft. Wayne 1976-77), Risk and Ins. Mgmt. Soc., Hartsmen, Soc. Preservation and Encouragement Barber Shop Quartet Singing in Am., Vocal Majority Chorus, Gt. No. Union Chorus, Sigma Tau Gamma. Home: 5 Henry Ranch Dr San Ramon CA 94583

VAUGHN, LINDA M. municipal official; b. Moline, Ill., Aug. 6, 1947; d. Merwin Perry and Margaret Anne (Larson) Baker; m. Jeffery M. Vaughn, Aug. 16, 1969; children: Jason P., Eric M. Student, Moline Inst. Commerce, 1965. Data entry clk. Farmall (Internat. Harvester), Rock Island, Ill., 1973-75, Ingersoll, Rockford, 1975-87; trustee Village of Machesney Park (Ill.), 1987-89, clk., 1989—. Guest columnist Post Jour., 1997—. Charter mem. Chamber Women's Network, Loves Park, Ill., 1995; sec. GPAC Sr. Ctr., Loves Park, 1997—; sec., treas. NIMCA, Regional Clk. Assn., Ill., 1995—. Mem. Northwestern Ill. Mcpl. Clks. Assn. (sec. 1990-92, treas. 1997-99), C. of C. (ambassador 1987—). Democrat. Roman Catholic. Avocations: writing, fishing, reading, walking, grandchildren. Home: 9519 Shore Dr Machesney Park IL 61115-2058 Office: Village Machesney Park 300 Machesney Rd Machesney Park IL 61115-2495

VAUGHN, MICHAEL S. criminal justice educator; s. Harley (Bud) Dewitt and Judith Ann Vaughn; m. Tzu-Hsiu Nancy Vaughn, Dec. 2, 1989; children: Rachel. PhD in Criminal Justice, Sam Houston State U., Huntsville, Tex., 1990—93. Assoc. prof. Ga. State U., Atlanta, 1993—. Book rev. editor, Jour. of Criminal Justice Edn. Acad. of Criminal Justice Scis., Greenbelt, Md., 1993—96; editor, police forum Police Sect., Acad. of Criminal Justice Scis., Greenbelt, Md., 1996—2001; editor, criminal justice rev. and internat. criminal justice rev. Ga. State U., Atlanta, 2001—; contbr., correctional health care report Civic Rsch. Inst., New York, 1999—. Contbr. articles. Named Outstanding Alumnus, Coll. of Criminal Justice, Sam Houston State U., 2002; recipient Outstanding Service award, Police Section, Acad. of Criminal Justice Sciences, 1998, Outstanding Paper, Acad. of Criminal Justice Scis., 1996. Mem.: Am. Assn. Univ. Profs., Am. Judicature Soc., Am. Psychology-Law Soc., Am. Soc. Criminology, Acad. Criminal Justice Scis. Avocation: reading. Office: Ga State Univ Criminal Justice PO Box 4018 Atlanta GA 30302-4018 Office Fax: 404-651-3658.

VAUGHN, PAMELA W. music educator; MusB, U. Wyo., 1973. Cert. music tchr. Vocal music tchr. Ralston (Nebr.) Pub. Sch., 1973-75, Millard Pub. Sch., Omaha, 1980-84; vocal accompanist Papillion (Nebr.) Pub. Sch., 1987—2001; pvt. piano tchr. Omaha, 1976—. Min. of music Presbyn. Ch., Omaha, 1977—87; choral dir. Trinity United Meth. Ch., Ralston, Nebr., 1987—97, dir. music ministries, Nebr., 1997—; All-State vocal accompanist Nebr. Music Educators Assn. , 1994—2001. Bd. mem. Nebr. Summer Music Olympics, 2000—. Mem. Nat. Music Tchrs. Assn., Nebr. Music Tchrs. Assn., Omaha Music Tchrs. Assn., Pi Kappa Lambda, Pi Kappa Pi. Methodist. Avocations: family history, grandchildren.

VAUGHN, RICHARD CLEMENTS, engineering educator; b. Ionia, Mich., Jan. 17, 1925; BA, Mich. State U., 1948; M Indsl. Engring., U. Toledo, 1956. EIT Profl. engr., Fla., Iowa. Various to indsl. engr. AP Parts Corp., Toledo, 1953—55; chief indsl. engr. Mather Spring Co., 1955; process engr. Ford Motor Co., Monroe, Mich., 1955—56; process engring. supr. Detroit Harvester Corp., Toledo, 1956—57. Asst. prof. U. Fla., Gainesville, 1957—62; assoc. prof. to ret. prof. Iowa State U., Ames, 1962—87. Author: (novels) (textbook) Legal Aspects of Engineering (6 edits.), 1962, Introduction to Industrial Engineering (3 edits.), 1967, Quality Assurance (2 edits.), 1974. Home: 1519 Harding Ave Ames IA 50010

VAUGHN, ROSELLA HARRIS, human relations professional; b. Statesville, N.C., May 4, 1934; d. Richard James and Mary Jane (Smith) Harris; m. Henry P. Pierce, Sept. 25, 1956 (dec. July 1978); children: Dyrel Pierce, Ledra P. Mesta, Phillip Oji Pierce; m. James Earl Vaughn, Sept. 20, 1983 (dec.); stepchildren: Sarah, Shirley, James E. Jr., Patricia. BA in Edn., Livingstone Coll., 1955; MA in gen. studies., George Washington U., 1975, postgrad., 1977-78. Card punch operator Nat. Security Agy., Washington, 1956-57, Dept. Motor Vehicles, Sacramento, 1957-59; substitute tchr. Calif. Pub. Schs., 1959-60; elm. sch. tchr. D.C. Pub. Schs., Washington, 1960-83; dir. employment tng. program YWCA, Lancaster, Pa., 1983-85; program coord. Lancaster Employment/Tng. Agy., 1985-87; human rels. rep. Lancaster County Human Rels. Commn., Lancaster, 1988—, mem. employment com., 1988—. Mem. employment adv. coun. Lancaster County Office of the Aging, 1989—. Bd. dirs. Lancaster Literacy Coun., 1987-88; active ptnrs. in edn. Sch. Dist. of Lancaster, 1991—, Cultural Coun. Lancaster County, 1990-91. Mem. Crispus Attucks Community Ctr. (pres. bd. dirs. 1985-87, outstanding svc. plaque 1989). Home: 7109 Lowen Rd Charlotte NC 28269-0194

VAUGHN, SUSAN MARIE, journalist, educator; b. Hastings, Nebr., Apr. 22, 1945; d. Philip S. and Berta I. Abrahamson; m. Thomas P. Vaughn (div. Sept. 10, 1982); children: Jeanne, Matthew. BA, Coe Coll., Cedar Rapids, Iowa, 1967; MS in Journalism, Columbia U., 1992. Reporter Hartford Courant , Manchester, Conn., 1971—75, Manchester (Conn.) Herald, 1976—79; mng. editor, reporter The Jours., Windsor, Conn., 1980—81; reporter, feature writer, copy editor Manchester Herald, 1984—87; news editor, reporter The Chronicle, Willimantic, Conn., 1987—91; reporter Jour. Inquirer, Manchester, 1992—97; news editor Bristol (Conn.) Press, 1997—98; copy editor The Advocate, Stamford, Conn., 1998—99; asst. prof. journalism Lynchburg (Va.) Coll., 2001—02. Mem. media careers adv. bd. Manchester C.C., 1989—94, mem. comm. program evaluation team, 1998; vis. asst. prof. journalism Iona Coll., New Rochelle, NY, 1999—2001. Contbr. newspaper article (Bus. award UP Internat. Cmty. Svc., 1988). Vol. Hartford Stage, 1984—89, Bushnell Auditorium, Hartford, 1995—99; pres., mem. Manchester Arts Coun., 1986—90; pres., mem. Acad. Music Vol., Lynchburg, Va., 2002; tchr. English as a Second Lang. Literacy Vols. Am., Stamford, 1999—2001. Fellow journalism, Finland Ministry of Fgn. Affairs, 1992. Mem.: Assn. Educators Journalism and Mass Comm., Soc. for Profl. Journalists, Coll. Media Advisers. Avocations: hiking, bicycling, photography, arts, travel. Office: Lynchburg Coll 1501 Lakeside Dr Lynchburg VA 24501 Business E-Mail: vaughn@lynchburg.edu.

VAUGHN, THOMAS JOSEPH, earth science educator, administrator; b. Lawrence, Mass., Dec. 23, 1944; s. Thomas Wilbur and Dorothy Agnes (Mallon) V.; m. Priscilla Margaret Bastian, June 30, 1973; children: Matthew Thomas, Judith Diane. BA in History/Geography, Mt. Carmel Coll., Niagara Falls, Ont., Can., 1968; AM in Geography, Boston U., 1972; MEd in Secondary Ednl. Adminstrn., U. Lowell, Mass., 1977; CAGS in Computers in Edn., Lesley U., Cambridge, Mass., 1985. Cert. tchr. earth sci., geography, history, cert. gen. supr., jr.-sr. h.s. prin., Mass. Tchr. earth sci. DeSales H.S., Louisville, 1968-69; tchg. fellow Boston U., 1969-71; liberal arts prof. Bryant-McIntosh Jr. Coll., Lawrence, 1971-72; asst. dir. project ESTEEM Harvard-Smithsonian, Cambridge, 1993; adult edn. instr. Arlington (Mass.)

Pub. Schs., 1985-90; instr. earth sci. Northeastern U., Boston, 1997—; earth sci. tchr., lead sci. tchr. Arlington H.S., 1972—. Telecomms. moderator Harvard U. Sci. Tchr. Network, Cambridge, 1986-89; chair study groups for sci. edn. reform Mass. Dept. Edn., Malden, 1995—, sci. tchr. leader, 1998. Co-author: Integrating Computers in Your Classroom: Middle and Secondary Science, 1994, Harvard Smithsonian Project IMAGE, 1997; presenter in field. Lector St. Theresa's Ch., Billerica, Mass., 1975—; trustee Billerica Pub. Libr., 1993—; mem. Billerica Friends of the Libr., 1995—. Recipient Pathfinder award in tech. Mass. Dept. Edn., 1991, Sci. Educator of Yr. award for Middlesex County, Mass. Assn. Sci. Tchrs., 1998, Presdl. award for excellence in tchg. math. and sci. NSF, 2000; Disting. Alumni award U. Mass., Lowell, 2000, Boston U., 2002; Tandy Tech. scholar, 1996, Disting. Alumnia award Boston U., 2002; inducted into Mass. Sci. Educators Hall of Fame, 1992; Tchr. Leadership Acad. of Mass., 2001. Fellow Tchr. Leadership Acad. Mass.; mem. Nat. Assn. Geosci. Tchrs. (regional pres.), Nat. Sci. Tchrs. Assn., Nat. Geog. Soc., Mass. Assn. Scis. Tchrs. (award sect.), Gamma Theta Upsilon (local pres.). Democrat. Roman Catholic. Avocations: computers, telecommunications and Internet, reading journals and books, walking. Office: Arlington HS 869 Massachusetts Ave Arlington MA 02476-4701 E-mail: tomv@arlington.k12.ma.us.

VAUGHN, WILLIAM PRESTON, historian, educator; b. East Chicago, Ind., May 28, 1933; s. James Carl and Georgiana (Preston) V.; m. Virginia Lee Meyer, June 10, 1961; 1 child, Rhonda Louise Horton. AB, U. Mo., Columbia, 1955; MA, Ohio State U., 1956, PhD, 1961. Instr. in history U. So. Calif., 1961-62; asst. prof. history U. N. Tex., Denton, 1962-65, assoc. prof., 1965-69, prof., 1969-91. Instr. Tex. Project, Malaysia, 1986, 88. Author: Schools for All: The Blacks and Public Education in the South, 1865-77, 1974, The Antimasonic Party in the United States, 1826-43, 1983; editor Transactions Tex. Lodge of Rsch., 1988—; contbr. numerous articles on black edn. masonry and polit. antimasonry to profl. jours. With arty. U.S. Army, 1956-57 Mem. SAR, SCV, So. Hist. Assn. (life), Historians Early Am. Republic, Blue Friars, Masons, Phi Beta Kappa, Phi Alpha Theta (manuscript competition winner 1972), Phi Delta Kappa. Republican. Episcopalian. Home: 908 Hilton Pl Denton TX 76209-8606

VAUGHN, WILLIAM WEAVER, retired lawyer; b. Los Angeles, Aug. 29, 1930; s. William Weaver and Josephine (Sweigert) V.; m. Claire Louise M'Closkey, June 2, 1962; children: Robert, Gregory, Elizabeth, Anthony, Christina, James. BA, Stanford U., 1952; LLB, UCLA, 1955. Bar: Calif. 1956. With O'Melveny & Myers, L.A., 1955-56, 57—, ptnr., 1964-96, of counsel, 1996—2002; ret., 2002. Served with U.S. Army, 1956-57. Recipient Learned Hand award Am. Jewish Com., 1991, Joseph A. Ball award for outstanding advocacy Brennan Ctr. for Justice, 1998. Fellow Am. Coll. Trial Lawyers (bd. regents 1992-95); mem. L.A. County Bar Assn. (trustee 1976-78, 80-82), L.A. County Bar Found. (bd. dirs. 1991-95), Assn. Bus. Trial Lawyers (bd. govs. 1980-82), Order of Coif, Calif. Club, Chancery Club I(pres. 1997-98). Office: O'Melveny & Myers 400 S Hope St Los Angeles CA 90071-2899

VAUGHT, RICHARD LOREN, urologist; b. Ind., Oct. 28, 1933; s. Loren Judson and Bernice Rose (Bridges) V.; widowed, July 1987; children: Megan, Niles, Barbara, Mary; m. Nancy Lee Gusa, Aug. 1992. AB in Anatomy and Physiology, Ind. U., 1955; MD, Ind. U., Indpls., 1958. Diplomate Am. Bd. Urology. Intern, then resident in gen. surgery U.S. Naval Hosp., St. Albans, N.Y., 1958-60, resident in urology, 1960-63; spl. fellow Sloan Kettering Meml. Hosp. for Cancer and Allied Diseases, N.Y.C., 1962; pediatric urology observer Babies Hosp., Columbia-Presbyn. Med. Ctr., 1962; head urology U.S. Naval Hosp., Beaufort, S.C., 1963-65, asst. chief urology, head pediatric urology San Diego, 1965-68; pvt. practice Plaza Urol., Sioux City; med. dir. dept. hyperbaric medicine St. Luke's Regional Med. Ctr., 1988-95. Pres., chmn. bd. dirs. Care Choices of Siouxland, Sioux City, 1987-94; med. dir. Male Impotence Clinic, Marian Health Ctr., Sioux City, 1995-97, Diagnostic Ctr. for Men of S.C., 1997-99. Organizer telecommunications system for deaf, Siouxland, 1983. Lt. comdr. USN, 1958-68. Fellow ACS, Internat. Soc. Cryosurgery, Am. Acad. Pediat.; mem. Am. Urol. Assn., Soc. Pediatric Urology, European Soc. Pediatric Urology (corr.), Undersea and Hyperbaric Medicine Soc., Am. Coll. Hyperbaric Medicine, Am. Soc. Laser Medicine and Surgery, Am. Lithotripsy Soc., Woodbury County Med. Soc. (pres.), Am. Confedn. Urologia, Am. Acad. Male Sexual Health, Sertoma (Sertoman of Yr. award 1983). Home: 111 Bushberry Way Greer SC 29650-2976 E-mail: rvaught100@aol.com.

VAUSE, EDWIN HAMILTON, research foundation administrator; b. Chgo., Mar. 30, 1923; s. Harry Russell and Sylvia Clair (Webster) V.; m. Harriet Evelyn Oestmann, June 30, 1951; children— Karen L., Russell E., Kurt H., Dirk C., Luke E. BS, U. Ill., 1947, MS, 1948; MBA, U. Chgo., 1952; D.Sc. (hon.), U. Evansville, 1977. Registered profl. engr., Ill., Ind. Engr., research dept. Standard Oil Co., Ind., 1948-52, asst. gen. foreman mfg. dept., 1952-57; dir. research adminstrn. Mead Johnson & Co., Evansville, Ind., 1957-60; v.p. Charles F. Kettering Found., Dayton, Ohio, 1960-66, v.p., adminstrn. dir., 1966-67, exec. v.p., 1967-71, v.p. for sci. and tech., 1971-88. Trustee The Found. Center, 1967-73; mem. adv. com. Acad. Forum, Nat. Acad. Scis. Vice-pres. Washington Twp. Bd. Edn., 1963-67; mem. Centerville-Washington Twp. Joint Planning Commn., 1967-68; mem. adv. bd. Center for Students Rights, Dayton, 1966-70; active Boy Scouts Am. Mem. Am. Inst. Chem. Engrs. (past chmn. Chgo. sect.), N.Y. Acad. Scis., Agrl. Research Inst., Nat. Industry State Agrl. Research Council. Clubs: Elks, Kiwanis (past pres.), Masons. Republican. Lutheran. Home: 11834 Calle Parral San Diego CA 92128-4534

VAUX JR. HENRY JAMES, economics educator; b. Portland, Oreg., Feb. 2, 1940; s. Henry James and Jean (Macduff) V.; m. Prindle Anders, June 19, 1964; children: Robert, Katherine. BA, U. Calif., Davis, 1962; MA, U. Mich., 1964, MS, 1968, PhD, 1973. Examiner U.S. Office Mgmt. and Budget, Washington, 1964-67; economist U.S. Nat. Water Commn., Arlington, Va., 1969-70; prof. econs. U. Calif., Riverside, 1970—, dir. water resources, 1986-93, assoc. v.p., 1992—. Pres. Nat. Inst. Water Resources, Washington, 1986-93; pres. bd. dirs. Water Edn. Found., Sacramento, 1990—; mem., chair water sci. and tech. bd. Nat. Rsch. Coun., 1994-2001; co-chair adv. bd. Rosenber Internat. Forum, Oakland, 1996—. Recipient Nat. Leadership award Univ. Coun. Water Resource Rsch., 1994. Mem. Cosmos Club. Office: U Calif Office Pres 1111 Franklin St Oakland CA 94607

VAVAGIAKIS, COSTA, artist, art educator; b. N.Y.C., Feb. 10, 1958; s. John Vavagiakis and Anna Glenjakis; m. Dana D. Calitri, May 29, 1988 (div. Aug. 1998). Student, Art Students League, N.Y.C., 1977—80, Nat. Acad. Design Sch. Fine Arts, 1977—80. Art tchr. 92nd St Y, N.Y.C., 1994—, Nat. Acad. Design Sch. Fine Arts, N.Y.C., 1994—, N.Y. Acad. Art, N.Y.C., 1997—, The Art Students League, N.Y.C., 1998—. One-man shows include Hackett-Freedman Gallery, San Francisco, 1998, 2000, Queens Mus. Art, Flushing, N.Y., 1999. Fellow Gregory M. Millard fellow, N.Y. Found. for the Art, N.Y.C., 2001; grantee Art grant, Pollock-Krasner Found., N.Y.C., 2000. Mem.: Art Students League N.Y. Home: PO Box 1103 Long Island City NY 11101-0103

VAVALA, DOMENIC ANTHONY, medical scientist, educator, retired air force officer; b. Providence, Feb. 1, 1925; s. Salvatore and Maria (Grenci) V. Certificate basic engring., Yale U. Army Specialized Training Program, 1944; BA, Brown U., 1947; MS, U. R.I., 1950; MA, Trinity U., San Antonio, 1954; PhD in Physiology, Accademia di Studi Superiori "Minerva", Italy, 1957; MEd, U. Houston, 1958; DSc (hon.), Nobile Accademia di Santa Teodora Imperatrice, Rome, 1966, DMS (hon.), 1970; DPH (hon.), Nobile Accademia di Santa Teodora Imperatrice, 1983; D Pedagogy (hon.), Studiorum Universitas Constantiniana of Sovrano Ordine Constantiniano di San Giorgio, Rome, 1976; EdD (hon.), Imperiale Accademia di San Cirillo, Pomezia, Italy, 1977; LittD, Univ. Internazionale Sveva "Frederick II", Bergamo, Italy, 1979; D Health Scis. (hon.), Johnson & Wales U., 1993; LLD (hon.), Fridericus II U., Capua, Italy, 1997; MD (hon.), Frederick II U., Providence, Rhode Island, 1999. Research asst. tumor research U. R.I., also asst. entomol. research, 1950; research asst. pharmacology Boston U. Sch. Medicine, 1950-51; commd. 2d lt. med. service USAF, 1951, advanced through grades to lt. col., 1968; physiologist cold injury research team Army Med. Research Lab., Osaka (Japan) Army Hosp., 1951-52; research aviation physiologist USAF Sch. Aviation Medicine, Randolph AFB, Tex., 1952-54, 3605th USAF Hosp., Ellington AFB, 1955-57, chief physiol. tng., 1957; cons. aviation physiology, film prodn. dept. U. Houston, 1956; research aviation physiologist, head acad. sect. dept. physiol. tng. USAF Hosp., Lackland AFB, Tex., 1957-58; vis. prof. physiology Incarnate Word Coll., San Antonio, 1958; research aviation physiologist, chief physiol. tng. comdr. 832d Physiol. Tng. Flight, 832d Tactical Hosp., Cannon AFB, N.Mex., 1958-65; adj. faculty mem. Eastern N.Mex. U., Portales, 1959-64; instr. adult edn. divsn. Clovis (N.Mex.) mcpl. schs., 1960; research aviation physiologist, comdr. 15th Physiol. Tng. Flight, 824th USAF Dispensary, Kadena Air Base, Okinawa, 1965-66; research scientist, directorate fgn. tech., aerospace med. div. Brooks AFB, Tex., 1966-68; chief R & D support and interface div., dep. dir. for fgn. tech., 1968-70; adj. instr. Johnson & Wales U., Providence, 1973-74; instr. humanities Johnson and Wales U., 1974-75, asst. prof. humanities, 1975-77, prof. health scis. and nutrition, 1977-93, prof. emeritus, 1993—, coord. biomed. and behavioral scis. Day Coll. divsn., 1973-75, psychology coord. vets. div. Coll. Continuing Edn., 1974-76, assoc. dean adj. faculty, 1975, dean faculty, 1975-77, coord. acad. devel., 1977-78, dir. mus. series, 1990—, curator Chapel Empress St. Theodora, 1992—. Pres. corp., chmn. bd. dirs. Sovereign Constantinian Order of St. George, Inc., R.I., 1986—; pres. corp., chmn. bd. dirs. The Noble Acad. of Empress St. Theodora of R.I., Inc., 1988—; instr. anatomy, physiology and med. terminology R.I. Hosp., Providence, R.I., 1987-90. Writer, producer: (TV Series) Your Body in Flight, Sta. KUHT, Houston, 1956; (TV series) Highway to Health, Okinawa, 1965; editor-in-chief: NADUS Jour., 1963-85; compiled and edited: Fifty Years of Progress of Soviet Medicine, 1917-67; abstractor, translator in medicine Chem. Abstracts Svc., Am. Chem. Soc., Ohio State U., 1963-74; editor: (Cath. parish newspaper) The Logos, 1965-66 (1st pl. 5th Air Force chapel printed news contest); contbr. articles to profl. jours. Trustee, Gov. Ctr. Sch., Providence, 1979-85; mem. scholarship com. St. Sahag and, St. Mesrob Armenian Apostolic Ch., Providence; choir master, music dir. Cannon AFB, N.Mex. Cath. Parish, 1958-65. Served with AUS, 1943-44. Recipient Disting. Svc. award Clovis (N.Mex.) Jaycees, 1959, Acad. Palms Gold medal Acad. Studi Superiori "Minerva", 1960, citation, chief chaplains USAF, 1970, commendation medal USAF, 1970, chief biomed. scientist insignia, biomed. scis. corps USAF Med. Svc., 1970, spl. faculty citation Johnson and Wales U., 1981, contbn. awd. doctoral program ednl. leadership Alan Feinstein Grad. Sch., Johnson and Wales U., Providence, RI, 1999; academician divsn. scis. Accademia di Studi Superiori "Minerva", 1960; Min. Plenipotentiary for U.S. of Nobile Accademia di Santa Teodora Imperatrice, Rome, 1967, rector pro tempore, 1980; decorated knight grand officer Merit Class, Sovereign Constantinian Order St. George, Rome, 1969, Knight of Grand Cross with Constantinian neckchain, Justice Class, Sovereign Constantinian Order St. George, 1969, Knight of Grand Cross Justice Class, Order St. John of Jerusalem, Knights of Malta, Bari, Italy, 1984, Knight of Grand Cross Justice Class, Order St. John of Jerusalem, Knights of Cyprus, Rhodes and Malta, Bari, 1984, Knight of Grand Cordon Justice Class, Order Teutonic Knights, Sao Paulo, 1986, Knight of Grand Cross Justice Class, Mil. Order St. Gereon, Sao Paulo, 1986, Knight of Grand Cross Justice Class, Mil. and Hospitalier Order St Jean d'Acre and St. Thomas, Capua, Italy, 1987, Knight of Grand Cross Justice Class, Mil. and Hospitalier Order St. Mary of Bethlehem, Capua, 1987; recipient Ednl. Professionalism award Domei Toastmasters Internat., 1965; named Magnificent Rector and Pres., The Constantinian U. (Studiorum Universitas Constantiniana), Italy, 1970, Marquis of Royal Throne of Swabia of Hohenstaufen Dynasty, Prince Jean von Schwaben, Bergamo, Italy, 1984, Duke of the New Rome of Imperial Dynasty of Amorium by His Imperial Highness Prince Don Francesco Amoroso d'Aragona, Capua, 2000. Fellow AAAS (emeritus), Tex. Acad. Sci., Royal Soc. Health (London; emeritus), Am. Inst. Chemists (emeritus); mem. Assn. Mil. Surgeons U.S. (life), Nat. Assn. Doctors U.S. (founder 1958, sec.-treas. 1958-85, editor-in-chief The NADUS Jour. 1963-68), Accademia di San Cirillo Italy (hon.), N.Y. Acad. Scis., Phi Sigma, Kappa Delta Pi, Phi Kappa Phi, Alpha Beta Kappa (charter mem., pres. R.I. Alpha chpt. Johnson & Wales U. 1984-92). Home: 30 Oaklawn Ave Apt 219 Cranston RI 02920-9319

VAVERE, ATIS, business and technology manager; b. Mora, Mn, Apr. 4, 1951; s. Margers and Vilma Vavere; children: Amy, Eric. BS CHEMISTRY (SUMMA CUM LAUDE), Univ. Of Wisconsin @ Eau Claire, Eau Claire, Wi, 1969—73; Ph. D. PHYSICAL CHEMISTRY, Iowa State University, Ames, Ia, 1973—78. Sr. research chemist MONSANTO COMPANY, St. Louis, 1978—80, research specialist, 1980—83; sr. research group leader MONSANTO ENVIRO-CHEM SYSTEMS, INC., 1983—90, technology manager Afghanistan, 1990—96; business and technology manager MONSANTO ENVIRO-CHEM SYSTEMS, INC, 1996—2002. Peer article reviewer JOURNAL OF CATALYSIS, 1980—81. Author: (scientific articles) JOURNAL OF CATALYSIS, 1981, (scientific article) , 1984, CHEMTECH, 1986, (historical/scientific article) SULFUR, 2000, (scientific research) PATENT, 1985, PATENTI, 1991. Mem.: NORTH AMERICAN CATALYSIS SOCIETY, AMERICAN CHEMICAL SOCIETY. Mem. Christian Ch. (Disciples Of Christ). Avocation: golf; travel; astronomy. Home: 1550 Rishon Hill Drive Saint Louis MO 6314663146-4928 Afghanistan Office: Monsanto Enviro-Chem Systems, Inc. P. O. Box 14547 Saint Louis MO 63178-4547 Office Fax: 314-275-5967. Personal E-mail: atisvavere@hotmail.com. Business E-Mail: atis.vavere@monsanto.com.

VAVROSKY, MARK JAMES, career officer, educator; b. Vancouver, Wash., July 4, 1962; s. Donald James and Edna Mae (Englehardt) V.; m. Connie Jean White Itatani, Nov. 27, 1981 (div. Jan. 1987); 1 child, Shannon Jean; m. Gail Cooper, July 7, 1990;children: Paige Marie, Cameron James. BA in Bus. Mgmt., Seattle U., 1984; MA in Edn., Chapman U., Concord, Calif., 1994. Asst. mgr. Household Fin. Corp., Oakland, Calif., 1985-86; commd. 2d lt. U.S. Army, 1985, advanced through grades to maj., 1989; pers. officer 185th Mill. Police Bn., Pittsburg, Calif., 1989-91; comdr. HHD 340th Forward Support Bn., San Lorenzo, 1991-95; asst. prof. mil. sci. Claremont (Calif.) McKenna Coll., 1995-97; personell officer 40th Infantry Divsn. Support Commd. (DISCOM), 1997-2000, Battalion OIC, 640th Divsn. Aviation Support Battalion, 2000—. V.p. Shadowood Homeowners Assn., Pleasant Hill, Calif., 1991-92. Decorated Meritorious Svc. medal, Army Commendation medal (6). Mem. Nat. Guard Assn. Calif. (treas. Diablo chpt. 1990-91, Sunburst chap. 1998-2002). Roman Catholic. Avocations: running marathons, cycling. Office: 640th DASB 854 E 7th St Long Beach CA 90813 E-mail: mark.vavrosky@ca.ngb.army.mil.

VAYANIAN, SOLARA ZAKELI, artist, educator; b. Chgo., June 14, 1947; d. Ralph William Forst, Marion Elizabeth Engel; children: Michael Paul Catlett, Noel Thomas Catlett. BA in Phys. Edn. and Dance, San Diego State U., 1975. Founder, dir. Winged Fire Prodns., Sedona, Ariz., 1978—; founder, facilitator Kinesio-Emotional Release System, 1978—; founder, pres. Compassionate Care Coalition, 2001—. Author: (novels) Time Dancer, 1972, The Stars Gave Passion, 1977, Octangle Blue, 1989, Time Out of Mind, 2000; author: (or co-author) (stage prodn.) Journey thru the Mask, The Doorway of the Heart. Founder, dir.Touch of Joy program Kachina Point Rehab. and Healthcare Ctr., Sedona. Recipient Barbara Marx Hubbard Women of Vision award for innovative social action, 1996. Achievements include development of of workable systems for healing, wholeness and human potential development through the arts, education, interactive community programs, performances and events. Avocations: reading, running, designing and sewing clothes, costumes. Office: Compassionate Care Coalition PO Box 622 Sedona AZ 86339

VAYDA, ANDREW P. human ecology and anthropology educator; b. Budapest, Hungary, Dec. 7, 1931; came to U.S., 1939; s. Sándor Vajda and Zelma Szentgyörgyi; m. Indah Setyawati, July 10, 1991 (div. July 1997). BA, Columbia U., 1952, PhD, 1956. From asst. prof. to assoc. prof. Columbia U., N.Y.C., 1960-68, prof., 1968-72, Rutgers U., New Brunswick, N.J., 1972—. Cons. World Wide Fund for Nature, Jakarta, Indonesia, 1992, 93, 98, Ford Found., Jakarta, 1981-84; disting. vis. scholar Ctr. for Internat. Forestry Rsch., Bogor, Indonesia, 1996. Author: (book) War in Ecological Perspective, 1976, (booklets) Bugis Settlers in East Kalimantan, 1996, Finding Causes of the 1997-98 Indonesian Forest Fires, 1998; editor-in-chief: (periodical) Human Ecology, 1971-77. Recipient Disting. Vis. Scholar award Ctr. for Internat. Forestry Rsch., 1996, Fulbright Lectr./Rsch. award USIA, 1989-90; vis. scholar grantee Ford Found., 1998; rsch. grantee NOAA, 2000—. Fellow AAAS, Am. Anthropol. Assn., Borneo Rsch. Coun., Inst. Human Ecology. Avocations: food, traveling, playing squash. Office: Rutgers U Dept Human Ecology New Brunswick NJ 08901 E-mail: vayda@aesop.rutgers.edu.

VAYDA, ROSE K. community volunteer; b. N.Y.C., Apr. 17, 1912; d. Max and Clara Kerner; widowed; children: Clara Kerner, Max Kerner, Rose, Sam, Sol, Ruth, Seymour, Harry, Kerner. Student, Washington Irving H.S., N.Y.C. Drama coach Clark Settlement House, N.Y.C., 1929; costumes person, extra Yiddish Art Theatre, 1930. Appeared in various films, TV commls., plays. Vol. Friendly Visitors, Miami, Fla., 1960, Hialeah (Fla.) Hosp., 1964-82, Lighthouse for Blind, Miami, 1985; vol. reader for the blind Broward C.C., Hollywood, Fla., 1993; active cancer support group Hollywood Med. Hosp. Recipient Cert. of Appreciation Mayor of Miami, 1985. Mem. Famous Poets Soc. (award 1996). Avocations: repertory theater, poetry group, piano. Home: 251 SW 132nd Way Apt H415 Pembroke Pines FL 33027-1673

VAYO, DAVID JOSEPH, composer, music educator; b. New Haven, Mar. 28, 1957; s. Harold Edward and Joan Virginia (Cassidy) V.; m. Marie-Susanne Langille, 2002; children: Rebecca Lynn, Gordon Francis. MusB, Ind. U., 1980, MusM, 1982; D of Musical Arts, U. Mich., 1990. Prof. Nat. U., Heredia, Costa Rica, 1982-84, Nat. Symphony Youth Sch., San Jose, Costa Rica, 1982-84; asst. prof. music Conn. Coll., New London, 1988-91, Ill. Wesleyan U. Sch. Music, Bloomington, 1991-95, assoc. prof., 1995-2000, prof., 2000—. Resident artist Banff Ctr. for Arts, 1992, 94, Va. Ctr. for Creative Arts, 1994, Centrum, Port Townsend, Wash., 1996; participating composer Internat. Soc. Contemporary Music-World Music Days, Yokohama, 2001, Mexico City, 1993, Internat. Double Reed Festival, Rotterdam, The Netherlands, 1995, Internat. Trombone Festival, 1997. Composer chamber composition Signals, 1997 (commd. by Koussevitzky Music Found. and Orkest de Volharding), Symphony: Blossoms and Awakenings, 1990 (performer St. Louis Symphony, Leonard Slatkin condr. 1993), Septet, 1998 (commd. by Southeastern Composers League), Eight Poems of William Carlos Williams for solo trombonist, 1994 (commd. by St. Louis Symphony), piano trio Awakening of the Heart (commd. Barlow Endowment for Music Composition), 1998; works pub. by MMB Music, Internat. Trombone Assn. Press and A.M. Percussion Publs. John Simon Guggenheim Meml. Found. fellow, 2001; Ill. Arts Coun. fellow, 2000. Mem. ASCAP (awards 1988—), Am. Music Ctr. (copying assistance grantee 1992), Coll. Music Soc. (presenter nat. conf. 1990, 94, 96), Soc. for Electro-Acoustic Music in U.S. (presenter nat. conf. 1989), Soc. Composers (membership chmn. 1990-2000, presenter nat. conf. 1990, 92, 95, 97, 98), Am. Composers Forum. Avocations: athletics, popular music, travel, reading, cooking. Office: Ill Wesleyan U Sch Music PO Box 2900 Bloomington IL 61702-2900 E-mail: dvayo@titan.iwu.edu.

VAZ, KATHERINE ANNE, language educator, writer; b. Castro Valley, Calif., Aug. 26, 1955; d. August Mark and Elizabeth (Sullivan) Vaz; m. Michael Trudeau, May 1, 1994. BA, U. Calif., Santa Barbara, 1977; MFA, U. Calif., Irvine, 1991. Assoc. prof. English U. Calif., Davis, 1995-99. Keynote spkr. Libr. of Congress, 1997; keynote spkr. lit. confs. U. Ariz., Ariz., U. Calif., Berkeley, U. Mass., Dartmouth U., Rutgers U.; mem. U.S. Presdl. del. to Expo 98/World's Fair, Lisbon, Portugal. Author: (novels) Saudade, 1994, Mariana, 1997, (short stories) Fado & Other Stories, 1997 (Drue Heinz Lit. prize, 1997). Grantee, Nat. Endowment Arts, 1993, Davis Humanities Inst., U. Calif., Davis, 1998—99. Mem.: PEN, Portuguese-Am. Leadership Coun. U.S., Authors Guild. Democrat. Roman Catholic.

VAZAKAS, MAURA FRAN, artist, music teacher; b. Bronx, N.Y., Mar. 24, 1950; d. Samuel Louis and Nita Saltzman; m. Stephen George Chatman, Aug. 19, 1972 (div. Jan. 1984); children: Rachel, Jessica; m. Thomas Lawrence Vazakas, June 21, 1984; children: Saul, Ben. BMus, Oberlin Coll., 1972; MMus, U. Mich., 1974. Piano tchr., 1972—; poetry editor The Pub., San Diego, 1997—. Artist Escondido Arts Partnership, Escondido, Calif., 1997-98, San Diego Art Inst., 1995-99; pianist U. Mich., New Music Ensemble, Ann Arbor, 1972-74; singer Vancouver Cantata Singers, B.C., Can., 1976-87. Author: (poetry) A Surrealist in Trouble, 1998, When Travel was Affordable, 1999, Salvador's Phone Book, 1999; representation, , , Represented in permanent collections Red Herring, San Francisco, Vivendi Universal, Paris, Sonten Enterprises, San Diego, g2 Galllery, Scottsdale, Ariz., So. Hych Gallery, N.Y.C., Galleria Dos , Palm Springs, Calif., Jan Baum Gallery, L.A., book, various newspapers, mags. and jours. Recipient hon. scholarship Julliard Sch. Music, 1966-68, Juror's Arts award San Diego Art Inst., 1996-99, NAPA award Clairemont Art Guild, 1996. Mem. Univ. City Women's Club (pres. 1991-92). Jewish. Avocations: piano performances, art museum outings, writing poetry. Home: 2924 Honors Ct San Diego CA 92122-2000 E-mail: mauravazakas@hotmail.com.

VAZIRANI-FALES, HEEA, legislative staff member, lawyer; b. Calcutta, India, Apr. 1, 1938; d. Sunder J. Vazirani; m. John Fales Jr., 1978; children: Deepika, Reetika, Ashish, Monika, Jyotika, Denise. AB, Guilford Coll., 1959; JD, Howard U., 1979. Staff/legis. dir. Montgomery County Del, Gen. Assembly of Md., 1981-87; legis. counsel to Congresswoman Constance A. Morella, U.S. Ho. of Reps., Washington, 1987-94, counsel subcom. on postal svc. com. govt. reform, 1995—2000, dep. staff dir. and counsel subcom. on D.C. govt. reform, 2000—01, counsel nd deputy dir. subcom. on D.C., 2001—. Mem. staff Vols. for Visually Handicapped, 1973-79, bd. dirs., 1979-81; bd. dirs. Manipal Edn. and Med. Found., 1970-92. Mem. Phi Delta Phi. Office: Subcom on DC B-349C Rayburn Bldg Washington DC 20515

VAZIRI, NOSRATOLA DABIR, internist, nephrologist, educator; b. Tehran, Iran, Oct. 13, 1939; came to U.S., 1969, naturalized, 1977; s. Abbas and Tahera Vaziri. MD, Tehran U., 1966. Diplomate Am. Bd. Internal Medicine, Am. Bd. Nephrology; cert. hypertension specialist Am. Soc. Hypertension. Intern Cook County Hosp., Chgo., 1969-70; resident Berkshire Med. Ctr., Pittsfield, Mass., 1970-71, Wadsworth VA Med. Ctr., L.A., 1971-72, UCLA Med. Ctr., 1972-74; prof. medicine U. Calif.-Irvine, 1979—, prof. physiology and biophysics, 2001—, chief nephrology and hypertension divsn., 1977—, dir. hemodialysis unit, 1977-94, vice chmn. dept. medicine, 1982-94, chmn. dept. medicine, 1994-98, chair faculty Coll. Medicine, 1998—2002. Sr. assoc. editor Jour. Spinal Cord Medicine; mem. editl. bd. Kidney Internat., Am. Jour. Nephrology, Nephron, Advances in Renal Replacement Therapies, Internat. Jour. Artificial Organs, Spinal Cord Medicine; contbr. numerous articles to med. jours. Mem. sci. adv. coun. Nat. Kidney Found., 1977—. Recipient Golden Apple award, 1977; named Outstanding Tchr. U. Calif., Irvine, 1975, 78, 79, 80, 82, Lauds and Laurels award for faculty achievement, 1999, Spirit of Nephrology award Nat. Kidney Found., 2002. Master: ACP; fellow: Am. Heart Assn. (fellow coun. high blood pressure rsch.); mem.: Assn. Profs. Medicine, Western Assn. Physicians, Am. Paraplegia Soc. (pres. 1992—94, Donald Munro award 2002), Am. Physiol. Soc., Am. Soc. Nephrology, Alpha Omega Alpha. Home: 66 Balboa Cv Newport Beach CA 92663-3226 Office: U Calif Irvine Med Ctr Div Nephrology Dept Medicine 101 The City Dr Orange CA 92868-3201 E-mail: ndvaziri@uci.edu.

VAZQUEZ, CARLOS MANUEL, law educator; b. Havana, Cuba, Jan. 22, 1958; came to U.S., 1962; s. Carlos Jesus and Lourdes Raida (Molina) V.; m. Mary Katherine Qualiana, Aug. 3, 1993; children: Elena Maria, Elias Mateo. BA, Yale U., 1979; JD, Columbia U., 1983. Bar: D.C. 1985, U.S. Ct. Appeals (D.C., 6th and 9th cirs.) 1985, U.S. Supreme Ct. 1989. Law clk. Legal Advisor's Office U.S. Dept. of State, Washington, 1983; law clk. to Judge Stephen Reinhardt U.S. Ct. Appeals (9th cir.) Calif., L.A., 1983-84; assoc. Covington & Burling, Washington, 1985-90; vis. assoc. prof. law Georgetown U. Law Ctr., 1990-91, assoc. prof. law, 1991-96, prof. law, 1996—. Contbr. articles to profl. jours. Mem. Inter-Am. Jud. com. Orgn. of Am. States, 2000—. Recipient Pro Bono Svc. award Internat. Human Rights Law Group, Washington, 1986. Mem. ABA, Am. Soc. Internat. Law, Hispanic Nat. Bar Assn., D.C. Bar (co-chair pub. internat. law com. 1995-2000). Roman Catholic. Avocations: travel, music, literature. Office: Georgetown Univ Law Ctr 600 New Jersey Ave NW Washington DC 20001-2022 E-mail: vazquez@law.georgetown.edu.

VÁZQUEZ, LOURDES, librarian, writer; b. P.R., P.R., May 26, 1949; d. William and Carmen Vázquez. BA, U. P.R., 1971, MLS, 1981; MA in Latin Am. and Caribbean Studies, NYU, 1985. Rsch. libr. N.Y. Pub. Libr., N.Y.C., 1981-83; dir. libr. svcs. McConnell Valdes Law Offices, 1987-94, Internat. Women's Tribune Ctr., 1994-97; Hostos C.C., Bklyn., 1997—; Africa, L.Am. and anthropology libr. Rutgers U., 1998—. Chmn. P.R. Adv. Com. on Librs.,

1992-94; co-coord. 1st and 2d Latin-Am. Book Fairs, 1985-87. Author: La rosa mecánica, 1991, Marina Arzola Biography, 1991, El amor Urgente, 1995, The Broken Heart, 1996, Historias de Pulgarcito, 1999; editor La Candelaria Series, 1995—; contbr. articles, essays to profl. jours. Mem. SALALM, Pen Club of P.R. (bd. dirs. 1991-94), Pen Am. Ctr., Poetry Project. Avocations: reading, museums, travel, movies. E-mail: lvazquez@rci.rutgers.edu.

VAZQUEZ, RICHARD MICHAEL, surgeon; b. Chgo., Dec. 24, 1944; MD, U. Ill., 1969. Diplomate Am. Bd. Surgery. Intern Presbyn.-St. Luke's Hosp., Chgo., 1969-70, resident, 1970-74; attending surgeon Northwestern Meml. Hosp.; asst. clin. prof. surgery Northwestern U. Med. Sch., 1981—. Cons. Ill. State Police, 1988-2002. Mem. ACS, Soc. Am. Gastrointestinal Endoscopic Surgery, Am. Coll. Phlebology (mem. website veincare com.) Office: 201 E Huron St Ste 11-250 Chicago IL 60611-2968 E-mail: drv@veincare.com., drv@gensurg.com.

VAZQUEZ, SUE ELLEN, elementary education educator; b. Rome, Aug. 2, 1951; d. Louis Frank and Eileen Louella (Hayes) Mercurio; children: Katie, Kristin; m. Kermith Vazquez, Feb. 17, 1995. AA, Mater Dei Coll., 1971; BA in Elem. Edn. and Sociology, SUNY, Potsdam, 1973, MS in Edn. and Learning Disabilities, 1987. Cert. in elem. education (nursery through grade 6), N.Y. Elem. tchr. Twin Rivers Elem. Sch., Massena, N.Y., 1973-88, Nightengale Elem. Sch., Massena, 1988—. Curriculum writer, rschr. Massena Ctrl. Schs., 1980—, AIDS adv. coun., 1987-91, student assistance program, 1994—, sci. curriculum, media coord., 1986. Co-author: (curriculum) Life Education for Children, 1980, Sexual Abuse Awareness for Educators, 1985, AIDS Awareness for Children, 1987; co-editor Immaculatan, 1970-71. Mem. NEA, Massena Tchrs. Fedn. (bldg. rep. 1978-80), Am. Fedn. Tchrs., Sci. Tchrs. Assn. of N.Y. State, North Country Colls. Internat. Reading Assn., Coll. Club of Massena, Massena Home Bur. (sec. 1975-77). Roman Catholic. Avocations: travel, music, lit., racquet sports, photography. Home: 11 Sharon Dr Massena NY 13662-1601 Office: Massena Ctrl Schs 84 Nightengale Ave Massena NY 13662-2538

VAZSONYI, ALEXANDER THOMAS, education educator; b. Traverse City, Mich., Oct. 16, 1964; AA, Northwestern Mich. Coll., 1987; BS, Grand Valley State U., 1989; MS, U. Ariz., 1993, PhD, 1995. Program coord. The U. of Ariz., Tucson, 1994—95; asst. rsch. scientist U. Ariz., 1995—96; asst. prof. Auburn U., Ala., 1996—2000, assoc. prof., 2000—. Cons. U. Ala., Tuscaloosa, 2001—, Kent State U., Ohio, 1999—2000. Contbr. articles. Faculty advisor Grad. Student Orgn., Auburn U., 2001—02. Nominee Disting. Alumna/Alumnus award, Grand Valley State U., 2000. Mem.: Soc. for Rsch. on Adolescence, Am. Soc. Criminology, Ctr. for the Advancement of Youth Health. Avocation: photography, music, travel. Office: Auburn Univ Dept Human Devel and Family Studies 284 Spidle Hall Auburn AL 36849

VAZSONYI, BALINT, concert pianist, television producer, political philosopher, columnist; b. Budapest, Hungary, Mar. 7, 1936; came to U.S., 1959; s. Miklos and Hedvig (Felsner) V.; m. Barbara Whittington, Feb. 26, 1960; 1 child, Nicholas. Artist Diploma, Franz Liszt Acad., Budapest, 1956; MMus, Fla. State U., 1960; PhD, U. Budapest, 1982. Concert and recording career, worldwide, 1948—; prof. music Ind. U., Bloomington, 1978-84; pres. Telemusic, Inc., 1983-98; sr. fellow The Potomac Found., McLean, Va., 1993—; dean of music New World Sch. of the Arts, 1993-95; dir. Ctr. of the Am. Founding, 1996—. Tchr. master classes in piano Yale, Harvard, New Eng. Conservatory, Dartmouth Coll. Author: Erno Dohnanyi, 1971, The Battle for America's Soul, 1995, America's 30 Years War: Who Is Winning?, 1998; author, producer, presenter TV biographies Beethoven, 1983, Mozart, Schubert, 1986, Brahms, 1987; first chronological cycle of Beethoven Sonatas, N.Y., 1976. Hon. Cultural Counselor of the Republic of Hungary, 1993-95; decorated Officers' Cross Order of the Republic of Hungary, 1999; recipient Americanism award DAR, 2000, Hon. Citizen of Indpls., 2000, Key to City of Charleston, W.Va., 2000. Office: The Potomac Found Ste 2A 1311 Dolley Madison Blvd Mc Lean VA 22101-3925 E-mail: bv@founding.org.

VAZZANA, JAMES ANTHONY, lawyer; b. Rochester, N.Y., Dec. 15, 1964; s. Joseph Anthony and Joan (Terrana) V.; m. Dina Gugino, June 29, 1991. BA, U. Rochester, 1987; JD, U. Dayton, 1990. Bar: N.Y. 1991, U.S. Dist. Ct. (we. dist.) N.Y. 1993. Assoc. Pauley and Barney, P.C., Rochester, N.Y., 1990-95, Law Office Brian J. Barney, Rochester, 1995, Woods, Oviatt, Gilman, Sturman & Clarke LLP, Rochester, 1995-2000; ptnr. Chamberlain, D'Amanda, Oppenheimer & Greenfield, 2000—. Fin. chmn. Com. to Return Supreme Ct. Justice Kenneth Fisher, Rochester, 1995, Com. to Re-elect Family Ct. Judge Anthony J. Sciolino, Rochester, 1996; chmn. Western N.Y. Citizens Rev. Panel for Child Protective Svcs. Mem. N.Y. State Bar Assn. (family law sect. 1991—, exec. com. 2000—), Monroe County Bar Assn. (fee arbitration com. 1994-97, juvenile law com. 1995-98, sec. family law sect. 1997, v.p. 1998, exec. coun. 1997), Italian Am. Businessmans Assn. (v.p. 1995-97, pres. 1998-2000), Theta Delta Chi Alumni Assn. Avocations: family, travel, golf, cooking, gardening. Office: Chamberlain D'Amanda Oppenheimer & Greenfield 1600 State St Rochester NY 14614 E-mail: jav@cdog.com.

VEACH, DANIEL LEE, editor; b. Erlanger, Ky., Oct. 17, 1948; s. Elbert Leslie and Anna Lee Veach; m. Susan Lynnette Shirley, Apr. 11, 1998. BA, Harvard U., 1972; MAT, Simmons Coll., 1975; MSLS, Clark Atlanta U., 1991. Exec. dir. Poetry Atlanta, Inc., 1985—; libr. Atlanta Univ. Ctr., 1992—; editor, pub. Atlanta Review, 1994—. Solo poetry recital Poetry Soc., London, 1998, Oxford (Eng.) U., 1998. Author: My Long Thigh Bone, 1984; author of poetry. Co-chair Harvard-Radcliffe SDS, Cambridge, Mass., 1970. Recipient Publ. in prize volume Sotheby's Internat. Poetry Competition, London, 1982. Mem. ALA, Ga. Libr. Assn. (bd. mem. 1996-97). Democrat. Avocations: playing clarinet and piano, composing. Office: Atlanta Review 2278 Vistamont Dr Decatur GA 30033-4704 E-mail: dan@atlantareview.com.

VEACH, ROBERT RAYMOND, JR. lawyer; b. Charleston, S.C., Nov. 28, 1950; s. Robert Raymond and Evelyn Ardell (Vegter) V.; m. Lori Sue Erickson, May 27, 1989. Student, St. Olaf Coll., 1968-70; BS in Acctg., Ariz. State U., 1972; JD, So. Meth. U., 1975. Bar: Tex. 1975, Nebr. 1975, U.S. Dist. Ct. Nebr. 1975, U.S. Dist. Ct. (no. dist.) Tex. 1975, Temporary Emergency Ct. Appeals 1975. Acctg. instr. Sch. Bus. So. Meth. U., Dallas, 1973-74; law clk. to Hon. Joe E. Estes U.S. Dist. Ct. No. Dist. Tex.-Temp. Emergency Ct. Appeals, 1975-76; assoc. Locke Purnell Boren Laney & Neely, 1976-80; v.p. The Lomas & Nettleton Co., 1980-83, Rauscher Pierce Refsnes, Inc., Dallas, 1983-87; pres. RPR Mortgage Fin. Corp., 1985-87; sr. shareholder Locke Purnell Rain Harrell, 1987-97; exec. v.p. Precision Imaging Solutions, Inc., 1998—; pvt. practice, 1998—. Allied mem. N.Y. Stock Exch., 1985-87; lectr. securities and banking confs.; bd. dirs. pvt. corps.; trustee Correctional Properties Trust (NYSE-CPV), chmn. audit and finance com., 1998—. Author legal articles. Dir. North Tex. affiliate Am. Diabetes Assn., Dallas, 1978-81; mem. Gov.'s Task Force Wash. State Housing Commn., 1982-83. Mem. ABA, State Bar of Tex., Nebr. State Bar Assn., Fed. Bar Assn., Dallas Bar Assn. Republican. Methodist. Avocations: golf, antique Am. firearms. Home: 4223 Brookview Dr Dallas TX 75220-3801 Office: 2911 Turtle Creek Blvd Ste 1240 Dallas TX 75219-6277

VEACO, KRISTINA, lawyer; b. Sacramento, Mar. 4, 1948; d. Robert Glenn and Lelia (McCain) V.; 1 child, Nina Katherine. BA, U. Calif., Davis, 1978; JD, Hastings Coll. Law, 1981. Legal adv. to commr. William T. Bagley Calif. Pub. Utilities Commn., San Francisco, 1981-86; sr. counsel Pacific Telesis Group, 1986-94; sr. counsel corp. and securities and pol. law AirTouch Comms., 1994-98; asst. gen. counsel, asst. sec. McKesson Corp., 1999—. Mem.: ABA, Am. Soc. Corp. Secs. (pres. San Francisco chpt. 2001—02, mem. adv. com., bd. dirs.), San Francisco Bar Assn., Phi Beta Kappa. Democrat. Episcopalian. Avocations: cooking, reading. Office: McKesson Corp 1 Post St Fl 29 San Francisco CA 94104-5233 E-mail: Kristina.veaco@mckesson.com.

VEAL, REX R. lawyer; b. Lafayette, Ga., May 2, 1956; s. Boyd Herman and Barbara Ann (Sharp) V.; m. Vicky Elizabeth Wilkins, Dec. 13, 1980; children: Matthew Aaron and Richard Andrew (twins). BA, U. Tenn., 1978, JD, 1980. Bar: Tenn. 1981, U.S. Dist. Ct. (ea. dist.) Tenn. 1981, U.S. Ct. Appeals (10th cir.) 1981, U.S. Ct. Appeals (6th cir.) 1984, U.S. Ct. Appeals (4th cir.) 1987, Ga. 1991, U.S. Dist. Ct. (no. dist.) Ga. 1991, U.S. Ct. Appeals (11th cir.) 1991, D.C. 1993, U.S. Dist. Ct. D.C. 1993, U.S. Ct. Appeals (D.C. and fed. cir.) 1993. Assoc. Finkelstein, Kern, Steinberg & Cunningham, Knoxville, Tenn., 1980-83; atty. FDIC, 1983-84, sr. atty., 1984-88, counsel liquidation Washington, 1988-89, assoc. gen. counsel, 1989-90; spl. counsel Resolution Trust Corp., 1989-90; ptnr. Powell, Goldstein, Frazer & Murphy, Atlanta and Washington, 1990-99, Kilpatrick Stockton LLP, Atlanta, 1999—. Lectr. in field. Contbr. articles to profl. jours. Mem. ABA, Tenn. Bar Assn., Ga. Bar Assn., Atlanta Bar Assn. Avocations: hiking, golf, collecting books. Home: 6201 Blackberry Hl Norcross GA 30092-1375 Office: Kilpatrick Stockton 1100 Peachtree St NE Ste 2800 Atlanta GA 30309-4501 E-mail: rveal@kilpatrickstockton.com.

VEALE, JOHN EDMOND (JACK VEALE), business executive; b. Winchester, Mass., July 12, 1954; s. Edmond John and Margaret Louise Veale; m. Laurie Jean Howard, Apr. 29, 1978; children: Alex, Jason. BSBA, Norwich U., 1976; MBA, Boise State U., 1987. With S.W. Hide Co., Boise, Idaho, 1976-88, acct., 1977-78, office mgr. corp. office, 1978-79, corp. contr., 1979-81, CFO, 1981-87; divsn. pres. N.W. Mgmt. Assocs., Gt. West Data Sys., 1981-84, CFO, 1984-88; v.p. Spicer Gas Co., Groton, Conn., 1988-90; mgr. Coastal Oil Corp., Revere, Mass., Hasbrouk Heights, N.J., 1990-92; pres. PTCFO, Inc., Conn., 1992—. Mem. bd. advisors Jackson Lumber and Millwork. Mem. Nat. Assn. Corp. Dirs. (chpt. pres.), Am. Soc. for Quality, Turnaround Mgmt. Assn. (bd. dirs.), Rotary Club Internat., Family Firm Inst., Nat. Ski Patrol, Norwich U. Alumni Assn. (bd. dirs.), Alpha Kappa Psi. Republican. Home: 48 Walkley Rd West Hartford CT 06119-1345 Office: PTCFO Inc 48 Walkley Rd Hartford CT 06119-1345

VEALE, TINKHAM, II, former chemical company executive, engineer; b. Topeka, Dec. 26, 1914; s. George W. and Grace Elizabeth (Walworth) V.; m. Harriett Alice Ernst, Sept. 6, 1941; children: Harriett Elizabeth Veale Leedy, Tinkham III, Helen Ernst Veale Gelbach. BS in Mech. Engring., Case Inst. Tech., 1937; LLD, Kenyon Coll., 1981. Registered profl. engr. With Gen. Motors Corp., 1937-38, Avery Engring. Co., 1939, Reliance Electric Co., 1940-41; asst. to pres. Ohio Crankshaft Co., 1942-46; gen. mgr. Tocco Co., 1947-51; pres. Ric Wil Corp., 1952-53, Alco Chem. Corp., 1954-56, dir., 1954-86. Spl. ptnr. Ball Burge & Kraus, investment bankers, 1957-60; chmn. bd. V. and V. Cos., Inc. and subs., Cleve., 1960-65, Alco Standard Corp. and subs., Valley Forge, Pa., 1965-86, Horsehead Industries, Inc. and subs., N.Y.C., 1981—2001, HTV Industries Inc. and subs., Cleve., 1978—; ptnr. Fair Elm Farm, 1948-2000, Kennedy Veale Stable, 1954-2000. Trustee Veale Charitable Found., 1966—. Recipient Silver Bowl award Case Inst. Tech., 1980; recipient Gold Medal Case Inst. Tech., 1982 Mem. Cleve. Engring. Soc., Nat. Soc. Registered Profl. Engrs., Newcomen Soc., Phi Kappa Psi. Home: PO Box 39 Gates Mills OH 44040-0039 Office: HTV Industries Inc PO Box 295 Gates Mills OH 44040-0295

VEANER, ALLEN BARNET, information science educator; b. Harrisburg, Pa., Mar. 17, 1929; s. Israel Ivan and Molly Samson Veaner; m. Rosalind Wilder Halevi, Mar. 29, 1953 (div. June 1971); children: Julie, Bonnie; m. Susan Paula Klement, Oct. 30, 1983. BA, Gettysburg Coll., 1949; MLS, Simmons Coll., 1960; MA, Hebrew Union Coll., Cin., 1969. Cataloguer Harvard U. Libr., Cambridge, Mass., 1957-59, head of photoduplication svc., 1959-64; head of acquisitions Stanford U. Librs., Palo Alto, Calif., 1964-67, asst. dir. of univ. librs., 1967-77; univ. libr. U. Calif., Santa Barbara, 1977-83; prin. Allen B. Veaner Assocs., Toronto, Ont., 1983-91; adj. prof. U. Ariz., Tucson, 1993—. Author: The Evaluation of Micropublications, 1971, Academic Librarianship in a Transformational Age, 1990; editor; Studies in Micropublishing, 1976; co-editor: Collaborative Library Systems Development, 1971; editor-in-chief Microform Rev., 1972-85. Sec. Summerset Homeowners Assn., Tucson, 1993—. 1st lt. U.S. Army, 1954-56. Mem. Am. Libr. Assn., Phi Beta Kappa. Avocations: airships and zeppelins, collecting works of Vladimir Nabokov, music. Home: PO Box 30786 Tucson AZ 85751

VEASEL, WALTER, minister, educator; b. Balt., Apr. 11, 1925; s. William Edward Veasel and Mary Lula (Boyd-Veasel) Ebert; m. Helen Ilene Gank; children: William, Holly, Bradley, Heide. ThB, Holmes Coll. of the Bible, 1947; BS in Elem. Edn., Towson State U., 1970; M in Ministries, Zion Sem., 1986. Ordained to ministry Pentecostal Holiness Ch., 1947; cert. tchr. Md. Tchr. Balt. City Schs., 1959-84; pastor Mid Atlantic Conf. Pentecostal Holiness Ch., 1948-54, Georgetown, D.C. and Daniels, Md., 1960-70, St. Catherines and London, Canada, 1955-59; founder, pastor Cmty. Ch., 1970-90; pastor emeritus Woodbridge Valley Ch. of God, 1990-94; prin. Tabernacle Christian Sch., Balt., 1988-94. Conf. Sunday sch. sec./treas.; conf. youth v.p.; conf. sec/treas., bd. dirs., 1950—70; instr. Tabernacle Bible Inst., 1970—75, Faith Sch. Theology, 1993. Trustee Full Gospel Pentecostal Ch., Ellicott City, 1999—; vol. nursing homes, reform schs. and prisons, 1948—; mem. adv. bd. Evangel Christian Acad., Balt., 1996—. Recipient Vols. cert., Ho. of Corrections, 1975—, Frederick Villa Nursing Home, 1980—. Republican. Home: 5025 Montgomery Rd Ellicott City MD 21043-6750 also: 638 Clark Lohr Rd Swanton MD 21561-2255

VEASEY, BYRON KEITH, information systems consultant; b. Washington, Mar. 17, 1957; s. Columbus Jr. and Joan Marie (Ingram) V. BS in Indsl. and Sys. Engring., U. So. Calif., 1979; MBA, Ball State U., 1982; M Mgmt. in Info. Sys., U. Dallas, 1989. Cert. quality analyst Quality Assurance Inst., computing profl. Inst. for Certification of Computer Profls. CIM engr. Mason & Hanger, Amarillo, Tex., 1983-87; bus. sys. analyst E-Sys., Garland, 1987-89; consulting mgr. Deloitte & Touche, Dallas, 1989-93; sr. cons. CSC, 1993-96; solutions mgr. AT&T, Chantilly, Va., 1996-97, Information Advantage, Vienna, 1997; info. sys. cons. DMR Consulting Group, Inc., Atlanta, 1997—. Mem. Dallas Heart Ball, 1991-92; mem. PM League Dallas Mus. of Art, 1992-93; bd. dirs. Dallas Wind Symphony, 1992; pres. Inst. of Indsl. Engrs., Dallas, 1992-93; v.p. programs Assn. for Sys. Mgmt., Dallas, 1991-93. Capt. USAF, 1979-82. Mem. Am. Legion. Republican. Avocations: theater, saxophone, chess, computers, travel. Home: 6917 Valley View Ln Apt 150 Irving TX 75039-2405 Office: Arthur Andersen 901 Main St Ste 6500 Dallas TX 75202

VEASEY, EUGENE NORMAN, state supreme court chief justice; b. Wilmington, Del., Jan. 9, 1933; s. Eugene E. and Elizabeth B. (Norman) V.; m. Suzanne Johnson, Aug. 4, 1956; children: Andrew Scott, Dluglas Ross, E. Norman Jr., Marian Elizabeth. AB, Dartmouth Coll., 1954; LLB, U. Pa., 1957. Bar: Del. 158, U.S. Supreme Ct. 1963. Dep. atty. gen. State of Del., 1961-62; chief dep., 1962-63; ptnr. Richards, Layton & Finger, Wilmington, Del., 1963-92; chief justice Del. Supreme Ct., 1992—. Contbr. articles to profl. jours. Bd. advisors U. Pa. Inst. for Law and Econs. Capt. Del. Air N.G., 1957-63. Fellow Am. Bar Found., Am. Coll. Trial Lawyers, Am. Intellectual Property Law Assn.; mem. Del. Bd. Bar Examiners (chmn. 1973-80), Del. Bar Assn. (pres. 1982-83, chmn. corp. law com. 1969-74, chmn. rules com. Del. Supreme Ct. 1974-80), ABA (chair bus. law sect. 1994-95, chair spl. com. on ethics 2000 1997—), Am. Law Inst. (bd. dirs. conf. chief jusice 1994-96, chair professionalism com. 1994-98, 1st v.p. 1998, pres.-elect 1998-99, pres. 1999-00), Nat. Ctr. State Cts. (chair bd. dirs. 1999-00). Republican. Episcopalian. Office: Del Supreme Ct PO Box 1997 Wilmington DE 19899-1997 E-mail: eveasey@state.de.us.

VEATCH, ELIZABETH WILSON, educational administrator; b. Bloomington, Ind., July 26, 1946; d. Henry Babcock and Mary Jane (Wilson) V. BA, Ind. U., 1968; MS, Georgetown U., 1970. Researcher Inter-Am. Found., Arlington, Va., 1971-73, program officer, 1973-86; asst. dir. Office of Fellowships and Grants, Smithsonian Instn., Washington, 1986-96; dir. Nat. Security Edn. Fellowship Program, Acad. Ednl. Devel., 1996—. Cons. Ford Found., N.Y.C., 1986-88, Inter-Am. Dialogue, Washington, 1990. Bd. dirs. Life Skills Ctr., Washington, 1988-96, Arlington County Community Found., 1991, fundraising com. Mem. Nat. Trust for Historic Preservation, Nat., Dem. Women's Club, Latin Am. Studies Assn. Democrat. Episcopalian. Office: NSEP/AED 1825 Connecticut Ave NW Washington DC 20009-5708 E-mail: eveatch@aed.org.

VEATCH, ROBERT MARLIN, philosophy educator, medical ethics researcher; b. Utica, N.Y., Jan. 22, 1939; s. Cecil Ross and Regina (Braddock) V.; m. Laurelyn Kay Lovett, June 17, 1961 (div. Oct. 1986); children: Paul Martin, Carlton Elliot; m. Ann Bender Pastore, May 23, 1987. BS, Purdue U., 1961; MS, U. Calif. at San Francisco, 1962; BD, Harvard U., 1964, MA, 1970, PhD, 1971; D Humanities (hon.), Creighton U., 1999. Teaching fellow Harvard U., 1968-70; research assoc. in medicine Coll. Physicians and Surgeons, Columbia U., 1971-72; assoc. for med. ethics Inst. of Society, Ethics and Life Scis., Hastings-on-Hudson, N.Y., 1970-75, sr. assoc., 1975-79; prof. med. ethics Kennedy Inst. Ethics Georgetown U., 1979—, prof. philosophy, 1981—, dir., 1989-96; adj. prof. depts. community and family medicine and ob/gyn, 1984—. Mem. vis. faculty various colls. and univs.; mem. gov. bd. Washington Regional Transplant Consortium, 1988—; bd. dirs. Hospice Care D.C., 1989-96, 97-99, pres., 1993-95; active United Network Organ Sharing Ethics Com., 1989-95. Author: Value-Freedom in Science and Technology, 1976, Death, Dying and the Biological Revolution, 1976, rev. edit., 1989, Case Studies in Medical Ethics, 1977, A Theory of Medical Ethics, 1981, The Foundations of Justice, 1987, The Patient as Partner, 1987; (with Sarah T. Fry) Case Studies in Nursing Ethics, 1987, rev. edit., 2000, The Patient-Physician Relationship: The Patient as Partner, Part 2, 1991; (with James T. Rule) Ethical Questions in Dentistry, 1993, (with Harley Flack) Case Studies in Allied Health Ethics, 1997, (with Paul DeVries and Lisa Newton) Ethics Applied, 2d. edit., 1999, (with Amy Haddad) Case Studies in Pharmacy Ethics, 1999, The Basics of Bioethics, 2000, Transplantation Ethics, 2000; editor or co-editor: Bibliography of Society, Ethics and the Life Sciences, 1973, rev. edit., 1978, The Teaching of Medical Ethics, 1973, Death Inside Out, 1975, Ethics and Health Policy, 1976, Teaching of Bioethics, 1976, Population Policy and Ethics, 1977, Life Span: Values and Life Extending Technologies, 1979, Cases in Bioethics From the Hastings Center Report, 1982, Medical Ethics, 1989, 2d edit., 1997, Cross Cultural Perspectives in Medical Ethics, 1989, rev. edit., 2000; (with Edmund D. Pellegrino and John P. Langan) Ethics, Trust, and the Professions, 1991; (with Tom L. Beauchamp) Ethical Issues in Death and Dying, 1996, (with Hans-Martin Sass and Rihito Kimura) Advance Directives and Surrogate Decision Making in Health Care: United States, Germany, and Japan, 1998, (with Albert R. Jonsen and LeRoy Walters) Source Book in Bioethics: A Documentary History, 1998; assoc. editor Encyclopedia of Bioethics, 1998; editl. bd. Jour. AMA, 1976-86, Jour. Medicine and Philosophy, 1980—, Harvard Theol. Rev., 1975—, Jour. Religious Ethics, 1981—; editl. adv. bd. Forum on Medicine, 1977-81; contbg. editor Hosp. Physician, 1975-85, Am. Jour. Hosp. Pharmacy, 1989-99; sr. editor Kennedy Inst. Ethics Jour., 1991—; contbr. articles to profl. jours. Mem. Soc. Christian Ethics. Office: Georgetown U Kennedy Inst Of Ethics Washington DC 20057-0001 E-mail: veatchr@georgetown.edu.

VEAZEY, DORIS ANNE, state agency administrator, retired; b. Dawson Spring, Ky., Feb. 16, 1935; d. Bradley Basil and Lucy Mable (Hamby) Sisk; m. Herman Veazey Jr., Aug. 15, 1964 (dec. Sept. 1987); 1 child, Vickie Dianne Veazey Kicinski. , Murray State U., 1952-54. Unemployment ins. examiner Dept. for Employment Svcs., Madisonville, Ky., 1954-73, unemployment ins. supr., 1973-85, field office mgr., 1985-96; ret., 1996. Bd. dirs., adv. bd. region II Vocat. Tech. Schs., Madisonville, 1988-92. Mem. Mayor's Work Force Devel. Com., 1993-96, Ky. Indsl. Devel. Com., 1992-96; dept. dir. Adult III Sunday Sch., 1994-96, ch. choir, 1990—; mem. staff devel. com. Madisonville First Bapt. Ch., 1997-99. Mem. Internat. Assn. of Pers. in Employment Svcs., Tenure, Order of Ky. Cols., Greater Madisonville C. of C. (dir. leadership 1988-93). Baptist. Avocations: reading, T.V., travel, photography. Home: 697 Brown Rd Madisonville KY 42431-2258

VEBLEN, THOMAS CLAYTON, management consultant; b. Hallock, Minn., Dec. 17, 1929; s. Edgar R. and Hattie (Lundgren) V.; m. Susan Alma Beaver, Sept. 1, 1950 (div. 1971); children: Kari Christen, Erik Rodli, Mark Andrew, Sara Catherine; m. Linda Joyce Eaton, Aug. 30, 1975; 1 child, Kristen Kirby. Student, U. Calif., Santa Barbara, 1950-51; BS, Calif. Poly. U., 1953; MS, Oreg. State U., 1955. Corp. v.p. Cargill, Inc., Wayzata, Minn., 1955-75; spl. asst. Sec. Interior, Washington, 1965; dir. food and agr. SRI Internat., Menlo Park, Calif., 1975-80; pres. Food Sys. Assocs., Inc., Washington, 1980-94; also bd. dirs. Food System Assocs., Inc.; chmn. Enterprise Cons., Inc., 1990—; dir. Georgetown Cons., Inc., 1993-95; convener The Superior Bus. Firm Roundtable, 1993—; chmn. Kirby Ventures LLC, Mpls., 1997—, Wyatt Ventures, LLC, Mpls. Mem. CMC Inst. Mgmt. Cons., 1988—97, pres. Washington chpt., 1991—93. Author: (with M. Nichols) The U.S. Food System, 1978; (with M. Abel) Creating a Superior National Food System, 1992, The Way of Business, 2000; editor Food System Update, 1986-95. Treas., bd. dirs. White House Fellows Assn., Washington, 1985; trustee Freedom from Hunger Found., Davis, Calif., 1980-99, chmn., 1986-89; bd. dirs. Patterson Sch., U. Ky., Lexington, 1976-99, Am. Near East Refugee Aid, 1994--. Recipient Presdl. Appointment White House Fellows Commn., Washington, 1965. Mem. Coun. on Fgn. Rels., Cato Inst., Cosmos Club. Episcopalian. Avocations: canoeing, gardening. Office: Enterprise Cons Inc 3105 Bloomington Ave South Minneapolis MN 55407 E-mail: superbizrt@aol.com.

VECCHIO, ROBERT PETER, business management educator; b. Chgo., June 29, 1950; s. Dominick C. and Angeline V.; m. Betty Ann Vecchio; Aug. 21, 1974; children: Julie, Mark. BS summa cum laude, DePaul U., 1972; MA, U. Ill., 1974, PhD, 1976. Instr. U. Ill., Urbana, 1973-76; mem. faculty dept. mgmt. U. Notre Dame, 1976—, dept. chmn., 1983-90, Franklin D. Schurz Prof. Mgmt., 1986—. Editor Jour. of Mgmt., 1995-2000. Fellow: APA, Am. Psychol. Soc., Soc. for Indsl. and Orgnl. Psychology; mem.: Mdiwest Psychol. Assn., Midwest Acad. Mgmt., Decision Scis. Inst., Acad. of Mgmt., Phi Eta Sigma, Delta Epsilon Sigma, Phi Kappa Phi. Home: 16856 Hampton Dr Granger IN 46530-6907 Office: U Notre Dame Dept Mgmt Notre Dame IN 46556

VECCHIOTTI, ROBERT ANTHONY, management and organizational consultant; b. N.Y.C., May 21, 1941; s. R. Lucien and Louise Victoria V.; m. Dorothea Irene Hoban, Oct. 12, 1963; children: John Robert, Rachel Irene, Sara Christine. BS, St. Peter's Coll., 1962; MA, Fordham U., 1964; PhD, St. Louis U., 1973. Lic. psychologist, Mo. Psychologist Testing and Advisement Ctr., NYU, Washington Sq. campus, 1964-65; group psychologist McDonnell Douglas, St. Louis, 1967-76, sr. bus. analyst, 1976-77, mgr. bus. planning, 1977-79; pres. Orgnl. Cons. Svcs., Inc., 1980—. Adj. assoc. prof. mgmt. Maryville Coll., St. Louis, 1975-81. Bd. dirs. Cath. Charities of St. Louis, 1981-86, Cath. Family Svc., 1986-2000, Mental Health Assn. St. Louis, 1989—, Sta. KWMU-FM, 1989-94. With U.S. Army, 1965-67. Mem. APA, Strategic Leadership Forum, Mo. Athletic Club, Rotary (past pres.). Office: Organizational Consulting Svcs Inc 230 S Bemiston Ave Ste 1107 Clayton MO 63105-1907

VECELLIO, LEO ARTHUR, JR. construction company executive; b. Beckley, W.Va., Oct. 26, 1946; s. Leo Arthur and Evelyn (Pais) V.; m. Kathryn Grace Cottrill, Nov. 29, 1975; children: Christopher Scott, Michael Andrew. BCE, Va. Poly. Inst. and State U., 1968; MCE, Ga. Inst. Tech., 1969; LLD, Northwood U., 1992. Sr. v.p. Vecellio & Grogan, Inc., Beckley, 1973-96, pres., CEO, chmn. bd. dirs., 1996—; mng. ptnr. Deerfield Property Assocs., 1988—, Vecellio Realty Co., 1990—; pres. Vecellio Realty Inc., 1997—; mng. ptnr. Orlando Property Assn. Ltd., 1997—, WRQ Property Assn. Ltd., 1997—. Pres. Vecellio Contracting Corp. and subs. (Ranger Constrn. Industries, West Palm Beach, PAVEX Corp., Deerfield Beach, White Rock Quarries, Miami 1990—), Fla., 1982—; bd. dirs. Nations Bank Palm Beach County (formerly Barnett Bank); founder, past dir. Gulf Nat. Bank, Sophia, W.Va.; founder, past dir. Nat. Bankers Trust, Beckley. Chmn. bd. dirs. Econ. Coun. Palm Beach County, Fla., 1985—, chmn.-elect, 1987, chmn., 1989; gov. Northwood U., West Palm Beach, 1985—; organizer, trustee Beckley Area Found., 1985; v.p., trustee Vecellio Family Found., Beckley, 1972-96, pres., trustee, 1996—; active Mini-Grace Commn., Fla. Coun. 100, 1989—, vice-chmn., 1991—; commn. dir., v.p. Criminal Justice Commn.; chmn. Budget Rev. Task Force, Budget Oversight Task Force; bd. dirs. Palm Beach County Cultural Coun. and Art Sch. Task Force, Fla. Coun. 100, Floridians for Better Transp., exec. com.; corporator Schepens Eye Rsch. Inst., Harvard U., 1993—; mem. engring. coun. 100 Va. Tech.; mem. pres.'s adv. bd. Ga. Inst. Tech., 2000—. Capt USAF, 1969-73. Recipient Free Enterprise medal Palm Beach Atlantic Coll., 1988. Mem. Am. Rd. and Transp. Builders Assn. (dir. 2000), Flexible Pavements Assn. (found, bd. dirs. 1979—), Contractors Assn. W. (bd. dirs. 1975—). Clubs: Mayacoo Lakes Country (West Palm Beach), Adios Golf (Coconut Creek, Fla.), Jupiter Hills (Fla.), Lost Tree. Republican. Roman Catholic. Avocations: golf, boating, skiing. Home: 771 Village Rd North Palm Beach FL 33408-3331 Office: Vecellio Contracting Corp PO Box 15065 West Palm Beach FL 33416-5065

VEDDER, RICHARD KENT, economics educator; b. Urbana, Ill., Nov. 5, 1940; s. Byron C. and Kathleen (Fry) V.; m. Karen Pirosko, June 18, 1968; children: Virin, Vanette. BA, Northwestern U., Evanston, Ill., 1962; MA, U.

Ill., 1963, PhD, 1965. Asst. prof. econs. Ohio U., Athens, 1965-69, assoc. prof. econs., 1969-74, prof. econs., 1974-85; economist Joint Econ. Com. of Congress, Washington, 1981-82; Dist. Prof. of econs. Ohio U., Athens, 1985—. Vis. prof. Claremont (Calif.) McKenna Coll., 1979-80, Econs. Inst. U. Colo., Boulder, 1979, 80, Washington U., St. Louis, 1995, 96. Author: American Economy in Historical Perspective, 1976, Can Teachers Own Their Own Schools?, 2000; co-author: (monograph) Poverty, Income Distribution, The Family and Public Policy, 1986, Out of Work: Unemployment and Government in Twentieth-Century America, 1993, rev. edit., 1997. Mem. Athens Bd. Edn., 1987-91; bd. dirs. Athens Community Music Sch., 1987-92. Recipient rsch. grants Earhart Found., 1970, 90, Rockefeller Found., 1974, Nat. Chamber Found., 1990, fellowship Inst. for Humane Studies, Palo Alto, Calif., 1983. Mem. Am. Econ. Assn., Econ. History Assn., Rotary. Republican. Presbyterian. Home: 7464 Ridgeview Cir Athens OH 45701-9005 Office: Ohio Univ Dept Econs Haning Hall Athens OH 45701

VEDENIAPIN, ANDREI B. psychiatrist, researcher; b. Ufa, Russia, Mar. 13, 1963; s. Boris N. Pavlov and Emma A. Vedeniapina; m. Yulia Yudokhina, 1996. MD, First Moscow Med. Inst., Moscow, Russia, 1985. Lic. psychiatrist, narcologist. Researcher First Moscow Med. Inst., Moscow, 1987—94; intern in neuropsychiatry NIAAA, St. Louis, 1994—95; rsch. assoc. Washington U., 1995—98, mgr. Project III Mo. Alcoholism Rsch. Ctr., 1999—. Contbr. articles. Recipient Young Scientist award, Ministry of Health of the USSR, 1988, 1989. Mem.: World Psychiatric Orgn. (mem. sect. psychophysiology), Soc. Psychophysiological Rsch. Achievements include development of for treatment of psychogenic headaches, stress evaluation. Office: Washigton U Sch Medicine 4625 Lindell Blvd 2nd Fl # 258 Saint Louis MO 63108 Office Fax: 314-454-0432. Business E-Mail: andrei@ethos.wustl.edu.

VEDOURAS, ANNA, federal lawyer; b. Cleveland, Ohio, Feb. 21, 1960; d. John and Emily (Peters) Vedouras. BA, U. Mich., 1981; JD, Cleve. State U., 1985. Bar: Ohio 1989. Atty. LIGHTNET, New Haven, 1985-86; contract adminstr. Constrn. Control Svcs., Inc., Boston, 1986-87; project mgr. Legal Support Svcs., 1987-89; sr. assoc. counsel Dept. of Defense, Cleveland, Ohio, 1989—. Pres. Young Friends Cleve. Mus. Art, 1993—95; trustee, v.p. Ctr. for Prevention of Domestic Violence, 1993—98; trustee Cleve. Play House, 1991—96; v.p. Cleve. Film Soc., 1993—, Cleve. Ctr. Contemporary Arts, 1996—2000, Spaces, 1999—; pres. Cleve. Mediation Ctr., 2001—; bd. dirs. Near West Theatre, 1996—2000. Recipient No. Ohio Live award of achievement, 1996, Disting. Fed. Svc. award, 1999; named one of 50 most interesting people Cleve. Mag., 1995; named Titan of Style, Sun Newspapers, 1995. Mem. Cleve. Bar Assn.

VEDROS, NEYLAN ANTHONY, microbiologist, educator; b. New Orleans, Oct. 6, 1929; s. Phillip John and Solange Agnes (Melancon) V.; m. Elizabeth Corbett, Apr. 9, 1955; children: Sally Ann, Philippa Jane. BS in Chemistry, La. State U., 1951, MS in Microbiology, 1957; PhD, U. Colo., 1960. Postdoctoral fellow Nat. Inst. Allergy and Infectious Diseases, U. Oreg., Portland, 1960-62; microbiologist Naval Med. Research Inst., Bethesda, Md., 1962-66; research microbiologist Naval Biosci. Lab., Oakland, Calif., 1966-67; assoc. prof. med. microbiology and immunology U. Calif., Berkeley, 1967-72, prof., 1972-91, prof. emeritus, 1991—. Dir. Naval Biosci. Lab., 1968-81; mem. expert panel on bacteriology WHO, 1972-91. Bd. trustees Alameda (Calif.) Library, 1973-78. Served to comdr. M.S.C. USNR, 1952-55, 62-67. Mem.: Internat. Assn. Aquatic Animal Medicine, Internat. Assn. Microbiol. Sci., Am. Soc. Microbiology. Home: 209 Almond Way Healdsburg CA 95448 E-mail: nvedros@earthlink.net.

VEE, RICHARD J. art educator; b. Detroit, Nov. 4, 1944; s. Frank V. Veselovsky, Henrietta E. Veselovsky. BFA, Wayne State U., 1967; MA, Ea. Mich. U., 1971. Mem.: NEA, Mich. Edn. Assn., Ky. Edn. Assn. Avocation: art. Home: 865 Darby Trace Winchester KY 40391

VEECH, RICHARD LEWIS, medical researcher, physician; b. Decatur, Ill., Sept. 19, 1935; s. G. Lewis and Jennie Edwards Veech; children: Jennifer Lally, Andrew, Thomas, George. BA, Harvard U., 1957, MD magna cum laude, 1962. USPHS fellow Harvard Med. Sch., Boston, 1962; intern, resident N.Y. Hosp./Cornell Med. Ctr., N.Y.C., 1962-64; clin. assoc. NIMH, Washington, 1964-66, med. officer, rschr., 1969-73; USPHS fellow dept. biochemistry Oxford (Eng.) U., 1966-69; chief lab. alcohol rsch. NIAAA, Washington, 1974-76; chief lab. of metabolism and molecular biology NIH/NIAAA, Rockville, Md., 1976-95, chief unit on metabolic control, 1995—. Mem. editl. bd. Jour. Biol. Chemistry, Bethesda, Md., 1975-80; cons. BTG Internat., London, 1995—. Contbr. over 250 articles to profl. jours., over 10 chpts. to texts and references. Trustee Found. for Advanced Rsch. in Med. Scis., Easton, Md., 1995—. Lt. comdr. USPHS, 1964-66. Recipient N.H. Hero's medal Manchester Union Leader, 1969, Rsch. medal Bly Found., 1974; John Douglas French Alzheimer's Found. grantee. Mem. Cosmos Club. Home: 712 Brent Rd Rockville MD 20850 Office: NIH/NIAAA 12501 Washington Ave Rockville MD 20852 Fax: (301) 443-0930.

VEEDER, NANCY WALKER, social work educator; b. Albany, N.Y., Mar. 17, 1937; d. Harold Gerit and Alice (Walker) V. AB, Smith Coll., Northampton, Mass., 1959; MS, Simmons Sch. Social Work, Boston, 1963; PhD, Brandeis U., 1974; MBA, Boston Coll., 1990. Prof., grad. sch. social work Boston Coll., Chestnut Hill, 1968—. Home: 53 Lake Ave Newton Center MA 02459-2110 E-mail: veeder@bc.edu.

VEEDER, PETER GREIG, lawyer; b. Pitts., Aug. 13, 1941; AB, Princeton U., 1963; JD, U. Pitts., 1966. Bar: Pa. 1966, D.C. 1976. Lawyer Thorp Reed & Armstrong, Pitts., 1970-99; of counsel Thorp, Reed & Armstrong LLP, 1999—. Office: Thorp Reed & Armstrong LLP 1 Oxford Ctr 301 Grant St Fl 14 Pittsburgh PA 15219-1425

VEENHUIS, PHILIP EDWARD, psychiatrist, educator, preventive medicine physician, administrator; b. Kalamazoo, Aug. 4, 1935; s. Claude Albert and Placide Mary (Steger) V.; m. Joanne Elizabeth Williams, Aug. 8, 1959; children: Mark Edward, Suzanne Marie. BA, Kalamazoo Coll., 1957; MD, U. Mich., 1961, MPH in Health Svcs. Adminstrn., 1990. Diplomate Am. Bd. Psychiatry; cert. of added qualifications in geropsychiatry; cert. in adminstrv. psychiatry; diplomate in pub. health and gen. preventive medicine Am. Bd. Preventive Medicine, 1997. Intern James Decker Munson Hosp., Traverse City, Mich., 1961-62; resident Lafayette Clinic Wayne State U., Detroit, 1962-65; dir. psychiat. edn. Med. Coll. Wis., Milw., 1970-73, acting chmn. dept. psychiatry, 1973-75, 82-86, dir. continuing edn. dept. psychiatry, 1975-86, dir. psychiat. tng., 1984-86; chmn. dept. psychiatry Providence Hosp., Southfield, Mich., 1986-93; med. dir. divsn. mental health/devel. disabil. subs. abuse N.C. Dept. Health and Human Svcs., Raleigh, 1993—. Assoc. prof. psychiatry Med. Coll. Wis., 1973-86; clin. prof. psychiatry Mich. State U., 1988-92, U. N.C., Chapel Hill, 1993—; clin. assoc. prof. Wayne State U., 1991-92 Contbr. articles to profl. jours. Served to lt. comdr. USNR, 1965-67. NIMH grantee, 1982-86. Fellow Am. Psychiat. Assn. (life), Am. Coll. Preventive Medicine; mem. AMA, North Psychiat. Assn., N.C. Med. Soc. Office: NC Dept Human Resources Divsn Mental Health 325 N Salisbury St Raleigh NC 27603-1388

VEERAVALLI, VENU, university educator; b. Rajahmundry, India, July 28, 1963; m. Starla Carpenter. PhD, University of Illinois, Urbana-Champaign, 1988—92. Assistant Professor Cornell University, Ithaca, NY, 1996—2000; Associate Professor University of Illinois, Urbana, IL, 2000—. Mem.: IEEE. Office: 128 CSL, University of Illinois 1308 West Main Street Urbana IL 61801 Office Fax: 217 244 1642. Personal E-mail: vvv@uiuc.edu. Business E-Mail: vvv@uiuc.edu.

VEGA, ALBERTO LEON, financial executive; b. Havana, Cuba, Apr. 11, 1947; came to U.S., 1961; s. Alberto Laureano and Ofelia Gregoria (Perez) V.; m. Rosa Maria Alvarez; children: Alberto Luis, Kevin David. BBA with honors, U. Miami, Fla., 1969. CPA, Fla. Sr. acct. Ernst & Whinney, Miami, 1969-73; asst. treas. Amcourt Systems, Inc., Coral Gables, Fla., 1973-74; v.p., chief fin. officer Heico Corp., Hollywood, 1974-82; sr. v.p., chief fin. officer Central Bancorp, Inc., Miami, 1982-84; sr. v.p. Pan Am. Banks, Inc., 1984-85; sr. v.p., chief fin. officer S. Floridabanc Fed. Savs. & Loan, Boca Raton, Fla., 1985-89, Ocean Bank, Miami, 1989—. Cons. in field. Mem. Fla. Inst. CPA's, Am. Inst. CPA's, Fin. Execs. Inst. Clubs: Exchange (Miami). Roman Catholic. Avocation: photography.

VEGA, BENJAMIN URBIZO, retired judge, television producer; b. La Ceiba, Honduras, Jan. 18, 1916; m. Janie Lou Smith, Oct. 12, 1989; AB, U. So. Calif., 1938, postgrad., 1939-40; LLB, Pacific Coast U. Law, 1941. Bar: Calif. 1947, U.S. Dist. Ct. (so. dist.) Calif. 1947, U.S. Supreme Ct. 1958. Assoc. Anderson, McPharlin & Connors, L.A., 1947-48, Newman & Newman, L.A., 1948-51; dep. dist. atty. County of L.A., 1951-66; judge L.A., County Mcpl. Ct., East L.A. Jud. Dist., 1966-86, retired, 1986; leader faculty seminar Calif. Jud. Coll. at Earl Warren Legal Inst., U. Calif-Berkeley, 1978. Mem. Calif. Gov.'s Adv. Com. on Children and Youth, 1968; del. Commn. of the Califs., 1978; bd. dirs. Los Angeles-Mexico City Sister City Com.; pres. Argentine Cultural Found., 1983. Recipient award for outstanding services from Mayor of L.A., 1973, City of Commerce, City of Montebello, Calif. Assembly, Southwestern Sch. Law, Disting. Pub. Service award Dist. Atty. L.A. Mem. Conf. Calif. Judges, Mcpl. Ct. Judges' Assn. (award for Outstanding Services), Beverly Hills Bar Assn., Navy League, L.A. County, Am. Judicature Soc., World Affairs Council, Rotary (hon.), Pi Sigma Alpha. Home: 101 California Ave Apt 1207 Santa Monica CA 90403-3525

VEGA, J. WILLIAM, aerospace engineering executive, consultant; b. Elizabeth, N.J., Jan. 30, 1931; s. John Charles and Margaret (Walker) V.; m. Carolyn Louise Burt, June 7, 1957 (div. 1976); children: Lynn Vega Membreño, Lore Vega Hynes, Susan; m. Pauline Anne Garner, Apr. 27, 1983. BSE, Princeton U., 1952, postgrad., 1955-56; MS, U.S. Internat. U., 1973. Sr. engr. Reaction Motors, Inc., Denville, N.J., 1956-58, Convair div. Gen. Dynamics, San Diego, 1958, project engr., sr. project engr., asst. chief engr., 1970-75, dir. advanced programs, 1975-83, v.p. advanced programs, 1983-88, v.p. rsch. and engring., 1988-90; cons. aerospace mgmt., 1991—. Past pres. bd. dirs. Durango (Colo.) Art Ctr.; pres. bd. dirs. Durango Cmty. Access TV; bd. dirs. Cmty. Found. of S.W. Colo.; bd. pres. Durango Cmty. Access TV. Lt. USN, 1952-55. Recipient Outstanding Vol. Fundraiser award State Colo., 1999. Fellow AIAA (assoc.); mem. Phi Beta Kappa. Avocations: skiing, boating, hiking, camping.

VEGA, JOSE GUADALUPE, psychologist, clinical director; b. June 4, 1953; s. Jose Guadalupe and Bertha (Saenz) V.; children: Lilian Anna, Jose Guadalupe III; m. Alberta L. Valdez, Oct. 5, 1990. BA, Pan Am. U., Edinburg, Tex., 1975; MA, U. Denver, 1976, PhD, 1979. Lic. psychologist, Colo., profl. counselor, Tex.; diplomate Am. Bd. Med. Psychotherapists, Am. Bd. Vocat. Neuropsychology, Am. Bd. Profl. Disability Cons., Am. Bd. Forensic Examiners, Am. Bd. Psychol. Specialties (forensic neuropsychology), Am. Bd. Profl. Neuropsychology; cert. adminstrn. Halste ad-Reitan Neuropsychology test batteries. With Oasis of Chandala, Denver, 1978-79, Maytag-Emrick Clinic, Aurora, Colo., 1979; psychologist Spanish Peaks Mental Health Ctr., Pueblo, 1980-85; pvt. practice Assocs. for Psychotherapy and Edn., Inc., 1985-86; co-owner Affiliates in Counseling, Psychol. Assessment & Cons., Inc., Pueblo, 1986-87; psychologist Parkview Psychol. Testing Clinic, 1987-93, Colo. Dept. Corrections, 1994-96; pvt. practice Pueblo, 1993—. State grievance bd. Psychology Augment Panel, 1988-95. Active Colo. Inst. Chicano Mental Health, Cmty. Youth Orgn., Boys Club Pueblo; mem. health and human svcs. com. City of Pueblo. Mem.: ACA, APA, Hispanic Neuropsychol. Soc., Nat. Hispanic Psychol. Assn., Colo. Psychol. Assn. (bd. dirs. non-metro rep. 1995—2000, pres.-elect 2000, pres. 2001—02, 2002—), Reitan Soc. (charter; v.p. 2000—02, pres. 2002—), Colo. Neuropsychol. Soc. (charter), Internat. Neuropsychol. Soc., Nat. Acad. Neuropsychology, Kappa Delta Pi, Phi Delta Kappa. Democrat. Roman Catholic. Office: 1301 W 17th St Pueblo CO 81003-1915 E-mail: drvega@aculink.net.

VEGA, MARYLOIS PURDY, journalist; b. Chgo., Nov. 4, 1914; d. William Thomas and Mary Helene (Buggy) Purdy; m. Carlos Juan Vega, Sept. 4, 1965. BA, U. Wis., Madison, 1935. With Time mag., N.Y.C., 1942-84; chief Letters to the Editor, 1951-67, chief editl. rsch., 1967-76, assoc. editor, 1976-84. Mem.: Overseas Press. Roman Catholic. Home: 303 Birchwood Southbury CT 06488-1378

VEGA, MATIAS ALFONSO, lawyer; b. Paris, Feb. 2, 1952; s. Matias Guillermo and Colette (Lafosse) V.; m. Carmella Margarita Kurczewski, Nov. 20, 1982; 1 child, Alexandra Lafosse. AB, Yale U., 1974; JD, Harvard U., 1977. Bar: N.Y. 1978, U.S. Dist. Ct. (so. and ea. dists.) N.Y. 1979, U.S. Supreme Ct. 1984, U.S. Ct. Appeals (6th and 9th cirs.) 1985, U.S. Dist. Ct. (no. dist.) Calif. 1985. Assoc. Curtis, Mallet-Prevost, Colt & Mosle, N.Y.C., 1977-85, ptnr., 1986—. Contbr. articles to profl. jours. Mem. ABA, Am. Soc. Internat. Law, N.Y. State Bar Assn. (chmn. com. Latin Am. law, internat. law and practice sect. 1987-90), Yale Club. Republican. Roman Catholic. Home: 31 Gedney Way Chappaqua NY 10514-1402 Office: Curtis Mallet-Prevost Colt 101 Park Ave Fl 34 New York NY 10178-0061 E-mail: matvega@msn.com., mvega@cm-p.com.

VEGA, RAYNETTE NORMA, hotel official; b. Kohala, Hawaii, Feb. 26, 1962; d. Antone Tony and Ramona Mona Vega. Student, Fayetteville (N.C.) Tech. Sch., 1980-81, Youth with a Mission, Sunland, Calif., 1982-83. Christian counselor Centrum of Hollywood, Calif., 1983-84; security officer Hawaii Protective Assn., Kamuela, 1984-87, Puakea Bay Ranch, Kapaau, Hawaii, 1987-93; concierge Hyatt Regency Waikoloa, 1988-89. Youth Christian counselor New Covenant Ch., Waimea, Hawaii, 1985-86. Author: (poetry) Rainbows of Poems from Heaven Above, 1987, Heart Beat in Love, 1993. Recipient Golden Poet award World of Poetry, 1987-91, award Poetry Acad., 1993, Poet of Merit award Internat. Soc. Poets, 1993, Internat. Hall of Fame, 1996. Avocations: jogging, tennis, reading, writing poetry.

VEGA, STEVE, poet; b. Manhattan, N.Y., Nov. 13, 1949; s. Exio Ocasio Vega; m. Veronica Gonzalez, Jan. 3, 1971; children: Katherine, James-Paul Christian, Diamond Zhane. Cert. in bus. mgmt., Marion Bus. Coll., 1973; cert., John Marshall Law Sch., 1977; cert. in corrections and probations svcs., Chgo. Loop Coll., 1986; BA, Coll. of Commr. Sci., 1995, M in Commr. Svc., 1996, postgrad., 1997; PhD, Lord Baden-Powell Coll., Lake Geneva, Wis., 1998; wilderness survival course, with APO wardogs, 1988; winter camping survival course, OKPIK, Woodstock, Ill., 1996; sea badge course, Great Lakes Navy Base, 1998. Adult probation officer Cook County, Ill., 1979-93; pub. safety officer, police-fireman aide Morton Grove (Ill.) emergency Svcs. and Disaster Agy., 1998—; CEO pvt. practice, 2002—. Union chief steward Cook County Adult Probation Dept., AFSCME, 1989—91; 1st v.p. AFSCME local 3486 APD officers, Chgo., 1991—92; cons. Chgo. Police Dept., FBI, U.S. Secret Svc.; dep. dir. Internat. Biog. Ctr., Cambridge, England, 2000; mem. steering com. Lord Baden-Powell U., 2002. Contbr. poetry to anthalogies; actor: (films) Music Box, Only the Lonely, Gladiator, Hero, Mo Money, Hoffa, Natural Born Killers, Mad Dog and Glory, Eye for and Eye (The Shadow of a Killer), Curly Sue, others; composer, rec. artist: songs The President Is Crying-September 11, 2001, 2001; writer, recorder World's First poetic musical World Trade Ctr. Tribute songs, 2001. Asst. coun. commn. Boy Scouts Am., Chgo., 1997, mem. ctrl. region com. Sea Scouting, 1998; vol., mem. com. City of Chgo. Health Sys. Agy., 1981—85. With USAF, 1970. Decorated Commendation medal USAF, knigth comdr. European Order Knighthood (Italy), 443d Svs. Squadron and Honor Guard USAF Mil. Aircraft Command; named World Poet, 1987—; named one of World's Great Living Poets, 1991; named to Hall of Fame, Lord Baden-Powell U., 2001, 2001; recipient Presdl. commendation, Pres. Ronald Reagan, 1987, 1988, Pres. George Bush, 1990, Arrowhead award, Boy Scouts Am., 1994. Mem.: ASCAP (composer, writer), Fraternal Order Police (officer 1988, sgt.-at-arms), Sovereign Mil. and Hospitaller Order St. George in Karinthia (titular head). Roman Catholic. Avocations: singing, composing, guitar, motorcycling, chess. Address: PO Box 221 Morton Grove IL 60053-0221 E-mail: steve_vega_records@yahoo.com.

VEGHTE, BILL, information technology executive; married; 1 child. BA with hon. in East Asian Studies, Harvard U. From product mgr. to corp. v.p. Microsoft, Redmond, Wash., 1990, corp. v.p. windows server group. Avocations: backcountry skiing, climbing, fishing. Office: One Microsoft Way Redmond WA 98052-6399*

VEHSE, ROBERT CHASE, management consultant, educator; b. Morgantown, W.Va., Sept. 9, 1936; s. Charles Henry and Edith Simmons Vehse; m. Terri Susan Lockart, Feb. 21, 1998; children: Kira Eliset, Megan Mariangela; m. Judith Carol Lawson, Aug. 26, 1961 (div. May 16, 1996); children: Daniel Remington, Deborah Vehse Lund. BA, W.Va. U., Morgantown, WV, 1954—58; MS, U. of Wis., Madison, WI, 1958—61; Ph. D, U. of Tenn., Knoxville, TN, 1968. Project Management Professional other. Mem. of the tech. staff AT&T Bell Labs, Reading, Pa., 1968—73, tech. supr., 1973—86, tech. dept. head, 1986—94, Lucent Technologies, Holmdel, NJ, 1994—96. Co-founder Connections Plus, Reading, Pa., 1992—2002. Contbr. articles to profl. jour. Squadron edn. officer U.S. Power Squadrons, Reading, Pa., 1971—74. Scholar Fulbright Scholorship, U.S Govt., 1971-1974. Mem.: Am. Phys. Soc. (life), W.Va. U. Phi Beta Kappa (hon.), U. of Tenn. Sigma Xi (hon.). Conservative-R. Episcopalian. Achievements include invention of Liquid Phase Epitaxy Apparatus. Avocations: music, sailing, teaching, church. Home: 353 Bald Eagle Drive Lancaster VA 22503 Personal E-mail: rvehse@rivnet.net.

VEHSLAGE, CAROLYN LEE, artist; b. N.J. BA in Econs. and Computer Sci., Lafayette Coll., 1983. Novell cert. netware engr. Mktg. mgr. Art Quilts at the Sedgwick, Phila., 2000—. Wall hanging, (original applique prize, 2000), framed quilted wall hanging, (first pl. adult amateur, 2000, first pl. miniatures, 2000), quilted wall hanging (commd. Pa. flower show vendor booth, 2001). Office: CLV Designs 24 Pine Glen Dr Sicklerville NJ 08081

VEIGEL, JON MICHAEL, science administrator; b. Mankato, Minn., Nov. 10, 1938; s. Walter Thomas and Thelma Geraldine (Lein) V.; m. Carol June Bradley, Aug. 10, 1962. BS, U. Washington, 1960; PhD, UCLA, 1965. Program mgr., congl. sci. fellow Office of Tech. Assessment, U.S. Congress, Washington, 1974-75; div. mgr. Calif. Energy Commn., Sacramento, 1975-78; asst. dir. Solar Energy Rsch. Inst., Golden, Colo., 1978-81; pres. Alt. Energy Corp., Rsch. Triangle Park, N.C., 1981-88, Oak Ridge (Tenn.) Associated Univs., 1988-96. Bd. dirs. Am. Coun. Energy Efficient Economy, Washington, Pacific Internat. Ctr. for High Tech. Rsch., Honolulu; cons. Sunhunner Assocs., LLC, 1996—. Contbr. articles to jours. Trustee Maryville Coll., 1990-96, Mendeleyev U., Moscow, Russia. 1st lt. USAF, 1965-68. Mem. AAAS (past mem. com. on sci. and engring. pub. policy, past chair). Avocations: photography. Office: SunRunner Assocs LLC 16259 W Spring Canyon Way Surprise AZ 85374-4961

VEIGELE, WILLIAM JOHN, physicist; b. N.Y.C., June 18, 1925; s. William John and Lena (Dorn) V.; m. Sue Jane Schwagerman, Jan. 25, 1956; children: William, Kris, Dyana, Lucy. BA, Hofstra U., 1949, MA, 1951; PhD, U. Colo., 1960. Instr. physics Williams Coll., Williamstown, Mass., 1951-52; instr. engring. and physics Hofstra U., Hempstead, N.Y., 1952-57; instr. physics U. Colo., Boulder, 1957-58; thermodynamicist Nat. Bur. Stds., Colo., 1958-59; prof., head dept. physics Parsons Coll., Iowa, 1960-61; sr. scientist Martin Marietta Aerospace Corp., Littleton, Colo., 1961-64; sr. scientist, program mgr. Kaman Scis. Corp., Colorado Springs, 1964-74; founder, pres. Resource Sci. Inc., 1974-78; program mgr., sr. scientist, product line mgr. Santa Barbara (Calif.) Rsch. Ctr., 1978-84; dept. dir. GRC, 1984-89; owner Astral Pub. Co., Santa Barbara, 1993—. Part-time lectr. physics U. Colo., Colorado Springs, 1966-77; part-time lectr., vis. assoc. prof. physics, nuc. and chem. engring., electrical computer engring., mech. and environ. engring. U. Santa Barbara, 1978-92; invitee Internat. Atomic Physics Conf., Gordon Rsch. Conf.; faculty affiliate atmospheric sci. Colo. State U.; sci. jour. referee Phys. Rev., Jour. Applied Physics, Jour. Chem. Physics, Am. Jour. Physics, Jour. Atmospheric Environment; cons. environ. divsn. County of Santa Barbara, Colo. Dept. Hwys., Denver, Med. Care and Rsch. Found., Denver, GRC, Santa Barbara, dept. elec. and computer engring. U. Calif. Santa Barbara, Raytheon Electromagnetics Sys. Divsn., Santa Barbara, SBRC, Goleta, Calif., Fairchild Camera and Instrument Corp., L.I., N.Y., owner Astral Pub. Co., Santa barbara, Calif., 1994—. Author: Golf Is Like Love, 1995, PC Patrol Craft of World War II, 1998, Best Time of Year, Chelydon Serpentina; contbr. numerous articles to profl. jours., mags. With USNR, 1943-46, with Res., 1947-68. NSF Sci. Faculty fellow; recipient hon. mention Writer's Digest Short Story Contest. Mem. AAAS, Am. Phys. Soc. (life), Am. Assn. Physics Tchrs., U.S. Naval Inst. (life), Navy League, Patrol Craft Sailors Assn. (life, bd. dirs.), PC 793 Assn. (pres., historian), Sigma Xi, Sigma Pi Sigma, Sigma Alpha. Avocations: golf, fishing, reading, travel, writing. Home: 333 Old Mill Rd Spc 324 Santa Barbara CA 93110-3655

VEILLE, JEAN-CLAUDE, maternal-fetal medicine physician, educator; b. France; came to U.S., 1982; m. Ann Veille; children: Olivier, Xavier, Patrique, Robert. BS, McGill U., 1971; MD, U. Montpellier, France, 1977. Fellow in maternal-fetal medicine Oreg. Health Scis., Portland, 1982-84; from asst. prof. to assoc. prof. Case Western Res. U., Cleve., 1984-90; chief maternal, fetal medicine Case Western Reserve U., 1989-90; assoc. prof., dir. maternal-fetal med. fellowship program Wake Forest U. Sch. Medicine, Winston-Salem, N.C., 1990-95, prof., 1995—, chief maternal-fetal medicine sect., 1997—2002; chmn. dept. ob-gyn. Albany (N.Y.) Med. Ctr. , 2002—. Contbr. articles to profl. jours. Grantee NIH, 1991-2002. Office: 47 New Scotland Ave Albany NY E-mail: veillej@mail.amc.edu.

VEIT, CLAIRICE GENE TIPTON, measurement psychologist; b. Monterey Park, Calif., Feb. 20, 1939; d. Albert Vern and Gene (Bunning) Tipton; children: Steven, Barbara, Laurette, Catherine. BA, UCLA, 1969, MA, 1970, PhD, 1974. Asst. prof. psychology Calif. State U., L.A., 1975-77, assoc. prof. psychology, 1977-80; rsch. psychologist The Rand Corp., Santa Monica, Calif., 1977—. Rsch. cons. NATO Tech. Ctr., The Hague, The Netherlands, 1980-81; faculty Rand Grad Sch., Santa Monica, 1993—. Developer subjective transfer function (STF) method to complex sys. analysis and the mental health inventory. Mem. LWV, NOW, Soc. Med. Decision-Making, Soc. for Judgement and Decision-Making, L.A. Opera League. Avocations: mountain climbing, playing piano, travel, music, theatre. Office: The Rand Corp 1700 Main St Santa Monica CA 90401-3297 E-mail: veit@rand.org.

VEIT, FRANCOIS, lawyer; b. Strasbourg, France, July 1, 1965; License in Philosophy, Sorbonne, Paris, 1987; Law Degree, Assas, Paris, 1990; LLM, Harvard, 1995. Mgr. Gide Loyrette Nouel, Prague, Czech Republic, 1999—. Office: Gide Loyrette Nouel Krakovska 9 Prague 1 Czech Republic

VEIT, KENNETH, dean, educator; DO, Phila. Coll. Osteo. Medicine, 1976. Med. dir. So. Huntington Co. Med. Ctr. , 1977—79; med. coord. Nat. Health Svc. Corp., Region III (USPHS) , 1980—81; chief clin. consultation br. U.S. Pub. Health Svc. , 1980—81; interim dean, asst. dean. gad. med. edn., dir. med. edn., chmn. divsn. cmty. medicine, dir. health care ctrs. Phila. Coll. Osteo. Medicine, dean, v.p. acad. affairs, 2002—. Lectr. in field; served numerous cmty. and govt. appts.; mem. several rev. bds. Recipient Humanitarian medal, USPHS, 1981. Office: 4170 City Ave Philadelphia PA 19131*

VEITCH, BOYER LEWIS, printing company executive; b. Phila., Oct. 20, 1930; s. Samuel Lewis and Agnes Mae (Bell) V.; m. Emmeline Barbara Smith, Nov. 22, 1952 (dec. Dec. 1994); children: William S., Nancy B., Thomas C.; m. Mary Chisholm Kiehn, Feb. 21, 1998. AB, Lafayette Coll., 1953; postgrad. Wharton Evening Sch., Acctg. and Fin., U. Pa., 1957-59. Advt. dir. Ware Bros. Co., Phila., 1956-62, v.p., 1962-69; salesman Zabel Bros. Co., 1969-75; chmn. Veitch Printing Corp., Lancaster, Pa., 1975—. Trustee Printers Disability Trust. Trustee Lafayette Coll., Easton, Pa., 1981-86, 87—, vice chmn. coll. rels. com., chmn. ann. fund, 1982-86, mem. fin. com., 1987-92, chmn. athletics and student affairs comn., 1992-97, mem. emeritus exec. com., 1997; mem. gen. adv. com. Lancaster County Career and Tech. Sch. System, 1996—; bd. dirs. Boys and Girls Club, Lancaster, 1980—, pres., 1990-92; dir. Boy's Club Lancaster Found., 1989—, pres., 1992—, elected to Boys and Girls Hall of Fame, 1999; dir. Gt. Valley Civic Assn., 1969-79; trustee Fulton Opera House Found., 1985-91, treas., 1987-89; bd. dirs. North Mus., 1992-94, Lancaster Airport Authority, 1994—, treas., 1994—; trustee PIA Disability Trust, 1994—; chmn. citizens for Schulze Com., Pa. 5th Congressional Dist., 1972-78; vestryman, sr. warden St. Peter's Ch. of Gt. Valley, 1972-78. Served with CIC, U.S. Army, 1954-56. Recipient Bronze Hope Chest award Nat. Multiple Sclerosis Soc., 1982, Nat. Svc. to Youth award Boys and Girls Clubs Am., 1992; named Small Bus. Person of Yr. Lancaster Co., 1991; named to Boys and Girls Club of Lancaster Alumni Hall of Fame, 1999, Graphic Arts Assn. Person of Yr., 2001; named Graphic Arts Assn. Person of Yr, 2001. Mem. SAR, Printing Industries Am. (dir. 1993-98), Graphic Arts Assn. (dir. 1980-98, chmn. 1990-92, Man of Yr. 2001), Lancaster C. of C. and Industry (dir. 1990-93), Lafayette Coll. Alumni Assn. (dir. 1974-78, pres. 1978-80), Pa. Economy League, Nat. Fedn. Ind. Bus., Phi Kappa Psi (past pres. and dir. chpt. alumni assn.). Clubs: Hamilton (bd. dirs. 1995—), Wash Day, Lancaster Country, Avalon Yacht, Lancaster Aero., Lancaster Pirates (first mate 2001—), Susquehanna Litho (dir. 1976-80, pres. 1979-80). Lodges: Rotary (Paul Harris fellow). Republican. Episcopalian. Home: 1044 Sylvan Rd Lancaster PA 17601-1933 also: 65 17th St E Avalon NJ 08202-2234 Office: Veitch Printing Corp 1740 Hempstead Rd Lancaster PA 17601-5889 E-mail: boygin@aol.com.

VEITCH, STEPHEN WILLIAM, investment counselor; b. Albuquerque, Aug. 19, 1927; s. Kenneth Easton and Edna (Miller) V.; B.A., U. N.Mex., 1949; LL.B., Stanford, 1957; student U. Nacional, Mex., 1949; m. Nancy Baker, June 28, 1951; children— Christopher Oxnard, Julia Blair. Bar: Calif., 1958. Probate adminstr. Wells Fargo Bank, San Francisco, 1957-59; sr. v.p. Van Strum & Towne, Inc., San Francisco, 1959-76, sr. v.p., 1976-82, pres., 1982-91, vice chmn, 1991-95, chmn., 1995. Mem. Guardsman, San Francisco, 1960—. With USNR, 1945-46; 1st lt. USAF, 1950-54. Mem. Am., San Francisco bar assns., Delta Theta Phi, Sigma Chi. Republican. Episcopalian. Clubs: Commonwealth, Pacific Union (San Francisco); Menlo Circus (Atherton, Calif.). Home: 33 Spencer Ln Atherton CA 94027-4038 Office: 505 Sansome St Ste 1001 San Francisco CA 94111-3134

VEITCH, THOMAS HAROLD, lawyer; b. Lake Odessa, Mich., June 9, 1938; s. Harold L. and Alice Lowe (Danes) V.; m. Ruta Purvins, 1963 (div. 1977); children: Kimura Lee, Gregory T.; m. Anne C. Veitch, Feb. 4, 1978; children: Stephanie Suzanne, Catherine. BS, Ctrl. Mich. U., Mt. Pleasant, 1960; JD, St. Mary's U., San Antonio, 1973. Bar: Tex. 1973. Mng. ptnr. Veitch & Britt PC, San Antonio, 1974-81; pres. Veitch & Assocs., 1981-95; ptnr. Soules & Wallace, 1995—. Dir. Tex. Legal Protection Plan, Austin, 1996—. Author: What You Need to Know to Settle With Insurance Companies, 1991, The Consultant's Guide to Litigation Services, How to be an Expert Witness, 1992. Bd. mem. Selective Svc., Local Bd. 113, 1982—; trustee San Antonio Rotary Youth Edn. Found., 1995—. Mem. Am. Assn. Ins. Mgmt. Cons. (dir. 1994—), CPCU Soc. (nat. com. mem. cons. and litigation sect. 1994—, pres. Alamo chpt. 1974), Assn. Atty.-Mediators (pres. 1996), San Antonio Bar Found. (trustee 1995—), St. Mary's Law Alumni Assn. (trustee 1996-2000), Rotary of San Antonio, Oak Hills Lions (pres. 1977), Sabor Toastmasters (pres. 1989). Avocations: golf, reading, travel, learning Spanish. Office: Soules & Wallace 100 W Houston St Ste 1500 San Antonio TX 78205-1433 E-mail: tveitch@soulesandwallace.com.

VEIZER, JÁN, geology educator; b. Pobedim, Slovakia, June 22, 1941; arrived in Can., 1973; s. Viktor and Brigita (Brandstetter) Veizer; m. Elena Ondrus, July 30, 1966; children: Robert, Andrew Douglas. Prom. Geol., Comenius U., Bratislava, Slovakia, 1964; RNDr, Comenius U., Bratislava, Slovak Republic, 1968; CSc, Slovak Acad. Sci., Bratislava, Slovakia, 1968; PhD, Australian Nat. U., Canberra, 1971. Asst. lectr. Comenius U., 1963-66; research scientist Slovak Acad. Sci., 1966-71; vis. asst. prof. UCLA, 1972; vis. rsch. scientist U. Göttingen, Fed. Republic Germany, 1972-73; rsch. scientist U. Tübingen, Fed. Republic Germany, 1973; from asst. prof. to full prof. U. Ottawa, Ont., Can., 1973—, rsch. chair NSERC/Noranda/Can. Inst. Advanced Rsch. Canada, 1997—; prof. Ruhr U., Bochum, Germany, 1988—; Disting. Univ. prof. U. Ottawa, 2001—. Cons. NASA, Houston, 1983—86; vis. prof., scholar Northwestern U., Evanston, Ill., 1983—87; vis. fellow Australian Nat. U., 1979; vis. prof. U. Tübingen, 1974; Lady Davis professorship Hebrew U., Jerusalem, 1987. Contbr. articles to profl. jours., chapters to books. Served to jr. lt. Med., 1965—66. Named Rsch. Prof. of Yr., 1987; recipient W. Leibniz prize, German Rsch. Found., 1992; fellow Humboldt, 1980, Killam Rsch., Can. Coun., 1986—88. Fellow: Geochem. Soc. Am., Geol. Soc. Am., Geol. Survey Slovak Rep. (Gold medal 2000), Geol. Soc. Can. (Past Pres. medal 1987, Logan medal 1995), Royal Soc. Can. (Willet G. Miller medal 1991, Bancroft medal 2000); mem.: Ski Club. Roman Catholic. Avocations: reading, hiking, skiing, history. Office: Dept Earth Scis U Ottawa Ottawa ON Canada K1N 6N5 also: Ruhr U Inst Geol Mineral Geophys Lehrstuhl Sedimentgeologie 44780 Bochum Germany

VEJVODA, EDWARD, aerospace company executive; b. N.Y.C., Apr. 18, 1924; s. Emil and Mary (Stuzinsky) V.; m. Mary Ellen Smith, June 12, 1949; children: Mary Diane, Karl Spencer, Gail Denise. BA in Chemistry, U. No. Colo., 1949, MA in Chemistry, 1951; postgrad., U. Denver, 1956-59. Analytical chemist Dow Chem. Co., Golden, Colo., 1952-60, mgr. rsch. and devel., 1961-64, 66-74; plutonium cons. ALKEM, Karlsruhe, Fed. Republic of Germany, 1964-65; dir. chem. ops. Rockwell Internat., Golden, 1975-85, exec. asst., 1986-87, ret., 1987; pvt. practice cons. Boulder, 1987—. Plutonium ops. cons. Rockwell Hanford Co., Richland, Wash., 1977-89; cons. SAIC, Germantown, Md., 1987-88, Los Alamos Tech. Assocs., 1989—. Patentee in field; contbr. articles to profl. jours. Served as sgt. AC, U.S. Army, 1943-46, PTO. Mem. Am. Chem. Soc. (awards com.), Inst. for Nuclear Materials Mgmt., Nat. Mgmt. Assn. (Excellence award 1986), Am. Legion, Sigma Xi. Lodges: Elks. Republican. Methodist. Avocations: hunting, fishing, boating.

VELA, LAURIE STORY, illustrator, writer, publisher, producer; b. Sacramento, Nov. 17, 1962; d. Harry and Hazel May (Triglia) Vela; m. Daniel Murphy; 1 child Jeremiah Vela-Murphy. AA in Comms., San Joaquin Delta Coll., Stockton, Calif., 1983; BA in Comms., U. Calif., Davis, 1990, MA in Edn., 1991. Tchg. asst. U. Calif., Davis, 1990—91; childcare specialist YMCA of the Redwoods, Boulder Creek, Calif., 1991—95; prin., performer, prodr. Laurie's Stories, Newtown Sq., Pa., 1992—. Cons., educator Loma Prieta (Calif.) Ind. Home Study, 1995—98, Green Valley Parent Co-Op Preschool, Palo Alto, Calif., 1996—98; presenter in field. Author, illustrator, prodr.: Leaping Literacy: Fun Phonics from A2Z, 1997, author, illustrator, prodr.: Laurie Story Audio Tapes, 1993—96, author, illustrator, prodr.: Environmental Musical Trilogy-Script's Castle, 1992, author, illustrator, performer, prodr.Leaping : Literacy Video Series, 12 shows, 2001—02, author, illustrator, performer, prodr.: Leaping Literacy Audio Series, 12 shows, 2002—; author: of more than 120 books. Recipient award for drama, Bank of Am., 1980. Mem.: Soc. Children's Book Authors and Illustrators, Children's Music Network, San Francisco Folk Music Club (children's activities coord. Camp Harmony 1994—). Avocations: nature, hiking, music, singing. Home and Office: Laurie's Stories 3514 Caley Rd Newtown Square PA 19073 E-mail: laurie@lauriestories.com.

VELARDE, HEIDE MARIE, publisher, writer; b. Honolulu, May 16, 1953; d. Margaret Curette, Nicholas Curette; m. Arthur Charles Velarde; children: Ryan, Aaron, Devin, Tori. Senior Clerk Typist Kelly Services, Kelly Girl Division, San Francisco, 1978—79; Accounting Technician Health and Human Services, Division of Accounting, Fiscal, and Budget Services, 1980—85; Data Entry /Clerk / Accounts Payable Kelly Services, Kelly Girl Division, Hayward, 1989—92; Publisher, Proprietor Crookbook Press, Union City, 1999—; Writer Amerecord, Hollywood, 2002—, Hilltop Records, Hollywood, 2002—. Author: A Fadeaway Dream of Justice to Redeem, 1999 (Certificate of Merit, 2000). Mem.: BMI. Avocation: reading, gardening, swimming. Home: 33244 Fourth Street Union City CA 94587-2104 Office: Crookbook Press 33244 Fourth Street Union City CA 94587-2104

VELARDO, JOSEPH THOMAS, molecular biology and endocrinology educator; b. Newark, Jan. 27, 1923; s. Michael Arthur and Antoinette (I.) V.; m. Forresta M.-M. Power, Aug. 12, 1948 (dec. July 1976). AB, U. No. Colo., 1948; SM, Miami U., Oxford, Ohio, 1949; PhD, Harvard U., 1952. Rsch. fellow in biology and endocrinology Harvard U., Cambridge, Mass., 1952-53; rsch. assoc. in pathology, ob-gyn. and surgery Harvard U. Sch. Medicine, Boston, 1953-55; asst. in surgery Peter Bent Brigham and Women's Hosp., 1954-55; asst. prof. anatomy and endocrinology Sch. Medicine, Yale U., New Haven, 1955-61; prof. anatomy, chmn. dept. N.Y. Med. Coll., N.Y.C., 1961-62; cons. N.Y. Fertility Inst., 1961-62; dir. Inst. for Study Human Reprodn., Cleve., 1962-67; prof. biology John Carroll U., 1962-67; mem. rsch. and edn. divs. St. Ann Ob-Gyn. Hosp., 1962-67, head dept. rsch., 1964-67; prof. anatomy Stritch Sch. Medicine Loyola U., Chgo., 1967-88, chmn. dept. anatomy Stritch Sch. of Medicine, 1967-73; v.p. Universal Rsch. Systems, Warren, Ohio, 1975—; pres. University Rsch. Systems, Lombard, 1979—, Internat. Basic and Biol.-Biomed. Curricula, Lombard, Ill., 1979—. Course moderator laparoscopy Brazil-Israel Congress on Fertility and Sterility, Brazil Soc. of Human Reprodn., Rio de Janeiro, 1973; mem. curriculum com. Yale U. Sch. Medicine, 1956—61, dir. exptl. mammalian labs., 1956—61; organizer, chmn. symposia in field. Author: (with others) Annual Reviews Physiology, Reproduction, 1961, Histochemistry of Enzymes in the Female Genital System, 1963, The Ovary, 1963, The Ureter, 1967, rev. edit., 1981; editor, contbr.: Endocrinology of Reproduction, 1958, The Essentials of Human Reproduction, 1958; cons. editor, co-author: The Uterus, 1959; contbr. Progestational Substances, 1958, Trophoblast and Its Tumors, 1959, The Vagina, 1959, Hormonal Steroids, Biochemistry, Pharmacology and Therapeutics, 1964, Human Reproduction, 1973; co-editor, contbr.: Biology of Reproduction, Basic and Clinical Studies, 1973; contbr. articles to profl. jours.; live broadcasts on major radio and TV networks on subjects of bioscis., biomed. careers and biomed. subjects; co-author, co-dir. med. movie on human reprodn. The Soft Anvil; life history and research highlights chronicled in The Endocrinologist, vol II, 2001. Apptd. U.S. del. to Vatican, 1964; charter mem. U.S. Rep. Presdl. Task Force, 1988—; charter mem. U.S. Rep. Nat. Senatorial Com., 1988—; mem. Rep. Senate Adv. Coun., 1997—; rep. U.S. Senate Inner Circle, 1988—, U.S. Rep. Senatorial Commn., 1991—. With USAAF, World War II, 1943-45. Decorated Presdl. Unit citation, 2 Bronze Stars; recipient award Lederle Med. Faculty Awards Com., 1955-58, Cert. of Achievement U.S. Rep. Nat. Senatorial Com., 1999, Disting. Alumni award, The William R. Ross award in sci., U. No. Colo., 1999; named hon. citizen City of Sao Paulo, Brazil, 1972; U.S. del. to Vatican, 1964. Fellow AAAS, N.Y. Acad. Scis. (co-organizer, chmn., consulting editor internat. symposium The Uterus), Gerontol. Soc., Pacific Coast Fertility Soc. (hon.); mem. French Nat. Soc. for Study of Sterility and Fertility (exec. hon. pres. IVth World Congress on Fertility and Sterility 1962), Am. Assn. Anatomists, Am. Soc. Zoologists, Soc. for Integrative and Comparative Biology (organizer symposium The Uterus), Am. Physiol. Soc. (vis. prof. 1962), Endocrine Soc., Soc. Endocrinology (Gt. Britain), Soc. Exptl. Biology and Medicine, Am. Soc. Study Sterility (Rubin award 1954), Internat. Fertility Assn., Pan Am. Assn. Anatomy (co-organizer symposium Reproduction 1972), Midwestern Soc. Anatomists (pres. 1973-74), Mexican Soc. Anatomy (hon.), Harvard Club, Sigma Xi, Kappa Delta Pi, Phi Sigma, Gamma Alpha, Alpha Epsilon Delta. Roman Catholic. Achievements include extensive original research and publications on the physiology and development of decidual tissue (experimental equivalent of the maternal portion of the placenta) in the rat; biological investigation of eighteen human adenohypophyses (anterior lobes of the human pituitary glands); induction of ovulation utilizing highly purified adenohypophyseal gonadotropic hormones in mammals; the pacemaker action of ovarian sex steroid hormones in reproductive processes; and the interaction of steroids in reproductive mechanisms. Office: 607 E Wilson Ave Lombard IL 60148-4062 *Personal philosophy: Success is best highlighted by the invincible instruments of character, truth, integrity, hard work, thinking, running the extra mile, leading or giving help where no other help seems forthcoming, recognizing the talents of our fellow man and lady, and above all, practicing of the Golden Rule.*

VELAYO, RICHARD SORIANO, psychologist, educator, researcher; s. Rodolfo Ratliff and Teresita Makasiar)Soriano) V. BA in Psychology and Behavioral Scis., De La Salle U., Manila, The Philippines, 1985; MA in Applied Behavior Analysis, U. Pacific, 1988; PhD in Psychology and Edn., U. Mich., 1993. Lectr. De La Salle U., Manila, 1985; grad. tchg. instr., rsch. assoc. U. Pacific, Stockton, Calif., 1986-88; grad. rsch. assoc. U. Mich., Ann Arbor, 1988-89, grad. tchg. instr., 1989-92; adj. asst. prof. Mont. State U., Bozeman, 1993-94; computer coord., assoc. prof. Dept. Psychology, Pace U., N.Y.C., 1994—. Assoc. editor Jour. Rsch. on Computing in Edn., 1994—; editl. bd. Internat. Jour. Instructional Media, 1994—; editor-in-chief Psych-Eye newsletter, 1996—. Pace U. scholar, 1995, 97 Mem. APA (Distinction in Rsch. award 1993), Am. Psychol. Soc., Am. Ednl. Rsch. Assn., N.Y. State Psychol. Assn., Coun. of Tchrs. of Undergrad. Psychology, Ea. Psychol. Assn., N.Y. Acad. Scis., Sigma Xi. Office: Pace Univ Dept Psychology 41 Park Row Rm 1324 New York NY 10038-1508 E-mail: rcgpsy@aol.com.

VELAZQUEZ, NYDIA M. congresswoman; b. Yabucoa, P.R., Mar. 28, 1953; Grad., U. P.R.; MA, NYU, 1976. Mem. 103rd-106th Congress from 12th N.Y. dist., Washington, 1992—; mem. banking and fin. svcs. com. 105th-106th Congress from 12th N.Y. dist., dem. mem. small bus. com. Ranking Dem. mem. of the Com. on Sml. Bus., 106th Congress. Office: US Ho of Reps 2241 Rayburn HOB Washington DC 20515-0001*

VELDE, JOHN ERNEST, JR. investment company executive; b. Pekin, Ill., June 15, 1917; s. John Ernest and Alga (Anderson) V.; m. Shirley Margaret Walker, July 29, 1940 (dec. 1969); 1 dau., Drew; m. Gail Patrick, Sept. 28, 1974 (dec. July 1980); m. Gretchen Swanson Pullen, Nov. 7, 1981. AB, U. Ill., 1938. Pres. Velde, Roelfs & Co., Pekin, 1955-60; dir. Herget Nat. Bank, 1948-75, Kroehler Mfg. Co., 1974-81; pres. Paisano Prodns., Inc., 1980-94, mng. ptnr., 1994—, The Gardner Partnership, 1994—. Trustee Pekin Pub. Library, 1948-69, Pekin Meml. Hosp., 1950-69, Everett McKinley Dirksen Rsch. Ctr., 1965-74, Am. Libr. Assn. Endowment, 1976-82, Joint Coun. Econ. Edn., 1977-83, Ctr. Am. Archeology, 1978-83, Western Heritage Mus., Omaha, 1994—; chmn. Am. Libr. Trustee Assn. Found., 1976; chmn. trustees, bd. dirs. Ctr. Ulcer Rsch. and Edn. Found., 1977-82; mem. bd. councilors Brain Rsch. Inst. UCLA, 1977-82; mem. Nat. Commn. on Libr. and Info. Sci., 1970-79; mem. adv. bd. on White House Conf. on Librs., 1976-80; bd. dirs. U. Ill. Found., 1977-83, Omaha Pub. Libr. Found., 1985-92, James Madison Coun. Libr. Congress, 1990—; vice chmn. U. Ill. Pres.' Coun., 1977-79, chmn., 1979-81, mem. fin. resources coun. steering com., 1976-78; mem. adv. coun. UCLA Grad. Sch. Libr. and Info. Sci., 1981-82; pres. Ill. Valley Library System, 1965-69; dir. Lakeview Ctr. for Arts and Scis., Peoria, Ill., 1962-73; mem. Nat. Book Com., 1969-74. Served as lt. (j.g.) USNR, World War II. Mem. Am. Libr. Trustee Assn. (regional v.p. 1970-72, chmn. internat. rels. com. 1973-76), Internat. Boy Scouts (Baden-Powell fellow 1987—), Kappa Sigma. Clubs: Chgo. Yacht, Internat. (Chgo.); California (Los Angeles); Outrigger Canoe (Honolulu); Thunderbird Country (Rancho Mirage, Calif.); Chaine des Rotisseurs, Chevaliers du Tastevin; Circumnavigators (N.Y.C.); Omaha, Omaha Country; Happy Hollow, Old Baldy (Saratoga, Wyo.), Eldorado Country (Indian Wells, Calif.). Home: 8405 Indian Hills Dr Omaha NE 68114-4099 also: 40-231 Club View Dr Rancho Mirage CA 92270-3527 also: 123 Arapahoe Dr Saratoga WY 82331

VELDEY, BONNIE, special education educator; b. Mpls., Jan. 24, 1960; d. George Joseph III and Ethel Annette Ackо;m. Steve Douglas Veldey, June 13, 1991; 1 child, Tyler George. AA, Inver Grove C.C., Inver Grove Heights, Minn., 1989; BA, Coll. St. Catherine, 1991; MA in Spl. Edn., U. St. Thomas, 1998. Sci. tchr. Roma (Tex.) Ind. Sch. Dist., 1991-92; spl. edn. tchr. Clark County Sch. Dist., Las Vegas, Nev., 1996-99; pvt. practice spl. edn. tchr. Mpls., 1999—2001; tchr. spl. edn. St. Louis Park (Minn.) Pub. Schs., 2001—. Democrat. Roman Catholic. Home: 4331 Minnehaha Ave Minneapolis MN 55406-3908

VELEZ, DIANA, historian, educator; b. N.Y.C., Mar. 11, 1949; d. Ismael Velez Rodriguez and Adorasion Pineiro Wiscovitch Velez. BA, CUNY, 1971; MA, PhD, Princeton U., 1977. Assoc. dir. Ctr. Latin Am. Studies U. Pitts., 1984-87; sr. program officer Tinker Found., N.Y.C., 1987-90; asst. dean arts & scis. U. Ctrl. Fla., Orlando, 1991-95, history faculty, 1995—. Doctoral fellowship Ford Found., 1971. Mem. Am. Hist. Assn., Soc. Spanish and Portuguese History, Conf. on Latin Am. History. Office: U Ctrl Fla History Dept PO Box 161350 Orlando FL 32816-1350 E-mail: velez@pegasus.cc.ucf.edu.

VELICER, JANET SCHAFBUCH, retired elementary school educator; b. Cedar Rapids, Iowa, Aug. 27, 1941; d. Allan J. and Geraldine Frances (Stuart) Schafbuch; m. Leland Frank Velicer, Aug. 17, 1963 (dec. Dec. 2000); children: Mark Allan, Gregory Jon, Daniel James. BS, Iowa State U., 1963, MS, 1966; cert. Elem. Edn., Mich. State U., 1976. Tchr. chemistry Prendergast High Sch., Upper Darby, Pa., 1964-65; tchr. home econs. Cardinal O'Hara High Sch., Springfield, 1965-66; substitute tchr. Pa., Mich., 1967-76; elem. tchr. Winans Elem. Sch., Waverly, Mich., 1976-78, Wardcliff Elem. Sch., Okemos, 1978-94; tchr. gifted and talented alternative program grades 4 and 5 Hiawatha Elem. Sch., 1994-95; tchr. grade 4 Wardcliff Elem. Sch., 1995-2001; ret., 2001. Computer coord., Great Books coord.; dist. com. mem. math, computer, substance abuse, cable TV, evaluation revision Okemos Pub. Schs., Instrnl. Coun.; del. Mich. Edn. Exch. Opportunity Program, Germany, 1999. Author: (video) Wardcliff School Documentary, 1982, The Integrated Arts Program of the Okemos Elementary Schools, 1983. Citizens adv. com. to develop a five-yr. plan, 1982-83, Bldg. utilization adv. com., 1983-84, Cmty. use of schs. adv. com., 1984-85, Strategic planning steering com., 1989-90, Taking our schs. into tomorrow com., 1990-91, Bonding election steering com., 1991; chmn. wellness com. Okemos Pub. Schs., 1993-95; bd. dirs. Okemos Music Patrons, 1981-86, pres., 1984-86; faculty rep. PTO; mem. leadership coun. Nat. Inst. Clin. Application Behavioral Medicine, 1998—; chaperone Okemos H.S. German Club Exch., 1987, Benton Cmty. H.S. Spanish Club Exch., Mex., 1995, Costa Rica, 1999, Spain, 2001. Recipient Classrooms of Tomorrow Tchr. award Mich. Dept. Edn., 1990. Mem. NEA, NAFE, Nat. Ret. Tchrs. Assn., Mich. Edn. Assn., Inst. Noetic Scis., Okemos Edn. Assn. (exec. coun.), Phi Kappa Phi, Mich. Coun. Tchrs. Math., Omicron Nu, Iota Sigma Pi. Democrat. Avocations: swimming, reading, hiking, travelogs, cultural events. Home: 2678 Blue Haven Ct East Lansing MI 48823-3804 E-mail: jvelicer@msu.edu.

VELICK, SIDNEY FREDERICK, research biochemist, educator; b. Detroit, May 3, 1913; s. Harry Alexander and Ella (Stocker) V.; m. Bernadette Stemler, Sept. 5, 1941; children: William Frederick, Martha Elizabeth. BS, Wayne State U., 1935; PhD, U. Mich., 1938. Research fellow parasitology Johns Hopkins U., 1939-40; research asso. chemistry Yale U., 1941-45; mem. biol. chemistry dept. Washington U. Sch. Medicine, St. Louis, 1946-63, prof. biol. chemistry, 1958-64; prof., head dept. biol. chemistry U. Utah Coll. Medicine, 1964-79, prof. emeritus, 1988—. Mem. biochemistry study sect. NIH. Assoc. editor: Archives Biochemistry and Biophysics; editorial bd.: Jour. Biol. Chemistry; contbr. papers on enzyme chemistry to tech. lit. Co-founder, pres. Alliance for the Mentally Ill Utah, 1980-85. Mem. NAS, AAAS, Am. Soc. Biol. Chemists, Am. Chem. Soc., Sigma Xi. Home: 4183 Parkview Dr Salt Lake City UT 84124-3436

VELIMIROVICH, BORIS, urologist; b. Pisek, Czech Republic, May 10, 1960; came to U.S., 1989; s. Alexandar M. and Ruzena (Supova) V.; m. Karina Skoczova, Dec. 10, 1988; children: Boris Milutin, Filip Alexandar, Ella Karina. MD, Charles U., Prague, Czech Republic, 1985, ECFMG, 1992. Diplomate Czechoslovak Bd. Pediatrics, Am. Bd. Urology. Pvt. practice pediat., Pisek, Czech Republic, 1987-89; resident in urology Emory U., Atlanta, 1992-96, chief resident urology, 1997-98; pvt. practice Urology Assocs. Middle Ga., P.C., Milledgeville, 1998-2000, Oconee Urology, P.C., 2000—. Fellow Am. Coll. Surgeons; mem. Am. Assn. Clin. Urologists, Am. Urol. Assn., Czech Urol. Soc. Home: 155 Lakecrest Dr NE Milledgeville GA 31061-9093 E-mail: bvelimi@alltel.net.

VELINOV, MILEN TODOROV, physician, researcher; b. Varna, Bulgaria; s. Todor Velinov and Rumiana Mincheva; m. Milena Moraru, Dec. 18, 1983; children: Yana, Philip. MD, Higher Med. Inst., Sofia, Bulgaria, 1986; PhD, Biomed. Inst., Sofia, 1995. Diplomate Am. Bd. Pediat. Rsch. asst. prof. Inst. Endocrinology, Sofia, 1987-91; fellow U. Conn. Health Ctr., Farmington., 1991-95; resident in pediat. N.Y. Meth. Hosp., Bklyn., 1995-98; rsch. sci. N.Y. State Inst. Basic Rsch., Staten Island, N.Y., 1998—; fellow clin. genetics Maimonides Med. Ctr., Bklyn., 1999—. Vis. fellow Genethon, Evry, France, 1993; instr. Biomed Inst., Sofia, 1993; adj. asst. pediat. N.Y. Hosp., 1997-98; lectr. genetics Maimonides Med. Ctr., 1999-2000. Contbr. med. articles to profl. jours. Recipient Clin. Rsch. award Soc. for Pediat. Rsch., 1994. Fellow Am. Acad. Pediatrics; mem. Am. Soc. Human Genetics, Prader-Willi Syndrome Assn. Avocations: sports, skiing, tennis. Office: NYS Inst for Basic Rsch 1050 Forest Hill Rd Staten Island NY 10314 E-mail: milen.velinov@omr.state.ny.us.

VELISARIS, CHRIS NICHOLAS, financial analyst; b. Berwyn, Ill., June 2, 1961; s. Nicholas Chris and Panagiota Nicholas (Georgiou) V.; m. Mary Elizabeth Vlahos, July 23, 1994; children: Christopher Nicholas, Madalyn Penelope. BS, U. Ill., 1983; MS, U. Wash., 1985; MBA, Dartmouth Coll., 1990; postgrad., U. Naples, Italy, 1991-94. Rsch. engr. Amoco Chem. Co., Naperville, Ill., 1983, 85-94; cons. Orco Ltd., Athens, 1989; rsch. mgr. U. Wash., Seattle, 1990-94; sr. staff specialist corp. fin. United Airlines, Chgo., 1994-99; project mgr. corp. fin. GATX Corp., 1999—. Founder, prin. officer Velisaris Investment Cons. Svcs., Inc., Brookfield, Ill., 1994—; cons. in field. Author: Proc. 31st Ann. Nat. Sampe Symp., 1986, Polymer Engrng. and Sci., 1986, 88, Proc. of the 5th European Conf. on Comp. Materials, 1992. Counselor Valleyview Correctional Ctr., Ill. Benedictine Coll., St. Charles, 1988; advisor Jr. Achievement of Chgo., Naperville, 1987-88. Mem. Tri-Orgn. of Amoco Corp. (dir. 1987-88). Greek Orthodox. Avocations: skiing, golf, tennis, chess, investing. Home: 59 Drexel Ave La Grange IL 60525-5845 Office: United Airlines WHQFT PO Box 66100 Chicago IL 60666-0100

VELLACOTT, MAURICE, member of parliament; b. Wadena, Can., Sept. 29, 1955; married; 4 children. B, Briercrest Sch.; M, Can. Theol. Sem.; D, Trinity Internat. U. Elected mem. Saskatoon Dist. Health Bd.; mem. House of Commons, Ottawa, Canada, 1997—, vice chair standing com. human resources develop. Can., dep. critic com. human resources develop. Can., mem. sub. com. status of persons with disabilities, dep. critic health, assoc. critic aboriginal affairs, co-chair all-party pro-life caucus. Mem. Can. Alliance Family Caucus; co-chair Stockwell Day Leadership Campaign, Saskatchewan. Mem.: Saskatchewan Landlard Assn., Saskatchewan Taxpayers Assn., Saskatoon C. of C., Toastmasters, Can. Club Saskatoon. Can. Alliance Caucus. Office: House of Commons 513 Confederation Bldg Ottawa ON K1A oA6 Canada Address: Unit 3-844 51st St Saskatoon SK 57K 5C7 Canada Office Fax: 613-992-3085., 306-975-4728. E-mail: vellam@parl.gc.ca.*

VELLEMAN, DANIEL JON, mathematics educator; b. Manhasset, N.Y., Aug. 10, 1954; s. Mortiz and Ruth V.; m. Shelley Lynne Jeffery, June 9, 1979. BA, Dartmouth Coll., 1976; PhD, U. Wis., 1980. Instr. U. Tex., Austin, 1980-83; asst. prof. Amherst (Mass.) Coll., 1983-87, assoc. prof., 1987-92, prof., 1992—. Author: How to Prove it, 1994, Which Way Did the Bicycle Go?, 1996, Philosophies of Mathematics, 2002; mem. editl. bd. Am. Math. Monthly, 1997—; editor: Dolciani Mathematical Expositions, 1999; contbr. Recipient grant NSF, 1982-83, 84-86, 86-87. Mem. Math. Assn. Am. (Lester R. Ford award 1994, Carl B. Allendoerfer Award 1996), Am. Math. Soc., Assn. Symbolic Logic. Office: Amherst Coll Dept Maths and Comp Sci Amherst MA 01002

VELLENGA, KATHLEEN OSBORNE, retired state legislator; b. Alliance, Nebr., Aug. 5, 1938; d. Howard Benson and Marjorie (Menke) Osborne; m. James Alan Vellenga, Aug. 9, 1959; children: Thomas, Charlotte Vellenga Landreau, Carolyn Vellenga Berman. BA, Macalester Coll., 1959. Tchr. St. Paul Pub. Schs., 1959-60, Children's Ctr. Montessori, St. Paul, 1973-74, Children's Ho. Montessori, St. Paul, 1974-79; mem. Minn. Ho. of Reps., 1980-94, mem. tax. com. and rules com., 1991—, chmn. St. Paul del., 1985-89, chmn. criminal justice div., 1989-90, chmn. crime and family law div., 1987-88, mem. Dem. steering com., 1987-94, chmn. judiciary, 1991, 92, chmn. edn. fin., 1992-93, 93-94. Mem. St. Paul Family Svcs. Bd., 1994-95; exec. dir. St. Paul/Ramsey County Children's Initiative, 1994-2000. Chmn. Healthstart, St. Paul, 1987-91; mem. Children, Youth and Families Consortium, 1995-99, Macalester Coll. Bd. Alumni, 1995-01; chair Minn. Higher Edn. Svcs. Coun., 2000—; mem. Citizen's League Bd., Minn., 1999—, State Commn. Cmty. Svc., 00—. Mem. LWV (v.p. St. Paul chpt. 1979), Minn. Women Elected Ofcls. (vice chair 1994). Democrat. Presbyterian.

VELMANS, LOET ABRAHAM, retired public relations executive; b. Amsterdam, Netherlands, Mar. 18, 1923; s. Joseph and Anna (Cohen) V.; m. Pauline Edith Van Hessen, Mar. 29, 1949; children: Marianne and Hester (twins), Jessica. Grad., U. Amsterdam, 1947. Info. officer Dutch Govt. in, Singapore, 1945-47; with Hill & Knowlton, Inc., 1953-86; v.p. Hill Knowlton Internat., Geneva, 1959-69, pres., 1960-74, vice chmn., 1969-76, pres. N.Y.C., 1976-86, chmn. bd., chief exec. officer, 1980-86. Contbr. articles on multinat. corps. to profl. jours. Bd. dirs. Lincoln Ctr. Inst., Bennington Coll., Boston Symphony Orch. Decorated Grande Ufficiale Order of Merit, Italy, 1989. Mem. Mid-Atlantic Club of N.Y. Inc. (pres. emeritus). Home: PO Box 178 Sheffield MA 01257-0178

VELTE, PAUL CHRISTIAN, IV, lawyer; b. Ft. Monmouth, N.J., Nov. 22, 1961; s. Paul Christian III and Carol Marie (Griffin) V. BA, North Tex. State U., 1985; JD, U. Tex., 1988. Atty., Austin, Tex., 1989—. Founder Peaceable Texans for Firearm Rights, Austin, 1994; dir., sec./treas. Am. Civil Rights League, Austin, 1994. Recipient Freedom Fighter award ABATE Tex., 1989. Mem. NRA, Gun Owners Am., Tex. Rifle Assn., Lawyer's 2d Amendment Soc. Avocations: computers, firearms, motorcycles. Office: 1122 Colorado St Ste 2320 Austin TX 78701-2132 Fax: 512-476-4974.

VELTMAN, JAY H. retired pediatrician; b. Grand Rapids, Mich., Oct. 3, 1929; s. Henry and Anna Veltman; m. Alberta Veltman, June 10, 1954; children: Jayne Gort, Lora Boogaard, Beth. AB, Calvine Coll., 1951; MD, U. Mich., 1955. Diplomate Am. Bd. Pediatrics. Pediatrician Childrens Hosp. Mich., Detroit, 1959-61; pvt. practice Grandville, 1961—2001. 1st lt. USN, 1957-59. Mem. AMA, Assn. Am. Physicians. Home: 3645 Wentworth Dr SW Wyoming MI 49509-3140

VELTMAN, MARTINUS J. retired physics educator; b. The Netherlands, 1931; PhD, U. Utrecht, The Netherlands, 1963. John D. MacArthur prof. physics U. Mich., Ann Arbor, now prof. emeritus. Recipient High Energy and Particle Physics prize, European Physics Soc., 1993, P.A.M. Dirac Medal and Prize, Internat. Ctr. for Theoretical Physics, 1996, Nobel prize in Physics, 1999. Office: U Mich Dept Physics 2477 Randall Lab 500 E University Ave Ann Arbor MI 48109-1120

VELZY, CHARLES O. mechanical engineer; b. Oak Park, Ill., Mar. 17, 1930; s. Charles R and Ethel B. V.; m. Marilyn A. Gilman, Aug. 17, 1957; children: Charles Mark, Barbara Helen, Patricia Ethel. BSM.E., U. Ill., 1953, BS in Civil Engring., 1960, MS in San. Engring., 1959. Registered profl. engr., N.Y., 11 other states. Design engr., project engr. Nussbaumer, Clarke & Velzy, N.Y.C., 1959-66; sec.-treas., dir. Charles R Velzy Assos., Inc., Armonk, N.Y., 1966-76; pres. Charles R. Velzy Assoc., Inc., 1976-92; v.p. Roy F. Weston Inc., 1987-92; pres. Charles O. Velzy, P.E., Lyndonville, Vt., 1992—. Contbr. articles to profl. jours. Mem. White Plains (N.Y.) Bldg. Code Appeals Bd., 1970-92. With U.S. Army, 1954-56. Recipient Disting. Alumnus award U. Ill., 1989. Fellow ASME (chmn. solid waste processing divsn 1973-74, mem. bd. rsch. and tech. dev. 1974-78, 2000—, bd. govs. 1983-84, pres. 1989-90, Centennial medal 1980, medal of achievement 1981, Dedicated Svc. award 1986), Am. Cons. Engrs. Coun.; mem. ASTM, ASCE (life), NSPE (Engr. of the Yr. 1980), Am. Acad. Environ. Engrs. (trustee 1984-87, treas. 1993-97, Stanley E. Kappe award 1998), Am. Water Works Assn. (life), Water Environ. Fedn., Air Waste Mgmt. Assn. Methodist. *After deciding on what is needed in a specific situation, based on the facts, establish your objectives and goals and persist to a successful conclusion.*

VENABLE, SUSAN CHRISTINE, artist; b. Long Beach, Calif., Dec. 30, 1944; d. Edwin Walter and Betty Ann (Justad) V.; m. Charles W. Vinick, Feb. 6, 1994; 1 child, Mern Kelsey Graefe. BFA magna cum laude, Calif. State U., Dominguez Hills, 1981; MFA, UCLA, 1984. Studio artist, Venice, Calif., 1975-98. One-woman shows include Marilyn Butler Fine Art, Scottsdale, Ariz., 1987, Maloney/Butler Gallery, Santa Monica, Calif., Tally Richards Gallery, Taos, N.Mex., 1989, Scottsdale Ctr. for the Arts, 1990, Rutledge Contemporary Art, Venice, 1991, Sun Art Mus., Sun City, Ariz., 1992, Howard Hughes Ctr., L.A., 1995; exhibited in group shows at Nancy Margolis Gallery, Portland, Maine, 1988, Palo Alto (Calif.) Cultural Ctr., 1988, Marilyn Butler Fine Art, Santa Fe, N.Mex., 1988, Lasorda/Iri Gallery, L.A., 1988, S.I.T.E., L.A., 1988, 89, Art L.A., 1989, 92, Boulder Ctr. for Visual Arts, 1989, Donna Rose Gallery, Sun Valley, Idaho, 1990, Nelson Fine Arts Ctr., Ariz. State U., Tempe, 1990, L.A. County Mus. of Art, 1991, Wyman Bldg., Mpls., 1992, Indigo, L.A., 1992, Brendan Walter Gallery, Santa Monica, 1993, N.I.C.A., Las Vegas, 1993, Gensler Assocs., Santa Monica, 1993, Valerie Miller Fine Arts, Palm Springs, Calif., 1993, Santa Monica Mus. of Art, 1994, Venice (Calif.) Art Walk, 1994, Nev. Inst. of Contemporary Art, Las Vegas, 1994, 95, 96, G.T. Gallery, Quechee, Vt., 1994, Mad River Post, Santa Monica, 1994, Steelcase, Pacific Design Ctr., L.A., 1995, MWP, Hollywood, Calif., 1995, Carthew Thompson, Beverly Hills, 1995; Valerie Miller Fine Art, Palm Desert, Calif., 1996, Joanne Chappell Gallery, San Francisco, 1996, S.O.F.A., Miami Beach, Fla., 1996, Art Network, Atlanta, 1996, Art Source, Indpls., 1996; represented in permanent pvt. and public collections. Faculty scholar UCLA, 1982. Home: 2323 Foothill Ln Santa Barbara CA 93105-2316

VENABLE, WILLIAM RALPH, III, marketing executive, finance executive; b. Kansas City, Mo., Mar. 18, 1959; s. William Ralph and Kathleen Loretta (Krivas) V. BS in Journalism, U. Kans., 1981; MBA in Mktg. and Fin., Rockhurst Coll., 1984; PhD, U. Mo., 2000. Film booker 20th Century Fox Film Corp., Kansas City, Mo., 1981-83; dir. alumni rels. Rockhurst Coll., 1983-86; fin. cons. Merrill Lynch, 1987-89; ops. mgr. AMC Entertainment, 1990-91; mktg. mgr. SecureAmerica, Omaha, 1991-92; event mgr. CCL-Hallmark Cards, Kansas City, 1993; dir. reseller rels. Ruf Strategic Solutions, Olathe, Kans., 1993-96; v.p., dir. database mktg. and strategies UMB Bank, N.A., Kansas City, Mo., 1997-2000; bus. integration mgr. portal strategy and devel. Sprint Corp., 2000—. Bd. dirs. Wilraven Capital Co., LLC; adv. bd. Barley's Ltd., 1995-97, LatAm Internat. Trading LLC; adv. dir. Marketsolutions LLC, 1995—, cons. River City Products, Inc., North Kansas City, 1986—. Author: (book) How to and Where of Kansas City Barbeque, 1989, Kansas City Barbeque Book, 1996; author, editor: (book) Absolute Barbeque, 1994. Founder O.E. Ellis Soc., Kansas City, 1984, Greater Omaha BBQ Soc., 1991, co-founder Students of the Social Sci. Consortium, Kansas City, 1996; co-chmn. Jazz Feast for Project ReStart, 1997-99, bd. dirs., 1999—; bd. dirs. Am. Cancer Soc., Kan sas City, 1983-88; mem. exec. programs adv. com. U. Mo., 1997-2000; rsch. com. In itiative for Competitive Inner Cities, Kansas City, Mo., 1996-98. Recipient Arthur Mag PhD fellowship U. Mo., 1996-97, Marjorie Powell Allen Grad. fellowship U. Mo., 1995-96. Mem. SAR (Kans. state treas. 1988), Greater Kansas City C. of C. Centurions (retreat chair 1986-87, steering com. 1994-95, 97-2000, alumni pres.-elect 1997-98, alum ni steering com. 1992-95, pres. 1999-2000), Centurions Found. (chmn. bd. 2001—), Native Sons of Kansas City, Univ. Club Kansas City (mem. house com. 1996-97, bd. dirs. 1997-99), Phi Kappa Sigma, Alpha Kappa Psi, Gamma Omicron Beta, University Senate. Republican. Roman Catholic. Avocations: writer, chef, historic renovator. Home: 8723 Aberdeen Dr Leawood KS 66206-1611 Office: Sprint MS KJOPKN0104 7500 W 110th Overland Park KS 66210 E-mail: wrvc57@umkc.edu.

VENABLE KING, GIOVAN, lawyer, minister; b. Winston-Salem, N.C., Dec. 10, 1956; d. Joel William and Jo Ann (Harbour) V. AB in Music magna cum laude, Dartmouth Coll., 1979; MDiv, Harvard U., 1983; JD, Stanford U., 1988. Bar: Calif. 1989, D.C. 1990, U.S. Supreme Ct. 1994; ordained minister Congregational Ch., 1984. Assoc. Wyman Bautzer Kuchel & Silbert, L.A., 1988-90; assoc. Gipson Hoffman & Pancione, 1990-92; pvt. practice, 1992—. Contbr. articles to profl. jours.; editor Cal West Congregationalist, 1990—; mem. Stanford Law Rev., 1987-89. Mem. The Ebell L.A., Phi Beta Kappa. Achievements include being the first woman ordained at the oldest Protestant Ch. in Southern California and the first woman to head a Southern California Congregational Church in 1992. Avocations: piano, running, travel, tennis. Office: 419 N Larchmont Blvd Los Angeles CA 90004-3013

VENDLER, HELEN HENNESSY, literature educator, poetry critic; b. Boston, Apr. 30, 1933; d. George and Helen (Conway) Hennessy; 1 son, David. AB, Emmanuel Coll., 1954; PhD, Harvard U., 1960; PhD (hon.), U. Oslo, 1981; D.Litt. (hon.), Smith Coll., 1980, Kenyon Coll., 1982, U. Hartford, 1985; DLitt (hon.), Union Coll., 1986, Columbia U., 1987, Washington U., 1991; D.Litt. (hon.), Marlboro Coll., 1989, Yale U., 2000; DHL (hon.), Dartmouth Coll., 1992, U. Mass., Amherst, 1992, Bates Coll., 1992, U. Toronto, Ont., Can., 1992, Trinity Coll., Dublin, Ireland, 1993, Fitchburg State U., 1990, U. Cambridge, 1997, Nat. U., Ireland, 1998, Wabash Coll., 1998, U. Mass, Dartmouth, 2000, Yale U., , 2000, U. Aberdeen, 2000, Tufts U., 2001. Instr. Cornell U., Ithaca, N.Y., 1960-63; lectr. Swarthmore (Pa.) Coll. and Haverford (Pa.) Coll., 1963-64; asst. prof. Smith Coll., Northampton, Mass., 1964-66; assoc. prof. Boston U., 1966-68, prof., 1968-85. Fulbright lectr. U. Bordeaux, France, 1968-69; vis. prof. Harvard U., 1981-85, Kenan prof., 1985—. Porter U. prof., 1990—, assoc. acad. dean, 1987-92, sr. fellow Harvard Soc. Fellows, 1981-93; poetry critic New Yorker, 1978-99; mem. ednl. adv. bd. Guggenheim Found., 1991-2001, Pulitzer Prize Bd., 1991-99. Author: Yeats's Vision and the Later Plays, 1963, On Extended Wings: Wallace Stevens' Longer Poems, 1969, The Poetry of George Herbert, 1975, Part of Nature, Part of Us, 1980, The Odes of John Keats, 1983, Wallace Stevens: Words Chosen Out of Desire, 1984; editor: Harvard Book of Contemporary American Poetry, 1985, Voices and Visions: The Poet in America, 1987, The Music of What Happens, 1988, Soul Says, 1995, The Given and the Made, 1995, The Breaking of Style, 1995, Poems, Poets, Poetry, 1995, The Art of Shakespeare's Sonnets, 1997, Seamus Heaney, 1998. Bd. dirs. Nat. Humanities Ctr., 1989-93. Recipient Lowell prize, 1969, Explicator prize, 1969, award Nat. Inst. Arts and Letters, 1975, Radcliffe Grad. Soc. medal, 1978, Nat. Book Critics award, 1980, Keats-Shelley Assn. award, 1994, Truman Capote award, 1996; Fulbright fellow, 1954, AAUW fellow, 1959, Guggenheim fellow, 1971-72, Am. Coun. Learned Socs. fellow, 1971-72, NEH fellow, 1980, 85, 94, Overseas fellow Churchill Coll., Cambridge, 1980, Charles Stewart Parnell fellow Magdalene Coll., Cambridge, 1996, hon. fellow, 1996—. Mem. MLA (exec. coun. 1972-75, pres. 1980), AAAL, English Inst. (trustee 1977-85), Am. Acad. Arts and Scis. (v.p. 1992-95), Norwegian Acad. Letters and Sci., Am. Philos. Soc. (Jefferson medal 2000), Phi Beta Kappa. Home: 54 Trowbridge St # 2 Cambridge MA 02138-4113 Office: Harvard U Dept English Barker Center Cambridge MA 02138-3929

VENEMAN, ANN M. federal official; b. Modesto, Calif., June 29, 1949; d. John G. and Nita D. (Bomberger) V. BA in polit. sci., U. Calif., Davis, 1970; M in pub. policy, U. Calif., Berkeley, 1971; JD, U. Calif., 1976. Bar: Calif. 1976, U.S. Supreme Ct. 1981. Atty. San Francisco Bay Area Rapid Transit Dist., 1976-78; dep. pub. defender City of Modesto, 1978-80; ptnr. Damrell, Damrell & Nelson, Modesto, 1980-86; asst. to adminstr. Fgn. Agrl. Svc., 1986-87, assoc. adminstr., 1987-89; dep. under-sec. Internat. Affairs and Commodity Programs, 1989-91; dep. sec. Dept. Agriculture, Washington, 1991-93; sec. Calif. Dept. Food and Agr., 1996-99, USDA, Washington, 2001—. Office: USDA Office Sec 14th & Independence Ave SW Washington DC 20250-0001*

VENERABLE, SHIRLEY MARIE, gifted education educator; b. Washington, Nov. 12, 1931; d. John Henry and Jessie Josephine (Young) Washington; m. Wendell Grant Venerable, Feb. 15, 1959; children: Angela Elizabeth Maria Venerable-Joyner, Wendell Mark. PhB, Northwestern U., 1963; MA, Roosevelt U., 1976, postgrad., 1985. Cert. in diagnostic and prescriptive reading, gifted edn., finger math., fine arts, Ill. Tchr. Lewis Champlin Sch., 1963-74, John Hay Acad., Chgo., 1975-87, Leslie Lewis Elem. Sch., Chgo., 1988-99, Robert Emmet Sch., Chgo., 1999—. Sponsor Reading Marathon Club, Chgo., 1991—; co-creator Project SMART-Stimulating Math. and Reading Techniques John Hay Acad., Chgo., 1987-90, curriculum coord., 1985-87; creative dance student, tchr. Kathryn Duham Sch., N.Y.C., 1955-56; creative dance tchr. Doris Patterson Dance Sch., Washington, 1953-55; recorder evening divsn. Northwestern U., Chgo., 1956-62; exch. student tchr. Conservatory Dance Movements, Chgo., 1958-59; art cons. Chgo. Pub. Sch., 1967. Author primary activities Let's Act and Chat, 1991-94, Teaching Black History Through Classroom Tours, 1989-90. Solicitor, vol. United Negro Coll. Fund, Chgo., 1994; sponsor Ward Reading Assn. Marathon, Chgo., 1991-94, 99; active St. Giles Coun. Cath. Women, 1985-96; vol. REAC Ctr. Programs Books, Info., Literacy and Learning, 1997-98. Recipient Meritorious award United Negro Coll. Fund, 1990, 94, Recognition award Alderman Percy Giles, Chgo., 1993. Mem.: ASCD (assoc. Recognition of Svcs. award 1989), Internat. Reading Assn., Nat. Women of Achievement Assn. (Chgo. chpt.), Phi Delta Kappa, Sigma Gamma Rho (Delta Sigma grad. chpt. 1963—93, Sigma chpt. 1992, Eta Xi Sigma chpt.), Eta Xi Sigma (Pearl award for excellence in edn. 1997). Roman Catholic. Home: 1108 N Euclid Ave Oak Park IL 60302-1219

VENET, CLAUDE HENRY, architect, acoustic engineer; b. Lyon, France, Aug. 10, 1946; came to U.S., 1981; s. René Joseph and Marcellé (Michel) V.; m. Valerie Picq, Sept. 22, 1997; children: Elle Cassiopée Mariana, Ulysse Luis Edouard. Dipl. electronic engr., ESTA, Rochefort, France, 1968; Lic. Physics, U. Paris, 1971; MArch, So. Calif. Inst. Architecture, 1986. U.K. mgr. Ling Dynamics/Altec, Royston, Eng., 1971-72; mng. dir. CVE Enterprises, London, 1972-75; sales dir. Macinnes/Amcron France, Paris, 1975-77; tech. dir. Audio Cons. Coordination, Rio de Janeiro, 1977-81; cons. Paramount (Sound) Films Corp., Glendale, Calif., 1981-82; pres. CV Acoustics, Arch. & Engring., Belleville, France, 1986-91, Archicoustics Inc., Miami and Rio de Janeiro, 1991—2002, Acoustinet Inc., Miami, 2002—. Lectr. U. Miami Sch. Architecture, 1995—. Vol. Architects Without Frontiers, Paris, 1990—. Named Outstanding Consulting Engr., Miami AIA. Mem. AIA, AAAS, Am. Inst. Physics, Acoustical Soc. Am., Nat. Coun. Acoustical Cons., Audio Engring. Soc., N.Y. Acad. of Sci., Order French Architects, Chamber French Cons. Engrs. Achievements include design of computer-driven, polymorphic, multiuse theatre with continuous variable acoustics/geometry; variable shape multi-acoustics recording studio design; more than 1000 consulting projects with including: Citicorp, Club Med, Credit Lyonnais, Disney, Eurodisney, Iguatemi Shopping Ctr., Brazil, Universal Studios, Miami Internat. Airport; international hotels and others. Office: 10650 NE 10th Ct Miami Shores FL 33138-2102

VENETSANOPOULOS, ANASTASIOS NICOLAOS, electrical engineer, educator; b. Athens, Greece, June 19, 1941; arrived in Can., 1968; s. Nicolaos Anastasios and Elli (Papacondilis) Venetsanopoulos. Diploma, Athens Coll., 1960; diploma in elec. and mech. engring., Nat. Tech. U., Athens, 1965, hon. doctorate, 1994; MS, Yale U., 1966, MPhil, 1968, PhD, 1969. Registered profl. engr., Greece, Ont. Asst. in instrn. engring. and applied sci. Yale U., 1966-68, research asst., 1968-69; lectr. U. Toronto, Ont., Can., 1968-69, asst. prof. elec. engring., 1970-73, assoc. prof., 1973-81, prof., 1981—, chmn. communications group dept. elec. engring., 1974-78, 81-86, assoc. chmn. elec. and computer engring., 1978-79, 97—, mem. elec. and computer engring. exec. com., 1981-86, 97—, mem. elec. engring. curriculum com., 1972-79. Acad. visitor Imperial Coll. Arts and Tech. U. London, 1979—80; vis. prof. Nat. Tech. U. Athens, 1979—80, Fed. U. Tech. Lausanne, Switzerland, 1986—87, Switzerland, 1993—94, U. Florence, Italy, 1987; cons. elec. engring. Consociates Ltd.; chmn. multimedia Bell-Can., 1999—; dean applied sci. & engring. U. Toronto, 2001—. Editor: Can. Elec. Engring. Jour., 1981—83; contbr. articles to profl. jours., chapters to books. Mem. allocations and agy. rels. com. United Cmty. Fund, Toronto, 1971—74; pres. Hellenic-Can. Cultural Soc., 1972—75; sec. gen. Greek Cmty. Met. Toronto, 1973—75. Recipient Excellence in Innovation award, Info. Tech. Rsch. Ctr., 1996; grantee Fulbright Travel, U.S., 1965, Def. Rsch. Bd. Can., 1972—75, UN, NSF, J. P. Bickell Found., Natural Scis. and Engring. Rsch. Coun. Can. Fellow: IEEE (fin. chmn. internat. symposium on circuit theroy 1973, tech. program chmn. internat. conf. comm. 1978, 1986, vice-chmn. Toronto sect. 1976—77, chmn. 1977—79, assoc. editor Transactions on circuits and sys. 1985—87, guest editor spl. 1987, tech. prgram chmn. internat. conf. on acoustics speech and signal proc 1991, Millenium medal 2001—), Can. Acad. Engring., Engring. Inst. Can.; mem.: Intercultural Coun. (chmn. ednl. com. 1971—80, sr. v.p. 1977—80), Am.-Hellenic Ednl. Progress Assn. (v.p. Toronto sect. 1973—75, pres. 1975—77), N.Y. Acad. Scis., Yale Sci. and Engring. Assn., Can. Soc. Elec. Engring. (chmn. Toronto sect. 1975—77, nat. dir. 1976—88, pres. 1983—86), Assn. Profl. Mech. Engrs. Greece, Assn. Profl. Elec. Engrs. Greece, Assn. Profl. Engrs. Ont., Tech. Chamber Greece, Sigma Xi. Office: U Toronto Dept Elec and Comp Engring Toronto ON Canada M5S 3G4

VENEY, M. BEATRICE, professional counselor; b. Leavensworth, Kans. m. Warren L. Veney. MA, Western Carolina U., 1985. Nat. cert. counselor. Counselor Sandhills C.C., Pinehurst, N.C., 1990-93; dir. Health Careers Opportunity Program No. Va. C.C., Annandale, 1993—. Cons. in field. Bd. dirs. Different Drum, Inc., Mt. Jezreel Bapt. Ch., Old Town, Alexandria, Va., Nat. Assn. Realtors; contractor Health Resource Svcs. Adminstrn. Milennium fellow Va. Collaborative Leadership Program, Richmond, 1999-2000. Mem. Am. Counseling Assn., Delta Sigma Theta. Baptist. Avocations: travel, reading, home decorating. Office: No Va CC 8333 Little River Turnpike Annandale VA 22003 Fax: 703-323-4576. E-mail: mveney@nvcc.vccs.edu.

VENEZKY, RICHARD LAWRENCE, English language educator; b. Pitts., Apr. 16, 1938; s. Bernard Jacob and Isabel (Zeisel) V.; m. Karen F. Gauz, Aug. 2, 1964; children: Dina Yael, Elie Michael. BEE, Cornell U., 1961, MA, 1962; postgrad., U. Calif., Berkeley, 1962-63; PhD, Stanford U., 1965. Sys. programmer, tech. writer Control Data Corp., Palo Alto, Calif., 1962-65; asst. prof. English and computer scis. U. Wis., Madison, 1965-69, assoc. prof. computer scis., 1969-74, prof., 1974-77, chmn. dept., 1975-77; Unidel prof. ednl. studies, prof. computer and info. sci., prof. linguistics U. Del., Newark, 1977—; Benton fellow in literacy U. Chgo., 1994-95. Vis. rsch. assoc. Tel Aviv U., 1969-70, rsch. fellow, 1973; cons. Oxford English Dictionary Supplement; dir. computing Dictionary of Old English, 1971— co-dir. for R & D Nat. Ctr. on Adult Literacy, 1990-95; scholar in residence U.S. Dept. Edn., 1997-98; sr. rschr/ OECD, 1999-01. Author: The Structure of English Orthography, 1970, Testing in Reading, 1974, Random House Spelling Across the Curriculum, 1988, The American Way of Spelling, 1999; co-author: A Microfiche Concordance to Old English, 1981, Letter and Word Perception, 1980, PRS-Pre-Reading Skills Program, 1985, The Subtle Danger, 1987, World of Reading, 1989, The Intelligent Design of Computer-Assisted Instruction, 1991; co-editor: Orthography, Reading and Dyslexia, 1980, Toward Defining Literacy, 1990, Literacy: An International Handbook, 1999; contbr. articles to profl. jours., chpts. to books. Chmn. edn. commn Madison Jewish Community Coun., 1973-77; v.p. Jewish Fedn. Del., 1986-89; regional chmn. Am. Profs. for Peace in Mid. East, 1968-73. Grantee Office of Edn., 1964-66, NSF, 1966-74, Nat. Inst. Edn., 1973-77, NEH, 1978-89, Office of Ednl. Rsch. and Improvement, Dept. Edn., 1990-95, Pew Charitable Trusts, 1995-97, Joyce Found., 1996-99. Fellow Am. Psychol. Soc.; mem. Am. Edn. Rsch. Assn., Internat. Reading Assn., Reading Hall of Fame (pres. 1996-97), Assn. Computing Machinery (Soc. Sci. Study of Reading, Disting. Fellow award, 1999). Democrat. Jewish. Home: 206 Hullihen Dr Newark DE 19711-3651 Office: U Del Room 211 Willard Hall Bldg Newark DE 19716-2999 E-mail: venezky@udel.edu.

VENGROW, MICHAEL IAN, neurologist; b. Brookline, Mass., Apr. 10, 1949; s. Max and Mary V.; m. Lucy Lee Smith, Aug. 4, 1979; children: Robert David, Mary Elizabeth. BS in Chemistry magna cum laude, U. Mass., 1971; MD, U. Mass., Worcester, 1977. Diplomate Am. Bd. Psychiatry and Neurology, Am. Bd. Clin. Neurophysiology, Am. Bd. Electrodiagnostic Medicine, Am. Acad. Pain Mgmt., Nat. Bd. Med. Examiners. Rsch. chemist, asst. KFA-Julich, West Germany, 1970; rsch. chemist, asst. biomed. svcs. divsn. Damon Corp., Needham, Mass., 1971-72; rsch. chemist, head Shrine Burn Inst., Boston, 1972-73; intern Naval Regional Med. Ctr., San Diego, 1977-78; battalion med. officer Third Combat Engr. Battalion, Third Marine Divsn., Okinawa, Japan, 1978-79; resident, chief resident in neurology Nat. Naval Med. Ctr., Bethesda, Md., 1979-82; fellow in clin. neurophysiology Walter Reed Army Med. Ctr., Washington, 1982-83; neurologist, head divsn. diagnostic neurophysiology Naval Hosp. San Diego, 1983-85; neurologist Neurology Ctr. No. Ariz., Flagstaff, 1985-96, Neurology Cons. of Dallas, 1996-98. Sr. reviewer Ariz. Long Term Care Sys., Phoenix, 1986-94; dir. Alzheimer's unit Kachina Point Health Ctr., Sedona, Ariz., 1986-93, dir. neurol. rehab. unit, 1989-93; dir. neurophysiology lab. Kingman Regional Med. Ctr., 1985-95, Flagstaff Med. Ctr., 1985-95, Cmty. Med. Edn. dir., 1988, chief medicine, 1989; mem. profl. adv. bd. Epilipsy Soc., Phoenix, 1987-96, Multiple Sclerosis Soc., Phoenix, 1989-96, Quantum Health Resources; cons. First Western Med. Group, Fresno, Calif., 1991-93, Long Term Care Program Ariz. Long Term Care System, 1987-95, Marcus J. Lawrence Hosp., Cottonwood, Ariz., Pub. Health Svcs. Hosp., Tuba City, Ariz.; ind. med. examiner, Ariz.; agreed med. examiner, qualified med. examiner, electromyographer BH Mgmt. Med. Group, Fresno, 1993—; instr. emergency medicine L.A. C.C. Overseas, Uniformed Svcs. U. Health Scis., Bethesda; clin. lectr. dept. neurology sch. health scis. U. Ariz., Tucson; clin. asst. prof. neurology U. Tex. Southwestern Med. Sch.; rschr. in field; presenter in field. Contbr. articles to profl. pubs. Bd. dirs. Flagstaff Symphony, 1991-94; sponsor Am. Youth Soccer Orgn., 1988-90. LCDR, USN, 1978-85, capt. M.C., USNR. Pub. Health scholar, 1975, State Bd. Higher Edn. Scholar, 1967-71, 75, Armed Forces Health Svcs. Profl. scholarship, 1975-77, Religious High Edn. scholar, 1965; recipient Navy commendation Operation Team Spirit, 1978, letter commendation Operation Desert Storm, 1991. Fellow Am. Acad. Neurology (govt. section), Am. EEG Soc. (practice com.), Am. Assn. Electrodiagnostic Medicine, Am. Electromyographic Soc.; mem. AMA, Ariz. Med. Assn., Tex. Med. Assn. (subcom. on accreditation, lectr. stroke project), Am. Mil. Surgeons U.S., Am. Epilepsy Soc., Uniformed Svcs. Neurology U.S., U.S. Navy Neurol. Soc., Am. Soc. Clin. Evoked Potentials, Am. Soc. Neuroimaging, Am. Med. EEG Assn., Naval Res. Assn, Am. Biographical Inst. Rsch. Assn., (life, dep. gov., bd. govs.), Am. Biographical Inst. (Man of Yr., 1992), Phi Eta Sigma, Phi Kappa Phi, Phi Beta Kappa. Avocations: scuba diving, rugby, bicycling, sailing, billiards. Home: 5977 Temple Dr Plano TX 75093-8707

VENINGA, JAMES FRANK, humanities educator, editor, author; b. Milw., Aug. 26, 1944; s. Frank and Otila Ann (Mauch) V.; m. Catherine M. Williams, Apr. 5, 1969; 1 child, Jennifer Elisa. BA, Baylor U., 1966; MTheol Studies, Harvard U., 1968; MA, Rice U., 1973, PhD, 1974. Instr. U. St. Thomas, Houston, 1971-73, asst. prof., 1974; asst. dir. Tex. Coun. for Humanities, Austin, 1975, exec. dir., 1976-97; pres., dir. Inst. for the Humanities at Salado, 1997-2000; CEO, campus dean U. Wis.-Marathon County, Wausau, 2000—. Dir. Nat. Fedn. State Humanities Couns., Washington, 1980-83; trustee Inst. for Humanities at Salado, Tex., 1980-85; vis. prof. Am. studies U. Tex., Austin, 1984, sr. lectr. Am. studies, 1986; vis. prof. Am. studies Baylor U., 1999. Author: The Humanities and Civic Imagination, 1999; editor: The Biographer's Gift, 1983, Vietnam in Remission, 1985, Standing with the Public, 1997; editor-in-chief Tex. Jour. Ideas, History and Culture, 1982-97. Recipient Baylor Man of Merit award Baylor U., 1985. Home: 309 Country Club Rd Schofield WI 54476 Office: U Wis 518 S 7th Ave Wausau WI 54401-5362

VENIT, MARK LOUIS, management consultant, author, lecturer; b. Phila., Dec. 5, 1948; s. Irving Gordon Venit and Mildred F. (Schnoll) Klugman; div.; children: Kyle, Gabriel. BA, Temple U., 1970, MPA, 1973, MBA, 1976. Pres. U.S. Advt. Corp., Broomall, Pa., 1974-83, Empire Specialty Printing Corp., Yeadon, 1976-82; v.p. Plymouth Mills Inc., N.Y.C., 1983-84; pres., chief exec. officer Roundtable Mgmt. Systems Ltd., U.S., Can., Ger., 1985—; exec. v.p. Talbot Street Pier Corp., Ocean City, Md., 1992—. Cons. in field. Author: Selling in Mexico: NAFTA and The Apparel Graphics Industry, 1994, The Business of Preprints, 1996, A Report to the Apparel Graphics Industry, 1997, Buffalo Bob and Howdy Doody, 1997; co-author: Textile Business, 1981; contbr. articles to profl. jours. Mem. Rep. City Exec. Com., Phila., 1970-72; mem. Del. County Rep. Exec. Com., 1975-90; treas. Del. County Libr. System, Media, 1978-85, Del. County chmn. Dole for Pres., 1988; mem. State of Md.'s Gov.'s Econ. Devel. Com., 1992—; mem. exec. bd. Temple Batyam, 1995—. Recipient Svc. to Industry award Gralla Pubs., Dallas, 1983-88. Mem. Screen Printing Assn. Internat. (Magnus award 1982), Apparel Graphics Inst. (pres. 1991—), Am. Soc. Assn. Execs., Rotary (Haverford Twp. dir. 1982-84, Man of Yr. 1984, Internat. Svc. award 1990), Masons (chmn. Masonic Edn. 1982-83), B'nai B'rith Youth Orgn. (Leadership award 1976), Variety Club (fund raising co-chair 1991, Award of Merit 1991, Amb. 1995—). Avocations: sand sculpture, piano, whitewater rafting, archaeology, psychic phenomena.

VENIT, WILLIAM BENNETT, electrical products company executive, consultant; b. Chgo., May 28, 1931; s. George Bernard and Ida (Schaffel) V.; m. Nancy Jean Carlson, Jan. 28, 1956; children: Steven Louis, Aprilann. Student, U. Ill., Champaign, 1949. Sales mgr. Coronet, Inc., Chgo., 1952-63, pres., chmn. bd. dirs., 1963-74, Roma Wire Inc., Chgo., 1971-74; chmn. bd. dirs. Swing Time #2, 1988-89; pres. Wm. Allen Inc., 1972-74; pres., chmn. bd. dirs. Wraprama Inc., 1988-95, Swag Lite, Inc., 1989—92. Pres. William Lamp Co., Inc., 1993, 97, William Wire Co., Inc., 1974-76; chmn. bd. dirs. MSWV, Inc., 1978—, pres. bd. dirs. 1985—; pres. Trio Steel Inc., Chgo., 1987-90; chmn. bd. Chgo. Lamp Works LLB, 1995, 98, chair 1996, 98; CEO Chgo. Chair Works, 1998, 2000, 2001; spl. cons. Roto Products, 1998—, DMSI Inc.; cons. Nu Style Lamp Shade, 2002—. Patentee Printed-Cir., 1964. With QMC AUS, 1949-52. Avocations: bicycling, golf. Home and Office: 323 Suwanee Ave Sarasota FL 34243-1930 E-mail: LampBill@aol.com.

VENKATA, SUBRAHMANYAM SARASWATI, electrical engineering educator, electric energy and power researcher; b. Nellore, Andhra Pradesh, India, June 28, 1942; came to U.S., 1968; s. Ramiah Saraswati and Lakshmi (Alladi) V.; m. Padma Subrahmanyam Mahadevan, Sept. 3, 1971; children: Sridevi Ramakumar, Harish Saraswati. BSEE, Andhra U., Waltair, India, 1963; MSEE, Indian Inst. Tech., Madras, 1965; PhD, U. S.C., 1971. Registered profl. engr., W.Va., Wash. Lectr. in elec. engring. Coimbatore (India) Inst. Tech., 1965-66; planning engr. S.C. Elec. & Gas Co., Columbia, 1969-70; postdoctoral fellow U. S.C., 1971; instr. elec. engring. U. Mass., Lowell, 1971-72; asst. prof. W.Va. U., Morgantown, 1972-75, assoc. prof., 1975-79; prof. U. Wash., Seattle, 1979-96; prof., chmn. dept. elec. and computer engring. Iowa State U., Ames, 1996—. Cons. Puget Sound Energy Co., Bellevue, Wash., 1980-93, GEC/Alsthom, N.Y.C., 1991-92; series editor, bd. dirs. PWS Pub. Co., 1991-98; affiliate prof. U. Wash., Seattle, 1997—; editor, IEEE Transactions on Power Systems, 1998-2000, IEEE/PES Rev. Letters, 1999—, Internat. Jour. Sys. Author: Introduction of Electrical Energy Devices, 1987; patentee adaptive var compensators, adaptive power quality conditioner, distribution reliability based design software. Advisor Explorers

Club, Morgantown, 1976-78; sec. Hindu Temple and Cultural Ctr. Pacific N.W., Seattle, 1990, chmn., 1991, 95; founding chmn. Hindu Temple and Cultural Ctr., Ames, Iowa, 1999—. Recipient W.Va. U. Assocs. award W.Va. U. Found., 1974, 78. Fellow IEEE (best paper award 1985, 88, 91, Outstanding Power Engring. Educator award 1996, chmn. power engring. edn. com. 2000—, Millenneum Medal award 2000); mem. Conf. Internat. des Grands Reseaux Electriques, IEEE Press for Power Series, 1998—, Sigma Xi, Tau Beta Pi, Eta Kappa Nu, Rotary. Democrat. Avocations: photography, tennis, table tennis. Home: 3109 Sycamore Rd Ames IA 50014-4510 Office: Dept Elec Computer Engring Iowa State U Ames IA 50011-3060 E-mail: venkata@iastate.edu.

VENKATACHALAM, KALLIDAIKURICHI, biochemist, educator, researcher; b. Kalakad, Tamilnadu, India, July 3, 1960; s. Kallidaikurichi Venkatraman and Vasanthalakshmi Venkatachalam; m. Usha Shankaranarayanan, June 16, 1988. BSc, MSc, Madurai Kamraj U.; BS, MS, Wash. State U.; PhD, Tex. A&M U., 1990. Postdoctoral fellow Baylor Coll. Medicine, Houston, 1990—93; rsch. fellow, scientist NIH, Bethesda, Md., 1993-99, mem. faculty in biochemistry FAES, 1996-99; assoc. prof. biochemistry Nova Southeastern U., Ft. Lauderdale, Fla., 1999—. Contbr. articles to profl. jours. Sec., v.p, pres., Indian Cultural Orgn., Houston. Rsch. grantee Great Lakes Ecology, 2000. Mem. AAAS, Am. Soc. Biochemistry and Molecular Biology, Am. Chem. Soc. Avocations: travel, study. Office: Nova Southwestern U 3200 S University Dr Fort Lauderdale FL 33328-2018 Fax: (954) 262-1802.

VENKATESH, PRASANA KRISHNAMURTHI, oil industry executive, researcher; b. Madras, India, July 17, 1966; s. Chinnaswami and Padmini Krishnamurthi. B Tech. Chem. Engring., Indian Inst. of Tech., Madras, India, 1983—87; MSChemE, MS in Ops. Rsch., Columbia U., 1987—89; PhD in Chem. Engring., U. Minn., Mpls., 1993—96. Chem. engr. Corp. Rsch., Exxon Rsch. and Engring. Co., Annandale, NJ, 1990—93; rsch. scientist Schlumberger-Doll Rsch., Ridgefield, Conn., 1997—99, sr. rsch. scientist, 1999—. Co-recipient NSF award, NSF, 1995—98; scholar Nat. Sci. Talent Sscholar, Government of India, 1983—87, vis. grad. scholar, Princeton U., 1989—90. Mem.: Soc. for Indsl. and Applied Math., Am. Phys. Soc. Hindu. Achievements include invention of Quantum Annealing for Global Optimisation, 2000; Density Functional Theory in Real Spaces, 2002. Avocations: literature, Indian- and Western-classical music. Office: Schlumberger-Doll Rsch 36 Old Quarry Rd Ridgefield CT 06877

VENNAT, MICHEL, lawyer, bank executive; b. Sept. 17, 1941; m. Marie-Anne Tawil; children: Catherine, Charles-Alexandre, Frédéric-André, Michèle-Anne, Philippe-Olivier. BA magna cum laude, Coll. Jean-de-Brébeuf, Montreal, Que., Can., 1960; LL.L., U. Montreal, 1963; MA, Oxford U., Eng., 1965. Bar: Que. 1966, Paris 1995; apptd. Queen's Counsel 1983, Officer of the Order of Can., 1995. Fgn. affairs officer Dept. External Affairs, Ottawa, Ont., Can., 1965; spl. asst. to Min. Fin., 1966-68; spl. asst. to Hon. Pierre E. Trudeau, Prime Min. of Can., 1968-70, spl. counsel, 1977; chmn. Can. Film Devel. Corp., Montreal, 1976-81; sr. ptnr. Stikeman, Elliott, 1970-90; pres. Dumez Investments Inc., 1986-87, Westburne Internat. Industries Ltd., 1987; vice chmn. United Westburne Inc., 1990, vice chmn., CEO, 1991-93, chmn., CEO, 1993-94, also bd. dirs.; pres. Bastos du Canada Limitée, 1987—, 2000, also bd. dirs.; sr. ptnr. Stikeman Elliot, Montreal, 1994-2000; pres., CEO bus. devel. Bank Canada, 2000. Chmn. Moody Industries Inc., 1998—2000; chmn. bd. dirs. Bus. Devel. Bank of Can.; lectr. in constl. law U. Montreal, 1970. Rhodes scholar, 1963-65. Mem. Barreau du Que., Barreau de Paris, Can. C. of C., French C. of C. (Can. bd. dirs.), Mt. Bruno Country Club, Hillside Tennis Club, Mt. Royal Club, Hermitage Club, Knowlton Golf Club, St. John Salmon Club, Montreal Badminton & Squash Club. Avocations: golf, tennis, skiing, fishing, hunting. Home: 619 Sydenham Ave Westmount QC Canada H3Y 2Z3 Office: Bus Devel Bank Can 5 Pl Ville Marie Ste 300 Montreal QC Canada H3B 5E7

VENNE, GEORGIA PACHECO, artist; b. Alamosa, Colo., Aug. 10, 1957; d. Joe Manuel and Cleo Maria (Espinoza) Pacheco; m. Robert J. Venne, July 29, 1952; 1 child, Leigh April. BA in Art cum laude, Adams State Coll., 1998. Bus. owner, Alamosa, 1985—; with interlibr. loan office Adams State Libr., 1996-98; artist Chamber Gallery, 1997-98; photographer Great Sand Dunes, 1998. Exhibited in group shows at Hatfield Gallery, 1998, Alamosa, 1998, Installation 214, 1998. Mem. Am. Youth Soccer Orgn. (coach 1992-94). Avocations: theater, concerts, photography, gardening, cooking. Home: 7991 S 103d Alamosa CO 81101

VENNERI, SAMUEL L. federal agency administrator; BS in Aerospace Engring., Pa. State U., 1969; MS in Engring. Sci., George Washington, 1975; postgrad., George Washington U. Prin. engr. Fairchild Space Electronics; aerospace asst. cons. Swales and Assocs.; program mgr. materials and structures divdn. Office Aeronautics and Space Tech. NASA, Washington, dir. spacecraft sys. divdn. Office Space Access and Tech., chief technologist, 1996—2000, assoc. adminstr. aerospace tech., 2000—. Office: NASA Hdqrs Mail Code R 300 E St SW Washington DC 20546

VENNING, ROBERT STANLEY, lawyer; b. Boise, Idaho, July 24, 1943; s. William Lucas and Corey Elizabeth (Brown) V.; m. Sandra Macdonald, May 9, 1966 (div. 1976); 1 child, Rachel Elizabeth; m. Laura Siegel, Mar. 24, 1979; 1 child, Daniel Rockhill Siegel. AB, Harvard U., 1965; MA, U. Chgo., 1966; LLB, Yale U., 1970. Bar: Calif., U.S. Dist. Ct. (no. dist.) Calif., 1971, U.S. Dist. Ct. (cen. dist.) Calif. 1973, U.S. Ct. Appeals (9th cir.) 1977, U.S. Supreme Ct. 1977, U.S. Ct. Appeals (fed. cir.) 1986, U.S. Ct. Appeals (D.C. cir.) 1987. Assoc. Heller Ehrman White & McAuliffe, San Francisco, 1970-73, 73-76, ptnr., 1977—, mem. exec. com., 1991-94. Vis. lectr. U. Wash., Seattle, 1973, Boalt Hall Sch. Law, U. Calif., Berkeley, 1982-85, 89, Sch. Bus., Stanford U., 1986-87. Editor Yale Law Jour., 1969-70. Early neutral evaluator U.S. Dist. Ct. (no. dist.) Calif., 1987—. Fellow Am. Bar Found. (life); mem. ABA, San Francisco Bar Assn. (past chair judiciary com.), CPR Inst. for Dispute Resolution, Olympic Club. Office: Heller White & McAuliffe 333 Bush St San Francisco CA 94104-2806

VENO, RONALD JAMES, JR. travel industry executive; b. Malden, Mass., Feb. 3, 1963; s. Ronald James and Jeanne (Greer) V.; m. Michele Carmelina Sipala, Aug. 12, 1989; children: Erica Joan, Ronald James III. BS, Westfield State Coll., 1985; MBA, Boston Coll., Chestnut Hill, Mass., 1993. Sales rep. Quikrete Co., Everett, Mass., 1987-88; area mgr. Sunoco, Providence, 1988-94; product mgr. Collette Tours, Pawtucket, R.I., 1994-96; dir. sales and mktg. Abercrombie and Kent Overseas, Oak Brook, Ill., 1996-98, v.p. sales and mktg., 1998—. Roman Catholic. Avocations: drawing, painting, fishing. Home: 14130 S Longview Ln Plainfield IL 60544-6010 Office: Abercrombie and Kent Overseas 1520 Kensington Rd Ste 212 Oak Brook IL 60523-2156

VENOSDEL, DANIEL PAUL, agricultural association administrator; b. Pittsfield, Ill., July 19, 1969; s. Danny Boy and Helen Jo Venosdel; m. Cynthia Kay Hallock, July 18, 1997. BS in Agrl. Bus., Calif. State U., Fresno, 1992. Com. mem. USDA, Sacramento, 1998; dir. Calif. Farm Bur. Fedn., 1995—. Polit. cons. ezgov.com, Atlanta, 2000; cons. Natural Resources Edn. Found., Elk Grove, Calif., 2000. Mem. Blood Ctr. Sacramento, 1995-2001; mem. Sacramento County Farm Bur., 1996-2001. Recipient Appreciation for Dedication to Govt. award USDA-Farm Svc. Agy., 1998. Mem. Sigma Alpha Epsilon. Avocations: sports, travel, outdoor activities, legislative process. Office: Calif Farm Bur Fedn 2300 River Plaza Dr Sacramento CA 95833 Office Fax: 916-561-5693. E-mail: pvenosdel@cfbf.com.

VENSON, LILY PRAGRATIS, journalist, lecturer; b. Chgo., Oct. 24, 1924; d. Peter Socrates and Rozina (Desillas) Pagratis; m. George John Venson, Oct. 15,1944 (dec. Mar. 1998); children: Virginia Venson Greninger, Perry George. AA, Wright College, 1943; student, U. Chgo., 1944. Reporter, feature writer, editl. writer Lerner Newspapers, Chgo., 1963-73; pub. info. officer Oak Forest (Ill.) Hosp., Health & Hosp. Governing Commn. Cook County, Cook County Hosp., Cook County Jail Hosp., 1973-75, chief pub. info., 1975-77; pub. info. officer Ill. Dept. of Children and Family Svcs., Chgo. and Springfield, Ill., 1980-91; journalism lectr. Columbia Coll., Chgo., 1997—; ind. journalist, 1999—. Mem. labor negotiating com. Chgo. chpt. Am. Newspaper Guild, Chgo., 1963-73; lectr. City Coll. Chgo., 1966; mem. exec. com. Health and Hosps. Governing Com. of Cook County, Chgo., 1975-77; editor Cook County News for Hotline Mag., Ill. Dept. Children and Family Svcs., 1985-90. Author poetry pub. in Internat. Libr. Poetry, 2000; contbr. articles to profl. jours. Mem. Hellenic Mus. And Cultural Ctr., 2002, Statue of Liberty-Ellis Island Found., Inc., 2002; election judge Cook County Bd. Elections, Chgo., 1996; mem. cts. and corrections com. Ill. Commn. Status of Women, Chgo. and Springfield, 1971—73. Recipient Civil Rights Brotherhood award Nat. Conf. Christians and Jews, 1965, 1st Pl. Cmty. Svc. award Am. Newspaper Guild, Chgo. chpt., 1970, Outstanding Reporting award Ill. Gov., 1972; nominee Pulitzer prize Columbia U., 1973. Mem.: Soc. Profl. Journalists, Ill. Woman's Press Assn. (chmn. Woman of Achievement 1971, co-sec. 1996, 1st pl. writing award 1968, 1st Pl. award 1989, 1990, 1991), Nat. Fedn. Press Women, St. Andrew Greek Orthodox Ch. Philoptohos Soc., Chgo. Headline Club. Home and Office: 3180 N Lake Shore Dr Apt 5D Chicago IL 60657-4849

VENTENILLA, AURORA CURAMEN, psychiatrist; b. San Jose, The Philippines, Nov. 7, 1939; came to U.S., 1968; d. Tereso and Petra (Patricio) Curamen; m. Doroteo Olba Ventenilla, Oct. 22, 1966; children: Anna, Enrique. MD, Manila Ctrl. U., 1963. Diplomate Am. Bd. Psychiatry and Neurology. Staff psychiatrist Cleve. VA Med. Ctr., 1974—96; contract psychiatrist COMPHEALTH, Salt Lake City, 1996—; staff psychiatrist Windsor Hosp., Chagrin Falls, Ohio, 1999—2001, Fremont Meml. Hosp., Chagrin Falls, 2000—, Ctr. for Families and Children, Chagrin Falls, 1999—. Chief of psychiatry 256 Gen. Hosp. U.S. Army Res., Parma, Ohio, 1986-92. Lt. col. U.S. Army Res., 1982-92. Decorated Army Commendation medal Operation Desert Storm, 1991. Mem. Am. Profl. Practice Assn., Assn. Philippine Physicians in Am., Assn. Philippine Physicians in Ohio. Home: 9826 Tamarack Trl Brecksville OH 44141-4109

VENTER, J. CRAIG, science foundation director; BS in Biochemistry, U. Calif., San Diego, 1972, PhD in Physiology and Pharmacology, 1975. Tchr. SUNY, Buffalo; with Roswell Pk. Meml. Inst.; sect. and lab chief Nat. Inst. Neurol. Disorders and Stroke NIH, Bethesda, Md., 1984-92; founder, chair, chief scientist The Inst. for Genomic Rsch., 1992—98; pres., chief sci. officer Celera Genomics Corp., Rockville, Md., 1998—2002; chmn. sci. adv. bd. Applera Corp., Norwalk, Conn. Bd. dirs. High Tech. Coun. Md.; mem. sci. adv. bd. ValiGene. Contbr. more than 160 articles to profl. jours. Recipient Beckman award, 1999, Chiron Corp. Biotech. Rsch. award, 1999. Fellow: AAAS, Am. Acad. Microbiology. Achievements include development of extensive rsch. in functional and comparative analysis of genome and gene products in viruses, eubacteria, pathogenic bacteria, archea and eukaryotes, both plant and animal including humans; first to fully sequence seven organisms; pioneered the use of automated gene sequencers; developed expressed sequence tags (ESTs); helped discover more than half of all human genes. Office: Applera Corp PO Box 5435 301 Merritt 7 Norwalk CT 06856-5435

VENTIMIGLIA, JOHN THOMAS, artist, art educator; b. Augusta, Maine, Jan. 12, 1943; s. William Anthony and Eleanor Margarite (Smith) V.; children: Timothy, August; m. Cheslye Larson, Feb. 11, 1995. Student, Skowhegan Sch. Painting & Sculpture, 1964; BFA, Syracuse U., 1965; MFA, Md. Inst. Coll. Art, Balt., 1967. Prof. 3 dimensional design, sculpture and drawing Maine Coll. Art, Portland, 1972—. Affiliated with Icon Gallery, Brunswick, Maine. Commissioned sculptures include Mt. Holyoke Coll., 1993-95, Cedars Nursing Home, 1992, Portland Pub. Libr., Portland Mus. Art. Advisor to restoration and preservaton com., Franklin Simmons' 1897 civil war monument The Lady of Victory, Portland, 1997. Recipient artist's residency Chateau de Rochefort-en-Terre, 1997. Home: 41 Pleasant Ave Portland ME 04103-3217 Office: MECA 97 Spring St Portland ME 04101-3933 E-mail: JVentimiglia@meca.edu.

VENTIMIGLIA, KATHARINE JANE GARVER, education educator; b. Muncie, Ind., Sept. 1, 1949; d. Edwin Gilmore and Sybil Marie (Daughtry) Garver; m. Joseph John Ventimiglia, June 17, 1972; children: Joseph Marc, Robert Edwin, Jeffrey Peter, Matthew Patrick. BA in Edn., NE La. U., 1971; MEd, Dowling Coll., 1991; postgrad., Hofstra U., 1999—. Cert. nursery and elem. tchr., Ill., N.Y. Tchr. Archdiocese of Chgo., 1971-72, Diocese of Bklyn., 1972-74; adj. asst. prof. coll. reading Suffolk C.C., Selden, N.Y., 1986-91, prof. reading, 1991—; asst. to dir. program learning disabled Dowling Coll., Oakdale, 1991-98, reading/learning disabilities specialist student support svc, 1993—, adj. lectr. edn., 1994-97; pvt. practice. Reading/learning disabilities specialist Dowling Coll., Oakdale, 1989—; presenter Literacy Vols. of Suffolk County, 1998; faculty child study dept. St. Joseph's Coll., Patchogue, N.Y. Author: (with others) Successful Strategies for Learning Disabled College Students: Reading, Writing and Reasoning, 1991. Treas. Sagamore Jr. H.S. PTA, Holtsville, N.Y., 1987-88, bd. dirs. 1986-89; treas. Gatelot Ave. PTA, Lake Ronkonkoma, N.Y., 1983-92, mem. exec. bd. 1979-92, project coord. Reading Is Fundamental, 1989-92. Mem. AAUW, DAR, Internat. Reading Assn., Orton Dyslexia Soc., Kappa Delta Pi, Alpha Upsilon Alpha. Avocations: teaching religious education, photography, reading, writing. Office: Dowling Coll Student Support Svcs Fortunoff Hall Rm 007 Oakdale NY 11769 also: Suffolk Community Coll Sagtikos Bldg Crooked Hill Rd Rm 201 Brentwood NY 11717-1005

VENTKER, DAVID NEIL, lawyer; b. Laredo, Tex., Feb. 6, 1957; s. David R. and Nancy M. (Sorenson) V.; m. Katherine Louise Wheeler, Oct. 1, 1983; children: Sarah, Emily. BA in Econs., Ohio State U., 1979, JD, 1982. Bar: Ohio 1982, Va. 1989, N.C. 1999, U.S. Ct. Mil. Appeals 1985. Commd. U.S. Navy, 1982, advanced through grades to lt. comdr., 1989, counsel defense S.C., 1983-85, counsel trial Sigonella, Italy, 1985-87; staff judge advocate Atlantic Fleet/NATO, 1987-89; ptnr. Huff, Poole & Mahoney, PC, 1999—2002; founder, prin. Ventker & Assocs., PLLC, Norfolk, Va., 2002—. Mem. Maritime Law Assn. of U.S. (procter in admiralty), Va. State Bar Assn. (counsel), N.C. State Bar Assn., Ohio Bar Assn., Internat. Assn. Def. Coun. Episcopalian. Office: Ventker & Assocs PLLC 101 W Main St Ste 4800 Norfolk VA 23510 E-mail: dventker@ventkerlaw.com.

VENTO, M. THÉRÈSE, lawyer; b. N.Y.C., June 30, 1951; d. Anthony Joseph and Margaret (Stechert) V.; m. Peter Michael MacNamara, Dec. 23, 1977; children: David Miles, Elyse Anne. BS, U. Fla., 1974, JD, 1976. Bar: Fla. 1977, U.S. Dist. Ct. (so. and mid. dists.) Fla. 1982, U.S. Ct. Appeals (5th and 11th cirs.) 1981, U.S. Supreme Ct. 1985. Clk. to presiding justice U.S. Dist. Ct. (so. dist.) Fla., Miami, 1976-78; assoc. Mahoney, Hadlow & Adams, 1978-79, Shutts & Bowen, Miami, 1979-84, ptnr., 1985-95; founding ptnr. Gallwey Gillman Curtis Vento & Horn, P.A., 1995—. Trustee Miami Art Mus., 1988—, v.p., 1999—; trustee The Beacon Coun., 1995-97, Law Sch. Alumni Coun., U. Fla., 1994—. Fellow Am. Bar Found.; mem. Dade County Bar Assn. (dir. young lawyers sect. 1978-83, editor newsletter 1981-83), Fla. Assn. for Women Lawyers, Fla. Bar Assn. (bd. govs., young lawyers div. 1983-85, civil procedure rules com. 1983-90, exec. coun. trial lawyers sect. 1996—), The Miami Forum (v.p. 1987-88, bd. dirs. 1989-91, co-pres. 2001-2002). Home: 3908 Main Hwy Miami FL 33133-6513 Office: Gallwey Gillman Curtis & Vento PA 200 SE 1st St Ste 1100 Miami FL 33131-1912 E-mail: TVento@GGCVH.com.

VENTOLA, DEAN SAMUEL, architect, architectural company executive; b. Montclair, N.J., Aug. 20, 1958; s. Nicholas Samuel and Josephine (Caputo) V. BArch, U. Md., 1982, BA with honors, 1983. Registered architect, Md., N.J., Pa., Va. Draftsman Associated Designers, Snow Hill, Md., 1981-82; draftsman designer Solar Design Group, Silver Spring, 1982-83; draftsman, designer Osman & Assocs., Reston, Va., 1983-85; draftsman/designer Grimm & Parker, Greenbelt, Md., 1985, project mgr., 1985-86; v.p., dir. design Milliner Constrn., Frederick, 1986-88, Md. registered architect, 1987, v.p., 1988-90; pres. Dean Ventola Architects, Damascus, 1990—. EEO officer HUD, Frederick, 1986—. Contbr. articles to profl. jours.; prin. designs include: Quad Home, 1985, New Market Shopping Ctr., 1986, New Market Texaco, 1987, Dearbought Exec. Complex, 1989, Westminster Self Storage, 1990, Copper Oaks Urban Design Guidelines, 1991, Pleasant Br. Wastewater Treatment Plant, 1992, Mt. Airy Bapt. Ch. renovations, 1992, Canam Steel addition, 1992, Clearspring Shopping Ctr., 1992, Windsor Knolls Recreation Ctr., 1993, Appler Recreation Ctr., 1994, Woodsboro Savs. Bank addition, 1994, Gettysburg Burger King, 1995, Mt. Airy Burger King, 1995, Monocacy Village Bank, 1996, Ridgeville Shopping Ctr., 1998, Myersville Burger King, 1998, Damascus Burger King, 1998, Cress Creek Villas, 1998, Bennigan's Restaurant, 2000; creator: (comic strip) Triangulations, 1997; work featured in Chespeake Home Mag., May/June 2001 issue. Recipient 1st place award of excellence in custom home design, 1989, 90. Mem. AIA, Nat. Bldg. Mus., Bldg. Ofcls. and Code Adminstrs. Assn. Republican. Avocations: art, architectural exhibits. Office: Dean Ventola Architects 23600 Cornerstone Ln Damascus MD 20872-2914

VENTRELLI, ANITA MARIE, lawyer; b. Berwyn, Ill., Apr. 20, 1964; d. Jose M. and Anita Marie (Loycano) Bolaños. AB, U. Mich., 1986; JD, DePaul U., 1989. Bar: Ill. 1990. Ptnr. Schiller DuCanto & Fleck, Chgo., 1997—. Fellow Am. Acad. Matrimonial Lawyers; mem. ABA, Ill. Bar Assn. Roman Catholic. Avocations: running, piano. Office: Schiller DuCanto & Fleck 200 N La Salle St Ste 2700 Chicago IL 60601-1098 E-mail: aventrelli@sdflaw.com.

VENTRES, DANIEL BRAINERD, JR. lawyer; b. Washington, Dec. 2, 1930; s. Daniel Brainerd and Sarah Helen (Dunlap) V.; m. Sarah Stevenson, May 22, 1954 (div. 1978); children: Katherine Ventres Canipelli, William Brainerd; m. Judith Martin, Dec. 27, 1984. BA in Bus. Adminstrn. and Econs., Ohio Wesleyan U., 1952; JD, George Washington U., 1957. Bar: Minn. 1960, U.S. Dist. Ct. Minn. 1965, U.S. Supreme Ct. 1969, U.S. Ct. Mil. Appeals 1972, U.S. Ct. Appeals (8th cir.) 1989. Appraiser, legal asst. Redevel. Land Agy., Washington, 1955-56; procurement and legal staff The Martin Co., Denver, 1957-59, Mpls. Honeywell Co., 1959-60; ptnr. Carlsen, Greiner & Law, Mpls., 1960-84, MacIntosh & Commers, Mpls., 1984-86; of counsel Gray, Plant, Mooty, Mooty & Bennett, PA, 1986-94, Gislason, Dosland, Hunter & Malecki, PA, Minnetonka, Minn., 1994-95; pvt. practice Mpls., 1995—. Assoc. counsel Amateur Athletic Union, Indpls., 1974-80, U.S. Swimming, Colorado Springs, Colo., 1978-80; chmn. ad hoc com. on dispute resolution alternatives in family law Minn. Supreme Ct., Mpls., 1993-96; adj. prof. family law Hamline U. Law Sch., St. Paul, 1993; referee settlement conf. program Hennepin County Dist. Ct., Mpls., 1994—; lectr. Nat. Bus. Inst. Seminars, 1994. Mem. Ind. Sch. Dist. 274 Bd. Edn., Hopkins, Minn., 1965-72; chmn., legis. coord. Suburban Sch. Dist. Joint Bd., Hopkins, 1972; v.p. adminstrn. U.S. Swimming Com.; U.S. swimming ofcl. Olympic Games, PanAm. Games, Aquatic World Games; chmn., dir. Minn. AAU swimming, Minn. AAU, 1968-80. Officer USMC, 1952-54; col. USMCR, 1972-78. Mem. ABA, FBA (bd. dirs., v.p. Minn. chpt. 1961—, Minn. rep. alternat dispute resolution com. 1995-96, chmn. subcom. on alternate dispute reolution practices, procedures and processes Minn. chpt. 1996—), Am. Acad. Matrimonial Lawyers, Am. Arbitration Assn. (arbitrator, mediator, evaluator Mpls. 1995-98), Minn. Bar Assn. (cert. arbitrator, mediator and evaluator, lectr. CLE 1988-95), Hennepin County Bar Assn., Masons. Office: 625 2d Ave S Ste 419 Minneapolis MN 55402

VENTRES, JUDITH MARTIN, lawyer; b. Ann Arbor, Mich., Feb. 10, 1943; d. D. Lawrence and Donna E. (Webb) Moran; children: Laura M. Buford, Paul M. Martin, A. Lindsay McGill; m. Daniel B. Ventres Jr., Dec. 27, 1984. BA, U. Mich., 1963; postgrad., U. Jean Moulin, Inst. du Droit, Lyon, France, 1981; JD, U. Minn., 1982. Bar: Minn. 1982, Fla. 1991, Colo. 1994, U.S. Tax Ct. 1989, U.S. Dist. Ct. Minn. 1989, U.S. Ct. Appeals (8th cir.) 1989. Tax supr., dir. fin. planning, asst. nat. dir. Coopers & Lybrand, Mpls., 1981-84; dir. fin. planning Investors Diversified Services subs. Am. Express, Mpls. and N.Y.C., 1984-85; sr. tax mgr., dir. fin. planning KPMG Peat Marwick Main & Co., Mpls., 1985-89; prin. Gray Plant Mooty Mooty & Bennett, P.A., 2000—02, Martin & Assocs., PA, Mpls., 1989—2000, 2002—. Faculty Minn. CLE, 1994; adv. bd. Nicollet/Ebenezer, 1996. Owner Alternatax, Inc. Mem. Mpls. C. of C. Campaign, Downtown Coun. Coms., Mpls., 1982-84, Metro Tax Planning Group, 1984-86, Mpls. Estate Planning Coun., 1985-99, Planned Giving Coun.; class chmn. fundraising campaign U. Minn. Law Sch., Mpls., 1985, 98; bd. dirs. Ensemble Capriccio, chmn. fundraising com., 1998—; usher Christ Presbyn. Ch., Edina, Minn., 1983—; mem. adv. coun. on planned giving ARC. Mem. ABA (task force on legal fin. planning), Minn. Bar Assn., Hennepin County Bar Assn., Fla. Bar Assn., Colo. Bar Assn., Minn. Soc. CPAs (instr. continuing legal edn. 1983-84, continuing profl. edn. 1982-86, individual, trust and estate provisions Tax Reform Act 1986, continuing legal edn. -estate planning 1994), Minn. Planned Giving Coun., Am. Assn. Ind. Investors (speaker), Am. Soc. CLUs, Minn. Soc. CLUs, Minn. Women Lawyers, Fla. Women Lawyers, Lex Alumnae, U. Mich. Alumni Assn. (coun. govs. 1989—, scholarship chmn.), U. Minn. Alumni Club (bd. dirs. 1996, coun. govs. 1988-96, pres., treas. mem. com.), Minn. World Trade Assn., Internat. Assn. Fin. Planners, Edina C. of C., Interlachen Club, Athletic Club, Lafayette Club, U. Minn. Alumni Assn. (mem. univ. issues com., nat. bd. dirs. 1996-99). Home: 1355 Vine Pl Mound MN 55364-9635 Office: Martin & Assoc PA 3800 W 80 St #270 Minneapolis MN 55431-

VENTRESCA, JOSEPH ANTHONY, energy coordinator; b. Lancaster, Ohio, Feb. 5, 1949; s. Giuseppe Attilio and Maria Artemia (Ciamacco) V.; m. Barbara Welling Hall, Dec. 18, 1982. BS in Math., Ohio U., 1971; MS in Environ. Sci., Miami U., Oxford, Ohio, 1978. Quality assurance insp. Phillips Roxanne Labs., Columbus, Ohio, 1972-74; teaching asst. Miami U., 1974-77; solar engr. Spectrum Solar Systems, Columbus, 1977; energy specialist State of Ohio, 1977-79; energy coord. City of Columbus, 1979—, project dir. DOE funded rsch., 1989—. Adj. tchr. architecture Miami U., 1988; mem. Columbus Weatherization Task Force, Renewable Energy Sources Fedn. Author: Budget Incentives for Municipal Energy Management, 1984, Before Ohio P.U.C., 1984; contbr. articles to profl. jours.; reviewer: The Columbus Energy Plan, 1981. Judge State Sci. Fair, Columbus, 1986-87; participant 1st U.S.-USSR Emerging Leaders Summit, 1988. Charles Kilbarger scholar, 1968-71; citation of Recognition Mayor of Columbus, 1988. Mem. Am. Soc. of Heating, Refrigeration, Airconditioning Engrs., Ohio Assn. of Energy Engrs. (bd. dirs. 1988), Nat. Assn. of Energy Engrs. (cert. indoor air quality), Ohio Pub. Facilities Maintenance Assn. (bd. dirs. 1988), Ohio Solar Energy Assn. (steering com. 1980). Avocations: sailing, windsurfing, camping. Home: 1640 W 3rd Ave Columbus OH 43212-2734 Office: City of Columbus Facilities 90 W Broad St Columbus OH 43215-4184

VENTRIGLIA, ANTHONY EMILO, mathematics educator; b. N.Y.C., June 20, 1922; s. Joseph and Anna Marie (Della Cava) V.; m. Lois E. Richter, June 27, 1953; children: Patricia Maguire, Linda Carella. AB, Columbia U., 1942; MSc, Brown U., 1943. Physicist N.A.C.A., Langley Field, Va., 1944-46; instr. Rutgers Univ., New Brunswick, N.J., 1947; instr. to asst. prof. to assoc. prof. Manhattan Coll., N.Y.C., 1947-92, adj. assoc. prof., 1992-95; ret., 1995. Cons. Environ. Engrs., N.Y.C. Social Sci. fellowship Social Sci. Rsch. Coun., Stanford U., 1954, Nat. Sci. fellowship Nat. Sci. Rsch. Coun., 1957. Mem. Am. Assn. of Math., Am. Math. Soc., Gamma Alpha (Cornell chpt.). Avocations: photography, cycling, hiking, theatre. Home: 1 Georgia Ave Bronxville NY 10708-6222

VENTRY, CATHERINE VALERIE, lawyer; b. Bronxville, N.Y., Feb. 19, 1949; d. Victor and Catherine Regina (Dillon) V. AB in Logic and Philosophy, Vassar Coll., 1971; postgrad., Boston U., 1972; JD, N.Y. Law Sch., 1978. Bar: N.Y. 1979, U.S. Dist. Ct. (so. and ea. dists.) N.Y. 1979. Adj. asst. prof. John Jay Coll. of Criminal Justice, N.Y.C., 1978-80; adj. asst. prof. bus. law Coll. Mount St. Vincent Lehman Coll., 1978-82; staff atty. City of N.Y. Dept. Housing Preservation and Devel. Litigation Bureau, 1981-84; pvt. practice N.Y., 1984—. Tax editor Prentice-Hall Pub. Co., Englewood Cliffs, N.J., 1980-81. Mem. N.Y. State Bar, Rockland County Women's Bar, Rockland County Bar Assn., MENSA. Avocations: rock music, song writing. Office: 873 Union Ave New Windsor NY 12553-5034

VENTRY, PAUL GUERIN, physician, government official; b. Ossining, N.Y., Sept. 1, 1934; s. Victor and Catherine (Dillon) V.; m. Betty Anne Baildon, Aug. 20, 1960. BS, Manhattan Coll., 1957; MD, Syracuse U., 1962. Diplomate Am. Bd. Profl. Disability Cons., Am. Bd. Forensic Medicine. Commd. 1st lt. U.S. Army, 1962; advanced through grades to lt. col., 1971; intern Walter Reed Gen. Hosp., 1962-63; resident, physician Pres. Eisenhower and Gen. Douglas McArthur, 1963-66; chief med. outptatient clinic, 1971; allergy cons. Surgeon Gen., Europe, 1967-70; chief medicine 47th Mobile Army Surg. Hosp., 1968-70; retired, 1971; chief adult svcs. Montgomery County (Md.) Health Dept., 1972; spl. dep. sheriff Montgomery County, 1972—; med. dir. Goddard Space Flight Ctr., NASA, 1973; ptnr. Med. Assocs., Washington, 1974. Med. dir. Civilian Employees Health Svc., Dept. Def., Washington, Walter Reed Army Med. Ctr., Pentgon Drug & Alcohol Program, Dept. Def. Blood Donor Program, Def. Intelligence Agy., 1975-83; prin. med. cons., sr. med. officer to Office HEarings and Appeals, Social Security Adminstrn., Arlington, Va., 1983—; asst. clin. prof. medicine George

Washington U., 1973-79; chief med. surg. cons., sr. med. officer in charge Social Security Adminstrn., 1983—; med. dir. Nat. Coun. Social Security Adminstrn. OHA, 1991, Am. Fedn. Govt. Employees #3615, 1991—, Nat. Coun. Social Security Employees, Am. Fed. Govt. Coun. 215; med. surg. cons. Wash. Hq. Svc. Dept. Def.; chief cons. med. surg. medicare fraud divsn. HHS Med. Dir. Contbr. articles to profl. jours. Immunology fellow, 1966, Allergy fellow, 1967. Fellow Am. Occupational Med. Assn., Am. Coll. Occupational and Environ. Medicine, Am. Acad. Disability Evaluating Physicians; mem. AMA, ACP, VFW, Fed. Physicians Assn. (treas.), Am. Pub. Health Assn., Am. Acad. Allergy, Royal Soc. Medicine, Brit. Allergy Soc., Am. Acad. Civil Svc. Physicians (treas.), Am. Coll. Physician Execs., Am. Bd. Forensic Examiners, Am. Legion, Assn. Mil. Surgeons, Mil. Dist. Washington Officers Assn., Nat. Fire Prevention Assn., Potomac C. of C., Washingtoin PErforming Arts Soc., D.C. Med. Soc., Montgomery County Med. Soc., Va. Med. Soc., Alpha Kappa Kappa. Home: 7813 Masters Dr Potomac MD 20854-3860

VENTURA, ANTHONY PAUL, artist, fine art educator; b. Southampton, N.Y., Jan. 24, 1927; s. Salvatore and Lillian (Morgan) V.; m. Barbara Jean Height, Apr. 9, 1961 (dec. May 1990); children: Tina, Mark, Paul. Student, Acad. of Arts, 1947-51, Pratt Inst., 1952-53, Art Students League, 1954-55. Tchr. Anthony Ventura Studio, Neptune, N.J., 1961—. Mem. traveling exhbns. Am. Watercolor Soc., N.Y.C., 1983; demonstrator Noyes Mus., Oceanville, N.J., 1988; mem. workshops Allendale (N.J.) Art Assn., 1990, Morristown (N.J.) Art Assn., 1993, 94. Contbr. articles to Watercolor 95, 98 mags., Best of Watercolor 97, Internat. Artist 99, (art video) Painting the Maine Coast, 1995; represented in permanent collections Winsor-Newton Co., 1975, Ft. Schyler Maritime Mus., 1986, Zhejiang Mus., China, 1993. With USN, 1945-46, PTO. Recipient Wells Stroud award AAPL, 1987, John Grabock award AAPL, 2001; Henry Gasser award NJ Watercolor Soc., 2001, Emil Carlson award Salmagundi Club, 2001, AAPL Grand. Nat. Pres.'s award, 2001, John O'Dwyer Meml. award Salmagundi Club, 2002. Mem. Guild Creative Art (adv. com. Shrewsbury, N.J. chpt. 1980-84), N.J. Waterco lor Soc. (exhbn. com. 1980-84, 2d v.p. 1982-84, 1st v.p. 1984-86, pres. 1987-88, jury of selection 1984-88, 94-97, 2000, jury of awards AAPh Grand Nat. 1996, Marian Price award 1993), Knickerbocker Artists (Knickerbocker Artist award 1985), Garden State Watercolor Soc. (jury of selection and awards Princeton, N.J. chpt. 1984-88, Warga award 1986), North Shore Art Assn., Hudson Valley Art Assn. (Transparent Watercolor award 1988), Salmagundi Club (Jane Impastato award 1990, Salmagundi award 1994, Top award 1998), N.J. Watercolor Soc. (Silver Medal 1995, 98, Doris D. Shoonmaker award 1999, Guild of Art 2000, Pres.'s award 2000.). Roman Catholic. Avocations: reading, travel, music, carpentry, photography. Home: 3430 Hwy # 66 Neptune NJ 07753

VENTURA, HECTOR OSVALDO, cardiologist; b. Buenos Aires, Mar. 21, 1951; came to U.S., 1981; s. Osvaldo Domingo and Nelida (Scocozza) V.; m. Laurie Anne Zeringue, Apr. 21, 1990; children: Austin Alejandro, Leighton Leandro, Kendra Mariel. BS, Nat. No. 10 Coll., Buenos Aires, 1968; MD, U. Buenos Aires, 1974. Diplomate Am. Bd. Internal Medicine with subspecialty in cardiovascular diseases. Resident in internal medicine Mil. Hosp., Argentina, 1975-78; rsch. fellow hypertension Ochsner Found., New Orleans, 1981-84; internal medicine resident Oschsner Found. Hosp., 1984-86, cardiology fellow, 1986-88; heart failure/heart transplant fellow Loyola U., Chgo., 1989; co-dir. heart failure heart transplant Oshsner Med. Inst., New Orleans, 1989-97, transplant adv. bd., 1992-97, ethics com., 1995-97; assoc. prof. medicine La. State U. Sch. Medicine; co-dir. advanced heart failure/cardiac transplant Tulane U. Med. Ctr., 1998-2000; prof. medicine Tulane U. Sch. Medicine, 2000—. Dir. cardiovasc. disease tng. program and edn. Ochsner Clinic Found., New Orleans, 2000—; jour. manuscript reviewer. Mem. editl. bd. Jour. Heart & Lung Transplantation, 1994; contbr. articles to profl. jours. 1st lt. Argentine Army, 1974-80. Ochsner Found. fellow, 1985-86. Fellow Am. Coll. Cardiology; mem. Am. Soc. Transplant (organ thoracic com. 1993—), Am. Heart Assn. Roman Catholic. Avocations: tennis, aerobic exercise. Home: 3746 Rue Chardonnay Metairie LA 70002-1500 Office: Ochsner Clinic Found 1514 Jefferson Hwy New Orleans LA 70121 E-mail: hventura@ochsner.org.

VENTURA, JACQUELINE N. nurse, researcher; b. Chgo., Sept. 17, 1942; d. Frank Joseph and Ellen Sarah (Healey) Ventura. Diploma, St. Francis Sch. Nursing, Evanston, Ill., 1963; BS, DePaul U., Chgo., 1967; MS, U. Wis., 1972, PhD, 1975-80. RN, Ill. Staff nurse Hines VA Hosp., Maywood, Ill., 1963-67; team leader US AID, Vinh Long, Vietnam, 1967-69; staff nurse Childrens Meml. Hosp., Chgo., 1969-70; clin. nurse specialist U. Wis. Hosps. and Clinics, Madison, 1972-75; nurse cons., instr. U. Wis. Sch. Nursing, 1975-78; asst. prof. nursing U. Calif., San Francsico, 1981-89, nurse rschr. dept. radiology, 1989-95; clin. rsch. assoc. Dendreon Corp., Seattle and Mountain View, Calif., 1996—2002. Recipient Civilian Svc. award Govt. of South Vietnam, 1969. Mem.: AAUW, Drug Info Assn., Women's Overseas League, Sigma Theta Tau. Home: 1530 5th Ave San Francisco CA 94122-3835 E-mail: jventura@dendreon.com.

VENTURA, JESSE (JAMES JANOS), governor; b. Mpls., July 15, 1951; s. George and Bernice Janos; m. Terry Ventura; children: Tyrel, Jade. Student, North Hennepin C.C. Profl. wrestler, 1973-84; ret.; gov. State of Minn., St. Paul, 1998—. Actor starring in several films including Predator; radio talk show host. Mayor City of Brooklyn Park, Minn., 1990-95; bd. advisors Make a Wish of Minn.; vol. football coach Champlin Park H.S. Served with USN, USNR. Mem. Am. Fedn. of TV and radio Announcers, Screen Actors Guild. Office: Office of the Governor State Capitol Rm 130 Saint Paul MN 55155-0001*

VENTURA, JOSE ANTONIO, industrial engineer, educator, researcher; b. Barcelona, Spain, Nov. 3, 1954; came to U.S., 1982; s. Jaime Ventura and Mercedes Valldosera; m. Marta Jaen, July 26, 1981; children: Marta, Laura, Luis. BS Engring., Poly. U. Barcelona, 1979; M Engring., U. Fla., 1984, PhD, 1986. Sys. analyst Nodec Informatica, Barcelona, 1979-80; asst. prof. Poly. U. Barcelona, 1980-82; rsch. asst. U. Fla., Gainesville, 1982-86; asst. prof. U. Mo., Columbia, 1986-89, Pa. State U., University Park, 1989-91, assoc. prof., 1991-95, prof. indsl. engring., 1995—. Vis. prof. U. Auckland, New Zealand, 1996; panelist, reviewer NSF, Washington, 1989—. Contbr. articles to profl. jours. Recipient Presdl. Young Investigator award NSF, 1990. Mem. Inst. Indsl. Engrs. (sr., divn. bd. dirs. 1991-94, chpt. pres. 1990-91, editor newsletter 1988-90, CIS award 1991), Inst. for Ops. Rsch. and Mgmt. Scis., N.Y. Acad. Scis. Achievements include decomposition and relaxation algorithms for nonlinear network optimization, CAD-based vision inspection systems; optimization techniques for just-in-time scheduling problems. Avocations: reading, travel, swimmming, tennis, soccer. Office: Pa State U 356 Leonhard Bldg University Park PA 16802-6817

VENTURI, ROBERT, architect; b. Phila., June 25, 1925; s. Robert C. and Vanna (Lanzetta) Venturi; m. Denise Lakofski, July 23, 1967; 1 child James Charles. Grad., Episcopal Acad., 1943; AB summa cum laude, Princeton U., 1947, MFA, 1950, DFA (hon.) , 1983, Oberlin Coll., 1977, Yale U., 1979, U. Pa., 1980; Laurea Honoris Causa in Architecture, U. Rome "La Sapienza", 1994. Designer firms of Oskar Stonorov, Eero Saarinen and Assos., Louis I. Kahn, 1950—58; ptnr. firm Venturi, Cope & Lippincott, Phila., 1958—61, Venturi and Short, Phila., 1961—64, Venturi and Rauch, Phila., 1964—80, Venturi, Rauch & Scott Brown, Phila., 1980—89, Venturi, Scott Brown and Assocs., Inc., 1989—; from asst. to assoc. prof. architecture U. Pa., 1957—65; Charlotte Shepherd Davenport prof. architecture Yale, 1966—70. With Payette Assocs., Yale U., 1998. Author: Complexity and Contradiction in Architecture, 1966, Complexity and Contradiction in Architecture, 2d edit., 1977; co-author (with Denise Scott Brown and Steven Izenour): Learning from Las Vegas, 1972, Learning from Las Vegas, 2d edit., 1977; co-author: (with Denise Scott Brown) A View from the Campidoglio, Selected Essays, 1953-84; author: Iconography and Electronics upon a Generic Architecture, 1996; author: (others, also articles) ;prin. works include Vanna Venturi House, Phila., 1961, Guild House, 1961, Humanities Bldg., SUNY, 1972, Franklin Ct., Phila., 1972, addition to Allen Meml. Art Mus., Oberlin Coll., 1973, Inst. for Sci. Info. Corp. Hdqs., Phila., 1978, Gordon Wu Hall, Princeton U., 1980, Seattle Art Mus., 1984, The Nat. Gallery, Sainsbury Wing, London, 1986, Fisher and Bendheim Halls, Princeton U., 1986, Gordon and Virginia MacDonald Med. Rsch. Labs. (with Payette Assocs.), UCLA, 1986, Charles P. Stevenson Jr. Libr., Bard Coll., 1989, Roy and Diana Vagelos Labs. IAST (with Payette Assocs.), U. Pa., 1990, Regional Govt. Bldg., Toulouse, France, 1992, Kirifuri Resort Facilities, Nikko, Japan, 1992, Trabant U. Ctr., U. Del., Newark, 1992, Meml. Hall Restoration and Addition, Harvard U., 1992, The Barnes Found. Restoration and Renovation, Merion, Pa., 1993, Disney Celebration (Fla.) Bank, 1993, Gonda (Goldschmied) Neuroscience and Genetics Rsch. Ctr. (with Lee, Burkhart, Liu Inc.), UCLA, 1993, Princeton Campus Ctr., Princeton U., 1996, Congress Ave. Bldg., Yale U. Sch. Medicine, 1998, (with Payette Assocs.) Master Plan and Buildings for U. Mich., 1997—. Trustee Am. Acad. Rome, 1966—71. Recipient Nat. Medal of Arts, 1992, Pritzker Architecture prize, 1991, Benjamin Franklin medal, The Royal Soc. for Encouragement of Arts, Mfrs. and Commerce, 1993; fellow Rome Prize Am. Acad., Rome, 1954—56. Fellow: AIA (award 1974, 1977, 1978), Accademia Nazionale di San Luca, Am. Acad. Arts and Scis., Am. Acad. of Arts and Letters, Am. Acad. in Rome, Royal Incorp. Architects of Scotland (hon.), Royal Inst. of Brit. Architects (hon.); mem.: Phi Beta Kappa. Office: Venturi Scott Brown & Assocs Inc 4236 Main St Philadelphia PA 19127-1603

VENTURO, FRANK ANGELO, communications educator, college offical; b. Gunnison, Colo., May 24, 1940; s. Peter J. and Theresa (Luchetta) V.; m. Margaret Patricia Palmer, July 1, 1967; children: Paul, Angela, Laura. BA, Western State Coll., Gunnison, 1964; MA, U. Colo., 1971, PhD, 1987. Tchr. English, speech South Routt County H.S., Oak Creek, Colo., spring 1965; tchr. speech and drama Grand Junction (Colo.) Ctrl. H.S., 1965-68; instr. comm. U. Colo., Boulder, 1969-71, St. Louis U., 1971-74; prof. comm. Western State Coll., Gunnison, 1974—, assoc. v.p. acad. affairs, 1991—, 1991-2000. Mediator, facilitator, arbitrator GV Assocs., Gunnison, 1988—; pres. Colo. Drama Speech Assn., 1978-79, Western State Coll. Edn. Assn., Gunnison, 1987-88. Chair Gunnison County Dems., 1981-84; mem. Gov.'s Econ. Adv. Coun., State of Colo., Denver, 1990-91; gov. appointee, mem. 7th Jud. Dist. Performance Review Com., 1995-2000, Colo. State Cts., 1995. Mem. Am. Assn. Higher Edn., Colo. Edn. Assn. (bd. dirs. 1988-92), Colo. Coun. Mediators and Mediation Orgns., Western State Coll. Alumni Assn. (pres. 1986-88). Democrat. Avocation: fly fishing. Home: 179 Tomichi Ln Gunnison CO 81230-9502 Office: Western State Coll Colo College Heights Gunnison CO 81231

VENZAGO, MARIO, conductor; b. Zurich, Switzerland, 1948; m. Marianne Skansi; children: Mario, Gabriel. Studied with, Hans Swarowsky, Vienna, 1973. Prin. guest conductor Malmo Symphony, Sweden; music dir. Basel Symphony Orch., Heidelberg Opera, 1986—89, Deutsche Kammerphilharmonic, 1989—92, Graz Opera Ho., 1990—95, Euskadi Nat. Opera, Spain, 1998—2001, Ind. Symphony Orch., 2002—. Guest conductor Berlin Philharmonic, Leipzig Gewandhaus Orchetser, London Philharmonic, City of Birmingham Symphony, Orchestre de la Suisse Romande , Tonhalle Orchestra Zurich , Tokyo's NHK Symphony, Berlin's Komische Oper, Salzburg Festival, Hannover Radio-Philharmonie, invited by Kurt Masur, Leipzig, Am. debut Hollywood Bowl, 1988, appeared N.J. Symphony, Ind. Symphony, Fla. Philharmonic, 1988; dir.: Balt. Symphony, 1995 (named artistic dir. symphony's summer festival , 2000); prin. conductor Winterthur City Orch. , Lucerne Opera Ho., Orchestre de la Suisse Romande. Recipient award, Diapason d'or, awards, Grand Prix du Disque, Edison prize. Office: Ind Symphony Orch 45 Monument Cir Indianapolis IN 46204-2919 Office Fax: 317-262-1159. Business E-Mail: iso@indyorch.org.*

VENZKE, KRISTINA LEA, academic administrator; b. Iowa City, Feb. 13, 1967; BA, U. Iowa, 1989; M in Internat. Adminstrn., Sch. Internat. Tng., 1995. Asst. study abroad advisor U. Iowa, Iowa City, 1991-92, project asst. for internat. edn., 1995-97; English tchr. Peace Corps, Chad, 1993-95. Dir. programs Humanities Iowa, 1998-2000; project coord. U. Iowa. Coll. Pub. Health, 2000—. Mem.: Iowa Peace Corps Assn. Office: 100 Oakdale Campus 222 IREH Iowa City IA 52242-5000 E-mail: kristina-venzke@uiowa.edu.

VÉR, ISTVÁN LÁSZLÓ, acoustical engineer, consultant; b. Tápiószecsö, Hungary, Dec. 22, 1934; came to U.S., 1965; s. István and Erzsebet G. (Darázs) V.; 1 child, Kristina M. BSEE, Tech. U., Budapest, 1956; MSEE, Tech. U., Aachen, Germany, 1960; PhD in Acoustics, Tech. U., Munich, 1963. R&D engr. Rohde and Schwarz, Munich, 1960-65; prin. cons. BBN Techs., Cambridge, Mass., 1965—. Author, editor: Noise & Vibration Engineering, 1992; holder patents. Recipient U.S. Sr. Scientist award Alexander von Humboldt Found., Germany, 1978, Best Paper award Am. Soc. Heating and Refrigeration Engring., 1979. Fellow Acoustical Soc. Am.; mem. Inst. Noise Control Engring. USA (dir. 1976-77), European Acoustics Assn. Avocations: literature, philosophy, travel, tennis. E-mail: iver@onemain.com.

VERA, ENRIQUE, psychiatrist; b. Buenos Aires, Dec. 3, 1939; came to U.S., 1964; s. Enrique and Nella (Pupulin) V.; m. Sara Grosso, June 13, 1964; children: Sylvia, Nancy, Henry. Grad. in edn., U. Buenos Aires, 1956, MD, 1964. Diplomate Am. Bd. Psychiatry and Neurology. Intern Detroit Meml. Hosp., 1964-65; resident U. Mo., 1968-71; dir. partial hospitalization and crisis unit Western Mo. Mental Health Ctr., Kansas City, 1971-76, dir. screening clinic, 1973-90, dir. psychotherapy unit, 1984-90, dir. forensic unit, 1986-88; grad. Topeka Inst. for Psychoanalysis, 1991; chief med. dir. Ctrl. Kansas City Mental Health Ctr., 1993-94; chief mental health clinic VA Outpatient Clinic, Ft. Myers, Fla., 1994-2000. Assoc. clin. prof. dept. psychiatry U. Mo., Kansas City. Author: Clinical responses to Disaster, 1989. Recipient award for crisis counseling HHS-USPHS, 1993. Mem. Am. Psychiat. Assn., Fla. Psychiat. Soc., Jackson County Med. Soc. Office: VA Outpatient Clinic 3033 Winkler Ext Fort Myers FL 33916-9413 E-mail: vera.enrique@bay-pines.va.gov.

VERAMALLAY, ASHTON ISARDATT, economist, educator; b. Albion Estate, Guyana, Mar. 2, 1940; s. Bonus David and Doris V.; m. Norma Surojni, Apr. 15, 1967; children: Stasia Ashmala, Shayne Ravin. BS in Econs., Sociology, U. Wis., La Crosse, 1970; MS in Econs., Iowa State U., 1972, PhD in Econs., 1976. Sr. master Belvedere Govt. Secondary Sch., Albion, 1963-67; asst. prof. W.Va. State Coll., Institute, 1976-77; from asst. prof. to prof. Ind. Univ. East, Richmond, 1977-90, prof., dir. Ctr. Econ. Edn., 1990—, chair bus. divsn., 1994—2001. Rsch. asst. Iowa State U., Ames, 1972-74, rschr., 1974-76; adv. bd. Small Bus. Devel. Ctr., Richmond, 1994—. Contbg. author: Encyclopedia of Keynesian Economics, 1997; contbr. articles to profl. publs. Mem. adv. bd. Richmond Hosp. Authority, 1995—; pres. ARC, Richmond, 1990; bd. dirs. Habitat for Humanity Greater Richmond, 1990—. Recipient Outstanding Svc. award Ind. Coun. Econ. Educators, 1979, Nat. Coun. Econ. Educators, 1983, 88, Sagamore of the Wabash award State of Ind., 1998. Mem. Internat. Atlantic Econ. Soc., Internat. Assn. Children's Social Econ. Edn. (editl. bd.), Am. Acon. Assn., Nat. Assn. Econ. Educators (mem. com. 1994—), Ea. Econ. Assn. (area rep.), Midwest Econ. Assn., Ind. Acad. Social Sci. (pres. 1992), AAUP, Kiwanis, Richmond C. of C. (edn. com. 1978-92, Dedicated Svc. and Leadership award 1993), Delta Mu Delta (nat. exec. coun.). Avocations: gardening, bicycling, reading, volleyball, cricket. Office: Indiana Univ E 2325 Chester Blvd Richmond IN 47374

VERANO, ANTHONY FRANK, retired banker; b. West Harrison, N.Y., Jan. 4, 1931; s. Frank and Rose (Viscomi) Verano; m. Clara Cosentino, July 8, 1951; children: Rosemarie, Diana Lynn. Student, Am. Inst. Banking, 1956-60, Bank Adminstrn. Inst., U. Wis., 1962-64, RCA Programmers Sch., 1965, Burroughs Programmers Sch., 1965, N.J. Bankers Data Processing Sch., 1966-68. With County Trust Co., White Plains, N.Y., 1949-61, sr. auditor, 1960-61; with State Nat. Bank Conn., Bridgeport, 1961—, auditor, 1962-79, exec. auditor, 1979—, Conn. Bank & Trust Co., 1983—; from v.p., auditor to sr. v.p., auditor Gateway Bank, Newtown, Conn., 1987-94, ret., 1996. Tchr. bank auditing Am. Inst. Banking, 1976-78. Mem. adv. bd. Norwalk Community Coll., 1968— . Served with USN, 1951-52. Mem. Bank Adminstrn. Inst. (dir. Stamford chpt. 1967-68, sec. Western Conn. chpt. 1968-69, treas. 1969-70, v.p. 1970-71, pres. 1971-72), Am. Acctg. Assn., Inst. Internal Auditors (cert. bank auditor, cert. bank compliance officer, cert. fin. svcs. auditor). Home: 224 Columbus Ave West Harrison NY 10604-2614 *It is difficult to define the elements of success. There are those who say success is achieved through drive and ambition only. However, those who have achieved their goals in life using only these two principles have probably destroyed more than they have created. Success, I feel, is achieved when drive and ambition are tempered with honesty, fairness, and respect for others. An individual must have a sense of dedication not only to his work and for those with whom he works but, most importantly, for those who work for him. This has been my philosophy in achieving my success.*

VERANT, WILLIAM J. state agency administrator; b. Washington, Dec. 19, 1941; m. Donna M. Verant; children: Bill Jr., Sharon. BSBA, Am. U. Various sr. mgmt. positions various comml. banks, savs. and loan and mortgage banks, Washington, Calif., N.Mex.; dir. fin. instns. divsn., regulation and licensing dept. State of N.Mex., Santa Fe, 1995—, acting dir. securities divsn. Avocation: restoring old cars. Office: State NMex PO Box 25101 725 Saint Michaels Dr Santa Fe NM 87504-7605

VERBA, BETTY LOU, real estate executive, investor; b. Cleve., Sept. 22, 1933; d. Albert Roy and Philomena (Weigel) Short; m. James Richard Verba, Sept. 11, 1954 (dec. Apr. 2001); children: Marilyn Danko, Christine Adkins, Patricia Zore, six grandchildren. Student, Miami U., Oxford, Ohio, 1952, Bowling Green State U., 1953. Lic. realtor, Ohio. Owner B&J Properties, 1963—; trustee Holiday Lakes Property Owners Assn., Willard, Ohio, 1973-77; realtor Realty One (formerly HGM/Hilltop), Parma Heights, 1977-94, Century 21 DePiero & Assocs., 1994—. Geneaologist (family history book) Short Family History, 1823-1973, Update, 1974-85. Mem. grand jury Cuyahoga County, 1990. Mem. Parma Genealogy Club (pres.). Democrat. Roman Catholic. Avocations: genealogy, world travel, photography (print and video), family activities. Home: 8800 Banner Ln Parma OH 44129-6072 Office: Century 21 De Piero and Assoc 5581 Ridge Rd Parma OH 44129-2372

VERBA, CYNTHIA, music history educator, academic administrator; b. N.Y.C., Apr. 4, 1934; d. Irving George and Frieda Winston; m. Sidney Verba; children: Margaret, Ericka, Martina. BA with honors, Vassar Coll., 1955; MA in Musicology, Stanford U., 1969; PhD in Musicology, U. Chgo., 1979. Instr. in music history Boston Conservatory Music, 1974-76; asst. dir. Office Career Svcs. Harvard U., 1978-83, assoc. dir. Office Career Svcs., 1984-86, dir. fellowships Grad. Sch. Arts and Scis., 1986—. Lectr. on gen. edn. Harvard U., 1978, 81, lectr. in music history ext. program, 1979—. Author: Music ant the French Enlightenment, 1993; contbr. articles to profl. jours. Danforth fellow U. Chgo., 1970-71, Bunting Inst. fellow Radcliffe Coll., 1987; summer grantee Nat. Found. Humanities, 1983. Mem. Am. Musicological Soc. (chair com. on acad. and nonacad. employment 1979-85). Avocations: hiking, piano. Office: Harvard U Grad Sch Arts and Scis 8 Garden St Cambridge MA 02138-3630 E-mail: cverba@fas.harvard.edu.

VERBA, SIDNEY, political scientist, educator; b. Bklyn., May 26, 1932; s. Morris Harold and Recci (Salman) V.; m. E. Cynthia Winston, June 17, 1955; children— Margaret Lynn, Ericka Kim, Martina Claire. BA, Harvard U., 1953; MA, Princeton U., 1955, PhD, 1959. Asst. prof. polit. sci. Princeton U., 1960-63, assoc. prof., 1963-64; prof. Stanford U., 1964-68, U. Chgo., 1968-72; prof. govt. Harvard U., 1972—, now Carl H. Pforzheimer prof., dir. univ. library, chmn. dept. govt., 1976-80, assoc. dean Faculty Arts and Scis., 1981—; dir. Harvard U. Library. Chmn. bd. dirs. Harvard U. Press, 1991—; chmn. policy com. Social Sci. Rsch. Coun., 1980-86; mem. Commn. on Behavioral and Social Scis., NRC, 1986-91; Commn. on Preservation and Access, chair com. on internat. conflict and cooperation, NRC, 1991-93; vis. com. MIT Polit. Sci. Dept.; bd. dirs. Social Sci. Rsch. Coun.; Tanner Lectr., Oxford, 1998. Author: Small Groups and Political Behavior, 1961, The Civic Culture, 1963, Caste, Race and Politics, 1969, Participation in America, 1972, Vietnam and the Silent Majority, 1972, The Changing American Voter, 1976, Participation and Political Equality, 1978, Injury to Insult, 1979, Introduction to American Government, 1983, Equality in America, 1985, Elites and the Idea of Equality, 1987, Designing Social Inquiry, 1994, Voice and Equality, 1995, The Private Roots of Public Action, 2001. Guggenheim fellow, 1980-81 Fellow Am. Acad. Arts and Scis.; mem. NAS (chair social and polit. sci. sect. 2002-), Am. Polit. Sci. Assn. (exec. coun. 1971-74, v.p. 1979-81, pres.-elect 1993-94, pres. 1994-95, Gladys Kammerer award 1972, Woodrow Wilson Found. award 1976, James Madison award 1993, Warren Miller award 2000), Internat. Studies Assn. (v.p. 1971-72). Jewish. Home: 142 Summit Ave Brookline MA 02446-2358 Office: Harvard U Library Dir Cambridge MA 02138

VERBOUT, JAMES PAUL, recreational therapist; b. Sterling, Ill., July 7, 1957; s. Louis Pius and Agnes (Rajnowski) V.; m. Loretta Margaret Jaquet, May 30, 1981; children: Kimberly Noel, Brandon James. BS in Therapeutic Recreation, U. Wis., LaCrosse, 1979; MA in Orgnl. Mgmt., U. St. Paul, 2002. Cert. therapeutic recreation specialist. Recreational therapist Glenwood (Iowa) State Hosp., 1979-80, Mayo Med. Ctr., Rochester, Minn., 1980—, program dir., clin. instr. Sch. Health Related Scis., 1988—, lead therapist, 1987-99, asst. supr. phys. medicine and rehab., 1999—. S.E. Minn. dir. Minn. Therapeutic Recreation steering com., Burnsville, 1988-90; v.p. Advanced Speech Interface Sys., 1993-94; mem. planning com., exhibit hall dir., co-emcee of event Disabled Outdoor Orgns. Recreation Symposium, 1997. Author: (with Robert Steuck) Activity Fun for You, 1983, (book chpt.) Consumer's Guide to Spinal Cord Injury, 2000; contbr. articles to profl. jours. Bd. dirs. Rochester Area Disabled Athletics and Recreation, Inc., 1986-95, vice sec., 1986-87, sec.-treas., 1988-90, v.p., 1991, pres., 1992-93, vol., 1986—; asst. coach Rochester Youth Baseball, 1995, Rochester Youth Soccer, 1995; vol. Rochester Youth Football, 1997-98; vol. Rochester Area Courage Daycamp, 1996-97; den rep. Cub Scouts Pack 210, 1993-94, pack sec., 1994-95; St. Mary's Hosp. chair United Way, 1994, rehab. rep., 1990-94; active Rochester Lourdes H.S. Band Boosters, 1998—, Baseball Boosters, 1998—. Recipient Spirit award Rochester Area Disabled Athletics and Recreation, 1989-90, Outstanding Bd. Mem. award Rochester Area Disabled Athletics and Recreation, 1995, Community-net Vol. award Internat. Yr. of the Vol., 2001. Mem. Am. Therapeutic Recreation Assn. (phys. medicine and rehab. network coord. com. chair 1997-99), Minn. Park and Recreation Assn., Nat. Closed Head Injury Found., State Closed Head Injury Found., S.E. Minn. Head Injury Support Group (charter mem., presenter 1982-94), Minn. Therapeutic Recreation Assn., Brain Injury Assn., Accessible Outdoor Recreation Assn. Am. (adv. bd. 1996-99), KC (3d degree). Democrat. Roman Catholic. Avocations: fishing, reading, bowling. Home: 4911 22nd Ave NW Rochester MN 55901-2033 Office: Mayo Med Ctr 200 1st St SW Rochester MN 55905-0001 E-mail: verbout.james@mayo.edu.

VERBOV, LEV FALKOVICH, metallurgical engineer, writer, translator; b. Leningrad, Russia, Jan. 10, 1937; came to U.S., 1977; s. Falka Shevelevich and Elka Abramovna Verbova; m. Larisa Ivanovna Fedkushova, Nov. 26, 1990; 1 child, Kristina Fedkouchova. MS in Metall. Engring., Tech. U., St. Petersburg, Russia, 1962. Sr. engr. All-Union Inst. Aluminum, Magnesium and Electrode Industry, St. Petersburg, 1962-77; engr.-scientist Aluminum Co. of Am., New Kensington, Pa., 1979-82; asst. editor Chem. Abstracts Svcs., Columbus, Ohio, 1985-87; cons. R&D scientist ECC Am., Inc., Sandersville, Ga., 1988-90; clk., team mem. Local Census Ctr., Bklyn., 1999-2000; freelance writer, 1966—; freelance translator, 1982—. Author: (books) Commercial Star, 1999, Swan Song of Ugly Duckling, 2000; composer: Solemn Melody, 1999; patentee in field. E-mail: lverbov@aol.com.

VERBURG, EDWIN ARNOLD, management consultant; b. Lakehurst, N.J., Oct. 6, 1945; s. Edwin Donald Verburg and Dorothy (Orrell) Hoodless; m. Joyce Elaine Majack, Sept. 14, 1968; children: Adelle Kristine, Wendi Elizabeth. BS, Calif. Polytech. U., 1968; M in City Planning, U. Calif., Berkeley, 1970; D in Pub. Adminstrn., George Washington U., 1975. Asst. planner City of Inglewood (Calif.), 1970-71; planner City of Glendale (Calif.), 1971-72; grad. assoc. U.S. Army Corps Engrs., Washington, 1974-75; mgr. fiscal analysis Met. Washington Council Govts., 1975-77; sr. program analyst U.S. Fish and Wildlife Service, Washington, 1977-79, asst. div. chief, 1979-80, div. chief, 1980-82, asst. dir. planning and budget, 1982-86, dep. asst. dir. policy budget and adminstrn., 1986-87; dir. office of fin. U.S. Dept. Treas., 1987-88, dir. fin. svcs. directorate, 1988-91, dir. fin. svcs. directorate, dep. CFO, 1991-95; assoc. adminstr. adminstrn. FAA, 1995-98; prin. ptnr. Avant Mgmt. Group, Inc., 1998-99; prin., fedn. govt. svcs. Kelly, Anderson & Assocs., 1999—. Author: Local State and Federal Fiscal Flows, 5 Vols., 1976; contbr. articles to fed. jours. Recipient Disting. Pub. Svc. award George Washington U., Sch. Bus. and Pub. Mgmt., 1994, Sec. of Treasury Disting Svc. award, 1995, Fin. Mgmt. Svc. Commrs. award, 1996. Mem. Am. Inst. Cert. Planners, Am. Planning Assn. (cert. govt. fin. mgr., Merit award Calif. chpt. 1973, First award Nat. Capital area chpt. 1980, Peer award for pub. svc. Dept. of Treasury 1990, sec. of treas. cert. appreciation 1991, Pres.'s

Meritorious Svc. award 1991, Commr.'s Citation Fin. Mgmt. Svc. 1996, Pres.'s award Combined Fed. Campaign 1997), Arlington Kiwanis (bd. dirs. 1999-2001, v.p. 2001-02, pres.-elect 2002-2003). Home: 538 N Oakland St Arlington VA 22203-2219

VERBY, JANE CRAWFORD, writer; b. La Crosse, Wis., Oct. 3, 1923; d. Clarence Horatio and Belva Gertrude (Hatch) Crawford; m. John Edward Verby, June 15, 1946; children: John Edward III, Steven, Ruth Davies, Karl. BA, Carleton Coll., 1945. Med. proofreader publs. dept. Mayo Clinic, Rochester, Minn., 1945-46; mem. staff Mpls. Star, 1946-47; tutor writing skills Onondaga Coll., Syracuse, N.Y., 1988. Co-author: How to Talk to Doctors, 1977; author: (novel) Patterns, 1986; contbr. articles to profl. publs. Recipient 2d prize award Cardiff Writing Cir., 1978. Mem. Nat. League Am. Pen Women (spkr., historian), Christian Writers Soc. (spkr.). Republican. Methodist. Avocations: walking, cycling, reading, grandchildren. Home: 9609 Washburn Ave S Minneapolis MN 55431-2460

VERCELLOTTI, JOHN RAYMOND, research chemist; b. Joliet, Ill., May 2, 1933; s. Joseph Francis and Mary Teresa (Walowski) V.; m. Sharon Cecile Vergez, Sept. 3, 1966; children: Ellen Theresa, Paul Auguste. BA, St. Bonaventure U., 1955; MS, Marquette U., 1960; PhD, Ohio State U., 1963. Lectr., rsch. assoc. Ohio State U., Columbus, 1963-64; asst. prof. Marquette U., Milw., 1964-67; assoc. prof. U. Tenn., Knoxville, 1967-70; prof. Va. Poly. Inst. & State U., Blacksburg, 1970-79; vis. prof. Inst. G. Ronzoni, Milan, Italy, 1977-78; sr. scientist Gulf South Res. Inst., New Orleans, 1980-85; rsch. chemist, rsch. leader So. Regional Rsch. Ctr. USDA, 1985-96, collaborator, 1999—. V.p. and sr. chemist V-Labs Inc., Covington, La., 1980-85, 96—; sr. rsch. advisor Sugar Processing Rsch. Inst., Inc., New Orleans, 1996-99, 01--; adj. prof. chemistry and physics S.E. La. U., Hammond, 1986—. Contbr. more than 200 articles to Elsevier & Am. Chem. Soc. Symposium Series; author, co-author numerous book chpts., 1960—; contbr. numerous articles to profl. jours. U. Tenn. minority colls. grantee, 1968-70, NSF grantee, 1964—. Mem. Am. Chem. Soc. (sec. 1968-90, Melville L. Wolfrom award 1994), Inst. Food Technologists; fellow Sigma Xi. Democrat. Roman Catholic. Achievements include research on food flavor quality and agricultural commodity utilization, origin of flavor from carbohydrates, lipid oxidation products, and peptides. Avocations: golfing, fishing, gardening, playing accordion. Home: 113 E 25th Ave Covington LA 70433-2819 Office: V-Labs Inc 423 N Theard St Covington LA 70433-2837 Business E-Mail: v-labs@v-labs.com.

VERCESI, HAYDÉE MARGARITA CHACHA, biomedical scientist; b. Bahia Blanca, Argentina, Sept. 24, 1959; arrived in U.S., 1988; d. Hector Vercesi and Elisa Martinez; m. Frederick Chanyapate Lahser, May 13, 1995; 1 child, Christopher Arthur Lahser-Vercesi. Vet. physician degree, U. Nacional del Centro, Argentina, 1983; MSc, Tex. A&M U., 1994. Technician Tex. A&M U., College Station, 1988-90, tchg. asst., 1990-94; rsch. technician Ctr. Behavioral Neurosci., SUNY, Stony Brook, 1995-97; rsch. coord. Mt. Sinai Med. Ctr., N.Y.C., 1997-99; assoc. scientist Schering Plough Rsch. Inst., Kenilworth, N.J., 1999—. Campaign coord. Amnesty Internat., 1991—, Ronkonkoma, N.Y., 1998. Avocations: flag collecting, writing, music, reading. Home: 183 Henshaw Ave Springfield NJ 07081 E-mail: haydee.vercesi@spcorp.com.

VERCOLLONE, CAROL FROST, clinical social worker, consultant; b. Ridgewood, N.J., Oct. 16, 1952; d. William Pepperell and Carol Anne (Norcross) Frost; m. Robert E. Vercollone, May 8, 1982. BA summa cum laude, U. Mass., 1974; MSW, U. Albany, 1978. Lic. social work, Mass. Social worker Whitney M. Young Health Ctr., Albany, N.Y., 1976-77; vol. counselor Rape Crisis Counseling Ctr., 1977-1978; intern family counselor Div. For Youth, Schenectady, N.Y., 1977-78; social worker Children's Health Program, Gt. Barrington, Mass., 1978-79; coord., asst. dir. Resolve, Inc., Arlington, 1979-83; psychotherapist Pastoral Counseling Ctr., Lowell, 1983-84; coord. spl. projects Resolve, Inc., Arlington, 1983-87; pvt. practice Stoneham, 1983—. Co-author: Understanding Artificial Insemination booklet, 1987. Bd. dirs. Resolve Bay State, 1986-89. Mem. NASW, Am. Fertility Soc., Open Door Soc., Friends Adoption. Address: 29 Cedar Ave Stoneham MA 02180-2420

VERDERBER, JOSEPH ANTHONY, capital equipment company executive; b. Nov. 30, 1938; s. Joseph Arthur and Dorothy Louise (Buchta) V.; m. Anita Barto, Sept. 10, 1960; children: Joseph Anthony, Lisa C., Paul A. BS in Mech. Engring., MIT, 1960, MS in Mech. Engring., 1961. Registered profl. engr., Ohio. Mgr. rsch. AM Internat., Cleve., 1964-70; dir. engring. Varityper div., East Hanover, N.J., 1971-73, product mgr., 1973-77, v.p. advanced bus. devel. multigraphics div. Mt. Prospect, Ill., 1977-81, gen. mgr. imaging systems group Bedford, Chgo., Mass., 1981, pres. East Hanover, N.J., 1982-88; corp. v.p. bus. devel. AM Internat., Inc., Chgo., 1988-89; pres. Am. Splty. Products, Dayton, Ohio, 1989-90, Barco Graphics, Inc., Dayton, 1990; v.p., gen. mgr. Gen. Scanning, Laser Sys. Divsn., Somerville, Mass., 1991-99; ret., 2000; CEO IBEX Process Tech., 2000. Lectr. Cleve. State U., 1962-67; chmn., SEMI New Eng. Forum, 1994-99. Recipient Karl Taylor Compton prize MIT, 1960; NSF fellow, 1961; named Inventor of Yr., AM Internat., Chgo., 1980. Mem. ASME, Nat. Printing Equipment and Supply Assn. (bd. dirs. 1986-88). E-mail: jverderber@aol.com.

VERDERY, DAVID NORWOOD, broadcast programming executive; b. Waco, Tex., Dec. 12, 1943; s. David Paul and Ruthe (McCawley) V.; m. Randy Lee Mahan, June 6, 1968 (div. 1970); 1 child, David Roderick. Student, Baylor U., 1961-64. Announcer KEFC, Waco, 1962-64; announcer, producer KHFI, Austin, Tex., 1964-65; announcer, prodn. dir. KIXL, Dallas, 1965-66; program dir. KVIL, 1967, KABL, San Francisco, 1968-69; nat. program coord. The McLendon Co., Dallas, 1969-73; v.p. programming TM Programming, 1973-80, Bonneville Broadcasting Sys., Northbrook, Ill., 1980-86; music dir. KBIG, L.A., 1985-95, asst. program dir., music dir., 1996-97, program dir., 1997; ret., 1998. Mem. Project Angel Food, L.A., 1992-94; mem. Permanent Charities Com., L.A., 1995-97, mem. Reading for the Blind, L.A., 1996-97; bd. dirs. Waco Civic Theatre, 1999-2001, v.p., 2000-01. Named Adult Contemporary Music Dir. of Yr., The Gavin Report, 1992, 93. Avocations: gourmet cooking, theater, travel, musical composing and arranging, magic. E-mail: wacodave@hot.rr.com.

VERDESCA, ARTHUR SALVATORE, internist, corporate medical director; b. Cliffside Park, N.J., May 25, 1930; s. Cosimo Theodore and Giulia Elvira (DeLipsis) V.; m. Ann Edith Copping, June 24, 1961; children: Stephen, Julia, Edith. AB, Columbia U., 1951, MD, 1955. Diplomate Am. Bd. Internal Medicine. Intern St. Luke's Hosp., N.Y.C., 1955-56, resident, 1956-57, 59-60, fellow Nat. Heart Inst., 1960-61; staff physician Western Electric, 1961-63, assoc. hdqrs. med. dir., 1963-65, hdqrs. med. dir., 1965-85; corp. med. dir. Am. Internat. Group, 1985—. Author: Live, Work and Be Healthy, 1980. Capt. USAF, 1957-59. Fellow ACP, Am. Acad. Occupational Medicine; mem. N.Y. Occupational Med. Assn. (pres. 1979-80). Roman Catholic. Avocation: crossword puzzle construction. Home: 19 Randolph Dr Morristown NJ 07960-5319 Office: Am Internat Group Inc 70 Pine St New York NY 10270-0002

VERDIER, DAVID D'OOGE, ophthalmologist, educator; b. Grand Rapids, Mich., Jan. 22, 1949; s. Leonard D'Ooge and Anita Beatrice (Carvalho) V.; m. Beverly Deane Johnson; children: Renée Leigh, Travis D'Ooge, Eric Leonard, Nora Claire. BA in Polit. Sci., U. Mich., 1971; MD, U. Mich. Med. Sch., 1977. Resident in family practice Med. U. S.C., Charleston, 1977-80; resident in ophthalmology Pitts. Eye and Ear, U. Pitts., 1980-83; corneal and external eye fellowship U. Iowa, Iowa City, 1983-84; pvt. practice med. and surg. ophthalmology Verdier Eye Ctr. P.C., Grand Rapids, Mich., 1984—; assoc. clin. prof. Mich. State U. Coll. Medicine, East Lansing, 1986—. Med. dir. Mich. Tissue Bank, Lansing, Mich., 1995-98, SEECOM, Mich., 1995—. Contbr. articles to profl. jours. and textbook chpts. Bd. dirs. East Grand Rapids (Mich.) Sch. Found., 1992-2000, Macatawa Bay Yacht Club, Holland, Mich., 1988-90, 94-95, Grand Rapids Art Mus., 1995-2001; bd. dirs. Macatawa Park Cottagers Assn., Holland, 1993-99, pres., 1993-98. Named to Galens Hon. Med. Soc., 1975-77. Mem. Mich. Ophthalmologic Soc (bd. dirs. 1994-2000), Mich. State Med. Soc. (del. 1993-2000). Home: 3043 Mary St SE Grand Rapids MI 49506-3150 Office: Verdier Eye Center PC 1000 E Paris Ave SE Ste 130 Grand Rapids MI 49546-3680

VERDILE, VINCENT PAUL, dean, emergency physician; b. Troy, N.Y., Aug. 13, 1955; s. Raphael Mario and Frances (Marinucci) V.; m. Louise Ann Wickware, Aug. 30, 1985. BS, Union U., 1977, MS, 1980; MD, Albany Med. Coll., 1984. Intern U. Pitts., 1984-85, resident in emergency medicine, 1985-87; assoc. med. dir. dept. pub. safety City of Pitts., 1985—93; flight physician Ctr. for Emergency Medicine, Pitts., 1988—93; chair. dept. of emergency med. Albany Med. Coll., 1993—2000, interim dean, 2000, dean, 2001—. Mem. adj. staff dept. emergency medicine Mercy Hosp., Pitts, 1987—93; med. dir., emergency med. technician Community Coll. Allegheny Coll., 1987—93; attending physician emergency dept. Presbyn.-Univ. Hosp., 1987—93; assoc. program dir. residency in emergency medicine Univ. of Pitts., 1987—93, asst. prof. medicine, 1987—93. Contbr. numerous articles to profl. jours. Mem. Soc. Acad. Emergency Medicine, Nat. Assn. Emergency Med. Svcs. Physicians (chmn. membership com. 1988—), Am. Coll. Emergency Physicians, Pa. chpt. Am. Coll. Emergency Physicians, Pa. State Med. Soc., Allegheny County Med. Soc., Am. Assn. Poison Control Ctrs. Roman Catholic. Office: Albany Med Coll 47 New Scotland Ave Albany NY 12208*

VERDINE, GREGORY LAWRENCE, chemist, educator; b. Somers Point, N.J., June 10, 1959; s. Richard Daniel and Therese Mary (Delaney) V.; m. Kasumi Koseki, Dec. 1, 1987; children: Vanessa Kaori, Lauren Arika, Erika Rose. BS, St. Joseph's U., Phila., 1982; MA, Columbia U., 1983, PhD, 1986; AB (hon.), Harvard U., 1995. Postdoctoral fellow MIT, Cambridge, Mass., 1986, 87, Harvard Med. Sch., Boston, 1987, 8; asst. prof. chemistry Faculty Arts and Scis. Harvard U., Cambridge, 1988-92, Thomas D. Cabot assoc. prof. chemistry, 1992-94, prof., 1994—. Sci. adv. bd. Ariad Pharms., Cambridge, 1992—, La Jolla (Calif.) Pharms., 1990—; cons. Hoffmann-LaRoche, Nutley, N.J., 1991—. Assoc. editor Chemistry and Biology, 1994—; contbr. numerous articles to profl. jours. Recipient Excellence in Chemistry award Zeneca Pharms., 1994; DuPont Young Faculty fellow, 1988, Searle scholar, 1990, Eli Lilly grantee, 1990, Alfred P. Sloan fellow, 1991, NSF Presdl. Young Investigator award, 1991, others. Mem. AAAS, Am. Chem. Soc. (Arthur C. Cope Scholar award 1994, Eli Lilly award 1995). Achievements include research in chemical genetics: the propagation, preservation and expression of genetic information. Office: Harvard U Dept Chemistry/Chem Bio 12 Oxford St Cambridge MA 02138-2902 Home: 7 Aileen Ter Gloucester MA 01930

VERDOL, JOSEPH ARTHUR, chemist; b. Chgo., Oct. 30, 1927; s. Joseph and Molly (Pangerl) Vrdolak; m. Elaine C. Glenn, July 7, 1973; children: David A., Lori. BS in Chemistry cum laude, U. Ill., 1951; PhD in Chemistry, Cornell U., 1955. Dir. polymer rsch. Sinclair Rsch., Harvey, Ill., 1963-68, v.p. N.Y.C., 1968-69; sr. v.p. Arco Tech. Inc., Phila., 1970-86; v.p. Arco Chem. Asia Pacific, Tokyo, 1980-86; pres. Chem. Tech. Worldwide Cons., N.Y.C., 1986—, Tasco Chem. USA. Former lectr. East-West trade Harvard U. Patentee in field of petrochemicals in Canada, Japan and Europe; Contbr. numerous articles to Ency. Polymer Sci. & Tech., Jour. Am. Chem. Soc., Oil & Gas Jour., Rubber Age, Rubber World, Harvard Revs. Lt. USMC, 1945-46, U.S. Army, 1950-51. Fellow Am. Inst. Chemists; mem. Am. Chem. Soc., AAAS. Roman Catholic. Achievements include patents in Petroleum, Polymer and Petrochemical fields, Methyl tertiarybutyl ether; invention of processes and new polymers which are used in petroleum refining, petrochemicals and chemical industry. Office: Chem Tech Worldwide 1641 3rd Ave Ste 16-he New York NY 10128-3623

VERDU, SERGIO, engineering educator; b. Barcelona, Spain, Aug. 15, 1958; came to U.S., 1980; s. Tomas Verdu and Visitacion Lucas; m. Mercedes Paratje, Jan. 19, 1982; 1 child, Ariana. Diploma telecomm. engr., Polytech. U. Barcelona, 1980; MS, U. Ill., 1982, PhD, 1984. Asst. prof. Princeton (N.J.) U., 1984-89, assoc. prof., 1989-92, prof., 1993—. Prin. investigator U.S. Office Naval Rsch., N.J. Dept. Higher Edn., U. S. Army Rsch. Office, N.J. Commn. Sci. and Tech., NSF, U.S.-Israel Binational Sci. Found.; vis. prof. U. Calif., Berkeley, 1998. Author: Multiuser Detection, 1998, Information Theory: Fifty Years of Discovery, 1999; mem. editl. bd. Transactions on Info. Theory, 1990-94; contbr. numerous articles to profl. jours, book chpts. Recipient Nat. U. prize Ministry Edn., Spain, 1982, Presdl. Young Invesitgator award NSF, 1988, Frederick E. Terman award Am. Soc. Engring. Edn., 2000. Fellow IEEE (Outstanding Paper award 1998, Millennium medal 2000); Info. Theory Soc. (v.p. 1995, pres. 1997, bd. govs. 1989—, Golden Jubilee Paper award 1998). Office: Princeton U Dept Elec Engring Princeton NJ 08544-0001 E-mail: verdu@princeton.edu.

VER DUIN, D'ARLENE K. research scientist; b. Grand Rapids, MI, Sept. 19, 1952; m. O. Lynn Sims, Mar. 15, 1996. BA in Sociology, U. North Tex., 1995, MPA, 1998. Rsch. scientist U. North Tex., Denton, 1999—. Mem. Am. Sociol. Assn., Pi Alpha Alpha (life). Democrat. Avocations: genealogy, needle arts, viola. Office: Univ North Tex Survey Rsch Ctr PO Box 310637 Denton TX 76203 E-mail: dverduin@scs.cmm.unt.edu.

VEREB, MICHAEL JOSEPH, retired pharmaceutical and cosmetic executive; b. Leechburg, Pa., Apr. 1, 1931; s. Michael Andrew and Mary Elizabeth (Chernay) V.; m. Joanne Maria Helms, Oct. 9, 1955; children: Kenneth Michael, Wayne William. BS in Indsl. Mgmt., Carnegie Mellon U., 1953; postgrad., U. Pitts., 1955-56, U. So. Ill., 1959. Registered profl. engr., Calif. Methods engr. Schenley (Pa.) Distillers, 1955-57; cons. EnServCo, Pitts., 1957-58; sr. indsl. engr. Olin Industries, Alton, Ill., 1958-59; mgr. indsl. engr. Ormet Aluminum subs. Olin Industries, Bucks Bottom, Ohio, 1959-66; resource mgr. Olin Aluminum, N.Y.C., 1966-67; dir. engring. Squibb Corp., New Brunswick, N.J., 1967-78, dir. facilities planning Lawrenceville, 1978-84; v.p. facilities planning Charles of Ritz Group, Ltd. div. Squibb Corp., Holmdel, 1984-87; div. mgr. pharms. Fluor Daniel, Inc., Marlton, 1988-97, cons., 1997; ret., 1997. Cons. EnServCo, Pitts., 1957-58, Pitman Moore div. of IMC, Washington Crossing, N.J.; rsch. coord. Lehigh U., Bethlehem, Pa., 1984-86. Inventor disposable containers. Coord. fund drives Carnegie Mellon U., Lawrenceville, N.J., 1973-83; 1st v.p. Raritan Valley Regional Chpt. C. of C., 1976-78. With U.S. Army, 1953-55. Mem. Inst. Indsl. Engring., Assn. Info. and Image Mgmt., Soc. Mfg. Engrs., Elks (v.p. 1960-66), Pi Kappa Alpha (v.p. 1952-53). Home: 5 Arncliffe Rise Medford NJ 08055-3337

VERED, RUTH, art gallery director, owner; b. Tel Aviv, Sept. 26, 1940; d. Abraham and Helen Rosenblum; children: Sharon, Oren. BA in Art History with honors, Bezalel U., Jerusalem, 1964. Freelance art cons., Israel and N.Y.C., 1965-75; dir. Vered Gallery, East Hampton, N.Y., 1977—. Exhibited at Vered Gallery. Sgt. paratroops Israeli Army, 1958-60. Home: 891 Park Ave New York NY 10021-0326 Office: Vered Gallery 68 Park Pl East Hampton NY 11937-2407 E-mail: vered@mindspring.com.

VEREEN, ROBERT CHARLES, retired trade association executive; b. Stillwater, Minn., Sept. 8, 1924; s. George and Leona Lucille (Made) Wihren; m. Rose Catherine Blair, Nov. 5, 1945; children: Robin, Stacy, Kim. Grad. high sch. Mng. editor Comml. West Mag., Mpls., 1946-50, Bruce Pub. Co., St. Paul, 1950-53, Nat. Retail Hardware Assn., Indpls., 1953-59; mng. dir. Liberty Distbrs., Phila., 1959-63; editor Hardware Retailing, Indpls., 1963-80; assoc. pub., dir. communications Nat. Retail Hardware Assn., 1980-84, sr. v.p., 1984-87; Vereen & Assocs., Mgmt., Mktg. Cons., 1987—. Lectr. mgmt. insts.; guest lectr. on distbn. pub.; co-founder U.S.A. Direct; co-founder, ptnr. Eurotrade Mktg., 1988—; ptnr. Hardlines Pers. Finders, 1987—. Author: (with Paul M. Doane) Hunting for Profit, 1965, The Computer Age in Merchandising, 1968, Perpetuating the Family-Owned Business, 1970, The How-To of Merchandising, 1975, The How-To of Store Operations, 1976, A Guide to Financial Management, 1976, Productivity: A Crisis for Management, 1978, Hardlines Rep Report Newsletter, 1984-94, Guidelines to Improve the Rep/Factory Relationships, 1992. Served with AUS, 1943-46. Mem. Am. Soc. Bus. Press Editors (dir., v.p. 1966-70), Soc. Nat. Assn. Publs. (dir., pres. 1970-75, chmn. journalism edn. liaison com. 1976-79), Toastmasters (v.p., treas., sec. 1955-59), Am. Hardware Mfrs. Assn. (co-founder, sec.-treas. Young Execs. Club 1958-.59, 63-65), Hardware-Housewares Packaging Expn. (founder 1960, chmn. com. packaging 1960-62, chmn. judging com. Hardware-Packaging Expn. 1975-78), Packaging Inst., Household Consumer Products Export Coun. (chmn. 1981-83), World-Wide DIY Coun. (exec. sec. 1981-99, dir. emeritus 1999—). Home and Office: 10769 Oriole Ct Indianapolis IN 46231-1006

VEREEN, WILLIAM JEROME, uniform manufacturing company executive; b. Moultrie, Ga., Sept. 7, 1940; s. William Coachman and Mary Elizabeth V.; m. Lula Evelyn King, June 9, 1963; children: Elizabeth King, William Coachman. BS in Indsl. Mgmt, Ga. Inst. Tech., 1963. With Riverside Mfg. Co., Moultrie, 1967—, from v.p. to exec. v.p., 1970-77, pres., 1977-84, pres., treas., CEO, 1984—; v.p., dir. Moultrie Cotton Mills, 1969—; exec. v.p. Riverside Industries, Inc., Moultrie, 1973-77, pres., 1977-84, CEO, 1984—, also dir. V.p. Riverside Uniform Rentals, Inc., Moultrie, 1971-80, pres., 1980-84, CEO, bd. dirs.; pres. Riverside Mfg. Co. (Ireland) Ltd., 1977—, Right Image Corp., Riverside Mfg. Co. GmbH, Germany, 1979—, also CEO, dir., 1984; pres., treas., CEO G.A. Rivers Corp., Riverside Mfg. Co. (U.K.) Ltd.; pres., treas. CEO, bd. dirs. Textile Clothing Tech. Corp.; chairholder Tyner eminent scholars, prof. coll. human scis. Fla. State U., 1993-94, mem. coll. human scis. devel. bd.; bd. dirs. Ga. Power Co., Gerber Sci., Inc., Blue Cross/Blue Shield Ga., Cerulean Cos., Inc., Trade and Tourism, Ga. Rsch. Alliance, Ga. Corp. Indsl. Devel.; mem. trilateral commn. apparel labeling NAFTA; so. regional adv. dir. Bank of Am. (GA) (formerly Nations Bank, N.A.; advisor textile and apparel tariffs and quotas U.S. Dept. State Bd.; mem. World Econ. Forum, Davos, Switzerland. Bd. dirs. Moultrie-Colquitt County (Ga.) Devel. Authority, 1973-77, Moultrie-Colquitt County United Givers, 1968-75, Moultrie YMCA, 1968-75, Colquitt County Cancer Soc., 1969-73; trustee Cmty. Welfare Assn. Moultrie, 1970—, Pineland Sch., Moultrie, 1971-75, Leadership Ga., 1972—, Ga. Coun. Econ. Edn.; trustee Am. Apparel Edn. Found.; adv. bd. Ga. Tech. sch. of textile and fiber engring.; elder 1st Presbyterian Ch. Capt. USMCR, 1963-67. Decorated Bronze Star with combat V, Purple Heart. Mem. Internat. Apparel Fedn. (2d v.p., 1st v.p., bd. dirs., exec. com., chmn. 1991-92), Am. Apparel Mfrs. Assn. (bd. dirs., exec. com., edn. found. com., 2d vice chmn., chmn. 1990-91), Nat. Assn. Uniform Mfrs. and Distbrs. (bd. dirs. 1988-91), Am. Apparel Edn. Found. (v.p., trustee), Capital City Club (Atlanta), Commerce Club (Atlanta), World Econ. Forum, Sunset Country Club, Ga. C. of C., Elks, Kiwanis, Sigma Alpha Epsilon. Home: 21 Dogwood Dr Moultrie GA 31768-6537 Office: PO Box 460 Moultrie GA 31776-0460

VERE HODGE, RICHARD ANTHONY, pharmaceutical executive, consultant; b. Burnham-on-Sea, Somerset, Eng., Dec. 27, 1943; s. Francis and Eleanor Mary Vere Hodge; married; 3 children. BA, Trinity Coll., Dublin, 1966; DPhil, Worcester Coll., Oxford, Eng., 1969. With Beecham Pharms. (then SmithKline Beecham Pharms., now GlaxoSmithKline), England, 1969-96, project mgr. human interferon project England, 1974-76, chief biochemist antiviral chemotherapy project England, 1981—92; loaned expert on famciclovir to World-wide Strategic Product Devel., 1993—96, assoc. dir., 1995—96; dir. Vere Hodge Antivirals Ltd., Reigate, Surrey, Eng., 1996—. Cons. Pharmasset, Inc., Atlanta, 2000—. Contbr. articles to profl. jours., chpts. to books; patent for treatment of latent infection of herpesvirus, 1999. Founding mem. Ch. Roof Fund Com., Leigh, Reigate, Surrey, Eng., 1989-99. Mem. Royal Soc. Chemistry, Am. Soc. Microbiology, Internat. Soc. Antiviral Rsch., The Chromatography Soc. Avocations: bell-ringing, gardening, hill walking. Office: Vere Hodge Antivirals Ltd Leigh Reigate Surrey RH2 8RD England E-mail: averehodge@aol.com.

VERFAILLIE, ROLAND BRUCE, mental health professional; b. Woodbury, N.J., Feb. 27, 1949; s. Roland Bird and Patricia Barbara Verfaillie; m. Donna L. Sessa, May 30, 1980; children: Loren, Eric. PhD, Trinity Coll., 2000. Pre-trial intervention specialist Fla. Dept. Corrections, West Palm Beach, 1973-76; forensic psychologist Lantana Correctional Inst., Dept. Corrections, Lantana, Fla., 1976—79; ctr. dir. the Counseling Ctr., Delray Beach, 1978-79; dir. cmty. mental health ctr. U.S. Dept. Def., Bad Hersfeld, Germany, 1980—83, supr. psychologist cmty. counseling svcs. Augsburg, Germany, 1983—84, dir. cmty. & family activities Augsburg mil. cmty., 1984—89; unit supr. adolescent substance abuse treatment program Savannas Hosp., Port St. Lucie, Fla., 1989—92; co-founder, exec. dir. Recovery Assics, Inc., 1992—. Adj. prof. Indian River C.C., Ft. Pierce, Fla., 1991—93, Fla. Atlantic U., Boca Raton, Fla., 1978, City Coll., Chgo., 1983—85, U. Md., 1985—88; spkr. in field; cons. Drug Free Workplace Programs, Treasure Coast, Fla., 1992—2001. Author: The Ashley Dancers, 1998, The Lie, 2000, Fast Track, 2001. Employee assistance provider Treasure Coast EAP, 1992—2001; chmn. task force Batterers Intervention Project, Treasure Coast, 1999—2001. Mem. Am. Counseling Assn., Am. Assn. Marriage & Family Counselors, Nat. Assn. Alcoholism and Drug Abuse Counselors, Fla. Alcohol & Drug Abuse Assn. Avocations: running, kayaking, hunting, writing. Home: 672 Cleveland Ave Stuart FL 34994 Office: Recovery Assocs Inc 8000 S US #1 Ste 202 Port Saint Lucie FL 34952 Personal E-mail: versessa@att.net.

VERGANO, LYNN (MARILYNN BETTE VERGANO), artist; b. N.Y.C., Nov. 14; d. George and Sis Anagnostis (Helaine Haas); children: Scott, Stephen, Sandy, Sefton. Student, Pratt Inst., 1959-60; BA, NYU, Heights, 1963; MA, NYU, 1964. Lectr. art Morris County Coll., 1982. Lectr. UN Pan Pacific and S.E. Asia Women's Assn., N.Y. chpt., 1996, 2001, AAUW, Caldwell, N.J. chpt. 1998, Nat. Soc. of Arts and Letters N.J. chpt. 1998,NSAL, 2001, AAUW, Somerset Hills, N.J. chpt., 2001; judge, art juror, critic. Author, illustrator: Paintings by Lynn Vergano, 1980, Paintings by Lynn Vergano, 1998; one-woman shows include Paper Mill Playhouse, N.J., 1976, 79, 83, Fairleigh Dickinson U., N.J., 1977, Drew U., N.J., 1977, Rutgers U., N.J., 1978-79, Hong Kong Arts Ctr., 1980, Am. Univ. Alumni, Bangkok, Thailand, 1980, Caldwell Coll., N.J., 1980, União Cultural Brasil-Estados Unidos, São Paulo, Brazil, 1982, Galleria Fenice, Venice, Italy, 1985, St. Sophia Mus., Istanbul, Turkey, 1988, Nat. Arts Club, N.Y.C., 1989, Centreplace, Hamilton, New Zealand, 1990, Women's Nat. Rep. Club, N.Y.C., 1997, UN Pan Pacific and S.E. Women's Assn., 2001; exhibited in group shows including Monmouth Mus., Lincroft, N.J., 1976, 77, 82, Morris Mus., Morristown, N.J., 1977, 78, N.J. State Capital Mus., Trenton, 1979, Macculloch Hall Hist. Mus., N.J., Morristown, 1984, 87, 89, 92, 96, Nat. Audubon Artists, N.Y.C., 1981, Salmagundi Club, N.Y.C., 1981, World Trade Ctr., N.Y., 1981, Nat. Arts Club, N.Y.C., 1981-99, Bergen Mus., Paramus, N.J., 1983, Lincoln Ctr., N.Y.C., 1987, Bklyn. Botanic Gardens, N.Y., 1987, Seton Hall U., South Orange, N.J., 1998, Johnson & Johnson, New Brunswick, N.J., 2000, others; exhbn. UN Pan Pacific and S.E. Asia Women's Assn.-N.Y. chpt. N.Y. Acad. of Sci., 1998, PP SEAWA, 2001, Nabisco World Hdqrs., Hanover, N.J., 1999, Reeves Reed Arboretum, Summit Coll. Club, 1999. Pres., chpt. charter mem., 1969-70, hon. mem. Welcome Wagon Club, Randolph, N.J., 1969—. Recipient UN 25th Anniversary Creative Writing award, 1970, John H. Miller award Morris County Coll., 1979, Grumbacher gold medallion, 1984, Torch award NYU, 1993. Mem. AAUW (hon.), Nat. Arts Club (exhibiting), Nat. Soc. Arts and Letters (exec. bd. N.J. chpt. 1979—), Federated Art Assns. N.J. (trustee 1982—, pres., chmn. bd. dirs. 1982-88, Heritage plaque 1989), N.Y. Acad. Scis., Kenilworth Art Assn. (hon.), Millburn-Short Hills Arts Ctr., Shanghai-Tiffin Club (hon., Disting. Svc. award 1998), Delta Kappa Gamma (N.Y.C. chpt., hon.).

VERGE, PIERRE, legal educator; b. Quebec City, Can., Jan. 9, 1936; s. Francis and Regina (Roy) V.; m. Colette Habel, June 29, 1963; children—Marc, Caroline, Louis. BA, Laval U., 1956, LL.L., 1959, LL.D., 1971; MA, McGill U., 1962, Cambridge U., 1977; LL.M., U. Toronto, 1968; 1971. Bar: Que. 1961, Queen's Counsel 1976. Pvt. practice law, Quebec City, Can., 1961-66; mem. faculty Laval U. Faculty of Law, 1966—; dean Laval U. Faculty of Law (Faculty of Law), 1973-77. Commonwealth fellow St. John's Coll., Cambridge U., 1977-78 Mem. Assn. Can. Law Tchrs. (pres. 1972-73, chmn. conf. law deans 1975-76), Que. Bar, Canadian Bar, Royal Soc. Can. Home: 2542 de la Falaise Sillery QC Canada G1T 1W3 Office: Cite Universitaire Universite Laval Quebec QC Canada

VERGHESE, ABRAHAM CHEERAN, internist, writer, educator; b. Addis Ababa, Ethiopia, May 30, 1955; came to U.S., 1980; s. George and Mary Verghese; children: Steven, Jacob. MD, Madras (India) U., 1979; MFA, U. Iowa, 1991; DSc (hon.), Swarthmore Coll., 2001. Diplomate Am. Bd. Internal Medicine, Am. Bd. Infectious Diseases, Geriatrics., and ulmonary Medicine. Intern Govt. Gen. Hosp., Madrass Med. Coll., 1979-80; resident, chief resident E. Tenn. State U., Johnson City, 1980-83, instr. in medicine, 1982-83, asst. prof. medicine, 1985-88, assoc. prof. medicine, 1988-90; tchg. asst. medicine Boston U., 1983-85; chief infectious diseases VA Med. Ctr., Johnson City, 1986-90, asst. chief medicine, 1988-90; vis. assoc. U. Iowa, Iowa City, 1990-91; prof. medicine Tex. Tech. U., El Paso, Tex., 1991—2002; chief infectious diseases Tex. Tech. Regional Acad. Health Ctr., 1991-97; prof. medicine, dir. Ctr. for Med. Humanities and Ethics, U. Tex. Health Scis. Ctr., San Antonio, 2002—. Author: My Own Country: A Doctor's Story of a Town and Its People in the Age of AIDS, 1994, (with others) Infection in the Nursing

Home, 1990. Named Tchr. of Yr. Internat. Medicine residents and Alpha Omega Alpha E. Tenn. State U., 1989; recipient James Michener fellowship to Writer's Workshop U. Iowa. Fellow ACP (publs. coms.), Royal Coll. Physicians Can., Infectious Diseases Soc. Am., Coll. Chest Physicians; mem. Am. Geriat. Soc., Am. Fedn. for Clin. Rsch., Am. Soc. Microbiology, Soc. for Exptl. Biology and Medicine. Office: UTHSCSA Mail Code 7730 7703 Floyd Curl Dr San Antonio TX 78229

VERGILIS, JOSEPH SEMYON, mechanical engineering educator; b. Odessa, Ukraine, Aug. 14, 1934; came to U.S., 1988; s. Semyon E. and Zinaida I. (Gleizerman) V.; m. Zhanna S. Berenfeld, Apr. 30, 1963; children: Helen, Irene. BS in Mfg. Engring., Poly. Inst., Odessa, 1958; PhD in Mech. Engring., Exptl. R&D Inst. Machine Tools, Moscow, 1973. Mfg. engr. Factory of Machine Tools, Odessa, 1958-66; sr. scientist R&D Inst. ENIMS, Moscow, 1966-87; cons. Beltran Assn., Inc., Bklyn., 1988-90; prof. mech. engring. Murray (Ky.) State U., 1990-92; cons. Russtrad, Inc., Richmond, Mass., 1992-93; prof. mech. engring. U. Turabo, Gurabo, P.R., 1993-94, CCNY, 1994—. Author: Fine-Boring Heads, 1972, Spindle Heads for Precision Tools, 1975; contbr. articles to profl. jours. Mem. ASME, Soc. Mfg. Engrs. (sr. mem.), Am. Soc. Engring. Edn. Republican. Jewish. Achievements include patents for tool holders for machine tools. Home: 868 E 24th St Brooklyn NY 11210-2822 Office: CCNY Convent Ave at 135 St New York NY 10031

VERGIN, TIMOTHY LYNN, commercial real estate appraiser, broker, investor; b. Watertown, Minn., Nov. 13, 1962; s. William Alfred and Carol Mae (Strecker) V.; m. Randi Noelle Spencer, May 9, 1987. AA in Bus. Adminstrn., North Hennepin Community Coll., Brooklyn Park, Minn., 1983; BS in Real Estate, St. Cloud State U., 1985. Lic. real appraiser, Minn., Wis., Colo.; cert. gen. real property appraiser, Minn. Appraiser Newcombe & Hansen Appraisals, Inc., Mpls., 1985-92, Diversified Real Estate Svcs., Inc., Mpls., 1992—; broker Realty World-Vergin, Buffalo, 1985-94; CFO, prin. Diversified Real Estate Svcs., Inc., Mpls., 1992—. Bd. dirs. Realty World-Vergin Corp.; bd. advs. Glaspoth, Inc., 2000-01; FKH Enterprises, Inc.; ptnr. Waverly Properties, LLP,1998—, Vandalia Assocs., LLP, 1993—, Stroman Constrn. and Design, Inc., 2000-01, Winner Ptnrs., 1998—; CEO Diversified Acquisitions, Inc., 1994—, Randeva Holdings LLP, 1999—; pres. ADN, Inc., 2000-02, bd. dirs.; CEO, T.L. Vergin Cons. and Mgmt., Inc., 2002--; real estate investor and cons. Treas. West Luth. H.S. Bd. Regents, 1997-2002. Scholar, Minn. Right of Way Appraisers, Mpls., 1985, St. Cloud State U., 1983. Mem. Appraisal Inst. Chgo., St. Cloud State Real Estate Alumni (exec. com. 1985, scholarship com. chmn. 1991-96), Phi Theta Kappa. Republican. Lutheran. Avocations: hunting, real estate and stock market investment, golf, weight-lifting. Home: 3115 Cahill Ave SE Buffalo MN 55313-5302 Office: Diversified Real Estate Svc 12 S 6th St Ste 520 Minneapolis MN 55402-1510

VERGNE, FRANÇOIS FREDERIC, lawyer; b. Paris, July 20, 1957; s. Robert Vergne and Raymonde Juéry; m. Caroline Raievski, July 1988; children: Dimitri, Thomas. Grad., Inst. d'Etudes Politiques de Paris, 1980; DEA-Droit, U. Paris I, 1983; LLM, U. Pa., 1984. Bar: Paris 1987. Assoc. Roquet Borde & Assocs., Paris, 1987—97, ptnr., 1997—99, De Pardieu Brocas Maffei & Leygonie, Paris, 1999—. Named Fulbright scholar, 1984. Mem.: Assn. des Anciens Scis. Po (dir. 1994—). Office: De Pardieu Brocas Maffei & Leygonie 64-66 Ave n Iena 75116 Paris France

VERGNES, BERNARD, information technology executive; Degree in Elec. Engring., Ecole Supérieure d'Electricité, Paris, 1968; MSc in Biomed. Engring., U. So. Calif.; diploma in Bus. Adminstrn., U. Catholique de Louvrain, Belgium. Mem. faculty Ecole Polytechnique, Montréal, Canada, 1968—70; founder Belgium subsidiary Modcomp., 1975—83; from gen. mgr. to chmn. emeritus Microsoft, Redmond, Wash., 1983—2000, chmn. emeritus, 2000—. Instr. U. Québec, Canada. Office: One Microsoft Way Redmond WA 98052-6399*

VERHAALEN, MARION, music educator; b. Milw., Dec. 9, 1930; d. Carl John Verhaalen and Agnes Rose Sieberlich. MusB, Alverno Coll., 1954; MusM, Cath. U., 1962; EdD, Columbia U., 1970. Music tchr., organist, Milw. and Elgin, Nebr., 1954-58; asst. prof. music Alverno Coll., Milw., 1958-78; instr. Wis. Conservatory Music, 1978—. Instr. various univs., conservatories, Brazil, 1973-90; cons., clinician Nat. and Internat. Piano Tchg. Founds. Editor: Musica Para Piano & Criando e Aprendendo, vols. 1-5, 1974-76; author: Keyboard Dimensions, 1984, Explorando Musica, 2 vols., 1988-90, Adult Piano Express, vols. 1-2, 1992, A Journey in Faith, 1997 (Gambinus award Milw. County Hist. Soc. 1998), Camargo Guarvieri Expressões de uma Vida, 2001; contbr. articles to profl. jours.; staff editor Musart mag., 1963-69; editor Notes of Interest newsletter, 1983-90; solo and two piano recitals with Milw. Cath. Symphony; composer vocal and choral works including Let Us Now Praise Water, 1979, Hymn of Glory, 1979, The Prairie Woman, 1979-81, Judith, 1981, Lord God, Let Your Spirit Come, 1981, Nunc Transitus, 1982, Marian Litany, 1987, Songs of the Way, 1990, Paean of Praise, 1992, On Children, 1994, Psalms, 1996, also compositions and arrangements for piano including Duets on Four Brazilian Songs, 1973, Modes in Miniature (collection), 1975, Concertino for Piano Solo, 1978, Songs from Brazil, 1981, Fantasy Suite, 1983, Johnny Has Gone for a Soldier, 1983, Folksongs of America, Set I and II, 1984, Canon in D for 8 hands, 1984, Canon in D for solo piano, 1984, Contemporary Christian Classics (collection), 1988, Suite for Friends, 1988, More Folk Songs from Here and There, 1993, 12 Bars of Blues, 1994, Solo Adventures I and II, 1997. Tchrs. Soll. scholar, 1969; grantee OAS, 1969-70, Wis. Arts Bd., 1981; Fulbright tchg. grantee, 1988; recipient Career Achievement award Milw. Panhellenic Assn., 1976, Outstanding Milw. Musician award Wis. Fedn. Music Clubs, 1980, Citation for Outstanding Svc. to Music Edn. in Wis., Wis. Fedn. Music Clubs, 1985. Mem. Wis. Music Tchrs. Assn. (editor newsletter 1997-99), MacDowell Club Milw., Delta Omicron (local and state chpt. pres. 1972-80, Outstanding Mem. award 1974). Avocations: travel, photography. Home: 2259 S 31st St Milwaukee WI 53215-2435 Office: Wis Conservatory Music 1485 N Prospect Ave Milwaukee WI 53202-3017

VERHALEN, ROBERT DONALD, consultant; b. Chgo., July 6, 1935; s. William Joseph and Pearl Evelyn (Anderson) V.; m. Phyllis Scandridge, Jan. 11, 1958; children: Elizabeth L., David S. BA, U. Iowa, 1963; MPH, U. N.C., 1965, DrPH, 1972. Expediter Fansteel Metall. Corp., North Chicago, Ill., 1957-58; tech. writer Collins Radio Co., Cedar Rapids, Iowa, 1958-59; rsch. aide Dept. Physics and Astronomy, Iowa City, 1960-63; sanitarian Lake County Health Dept., Waukegan, Ill., 1963-64; cons. safety mgmt. Ga. Dept. Pub. Health, Atlanta, 1965—67; instr. U. N.C., Chapel Hill, 1968-70; chief task force Pres.'s Commn. on Product Safety, Washington, 1969-70; asst. dir. Bur. Product Safety FDA, 1970-73; assoc. dir. U.S. Consumer Product Safety Commn., 1973-95; pres. Verhalen & Assocs., McLean, Va., 1995—; gen. ptnr. advotec Investment Ltd. Partnership, 1997—; chmn. Elmstreet Tech. Group, 1999—. Pres.-elect found. bd. Sch. Pub. Health U. N.C., Chapel Hill, 2000—, guest lectr., 1975—, Walter Reed Army Med. Ctr., Washington, 1982—. Mem. editorial bd. Jour. Safety Rsch.; developer Nat. Electronic Injury Surveillance System; contbr. articles to profl. jours. Sgt. USMC, 1953-57. Mem. Am. Coll. Epidemiology, Soc. Epidemiologic Rsch., Am. Pub. Health Assn., Am. Statis. Assn., Sr. Exec.'s Assn. (charter), Sr. Exec. Svc. Lutheran. Avocation: sailing. Home: 640 Live Oak Dr Mc Lean VA 22101-1563 Office: Verhalen & Assocs 6867 Elm St Ste 300 Mc Lean VA 22101-3871 E-mail: verhalenr@aol.com.

VERHEIDE, TARA COLLEEN, artist, educator; b. Schenectady, N.Y., Jan. 19, 1961; d. James Vincent Scripa and Jane Charlotte (Sinclair) Verheide. BFA in Sculpture, SUNY, New Paltz, 1984; MA in Edn. Curriculum and Design, Castleton State Coll., 1993. Instr. dance and visual art Main Street Arts Ctr., Saxton's River, Vt., 1989-92; art tchr. Springfield (Vt.) H.S., 1991-92; instr. skills for ind. Adult Svcs., Springfield, 1993—; instr. welding StepUp for Women in the Trades, Rutland, 1995—. Spl. evaluator Vt. State Colls., Waterbury, 1993; mem. artist com. Chaffee Ctr. Visual Arts, Rutland, 1994—; instr. drawing C.C. Vt., Rutland, 1994—; prof. intro to studio arts, art in dialogue, visual comm. Castleton (Vt.) State Coll ., 1997—; instr. welded sculpture , Springfield Tech. Ctr. One-woman shows included in Chaffee Visual Arts Ctr., Vt., 1990, Beside Myself Gallery, Vt., 1993; group shows include Helio Gallery, N.Y.C., 1990, Stamford (Conn.) Art Mus., 1991, Moonbrook ARt Gallery, Vt., 1984, Helen Day Art Ctr., Vt., 1989, Coll. of Atlantic, Maine, 1998, Castleton State Coll., Vt., 1998, Canal St. Gallery, Mass., 1998, 99, Webster Coll. Gallery, St. Louis, 1998. Recipient Disting./Creative Expression with Color award Stamford Art Mus., 1991, Grumbacher award Grumbacher Co., 1991. Avocations: dance, choreography, art performance, visual communications studies and research, semiotic art analysis. Home: RR 1 Box 1400 Ludlow VT 05149-9801 Office: Fine Arts Ctr Castleton State Coll Castleton VT 05735 E-mail: bonefarmproductions@yahoo.com.

VERHESEN, ANNA MARIA HUBERTINA, counselor; b. Heerenveen, Friesland, Netherland, Dec. 6, 1932; came to U.S., 1968; d. Hendrikus H. and Henrika C. (Kluessjen) V. BS, Mercy Coll. of Detroit, 1981; MA, Sienna Height, Adrian, Mich., 1992. Childcare worker Schiedam, Netherland, 1952-54; social worker Rotterdam Halfweg, Netherland, 1954-59; childcare worker Mt. St. Ann's Home, Worcester and Lawrence, Mass., 1968-70; chem. dependency social worker St. Vincent Med. Ctr., Toledo, 1970-75; social worker St. Joseph Hosp., Nashua, N.H., 1975-78; vocation dir. Grey Nuns, Lexington, Mass., 1978-79; coord. community svcs. St. Vincents Med. Ctr., Toledo, 1981-91; pvt. practice clin. therapist Sylvania, Ohio, 1992—. Alcohol/drug addiction/mental health counselor for ex-prisoners; founder St. Vincent Med. Ctr. Alcoholism Detox and Rehab. Unit, Toledo, 1970-75. Co-founder Transitional Residences for the Homeless, Toledo, 1981-90, Ohio Coalition for the Homeless, Columbus, 1982-89; co-founder of a home for persons with AIDS; co-chair City of Toledo Housing Policy, 1985-90; coord. Housing Now, Toledo, 1988-90. Recipient Woman of Achievement award Women in Communication, Toledo, 1986, Spirit of '87 award N.W. Ordinance and U.S. Constn. Bicentennial Commn., Toledo, 1987, Gov.'s Spl. Recognition award, 1988, Man for Others award St. John's High Sch., 1991; named Woman of Toledo, St. Vincent Med. Ctr. Aux., 1988, Ohio Ho. of Reps., 1987; featured in various mags. Roman Catholic. Home: 2015 N Mccord Rd Apt 127 Toledo OH 43615-3071 Office: Elliott and Assocs Inc 5600 Monroe St Sylvania OH 43560-2731 E-mail: hubertina@toast.net.

VERHEY, JOSEPH WILLIAM, psychiatrist, educator; b. Oakland, Calif., Sept. 28, 1928; s. Joseph Bernard and Anne (Hanken) V.; BS summa cum laude, Seattle U., 1954; MD, U. Wash., 1958; m. Darlene Helen Seiler, July 21, 1956. Intern, King County Hosp., Seattle, 1958-59; resident Payne Whitney Psychiatric Clinic, N.Y. Hosp., Cornell Med. Center, N.Y.C., 1959-62, U. Wash. Hosp., Seattle, 1962-63; pvt. practice, Seattle, 1963-78; mem. staff U. Providence Hosp., 1963-78, Fairfax Hosp., 1963-78, VA Med. Center, Tacoma, 1978-83, chief inpatient psychiatry sect., 1983—; clin. instr. psychiatry U. Wash. Med. Sch., 1963-68, clin. asst. prof. psychiatry, 1968-82, clin. assoc. prof., 1982—; cons. psychiatry U.S. Dept. Def., Wash. State Bur. Juvenile Rehab.; examiner Am. Bd. Psychiatry and Neurology. Diplomate Am. Bd. Psychiatry and Neurology. Fellow N. Pacific Soc. Psychiatry and Neurology, Am. Psychiat. Assn.; mem. AMA, Am. Fedn. Clin. Rsch., World Fedn. Mental Health, Soc. Mil. Surgeons of U.S., Wash. Athletic Club, Swedish Club (life). Home: 1100 University St Seattle WA 98101-2848 Office: Va Med Ctr Tacoma WA 98493-0001

VERING, JOHN ALBERT, lawyer; b. Marysville, Kans., Feb. 6, 1951; s. John Albert and Bernadine E. (Kieffer) V.; m. Ann E. Arman, June 28, 1980; children: Julia Ann, Catherine Ann, Mary Ann. BA summa cum laude, Harvard U., 1973; JD, U. Va., 1976. Bar: Mo. 1976, U.S. Dist. Ct. (we. dist.) Mo. 1976, U.S. Ct. Appeals (10th cir.), 1980, U.S. Ct. Appeals (4th cir.) 1987, Kans. 1990, U.S. Dist. Ct. Kans. 1990; arbitrator, mediator. Assoc. Dietrich, Davis, Dicus, Rowlands, Schmitt & Gorman, Kansas City, Mo., 1976-81, ptnr., 1982—. Editor: U. Va. Law Rev., 1974-76. Bd. dirs. Greater Kansas City YMCA Southwest Dist., 1987. Mem.: Harvard Club (adv. bd. schs. com. Kans. City 1977—2002, v.p. 1981—82, 1992—93, pres. 1994—96, mem. adv. bd. 1996—2002). Democrat. Roman Catholic. Home: 1210 W 68th Ter Kansas City MO 64113-1904 Office: Armstrong Teasdale LLP 2345 Grand Blvd Ste 2000 Kansas City MO 64108-2617 E-mail: jvering@armstrongteasdale.com.

VERINK, ELLIS DANIEL, JR. metallurgical engineering educator, consultant; b. Peking, China, Feb. 9, 1920; s. Ellis Daniel and Phoebe Elizabeth (Smith) V.; m. Martha Eulala Owens, July 4, 1942; children: Barbara Ann, Wendy Susan. BS, Purdue U., 1941; MS, Ohio State U., 1963, PhD, 1965. Registered profl. engr., Fla., Pa., Calif. Mgr. chem. sect., sales devel. divsn. Alcoa, New Kensington, Pa., 1946-59, mgr. chem. and petroleum indsl. sales Pitts., 1959-62; assoc. prof. metall. engring. U. Fla., Gainesville, 1965-68, prof. materials sci. and engring., 1968—, disting. svc. prof., 1984-91, prof. emeritus, 1991—; pres. Materials Cons., Inc., 1970—. Cons. Aluminum Assn., Washington, 1966-84; mem. U.S. nuclear waste tech. rev. bd., 1989-97. Author: Corrosion Testing Made Easy, The Basics, 1993; editor: Methods of Materials Selections, 1968, Material Stability and Environmental Degradation, 1988; contbr. articles to profl. jours. Pres. Gainesville YMCA, 1977. Recipient Sam Tour award ASTM, 1979, Donald E. Marlowe award Am. Soc. Engring. Edn., 1991; recipient Disting. Alumnus award Ohio State U., 1982, Disting. Faculty award Fla. Blue Key, 1983; named Tchr.-Scholar of Year U. Fla., 1979 Fellow Metall. Soc. of AIME (pres. 1984, Educator of Yr. award 1988), Am. Soc. Materials Internat., Nat. Assn. Corrosion Engrs. Internat. (bd. dirs. 1984-87, Willis Rodney Whitney award; mem. Masons, Shriners, Kiwanis, Sigma Xi, Tau Beta Pi. Republican. Presbyterian. Office: U Fla Dept Materials Sci Eng Gainesville FL 32611 Home: Apt M224 7805 NW 28th Pl Gainesville FL 32606-8659

VERKRUIJSSE, PIETER JOZIAS, classicist, educator; b. Groede, The Netherlands, Jan. 27, 1943; s. Jannis Abraham Verkruijsse and Maria Herrebout; m. Johanna H.T.J. de Feyter, Mar. 15, 1968 (div. 1985); 1 child, Elisabeth Maria. PhD, U. Amsterdam, 1983. Tchr. Dutch lit. U. Amsterdam, 1968—. Editor (periodical) Neder-L, 1996—. Avocations: bibliography, palaeography, archivist. Home: 6 Weissenbruchlaan NL 2421 Nieuwkoop Netherlands Office: U Amsterdam 134 Spuistraat NL1012VB Amsterdam Netherlands E-mail: piet.verkruijsse@hum.uva.nl.

VERMA, ASHOK, neurologist, researcher; b. Jaipur, Raj, India, Aug. 30, 1954; arrived in U.S., 1988; s. Ram Karan and Jaya Devi; m. Usha Chhikara-Verma, May 17, 1981; children: Nupur, Neil, Nipun. MB BChir, SMS Med. Coll., Jaipur, 1977, MD, 1980; DM, All India Inst. Med. Sci., New Delhi, 1984. Lectr. neurology All India Inst. Med. Sci., New Delhi, 1984—85, asst. prof. neurology, 1985—94; instr. neurology U. Miami Sch. Medicine, 1995—97, asst. prof. neurology, 1998—2000, assoc. prof. neurology, 2001—. Attending neurologist Jackson Meml. Hosp./U. Miami, 1995—; staff neurologist Miami VA Med. Ctr., 1995—; asst. dir. neurology residency program U. Miami, 1999—. Editor: Yearbook of Neurology and Neurosurgery, 2000—; author: 9 book chpts.; contbr. Recipient 3 Acad. Gold medals, Indian Med. Assn., 1978, Pharmacia and Upjohn Young Investigator award for outstanding rsch., 1996; fellow JE Fogarty Internat. fellow, NIH, 1988, VA fellow in neurotraining, Dept. VA Affairs, 1995. Fellow: Am. Assn. Electrodiag Med.; mem.: Am. Acad. Neurology, Neurology Soc. India (life). Avocations: tennis, reading. Office: U Miami Sch Medicine Dept Neurology Ste 701 1150 NW 14th St Miami FL 33136

VERMA, DINESH CHANDRA, computer scientist, writer; b. Deoria, Uttar Pradesh, India, Nov. 16, 1965; s. Suresh Chandra Verma and Chanda Devi; m. Paridhi Verma; children: Archit, Riya. B of Tech., Indian Inst. Tech., Kanpur, Indi7, 1987; MS in Mgmt. of Tech., Poly. U., 1998; PhD, U. Calif., Berkeley, 1992. Rschr. IBM Thomas J. Watson Rsch. Ctr., Hawthorne, NY, 1992—95, Philips Rsch., Briarcliff Manor, 1995—97; rschr., rsch. mgr. IBM Thomas J. Watson Rsch. Ctr., Hawthorne, 1997—. Author: (book) Supporting Service Level Agreements on IP Networks, 1999 (President's Gold medal (India) , 1987), Policy Enabled Networking, 2000, Content Distribution Networks, 2002; contbr. sci. and tech. articles to profl. jours. Mem.: IEEE (vice chair tech. com. on computer comms.). Hindu. Achievements include patents for computers. Avocations: swimming, gardening, folk tales. Office: IBM Thomas J Watson Rsch Ctr PO Box 704 Yorktown Heights NY 10598 Office Fax: 914-784-6205. Business E-Mail: dverma@us.ibm.com.

VERMA, INDER M. biochemist; b. Sangrur, Punjab, India, Nov. 28, 1947; MSc, Lucknow U., India, 1966; PhD in Biochemistry, Weizmann Inst. Sci., Rehovot, Israel, 1971. From asst. prof. to assoc. prof. Salk Inst., 1974-83; sr. mem. Molecular Biology & Virology Lab, 1983-85; prof. Molecular Biology, 1985-95; prof. Lab. Genetics Salk Inst., 1995—. Fellow Jane Coffin Childs Meml. Fund, 1970-73; Reverend Soloman B. Caulker Meml. fellow, 1967-70; adj. assoc. prof. U. Calif. San Diego, 1979-83, adj. prof. Biology, 1983—; mem. Virology Study Sec., 1981-85, elected mem., Inst. of Medicine, 1999. Recipient medal Outstanding Scientist N. Am. Scientists of Indian Origin, 1985-86; merit award NIH, 1987, outstanding investigator award, 1988; bd. trustees Salk Inst., 1989-91 & 94—; mem. acad. coun., 1989—; vchmn. Fac. and Acad. coun., 1989-90 & 94-95; chmn., 1991-92 & 96-97; prof. Molecular Biology, Am. Cancer Soc., 1990; lectr. Purdue U., 1991, Sch. Med. Vanderbilt U., 1992, TATA Meml. Hosp., Bombay, India, 1992, U. Chgo., 1992, Queenstown, New Zealand, 1993, N.Y.U., 1993, Bar-Ilan U., Ramat Gan, Israel, and others. Mem. Nat. Acad. Sci., Am. Cancer Soc. Office: Salk Inst Biol Studies 10010 N Torrey Pines Rd La Jolla CA 92037-1099*

VERMA, SATYA BHUSHAN, optometrist, educator; b. Multan, Punjab, India; s. Hari C. and Satwanti (Girdhar) V.; m. Asha C. Valecha, Dec. 28, 1974; children: Pooja, Kajal. DR OPT, Sch. Optometry GEH, Aligarh, India, 1964; BA, Delhi U., 1968; AO, U. Calif. Berkeley, 1971; OD, Pa. Coll. Optometry, 1975. Diplomate Am. Acad. Optometry, Pub. Health and Environ. Optometry. Refractionist Eye Dept. Willingdon Hosp., New Delhi, India, 1967-70; assoc. Sch. Optometry U. Calif., Berkeley, 1970-71; assoc. Pa. Coll. Optometry, Phila., 1971-75, asst. prof., 1976—. Cons. East Coast Migrant Health, Washington, 1990—. Contbr. chpts. in books and articles to profl. jours. Bd. dirs. Bridgeport-Upper Merion Lions Club, pres. 1987; chair scholarship com. AIP Found., Morrestown, N.J., 1994—; del. White House Conf. on Aging, 1995. Named Optometrist of Yr., Am. Optometric Assn., 1998; recipient Disting. Svc. award Prevent Blindness Am., 1998, Disting. Practitioner in Optometry The Am. Acads. of Practice, 2000. Fellow Am. Acad. Optometry; mem. APHA (chair vision care sect.), Nat. Coun. Aging (bd. dirs., exec. com., chair-elect health promotion inst.), Nat. Vol. Orgn. for Ind. Living for Aging (chair 1992-94), Pa. Optometric Assn. (pres. 1996, past pres. 1997—, OD of Yr. 1997, 86, George Gottschalk Meml. award 1985), Chester-Delaware County Optometric Soc. (pres. 1982-84, OD of Yr. 1997, 86). Democrat. Hindu. Avocations: golf, tennis. Office: Pa Coll Optometry 8360 Old York Rd Elkins Park PA 19027-1516 E-mail: satya@pco.edu.

VERMA, SURJIT KUMAR, retired school system administrator; b. India, May 17, 1940; arrived in Canada 1966; s. Sohara Lal and Gian Devi V.; m. Raj Verma; 1 child, Soania. MEd, St. Francis Xavier U., N.S., 1975; postgrad., Dalhousie U., N.S., U. Ottawa, Ont., Can, 1979. Cert. tchr. Nova Scotia. Sci. dept. head Halifax County Bedford Dist. Sch. Bd., N.S., Canada, 1968-88, curriculum supr. Canada, 1988-94; ret., 1995. Served on C.T.F. Project Overseas Can. Teams, W.I., Nigeria, 1976, 77; mem. provincial sci. task force, biology rev. com., elem. sci. Nova Scotia Dept. Edn.; mem. Internat. Sci. Symposium, 1979; mem. selection panel PromoSci. Program. Natural Scis. and Engring. Rsch. Coun. of Can.; mem. exec. coun. N.S. Inst. Sci.; worksop presenter numerous sci. workshops. Contbr. to profl. jours. Chmn. First Metro Halifax Dartmouth Reg Sci. Fair, 1975; co-chmn. Canada Wide Sci Fair, 1984. Recipient Sci. Tchg. Achievement Recognition award U.S. Nat. Sci. Tchrs. Assn. and Am. Gas Assn., 1993, Profl. Devel. award N.S. Tchrs. Union, Tchg. Excellence in Sci., Tech. and Math. award Prime Min. Can., 1993, 94, Sci. on Display award NASCO, 1993-94, Outstanding Achievement in Sci. Edn. award Halifax County Sch. Bd., 1993, Surjit Verma award for tchg. excellence created in his honor Halifax County Bedrod Dist. Sch. Bd., 1994, Michael Smith award Industry Can., 1996; U. Ottawa fellow, 1979, Dalhousie U. grad. fellow, 1980, Math. Sci. Tech. Edn. fellow Royal Bank Queen's U., 1994; Dalhousie U. Rsch. Devel. grantee, 1979; N.S. Tchrs. Union scholar, 1979; Can./N.S. Tech. Devel. grantee, 1995. Mem. Nova Scotia Inst. Sci. (coun. mem.), Natural Sci. and Engring. Rsch. Coun. (mem. selection panel promosci. project). Avocations: jogging, yoga. Home: 49 Rosewood Ave Timberlea NS Canada B3T 1C6 E-mail: rsverma@globalserve.net.

VERME, DANTE AMERICO, statistician, educator; b. Lima, Peru, July 28, 1953; s. Dante Antonio and Carmen Victoria Verme; m. Sonia Verme, Aug. 7, 1985; children: Dante Jorge, Katerina Marie. PhD Math. Stats., George Wash. U., Washington, DC, 1990, MS Applied Stats., 1983; BS Economics, Universidad Del Pacifico, Lima, Peru, 1976. Assoc. educator Dept. of Epidemiology and Biostatistics, Washington, 1997—; asst. rsch. educator The Biostatistics Ctr., Rockville, Md., 1990—97, rsch. assoc., 1989—90. Guest lectr. Instituto de Cardiologia Juana Caral, Corrientes, Argentina, 2000. Contbr. articles to profl. jour. Recipient Excellence in Tchg. Award, Sch. of Pub. Health and Health Services, 1997, 1998, 1999, 2000, 2002. Mem.: Am. Statis. Assn. Avocations: swimming, raquetball. Office: Washington State University 2300 I Street NW Suite 125 Washington DC 20037-2336

VERMEER, MAUREEN DOROTHY, sales executive; b. Bronxville, N.Y., Mar. 21, 1945; d. Albert Casey and Helen (Valentine Casey) Vermeer; m. John R. Fassnacht, Feb. 11, 1966 (div. 1975); m. George M. Dallas Peltz IV, Oct. 26, 1985. Grad., NYU Real Estate Inst., 1976. Lic. real estate broker, notary pub., N.Y. With Douglas Elliman, N.Y.C., 1965-74, mgmt. supr., 1974-78, v.p., 1978-83; real estate broker Rachmani Corp., 1983-84; v.p. sales and mktg. Carol Mgmt. Corp., 1984-90; v.p. mktg. The Sunshine Group, 1990; v.p., sec., bd. dirs. H.J. Kalikow & Co., 1991—. Mem. Real Estate Bd. N.Y. (bd. dirs., residential mgmt. com.), Assn. Real Estate Women (bd. dirs. charitable fund). Republican. Presbyterian. Avocations: skiing, scuba diving. Home: 111 Broadway Norwood NJ 07648-1412 Office: H J Kalikow & Co 101 Park Ave Fl 25 New York NY 10178-0002

VERMEIL, DICK, professional football coach; b. Calistoga, Calif. m. Carolyn Drake; two sons. Head coach Phila. Eagles, 1976—82; football coach St. Louis Rams, 1997-2000; pub. spkr. Nationwide Spkrs. Bur., Beverly Hills, Calif., 2000—01; head coach Kansas City Chiefs, 2001—. Career highlights include: coaching 1999-2000 Super Bowl XXXIV championship season, St. Louis Rams, becoming the oldest coach in NFL history to win a Super Bowl; tv analyst with CBS, ABC. Named Coach of Yr. on four levels, high sch., jr. coll., nat. collegiate Divsn. I, NFL; named first fulltime spl. teams coach in NFL history with Rams, under head coach George Allen, 1969. Office: Kansas City Chiefs One Arrowhead Drive Kansas City MO 64129*

VERMEL, PAUL, conductor; b. Paris, France, Feb. 19, 1924; s. Naoum and Marguerite V.; m. Carolyn Paulin, Mar. 25, 1978; Valerie Jones. Diploma in orch. conducting, Juilliard Sch. Music, 1951; D, Nasson Coll., 1975. Music dir. conductor Fresno (Calif.) Philharmonic, 1959-66, Music in Maine, Bangor-Portland, 1966—69, Portland Symphony, 1967—95; prof. music U. Ill., Urbana, 1974-94; music dir. conductor Champaign-Urbana Symphony, 1974-94, Northwest Symphony, Des Plaines, Ill., 1994—, N. Suburban Symphony, Lake Forest, 1997—. Faculty Conductors Inst., Columbia, S.C., 1992—; dir. conducting program Aspen Music Festival, 1978-92. Contbr. articles to profl. jours. Recipient Koussevitzky Conducting award, Berkshire Music Ctr., Lenox, Mass., 1954; Ford Found. grantee, Balt., 1963. Avocations: reading, painting, swimming, photography.

VERMETTE, RAYMOND EDWARD, clinical laboratories administrator; b. Lewiston, Maine, June 30, 1942; s. Edward Louis and Anna Lucy (Raymond) V.; m. Ernestine Pero, Dec. 29[8], 1963; children: Tamara, Gregory. BS in Bacteriology, U. Maine, 1964; MS in Biochemistry, U. Wis., 1966; MBA, Temple U., 1973; master tchr.'s cert., Cath. Diocese Boston, 1981. Cert. in pers. mgmt., Va. Supr. animal toxicology Hazleton Labs., Vienna, 1967-71; pers. mgr. Damon Clin. Lab., Phila., 1971-73, ops. mgr., 1973-75, gen. mgr. Needham Heights, Mass., 1975-90; v.p. ops. Damon Corp., 1983-87, corp. v.p., 1987-89, sr. v.p., 1990=93; sr. v.p., gen. mgr. Corning/MetPath, Westwood, Mass., 1994-95; ret., 1995. Vis. lectr. fin. mgmt. and bus. adminstrn. Framingham State Coll., 1978—84; instr. mgmt. Newbury Jr. Coll., Boston, 1976—79; health care mgmt. cons., 2001—. Author: (with B. Kliman and E. Kolowrat) What You Should Know About Medical Lab Tests, 1979. V.p. fin. com., Framingham, Mass., 1982—84; mem. capital budget com. Town of Framingham, 1987; mem-elect Framingham Town Meeting, 1987—90, Govt. Study Com., 1995—97, mem. fin. com., 1997—2001; chmn. bd. religious edn. Cath. Ch., Framingham, 1981—84, co-chmn. pre-marriage preparation coun., 1981—99, organist, 1979—. Democrat. Home: 11 Willowbrook Dr Framingham MA 01702-5515

VERMEULE, CORNELIUS CLARKSON, III, museum curator; b. Orange, N.J., Aug. 10, 1925; s. Cornelius Clarkson, Jr. and Catherine Sayre (Comstock) V.; m. Emily Dickinson Townsend, Feb. 2, 1957 (dec. Feb. 6, 2001); children— Emily D. Blake, Cornelius Adrian Comstock. Grad., Pomfret Sch., 1943; AB, Harvard, 1949, MA, 1951; PhD, U. London, Eng., 1953; DHL (hon.), Boston Coll., 1995. Instr. fine arts, then asst. prof. U. Mich., 1953-55; asst. prof. classical archaeology Bryn Mawr (Pa.) Coll., 1955-57; curator classical art Mus. Fine Arts, Boston, 1956-96, curator emeritus, 1996—, acting dir., 1972-73; assoc. curator coins Mass. Hist. Soc., 1965-71, curator, 1971—. Lectr. fine arts Smith Coll., 1960-64, Boston U., Harvard, Wellesley Coll.; vis. prof. Yale, 1969-70, 72-73; Thomas Spencer Jerome lectr. U. Mich., 1975-76; vis. prof. Boston Coll., 1978-97; vis. prof. U. Aberdeen, Scotland, 1993; pres. Internat. Com. to Save Jewish Catacombs of Italy, 1980-84, chmn., 1984-98, dir. 1998-2000; cons. classical art Worcester Art Mus., 1998-2001. Author: (with N. Jacobs) Japanese Coinage, 1948, 2d edit., 1972, Bibliography of Applied Numismatics, 1956, The Goddess Roma, 1959, 2d edit., 1974, Dal Pozzo-Albani Drawings, 1960, European Art and the Classical Past, 1964, Drawings at Windsor Castle, 1966, Roman Imperial Art in Greece and Asia Minor, 1968, Polykleitos, 1969, Numismatic Art in America, 1971, (with M. Comstock) Greek Etruscan and Roman Bronzes, 1972, (with N. Neuerburg) Catalogue of the Ancient Art in the J. Paul Getty Museum, 1973, Greek and Roman Sculpture in Gold and Silver, 1974, Greek and Roman Cyprus, 1976, (with M. Comstock) Sculpture in Stone, 1976, Greek Sculpture and Roman Taste, 1977, Roman Art: Early Republic to Late Empire, 1978, (with A Herrmann) The Ernest Brummer Collections, Vol. II, 1979, Greek Art: Socrates to Sulla, 1980, The Jewish Experience in Roman Art, 1981, Masterpieces of Greek and Roman Sculpture in America, 1982, Greek Art: Prehistoric to Perikles, 1982, Numismatic Studies, 1983, Alexander the Great Conquers Rome, 1985, The Cult Images of Imperial Rome, 1986, Numismatic Art of the Greek Imperial World, 1987, Philatelic Art in America, 1987, (with M. Comstock) Sculpture in Stone and Bronze, 1988, (with A. Brauer) Stone Sculptures, The Greek, Roman and Etruscan Collections of the Harvard University Art Museums, 1990, (with others) Le Sport dans la Grèce Antique, 1992, Du Jeu à la Compétition, 1992, (with others) El Deporte en la Grecia Antigua, La génesis del olimpismo, 1992-93, (with others) Vase-Painting in Italy, 1993; editl. bd. Minerva, 2002—. Trustee Cardinal Spellman Philatelic Mus., 1980-93. Served to 1st lt. AUS, 1943-47. Recipient Bicentennial medal Boston Coll., 1976; Fulbright fellow, 1951-53; Guggenheim fellow, 1968 Fellow AAAS, Am. Numis. Soc. (life), Royal Numis. Soc., Soc. Antiquaries; mem. Coll. Art Assn. (life), Archaeol. Inst. Am. (life) German Archaeol. Inst., Holland Soc. N.Y., Colonial Lords of Manors in Am., Mass. Hist. Soc. (hon.); Tavern Club (medalist 1986, Boston). Home: 47 Coolidge Hill Rd Cambridge MA 02138-5509 Office: Mus Fine Arts 465 Huntington Ave Boston MA 02115-5597 *To teach, collect and record the past, as exemplar for the present, as prologue to the future, can there be any better use of a historian's and archaeologist's professional life?.*

VERMILLION, ROBERT LEE, obstetrician, gynecologist; b. Beckley, W.Va., July 31, 1942; s. Thomas Uriah and Emily Rebecca (Hogg) V.; m. Constance Ann Hicks, June 23, 1973; children: Jason, Jennifer. BS, U. Md., 1964; MD, Med. Coll. of Va., 1968. Intern Johns Hopkins Hosp., Balt., 1968-69, resident in ob-gyn., 1969-71, 73-74; asst. prof. ob-gyn U. South Fla., Tampa, 1974-76; practice medicine specializing in ob-gyn Roanoke, Va., 1977—. Served to maj. U.S. Army, 1971-73. Fellow Am. Coll. Ob-Gyn; mem. AMA, Med. Soc. Va., Am. Fertility Soc., South Atlantic Assn. Ob-Gyn, Va. Ob-Gyn Soc. Presbyterian. Office: 21Highland Ave Ste 200 Roanoke VA 24013-2254

VERMILYE, PETER HOAGLAND, banker; b. N.Y.C., Jan. 17, 1920; s. Herbert Noble and Elise Tace (Hillyer) V.; m. Lucy Shaw Mitchell, Oct. 14, 1950; children: Peter H., Dana R., Andrew R., Mary S. AB, Princeton U., 1940. V.p. pension investments J.P. Morgan & Co. and Morgan Guaranty Trust, 1940-64; ptnr. State St. Research & Mgmt., Boston, 1965-69; pres. Alliance Capital Mgmt., N.Y.C., 1970-77; sr. v.p., chief investment officer Citibank, 1977-84; chmn. Baring Am. Asset Mgmt., Boston, 1984-89; sr. advisor Baring Asset Mgmt., 1990-95, Harbor Capital Mgmt., Boston, 1996—. Chmn. emeritus Huntington Theatre, 1989-96; bd. dirs. Engelhard Hanovia, Breadstreet Holdings Corp. Trustee Boston U., 1970—. Mem.: Brook, Somerset, Myopia. Home: 157 School St Manchester MA 01944-1236 also: 107 Chestnut St Boston MA 02108-1038 Office: Harbor Capital Mgmt 125 High St Fl 26 Boston MA 02110-2704

VERMILYEA, STANLEY GEORGE, prosthodontist, educator; b. Portland, Oreg., Jan. 29, 1946; s. Stanley Edmonds and Hattie Willamina (Bittner) V.; m. Barbara Jean Koester Ternus, June 23, 1967 (div. Dec. 1979); 1 child, Sheryl Eileen; m. Ileana Esther Villamarzo, July 3, 1980; 1 child, Michael Enrique. BS, Portland State Coll., 1970; DMD, U. Oreg., Portland, 1971; MS in Dental Materials, U. Mich., 1976; cert. in prosthodontics, Walter Reed Army Med. Ctr., Washington, 1985. Diplomate Am. Bd. Prosthodontics. Commd. 2d lt. U.S. Army, 1971, advanced through grades to col., 1985, dentist, 1971-76; rschr. dental materials U.S. Army Inst. Dental Rsch., Washington, 1976-80, chief dental materials rsch., 1980-83; prosthodontist U.S. Army, various locations, 1983-89, co-dir. residency in prosthodontics Washington, 1989-92, ret., 1992; asst. prof. Coll. Dentistry Ohio State U., Columbus, 1992-95, chmn. primary care, 1996—, assoc. dean clin. affairs, 2001—. Contbr. chpt. to book and articles to profl. jours. Fellow Am. Coll. Prosthodontists, Acad. Gen. Dentistry; mem. Internat. Assn. Dental Rsch. Achievements include research on the corrosion characteristics of dental alloys as well as the compositions and microstructural features of dental materials. Office: Ohio State U Coll Dentistry 305 W 12th Ave Columbus OH 43210-1267 E-mail: vermilyea.1@osu.edu.

VERMYLEN, PAUL ANTHONY, JR. oil company executive; b. N.Y.C., Dec. 5, 1946; s. Paul Anthony and Nancy Primrose (Barr) V.; m. Robin S. Collins, Jan. 24, 1970; children: Robert T.C., Nancy Barr, Sarah Morgan, Paul Anthony III. AB, Georgetown U., 1968; MBA, Columbia U., 1971. V.p. Citibank N.A., N.Y.C., 1971-78; treas. Commonwealth Oil Refining Co., San Antonio, 1978-81, v.p. fin., chief fin. officer, 1981-82; v.p., chief fin. officer, dir. Meenan Oil Co., Inc., Syosset, NY, 1982—91, pres., 1992—2001, Meenan Oil Co., L.P., 1992—2001. Bd. dirs. Petroleum Industry Rsch. Found., 1992—. Bd. dirs. Huntington Arts Coun., N.Y., 1983-89, v.p., 1986-87, pres., 1987-89; bd. dirs. Cold Spring Harbor Whaling Mus., 1995-2000; bd. advisors Cold Spring Harbor Lab. DNA Learning Ctr., 1991-2000; bd. regents Georgetown U., Washington, 1997—. Mem. Empire State Petroleum Assn. (bd. dirs. 1994-2001), Cold Spring Harbor Beach Club, Seawanhaka Corinthian Yacht Club, N.Y. Yacht Club. Office: 6900 Jericho Tpke Syosset NY 11791-4499

VERNA, MARIO, surgeon; b. Buenos Aires, May 12, 1937; came to U.S., 1963; s. Carmelo and Raquel P. (Vitale) V.; m. Ana E. Blanc, June 9, 1963; children: Mario F., Paul, Matias A. MD, U. Buenos Aires, 1961. Diplomate, Am. Bd. Surgery. Intern Hackensack (N.J.) Hosp., 1963-64, resident in surgery, 1964-68; pvt. practice Hackensack. Mem. med. staff Hackensack Med. Ctr., chief oncology sect., dept. surgery, 1990—, chmn. cancer com. and tumor bd., 1978—, chmn. med. bd., 1990; dir. Inst. for Breast Care, Hackensack U. Med. Ctr., 1995—; dir. surg. edn. Policlinico Ferroviario, Mendoza, Argentina, 1972-76; chief instr. surgery U. Cuyo, Argentina, 1974-75; clin. asst. prof. surgery Coll. Medicine and Dentistry N.J./M.J. Med. Sch., 1980—; lectr. at profl. meetings. Contbr. to med. publs. Fellow ACS, Argentine Assn. Surgery. Roman Catholic. Avocation: scuba diving. Home: 10 Depeyster Ave Tenafly NJ 07670-2208 Office: 20 Prospect Ave Ste 516 Hackensack NJ 07601

VERNARELLI, MICHAEL JOSEPH, economics educator, consultant; b. Rochester, N.Y., Nov. 24, 1948; s. S. John and Angelica Dolores (Morabito) V.; m. Joan Ann Taylor, Oct. 4, 1975; children: Jacqueline Andrea, Laurel Aileen. BA in Econs., U. Mich., 1970; MA in Econs., SUNY, Binghamton, 1974, PhD in Econs., 1978. Account analyst Travelers Ins. Co., Rochester, 1970-71; rsch. assoc. Ctrl. Adminstrn. SUNY, 1975-76; prof. econs. Rochester Inst. Tech., 1976—, chmn. dept., 1987—. Cons. econs. Rochester Downtown Devel. Corp., 1980; rsch. economist divsn. housing rsch. HUD, Washington, 1980-81, vis. scholar, 1980; pres., forensic economist Rochester Econ. Cons., 1983—; vis. prof. U.S. Bus. Sch. in Prague, 1992-96. Contbg. author: Federal Housing Policy and Desegregation, 1986. Mem. Brighton (N.Y.) Bd. Archtl. Rev., 1990-91, mem. planning bd., 1991-98. Recipient Eisenhart award Rochester Inst. Tech., 1987; grantee SUNY, Binghamton, 1974. Mem. Am. Econ. Assn., Nat. Assn. Forensic Economists, Ea. Econ. Assn., Greater Rochester C. of C. (panel mem. bus. trends com. 1987—), Omicron Delta Epsilon. Roman Catholic. Avocation: golf. Home: 133 Esplanade Dr Rochester NY 14610-3325 Office: Rochester Inst Tech Rochester NY 14623-0887

VERNAVA, ANTHONY MICHAEL, lawyer; b. N.Y.C., May 13, 1937; s. Michel Antonio Vernava and Ana Avellina Guerriero. BS, Georgetown U., 1959; JD, Harvard U., 1962; LLM, NYU, 1965; MA in L.Am. Studies/Internat. Fin., George Washington U., 1999. Bar: N.Y. 1962, U.S. Dist. Ct. (so. and ea. dists.) N.Y. 1963, U.S. Ct. Appeals (2nd cir.) 1963, Mich. 1965, U.S. Dist. Ct. (ea. dist.) Mich. 1966, U.S. Tax Ct. 1966, U.S. Supreme Ct. 1966, Ill. 1973. Atty. Reid & Priest, N.Y.C., 1962-63, IBM Corp., Armonk, N.Y., 1963-65; assoc. prof. Wayne State U., Detroit, 1965-68, prof., 1968-72; pvt. practice law Detroit and Chgo., 1972-75; prof. law So. Meth. U., Dallas, 1975-76; prof. law, consulting atty. U. Detroit Sch. Law, 1976-95; pvt. practice internat. cons. Fairfax, Va., 1995—. Arbitrator Mich. Employment Rels. Commn., Detroit, 1988-95. Contbr. articles to profl. jours. Mem. ABA, N.Y. State Bar. Avocations: international travel, pre-Colombian civilizations, boating, hiking. Office: PO Box 99 Oakton VA 22124-0099

VERNER, JAMES MELTON, lawyer; b. Selma, Ala., Sept. 19, 1915; s. Singleton Foster and Jennie (Harris) V.; m. Gretchen Gores, Aug. 12, 1939; children: Ann Verner Picardo, James Singleton, William Melton. Student, Biltmore Coll., 1932-34; AB, U. N.C., 1936, LL.B., 1938. Bar: N.C. 1938, Tenn. 1947, D.C. 1950, Va., 1986. Assoc. firm Gover & Covington, Charlotte, N.C., 1938; law clk. atty. gen., 1938-40; atty. CAB, Washington, 1940-43; asst. gen. counsel Chgo. & So. Airlines, Memphis, 1946-47; atty. Air Transport Assn. Am., Washington, 1947-49; hearing examiner CAB, 1949-50, exec. asst. to chmn., 1950, exec. dir., 1950-53; atty. Turney & Turney, 1953-60, ptnr., 1954-60; ptnr. firm Verner, Liipfert, Bernhard, McPherson & Hand, Chartered (and predecessor firms), 1960-88, hon. mem. bd. dirs., 1988—. Assoc. editor: N.C. Law Rev, 1937-38. Former mem., chmn. policy bd. Legal Counsel for Elderly, Washington. Served as lt. (j.g.) USNR, 1943-46; legal officer Naval Air Transport Svc., 1945-46. Mem. ABA, Order of Golden Fleece, Cosmos Club (Washington). Home: 900 N Taylor St # 2104-2106 Arlington VA 22203-1858 Office: 901 15th St NW Washington DC 20005-2327 *My belief is that if you treat other people fairly and trust them, you will seldom be disappointed and will be the better for it.*

VERNEY, RICHARD GREVILLE, paper company executive; b. Providence, Aug. 24, 1946; s. Gilbert and Virginia Ruth (Piggott) V.; m. Dorothy Howard, Aug. 26, 1967; children: Virginia F., Elizabeth I., Heather B., Eric B. AB, Brown U., 1968. Mgmt. trainee Monadnock Paper Mills, Bennington, N.H., 1969-70, asst. gen. mgr., 1970, exec. v.p., 1970-76, pres., 1977-85, chmn., CEO, 1978—, Monadnock Non-Wovens, LLC, 1998—. Mem. exec. com. Crotched Mt. Found., Greenfield, NH, 1974—87, trustee, 1974—, St. George's Sch., Newport, RI, 1978—93, chmn., 1985—89, hon. trustee, 1993—2000, Monadnock Cmty. Hosp., 1993—2000, v.p., 1997—99; trustee Nantucket Conservation Found., Inc., 1994—, pres., 1998—. Mem. Am. Forest and Paper Assn. (bd. dirs. 1991-98, chmn. splty. packaging and indsl. divsn. 1984-85, chmn. exec. bd. pulp consumers divsn. 1980-82, chmn. cover and text exec. com. 1989-91), Bus. Industry Assn. N.H. (bd. dirs. 1991—, mem. exec. com. 1998—), Sales Assn. Paper Industry, Boston Paper Trade Assn. (pres. 1985-86), Algonquin Club (Boston), Nantucket Yacht Club (Mass.), N.Y. Yacht Club (N.Y.C.). Republican. Episcopalian. Home: PO Box 145 The Verney Farm Bennington NH 03442-0145 Office: Monadnock Paper Mills Inc 117 Antrim Rd Bennington NH 03442-4205

VERNICK, JEFFREY FRANCIS, county official; b. Elizabeth, N.J., June 26, 1965; s. Arnold Sander and Lynne Beatrice Vernick. BA in Econs., McGill U., Montreal, Que., Can., 1988. Cert. Am. Inst. Cert. Planners; lic. profl. planner, N.J. Transp. analyst trainee N.J. Dept. Transp., Trenton, 1988-90; transp. planner Permanent Citizens Adv. Com., N.Y. Met. Transp. Authority, N.Y.C., 1990-93, Ebasco Infrastructure (now Raytheon Infrastructure Svcs.), N.Y.C., 1993-94, Parsons Brinckerhoff, Inc., Princeton, N.J., 1994-98; supervising transp. planner Monmouth County (N.J.) Planning Bd., Freehold, 1998—. Asst. N.J. Transit, Newark, summers, 1985, 86; train crew mem. New Hope (Pa.) and Ivyland (Pa.) R.R., 1998—; cert. employment trip reduction program N.J. Dept. Transp., Trenton, 1993—. Project leader, designer Dept. Level Libr. On-Line Catalog and Info. Sys., 1994-96 (quality improvement award 1996). Mem. Am. Planning Assn., Transp. Rsch. Bd. Jewish. Avocations: industrial archaeology, history, travel, transportation research, athletics. Home: 8-3 Deptford Ct Freehold NJ 07728-3915 Office: Monmouth County Planning Bd 1 E Main St Freehold NJ 07728-2278 E-mail: JVhotrail@aol.com.

VERNIERO, PETER G. state supreme court justice; married; 2 children. BA summa cum laude, Drew U., 1981; JD, Duke U., 1984. Law clk. to Justice Robert L. Clifford, 1984; with Pitney, Hardin, Kipp & Szuch, Morristown, NJ, 1985—87; dir. Herold & Haines P.A., Warren; chief counsel, chief of staff Gov. Christine Whitman, Trenton; atty. gen. State of N.J., 1996—99; assoc. justice N.J. Supreme Ct., 1999—. Adj. prof. bus. law County Coll. Morris, 1986. Exec. dir. Rep. State Com., 1989—90. Office: NJ Supreme Ct Hunterdon County Justice Ctr 65 Park Ave Flemington NJ 08822-0970*

VERNON, ALEJANDRA, artist; b. Reading, Pa., Sept. 6, 1944; Solo exhibit Newton (Mass.) Free Libr., 2000; exhibited in group shows at Ankrum Gallery, L.A., 1969-76, L.A. Art Assn., 1967-82, Chameleon Gallery, Newburyport, Mass., 1996—, Mercury Gallery, Boston, 1997—, Cambridge Art Assn. Nat. Prize Show, Boston, 1999, Alpers Fine Art, Andover, Mass., 2000, Icaro Gallery, Long Beach, Calif., 2002—. Recipient Sagendorph meml. prize Yankee Mag., 1999. Mem. Copley Soc. Boston. Home: 6481 Atlantic Ave # N219 Long Beach CA 90805 E-mail: avernon@avernon.com.

VERNON, CARL ATLEE, JR. retired wholesale food distributor executive; b. Topeka, Aug. 15, 1926; s. Carl Atlee and Capitola May (Jarboe) V.; m. Marion Leila Colton, May 7, 1950; children— Mary Catherine, Matthew Fowler, Susan Elizabeth BS, Yale U., 1947. Merchandising mgr. Fleming Cos., Topeka, 1957-61, dir. merchandising, 1961-66, dir. info. services, 1966-72, v.p. info. services, 1972-74, v.p. regional systems, 1974-79, sr. v.p. mktg. services Oklahoma City, 1979-88. Chmn. Shawnee County chpt. ARC, Topeka, Kans., 1957-58. Served to ensign USNR, 1944-46 Republican. Episcopalian. Avocations: golf; gardening; travel.

VERNON, DARRYL MITCHELL, lawyer; b. N.Y.C., May 4, 1956; s. Leonard and Joyce (Davidson) V.; m. Lauren Lynn Bernstein, Aug. 21, 1982. BA in Math., Tufts U., 1978; JD, Yeshiva U., 1981. Bar: N.Y. 1982, U.S. Dist. Ct. (so. and ea. dists.) N.Y. 1982, U.S. Ct. Appeals (2d cir.) 1987. Assoc. Hochberg & Greenberg, N.Y.C., 1981-82; ptnr. Greenberg & Vernon, 1982-83, Law Offices of Darryl M. Vernon, N.Y.C., 1983—; pres., ptnr. Vernon & Ginsburg, LLP, 1989—. Spkr. in field. Contbr. articles to profl. jours. Samuel Belkin scholar Yeshiva U., 1979. Mem. Assn. Bar City N.Y. (com. legal issues pertaining to animals). Office: 261 Madison Ave New York NY 10016-2303

VERNON, DORIS SCHALLER, retired writer; b. Petoskey, Mich., Mar. 7, 1915; d. Harve and Edna (Covey) Fredericksen; m. William Albert Schaller, Oct. 18, 1938; children: Kirk, Karen, Brent. Student, Cleary Coll., 1936-37, North Cen. Mich. Coll., 1960-61, 66-69. Sec. Mr. Beebe, Dean Freshman Coll., Petoskey, Mich., 1934-35, Dr. Dean C. Burns, Burns Clinic, Petoskey, 1937-38; with Probate and Juvenile Ct. Register, 1956-60; sec. bd. No. Mich. Rev., Inc., Mich., 1960-93; ret., 1996. Bd. dirs., Petoskey Friendship Ctr., gardening com., 2001—. Contbr. travel stories to profl. publs. Cub scout leader, Petoskey; treas. Camp Daggett Bd.; pres. Bus. and Profl. Women's Club, Petoskey, 1974-75; state bd. Don't Waste Mich., Riga and Lansing, 1989—, bd. dirs. No. bd., 1988—; civic gardening chair Petoskey Area Garden Club, sec., 1986; program chair Keenagers, First Christian Ch.; choir mem. First Christian Ch.; dir. Friendship Chorus for Care Ctrs. Singing Monthly Programs, Emmet County; bd. dirs. Friendship Ctr. Petosky, Mich., 1997-2001. Recipient cert. of commendation Guardian of the Earth, No. Mich., 1997. Avocations: square dancing, quilting. Home: 1028 Hoffman St Petoskey MI 49770-3213

VERNON, HEIDI, international business educator; b. Washington, Mar. 3, 1938; d. Raymond and Josephine (Stone) V.; m. Lawrence N. Wortzel, Dec. 23, 1956 (dec. Feb. 1996); children: Joshua C., Jennifer R. Stiller; m. F. Gerard Adams, Oct. 12, 1997. AB, Rutgers U., 1960; AM, Boston U., 1978, PhD, 1980. Owner Heidi Wortzel's Cooking Sch., Newton, Mass., 1970-75; prof. Northeastern U., Boston, 1980—. Sr. prof. Prasetiya Mulya Grad. Sch. Mgmt., Jakarta, Indonesia, 1987—; sr. cons. Global Resources, Corona de Mar, Calif., 1992—. Author: Business and Society, 1990, 6th edit., 1998, Lowell: The Corporations and the City, 1992; co-author: Strategic Management in the Global Environment, 1989, 3rd edit., 1997. Fellow Ea. Acad. Mgmt., 1994. Mem. Eastern Acad. Mgmt. (bd. mem., sec. 1988-91), Acad. Mgmt. (divsn. chair 1992), Acad. Internat. Bus. Democrat. Avocations: cooking, photography, gardening. Home: 39 Stafford Rd Newton MA 02459-1818 Office: Northeastern Univ 313 Hayden Boston MA 02115 E-mail: h.vernon@neu.edu.

VERNON, LAWRENCE GORDON, librarian; b. May 19, 1937; s. Angus Vernon and Anna Drucilla (Elliott) Vernon gabourel; m. Crystal Yvonne Gibson, July 18, 1959; children: Marlon, Dylan, Karen. Assoc., Brit. Libr. Assn. Corr. Course, London, 1959-63. Libr. asst. Nat. Libr. Svc., Belize, 1956-58, jr. asst. libr. Belize, 1958-66, asst. libr. Belize, 1966-76, sr. libr. Belize, 1976-78, chief libr. Belize, 1978-92; asst. libr. Univ. Coll. Belize, 1992, libr. dir., 1993-96, assoc. libr., 1996—. C0-author: Among My Souvenirs, 1966. Sec. bd. govs. Excelsior Cmty. H.S., Belize City, 1979; vice-chmn. Coun. of Vol. Social Svcs., 1986, rec. sec., 1989; chmn. Belize Scholarship Com., 1983. Mem. Belize Libr. Assn. (treas. 1978). Methodist. E-mail: lvernon@UB.edu.bz.

VERNON, LILLIAN, mail order company executive; b. 1927; d. Herman and Erna Menasche; m. Paolo Martino; children: Fred, David. DCS(hon.) , Mercy Coll., Dobbs Ferry, N.Y., 1984, Coll. New Rochelle; DSc in Bus. Adminstrn. (hon.) , Bryant Coll.; LLD (hon.) , Baruch Coll.; LHD (hon.) , Old Dominion U.; DCS (hon.) , Mercy Coll.; DCS Coll. New Rochelle (hon.); D. in Bus. Adminstrn. (hon.) , Bryant Coll.; LLD (hon.) , Baruch Coll. Chmn., CEO Lillian Vernon, New Rochelle, NY, 1951—. Lectr. in field. Contbr. articles to profl. jours. Trustee Coll. Human Svcs., Bryant Coll.; mem. adv. bd. Giraffe Project Girl Scout Coun. Tidewater; mem. adv. bd. Women's News; mem. bd. overseers Columbia U. Bus. Sch., NYU; mem. adv. com. Citizens Amb. Program; mem. bus. com. Met. Mus. Art; bd. govs. The Forum; mem. nat. com. The Kennedy Ctr. for Performing Arts, Washington; active The Ellis Island Reopening Com.; Bd. dirs. Westchester County, Ctr. Preventive Psychiatry, Va. Opera, Children's Mus. Arts, Retinitis Pigmentosa Found. Named Va. Press Women Newsmaker of Yr., woman of Yr., Women's Direct Response Group and Westchester County Fedn. Women's Clubs, Hampton Rds. Woman of Yr., So. New Eng. Entrepreneur of Yr.; named to Acad. Women Achievers, YWCA, Direct Mktg. Assn. Hall of Fame, Conn. Women's Hall of Fame; recipient Disting. Achievement award, Lab. Inst. Merchandising, Entrepreneurial award, Women's Bus. Owners of N.Y., 1983, Bravo award, YWCA, Woman of Achievement award, Woman's NEws, Nat. Hero award, Big. Bros./Big Sisters, Legend in Leadership award, Emory U., A Woman Who Has Made a Differene award, Inter. Womens Forum, medal of honor, Ellis Island, Bus. Leadership award, Gannett Newspapers, Outstanding Bus. Leader award, Northwood Inst., Congl. Record Commendation award, Crystal award, Coll. Human Svcs., City of Peace award, Bonds of Israel, Svc. award, Sr. Placement Bur., Excellence award, Westchester Assn. Women Bus. Owners, Commendation in Cong. Record, Magnificent Seven award, Bus. and Profl. Women, Woman of Distinction award, Birmingham So. Coll. Mem.: Nat. Retail Fedn. (bd. dirs.), Women's Forum, Com. of 200, Am. Stock Exch. (listed co. adv. com.), Am. Bus. Conf. (dir.), Lotos Club. Office: Lillian Vernon Corp 1 Theall Rd Rye NY 10580-1450 Office Fax: 914-925-1502.

VERNON, STEPHEN EDWARD, pathologist; b. Dayton, Ohio, Nov. 25, 1949; s. Marvin and Catherine (Richard) V. BA in Zoology, U. South Fla., 1971, MD, 1974. Diplomate Am. Bd. Pathology; bd. cert. anatomic and clin. pathology, 1979, immunopathology, 1983, cytopathology, 1997. Intern Loma Linda (Calif.) U. Med. Ctr., 1975-76; resident in pathology UCLA, 1977-79; staff pathologist St. Francis Hosp., Miami Beach, Fla., 1979-85; pathologist East Point Hosp., Lehigh Acres, 1985-86; assoc. med. examiner Dist. 21, Ft. Myers, 1985-86; sr. attending pathologist Mercy Hosp., Miami, 1986—, dir. med. edn., 1989-95; clin. asst. prof. pathology U. Miami Sch. Medicine, 1998—. Inspector Coll. Am. Pathologists, 1980—. Editor-in-chief Jour. Mercy Medicine, 1992-95, Miami Medicine, 1995-97; contbr. articles to profl. jours. Am. Cancer Soc. fellow, 1978-79. Fellow Coll. Am. Pathologists (del. 1986—, spokesperson 1987—); mem. Fla. Med. Assn. (accreditation com. 1989—), Fla. Soc. Pathologists (pres. 1988-89), South Fla. Soc. Pathologists (pres. 1993-94), South Fla. Cytometry Grup (founder, charter officer). Achievements include research in immunohistochemistry and pathology. Office: U Miami Sch Medicine Dept Pathology D-33 PO Box 16960 Miami FL 33101-6960

VERNON, WESTON, III (WES VERNON), broadcaster, writer, actor; b. N.Y.C., Aug. 23, 1931; s. Weston, Jr. and Adelaide (Neilson) V.; m. Alida Steinvoort, Oct. 5, 1951; children: Rosanne, Weston IV, Diane, John Randall. Student, Utah State U., 1949-50, Brigham Young U., 1953-54. Early broadcasting career on staff of radio stas., in Utah and Wyo., 1950-54; news and announcer KBMY, Billings, Mont., 1954-63; news dir., polit. specialist KSL Radio-TV, Salt Lake City, 1963-68; bur. chief Bonneville Internat. Corp., Washington, 1968-72; corr. CBS Radio Stas. News Svc. CBS Radio, 1972-97; host CBS Crosstalk, 1975-97. Columnist The High Green, The Timetable, Washington corr. NationalCorridors.org, NewsMax.com, Trains.com. Bd. dirs. Winding-Orchard Citizens Assn., Wheaton-Glenmont, Md., 1974-77, 86—, pres., 1975-76. Served with AUS, 1951-52. Recipient Journalism awards Mont. A.P. Press Stas., 1960, Journalism awards Utah Bar Assn., 1965, Journalism awards Utah Broadcasters Assn., 1965-66, Nat. Press Club. Mem. SAG, AFTRA (exec. bd. Balt.-Wash. local 1997—), Am. Legion (comdr. Yellowstone Post 4 1962-63), Chesapeake Rlwy. Assn. (pres. 1992-94, bd. dirs.). Office: 1605 Billman Ln Silver Spring MD 20902-1417

VERO, RADU, freelance medical and scientific illustrator, educator, writer, consultant; b. Bucharest, Romania, Oct. 20, 1926; came to U.S., 1973; s. Leon and Bella Sylvia (Spiegler) V.; m. Susan Ezpeleta D'Aste. BA, Inst. Architecture, Bucharest, 1951. Freelance illustrator, Bucharest, 1952-61, Israel, 1961-73, N.Y.C., 1973—. Mem. faculty Fashion Inst. Tech., N.Y.C., 1982—; discoverer novel set of curves (cubals) in analytic geometry. Author: Understanding Perspective, 1980, Airbrush, 1982, Airbrush 2, 1984. Recipient illustration award N.Y. Acad. Scis., 1975, Vargas award, 1997. Mem. N.Y. Acad. Scis.

VERON, J. MICHAEL, lawyer, writer; b. Lake Charles, La., Aug. 24, 1950; s. Earl Ernest and Alverdy (Heyd) V.; m. Melinda Anne Guidry, Jan. 2, 1993; children: John Heyd, Katharine Leigh, Dylan Michael Earl. BA, Tulane U., 1972, JD, 1974; LLM, Harvard U., 1976. Bar: La. 1974, U.S. Dist. Ct. (we. dist.) La. 1977, U.S. Dist. Ct. (ea. dist.) La. 1979, U.S. Dist. Ct. (mid. dist.) La., 1983, U.S. Dist. Ct. (ea. dist.) Tex. 1992), U.S. Ct. Appeals (5th cir.) 1981, U.S. Ct. Appeals (fed. cir.) 1996, U.S. Tax Ct. 1988. Law clk. to presiding justice La. Supreme Ct., New Orleans, 1974-75; sole practice Lake Charles, 1976-78; ptnr. Scofield, Gerard, Veron, Singletary & Pohorelsky (formerly Scofield, Gerard, Veron, Hoskins & Soileau), 1978—. Instr. legal method and rsch. Boston U., 1975-76; lectr. environ. law McNeese State U., 1976-79; faculty Tulane Trial Adv. Inst., 1980; adj. prof. La. State U. Sch. Law, 1993-2000. Author: The Greatest Player Who Never Lived, 2000, The Greatest Course That Never Was, 2001; mem. bd. editors Tulane Law Rev., 1972-73, assoc. editor, 1973-74. Mem. athletic adv. com. Tulane U., 1983-86; pres. Krewe of Barataria, 1980-86. Named to La. State U. Law Ctr. Hall of Fame, 1993. Mem. U.S. Golf Assn. (sectional affairs com.), La. Golf. Assn. (bd. dirs., pres. 1990), Order of Coif, Maritime Law Assn., Lake Charles Country Club (pres. 1986). Roman Catholic. Avocations: golf, gin rummy, athletics. Home: 9 Par Dr Lake Charles LA 70605-5925 Office: Scofield Gerard Veron Singletary & Pohorelsky 1114 Ryan St Lake Charles LA 70601-5252 E-mail: mveron@sgvsp.com.

VERONA, MONICA J. concert pianist, educator; b. Milw., July 2, 1956; d. Emanuel A. and Winifred M. V. BA in Italian and Art History, U. Wis., Milw., 1982; MusM, Manhattan Sch. Music, 1984; Performer's Cert. Degree, No. Ill. U., 1987; doctoral student, Manhattan Sch. Music, 1985-92. Teaching asst. piano and chamber music No. Ill. U., DeKalb, 1984-85; piano faculty The Fleming Sch., N.Y.C., 1987-90, The Calhoun Sch., N.Y.C., 1989—, Bklyn. Coll. Preparatory Ctr. for the Performing Arts, 1992—, The Trevor Day Sch., 1996—, Bloomingdale Sch. of Music, 1999—. Sub. tchr. in solo and duo piano lit. Manhattan Sch. of Music Preparatory Divsn., 1987. Author: J.S. Bach's Chromatic Fantasy and Fugue: A Study of Virtuoso Keyboard Forms From the 16th to 18th Centuries, 1995; solo performances include: Met. Mus. Art, Salzburg Festival, Ravinia Festival, U.S. Dept. Interior/Am. Landmarks Festival, New Rochelle Pub. Libr. Series, Manhattan Sch. Music, Steinway

Hall, N.Y.C., Klavierhaus, N.Y.C., Nicholas Roerich Mus., Bklyn. Coll., No. Ill. U., PBS TV Milw., U. Wis., Goeth Inst. Milw., Park Ave. Christian Ch. Recital Series, N.Y.C., St. Paul's Recital Series, Nyack, N.Y., St. Peter's Concert Series at Citicorp, N.Y.C., Milw. Cath. Symphony Orch., Donnell N.Y. Pub. Lib. Series, Charles Allis Art Mus., Milw., Katonah Village Recital Series; chamber music performances include: Manhattan Sch. Music, No. Ill. U., Goethe Inst., Met. Mus. of Art, N.Y., others; participant numerous music festivals. Recipient numerous sholarships, 1975-87, first prize Nat. Fedn. Music Clubs Competition, 1976, third prize Mu Phi Epsilon Scholarship Competition, 1977, first prize Ida Schroeder Found. Scholarship Competition, 1978. Mem. Mu Phi Epsilon (prs. N.Y.C. 1998—). Roman Catholic. Avocation: gardening, drawing. Home and Office: 45 Tiemann Pl Apt 5M New York NY 10027-3327

VERONIS, GEORGE, geophysics educator; b. New Brunswick, N.J., June 6, 1926; s. Nicholas Emmanuel and Angeliki (Efthimakis) V.; m. Anna Margareta Olsson, Nov. 8, 1963; m. Catherine Elizabeth, Jan. 29, 1949 (div. Nov. 1962); children— Melissa, Benjamin. A.B., Lafayette Coll., 1950; Ph.D., Brown U., 1954; M.A. (hon.), Yale U., 1966; DSc (hon.) Lafayette Coll. 1997. Staff meteorologist Inst. Advanced Study, Princeton, 1953-56; staff mathematician Woods Hole Oceanographic Inst., Mass., 1956-64, mem. staff, dir. geophys. fluid dynamics summer program, 1959—, assoc. prof. MIT, Cambridge, 1961-64, research oceanographer, 1964-66; prof. geophysics and applied sci. Yale U., New Haven, 1966— , Henry Barnard Davis prof., 1985— , chmn. geology and geophysics, 1976-79, dir. applied math, 1979-93. Editor Jour. Marine Rsch., 1973—; contbr. articles to profl. jours. Served with USN, 1943-46. Fellow Am. Acad. Arts and Scis., Am. Geophys. Union; mem. NAS, Norwegian Acad. Scis. (Robert L. and Bettie P. Cody award 1989, Henry Stommel Rsch. award 1997). Greek Orthodox. E-mail: george.veronis@yale.edu.

VERONIS, PETER, publisher; b. New Brunswick, N.J., June 15, 1923; s. Nicholas M. and Angeliki (Efthemakis) V.; m. Dorothy E. White, Sept. 8, 1947; 1 dau., Judith Anne Veronis Rodgers. Student, Columbia U., 1951-54. Nat. advt. mgr. Springfield (Mass.) Newspapers, 1954-57; v.p., gen. sales mgr. Ridder Johns Co., N.Y.C., 1957-62; corp. exec. Curtis Pub. Co., 1963-64; assoc. sales mgr. Look mag., 1964-68; v.p., advt. dir. Psychology Today mag., 1968-71; v.p. advt. Saturday Rev., N.Y.C., 1971-73; pub. Book Digest, 1973-80; pres. PV Pub. Inc., 1980-81, Conn., 1988—; v.p., founder and dir. CBS Mag. Network, N.Y.C., 1981-85, pres., 1985-87, Diamandis Mag. Network, 1987-88. Served with USN, 1941-51. Home: 42 Thornwood Rd Stamford CT 06903-2613 E-mail: pveronis@aol.com.

VERPLANCK, WILLIAM SAMUEL, psychologist, educator; b. Plainfield, N.J., Jan. 6, 1916; s. William Samuel and Kathryn (Tracy) V. BS, U. Va., 1937, MA, 1938; PhD, Brown U., 1941. Asst. prof. Ind. U., 1946-50; asst. prof. Harvard, 1950-55, acting asso. prof., 1955-56; research asso. Stanford U., 1956-57; asso. prof. Hunter Coll., 1957-59; prof. U. Md., 1958-62; prof. psychology U. Tenn., 1963-81, head dept., 1963-73; founder, chmn. Resource Assocs., Inc., 1980-88. Bd. dirs. Cambridge Ctr. for Behavioral Sci., 1990-93. Author: (with others) Modern Learning Theory, 1953. Bd. trustees Cambridge Ctr. Behavioral Studies, 1995-2000. Served to lt. USNR, 1943-46. Recipient travel grant Am. Philos. Assn., 1953 Fellow APA, Am. Psychol. Soc., Assn. Study Animal Behavior, AAAS; mem. Ea. Psychol. Assn., Psychonomic Soc. (founder, past sec.-treas., bd. govs.), Sigma Xi, Sigma Alpha Epsilon. E-mail: wverplan@utk.edu./wverplan.com. *The history of psychology is largely constituted of a succession of fads overlying the continuity given by a few plausible technological methods which have been progressively misapplied, with little critical concern for their social, political or scientific consequences.*

VERRELLI, ANTHONY LOUIS, lawyer; b. Bronx, Feb. 19, 1967; s. Sebastiano and Josephine V.; m. Sungho Pak, Feb. 16, 1997. BA cum laude, Iona Coll., 1989; MA summa cum laude, St. John's U., 1991; JD, Seton Hall U., 1994. Bar: N.J. 1994, N.Y. 1995, U.S. Dist. Ct. (so. and ea. dists.) N.Y. 1995. Atty. pvt. practice, Bronx, 1994—. St. John's U. Grad. Sch. scholar, Jamaica, N.Y., 1991. Mem. N.Y. State Trial Lawyers Assn., Bronx County Bar Assn. Avocations: soccer, hiking, golf. Office: 2701 Williamsbridge Rd Bronx NY 10469-4109 E-mail: AVerrelliEsq@aol.com.

VERRETT, SHIRLEY, soprano; b. New Orleans, May 31, 1931; d. Leon Solomon and Elvira Augustine (Harris) V.; m. Louis Frank LoMonaco, Dec. 10, 1963; 1 dau., Francesca. AA, Ventura (Calif.) Coll., 1951; diploma in voice (scholarship 1956-61), Juilliard Sch. Music, 1961; MusD (hon.), Coll. Holy Cross, Mass., 1978. CPA, Cert. real estate broker. James Earl Jones disting. univ. prof. voice U. Mich. Sch. Music, 1996—. Mem. adv. bd. Opera Ebony. Recital debut Town Hall, N.Y.C., 1958; appeared as Irina in Lost in the Stars, 1958; orchestral debut Phila. Orch., 1960; operatic debut in Carmen, Festival of Two Worlds, Spoleto, Italy, 1962; debuts with Bolshoi Opera, Moscow, 1963, N.Y.C. Opera, 1964, Royal Opera, Covent Garden, 1966, Maggio Fiorentino, Florence, 1967, Met. Opera, 1968, Teatro San Carlos, Naples, 1968, Dallas Civic Opera, 1969, La Scala, 1970, Vienna State Opera, 1970, San Francisco Opera, 1972, Paris Opera, 1973, Opera Co. Boston, 1976, Opera Bastille, Paris, 1990; guest appearances with all major U.S. symphony orchs.; toured Eastern Europe and Greece with La Scala chorus and orch., 1981; TV debut on Ed Sullivan Show, 1963; TV performances include: Great Performances series, live performance of Macbeth at La Scala, Santuzza in Cavalleria Rusticana; film debut Maggio Musicale, 1989, Macbeth, 1986; rec. artist, RCA, Columbia, ABC (Westminster), Angel Everest, Kapp, Philips Records and Deutsche Grammophon. Recipient Marian Anderson award, 1955, Nat. Fedn. Music Clubs award, 1961, Walter Naumberg award, 1958, Blanche Thebom award, 1960; named Chevalier Arts and Letters (France), 1970, Commandeur, 1984; John Hay Whitney fellow, 1959; Ford Found. fellow, 1962-63; Martha Baird Rockefeller Aid to Music Fund fellow, 1959-61; grantee William Matteus Sullivan Fund, 1959; grantee Berkshire Music Opera, 1956; recipient Achievement award Ventura Coll., 1963, Achievement award N.Y. chpt. Albert Einstein Coll. Medicine, 1975; 2 plaques Los Angeles Sentinel Newspaper, 1960; plaque Peninsula Music Festival, 1963; Los Angeles Times Woman of Yr. award, 1969 Mem. Mu Phi Epsilon. Office: Herbert Breslin Inc 6124 Liebig Ave Bronx NY 10471-1008 also: U Mich Sch Music 1100 Baits Dr Ann Arbor MI 48109-2085

VERRILL, CHARLES OWEN, JR. lawyer; b. Biddeford, Maine, Sept. 30, 1937; s. Charles Owen and Elizabeth (Handy) V.; m. Mary Ann Blanchard, Aug. 13, 1960 (dec.); children: Martha Anne, Edward Blanchard, Ethan Christopher, Elizabeth Handy, Matthew Lawton, Peter Goldthwait; m. Diana Baber, Dec. 11, 1993. AB, Tufts U., 1959; LLB, Duke U., 1962. Bar: D.C. 1962. Assoc. Weaver & Glassie, 1962-64, Barco, Cook, Patton & Blow, 1964-66, ptnr., 1967, Patton, Boggs & Blow, 1967-84, Wiley, Rein & Fielding, Washington, 1984—. Adj. prof. internat. trade law/internat. bus. transaction Georgetown U. Law Ctr., Washington, 1978—, Charles Fahy Disting. adj. prof., 1993; vis. sr. lectr. internat. trade law Duke U. Law Sch., 1998—; conf. chmn. The Future of Internat. Steel Industry, Bellagio, Italy, 1984, U.S. Agenda for Uruguay Round, Airlie House, Warrenton, Va., 1986, Polish Joint Venture Law, Cracow, Poland, 1987, Internat. Steel Industry II, Bellagio, 1987, Bulgaria and the GATT, Washington, 1977; chair, spkr. Protection of Intellectual Property from Theft and Piracy Abroad Southwestern Legal Found. Fgn. Investment Symposium, 1995, chair, panel on NAFTA 2 1/2 Years Later, 1996. Local dir. Tufts U. Ann. Fund, 1965-69; mem. Duke Law Alumni Coun., 1972-75; trustee Internat. Law Inst., 1981—, chmn. bd. trustees, 1983-87; apptd. to roster of dispute settlement panelists World Trade Orgn., 1995, 97; chmn. adv. bd. Inst. for Advancement of Svc., 1997—; mem. adv. com. rules U.S. Ct. Internat. Trade, 1998—; chmn. D.C. Cable Television Adv. Com., 1999—; mem. bd. visitors Duke U. Law Sch., 2000—; mem. nat. adv. bd. Nat. Resources Coun. Maine, 2002—. Mem. ABA, Internat. Bar Assn., D.C. Bar Assn., Order of Coif, Theta Delta Chi, Phi Delta Phi, Met. Club (Washington), Chevy Chase Club (Md.), Tarratine Club (Dark Harbor, Maine). Home: 3000 Q St NW Washington DC 20007-3080 Office: 1776 K St NW Washington DC 20006-2304 E-mail: cverrill@wrf.com.

VERRILL, F. GLENN, advertising executive; b. N.Y.C., Dec. 17, 1923; s. Ralph Francis and Rose (Verner) V.; m. Jean Demar, Aug. 25, 1946; children: Gary, Joan. AB, Adelphi Coll., 1949; A.M., Harvard U., 1950. With Batten, Barton, Durstine & Osborn, Inc., 1952—, v.p., 1964; creative dir. Batten, Barton, Durstine & Osborn, Inc. (Burke Dowling Adams div.), Atlanta, 1965-70, exec. v.p., gen. mgr., 1970-71, pres., 1971-88, chmn., 1988—, also dir. parent co. Author: Advertising Procedure, 1983, rev. edit., 1986, 88. Mem. adv. bd. U. Ga.; vice chmn. bd. overseers Coll. Bus. Adminstrn., Ga. State U.; bd. dirs. Atlanta Humane Soc., pres., 1980-81; chmn. Advanced Advt. Inst. Atlanta, 1981; mem. Peabody award com., 1984—; bd. dirs. Atlanta Coll. of Art, 1990. With USAAF, 1943-46. Mem. Am. Assn. Advt. Agys. (nat. dir. 1973—) Clubs: Atlanta Athletic, Cherokee, Harvard (Atlanta). Episcopalian. Home: 2600 W Wesley Rd NW Atlanta GA 30327-2036 Office: BBDO Inc 3620 Cloudland Dr NW Atlanta GA 30327-2908

VERRILL, JOHN HOWARD, museum director; b. Biddeford, Maine, June 17, 1947; s. Charles Owen and Elizabeth Martha (Handy) V.; m. Carol Christine Cory, Sept. 8, 1967; 1 child, Nathan Lawrence. BA, Campbell U., 1969. Tchr. St. Mary's County Schs., Leonardtown, Md., 1969-73; sales mgr. Kable News Co., N.Y.C., 1973-79; contract adminstr. Fischbach and Moore, L.K. Comstock, Lanham, Md., 1979-83; agrl. entrepreneur Jubilee Farm, Hebron, 1983-87; mus. mgr. NASA, Wallops Island, Va., 1985; exec. dir. Purnell Mus., Snow Hill, Md., 1986-93, Ea Shore of Va. Hist. Soc., Onancock, Va., 1993—. Faculty mem. Seminar for Hist. Adminstrn. at Colonial Williamsburg, 1999-2000. Editor: (book) Trustee, Board Member Handbook, 1995. Pres. Wicomico County Fair, Salisbury, Md., 1986, S.E. Shore Travel Coun., Salisbury, 1988, Lions Club, Hebron, Md., 1991; active Hist. Adminstrn. 1999-2000. Recipient Gov.'s citation, Maryland Gov. Schaeffer, 1994. Mem. Am. Assn. Mus., S. Ea. Mus. Conf. (mentor 1994)), Va. Assn. Mus. (mentor 1997), Am. Assn. State and Local History, Small Mus. Assn. (chmn. 1990, bd. dirs. 1997—), Rotary Club Melfa, Va. (pres. 1995), Ea. Shore Barrier Islands Ctr. (bd. dirs. 1995—). Episcopalian (Lay Eucharistic Minister). Avocations: home restoration, gardening, boating, travel. Office: Ea Shore Va Hist Soc PO Box 193 Onancock VA 23417-0193 E-mail: kerr@esva.net.

VERRILLO, RONALD THOMAS, neuroscience educator, researcher; b. Hartford, Conn., July 31, 1927; s. Francesco Paul and Angela (Forte) V.; m. Violet Silverstein, June 3, 1950; children: Erica, Dan, Thomas. BA, Syracuse U., 1952; PhD, U. Rochester, 1958. Asst. prof. Syracuse U., 1957-62, rsch. assoc., 1959-63, rsch. fellow, 1963-67, assoc. prof., 1967-74, prof., 1974-94, prof. emeritus, 1995—, assoc. dir. Inst. Sensory Rsch., 1980-84, dir., 1984-93, dir. grad. neurosci. program, 1984-93. Advisor com. on hearing, bioacoustics and biomechanics NRC. Author: Adjustment to Visual Disability, 1961 (award 1962); contbr. chpts. to books, articles to profl. jours. With USN, 1945-46. Fellow Am. Found. for Blind, 1956, NATO, 1970; grantee NSF, 1969-72, 84-87, NIH, 1972—; recipient Internat. Sensory Aids award, 1998. Fellow Acoustical Soc. Am. (Silver medal 1999); mem. Soc. for Neurosci., N.Y. Acad. Scis., Sigma Xi (Rsch. award 1982). Home: 312 Berkeley Dr Syracuse NY 13210-3031 Office: Syracuse U Inst Sensory Rsch 621 Skytop Rd Syracuse NY 13244-5290 E-mail: ron_verrillo@isr.syr.edu.

VERRONE, PATRIC MILLER, lawyer, writer; b. Glendale, N.Y.C., Sept. 29, 1959; s. Pat and Edna (Miller) V.; m. Margaret Maiya Williams, 1989; children: Patric Carroll Williams, Marianne Emma Williams, Theodore Henry Williams. BA, Harvard U., 1981; JD, Boston Coll., 1984. Bar: Fla. 1984, Calif. 1988, U.S. Dist. Ct. (mid. dist.) Fla. 1984, U.S. Dist. Ct. (ctrl. dist.) Calif. 1995, U.S. Ct. Appeals (9th cir.) 1995. Assoc. Allen, Knudsen, Swartz, DeBoest, Rhoads & Edwards, Ft. Myers, Fla., 1984-86; writer The Tonight Show, Burbank, Calif., 1987-90. Adj. prof. Loyola Law Sch., LA, 1998—2000. Dir., producer, writer The Civil War--The Lost Episode, 1991; writer The Larry Sanders Show, 1992-94, The Critic, 1993-95; producer, writer The Simpsons, 1994-95, Muppets Tonight!, 1995-97 (Emmy award Best Children's Program 1998), Pinky and the Brain, 1998, Futurama, 1998-2002 (Environ. Media award 2000, Emmy nominee 1999, 2001, 2002); editor Harvard Lampoon, 1978-84, Boston Coll. Law Rev., 1983-84, Fla. Bar Jour., 1987-88, L.A. Lawyer, 1994—; issue editor: Ann. Entertainment Law Issue, 1995-2002; contbr. articles to profl. jours. including Elysian Fields Quar., Baseball and the American Legal Mind, White's Guide to Collecting Figures, written by, Frank Sinatra: The Man, The Music, The Legend. Bd. dirs. Calif. Confedn. of Arts, 1994-98, Mus. Contemporary Art, 1994-95. Mem. ABA (vice-chair arts, entertainment and sports law com. 1995-96), Calif. Bar, Calif. Lawyers for Arts, L.A. County Bar Assn. (sec. barristers exec. com., chair artists and the law com., steering com. homeless shelter project, intellectual property and entertainment law sect., state appelate jud. evaluation com., legis. activity com.), Fla. Bar Assn., Writers Guild Am. West (exec. com. animation writers caucus, bd. dirs. 1999-2001, sec., treas., 2001-, membership com. 1999-2001, fin. com. 1999-2001, legis. support com., 2001 contract negotiating com., chair organizing com. 2001-, animation writing award animation writers caucus), Harvard Club Lee County (v.p. 1985-86), Harvard Club So. Calif. Republican. Roman Catholic. Avocations: baseball, history. Home and Office: PO Box 1428 Pacific Palisades CA 90272-1428

VERRY, WILLIAM ROBERT, retired mathematics researcher; b. July 11, 1933; s. William Richard and Maurine Houser (Braden) V.; m. Bette Lee Ronspiess, Nov. 20, 1955 (div. 1981); children: William David, Sandra Kay Verry Londregan, Steven Bruce, Kenneth Scott; m. Jean Elizabeth Morrison, Oct. 16, 1982; step-children: Lucinda Jean Hale, Christine Carol Hale Fortner, Martha Jean Johnson, Brian Kenneth Lackey, Robert Morrison Lackey. BA, Reed Coll., 1955; BS, Portland State U., 1957; MA, Fresno State U., 1960; PhD, Ohio State U., Columbus, 1972. Instr. chemistry Reedley (Calif.) Coll., 1957-60; ops. rsch. analyst Naval Weapons Ctr., China Lake, Calif., 1960-63; ordnance engr. Honeywell Ordnance, Hopkins, Minn., 1963-64; sr. scientist Litton Industries, St. Paul, 1964-67; project mgr. Tech. Ops., Inc., Alexandria, Va., 1967-70; rsch. assoc. Ohio State U., Columbus, 1970-72; prin. engr. Computer Sci. Corp., Falls Church, Va., 1972-77; mem. tech. staff MITRE Corp., Albuquerque, 1977-85; C3 program dir., assoc. prof. math. sci. Clemson U., S.C., 1985-87; dep. dir. Riverside Rsch. Inst., Rosslyn, Va., 1987-91; mgr. Hillcrest Gardens, Livermore, Calif., 1992-98, ret., 1998. Founder, minister Christian Love Ctr.; founder, v.p. Interfaith Sharing, Inc., 1994-98. Mem. Inst. for Ops. Rsch. and the Mgmt. Scis. Home: PO Box 765 24 Snowden Cutoff Rd White Salmon WA 98672 E-mail: billverry@gorge.net.

VERSCH, ESTHER MARIE, artist; b. Santa Monica, Calif., May 27, 1927; d. Claro Contreras Santellanes and Juana Hernandez; m. Chester Ray Fraelich, Nov. 14, 1943 (div. Nov. 1964); children: Joe Fraelich, Diane Fraelich Foster Preston; m. Terry Lee Versch, June 21, 1969; stepchildren: Fred, Roman, Joseph, Terry Jr., Michael. Student, East L.A. Coll., Pasadena City Coll. Lic. vocat. nurse. Nurse pvt. dr.'s office, L.A., 1968-69, U. So. Calif. Med. Ctr., 1963-68; artist Altadena, Calif., 1972—. Artist: (front cover) Library Services L.A., 1983, Christmas card for Western Greeting Inc., (back cover) Moccasin Tracks, 1984-85; one woman shows include Republic Fed. Savings, Altadena, Calif., Pasadena Pub. Libr., Whites Art Store and Gallery, La Canada, Calif., 1979, Windmill Gallery, 1985; group exhibitions: Women Artists of the West Internat. Exhibition and Sale, Cody Western and Wildlife Classyc, 1979, Nat. Cowgirl Hall of Fame, Hereford, Tex., 1978, Beauty for the Beast Benefit, 1980, Ducks Unltd. Invitational Art Show, Taylor, Mich., 1986-87, Lawrence (Kans.) Indian Art Show, Mus. Anthropology, 1989-90, Snake River Showcase, Lewiston, Idaho, 1992, Women Artists of the West, 1992, 98, 99, Death Valley 49's Invitational Art Show, 1994-2000, 2001, George Ohr Cultural Arts and Cultural Ctr., Biloxi, Miss., 1998, Western and Wildlife Invitational Art Show, Estes Park, Colo., 2000, WAOW Art Show Pinedale, Wyo, 2002, Art and Music Festival, Dublin, Ohio, 2002; collections: Johnson Humrick House Mus., Coshocton, Ohio, and other private collections; illustrator back cover Moccasin Tracks, 1984-85. Vol. nurses aide City View Hosp., L.A., 1960-63; vol. Arroyo Rep., Pasadena, Calif., St. Luke Hosp., Pasadena, 1990-94, flu immunization ARC, 1977-78. Recipient Gold medal for watercolor San Gabriel Fine Arts, 1979, Best of Show award for watercolor Am. Indian and Western, 1990, Hon. mention San Gabriel Fine Arts, 1990, 3rd Place Watercolor Women Artists of the West Saddle Back Art Gallery, 1982. Mem. Women Artists of the West (emeritus mem., treas., asst. sec., editor West Wind, membership chmn.), Ohio Art League, Coshocton Art Guild. Republican. Roman Catholic. Avocations: walking, gardening, sewing. E-mail: everschart@newsguy.com.

VERSCHAEGEN, CLAIRE FLORENCE, oncologist; b. Brussels, Nov. 6, 1957; came to U.S., 1985; m. Murthy Ram, July 24, 1987; children: Victor, Adeline. MS, U. Libre Bruxelles, Brussels, 1980, MD, 1982. Diplomate Am. Bd. Internal Medicine, Am. Bd. Med. Oncology. Resident in internal medicine Inst. Bordet, Brussels, 1982-85; postdoctoral fellow Stehlin Found., Houston, 1985-88; resident in internal medicine U. Tex. Health Sci. Ctr., 1988-91; fellow in med. oncology M.D. Anderson Cancer Ctr., 1992-95, instr., asst. internist, 1995-97, asst. prof., 1997—. Mem. steering com. Physician Oncology Edn. Program, Austin, Tex., 1996—2001; fellow in internal medicine U. Libre Bruxelles, Belgium, 1991—92. Fellow Fulbright Found., 1985, Belgian Am. Edn. Found., 1985; recipient Occino-Kernkamp prize Belgian AUW, 1986. Fellow ACP, Am. Coll. Internal Physicians, Tex. Med. Assn.; mem. Am. Soc. Clin. Oncology, Am. Assn. for Cancer Rsch. Fax: 713-745-1541. E-mail: c.verschraegen@usa.net.

VERSCHOOR, CURTIS CARL, business educator, consultant; b. Grand Rapids, Mich., June 7, 1931; s. Peter and Leonene (Dahlstrom) V.; m. Marie Emilie Kritschgau, June 18, 1952; children— Katherine Anne, Carolyn Marie, John Peter, Carla Michelle. BBA with distinction, U. Mich., 1951, MBA, 1952; EdD, No. Ill. U., 1977. CPA; cert. mgmt. acctg., cert. fin. planner, cert. fraud examiner, cert. internal auditor; chartered fin. cons. Pub. accountant Touche, Ross, Bailey & Smart (C.P.A.'s), 1955-63; with Singer Co., 1963-68, asst. controller, 1965-68; controller Colgate-Palmolive Co., 1968-69; asst. controller bus. products group Xerox Corp., 1969-72; controller Baxter Internat., 1972-73; v.p. finance Altair Corp., Chgo., 1973-74; prof. DePaul U., 1974-94, ledger and quill alumni rsch. prof., 1994—; pres. C.C. Verschoor & Assocs., Inc., 1981—. Part-time instr. Wayne State U., 1955-60; author audit com. briefings. Author: Audit Committee Briefing: Understanding the 21st Century Audit Committee Governance Roles, 2000, Audit Committee Briefing: Facilitating New Audit Committee Responsibilites, 2001; contbg. editor: Jour. Accountancy, 1961-62, Jour. Internal Auditing, 1985—, Strategic Fin.; editl. adv. bd. Acctg. Today, 1991—. Trustee Hektoen Inst. Med. Rsch., Chgo., 1996—. Served with AUS, 1953-55. Recipient Elijah Watts Sells award Am. Inst. C.P.A.'s, 1953 Mem. AICPA, Fin. Execs. Inst., Am. Acctg. Assn., Inst. Mgmt. Accts., Inst. Internal Auditors, Nat. Assn. Corp. Dirs., Beta Gamma Sigma, Beta Alpha Psi, Delta Pi Epsilon, Phi Kappa Phi, Phi Eta Sigma. Home: 231 Wyngate Dr Barrington IL 60010-4840 Office: DePaul Univ One E Jackson Blvd Chicago IL 60604-2287 E-mail: cverscho@condor.depaul.edu.

VERSFELT, DAVID SCOTT, lawyer; b. Mineola, N.Y., Feb. 17, 1951; s. William H. and Ruth (Gerland) V.; m. Mary Deborah Garber, Aug. 31, 1974; children: Christopher L., William S., Kathryn H. AB, Princeton U., 1973; JD, Columbia U., 1976. Bar: N.Y. 1977, U.S. Dist. Ct. (so. and ea. dists.) N.Y. 1977, U.S. Ct. Appeals (D.C. cir.) 1979, U.S. Ct. Appeals (2d and 7th cirs.) 1980, U.S. Supreme Ct. 1980, U.S. Ct. Appeals (9th cir.) 1981, U.S. Ct. Appeals (3d cir.) 1982, Ct. Internat. Trade 1990, U.S. Ct. Appeals (fed. cir.) 1994, U.S. Ct. Appeals (6th cir.) 1996. Mem. Coun. of Community Law Office; vol. div. Legal Aid Soc., N.Y.C., 1985-88; dir. Partnership for a Drug-Free Am., 1989—. Mem. ABA, Assn. Bar City N.Y. (com. on state legislation 1983-85), Phi Beta Kappa. Office: Kirkpatrick & Lockhart LLP 599 Lexington Ave New York NY 10022-6030 E-mail: dversfelt@kl.com.

VERSHBOW, ALEXANDER R. diplomat; m. Lisa Vershbow; two children. BA in Russian and East European Studies, Yale Coll., 1974; MS in Internat. Rels., Columbia U., 1976. Various fgn. svc. positions, 1977—; dir. Office of Soviet Union Affairs U.S. Dept. of State, 1988-91; prin. dep. asst. Sec. of State for European and Can. Affairs, 1993-94; spl. asst. to pres. and sr. dir. European Affairs Nat. Security Coun., 1995-97; U.S. amb. NATO and permanent rep. to North Atlantic Coun., 1998—. Mem. Pres.'s delegation for NATO's 50th ann. Summit, Washington, 1999; involved in devel. of U.S. and NATO policy on Kosovo, others. Contbr. articles to profl. jours. Recipient Anatoly Sharansky Freedom award Union of Couns. of Soviet Jews, 1990, 1st ann. Joseph J. Kruzel award, Sec. of Def. William Cohen, 1997. Office: U.S. Embassy in Moscow Bolshoy Devyatinskiy Pereulok No.8 121099 Moscow Russia

VERSIC, LINDA JOAN, nurse educator, research company executive; b. Aug. 27, 1944; d. Robert and Kathryn I. (Fagird) Davies; m. Ronald James Versic, June 11, 1966; children: Kathryn Clara, Paul Joseph. RN, Johns Hopkins Sch. of Nursing, 1965; BS in Health Edn., Ctrl. State U., 1980; MS in Edn., Nova S.E.U., 2000. Asst. head nurse Johns Hopkins Hosp., Balt., 1965—67; staff Nurse Registry Miami Valley Hosp., Dayton, Ohio, 1973—90; instr. Miami Jacobs Jr. Coll. Bus., 1977—79; pres. Ronald T. Dodge Co., 1979—86, chmn. bd., 1987—; chmn. bd. dirs. A-1 Travel, Inc. Instr. Warren County (Ohio) Career Ctr., 1980—84, coord. diversified health occupations, 1984—. Coord. youth activities, mem. steering com. Queen of Apostles Cmty.; active Miami Valley Mil. Affairs Assn., Glen Helen, Friends of Dayton Ballet, Dayton Art Inst., Cin. Art Mus. Recipient Excellence in Tchg. award, 1992, award for Project Excellence, 1992. Mem.: Am. Vocat. Assn., Ohio Vocat. Assn., Welsh Soc. Cin., Yugoslav Club of Greater Dayton, Johns Hopkins Club, Vocat. Indsl. Clubs Am. (chpt. advisor 1982—). Roman Catholic. Home: 1601 Shafor Blvd Dayton OH 45419-3103 Office: Ronald T Dodge Co PO Box 41630 Dayton OH 45441-0630

VER STEEG, CLARENCE LESTER, historian, educator; b. Orange City, Iowa, Dec. 28, 1922; s. John A. and Annie (Vischer) Ver S.; m. Dorothy Ann De Vries, Dec. 24, 1943; 1 child, John Charles. AB, Morningside Coll., Sioux City, Iowa, 1943; MA, Columbia U., 1946, PhD, 1950; LHD, Morningside Coll., 1988. Lectr., then instr. history Columbia U., N.Y.C., 1946-50; mem. faculty Northwestern U., Evanston, Ill., 1950—, prof. history, 1959—, dean grad. sch., 1975-86. Vis. lectr. Harvard U., 1959-60; mem. council Inst. Early Am. History and Culture, Williamsburg, Va., 1961-64, 68-72, chmn. exec. com., 1970-72; vis. mem. Inst. Advanced Study, Princeton, N.J., 1967-68; chmn. faculty com. to recommend Master Plan Higher Edn. in Ill., 1962-64; mem. Grad. Record Exam. Bd., 1981-86, chmn., 1984-86; bd. dirs. Ctr. for Research Libraries, 1980-85, Council Grad. Schs. in U.S., 1983-87; pres. Assn. Grad. Schs., 1984-85; mem. steering com. Grad. Research Project, Consortium on Financing Higher Edn., 1981-85; mem. working group on talent Nat. Acad. Scis., 1984-87; mem. Higher Edn. Policy Adv. Com. to OCLC, Online Computer Library Ctr., 1984-87. Author: Robert Morris, Revolutionary Financier, 1954, A True and Historical Narrative of the Colony of Georgia, 1960, The American People: Their History, 1961, The Formative Years, 1607-1763, 1964 (Brit. edit.), 1965, The Story of Our Country, 1965, (with others) Investigating Man's World, 6 vols., 1970, A People and a Nation, 1971, The Origins of a Southern Mosaic: Studies of Early Carolina and Georgia, 1975, World Cultures, 1977, American Spirit, 1982, rev. edit., 1990; sr. author: Heath Social Studies, 7 Vols., 1991, Planning at Northwestern University in the 1960s, 1993; editor: Great Issues in American History, From Settlement to Revolution 1584-1776, 1969; editl. cons.: Papers of Robert Morris, vols. I-IX, 1973-99; contbr. articles to profl. jours. Served with USAAF, 1942-45. Decorated Air medal with 3 oak leaf clusters; 5 Battle Stars; Social Sci. Research Council fellow, 1948-49, George A. and Eliza Gardner Howard Found. fellow, 1954-55, Huntington Library research fellow, 1955, Am. Council Learned Socs. sr. fellow, 1958-59, Guggenheim fellow, 1964-65, NEH sr. fellow, 1973; Northwestern U. Clarence L. Ver Steeg Professorship established in his honor, 1997. Mem. AAUP, Am. Hist. Assn. (nominating com. 1965-68, chmn. 1967-68, Albert J. Beveridge prize 1952, hon. mention 1991 Eugene Asher Disting. Teaching award), Orgn. Am. Historians (editorial bd. Jour. Am. History 1968-72), So. Hist. Assn. (nominating com. 1970-72). Presbyterian. Home: Apt 311 Two Arbor Ln Evanston IL 60201-4216 Office: Northwestern Univ Dept History Evanston IL 60208-0001 E-mail: c-ver@nww.edu.

VER STEEG, DONNA LORRAINE FRANK, nurse, sociologist, educator; b. Minot, N.D., Sept. 23, 1929; d. John Jonas and Pearl H. (Denlinger) Frank; m. Richard W. Ver Steeg, Nov. 22, 1950; children: Juliana, Anne, Richard B. BSN, Stanford, 1951; MSN, U. Calif., San Francisco, 1967; MA in Sociology, UCLA, 1969, PhD in Sociology, 1973. Clin. instr. U. N.D. Sch. Nursing, 1962-63; USPHS nurse rsch. fellow UCLA, 1969-72; spl. cons., adv. com. on physicians' assts. and nurse practitioner progs. Calif. State Bd. Med. Examiners, 1972-73; asst. prof. UCLA Sch. Nursing, 1973-79, assoc. prof., 1979-94, asst. dean, 1979-81, chmn. primary ambulatory care, 1976-87, assoc. dean, 1983-86, prof. emeritus, chair primary care, 1994-96, prof. emeritus, 1996—. Co-prin. investigator PRIMEX Project Family Nurse Practitioners, UCLA Ext., 1974—76; assoc. cons. Calif. Postsecondary Edn. Commn., 1975—76; spl. cons. Calif. Dept. Consumer Affairs, 1978; accredited visitor Western Assn. Schs. and Colls., 1985; mem. Calif. State Legis. Health Policy Forum, 1980—81; mem. nurse practitioner adv. com. Calif. Bd. RNs, 1995—97; mem. Edn. Industry Interface, Info. Devel. Mktg. Sub Coms., 1995—99, recruitment, 1999—2001; archivist Calif. Strategic Planning Com. Nursing/Colleagues in Caring Project, 1995—. Contbr. chpts. to profl. books, articles to profl. jours. Recipient Leadership award Calif. Area Health Edn. Ctr. Sys., 1989, Commendation award Calif. State Assembly, 1994; named Outstanding Faculty Mem., UCLA Sch. Nursing, 1982. Fellow Am. Acad. Nursing; mem. AAAS, AAUW, ANA (pres. elect Calif. 1977-79, pres. Calif. 1979-81), Calif. Chpt. ANA Calif. (interim chair Calif. 1995-96), Nat. League Nursing, Calif. League Nursing, N.Am. Nursing Diagnosis Assn., Am. Assn. History Nursing, Stanford Nurses Club, Sigma Theta Tau (Alpha Eta chpt. Leadership award Gamma Tau chpt. 1994), Sigma Xi. Home: 708 Swarthmore Ave Pacific Palisades CA 90272-4353 Office: UCLA Sch Nursing Box 956917 Los Angeles CA 90095-6917

VERSTEGEN, DEBORAH A. policy and finance educator; b. Neenah, Wis., Oct. 27, 1946; d. Gerald C. and Margaret A. (Lamers) V. BA, Loretto Heights Coll., 1969; EdM, U. Rochester, 1972; MS, U. Wis., 1981, PhD, 1983. Adminstr. Iditarod Area Sch. Dist., McGrath, Alaska, 1976-79; rsch. asst., fellow Wis. Ctr. for Edn. Rsch., 1981-84; dir. asst. prof. mid-mgmt. program U. Tex., Austin, 1984-86; asst. prof. edn. in policy and finance U. Va., Charlottesville, 1986-91, assoc. prof. edn. in policy and finance, 1992-99, prof., 2000—. Rsch. assoc. Oxford U., Eng., 1991; adv. bd. U.S. Dept. Edn., 1989-92. Author over 160 books, reports, chpts., articles and revs., latest being The Impacts of Litigation and Legislation on Public School Finance, 1990, Spheres of Justice in Education, 1991; editor Jour. Edn. Fin., 1990-93, editor edn. policy, 1993—. Treas. LVW, 1986, mem. Va. state bd., 1995—97, Va. edn. chair, 1993—2001. Mem.: AAUP (exec. bd. Va. 1999—, pres.-elect 2002), U. Coun. on Ednl. Adminstrn. (adv. bd. fin. ctr., disting. svc. award 1991), Women Edn. Leaders Va. (chair 1988, pres. 1999—2000, founder), Am. Ednl. Rsch. Assn., Am. Ednl. Fin. Assn. (bd. dir., disting. svc. award 1989), Phi Kappa Phi, Phi Delta Kappa. Home: 2156 Timber Mdws Charlottesville VA 22911-7231 Office: U Va Curry Sch Edn Ruffner Hall 405 Emmet St S Charlottesville VA 22903-2424 E-mail: dav3e@virginia.edu.

VERTES, AKOS, chemist, educator; b. Budapest, Hungary; PhD in Chemistry, Eotvos Lorand U., 1979. Assoc. prof. George Washington U., Washington, 1991—2000, prof., 2000—. Dep. chair George Washington U., 1997—; contractor Naval Rsch. Lab., Washington, 1993—; lectr. in field. Editor: Laser Ionization Mass Analysis, 1993; mem. editl. bd. Laser Interactions with Materials, 2002—. Mem.: AAAS, Hungarian Acad. Scis. (Dr. award 2001, mem. gen. assembly 2001), Am. Soc. Mass Spectrometry, Am. Chem. Soc., Baltimore-Washington Area Mass Spectrometry Discussion Group (chair 1998—99). Office: George Washington Univ Dept Chemistry 725 21st Street NW Washington DC 20052 Office Fax: 202-994-5873. Business E-Mail: vertes@gwu.edu.

VERTREACE-DOODY, MARTHA MODENA, English educator, poet; b. Washington, Nov. 24, 1945; d. Walter Charles and Modena Kendrick Vertreace; m. Timothy S. Doody. BA, D.C. Tchrs. Coll., 1967; MA, Roosevelt U., 1972, MPH, 1973; MS, Mundelein Coll., 1981; MFA, Vermont Coll., 1996. Tchr. English Roosevelt H.S., Gary, Ind., 1967-72; Disting. prof. English Kennedy-King Coll., Chgo., 1976—. Adv. bd. mem. City Mag., Chgo., 1984-86, Seams Mag., Chgo., 1986-87; poetry fellow Hawthornden Internat. Retreat for Writers, Lasswade, Scotland, 1992, 93, Writers Ctr., Dublin, Ireland, 1993; adj. prof. English Columbia Coll., Chgo., 1993—. Author: Second House from the Corner, 1986, Under a Cat's-Eye Moon, 1991, Kelly in the Mirror, 1993, Oracle Bones, 1994, Cinnabar, 1995, Light Caught Bending, 1995, Maafa: When Night Becomes a Lion, 1996, Second Mourning, 1998, Smokeless Flame, 1998, Dragon Lady: Tsukimi, 1999; editor: Class Act mag., 1988-91. Contest judge White Eagle Coll. Press, Ill., 1994, Triton Coll., 1994; poet-in-residence St. Thomas the Apostle Cath. Ch., Chgo., 1996; mem. Harper Square Adv. Bd., Chgo., 1997. Mem. MLA, Soc. for the Study Midwestern Lit., Soc. Writers Children's Lit., Ill. Assn. Tchrs. English, Midwest Regional Conf. Tchg. English in Two-Yr. Coll. Democratic Socialist. Roman Catholic. Avocations: travel, writing poetry, music. Home: 5232 S Greenwood Ave Chicago IL 60615-4316 Office: Kennedy-King Coll 6800 S Wentworth Ave Chicago IL 60621-3728

VERTS, LITA JEANNE, university administrator; b. Jonesboro, Ark., Apr. 13, 1935; d. William Gus and Lolita Josephine (Peeler) Nash; m. B. J. Verts, Aug. 29, 1954 (div. 1975); 1 child, William Trigg. BA, Oreg. State U., 1973; MA in Lingustics, U. Oreg., 1974; postgrad., U. Hawaii, 1977. Librarian Forest Research Lab., Corvallis, Oreg., 1966-69; instr. English Lang. Inst., 1974-80; dir. spl. svcs. Oreg. State U., 1980-96, faculty senator, 1988-96; ret., 1996. Editor ann. book: Trio Achievers, 1986, 87, 88; contbr. articles to profl. jours. Precinct com. Rep. Party, Corvallis, 1977-80; adminstrv. bd. 1st United Meth. Ch., Corvallis, 1987-89, mem. fin. com., 1987-93, tchr. Bible, 1978—; bd. dirs. Westminster Ho., United Campus Ministries, 1994-95; adv. coun. Disabilities Svc., Linn, Benton, Lincoln Counties, 1990-99, vice-chmn., 1992-93, chmn. 1993-94; citizen adv. bd. on Transit, 1998—, intercity steering com., 1999—, Corvallis Downtown Parking Commn., 1999—; Oreg. Long-term Care Ombudsman, 1999—. Mem. N.W. Assn. Spl. Programs (pres. 1985-86), Nat. Coun. Ednl. Opportunities Assn. (bd. dirs. 1984-87), Nat. Gardening Assn., Alpha Phi (mem. corp. bd. Beta Upsilon chpt. 1990-96). Republican. Methodist. Avocations: gardening, photography, golf. Home: 530 SE Mayberry Ave Corvallis OR 97333-1866 Office: Spl Svcs Project Waldo 337 OSU Corvallis OR 97331 E-mail: vertsl@ucs.orst.edu.

VERVERS, BEVERLY JOAN, career development administrator; b. Paterson, N.J., June 13, 1953; d. Charles John and Helen V. BA, Ramapo Coll., Mahwah, N.J., 1975; MA, Montclair State Coll., Upper Montclair, N.J., 1990. Nat. cert. counselor; lic. profl. counselor, N.J.; cert. profl. counselor, Ariz. Program asst. Planned Parenthood, Boonton/Morristown, N.J., 1974-78; employment interviewer N.J. State Employment Svc., Passaic, 1977-83; employment placement specialist Bergen Cmty. Coll., Paramus, N.J., 1983-85; asst. dir. cooperative edn. Montclair State U., Upper Montclair, 1985—. Mem. ACA, Nat. Career Devel. Assn., Coop. Edn. Assn., Mid. Atlantic Career Counseling Assn. Office: Ctr for Cmty-Based Learning Montclair State U Upper Montclair NJ 07043 E-mail: verversb@mail.montclair.edu.

VERVILLE, ELIZABETH GIAVANI, federal official; b. N.Y.C., July 13, 1940; d. Joseph and Gertrude (Levy) Giavani. BA, Duke U., 1961; LLB, Columbia U., 1964. Bar: Mass. 1965, U.S. Supreme Ct. 1970, D.C. 1980. Assoc. Snow Motley & Holt, successor Gaston Snow & Ely Bartlett, Boston, 1965-67; asst. atty. gen. Commonwealth of Mass., 1967-69; atty. advisor for African affairs U.S. Dept. State, Washington, 1979-72, asst. legal adviser for East Asian and Pacific affairs, 1972-80, dep. legal adviser, 1980-89; dep. asst. sec. state Bur. Politico-Mil. Affairs Bur. Politico-Mil. Affairs, 1989-92, sr. coord., 1992-95; dir. for global and multilateral affairs Nat. Security Coun., Washington, 1995-98; dep. dir. Critical Infrastructure Assurance Office, 1998-2000; spl. rep. Bur. Narcotics and Law Enforcement, 2000-01; acting dep. asst. sec. Bur. Internat. Narcotics and Law Enforcement, Dept. State, 2001—. Recipient presdl. rank of meritorious exec., 1985, 90, presdl. rank disting. exec., 1988. Mem. Am. Soc. Internat. Law, Coun. on Fgn. Rels. Home: 3012 Dumbarton Ave NW Washington DC 20007-3305 Office: Bur Internat Narcotics & Law Enforcement State Dept Washington DC 20520-0001 E-mail: e.verville@state.gov.

VESCOVO, DIANE KIRKLAND, federal judge; b. 1955; BA summa cum laude, U. Va., 1976; JD, Memphis State U., 1980. Bar: Tenn. 1980. Atty. Lloyd C. Kirkland, Jr., Memphis, 1981-87, Internat. Paper Co., Memphis, 1987-92, Wolff, Ardis, P.C., Memphis, 1992-95; magistrate judge U.S. Dist. Ct. (we. dist.), 1995—. Mem. Phi Beta Kappa. Office: US Dist Ct 341 Federal Bldg 167 N Main St Memphis TN 38103-1816 Fax: 901-495-1387.

VESELINOVIČ, DRAŠKO, stock exchange executive; b. Ljubljana, Slovenia, Feb. 26, 1959; s. Branko and Breda (Pokorn) V.; 1 child, Eva. M of Internat. Fin., U. Ljubljana, 1986, DSc in Econs., 1996. Fgn. exch. dealer Ljubljanska Bank, fgn. exch. and internat. treasury mgr.; assoc. prof. Faculty of Econs.; fin. adviser Slovene Govt.; CEO Ljubljana Stock Exch., gen. mgr., 1993—. Founder The Yugoslav Stock Exch., 1989. Author: Foreign Exchange in Developed World & in Yugoslavia, 1988, Foreign Exchange Trading, 1991, Stock Exchange Handbook, 1991, 95, Options and Other Derivative Financial Instruments, 1998, Aphorisms, 1996; author over 100 articles. Mem. Tennis Assn. Slovenia (pres.) Avocations: tennis, music. Office: Ljubljana Stock Exchange Inc Slovenska c 56 1000 Ljubljana Slovenia E-mail: drasko.veselinovic@ljse.si.

VESELL, ELLIOT SAUL, pharmacologist, educator; b. N.Y.C., Dec. 24, 1933; s. Harry and Evelyn (Jaffe) V.; m. Kristen Paige Peery, Mar. 24, 1968; children: Liane Clark, Hilary Peery. AB, Harvard U., 1955, MD, 1959; DSc (hon.), Phila. Coll. Pharmacy & Sci., 1988; PhD, Philipps U., Marburg, Germany, 1991. Intern, children's med. svc. Mass. Gen. Hosp., Boston, 1959-60; rsch. assoc. Rockefeller U., N.Y.C., 1960-62; resident in medicine Peter Bent Brigham Hosp., Boston, 1962-63; clin. assoc. Nat. Inst. Arthritis and Metabolic Diseases, NIH, Bethesda, Md., 1963-65; head sect. pharmacogenetics Nat. Heart Inst., NIH, 1965-68; Evan Pugh prof. pharmacology Pa. State U., Hershey, 1968—, asst. dean grad. edn., 1973-96, chmn. dept. pharmacology Coll. Medicine, 1968—2000, 1980—, Bernard B. Brodie prof., 1991—. Frohlich vis. prof. Royal Soc. Medicine, 1985, Pfizer vis. prof., Burroughs Wellcome vis. prof. Editor: The Life and Works of Thomas Cole, 1964, Progress in Basic and Clinical Pharmacology, 1990, numerous others; contbr. numerous articles to profl. jours. Recipient Von Humboldt award, 1988. Fellow AAAS, Royal Soc. of Medicine; mem. Assn. Am. Physicians, Am. Soc. for Clin. Investigation, Am. Soc. Pharmacology and Exptl. Therapeutics (sec.-treas. 1995-98, Exptl. Therapeutics award 1971, Harry Gold award in clin. pharmacology, 1985), Am. Coll. Clin. Pharmacology (pres. 1980-82, Disting. Investigator award 1999), Am. Soc. Clin. Pharmacology and Therapeutics (Oscar B. Hunter Meml. award 1991). E-mail: esv1psu.edu. Office: Pa State U Coll Medicine Dept Pharmacology PO Box 850 Hershey PA 17033-0850

VESELY, TORI ANN, lawyer; b. Portage, Wis., Aug. 24, 1965; d. Paul R. and Claudia K. Vesely. BA in Polit Sci., Carthage Coll., 1987; JD, Marquette U., 1990. Bar: Wis., 1990, U.S. Dist. Ct. (ea. and we. dists.) Wis. 1990. Asst. corp. counsel Sauk County, Baraboo, Wis., 1993—. Vol. Spl. Olympics, Merrill, Wis., 1991. Mem. State Bar Wis., Wis. Child Support Enforcement Assn., Sauk County Bar Assn. Office: Sauk Co Child Support Agy 515 Oak St Baraboo WI 53913-2416 E-mail: tvesely@co.sauk.wi.us.

VESETH, MICHAEL AARON, economics educator; b. Tacoma, Wash., Nov. 4, 1949; s. Einar Melven and Mary Jane (Morgan) V.; m. Sue Ann Trbovich, July 24, 1976. BA, U. Puget Sound, 1972; M.S., Purdue U., 1974, PhD, 1975. Research assoc. Adv. Commn. on Intergovtl. Relations, Washington, 1974-75; asst. prof. econs. U. Puget Sound, Tacoma, 1975-80, assoc. prof., 1980-87, prof., 1987-93, dir. internat. polit. economy program, 1993—. Author: Public Finance, 1984; Introductory Macroeconomics, 1980, 81, 84; Introductory Microeconomics, 1981; Introductory Economics, 1981; Coursebook for Economics, 1981; Economics: Cost and Choice, 1987; Mountains of Debt, 1990; Introduction to International Political Economy, 1996, 2001; Selling Globalization, 1998; New York Times: The Rise of the Global Economy, 2002.

VESEY, MARY FRANCES, writer, educator; b. Providence, July 11, 1965; d. Joseph Rosario and Mary Alice Perroni. BA, W.Va. U., 1988; MA, R.I. Coll., 1997. Cert. tchr. secondary English R.I., Mass. Tchr. Bristol (R.I.) County Pub. Schs., 1989—94; English tchr. St. Mary Sch., Providence, 1994—96; tchr. Blessed Sacrament Sch., 1996—98. Facilitator ednl. studies Diocese Providence Cath. Schs., 1994—95, spelling bee judge, 1996—98; STAR team dirs., program dir. Greater Providence YMCA, 1995—96. Author: (book) The Confessions of citizen g, 2002; contbr. poetry to publs. Fundraiser Greater Providence YMCA, 1994—98, United Way, Providence, 1995—96. Mem.: New Eng. Masters Swim Club (All-Am. swimmer 1996, World Ranked Masters swimmer 1996), Golden Key, Phi Beta Kappa.

VESPA, NED ANGELO, photographer; b. Streator, Ill., May 31, 1942; s. Ned James and Evelyn Blanche (Flanigan) V.; m. Carol DeMasters, Sept. 11, 1976; 1 child, Nicole Marie; 1 son by previous marriage, James Paul. BS, So. Ill. U., 1965. Photographer Milw. Jour. Co., 1965-95, Milw. Sentinel, 1965-95; ret., 1995; freelance, 1995—. Mem. Nat. Press Photographers Assn., Wis. News Photographers Assn. (past pres.), Milw. Press Photographers. Home: 38309 Genesee Lake Rd Oconomowoc WI 53066-8614

VESPER, ETHEL ROSE, language educator, consultant; d. Eugene and Celia Blum; m. Donald Robert Vesper, Apr. 10, 1960 (div. 1980); children: Tina, Patrick. BS in Edn., U. Kans., 1960; MA in Linguistics, U. Calif., Davis, 1969; PhD in Anthropology, U. Mo., 1976; MA in Ministry, Seattle U., 1985. CEO, primary cons. NorWeskan Assocs., Seattle, 1978—; asst. prof. anthropology dept Phillips U., Enid, Okla., 1980—84, dir. ESL program, 1980—84; lead & trainer, panel maintenance Boeing Co., Seattle, 1986—96, edn., tng. DCAC/MRM, 1996—99, orgnl. devel. advisor, 1996—2000, coord., employee devel. Maintenance Engring. & Publs., 1999—2002; online facilitator U. Phoenix, 2000—. Instr. Skagit Valley C.C., Langley, Wash., 1984—90, U. Phoenix, 1999—. Author: (book) Intro Linguistics: A Text for High School Students, 1965; author: (with Don R. Vesper) Change in language situation and attitudes in a multilingual society, 1975. Vol. chaplain Wash. State Reformatory, Monroe, 1984—; min. St. James Cath., Seattle, 2000—, mem. operation nightwatch, 1995—; coord., Eucharistic min. Cabrini Pastoral Care Swedish Hosp./St. James Cath., 2001—; vol. chaplain Monroe Correctional Complex, Twin Rivers Unit. Named Vol. of the Yr., Wash. State, Dept. Corrections, 1999-2000; fellow Nat. Fgn. Lang., NSF, 1971-71; 1972-73, Grad. Traineeship, 1973-1974; grantee, 1974-76. Fellow: Am. Anthropology Assn. Roman Catholic. E-mail: e.vesper@worldnet.att.net.

VESSEL, ROBERT LESLIE, lawyer; b. Chgo., Mar. 21, 1942; s. Louis Frank and Margaret Ruth (Barber) V.; m. Diane White, Oct. 12, 1966; m. Lise Vessel, Dec. 19, 1992. BA, U. Ill., 1964; JD, Seton Hall U., 1973; LLM in Taxation, U. Miami, Coral Gables, Fla., 1980. Bar: N.J. 1973, Fla. 1981, U.S. Dist. Ct. (so. and mid. dists.) Fla. 1981, U.S. Ct. Appeals (11th cir.) 1981; bd. cert. civil trial, Fla. Assoc. Bennett & Bennett P.A., East Orange, N.J., 1973-76; ptnr. Kantor & Vessel, P.A., Wayne, 1976-81; assoc. Haddad Josephs & Jack, P.A., Coral Gables, Fla., 1981-85; ptnr. Mitchell Alley Rywant & Vessel, Tampa, 1985-89, Moffitt & Vessel, P.A., Tampa, 1989-94, Vessel & Morales, P.A., Tampa, 1994-99. With USNR, 1964-66. Mem. Assn. Trial Lawyers Am., Nat. Inst. Trial Advocacy, Acad. Fla. Trial Lawyers, Hillsboro County Bar Assn. Avocation: sailing. Office: Robert L Vessel PA 1100 W Kennedy Blvd Tampa FL 33606-1966 E-mail: veslaw@msn.com.

VESSEY, JOHN WILLIAM, JR. army officer; b. Mpls., June 29, 1922; s. John William and Emily (Roche) V.; m. Avis Claire Funk, July 18, 1945; children: John William, David, Sarah. BS, U. Md., 1963; MS, George Washington U., 1967; LLD, Concordia Coll., St. Paul, 1978, U. Md., 1983, Concordia Sem., St. Louis, 1983; DMS (hon.), Norwich U., Northfield, Vt., 1985; grad., Command and Gen. Staff Coll., 1958, Indsl. Coll. Armed Forces, 1966. Commd. 2nd lt. U.S. Army, 1944, advanced through grades to gen., 1976; comdr. U.S. Army Support Command Thailand, 1970-71; chief Mil. Assistance Adv. Group Laos, 1972-73; dir. ops. Dept. Army Washington, 1973-74; comdr. 4th Inf. Div. Ft. Carson, Colo., 1974-75; dep. chief of staff-ops. Dept. Army Washington, 1975-76; comdr.-in-chief UN Command/U.S. Forces in Korea Seoul, 1976-79; comdr.-in-chief Republic of Korea/U.S. Combined Forces Command, 1978-79; vice chief of staff U.S. Army Washington, 1979-82; chmn. Joint Chiefs of Staff, 1982-85; ret. U.S. Army, 1985; presdl. emissary to Hanoi for POW/MIA matters, 1987-93. Bd. dirs. Nat. Flag Day Com.; mem. bd. vistors UMUC; chmn. bd. Ctr. Preventive Action, Def. Sci. Bd. Decorated D.S.C., Def. D.S.M., D.S.M., AF D.S.M., Navy D.S.M., Legion of Merit, Bronze Star, Air medal, Joint Svcs. Commendation medal, Army Commendation medal, Purple Heart (U.S.), Presdl. Medal of Freedom, decorated by govts. of Austria, Belgium, Chile, Colombia, Germany, France, Greece, Honduras, Korea, Luxembourg, Norway, Pakistan, Saudi Arabia, Spain, Thailand, Uruguay; recipient State of Minn. Disting. Svc. medal, Excellence in Diplomacy award Am. Acad. of Diplomacy, Sylvanus Thayer award USMA, Alumni Achievement award and Disting. Pub. Svc. award George Washington U., Disting. Alumnus award U. Md., Golden Plate award Am. Acad. Achievement, Adm. John M. Will award N.Y. Coun. Navy League, hon. award Nat. League Families. Mem. VFW (Eisenhower medal), Assn. U.S. Army (George Marshall medal), Army Aviation Assn., U.S. Armor Assn., Coun. Fgn. Rels. (chair bd. dirs. ctr. for prevention action), Phi Kappa Phi. Lutheran.

VESSOT, ROBERT FREDERICK CHARLES, physicist, researcher; b. Montreal, Que., Can., Apr. 16, 1930; s. Robert Charles Ulysses and Marguerite Yvonne (Giauque) V.; m. Norma Newman Wight, Apr. 18, 1959; children: Judith Norma, Margaret Anne, Nancy Elizabeth. BA, McGill U., 1951, B.Sc., 1954, PhD, 1956. Mem. research staff MIT, 1956-60; mgr. Maser Research and Devel., Varian Assos., Hewlett Packard, Beverly, Mass., 1960-69; sr. physicist Harvard-Smithsonian Center for Astrophysics, Cambridge, 1969-2001, rsch. assoc., 2002—. Contbr. articles to profl. jours.; patentee in field. Served with RCAF, 1951-53. Recipient medal for outstanding sci. achievement NASA, 1978, I.I. Rabi award IEEE, 1993. Fellow Am. Phys. Soc.; mem. Eastern Yacht Club. Office: 60 Garden St Cambridge MA 02138-1516 E-mail: rvessot@cfa.harvard.edu.

VESSUP, JOLENE ADRIEL, pastoral counselor, researcher, marketing professional, researcher; b. Lynwood, Calif., Oct. 26, 1951; d. Johannes Baltezar and Ellene Ernestine (Cravens) Vessup. BA, U. So. Calif., 1973. Choir dir., singer, sales girl Bethel Apostolic Faith Ch., San Bernardino, Calif., 1961-69, Sunday sch. tchr., cook, 1962-69, reading tutor, 1977-78; speech tutor, rsch. asst., pub. rels. spkr. U. So. Calif. and Pacific H.S., L.A. & San Bernardino, 1969-73; dispatcher bookeeping, 1971—73, 1973—; exec. pres. Craftors/The Dir. Co. , 1973—, salesperson, 1973—; peer counselor Postgrad. Rehab. Ctr., N.Y.C., 1974-95; early childhood devel. vol. Calif. State U., L.A., 1975-79; spl. edn. tchr.'s asst. San Bernardino Unified Sch. Dist., 1979-80; unlicensed missionary Greater Refuge Temple Ch., N.Y.C., 1996—. Rschr. chs. and religious edn., acctg. and bus. mktg. Mem. ARC. Mem. AAUW, Nat. Geog. Soc., Wildlife Conservation Soc., Smithsonian Instn. Press, Stuttering Found. Am., Nat. Conservancy, Nat. Trust Found. Avocations: writing, counseling, teaching, handball, reading. Home: JAF Box 8316 New York NY 10001-9999 Office: PO Box 8613 New York NY 10116-8613

VEST, GAYLE SOUTHWORTH, obstetrician and gynecologist; b. Duluth, Minn., Apr. 7, 1948; d. Russell Eugene and Brandon (Young) Southworth; m. Steven Lee Vest, Nov. 27, 1971; 1 child, Matthew Steven. BS, U. Mich., 1970. Diplomate Am. Bd. Ob-Gyn. Intern in ob-gyn. Milw. County Gen. Hosp., 1974-75, So. Ill. U. Sch. Medicine, 1975-78; pvt. practice Chapel Hill (N.C.) Ob-Gyn., 1978-80; asst. attending physician dept. ob-gyn. U. N.C. Sch. Medicine, Chapel Hill, 1978-80; clin. assoc. dept. ob-gyn. Duke U. Med. Ctr., Durham, N.C., 1978-80; pvt. practice Big Stone Gap (Va.) Clinic, 1980-88, Norwise Ob-Gyn. Assocs., Norton, Va., 1988—. Fellow: ACOG; mem.: Wise County Med. Soc., Med. Soc. Va., Va. Ob-Gyn. Soc., Christian Med. and Dental Assn., Am. Soc. Reproductive Medicine. Avocations: skiing, kayaking, travel. Office: Norwise Ob-Gyn Assocs 102 15th St NW Ste 301 Norton VA 24273-1616

VEST, GEORGE SOUTHALL, retired diplomat; b. Columbia, Va., Dec. 25, 1918; s. George Southall and Nancy Margaret (Robertson) V.; m. Emily Barber Clemons, June 21, 1947; children— Jeannie, George, Henry BA, U. Va., 1941, MA, 1947. Fgn. service duty SHAPE and NATO, Quito, Ottawa, Paris; dir. bur. polit. mil. affairs Dept. State, asst. sec. of state for European affairs, 1977-81; ambassador to European Communities Brussels, 1981-85; dir. gen. Fgn. Svc. Dept. State, Washington, 1985-89, career amb., 1987-89, ret., 1989. Served to capt. U.S. Army, 1941-46, ETO Mem. Phi Beta Kappa Episcopalian. Avocations: bicycling, gardening. Home: 5307 Iroquois Rd Bethesda MD 20816-3104

VEST, HYRUM GRANT, JR. retired horticultural sciences educator; b. Salt Lake City, Sept. 23, 1935; s. Hyrum and Josephine Gwendolyn (Lund) V.; m. Gayle Pixton, Sept. 18, 1958; children: Kelly, Lani, Kari, Kamille, Kyle. BS, Utah State U., 1960, MS, 1964; PhD, U. Minn., 1967. Pathologist, agronomist U.S. Dept. Agr., Beltsville, Md., 1967-70; vegetable breeder Mich. State U., East Lansing, 1970-76; dept. head dept. hort. and landscape architecture Okla. State U., Stillwater, 1976-83; head dept. hort. scis. Tex A & M U., College Station, 1983-89; head dept. plants, soils and biometeorology Utah State U., Logan, 1989-95, assoc. dir. Utah Agrl. Experiment Sta., 1995-2000; mem. Nat. Plant Genetics Resource Bd., Washington, 1982-88; ret., 2000. Served to 1st lt. U.S. Army, 1960-63. Univ. research fellow Utah State U., 1963-64 Fellow Am. Soc. Hort. Sci. Republican. Mem. Lds Ch. Home: 368 Spring Creek Rd Providence UT 84332-9432 E-mail: gvest@cc.usu.edu.

VEST, JAMES MURRAY, foreign language and literature educator; b. Roanoke, Va., Mar. 27, 1947; s. Eddie Lewis and Irene (Cannaday) V.; m. Nancy Foltz, June 6, 1970; 1 child, Cecelia. BA, Davidson (N.C.) Coll., 1969; MA, Duke U., 1971, PhD, 1973. From asst. to assoc. prof. Rhodes Coll., Memphis, 1973-91, chmn. French dept., 1983-98, prof., 1991—, head French program, 1984-98. Adminstr. Rhodes in Paris Program, France, 1978-87; organizer faculty teaching seminars, 1988—. Author: The French Face of Ophelia, 1989, The Poetic Works of Maurice de Guérin, 1991; contbr. articles to profl. jours. Chmn. Urban Outreach Commn., Memphis, 1978-81; leader youth groups, 1983—. Capt. U.S. Army Res., 1973—. Recipient campus svc. award Sears-Roebuck, 1990, Outstanding Teaching award Clarence Day Found., Memphis, 1984, Am. Assn. Higher Edn., 1988; Woodrow Wilson fellow, 1971, NDEA Title IV fellow, 1969. Mem. MLA, So. Atlantic Modern Lang. Assn., Am. Assn. of Tchrs. of French, Am. Coun. Teaching Fgn. Lang. Avocations: cinema, hiking. Office: 2000 N Pkwy Rhodes C Memphis TN 38112

VEST, STEVEN LEE, gastroenterologist, hepatologist, internist; b. Mpls., July 30, 1948; s. Lee Herbert and Marian Mize (Rains) V.; m. Gayle Maureen Southworth, Nov. 27, 1971; 1 child, Matthew Steven. BA, U. Minn., 1970, MD, 1974. Diplomate Am. Bd. Internal Medicine, Am. Bd Gastroenterology. Intern internal medicine Milw. County Hosp., 1974-75; resident internal medicine So. Ill. U., Springfield, 1975-77; fellow in gastroenterology and hepatology Duke U. Med. Ctr., Durham, N.C., 1978-80; gastroenterology-hepatology and internal medicine cons. Lonesome Pine Hosp., Big Stone Gap, Va., 1980—; gastroenterology and internal medicine cons. St. Mary's Hosp., Norton, 1983—, Norton Community Hosp., Norton, Va., 1985—. Chmn. med. care evaluation, Lonesome Pine Hosp., Big Stone Gap, 1984-88, chmn. pharmacy, therapeutics & transfusion com., 1992-94; chief of medicine Norton Cmty. Hosp., 1991-93, 97-99, exec. com., 1991-93, 97-99, credentials com., 1995-97, bylaws com., 1996-97. Fellow ACP-Am. Soc. Internal Medicine, Am. Coll. Gastroenterology; mem. Am. Gastroent. Assn., Am. Soc. Internal Medicine, Va. Med. Soc. (state del. 1992), Wise County Med. Soc. (treas. 1984-86, v.p. 1991-92, pres. 1992-93), Am. Assn. Christian Counselors, Wise County C. of C. Methodist. Avocations: kayaking, jogging, skiing, photography, karate. Home: Powell Valley 1800 Egan Rd Big Stone Gap VA 24219-4224 Office: NCH Med Arts Bldg #2 98 15th St NW Ste 202 Norton VA 24273-1600

VESTAL, JUDITH CARSON, occupational therapist; b. Memphis, Dec. 22, 1939; d. Carl Thomas and Emma Winifred (Stewart) Carson; m. Tommy Vestal, June 22, 1974. BS in Elem. Edn., U. Tenn., 1961; BS in Occupl. Therapy, Washington U., St. Louis, 1964; MA in Guidance and Counseling, La. Tech. U., 1978; PhD, Tex. Woman's U., 1997. Cert. occupl. therapist, La. Occupl. therapist Sewall Rehab. Ctr., Denver, 1964-67, Whittington Hosp., London, 1967-70, The London Hosp., 1970-74, N.W. La. Rehab., Shreveport, 1975-77, Caddo Bossier Assn. for Retarded Children, Shreveport, 1977-81, La. State U. Med. Ctr., Shreveport, 1981-87, asst. prof. occupl. therapy, 1986-92, assoc. prof. clin. occupl. therapy, 1992—; program dir. occupl. therapy Sch. Allied Health Profls. La. State U. Health Scis. Ctr., 2001—. Editl. bd. Am. Jour. Occupl. Therapy, 1984-87; contbr. articles to profl. jours. Bd. dirs. Children's Learning Ctr., Shreveport, 1980-89; mem. Spl. Edn. Adv. Coun., Shreveport, 1985-91; mem., sec. vestry Ch. of Epiphany, Shreveport, 1992-96. Mem.: Mental Health Assn. Caddo-Bossier (bd. dirs. 2001—), Internat. Soc. for Alternative and Augmentative Comm., Neurodevelopmental Treatment Assn., Soc. for Rsch. in Child Devel., La. Occupl. Therapy Assn. (v.p. 1983—86, pres. 1986—90, Pres.'s award 1991, Award of Merit 1994, Svc. award 2002), Am. Occupl. Therapy Assn. (sec. com. on state assn. pres. 1989—92, Svc. award 1992), Phi Kappa Phi. Reformed Episcopal Ch. Avocations: reading, travel, music. Home: 176 Preston Ave Shreveport LA 71105-3306 Office: Louisiana State Univ Health Scis Center Sch Allied Health Prof 1501 Kings Hwy Shreveport LA 71130-3932

VESTAL, LOWELL A. real estate manager; b. Horton, Kans., July 20, 1934; s. Ralph Morcel and Rachel Gertrude (Bragdon) V. BA, U. Nebr., 1956. Sales coord. Ea. Nebr. Pub. Power Dist., Syracuse, Nebr., 1959; mng. editor Nebr.

Rural Elec. Assn., Lincoln, 1960-71; self-employed real estate mgr., 1971—. Mem. Lancaster County Rep. Ctrl. Com., Lincoln, 1973-82, Nebr. Rep. Ctrl. Com., 1980-82. Capt. USAR, 1956-67. Mem. Real Estate Owners and Mgr. Assn. (pres. 1990-91), Kiwanis, Masons (editor Masonic News 1989-2001), Order of the Ea. Star, Hiram Club. Republican. Presbyterian. Avocations: travel, photography. Home: 1330 Furnas Ave Lincoln NE 68521-2262

VESTAL, MARILYN ANITA, writer, researcher, educator; b. Pitts., May 28, 1950; d. Elmo Foucheaux and Mary Alice (Hayes) Vestal; 1 child, Daven Remley. BS in Child and Family Devel., Va. Tech. Inst., 1974; MBA in Mgmt., Tex. Tech. U., 1980; PhD Conflict Management, Nova Southeastern U., 2001. Vol. Peace Corps, Dominican Republic, 1974-76; child devel. tng. specialist Tex. Tech. U., Lubbock, 1977-80; methods analyst supr. Cmty. Progress Coun., York, PA., 1980-81; program adminstr. East Coast Migrant Head Start Project, 1982-84; mgmt./fiscal specialist, data mgmt. project coord. Head Start Resource and Tng. Ctr., U. Md., 1984-87; exec. dir. Child Care Cons., Inc., Pa., 1987-90; mgmt. cons., 1990—2002; mediator, 1999—2002; self employed mgmt cons. and mediator, 2000—02. Asst. prof. human resources mgmt. Webber Coll., 1993-97, assoc. professor, mgmt. orgn. devel. Eastern Mennonite Univ., 2000—02, adj. prof. Nova Southeastern Univ., 2001-2002; cons. S.C. Ednl. TV, 1992-96, U. Md., Head Start Resource and Tng. Ctr., 1988-92, South Fla. C.C., 1995, Region IV Mgmt. Inst., Tuskegee U., 1995, DHHS/Adminstrn. on Children and Families, Washington, 1991—, Wheelock Coll., 1997-98, Aspen Sys., among others; presenter numerous papers at confs., workshops. Facilitator Wellspring Retreat, Family Enrichment Ctr., Archdiocese of Miami, 1998-2002; arbitrator Nat. Assn. Securities Dealers, 1998-2002; mem. Nat. Peace Corps Assn., Soc. for Assn. Human Resources Mgmt., 2001-2002, Consortrum on Peace Rsch., Ed., Devel., 2000-2002; mem., bd. dirs. Child Care Cons., Inc., York, 1990-91, bd. pres. Medication Services Conflict Resolution, 2000-2002; bd. dirs. Atkins House, York, 1989-90. Recipient Margaret Sangar award Planned Parenthood, 1975, Beyond War award, 1987, Cert. Recognition Dept. Interior, 1976. Mem. Broward County Mediators Assn. Roman Catholic. Avocations: tennis, travel, culture. E-mail: anitavestal@aol.com.

VETERE, RICHARD, scriptwriter, writer, educator; b. N.Y.C., Jan. 15, 1952; s. Albert Vetere and Angelina Guiliano. BA, St. John's U., 1973; MA of English Lit., Columbia U., 1974. Prof. media dept. CUNY/Queens Coll., N.Y.C., 1985—. Recipient New Century playwriting award; grantee, Cultural Coun. Found./CETA, 1980, Mary Roberts Found. grantee for playwriting, 1976. Mem.: Poets and Writers, Authors Guild, Writers Guild Am., Dramatist Guild. Roman Catholic. Home: 53-40 62d St Flushing NY 11378 E-mail: vetrich88@aol.com.

VETSCHER, TIMOTHY JOHN, reporter, anchor on TV news show; b. St. Paul, Mar. 4, 1976; s. John T. and Mary J. V. BA, Marquette U., 1998. Writer WDJT-TV, Milw., 1997; reporter KSAX-TV, Alexandria, Minn., 1998; reporter, anchor KLKN-TV, Lincoln, Nebr., 1999; news reporter WHBQ-TV, Fox 13, Memphis, 1999—. Columnist Marquette Tribune, 1996-98; talk show host WMUR Radio. Recipient Best Investigative Story award Nebr. AP, 2000. Mem. Soc. Profl. Journalists, Radio and TV News Dirs. Assn. Democrat. Roman Catholic. Avocations: golf, reading, travel, opera. Home: 535 Kenneland Ct Apt 206 Cordova TN 38018-2209 Office: WHBQ-TV 485 S Highland St Memphis TN 38111-4391 E-mail: timothy376@aol.com.

VETTEL, NIKI MARCIA (MONICA MARCIA SCHER), broadcasting executive; b. N.Y.C., Oct. 23, 1951; d. William and Helen (Wurth) S.; m. Richard Vettel, Feb. 11, 1995. BA magna cum laude, SUNY, Buffalo, 1973, MA, 1977. Coord. pub. info. Citizens for Quality Edn., Buffalo, 1978-79; coord. instructional TV WNED-TV, 1979-83; dir. program info. Ea. Ednl. TV Network, Boston, 1983-86, asst. dir. program acquisition, 1986-89; v.p. Nat. Syndication, Am. Program Svc., 1989-92; v.p. program and devel. Am. Program Svc., 1992-97, sr. v.p., program devel., 1997—98; sr. mktg. cons., sr. project cons. Unitech Sys., Winthrop, 1998—; pres. Realitycheck Media Cons., 1998—. Instr. Niagara C.C., Niagara Falls, N.Y., 1976-77, Mass. C.C., 1998; instr., lectr. dept. comms. SUNY, Buffalo, 1977-79; instr. Empire State Coll., Buffalo, 1977-78. Avocation: horsemanship. Home: 1 Seal Harbor Rd # 508 Winthrop MA 02152-1025 Office: RealityCheck Media 1 Seal Harbor Rd Apt 508 Winthrop MA 02152-1025

VETTER, JAMES GEORGE, JR. lawyer; b. Omaha, Apr. 8, 1934; s. James George and Helen Louise (Adams) V.; m. Mary Ellen Froelich, June 25, 1960; 1 child, James G. III. BS, Georgetown U., 1954; JD, Creighton U., 1960. Bar: Nebr. 1960, Tex. 1967. Counsel IRS, Washington, 1960-64, Dallas, 1964-67; practiced in, 1967—; sr. ptnr. Vetter, Bates, Tibbals, Lee & DeBusk P.C., 1979-89; mem. Godwin & Gruber, P.C., 1989—, mng. dir., 1994-98. Lectr. taxation seminars; bd. dirs. Pilgrim's Pride Corp., AFV Energy, Inc., VLSIP Techs., Inc. Contbr. articles to profl. jours. Asst. sgt.-at-arms Tex. Dem. Conv., 1968; advisor selection com. Georgetown U., 1970-85; scoutmaster Boy Scouts Am., 1974-75; trustee St. Monica Sch. Endowment Trust, 1999—. With USAF, 1954-57; capt. USAFR, ret. Fellow Tex. Bar Found.; mem. Nebr. Bar Assn., State Bar Tex. (cert. tax law 1983—), Coll. State Bar Tex., Dallas Bar Assn. (chmn. fee disputes com. 1985, chmn. publs. com. 1988, chmn. pictoral directory com. 1993), Real Estate Fin. Execs. Assn. (pres. 1982-83), Cash Alliance (pres. 1987-88), Creighton U. Alumni Assn. (pres. Dallas-Ft. Worth 1969-70), Ctrl. Dallas Assn. (bd. dirs. 1994-95), Park Cities Club, Delta Theta Phi. Roman Catholic. Home: 11023 Rosser Rd Dallas TX 75229-3915 Office: Godwin & Gruber PC 1201 Elm St Ste 1700 Dallas TX 75270 E-mail: jvetter@godwingruber.com.

VETTER, RICHARD JAMES, health physicist; b. Castlewood, S.D., July 17, 1943; s. Ralph E. and Mary E. (Reitzel) V.; m. Janice M. Haberly, Mar. 13, 1965; children: Stephanie, Pamela. BS, S.D. State U., 1965, MS, 1967; PhD, Purdue U., 1969. Asst. prof. Point Park Coll., Pitts., 1969-70, Purdue U., West Lafayette, Ind., 1970-75, assoc. prof., 1975-79, prof., 1979-80, asst. radiation safety officer, 1970-80; radiation safety officer Mayo Found., Rochester, Minn., 1981—; prof. Mayo Med. Sch., 1981—; head sect. occupational safety Mayo Found., 1990-2000, med. dir. safety, 2000—. Dir. Minn. Safety Coun., Mpls., 1991-2000. Contbr. articles to profl. jours. Mem. Am. Assn. Physicists of Medicine, Am. Acad. Health Physics (dir. 1999—), Internat. Radiation Protection Assn., Soc. Nuclear Medicine, Health Physics Soc. (dir. 1986-88, editor jour. 1988-88, editor-in-chief 1988-94, pres. 1996-97), Nat. Coun. on Radiation Protection and Measurements (councilman 1998—), Am. Bd. Med. Physics (dir. 1998-2000), Am. Bd. Health Physics (dir. 1998—). Lutheran. Avocations: canoeing, fishing, cross-country skiing. Office: Mayo Clinic B28 Medical Scis Rochester MN 55905-0001 E-mail: rvetter@mayo.edu.

VETTER, VICTORIA L. pediatrician, educator, cardiologist; b. Louisville, Aug. 15, 1946; d. Albert Elmo and Mildred Irene (Burden) Vetter; m. Anthony S. Jennings, June 8, 1974; children: Jennifer, Jonathan, Jason. BA in Chemistry, U. Ky., 1968, MD, 1972. Bd. cert. Am. Bd. Pediat. in Pediat. and Pediat. Cardiology. Intern pediat. Johns Hopkins Hosp., Balt., 1972—73, resident pediat., 1973—74; sr. resident pediat. Vanderbilt U. Hosp., Nashville, 1974—75; fellow pediat. cardiology The Children's Hosp. Phila., 1975—78, asst. cardiologist, 1978—82, assoc. cardiologist, 1982—89, sr. cardiologist, 1989—, dir. pediat. electrophysiology lab., 1978—95, dir. pediat. electrocardiography lab., 1978—, chief divsn. cardiology, 1993—; sr. physician dept. pediat. U. Pa. Sch. Medicine, 1989—. Instr. pediat. U. Pa. Sch. Medicine, 1978, asst. prof. pediat., 1978—81, prof. pediat., 1999—; asst. prof. pediat. The Children's Hosp. Phila., U. Pa. Sch. Medicine, 1981—87, assoc. prof. pediat., 1987—99; lectr. in field. Sci. reviewer: jours. Circulation, sci. reviewer: jours. Am. Jour. Cardiology, sci. reviewer: jours. Jour. Am. Coll. Cardiology, sci. reviewer: jours. Pediat. Cardiology, sci. reviewer: jours. Pacing and Clin. Electrophysiology, sci. reviewer: jours. Pediat. Rsch., sci. reviewer: jours. Clin. Pediat., sci. reviewer: jours. Annals of Internal Medicine, sci. reviewer: jours. New Eng. Jour. Medicine, sci. reviewer: jours. Jour. Cardiovasc. Electrophysiology, sci. reviewer: jours. Jour. Pediat., sci. reviewer: jours. Am. Jour. Diseases of Children, sci. reviewer: jours. Pediat. Emergency Care; contbr. chapters to books, articles and abtracts to jours. Grantee in field. Fellow: Am. Coll. Cardiology (mem. emergency cardiac care com. 1992—98, mem. pediat. cardiology com. 1994—96, mem. 1996 annual sci. session program com. 1995—96, mem. credentials com. 1997—2000), Am. Acad. Pediat. (mem. exec. com. pediat. cardiology subsect. 1989—92, Young Investigator award sect. on cardiology 1978); mem.: AMA, John Morgan Soc., Phila. Arrhythmia Group, Pediat. Arrhythmia Group (mem. steering com.), Phila. County Med. Soc., Internat. Registry for Drug-Induced Arrhythmias (mem. sci. adv. com.), Sudden Arrhythmia Death Syndromes Found. (mem. sci. adv. bd.), Cardiac Arrhythmias Rsch. and Edn. Found., Inc. (mem. sci. adv. bd., Heart of the Child award 1996), N.Am. Soc. Pacing and Electrophysiology (mem. annual sci. sessions program com. 1998—2001, mem. pediat. com. 1998—2001), Pediat. Electrophysiology Soc., Am. Heart Assn. Coun. on Cardiovasc. Disease in the Young (mem. exec. com. 1993—98, mem. com. on tng. in pediat. cardiology 1994—96, mem. com. on electrocardiography and arrhythmias 1995—97, mem. membership com. 1996—97, chair Rashkind lecture selection com.), Am. Heart Assn. (med. spokesperson), Am. Heart Assn. Southeastern Pa. Affiliate (mem. rsch. peer rev. com. 1987—92, program chairperson 1988—90, v.p. 1989—90, pres.-elect 1990—91, pres. 1991—92, past-pres. 1992—93, mem. exec. com. 1988—93, mem. bd. dirs. 1993—96, mem. bd. govs. 1994—96, mem. pediat. sub-com. cardiac support coalition 1997—, post-doctoral fellow 1976—77, 1978—79), Alpha Omega Alpha, Phi Beta Kappa. Home: 110 Willow Way Cherry Hill NJ 08034-3049 Office: The Childrens Hosp Phila 34th St and Civic Center Blvd Philadelphia PA 19104

VETTERLING, MARY-ANNE, Spanish language and literature educator; b. Cleve., Aug. 7, 1948; d. Thomas James and Catherine (Manning) Lee; m. William Thomas Vetterling, Aug. 18, 1973. BA magna cum laude, Smith Coll., 1970; AM, Harvard U., 1971, PhD, 1977. Teaching fellow Harvard U., Cambridge, Mass., 1972-76; instr. Northeastern U., Boston, 1976-77, asst. prof. Spanish & Portuguese, 1977-83; tchr. Spanish Buckingham Browne & Nichols, Cambridge, 1983-84; asst. prof. Spanish Regis Coll., Weston, Mass., 1984-88, assoc. prof. Spanish, 1988-95, prof. Spanish, 1995—. Editor MaFLA Newsletter; author bibliography, articles. Sec. Paint Rock Pool, Lexington, Mass., 1989-92. Recipient honor Woodrow Wilson Found., 1970, Alfonso X the Wise award, 1998. Mem. MLA, Am. Assn. Tchrs. Spanish & Portuguese (chpt. treas., editor, pres., se c. bd. dirs. 1977—, exec. coun. 1997-99), Phi Beta Kappa. Avocations: stamp collecting, amateur radio. Office: Regis College Dept Spanish 235 Wellesley St Weston MA 02493-1571 E-mail: mav@regiscollege.edu.

VEZERIDIS, MICHAEL PANAGIOTIS, surgeon, educator; b. Thessaloniki, Greece, Dec. 16, 1943; came to U.S., 1974; s. Panagiotis and Sofia (Avramidis) V.; m. Therese Mary Statz; children: Peter Statz, Alexander Michael. MD, U. Athens, 1967; MA (hon) ad eundem, Brown U., 1989. Diplomate Am. Bd. Surgery. Fellow surg. rsch. Harvard Med. Sch./Mass. Gen. Hosp., Boston, 1974-77; resident U. Mass., Worcester, 1977-80; fellow in surg. oncology Roswell Park Meml. Inst., Buffalo, 1980-81, attending surgeon, 1981-82; staff surgeon VA Med. Ctr., Providence, 1982-84; asst. prof. surgery Brown U., 1982-88; chief surg. oncology VA Med. Ctr., 1984—, assoc. chief surgery, 1986-98, chief surgery, 1998—; cons. in surgery R.I. Hosp., 1987—; surg. oncologist Roger Williams Med. Ctr., 1989—; assoc. dir. div. surg. oncology Brown U., 1989—, assoc. prof. surgery, 1988-94, prof., 1994—; prof. surgery Boston U. Sch. Medicine, 1999—. Chmn. profl. edn. com. R.I. divsn. Am. Cancer Soc., Providence, 1987-89, pres.-elect 1989-91, pres. 1991-93, del. dir. to nat. bd. dirs., 1993-96, mem. Nat. Assembly of the Am. Cancer Soc., 1997—, bd. dirs. New Eng. divsn., 1997-2001, chief med. officer New Eng. divsn., 1999-2001; chmn. R.I. State Cancer Liaison Program ACS, 1999—; vis. prof. U. Patras (Greece) Med. Sch., 1988; mem. sci. adv. com. Clin. Rsch. Ctr., Brown U., Providence, 1989-91. Contbr. articles to profl. jours. and chpts. in med. books. Mem. parish coun. Ch. of Annunciation, Cranston, R.I., 1985-91; v.p. Hellenic Cultural Soc. Southeastern New Eng., Providence, 1987-89. Decorated Navy Commendation medal; named Profl. Fed. Employee of Yr., R.I. Fed. Exec. Coun., 1987; recipient St. George medal Am. Cancer Soc.; Merit Rev. Cancer Rsch. grantee VA, 1983-89. Fellow ACS (treas. R.I. chpt. 1996-2000, pres.-elect 2000-2002, pres. 2002-); mem. Soc. Surg. Oncology, Assn. for Acad. Surgery, Am. Soc. Clin. Oncology, N.Y. Acad. Scis. (life), Soc. for Surgery Alimentary Tract, Am. Assn. for Cancer Rsch., Collegium Internat. Chirurgiae Digestivae, Assn. Mil. Surgeons U.S., Soc. for Metastasis Rsch., New Eng. Cancer Soc., New Eng. Surg. Soc., Quidnessett Country Club. Greek Orthodox. Avocations: classical music, reading, fencing, tennis, squash, cross-country skiing. Home: 50 Limerock Dr East Greenwich RI 02818-1643 Office: Roger Williams Med Ctr 825 Chalkstone Ave Providence RI 02908-4728 E-mail: michael_vezeridismd@med.va.gov.

VEZNEDAROGLU, KINCAL, social worker; b. Izmir, Turkey, Feb. 5, 1936; came to U.S., 1959; d. Mustafa Haydar and Sabina (Yurd) Nazli; m. Muhtesem Veznedaroglu, Oct. 11, 1960; children: Ismail, Leyla, Erol. BA, Am. Coll. for Girls, 1957; MSW, Smith Coll., 1961. Bd. cert. diplomate in clin. social work; lic. social worker, N.Y. Staff social worker Winnipeg (Manitoba, Can.) Gen. Hosp., 1961-65; acting dir., supr., clin. social worker Wyoming County Mental Health Clinic, Warsaw, 1981-89. Cons. in field. Mem. NASW, N.Y. State Soc. Clin. Social Work Psychotherapists, Am. Orthopsychiat. Assn., Inc. Avocations: tennis, swimming. Home: 3240 Bermuda Isle Cir Apt 915 Naples FL 34109-3215

VEZVAEI, MAHBOBEH, mathematics educator; b. Tehran, Iran, Oct. 3, 1952; came to U.S., 1978; d. Hosain and Ehteram (Ghaderi) V.; m. Mosthea Rahmani, June 21, 1978; children: Rouhollah, Mona, Mariam, Haumed. MS, Informatic Inst., Tehran, 1978, Case Western Res. U., 1983, PhD, 1987. Cert. healthcare nursing. H.S. tchr., Tehran, 1972-75; instr. Ertebatat U., 1978; dir. divsn. statistics Bonyad Khayria, 1975-78; cons. Case Western Res. U., Cleve., 1986; lectr. Kent State U., Kent, Ohio, 1983-99, asst. prof., 1999—. Rschr. in field. Recipient grad. assistantship Case Western Res. U., 1979-82. Mem. Am. Statis. Assn., Iranian Statis. Assn., Assn. of Women in Math. Avocations: reading, walking, cooking, being with family, sewing. Office: Kent State Univ Dept Math Scis Kent OH 44242-0001 E-mail: vezvaei@mcs.kent.edu.

VIANCO, PAUL THOMAS, metallurgist; b. Rochester, N.Y., Dec. 28, 1957; s. George William and Josephine Rose (Sardisco) V.; m. Karen Elaine Claghorn; children: Maria Elaine, Sara Leslie. BS in Physics, SUNY, 1980; MS in Mech. and Aeronautical Engring., U. Rochester, 1981, PhD in Materials Sci., 1986. Sr. mem. tech. staff Sandia Nat. Labs., Alburquerque, 1987—. Mem. ASME, Am. Welding Soc. (chmn. subcom. 1992—), ASM Internat., The Metall. Soc., Surface Mount Tech. Assn. (sec. to bd. dirs.). Home: 4012 Shenandoah Pl NE Albuquerque NM 87111-4158 Office: Sandia Nat Labs PO Box 5800 Albuquerque NM 87185-0100

VIANDS, DONALD REX, plant breeder and educator; b. Riverdale, Md., Apr. 1, 1952; s. Walter Leroy and Lydia (Zeh) V.; m. Janice Ann Ruppelt, Aug. 7, 1976; children: Jamie Christopher, April Suzanne. BS in Agronomy, U. Md., 1974; MS in Plant Breeding, U. Minn., 1977, PhD in Plant Breeding, 1979. Undergrad. rsch. asst. U. Md., College Park, 1969-74; grad. rsch. asst. U. Minn., St. Paul, 1974-79; asst. prof. Cornell U., Ithaca, N.Y., 1979-85, assoc. prof., 1985-92, prof., 1992—, assoc. dir. acad. programs, 1995—. Mem. adv. com. biotech. sci. adv. com. EPA, Washington, 1987-95; mem. steering com. N.Y. State North Country Devel. Program, 1990-99; adv. N.Y. State Forage and Grassland Coun., 1984-90, Alfalfa Crop Adv. Com., 1984-92. Contbr. articles to profl. jours., chpts. to books. Sunday sch. tchr. People's Bapt. Ch., Newfield, N.Y., 1988-2000, deacon, 1988-90, 93-98, Awana comdr., 1993-2000. Named Most Influential Faculty Mem. for Merrill Presdl. Scholar, Cornell U., 1991. Mem. Am. Soc. Agronomy (N.E. regional coord. mem. com. 1998-99), Crop Sci. Soc. Am., Am. Seed Trade Assn. (mem. minimum distance com. 1988-94), N.Am. Alfalfa Improvement Conf. (sec. 1984-86, v.p. 1986-88, pres. 1988-90), Ea. Forage Improvement Conf., Am. Forage and Grassland Coun. Republican. Achievements include development of 11 alfalfa varieties and 1 birdsfoot trefoil variety. Office: Cornell Univ Office Acad Programs 155 Roberts Hall Ithaca NY 14853-5905 E-mail: drv3@cornell.edu.

VIANI, JAMES LAURENCE, lawyer; b. Kincaid, Ill., Dec. 24, 1932; s. Frank Jerome and Alfonsina V.; m. Virginia Lee Wilson, Dec. 27, 1958; children: Theresa, Diana, Deborah. BS, Millikin U., 1954; LLB, Wash. U., St. Louis, 1957. Bar: Ill. 1957, Mo. 1957. Assoc. Blackmar, Swanson, Midgley, Jones & Eager, Kansas City, Mo., 1958-59, Stinson, Mag & Fizzell, Kansas City, 1960-62; ptnr. Stinson, Mag & Fizzel, 1962-87, chmn. corp. dept., 1979-87, cons. ptnr., 1988-92. Br. bd. chmn. YMCA, Kansas City, 1979-81. With U.S. Army, 1957-63. Mem. ABA, Phi Kappa Phi, Order of the Coif. Republican. Avocations: hiking, reading, farming. Home: 11106 Belleview Ave Kansas City MO 64114-5115

VIANI, ROLANDO MARIO, pediatrician, researcher; b. Lima, Peru, Nov. 10, 1956; arrived in US, 1991; s. Mario and Nelly (Velarde) Viani; m. Maria B E Kraft, Dec. 26, 1986; children: Phillip, Nicholas. MD, U. Peruana Cayetano Heredia, Lima, 1984; MTP, Liverpool Sch. Tropical Med., 1990. Diplomate Am Bd Pediatrics, Am. Bd. Pediat. Infectious Diseases. Intern U. Peruana Cayetano Heredia, 1983-84; resident Univ. Hosp., Lima, 1986-89; from resident to fellow SUNY Health Sci. Ctr., Bklyn., 1991-95; rsch. fellow U. Calif. San Diego, La Jolla, 1995-97, clin. instr. dept. pediat. Sch. Medicine, 1997-98; asst. clin. prof. pdiatrics U. Calif. San Francisco-Fresno Med. Edn. Program, 1999-2001; dir. pediatric spl. svc. Sequoia Cmty. Health Found., Fresno, 1999-2001; asst. clin. prof. pediats. U. Calif., San Diego, 2001—. Mem.: Pediatrics Infectious Disease Soc Am, Am Acad Pediatrics. Office: U Calif San Diego Stein Clin Rsch Bldg Rm 434 9500 Gilman Dr MC 0672 La Jolla CA 92093-0672 E-mail: rviani@ucsd.edu.

VICARI, ANDREW, artist; b. Port Talbot, Wales, Apr. 20, 1938; s. Vittorio Vicari and Italia Bertani. Student, Slade Sch. of Art, London, 1951-53. Represented in many permanent and pvt. collections including: Dallas Mus. Fine Arts, Nat. Libr. Wales, Mus. Tel-Aviv, Contemporary Arts Soc. Great Britain, Tate Gallery, Columbus Mus. Fine Arts, Poldi Pezzoli Mus., Milan, Mus. Petit Palais, Modern Art, Geneva, David Lloyd Kreeger Coll., Washington, IBM Coll. Armonk, N.Y., Palais Princier, Monoco; group exibs. include: Retrospective Chinese Ministry of Culture, Palais des Beaux Arts, Beijing, 1995, From War to Peace in the Gulf, Vicari Opus of 225 paintings, 1990-2000, Ministry of the Interior, Paris, 2000, many others; commd. paintings include: King of Saudi Arabia, Interpol and CRS France; author: Triumph of the Bedouin, 1984; illustrator: (poems) From the Orient and the Desert, 1984, La Vigonade a Vicari (by Louis Pauwels), 1989, (BBC film) Outrageous Fortune, 1997, the Mystery of Memory, 2002. World patron Beacon Millenium Trust. Decorated Chevalier Order of Merit (Monaco); brigadier d'honneur Compagnie Republicaine de Securite (France); recipient European Beaux Arts prize, 1995; recipient Beaux Arts prize European Parliament and Coun. Europe, 1995. Fellow London Zool. Soc.; mem. East India & Pub. Schs. Club (London), Cardiff (Wales) & County Club, Bristol Channel Yacht Club, Lords Cricket Ground London, Rotary Internat. Avocations: tennis, running, gourmet cuisine. Home: The East India Club 16 St James' Square London SW1Y 4LH England

VICARY, WILLIAM CHARLES, JR. director sales and marketing; b. Dearborn, Mich., Nov. 27, 1956; s. William Charles and Nancy Jane (Ternes) V.; m. Sandra Kay Leach, Mar. 24, 1990. AS in Liberal Arts, Henry Ford C.C., 1977; BS in Packaging Engring., Mich. State U., 1980. Packaging engr. GM, Dayton, Ohio, 1980-83, Sanders Assoc., Nashua, N.H., 1983-84; corp. packaging engr. Mack Trucks, Inc., Allentown, Pa., 1984-86; mktg. coord. Fluor Daniel, Inc., Greenville, S.C., 1986-91; mgr. bus. devel. Simons Engring., 1991-95; venue coord. and cons. ACOG and Planit Sports, 1996-97; dir. food & beverage Sverdrup Facilities Inc., St. Louis, 1997-98; dir. corp. mktg. and sales SSOE Inc., Toledo, 1998—. Venue coord-yatching Atlanta Com. for Olympic Games, Savannah, Ga., 1996; pres. Planit Sports & Events, Greer, S.C., St. Louis, 1995—. Co-chairperson & founder Golf for Greenville, 1990, 91. Mem. KC. Avocations: golf, boating music art. Home: 8324 Country Brook Dr Holland OH 43528-9165 Office: SSOE Inc 1001 Madison Ave Ste A Toledo OH 43624-1585 Fax: (419) 255-6101.

VICE, CHARLES LOREN, electromechanical engineer; b. LaVerne, Okla., Jan. 2, 1921; s. Cyrus Christopher and Ethel Sewatch (Hoy) V.; m. Katherine Margaret Maxwell, July 14, 1949; children: Katherine Lorene, Charles Clark, Ann Marie. Cert., Oreg. State U., 1944, BSME, 1947; postgrad., U. So. Calif., 1948-55. Registered profl. engr., Calif. Mgr. magnetic head divsn. Gen. Instrument Corp., Hawthorne, Calif., 1959-62; sr. staff engr. magnetic head divsn. Ampex Corp., Redwood City, 1962-66; chief mech. engr. Collins Radio Corp., Newport Beach, 1967-69; pres. FerraFlux Corp., Santa Ana, 1970-78; sr. staff engr. McDonnell Douglas Computer Systems Co., Irvine, 1979-89, Santa Ana, 1989, ret., 1989. Cons. Teac Corp. Japan, 1974-78, Otari Corp. Japan, 1975-77, Univac Corp., Salt Lake City, 1975-76, Crown Radio Corp. Japan, 1979-80, Sabor Corp. Japan, 1982, Empire Corp., Tokyo, 1987-89, DIGI SYS Corp., Fullerton, Calif., 1988-89, Puritan Bennett Aerosystems, El Segundo, Calif., 1989-94, Avox Corp., Van Nuys, Calif., 1995—. Patentee in field. With U.S. Army Engrs., 1943-46. Decorated Bronze Star. Mem. NSPE, Toastmasters. Republican. Avocations: piano, singing. Office: Precision Cons Inc 5902 E Bryce Ave Orange CA 92867-3305 Fax: (714) 998-0846. E-mail: clvice@cs.com.

VICE, ROY LEE, history educator; b. Lynchburg, Va., Oct. 12, 1950; s. Cline Lowell and Ruth Burchell (Newman) V. BA in History, BS in Physics, Carson-Newman Coll., 1972; MA in History, U. Chgo., 1976, PhD in History, 1984. Lectr. Continuing Edn. program U. Chgo., 1985-86, 87-88, rare books asst. univ. librs., 1986; asst. prof. Pacific Luth. U., Tacoma, 1986-87, Clemson (S.C.) U., 1988-90, Wright State U., Dayton, Ohio, 1990-95, assoc. prof., 1995—. Contbr. articles to profl. jours. Vol. tutor CYCLE Cabrini-Green Projects, Chgo., 1981—86; vol. lectr. LaSalle St. Ch., 1989—98, 2000—01. With U.S. Army, 1972—74. Mem. Am. Hist. Assn., 16th Century Studies Conf. Democrat. Baptist. Home: 229 E 2nd St Dayton OH 45402-1719 Office: Wright State U Dept History 3640 Colonel Glenn Hwy Dayton OH 45435-0001 E-mail: roy.vice@wright.edu.

VICE, SUSAN F. medicinal chemist; b. Oshawa, Ont., Can., Apr. 19, 1956; m. Andrew S. Thompson, Nov. 27, 1987. BS in Chemistry, U. We. Ont., London, Can., 1980; PhD, U. Waterloo, Ont., 1984. Postdoc. fellow U. Calif., Irvine, 1984—86; rsch. scientist Polysar Ltd., Sarnia, 1986—88; sr. prin. scientist Schering Plough Rsch. Inst., Kenilworth, NJ, 1988—2000. Contbr. articles. Fellow Charles S. Humphrey grad. fellow, Guelph-Waterloo Ctr. Grad. Work in Chemistry, 1983, postdoc. fellow, Natural Scis. and Engring. Rsch. Coun., 1984—86, inds. postdoc. fellow, 1986; scholar, 1981—84. Mem.: Chem. Inst. Can./Soc. Chemistry, Am. Chem. Soc. Home: 1144 Sawmill Rd Mountainside NJ 07092-2213

VICENS, GUILLERMO JUAN, engineering executive; m. Marti Vicens; four children. BSCE, MIT, 1970, MSCE, 1972, PhD in Water Resources, 1974; postgrad., Babson Coll. Diplomate Am. Acad. Environ. Engrs.; registered profl. engr., Maine, Mass., N.H. Sr. v.p. Camp Dresser & McKee Inc., Cambridge. Bd. dirs. Am. Coun. Egring. Cos., former chmn. environ. com. Former mem., chmn. North Andover (Mass.) Conservation Commn. Mem. ASCE, Am. Water Works Assn., Water Environment Fedn., Am. Geophys. Union, Am. Inst. Hydrology (cert. hydrologist, gen. chmn. organizing com. annual meeting 1996). Office: Camp Dresser & McKee Inc 50 Hampshire St Cambridge MA 02139

VICENZI, ANGELA ELIZABETH, nursing researcher; b. N.Y.C., Aug. 19, 1938; d. Peter Christiaan and Angeline Elizabeth (Rudtke) Richard; m. Richard Emil Vicenzi, Nov. 11, 1961; children: Richard Martin, Paul Andrew, Stephen Mark, Douglas Emil. Diploma, St. Vincent's Hosp. Sch. Nursing, N.Y.C., 1959; BSN, Western Conn. State U., 1977; MEd in Cmty. Health Nursing, Columbia U., 1980, EdD in Health Edn., 1984. Pub. health nurse City of N.Y., 1960-61; pediat. staff nurse Norwalk (Conn.) Hosp., 1970-73; profl. nurse traineeship Columbia U. Tchrs. Coll., N.Y.C., 1978-80; clin. instr. Norwalk C.C., 1977-78; asst. prof. Sacred Heart U., Fairfield, Conn., 1980-83; from. asst. prof. to assoc. prof. So. Conn. State U., New Haven, 1985-95, prof., 1995-2000, prof. emeritus, 2000; prof. Western Conn. State U., 2001—02. Cons. Corp. Health Cons., Norwalk, 1980-90; pres. faculty senate So. Conn. State U., 1991-94. Editor, pub. Complexity & Chaos in Nursing Jour., 1994—; contbr. articles to profl. jours. Mem. St. Jerome Parish Coun., Norwalk, 1995-97. Recipient Virginia A. Henderson award Conn. Nurses Assn., 1996; grantee Conn. State U., 1994-95, Profl. Nurse Traineeship grantee Health and Human Svcs., 1991-94. Mem. AAUP (treas. So. Conn. State U. chpt. 1995-97, pres. 1998-2000), Assn. Cmty. Health Nursing Educators (program chmn. 1995), Mu Beta, Sigma Theta Tau (pres. 1992-94).

VICHIOLA, CHRISTOPHER MICHAEL, educator, writer; b. Bridgeport, Conn., Apr. 27, 1959; s. Michael Richard and Delores (Distaci) Vichiola; m. Tracey Vichiola, Nov. 12, 1997; children: Michael, Christopher , Anthony. *Grandfather Michael Vichiola came from Italy to Bridgeport, Connecticut. He had 8 children: Michael, Jr., Arthur, Raymond, Robert, Ronald, John, Laura and Lucille. Michael Vichiola, Jr., who was a sheet metal worker, married Delores Distaci, a teacher. Their son, Christopher Michael Vichiola, is married to Tracey, daughter of Marion and Lee White. Tracey works as a health care professional, martial artist and a teacher for the Center for Action. Christopher Michael Vichiola, Jr., was born September 17, 1998.* AS, Western Conn. State U., 1981, BA, 1983; grad., Colonel James "Bo" Gritz's Spec. Forces Green Beret On-Field Med. Surg. Sch. Cert. nursing asst. Martial arts tchr. Am. Bujinkan Dojo, Danbury, Conn., 1993—; tchr., distbr. Ctr. for Action, Kamiah, Idaho, 1997—; with Home Depot, 1998—, A&P Foodmart, 1999. Educator, cons. Primerica Fin. Svcs., Danbury, 1997—; educator Christic Inst. Law Firm, Washington, 1995—. *Christopher Michael Vichiola served as a key supporter and educator of the Christic Institute Law Firm's Iran-Contra LA Penca Lawsuit. As a martial arts expert, Mr. Vichiola performed exceptional displays of strength such as walking over burning hot coals and not getting injured. During Colonel Gritz's special Forces Training, Mr. Vichiola performed major surgery by extracting bullets out of injured animals.Mr.Vichiola,during Navy Seal Training mapped out underwater location for demolition.* Author: Above the Law - The Real Story's Files, 1995, Above the Law Part II, 1995, The Real Story of Christopher Vichiola and Colonel Gritz, 1997, The Real Story of Christopher Vichiola's and Colonel Gritz's Training, 1997. Educator Rev. Jesse L. Jackson's Rainbow Coalition, Washington, 1992—, Mayor Eugene Eriquez Dem. Party, Danbury, 1987—, Rep. Jack Brooks, 1991—, Gov. Michael Dukakis, 1989—. Black belt in Ninjutsu, 1997; recipient Eagle award Col. James "Bo" Gritz, 1997, Spike Navy Seal Scuba badge Col. James "Bo" Gritz, 1997. Avocations: camping, scuba diving, basketball, football, martial arts. Home: 48 Candlewood Lake Rd S Apt 3 New Milford CT 06776-4562

VICK, AARON CONLEY, contractor, consultant; b. Raleigh, N.C. s. William C. and Opal Vick; m. Julia Polloni, Aug. 2, 1975; children: Daniel Christopher, Carl Andrew. AA, Louisburg (N.C.) Coll., 1974; BSCE, N.C. State U., 1978, MS in Mgmt., 2000. Various positions constrn. cos., 1970—78; estimator, project mgr., 1978—87; v.p. Wm. C. Vick Constrn. Co., 1987—. Home: 4609 Whitmire Pl Raleigh NC 27612 Office: 3930 Western Blvd Raleigh NC 27606

VICK, COLUMBUS EDWIN, JR. retired civil engineering design firm executive; b. Jacksonville, Fla., Nov. 8, 1934; s. Columbus Edwin Sr. and Lucretia (Dean) V.; m. Laura Anne McGowan, Mar. 28, 1964; children: Jennifer, Carolyn, Elizabeth. BSCE, N.C. State U., 1956, MSCE, 1960. Registered profl. engr., 15 states. Rsch. asst. N.C. State Civil Engring. Dept., Raleigh, 1958-60; transp. planning engr. Harland Bartholomew & Assocs., Memphis, 1960-64, office and project mgr. Raleigh, 1964-67; prin., co-founder Kimley-Horn and Assocs. Inc., 1967-72, pres., 1972-92; chmn., 1992-2000. Bd. dirs. Wachovia Bank, Design Profls. Coalition Am. Cons. Engrs. Coun. Co-author: North Carolina Atlas; contbr. articles to profl. jours. Past pres., bd. dirs. N.C. State U. Engring. Found.; past pres. bd. assocs. Meredith Coll.; past dir. N.C. State U. Alumni Assn.; bd. visitors N.C. State U.; past 2d v.p. Bapt. State Conv. of N.C.; bd. dirs. Assoc. Bapt. Press, Bibl. Recorder; trustee Kenan Inst. for Engring. Tech. and Sci., Gardner Webb U., Meredith Coll.; mem. bd. advisors Wake Forest U. Sch. Divinity. Named Disting. Engring. alumnus N.C. State U., 1991. Fellow ASCE (Outstanding Young Engr. award ea. br. N.C. sect. 1966), Inst. Transp. Engrs. (Oustanding Individual Activity award so. sect. 1978, Disting. Svc. award so. sect. 1981, Lifetime Svc. award N.C. sect. 1995); mem. NSPE (Disting. Svc. award), Am. Con. Engrs. Coun., Am. Inst. Cert. Planners, Profl. Svcs. Mgmt. Assn. (Coll. of Fellow), N.C. Soc. Engrs. (Outstanding Engring Achievement award 1992). Baptist. Home: 2205 Nancy Ann Dr Raleigh NC 27607-3318 Office: Kimley-Horn and Assocs Inc 3001 Weston Pky Cary NC 27513-2301 E-mail: ed.vick@kimley-horn.com.

VICK, EDWARD HOGE, JR. advertising executive; b. N.Y.C., Feb. 27, 1944; s. Edward Hoge and Margaret Jane (Sprankle) V.; m. Nancy Jane Newcomer; Children: Joshua D., Charlie, Jane. AB, U. N.C., 1966; MS, Northwestern U., 1971. With Benton & Bowles, Inc., N.Y.C., 1971-75, Ogilvy & Mather, Inc., N.Y.C., 1975-83; exec. v.p., dir. account service Ammirati & Puris Inc., 1983-85, pres., chief operating officer, 1985-90; pres., CEO Levine, Huntley, Vick & Beaver, N.Y.C., 1990-94, Young & Rubicam N.Y., 1994-96, chmn., CEO, 1997—. Author: An Examination of the Creative Process, 1971. Bd. vis. U. N.C. Decorated Bronze Star (2). Mem. Am. Assn. Advt. Agys. (bd. dirs.), Advt. Edn. Found. (bd. dirs.), St. Andrew's Soc. Republican. Presbyterian. Home: 501 Guard Hill Rd Bedford NY 10506 Office: Young & Rubicam 285 Madison Ave New York NY 10017

VICK, JAMES ALBERT, publishing executive, consultant; b. Norwalk, Conn., Feb. 5, 1945; s. James Albert and Madeline (Mayhew) V.; m. Deborah M. Ashley, Dec. 23, 1964 (div. Oct. 1974); children: James Ashley, Guy Robert; m. Susan Jane Collins, May 14, 1977; 1 child, Jonathan Scott. BS, Boston U., 1967. Dist. mgr. McGraw Hill Pub. Co., N.Y.C., 1969-75, Cahners Pub. Co., N.Y.C., 1975-79; mgr. advt. ASCE, 1979-82; v.p. mktg. Bill Communications, 1982-87; pub. Thomas Pub. Co., 1987-95; v.p. Web Property Devel. Poppe Tyson, 1995-96; exec. v.p. sales/mktg. Lawyers Weekly Publs., Boston, 1996-98; v.p. publ. Phillips Publ./KIPI, White Plains, N.Y., 1998-2000; pub., staff dir. IEEE Spectrum Mag., N.Y.C., 2000—. Cons. Carvajal, Calle, Columbia, 1984, McLarens, London, 1987. Capt. USAR, 1967-70, Vietnam. Mem. IEEE (comms. soc., computer soc.), Bus. Mktg. Assn. (cert. bus. communicator), Am. Bus. Press (pubs. com.), Soc. Plastics Engrs., Pharm Ad Club, Princeton Club, Port Royal Golf Club, Elks. Episcopalian. Avocations: golf, sailing, antique restoration. Home: 473 Judd Rd Easton CT 06612 Office: IEEE Spectrum Mag 3 Park Ave Ste 1701 New York NY 10016-5997 Fax: (914) 328-9093. E-mail: j.vick@ieee.org.

VICK, JEFFREY HARRISON, music educator, musician; b. Denver, Nov. 5, 1965; s. Donald James and Sharlene Marie (Savage) Vick; m. Jacquelyn Campeau, Nov. 20, 1999; 1 child Teresa Irene. BS in Music, U. Ariz., 1989; MEd in Music, Mont. State U., 1991. Cert. music tchr. grades K-12 Mont., secondary tchr. grades 7-12, secondary tchr. music, Office of Pub. Instrn., State Mont. Music educator Bozeman (Mont.) Pub. Schs., 1990—91, Willow Creek (Mont.) Sch., 1991—92, Anderson Sch. Dist. #41, Bozeman, 1993—. Pvt. percussion tchr., Bozeman, 1989—; prin. timpanist and percussionist Bozeman Symphony Orch., 1989—, Intermountain Opera Assn., Bozeman, 1990—, Mont. Ballet Co., Bozeman, 1993—; prin. timpanist Mont. Summer Symphony, Helena, 1998—; libr., coach Ann. Chamber Music Festival, Mont. State U., Bozeman, 1990—, mem.a dv. bd. , 1998—; adj. instr. music Mont. State U., Bozeman, 1992—96; founding dir. PercOrchestra (Percussion Quartet), Bozeman, 2000—. Composer: (band composition) Theme and Variations, 1984, (percussion composition) Escalation and Denovement, 1985, (Gamelan Composition) Permulaan Baru, 2001, Musik Percobaan, 2001, Baru Saja Lahir, 2002; editor: (Newsletter) Montana Percussion News, 1998—2002; musician: (Concerto with Orchestra) MILHAUD: Concerto for Percussion, 1991, (Chamber Recital) Nat. Arts Festival - Grahamstown, S.A., 1992, (Concerto with Orchestra) SVOBODA: Concerto for Marimba, 1996, (Chamber Recital with Cascade Quartet) KULESHA: Quintet-Sonata, 1998, (Chamber Recital with Mistral Duo) UNG: Spiral, 1999, (Concerto with Percussion Ensemble) MCCARTHY: Concerto for Marimba, Percussion and Synthesizers, 2001. Recipient Individual Artist Fellowship award, Mont. Arts Coun., 1992—93. Mem.: NEA, Mont. Music Educators Assn., Music Educators Nat. Conf., Percussive Arts Soc. (sec. Ariz. chpt. 1986—87, v.p. Ariz. chpt. 1987—88, sec. Mont. chpt. 1998—2002), Am. Fedn. Musicians (exec. bd. local 709 1996—99, pres. local 709 1999—2002), Phi Delta Kappa (profl. rsch. grant 1999). Avocations: collecting instruments and masks, photography, world music. Home: 529 South Black Ave Bozeman MT 59715-5301 Office: Anderson Sch Dist #41 10040 Cottonwood Rd Bozeman MT 59718 Personal E-mail: jvick@metnet.state.mt.us.

VICK, MARIE, retired health science educator; b. Saltillo, Tex., Jan. 22, 1922; d. Alphy Edgar and Mollie (Cowser) Pitts; m. Joe Edward Vick, Apr. 5, 1942; children: Mona Marie, Rex Edward. BS, Tex. Woman's U., Denton, 1942, MA, 1949. Tchr. Coahoma (Tex.) High Sch., 1942-43, Santa Rita Elem. Sch., San Angelo, Tex., 1943-45, Crozier Tech. High Sch., Dallas, 1946-47, Monroe Jr. High Sch., Omaha, 1947-48; instr. Tex. Woman's U., Denton, 1948-50; tchr. San Angelo (Tex.) Jr. High Sch., 1957-58, San Angelo (Tex.) Sr. High Sch., 1957-58, Harlingen Bonham Elem. Sch., 1958-59, Harlingen (Tex.) High Sch., 1959-62; prof. health sci. Coll. Edn. U. Houston, 1962-80. Author: A Collection of Dances for Children, 1970; Health Science in the Elementary School, 1979; contbr. articles to profl. jours.; artist in oil, watercolor and acrylic. Mem. exec. bd. Health Care Task Force of Walker County. Recipient Cert. of Achievement, Tex. Commn. Intercollegiate Athletics for Women, 1972, Research Service award Tex. Cancer Control Program, 1978-79, Plaudit award Nat. Dance Assn., 1982, Disting. Service award Pan Am. U., 1983, Service citation Am. Cancer Soc., Cert. of Appreciation, Tex. div. Am. Cancer Soc., 1980; Favorite Prof. honoree Cap and Gown Mortar Bd., U. Houston, 1974. Mem. AAHPERD (dance editor 1971-74), NEA, AARP (chmn. legis. com. Huntsville chpt. 1988-90, bd. dirs., liaison person Walker County commrs. 1989-90, chmn. cmty. svc. project Walker County Unpaved Rd. Survey, 1989, mem. exec. bd. 1992—), Am. Sch. Health Assn., So. Assn. Health, Phys. Edn. Coll. Women (sec. dance sect. 1970-73), Tex. State Tchrs. Assn. (sect. chmn. 1964-65), Tex. Assn Health, Phys. Edn. and Recreation (chmn. dance sect. 1968-69), Tex. Assn. Coll. Tchrs., Nat. Ret. Tchrs. Assn. (legis. chmn. 1988-89), Tex. Assn. Ret. Tchrs., Property Owners Assn. (organizer, 1st pres.), U. Houston Assn. Ret. Profs., Tex. Women's U. Nat. Alumnae Assn. (life). Democrat. Methodist. Home: 411 Obannon Ranch Rd Huntsville TX 77320-1574

VICK, MAURICE MCCALL, JR. urologist; b. Baton Rouge, Jan. 26, 1940; s. Maurice Sr. and Louise Whitfield (Cannon) V.; m. Myrtle G., June 9, 1962 (div. Sept. 1989); children: Mackie, Randy, Michael; m. Charlotte Olive, Sept. 23, 1989; children: David, Ben, Jen. BS, La. State U., 1961, MD, 1965. Intern, resident Charity Hosp., New Orleans, 1970; urologist pvt. practice, Baton Rouge, 1972-92, retired, 1992; with Cellular one, Ind. & Ill, 1989-92, Fla. Telecommunications, Inc., Orlando, 1990—; owner Vick Devel., Inc., Sarasota, Fla., 1992—. Bd. dirs. St. Joseph Children's Home, Baton Rouge, 1976-78; chmn. med. divsn. United Givers Fund, Baton Rouge, 1978-79; bd. dirs. Eddy Toussaint Ballet, Sarasota, 1994-95, Sarasota Symphony, 1995—. Lt. comdr. USPHS, 1970-72. Mem. AMA, Am. Urological Assn., Am. Lithotripsy Soc., La. State Med. Assn., Southeast sect. Am. Urological Assn., East Baton Rouge Med. Assn., Phi Kappa Phi, Alpha Omega Alpha. Republican. Episcopalian. Avocations: boating, fishing, tennis. Office: PO Box 6119 Sarasota FL 34278-6119

VICK, MICHAEL, football player; b. Newport News, Va. , June 26, 1980; Attended , Va. Tech. Football player Atlanta Falcons, 2001—. Office: Atlanta Falcons 4400 Falcon Pkwy Flowery Branch GA 30542*

VICK, NICHOLAS A. neurologist; b. Chgo., Oct. 3, 1939; MD, U. Chgo., 1965. Diplomate Am. Bd. Neurology. Intern U. Chgo. Hosps., 1965, resident in neurology, 1966-68; fellow in neurology NIH, Bethesda, Md., 1968-70; staff Evanston (Ill.) Hosp., 1975—; prof. neurology Northwestern U. Med. Sch., Evanston, Ill., 1978—. Office: Evanston Hosp Dept Neurology 2650 Ridge Ave Evanston IL 60201-1781*

VICK, SUSAN, playwright, educator, director, actress; b. Raleigh, N.C., Nov. 4, 1945; d. Thomas B. Jr. and Merle (Hayes) V. MFA, So. Meth. U., 1969; PhD, U. Ill., 1979. Prof. drama and theatre, dir. theatre Worcester (Mass.) Poly. Inst., 1981—; playwright Excuse Me For Living Prodns., Cambridge, 1989—, Festival Fringe, Edinburgh, 1989—. Playwright Ensemble Studio Theatre, N.Y.C., 1981-83; founder WPI Ann. New Voices Festival of Original Plays, 1982. Editor: (2 vols.) Playwrights Press, Amherst, 1988—; playwright: When I Was Your Age, 1982, Ord-Way Ames-Gay, 1982, Investments, 1985, Half Naked, 1989, Quandary, 1983, Meat Selection, 1984, Give My Love to Everyone But, 1989; appeared in plays including Rip Van Winkle, 1979, Why I Live at The P.O., 1982, The Play Group, 1984-85, Present Stage, 1985, Sister Mary Ignatius Explain It All, 1986, Wipeout, 1988, Bogus Joan, 1992-93; dir. play Give My Love to Everyone But, 1990 (Edinburgh Festival); theatre editor: Sojourner The Women's Forum, 1995-98; dramaturg, script cons. Clyde Unity Theatre, Glasgow, Scotland, 1992-93, 1999-2000. Dir., Women's Community Theatre, Amherst, 1981-84, Upstart, Wis., 1994. Faculty fellow U. Ill., 1976-77, Bd. of Trustees Award for Outstanding Tchg., Worcester Poly. Inst., 1997. Mem. U.S. Inst. for Theatre Tech., Nat. Assn. Schs. of Theatre, New Eng. Theatre Conf., Inc., Drama League, Dramatists Guild (assoc.), Soc. Stage Dirs. and Choreographers (assoc.), U.S. Inst. Theatre Tech., New England Theatre Conf., Nat. Assn. Schs. Theatre, Alpha Phi Omega (Svc. to Students award 1996). Avocations: puppets, frogs, travel. Office: Worcester Poly Tech Inst 100 Institute Rd Worcester MA 01609-2247

VICKER, RAY, writer; b. Wis., Aug. 27, 1917; s. Joseph John and Mary (Young) V.; m. Margaret Ella Leach, Feb. 23, 1944. Student, Wis. State U., Stevens Point, 1934, Los Angeles City Coll., 1940-41, U.S. Mcht. Marine Officers' Sch., 1944, Northwestern U., 1947-49. With Chgo. Jour. Commerce, 1946-50, automobile editor, 1947-50; mem. staff Wall St. Jour., 1950-83, European editor Eng., 1960-75, sr. internat. editor Eng., 1975-83. Sr. internatl. ediotr, 1975-83. Author: How an Election Was Won, 1962, Those Swiss Money Men, 1973, Kingdom of Oil, 1974, Realms of Gold, 1975, This Hungry World, 1976, Dow Jones Guide to Retirement Planning, 1985, The Informed Investor, 1990; also numerous articles. Served with U.S. Merchant Marine, 1942-46. Recipient Outstanding Reporting Abroad award Chgo. Newspaper Guild, 1959; Best Bus. Reporting Abroad award E. W. Fairchild, 1963, 67; hon. mention, 1965; Bob Considine award, 1979; ICMA Journalism award, 1983 Mem. Soc. Profl. Journalists, Authors Guild. Clubs: Overseas Press (Reporting award 1963, 67) (N.Y.C.); Press (Chgo.). Roman Catholic. Home and Office: Apt 15201 7500 N Calle Sin Envidia Tucson AZ 85718-7375

VICKERS, GEORGE ROSS, non-profit organization executive, sociology educator; b. Evanston, Ill., Dec. 26, 1943; s. George Warren and Frances Louise (Ross) V.; m. Elizabeth Ann Levy, Jan. 26, 1979 (div. 1997). Student, Northwestern U., 1966-68; MA, Washington U., 1970, PhD, 1973. Staff sociologist Russell Sage Found., N.Y.C., 1973-75; prof. Bklyn. Coll. and the Grad. Ctr., CUNY, N.Y.C. and Bklyn., 1975-97; exec. dir. Washington Office of Latin Am., 1993—2001, also bd. dirs.; regional dir. for Latin Am. Open Society Inst., 2002—. Bd. dirs. Resist Found., Cambridge, Mass., Inst. for Ctrl. Am. Studies, N.Y.C., Hemisphere Initiatives, Cambridge. Author: The Formation of the New Left, 1975, Prologue to Sociology, 1977. Mem. presdl. del. to observe the elections in El Salvador, Pres. of the U.S., El Salvador, 1994; U.S. Spl. Ambassador to Guatamala, 2000. Mem. Am. Sociol. Assn., L.Am. Studies Assn. (chair com. on acad. freedom and human rights 2002--). Avocation: running. E-mail: gvickers@sorosny.org.

VICKERS, MARK STEPHEN, business educator, travel industry executive, sculptor, painter; b. Vallego, Calif., Sept. 11, 1957; s. John Frederick and Anna Ruth (Boschell) V. BA in Bus. Adminstrn., Azusa Pacific U., 1979; grad. studies, U. Bourgogne, Dijon, France, 1986-87. Dir. public relations Azusa Pacific div. Bus., 1977-78; copywriter Pennington, Inc., Fullerton, Calif., 1978; dir. communications Glendora (Calif.) C. of C., 1979; asst. mgr., dir. public relations Burbank (Calif.) C. of C., 1979-82, exec. dir., 1982-84; v.p. Astra Tours and Travel, Los Angeles, 1984-86; custom group cons. Marquis Tours, Vallejo, 1987—; bus. instr. St. Patrick's High Sch., 1987—; pres. US Sportsmarque, 1987—. Author: Selling Art on the Internet, 2000, Right-Brained Guide to a Left-Brained Industry, 2002; columnist, poet and contbg. editor Calif. Chamber Execs. Assn. Newsletter and Burbank Bus. Today mag. Coordinator Burbank Trade Fair Festival. Recipient Eagle Scout award Boy Scouts Am., 1971; Bus. award Bank of Am., 1975; Outstanding Young Man of Am. award U.S. Jaycees, 1982; Calif. State Senate Resolution award, 1984. Mem. Am. Chamber Execs. Assn., Calif. Chamber Execs. Assn., Los Angeles Public Interest Radio and TV Ednl. Soc. Clubs: Toastmasters (Burbank); San Fernando Valley Press (pres.).

VICKERS, MARY LOUISE, financial analyst; b. Cleve., June 28, 1948; d. Paul Orland and Margaret Corrine (Wolfe) V. AA, David N. Meyers Coll. (formerly Dyke Coll.), 1968, BSBA, 1986. Traffic coord. Sta. WDBN-Radio, Inc., Medina, Ohio, 1968-73; exec. sec. Newspaper Enterprise Assn., Cleve., 1974-76; adminstrv. sec. Eaton Corp., 1976-84, exec. sec., 1984-86, exec. asst., 1986—2000, analyst investor rels., 2001—. Mem. 150th ann. com. David N. Meyers Coll. Mem. Nat. Hemi Owners Assn., David N. Meyers Coll. Aumni Assn. (pres. 1998-99). Avocations: gardening, reading, hot rod automobiles. Home: 4343 N Miami Dr Parma OH 44134-6217 Office: Eaton Corp Eaton Ctr Cleveland OH 44114

VICKERS, NANCY J. academic administrator; BA, Mt. Holyoke Coll., 1967, LHD (hon.), 1999; MA, Yale U., 1971, PhD, 1976. Prof. French and Italian Dartmouth Coll., 1973-87; prof. French, Italian, and comparative literature U. Southern Calif., 1987-97, dean curriculum and instrn. Coll. Letters, Arts and Scis., 1994-97; pres. Bryn Mawr Coll., 1997—. Vis. prof. Harvard U., U. Pa., UCLA; vis. fellow Princeton U.; mem. bd. councillors Coll. Letters, Arts and Scis., U. So. Calif., 1997—; bd. dirs. Bryn Mawr Bank Corp; bd. governors of the Univ. of California Humanities Rsch. Institute; Council Dante Soc. of Am. Recipient Presidential Medal for Outstanding Leadership and Achievement, Dartmouth Coll., 1991 Office: Bryn Mawr Coll 101 N Merion Ave Bryn Mawr PA 19010-2899

VICKERS, ROGER SPENCER, physicist, environmental mapping director; b. Hitchin, Hertfordshire, Eng., Nov. 13, 1937; came to U.S., 1963, naturalized, 1974; s. John Hector and Corona (McCarthy) V.; m. Solvi Loken, May 18, 1968; children: Michelle, Jacqueline, Kevin. BSc with honors, Southampton U., Eng., 1959, PhD, 1963. Physicist Ill. Inst. Tech. Research Inst., Chgo., 1963-66; rsch. assoc. Stanford U., 1966-68; v.p. sci. and applications E.R.A., Inc., Houston, 1969-70; assoc. prof. elec. engrng. Colo. State U., 1970-73; dir. advanced radar program SRI Internat., Menlo Park, Calif., 1973-98; dir. Environ. Mapping-Can., Vancouver, B.C., 1998—, Internat. Radar Cons. Inc., Redwood City, Calif., 2000—. Cons. NSF. Mem. IEEE. Home: 171 Main St # 252 Los Altos CA 94022 E-mail: rvickers@em-canada.com.

VICKERS, STANLEY, biochemical pharmacologist; b. Blackpool, Eng., Sept. 27, 1939; came to U.S., 1962, naturalized, 1979; s. Norman Stanley and Hannah (Snape) V.; m. Florence Margaret Foster, Jan. 6, 1975. BSc external, London U., 1962; PhD, SUNY, Buffalo, 1967. Fellow U. Kans., Lawrence, 1966-69; sr. rsch. pharmacologist Merck & Co., West Point, Pa., 1969-71, rsch. fellow, 1971-81, sr. rsch. fellow, 1981-2001. Assoc. editor Current Drug Metabolism, 1999-2001; contbr. articles to profl. jours.; patentee in field. Mem. AAAS, Am. Assn. Pharm. Scis., Am. Soc. Pharmacology and Exptl. Therapeutics, Am. Chem. Soc., N.Y. Acad. Scis., Internat. Soc. for Study of Xenobiotics. Avocations: golf, skiing, health club activities.

VICKERY, ANN MORGAN, lawyer; b. Anderson, S.C., June 25, 1944; d. Joseph Harold and Doris (Rogers) Morgan; m. Raymond Ezekiel Vickery, Jr., June 23, 1979; children: Raymond Morgan, Philip Dickens. AB History, Mary Baldwin Coll., 1965; JD, Georgetown U., 1978. Bar: D.C. 1978. Elem. sch. tchr., Chesterfield County, Va., 1965-66; legal publs. specialist Nat. Archives and Record Svc., Washington, 1966-69; speech writing staff to Pres., rsch. asst., chief rschr., staff asst. The White House, 1969-74; summer clerk Graham & James, 1975; various positions Dept. Treasury, 1975-78; atty. Hogan & Hartson, LLP, 1978—. Health group dir. Hogan and Hartson, LLP, Washington, 1991—, exec. com., 1992-95, 96-99, Washington office mng. ptnr., 1999—; outside legal counsel Nat. Hospice and Palliative Care Orgn., 1982—(named Woman of the Yr. 1986); spkr. in field. Contbr. articles to profl. jours. Dir. Hospice No. Va., Arlington, 1987-93; trustee Nat. Hospice Found., 1996—. Mem. ABA, Am. Health Lawyers Assn., D.C. Bar, Health on Wednesday, Phi Alpha Theta. Office: Hogan & Hartson LLP Columbia Square 555 13th St NW Ste 800E Washington DC 20004-1161

VICKERY, BYRDEAN EYVONNE HUGHES (MRS. CHARLES EVERETT VICKERY JR.), retired library services administrator; b. Apr. 18, 1928; d. Roy Franklin and Margaret Cordelia (Wood) Hughes; m. Charles Everett Vickery, Jr., Nov. 5, 1948; 1 child, Camille. Student, Flat River (Mo.) Jr. Coll., 1946-48; BS in Edn., S.E. Mo. State Coll., 1954; MLS, U. Wash., 1964; postgrad., Wash. State U., 1969-70. Tchr. Ironton (Mo.) Pub. Schs., 1948-56; elem. tchr. Pasco (Wash.) Sch. Dist. 1, 1956-61, jr. high sch. libr., 1961-68, coord. librs., 1968-69; asst. libr. Columbia Basin Cmty. Coll., Pasco, 1969-70; head libr., dir. Instructional Resources Ctr., 1970-78, dir. libr. svcs., 1979-87, assoc. dean libr. svcs., 1987-90, ret., 1990; owner Vickery Search & Research, 1990-99. Chmn. S.E. Wash. Libr. Svc. Area, 1977-78, 88-90; bd. dirs. Pasco-Kennewick Cmty. Concerts, 1977-88, pres., 1980-81, 87-88, Pasco-Kennewick Cmty. Concerts, treas., 1991-99; bd. dirs. Mid-Columbia Symphony Orch., 1983-89; trustee Wash. Commn. Humanities, 1982-85; bd. mem. Arts Coun. Mid-Columbia Region, 1991-93. Author, editor: Library and Research Skills Curriculum Guides for the Pasco School District, 1967; author (with Jean Thompson), also editor Learning Resources Handbook for Teachers, 1969. Recipient Woman of Achievement award Pasco Bus. and Profl. Women's Club, 1976. Mem. ALA, AAUW (2d v.p. 1966-68, corr. sec. 1969), Wash. Dept. Audio-Visual Instrn., Wash. Libr. Assn., Am. Assn. Higher Edn., Wash. Assn. Higher Edn., Wash. State Assn. Sch. Librs. (state conf. chmn. 1971-72), Tri-Cities Librs. Assn., Wash. Libr. Media Assn. (community coll. levels chmn. 1986-87), Am. Assn. Rsch. Libr., Soroptimist Internat. Assn. (rec. sec. Pasco-Kennewick chpt. 1971-72, treas. 1973-74, pres. 1978-80, v.p. 1989-90, treas. 1991, found. & awards chmn. 1995-96), Columbia Basin Coll. Adminstrs. Assn. (sec.-treas. 1973-74), Pacific N.W. Assn. Ch. Libr., Women in communications, Pasco Bus. and Profl. Women's Club, PEO-HJ (corr. sec. 2002-), Gen. Fedn. Women's Clubs of Mo., Beta Sigma Phi, Delta Kappa Gamma, Phi Delta Kappa (sec. 1981-82, Outstanding Educator award 1983).

VICKERY, EDWARD DOWNTAIN, lawyer; b. Fort Worth, Tex., May 1, 1922; s. Charles Richard and Margaret May Vickery; children: Anne Vickery Stevenson, E.D. Jr. AS, North Tex. Agrl. Coll., 1941; BA, U. Tex., 1947, JD with honors, 1948. Bar: Tex. 1948, U.S. Dist. Ct. (so. dist.) Tex. 1948, U.S. Ct. Appeals (5th cir.) 1950, Bd. Immagration Appeals 1952, U.S. Supreme Ct. 1953. From assoc. to sr. ptnr. Royston, Rayzor, Vickery & Williams, Houston, 1948-55, sr. ptnr., 1955-98, of counsel, 1999—. Chmn. bd. dirs. First Nat. Bank Bellaire, Tex. Coastal Bank, Katy Bank, Tradition Bank, Houston. Deacon First Presbyn. Ch., Houston, 1958-64, elder 1965-94; mem. Brazos Presbyn. Ch., 1972-77, chmn. 1976-77; bd. trustees Austin (Tex.) Presbyn. Theol. Sem., 1976-85, 86-95, v. chmn. 1978-83, chmn. 1983-85, 89-95; bd. trustees Tex. Presbyn. Found. 1978-85. Fellow Am. Coll. Trial Lawyers, Internat. Acad. Trial Lawyers (Am. chpt.); mem. Internat. Assn. Ins. Counsel, Am. Judicature Soc., Maritime Law Assn. U.S. (exec. com. 1977-80), Hist. Soc. Supreme Ct. U.S., Tex. Assn. Def. Counsel (bd. dirs. 1965-67), Tex. Bar Found. (Houston chpt.), Tulane Admiralty Law Inst. (program, planning com., adv. bd., 1965-92), Propellor Club U.S. (nat. pres. 1965-66, 66-67, nat. first v.p. 1964-65, nat. exec. com. 1961-85, port of Houston pres. 1961-62), U. Tex. Littlefield Soc., Chancellor's Coun., T Assn., Longhorn Found., Law Sch. Found., Mariners Club, Houston Club, Lakeside Country Club. Home: 610 Wellesley Dr Houston TX 77024-5507 Office: Royston Rayzor Vickery & Williams LLP 1001 McKinney Ste 1100 Houston TX 77002-6418 E-mail: ed.vickery@roystonlaw.com.

VICKERY, EUGENE BENTON, JR. lawyer; b. New Orleans, Nov. 23, 1936; s. Eugene Benton and Esther (Cleveland) V.; m. Anne Saunders Porteous, Aug. 25, 1961; children: Eugene Benton III, Saunders P., Ninette C., William A. AB, Williams Coll., 1962; JD, Loyola U., New Orleans, 1967. Bar: La. 1967, U.S. Dist. Ct. (ea. and we. dists.) La. 1967, U.S. Ct. Appeals (5th cir.) 1967. Supr. computer sys., sr. tech. programmer Shell Oil Co., New Orleans Data Ctr., 1962-67; jr. ptnr. Porteous, Toledano, Hainkel & Johnson, New Orleans, 1968-73; ptnr. Sutterfield & Vickery, 1974-82; sole practice, 1982—. Procurator-adv. Met. Tribunal for Archdiocese of New Orleans. Trustee St. George's Epis. Sch., 1975-83, chmn., 1978-79; mem. La. Landmarks Soc., Met. Crime Commn., Uptown Neighborhood Improvement Awsn., New Orleans and River Region C. of C. Served with U.S., 1956-59. Mem. ABA, La. Bar Assn., New Orleans Bar Assn., La. Assn. Def. Counsel, New Orleans Assn. Def. Counsel, Def. Rsch. Inst., Am. Judicature Soc., Am. Arbitration Assn. (panel of arbitrators 1968—), Notaries Assn. New Orleans, Boston Club, La. Club, Williams Club (N.Y.C.), Delta Phi. Republican. Roman Catholic. Home and Office: 5526 Chestnut St New Orleans LA 70115-3109 E-mail: genevickery@alumm.williams.edu.

VICKERY, JON LIVINGSTONE, neurologist; b. Freeport, Ill., May 30, 1955; s. Eugene Livingstone and Millie Margaret (Cox) V.; m. Diane Antoinetti; children: Daniel Scott, John Michael. BA, Northwestern U., 1976; MD, U. Ill., Chgo., 1980. Diplomate Nat. Bd. Med. Examiners. Resident in neurology U. Va., Charlottesville, 1980-84; staff neurologist Pinnacle Health

Sys., Harrisburg, Pa., 1984—; ptnr. Pa. Neurol. Assocs., Lemoyne, 1984—; assoc. prof. of medicine Hershey Med. Ctr., Pa. State U., 1984-99; chief of medicine Holy Spirit Hosp., Camp Hill, Pa., 1992-95. Asst. coach Dickinson Coll. Fencing Team. Fellow Am. Acad. Neurology; mem. AMA, Dauphin County Med. soc. (del. 1985—), U.S. Fencing Coaches Assn., U.S. Fencing Assn., U.S. Fencing Coaches Assn. (cert. moniteur de armes), Am. Orchid Soc. (cert. judge, mem. conservation com, 1989-91), Beaufort Hunt Club (bd. dirs.), Masons, Shriners. Avocations: fencing, photography, raising orchids, theater. Office: Pa Neurol Assocs 108 Lowther St Lemoyne PA 17043-2012

VICKERY, RAYMOND EZEKIEL, JR. international business consultant, lawyer; b. Brookhaven, Miss., Apr. 30, 1942; s. Raymond Ezekiel and Clarene Helen (Dickens) V.; m. Raymond Clair Brown, Dec. 23, 1967 (div. June 1976); m. Ann Morgan, June 25, 1979; children: Raymond Morgan, Philip Dickens. AB, Duke U., 1964; postgrad., U. Sri Lanka, 1964-65; LLB, Harvard U., 1968. Assoc. Hogan & Hartson, Washington, 1968-77, ptnr. McLean, Va., 1985-93, Johnson & Vickery, Vienna, 1977-81, Reed Smith Shaw & McClay, McLean, 1981-85; asst. sec. for trade devel. U.S. Dept. Commerce, Washington, 1993-97; pvt. practice, 1997—2000; of counsel Kile, Goekjian, Lerner & Reed, 1999—. Adj. prof. internat. transactions George Mason U., Fairfax, Va., 1997—. Contbr. articles to profl. jours. Del. Va. Gen. Assembly, Richmond, 1974-80; mem. Dem. Com., Fairfax County, Va., 1971-93; Dem. nominee for Congress, Va., 1992; mem. State Ctrl. Com., Va., 1993; mem. Libr. Bd., Fairfax County, 1972-74. Fulbright scholar, 1964. Mem. ABA, Va. Bar Assn., D.C. Bar Assn., City Club. Phi Beta Kappa, Omicron Delta Kappa. Baptist. Avocations: fishing, horseback riding. Home: 2733 Willow Dr Vienna VA 22181-5310 Office: 1101 Pennsylvania Ave NW Washington DC 20004-2514

VICKERY, ROBERT BRUCE, oil industry executive, consultant; b. Shreveport, La., Aug. 25, 1938; s. Wilbur Claude and Clara Louise (Powell) V.; m. Margaret Lynn Gray, April 6, 1961; children: Joy Lynn, Andrew Gray, William Charles. Degree in Petroleum Engring., Colo. Sch. Mines, 1962; degree in Arctic Engring., U. Alaska, 1974. Petroleum engr. Pan Am. Petroleum Corp., Worland, Wyo., 1962-64; v.p. ops. Vickery Drilling Co., Inc., Evansville, Ind., 1964-73; mgr. drilling BP Alaska, Inc., Sohio-BP, Sohio Petroleum Corp., Anchorage, 1973-80; chmn. Artic Alaska Drilling Co., Inc., 1980-85; pres. Walker Energy Ptnrs., Houston, 1986-87, Refuge Exploration, Inc., Houston, 1988-99, Owensboro, Ky., 1988-99; ptnr. Presco Western LLC, Denver, 1998—. Author: World Oil, 1982. Pres. Boys Club of Alaska, 1978-80; trustee Boys Clubs Am., 1980-87; Alaska fin. chmn. Re-election of Pres. Reagan Com., 1984. Recipient Alaska Engr. of the Year award SPE of AIME, 1982. Mem. Soc. Petroleum Engrs., Ky. Oil and Gas Assn. (dir. 1993-2000), Ill. Oil and Gas Assn. (dir. 1993-2000). Office: Presco Western LLC 1775 Sherman St Ste 2950 Denver CO 80203-4345 E-mail: vicvickery@cs.com.

VICKERY, WILLIAM, arts administrator; B, M, Juilliard Sch.; studies with the late Roger Smith. Dir. music program NEA, Washington, 1987-89; pres., mng. dir. The St. Paul Chamber Orch., 1989—93; exec. dir. Ark. Symphony Orch., Little Rock. Asst. dean Aspen Music Sch.; orch. mgr. Juilliard Sch., guest lectr.; mem. Seaver/NEA Condr.'s Award panel. Performances with the Met. Opera Orch., the Greenwich (Conn.) Philharm., and in N.Y.C. Former exec. v.p. Aspen Music Festival; mem. adv. com. Minn. Chorale. Recipient Yamaha Internat. award. Office: Ark Symphony Orch 2417 N Tyler St Little Rock AR 72207-3740*

VICKREY, HERTA MILLER, microbiologist; b. San Gregorio, Calif. d. John George and Hertha Lucy Miller; m. William David Vickrey; children: Ellean H., Carlene L. Smith, Corrine A. Pochop, Arlene A.; m. Robert James Fitzgibbon, Dec. 28, 1979. BA, San Jose State U., 1957; MA, U. Calif., Berkeley, 1963, PhD in Bacteriology and Immunology, 1970. Cert. immunologist, pub. health microbiologist, clin. lab. scientist. Pub. health microbiologist Viral & Rickettsial Diseases Lab., Calif. State Dept. Pub. Health, Berkeley, 1958-60, 61-62, 1964; postgrad. rsch. bacteriologist dept. bacteriology U. Calif., 1963-64; bacteriologist Children's Hosp. Med. Ctr. No. Calif., Oakland, 1958-70; asst. prof. U. Victoria, B.C., Can., 1970-72; rsch. assoc. rsch. dept. Wayne County Gen. Hosp., Wayne, Mich., 1972-83; lab. supr. med. rsch. and edn. U. Mich., Ann Arbor, 1977-83; pub. health lab. dir. Shasta County Pub. Health Svcs., Redding, Calif., 1983-84; sr. pub. health microbiologist Tulare County Pub. Health Lab., Tulare, 1984—, tech. supr. Visalia, 1992-93; med. technologist Hillman Health Clin. Lab., Tulare, 1994-96, clin. lab. scientist, 1996—. Vis. scientist MIT, Cambridge, 1982; organizer, lectr. mycology workshop Tulare County Health Dept. Lab., Visalia, 1988; USPHS trainee U. Calif., Berkeley, 1965, 66. Author: Isolation and Identification of Mycotic Agents, 1987-88; contbr. articles to profl. jours. Fundraiser Battered Women's Shelter, Redding, 1983, Real Opportunities for Youth, Visalia, 1985, 86, Open Gate Ministries, Dinuba, Visalia, 1987-94, 97-99. Fellow NIH, 1966-69, Dr. E.E. Dowdle rsch. fellow, U. Calif., 1969-70; grantee U. Victoria, 1970-72, Med. Rsch. and Edn. and Med. Adminstrn., U. Mich., 1973-83. Mem. No. Calif. Assn. Pub. Health Microbiologists, Calif. Scholarship Soc., Am. Soc. Clin. Pathologists (assoc.), Phi Beta Kappa, Delta Omega, Phi Kappa Phi, Beta Beta Beta. Avocations: biking, hiking, swimming. Home: 3505 W Campus Dr Apt 5 Visalia CA 93277-1869 Office: Tulare County Pub Health Lab 1062 S K St Tulare CA 93274-6421

VICKREY, ROBERT FISCHER, newspaper and broadcasting executive; b. Mendota, Ill., May 21, 1944; s. Gail Sabin and Marie Augusta (Fischer) V.; m. Barbara Ann Harmon, May 30, 1970; 1 son, Robert James. Student, Ill. Valley Community Coll., 1963-64, Dana Coll., 1964. Account exec. Daily News Tribune, La Salle, Ill., 1968-71, La Salle County Broadcasting Corp., La Salle, 1971-72, sales mgr., 1972-84, v.p., 1984—, Daily News-Tribune, 1985—, Miller Group Media, 1992—. Bd. dirs. Tri-County Fin. Group, 1st State Bank-Mendota Ill.; founder, v.p. No. Ill. Indsl. Devel. Corp., 1985-86; founder, pres. Ill. Econ. Devel. Coun., 1997—. Mem. pub. relations com. Starved Rock Area coun. Boy Scouts Am., 1972—76; pres. Ill. Econ. Devel. Coun., 1999—; chmn. LaSalle County Rep. Ctrl. Com.; dep. state ctrl. committeeman Ill. Rep. Party; bd. dirs. United Way of Ill. Valley, 1973—75, mem. pub. rels. com., 1980—82; bd. dirs. Ill. Gaming Bd., 1992—, Canal Corridor Assn., 1996—; chmn. Ill. Gaming Bd., 1999—2000; bd. trustees U. Ill., 2001—. Served with U.S. Army, 1966—68. Decorated Army Commendation medal. Mem. Nat. Assn. Broadcasters, Ill. Valley Area C. of C. (past pres.), Wilde Waters YAcht Club (Ottawa, Ill.), Governor's Club (Ill.), Elks, AMVETS (life). Home: 902 16th St Peru IL 61354-1821 Office: 426 2nd St La Salle IL 61301-2334

VICTOR, JAY, retired dermatologist; b. Detroit, Dec. 4, 1935; s. Ben and Pauline (Meisel) Victor; m. Elana S. Lepler, Mar. 1965 (div. Aug. 1977); children: Pamela C., Daryl B.; m. Marianne Cook, Sept. 4, 1978; children: Jonah A., Lauren. BA, U. Mich., 1958, MD, 1962. Diplomate Am. Bd. Dermatology. Intern Henry Ford Hosp., Detroit, 1962-63, resident in dermatology, 1963-66; asst. prof. dermatology Wayne State U. Sch. of Medicine, 1968—; pvt. practice in dermatology Allen Park, 1966—2001; ret., 2001. Mem. active staff Oakwood Hosp., Dearborn, Mich., 1967—, emeritus staff, Mich.; courtesy staff Detroit Med. Ctr., 1967—; cons. Heritage Hosp., Taylor, Mich., 1980—. Fellow: Am. Acad. Dermatology; mem.: AMA, Mich. Dermatology Soc., Wayne County Med. Soc., Mich. State Med. Soc. (del. 1980—). Jewish. Avocations: skiing, running, bicycling, sports.

VICTOR, JEFFREY SPENCER, sociology educator; b. N.Y.C., Oct. 1, 1941; s. Bert Lawrence and May Victor; m. Michele Marie Honoré, July 17, 1965; 1 child, Mathieu. BS in Social Studies Edn., SUNY, Oneonta, 1963; postgrad., U. Md., 1963-65; MS in Sociology and Psychology, SUNY, Buffalo, 1969, PhD in Sociology, 1974. Prof. sociology Jamestown (N.Y.) C.C., 1965—. Mem. adv. bd. False Memory Syndrome Found., Phila., 1992—. Author: Human Sexuality, 1980, Satanic Panic, 1993; also articles. Recipient Chancellor's award for teaching excellence SUNY, 1988, H.L. Mencken Book Awd., 1994. Mem. Internat. Soc. for Contemporary Legend Rsch. Unitarian Universalist. Home: 30 Hillcrest Ave Jamestown NY 14701-6118 Office: Jamestown CC 525 Falconer St Jamestown NY 14701-1920 E-mail: JeffVictor@mail.sunyjcc.edu.

VICTOR, LORRAINE CARP;, critical care nurse; b. Duluth, Minn., June 14, 1953; d. George E. and Phyllis M. (Pierce) Drimel; m. Robert G. Victor BA in Nursing, Coll. St. Scholastica, 1975; MS in Nursing, U. Minn., 1984; postgrad., Coll. St. Catherine. Cert. regional trainer for neonatal resuscitation program, neonatal clin. nurse; cert. critical care clin. nurse specialist. Staff nurse St. Mary's Hosp., Rochester, Minn., 1975-79, 80-81, U. Wis. Hosp., Madison, 1979-80, U. Minn. Hosps., Mpls., 1981-84, 85-86; clin. instr. neonatal ICU, Children's Hosp., St. Paul, 1984-86; clin. nurse specialist neonatal ICU, Orlando (Fla.) Regional Med. Ctr., 1986-88, Children's Hosp., St. Paul, 1988—2001; neonatal nurse practitioner Children's Hosp. , 2001—. Mem. AACN (Critical Care Nurse of Yr. award Greater Twin Cities chpt. 1992, cert. NICU clin. nurse specialist, cert. neonatal nurse practitioner), Nat. Cert. Corp. (cert. in neonatal intensive care nursing), Nat. Assn. Neonatal Nurses, Sigma Theta Tau. Office: Children's Hosps & Clinics St Paul Birth Ctr 345 Smith Ave N Saint Paul MN 55102-2369

VICTOR, MICHAEL GARY, lawyer, physician; b. Detroit, Sept. 20, 1945; s. Simon H. and Helen (Litsky) V.; children: Elise Nicole, Sara Lisabeth. Bar: Ill. 1980, U.S. Dist. Ct. (no. dist.) Ill. 1980, U.S. Ct. Appeals (7th cir.) 1981; diplomate Am. Bd. Legal Medicine. Pres. Advocate Adv. Assocs., Chgo., 1982-95; asst. prof. medicine Northwestern U. Med. Sch., 1982—; pvt. practice law Barrington, Ill., 1982—; lectr. U. Ill., Chgo., 1999—. Dir. emergency medicine Loretto Hosp., Chgo., 1980-85, chief. sect. of emergency medicine St. Josephs Hosp., Chgo., 1985-87; v.p. Med. Emergency Svcs. Assocs., Buffalo Grove, Ill., 1989; v.p. MESA Mgmt. Corp.; of counsel Bollinger, Ruberry & Garvey, Chgo. Author: Informed Consent, 1980; Brain Death, 1980; (with others) Due Process for Physicians, 1984, A Physicians Guide to the Illinios Living Will Act, The Choice is Ours!, 1989. Recipient Service awards Am. Coll. Emergency Medicine, 1973-83. Fellow Am. Coll. Legal Medicine (bd. govs. 1996-97, alt. del. to AMA House of Dels. 1996-97), Chgo. Acad. Legal Medicine; mem. Am. Coll. Emergency Physicians (pres. Ill. chpt. 1980, med.-legal-ins. council 1980-81, 83-84), ABA, Ill. State Bar Assn., Am. Soc. Law and Medicine, Chgo. Bar Assn. (med.-legal council 1981-83), AMA, Ill. State Med. Soc. (med.-legal council 1980-86, 88), Chgo. Med. Soc. Jewish. Home and Office: 153 Aberdour Ln Palatine IL 60067-8001 E-mail: mgv@merle.acns.nwu.edu.

VICTOR, RICHARD STEVEN, lawyer; b. Detroit, Aug. 3, 1949; s. Simon H. and Helen (Litsky) V.; m. Denise L. Berman, Nov. 26, 1978; children: Daniel, Ronald, Sandra. Bar: Mich. 1975, U.S. Dist. Ct. (ea. dist.) Mich. 1975. Assoc. Law Offices of Albert Best, Detroit, 1975; ptnr. Best & Victor, Oak Park, Mich., 1976-80; sole practice, 1981-85; ptnr. Law Offices of Victor, Robbins and Bassett and predecessor firms, Birmingham, Mich., 1986-93, Victor and Robbins and predecessor firms, Birmingham, 1993-98, Bloomfield Hills, Mich., 1998-2000; pvt. practice Richard S. Victor, PLLC, 2000—. Instr. in family law Oakland U., Rochester, Mich., 1976—; bd. dirs. Agy. for Jewish Edn., 1990; legal advisor family law Sta. Ask the Lawyer WXYT radio. Author: (column) Legally Speaking, Stepfamily Bull., 1984—; author, genera editor: Michigan Practitioners Series: Family Law and Practice, 1997; tech. advisor Whose Mother Am I? Aaron Spelling Prodns./ABC Movies; bd. editors Mich. Lawyers Weekly newspaper, 2000. Mem. community adv. bd. Woodland Hills Med. Ctr., 1981—; v.p. Bloomfield (Mich.) Sq. Homeowners Assn., 1985—, pres. 1988; chmn. legis. com. Birmingham Schs. PTA, 1987—. Recipient Award of Meritorious Svc. to the Chldren of Am., Nat. Coun. of Juvenile and Family Ct. Judges, 1993, Child Advocate of Yr. award Chld Abuse and Neglect Coun., 1994, Disting. Svc. award Oakland County Bar Assn., 1994, Lifetime Achievement award State Bar Mich., 1999, Disting. Alumni Award Nat. Alumni Assn. of Mich. State U.-Detroit Coll. of Law, 2000. Fellow Mich. State Bar Found., Am. Acad. Matrimonial Lawyers (bd. mgrs. Mich. chpt. 1999—, com. chair); mem. ABA (expert lectr. sem. 1988, exec. com. on custody 1989—), Mich. Bar Assn. (treas. family law sect. 1987-88, sec. 1988-89, chmn. continuing legal edn. com. family law sect., 1986-90, corr. sec. 1988-89, chmn. elect 1989-90, chmn. family law sect. 1990-91, Appreciation award from family law sect. 1987-89, Lifetime Achievement award family law sect. 1999, co-founder SMILE), Oakland County Bar Assn. (chmn. lawyer's admission com. 1981, unauthorized practice of law 1982, oldtimer's night 1984-85, speakers bur. 1985), Family Law Coun. (chmn. legis. com.), Grandparent Rights Orgn. (founder, exec. dir. 1984—, newsletter editor), B'nai B'rith Barristers. Jewish. Avocation: playing piano. Office: Law Offices of Richard S Victor PLLC 100 W Long Lake Rd Ste 250 Bloomfield Hills MI 48304-2721 E-mail: rsvlaw@aol.com.

VICTOR, ROBERT EUGENE, real estate corporation executive, lawyer; b. N.Y.C., Dec. 17, 1929; s. Louis and Rebecca (Teitelbaum) V.; m. Dorothy Saffir, Oct. 14, 1951; children— Priscilla Saffir Victor Faubel, Pandora Saffir. LL.B., St. John's U., 1953, JD, 1968. Bar: N.Y. bar 1953, Calif. bar 1965. With firm Szold and Brandwen, N.Y.C., 1953-54; atty. Dept. Army, Phila., 1955-56; with Hughes Aircraft Co., Culver City, Calif., 1956-62; v.p., gen. counsel Packard Bell Electronics Corp., Los Angeles, 1962-70; sr. v.p., gen. counsel Cordon Internat. Corp., 1970-78; also dir.; gen. counsel Am. Harp Soc., 1969-85; pres. Vanowen Realty Corp., 1978-93, also dir. Mem. Los Angeles County Bar Assn. Clubs: Masons. Office: 722 Walden Dr Beverly Hills CA 90210-3125

VICTOR, RONALD JOSEPH, JR. banking professional; b. Sewickley, Pa., Oct. 30, 1964; s. Ronald Joseph Sr. and Nancy Carol (Kniess) V. BSBA, Robert Morris Coll., Pitts., 1987. Remittance processing operator Mellon Bank, N.A., Pitts., 1983-84, mini-computer operator, 1984-85, sr. mini-computer operator, 1985-87, systems specialist, 1987-92, conversion coord., 1992-93, mgr. data capture unit of wholesale lockbox, 1993-94, asst. gen. mgr. remittance processing, 1994-95; intern Profl. Mgmt. Svcs., Carnegie, Pa., 1985-86; asst. v.p., product design mgr. PNC Bank, Pitts., 1995-98; v.p., sr. product mgr. Mellon Bank, 1998-99, v.p., product line mgr., 1999—. Mem. Assn. for Info. and Image Mgmt., Assn. for Work Process Improvement, Banctec Sys. User Assn. (pres. bd. dirs.), Assn. Fin. Profls., Banctel Sys. User Assn. Democrat. Roman Catholic. Avocations: hockey, softball, boating, sports memorabilia. Home: 21 Downs Dr Coraopolis PA 15108-3607 Office: Mellon Bank 3 Mellon Bank Ctr # 153-3415 Pittsburgh PA 15259-0001 E-mail: VIC0625@aol.com.

VICTOR, WILLIAM WEIR, retired telephone company executive, consultant; b. Marshall, Ill., Apr. 16, 1924; s. Sturges L. and Esther (Weir) V.; m. Patricia Kelly, Sept. 7, 1946; children: William K., Jill Victor Buelsing, D. Gregory. Student, U. Okla., 1943-44; EE, U. Cin., 1948, U. Ill., 1949. Various positions Cin. Bell Telephone, Ohio, 1947-69, v.p., 1972-85, sr. v.p., 1986-87; v.p. 195 Corp., N.Y., 1969-72. Bd. dirs. Skidmore Sales and Distbn. Co. Trustee Goodwill Industries, Cin., 1973-91, WCET Ednl. TV Found., Cin., 1972-86, Bethesda Hosp., Cin., 1978, Herman Schneider Found., Cin., 1983, Armstrong Chapel Found., 1992; trustee, v.p. Millcreek Valley Conservancy Dist., 1990-99. Sgt. USAR, 1943-45, ETO; lt. col. USAR, ret. Mem. IEEE, Engring. Soc. Cin., Cin. Country Club. Home: 5440 Windridge Ct Cincinnati OH 45243-2967 E-mail: wwvic@aol.com.

VICTORICA, BENJAMIN EDUARDO, pediatrician, educator; b. Mendoza, Argentina, June 9, 1936; came to U.S., 1964; s. Benjamin and Georgina (Roman) V.; m. Blanca Elsa Caballero, June 1963; children: Maria Fernanda, Benjamin Eduardo, Monica. BS, Nat. Coll. A. Alvarez, 1952; MD, U. Cuyo Med. Sch., 1962. Diplomate Am. Bd. Pediatrics, Am. Bd. Pediatric Cardiology. Intern St. Benedict's Hosp., Ogden, Utah, 1963-64; resident in pediatrics U. Fla. Coll. Medicine, Gainesville, 1964-66, chief resident in pediatrics, 1966, instr., spl. trainee divsn. cardiology dept. pediatrics, 1967-70, asst. prof. pediatrics, 1970-74, assoc. to profl. pediatrics, 1974-90, Va. Root Sutherland prof. of pediatric cardiology, 1991—. Cons. Divsn. Children's Med. Svcs., Fla., 1971—; med. dir. CV tech. U. Fla., 1976-85; med. dir. heart sta. Shands Hosp., Gainesville, 1977-94, med. dir. cardiac catheter lab., 1994-99. Author: Heart Disease in Children, 1977, 84, Problems in Critical Care, 1987, Diagnostic in Therapeutic Cardiac Care, 1989; editor: Pediatric Cardiology: A Problem Oriented Approach, 1993. Fellow Am. Acad. Pediatrics, Am. Coll. Cardiology. Republican. Roman Catholic. Avocations: travel, golf. Office: U Fla Coll Medicine Gainesville FL 32610 E-mail: bvictorica@aol.com.

VICTORIO, LORA JANE, newswriter, producer; b. Panorama City, Calif., May 16, 1979; d. Villamor and Leticia V. BA in Journalism, Pepperdine U., 2001. Writer Ultimate TV, Encino, Calif., 1998-99; web designer Pepperdine U., Malibu, 1998-2001; writer, prodr. ABC Network NewsOne, L.A., 1999—2002; prodr. Network News Svc., 2001—; asst. budget editor City News Svc., 2002—. Editor Graphic newspaper, 2001 (best layout and design award), Currents Mag., 2001. Mem. Soc. Profl. Journalists, Evang. Press Assn., Asian-Am. Journalists, Golden Key. Avocations: reading, writing, painting, volleyball. Fax.

VICTORSON, MICHAEL BRUCE, lawyer; b. Fairmont, W.Va., July 13, 1954; s. Morton Jerome and Deborah (Jacobson) V.; m. Janet Harris, Mar. 8, 1981; children: David Solomon, Sara Lorraine. BA, W.Va. U., 1976, JD, 1979. Bar: W.Va. 1979, U.S. Dist. Ct. (so. and no. dists.) W.Va. 1979, U.S. Dist. Ct. (ea. dist.) Ky. 1986, U.S. Ct. Appeals (4th cir.) 1980, U.S. Supreme Ct., 1992. Assoc. Love, Wise, Robinson and Woodroe, Charleston, W.Va., 1979-83, Robinson & McElwee LLP, Charleston, 1983-84, ptnr., 1985-99; mem. Jackson Kelly PLLC, 1999—. Spkr. in field. Contbr. articles to profl. jours. Chmn. appeal bd. U.S. Selective Svc. System, So. Dist. W.Va., Charleston, 1983—; lawyers' chmn. United Way Kanawha Valley, Charleston, 1988-92, chmn. profl. divsn., 1992-93, admissions com., 1990-92; treas., bd. dirs. Med. Eye Bank W.Va., Charleston, 1989—, treas., 2000—; bd. dirs. Sunrise Collectors Club, 2002—; trustee B'nai Jacob Synagogue, 1992-94, v.p. 1997-2001, pres. 2001-; trustee Federated Jewish Charities of Charleston, Inc., 1998—, vis. com. W.Va. U. Coll. Law, 1996-2000. Mem. ABA, Internat. Assn. Jewish Lawyers and Jurists, Am. Law Firm Assn. (products liability steering com., bd. dirs. 1998-99), W.Va. Bar Assn., W.Va. State Bar Assn., Kanawha County Bar Assn., Def. Rsch. Inst., Def. Trial Counsel W.Va. (charter, bd. govs. 1992-98), Order of Coif, Phi Beta Kappa, Phi Delta Phi, Phi Kappa Phi, Pi Sigma Alpha. Office: Jackson Kelly PLLC PO Box 553 Charleston WV 25322-0553 E-mail: mvictorson@jacksonkelly.com.

VICTORY, JEFFREY PAUL, state supreme court justice; b. Shreveport, La., Jan. 29, 1946; s. Thomas Edward and Esther (Horton) V.; m. Nancy Clark Victory, Jan. 20, 1973; children: Paul Bradford, William Peter, Christopher Thomas, Mary Katherine. BA in History and Govt., Centenary Coll., 1967; JD, Tulane U., 1971. Bar: La. 1971. Ptnr. Tucker, Jeter, Jackson & Victory, Shreveport, 1971-82; dist. ct. judge 1st Jud. Dist. Ct., 1982-90; appellate judge 2d Circuit Ct. of Appeal, 1991-95; assoc. justice Supreme Ct. La., 1995—. Bd. dirs. CODAC Drug Abuse, Shreveport; mem. La. Sentencing Commn. La. NG, 1969-75. Mem. ABA, Shreveport Bar Assn., La. Bar Assn. Republican. Baptist. Avocations: tennis, motorcycles, classic cars. Office: Supreme Ct 301 Loyola Ave New Orleans LA 70112-1814*

VICTORY, NANCY, federal agency administrator; BA, Princeton U.; JD, Georgetown U. Ptnr. Wiley, Rein & Fielding, Washington; asst. sec. for comm. and info. Dept. Commerce, 2001—, adminstr. Nat. Telecom. and Info. Adminstrn., 2001—. Office: Dept Commerce Nat Telecom and Info Adminstrn 14th & Constitution Ave NW Washington DC 20230*

VIDA, DIANE, high school administrator; b. Chgo. d. Michael Paul and Mary Vida. BA, Western Ill. U., Macomb; MA, Roosevelt U., Chgo.; EdD, Drake U. Tchr. English Grant Cmty. Sch. Dist. 124, Fox Lake, Ill., 1978-85, dir. humanities, adminstr., 1985—, tchr. sci., 1989-90, curriculum coord., 1990-96, gifted coord., 1990—. Bd. mem. Lake County Gifted Adv. Coun., 2000—. Recipient Those Who Excel award ISBE, Springfield, Ill., 1994-95, Women in Achievement award YMCA Lake County, Ill., 1995; named Educator of the Month, Coca Cola, Waukegan, Ill., 1994-95. Mem. Nat. Coun. Tchrs. of English, Ill. Assn. Tchrs. of English, Ill. Prins. Assn., Lake County Bus. and Profl. Women, Lake County Curriculum Resource Coun. (exec. bd. 1996—). Office: Grant Cmty H S Dist 124 285 E Grand Ave Fox Lake IL 60020-1634

VIDA, STEPHEN ROBERT, environmental engineer; b. N.Y.C., Feb. 13, 1951; s. Stephen Robert and Anna (Leszkovics) V.; m. Louisa Kramer, June 29, 1974; children: Robert Marc, Kristine Michelle. B of Engring., Manhattan Coll., 1973, M of Environ. Engring., 1975; MBA, NYU, 1984. Registered profl. engr. Environ. engr. Havens and Emerson, Saddle Brook, N.J., 1973-75, U.S. EPA, N.Y.C., 1975-81; exec. dir. Two Bridges Sewerage Authority, Lincoln Park, N.J., 1981-82; cons. Coopers and Lybrand, N.Y.C., 1982-87; mgr. Ernst and Young, 1987-91; environ. engr. U.S. EPA, 1991—. Commr., bd. dirs. Syosset (N.Y.) Soccer Club, 1988-97; boys select program dir. L.I. Jr. Soccer League, 1998-2001; boys state soccer program adminstr. Eastern N.Y. Youth Soccer Assn., 2001—. Recipient fellowship U.S. EPA, 1973. Mem. NSPE (advisor scholarship com. Nassau County 1975-82, N.Y. state level 1990-91), Tau Beta Pi, Chi Epsilon. Home: 19 Lilac Dr Syosset NY 11791-2814 E-mail: vida.stephen@epa.gov.

VIDAILLET, HUMBERTO J., JR. physician, researcher; b. Santiago, Cuba, Sept. 24, 1954; came to U.S., 1968; s. Humberto J. and Caridad Vidaillet; m. Debbie Vidaillet, June 6, 1981; children: Kelsey, Daniel, Corbin. MD, U. Okla., 1981. Resident in internal medicine Mayo Clinic, Rochester, Minn., 1981-84; tng. in cardiology/electrophysiology Duke U. Med. Ctr., Durham, N.C., 1984-87; dir. cardiac electrophysiology Marshfield (Wis.) Clinic, 1987—; assoc. clin. prof. medicine U. Wis. Sch. Medicine, Madison, 1994-2000, clin. prof. medicine, 2000—. Prof. medicine U. Chile Sch. Medicine, 1994; cons. prof. medicine Inst. Med. Sci., Sch. Medicine, Medellin, Colombia, 1999; med. dir. arrhythmia svcs. St. Joseph Hosp., Marshfield, 1992—. Contbr. articles to profl. jours. Mem. parish coun. Our Lady of Peace Cath. Ch., Marshfield, 1996—; bd. dirs. Univ. Found., U. Wis., Marshfield; elected clin. physician rep. to bd. trustees Marshfield Rsch. Found., 2000-2003; cons. to pharm. and med. device industry; coord., local prin. investigator clin. trials of med. rsch. Am. Heart Assn. sr. investigator award, 1997. Fellow ACP (chair internat. com. 1989-92, winner clin. paper competition 1984, 86, 87, mem. faculty ann. sci. sessions), Am. Coll. Cardiology (sr. investigator award, 2000), Am. Coll. Chest Physicians; mem. N.Am. Soc. Electrophysiology and Pacing (faculty ann. sci. sessions), Internat. Netsuke Collectors Soc. Office: Marshfield Clinic 1000 N Oak Ave Marshfield WI 54449-5702 E-mail: vidaillh@mfldclin.edu.

VIDAL, ALEJANDRO LEGASPI (ANDY VIDAL), architect; b. Kawit, Cavite, The Philippines, May 3, 1934; came to U.S. 1954; s. Antonio and Patrocinia Santonil (Legaspi) V.; m. Fe Del Rosario, Aug. 16, 1962; 1 child, Alex Anthony. BS in Architecture, Mapua Inst. Tech., 1962. Registered arch., The Philippines. Prin. A.L. Vidal Arch., Manila, The Philippines, 1962-63; staff arch. Vinnell Wall & Green, Agana, Guam, 1963-64; project engr. Dillingham Corp. of Nevada, Hawaii and Guam, 1964-74; sr. project mgr., preconstrn. svc. mgr. Fletcher-Pacific Constrn. Co. Ltd., Honolulu, 1974-96; prin. A.L. Vidal Constrn. Cons., 1996-2000, A.L. Vidal Arch., Cavite, The Philippines, 1996-2000. Designer, builder first application of integrated aluminum forming sys. for high rise concrete construction. Active Rep. Presdl. Task Force, Washington, 1980-88, Rep. Senatorial Com., Washington, 1980-88. With USN, 1954-58, Korea. Mem. VFW (life), Am. Mgmt. Assn., Soc. Am. Mil. Engrs., Am. Legion, U. Hawaii Found., Chancellor's Club, Disabled Am. Vets., Comdrs. Club. Roman Catholic. Avocations: golf, swimming, volunteer work. Home: 1051 Kaluanui Rd Honolulu HI 96825-1321 E-mail: avidal96825@yahoo.com.

VIDAL, DAVID JONATHAN, insurance company executive, journalist; b. Bayamón, P.R., Oct. 11, 1946; s. Jesus Maria and Ercira Audacia (Mejia) V.; m. Watuza Leal, Jan. 25, 1975; 1 child, Katalyn. AB cum laude, Princeton U., 1968; student, Sch. Advanced Internat. Studies, Washington, 1982-83; MBA, Columbia U., 1991. Reporter The Caracas (Venezuela) Daily Jour., 1969-70; reporter, news editor AP, Caracas, N.Y., Sao Paulo, 1970-73, corr. Brasilia, Brazil, 1973-75; reporter, bur. chief N.Y. Times, N.Y.C. and Rio de Janeiro, 1975-80; spl. asst., White House fellow Dept. State, Washington, 1980-81; cons. U.S. AID, 1981-82; dept. mgr. task force Pres.'s Pvt. Sector Survey on Cost Control, 1982-83; exec. dir. Nat. Commn. Secondary Schooling for Hispanics, 1983-84; dir. pub. affairs N.Y.C. Partnership, 1984-85; asst. v.p. Continental Ins., N.Y.C., 1985-95; v.p. Coun. on Fgn. Rels., 1995-97; dir. rsch. global corp. citizenship The Conf. Bd., 1997—; pub. Across the Board, 2001—. Adj. prof. journalism Columbia U. Grad. Sch. Journalism, N.Y.C., 1985-86; bd. dirs. Pub. Affairs Coun., Washington, 1988-95; trustee Found. for Pub. Affairs, Washington, 1989-95; mem. Contbns. Adv. Group, 1988-95, chmn., 1994-95; mem. corp. adv. group Schomburg Ctr. for Rsch. in Black Culture, 1988-95, Ad Hoc Com. on Charter Revision, 1988, Nat. Hispanic Agenda, 1988; mem. adv. group Latino Leadership Fund, 1991-95; vice-chmn. Nat. Civic League, 1999—. Author newspaper series N.Y. Times, 1980; contbr. articles and reports in field. Trustee N.Y. Theol. Sem., N.Y.C., 1990—; elder, trustee West End Presbyn. Ch., N.Y.C., 1986—; mem. Coun. of Fgn. Rels.; prin. Coun. for Excellence in Govt., Washington, 1992—; dir. Coun. on Internat. Ednl. Exchange, N.Y.C., 1997—. Recipient Hispanic Achievement award Wall Street chpt. IMAGE, N.Y.C., 1989; Fulbright scholar, Washington and Venezuela, 1968. Mem. N.Y. Regional Assn. Grantmakers (dir., sec.

1988-95), Nat. Inst. Industry Assn. (corp. adv. group 1990-95), Nat. Civic League, Internat. Platform Assn., Coun. on Fgn. Rels. Democrat. Office: The Conf Bd 845 3rd Ave New York NY 10022-6601 E-mail: david.vidal@conference-board.org.

VIDAL, MAUREEN ERIS, English language educator, actress; b. Bklyn., Mar. 18, 1956; d. Louis and Lillian (Kaplan) Hendelman; m. Juan Vidal, June 25, 1974 (div. Sept. 1981); m. Guillermo Eduardo Uriarte, Dec. 22, 1986. BA, Bklyn. Coll., 1976, MS, 1981. English tchr. N.Y.C. Bd. Edn., 1976-97, co-chair women's history dept., 1995-99, chair, 1999—, dean, 1997—. Mem. PETA Humane Soc. Mem.: AFTRA, Nat. Anti-Vivesection Soc., Doris Day Animal League, Heights Players Theater Co. (actress, arranger theatrical performance for residents of homeless shelters 1986—, exec. bd., sec. 1993—), Delta Psi Omega. Avocations: world traveling, white water rafting, scuba diving, sky diving, theater. Home: 3380 Nostrand Ave Brooklyn NY 11229-4056 Office: I S 318 101 Walton St Brooklyn NY 11206-4311 also: Heights Players 26 Willow Pl Brooklyn NY 11201-4513 E-mail: MVidal4942@aol.com.

VIDAL, PEDRO JOSE, foreign language educator; b. Caracas, Venezuela, Jan. 28, 1955; s. Pedro Jose and Carmen Alicia (Jaimes) Vidal; m. Aura Violeta Urbina-Vidal, Feb. 4, 1971; children: Pedro III, Phelipe Gabriel, Theodore Vidal. BALA cum laude, Am. U., 1984, MA in Spanish Studies, 1986; postgrad., Md. U., 1991-97. Lectr. U.S. Dept. of State/The Fgn. Svc. Inst., 1983-93, Am. Inst. for Free Labor Devel., White Oak, Md., 1983-93, Bus. Coun. for Internat. Understanding Inst., Washington, 1990-95; instr. Am. U., 1990-95; lectr. LTB Inc., 1995—; instr. Spanish and Latin Am. studies Bowie (Md.) State U., 1995—. Adj. prof. Am. U., 1985-90, 95-96; program coord. Bus. Coun. for Internat. Understanding Inst., 1988-90, instr. 1983-88; internat. coord. The George Washington U., Washington, 1982-85. Reviewer text books in field. Mem. MLA, AAUP, Latin Am. Studies Assn., Pi Sigma Alpha. Democrat. Roman Catholic. Avocations: computer, Bonsais, painting and drawing, fiction writing. Home: 4800 Kemper St Rockville MD 20853-2917 Office: Bowie State U Bowie MD 20719 E-mail: pvidal@BowieState.edu.

VIDAL, RONALD ANTHONY, otolaryngology; b. N.Y.C., 1951; MD, SUNY, 1977. Diplomate Am. Bd. Otolaryngology. Resident in gen. surgery Millard Fillmore Hosp., Buffalo, 1977-79; resident in otolaryngology U. Affiliated Hosp., 1979-82; ptnr. Assocs. Clinton, 1983—, mem. mgmt. com., 1996-2000; pres. med. staff Mercy Health Ctr., Clinton, Iowa, 1994-95; chmn. mgmt. com. Assocs. Clinton, 1999-2000; chmn. dept. surgery and chmn. credentials com. Samaritan Health Sys. Mercy Med. Ctr., Clinton, Iowa, 1997. Bd. dirs. Gateway Physician Hosp. Orgn. Mem. ACS, IMS, Am. Acad. Otolaryngology Head and Neck Surgery. Office: Springdale Dr & 13th Ave N Clinton IA 52732

VIDELL, JARED STEVEN, cardiologist; b. Phila., Apr. 9, 1947; s. Harry and Rose (Malken) V.; m. Cyla Trocki, Dec. 27, 1969; children: Haviv Elana, Mikhael Alon, Samara Pilar. BEd, U. Miami, 1969; DO, Phila. Coll. Osteo. Medicine, 1976. Resident and chief resident in internal medicine Atlantic City (N.J.) Med. Ctr., 1976-79; fellow in cardiovascular diseases Albert Einstein Med. Ctr., Phila., 1979-81; rsch. fellow in nuclear cardiology Deborah Heart and Lung Ctr., Browns Mills, N.J., 1981-82, dir. employee health svcs., 1982-84; asst. dir. cardiology Pritikin Longevity Ctr., Downington, Pa., 1984-87; cardiologist, dir. clin. lab. Physician Care, P.C., Towanda, 1987-90; from co-chmn. intensive care to dir. cardiac stress lab. Meml. Hosp., 1987-90; dir. house staff, intensive/cardiac care Lower Bucks Hosp., Bristol, Pa., 1992-94; dir. house staff ICU-CCU North Phila. Health Systems, 1994-97; med. dir. North Phila. Health Sys. Girard Med. Ctr., 1997—, chmn. clin. medicine, 1997—. Med. dir. Am. Cancer Soc. chpt., 1989-90; state peer rev. KEPRO, 1989-90. Contbr. rsch. articles to profl. jours. Maj. M.C. USAR, Maj. USMC Res. Fellow: Am. Coll. Angiology; mem.: AMA, Nat. Assn. Managed Care Physicians, Alumni Assn. Phila. Coll. Osteo. Medicine, Phila. County Med. Soc., Pa. Med. Soc., Am. Soc. Law, Medicine and Ethics, Internat. Platform Assn., Am. Coll. Physician Execs., INternat. Soc. Endovascular Surgery, Internat. Soc. Internal Medicine, Am. Soc. Internal Medicine, Am. Coll. Chest Physicians. Jewish. Avocations: squash, cycling, cross country skiing, traveling, fishing. Home: 408 N Exeter Ave Margate City NJ 08402-1868

VIDERMAN, LINDA JEAN, paralegal, corporate executive; b. Follansbee, W.Va., Dec. 4, 1957; d. Charles Richard and Louise Edith (LeBoeuf) Roberts; m. David Gerald Viderman Jr., Mar. 15, 1974; children: Jessica Renae, April Mae, Melinda Dawn. AS, W.Va. No. C.C., 1983; cert. income tax prep., H&R Block, Steubenville, Ohio, 1986. Cert. surg. tech., fin. counselor; lic. ins. agt. Food prep. pers. Bonanza Steak House, Weirton, W.Va., 1981—83; ward clk., food svcs. Weirton Med. Ctr., 1982—84; sec., treas. Mountaineer Security Systems, Inc., Wheeling, W.Va., 1983—86; owner, operator The Button Booth, Colliers, 1985—; paralegal, adminstr. Atty. Dominic J. Potts, Steubenville, Ohio, 1987—92; gen. ptnr., executrix Panhandle Homes, Wellsburg, W.Va., 1988—96; sec.-treas., executrix Panhandle Homes, Inc., 1996—; ins. agt. Milico, Mass. Indemnity, 1991—92, L&L Ins. Svcs., 1992—94; paralegal Atty. Fred Risovich II, Weirton, 1991—93; sec. The Hon. Fred Risovich II, Wheeling, 1993; paralegal atty. Christopher J. Paull, Wellsburg, W.Va., 1993—; owner Wellsburg Office Supply, 1993—94; owner, operator Viderman Child Care Svcs. Co., Wellsburg, 1997—; owner, dir. Viderman & Assocs., 1997—. Notary pub., 1991—. Contbr. articles to profl. jours.; author numerous poems. Chmn. safety com. Colliers (W.Va.) Primary PTA, 1985-87; founding mem. Brooke County Homeschoolers/Panhandle Homeschoolers Assn., 1999; editor Panhandle Homeschoolers Newsletter, 2000; mem., sec. LaLeche League, Steubenville, Ohio, 1978-80; vol. counselor W.Va. U. Fin. Counseling Svc., 1990—; IRS vol. Vol. Income Tax Assistance Program, 1991—. Mem. W.Va. Manufactured Housing Assn. (bd. dirs. 2001-), W.Va. Writers Assn., Legal Assts. of W.Va., Inc., Am. Affiliate of Nat. Assn. Legal Assts., W.Va. Trial Lawyers Assn., Wellsburg Art Assn., Brooke County Genealogical Soc., Phi Theta Kappa. Jehovah'S Witness. Avocations: Christian ministry, home computing, camping, genealogy, home schooling. Home: RR2 Box 28 Wellsburg WV 26070-9500 Office: Panhandle Homes Inc RR 2 Box 27A Wellsburg WV 26070-9500 E-mail: lviderman@aol.com.

VIE, GEORGE WILLIAM, III, lawyer; b. Tampa, Fla., Mar. 21, 1961; s. George William Jr. and Cheri Ann (Bass) V. BS magna cum laude, U. Houston, Clear Lake, Tex., 1985; JD, U. Tex., 1988. Bar: Tex. 1989, U.S. Dist. Ct. (so. dist.) Tex. 1990, U.S. Ct. Appeals (5th cir.) 1990, U.S. Mil. Ct. Appeals 1995, U.S. Supreme Ct. 1995; bd. cert. civil appellate law Tex. Bd. Legal Specialization. Legal asst. Bankston, Wright & Greenhill, Austin, Tex., 1985-89, atty., 1989-90; ptnr. Mills Shirley, Galveston, Tex., 1990—. Spkr. in field. Contbr. articles to legal publs. Fellow Tex. Bar Found.; mem. FBA, State Bar Tex., Phi Kappa Phi, Sigma Phi Epsilon. Office: Mills Shirley 2228 Mechanic St Ste 400 Galveston TX 77550-1591 E-mail: gvie@millshirley.com.

VIEBAHN, FRED, writer, journalist; b. Gummersbach, Germany, Apr. 16, 1947; came to U.S., 1976; s. Hans and Elisabeth (Marx) V.; m. Rita F. Dove, Mar. 23, 1979; 1 child, Aviva Chantal. Student, U. Cologne, Germany, 1966-71. Freelance journalist, 1966—. Vis. assoc. prof. German, U. Tex., Austin, 1977, Oberlin (Ohio) Coll., 1977-79; adj. prof. creative writing Ariz. State U., Tempe, 1981-89; scholar in residence, U. Va., Charlottesville, 1989—; adv. bd. Ploughshares Mag., Boston, 1990—. Author: Die Schwarzen Tauben, 1969 (German Book of the Month award Nov. 1969), Das Haus Che, 1973, Larissa, 1976, Die Fesseln der Freiheit, 1979, The Stain, 1988; editor: The Image of America in Contemporary German Writing, 1983. Chmn. Young Socialists, Castrop-Rauxel, Germany, 1972-73. bd. dirs. Social Dem. Party, Castrop-Rauxel, 1972-73. Recipient Lit. prize City of Cologne, 1973, John Nims Translation prize Poetry Mag., 1999; Internat. Travel fellow West German Fgn. Ministry, 1976, Fulbright fellow U. Iowa, 1976, Lit. fellow City West Berlin, 1980; Mishkenot Sha'ananim Residency, City of Jerusalem, 1979. Mem. Assn. German Writers (bd. dirs. 1974-76), Internat. PEN Club. Avocations: photography, videography. Office: Dept English Univ Va 219 Bryan Hall Charlottesville VA 22903

VIEGAS, LOUIS PAUL, real estate salesperson, retired postmaster; b. Bklyn., Aug. 24, 1940; s. Jack and Antoinette (Cappiello) V.; m. Charlotte Sonia Storey, May 28, 1967; children: Cindy, Tracy. AAS. in Bus., N.Y. Inst. Tech., 1978, BS in Bus., 1979; postgrad., St. John's U., Queens, N.Y., 1987. Lic. real estate assoc. Traffic asst. Berkshire Chem. Corp., N.Y.C., 1956-59; engrng. aide Bd. Higher Edn., 1959-61; letter carrier U.S. Postal Svc., Bklyn., 1961-68, supr., 1968-79, area mgr., 1979-82, mgr., deliveries & collections, 1982-85, dir. city ops., 1985-87, postmaster N.Y., 1987-92; ret., 1992; cons. U.S. Postal Svc., N.Y.C., 1995-99; sales assoc. Sung and Assocs. Real Estate Corp., 2000—. Mem. Northeast Region Speakers Bur., N.Y., N.J., New Eng., 1985—. Mem. Assn. for the Help Retarded Children, Nassau County, N.Y., 1974-89, Valley Stream Civilian Patrol, Valley Stream, N.Y., 1984-86, Nassau County Foster Parents Assn., 1982-87. Named Man of Yr. Holy Name Soc. Bklyn., 1986, Christopher Columbus Assn., Bklyn., Staten Island, 1987, Bklyn. Jewish Postal Workers Welfare League, 1989. Mem. Nat. League Postmasters of U.S., Nat. Assn. Postal Suprs., Sons of Italy. Republican. Roman Catholic. Avocation: photography. Office: Sung and Assocs Real Estate Corp 31 W Merrick Rd VAlley Stream NY 11580-9998 E-mail: lou@barps.com.

VIEGELAHN, MARCIA ELIZABETH, music educator; b. Stanton, Mich., May 1, 1940; d. Eldon Ward and Esther Elizabeth (Chapin) Jones; m. Gary Lee Viegelahn, June 18, 1966 (dec. Nov. 1991). Diploma, Moody Bible Inst., 1962; B in Music Edn., U. Mich., 1964; M in Music Edn., No. Mich. U., 1975. Cert. tchr., Mich. Music educator Van Buren County Pub. Schs., South Haven, Mich., 1964-66, Calumet (Mich.) Pub. Schs., 1966-72; pvt. music tchr. Lake Linden, Mich., 1972—. Choir dir. Reformed Ch., South Haven, Mich., 1964-66, First Bapt. Ch., Calumet, Mich., 1966-80; music educator Lake Linden Hubbell Schs., 1987-92. Mem. Mich. Music Tchrs. Assn., Lake Superior Music Tchrs. Assn. (sec. 1990-92, pres. 1993—). Republican. Baptist. Avocations: sewing, knitting. Home: 27570 W 34th St Lake Linden MI 49945-1331

VIEHE, KARL WILLIAM, mathematics educator, lawyer, investment banker; b. Allentown, Pa., Aug. 12, 1943; s. John Sage and Margaret (Higgs) V. BA in Govt. and Econs., Am. U., 1965, MA in Econs., 1968; JD, Howard U., 1981; MLT in Taxation, Georgetown U., 1982. Bar: D.C. 1983, U.S. Tax Ct. 1984, U.S. Ct. Internat. Trade 1988, U.S. Ct. Appeals (4th cir.) 1988, U.S. Ct. Appeals (D.C. cir.) 1985, U.S. Supreme Ct. 1988. Instr. math. and Russian lang. St. Albans Sch., Washington, 1968-69; pres., CEO Investment-Futures Group, 1968-84; prof. math. and stats. U. D.C., 1971—. Gen. counsel Promstroy Bank Russia, 1996-97; adj. prof. internat. law and fin. Am. U., 1972—; adj. prof. internat. law and bus. George Washington U., 1986—; internat. advt. dir. Washingtonian Mag., 1972-75; mgmt. program chmn. Fla. Inst. Tech., 1983-85; adj. faculty Internat. Law Inst., Washington, 1986—, Internat. Devel. Law Inst., Rome, 1987—; v.p., gen. counsel James A. Tilley Co., Investment Bankers, Washington, Moscow, 1994-95; chmn., CEO Horizons-Northstar Capital Mgmt. Co., Washington, 1995-97; gen. counsel U.S. Congrl. Philharmonic Orch., 1998-99; co-chmn. U.S. IRS Ann. Conf. on Current Issues in Internat. Taxation, 1986-88, Dept. Commerce Ann. Conf. on Current Issues in Internat. Trade, 1994-97; internat. adv. bd. McGeorge Sch. Law, 1987—; presenter in field. Contbr. articles to profl. jours. Vice-chmn. bd. dirs., gen. counsel U.S. Congrl. Philharmonic Soc. Mem. ABA, Am. Econ. Assn., Am. Fin. Assn., Am. Arbitration Assn. (comml. panel, internat. panel), Washington Fgn. Law Soc. (bd. dirs.), D.C. Bar Assn., U.S. Congl. Philharmonic Soc. (vice-chmn. bd. govs.). Avocations: piano, photography, triathlons, marathons, tennis. Home: 2401 H St NW Apt 707 Washington DC 20037-2581 Office: Horizons & Northstar Capital Mgmt Co 1700 Pennsylvania Ave NW Washington DC 20006-4704

VIEHE, RICHARD B. medical association administrator; m. Margaret Viehe; children: Anne, Thomas, Andrew. BS, Cornell U.; postgrad., Calif. Coll. Podiatric Medicine. Resident in podiatry Lincoln Cmty. Hosp., Calif.; pvt. practice; staff physician Children's Hosp. of Orange County; Coastal Cmtys. Hosp., Santa Ana; Coll. Hosp., Costa Mesa; Fountain Valley Cmty. Hosp.; Hoag Meml. Presbyn. Hosp., Newport Beach; St. Joseph Hosp., Orange County, & Western Med. Ctr., Santa Ana; pres. Am. Podiatric Med. Assn. Mem.: Orange County Podiatric Med. Assn. (past pres.), Calif. Podiatric Med. Assn. (past pres.), Alpha Gamma Kappa, Pi Delta. Office: Am Pediat Med Assn 9312 Old Georgetown Rd Bethesda MD 20814*

VIEIRA, KAREN ELIZABETH, human resources professional; b. London, Sept. 20, 1969; came to U.S., 1982; d. Winston Osbert and Faye Allison (Vierira) V. BS in Pers., Indsl. Rels., Norfolk State U., 1990; MA in Human Resources Devel., 1997. Mgr. Cup Temporaries, Inc., Washington, 1989-91; office mgr. Allan B. Williams & Assocs., 1991; sec. pers. office George Washington U., 1991—; sr. human resources officer Acad. for Ednl Devel, 1996—. Retail sales clk. Kids "R" Us, 1987—. Mem. NAFE, Soc. for Human Resources Mgmt., Black Human Resources Network, Employment Mgmt. Assn. Office: Acad for Ednl Devel 1825 Connecticut Ave NW Washington DC 20009-5708

VIEIRA, LINDA MARIE, medical administrator, endoscopy nurse; b. San Jose, Calif., July 8, 1961; d. Albert Sequeira and Catherine Marie (Souza) Vieira; m. John Bettencourt Ramos, June 12, 1982 (div. July 1993). AA, De Anza Coll., 1986; BA, St. Mary's Coll. Calif., Moraga, 1988; AS in Nursing, De Anza Coll., Cupertino, Calif., 2000. RN, Calif.; cert. gastrointestinal clinician. Endoscopy technician O'Connor Hosp., San Jose, 1979-94; nurse endoscopy Good Samaritan Health Sys., Los Gatos, Calif., 1994—, Regional Med. Ctr. San Jose (formerly Alexian Bros. Hosp.), San Jose, 1995—; adminstrv./tech. coord. South Bay Endoscopy Ctr., 1997—; sec.-treas. Vieira Enterprises, Santa Clara, 1999—; nurse GI Lab./Santa Clara Valley Med. Ctr., San Jose, 2001. Aerobic instr. Mountain View (Calif.) Athletic Club, 1984-95, Decathlon Club, Santa Clara, 1991—, Golds Gym, Mountain View, 1994—, Club One@Silicon Valley Athletic Club, 1995-2000. Contbr. articles to profl. jours. Vol. O'Connor Hosp., 1975-79; active campaign Santa Clara City Council, 1980-81; class rep. DeAnza Coll. Inter Club Coun., 1999. Fellow: Luso Am. Fraternal Fedn. (state youth pres. 1979—80, youth leader local coun. Santa Clara Mountain View 1979—87, founder, organizer Mountain View-Santa Clara chpt. 1980, pres. local region 1980—84, state 20-30 pres. 1984—85, state dir. youth programs 1988—94, state dir. 1994—2000, chair youth dirs. 1998—99, state outside guard 2000—, scholar 1979), Soc. Espspirito Santo of Santa Clara, No. Soc. Gastrointestinal Assts., Irmandade Da Festa Do Espirto Santo (sec. 1974—85, queen 1975—76), Soc. Gastrointestinal Assts.; mem.: Am. Coun. Exercise (cert. aerobics instr. 1991—). Republican. Roman Catholic. Avocations: aerobic dance, weight lifting, gardening, wine tasting. Home: 911 Fairfield Ave Santa Clara CA 95050 Office: South Bay Endoscopy Ctr 455 Oconnor Dr Ste 340 San Jose CA 95128-1644 Fax: 408-283-3718. E-mail: sbec@silcon.com.

VIENER, JOHN D. lawyer; b. Richmond, Va., Oct. 18, 1939; s. Reuben and Thelma (Kurtz) V.; m. Karin Erika Bauer, Apr. 7, 1969; children: John D. Jr., Katherine Bauer Viener Riordan. BA, Yale U., 1961; JD, Harvard U., 1964. Bar: N.Y. State 1965, U.S. Supreme Ct. 1970, U.S. Dist. Ct. (so. dist.) N.Y. 1974, U.S. Tax Ct. 1975. Assoc. Satterlee, Warfield & Stephens, N.Y.C., 1964-69; sole practice, 1969-76; sr. ptnr. Christy & Viener, 1976-98, Salans, Hertzfeld, Heilbronn, Christy & Viener, N.Y.C., 1999-2000; prin., dir. BFD Capital Beteiligungs GmbH, 2001—. Dir. Beteiligungs GmbH, 2001—; founder, bd. dirs., gen. counsel Foxfire Fund, Inc., 1968—88; gen. counsel, bd. dirs. Landmark Communities, 1970—, Am. Continental Properties Group, 1978—, NF&M Internat., Inc., 1976—, Singer Fund, Inc., 1979—, Immunotherapy, Inc., 1997—99, Tupper Broadcasting Group Cos., 1996—, Viener Found., 1991—; gen. counsel Nat. Cancer Found. Cancer Care, 1982—85, Troster, Singer & Co., 1970—77; bd. dirs. Gen. Financiere Immob. et Commer. S.A., 1985—89; spl. counsel fin. instns., investment banking and securities concerns; real estate and tax advisor. Bd. dirs. York Theatre Co., 1999-2001, The N.Y. Pops, 1999-2002. Mem. Meeker Brook Sporting Assn., Fairfield County Hounds, Manursing Island Club, Washington Club, Palm Beach Polo. also: 650 Park Avenue New York NY 10021 Office: 620 5th Ave New York NY 10020-2402

VIERCK, CHARLES JOHN, JR. neuroscience educator, scientist; b. Columbus, Ohio, July 6, 1936; s. Charles John and Esther (Amadon) V.; m. Cheryl Stogner; children: Kenneth Christopher, Karl Frederick. B.Sc., U. Fla., 1959, M.Sc., 1961, PhD, 1963. Postdoctoral fellow U. Pa., Phila., 1963-65; asst. prof. U. Fla., Gainesville, 1965-71, assoc. prof., 1971-77, prof., 1977—. Adj. prof. U. N.C., Chapel Hill, 1977— ; dir. Ctr. Neurobiol. Scis. U. Fla., Gainesville Editor: (textbook) Basics of Neuroscience, 1974; contbr. articles to profl. jours., also chpts. to books; mem. editorial bd. Somatosensory Motor Research, Am. Pain Soc. Jour. Grantee NIH, NIMH, NSF, VA, 1966— Mem. Soc. Neurosci., Internat. Assn. Study Pain Democrat. Avocations: jazz, golf. Home: 9331 NW 15th Pl Gainesville FL 32606-5580 Office: U Fla PO Box 100244 Gainesville FL 32610-0244 E-mail: vierck@ufbi.ufl.edu.

VIERECK, PETER, poet, historian, educator; b. N.Y.C., Aug. 5, 1916; s. George S. and Margaret (Hein) V.; m. Anya de Markov, June 1945 (div. May 1970); children: John-Alexis, Valerie Edwina (Mrs. John Gibbs); m. Betty Martin Falkenberg, Aug. 30, 1972. BS summa cum laude, Harvard U., 1937, MA, 1939, PhD, 1942; Henry fellow Christ Ch., Oxford (Eng.) U., 1937-38; LHD (hon.), Olivet Coll., 1959. Teaching asst. Harvard, 1941-42, instr. German lit., tutor history and lit. dept., 1946-47; instr. history U.S. Army U., Florence, Italy, 1945; asst. prof. history Smith Coll., 1947-48, vis. lectr. Russian history, 1948-49; assoc. prof. Modern European, Russian history Mt. Holyoke Coll., 1948-55, prof., 1955—. Vis. lectr. Am. Culture Oxford U., 1953; Whittal lectr. in poetry Library of Congress, 1954, 63, 79; Fulbright prof. Am. poetry and civilization U. Florence, Italy, 1954-56; Elliston chair poetry lectr. U. Cin., 1956; vis. lectr. U. Calif. at, Berkeley, 1957; Disting. William R. Kenan prof. Mt. Holyoke Coll., 1979— ; Charter mem. Council Basic Edn.; vis. poet Russian-Am. cultural exchange program Dept. State, USSR, 1961; vis. research scholar 20th Century Fund, USSR, 1962-63; vis. scholar Rockefeller Study Center at Bellagio, Italy, 1977; vis. artist and scholar Am. Acad. in, Rome, 1949-50, 78; dir. poetry workshop N.Y. Writers Conf., 1965-67; research fellow Huntington Library, San Marino, Calif., 1978. Author: Metapolitics— From the Romantics to Hitler, 1941 (Swedish edit., 1942, Italian, 1948), rev. edit., 2002, Terror and Decorum, poems, 1948, reprinted, 1972, Who Killed the Universe, novelette included in anthology New Directions Ten, 1948, Conservatism Revisited-The Revolt Against Revolt 1815-1949, 1949 (English edit, 1950), Strike Through the Mask, New Lyrical Poems, 1950, reprinted, 1972, The First Morning: New Poems, 1952, reprinted, 1972, Shame and Glory of the Intellectuals, 1953, rev. edit., 1965, reprinted 1978, Dream and Responsibility, The Tension Between Poetry and Society, 1953, The Unadjusted Man; a New Hero for Americans, 1956, reprinted, 1973, Conservatism: From John Adams to Churchill, 1956, reprinted, 1978, The Persimmon Tree, poems, 1956, Inner Liberty, The Stubborn Grit in the Machine, 1957, The Tree Witch: A Verse Drama, 1961, reprinted, 1973, Meta-politics, The Roots of the Nazi Mind, 1961, rev. expanded edit. 1965, Conservatism Revisited and The New Conservatives: What Went Wrong; rev. paperback edits., 1962, 65, reprinted hardcover, 1978, New and Selected Poems, 1932-67, 1967, Archer in the Marrow: The Applewood Poetry Cycles of 1967-87, 1987, Tide & Continuities: Last & First Poems, 1995; also author of selections in symposium books Towards a World Community, 1950, Midcentury American Poets, 1950, Arts in Renewal, 1951, The New American Right, 1955, Education in a Free Society, 1958, The Radical Right, 1962, Soviet Policy Making, 1967, Outside Looking In, 1972, A Question of Quality, 1976, The Southern California Anthology, 1987, rev. edits., 1987, 89, Decade: New Letters Anthology of the 80s, 1990; contbr. essays, poems to popular mags., and profl. jours., monograph on Conservatism in Ency. Brit., 1974. Sgt. U.S. Army, 1943-45, Africa and Italy. Decorated 2 battle stars; awarded Tietjens prize for poetry, 1948, Pulitzer prize for poetry, 1949; recipient Most Disting. Alumnus award Horace Mann School for Boys, 1958, Poetry Translation award Translation Center, Columbia U., 1978, Sadin poetry prize N.Y. Quar., 1977, Golden Rose award New Eng. Poetry Club, 1981, Varoujan prize, 1983, New Eng. Poetry Club prize, 1998, Anne Sexton prize Agni mag., 1999; Guggenheim fellow Rome, 1949-50; Rockefeller Found. rschr. in history Germany, summer 1958; NEH sr. rsch. fellow USSR, 1969; Mass. Artists Found. fellow, 1978 Mem. Am. Hist. Assn., Oxford Soc., Poetry Soc. Am., P.E.N., Phi Beta Kappa. Clubs: Harvard (N.Y.C. and London); Bryce (Oxford, Eng.). Home: 12 Silver St South Hadley MA 01075-1616 *After 84 years of books, scars, and sugar plums, my rock-bottom thought on life is a line of Vachel Lindsay: "Courage and sleep are the principal things.".*

VIERRA, DEBORAH, critical care, community health nurse; b. Yonkers, N.Y., July 2, 1957; d. Alfred and Amelia (Schurko) Kuropatwa; m. Joseph J. Vierra Jr., Dec. 13, 1979. AAS, Westchester Community Coll., 1984; postgrad., Coll. Mt. St. Vincent, Coll. of New Rochelle, U. Del., 1995—. Cert. clin. drug toxicology, respiratory care, cardiac care, intravenous therapy, rehabilitation, chemotherapy; cert. instr. ACLS, pediatric ALS. Staff nurse United Hosp., Portchester, N.Y., 1984-85, Bellevue Hosp., N.Y.C., 1985-87; rsch. nurse N.Y. Med. Coll., Valhalla, 1987-88; home care coord., asst. patient care coord. emergency dept. Our Lady of Mercy Med. Ctr., Bronx, N.Y., 1988-90; dir. care nurse Montifiore Home Health Agy., 1990-92; direct care nurse Wayne Meml. Home Health Agy., Hawley, Pa., 1992-95, supr., 1995-99; perdiem emergency rn. Arden Hill Hosp., Goshen, N.Y., 1999; part-time home health nurse Montefiore Home Health Agy., Bronx, 1999—; full time health/wellness mgr. Delaware Valley Job Corps, Callicoon, NY, 2001—. Ptnr. D&C Dunnit, Creative Ceramics, Creative Artwork, Nat. Honor Soc. With U.S. Army, 1977-80. Mem. ANA, Golden Key. also: D & C Dunnit RR 1 Box 477-A Hawley PA 18428 E-mail: dcdunnit@ltis.net.

VIERTEL, GEORGE JOSEPH, lawyer, arbitrator, mediator, consulting engineer; b. N.Y.C., June 10, 1912; s. William and Marie Dorothy (Reichert) V.; 1 child, Elise V. Robertson. BSCE, NYU, 1934; LLB, LaSalle U., Chgo., 1952; cert., Old Dominion U., 1963; student, Alliance Francaise, Paris, 1971; JD (hon.), Bernadean U., 1973; PhD (hon.), USUA, 1977. Bar: Va. 1954, D.C., 1972, Md., 1981, U.S. Dist. Ct. (ea. dist. Va.) 1954, U.S. Ct. Appeals (4th cir.) 1954, U.S. Tax Ct. 1954, U.S. Supreme Ct. 1957, U.S. Claims Ct. 1961, U.S. Dist. Ct. Hawaii 1962, U.S. Ct. Appeals (9th cir.) 1963, U.S. Dist. Ct. (D.C. dist.) 1972, U.S. Ct. Appeals (7th cir.) 1972, U.S. Ct. Appeals (D.C. cir.) 1973, Ct. Appeals Md. 1981, U.S. Ct. Mil. Appeals 1973, U.S. Dist. Ct. Md. 1981; registered profl. engr. Md., Va., D.C., N.Y., Wis.; cert. expedited dispute settler; cert. arbitrator Superior Ct. D.C.; lic. real estate broker, Md. Freelance constrn. estimator, 1952-57; asst. engr. N.Y.C. Housing Authority, 1934, Bd. Transp. N.Y.C, 1933-34; supr. constrn. M. Shapiro & Son, N.Y.C.; engr. N.Y.C. Bd. Water Supply; asst. resident engr. Langley Field Sta., Va.; civil engr. Nat. Adv. Com. for Aeronautics (now known as NASA), Langley Field, 1940-48; assoc. Williams, Coile, Blanchard, Architects and Engrs., Newport News, Va., 1948-50; ptnr., chief engr. Assoc. Architects and Engrs., 1950-61; asst. to dir. Office of Constrn. and Facility Mgmt. U.S. Dept. Energy, Washington, 1977-79; sole practice law Va., 1954—, Washington, 1972—, Md., 1981—. Arbitrator, mediator D.C. Superior Ct., Balt. City Cir. Ct., among others. Contbr. articles to profl. jours. Lt. U.S. Army Corps Engrs., 1934-39. Fellow ASCE (life, pres. local chpt. 1965-67); mem. Bar Assn. Montgomery County, Assn. for Conflict Resolution. Home: 4407 Pinetree Rd Rockville MD 20853-1320 Office: 9525 Georgia Ave Ste 105 Silver Spring MD 20910-1439

VIESSMAN, WARREN, JR. academic dean, civil engineering educator, researcher; b. Balt., Nov. 9, 1930; s. Warren and Helen Adair (Berlinckee) V.; m. Gloria Marie Scheiner, May 11, 1953 (div. Apr. 1975); children: Wendy, Stephen, Suzanne, Michael, Thomas, Sandra; m. Elizabeth Gertrude Rothe, Aug. 8, 1980; children: Heather, Joshua. B in Engrng., Johns Hopkins U., 1952, MS in Engrng., 1958, DEng, 1961. Registered profl. engr., Md. Engr. W. H. Primrose & Assocs., Towson, Md., 1955-57; project engr. Johns Hopkins U., Balt., 1957-61; from asst. to assoc. prof. N.Mex. State U., Las Cruces, 1961-66; prof. U. Maine, Orono, 1966-68, U. Nebr., Lincoln, 1968-75; sr. specialist Libr. Congress, Washington, 1975-83; prof., chmn. U. Fla., Gainesville, 1983-90, assoc. dean for rsch. and grad. study, 1990-91, assoc. dean for acad. programs, 1991—. Vis. scientist Am. Geophys. Union, 1970-71; Maurice Kremer lectr. U. Nebr., 1985, 2001; lectr. Harvard U. Water Policy Seminar, 1988; Wayne S. Nichols Meml. Fund lectr. Ohio State U., 1990; mem. steering com. on groundwater and energy U.S. Dept. Energy, 1979-80; mem. task group on fed. water rsch. U.S. Geol. Survey, 1985-87; mem. com. of water sci. and tech. bd. NAS, 1986-90; mem. water resources working group Nat. Coun. on Pub. Works Improvement, 1987; chmn., chief of engrs. Environ. Adv. Bd., Washington, 1991-93; chmn. solid and hazardous waste mgmt. adv. bd. State U. Sys. Fla. Co-author: Water Supply and Pollution Control, 1993, Water Management: Technology and Institutions, 1984, Introduction to Hydrology, 1996; contbr. over 167 articles to profl. jours. Mem. Water Mgmt. Com., Gainesville, 1983-88, Fla. Environ. Efficiency Study Commn., 1986-88. 1st lt. U.S. Army C.E., 1952-54, Korea. Recipient Comdr.'s award for pub. svc. U.S. Dept. Army, 1993. Fellow ASCE (hon.

mem., Julian Hinds award 1989), Am. Water Resources Assn. (nat. pres. 1990, Icko Iben award 1983, Henry P. Caulfield Jr. medal 1996), Univs. Coun. on Water Resources (pres. 1987, Warren A. Hall medal 1994), Sigma Xi, Tau Beta Pi. Avocations: scuba diving, woodworking. Office: U Fla Coll Engring PO Box 116550 Gainesville FL 32611-6550 E-mail: wvies@eng.ufl.edu.

VIEST, IVAN M(IROSLAV), consulting structural engineer; b. Bratislava, Slovakia, Czechoslovakia, Oct. 10, 1922; came to U.S., 1947, naturalized, 1955; s. Ivan and Maria (Zacharova) V.; m. Barbara K. Stevenson, May 23, 1953. Ing., Slovak Tech. U., Bratislava, 1946; MS, Ga. Inst. Tech., 1948; PhD, U. Ill., 1951; D (hon.) , Kosice Tech. U., 2002. Registered profl. engr., Pa. Research asst. U. Ill., Urbana, 1948-50, research assoc., 1950-51, research asst. prof., 1951-55, research assoc. prof., 1955-57; bridge research engr. Am. Assn. State Hwy. Ofcls., Nat. Acad. Scis., Ottawa, Ill., 1957-61; structural engr. Bethlehem Steel Corp., Pa., 1961-67, sr. structural cons., 1967-70, asst. mgr. sales engring. div., 1970-82; pvt. cons. structural engr. IMV Cons., 1983—. Lectr. in field. Author: Composite Construction, 1958, History of Engineering Foundation, 1991, Composite Construction--Design for Buildings, 1997, Seventy-Five Years of the Lehigh Valley Section, 1997. Recipient Constrn. award Engring. News Record, 1972; named to Hall of Fame, Ga. Inst. of Tech., 1998. Fellow AAAS, Am. Concrete Inst. (Wason Rsch. medal 1956); mem. NAE, ASCE (hon., v.p. 1973-75, Rsch. prize 1958, Ernest E. Howard award 1991), Internat. Assn. Bridge and Structural Engring., Transp. Rsch. Bd. (emeritus 1999—), Czechoslovak Soc. Arts and Scis. (exec. v.p. 1992-93), Earthquake Engring. Rsch. Inst., Saucon Valley Country Club (Bethlehem). Achievements include research, numerous rsch. publs. on various aspects of steel and concrete structures, especially bridges and bldgs., to profl. jours.

VIETH, GIFFORD DUANE, lawyer; b. Omaha, Sept. 20, 1923; s. Walter E. and Irene E. (Horn) V.; m. Jane G. Richardson, Feb. 16, 1952; children: Peter D., Robert R., Jane G. BA, U. Iowa, 1947, JD, 1949. Bar: Iowa 1949, D.C. 1949, U.S. Dist. Ct. Iowa 1953, U.S. Dist. Ct. Md. 1955, U.S. Ct. Claims 1958, U.S. Ct. Appeals (3d cir.) 1960, U.S. Dist. Ct. (ea. dist.) Wis. 1965, U.S. Supreme Ct. 1966, U.S. Ct. Appeals (2d cir.) 1970, U.S. Ct. Appeals (7th cir.) 1971. Ptnr. Arnold & Porter, Washington, 1949—. Mem. D.C. Commn. on Budget and Financial Priorities, 1989-90. Trustee Iowa Law Sch. Found., Iowa City, 1971-88, Fed. City Council, Washington, 1972—. With USAAF, 1942-45, ETO. Mem. ABA, D.C. Bar Assn., Iowa State Bar Assn., Columbia Country Club, Burning Tree Club, Met. Club. Lutheran. Avocation: golf. Home: 4407 Chalfont Pl Bethesda MD 20816-1812 Office: Arnold & Porter 555 12th St NW Ste 1202 Washington DC 20004-1200

VIETOR, HAROLD DUANE, federal judge; b. Parkersburg, Iowa, Dec. 29, 1931; s. Harold Howard and Alma Johanna (Kreimeyer) V.; m. Dalia Artemisa Zamarripa Cadena, Mar. 24, 1973; children: Christine Elizabeth, John Richard, Greta Maria. BA, U. Iowa, 1955, JD, 1958. Bar: Iowa 1958. Law clk. U.S. Ct. Appeals 8th Circuit, 1958-59; ptnr. Bleakley Law Offices, Cedar Rapids, Iowa, 1959-65; judge Iowa Dist. Ct., 1965-79, chief judge, 1970-79; U.S. dist. judge U.S. Dist. Ct. for So. Dist. Iowa, Des Moines, 1979-96, chief judge, 1985-92, sr. U.S. dist. judge, 1997—. Lectr. at law schs., legal seminars U.S. and Japan. Contbr. articles to profl. jours. in U.S. and Japan. Served with USN, 1952-54. Mem. ABA, Iowa Bar Assn. (pres. jr. sect. 1966-67), Iowa Judges Assn. (pres. 1975-76), 8th Cir. Dist. Judges Assn. (pres. 1986-88). Office: US Dist Ct 221 US Courthouse 123 E Walnut St Des Moines IA 50309-2035

VIETS, ELAINE FRANCES, writer; b. St. Louis, Feb. 5, 1950; d. Henry Frederick and Elaine Frances Viets; m. Don Crinklaw, Aug. 6, 1971. BJ, U. Mo., 1972. Columnist St. Louis Post-Dispatch, 1979-95, United Media, N.Y.C., 1996-2000. Tchr. writing seminars Broward Libr., Fla. Ctr. for the Book, 1998-99, St. Louis Pub. Libr., 1999. Author: (mystery novels) Backstab, 1997, Rubout, 1998, Pink Flamingo Murders, 1999, (humor) How to Commit Monogamy, 1997, Doc in the Box, 2000. Recipient Emmy award St. Louis chpt. NATAS, 1989, 90; named Fla. Au. of Yr., Pompano Beach Friends of the Libr., 2000. Mem. Mystery Writers of Am. (bd. dirs., sec. Fla. chpt. 1999-00, pres. Fla. chpt. 2000, dir.-at-large 2002, Edgar com. best novel 1999, chair Edgar com. best first novel 2002), Sisters in Crime (bd. dirs.). Avocations: reading, walking, weight training. E-mail: eviets@aol.com.

VIETS, HERMANN, college president, consultant; b. Quedlinburg, Fed. Republic Germany, Jan. 28, 1943; came to U.S., 1949, naturalized, 1961; s. Hans and Herta (Heik) V.; m. Pamela Deane, June 30, 1968; children: Danielle, Deane, Hans, Hillary BS, Polytech. U., 1965, MS, 1966, PhD, 1970. Fellow von Karman Inst., Brussels, 1969-70; group leader Wright-Patterson AFB, Dayton, Ohio, 1970-76; prof. Wright State U., 1976-81; assoc. dean W.Va. U., Morgantown, 1981-83; dean U. R.I., Kingston, 1983-91; pres. Milw. Sch. Engring., 1991—. Chmn. bd. dirs. Precision Stampings, Inc., Beaumont, Calif., 1977—; bd. dirs. Gehl Co., West Bend, Wis., Astro Med, Inc., West Warwick, R.I., Wenthe-Davidson Engring. Co., New Berlin, Wis., Max Kade Inst. for German-Am. Studies, Discovery World, Milw. County Rsch. Park Corp.; cons. USAF Aero Propulsion Lab., Dayton, 1976-80, Covington & Burling, Washington, 1976-77; cons. in field. Patentee in aero. field; contbr. numerous articles to profl. jours. Mem. Greater Milw. Com.; dir. Competitive Wis., Gov. Regional H.S. Excellence Co., 1994, Gov.'s Export Strategy Commn., 1994; trustee Pub. Policy Forum. Recipient Tech. Achievement award USAF, 1974, Sci. Achievement award, 1975, Gov.'s Sci. and Tech. award State of R.I., 1987, Goodrich Pub. Svc. award, 1990, Citation R.I. Legislature, 1987, 90, 91, Outstanding Alumnus award aerospace engring. dept. Poly. U., 1994; Disting. Alumnus Poly. U., 1995, Engr. of Yr. award Engrs. and Scientists of Milw., 1997; named Hon. Citizen Fachhochschule Luebeck, Germany, 1998; postdoctoral fellow NATO, 1969-70, NASA, 1965-69. Fellow AIAA (assoc., acad. affairs com. 1998—, Best Tech. Paper award Allegheny-Pitts. sect. 1982); mem. German Assn. for Luft and Raumfahrt, German-Am. Heritage Soc. (bd. dirs.), Nat. Assn. Independent Coll. and Univ. (bd. dirs.), Am. Soc. Engring. Edn., Japan-Am. Soc. (bd. dirs. 1994), Soc. Mfg. Engrs., Rotary, Sigma Xi, Phi Kappa Phi, Tau Beta Pi, Sigma Gamma Tau. Avocations: antique automobiles, beer steins, Notgeld currency. Home: 4216 N Lake Dr Milwaukee WI 53211-1722 Office: Milw Sch Engring 1025 N Broadway Milwaukee WI 53202-3109

VIETZKE, WESLEY MAUNDER, internist, educator; b. Ft. Defiance, Ariz., Jan. 1, 1938; s. Paul Carl Franz and Alice Rose (Maunder) V.; m. Barbara Joan Feroe, Apr. 2, 1966; children: Gay Elizabeth, Robert Paul. BA, DePauw U., 1959; MD, Johns Hopkins U., 1963. Diplomate Am. Bd. Internal Medicine. Intern Grace-New Haven Hosp., 1963-64; resident Yale-New Haven Hosp., 1964-65, 67-68; asst. prof. medicine U. Conn., Farmington, 1969-70, assoc. dean, 1971-75; asst. clin. prof. medicine Yale U., New Haven, 1975—. Asst. to dir. health plan Yale U., 1981-84; physician in charge Kaiser Permanente, Stamford, Conn., 1986-90. Contbr. articles to profl. jours. Lt. comdr. USPHS, 1965-67. Fellow ACP; mem. Phi Beta Kappa, Alpha Omega Alpha. Democrat. Avocations: oil painting, travel. Home and Office: 15 W Haycock Point Rd Branford CT 06405-5307 E-mail: wesley.vietzke@snet.net.

VIEWEG, BRUCE WAYNE, mental health researcher; b. Westminster, Mass., July 30, 1947; s. Herman C. and Ardath (Woollacott) V.; m. JoAnne Rawlings, Dec. 19, 1970; children: Emily, Anna. BMus Ed, U. Lowell, 1969; MSEd, So. Ill. U., 1975. Tchr. Hampshire Country Sch., Rindge, NH, 1969—71; rsch. technician U. Mo. Inst. Psychiatry, Columbia, 1972—75, rsch. specialist, 1975—80, rsch. asst., 1980—84, rsch. assoc., 1984—94, dir. computer lab., 1987—94; dep. dir. for quality of treatment Mo. Dept. of Mental Health, Jefferson City, 1994—95, dir. of office of info. systems, 1995—99, chief info. officer, 1999; dir. IT svcs. for health scis. St. Louis U., 1999—2000, asst. v.p. application svcs., info. tech. svcs., 2000—02, assoc. v.p. application svcs., info. tech. svcs., 2002—. Author: (with others) many sci. books; contbr. articles profl. jours. Treas. Hand in Hand Presch., St. Charles, Mo., 1980; pres. Becky-David Elem. Sch. PTO, St. Charles, 1988, 89; long-range planning coun. Francis Howell Sch. Dist., 1988-94, long-range study com. on tech.,1990, long range task force on faculty compensation, 1990, mem. bd. edn., 1992-94, pres. 1993; steering com. Knights of Excellence North H.S., 1990; bd. dirs. Crider Mental Health Ctr., 2001-, Cmty. Health Charities of Kans. and Mo. Recipient Howell of Fame award Francis Howell Sch. Dist., 1990. Mem. Silver Key. Avocations: personal computing, reading. Home: 6 Regatta Bay Ct Lake Saint Louis MO 63367-2246 Office: St Louis U 3694 W Pine Mall Saint Louis MO 63108 E-mail: viewegbw@slu.edu.

VIEZER, TIMOTHY WAYNE, economist; b. Cleve., Jan. 13, 1959; s. Lawrence Stephen and Elaine Pearl (Thompson) V.; m. Jody Claire Russell, Oct. 14, 1988 (div. Aug. 1993); 1 child, Jessica Marlene; m. Joani Sue Yoakum, Sept. 21, 1996. BBA, BA with honors, Kent State U., 1982, MA in Econs., 1987, MA, 1989; PhD in Agrl. Econs., Ohio State U., 1998. Adminstrv. asst. Arthur Andersen & Co., Cleve., 1985; corp. economist Centerior Energy Corp., 1985-90; grad. teaching assoc. Ohio State U., Columbus, 1990-91; grad. rsch. assoc. Nat. Regulatory Rsch. Inst., 1991-93; asst. economist Huntington Nat. Bank, 1991-92; portfolio analyst State Tcrhs. Retirement System of Ohio, 1993-99; investment analyst Sch. Employees Retirement Sys. Ohio, 1999—. Instr. econs. Cuyahoga C.C., Parma, Ohio, 1989-90; lectr. Baldwin-Wallace Coll., Berea, Ohio, 1989-90, Ohio Dominican Coll., Columbus, 1991, Capital U., 1991—, Columbus State C.C., 1992—, Otterbein Coll., 1993—, Franklin U., 1994—. Co-author: The Soviet Occupation of Afghanistan, 1986. Named one of Outstanding Young Men of Am. U.S. Jaycees, 1981. Mem. Am. Econ. Assn., Nat. Assn. Bus. Economists, Internat. Assn. Bus. Forecasting (asst. sec. 1986, bd. dirs. 1987), Columbus Assn. Bus. Economists (pres.), Am. Real Estate Soc. Roman Catholic. Home: 231 E Como Ave Columbus OH 43202-1212

VIG, VERNON EDWARD, lawyer; b. St. Cloud, Minn., June 19, 1937; s. Edward Enoch and Salley Johanna (Johnson) V.; m, Susan Jane Rosenow, June 10, 1961; 1 child, Elizabeth Karen. BA, Carleton Coll., 1959; LLB, NYU, 1962, LLM, 1963; postdoctoral studies, Univ. Paris, Fac. de Droit, 1964. Bar: N.Y. 1962; avocat, Paris, 1992. Assoc. Cleary, Gottlieb, Steen & Hamilton, Paris, 1964, Donovan, Leisure, Newton & Irvine, N.Y.C. and Paris, 1965-72, ptnr., 1972-86, LeBoeuf, Lamb, Greene & MacRae, N.Y.C., 1986—2001, of counsel, 2002—. Sr. warden Grace Ch., Bklyn., 1986-2001. George F. Baker scholar, Fulbright scholar, 1963-64, Ford Found. scholar, 1963-64. Mem. ABA (internat. and antitrust sects.), N.Y. State Bar Assn. (chmn. antitrust sect. 1987-88), Assn. of Bar of City of N.Y., Internat. Bar Assn., Union Internat. des Avocats, Heights Casino (bklyn.), Merriewold Club (Forestburgh, N.Y., bd. dirs. 1985-91). Episcopalian. Office: LeBoeuf Lamb Greene & MacRae 125 W 55th St New York NY 10019-5369 E-mail: vvig@llgm.com.

VIGDOR, JAMES SCOTT, distribution executive; b. Bklyn., Oct. 12, 1953; s. Irving and Betty Jean (Wolkenbrod) V.; 1 child, Rachel Dyan. BA, Ohio State U., 1975. Regional distbn. mgr. Gestetner Corp., L.A., 1979-83; asst. ops. mgr. Wall-Pride, Inc., Van Nuys, Calif., 1983-88; ops. mgr. Opportunities for Learning, Inc., Chatsworth, 1988-89; dir. ops. Image Entertainment, 1989-91; ops mgr. Cal-Abco and Legend Computer Products, Woodland Hills, Calif., 1991-95; dir. ops. HW Electronics, Van Nuys, 1995-97; v.p. ops. ImpresTech., Wareforce, Inc./Advanced Optical Distbn., Encino, 1997-99; dir. ops. Fairchild Fasteners, Simi Valley, 1999—. Office: Fairchild Fasteners 3990A Heritage Oak Ct Simi Valley CA 93063 E-mail: jvigdor@worldnet.att.net., jimvigdor@fairchilddirect.com.

VIGEANT, SHAWN PATRICK, oil industry executive; b. New Bedford, Mass., Oct. 14, 1970; s. Roland Richard and Lea Andrews Vigeant; m. Kristin Lynn Whiteside; children: Ryan. BS in Ocean Engring., Fla. Inst. Tech., 1993. Cert. engr.-in-tng., Tex. Marine project geophysicist Digicon Geophys. (Veritas DGC), Houston, 1993—94; mech./ops. engr. Diamond Offshore Drilling, Inc., 1994—95, project engr., 1995—97, sr. subsea /mech. engr., 1997—98, mgr. contract svcs., 1998—99, mgr. contracts and mktg. dept., 1999—. Spkr. confs. in field. Contbr. articles to profl. jours. Team capt. /corp. leader Juvenile Diabetes Rsch. Found., Houston, 1999—. Mem.: Am. Petroleum Inst., Soc. Naval Archs. and Marine Engrs., Am. Assn. Drilling Engrs., Soc. Petroleum Engrs., Internat. Assn. Drilling Contractors. Presbyterian. Avocations: church, golf, softball, running, hunting. Office: Diamond Offshore Drilling Inc. 15415 Katy Fwy Suite 100 Houston TX 77094 Office Fax: 281-492-5310. Business E-Mail: svigeant@dodi.com.

VIGEN, JAMES BRUCE, minister, theologian; b. Chgo., Sept. 1, 1950; s. Oscar Clarence and Lois (Ander) V.; m. JoAnne Albing, Dec. 16, 1953; children: Katrina, Olav, Corinne. BA, Va. Commonwealth U., 1973; MDiv, Trinity Theol. Sem., Columbus, Ohio, 1977; MST, Yale U., 1978; PhD, Luth. Sch. Theology Chgo., 1991. Missionary pastor Evang. Luth. Ch. Am., Ft. Dauphin, Tulear, Madagascar, 1978-83; founder, dean Behaza (Tulear) Regional Theol. Sem., 1983-85; prof. systematic theology Ivory Theol. Sem., Fianarantsoa, Madagascar, 1988-89, acting dean Madagascar, 1989-90, assoc. dean, chair ch. history Madagascar, 1990-91; chmn. mission, liaison to ch. Malagasy Luth. Ch., Antananarivo, Madagascar, 1992-96; pastor Ascension Luth. Ch., Binghamton, N.Y., 1996-99; pastor, mem. adj. faculty Sch. Mission and Theology Stavanger (Rogaland, Norway) Internat. Ch., 1999—2002; dir. Lutheran Advocacy Ministry, 2002—. Mem. edn. com. Stavanger Internat. Sch., Rogaland, 2000—. Author: Madagascar and Christianity, 1993, Norwegian American Studies, Vol. 34, 1995, Christianity in the South of Madagascar, 1996; also articles. Decorated Chevalier, Govt. of Madagascar, 1997. Mem. Am. Acad. Religion, Am. Soc. Missiology, Norwegian-Am. Hist. Soc., Luth. Hist. Soc. Getysburg. Democrat. Avocations: walking, gardening. Home and Office: Holy Trinity Lutheran Church 2723 Clark Ave Raleigh NC 27607-7199 E-mail: htlcraleigh@worldnet.att.com.

VIGEN, KATHRYN L. VOSS, nursing administrator, educator; b. Lakefield, Minn., Sept. 24, 1934; d. Edward Stanley and Bertha C. (Richter) Voss; m. David C. Vigen, June 23, 1956 (div. 1977); children: Eric. E., Amy Vigen Hemstad, Aana Marie. BS in Nursing magna cum laude, St. Olaf Coll., 1956; MEd, S.D. State U., 1975; MS, Rush U., 1980; PhD, U. Minn., 1987. RN. Staff nurse various hosps., Mpls, Boston, Chgo., 1956-68; nursing instr. S.E.A. Sch. Practical Nursing, Sioux Falls, S.D., 1969-74; statewide coord. upward mobility in nursing Augustana Coll., 1974-78; cons./researcher S.D. Commn. Higher Edn., 1974-79; gov. appointed bd. mem. S.D. Bd. Nursing, 1975-79; RN upward mobility project dir., chair/dir. div. of nursing Huron Coll. S.D. State U., 1978-79, mobility project dir., 1980-84; head dept. nursing, assoc. prof. Luther Coll., Decorah, Iowa, 1984-94; prof. nursing Graceland Coll., Independence, Mo., 1994-2001; dir., dean Sch. Nursing, North Park U., Chgo., 2001—. Cons. in field; developer outreach MSN programs Graceland Coll.; governing bd. mem. Midwest Alliance in Nursing, S.D. and Iowa, 1984-92, Mo., 1998—; founder Soc. for Advancement of Nursing, Malta, 1992; developer Health Care in the Mediterranean Study Abroad Program, Greece and Malta, 1994, 96, 98; developer summer internship for Maltese nursing students Mayo Med. Ctr. and Luther Coll.; presenter on internat. collaboration with Malta for nursing leadership 2d Internat. Acad. Congress on Nursing, Kansas City, 1996; presenter in field. Author: Role of a Dean in a Private Liberal Arts College, 1992; devel. and initiated 3 nursing programs in S.D., 1974-84 (named Women of Yr., 1982). Lobbyist Nursing Schs. in S.D., 1974-79; task force mem. Sen. Tom Harkin's Nurse's Adv. Com., 1986-94. Fellow to rep. U.S.A. ANA cand. in internat. coun. nursing 3M, St. Paul, 1978; recipient Leadership award Bush Found., St. Paul, 1979; Faculty fellow Minn. Area Geriatric Edn. Ctr. U. Minn., 1990-91; recipient Fulbright award Malta Coun. Internat. Exch. of Scholars, Washington, 1992—. Mem. AAUW, ANA, AACN (hon. mem.), Am. Assn. Colls. Nursing (hon., exec. devel. subcom. 1990—, Hon. Mem. award), Internat. Assn. Human Caring, Iowa Nurse's Assn. (bd. dirs. 1989-92, mem. nursing edn. com. 1989—, co-pres. 1989—), Midwest Alliance in Nursing (gov. bd. rep. Iowa 1989-92, chair membership com. 1989-92, Mo., 1998—, S.D. gov. bd. rep. 1984-86, Rozella Schlotfeldt Leadership award 1993), Iowa Acad. Sci., Iowa Assn. Colls. Nursing Soc., Gerontol. Soc. Am., Am. Assn. Colls. Mich., Rotary, Sigma Theta Tau. Democrat. Lutheran. Avocations: singing, travel and other cultures, meeting people, sailing, reading. Home: 5360 N Lowell Ave # 412 Chicago IL 60630 Office: North Park U 3225 W Foster Ave Chicago IL 60625

VIGIER, FRANÇOIS CLAUDE DENIS, city planning educator; b. Geneva, Oct. 14, 1931; s. Eugene Henri Rene and Françoise (Dupuy) V. BArch, MIT, 1955; M in City Planning, Harvard U., 1959, PhD, 1967. Architect UN Relief and Works Agy., Jordan, 1955-57; designer Town Planning Cons., Cambridge, Mass., 1957-58; mem. faculty Harvard Grad. Sch. Design, 1960—, prof. city planning and urban design, 1968-85, Charles Dyer Norton prof. regional planning, 1985—, dir. Ctr. Urban Devel. Studies, 1987—, chmn. spl. programs, 1982-86, chmn. dept. urban planning and design, 1992-98. Vis. lectr. art Dartmouth Coll., 1962, 64; vis. critic urban design U. N.C., 1963; cons. Ford Found. Latin Am. program, 1964-65, Ednl. Svcs., Inc., 1966; dir. Harvard Ctr. Environ. Design Studies, 1967-69; pres. Nash-Vigier Inc., Cambridge, 1965-91. Author: Change and Apathy: Liverpool and Manchester During the Industrial Revolution, 1970, Housing in Tunis, 1987; contbr. articles to various periodicals. Decorated Knight, Order of Merit, France, 1995. Mem. Am. Inst. Cert. Planners, Am. Planning Assn. Home: 27 Fayerweather St Cambridge MA 02138-3329 E-mail: FVigier@gsd.harvard.edu.

VIGIL, DANIEL AGUSTIN, academic administrator; b. Denver, Feb. 13, 1947; s. Agustin and Rachel (Naranjo) V.; m. Claudia Cartier. BA in History, U. Colo., Denver, 1978, JD, 1982. Bar: Colo. 1982, U.S. Dist. Ct. Colo. 1983. Project mgr. Mathematics Policy Rsch., Denver, 1978; law clk. Denver Dist. Ct., 1982-83; ptnr. Vigil and Bley, Denver, 1983-85; asst. dean sch. law U. Colo., Boulder, 1983-89, assoc. dean sch. law, 1989—. Apptd. by chief justice of Colo. Supreme Ct. to serve on Colo. Supreme Ct. Ad Hoc Com. on miniority participation in legal profession, 1988-94; adj. prof. U. Colo. Sch. Law; mem. Gov. Colo. Lottery Commn., 1990-97; mem. Colo. Supreme Ct. Hearing Bd., 1998—; mem. atty. regulatory adv. com. Colo. Supreme Ct., 2002—. Editor (newsletter) Class Action, 1987-88; co-editor (ethics com. column) Colo. Lawyer, 1995-97. Bd. dirs. Legal Aid Soc. Met. Denver, 1986-99, chmn. bd. dirs., 1998-99; past v.p. Colo. Minority Scholarhip Consortium, pres. 1990-91; bd. trustees Colo. Atty.'s Fund for Client Protection, 2001—, Boulder Bar Found., 2000—; mem. Task Force on Community Race Rels., Boulder, 1989-94; past mem. jud. nomination rev. com. U.S. Senator Tim Wirth; chmn. bd. dirs. Colo. Legal Svcs., 2000-. Mem. Colo. Bar Assn. (mem. legal edn. and admissions com. 1989-94, chmn. 1989-91, bd. govs. 1991, 97—), Hispanic Nat. Bar Assn. (chmn. scholarship com. 1990-95), Colo Hispanic Bar Assn. (bd. dirs. 1985-89, pres. 1990), Denver Bar Assn. (joint com. on minorities in the legal profession), Boulder County Bar Assn. (ex-officio mem., trustee), Inns of Ct. (Penfield Tate chpt.), Phi Delta Phi (faculty sponsor). Roman Catholic. Avocations: skiing, cosmology. Home: 828 3d Ave PO Box 518 Lyons CO 80540-0518 Office: U Colo Sch Law PO Box 401 Boulder CO 80303 E-mail: Daniel.Vigil@colorado.edu.

VIGIL, EUGENE LEON, federal agency administrator, cell biologist, retired; b. Chgo., Mar. 14, 1941; s. Marcelo Raymond and Anna (Lewus) V.; m. Suan M. Davis, Jan. 22, 1963 (div. Sept. 1989); children: Michael, Jennifer, Aimee; m. Marcia Janice Holden, Apr. 18, 1993. BS, Loyola U., 1963; MS, U. Iowa, 1965, PhD, 1967. NIH postdocturl fellow U. Wis., 1967-69; pub. health trainee U. Chgo., 1969-71, Danforth tutor, 1970; asst. prof. Marquette U., Milw., 1971-79, U. Md., College Park, 1979-81, rsch. assoc., 1981-88; plant physiologist USDA/ARS, Beltsville, Md., 1988-95; program dir. NIH, Bethesda, 1995-98, sci. rev. adminstr., 1998—, ret., 2001. Program chmn. Histochem. Soc., N.Y.C., 1976-79, councilor 1979-82; study sect. mem. cell biology NSF, Washington, 1983-87; mem. minority affairs com. Am. Soc. Cell Biology, Bethesda, 1991-97; chmn. min. affr com., mem. exec. com. Am. Soc. Plant Physiology, Rockville, Md., 1995-97. Author, editor: Botanical Cytochemistry, 1980. Pres. Milw. Hort. Soc.; precinct chmn. Rep. Party, Chgo. Predoctoral fellow NIH, U. Iowa, Iowa City, 1966, fellow German Acad. Exch., Munich, 1975; grantee NATO, Munich and Heidelberg, Germany, 1976, NSF, 1979. Mem.: Internat. League Antiquarian Booksellers, Antiquarian Booksellers Assn. Am., Rotary (group sec. Beltsville, Md. 1998—99, pres.-elect 1999—, pres. 2000—02). Home: 4606 Brandon Ln Beltsville MD 20705-2603 E-mail: vigile@kreative.net.

VIGIL, HENRY P. information technology executive; BA in Philosophy, MBA, Stanford U. From dir. mktg. to corp. v.p. Microsoft, Redmond, Wash., 1990, corp. v.p. consumer strategy & partnerships. Bd. dir. Artist Trust. Founder City Yr. Seattle. Office: One Microsoft Way Redmond WA 98052-6399*

VIGIL-GIRON, REBECCA, state official; b. Taos, N.Mex., Sept. 4, 1954; d. Felix W. and Cecilia (Santistevan) Vigil; m. Rick Giron; 1 child, Andrew R. AA in Elem. Edn., N.Mex. Highlands U., 1978, BA in French, 1991. Sec., project monitor, customer svc. rep. Pub. Svc. Co. N.Mex., 1978-86; sec. of state N.Mex., 1987-90, 98—; exec. dir. N.Mex. Commn. Status of Women, 1991; electoral observer UN, Angola, Africa, 1992, Internat. Found. Electoral Sys., Dominican Republic, 1994, Equatorial Guinea, Africa, 1996, Washington, 1996. Participant AMPART, Mex., 1991. Dem. nominee U.S. Ho. Reps., 1990. Named among 100 MOst Influential Hispanics in Nation, Hispanic Bus. Mag., 1990; recipient Trio Achievers award S.W. Assn. Student Assistance Programs, 1993, Gov.'s award Outstanding N.Mex. Women, 1994. Mem. Albuquerque Hispano C. of C. (membership rep., sr. sales mktg. rep., corp. rels. coord.) Office: Office of the New Mexico Secretary of State State Capitol North Annex, Suite 300 Santa Fe NM 87503*

VIGLIOTTI, PATRICIA NOREEN, welder, sculptor; b. Poughkeepsie, N.Y., May 13, 1955; d. James George and Florence Violet (Terwilligar) Dingee; Grad. h.s., Stratsbough. Welder Argos Inc., Brester, N.Y., 1989—; owner Vigliotti Sculpture Gallery & Studio, Balwinville. One woman shows include Ward Lawrence, N.Y.C., Gallery 84; exhibited in group shows at Tannery Brook Collections Gallery, Woodstock, N.Y., Samagundi Club Galleries, New Rochell Art Assn. (hon. mention), Gregg Chim Gallery, 1992, Conn. Acad. of Fine Arts, 1992, Orgn. of Ind. Artists, N.Y.C., represented in Providence Town of Mass. by Ester Lastique; featured as a sculptor in New Art International, 1997-98. Avocations: raising cockatiels and iguanas. Home: 4 Locust St Apt E Fishkill NY 12524

VIGNERON, ALLEN HENRY, theology educator, rector, auxiliary bishop; b. Mt. Clemens, Mich., Oct. 21, 1948; s. Elwin E. and Bernadine K. (Kott) V. AB in Philosophy, Sacred Heart Sem., Detroit, 1970; STL in Fundamental Theology, Pontifical Gregorian U., 1977; PhD in Philosophy, Cath. U. Am., 1987. Ordained deacon Roman Cath. Ch., 1973, ordained priest, 1975, titular bishop, 1996. Assoc. pastor Our Lady Queen of Peace Ch., Harper Woods, Mich., 1975-79; asst. prof. philosophy and theology Sacred Heart Major Sem., Detroit, 1985—; addetto of the secretariat of his Holiness the Pope The Holy See, Vatican City, 1991-94; rector, pres. Sacred Heart Major Sem., Detroit, 1994—; auxiliary bishop Archdiocese of Detroit, 1996—. Adj. prof. theology Pontifical Gregorian U., Rome, 1992-94. Office: Sacred Heart Major Sem 2701 W Chicago Detroit MI 48206-1704

VIGNESWARAN, WICKII THAMBIAH, cardiothoracic surgeon, educator; b. Jaffna, Sri Lanka, Jan. 25, 1955; came to U.S., 1991; s. Murugesu and Raja Poopathy (Nagalingam) Thambiah; m. Jnanarupy Thillainayagam, Dec. 3, 1984; children: Yalini, Hari, Janani. MB BChir, U. Sri Lanka, Peradeniya, 1978. Advanced cardiothoracic surg. fellow Mayo Clinic, Rochester, Minn., 1991-93; dir. gen. thoracic surgery U. Ill.-Chgo. Med. Ctr., 1994-98; dir. thoracic organ, dir. cardiothoracic transplant U. Ill.-Chgo., 1994-98; chief cardiothoracic surgery Westside VA Med. Ctr., Chgo., 1994-98; attending assoc. Michael Reese Hosp., 1994-98; courtesy staff Mercy Hosp. Med. Ctr., 1994-98; staff mem. Hines VA Med. Ctr., 1998—; chief thoracic surgery Loyola U. Med. Ctr., Maywood, Ill., 1998—, dir. lung transplantation, 1998—. Mem. exec. com. Tamil-Nadu med. grads., Chgo., 1996-98; faculty advisor Hindu Student Coun., U. Ill.-Chgo., 1996-98. Contbr. numerous articles to med. jours. including Thorax, Jour. Cardiovasc. Surgery, Jour. Clin. Transplantation. Sen. U. Ill.-Chgo., Champaign and Rockford, Ill., 1996-98; chmn. cardiothoracic subcom. Regional Organ Bank of Ill., Chgo., 1996-97. Recipient Trainee Investigator award Midwestern Award Cen. Soc. for Clin. Investigation and Am. Fedn. for Clin. Rsch., 1993, Young Investigator award DuPont Pharm./ACP, 1993. Fellow ACP, Royal Coll. Surgeons Edinburgh, Royal Coll. Physicians and Surgeons Can., ACS, Internat. Coll. Surgeons; mem. AAAS, Internat. Soc. Heart and Lung Transplantation (coun. mem. for pulmonary transplantation, coun. mem. for basic sci. and pathology), Internat. Soc. for Diseases of the Esophagus, Internat. Surg. Soc., Royal Coll. Surgeons and Physicians London, Royal Coll. Surgeons Eng., Brit. Thoracic Soc., Soc. Cardiothoracic Surgeons of Gt. Britain and Ireland, Am. Fedn. for Clin. Rsch., Am. Thoracic Soc., Soc. Thoracic Surgeons, Ill. Thoracic Surg. Soc. (pres. 2001), N.Y. Acad. Sci., Gen. Thoracic Surgery Club, Chgo. Surg. Soc., N.Am. Tamils Sci. and Tech. Soc. Hindu. Avocation: traveling, martial arts, nature. Office: Loyola U & Stritch Sch of Medicine 2160 S 1st Ave Maywood IL 60153-3304 E-mail: wvignes@wpo.it.luc.edu.

VIGODA, ABE, actor; b. N.Y.C., Feb. 24, 1921; s. Samuel and Lena (Moses) V.; m. Beatrice Schy, Feb. 24, 1968; 1 dau., Carol. Student, Theatre Sch. Dramatic Arts, Am. Theatre Wing. Actor in numerous Broadway prodns. including The Man in The Glass Booth, 1968, Tough to Get Help, 1972, Marat-Sade, 1967, Inquest, 1970, Arsenic and Old Lace, 1986; film appearances include: The Godfather, 1972, Part II, 1974, The Don is Dead, 1973,

Newman's Law, 1973, The Cheap Detective, 1978, Prancer, 1990, Look Who's Talking, 1990, Joe Versus the Volcano, 1991, Keaton's Cop, 1991, Taking Gary Feldman, 1992, Sugar Hill, 1993, North, 1994, Love is All There Is, 1996, Good Burger, 1997, Me and the Gods, 1997, A Brooklyn State of Mind, 1997, Just the Ticket, 1999, Chump Change, 1999, (voice) Batman: Mask of the Phantasm, 1993; TV appearances include Barney Miller 1975-79 (Emmy award nomination 1975-76, 76-77), Fish, 1977-78, Murder She Wrote, MacGyver, Wings, Law and Order, Mad About You, Diagnosis Murder, Weird Science, Touched by an Angel, Viva Variety, The Norm Show; TV films include The Devil's Daughter, 1973, Toma, 1973, The Story of Pretty Boy Floyd, 1974, Having Babies, 1976, How To Pick Up Girls, 1978, The Comedy Company, 1978, Death Car on The Freeway, 1979, Gridlock, 1980, Witness to the Mob, 1998, others. Mem. Actors Equity Assn., Screen Actors Guild, AFTRA. *When I was a young man I was told success had to come in my youth. I found this to be a myth. My experiences have taught me that if you deeply believe in what you are doing, success can come at any age.*

VIGTEL, GUDMUND, museum director emeritus; b. July 9, 1925; came to U.S., 1948, naturalized, 1966; s. Arne Jonsen and Elisabeth (Petri) V.; m. Solveig Lund, 1951 (div. 1964); 1 child, Elisabeth; m. Carolyn Gates Smith, July 18, 1964; 1 child, Catherine Higdon. BFA, U. Ga., 1952, MFA, 1953; DFA (hon.), Atlanta Coll. Art, 1991. Adminstrv. asst. Corcoran Gallery Art, Washington, 1954-61, asst. dir., 1961-63; dir. High Mus. Art, Atlanta, 1963-91, dir. emeritus, 1991—. Contbr. articles and essays to profl. publs. With Royal Norwegian Air Force, 1944-45. Decorated Chevalier des Arts et Lettres, Min. of Culture, France, 1985; recipient Order of Merit 1st Class, Fed. Republic Germany, 1989. Home: 2082 Golfview Dr NW Atlanta GA 30309-1210

VIIL, HEINO, retired engineer; b. Riisipere, Estonia, Dec. 18, 1919; arrived in U.S., 1951; s. Johannes Friedrich and Pauline (Jahnsohn) Viil; m. Ella Toomet, Apr. 30, 1941 (div. 1949); m. Mirdza Berzins, July 25, 1953; children: Brunolf, Silvia. PhD, Albert-Ludwigs U., Freiburg, West Germany, 1950; BS, Drexel U., Phila., 1962; MS, George Washington U., 1967, SUNY, Buffalo, 1974. Preliminary engr. Proctor & Schwartz, Phila., 1951—62; rsch. engr. Robertshaw, King of Prussia, 1962—63; ops. analyst Vitro Labs., Silver Spring, Md., 1963—68; devel. engr. Bell Aerospace Co., Buffalo, 1968—74; sr. engr. Singer, Kearfott, Wayne, NJ, 1974—78; sr. mem. tech. staff ITT Def. Comms. Divsn., Nutley, 1978—94; ret., 1994. Mem.: Alpha Sigma Lambda. Home: 543 Main St Little Falls NJ 07424-2448

VIJAY, P. V. engineering educator; b. Bangalore, Karnataka State, India, June 22, 1967; s. B. S. VenkataRayappa and N. Anjana; m. Sucharitha Bachanna; children: Aishwarya. M in Structural Engring., Bangalore U., 1991, W.Va. U., 1995, PhD, 1998. Lectr. MSR Inst. Tech., Bangalore, 1991—93; engring. scientist Constructed Facilities Ctr. W.Va. U., Morgantown, 1999—2000, asst. prof. (rsch.) dept. civil engring., 2000—. Contbr. articles and papers to profl. jours. Grantee, FHWA, WVDOT, Army Corps Engrs., 1999, 2000, 2001. Mem.: ASCE, ACI (reviewer jour. papers). Office: W Va U Dept Civil Engring Coll Engring Morgantown WV 26505 Personal E-mail: pvvijaypv@yahoo.com.

VIJAYAKUMAR, RAJAGOPAL, filter industry executive; b. Madras, India, Jan. 8, 1950; came to the U.S., 1975; s. Arum Visvanathan and Bhama (Rajan) Rajagopal; m. Sarojini Sockalingam, June 21, 1972; children: Vinod, Gayathri, Savithri. BSME, U. Madras, 1971; MSME, U. Minn., 1977, PhD in Mech. Engring., 1982. Exec. in tng. Easun Group, Madras, 1971-73; works mgr. Torrance & Sons, 1973-75; rsch./tchg. asst. U. Minn., Mpls., 1976-82; sr. scientist, mgr. CE-Environ., Camarillo, Calif., 1982-89; dir. engring. and R&D Cambridge Filter Corp., Syracuse, N.Y., 1989-91; spl. project mgr. Racal Health and Safety, 1991-93; dir. mktg. Hollingsworth & Vose, West Groton, Mass., 1993-2001; v.p. tech. and mktg. Air Techniques Internat., 2001—. Contbr. articles to profl. jours. Mem. ASME, Inst. Environ. Sci. (chair working group 1989—), U.S. Rowing Assn. (vol., coach). Avocations: carpentry, rowing, photography. Home: 3928 Willowbrook Ln Liverpool NY 13090-3156 Office: Air Techniques Internat 11403 Cronridge Dr Owings Mills MD 21117 E-mail: vvvijay@aol.com.

VIJAYARATNAM, KANAPATHIPILLAI, civil and environmental engineer, consultant, director; b. Analaitivu, Sri Lanka, May 10, 1948; arrived in Eng., 1979, naturalized, 1990; s. Kathirvelu Kanapathipillai and Parvathy Ponniah; m. Sakuntala Mylwaganam, Oct. 31, 1979. BSc in Engring. with honors, U. Ceylon, Peradeniya, 1971; M Engring., Asian Inst. Tech., Bangkok, 1977; MSc in Pub. Health Environ. Engring., Imperial Coll. U. London, 1982; cert. sustainable bus. challenge, World Bus. Coun. Sustainable Devel., 1999. Chartered engr., U.K. Instr. civil engring. U. Ceylon, Peradeniya, 1972; civil engr. Mahaweli Devel. Bd., Colombo, Sri Lanka, 1972-75, Renardet Engring., Singapore, 1977-80; engr. Chanton Engring. Ltd., Middlesex, U.K., 1984-85, S.P. Collins Assocs., Cambridge, U.K., 1985-86; cons. civil engr. Coulsdon, U.K., 1986-88; sr. engr. Neilcot Constrn. Ltd., Kent, U.K., 1988-90; engr. clean water dept. Binnie & Ptnrs., Cons. Engrs., Redhill, U.K., 1990-94; sr. engr. grade 1 SMHBinnie Cons. Engrs., K.L., Malaysia, 1995-96; dep. project mgr., prin. engr. S.S.P. Consulting Engrs., Kuala Lumpur, Malaysia, 1996-97, engring. cons. Malaysia, 1998-99; mng. dir. Rosebury Cons., Ltd., 1999—. Bd. dirs. AITA-NET (Europe), Ltd., AITA-NET Ltd.; engring. cons., Civil, Water & Environ. Engring. Projs., 1998-99, exec. dir. AITA-Net (Europe), Internat. Cons. Consortium, 2001—, participant, presenter various internat. confs. and seminars, Am. (Orlando, Pitts., MIT, Las Vegas), U.K. (London, Oxford, Newcastle), Europe (Netherlands, Sweden, Switzerland, Italy), Asia (Malaysia, Singapore, Thailand, Australia). Orig. contbr. to re-engring. of water ind. orgs., Broader Edu. of Civil Engs. in 21st Century, Cost and Performance Optimization of Water Treatment System (conceptual and mathematical), 1982, Sustainable Development of Infrastructure in Water and Environ. Engring., 1996, Environmentally Sound Dam and Water Power Devel., 1995, Emergence and Complexity in Urban Environmental Engring Mgmt. in 21st Century, 1999, Environ. Engring. Edn. in 21st Century, 1999, and Future Dir. Tech. Edn. in Asia, 1999, Project Mgmt. Water Supply and Treatment Projects in Asia, 1995, Future Direction Engrin. Edn. for a Sustainable World in the New Millenium, 2000, Sustainable Water Supply for City, 2001, Sustainable Waste Management, 2001. Contbr. articles, tech. papers to profl. jours. U.K. Govt. scholar, 1976-77; NATO Advanced Inst. grantee, 1981, UNESCO/Colo. State U. grantee, 1981; named one of 500 Leaders of New Century, 1999, Asians in Millennium, 100 Eminent Tamils of 20th Century. Mem. AAAS, ASCE, UNESCO, Instn. Civil Engrs. London, Internat. Water Assn., Internat. Assn. Hydraulic Rsch. and Engring., Internat. Assns. Water Resources, Water Power, Soc. of Risk Analysis, Internat. Coun. on Systems Engring., Am. Water Resources Assn., Brit. Assn. Advancement of Sci. Avocations: golf, travel, reading, writing, fine arts. Home: 1 Ashcroft Rise Coulsdon Surrey CR5 2SS England E-mail: vijay@vijayaratnam.com.

VIJUK, MICHAEL, business management educator; b. Chgo., July 15, 1954; m. Beth Lynn Krueger, June 1, 1996. BA, Carthage Coll., 1976; MBA, Roosevelt U., 1977. Buyer Goldblatt Bros., Chgo., 1977-80; mem. mgmt. faculty William R. Harper Coll., Palatine, Ill., 1981—. Trustee McHenry C.C., Ill., 2001. Mem. Ill. C.C. Faculty Assn. (exec. bd. dirs. 2001). Avocations: woodworking, golf. Office: William R Harper Coll Dept Bus Mgmt Palatine IL 60067 E-mail: mvijuk@harper.cc.il.us.

VIJVERBERG, WIM PETRUS MARIA, economics educator; b. The Hague, The Netherlands, Sept. 30, 1955; came to U.S., 1977; s. Wilhelmus P.M. and Apollonia E. (Barendse) V.; m. Chu-Ping Chen, May 26, 1981; children: Michelle, Andrea, William. BA, Erasmus U. of Rotterdam, The Netherlands, 1975; MA, U. Pitts., 1979, PhD, 1981. Postdoctoral fellow Yale U., New Haven, 1981-84; vis. asst. prof. econs. U. Hawaii at Manoa, Honolulu, 1984-85; asst. prof. Ill. State U., Normal, 1985-86; asst. prof. econs. and polit. economy U. Tex. at Dallas, Richardson, 1986-91, assoc. prof., 1991-97, prof., 1997—. Cons. The World Bank, Washington, 1985-91, 94-96. Contbr. articles to profl. jours., 1980—. Deacon, Calvary Chapel Assembly of God, Richardson, 1991—. Andrew Mellon Found. predoctoral fellow, Pitts., 1979-81. Mem. Am. Econ. Assn., Econometric Soc. Office: Univ Tex Dallas Sch Social Sci 2601 N Floyd Rd Richardson TX 75080-1407

VIKEN, MARK, information technology executive; m. Kathryn Viken; 3 children. AA, Harper Coll. Sales mgmt. positions consumer electronics retailer, Chgo.; key accounts sales person Sony Electronics Inc., 1981, v.p. sales office, v.p. mktg. gen. audio, mgmt. positions consumer audio/video group, sr. v.p. personal audio/video mktg., sr. v.p. divsn. digital imaging, pres. Personal Network Solutions Co., sr. v.p. divsn. info. tech. products. Office: Sony Electronics 1 Sony Dr Park Ridge NJ 07656*

VIKTORA, RICHARD EMIL, lawyer; b. Chgo., July 1, 1943; s. Emil J. and Lillian B. (Smatlak) V.; m. Anne Marie Kus, Feb. 20, 1971. BS, U. Ill., 1965; JD, John Marshall Law Sch., 1969. Bar: Ill. 1969, U.S. Dist. Ct. (no. dist.) Ill. 1969, U.S. Ct. Appeals (7th cir.) 1970, U.S. Supreme Ct. 1975, N.Y. 1981, U.S. Dist. Ct. (so. and ea. dists.) N.Y. 1983. Assoc. Menk, Johnson & Bishop, Chgo., 1969-73; litigation group counsel, regulatory counsel, asst. sec. G.D. Searle & Co., Skokie, Ill., 1973-80; asst. sec., dir. gen. svcs. Revlon, Inc.; asst. sec. Revlon Group, Inc., N.Y.C., 1980-92; gen. counsel Skidmore, Owings & Merrill LLP, 1992—. Lawyer; b. Chgo., July 1, 1943; s. Emil J. and Lillian B. (Smatlak) V.; m. Anne Marie Kus, Feb. 20, 1971. B.S., U. Ill., 1965; JD, John Marshall Law Sch., 1969. Bar: Ill. 1969, U.S. Dist. Ct. (no. dist.) Ill. 1969, U.S. Ct. Appeals (7th cir.) 1970, U.S. Supreme Ct. 1975, N.Y. 1981, U.S. Dist. Ct. (so. and ea. dists.) N.Y. 1983. Assoc. Menk, Johnson, & Bishop, Chgo., 1969-73; instr. John Marshall Law Sch., Chgo., 1970-73; litigation group counsel, regulatory counsel, asst. sec. G.D. Searle & Co., Skokie, Ill., 1973-80; asst. sec., dir. gen. svcs. Revlon, Inc., also asst. sec. Revlon Group, Inc., N.Y.C., 1980-92; gen. counsel Skidmore Owings & Merrill LLP, N.Y.C., 1992—. Zoning adminstr. Village of Bartlett (Ill.), 1974, chmn. Plan Commn., 1975, trustee, 1975-79. Mem. ABA, Ill. State Bar Assn., Chgo. Bar Assn., Def. Research Inst., Am. Corp. Counsel Assn., Assn. Trial Lawyers Am., Def. Assn. N.Y., Assn. of Bar of City of N.Y., Westchester-Fairfield Corp. Counsel Assn., Order of John Marshall Law Sch., Delta Theta Phi (scholar Key), Anvil Club (East Dundee, Ill.), Masons. Republican. Roman Catholic. Zoning adminstr. Village of Bartlett, Ill., 1974, chmn. Plan Commn., 1975, trustee, 1975-79. Mem. ABA, Ill. State Bar Assn., Chgo. Bar Assn., Def. Rsch. Inst., Am. Corp. Counsel Assn., Assn. Trial Lawyers Am., Def. Assn. N.Y., Assn. of Bar of City of N.Y., Westchester-Fairfield Corp. Counsel Assn., Order of John Marshall Law Sch., Delta Theta Phi (scholar Key), Anvil Club (East Dundee, Ill.), Masons. Republican. Roman Catholic. Home: 11 Saddle Hill Ln Stamford CT 06903-2309 Office: Skidmore Owings & Merrill LLP 14 Wall St New York NY 10005-2101 E-mail: richard.e.viktora@som.com.

VILA, ADIS MARIA, corporate executive, former government official, lawyer; b. Cuba, Aug. 1, 1953; came to U.S., 1962; d. Calixto Vila and Adis C. Fernandez. BA with distinction, Rollins Coll., 1974; JD with honors, U. Fla., 1978; LLM with high honors, Institut Universitaire de Hautes Estudes Internationales, Geneva, 1981; MBA, U Chgo., 1997. Bar: Fla. 1979, D.C. 1984. Assoc. Paul & Thomson, 1979-82; White House fellow Office Pub. Liaison, Washington, 1982-83; spl. asst. to sec. state for inter-Am. affairs Dept. State, 1983-86; dir. Office of Mex. and Caribbean Basin, Dept. Commerce, 1986-87; sec. Dept. Adminstrn., State of Fla., 1987-89; asst. sec. for adminstrn. USDA, Washington, 1989-91; vis. asst., prof. Fla. Internat. U., 1993-94; vis. fellow Nat. Def. U., Washington, 1992-93; v.p. internat. devel. The Vigoro Corp., Chgo., 1994-95; v.p. govt. affairs regulatory policy, Carribean & Latin Am. Nortel Networks, 1997-2000; pres., CEO Vila & Assocs., 2001—02; v.p. external affairs Miami Dade C.C., Fla., 2002—. Mem. adv. bd. Americas, Global Asset Mgmt. Fund, 1999—. Trustee So. Ctr. for Internat. Studies, 1987—. Named one of 100 Most Influential Hispanics, 1988; Paul Harris fellow Rotary Internat., 1983, U.S.-Japan Leadership fellow, 1991-92, Eisenhower Exch. fellow, Beca Fiore, Argentina, 1992. Mem. Dade County Bar Assn. (bd. dirs. young and lawyers sect. 1979-87), Coun. Fgn. Rels. (term mem. 1987-92), Internat. Women's Forum, Am. Coun. Young Polit. Leaders (bd. dirs. 1984—), Women Execs. in State Govt. (bd. dirs. 1987-89). Republican. Roman Catholic. Avocations: tennis, skiing, golf, theater, arts. E-mail: adisvila@aol.com.

VILA, ROBERT JOSEPH, television host, designer, real estate developer; b. Miami, Fla., June 20, 1946; s. Roberto and Esperanza (Robles) V.; m. Diana Barrett, Oct. 3, 1975; children: Christopher, Monica, Susannah. AA in Architecture, Miami Dade Jr. Coll., 1966; BS in Journalism, U. Fla., 1969. Editor English Lang. Cons., Stuttgart, Fed. Republic of Germany, 1971; stagehand Wurttemburg State Theatre, 1972; project mgr. Barrett Assocs., Boston, 1973-74; pres. R.J. Vila, Inc., 1975-85; host This Old House Sta. WGBH-TV, 1978-89; host Bob Vila's Home Again, Cape Cod and Chgo., 1990—, Martha's Vineyard and Malibu, Calif., 1991-92. Author: This Old House, 1980, Bob Vila's This Old House, 1982, Guide to Building Materials, 1986, Guide to Buying Your Dream House, 1990, Bob Vila's Tool Box, 1993, Bob Vila's Guide to Historic Homes of New England, 1993, Bob Vila's Guide to Historic Homes of the South, 1993, Bob Vila's Guide to Historic Homes of the Mid-Atlantic, 1993, Bob Vila's Workshop, 1994, Bob Vila's Guide to Historic Homes of the Midwest and Great Plains, 1994, Bob Vila's Guide to Historic Homes of the West, 1994, (A&E Special) Bob Vila's Guide to Historic Homes, 1996, Bob Vila's American Home mag., 1996. Bd. dirs. Plimouth Plantation, Plymouth, Mass., Nat. Alliance to End Homelessness, Washington. Emmy award New England Region, 1979, Nat., 1985. Mem.: Screen Actors Guild, Am. Fedn. TV Radio Artists, Friars Club (N.Y.C.). Roman Catholic. Avocations: sailing, fishing, cycling, gardening, woodworking. Office: BVTV Inc 115 Kingston St Boston MA 02111 Fax: (617) 547-1932.

VILA-BARNÉS, GLADYS, language educator; b. San Juan, P.R., Feb. 4, 1943; d. José Vila, Gladys Barnés; m. Dimas Pagán, Dec. 15, 1972; 1 child Amarilis Pagán Vila. BA magna cum laude, U. P.R., 1963; MA, NYU, 1965; PhD, U. P.R., 1982; postgrad., Universidad Central, Madrid, 1966—68. Music tchr. Central H.S., PR, 1966; tchr. Republica de Colombia H.S., 1969; instr. Spanish as a second lang. U. P.R., San Juan, 1969—77; instr. P.R. Jr. Coll., 1969—71; prof. Interam. U., San Juan, 1971—. Mem. Com. to Commemorate the 500th Anniversary of Discovery of P.R., 1993. Author: Significado y coherencia del universo namativo de Augusto Roa Bastos, 1984; co-author: Fundamentos de la Lengua española, 1985, Personalidad y Literatura puertorrigueñas, 1997. Mem. panel literary awards U. P.R., Recinto Ciencias Medicas, 1994; mem. panel lit.awards Interam. U., San Juan, 1994. Recipient Spl. award for El Caribe: Encuenho Cultural, Interam. U., 1985, Spl. award for Personalidad y Lit. puertorriguеñas, 1985. Mem.: MLA, L.Am. Studies Assn., Amnesty Internat. Roman Catholic. Avocations: piano, oil painting.

VILAR, ALBERTO W. investment company executive; b. N.J. Bachelor's degree, Washington and Jefferson Coll.; Master's degree, Iona Coll. Co-founder, pres., profile mgr. Amerindo Investment Advisors, San Francisco, 1980. Active in philanthropic, healthcare, and cultural endeavors; founder Alberto Vilar Global Fellows in the Performing Arts. Office: Amerindo Investment Advisors Ste 2300 1 Embarcadero Ctr San Francisco CA 94111

VILARDEBO, ANGIE MARIE, management consultant, parochial school educator; b. Tampa, Fla., July 15, 1938; d. Vincent and Antonina (Fazio) Noto; m. Charles Kenneth Vilardebo, June 26, 1960; children: Charles, Kenneth, Michele, Melanie. BA, Notre Dame Md., 1960; postgrad., Rollins Coll., 1980. Cert. tchr., Fla. Tchr. Sea Park Elem. Sch., Satellite Beach, Fla., 1960-61; office mgr. Computer Systems Enterprises, 1973-76; artist, 1976-79; employment counselor Career Cons., Melbourne, Fla., 1979-80; tchr. Our Lady of Lourdes Parochial Sch., 1980-89, 93-98; pres. Consol. Ventures, Inc., Satellite Beach, 1989—, Versatile Suppliers, Inc., Satellite Beach, 1989-93. Prin. search com. Diocese of Orlando, Fla., 1989-90. Patentee personal grading machine. V.p. Jaycees, Satellite Beach, 1976-77, pres., 1977-78. Recipient 1st Place Art award Fla. Fedn. Woman's Clubs, 1978, 2nd Place Art award, 1979, Honorable Mention, 1980. Mem. Satellite Beach Woman's Club, Paper Chaser's Investment Club, Brevard Arts Ctr. & Mus., Space Coast Art League (social chmn. 1987—), CompuVest Investment Club. Roman Catholic. Avocations: bridge, writing, reading, oil painting, entrepreneurship. Home and Office: 100 Riverside Dr Apt 706 Cocoa FL 32922-7866

VILARDI, AGNES FRANCINE, real estate broker; b. Monson, Mass., Sept. 29, 1918; m. Frank S. Vilardi, Dec. 2, 1939 (dec.); 2 children. Cert. of Dental assisting, Pasadena Jr. Coll., 1954. Lic. real estate broker. Real estate broker, owner Vilardi Realty, Yorba Linda, Calif. Cons. in property mgmt. Mem. Am. Dental Asst. Assn., North Orange County Bd. Realtors (sec./treas. 1972), Yorba Linda Country Club, Desert Princess Country Club. Home and Office: 18982 Villa Ter Yorba Linda CA 92886-2610

VILARDI, CHARLES RONALD, assistant principal; b. Patterson, N.J., Oct. 30, 1970; s. Richard Joseph and JoAnn Barbara (Anthony) V.; m. Tracy Lynn Blatchford, July 31, 1993; children: Carly Marie, Nicholas Anthony. AA, Edison C.C., Ft. Myers, Fla., 1991; BS in Elem. Edn., U. South Fla., 1993, MEd in Ednl. Leadership, 1997. Aide City of Cape Coral, Fla., 1986-88, counselor, 1988-93, dir. summer programs, 1993-99, asst. prin., 1999—; tchr. emotionally handicapped Lee County Sch. Bd., Ft. Myers, Fla., 1993-94, tchr. 1st grade, 1994-97, tchr. 4th grade, 1997-99. Sch. adv. chairperson Gulf Elem., Cape Coral, 1995-98, grade level chairperson, 1995-97; mem. tech. com., 1995, 97, sch. improvement com., 1996-99, chairperson 5 star award com., 1997-99; mem. Lee County Quality Improvement Com.. Mem. ASCD, Nat. Coun. Tchrs. of English. Avocations: cooking, swimming, vacationing. Office: North Ft Myers Acad for Arts 1856 Suncoast Ln Fort Myers FL 33917-1838 E-mail: chuckv@lee.k12.fl.us.

VILAS, FAITH, aerospace scientist; b. Evanston, Ill., Apr. 14, 1952; d. Jack Jr. and Faith McCrea (Lehman) V.; m. Larry Wayne Smith, July 5, 1986. BA, Wellesley (Mass.) Coll., 1973; MS, MIT, 1975; PhD, U. Ariz., 1984. Sr. rsch. asst. Cerro Tololo Inter-Am. Obs., La Serena, Chile, 1975-77; sr. assoc. scientist Lockheed Electronics Co., Houston, 1977-78; vis. rsch. scientist NRC, Johnson Space Ctr., 1984-85; space scientist NASA, Johnson Space Ctr., 1985—2001; acting Discovery program scientist NASA Hdqs., Washington, 2001—. Editor: (with C.R. Chapman and M.S. Matthews) Mercury, 1988; mem. editl. bd. Icarus, 2001—. Bd. dirs. Vatican Observatory Found., 1996—. Mem. Am. Astron. Soc. (div. planetary scis. nominating com. 1988-91, sec. 1992-95, vice chmn. 1995-96, chmn. 1996-97, prize com. chmn. 1997-98), Johnson Space Ctr. Nat. Mgmt. Assn. (chair Am. enterprise com. 1987-88, Shield Excellence award 1988). Episcopalian. Avocations: traveling, flying, emergency medicine. Office: NASA Hdqrs Code SE 300 E St SW Washington DC 20546 E-mail: faith.vilas@hq.nasa.gov.

VILCEK, JAN TOMAS, immunologist, medical educator; b. Bratislava, Czechoslovakia, June 17, 1933; came to U.S., 1965, naturalized, 1970. s. Julius and Friderika (Fischer) V.; m. Marica F. Gerhath, July 28, 1962 MD, Comenius U., Bratislava, 1957; CSc (PhD), Czechoslovak Acad. Sci., Bratislava, 1962. Fellow Inst. Virology, Bratislava, 1957-62, head of lab., 1962-64; asst. prof. microbiology NYU Med. Ctr., N.Y.C., 1965-68, assoc. prof., 1968-73, prof., 1973—. Chmn. nomenclature com. WHO, 1981—86; mem. adv. com. Cancer Soc., 1981—87, chmn., 1983; mem. sci. adv. bd. Max Planck Inst., Munich, 1987—95; pres. The Friderika Fischer Found., 2000—. Author: Interferon, 1969; editor in chief Archives of Virology, 1975-86, Cytokine and Growth Factor Revs., 1995—; editor: Interferons and the Immune System, 1984, Tumor Necrosis Factor: Structure, Function and Mechanism of Action, 1991, Cytokine Reference, 2000; mem. editl. bd. Virology, 1979-81, Archives of Virology, 1986-92, Infection and Immunity, 1983-85, Antiviral Rsch., 1984-88, Jour. Interferon and Cytokine Rsch., 1988—, Jour. Immunological Methods, 1986—, Natural Immunity and Cell Growth Regulation, 1986-92, Jour. Immunology, 1987-89, Lymphokine Rsch., 1987-94, Jour. Biol. Chemistry, 1988-90, ISI Atlas Sci., Immunology, 1988-89, Jour. Cellular Physiology, 1988—, Cytokine, 1989—, Biologicals, 1989-95, Acta Virologica, 1991—, Internat. Archives of Allergy and Immunology, 1992-98, Folia Biologica, 1993-96, Cellular Immunology, 1993-96, Jour. of Inflammation, 1994-97, Cytokines, Cellular & Molecular Therapy, 1998—; contbr. articles to profl. jours.; co-inventor of anti-inflammatory drug infliximab used in rheumatoid arthritis and Crohn's disease. Mem. rev. panel Israel Cancer Rsch. Fund, 1993-96; mem. fellowship rev. com. Am. Heart Assn., 1992-94. Recipient Rsch. Career Devel. award, USPHS, 1968—73, Recognition award, Japanese Inflammation Soc., 1989, Outstanding Investigator award, Nat. Cancer Inst., NIH, 1991—98, Elliott Osserman award for disting. svc. in support of cancer rsch., 1996, Disting. Alumnus award and medal, Comenius U., Bratislava, 2001; grantee, USPHS, numerous other orgns. Fellow AAAS; mem. Soc. Gen. Microbiology, Am. Soc. Microbiology, Am. Assn. Immunologists, Internat. Soc. Interferon Rsch., Czech Immunology Soc., Internat. Cytokine Soc. (pres. 1997-98), Czechoslovak Soc. for Microbiology. Office: NYU Med Ctr 550 1st Ave New York NY 10016-6402 E-mail: jan.vilcek@med.nyu.edu.

VILCHES-O'BOURKE, OCTAVIO AUGUSTO, accounting company executive; b. Havana, Cuba, Aug. 15, 1923; came to the U.S., 1962, naturalized, 1967; s. Bartolome and Isabel Susana (O'Bourke) Vilches; m. Alba Del Valle Junco, July 24, 1954; 1 son, Octavio Roberto. CPA, U. Havana, 1949, JD, 1951, PhD in Econ. Scis., 1953. Owner Octavio Vilches & Assocs., Havana, 1949-61; comptr. United R.R. of Cuba, 1950-53; cons. econ. affairs Cuban Dept. Labor, Havana, 1953; auditor Cuban Dept. Treasury, 1952-59; pres. Roble Furniture, Inc., San Juan, P.R., 1963-65; owner Hato Rey, P.R., 1963—; pres. Mero Constrn. Corp., San Juan, 1973. Mem. Circulo Cubano P.R., Colegio Contadores Publicos en el Exilio, Colegio Abogados en el Exilio, Cuban Nat. Bar Assn., Nat. Soc. Pub. Accts., Am. Club (Miami, Fla.). Republican. Home: Golden Gate 146 Turquesa St San Juan PR 00920 Office: Condominio El Centro II Ste 1402 Hato Rey PR 00920 Address: PO Box 190300 San Juan PR 00919-0300

VILCHEZ, RICARDO S. library supervisor; b. Masaya, Nicaragua, Jan. 20, 1953; s. Adrian Zamora and Maria M. Vilchez; children: Ricardol E., Nidia E. BA, Fordham U., 1990; MBA, CES, Managua, Nicaragua, 1978; diploma, Inst. of Christian Econs., 1982; MLS, Pratt Inst., Bklyn., 1995. With Nat. Police Nicaragua, Managua, 1968-72; presdl. asst. Govt. Nicaragua, 1972-74; libr. asst. Ctrl. Bank Libr., Managua, 1974-75; asst. presdl. office Ctrl. Bank Managua, 1975-79; libr. supervisor Fordham U., N.Y.C., 1989—. Editor (CD) Los Motivos Del Lobo, 2000. V.p. Nicaraguan Children's Found., N.Y.C., 1999—; cultural dir. Nicaraguan Support Group, N.Y.C., 1999—; pres. Comision Hispana Pro Obra Rubén Dario N.Y., 1998—. Mem. Am. Libr. Assn., Am. Soc. Info. Sci., Libr. Congress. Republican. Roman Catholic. Avocations: cultural activities, travel, walking, rare books, community activities. Home: 13 Van Pelt Ave Staten Island NY 10303-2478 Office: Fordham U 113 W 60th St New York NY 10023-7484

VILE, SANDRA JANE, leadership training educator; b. Oceanside, N.Y., Oct. 4, 1939; d. John Oliver and Roberta May (Wood) Ryan; m. Joseph Charles Vile, June 27, 1964; children: Jonathan Charles, Susan Jane. BS in Christian Edn. cum laude, Nyack Coll., 1961; MS in Edn., SUNY, Oneonta, 1963; diploma, Childrens Ministries Inst., Warrenton, Mo., 1974; Cert. in Visual Comm., Faith Venture Visuals, Inc., Lititz, Pa., 1979. Cert. elem. tchr., N.Y. Tchr. Hudson (N.Y.) City Sch. Dist., 1961-64, South Orangetown Ctrl. Sch. Dist., Orangeburg, N.Y., 1964-67; local dir. Child Evangelism Fellowship of Empire State, Afton, 1972-88, state tng. instr., 1988-92; leadership tng. instr. Child Evangelism Fellowship, Inc., Warrenton, 1992—. Vis. lectr. Nyack (N.Y.) Coll., 1967; tng. cons. Faith Venture Visuals, Inc., 1980-96. Contbr.: Children's Ministry Resource Bible, 1993. Lay leader Teen Missions, Inc., Merritt Island, Fla., 1982. Recipient Alumna of Yr. award Faith Venture Visuals, Inc., 1993. Mem. Pro Merito Soc., Logicians Soc. Avocations: computers, travel, counted cross-stitch. Home and Office: 270 Route 27B Hudson NY 12534-3919

VILENCHIK, MICHAEL MARC, biophysicist, bio-oncologist, physician, virologist, radiobiologist; b. Brjansk, Russia, May 30, 1938; s. Marc and Grunja G. (Smoljakova) V.; m. Valentina I. Vasilieva, Jan. 12, 1964 (div. 1967); 1 child, Joan; m. Julia N. Runova, Mar. 6, 1968 (div. 1971); 1 child, Vera. MD, 1st Med. Inst., St. Petersburg, Russia, 1961; PhD, Inst. Virology, Moscow, 1967. Postgrad. rsch. Inst. Virology, Moscow, 1963-66; rsch. scientist, sr. biophysicist, sr. resident Inst. Biophysics, Pushchino, Moscow, 1966-90; vis. scientist Med. Rsch. Coun., Didcot, England, 1990—; rschr. Inst. for Environ. Rsch., Tel Aviv, 1991; rsch. scholar SUNY Health Sci. Ctr., Syracuse, 1991-93, Cornell U., Ithaca, N.Y., 1993-94; rsch. scientist Longevity Achievement Found. and Sally Balin Med. Ctr., Media, Pa., 1994—. Author: Biological Fundamentals of Aging and Longevity, 1976, 87, 89, Radiobiological Effects and Environment, 1983, 91, The Rules of Molecular-Genetic Action of Chemical Carcinogens, 1977, Dynamic DNA Instability and the Late Radiobiological Effects, 1987, Modification of Carcinogenic and Antitumor Actions of Ionizing Radiation, 1985; contbr. articles to profl. jours., also to Ency. Gerontology, Vol. 2, Acad. Press, 1996, others; monographs in fields of biophysics of aging and carcinogenesis; mechanisms of radiation effects and biophyisics of the genome.

VILES, HENRY, pathologist; b. Cali, Colombia, Dec. 24, 1938; s. Pedro and Tulia V.; m. Mary Jo Oliver, Oct. 10, 1980; children: Maurice Andres, Tabatha, Joshua. MD, U. del Valle, Colombia, 1968. Diplomate Am. Bd. Pathology. Rotating intern Hosp. U. del Valle, Cali, 1967-68; resident in pathology Stamford (Conn.) Hosp., 1971-75, chief pathology resident, 1975-76; dir. labs. Mayfield (Ky.) Cmty. Hosp.Columbia Pinelake Regional Hosp., 1976—. Fellow AAAS, Coll. Am. Pathologists, Am. Soc. Microbiology. Home: 309 Lakeview Dr Mayfield KY 42066-4765 Office: 1099 Medical Center Dr Mayfield KY 42066-1159

VILESOV, ANDREY FEDOROVITCH, research physical chemist; b. St. Petersburg, Russia, Nov. 6, 1958; s. Fedor I. and Vera K. (Adamchuk) V.; m. Alla V. Barkova, Dec. 24, 1995. Diploma, St. Petersburg State U., 1982, PhD, 1985. Rschr. Inst. Physics St. Petersburg State U., 1985-90; rschr. Max-Planck Inst fur Strömungsforschung, Goettingen, Germany, 1991-99; assoc. prof. U. So. Calif., L.A., 2000—. Contbr. articles to sci. jours. Recipient Alexander von Humboldt fellowship, Germany, 1991-92, Max-Planck Soc. fellowship, Germany, 1993-95, Habilitaiton fellowship German Rsch. Soc., 1996-98. Office: Dept Chemistry Univ So Calif Los Angeles CA 90089 E-mail: vilesov@usc.edu.

VILK, VICTOR JOSEPH, retired radiologist; b. Butte, Mont., Aug. 16, 1929; BS, U. Mont., 1952, MS in Microbiology, 1954; MD, U. Md., 1962. Diplomate Am. Bd. Radiology. Intern St. Lukes Hosp., Denver, 1962-63, resident, 1963-65, Tumor Inst. Swedish Hosp., Seattle, 1965-66; fellow St. Luke's Hosp., Denver, 1966-67. Mem. AMA, Am. Coll. Radiology, Oreg. Med. Assn.

VILLA, JOHN KAZAR, lawyer; b. Ypsilanti, Mich., June 9, 1948; s. John Joseph and Susie (Hoogasian) V.; m. Ellen A. Edwards, June 3, 1990. AB, Duke U., 1970; JD, U. Mich., 1973. Bar: D.C. 1973. Trial atty. U.S. Dept. Justice, Washington, 1973-77; assoc. Williams & Connolly, 1977-81, ptnr., 1981—. Author: legal treatises. Office: Williams & Connolly 725 12th St NW Washington DC 20005-5901

VILLABLANCA, JAIME ROLANDO, medical neuroscientist, educator; b. Chillán, Chile, Feb. 1929; came to U.S., 1971; naturalized, 1985; s. Ernesto and Teresa (Hernàndez) V.; m. Guillermina Nieto, Dec. 3, 1955; children: Amparo C., Jaime G., Pablo J., Francis X., Claudio I. Bachelor in Biology, Nat. Inst. Chile, 1946; licentiate medicine, U. Chile, 1953, MD, 1954. Cert. neurophysiologist. Rockefeller Found. postdoctoral fellow in physiology John Hopkins and Harvard Med. Schs., 1959-61; Fogarty internat. rsch. fellow in anatomy UCLA, 1966-68, assoc. research anatomist and psychiatrist, 1971-72; assoc. prof. psychiatry and biobehavioral scis. UCLA Sch. Medicine, 1972-76; prof. psychiatry and biobehavioral scis. UCLA, 1976—, prof. neurobiology, 1977—. Mem. faculty U. Chile Sch. Medicine, 1954-71, prof. exptl. medicine, 1970-71; vis. prof. neurobiology Cath. U. Chile Sch. Medicine, 1974; cons. in field. Author numerous rsch. papers, book chpts., abstracts; chief regional editor Developmental Brain Dysfunction, 1988-99. Decorated Order Francisco de Miranda (Venezuela); recipient Premio Reina Sofia, Madrid, 1990, Lifetime Achievement award UCLA Sch. Medicine, 2001; fellow Rockefeller Found., 1959-61, Fogarty Internat. Rsch. fellow NIH, 1966-68; grantee USAF Office Sci. Rsch., 1962-65, Found. Fund Rsch. Psychiatry, 1969-72, USPHS-Nat. Inst. Child Human Devel., 1972-96, USPHS-Nat. Inst. Drug Abuse, 1981-85, USPHS-Nat. Inst. Neurol. Disorders and Stroke, 1988-92, Fgn. Scientist Traveling grant Tokyo Met. Govt., 1995. Mem. AAAS, AAUP, Am. Assn. Anatomists, Mental Retardation Rsch. Ctr., Brain Rsch. Inst., Internat. Brain Rsch. Orgn., Am. Physiol. Soc., Soc. for Neurosci., Assn. Venezolana Padres de Niños Excepcionales, Soc. Child and Adolescent Psychiatry and Neurology (Chile, hon.), Sigma Xi. Home: 200 Surfview Dr Pacific Palisades CA 90272-2911 Office: UCLA Dept Psychiatry & Biobehavioral Scis Los Angeles CA 90024-1759 E-mail: jvillablanca@mednet.ucla.edu.

VILLA-KOMAROFF, LYDIA, molecular biologist, educator, university official; b. Las Vegas, N.Mex., Aug. 7, 1947; d. John Dias and Drucilla (Jaramillo) V.; m. Anthony Leader Komaroff, June 18, 1970. BA, Goucher Coll., 1970; PhD, MIT, 1975; DSc (hon.), St. Thomas U., 1996, Pine Manor Coll., 1997; PhD (hon.), Goucher Coll., 1997. Rsch. fellow Harvard U., Cambridge, 1975-78; asst. prof. dept. microbiology U. Mass. Med. Ctr., Worcester, 1978-81, assoc. prof. dept. molecular genetics micro, 1982-85; assoc. prof. dept. neurology Harvard Med. Sch., Boston, 1986-95; sr. rsch. assoc. neurology Children's Hosp., 1985-95, assoc. dir. mental retardation rsch. ctr., 1987-94; prof. dept. neurology Northwestern U., Evanston, Ill., 1995—, assoc. v.p. rsch., 1995-97, v.p. rsch., 1998—. Mem. mammalian genetics study sect. NIH, 1982-84, mem. reviewers rsch., 1989, mem. neurol. disorders program project rev. com., 1989-94; mem. adv. bd. Biol. Scis. Directorate, NSF, 1994-99; mem. bd. dirs. Nat. Ctr. Genome Rsch., 1995-2000, AAAS, 2000—; mem. adv. coun. Nat. Inst. Neurol. Disorders and Stroke, NIH, 2000—. Contbr. articles and abstracts to profl. jours.; patentee in field. Recipient Hispanic Engr. Nat. Achievement award, 1992, Nat. Achievement award Hispanic Mag., 1996; inducted Hispanic Engr. Nat. Achievement Hall of Fame, 1999; Helen Hay Whitney Found. fellow, 1975-78; NIH grantee, 1978-85, 89-96. Mem. Am. Soc. Microbiology, Assn. for Women in Sci., Soc. for Neurosci., Am. Soc. Cell Biology, Soc. for Advancement Chicanos and Native Ams. in Sci. (founding, bd. dirs. 1987-93, v.p. 1990-93), Office: Northwestern U 633 Clark St Evanston IL 60208-0001 E-mail: LVK@northwestern.edu.

VILLALOBOS, RAUL, lawyer; b. El Paso, Tex., Feb. 23, 1931; s. Pablo and Pilar O. Villalobos; m. Glenda Charlene Allen. BBA, U. Tex., El Paso, 1972; JD, U. Houston, 1973. Bar: Tex., U.S. Supreme Ct., U.S. Dist. (so. and we. dist.) Tex., U.S. Tax Ct. Counsel IRS, Houston, 1973, State Securities Bd., Houston, 1974. With U.S. Army, 1951-53. Home: 9003 Magnetic St El Paso TX 79904-1020

VILLALON, DALISAY MANUEL, nurse, real estate broker; b. Angat, Bulacan, Philippines, Apr. 27, 1941; came to U.S., 1967; d. Federico Manuel and Librada (Garcia) Manuel; divorced; children: Ricky, May, Liberty, Derrick, Dolly Rose. BS in Nursing, Manila Cen. U., 1961; postgrad. in nursing, U. Ill., Chgo., 1972-74. RN, Ill. Instr. nursing Cen. Luzon Sch. Nursing, Philippines, 1966-67; staff nurse St. Alexis Hosp., Cleve., 1968-70, Augustana Hosp., Chgo., 1972-74; nurse mgr. Holy Child Med. Clinic, 1976-80; nurse auditor 1st Health Care, Rosemont, Ill., 1982-83; dir. nurses North Shore Terr., Waukegan, 1983-90, Carlton House, 1991-94. Columnist Philippine News. Bd. dirs. Filipino Am. Coun., Chgo., 1978-80, v.p., 1980-82; bd. dirs. Asian Human Svcs., Chgo.; pres. Am.-Filipino Profl. Civic Alliance, Chgo., 1984-90, Philipino-Am. United for Svc.-Oriental Objective, 1991—; chmn. Philippine Week Com., 1979; past v.p. Filipino Ams. Concerned for Elderly; trustee Rizal-MacArthur Found.; past v.p. Filipino Svc. League, 1989-91; past exec. v.p. Asian Festival, Inc.; past chmn. various civic coms.; mem. Asian-Am. Adv. Coun. Mayor Daley, 1989-97. Recipient Cert. Appreciation Rizal-MacArthur Found., 1977, Most Outstanding Filipino in Midwest award Cavite Assn. Am., 1980, Outstanding Community Svc. Appreciation award Filipino Am. Coun., 1981, 89, NGHIA Sinh Internat., Inc., 1989, Outstanding Svc. award Asian-Am. Coaliton, 1989, Outstanding Contrn. award Dirs. Nursing and Adminstrs. Conf., 1988; named to Filipino Hall of Fame for comty. svc., 1996 Phil Reports TV. Mem. Ill. Nurses Assn. (bd. dirs., dist. senator 1989-91, human rights and ethics commn. 1990-91), Philippine Med. Assn. Aux. (pres. 1980, Outstanding Leadership award 1989), Chgo. Med. Soc. Aus. (v.p. 1980), Chgo. Philippine Lioness Club (pres. 1983-84, Outstanding Svc. award 1985), Filipino Woman's Club Chgo. (Outstanding Woman in Leadership 1992, Chgo. Filipino Hall of Fame award 1998), Filipino Am. Polit. Assn. Democrat. Roman Catholic. Home: 1070 Sanders Rd Northbrook IL 60062-2904 Office: Vitas Health Care Corp Vitas Innovative Care 700 N Sacramento Chicago IL 60612 E-mail: delyvillalon@netzero.net.

VILLANO, PETER F. state legislator; b. New Haven; m. Florence Roome; 4 children. BA, U. Pa. Mem. Conn. Congl. Staff, 1974-81; mayor Town of Hamden (Conn.), 1981-85; legis. liaison State Dept. Aging, Hamden, 1987-91; mem. dist. 91 Conn. Ho. of Reps., 1993—. Mem. Hamden Town Com. Mem. Edgehill Nieghborhood Assn. Mem. Conn. Audubon Soc., Am. Mus. Natural History. Address: 133 Armory St Hamden CT 06517-4005

VILLARAN, YURI, physician, medical educator; b. Lima, Peru, Dec. 23, 1962; came to U.S., 1988; s. Pedro Jorge and Celia Eufrasia V.; m. Teresa René, July 2, 1993. MD, U. Peruana Cayetano Heredia, Lima, Peru, 1980-88. Diplomate Am. Bd. Internal Medicine, Am. Bd. Pulmonary Medicine, Am. Bd. Critical Care Medicine; cert. ACLS, BCLS, ednl. comm. for fgn. med. grads.; cert. nutrition specialist. Transitional internship Sch. Medicine U. Peruana Cayetano Heredia, Lima, Peru, 1987-88; clin. clk. internal medicine Jackson Meml. Med. Ctr. U. Miami, 1988-89; intern in internal medicine So. Ill. U., Springfield, 1989-90, resident in internal medicine, 1990-92; fellow in pulmonary, critical care medicine U. Ky. Med. Ctr., Lexington, 1992-95; clin. instr. pulmonary, critical care medicine, 1995-96; clin. fellow postdoct. scholar lung transplantation U. Ky. Med. Ctr., Lexington, 1995-96; staff physician Pulmonary and Critical Care Medicine Primary Care Svcs. Lexington Fayette County Health Dept., 1996-98; pvt. practice, 1998—. Mem. staff Samaritan Hosp. Lexington, St. Joseph Hosp. Lexington, St. Joseph Hosp., East Lexington, Ctrl. Bapt. Hosp., Lexington; lectr. in field. Contbr. numerous articles to profl. jours. Fellow ACP, Am. Coll. Chest Physicians; mem. AMA, Am. Thoracic Soc., Internat. Soc. Heart-Lung Transplantation, Peruvian Med. Soc., Ky. Thoracic Soc. (mem. conf. program com. 1996, 97), Soc. Critical Care Medicine, Lexington Med. Soc., Am. Soc. Parenteral and Enteral Nutrition, Am. Coll. Nutrition. Office: Pulmonary Assocs 166 Pasadena Dr Lexington KY 40503-2907 Fax: 859-277-9699.

VILLARI, JACK C. performing arts executive, arts entrepreneur; b. Cleve., Nov. 18, 1938; s. Sam and Grace (Zingale) V.; m. Kathleen R. Sims, Sept. 25, 1965; children: Maria, Brian. BA, Govs. State U., University Park, Ill., 1978. Singer, producer musical revues, supper clubs, broadway musicals, U.S., 1958-70; pres. Am. Dance Ctr., Olympia Fields and Orland Park, Ill., 1971—; artistic dir. Am. Dance Ctr. Regional Ballet Co., 1973—. Dance adminstrv. dir. Prairie State Coll., Chicago Heights, Ill., 1979-98, Govs. State U., University Park, Ill., 1971-76, Chgo. Conservatory Coll., Chgo., 1977-79; prodn. asst. Warner Bros. Hanna-Barbera, Walt Disney Prodns. Author: Official Guide to Disco Dance Steps, 1978; created original ballet "Hansel and Gretel", 1976; creator dinner/show Holliday Fantasy, 2000 (award); asst. choreographer USO Tour to the Far East, 1970. Estab. continuing dance classes Cmty. Recreation Depts., Olympia Fields, Crete, Frankfort Sq., Oak Forest, Hazel Crest, Park Forest, Oak Lawn, Mokena, Homewood-Flossmoor, Tinley Park, Palos Park, Palos Hills, Sauk Village; prodn. coord. Urban Gateways, Chgo. With U.S. Army, 1961-67. Grantee Midwest Suburban Pub., 1973—, Ill. Arts Coun., 1982 and 1986, ARCO Corp., 1984, Target, 1995—, City Proclamation, 1996; recipient congrl. cert. Ill., 1984, Internat. Gold Medal Ballet Bolshoi Soloists Ballet and Cultural Exch., 1978; named Outstanding Dance Educator Am., Dance Mag., 1980. Mem. Prairie State Coll. Performing Arts Coun. (mem. adv. com. 1985-92), Morality in Media. Roman Catholic. Avocation: song-writing. Home: 1037 Wingate Rd Olympia Fields IL 60461-1604 Office: Am Dance Ctr 1933 Ridge Rd Homewood IL 60430-1904 also: 10464 W 163d Pl Orland Park IL 60467

VILLARREAL, CARLOS CASTANEDA, engineering executive; b. Brownsville, Tex., Nov. 9, 1924; s. Jesus Jose and Elisa L. (Castaneda) V.; m. Doris Ann Akers, Sept. 10, 1948 (dec. 1995); children: Timothy Hill, David Akers. BS, U.S. Naval Acad., 1948; MS, U.S. Navy Postgrad. Sch., 1950; LLD (hon.), St. Mary's U., 1972. Registered profl. engr. Commd. ensign U.S. Navy, 1948, advanced through grades to lt., 1956; comdg. officer U.S.S. Rhea, 1951, U.S.S. Osprey, 1952; comdr. Mine Div. 31, 1953; instr. elec. engring. U.S. Naval Acad., 1955; resigned, 1956; mgr. marine and indsl. operation Gen. Electric Co., 1956-66; v.p. mktg. and adminstrn. Marquardt Corp., 1966-69; head Urban Mass Transit Adminstrn., Dept. Transp., Washington, 1969-73; commr. Postal Rate Commn., 1973-79, vice chmn., 1975-79; v.p. Washington ops. Wilbur Smith and Assocs., 1979-84, sr. v.p., 1984-86, exec. v.p., 1987—, also bd. dirs. Lectr. in field; mem. industry sector adv. com. Dept. Commerce; mem. sect. 13 adv. com. Dept. Transp., 1983-86; tchr. U.S. Naval Acad., 1954-56. Contbr. to profl. jours. Mem. devel. com. Wolftrap Farm Park for the Performing Arts, 1973-78; mem. council St. Elizabeth Ch., 1982-86, chmn. fin. com.; mem. bd. edn. St. Elizabeth Sch.; bd. dirs. Assoc. Catholic Charities, 1983-86; mem. fin. com. Cath. Charities, U.S.A.; mem. John Carrol Soc. Decorated knight Sovereign Mil. Hospitaller Order St. John of Jerusalem of Rhodes and Malta, 1981, Knight Equestrian Order of the Holy Sepulchre of Jerusalem, 1995; recipient award outstanding achievement Dept. Transp. Fellow ASCE, Am. Cons. Engrs. Coun. (vice chmn. internat. com.); mem. IEEE, NSPE (pres. D.C. soc. 1986-87, bd. dirs. 1988-91), Am. Pub. Transit Assn., Soc. Naval Architects and Marine Engrs., Soc. Am. Mil. Engrs., Am. Rds. and Transp. Builders Assn. (chmn. pub. transp. adv. coun.), Transp. Rsch. Bd., Washington Soc. Engrs., Internat. Bridge, Tunnel and Turnpike Assn., Inst. World Politics, Inst. Traffic Engrs., Intelligent Transp. Soc. Am. (chmn. fin. com., bd. dirs.), Univ. Club, Army-Navy Club (pres.). Republican. Roman Catholic. Office: Wilbur Smith Assocs 2921 Telestar Ct Falls Church VA 22042-1205 E-mail: cvillarreal@wilbursmith.com.

VILLARREAL, FERNANDO MARIN, lawyer; b. Mathis, Tex., Oct. 2, 1956; s. Pablo and Dora Villarreal; m. Yvonne Dominguez, Sept. 30, 1995; 1 child, Analisa Yvonne. AA, McLennan C.C., Waco, Tex., 1977; BBA, Baylor U., 1979; JD, U. Houston, 1983. Bar: Tex. 1983. Pvt. practice, Waco, Tex., 1983—. Justice of peace, McLennan County, Waco, 1992—. V.p. McLennan County Dem. Com., Waco; past pres. League United L.Am. Citizens, Waco. Mem. McLennon County Bar Assn. (bd. dirs.). Democrat. Roman Catholic. Avocations: reading, walking, gardening. Office: 3305 Robinson Dr Ste B Waco TX 76706

VILLARREAL, JUAN DE DIOS, management consultant; b. Monterrey, Mex., May 30, 1972; came to U.S., 1994; s. Amado and Maria Aurora (Gonzalez) V. BSc in Mech. and Elec. Engring., Inst. Tech. & Superior Studies, Monterrey, 1993; MBA. Staff cons. Kurt Salmon Assocs., Miami, Fla., 1994-99; pres. J.D. Villarreal, Ops. Mgmt. Cons., 2000—. Roman Catholic. Avocations: soccer, running, reading. Home: Tucan 354 Country Tesoro Monterrey 64850 Mexico Office: 1209 San Dario Ave PMB 4-735 Laredo TX 78040-4505 E-mail: jdv@jdvillarreal.com.

VILLARRUBIA, JAN, playwright, educator; b. New Orleans, Apr. 11, 1948; d. Forrest and Audrey Levy B.; m. Ernest Charles Merrell, Aug. 18, 1978 (div. Jan. 2001); 1 child, Forrest. BA, La. State U., 1970, MA, 1971. Poet in residence, New Orleans, 1984-88, 91-00; New Orleans area creative writing advisor Country Day Creative Arts Program, Metairie, 1985—86, 1991—2002; project dir. DramaRama, Inc., New Orleans, 1993-95; vis. poet/playwright in residence Country Day Sch., Metairie, 2000—. Author: (plays) Miz Lena's Backyard, 1994, Odd Fellows, 1996. Mem. Dramatists Guild, Contemporary Arts Ctr. (bd. dirs. 1990-93), Alternate Roots, Poets and Writers. Democrat. Avocations: birding, crafts, dance, world religions. Office: Country Day Sch 300 Park Rd Metairie LA 70005 E-mail: jvilla@yahoo.com .

VILLARS, JILL ANNETTE, webmaster; b. Frankfort, Ind., Apr. 14, 1971; d. Robert Glenn and Nancy Jeanne (Emans) V. BA, Purdue U., 1993; MLS, M Info. Sci., Ind. U., Indpls., 2002. Lic. tchr., Ind. Adminstrv. asst. Melanie Sanders, MD, Indpls., 1994-97; comm./data specialist St. Elizabeth Ann Seton Hosp., Carmel, 1988—2001; webmaster St. Vincent Hosp., Indpls., 2001—. Bd. dirs. Iris and Co., Indpls., 1996—. Mem.: Web Design and Developers Assn., HTML Writers Guild, World Orgn. Webmasters, Internat. Assn. Webmasters, Sigma Kappa Alumna. Republican. Presbyterian. Avocations: genealogy. Office: St Vincent Hosp 2001 W 86th St Indianapolis IN 46240 E-mail: javillar@stvincent.org.

VILLASENOR, BARBARA, book publisher; b. L.A., Sept. 17, 1946; d. Charles Belmont and Zita (Lewis) Block; m. Victor Edmundo Villasenor, Dec. 29, 1974 (div. Dec. 1999); children: David Cuauhtemoc, Joseph Edmundo. BA in Sociology, U. Calif., Berkeley, 1967; postgrad., Radcliffe coll., 1967. Media buyer Diener Hauser Greenthal, L.A., 1971-76; editor Charles Pub., Oceanside, Calif., 1976-87, pub., 1987—. Ptnr. Strategies, San Diego, 1998—99; breath worker Heart to Heart, San Diego, 1988—94; event coord. Snow Goose Global Thanksgiving, Oceanside, 1992—; mem. Interfaith Alliance, San Diego, 1996—. Recipient award, Small Press Mag., 1996. Mem.: San Diego Pub. Alliance, San. Diego Book Forum. Democrat. Avocations: creative expression, peace in the Mid. East. Office: Charles Publishing 1308 Stewart St Oceanside CA 92054-5448

VILLAVASO, STEPHEN DONALD, lawyer, urban planner; b. New Orleans, July 12, 1949; s. Donald Philip and Jacklyn (Tully) V.; m. Regina Smith, Apr. 17, 1971; children: Christine Regina, Stephen Warner. BS in Econs., U. New Orleans, 1971, M in Urban and Regional Planning, 1976; JD, Loyola U., New Orleans, 1981. Bar: La. 1982; recognized ct. expert in land use, planning and zoning. Urban and regional planner Barnard & Thomas, New Orleans, 1976-78; dir. analysis and planning Office of Mayor, City of New Orleans, 1978-81; counsel for planning and devel. Office of City Atty., City of New Orleans, 1983-84; dir. planning and environ. affairs Tecon Realty, New Orleans, 1981-83; v.p. for planning and project mgmt. Morphy, Makofsky, Mumphrey & Masson, 1984-89; bus. devel. mgr. Waste Mgmt., Inc., 1989-96; pres. Villavaso & Assocs., LLC, 1996—, Brownfields Redevel. Profls. LLC, New Orleans, 2000—. Bd. dirs. Regional Loan Corp.; guest lectr., adj. prof. Coll. of Urban and Pub. Affairs, U. New Orleans, 1976—; spl. instr. grad. studies in urban planning So. U. New Orleans, 1987—. Bd. dirs. New Orleans Traffic and Transp. Bur., 1981-86, Riverfront Awareness, New Orleans, 1984-86; bd. dirs. Vols. Am. Greater New Orleans, 1987-96, vice chmn., 1990, chmn. bd., 1992-95. With USN, 1971-74. Named one of Outstanding Young Men of Am., 1980, 82. Mem. ABA, Am. Inst. of Cert. Planners, Am. Planning Assn. (pres. La. div. 1980-84, disting. svc. award 1985), Urban Land Inst., La. Bar Assn., U. New Orleans Alumni Assn. (bd. dirs. 1990—), Phi Kappa Phi, Delta Sigma Pi (pres. 1971), Omicron Delta Kappa. Democrat. Roman Catholic. Avocations: philately, camping, travel. E-mial. Home: 6304 Beauregard Ave New Orleans LA 70124-4502 E-mail: villavaso.assoc.llc@worldnet.att.net.

VILLAVECES, JAMES WALTER, allergist, immunologist; b. San Luis Obispo, Calif., Nov. 4, 1933; s. Robert and Solita (Combariza) V. BA, UCLA, 1955; MD, U. Calif. Med. Sch., 1960. Cert. Am. Bd. Allergy and Immunology. Intern Sawtelle VA Hosp., L.A., 1960-61; preceptorship in adult allergy L.A. County Hosp., Los Angeles, 1964-66; fellow in allergy White Meml. CCM, L.A., 1966-67; chief allergy divsn. Ventura (Calif.) Med. Ctr., 1969-87; practice medicine specializing in allergy-immunology Ventura, 1984—. Inventor, cons. Lifelike Products Inc., 2001-02; cons. Bio-Dynamics Co., Ventura, 1975-80, Norwich-Eaton and Pharmacia and 3M, Ventura, 1980-85; founder botanical weed allergy walks, 1970; producer Ventura County cities street-tree guide for asthma patients; pharmacy and therapeutics com. Wellpoint (Blue Cross Calif.) Inc., 1995-99, former cons. and lectr. in field. Writer, prodr., editor films; contbr. articles on biology of pollens and molds of Ventura County to profl. jours.; patentee in field. Bd. dirs. Am. Lung Assn., Ventura, 1969-85, pres., 1974, advisor air pollution control com., 1971-74; judge Ventura Sci. Fair, 1970-85. Recipient Commendation, County Bd. Suprs., Ventura, 1974. Fellow Am. Acad. Allergy, Am. Coll. Allergists; mem. Calif. Soc. Allergy-Immunology, Calif. Med. Assn., Ventura County med. Assn., Gold Coast Tri-County Allergy Soc. (pres. 1987, bot. surgery for allergic plants 2002), CAL Club (hon.), Ventura County Sports Hall of Fame (mem. founding bd.), Mensa. Republican. Avocations: writing, photography, lecturing, pistol target shooting, fishing. Home: 928 High Point Dr Ventura CA 93003-1415 Office: Dudley Profl Ctr 4080 Loma Vista Rd Ste M Ventura CA 93003-1811 E-mail: jvillavece@aol.com.

VILLAVERDE, ROBERTO, civil engineer; b. Chihuahua, Mex., Aug. 14, 1945; came to U.S., 1975; s. Jesus and Carolina (Lazo) V.; m. Phyllis Arlene Potocky, June 21, 1980; children: Derrick Anton, Carlina Jeanette. BS, U. Chihuahua, 1968; MS, Nat. U. Mex., Mexico City, 1971; PhD, U. Ill., 1980. Reg. civil engr., Calif. Asst. prof. San Diego State U., 1980-81; rsch. prof. nat. U. Mex., Mexico City, 1981-82; asst. prof. U. Calif., Irvine, 1983-88, assoc. prof., 1988-96, prof., 1996—. Co-author: International Handbook of Seismic Resistance Design, 1993; contbr. articles to profl. jours. Recipient Faculty Devel. award San Diego State U., 1981, Career Devel. award U. Calif., 1986, Outstanding Contbn. to Undergrad. Rsch. award U. Calif., Irvine, 1996; OTCA scholar, 1971; Faculty Rsch. fellow U. Calif., 1985. Mem. Am. Soc. Civil Engrs., Earthquake Engring. Rsch. Inst., Seismological Soc. Am. Roman Catholic. Office: U Calif Civil Engring Dept Irvine CA 92697-0001

VILLECCO, JUDY DIANA, substance abuse, mental health counselor, director; b. Knoxville, Tenn., Jan. 19, 1948; d. William Arthur and Louise (Reagan) Chamberlain; m. Tucker, June 10, 1965 (div. 1974); children: Linda Louise (Tucker) Smith, Constance Christine Lehman; m. Roger Anthony Villecco, May 3, 1979. BA in Psychology, U. West Fla., 1988, MA in Psychology, 1992. Lic. mental health counselor, Fla.; cert. addiction profl., Fla.; internat. cert. alcohol and drug counselor. Counselor Gulf Coast Hosp., Ft. Walton Beach, Fla., 1986-87; peer counselor U. West Fla., 1987-89; family and prevention counselor Okaloosa Guidance Clinic, 1988-89; family svc. dir. Anon Anew of Tampa (Fla.), Inc., 1989-91; dir. Renew Counseling Ctr., Ft. Walton Beach, 1990-92; substance abuse dept. dir. Avalon Ctr., Milton, Fla., 1992-93; adult coord. Partial & Rivendell, Ft. Walton Beach, 1994-95; pvt. practice Emerald Coast Psychiat. Care, P.A., Fort Walton Beach, 1994-95, Associated Psychotherapists, Ft. Walton Beach, 1995-97; with Aegis Behavioral Care, 1997-99; pvt. practice, 1999—. Co-founder, pres. Villecco Rsch. Corp.; internat. substance abuse counselor ; dir. and presenter in field. Author: Co-dependency Treatment Manual, 1992; creator Effective Treatment for Codependants, 1992. Named Outstanding Mental Health Profl. of Yr. Mental Health Assn., 1994. Mem. Internat. Assn. for Offender Counselors, Fla. Alcohol, Drug, Substance Abuse Assn. (bd. dirs., regional rep., Regional Profl. of Yr. 1992-93, 95-96), Am. Counseling Assn., Internat. Assn. for Marriage and Family Counseling, 1997-98, Phi Theta Kappa, Alpha Phi Sigma. Avocations: crafts, grandchildren, travel. Office: Ste 37 348 Miracle Strip Pkwy SW Fort Walton Beach FL 32548-5200

VILLELLA, EDWARD JOSEPH, ballet dancer, educator, choreographer, artistic director, performing arts administrator; b. L.I., N.Y., Oct. 1, 1936; s. Joseph and Mildred (DeGiovanni) V.; m. Janet Greschler (div. Nov. 1980); 1 child, Roddy; m. Linda Carbonetta, Apr. 1981; children: Christa Francesca, Lauren. BS in Marine Transp., N.Y. State Maritime Coll., 1957; LHD (hon.) , Boston Conservatory, 1985, hon. degree, Union Coll., Schenectady, N.Y., 1991; DHL (hon.) , St. Thomas U., Miami, Fla., 1994, U. S.C., 1997; DFA (hon.) , SUNY Maritime Coll., Bronx, 1998; Doctor (hon.) , Fla. Atlantic U., 2000, U. N.C., Asheville, 2002, Coll. Charleston, 2002. Mem. N.Y.C. Ballet, 1957, soloist, 1958-60, prin. soloist, 1960-83; artistic dir. Ballet Okla., Oklahoma City, 1983-86; founding artistic dir., CEO Miami (Fla.) City Ballet, 1985—. Vis. artist U.S. Mil. Acad., West Point, 1981-82, Harvard U., 1999-2000; vis. prof. dance U. Iowa, 1981; resident Heritage chair arts and cultural criticism George Mason U.; Dorothy F. Schmidt artist-in-residence Coll. of Arts & Letters. Performed dances in Symphony C, Scotch Symphony, Western Symphony, Donizetti Variations, Swan Lake, La Source, The Nutcracker, Agon, Stars and Stripes, The Prodigal Son; premiered in Balanchine works including The Figure in the Carpet, 1960, Electronics, 1961, A Midsummer Night's Dream, 1962, Bugaku, 1963, Tarantella, 1964, Harlequinade, 1965, The Brahms-Schoenberg Quartet, 1966, Jewels, 1967, Symphony in Three Movements, 1972, Schéhérazade, 1975; choreography includes Narkissas, 1966, Shostakovitch Ballet Suite, 1972, Shenandoah, 1972, Gayane Pas de Deux, 1972, Salute to Cole, 1973, Sea Chanties, 1974, Prelude, Riffs and Fugues, 1980; TV appearances include The Ed Sullivan Show, Bell Telephone Hour, Mike Douglas Show, (TV spl.) Harlequin, 1975 (Emmy award), summer theaters, festivals, U.S. and abroad, 1957—; co-author: (autobiography) Prodigal Son, 1991. Mem. Nat. Coun. of Arts, 1968-74; chmn. Commn. for Cultural Affairs City N.Y., 1978; bd. visitors N.C. Sch. for the Arts; mem. dance adv. panel Nat. Endowment for Arts; trustee Wolf Trap Found. for the Arts. Robert J.H. Kiphuth fellow Yale U., 2001; recipient Dance Mag. award, 1964, Lions of the Performing Arts award N.Y. Pub. Libr., 1987, Capezio Dance award, 1989, Gold medal Nat. Soc. Arts and Letters, 1990, William G. Anderson merit award AAHPERD, 1991, Nat. Medal of Arts award 1997, Kennedy Ctr. Honors, 1997, Cultural Svc. award Bklyn. Ctr. for Performing Arts at Bklyn. Coll., 1998; named Miamian of Yr., UNICO Nat., 1993; named to Fla. Artists Hall of Fame, 1997, Dorothy F. Schmidt Artist-in-Residence Dorothy F. Schmidt Coll. Arts and Letters, 2000-01, Am.'s Irreplaceable Dance Treasures: The First 100; Robert J. H. Kiphuth fellow Yale U., 2001.

VILLEMEZ, CLARENCE LOUIS, biologist, educator; b. Port Arthur, Tex., Sept. 6, 1938; s. Clarence Louis and Winnie Teresa Villemez; m. Barbara Elizabeth Griffin, May 22, 2000; children: Louis, Adele. AB, Harvard U., 1958; MS, Purdue U., 1961, PhD, 1962. Asst. prof. Purdue U., West Lafayette,

Ind., 1962—65; asst. rsch. biochemist U. of Calif., Berkeley, Calif., 1965—66; rsch. assoc. in chemistry U. of Colo., Boulder, Colo., 1966—67; from asst. prof. to assoc. prof. Ohio U., Athens, Ohio, 1967—72; from assoc. prof. to prof. of biochemistry & chemistry U. of Wyo., Laramie, Wyo., 1972—. Vis. prof. microbiology U. Tex. Med. Sch., Dallas, 1979—80. Contbr. chapters to books, articles to profl. jours. Pres. ACLU, Wyo., 1980—83. Grantee, NIH, NSF, Atomic Energy Commn., WHO. Mem.: AAAS, Am. Assn. for Cell Biology, Am. Soc. for Biochemistry & Molecular Biology. None. Avocations: sports, hunting, fly fishing, chess, poker. Home: 2132 Rainbow Avenue Laramie WY 82070 Office: University of Wyoming Department of Molecular Biology Laramie WY 82071-3944 Home Fax: 307-766-3875; Office Fax: 307-766-3875. Personal E-mail: villemez@uwyo.edu. E-mail: villemez@uwyo.edu.

VILLERS, PHILIPPE, mechanical engineer; b. Paris, June 20, 1935; came to U.S., 1940, naturalized, 1946; s. Raymond and Garda (Schmidt) V.; m. Annie Louise Young, July 13, 1957 (div. 1973); children: Jocelyn Anne (dec.), Renata Jane; m. Katherine Stephan, 1973; children: Noel Stephan, Carolyn Grace. AB in Applied Scis. cum laude, Harvard U., 1955; SM in Mech. Engring, MIT, 1960. Mem. mfg. tng. program Gen. Electric Co., 1955-58; project engr. Perkin-Elmer Corp., Wilton, Conn., 1959-62; project engr. Apollo Antenna pointings sensor Barnes Engring. Co., Stamford, 1962-65; project mgr. Advanced Products Center, Link Group, Gen. Precision, Inc., Binghamton, N.Y., 1965-67; mgr. advanced products Concord Control, Inc., Boston, 1967-69; co-founder, sr. v.p., dir. Computervision Corp., Bedford, Mass., 1969-80; founder, pres., dir. Automatix, Inc., Billerica, 1980-84; chmn. bd. Automatix Inc., 1984-86; founder, pres., dir. Cognition Inc., 1985-88. Bd. dirs. Xyvision, Inc., Wakefield, Mass., chmn., Mass., 1992—94; bd. dirs. Conflict Mgmt. Group, Cambridge, Mass., Quitnet, Inc., Boston, Cambridge Incubator, Grainpro Inc., Concord, Mass., pres., Mass., 1996—. Patentee process welding aluminum liners to steel surfaces, horizon sensor for visible wavelength, infrared roughness testing instrument, improved thermopile constrn. thermal die marker; pioneer design and feasibility solar sail applications for interplanetary probe propulsion and stblzn. Mem. Dem. Town Com., Wilton, Conn., 1963, Concord, Mass., 1978—, chmn., 1984-96; mem. Harvard Com. on Univ. Resources, 1981-92; mem. various vis. coms. MIT, 1981-91; mem. vis. com. Nat. Bur. Standards, 1981-84; trustee U. Lowell, 1985-91; founder, pres. Families U.S.A. Founds. (formerly Villers Found.), Washington, 1981—, Bay State Retiree Vol. Coun., Concord, 1989-92; del. Dem. Nat. Conv., 1988, 92. NSF grad. fellow, 1959-60. Mem. IEEE, ASME, Amnesty Internat. (bd. dirs. 1990-96, ombudsman 1992-96, exec. com. 1994-96, leadership coun. 1995—, coord. group 15 1998—), Soc. Mfg. Engrs., ACLU (pres. com. 1981—, bd. dirs. Physicians for Human Rights 1991-94), Unitarian-Universalist Assn. (pres. coun. 1982-86), Sigma Xi. Home: 20 Whits End Rd Concord MA 01742-5411 Office: 200 Baker Ave Ste 309 Concord MA 01742-2170 E-mail: pvillers@igc.org.

VILLET, BARBARA, writer; b. Oceanside, N.Y., Feb. 6, 1931; d. Thomas L. Cummiskey and Cecelia A. Fitzpatrick; m. Charles Grey Villet (dec.); 1 child, Ann C. Villet-Lagomarsino. AB, Middlebury Coll., 1952; AMT, Harvard U., 1953. Editor, reporter Radio Free Europe, N.Y.C., 1953-55; tchr. Valley Stream (N.Y.) C. High, 1955-56; reporter, editor, writer Life Mag., N.Y.C., 1956-72; freelance writer, 1972—. Author: (books) Those Whom God Chose, 1965, Blood River, 1980, (nonfiction book) Head Nurse, 1972; contbr. articles to popular mags. Trustee Middlebury Coll., 1970-75, overseer, 1975—; bd. dirs. Unity House, Troy, N.Y., 1998—. Avocations: painting, golf, travel. Home: 208 Eagleville Rd Shushan NY 12873-2007 E-mail: villetb@sover.net.

VILLFORTH, JOHN CARL, health physicist; b. Reading, Pa., Dec. 28, 1930; s. Carl and Grace L. (Fichthorn) V.; m. Joanne E. Heine, Sept. 12, 1953; children: Mary Jane Smith, Elaine, Jennifer Veazy. BS in San. Engring., Pa. State U., 1952, MS, 1954; MS in Physics, Vanderbilt U., 1958. Cert. Am. Bd. Health Physics. With USPHS, 1961-90; dir. Ctr. for Devices and Radiol. Health, 1969-90, asst. surgeon gen., 1972-90, chief engr., 1985-89; pres. Food and Drug Law Inst., Washington, 1990—2001. Bd. dirs. Vasogen Inc., EduNeering Inc. Served to capt. USAF, 1954-61. Recipient Meritorious Svc. medal USPHS, 1974, D.S.M., 1980, 84, Outstanding Svc. medal, 1986, Outstanding Engring. Alumnus award Pa. State Univ., 1987, U. Alumni Fellow, Pa. State U., 2002, Sec. Recognition award Dept. Health and Human Svcs., 1987, FDA Disting. Alumni award, 2000. Mem.: USPHS Commd. Officers Assn. (chmn. bd. dirs. 1999—2000), Regulatory Affairs Profl. Soc., Internat. Radiation Protection Assn., Assn. Food and drug Ofcls., Health Physics Soc. (pres. 1976—77, Elda Anderson award 1970). E-mail: jcvillforth@erols.com. *Understand the problem! Too much energy is wasted and too many relationships are strained because we fail to understand the underlying problem before we embark on a solution.*

VILLOCH, KELLY CARNEY, art director; b. Kyoto, Japan, July 22, 1950; d. William Riley and stepdaughter Hazel Fowler Carney; m. Joe D. Villoch, Aug. 9, 1969; children: Jonathan, Christopher, Jennifer. A in Fine Arts, Dade C.C., Miami, Fla., 1971; student, Metro Fine Arts, 1973-74, Fla. Internat. U., 1985-88. Design asst. Lanvin, Miami, 1971—74, Fieldcrest, Miami, 1974-77; art dir. Advercolor, 1977-78; art dir. copywriter ABC, 1978-89; writer Armed Forces Radio & TV Network; multimedia dir. ADVITEC, 1989-91; art dir. writer Miami Write, 1979—89; owner Beach Point Prodns., 1992—; editor-in-chief L'Avenue Mag., 1998—. Lectr. Miami Dade C.C., cons. Studio Masters, North Miami, 1979-89; writer Lucent Techs., Telephonetics, Algorhythm, Inter-tel, 1997—; creative mktg. dir. Raintree Media, 2000. Prin. works include mixed media, 1974 (Best of Show 1974), pen and ink drawing, 1988 (Best Poster 1988); writer, dir., editor, prodr. (video film): Bif, 1988, Drink + Drive = Die, 1994; writer, dir., prodr. (pub. svc. announcement) Reading is the Real Adventure, 1990; film editor Talent Times Mag.; author: Winds of Freedom, 1994; art dir., exec. com. Miami Hispanic Media Conf., 1992, 93, 94; editor-in-chief, film editor: In Grove Miami Mag., 1994-96; webmaster, web content provider, website design cons., writer, graphic artist Guru Comms., 1996; editor-in-chief In Grove Miami Mag., 1994-96, L'Avenue Mag., Miami Mag., Fla. Journey and Miami Guide, 1998-99, Paladar mag., 2002, Decasa mag., 2002, Flash Animation: Passionate Nomad-A Journey Through Cairo, 2002; web content provider WEBCOM; webmaster Guru Comm., 1996, Miami Metro Mag., 2000; sr. editor Channels Intl. Mag., 2001; web site designer, multimedia dir. State of Fla. grantee LimeLite Studios, Inc., 1990, William Douglas Pawley Found. grantee, Frances Wolfson scholar, Cultural Consortium grantee, 1993. Mem. Am. Film Inst., Phi Beta Kappa. Avocations: animation, printmaking, skin diving, boating, painting. E-mail: beachn@worldnet.att.net.

VILLWOCK, KENNETH JAMES, procurement executive; b. Coral Gables, Fla., Jan. 9, 1953; s. Homer Samuel Short and Anna (Pierce) Villwock; m. Martha Lemus Medina, June 12, 1977; children: Theodore Elliott, Joshua James. BA, Golden Gate U., 1976; Th.M., Dallas Sem., 1980; MBA, North Tex. State U., 1985. Cert. purchasing mgr. Telemetry repair Kentron Hawaii, Ltd., Edwards AFB, Calif., 1975-76; subcontractor Dallas, 1976-80; fin. analyst, mgr. US Mktg., Unisys, 1980-83, fin. ops. mgr., 1984-85; cash mgr. Corp. Treasury Unisys, Blue Bell, Pa., 1986-88; dir. pricing and bus. analysis U.S. Mktg., Unisys, 1989; dir. fin. and procurement, global customer svcs. Unisys, 1990-95; dir. worldwide procurement Global Customer Svc., Unisys, 1996-97; dir. Global Re-Sale Procurement, Unisys, 1998-2000; pres. Emeritor, Inc., Upper Gwynedd, Pa., 2000—01; dir. global procurement Cendian Corp., Atlanta, 2001—. Fin. planner Fin. Planning Source, Dallas, 1984-87. Youth dir. Scofield Meml. Ch., Dallas, 1979; Bible tchr. various chs., Dallas, Souderton, Pa., 1972-95; referee Whitpain Soccer Assn., Blue Bell, 1988-90; ranger Boys Brigade, Souderton, 1990-93; elder Calvary Ch. of Souderton, 1992. Staff sgt. USAF, 1971-75. Mem. Nat. Assn. Purchasing Mgmt. Republican. Avocations: Biblical studies, skiing, golf, tennis. Home: 100 Savannah Estates Dr Atlanta GA 30350- Office: Cendian Corp Six Concourse Pkwy Ste 2800 Atlanta GA 30328-0747 E-mail: Jim.Villwock@cendian.com.

VILNROTTER, VICTOR ALPÁR, research engineer; b. Kunhegyes, Hungary, Nov. 8, 1944; came to U.S., 1957; s. Nicholas and Aranka (Vidovits) V.; m. Felicia D'Auria, Jan. 20, 1974; children: Katherine, Brian. BSEE, NYU, 1971; MS, MIT, 1974; PhD in EE, U. So. Calif., L.A., 1978. Teaching asst. MIT, Cambridge, Mass., 1972-74; rsch. engr. Jet Propulsion Lab., Pasadena, Calif., 1979—. Contbr. articles to profl. jours.; patentee in field. Mem. IEEE (referee in communications soc. 1980—), N.Y. Acad. Scis., Sigma Xi, Eta Kappa Nu. Achievements include development and demonstration of real-time array-feed antenna compensation system for future deep-space missions; development of robust receiver structures for autonomous monitoring of spacecraft beacon signals; optimum frequency estimators for use during high-dynamic spacecraft maneuvers such as orbit-insertion, and development of optimum receivers for tracking and detecting very weak radio frequency and optical signals from deep space; research in quantive detection of optical signals; research of novel algorithms for phasing and beam forming of large anays. Home: 1334 Greenbriar Rd Glendale CA 91207-1254

VILSACK, THOMAS, governor; b. Dec. 13, 1950; adopted s. Bud and Dolly Vilsack; m. Christie Bell, Aug. 1973; children: Jess, Doug. B.History, Hamilton Coll., Clinton, N.Y., 1972; JD, Union U., 1975. Pvt. practice, Mt. Pleasant, Iowa, 1975—87; senator State of Iowa, 1992-98, gov., 1999—. Mayor City of Mt. Pleasant, 1987-92; bd. dirs. United Way, Mt. Pleasant. Mem. Mt. Pleasant C. of C. (pres.), Rotary (pres.). Office: Office of the Governor State Capitol Bldg Des Moines IA 50319-0001*

VILTER, RICHARD WILLIAM, physician, educator; b. Cin., Mar. 21, 1911; s. William Frederick and Clara (Bieler) V.; m. Sue Potter, Aug. 17, 1935; 1 son, Richard William (dec.). AB, Harvard U., 1933, MD, 1937. Diplomate: Am. Bd. Internal Medicine. Intern, resident internal medicine Cin. Gen. Hosp., 1937-42, founding dir. divsn. hematology/oncology, 1945-56, asst. dir. dept. internal medicine, 1953-56, dir., 1956-78; assoc. prof. medicine U. Cin. Coll. Medicine, 1948-56, Gordon and Helen Hughes Taylor prof., 1956-78, prof. medicine on spl. assignment, 1978-81, prof. medicine emeritus, 1981—, asst. dean, 1945-51. Cons. VA, 1947—; cons. hematology Good Samaritan Hosp., Cin.; cons. physician Christ, Drake hosps., Cin.; mem. sci adv. bd. Nat. Vitamin Found., 1953-56; spl. cons. nutrition and anemias in Egypt WHO, 1954; cons. Pan Am. Sanitary Bur. Anemias of Kashiorkor in Guatemala and Panama, 1955; mem. Am. Cancer Soc. Com. on Investigation and Therapy of Cancer, 1960-64, chmn. 1964; chmn. hematology sect. NIH, 1965-69, nat. adv. com. anemia malnutrition Rsch. Ctr. Chiengmai, Thailand, 1967-75. Assoc. editor Jour. Clin. Investigation, 1951-52; contbr. to profl. publs. Recipient Joseph Goldberger award AMA, 1960, Daniel Drake medal U. Cin., 1985, Golden Apple award U. Cin., 1985, award for excellence U. Cin., 1990, Daniel Drake Humanitarian award Acad. Medicine, Cin., 1991, 1st recipient U. Cin. Coll. Medicine Lifetime Tchg. award, 1995; Richard W. and Sue P. Vilter endowed professorship U. Cin. Coll. Medicine est. and funded 1999. Master ACP (past gov. Ohio bd. regents, sec. gen. 1973-78, pres.-elect 1978-79, pres. 1979-80, pres. emeritus 1984); mem. Federated Coun. for Internal Medicine (chmn. 1979-80), Clin. and Climatol. Assn. (v.p. 1982-83), Assn. Am. Physicians, Am. Soc. Clin. Nutrition (pres. 1960-61), Am. Soc. Clin. Investigation, Ctrl. Soc. Clin. Rsch. (coun. mem. 1957-60), Am. Soc. Hematology, Am. Bd. Nutrition, Internat. Soc. Hematology, Cin. Lit. Club (pres. 1990-91), Phi Beta Kappa, Alpha Omega Alpha, Nu Sigma Nu. Home: 5 Annwood Ln Cincinnati OH 45206-1419 Office: U Cin Med Ctr Cincinnati OH 45267-0001 E-mail: vilterr@ucmail.uc.edu.

VIMONT, RICHARD ELGIN, lawyer; b. Lexington, Ky., Aug. 3, 1936; s. Richard Thompson and Christine Frazee (Anderson) V.; m. Louise Marie Salyer, Sept. 20, 1960; children: Richard Thompson II, Margaret Anderson; m. 2d, Martha Jane Murray, Nov. 13, 1982 (div.); m. Mary Ann Farley, May 31, 1997. BS, U. Ky., 1958, JD, 1960. Bar: Ky. 1960, U.S. Dist. Ct. (ea. dist.) Ky. 1964, U.S. Ct. Appeals (2d and 6th cirs.) 1964, U.S. Supreme Ct. 1966, U.S. Ct. Appeals (2d cir.) 1998. Assoc. Brown, Sledd and McCann, 1960-64; ptnr. Core, Vimont and Combs, 1964-68, Breckenridge, Vimont and Amato, 1968-70, Anggelis, Vimont and Bunch, 1970-78, Vimont and Wills PLLC, Lexington, 1978—, mng. mem., 1998—. Asst. commonwealth atty., 1973-75; vis. prof. Transylvania U., 1978-80, Midway Coll., 1992; bd. dirs. Equitania Ins. Co.; mng. dir. Equitania Ins. Co., 1990-93, pres., CEO, 1993-95; gen. counsel Pavenstedt Pauli (U.S.A.), Inc., 1990-92; adj. prof. U. Kent. Coll. of Law, 1998. City commr., Lexington, 1971-72; chmn. Lexington Mounted Police Bd., chair, 1997-2000; bd. dirs. Ky. World Trade Ctr., 1990-97, Lexington Ballet Co., 1989-90; ch. parliamentarian Christian Ch. (Disciples of Christ). Fellow U. Ky., U. Kent. Mem. ABA, Am. Acad. Trial Attys., Ky. Bar Assn., Ky. Acad. Trial Attys., Fayette County Bar Assn., Lexington C. of C., Thoroughbred Club of Am., Lexington Polo Club, Spindletop Hall Club (bd. dirs. 1978-81, 86-90), Rotary (sec. Lexington endowment 1994-97, Paul Harris fellow). Democrat. Office: 155 E Main St Fl 3 Lexington KY 40507-1300

VINAR, BENJAMIN, lawyer; b. Rock Island, Ill., Apr. 10, 1935; s. Isidore and Bessie (Shaman) V.; m. Rochelle Weinfeld, June 17, 1962; children: Jacqueline, Dov, Elana, Daniella. BA, U. Ill., 1957; LLB, NYU, 1960. Bar: N.Y. 1961, U.S. Dist. Ct. (so. dist.) N.Y. 1962, U.S. Ct. Appeals (2nd cir.) 1964, U.S. Supreme Ct. 1966, U.S. Dist. Ct. (ea. dist.) N.Y. 1971. Assoc. Donovan, Leisure, Newton & Irvine, N.Y.C., 1961-71; pvt. practice, 1971-76, Garden City, N.Y. and N.Y.C., 1986—; ptnr. Siff & Newman, P.C., N.Y.C., 1976-86. Contbr. articles to profl. jours. Mem. nat. law com. Anti-Defamation League, N.Y.C., 1975-2000; pres. Queens Jewish Community Coun., N.Y.C., 1979-81, Young Israel of Queens Valley, N.Y.C., 1984-86; v.p. Nat. Coun. Young Israel, 1986-90, YM-YMHA of No. Queens, N.Y.C., 1989-91; bd. dirs. Met. Coun. on Jewish Poverty, N.Y.C., 1984-89. Mem. ABA, Nassau Bar Assn. (chair appellate practice com.), NYU Law Rev. Alumni Assn. (pres. 1981-83), Order of Coif, Phi Beta Kappa, Phi Kappa Phi. Democrat. E-mail: bvinar@compuserve.com.

VINCE, CLINTON ANDREW, lawyer; b. Bklyn., May 31, 1949; s. Tibor Andrew and Priscilla (Ward) V.; divorced; children: Matthew McHale, Jennifer Anne. AB, Trinity Coll., 1971; JD, Georgetown U., 1974. Bar: N.Y. 1975, U.S. Dist. Ct. (so. and ea. dists.) N.Y. 1975, U.S. Ct. Appeals (2nd cir.) 1975, D.C. 1976, U.S. Dist. Ct. D.C. 1976, U.S. Ct. Appeals (D.C. and 8th cirs.) 1976, U.S. Supreme Ct. 1979, U.S. Ct. Appeals (4th and 11th cirs.) 1984, U.S. Ct. Appeals (5th cir.) 1985, U.S. Ct. Appeals (10th cir.) 1988. Ptnr. Verner, Liipfert, Bernhard, McPherson & Hand, Washington, 1984—2001; ptnr., dir. energy group Sullivan & Worcester, LLP, 2001—. Chief energy cons. City of New Orleans, 1983—; gen. counsel Southeastern Power Resources Com., Tucker, Ga., 1986—. Contbr. articles to profl. jours. Bd. dirs. Fed. City Coun., bd. trustees Keystone Energy; treas. bd. dirs. The Writers Ctr., One Voice. Mem. ABA, ATLA, Fed. Energy Bar Assn. (chmn. bd. dirs., chair Fed. Energy Law Jour. Found.), D.C. Bar Assn., Ctr. Strategic and Internat. Studies (mem. roundtable), Econ. Club Washington, City Tavern Club, Cosmos Club. Avocations: sailing, skiing, tennis, literature, writing. Office: Sullivan & Worcester LLP 1666 K St NW Ste 700 Washington DC 20006 E-mail: cvince@sandw.com.

VINCELLI, PATRICK THOMAS, human resources specialist; b. St. Paul, Feb. 24, 1946; s. Patrick Joseph and Ruth Lillian Vincelli; m. Gayle Margaret Lichliter, June 19, 1971; children: Anthony James, Todd Patrick. BS in Sociology, St. John's U., Collegeville, Minn., 1968; MA in Indsl. Rels., U. Minn., 1972. Adminstr. human resources Control Data/No. States Power, Mpls., 1972—79; mgr. human resources Control Data, 1979—82, mgr. staffing svcs., 1982—88, mgr. human resources, 1988—90; dir. human resources Fredrickson & Byron, P.A., 1990—96, Zytec Corp., Eden Prairie, 1996—99; v.p. human resources Artesyn Technologies, 1999—. Author: Metropolitan Area Golf Course Director, (poetry) The Eternal Want, 1964, An Apathetic Love, 1999. Coach youth league Burnsville Athletic Club, 1986—89; mem. fin. and pers. coun. Mary, Mother of the Ch., Burnsville, Minn., 1990—, caregiver, Stephen's Ministry, 1992—97; com. mem. Bloomington Edn. and Employer Exchange, 1986—87. Cpl. U.S. Army, 1968—70. Recipient Recognition for Minority Scholarship Program, Assn. of Legal Adminstrs., 1993. Mem.: U. Minn. Alumni Assn., Indsl. Rels. Alumni Assn. (exec. program chair 1970—), Soc. for Human Resource Mgmt. Republican. Roman Catholic. Avocations: golf, travel, fitness. Mailing: Artesyn Technologies 7575 Market Place Dr Eden Prairie MN 55344

VINCENT, ADELE JUDITH, foundation adminstrator; b. Ashton-Under-Lyne, Lancashire, Eng., May 10, 1935; d. Ian MacDonald and Marian (Leech) Bagnall; m. Charles Geoffrey Vincent, Apr. 24, 1965; children: Wendy Anne, Christopher Loy, Mary Jane. BA with honors, Oxford (Eng.) U., 1957, MA, 1961. Staff writer The Observer, London, 1957-64, The N.Y. Times, N.Y.C., 1964-65; edit. writer The Courier-Jour., Louisville, 1971-78; program officer, assoc. dir. Cummins Engine Found., Columbus, Ind., 1981—. Mem. adv. council PreCollegiate Edn. Group, Council on Founds., Washington, 1983-85. Contbr. numerous articles to profl. jours. Mem. bd. women Founds./Corp. Philanthropy, 1985—. Mem. LWV (pres. Columbus chpt. 1983-85. Democrat. Episcopalian. Home: 4873 E Windsor Ln Columbus IN 47201-9650 Office: Cummins Engine Found PO Box 3005 Columbus IN 47202-3005

VINCENT, CHARLES EAGAR, JR. sports columnist; b. Beaumont, Tex., Mar. 24, 1940; s. Charles Eagar and Hazel Ruth (Balston) V.; m. Mary Jacquelyn Bertman, Aug. 8, 1959 (div. Jan. 1969); children: Lisa Marie, Dixie Ann, Charles Joseph, John Patrick; m. Patricia Helene Skinner, Mar. 28, 1970 (div. Apr. 1985); 1 child, Susanna Lee; m. Karen Judith Peterson, Aug. 17, 1985. Student, Victoria Coll., 1958-59. Reporter Victoria (Tex.) Mirror, 1958-59, Taylor (Tex.) Daily Press, 1959-60; sports writer Beaumont (Tex.) Jour., 1960-62; sports editor Galveston (Tex.) Tribune, 1962-63; sports writer San Antonio Express-News, 1963-69, Sandusky (Ohio) Register, 1969-70, Detroit Free Press, 1970-85, sports columnist, 1985-99. Author: Welcome to My World, 1994, Broken Wings, 1998; co-author: (with Richard Bak) The Corner, A Century of Memories at Michigan and Trumbull, 1999. Recipient 4th Pl. award Nat. AP Sports Editors, 1981, 5th Pl., 1989, 92, Sister Mary Leila Meml. award, 1991, Mich. Columnist of Yr. award, 1991, 97; Afro-Am. Night honoree, 1991, Mich. Writer of the Yr. Nat. Sportscasters and Sportswriters, 1998. Mem. Baseball Writers Assn. Am. Avocations: traveling, cooking, geneology. E-mail: Vincentcharlie@hotmail.com.

VINCENT, DAVID RIDGELY, management consulting executive; b. Detroit, Aug. 9, 1941; s. Charles Ridgely and Charlotte Jane (McCarroll) V.; m. Margaret Helen Anderson, Aug. 25, 1962 (div. 1973); children: Sandra Lee, Cheryl Ann; m. Judith Ann Gomez, July 2, 1978; 1 child, Amber; stepchildren: Michael Jr., Jesse Joseph Flores (dec.). BS, BA, Calif. State U., Sacramento, 1964; MBA, Calif. State U., Hayward, 1971; PhD, Somerset U., 1991. Cert. profl. cons. to mgmt., 1994. Sr. ops. analyst Aerojet Gen. Corp., Sacramento, 1960-66; contr. Hexcel Corp., Dublin, 1966-70; mng. dir. Memorex, Vienna, Austria, 1970-74; sales mgr. Ampex World Ops., Friebourg, Switzerland, 1974-76; dir. product mgmt. NCR, Sunnyvale, Calif., 1976-79; v.p. Boole & Babbage Inc., 1979-85; gen. mgr. Inst. Info. Mgmt., Sunnyvale Calif., Calif., 1979-85; pres., CEO The Info. Group, Inc., Santa Clara, 1985—. Author: Perspectives in Information Management, Information Economics, 1983, Handbook of Information Resource Management, 1987, The Information-Based Corporation: stakeholder economics and the technology investment, 1990, Reengineering Fundamentals: Business Processes and the Global Economy, 1994-96; contbr. monographs and papers to profl. jours. U.S. Soccer Fedn. soccer referee emeritus. Mem.: Am. Mktg. Assn., Nat. Investor Rels. Inst., Assn. Fin. Profls., Product Devel. and Mgmt. Assn., World Future Soc., Soc. Competitive Intelligence Profls., Am. Electronics Assn., Nat. Alliance Bus. Econs. (chair bus. devel. com.). Home: 2803 Kalliam Dr Santa Clara CA 95051-6838 Office: The Info Group Inc 4675 Stevens Creek Blvd Ste 100 Santa Clara CA 95051-6763

VINCENT, FREDERICK MICHAEL, SR. neurologist, educational administrator; b. Detroit, Nov. 19, 1948; s. George S. and Alyce M. (Borkowski) V.; m. Patricia Lucille Cordes, Oct. 7, 1972; children: Frederick Michael Jr., Joshua Peter, Melissa Anne. BS in Biology, Aquinas Coll., 1970; MD, Mich. State U., 1973. Diplomate Am. Bd. Psychiatry and Neurology, Am. Bd. Electrodiagnostic Medicine, Nat. Bd. Med. Examiners, Am. Bd. Forensic Medicine, Am. Bd. Clin. Neurophysiology. Intern St. Luke's Hosp., Duluth, Minn., 1974-75; resident in neurology Dartmouth Med. Sch., Hanover, N.H., 1975-77, instr. dept. medicine, chief resident neurology, 1977-78; chief neurology sect. Munson Med. Ctr., Traverse City, Mich., 1978-84; asst. clin. prof. medicine and pathology Mich. State U., East Lansing, 1978-84, chief sect. neurology Coll. Human Medicine, 1984-87, clin. prof. psychiatry and internal medicine, 1989—, clin. prof. medicine, 1990—, clin. prof. neurology and ophthalmology, 2000—; pvt. practice Lansing, Mich., 1987—. Clin. and rsch. fellow neuro-oncology Mass. Gen. Hosp., Boston, 1985; clin. fellow in neurology Harvard Med. Sch., Boston, 1985; cons. med. asst. program Northwestern Mich. Coll., Traverse City, 1983—84; neurology cons. radio call-in show Sta. WKAR , East Lansing, 1984—2000, Sta. WCMU-TV, 1987, 1993—. Author: Neurology: Problems in Primary Care, 1987, 2d edit., 1993; contbr. more than 80 articles to sci. and profl. jours. Fellow NSF, 1969, Nat. Multiple Sclerosis Soc., 1971. Fellow: ACP, Am. Assn. Electrodiagnostic Medicine (computer electronics com. 1995—98, profl. practice com. 1999—2000, practice rev. panel 2000—), Am. Acad. Neurology (program accreditation devel. subcom. 1993—2001), Am. Bd. Forensic Examiners, Am. Heart Assn.; mem.: Am. Coll. Legal Medicine, Am. Soc. Neurorehab., Soc. for Neuro-Oncology, Movement Disorders Soc., Am. Clin. Neurophysiology Soc., Am. Fedn. Clin. Rsch., Am. Soc. Clin. Oncology, Am. Acad. Clin. Neurophysiology, Soc. Neuro-Oncology, Univ. Club, Alpha Omega Alpha. Roman Catholic. E-malk. Office: 1515 Lake Lansing Rd Ste F1 Lansing MI 48912-3752 E-mail: vincen11@msu.edu.

VINCENT, HAL WELLMAN, marine corps officer, investor; b. Pontiac, Mich., Sept. 27, 1927; s. Harold and Glenda (Wellman) V.; m. Virginia Bayler, June 9, 1951; children: David B., Dale W., Deborah K. Vincent Minder. Student, Navy V-5 program Western Mich. Coll./Colgate U., 1945; BS, U.S. Naval Acad., 1950; postgrad., Marine Officers Basic Sch., 1950, Flight Sch., 1952, Test Pilot Sch., 1955, Navy Fleet Air Gunnery Sch., 1958, Air Force Fighter Weapons Sch., 1959, Marine Corps Command and Staff Coll., 1964, Indsl. Coll., 1969, Marine Air Weapons Tng. Unit, 1972. Cert. flight and instrument instr. Commd. 2d lt. U.S. Marine Corps, 1950, advanced through grades to maj. gen., 1974; rifle and machinegun platoon comdr. Camp Lejeune, N.C., 1951; fighter pilot El Toro, Calif. and, Korea, 1953-54; test pilot Flight Test Div., Patuxent River, Md., 1955-57; ops. officer, squadron asst. and fighter pilot El Toro, 1958-59; conventional weapons project test pilot Naval Air Weapons Test Ctr., China Lake, Calif., 1960-62; squadron ops. and exec. officer El Toro and Japan, 1962-64; aviation specialist Marine Corps amphibious warfare presentation team and staff officer Quantico, Va., 1965-66; comdg. officer 2d Marine Aircraft Wing fighter-attack squadron, Beaufort, S.C., 1967-68; exec. officer Marine Aircraft Group, Vietnam, 1969; logistics staff officer Fleet Marine Force Pacific, Hawaii, 1970-72; comdg. officer Marine Aircraft Group, Yuma, Ariz., 1972-73; chief of staff 3d Marine Aircraft Wing, El Toro, 1973-76; dep. chief. of staff plans and policy to Comdr. in Chief Atlantic, Norfolk, Va., 1976-78; comdg. gen. 2d Marine Aircraft Wing, Cherry Point, N.C., 1978-80; dep. comdg. gen. Fleet Marine Force Atlantic, Norfolk, 1980-81; ret., 1981; pvt. investor, 1981—. Flight test pilot; preliminary pilot, evaluator new mil. aircraft. Contbr. numerous articles on tactics and conventional weapons delivery, flight test stability and control to various mil. publs. Decorated Legion of Merit with 2 gold stars, D.F.C., Bronze Star with combat V, Air medal with star and numeral 14, Joint Svcs. Commendation medal U.S., Honor medal 1st class, Cross of Gallantry with gold star (Republic of Vietnam). Mem. SAR, Soc. Exptl. Test Pilots, Early Pioneer Naval Aviators, Marine Corps Aviation Assn., Mach 2 Club, Marbella Country Club. Achievements include invention of triple ejector rack for delivery of conventional bombs, 1961; devel. of fighter tactics in F8 and F4 aircraft, 1958-69; flew 165 models of fgn. and U.S. mil. aircraft; flew 8 models of fixed wing and helicopters on 242 combat missions; first Marine to fly MACH-2. E-mail: hwvincent@webtv.net. *In all 36 years in the service I am convinced that war is bad, and little is accomplished in the long term by warfare. However when National policy dictates a war, then we must not limit what can be done. We must win! My thought then remains: "Winning isn't everything, it's the only thing!" When I must go to battle I want to be allowed to "fight to win".*

VINCENT, JAMES LOUIS, biotechnology company executive; b. Johnstown, Pa., Dec. 15, 1939; s. Robert Clyde and Marietta Lucille (Kennedy) V.; m. Elizabeth M. Matthews, Aug. 19, 1961 (div. 1998); children: Aimee Archelle, Christopher James; m. Joyce Anne Fitzgibbons, Dec. 30, 1999. BSME, Duke U., 1961; MBA in Indsl. Mgmt., U. Pa., 1963; DBA (hon.), U. New Haven, 1998. Mgr. Far East div. Tex. Instruments, Inc., Tokyo, 1970-72; pres. Tex. Instrument Asia, Ltd., 1970-72; v.p. diagnostic ops., pres. diagnostics div. Abbott Labs., North Chgo., Ill., 1972-74, group v.p., bd. dirs., 1974-81, exec. v.p., COO, bd. dirs., 1979-81; corp. group v.p., pres. Allied Health and Sci. Products Co. Allied Corp., Morristown, N.J., 1982-85; CEO Biogen, Inc., Cambridge, Mass., 1985-97, 1999—2000, chmn. bd., 1997—2002; ret., 2002. Bd. dirs. Found. for Nat. Tech. Trustee Duke U., Com. for Econ. Devel.; bd. overseers Wharton Grad. Bus. Sch., U. Pa.; bd. dirs. Mass. chpt. Nat. Multiple Sclerosis Soc. Recipient Young Exec. Achievement

Young Execs. Club, Chgo., 1976, Disting. Alumni award Duke U., 1988, Biotech. award Wall St. Transcript, 1997. Mem. Mass. Bus. Roundtable, The Comml. Club Boston, Algonquin Club Boston, The Links (N.Y.C.). Republican. Presbyterian. Office: Biogen Inc 14 Cambridge Ctr Cambridge MA 02142-1481

VINCENT, JOHN BERTRAM, chemist, educator; b. Cape Girardeau, Mo., July 10, 1962; s. Jack Donald and Patricia Illers Vincent; m. Sharon Ellen Nevels; children: Allisa, Christina. BS, Murray (Ky.) State U., 1984; PhD, Ind. U., 1988. Postdoctoral rsch. assoc. U. Va., Charlottesville, 1988-90, NIH postdoctoral fellow, 1990-91; asst. prof. chemistry U. Ala., Tuscaloosa, 1991-96, assoc. prof., 1996-2001, prof., 2001—. Contbr. over 150 articles and abstracts to profl. jours. Recipient Outstanding Commitment to Tchg. award U. Ala. Alumni Assn., 1999, Outstanding Honor Program Faculty award U. Ala. Honors Student Assn., 1998. Mem. Am. Diabetes Assn., Ala. Acad. Sci., Coun. on Undergrad. Rsch., Soc. Biol. Inorganic Chemistry, Am. Chem. Soc. (sec. Ala. sect. 1996-97). Presbyterian. Home: 716 53d Ct E Tuscaloosa AL 35404 Office: U Ala Dept Chemistry Tuscaloosa AL 35487-0336 Fax: (205) 348-9104. E-mail: nevels@dbtech.net., jvincent@bama.ua.edu.

VINCENT, MARY LILLIAN CARTER, librarian; b. Sandersville, Ga., Nov. 30, 1931; d. Virgil and Mamie (Etheridge) Carter; m. Timothy Vincent, Jan. 29, 1965; 1 stepchild, Renee. BA, Fordham U., 1977; MS, Pratt Inst., 1986, MLS, 1988. Owner, operator Pin & Curl Beauty Salon, Bklyn., 1959-72; data processing supr., operator Statis. Tabulating Corp., N.Y.C., 1957-75; dir. Bethel at Weeksville, Child Devel. Ctr., Bklyn., 1975-80; media technician Pratt Inst., 1981-88, asst. dir. multi media svcs., 1988-89, dir., 1989—. Author manual, 1980. Trustee Weeksville Soc., Bklyn., 1978-91, treas. bd. trustees, 1980-91. Mem. AAUW, Assn. for Ednl. Comm. and Tech.-Minorities in Media, African Am. Mus. Assn., Black Alumni of Pratt. Avocations: music, writing, travel, history. Office: Pratt Inst 200 Willoughby Ave Brooklyn NY 11205-3899

VINCENT, MICHAEL PAUL, plastic surgeon; b. Ottawa, Ontario, Can., Aug. 8, 1950; s. Dale Leon and Mildred (Havird) V.; m. Mary Margaret Glennon, July 28, 1973; children: Kathryn Blair, Jonathan Michael, Marc Andrew, Caroline Wyatte. BA, Duke U., 1972, MD, 1976. Diplomate Am. Bd. Surgery, Am. Bd. Plastic Surgery. Internship in surgery Bethesda Naval Hosp., Bethesda, Md., 1976-77, gen. surgery residency, 1977-81; plastic surgery and hand surgery fellowship Eastern Va. Sch. of Medicine, Norfolk, Va., 1982—84; chief, plastic surgery Nat. Naval Med. Ctr., Bethesda, 1984-92; plastic surgeon pvt. practice, Rockville, Md., 1992—. Assoc. prof. of clin. surgery, Uniformed Svcs. U. of the Health Scis., Bethesda, 1989—; clin. cons. plastic surgery NIH, 1987—; chief plastic surgery Shady Grove Adventist Hosp., Holy Cross Hosp.; also speaker, advisor. Contbr. chpts. to books: Eyelid Reconstruction, 1987, 91, 92, Ptosis Surgery, 1988; contbr. chpt. to book and articles to profl. jours.; co-editor Flap Dissection Workshop, 1984; prodr. (video) Breast Reconstruction and the Tram Flap, 1990. Active Operation Smile, Washington, 1986—, St. Francis Episcopal Ch., Potomac, Md., 1986—; founding med. advisor My Image After Breast Cancer. With USN, 1972-92, vet. Operation Desert Shield/Storm. Recipient Physician Recognition award, AMA. Fellow ACS; mem. Plastic Surgery Ednl. Found., Am. Soc. Plastic Surgeons (former mem. bd. dirs.), Am. Soc. Aesthetic Plastic Surgery, Nat. Capital Soc. Plastic Surgeons, Montgomery County Med. Soc., Phi Beta Kappa. Episcopal. Avocations: tennis, jogging, golf. Home: 11812 Piney Glen Ln Potomac MD 20854-1413 Office: Ambulatory Plastic Surgery Ctr 9715 Med Ctr Dr Ste 315 Rockville MD 20850 Fax: 301-738-7920. E-mail: vincent_michael@msn.com.

VINCENT, NORMAN FULLER, broadcasting executive; b. Boston, Oct. 5, 1930; s. Norman Harrison and Marian Bernice (Fuller) V.; m. Karen Ann Walter, June 21, 1969. BA, Denison U., 1953. Sales mgr. Sta. WMBR, Jacksonville, Fla., 1956-62; gen. mgr. Sta. WZOK, 1962-66; owner, pres. Norm Vincent Sound Recording Studios, Inc., 1966-75; dir. radio ops. Sta. WJCT, 1975-91; announcer, narrator radio, TV film and video, talking books, 1991—. Producer, host (radio): Swing Time with Norm Vincent, 1992—. Served with USN, 1953-56; to comdr. USNR, 1958-80. Mem.: Advt. Fed. Am., Jacksonville C. of C. (armed svcs. com.), Navy League, Exch. Club, Sigma Alpha Epsilon. Republican. Episcopalian. Home: 2110 The Woods Dr Jacksonville FL 32246-1016

VINCENT, NORMAN L. retired insurance company executive; b. Milw., July 21, 1933; s. Victor V. Vincent and Hilda I. (Boedecker) Vincent Patlow; m. Arlene Page, Jan. 31, 1953 (div. 1978); children: J. Todd, Meg; m. Donna Jean Doll, Aug. 8, 1980. BS, U. Wis., 1957; MS, Purdue U., 1958, PhD, 1960. Diplomate Am. Bd. Profl. Psychology; registered psychologist., Ill., C.P.C.U., C.L.U. Supr. agy. research State Farm Ins. Cos., Bloomington, Ill., 1960-63, dir. agy. research., 1963-66, asst. v.p. agy., 1966-69, asst. v.p. exec., 1969-70, v.p. data processing, 1970-94; systems v.p., 1994-95. Pres. Bloomington Bd. Edn., 1974-77; bd. dirs. YMCA, Bloomington, 1971-85. Served with M.I. U.S. Army, 1953-55. Mem. AAAS Home: W332 N 5861 Meadowlark Ct Nashotah WI 53058-9528

VINCENT, THOMAS JAMES, retired manufacturing company executive; b. Balt., Mar. 17, 1934; s. Thomas Alonzo and Helen Geraldine (Cloman) V.; divorced; children: Wayne S., Robin K. MS, MIT, 1968. Div. gen. mgr. Fairchild Industries, St. Augustine, Fla., 1969-72; pres. T.J. Vincent Properties Ltd., 1972-75, Pacific Concrete & Rock Co., Honolulu, 1975-77, Ramsey Engrng. Co., St. Paul, 1977-80, Kobe Inc., Los Angeles, 1980-84, Milchem Inc., Houston, 1984-85, York (Pa.) Internat. Corp., 1985-88, also bd. dirs., cons.; chmn., CEO Hawaii Seafood Growers, Inc., Kahuku, 1990-92. Author: Fairplan, 1962. Founder, pres. Thomas J. Vincent Found. Inc., Kaneohe, Hawaii, 1990—; founder, v.p., treas. Winter Park (Fla.) Family Health Ctr., Inc., 1995—. Named one of Outstanding Young Men in Am., Jaycees, 1965; Alfred P. Sloan fellow MIT, 1967; recipient Research for Progress Achievement award, 1972. Avocations: deep sea fishing, orchid growing. Home and Office: 44-447 Kaneohe Bay Dr Kaneohe HI 96744

VINCENT, THOMAS LANGE, educator; b. Sept. 16, 1935; MS, Oreg. State U., 1960; PhD, U. Ariz., 1963. Prof. U. Ariz., Tucson, 1963—91, prof. emeritus, 1991—. Home: 5225 W Lazy C Dr Tucson AZ 85745-9052

VINCENTI, MICHAEL BAXTER, lawyer; b. Balt., Dec. 28, 1950; s. Rudolph and Betty (Jones) V.; m. Patricia Lynn Bishopp, Apr. 14, 1984; children: Sarah, Elizabeth. BA, Johns Hopkins U., 1972; JD, NYU Sch. Law, 1975. Bar: Ill. 1975, Ky. 1979; cert. comml. investor, Ky. Assoc. Sonnenschein, Nath & Rosenthal, Chgo., 1975-79; from assoc. to ptnr. Wyatt, Tarrant & Combs, Louisville, 1979—. Guest instr. Jefferson Cmty. Coll., Louisville, 1988-98. Sec., gen. counsel Louisville Sci. Ctr., 1993—; dir., counsel bd. trustees Chance Sch., Louisville, 1995-98. Mem. ABA, Internat. Coun. Shopping Ctrs., Ill. Bar Assn., Am. Land Title Assn. (lender's counsel group), Am. Coll. Real Estate Lawyers, Am. Coll. Mortgage Attys., Ky. Bar Assn., Louisville Bar Assn., Rotary, Louisville Boat Club, Lex Mundi. Episcopalian. Avocations: squash, racquetball, tennis, travel, reading. Office: Wyatt Tarrant & Combs 500 W Jefferson St Ste 2700 Louisville KY 40202-2898 Fax: 502-589-0309. E-mail: mvincenti@wyattfirm.com.

VINCENTI, SHELDON ARNOLD, law educator, lawyer; b. Ogden, Utah, Sept. 4, 1938; s. Arnold Joseph and Mae (Burch) V.; children: Matthew Lewis, Amanda Jo. AB, Harvard U., 1960, JD, 1963. Bar: Utah 1963. Sole practice law, Ogden, 1966-67; ptnr. Lowe and Vincenti, Ogden, 1968-70; legis. asst. to U.S. Rep. Gunn McKay, Washington, 1971-72, adminstrv. asst., 1973; prof., assoc. dean U. of Idaho Coll. of Law, Moscow, Idaho, 1973-83, dean, prof. law, 1983-95, prof. law, 1995—. Home: 2480 W Twin Rd Moscow ID 83843-9114 Office: U Idaho Coll Law 6th & Rayburn St Moscow ID 83843

VINCENTI, WALTER GUIDO, aeronautical engineer, emeritus educator; b. Balt., Apr. 20, 1917; s. Guido A. and Agnes (Nicolini) V.; m. Joyce H. Weaver, Sept. 6, 1947; children— Margaret Anna, Marc Guido. AB, Stanford U., 1938, Aero. Engr., 1940. Aero. research scientist NACA, 1940-57; prof. aero. and astronautics and history of tech. Stanford U., 1957-83, prof. emeritus, 1983—. Cons. to industry, 1957—; mem. adv. panel engrng. sec. NSF, 1960-63. Author: (with Charles H. Kruger, Jr.) Introduction to Physical Gas Dynamics, 1965, (with Nathan Rosenberg) The Britannia Bridge, 1978, What Engineers Know and How They Know It, 1990; also papers.; co-editor (with Milton Van Dyke) Annual Review of Fluid Mechanics, 1970-76. Served with USN, 1945-46. Recipient Gold medal Pi Tau Sigma, 1948, Engr.-Historian award ASME, 1997; Rockefeller Pub. Service award, 1956; Guggenheim fellow, 1963 Fellow AIAA; mem. Internat. Acad. Astronautics (corr.), Soc. History Tech. (Usher prize 1984, Leonardo da Vinci medal 1998), Nat. Acad. Engrng., Newcomen Soc., Phi Beta Kappa, Sigma Xi, Tau Beta Pi. Home: 13200 E Sunset Dr Los Altos CA 94022-3427 Office: Stanford U Stanford CA 94305 E-mail: sts@stanford.edu.

VINCI, JOHN NICHOLAS, architect, educator; b. Chgo., Feb. 6, 1937; s. Nicholas and Nicolina (Camiola) V. B.Arch., Ill. Inst. Tech., 1960. Registered architect, Ill., Mo., Mich., Pa., NCARB. Draftsman Skidmore, Owings, Merrill, Chgo., 1960-61; with City of Chgo., 1961; stencil restorer Crombie Taylor, Chgo., 1961-62; designer Brenner, Danforth, Rockwell, 1962-68; architect Vinci, Inc., 1977-95; ptnr. Vinci/Hamp, Architects, Inc., 1995—; lectr. Roosevelt U., 1969-72, Ill. Inst. Tech., Chgo., 1972-90, adj. prof., 1999. Author: (booklet) Trading Room-Art Inst. Chgo., 1977; contr. articles to profl. jours.; exhbn. designer. Bd. dirs. Music of Baroque, Chgo., 1976-87, Campbell Ctr. Found.; mem. adv. com. Commn. on Chgo. Archtl. and Hist. Landmarks, 1971-83; exec. sec. Richard Nickel Com, Chgo., 1972—; chmn. Howard Van Doren Shaw Soc., 1994-2001; internat. arts adv. coun. Wexner Ctr. for the Arts, 1994—; mem. Landmark Preservation of Ill. Fellow AIA; mem. Soc. Archtl. Historians, Frank Lloyd Wright Home and Studio Found., Art Inst. Chgo., The Corp. of YADDO, Chgo. Hist. Soc., Arts Club of Chgo. Roman Catholic. Home: 3152 N Cambridge Ave Chicago IL 60657-4613 Office: Vinci/Hamp Architects Inc 1147 W Ohio St Chicago IL 60622-6472

VINCIGUERRA, SALVATORE, music educator; b. Miami, June 3, 1974; s. Anthony Vinciguerra and Genevieve Campo-Vinciguerra. BS Music Edn., Troy State U., 1997; MA Music Edn., Valdosta State U., 1999. Cert. tchr. Ala, 1997, Ga., 1997, Fla., 2000. Dir. orchs. Pointe South Mid. Sch., Jonesboro, Ga., 1998—99; string orch. specialist, brass instr. Ala. Sch. Fine Arts, Birmingham, 1999—2000; string orch. specialist/ dir. orchs. Hillsborough County Pub. Schs./Wharton H.S., Tampa, 2000. Mem.: Nat. Educators Assn., Internat. Trumpet Guild, Fla. Orch. Assn., Music Educator's Nat. Conf. Democrat. Roman Catholic. Avocation: painting, composing music, arranging music, playing the piano, trumpet and violin, gardening.

VINCIGUERRA, THOMAS MICHAEL, chemical engineer; b. Beaver Falls, Pa., Apr. 22, 1953; s. Stephen H. and Gloria I. (Casiato) V.; m. Joan Knueven, Sept. 13, 1980; children: Lisa, Janna. BSChemE summa cum laude, U. Cin., 1976. Project engr. Merrell Nat. Labs., Cin., 1976-78, asst. dir. prodn., 1978-80; prodn. mgr. Merrell Dow Pharms., Inc., 1980-84, environ. engr., 1984-89; supr. environ. svcs. Marion Merrell Dow, Inc., 1989-91, mgr. environ. svcs. and indsl. hygiene, 1991-92; mgr. dry products mfg. Hoechst Marion Roussel, Inc., 1992-95, dir. mfg., 1995-96, dir. faccilities mgmt., 1996—. Mem. Reading Schs. and Merrell Ptnrship. in Edn. Daycare Com., Cin., 1988-91; mem. steering com., 1991-93, head steering com., 1993—, coord. Engrng. Cooperative Edn. Prog., 1996—. Counselor Jr. Achievement, Cin., 1988; coach Youth Soccer, Cin., 1988—; mem. Hamilton County (Ohio) Emergency Planning Com., 1989-92. Recipient special recognition New Richmond (Ohio) High Sch., 1990. Mem. Am. Inst. Chem. Engrs. Avocation: photography. Office: Marion Merrell Dow Inc 2110 E Galbraith Rd Cincinnati OH 45237-1625

VINCOLI, JEFFREY WAYNE, safety and environmental engineering executive; b. Port Chester, N.Y., May 18, 1959; s. Joseph and Carmela Mildred (Smeriglio) V.; m. Rosemary Berry Bowling, Sept. 29, 1984. AS in Flight Tech., Fla. Inst. Tech., 1979, BS in Air Commerce, 1981; MS in Aero. Sci., MBA in Aviation Mgmt., Embry Riddle Aero. U., 1984. Safety engr. United Space Boosters, Inc., Kennedy Space Ctr., Fla., 1981-83; safety insp. EG&G Fla., Inc., 1983-85; sr. safety engr. McDonnell Douglas, Titusville, Fla., 1985-88, Cape Canaveral, 1988-95; pres. J.W. Vincoli & Assocs., Titusville, 1993—. Cons. in field. Author: Basic Guide Series, 1993-95; contbr. articles to profl. jours. Mem. Rep. Nat. Com., Washington, 1988, Fla. Assn. for Auto Safety Now, Tallahassee, 1986-88; mem., advisor Community Coalition for Seat Belt Usage, Brevard County, Fla., 1986-87; advisor Mayor's Com. on Drug Abuse, Titusville, Fla., 1987-88; mem. safety and health del. to USSR, Am. People Amb. Program, 1991, del. to People's Rep. China, 1993, Vietnam, 1995. Recipient Significant Achievement award Canaveral Coun. Tech. Socs., 1987. Mem. AIAA, Nat. Environ. Health Assn., Cape Canaveral Am. Soc. Safety Engrs. (profl., pres. 1986-88, tech. writing excellence award 1988, safety profl. of yr. 1987, 93), Am. Indsl. Hygiene Assn. (assoc.), Nat. Safety Coun., System Safety Soc. (mgr. of yr. 1993). Republican. Roman Catholic. Avocations: weightlifting, walking, wood carving, writing. Home: 7786 Windover Way Titusville FL 32780-3703 Office: J W Vincoli & Assocs 7786 Windover Way Titusville FL 32780-3703

VINDERSCHMITT, BERNARD V. data processing executive; MSEE, U. Pa.; MBA, Rider U. Various positions RCA; past v.p., gen. mgr. Zilog; CEO Xilinx, 1984—96, chmn. bd., 1996—. Office: Xilinx Inc. 2100 Logic Dr San Jose CA 95124-3400 Office Fax: 408-559-7114.

VINECOUR, ONEIDA AGNES, nurse; b. Port Arthur, Tex., Oct. 15, 1917; d. Ernest Eugene and Gertrude Mary (Wooldridge) Thorn; m. Seymour Vinecour, Jan. 14, 1943 (dec. 1976); children: Seymour Jacob, Rebecca Leah. Diploma, St. Mary's Hosp. Sch. Nursing, Port Arthur, 1939; postgrad., cert. Surg. Tech., Anesthesia, Cook County Hosp., 1939-40; postgrad. U. Chgo., 1939-40, Tex. Coll. Mines, 1943, U. Tex. Health Ctr. R.N., cert. occupational audiometric technician, occupl. spirometric technician. Operating room supr., instr. Schumpert Meml. Hosp., Shreveport, La., 1940-41; anesthetist St. Joseph Hosp., Albuquerque, 1941-42; operating room supr., instr. Lynn City Hosp. (Mass.), 1946-48; staff anesthetist St. Mary's Hosp., Port Arthur, Tex., 1951-53, in service dir., 1971-73; staff nurse Tyler County Hosp., Woodville, Tex., 1964-65; dept. head, supr. Park Pl. Hosp., Port Arthur, 1965-71; operating room supr. Mid-County Hosp., Nederland, Tex., 1973-81; staff nurse Baptist Meml. Hosp., Beaumont, Tex., 1973-81; part time staff Health Care Svcs., Port Arthur, 1983—; indsl. nurse Synpol Inc., 1984-86; staff nurse Texaco Chem. Plant, Port Arthur, 1986-92, Olsten Health Care Svcs., 1992—, staff nurse Huntsman Petro-Chem. Corp., 1996—. Served as officer U.S. Army Nurse Corps, 1942-46. Mem. Am. Nurses Assn., Mass. Nurses Assn., Tex. State Nurses Assn., Assn. Occupational Health Nurses. Republican. Methodist. Home: 2502 Glenwood Dr Port Arthur TX 77642-2639

VINER, NICHOLAS ANDRÉ, physician, urologist; b. Bridgeport, Conn., Jan. 10, 1942; AB, Holy Cross Coll., 1964; MD, Vanderbilt U., 1968. Diplomate Am. Bd. Urology. Rotating intern Greenwich (Conn.) Hosp., 1968-69, resident in gen. surgery, 1969-70; resident in urology Vanderbilt U., 1970-74; chief of urology Scott AFB, Belleville, Ill., 1974-76, Bridgeport Hosp., 1983—. Pres. Bridgeport Health Network, 1990-95. Maj. USAF, 1974-76. Fellow ACS. Avocations: hiking, biking, theater, cooking, travel, photography. Office: Urol Assocs of Bridgeport 160 Hawley Ln Trumbull CT 06611-5300

VINER, PETER, communications executive; 1 child, Christine. Profl. Mgmt., Harvard, 1980. Cert. Can. Advertising Agy. Practitioner, 1970. Exec. v.p. Telemedia, Inc., 1984-88; pres. Telemedia Comms. Ontario, Inc., 1980-84, CKVU TV, Vancouver, 1974-80; with CanWest Global Comm. Corp., Toronto, Man., 1974—, CEO, 1997-99, vice-chmn., 1999—. Office: CanWest Global Comm Corp 81 Barber Green Rd Toronto ON Canada M3C 2A2 E-mail: pviner@globaltv.ca.

VINES, HENRY ELLSWORTH, III, accountant, lawyer, financial planner; b. Chgo., Apr. 17, 1950; s. Henry Ellsworth and Verle (Low) V.; m. Ethel Melton (div. 1977); 1 child, Tiffany Layne; m. Cindy Lou Rich, Jan. 5, 1985; 1 child, Sasha Teresa Root. BS, Menlo Sch. Bus. Adminstrn., 1972; MBA, Golden Gate Grad. Sch., 1985; CFP, Coll. Fin. Planning, Denver, 1987; JD, William F. Taft Law Sch., 1994; LLM, Wash. Sch. Law, 1998. Bar: Calif. 1996; CPA, Calif.; certified CFP. Asst. contr. Legallet Tanning, San Francisco, 1973-79; auditor Martin Schoonover & Paddock, Orange, 1980-82; tax mgr. Helsley Mulcahy & Fesler, Santa Ana, 1982-85; v.p. fin. Catalina Furniture Co., Fullerton, 1985-94; CFO Precision Concepts, Anaheim, 1987-93; pvt. practice in tax preparation Orange, 1985—; CFO M.E. Woodworking, Riverside, 1989-93, Textured Design Furniture, Anaheim, 1994-95; corp. and tax atty. in pvt. practice, Irvine, Calif., 1996—. Contbr. articles in field. Mem. ABA, AICPA, Calif. Inst. CPAs, Foster City Tennis Club (pres. 1977), San Mateo Tennis Club (pres. 1978), Irvine Spectrum Toastmasters (pres. 2000-01). Republican. Avocations: tennis, golf. Home: 130 N Windy Pointe Orange CA 92869-2400 Office: Ste 300 8 Corporate Park Irvine CA 92606-5196

VINES, SUE ANN, small business owner; b. Cin., July 30, 1946; d. Edward and Frances M.K. (Lamb) Franz; m. Steven Richard Vines, June 8; children: William, Wayne, Jeanny, James, Heather. Registered nat. environ. profl.; registered environ. assessor., Calif. Environ. specialist Gibson Oil Refining Co., Inc., Bakersfield, Calif., 1983-93; owner, mgr. Susieq's Claythings, 1993—. Bd. dirs. Kern County Sci. Found., Bakersfield; adv. bd. Bur. Land Mgmt., Bakersfield, 1990-93; chmn. steering com. Hazardous Waste Assn. Calif., Bakersfield, 1987-94. Mem. Kern County Household Hazardous Waste Com., Bakersfield, 1990-91, Pauline Larwood's Breakfast Coun., Bakersfield. Recipient Pres. award Hazardous Waste Assn. Calif., Bakersfield, 1991. Mem. Air and Waste Mgmt. Assn., Golden Empire Safety Soc., Kids Saving Earth (leader), Mensa. Office: Susieq's Claythings 7104 Azalea Ave Bakersfield CA 93306-4713

VINET, GEORGE ELLSWORTH, JR. foundation administrator; b. S.I., N.Y., Feb. 26, 1955; s. George E. and Mildred F. (Addish) V. AA, Coll. S.I., 1975, diploma in sec. sch. adminstrn. & suprv., 1981; BS in Health Sci., Bklyn. Coll., 1977; MS, Hunter Coll., 1979. Cert. health and phys. educator, secondary sch. adminstr., supr., health edn. specialist, N.Y., N.J. With Curtis H.S., S.I., N.Y., 1990—. Exec. bd. S.I. council Boy Scouts Am., 1974—; water safety com. S.I. chpt. ARC, 1970—, water safety instr., trainer, 1981—. Recipient Svc. medal ARC, 1981, Silver Beaver award Boy Scouts Am., 1992, Wm. Sprugeon award for long, outstanding svc. to exploring, 1997, Vigil Honor from Honor Campers, Order of the Arrow, 1995, St. George award for long, outstanding svc. to cath. scouting CYO-Arch. N.Y., 2001. Mem. AAHPERD, Aquatics Coun. (master aquatic clinician 1993—). Home: 4 Hardy Pl Staten Island NY 10308-2253 Office: Curtis High Sch 105 Hamilton Ave Staten Island NY 10301-1610

VINET, LUC, physicist; b. Montreal, Apr. 16, 1953; s. Jean and Françoise (Ouellette) V.; m. Letitia Muresan, May 19, 1989; children: Jean-François, Laurent, Stéphane, Sophie Andrée. BSc, U. Montreal, 1973, MSc, 1974, PhD, 1980; D. U. P.& M. Curie, Paris, 1979. Rsch. assoc. MIT, Cambridge, 1980—82; rsch. fellow, asst. prof., assoc. prof. U. Montreal, Canada, 1982—92, prof. physics, 1992—99; vice prin. (acad.) McGill U., Montreal, 1999—2001, provost, vice prin. (acad.), 2001—. Invited prof. U. Cath. de Louvain, 1980-81; vis. scholar MIT, Cambridge, 1987; vis. prof. UCLA, 1989-90; dir. Ctr. Rsch. Math., Montreal, 1993-99. Editor: Particle Physics and Quantum Field Theory, 1995, Symmetries and Integrability of Difference Equations, 1995, Quantum Groups Integrable Models and Statistical Systems, 1993, Group Theoretical Methods in Physics, 1989. Grantee FCAR, 1984—, NSERC, 1982—, rsch. fellow, 1982-92. Mem. APS, AMS, SIAM, CAP, CMS. Achievements include contributions in theoretical physics and mathematics - symmetry studies of difference equations; algebraic interpretation of q-special functions using quantum groups; applications of Berry potentials in the nuclear collective model; identification of Lie superalgebras as dynamical algebras in quantum mechanics; development of dimensional reduction in Yang Mills theories.

VINING, DANIEL RUTLEDGE, economics educator; b. Birmingham, Ala., Aug. 12, 1908; s. George Joseph and Margaret Olivia Vining; m. Margaret McClanahan, June 17, 1936 (dec.); children: George Joseph III, Daniel Rutledge Jr. BBA, U. Tex., 1931, MA, 1935; PhD, U. Chgo., 1944. Prof. econs. Westminster Coll., Fulton, Mo., 1935-38; instr. econs. and stats. U. Ark., Fayetteville, 1938-40, asst. prof. econs. and stats., 1941-43, assoc. prof., 1944; prof. econs. U. Va., Charlottesville, 1945—. Statistician Fed. Res. Bank Atlanta, 1941; rsch. asst. Nat. Bur. Econ. Rsch., N.Y.C., 1948-49; vis. prof. Columbia U., N.Y.C., summer 1949, U. Calif. Berkeley, summer 1956, U. Minn., Mpls., summer 1956; chmn. Sch. Bus. Adminstrn., Charlottesville, 1952-54. Author: On Appraising the Performance of an Economic System, 1984; contbr. articles to profl. jours. Ford Found. Faculty Rsch. fellow, Charlottesville, 1956-57, So. Regional Sci. Assn. fellow, Atlanta, 1987. Mem. Am. Econ. Assn., Am. Stats. Assn., Regional Sci. Assn. Episcopalian. Avocation: farming. Home: Dunlodge PO Box 5020 Charlottesville VA 22905-5020

VINING, JOSEPH (GEORGE JOSEPH VINING), law educator; b. Fulton, Mo., Mar. 3, 1938; s. D. Rutledge and Margaret (McClanahan) V.; m. Alice Marshall Williams, Sept. 18, 1965; children: George Joseph IV, Spencer Carter. BA, Yale U., 1959, Cambridge U., 1961, MA, 1970; JD, Harvard U., 1964. Bar: DC 1965. Atty. Office Dep. Atty. Gen., Dept. Justice, Washington, 1965; asst. to exec. dir. Nat. Crime Commn., 1966; assoc. Covington and Burling, Washington, 1966-69; asst. prof. law U. Mich., 1969-72, assoc. prof., 1972-74, prof., 1974-85, Hutchins prof., 1985—. Sir Edward Youde prof., Hong Kong, 2002. Author: Legal Identity, 1978, The Authoritative and the Authoritarian, 1986, From Newton's Sleep, 1995. NEH sr. fellow, 1982-83, Bellagio fellow Rockfeller Found., 1997. Fellow Am. Acad. Arts and Scis.; mem. ABA, D.C. Bar Assn. Am. Law Inst., Century Assn. Office: U Mich 964 Lega Rsch Ann Arbor MI 48109-1215

VINKEMULDER, H. YVONNE, retired lawyer; b. Grand Rapids, Mich., Aug. 21, 1930; d. Arthur and Frances (DeWitt) V. Student, Calvin Coll., 1948-50, Blodgett Hosp. Sch. Nursing, 1950-52; BA, Trinity Coll., 1956; JD, U. Miami, Coral Gables, Fla., 1983. Bar: Wis. 1983. Staff nurse Little Traverse Hosp., Petoskey, Mich., 1952-53, Swedish Covenant Hosp., Chgo., 1953-55; campus nurse Trinity Coll., 1955-57; head nurse Colo. Coll., Colorado Springs, 1957-61; sec. Inter-Varsity Christian Fellowship, Chgo., 1961-65, asst. to dir. devel. Chgo. and Madison, Wis., 1965-74, dir. devel. Madison, 1974-80, dir. planned giving, 1979-81, 90-96, gen. counsel, 1983-96; ret., 1996. Cons. in devel. various orgns., 1976-80; cons. not-for-profit orgn., 1990-2000; lectr. internat. law Fgn. Language Inst., Tianjin, China, 1989. Columnist The Branch, 1976-79; contbg. author: A Guide to Wisconsin Non Profit Corporations, 1990; contbr. articles to mags. Bd. dirs. Internat. Fellowship of Evang. Students, Inc., Boston, 1975-85, Schloss Mittersill Christian Conf. Inc., Madison, 1985-93, 94-2002, Family Rsch. Inst., Madison, 2000—; clk. Faith Bapt. Ch., Madison, 1985-95; mem. stds. com. Evang. Coun. Fin. Accountability, 1989-96; mem. steering com. Evang. Legal Forum, 1988-90, gen. bd. Buckeye Evang. Free Ch., 1999-2000, Door Creek Ch., 2000-02; legal cons., religious orgns., 1999—. Mem. Wis. State Bar Assn. Mem. Evang. Free Ch. Home: PO Box 751 Penney Farms FL 32079- E-mail: vinkemulder@juno.com.

VINKEN, PIERRE JACQUES, neurosurgeon, publishing executive; b. Nov. 25, 1927; MD, U. Utrecht, The Netherlands, 1955; postgrad. in psychiatry, neurolology, and neurosurgery, U. Amsterdam, 1957-63; hon. Dr., U. Paris, 1981. Staff neurosurgeon Univ. Clinic, Amsterdam, 1964-69; pres., chief editor Excerpta Medica Found., Amsterdam and Princeton, N.J., 1962-88; mng. dir. Elsevier Pub. Co., Amsterdam, 1972-78, chmn. bd. dirs., 1979-95, Reed Elsevier, London, 1993-95. Chmn. supervising bd. Halder Holdings, The Hague, Blue Horse Prodns., Rotterdam, Medialand, Amsterdam, Optas, Rotterdam, Trust Theater Co.; bd. dirs. Wereldhave Investment Co., The Hague, Logica, London, Rotterdam, Aalberts Industries, Driebergen, Revisor, Amsterdam, Nat. Acad. Arts, Amsterdam, Internat. Rights-Collecting and Distbns. Agy.; prof. med. database informatics U. Leyden, 1975-93; mem. Nat. Sci. Policy Coun., The Hague, 1983-90; chmn. Netherlands del. Intergovtl. Unisist Conf., Paris, 1970; mem. Netherlands Unisist Commn., 1971-79. Founder, editor-in-chief: Handbook of Clinical Neurology, 77 vols.; editor sci. books; contbr. articles to profl. jours. Chmn. Netherlands Commn. Bibliography and Documentation, 1972-81; pres. Internat. Congress Patient Counselling, 1976-79; chmn. The Lancet, London, 1991-95; chmn. Hiscom, Leyden, 1987-98; bd. dirs. Pearson, London, 1988-91, The Economist, London, 1989-92; chmn. Mees Pierson Bank, Amsterdam, 1994-97; dep. chmn. European Pubs. Coun., mem. soc. adv. coun. Tinbergen Inst., Rotterdam, 1996-2000 Recipient Royal Netherlands Acad. Sci. award, 1997. Mem. European Info. Providers Assn. (pres. 1980-83), Neurol. Soc. India (hon.), French Neurol. Soc. (hon.), Amsterdam Neurol. Soc. (hon.), Peruvian Soc. Psychiat. Neurology and Neurosurgery (hon.), Netherlands Rep. Soc. (founder

1996), Order Hipolitó Unanue (Peru, commdr.), Order of Netherlands' Lion (Knight), Order of Orange Nassau (Netherlands, commdr.). Home: 142 Bentveldsweg 2111 EE Aerdenhout Netherlands

VINORES, STANLEY ANTHONY, ophthalmology educator; b. Pottsville, Pa., July 7, 1950; s. Stanley Matthew and Betty Olive (Taylor) V.; m. Ann Louise Musgrove, Oct. 12, 1977; children: Melissa, Tammi, Charles, Erie. BS in Zoology, Pa. State U., 1972; PhD in Zoology, U. Tex., 1976. Postdoctoral fellow in biochem. pathology Ohio State U., Columbus, 1977-78; staff fellow devel. neurobiology NIH, Bethesda, Md., 1978-81; rsch. assoc. Inst. Cancer Rsch.-Fox Chase, Phila., 1981-82; rsch. asst. prof. neuropathology U. Va. Sch. Medicine, Charlottesville, 1982-85, rsch. asst. prof. ophthalmology, 1985-91; asst. prof. ophthalmology Johns Hopkins U. Sch. Medicine, Balt., 1991-92, assoc. prof., 1992—. Ad hoc reviewer visual scis. C study sect. Nat. Eye Inst., NIH, Bethesda, 1996; grant reviewer NSF, U. Mich. Diabetes Ctr., Fight for Sight; reviewer 17 sci. jours. Youth recreation league coach, 1991—; treas. Cub Scouts Am., Randallstown, 1992-93; lector St. Alphonsus Ch., Woodstock, Md., 1994-2000. Grantee NIH, 1985—, 89-91, 92—; recipient Lew R. Wasserman Merit award. Mem. Assn. Rsch. in Vision and Ophthalmology, Soc. Neurosci., N.Y. Acad. Scis., Histochem. Soc., Internat. Soc. Eye Rsch., Am. Soc. Investigative Pathology, Am. Diabetes Assn., Fedn. Am. Soc. Experimental Biology, Internat. Soc. Molec. Morph., Internat. Brain Rsch. Orgn., World Fedn. Neuroscientists. Roman Catholic. Avocations: sports, outdoors. Home: 9518 Meadows Farm Dr Owings Mills MD 21117 Office: Johns Hopkins U Sch Med 825 Maumenee Bldg 600 N Wolfe St Baltimore MD 21287-0005

VINROOT, RICHARD ALLEN, lawyer, mayor; b. Charlotte, N.C., Apr. 14, 1941; s. Gustav Edgar and Vera Frances (Pickett) V.; m. Judith Lee Allen, Dec. 29, 1964; children: Richard A., Laura Tabor, Kathryn Pickett. BS in Bus. Adminstrn., U. N.C., 1963, JD, 1966. Bar: N.C. 1966, U.S. Dist. Ct. (ea., mid. and we. dists.) N.C. 1969, U.S. Ct. Appeals (4th cir.) 1969. Ptnr. Robinson, Bradshaw & Hinson, P.A., Charlotte, 1969—. Mayor City of Charlotte, 1991-95; bd. dirs. Martin-Marietta Materials Inc. Tchr. sr. h.s. sunday sch. Myers Park Presbyn. Ch., 1970—, ruling elder, 1970-76, 78-84, 96—, chmn. of session, 1984; mem. Charlotte City Coun., 1983-91. With U.S. Army, 1967-68, Vietnam. Recipient Bronze Star, 1968; named Mcpl. Leader of the Yr. Am. City & County Mag., 1995. Mem. ABA, VFW, N.C. Bar Assn., Mecklenburg County Bar Assn. (sec. 1976, bd. dir. 1970-76), Mecklenburg County Vietnam Vets. Assn., Mecklenburg County Eagle Scouts Assn., Am. Legion, Phalanx Lodge Mason.. Republican. Presbyterian. Office: Robinson Bradshaw & Hinson PA 1900 Independence Ctr 101 N Tryon St Ste 1900 Charlotte NC 28246-0103

VINSON, BROOKE EUGENE, investment company executive; b. Decatur, Ill., Oct. 10, 1964; s. Donald Eugene and Georgia Luverne Vinson. BA in Econs., Ill. State U., Normal, 1987. Investment rep. Edward D. Jones & Co., Durango, Colo., 1993-96; fin. cons. Merrill Lynch, 1996-97; v.p. Wells Fargo Investments, 1997—2000; registered prin. LPL Investments, 2000—. Coach Durango Youth Soccer, 1995—; bd. mem. United Way/S.W. Colo., Durango, 1995. Acad. scholar Ill. State Gen. Assembly, 1982. Mem. Internat. Assn. Fin. Planners, Inst. CFPs (accredited asset mgmt. specialist), Rotary Internat., Durango C. of C. Avocations: travel, tennis, softball. Office: 700 Main Ave Durango CO 81301 Home: PO Box 4516 Durango CO 81302-4516

VINSON, DANNY STEVE, musician, music educator; b. Overton, Tex., July 13, 1957; s. Don Ray Vinson and Gaynell Greer; m. Brenda Lynn Blakely, Apr. 14, 1994; children: Lillian Musetta, Evelyn Gaynell, Emily Merryweather. Assoc. of Fine Arts, Kilgore Coll., Tex., 1977; MusB in Edn., U. North Tex., 1982; MS in Music Edn., U. Ill., 1983. Cert. tchr. K-12 Tex. Musician USCG Band, New London, Conn., 1984—; instr. trombone and euphonium U. R.I., Kingston, 1994—; lectr. music U. Conn., Storrs, 1997—. Clinician various state music educators confs., 1988—, Hude Low Brass Workshop, Hude, Germany, 2001—. Chief musician USCG, 1984—2002, USCG Acad., New London, CT. Mem.: SCV (life), NRA (life), Music Educators Nat. Conf., Internat. Tuba Euphonium Assn. (life), Phi Mu Alpha Sinfonia. Conservative. Avocations: outdoor cooking, wine, marksmanship, Civil War history. Home: PO Box 1151 Groton CT 06340 Office: USCG Band 15 Mohegan Dr New London CT 06320

VINSON, JAMES SPANGLER, academic administrator; b. Chambersburg, Pa., May 17, 1941; s. Wilbur S. and Anna M. (Spangler) V.; m. Susan Alexander, Apr. 8, 1967; children: Suzannah, Elizabeth. BA, Gettysburg Coll., 1963; MS, U. Va., 1965, PhD, 1967. Asst. prof. physics MacMurray Coll., Jacksonville, Ill., 1967-71; asso. prof. physics U. N.C., Asheville, 1971-78, prof. physics, 1974-78, chmn. dept. physics, dir. acad. computing, 1974-78; prof. physics, dean Coll. Arts and Scis. U. Hartford (Conn.), 1978-83; v.p. acad. affairs Trinity U., San Antonio, 1983-87; pres. U. Evansville, Ind., 1987-2001, pres. emeritus, 2001—. Computer cons. Contbr. articles to profl. jours. Mem. Am. Phys. Soc., World Future Soc., AAAS, Am. Assn. for Advancement of Humanities, Am. Assn. for Higher Edn., Am. Assn. Physics Tchrs., Phi Beta Kappa, Sigma Xi, Phi Sigma Kappa. Methodist.

VINSON, LAURENCE DUNCAN, JR. lawyer; b. Gadsden, Ala., Mar. 17, 1947; BS with hons., U. Ala., Tuscaloosa, 1969; JD, U. Ala., 1973. Bar: Ala., U.S. Dist. Ct. (no., mid. and so. dists.) Ala., U.S. Ct. Appeals (11th cir.), U.S. Supreme Ct. Assoc. Bradley Arant Rose & White, LLP, Birmingham, Ala., 1973-79, ptnr., 1979—. Bar: Ala. 1973, U.S. Dist. Ct. (no. dist.) Ala. 1973, U.S. Supreme Ct. 1977, U.S. Ct. Appeals (11th cir.) 1981, U.S. Dist. Ct. (so. dist.) Ala. 1989, U.S. Dist. Ct. (mid. dist.) Ala. 1991. Chmn. Ala. Uniform Comml. Code Revisions Coms., Arts 3, 4, 4A and 9. Mem. ABA, Birmingham Bar Assn., Ala. State Bar, Ala. Law Inst., Order of Coif, Phi Beta Kappa, Omicron Delta Kappa. Office: Bradley Arant Rose & White LLP One Federal Pl 1819 5th Ave N Birmingham AL 35203-2736

VINSON, LEILA TERRY WALKER, retired gerontological social worker; b. Lynchburg, Va., July 28, 1928; d. William Terry and Ada Allen (Moore) Walker; m. Hughes Nelson Vinson, Aug. 11, 1951; children: Hughes Nelson, William Terry. Student, Agnes Scott Coll., 1946-48; BA, U. Ala., Tuscaloosa, 1950; postgrad., U. Ala., Birmingham, 1980-81, U. Va., 1950-51. Cert. gerontol. social worker, Ala. Tchr. English and Latin Marion County Bd. Edn., Hamilton, Ala., 1952-59; social worker I Marion County Dept. Pensions and Security, 1963-72, gerontol. social worker II, 1972-85; ret., 1985. Bd. dirs. Marion County Dept. Human Resources, 1985—; bd. mem. Clye Nix Libr., Bevill Coll. Cmty. Theatre, 1992—; spkr. gen. subjects. Recipient Ala. Woman Committed to Excellence award Tuscaloosa coun. Girl Scouts U.S., 1987; named Mrs. Marion County, PTA, Gwin, Ala., 1969, Woman of Yr. Town of Hamilton, 1980, New Retiree of Yr. Ala. Ret. State Employees Assn., 1988, Woman of Yr. BPW, 1985; Gessener Harrison fellow U. Va., 1950-51. Mem. AAUW, DAR (flag chmn. Bedford chpt. 1988-90), UDC, Bus. and Profl. Women's Club (dist. dir. 1984-86, Outstanding Dir. award 1986), Ala. Fedn. Women's Club. Home: PO Box 1112 Hamilton AL 35570-1112 also: Military Rd Hamilton AL 35570

VINSON, NATHAN, retired marketing professional, retired arbitrator; b. Detroit, Aug. 29, 1937; s. Adam and Annie K. Vinson; m. Nora L. Vinson, June 20, 1961; children: Tyrone E., Kimberly D. Student, Wayne State U., 1970, Henry Ford C.C., Dearborn, 1973; cert. completion, U. Wis., 1974. Owner, mgr. Vince's Record Shop, 1970—80; pres. Dash Club, Inc., 1986—95; arbitrator Better Bus. Bur., 1990—; pres., CEO Vince's Mktg. and Real Estate Mgmt., Inc., 1990—. Pres. bd. dirs. Phoenix Job Devel. Svcs., Inc., Holbrook Ave. Fed. Credit Union. State coord. for cmty. ops. AARP, 1996—2000, liaison to labor and religious groups, 2000—; active Greater New Mt. Moriah Bapt. Ch., Detroit. Mem.: NAACP (life), Nat. Panel Consumer Arbitrators, Coalition Black Trades Unionists, N.W. Lions Club. Democrat. Home: PO Box 34603 Detroit MI 48234 Office: Holbrook Fed Credit Union 2112 Holbrook Ave Hamtramck MI 48212

VINSON, WILLIAM THEODORE, lawyer, diversified corporation executive; BS, USAF Acad., 1965; JD, UCLA, 1969. Bar: Calif. 1970. Judge advocate USAF, 1970-74; trial counsel Phillips Petroleum, San Mateo, Calif., 1974-75; atty. Lockheed Corp., Westlake Village, 1975-90, v.p. & sec., 1990-92, v.p., gen. couns., 92-95; v.p., chief counsel Lockheed Martin Corp., 1995-98; cons. Lockheed Corp., 1998; dir. Siemens Govt. Svcs., Inc., 2001—. Bd. dirs. Westminster Free Clinic, 2001—. Office: 5560 E Napoleon Ave Oak Park CA 91377-4746

VINTON, BOBBY (STANLEY ROBERT VINTON), entertainer; b. Canonsburg, Pa., Apr. 16; s. Stanley and Dorothy (Studzenski) V.; m. Dolly Dobbin, Dec. 17, 1962; children: Robert, Kristin, Christopher, Jennifer, Rebecca. Student, Duquesne U., Pitts. Leader own band, singer, nightclub entertainer Blue Velvet Theater, Branson, Mo. Owner Tapestry Record Co., Feather Music Pub. Co., Acacia Music Pub. Co.; performer Blue Velvet Theatre, Branson, Mo.; tours throughout the U.S. Appearances on TV in Bobby Vinton Show, 1975, also numerous guest appearances; single Gold records include Roses Are Red, Blue on Blue, Blue Velvet, Mr. Lonely, I Love How You Love Me, My Melody of Love; rec. artist Epic; dramatic roles in films Surf Party, Big Jake, 1971, The Train Robbers, 1973, also on TV; author (autobiography) Polish Prince; albums include Geatest Polka Hits of All Time, 1991, Timeless, Mr. Lonely: His Greatest Songs Today, 1991, (with George Burns) As Time Goes By, 1992. Served with U.S. Army. Named Number One Male Vocalist, Cash Box mag., 1965; Most Played Rec. Artist, Billboard mag., 1965. Address: PO Box 6010 Branson MO 65615-6010

VINZ, FRANK LOUIS, electrical engineer; b. Laredo, Tex., Jan. 5, 1932; s. Louis and Margaret Reeves (Schaer) V.; m. Mary Marguerite Harlow, June 24, 1956; children: Laura Lee, Susan Elizabeth, Bradley Louis. BSEE, Tex. A&M U., 1953; MSEE, USAF Inst. Tech., 1963; postgrad. in Elec. Engring., U. Tenn., 1967. Cert. FAA flight instr. Officer USAF, 1953-58; project officer Air Force Armament Ctr., 1955-58; electronic engr. Army Ballistic Missile Agy., Redstone Arsenal, Ala., 1958-60; engring. supr. Marshall Space Flight Ctr. NASA, Huntsville, 1960-89; prin. engr. BDM Internat., Inc., 1989-91; sr. engr. Loral AeroSys divsn., 1991-94; software engr. Boeing Space Sta., 1995—. Participant Apollo/Saturn, space shuttle, space sta., nat. missile def. programs NASA Contbr. articles to Jour. Inst. Navigation, SPIE Symposium on Intelligent Robots. Trustee, chmn. Presbyn. Ch., Huntsville, 1974-76, elder, 1959-63, 78-81, 83-85. Grad. sch. scholarship NASA-MSFC, U. Tenn., 1966-67. Mem. AIAA (com. for flight simulation), Huntsville Assn. Tech. Socs. (pres. 1995-96), U.S. Power Squadrons (squadron comdr. 1984-86), Tau Beta Pi. Home: 1006 San Ramon Ave SE Huntsville AL 35802-2659 E-mail: frank.l.vinz@boeing.com.

VIOLA, BILL, artist, writer; b. N.Y.C., Jan. 25, 1951; s. William John and Wynne Viola; m. Kira Perov; children: Blake, Andrei. BFA, Syracuse U., 1973, DFA, 1995, Sch. Art Inst. Chgo., 1997, Calif. Coll. Arts & Crafts, Oakland, 1998, Mass. Coll. Art, 1999, Calif. Inst. of the Arts, Valencia, 2000, U. Sunderland, Eng., 2000. Tech. dir. Art/Tapes/22 Video Studio, Florence, Italy, 1974-76; artist-in-residence Sta. WNET, N.Y.C., 1976-83, Sony Corp., Atsugi Labs., Japan, 1980-81, San Diego Zoo, 1984; instr. Calif. Inst. of Arts, Valencia, 1983; represented by Anthony d'Offay Gallery, London, James Cohan Gallery, N.Y.C. Solo exhbns. include The Kitchen Ctr., N.Y., 1974, Everson Mus. Art, Syracuse, N.Y., 1975, Mus. Modern Art, N.Y.C., 1979, 87, Whitney Mus. Art, N.Y.C., 1982, Musee d'Art Moderne, Paris, 1983, Mus. Contemporary Art, L.A., 1985, Fukui Prefectural Mus. Art, Fukui City, Japan, 1989, Staditsche Kunsthalle Düsseldorf, 1992, Moderna Musee, Stockholm, 1993, Museo Nacional Centro de Arte Reina Sofia, Madrid, 1993, Musee Cantonal des Beaux-Arts, Lausanne, Switzerland, 1993, Whitechapel Art Gallery, London, 1993, Tel Aviv Mus. Art, 1994, Musée d'Art Contemporain, Montreal, 1993, Centro Cultural/Banco de Brazil, Rio de Janeiro, 1994, 46th Venice Biennale, 1995, Festival d'Automne Paris, 1996, Bill Viola: A 25 Year Survey Exhbn., Whitney Mus. Am. Art, N.Y., travels to Whitney Mus. Am. Art, 1997, L.A. County Mus. Am. Art, 1998, Stedelijk Mus., Amsterdam, 1998, Mus. Pur Moderne Kunst and Shirnkunstalle Dominkankloister, Germany, 1999, San Francisco Mus. Modern Art, 1999, Art Inst. Chgo., 1999-2000, 2KM, Karlsruhe, Germany, 2000, James Cohan Gallery, N.Y., 2000, Anthony d'Offay Gallery, London, 2001, Bill Viola: Going Forth By Day, Deutsche Guggenheim Berlin, 2002; group exhbns. include De Saisset Art Gallery and Mus., Santa Clara, Calif., 1972, Whitney Mus. Am. Art, 1975-87, 89, 93, Stedelijk Mus., Amsterdam, 1984, Carnegie Mus. Art, Pitts., 1988, Kölnischer Kunstverein, Cologne, Germany, 1989, Israel Mus., Jerusalem, 1990, Musée Nat. d'Art Moderne, Ctr. Georges Pompidou, Paris, 1990, Martin Gropius Bau, Berlin, 1991, Mus. Moderne Kunst, Frankfurt, Germany, 1991, Royal Acad., London, 1993, Denver Art Mus., Columbus (Ohio) Art Mus., 1994, Anthony d'Offay Gallery, London, 1995, Mus. Modern Art, N.Y.C., 1995, Tate Gallery, London, 1995, Albright-Knox Art Gallery, 1996, Fabric Workshop, Phila., 1997, MOMA, N.Y., 1999, La Beauté, Found Cartier, 2000, Tate Modern, London, 2000, Nat. Gallery, London, 2000, James Cohan Gallery, NY, 2001; spl. screening film: Dèserts, Vienna, Austria, 1994, WhiteCahpel Art Gallery, London, 2001, 49th Venice Biennale, 2001, Perth Festival, Australia, 2001, Commune di Ferrara, Italy, 2001, Musse d'Art Contemporian de Montreal, Canada, 2001; commns. include The Stopping mind, Mus. Moderne Kunst, Frankfurt, 1991, Nantes Triptych, Dèlegation aux Arts Plastiques, Nantes, France, 1992, Slowly Turning Narrative, Isnt. Comtemporary Art, Phila., Va. Mus. Fine Art, Richmond, 1992, Tiny Deaths, Biennale d'Art Contemporain de Lyon, France, 1993, Dèserts, Konzerthause, Vienna, 1994, 3e Biennale d'Art contemporaire de Lyon, Musèe d'art contemporain, Lyon, France, 1995, Helaba Main Tower, Frankfurt, Germany, 2000, Gotesborgs Musiken, Sweden, 2001, Deserts, Konzerthaus, Vienna, 2001, Deserts, Carnigie Hall, New York, 2001, Deserts, Royal Festival Hall, London, 2001, Deserts, IRCAM, Centre Pomidou Main Hall, Paris, 2001, others; composer: (album) David Tudor-Rainforest IV, 1981; (video) Chott el-Djerid, Anthem, 1983, Hatsu-Yume, 1981, The Reflecting Pool, 1977-79, The Space Between the Teeth, 1976, Bill Viola: Selected Works, 1986, I Do Not Know What It Is I Am Like, 1986, The Passing, 1991, The City of Man, 1989, Nantes Triptych, 1992, Slowly Turning Narritive, 1992, Tiny Deaths, 1993, The Greetings, 1995, The Crossing, 1996, The Quintet of Remembrance, 2000, The Quintet of the Unseen, 2000, The Quintet of the Astonished, The Qyuintet of the Silent, 2000, Surrender, 2001, Catherine's Room, 2001, Five Angles for the Millenium, 2001, Going Forth By Day, 2002. Japan/U.S. Creative Arts fellow NEA, 1980, Rockefeller Found. Video Artist fellow, 1982, Visual Artist fellow NEA, 1983-89, Guggenheim Meml. Found. fellow, 1985, Intercultural Film/Video fellow Rockefeller Found., 1991; recipient Jury prize U.S. Film and Video Festival, 1982, Grand prize, 1983, Jury prize Video Culture/Can., 1983, Grand prize for video art, 1984, First prize for video art Athens (Ohio) Film/Video Festival, 1984, Maya Deren award Am. Film Inst., 1987, First prize Festival Internat. d'Art Video et des Nouvelles Images Electroniques de Locarno, 1987, John D. and Catherine T. MacArthur Found. award, 1989, Skowhegan medal, 1993, First prize Festival Internat. de Video, Cidade de Vigo, Spain, 1993, Medienkunstpreis, Siemens Kulturprogramm and Zentrum fur Kunst und Medientechnologie, Germany, 1993; scholar-in-residence The Getty Rsch. Inst. for History of Art and Humanities, L.A., 1998. Office: 282 Granada Ave Long Beach CA 90803 E-mail: info@billviola.com.

VIOLA, MARY JO, art history educator; b. Yonkers, N.Y., July 25, 1941; d. William F. and May (Cleary) O'Connor; m. Jerome Joseph Viola, June 21, 1967 (dec. Feb. 1990). BA in Fine Arts, Coll. of Mt. St. Vincent, 1963; MA in Art History, NYU, 1966; MPhil in Art History, CUNY, 1983, PhD in Art History, 1992. Art history tchr. Georgian Ct. Coll., N.J., 1965-66, Hollins Coll., Roanoke, Va., 1966-67, Marymount Coll., Tarrytown, N.Y., 1967-71, Baruch Coll., CUNY, N.Y.C., 1974-97, Bklyn. Coll., 1990-97, Parsons Sch. of Design, N.Y.C., 1991-93, Rutgers U., 1993-95, Bronx C.C. CUNY, 1997—. Curator exhbns. Baruch Coll. Gallery, N.Y.C., 1987-88. Editor: A World View of Art History, 1985; art exhibited at Tribes Gallery, N.Y.C., 1996; creater ednl. videos. Rschr. for ethnic festivals, N.Y.C., 1993—. Fellow Nat. Trust for Hist. Preservation, 1964, Marymount Coll., 1970, Boston Mus. Fine Arts/CUNY, 1978, Luce Found., 1988. Mem. Coll. Art Assn., Historians of Am. Art, City Lore. Avocations: tai chi, Argentine tango, ballroom dance. Home and Office: 37 Roosevelt St Yonkers NY 10701-5823

VIOLANTE, JOSEPH ANTHONY, lawyer; b. Jersey City, June 15, 1950; s. Carmine Joseph and Rosa (Cardillo) V.; m. Linda Lee Munn, July 5, 1972; children: Joseph Anthony II, Christy Anne, Gina Lee. Student, St. Peter's Coll., Jersey City, 1972-74; BA, U. N.Mex., 1975; JD, U. La Verne (Calif.), 1980. Bar: Calif. 1981, D.C. 1990, U.S. Dist. Ct. (cen. dist.) Calif. 1982, (6th dist.) Ohio 1992, U.S. Ct. Appeals (fed. cir.) 1990, U.S. Ct. Appeals (D.C. cir.) 1991, U.S. Ct. Vets. Appeals 1990. Sole practice, Thousand Oaks, Calif., 1981-85; atty., cons. Bd. Vet. Appeals, Washington, 1985-90; staff counsel DAV, 1990-92, legis. counsel, 1992-96, dep. nat. legis. dir., 1996-97, nat. legis. dir., 1997—. Mem. adv. com. Bowie Cable T.V., 1989-91, bd. dirs., 1992-94. Co-host cable TV show Vets. Forum, 1991-94. Asst. coach Am. Youth Soccer Orgn., Thousand Oaks, 1981-84, Little League, Thousand Oaks, 1981-84; del. John Glenn Calif. Dem. Presdl. Primary, Thousand Oaks, 1984; active campaign Combined Fed., Washington, 1985; mem. presdl. del. Prisoners of War/Missing in Action, Southeast Asia, 1996. With USMC, 1969-72. Mem.: FBA (vets. com. 1991—92, at-large bd. mem., contbg. writer Tommy), KC, ABA (vice chmn. vets. benefit com. 1991—98), DAV (life; comdr. 1990—91), Coun. of 2,000, Nat. Italian-Am. Found. (nat. mentors program), Italian-Am. Bar Assn., DC Bar Assn., Fed. Cir. Bar Assn. (chmn. vets appeal com. 1992—96, chmn. legis. com. 1996—2001, bd. govs. 2001—), Calif. Bar Assn., Nat. Found. Women Legislators (bd. mem.), VFW (life; comdr. 1984—85), 2d Bn. 4th Marine Assn., Marine Corps League, Italian-Am. War Vets., Am. Legion, 3d Marine Divsn. Assn. (life). Democrat. Roman Catholic. Avocations: collecting coins, soccer, softball, reading. Home: 2515 Ann Arbor Ln Bowie MD 20716-1562 Office: DAV Nat Svc & Legis Hdqrs 807 Maine Ave SW Washington DC 20024-2410

VIOLENUS, AGNES A. retired school system administrator; b. N.Y.C., May 17, 1931; d. Antonio and Constance Violenus. BA, Hunter Coll., 1952; MA, Columbia U., 1958; EdD, Nova U., 1990. Tchr. N.Y. State Day Care, N.Y.C., 1952-53, N.Y.C. Bd. Edn., 1953-66; asst. prin. N.Y.C. Elem. and Jr. H.S., 1966-91; student tchr. supr. dept. edn., adj. lectr. CCNY, 1997—. Adj. instr. computer dept. continuing edn. divsn. York Coll., N.Y.C., 1985-88, Hunter Coll., N.Y.C., 1998—; adj. instr. tchr. mentor program grad. edn. divsn. CCNY, 1990-91; reviewer ednl. and instrnl. films; judge news and documentary Emmy awards NATAS, 1995, 97, 2000. Co-author: LOGO: K-12, 1980; contbr. articles to profl. jours. Mem. mid-Manhattan br. NAACP, mem. com. on Afro-Am. acad., cultural, and tech. olympics; life mem. Girl Scouts U.S., N.Y.C.; bd. visitors Manhattan Psychiat. Ctr., 1995, pres., 2000, chair 1999—; vol. advisor math., sci., computers Workshop Ctr., CCNY, 1995-97; bd. dirs. Hunter Coll. Scholarship and Welfare Fund. Recipient Dedicated Svc. award Coun. Suprs. and Adminstrs., Appreciation award Aerospace Edn. Assn., 1985, Significant Contbn. award Am. Soc. for Aerospace Edn., 1985, Leaders' Day Cert. of Appreciation, Girl Scouts U.S., 1997. Mem. ASCE, AAUW, Am. Ednl. Rsch. Assn., Assn. Advancement of Computing in Edn., Assn. Computers in Math. and Sci. Tchg., Soc. for Info. Tech. and Tchr. Edn., Assn. for Women in Sci., Nat. Tech. Assn., N.Y. Acad. Scis. (scientists in schs. program 1995), Nat. Assn. Negro Bus. and Profl. Women's Clubs (scholarship com. 1989—, family math. com. 1995, rec. sec. 1994-95, profl. award 1997), Nat. Black Child Devel. Inst. (bd. dirs. 1991—, sci. exhibit com. 1995, v.p. 1999, co-chair program 1999, 2000, pub. policy com. 1991—, Bridge Bldr.'s award 1995), Pub. Edn. Assn. (mem. good schs. exch. com. 1990), Schomburg Ctr. Rsch. in Black Culture Schomburg Corp. (vols. adv. com. 1992—, bd. trustee, co-chair corp. task force on African-Am. in math., sci. and tech. 1992—, pres. 1995-98, treas. 1999-2000), Doctorate Assn. N.Y. Educators, N.Y. Alliance Black Sch. Educators, Hunter Coll. Alumni Assn. (bd. dirs. 1993—, rec. sec. 1996-99, treas. 1999—, named to Hall of Fame 1998), Bank St. Alumni Coun. Greater N.Y. (asst. sect. 1991-93), Wistarians Alumni Hunter Coll. (exec. com. 1990—, pres. 1990-94). Democrat. Roman Catholic. Avocations: aeronautics and space science, music, collecting black education memorabilia, instructing survival strategies and techniques for women and children, family genealogy.

VIOLET, WOODROW WILSON, JR. retired chiropractor; b. Sept. 19, 1937; s. Woodrow Wilson and Alice Katherine (Woods) V.; m. Judith Jane Thatcher, June 15, 1963; children: Woodina Lonize, Leslie Alice. Grad. with honors, U.S. Army Med. Svc. Sch., 1955; student, Ventura Coll., 1961-62; grad., L.A. Coll. Chiropractic, 1966. Pvt. practice chiropractic medicine, Santa Barbara, Calif., 1966-73, London, 1973-74, Carpinteria, Calif., 1974-84. Past mem. coun. roentgenology Am. Chiropractic Assn. Former mem. Parker Chiropractic Rsch. Found., Ft. Worth. With USAF, 1955-63. Recipient award merit Calif. Chiropractic Colls., Inc., 1975, cert. of appreciation Nat. Chiropractic Antitrust Com., 1977. Mem. Nat. Geog. Soc., Delta Sigma. Patentee surg. instrument. Home: 210 N Mall Dr Unit 140 Saint George UT 84790-1477 E-mail: jjv@redrock.net.

VIOLETTE, DIANE MARIE, small business owner, freelance editor; b. Pontiac, Mich., Apr. 19, 1958; d. Bernard Desmond and Mary Virginia V.; m. Glenn Martin Payette, Apr. 18, 1987. BA in Journalism, Mich. State U., 1980; cert. in govt. contracts and mgmt., UCLA, 1987; MBA summa cum laude, Calif. State U., Northridge, 1991. Contract adminstr. Def. Contract Adminstrn. Services Mgmt. Area, Van Nuys, Calif., 1980-84, adminstrv. contract officer, 1984-87; pres. cons., editing Diane Violette & Assocs., 1987—; owner Editmaster, 1999—. Contbr. articles to profl. jours. Mem. Nat. Contract Mgmt. Assn. Avocations: reading, cooking, travel, film, walking.

VIOLETTE, GLENN PHILLIP, transportation engineer; b. Hartford, Conn., Nov. 15, 1950; s. Reginald Joseph and Marielle Theresa (Bernier) B.; m. Susan Linda Begam, May 15, 1988. BSCE, Colo. State U., 1982. Registered profl. engr., Colo. Engring. aide Colo. State Hwy. Dept., Glenwood Springs, Colo., 1974-79, hwy. engr., 1980-82, Loveland, 1979-80, project engr. Glenwood Canyon, 1983-97; resident engr. Colo. State Dept. Transp., Craig, 1998—. Guest speaker in field. Contbg. editor, author, photographer publs. in field. Recipient scholarship Fed. Hwy Adminstrn., 1978. Mem. ASCE, Amnesty Internat., Nat. Rifle Assn., Siera Club, Audubon Soc., Nature Conservancy, World Wildlife Fund, Cousteau Soc., Chi Epsilon. Office: Colo Dept Transp 270 Ranney St Craig CO 81625-2840 E-mail: glenn.violette@dot.state.co.us.

VIORST, JUDITH STAHL, author; b. Newark, Feb. 2, 1931; d. Martin Leonard and Ruth June (Ehrenkranz) Stahl; m. Milton Viorst, Jan. 30, 1960; children: Anthony Jacob, Nicholas Nathan, Alexander Noah. BA, Rutgers U., 1952; grad., Washington Psychoanalytic Inst., 1981. Author: (children's books) Sunday Morning, 1968, I'll Fix Anthony, 1969, Try It Again Sam, 1970, The Tenth Good Thing About Barney, 1971 (Silver Pencil award 1973), Alexander and the Terrible Horrible No Good Very Bad Day, 1972, My Mama Says There Aren't Any Zombies, Ghosts, Vampires, Creatures, Demons, Monsters, Fiends, Goblins or Things, 1973, Rosie and Michael, 1974, Alexander, Who Used to Be Rich Last Sunday, 1978, The Good-Bye Book, 1988, Earrings!, 1990, The Alphabet From Z to A (with Much Confusion on the Way), 1994, Alexander, Who's Not (Do You Hear Me? I Mean It!) Going to Move, 1995, Super-Completely and Totally the Messiest, 2001; (poetry) The Village Square, 1965-66, It's Hard to Be Hip Over Thirty and Other Tragedies of Married Life, 1968, People and Other Aggravations, 1971, How Did I Get to Be Forty and Other Atrocities, 1976, If I Were in Charge of the World and Other Worries, 1981, When Did I Stop Being Twenty and Other Injustices, 1987, Forever Fifty and Other Negotiations, 1989, Sad Underwear and Other Complications, 1995, Suddenly Sixty and Other Shocks of Later Life, 2000; (with Milton Viorst) The Washington Underground Gourmet, 1970, Yes Married, 1972, A Visit From St. Nicholas (To a Liberated Household), 1977, Love and Guilt and the Meaning of Life, Etc., 1979, Necessary Losses, 1986, Murdering Mr. Monti, 1994, Imperfect Control, 1998, Your'e Officially a Grown-Up, 1999; (musical) Love and Shrimp (book and lyrics), 1990; (HBO children's movie) Alexander and the Terrible, Horrible, No Good, Very Bad Day (book and lyrics), 1990, children's stage musical, 1998. Recipient Emmy award for poems used in Anne Bancroft Spl., 1970. Jewish.

VIORST, MILTON, writer; b. Paterson, N.J., Feb. 18, 1930; s. Louis and Betty (LeVine) V.; m. Judith Stahl, Jan. 30, 1960; children— Anthony, Nicholas, Alexander. BA summa cum laude, Rutgers U., 1951; student (Fulbright scholar), U. Lyon, France, 1952; MA, Harvard U., 1955; MS, Columbia U., 1956. Reporter Bergen (N.J.) Record, 1955-56, Newark StarLedger, 1956-57, Washington Post, 1957-61; Washington corr. N.Y. Post, 1961-64; syndicated columnist Washington Evening Star, 1971-75; staff writer The New Yorker, N.Y.C., 1987-93; Ferris prof. journalism Princeton (N.J.) U., 1995-96. Lectr. in field. Author: Hostile Allies: FDR and deGaulle, 1965, Great Documents of Western Civilization, 1965, Fall from Grace: The Republican Party and the Puritan Ethic, 1968, Hustlers and Heroes, 1971, Fire in the Streets: America in the 1960's, 1980, Making a Difference: The Peace Corps at Twenty-five, 1986, Sands of Sorrow: Israel's Journey from Independence, 1987, Reaching for the Olive Branch: UNRWA and Peace in the Middle East, 1990, Sandcastles: The Arabs in Search of the Modern World, 1994, In the Shadow of the Prophet: The Struggle for the Soul of Islam, 1998, What

Shall I Do With This People? Jews and the Fractious Politics of Judaism; also articles.; contbg. corr. Washington Quar. Chmn. Fund for Investigative Journalism, 1979-78; bd. dirs. Georgetown Day Sch., 1977-80; mem. nat. adv. com. Middle East Policy Coun. Served as officer USAF, 1952-54. Recipient Columbia Journalism Alumni award, 1992; Woodrow Wilson sr. fellow, 1973-79, Alicia Patterson fellow, 1979; Middle East Inst. sr. scholar. Mem. PEN, Soc. Profl. Journalists, Author's Guild, Coun. on Fgn. Rels., Am. Peace Now, Phi Beta Kappa. E-mail: mviorst@aol.com.

VIRASCH, RIJ LEE, surgeon; b. Thailand, 1945; MD, Chiengmai Hosp. U., 1969. Diplomate Am. Bd. Surgery. Intern St. Joseph Hosp., Chgo., 1970-71, resident in surgery, 1971-75, staff, 1975—. Fellow Ill. Coll. Surgeons; mem. AMA, Ill. State Med. Soc. Office: 2800 N Sheridan Rd Ste 510 Chicago IL 60657-6157

VIRELLI, LOUIS JAMES, JR. lawyer; b. Phila., Nov. 4, 1948; s. Louis James and Elsie Antoinette (Colombo) V.; m. Barbara Ann Rotella, Aug. 22, 1970; children: Louis J. III, Christopher F. BE in Mech. Engring., Villanova U., 1970; JD, U. Tenn., 1972. Bar: Pa. 1973, U.S. Patent and Trademark Office, 1973, U.S. Ct. Customs and Patent Appeals 1974, U.S. Dist. Ct. (we. dist.) Pa. 1976, U.S. Dist. Ct. (ea. dist.) Pa. 1977, U.S. Ct. Appeals (9th cir.) 1980, U.S. Ct. Appeals (D.C. cir.) 1982, U.S. Supreme Ct. 1982. Patent atty. Sperry New Holland Co., New Holland, Pa., 1973-74; assoc. counsel Westinghouse Co., Pitts., 1974-76; assoc. Paul & Paul, Phila., 1976-80, ptnr., 1980-84; patent counsel Nat. Starch and Chem. Co., Bridgewater, N.J., 1984-88, asst. gen. counsel, intellectual property, 1988-92, gen. counsel, intellectual property, 1992-95; asst. gen. counsel Patents Unilever U.S., Inc., Edgewater, 1988-95; v.p. gen. patent counsel Unilever N.V., P.L.C., 1995-96, sr. v.p., gen. patent counsel, 1997—. Arbitrator U.S. Dist. Ct. (ea. dist.) Pa., Phila., 1982-84. Mem.: ABA, Assn. Corp. Patent Counsel (treas., v.p.), Phila. Patent Law Assn., NJ Patent Law Assn. Office: Unilever US Inc 45 River Rd Edgewater NJ 07020-1017 also: Unilever PLC Unilever House Blackfriars London England E-mail: louis.virelli@unilever.com.

VIRGO, JOHN MICHAEL, economist, researcher, educator; b. Prestbury Village, Eng., Mar. 11, 1943; s. John Joseph and Muriel Agnes (Franks) V.; m. Katherine Sue Ulmrich, Sept. 6, 1980; 1 child, Debra Marie Riekstins. BA, Calif. State U., Fullerton, 1967, MA, 1969, Claremont Grad. U., 1971, PhD, 1972. Instr. econs. Whittier (Calif.) Coll., 1970-71, Calif. State U., Fullerton and Long Beach, 1971-72, Claremont (Calif.) Grad. Sch., 1971-72; asst. prof. econs. Va. Commonwealth U., Richmond, 1972-74; assoc. prof. mgmt. So. Ill. U., Edwardsville, 1975-83, prof., 1984—. Bd. dirs., founder Internat. Health Econ. & Mgmt. Inst., Edwardsville, 1983-87. Author: Legal & Illegal California Farmworkers, 1974; author, editor: Health Care: An International Perspective, 1984, Exploring New Vistas in Health Care, 1985, Restructuring Health Policy, 1986; founder, editor-in-chief Internat. Advances in Econ. Rsch.; contbr. articles to profl. jours. Served with USN, 1965-68. Mem. AMA, Am. Econ. Assn., Am. Soc. Assn. Execs., Internat. Atlantic Econ. Soc. (founder, exec. v.p., mng. editor Atlantic Econ. jour. 1973—), European Econ. Assn., Allied Social Scis. Assn. (chmn. exec. confs. 1982-84), Western Econs. Assn., Western Econ. Assn., So. Econs. Assn., Media Club (St. Louis). Democrat. Roman Catholic. Avocations: tennis, skiing. Home: 5277 Lindell Blvd Saint Louis MO 63108-1223 Office: Internat Atlantic Econ Soc 2nd Fl 4949 W Pine Blvd Saint Louis MO 63108-1431

VIRGO, KATHERINE SUE, health services researcher; b. East Alton, Ill., Feb. 14, 1959; d. John William and Doris Ann (Spencer) Ulmrich; m. John Michael Virgo, Sept. 6, 1980. BSBA, So. Ill. U., 1981, MBA, 1983; PhD in Health Svcs. Rsch., St. Louis U., 1991. From asst. coord. to exec. adminstr. Atlantic Econ. Soc., Edwardsville, Ill., 1978-86; co-founder, exec. adminstr. Internat. Health Econs. and Mgmt. Inst., 1983-87; health sci. specialist VA Med. Ctr., St. Louis, 1986-93, clin. rsch. coord., 1993—; asst. prof. St. Louis U., 1991-96, assoc. prof., 1996-2001, prof., 2001—. Bd. dirs. Internat. Health Econs. and Mgmt. Inst., Edwardsville, 1983-87. Assoc. editor Atlantic Econ. Jour., 1994—; dep. editor Internat. Advances in Econ. Rsch., 1995—; co-editor Cancer Patient Follow-Up, 1997; ad hoc reviewer Jour. of the AMA, 1995-96, Med. Care, 1995—, Women's Health Issues, 2000-01, Jour. Spinal Cord Medicine, 2002—; contbr. numerous articles to profl. jours. Mem. St. Louis Cathedral Basilica Choir. VA grantee. Mem.: APHA, Am. Paraplegia Soc., Health Econs. Rsch. Orgn., Acad. for Health Svcs. Rsch. and Health Policy, Am. Soc. Clin. Oncology, Internat. Health Econs. Assn. Democrat. Roman Catholic. Avocations: singing, piano, reading, swimming. Home: 5277 Lindell Blvd Saint Louis MO 63108-1223 Office: VA Med Ctr 112JC 915 N Grand Blvd Saint Louis MO 63106-1621 E-mail: virgoks@slu.edu.

VIRGO, MURIEL AGNES, swimming school owner; b. Liverpool, Cheshire, Eng., Apr. 3, 1924; d. Harold Thornhill and Susan Ann (Duff) Franks; m. John Virgo, Aug. 13, 1942; children: John Michael, Angela Victoria, Barbara Ann, Collin Anthony, Donna Marie. Grad. parochial schs. Co-owner Virgo Swim Sch., Garden Grove, Calif., 1967—. Mem. Ancient Mystical Order Rosae Crucis, Traditional Martinist Order. Republican. Roman Catholic. Avocation: ballroom dancing. Home: 12751 Crestwood Cir Garden Grove CA 92841-5250 Office: Virgo Swim Sch 12851 Brookhurst Way Garden Grove CA 92841-5205

VIRK, RACHEL LEWIS, lawyer; b. Lowell, Mass., Nov. 22, 1961; d. Gary Lee and Diane Lewis; m. Vijay Vir Singh Virk, Sept. 22, 1996. Bar: Va. 1989. Atty. Robert A. Ades & Assocs. PC, Springfield, Va., 1990-99, Plofchan & Assocs, Sterling, 1999—. Office: Plofchan & Assocs 46308 Cranston St Ste 225 Sterling VA 20165-7239 E-mail: rvirk@plofchanlaw.com.

VIRKHAUS, TAAVO, symphony orchestra conductor; b. Tartu, Estonia, June 29, 1934; came to U.S., 1949; s. Adalbert August and Helene Marie (Sild) V.; m. Nancy Ellen Herman, Mar. 29, 1969. MusB U. Miami, 1955; MusM Eastman Sch. of Music, Rochester, 1957, DMA, 1967. Dir. music U. Rochester (N.Y.), also assoc. prof. Eastman Sch., Rochester, 1967-77; music dir., condr. Duluth (Minn.) Superior Symphony Orch., 1977-94; guest condr. Rochester Philharm., Minn. Orch., Balt. Symphony, Vancouver Symphony and others, 1972—; music dir., condr. Hunstville (Ala.) Symphony Orch., 1989—; guest condr. at Tallinn, Estonia, 1978, 88, 90, 92, 93, 94; lectr. U. Minn.-Duluth, U. of Wis.-Superior. With U.S. Army, 1957-58, USAR, 1957-61. Recipient Howard Hanson Composition award, 1966, Am. Heritage award JFK Libr. for Minorities, 1974; Fulbright scholar, Musikhochschule, Cologne, 1963. Mem. Am. Symphony Orch. League, Condrs. Guild, Am. Fedn. of Musicians. Composer: Violin Concerto, 1966, Symphony No. 1, 1976, Symphony No. 2, 1979, Symphony No. 3, 1984, Symphony No. 4, 1989, Symphony No. 5, 1994, Violin Concerto No. 2, 1995. Republican. Lutheran. E-mail: tvirkhaus@knology.net.

VIRKLER, MARK WILLIAM, religious educator; b. Lowville, N.Y., Mar. 25, 1952; s. Clayton Einbeck and Lillian Amelia V.; m. Patricia Claire, Dec. 16, 1972; children: Charity, Joshua. BA, Roberts Wesleyan Coll., 1974; ThM, Miami Christian U., 1985; PhD, Carolina Christian U., 1994. Youth pastor Avon (N.Y.) Wesleyan Ch., 1971-74; asst. prof. Yorkshire (N.Y.) Free Meth. Ch., 1975; assoc. pastor Curriers (N.Y.) Cmty. Ch., 1976; founding pastor Pioneer Christian Fellowship, Arcade, N.Y., 1976-82; asst. pastor Full Gospel Tabernacle, Orchard Park, 1982-89; pres. Communion with God Ministries, Elma, 1989—. Pres. Christian Leadership U., Elma, 1994—, Covenant Enterprises, Elma, 1994—; dir. Christian Restoration Fellowship Internat., Elma, 1998—. Author: Communion With God, 1983, Dialogue With God, 1985, Counseled By God, 1989, Naturally Supernatural, 1990, Go Natural, 1994. Avocations: reading, writing, researching, family time. Office: Communion with God Ministries 1431 Bullis Rd Elma NY 14059-9656 E-mail: mark@cluonline.com.

VIROSTEK, ROBERT JOSEPH, physician; b. Braddock, Pa., July 4, 1938; AB, Dartmouth Coll., 1960; MD, U. Cin., 1963. Intern Harrisburg Gen. Hosp., 1963-64, resident, 1964-67; dept. head Champlain Valley Physicians Hosp. Med. Ctr., Plattsburgh, N.Y., 1990-91, pres. med. staff, 1997-99; assoc. prof. U. Vt. Med. Sch., 1997—; pvt. practice; v.p. med. staff Champlain Valley Physicians Hosp. Med. Ctr., 2001—. Mem. Upper Hudson Prenatal Svcs. Network. Mem. AAGL, ACOG, AFS, AIUM, AMA. Office: Lake Champlain ObGyn PC 206 Cornelia St Ste 306 Plattsburgh NY 12901-2789

VIRTEL, JAMES JOHN, lawyer; b. Joliet, Ill., May 15, 1944; BA cum laude, Loras Coll., 1966; JD cum laude, St. Louis U., 1969. Bar: Mo. 1969, Ill. 1969. Atty. Armstrong, Teasdale, Schlafly & Davis (now called Armstrong Teasdale LLP), St. Louis, 1976—. Adj. prof. law St. Louis U., 1995-99; regent Loras Coll., Dubuque, Iowa, 1996—. Editor: St. Louis U. Law Jour., 1968-69. Fellow Am. Coll. Trial Lawyers; mem. Ill. State Bar Assn., Mo. State Bar Assn. Office: Armstrong Teasdale LLP 1 Metropolitan Sq Ste 2600 Saint Louis MO 63102-2740 E-mail: jvirtel@armstrongteasdale.com.

VISBAL, KRISTEN ELIZABETH, sculptor; b. Montevideo, Uruguay, Dec. 3, 1962; (parents Am. citizens); d. Ralph Albert and Elizabeth Krystyniak Visbal. Student, U. Ariz., 1980—82, U. Md., 1983—84; BA in Art summa cum laude, Salisbury (Md.) State U., 1995. Apprentice lost wax fine art casting Johnson Atelier Foundry, Mercerville, N.J., 1995-98; owner, mgr. Visbal Fine Bronze Sculpture, Lewes, Del., 1998—. Exhibitions include Extension Gallery, Mercerville, 1997, Salisbury State U., 1995, 1999, 2000, Lincoln Ctr., N.Y.C., 1997, Rehoboth (Del.) Art League, 1998, 2000, Gov.'s Mansion, Dover, Del., 1999, Brookgreen Gardens Curator's Auction, Murrells Inlet, S.C., 1998—2002, Ward Mus., Salisbury, Md., 1999, Easton (Md.) Waterfowl Festival, 1999, 2001, exhibitions include Chadds Ford (Pa.) Inn, 2000, exhibitions include Art by the Sea, Juno Beach, Fla., 2001, Pen and Brush Club, N.Y.C., 2000—02, Nat. Sculpture Soc., 2001, Nat. Arts Club, 2001; artist (pub. commns.) Passing the Torch (Olympic Gold medalist Bob Hayes), Jacksonville, Fla., Sea Express (Boy on Dolphin), Jacksonville Beach, Fla., Girl Chasing Butterflies, Plainsboro, N.J. Grantee, State of Del., 1992. Mem. Nat. Sculpture Soc. (colleague), Catharine Lorillard Wolfe Arts Club (assoc.), Nat. Mus. Women in Arts, Internat. Sculpture Ctr., Pen and Brush Club (resident assoc.). Avocations: biking, swimming. Office: Visbal Fine Bronze Sculpture 42 Nassau Commons Lewes DE 19958 Fax: 302-645-7884. E-mail: kristen@visbalsculpture.com.

VISCARDI, PETER G. insurance company executive; b. N.Y.C., Dec. 28, 1947; s. Peter and Louise (Johnson) Viscardi; m. Margaret E. McGowan, Sept. 11, 1971 (div. 2001); children: Margaret, Peter. BA, Hunter Coll., 1970. CPCU. Ins. mgr. Jaffie Contracting Co., Inc., N.Y.C., 1971-73; ins. adminstr. Otis Elevator Co., 1973, supr. ins. adminstrn., 1974; dir. adminstrn. Finsure divsn. Studebaker-Worthington, Inc., 1975-78, corp. risk mgr./exec. v.p., chief oper. officer, 1978-80; mgr. corp. ins. Fortune Brands, Inc. (formerly Am. Brands), 1980-81, mgr. corp. ins. and real estate, 1981-87, dir. corp. ins. Old Greenwich, Conn., 1987-90, dir. risk mgmt. and environ. affairs, 1990-99. Cons. Shirley, NY, 2000—. Mem. editl. bd.: Risk and Benefits Mag., 1987—89, mem. editl. bd.: , 1991—92, instnl. investor adv. bd.:. Mem. adv. bd. ACE Bermuda, 1999—. Mem.: Air and Waste Mgmt. Assn., Nat. Assn. Environ. Mgrs., Nat. Assn. Mfrs. (risk mgmt. and environ. quality coms. 1990—99), Risk and Ins. Mgmt. Soc., Am. Mgmt. Assn. (ins. and risk mgmt. coun.), Soc. CPCUs. E-mail: peviscardi@cs.com.

VISCHER, HAROLD HARRY, manufacturing company executive; b. Toledo, Oct. 17, 1914; s. Harry Philip and Hazel May (Patterson) V.; m. DeNell Meyers, Feb. 18, 1938; children: Harold Harry, Robert P., Michael L. BBA, U. Toledo, 1937. With Ohio Bell Telephone Co., 1937-38; with Firestone Tire & Rubber Co., Toledo, 1948-61, nat. passenger tire sales mgr., 1953-57, dist. mgr., 1957-61; with Bandag Inc., Muscatine, Iowa, 1961-80; exec. v.p., pres. Bandag Inc. (Rubber and Equipment Sales group), 1975-80; also dir.; pres., gen. mgr. Hardline Internat., Inc., Jackson, Mich., 1980-82; chmn. Tred-X Corp., 1982—. Mem. City Council, Muscatine, 1964-76; chmn., mem. Dist. Export Council Iowa, 1964-81; chmn. Muscatine United Way, 1969-70; mem. adv. bd. Engring. Coll. Iowa State U., 1970-81; mem. Muscatine Light & Water Bd., 1979-80. Elected to Nat. Tire Dealers and Retreaders Assn. Hall of Fame, 1988, to Internat. Tire Retreading and Repairing Hall of Fame, 1990. Mem. Nat. Tire and Retreaders Suppliers Group Assn. (chmn. 1979-80, exec. com. 1977-80), Tire Retread Info. Bur. (exec. com. 1974-81), Am. Retreading Assn. (adv. bd. 1970-72), Retreading Industry Assn., Industry Man of Yr. 1979), Christian Business men's Com., Gideons, Rotary. Republican. Home: 13500 Vischer Rd Brooklyn MI 49230-9022

VISCLOSKY, PETER JOHN, congressman, lawyer; b. Gary, Ind., Aug. 13, 1949; s. John and Helen (Kauzlaric) V. BS in Acctg., Ind. U.-Indpls., 1970; JD, U. Notre Dame, 1973; LL.M. in Internat. and Comparative Law, Georgetown U., 1983. Bar: Ind., D.C., U.S. Supreme Court. Legal asst. Dist. Atty.'s Office, N.Y.C., 1972; assoc. Benjamin, Greco & Gouveia, Merrillville, Ind., 1973-76, Greco, Gouveia, Miller, Pera & Bishop, Merrillville, 1982-84; assoc. staff appropriations com. U.S. Ho. of Reps., Washington, 1976-80, assoc. staff budget com., 1980-82; mem. U.S. Congress from 1st dist. Ind., 1985—; mem. appropriations com., subcoms. treasury, postal svc., gen. govt. and military constrn. Democrat. Roman Catholic. Office: US House of Reps 2313 Rayburn Hob Washington DC 20515-1401 also: 701 E 83d Ave Ste 9 Merrillville IN 46410*

VISCO, FERDINAND JOSEPH, cardiologist, educator; b. Bklyn., July 8, 1941; s. Joseph Thomas and Susan (Baratta) V.; m. Laurie Judith Glass, Sept. 18, 1983; 1 child, Melissa; children by previous marriage, Ruth, Joseph, Jennifer. BS in Biology, Fairfield U., 1963; MD, U. Padua, Italy, 1969. Diplomate in internal medicine and cardiovasc. disease Am. Bd. Internal Medicine; diplomate Am. Bd. Nuclear Cardiology, Nat. Bd. Echocardiography; lic. physician and surgeon, N.Y. Intern Flushing (N.Y.) Hosp., 1969-70; jr. and sr. resident medicine Cath. Med. Ctr., Queens Hosp. Ctr., Jamaica, N.Y., 1970-72; fellow cardiology Nassau County Med. Ctr., East Meadow, 1972-74; dir. medicine Freeport (N.Y.) Hosp., 1975; instr. medicine SUNY, Stony Brook, 1973-75, Albert Einstein Coll. Medicine, Bronx, N.Y., 1975-78, asst. prof. medicine, 1978-2001; attending physician St. John's Queens Hosp., Cath. Med. Ctr., Bklyn., 1996—, dir. non-invasive cardiology lab., 1996—; assoc. dir. cardiology Bronx Lebanon Hosp., 1993-96; dir. Non-Invasive Cardiology Lab, 1975-96; asst. prof. medicine N.Y. Med. Coll., Valhalla, N.Y., 2001—. Fellow Am. Coll. Cardiology, ACP, Coun. Clin. Cardiology; mem. Am. Soc. Echocardiography, Am. Soc. Nuc. Cardiology. Avocations: computers, ham radio, golf. Office: St Johns Queens Hosp Divsn Cardiology 90-02 Queens Blvd Elmhurst NY 11373 E-mail: fjvisco@aol.com.

VISCOMI, B. VINCENT, civil engineer; b. Phila., Sept. 21, 1933; s. Joseph and Rose (Sidoti) V.; m. Mary Hughes, Feb. 15, 1958; children: Vincent Andrew, Christopher Michael, Roseann Marie. BS in Mech. Engring., Drexel U., 1956; MS in Mech. Engring., Lehigh U., 1957; PhD in Civil Engring., U. Colo., 1968. Nuclear reactor engr. Phila. Electric Co., 1957-64; Simon Cameron Long prof. civil and environ. engring. Lafayette Coll., Easton, Pa., 1964—. Mem. Commn. on Higher Edn., 1982—. Patentee in field. Pres. Easton Bd. Health, 1972-78. Served to 1st lt. U.S. Army, 1957-64. Recipient Jones Faculty award, 1969, Superior Teaching award Student Body Lafayette Coll., 1974, 78, award Charles and Mary Lindback Found. for Superior Teaching, 1976, Thomas and Laura Jones award for scholarship, 1997. Mem. ASCE (past pres.), Am. Soc. Engring. Edn., N.Y. Acad. Scis., Am. Nuclear soc., Phi Beta Kappa, Sigma Xi, Phi Kappa Phi, Tau Beta Pi. Home: 127 High St Easton PA 18042-1609 Office: Dept Civil Engring Lafayette Coll Easton PA 18042 E-mail: viscomib@lafayette.edu.

VISCOUNTY, PERRY JOSEPH, lawyer; b. Orange, Calif., Sept. 29, 1962; s. Thomas Alexander and Terry Lea V.; m. Mary Katherine Powell, July 24, 1993; children: John H., Matthew W., Claire E., William J. BS, U. Southern Calif., 1984, JD, 1987. Bar: Calif. 1987, U.S. Dist. Ct. (no., ea., ctrl. and so. dist.) Calif. 1987, U.S. Ct. Appeals (9th cir.) 1987, U.S. Ct. Appeals (fed. cir.) 1995, U.S. Supreme Ct. 1995. Ptrn. Sheppard, Mullin, Richter & Hampton, Costa Mesa, Calif., 1987-98; ptnr. Latham & Watkins, 1998—. Author: Trade Secrets Practice in California, 1996; contbr. articles to profl. jours and newspaper. Mem. Internat. Trademark Assn. (meetings com.), Calif. State Bar (founder, edn. com. 1993), Orange County Patent Law Assn. (chmn. trade secret com.), Orange County Bar Found. (Willey W. Manuel Pro Bono award, 1993, Svcs. award, 1994), Young Exec. Am. (nat. bd. dir. 1997, bd. dir. 1996-97. Avocations: golf, tennis, volleyball and reading. Office: Latham & Watkins 650 Town Center Dr Ste 2000 Costa Mesa CA 92626-1925

VISCOVICH, SIR ANDREW JOHN, educational management consultant; b. Oakland, Calif., Sept. 25, 1925; s. Peter Andrew and Lucy Pauline (Razovich) V.; m. Roen Shirley Mulvana, Apr. 19, 1952 (div. Feb. 1985); children: Randal Peter, Andra Clair; m. Elena Beth Wong, Apr. 28, 1991; 1 child, Alison Wong. BA, U. Calif., Berkeley, 1949; MA, San Francisco State U., 1960; EdD, U. Calif., Berkeley, 1973; cert. labor dispute resolution, Golden Gate U., 1976. Assoc. supt. Oakland Unified Sch. Dist., Calif., 1970-77; supt. Palm Springs (Calif.) Unified Sch. Dist., 1976-79, Garvey Sch. Dist., Rosemead, Calif., 1979-88, Berkeley (Calif.) Unified Sch. Dist., Stockton, 1988-90; pres. Ctr. for Ednl. Rsch. in Adminstrn., 1990—. Adj. prof. U. Calif., Berkeley, 1965-67, Calif. State U., Hayward, 1970-76, L.A., 1971-8; exec. dir. Marcus Foster Edn. Found., Oakland, 1975-76; cons. Spanish Ministry Edn., 1987—, Republic of China Ministry Edn., Taipei, Taiwan, 1986-89, Croatian Ministry Edn., Zagreb, 1993—, Marriott Sch. Svcs, 1992—, CSHQH, Idaho; pre-sch. dir. Oakland Unified Sch. Dist., 1974-76; asst. dir. Bay Area Bilingual Edn. League, 1971-75; dir. Bay Area Tchr. Ctr., 1974, asst. dir. Far West Ednl. Lab., 1974; adj. assoc. prof. Calif. State U. at L.A.and Hayward, U. South Fla., U. Oreg., Coll. of Holy Names; exec. dir. ANRO Cons., Inc., Calif., 1973-82; state adminstr. Coachella Unified Sch. Dist., Thermal, Calif., 1992; nat. dir. supt. consulting svcs. Sodexho Marriott Corp., 1992-99. Author: Language Programs for the Disadvantaged, 1965, R.E.S. Plus, 1978; contbr. The School Principal, 1978. Chair United Way, Pasadena, Calif., 1985; pres. Croatian Scholarship Found., San Ramon, Calif., 1993-94. Served to ens. USNR, 1959-64. Recipient award for innovations in alternative schools Behavioral Rsch. Lab., San Francisco, 1973; named Knight of Civil Order of Merit King Juan Carlos of Spain, 1990. Mem. Am. Mgmt. Assn., Am. Assn. Sch. Adminstrs., Assn. Calif. Sch. Adminstrs., Calif. City Sch. Supts., Calif. Tchrs. Assn. (John Swett award 1978), Tau Kappa Epsilon. Avocations: golf, reading, travel. ultralite flying. Home: 3754 Fort Donelson Dr Stockton CA 95219-3211

VISCUSI, W(ILLIAM) G. KIP, economics educator; b. Trenton, N.J., Oct. 3, 1949; s. William Edward and Evelyn (Martin) V.; m. Catherine Makdisi, Sep. 26, 1972; children: Kira Margaret, Michael Kip. AB summa cum laude, Harvard U., 1971, MPP, 1973, AM, 1974, PhD, 1976. Prof. econs. Northwestern U., Evanston, Ill., 1976-80, 85-88; dep. dir. White House Council on Wage and Price Stability, Washington, 1979-81; prof. econs. Duke U., Durham, N.C., 1981-85; John M. Olin prof. econs. U. Chgo., 1985-86; George G. Allen prof. econs. Duke U., Durham, N.C., 1988-96; John M. Olin prof. law and econs. Harvard Law Sch., 1995, John F. Cogan Jr. prof. law and econs. Mass., 1996—. Rsch. assoc. Nat. Bur. Econ. Rsch., 1978—, Nat. Commn. for Employment Policy, 1981; mem. EPA Sci. Adv. Bd., 1986—, econs. bd., 1992—, Clean Air Act, 1992—, Nat. Acad. Sci. Panel, 1978-79; cons. U.S. Gen. Acctg. Office, 1981-85, Dept. Justice, 1986-87, 89-91, U.S. Office Mgmt. and Budget, 1983; assoc. reporter Am. Law Inst., 1986-91; adj. fellow in civil justice manhattan Inst., 1987—; inaugural speaker Geneva Risk Econ. Lectrs., Geneva Assn. Risk and Ins., 1989; John R. Commons lectr. U. Wis., 1990; Ayne Ryde lectr. Lund U., Sweden. Author: Employment Hazards, 1979 (Wells prize 1977), Risk by Choice, 1983, Regulating Consumer Product Safety, 1984, Learning About Risk, 1987, Reforming Products Liability, 1991, Fatal Tradeoffs, 1992, Smoking, 1992; editor Jour. Risk and Uncertainty; contbg. editor Regulation mag.; assoc. editor Internat. Rev. of Law Econs., Geneva Papers on Risk and Ins. Theory, Jour. Regulatory Econs., Jour. Environ. Econs. and Mgmt., J Risk and Ins., Rev. Econs. and Stats., Am. Econ. Rev., Managerial and Decision Econs. Recipient Article of the Yr. award Econ. Inquiry, 1988, Book of the Yr. awards Am. Risk and Ins. Assn., 1992, 93, 94. Mem. Am. Econs. Assn., Econometric Soc., Assn. Environ. and Resource Economists, Assn. for Pub. Policy Analysis and Mgmt., So. Econs. Assn. We. Econs. Assn., Managerials and Decision Econs. Roman Catholic. Office: Harvard Law Sch Hauser 302 Cambridge MA 02138

VISEK, ALBERT JAMES, retired computer engineer; b. Phila., July 7, 1934; s. Albert John and Rose (Schlacta) V.; m. Patricia Ann Mullen, Aug. 25, 1962; children: Patrick Albert, Kelly Ann. BS in Physics and Electronics, LaSalle Coll., 1968; MBA, Temple U., 1978. Project engring. mgr., test dir. spl. projects GE Co., Phila., 1961-73; mgr. EMI/EMC Group Sperry Corp. Hdqtrs., Blue Bell, Pa., 1973-86; program coord. Tempest Def. Systems Div., Great Valley, 1986-87; mgr. product engring. and environ. support Info. Systems Group, Exton, 1987-89; OEM product quality staff engr. Personal Workstation Div., Flemington, N.J., 1990-92; staff engr. Power Supply Engring. Group Computer Systems Group, Tredyffrin, Pa., 1992-98; with Unisys Corp., Blue Bell, 1973-98; pvt. tech. cons., 1998—. Co-founder, dir. engring., cons. Computer Room Specialists, Bethlehem, Pa., 1989-92; co. rep., vice-chmn. CBEMA trade assn.; presenter tech. papers in field, seminars and confs. in field. With USN, 1957-59. Mem. IEEE (presenter paper symposium 1986), Nat. Assn. Radio and Telecomm. Engrs. (cert. electromagnetic compatibility engr.) Roman Catholic. Avocations: fishing, boating, travel, cooking, reading. Home and Office: 1306 Hartranft Ave Fort Washington PA 19034-1604 E-mail: alvisek@aol.com.

VISHNEVSKY, VALENTINA MICHAILOVNA, pianist, ballet consultant; b. Rostow, USSR; came to U.S., 1949; d. Michael and Vassa (Velikopolskaya) Cherednichenko; m. Vadim Vitali Vishnevsky, Mar. 9, 1952 (dec.). Degree, Konservatorium, Heidelberg, Fed. Republic Germany, 1949. Prin. pianist Am. Ballet Theater Sch., N.Y.C., 1951-82; pianist Alvin Ailey Dance Sch., 1983; ballet cons., mem. adv. bd. Vero Beach (Fla.) Ballet Co., Vero Beach, Fla., 1984—. Pianist 1st Internat. Ballet Competition, 1979. Pianist: (film) First Position, 1973, (album series) Ballet Class, 1963-79, (TV show) Today, 1972.

VISION, BLANCHE STEIN, retired judge; b. Chgo., Apr. 4, 1922; d. Abe and Ida (Mash) Stein; m. Philip H. Vision, Sept. 30, 1967 (dec. Mar. 1997). BA, U. Chgo., 1943; JD, Columbia U., 1948. Bar: Oreg. 1949, D.C. 1950, U.S. Ct. Appeals (7th cir.) 1967. House counsel Goldblatt Bros. Dept. Stores, Chgo., 1950-51; dir. sta. rels. Keystone Broadcasting System, 1952-60; sr. atty. FTC, 1961-80; adminstrv. law judge Office Hearings and Appeals. Social Security Adminstrn., 1980-83. Arbitrator Better Bus. Bur. Greater Chgo., 1970-80; judge Judicate Nat. Pvt. Ct. Sys., 1987-92. Bd. dirs. Property Owners and Residents Assn., Sun City West, Ariz., 1985, Sun Cities Art Mus., 1985, Sun Cities Transit System, Inc., 1985-89, Sun Cities Symphony Guild, 1987-88, Sun Cities Symphony Assn., 1987-89, Sun Health Found. Aux., 1988. Recipient FTC Meritorious Svc. award. Mem. ABA, AAUW (v.p. Sun City West chpt. 1984), D.C. Bar Assn., Am. Arbitration Assn. (panel of arbitrators), Phi Beta Kappa. Home: 13225 W Castlebar Dr Sun City West AZ 85375-2502

VISKANTA, RAYMOND, mechanical engineering educator; b. Lithuania, July 16, 1931; came to U.S., 1949, naturalized, 1955; s. Vincas and Genovaite (Vinickas) V.; m. Birute Barbara Barpsys, Oct. 13, 1956; children: Renata, Vitas, Tadas. BSME, U. Ill., 1955; MSME, Purdue U., 1956, PhD, 1960; DEng (hon.), Tech. U. Munich, 1994. Registered profl. engr., Ill. Asst. mech. engr. Argonne (Ill.) Nat. Lab., 1956-59, student rsch. assoc., 1959-60, assoc. mech. engr., 1960-62; assoc. prof. mech. engring. Purdue U., West Lafayette, Ind., 1962-66, prof. mech. engring., 1966-86, Goss disting. prof. engring., 1986—. Guest prof. Tech. U. Munich, Germany, 1976-77, U. Karlsruhe, Germany, 1987; vis. prof. Tokyo Inst. Tech., 1983. Contbr. over 500 tech. articles to profl. jours. Recipient Sr. U.S. Scientist award Alexander von Humboldt Found., 1975, Sr. Rsch. award Am. Soc. Engring. Edn., 1984, Nusselt-Reynolds prize, 1991, Thermal Engring. award for Internat. Activity, Japan Soc. Mech. Engrs., 1994, Alumni award for Disting. Svc. U. Ill.-Urbana-Champaign, 2000; Japan Soc. for Promotion of Sci. fellow, 1983. Fellow ASME (Heat Transfer Meml. award 1976, Max Jakob Meml. award 1986, Melville medal 1988), AIAA (Thermophysics award 1979); mem. AAAS, NAE, Acad. Engring. Scis. Russian Fedn. (fgn.), Lithuanian Acad. Scis. (fgn.), Sigma Xi, Pi Tau Sigma, Tau Beta Pi. Home: 3631 Chancellor Way West Lafayette IN 47906-8809 Office: Purdue Univ 1288 Mechanical Engineering West Lafayette IN 47907-1288 E-mail: rviskanta@earthlink.net., viskanta@ecn.purdue.edu.

VISOCKI, NANCY GAYLE, electronic commerce consultant; b. Dumont, N.J., May 13, 1952; d. Thomas and Gloria Visocki. BA in Maths., Manhattanville Coll., 1974; MS in Ops. Rsch. and Stats., Rensselaer Poly. Inst., 1977. Rsch. asst. Coll. Physicians and Surgeons Columbia U., N.Y.C., 1974-75; programmer analyst R. Shriver Assocs., Parsippany, N.J., 1977-79; sr. tech. rep. GE Info. Svcs. Co., East Orange, 1979-81, mgr. project office Morristown, 1981-83, tech. dir., 1983-87, tech. mgr., 1988-89, area mgr. sys. devel. and consulting Parsippany, 1989-92, area tech. mgr. sys. devel. and cons., Fin. Info. Sys., 1992-93, sr. cons. info. svcs., 1993-98, project mgr. e-commerce sys. integration, 1998-2000; mgr. Major e-commerce Applications Practice,

2000—. Active Western Hills Christian Ch., Tranquility, N.J., 1986—; vol. Women's Ctr., Hackettstown, N.J., 1989-93; class fundraising and gift chmn. Rensselaer Poly. Inst., Troy, N.Y., 1991-95; vol. Elfun Soc., 1981—. Manhattanville Coll. grantee, Purchase, N.Y., 1970-71; tuition fellow Rensselaer Poly. Inst., 1975-77. Mem. NAFE, Elfun, Women of Accomplishment. Avocations: tai chi, rollerblading, hiking, bicycling, reading. Office: GE Info Svcs Co 20 Waterview Blvd Ste 302 Parsippany NJ 07054-1229

VISSER, RICHARD EDGAR, minister; b. South Weymouth, Mass., Apr. 28, 1937; s. Edgar and Marjorie (McPhee) V.; m. Carol Naomi Edwards, June 21, 1958; children: Andrew, Thomas, Peter. AB, Gordon Coll., 1958, BS, 1959; BD, Gordon Div. Sch., 1962, MRE, 1965; D Ministry, Asbury Theol. Sem., 1983. Ordained to ministry Am. Bapt. Chs. in U.S.A., 1962. Pastor Acton-Milton Mills Bapt. Ch., Milton Mills, N.H., 1962-65; First Bapt. Ch., Derry, 1966-69; min. edn. Peters Creek Bapt. Ch., Library, Pa., 1969-73; pastor 1st Bapt. Ch., Warren, 1973-79, min. ch. edn. and music St. Albans, W.Va., 1980-83, pastor Waynesburg, Pa., 1983—. Pres. Clergymen's Assn. of Derry, 1967-69; founder, chmn. Pitts. Ch. Edn. Conv., 1972-73; clk. Pitts. Bapt. Assn., 1971-73; pres. Ministerial Assn., Warren, 1975-76, St. Albans, 1982-83, Waynesburg, 1988-90, 99-2001; moderator Ten Mile Assn. Waynesburg, 1985-87; pres., Ten Mile Assn. Mins. and Spouses, 2001—; co-founder, vice chmn. Ten Mile and Monogahela Assns. Lic. Lay Pastor Tng. Program, 1988-90; chairperson Am. Bapt. Ch. Leadership Inst. Western Pa., 1993-2002; pres. Am. Bapt. Chs. of Pa. and Del., 1991-92, chmn. Sunday Sch. team, 1987-90, exec. com., 1987-94, 1997-2002; mem. gen. bd., bd. ednl. ministries Am. Bapt. Chs. U.S.A., 1997-2002, mem. com. of 100 for Renewal, 1992-98; mem. Ministers and Missionaries Benefit Bd., 1999-2002, mem. comms. com., 1999-2002, chmn. benefits com., 2000-2002. Founder, chmn. Warren (Pa.) Community Chorus, 1974-78; pres. Warren County Health and Welfare Coun., 1975-77; chmn. Forest-Warren Counties Human Svcs. Adv. Commn., 1978-79; co. chmn. Greene County Human Svcs. Adv. Commn., Pa., 1988-96, vice chmn., 2000—, chmn. mental health com., 2000—, mem. sr. outreach and referral com.; chmn. Greene County chpt. ARC, 1989-91; bd. dirs. Greene County Meml. Hosp., 1989—; bd. dirs. Comty. Found. Greene County, 2000—, vice chmn. 2001—. Recipient Apollo award Alderson-Broaddus Coll., Philippi, W.Va., 1995. Mem. Am. Bapt. Mins. Coun. (Excellence in Ministry award 2000, v.p. Pa. and Del. chpt. 1978-79), Rotary (v.p. Waynesburg Club 1990-91, pres. 1991-92). Avocations: walking, reading, singing. Home: 711 2nd Ave Waynesburg PA 15370-1162 Office: 1st Bapt Ch 303 W High St Waynesburg PA 15370-1209 E-mail: firstbaptist@alltel.net. *I feel that sometimes people avoid leadership roles because they can be demanding. I do not seek leadership roles, but when I see needs and suggest possible solutions, these roles often seem to find me. I have found that an open, ordinary person such as I can make a difference and enjoy some rich rewards.*

VISSER, VALYA ELIZABETH, physician; b. Chgo., Oct. 2, 1947; d. Roy Warren and Tania Eugenia (Morozoff) Nelson; children: Kira Elizabeth Visser, Michael Philip Visser. BS, Iowa State U., 1968; MD, U. Iowa, 1973. Diplomate Am. Bd. Pediatrics, Sub-Bd. Neonatal-Perinatal Medicine. Resident pediatrics U. Iowa Hosps. and Clinics, Iowa City, 1976; fellow neonatology Children's Mercy Hosp., Kansas City, 1978; asst. prof. pediatrics U. Kans. Sch. Medicine, 1978-81; staff pediatrician U.S. Army Med. Corps., Ft. Bragg, N.C., 1981-83; attending neonatologist Carolinas Med. Ctr., Charlotte, 1983—. Chair dept. pediatrics Carolinas Med. Ctr., Charlotte, 1999—; conf. chair Extracorporeal Life Support Orgn., Ann Arbor, Mich., 1993-95. Major Med. Corps., 1981-83. Fellow Am. Acad. Pediatrics. Mem. Unitarian-Universalist Ch. Avocations: parenting, music. Office: Carolinas Med Ctr Dept Pediatrics PO Box 32861 Charlotte NC 28232-2861

VISSICCHIO, ANDREW JOHN, JR. linen service company executive; b. N.Y.C., Dec. 21, 1941; s. Andrew John and Ann (Renna) V.; m. Patricia Ann Hunken, Jan. 18, 1964; children: Andrew John III, Douglas David. BS in Bus., L.I. U., 1963; postgrad., A.T. Roth Grad. Sch. Bus., 1963-64, Harvard U., 1995, 98. Gen. mgr. Allied Coat & Apron, Bklyn., 1963-72; ops. officer N.Y. Ocean Sci. Lab., Montauk, N.Y., 1972-76; gen. mgr. Am. Svc. Corp., Miami, Fla., 1976-79, dist. mgr., 1979-83, v.p. ops., 1983-87; gen. mgr. Nat. Linen Svc., West Palm Beach, Fla., 1987-88, dist. mgr. Atlanta, 1988-90, v.p., gen. mgr. linen supply divsn., 1990-94, regional v.p., 1994-96; v.p. FDR Svcs. Group, Hempstead, N.Y., 1997-99; regional v.p. Video Save Inc., N.Y.C., 2000-01. Author: A Book of Simple Poems; Pianist recital Carnegie Hall, 1956, 57. Mem. fin com. City of Boca Raton. Recipient Dedicated Svc. award Montauk Fire Dept., 1976, Milliken award New Prodn. Devel. in Textile Rental Industry, 1996; Meadowbrook Bank scholar L.I. U., 1962-63. Mem. Textile Rental Svc. Assn. (strategic com. 1984-86), S.Am. Explorers Club, Am. Orchid Soc., Boca Raton Orchid Soc. (fin. com.), Coalition for Species Orchid. Republican. Roman Catholic. Avocations: collecting and growing orchids, writing poetry, boating, fishing, classical music-opera. Home: 2350 NW 38th St Boca Raton FL 33431-5439

VISTE, ARLEN ELLARD, chemistry educator; b. Austin, Minn., Aug. 13, 1936; s. Arthur E. and Edith L. (Kehret) V.; m. Elizabeth Ann Lindbeck, June 14, 1959; children: Solveig, David, Mark. BA, St. Olaf Coll., 1958; PhD, U. Chgo., 1962. Asst. prof. chemistry St. Olaf Coll., Northfield, Minn., 1962-63; NSF fellow Columbia U., N.Y.C., 1963-64; asst. prof. Augustana Coll., Sioux Falls, S.D., 1964-68, assoc. prof., 1968-73, prof., 1973—, prof. emeritus, 2002—. Contbr. articles to profl. jours. Mem. Am. Chem. Soc., Royal Soc. Chemistry (London), S.D. Acad. Sci., Midwest Assn. Chemistry Tchrs. in Liberal Arts Colls., Phi Beta Kappa, Sigma Xi. Home: 1500 W 30th St Sioux Falls SD 57105-3622 Office: Augustana Coll Chemistry Dept Sioux Falls SD 57197-0001

VISWANATHAN, RAJU RAMACHANDRAN, physicist; b. New Delhi, July 29, 1963; arrived in Singapore, 1994; s. C.V. and Kalpagam (Kothandaraman) R.; m. Ranjitha Viswanathan, July 4, 1991; children: Sneha, Preeti. B of Tech., Indian Inst. Tech., Madras, 1984; PhD, U. Fla., 1989. Scientist Ctr. Artificial Intelligence & Robotics, Bangalore, India, 1992-94; sr. scientist Ctr. Info.-enhanced Medicine, Singapore, 1994—. Vis. scientist Internat. Ctr. Theoretical Physics, Trieste, Italy, 1989-91. Contbr. articles to profl. jours. John Slater fellow, U. Fla., Gainesville, 1984-89. Mem. AAAS, IEEE, Indian Acad. Scis. Avocations: reading, music, travel, cooking. Office: Ctr Info-enhanced Medicine 10 Sci Park Rd No 03-14 Singapore 117684 Singapore

VISWANATHAN, RAMASWAMY, physician, educator; b. Coimbatore, India, Aug. 20, 1949; came to U.S., 1972; s. Thiruvalangadu and Bhavani Krishnamurthy Ramaswamy; m. Kusum Ramakrishna, June 15, 1980; children: Vikram, Vivek, Vidya. MB, BS, U. Madras, 1972; D of Med. Sci., SUNY, 1989. Diplomate Am. Bd. Psychiatry and Neurology, geriatric psychiatry, addiction psychiatry, Am. Bd. Internal Medicine. Med. intern Bklyn.-Cumberland Med. Ctr., 1972-73; resident in internal medicine L.I. Jewish-Hillside Med. Ctr.-Queens Hosp. Ctr. Affiliation, N.Y.C., 1973-74; resident in psychiatry SUNY Health Sci. Ctr., Bklyn., 1974-77, fellow in psychosomatic medicine, 1976-78, fellow in research tng. in psychiatry, 1977-79, mem. staff, 1978—, clin. asst. prof. psychiatry, 1979-87, instr. in medicine, 1979—, clin. assoc. prof., 1987-90, assoc. prof. clin. psychiatry, 1990—, assoc. dir. med.-psychiat. liaison svc., 1981-83, 84-97, acting dir., 1983-84, dir., psychiat. liaison svc., 1998—, med. dir. Anxiety Disorders Clinic, 1982—, mem. com. cancer edn. and preventive oncology, 1983-92, dir. course on life-threatening illness, dying and death, 1984-89, dir. med. interviewing course, 1985-89, dir. doctor-patient relationship course, 1989-90, dir. intro. to clin. medicine-human dimension course, 1990-98, cons. AIDS unit, 1989—, with student evaluation and promotion com., 1989-94, with course dirs.' com., 1989-98; mem. exec. com. Univ. Hosp., 1992-96; internal medicine residency program rev. com. SUNY Health Sci. Ctr., 1994—; cons. Bklyn. VA Med. Ctr., 1986-89; pvt. practice medicine specializing in psychiatry, psychosomatic medicine, behavior therapy, hypnosis and sex therapy Bklyn., 1978—. Mem. task force on doctoring experience curricular reform, 1997—. Contbr. articles to profl. jours. Curriculum coun. Herricks Pub. Sch. Dist., 1992-95. Fellow ACP, Am. Psychiat. Assn. (dep. rep. Asian-Am. caucus 1996-99, RG rep. 1999—, assembly com. on procedures, 1997—, com. on consultation, liaison psychiatry and primary care edn. 1992-98, coun. on internat. affairs 1992-95, 97—, nominating com. 1997-98, assembly com. on planning 1998—, cert. excellence in med. evaluation 1999), Indian Psychiat. Soc. (life), Acad. Psychosomatic Medicine; mem. AMA, Bklyn. Psychiat. Soc. (councillor, pres. elect 1988-90, pres. 1990-92, chmn. com. on AIDS, 1990-92, chmn. com. on consultation-liaison psychiatry 1990-92, chmn. disaster response com. 1991-92, chmn. legis. and pvt. practice com. 1992-96, chmn. legis. com. 1996—, chmn. internat. affairs com. 1992-94), Am. Acad. Psychiatry and the Law (rsch. com. 1998—, internat. rels. com. 1998—, Assn. Advancement Behavior Therapy, Soc. Liaison Psychiatry (bd. dirs. 1986-90, 93-96, sec. 1987-88), Anxiety Disorders Assn. Am., N.Y. State Psychiat. Assn. (com. on govt. health programs 1988-94, task force on practice guidelines, legis. com., chmn. edn. com. 1992-96), Soc. Exploration Psychotherapy Integration, Indo-Am. Psychiat. Assn. (founder, life, exec. com. 1979-85, 92—, sec. 1992-94, pres.-elect 1994-96, pres. 1996-98, Sci. and Svc. award 1990). Office: SUNY Health Sci Ctr 450 Clarkson Ave # 127 Brooklyn NY 11203-2056

VITA, STEVEN, poet; b. Chgo., July 16, 1960; s. John and Rosemarie V. BA in Art and English, Denison U., 1982; MFA in English, CUNY, 1985. Founder, editor Veery, Chgo., 1991—. Author: The Heart of Tents, 1991. Mem. Am. Philos. Assn. Office: VEERY 333 N Michigan Ave Ste 2032 Chicago IL 60601-4102

VITAGLIANO, KATHLEEN ALYCE FULLER, secondary education educator; b. Oneida, N.Y., May 3, 1949; d. Allen Herbert and Phyllis Ann (Fearon) Fuller; m. Gene Angelo Vitagliano, Feb. 10, 1973 (div. 1998); children: Marissa Ariana, Marc Anthony, Michael Allen. BA in English, SUNY, Buffalo, 1971, EdM in English Education, 1973; cert. creative studies, SUC, Buffalo, 1990. Cert. secondary English tchr. N.Y., sch. dist. adminstr., N.Y. Tchr. English grades 7-12 Buffalo Pub. Schs., N.Y., 1972-93, 95-97, tchr. of gifted grades 5-8, 1992-97; magnet sch. tchr. specialist Campus West Sch., Buffalo, 1993-95; asst. prin. Kensington H.S., 1997—2001, Grover Cleveland H.S., Buffalo, 2001—. Facilitator Creative Problem Solving, 1990—; workshop presenter Buffalo Tchr. Ctr., N.Y., 1992—. Singer Buffalo Philharm. Chorus, N.Y., 1973—; mem. Just Buffalo Literary Ctr., 1991—; del. Buffalo Tchrs. Fedn., 1992-97; bd. dirs. Parent, Tchr. and Student Cmty. Orgn. of City Honors Sch., 1993-97, v.p., 1994-97; mem. Ednl. Leadership Buffalo, Class of 1998, supt. adv. com., 2000—; choir Westminster Presbyn. Ch., 1998—. Grantee NEH, 1985; recipient Pathfinders award for sch./bus. partnership, 1995; Western N.Y. Writing Project fellow Canisius Coll., 1990, 95, 99; poetry collection editor 1995, 2002. Mem. ASCD, N.Y. State English Coun. (Tchr. of Excellence award 1991), Nat. Coun. Tchrs. English, Secondary Asst. Prins. Assn. (sec. 1998-2001), Grad. Sch. Edn. Alumni Assn. SUNY Buffalo, Creative Edn. Found., Creative Studies Alumni Assn. State U. Coll. Buffalo (newsletter editor 1991-95, v.p. 1992-96), Advocacy for Gifted and Talented Edn. N.Y., Internat. Creativity Network, Phi Delta Kappa. Avocations: singing, writing poetry, drama, reading. Home: 343 Sanders Rd Buffalo NY 14216-1420 Office: Grover Cleveland HS 110 14th St Buffalo NY 14213 E-mail: vitagliano@earthlink.net.

VITAGLIANO, PASQUALE ANDREW, orthodontist, educator; b. Bklyn., Dec. 15, 1940; s. Joseph Pasquale and Caroline Antoinette (Sessa) V.; m. Genevieve Marie Vitaliano, Jne 11, 1966; children: Joseph, Marissa. BA, NYU, 1962, DDS, 1966; MS in Dentistry, Fairleigh Dickinson U., 1971. Diplomate Am. Bd. Orthodontics, Coll. Bd. of Orthodontics. Assoc. prof. Stony Brook (N.Y.) U., 1972-95; attending orthodontist L.I. Jewish Hosp., New Hyde Pk., N.Y., 1978—, Good Samaritan Hosp., West Islip, 1978—. Contbr. articles to profl. jours. Mem. exec. com. L.I. Aquarium, Bayshore, N.Y., 1997—; interviewer Duke U., Durham, N.C., mem. parent fund raising com., 1987—. Capt. U.S. Army, 1967-69. Recipient commendation U.S. Army, 1968. Fellow Am. Bd. Orthodontics; mem. ADA, Am. Orthodontic Assn., Strang Tweed (Eastern) Assn. Orthodontics (exec. bd.), Nassau County Dental Soc., Internat. Fedn. Dentists, Omicron Kappa Upsilon. Avocations: fly fishing, biking, equestrian activities, boating. Office: Massapequa Orthodontic Assocs 847 N Broadway Massapequa NY 11758-2338

VITAL, PATRICIA BEST, lawyer; b. Pitts., Mar. 26; d. Clarence D. and Billie Lorraine (Wilson) B.; m. Leo Vital, Mar. 30. BA magna cum laude, U. Tenn., Chattanooga, 1989; JD with honors, U. Tenn., 1992. Bar: Ga. 1994, Tenn. 1993, U.S. Dist. Ct. (ea. dist.) Tenn. 1993, U.S. Dist. Ct. (no. dist.) Ga. 1995, U.S. Ct. Appeals (6th cir.) 1993, U.S. Ct. Appeals (11th cir.) 1995, U.S. Supreme Ct. 1996. Legal asst. Gleason & Assoc. Law Firm, Rossville, Ga., 1981-82; med. staff coord. Hutcheson Med. Ctr., Ft. Oglethorpe, 1982-86; rsch. asst. U. Tenn. Law Coll., Knoxville, 1991-92; from law clk. to assoc. atty. Lusk, Carter & McGehey, Chattanooga, 1990-93; pvt. practice, 1993—; mediator, arbitrator Vital Dispute Resolution Svcs., 1996—. Law clk. Hamilton County Attys. Office, Chattanooga, summer 1990; devel. coun. co-chair class 1992 U. Tenn. Coll. Law, alumni network mentoring program, 1995—, deans cir., 1992—; pres. adult scholars program U. Tenn., Chattanooga, 1988-89, adult scholars program adv. coun., scholarship com., 1994—; presenter in field; adj. prof. pre-trial litigation, legal asst. studies program U. Tenn., fall, 1997; instr. Law Sch. Admission Test preparation course KAPLAN, Inc., 1999-2000; commn. continuing legal edn. and specialization Tenn. Supreme Ct., 1996-2001; panel mediator, arbitrator (Ea. and Mid. dists.) Tenn. Fed. Mediation Programs, U.S. Dept. Justice, Key Bridge Found., Am. with Disabilities, Chattanooga Better Bus. Bur., Coun. Better Bus. Burs. AutoLine Arbitration, Hamilton County Tenn. Divorce Mediation, Am. Health Lawyers ADR Svc.; mem. panel, chair arbitration panel Nat. Assn. Securities Dealers. Co-author: Tennessee Alternative Dispute Resolution Handbook, 1997; contbr. articles to profl. jours. Mentor Hamilton County Bd. Edn., 1995-96; cmty. resource person Ooltewah Middle and Chattanooga Phoenix Middle Schs., 1994-96; capt. attys. team presch. phon-a-thon Siskin Found., 1994-95; mem. Chattanooga Chamber Found. Leadership Chattanooga Class, 1997-98; nat. adv. bd. Ctr. for Enterprise Edn., Peabody Coll. Edn., Vanderbilt U., 1998-2000. Mem. ABA (ethics 2000 adv. coun. 1998, dispute resolution sect. Boston Conf. Planning Com. 1998-2000, co-chair dispute resolution sect. State and Local Bar Com. 1998-2000), AAUW, Fed. Bar Assn., Nat. Inst. Dispute Resolution, Nat. Assn. Mediators in Edn., Am. Health Lawyers Assn., Nat. Assn. Women Bus. Owners (local chpt. bd. dirs. 1994), Am. Soc. Law, Medicine and Ethics, Tenn. Bar Assn. (com. chair, sec. and spkr. ho. of dels. 1995—, com. chair law related edn. 1996-97, bd. dirs. law office tech. and mgmt. 1994-96, sec-treas., chair-elect, chair dispute resolution sect. 1995-98, Merit award 1995, mem. editl. bd. TBALink), Mediation Assn. Tenn. (chair continuing mediation edn., curriculum com. 1996-98), Tenn. Trial Lawyers Assn., Tenn. Assn. Med. Staff Svcs., Nat. and Tenn. Assn. Ptnrs. in Edn., Ga. State Bar Assn., Chattanooga Bar Assn. (bd. govs. 1996-97, chair bd. govs. task force on the future Tenn. judicial sys. 1995-96, centennial planning com. 1996-97, chair continuing legal edn. com. 1994-95, chair ethics rules rev. com. 1998-99, chair dispute resolution com. 1998—, First Beyond the Call of Duty award 1995), Chattanooga Trial Lawyers Assn. (dir., gov. bd. 1995-2000), Southeast Tenn. Lawyers Assn. Women (dir. at-large 1996-97), Better Bus. Bur., S.E. Tenn. Coun. on Children & Youth, Chattanooga Area C. of C., Phi Delta Phi. Avocations: whitewater rafting, mountain hiking, aerobics, reading. Office: Vital Law Offc & Dispute Resolution Svcs James Bldg Ste 801 735 Broad St Chattanooga TN 37402-1804 Fax: (423) 267-2376. E-mail: bestlaw@mindspring.com.

VITALE, ALISHA RENEE, research associate; b. Decatur, Ga. d. Joseph Henry Frohock and Sheryl Louise Coffy; m. John Anthony Vitale III, Dec. 29, 1997. AA, St. Petersburg Jr. Coll., 1995; BS in Edn. magna cum laude, U. South Fla., 1998, MA in Mental Health Counseling, 2000; student in Comm., U. S. Fla. Rsch. assoc. Inst. for Instrnl. Rsch. and Practice, Tampa, Fla., 2001—. Big sister Big Bros./Big Sisters, Largo, Fla., 1995—. Mem.: Nat. Comm. Assn., Humanists of Fla., Chi Sigma Iota. Democrat. Office: U South Fla Inst Instrnl Rsch/Practice 4202 E Fowler Ave HMS 401 Tampa FL 33620 E-mail: alisha@iirp.coedu.usf.edu.

VITALE, ANNA M. travel, construction and real estate management executive; b. Newark, July 17, 1942; d. Andrew and Pearl (Chelak) Franchak; m. Frederick R. Vitale, May 7, 1961; children: F. Richard, J. Steven, J. Christipher. Attended Trenton State Coll., 1967-68. Vice pres. Vitran, Inc., Allentown, N.J., 1972-80, pres., 1980—, also dir.; ptnr. Hampton Manor Ltd., Mt. Holly, N.J., 1983—, also dir.; pres. Travel World Corp., Mt. Holly, N.J., 1989—; mgr., owner LaChez Salon, Allentown, 1966-76, Colonial Manor Salon, Jacobstown, N.J., 1977-88. Mem. U.S. Trotting Assn., N.J. and Pa. Racing Commn., Am. Soc. Noteries, Internat. Platform Assn. Home: 8 Patty Dr Wrightstown NJ 08562-2218

VITALE, GERALD LEE, financial services executive; b. Chgo., Apr. 3, 1950; s. Le Roy Allen and Gilda Leanora (Rasori) V. BS in Psychology, Loyola U., Chgo., 1972. Fin. mgr. Mellon Fin., Chgo., 1973-76; credit mgr. Kemper Ins. Co., 1976-78; pres., CEO Tribune Employees Credit Union, 1978-96. Pres. NCR Credit Union User Group, Dayton, Ohio, 1984-91; CEO, Gerald Equity Resources, Inc., 1996—; mem. adv. bd. Ill. Gov.'s Credit Union, 1993-98; dir. fin. Rush Cancer Inst., 2000-2001. *Gerald Vitale is President of Garfield Equity Resources, a firm that specializes in providing financial investment advice for the new economy. He has over twenty years experience in Financial Services Management. He has served as president of the Tribune Company Credit Union, Financial Director of the Rush Cancer Institute, and Finance Manager at Mellon Financial Services. Mr. Vitale is well known in Chicago as co-host of the CLTV program "Watch Your Wallet." He has served numerous organizations as a member of their Board of Directors, including the Illinois Credit Advisory Board (1993-1998).* Co-host Chicagoland Cable (CLTV) TV Fin. Reports, Tribune Broadcasting, 1993-96. Mem. Habitat for Humanity, 1998—, Nat. Rep. Senatorial Com., 2002, Heritage Found., 2002—; counselor youth motivation Chgo. C. of C. and Industry, 1980—97, mem. adv. bd., 1984—96; counselor Hire the Future, 1988—96; vol. Red Cloud Athletic Assn., 1993—2000, Friends of Providence-St. Mel, 1993—; mem. Chgo. Coun. Fgn. Rels., 1995—98; mem. Coun. of 1000 Nat. Italian-Am. Found., 1995—99, Humane Soc. U.S., 1997—; mem. fin. svcs. com. Exec. Club City of Chgo., 1993—99; mem. Ctr. Study of Presidency, 1993—97, Filene Inst., 1992—96, Ill. Arts Alliance, 1996—98, GOP Action Com., 1992—97. Recipient award, Eisenhower Commn., 2002. Mem.: Greater Garfield C. of C. (bd. dirs. 1992—95), The Carter Ctr., Am. Enterprise Inst., Nat. Assn. Investors (corp. mem. 1999—), Nat. Assn. State Chartered Credit Unions (bd. dirs. 1995—97, region V dir.), Midwest Assn. Credit Unions (bd. dirs. 1992—96), Am. Mgmt. Assn., Sky Line Club, Monroe Club (bd. dirs. 1995—99). Roman Catholic. Avocations: hiking, rowing, long-distance walking. Home: 1636 N Wells St Apt 2410 Chicago IL 60614-6020 Office: GER Inc 1636 N Wells St Apt 2410 Chicago IL 60614-6020 E-mail: gerinc@aol.com.

VITALE, MAGDA, artist; b. N.Y.C., July 20, 1939; d. John and Tomasita (Couso) Reyes; m. Robert James Vitale, Dec. 23, 1957 (dec. Sept. 1990); children: Pamela, Robert, John. BFA, Moore Coll. Art, Phila., 1980; student, Barnes Found., Merion, Pa., Skowhegan (Maine) Sch. Painting and Sculpture. One-woman shows include Nexus Gallery, Phila., 1982, 84, St. Joseph's U., Phila., 1983, U. Pitts. Gallery, 1987, Camden County Coll., Blackwood, N.J., 1988, Am. Embassy, Brussels, 1989, Del. Art Mus., Wilmington, 1989, Moore Coll. Art, Phila., 1989, Cabrini Coll., Radnor, Pa., 1989, Trenton (N.J.) City Mus., 1989, Becton Hall Gallery, Fairleigh Dickinson U., Rutherford, N.J., 1991, No. Ind. Arts Assn. William J. Bachman Gallery, Munster, Ind., 1992, Henri Gallery, Washington, 1991; exhibited in group shows the most recent being Schomarie County Arts Gallery, Cobleskill, N.Y., 1990, Nexus Gallery, 1990, Zepher Gallery, Louisville, 1990, Schoharie County Arts Gallery, Cobleskill, N.Y., 1990, Henri Gallery, Washington, 1991, 93, Zoller Gallery, Pa. State U., 1991, 93, Wilkes Barre (Pa.) U., 1991, Erie (Pa.) Art Mus., 1992, Boyle (Ireland) Arts Festival, 1993, Islip (N.Y.) Art Mus., 1993, Am. Embassy, Dublin, Ireland, 1993; traveling exhbn. Ballycastle, Limrick, Dublin, Republic of Ireland; works represented in permanent collections including Best Products, Inc., 1838 Investment Advisers, N.J. Power and Light, Carnegie Ctr., Princeton, N.J., Islip Art Mus., Embassy Dublin, Balenglen Arts Found., Ballycastle. Recipient Purchase prize Delaware County C.C., 1976, Scholarship Skowehegan (Maine) Sch. Painting and Sculpture, 1979, Expo V award Northport (N.Y.) Galleries, 1986, Fellowship award Ballingen Found., Bally Castle, Ireland, 1992. Home: 12 Springton Lake Rd Media PA 19063-1824

VITALE, PAUL, accountant; b. Bklyn., Oct. 7, 1958; s. Joseph A. and Joan J. (Pecoraro) V.; m. Marie N. Barbieri, Mar. 28, 1982; children: Michelle, Stephen, Jaclyn. BS in Acctg. magna cum laude, St. John's U., 1979. CPA, N.Y. Sr. mgr. Arthur Andersen & Co., Melville, N.Y., 1979-90; v.p. fin., treas., sec. Barron's Ednl. Series, Inc., Hauppauge, 1990-93; sole practice in pub. acctg. Garden City, 1993-98; contr. ARC in Greater N.Y., 2002. CFO, treas. Comml. Capital Corp., Comcap Holding Corp., 1998-2001. Bd. dirs., treas. North Shore Child and Family Guidance Assn., 1995, Garden City Cmty. Fund., 2000; controller Am. Red. Cross Greater NY, 2002-. Named Outstanding Young Man Am., 1985; recipient Regents scholarship N.Y. State Dept. Edn., 1976, St. John's U. Scholastic Excellence award, 1976. Mem. AICPA, N.Y. State Soc. CPAs (instr. Suffolk County chpt. 1991, 92), Fin. Exec. Internat., Mineola-Garden City Rotary Club (bd. dirs. 1996). Avocations: golf, collectibles. E-mail: MPMSJK@aol.com.

VITALI, GREGORY S. (GREG), state legislator; b. Havertown, Pa., June 4, 1956; 1 child, Sarah. BS cum laude, Villanova U., 1978, JD, 1981. Rep. Dist. 166 State of Pa., 1993—. Address: 1001 Darby Rd Havertown PA 19083-3818

VITALIANO, PETER PAUL, medical educator, researcher; b. Hazleton, Pa. s. Salvatore and Mary (Gaudio) V. BA, Queens Coll., 1969; MS, Syracuse U., 1973, Ph, 1975; postdoct., Fla. State U., 1976, U. Wash., 1977. Rsch. assoc. U. Wash., Seattle, 1978, from asst. to prof., 1979-88, prof., 1988—. Editor: Annals of Behavioral Medicine, 1997; mem. editl. bd.: Psychoneuroendocrinologym 1985—, Health Psychology, 1996—, Internat. Behavioral Medicine, 1999; contbr. 180 articles to profl. jours. Grantee Nat. Inst. Aging, 1986-89, 94-99, Nat. Inst. Mental Health, 1988-93, 98—. Fellow Am. Psychol. Assn., Soc. Beahvioral Medicine, Gerontol. Soc. Am.; mem. Acad. Behavioral Medicine Rsch. (coun.). Avocations: art, nature, music. Office: U Wash PO Box 356560 Seattle WA 98195-6560

VITANIEMI, LISA DAWN, computer coordinator; b. Greencastle, Ind., Mar. 11, 1961; d. David C. and Patricia E. Bombei; m. Steven R. Vitaniemi, Jan. 20, 1966; 1 child, Jennifer Puckett. B in Bus. Edn., Ind. State U., Terre Haute, 1990, MEd, 1995. Tchr., computer coord. Georgetown (Ill.) -Ridge Farm High Sch., 1990—. Tchr., leader Cayuga (Ind.) Christian Ch., 1998-01. Recipient Award of Distinction Ill. State Bd. Edn., 2000, 02, Golden Ruler award Regional Office Edn., 1996, Connections award, Ill. State Bd. Edn., 1995. Office: Georgetown-Ridge Farm High Sch 500 Mulberry Georgetown IL 61846 Fax: 217-662-3404.

VITEK, RICHARD KENNETH, scientific instrument company executive; b. Chgo., Feb. 1, 1935; s. Martin and Mildred (Veverka) V.; m. Marilyn W. Young, June 23, 1956; children: Christine, Debra, Evelyn. AB, Albion Coll., 1956; MS, U. Mo., 1958, profl. degree in chemistry, 1994. Rsch. chemist Allied Chem. Corp., Morristown, N.J., 1958-64, AEC/Nat. Lead Co., Cin., 1957; sales mgr. Aldrich Chem. Co., Inc., Milw., 1964-66, dir. mktg., 1966-68; pres., chmn. Camag, Inc., 1968-79, Fotodyne Inc. and Variquest Techs., Inc., Hartland, Wis., 1980—. Contbr. articles to profl. jours. and books. Co-founder Chem. Rsch. Found.; Florentine Opera Co.; bd.dirs. various civic and indsl. orgns.; chmn. bd. trustees, pres. U. Mo., Rolla; trustee Opera Am. Recipient Disting. Alumni award Albion Coll., 1994, Disting. Alumni Achievement award U. Mo., 1998. Mem. Am. Chem. Soc., Coun. Ind. Mgrs., Wis. Acad. Scis., Arts and Letters, Ind. Bus. Assn. Wis., Wis. Bus. Assn. Independent Republican. Congregationalist. Achievements include 8 patents; discovery of Bismuth Dimethyglyoxime and F3NO. Office: PO Box 704 Brookfield WI 53008

VITEK, VACLAV, materials scientist; b. Olomouc, Czechoslovakia, Sept. 10, 1940; came to U.S., 1978; s. Josef and Ruzena V.; m. Ludovita Stankovicova, Aug. 5, 1972; children: Adrian Joseph, Clementine Mary. BSc in Physics, Charles U., Prague, 1962; PhD in Physics, Czechoslovakian Acad. Scis., Prague, 1966; hon. doctorate, Tech. U. Brno, 1999. Research assoc. dept. metall. materials sci. and research fellow Wolfson Coll., Oxford (Eng.) U., 1967-75; research officer Central Elec. Research Labs., Central Elec. Generating Bd., Leatherhead, Eng., 1975-78; prof. materials sci. and engring. U. Pa., 1978—. Vis. prf. U. Groningen, The Netherlands, 1985-86. Recipient Humboldt award for sr. scientists, Germany, 1992-93, Acta metallurgica Gold medal, 1996, Mach medal Czech Acad. Scis., 1999. Fellow Inst. Physics (London), Am. Soc. Metals Internat., Metals, Minerals Materials Soc.; mem. Am. Phys. Soc., Materials Rsch. Soc. Office: U Pa Dept Materials Sci and Engring 3231 Walnut St Philadelphia PA 19104-6202 E-mail: vitek@lrsm.upenn.edu .

VITETTA, ELLEN SHAPIRO, microbiologist educator, immunologist; BA, Conn. Coll.; MS, NYU, 1966, PhD, MD, 1968. Prof. microbiology Southwestern Med. Sch., U. Tex., Dallas, 1976—; dir. Cancer Immunobiology Ctr., U. Tex., 1988—; Sheryle Simmons Patigian Disting. chair in cancer immunobiology Southwestern Med. Sch., U. Tex., 1989—. Bd. sci. coun. NCI Cancer Treatment Bd., 1993; sci. adv. bd. Howard Hughes Med. Inst., 1992—; Kettering selection com. GM Cancer Rsch. Foun., 1987-88; task force NIAID in Immunology, 1989-90; mem. sci. bd. Ludwig Inst., 1983—. Mem. editl. bd.: Advances in Host Defense Mechanisms, 1983—, Annual Review of Immunology, 1991—, Bioconjugate Chemistry, 1989-93, Cellular Immunology, 1984-93, Current Opinions in Immunology, 1992—, FASEB Journal, 1987—, Internat. Jour. of Oncology, 1992—, Internat. Soc. Immunopharmacology, 1989—, Jour. of Immunology, 1975-78, Molecular Immunology, 1978-93; assoc. editor Cancer Research, 1986—; Immunochemistry sect. editor: Jour. of Immunology, 1978-82; co-editor in chief: Therapeutic Immunology, 1992—. Recipient Women's Excellence in Sci. award Fedn. Am. Soc. Exptl. Biology, 1991, Taittinger Breast Cancer Rsch. award Komen Found., 1983, Pierce Immunotoxin award, 1988, NIH Merit award, 1987—, U. Tex. Southwestern Med. Sch. Faculty Teaching awards 1989, 91, 92, 93, 94, FASED Excellence in Sci. award, 1991, Abbot Clinical Immunology award Am. Soc. Microbiologists, 1992, Past State Pres. award Tex. Fed. Bus. Profl. Women's Club, 1993, Richard and Hinda Rosenthal Found. award Am. Assn. Cancer Rsch 1995, Charlotte Friend award Am. Assn. Cancer Rsch., 1995. Mem. Am. Assn. Immunologists (pres. 1994), Nat. Acad. Scis., Am. Acad. Microbiology (hon.). Achievements include co-discovery of IL-4, development of immunotoxins and identification of IgD on murine B cells. Office: Univ of Texas Cancer Immunobiol Ctr 6000 Harry Hines Blvd Dallas TX 75235-5303 Address: Scottdale Conference 6914 Pemberton Dr Dallas TX 75230-4260 E-mail: ellen.vitetta@utsoutheastern.edu.

VITKOWSKY, VINCENT JOSEPH, lawyer; b. Newark, Oct. 3, 1955; s. Boniface and Rosemary (Ofack) V.; m. Mary Gunzburg, May 16, 1981 (div. 1997); children: Vincent Jr., Victoria; m. Pandora Strasler, Sept. 18, 1999. BA, Northwestern U., 1977; JD, Cornell U., 1980. Bar: NY 1981. Assoc. Hart and Hume, N.Y.C., 1980-84, Kroll & Tract, N.Y.C., 1984-87; of counsel Nixon, Hargrave, Devans & Doyle, 1988-89; ptnr. Buchalter, Nemer, Fields & Younger, 1990-95, Edwards & Angell LLP, N.Y.C., 1996—. Mem. panel arbitration London Ct. Internat. Arbitration; lectr. in field. Contbr. articles to profl. jours. Mem. ABA (com. chmn.), Am. Arbitration Assn. (inernat. panel arbitrators), Internat. Bar Assn. (com. officer), Internat. Law Assn., Assn. Bar City of N.Y., Cornell Club, Human Rights Watch, IBA Human Rights Inst. (officer, com. on interventions and trial observations), Lawyers Com. for Human Rights. Home: 422 E 72d St Apt 15E New York NY 10021 Office: Edwards & Angell LLP 750 Lexington Ave Fl 12 New York NY 10022-1253

VITRAC, JEAN-JACQUES CHARLES, international business consultant; b. Paris, May 31, 1942; came to U.S., 1972; s. Jean Bernard Vitrac and Paulette Aimée (Buisson) Mannerheim; m. Roswitha Kahling, Sept. 11, 1965; children: Emmanuel, François, Catherine. Diploma, Faculty of Law, Aix, France, 1963; post grad. in mktg., Institut National Du Marketing, Paris, 1972; post grad. in econ. scis., Institut Superieur Sciences Economiques, Paris, 1979. Devel. officer Europe-Africa Internat. Jaycees, Geneva, 1968-70; dir. econ. affairs Internat. Jaycees, Coral Gables, Fla., 1970-72; mktg. cons. Bernard Krief Internat., Paris, 1973-79; strategy cons. Euro-PacRim Internat., Walnut Creek, Calif., 1980—. Owner Domaine Becquet Winery, Valley Springs, Calif.; chair task force on multinat. strategies Ctrl. Bank of France, Paris, 1974-78; mktg. cons. Aérospatiale, Paris, 1978; bd. dirs. Capsule Française Inc., Napa, Calif.; asst. prof. mktg. Inst. Français de Gestion, Paris, 1973-79; U.S. chmn. L'Entreprise Demain, Brussels, 1982-98; no. Calif. chmn. World Tech. Execs. Network, 1987-90. Author: Discover Export, 1974; co-author: Doing Business in California, 1989; editor World Tech. Execs. Network Review, 1989-90. Bd. dirs. E. Bay Internat. Trade Coun., 1996-97; chair parish coun. St. Patrick's Ch., 1998, 99; trustee Mark Twain St. Joseph's Hosp. Found., 1999—, exec. bd. mem., pub. rels. com. co-chair, 2000—; elected to Calaveras County Rep. Ctrl. Com., 2001. Named knight Equestrian Order of Holy Sepulchre of Jerusalem. Mem. KC (dep. grand knight 1998, treas. 1999-2001, Grand Knight 2001-2002), Am. Assn. Polit. Cons., Art Ranaissance Found. (hon., chair Calif. chpt. 1994—), Classical Philharmonic (v.p. 1995-96), Cal-France Coun. (v.p. 1996-97), Kiwanis Internat (gov.'s cabinet, dir. com. svc. 1996-97), French War Vets. (No. Calif. chpt. pres. 1996-97), Napa Kiwanis Club (disting. pres. 1993, bd. dirs. Calif.-Nev.-Hawaii Found. 1996-98), Wine Inst., Calaveras Wine Assn., West Calaveras Rotary (pres. 2000-2001). Republican. Roman Catholic. Home: Becket's Ranch PO Box 467 Valley Springs CA 95252 Office: Euro PacRim Int Corp 2173 Hwy 12 East PO Box 1418 Valley Springs CA 95252-1418

VITT, DAVID AARON, medical manufacturing company executive; b. Phila., Aug. 3, 1938; s. Nathan and Flora B.; m. Renee Lee Salkever, Oct. 20, 1963; children: Nadine Lori Einiger, Jeffrey Richard. BS, Temple U., 1961. Sales engr. X-Ray Corp., Phila., 1961-65, Midwest Am., Chgo., 1965-67, product mgr., 1967-68, product mgr. regional sales, 1968-70; dir. mktg. Valtronic & Living Wills, Bronx, N.Y., 1970-74; v.p. Siemens Med. Systems Inc. gen. mgr. dental div., Iselin, N.J., 1974-86, past corp. v.p.; CEO, pres. Pelton & Crane, Charlotte, N.C., 1986-89; v.p. govt. sales Siemens Med. Systems Corp. Officers, ret., 1994; founder, pres., CEO D.A.V., Inc., 1995—; founder, co-owner RealDental.com. Pres. Denx Am. Inc., 1998; industry rep. to Am. Nat. Standards Inst.; co. rep. U.S.-USSR Trade and Econ. Coun.; co-founder Enter Am. Group Exec. Consultants. Bd. dirs. Am. Fund for Dental Health; apptd. mem. Charlotte Mecklenburg Community Relations Com.; mem. bd. visitors, bd. vis. U. N.C., Charlotte; officer, mem. exec. com. Jr. Achievement. Served in USAR, 1961-68. Mem. Am. Mgmt. Assn. (bd. dirs. N.J. chpt.), Am. Mktg. Assn., Am. Dental Trade Assn. (bd. dirs.), Dental Mfrs. Am. (past pres.), Am. Acad. Dental Radiology, Charlotte C. of C. (bd. advisors), Acad. Gen. Dentists (bd. mem. found.), Masons (32 deg.), Shriners. Republican.

VITT, SAMUEL BRADSHAW, communications media services executive; b. Greensboro, N.C., Oct. 23, 1926; s. Bruno Caesar and Gray (Bradshaw) V.; m. Marie Foster, Oct. 30, 1955; children: Joanne Louise, Michael Bradshaw, Mark Thomas. AB, Dartmouth Coll., 1950. Exec. asst. TV film CBS, N.Y.C., 1950-52; broadcast media buyer Benton & Bowles, Inc., 1952-54, Biow Co., N.Y.C., 1954-55, assoc. account exec., 1955-56; advt. dir. Banking Law Jour., 1955-69; broadcast media buyer Doherty, Clifford, Steers & Shenfield, Inc., N.Y.C., 1956-57, media supr., 1958-59, v.p., media supr., 1960, v.p., assoc. media dir., 1960, v.p., media dir., 1960-63, v.p. in charge media and broadcast programming, 1963-64; v.p., exec. dir. media-program dept. Ted Bates & Co., Inc., 1964-66, sr. v.p., exec. dir. media-program dept., 1966-69; dir. Advt. Info. Services, Inc., 1964-65; founder, pres. Vitt Media Internat., Inc., N.Y.C., 1969-81, chmn., CEO, 1982-91, chmn. emeritus, 1991—. Lectr. in field, 1967—; lectr. advt. media NYU, 1973, 74, Am. Mgmt. Assn., 1974, 75, Assn. Nat. Advertisers, 1967, 69, 70, Advt. Age Media Workshop, 1975. Media columnist Madison Ave, 1963-68; editorial cons. Media/Scope, 1968-69; contbr. Advertising Procedure, 1969, rev. edit., 1973, 5th, 6th, 7th edits., 1977, Exploring Advertising, 1970; contbg. editor Handbook of Advertising Management, 1970; contbg. editor Nation's Bus., Broadcasting, Variety, Anny, TV/Radio Age, Sponsor, Printer's Ink; producer rec. album The Body in the Seine; cover story guest editor Media Decisions, 1967. Chmn. radio-TV reps. divsn. Greater N.Y. Fund, 1962, chmn. consumer pub. divsn., 1963; mem. Nat. UN Day Com., 1973, vice chmn., 1974, assoc. chmn. 1975, co-chmn., 1976-77; bd. dirs. UN Assn. Am., 1977; bd. dirs., chmn. Rsch. Inst. Hearing and Balance Disorders Ltd., 1979—; mem. advt. adv. com. The Acting Com., 1984; mem. Pres. Reagan's Joint Presdl. Congl. Steering Com., 1982, Bush Presdl. Roundtable, 1990—. Served to Lt. (j.g.) USN, 1944-46. Recipient Media awards Sta. WRAP, Norfolk, Va., 1962, award of Merit Greater N.Y. Fund, 1963, Gold Key Advt. Leadership award Sta. Reps. Assn., 1967, ann. honors Ad Daily, 1967, Cert. Merit Media/Scope, 1967, 69, Creative Pub. Statement Concerning Advt. award, Cert. of Appreciation, U.S. Congress, 1993, Rep. Congl. Order Liberty, Nat. Rep. Congl. Com., 1993, Order of Merit, Nat. Rep. Senatorial Com., 1994, Rep. Presdl. award Pres. Ronald Reagan and Rep. Senate Leadership, 1994, (with wife) Rep. Senatorial Medal of Freedom, 1994; (with wife) named one of 10 Best Dressed Men in Advt. Cmty., Gentlemen's Quar., 1979; honoree (with wife) New Rochelle Hosp. Med. Ctr. Centennial Waldorf-Astoria Gala, 1992. Mem. Am. Assn. Advt. Agys. (broadcast media com. dir. corr. 1958-63, media operating com. on consumer mags. 1964-65), Internat. Radio and TV Soc. (time-buying and selling seminar com. dir. 1961-62), Internat. Radio and TV Found. (faculty seminar 1974), Nat. Acad. Arts Sci. (mem. com. dir.), Media Dirs. Coun., Sigma Alpha Epsilon, Manor Park Beach Club, N.Y. Athletic Club, Roxbury Run Club (N.Y., Denver). Presbyterian. Avocations: tennis, skiing, golf, swimming, chess. Home: 1272 W Main St Ste 3 Newark OH 43055-2080

VITTER, DAVID, congressman; b. May 15, 1961; m. Wendy Baldwin; children: Sophie, Lise and Airey (twins). BA magna cum laude, Harvard U.; MA in History/Econs. with highest honors, Oxford U.; JD with honors, Tulane U. Bus. atty., La.; mem. La. Ho. of Reps., 1971-99, U.S. Congress from 1st. dist. La., 1999—, mem. transp. and judiciary com., govt. reform com., 1999—. Adj. prof. law Tulane U., Loyola U., New Orleans. Articles editor Tulane Law Rev. Lecotr, St. Francis Xavier Cath. Ch., Metairie, La. Rhodes scholar. Mem. Phi Beta Kappa. Republican. Office: 414 Cannon House Ofc Bldg Washington DC 20515-0551*

VITTI, ANTHONY MARK, secondary education educator; b. Stamford, Conn., Sept. 6, 1961; s. Anthony Frank and Joanne Marie (Milano) V. BS, Conn. State U., 1984; student, Mt. St. Mary's Sem., Emmitsburg, Md., 1987-89; MS in Instrnl. Leadership, Nat. U., 1996. Cert. tchr. Dir. edn., dir. music Diocese St. Petersburg, Fla., 1984-86; behavior mgmt. specialist Savannah (Ga.) Chattam Schs., 1986—; designated mentor tchr. Poway (Calif.) Unified Schs., 1990—. Poet, songwriter. Coord. March of Dimes, San Diego, 1994—. Named Tchr. of Yr., Poway Unified Schs., 1995. Mem. ASCD, Nat. U. Alumni Assn. (Pres. award 1993), Danbury H.S. Alumni Assn. (George W. Perry award 1978), KC, Elks (scholar 1986). Avocations: weight training, distance biking, cooking, writing poetry. Home: 8375 Entreken Way San Diego CA 92129-4405 Office: Poway Unified Schs 13626 Twin Peaks Rd Poway CA 92064-3034 E-mail: markalonzo@home.com.

VITTONE, BERNARD JOHN, psychiatrist, researcher; b. Latrobe, Pa., Oct. 5, 1951; s. Felix Edward and Jessie (Mosso) V.; children: Matthew, Victoria. BS in Psychology, Georgetown U., 1969-73, DMS, 1973-77. Diplomate Am. Bd. Psychiatry and Neurology. Intern in flexible medicine, then resident in psychiatry St. Vincent's Hosp and Med. Ctr., N.Y.C., 1977-82; resident in ophthalmology Wills Eye Hosp., Phila., 1978-79; staff psychiatrist Phila. State Hosp., 1979; med. staff fellow NIMH, Bethesda, Md., 1982-84; dir. Nat. Ctr. for Treatment of Phobias, Anxiety, and Depression, Washington, 1985—. Cons. Roundhouse Sq. Psychiat. Ctr., Alexandria, Va., 1984-85; guest rschr. NIMH, 1984-93; mem. tng. com. St. Vincent's Hosp. and Med. Ctr., N.Y.C., 1980-81; mem. attending staff Dominion Hosp., 1991-92; mem. faculty Washington Sch. Psychiatry, 1997—; featured expert Nightline, Washington Post, Newsweek, numerous other TV and newspaper pieces. Contbg. author to profl. jours. and books. Mem. instnl. rev. bd. Inst. for Behavior and Health, Rockville, Md., 1988-91; dir. adv. bd. Am. Against Drugs, 1990-94. Recipient Outstanding achievement award in microbiology, Georgetown Univ., 1976; named Top Washington Psychotherapist, Washingtonian mag., 1998. Mem. AMA, Am. Psychiat. Assn., Washington Psychiat. Soc., Anxiety Disorders Assn. of Am., Alpha Omega Alpha. Avocations: tennis, table tennis, billiards, swimming, darts. Office: NCTPAD 2423 Pennsylvania Ave NW Washington DC 20037-1718

VITULLI, WILLIAM FRANCIS, psychology educator, retired; b. Bklyn., July 17, 1936; s. William S. and Sadie Rosaria (Stallone) V.; m. Betty Jean Sheubrooks, June 15, 1961; children: Paige Vitulli Baggett, Quinn Anthony, Sherik Vitulli Butler. BA, U. Miami, 1961, MS, 1963, PhD, 1966. Lic. psychologist, Ala. Grad. asst. U. Miami, Coral Gables, Fla., 1961-65; asst. prof. psychology U. South Ala., Mobile, 1965-69, assoc. prof., 1969-75, prof., 1975-2001, chair sr. faculty caucus, 1999, emeritus prof., 2001—. V.p. Ala. Bd. Examiners in Psychology, Montgomery, 1982-84; rsch. cons. Drug Edn. Coun., Mobile, 1988-94. Mem. editl. bd. Jour. Sport Behavior, 1978—; cons. editor Jour. Genetic Psychology, 1999—; contbr. articles to profl. jours. Mem. adv. bd. Contact Mobile, 1987-92. Named Prof. of Quar., Alpha Lambda Delta, Faculty Mem. of Yr., 1993-94; recipient Outstanding Prof. award Alumni Assn., 1994; named to Golden Key Nat. Honor Soc., 200. Mem. APA, Southeastern Psychol. Assn., Ala. Psychol. Assn. (pres. 1975), Italian-Am. Cultural Soc. South Ala. (chair hist.-cultural com. 1982), Sigma Xi (pres.-elect U. South Ala. chpt. 1996-97), Psi Chi (faculty adviser U. South Ala. chpt. 1972-80, chair sr. faculty caucus U. South Ala. 1999-00). Roman Catholic. Avocations: jogging, athletics research and analysis, fishing. Home: 2025 Maryknoll Ct Mobile AL 36695-3829 E-mail: wvitulli@usouthal.edu.

VITULLO, ANTHONY JOSEPH, communications industry executive; b. Phila., July 18, 1948; s. Gennaro Anthony and Anna Theresa (Lariccia) V.; m. Marlene L. Ciliberti, June 20, 1970; children: Anthony J. Jr., Michael A. BS in Acctg., St. Joseph's U., Phila., 1970, MBA, 1986, postgrad., 2000—. CPA, Pa., N.J. Sr. acct. Laventhol and Horwath, Phila., 1970-73; dir. internal audit Nat. Student Mktg. Corp., Chgo., 1973-75; v.p. fin. Capital Equipment Leasing Corp., Phila., 1975-80, Geriatric and Med. Ctrs. Inc., Phila., 1980-81, Horsham Psychiat. Group Inc., Ambler, Pa., 1981-83; pvt. practice, Medford, N.J., 1983-86; v.p. fin., CFO, Vineland (N.J.) Transit Mix Concrete Co. Inc., 1986-90, Scancem Industries, Inc., Marlton, N.J., 1990-93; v.p., CFO, The Vineland Group, 1993-95; v.p., CFO Audio & Video Labs. Inc. trading as Disc Makers, Pennsauken, 1995-97, CFO, Arcnet, LLC, Holmdel, 1997—. Chmn. parish fin. com. St. Mary of Lakes Ch., Medford, 1983—; pres. Music Boosters, Holy Cross H.S., 1995-97, mem. prin.'s adv. coun., 1995-97; trustee Laurel Creek Condominium Assn., 2000, pres., 2001—. Fellow N.J. Soc. CPAs; mem. AICPA, Pa. Inst. CPAs. Roman Catholic. Avocations: coaching youth, bowling, racquetball, music recording and performance. Office: Arcnet LLC Bldg 2 670 N Beers St Ste 2 Holmdel NJ 07733-1527

VITULLO, B. BENNY, pediatrician, neonatologist, educator; b. Montreal, Que., Can., June 6, 1950; came to U.S., 1992; m. Geri Morris, Aug. 28, 1976; children: Jennifer, Dayna, Marie. BSc, Loyola Coll., 1971; MD, McGill U., 1975. Diplomate Am. Bd. Pediatrics. Intern, resident, then fellow Montreal Children's Hosp., 1975-80; clin. asst. prof. U. Rochester, NY, 1998—; dir. nurseries Parkridge Hosp., 1999—. Fellow Royal Coll. Physicians Can., Am. Acad. Pediat. Avocations: fishing, sailing, train models. Office: Pky Pediat 353 Island Cottage Rd Rochester NY 14612-2308

VITVITSKY, JACK, physician assistant; b. White Plains, N.Y., Mar. 8, 1945; s. Alexander Jack and Helen Louise Virginia (Rider) V. BS, U. Rochester, 1968; AAS, Cuyahoga C.C., Cleve., Ohio, 1978; postgrad., SUNY, Plattsburgh, 1964-66, 73-74, Liberty U., 1994—. Cert. first aid and CPR instr. ARC; cert. EMT instr. N.Y.; cert. ground and flight instr., multi-engine instr., written test examiner FAA. Physician's asst. Planned Parenthood No. N.Y., 1979-84, Dr. David P. Gorman, Malone, N.Y., 1980-81, N.Y. State Dept. Corrections, Dannemora, 1981-84, N.Y. State Office Mental Retardation and Devel. Disabilities, Tupper Lake, 1984-85, N.Y. State Dept. Corrections, Raybrook, NY, 1985—2002; ret., 2002; owner Adirondack Computer Testing Ctr., 1996—; assoc. sales rep. Primerica Fin. Svcs., Plattsburg, NY, 2002—. Contbr. articles to profl. jours. Active Lake Placid Vol. Ambulance Svc., Inc., 1975—, Nat. Ski Patrol System, 1975—; mem. aviation explorer program Boy Scouts Am. With U.S.Army Res., 1981-84, N.Y. Army N.G., 1984—. Mem. Am. Acad. Physician Assts. (cons. minority affairs com. 1999—), N.Y. State Soc. Physician Assts., Soc. Army Physician Assts. (del. to Am. Acad. Physician Assts. Ho. of Dels.), Adirondack Soc. Physician Assts. (sec. 1996—), Mid-Hudson Assn. Physician Assts., Fellowship Christian Physician Assts. (sec. 1992-97), Exptl. Aviation Assn., Aircraft Owners and Pilots Assn., U.S. Army Flight Soc. of Flight Surgeons, NRA, Gun Owners Am. Republican. Avocations: snowshoeing, skiing, writing, woodworking, equine activities. Home: 451 Old Military Rd Lake Placid NY 12946-1824 Office: NY Army NG 147 Warren St Glens Falls NY 12801 also: Adirondack Computer Testing Ctr Adirondack Regional Airport Box 209A Saranac Lake NY 12983

VIVARELLI, DANIEL GEORGE, SR. special education and learning disabilities educator, consultant; b. Vineland, N.J., May 25, 1947; s. Daniel Thomas and Lillian Rachel (Johnson) V.; m. Judith Alice Moses, July 12, 1969; children: Cara Marie, Daniel George Jr. BA in Spl. Edn., Trenton State Coll., 1969; MEd in Learning Disabilities, Glassboro (N.J.) State Coll., 1972, postgrad., 1986. Cert. prin./supr., N.J.; cert. tchr. of handicapped, N.J., learning disabilities tchr./cons., N.J. Tchr. of handicapped Vineland Pub. Schs., 1969-72, learning disabilities tchr., cons., 1972-75, Camden County Tech. Schs., Sicklerville, N.J., 1975—, chmn. child study team, 1978—; Bd. mem. County Tech. Education Cntr. , Cumberland, 2002. Past mem. Vineland Bd. of Edn.; mem. Luth. Ch. of the Redeemer Mem. Collegiate Basketball Ofcls. Assn., Vocat. Indsl. Clubs Am., Home: 114 Sycamore Ln Vineland NJ 08361-2953 Office: Camden County Tech Schs 343 Berlin Cross Keys Rd Sicklerville NJ 08081-4000 E-mail: dvivarelli@ccts.tec.nj.us.

VIVONA, DANIEL NICHOLAS, chemist; b. Chgo., Apr. 13, 1924; s. Daniel and Mary Rose (Lomonico) V.; m. Helen Mary Belanger, Sept. 14, 1950; 1 child, Daniel Maurice. Student, Chgo. City Coll., 1941-42; BA, U. Maine, 1951; MS, Pa. State U., 1953; postgrad., Purdue U., 1953-56. Instr. chemistry Purdue U., Lafayette, Ind., 1955-56; with Minn. Mining and Mfg. Co., St. Paul, 1956-86, sr. chemist, 1969-79, info. scientist, 1979-81, quality assurance sr. chemist, 1981-86, cons., 1986—. With USAAF, 1943-45. Decorated Air medal with oak leaf clusters, DFC. Dow Corning fellow, 1952-53. Mem. Am. Chem. Soc., Phi Beta Kappa. Roman Catholic. Home: 3253 Kraft Cir N Lake Elmo MN 55042-9720 Office: Beta of Dan Vivona PO Box 128 Lake Elmo MN 55042-0128

VIZARD, MICHAEL, periodical editor; Editor PC Week, Computerworld, Digital Review; editor news InfoWorld, 1995-97, v.p. news, 1997, editor-in-chief. Office: InfoWorld Pub 155 Bovet Rd Ste 800 San Mateo CA 94402-3150*

VIZCAINO, HENRY P. mining engineer, consultant; b. Hurley, N.Mex., Aug. 28, 1918; s. Emilio D. and Petra (Perea) V.; m. Esther B. Lopez, Sept. 16, 1941; children: Maria Elena, Rick, Arthur, Carlos. BS in Engring., Nat. U., Mexico City, 1941; geology student, U. N.Mex., 1951-54. Registered profl. engr. With Financiera Minera S.A., Mexico City, 1942-47; gen. mgr. Minas Mexicanas S.A., Torreon, Mex., 1947-51; exploration engr. Kerr McGee Corp., Okla., 1955-69; cons. Albuquerque, 1969-75, 84—; regional geologist Bendix Field Engring., Austin, Tex., 1976-79, staff geo-scientist Grand Junction, Colo., 1979-81; sr. geologist Hunt Oil Co., Dallas, 1981-84. Contbr. articles to profl. publs. Mem. AIME, Internat. Platform Assn., Aircraft Owners and Pilots Assn., Rotary, Elks. Republican. Congregationalist. Address: 12332 Los Arboles Ave NE Albuquerque NM 87112-2079

VIZQUEL, OMAR ENRIQUE, professional baseball player; b. Caracus, Venezuela, Apr. 24, 1967; Grad. high sch., Caracus. With Seattle Mariners, 1989-93; shortstop Cleve. Indians, 1994—. Recipient Winner Am. League Golden Glove, 1993-96. Office: Cleve Indians 2401 Ontario St Cleveland OH 44115-4003*

VIZY, KALMAN NICHOLAS, research physicist, educator; b. Gyor, Hungary, July 7, 1940; came to U.S., 1954, naturalized, 1962; s. Joseph and Helen Julianna (Meleg) V.; m. Mary Anne Smith, Aug. 31, 1968; children: Anne Katharine, Edward Kalman. B Engring. Sci., Cleve. State U., 1964; MS, John Carroll U., 1967; PhD, Walden U., 1990. Registered profl. engr., N.Y. Apprentice design engr. Warner & Swasey, Cleve., 1959-64; tchr., head dept. scis. Byzantine Ednl. Ctr., Parma, Ohio, 1964-67; rsch. physicist Eastman Kodak Rsch. Labs., Rochester, N.Y., 1967-79, corp. tech. and sci. advisor, 1080-91, worldwide tech. lectr., 1980—. Adj. prof. physics Rochester Inst. Tech., 1968—, Roberts Wesleyan Coll., 1993—; adj. asst. prof. radiology U. Rochester Med. Ctr., 1990—. Mem. Rochester-Rennes Sister Cities Com., 1977—. Recipient Excellence in Tchg. award Rochester Inst. Tech., 1980. Mem. ASME, NSPE, Am. Soc. Photogrammetry (cert. photogrammetrist, autometric award 1975), N.Y. State Soc. Profl. Engrs., Am. Assn. Physics Tchr., Am. Assn. Physicists in Medicine, Optical Soc. Am. (house chmn. 1975), Am. Phys. Soc., Soc. Photog. Scientists and Engrs. (inter-soc. rep. 1975-79), Soc. Info. Displays, Am. Coll. Radiology, Rochester Acad. Scis. (v.p. 1993-98), Health Physics Soc. (pres. 1999-00). Achievements include inventions in field. Home and Office: 16 Clearview Dr Spencerport NY 14559-1118

VIZZINI, CAROL REDFIELD, symphony musician, music educator; b. San Diego, Jan. 3, 1946; d. Ernest Sylvester and Eleanor Diana (Soneson) Redfield; m. Edward Tracy Browning (div. 1981); children: Victor, Charlotte; m. Joseph Russell Vizzini, Apr. 12, 1997. MusB, Phila. Musical Acad., 1968. Prin. cellist Somerset Hills Symphony, Basking Ridge, N.J., 1971-81, New Philharm. of N.W. N.J., Morristown, 1978-87; asst. prin. cellist Princeton (N.J.) Chamber Symphony, 1985-95; prin. cellist Orch. St. Peter-by-the-Sea, Point Pleasant, N.J., 1987-92; instr. in cello Westminster Conservatory, Rider U., Princeton, 1987—, head string dept., 1992—. Chamber music coach Vt. Music and Arts Ctr., Lyndonville, 1980-81; coach Greater Princeton Youth Orch., 1989-92; chamber music coach N.J. Youth Symphonies, Summit, 1989—; chamber music count. Westminster Conservatory, 1991-98. Author: Cello Scales, Volume One (One and Two Octave Scales), 1997, Cello Scales, Volume Two (Three and Four Octave Scales), 2000. Mem. Am. String Tchrs. Assn., Am. Fedn. Musicians, Music Tchrs. Nat. Assn. (string coord. 1989-93). Avocations: gardening, fly fishing, travel. Office: Westminster Conservatory of Music Rider Univ 101 Walnut Ln Princeton NJ 08540-3819 E-mail: cjvizzini@earthlink.com.

VLACH, JEFFREY ALLEN, environmental specialist; b. Detroit, May 18, 1953; s. Robert Allen and Virginia Mae (Melton) V.; m. Diane Kay Daugherty, Oct. 27, 1984; children: Elizabeth Daugherty, Meredith Anna. BS, Purdue U., 1975. Environ. specialist D.E. McGillem and Assocs., Inc., Indpls., 1975-80, United Cons. Engrs., Inc., Indpls., 1980-88, Beam, Longest & Neff, LLC, Indpls., 1988—; chief environ. analysis mgr./assoc. Cmty. Transp. Solutions, Inc., Louisville, 1998—. Asbestos bldg. inspector, mgmt. planner EPA, 1989. Conservation coord. Amos Butler chpt. Nat. Audubon Soc., Indpls., 1980-82. Recipient Engring. Excellence Merit award Consulting Engrs. Ind., Inc., 1997; named Eagle Scout Boy Scouts Am., 1969. Mem. ASCE (affiliate), Nat. Wildlife Fedn., Natural Resources Def. Coun., Nat. Assn. Environ. Profls. Office: Beam Longest & Neff LLC 8126 Castleton Rd Indianapolis IN 46250-2099 E-mail: jvlach@b-l-n.com.

VLACH, JIRI, electrical engineering educator, researcher; b. Prague, Czechoslovakia, Oct. 5, 1922; emigrated to Can., 1969; s. Frantisek and Bozena (Papouskova) V.; m. Dagmar Gutova, Oct. 22, 1949; 1 son, Martin. Dipl.eng., Tech. U. Prague, 1947, C.Sc., 1957. With Research Inst. for Radio Communications, Prague, 1948-67, head math. dept., until 1967; vis. prof. U. Ill., Urbana, 1967-69; prof. elec. engring. U. Waterloo (Ont., Can.), 1969—. Author: Computerized Approximation and Synthesis of Linear Networks, 1969, (with others) Computer Methods for Circuit Analysis and Design, 1983, 2nd edit., 1994, Basic Network Theory with Computer Applications, 1992; assoc. editor IEEE Trans. on Circuits and Systems, 1979-80, 87-88, 98—. Fellow IEEE (life); mem. Eta Kappa Nu Home: 355 Craigleith Dr Waterloo ON Canada N2L 5B5 Office: U Waterloo 200 University Ave West Waterloo ON Canada N2L 3G1

VLACHOS, DIONISIOS GERASIMOS, science educator; b. Athens, Greece, July 11, 1964; came to U.S., 1987; s. Gerasimos and Elizabeth Vlachos; m. Menexia N. Tsoubeli, July 8, 1989; children: Mino, Elli. Diploma, Nat. Tech. U. Athens, 1987; MS, U. Minn., 1990, PhD, 1992. Rsch. assoc. Army High Performance Computing Rsch. Ctr., Mpls., 1992-93; asst. prof. U. Mass., Amherst, 1993-98, assoc. prof., 1998-2000; prof. chem. engring. U. Del., Newark, 2000—. Advisor, indsl. cons. U. Mass., Amherst, 1993-99. Young Investigator grantee Office of Naval Rsch., 1996, career grantee NSF, 1997. Mem. AIChE (assoc. mem., sessions organizer 1991-99), Am. Chem. Soc., Combustion Inst., New Eng. Catalysis Soc. (sec. 1995-97). Office: U Del Dept Chem Engring 325 Colburn Lab Newark DE 19716-3110 Fax: 413-545-1647. E-mail: vlachos@che.udel.edu.

VLACHOS, PETER GEORGE, economics educator; b. Apr. 4, 1944; s. George Peter and Thelma Lucille (Ridenour) Vlachos. BA, U. Cin., 1966, MA, 1967, PhD, 1969. Econ. affairs officer UN, Bangkok, 1975; assoc. prof. econs. and quantitative methods U. Hawaii, Honolulu, 1969—83; prof. Shanghai Inst. Internat. Econ. Mgmt., 1984—; staff planner City and County of Honolulu Dept. Gen. Planning, 1986, Hawaii State Dept. Land and Natural Resources, 1987—88; mgr. customer support Chase Manhattan Bank, NY, 1989—90; ind. economist, 1983—. Cons. in field; vis. prof. Waseda U., Tokyo, 1973, Aoyama Gakuin Daigaku, Tokyo, 1977, Xavier U., Cin., 1973, Cin., 77, Roosevelt U., Honolulu, 1986—89, Wright State U., Dayton, 1989—; coord. U.S. Bur. Census, Dayton and Springfield, Ohio, 2000. Editor:

Jour. Readings in Managerial Econs., 1975; contbr. articles to profl. jours. Vol. Atherton br. YMCA, Honolulu, 1971—84; mem. Neighborhood Bd. 8, Neighborhood Commn., 1979—81. Grantee, U. Hawaii, U. Cin., Saudi Arabian Govt. Mem.: NEA, AAUP, Hawaii Edn. Assn., Western Econ. Assn., Am. Econ. Assn. Eastern Orthodox. E-mail: pvlachos45402@yahoo.com.

VLAD, LUIGINA DOROTI, endocrinologist; b. Constanta, Romania, May 10, 1962; came to U.S., 1990; d. Horia and Elena Vlad; m. Sheldon Grodsky, Jan. 31, 1999; 1 child, Philip Grodsky. MD, Inst. Medicine and Pharmacy, Bucharest, 1987. Bd. cert. FLEX; bd. cert. in internal medicine and endocrinology, diabetes, and metabolism. Resident Cmty. Hosp., Constanta, 1987-89, St. Barnabas Med. Ctr., Livingston, N.J., 1993-96; fellow in endocrinology and metabolism SUNY-Downstate, Bklyn., 1996-98; physician Joslin Ctr. for Diabetes, Livinston, 1998—. Recipient Leia Marcovici M.D. Meml. award, 1994-95, Albert N. Siegel M.D. Meml. award, 1995-96; Resident Rsch. scholar, 1994-95, 95-96. Avocations: reading, music. Office: Joslin Ctr for Diabetes 200 S Orange Ave Livingston NJ 07039-5817 E-mail: lvlad@sbhcs.com.

VLADECK, BRUCE CHARNEY, health services administrator, policy educator; b. N.Y.C., Sept. 13, 1949; s. Stephen Charney and Judith (Pomarlen) V.; m. Fredda Wellin, Aug. 5, 1973; children— Elizabeth Charney, Stephen Isaiah, Abigail Sarah. BA, Harvard U., 1970; MA, U. Mich, 1972, PhD in Polit. Sci., 1973. Assoc. social scientist N.Y.C.-Rand Inst., 1973-74; asst. prof. Columbia U., N.Y.C., 1974-78, assoc. prof., 1978-79; asst. commr. health planning and resources devel. N.J. Dept. Health, Trenton, 1979-82; asst. v.p. Robert Wood Johnson Found., Princeton, N.J., 1982-83; pres. United Hosp. Fund, N.Y.C., 1983-93; adminstr. HCFA, Washington, 1993-97; prof. health policy and geriatrics Mt. Sinai Med. Ctr., N.Y.C., 1997—. Sr. v.p. policy Mt. Sinai-N.Y. U. Health, 1998—; mem. N.Y. State Coun. on Health Care Financing, Albany, 1978-92; mem. com. on nursing home regulation Inst. Medicine, Washington, 1983-85, chmn. com. on health care for homeless people, 1986-88, mem. prospective payment assessment com., 1986-93; mem. Nat. Bipartisan Commn. on Future of Medicare, 1997-98. Author: Unloving Care: The Nursing Home Tragedy, 1981. Contbr. numerous articles to profl. publs. Fellow N.Y. Acad. Medicine; mem. Inst. Medicine, Nat. Acad. Scis., Phi Beta Kappa. Home: 1212 5th Ave New York NY 10029-5210 Office: Mt Sinai Med Ctr Box 1062 1 Gustave Levy Pl New York NY 10029 E-mail: bruce.vladeck@mountsinai.org.

VLADEM, PAUL JAY, investment advisor, broker; b. Chgo., Apr. 5, 1952; s. Arthur I. and Elaine A. (Ascher) V.; m. Sondra Joyce Berman, Dec. 27, 1981; children: Ashley Sherree, Evan David. BSBA with honors and high distinction, U. Ill., Chgo., 1974. Lic. brokerage securities, Fla., Ill., Ariz., Conn., Ga., Ind., N.C., Colo., Md., Nev., N.Y., Ohio, Calif., Utah; registered investment advisor; lic. ins. agt., Fla., Ill., Ind., Utah, Conn.; CPA, Fla., Ill.; lic. real estate agt., Fla. In charge acct. Peat Marwick, Fort Lauderdale, Fla., 1974-76; mgr. McGladrey & Pullen, CPA, 1976-85; sr. v.p. fin. Integrated Resources formerly Easter Kramer, Boca Raton, Fla., 1985-89; pres. Associated Investor Svcs., Fort Lauderdale, 1989—. Bd. dirs. Israel Bonds, Ft. Lauderdale, 1994, Jewish Family Svc., Ft. Lauderdale, 1993; chmn. CPA Com. on Israel Bonds, Ft. Lauderdale, 1994, mem. prof. adv. com., 1992—. Named One of Top Ten Brokers of Yr. Registered Rep. Mag., 1994. Mem. AICPA (personal planning divsn.), Fla. Inst. CPAs (mem. personal fin. planning com., 1985), Internat. Platform Assn. Democrat. Jewish. Avocations: tennis, basketball, attending sporting events. Home: 6508 NW 103rd Ln Parkland FL 33076-2934 Office: Associated Investor Svcs 2699 Stirling Rd Ste A200 Fort Lauderdale FL 33312-6583 E-mail: Paul@afc-ais.com.

VLADUTIU, ADRIAN O. clinical pathologist, pathology educator; b. Bucharest, Romania, Aug. 5, 1940; came to U.S., 1969, naturalized 1974; s. Octavian and Veturia (Chirescu) V.; m. Georgirene D. Therrien; children: Christina Lynn, Catherine Joy. MD, Sch. Medicine, Bucharest, 1962; PhD, Sch. Medicine, Jassy, Romania, 1968. Diplomate Am. Bd. Pathology. Asst. prof. physiopathology Sch. Medicine, Bucharest, 1968-71; assoc. prof. pathology SUNY Sch. Medicine, Buffalo, 1978-81, prof. pathology, 1981—; pathologist Buffalo Gen. Hosp., 1974—, dir. clin. labs., 1982—, prof. microbiology, 1982—, prof. medicine, 1985—. Cons. Niagara Falls (N.Y.) Meml. Hosp., 1976-82, Tri-County Hosp., Gowanda, N.Y., 1991-93; acting head dept. pathology Buffalo Gen. Hosp., 1985-86. Contbr. articles to profl. jours., chapters to books. Med. Rsch. Coun. Can. fellow, 1968, Buswell fellow, 1969; recipient rsch. award NIH, 1985. Fellow: ACP, Nat. Acad. Clin. Biochemistry, Coll. Am. Pathologists; mem.: Am. Soc. Investigative Pathology, Am. Soc. Immunologists. Achievements include first demonstration of the association of autoimmunity with major histocompability antigens. Home: 80 Oakview Dr Buffalo NY 14221-1420

VLAOVIC, MILAN STEPHEN, pathologist; b. Novi Sad, Yugoslavia, Feb. 1, 1936; came to U.S., 1970; s. Stevan and Olga (Kantardzic) V.; m. Sharon Helen Rabatich, July 24, 1969; children: Stevan Alexander, Sofija Ann, Peter Michael. DVM, U. Belgrade, Yugoslavia, 1961; MS, U. Sask., Saskatoon, Can., 1970; postgrad., Wash. State U., 1970-71; PhD, U. Mo., 1974. Veterinarian Prosina, Beli Manastir, Yugoslavia, 1961-63; head technologist Banatski Karlovac (Yugoslavia) Meat Plant, 1963-65; pvt. practice vet. medicine various cities, Fed. Republic Germany, 1965-67; insp. various meat plants, Winnipeg, Man., Can., 1967-68; mgr. Frederick (Md.) Cancer Rsch. Ctr., 1974-77; toxicologic pathologist Indsl. Bio-Test, Decatur, Ill., 1977-78; mgr. toxicology support Eastman Kodak Co., Rochester, N.Y., 1978-97; cons. in toxicology and pathology, 1997—. Mem. Soc. Toxicologic Pathologists, Soc. Vet. Immunologists. Serbian Orthodox. Avocation: tennis. Home: PO Box 1129 Charles Town WV 25414-7129

VLASAK, WALTER RAYMOND, state official, human resource manager; b. Hartsgrove, Ohio, Aug. 31, 1938; s. Raymond Frank and Ethel (Chilan) V.; m. Julia Andrews, Feb. 25, 1966; children: Marc Andrew, Tanya Ethel. BSBA, Kent State U., 1963; MA, U. Akron, 1975. Commd. 2d lt. U.S. Army, 1963; platoon leader, anti-tank platoon leader and battalion adjutant 82d Airborne Div., 1963-65; combat duty Viet Nam, 1965-66, 68-69; exec. officer, co. comdr. and hdqrs. commandant of the cadre and troops U.S. Army Sch. Europe, Oberammergau, Fed. Republic Germany, 1966-68; asst. prof. Mil. Sci. Kent (Ohio) State U., 1970-74; infantry battalion exec. officer 9th Infantry Div., Ft. Lewis, Wash., 1976-77, orgnl. effectiveness cons. to commanding gen., 1977-79, brigade exec. officer, 1980-82; orgnl. effectiveness cons. to commanding gen. 8th U.S. Army, U.S. Forces, Korea, 1979-80; advanced through ranks to lt. col. U.S. Army, 1980, ret., 1984; pres. Comsult, Inc., Tacoma, 1984—; mgr. employee devel. tng. dept. social and health svcs. State of Wash., 1985—. Decorated Legion of Merit, Bronze Star with V device and two oak leaf clusters, Air medal, Purple Heart, Vietnamese Cross of Gallantry with Silver Star. Mem. Am. Soc. for Tng. and Devel., Assn. U.S. Army (bd. dirs. Tacoma 1984—). Avocations: hiking, camping, fishing. Home: 10602 Hill Terrace Rd SW Tacoma WA 98498-4337 Office: State Wash Dept Social & Health Svcs 8425 27th St W Tacoma WA 98466-2722 E-mail: wrvlasak@qwest.net.

VLAVIANOS, JOHN G. retired federal agency administrator; b. Athens, Greece, Oct. 10, 1933; came to U.S., 1951; s. George and Maria (Rudolph) V.; m. Lina T. Skucas. Bachelor Mech. Engring., NYU, 1956. Marine applications engr. Worthington Pump Co., Inc., Harrison, N.J., 1956-60; supt. engr. Hellenic Lines, Ltd., N.Y.C., 1960-63; sr. supr. planning dept., electric boat div. Gen. Dynamics Corp., Groton, Conn., 1963-68; mgr., European marine div. Worthington Pump Co., Inc., Hamburg, Germany, 1968-72, v.p., Europe, Africa, Middle East London, 1972-77; v.p. internat. Balt. Aircoil Co., Inc., Jessup, Md., 1977-80; dir. exports devel. office U.S. Dept. Commerce, Washington, 1980-86, dir. trade events div., 1986-91, U.S. and fgn. comml. svc. dir. ops. western hemisphere, 1991-95, dir. ops. East Asia/Pacific, 1995-97; ret., 1997. Avocations: sailing, photography, swimming, travel. Home: 478 Old Orchard Cir Millersville MD 21108-2009 E-mail: vlavianos@usa.net.

VLCEK, DONALD JOSEPH, JR. food distribution company executive, consultant, business author, executive coach; b. Chgo., Oct. 30, 1949; s. Donald Joseph and Rosemarie (Krizek) V.; m. Claudia Germain Meyer, July 22, 1978 (div. 1983); 1 child, Suzanne Mae; m. Valeria Olive Russell, Nov. 11, 1989; children: James Donald, Victoria Rose. BBA, U. Mich., 1971. Cert. facilitator Adires Inst. Gen. mgr. Popps, Inc., Hamtramck, Mich., 1969-76; pres. Domino's Pizza Distbn. Corp., Ann Arbor, 1978-93, chmn., 1993-94, also bd. dirs.; pres. Don Vlcek & Assocs., Ltd., Plymouth, 1994—; CEO Beaver Buddies, LLC; master franchisee Beaver Tails Can., Inc., Mich., Ind., Ill., Ohio, Wis. Profl. speaker, personal coach, seminar leader, bus. cons., workshop facilitator; trustee Domino's Pizza Ptnrs. Found.; bd. dirs. RPM Pizza Inc., Gulfport, Miss., Dimango Corp., South Lyon, Mich.; sr. v.p. distbn. and tech. Domino's Ohio Commissary, Zanesville; pres. Morel Mountain Corp.; judge 1994 Duck Stamp contest U.S. Dept. Interior, Jr. Fed. Duck Stamp Contest, 1995; bd. dirs. Beaver Tails Can. Author: The Domino Effect, 1992 (Best of Bus. award ALA 1992, Soundview's Top 30 Business books of 1993), SuperVision, 1997, Job Planning and Review System Manual, 1997, 2001; (audio cassette tape series Super Vision; contbr. articles to profl. jours. Bd. dirs. Men's Hockey League of Oak Park, Mich., 1973-78; asst. coach Redford Scorpions Jr. Travel Hockey Team. Named Person of Yr. Bd. Franchises, Boston, 1981; recipient Teal award Ducks Unltd., 1992, State Major Gifts Chmn. award, 1992, 93, State Chmn.'s award, 1992, State Major Gifts award, 1994. Mem. Am. Soc. of Tng. Dirs., Mich. Steelheaders Assn. (life), Ducks Unltd. (life, Domino's Pizza chpt. treas., sponsor, chmn. 1988—, Mich. state bd. dirs., life sponsor, chmn. 1989, 91-92, state trustee 1992-98, hon. trustee 2001—, chmn. exec. com. 1992-94, major gifts chmn. 1993-98, chmn. strategic devel. com. 1994, sponsor in perpetuity Grand Slam Life, Heritage sponsor), Mich. United Conservation Club (life), Whitetails Unltd. (life), Pheasants Forever (life), Midstates Masters Bowling Assn. (bd. dirs. 1976-85), Barton Hills Country Club (golf com., capt. dist. team), U. Mich. Alumni Assn. (life), Domino's Lodge/Drummond Island Wildlife Habitat Found. (pres., chmn. bd.), Vlcek Family Wildlife Found. (pres., chmn. bd.), Elks (life), Die Hard Cubs Fan Club, Greater Detroit C. of C., Profl. Spkrs. Assn. of Mich. (bd. dirs. 1997-99), Mich. Soc. Assn. Execs., Sm. Bus. Assn. Mich., Nat. Spkrs. Assn., Profl. Spkrs. Ill. (profl.), Internat. Coaching Fedn. (cert. master), Am. Soc. Tng. Dirs. Republican. Roman Catholic. Avocations: hunting, fishing, hockey, collecting wildlife art, coins, and sports cards and memorabilia. Home: 9251 Beck Rd N Plymouth MI 48170-3336 Office: Don Vlcek & Assoc Ltd PO Box 701353 Plymouth MI 48170-0963

VLECK, KAREN L. radiologist; b. Balt., Feb. 28, 1950; d. Fred Charles Vleck and Norma Louise Ledbetter; m. Charles Wayne Maloney, Apr. 29, 1972 (div. June 1981). BFA, Va. Commonwealth U., 1972. Cert. radiation therapist Md., 1991, RTT Md., 1992. Radiation therapist Equimed, Balt., 1992—94, Radamerica, Balt., 1997—99, Johns Hopkins Hosp., Balt., 2001—. Childrens books. Grantee Senatorial grant, State Senator, 1990—92. Mem.: DAR, Am. Soc. Radiologic Techs. Achievements include patents for on toothfairy pillows; on bookties. Avocations: seamstress, candy maker, gardener. Home: 5 Glendorian Ct Cockeysville MD 21030-2407

VLIET, ANDREW J. science organization executive; b. Honolulu, Oct. 4, 1964; s. Andrew J. and Charlotte M. Vliet; m. Ingrid M. Nicholson, Sept. 17, 1987; 1 child, Naomi. BSc, U. Mont., 1986; PhD, U. Oxford, Eng., 1989. Commd. 2d lt U.S. Army, 1986-95, advanced through grades to maj., 1995; program mgr. USAR, Ft. Bliss, Tex., 1995-99, dir. plans and programs analysis, 1996-99; sr. biologist GeoMarine, Inc., El Paso, 1995; program mgr. Sci. Applications Internat. Corp., Carson City, Nev., 1999—. Maj. U.S. Army, 1986-95. Office: Sci Applications Internat Corp 111 W Telegraph St Ste 100 Carson City NV 89703

VLODAVER, ZEEV A. cardiologist; b. Lomas de Zamora, Argentina; came to U.s., 1970; s. Marcos Vlodaver and Dora Weledniger; m. Dalia Puterman, July 3, 1962; children: Aner, Sagit, Royee. MD, Buenos Aires U., 1956. Fellow in cardiology Tel Aviv U., 1969; sr. rsch. assoc. cardiolovasc. pathology rsch. United Hosp., St. Paul, 1970-80; med. dir. non invasive cardiology Unity Hosp., Fridley, Minn., 1977—; clin. assoc. prof. U. Minn., Mpls., 1982—. Author: Coronary Art in Congenital Heart, 1975, Coronary Heart Disease, 1976; contbr. ; chief editor: Med. Jour. of Allina, 1992—99 (Clarion award, 92). Fellow Am. Coll. Cardiology, Am. Heart Assn. Avocations: jogging, travel, archeology, classical music. Home: 6 Edgcumbe Pl Saint Paul MN 55116-2308 Office: Unity Hosp-Allina 650 Osborne Rd NE Fridley MN 55432-2762

VO, EVANLY, physicist; b. Quang Ngai, Ctrl., Vietnam, Nov. 15, 1965; parents Kim Vo and Quy Thi Nguyen; m. Quynh-Giao Thi Nguyen, May 23, 1998; 1 child, Jennifer Nguyen Vo. BS, U. New Orleans, 1993; PhD, U. Houston, 1997. Tchg. asst. U. Houston, 1994-95, rsch. asst., 1995-97; postdoc. scientist U. Calif., Riverside, 1998; rsch. chemist Nat. Inst. Occupl. Safety and Health, Morgantown, W.Va., 1998—2002, phys. scientist Pitts., 2002—. Contbr. articles to profl. jours. Recipient tchg. asistantship award U. Houston, 1994-95. Mem. ACS, Golden Key, Phi Kappa Phi, Alpah Theta Epsilon. Avocations: tennis, soccer. Home: 8346 Neff St Houston TX 77036 Office: CDC/NIOSH/DSR/PTB Mailstop G800 1095 Willowdale Rd Morgantown WV 26505 Fax: (304) 285-6047. E-mail: eav8@cdc.gov.

VO, HIEU N. intern architect; b. Cantho City, Cantho, Vietnam, June 2, 1963; s. Tan T. Vo, Tiet L. Lam; m. Hanh T. none. AA, L.A. Pierce Coll., 1994; BArch (hon.) , Calif. State Poly. U., 1998. Project mgr. Underwood Assocs. Architects, Decatur, Ala., 1998—99, L. Hughes Assoc. Architects, Huntsville, 2000—. Named to The Talent Roster for Disting. Acad. Performance, The Coll. Bd.s Coll. Scholarship Svc., 1993; recipient Concour d'Elegance, Calif. State Poly. U. Coll. of Environ. Design, 1998. Mem.: AIA (assoc.), Golden Key (life; California State Polytechic University, Pomona, Outstanding Achievement Scholastic and Excellent 1997). Home: 429 Barrington Hills Dr Madison AL 35758 Personal E-mail: HVO24@aol.com.

VO, HUU DINH, pediatrician, educator; b. Hue, Vietnam, Apr. 29, 1950; came to U.S., 1975; s. Chanh Dinh and Dong Thi (Pham) V.; children: Katherine Hoa-An, Karyn Bao-An. MD, U. Saigon, 1975. Diplomate Am. Bd. Pediat. Adminstr. bilingual vocat. tng. Cmty. Care and Devel. Svc., L.A., 1976-77; resident in pediat. Univ. Hosp., Jacksonville, Fla., 1977-80; physician, surgeon, chief med. officer Lanterman Devel. Ctr., Pomona, Calif., 1980-92, chief med. staff, 1984-88, coord. med. ancillary svc., 1984-88, 91—; physician Pomona Valley Cmty. Hosp., 1988-90; asst. clin. prof. Loma Linda (Calif.) Med. Sch., 1985-92; chief med. officer So. Reception Ctr. and Clinic., Norwalk, Calif., 1992-98; physician, surgeon F.C. Nelles Youth Facility, 1998—. Bd. dirs. Pomona Med. Clinic Inc. Radio talk show host (weekly), 1997—. Pres. Vietnamese Cmty. Pomona Valley, 1983-85, 87-95, 99—, chmn., 1993-95; nat. co-chair mem. Vietnamese Am. Cmty. in U.S.A., 1993-95, chmn., bd. comptrollers, 1998—; bd. dirs. YMCA, Pomona, 1988-92, Sch.-Cmty. Partnership, Ponoma, 1988-92, ARC-Pomona chpt., 1995—. Mem. AMA (Physician recognition award 1989, 1992, 98), L.A. Pediat. Soc., Vietnamese-Am. Physicians Assn. La. and Orange County (founding mem., sec. 1982-84, bd. dirs. 1987-90). Republican. Buddhist. Avocations: tennis, soccer, reading, singing, music. Home: 23690 Ridgecrest Ct Diamond Bar CA 91765 Office: Pomona Med Clinic 1182 E 40th Ave Pomona CA 91767 E-mail: drhuuvo@hotmail.com.

VO, NGHIA VAN, materials scientist, electrical engineer; b. Saigon, Vietnam, July 18, 1969; arrived in United States, 1997; s. Nga Van Vo and Hoa Thi Do. BSc in Computer Sci. and Applied Math., U. Adelaide, Australia, 1992, BEE, 1993, BSc in Exptl. Physics with honors, 1994; PhD in Materials Engring., U. Wollongong, NSW, Australia, 1997. Solid state devices engr. CSIRO, Australia Telescope Nat. Facility, Marsfield, NSW, 1991-92; radio astronomer U. Adelaide, 1993-94; sr. advisor, mentor Wegrona Coll., Wollongong, 1994-96; materials rschr. inst. Materials Tech. and Mfg., 1994-97; rsch. scientist, fellow Los Alamos (N.Mex.) Nat. Lab., 1997-98; materials scientist Intermagnetics Gen. Corp., Schenectady, NY, 1998—2001; lead engr. Gen. Electric Power Sys., 2001—. Referee Philos. Mag. B, 1997—, Jour. Superconductivity, 1997—, Jour. Materials Rsch., 1997—, Superconductor Sci. and Tech., 1997—. Contbr. numerous articles to profl. jours. Rsch. fellow Los Alamos Nat. Lab., 1997, NRIM Japan, 1997. Mem. IEEE, AIME, Materials Rsch. Soc. Avocations: classical guitar, swimming, music, reading, martial arts.

VOCE, JOAN A. CIFONELLI, retired elementary school educator; b. Utica, N.Y., Mar. 22, 1936; d. Albert and Theresa (Buono) Cifonelli; m. Eugene R. Voce Sr., Aug. 16, 1958; children: Eugene R. Jr., Lisa V. Stewart, Mark L., Daniel A. BS in Elem. Edn., Coll. St. Rose, Albany, N.Y., 1958; MS in Elem. Edn., SUNY, Cortland, 1981. Elem. tchr. Utica (N.Y.) Pub. Schs., 1958-59, 61-62, 64-67; tchr. Deerfield Elem. Sch., Whitesboro (N.Y.) Ctrl. Sch. Dist., Utica, 1968-91. Active YWCA. Mem. AAUW (Mohawk Valley br.), N.Y. State United Tchrs., Whitesboro Ret. Tchrs. Assn., Am. Italian Heritage Assn., Am. Assn. Ret. Persons, Oneida County Ret. Tchrs. Assn. (sec.), N.Y. State Ret. Tchrs. Assn., Coll. of St. Rose Alumni Assn., Utica Symphony League, Mohawk Valley Performing Arts, Pelican Bay Country Club (Daytona Beach, Fla.), Skenandoa Golf and Country Club (Clinton, NY), Alpha Delta Kappa (v.p. 1974-76, pres. 1976-78, corr. sec. 1972-74, rec. sec. 1986-88, 90-91). Avocations: reading, travel, golf, gourmet cooking, theatre. Home: 314B Clinton St Whitesboro NY 13492-2517 also: 201 Surf Scooter Dr Daytona Beach FL 32119 E-mail: jgvoce@webtv.net.

VOCHT, MICHELLE ELISE, lawyer; b. Detroit, Sept. 27, 1956; BA with honors, U. Mich., 1978; JD, Wayne State U., 1981. Bar: Mich., U.S. Dist. Ct. (ea. and we. dist.) Mich., U.S. Ct. Appeals (6th cir.), 1981. V.p., treas. Roy, Shecter & Vocht PC, Detroit, Bloomfield Hills, Mich., 1981—. Pro bono teaching faculty Detroit chpt. Fed. Bar Assn.; mediator Mediation Tribunal Wayne County Cir. Ct., 1989—; pre-sentencing probation officer 48th Dist. Ct., 1989-90. Mem. com. for re-election Mich. Supreme Ct. Justice, 1986; mem. Rep. Assembly, Oak County, 1992-99—; exec. bd. Birmingham Women's Community Ctr., 1987-88; bd. dir. Community Adv. Bd.-Arbor Clin. Group, Inc., 1989-91; mem. drug and alcohol abuse spl. task force County of Oakland, 1989-90. Mem.: ATLA, Internat. Platform Assn., Oakland Trial Lawyers Assn. (bd. dirs. 1982—84, 1988—, sec. 1990—, v.p. 1991—92, pres. 1992—95), Mich. Employment Law Assn., State Bar Assn. Mich. (sec. 1982—83, hearing and panelist atty. discipline bd. 1982—, state ct. adminstrn. commn. 1996—), Am. Inns of Ct. (barrister 1984—87), Indsl. Rels. Rsch. Assn., USTA (sect. umpire 2000—, sect. referee 2001—). Roman Catholic. Avocations: hiking, history, humanities, sciences, tennis. Home: 901 N Adams Rd Birmingham MI 48009-5646 Office: Roy Shecter & Vocht PC 36700 Woodward Ave Ste 205 Bloomfield Hills MI 48304-0930 E-mail: vocht@rsmv.com.

VODRA, RICHARD EARLE, financial planner; b. Portland, Oreg., Mar. 12, 1948; s. Victor H. and Marjorie W. Vodra. BA, Coll. of Wooster, 1969; JD, Yale U., 1972. CFP. Assoc. nat. dir. Cystic Fibrosis Found., Rockville, Md., 1978-84; spl. expert Nat. Heart, Lung and Blood Inst., Bethesda, 1984-85; fin. planner Fin. Svc. Group, Vienna, 1985-87, Mason Assocs., Herndon, 1987-92, Acacia Group, Fairfax, 1992-97, Legacy Advisors, McLean, 1997—. Author: Health/Medicine Legislation: How It Works, 1980, Enough Money, 2001; contbr. articles to profl. publs. Mem. Fin. Planning Assn. (nat. capital chpt. pres. 1997), Nazrudin Project. Home: 6827 Montivideo Square Ct Falls Church VA 22043-1657 E-mail: rvodra@legacy-advisors.com.

VODYANOY, VITALY JACOB, biophysicist, educator; b. Kiev, Ukraine, USSR, June 2, 1941; came to U.S., 1979; s. Jacob and Vera (Reznik) V.; m. Galina Rubin, Apr. 22, 1967; 1 child, Valerie. MS in Physics, Moscow Physical Engring. Inst., 1964; PhD in Biophysics, Agrophysical Rsch. Inst., Leningrad, USSR, 1973. Asst. prof. Inst. of Semiconductors, Leningrad, USSR, 1965-72; assoc. prof. A.F. Ioffe Physicotech. U., 1972-78; sr. rsch. scientist NYU, 1979-82; rsch. assoc. U. Calif., Irvine, 1982-89; assoc. prof. Auburn (Ala.) U., 1989-93, prof., 1993—. Ad hoc reviewer NSF, Washington, 1985—; dir. Biosensor Lab. of Inst. for Biol. Detection Sys. Author: (with others) Membrane Biophysics, 1971, Physics of Solid State and Neutron Scattering, 1974, Receptors Events and Transduction Mechanisms in Taste and Olfaction, 1989, Molecular Electronics: Biosensors and Biocomputers, 1989, Central Nervous System Neurotransmitters and Neuromodulators, 1994; contbr. more than 70 articles to profl. jours.; inventor device for film deposition, methods for forming monolayers. Grantee NSF-U. Calif., 1982-85, 85-88, U.S. Army Rsch. Office, 1985-88, U. Calif., 1986-88, 88-92, U. Calif., FAA, 1993-97, 2001-04, Battelle, 1997-2000, NSF, 1998-2000, Auburn U., DARPA, 2000—, TSWG, 2002—, others. Mem. AAAS, Am. Phys. Soc., Biophys. Soc., Fedn. Am. Socs. for Exptl. Biology, Phi Beta Delta, Phi Zeta. Republican. Jewish. Avocation: medical herbs. Home: 541 Summertrees Dr Auburn AL 36832-6766 Office: Auburn U Coll of Vet Medicine 212 Greene Hall Auburn AL 36849-6121 E-mail: vodyavi@vetmed.auburn.edu.

VOEGELI, VICTOR JACQUE, history educator, dean; b. Jackson, Tenn., Dec. 21, 1934; s. Victor Jacque Voegeli and Winnie (Lassiter) Voegele; m. Anna Jean King, Oct. 14, 1956; children: Victor Jacque, Charles Lassiter. BS, Murray State Coll., 1956; MA, Tulane U., 1961, PhD, 1965. Instr. history Tulane U., 1963-65, asst. prof., 1965-67; asst. prof. history Vanderbilt U., 1967-69, assoc. prof., 1969-73, prof. history, 1973-98, chmn. history dept., 1973-76, dean Coll. Arts and Sci., 1976-92, acting dean Coll. Arts and Sci., 1996-97, prof. emeritus, dean, 1998—. Author: Free But Not Equal: The Midwest and the Negro During the Civil War, 1967. Served with U.S. Army, 1956-58. Nat. Endowment Humanities grantee, 1969-70, 72 Mem. So. Hist. Assn. Address: 2110 Golf Club Ln Nashville TN 37215-1224

VOELKER, ESTELLE ROSE, software engineer, educator; b. Bozeman, Mont., July 20, 1936; d. Stanley Walter and Dorothy May (Bennette) V.; m. LaVerne A. Neuharth, Oct. 6, 1956 (div. Nov. 1965); 1 child, Paul Stanley; m. Robert J. Grove, Apr. 5, 1975 (div. Oct. 1984); m. Edgar J. Spencer, May 19, 1990 (dec. July 1998). BS in Math., N.D. State U., 1964. Tchr. math. Crookston (Minn.) Pub. Sch., 1964-65; software engr. Gen. Dynamics, San Diego, 1967-91. Democrat.

VOELKER, JOSEPH L. neurosurgeon; b. Sept. 11, 1955; AB, Ind. U., Bloomington, 1977; MD, Ind. U., Indpls., 1981. Resident in neurosurgery Ind. U. Sch. Medicine, Indpls., 1982-88; fellow in vascular neurosurgery U. Western Ont., London, Can., 1990-91; asst. prof. neurosurgery W.Va. U. Sch. Medicine, Morgantown, 1991-98, assoc. prof. neurosurgery, 1998—. Contbr. chpts. to books. Bd. dirs. head injury edn. program Think First of W.Va., Morgantown, 1993—. Office: W Va U Sch Medicine Dept Neurosurgery Morgantown WV 26506

VOELKER, MARGARET IRENE (MEG VOELKER), gerontology, medical, surgical nurse; b. Bitburg, Germany, Dec. 31, 1955; d. Lewis R. and Patricia Irene (Schaffner) Miller; 1 child, Christopher Douglas. Med. Office Asst., Clover Park Vocat.-Tech., Tacoma, Wash., 1975, diploma in practical nursing, 1984; ASN, Tacoma C.C., 1988; BSN, U. Wash., Tacoma, 1995. Cert. ACLS, PALS. Nursing asst. Jackson County Hosp., Altus, Okla., 1976-77; receptionist Western Clinic, Tacoma, 1983; LPN, Tacoma Gen. Hosp., 1984-88, clin. geriatric nurse, 1988-90, clin. nurse post anesthesia care unit perioperative svcs., 1990—, pre-admit clinic nurse, 1995—96, mem. staff nurse coun., 1990-91, procedural sedation nurse, 1996—99, mem. clin. practice coun., 1998-99, interventional radiology nurse, 1999—2000, conscious sedation/staff nurse PACU, 2000—01; head nurse gen. surgery clinic, assoc. investigator Madigan Army Med. Ctr., Ft. Lewis, Wash., 2001—. Editor NPANA newsletter, 1997-99. Recipient G. Corydon Wagner endowment fund scholarship. Mem. Am. Soc. PeriAnesthesia Nurses, N.W. PeriAnesthesia Nurses Assn., U. Wash. Alumni Assn. (life), Phi Theta Kappa, Sigma Theta Tau. E-mail: Braunys@aol.com.

VOELL, RICHARD ALLEN, retired private investor; b. Chgo., Dec. 29, 1933; s. John Herman and Esther Frances (Anderson) V.; m. Virginia Charlotte Broderick, Dec. 20, 1958; children: David Broderick, Gregory Jon, Jeffrey Scott. BA, U. Ill., 1956; MBA, U. Hawaii, 1960. With Beatrice Foods Co., Chgo., 1958-79, group mgr. recreational products group, 1971-73, corp. v.p., 1973-75, vice chmn., 1975-79; pres., chief operating officer Penn Central Corp., Greenwich, Conn., 1979-81, chief exec. officer, 1981; pres., chief exec. officer The Rockefeller Group, N.Y.C., 1982-95. Chmn. Harbor Rock Corp.; mem. adv. bds. Fiat and Club Med; mem. bds. SPA Exor and Con Edison; vice chmn. N.Y.C. Partnerships. Chair nominating com. Wildlife Conservation Soc.; chmn. Bus. Coun. for UN, 1982-97; mem. adv. bd. Ctr. for Sustainable Fisheries—Rosentiel Sch. Marine and Atmospheric Sci. 1st lt. AUS, 1956-58. Mem. UN Assn. (vice chmn.), Chief Execs. Orgn., Coun. on Fgn. Rels., Econ. Club N.Y. (past chmn.), Rockefeller Ctr. Club, Greenwich (Conn.) Country Club, Riverside (Conn.) Yacht Club, Chgo. Club, U. Ill. Founders Club. E-mail: pigoose@aol.com.

VOELLER, JOHN GEORGE, engineer; b. Denver; s. John George and Catherine Eunice V.; m. Sheila Kay Voeller, Oct. 19, 1951. BME, Ga. Tech. U., 1971. Registered profl. engr., Kans., Mich. Field engr. Westinghouse, N.Y.C., 1971-73, start-up engr. Atlanta, 1973-74; nuclear stree engr. Black and Veatch, Kansas City, Mo., 1974-77, dir. engring. info. tech., 1977-88, ptnr. in charge of info. tech., 1989-94, chief tech. officer, 1994-95, chief knowledge officer, chief tech. officer, 1997—. Bd. dirs. e-Builder, Boca Raton, Fla., Design Build Ptnrs., N.Y.C., CERF; adv. bd. CII, Austin, Tex. Author: (3 vol. set) I.T. User Survival Guide, 1986-94; patentee in field. Recipient Enterprise Value award CIO Mag., 1997, Ed Forrest award AEC Systems Conv., 1999. Mem. AAAI, AAAS, ACM, IEEE Computer Soc. Avocations: astronomy, die cast, music, exotic car history, robotics. Office: Black and Veatch 11401 Lamar Overland Park KS 66211

VOELLER, NANCY DARLENE, secondary school educator; b. Rapid City , S.D., Aug. 10, 1973; d. William John and Bonnie Jo Simpson; m. Scott Alan Voeller; children: John. BS in Edn., No. State U., 1999. Cert. tchr. S.D. Author poetry. Mem.: Internat. Soc. Poets (life).

VOELLGER, GARY A. business consulting executive, retired air force officer; BS in Indsl. Rels. Pers. Mgmt., San Jose State U., 1967; grad., Squadron Officer Sch., 1971; M in Psychology, Peperdine U., 1976; grad., Air Command Staff Coll., Maxwell AFB, 1979, Air War Coll., 1988; cert. in Joint Flag Officer War Fighting, Maxwell AFB, 1997; cert.in sr. mgrs. govt. seminar, Harvard U., 1997. Commd. 2d. lt. USAF, 1967, advanced through grades to maj. gen., 1996; pers. officer 379th Combat Support Grp., Wurtsmith AFB, Mich., 1967-69; undergrad. navigator trng. Mather AFB, Calif., 1969-69; weapons sys. officer 46th Tactical Fighter Squadron, MacDill AFB, Fla., 1970-70; weapons syss. officer 91st Tactical Fighter Squadron, Royal Air Force Bentwaters, Eng., 1970-72; undergrad. pilot tng. Laredo AFB, Tex., 1972; F-111 transition tng. Nellis AFB, Nev., 1973-73; F-111 pilot 428th Tactical Fighter Squadron, Takhli Royal AFB, Thailand, 1973-74; F-111 instr. pilot, flight comdr., standardization and evaluation flight examiner 523rd Tactical Fighter Squadron, 27th Tactical Fighter Wing, Cannon AFB, N.Mex., 1974-79; air ops. staff officer, politico-mil. affairs officer, asst. dep. dir. Joint Nat. Security Coun. Matters Hdqs. USAF, Washington, 1980-84; comdr. 55th Tactical Fighter Squadron, Royal Air Force, Upper Heyford, Eng., 1984-87; asst. dep. comdr. ops. 20th Tactical Fighter Wing; dep. comdr. ops. 4450th Tactical Group, Nellis AFB, Nev., 1988-89, vice comdr., 1989-90; comdr. 552nd Air Control Wing, Tinker AFB, Okla., 1990-92, Coll. Aerospace Doctrine, Rsch. and Edn., Air U., Maxwell AFB, Ala., 1992-93, 43rd Air Refueling Wing, Malmstrom AFB, Mont., 1993-94, 92nd Air Refueling Wing, Fairchild AFB, Wash., 1994-95, 437th Airlift Wing, Charleston AFB, S.C., 1995-96; dir. ops. Hdqs. Air Mobility Command, Scott AFB, Ill., 1996-98; NATO force comdr. Hdqs. NATO Airborne Early Warning Force, Mons, Belgium, 1998-2000; ret. USAF; prin. Booz Allen & Hamilton, O'Fallon, Ill. Decorated D.D.S.M., Legion of Merit with oak leaf Cluster, Bronze Star medal, Meritorious Svc. medal with two oak leaf clusters, Air medal with oak leaf cluster, Armed Forces Expeditionary medal, Rep. Vietnam Gallantry Cross with Palm. Office: Booz Allen & Hamilton Inc 1728 Corporate Crossing O'Fallon IL 62269

VOELTE, DONALD R. energy company executive; b. Omaha, Dec. 17, 1952; s. Donald R. Sr. and Iryl Verlene (Hunter) V.; m. Nancy Alison Keegan, June 30, 1990; 1 child, Kevin. BS in Civil Engring., U. Nebr., 1975; postgrad., U. Houston, 1977-78. Producing mgr. Mobil Exploration & Producing U.S., Inc., Houston, 1987-88, planning mgr. U.S. Dallas, 1988-90; plannng mgr. Mobil Corp., Fairfax, Va., 1990-92, v.p. supply and transp., 1992-94, v.p. U.S. mktg., 1994, pres. producing and exploration ventures, 1994-97; sr. v.p. planning Atlantic Richfield (Arco), L.A., 1997-98, exec. v.p. internat. exploration and producing, 1998-2000; CEO Chroma Energy, Houston, 2001—. Bd. dirs. Rand Corp., Third Wave Ventures, Chroma Energy, F-W Oil Exploration LLC. Mem. ASCE, Am. Soc. Petroleum Engrs. Republican. Avocations: golf, skiing, hunting, painting. Home: 2197 Sheringham Ln Los Angeles CA 90077-1358 Fax: (310) 472-8902. E-mail: dvoelte@aol.com.

VOGE, VICTORIA MAE, occupational medicine physician; b. Mpls., June 27, 1943; d. Donald Oscar and Veryl Shirley (Harms) V.; m. Gerald Ralph Black, Jan. 10, 1976; children: Robert, John, Katherine, Kimberly. BA, U. Minn., 1964; MD, Nat. Autonomous U. of Mex., 1971; MPH, Johns Hopkins U., 1977, Med. Coll. Wis., 1990. Diplomate Am. Bd. Preventive Medicine. Commd. lt. USN, 1972, advanced through grades to comdr., 1981; intern Naval Hosp., Phila., 1972-73; resident Naval Aerospace Med. Inst., Pensacola, Fla., 1975-78; aerospace medicine specialist USN, 1972-96; with occupl. medicine Med. Coll. Wis., Milw., 1986-90; head acceleration physiology Naval Air Devel. Ctr., Warminster, Pa., 1973-76; head aeromed. divsn. Naval Safety Ctr., Norfolk, Va., 1978-81; sr. flight surgeon Naval Hosp., Agana, Guam, 1981-83; chief mil. med., chief occupl. med., chief aviation med. Corpus Christi Naval Hosp., 1984-88; chief flight surgeon Naval Air Devel. Ctr., Warminster, 1988-91; rschr. air crew stds. Armstrong Lab., Brooks AFB, Tex., 1991-96; cons. in occupl. medicine, 1996—; head occupl. medicine Meml. Med. Ctr., Port Lavaca, Tex., 1998—2001; cons. in field. Contbr. articles to profl. jours. Recipient Wiley Post award for aerospace physiology, 1980, Ashton Graybiel award for outstanding contributions to aerospace medicine lit., 1998. Fellow: Aerospace Human Factors Assn., Am. Coll. Occupl. and Environ. Medicine, Am. Coll. Preventive Medicine, Aerospace Medicine Assn., Internat. Acad. Aviation and Space Medicine; mem.: Tex. Med. Assn., So. Med. Assn. Mem. Lds Ch. Avocations: scuba diving, flying, travel. Home: 15068 FM 766 Gonzales TX 78629-9403 E-mail: vmvoge@gvtc.com.

VOGEL, ARTHUR ANTON, clergyman; b. Milw., Feb. 24, 1924; s. Arthur Louis and Gladys Eirene (Larson) V.; m. Katharine Louise Nunn, Dec. 29, 1947; children: John Nunn, Arthur Anton, Katharine Ann. Student, U. of South, 1942-43, Carroll Coll., 1943-44; B.D., Nashotah House Theol. Sem., 1946; MA, U. Chgo., 1948; PhD, Harvard, 1952; S.T.D., Gen. Theol. Sem., 1969; D.C.L., Nashotah House, 1969; D.D., U. of South, 1971. Ordained deacon Episcopal Ch., 1946, priest, 1948; teaching asst. philosophy Harvard, Cambridge, Mass., 1949-50; instr. Trinity Coll., Hartford, Conn., 1950-52; mem. faculty Nashotah House Theol. Sem., Nashotah, Wis., 1952-71, asso. prof., 1954-56, William Adams prof. philosophical and systematic theology, 1956-71, sub-dean Sem., 1964-71; bishop coadjutor Diocese of West Mo., Kansas City, 1971-72, bishop, 1972-89; rector Ch. St. John Chrysostom, Delafield, Wis., 1952-56; dir. Anglican Theol. Rev., Evanston, Ill., 1964-69; mem. Internat. Anglican-Roman Cath. Consultation, 1970-90, Nat. Anglican-Roman Catholic Consultation, 1965-84, Anglican chmn., 1973-84; mem. Standing Commn. on Ecumenical Relations of Episcopal Ch., 1957-79; mem. gen. bd. examining chaplains Episcopal Ch., 1971-72. Del. Episcopal Ch., 4th Assembly World Council Chruches, Uppsala, Sweden, 1968, and others. Author: Reality, Reason and Religion, 1957, The Gift of Grace, 1958, The Christian Person, 1963, The Next Christian Epoch, 1966, Is the Last Supper Finished?, 1968, Body Theology, 1973, The Power of His Resurrection, 1976, Proclamation 2: Easter, 1980, The Jesus Prayer for Today, 1982, I Know God Better Than I Know Myself, 1989, Christ in His Time and Ours, 1982, God, Prayer and Healing, 1995, Radical Christianity and the Flesh of Jesus, 1995; editor: Theology in Anglicanism, 1985; contbr. articles to profl. jours. Vice chmn. bd. dirs. St. Luke's Hosp., Kansas City, Mo., 1971, chmn., 1973-89. Research fellow Harvard, 1950 Mem. Am. Philos. Assn., Metaphys. Soc. Am., Soc. Existential and Phenomenological Philosophy, Catholic Theol. Soc. Am. Home: 524 W 119th Ter Kansas City MO 64145-1043

VOGEL, CARL-WILHELM ERNST, biomedical scientist, clinical pathologist; b. Hamburg, Germany, Mar. 9, 1951; came to U.S., 1979; s. Erich Hermann Walter and Lisbeth Klara (Barbulla) V.; m. Candice G. McMullan, 1989. MD, U. Hamburg (Germany), 1976; diploma in biology, 1980, PhD in Biochemistry, 1986. Diplomate Am. Bd. Pathology; cert. Bd. Lab. Medicine and Bd. Med. Biochemistry (Germany). Predoctoral rsch. fellow Tropical Inst., Hamburg, 1973-75; intern Univ. Hosps., Hamburg and Kiel, Germany, 1976-78; postdoct. rsch. fellow Rsch. Inst. Scripps Clinic, La Jolla, Calif., 1979-82; asst. prof. biochemistry and medicine Georgetown U., Washington, 1982-87, assoc. prof., 1987-91, adj. prof., 1991-99, resident in medicine, pathology, allergy/immunology, 1984-86, 88-89; prof., chmn. dept. biochemistry and molecular biology U. Hamburg, Germany, 1990-99; prof. pathology U. Hawaii John A. Burns Sch. Medicine, Honolulu, 1999—, dir. Cancer Rsch. Ctr., 1999—. Mem. Vincent T. Lombardi Cancer Rsch. Ctr., Washington, 1982-92; mem. Internat. Ctr. for Interdisciplinary Studies of Immunology, Washington, 1982-94, sci. dir., 1987-91; vis. prof. pathology and lab. medicine Ind. U.-Purdue, Indpls., 1996-97; mem. examiner Bd. Lab. Medicine (Germany), 1991-99, Bd. Med. Biochem. (Germany), 1998-99; cons. to biomed. corps. Mem. editl. bd. Jour. Devel. and Comparative Immunology, 1984-96. Recipient Nat. Cancer Inst./NIH Rsch. Career Devel. award; overseas rsch. fellow Studienstiftung des Deutschen Volkes, 1978-79, U.S.A. rsch. fellow Deutsche Forschungsgemeinschaft, 1980-82; NIH rsch. grantee, 1983-94, 99—. Fellow Am. Soc. Clin. Pathology, Coll. Am. Pathologists; mem. AMA, AAAS, Am. Chem. Soc., Gesellschaft Biologische Chemie, Am. Soc. Microbiology, Am. Assn., Immunologists, Am. Soc. Biochemistry and Molecular Biology, Am. Assn. Cancer Rsch., Am. Soc. Clin. Oncology, Am. Soc. Tropical Medicine and Hygiene, Internat. Soc. Devel. and Comparative Immunology, Am. Fedn. Med. Rsch., Gesellschaft Immunologie, Gesellschaft Deutscher Chemiker, Am. Soc. Clin. Investigation, Am. Soc. Investigative Pathology, German Soc. Cell Biology, German Soc. Lab. Medicine, Japanese Biochem. Soc., Australasian Soc. Immunology, Japanese Cancer Assn., German Cancer Soc., European Assn. Cancer Rsch., Hawaii Med. Assn., Sigma Xi. Office: Cancer Rsch Ctr Hawaii 1236 Lauhala St Honolulu HI 96813-2424 Fax: 808-586-3052. E-mail: cvogel@crch.hawaii.edu.

VOGEL, CEDRIC WAKELEE, lawyer; b. Cin., June 4, 1946; s. Cedric and Patricia (Woodruff) V. BA, Yale U., 1968; JD, Harvard U., 1971. Bar: Ohio 1972, Fla. 1973, U.S. Tax Ct. 1972, U.S. Supreme Ct. 1975. Ptnr. Vogel, Heis, Wenstrup & Cameron, Cin., 1972-96; sole practice, 1997—. Bd. dirs. Pro Srs., 1994—. Chmn. mem.'s com. Cin. Art Mus., 1987-88; chmn. auction Cin. Hist. Soc., 1985; local pres. English Speaking Union, 1979-81, nat. bd. dirs., 1981; chmn. Keep Cin. Beautiful, Inc., 1994-96; active Bravo! Cin. Ballet, 1989; chmn. Act II Nutcracker Ball, 1987-88; bd. dirs. Merc Libr., 1991-98; bd. dirs. Cin. Preservation Assn., 1990-93, Cin. Opera Guild, 1997-99; vice chmn. Children's Heart Assn. Reds Rally, 1989; bd. dirs. Cin. Country Day Sch., 1983, pres. Alumni Coun. and Ann. Fund, 1983. Mem. Cin. Bar Assn., Fla. Bar Assn., Harvard Law Sch. Assn. Cin. (pres. 1997-99, Heimlich Inst. (trustee 1987-2001), Yale Alumni Assn. (del. 1984-87), Cin. Yale Club (pres. 1980-81, 96-97), Cincinnatus, The Lawyers Club Cin. (pres. 1995), Harvard Club of Cin. (bd. dirs. 1996-98, pres. 1999-2000). Republican. Home: 2270 Madison Rd Cincinnati OH 45208-2659 Office: 817 Main St Ste 800 Cincinnati OH 45202-2183

VOGEL, DAVID SETH, lawyer; b. N.Y.C., July 11, 1955; s. Joshua Selig and Muriel Rita Vogel; m. Patrice Louise Jaxon; children: Claire, Jack. AB, Amherst Coll., 1973—77; JD magna cum laude, Boston U., 1979—82. Law clerk Hon. Frank M. Johnson, Jr., 11th Circuit Ct. of Appeals, Montgomery, Ala., 1982—83; assoc. Perkins Coie Law Firm, Seattle, 1983—84; dep. prosecutor King County Prosecutor's Office, 1984—89; assoc. Levinson Friedman Law Firm, 1989—92; prin. Law Offices of David S. Vogel, 1992—. Pres. Vashon-Maury Island Cmty. Coun., Vashon Island, Wash., 1986—93, bd. mem., 1985—2000, Vashon Household, Vashon Island, 1996—2002; chair Vashon Town Plan Com., 1992—96. Recipient Cmty. Svc. award, Vashon-Maury Island Audubon Soc., 1994, Pilchuck Audubon Soc., 1997. Mem.: ABA, Wash. Assn. Criminal Defense Lawyers, Brain Injury Assn., Wash. State Trial Lawyers Assn., Assn. of Trial Lawyers of Am., Wash. State Bar Assn., Seattle-King County Bar Assn., WSTLA Eagles. Liberal. Jewish. Avocations: fishing, hiking, camping. Office: Law Offices of David Vogel 2025 First Ave Penthouse Ste A Seattle WA 98121 Office Fax: 206-448-7950. Personal E-mail: dsvogel@earthlink.net.

VOGEL, DONALD STANLEY, gallery executive, artist; b. Oct. 20, 1917; s. Walter Frederick and Francis Osborne (Talmadge) V.; m. Margaret Katherine Mayer, Oct. 14, 1947 (dec. June 1974); children: Eric Stefan, Kevin Eliot, Katherine Barley; m. Erika Kjar Farkac, Oct. 4, 1980. Student, Chgo. Art Inst., 1936. With WPA Easel Project, Chgo., 1940; tech. dir. Dallas Little Theatre, 1942-43; dir. Betty McLean Gallery, Dallas, 1951-54; dir., owner Valley House Gallery, 1954—. Dir., ptnr. Main Place Gallery, Dallas, 1968-70. Author: (with Margaret Mayer) Aunt Clara: The Paintings of Clara McDonald Williamson, 1966, Charcoal and Cadmium Red, 1989, Not for Revenge, 1991, King of the Hill, 1991, Transcendent Collector, 1992, Drawing for Paintings, 1992, The Untold Studio Secret, A Fantasy, 1992, The Boardinghouse, 1995, Prime Targets, 1996, Seeking the Intangible, 1996, (autobiography) Memories and Images, 2000, (short story) I Woke Up Dead, 1999, Once Upon Death, 2000, The Seekers, Retrospective Exhbn. for 5 museums with 120-page catalog; also essays and catalogs. Recipient Dallas Visual Art Ctr. Legend award, 1999. Mem. Art Dealers Assn., Am. Inc. Avocations: travel, swimming. Office: 6616 Spring Valley Rd Dallas TX 75254-8635 E-mail: gallery@valleyhouse.com.

VOGEL, EZRA F. sociology educator; b. Delaware, Ohio, July 11, 1930; s. Joseph H. and Edith (Nachman) V.; m. Suzanne Hall, July 5, 1953 (div.); children: David, Steven, Eva; m. Charlotte Ikels, Nov. 3, 1979. BA, Ohio Wesleyan U., 1950; MA, Bowling Green State U., 1951; PhD, Harvard U., 1958; LittD (hon.), Kwansai Gakuin, 1980, Wittenberg Coll., 1981, Bowling Green State U., 1982, U. Md., 1983, Albion Coll., 1988, Chinese U., Hong Kong, 1992, Ohio Wesleyan, 1996; LittD (hon.) , U. Mass., Lowell, 1996, Yamaguchi U., 1998, Monterrey Inst., 2002. Rsch. fellow Harvard (for work in Japan), 1958-60; asst. prof. Yale U., 1960-61; rsch. assoc., lectr. Harvard U., 1961-67, prof., 1967—, Henry Ford II rsch. prof. social scis., 1990—, assoc. dir. East Asian Rsch. Ctr., 1967-73, dir., 1973-77, chmn. council East Asian studies, 1977-80, dir. program on U.S.-Japan relations, 1980-87, hon. chmn. program on U.S.-Japan rels., 1988—, mem. faculty council, 1981-84; nat. intelligence officer for East Asia Nat. Intelligence Coun., 1993-95, dir. Fairbank Ctr. East Asian Studies, 1995-99; dir. Asia Ctr. Harvard U., 1997-99, rsch. prof., 2000—. Mem. Joint Com. on Contemporary China, 1968-75, Com. on Scholarly Communication with Peoples Republic China, 1973-75, Joint Com. Japanese Studies, 1977-79 Author: Japan's New Middle Class, 1963, Canton Under Communism, 1969, Japan As Number One, 1979, Comeback, 1985, The Impact of Japan on a Changing World, 1987, One Step Ahead in China, 1989, The Four Little Dragons, 1991, Is Japan Still Number One?, 2000; editor: (with Norman W. Bell) A Modern Introduction to the Family, 1960, Modern Japanese Organization and Decision-Making, 1975, (with George Lodge) Ideology and National Competitiveness, Living With China, 1997. Trustee Ohio Wesleyan U., 1970-75, 80-94. Served with AUS, 1951-53. Recipient Harvard faculty prize for book of year, 1970, Japan Found. prize, 1996, Japan soc. prize 1998; Guggenheim fellow, 1972 Mem. Assn. Asian Studies (bd. dirs. 1970-72), Am. Acad. Arts and Scis. Home: 14 Sumner Rd Cambridge MA 02138-3018 E-mail: efvogel@fas.harvard.edu.

VOGEL, H. VICTORIA, psychotherapist, trauma, post-traumatic stress disorder and addiction recovery counselor and educator, author; BA, U. Md., 1968; MA, NYU, 1970, 75; MEd, Columbia U., 1982, postgrad., 1982—; cert., Am. Projective Drawing Inst., 1983; CASAC, New Sch. U. for Social Rsch., 2000. Diplomate Am. Acad. Experts in Traumatic Stress; cert. addiction recovery counselor, expert in traumatic stress, alcohol and substance abuse counselor, addictions treatment, addiction counseling alcohol and substance abuse. Art therapist Childville, Bklyn., 1962-64; tchr. Montgomery County (Md.) Jr. H.S., 1968-69; with H.S. divsn. N.Y.C. Bd. Edn., 1970—; guidance counselor, instr., psychotherapist in pvt. practice. Guidance counselor, instr., psychotherapist in pvt. practice; clin. counseling cons. psychodiagnosis and devel. studies, art/play therapy The Modern Sch., 1984—; art/play therapist Hosp. Ctr. for Neuromuscular Disease and Devel. Disorders, 1986—; employment counselor-adminstr. N.Y. State Dept. Labor Concentrated Employment Program, 1971-72; intern psychotherapy and psychoanalysis psychiat. divsn. Ctrl. Islip Hosp., 1973-75, Calif. Grad. Inst., L.A.; intern psychol. counseling and rehab. N.J. Coll. Medicine, Newark, 1979. Author: The Never Ending Story of Alcohol, Drugs and Other Substance Abuse, 1992, Variant Sexual Behavior and the Aesthetic Modern Nudes, 1992, Psychological Science of School Behavior Intervention, 1993, Joycean Conceptual Modernism: Relationships and Deviant Sexuality, 1995, Electronic Evil Eyes, 1995 (U.S. Cert. of Recognition, 1996), Psychological Paradigms of Alcohol Violence Suicide Trauma Addiction Variant Pathologies PTSD and Schizophrenia, 1999. Mem. com. for spl. events NYU, 1989; participant clin. and artistic perspectives Am. Acad. Psychoanalysis Conf., 1990, participant clin. postmodernism and psychoanalysis, 1996; aux. police officer N.Y. Police Dept., 1994—; chair bylaws com. Columbia U., 1995—. Mem.: ACA, AAAS, APA, Tchrs. Coll. Adminstrv. Women in Edn., Assn. Humanistic Psychology (exec. sec. 1981), Art/Play Therapy, N.Y. Art Tchrs. Assn., Am. Acad. Experts Traumatic Stress (diplomate in expert traumatic stress), Am. Soc. Group Psychotherapy and Psychodrama (publs. com. 1984—), Am. Orthopsychiat. Assn., Am. Psychol. Soc., Phi Delta Kappa (editor chpt. newsletter 1981—84, exec. sec. Columbia U. chpt. 1984—, chmn. nominating com. for chpt. officers 1986—, rsch. rep. 1986—, pub. rels. exec. bd. dirs. 1991, NYU chpt. v.p. programs 1994—).

VOGEL, HENRY ELLIOTT, retired university dean and physics educator; b. Greenville, S.C., Sept. 16, 1925; s. Henry Lamprecht and Alice (Cousins) V.; m. Barbara Argyle Gladden, Aug. 16, 1953; children: Alisabeth, Henry L. II, Barbara Alice, Susan Marie. BS, Furman U., 1948; MS, U. N.C., 1950, PhD, 1962. Instr. dept. physics Clemson (S.C.) U., 1950-52, asst. prof. physics, 1952-59, assoc. prof., 1959-65, prof., 1965-67, prof., head physics dept., 1967-71; prof., dean Clemson (S.C.) U. Coll. Scis., 1971-87, prof. physics, 1987-90, dean emeritus, prof. emeritus dept. physics and astronomy, 1990—. Mem. S.C. ad hoc com. for NSF exptl. program to stimulate competitive research, 1978-87; mem. tech. adv. bd. S.C. Research Authority, 1984-87. Served with AUS, 1943-45. Decorated Bronze Star, Purple Heart. Mem. Am. Phys. Soc., Am. Assn. Physics Tchrs., Sigma Xi, Sigma Pi, Alpha Epsilon Delta. Address: 222 Wyatt Ave Clemson SC 29631-3003 E-mail: henryvgl@aol.com.

VOGEL, HOWARD STANLEY, lawyer; b. N.Y.C., Jan. 21, 1934; s. Moe and Sylvia (Miller) V.; m. Judith Anne Gelb, June 30, 1962; 1 son, Michael S. BA, Bklyn. Coll., 1954; JD, Columbia U., 1957; LLM in Corp. Law, NYU, 1969. Bar: N.Y. 1957, U.S. Supreme Ct. 1964. Assoc. Whitman & Ransom, N.Y.C., 1961-66; with Texaco Inc., 1966-99, gen. atty., 1970-73, assoc. gen. counsel, 1973-81, gen. counsel Tex. Philanthropic Found. Inc., 1979-82; gen. counsel Jefferson Chem. Co. Texaco Chems. Can. Inc., 1973-82; assoc. gen. tax counsel, gen. mgr. adminstr. Texaco Inc., White Plains, N.Y., 1981-99; counsel Allegaert Berger & Vogel LLP, N.Y.C., 1999—. Gen. tax counsel Texaco Found. Inc., 1995-99; pres., dir. 169 E. 69th Corp., 1981—. Served to 1st lt. JAGC, U.S. Army, 1958-60. Mem. ABA, Aassn. Bar City N.Y., Fed. Bar Coun., Assn. Ex-Mems. of Squadron A., Princeton Club (N.Y.C.). Home: 169 E 69th St Apt 9D New York NY 10021-5163 Office: 18th Fl 111 Broadway Fl 18 New York NY 10006-1901 E-mail: hvogel@abv.com.

VOGEL, JOHN WALTER, lawyer; b. Dansville, N.Y., Sept. 19, 1948; s. Walter Earl and Betty (Elston) V.; m. Pamela Hill; children: Michael John, Jennifer Alexandra. BA, SUNY, Albany, 1970; JD, Syracuse U., 1976. Bar: N.Y. 1976, U.S. Dist. Ct. (we. dist.) N.Y. 1979, U.S. Tax Ct. 1980, U.S. Supreme Ct., 1980, U.S. Dist. Ct. (no. dist.) N.Y. 1985, U.S. Ct. Appeals (2d cir.) 1985. Assoc. Edward J. Degnan Law Offices, Canisteo, NY, 1976-77; atty. N.Y. State Dept. Agrl. & Markets, Albany, 1977-78; sole practice law Dansville, 1978—. Legal counsel Dansville Econ. Devel. Corp., 1983—; atty. Livingston County Habitat for Humanity, N.Y. State Festival of Balloons. Dir. Livingston County (N.Y.) Drug Abuse Prevention Council, 1981-82. Served with U.S. Army, 1970-73. Mem. N.Y. State Bar Assn., Livingston County Bar Assn. (sec., treas. 1980-82, v.p. 1984-85, pres. 1985-86), Dansville C. of C. (bd. dirs. 1985—). Republican. Methodist. Home: 261 Main St Dansville NY 14437-1111 Office: 125 Main St Dansville NY 14437-1611

VOGEL, JULIUS, retired consulting actuary; b. N.Y.C., Jan. 22, 1924; s. Max and Bertha V.; m. Corinne Iskowitz, Mar. 11, 1947; children: Robert, Charles. BA, Bklyn. Coll., 1943. With Prudential Ins. Co. Am., Newark, 1946-82, sr. v.p., chief actuary, 1977-82; chmn. Pruco Services Inc., 1979-82, Prudential's Gibraltar Fund, 1980-82. Served with U.S. Army, 1944-46. Recipient Disting. Public Service award Dept. Navy, 1976 Fellow Soc. Actuaries (pres. 1979-80); mem. Am. Acad. Actuaries.

VOGEL, MICHAEL N. journalist, writer, historian; b. Buffalo, May 26, 1947; s. Ralph John and Florence Helen (Pohlmann) V.; m. Stasia Zoladz, Aug. 28, 1971; children: Charity Ann, Rebecca Marie, Alex Christian. BA in English, Canisius Coll., 1969; MA in English, So. Ill. U., 1970. Journalist Buffalo News, 1970—, dep. editl. page editor. Assoc. prof. journalism Buffalo State U. Coll., 1979-80. Author: Maritime Buffalo, 1990, Echoes in the Mist, 1991, America's Crossroads, 1993. Pres. Buffalo Lighthouse Assn., Inc., 1985—; co-founder St. Michael's Sch. at Greycliff, Derby, N.Y., 1987; pres. Buffalo Newspaper Guild, 1994-96; bd. dirs. Landmark Soc. Niagara Frontier, 1990-91, Western N.Y. Heritage Inst., 1994-98, Friends of N.Y. State Newspaper Project, 1996—; pres. Am. Lighthouse Coord. Com.; founding trustee Nat. Lighthouse Ctr. and Mus.; adv. bd. Great Lakes Lighthouse Mus. 1st lt. U.S. Army, 1971-73. Recipient numerous awards including One to One Media award, 1978, 79, Newspaper Editorial Workshop award, 1979-80, N.Y. State AP award, 1982-90, Am. Planning Assn. award, 1987. Mem. U.S. Lighthouse Soc., Gt. Lakes Hist. Soc., Buffalo & Erie County Hist. Soc. (Augspurger award 1989, Niederlander award 1990), Buffalo Mus. Sci. Roman Catholic. Avocations: sailing, photography, reading. Home: 6540 Lake Shore Rd Derby NY 14047-9755 Office: Buffalo News PO Box 100 Buffalo NY 14240-0100

VOGEL, NADINE ORSOFF, diversified financial services company executive; b. Bronx, N.Y., Oct. 21, 1963; d. Eli H. and Phyllis S. (Landskroner) Orsoff; m. Douglas Albert Vogel, June 15, 1985; children: Gretchen Ashley, Rachel Shayla. Student, U. South Fla., 1981-83; BS, Coll. of Charleston, 1985; MBA, Golden Gate U., 1987. Account rep., asst. mgr. Met Life, L.A., 1987-89, br. agy. mgr., 1989-93, account exec., 1993-98, asst. v.p. mktg., 1998—; founder Spl. Needs Adv. for Parents, 1993—2001, v.p. mktg., 2001—. Nat. advisor, spkr., author on spl. needs planning; mem. corp. exec. bd. Ins. Adv. Bd. Featured on Lifetime Live, Lifetime Channel, Pure Oxygen, Oxygen TV. Named Mothers We Love top 25 list, Working Mother Mag., 2000, Fast 50 innovator, Fast Co. mag., 2002; recipient Mothering that Works award, Working Mother Mag., 2000. Mem.: Corp. Leadership Coun., Exec. Women N.J., Nat. Orgn. Rare Disorders. Avocations: piano, guitar, swimming, working out. Office: Harborside Fin Ctr 600 Plz II 6th Fl Jersey City NJ 07311-1103

VOGEL, NELSON J., JR. lawyer; b. South Bend, Ind., Oct. 13, 1946; s. Nelson J. and Carolyn B. (Drzewiecki) V.; m. Sandra L. Cudney, May 17, 1969; children: Ryan C., Justin M., Nathan J., Lindsey M. BS cum laude, Miami U., Oxford, Ohio, 1968; JD cum laude, U. Notre Dame, 1971. Bar: Ind. 1971, Mich. 1971, U.S. Dist. Ct. (no. dist.) Ind. 1971, U.S. Tax Ct. 1972, U.S. Ct. Appeals (5th cir.) 1975, U.S. Ct. Claims 1980; CPA, Ind. Acct. Coopers & Lybrand, South Bend, 1969-71; assoc. Barnes & Thornburg, 1971-76, ptnr., 1977—. Lectr. U. Notre Dame, South Bend, 1971, 74-80; instr. Ind. U., South Bend, 1971-74; bd. advisors Goshen Coll. Family Bus. Program, 1993-99; vice-chair Barnes & Thornburg, 2001—, mng. ptnr. South Bend office, 2001—; trustee Project Future, St. Joseph Co., 2002—. Pres. Big Bros., Big Sisters, South Bend, 1978-79; bd. pres. South Bend Regional Mus. Art, 1984-86; mem. ethics com. Meml. Hosp., South Bend, 1986-94. Mem. Nat. Employee Stock Ownership Plan Assn. (sec.-treas. Ind. chpt. 1993-95), Am. Assn. Atty.-CPAs, Nat. Assn. State Bar Tax Sec. (exec. com. 1982-84), Ind. State Bar Assn. (chmn. taxation sect. 1981-82, Citation of Merit 1979), Ind. Assn. Mediators, Mich. Bar Assn. (tax sect.), Ind. State H.S. Hockey Assn., Inc. (bd. dirs. 1998-2001, treas. 1998-2001), Michiana World Affairs Coun. (bd. dirs. 1992-96), Michiana World Trade club (bd. dirs. 1992-96), Mental Health Assn. St. Joseph County (bd. dirs. 1997-2001). Home: 1146 Dunrobbin Ln South Bend IN 46614-2150 Office: Barnes & Thornburg 600 1st Source Bank 100 N Michigan St Ste 600 South Bend IN 46601-1632 E-mail: nvogel@btlaw.com.

VOGEL, PAULA ANNE, playwright; b. Washington, Nov. 16, 1951; d. Donald Stephen and Phyllis (Bremerman) V. BA, Cath. U., 1974; doctoral studies, Cornell U., 1974-77. Instr. theatre and women's studies Cornell U., Ithaca, N.Y., 1978-81; prodn. supr. Theatre on Film & Tape, N.Y.C., 1983-85; prof. Creative Writing Program, Brown U., Providence, 1985—. Author various plays including The Oldest Profession, 1990, The Baltimore Waltz, 1989, And Baby Makes Seven, 1986, Desdemona, 1985, Meg, 1977 (Nat. Playwright award Am. Coll. Theatre Festial), Oldest Profession, 1980. Author various plays including Desdemona, 1985, And Baby Makes Seven, 1984, The Baltimore Waltz, 1992 (Obie award for best play 1992), The Oldest Profession, 1988, Hot 'N' Throbbing, 1994, The Mineola Twins, 1996, How I Learned to Drive, 1996 (Pulitzer prize 1998). Recipient Bunting award Radcliffe-Harvard Colls., 1990, Pew Charitable Trust Sr. Residency award, 1995, Obie award for best play, 1997, N.Y. Drama Critics Drama Desk award for best play, Lorteland Outer Critics award for Best Play, Laura Pels award, 1999; Fund for New Am. Plays grantee, 1994; Playwright fellow NEA, 1981, 90; Guggenhei fellow, 1995. Fellow MacDowell Colony; mem. New Dramatists. Office: Brown U PO Box 1852 Providence RI 02912-1852*

VOGEL, RICHARD WIEDEMANN, business owner, ichthyodynamicist, educator; b. N.Y.C., Apr. 12, 1950; s. Jack and Edna Jeanne (Wiedemann) V.; m. Pamela Jane Gordon, Aug. 7, 1974; children: Amy Jane, Katy Lynn, Gina Marie, Krista Jeanne. Postgrad. Owner, operator ichthyol. rsch. and comml. fishing vessel, Santa Barbara, Calif., 1973-88; designer advanced hydrodynamic curvature Clark Foam Factory, Laguna Beach, 1994—. Lectr. Surfrider Found. Conf., U. Calif., San Diego, 1994. Inventor in field. Episcopalian. Avocations: music, athletic tng. and fitness. Office: Ichthyodynamics PO Box 1167 Hanalei HI 96714-1167

VOGEL, ROBERT, retired lawyer, educator; b. Coleharbor, N.D., Dec. 6, 1918; s. Frank A. and Louella (Larsen) V.; m. Elsa Mork, May 29, 1942; children: Mary Lou, Sarah May, Frank, Robert. BS, U. N.D., 1939; LL.B., Mpls. Coll. Law, 1942. Bar: N.D. 1943. Practiced in Garrison, 1943-54; state's atty. McLean County, 1948-54; U.S. atty. Fargo, 1954-61; mem. Vogel, Bair & Brown, Mandan, N.D., 1961-73; justice N.D. Supreme Ct., 1973-78; prof. U. N.D. Law Sch., Grand Forks, 1978-95; ret., 1997. Democratic candidate for U.S. Ho. of Reps., 2d Dist. N.D., 1962; mem., sec. Nonpartisan League State Exec. Com., 1952; mem. N.D. Parole Bd., 1966-73. Fellow Am. Bar Found. Home: 524 Harvard St Grand Forks ND 58203-2845 E-mail: rv5740@wiktel.com.

VOGEL, ROBERT LEE, college administrator, clergyman; b. Phillipsburg, Kans., Sept. 27, 1934; s. Howard and Marie V.; m. Sally M. Johnson, June 3, 1956; children— Susan, Kirk BA, Wartburg Coll., 1956; B.D., M.Div., Wartburg Theol. Sem., 1960, D.D. (hon.), 1976. Ordained to ministry Am. Lutheran Ch., 1960. Organizing pastor Faith Luth. Ch., Golden, Colo., 1960-65; regional dir. div. youth activity Am. Luth. Ch., Chgo., 1965-67, dir. parish resources, div. youth activity Mpls., 1967-69; sr. pastor Our Savior's Luth. Ch., Denver, 1969-73; exec. asst. to pres. Am. Luth. Ch., Mpls., 1973-80; pres. Wartburg Coll., Waverly, Iowa, 1980-98; interim pres. Grand View Coll., 1999. V.p. Internat. Luther League, Am. Luth. Ch., 1953-58, pres., 1958-60; ofcl. observer Luth. World Fedn. Assembly, 1957; mem. com. on laity Am. Luth. Ch., 1964-67. Mem. nominating com., theol. edn. coord. com. Evang. Luth. Ch. Am., 1996—. Recipient Alumni citation Wartburg Coll., 1978 Mem. Coun. Ind. Colls., Iowa Assn. Ind. Colls. and Univs. (chmn. bd. 1987-88), Luth. Ednl. Conf. N. Am. (pres. 1988-89), Nat. Assn. Ind. Colls. and Univs. (commn. mem.). Home and Office: 900 Saint Paul St Denver CO 80206-3940

VOGEL, RONALD BRUCE, food products executive, real estate broker; b. Vancouver, Wash., Feb. 16, 1934; s. Joseph John and Thelma Mae (Karker) V.; m. Carol Vandecar, Mar. 16, 1958; children: Joseph S., Rhonda L., Theresa J., Denise R.; m. Donita Dawn Schneider, Aug. 8, 1970 (dec. June 1974); 1 child, Cynthia Dawn. BS in Chemistry, U. Wash., 1959. Glass maker Penberthy Instrument Co., Seattle, 1959-60; lab. technician Gt. Western Malting Co., Vancouver, 1960-62, chief chemist, 1962-67, mgr. corp. quality control, 1967-72, mgr. customer svcs., 1972-77, v.p. customer svcs., 1977-79, v.p. sales, 1979-84, gen. mgr., 1984-89, pres., CEO, 1989-95; ret. Gen. ptnr. Rou Vogel Family Partnership. Chmn. bd. dirs. Columbia Empire Jr. Achievement, Portland, Oreg., 1991-92. With U.S. Army, 1954-56. Recipient numerous awards. Mem. Master Brewers Assn. Am. (pres. 1996), Am. Malting Barley Assn. (chmn. 1984-86, 89-91), Vancouver C. of C. (chmn. 1991-93), Applied Phytologics, Inc. (bd. dirs.). Office: 54 317 NE 104th Ave Vancouver WA 98664

VOGEL, STEVEN MICHAEL, philosopher, educator; b. N.Y.C., Feb. 21, 1954; s. Amos and Marcia V.; m. Jane Ann Henderson, June 18, 1988; children: Anna, Jesse. Ba, Yale U., 1975; MA, Boston U., 1977, PhD, 1984. From asst. prof. philosophy Denison U., Granville, Ohio, 1984-90, assoc. prof., 1990-96, prof., 1996—, chair dept. philosophy, 1992-97, 2000—. Author: Against Nature, 1996. Mem. Am. Philos. Assn., Soc. Phenomenology & Existential Philosophy. Office: Dept Philosophy Denison Univ Granville OH 43023

VOGEL, SUSAN CAROL, nursing administrator; b. Hartford, Conn., Oct. 9, 1948; d. Morton B. and Esther (Riback) Worshoufsky. Diploma in nursing, Grace Hosp., New Haven, 1969; B in Healthcare Mgmt., U. La Verne, 1991, M in Health Adminstrn., 1994. RN, Calif.; cert. nephrology nurse, Nephrology Nurse Cert. Bd. Oper. rm. nurse New Britain (Conn.) Gen. Hosp., 1970-72; staff nurse oper. rm. Parkview Cmty. Hosp., Riverside, Calif., 1972-74; staff nurse dialysis, IV team Cedars-Sinai Med. Ctr., L.A., 1974-82; clin. nurse III dialysis UCLA, 1982-88; nurse mgr. inpatient dialysis UCLA Med. Ctr., 1988-93; adminstr. South Valley Regional Dialysis Ctr., Encino, Calif., 1993—; pres. Renal Replacement Therapies, Inc. Bd. dirs. End Stage Renal Disease Network 18. Author: (with others) Review of Hemodialysis for Nurses and Dialysis Personnel, 1993, 99, Vascular Access, Principles & Practices, 3rd edit., 1996; editor Nephrology Nursing Jour., 2000-02. Mem. med. rev. bd. End Stage Renal Disease Network 18, 1996-2000, Calif. Dialysis Coun., 1998—. Mem. NAFE, Am. Orgn. Nurse Execs., Am. Nephrology Nurses Assn. (pres. L.A. chpt. 1990-92, 96-98, nat. chairperson hemodialysis spl. interest group 1993-95), Nat. Kidney Found. Avocations: traveling, skiing. Office: South Valley Regional Dialysis Ctr 17815 Ventura Blvd Ste 100 Encino CA 91316-3600

VOGEL, THOMAS TIMOTHY, surgeon, health care consultant, lay church worker; b. Columbus, Ohio, Feb. 1, 1934; s. Thomas A. and Charlotte A. (Hogan) V.; m. M.M. Darina Kelleher, May 29, 1965; children: Thomas T., Catherine D., Mark P., Nicola M. AB, Coll. of Holy Cross, 1955; MS, Ohio State U., 1960, PhD, 1962; MD, Georgetown U., 1965. Pvt. practice surgery, Columbus, 1971-2001; chmn. liturgy com., pres. parish coun. St. Catharine Parish, 1971-73; chmn. diocesan adminstrn. com. Diocesan Pastoral Coun., 1972-73, chmn., 1973-75; vice prefect Sodality of Holy Cross, 1953-55; mem. Ohio Bishop's Adv. Coun., Columbus, 1976-79. Clin. asst. prof. surgery Ohio State U., Columbus, 1974—; past trustee Peer Rev. Sys., Inc.; assoc. med. dir. United Health Care, Columbus, 1997-2000; cons. Rehabilitation Svcs.; commr., surveillance utilization rev. mem. Medicaid, State of Ohio, 1998-2000; assoc. med. dir. Palmetto GBA, 1999—. Contbr. articles to profl. jours. Bd. dirs. St. Vincent's Children's Ctr., 1975-83, chmn., 1981-82; past chmn. bd. trustees St. Joseph Montessori Sch. Named Knight of the Holy Sepulchre, Equestrian Order of the Holy Sepulchre of Jerusalem, 2001; recipient Layman's award, Columbus Ea. Kiwanis, 1972. Mem. ACS, Am. Physiol. Soc., Assn. for Acad. Surgery, Ohio State Med. Assn. (del. 1993—), Sigma Xi, Delta Epsilon Sigma. Roman Catholic. Home: 247 S Ardmore Rd Columbus OH 43209-1701 Office: 621 S Cassingham Rd Columbus OH 43209-2403 E-mail: vogel.3@osu.edu.

VOGEL, VICTOR GERALD, medical educator, researcher; b. Bethlehem, Pa., Mar. 14, 1952; s. Victor Gerald Jr. and Margaret Moser (Smith) V.; m. Saralyn Sue Schaffner, June 25, 1977; children: Heather Marie, Christiaan Keith. Diplomate Am. Bd. Internal Medicine, Am. Bd. Preventive Medicine, Nat. Bd. Med. Examiners. Resident in internal medicine Balt. City Hosps., 1978-81; fellow in med. oncology Johns Hopkins Oncology Ctr., Balt., 1983-86; Andrew W. Mellon fellow Johns Hopkins Sch. Hygiene Pub. Health, 1984-86; asst. prof. medicine and epidemiology U. Tex./M.D. Anderson Cancer Ctr., Houston, 1986-93, assoc. prof. clin. cancer prevention, 1993-95; asst. prof. epidemiology U. Tex. Sch. Pub. Health, 1987-95; prof. medicine and epidemiology U. Pitts. Cancer Inst./Magee-Womens Hosp., 1996—, dir. MAGEE/UPCI breast cancer program, 1996—. Epidemiologist Tex. breast screening project Am. Cancer Soc., 1986-93; mem. data and safety monitoring bd. Women's Health Initiative, NIH, 1994—; bd. dirs. Nat. Surg. Adjuvant Breast and Bowel Project Found., Inc., 1997—, AMC Cancer Ctr., Denver, 1996-99; protocol chmn. Nat. Cancer Inst. Study of Tamoxifen and Raloxifene. Contbr. articles to profl. jours. Founding mem. Nat. Surg. adjuvant Breast and Bowel Project Found., Inc. Served with USPHS, 1981-83. Named Med. Vol. of Yr., Am. Cancer Soc., 1983, award 1987, career devel. award, 1990-93; fellow Susan G. Komen Breast Cancer Found., 1990-93. Fellow Am. Coll. Preventive Medicine, ACP; mem. Am. Soc. Clin. Oncology, Am. Soc. Preventive Oncology, Christian Med. and Dental Assn., Am. Assn. Cancer Rsch. Republican. Presbyterian. Avocation: flying. Office: University of Pittsburgh Cancer Inst Magee-Womens Hosp 300 Halket St Rm 3524 Pittsburgh PA 15213-3108 E-mail: vvogel@mail.magee.edu.

VOGEL, WERNER PAUL, retired machine company executive; b. Louisville, June 15, 1923; s. Werner George and Emma (Bartman) V.; B. Mech. Engring., U. Louisville, 1950; m. Helen Louise Knapp, Oct. 2, 1954. With Henry Vogt Machine Co., Louisville, 1942-86, asst. plant supt., 1957-60, plant supt., 1961-73, v.p., 1974-86. Trustee, City of Strathmoor Village, Ky., 1959-61; clk. City of Glenview Manor, Ky., 1967-73, trustee, 1974-75, treas. 1986-89; bd. dirs. Louisville Protestant Altenheim, 1979-90, pres., 1985-90, ret.; mem. adv. coun. Lindsey Wilson Coll., 1988—. Served with USAAF, 1944-46. Mem. ASME, Tau Beta Pi, Sigma Tau. Republican. Methodist. Home: 29 Glenwood Rd Louisville KY 40222-6168

VOGEL, WILLIAM DICKERMAN, telecommunications executive; b. N.Y.C., Oct. 21, 1961; s. Ralph B. and Mabel (Harris) V.; m. Mary Anne Taylor. AB, Harvard Coll., 1984. CFA. Rsch. asst. George W. Ball, Princeton, N.J., 1986; corp. search cons. Korn/Ferry Internat., Hong Kong, 1987; equity rsch. analyst The Boston Co., Boston, 1988-93; telecom. analyst Nat. West Securities, N.Y.C., 1993-95; sr. v.p., head telecomm. equity rsch. Dillon, Read & Co., 1996; mng. dir., head telecomm. equity rsch. NationsBanc Montgomery Securities, 1997-98; sr. v.p. strategic planning Winstar Comm., 1999-2000; ind. cons., 2000—. Author: Strategic Assessment, Regional Bell Telephone Cos., 1994. Trustee St. Paul's Sch., Concord, N.H. Mem. Assn. Investment Mgmt. and Rsch., Boston Security Analysts Soc., N.Y. Soc. Security Analysts, New Eng. Hist. and Geneal. Soc. Avocations: tennis, skiing, mountain biking, geneal. rsch.

VOGELEY, CLYDE EICHER, JR. engineering educator, artist, consultant; b. Pitts., Oct. 19, 1917; s. Clyde Eicher and Eva May (Reynolds) V.; m. Blanche Wormington Peters, Dec. 15, 1947; children: Eva Anne, Susan Elizabeth Steele. BFA in Art Edn., Carnegie Mellon U., 1940; BS in Engring. Physics, U. Pitts., 1944, PhD in Math., 1949. Art supr. Pub. Sch. System, Spingdale, Pa., 1940-41; rsch. engr. Westinghouse Rsch. Labs., East Pitts., 1944-54; adj. prof. math. U. Pitts., 1954-64; sr. scientist Bettis Atomic Power Lab., West Mifflin, Pa., 1956-59, supr. tech. tng., 1959-71; mgr. Bettis Reactor Engring. Sch., 1971-77, dir., 1977-92; cons. U.S. Dept. Energy, Washington, 1992-95. Cons. Bettis Atomic Power Lab., W. Mifflin, 1954-56; U.S. Navy Nuclear Power Schs., Mare Island, Calif., Bainbridge, Md., 1959-69. Author: (grad. sch. course) Non-linear Differential Equations, 1954; (rev. text) Ordinary Differential Equations, Rev. edit. 5, Shock and Vibration Problems, Rev. Edit. 6, 1991; rsch. report distributed to Brit., Can. and U.S. Govts. for use in design of airborne radar systems, 1944; oil painting represented in permanent Latrobe collection; acrylics, water colors and Christmas card designs in several pvt. collections; oil painting included in Barbara H. Nakle's A Unique Vision of Art, 1997, water color included in collection Superior Ct. of Pa. 1999. Pres., trustee Whitehall (Pa.) Pub. Libr., 1985. Recipient letter of commendation naval reactors br. USN, 1992. Mem. IEEE (life), Am. Phys. Soc., Assoc. Artists Pitts. (hon.), Pitts. Watercolor Soc., Sigma Xi, Sigma Pi Sigma, Sigma Tau. Presbyterian. Achievements include patents for Automatic Continuous Wave Radar Tracking System, Modulating Signals Passing Along Ridged Waveguides, Ridged Waveguide Matching Device, Method for Joining Several Ridged Waveguides, Antenna Feed Modulation Unit, others. Home: 185 Peach Dr Pittsburgh PA 15236-2145 *My life as an artist, scientist, and teacher has been a wonderful journey - made richer by my family, teachers, friends, colleagues, and students. It has never seemed like work.*

VOGELGESANG, SANDRA LOUISE, business executive, writer; b. Canton, Ohio, July 27, 1942; d. Glenn Wesley and Louise (Forry) Vogelgesang; m. Geoffrey Ernest Wolfe, July 4, 1982. BA, Cornell U., 1964; MA, Tufts U., 1965, MA in Law and Diplomacy, 1966, PhD, 1971. With Dept. State, Washington, 1975-97, policy planner for sec. state and European Bur., 1975-80, dir. Econ Policy Office, Orgn. Econ. Coop. and Devel., 1981-82, econ. minister U.S. Embassy, Ottawa, Can., 1982-86, dep. asst. sec. Internat. Orgn. Affairs Bur., 1986-89; dep. asst. adminstr. Office Internat. Activities Environ. Protection Agy., 1989-92; with Dept. State, 1992; sr. policy advisor Agy. for Internat. Devel., 1993; U.S. amb. to Nepal Dept. State, Washington, 1994-97; pres. Everest Assocs. and Himalaya, 1997—. Bd. dirs. Ctr. for Econ. Devel. and Population Activities; mem. women and conservation com. World Wildlife Fund, 1997—, mem. Nat. Coun., 1999—; bd. advisors Am.'s Soc., N.Y.C., 1986—89; mem. Pres.'s Coun. of Cornell Women Cornell U., 1998—; adv, com. Dept. of Treasury com. on Internat. Child Labor Enforcement, 1999—. Author: Long Dark Night of the Soul, The American Intellectual Left and the Vietnam War, 1974, American Dream-Global Nightmare: The Dilemma of U.S. Human Rights Policy, 1980. Bd. dirs. Crafts Ctr., 1999-2000. Recipient Meritorious Service awards, 1973, 74, 82, 83, 86, Disting. Honor award, 1976 Dept. State, Pres.' Disting. Service award, 1985. Mem. Council on Fgn. Relations. Office: 9009 Charred Oak Dr West Bethesda MD 20817-1923 E-mail: everest.associates@erols.com.

VOGELMAN, JOSEPH HERBERT, scientific engineering company executive; b. N.Y.C., Aug. 18, 1920; s. Jacob and Sabina (Weingarten) V.; m. Norma Schneider, Dec. 8, 1946; children: Jeffrey Allan, Leslie Sue, Linda Leigh. BS, CCNY, 1940; M.E.E., Poly. Inst. Bklyn., 1948, D.Elec. Engring., 1957. Registered profl. engr., N.Y., N.J. Project engr. Signal Corps Engr. Labs., Belmar, N.J., 1943-45; chief devel. br. Watson Labs., Eatontown, 1945-50; chief scientist Rome Air Devel. Center, Griffiss AFB, N.Y., 1951-52, chief electronic warfare lab., 1953-56, dir. communications, 1956-59; v.p., dir. Capehart Corp., N.Y.C., 1959-64; dir. electronics Chromalloy Am. Corp., 1964-67, gen. mgr. pocket fone div., 1966-67, v.p., 1967-73; v.p., dir. Cro-Med Bionics Corp., 1968-73; vice chmn. bd., dir. Laser Link Corp., 1968-73; chief scientist, dir. Orentreich Found. for Advancement Sci., 1973—; pres. Vogelman Devel. Corp., 1973—. Chmn. tech. adv. com. Compupix, Inc., 1984-86. Contbr. articles to profl. jours. and encys.; patentee in field. Served with AUS, 1942-43. Recipient Outstanding Performance award USAF, 1957 Fellow AAAS, IEEE; mem. Titulaire, Societe Francaise de Electroniciens et des Radio Electriciens, N.Y. Acad. Scis., Sigma Xi, Eta Kappa Nu. Home: 48 Green Dr Roslyn NY 11576-3221 Office: 910 5th Ave New York NY 10021-4155 E-mail: dr.jhv@juno.com.

VOGELMAN, LAWRENCE ALLEN, law educator, lawyer; b. Bklyn., Feb. 24, 1949; s. Herman and Gertrude (Wohl) V.; m. Deborah Malka, Jan. 24, 1971 (div. Aug. 1980); m. Marcia Sikowitz, Mar. 3, 1985 (div. Nov. 1999). BA, Bklyn. Coll., 1970; JD, Bklyn. Law Sch., 1973. Bar: N.Y. 1974, U.S. Dist. Ct. (so. and ea. dists.) N.Y. 1975, U.S. Ct. Appeals (2d cir.) 1975, U.S. Ct. Appeals (3d cir.) 1983, U.S. Supreme Ct. 1983, N.H. 1994, U.S. Dist. Ct. N.H. 1994, U.S. Ct. Appeals (1st cir.) 2001. Trial atty. Legal Aid Soc., N.Y.C., 1973-77; assoc. appellate counsel Criminal Appeals Bur., 1977-78; clin. prof. law Yeshiva U. Benjamin N. Cardozo Sch. Law, 1979-93; dep. dir. N.H. Pub. Defender, Concord, N.H., 1993-97; coun. Shuchman, Krause-Elmslie, P.L.L.C., 1997—. Adj. prof. law Franklin Pierce Law Ctr., 1994-98; faculty Inst. for Criminal Def. Advocacy, 1995—; program dir. Max Freund Litigation Ctr., 1984—; team leader Emory U. Trial Techniques Program, Atlanta, 1981-89, N.J. region, Nat. Inst. Trial Advocacy, 1997—; faculty N.E. region, Nat. Inst. Trial Advocacy, 1985—, Tom C. Clark Ctr. for Advocacy, Hofstra U. Sch. Law, 1985—, Legal Aid Socs. Trial Advocacy Program, 1986-89, Widener U. Law Sch. Intensive Trial Program, 1987-91, U. San Francisco Intensive Trial Advocacy Program, 1991—; mem. indigent's assigned counsel panel, appellate div. First Dept., N.Y.C., 1979-94; crminal justice act panel U.S. Dist. Ct. (so. and ea. dists.) N.Y., 1985-94, dist. N.H., 1997—; adminstrv. law judge N.Y.C. Environ. Control Bd., 1980-81. Author, editor: Cases and Materials on Clinical Legal Education, 1979; editor revisions to Eyewitness Identification. Pres. bd. trustees Woodward Park Sch., 1990—94; bd. dirs., legal coun. N.H. Civil Liberties Union. Fellow Am. Bd. Criminal Lawyers; mem. Assn. of Bar of City of N.Y., Assn. of Legal Aid Attys. (exec. v.p. 1977-78, exec. com. 1984-86, bargaining com. chairperson 1974-79), Soc. Am. Law Tchrs., Assn. Trial Lawyers Am (exec. com. civil rights sect.), Nat. Assn. Criminal Def. Lawyers (bd. dirs.), N.H. Bar Assn. (ethics com. 1995—, dispute resolution com. 1999—, bd. law examiners 1999—), N.H. Assn. Criminal Def. Lawyers, N.Y. State Defenders Assn., Order of Barristers, Am. Inns of Ct. (master Daniel Webster Inn of Ct.), Fortune Soc. (exec. com., bd. dirs.). Democrat. Jewish. Achievements include notable cases such as: People vs. Joel Steinberg, represented co-defendant, Hedda Nussbaum in homicide death Lisa Steinberg; U.S. vs. Falvey, in which Irish Rep. Army supporters were acquitted of gun running because of knowledge and approval of CIA; Bell vs. Coughlin, which involved highly publicized homicide of 2 N.Y. police officers; People vs. Roche, which established agy. def. to drug sale in State of N.Y.'s highest ct.; U.S. vs. Joseph, which appealed convictions in Brinks case. Home: 22 Cedar Point Rd Durham NH 03824 Office: Shuchman & Krause-Elmslie PLLC PO Box 220 Exeter NH 03833-0220 E-mail: lav@sisna.com., larryvpd@aol.com.

VOGEL-SPROTT, MURIEL DORIS, psychology educator, researcher; b. Waterloo, Can., Aug. 20, 1934; d. Henry and Anne Ellen (Stroh) V.; m. David Arthur Sprott, Dec. 16, 1961; children: Anne Ellen, Jane Barry. BA, McMaster U., Can., 1955; MA, U. Toronto, 1957; PhD, 1960. Rsch. assoc. Addiction Rsch. Found., Toronto, 1959-61; asst. prof. psychology U. Waterloo, Canada, 1961-65; assoc. prof., 1965-69; prof., 1969-96; rsch. prof., 1996-97; disting. prof. emerita, 1997—. Author: Alcohol Tolerance and Social Drinking, 1992; contbr. numerous chpts. and rsch. papers in profl. publs. in field. Recipient Rsch. award AA Found. for Traffic Safety, 1988; named Disting. Psychopharacologist, Can. Psychol. Assn., 1988, grantee Govt. and Pvt. agys. in Can. and USA. Fellow APA, Can. Psychol. Assn., Psychonomic Sci. Office: Dept Psychology University of Waterloo Waterloo ON N2L3G1 Canada E-mail: mvogel@watarts.uwaterloo.ca.

VOGELSTEIN, BERT, oncology educator; BS, U. Pa., 1970; MD, Johns Hopkins U. Rsch. assoc. Nat. Cancer Inst., 1976—78; Clayton prof. oncology Johns Hopkins U. Sch. Medicine, Balt., 1978—, prof. pathology. Advisor NIH Sci. Rev. Groups, Nat. Cancer Inst. Assoc. editor: Genes, Chromosomes and Cancer, mem. bd. reviewing editors: Sci. mag.; contbr. articles to profl. jours. Recipient Anne & Jason Farber Lecture award, Am. Acad. Neurology, 1991, Internat. award, Gairdner Found., 1992, Medal of Honor, Am. Cancer Soc., 1992, Richard Lounsbery award, NAS, 1993, Baxter Rsch. award, Assn. Am. Med. Coll., 1994, G.H.A. Clowes Meml. award, Am. Assn. Cancer Rsch., 1995, laureates Passano Found., 1994. Mem.: NAS, Inst. Medicine, Am. Acad. Arts and Scis. Achievements include revolutionizing our understanding of complex genetic mutations that occur when an normal bowel epithelial cell is transformed into a malignant cell. Office: Johns Hopkins U Sch Med Dept Oncology 424 N Bond St Baltimore MD 21231-1000*

VOGELZANG, JEANNE MARIE, professional association executive, attorney; b. Hammond, Ind., Apr. 15, 1950; d. Richard and Laura Ann (Vanderaa) Jabaay; m. Nicholas John Vogelzang, May 17, 1971; children: Nick, Adam, Tim. BA, Trinity Christian Coll., Palos Heights, Ill., 1972; MBA, U. Minn., 1981; JD, U. Chgo., 1987. Bar: Ill. 1987; CPA, Ill.; cert. assn. exec. Tchr. Timothy Christian H.S., Elmhurst, Ill., 1972-74; tchg. assoc. in fin. U. Minn., Mpls., 1980-81; fin. analyst Quaker Oats Co., Chgo., 1982-84; assoc. Baker & McKenzie, 1987-89, Jenner & Block, Chgo., 1989-91; pres., owner J.M. Vogelzang & Assocs., Western Springs, Ill., 1991-99; exec. dir. Structural Engrs. Assn. Ill., Chgo., 1992—, Nat. Coun. Structural Engrs. Assns., Chgo., 1996—; pub., editor Structure mag., 1996—. Com. mem. Western Springs Planning Commn., 1991—95; village trustee Village of Western Springs, 1995—99, chmn. fin., chmn. gen. govt. com.; mem. adv. bd. Coll. DuPage Internat. Trade Ctr., Glen Ellyn, 1992—94; bd. dirs., mem. acad. affairs com., planning com., exec. com. sec. Trinity Christian Coll., 1992—98; mem. trustees' evaluation com. Christian Ref. Ch. N.Am., 1998—; treas. The Tower Party of Western Springs, 1999—2001; mem. jud. code com. Christian Reformed Ch. N.Am., Grand Rapids, Mich., 1991—97; bd. dirs. Austin Christian Law Ctr., Chgo., 1989—92, Barnabas Found., Palos Heights, 1989—95, Ctrl. Park Chapel, Holland, Mich., 2002—. Fellow Ill. Lincoln Excellence in Pub. Svc., 1999. Mem. ABA, Am. Soc. Assn. Execs., Ill. Bar Assn., Chgo. Bar Assn., Elim Work Svcs. Bus. Roundtable. Mem. Christian Reformed Ch. Office: 203 N Wabash Ave Ste 2010 Chicago IL 60601-2418

VOGL, LAUREL COVINGTON, artist, educator; b. Huntington Park, Calif., May 8, 1942; d. Raymond A. and Sue (Kunicki) Covington; m. Christopher John Vogl, Apr. 5, 1969. BFA, U. So. Calif., L.A., 1964; MFA, Claremont Grad. Sch., 1968. Cert. tchr. art K-12, Calif., Colo. Tchr. art Edison Jr. H.S., L.A., 1964-66; elem. tchr. art Pomona (Calif.) Unified Schs., 1966-67; tchr. art Murray (Ky.) State U., 1968-70, Newton Jr. H.S., Littleton, Colo., 1972-75; prof. art Ft. Lewis Coll., Durango, 1976—, chair dept. art, 1997—. Juror art exhbns. Colo., N.Mex., 1981—. One-woman shows include Ft. Lewis Coll. Art Gallery, 1996, 99, 2001; exhibited watercolor painting numerous internat. juried exhbns., 1991—; artwork pub. books: Splash IV, 1996, Best of Watercolor, 1996, Best of Watercolor Composition, 1997, Splash V, 1998, Best of Watercolor 3, 1999, Splash VI, 1999; represented in permanent collections Hutcheson Cancer Ctr., Wash. Bd. dirs. Arts Force, Durango, 1991-99; mem. organizing com. Very Spl. Arts Durango, 1981-86. Recipient Foster award Watercolor West, Brea, Calif., 1996, Purchase award N.W. Watercolor Soc./Hutcheson Cancer Ctr., Wash., 1992, Richeson award San Diego Watercolor Soc., 1994. Mem. Nat. Watercolor Soc., Am. Watercolor Soc., Colo. Watercolor Soc., Rocky Mountain Nat. Watermedia, Western Colo. Watercolor Soc. (Bd. of Dirs. award 1991), Colo. Art Edn. Assn. (higher edn. rep. 1988-91), Intermountain Weavers Guild (bd. dirs. 1983-84), Nat. Art Edn. Assn. Home: 333 Northeast Cir Durango CO 81301-8426 Office: Fort Lewis College Dept Art Durango CO 81301 E-mail: vogl_l@fortlewis.edu.

VOGL, OTTO, polymer science and engineering educator; b. Traiskirchen, Austria, Nov. 6, 1927; came to U.S., 1953, naturalized, 1959; s. Franz and Leopoldine (Scholz) V.; m. Jane Cunningham, June 10, 1955; children: Eric, Yvonne. PhD, U. Vienna, 1950; Doctorate (hon.), U. Jena, Germany, 1983, Poly. Inst., Iasi, Romania, 1992, Osaka U., Japan, Slovak Acad. Scis., 2001. Instr. U. Vienna, 1948-55; research asso. U. Mich., 1953-55, Princeton U., 1955-56; scientist E.I. Du Pont de Nemours & Co., Wilmington, Del., 1956-70; prof. polymer sci. and engring. U. Mass., 1970-83, prof. emeritus, 1983—; Herman F. Mark prof. polymer sci. Poly. U., Bklyn., 1983-95, prof. emeritus, 1996—. Guest prof. Kyoto U., 1968, 80, Osaka U., 1968, 96, Royal Inst. Stockholm, 1971, 87, U. Freiburg, Germany, 1973, U. Berlin, 1977, Strasbourg U., 1976, Tech. U. Dresden, 1982, Wuhan (China) U.; Monbusho prof. Kyoto Inst. Technology, Japan, 1996; guest Soviet Acad. Sci., 1973, Polish Acad. Sci., 1973, 75, Acad. Sci. Romania, 1974, 76; cons. in field. Chmn. com. on macromolecular chemistry Nat. Acad. Sci. Author: Polyaldehydes, 1967, (with Furukawa) Polymerization of Heterocyclics, 1973, Ionic Polymerization, 1976, (with Simionescu) Radical Co and Graftpolymerization, 1978, (with Donaruma) Polymeric Drugs, 1978, (with Donaruma and Ottenbrite) Polymers in Biology and Medicine, 1980, (with Goldberg and Donaruma) Targeted Drugs, 1983, (with Immergut) Polymer Science in the Next Decade, 1997, (with Kitayama and Hatada) Macromolecular Design of Polymeric Materials; contbr. articles to profl. jours. Recipient Fulbright award, 1976, Humboldt prize, 1977, Chemistry Pioneer award, 1985, Gold medal City of Vienna, Austria, 1986, Exner medal, 1987, Mark medal, 1989, Honor Ring, City of Traiskirchen, 1989; Japan Soc. Promotion of Sci. sr. fellow, 1980, golden hon. diploma U. Vienna, 2000, Hon. Cross of Arts and Scis., Rep. of Austria, 2000, Herman F. Mark award Am. Chem. Soc., 2000. Fellow AAAS; mem. Am. Chem. Soc. (chmn. div. polymer chemistry 1974, chmn. Conn. Valley sect. 1974, award applied polymer chemistry 1990), Am. Inst. Chemistry (chmn. Pioneer Award 1985), Austrian Chem. Soc. (hon.), Japanese Soc. Polymer Sci. (award 1991), N.Y. Acad. Sci., Austrian Acad. Sci., Royal Swedish Acad. Sci., Pacific Polymer Fedn. (pres.), Slovak Chem. Soc. (hon. mem.), Croatian Chem. Soc. (hon. mem.), Soc. Polymer Sci. Japan (life), Sigma Xi. Home: 12 Canterbury Ln Amherst MA 01002-3536 Office: U Mass Dept Polymer Sci and Engring Amherst MA 01003-4530 E-mail: vogl@polysci.umass.edu., voglotto@aol.com.

VOGT, ALBERT RALPH, forester, educator, program director; BS in Forest Mgmt., U. Mo., 1961, MS in Tree Physiology, 1962, PhD in Tree Physiology, 1966. Instr. in dendrology U. Mo., Columbia, 1965-66; asst. prof. rsch. tree physiology Ohio State U., 1966-69, assoc. prof., assoc. chmn. rsch. and adminstrn. forestry, 1969-76, prof., chmn. dept. adminstrn. and tchg. forestry, 1976-85; prof., dir. sch. natural resources U. Mo., 1985—. Pres Nat Asn Prof Forestry Schs and Cols, 1998—2000; mem Mo Forest Heritage Initiative, Gov's Task Force Environ Educ, Mo Gov's Energy Coalition, Mo Citizen's Comt Soil, Water, and State Parks; co-chair steering comt 3d Forestry Educ Symp, 1991; co-chair external rev dept forestry So Ill Univ, Carbondale, 1993; co-chair sch forest resources Pa State Univ, 1995; chair external rev forestry Univ Wis, Madison, 1997. Office: U Mo Sch Natural Resources 103C Natural Resources Bldg Columbia MO 65211-0001 E-mail: vogta@missouri.edu.

VOGT, ALISON WOODIN, physician; b. Utica, N.Y., Jan. 2, 1964; d. William Jackson Jr. and Joanna (Johnson) Woodin; m. Eric James Vogt, Oct. 22, 1994. BA, Williams Coll., 1985; MD, Dartmouth Coll., 1991. Diplomate Am. Bd. Anesthesiology. Chief resident in anesthesiology U. Rochester, N.Y., 1994-95, fellow in ambulatory anesthesia, 1996, sr. instr., 1996, asst. prof. NY, 1996-99, clin. asst. prof., 1999—; chief of anesthesia Lattimore Cmty. Surgictr., Rochester, 1997-2000, med. dir., 2000—. Contbr. articles to profl. jours. Mem.: AMA, N.Y. State Soc. Anesthesiologists (mem. com. on continuous quality improvement and peer rev. 1996—2001), Soc. for Ambulatory Anesthesiology (mem. com. on freestanding surgictrs. 1997—2000, mem. com. on fin. and budget 1997—2001, Resident Travel award 1995), Am. Soc. Anesthesiology, Alpha Omega Alpha. Office: Highland Hosp Dept Anesthesiology 1000 South Ave Rochester NY 14620-2782

VOGT, ERICH WOLFGANG, physicist, academic administrator; b. Steinbach, Man., Can., Nov. 12, 1929; s. Peter Andrew and Susanna (Reimer) V.; m. Barbara Mary Greenfield, Aug. 27, 1952; children: Edith Susan, Elizabeth Mary, David Eric, Jonathan Michael, Robert Jeremy. BS, U. Man., 1951, MS, 1952; PhD, Princeton U., 1955; DSc (hon.), U. Man., 1982, Queen's U., 1984; LLD (hon.), U. Regina, 1986; DSc (hon.), Carleton U., 1988, U. B.C., 1999; LLD (hon.), Simon Fraser U., 1996. Rsch. officer Chalk River (Ont.) Nuclear Labs., 1956-65; prof. physics U. B.C., Vancouver, 1965-95, prof. emeritus, 1995—, assoc. dir. TRIUMF Project, 1968-73, dir. TRIUMF Project, 1981-94, v.p. univ., 1975-81; chmn. Sci. Council B.C., 1978-80. Co-editor: Advances in Nuclear Physics, 1968—; Contbr. articles to profl. jours. Decorated officer Order of Can.; recipient Centennial medal of Can., 1967 Fellow Royal Soc. Can., Am. Phys. Soc.; mem. Can. Assn. Physicists (past pres., gold medal for achievement in physics 1988). Office: Triumf 4004 Wesbrook Mall Vancouver BC Canada V6T 2A3

VOGT, EVON ZARTMAN, JR. anthropologist, writer; b. Gallup, N.Mex., Aug. 20, 1918; s. Evon and Shirley (Bergman) V.; m. Catherine Christine Hiller, Sept. 4, 1941; children— Shirley Naneen (Mrs. Geza Teleki), Evon Zartman III, Eric Edwards, Charles Anthony. AB, U. Chgo., 1941, MA, 1946, PhD, 1948. Instr. Harvard U., 1948-50, asst. prof., 1950-55, assoc. prof., 1955-59, prof. anthropology, 1959-89, prof. emeritus, 1989—, dir. Harvard Chiapas project, 1957—, chmn. dept. anthropology, 1969-73, master Kirkland House, 1974-82; asst. curator Am. ethnology Harvard (Peabody Mus.), 1950-59, curator Middle Am. ethnology, 1960-89, hon. curator Middle Am. ethnology, 1990—. Vis. prof. U. Hawaii, 1972; Mem. div. anthropology and psychology NRC, 1955-57 Author: Navaho Veterans, 1951, Modern Homesteaders, 1955, (with W.A. Lessa) Reader in Comparative Religion, 1958, (with Ray Hyman) Water Witching U.S.A., 1959, 3d edit., 2000, Zinacantan: A Maya Community in The Highlands of Chiapas, 1969 (Harvard Press Faculty prize Sahagun prize 1969), The Zinacantecos of Mexico: A Modern Maya Way of Life, 1970, 2d edit. 1990, Tortillas for the Gods: A Symbolic Analysis of Zinacanteco Rituals, 1976, 2d edit., 1993, Fieldwork Among the Maya: Reflections on The Harvard Chiapas Project, 1994; editor: Desarrollo Cultural de Los Mayas, 1964, Los Zinacantecos, 1966, People of Rimrock, 1966, Handbook of Middle American Indians, vols. 7 and 8, 1969, Aerial Photography in Anthropological Field Research, 1974, (with Richard M. Leventhal) Prehistoric Settlement Patterns, 1983. Served from ensign to lt. USNR, 1942-46. Decorated Order Aztec Eagle Mexico; fellow Center for Advanced Study in Behavioral Sci., 1956-57 Fellow Am. Acad. Arts and Scis. (councilor 1974-78), Am. Anthrop. Assn. (exec. bd. 1958-60); mem. NAS (chmn. anthropology sect. 1981-84, class V behavioral and social scis. 1986-89), Am. Philos. Soc., Soc. Am. Archaeology, Royal Anthrop. Inst. Gt. Britain and Ireland, Am. Ethnological Soc., Tavern Club. Home: 14 Chauncy St Cambridge MA 02138-2528 Office: Peabody Museum 35C Harvard Univ Cambridge MA 02138-6437

VOGT, EVON ZARTMAN, III (TERRY VOGT), merchant banker; b. Chgo., Aug. 29, 1946; s. Evon Zartman Jr. and Catherine C. (Hiller) V.; m. Mary Hewit Anschuetz, Sept. 26, 1970; 1 child, Elizabeth Christine. AB, Harvard U., 1968; MBA, U. Colo., 1976. Vol., then staff mem. U.S. Peace Corps., Brazil, 1968-72; v.p. Wells Fargo Bank, Sao Paulo, Brazil, 1977-81; mng. dir. Wells Fargo Internat. Ltd., Grand Cayman, 1982-84; mgr. global funding Wells Fargo Bank, San Francisco, 1984-86; pres. ARBI Transnat., Inc., 1986—2002; dep. dir. gen. Inter-Am. Inst. Coop. on Agr., San Jose, Costa Rica, 2002—. Bd. dir. Magtech Ammunition Co., Inc., Centerville, Minn. Bd. dirs. Internat. Diplomacy Coun., San Francisco, 1990-98, 2000—2002, pres. 1995-97; active No. Calif. C.A.R.E. Found., 1993-95, The Mex. Mus., 1994-96; bd. dirs. World Affairs Coun. of No. Calif., 1996—2002. Recipient Order of Rio Branco, Brazilian Govt., 1996. Mem. Brazil Soc. No. Calif. (pres. 1989-94), Pan Am. Soc. Calif. (bd. dirs., pres. 1991-94), World Affairs Coun. No. Calif. (bd. dirs.). E-mail: terry.vogt@iica.ac.cr.

VOGT, HARRY BRUCE, physician; b. Yankton, S.D., Dec. 9, 1948; s. Harry August and Audrey Martha Vogt; m. Judith Gail, Aug. 7, 1971; children: Christopher, Scott, Jeremy. BA in Biol. Sci., U. S.D., 1971, BS in Medicine, 1972; MD, U. Nebr., 1974. Diplomate Am. Bd. Family Practice. Intern, resident Sioux Falls Family Practice Residency Program, 1974-77; pvt. practice Ctrl. Plains Clinic, Sioux Falls, S.D., 1977-81; assoc. dir. Sioux Falls Family Practice Residency, 1981-89; acting dir. Sioux Falls Family Practice, 1982-83; dir. med. edn., dir. transitional yr. residency McKennan Hosp., 1989-92; dir. intro. clin. medicine U. S.D., Sioux Falls, 1988-96, dean grad. med. edn., 1989-96, dir. transitional yr. residency program, 1992-98, chair dept. family medicine, 1996—, Anton Hyden Meml. Disting. prof., 1997. Gov.'s health adv. com. State S.D., Pierre, 1997—. Author: Lower Respiratory Infection, 1995; editor S.D. Acad. Family Physicians News, 1993-97; guest editor Primary Care, 1990. Pres. United Day Care Ctr., Sioux Falls, 1991, U. S.D. Sch. Medicine Alumni Found., Sioux Falls, 1992—93; trustee emeritus U. S.D. Found., Vermilion, 1993; sec.-treas. U. S.D. Sch. Medicine Alumni Found., Sioux Falls, 2001—. Recipient Merit award S.D. Acad. Family Physicians, 1995, 96. Fellow Am. Acad. Family Physicians; mem. Nat. Bd. Med. Examiners (computer based case simulation com. 1999-2001), Assn. Am. Med. Colls. (group ednl. affairs), Soc. Tchrs. Family Medicine, Alpha Omega Alpha. Democrat. Methodist. Avocations: reading, tennis, golf, fishing, movies. Office: U SD Sch Medicine 1400 W 22nd St Sioux Falls SD 57105-1505 E-mail: hvogt@usd.edu.

VOGT, HARTMUT, education educator; b. Berlin, Oct. 18, 1923; s. Alfred and Luise (Thiele) V.; m. Helga Hellebrand, July 16, 1952. State exam for tchr., U. Berlin, 1950, PhD, 1956. State tchr., Berlin, 1950-51; from lectr. to asst. prof. Univs. Berlin, Tübingen, Marburg, Fed. Republic Germany, 1951-70; full prof. U. Dortmund, Fed. Republic Germany, 1970-89, prof. emeritus Fed. Republic Germany, 1989—. Author several books in field; contbr. articles to profl. jours. 1st lt. German Air Force, 1941-45. Mem. Flying Club. Avocation: piloting. Home: Otterbach 80 H 18 D-53902 Bad Muenstereifel Germany Office: Univ Dortmund Emil-Figge-Strasse 50 D-44221 Dortmund 50 Germany

VOGT, MARGARET MARY, kitchen designer; b. Cleve., Oct. 24, 1955; d. J. William and Margot C. V.; m. Bruce E. Burns, June 25, 1977 (div. Oct. 1992). BA, Notre Dame Coll. Ohio, South Euclid, 1977. Interior designer, Chagrin Falls, Ohio, 1977-85; kitchen designer The Cabinet Ctr., Richmond Heights, 1985-88, 89-92, Falls Kitchens, Chagrin Falls, 1988-89, Siematic, Cleve., 1992-93, show room mgr. Charlotte, N.C., 1993-94; lead kitchen designer The Home Depot, Gastonia, NC, 1995—2002; kitchen cons., 2002—. Mem. Am. Soc. Interior Designers (affil., designer Designer Showcase, Gastonia 1995, Charlotte 1999, Nat. Kitchen and Bath Assn.(cert., sec. Carolinas chpt. 1994-95, treas. 1995-97, v.p. programs 1997-99, pres. 2000-01, v.p. profl. devel. 2002—, v.p. comm.), Nat. Kitchen and Bath Assn. (v.p. programs 1991-93, Ohio chpt. treas. 1989-91). Avocations: gardening, cooking.

VOGT, ROCHUS EUGEN, physicist, educator; b. Neckarelz, Germany, Dec. 21, 1929; came to U.S., 1953; s. Heinrich and Paula (Schaefer) V.; m. Micheline Alice Yvonne Bauduin, Sept. 6, 1958; children: Michele, Nicole. Student, U. Karlsruhe, Germany, 1950-52, U. Heidelberg, 1952-53; SM, U. Chgo., 1957, PhD, 1961. Asst. prof. physics Calif. Inst. Tech., Pasadena, 1962-65, assoc. prof., 1965-70, prof., 1970—, R. Stanton Avery disting. svc. prof., 1982—, chmn. faculty, 1975-77, chief scientist Jet Propulsion Lab., 1977-78, chmn. div. physics, math. and astronomy, 1978-83, acting dir. Owens Valley Radio Obs., 1980-81, v.p. and provost, 1983-87. Vis. prof. physics MIT, 1988-94; dir. Caltech/MIT Laser Interferometer Gravitational Wave Observatory Project, 1987-94. Author: Cosmic Rays (in World Book Ency.), 1978, (with R.B. Leighton) Exercises in Introductory Physics, 1969; contbr. articles to profl. jours. Fulbright fellow, 1953-54; recipient Exceptional Sci. Achievement medal NASA, 1981, Profl. Achievement award U. Chgo. Alumni Assn., 1981. Fellow AAAS, A. Phys. Soc. Achievements include research in astrophysics and gravitation. Office: Calif Inst Tech Dept Physics 103-33 Pasadena CA 91125-0001 E-mail: vogt@caltech.edu.

VOHS, JAMES ARTHUR, health care program executive; b. Idaho Falls, Idaho, Sept. 26, 1928; s. John Dale and Cliff Lucille (Packer) Vohs; m. Janice Hughes, Sept. 19, 1953 (dec. Oct. 1999); children: Lorraine, Carol, Nancy, Sharla. BA, U. Calif., Berkeley, 1952; postgrad., Harvard Sch. Bus., 1966. Employed by various Kaiser affiliated orgns., 1952—92; chmn., pres., CEO Kaiser Found. Hosps. and Kaiser Found. Health Plan, INc., Oakland, Calif., 1975—92, chmn. emeritus; chmn. bd. dirs. Holy Names Coll., 1981—92; chmn. Marcus Foster Inst., 1981—. Chmn. Fed. Res. Bank San Francisco, 1991—94. Mem. Oakland Bd. Port Commrs., 1993—96; bd. dirs. Oakland-Alameda County Coliseum Complex, 1986—96, Bay Area Coun., 1985—94, chmn., 1991—92. With U.S. Army, 1946—48. Mem.: Inst. Medicine NAS.

VOIGES, PAUL JOEL, accountant; b. N.Y.C., Feb. 4, 1943; s. Gunther William and Beatrice Pearl (Glantz) V. BA, Wagner Coll., 1972; M Fin., N.Y. Inst. Tech., 1978. Acctg. clk. Appeal Printing Co., Inc., N.Y.C., 1960-65, asst. acctg. mgr., 1969-72; acctg. mgr. Simplicity Pattern Co., Inc., 1972-75, asst. tax mgr., 1975-79, acctg. mgr., asst. tax mgr., 1979-82; chief acct., tax mgr. Appeal Printing Co., Inc., 1986-88; ins. mgr., account mgr. Lockwood Kessler & Bartlett, Inc., L.I., N.Y., 1988—. Pvt. practice acctg. and tax preparation, L.I., 1977—. Sgt. USAF, 1965-69, Vietnam. Mem. Tau Kappa Epsilon. Home: PO Box 3084 Patchogue NY 11772

VOIGT, BARTON R. state supreme court justice; BA and MA in Am. History, law degree, U. Wyo. Atty., Thermopolis, Wyo.; former Hot Springs County atty.; former county ct. judge Gillette, Wyo.; former dist. judge Douglas; justice Wyo. Supreme Ct., 2001—. Office: 2301 Capitol Ave Cheyenne WY 82001 Office Fax: 307-777-6129.*

VOIGT, DAWN ALISE, college program administrator, consultant; b. Caledonia, Minn., Jan. 26, 1960; d. Merlin Otto and Evangeline Martha Voigt. Student, U. London, 1980-81; BA in Psychology and Sociology, Winona (Minn.) State U., 1982; MA in Indsl. and Orgnl. Psychology, DePaul U., 1989, PhD in Indsl. and Orgn. Psychology, 1993. Rschr. Johnson O'Connor Rsch. Found., Chgo., 1989-92; rsch. coord. Jewish Vocat. Svc., 1989-92; human resource assessor Stephen A. Laser and Assocs., 1990-92; sr. test and measurement specialist Med. Coll. Wis., Milw., 1992-94; assessment and grants mgr. Family Svc. of Milw., 1995-97; adminstr., edn. coord. Walker's Point Ctr. for the Arts, Milw., 1997-98; program devel. and evaluation coord. Waukesha (Wis.) County Tech. Coll., 1998—. Cons. Milw. Mental Health Consultants, 1997—. Project analyst Home Visitation Developmental Assessment Scale, 1996. Vol. Jobs for Youth, Inc., Chgo., 1988—92; bd. dirs. Walker's Point Ctr. for the Arts, Milw., 1999—, chair edn. subcom., 1999—2001, v.p. adminstrn., 2001—. Mem. APA. Avocations: origami and paper arts, gardening, sewing, outdoor activities. Home: 2672 N 67th St Wauwatosa WI 53213-1461 Office: Waukesha County Tech Coll 800 Main St Pewaukee WI 53072-4601

VOIGT, ELLEN, literature educator; BA, Converse Coll.; MFA, U. Iowa. Prof. poetry MIT; prof. Goddard Coll., Warren Wilson Coll., Asheville, NC, 1981—. Tchr. Bread Loaf Writers' Conf., Aspen Writer's Conf., Ind. Writers' Conf., Napa Writer's Conf., Catskills Writers' Conf., RopeWalk Writers' Conf. Author: (poems) Claiming Kin, 1976, The Forces of Plenty, 1983, The Lotus Flowers., 1987, Two Trees, 1992, Shadows of Heaven, 2002, (sonnet) Kyrie, 1995 (Nat. Book Critics' Circle award finalist, Teasdale Poetry prize); co-editor (with Gregory Orr): Poets Teaching Poets: Self and the World; author: The Flexible Lyric, 2001. Fellow, Acad. Am. Poets, 2002; grantee, Vt. Coun. Arts, NEA, Guggenheim Found. Office: Warren Wilson Coll PO Box 9000 Asheville NC 28815*

VOIGT, RICHARD, lawyer; b. Oskaloosa, Iowa, Jan. 20, 1946; s. Franz Otto Wilhelm and Minni (Heilbrunn) V.; m. Annemarie H. Riemer, Oct. 2, 1976; children: Samuel, Nicholas. BA, Conn. Wesleyan U., 1968; JD, U. Va., 1974. Bar: Va. 1974, U.S. Dist. Ct. (ea. dist.) Va. 1979, Conn. 1981, U.S. Dist. Ct. Conn. 1982, U.S. Ct. Claims 1982, U.S. Ct. Appeals (4th cir.) 1982. Assoc. counsel regional litigation Solicitor's Office Osha Div., 1978-80; staff atty. U.S. Dept. Labor, Washington, 1974-78; prin. Siegel, O'Connor, Schiff, Zangari & Kainen, P.C., 1981-88, 87-88; ptnr. Cummings & Lockwood, Hartford, 1988—. Contbg. author: ABA Treatise on Occupational Safety and Health Law, 1988; contbr. articles to profl. jours. Bd. dirs. Urban League Greater Hartford, 1984-88, Isnt. for Non-Profit Tng. and Devel., 1991-95, Hartford Proud and Beautiful, 1995—, Greater Hartford Arts Coun., 2001—. Mem. ABA (labor and employment law sect., OSHA com., litigation sect.), Conn. Bar Assn. (labor employment law sect., employment discrimination com., com. on alternative dispute resolution). Avocations: acrylic design, history, sports. Office: Cummings & Lockwood 36th Floor Cityplace I Hartford CT 06103

VOIGT, STEVEN RUSSELL, lawyer; b. Geneva, Dec. 29, 1952; s. James Leroy and Martha Anne (Erikson) V.; m. Barbara Jeane Molcyk, Apr. 23, 1983; children: Kelsey Marie, Katelyn Anne. BS, U. Nebr., 1975, JD, 1978. Bar: Nebr. 1978, U.S. Dist. Ct. Nebr. 1978, U.S. Tax Ct. 1980. Assoc. Nye, Hervert, Jorgensen & Watson, Kearney, Nebr., 1978-80; ptnr. Giese, Butler & Voigt, 1980-82, Butler & Voigt, Kearney, 1982-85, Butler, Voigt & Brewster, Kearney, 1985-97, Butler, Voigt & Stewart P.C., Kearney, 1997—. Bd. dirs. Western Nebr. Legal Svcs., Scottsbluff, pres. bd. 1997—; pub. defender County of Kearney, Minden, Nebr., 1982—; pres. Nebr. Lawyers Trust Account Found., Lincoln, 1986-90. Mem. ABA (exec. coun. young lawyers div. 1985-86), Assn. Trial Lawyers Am., Nebr. State Bar Assn. (vice chair judiciary com.), Nebr. Criminal Defense Atty's. Assn., Sertoma (pres. Kearney chpt. 1983-84), Kearney Country Club (pres. of bd. dirs. 1995), Masons, Shriners. Avocations: golf, bicycling. Home: 5207 Avenue G Pl Kearney NE 68847-8598 Office: Butler Voigt & Stewart PC 2202 Central Ave Ste 200 Kearney NE 68847-5359

VOINOVICH, GEORGE V. senator, former mayor and governor; b. Cleve., July 15, 1936; m. Janet Voinovich; 3 children. BA, Ohio U., 1958; JD, Ohio State U., 1961; LL.D. (hon.), Ohio U., 1981. Bar: Ohio 1961, U.S. Supreme Ct. 1968. Asst. atty. gen. State of Ohio, 1963-64; mem. Ohio Ho. of Reps., 1967-71; auditor Cuyahoga County, Ohio, 1971-76; commr., 1977-78; lt. gov. State of Ohio, 1979; mayor City of Cleve., 1979-89; gov. State of Ohio, 1991-98; U.S. senator from Ohio, 1999—. Pres. Nat. League Cities, 1984-85; trustee U.S. Conf. Mayors; chmn. Midwestern Govs. Conf., 1991-92, Coun. Gt. Lakes Govs., 1992-94. Recipient cert. of Merit award Ohio U., Humanitarian award NCCJ, 1986; named one of Outstanding Young Men in Ohio Ohio Jaycees, 1970; one of Outstanding Young Men in Greater Cleve. Cleve. Jaycees; Disting. Urban Mayor award Nat. Urban Coalition, 1987; named to All-Pro City Mgmt. team City & State Mag., 1987. Mem. Rep. Govs. Assn. (vice chmn. 1991-92, chmn. 1992-93), Nat. Govs. Assn. (chmn. edn. action team on sch. readiness 1991, chmn. child support enforcement work group 1991-92, mem. strategic planning task force 1991-92, mem. human resources com. 1991—, co-chmn. task force on edn. 1992-93, mem. exec. com. 1993—, co-lead gov. on fed. mandates 1993—, chmn. 1997-98), Omicron Delta Kappa, Phi Alpha Theta, Phi Delta Phi. Republican. Office: US Senate 317 Hart Bldg Washington DC 20510-0001*

VOITLE, ROBERT ALLEN, college dean, physiologist; b. Parkersburg, W.Va., May 12, 1938; s. Ray Christian and Ruby Virginia (Hannaman) V.; m. Linda Ellen Loveday, Dec. 5, 1975; children: Robert Allen, Elizabeth Anne, Christian Blair, Vanessa Virginia. BS, W.Va. U., 1962; MS, W.Va., 1965; PhD, U. Tenn., 1969. Asst. in poultry U. Tenn., Knoxville, 1965-69; asst. prof. physiology U. Fla., Gainesville, 1969-75, assoc. prof., 1975-79; prof., head dept. poultry Calif. Poly. State U., San Luis Obispo, 1979-81; assoc. dean Coll. Agr., Auburn U., Ala., 1981-00, prof. poultry sci., 2000—. Cons. Columbia Bank for Coops., S.C., 1972 Contbr. articles to sci. jours. Pres., other offices Alachua County Fair Assn., Gainesville, 1969-79. Recipient Pub. Service award Alachua County Commn., 1975; recipient Tchr. of Yr. award U. Fla., 1977, Golden Feather award Calif. Poly. Inst., 1982 Mem. Poultry Sci. Assn., So. Poultry Sci. Assn., Gainesville Jaycees (JCI senatorship), Sigma Xi, Gamma Sigma Delta Clubs: Elks. Episcopalian. Home: 2247 Longwood Dr Auburn AL 36830-7105 Office: Auburn U Coll Agr Auburn AL 36849 E-mail: rvoitle@ag.auburn.edu.

VOJCANIN, SAVA ALEXANDER, lawyer; b. Oak Lawn, Ill., Oct. 15, 1964; s. Jovan and Lili (Yovanovich) V. Diplomate, Culver Mil. Acad., 1981; BA with distinction, DePauw U., 1985; JD, Washington U., 1988. Bar: Ill. 1988, U.S. Dist. Ct. (no. dist.) Ill. 1989, U.S. Dist. Ct. (no. dist.) Tex. 1996. Assoc. Schaffenegger, Watson & Peterson Ltd., Chgo., 1988-91, Clausen Miller P.C., Chgo., 1991-98, ptnr., 1999—, shareholder, 2002—. Editor: Law, Culture and Values, 1989. Mem. Mayor's Adv. Coun. on Immigrant and Refugee Affairs, Chgo., 1992-97; trustee St. Basil Orthodox Ch. of Lake Forest, 1997—, sec. bd. trustees, 1999-2002, nominating com., 2002--. Mem.: Chgo. Bar Assn., Serbian Bar Assn. (bd. dirs., treas. 1999—2000, sec. 2000—01, v.p. 2001—02, pres. 2002—). Orthodox. Office: Clausen Miller PC 10 S LaSalle St Chicago IL 60603-1098 E-mail: svojcanin@clausen.com.

VOJTA, PAUL ALAN, mathematics educator; b. Mpls., Sept. 30, 1957; s. Francis J. and Margaret L. V. B in Math., U. Minn., 1978; MA, Harvard U., 1980, PhD, 1983. Instr. Yale U., New Haven, 1983-86; fellow Math. Scis. Rsch. Inst., Berkeley, Calif., 1986-87, Miller Inst. for Basic Rsch., Berkeley, 1987-89; assoc. prof. U. Calif., 1989-92, prof., 1992—. Mem. Inst. for Advanced Study, Princeton, 1989-90, 96-97. Author: Diophantine Approximations and Value Distribution Theory, 1987. Recipient perfect score Internat. Math. Olympiad, 1975. Mem. Am. Math. Soc. (Frank Nelson Cole Number Theory prize 1992), Math. Assn. Am., Phi Beta Kappa, Tau Beta Pi. Avocations: computer, skiing. Office: Univ Calif Dept Math 970 Evans Hall # 3840 Berkeley CA 94720-3840

VOKETAITIS, ARNOLD MATTHEW, bass-baritone, educator; b. East Haven, Conn., May 11, 1930; s. Mathew Joseph and Agnes Mary (Pilvelis) V.; m. Marion Lee Dever, June 1959 (div. 1967); children: Arnold Mathew Jr., Paul Stanley; m. Nijole Lipciute, Sept. 6, 1968. BS in Bus. Adminstrn, Quinnipiac Coll., 1954; postgrad., Yale U. Dir. opera program De Paul U., Chgo., 1987-89. Lectr. techniques for mus. stage, author singing technique Northwestern U., Evanston, Ill., 1986; mem. adv. panels in music and ethnic affairs Ill. Arts Coun.; mem. panel for opera and mus. theatre NEA; faculty mem. Brevard (N.C.) Summer Music Ctr., 1987, 88; artist-in-residence for opera and voice Auburn U., Ala., 1990-93; artist/mgr. for pianists, formed Keyboard Artists Internat., 1998. Condr. master classes in singing; author on voice technique; operatic debut with N.Y.C. Opera, 1958, European debut at Liceo, Barcelona, Spain, 1968; mem. Met. Opera Nat. Co., appeared with maj. operatic and symphonic orgns. in U.S., Can., Mex., Cen. Am., S.Am., Lyric Opera of Chgo., 1966-84, 89, rec. artist for Desto, Vox, Columbia, RCA; recitalist appearances on Pay-TV; classical soloist U.S. Army Band, Washington. Served as sgt. U.S. Army, 1954-56. Recipient 1st place award, Conn. Opera Assn. auditions, 1957, Rockefeller Found. award, 1964, Lithuanian Man of Yr. award, 1990, Disting. Alumni award, Quinnipiac U., 1991. Mem. AFTRA, Am. Guild Mus. Artists (life), Actors Equity. Avocations: golfing, fishing, theater. *I have felt very strongly over the years that opera was written to be enjoyed, not revered, and that it cried out to be acted as well as sung. With television's influence on the viewer, necessity became reality and my hopes are being realized.*

VOLAKIS, JOHN LEONIDAS, engineering educator; b. Chios, Greece, May 13, 1956; came to U.S., 1973; s. Leonidas I. and Maria L. (Makarigakis) V.; m. Maria I. Papouras, 1985; children: Leo, Alexandro. BE summa cum laude, Youngstown State U., 1978; MS, Ohio State U., 1979, PhD, 1982. Mem. tech. staff Rockwell Internat., Columbus, Ohio, Lakewood, Calif., 1982-84; asst. prof. elec. engring. and computer sci. U. Mich., Ann Arbor, 1984-89, assoc. prof., 1989-94, prof. computer sci., 1994—, prof. elec. engring., dir. radiation lab, 1998-2000. Gen. chmn. IEEE Antennas and Propagation Internat. Symposium and Radio Sci. Meeting, 1993; mem. tech. coms. COMPUMAG Conf., 1994, 95, 98, Advanced Computational Electromagnetics Conf., 1995, 96; mem. Senate Assembly, U. Mich. rsch. policies and acad. affairs coms., 1994-97, elec. engring. dept. exec. com., 1997-99, grad. divsn. com., 1990—. Co-author: (books) Approximate Boundary Conditions in Electromagnetics, 1995, Finite Element Methods for Electromagnetics, 1998; contbr. chpts. or articles to 20 other books, 185 articles to refereed jours., 220 tech. papers to sci. symposiums or confs.; assoc. editor IEEE Antennas and Propagation Transactions, 1989-93, IEEE Antennas and Propagation Mag., 1992—. Radio Sci., 1994-97, Jour. Electromagnetics Waves and Applications, 1995—; co-inventor slot spiral antenna with integrated balun and feed, patent pending. Fellow IEEE (numerous coms. including adminstrv. com. 1996-99. past chmn. antennas symposium); mem. Internat. Union of Radio Sci., Sigma Xi, Phi Kappa Phi, Tau Beta Pi. Office: U Mich 1301 Beal Ave Ann Arbor MI 48109-2122

VOLANSKI, JOSEPH JAMES, retailer; b. Painesville, Ohio, Oct. 21, 1930; s. Joseph Volanski and Mary Kovacs; m. Theresa Marie Garzia, July 26, 1952; children: Thomas, Donna, Cheryl, Karen. Grad. H.S., Harding H.S., Fairport Harbor, Ohio, 1948. Owner, operator Chardon (Ohio) Beverage Store, 1955—; owner Voco Marine Model, Painesville, 1979—. Model freighters represented in permanent collections of 6 nat. marine museums; host Capt. Joe Musical Cruises WATJ-1560 AM, Chardon, 1994—. Chmn. Painesville Twp. Zoning Bd. With USN, 1950-54. Mem. Toastmasters. Home: 355 Barrington Ridge Rd Painesville OH 44077-1505 Office: Voco Marine Model 355 Barrington Ridge Rd Painesville OH 44077-1505

VOLBERDING, PAUL ARTHUR, academic physician; b. Rochester, Minn., Sept. 26, 1949; s. Walter A. and Eldora M. (Prescher) V.; m. Juline Christofferson, June 15, 1971 (div. June 1976); m. Mary M. Cooke, June 6, 1980; children: Alexander, Benjamin, Emily. AB, U. Chgo., 1971; MD, U. Minn., 1975. Resident in internal medicine U. Utah, Salt Lake City, 1975-78; fellow in oncology U. Calif., San Francisco, 1978-81; dir. med. oncology San Francisco Gen. Hosp., 1981—, dir. AIDS program, 1983—; dir. Ctr. for AIDS Rsch. U. Calif., San Francisco, 1988—, prof. medicine, 1990—. Bd. dirs. Dignity Ptnrs. Inc., 1996—; elected mem., Inst. of Medicine, 1999. Editor: Medical Management in AIDS, 1986; editor Jour. of AIDS, 1990—. Fellow ACP, AAAS; mem. Internat. AIDS Soc. (founder, chmn. bd.). Office: U Calif San Francisco San Francisco AIDS Program 995 Potrero Ave San Francisco CA 94110-2859*

VOLBERG, HERMAN WILLIAM, electronics engineer, consultant; b. Hilo, Hawaii, Apr. 6, 1925; s. Fred Joseph and Kathryn Thelma (Ludloff) V.; m. Louise Ethel Potter, Apr. 26, 1968; children: Michael, Lori. BSEE, U. Calif., Berkeley, 1949. Project engr. Naval Electronics Lab., San Diego, 1950-56; head solid state rsch. S.C. div. Gen. Dynamics, 1956-60; founder Solidyne Solid State Instruments, La Jolla, 1958-60; founder, v.p. electronics divsn. Ametek/Straza, El Cajon, 1960-66; founder, cons. H.V. Cons., San Diego, 1966-69; sr. scientist Naval Ocean Systems Ctr., Oahu, Hawaii, 1970-77; chief scientist Integrated Scis. Corp., Santa Monica, Calif., 1978-80; founder, pres. Acoustic Sys. Inc., Goleta, 1980-84, Invotron, Inc., Murray, Utah, 1984—; sr. scientist Reson, Inc., Santa Barbara, Calif., 1992—. Cons. Lockheed-Martin, 1985—, U. Utah Ctr. for Engring. Design, 1991; cons. on autonomous underwater vehicle sonar systems Mitsui/U. Tokyo, 1992; lectr. solid state course UCLA and IBM, 1956-62; instr. Applied Tech. Inst., Columbia, Md., 1988—; contbr. to undersea acoustical rsch. and devel. programs European Union, 1990—; dir. program in sci., tech., environ. policy Woodrow Wilson Sch. Princeton U. Contbr. articles to IRE Bull., IEEE Ocean Electronics Symposium, IEEE/MTS Oceans, UDT Conf. Procs. Mem. adv. panels for advanced sonar systems and for high resolution sonars, USN, 1970-77. 1st lt. U.S. Army, 1944-47, ETO. Recipient award of merit Dept. Navy, 1973, 94. Mem.: NRA, AAAS, IEEE (life), Math. Assn. Am., N.Y. Acad. Scis., Acoustical Soc. Am., Libr. Congress Assocs. (charter), Marine Tech. Soc., Mine Warfare Assn., U.S. Naval Inst., Planetary Assn., Old Crows, Am. Legion, Elks, Masons. Achievements include patents for device for detecting and displaying the response of tissue to stimuli, high rate neutralizer (HIRAN), crane high-voltage sensing system. Home and Office: 41 W 6830 S Murray UT 84107-7124 E-mail: hwv@aros.net.

VOLBORTH, ALEXIS VON, geochemist, geological engineering educator; b. Viipuri, Finland, July 11, 1924; came to U.S. 1955, naturalized; m. Nadia Hasso, 1947; children: Tatyana, Swetlana, Maria, Gregory, Anna, Nicholaus H.W., Elisabeth. PhC, U. Helsinki, 1950, PhLic and PhD in Geology-Mineralogy, 1954. Mineralogist, rsch. assoc., assoc. prof., prof. U. Nev., Reno, 1956-68; Killam vis. prof. geology, Killam rsch. prof. Dalhousie U., Can., 1968-72; vis. prof. NASA Lunar Sci. Inst., U. Houston, 1972-73; vis. rsch. chemist U. Calif., Irvine, 1973-76; prof. geology and chemistry N.D. State U., 1975-78; prof. geology, scientist Nucleaar Radiation Ctr., Wash. State U., Pullman, 1978-79; prof. geochemistry and chemistry Mont. Coll. Mineral Sci. and Tech., Butte, 1979-94, prof. geol. engring., 1987-92, dir. accelerator lab., 1983-86, sr. radiation safety officer, 1983-86; prof. emeritus Mont. Tech./U. Mont., 1995—. Prin. investigator Stoichiometry Study Lunar Rocks, NASA, 1972-73; cons. AEC, 1961-63, NASA, 1965-73, Anaconda Co., 1968, Atomic Energy Orgn. Iran, 1975, King Abdul Aziz U., Jeddah, Saudi Arabia, 1975-76, Johns Manville Corp., Chevron, 1980-83, Pegasus Gold Inc., 1987, Placer Dome Inc., Echo Bay, Inc., 1990; U.S. rep., del. 2d Conf. on Natural Reactors, IAEC, Paris, 1977; U.S. rep. Internat. Geol. Correlation Program, 1990-96; interpreter, Russian translator in Soviet Siberia for U.S. and Can. mining cos., 1990-96. Contbr. articles to profl. jours. Traveling rsch. fellow Outokumpu Found., U. Vienna, U. Heidelberg, 1954-55, Hoover fellow Calif. Inst. Tech., 1955-56, sr. fellow Australian Acad. Sci., 1965, fellow Guggenheim Found., 1965-66; fossil Elkoceras Volborthi named in his honor. Fellow Mineral. Soc. Am., Am. Inst. Chemists; mem. Am. Chem. Soc., Am. Nuclear Soc., Soc. Econ. Geologists, Internat. Precious Metals Inst. Home and Office: PO Box 80 Dayton MT 59914-0080

VOLCIAK-RADAI, JOSEPHINE CELIA, business owner, editor, columnist, poet, writer, vocalist; b. Hertfordshire, Hitchin, Eng., Nov. 19, 1945; came to U.S., 1946; d. John and Rosina Lillian (Miller) Volciak; children: Josette Linda Radai, Jacqueline Jeanne Shaw. Diploma, Hazleton (Pa.) Sr. High Sch., 1963; student, N. Harris C.C., Houston, 1980. Owner daycare facility, 1972—; columnist state and local newspapers, 1976-79; columnist, bull. editor Humble Observer-GS Corner, Kingwood, Tex., 1990—. Cons. Soft Spin Press Publ., Manhattan Beach, Calif., 1985; pres. Haiku and You Poetry Group, Kingwood and Humble, Tex., 1987-89; spkr. in field. Author: (poems) Thorned Rose, 1999, (book) Thorned Rose, 1999; editor: (poets' newsletter) The Grapevine, 1990-98; cons. poetry editor: Innisfree Literary Jour., 1989-92, poetry editor, 1992-95; creator: (tv series) Poetry Break KT-TV Channel 14, Kingwood, Tex. Founding rep., del. Lake Houston Literary Arts Coun., Kingwood, Tex., 1996; chmn. cultural arts Spring Branch (Tex.) Sch. Dist. PTA, 1976-77. Recipient 3rd Place award in watercolor Women's Club Lebanon, Pa. Mem.: Kingwood Poets Soc. (founder 1990, pres. 1990—99, 2002—), Literary Focus (Disting. Mention Spl. Poetry award 1990), Internat. Soc. Poets (Internat. Recognition award 1990, Poet of Yr. 1997, Internat. Poet Merit award 2001, Poet of Yr. 2002), World of Poetry Orgn. (Golden Poet award 1990, 1992), Poetry Soc. Tex., Tex. State Poetry Soc. (bull. editor 1993), Poetry Soc. Tex. (councillor 1994—, Ann. award 1996, Beaumont prize 1996, Castle award 1996), Am. Acad. Poets, Nat. Fedn. Poetry Socs., Nat. Soc. Womens Clubs. Avocations: drawing with charcoal, watercolors, ceramics, embroidery, collecting antique books.

VOLCKER, PAUL A. economist; b. Cape May, N.J., Sept. 5, 1927; s. Paul A. and Alma Louise (Klippel) V.; m. Barbara Marie Bahnson, Sept. 11, 1954 (dec. June 1998); children: Janice, James. AB summa cum laude, Princeton U., 1949, LLD (hon.), 1982; MA, Harvard U., 1951, LLD (hon.), 1985. Economist Fed. Res. Bank N.Y., 1952-57, pres., 1975-79; economist Chase Manhattan Bank, N.Y.C., 1957-61, v.p., dir. planning, 1965-68; with Dept. Treasury, Washington, 1961-65, 69-74, dep. under sec. monetary affairs, 1963-65, under sec., 1969-74; chmn. bd. govs. Fed. Res. Bd., 1979-87. Prof. internat. econ. policy Princeton U., 1988-95; chmn. Nat. Commn. on Pub. Svc., 1987-90, Internat. Acctg. Stds. Com., Trilateral Commn., 1990-2001, Internat. House & Fin., Svcs. Vol. Corps; ; bd. dirs. Prudential Ins. Co.; overseer TIAA-CREF. Sr. fellow Woodrow Wilson Sch. Pub. and Internat. Affairs, 1974-75. Mem. Am. Coun. Germany (dir.), Japan Soc. (dir.), Inst. Internat. Econs. (dir.), Group of Thirty (dir.).

VOLDMAN, STEVEN HOWARD, electrical engineer; b. Rochester, N.Y., Sept. 8, 1957; s. Carl Jerome and Blossom (Passer) V.; m. Annie Curry Brown, July 1986; children: Aaron Samuel, Rachel Pesha. BS, U. Buffalo, 1979; MS, MIT, 1981, EE, 1982; MS in Engring. Physics, U. Vt., 1986, PhD, 1991; postgrad., IBM, 1988-91. Engring. asst. R.E. Ginna Nuclear plant Rochester Gas & Electric, N.Y., 1977, 78; rsch. assoc. MIT, Boston, 1979-81, rsch. assoc. high voltage rsch. lab., 1981-82; staff level engr. IBM, Burlington, Vt., 1982—, 4-Mb DRAM devel. staff, 1985-88, 16-Mb DRAM devel. staff, 1991-93, 0.25 um advanced logic devel., 1993—, 0.15 um development, SOI devel., SIGE devel., SEMATECH esd testors and testing chmn., 1997—, SiGe devel., 2000—, SiGeC devel., 2001—. Adv. engr. IBM, 1993—; bd. dirs. Conf. on Judaism in Rural New Eng., Inc.; mem. tech. program com. Elec. Overstress/Electrostatic Discharge Symposium, 1993—, Internat. Reliability Physics, Symposium; coord. SEMATECH Electrostatic Discharge tech. benchmarking group, 1996—, Integrated Reliability Workshop, 1999—, Internat. Reliability Physics Symposium, 2002— Elec. Overstress/Electrostatic Discharge Symposium, 1998—, tech. program chmn., 2000, steering com. 2000, bd. dirs., 2001—, mem. steering com., 2001, vice chmn. 2001, gen. chmn., 2001—; tech. com. Internat. Reliability Physics Symposium; liaison SEMATECH/ESDA; chmn. EOS/ESD Device Testing Std. Com. on Transmission Line Pulse, 2001—; tech. steering com. Internat. Phys. and Failure Analysis Symposium, 2001—. Contbr. articles to Internat. Electron Device Meeting, Conf. on Elec. Insulation and Dielectric Phenomena, Transaction Elec. Devices, Computational Method in Elec. Engring., Numerical Analysis of Sem. Devices and Integrated Crcts., Device Rsch. Conf., Electrochem. Soc., Internat. Conf. on Microelectronic Test Structures, IEEE Transaction on Nuclear Sci., ECS Low Temperature Procs., Jour. Applied Physics, Jour. Electrostats. Discharge and Elec. Overstress Conf. Procs., Sci. Am.; more than 105 patents in field. Bd. dirs. Ohavi Zedek Synagogue, 1986—90, bd. govs., 2001—; bd. dirs. U. Vt. Hillel, 1999—. Mem. IEEE (sr., mem. tech. steering com. internat. phys. and failure analysis), Electrostatic Discharge Assn. (bd. dirs. 2001—, stds. com. chmn. transmission line pulse device 5.5 2001—, mem. edn. com., bd. dirs., symposium gen. chmn.), Sigma Xi, Phi Eta Sigma, Tau Beta Pi. Democrat.

VOLDMAN, YAKOV, conductor, music educator; b. Moldova, USSR, Jan. 21, 1944; s. Ihil and Fanya Voldman; m. Raisa Bonduriaskaya, July 3, 1971; 1 child Zorrik. BD in Violin Performance Tchg., Sch. Music, Chernovitsy, USSR, 1962; MD in Concert Performance, State U. Art and Music, Kishinev, USSR, 1967; postgrad., Moscow State Cons., 1972—73, PhD in Music, 1985. Asst. concert master State Symphony Orch., Kishinev, 1967—80; prof. violin Kishinev State Obs., 1970—89; tchr. Bloomington (Ind.) Sch. Music, 1972—73; condr. tchr. Sault Ste. Marie summer sch., Canada, 1993; violinist Baton Rouge Symphony Orch., 1992—; asst. prof. violin, orch. condr. Southeastern La. U., Hammond, 1993—, music dir. string acad., 1995—. Mem.: LMTNA, MTNA. Home: 6 Balmoral Cir Hammond LA 70401

VOLENIK, JAMES EDWARD, music educator; b. Detroit, Oct. 19, 1959; s. Donald Arthur and Marianne Louise Volenik. BA Music Ed., Youngstown State Univ., Youngstown, OH, 1977—82; MA Ed., Coll. of Mt. St. Joseph, Cincinnati, OH, 1989. Dir. bands Canfield Village Mid. Sch., Canfield, Ohio, 1985—. Pres. dist. v Ohio Music Educators Assn., Canfield, Ohio, 2001—; pres. Canfield Edn. Assn., Canfield, Ohio, 1995—96. Recipient Tchr. of the Yr., Youngstown Area Arts Coun., 1998, Martha Holden Jennings Scholar, 2000. Mem.: Ohio Music Educators Assn., Music Educators Nat. Conf., Phi Beta Mu. Home: 1781 South Raccoon Rd Youngstown OH 44515-4727 Office: Canfield Village Middle School 42 Wadsworth St Canfield OH 44406 E-mail: canf_jv@access-k12.org.

VOLENTINE, RICHARD J., JR. lawyer; b. Tampa, Fla., Apr. 2, 1955; s. Richard J. Sr. and Mary Francis (Shaw) V.; m. Susan Ruth Zimmerman, May 16, 1981; children: Rachel Elizabeth, Scott Thomas, Melissa Mary. BS, Spring Hill Coll., 1977; JD, U. Ala., 1980. Bar: Ala. 1980, Mo. 1982, Fla. 1984. Staff atty. Ala. Jud. Coll., Tuscaloosa, 1980-81; staff counsel Citicorp Person-to-Person, Inc., St. Louis, 1982; regional counsel Citicorp Person-to-Person Corp., Tampa, 1982-84; asst. gen. counsel Citicorp Savs. Fla., Miami, 1984-85; assoc. counsel Nationwide Capital Corp., Atlanta, 1985-86; regional atty. FDIC, 1986-88; gen. counsel, v.p. Altus Bank, Mobile, Ala., 1988-90; v.p., assoc. gen. counsel Chase Home Mortgage Corp., Tampa, Fla., 1990-91; sr. v.p., chief legal officer Prudential Bank, Atlanta, 1991—. Mem. ABA, Am. Corp. Counsel Assn., Ala. Jud. Coll. Faculty Assn. (hon.). Republican. Roman Catholic. Avocations: playing golf and other sports, photography, writing. Home: 2688 Tritt Springs Dr Marietta GA 30062-5268 Office: Prudential Bank 1 Ravinia Dr Ste 1000 Atlanta GA 30346-2103

VOLGY, THOMAS JOHN, political science educator, organization official; b. Budapest, Hungary, Mar. 19, 1946; BA magna cum laude, Oakland U., 1967; MA, U. Minn., 1969, PhD, 1972. Prof. polit. sci. U. Ariz., Tucson; dir. U. Teaching Ctr.; mayor City of Tucson, 1987-91. Exec. dir. Internat. Studies Assn., 1995—; chmn. telecom. com. U. Conf. Mayors, 1988—; Dem. nominee for congress, 1998; cons. H.S. curriculum project Ind. U. Author: Politics in the Trenches, 2001; co-author: The Forgotten Americans, 1992; editor: Exploring Relationships Between Mass Media and Political Culture: The Impact of Television and Music on American Society, 1976; contbr. articles to profl. jours.; producer two TV documentaries for PBS. Mem. Nat. Women's Polit. Caucus Conv., 1983, U.S. Senate Fin. Com., 1985, U.S. Ho. of Reps. Telecomm. Com., 1988—, Polit. Sci. Adminstrn. Com., 1986, Gov.'s Task Force on Women and Poverty, 1986, United Way, 1985-87; bd. dirs. Honors Program, 1981—, U. Teaching Ctr., 1988—, Tucson Urban League, 1981, Ododo Theatre, 1984, So. Ariz. Mental Health Care Ctr., 1987, Nat. Fedn. Local Cable TV Programmers; chmn. Internat. Rels. Caucus, 1981, 86—, Transp. and Telecommunications Com. Nat. League Cities, 1986, 88-91. NDEA scholar, 1964-76; NDEA fellow, 1967-70; recipient Oasis award for oustanding prodn. of local affairs TV programming; named Outstanding Young Am., 1981, Outstanding Naturalized Citizen of Yr., 1980; faculty research grantee U. Ariz., 1972-75, 77-78. Mem. Pima Assn. Govts., Nat. Fedn. Local Cable Programmers. Democrat. Jewish. Office: U Ariz Polit Dept Sci Tucson AZ 85721-0001

VOLICER, LADISLAV, physician, educator; b. Prague, Czechoslovakia, May 21, 1935; came to U.S., 1969, naturalized, 1977; s. Ladislav and Vilma (Molnarova) V.; m. Olga Holeckova, July 14, 1959 (div. 1970); children: Irena, Katerina; m. Beverly J. Beers, May 20, 1972 (div. 1998); children: Zuzka, Marika, Nadine. MD, Charles U., Prague, 1959; PhD in Pharmacology, Czechoslovak Acad. Scis., Prague, 1964. Research assoc. Czechoslovak Acad. Sci., Prague, 1966-68; research asst. prof. U. Munich, Fed. Republic Germany, 1968-69; from asst. to assoc. prof. pharmacology Boston U. Sch. Medicine, 1969-77, asst. prof. medicine, 1975—, prof. pharmacology, 1977—, prof. psychiatry, 1985—, mem. inst. rev. bd., 1975-78. Clin. pharmacologist E.N. Rogers Meml. Vets. Hosp., Bedford, Mass., 1980-87, dep. dir. Geriatric Research Edn. Clin. Ctr., 1987-92, clin. dir., 1992—; mem. drug formulary com. State Mass., Boston, 1977-83; mem. inst. rev. bd. McLean Hosp., Belmont, Mass., 1980—, rsch. psychiatrist, 1997—. Editor: Clinical Aspects of Cyclic Nucleotides, 1977, Clinical Management of Alzheimer's Disease, 1988, Hospice Care for Patients with Advanced Progressive Dementia, 1998; Enhancing Quality of Life in Advanced Dementia, 1999, Management of Challenging Behaviors in Dementia, 2000; contbr. papers to profl. publs. Grantee Nat. Inst. Aging, 1986—, Nat. Inst. Alcoholism and Alcohol Abuse, 1972-79, Nat. Inst. Drug Abuse, 1973-78, Merck, Sharp & Dohme, 1971; recipient Alcoholism Research award VA, 1979-85. Fellow Gerontol. Soc. Am., Am. Acad. Nursing; mem. Am. Geriatric Soc., Am. Med. Dirs. Assn. Democrat. Unitarian Universalist. Office: EN Rogers Meml Vets Hosp 200 Springs Rd Bedford MA 01730-1114 Home: 17 Winsor Rd Billerica MA 01821-3717

VOLIN, SUZANNE, former laboratory administrator; b. Detroit, Sept. 27, 1921; d. Kean Leo and Mignonne Bader Cronin; m. Verlynne Vincent Volin, Sept. 8, 1945; children: Suzanna, James, Virginia, Mignonne, André, Richard, Michelle, John. BA, U. Western Ont., London, Can. With Providence Hosp., Detroit, Childrens Hosp., Detroit, Evanston (Ill.) Clin. Lab., Detroit. Fellowship grantee Sioux Falls Branch STate. Mem. AAWU (ednl. rsch. and project grantee), Am. Soc. Clin. Pathologists (cert. med. technologist). Republican. Roman Catholic. Avocations: bridge, traveling, golf, tennis. Home: 1325 S 2nd Ave Sioux Falls SD 57105-1907

VOLIVA, SHARON LEE (SHARON LEE GROSSMAN), community volunteer, child and education advocate; b. Chgo., Feb. 27, 1944; d. Andrew Edward Grossman and Gertrude Rose (Mallory) Grossman Kvasnicka; m. Benjamin Harrison Voliva Jr., July 23, 1966; children: Annette L. Voliva DeLaCroix, Alan L., Andrea E. Voliva Krainik, Cheryl L. Voliva Merritt, Benjamin H. III. Contbr. articles to profl. jours. Mem. bd. edn. Thornton Twp. High Schs. Dist. 205, 1985—; bd. dirs. Dolton-Riverdale United Way, Ill. Learning Partnership; v.p. Coalition for Ednl. Rights; trustee Ivanhoe United Meth. Ch.; dist. 19 legis. asst. Ill. PTA; state bd. mgrs. Ill. Congress Parents and Tchrs., legislation chmn./lobbyist; mem. exec. bd. dirs. South Met. Assn. for Low Incidence Handicapped; chmn. Parents March for Sch. Funding. Recipient Appreciation award South Cook County Girl Scouts, 1977, Thanks Badge award, 1980, Outstanding Community Svc. award Riverdale-Dolton Jaycees, 1978, WTTW Svc. Appreciation plaque, 1975, 76, 77, WTTW Chmn.'s Gavel award, 1978, Pres.'s award for Svc. United Way, 1989. Mem. Nat. Congress Parents and Tchrs. (life), Nat. Congress of Parents and Tchrs. (life). Methodist. Avocations: oil painting, ceramics. Home: 10 W Sibley Blvd Dolton IL 60419-1513

VOLK, CECILIA ANN, elementary education educator; b. Greensburg, Ind., Mar. 8, 1956; d. Paul George and Ruth (Martin) Volk. BS, Purdue U., 1978; MA in Edn., Ball State U., 1984. Cert. K-Primary tchr., Ind. Tchr. spl. edn. Greensburg Cmty. Schs., 1978-79; tchr. Decatur County Day Care, Greensburg, 1979-81; tchr. 1st grade St. Louis Sch., Batesville, Ind., 1983-91, kindergarten tchr., 1991—, tchr. kindergarten, 1991—. Mem. ASCD, Am. Assn. Family and Consumer Scis., Nat. Assn. Edn. Young Children, Ind. Assn. Edn. Young Chidren, Nat. Coun. Tchrs. Math., Ind. Home Econs. Assn., Nat. Cath. Ednl. Assn., Purdue Alumni Assn., Delta Kappa Gamma. Home: 1035 N Broadway St Greensburg IN 47240-1309 Office: St Louis Sch 17 E Saint Louis Pl Batesville IN 47006-1397

VOLK, CHRISTIAN J. microbiologist, research scientist; b. LeCreusot, Saone-et-Loire, France, Apr. 3, 1965; s. Joseph M. and Liliane J. Volk; m. Catherine B. Volk, Aug. 8, 1992; children: Vincent, Claire. Degree in biology, Inst. U. de Technologie, Dijon, France, 1985; degree in agrl. enginring., Ecole Nat. Ingen. des Travaux, Dijon, France, 1988; PhD in Environ. Sci., Ecole Nat. des Ponts et Chaussees, Paris, 1994. Rsch. engr. Compagnie Generale des Eaux, Maisons, France, 1990-93; rsch. assoc. Am. Water Works Svc. Co., Belleville, Ill., 1994-97; water quality specialist Ind.-Am. Water Co., Muncie, Ind., 1997—. Reviewer Jour. Water Rsch,. 1999—; mem. com. Std. Methods, Denver, 1996—. Contbr. . Mem. Am. Water Works Assn. (project adv. com. 1999—, grantee 1996—), Am. Soc. for Microbiology, Internat. Water Assn. Home: 2013 W Bryden Muncie IN 47304 Office: Ind Am Water Co PO Box 1152 1420 S Burlington Dr Muncie IN 47308-1152 E-mail: cvolk@amwater.com.

VOLK, KENNETH HOHNE, lawyer; b. Hackensack, N.J., Nov. 8, 1922; s. Henry L. and Constance (Brady) V.; m. Joyce Geary, May 11, 1954; children: Christopher H., Cynthia. BS, U.S. Naval Acad., 1946; LLB, Yale U., 1953. Ptnr. Burlingham, Underwood, N.Y.C., 1955-92; of counsel McLane, Graf, Raulerson & Middleton, Portsmouth, N.H., 1992—. Speaker various symposia and confs. on maritime law. Assoc. editor Am. Maritime Cases; contbr. articles to profl. jours. Pres. Maritime Assocs., N.Y.C., 1967-68; chmn. bd. dirs. Seamen's House YMCA, N.Y.C., 1971-76; sec., bd. dirs. Seamen's Ch. Inst., N.Y.C., 1977-92; bd. dirs. Strawbery Banke Mus., Portsmouth, N.H.; mem. adv. bd. Tulane Admiralty Law Inst.. Fellow Am. Bar Found., Am. Coll. Trial Lawyers; mem. ABA, Assn. Bar of City of N.Y., Maritime Law Assn. U.S. (exec. com. 1977-80, pres. 1990-92), Comite Maritime Internat. (titulary mem.), Quaker Hill Country Club (pres. 1976-78). Republican. Espicopalian. Avocations: reading, hiking, fishing. Office: McLane Graf Raulerson 10 Pleasant St Portsmouth NH 03801

VOLK, KRISTIN, advertising agency executive; b. Phila., Feb. 26, 1953; d. Richard H. and Doris (Colasanti) V. BS in Biology, Tufts U., 1976; MPH, Boston U. Sch. Med., 1981. Rsch. technician Beth Israel Hosp., Boston, 1976; rsch. asst. Dana-Farber Cancer Inst., 1976-78; sr. rsch. asst. Beth Israel Hosp., 1978-81; rsch. supr. Schneider Parker Jakuc Advt., 1981-86; v.p., assoc. rsch. dir. HBM/Creamer, 1986-88, Della Femina McNamee, Boston, 1988-90; v.p., dir. rsch. Lawner Reingold Britton & Ptnrs., 1990-93; sr. v.p., dir. consumer insight group Arnold Fortuna Lawner & Cabot, 1993-95; exec. v.p., dir. consumer insight group Arnold Comm., Inc., 1995-99; exec. v.p., dir. strategic planning Deutsch Boston, 1999—2001; exec. v.p., chief mktg. officer Arnold Worldwide, N.Y.C., 2001—. Guest lectr. colls. and univs., Boston. Contbr. articles to profl. jours. Mem. Am. Assn. Advt. Agencies (account planning group com., chmn. conf. 1998), Ad Club Boston. Home: 180 W 20th St Apt 10F New York NY 10011

VOLK, NORMAN HANS, financial executive; b. N.Y.C., Jan. 10, 1935; s. Hans and Mary (Zurl) V.; m. Karlyn Schram, Aug. 17, 1959; children: Kari, Heidi, Jenny. BA, Valparaiso (Ind.) U., 1957; MA, Marquette U., Milw., 1959. Dir. pub. rels. Wagner Coll., N.Y.C., 1961-62; asst. to owner Alan M. Wood, 1962-72; sr. v.p. Bessemer Trust Co., 1972-85; pres. Chamberlain & Steward, 1985—. Trustee John Hartford Found., N.Y.C., 1979—. With U.S. Army, 1959-61. Mem. Univ. Club, Univ. Glee Club of N.Y.C., Doubles Club. Lutheran. Home: 445 Walton Rd Maplewood NJ 07040-1119 Office: 400 Park Ave New York NY 10022-4406

VOLK, PATRICIA GAY, fiction writer, essayist; b. N.Y.C., July 16, 1943; d. Cecil Sussman and Audrey Elaine (Morgen) Volk; m. Andrew Blitzer, Dec. 21, 1969; children— Peter Morgen, Polly Volk BFA cum laude, Syracuse U., 1964; student, Sch. Visual Arts, N.Y.C., 1968, New Sch., 1975, Columbia U., 1977-88. Art dir. Appelbaum & Curtis, N.Y.C., 1964-65, Seventeen Mag., Triangle Publs., N.Y.C., 1966-68; copywriter Doyle, Dane, Bernbach, Inc., 1969-88, also sr. v.p., creative mgr., 1969-87, sr. v.p.- assoc. creative dir., 1987-88; columnist N.Y. Newsday, 1995-96; fiction instr. Yeshiva Coll. Fiction instr. Playwrights Horizon Theater Sch., Marymount Coll. Author: The Yellow Banana, 1985 (Word Beat Press Fiction Book award 1984), White Light, 1987, All it Takes, 1990, Stuffed: Adventures of a Restaurant Family, 2001; contbr. articles to N.Y. Times mag., Redbook, Allure, Mirabella, Family Circle, The New Yorker, The Atlantic, Playboy, others; contbr. short stories to popular and small press publs. and anthologies. Recipient Stephen E. Kelly award, 1983, Various Andy, Clio, Effie and One Show awards, 1970—88, Yaddo fellow, 1983, 1999, MacDowell fellow, 1984, 2000. Mem.: PEN, Author's Guild, Juliana Berner's Anglers.

VOLK, PAUL S. lawyer; b. Concord, Mass., Aug. 6, 1957; s. Paul and Amaryllis Ann V.; m. Deborah Ann Pensack, Feb. 13, 1982. BA cum laude, U. Vt., 1980; JD summa cum laude, New England Sch. Law, 1986. Bar: Vt. 1987, U.S. Dist. Ct. Vt. 1987, U.S. Ct. Appeals (2d cir.) 1991, U.S. Dist. Ct. (no. dist.) N.Y. 1995. Assoc., contract pub. defender Blodgett & Watts, Burlington, Vt., 1986-89; ptnr. Blodgett, Watts & Volk, P.C., 1989—. Supervising atty. student legal svc. U. Vt., Burlington, 1988—. Mem. ACLU (dir. 1994-00), Vt. Bar Assn. (mem. criminal law com.), Vt. Assn. Criminal Def. Lawyers (dir. 1991—, pres. 1998). Democrat. Avocations: downhill skiing, tennis, golfing, mountain sports, music. Office: Blodgett Watts & Volk PC PO Box 8 Burlington VT 05402-0008

VOLK, STEPHEN RICHARD, company executive, lawyer; b. Boston, Apr. 22, 1936; s. Ralph and Miriam (Rose) V.; m. Veronica J. Brown, June 19, 1959 (dec. Feb. 1989); children: Jeffrey A., Andrew M., Michael J.; m. Diane Kemelman, Apr. 22, 1990; 1 child, Anne. Student, Dartmouth Coll., 1957; JD, Harvard U., 1960. Bar: N.Y. 1961. Assoc. Shearman & Sterling, N.Y.C., 1960-68, ptnr., 1968—, dep. sr. ptnr., 1988-91, sr. ptnr., 1991—2001; vice chmn. Credit Suisse First Boston, 2001—02, chmn., 2002—. Bd. dirs. ContiGroup Cos. Inc. Bd. dirs. Consol. Edison, Inc., 1996; trustee Consol Edison Co. N.Y.C., Inc., 1998, Harvard Law Sch. Assn., N.Y.C., 1999; mem. dean's adv. bd. Harvard Law Sch., 1997. Fellow Am. Bar Found.; mem. ABA (com. on securities regulation 1974), Assn. Bar City N.Y., Coun. on Fgn. Rels., Univ. Club, Phi Beta Kappa. Office: 11 Madison Ave 27th Fl New York NY 10010-3629

VOLK, THOMAS, accountant; b. Stuttgart, Germany, July 30, 1970; came to U.S., 1971; s. Earl Walter and Erika (Theilmann) V. BS in Acctg. and Criminal Justice, U. Scranton, 1993, MBA in Acctg. and Finance, 1995. Asst. mgr. Catholic Youth Ctr., Scranton, Pa., 1990-93; acct. Internat. Soc. Animal Rights, Clarks Summit, 1993-94; head acct. Diocesan Guild Studios, Scranton, 1994—. Vol. Catholic Youth Ctr., Scranton, 1993—, Jr. Achievement Northeast Pa. Mem. Inst. Mgmt. Accts. Home: PO Box 761261 San Antonio TX 78245-6261 Office: Diocesan Guild Studios 400 Wyoming Ave Ste 1 Scranton PA 18503-1272

VOLKENING, THOMAS CHARLES, engineering librarian; b. Port Huron, Mich., Mar. 11, 1950; s. Burt Austin and Carol Louise (Pepper) V. BA in biology, Oakland U., 1972; MLS, Western Mich. U., 1976. Pub. svcs. libr. U. Detroit, 1977-84; engring. libr. Mich. State U., E. Lansing, 1984—. Mem. Am. Soc. Engring. Edn. (engring. librs. divsn.), Mich. Libr. Assn. Avocations: gardening, science fiction. Office: Mich State U Engring Libr East Lansing MI 48824

VOLKER, DALE MARTIN, state legislator, lawyer; b. Lancaster, NY, Aug. 2, 1940; s. Julius J. and Loretta (O'Neill) Volker; m. Carol A. Suchyna, Nov. 28, 1970; children: Martin Andrew, Mark Dale, Meredith Ann. BA, Canisius Coll., 1966; JD, SUNY, Buffalo, 1966. Bar: NY 1967. Police officer Village of Depew, NY, 1966—72; assemblyman NY State Assembly, Albany, 1972—74; mem. NY State Senate, 1975—, Fowler and Volker, Lancaster. Mem.: Erie County Bar Assn., Eagles, Moose, Elks. Republican. Roman Catholic. Home: 92 Center Dr Depew NY 14043-1706 Office: 708 Legislative Office Bldg Albany NY 12247 Address: 5441 Broadway St Lancaster NY 14086-2123 E-mail: volker@senate.state.ny.us.

VOLKERING, MARY JOE, special education educator; b. Covington, Ky., Mar. 13, 1936; d. Everett Thomas and Edna Mae (Bohmer) Foley; m. Jack Lawrence Volkering, Aug. 19, 1961 (dec. Jan. 11, 1989); 1 child, Tara. BA, Thomas More Coll, 1961; MEd, U. Cin., 1977. Cert. educator of mentally handicapped, Ohio, Ky. Asst. engr. AT&T Co., Cin., 1956-63; tchr. severe & profound Comprehensive Care, Covington, Ky., 1970-76; tchr. mentally retarded Riverside Good Counsel Sch., Ft. Mitchell, 1976-79; tchr. trainable handicapped Covington (Ky.) Ind. Sch., 1979-99, spl. edn. cons., 1999—. Bd. dirs. No. Ky. Assn. for Retarded, Covington, 1980—; adj. prof. No. Ky. U., Highland Heights, 1987-88. Leader Girl Scout Troop, Ft. Wright, Ky., 1973. Named John Bauer Spl. Edn. Tchr. of the Yr. North Ky. Assn. Retarded, 1979, Tchr. of the Yr. G.O. Swing Sch., Covington Ind. Schs., 1986, Golden Apple Nominee Tchr., Ky. Post and Jaycees, 1988. Mem. No. Ky. Assn. Retarded (treas. 1984-86, sec. 1980-82). Democrat. Roman Catholic.

VOLKHARDT, JOHN MALCOLM, food company executive; b. Chester, Pa., Apr. 13, 1917; s. George Thomas and Evelyn (Mitchell) V.; m. Linda J. Volkhardt; children: Michael, Jacqueline, Janet, Dana. AB cum laude, Brown U., 1939. Product mgr. Vick Chem. Co., N.Y.C., 1939-48; gen. mgr. Northam Warren Co., Stamford, Conn., 1948-56, Rit div. Best Foods Co., N.Y.C., 1956-58; with Best Foods div. CPC Internat. Inc., Englewood Cliffs, N.J., 1958-78, exec. v.p., 1968-71, pres., 1971-78; pres. North Am. div. CPC Internat. and exec. v.p. CPC Internat., 1978-82, group v.p., 1979; v.p. CPC, 1971-78, dir., 1977-82; pres., chmn. Full Circle Corp., Moss Creek, 1985-91; pres. Water Oak Utility, 1985-91. Chmn. bd. Keep Am. Beautiful, Inc., 1979-82, chmn. bd. trustees, 1982. Recipient Herbert Hoover award Nat. Assn. Wholesale Grocers Am.; honoree Nat. Jewish Hosp., 1976. Mem. Phi Beta Kappa.

VOLKMAN, ALVIN, physician, research scientist, educator, retired; b. Bklyn., June 10, 1926; s. Henry Phillip and Sarah Lucille (Silverstein) V.; m. Winifred Joan Grinnell, June 12, 1947 (div. Aug. 1967); children: Karl Frederick, Nicholas James, Rebecca Jane Evans, Margaret Rose Werrell, Deborah Ann Falls; m. Carol Ann Fishel, Jan 26, 1973 (dec. Sept. 1992); 1 child, Natalie Fishel; 1 stepchild, Jeffrey C. Moore; m. A. Suzanne Hiss, Oct. 6, 1997. BS, Union Coll., 1947; MD, U. Buffalo, 1951; D in Philosophy, U. Oxford, Eng., 1963. Diplomate Nat. Bd. Med. Examiners, Am. Bd. Pathology. Intern Mt. Sinai Hosp., Cleve., 1951-52; rsch. fellow dept. anatomy Western Res. U. Sch. Medicine, 1952-54; resident, then sr. resident, then asst. in pathology Peter Bent Brigham Hosp., Boston, 1956-60; asst. prof. pathology Columbia U. Coll. Physicians and Surgeons, 1960-66; asst. mem., then assoc. mem. Trudeau Inst., Saranac Lake, N.Y., 1966-67; prof. dept. pathology East

Carolina U. Sch. Medicine, Greenville, N.C., 1977—, acting chmn. dept. pathology, 1989-90, asoc. dean for rsch. and grad. studies, 1989-95, prof. emeritus, 1995—, ret., 1999. Mem. NIH study sect. immunological scis., 1975-79, chmn., 1977-79. Contbr. articles to sci. jours. Served to lt. USNR, 1954-56. Am. Cancer Soc. scholar, 1961-63, Arth and Rheumat Found. fellow, 1952-54. Mem. AAAS, Am. Soc. Investigative Pathology, Am. Assn. Immunologists, Am. Soc. Hematology, Reticuloendothelial Soc., Am. Soc. Microbiologists, N.Y. Acad. Scis., Soc., Leukocyte Biology (hon. life). E-mail: alphavic@earthlink.net.

VOLKOW, NORA DOLORES, psychiatrist, scientist; b. Mexico City, Mar. 27, 1956; m. Steven Adler. BA, Modern Am. Sch., Mexico City, 1974; MD, Nat. U. Mex., 1980; postgrad. in Psychiatry, NYU, 1980-84. Diplomate Am. Bd. Psychiatry and Neurology. Rsch. asst. Registro Nacional de Anat. Path., Mexico City, 1975-76, Miles Lab. Exp. Therap., Mexico City, 1977-78; intern St. Anne Psychiat. Hosp., Paris, 1979-80; rsch. collaborator dept. chemistry BNL, Upton, N.Y., 1981-87; asst. prof. U. Tex. Med. Sch., Houston, 1984-87; attending physician psychiat. unit Herman Hosp., 1985-87; assoc. scientist dept. medicine Brookhaven Nat. Lab., Upton, N.Y., 1987-89, scientist dept. medicine, 1989—; assoc. prof. dept. psychiatry SUNY, Stony Brook, 1991—; dir. Nuclear Medicine Brookhaven Nat. Lab, 1994—; dir, NIDA/DOE Imaging Ctr. Brookhaven Nat. Lab., 1997—, assoc. lab. dir. life sciences, 1999—; assoc. dean, Sch. Med. SUNY, Stony Brook at Brookhaven Nat. Lab., 1997—. Mem. Adv. Com. for Minority Tng. in Psychiatry, Washington, 1991—; mem. study sect. in clin. neuroscis. NIH, Washington, 1992—; elected mem., Inst. Medicine, 2000. Co-editor: Positron Emission Tomography in Schizophrenia Research, 1991. Recipient Premio Robins award U. Mex., 1978, Premio Gabino Barrera award U. Mex., 1981, Laughlin fellowship Am. Coll. Psychiatry, 1984, Scanditronix scholarship , 1985. Office: Brookhaven Nat Lab Med Dept 30 Bell Ave Upton NY 11973*

VOLKWEIN, VASILIKI ANGELOPOULOS, academic administrator, educator; b. Deposit, N.Y., Mar. 4, 1938; d. Angelos Adam and Maria Stamatakou Angelopoulos; m. James Fredericks Volkwein, June 23, 1963; children: Edward Angelos, James Fredericks Jr. AB magna cum laude, Syracuse U., 1959; MEd, Cornell U., 1964; MS, U. Albany, 1996. Tchr. English, Chenango Valley Ctrl. Sch., Binghamton, N.Y., 1959-66; instr. English edn. Cornell U., Ithaca, 1966; tchr. English, Voorheesville (N.Y.) Jr.-Sr. H.S., 1973-99; ret., 1999. Coord. dist. humanities Voorheesville Ctrl. Sch., 1990-93, chmn. English dept., 1992-99; supr. student tchrs. U. Albany, 1992-99; lectr. China Inst., 1988; cons. in field. V.p. Cornell Alumni Club, Schenectady, 1972-73, pres., 1973-74; alumni interviewer Cornell Secondary Schs. Com., Albany, 1968-99; Sunday sch. tchr. St. Sophia Greek Orthodox, Albany, 1968-78; chmn. Capital Dist. Humanities Com., 1990-93. Mem. N.Y. State English Coun., N.Y. State United Tchrs., Phi Beta Kappa. Democrat. Greek Orthodox. Avocations: reading, playing piano, swimming, biking, writing.

VOLL, JOHN OBERT, history educator; b. Hudson, Wis., Apr. 20, 1936; s. Obert Frank and Ruth Olivia (Seaberg) V.; m. Sarah Lynne Potts, June 12, 1965; children: Sarah Layla, Michael Obert. AB summa cum laude, Dartmouth Coll., 1958, PhD (Ford Found. fellow), 1969; AM (Danforth fellow), Harvard U., 1960. Instr. history U. N.H., Durham, 1965-69, asst. prof., 1969-74, assoc. prof., 1974-82, prof., 1982-95, chair dept., 1988-91; prof. Georgetown U., Washington, 1995—, dep. dir. Ctr. for Muslim-Christian Understanding, 1996—. Mem. history and social scis. adv. com. Coll. Bd. 1983-86, chmn. European history and world cultures achievement test com., 1985-88; tchg. fellow Harvard U., 1969. Author: Historical Dictionary of the Sudan, 1978, 2nd edit., 1992, Islam Continuity and Change in the Modern World, 2nd edit., 1994; (with others) The Sudan: Unity and Diversity, 1985, Eighteenth Century Renewal and Reform in Islam, 1987, Sudan: State and Society in Crisis, 1991, Islam and Democracy, 1996, Makers of Contemporary Islam, 2001; contbr. articles to profl. jours. Mem. bd. Ecumenical Ministry U. N.H., 1974-78, pres., 1975-77; chmn. social action Durham Cmty. Ch., 1974-75, mem. ch. coun., 1977-78, deacon, 1986—. Sheldon traveling fellow, 1960-61, U. N.H. summer fellow, 1969, 89, NEH fellow, 1971-72, Fulbright faculty rsch. abroad fellow, 1978-79, Inst. Advanced Studies fellow Hebrew U., 1984-85; recipient Egyptian Presdl. medal, 1991. Mem. Am. Coun. Learned Socs. (del. 1989-96, del. exec. com. 1989-92, bd. dirs. 1990-92), New England Hist. Assn. (sec. 1975-78, v.p. 1981, pres. 1982), Sudan Studies Assn. (bd. dirs. 1981-82, co-exec. dir. 1990-94), N.H. Coun. on World Affairs (bd. dirs. 1978-95), Am. Hist. Assn. (chmn. program com. 1999), Mid. East Studies Assn. (bd. dirs. 1987-89, pres. 1992-93), Am. Coun. for Study of Islamic Socs. (bd. dirs. 1989—, v.p. 1989-91), N.H. Humanities Coun. (bd. dirs. 1991-95). Mem. United Ch. of Christ. Home: 4000 Cathedral Ave NW Apt 652B Washington DC 20016-5205 Office: Ctr Muslim Christian Understanding Georgetown U Washington DC 20057-0001 E-mail: vollj@georgetown.edu.

VOLL, SARAH POTTS, economic consultant; b. Wilmington, Del., Nov. 13, 1942; d. Robert Curtis and Dorothy Ruth (Counahan) Potts; m. John Obert Voll, June 12, 1965; children: Sarah Layla, Michael Obert. BA, Goucher Coll., Towson, Md., 1964; AM, Harvard U., 1966; PhD, U. N.H., 1977. Exec. sec. N.H. Council on World Affairs, Durham, 1966-68; mem. N.H. Ho. of Reps., Concord, 1977-78; ind. econ. cons. U.S. Agy. Internat. Devel., Ford Found., Middle East Adv. Group, Cairo, Egypt, 1978-79; dist. mgr. U.S. Census Bur. 1st Congl. Dist. N.H., Portsmouth, 1979-80; asst. budget dir. Office of Gov., Concord, N.H., 1980-81; chief economist N.H. Pub. Utilities Commn., 1981-94, exec. dir., sec., 1994-96; sr. cons. Nat. Econ. Rsch. Assocs., Washington, 1996-99, v.p., 1999—. Mem. rsch. adv. com. Nat. Regulatory Rsch. Inst., 1988-92, chair, 1990-92; mem. Durham Town Coun., 1988-93, chair, 1992-93; treas. United Campus Ministry to the U. N.H., 1990-96, chmn. New Eng. Exec. Dir.; lectr. Regulatory Rsch. Program, 1987-96. Author: Plough in Field Arable, 1980, N.H. Regulatory Handbook for Small Scale Electric Producers; co-author: The Sudan: Unity & Diversity, 1985; contbr. articles to profl. jours. Mem. Durham Budget Com., 1977-78, 87-88; co-chmn. Pres. Jimmy Carter Primary campaign for Towns of Durham, Lee and Madbury, 1975-76; sec. Strafford County Dems., 1977-78; chmn. bd. stewards Cmty. Ch. of Durham, 1984-86, mem. Diaconate, 1994-96; mem. staff subcom. on econs. and fin. Nat. Assn. Regulatory Utility Commrs., 1986-94, task forces on electric cost allocation, rate design and least cost planning, mem. staff subcom. on water, 1993-96, mem. staff subcom. on exec. dirs., 1994-96. Harvard U. fellow, 1964-65, Nat. Def. for Language fellow Harvard U., 1965-66. Mem. Internat. Assn. Energy Economists, Am. Econs. Assn. (transp. and pub. utilities group), Mid. East Studies Assn., Sudan Studies Assn. (co-exec. dir., treas. 1990-94), DAR (chpt. regent 1976-80, state sec. 1980-83, 93-95, state treas. 1983-86, state chaplain 1995-98, chair mus. com. 1998—), State Officers Club (v.p. 1988-90, pres. 1990-92), Phi Beta Kappa. Democrat. Mem. United Ch. of Christ. Home: 4000 Cathedral Ave NW Apt 652B Washington DC 20016-5205 E-mail: sarah.voll@nera.com.

VOLLBRECHT, EDWARD ALAN, school superintendent; b. Freeport, N.Y., July 22, 1941; s. Edward Chester and Lillian Elizabeth (Heinecke) V.; m. Catherine Ann Salgado, Dec. 2, 1977; 1 child, Matthew Grayson. BS, SUNY, New Paltz, 1963; MS, Hofstra U., 1968; PhD, Walden U., Naples, Fla., 1973. Adminstrv. asst. Pearl River (N.Y.) Sch. Dist., 1968-70, asst. prin., 1970-71; prin. Mark Twain Mid. Sch., Yonkers, N.Y., 1971-73; asst. dir. mid. schs. Yonkers Pub. Schs., 1973-74, dir. secondary edn., 1974-75; asst. supt. Bethlehem (Pa.) Area Sch. Dist., 1975-78; supt. schs. South Williamsport (Pa.) Area Sch. Dist., 1978-84, N.W. Area Sch. Dist., Shickshinny, Pa., 1984-88, Everett (Pa.) Area Sch. Dist., 1988—. Cons. New Eng. Sch. Devel. Coun., Boston, 1973-75; adj. prof. Manhattan Coll., N.Y.C., 1975-76, Lehigh U., Bethlehem, 1978-79. Mem. Everett Area Indsl. Devel. Corp., 1988—, Wet Providence Indsl. Devel. Authority, Bedford County Devel. Authority, Bedford County Devel. Assn., Bedford County Planning Commn.; exec. bd. Shippensburg Sch. Study Coun., Pa. State Sch. Study Coun. Educator of Yr., 1998, Svc. for Youth award YMCA, Yonkers, 1975. Mem. ASCD, Am. Assn. Sch. Adminstrs., Pa. Assn. Sch. Adminstrs., Pa. Assn. Rural and Small Schs. (exec. bd.), Pa. Sch. Bds. Assn., Bedford County Ednl. Found., Allegany C.C. Found., Lions, Rotary, Naurashank, Phi Delta Kappa. Republican. Roman Catholic. Home: 415 Locust Ct Everett PA 15537 Office: Everett Area Sch Dist 427 E South St Everett PA 15537-1275

VOLLEN, ROBERT JAY, lawyer; b. Chgo., Jan. 23, 1940; s. Ben N. and Rose (Belonsky) V.; m. Judith Paula Spector, Aug. 12, 1961; children: Steven, Neil, Jennifer. AB, U. Mich., 1961; JD, U. Chgo., 1964. Bar: Ill. 1964, D.C. 1965, U.S. Supreme Ct. 1975. Atty. appellate sect. Civil Div., U.S. Dept. Justice, Washington, 1964-65; asso. firm Schiff Hardin & Waite, Chgo., 1965-70, partner firm, 1971-72; gen. counsel BPI (Bus. and Profl. People for Pub. Interest), Chgo., 1972-83; ptnr. Schwartz & Freeman, 1983-87. Mem. vis. com. U. Chgo. Law Sch., 1978-81. Mem. Chgo. Council Lawyers (gov. 1972-76, 79-81), ABA (ho. of dels. 1974-76) Home: 2 Kingswood Ct Deerfield IL 60015-1912 E-mail: rvollen@aol.com.

VOLLMER, HELEN, public relations executive; B Journalism, M Radio/TV/Film, U. Tex. Copywriter for maj. retail outlet; acct. exec. Ruder & Finn; v.p., mgr. client rels. Bozell & Jacobs Pub. Rels.; CEO Vollmer Pub. Rels. Office: Vollmer Pub Rels 800 Travis, Ste 501 Houston TX 77002-5706*

VOLLMER, HOWARD ROBERT, artist, photographer; b. St. Paul, Dec. 16, 1930; s. Herbert Lenard and Elfreida Wilhelmena Elizabeth (Rubbert) V.; m. Velma Martin, Feb. 10, 1951; children: Mark David, Lori Lynn. BA, Hamline U., 1957; MA, Ariz. State U., 1968; postgrad., U. Minn., 1970-85. Screen print rsch. developer 3M Co., St. Paul, 1948-51; tchr. art ESL, St. Paul Pub. Schs., 1957-87; corp. product analyst, treas. Gateway Labs., Golden Valley, Minn., 1975-78; owner, photographer, artist Remember Art and Photog. Svcs., White Bear Lake, 1980—; owner, photographer, artist, writer Image Concepts, Florence, Ariz. Creator, co-presenter TV program Crafts in Edn., Sta. KTCA-TV, St. Paul, 1959. Author, illustrator: Chipmunk Children's Book, 1995. Chmn. White Bear Arts Coun., 1975-80; bd. dirs. Florence Gardens Mobile Home Assn. Sgt. USAF, 1951-52. Nat. Experienced Tchrs. Art fellow, 1967-68. Mem. Nat. Art Edn. Assn., St. Paul Fedn. Tchrs. Democrat-Farmer-Labor Party. Lutheran. Avocations: nature, hiking, woodworking, collecting stamps. E-mail: hofmiler@casagrande.com.

VOLLMER, JAMES E. high technology management executive; b. Phila., Apr. 19, 1924; s. Edward L. and Elizabeth (MacMichael) V.; m. Mary Campolieto, Nov. 16, 1946 (dec. July 1992); children: Jamie, Kurt, Kimarie; m. Avalon E. Kolar, Jan. 27, 1994. BS, Union Coll., Schenectady, 1945; MA, Temple U., Phila., 1951, PhD, 1956; grad., Advanced Mgmt. Program, Harvard U. Bus. Sch., 1971. Instr. physics Temple U., 1946-51; research supr. Honeywell Corp., Phila., 1952-59; with RCA, 1959—, dir. Advanced Tech. Labs., Camden, N.J., 1959-72, div. v.p., gen. mgr. Govt. Systems Group, N.J., 1972-79, corp. group v.p. Govt. Systems Div., Comml. Communications Div. and Picture Tube Div. Cherry Hill, 1979-83, corp. sr. v.p. Princeton, 1983-84; pres. James Vollmer Assocs. Inc., Jupiter Inlet Colony, Fla., 1984-89. Disting. lectr. Am. Soc. Engring. Edn., 1972 Author; patentee in field. Vice pres. Palm Beach County (Fla.) United Way, 1974-75; exec. adv. council Fla. Atlantic U., Boca Raton, Fla., 1974-75; vice chmn. campaign Camden County (N.J.) United Way, 1980; bd. dirs. W. Jersey Hosp., Camden, 1980; bd. govs. Franklin Inst., Phila., 1980; chmn. bd. Bartol Rsch. Found., 1980-87. With USNR, 1943-45. Fellow IEEE, AAAS; mem. Am. Phys. Soc., Nat. Security Indsl. Assn. (nat. trustee, past pres. Phila. chpt.), World Affairs Coun. Phila. (bd. dirs. 1982-85), Navy League (life), S. Jersey C. of C. (dir. 1975-77), Tequesta Country Club, Phi Beta Kappa, Sigma Xi, Sigma Pi Sigma, Eta Kappa Nu. Home: 212 Turtle Creek Dr Tequesta FL 33469-1545 *Management is the process of making decisions in the presence of uncertainty. Success comes to those who recognize this and correctly evaluate their uncertainty tolerance, and work to maximize it.*

VOLLMER, RICHARD WADE, federal judge; b. St. Louis, Mar. 7, 1926; s. Richard W. and Beatrice (Burke) V.; m. Marilyn S. Stikes, Sept. 17, 1949. Student, Springhill Coll., 1946-49; LLB, U. Ala., 1953. Bar: Ala. 1953, U.S. Dist. Ct. (so. dist.) Ala. 1956, U.S. Ct. Appeals (5th cir.) 1963, U.S. Ct. Appeals (11th cir.) 1983. Sr. judge U.S. Dist. Ct. (so. dist.) Ala., 1990—. Mem. Mobile Bar Assn. (pres. 1990), Rotary (Paul Harris fellow 1988). Roman Catholic.

VOLLUM, ROBERT BOONE, management consultant; b. Abington, Pa., Sept. 13, 1933; s. Charles Milton and Marion (Yocum) V.; m. Gayle Lorraine Timmerman, July 8, 1956; children: Robert Boone III, Jeffrey Charles. BS in Engring. and Sci., U.S. Naval Acad., 1955. Sr. cons., group leader Stevenson, Jordan & Harrison, Inc., N.Y.C., 1959-65; asst. to pres., plant supt., sales engr. W.L. Gore & Assocs., Inc., Newark, 1965-69; gen. mgr. Philmont Pressed Steel subs. Gulf & Western Industries, Inc., Bethayres, Pa., 1969-72, Air Shields div. Narco Sci. Industries, Inc., Hatboro, 1972-75; pres. Advanced Airflow Tech., Inc., Warminster, 1975-76, R.B. Vollum & Assocs., Huntingdon Valley, 1986—, RBV Mktg. Inc., Willow Grove, 1992—; chmn. bd. dirs., CEO SFM Technologies, 1994—. Prin. mfg. cons. Sperry Corp., Blue Bell, Pa., 1976-84; dir. cons. Creative Output, Inc., Milford, Conn., 1984-86; spkr. in field. Contbr. articles to profl. jours. Bd. dirs. Upper Moreland Little League, 1965-76. Served to lt. USN, 1955-59. Fellow Am. Prodn. and Inventory Control Soc. (chpt. pres. 1984-85); mem. soc. Mfg. Engrs (sr. mem.), Computer and Automated Systems Assn. (sr. mem.). Republican. Episcopalian. Home: 525 Overlook Ave Willow Grove PA 19090-2818 Office: PO Box 206 Huntingdon Valley PA 19006-0206 E-mail: rbvollum@rbvollum.com.

VOLMAN, DAVID HERSCHEL, chemistry educator; b. Los Angeles, July 10, 1916; s. Carl Herman and Blanche (Taylor) V.; m. Ruth Clare Jackson, Sept. 15, 1944; children: Thomas Peter, Susan Frances, Daniel Henry. BA, UCLA, 1937; MS, 1938; PhD (Standard Oil Co. fellow), Stanford U., 1940. Mem. faculty U. Calif.-Davis, 1940-41, 46—, prof. chemistry, 1956-87, emeritus prof. chemistry, 1987—, chmn. dept., 1974-81, chmn. Acad. Senate, 1971-72; research chemist OSRD, 1941-46; research fellow Harvard U., 1949-50. Vis. prof. U. Wash. 1958 Editor: Advances in Photochemistry, 1983-98; mem. editorial bd. Jour. Photochemistry and Photobiology, 1972-98; contbr. articles to profl. jours. Grantee Research Corp. Am.; Grantee NIH; Grantee U.S. Army Research Office; Grantee NSF; Guggenheim fellow, 1949-50 Mem. Am. Chem. Soc., AAUP, Inter-Am. Photochem. Soc., Assn. Harvard Chemists, Sigma Xi. Office: U Calif Davis Dept Chemistry 1 Shields Ave Davis CA 95616

VOLMER, SUZANNE, artist; b. Montpelier, Vt., Nov. 25, 1956; d. William S. and Carolyn Lawton Volmer. BFA with honors, Pratt Inst., 1979. Writer, art critic Arts Mag., N.Y.C., 1982-84; instr. RISD, Providence, 1985-89; arts adv. bd. Warwick (R.I.) Mus., 1989-92; guest artist Mass. Coll. Art, Boston, 1995-96. One-woman shows include Hydrangea House Gallery, Newport, R.I., 1992, Newport Art Mus., 1996; group exhbns. include Twining Gallery, N.Y.C., 1987, RISD, Providence, 1988, 89, Galerie Schneider, Freiburg, Germany, 1988, Mannheim Mus., Germany, 1989; represented by Galerie Ortillés-Fourcat, Paris. Recipient 1st prize juried sr. fine art show Pratt Inst., Bklyn., 1979. Home: 25 Livingston St Lincoln RI 02865-1920 Studio: 702 Great Rd Lincoln RI 02865-1421 E-mail: suzannevolmer@yahoo.com.

VOLMERT, DEBORAH JEAN, lawyer; b. Belleville, Ill., June 9, 1968; d. David A. and Mary Faye Mehrmann; m. Douglas Ambrose Volmert, May 20, 1995; children: Brett Douglas, Luke David. BS, Truman State U., 1990; JD, Washington U., 1993. Bar: Ill. 1993, U.S. Dist. Ct. (so. dist.) Ill. 1993, Mo. 1994, U.S. Ct. Appeals (7th cir.) 1995, U.S. Dist. Ct. (ea. dist.) Mo. 1997. Atty. Thompson & Mitchell, Belleville, Ill., 1993-97, The Stolar Partnership, Belleville, 1997—. Sec. Belleville Main St., Inc., 1998—, also bd. dirs. Bd. dirs. Hoyleton (Ill.) Youth and Family Svcs., 1995—. Mem. ABA, Nat. Assn. Bond Lawyers, Ill. State Bar Assn., Monroe County Bar Assn. (pres. 1997-98), St. Clair County Bar Assn. Office: The Stolar Partnership PO Box 484 Belleville IL 62222-0484

VOLOKH, EUGENE, law educator; b. Kiev, Ukraine, Feb. 29, 1968; arrived in U.S., 1975; BS, UCLA, 1983, JD, 1992. Law clk. Judge Alex Kozinski, U.S. Ct. Appeals, Pasadena, Calif., 1992—93, Justice Sandra Day O'Connor, Washington, 1993—94; prof. law UCLA, 1994—. Author: (textbook) The First Amendment: Problems, Cases and Policy Arguments, 2001. Legal advisor Yes on Prop. 209 Anti-Race-Preference Campaign, 1995—96. Mem.: Federalist Soc. (Free Speech Practice Group exec. com. 1998). Conservative. Office: UCLA Sch Law 405 Hilgard Ave Los Angeles CA 90095

VOLPE, ANGELO ANTHONY, former university president, chemistry educator; b. Nov. 8, 1938; s. Bernard Charles and Serafina (Martorana) V.; m. Jennette Murray, May 15, 1965. BS, Bklyn. Coll., 1959; MS, U. Md., 1962, PhD, 1966; M in Engring. (hons.), Stevens Inst. Tech., 1975. Rsch. chemist USN Ordnance Lab., Silver Spring, Md., 1961-66; from asst. prof. to prof. chemistry Stevens Inst. Tech., Hoboken, N.J., 1966-77; chmn. dept. chemistry East Carolina U., Greenville, N.C., 1977-80, dean Coll. Arts and Scis., 1980-83, vice chancellor for acad. affairs, 1983-87; pres. Tenn. Technol. U., Cookeville, 1987-2000, pres. emeritus, 2000—. Adj. prof. textile chem. N.C. State U., Raleigh, 1978-82; guest lect. Plastics Inst. Am., Hoboken, 1967-82. Contbr. articles to profl. jours. Recipient Ednl. Svc. award Plastics Inst. Am., 1973; named Freygang Outstanding Tchr., Stevens Inst. Tech., 1975. Mem. Am. Chem. Soc., Tenn. Acad. Scis., Sigma Xi, Phi Kappa Phi. Democrat. Roman Catholic. Avocations: golf, reading. Home: 734 Loweland Rd Cookeville TN 38501-2888 E-mail: avolpe@tntech.edu.

VOLPE, EDMOND L(ORIS), college president; b. New Haven, Nov. 16, 1922; s. Joseph D. and Rose (Maisano) V.; m. Rose Conte, May 20, 1950; children: Rosalind, Lisa. AB, U. Mich., 1943; MA, Columbia U., 1947, PhD, 1954. Instr. N.Y. U., 1949-54; mem. faculty City Coll. N.Y., 1954-74, prof. English, 1964-74, chmn. dept., 1964-70; pres. Richmond Coll., 1974-76, Coll. S.I., 1976-94. Fulbright prof. Am. lit., France, 1960-61 Author: A Reader's Guide to William Faulkner, 1964; also anthologies and coll. text books.; Co-editor: Eleven Modern Short Novels. Bd. dirs. Staten Island United Way, 1975—, S.I. council Boy Scouts Am., 1977-84, S.I. Doctors Hosp., 1977-78, Snug Harbor Cultural Ctr., 1978-83, St. Vincent's Hosp., 1979—; mem. N.Y.C. Mayor's Commn. on Bias, 1986-88. With AUS, 1943-46. Recipient Commendatore Order of Merit, Republic of Italy, Cmty. Svc. award Italian Club S.I., Humanitarian award S.I. Jewish Found. Sch., Mills G. Skinner award S.I. br. N.Y. Urban League, Christopher Columbus award Columbian Assn. Bd. Edn., Disting. Cmty. Svc. award YMCA, Cmty. Svc. award S.I. Women's divsn. Am. Com. on Italian Migration, Outstanding Achievement award Guiseppe Mazzini Lodge of Sons of Italy; named Educator of Yr. Am. Legion Richmond County. Mem. MLA, Am. Studies Assn., Assn. Dept. English (exec. com. 1969-71), Am. Assn. State Colls. and Univs. (task force ednl. opportunites for the aging, research and liason com., com. internat. programs, health affairs com.), Am. Assn. Higher Edn., Am. Assn. Colls. for Tchr. Edn., Am. Assn. Univ. Profs., Am. Council Edn., Am. Studies Assn., Assn. Colls. and Univs. N.Y., Assn. Depts. of English (nat. exec. com.), Coll. English Assn. (nat. bd. dirs.), Consortium Internat. Programs, Inst. Internat. Edn., Inc., Middle States Assn. Colls. and Schs. Clubs: Andiron N.Y. (pres. 1972-75).

VOLPE, EILEEN RAE, special education educator; b. Fort Morgan, Colo., Aug. 23, 1942; d. Earl Lester and Ellen Ada (Hearting) Moore; m. David P. Volpe, July 28, 1965 (div. 1980); children: David P. Jr., Christina Marie. BA, U. No. Colo., 1964, MA, 1978. Cert. fine art tchr., learning handicapped specialist, resource specialist. 5th grade tchr. Meml. Elem. Sch., Milford, Mass., 1967-68; fine arts jr./sr. high tchr. Nipmuc Regional Jr. Sr. H.S., Mendon, 1968-69; spl. edn. tchr. Saugus (Calif.) H.S., 1979—98, Valencia (Calif.) H.S., 1998—. Publicity dir. Sacred Heart Ch., Milford, Mass., 1974-75, float coord. bicentennial parade, 1975. Author: (poetry) Seasons to Come, 1994, Best Poems of 1997, The Other Side of Midnight, 1997, Best of 2001 Poems; contbr. to Best of Millennium Poetry, 1999-2000, Best of 2002 Poems. Mem. Calif. Tchr. Assn., Coun. for Exceptional Children, DAR, Phi Delta Kappa, Kappa Delta Pi. Republican. Avocations: arts and crafts, photography, travel, doll collecting and creation. Office: Valencia HS 27801 Dickason Dr Valencia CA 91355-4012

VOLPE, ELLEN MARIE, secondary school educator; b. Bronx, N.Y., Aug. 2, 1949; d. George Thomas and Mary (Popadinecz) Soloweyko; m. Ronald Edward Volpe, May 22, 1971; children: Keith, Daniel, Christopher, Stephanie. BBA, Pace U., 1971; MA in Teaching, Sacred Heart U., 1986. Tchr. Conn. Bus. Inst., Stratford, 1979-80, Katherine Gibbs Sch., Norwalk, Conn., 1980-89; adj. instr. So. Cen. Community Coll., New Haven, 1986-87, Salt Lake C. C., Phillips Jr. Coll., Salt Lake City, 1992-93; instr. Bryman Sch., 1990-92; tchr. Indian Hills Mid. Sch., Sandy, Utah, 1993-99, vocational dept. chmn.; tchr. MaST Cmty. Charter Sch., Phila., 1999-2001. Bus. team leader reaccreditation and tech. coms. Indian Hills Mid. Sch., 1996, vocat. dept. chair; mem. curriculum rev. com. Katharine Gibbs Sch., 1989-90. Avocations: ceramics, gardening. Home: 51 West St Warwick NY 10990-1432 E-mail: compteach50@hotmail.com.

VOLPE, ERMINIO PETER, biologist, educator; b. N.Y.C., Apr. 7, 1927; s. Rocco and Rose (Ciano) Volpe; m. Lesley D. Volpe, 1992; children: Laura Elizabeth, Lisa Lawton, John Peter. BS, CCNY, 1948; MA, Columbia U., 1949, PhD (Newberry award 1952), 1952. Asst. zoologist Columbia U., N.Y.C., 1948-51; instr. biology CCNY, 1951-52; asst. prof. zoology Newcomb Coll., Tulane U., 1952-81, chmn. dept. zoology, 1954-64, 64-66, 69-79, W.R. Irby disting. prof. biology, 1979-81, assoc. dean Grad. Sch., 1967-69; prof. basic med. scis. (genetics) Mercer U. Sch. Medicine, Macon, Ga., 1981—. Cons. Nat. Commn. for Undergrad. Edn. in Biol. Scis., 1964-71; mem. steering com. Biol. Scis. Curriculum Study, 1966-70; panelist NRC, 1967-70; mem. U.S. Nat. Commn. for UNESCO, 1968-72; regional lectr. Sigma Xi, 1970-72; lectr. Elderhostel, 1988-98; chmn. Advanced Placement Test in Biology, Ednl. Testing Service, 1975-80. Author: (textbook) Understanding Evolution, 2000, Human Heredity and Birth Defects, 1971, Patterns and Experiments in Developmental Biology, 2001, Man, Nature, and Society, 1975, The Amphibian Embryo in Transplantation Immunity, 1980, Biology and Human Concerns, 1993, Patient in the Womb, 1984, Test-Tube Conception: A Blend of Love and Science, 1987; mem. editl. bd. jour. Copeia, 1962-63; assoc. editor Jour. Exptl. Zoology, 1968-76, 84-85; editor jour. Am. Zoologist, 1975-80; contbr. articles to profl. jours. Served with USNR, 1945-46. Fellow AAAS; mem. Genetics Soc. Am., Am. Soc. Zoologists (pres. 1981), Am. Soc. Naturalists, Soc. Devel. Biology, Soc. Study Evolution, Am. Soc. for Cell Biology, Am. Soc. Human Genetics, Phi Beta Kappa (v.p. Tulane U. chpt. 1962), Sigma Xi (pres. Tulane U. chpt. 1964, faculty award 1972.) Home: 1105 Bond St Macon GA 31201-1602 Office: Mercer Univ Sch Medicine 1550 College St Macon GA 31207-1500

VOLPE, EUGENE ARNOLD, immunologist, researcher; b. Moscow, Oct. 31, 1947; arrived in Latvia, 1966; came to U.S., 2000; s. Arnold Maxim and Olga Pavel (Nikitina) V. MS in Medicine, Riga (Latvia) Med. Inst., 1972; postgrad., USSR Acad. Med. Scis., Moscow, 1972-75, PhD in Medicine, 1976; postgrad., Polit. U. Riga, 1984-85; MD, Inst. Exptl. Clin. Medicine, Riga, 1992, Dr. habil. medicine, 1997. Postdoctoral rsch. fellow in natural antitumor resistance N.N. Blokhin Ctr. for Cancer Rsch., Moscow, 1989-95; jr. rschr. scientist Inst. Exptl. and Clin. Medicine, Riga, 1975-80, sr. rsch. scientist, 1981-94, leading rsch. scientist, 1994-99, D habil. medicine, 1997; sr. scientist, assoc. investigator dept. exptl. hematology, tumor immunologist St. Jude Children's Rsch. Hosp., Memphis, 2000—. Mem. sci. group leaderships Lab. Host Biostimulators, Dept. Oncology, Inst. Exptl. and Clin. Medicine, Riga, 1981—; vis. scientist Mario Negri Inst. for Pharmacol. Rsch., Milan, 1996, St. Jude's Children's Rsch. Hosp., Memphis, 2000; mem. coun. for Theses Habilitation and Promotion, Univ. Latvia, Riga (specialty theoretical medicine), rsch. bd. advisors The Am. Biog. Inst., Inc., Raleigh, N.C. Contbr. articles to sci. jours. Named Sr. Rsch. Worker, USSR Highest Attestation Com., 1983; recipient diploma Red Cross Soc., 1975, Award for Profl. Excellence, 1975, Badge of Honor for Profl. Achievements, 1977, travel award Ares-Serono Found., Switzerland, 1991, Travel award Belgian Assn. Against Cancer, 1993, Mr. George Soros' Internat. Sci. Found., Single award for profl. achievements, 1993, Travel Fund award 4th Internat. TNF Congress, The Netherlands, 1994, Travel award Novartis Internat. AG, Switzerland, 1997, Travel award Soros Found.-Latvia, 1997, Silver medal award 2000 Outstanding Achievements, U.K., 1997, Travel award Immuno-Designed Molecules Ltd., France, 1998; long-term rsch. grantee Latvian Coun. Sci., 1994, Mr. George Soros' Internat. Sci. Found., 1994; Paolo Baffi Study grantee European Sch. Oncology, Italy, 1996. Mem. Internat. Soc. for Preventive Oncology (travel award 1994), Baltic Immunol. Soc., European Assn. for Cancer Rsch. (travel awards 1991, 93, 94, 98), European Macrophage Soc., Soc. Exptl. Biology and Medicine, Soc. Leukocyte Biology (travel award 1997, 99), N.Y. Acad. Sci. Avocations: bookbinding, classic and modern poetry, literature, Impressionism and avant-garde painting, traveling. Office: St Jude Chldrns Rsch Hosp Dept Molec Pharm 332 N Lauderdale St Memphis TN 38105-2729 E-mail: eungnevolpe@yahoo.com.

VOLPE, JOSEPH JOHN, pediatric neurologist, educator; b. Salem, Mass., Dec. 17, 1938; s. John Rosario and Anne Eleanor (Femino) V.; m. Sara Lee Solov, June 2, 1980; children from previous marriage: Joanna Marie, Joseph

Anthony, John Matthew. BA, Bowdoin Coll., 1960; MD, Harvard U., 1964. Diplomate Am. Bd. Pediatrics, Am. Bd. Neurology and Psychiatry with spl. competence in child neurology. Pediatric intern Mass. Gen. Hosp., Boston, 1964-65, pediatric resident, 1965-66, neurology and pediatric resident, 1968-71; rsch. assoc. Nat. Inst. Child Health and Human Devel., Bethesda, Md., 1966-68; asst. prof. pediatrics and neurology Washington U. Med. Sch., St. Louis, 1971-76, assoc. prof. pediatrics and neurology, 1976-79, prof. pediatrics and neurology, 1979—, prof. biol. chemistry, 1980-90, dir. div. pediatric neurology, 1984-90; Bronson Crothers prof. neurology Harvard Med. Sch., Boston, 1990—; neurologist in chief Children's Hosp., 1990—. Author: Neurology of the Newborn, 1981, 4th edit., 2000; contbr. over 300 articles to profl. jours. Capt. USPHS, 1966-68. Recipient Weinstein-Goldensohn award United Cerebral Palsy Assn., 1985; rsch. grantee NIH, 1973—, March of Dimes Nat. Found., 1985-87. Mem. Nat. Acad. Scis. Inst. Medicine. Office: Children's Hosp 300 Longwood Ave Boston MA 02115-5737

VOLPE, PETER ANTHONY, surgeon; b. Columbus, Ohio, Dec. 17, 1936; s. Peter Anthony and Jeanette Katherine (Volz) V.; m. Suzanne Stephens, Sept. 5, 1959 (div. 1977); children: John David, Michael Charles; m. Kathleen Ann Townsend, Mar. 28, 1978 (div. 1999); 1 child, Mark Christopher; m. Theresa Ann Morse, Aug. 27, 2000. BA cum laude, Ohio State U., 1958, MD summa cum laude, 1961. Diplomate Am. Bd. Surgery, Am. Bd. Colon and Rectal Surgery (pres. 1988). Pvt. practice, San Francisco, 1969—; sr. ptnr. Volpe, Chui, Abel, Yee, Sternberg, 1987—; clin. prof. surgery U. Calif., 1995—. Asst. clin. prof. surgery U. Calif., San Francisco, 1972-95, clin. prof., 1995—; chmn. dept. surgery St. Mary's Hosp. and Med. Ctr., San Francisco, 1978-90. Contbr. articles to profl. jours. Lt. USN, 1962-64. Fellow ACS (bd. govs. 1988-94), Am. Soc. Colon and Rectal Surgeons (treas. 1985-89, pres. 1990); mem. San Francisco Surg. Soc., San Francisco Med. Soc. Republican. Roman Catholic. Office: Volpe Chiu Abel and Yee Sternberg 3838 California St San Francisco CA 94118-1522

VOLPE, RALPH PASQUALE, insurance company executive; b. Souderton, Pa., Sept. 20, 1936; s. Pasquale S. and Katie M. (Hartzell) V.; m. Marie F. Romano, Feb. 6, 1962; children: William, Anthony, Lynda. BA in Polit. Sci., Pa. State U., University Park, 1963. Claim cons. Aetna Life & Casualty Co., King of Prussia, 1964-97; litig. cons. Hartford Ins., 1998—. Mem. Upper Merion Twp. Bd. Suprs., 1974-79, 82-87, 94—, chmn., 1984, 86, 87, 96, 97, vice chmn., 1985, 95, 2d. v.p. Montgomery County Assn. Twp. Ofcls., 1995-97, pres., 1997-99, past pres., 1999-2001; mem. exec. bd. Greater Valley Forge Transp. Mgmt. Assn., 1994—; mem. Upper Merion Govt. Study Commn., 1974, Rt. 202 Exec. Com., 1994—; chmn. Upper Merion Dems., 1980-81; chmn. Montgomery County Dem. Campaign, 1975; chmn. blue ribbon panel Montgomery County Waste Sys. Authority, 1997-98. With U.S. Army, 1959-61. Recipient Good Govt. award Upper Merion Jaycees, 1977, Excellence in Govt. award King of Prussia C. of C., 1997. Mem.: Southeastern Assn. Twp. Ofcls., Pa. State Assn. Twp. Suprs. (chmn. resolution-legislation com. 2002—, chmn. rules com. 1997—2000), Valley Forge Hist. Soc., Chapel Four Chaplains, Legion (hon.), Valley Forger Order Sons of Italy in Am. # 1776, Optimists. Republican. Roman Catholic. Home: 240 Strawberry Ln King Of Prussia PA 19406

VOLPE, RICHARD GERARD, insurance accounts executive, consultant; b. Sewickley, Pa., Apr. 10, 1950; s. Ralph Carl and Louise P. (Cosentino) V.; m. Janet Lynn Henne, May 10, 1986; 1 child, John Ralph. BA, Vanderbilt U., 1972. CPCU. Trainee, asst. mgr. Hartford (Conn.) Ins. Group, 1973-74; v.p. sales Roy E. Barker Co., Franklin, Tenn., 1975-80; asst. v.p., product mgr. comml. ins. Nat. Farmers Union Ins., Denver, 1980-82; prin. R.G. Volpe & Assocs, 1982-85; acct. exec. Millers Mut. Ins., Aurora, Colo., 1985-89; pres, CEO AccuSure, Inc., Arvada, 1989—; acct. exec. J.R. Misken, Inc., Denver, 1990-92, The Prudential, Colorado Springs, 1992-2001; sr. fin. rep. Principal Fin., Denver, 2001—. Edn. chmn. Insurors Tenn., Nashville, 1978-79; new candidate chmn. Mid-Tenn. chpt. CPCU, Nashville, 1979-80; cons. Bennett Nat. Bank Colo., mktg. mgr., 1989-90; cons. Colo. Plains Ins., Inc., 1987-90. Contbr. articles to profl. jours. Dem. chmn. Williamson County, Tenn., 1979; campaign mgr. legis., Franklin, 1979-98; legis. chmn. Centennial Life Underwriters, 1998, 2000, 02; del. Rep. State Caucus, 1998, 2000; mem. dist. com. Arapaho Dist., Denver Area coun. Boy Scouts Am., 2000. Named Hon. Col. Gov. Tenn., 1979. Fellow Life Underwriters Tng. Coun.; mem. Soc. Property and Casualty Underwriters, Centennial Life Underwriters, Million Dollar Roundtable (qualifying mem.), South Metro Denver C. of C., Order of the Arrow. Roman Catholic. Avocations: skiing, camping, hiking, biking, sailing. Home: 10908 Snow Cloud Trl Littleton CO 80125-9210 Office: Principal Fin 7600 E Eastman Ave Ste 300 Denver CO 80231 also: Prin Fin 7600 E Eastman Ave Ste 300 Denver CO 80231 Fax: 303-751-1214. E-mail: volpe.richard@principal.com.

VOLPÉ, ROBERT, endocrinologist, researcher, educator; b. Toronto, Ont., Can., Mar. 6, 1926; s. Aaron G. and Esther (Shulman) V.; m. Ruth Vera Pullan, Sept. 5, 1949 (dec. Jan. 1997); children: Catherine, Elizabeth, Peter, Edward, Rose Ellen. MD, U. Toronto, 1950. Intern U. Toronto, 1950-51, resident in internal medicine, 1951-52, 53-55, fellow in endocrinology, 1952-53, NRC fellow, 1955-57, sr. rsch. fellow dept. medicine, 1957-62, McPhedran fellow, 1957-65, from asst. prof. to prof., 1962-92, prof. emeritus, 1992—, dir. divsn. endocrinology and metabolism, 1987-92, chmn. centennial com., 1987-88; attending staff St. Joseph's Hosp., Toronto, 1957-66; active staff Wellesley Hosp., 1966-2000, St. Michael's Hosp., Toronto, 2000—; dir. endocrinology rsch. lab. Wellesley Hosp., 1968-97, physician-in-chief, 1974-87. Trans-Atlantic vis. prof. Caledonia Endocrine Soc., 1985; Hashimoto Meml. lectr. Kyushu U., Fukuoka, Japan, 1992; K.J.R. Wightman vis. prof. Royal Coll. Physicians, Can., 1994; celebratory lectr. commemorating 200th anniversary of birth of Robert Graves, Dublin, Ireland, 1996. Author: Systematic Endocrinology, 1973, 2nd edit., 1979, Thyrotoxicosis, 1978, Auto-immunity in the Endocrine System, 1981, Auto-immunity and Endocrine Disease, 1985, Thyroid Function and Disease, 1987, Autoimmune Diseases of the Endocrine System, 1990, The Autoimmune Endocrinopathies, 1999; past editl. bd. mem. Jour. Clin. Endocrinology and Metabolism, Clin. Medicine, Clin. Endocrinology, Annals Internal Medicine, Endocrine Pathology, American Journal of Physiology, Opinions in Endocrinolgy Metabolism, Thyroid; mem. editl. bd. Jour. Royal Soc. Medicine; contbr. over 320 articles to profl. jours. Nat. med. advisor Thyroid Found. Can., 1990—. Served with Royal Can. Naval Vol. Res., 1943-45 Recipient Goldie medal for med. rsch. U. Toronto, 1971, Novo-Nordisk prize Irish Endocrine Soc., 1990; Med. Rsch. Coun. Can. grantee, 1960-97. Master ACP (gov. for Ont. 1978-83); fellow Royal Coll. Physicians Can. (coun. 1988-96, chmn. ann. meetings com. 1988-94, sci. program com. 1988-94, chmn. rsch. com. 1994-96, v.p. medicine 1994-96), Royal Coll. Physicians Edinburgh and London, Royal Soc. Medicine (editl. bd.); mem. AAAS, Can. Soc. Endocrinology and Metabolism (past pres., Sandoz prize lectr. 1985, Disting. Svc. award 1990), Toronto Soc. Clin. Rsch. (Baxter prize lectr. 1984), Can. Soc. Clin. Investigation (Disting. Svc. award 1998), Am. Thyroid Assn. (pres. 1980-81, Disting. Scientist award 1991), Assn. Am. Physicians, Endocrine Soc., Am. Fedn. Clin. Rsch., Can. Soc. Nuclear Medicine (Jamieson prize lectr. 1980), Can. Inst. Acad. Medicine, N.Y. Acad. Sci., European Thyroid Assn. (corr.), L.Am. Thyroid Assn. (corr.), Soc. Endocrinology and Metabolism of Chile (hon.), Caledonia Soc. Endocrinology (hon.), Japan Endocrine Soc. (hon., gold medal 1986), Alpine Ski Club (bd. dirs. 1987-89), U. Toronto Faculty Club. Home: 400 Walmer Rd Apt 1829 Toronto ON Canada M5P 2X7 Office: 600 Sherbourne Ste 211 Toronto ON Canada M4X 1W4 E-mail: robertvolpe@sympatico.ca. *Rigid adherence to high standards and integrity is essential. Do what is worth doing now, not tomorrow.*

VOLPE, THOMAS J. advertising executive; b. Bklyn., Dec. 22, 1935; s. John G and Josephine (Fontana) Volpe; m. Anita Mazzei, Nov. 24, 1957; children: Lisa, Lori, John. BS in Econs., Bklyn. Coll., 1957; MBA, CCNY, 1965; hon. degree, St. Francis Coll., 1997. Mgr. Deloitte Haskins & Sells, N.Y.C., 1957-70; v.p., treas. Colgate Palmolive Co., 1970-85; sr. v.p., fin. ops. Interpublic Group of Cos., 1986—2001. Bd. dirs. Am. Tech. Ceramics, Rent-A-Wreck, Indust Leaders Fund. Bd dirs Multiple Sclerosis Soc, New York, NY, 1979—, vice chair; trustee St. Francis Coll., Bklyn., 1971—, chmn. bd. trustees. Mem.: NY State Soc CPAs (comt chmn), Fin Execs Inst (comt chmn, pres NY chpt 1995). Office: Babcock & Brown 599 Lexington Ave New York NY 10022 E-mail: tomv@babcockbrown.com.

VOLPERT, RICHARD SIDNEY, lawyer; b. Cambridge, Mass., Feb. 16, 1935; s. Samuel Abbot and Julia (Fogel) V.; m. Marcia Flaster, June 11, 1958; children: Barry, Sandy, Linda, Nancy. BA, Amherst Coll., 1956; LL.B. (Stone scholar), Columbia U., 1959. Bar: Calif. bar 1960. Atty. firm O'Melveny & Myers, Los Angeles, 1959-86, ptnr. L.A., 1967-86, Skadden, Arps, Slate, Meagher & Flom, L.A., 1986-95, Munger, Tolles & Olson, L.A., 1995—. Pub. Jewish Jour. of Los Angeles, 1985-87 . Editor, chmn.: Los Angeles Bar Jour, 1965, 66, 67, Calif. State Bar Jour, 1972-73. Chmn. cmty. rels. com. Jewish Fedn.-Coun. L.A., 1977-80; bd. dirs. Jewish Fedn.-Coun. Greater L.A., 1976-99, v.p., 1978-81; pres. Los Angeles County Natural History Mus. Found., 1978-84, trustee, 1974—, chair bd. dirs., 1992-97, pres., bd. govs., 1997—; chmn. bd. councilors U. So. Calif. Law Ctr., 1979-85; vice chmn. Nat. Jewish Cmty. Rels. Adv. Coun., 1981-84, mem. exec. com., 1978-85; bd. dirs. U. Judaism, 1973-89, bd. govs., 1973-89; bd. dirs. Valley Beth Shalom, Encino, Calif., 1964-88; mem. capital program major gifts com. Amherst Coll., 1978-86; bd. dirs., mem. exec. com. L.A. Wholesale Produce Market Devel. Corp., 1978-95, v.p., 1981-93, pres. 1993-96; mem. exec. bd. L.A. chpt. Am. Jewish Com., 1967-2002, pres., 1999—; vice-chmn. Los Angeles County Econ. Devel. Council, 1978-81; bd. dirs. Jewish Cmty. Found., 1981—, Brandeis-Bardin Inst., 1995-2000; mem. Pacific S.W. regional bd. Anti Defamation League B'nai B'rith, 1964—. Named Man of Year, 1978 Fellow Am. Bar Found.; mem. Los Angeles County Bar Assn. (trustee 1968-70, chmn. real property sect. 1974-75), Los Angeles County Bar Found. (trustee 1977-80, 96-99), Calif. Bar Assn. (com. on adminstrn. justice 1973-76), Am. Coll. Real Estate Lawyers (bd. govs. 1996-99), Anglo-Am. Real Property Inst. (treas. 1995-98), Amherst Club of So. Calif. (dir. 1968-85, pres. 1972-73), City Club (L.A.). Jewish. Home: 16055 Royal Oak Rd Encino CA 91436-3913 Office: Munger Tolles & Olson 355 S Grand Ave 35th Fl Los Angeles CA 90071-1560 E-mail: volpertrs@mto.com.

VOLTZ, STERLING ERNEST, physical chemist, researcher; b. Phila., Apr. 17, 1921; s. Harry John and Gertrude Irene (Derr) V.; m. Betty Morgan, Nov. 6, 1943; children: Sandra Elizabeth, Karen Lee. BA, Temple U., 1943, MA, 1947, PhD, 1952. Rsch. chemist Houdry Process Corp., Linwood, Pa., 1951-58; group leader Sun Oil Co., Marcus Hook, 1958-60; supervising engr. GE, Phila., 1960-62, cons. liaison scientist Valley Forge, Pa., 1962-68; rsch. assoc. Mobil Rsch. & Devel. Corp., Paulsboro, N.J., 1968-80, adminstrv., 1980-86; pvt. practice Media, Pa., 1986—. Contbr. articles to Jour. Phys. Chem., Jour. Am. Chem. Soc., Jour. Organic Chemistry, Analytical Chemistry, Jour. Soc. Automotive Engrs., Jour. Chem. and Engring. Data, Jour. Am. Inst. Chem. Engrs. and others. Lt. (j.g.) USN, 1943-46, ETO. Mem. AAAS, Am. Chem. Soc. (Phila. sect.), Catalysis Soc., Catalysis Club. Phila. (sec.-treas., chmn., dir. 1957-60), Am. Legion, Disabled Am. Vets., Sigma Xi. Achievements include 23 patents for Simulation of Catalytic Cracking Process, for Compatible Mixtures of Coal Liquids and Petroleum Based Fuels, for Reactivation of Automotive Exhaust Oxidation Catalyst, for Increasing Antiknock Value of Olefinic Gasoline, for Preparation of Aromatic Hydrocarbons, for Process for Dehydrocyclizing Heterocyclic Organic Compounds, for Alumina Stabilized by Thoria to Resist Alpha Alumina Formation, for Method of Treating Chromium Oxide, others; invention of plastic dry bag; co-development of commercial methanol-to-gasoline process, of fuel cell for space power applications, including first successful operation in space flight; development of catalysts and processes for petroleum and petrochemical conversions, of electronic apparatus to measure dielectric properties during oxidation reactions and establish reaction kinetics; establishment of relationship between catalytic properties, surface chemistry, and semiconductivity properties of metal oxide catalysts; research on catalytic systems for automotive emissions control including kinetic model of oxidation of carbon monoxide and hydrocarbons. Home: 6 E Glen Cir Media PA 19063-4712

VOLZ, ANNABELLE WEKAR, learning disabilities educator, consultant; b. Niagara Falls, N.Y., May 24, 1926; d. Fred Wekar and Margaret Eleanor (McGillivray) Wekar Treadwell; m. William Mount Volz, May 9, 1958; children: Amy D., William M. Jr. BA, Seton Hill Coll., 1948; MS in Elem. Edn., N.Y. State Univ. Coll., 1956. Cert. learning disabilities cons. N.J. Georgian Ct. Coll., 1981. Lab. technician Moore Bus. Forms Inc., Niagara Falls, 1948-50, Niagara Falls Health Dept., 1950-53; tchr. Niagara Falls Bd. Edn., 1953-56, Am. Dependent Sch., Ashiya, Japan, 1956-58, Mehlville Bd. Edn., St. Louis County, Mo., 1968-70, U.S. Dependent Schs. European Theatre, Weisbaden, Fed. Republic of Germany, 1970-74; para-profl. Medford (N.J.) Bd. Edn., 1978-81; learning disabilities tchr., cons. Southampton Bd. Edn., Vincentown, N.J., 1981-91. Mem. Womens Fin. Info. Program, Burlington County, 1990-91. Mem. LWV (N.C. chpt., Winston-Salem chpt. 1993-99, sec. 1994-96, mem. chair 199 6-99, voter's guide chair 1996, 98, LWV Piedmont chpt.), AAUW (N.J. chpt. Medford chpt. 1982-91, N.C. Winston Salem chpt. 1992—, treas. 1993-2000), Nat. Retired Edn. Assn., N.J. Retired Edn. Assn., Assn. Learning Cons., Seton Hill Alumnae Assn., Kappa Delta Pi. Home: 5080 Mountain View Rd Winston Salem NC 27104-5110

VOLZ, CHARLES HARVIE, JR. lawyer; b. Richmond, Va., Sept. 15, 1925; s. Charles Harvie and Mary V. (Mallory) V.; m. Constance A. Lewis, July 30, 1976; children: Charles Harvie III, Judith C. BS, U. Ala., 1950, JD, 1951. Bar: Ala. 1951, U.S. Dist. Ct. Ala., U.S. Ct. Appeals (5th cir.), U.S. Ct. Mil. Appeals, U.S. Ct. Appeals (11th cir.), U.S. Supreme Ct. 1962. Spl. agt. FBI, 1951; claim mgr. Allstate Ins. Co., 1952-54; claims atty. State Farm Ins. Co., 1954-57; ptnr. Roberts, Orme & Volz, 1957-59; sole practice Montgomery, 1961-63; asst. dir. Dept. Indsl. Rels., State of Ala., 1959-63; pntr. Volz, Capouano, Wampold & Prestwood, 1963-84, Volz & Volz, 1984-95, Volz, Prestwood & Hanan, 1995—. Note editor Ala. Law Rev., 1950-51. Campaign dir. March of Dimes, 1958, Am. Cancer Soc., 1967; exec. sec. Gov.'s Com. on Employment of Physically Handicapped, 1959-62; mem. Pres.'s Com. on Employment of Physically Handicapped, 1959-62; pres., bd. dirs. Montgomery chpt. Am. Cancer Soc. 2nd lt. USAAF, 1943-45. Recipient Outstanding Service award Am. Cancer Soc., 1967 Mem. ATLA (state committeeman 1973-75), Am. Arbitration Assn. (mem. nat. panel), ABA, Ala. Bar Assn., Ala. Trial Lawyers Assn., Farrah Law Soc., Montgomery Country Club, Masons, Kiwanis, Phi Alpha Delta. Methodist. Home: 1638 Cobblestone Ct Montgomery AL 36117-1713 Office: 350 Adams Ave Montgomery AL 36104-4204

VOLZ, ELIZABETH LANGWORTHY, social worker, educator; b. Cambridge, Mass., Dec. 16, 1967; d. Christofer Volz and Jennifer E. (Langworthy) Hansen; m. Ira Dale Price, June 4, 1991; children: Alexander I. Volz-Price, Wesley D. Volz-Price, Ian I. Volz-Price, Jennifer E. Volz-Price. BA in Polit. Sci. and Women's Studies, Swarthmore Coll., 1990. Cert. social worker, N.J. Counselor Cherry Hill (N.J.) Women's Ctr., 1987-91, Northeast Women's Ctr., Phila., 1990-91; instr., program coord. Glassboro People in Transition, 1995—98; svcs. coord. Glassboro Housing Authority, 1995—. Mem. N.J. Commn. on Women, 2002—. Mem. NOW (v.p. N.J. 1995-98, pres. 1998—). Office: NOW 110 State St Trenton NJ 08608

VOLZ, WILLIAM HARRY, law educator, administrator; b. Sandusky, Mich., Dec. 28, 1946; s. Harry Bender and Belva Geneva (Riehl) V. BA, Mich. State U., 1968; MA, U. Mich., 1972; MBA, Harvard U., 1978; JD, Wayne State U., 1975. Bar: mich. 1975. Atty. pvt. practice, Detroit, 1975-77; mgmt. analyst Office of Gen. Counsel, HEW, Woodlawn, Md., 1977; from asst. to dean Wayne State U., Detroit, 1978—86, dean, 1986—95; dir. Ctr. for Legal Studies Wayne State U. Law Sch., 1996-97. Cons. Merrill Lynch, Pierce, Fenner & Smith, N.Y.C., 1980-93, City of Detroit Law Dept., 1982, Mich. Supreme Ct., Detroit, 1981; ptnr. Mich. CPA Rev., Southfield, 1983-85; expert witness in product liability, comml. law and bus. ethics; pres. Wedgewood Group. Author: Managing a Trial, 1982; contbr. articles to legal jours.; mem. editl. bds. of bus. and law jours. Internat. adv. bd. Inst. Mgmt., I. L'viv, Ukraine, Legal counsel Free Legal Aid Clinic, Inc., Detroitm 1976—, Shared Ministries, Detroit, 1981, Sino-Am. Tech. Exch. coun., China, 1982; chair advt. rev. panel BBB, Detroit, 1988-90; pres. Mich. Acad. Sci., Arts and Letters, 1995-96, 98-2000, bd. dirs.; pres. Common Ground, PLAYERS; bd. dirs. Greater Detroit Alliance Bus., Olde Custodian Fund. Mem.: ABA, The Wedgewood Group (pres.), Players, Amateur Medicant Soc. (commissionaire 1981—85), Harvard Bus. Sch. Club Detroitm, Econ. Club Detroit, Detroit Athletic Club, Beta Alpha Psu, Alpha Kappa Psi, Golden Key. Mem. Reorganized Lds Ch. Home: 3846 Wedgewood Dr Bloomfield Hills MI 48301-3949 Office: Wayne State U Sch Bus Adminstrn Cass Ave Detroit MI 48202 E-mail: w.h.volz@wayne.edu.

VON ANDRIAN, ULRICH HANS, pathology educator; b. Munich, Aug. 15, 1963; came to U.S., 1989; s. Henrich M. and Dagmar U. (Helm) von A.; m. Laila Goodarzi, Aug. 21, 1992. MD, Ludwig Maximilians U., Munich, 1989, PhD, 1992. Postdoctoral fellow La Jolla (Calif.) Inst. for Exptl. Medicine, 1989-91, Stanford U., 1992-94; vis. scholar Ames. Dept., U. Calif., San Diego, 1989-91; asst. prof. pathology Harvard Sch. Medicine, 1994—; jr. investigator Ctr. for Blood Rsch., Boston, 1994—. Contbr. articles to profl. jours. including PNAS, Cell, others. Rsch. grantee Gerrnan Rsch. Assn. (DFG), 1992-94, NIH, 1996—. Mem. Microcirculatory Soc. Achievements include the molecular analysis of white blood cell adhesion and migration in the cardiovascular system. Office: Ctr Blood Rsch 200 Longwood Ave Boston MA 02115-5701

VON ARX, DOLPH WILLIAM, food products executive; b. St. Louis, Aug. 30, 1934; s. Adolph William and Margaret Louise (Linderer) von A.; m. Sharon Joy Landolt, Dec. 21, 1957; children: Vanessa von Arx Gilvarg, Eric S., Valerie L. BSBA, Washington U., St. Louis, 1961; LHD, St. Augustine Coll., 1988. Account exec. Compton Advt., N.Y.C., 1961-64; v.p. mktg. Ralston Purina Co., St. Louis, 1964-69; exec. v.p. mktg. Gillette Personal Care Div., Chgo., 1969-72; exec. v.p. gen. mgmt. group T.J. Lipton Inc., Englewood Cliffs, N.J., 1973-87; pres., chief exec. officer R.J. Reynold Tobacco Co., Winston-Salem, N.C., 1987-88; chmn., chief exec. officer Planters LifeSavers Co., 1988-91. Bd. dirs. Interat. Multi Food, Mpls., Ive Mackenzie, Toronto, Boca Raton, Fla., No. Trust Fla. Corp., Miami, Cree Rsch. Inc., Durham, N.C., Ruby Tuesday Inc., BMC Fund Inc., Adhesion Techs., Inc., Charlotte, N.C.; chmn. Morrison's Restaurant Atlanta, 1996-98. Bd. visitors U. N.C., 1988-92; chmn. bd. trustees Wake Forest U. Grad. Sch. Mgmt., 1988-96; pres. bd. trustees N.C. Dance Theater, Winston-Salem, 1989-90; bd. dirs. Forsyth Meml. Hosp., 1988-92, Naples Conservancy, Naples Philharmonic Ctr. for Arts, Florida Arts Coun., Reynolds Mus. Am. Art, Naples Cmty. Hosp., chmn., 1994-99, bd. dirs. health care sys., chmn., 1995—. Mem. Belle Haven Club (Greenwich) (bd. dirs. 1983-87), Naples Yacht Club, Univ. Club (N.Y.C.), Linville Ridge Country Club (Linville, N.C.), Royal Poinciana Club (Naples, Fla.), Port Royal Club (Naples). Avocation: tennis. Home: 3663 Rum Row Naples FL 34102

VON BEHREN, RUTH LECHNER, adult day health care specialist, retired; b. Dubuque, Iowa, Apr. 10, 1933; d. Adolph J. and Elva M. (Fedeler) Lechner; m. Donald O. Von Behren, Dec. 16, 1952 (div. 1965); children: Debi, Jerry, LuAnn. BS, Ill. State U., 1965, MA, 1968; PhD, U. Calif., Davis, 1972. Tchr. Centennial Sch., El Paso, Ill., 1962-65; grad. asst. Ill. State U., Normal, 1967-68; assoc. in History U. Calif., 1968-71; rsch. asst. Calif. Health and Welfare Agy., Sacramento, 1972-74; asst. prof. Sacramento State U., 1970-71, 78-79; analyst Calif. Dept. Health Svcs., Sacramento, 1974-75, sect. chief adult day health care, 1975-80; project dir. State Health and Welfare Agy., 1980-82; adult day health care specialist On Lok Sr. Health Svcs., San Francisco, 1982-95; ret., 1995. Cons. adult day health care various orgns. Author: Adult Day Care in America, 1986, Adult Day Care: A Program for the Functionally Impaired, 1989, (with others) Planning and Managing Adult Day Care, 1989; contbr. articles to profl. jours. Sec. Yolo County Hist. Soc., Woodland, Calif., 1976-80; dir. Yolo County Mus. Assocs., Woodland, 1980-82. Recipient Adult Day Health Care Tech. Assistance award Kaiser Found., 1983-86, Rural Adult Day Care Model award Sierra Found., 1988-89. Mem. Nat. Coun. on Aging, Inc., Nat. Inst. on Adult Day Care (chair 1988-90, Ruth Von Behren award for Outstanding Dedication to Growth and Devel. of Adult Day Care, Nat. Inst. on Adult Day Care, 1992), Phi Alpha Theta, Alpha Phi Gamma, Alpha Psi Omega, Kappa Delta Phi, Phi Kappa Phi. Avocations: reading, bird-watching, opera, antiques and collectibles. Home: 1813 Chapman Pl Davis CA 95616-1455

VON BER, INA, finance educator, psychologist; BA cum laude, USIU, San Diego, 1984; MA, USIU, 1985, PhD, 1987. Cert. in bus. mgmt. with specialization in leadership. Dir. La Jolla (Calif.) Inst. for Psychology, 1987—92; exec. and mgmt. cons. various, San Diego, 1987—; prof. mgmt., internat. bus. Webster U., 1997—. Exec. bd., program co-chair World Affairs Coun. Mem. exec. bd., program co-chair World Affairs Coun., San Diego, 1999—; bd. dirs. La Jolla Social Svc. League, 2000—01. Avocations: skiing, tennis, golf, art, travel.

VON BERNUTH, CARL W. lawyer, diversified corporation executive; b. Feb. 2, 1944; BA, Yale U., 1966, LLB, 1969. Bar: N.Y. 1970, Pa. 1990. Corp. atty. White & Case, 1969-80; assoc. gen. counsel Union Pacific Corp., N.Y.C., 1980-83, dep. gen. counsel fin. and adminstrn., 1984-88, v.p., gen. counsel Bethlehem, Pa., 1988-91, sr. v.p., gen. counsel, 1991-97, sr. v.p., gen. counsel and sec. Omaha, 1997—. Mem. Am. Corp. Counsel Assn., Practicing Law Inst. Office: Union Pacific Corp 1416 Dodge St Rm 1230 Omaha NE 68179-0001

VON BERNUTH, ROBERT DEAN, agricultural engineering educator, consultant; b. Del Norte, Colo., Apr. 14, 1946; s. John Daniel and Bernice H. (Dunlap) von B.; m. Judy M. Wehrman, Dec. 27, 1969; children: Jeanie, Suzie BSE, Colo. State U., 1968; MS, U. Idaho, 1970; MBA, Claremont (Calif.) Grad. Sch., 1980; PhD in Engring., U. Nebr., 1982. Registered profl. engr., Calif., Nebr. Agrl. product mgr. Rain Bird Sprinkler Mfg., Glendora, Calif., 1974-80; instr. agrl. engring. U. Nebr., Lincoln, 1980-82; from assoc. prof. to prof. U. Tenn., Knoxville, 1982-90; prof. Mich. State U., East Lansing, 1990—, chmn., 1992-96. V.p. Von-Sol Cons., Lincoln, 1980-82; prin. Von Bernuth Agrl. cons., Knoxville, East Lansing, 1982—. Patentee in field. With USNR, 1970—98, Vietnam. Decorated DFC (2); recipient Disting. Naval Grad. award USN Flight Program, Pensacola, Fla., 1970. Fellow Am. Soc. Agrl. Engrs.; mem. ASCE, Irrigation Assn. (Person of Yr. 1994), Naval Res. Assn. Avocations: flying, skiing, antique tractors. Office: Mich State U Dept Constrn Mgmt 213 Farrall Hall East Lansing MI 48824-1323

VON BRANDENSTEIN, PATRIZIA, production designer; Prodn. designer The Mirisch Agy., L.A., 1978—. Prodn. designer films including Heartland, 1979, Breaking Away, 1979, Ragtime, 1981 (Academy award nomination best art direction 1981), Silkwood, 1983, Amadeus, 1984 (Academy award best art direction 1984), A Chorus Line, 1985, The Money Pit, 1986, No Mercy, 1987, The Untouchables, 1987 (Academy award nomination best art direction 1987), Working Girl, 1988, The Lemon Sisters, 1990, Postcards From the Edge, 1990, Billy Bathgate, 1992, Sneakers, 1992, Leap of Faith, 1993, Six Degrees of Separation, 1993, The Quick and the Dead, 1995, Just Cause, 1995, The People vs. Larry Flynt, 1996, A Simple Plan, 1998, Man on the Moon, 1999, Shaft, 2000, A Few Good Years, 2002, The Emperor's Club, 2002; costume designer films including Between the Lines, 1977, Saturday Night Fever, 1977, A Little Sex, 1982.

VON BRAUN, CURT, aerospace engineer; b. Royal Oak, Mich., Nov. 16, 1962; s. Magnus and Nathalie von Braun; m. Christine Guarisco, May 21, 1988; children: Katie Elizabeth, Christoph Maximilian. BS, Ariz. State U., 1985; MS, U. Mich., 1986; PhD, U. Tex., 1991. Instr. dept. aerospace engring. U. Tex., Austin, 1987-91; mem. rsch. staff Deutsches Geodaetisches Forschungsinstitut, Oberpfaffenhofen, Germany, 1992-93, GeoForschungsZentrum, Potsdam, Germany, 1993; mem. tech. staff MIT Lincoln Lab., Lexington, Mass., 1994-99, group leader, 1999—. Contbr. numerous papers to profl. confs., articles to profl. jours. including Jour. Guidance, Control and Dynamics, others. Pres. engring. coll. coun. Ariz. State U., Tempe, 1984, mem., 1982-85. Milo Oliphant fellow U. Mich., 1986, Regent's fellow U. Mich., 1985; recipent Tchg. Excellence award U. Tex. Coll. Engring., 1990, Disting. Achievement award Ariz. State U. Coll. Engring., 1984. Mem. AIAA, Golden Key, Tau Beta Pi, Pi Tau Sigma, Phi Kappa Phi. Avocations: real estate investment, carpentry, travel. Home: 49 Lexington St Burlington MA 01803 Office: 244 Wood St Lexington MA 02420-9185 E-mail: braun@ll.mit.edu.

VON BRAUN, PETER CARL MOORE STEWART, business executive; b. Greenwich, Conn., June 24, 1940; s. Carl Conrad and Martha Irwin (Moore) von B.; m. Elisabeth Esser, July 1, 1967 (div. Dec. 1980); m. Denene Jensen, Sept. 26, 1987; children: Christina Stewart, Alexander Stewart. BA with high honors, Yale U., 1964; PhD summa cum laude, U. Cologne, 1966. Assoc. McKinsey & Co., Inc., N.Y.C., 1966-72, prin., 1972-77; chief internat. program devel. Order of St. John, London, 1977-80; exec. dir. Sight Programme, London and Sultanate of Oman, 1977-84; mng. ptnr. Leyton Assocs., Greenwich, 1980—; chmn., CEO Am. Microtrace Corp., Virginia Beach, Va., 1987-95, RusPetrol (USA), LLC, Greenwich, Conn., 1989-99. Mng. dir. LabelADD, LLC, Greenwich, Conn., 1987—; chmn. Leix LLC,

Riverside, Conn., 2000—, Best Candle Co., Riverside, Conn., 2001—. Author: Die Verteidigung Indiens, 1968, How to Save a Life, 1977, How to Save An Eye, 1981; contbr. articles to profl. jours.; producer (film) How to Save a Life, 1977. Chmn. Battle Harbour Found., Greenwich, 1972—; vestryman Trinity Parish, N.Y.C., 1977-84; chmn. Anglican Svc. Tng. & Relief Orgn., London, 1986—; bd. dirs. Presiding Bishop's Fund, N.Y.C., 1977-81; mem. exec. bd. Greenwich Coun. Boy Scouts Am. With USN, 1956-58, U.S. Army, 1958-64. Decorated knight of grace and knight of justice Order of St. John, companion with star Order of Merit (Cyprus), other fgn. and U.S. decorations; Fulbright scholar, 1964-66. Mem.: Cavalry, Guards Polo (London); N.Y. Yacht (N.Y.C.), Yale Club, Indian Harbor Yacht Field Club (Greenwich, Conn.), Battle Harbour Yacht (Newfoundland, Can.), Commodore, Stewart Soc. (Edinburgh). Republican. Episcopalian. Avocations: sailing, military history, cooking. Home: 36 Zaccheus Mead Ln Greenwich CT 06831-3753

VON BRIESEN, EDWARD FULLER, builder, real estate developer; b. Glen Cove, N.Y., Sept. 21, 1948; s. Hans and Elizabeth Schermerhorn (Suydam) von B.; m. Alice Ruth Marvin. BSEE, Tufts U., 1970. Engr. L.I. Lighting Co., Hicksville, N.Y., 1970-72; pres. Briesmar Inc., Oyster Bay, 1973-82, Breza Enterprises Inc., Oyster Bay, 1982—. Road commr. Inc. Village of Oyster Bay Cove, 1981-97; sec. Grenville Baker Boys and Girls Club, Locust Valley, N.Y., 1996—, treas.; pres. L.I. Lead Assessment and Control, Inc., 1996—; bd. dirs. Nassau County chpt. ARC, 1998—. Mem.: Piping Rock (Locust Valley, N.Y.). Republican. Episcopalian. Avocations: flying, restoring antique autos. Home and Office: 133 Horseshoe Rd Mill Neck NY 11765-1006

VON BURG, FREDERICK E., SR. secondary school educator, writer; b. Biel, Switzerland, Feb. 22, 1934; arrived in U.S., 1942; s. Emil and Frieda Von Burg; m. Loretta Sauls, Aug. 25, 1962; children: Gregory, Paul, Frederick Jr. BS in Edn., St. John's U., 1961, MS in Edn., 1965. Cert. secondary sch. prin., supr., English tchr. N.Y., 1965. English tchr. Levittown (N.Y.) Schs., 1961—64, Sch. Dist. #13, S. Huntington, NY, 1964—66, Levittown (N.Y.) Schs., 1966—92; Tutor Creative Tutoring, Plainview, NY, 1992—95. Camp counselor and supr. Various camps, NY, 1952—79. Author: Raising Your Future, 2000, Keepy My White Sneakers, Kit Carson, 2002. Achievements include development of new names for Jean Plaget's Periods of Development. Avocations: canoeing, hiking, skiing.

VON BURG, MARY M. retired advocate, social services administrator; b. Montezuma, Ind., Feb. 13, 1937; d. Jesse and Gertrude (Wilburn) Thomas.; m. Raymond E. Von Burg, Feb. 28, 1958; 1 child, Raymond E. BS in Secondary Edn., Ind. U., Indpls., 1980; MS in Counseling and Student Pers., Ind. U., 1984, postgrad., 1989—. Sec., treas. Brownsburg H.S., 1972-79; rsch. asst., faculty sec. Sch. Pub. & Environ. Affairs, Ind. U., Indpls., 1980-81; adminstrv. sec. dean's office Sch. Medicine, Ind. U., 1981-85; counseling Marion County Prosecutor's Alternative Runaways Program, 1984-85; instr. Ind. U., Indpls., 1984-85, adminstrv. coord. cmty. child abuse project Sch. Medicine Dept. Pediats., 1985—; exec. sec. dept. pediatrics Sch. Medicine Ind. U., 1985-88; project mgr. Regionalization Care for Abused Children, 1988—. Coord. adminstrn. Cmty. Child Abuse Project., 1985—, Liaison Child Abuse Forum, Indpls., 1988—; mem. com. Child Advocacy Ind. U. Hosp., Indpls., 1989—; delegation to Russia and Lithuania Citizen Amb. Program People to People Internat., 1994; pres. Domestic Violence Network, 1994-97. Contbr. numerous articles to profl. jours. Mem. violence awareness com. Wishard Meml. Hosp., 1995-99; chair battered women's protocol com. Marion County, 1994-99, statewide tng. domestic violence/child abuse, 1994-99, mem. prevention of child abuse and neglect through dental awareness coalition, 1994-99; chair Marion County Ind. Hosp. Liaison Child Abuse, 1987-99, Sch. Liaison Child Abuse Forum, 1992-99; mem. Domestic Violence Network, 1989-99 (pres. 1989-97); coord. Marion County Child Fatality Review Team, 1994-99. Avocations: travel, photography, writing, boating, scuba diving. E-mail: mvonburg@msn.com.

VON CAMPE, HILMAR A. investment company executive, writer; b. Halle, Germany, Apr. 11, 1925; came to U.S., 1990; s. Alfred and Margarete von C.; m. Ubaldina Angelica Gamio, Dec. 1, 1972; children: Stefan, Sabrina. Diplom, Hamburg (Germany) U., 1950. Bd. mem. Moral Rearmament Germany, L.Am., 1958-69; asst. to pres. Adela Investment Co., Lima, Peru, 1971-72, regional mgr. Kingston, Jamaica, 1973-76; mgr. Cotinco, S.A., Mexico City, 1977-79; exec. dir. Formamex S.A. de CV, 1980-92; owner 5 Continents, Inc., Colorado Springs, Colo., 1993—. Author: Feigheit und Anpassung, 1989, Moral Meltdown, 2001, Connecting with the Power of God, 1996, Deutschland im Globalen Bürgerkrieg, 2002. Bd. mem. Berlin Sculpture Fund, Inc. Decorated Iron Cross, Assault Medal. Mem. Am. Ret. Officers Assn., Order of St. John (knight). Lutheran. Office: Five Continents PO Box 60326 Colorado Springs CO 80960-0326 E-mail: voncampe@aol.com.

VON DASSANOWSKY, ELFI (ELFRIEDE MARIA VON DASSANOWSKY), film producer, educator, vocalist; b. Vienna, Austria, Feb. 2, 1924; d. Franz Leopold and Anna (Grünwald-Esterhazy) von Dass.; 3 children. Diploma, Hochschule für Musik und darstellende Kunst, Vienna, 1944; vocal studies with Paula Mark-Neusser, piano studies with Emil von Sauer. Actress in Austrian theater and film, 1946-53; broadcast announcer Forces Broadcasting, Central Europe, Vienna, BBC, Vienna; co-founder, prodr. Belvedere Film Studio, Austria, 1946; adminstr., casting dir. Phoebus Internat. Film, Germany, 1951; pres. Belvedere Film Productions, L.A., 1999—. Various business activities, 1968-90, music coach for film dir. Karl Hartl and Actor Curd Jurgens, 1941-42; vocal coach, piano classes, N.Y., Hollywood, 1955-67; faculty mem., cons. numerous internat. acads. and cultural orgns.; star contract UFA Studios, Berlin, 1944. Opera debut as Susanne in Le Nozze di Figaro, St. Pölten, 1946; guest appearances in Vienna, St. Pölten, Hamburg, Flensburg, Munich, 1946-53; prin. roles soprano and mezzo include Agathe in Freischütz, Mimi in Boheme, Hansel and Gretel, Lola in Cavalleria Rusticana, Orlofsky in Fledermaus; numerous leading roles in Viennese operetta; spl. vocal and piano recitals for Allied high Command Europe, 1947-49; European radio performances as singer and pianist, Co-Producer: Die Glücksmühle, 1947, Wer küsst Wen?,1947, Der Leberfleck, 1948, Dr. Rosin, 1949, Märchen vom Glück, 1949; exec. prodr. Semmelweis, 2001. Decorated Chevalier, Ordre des Arts et des Lettres, France, 2001, Order of Merit in Gold, City of Vienna, 2002; recipient Accademica Honoris Causa Accademia Culturale d'Europe, 1990, Order of Merit in Gold, Austria, 1991, Gold Medallion City of Vienna, 1996, Honor City of L.A., 1996, Mozart medal UNESCO, 1997, medal of honor Austrian Film Archives, 1998; named Elfriede von Dassanowsky Day Calif. State Senate, 1996; granted title of Prof. by Austrian Pres., 1998, Women's Internat. Ctr. Living Legacy award, 2000. Mem. Austrian Am. Film Assn., Assn. Austrian Film Producers, Women's Internat. Ctr., U.S. National Women's Hall of Fame, Friends of L.A. Philharm. Roman Catholic. Home and Office: 13052 Moorpark St Ste 203 Studio City CA 91604-5003 E-mail: Belvederefilm@yahoo.com.

VONDERBRINK, GERALD WILLIAM, retired academic administrator, property manager; b. Cin. s. Richard Bernard and Marguerite Grady Vonderbrink; widowed; children: David Jerome, Diane Edwards, Philip Gerald, Joseph Paul. BSBA, Xavier U., 1950; MBA, U. Dayton, 1966. Jr. acct. Alexander Grant, Cin., 1950-51; sr. acct. Hathaway & Hathaway, 1951-54; contr. Aerosonic Instrument Co., 1954-56; fin. analyst GE, 1956-57; contr. Coll. Conservatory of Music, 1958-61; v.p. fin. affairs U. Dayton, Ohio, 1961-92, asst. exec. v.p., 1993-98. Contbr. articles to profl. jours. Pres. Ohio Assn. Coll. and Univ. Bus. Officers, 1967-68; sec./treas. Ctrl. Assn. Coll. and Univ. Bus. Officers, 1968-69; mem. fin. aid com. Nat. Assn. Coll. and Univ. Bus. Officers, Washington, 1978; chmn. bd. dirs. U. Dayton Libr. Advancement Assn., 1999—; treas. bd. dirs. Places, Inc., Dayton, 1999-2001; bd. dirs. Dakota Ctr., Dayton, 1999-2001, Caring Families, Inc., Dayton, 1996-2001. Cpl. U.S. Army Signal Corps, 1946-48, Japan. Democrat. Roman Catholic. Avocations: tennis, bridge.

VONDER HAAR, THOMAS H. meteorology educator; b. Quincy, Ill., Dec. 28, 1942; m. Dee M. Clark, 1980; children: Kim, Kurt, Nicholas, Krista, Matthew. BS, St. Louis U., 1963; MS, U. Wis., 1964, PhD in Meteorology, 1968. Assoc. scientist meteorology Space Sci. & Engring. Ctr. U. Wis., Madison, 1968-70; assoc. prof. meteorology Colo. State U., Ft. Collins, 1970-77, prof. atmospheric sci., 1977—, univ. disting. prof., 1994, head dept. atmospheric sci., 1974-84, acting dean Coll. Engring., 1981-82. Cons. U.S. Army, ITT Aerospace, Sci. and Tech. Corp., World Meteor Orgn. UN, Ball Aerospace Corp., 1969—. Mem. Am. Meteorol. Soc., Sigma Xi. Office: Coop Inst Rsch in Atmosphere Colo State U Fort Collins CO 80523-1375

VON DER HEYDEN, KARL INGOLF MUELLER, manufacturing executive; b. Berlin, July 18, 1936; arrived in U.S., 1957, naturalized, 1967; s. Werner and Erika (Mueller) von der Heyden; m. Mary Ellen Terrell, Aug. 17, 1963; children: Ellen, Eric. Student, Free U., Berlin, 1959-61; BA, Duke, 1962; MBA, U. Pa., 1964. CPA Pa. Mgmt. trainee Berliner Bank, Berlin, 1955-57; sr. staff acct. Coopers & Lybrand, Phila., 1963-66; asst. comptr., corporate comptr. Pitney-Bowes, Inc., Stamford, Conn., 1966-74; v.p., contr. PepsiCo, Inc., Purchase, 1974-77; vice-chmn. PepsiCo, Inc., 1996-2001; v.p. fin. Pepsi-Cola Co., 1977-79, v.p. mfg., 1979-80; v.p. fin., treas. H.J. Heinz Co., Pitts., 1980-83, sr. v.p. fin., CFO, also bd. dirs., 1983-89; exec. v.p., CFO RJR Nabisco Inc., N.Y.C., 1989-93, co-chmn., CEO, 1993; pres., CEO Metallgesellschaft Corp., 1993-94; sr. advisor Clipper Group, 1994-97. Chmn. Fin. Acctg. Stds. Adv. Coun., 1995—96; bd. dirs. AstraZeneca PLC, Federated Dept. Stores, Inc., Aramark Corp. Trustee Duke U., Am. Acad., Berlin. Mem.: Field Club (Greenwich, Conn.), Univ. Club (N.Y.C.). Home: 15 Khakum Wood Rd Greenwich CT 06831-3728 Office: Ste 100 2 Sound View Dr Greenwich CT 06830

VON DER HEYDT, JAMES ARNOLD, federal judge; b. Miles City, Mont., July 15, 1919; s. Harry Karl and Alice S. (Arnold) von der H.; m. Verna E. Johnson, May 21, 1952. BA, Albion (Mich.) Coll., 1942; JD, Northwestern, 1951. Bar: Alaska 1951. Pvt. practice, Nome, 1953-59; judge superior ct. Juneau, Alaska, 1959-66; from judge to sr. judge U.S. Dist. Ct. Alaska, 1966—; U.S. commr. Nome, 1951—; U.S. atty. div. 2 Dist. Alaska, 1951-53; mem. Alaska Ho. of Reps., 1957-59. Author: Mother Sawtooth's Nome, 1990, Alaska, The Short and Long of It, 2000. Pres. Anchorage Fine Arts Mus. Assn. Recipient Disting. Alumni award Albion Coll., 1995. Mem. Alaska Bar Assn. (mem. bd. govs. 1955-59, pres. 1959-60), Am. Judicature Soc., Masons (32d degree), Shriners, Phi Delta Phi, Sigma Nu. Clubs: Mason (32 deg.), Shriner. Avocation: researching Arctic bird life, creative writing. Office: US Dist Ct 222 W 7th Ave Box 40 Anchorage AK 99513-7564

VONDRACEK, BETTY SUE, interior designer, remodeling contractor, real estate agent; b. Tulsa, Aug. 27, 1938; d. John Carson and Susan Elizabeth (Nall) Bumgarner; m. Rudy J. Vondracek, Feb. 4, 1961 (dec. Sept. 1990); children: Richard, John (dec.), Vikki. BFA, U. Kans., 1960. Lic. interior designer; lic. real estate agt. Comml. artist Hall & Floyd Advt., Tulsa, 1960-62; freelance artist El Dorado, Ark., 1962-67, Chgo., 1967-69; interior designer Jeanette Ford Interiors, Dallas, 1974-76; owner, designer, contractor Bee Vee Studio, 1976—; real estate agt. Mahoney Realty Svcs., 1992—. Mem. grievance com. Greater Dallas Bd. Realtors, 1992—; mem. Dallas Supts. Adv. Com. Designer Scottish Rite Hosp. Parade of Homes, 1984, March of Dimes Holiday Tour of Homes, 1985-86, Christmas at DeGolyer, 1988-90, Dallas Symphony Showhouse, 1985, 87, 89, 92. Elected ofcl. Dallas Ind. Sch. Dist., 1986-92; pres. West-Lake Rep. Women, Dallas, 1975-77, 92-94; chmn. bd. dirs. Am. Heart Assn., Dallas, 1990-91, Tex. chpt. bd. dirs., 1990—, chmn. bd. Tex. affiliate, 1996—, chmn. capital campaign, chmn. pub. affairs; mem. edn. com. Women's Coun. Dallas County. Recipient Dwight D. Eisenhower award Am. Heart Assn., 1993, Douglas S. Perry Vol. of Yr., Am. Heart Assn., 1990, Key Communicator award Tex. Sch. Pub. Rels., 1984, Disting. Svc. award Nat. Com. for Citizens in Edn., 1984. Mem. Am. Soc. Interior Designers. Roman Catholic. Avocations: painting, gardening, cooking, skiing. Office: Bee Vee Studio 6215 Chesley Ln Dallas TX 75214-2118

VONDRACEK, M. JON, communications executive; b. Chgo., Oct. 23, 1938; s. Milo J. and Genevieve H. V.; m. Elisabeth B. Vondracek, May 8, 1965. BA, Lawrence U., 1964. Journalist Wash. Post, N.Y. Times, Time Mag., Wash. D.C., 1961—66; sec., dir. comm. Georgetown U. Ctr. for Strategic & Internat. Studies, 1966—86; v.p. corp. pub. affairs Young & Rubicam, N.Y.C., 1986—87; adv. to the pres. Ctr. for Strategic & Internat. Studies, Wash., DC, 1987—89; v.p. The Johnson Found., Racine, Wis., 1989—95; v.p. external rels. CSIS, 1995—2000, v.p. and advisor to pres., 2000—. Trustee Lawrence U., 1998—; mng. dir., advisor to Pres. World Affairs Coun. Washington, D.C., 2001— Mem. Nat. Press Club, Metropolitan Club of Wash., Union League Club of N.Y., Univ. Club of Wash., Racine Yatch Club. Office: CSIS 1800 K St NW Ste 400 Washington DC 20006-2294 E-mail: mjvondracek@csis.org.

VON DRACHENFELS, SUZANNE HAMILTON, writer; b. L.A., May 26, 1928; d. Augustus Adolphus and Floribel Hargett (Kelly) Hamilton; m. James True Luscombe, July 14, 1950 (div. 1969); children: James Hamilton Luscombe, Kelly Ann Luscombe, Elizabeth Scott Buckingham, Patricia Jane Pecoulas; m. Louis Wood Robinson, Aug. 1972 (div. 1988); m. Alec Verner, Baron von Drachenfels, Aug. 14, 1990 (dec. Aug. 2000). BS, U. So. Calif., 1950. Tabletop cons., spkr. Fitz & Floyd, Dallas, 1983-90; contbg. editor Giftware News, Chgo., 1987-91. Author: The Art of the Table, 2000. Vol., mem. bd. Jr. League Pasadena, 1958-83, Nat. Charity League, San Marino area chpt., 1970-79; docent Huntington Libr. & Art Gallery, San Marino, 1962-68, L.A. County Mus. of Art, 1969-74; pres. Jr. League Sustainers, Pasadena, 1977. Republican. Episcopalian. Avocations: study of and collecting Oriental porcelain, reading history of tableware and table manners, travel. Home: 149 Littlefield Rd Monterey CA 93940-4917 E-mail: tabltalk@pacbell.net.

VON DREHLE, RAMON ARNOLD, lawyer; b. St. Louis, Mar. 12, 1930; s. Arnold Henry and Sylvia E. (Ahrens) Von D.; m. Gillian Margaret Turner, Sept. 13, 1980; children by previous marriage: Carin L., Lisa A., Courtney A. BS, Washington U., St. Louis, 1952; JD, U. Tex., Austin, 1957; postgrad, Parker Sch. Internat. Law, Columbia U., 1965. Bar: Tex. 1956, Mich. 1957, U.S. Supreme Ct. 1981. Sr. atty. Ford Motor Co., Dearborn, Mich., 1957-67; assoc., asst. gen. counsel Ford of Europe, Inc., Brentwood, Essex, Eng., 1967-75, v.p., gen. counsel, 1975-79; v.p. legal Ford Motor Credit Co., Dearborn, 1979-87; v.p., gen. counsel Am. Road Ins. Co., 1979-87; exec. dir. legal affairs Ford Fin. Services Group, 1987-91; leader in residence Walsh Coll., Mich., 1992. Panelist large complex case program Am. Arbitration Assn., 1993—; advisor to Czech Republic Ministry of Privatization, Prague, 1993-94; leader Russian Def. Conversion Project, 1995-96; lectr. in Ea. Europe, 1995; pres. Focus Internat. LLC, 1995—. Article editor: Tex. Law Rev, 1956-57. Trustee Birmingham Unitarian Ch., 1966-67. Served to 1st lt. AUS, 1952-54, Korea. Mem. ABA, Mich. Bar Assn., Tex. Bar Assn., Internat. Bar Assn., Am. Fin. Svcs. Assn. (chmn. 1990-91, bd. dirs. 1981-91), Fin. Svcs. Coun. (bd. dirs. 1987-91), Washington U. Alumni Club Detroit (past pres.), Order of Coif, Tower Club (Tysons, Va.), Confrèrie des Chevilier du Tastevin (France, Washington), Capitol Hill Club (Washington), Royal Automobile Club (London), Cosmos Club (Washington). Mem. Christ Ch. Home and Office: 519 Princess St Alexandria VA 22314-2332 E-mail: rvond2@aol.com.

VONDRUSKA, ELOISE MARIE, librarian; b. Chgo., Sept. 13, 1950; d. George A. and Irene L. Klebba; m. Richard J. Vondruska, Aug. 11, 1972. BA, Loyola U., Chgo., 1972; MS, U. Ill., 1973. Acquisitions librarian Parkland Coll., Champaign, Ill., 1973-79, tech. svcs. librarian, 1979-83; serials cataloger Arlington Heights (Ill.) Meml. Library, 1983-85; authorities librarian Northwestern U., Evanston, Ill., 1985-87; rsch. adminstr. Dastrup/Vondruska Assocs., Chgo., 1987-91. Head catalog dept. Northwestern U. Sch. Law Libr., 1989-97, assoc. dir. for bibliog. svcs., 1997—. Ill. State scholar, 1968-72, DePaul U. scholar, 1968; Katharine L. Sharp fellow, 1972. Mem. ALA, Am. Assn. Law Librs., Chgo. Assn. Law Librs., Ill. Libr. Assn. (bd. dirs. 1983, 85-86), Beta Phi Mu. Avocations: travel, golf, films. Office: 357 E Chicago Ave Chicago IL 60611-3059

VON ESCHEN, ROBERT LEROY, electrical engineer, consultant; b. Glasgow, Mont., Oct. 3, 1936; s. Leroy and Lillian Victoria (Eliason) Von E.; m. Carolyn Kay Frampton, Dec. 14, 1965 (dec. Feb. 1999); children: Eric Leroy, Marc Alfred. BSEE, Mont. State U., 1961; postgrad., U. Liberia, Lakeland C.C., Glendale C.C. Registered profl. engr., Pa. Hydro constrn. engr. U.S. Army Corps of Engrs., Mont. and S.D., 1961-62; hdqrs. chief engr. Eagle Constrn. Co., Colo., 1962; resident transp./distbn. elec. engr. Stanley Cons., Inc., West Africa, 1962-63, hydro cons., startup engr. West Africa, 1965-66; with Stanley Cons., 1962-68, Gilbert Assoc./United Energy Svc., 1968-92; performance based assessment program sect. engr., maintenance planning engr., condition assessment survey sec. mgr. Gilbert Assocs., Inc., Tex., 1992—. Bd. dirs. Kidsworld Multimedia; cons. engr. fossil power plant, Ky., Colo., Mo., Korea; site project mgr., Ariz., Aruba; nuclear constrn. startup engr., Pa., Ala., Ohio; safety sys. functional inspector, Calif., Wis., Oreg.; performance based assessment program project mgr., Tex.; tech. cons. World Bank, Liberia; engring. cons. USN, Manila, 1967; founding dr. Madison Comptr. Soc., Ohio, 1983-85; v.p., dr. Boy Scouts Am., 1981-84. Founder, dir. Madison (Ohio) Computer Soc., 1983-85; v.p., bd. dirs. N.E. coun. Boy Scouts Am., Painesville, 1983-85. Recipient Silver Beaver award Boy Scouts Am., 19 other awards. Mem. IEEE, NRA, NPSE, NARP, Soc. Am. Mil. Engrs., Nat. Def. Indsl. Orgn., Profl. Engring. Soc. Ohio, Profl. Engring. Soc. Tex., Masons (life), Shriners. Avocations: target and skeet shooting, constrn. design, computers, electronics. Home: 3445 Gladstone Ln Amarillo TX 79121-1525 Office: Mason & Hanger Mason Corp PO Box 30020 Amarillo TX 79120-0020

VON ESSEN, THOMAS, protective services official; b. Bklyn. m. Rita Von Essen; children: Pamela, Erica, Marc, Tom. BA in Econs., St. Francis Coll. Bklyn.; MEd, C.W. Post; grad., N.Y.C. Fire Dept. Sch., 1970. Firefighter Fire Dept. N.Y.C., 1970-85; from del. to pres. N.Y.C. Firefighters, 1985-96; commr. Fire Dept. N.Y.C., 1996—. Office: Fire Dept NY 9 Metrotech Ctr Brooklyn NY 11201-5431 Fax: 718-999-1031.

VON FETTWEIS, YVONNE CACHÉ, archivist, historian; b. L.A., Nov. 28, 1935; d. Boyd Eugene and Georgette Louisa (Tilmann) Adams; m. Maurice Lee Caché, Jan. 8, 1955 (div. 1962); children: Maurice C.B. II, Michele-Yvonne (Mrs. Vernon Young Sr.); m. Rolland Phillip von Fettweis, July 22, 1967. BA, Wagner Coll., 1954; postgrad, Am. U., 1973, Bentley Coll., 1981. Legal sec., asst. Judge, Davis, Stern, Orfinger & Tindall, Daytona Beach, Fla., 1961-66; head rec. sect., bd. dirs. 1st Ch. Christ Scientist, Boston, 1969-71, rsch. assoc., 1971-72, adminstrv. archivist, 1972-78, sr. assoc. archivist, 1979-84, records adminstr., 1984-91, div. mgr. records mgmt./orgnl. archives, 1991-92, divsn. mgr. ch. history, 1992—, divsn. mgr. ch. history and healing ministry, 1995; divsn. mgr. ch. history, 1995-96; ch. historian 1st Ch. Christ Scientist, Boston, 1996—. Cons. Christian Sci. Bd. Dirs., 1999—, pres. of Mother Ch., 2002-; mem. Religious Pub. Rels. Coun. Co-author: Mary Baker Eddy: A Lifetime of Healing, 1996, Mary Baker Eddy: Christian Healer, 1997, The New Woman and the New Church: The Lincoln Women, 2001. Trustee Ch. Hist. Trust, 1995—; exec. sec. Volusia County Goldwater campaign, Daytona Beach, 1964; mem. Christian Sci. Bd. Lectureship, 1998. Mem. Soc. Am. Archivists (editor The Archival Spirit), Automated Records and Techniques Task Force, Am. Mgmt. Assn., Orgn. Am. Historians, Ctr. for Study Presidency, Religious Pub. Rels. Coun., New Eng. Archivists, Assn. Records Mgrs. and Adminstrs. (bd. dirs. 1983—), Assn. Coll. and Rsch. Librs., Bay State Hist. League, Order Ea. Star, Order Rainbow (bd. dirs. 1972-77). Republican. Christian Scientist. Home: 147 Bosarvey Dr Ormond Beach FL 32176-6662 Office: 1st Ch Christ Sci 175 Huntington Ave # A240 Boston MA 02115-3117

VON FISCHER, GEORGE HERMAN, social psychologist, unified social systems scientist, management consultant, planning and data processing executive; b. Cin., Oct. 24, 1935; s. George Henry and Dorothea Ann (Steffens) Von F.; m. Patricia L. Seward, June 21, 1961 (div. 1981); children: Gary L., Michael L. BBA, U. Cin., 1962, PhD, 1984; MA, U. Akron, 1968. CPA, Ohio. Auditor Arthur Young & Co., Cin., 1959-61; systems analyst AVCO Corp., 1961-63; exec. dir. long-range planning The Hoover Worldwide Corp., Canton, Ohio, 1964-71; instr. U. Cin., U. Akron, Kent State U., Edgecliff Coll., 1972-78; asst. prof. No. Ky. U., Highland Heights, 1978-80; dir. MIS Cin. Electronics, 1980-81; mgmt. cons. New Eng. Trade Adjustment Assistance Ctr., Boston, 1982; chief contractor ADP Evaluation Divsn., Def. Contract Mgmt. Dist. N.E., 1983-97; ret., 1997. Contbr. articles to profl. jours. Mem. corp. planning adv. com. Cleve. State U., 1968; mem. long-range planning adv. com. U. Cin., 1973-74; reader Recording for the Blind, Cambridge, Mass., 1992—; mem. Satuit Concert Band, Milton Concert Band, Canton Am. Legion Post Band, German Double Eagle Band. With U.S. Army, 1954-56. Named Best Actor of Yr. Ohio Com. Theater Orgn., 1968; fellow U. Cin., 1972-73. Mem. AAAS, Union of Concerned Scientists, Alpha Kappa Delta. Achievements include development of documentation and methodological procedures for government oversight of contractor IRM operations, management and facilities; research in unified social science; facilitation in implementing total quality management in the federal government. Home: 570 Massachusetts Ave Boston MA 02118-1402 Office: 395 Summer St Boston MA 02210-1719

VON FRAUNHOFER-KOSINSKI, KATHERINA, bank executive; b. N.Y.C. m. Jerzy Kosinski, Feb. 15, 1987 (dec. May 3, 1991). Student, St. Joseph's Convent, London, Clark's Coll. Various positions Robert W. Orr & Assocs., N.Y.C., 1954-55; with traffic dept. Compton Advt., Inc., 1956-63; acct. exec. J. Walter Thompson Co., 1963-69; product mgr. Natural Wonder line Revlon Co., N.Y., 1969-71; pres. Scientia Factum, Inc., N.Y.C., 1971—, Polish Am. Resources Corp., N.Y.C., 1992—, pres., CEO, 1992—; founder, CEO, pres. Polish Am. Techs., L.P., 1992—; chmn. bd. dirs. Am. Bank in Poland/AmerBank, Warsaw, 1991—2001, bd. dirs., 2001—. Co-founder Westchester Sports Club. Assoc. fellow Timothy Dwight Coll./Yale U., 1997—. Avocations: skiing, horse/polo, swimming, photography. Home: 60 W 57th St New York NY 10019-3909

VON FRIEDERICHS-FITZWATER, MARLENE MARIE, health communication scholar and researcher; b. Beatrice, Nebr., July 14, 1939; d. Paul M. and Velma B. (von Friederichs) Fitzwater; children: Richard Nielson, Kevin T. Young, James L. Nielson, Paul M. Nielson. BS, Westminster Coll., 1981; MA, U. Nebr., Omaha, 1981; PhD, U. Utah, 1987; cert. in death edn., Prague U., 1982. Various pub. rels., writing and editing positions, 1957-78; teaching fellow in comm. U. Nebr., Omaha, 1978-83, U. Utah, Salt Lake City, 1978-83; asst. prof. mass comm. U. So. Colo., Pueblo, 1983-85; prof. comm. studies Calif. State U., Sacramento, 1985—, chair comm. studies, 1996-2000; assoc. clin. prof. family practice Sch. Medicine U. Calif., Davis, 1987—. Condr. workshops on communication skills for health care profls. Bergan Mercy Hosp., Omaha, 1980-81, Mercy Care Ctr., Omaha, 1980-81, Am. Cancer Soc., 1981-82, Hospice of Salt Lake, Utah, 1981-82; condr. seminars, workshops and courses on health communication, death and dying, patient edn. and compliance, other related topics, 1983—; presenter in health communication various profl. orgn. meetings and confs., 1981—; dir., co-founder The Health Communication Rsch. Inst., Sacramento, 1988—. Contbr. articles to profl. jours. Trainer United Way, Sacramento, project mgr., 1986—; pres. bd. dirs. Hospice Care Sacramento, Inc., 1986-87; instr. vol. tng. program Hospice Consortium Sacramento; hospice vol. 1980—. Recipient Lifetime Achievement award Sacramento Pub. Rels. Assn., also numerous state, regional and nat. awards for writing, editing, publ. design and photography. Fellow Am. Acad. on Physician & Patient; mem. Internat. Communication Assn. (health communication div., newsletter editor 1987-89, sec. 1989-91), AAUP, Assn. Behavioral Scis. and Med. Edn., Assn. Women in Sci., Pub. Rels. Soc. Am. (bd. dirs. Calif. Capital chpt. 1987-91), Soc. Tchrs. Family Medicine, Soc. Health Care Pub. Rels. and Mktg. No. Calif. Home: 5020 Hackberry Ln Sacramento CA 95841-4765 Office: Calif State U Communication Studies Dept 6000 J St Sacramento CA 95819-2605 E-mail: fitzwaterm@csus.edu., fitzm@heri.com.

VON FURSTENBERG, BETSY, actress, writer; b. Neiheim Heusen, Germany, Aug. 16, 1931; d. Count Franz-Egon and Elizabeth (Johnson) von F.; m. Guy Vincent de la Maisoneuve (div.); 2 children.; m. John J. Reynolds, Mar. 26, 1984. Attended Miss Hewitt's Classes, N.Y. Tutoring Sch.; prepared for stage with Sanford Meisner at Neighborhood Playhouse. Made Broadway stage debut in Second Threshold, N.Y., 1951; appeared in Dear Barbarians, 1952, Oh Men Oh Women, 1954, The Chalk Garden, 1955, Child of Fortune, 1956, Nature's Way, 1957, Much Ado About Nothing, 1959, Mary Mary, 1965, Paisley Convertible, 1967, Avanti, 1968, The Gingerbread Lady, 1970 (toured 1971), Absurd Person Singular, 1976; off Broadway appearances include For Love or Money, 1951; toured in Petrified Forest, Jason and Second Man, 1952; appeared in Josephine, 1953; subsequently toured, 1955; What Every Woman Knows, 1955, The Making of Moo, 1958 (toured 1958), Say Darling, 1959, Wonderful Town, 1959, Season of Choice, 1959, Beyond Desire, 1967, Private Lives, 1968, Does Anyone Here Do the Peabody, 1976; appeared in Along Came a Spider, Theatre in the Park, N.Y.C., 1985; appeared in film Women Without Names, 1950; TV appearances include Robert Montgomery Show, Ed Sullivan Show, Alfred Hitchcock Presents, One Step

Beyond, The Mike Wallace Show, Johnny Carson Show, Omnibus, Theatre of the Week, The Secret Storm, As the World Turns, Movie of the Week, Your Money or Your Wife, Another World; writer syndicated column More Than Beauty; contbr. articles to newspapers and mags. including N.Y. Times Sunday Arts and Leisure, Saturday Rev. of Literature, People, Good Housekeeping, Art News, Pan Am Travel; co-author: (novel) Mirror, Mirror, 1988. Avocations: tennis, painting, photography.

VON FURSTENBERG, GEORGE MICHAEL, economics educator, researcher; b. Germany, Dec. 3, 1941; came to U.S., 1961; s. Kaspar Freiherr and Elisabeth Freifrau (von Boeselager) von F.; m. Gabrielle M. Freiin Koblitz von Willmburg, June 9, 1967; 1 child, Philip G. PhD, Princeton U., 1967. Asst. prof. econs. Cornell U., Ithaca, N.Y., 1966-70; assoc. prof. econs. Ind. U., Bloomington, 1970-73, prof., 1976-78, Rudy prof. econs., 1983—; Robert Bendheim prof. econ. and financial policy Fordham U., N.Y.C., 2000—; sr. staff economist Council Econ. Advisors, Washington, 1973-76; div. chief research dept. IMF, 1978-83. Project dir. Am. Coun. Life Ins., Washington, 1976-78; sr. advisor Brookings Instn., Washington 1978-90; vis. sr. economist planning and analysis staff Dept. State, Washington 1989-90; Bissell-Fulbright vis. prof. Can.-Am. rels. U. Toronto, 1994-95. Contbg. author, editor: The Government and Capital Formation, 1980, Capital, Efficiency and Growth, 1980, Acting Under Uncertainty: Multidisciplinary Conceptions, 1990, Regulation and Supervision of Financial Institutions in the NAFTA Countries and Beyond, 1997; editor: International Money and Credit: The Policy Roles, 1983; co-author: Learning from the World's Best Central Bankers, 1998; assoc. editor Rev. of Econs. and Stats., 1987-92, Open Econs. Rev., 1997—; contbr. articles to profl. jours. Fulbright grantee to Poland, 1991-92. Mem. N.Am. Econs. and Fin. Assn. (pres. 2000), Am. Econ. Assn. Roman Catholic. Avocations: tennis, sailing. Office: Indiana U Dept Economics Wylie Hall Bloomington IN 47405

VON GENCSY, EVA, dancer, choreographer, educator; b. Csongrad, Hungary, Mar. 11, 1924; arrived in Can., 1948; d. Joseph and Valery Von G.; m. John S. Murray, May 13, 1957 (div. 1967). Student V.G. Troyanoff, Russian Ballet Acad., Budapest, Hungary, 1934-41, Szineszegyesuleti Iskola Theatre Sch., 1941-44; diploma, Royal Acad. Dance, London, 1953. Solo debut Salzburg (Austria) Landes Theatre, 1945-47; soloist Royal Winnipeg (Can.) Ballet, 1948-53; with Ballets Chiriaeff TV Co. (now Les Grands Ballet Canadiens), 1953-57, TV performer, 1957-70. Jazz instr. Banff Sch. Fine Arts, summers 1962-75; founder, dir. jazz workshop Saidye Bronfman Ctr., Montreal, Que., Can., 1965-72; with Les Grands Ballets Canadiens, 1962-72; co-founder, artistic dir., resident choreographer Les Ballets Jazz de Montreal Sch. and Co., 1972-79; guest tchr. Can., U.S.A., Europe, Malta, Marrocco, 1979-97; choreographer; adjudicator dance festivals. Past bd. dirs. Dance in Can. Recipient Best Dancer award French TV, 1967, Queen's medal, 1977, Lifetime Achievement award U. Que., Montreal, 1997, Rossetti Lifetime Achievement award, 1997. Mem.: Equity (hon.). Home: Apt 508 3650 Rue de la Montagne Montreal QC Canada H3G 2A8

VON GIERKE, HENNING EDGAR, biomedical science educator, former government official, researcher; b. Karlsruhe, Germany, May 22, 1917; arrived in U.S., 1947, naturalized, 1977; s. Edgar and Julie (Braun) Von Gierke; married; 2 children. Dipl. Ing., Karlsruhe Tech., 1943, Dr. Engr., 1944. Asst. in acoustics Karlsruhe Tech., 1944—47, lectr., 1946; cons. Aerospace Med. Research Labs, Wright-Patterson AFB, Ohio, 1947—54, chief bioacoustics br., 1954—63, dir. biodynamics and bionics div., 1963—88; assoc. prof. Ohio State U., 1963—88; clin. prof. Wright State U., 1980—. Mem. com. hearing bioacoustics and biomechanics NRC, 1953—93, chmn., 1990—93, bioastronaut com., 1959—61; mem. adv. com., flight medicine and biology NASA, 1960—61. Author numerous tech. publs., book chpts.; patentee in field. Fellow: Am. Inst. Med. and Biol. Engrng., Coll. Fellows, Aerospace Med. Assn. (v.p. 1966—67, E. Liljenkrantz award 1966, A.D. Tuttle award 1974), Inst. Environ. Scis. (hon.), Acoustical Soc. Am. (pres. 1979—80, Silver medal 1981, Gold medal 1999); mem.: Internat. Acad. Astronautics, Mil. Audiology Assn. (hon.), Biomed. Engrng. Soc., Inst. Noise Ctrl. Engrng., Internat. Acad. Aviation and Space Medicine, NAE. Achievements include research in bioacoustics, acoustics, biomechanics and bioengring. Home: 1325 Meadow Ln Yellow Springs OH 45387-1219

VON GIZYCKI, ALKISTIS ROMANOFF, research scientist, educator, scholar, writer; b. Famagusta, Cyprus; came to U.S. in 1967. d. Costas and Evangelia Lillian Victoria Kyprianou; m. Nicholas Romanoff, 1977 (dec.); m. Walter Von Gizycki, Sept. 19, 1981 (div. Dec. 1992); children: Bernard, Elsa. BA with honors, RMWC, Lynchburg, Va., 1967-71; MA in Psychology, New Sch. U., 1976-78. Educator, counselor Bilingual Bd. Edn., Nicosia, Cyprus, 1971-86; bus. devel. Bucci Trading Co., Cyprus, 1981-86; rschr., writer freelance, 1986—. Officer ch. bd. Fifth Ave. Presbyn. Ch. 19979—; vol. ch. and civic leader. Fulbright grantee; recipient Gen. Excellence award Am. Acad., Nicosia, Cyprus, 1967, Vol. award J.P. Morgan Chase Found., 1995, Outstanding Performance award J.P. Morgan Chase, 1997. Mem. NOW, N.Y. Acad. Scis. (assoc.), Am. Psychol. Assn., Am. Assn. U. Women. Avocations: theater, films, reading, music, ballet. Home: 1756 W 1st St Brooklyn NY 11223-1726 E-mail: alk12345@aol.com.

VON GONTEN, KEVIN PAUL, priest, liturgist, theologian; b. Bklyn., Mar. 21, 1949; s. Joseph William and Marion Von G. BA in Religious Studies, St. Francis Coll., Bklyn., 1979; AM in Hist. Theology, Fordham U., 1982; STM, Gen. Theol. Sem., N.Y.C, 1987. Ordained to ministry Episcopal Ch. as deacon, 1987, as priest, 1987. Prof. St. Francis Coll., Bklyn., 1982-87; asst. pastor St. Gregory's Ch., Parsippany, N.J., 1985-87; assoc. rector St. Stephen's Ch., Port Washington, N.Y., 1987-89; vicar All Souls Ch., Stony Brook, 1989—. Prof. George Mercer Sch. Theology, Garden City, N.Y.; chmn. Diocesan Commn. on Liturgy, 1989-99; dir. exploration of ministry program Diocese of L.I., 1987-2000; asst. sec. trustees Diocese of L.I., 1995-98; pres. bd. mgrs. Camp DeWolfe, 1995-97; sec. of conv. Diocese of L.I., 1993-99, chair dept. mission, 1998—. Author: The Great Vigil of Easter. Active N.Y. State Firefighter. Mem. Am. Acad. Religion, Nat. Assn. for the Catechumenate, Coll. Theology Soc., Theta Alpha Kappa. Office: All Souls Ch 10 Mill Pond Rd Stony Brook NY 11790-1816 E-mail: frkpv@optonline.net.

VON HAGEN, MARK LOUIS, historian, educator; b. Cin., July 21, 1954; s. Daniel William Von Hagen, Martha Berta Von Hagen; life ptnr. Johnny Roldan-Chacon. BS in Fgn. Svc., Georgetown U., 1976; MA in Slavic Lang. & Lit., Ind. U., 1978; PhD in History & Humanities, Stanford U., 1984. Dir. Harriman inst. Columbia U., 1985—2001, prof. history, 1985—. Cons. Primary Source Microfilms, Woodbridge, NY, 1986—. Author: Soldiers in the Proletarian Dictatorship, 1990; editor: After Empire, 1997; mem. editl. bd.: Ab Imperio, 2000—, mem. editl. bd.: Kritika, 2000—. Fellow, Fulbright Fellows-IREX, 1982—83, Social Sci. Rsch. Coun., 1986, Alexander-von-Humboldt Stiftung, 1991; grantee The Russian-Ukrainian Encounter grant, Nat. Endowment for the Humanities, Alexander-von-Humboldt Found., 1994—96, History of Human Rights Movement in the Era of Sakharov grant, Ford Found., Empire and Region: The Russian Case grant, 1997—2002. Mem.: Shevchenko Sci. Soc., Am. Assn. for the Advancement of Slavic Studies (bd. dir. 2000—), Coun. on Fgn. Rels., Internat. Assn. of Ukrainists (v.p. 1999—2002). Office: Dept of History Columbia University Fayerweather 611 New York NY 10027 Personal E-mail: markvh@rcn.com. Business E-Mail: mlv2@columbia.edu.

VON HAKE, MARGARET JOAN, librarian; b. Santa Monica, Calif., Oct. 27, 1933; d. Carl August and Inez Garnet (Johnson) von Hake BA, La Sierra U., 1955; MS in Library Sci., U. So. Calif., 1963. Tchr. Newbury Park (Calif.) Acad., 1955-60, librarian, 1957-60; circulation librarian Columbia Union Coll., Takoma Park, Md., 1962-67, library dir., 1967—, assoc. prof., 1990—. Mem. ALA, Md. Libr. Assn., Congress of Acad. Libr. Dirs. of Md. (exec. dir. 1999-00), Md. Ind. Coll.and Univ. Assn. Libr. Dirs. Round Table (chair 1996-98), Assn. Seventh Day Adventist Librs. (newsletter editor 1981-83, pres. 1989-90), Master Chorale Washington, Sligo Federated Music Club (pres. 1988-89). Republican. Office: Columbia Union Coll 7600 Flower Ave Takoma Park MD 20912-7796

VON HERRMANN, DENISE KEEFER, educator; b. Atlanta, Sept. 24, 1962; d. Clyde Andrew and Dolores Jean (Mahanna) Keefer; m. Andrew Benjamin von Herrmann, Aug. 18, 1990; 1 child, Joshua. BA, Washington and Jefferson Coll., 1984; MA, Jacksonville State U., 1989; postgrad., U. Ala., 1990—. Pub. relations dir. Dalton Jr. Coll., Dalton, Ga., 1985; bus. writer Marietta Daily Jour., Marietta, 1985-86; freelancer Atlanta, 1986; box office mgr., promotions dir. Jacksonville State U. Drama, Jacksonville, Ala., 1987-90; instr. DeKalb Coll., Atlanta, 1990-91, 93—, U. Ala., 1991-93. Instr. Job Tng. Partership Act Programs, Dalton, 1985; seminar leader Non-Profit Orgn. Assn., Morrow, Ga., 1986. Pub. rels. asst. United Way Cobb County, Marietta, 1985-86; campaign staffer Browder for Congress campaign, Anniston, Ala., 1989; registrar The Civics Bee sponsored by Closeys Found., 3d Congl. Dist., Ala., 1989; mem. Red Cross Flood Force Telephone Bank, Atlanta, 1994. Mem. Am. Polit. Sci. Assn., So. Polit. Sci. Assn., Kappa Kappa Gamma (charter mem. Washington, Pa. and alumnae clubs in Ga., faculty adv. U. Ala. 1993). Avocations: acting, aerobic dance, gourmet cooking.

VON HERZEN, RICHARD PIERRE, research scientist, consultant; b. L.A., May 21, 1930; s. Constantine Pierre Von Herzen and Elizabeth Martha (Hevener) Hough; m. Janice Elaine Rutter, Mar. 8, 1958; children— Brian P., Carol E. BS, Calif. Inst. Tech., 1952; MA, Harvard U., 1956; PhD, UCLA, 1960. Asst. rschr. Scripps Inst. Oceanography, LaJolla, Calif., 1960-64, vis. investigator, lectr., 1974-75; dep. dir. Office Oceanography UNESCO, Paris, 1964-66; assoc. to sr. scientist Woods Hole Oceanog. Inst., Mass., 1966-96, emeritus, 1996—, chmn. dept. geology and geophysics, 1982-85. Contbr. articles to profl. jours. With U.S. Army, 1953-55. Fellow Am. Geophys. Union (assoc. editor Jour. Geophys. Rsch. 1969-71, Ewing medal 1998). Avocations: travel; sailing; biking. Home: PO Box 271 Woods Hole MA 02543-0271 Office: Woods Hole Oceanog Inst Woods Hole MA 02543

VON HILSHEIMER, GEORGE EDWIN, III, neuropsychologist; b. West Palm Beach, Fla., Aug. 15, 1934; s. George E. Jr. and Dorothy Sue (Bridges) Von H.; m. Catherine Jean Munson, Dec. 27, 1968 (div. Oct. 1987); children: Dana Germaine, George E. IV, Alexandra; m. Jonnie Mae Warner, June 29, 1991. BA, U. Miami, 1955; PhD, Saybrook Inst., 1977. Diplomate Acad. Psychosomatic Medicine, Am. Bd. Behavioral Medicine, Am. Acad. Pain Mgmt., Am. Bd. Cert. Managed Care Providers, Am. Acad. Psychol. Treating Addiction, Nat. Register Neurofeedback. Sr. minister Humanitas, N.Y.C., 1959-64; cons. Pres. Kennedy's Commn. Nat. Vol. Svc., Juv. Del., Migratory Labor, 1963-64; headmaster Summerlane Sch., North Branch, N.Y., 1964-69; supt. Green Valley Sch., Orange City, Fla., 1969-74; neuropsychologist Growth Insts., Twyman's Mill, Va., 1974-79, Growth Inst., DeLand, Fla., 1980-82; assoc. health prof. Maitland, 1982-98; pvt. practice biofeedback trainer and hypnotist, 1998—. Cons. Sci. Adv. Bd. EPA, Washington, 1974-84; chmn. Certification Bd., Internat. Coll. Environ. Medicine, 1991-94; mem. Bd. Assn. Diagnostic Efficiency and Brief Therapy, dir. curriculum, 1993-94. Author: How to Live With Your Special Child, 1970, Understanding Problems of Children, 1975, Allergy, Toxins and the LD Child, 1977, Psychobiology of Delinquents, 1978, Depression Is Not a Disease, 1989, Brief Therapy, 1993, Brief Therapy: Antecedent Scientific Principles, 1994; editor Human Learning, Washington, 1974-94; editor: Jour. of ANT, ANT Trails, 1998—. Mem. spl. bd. Fla. Symphony Orch., 1992-93. With mil. intelligence U.S. Army, 1957-59. Fellow Royal Soc. Health (life), Internat. Coll. Applied Nutrition, Acad. Psychosomatic Medicine; mem. Assn. Neurotrainers (pres. 1998), Toastmasters, Phi Kappa Phi, Omicron Delta Kappa, Alpha Sigma Phi. Mem. Ch. of Brethren. Achievements include establishment of minor physical anomalies as significant predictor of physical and mental disease; demonstrated that treatment by neurofeedback significantly reduced criminal recidivism and that delinquency is a function of physical disease; demonstrated that ADHD and pain respond to neurofeedback; introduced treatment of schizophrenia by neurofeedback through Electro Dermal Response; introduced treatment of irritable bowel syndrome by neurofeedback; contributor to proof that alcoholism responds to EEG biofeedback. Office: AAT 125 S Swoope Ave Ste 109 Maitland FL 32751-5784 E-mail: drvonh@mindspring.com.

VON HIPPEL, ERIC ARTHUR, innovation educator; b. Boston, Aug. 27, 1941; s. Arthur Robert and Dagmar von Hippel; m. Jessie Roberta Janjigian; children: Christiana Dagmar, Eric James. BA, Harvard U., Cambridge, Mass., 1964; MS, MIT, 1966; PhD, Carnegie-Mellon U., Pitts., 1973. Engrng. mgr. Graphic Sciences, Inc, Danbury, Conn., 1966—69; cons. McKinsey and Co., N.Y.C., 1970—72; prof. Sloan School of Management, MIT, Cambridge, 1973—. Pres. Lead User Concepts Inc, Cambridge, 1996—. Author: (Book) The Sources of Innovation, 1988; contbr. articles to scholarly jours. Named Sir Walter Scott Disting. Prof., Australian Grad. Sch. Mgmt., 1997—98; grantee Scholarly Rsch. grantee, NSF, Alfred P. Sloan Found., 3M; Nortel Networks; NYNEX; Xerox; Bush,Boake,Allen,Bell-Atlantic, Fellow, Canadian Inst. for Advanced Rsch., 1995—97. Achievements include patents for facsimile technology. Avocation: industrial archaeology. Office: MIT Rm E52-566 50 Memorial Dr Cambridge MA 02141

VON HIPPEL, PETER HANS, chemistry educator, molecular biology researcher; b. Goettingen, Germany, Mar. 13, 1931; came to U.S., 1937, naturalized, 1942; s. Arthur Robert and Dagmar (franck) von H.; m. Josephine Baron Raskind, June 20, 1954; children: David F., James A., Benjamin J. BS, MIT, 1952, MS, 1953, PhD, 1955. Phys. biochemist Naval Med. Research Inst., Bethesda, Md., 1956-59; from asst. prof. to assoc. prof. biochemistry Med. Sch. Dartmouth Coll., 1959-67; prof. chemistry, mem. Inst. Molecular Biology U. Oreg., 1967-79, dir. Inst. Molecular Biology, 1969-80, chmn. dept. chemistry, 1980-87; rsch. prof. chemistry Am. Cancer Soc., 1989—. Chmn. biopolymers Gordon Conf., 1968; mem. trustees vis. com. biology dept. MIT, 1973-76; mem. bd. sci. counsellors Nat. Inst. Arthritis, Metabolic and Digestive Diseases, NIH, 1974-78, mem. coun. Nat. Inst. Gen. Med. Scis., 1982-86, mem. dir.'s adv. com., 1987-92; mem. sci. and tech. ctrs. adv. com. NSF, 1987-89; bd. dirs. Fedn. Am. Socs. for Exptl. Biology, 1994-98; mem. NIH-CSR panel on boundaries for sci. rev., 1998—. Mem. editl. bd. Jour. Biol. Chemistry, 1967-73, 76-82, Biochem. Biophys. Acta, 1965-70, Physiol. Revs., 1972-77, Biochemistry, 1977-80, Trends in Biochem. Soc., 1987—, Protein Sci., 1990-95; editor Jour. Molecular Biology, 1986-94; contbr. articles to profl. jours., chpts. to books. Lt. M.S.C. USNR, 1956-59. Recipient Merck award Am. Soc. Biochem. and Molecular Biology, 2000; NSF predoctoral fellow, 1953-55; NIH postdoctoral fellow, 1955-56; NIH sr. fellow, 1959-67; Guggenheim fellow, 1973-74 Fellow Am. Acad. Arts and Scis.; mem. AAAS, Am. Chem. Soc., Am. Soc. Biol. Chemists, Biophys. Soc. (mem. coun. 1970-73, pres. 1973-74), Nat. Acad. Scis., Fedn. Biochem. and Molecular Biology, Am. Scientists, Sigma Xi. Home: 1900 Crest Dr Eugene OR 97405-1753

VON HOELLE, JOHN JACOB LEWIS, publisher, commercial developer; b. Miami, Fla., Sept. 21, 1940; s. John Charles and Susan Ann (Lewis) von H.; m. Jan Behringer, Oct. 7, 1961; children: Eric, Christopher, Thimothy, Andrew, Ellen. MS, U. Cambridge, Eng., 1966. V.p. MNI Corp., N.Y.C., 1969-79, McCall's Publs., N.Y.C., 1979-81; pres. Dyne-Am. Publs., Wilmington, 1981-95; dir. publs. Oak Knoll Press, New Castle, Del., 1995—. Bd. dirs. St. Paul's Bibliographies, Winchester, U.K., Agamemnon Corp., Wilmington, Del; cons. Smithsonian Instn., Washington; spkr. internat. antiquarian and pub. convs., 1980—. Author: Collector's Encyclopedia, 1983, 1984, 1986, Sound and Glory, 1990, Godfather of the Brandywine, 1994, Tales of the Eastern Shore, 1995, The Lewis Chronicles, 1996, In Search Of, 1999, The Silence of Them, 2000, various other books on history, biography and short stories; editor, co-pub.: The British Libr., 1995—, editor, co-pub.: Libr. of Congress, 2000—. Pres. Kiwanis, Wilmington, 1973. Lt. col. USAF, 1958-62, USAFR, 1964-91. Recipient N.Y. award for scholarship and rsch. TCI, 1986, Taylor-Peabody award in Am. lit., 1995. Mem. Assn. Am. Pubs., Nat. Writers Assn., Internat. Assn. Fgn. War Corrs., Assn. Former Intelligence Officers (Washington, D.C.), Royal Cambrian Geneal. Soc. Avocations: writing, Mayan and Mesopotamian archaeology, collecting Cold War espionology books and cuneiform tablets. Office: Oak Knoll Press 310 Delaware St New Castle DE 19720-5037

VON HOFFMAN, NICHOLAS, writer, former journalist; b. N.Y.C., Oct. 16, 1929; s. Carl and Anna (Bruenn) von H.; m. Ann Byrne, 1950 (div.); children: Alexander, Aristodemos, Constantine; m. Patricia Bennett, 1979 (div.). Grad., Fordham Prep. Sch., 1948. Assoc. dir. Indsl. Area Found., Chgo., 1954-63; mem. staff Chgo. Daily News, 1963-66, Washington Post, 1966—76; columnist N.Y. Observer, 1993—; contbg. writer Archtl. Digest, 1996—. Author: Mississippi Notebook, 1964, Multiversity, 1966, We Are The People Our Parents Warned Us Against, 1968, Two, Three, Many More, 1969, Left at The Post, 1970, (with Garry Trudeau) Fireside Watergate, 1973, Tales From the Margaret Mead Taproom, 1976, Make-Believe Presidents: Illusions of Power from McKinley to Carter, 1978, Organized Crimes, 1984, Citizen Cohn, 1988, Capitalist Fools, 1992; also articles.

VON HOLDEN, MARTIN HARVEY, psychologist; b. Bronx, N.Y., May 29, 1942; s. Leon and Gertrude (Fishbein) Von H.; m. Virginia T. Brown, Dec. 17, 1971; 1 child, Mark Walter; children by previous marriage: Sandi Gwen Bitton, David Lawrence; 1 stepchild, Theresa Ann Brilli-Rogers. BA, NYU, 1964; MA, U. Toledo, 1965; D Pub. Adminstrn., NYU, 1981. Sr. psychologist N.Y. State Dept. Mental Hygiene, Rockland State Hosp., Orangeberg, 1966-67, team leader, 1970-71, dir. interdisciplinary tng. team, 1971-73; chief of service Metro Unit Harlem Valley Psychiat. Ctr., Wingdale, N.Y., 1973-74, dep. dir. programs, 1974-75; dep. dir. treatment svcs. Pilgrim Psychiat. Ctr., West Brentwood, 1975-76; dir. Matteawan State Hosp., Beacon, 1977, Ctrl. N.Y. Psychiat. Ctr., Marcy, 1977-82; exec. dir. Rochester (N.Y.) Psychiat. Ctr., 1982-97; privatization project mgr. Fla. Dept. Children & Families, Tallahassee, 1997-98; from svc. team coord. to adminstr. G. Pierce Wood Meml. Hosp., Arcadia, 1998-2000; adminstr. G. Pierce Wood Meml., 2000—02; ops. mgmt. cons. mgr. DeSoto Juvenile Correctional Facility, 2002—. Assoc. dir. Inst. Motivation Rsch., Croton-on-Hudson, N.Y., 1965-73; dir. Martin H. Von Holden Assocs., motivation rsch., Fairlawn, N.J., 1970-74; cons. psychologist, group therapist Green Haven Correctional Facility, Stormville, N.Y., 1970-77; cons. psychologist, group therapist Auburn (N.Y.) Correctional Facility, 1977-94, Butler Correctional Facility, 1994-96, Willard Drug Treatment Ctr., 1997; clin. assoc. prof. dept. psychiatry Sch. Medicine, U. Rochester, 1983-97; spkr. nat. and internat. profl. confs. including 2nd World Congress on Prison Health Care, 1983. Contbr. articles to profl. jours. Mem. adv. coun. N.Y. State Commn. Quality Care to Mentally Disabled, 1989-97. Capt. MSC, U.S. Army, 1967-70. Recipient James Gordon Bennett prize NYU, 1964, Outstanding Achievement award United Way of N.Y. State, 1994. Fellow Am. Assn. Mental Health Adminstrs. (cert. mental health adminstr.); mem. Am. Psychol. Assn., Am. Correctional Assn., Am. Assn. Correctional Psychologists, Assn. Facility Dirs. N.Y. State Office Mental Health (pres. 1984-85), Order of Arrow, Psi Chi Jewish. Home: 1250 Peppertree Ln Port Charlotte FL 33952-1357

VON HONTS, JACQUELINE JAY, artist, educator; b. San Antonio, Nov. 25, 1940; d. Emory Ralph and Helen Marie (Elder) Honts. BA in Painting, Trinity U., 1957; cert. in illustration, layout and design, Parsons Sch. of Design, 1959; MFA, U. Ams., 1964; PhD in Interrelated Studio Arts, N.Y. U., 1987; cert. in illustration, layout and design, Parsons Sch. of Design. Instr. San Antonio Coll., 1967-73, St. Mary's U., San Antonio, 1969-82, State U. N.Y., Buffalo, 1974-76, Niagara C.C., Niagara Falls, 1975, Dallas Independent Sch. Dist., 1981-82, San Antonio Mus. Art, 1994, 95, instr., adminstr., 1989, 91, 93-95, Trinity U., San Antonio, 1996, Northside Sch. Dist., 1997; art dir., owner Love Tex. Gallery SA Internat. Airport, 1982-99. Sr. artist Family Circle Mag., N.Y.C., 1959-62; asst. promotional dir. Better Homes and Gardens, N.Y.C., 1974-75; spkr. in field. Prin. work include sculptures Lake Travis, Austin, Tex., Hemisfair Playground, San Antonio, Colonial Hills Meth. Ch., and several private collections; executed murals Internat. Ptnrs. Ams. Internat. Conf., San Antonio, 1981, Modern Pentathlon Olympic Ctr., L.A., 1984, Am. Women in Radio and TV Nat. Conv., San Antonio, Trade Through the Ages Internat. Conv., San Antonio, Univ. Health Sys. Hosp.; one woman show include Instituto Mexicano-Norteamericaon de Relaciones Culturales, Mexico City, Am. Haus, West Berlin, McNay Mus., San Antonio, MGM Grand Hotel, Las Vegas, Nev., SOHO Gallery, N.Y.C., Art League Gallery, San Antonio, Gallery One, N.Y., Rockport Ctr. for the Arts, Tex.; exhibited in group shows at Intstituto Peruano-Norteamericano, Lima, Peru, Bright Shawl, San Antonio, Witte Mus., San Antonio, Ursuline Gallery, San Antonio, Jacob Javits Ctr., N.Y.C.; comml. artist for Bapt. Radio-TV Commn., Ft. Worth, Sta. KXAS-TV, Dallas, Sta. WFAA-TV, Dallas, Dem. Nat. Conv., 1976, TV News Network, Morristown, N.J., Sta. WBEN-TV, Buffalo; ct. rm. artist Watergate Trial N.Y. Times. Cover designer Bapt. Sunday Sch. Bd., Nashville, Tenn. Recipient Benedictine Liqueur award Jules Wile Sons, 1977, 1st prize in sculpture Dallas Art Edn. Assn., 1981; named one of Outstanding Young Women in Tex., 1970; grantee HEB, 1996, U.S. State Dept., 1989; scholar Ford Salute to Edn., 1994, 95, 96, San Antonio Tchrs. Coun., San Antonio Dept. Arts and Cultural Affairs. Mem. Tex. Ptnrs. of the Ams. (dir. cultural 1972-98), San Antonio Art League. Baptist. Home: PO Box 13023 San Antonio TX 78213-0023

VONK, HANS, conductor; b. Amsterdam, The Netherlands, June 18, 1942; s. Frans Vonk; m. Jessie Folkerts. Degree in Music, Ignatius Coll., Amsterdam; Degree in Law, City U., Amsterdam, 1964; trained with Franco Ferrara, 1964-66. Condr. Nat. Ballet, Amsterdam, 1966-69; asst. condr. Concertgebouw Orch., 1969-73; condr. Radio Philharm. Orch., Hilversum, The Netherlands, 1973-79; chief condr. Netherlands Opera, Amsterdam, 1976-85, Residentie Orkestra, Den Haag, 1980-91, Staatskapelle, Dresden, Germany, 1985-90; assoc. condr. Royal Philharmonic, London, 1976-79; chief condr. Radio Symphonie Orch., Cologne, Germany, 1991-97; music dir., condr. St. Louis Symphony, 1996—. Prin. guest condr. Netherlands Radio Philharm.; guest condr. l'Orchestre Nat. de France, Oslo Philharmonic, London Symphony, Norddeutsche Rundfunk, London Philharmonic, English Chamber Orch., Phila. Orch., Minn. Orch., Nat. Symphony Orch., Detroit Orch., Montreal Orch., Dallas Orch., Seattle Orch., Cleve. Orch., Boston Symphony Orch., Pitts. Orch., San Francisco Orch., Houston Orch., Balt. Orch., Mostly Mozart Festival Orch.; opera condr. La Scala, Rome, 1980, 88, Netherlands Opera, Dresden State Opera. Recs.: (with Christian Zacharias) 5 Beethoven piano concertos, Mozart overtures, The Nutcracker (Tchaikovsky), Der Rosenkavalier, Schumann symphonies and concertos, Bruckner Symphonies 4 and 6. Office: St Louis Symphony Orch Powell Symphony Hall 718 N Grand Blvd Saint Louis MO 63103-1011 also: care IMG Artists North AM 22 E 71st St New York NY 10021-4975*

VON KALINOWSKI, JULIAN ONESIME, lawyer; b. St. Louis, May 19, 1916; s. Walter E. and Maybelle (Michaud) von K.; m. Penelope Jayne Dyer, June 29, 1980; children by previous marriage: Julian Onesime, Wendy Jean von Kalinowski. BA, Miss. Coll., 1937; JD with honors, U. Va., 1940. Bar: Va. 1940, Calif. 1946. Assoc. Gibson, Dunn and Crutcher, L.A., 1946-52, ptnr., 1953-85, mem. exec. com., 1962-82, adv. ptnr., 1985—; CEO, chmn. Litigation Scis., Inc., Culver City, Calif., 1991-94, chmn. emeritus Torrance, 1994-96, Dispute Dyamics, Inc., Torrance, 1996-2000. Instr. Columbia Law Sch., Parker Sch. Fgn. and Comparative Law, summer 1981; instr. antitrust law So. Meth. Sch. of Law, summer 1982-84, bd. visitors, 1982-85; v.p., bd. dirs., dir. W.M. Keck Found.; mem. faculty Practising Law Inst., 1971, 76, 78, 79, 80; instr. in spl. course on antitrust litigation Columbia U. Law Sch., N.Y.C., 1981; mem. lawyers dels. com. to 9th Cir. Jud. Conf., 1953-67; UN :xpert Mission to People's Republic China, 1982. Contbr. articles to legal jours.; author: Antitrust Laws and Trade Regulation, 1969, desk edit., 1981; gen. editor: World Law of Competition, 1978, Antitrust Counseling and Litigation Techniques, 1984; gen. editor emeritus Antitrust Report. With USN, 1941-46, capt. Res. ret. Fellow Am. Bar Found., Am. Coll. Trial Lawyers (chmn. complex litigation com. 1984-87); mem. ABA (ho. of dels. 1970, chmn. antitrust law sect. 1972-73), State Bar Calif. (Anti-Trust Lawyer of Yr. award 2000), L.A. Bar Assn., U. Va. Law Sch. Alumni Assn. (mem. deans adv. coun.), Calif. Club, L.A. Country Club, La Jolla Beach and Tennis Club, Phi Kappa Psi, Phi Alpha Delta. Republican. Episcopalian. Home: 12320 Ridge Cir Los Angeles CA 90049-1151 Office: 12320 Ridge Cir Los Angeles CA 90049-1151 E-mail: JOvonK@aol.com.

VON KANN, CLIFTON FERDINAND, aviation and space executive, software executive; b. Boston, Oct. 14, 1915; s. Alfred and Lyllian (Kaufman) von K.; m. Sallie Emery Flint, Oct. 6, 1938 (div. May 1965); children: Curtis Emery, Lisa Christine; m. Kathryn Heyne, July 18, 1965. AB cum laude, Harvard U., 1937, MBA, 1948, D in Aero. Sc. (hon.), 1984; grad., Arty. Sch., 1942, Command and Gen. Staff Sch., 1945, Armed Forces Staff Coll., 1954, Nat. War Coll., 1957. Commd. 2d lt., F.A. U.S. Army, 1938, advanced through grades to maj. gen., 1962; various combat assignments, North Africa, Sicily and Italy, 1942-45; mem. War Dept. gen. staff, 1945-46; with Office Comptr., Dept. of Army, 1948-51; with CIA, 1951-53; comdg. officer 7th Inf. Div. Arty., 8th Army, 1954; with Korean Mil. Adv. Group Korea, 1954-55; with Hdqrs. Army Forces Far East and 8th Army, Japan, 1955-56; asst. div. comdr. 82d Airborne Div. Ft. Bragg, N.C., 1957-59; dir. army aviation Dept. Army, 1959-61; J-3 U.S. Strike Command, Tampa, Fla., 1961-62; comdg. gen. 1st cavalry div. Korea, 1962-63; comdg. gen. U.S. Army Aviation Ctr. Ft. Rucker, Ala., 1963-65; ret., 1965; v.p. ops. and engring. Air Transport Assn. Am., 1965-70, sr. v.p. ops. and airports, 1970-80; pres. Nat. Aeron. Assn., 1980-89; chmn. bd. Nat. Aeronautic Assn., 1989-90, chmn. emeritus, 1992—. Decorated Silver Star, Legion of Merit; Cross of Mil. Valor (Italy); recipient Charles Edwin Webb Meml. medal Pa. Mil. Coll., 1964, mil. rev. award Command and Gen. Staff Coll., 1964, Clifford W. Henderson award for achievement, 1990, Dept. Transp./FAA award for disting. svc., 1990. Mem. Am. Helicopter Soc. (chmn. bd. 1962-63, pres. 1961-62), World Aerospace Edn. Assn. (bd. dirs. 1987-93, pres. 1990-91, Fedn. Aeronautique Internat. (v.p. 1980-88, pres. 1988-90), Black Tie Club (Washington; pres. 1978-79), Aero Club (Washington; pres. 1969), Harvard Varsity Club (Cambridge), Met. Club (Washington), Nat. Aviation Club (pres. 1974-75). Clubs: Harvard Varsity (Cambridge); Metropolitan, Nat. Aviation (pres. 1974-75). Home and Office: Apt 502 4200 Massachusetts Ave NW Washington DC 20016-4752 E-mail: cvonkann@aol.com.

VON KENNEL, GARY PHILLIP, marketing company executive; b. cin, Aug. 17, 1948; s. Harry Phillip and Dorothy (Lanzer) Von K.; m. Jane Louise Endean, June 27, 1970; children: Andrew Phillip, John Benjamin. BA, U. Ky., 1971. Sales trainee Gillette-Personal Care Co., Cin., 1972-74, sales rep., 1972-74, project mgr. graphics Boston, 1975-77; mgr. brand promotions Miller Brewing Co., Milw., 1977-80; v.p. Target Mktg., Chgo., 1980-81; pres. Promotional Services Group, Dallas, 1981-86, Multi-Dimension Mktg., Inc., Dallas, 1986-99; CEO TLP Inc., Dallas, 1999—. Presbyterian. Home: 6032 Deloache Ave Dallas TX 75225-2809 Office: TLP Inc Dallas Harwood Ctr 1999 Bryan St Fl 28 Dallas TX 75201-6868*

VON KEUDELL, RENATE, language educator; b. Lübeck, Germany; arrived in U.S., 1962; AA, William Rainey Harper Coll., 1974; BA, Elmhurst Coll., 1976; MA, Northwestern U., 1977. Instr. German, French, ESL William Rainey Harper Coll., Palatine, Ill., 1978—92, assoc. prof., chair German dept., 1993—. Author: (textbook) Exercies in German Grammar, 1995, A Journey in German, 1999. Mem.: MLA, Chgo. Coun. Fgn. Rels., Goethe Inst. Chgo., Am. Assn. Tchrs. German. Avocations: reading, writing, travel, walking, opera. Office: William Rainey Harper Coll 1200 W Algonquin Rd Palatine IL 60067

VON KLEMPERER, KLEMENS, historian, educator; b. Berlin, Nov. 2, 1916; came to U.S., 1938; s. Herbert O. and Frieda (Kuffner) Von K.; m. Elizabeth Lee Gallaher, Dec. 19, 1953; children— Catharine Lee, James Alfred Abitur, Französisches Gymnasium, Berlin, 1934; MA, Harvard U., 1940, PhD, 1949; MA, Cambridge U., 1974. Vis. prof. Stanford U., Palo Alto, Calif., 1960; prof. history Bonn U., Fed. Republic Germany, 1963-64; L. Clark Seelye prof. history Smith Coll., Northampton, Mass., 1960-87, prof. emeritus, 1987—. Vis. prof. Amherst (Mass.) Coll., 1989, 91, 96; vis. fellow Trinity Coll., Oxford, Eng., 1982. Author: Germany's New Conservatism, 1957, Mandate for Resistance, 1969, Ignaz Seipel: Christian Statesman, 1972, German Resistance Against Hitler: The Search for Allies Abroad 1938-1945, 1992, The German Incertitudes, 1914-1945, 2000; editor: A Noble Combat. The Letters of Shiela Grant Duff and Adam von Trott, 1988, "Für Deutschland" Die Männer des 20 Juli, 1994; contbr. articles to profl. jours. Served with AUS, 1943-46, ETO Recipient Austrian Cross of Honor for Sci. and Art 1st class, 1997; Guggenheim Found. fellow, 1957-58; Fulbright fellow, 1957-58, 63-64; Overseas fellow Churchill Coll., Cambridge, Eng., 1973-74; Inst. for Advanced Study fellow, Berlin, 1986; Am. Philos. Soc. grantee, 1977-78, Am. Council of Learned Socs. grantee, 1978-79 Mem. Am. Hist. Soc. (chmn. conf. group for central European history 1982-83) Clubs: Century (N.Y.C.). Avocations: playing recorder; mountaineering; hiking. Home: 23 Washington Ave Northampton MA 01060-2822 Office: Smith Coll Northampton MA 01063-0001

VON KOHORN, BARON RALPH STEVEN, retired investment banker, author; b. Chemnitz, Germany, Dec. 14, 1919; arrived in N.Z., 1963; s. Baron Oscar and Valerie (Wirth) von K.; m. Jillian Annette Bussell, Feb. 25, 1967; children by previous marriage: Karen Janne, Kirk Steven. Student, U. So. Calif., U. Mich. Dep. chmn. various world wide bus. orgns., 1945-62; ret. Settlor von Kohorn Family Trust Controlling Genrock Group of Cos., N.Z. and Australia. Author: Abstract Paintings by Forty New Zealand Artists, 1966; What You Always Wanted to Know about Single Sideband Radio and Never Dared to Ask, 1976, VHF/FM Marine Radio, 1977, Columbia Cruises South, 1977, Columbia Cruises North, 1978, Management of a General Ancillary Licence for Clubs, 1978, Your Guide to Marine Search and Rescue, 1980; co-author, cartographer: A Cruising Man's Guide to the Marlborough Sounds, 1979, A Cruising Guide-Cape Palliser to Marlborough Sounds and Tasman Bay, 1982, The Sounds Crusing Guide, including Cape Palliser to Farewell Spit, 1986, The Cohorn Clan, 1987, The Cohorn Clan 2, 1988, New Zealand Cruising Guide-Central Area, 1989, 2d edit., 1994, 3rd edit., 1999, The Cohorn Clan 3, 1996. Founding sr. v.p., dir. Am. C. of C., 1965-74; bd. dirs. Am. Edn. Found. (Fulbright), 1965-94, Kennedy Meml. Fellowship, 1972-94, East-West Ctr., Honolulu, 1972-78; selector Eisenhower Fellowships, 1966-68, 78, 81, 86; trustee Wellington Visual Arts Trust, 1968-72, Found. for Newborn Child, 1977-96, N.Z. Oral History Archives, 1981-94, Wellington Maritime Mus., 1989-96, founder, pres.; trustee, dir. N.Z. Sports Found., 1977-85, gov., 1986-94, hon. life mem.; nat. treas. N.Z. Water Safety Coun., 1979-87, Small Boat Safety Com., 1977-90; com. chmn. N.Z. Yachting Fedn., hon. life mem. Recipient Graham Hayter trophy, 1973-74, 78-79; Lane Bryant Internat. Vol. award, 1969, Water Safety award Minister of Internal Affairs, 1987, Merit award Minister of Transport, 1987, Outstanding Vol. Svc. award Wellington, N.Z., 1987, Tribute of Appreciation award U.S. Govt., 1987, N.Z. Yacht Cruising award. Fellow Inst. Dirs. (London), N.Z. Inst. Mgmt. (counselor); mem. Royal Yachting Assn. (London, life), Past Commodores Assn. N.Z. (pres.), Internat. Order Past Commodores (internat. v.p. 1982-93, v.p. emeritus 1993—, hon. life mem., patron 1996), N.Z. Am. Assn., Wellington Planetarium Soc. (life, vice-chmn. 1968-73), Inst. Advanced Motorists (life, vice-chmn. 1969-73), Mus. Wellington (life, boardroom named in his honor), Nat. Press Club, Wellesley Club (Wellington), Tattersalls Club (Sydney), U. Club, Royal N.Z. Yacht Club, Royal Port Nicholson Yacht Club (life), Mana Cruising Club (life, past commodore) Home: Herbert Gardens 186 The Terrace Wellington New Zealand Home (Summer): 122 Alexandra Parade Alexandra Headland QLD 4575 Australia

VON KRENNER, WALTHER G. artist, writer, art consultant and appraiser; b. West Germany, June 26, 1940; s. Frederick and Anna-Marie (von Wolfrath) von K.; m. Hana Renate Geue, 1960; children: Michael P., Karen P. Student, Buddhist U., Bangkok, Thailand; field rschr., student, Cambodia. Curator, v.p. Gallery Lahaina, Maui, Hawaii; pres. Internat. Valuation Honolulu, 1973-80; owner Al Hilal Arabians, Mont.; instr. aikido, 1962—; founder, dir. Sandokan Aikido Schs., 1981. Named to U.S. Martial Arts Hall of Fame. Mem. Am. Soc. Appraisers (sr. mem.; pres., dir.). Avocation: aikido (8th degree black belt). Home: PO Box 1338 Kalispell MT 59903-1338 E-mail: tasis@digisys.net.

VON KUTZLEBEN, BERND EBERHARD, nuclear engineer; b. N.Y.C., May 23, 1950; s. Siegfried Edwin and Ursula Herta (Klotz) von K.; m. Susan Eileen Thrane, Feb. 12, 1983 (div. 1991); children: John Hays Morgan, Alexander Joachim, Eric Raymond; m. Carolyn Alice Hays, Dec. 5, 1991. BS in Physics, U. Hamburg, 1974; BS in Physics Engring., Fachhochschule Wedel, 1976, MS, 1979. Nuc. test engr. Combustion Engring., Windsor, Conn., 1979-82, sr. nuc. test engr., 1982-85, nuc. test cons., 1985-90, nuc. test mgr., 1991-92, resident nuc. engring. mgr. Republic of Korea, 1992-95; nuc. engring. mgr. ABB Combustion Engring., Windsor, Conn., U.S., 1996-2000; mgr. equipment supply YGN 5&6 nuc. project Westinghouse Electric Co., 2000—01, asst. project mgr. YGN 5&6 nuc. project, 2001—. V.p. Treetop Water Corp., Ft. Worth, 1990—. Mem. U.S. Nuc. Soc. Republican. Avocations: cooking, travel, foreign cultures and customs. Home: 35 Anvil Dr Avon CT 06001-3218 E-mail: bernievk@attbi.com., bernie.von_kutzleben@us.westinghouse.com.

VON LINSOWE, MARINA DOROTHY, information systems consultant; b. Indpls., July 21, 1952; d. Carl Victor and Dorothy Mae (Quinn) von Linsowe; m. Clayton Albert Wilson IV, Aug. 11, 1990; children: Kira von Linsowe Parker, Lara Carla von Linsowe-Wilson, Tami Cheri von Linsowe-Wilson. Student Am. River Coll., Portland State U. Cert. Prodn. and Inventory Mgmt. Verbal operator Credit Bur. Metro, San Jose, Calif. and Portland, Oreg., 1970-72; computer clk. Security Pacific Bank, San Jose, 1972-73; proof operator Crocker Bank, Seaside, Calif., 1973-74; proof supr. Great Western Bank, Portland, 1974-75; bookkeeper The Clothes Horse, Portland, 1976-78; computer operator Harsh Investment Co., Portland, 1978-79; data processing mgr. Portland Fish Co., 1979-81; data processing mgr. J & W Sci. Inc., Rancho Cordova, Calif., 1981-83; search and recruit specialist, data processing mgr. Re:Search Exec. Recruiters, Sacramento, Calif., 1983; sr. systems analyst Unisys Corp. (formerly Burroughs), 1983-91; sr. systems cons. FileNet Corp., Portland, Oreg., 1991-92; owner Optimal System Svcs., Portland, Oreg., 1992—; bus sys. analyst, software design and devel., mfg. specialist Portland. First violinist Am. River Orch. Recipient Bank of Am. Music award, 1970. Mem. NAFE, Am. Prodn. and Inventory Control Soc. (cert.), Am. Mgrs. Assn., MENSA, Data Processing Mgmt. Assn. Republican. Lutheran. Address: 3280 SW 170th Ave Apt 1780 Beaverton OR 97006-8612

VON MANDEL, MICHAEL JACQUES, lawyer; b. Yokohama, Japan, Oct. 20, 1941; came to the U.S., 1946; s. Michael Maximillan and Suzanne (Jacques) V.M.; m. Mary Denise Bienvenue, Dec. 22, 1984; 1 child, Michelle Denise. AB in Econs., Georgetown U., 1964; JD, Cath. U., 1968; LLM in Taxation, NYU, 1970. Bar: Washington 1969, Conn. 1969, U.S. Supreme Ct. 1972, Ill. 1976, U.S. Dist. Ct. (no. dist.) Ill. 1976, U.S. Ct. Appeals (7th cir.) 1976, Fla. 1977. Trial atty. FTC, Washington, 1968-69; trial atty. tax divsn. U.S. Dept. Justice, 1970-76; pvt. practice Chgo., 1976-93; ptnr. Von Mandel & Von Mandel, 1994—. Adj. prof. grad. tax program DePaul U., Chgo., 1980-83. Contbr. chapters to books. Mem. ABA (tax and litigation sects. 1976—), Chgo. Bar Assn. (fed. tax com. 1976—), Fed. Bar Assn. (bd. dirs. 1981-93), Seventh Cir Bar Assn., Union League Club. Roman Catholic. Address: 79 W Monroe St Ste 1000 Chicago IL 60603-4901 E-mail: mvmtax@aol.com.

VON MEHREN, ARTHUR TAYLOR, lawyer, educator; b. Albert Lea, Minn., Aug. 10, 1922; s. Sigurd Anders and Eulalia Marion (Anderson) von M.; m. Joan Elizabeth Moore, Oct. 11, 1947; children— George Moore, Peter Anders, Philip Taylor S.B., Harvard U., 1942, LL.B., 1945, PhD, 1946; Faculty of Law, U. Zurich, 1946-47; Faculte de Droit, U. Paris, 1948-49; Doctor iuris (h.c.), Katholieke U., Leuven, 1985, U. Pantheon-Assas (Paris II), 2000. Bar: Mass. 1950, U.S. Dist. Ct. Mass. 1980. Law clk. U.S. Ct. Appeals (1st cir.), 1945-46; asst. prof. law Harvard U., 1946-53, prof., 1953-76, Story prof., 1976-93, prof. emeritus, 1993—, dir. East Asian legal studies program, 1981-83; acting chief legislation br., legal div. Occupation Mil. Govt. U.S.,Germany, 1947-48, cons. legal div., 1949. Tchr. Salzburg Seminar in Am. Studies, summers 1953, 54; Fulbright research prof. U. Tokyo, Japan, 1956-57, Rome, Italy, 1968-69; cons. legal studies Ford Found., New Delhi, 1962-63; vis. prof. U. Frankfurt, summer 1967, City Univ. Hong Kong, 1995; Ford vis. prof. Inst. Advanced Legal Studies, U. London, 1976; assoc. prof. U. Paris, 1977; Goodhart prof. legal sci. U. Cambridge, 1983-84, fellow Downing Coll., 1983-84, hon. fellow, 1984—; fellow Wissenschaftskolleg zu Berlin, 1990-91. Author: The Civil Law System: An Introduction to the Comparative Study of Law, 1957, 2d edit. (with J. Gordley), 1977, Law in the United States: A General and Comparative View, 1988; co-author: The Law of Multistate Problems: Cases and Materials in the Conflict of Laws, 1965, Conflict of Laws: American, Comparative, International, 1998, International Commercial Arbitration, 1999; mem. editl. bd. Am. Jour. Comparative Law, 1952-86; contbr. articles to profl. jours.; editor: Law in Japan-The Legal Order in a Changing Soc., 1963; mem. editorial com. Internat. Ency. Comparative Law, 1969—. Mem. U.S. Del. Hague Conf. pvt. internat. law, 1966, 68, 76, 80, 85, 93, 96, 2001. Named to Order of the Rising Sun, golden rays Japanese Govt., 1989; Guggenheim fellow, 1968-69; inst. fellow Sackler Inst. Advanced Studies, 1986-87. Mem. ABA (Leonard J. Theberge Award for Pvt. Internat. Law 1997, Sect. of Internat. Law and Practice), Am. Acad. Arts and Scis., Internat. Acad. Comparative Law, Institut de Droit Internat., Japanese Am. Soc. Legal Studies, Am. Soc. Comparative Law (bd. dirs., former pres.), Am. Soc. Polit. and Legal Philosophy, Institut Grand-Duchal (corr.), Phi Beta Kappa. Office: Harvard Law Sch/ AR-231 1545 Massachusetts Ave Cambridge MA 02138-2903 E-mail: vonmehre@law.harvard.edu.

VON MEHREN, GEORGE M. lawyer; b. Boston, Nov. 2, 1950; s. Arthur Taylor and Joan Elizabeth (Moore) von M.; children: Paige Elizabeth, Reed Carl. AB, Harvard U., 1972, JD, 1977; BA, Cambridge U., Eng., 1974, MA, 1985. Bar: Ohio 1977. Assoc. Squire, Sanders & Dempsey, Cleve., 1977-86, ptnr., 1986—, mem. mgmt. com., 1990-93, co-chmn. internat. litig. practice group, 1998—. Mem. adv. com. U.S. Dist. Ct. (no. dist.) Ohio, 1991-95; del. 59th Conf. of the Sixth Jud. Cir. of the U.S. Co-author: Non-US Firms, How to Enforce Your Foreign Trade Secrets in the US, United States Ligigation Yearbook, 1999; editor: Harvard Law Rev., 1975-77. Trustee Rainbow Children's Mus., 1998—2001, Beck Ctr. for the Arts, 1999—2001. Mem.: Union Club. Office: Squire Sanders & Dempsey 127 Public Sq Ste 4900 Cleveland OH 44114-1304

VON MEHREN, ROBERT BRANDT, lawyer, retired; b. Albert Lea, Minn., Aug. 10, 1922; s. Sigurd Anders and Eulalia Marion (Anderson) von M.; m. Mary Katharine Kelly, June 26, 1948 (dec. Mar. 1985); children: Carl S., John M., Katharine, Jane, Margaret; m. Susan Heller Anderson, Apr. 2, 1988. BA summa cum laude with philosophical oration, Yale U., 1943; LLB magna cum laude, Harvard U., 1946. Bar: N.Y. 1946, U.S. Supreme Ct. 1954. Law clk. to Judge Learned Hand U.S. Ct. Appeals (2d cir.), 1946-47; law clk. to Assoc. Justice Stanley Reed U.S. Supreme Ct., 1947-48; assoc. Debevoise & Plimpton, N.Y.C., 1946, 48-57, ptnr., 1957-93, of counsel, 1994-95, ret., 1995. Arbitrator in internat. and other matters; sr. lectr. in law Wharton Sch. U. Pa., Phila., 1985-86; legal counsel Prep. Commn. for Internat. Atomic Energy Agy., N.Y.C., 1956-57; trustee Practising Law Inst., N.Y.C., 1972-96, emeritus, 1996, pres., 1979-86, chmn. bd., 1986-96. Bd. editors Harvard Law Rev., 1944-46, Am. Jour. Internat. Law, 1981-89, hon. editor, 1990-2000; contbr. articles to profl. jours. Trustee Axe Houghton Found., N.Y.C., 1965—; bd. dirs. Legal Aid Soc., N.Y.C., 1966-70; pres. Harvard Law Sch. Assn. N.Y., 1982-83. Mem. Assn. Bar City N.Y., Internat. Law Assn. (vice chmn. 1989—, pres. Am. br. 1978-86, chmn. exec. com. 1986-92), Coll. of Comml. Arbitrators, Coun. on Fgn. Rels., Univ. Club, Century Assn. N.Y.C. Home: 925 Park Ave New York NY 10028-0210 Office: 919 3rd Ave 46th Fl New York NY 10022

VON MERING, OTTO OSWALD, anthropology educator; b. Berlin, Germany, Oct. 21, 1922; came to Switzerland, 1933, to U.S., 1939, naturalized, 1954; s. Otto O. and Henriette (Troeger) von M.; m. Shirley Ruth Brook, Sept. 11, 1954; children: Gretchen, Karin, Gregory, Hilary, Celia. Grad., Belmont Hill Sch., 1940; BA in History, Williams Coll., 1944; PhD in Social Anthropology, Harvard U., 1956. Instr. Belmont Hill Sch., Belmont, Mass., 1945-47, Boston U., 1947-48, Cambridge Jr. Coll., 1948-49; rsch. asst. lab. social rels. Harvard U., 1950-51, Boston Psychopathic Hosp., 1951-53; Russell Sage Found. fellow N.Y.C., 1953-55; asst. prof. social anthropology U. Pitts. Coll. Medicine, 1955-60, assoc. prof., 1960-65, prof. social anthropology, 1965-71; prof. child devel. and child care U. Pitts. Coll. Allied Health Professions, 1969-71; prof. anthropology and family medicine U. Fla., 1971-76, prof. anthropology in ob-gyn, 1979-84, prof. anthropology and gerontology, 1986-96, prof. anthropology and gerontology emeritus, 1998, joint prof. dept. medicine, coll. medicine, 1994-96. Lectr. Sigmund Freud Inst., Frankfurt, Germany, 1962-64, Pitts. Psychoanalytical Inst., 1960--71, Interuniv. Forum, 1967-71; tech. adviser Maurice Falk Med. Fund, 1964-75; Fulbright vis. lectr., 1962-63; Richard-Merton guest prof. Heidelberg U., Germany, 1962-63; vis. prof. Dartmouth, 1970-71; vis. lectr. continuing edn. Med. Coll. of Pa., 1990-92, vis. lectr. U. Sheffield, Eng., Fall, 1995, U. Liverpool, 1995, U. Augsburg, 1997, U. Heidelberg, fall 1997; hon. vis. prof. U. Coll. London Med. Sch., fall 1997; bd. dirs. Tech. Assistance Resource Assocs., U. Fla., 1979-84; supr. grad. study program Ctr. Gerontologic Studies, U. Fla., 1983-85, assoc. dir. 1985-86, dir. 1986-96, prof. emeritus 1998; mem. coordinating com. Geriatric Edn. Ctr., Coll. of Medicine, U. Fla., 1986-96; mem. med. selection com. Coll. Medicine U. Fla., 2000—; mem. nat. tech. expert panel on long-term care Health Care Financing Adminstrn., Washington; chair, mem. adv. bd. Internat. Exchange Ctr. on Gerontology State U. System of Fla., 1987-92; adv. bd. Second Season Broadcasting Network, Palm Beach, Fla., 1989-92, Fla. Policy Exch. Ctr. on Aging, State U. System Fla., 1991-95, Assoc. Health Industries of Fla., Inc., Nat. Shared Housing Resource Ctr., Balt.; cons. mental hosps. Author: Remotivating the Mental Patient, 1957, A Grammar of Human Values, 1961, (with Mitscherlich and Brocher) Der Kranke in der Modernen Gesellschaft, 1967, (with Kasdan) Anthropology in the Behavioral and Health Sciences, 1970, (with Maria Alvarez) Aging, Demography and Well-Being in Latin America, 1989; (with R. Binstock and L. Cluff) The Future of Long Term Care, 1996; also articles; commentary editor: Human Organization, 1974-76; corr. editor Jour. Geriatric Psychiatry; mem. editl. bd. Med. Anthropology, 1976-84, Ednl. Gerontology, 1990-2002, Australasian Leisure for Pleasure Jour., 1995-2000, Jour. Cross-Cultural Gerontology, 1996-2002. Mem. nat. adv. bd. Nat. Shared Housing Resource Ctr., 1994-95; pres. Dedicated Alt. Resources for the Elderly, 1996-98; mem., bd. dirs. No. Ctrl. Fla. chpt. Alzheimer's Assn., 1996—; bd. dirs. Shepherd's Ctrs. Am., Gainesville, 1998-2000. Recipient Fulbright-Hayes Travel award, 1962-63; grantee Wenner-Gren Found., N.Y., 1962-63, Am. Philos. Soc., 1962-63, Maurice Falk Med. Fund, 1970-71, US-DHHS, 1979-83, Walter Reed Army Inst. Rsch., 1987-91. US-ADA/Fla. Dept. of Elder Affairs, 1993-94; spl. fellow NIMH, 1971-72. Fellow AAAS, Am. Anthrop. Assn. (mem. James Mooney award com. 1978-81, vis. lectr. 1961,-62, 71-74, 91-92), Am. Gerontol. Soc., Royal Soc. Health, Acad. Psychosomatic Medicine, Am. Ethnological Soc., Soc. Applied Anthropology, Royal Anthrop. Inst.; mem. Assn. Am. Med. Colls., Assn. Anthrop. Gerontol. (pres.-elect 1991-92, pres. 1992-93), Am. Fedn. Clin. Research, Am. Public Health Assn., Canadian Assn. Gerontology, British Soc. Gerontology, Med. Group Mgmt. Assn., World Fedn. Mental Health, Internat. Assn. Social Psychiatry (regional counselor 1973-81), Internat. Hosp. Fedn., Help Age Internat. (London). Home: 818 NW 21st St Gainesville FL 32603-1027 Office: U Fla Dept Anthropology Turlington Hall Gainesville FL 32611 *Three guides to conduct I value most: always search for the best fit of fact, argument, and experience. Every first remedy must be amended quickly. When the past disturbs the present, more work on the future is needed.*

VONNEGUT, KURT, JR. writer; b. Indpls., Nov. 11, 1922; s. Kurt and Edith Sophia (Lieber) V.; m. Jane Marie Cox, Sept. 1, 1945 (div. 1979); children: Mark, Edith, Nanette; adopted nephews: James, Steven and Kurt Adams; m. Jill Krementz, 1979, 1 child, Lily. Student, Cornell U., 1940-42, U. Chgo., 1945-47, MA in Anthropology, 1971. Reporter Chgo. City News Bur., 1946; pub. relations with Gen. Electric Co., 1947-50; free-lance writer N.Y.C., 1950-65, 74—; lectr. writers workshop U. Iowa, Iowa City, 1965-67; lectr. in English Harvard U., Cambridge, Mass., 1970; disting. prof. CCNY, 1973-74. Author: (novels) Player Piano, 1951, Sirens of Titan, 1959, Mother Night, 1961, Cat's Cradle, 1963, God Bless You, Mr. Rosewater, 1964, Slaughterhouse-Five, 1969, Breakfast of Champions, 1973, Slapstick, or Lonesome No More, 1976, Jailbird, 1979, Deadeye Dick, 1982, Galápagos, 1985, Bluebeard, 1987, Hocus Pocus, 1990, Timequake, 1997, (collected stories) Welcome to the Monkey House, 1968; (play) Happy Birthday, Wanda June, 1970; (TV Script) Between Time and Timbuktu or Prometheus-5, 1972; (essays) Wampeters, Foma and Granfalloons, 1974; (Christmas Story with illustrations by Ivan Chermayeff) Sun Moon Star, 1980; (autobiographical collage) Palm Sunday, 1981, (collection of speeches and essays) Fates Worse Than Death, 1991, Timequake, 1997, (collection of short stories) Bagombo Snuff Box, 1999; also short stories, articles, revs. Served with inf. AUS, 1942-45. Guggenheim fellow, 1967-68. Mem. Nat. Inst. Arts and Letters (recipient Lit. award 1970). Office: c/o Donald C Farber Jacob Medinger & Finnegan LLP 1270 Avenue of the Americas New York NY 10020 Fax: (212) 332-7235. E-mail: Donaldc14@aol.com.

VONNIEDA, JEAN LORAYNE, infection control practitioner; b. Reading, Pa., Aug. 27, 1952; d. Claude E. Sr. and Miriam K. (Mohn) Keim; m. Richard VonNieda, Feb. 27, 1981; 1 child, Jenny Beth Miller. Diploma, Reading Hosp., 1973; BSN summa cum laude, Kutztown (Pa.) U., 1991. Cert. in infection control, 2001. Staff nurse Reading Hosp., 1973-74, staff nurse ICU/CCU, 1975-76; charge nurse ICU/Emergency Rm. Martin Luther Hosp., Anaheim, Calif., 1976-77; staff nurse ICU/CCU Phoenixville (Pa.) Hosp., 1979-80; staff nurse/patient edn. resource nurse Reading Hosp., 1980-92, nurse mgr. med./surg., infectious disease specialty, 1992-99, infection control practitioner, 1999—. Mem.: Assn. for Profls. in Infection Control and Epidemiology (poster presenter San Diego 1998, East Ctrl. Pa. chpt. bd. dirs. 2002—), Kutztown U. Nursing Honors Soc. (past sec.), Xi Omega, Sigma Theta Tau (bd. dirs., publicity chairperson, newsletter editor). Home: 601 El Hatco Dr Temple PA 19560-1109 E-mail: rphilphan1@aol.com., vonniedaj@readinghospital.org.

VON RAFFLER-ENGEL, WALBURGA (WALBURGA ENGEL), linguist, cross-cultural communications specialist, lecturer, writer; b. Munich, Germany, Sept. 25, 1920; came to U.S., 1949, naturalized, 1955; d. Friedrich J. and Gertrud E. (Kiefer) von R.; m. A. Ferdinand Engel, June 2, 1957; children: Lea Maxine, Eric Robert von Raffler. DLitt, U. Turin, Italy, 1947; MS, Columbia U., 1951; PhD, Ind. U., 1953. Free-lance journalist, 1949-58; mem. faculty Bennett Coll., Greensboro, N.C., 1953-55, U. Charleston (formerly Morris Harvey Coll.), W.Va., 1955-57, Adelphi U., CUNY, 1957-58, NYU, 1958-59, U. Florence, Italy, 1959-60, Istituto Postuniversitario Orgn. Aziendale, Turin, Italy, 1960-61, Bologna Center of Johns Hopkins U., 1964; assoc. prof. linguistics Vanderbilt U., Nashville, 1965-77, prof. linguistics, 1977-85, prof. emerita, sr. rsch. assoc. Inst. Pub. Policy Studies, 1985—, dir. linguistics program, 1978—85; chmn. com. on linguistics Nashville U. Ctr., 1978—85; Italian NSF prof. Psychol. Inst. U. Florence, Italy, 1986-87; prof. NATO Advanced Study Inst., Cortona, Italy, 1988; pres. Kinesics Internat., 1988—. Vis. prof. linguistics Shanxi U., Peoples Republic China, 1985; vis. prof. U. Ottawa, Ont., Can., 1971-72, Lang. Scis. Inst., Internat. Christian U., Tokyo, 1976; grant evaluator NEH, NSF, Can. Coun.; manuscript reader Ind. U. Press, U. Ill. Press, Prentice-Hall; advisor Trinity U., Simon Frazer U.; lectr. in field; dir. internat. seminar Cross-Cultural Comm., 1986-87; mem. Ctr. for Global Media Studies, 1999; State Dept. Italy del. to Congress of the Hague. Author: Il prelinguaggio infantile, 1964, The Perception of Nonverbal Behavior in the Career Interview, 1983, The Perception of the Unborn Across the Cultures of the World, Japanese edit., 1993, English edit., 1994 (transl. into Chinese), A Traveler's Guide to Cross-Cultural Business Communications, 2000; co-author: Language Intervention Programs, 1960-75; editor, co-editor 12 books; author films and videotape; contbr. of 500 articles to profl. jours. in Engish, Itialian, French, German. Grantee Am. Coun. Learned Socs., NSF, Can. Coun., Ford Found., Kenan Venture Fund, Japanese Ministry Edn., NATO, UNESCO, Finnish Acad., Meharry Med. Coll., Internat. Sociol. Assn., Internat. Coun. Linguists, Tex. A&M U., Vanderbilt U., others. Mem. AAUP, Internat. Linguistic Assn., Linguistic Soc. Am. (chmn. Golden Anniversary film com. 1974, emerita 1985—), Linguistic Assn. Can. and the U.S., Internat. Assn. for Applied Linguistics (com. on discourse analyses, sessions chmn. 1978), Lang. Origins Soc. (exec. com. 1985-97, chmn. internat. congress, 1987), Internat. Sociol. Assn. (rsch. com. for sociolinguistics, session co-chmn. internat. conf. 1983, session chmn. profl. conf. 1983), Internat. Coun. Psychologists, Internat. Assn. for Intercultural Comms. Studies, Internat. Assn. for Study of Child Lang. (v.p. 1975-78, chmn. internat. conf. Tuscan Acad. Scis., Florence, Italy 1972), Inst. for Nonverbal Comm. Rsch. (workshop leader 1981), Southeastern Conf. on Linguistics, 1980— (hon. mem. 1985—), Semiotic Soc. Am. (organizing com. Internat. Semiotics Inst. 1981), Nat. Assn. Scholars, Tenn. Assn. Scholars (bd. dirs. 1998-99), Internat. Assn. for Intercultural Comms. Studies (panel organizer 1999), United Europe Movement (sect. chmn. 1944-45), Internat. Comm. Assn., Internat. Pragmatics Assn. Achievements include being instrumental in forcing Vanderbilt U. to enroll women on an equal basis with men. Home and Office: 2455 Brighton Oaks San Antonio TX 78231 *In the social sciences theories come and theories go. Carefully collected and objectively analyzed data are useful for generations and the cleanest research design in the lab does not equal a moderately neat design in the naturalistic setting.*

VON RECUM, ANDREAS F. veterinarian, bioengineer; b. Dillingen, Bavaria, Germany, July 5, 1939; came to U.S., 1971; s. Bogdan Freiherr and Ilse Freifrau (von Rosenberg) von R.; m. Grudrun F. Bredenbröker-Hardt, Oct. 2, 1965; children: Derik F., Vera F., Uta F., Horst F., Thomas F., Elsa F. BS, U. Giessen, 1965; DVM, Free U. Berlin, 1968, PhD, 1969; PhD in Vet. Surgery, Colo. State U., 1974. Practitioner farm animal medicine and surgery, Meitingen, Germany, 1968-69; clin. staff small animal clinic Free U. Berlin (Germany), Coll. Vet. Medicine, 1969-72; rsch. asst. surg. lab. Colo. State U., Coll. Vet. Medicine, Ft. Collins, 1972-74; dir. surg. rsch. lab. Sinai Hosp. Detroit, 1975-77; prof. dept. bioengring. Clemson (S.C.) U., 1978-93, head dept. bioengring., 1982-93; chmn. bioengring. alliance S.C. Coll. Engring., Clemson U., 1984-88; scientific staff Shriners Hosp., Greenville, S.C., 1989-95; prof. Hunter endowed chair bioengring. Clemson U. Coll. Engring.,

1993-97; assoc. dean rsch., prof. Ohio State U., Columbus, 1997—. Mem. coll. exec. com. Coll. Vet. Medicine, Free U., Berlin, 1970-71; adj. assoc. prof. comparative surgery Wayne State U. Sch. Medicine, Dept. Comparative Medicine, 1975-77; adj. prof. surgery U. S.C. Sch. Medicine, 1984—, Med. U. S.C., 1987-97; adj. prof. biomaterials Coll. Dentistry, U. Nijmegen, 1993—; chair internat. liaison com. World's Biomaterials Socs., 1996-2000; cons. in field. Editor Jour. Investigative Surg., 1991-97; patentee in field. Recipient Fulbright Scientist award, 1990-91, Alexander von Humboldt Sr. Scientist award, 1990-91; nat. and internat. fellow Biomaterials Sci. and Engring., 1996. Mem. AVMA, Am. Soc. Lab. Animal Practitioners, Blue Ridge Vet. Med. Assn. (pres. 1984), Soc. Biomaterials (asst. editor 1986—, editl. bd. 1983, program chmn. 1990, sec.-treas. 1990-92, pres. 1993-94), Internat. Soc. Artificial Internal Organs, Am. Soc. Artificial Organs, Am. Heart Assn., Acad. Surg. Rsch. (founder 1982, pres. 1982-83, newsletter editor 1982-85), Biomed. Engring. Soc., Am. Soc. Engring. Edn., Assn. Advancement Med. Instrumentation. Presbyterian. Office: Ohio State U Coll Vet Medicine 1900 Coffey Rd Columbus OH 43210-1006 E-mail: vonrecum.1@osu.edu.

VON REIS CORNELL, SONJA MARGARETHA, artist; b. Gothenburg, Sweden, Nov. 19, 1925; came to the U.S., 1948; d. James Adolf Helmer and Iris Margaretha (Malmstrom) von R.; m. Lorain Dale Cornell, Oct. 29, 1949 (dec. Dec. 1988); children: Charles Peter, Susan Christina, Sonja Elizabeth. BA, Mich. State U., 1969, MA, 1970, MFA, 1975. Interpreter Gen. Motors Overseas, Detroit, 1948-49; tchr. art and humanities Dewitt (Mich.) Pub. Schs., 1970-88. Instr. evening coll. Mich. State U., East Lansing, 1975-76; mem. Art Scholarships, Lansing, 1985-90; jurying Lansing Art Guild, Mich., 1990—, East Lansing Arts Orgn., 1991—. One person shows include Prints Ancient and Modern, East Lansing, Okemos (Mich.) Community Ch., Jacobsons', East Lansing, Creative Arts Gallery, Mt. Pleasant, Mich., Lansing Art Gallery, others; group shows include Art Now, Goteborg, Sweden, Katharine Rich Perlow Gallery, N.Y.C., Foster/White Gallery, Seattle, others; collections include Wharton Ctr., East Lansing, Phillips Petroleum Corp., Bartlesville, Okla., Ceco Corp., Chgo., Mich. Edn. Assn., East Lansing, others. Mem. Friend of Kresge Art Mus., East Lansing, 1975—. Mem. NEA, Swedish Internat. Edn. Assn., Mich. Edn. Assn., Detroit Swedish Coun., Jenny Lind Club Mich. Avocations: travel, opera, books.

VONRENTZELL, ELIZABETH, pharmaceutical executive; d. Richard E. vonRentzell and Kathryn S. vonRentzel. Student, Northwestern U., 1996—98, U. of Nebr., 1995—2000. Gatehouse attendant Residence Inn by Marriott, Lincoln, Nebr., 1993—97; credit rep. Nat. Bank of Commerce, 1997—97; archive asst. Northwestern U., Evanston, Ill., 1997—98; adminstrv. asst. M E Group, Lincoln, 1998; aversions rep. Unipac, 1998—99; pub. area coord. iUniverse, 1999—2000; document assoc. Gilead Sciences, Boulder, Colo., 2001; patient care technician Spalding Rehab., Aurora, 2001; document assoc. OSI Pharmaceuticals, Boulder, 2002—. Prodr.: (website publication) The Reader's Take, 2002. Vol. Internat. English Ctr., Boulder, 2002, Boulder County AIDS Project, 2002; team capt., vol. Am. Cancer Soc., Longmont, 2001—02; vol. Denver Botanic Gardens, 2002—02, Women's Bean Project, Denver, 2001—02; grant writer Mary Weslin Homes, 2002; tchr., editor Asian Cultural Cmty. Ctr., Lincoln, 1998—99; pres., sec. U. Alliance for Life, Evanston, 1996—98; pres. SMArTeams, 1996—98; outreach officer Soc. of Women Engineers, 1996—98; account exec. AdShop, Am. Mktg. Assn., 1997—98; vol. Wagner Health Ctr., 1996—98, Ten Thousand Villages, Evanston, 1998—98. Mem.: NAFE, Internat. Soc. Six Sigma Professionals, Assn. Psychosocial Nurses, Drug Info. Assn. (spl. interest area com. 2002—02), Am. Med. Writers Assn. Republican. Roman Catholic. Avocations: travel, jogging. Home: 1366 Garfield St # 303 Denver CO 80206 Office: OSI Pharms 2860 Wilderness Pl Boulder CO 80301 Personal E-mail: lizmvr@yahoo.com. E-mail: evonrentzell@osip.com.

VON RHEIN, JOHN RICHARD, music critic, editor; b. Pasadena, Calif., Sept. 10, 1945; s. Hans Walter and Elsa Maryon (Brossmann) von R. AA, Pasadena City Coll., 1965; BA in Eng., UCLA, 1967; BA in Music, Calif. State U., Los Angeles, 1970. Music reviewer Hollywood (Calif.) Citizen-News, 1968-70; music editor and critic, dance critic Akron (Ohio) Beacon Jour., 1971-77; music critic Chgo. Tribune, 1977—; prof. music appreciation Rio Hondo Jr. Coll., Calif., 1970-71. Lectr., TV host, rec. annotator. Author (with Andrew Porter): Bravi; contbr. revs. and articles to , , , , . Music Critics Assn.-Kennedy Center for Performing Arts fellow, 1972, 75; recipient Peter Lisagor award Soc. Profl. Journalists, 1999. Mem. Music Critics Assn. (edn. com., dir. 1988), Ravinia Critics Inst. (dir. 1988). Office: Chgo Tribune Co 435 N Michigan Ave Chicago IL 60611-4066 E-mail: jvonrhein@tribune.com.

VON ROENN, KELVIN ALEXANDER, neurosurgeon; b. Louisville, Dec. 5, 1949; s. Warren George and Catherine Jean (Bauer) Von R.; m. Jamie Hayden, June 24, 1979; children: Erika Marie, Lisa J., Alexander H., Karl G. BS, Xavier U., 1971; MD, U. Ky., 1975. Diplomate Am. Bd. Neurol. Surgery. Instr. neurosurgery Rush-Presbyn. St. Luke's Med. Ctr., Chgo., 1980-83, asst. prof. neurosurgery, 1983—; vice chmn. dept. of neurosurgery Rush-Presbyn. St Luke's Med. Ctr., 2000—; cons. neurosurgery Shriner's Hosp. for Crippled Children, 1988—, attending neurosurgeon, 1990—, program dir. neurosurg. resident edn., 1997—2002; dir. brain tumor clinic Rush Cancer Ctr., 1997—, residency program dir. neurosurgery, 2002. Lectr. sect. of neurosurgery U. Ill. Coll. Med., 1996-2002; vol. attending Cook County Hosp., Chgo., 1996-; attending neurosurgeon U. Ill., 1997, 98, 99, 2000. Named one of Outstanding Young Men of Am., 1986. Fellow ACS; mem. Congress Neurologic Surgeons, Am. Assn. Neurol. Surgeons, Ill. Neurosurg. Soc. (v.p. 1994-95, pres. 1995-96), Alpha Sigma Nu, Alpha Omega Alpha. Avocations: opera, gardening, fishing. Office: Chgo Inst Neurosurgery and Neurorsch 1725 W Harrison St Ste 1115 Chicago IL 60612-3835

VON ROSEN, RÜDIGER, stock exchange executive; b. Grocholin, June 21, 1943; Diploma, U. Frankfurt, 1970; PhD, 1973. With Deutsche Bundesbank, 1974-86; exec. vice-chmn. Fedn. German Stock Exchanges, 1986-93; speaker bd. mng. dirs. Frankfurter Wertpapierbörse AG, Frankfurt, 1990-92; mem. bd. mng. dirs. Deutsche Börse AG, 1993-94, mng. dir., 1995—, Deutsche Aktieninstitut EV, Frankfurt. Hon. prof. Frankfurt U., 1998. Office: Deutsches Aktieninstitut EV Boersenplatz 5 D-60313 Frankfurt Am Main Germany

VON RYDINGSVARD, URSULA KAROLISZYN, sculptor; b. Deensen, Germany, July 26, 1942; came to U.S., 1950; d. Ignacy and Konegunda (Sternal) Karoliszyn; m. Paul Greengard. BA, MA, U. Miami, Coral Gables, Fla., 1965; postgrad., U. Calif., Berkeley, 1969-70; MFA, Columbia U., 1975; PhD (hon.), Md. Inst. Art, 1991. Instr. Sch. Visual Arts, N.Y.C., 1981-82; asst. prof. Pratt Inst., Bklyn., 1978-82, Fordham U., Bronx, N.Y., 1980-82; assoc. prof. Yale U., New Haven, 1982-86; prof. grad. divsn. Sch. Visual Arts, N.Y.C., 1986—. One-woman shows include Laumeier Sculpture Gallery, St. Louis, 1988, Capp St. Project San Francisco, 1990, Lorence-Monk Gallery, N.Y.C., 1990-91, Zamek Ujazdowski Contemporary Art Ctr., Warsaw, Poland, 1992, Storm King Art Ctr., Mountainville, N.Y., 1992-94, Galerie Lelong, N.Y.C., 1994, Weatherspoon Art Gallery, Grensboro, N.C., 1994, Univ. Gallery, Amherst, 1995, Mus. Art, Providence, 1996, Mus. Art R.I. Sch. Design, Providence, 1996, Yorkshire Sculpture Pk., Wakefield, England, 1997, Nelson-Atkins Mus., Kansas City, Mo., 1998, Madison (Wis.) Art Ctr., 1998, Chgo. Cultural Ctr., 1998, Indpls. Mus. Art, 1999, The Contemporary Mus., Honolulu, 1999, Barbara Krakow Gallery, Boston, 1999, Galerie Lelong, Zurich, 2000, N.Y.C., 2000, Doris C. Freedman Plz., Ctrl. Pk., N.Y.C., 2000, Neuberger Mus. Art, SUNY, Purchase, 2002; exhibited in group shows at Contemporary Arts Ctr., Cin., 1987, Damon Brandt Gallery, N.Y.C., 1989, Met. Mus. Art, N.Y.C., 1989-93, Whitney Mus. Contemporary Art, 1990, Cultural Ctr., Chgo., 1991, Ctrl. Bur. Art Exhbns., Warsaw and Krakow, Poland, 1991, The Cultural Space/Exit Art, N.Y.C., 1992, Galerie Lelong, N.Y.C., 1993, Denver Art Mus. and Columbus Art Mus., 1994—, others; outdoor exhbns include Pelham Bay Park, Bronx, N.Y., 1978, Neuberger Mus., Purchase, N.Y., 1979, Artpark, Lewiston, N.Y., 1979, Laumeier Sculpture Park, St. Louis, 1989-94, Walker Art Ctr., Mpls., 1990-93, Oliver Ranch, Geyserville, Calif., Storm King Art Ctr., Mountainville, N.Y., 1992-93; contbr. articles to profl. jours. Fulbright Hays travel grantee, 1975; grantee N.Y. State Coun. Arts, Am. the Beautiful Fund, Nat. Endowment for Arts, Creative Artists Program Svc.; Griswald traveling grantee Yale U., 1985; Guggenheim fellow, 1983-84; Nat. Endowment for Arts individual artists grantee, 1986-87; recipient Acad. award in Art, Am. Acad. Arts and Letters, 1994, Alfred Jurzykowski Found. Fine Arts award, 1996, Joan Mitchell award, N.Y., 1997. Studio: 429 S 5th St Brooklyn NY 11211-7425 E-mail: art@galerielong.com.

VON SAUERS, JOSEPH F. lawyer; b. N.Y.C. s. Joseph F. and Margaret von Sauers; m. June A. von Sauers. BEE, Manhattan Coll., 1980; MBA, Pepperdine U., 1987; JD, Southwestern U., 1991; LLM, Columbia U., 1995; DBA, North Central U., 2001. Bar: Calif. 1992, D.C. 1993, Minn. 1993, Tex. 1993, Colo. 1994, U.S. Patent and Trademark Office. Contracts negotiator Hughes Aircraft Co., El Segundo, Calif., 1985-92; atty. Jones, Day, Reavis & Pogue, Dallas, 1992-94, Loeb & Loeb, LLP, L.A., 1995-97, Gray, Cary, Ware & Freidenrich, Palo Alto, Calif., 1997-98; dep. gen. coun. Roland Corp. U.S., L.A., 1998—. Active Calif. Lawyers for Arts, L.A., 1996; guest spkr. Loyola U., L.A., 1996. Contbr. articles to profl. jours. Mem. Am. Legion. Comdr. USNR. Recipient Kuwait Liberation medal Saudi Arabian/Kuwaiti Govts., 1992, 96; Wildman scholar Southwestern U., 1987-91. Mem. Naval Res. Assn., L.A. County Bar Assn. Avocations: sailing, golf, tennis.

VON SCHACK, WESLEY W. energy services company executive; b. N.Y., 1944; married. AB, Fordham U., 1965; MBA, St. John's U., Jamaica, N.Y., 1971; doctorate, Pace U., 1990. Chmn., CEO, pres. DQE, Pitts., 1986-96, ret., 1996; chmn., pres., CEO N.Y. State Electric and Gas Corp., Binghamton, 1996-99, chmn. bd. dirs., 1999—; chmn., pres., CEO Energy East Corp., Albany, N.Y., 1998—. Bd. dirs. Mellon Fin. Corp., Mellon Bank, N.A., RTI Internat. Metals, Inc., The Peconic Land Trust, AEGIS Ins. Svcs., Inc., Am. Gas Assoc, The Gettysburg Nat. Battlefield Mus. Found., Fordham Univ. Vice chmn. bd. The Peconic Land Trust; bd. dirs. Am. Gas Assn. Found. Mem.: Am. Gas Assn. (bd. dirs.). Office: Energy East Corp PO Box 12904 Albany NY 12212-2904

VONSCHLEGEL, PATRICIA, artist; b. Fayetteville, N.C., Aug. 3, 1941; d. Robert Blackburn and Margaret (Scull) Slagle; m. John Lee Jordan, July 16, 1960 (div. Feb. 1975); children: John Christopher Jordan, Lisa Nicole Jordan. B of Creative Arts, U. N.C., Charlotte, 1978. Tchr. aide Children's Adventure, Nederland, Colo., 1978; kindergarten tchr. Charlotte Acad., 1980-81; tchr., supr. San Francisco Head Start, 1981-82; art tchr. Our Lady of Consolation, Charlotte, 1982-83. Exhbns. include McKnight Gallery/U. N.C., 1978, Charlotte Printmakers, 1978, Princeton U., 1979, Davis (Calif.) Art Fair, 1982, Queens Gallery Group Show, Charlotte, 1983, Springs Mills Show, Lancaster, S.C., 1987, Art on the River, Savannah, Ga., 1989, Ann Gleason Interiors, Savannah, 1989, Spotlight on So. Artists, Atlanta, 1991, 92, 93, 94, 95, Coastal Nat., St. Simon Island, Ga., 1992, The Checkered Moon Gallery, 1993, Evening of the Arts/Hilton Head Island, S.C., 1992, 93, 94, 95, 96, Tin Can Alley Exhibit/Self Ctr.,Hilton Head, 1996; solo show at Patton and Howell, Savannah, 1990; contbr. to publd. Sanskrit, So. Accent. Roman Catholic. Avocations: theater, symphony, reading. Home: 322 E Taylor St Apt 1207 Savannah GA 31401-5059

VONSCHULZE-DELITZSCH, MARILYN WANDLING (LADY VONSCHULZE-DELITZSCH), artist, writer; b. Alton, Ill., May 16, 1932; d. Ralph Marion and Mary Mildred (Branson) W.; m. Sir Georg W.W. Herzog VonSchulze-Delitzsch; children: Jeffrey, Douglas, Pamela. Student, Monticello Coll., Godfrey, Ill, 1950-51, U. Ill., 1951-53; BA in Art, Webster U., St. Louis, 1968; MA Edn. in Art Edn., Washington U., St. Louis, 1975. Cert. tchr. art Kindergarten-Grade 12, Mo. 4th grade tchr. Alton (Ill.) Pub. Schs., 1961-62; art. buying dept. Gardner Advt. Co. Inc., St. Louis, 1962-63; art tchr. mid. sch. Lindbergh Sch. Dist., 1968-75; cons., designer V.P. Fair, Inc., 1982; adminstrv. asst. to headmaster, coll. counseling dept. John Burroughs Sch., 1979-82; dir. pub. rels. and advt. Dance St. Louis, 1983-85; freelance art and design St. Louis, 1970—; tchr. art mid. sch. St. Louis Pub. Schs., 1987-90, tchr. art Elem. Magnet Sch. for Visual and Performing Arts, 1990-98. Tchr. drawing and painting Summer Arts Inst., St. Louis Pub. Schs., 1992, graphic arts designer, cons. comty. affairs divsn., 1985-96, sch. vol. divsn., 1990-92, Webster Groves (Mo.) Sch. Dist., 1989-90, Pub. Sch. Retirement Sys., St. Louis, 1991; implementer classroom multi-cultural art edn. projects, 1987-98; summer participant Improving Visual Arts Edn., Getty Ctr. for Edn. in Arts, 1990; book illustrator-McGraw Hill Inter-Americana de Mexico, Mexico City, 1994-95, Simon & Schuster, Mexico City. Designer (cover and icons) English Language Teaching Text, 1996; designer Centennial Logo for St. Louis Pub. Schs. Sesquicentennial, 1988; painter, designer murals for Ctrl. Presbyn. Ch. Nursery, 1978-79, St. Nicholas Greek Orthodox Ch., 1980; designer two outdoor villages VP Fair, Arch Grounds, St. Louis, 1982; published writer. Patron St. Louis Symphony Orch. Recipient merit and honor awards Nat. Sch. Pub. Rels. Assn., 1990, 91, 92, 93, 95, Mo. Sch. Pub. Rels. Assn., 1989-90, 91, 92, 93. Mem. St. Louis Art Mus., PEO Sisterhood, Nat. Soc. DAR, Colonial Dames of 17th Cent., United Daus. of Confederacy, Chi Omega Alumnae. Avocations: Native American arts and culture, paintings, drawings, portraits. E-mail: tulipsaintlouis@earthlink.net.

VON SEGGERN, KRISTEN L. executive; b. Syracuse, N.Y., Sept. 15, 1968; d. Walter Ernst Von Seggern and Sydney Demers Radka. BS in Biotech., Rochester Inst. Tech., 1990; MPH, U. Conn., 1997; MBA, Rutgers U., 2000. Clin. rsch. assoc. Parexel Internat., Waltham, Mass., 1990-95; assoc. clin. scientist Bristol Myers Squibb, Wallingford, Conn., 1996-97, assoc. mgr. Plainsboro, N.J., 1997-98, mgr., 1998-99, assoc. dir., 1991-2000, catagory leader Princeton, 2000-01, dir. bus. devel. NJ, 2001—. Mem. Jr. League Greater Princeton. Home: 13 Woodmont Dr Lawrenceville NJ 08648 Office: Bristol Myers Squibb Rte 206 and Provinceline Rd Princeton NJ 08540

VON STUDNITZ, GILBERT ALFRED, state official; b. Hamburg, Germany, Nov. 24, 1950; came to U.S., 1954. s. Helfrid and Rosemarie Sofie (Kreiten) von S.; m. Erica Lynn Hoot, May 26, 1990. BA, Calif. State U., L.A., 1972. Adminstrv. hearing officer State of Calif., Montebello, 1987-91, mgr. III driver control policy unit Dept. Motor Vehicles Sacramento, 1991-93; ops. mgr. Driver Safety Review, 1993-95; contract mgr. State Dept. Health Svcs., 1995-97; staff mgr. licensing ops. policy Dept. Motor Vehicles, Sacramento, 1997-2000; Welfare-to-Work regional mgr. State Health and Human Svcs. Agy., 2000—. Author: Aristocracy in America, 1989; editor publs. on German nobility in U.S., 1986—. Active L.A. Conservancy, West Adams Heritage Assn., dir., 1989-91. Fellow: Entente Cordiale for Chivalric and Heraldic Traditions, Am. Soc. for Chivalric Rsch. (hon.); mem.: Nat. Assn. Managed Care Regulators, Driver Improvement Assn. Calif. (v.p. 1992—96, dir. media rels. 1996—), Calif. State mgrs. Assn., Orders and Medals Soc. Am., Sierra Club, Assn. German Nobility in N.Am. (pres. 1985—), Benicia Hist. Soc., Intertel, Mensa, Phi Sigma Kappa (v.p. chpt. 1978). Roman Catholic. Avocations: genealogical research, collecting. Home: 1101 W 2nd St Benicia CA 94510-3125

VON TAAFFE-ROSSMANN, COSIMA T. physician, writer, inventor; b. Kuklov, Austria, Nov. 21, 1944; came to U.S., 1988; d. Theophil and Marianna Hajossy; m. Charles Boris Rossmann, Oct. 19, 1969; children: Nathalie Nissa Cora, Nadine Nicole Nora. MD, Purkyne U., Brno, Czechoslovakia, 1967. Intern Valtice (Austria) Stadt Wien Krankenhaus, 1967-68, resident ob-gyn, 1968-69; med. researcher Kidney Disease Inst., Albany, N.Y., 1970-71; resident internal medicine Valtice Gen. Hosp., 1972-73; gen. practice Nat. Health System, Austria, 1973-74; pvt. practice West Germany, 1974-80; med. officer Baragwanath Hosp., Johannesburg, South Africa, 1984-85, Edendale Hosp., Pietermaritzburg, South Africa, 1985-86; pvt. practice Huntingburg, Ind., 1988-90, Valdosta, Ga., 1990—. Med. researcher, 1966—. Contbr. articles on medicine to profl. jours.; inventor, patentee in field. Office: 2000 N Patterson St Valdosta GA 31602-2945

VON TERSCH, LAWRENCE WAYNE, electrical engineering educator, university dean; b. Waverly, Iowa, Mar. 17, 1923; s. Alfred and Martha (Emerson) Von T.; m. LaValle Sills, Dec. 17, 1948; 1 son, Richard George. BS, Iowa State U., 1943, MS, 1948, PhD, 1953. From instr. to prof. elec. engring. Iowa State U., 1946-56; dir. computer lab. Mich. State U., 1956-83, prof. elec. engring., chmn. dept., 1958-65, assoc. dean engring., 1965-68, dean, 1968-89, dean emeritus, 1989—. Author: (with A. W. Swago) Recurrent Electrical Transients, 1953. Mem. IEEE; mem. Sigma Xi, Tau Beta Pi, Eta Kappa Nu, Phi Kappa Phi, Pi Mu Epsilon Home: 4282 Tacoma Blvd Okemos MI 48864-2734 Office: Michigan State U Coll Engring East Lansing MI 48823 E-mail: vontersc@egr.msu.edu.

VON THURN, JELENA, health science specialist; b. Skopje, Macedonia, Yugoslavia, Jan. 1, 1939; came to U.S., 1972; d. Miladin and Hedy (Hem) M.; m. Ernst Anzbock, Dec. 14, 1959 (div. 1971); children: Harald, Evelyn; m. Ranko Caric, Nov. 3, 1973 (div. 1980); 1 child, Peter. Student, Molloy Coll., 1979-81, L.I. U., 1981-82, Rockland C.C., 1985, Vt. Coll., 1985-86, Orange County C.C., 1988, Empire State Coll., 1990—. Ordained to ministry Universal Spiritualist Assn. U.S.A., 1985; lic., real estate agt., N.Y.; registered and cert. reflexologist, N.Y. Owner Walter's Bake Shop, 1973-79; nurse's aide Hillside Manor, 1980; clerical worker Molloy Coll., 1980-81, L.I. U., 1981-82; chiropractor asst. Steven R. Siegel D.C., 1982; owner Linden Motel, 1983; lectr. on Shiatsu and reflexology New Age Ctr., 1985-86; v.p., min. Universal Ctr. New Age Consciousness, Inc., Milford, Pa., 1985—; with Abatelli Realty, 1988; owner Athena Spa, 1993-94, Jelena's Skin Care and Anti-Aging Clinic, Carmel, Calif., 1998—; esthetician The Spa, Pebble Beach, 1999. Gen. agt. Intern Cons. Exchange, San Diego, Calif., 1986; spa and skincare therapist, Pebble Beach, Calif., 1995, Carmel Valley Ranch, 1995, Hyatt Regency, 1996. Mem. Alliance of Massage Therapists, Inc., Universal Spiritualist Assn., Assoc. Bodywork and Massage Profls., Carmel Art Assn. Avocations: oil painting, piano, guitar, dancing, estate auctions.

VON TILSIT, HEIDEMARIE, information management specialist; b. Heinrichswalde, Germany, Sept. 26, 1944; came to U.S., 1967; d. Heinz and Kaethe Krink; m. Leonard Wierzba, May 14, 1969 (div. 1980). Buchhandel, Dt. Buchh. Schule, Kiel, Germany, 1965; profl. cert., Coll. of Further Edn., Oxford, Eng., 1966; BA, Calif. State U., Fullerton, 1979. Library asst. Allergan, Inc., Irvine, Calif., 1975-76; info. analyst Allergan Pharms., 1976-79, library supr., 1979-81, mgr. corp. info. ctr., 1982-98; dir. Corp. Info. Ctr., 1999—. Cons. in field; owner, pres. Unitran, Corona, Calif., 1980—; adv. bd. Coil & Assocs. Career Cons., Orange, Calif., 1987—; adv. bd. for univ.-industry rsch. and tech. U. Calif., Irvine, 1992-99; adv. bd. Sch. Libr./Info. Sci., Continuing Edn., Calif. State U., Fullerton. Editor/writer articles sci. and information mgmt. Vol. AIDS Svcs. Found., 1994—; bd. mem. Elections Com. of the County of Orange, 1998; mem. Eleanor Roosevelt Dem. Club, 1996—; co-chair Inland Empire Lesbian & Gay Dem. Club, 1997—; regional rep. Calif. Alliance for Pride and Equality (CAPE) 1998-01; mem. Riverside County Dem. Ctrl. Com., 2000—. Mem. Am. Soc. Info. Sci., Spl. Librs. Assn., Pharm. Edn. & Rsch. Inst. (com. info. mgmt. sect. 1985-99), Drug Info. Assn. (mem. adv. bd. info. mgmt. sect. 2000—). Democrat. Avocations: civil rights, political action, dramatic arts, horseback riding, sporting clays. Home: 1543 San Rafael Dr Corona CA 92882-3795 Office: Allergan Inc 2525 Dupont Dr Irvine CA 92612-1599 E-mail: von-tilsit_heidi@allergan.com.

VON TUNGELN, GEORGE ROBERT, retired university administrator, economics consultant; b. Golconda, Ill., July 18, 1931; s. Cecil Ernest and Rachel Elizabeth (Wright) von T.; m. Marilyn Ruth Burris, Nov. 6, 1955; children— Stuart, Cheryl, Brenda, Sonya, Eric. BS, So. Ill. U., 1951, MS, 1956; PhD, U. Ga., 1974. Asst. mgr. exptl. farms So. Ill. U., Carbondale, 1951-52; instr., research asst. Pa. State U., 1955-58; asst. prof. to prof. agrl. sci. Clemson (S.C.) U., 1958-85, asst. to dean internat. programs, 1977-85; cons. econs. and internat. econ. devel. El Paso, 1985—. Pres. P.T.O., 1973 Contbr. articles to profl. jours. Served with AUS, 1952-54. Mem. Assn. U.S. Univ. Dirs. Internat. Agrl. Programs, Partners of Americas, West Tex. Football Officials Assn., Phi Kappa Phi, Gamma Sigma Delta. Clubs: S.C. Football Ofcls. Assn, Sertoma (chmn. bd. 1972). Republican. Baptist. Home and Office: 547 Cocula Ave El Paso TX 79932-2731

VONTUR, RUTH POTH, retired elementary school educator; b. Beeville, Tex., Sept. 10, 1944; d. Robert Bennal and Ruth (Matejek) Poth; m. Robert F. Vontur, Aug. 8, 1964; children: Catherine Anne, Craig Robert, Cynthia Anne. BS in Edn., Southwest Tex. State U., 1966. Cert. health and phys. edn. tchr., biology tchr. Tex. Teachng asst. Blessed Sacrament Confraternity Christian Doctrine, Poth, Tex., 1958-64; phys. edn. tchr. Judson Ind. Sch. Dist., Converse, 1966-68, St. Monica's Altar Soc. (Coun. of Cath. Women), Converse, 1974-96; substitute tchr. St. Monica's Confraternity Christian Doctrine, 1971—. Judson Ind. Sch. Dist., San Antonio, 1972-75, 80-81, phys. edn. tchr. Converse, 1966-68, 81-2000; ret., 2000. County adv. bd. Am. Heart Assn., San Antonio, Tex., 1985-88, jump rope for heart coord., 1984-2000, heart ptnr., 1992-2000 (recognized Tex. Jump Rope for Heart Pioneer, 1999); mentor Converse Elem. Sch., 1998—, outstanding mentor, 2000-01. Pres. St. Monica's Coun. Altar Soc., Converse, 1975; mem. St. Monica's Altar Soc., 1974-96; sponsor Young Astronauts, 1993-2000, Hall Patrol, 1990-93, 96-2000, Flag Patrol, 1996-2000; contact person elem. phys. edn. Judson ISD, 1982-96. Recipient award Tex. Pioneer Jump Rope for Heart, AHA, 1999. Mem.: Randolph Area Ret. Educators. Roman Catholic. Avocations: oil painting, tee shirt painting, sewing, home decorating, gardening. Home: 105 Norris Dr W Converse TX 78109-1905 E-mail: ruthv3000@aol.com.

VONTZ, C. GREGORY, pharmaceutical executive; BS in Chemistry, U. Fla. With Merck, Sharp, Dohme; various strategic bus., sales, mktg. positions including dir. new markets and health care policy Genentech, 1987—99; exec. v.p., chief comml. officer Connetics, COO. Office: Connetics Corp 3290 West Bayshore Rd Palo Alto CA 94303*

VONTZ, THOMAS SCOTT, education educator; b. McCook, Nebr., Sept. 9, 1965; s. Lawrence Raymond and Marilyn Joyce (Wood) V.; m. Dawn Renee Vontz, Feb. 22, 1992; children: Gabrielle Rae, Victoria Lauren, Madeline Lee, Alexander James. BS, U. Nebr., Lincoln, 1992, M.Secondary Tchg., 1993; PhD, Ind. U., 2000. Secondary social studies tchr. Lincoln Pub. Schs., 1993-96; assoc. instr. tchr. edn. Ind. U., Bloomington, 1996-01, staff asst. Social Studies Devel. Ctr., 1996-01, dir. Ind. program law-related edn., 1998-01; asst. prof. Rockhurst U., Kansas City, Mo., 2001—. Dir. Ind. Program Law Related Edn., 1998-2001; state coord. We the People..., The Citizen and the Constitution, 1998, state coord., project citizen, 1998-01, dist. coord. Kans. We the People; rsch. assoc. Ind. U., 2000-01. Author: Project Citizen and the Civic Development of Adolescent Students in Indiana, Latvia and Lithuania, 2000; editor: Resources on Law-Related Education, 1997. James Madison Meml. fellow, 1993, Ind. U. Grad. fellow, 1996, 97. Mem. Nat. Coun. Social Studies, Nat. Coun. for History of Edn., Ind. Coun. for Social Studies (bd. dirs.), John Dewey Soc., Midwestern Ednl. Rsch. Assn. (session chair 1996), Phi Delta Kappa, Pi Lambda Theta. Roman Catholic. Avocations: fishing, hunting, reading, golf. Office: 1100 Rockhurst Rd Kansas City MO 64110- Home: 7636 N Wabash Ave Kansas City MO 64118-2060

VON UNRUG, THOMAS PAUL, physician, lab administrator; b. Cracow, Poland, Apr. 19, 1966; came to U.S., 1978; s. Konstanty and Maria Von Unrug; m. Carmen Esther de Pablo, July 1, 1995; 1 child, Carmen-Maria. BS, BA, U. Ky., 1989, MD, 1994. Diplomate Am. Bd. Internal Medicine. Intern Chandler Med. Ctr., Lexington, Ky., 1994-95, resident, 1995-97; attending physician, lab. dir. Von Unrug Med. Group, 1997—. Mem. reader adv. bd. Mayo Clinic Procs., 1998—; mem. quality improvement com. Advantage Care, Lexington, 1998—; mem. exec. com. Family Health Physicians, Lexington, 1998—; regional exec. dir., med. dir. Sunrise Nursing Homes, Lexington, 1999—; asst. prof. internal medicine U. Ky., Lexington, 1999—. Clinic vol. Salvation Army, Lexington, 1993; vol. physician St. Joseph Hosp. Med. Clinic, Lexington, 1997—. Travelling scholar Internat. Students Office, 1986. Fellow U. Ky. Fellow Soc.; mem. U. Ky. Med. Alumni Assn., Rotary. Roman Catholic. Avocations: photography, skiing, travel, collecting Nazca culture. Office: Von Unrug Med Group 1401 Harrodsburg Rd Ste B299 Lexington KY 40504-3747

VON WALDOW, ARND N. lawyer; b. Moenchen-Gladbach, Germany, Mar. 15, 1957; came to U.S., 1966; s. Hans Eberhard and Brigitte H. (Schulze-Kadelbach) von W.; m. Esther R. Haguel, May 25, 1987; children: Rachel J., Danielle M. BA, Syracuse U., 1980; JD, U. Pitts., 1983. Bar: La. 1983, Pa. 1989. Assoc. Sessions & Fishman, New Orleans, 1983-90, Eckert, Seamans, Cherin & Mellott, Pitts., 1990-91; ptnr. Meyer, Darragh, Buckler, Bebenek & Eck, 1991-99, Reed, Smith, Shaw & McClay, Pitts., 1999—. Mem. Product Liability Adv. Coun., Chgo., 1991—. Mem. ABA, Def. Rsch. Inst., Phi Beta Kappa. Home: 1738 Hempstead Ln Pittsburgh PA 15241-1376 Office: Reed Smith Shaw & McClay 435 6th Ave Ste 2 Pittsburgh PA 15219-1886

VOOGT, JAMES LEONARD, medical educator; b. Grand Rapids, Mich., Feb. 8, 1944; married; 3 children. Student, Calvin Coll., 1962-64; BS in Biological Sci., Mich. Tech. U., 1966; MS in Physiology, Mich. State U., 1968, PhD in Physiology, 1970. Fellow, lectr. dept. physiology U. Calif., San Francisco, 1970-71; asst. prof. dept. physiology and biophysics U. Louisville

Sch. Medicine, 1971-77, assoc. prof. dept. physiology and biophysics, 1977; assoc. prof. dept. physiology U. Kans. Sch. Medicine, 1977-82, prof. physiology, 1982—. Assoc. dean rsch. U. Kans. Sch. Medicine, 1982—84, acting chmn. dept. physiology, 1993—2001; vis. prof. Erasmus U., 1985. Mem. editl. bd. Endocrinology, 1984-86, 89-92, Am. Jour. Physiology, 1984-88, Doody's Jour., 1995-98; ad hoc reviewer Neuroendocrinology, Sci., Biology of Reproduction, Life Scis., Jour. Endocrinology, Molecular Cellular Neurosci., Procs. Soc. Exptl. Biology and Medicine, biochm. endocrinology study sect. NIH, 1992, reproductive endocrinology study sect., 1994-98; reviewer grants NSF; editor sci. procs. Rsch. Week, 1982-83; contbr. over 120 articles to profl. publs., 4 chpts. to books. Grantee NIH, 1972-85, 88—, NSF, 1985-86, 91-94, Ctr. on Aging, 1988, Nat. Inst. Drug Abuse, 1991-93; fellow Japan Soc. Promotion of Sci., 1993; recipient Outstanding Young Alumni award Mich. Tech. Univ., 1974, Honors in Edn., Med. Student Voice, 1990; inducted Mich. Tech. U. Acad. of Scis. and Arts, 2000. Mem. AAAS, Endocrine Soc., Internat. Soc. Neuroendocrinology (charter mem.), Am. Physiol. Soc. (pub. affairs adv. com. 1983-87) Soc. Neuroscis., Phi Kappa Phi, Sigma Xi. Office: Dept Molecular and Integrative Physiology U Kans Med Ctr 3901 Rainbow Blvd Kansas City KS 66160-0001

VOOK, FREDERICK LUDWIG, physicist, consultant; b. Milw., Jan. 17, 1931; s. Fred Ludwig and Hedwig Anna (Werner) V.; m. Frederica Jean Sandin, Aug. 16, 1958; children: Eric Robert, Dietrich Werner. BA with honors, U. Chgo., 1951, BS, 1952; MS, U. Ill., 1954, PhD in Physics, 1958. With Sandia Labs., Kirtland AFB East, N.Mex., 1958-94; div. supr., 1962-71; mgr. dept. research, 1971-78; dir. research, 1978-94; pvt. cons. Albuquerque, 1994—. Editor: Radiation Effects in Semiconductors, 1968; co-editor: Applications of Ion Beams to Metals, 1974. Mem. coll. engring. adv. bd. U. Ill.; mem. policy bd. Nat. Nanofabrication Facility Cornell U.; mem. basic energy sci. adv. com. Panel on Value of Basic Rsch; mem. Okla. State Univ. Ctr. for Laser and Photonics Rsch. adv. bd. U. Chgo. and U. Ill. scholar and fellow. Fellow Am. Phys. Soc.; mem. IEEE (sr. mem.), Böhmische Physikalische Gesellschaft, Phi Beta Kappa, Sigma Xi. E-mail: fandfvook@msn.com.

VOORHEES, DAVID WILLIAM, editor, historian; b. Jersey City, Sept. 20, 1947; s. William Franklin Jr. and Irma Rose (Grissom) V. BA, NYU, 1974, MA, 1977, PhD, 1988. Reference history mng. editor Charles Scribner's Sons, N.Y.C., 1976-83; co-editor Papers of William Livingston, 1983-88; dir. The Papers of Jacob Leisler project Nat. Hist. Publs. and Records Commn., 1988—; editor-in-chief de Halve Maen, 1990—. Rsch. asst. Bur. Applied Social Rsch. Columbia U., Metropolitan Mus. Art; instr. history NYU; mem. edn. and history com. Hist. New Amsterdam, 1999—. Author: Centennial History of the Holland Society of New York, 1985; editor: Concise Dictionary of American History, 1983; compiler: Concise Dictionary of Huguenot Ancestors, 1985; mng. editor: Ency. Am. Fgn. Policy, 1978 (Am. Libr. Assn. award, Choice Mag. award 1980), Ency. Am. Econ. History, 1980 (Am. Libr. Assn. award 1980, Choice Mag. award 1980), Album of Am. History, 1981, Dictionary of Am. Biography: Supplement VII, 1981, Dictionary of Am. Biography: Biog. Index Guide, 1981, Ency. Am. Govt. and Politics, 1984; assoc. editor: Dictionary Am. History, 1976, Am. Writers, 1979, 81, Brit. Writers, 1979, 80, 81, Concise Dictionary Am. Biography, 1980, Dictionary Sci. Biography, 1970-81, Dictionary of Middle Ages, 1984, Ency. Am. Jud. Sys., 1987; transl., editor: Records of the Reformed Protestant Dutch Church of the Town of Flatbush in Kings County, vol. 1, 1998; contbr. numerous articles to history publs., conf. presentations. Bd. dirs. Friends of First Presbyn. Ch., Hudson, NY. Recipient N.Y. State Hist. Assn. Manuscript award, 1990, Hendricks Manuscript award Friends of New Netherland, 1990, Huguenot Soc. Am. medal, 1993, N.Y. State Libr. Rsch. Residency award, 1995, Alice P. Kenney award Friends of New Netherland, 1998; named N.Y. State Coun. Humanities spkr., 1996—; grantee Am. Philos. Soc., 1989, Am. Coun. Learned Socs., 1990; Gilder Lehrman fellow, 2000. Fellow Huguenot Soc. Am.; mem. Am. Hist. Assn., Assn. Documentary Editors, N.Y. Hist. Soc., N.Y. Geneal. and Biog. Soc., Columbia County (NY) Hist. Soc. (bd. dirs.), Holland Soc. N.Y. (trustee 1980—, Gold medal 1995), St. Nicholas Soc. (trustee 1985—). Liberal. Presbyterian. Avocations: swimming, hiking, drawing, painting. Home: PO Box 755 234 Union St Hudson NY 12534 Office: The Holland Soc NY 122 E 58th St Rm 204 New York NY 10022-1941 E-mail: david.voorhees@nyu.edu.

VOORHEES, JAMES DAYTON, JR. lawyer; b. Haverford, Pa., Nov. 14, 1917; s. James Dayton Voorhees and Elsa Denison Jameson; m. Mary Margaret Fuller, Sept. 5, 1942 (dec. Apr. 1991); children: J. Dayton III, Susan F. Voorhees-Maxfield, Jane Voorhees Kiss. BA, Yale U., 1940; JD, Harvard U., 1943. Bar: N.H. 1947, Colo. 1948, U.S. Dist. Ct. Colo. 1948, U.S. Ct. Appeals (10th cir.) 1949, U.S. Ct. Appeals (5th cir.) 1956, U.S. Supreme Ct. 1960. Assoc. Johnson & Robertson, Denver, 1947-50; atty. Conoco Inc., 1950-56; ptnr. Moran, Reidy & Voorhees, 1956-78, Kutak, Rock & Huie, Denver, 1978-80; ptnr., counsel Davis, Graham & Stubbs, 1980—. Mem. Denver Bd. Edn., 1965-71, pres. 1967-69. Lt. comdr. USNR, 1941-46, ATO, PTO. Mem.: ABA, Denver Bar Assn., Colo. Bar Assn., University Club, Denver Country Club. Republican. Avocation: golf.

VOORHEES, KENT JAY, chemist; b. Provo, Utah, Sept. 7, 1943; s. Melrose and Beulah Madge (Hansen) V.; m. Tamara Lee Lasson, June 9, 1966; children: Christian Ward, Danielle Kay. BS, Utah State U., 1965, MS, 1968, PhD, 1970. Fellow Mich. State U., East Lansing, 1970-72; instr. U. Utah, Salt Lake City, 1971-73, asst. rsch. prof., 1973-76, assoc. rsch. prof., 1976-79; asst. prof. Colo. Sch. Mines, Golden, 1979-83, assoc. prof., 1983-86, prof., 1986—. Cons. 1979—; scientific adv. bd. Colo. Health Care, Denver, 1997—; bd. dirs. Petrex, Golden, 1982-86; editorial bd. Analytical Pyrolysis, Amsterdam, The Netherlands, 1988-2000, editor, Analytical Pyrolysis, 2001—. Author: Analytical pyrolysis, 1982; contbr. articles to profl. jours. Recipient Rsch. award, Am. Chem. Soc., 1995, Orise Faculty fellow, Food and Drug Adminstrn., 1995, R&D 100 award, Utah State U., 2000, Disting. Alumni award, Utah State U., Dept. Chemistry, 2001. Mem. ACS (nominations and elections com. 1988-92, coun. policy com. 1999—), Colo. Am. Chem. Soc. (councilor 1981—), Am. Soc. Mass Spectrometry. Avocations: golf, fishing, boating. E-mail: kvoorhee@mines.edu.

VOORHEES, STEPHANIE ROBIN NEE FAUGHT, retired art educator; b. Indpls., Dec. 18, 1951; d. Edward Francis and Dorothy Marie (Teague) F.; m. James Osborn Voorhees, June 19, 1999. BFA, Montclair (N.J.) State U., 1973, postgrad., 1974-76. Substitute tchr. Woodbridge (N.J.) Twp. Bd. of Edn., 1971-73, elem. art tchr., 1973-84, 85-86; middle sch. art tchr. Colonia (N.J.) Middle Sch., 1984-85; high sch. art tchr. Woodridge HS, 1986—90; middle sch. art tchr. Avenel (N.J.) Middle Sch., 1990-94; art tchr. John F. Kennedy H.S., Iselin, N.J., 1994-98, ret., 1998. Spkr. Woodbridge River Watch, 1991; pvt. art tchr., 1983-93; yearbook advisor Woodbridge H.S., 1989-90, Avenel Mid. Sch., 1991-94, John F. Kennedy H.S., 1995-98; play set designer, 1989, 94-97. Illustrator: Care of the Lower Back, 1975, Touching All the Bases, 1993; profl. muralist. Campaign vol. Rep. Party, Woodbridge, 1992; sec. to the producer Fgn. Broadcast Svc. Dem./Rep. Nat. Convs., Miami, 1972. Recipient Gov.'s Tchr. Recognition award NJ State Dept. of Edn., 1992, Excellence in Edn. award Woodbridge C. of C., 1992. Mem. AAUW, Woodbridge Twp. Fedn. of Tchrs. (v.p. 1980-83, pres. 1983-95, Cert. of Merit, 1982), Art Educators of N.J., Met. Mus. of Art, Manatee County Vet.'s Coun. (sr. v.p.), Ecology Club (advisor 1990-94), Am. Legion Post 325 Ladies Aux. (historian 2000-01, treas. 2001—), Am. Legion Post 325 (sec., treas.), Cabane 880 (historian 2000-01, garde de la port 2001-02), VFW Post 10141 Ladies Aux. (sec.). Baptist. Avocations: singing, playing piano, dancing, writing, cruise travel. Home: 29 River Isles Bradenton FL 34208-9003

VOORHESS, MARY LOUISE, pediatric endocrinologist; b. Livingston Manor, N.Y., June 2, 1926; d. Harry William and Helen Grace (Schwartz) V. RN, City Hosp. Sch. Nursing, Binghamton, N.Y., 1946; BA in Zoology, U. Tex., 1952; MD, Baylor Coll., Houston, 1956. Diplomate Am. Bd. Pediatrics and Pediatric Endocrinology. Rotating intern Albany (N.Y.) Med. Ctr., 1956-57, asst. resident pediatrics, 1957-58, chief resident pediatrics, 1958-59; rsch. fellow pediatric endocrinology and genetics SUNY Health Sci. Ctr., Syracuse, 1959-61, asst. prof. pediatrics, 1961-65, assoc. prof. pediatrics, 1965-70, prof. pediatrics, 1970-76, SUNY Sch. Medicine and Biomed. Scis., Buffalo, 1976-91, prof. pediatrics emeritus, 1991—; co-chief div. endocrinology Children's Hosp. Buffalo, 1976-91; retired, 1997. Ad hoc reviewer Jour. Pediatrics, Pediatrics, Am. Jour. Diseases Children, other. Contbr. sci. articles to profl. jours., chpts. to books. Mem. adv. bd. Interim Healthcare inc., 1991-97; mem. devel. coun. Children's Hosp. Buffalo Found., 1991-97; med. dir. Children's Growth Found., Buffalo, 1976-97; cmty. advisor Assn. for Rsch. Childhood Cancer, Buffalo, 1990-97. Recipient rsch. career devel. award Nat. Cancer Inst., 1961-71, Dean's award SUNY Sch. Medicine and Biomed. Scis., 1991. Fellow Am. Acad. Pediatrics, AAAS; mem. Soc. Pediatric Rsch. (emeritus), Am. Pediatric Soc. (emeritus), Endocrine Soc. (emeritus), Lawson Wilkins Pediatric Endocrine Soc. (emeritus), Phi Beta Kappa, Alpha Omega Alpha. Presbyterian. Home: 6311 Chiswick Park Williamsburg VA 23188-6369 E-mail: mlv6311@widomaker.com.

VOORHIS, ROGER JOSEPH, consumer products company executive; b. Somers Point, NJ, Aug. 16, 1953; s. Roger Joseph and Emma Mae Voorhis; m. Christine Anne Holmbraker. BS in Mech. Engring., Syracuse U., 1975, MS in Mech. Engring., 1977. Registered profl. mech. engr., N.Y. Project engr. rsch. divsn. mech. sys. group United Technologies, Carrier Corp., Syracuse, NY, 1977—82, sr. rsch. engr. rsch. divsn. mech. sys. group, 1982—84, program mgr. residential products divsn. split sys. products, 1984—85, program mgr. residential products variable speed tech., 1985—86, program mgr. electronic controls engring., 1986—87, program mgr. corp. engring. svcs., 1987—90, dir. advanced sys. group, 1990—96; dir. engring. minisplit products Am. Std. Inc., Trane Internat. Unitary Sys., Hong Kong, 1996—99; dir. engring. Am. Std. Inc., Trane Internat. Unitary Systems, Brussels, 2000—01; dir. product devel. Am. Std. Inc., Trane Commerical Sys., Global Unitary Products, Clarksville, Tenn., 2001—. Contbr. articles to profl. jours. Mem.: ASHRAE. Achievements include patents for new testing and rating procedures for seasonal performance of heat pumps with variable speed compressors; refrigerant metering in variable flow systems; defrost control for variable speed heat pump; heat pump charging; control module cooling. Office: Trane Air Conditioning Co 2701 Wilma Rudolph Blvd Clarksville TN 37040 Office Fax: 931-648-5901. Personal E-mail: chrisNroger@charter.net. Business E-mail: Roger.Voorhis@trane.com.

VOORLAS, STEPHANIE KATHERINE, freelance/self-employed writer, photographer; b. Racine, Wis., Apr. 1, 1951; d. Peter Harry Voorlas and Athena Callas. BA in Social Anthropology, U. Beirut, Lebanon, 1974; BA in Arabic Studies, U. Utah, 1993. Freelance writer, photographer. Contbr. articles. Tibetan Buddhist. Avocations: skiing, mountaineering. Home: PO Box 527 Silverton CO 81433

VOORSANGER, BARTHOLOMEW, architect; b. Detroit, Mar. 23, 1937; s. Jacob H. and Ethel A. (Arnstein) V.; m. Lisa Livingston, 1964; m. Catherine Hoover, Sept. 10, 1983 (dec. Dec. 2001); children: Roxanna Virginia (dec.), Matthew Ansley. AB cum laude, Princeton U., 1960; diplome, Fontainebleau, 1960; MArch, Harvard U., 1964. Assoc. Vincent Ponte, Montreal, Que., Can., 1964-67, I.M. Pei & Ptnrs., 1968-78, dir. Iran, 1975-78; co-chmn. Voorsanger & Mills (Architects), N.Y.C., 1978-90; founder, prin. Voorsanger & Assocs., Architects, 1990—; founder Taylor/Voorsanger Urban Designers, 1991. Lectr. Bennington (Vt.) Coll., U. Pa., Columbia U., Harvard U.; guest critic, lectr. Yale U., Pratt Inst., CUNY, R.I. Sch. Design, U. Cin., Syracuse U., U. Tex., Arlington; mem. adv. bd. Parson Sch. Architecture; mem. archtl. rev. panel Port Authority of N.Y. & N.J.; advisor to Samsung Corp., Korea. Exhbns. include: NYU, Archtl. Assn., London, Harvard Grad. Sch. Design, Vacant Lots Housing Study, N.Y., Deutsches Architeckur Mus., Frankfurt, Mus. Finnish Architecture, Avery Lib.Centennial Exhbn. Columbia Univ., Helsinki, Bklyn. Mus.; major projects include: Le Cygne Restaurant, Neiman houseboat, NYU Midtown Ctr., NYU Bus. Sch. Library, La Grandeur housing, NYU dormitories, Hostos Community Coll., N.Y.; finalist Bklyn. Mus. masterplan internat. competition, expansion and master plan Pierpont Morgan Libr., Wethersfield Carriage Mus., America, N.Y.; Montana and Wyoming Residences; Advanced Tng. Ctr., NYU, New York Apt., N.Y.C., Riverdale (N.Y.) Jewish Ctr.; fellow J. Pierpont Morgan Libr., N.Y., Asia Soc., NY, Brody Residence, VA, Daniels/Falks Residence, Ariz., Port Authority N.Y./N.J. Air Traffic Control Towers, Bayly Art Mus., U. Va. Mem. vis. com. R.I. Sch. Design, U. Tex., Arlington; mem. N.Y. Hist. Soc., also mem. archtl. cir. steering com.; chmn. bd. advisors Temple Hoyne Buell Ctr., Study Am. Architecture, Columbia U., N.Y.C., 1989—; mem. adv. bd. Parsons Sch. Architecture; chair archtl. rev. panel Port Authority N.Y. and N.J.; bd. dirs. Worldesign Found.; mem. Regent's Panel N.Y. State U., N.Y. State Regents' Com. on Schs; pres. N.Y. Found. for Architecture 2000-2001. 1st lt. U.S. Army, 1960-61. Recipient Cannon prize NAD, awards N.Y.C. chpt. AIA, AIA/Better Homes, Bard City Club, Interiors mag., Stone Inst., AIA/Libr., Lumen, Pratt Inst., NYU, N.Y.C. Art Commn. Fellow: AIA ((numerous offices, including pres. N.Y.C. chpt.) 1987, Nat. Honor award, N.Y. State award); mem.: Alumni Coun. Grad. Sch. Design Harvard ((editl. bd. Harvard Design mag.)), Wadawanuck Club, Century Assn., Sir John Soane Mus. Found., Archtl. League N.Y.C. ((bd. dirs.)), Ellis Island Yacht Club (commodore 2001—). Office: 246 W 38th St Fl 14 New York NY 10018-5805

VORA, ASHOK, financial economist; b. Bombay, India, July 19, 1947; came to U.S., 1970; s. Kevalchand and Laxmi (Mehta) V.; m. Rama Kata, Dec. 12, 1982; children: Anjali Serena, Amit Raunak. B.Sc., U. Bombay, 1967; MBA, Indian Inst. Mgmt., 1970; PhD, Northwestern U., 1973. Asst. to chmn. Vora Automotives Ltd., Bombay, 1963-67, dir., 1967-70; asst. prof. fin. CUNY, 1973-80; vis. asst. prof. fin. U. Wis., Madison, 1977; vis. assoc. prof. fin. Northwestern U., Evanston, Ill., 1979-80; assoc. prof. fin. CUNY, 1980-84, prof. fin., 1984—; dir. fin. rsch. Fed. Home Loan Mortgage Corp., Reston, Va., 1987-88; vis. prof. fin. Hofstra U., Hempstead, N.Y., 1990-91. Cons. in field. Contbr. articles to profl. jours. Mem. Am. Econ. Assn., Am. Fin. Assn., Fin. Mgmt. Assn., So. Fin. Assn., S.W. Fin. Assn., Western Fin. Assn., Mensa, Nat. Wildlife Fedn., Beta Gamma Sigma. Office: CUNY Dept Econs 17 Lexington Ave New York NY 10010-5518

VORA, MANU KISHANDAS, chemical engineer, quality consultant; b. Bombay, India, Oct. 31, 1945; s. Kishandas Narandas and Shantaben K. (Valia) V., m. Nila Narotamdas Kothari, June 16, 1974; children: Ashish, Anand. BSChemE, Banaras (India) Hindu U., 1968; MSChemE, Ill. Inst. Tech., Chgo., 1970, PhD in ChemE, 1975; MBA, Keller Grad. Sch. Mgmt., Chgo., 1985. Grad. asst. Ill. Inst. Tech., 1969-74; rsch. assoc. Inst. Gas Tech., Chgo., 1976-77, chem. engr., 1977-79, engring. supr., 1979-82; mem. tech. staff AT&T Bell Labs. (now Lucent Techs.), Holmdel, N.J., 1983-84, Naperville, Ill., 1984—, mgr. customer sasfisfaction, 1990-96, voice of the customer mgr., 1997-2000; pres., CEO Bus. Excellence, Inc., 2000—. Adj. faculty mem. Ill. Inst. Tech., Chgo., part-time, 1993—; spkr. in field. Invited editor Internat. Petroleum Encyclopedia, 1980. Chmn. Save the Children Holiday Fund Drive, 1986-99; trustee Avery Coonley Sch., Downers Grove, Ill., 1987-91; pres., dir. Blind Found. for India, Naperville, 1989—. Recipient Non-Supervisory AA award Affirmative Actions Adv. Com., 1987, 92, 97, Outstanding Contbn. award Asian Am. for Affirmative Actions, 1989, Disting. Svc. award Save the Children, 1990, Ann. Merit award Chgo. Assn. Tech. Socs., 1992. Fellow Am. Soc. Quality Control (standing rev. bd. 1988—, editl. re. bd. 1989, tech. media com. 1989, mixed media rev. bd. 1994, nat. quality month regional planning com. 1989-94, nat. cert. com. 1989-94, chmn. cert. process improvements subcom. 1990-94, testimonial awards 1995, 96, 2001, 02, exec. bd. Chgo. sect., vice chmn. sect. affairs 1993-94, sect. chmn. 1994-95, nat. dir. at large, 1996-98, nat. dir. 1998-2000, v.p. 2000-2002, vice chmn. investing in quality capital campaign, spl. award 1991, Century Club award 1992, Founders' award 1993, Joe Lisy Quality award 1994, Grant medal 2001); mem. Ill. Team Excellence award (chief judge 1993-99, steering com. 1993-99, award). Hindu. Avocations: reading, photography, travel, philanthropic activities. Home: 1256 Hamilton Ln Naperville IL 60540-8373 Office: Bus Excellence Inc PO Box 5585 Naperville IL 60567-5585 E-mail: manuvora@b-einc.com.

VORCE, MICHAEL EUGENE, music educator; b. Granite City, Ill., Sept. 19, 1953; s. Leonard Eugene and Doris June Vorce; m. Debra Dee Godsey, Jan. 10, 1981; children: Madrigal Renee Vorce Brown, Jonathan Michael Vorce, Brian Patrick Vorce; m. Debra Ann Peacher, Aug. 30, 1974 (dec. June 28, 1978). BS, U. of Mo. Columbia, Columbia, MO, 1980—84. Program dir. Coordinated Youth & Human Services, Granite City, Ill., 1987—91; educator Francis Howell Sch. Dist., St. Charles, Mo., 1991—93; music educator Granite City Pub. Schools, Granite City, Ill., 1993—2002. Faculty advisor Tri-M Music Honor Soc., Granite City, Ill., 1997—; choral dir. Coolidge Mid. Sch., Granite City, Ill., 1997—, yearbook advisor, Ill., 1994—98; asst. band dir. Francis Howell Sch. Dist., St. Charles, Mo., 1991—93. Composer: (music) Choral Works For Worship, Songs for Worship, Woodwind Quartet. Musician Alton First So. Bapt. Ch., Alton, Ill., 2001; mem. Alton Mcpl. Band, 2002, Rotary Club, Alton, 2002. Recipient First Superior Rating, Ill. Grade Sch. Music Assn. Contest, 1999-2002, Second Pl., Greater St. Louis Marching Compitition, 1992. Mem.: Music Educators Nat. Conf., Am. Choral Directors Assn., Tri-M Music Honor Soc., Phi Mu Alpha Sinfonia. Independent. Southern Baptist. Avocations: motorcycling, working out, working out, working out, working out. Home: 1116 Washington Avenue Alton IL 62002 Office: Coolidge Middle School 3231 Nameoki Road Granite City IL 62040 Personal E-mail: gcmusicteacher@charter.net.

VORIS, DAVID CLARENCE, retired neurosurgeon; b. Aug. 24, 1923; BA, U. Ill., 1947, BS, 1948, MD, 1951. Diplomate Am. Bd. Neurologic Surgery. Intern Cook County Hosp., Chgo., 1951-52; fellow in neurol. surgery Mayo Clinic, Rochester, Minn., 1952-56; resident in neurol. surgery Mercy Hosp., Chgo., 1957, neurologic surgeon, 1957-85; ret., 1985. Clin. prof. neurologic surgery U. Ill. Coll. Medicine; attending neurosurgeon Mercy Hosp., Stanthony Hosp., MacNeal Meml. Hosp., Cook County Hosp., Hines VA Hosp. Mem. ACS, AMA, Am. Assn. Neurosurgens, Chi Med. Soc., Ill. Med. Soc., Chi Neurologic Soc., Ctrl. Neurosurgical Soc. Home: 4189 S 400 W Hanover IN 47243-9112

VORPAGEL, WILBUR CHARLES, historical consultant; b. Milw., Feb. 26, 1926; s. Arthur Fred and Emma (Hintz) V.; Betty J. Hoch, June 19, 1952; stepchildren: Jerry L., Sharon Belveal Sullenberger. Student Army specialized tng. program, U. Ill., 1943-44; BBA, U. Wis., 1949; MBA, U. Denver, 1953. Cert. tchr., Colo. Instr. Montezuma County High Sch., Cortez, Colo., 1949-51; coord. bus. edn. Pueblo (Colo.) Pub. Schs., 1951-56; pvt. practice bus. cons. Pueblo and Denver, 1956—. Tchr. bus. edn. Emily Griffith Opportunity Sch., Denver, 1959-69; various positions with Denver & Rio Grande Western R.R. Co., Denver, 1959-88; cons. in field. Bd. dirs. Colo. Ret. Sch. Employees Assn., Denver, 1988—; rep. Custer Battlefield Hist. & Mus. Assn. Sgt. U.S. Army, 1944-46, ETO. Mem. Augustan Soc., St. John Vol. Corp., S.E. Colo. Geneal. Soc., Rio Grande Vets. Club (bd. dirs. Pueblo chpt.), Biblical Archaeol. Soc. (contbg. writer), Nat. Huguenot Soc., Colo. Huguenot Soc. (organizing pres. 1979-95), 70th Inf. Divsn. Assn., Shriners, Masons. Republican. Mem. Christian Ch. Avocations: archeo-astronomy, militaria, numismatics, autographs, incunabula. Home and Office: 335 Davis Ave Pueblo CO 81004-1019 *Personal philosophy: We really live twice when we can enjoy the past and the present. Born into a world unbidden, assailed by forces beyond our ken, carried out protesting - life is still worth living. The best is yet to come.*

VORT, ROBERT A. lawyer; b. Newark, Sept. 24, 1943; s. Saul S. and Ruth J. (Jacobson) Vort; m. Elizabeth Hornstein, June 25, 1968 (div. Nov. 1979); m. Marcelle Greenstein, Nov. 18, 1979 (div. Jan. 1991); children: Joel, Abigail, Rebecca; m. Tina Kruh, Feb. 4, 1996; 1 child Hannah. BS in Econs., U. Pa., 1965; JD, Columbia U., 1968. Bar: N.J. 1968, N.Y. 1970, U.S. Ct. Appeals (2d and 3d cirs. 1975), U.S. Ct. Appeals (9th cir.) 1980, U.S. Ct. Appeals (5th cir.) 1981, U.S. Ct. Appeals (fed. cir.) 1984, U.S. Dist. Ct. N.J. 1968, U.S. Dist. Ct. (so. and ea. dists.) N.Y. 1984, U.S. Supreme Ct. 1977. Law clk. to Hon. Theodore I. Botter Superior Ct. of N.J., 1968-69; assoc. Davis & Cox, 1969-71, Israel B. Greene, 1971-73; sole practitioner, 1973-82; ptnr. Balk, Goldberger, Seligsohn, O'Connor & Rhatican, 1982-84, Kirsten, Friedman & Cherin, 1986; pvt. practice, 1984-85, 87-88; ptnr. Goldberg, Mufson & Spar, West Orange, N.J., 1988-91; counsel Donald Friedman, 1991-92; pvt. practice Tenafly, N.J., 1997—; ptnr. Pearce, Vort & Fleisig LLC, Hackensack, 2001—. Mem. ABA (litigation sect., family law sect., legal econs. sect.), N.J. State Bar Assn. (appellate practice subcom.), Bergen County Bar Assn. Office: Pearce Vort & Fleisig LLC Court Plaza North 25 Main St Hackensack NJ 07601 E-mail: rvort@pearcelawl.com.

VORWERK, ETTA CHARLSIE, artist; b. Tennga, Ga., Jan. 28, 1934; d. James A. and Hester L. (Davis) Pritchett; m. Norman T. Vorwerk, Feb. 9, 1956; children: Karl, Lauren, Michael. AB, Ga. Coll. for Women, Milledgeville, 1955. Billboard design artist Vanesco Poster, Chattanooga, 1955; cartographic draftsman TVA, 1955; fashion illustrator Loveman's, 1956; freelance comml. artist Chattanooga, Charleston, S.C., 1957—; pvt. art instr. for children and adults, 1966—; art instr. continuing edn. Charleston So. U., 1979-82. Exhbn. chmn. Charleston Artist Guild, Summerville Artist Guild; chair Flowertown Festival, Summerville, S.C., 1972-98; co-coord. Picolo-Spoleto Outdoor Art Exhibit, City of Charleston, 1983-98, others. Illustrator: (jokes) Tales and Taradiddles, (elem. book) St. Paul's Epitahs, others. Mem. Bd. Archtl. Rev., Summerville, 1976—; mem. women's bd. St. Paul's Ch., Summerville, 1968-84; active Boy Scouts Am., Girl Scouts U.S.; vol. Mental Health Clinic. Recipient art show ribbons. Mem. Charleston Artist Guild, Summerville Artist Guild. Episcopalian. Avocations: gardening, cooking, sewing, photography, nature. Home and Office: 315 W Carolina Ave Summerville SC 29483-4358

VORYS, ARTHUR ISAIAH, lawyer; b. Columbus, Ohio, June 16, 1923; s. Webb Isaiah and Adeline (Werner) V.; m. Lucia Rogers, July 16, 1949 (div. 1980); children: Caroline S., Adeline Vorys Cranson, Lucy Vorys Noll, Webb I.; m. Ann Harris, Dec. 13, 1980. BA, Williams Coll., 1945; LLB, JD, Ohio State U., 1949. Bar: Ohio 1949. From assoc. to ptnr. Vorys, Sater, Seymour & Pease LLP, Columbus, 1949-82, sr. ptnr., 1982-93, of counsel, 1993—. Supt. ins. State of Ohio, 1957-59; bd. dirs Vorys Bros., Inc., others. Trustee, past pres. Children's Hosp., Greenlawn Cemetery Found.; trustee, former chmn. Ohio State U. Hosps.; regent Capital U.; del. Rep. Nat. Conv., 1968, 72. Lt. USMCR, World War II. Decorated Purple Heart. Fellow Ohio State Bar, Columbus Bar Assn.; mem. ABA, Am. Judicature Soc., Rocky Fork Headley Hunt Club, Rocky Fork Hunt and Country Club, Capital Club, Phi Delta Phi, Chi Psi. Home: 5826 Havens Corners Rd Columbus OH 43230-3142 Office: Vorys Sater Seymour & Pease LLP PO Box 1008 52 E Gay St Columbus OH 43216-1008

VOS, HUBERT DANIEL, private investor; b. Paris, Aug. 2, 1933; s. Marius and Aline (Porge) V.; m. Susan Hill, Apr. 18, 1958; children: Wendy, James. BA, Institut d'Etudes Politiques, U. Paris, 1954; M in Pub. Adminstrn., Princeton U., 1956. Internal auditor Internat. Packers Ltd., 1957-61, dir. fin., 1962-64; asst. to contr. Monsanto Co., 1964-66, contr. internat. div., 1966-69; v.p. planning and fin. Smith Kline Corp., 1969-72; sr. v.p. fin. Comml. Credit Co., Balt., 1972-74; sr. v.p. fin. and adminstrn., dir. Norton Simon Inc., N.Y.C., 1974-79; sr. v.p. fin., dir. Becton Dickinson and Co., Paramus, N.J., 1979-83; pres. Stonington Capital Corp., Santa Barbara, Calif., 1984—. Bd. dirs. Rowe Price New Era Fund Inc., New Horizons Fund Inc., Equity Income Fund Inc., Capital Appreciation Fund, Inc., Sci. and Tech. Fund, Inc., Small Capital Appreciation Fund, Inc., Balanced Fund, Inc. Bd. dirs. Surg. Eye Expdns. Internat. Mem. Am. Mgmt. Assn. (gen. mgmt. coun.), La Cumbre Golf and Country Club. Home: 800 Via Hierba Santa Barbara CA 93110-2222

VOSBECK, ROBERT RANDALL, architect; b. Mankato, Minn., May 18, 1930; s. William Frederick and Gladys (Anderson) V.; m. Phoebe Macklin, June 21, 1953; children: Gretchen, Randy, Heidi, Macklin. BArch, U. Minn., 1954. Various archtl. positions, 1956-62; ptnr. Vosbeck-Vosbeck & Assocs., Alexandria, Va., 1962-66, VVKR Partnership, Alexandria, 1966-79; exec. v.p. VVKR Inc., 1979-82, pres., 1982-88; prin. Vosbeck/DMJM, Washington and Alexandria, Va., 1989-94; v.p. DMJM Arch. and Engring., 1990-94; pvt. practice archtl. cons., 1994—. Mem. Nat. Capital Planning Commn., 1976-81, U.S./USSR Joint Group on Bldg. Design and Constrn., 1974-79; mem. Nat. Park System Adv. Bd., 1984-88. Archtl. works include Pub. Safety Ctr., Alexandria, Va., 1987, Yorktown (Va.) Visitors Ctr. 1976, Frank Reeves Mcpl. Office Bldg., Washington, 1986, Fed. Bldg., Norfolk, Va., 1979, Jeff Davis Assocs. Office Complex, Arlington, Va., 1991, Westminster Continued Care Retirement Community, Lake Ridge, Va., 1993. Pres. Alexandria Jaycees, 1960-61; v.p. Va. Jaycees, 1962-63; pres. Alexandria Ch. of Com., 1974-75. Engring. officer USMC, 1954-56. Recipient Plaque of Honor, Fedn. Colegios Architects, Republic of Mexico, Alumni Achievement award U. Minn. Coll. Arch., 2001, hon. fellowship Colegios Architects of Spain, Royal Archtl. Inst. Can., Soc. Architects of Mex.; named Outstanding Young Man in Va., 1963, Acadamecian, Internt. Acad. Arch. Fellow AIA (bd. dirs. 1976-78, v.p. 1979-80, pres. 1981), Internat. Union Architects (coun. 1981-87), Nat. Trust Hist. Preservation. Presbyterian. Home and Office: 770 Potato Patch Dr Unit A Vail CO 81657-4462 E-mail: vosbeckr@cs.com.

VOSBECK, WILLIAM FREDERICK, JR. architect; b. Mankato, Minn., May 13, 1924; s. William Frederick and Gladys (Anderson) V.; m. Elizabeth Just, Aug. 2, 1947; children: Lee, William Frederick III, Lynn, James Stephen. Student, U. Notre Dame, 1943, Cornell U., 1945; BArch, U. Minn., 1947. Ptnr. Vosbeck & Ward, Alexandria, Va., 1957-62, Vosbeck Vosbeck & Assos. (changed to Vosbeck Vosbeck Kendrick Redinger, Architects, Engrs., Planners), Alexandria, 1962-68; chmn. bd. dirs. VVKR, Inc. Bd. dirs. Dominion Resources Va. Power, Crestar Fin. Corp. Mem. Gov.'s Com. Employment Handicapped, 1973; trustee Va. Found. Ind. Colls., Va. Mus. Fine Arts, Va. C. of C.; mem. Alexandra Hosp. Bd., pres., 1970. With USMCR, 1943-50. Recipient Wash. Acad. Sci. Nat. Capital award for achievement in arch., Nat. Rehab. Assn. citation tech. svcs., Gargoyle award, T. David Fitz-Gibbon Archt. Firm awrd, numerous honor and merit awards Va. Soc. AIA, Va. Mus. Fine Arts, Outstanding Achievement award Engring. News Record, 1977. Fellow AIA (pres. Va. chpt. 1971). Clubs: Belle Haven Country, Cosmos, Rotary. Home: 7512 Fort Hunt Rd Alexandria VA 22307-1924 Office: Vosbeck Assocs 211 N Union St Alexandria VA 22314-2643 Fax: 703 683-4707.

VOSBURG, BRUCE DAVID, lawyer; b. Omaha, June 17, 1943; s. Noble Perrin and Dena V. (Ferrari) V.; m. Susan Simpson, May 27, 1972; children: Margaret Amy, Wendy Christine, Bruce David. BA, U. Notre Dame, 1965; BSME, 1966; JD, Harvard U., 1969. Bar: Nebr. 1969, Ill. 1970, U.S. Supreme Ct. 1974. Law clk. U.S. Dist. Ct. Nebr., 1969-70; assoc. Kirkland & Ellis, Chgo., 1970-72; ptnr. Fitzgerald & Schorr, Omaha, 1972—. Author: Financing Small Businesses, 1981, Securities Law Practice, 1987, Securities Law-Going Public, 1989, Trade Secret Protection, 1994, Protecting Intellectual Property, 1998, Intellectual Property Law, 1998. Pres. Children's Crisis Ctr., 1984-85, bd. dirs., 1973-84; pres. Nebr. Tennis Assn., 1976-77; mem. Leadership Omaha, 1979; chmn. bd. dirs. City of Omaha Parks and Recreation, 1985-92; founding dir. Friends of the Parks, 1988; bd. dirs. Omaha Pub. Libr. Found., 1997—, pres., 1999—; bd. dirs. Western Heritage Mus., 1998—. Fellow Nebr. Bar Found.; mem. ABA, Nat. Assn. Bond Attys., Nebr. Bar Assn. (chmn. securities com.), Omaha Bar Assn. (exec. coun. 1983-86), Rotary (dir. 1993—), Mo. Valley Tennis Assn. (chmn. grievance com. 1978—), Am. Intellectual Property Lawyers Assn., Tau Beta Pi. Republican. Roman Catholic. Office: Ste 400 13220 California St Omaha NE 68154-5228

VOSBURG, SUZANNE K. research scientist; b. Salamanca, N.Y., Oct. 15, 1965; d. John F. and Karen B. Vosburg. BA, U. Mich., 1988; MS, SUNY, Buffalo, 1992; PhD, U. Bergen, Norway, 1998. Grad. and rsch. asst. Ctr. for Studies in Creativity, Buffalo, 1990-93; jr. rsch. fellow U. Bergen, 1993, asst. prof., 1994-95; rsch. asst. N.Y. Hosp.-Cornell Med. Ctr., White Plains, 1996-98; rsch. scientist N.Y. State Psychiat. Inst., N.Y.C., 1998-99, programmer, analyst, 1999-2000, rsch. scientist, 2000—. Contbr. articles to profl. jours., chpt. to book. Grantee U. Tromso, Norway, 1995. Mem. APA, Am. Psychol. Soc. Avocations: music, yoga, bicycling. Office: NY State Psychiat Inst Substance Abuse Rot Unit 120 1051 Riverside Dr New York NY 10032-1013 E-mail: vosburg@pi.cpmc.columbia.edu.

VOSE, MORTON, II (SETH MORTON VOSE II), art appraiser; b. Brookline, Mass. s. Robert Churchill Vose and Sarah Helen Williams; m. Ruth Denny Vose, Sept. 7, 1940; children: Ruth Storrow, Virginia Williams Vose, Seth Morton III. AB, Harvard U., 1931. Pres. Vose Galleries Boston, Inc., 1965—76, Vose Archive, Brookline, 1982—98. Mem. adv. bd. Art Gallery, U. N.H., Durham, Mead Art Mus., Amherst (Mass.) Coll., Hunter Mus. Art, Chattanooga; proprietor Redwood Libr. and Athenaeum, Newport, RI, 1958—. Trustee Brookline Pub. Libr.; mem. BiCentennial Commn. Capt. Mass. State Guard. Mem.: R.I. Hist. Soc., N.H. Hist. Soc., Mass. Hist. Soc., Brookline Hist. Soc., Boston Athenaeum. Republican. Home: 1010 Waltham St Lexington MA 02421

VOSEVICH, KATHI ANN, writer, editor, scholar; b. St. Louis, Oct. 12, 1957; d. William and Catherine Mildred (Kalinowski) V.; m. James Hughes Meredith, Sept. 6, 1986. AB with honors, St. Louis U., 1980, MA, 1983; PhD, U. Denver, 1988. Tchg. fellow St. Louis U., 1980-83, acad. advising fellow, 1983-84; tchg. fellow U. Denver, 1985-87; prof. ESL, BNM Talensch., Uden, The Netherlands, 1988-91; instr. English, mentor U. Ga., Athens, 1992-94; vis. asst. prof. Colo. Coll., Colorado Springs, 1994; sr. tech. writer and editor Titan Client/Server Techs., 1994-96, head documentation, libr., 1996-97; documentation mgr. Beechwood, 1997-98, tech. mgr., 1998-99; tech. writer Microsoft, Redmond, Wash., 1999-2000; documentation and process mgr. Sprint, Denver, 2000; practice and group mgr. e-business Sprint Corp., 2000—. Forensic judge USAF Acad., Colo., 1987-88; edn. officer Volkel (The Netherlands) Air Base, 1988-91; instr. English European divsn. U. Md., The Netherlands and Belgium, 1989-91. Author: Customer Care User's Guide, 1996, Interview with Joseph Heller, 1999, Conversations with Joseph Heller in Understanding the Literature of World War II, 1999, Office Update, 1999-2000, Tutoring the Tudors, 2000; editor: Subscription Services System Documentation, 1996, Titan Process Documentation, 1994-96; copy editor: Language, Ideas, and American Culture; War, Literature and the Arts; contbr. over 100 electronic texts and articles to profl. jours. Colo. scholar U. Denver, 1985-86, grad. dean scholar, 1988; NEH fellow U. Md., 1994 Mem. MLA, Phi Beta Kappa, Alpha Sigma Nu. Roman Catholic. Avocations: writing, drawing, raising Bernese mountain dogs. Office: Sprint Ste 1100 1099 18th St Denver CO 80202

VOSHEL, ELIZABETH HARBECK, social worker, educator; b. Grand Haven, Mich., Oct. 2, 1951; d. Eugene Orr and Sarah Page Harbeck; m. Geoffrey Allen Voshel, Apr. 7, 1973; children: Justin, Kathleen. BA, Alma Coll., Alma, MI, 1973; Master of Social Work, Western Mich. U., Kalamazoo, 1978. Cert. Social Worker NASW Acad. of Cert. Social Work, 1980. Head educator Battle Creek Day Care Ctr., Battle Creek, Mich., 1974—75; exec. dir. Battle Creek Cay Care Ctr., 1975—76; clin. social worker VA Med. Ctr., 1978—92, supervisory social worker, 1992—2000; coord. of field edn. Sch. of Social Work, Kalamazoo, 2000—. Chairperson NASW, Lansing, Mich., 1996—2002, mem., Mich., 1992—96, vice-president fo standards & services, Mich., 1978—2002. Author: (presentation / workshop) Canadian Schools of Social Work. Recipient Project Charlie / Peaceful Partners, Kalamazoo, MI, 2001. Episcopalian. Avocations: walking, reading, computers, computers, computers. Office: WMU School of Social Work 1903 West Michigan Avenue Kalamazoo MI 49008-5354 Office Fax: 616-387-3183. E-mail: elizabeth.voshel@wmich.edu.

VOSKA, KATHRYN CAPLES, consultant, facilitator; b. Berkeley, Cal., Dec. 26, 1942; d. Donald Buxton and Ellen Marion (Smith) Caples; m. David Karl Nehrling, Aug. 15, 1964 (div. Nov. 1980); children: Sandra E. Nehrling, Barbara M. Nehrling, Melissa A. Nehrling-Holmgren; m. James Edward Voska, Aug. 31, 1985. BS, Northwestern U., 1964; MS, Nat.-Louis U., 1989. Cert. teacher, Ill.; cert. career mgmt. fellow practitioner Internat. Bd. for Career Mgmt. Cert. Tchr. pub. schs., Northbrook and Evanston, Ill., 1964-65; acting phys. dir. YWCA, Evanston, 1975; quality control technician Baxter Travenol, Morton Grove, 1978-80; sr. quality assurance analyst Hollister Inc., Libertyville, 1980-85; info. ctr. trainer, tech. training mgr. Rand McNally, Skokie, 1985-92; cons., facilitator Capka & Assocs., Skokie and Kansas City, 1992—; dir. edn. Nat. Office Machine Dealers, 1992-94; career and mgmt. cons. Right Mgmt. Cons., Overland Park, Kans., 1994—. Pvt. practice estate conservator; bd. dirs. Coro/Kansas City, 1996—. Telephone worker Contact Chgo. Crisis Hotline, 1989-90; CPR instr. trainer Amer. Heart Assn., Chgo., 1977-89; aquatic dir. YMCA, Evanston, Ill., 1969-80; rep. Alumnae Panhellenic Coun., Evanston, 1969-75; grad. Leadership Overland Park, 1996, mem. 15th anniv. special task force. Mem. ASTD (bd. dirs. Kansas City chpt. 1997-99), ASCD, Soc. Human Resource Mgmt., Midwest Soc. Profl. Cons., Assn. for Mgmt. Orgn. Design, Chgo. Orgn. Data Processing Educators, Chgo. Computer Soc., Info. Ctr. Exch. of Chgo., Assn. Quality and Participation, Am. Soc. for Quality (teller N.E. Ill. sect. 1982-84), Internat. Soc. for Performance Improvement, Internat. Assn. Career Mgmt. Profls. (founding pres. Kansas City chpt., nat. bd. mem. 2000—, nat. bd. v.p. 2002—), The Learning Resource Network. Presbyterian. Avocations: scuba diving, swimming, hiking, camping, traveling. Home: 1001 E 118th Ter Kansas City MO 64131-3828 Office: Right Mgmt Cons 7300 W 110th St Ste 800 Overland Park KS 66210-2387 E-mail: kathy.voska@right.com., kvoska@kc.rr.com.

VOSLER PETRELLA, BRENDA GAYLE, family nurse practitioner, educator, researcher; b. Beaver Falls, Pa., Sept. 18, 1964; d. Gale Carlton and Donna Jeanne (Gibson) V. AD with distinction, Kent State U., East Liverpool, Ohio, 1985; BS, Pa. State U., Beaver, 1990; BSN with high distinction, Pa. State U., 1991; MSN, LaRoche Coll., Pitts., 1997. Cert. emergency med. technician, emergency nurse, ACLS instr.; CRNP. Assoc. instr. Ctr. for Emergency Medicine, Pitts., 1992-96; staff nurse in emergency dept. U. Pitts. Med. Ctr., 1988-97; family nurse practitioner Tri States Surg. Assocs., 1997—2001, CRNP Heritage Valley Health System, The Med. Ctr., Beaver and Sewickley Valley Hosp., 2001—; part-time nursing instr. Beaver County C.C., 2001—. Nurse on disaster mgmt. team U.S. Govt., Pitts., 1997—; pres., program coord. therapeutic riding program Windwalker Farm, Inc., 1992—; assoc. prof. Duquesne U., 2000—. Mem. Emergency Nurses Assn., Sigma Theta Tau. Home: 190 Fredrickstown Rd Midland PA 15059-2204

VOSS, ANNE COBLE, nutritional biochemist; b. Richmond, Ind., Aug. 22, 1946; d. James Richard and Helen Lucille (Hoyt) Coble; m. Harold Lloyd Voss, July 20, 1969; children: Daniel, Jordan Matthew, Sarah Georgette. BS, Ohio State U., 1968, PhD, 1984. Registered dietitian. Therapeutic dietitian Johns Hopkins Hosp., Balt., 1968-69; clin. instr. Ohio State U. Hosps., Columbus, 1969-70; clin. dietitian U.S. Army Med. Clinic, Rothwesten, Fed. Republic Germany, 1970-72; clin. rsch. monitor Ross Labs., Columbus, 1978-79; rsch. asst. Ohio State U., 1979-84, rsch. assoc., lectr., 1985-91; mgr. outcomes rsch. Ross Products divsn. Abbott Labs., Ohio, 1992—. Adj. asst. prof. Otterbein Coll., Westerville, Ohio, 1990-93; nutrition advisor Ohio Dental Assn., Columbus, 1977-93, ADA, Chgo., 1987-93; cons. Ohio Bd. Dietetics, Columbus, 1989-93; vis. scientist Rikshospitalet, Oslo, Norway, 1992. Author: Polyunsaturated Fatty Acids and Eicosanoids, 1987; author, editor: Nutrition Perspectives, 1990, 91, 2d edit., 1993; contbr. articles to profl. jours. Mem. exec. bd. Aux. to Ohio Dental Assn., Columbus, 1979-95; bd. dirs. Ohio Dental Polit. Action Com., Columbus, 1989-92, YWCA, Columbus, 1990-93; Gov.'s appointee, chmn. Ohio Bd. Dietetics. Recipient award Clement Found., Westerville, 1991, Disting. Alumni award Ohio State U., 1996; Nutrition Edn. in Tng. grant Ohio Dept. Edn., Columbus, 1978. Mem. Am. Dietetic Assn., Ohio Dietetic Assn., Med. Dietetics Assn. (founding mem., pres., v.p., sec. 1978—), Ohio Coun. Against Health Fraud (founding mem., bd. govs. 1987—), Ohio Nutrition Coun. (exec. bd. 1987-94), Columbus Dietetic Assn., Sigma Xi, Sigma Delta Epsilon (sec. 1985—). Methodist. Avocations: gardening, cooking, sewing, skiing. Home: 1526 Bridgeton Dr Columbus OH 43220-3908 Office: Abbott Labs Ross Products Divsn 625 Cleveland Ave Columbus OH 43215-1754

VOSS, DENNIS F. priest; b. Germantown, Ill., May 30, 1938; s. Lawrence B. and Marie E. (Schomaker) Voss. BA, St. Mary of the Lake, Mundelein, Ill., 1960; ThM, St. Mary of the Lake Sem., Mundelein, Ill., 1963; Lic.in Sacred Theology, St. Mary of the Lake Sem., 1964. Priest Roman Cath. Ch.; cert. grief counselor Ill., 1990. Assoc. pastor St. Peter's Cathedral, Belleville, Ill., 1964—69, St. Albert the Great Ch., Fairview Hts., 1969—71; pastor St. Cyril Ch., East St. Louis, 1971—73, St. Mary Ch., Centralia, 1973—78, St. Stephen Ch., Flora, 1978—79; assoc. pastor St. Peter's Cathedral, Belleville; chaplain St. Elizabeth Hosp.; pastor St. Liborius Ch., St. Libory, Ill., St. Anthony Ch., Lively. Chair ethics com. St. Elizabeth Hosp., Belleville, 1989—2000, grief counselor, 2000, mental health counselor, 1982—2000; mem. ethics com. Hospice of So. Ill., 1998—; chair ethics com. Gateway Cath. Ethics Network, 1997—2000. Mem.: Assn. of Grief Counselors and Educators. Roman Catholic. Avocations: gardening, fishing. Home and Office: 911 Sparta St Saint Libory IL 62282

VOSS, EDWARD WILLIAM, JR. immunologist, educator; b. Chgo., Dec. 2, 1933; s. Edward William and Lois Wilma (Graham) V.; m. Virginia Hellman, June 15, 1974; children: Cathleen, Valerie. AB, Cornell Coll., Iowa, 1955; MS, Ind. U., 1964, PhD, 1966. Asst. prof. microbiology U. Ill., Urbana, 1967-71, assoc. prof., 1971-74, prof., 1974-98, prof. emeritus, 1999—, adj. prof. dept. vet. pathobiology, 2001—, dir. cell sci. ctr., 1988-94, Coll. Liberal Arts and Scis. Jubilee prof., 1990. Rev. panel on molecular biology-gene structure USDA, Washington, 1985-86, U.S. Dept. Energy Rsch., 1994; panel mem. in biol. scis. NSF Minority Grad. Fellowships, Washington, 1986-88; sci. adv. bd. Biotech. Rsch. and Devel. Corp., 1989—; mem. Peer Review Com. AHA, 1993-96; study sect. innovation grant program for approaches in HIV vaccine rsch. NIH, 1997; adj. prof. U. Hawaii, Manoa, 1999-2001, Coll. Vet. Medicine, 2001-. Author, editor: Fluorescein Hapten: An Immunological Probe, 1984, Anti-DNA Antibodies in SLE, 1988; adv. editor: Immunochemistry, 1975-78, Molecular Immunology, 1980— ; mem. editorial bd.: Applied and Environ. Microbiology, 1979— ; contbr. articles to profl. jours. Apptd. to pres.'s coun. U. Ill. Found., 1995. Served with U.S. Army, 1956-58. NIH fellow, 1966-67, NSF fellow, 1975-77; NIH grantee, 1967—, NSF grantee, 1967—; recipient Disting. Lectr. award U. Ill., 1983; named 1st James R. Martin Univ. scholar, 1994; recipient Exemplary Contbn. award Lupus Found. Am., 1994. Ednl. Aid award E.I. DuPont, 1994, 95. Fellow Am. Inst. Chemists; mem. AAAS, Fedn. Am. Scientists, Am. Assn. Immunologists, Am. Assn. Biol. Chemists, Reticuloendothelial Soc., Am. Lupus Soc. (hon. bd. dirs. Cen. Ill. chpt. 1986—, named to Nat. Lupus Hall of Fame 1988, Cmty. Svc. award 1996), N.Y. Acad. Scis., U.S. Pharmacopeial Conv., Inc., Nat. Geog. Soc., Am. Chem. Soc. (tour speaker 1984-87), Protein Soc., Sigma Xi. Home: 2207 Boudreau Cir Urbana IL 61801-6601 Office: Dept Vet Pathobiology Coll Vet Medicine 2522 VMBSB 2001 South Lincoln Ave Urbana IL 61802 E-mail: e-voss1@life.uiuc.edu. *Perserverance, determination and sacrifice only when coupled to appropriate goals in basic research and teaching yield results that justify the effort and commitment.*

VOSS, JACK DONALD, international business consultant, lawyer; b. Stoughton, Wis., Sept. 24, 1921; s. George C. and Grace (Tusler) V.; m. Mary Josephine Edgarton, May 7, 1955; children: Julia, Jennifer, Andrew, Charles. Ph.B., U. Wis., 1943; JD, Harvard U., 1948. Bar: Ill. 1949, Ohio 1963. From assoc. to ptnr. Sidney & Austin predecessor firm, Chgo., 1948-62; gen. counsel Anchor Hocking Corp., Lancaster, Ohio, 1962-67, v.p., gen. counsel, 1967-72, gen. mgr. internat., 1970-86; pres. Anchor Hocking Internat. Corp., 1972-86; mng. ptnr. Voss Internat., 1986—. Chmn. Internat. Coun. Conf. bd., 1985-87. Mem. Fairfield County Rep. Ctrl. and Exec. Com.; pres. Fairfield Heritage Assn., 1966-69; v.p. Lancaster Community Concert Assn., 1965-73; trustee, chmn. Ohio Info. Com. With USNR, 1943-46, ATO, MTO, PTO. Mem. ABA (internat. law & practice and bus. law sects.), Ohio Bar Assn. (chmn. corp. counsel sect. 1966), Columbus Bar Assn., Chgo. Bar Assn., Fairfield County Bar Assn., Licensing Execs. Soc., Am. Arbitration Assn. (panel mem.), Ctr. for Internat. Comml. Arbitration (panel mem.), Harvard Law Sch. Assn., Ohio Mfrs. Assn. (trustee, v.p. 1970-72), Symposiarch, Alpha Chi Rho. Clubs: Rotary (pres. Lancaster 1968), Racquet (Chgo.); Landsdowne (London). Lutheran. Home: PO Box 0624 Lancaster OH 43130-0624 Office: Voss Internat 212 S Broad St Lancaster OH 43130-4381

VOSS, JAMES S. astronaut; b. Cordova, Ala., Mar. 3, 1949; m. Suzan Curry; 1 child. BSc in Aerospace Engring., Auburn U., 1972; MSc in Aerospace Engring., U. Colo., 1974, PhD (hon.) , 2000. Commd. 2d lt. U.S. Army, advanced through grades to col., various assignments; vehicle integration test engr. NASA, Houston, 1984—87, astronaut, 1988—. Astronaut Space Shuttle Atlantis, 1991, Space Shuttle Discovery, 1992, Space Shuttle Endeavour, 1995, Space Shuttle Atlantis, 2000, Space Shuttle Discovery, lived on Internat. Space Sta., 2001. Decorated Def. Meritorious Svc. medal U.S. Army, Def. Superior Svc. medal, Def. Meritorious Svc. medal. Avocations: woodworking, skiing, softball, racquetball, scuba diving. Office: Astronaut Office CB NASA Johnson Space Center Houston TX 77058*

VOSS, JANICE E. astronaut; b. South Bend, Ind., Oct. 8, 1956; d. James R. and Voss. Student, U. Okla., 1973—75; BSc in Engring Sci., Purdue U., 1975; MSc in Elec. Engring., MIT, 1977; student, Rice U., 1977—78; PhD in Aero. & Astronautics, MIT, 1987. Co-op NASA, Houston, 1973—75, crew tnr., 1977—87; with Orbiatl Sci. Corp., 1987—90; astronaut NASA, 1991—. Astronaut space mission on STS-57, 1993, space mission on STS-63, 1995; payload comdr. space mission on STS-83, 1997; astronaut space mission on STS-94, 1997, space mission on STS-99, 2000. Fellow, NSF, 1976, Howard Hughes fellow, 1981, Zonta Amelia Earhart fellow, 1982. Mem.: AIAA. Avocations: reading, dancing, volleyball, flying. Office: Astronaut Office CB NASA Johnson Space Center Houston TX 77058*

VOSS, JERROLD RICHARD, city planner, educator, university official; b. Chgo., Nov. 4, 1932; s. Peter Walter and Annis Lorraine (Hayes) V.; m. Jean Evelyn Peterson, Aug. 21, 1954; children— Cynthia Jean, Tania Hayes. B.Arch., Cornell U., 1955; M. City Planning, Harvard U., 1959; PhD (Bus. History fellow, Univ. fellow, IBM fellow), 1971. Asst. prof. U. Calif., 1960-61; asst. prof., asso. prof. U. Ill., 1961-69; asso. prof. Harvard U., 1969-71; prof. city and regional planning Ohio State U., Columbus, 1971—, chmn. dept. city and regional planning, 1971-79; dir. Ohio State U. (Knowlton Sch. Architecture), 1981-96, prof., 1996-2000, dir., prof. emeritus, 2000—. UN advisor to Govt. Indonesia, 1964-65; social affairs officer UN Secretariat, 1970-71; project mgr. UN Task Force on Human Environment, Thailand, 1975-76; dir. rsch. and devel. UN Ctr. for Human Settlements (Habitat), 1979-81; cons. Ill. Dept. Devel., J.S. Bolles & Assocs., UN Office Tech. Cooperation, UN Devel. Program, AID, Bechtel Nat. Inc., other pvt. and pub. orgns.; mem. external examiners team United Arab U., 1992—. Author: Human Settlements: Problems and Priorities; Contbr. articles to profl. jours. Mem. pub. policy com. Smithsonian Instn., 1970-73; bd. dirs. Champaign County United Community Council, 1965-69, Columbus Theatre Ballet Assn., 1972-75. Served to 1st lt. U.S. Army, 1955-57. Mem. Acad. for Contemporary Problems (asso.), Am. Am. Inst. Planners, Am. Soc. Engring. Edn., Internat. Center for Urban Land Policy (London). Office: 190 W 17th Ave Columbus OH 43210-1320

VOSS, LINDA I. automotive company executive; b. Pigeon, Mich., Dec. 4, 1959; d. Edward Robert and Pearl Irene (Riffel) Ulrich; m. Timothy Allan Voss, Aug. 9, 1980; 1 child, Jason Adam. BS in Mgmt., Oakland U., Rochester, Mich., 1982; MBA in Fin., U. Mich., 1986. Student asst. Oakland U., Rochester, 1981; acct. GMAC, Detroit, 1982-84, fin. analyst, 1985-87, asst. mgr., 1988-89, mgr., 1989-90; mem. fin. staff GM, 1990-91; credit analysis mgr. GMAC, 1992-93, fin. planning mgr., 1993-94, asst. treas., 1995-96, fin. dir., 1996-97; CFO, exec. v.p. Nuvell Fin. Svcs./Credit Corp., Little Rock, 1997—. Bd. dirs. Nuvell Fin. Svcs., Saab Fin. Svcs. Corp. Author fin. software, 1988. Tchr. St. John Sunday Sch., Rochester, 1987-91; coach Rochester YMCA, 1988-91; mem. Ark. Sales Tax Adv. Com., 2000. GM fellow, 1984. Mem. Fin. Mgmt. Assn., Golden Key, Beta Gamma Sigma. Lutheran. Avocations: antiques, golf, piano. Home: 2216 Beckenham Cv Little Rock AR 72212-3230 Office: Nuvell Financial Services 17500 Chenal Pkwy Ste 200 Little Rock AR 72223-3911 E-mail: lvoss@nuvell.com.

VOSS, OMER GERALD, truck company executive; b. Downs, Kans., Sept. 14, 1916; s. John and Grace (Bohlen) V.; m. Annabelle Katherine Lutz, June 20, 1940; children— Jerrol Ann, Omer Gerald. AB, Ft. Hays (Kans.) State Coll., 1937; JD, U. Kans., 1939. Bar: Kans. bar 1939. With Internat. Harvester Co., 1936-79, v.p. farm equipment div., 1962-66, exec. v.p., dir., 1966—, vice chmn., 1977-79. Served with USAAF, 1943-46. Mem.: Chicago, Commercial, Westmoreland Country.

VOSS, REGIS DALE, agronomist, educator; b. Cedar Rapids, Iowa, Jan. 4, 1931; s. Francis Joseph and Mary Valeria (Womichil) V.; m. Margaret Anne Mitchell, Nov. 24, 1956; children: Lori Anne, John Patrick, David James. BS, Iowa State U., 1952, PhD, 1962. cert. profl. agronomist. Agriculturist Tenn. Valley Authority, Muscle Shoals, Ala., 1962-64; prof. Iowa State U., Ames, 1964-99, prof. emeritus, 1999—. Co-contbr. chpt. to: Fertilizer Technology and Use, 1985, Soil Testing and Plant Analysis, 1990; assoc. editor Jour. Prodn. Agr., 1988-92. Pres. FarmHouse Frat. Alumni Assn. Bd., Ames, 1990. 1st lt. USAF, 1952-56, Korea. Recipient Burlington No. Found. award Iowa State U., 1990, disting. svc. award Iowa State U. Ext., 1996, Iowa Master Farmer Exceptional Svc. award, 1998. Fellow AAAS, Am. Soc. Agronomy (bd. dirs. 1976-78, Agronomic Extension Edn. award 1984, Agronomic Achievement award 1989, Werner L. Nelson award 1992), Soil Sci. Soc. Am. (bd. dirs. 1980-83). Republican. Roman Catholic. Achievements include development of field laboratory for training of crop advisors on diagnosis of crop problems; research on effects of soil amendments on chemical indices and crop yields and economic analysis of crop yield. Office: Iowa State Univ Agronomy Hl Ames IA 50011-0001

VOSS, TERENCE J. human factors scientist, educator; b. Cin., June 29, 1942; s. Harold A. and Marguerite (Canavan) V.; m. Charmaine E. Wilson, Sept. 3, 1983. BA, SUNY, Geneseo, 1965; MA, Fla. Atlantic U., 1972; postgrad., U. Mont., 1973-78. Cert. profl. ergonomist. Dept. dir., sr. staff scientist Essex Corp., Alexandria, VA., 1980-88; sr. human factors scientist Advanced Resources Devel. Corp., Columbia, Md., 1988-90; lead human factors scientist, fellow engr. Westinghouse Savannah River Co., Aiken, S.C., 1990-97, Westinghouse Safety Mgmt. Solutions, LLC, Aiken, 1997—. Cons. in field; mem. adj. faculty psychology dept. DePaul U., Chgo., 1990; human factors cons. U.S. Dept. Energy, 1990—. Contbr. articles to profl. jours. Mem. Citizens for Nuclear Tech. Awareness. Named Citizen Amb., People to People Internat., 1985, 97. Mem. IEEE, (nuclear power engring. com., chair subcom. for human factors, control facilities and reliability), Am. Nuclear Soc., Human Factors and Ergonomics Soc., Sci. Rsch. Soc. N.Am., Sigma Xi. Achievements include contributions resulting in improvements to nuclear facilities and national consensus standards thereby reducing human error, facilitating human behavior and increasing operator and public safety. Home: 203 Trafalgar St SW Aiken SC 29801-3745 Office: Westinghouse Safety Mgmt Solutions LLC PO Box 5388 Aiken SC 29804-5388

VOSS, WILLIAM CHARLES, retired oil company executive; b. Buffalo, Sept. 22, 1937; s. William T. and Dorathea S. (Grotke) V.; m. Marilyn Erickson, Sept. 6, 1958; children: William, John, Douglas. AB with honors, Harvard U., 1959, MBA with honors, 1961. With Northwestern Refining Co., St. Paul Park, 1961-70, v.p. adminstrn., 1969-71; with Ashland Oil Inc., Ky., 1971-89, v.p., 1973-79, adminstrv. v.p., 1979-80, sr. v.p., group operating officer, 1980-89; pres. Ashland-Warren Inc., 1979-83, APAC, Inc., 1980-82, 83-86. Mem. Am. Chem. Soc. Republican. Home: 6756 N Fleur de Lane Stone Lake WI 54876

VOSSLER, JOHN ALBERT, civil engineer; b. Newburgh, N.Y., Oct. 9, 1925; s. Vernon Martense and Frieda (Bachmann) V.; m. Betiejean Sleight Erts, Sept. 4, 1948; children: Karen Ann, Susan Jean. BS in Structural Engring., U. Mich., 1951. Registered profl. engr., N.Y., Conn. Structural engr. Marine div. Maxon Constrn. Co., Tell City, Ind., 1953-56; staff engr. Systems Mfg. div. IBM, Poughkeepsie, N.Y., 1956-68; project mgr. Real Estate & Constrn. div. IBM, Stamford, Conn., 1968-88; adv. engr. Gen. Systems div. IBM, Hopewell Junction, N.Y., 1988-89; dir. devel. Getter, Segner & Gironda, P.E., P.C., Valhalla, 1989-93; prin. John A. Vossler Assocs., Danbury, Conn., 1988—. Pres. JAVAssociates, LLC, Danbury, Conn. Bd. dirs. Lake Pl. Condo Assn., 1989-95; dir. mems. adv. coun. St. George's Club, Bermuda. With U.S. Army, 1944-46, PTO; 1st lt. USAF, 1951-53. Mem. ASCE, NSPE, Conn. Soc. Profl. Engrs., Conn. Engrs. in Pvt. Practice, Am. Radio Relay League (lic. amateur K2BGU). Home: 12-147 Boulevard Dr Danbury CT 06810-7223 Office: JAVAssociates LLC 12-147 Boulevard Dr Danbury CT 06810-7223 E-mail: jvossler@javassociates.com.

VOSSOUGHI, SHAPOUR, chemical and petroleum engineering educator; b. Siahkal, Gilan, Iran, June 25, 1945; s. Mirza Aghasi and Ghamar Talat (Farahpour) V.; m. Ziba Mani, Nov. 6, 1973; children: Anahita, Sarah, Nadia. Grad. diploma, McGill U., Montreal, Can., 1971; MSc., U. Alta., Edmonton, Can., 1973, PhD, 1976. Instr. Arya-Mehr U., Tehran, Iran, 1967-70; rsch. assoc. U. Kans., Lawrence, 1976-77, asst. scientist, 1977-78; sr. scientist Nat. Iranian Oil Co., Tehran, 1978-79; asst. scientist U. Kans., Lawrence, 1979-81, assoc. scientist, 1981-82, assoc. prof., 1982-94, prof., 1994—. Researcher Shell Rsch. Ctr., Rijswijk, the Netherlands, 1978-79; sabbatical researcher Elf Aquitaine, Pau, France, 1989-90; tech. presenter in field; cons. for UN, Nat. Iranian Oil Co. and U. of Petroleum Industry, Ahwaz, Iran. Contbr. over 30 publs. to profl. jours. including Can. Jour. Chem. Engring., Jour. Can. Petroleum Tech., Soc. Petroleum Engrs. Jour., Jour. Thermal Anal., Indsl. Engring. Chem. Fundamentals, Trans. Soc. Petroleum Engrs., Thermochimica Acta, Chem. Engring. Commun., SPE Reservoir Engring., Jour. Petroleum Sci. and Engring. Faculty fellow EXXON Edn. Found., 1982-85; rsch. grantee Columbian Resources Inc., Topeka, 1989, U. Kans., 1983-89, Dept. of Energy, 1982-84, 92—, Core Labs., 1980-81. Mem. Soc. Petroleum Engrs., Am. Inst. Chem. Engrs., N.Am. Thermal Analysis Soc., Soc. of Rheology, Sigma Xi. Achievements include patent in field. Home: 1035 Lakecrest Rd Lawrence KS 66049-3321 Office: U Kans 4006 Learned Hall Lawrence KS 66045-7526 E-mail: shapour@ku.edu.

VOSTIAR, JOHN, telecommunications industry executive; b. Newark, Mar. 2, 1949; s. Peter and Anna (Glogoski) V. AS in Edn., Essex County Coll., 1970; BA in Psychology, William Patterson Coll., 1976; M of Spl. Studies in Applied Comm., U. Denver, 1991. Test desk tech. N.J. Bell, Newark, 1972-78, Mountain Bell, Denver, 1978-80; comm. tech. AT&T Long Line, 1980-82; supr. engr. AT&T Transmission Systems, San Fransicso, 1982-83; comm. tech. AT&T, Denver, 1983-94, ATT Internat., 1994-98; with consumer LD AT&T, 1998-2000; design engr. AT&T Quest, Denver, 2000; circuit design engr. 360 network, Broomfield, 2000—21. Union steward Comm. Worker Am., Denver, 1981-83. Editor: Comm. Worker Am. paper, 1982-83. Mem. Colo. Tai Chi Soc., U. Denver Alumni Assn. Avocations: tai chi, reading, hiking, skiing, yoga. Office: AT&T Internat 2535 E 40th Ave Rm D32 Denver CO 80205-3601 Home: Apt D 5534 W Canyon Trl Littleton CO 80128-8400 E-mail: JohnVostiar@att.net.

VOTAW, CARMEN DELGADO, civic association executive; b. Humacao, P.R., Sept. 29, 1935; d. Luis Oscar Delgado and Candida Paz Ruiz; m. Gregory B. Votaw, Oct. 10, 1960; children: Stephen Gregory, Michael Albert, Lisa Juliette. Diploma in sec. scis., U. P.R., Rio Piedras, 1954; BA in Internat. Studies, Am. U., 1983, postgrad.; D (hon.), Hood Coll., 1982. Fed. programs specialist Office Commonwealth P.R., Washington, 1972-76; co-chair Nat. Adv. Com. on Women, 1977-79; pres. Inter-Am. commn. women Orgn. Am. States, Washington, 1978-80; v.p. Info. Svcs. for Latin Am., 1981-84; adminstrv. asst. congressman Jaime B. Fuster U.S. Ho. Reps., 1985-91; Washington rep., dir. govt. rels. Washington office Girl Scouts USA, 1991-97; dir. govt. rels. United Way Am., 1997-98; sr. v.p. Alliance for Children and Families, 1998—. Pub. mem. fgn. svc. selection bd. U.S. Dept. State, 1976, U.S. rep. to Inter-Am. Commn. Women and exec. com., 1977-81; mem. trial ct. judicial nominating commn. Dist. 11, State Md.; bd. dirs. Inter-Am. Inst. Human Rights, Congl. Hispanic Caucus Inst.; seminar participant Aspen Inst.; participant numerous nat. and internat. forums, coms., meetings; chair Nat. Coalition for Women and Girls in Edn., Policy Coun. of Nat. Assembly Human Svcs. Orgns.; mem. ind. sector's govt. rels. com.. Author: Some Biographical Profiles, 1978, Puerto Rican Women, 1995; contbr. articles to profl. jours.; translator publs. in English and Spanish. Trustee Pan Am. Devel. Found.; exec. com., chair program com. Girl Scouts U.S.A.; mem. world confs. on women UN, Mex., 1975, Denmark, 1980, Kenya, 1985, China, 1995, U.S., 2000. Recipient Recognition and Appreciation award Nat. Assn. Cuban-Am. Women, 1978, Appreciation scroll U.S. Army, 1981, Ann. Hispanic Svc. award Coalition Fed. Hispanic Employee Orgns., 1982, Contbn. award Nat. Inst. for Women of Color, 1982, Svc. to Women award Federally Employed Women, 1984, Excellence in Svc. to Cmty. award Inst. P.R. N.Y., 1986, Outstanding Achievement award Nat. Coun. Hispanic women, 1991, Civil Rights award NASA, 1994, Primeras award Mex.-Am. Women's Nat. Assn., 2000, Nat. Hispanic Heritage award Nat. Hispanic Heritage Found., 1996; named One of Top 100 Hispanic Women in Comm., Hispanic USA Mag., 1987; inducted into Md. Women Hall of Fame, 1992. Mem. LWV (v.p., bd. dirs. overseas edn. fund, 1964-81), Nat. Conf. Puerto Rican. Women (pres. D.C. chpt. 1975, nat. pres. 1976-78, Svc. award D.C. chpt. 1976, Advancement of Women award 1980, Achievement award 1983), Nat. Women's Conf. Com., Nat. Women's Polit. Caucus (adv. com.), World Assn. Girl Guides and Girl Scouts (trainer western hemisphere 1984, 86, co-chair world conf. 1987, chair western hemisphere com. 1990-91), Mid. Atlantic Equity Consortium, Pub. Mems. Assn. Fgn. Svc., Coun. on Fgn. Rels., Soc. for Internat. Devel., Latin Am. Studies Assn., Caribbean Studies Assn., UN Assn. Democrat. Episcopalian. Home: 6717 Loring Ct Bethesda MD 20817-3148 Office: Alliance Children Families 1701 K St NW Ste 200 Washington DC 20006-1523 E-mail: cdelgadovo@aol.com., cvotaw@alliance1.org.

VOTAW, JOHN FREDERICK, educational foundation executive, educator; b. Richmond, Va., May 9, 1939; s. Frederick Lee and Katherine (B.) V.; m. Joyce Marie Miller, June 8, 1961; children: Laura, Cynthia, Mary, John Jr. BS, U.S. Mil. Acad., 1961; MA in History, U. Calif., Davis, 1969; grad., U.S. Army Colls., 1970, 85; PhD in History, Temple U., 1991. Commd. 2d lt. U.S. Army, 1961, advanced through grades to lt. col., 1976; comdr. Company C 1st bn. 69th Armor U.S. Army, Hawaii, 1964-65; comdr. Troop A 1st Squadron 11th ACR U.S. Army, South Vietnam, 1966-67, comdr. C&C Squadron 11th ACR Germany, 1975-77; asst. prof. history U.S. Mil. Acad., West Point, N.Y., 1970-73, asst. dean for plans and programs, 1980-81, asst. prof., 1981-82; dep. dir. U.S. Army Mil. History Inst., Carlisle Barracks, Pa., 1983-86; ret. U.S. Army, 1986; dir. First Divsn. Mus., Wheaton, 1986—; exec. dir. Cantigny First Divsn. Found., 1991—. Adj. asst. prof. history Dominican U. (formerly Rosary Coll.), River Forest, Ill., 1991-98, adj. assoc. prof. history, 1998—; dir. Col. Robt. R. McCormick Rsch. Ctr., Wheaton, 1991—; series editor Cantigny Mil. History Series. Contbg. author: The D-Day Ency., 1993, The Ency. of Am. Wars - The First World War, 1994, The European Powers in the First World War: An Ency., 1996, Encyc. of the Vietnam War, 3 vols., 1998, A Guide to the Study and Use of Military History, 1979, History in Dispute, vol. 5; contbr. articles to profl. jours. Mem. adv. com. Ctr. for the Study of Force and Diplomacy, Temple U., 1996—. Decorated Legion of Merit, Bronze Star with "V" device, Purple Heart (3 awards) and others. Mem. Am. Hist. Assn., Orgn. Am. Historians, Soc. for Mil. History (trustee 2001—), Am. Assn. Mus., U.S. Naval Inst. (life), U.S. Army War Coll. Alumni Assn. (life), Ret. Officers Assn. (life), Disabled Am. Vets., Assn. Grads. U.S. Mil. Acad., U. Calif. Davis Alumni Assn. (life), Am. Vets. (life), Am. Legion (life), Kiwanis (Wheaton club 1986—, pres. 1991-92), Phi Alpha Theta, Phi Kappa Phi (life). Avocations: reading, writing, classical music, golf. Office: First Divsn Mus at Cantigny 1 S 151 Winfield Rd Wheaton IL 60187-6097 E-mail: jvotaw@tribune.com.

VOTH, ALDEN H. political science educator; b. Goessel, Kans., May 4, 1926; s. John F. and Helena (Hildebrandt) V.; m. Norma E. Jost, Aug. 18, 1956; children: Susan, Thomas. BA, Bethel Coll., 1950; MS in Econs., Iowa State U., Ames, 1953; PhD in Internat. Rels., U. Chgo., 1959. Assoc. prof. polit. sci. Upland (Calif.) Coll., 1960-63; prof. polit. sci. San Jose (Calif.) State U., 1963-65, 67-91, prof. emeritus, 1991—. Vis. prof. polit. sci. Am. U. in Cairo, 1965-67. Author: Moscow Abandons Israel, 1980, (with others) The Kissinger Legacy, 1984. Trustee Pomona (Calif.) Valley Am. Assn. UN, 1963; participant China Ednl. Exch., 1996. Am. U. in Cairo Rsch. grantee, 1966; Nat. Coun. on U.S.-Arab Rels. fellow, 1990—. Home: 1385 Kimberly Dr San Jose CA 95118-1426 Office: San Jose State U One Washington Sq San Jose CA 95192 E-mail: ahvoth@aol.com.

VOUDOUKIS, IGNATIOS JOHN, internist, cardiologist; b. Skalohorion, Lesvos, Greece, July 8, 1927; came to U.S., 1955; s. John Ignatios and Christina (Hatzilias) V.; m. Penny Christakos, July 15, 1962; 1 child, Christine Antoinette. MD, Nat. U. Athens, 1954. Intern Meml. Hosp., Albany, N.Y., 1955-56; resident Episcopal Hosp., Phila., 1956-58, Hahnemann Med. Coll. and Hosp., Phila., 1958-59; fellow in cardiology Jackson Meml. Hosp. and U. of Miami, Fla., 1959-61, Jewish Gen. Hosp., Montreal, 1961-63; rsch. assoc. in cardiology Maine Med. Ctr., Portland, 1963-64; assoc. physician Henry Ford Hosp., Detroit, 1964-67; adj. instr. medicine Wayne State U., 1969, clin. asst. prof. medicine, 1973, clin. assoc. prof. internal medicine, 1981—; pvt. practice, 1967—. Active staff Harper Hosp., Detroit, Hutzel Hosp., Detroit. Mem. lab. facilities coun. Dept. Pub. Health, State of Mich., 1968-74; pres. Hypertension Coord. and Planning Coun. of Southeastern Mich., 1974. Recipient St. Paul Medallion, Greek Orthodox Diocese and Archdiocese of N. and S. Am., Detroit, 1986. Fellow ACP, Am. Coll. Angiology; mem. Am. Soc. Nephrology, Am. Soc. Hypertension (charter), Hellenic Univ. Club (pres. 1968-69), Detroit Athletic Club. Greek Orthodox. Office: Hutzel Hosp Profl Bldg 4727 Saint Antoine St Ste 402 Detroit MI 48201-1461

VOWLES, RICHARD BECKMAN, literature educator; b. Fargo, N.D., Oct. 5, 1917; s. Guy Richard and Ella (Beckman) V.; m. Ellen Noah Hudson, Aug. 1, 1942 (div. 1969); children: Elizabeth Ellen, Richard Hudson. BS, Davidson Coll., 1938; postgrad., U. N.C., 1938-39, U. Stockholm, 1939-40; MA, Yale U., 1942, PhD, 1950. Engr. Hercules Powder Co., Wilmington, Chattanooga, 1941-43; chemist Rohm & Haas, Knoxville, Tenn., 1943-44; econ. cons. War Dept., 1944; Am. vice consul Gothenburg, Sweden, 1945-46; asst. prof. English Southwestern U., Memphis, 1948-50, Queens U., N.Y.C., 1950-51; asso. prof. English U. Fla., 1951-60; prof. Scandinavian and comparative lit. U. Wis., Madison, 1960-85, prof. emeritus, 1985—, chmn. comparative lit., 1962-63, 64-67, 71-72, chmn. Scandinavian studies, 1977-80. Am. specialist in Scandinavia Dept. State, summer 1963; vis. prof. N.Y.U., summer 1964, U. Helsinki, Finland, spring 1968, Stockholm, 1969; lectr., Sydney, Australia, 1975, Paris, 1975; master ceremonies Santa Fe Scandinavian Film Festival, 1984 *Introduced many Scandinavian authors to an American readership: Karin Boye, Artur Lundkvist, Harry Martinson, Gunnar Ekelöf, Johannes Edfeldt, Stig Dagerman, Martin A. Hansen, H.C. Branner, among others; continues to make discoveries, for example the Chippewa half-sister of the Danish author Karen Blixen, of Out of Africa fame, unknown to her; is researching the Danish influence on the American labor movement (Laurence Gronlund, The Cooperative Commonwealth, 1884).* Editor: Eternal Smile, 1954, Dramatic Theory, 1956, Comparatists at Work, 1968; Adv. editor: Nordic Council Series, 1965-70, Herder Ency. of World Lit; contbr. articles to profl. jours. Am.-Scandinavian Found. fellow Stockholm, 1939-40, Lassen fellow Am. Scandinavian Found., 1986; Fulbright fellow Copenhagen, 1955-56; Strindberg fellow Stockholm, 1973; Swedish govt. research award, 1978; Norwegian Govt. fellow, summer 1978 Mem. Modern Lang. Assn., Soc. Advancement Scandinavian Study (mem. exec. com.), Internat. Comparative Lit. Assn., Am. Comparative Lit. Assn. (adv. bd.), Strindberg Soc., Phi Beta Kappa. Home: 1115 Oak Way Madison WI 53705-1420

VOYCHECK, GERALD LOUIS, nursing home administrator, social worker; b. Wilkes-Barre, Pa., Mar. 10, 1944; s. Martin Vojcik and Lottie (Lukashefska) V. BA, Quincy Coll., 1968; MA, Sangamon State U., 1981; postgrad., So. Ill. U., 1981-82. Joined Franciscan Bros. Holy Cross., 1964. Tchr. St. James Trade Sch., Springfield, Ill., 1968-71; evening librarian Springfield Coll., 1968-69; cataloger St. Francis Convent, Springfield, 1971-72; worker child care Lt. Joseph P. Kennedy, Palos Park, Ill., 1972-73; technician mental retardation Good Shepherd Manor, Momence, 1973-75; asst. adminstr. Bro. James Ct., Springfield, 1975-76, adminstr., 1976-79, 96—, social worker, 1979—; exec. dir. Springfield Devel., 1985-86. Instr. Lincoln Land Community Coll., Springfield, 1981—; interpreter Ill. Dept. Mental Health, Springfield, 1986; sec. Franciscan Bros. Holy Cross, 1973-76, bd. dirs., 1985—. Vol. Acquired Immune Deficiency Disease, sexual assault counseling. Mem. Polish Nat. Alliance. Republican. Roman Catholic. Avocations: fgn. langs., food microbiology, horticulture. Home: 2500 Saint James Rd Springfield IL 62707-9736 Office: Brother James Ct Sangamon Avenue Rd Springfield IL 62707-9731

VOYIADJIS, GEORGE ZINO, civil engineer, educator; b. Cairo, Egypt, Dec. 15, 1946; s. Zino Dimitri and Eleni (Mavridou) V.; m. Christina George Tziortzi, Nov. 4, 1978; children: Helena G., Andrew G. BSc with highest honors, Ain Shams U., Cairo, 1969; MSc, Calif. Inst. Tech., 1970; DSc, Columbia U., 1973. Reg. eng. in tng., 1981. Sr. stress analyst Nuclear Power Svcs., Inc., N.Y.C., 1973-75, EBASCO Svcs., Inc., N.Y.C., 1975; assoc. prof. U. Petroleum and Minerals, Dhahran, Saudi Arabia, 1975-80; Boyd prof. civil engrng. La. State U., Baton Rouge, 1980—, acting assoc. dean Grad. Sch., 1992-94, chmn., Bingham C. Stewart Disting. prof. dept. civil and environ. engrng., 2001—. Editor: Mechanics of Material Interfaces, 1986, Advances in the Theory of Plates and Shells, 1990, Microstructural Characterization in Constitutive Modeling of Metals and Granular Media, 1992, Damage in Composite Materials, 1993, Advances in Damage Mechanics: Metals and Metal Matrix Composites, 1999; contbr. over 100 articles on mech. behavior of solids to profl. publs. Recipient best paper prize Canadian Soc. Mech. Engrng. Transactions, 1984. Fellow ASCE, ASME, Am. Acad. Mechanics; mem. Am. Soc. Engrng. Educators, Soc. Engrng. Sci., Sigma Xi. Democrat. Achievements include study of modeling mechanical behavior of metals and metal matrix composites; refined theory of plates and shells and numerical simulation of elasto-plastic contact problems and damage mechanics. Home: 12718 N Oak Hills Pky Baton Rouge LA 70810-3243 Office: La State U Dept Civil & Environ Engrng 3508-B CEBA Bldg Baton Rouge LA 70803 Fax: 225-578-9176. E-mail: voyiadjis@eng.lsu.edu.

VOYLES, RICHARD MEREDITH, electrical engineer; b. Indpls., Feb. 21, 1962; s. Richard Meredith Sr. and Mabel (Livezey) V.; m. Kathleen Marie Lawless, Nov. 24, 1984; children: Caroline Halley, Sarah Allison, Meredith Kathleen. BSEE, Purdue U., 1983, postgrad., 1983-84, Carnegie Mellon U., 1990—; MSMSE, Stanford U., 1987-89. Engr. Dart Controls, Zionsville, Ind., 1981-83; robotics intern artificial intelligence lab. MIT, Cambridge, Mass., 1983; mfg. engr. IBM Corp., Endicott, N.Y., 1984-87; rsch. asst. Stanford Robotics Lab., Calif., 1987-89; rsch. scientist Integrated Systems Inc., Santa Clara, 1989-90; founder, pres. Trident Robotics and Rsch., Inc., Wexford, Pa., 1990—; co-founder, v.p. rsch. Vigilant Technologies Inc., San Jose, 1992-93. Sta. mgr. WRFL-FM, West Lafayette, Ind., 1982-83; instr. Broome Community Coll., Binghamton, N.Y., 1986. Editor Purdue Engr. Mag., West Lafayette, 1982-83; contbr. articles to profl. jours. Wrestling coach Tecumseh Jr. High Sch., Lafayette, Ind., 1982-83; wrestling asst. Union Endicott (N.Y.) High Sch., 1984-86. Fessenden-Trott scholar Purdue U., 1983, Purdue 500, 1981-82; Nat. Def. Sci. and Engrng. fellow, 1990. Mem. IEEE, Am. Soc. Engrng. Edn., Am. Mensa, Planetary Soc., Eta Kappa Nu. Presbyterian. Avocations: electronics, photography, astronomy, triathlon, decathlon. Office: Trident Robotics and Rsch Inc 2516 Matterhorn Dr Wexford PA 15090-7962

VRABLIK, EDWARD ROBERT, import/export company executive; b. Chgo., June 8, 1932; s. Steven Martin and Meri (Korbel) V.; m. Bernice G. Germer, Jan. 25, 1958; children: Edward Robert, II, Scott S. BS in Chem. Engrng, Northwestern U., 1956; MBA, U. Chgo., 1961; postgrad., MIT, 1970. Registered profl. engr., Ill. Dir. indsl. mktg. Eimco Corp., 1956-61; dir. indsl. mktg. and planning Swift & Co., Chgo., 1961-68; v.p., gen. mgr. Swift Chem. Co., 1968-73; pres., chief exec. officer Estech Gen. Chems. Corp., 1973-86; pres. Kare Internat. Inc., 1986—. Pres. Julius and Assocs., Inc., Kare Internat., Inc.; bd dirs. Potash Phosphate Inst., Consol. Fertilizers, Ltd.; mem. mgmt. com. Esmark Inc., Korbel, Inc., Mister Lawn Care, Inc. Author; patentee in field. Bd. dirs., v.p. Northwestern U. Tech. Inst.; trustee Future Farmers Am. Mem. Internat. Superphosphate Mfrs. Assn. (dir.), Am. Inst. Chem. Engrs., Fertilizer Inst. (dir.) Clubs: Butler Nat. (Oak Brook, Ill.). Lutheran. Home: 631 Thompsons Way Palatine IL 60067-4653 Office: 141 W Jackson Blvd Chicago IL 60604-2992

VRANA, VERLON KENNETH, retired professional society administrator, conservationist; b. Seward, Nebr., June 25, 1925; s. Anton and Florence (Walker) V.; m. Elaine Janet Flowerday, June 5, 1949; children: Verlon Rodney, Timothy James, Carolyn Elaine, Jon David. Student, U. Nebr., 1959-62; BBA, George Washington U., 1967, MBA, 1970; mgmt. course, Harvard U., 1979. Field technician Soil Conservation Svc., USDA, Seward, 1948-58, watershed planner, cons. Lincoln, Nebr., 1958-62, mem. pers. staff Washington, 1962-72, dir. pers. div., 1972-76, asst. adminstr. for mgmt., 1976-79, assoc. dep. chief for adminstrn., 1979-80; chief planning div. Nebr. Natural Resources Com., Lincoln, 1980-88; owner-farmer Blue Ridge Farm, Seward, 1980-89; exec. v.p. Soil and Water Conservation Soc., Ankeny, Iowa, 1989-91; pres. Vrana Assocs., Seward, Nebr., 1992—. Bd. dirs., sec. N.E. Natural Resources Dist., York, Nebr., 1988-89; bd. dirs. Cattle Nat. Bank and Trust, Seward; alt. dir. Renewable Natural Resources Foun., Washington, 1989-91. Contbr. articles to jours. in field. Mem. Com. on Ministry Presbyn. Ch. U.S.A., 1986-89, elder, 1970—; vice moderator Homestead Presbytery, 1989; treas. Nebr. Soil and Water Conservation Found., 1992-97; mem. Seward City Coun., 1998—. Recipient N.E. Centennial Grass Seeding award N.E. Centennial Commn., Lincoln, 1967, N.E. Soil Steward award N.E. Natural Resources Commn., Lincoln, 1986. Fellow Soil and Water Conservation Soc. (pres. N.E. Coun. 1986, Presdl. citation 1989), Isaac Walton League (dir. Seward chpt. 1984-89), Nat. Wildlife Fedn. (soil conservationist of yr. award 1987), Seward Grange (officer 1984-89, 92-99), Shriner, Kiwanis (Disting. Pres. Seward chpt. 1996-97). Home and Office: Vrana Assocs 131 N 1st St Seward NE 68434-2130 E-mail: vv21929@alltel.net.

VRANICAR, GREGORY LEONARD, lawyer; b. Milw., June 28, 1950; s. Leonard B. and Margery Jean (Anderson) V.; m. Marilyn J. Vrbenec, May 1, 1982; children: Mark A., David G. BA, Grinnell Coll., 1972; JD, U. Iowa, 1975. Bar: Iowa 1975, Mo. 1978, U.S. Dist. Ct. (we. dist.) Mo. 1978, U.S. Ct. Appeals (8th cir.) 1980, U.S. Ct. Appeals (10th cir.) 1983. Assoc. Rich, Granoff, Levy & Gee, Kansas City, Mo., 1978-83, ptnr., 1983-90, Seigfreid, Bingham, Levy, Selzer & Gee, Kansas City, 1990-94; fund devel. dir. Midwest Christian Counseling Ctr., 1994-95, acting exec. dir., 1996-97, exec. dir., 1997—. Dir. Coterie Theatre, Inc., Kansas City, 1988-94, pres., 1991-92; pres. Sr. Companion Program, Kansas City, 1987-88, adv. coun., 1985—; mem. peace and social justice com. Cure of Ars Ch., Leawood, Kans., 1990—; alumni bd. Grinnell Coll., 1993—. Capt. USAF, 1975-78. Democrat. Roman Catholic. Avocations: jogging, swimming. Home: 9726 Aberdeen St Shawnee Mission KS 66206-2149 Office: Midwest Christian Couseling Ctr 4520 Madison Ave Ste 301 Kansas City MO 64111-3541

VRANISH, JOHN MICHAEL, electrical engineer, researcher; b. Brainerd, Minn., May 20, 1939; s. John Paul and Louise Ann (Jenkins) V.; m. Dorothy Jean Ward, June 27, 1980; children: John Christopher, Anthony Brian. BS, U.S. Mil. Acad., 1962; MSEE, George Washington U., 1973. Staff engr. robotics rsch. Naval Surface Weapons Ctr., White Oak, Silver Spring, Md., 1971-82, Nat. Bur. Standards, Gaithersburg, 1982-86; staff engr. space mechanisms and space robotics Goddard Space Flight Ctr., Greenbelt, 1986—. Mem. tech. task force Office of Sec. Def., 1981-82, fact finding com., 1981; cons. U.S. Congress, 1983, 87, 96; spkr. in field. Inventor capaciflector, 3-D sprags, carrier-less anti-backlash transmission, robotic deriveter, magnetostrictive direct drive rotary motor, spin bearings, continuously variable planetary transmission, gear bearings, flexure wedges, 3-D interactive display, screw locking "clickless" wrench; patentee, licensor in field; contbr. articles to books, jours. and various publs. Capt. U.S. Army, 1962-70. Mem. Robotics Internat. of Soc. Mfg. Engrs. (charter, award 1981). Holder world record for precision non contact robotic assembly in space. Avocations: sports, physical fitness, military history. Home: 900 Truro Ln Crofton MD 21114-1207 Office: NASA/Goddard Space Flight Ctr Code 544 Greenbelt MD 20771-0001 E-mail: jvranish@mscmail.gsfc.nasa.gov., jmvranish@home.com.

VRATIL, KATHRYN HOEFER, federal judge; b. Manhattan, Kans., Apr. 21, 1949; d. John J. and Kathryn Ruth (Fryer) Hoefer; children: Alison K., John A., Ashley A. BA, U. Kans., 1971, JD, 1975; postgrad., Exeter U., 1971-72. Bar: Kans. 1975, Mo. 1978, U.S. Dist. Ct. Kans. 1975, U.S. Dist. Ct. (we. dist.) Mo. 1978, U.S. Dist. Ct. (ea. dist.) Mo. 1985, U.S. Ct. Appeals (8th cir.) 1978, U.S. Ct. Appeals (10th cir.) 1980, U.S. Ct. Appeals (11th dist.) 1983, U.S. Supreme Ct., 1995. Law clk. U.S. Dist. Ct., Kansas City, Kans., 1975-78; assoc. Lathrop Koontz & Norquist, Mo., 1978-83; ptnr. Lathrop & Norquist, 1984-92; judge City of Prairie Village, Kans., 1990-92. Bd. dirs. Kans. Legal Bd. Svcs., 1991-92. Bd. editors Kans. Law Rev., 1974-75, Jour. Kans. Bar Assn., 1992—. Mem. Kansas City Tomorrow (XIV); bd. trustees, shepherd-deacon Village Presbyn. Ch.; nat. adv. bd. U. Kans. Ctr. for Environ. Edn. and Tng., 1993-95; bd. dirs. Kans. Legal Svcs., 1991-92. Fellow Kans. Bar Foun., Am. Bar Found.; mem. ABA (edtl. bd. Judges Jour. 1996—), Am. Judicature Soc., Nat. Assn. Judges, Fed. Judges Assn., Kans. Bar Assn., Mo. Bar Assn., Kansas City Met. Area Bar Assn., Wyandotte County Bar Assn., Johnson County Bar Assn., Assn. Women Judges, Lawyers Assn. Kansas City, Supreme Ct. Hist. Soc., Kans. State Hist. Soc., U. Kans. Law Soc. (bd. govs. 1978-81), Kans. U. Alumni Assn. (mem. Kansas City chpt. alumni bd. 1990-92, nat. bd. dirs. 1991-96, bd. govs. Adams Alumni Ctr. 1992-95, mem. chancellor's club 1993—, mem. Williams ednl. fund 1993—, mem. Jayhawks for higher edn. 1993-95), Homestead Country Club Prairie Village (pres. 1985-86), Native Sons and Daus of Kans. (life), Rotary, Jr. League Wyandotte and Johnson Counties, Order of Coif, Kans. Inn of Ct. (master 1993—, pres. 1999-2000), Phi Kappa Phi. Republican. Presbyterian. Avocations: cycling, sailing. Office: 511 US Courthouse 500 State Ave Kansas City KS 66101-2403

VREDEVOE, DONNA LOU, research immunologist, microbiologist, educator; b. Ann Arbor, Mich., Jan. 11, 1938; BA in Bacteriology, UCLA, 1959, PhD in Microbiology, 1963. USPHS postdoctoral fellow Stanford U., 1963-64; instr. bacteriology UCLA, 1963, postgrad.rsch. immunologist dept. surgery Ctr. Health Scis., 1964-65, asst. research immunologist dept. surgery Center Health Scis., 1964-67; asst. prof. Sch. Nursing, Center Health Scis., 1967-70, asso. prof., 1970-76, prof., 1976—, asso. dean Sch. Nursing, 1983-85, acting assoc. dean Sch. Nursing., 1985-86, asst. dir. space planning Cancer Center, 1976-78, dir. space planning, 1978-90, cons. to lab. nuclear medicine and radiation biology, 1967-80; acting dean Sch. Nursing Center Health Scis., 1995-96. Chair UCLA Acad. Senate, 1999-2000; vice chancellor acad. personnel UCLA, 2001—. Contbr. articles to profl. publs. Postdoctoral fellow USPHS, 1963-64; Mabel Wilson Richards scholar UCLA, 1960-61; research grantee Am. Cancer Soc., Calif. Inst. Cancer Research, Calif. div. Am. Cancer Soc., USPHS, Am. Nurses Found., Cancer Research Coordinating Com. U. Calif., Dept. Energy, UCLA. Mem Am. Soc. Microbiology, Am. Assn. Immunologists, Am. Assn. Cancer Research, Nat. League Nursing (2d v.p. 1979-81), Sigma Xi, Alpha Gamma Sigma, Sigma Theta Tau (nat. hon. mem.) Office: UCLA Chancellor's Office 2147 Murphy Hall PO Box 951405 Los Angeles CA 90095-1405

VREE, ROGER ALLEN, lawyer; b. Chgo., Oct. 2, 1943; s. Louis Gerard and Ruby June (Boersma) V.; m. Lauren Trumbull Gartside, Mar. 29, 1969; children: Jonathan Todd, Matthew David. BA, Wheaton Coll., 1965; MA, Stanford U., 1966, JD, 1969. Bar: Ill. 1969, U.S. Dist. Ct. (no. dist.) Ill. 1969. Assoc. Sidley & Austin, Chgo., 1969—75; ptnr. Sidley Austin Brown & Wood, 1975—. Mem.: ABA, Univ. Club (Chgo.). Office: Sidley Austin Brown & Wood Bank One Plz 10 South Dearborn Chicago IL 60603-2000 E-mail: rvree@sidley.com.

VREELAND, JAMES RAYMOND, political science educator; b. N.Y.C., Dec. 14, 1971; s. James Joseph and Joan Angela Vreeland. PhD, NYU, 1999. Asst. prof. polit. sci. Yale U., New Haven, 1999—, dir. undergrad. studies Internat. Studies Program, 2000—. Author: The IMF and Economic Development, 2002. Mem. Am. Polit. Sci. Assn. Office: 124 Prospect St New Haven CT 06511-3741 Office Fax: 203 432 6196. E-mail: james.vreeland@yale.edu.

VREELAND, ROBERT WILDER, retired electronics engineer; b. Glen Ridge, N.J., Mar. 4, 1923; s. Frederick King and Elizabeth Lenora (Wilder) V.; m. Jean Gay Fullerton, Jan. 21, 1967; 1 son, Robert Wilder. BS, U. Calif., Berkeley, 1947. Electronics engr. Litton Industries, San Carlos, Calif., 1948-55; sr. devel. electronics engr. U. Calif. Med. Ctr., San Francisco, 1955-89; ret. Cons. electrical engrng; speaker 8th Internat. Symposium Biotelemetry, Dubrovnik, Yugoslavia, 1984, RF Expo, Anaheim, Calif., 1985, 86, 87. Contbr. articles to profl. jours., also to internat. meetings and symposiums; patentee in field. Recipient Chancellor's award U. Calif., San Francisco, 1979; cert. appreciation for 25 years' service U. Calif., San Francisco, 1980. Mem. IEEE, Am. Radio Relay League (pub. svc. award 1962). Home: 45 Maywood Dr San Francisco CA 94127-2007

VREELAND, RUSSELL GLENN, accountant, consultant; b. Princeton, N.J., Apr. 27, 1960; s. Glenn Earl and Barbara Ann (Jungels) V.; m. Traci Ann Harbold, Dec. 17, 1988; children: Hans Russell, Anna Patricia. BSBA, Bloomsburg (Pa.) U., 1982. CPA, Pa., Md.; accredited in bus. valuations AICPA. Sr. acct. Louis H. Linowitz & Co., Trenton, N.J., 1982-85; tax supr. Horty & Horty, P.A., Wilmington, Del., 1985-87; tax mgr. Stewart Waddell & Co. P.A., Columbia, Md., 1988-92; assoc. in charge of tax Hillman & Glorioso, P.L.L.C., Vienna, 1993-98; ptnr. Vreeland & Assocs., LLC, 1998—, Vreeland & Co., Ltd., 2001—. Speaker in field. Author: Foreign Sales Corporations - A Primer, 1992, Exporting-Are You Ready?, 1993; contbr. articles to profl. jours. Chmn. fin. com. Woodland Village Condominium Assn., 1989-90; mem. Sykesville (Md.) Econ. Devel. Commn., 1998-2001, Sykesville Budget Com., 1999, chair, 2000–; mem. Sykesville Capital Improvement Com., 1999, chair, 2000—; mem. Sykesville Town Coun., 2000—, Sykesville Historic Dist. Commn. 2002–; co-chair fin. com. Messiah Luth. Ch., 2000—. Mem. AICPAs (tax. divsn., mgmt. consulting svcs. divsn., adv. group mem. partnership taxation com. 1997-98, accredited in bus. evaluations, apptd. mem. partnership taxation com. 1998-99), Md. Assn. CPAs (fed. taxation com. 1990-91), Inst. Bus. Appraisers. Republican. Lutheran. Office: Vreeland & Assocs LLC 7200 Norris Ave Sykesville MD 21784-6642 E-mail: rgv_cpa@msn.com.

VREELAND, VICTORIA LYNN, lawyer; b. Ravenna, Nebr., Nov. 7, 1948; d. Nelson Eugene Vreeland and Bernice Schmale Sadler; children: Ted Mansfield, Aleksander Ferguson, Cole. BA, Ea. Wash. U., 1972; JD, Gonzaga U., 1976. Bar: Wash. 1976. Jud. clk. Wash. State Ct. of Appeals, Spokane, 1976-78; asst. atty. gen. State of Wash., Seattle, 1978-83; ptnr. Gordon Thomas Honeywell, 1983—. Contbr. articles to profl. jours. Mem. Wash. State Bar Assn. (gov. 1999—), Wash. State Trial Lawyers Assn. (dir. 1994-98). Avocation: pianist. Office: Gordon Thomas Honeywell 2100 One Union Sq Seattle WA 98101

VREELAND-FLYNN, TRACY LYNN, elementary education educator; b. San Antonio, Oct. 18, 1966; d. James Chester and Mary Lou (Meighan) V.; m. Russell Brian Flynn; 1 child, Brian Russell Flynn. BS in Edn., Shippensburg (Pa.) U., 1989; MEd, St. Francis Coll., Loretto, Pa., 1994. women's and men's varsity asst., swim team coach Altoona Area H.S., 1991-92. Tchr. Altoona (Pa.) Area Sch. Dist., 1990—, tchr. 3d grade, 1990—96, tchr. 4th grade, 1996-98, tchr. 6th grade, 1998-99, tchr. 5th-6th grade, 1999—, webmaster, 1998—. Computer trainer; dist.-wide tech. coord. com. Altoona Area Sch. Dist.; parent-cmty. study team ACT 178 dist. com. Outcomes Bd. Edn.; tchr. computer camps Altoona Area Sch. Dist., 1993-96; instr. in field. Mem. NEA, ASCD, Nat. Reading Assn., Pa. State Edn. Assn., Altoona Area Edn. Assn. Republican. Roman Catholic. Home: 4 Woodland Terrace Duncansville PA 16635 Office: Juniata Elem Sch 418 8th Ave Juniata Altoona PA 16601-5718 E-mail: trflynn@pennwoods.net.

VREMAN, ANNA AURORA, artist, technical writer; b. Miami, Fla., July 8, 1956; d. Gerhard Jan Willem and Josina Hendrika (Schouten) V.; m. Lowell B. Symmes, Feb. 16, 1996. BS in Elec. Engring., U. Vt., Burlington, 1983. Electronics technician IBM Corp., Essex Junction, Vt., 1976-83, elec. engr., 1983-90; tech. writer United Engrs., 1991-92; tech. writer, cons., owner Lamoille Valley Tech. Svcs., Milton, 1990—; artist, 1999—. Mem. No. Vt. Artists Assn. (bd. dirs. 1997-2000). Office: Lamoille Valley Tech Svcs 623 W Milton Rd Milton VT 05468-3396

VRETTOS, ATHENA, literature educator; b. Oakland, Calif., Feb. 11, 1960; d. Spyros Vrettos and Margaret Vrettos Gannon; m. Christopher Flint, May 13, 1989; 1 child Gray Flint-Vrettos. BA, Vassar Coll., 1981; MA, U. Pa., 1984, PhD, 1988. Asst. prof. English lit. U. Mich., Ann Arbor, 1988—95; assoc. prof. Case Western Res. U., Cleve., 1996—. Dir. grad. studies Case Western Res. U., Cleve., 1999—. Author: Somatic Fictions, 1995. Fellow, Am. Coun. Learned Socs., 1989—90, NEH, 1995—96, John Simon Guggenheim Found., 1996—97. Mem.: MLA. Office: Case Western Res U Dept English 10900 Euclid Ave Cleveland OH 44109

VRIS, THOMAS W. surgeon; b. Elkins, W.Va., Apr. 27, 1951; s. Thomas and Barbara (Johns) V.; children: Tracy, Courtney. BA, Columbia U., 1973; MD with honors, NYU, 1979. Diplomate Am. Bd. Otolaryngology. Resident Harvard Sch. Medicine, Boston, 1979-81, Yale U., New Haven, 1982-85; fellow in plastic surgery, Heiden, Switzerland, 1985; attending surgeon, chief ENT and facial plastic surgery Norwalk (Conn.) Hosp., 1985—; pvt. practice Yale U., New Haven, 1985—; asst. chief of staff Norwalk Hosp., 2002—. Mem. tchg. staff Sch. Medicine Yale U., New Haven. Mem. Norwalk Med. Soc. (treas. 1991-92, pres. 1994-95), Columbia Club, Am. Acad. Otolaryngohology Head and Neck Surgery, Saugatuck Harbor Yacht Club. Republican. Episcopalian. Office: 10 Mott Ave Ste 3-1 Norwalk CT 06850-3348

VRONSKIY, VADIM VIKTOROVICH, financial company executive; b. Khabarovsk, Russia, Apr. 15, 1969; s. Viktor Antonovich and Galina Grigorevna (Avramenko) V.; m. Yelena Anatolyevna Nadezhdina, Sept. 11, 1993; 1 child, Vronskiy Vladlen. BS in Econs., Mil. Acad., Volsk, Russia, 1991; MA with highest honors, Internat. Bus. Mgmt. Sch., Zurich, 2000. Sr. acct. Russian Force Mil. Corps., Tajikistan, 1991—92; sr. control acct. comml. bank Somon Bank, Tajikistan, 1992—94; fin. analyst Central-Asian-Am. Enterprise Fund, Uzbekistan, 1994—97; fin. dir. Medstar Trading Ltd., Moscow, 1997—99; portfolio auditor State St. Investment Bank, Boston, 1999—2001, sr. auditor, 2001—. Cons. in field. Lt. Russian Mil., 1991-92. Avocations: swimming, tennis, shooting, cycling. E-mail: yeleng@msn.com., ysa-vvv@yahoo.com.

VRSCAK, WILLIAM MARTIN, artist, art educator; b. Pitts., Oct. 31, 1939; s. Nicholas and Mary Helen (Buchlmeyer) V.; m. Marlene Suresky, July 1, 1977. Student, Ivy Sch. Art, Pitts., 1964-67. Print prodn. mgr. Fuller, Smith & Ross, Pitts., 1966-75, Creamer, Inc., Pitts., 1975-84; artist, illustrator, 1984—. Tchr. seminars and classes Pitts. Ctr. for Arts, 1989—, James Madison U., harrisonburg, Va., 1995, Sweetwater Art Ctr., Sewickley, Pa., 1988—, Niagara Frontier WS, Buffalo, N.Y., 1988-91, Touchstone Ctr. for Crafts, Elliotsville, Pa., 1992—, Rochester (N.Y.) Art Club, 1991, Southwest Artists, Ft. Worth, 1995, Jade Fon Workshops, Monterey, Calif., 1996—, Maine Art Workshops, Port Clyde, 1996-99, numerous art groups in the mid-Atlantic region. Solo exhbns. include Renaissance Gallery, Pitts., 1986, Country Studio, Hadley, Pa., 1986, Art Inst. Pitts., 1986, Davis and Elkins (W.Va.) Coll., 1990, La Roche Coll., Pitts., 1994, Water St. Gallery, Saugatuck, Mich., 1992, 95, 98; group exhbns. include Am. Watercolor Soc., 1986, 88, 89, 90, Audubon Artists' Nat. Exhbn., N.Y.C. (Silver medal 1988, Sadie and Max Tesser award 1989), Rocky Mountain Nat. Watermedia Exhibit, Golden, Colo. (Grunbacher award 1987), Adirondacks Nat. Exhbn. Am. Watercolors, Old Forge, N.Y. (Garnet award 1987, Juror's award 1991), Midwest Watercolor Soc., Green Bay, Wis. (Spl. Merit award 1988), Ky. Watercolor Soc. Aqueous, Louisville (Reliance Universal Merit award 1987, Mike Heuman Purchase award 1987), Pitts. Watercolor Soc. Aqueous Ann. (PWS award 1987, Best of Show 1989, Juror's award 1994, Merit award 1996), Always a River Invitational Exhbn., 1991; represented corp. collections Westinghouse Corp., Koppers Corp., WTAE Broadcasting, Blue Cross Western Pa., Earnst & Young, Inc., PNC Corp., Davis & Elkins U.; contbr. illustrations to mags. and books. Winner Treasures of Pitts. Outdoor Board Competition, 1987. Mem. Am. Watercolor Soc., Audubon Artists, Pitts. Watercolor Soc. Home: 418 Teece Ave Pittsburgh PA 15202-3222

VU, ERIC TIN, neurobiologist, researcher; b. Saigon, Vietnam, Apr. 8, 1963; came to U.S., 1975; s. Van and Bich-Chi (Ha) Vu-Thuong; m. Ngoc Hong Vo, June 2, 1999. BA, U. Tex., 1985; PhD, UCLA, 1990. Postdoctoral fellow Calif. Inst. Tech., Pasadena, 1991-93, sr. rsch. fellow, 1994-95; staff scientist Barrow Neurol. Inst., Phoenix, 1995—. Author: (with others) Frontiers in Crustacean Neurobiology, 1990; contbr. articles to profl. jours. U. Tex. Disting. scholar, 1983-85; Chancellor's fellow UCLA, 1985, NSF fellow, 1986, Alfred P. Sloan Rsch. fellow, 1996; recipient Nat. Rsch. Svc. award NIH, 1991, Capranica Found. Prize in Neuroethology, 1995. Mem. Soc. for Neuroscience, Internat. Soc. for Neuroethology, Internat. Brain Rsch. Orgn., Soc. Neural Control Movement. Office: Barrow Neurol Inst Divsn Neurobiology 350 W Thomas Rd Phoenix AZ 85013-4409

VU, JOSEPH DUONG, financial educator; b. Hanoi, Vietnam, Mar. 13, 1952; s. Phuong and Nhan (Trinh) V.; m. Huyen Tran T. Do, July 1, 1978; children: Christine, Daniel. BBA, Ohio U., 1973; MBA, U. Chgo., 1975, PhD in Fin., 1984. Asst. prof. Loyola U., Chgo., 1981-85, U. Ill., Chgo., 1985-88; assoc. prof. fin. DePaul U., 1988—. Author: Investment Management, 1993. Mem. Am. Fin. Assn., Vietnamese Assn. Ill. (pres. 1993-98). Avocation: tennis. E-mail: jvu@condor.depaul.edu.

VU, QUAT THUONG, electrical engineer; b. Vietnam, Aug. 5, 1944; came to U.S., 1988; s. Mao Quy and Phung Thi Vu; children: Hien T., Duc T. BSEE, U. Ky., 1965; MSEE, Calif. Inst. of Tech., 1967, PhDEE, 1970. Dean MINH-DUC U. Coll. Engring., Saigon, Vietnam, 1971-75; rschr. Hochiminh City, Vietnam, 1977-87, CNRS-CRN, Strasbourg, France, 1987-88, Calif. Inst. of Tech., Pasadena, 1989-90, Intel Corp., Santa Clara, Calif., 1990—. Achievements include several patents in field. Office: Intel Corp M/S SC1-03 3065 Bowers Ave Santa Clara CA 95054-3293 E-mail: quat.t.vu@intel.com.

VUCKOVIC, ALEXANDER, psychiatrist; b. Belgrad, Yugoslavia, Aug. 28, 1955; came to the U.S., 1963; s. Vladeta and Mila (Pavlovic) V.; children: Alexander Daniel, Elizabeth Marie. BS summa cum laude, U. Notre Dame, 1977; MD, Harvard U., 1981. Diplomate Am. Bd. Psychiatry and Neurology. Asst. psychiatrist McLean Hosp., Belmont, Mass., 1985—, assoc. psychiatrist, 1999—; med. dir. The Pavilion, McLean Hosp., 1999—; instr. Harvard Med. Sch., Boston, 1985—2001, clin. asst. prof., 2001—. Pres. Crimson Mental Health Assocs., Inc., Belmont, 1993-95. Co-author: Under Observation, 1994; editor: The Angels of Madness, 1992. Mem. AMA, Am. Psychiat. Assn., Phi Beta Kappa. Avocations: writing, running, reading. Office: 115 Mill St Belmont MA 02478-1041

VUCUREVICH, CONSTANCE LANE, investment executive; b. Lynchburg, Va., Nov. 9, 1946; d. Landon Bell and Frances Nelson (Mathews) Lane; m. James Wilson Stanfield, Feb. 2, 1968 (div. July 1980); children: James Wilson Stanfield III, Amanda Page Stanfield; m. John Thomas Vucurevich, Oct. 1, 1988. Student, Sweet Briar Coll., 1965-68; BSBA in Mktg./Mgmt., Nat. Coll., Rapid City, S.D., 1984. Registered securities broker. Investment exec. Piper Jaffray & Hopwood, Rapid City, 1984-87; investment executive Wheat First Securities, Richmond, Va., 1987-88; asst. v.p. Piper Jaffray, Inc., Rapid City, 1988—. Founder, dir., v.p., sec. L.B. Lane Family Found., Hickory, N.C., 1988—; bd. dirs. John T. Vucurevich Found., Rapid City, 1991—, Rapid City Boys Club, 1991—, Rapid City YMCA, 1994—, Rapid City Regional Hosp., 1994—; grad. Leadership Rapid City, 1985; mem. Mayor's Econ. Devel. Com., Rapid City, 1990; mem. choir Emmanuel Episc. Ch., 1982—. Recipient Philanthropist of Yr. award Gov. of S.D., Pierre, 1992. Mem. Womens Network. Republican. Episcopalian. Avocations: swimming, hiking, entertaining, singing, hot air ballooning. Office: Piper Jaffray Inc 726 St Joe St Rapid City SD 57701-2785 Home: 23032 Thunderhead Falls Rd Rapid City SD 57702-8525

VUILLEUMIER, FRANÇOIS, curator, biologist, ornithologist, educator; b. Berne, Switzerland, Nov. 26, 1938; came to U.S., 1961; U.S., naturalized, 2000. s. Willy Georges and Denise Geneviève (Privat) V.; m. Patricia Beryl Simpson, 1964 (div. 1971); m. Bonita Rae Johnson, 1972 (div. 1981); children: Alexis Brendan, Claire Anne; m. Rebecca Branch Finnell, Feb. 26, 1983; 1 child, Isabelle Finnell. Licence es sciences naturelles, U. Geneva, Switzerland, 1961; PhD, Harvard U., 1967. Instr. U. Mass., Boston, 1966-67, asst. prof., 1967-70, assoc. prof., 1971; prof. U. Lausanne, Switzerland, 1971-72; sr. researcher Marine Biol. Sta., Roscoff, France, 1972-73; assoc. curator Am. Mus. Natural History, N.Y.C., 1974-79, curator, 1979—. Dir. Inst. Animal Ecology, U. Lausanne, 1971-72; vis. prof. U. Paris, 1973-74, U. of the Andes, Mérida, Venezuela, 1981; adj. prof. CUNY, 1978—; summer faculty Coll. of the Atlantic, Maine, 1987-92, 95, 99, 2000; chmn. Dept. Ornithology, Chapman Fund, Am. Mus. Natural History, 1987-92; plenary lectr. XX Internat. Ornithol. Congress, South Africa; leader ornithol. expeditions, Ecuador, Venezuela, Peru, Bolivia, Argentina, Chile, New Britain, New Caledonia; cruise lectr. North Pole, Antarctica, Galapagos, Falkland Islands, New Guinea. Co-author: High Altitude Tropical Biogeography, 1986; mem. editl. bd., book rev. editor Ornitologia Neotropical, El Hornero, Ararajuba Anales del Instituto de la Patagonia, Rivista Italiana di Ornitologia, Zoosystema, Revue d'Ecologie, Revista Chilena de Ornitologia; contbr. more than 245 articles to profl. jours. Chapman fellow Am. Mus., 1967-68. Fellow AAAS, Am. Ornithologists Union; mem. Internat. Coun. for Bird Preservation (bd. dirs. Pan-Am. sect.), Soc. Italiana Sci. Nat., French Ornithol. Soc. (corr.), Soc. for Study of Evolution, Neotropical Ornithol. Soc., Union Chilean Ornithologists, Assn. Ornitológica del Plata, Swiss Soc. for the Study and Protection of Birds, Zeiss Hist. Soc., Neotropical Ornithological Soc. (pres. 1999—). Avocations: painting, reading, fgn. langs., cooking, collecting vintage binoculars. Office: Am Mus Natural History Central Pk West At 79T St New York NY 10024

VUJOVIC, MARY JANE, education and employment training planner; b. Huntington, N.Y., Dec. 3, 1951; d. Carl David Brell, Sr. and Alice Lucille (Hanson) B. BS in Psychology cum laude, U. Wash., 1973, postgrad., 1980-84. Spl. edn. tchr. Town of Huntington, 1972; adminstrv. asst. Daishowa Am. Corp., Seattle, 1973-74; with King County Work Tng. Program, 1973-85, records sect. mgr., 1977-84, contracts mgr., 1984-85; tech. cons., program mgr. Refugee Ctr. of Clark County, Vancouver, Wash., 1985-87; instr., counselor S.W. Wash. Pvt. Industry Coun., 1986-87; planner Wash. Human Devel., Seattle, 1987, dir. planning and MIS, 1987-94; tech. cons. SJL and Assocs., 1990—; dir. prog. devel. and evaluation Yakima Valley Opportunities Industrialization Ctr., 1994-2000; dir. devel. and adminstrn. Snohomish County Workforce Devel. Coun., 2000—. Mem. planning and adv. com. Seattle-King County Pvt. Industry Coun., 1987-94; mem. Partnership for Tng. and Employment Careers, Washington, 1991-94. Bd. dirs. Slavia, Seattle, St. James Refugee Program, Seattle, 1993-95. Mem. Phi Beta Kappa. Avocation: South Slavic dance and cultural preservation. Office: Snohomish County Workforce Devel Coun 917 134th St SW Everett WA 98204-9377 E-mail: maryjane@snonet.org.

VUKSANOVIĆ, MIRO, library director, writer; b. Krnja Jela, Montenegro, May 4, 1944; s. Milutin and Koja (Grdinić) V.; m. Milana Dzuver; children: Danilo, Jelena. Grad., U. Belgrade, Yugoslavia, 1969. Secondary sch. tchr. Tech. Sch., Sombor, Yugoslavia, 1970-75; dir. City Libr. Karlo Bijelicki, 1975-88, Biblioteka Matice srpske, Novi Sad, Yugoslavia, 1988—. Author: (novels) Kletva Peka Perkova, 1977, Gradista, 1989, Daleko bilo, 1995, Semolj gora, 2000; (short stories) Gorske oci, 1982, Nemusti jezik, 1984, Vucji tragovi, 1987; (poems) Tamooni, 1992, Moracnik, 1994, Točilo, 2001; and other writings. Recipient Miroslavljevo jevandelje, Meml. of Vuk, Politika, Borba, Assn. of Writers of Vojvodina. Mem. Assn. of Writers (pres. 1985-86), Fedn. Socs. of Writers Belgrade (pres. 1984-86), Fedn. Socs. of Librs. Yugoslavia (pres. 1985-87), Fedn. Nat. Librs. (pres. 1988-92), Serbian Sci. and Cultural Soc. Matica srpska (collaborator 1988, mem. adminstrv. com. 1988). Office: Matice Srpske Libr Matice Srpske 1 21000 Novi Sad Yugoslavia

VUKSTA, MICHAEL JOSEPH, surgeon; b. Pitts., Apr. 25, 1926; s. Michael and Mary Sarah (Hanulya) V.; m. Dorothy Ann Bosak, Sept. 12, 1953; children: Patricia, Michael, Carol, Janet. BA, Youngstown State U., 1949; MD, Ohio State U., 1957. Diplomate Am. Bd. Surgery. Enlisted USN, advanced through grades to capt., 1974; intern St. Elizabeth Hosp., Youngstown, Ohio, resident in gen. surgery, 1958-62; pvt. practice gen. surgery, 1962-89; head blue team surgery Oak Knoll U.S. Naval Hosp., Oakland, Calif., 1989-93; assoc. prof. surgery NEOUCOM. Capt. USN retired. Fellow ACS, Am. Coll. Sports Medicine, Southwestern Surg. Congress; mem. Nat. Athletic Trainers Assn. (advisor). Byzantine Catholic. Home: 131 Lovett Pl Pensacola FL 32506-5265

VULEVICH, EDWARD, JR. prosecutor; b. Nov. 5, 1933; s. Edward J. and Minnie R. V.; m. Diane Misko; children: Erin, Jan, John. AB, U. Ala., 1955, JD, 1957. Bar: Ala., U.S. Supreme Ct., U.S. Ct. Appeals (11th cir.) Ala., U.S. Ct. Appeals (5th cir.) Ala. Atty. U.S. Dept. Justice, Mobile, Ala., 1969—, chief civil divsn. Office: US Attys Office 63 S Royal St Mobile AL 36602-3245

VULGAMORE, MELVIN L. retired college president; b. Springfield, Ohio, July 19, 1935; s. Leo Beeman and Della Marie (McCoy) V.; m. Ethelanne Oyer, Feb. 17, 1957; children: Allison Beth, Sarah Faith Vulgamore Evans. BA with honors, Ohio Wesleyan U., 1957; BD, Harvard U., 1960; PhD, Boston U., 1963. Chmn., prof. religion Ohio Wesleyan U., Delaware, 1962-78, assoc. dean faculty, 1972-73, dean acad. affairs, 1973-78; v.p., provost U. Richmond, Va., 1978-83; pres. Albion Coll., Mich., 1983-97, chancellor, 1997—; ret., 1998. Vis. prof. Am. U. Beirut, 1971-72; vis. scholar Harvard U., 1995. Contbr. articles to profl. jours. Trustee Howe Mil. Sch., Ind., 1984-97; mem. Mich. Coun. for Humanities, 1985-89, 96-97. Mem. Am. Acad. Religion, Tillich Soc. N.Am., Harvard Faculty Club, St. Botolph Club, Nat. Press Club, Phi Beta Kappa, Omicron Delta Kappa, Delta Sigma Rho, Pi Sigma Alpha. Avocations: bicycling, tennis, classical music, antique collecting and refinishing. Home: 27 Pleasant St New London NH 03257-4817

VUNJAK-NOVAKOVIC, GORDANA, chemical engineer, educator; b. Belgrade, Yugoslavia, Aug. 26, 1948; came to U.S., 1993; d. Vlajko and Mila (Simeunovic) Vunjak; m. Branko Novakovic, Oct. 27, 1974; 1 child, Stasha. BS, U. Belgrade, 1972, MS, 1975, PhD, 1980. From asst. prof. to prof. chem. engring. Belgrade U., 1981—. Adj. prof. chem. engring. Tufts U., Boston, 1994—; from rsch. scientist to prin. rsch. scientist MIT, Cambridge, Mass., 1992—. Contbr. over 140 articles to sci. jours. and books. Fulbright Found. fellow, 1986-87. Fellow: Am. Inst. Med. and Biomed. Engring.; mem.: AIChE, AAAS, Soc. for Vitro Biology, Materials Rsch. Soc., Fulbright Scholars. Avocations: literature, classical music, film, travel. Office: MIT E25-330 77 Massachusetts Ave Cambridge MA 02139-4301 E-mail: gordana@mit.edu.

VY, LE K. education educator; b. Saigon, Vietnam, June 28, 1964; arrived in U.S., 1992; s. Ngoc Le, Thuan Dao. BS, Hochiminh City Normal U., 1986; PhD, U. Utah, 1995. Asst. prof. U. Mo., Rolla, 1996—2002, assoc. prof., 2002—. Author: Global Bifurcation in Variational Inequalities, 1997 (Campus Author of the Month, 1999). Grantee, U. Mo., 1997. Office: Dept Math and Stats U Mo Rolla Rolla MO 65409

VYAS, YATIN M. pediatrician; b. Rajkot, India, July 30, 1963; s. Mahendra M. and Mandakini M. (Thakar) V. MBBS, B.J. Med. Coll., Ahmedabad, Gujarat, India, 1986, MD, 1990. Cert. pediat., 1995. Intern Civil Hosp.-B.J. Med. Coll., 1986-87, resident in pediat., 1987-90; attending staff Fed. Health Orgn. Hosp., Kalol, India, 1991-93; resident in pediat. Bellevue Hosp.-NYU Sch. Medicine, N.Y.C., 1993-95; fellow in pediat. hematology-oncology Meml. Sloan-Kettering Cancer Ctr., 1995-98, spl. fellow pediat. hematology-oncology, 1998-99; rsch. fellow dept. human immunogenetics Sloan-Kettering Inst. for Cancer Rsch., 1999-2000, rsch. assoc., 2001—. Mem. Am. Soc. Hematology, Am. Soc. Clin. Oncology, Am. Acad. Pediat. Am. Assn. Cancer Rsch. Home: Apt 16-G 1233 York Ave New York NY 10021-6306 E-mail: vyasy@mskcc.org.

VYAVAHARE, NARENDRA R. biomedical researcher, educator; b. Pune, Maharashtra, India, Jan. 21, 1963; arrived in U.S., 1991; s. Rajaram V. Vyavahare, Pramila R. Vyavahare; m. Shobha Narendra Kulkarni; children: Medha, Teja. BS, U. Pune, India, 1983, MS, 1985, PhD, 1990. Post-doctoral fellow Rutgers U., New Brunswick, NJ, 1991—93; rsch. investigator U. Mich., Ann Arbor, 1993—97; rsch. asst. prof. U. Pa., Phila., 1997—99; dir. Cardiovasc. Implant Rsch. Lab. Clemson (S.C.) U., 1999—. Cons. St. Jude Meds., St. Paul, 1999—2000. Contbr. articles to profl. jours. Recipient Scientist Devel. award, Nat. Am. Heart Assn., 1998—2002, Rsch. Investigator award, NIH, 2000—, Rsch. Infrastructure award, 2002—. Mem.: Soc. for Biomaterials (assoc.; sec. cardiovasc. biomaterials spl. interest group 2001—02). Achievements include patents for hydrogel compositions for controlled delivery of virus vectors and methods of use thereof. Office: Clemson Univ Bioengring Dept 501 Rhodes Hall Clemson SC 29634 Office Fax: 864-656-4466. Personal E-mail: narenv@clemson.edu. Business E-Mail: narenv@clemson.edu.

VYAZOVKIN, SERGEY, chemist, educator; b. Kazan, Russia, Feb. 20, 1960; came to U.S., 1995; s. Valentin and Irma Vyazovkin; m. Sasha Vyazovkin, Oct. 1, 1983; 1 child, Polina. BS, Belorussian U., Minsk, 1982, PhD in Chemistry, 1989. Rsch. prof. U. Utah, Salt Lake City, 1998—2001; prof. U. Ala., Birmingham, 2001—. Lise Meitner Rsch. fellow Austrian Rsch. Fund, 1992, 93, NATO rsch. fellow, 1994. Mem. NATAS. Office: U Ala Dept Chemistry 901 S 14th St Birmingham AL 35294

VYDARENY, JOHN RICHARD, dermatologist; b. Battle Creek, Mich., Jan. 23, 1938; m. Kay Herzog, June 9, 1968 (div. Mar. 1990); children: Kimberly Ann, Todd Richard, Kris Michael. AB, Albion (Mich.) Coll., 1960; MS, U. Ill., 1962; MD, U. Mich., 1968. Diplomate Am. Bd. Dermatology. Intern Blodget Meml. Med. Ctr., Grand Rapids, Mich., 1968-69; gen. med. officer USAF, Calif., 1969-71; resident in dermatology Duke U. Med. Sch., Durham, N.C., 1971-74; pvt. practice Grand Rapids, Mich., 1974—. Capt. USAF, 1969-71. Decorated Bronze Star, USAF, Vietnam, 1969-70; named Tchr. of Yr., dept. internal medicine Blodgett Hosp., Grand Rapids, 1996-97. Fellow Am. Acad. Dermatology; mem. Mich. Dermatol. Soc., Chgo. Dermatol. Soc., Soc. Pediat. Dermatology, Wilderneu Med. Soc. Avocations: hiking, cross-country skiing, biking. Office: 1900 Wealthy St SE Grand Rapids MI 49506-2969

VYKUKAL, EUGENE LAWRENCE, wholesale drug company executive; b. Caldwell, Tex., June 26, 1929; s. Henry J. and Anna P. (Polansky) V.; m. Judith Anderson, Jan. 1, 1977; children— Anna K., Mark Roman, Laura Roman, Geni. BS in Pharmacy, U. Tex., Austin, 1952. Pharmacist Scarborough's Pharmacy, Baytown, Tex., 1952-53; pharmacist Gene Vykukal's Pharmacy, Clifton, 1953-57; with Southwestern Drug Corp. (name now Bergen Brunswig Drug Co.), 1957-86; gen. sales mgr. Southwestern Drug Corp., Dallas, 1966-67, v.p., dir. sales, 1967-75, exec. v.p., dir. sales, 1975-81, exec. v.p., 1980-81, pres., chief exec. officer, 1981-86, vice chmn., 1985-86, dir., 1966-86; asst. dean for devel., lectr. Coll. Pharmacy U. Tex., Austin, 1991—, mem. adv. coun. Pharm. Found., chmn., 1978—; sr. v.p. profl. affairs Bergen Brunswig Corp., Bergen Brunswig Drug Co., 1986—. Mem. centennial endowment com. U. Tex., 1980— ; bd. dirs. Baylor U. Med. Center Found., Dallas; mem. indsl. adv. coun. Coll. Pharmacy, U. Ky., 1990—. Recipient Disting. Alumni award U. Tex. Coll. Pharmacy, 1979, William J. Sheffield Disting. Alumni award U. Tex. at Austin Coll. Pharmacy, 1987, Legend of Pharmacy award U. Tex. Coll. Pharmacy Alumni Assn., 1997. Mem. Nat. Wholesale Druggists Assn. (chmn. sales mgmt. com. 1972-73, dir. 1980—, chmn. bd. 1985-86, 1st vice chmn. 1983—, chmn. exec. com. 1987—, Timothy Barry award 1990), Am. Pharm. Assn., Tex. Pharm. Assn. (long range planning com. 1983—), Wholesale Druggist Assn. Tex. (pres. 1978-79), Drug Travelers Assn. Tex. (pres. 1977-78), Sales and Mktg. Execs. Dallas (dir. 1971-72). Roman Catholic. Office: U Tex Coll Pharmacy Pharmacy Bldg Austin TX 78712-1074 *The quality of life in our great country has been enhanced by the tremendous strides made in our health care delivery system over the past three decades. To have served in the pharmaceutical segment has been very rewarding.*

VYN, KATHLEEN A. small business owner; b. Toledo, Aug. 25, 1949; d. John and Patty Vyn; m. Daniel D. Glicken, 1987. BA in English, No. Ill. U., 1972; MA in Creative Writing, San Francisco State U., 1985. Writer/naturalist Lake County Forest Preserve Dist., Deerfield, Ill., 1972-74; reporter News & Advertiser Pub., Highland Park, 1974-76; pres. Kathleen Vyn Assocs., Chgo., 1981—. Author: The Prairie Community, 1978, Spring in the High Sierras, 1980; editor "Stet", Chgo., 1987-88. Writing fellow Ragdale Found., 1979, Ossabaw Island, Ga., 1980, Va. Ctr. for the Creative Arts, 1980. Mem. Mag. Writers Chgo. (organizing com. 1991-92), Ill. Women's Press Assn., Ind. Writers of Chgo. Office: Kathleen Vyn Assocs 1429 W Rosemont Ave Chicago IL 60660-1319 E-mail: kglick@aol.com.

WAALAND, IRVING THEODORE, retired aerospace design executive; b. Bklyn., July 2, 1927; s. Trygve and Marie Waaland; m. Helen Rita Katz, Apr. 7, 1961; children: Theodore, Neil, Elizabeth, Scott, Diane. B of Aero. Engring. magna cum laude, NYU, 1953. Project engr. Grumman Corp., Bethpage, N.Y., 1953-74; v.p., B-2 Chief Designer Northrop Corp., Pico Rivera, Calif., 1974-93. Patentee in field. With USAF, 1946-48. Fellow AIAA (Aircraft Design award 1989, Aircraft Design cert. merit 1989, Wright Bros. lectr. in Aeronautics 1991); mem. NAE, Am. Def. Preparedness Assn. (Leslie E Simon award 1990), SAE (Aerospace Engring. Leadership award 1993). Home: 1132 La Limonar Rd Santa Ana CA 92705-2354 E-mail: iwaaland@cox.net.

WAAS, ANDREA SUE, nonprofit foundation administrator; b. Kansas City, Mo., Mar. 5, 1958; d. Willis Albert Waas. BS in Journalism, U. Kans., 1980; MBA, Cardinal Stritch Coll., 1990. Founder Wings of Light, Inc., Phoenix, 1995—. Contbr. Wings newsletter. Mem. Am. Soc. Assn. Execs. Avocation: flying. Office: Wings of Light Inc PMB 448 16845 N 29th Ave # 1 Phoenix AZ 85053 E-mail: awaaswings@aol.com.

WABER, HARRY EDWARD, insurance agency executive; b. Phila., May 2, 1911; s. Max and Hattie (Sonnenfeld) W.; m. Raechal Kravitz, Oct. 8, 1935 (dec.); children: Beth Rebecca Love, Michael David. BS in Econs., U. Pa., 1933. With Montgomery Scott & Co., Phila., 1933-35, Waber & Co., 1935-56, Waber-Odell, 1956-75, Trio Mgmt., 1963-75; founder, chmn. Main Line Agy., Inc., Wynnewood, Pa., 1960—. Founder Montgomery Gen. Agy., Inc., Wynnewood, 1962; underwriting mem. Lloyds, 1977—. Trustee Fedn. Jewish Agys.; vice chmn. Allied Jewish Appeal; bd. dirs. Akiba Acad., Torah Acad., Phila. Jewish Archives Ctr., Beth Jacobs Schs.; bd. govs. Greenhill condominium Assn.; treas. Lower Merion Cmty. Watch. With U.S. Army, 1943-46. Decorated Army Commendation medal; recipient cert. of merit Big Bros., 1961; C.P.C.U. Mem. Soc. Chartered Property and Casualty Underwriters, Locust Club, White Manor Country Club (past pres.), Bryn Mawr Kennel Club (past gov.), B'nai Brith, Bala Golf Club. Home: 1001 City Ave Apt Wa-704 Wynnewood PA 19096-3938

WABLER, ROBERT CHARLES, JR. retail, restaurant and distribution executive; b. Dayton, Ohio, Dec. 14, 1948; s. Robert Charles Sr. and Eileen Marie (Langen) W.; m. Linda Adele Rayburn; 1 child, Robert Charles III. BS in Acctg. cum laude, U. Dayton, 1971; MS in Acctg. magna cum laude, U. Ga., 1976. Sr. auditor Touche Ross and Co., Dayton, 1971-73; internal auditor So. Company Services, Atlanta, 1974-75; acctg. mgr. Rich's div. Federated Dept. Stores, 1976-77; dir. auditing Munford, Inc., 1977-81, v.p., controller, 1982-83, v.p. fin. analyses, 1983-86; v.p. adminstrn. World Bazaar div. Munford, Inc., 1981-82, sr. v.p. fin., 1986-89; sr. v.p. fin. and adminstrn., sec. The Athlete's Foot Group, Inc., 1989-93; exec. v.p., CFO, treas. Just For Feet Inc., Birmingham, Ala., 1993-97; sr. v.p., CFO The Johnny Rockets Group, Inc.,

Irvine, Calif., 1997-98; prin. Sofas & Seats, Atlanta, 1998—. Author: The Minimum Expenses Needed Technique, 1985. Mem. AICPA, Ga. Soc. CPAs, Inst. Internal Auditors, Assn. Systems Mgmt., EDP Auditor Assn. (bd. dirs. 1978-79).

WACHA, SANDRA J. musician, educator; b. Ottumwa, Iowa, July 23, 1943; d. Earl William and Lois Katherine Lanz; m. Howard Willis Moore Jr., Apr. 27, 1968 (dec. Aug. 1984); children: Michael Howard, Jeffrey Allen; m. Richard Stoner Wacha, June 1, 1991; children: Heather Gayle, Richard C. B of Music Edn., Drake U., 1966; M of Music, U. Nebr., 1991. Prin. flutist Des Moines (Iowa) Symphony Orch., 1969-99; instr. flute Simpson Coll., Indianola, Iowa, 1998—99; tchr. music pvt. studio Des Moines, 1969—. Flutist Westminster Chamber Orch., Des Moines, 1996—, Brandenburg Ensemble, 1989-2000, Odyssey Trio, 1996—, Amadeus Woodwind Quintet, Des Moines, 1994-99. Flutist (CD) Winter White, 1998, Always Autumn, 1999, Sensations of Summer, 2002. Fellow Fortnightly Mus. Club (pres. 1996-98); mem. Sigma Alpha Iota. Avocations: piano, in-line skating, swimming. Home: 6004 N Waterbury Rd Des Moines IA 50312-1344

WACHAL, ROBERT STANLEY, linguistics educator, consultant; b. Omaha, Mar. 13, 1929; s. Stanley William and Marie Frances (Rokusek) W.; m. Jane McCune, Sept. 15, 1968. BA, U. Minn., 1952; MS, U. Wis., 1959, PhD, 1966. Tchr. Mound Sch. Dist., Minn., 1955-59; faculty mem. U. Iowa, Iowa City, 1964—, prof. linguistics, 1975-97, prof. emeritus, 1997—, chmn. dept., 1975-81; cons. Am. Coll. Testing Program, 1981-95, Ednl. Testing Svc., Princeton, N.J., 1996, NSF, Washington, 1975-90, Can. Council, Ottawa, Ont., 1975-80, Nat. Endowment for Humanities, N.Y.C., 1978, 93. Mem. editl. adv. com. Am. Speech, 1988-93. Compiler, editor: Abbreviations Dictionary, 1999. Fulbright prof. Athens, Greece, 1966-67; research grantee U.S. Office Naval Research, 1969-72, Can. Med. Research Council Victoria, B.C., 1967-74 Fellow Acad. Aphasia; mem. Am. Dialect Soc., Dictionary Soc. N.Am. Home: 8 Woodland Hts NE Iowa City IA 52240-9136

WACHBRIT, JILL BARRETT, accountant, tax specialist; b. Ventura, Calif., May 27, 1955; d. Preston Everett Barrett and Lois JoAnne (Fondersmith) Batchelder; m. Michael Ian Wachbrit, June 21, 1981; children: Michelle, Tracy. AA, Santa Monica City Coll., 1975; BS, Calif. State U., Northridge, 1979; M in Bus. Taxation, U. So. Calif., 1985. CPA. Supervising sr. tax acct. Peat, Marwick, Mitchell & Co., Century City, Calif., 1979-82; sr. tax analyst Avery Internat., Pasadena, 1982-83; tax mgr., asst. v.p. First Interstate Leasing, 1983-88; v.p. Security Pacific Corp., L.A., 1988-92; tax mgr., acct. El Camino Resources Ltd., Woodland Hills, Calif., 1992-95; tax mgr. Herbalife Internat. of Am., Century City, 1995-97; sr. tax mgr. PMC, Inc., Sun Valley, 1997—. Republican. Jewish. Avocations: reading, travel, collecting. E-mail: jillw@pmcglobalinc.com.

WACHENFELD, WILLIAM THOMAS, lawyer, foundation executive; b. Orange, N.J., Feb. 9, 1926; s. William A. and Ann (Weir) W.; children: William S., Robin A., John C. AB, Tufts U., 1947; LL.B., Duke U., 1950. Bar: N.J. 1949. Since practiced in Newark; mem. firm Lum, Biunno & Tompkins, 1957-58; pres. Charles Hayden Found., N.Y.C., 1968-97, chmn., 1997-99; prof. law jersey City divsn. Jersey City div. Rutgers U., 1954-56; v.p., assoc. gen. counsel Prudential Ins. Co. Am., 1965-84; of counsel Tompkins, McGuire & Wachenfeld, Newark, 1984-00. Pres. Essex County Park Commn., 1960-65, Newark Acad., 1972-80; commr. pub. affairs, Orange, 1956-58; mem. N.J. Econ. Devel. Coun., 1980-88, 91-94; bd. govs. N.J. Hist. Soc., 1981-83; mem. adv. bd. Wildlife Conservation Soc., 1983-93; trustee Liberty Sci. Ctr., 1988-93. Fellow Am. Bar Found.; mem. ABA, N.J. Bar Assn., Essex County Bar Assn., N.Y. Regional Assn. Grantmakers (bd. dirs. 1992-97), Eastward Ho Country Club, HC Yacht Club (commodore 1992-97). Home: 174 Sea Pine Rd North Chatham MA 02650-1077 Office: Tompkins McGuire & Wachenfeld 4 Gateway Ctr 100 Mulberry St Newark NJ 07102-4004

WACHEWSKI, ROBERT THOMAS, health facility administrator; b. Bklyn., May 29, 1952; s. Henry and Sophie (Kaptur) W. BBA, Baruch Coll., 1975; MPA, NYU, 1981. Mgr. fed. funding City of N.Y. Dept. Mental Health, N.Y.C., 1976-80; assoc. dir. fin. Bronx-Lebanon Hosp. Ctr.-Crotona Park Cmty. Mental Health, 1980-82; dir. fin. Maimonides Cmty. Mental Health Ctr., Bklyn., 1982-86; assoc. adminstr. dept. psychiatry Maimonides Med. Ctr., 1986-90, asst. dir. fin., 1990-92, asst. v.p., 1992—2001, assoc. v.p. for grants and govt. contracts, 2001—. Bd. dirs., treas. The Heights Players, Inc., Bklyn., 1992—. Co-prodr. various plays and musicals, 1992—. Bd. dirs., treas. 66 Orange St. Housing Corp., Inc., Bklyn., 1999—; bd. dirs. A.T. White Cmty. Ctr., Inc., Bklyn., 2000—. Mem. Healthcare Fin. Mgmt. Assn. Democrat. Home: 66 Orange St Apt 4A Brooklyn NY 11201-1738 Office: Maimonides Med Ctr 4802 10th Ave Brooklyn NY 11219-2844

WACHMAN, MARVIN, former university president and chancellor; b. Milw., Mar. 24, 1917; s. Alex and Ida (Epstein) W.; m. Adeline Lillian Schpok, Apr. 12, 1942; children: Kathleen M., Lynn A. BS, Northwestern U., 1939, MA, 1940; PhD, U. Ill., 1942; LLD (hon.), U. Pa., 1964, Lincoln (Pa.) U., 1970, Del. Valley Coll. Sci. and Agr., 1973, Med. Coll. Pa., 1982, Bloomfield Coll., 1987, Albright Coll., 1991; DHL (hon.), Gratz Coll., 1973; LittD (hon.), Jewish Theol. Sem. Am., 1973, Drexel U., 1980; LHD (hon.), Colgate U., 1975, Widener U., 1976; DSc (hon.), Thomas Jefferson U., 1980; LHD, U. New Eng., 1997; DHL, Phila. Coll. Textiles and Sci., 1999. Asst. in history U. Ill., 1940-42; instr. Biarritz Am. U., Biarritz, France, 1945-46; vis. asst. prof. San Diego State Coll., summer 1948, U. Minn., 1950; assoc. prof. history U. Md. in Europe, 1952-53; from instr. to prof. Colgate U., 1946-61, dir. upper class core program, 1956-61; pres. Lincoln (Pa.) U., 1961-70; v.p. acad. affairs Temple U., 1970-73, pres., 1973-82, chancellor, 1982-2000, Dir. Salzburg Seminar in Am. Studies, 1958-60, pres. Fgn. Policy Rsch. Inst., 1983-89; acting exec. dir. Pa. Higher Edn. Assistance Agy., 1989; acting pres. Phila. Coll. Textiles and Sci., 1991; pres. Albright Coll., 1991-92. Past chmn. Nat. Ctr. for Higher Edn. Mgmt. Sys.; specialist in Africa for State Dept., 1965, 68; mem. adv. coun. World Learning, Inc.; mem. Colgate Nat. Coun.; dir., co-chair COLLEGIS Edouprise, Inc.; dir. emeritus Germantown Ins. Co. Author: History of Social-Democratic Party of Milwaukee, 1897-1910, 1945; contbr. articles to profl. jours. and newspapers, also chpts. in books. Mem. adv. coun. Greater Phila. Urban Affairs Coalition, World Affairs Coun.; vice chair Fgn. Policy Rsch. Inst.; hon. dir. Phila. Contributionship; trustee emeritus Balch Inst. Ethnic Studies; mem. bd. overseers Coll. V.I.; hon. trustee Albright Coll.; hon. life trustee Temple U.; alumni regent Phila. area Northwestern U. With U.S. Army, 1942—46. Mem. NAACP, Am. Studies Assn. (past mem. exec. com.), AAUP (past pres. Colgate U. chpt.), Am. Hist. Assn., ACLU, Pa. Assn. Colls. and Univs. (past chmn., pres. 1993), Phi Beta Kappa. Office: Temple U Philadelphia PA 19122-6096 E-mail: mwachman@vm.temple.edu.

WACHNER, LINDA JOY, apparel marketing and manufacturing executive; b. N.Y.C., Feb. 3, 1946; d. Herman and Shirley W.; m. Seymour Applebaum, Dec. 21, 1973 (dec., 1983) BS in Econs. and Bus., U. Buffalo, 1966. Buyer Foley's Federated Dept. Store, Houston, 1968-69; sr. buyer R.H. Macy's, N.Y.C., 1969-74; v.p. Warner divsn. Warnaco, Bridgeport, Conn., 1974-77; v.p. corp. mktg. Caron Internat., N.Y.C., 1977-79; chief exec. officer U.S. divsn. Max Factor & Co., Hollywood, Calif., 1979-82, pres., chief exec. officer, 1982-83, Max Factor & Co. Worldwide, 1983-84; mng. dir. Adler & Shaykin, N.Y.C., 1985-86; pres., CEO, chmn. Warnaco Inc., 1986—. Bd. dirs. Applied Graphics Tech., N.Y. Stock Exch. Presdl. appointee Adv. Com. for Trade, Policy, Negotiations; trustee U. Buffalo Found., Carnegie Hall, Aspen Inst.; bd. overseers Meml. Sloan-Kettering Cancer Ctr. Recipient Silver Achievement award L.A. YWCA; named Outstanding Woman in Bus. Women's Equity Action League, 1980, Woman of Yr., MS. Mag., 1986, one of the Yr.'s Most Fascinating Bus. People, Fortune Mag., 1986, one of 10 Most Powerful Women in Corp. Am., Savvy Woman Mag., 1989, 90, Am.'s Most Successful Bus. Woman, Fortune Mag., 1992, Queen of Cash Flow, Chief Exec. Mag., 1994. Mem. Am. Mgmt. Assn., Am. Apparel Mktg. Assn. (bd. dirs.), Bus. Roundtable, Coun. on Fgn. Rels. Republican. Jewish. Office: Warnaco Inc/Authentic Fitness Corp 90 Park Ave New York NY 10016-1301

WACHOB, TOM WEBB, JR. retired obstetrician-gynecologist; b. El Paso, Ill., July 16, 1923; s. Tom Webb and Esther Della (Cooper) W.; m. Patricia Klemm, June 20, 1944 (div. 1952); children: William K., Robert T.; m. Susan Ann Niederwimer, Nov. 15, 1952 (dec. May 1992); children: Carol Ann, Thomas S., James C.; m. Dorothy Boyd Gray Riggin, June 12, 1996. BS, Ill. Wesleyan U., 1944; MD, U. Ill., 1946. Diplomate Am. Bd. Ob-Gyn. Rotating intern St. Elizabeth Hosp., Lafayette, Ind., 1946-47; resident in ob-gyn. St. Louis City Hosp., 1949-50, St. Elizabeth Hosp., Lafayette, 1950-52; with So. Clin., Texarkana, 1952-54, Howard Comty. Hosp., Kokomo, Ind. Mem. ACOG, AMA, Cen. Assn. Obstetricians and Gynecologists, Ind. Ob-Gyn. Soc. (pres. 1968), Kokomo Rotary Club (pres. 1965), Belleair Country Club, Kokomo Country Club. Republican.

WACHOWIAK, MARK, biomedical engineer, researcher, computer scientist, researcher; b. Buffalo, N.Y., Aug. 20; s. Paul Peter Wachowiak and Lorraine Mary Browarek. BS, U. Louisville, 1994, MS, 1997. Rsch. assoc. Frazier Rehab. Ctr., Louisville, 1996—2000; instr. U. Louisville, 2000—01, univ. fellow, 1998—. Instr. Bellarmine U., Louisville, 1999—2000; instr., cons. U. Louisville, 2000. Contbr. chapters to books, articles to profl. jours. Mem.: IEEE. Avocations: guitar, music, philosophy, foreign languages, literature. Office: Dept Computer Engring and Computer Sci Univ Louisville Louisville KY 40292

WACHOWSKI, ANDY, film director; b. Chgo., Dec. 29, 1967; Motion picture dir., writer, prodr. (With brother Larry) exec. prodr., writer, dir. films Bound, 1996, The Matrix, 1999 (Internat. Fantasy Film award 1999), Assassins, 1995 (story). Office: EON Entertainment 400 Warner Blvd Bldg 81 Burbank CA 91522-0001*

WACHOWSKI, LARRY, film director; b. Chgo., June 21, 1965; Motion picture dir., writer, prodr. (With brother Andy) exec. prodr., writer, dir. films Bound, 1996 (Internat. Fantasy Film award 1997), The Matrix, 1999, Assassins, 1995 (story). Office: EON Entertainment 4000 Warner Blvd # 81 Burbank CA 91522-0001*

WACHS, ETHEL, secondary education educator, fine arts teacher; b. N.Y.C., Dec. 26, 1933; d. Max and Dora Katzman; m. Paul Philip Wachs, (dec. Nov. 1981); 1 child, Myrna. BA, Bklyn. Coll., 1968, MA, MS, Bklyn. Coll. Tchr. fine art Bd. Edn., N.Y.C., 1959—. Adj. prof. art adult edn. divsn. Bklyn. (N.Y.) Coll., 1968-95. Author: Lesson Plans for Art Teacher, 1967. Recipient Lone Star Industries award Silvermine Guild, New Canaan, 1976, Old Saybrook Spl. award Old Saybrook, Conn., 1980, Audubon medal of honor for aquamedia Audubon Artists, N.Y., 1982, Philip Isenberg award Audubon Artists, 1996, Savoir Faire Paper award Audobon Artists, 1999. Mem. Audubon Artists, Artists Equity, Nat. Assn. Women Artists (Martha Reed Meml. award 1991). Avocation: collecting American art. Home: 20 E 9th St New York NY 10003-5944 Office: H S Health Professions 345 E 15th St New York NY 10003-4002 E-mail: achsw@aol.com.

WACHS, ISRAEL EPHRAIM, chemical engineering educator; b. Jan. 28, 1950; s. Muni M. and Rose (Wites) W.; m. Gale S. Gavil, Dec. 29, 1973; children: Heidi L., David J. BE in Chem. Engring., CUNY, 1973; MS in Chem. Engring., Stanford U., 1974, PhD in Chem. Engring., 1978. Staff engr. Exxon Rsch. & Engring. Co., Clinton, N.J., 1977-86; prof. chem. engring. Lehigh U., Bethlehem, Pa., 1987—. Cons. chem., petroleum, environ. and materials industries , 1987—; vis. fellow divsn. chemistry and chem. engring. Calif. Inst. Tech., Pasadena, 1986; dept. chem. engring. Princeton (N.J.) U. , Princeton, NJ, 1993; lectr. Netherlands Inst. Catalysis , 1994; co-chmn. 4th Internat. Symposium on Group Five Compounds , 1999—2002; mem. internat. adv. bd. Internat. Symposium on Nb Compounds , 1992—95. Editor: Characterization of Catalytic Materials, 1992; guest editor: Catalysis Today, special issue, vol. 51, 1999; contbr. articles to profl. jours.; patentee in field; editl. adv. bd. Catalysis Today, 1996—, Rsch. Chem. Intermediates, 1997—, Catalysis Letters, 1999—, Topics in Catalysis, 1999—. Recipient Parravano Meml. award for excellence in catalysis rsch. Mich. Catalysis Soc., 1991, Career Achievement award Engring. Sch. Alumni of City Coll. CUNY, 1992, EPA Clean Air Excellence award, 2001. Mem. Am. Inst. Chem. Engrs., ACS (symposia adv. bd. coloid and surface chemistry divsn. 1999—), N.Am. Catalysis Soc. (organizing com. and dir. Kokes student travel awards 16th meeting 1999, co-dir. Kokes student travel awards 17th meeting 2001), Materials Rsch. Soc., Catalysis Soc. Met. N.Y. (chmn. elect 1990-91, chmn. 1991-92, bd. dirs. 1992-95, 96-99, award for excellence in catalysis 1996), Internat. Symposium on Group Five Elements (mem. internat. adv. bd. 1995—). Office: Lehigh U Dept Chem Engring Iacocca Hall 111 Research Dr Bethlehem PA 18015-4732 E-mail: iew0@lehigh.edu.

WACHS, MARTIN, urban planning educator, author, consultant; b. N.Y.C., June 8, 1941; s. Robert and Doris (Margolis) W.; m. Helen Pollner, Aug. 18, 1963; children: Faye Linda, Steven Brett. BCE, CUNY, 1963; MS, Northwestern U., 1965, PhD, 1967. Asst. prof. U. Ill., Chgo., 1967-69, Northwestern U., Evanston, Ill., 1969-71; assoc. prof. urban planning UCLA, 1971-76, prof., 1976-96; dir. U. Calif. Transp. Ctr., 1996-99; prof. civil and environ. engring. and city/regional planning U. Calif., Berkeley, 1996—, dir. Inst. Transp. Studies, 1999—. Vis. disting. prof. Rutgers U., New Brunswick, N.J., 1983-84; mem. exec. com. Transp. Rsch. Bd., 1995—, chmn., 2000; vis fellow Oxford (Eng.) U., 1976-77. Author: Transportation for the Elderly: Changing Lifestyles, Changing Needs, 1979, Transportation Planning on Trial, 1996, also numerous articles; editor: Ethics in Planning, 1984, The Car and the City, 1992. Mem. steering com. L.A. Parking Mgmt. Study, 1976-78; bd. dirs. L.A. Commuter computer, 1978-94, mem. Calif. Commn. on Transp. Investment, 1995. Served to capt. Ordnance Corps, U.S. Army, 1967-69. Recipient Pike Johnson award Transp. Rsch. Bd., 1976, Disting. Tchg. award UCLA Alumni Assn., 1986, Disting. Planning Educator award Calif. Planners Found., 1986; Guggenheim fellow, 1977; Rockefeller Found. humanities fellow, 1980. Fellow: Am. Inst. Cert. Planners, Am. Coun. Edn.; mem.: ASCE, Inst. Transp. Engrs. Jewish. Home: 1106 Grizzly Peak Blvd Berkeley CA 94708-1704 Office: U Calif Berkeley Inst Transp Studies 109 Mclaughlin Hall Berkeley CA 94720-1720 E-mail: mwachs@uclink4.berkeley.edu.

WACHS, MELVIN WALTER, government official; b. Detroit, Dec. 5, 1930; s. Harry H. and Gussie E. Wachs; B.A., U. Mich., 1952, M.A., 1954; postgrad. U. Chgo., 1955, Cornell U., 1954-56; diploma Indsl. Coll. Armed Forces, 1960; Ph.D., Am. U., 1968; diploma Nat. Def. U., 1986. Various research and teaching positions, 1954-58; asst. prof. polit. sci., chmn. Asia program Western Mich. U., Kalamazoo, 1959-62; asso. dir. Exec. Insts., Office Career Devel., CSC, 1962-64, asso. dir. ednl. resources, 1964-66; prof. polit. sci., advanced program in govtl. studies U. Okla., 1965— ; prof. bus., mgmt. and public adminstrn. Central Mich. U., 1975— ; acting chief planning br. NIMH, 1966-68; dir. Community Devel. and Tng. div. HUD, 1968-72, sr. program officer community planning and devel., 1972-82, dir. intergovtl. programs div., 1982— , coastal zone mgmt. programs coordinator, 1978-82; staff dir. subcom. on sci. manpower Pres.'s Sci. Adv. Com., 1962-65; mem. Fed. Interagy. Com. on Edn., 1968— , mem. subcom. on energy and environ., 1981— , early childhood edn., 1986— ; mem. White House Energy Task Force, 1977— . Treas., Chevy Chase Gardens Citizens Assn., 1975-78; chmn. West Drummond Citizens Assn., 1978— . Social Sci. Research Council fellow, 1955; Ford Found. fgn. area fellow, 1956-58; Carnegie Corp. grantee, 1960-61. Mem. AAAS (book rev. editor Sci. Books and Films), Am. Polit. Sci. Assn., Am. Soc. Public Adminstrn., Am. Soc. Planning Ofcls., Am. Public Health Assn. Author reports and articles; editor: (with others) Dictionary of Political Science, 1964; Interagency Energy Impact Series, 1976— ; Rapid Growth from Energy, 1976; Ann. Report to Congress on Community Development Programs, 1982— ; also others. Office: Hud Washington DC 20410-0001

WACHS, SAUL PHILIP, Jewish education educator; b. Phila., Dec. 24, 1931; s. Abraham and Annette (Schaller) W.; m. Barbara Ruth Eidelman, Jan. 27, 1957 (dec. 1997); children: Sharona Rachel, Hillel Eliezer, Devorah Leah, Aviva Marcia (dec.); m. Diane Ruth Cover, Feb. 6, 2000. Hebrew tchr. diploma, Gratz Coll., 1951; BS in Edn., Temple U., 1953; BRE, Jewish Theol. Sem., 1956, B in Sacred Music, 1959, D Pedagogy (hon.), 1989; MA, Ohio State U., 1966, PhD, 1970. Dir. edn. Congregation Tifereth Israel, Columbus, Ohio, 1960-70, Park Ave Synagogue, N.Y.C., 1970-72; asst. prof., dir. Jewish edn. program Brandeis U., Waltham, Mass., 1972-75; dean Gratz Coll., Phila., 1975-80, Rosaline B. Feinstein prof. of Jewish edn., chair dept., 1980—. Bd. dirs. Jewish Edn. Assembly, N.Y.C., 1965-70, Akiba, Merion, Pa., 1975—, Beth Hillel-Beth El, Wynnewood, Pa., 1984-88, Coun. for Jewish Edn., N.Y.C., 1970-74; vis. lectr. Hebrew U., 1986-89, tutor, 1988-89, vis. rschr., 1985; vis. professorial lectr. Am. U.-George Washington U.; vis. prof. Jewish Theol. Sem. Am.; vis. instr. Coll. of Jewish Studies, Cleve., 1965-69; cons. United Synagogue Dept. Edn., 1980—, Herzlia United Schs., Cape Town, 1989—; mem. ethical adv. com. Jewish Family and Children's Svc., Phila.; vis. prof. Balt. Hebrew U., 1998-2000, U. Judaism, 1998-, Jewish Theol. Sem., 1998,. Co-author texts: Judaism, 1979, Jewish Education, 1991, also curriculum materials; contbr. articles to religious publs. Mem. Soviet Jewry com. Phila Jewish Community Rels. Coun.; bd. dirs. Akiba Hebrew Acad., 1992—. Recipient Aaron Zacks award Am. Assn. for Jewish Edn., 1959, Behrman House award for lifetime achievement Jewish Educators Assembly, 1995, Ateret Kavod award United Synagogue. Mem. ASCD, Coalition for Jewish Edn., Assn. for Jewish Studies, Assn. Instns. of Higher Learning in Jewish (past pres.), Phi Delta Kappa. Home: 346 E Lancaster Ave Apt 102 Wynnewood PA 19096-2221 Office: Gratz Coll Melrose Avenue Rd Philadelphia PA 19126 E-mail: wachscover@home.com., swachs@gratz.edu. *"Happiness consists of the fulfillment of the need to be needed." (Abraham Joshua Heschel). Teaching can make a person happy because a teacher is needed.*

WACHSMAN, HARVEY FREDERICK, lawyer, neurosurgeon; b. Bklyn., June 13, 1936; s. Ben and Mollie (Kugel) W.; m. Kathryn M. D'Agostino, Jan. 31, 1976; children: Dara Nicole, David Winston, Jacqueline Victoria, Lauren Elizabeth, Derek Charles, Ashley Max, Marea Lane, Melissa Roseanne. BA, Tulane U., 1958; MD, Chgo. Med. Sch., 1962; JD, Bklyn. Law Sch., 1976. Bar: Conn. 1976, N.Y. 1977, Fla. 1977, D.C. 1978, U.S. Supreme Ct. 1980, Pa. 1984, Md. 1986, Tex. 1987, cert.: Am. Bd. Legal Medicine, Am. Bd. Profl. Liabiloty Attys.; diplomate Nat. Bd. Med. Examiners. Intern surgery Kings County Hosp. Ctr., Bklyn., 1962-63; resident in surgery Kingsbrook Med. Ctr., 1964-65; resident in neurol. surgery Emory U. Hosp., Atlanta, 1965-69; practice medicine specializing in neurosurgery Bridgeport, Conn., 1972-74; sr. ptnr. Law Offices of Harvey F. Wachsman, MD, JD, LLP, Great Neck, NY, 2001—; of counsel firm Queller, Fisher, Dienst, Serrins, Washor & Kool, LLP, N.Y.C., of counsel. Trustee SUNY, chmn. health sci. and hosp. com.; pres., CEO Found. Excellence & Ethics in Medicine. Author: American Law of Medical Malpractice, Vol. I, 1980, 2d edit., 1992, American Law of Medical Malpractice, Vol. II, 1981, 2d edit., 1993, American Law of Medical Malpractice, Vol. III, 1982, 2d edit., 1994, Cumulative Supplement to American Law of Medical Malpractice, 1981, 82, 83, 84, 85, American Law of Medical Malpractice, 2d edit., Vols. I, II and II, Lethal Medicine, 1993; mem. editl. bd. Legal Aspects of Med. Practice, 1978-82. Trustee SUNY, chmn. health sci. and hosp. com. Fellow: Assn. Trial Lawyers Am., Royal Soc. Medicine (London), Royal Soc. Arts (London), Am. Coll. Legal Medicine (mem. bd. govs. 1986, chmn. edn. com. 1983—, chmn. 1985, chmn. nat. meeting New Orleans 1988, nat. meeting, bd. dirs. ACLM Found.), Royal Soc. Medicine; mem.: ABA, Nassau-Suffolk Trial Lawyers Assn., Fairfield County Med. Soc., Nassau County Bar Assn., Pa. Trial Lawyers Assn., Tex. Trial Lawyers Assn., Md. Trial Lawyers Assn., Fla. Acad. Trial Lawyers, Conn. Trial Lawyers Assn., N.Y. Trial Lawyers Assn., N.Y. Acad. Scis., D.C. Bar Assn., Fla. Bar Assn., Conn. Bar Assn., N.Y. Bar Assn., Congress Neurol. Surgeons, Cosmos (Washington), Cosmos Club (Washington). Office: 1010 Northern Blvd Ste 208 Great Neck NY 11021 also: 233 Broadway New York NY 10000 E-mail: hwachsman@quellerfisher.com. *In my pursuit of knowledge and excellence in the fields of neurosurgery and the law, I have found that arming oneself with the power of knowledge is truly the key to helping others. Let one's goal in life be to help others, and he shall always find fulfillment, challenge and hope.*

WACHSMUTH, ROBERT WILLIAM, lawyer; b. Crowell, Tex., Jan. 20, 1942; s. Frederick W. and Dorothy (McKown) W.; m. Karin Lynn Kusiak, Dec. 11, 1999; children: Wendi Leigh, Ashley Beth Bass, Matthew McKown, Daniel Kusiak. BA, U. Tex., 1965, JD, 1966, grad. bus. sch., 1976. Bar: Tex. 1966, U.S. Dist. Ct. (we. dist.) Tex. 1970, U.S. Ct. Appeals (5th cir., 11 cir.) 1975, U.S. Supreme Ct. 1979, U.S. Dist. Ct. (so. dist.) Tex. 1987. Assoc. Foster, Lewis, Langley, Gardner and Banack, San Antonio, 1969-73; of counsel H.B. Zachry Co., 1973-79; ptnr. Johnson, Johnston, Bowlin, Wachsmuth and Vives, 1973-79, Kelfer, Coatney & Wachsmuth, San Antonio, 1979-81, Kelfer, Coatney, Wachsmuth & Saunders, San Antonio, 1981-83, Brock & Kelfer, P.C., San Antonio, 1983-88, Coatney & Wachsmuth, P.C., San Antonio, 1989-92, Gendry, Sprague & Wachsmuth, P.C., San Antonio, 1992-94, The Kleberg Law Firm, P.C., San Antonio, 1994—. Panel arbitrators Bexar County Arbitration Program, San Antonio, 1988; instr. San Antonio Jr. Coll., 1972-74; bd. cert./civil trial law Tex. Bd. Legal Specialization, 1981—; mem. faculty constrn. mgmt. and contrn. exec. program Tex. A&M U. Contbr. articles to profl. jours. Bd. dirs. Halfway House San Antonio, San Antonio and South Tex. br. Jr. Achievement, 1997—. Capt., mil. judge USMCR, 1966-69, Vietnam. Fellow Tex. Bar Found., Coll. of the State Bar; mem. ABA (vice chmn. comms. industry com. antitrust law sect. 1998-2001, mem. steering com. divsn. VIII forum on constrn. industry 1999—), State Bar of Tex. (bd. dirs., treas., sec., vice chmn. constrn. law sect. 1989-92, chmn. 1992-93), Am. Arbitration Assn. (panel of arbitrators, panel of mediators), San Antonio Bar Assn. (chmn. alternative dispute resolution com.), Fed. Bar Assn., Am. Subcontractors Assn. (gen. counsel San Antonio chpt. 1984-92), Assn. Gen. Contractors (gen. counsel San Antonio chpt. 1995—), Plaza Club (social com.), Masons, Scottish Rite, Shriners, Optimists (pres. 1977-78).Jr. Achievement (San Antonio and So. Tex., dir. 1997—). Republican. Episcopalian. Avocations: hunting, skiing, spectator sports, fishing, golf. Office: The Kleberg Law Firm PC 112 E Pecan St Ste 1300 San Antonio TX 78205-1538 E-mail: rwachsmuth@kleberg.com.

WACHSTEIN, JOAN MARTHA, dental hygienist; b. Phila., Nov. 12, 1941; d. Milton and Mabel Louise (Friedman) Hertzfeld; m. Mortimer Berwyn Wachstein, July 14, 1962 (dec. 1989); 1 child, Esther Lynn. RDH, Temple U., Phila., 1961. Registered dental hygienist; cert. gerontology referral Union Am. Hebrew Congregations and Hebrew Union Coll. Jewish Inst. Religion. Dental hygienist Dr. M.B. Wachstein, Newark, 1970-89; pres. Jewish Family Svc. of Del., 1992—94, Aux. of Miltion & Hattie Kutz Home , 1985—97; campaign mgr. Milton and Hattie Kutz Home for Capital Campaign, 1995; pres. Milton and Hattie Kutz Home, Inc., 1999—99. Bd. dirs. Jewish Fedn. Del., 1994—97, 1999, mem. exec. com., 1992—93, mem. Jewish Cmty. endowment com., 1993—99; mem. Mid-Atlantic coun. Union Am. Hebrew Congregations, 1981—, vice chair biennial program com., 1990—92, chair, 1992—94, bd. dirs., 1994—, v.p., 1992—98, pres., 1998—2002; trustee Union of Am. Hebrew Congregations, 1994—, mem. com. on Jewish family concerns, 1997—, mem. commn. on religious living, 1998, mem. outreach commn. exec. com., chair com. on older adults, 1996—2000, com. on small congregations, 2000—02, biennial program com., 2000—02, budget com., 2000—03, chair task force adult care facilities, 2001; mem. Women of Reform Judaism, Fedn. Temple Sisterhoods, 1975—97, v.p., 1987—89, 1989—91, 1991—93, mem.-at-large bd. dirs., 1993—97; pres. Beth Emeth Sisterhood, 1968—70; mem. jr. bd. Christiana Care Del., Inc.; apptd. commn. adult entertainment establishments State of Del., 1993—2001; mem. N.Am. bd. World Union Progressive Judaism; mem. exec. com. ARZA/World Union N.Am., 1999—; chair Women for Carper com. for Gov. State of Del., 1993—96; co-chmn. Women for Minner for Gov., State of Del., 2001—; vol. ombudsman State of Del. Divsn. Svcs. for Aging Adults and Adults with Phys. Disabilities, 2000—02; pres. Jewish Family Svc. of Del., 1992—94; pres. aux. Milton and Hattie Kutz Home, 1985—87; pres. Kutz Home, Inc., 1997—99; bd. dirs. Jewish Fedn. Del., 1991—92, Assn. Jewish Families and Children, 1995—99. Recipient Community Builder award NCCJ, 1985, Keva cert. Ctrl. Conf. Am. Rabbis and Nat. Assn. Temple Educators. Mem.: Orgn. for Ednl. Resources and Tech. Tng., Nat. Coun. Jewish Women, Hadassah, Jewish Women Internat., Temple U. Dental Hygiene Alumni Assn. Jewish. Home: 3331 Silverside Rd Wilmington DE 19810-4804 Fax: 302-478-5157. E-mail: JWachs3331@aol.com.

WACHSTETER, GEORGE, illustrator; b. Hartford, Conn., Mar. 12, 1911; s. Josef and Therese (Weiss) W.; m. Thelma Altshuler, July 29, 1939 (dec. 1991). Ed. pub. schs., Hartford. Illustrator Major Advt. Agys, Theatre and Motion Picture Prodns., 1936—, CBS, NBC, ABC Radio and TV Networks, 1937-70; weekly illustrator and caricature to drama pages N.Y. Herald Tribune, 1941-50; contbr. illustration and caricature to drama and polit. pages N.Y. Times, 1938-50; caricaturist Theatre Guild On The Air, U.S. Steel, 1945-63; artist TV section N.Y. Times, 1950-51; featured drama artist N.Y. Jour. Am., 1956-63, artist TV mag. covers, 1958-63, Hearst Syndicate, 1963-65; drama artist N.Y. World Telegram, 1964-66; syndicated feature illustrator Hallmark TV Drama Series, 1964-69. Illustrator, caricaturist (book) NBC Book of Stars, 1957; portrait Taft Meml. Fund Campaign, 1956; numerous work in pub. and pvt. collections. Jewish. Home: 85-05 Elmhurst Ave Elmhurst NY 11373-3357

WACHTEL, JOHN STEVEN, obstetrician, gynecologist; b. Chgo., Oct. 18, 1950; s. Hans and Lillian (Kriloff) W.; m. Mary Louise Lee, June 24, 1973; children: Hanna, Josh, Leah, Noah. BS, Stanford (Calif.) U., 1972; MD, U. Calif., San Diego, 1976. Diplomate Am. Bd. Ob-Gyn. Intern U. Calif. San Diego, La Jolla, 1976-77; resident in ob-gyn. Stanford U., 1977-80, clin. prof.; obstetrician Stanford U. Hosp., 1980—. Mem. AMA, Am. Coll. Ob-Gyn., Calif. Med. Assn., San Mateo County Med. Soc., Santa Clara County Med. Soc. Office: Menlo Med Clinic 1300 Crane St Menlo Park CA 94025-4283

WACHTEL, JOSEPH HEINDEL, sculptor; b. Gura-Putila, Ukraine, Apr. 12, 1914; came to U.S., 1962; s. Israel and Shendel W.; m. S. Pouse (dec. 1991); 1 child, Peter L. Student, Palm Beach (Fla.) C.C., 1983, 1999. Mech. technician, Czernovitz, Ukraine, 1933—41; with Ukraine mil., 1941—62; pres. Salisbury Fashion, N.Y.C., 1968-78; quality control Space Legs, 1979-88. Author: Escape from the Hounds of Hell, 1993. Sculptures on permanent display at Temple Beth Tikvah, Lake Worth, Fla., Yad Vashem, Jerusalem, Nat. Holocaust Mus., Washington, Mus. of Tolerance, L.A. Mem. B'nai B'rith, Holocaust Survivors Orgn. Democrat. Jewish. Avocations: fishing, walking, reading. Home: 313 Knotty Pine Cir Apt A-2 Lake Worth FL 33463-9053

WACHTEL, NORMAN JAY, lawyer; b. N.Y.C., June 1, 1941; s. A. Allen and Lillian (Rolnik) W.; m. C. Robin Fixler, June 12, 1969; children: Jonathan, Charles. AB, U. Pa., 1963, LLB, 1966; LLM, Boston U., 1967. Bar: N.Y. 1967. Assoc. Demov, Morris & Hammerling, N.Y.C., 1966-78, ptnr., 1978-87, Rogers & Wells, N.Y.C., 1987-96, of counsel, 1996-99, Clifford, Chance, Rogers & Wells, N.Y.C., 1999—. Bd. advisors 1st Am. Title Ins. Co. N.Y., 1982—. Author: (chpt.) Real Estate Titles, 1984. Office: Rogers & Wells 200 Park Ave Ste 5200 New York NY 10166-0005 E-mail: dex1125@aol.com., norman.wachtel@cliffordchance.com.

WACHTELL, ESTHER, non-profit management executive, consultant; b. June 30; m. Thomas Wachtell, Jan. 27; children: Roger Bruce, Wendy Anne, Peter James. BA in Phil., Conn. Coll.; MA in Literature, Cornell U. Pres. Music Ctr. of Los Angeles County; founder, pres. The Wachtell Group, TWG, Inc. Lectr. UCLA Grad. Sch. of Mgmt. Bd. visitors George L. Graziadio Sch. of Bus. Pepperdine U.; bd. dirs. The Ventura County Mus. of History and Art; chair U. So. Calif Ctr. Philanthropy and Pub. Policy; bd. dirs. Children's Hosp. L.A. Mem.: Regency Club (bd. dirs.). Fax: 805-649-3303.

WACHTLER, SOL, law educator, retired judge, arbitration corporation executive, writer; b. N.Y.C., Apr. 29, 1930; s. Philip Henry and Fay (Sobel) W.; m. Joan Wolosoff, Feb. 23, 1952; children: Lauren Jane, Marjorie Dru, Alison Toni, Philip Henry. BA, Washington and Lee U., 1951, LLB, 1952, postgrad., 1980, LLD (hon.), 1981, New Eng. Sch. Law, 1978, Bklyn. Law Sch., 1978, Hofstra U., 1980, SUNY, 1981, Syracuse U., Dowling Coll., 1990, Thomas M. Cooley Law Sch., 1990, New. Eng. Law Sch.; LHD (hon.), LIU, Coll. of St. Rose. Bar: N.Y. 1956. Justice N.Y. State Supreme Ct., 1968-72; judge N.Y. State Ct. Appeals, Albany, 1972-84; chief judge State of N.Y., 1985-93; prof. law Touro Law Sch., 1997—. Guest lectr. Bklyn. Law Sch., Hofstra Law Sch., Yale U. Sch. Law, Albany Law Sch., St. John's Law Sch., 1968-77, USIA, Munich, Germany, 1973, Stuttgart, Germany, 1977, U. Leyden, Amsterdam, Stockholm, 1988, Madrid, 1989; chmn. N.Y. State Fair Trial/Free Press Conf., N.Y. State Commn. on Bicentennial of U.S. Constitution.; bd. dirs. Confs. Cief Justices; mem. Nat Jud. Coun. Author: After the Madness, 1997; critic-at-large New Yorker mag., 1996; contbr. articles to legal jours. Councilman Town of North Hempstead, N.Y., 1963-65, chief exec., 1965-67; mem. Nassau County Bd. Suprs., 1965-67, chmn. com. pub. safety, 1965-67; trustee L.I. Jewish-Hillside Med. Ctr., 1970-98, L.I. U.; exec. com. North Shore L.I. Jewish Health Sys., 1998—; bd. overseers Nelson A. Rockefeller Inst. Govt.; dist. chmn. Boy Scouts Am., 1968-69; trustee Cerebral Palsy Assn., Assn. for Help of Retarded Children, 1966-67. Mem. Am. Law Inst., Assn. N.Y. State Supreme Ct. Justices, ABA, N.Y. State Bar Assn., Nassau County Bar Assn., Order of Coif, Phi Delta Phi. Jewish. Home: 10 Stonehill Dr N Manhasset NY 11030-4438 E-mail: SWCADRE@aol.com. *As a people, we are fond of the observation that ours is a nation of laws and not of men. It too, like the words of our great laws, seems to lend security, a sense of certainty, and a predictability to the paths we travel. In the law particularly, the thought that past generations have separated right from wrong and good from evil can be comforting. Yet, here again, if we will just scratch the surface, we will find that the greatest responsibility for our national welfare does not rest with statutes carved in stone but with the principles, conscience, and morality of the individuals who constitute this generation.*

WACHTMANN, LYNN R. state legislator; m. Trudy Blue; children: Cory, Aaron. Grad., Four County Joint Vocat. Sch. Owner, pres. Maumee Valley Bottlers, Inc., Napoleon, Ohio; ptnr. Culligan Water Conditioning; former councilman City of Napoleon; mem. Ho. of Reps., Ohio, 1985—98, Ohio Senate from 1st dist., Columbus, 1999—, chmn. health, human svcs. and aging com., mem. energy, natural resources, environment, highways and transp., ins., commerce and labor coms. Vol. fundraiser Crisis Pregnancy Ctrs. of N.W. Ohio, Bryan; vol. Orphan Grain Train; mem. Rep. Ctrl. Com.; Sunday sch. tchr., usher St. Paul Luth. Ch.; bd. dirs. Ohio Water Quality Assn. Named Nat. Legislator of Yr., Am. Legis. Exch. Coun., 1994, State Legislator of Yr., Nat. Retail Fedn., 1996, Legislator of Yr., Am. Legion; recipient Bobcat Legis. award, 1993, Watchdog of the Treasury award, United Conservatives of Ohio, Oustanding Freshman Legislator of Yr. award, 2000, Grad. Wall of Fame award, Four County Joint Vocat. Sch., 1997, Legislator of Yr. Defender of Life award, Ohio Right to Life, 1997, Conservation Legis. award, League of Ohio Sportsmen Nat. Wildlife Fedn., 1997, Guardian of Small Bus. award, Nat. Fedn. Ind. Bus., 1998. Mem.: NRA, Ohio Twp. Assn., Nat. Assn. Sportsman Legislators, Am. Legis. Exch. Coun. (state chmn.), Ohio Right to Life Soc., Gideon's Internat., Ohio Farm Bur., Pheasants Forever, Ducks Unlimited. Republican. Office: Rm # 040 Senate Bldg Columbus OH 43215

WACHTMEISTER, COUNT WILHELM H. F. diplomat; b. Vanas, Sweden, Apr. 29, 1923; s. Gustaf and Margaretha (Trolle) W.; m. Ulla Leuhusen, 1947; children: Anna, Erik. LLD, U. Stockholm, Sweden, 1946. Attache Swedish Ministry for Fgn. Affairs, 1946-47; attache Swedish Embassy, Vienna, Madrid and Lisbon, 1947-50; 2d sec. Swedish Ministry Fgn. Affairs, Stockholm, Sweden, 1950-55; 1st sec. Swedish Embassy, Moscow, 1955-58; personal asst. to UN Sec. Gen., 1958-61; head UN sect. Fgn. Ministry, Stockholm, 1962-65, dep. under-sec. polit. affairs, 1965-66; ambassador to Algeria Swedish Embassy, 1966-67; under-sec. for polit. affairs Swedish Ministry Fgn. Affairs, Stockholm, 1968-74; Swedish ambassador to U.S. Swedish Embassy, Washington, 1974-89; dean diplomatic corps in Washington, 1986-89. Sr. advisor to chmn. AB Volvo, 1989-94. Mem. Soc. Cin. (France), New World Found. (chmn.), Swedish-Am. C. of C. (chmn. 1993-95), Met. Club of Washington, Fed. City Club, Washington, Sällskapet, Stockholm. Avocation: tennis. Address: Karlavogen 59A SE 11449 Stockholm Sweden Fax: (202) 966-8116.

WACKENHUT, RICHARD RUSSELL, security company executive; b. Balt., Nov. 11, 1947; s. George Russell and Ruth Johann (Bell) W.; m. Mariane Hutson Ball, Mar. 13, 1971 (div. May 2000); children: Jennifer Anne, Lisa Renee, Ashley Elizabeth, Lauren Hutson. BA in Polit. Sci., The Citadel Mil. Coll., 1969; grad. bus. sch. advanced mgmt. program, Harvard U., 1987. With Wackenhut Corp., Coral Gables and Palm Beach Gardens, Fla. and Columbia, S.C., 1973—, v.p. ops. Coral Gables, 1981-82, sr. v.p. domestic ops., 1982-83, sr. v.p. ops., 1983-86, pres., COO, 1986-99, vice chmn., pres., COO, 1999—, vice chmn., pres., CEO, 2000, also bd. dirs. various subs. Past bd. dirs. Assoc. Industries of Fla.; former mem. The Citadel Adv. Coun. Mem. Internat. Assn. Chiefs Police, Internat. Security Mgmt. Assn., Am. Soc. Indsl. Security. Republican. Christian Scientist. Avocations: racquetball, jogging, boating. Office: Wackenhut Corp 4200 Wackenhut Dr Ste 100 Palm Beach Gardens FL 33410

WACKER, SUSAN REGINA, creative design director; b. Red Bank, N.J., Apr. 29, 1954; d. Durward Richard and Margaret Rose (Williams) W. BFA, Pratt Inst., 1978, cert. computer graphics/electronic pub., 2001. Asst. art dir. Lesley-Hille Inc., N.Y.C., 1975-79; art dir. Kasica, Lefton, Brown, Inc., 1979-80, Marinelli & Hnath Assocs., Inc., N.Y.C., 1980-82; sr. design dir. Elizabeth Arden Co., 1982-99; art dir. L'Oreal Retail Divsn., 2000—02. Exhibited at The Nature of Diamonds, Mus. Natural History, N.Y.C., 1997-98; patentee in field. Recipient (4) DESI awards, 1980, ANDY award, 1980, Fragrance Found. award, 1988, 91, 92, Silver award N.J. Packaging Execs. Club, 1990, ADDY Excellence citation, 1991, Edison Best New Products Gold Medal award, 1991, (2) Gold awards Nat. Paperbox & Packaging Assn., 1992, (2) Gold awards, 1994, Silver award Paperboard Packaging Coun., 1993, Excellence award, 1993, Silver Excellence award Nat. Paperbox & Packaging Assn., 1993, (10) Silver Excellence awards, 1994, Mobius 1st Place Statuette award, 1995, Gold award Nat. Paperboard Coun., 1995, Prix Francois 1st de L'Emballage de Luxe, 1995, OMA Gold award, 1995, Oscar de L'Emballage Prestige à Lyon, 1995, Mobius award First Place Statuette for Elizabeth Taylor's Black Pearls perfume product line/package design, 1996, OMA Gold award for Elizabeth Arden's 5th Avenue tester display, 1996, OMA Bronze award for Elizabeth Taylor's Black Pearls tester display, 1996, Lagerfeld, Jako Mchdsg., 1998, CPC "Package of the Month" (October), Elizabeth Arden's 5th Avenue fragrance line, 1996, Natl. Paperboard Packaging Conc. award, 1996, OMA Bronze award Lagerfeld JAKO Merchandising Program, 1998. Mem. Internat. Perfume Bottle Assn., Cosmetic Exec. Women Found., Fashion Group Internat. Avocations: skiing, tennis, horseback riding, photography. E-mail: srwacker@aol.com.

WACKER, WARREN ERNEST CLYDE, physician, educator; b. Bklyn., Feb. 29, 1924; s. John Frederick and Kitty Dora (Morrissey) W.; m. Ann Romeyn MacMillan, May 22, 1948; children: Margaret Morrissey, John Frederick. Student, Georgetown U., 1946-47; MD, George Washington U., 1951; MA (hon.), Harvard, 1968. Intern George Washington U. Hosp., 1951-52, resident in internal medicine, 1952-53; resident Peter Bent Brigham Hosp., Boston, 1953-55; Nat. Found. Infantile Paralysis fellow, 1955-57; investigator Howard Hughes Med. Inst., Boston, 1957-68; from faculty to prof. hygiene Harvard U., Cambridge, 1955-71, assoc. prof. medicine, 1968—71, 1971—89, Henry K. Oliver prof. hygiene emeritus, 1995, acting master Mather House, 1974-75, acting master Kirkland House, 1975-76, master Cabot House, 1978-84; sr. med. cons. Risk Mgmt. Found., Cambridge, 1992—. Dir. health svcs. Harvard U., Cambridge, 1971-89; vis. scholar St. Mary's Hosp. Med. Sch., 1964; vis. prof. U. Tel Aviv, 1981; chmn. bd. Applied Mgmt. Sys., Burlington, Mass., 1982-97, Millipore Corp., Bedford, Mass., 1971-94. Author: Magnesium and Man, 1981; sec., editorial adv. bd.: Biochemistry, 1962-76; assoc. editor: Magnesium; mem. editl. bd. Toxiogical and Environ. Chemistry; contbr. articles to med. and sci. jours. Vestryman St. Paul's Episc. Ch., Brookline, Mass., 1965-68, 76-79, 91-94; bd. dirs. Harvard Cmty. Health Plan, Boston, 1973-84, mem. fin. com., 1984-86, mem. corp., 1986-96; bd. dirs. Bishop Rhinelander Found., Cambridge, 1973-76, 78-84, Controlled Risk Ins. Co., 1976-78; pres. bd. overseers Peter Bent Brigham Hosp., Boston, 1979-84; trustee Brigham and Women's Hosp., Boston, 1984-89,Risk Mgmt. Found., 1979-92; mem. mgmt. bd. MIT, 1985-95; mem. corp. Mt. Auburn Hosp., Cambridge, 1986—; mem. adv. bd. hospitality program Episc. Diocese Mass., 1989-95. 1st lt. USAAF, 1942-45. Decorated Air medal, D.F.C., Liberation medal (Greece); named Disting. Alumnus, George Washington U., 1963; recipient Cert. of Merit, Soc. Magnesium Research, 1985. Mem. AMA, Am. Chem. Soc., Am. Soc. Biol. Chemistry, Am. Soc. Clin. Investigation, Mass. Med. Soc., A.C.P., Am. Coll. Health Assn. (pres. 1981, Boynton award 1986), Biochemistry Soc. (London), Am. Coll. Nutrition, Sigma Xi, Alpha Omega Alpha, Harvard Club (Boston). Home: 91 Glen Rd Brookline MA 02445-7764 Office: Risk Mgmt Found 101 Main St Cambridge MA 02142-1519 E-mail: wwacker@rmf.harvard.edu.

WACKERBAUER, RENATE ANNA, physicist; b. Geisenhausen, Bavaria, Germany, Sept. 23, 1963; came to U.S., 1998; d. Rudolf and Anna Wackerbauer. Diploma in physics, Tech. U. Munich, 1990, vordiploma in physics, 1985; PhD in Physics (Nonlinear Dynamics), Ludwig-Maximilian U., Munich, 1995. Rsch. scientist Max-Planck-Inst. Extraterrestrial Physics, Munich, 1990-96, Max-Planck Inst. Complex Systems, Dresden, Germany, 1996-98, W.Va. U., Morgantown, 1998-2001; asst. prof. physics U. Alaska, Fairbanks, 2001—. Presenter 5th United European Gastroenterology Week, Paris, 1996; poster presenter internat. confs.; session chair Chaos Conf., Munich, 1993; conf. organizer Physics Session, Nat. Summer Sch. on Complex Systems, Tutzing, Germany, 1995; invited spkr. numerous instns., 1988—. Contbr. articles to profl. jours., including Chaos, Phys. Rev. Letters, Phys. Rev. E, Gastroenterology, Gut, others; contbr. chpts. to books. Fellow Max-Planck Soc., 1994. Mem. Am. Phys. Soc. (divsn. biol. physics, group statis. and nonlinear physics), German Phys. Soc. (divsn. condensed matter physics). Achievements include research in modeling of biological systems: neuron models, plasmodium; spatiotemporal complexity in reaction-diffusion systems, population dynamics; stochastic dynamical systems with few/many degrees of freedom: stabilization and synchronization phenomena, noisy neuronal assemblies, small-world topology; nonlinear time-series/image analysis; applications to natural systems. Avocations: ceramics. Office: U Alaska Dept Physics PO Box 755920 Fairbanks AK 99775-5920

WACKER-BRAWLEY, MARGARET, communications executive; b. Dec. 12, 1951; d. Warren Ernest Clyde and Ann Romeyn (MacMillan) W.; m. Richard Warren Brawley, Feb. 26, 1994. BA, Carnegie Mellon U., 1974. Promotion specialist Millipore Corp., Bedford, Mass., 1974-77, dir. comm. Lab. Products divsn., 1981-82, corp. comm. mgr., 1982-88, human resources project mgr., 1989-93, sr. acct. mgr. biosci. divsn., 1993-94, mgr. tech. pubs. and life sci. promotion, lab. & health care products divsn., 1994-95, mgr. mktg. comm., analytical products divsn., 1995—; dir. advt. IVAC divsn. Eli Lilly Co., San Diego, 1977-79, dist. sales mgr. L.A., 1979-80; bus. unit mgr. Sage divsn. Orion Rsch., Cambridge, Mass., 1980-81. Counselor to handicapped individuals in bus. Democrat. Episcopalian. Avocations: computer aided illustration, graphic design and desktop publishing, collage. Home: The Brook House 77 Pond Ave Apt 701C Brookline MA 02445-7114 Office: Millipore Corp 80 Ashby Rd Bedford MA 01730-2271 E-mail: rwbmwb@rcn.com.

WACKYM, PHILLIP ASHLEY, surgeon, researcher, otolaryngologist; b. Balt., Dec. 25, 1957; s. Phillip Adeeb and Elsie Jean W.; m. Jeremy JoAlice Miller, July 25, 1983; 1 child, Ashton Rhys. BA in Chemistry, Calif. State U., Fullerton, 1980; MD, Vanderbilt U., 1985. Diplomate Am. Bd. Otolaryngology, 1992 (guest examiner 1994-96). Resident in surgery UCLA Med. Ctr., L.A., 1985-86, resident in neurosurgery, 1986-87, resident in head and neck surgery, 1987-91; asst. prof. surgery UCLA Sch. Medicine, 1991-95; fellow otology, neuro-otology and skull base surgery U. Iowa, Iowa City, 1991-92, vis. asst. prof. otolaryngology, 1991-92; assoc. prof. Mt. Sinai Sch. of Medicine, N.Y.C., 1995-98; prof./chmn. dept. otolaryngology and communication scis. Med. Coll. Wisc., Milwaukee, 1998—, chief divsn. otology and neuro-otologic skull base surgery, 1998—. Chief ear service Mt. Sinai Med. Ctr. N.Y.C., 1995-98, dir. molecular biology lab., 1995-98, bd. dirs. Assn. Attending Staff, 1995-98; mem. hearing study sect., Ctr. for Sci. Revs., NIH, Bethesda, Md. , 1996-2000. Author: (thesis) Laryngoscope, 1996 (Fowler award 1997); mem. editl. bd. Laryngoscope, 1996—. Recipient Clin. Investigator award Nat. Inst. Deafness and Other Comm. Disorders/NIH, Los Angeles, 1991-95, First Ind. Rsch. and Transition award, 1995—, Baron Rsch. award Triological Soc., We. sect., 1990, 93; Torok award Am. Neurotology Soc., 1993; Honor award Am. Acad. Otolaryngology Head and Neck Surgery, 1998. Fellow ACS, Am. Laryngol., Rhinol. & Otologic Soc., N.Y. Acad. Sci.; mem. Am. Otologic Soc., Am. Acad. Otolaryngology Head and Neck Surgery Found. (chmn. grants and prizes com. 1997-2000). Episcopalian. Achievements include: 104 jour. publs., 17 textbook chpts., 1 videotape, 52 invited presentations, 40 submitted presentations. Office: Dept Otolaryngology Med Coll Wisc 9200 W Wisconsin Ave Milwaukee WI 53226-3522 E-mail: wackym@mcw.edu.

WACTAWSKI-WENDE, JEAN, epidemiologist, educator, researcher; d. John Stanley Wactawski and Elizabeth Louise Ramsay; m. Karl Edward Wende, 1989; children: Alexandra Grace, Marilyn Elizabeth. BA in Biology, Canisius Coll., 1981; MS in Natural Scis., U. Buffalo, 1983, PhD in Epidemiology, 1989. Rsch. scientist Roswell Park Cancer Inst., Buffalo, 1982-89; clin. asst. prof. U. Buffalo, 1989-98, asst. prof., 1998—. Mem. faculty coun. U. Buffalo Sch. Medicine, 1994—. Contbr. articles to sci. and profl. jours. Bd. dirs. Niagara Hospice, Niagara County Bd. Health, N.Y., 1996-2002. Grantee Women's Health Initiative, NIH, 1993—, U.S. Army, 1996-2001, Women's Health Inst., 1995—, NIDR, 2002-. Mem. Am. Coll. of Epidemiology, Soc. for Epidemiologic Rsch., Soc. for Bone and Mineral Rsch. Presbyterian. Avocations: golf, sailing. Office: U Buffalo Sch Medicine 270 Farber Hall 3435 Main St Buffalo NY 14214-3001 E-mail: JWW@Buffalo.edu.

WADDELL, ELLIOT DEAN, civil engineer, consultant; b. Sioux City, Iowa, Aug. 4, 1956; s. Duwane Blair and Beverly Delight (Hughes) W.; m. Lauri Lane Ryan, Aug. 7, 1976; children: Rebeka Lane, Tamara Ann, Jaquilyn Rae, Beau Elliot. BS in Engring. Ops., Iowa State U., 1978. Registered profl. engr., Iowa, Nebr., S.D. Engr. in tng. Schlotfeldt Engring., Webster City, Iowa, 1978-80; project engr. Flannery Engring., Elk Point, S.D., 1980-83; engr., owner Five States Engring., Westfield, Iowa, 1983—. Leader, youth com. rep. 4-H, Plymouth County, Iowa, 1988-93; steering com., Planca team Cursillo, Iowa, 1990—; adult leader Teens Encounter Christ, Iowa, 1992—; active Akron First Ch. of Christ; state lay dir. Western Iowa Walk to Emmaus. Mem. Iowa Soc. Solid Waste Operators (tech. com.), Iowa Assn. Gen. Contractors. Republican. Achievements include development of economical methods to recycle in rural communities with primary utilization on existing local infrastructure, develop safe drinking water for public, develop unique on-site treatment methods at chemical spill sites. Avocations: youth leadership, church leadership, community service. Home and Office: 19481 Echo Rd Westfield IA 51062-8520

WADDELL, PHILLIP DEAN, lawyer; b. Covington, Ky., Nov. 14, 1948; s. Ewell Edward and Sarah Isobel (Dean) W.; m. Jill Annette Tolson, Aug. 23, 1975; children: Nathan Ewell, James Seth. BA, Centre Coll. Ky., 1971; JD, No. Ky. U., 1982. Bar: Ky. 1982, Ohio 1983, Tenn. 1986. V.p., mgr. escrow Eagle Savings Assn., Cin., 1973-83; v.p. Union Planters Nat. Bank, Memphis, 1983-84; sr. v.p., liason First Nat. Bank & Trust Co., Oklahoma City, 1984-86; sr. v.p., sec., gen. counsel First Mortgage Strategies Group, Inc., Memphis, 1986-92; atty. pvt. practice, 1992—. Mem. ABA, Am. Judicature Soc., Ky. Bar Assn., Tenn. Bar Assn. Lodges: Kiwanis. Republican. Presbyterian. Home: 2095 Allenby Rd Memphis TN 38139-4343 Office: 3169 Professional Plz Ste 2 Germantown TN 38138-7917

WADDELL, WILLIAM JOSEPH, pharmacologist, toxicologist; b. Commerce, Ga., Mar. 16, 1929; s. John Daniel and Lillian Marie (Vollrath) W.; m. Grace Carolyn Marlowe, Oct. 19, 1974; children: William Joseph, James Glenn, Martin Christie, Amy Alison. AB in Chemistry, U. N.C., 1951, MD, 1955. Postdoctoral research fellow U. N.C. Sch. Medicine, 1955-58, asst. prof. pharmacology, 1958-62, asso. prof., 1962-72; asso. prof. oral biology U. N.C. Sch. Medicine (Dental Research Center), 1967-69, prof., 1969-72, asso. dir., 1968-72; prof. pharmacology U. Ky. Coll. Medicine, Lexington, 1972-77; prof., chmn. dept. pharmacology and toxicology U. Louisville, 1977-97, emeritus chmn., 1997—, prof. emeritus, 1998—. Centennial Alumni Disting. vis. prof. U. N.C. Sch. Medicine, 1979 Contbr. articles to profl. jours. Fellow Acad. Toxicological Scis.; mem. Am. Soc. for Pharmacology and Exptl. Therapeutics, Am. Physiol. Soc., Am. Teratology Soc., Internat. Soc. for Study Xenobiotics, Soc. for Exptl. Biology and Medicine, Soc. Toxicology, Sigma Xi. Home: 14300 Rose Wycombe Rd Prospect KY 40059-9024 Office: U Louisville Dept Pharmacology Louisville KY 40292-0001 E-mail: bwaddell@louisville.edu.

WADDEN, CHRISTOPHER DAVID, food products executive; b. Ridgewood, N.J., Feb. 25, 1959; s. Robert Vincent and Mary Elizabeth (Townley) W. BSME, Tex. A&M U., 1981. Registered profl. engr., Tex. Ind. spl. project engr. Dresser Magcobar, Houston, 1981-83; staff engr. Nabisco Brands (Nat. Biscuit Co.), 1983-84, mechanical supt. St. Louis, 1984-85, sr. project engr. East Hanover, N.J., 1985-86, shift mgr. Houston, 1986-88, ops. mgr. San Francisco, 1988-89, mfg. mgr. Chgo., 1989-91; gen. mgr. Yili Nabisco Biscuit and Food Co., Ltd., Beijing, 1991-95; pres. F.W.C. Internat., Lighthouse Point, Fla., 1995-2000; gen. mgr. Laguna Cookie Co., Tustin, Calif., 2000—01, Organic Milling Co., San Dimas, 2001—. Contbg. author: Cookie and Cracker Manufacturing, 1990. Rep. com. mem., Lisle, Ill., 1990. Roman Catholic. Avocations: aviation, oenology, acting, writing. Office: 2172 Loggia Newport Beach CA 92660-9041

WADDEN, RICHARD ALBERT, environmental engineer, educator, consultant, research director; b. Sioux City, Iowa, Oct. 3, 1936; s. Sylvester Francis and Hermina Lillian (Costello) W.; m. Angela Louise Trabert, Aug. 9, 1975; children: Angela Terese, Noah Albert, Nuiko Clare Student, St. John's U., Collegeville, Minn., 1954-56; BS in Chem. Engring., Iowa State U., 1959; MS in Chem. Engring, N.C. State U., 1962; PhD in Chem. and Environ. Engring., Northwestern U., 1972. Registered profl. engr., Ill.; cert. indsl. hygienist. Engr. Linde Co., Tonnawanda, N.Y., 1959-60, Humble Oil Co., Houston, 1962-65; instr. engring. Pahlavi U. Peace Corps, Shiraz, Iran, 1965-67; tech. adviser Ill. Pollution Control Bd., Chgo., 1971-72; asst. dir. Environ. Health Resource Ctr. Ill., 1972-74; asst. prof. environ. and occupational health scis. Sch. Pub. Health U. Ill.-Chgo., 1972-75, assoc. prof., 1975-79, prof., 1979—, dir., 1984-86, 88-92; dir. Office Tech. Transfer U. Ill. Ctr. for Solid Waste Mgmt. and Resch., 1987-92; dir. indsl. hygiene and hazardous waste tng. programs Occupl. Safety and Health Ctr., U. Ill.-Chgo., Chgo. Vis. scientist Nat. Inst. Environ. Studies, Japan, 1978-79, invited scientist, 1983, 84, 88; cons. air pollution control, health implications of energy devel., indoor air pollution; vis. scholar dept. civil engring. Northwestern U., Evanston, Ill., 1997. Author: Energy Utilization and Environmental Health, 1978, (with P.A. Scheff) Indoor Air Pollution, 1983, Engineering Design for Control of Workplace Hazards, 1987; contbr. numerous articles to profl. publs. Sr. Internat. fellow Fogarty Internat. Ctr.-NIH, 1978-79, 83; WHO fellow, 1984. Mem. AIChE, Am. Chem. Soc., Am. Acad. Environ. Engrs. (diplomate), Am. Acad. Indsl. Hygiene (diplomate), Air and Waste Mgmt. Assn., Am. Indsl. Hygiene Assn., Am. Conf. Govtl. Indsl. Hygienists. Office: U Ill m/c 922 2121 W Taylor St Chicago IL 60612-7260

WADDEN, THOMAS ANTONY, psychologist, educator; b. Richmond, Va., Sept. 3, 1952; s. Thomas Antony Jr. and Mary Lloyd (Cradock) W.; m. Jan Robin Linowitz, Nov. 11, 1984; children: David Joseph, Michael James, Steven Zachary. AB magna cum laude, Brown U., 1975; PhD, U. N.C., 1981; MA (hon.), U. Pa., 1994. Psychology intern Boston VA Med. Ctr., 1980-81; instr. in psychology U. Pa. Sch. Medicine, Phila., 1981-82, asst. prof. psychology, 1982-87, assoc. prof. psychology, 1987-91, prof. psychology, 1994—; prof. psychology, dir. clin. tng. Syracuse (N.Y.) U., 1992-93. Clin. dir. Obesity Rsch. Group, U. Pa., Phila., 1983-91, dir. Weight and Eating Disorders Program, 1994—; dir. Ctr. for Health and Behavior, Syracuse U., 1992-93. Author (with K.D. Brownell): LEARN PRogram for Weight Control, 1998; assoc. editor: Annals of Behavioral Medicine, 1990—93, mem. editl. bd.: Internat. Jour. Eating Disorders, mem. editl. bd.: Jour. Cons. and Clin. Psychology, mem. editl. bd.: Obesity Rsch.; editor (with T.B. Vanltallie): Treatment of the Seriously Obese Patient, 1992; editor: (with A.J. Stunkard) Obesity: Theory and Therapy, 1993, Handbook of Obesity Treatment, 2002; contbr. chapters to books; writer: numerous sci. papers. Recipient Nat. Rsch. Svc. award NIMH, 1983-85, Rsch. Scientist Devel. award, 1987-91, 94—. Mem. APA, Soc. Behavioral Medicine (bd. dirs. 1987-90), Assn. for Advancement of Behavior Therapy (New Rschr. award 1986), Acad. Behavioral Medicine, Germantown Cricket Club, Cosmos Club, Phi Beta Kappa, Sigma Xi. Democrat. Avocations: tennis, squash, symphonic music, guitar. Home: 433 Bolsover Rd Wynnewood PA 19096-1301 Office: U Pa Ste 3029 3535 Market St Philadelphia PA 19104-2641 E-mail: wadden@mail.med.upenn.edu.

WADDINGTON, BETTE HOPE (ELIZABETH CROWDER), violinist, educator; b. San Francisco; d. John and Marguerite (Crowder) Waddington. BA in Music, U. Calif., Berkeley, 1945, postgrad., Julliard Sch. Music, 1950, San Jose State Coll., 1955; MA in Music and Art, San Francisco U., 1953; studied with, Joseph Fuchs, Melvin Ritter, Frank Gittelson, Felix Khuner, Daniel Bonsack, D.C. Dounis, Naoum Blinder, Eddy Brown. Cert. gen. elem. and secondary tchr., Calif.; life cert. music and art for jr. coll.; cert. in librarianship for elem. sch. to jr. coll., Calif. Violinist Erie (Pa.) Symphony, 1950-51, Dallas Symphony, 1957-58, St. Louis Symphony, 1958-95. Toured alone and with St. Louis Symphony U.S., Can., Middle East, Japan, China, England, Korea, Europe, Africa; concert master Peninsula Symphony, Redwood City and San Mateo, Calif., Grove Music Soc., N.Y.C.; violinist St. Louis Symphony, 1958-95, violinist emeritus; numerous recs. St. Louis Symphony, 1958—. Julliard Sch. Music scholar 1950, San Jose State Coll. scholar 1955.. Mem. Am. String Tchrs. Assn., Am. Musicians Union (life, St. Louis and San Francisco chpts.), U. Calif. Alumnae Assn. (life, Berkeley), San Francisco State U. Alumni Assn. (life), San Jose State U. Alumni Assn. (life),

Sierra Club (life), Alpha Beta Alpha. Avocations: travel, art, archeology, history, drawing, painting. Office: St Louis Symphony Orch care Powell Symphony Hall 718 N Grand Blvd Saint Louis MO 63103-1011

WADDINGTON, IRMA JOANN, music teacher; b. Nokomis, Ill., June 7, 1929; d. Albert William and Rose Minnie (Hueschen) Miller; m. Ralph Roger Waddington, Nov. 3, 1946; children: Joann, Janet, Jennifer. Cert. piano, organ Ill. State Music Tchrs. Assn. Music tchr. pvt. studio, Pana, Ill., 1957—; ch. organist, choir dir. St. Paul Lutheran Ch., 1957—; keyboard player Waddington Trio, 1987—98, 2000—02. Composer: Memories of Kerri, 1983, Rejoice! Rejoice!, 1993, Praise! Praise!, 1993. Organist Rotary Club, Pana, 1985—, sr. citizens, Pana, 1970—, local nursing homes, Pana, 1974—. Named Best Piano Teacher, Decatur (Ill.) Herald & Review, 1987, Member of Yr. Decatur Area Music Tchrs. Assn., 1997. Mem. Am. Fedn. Musicians (pres., 1965-68), Music Tchrs. Nat. Assn., Decatur Area Music Tchrs. Assn. (pres. 1983, 84, 90, 94, 95, clinician, 1979—), Ill. Music Tchrs. Assn. (clinician 1991 conv.). Republican. Lutheran. Avocations: travel, golf. Home: 709A Kitchell Ave Pana IL 62557-1875

WADDINGTON, RAYMOND BRUCE, JR. English language educator; b. Santa Barbara, Calif., Sept. 27, 1935; s. Raymond Bruce and Marjorie Gladys (Waddell) W.; m. Linda Gayle Jones, Sept. 7, 1957 (div.); children: Raymond Bruce, Edward Jackson; m. Kathleen Martha Ward, Oct. 11, 1985 BA, Stanford U., 1957; PhD, Rice U., 1963; postdoctoral (Univ. fellow in Humanities), Johns Hopkins U., 1965-66. Instr. English U. Houston, 1961-62; instr. U. Kans., 1962-63, asst. prof., 1963-65; asst. prof. English lit. U. Wis., Madison, 1966-68, assoc. prof., 1968-74, prof., 1974-82; prof. English lit. U. Calif., Davis, 1982—. Author: The Mind's Empire, 1974; co-editor: The Rhetoric of Renaissance Poetry, 1974, The Age of Milton, 1980, The Expulsion of the Jews, 1994; mem. editl. bd. The Medal, 1991, Renaissance Quar., 2000; sr. editor: Sixteenth Century Jour.; editor: Garland Studies in the Renaissance. Huntington Library fellow, 1967, 75; Inst. Research in Humanities fellow, 1971-72; Guggenheim fellow, 1972-73; NEH fellow, 1977, 83; Newberry Library fellow, 1978; Am. Philos. Soc. grantee, 1965. Mem. Renaissance Soc. Am., Milton Soc. Am., Am. Numismatic Soc., 16th Century Studies Conf. (pres. 1985), Brit. Art Medal Soc., Logos Club. Home: 39 Pershing Ave Woodland CA 95695-2845 Office: U Calif Dept English Davis CA 95616 E-mail: rbwaddington@ucdavis.edu.

WADDLE, JOHN FREDERICK, former retail chain executive; b. Somerset, Ky., July 1, 1927; s. Lewis Everett and Anna Hail (Prather) W.; m. Catherine Joan Osborn, June 3, 1977; children: Lewis Victor, Joan Catherine, John Frederick. BS, U. Ky., 1949; MS, NYU, 1952. With Sears, Roebuck and Co., Chgo., 1949-85, nat. mgr. toys, 1969-72, asst. to sr. exec. v.p. merchandising, 1972-76, group nat. merchandising mgr., 1977-78, v.p. children's apparel, 1978-82; mng. dir., exec. v.p. Sears World Trade, Inc., Chgo., 1982-85. Served with USN, 1945-46. Republican. Presbyterian. E-mail: cathwaddle@aol.com.

WADDY, LAWRENCE HEBER, religious writer; b. Sydney, Australia, Oct. 5, 1914; came to U.S., 1963; s. Percival Stacy and Etheldred (Spittal) W.; m. Laurie Hancock, July 10, 1972. BA, Oxford (Eng.) U., 1937, MA, 1945. Asst. master Winchester Coll. Eng., 1938-42; headmaster Tonbridge Sch., Eng., 1949-62; edn. officer BBC, Eng., 1962-63; chaplain The Bishop's Sch., La Jolla, Calif., 1963-67; lectr. in Greek and Latin lit. U. Calif., San Diego, 1969-80; vicar Ch. of Good Samaritan, University City, Calif., 1970-74; hon. asst. St. James By The Sea Episcopal Ch., La Jolla, 1975—. Author: Pax Romana & World Peace, 1950, The Bible as Drama, 1975, Drama in Worship, 1978, Symphony, 1976, A Parish By the Sea, 1988, Shakespeare Remembers, 1994, First Bible Stories, 1994, Florence Nightingale, 1996. Chaplain, British Navy, 1942-46. Recipient Drama 1st prize BBC, 1964. Republican. Home: 5910 Camino De La Costa La Jolla CA 92037-6550

WADDY, PATRICIA A. architectural history educator; b. Cannelton, Ind., July 29, 1941; d. Luther and Gertrude Viola (Brandyberry) W. BA, Rice U., 1963; MA, Tulane U., 1965; PhD, NYU, 1973. Vis. lectr. Carnegie-Mellon U., Pitts., 1970-71, asst. prof., 1971-77; assoc. prof. archtl. history Syracuse (N.Y.) U., 1977-91, prof., 1991—. Vis. lectr. Cornell U., Ithaca, N.Y., 1977, vis. assoc. prof., 1980. Author: Seventeenth-Century Roman Palaces: Use and The Art of the Plan, 1990 (Alice Davis Hitchcock award 1992); co-author: (with D. DiCastro and A.M. Pedrocchi) Il Palazzo Pallavicini Rospigliosi e la Galleria Pallavicini, 2000; editor Nicodemus Tessin the Younger, Traicté dela decoration interieure (1717), 2002. Fulbright grantee, Rome, 1968-69; fellow Am. Acad. in Rome, 1970, Nat. Humanities Ctr., 1984-85, Samuel H. Kress sr. fellow Nat. Gallery Art, 1994-95, NEH fellow, 1998-99, Guggenheim fellow, 1999-00, Am. Coun. Learned Soc. fellow, 1978. Mem. Soc. Archtl. Historians (book rev. editor Jour. 1985-88, editor 1990-93, 2d v.p. 1993-94, 1st v.p. 1994-96, pres. 1996-98), Coll. Art Assn., Renaissance Soc. Am. Office: Syracuse U Sch Architecture Syracuse NY 13244-1250 E-mail: pwaddy@syr.edu.

WADE, BEN FRANK, college administrator; b. Roanoke, Va., July 20, 1935; s. Frank Hart and Clyde Temple (Weaver) W.; m. Janice Marie Wine, June 14, 1958; children— Andrea Marie, Laurel Faye BA, Bridgewater Coll., 1957; MDiv cum laude, United Theol. Sem., 1960; STM, Boston U., 1961; MS, Columbia U., 1966; PhD, Hartford Sem. Found., 1966. Prof. Shenandoah Coll., Winchester, Va., 1963-65, United Theol. Sem., Dayton, Ohio, 1965-69, James Madison U., Harrisonburg, Va., 1969-71; acad. dean Brevard Coll., N.C., 1971-73, Fla. So. Coll., Lakeland, Fla., 1973-77; pres. Westmar Coll., LeMars, Iowa, 1977-79; provost Bridgewater Coll., Va., 1979-85; v.p., acad. dean Fla. So. Coll., Lakeland, Fla., 1985-96, v.p., dean emeritus, 1996—. Mem., chmn. accreditation visit teams So. Assn. Colls. and Schs., State Council Higher Edn. Va.; vis. lectr., cons. Divsn. chmn. YMCA Capital Funds Campaign, Lakeland, Fla., 1975; ret. mem. Fla. Annual Conf., United Meth. Ch. Named Disting. Alumnus, Bridgewater Coll., 1994, Hon. Alumnus, Fla. So. Coll., 1996; Hartzler fellow Hartford Sem. Found., 1961-62, 62-63. Mem. Theta Chi Beta, Phi Eta Sigma, Omicron Delta Kappa. Avocations: breadmaking; saddle horses; music. Home: 3733 Highland Fairways Blvd Lakeland FL 33810-5765

WADE, DAVID C. artist; b. Salt Lake City, Feb. 26, 1952; s. Homer E. and Margaret Wade; m. Julie Hayes; children: Madison. Artist, Salt Lake City, 1976—98, Cokeville, Wyo., 1998—. Art instr., Jackson, 2000. Recipient Migratory Bird award, Arts for the Parks, 1999, Wildlife award, Art for the Parks, 2000. Home: P.O. Box 275 Cokeville WY 83114 Personal E-mail: dwade@allwest.net.

WADE, DAVID STUART, surgeon; b. Guthrie, Okla., July 21, 1955; MD, Uniformed Svcs. U. Health Sci., 1981. Diplomate Am. Bd. Surgery. Intern Naval Hosp., Bethesda, Md., 1981, resident in gen. surgery Portsmouth, 1982-86; fellow in surg. oncology Roswell Park Meml. Inst., Buffalo, 1987-89; from head dept. surgery to dir. surg. svc. Naval Hosp., Oakland, Calif., 1992-95; head dept. surgery Nat. Naval Med. Ctr., Bethesda, 1996, chief clin. staff, 1997-99, dep. comdr., 1999-2000; dep. for edn., tng. and pers. Bur. of Medicine, 2000-01; comdg. officer Naval Sch. Health Scis., Bethesda, 2001—02; fleet surgeon Cmdr. in Chief, U.S. Naval Forces, Europe (CINCUSNAVEUR), 2002—. E-mail: davidswade2002@yahoo.com.

WADE, EDWIN LEE, author, lawyer; b. Yonkers, N.Y., Jan. 26, 1932; s. James and Helen Pierce (Kinne) W.; m. Nancy Lou Sells, Mar. 23, 1957; children: James Lee, Jeffrey K. BS, Columbia U., 1954; MA, U. Chgo., 1956; JD, Georgetown U., 1965. Bar: Ill. 1965. Fgn. svc. officer U.S. Dept. State, 1956-57; mktg. analyst Chrysler Internat., S.A., Switzerland, 1957-61; intelligence officer CIA, 1961-63; industry analyst U.S. Internat. Trade Commn., 1963-65; gen. atty. Universal Oil Products Co., Des Plaines, Ill., 1965-72; atty. Amsted Industries, Inc., Chgo., 1972-73; chief counsel dept. gen. svcs. State of Ill., Springfield, 1973-75; sr. atty. U.S. Gypsum Co., Chgo., 1975-84; gen. atty. USG Corp., 1985, corp. counsel, 1986, asst. gen. counsel, 1987, corp. sec., 1987-90, corp. sec., asst. gen. counsel, 1990-93; prin. Edwin L. Wade, 1993-95; instr. Roosevelt U., Chgo., 1995-96. Author: (books) Constitution 2000: A Federalist Proposal for the New Century, 2000, Talking Sense at Century's End: A Barbarous Time...Now What?, 2000; editor: Let's Talk Sense, A Pub. Affairs Newsletter, 1994-98. Fellow Chgo. Bar Assn. (life); mem. ABA, Ill. Bar Assn., Am. Philatelic Soc., Royal Philatelic Soc. Can. Home: 434 Mary Ln Crystal Lake IL 60014-7257 Office: Let's Talk Sense Publishing Co PO Box 6716 Chicago IL 60680-6716 E-mail: edwade@mymailstation.com.

WADE, ERNESTINE, public health nurse; b. Franklin, La., Aug. 18, 1941; d. Phillip and Emma (Bettis) Miller; m. James Wade Jr., Dec. 25, 1965; 1 child, Kevin Troy. ASN, Lamar U., 1980. Nurse asst. U. Tex., Galveston, 1961; pharmacy technician St. Mary Hosp., Port Arthur, Tex., 1963-64, lic. vocat. nurse, 1967-80, RN, 1980-81, Bapt. Hosp., Beaumont, 1981-82, UpJohn Home Health Agy., Port Arthur, 1982-83, Pub. Health Dept., Port Arthur, 1983-96; dir. health Port Arthur City Health Dept., 1996—. Mem. Star Enterprise Corp., Port Arthur, 1996—, UpJohn Healthcare, 1981-83, Port Arthur Ind. Sch. Dist. Head-Start, 1994-96. Mem. Southeast Tex. Nursing Assn. Avocations: reading, walking. Home: 4918 Austin Ave Port Arthur TX 77640-2505 Office: Port Arthur City Health Dept 603 5th St Port Arthur TX 77640-6540

WADE, GLEN, electrical engineer, educator; b. Ogden, Utah, Mar. 19, 1921; s. Lester Andrew and Nellie (Vanderwerff) W.; m. LaRee Bailey, Mar. 20, 1945; children: Kathleen Ann, RaLee, Lisa Jean, Mary Sue. BS in Elec. Engring, U. Utah, 1948, MS, 1949; PhD, Stanford U., 1954. Research group leader, asso. prof. elec. engring. Stanford U., 1955-60; asso. dir. engring., microwave and power tube div. Raytheon Co., 1960-61, asst gen. mgr. research div., 1961-63; dir. Sch. Elec. Engring., Cornell U., 1963-66, J.P. Levis prof. engring., 1963-66; prof. elec. engring. U. Calif. at Santa Barbara, 1966—. Indsl. advisor U. R.I., 1961-63; vis. lectr. Harvard, 1963; cons. to industry, 1956—; vis. prof. Tokyo U., 1971; Fulbright-Hays lectr., Spain, 1972-73; cons. mem. Dept. Def. Adv. Group Electron Devices, 1966-73; Spl. Chair prof. Nat. Taiwan U., 1980-81, internationally renowned fgn. scholar lectureship, 1988; UN vis. prof. Nanjing Inst. Tech., 1986; UN vis. prof. S.E. U. People's Republic of China, 1989, Nat. Com. Sci. and Tech. vis. prof. U. Guanajuato, Mex., 1994—; elected mem. The Electromagnetics Acad., 1990. Editor: Transactions on Electron Devices, 1961-71, IEEE Jour. Quantum Electronics, 1965-68; series editor: Harcourt Brace Jovanovich, 1964—; contbr. articles to profl. jours. U.S. del. Tech. Cooperation Program internat. meeting, 1970. Served with USNR, 1944-46. Recipient ann. award Nat. Electronics Conf., 1959, Outstanding Teaching award Acad. Senate, U. Calif., Santa Barbara, 1977, Prof. of Yr. award U. Calif. at Santa Barbara Mortar Bd. Sr. Honor Soc., 1988, Hon. Chairmanship award Twentieth Acoustical Imaging, 1992, Disting. Alumnus award Engring. Coll. U. Utah, 1998. Fellow IEEE (life; mem. adminstrv. com. profl. group election devices 1960-71, mem. publs. bd., chmn. info. processing com., mem. exec. com. 1971-72, dir. 1971-72, chmn. ednl. activities bd. 1971-72, editor proc. 1977-80, Centennial award 1984, Millennium medal 2000); mem. Am. Phys. Soc., Phi Kappa Phi, Tau Beta Pi, Sigma Xi, Eta Kappa Nu (Outstanding Young Elec. Engr. award 1955) Home: 1098 Golf Rd Santa Barbara CA 93108-2411 E-mail: wade@ece.ucsb.edu.

WADE, JAMES O'SHEA, editor and writer; b. Atlanta, June 17, 1940; s. Richard J. and Mary Clare (O'Shea) W.; m. Linda Norman, June 19, 1971; 1 child, Christopher Scott. AB magna cum laude, Harvard U., 1962. Editor Blaisdell Pub. Co., N.Y.C., 1963-65; asst. to pres., sr. editor Macmillan Co., 1966-69; editor-in-chief World Pub. Co., 1969-71; v.p., editorial dir. David McKay Co., 1971-74; founder, pres. Wade Pub. Co., Inc., N.Y.C., 1975-78; exec. v.p. Rawson, Wade Pubs., Inc., 1978-82; sr. editor Crown Pubs., Inc., 1982-85, exec. editor, 1985-95, v.p., 1988-95; with Ind. Editors Group, 1996—. Mem. Century Club (N.Y.C.), Iroquois/D.U. Club (Harvard), Hasty-Pudding Inst. 1770 (Harvard U.). Democrat. Home and Office: 1565 Baptist Church Rd Yorktown Heights NY 10598-5812 E-mail: jedit@westnet.com.

WADE, JEFFREY LEE, lawyer; b. Louisville, Oct. 5, 1946; s. Louis Harold and Lelia May (Powell) W.; divorced; children: Jody Martin, Betsy Ellen, Anna Lee. BA in Arts and Scis., U. Ky., 1968; MSW, Fla. State U., 1973; JD, U. Louisville, 1982. Bar: Ky. 1982, U.S. Dist. Ct. (we. dist.) Ky. 1985, U.S. Dist. Ct. (ea. dist.) Ky. 1991, U.S. Tax Ct. 1985, U.S. Ct. Appeals (6th cir.) 1985, U.S. Supreme Ct. 1992. Social worker Ky. Dept. Child Welfare, Lexington, 1969-71; cons. Fla. Drug Abuse Program, Tallahassee, 1973; mgmt. cons. Resource Planning Corp., Washington, 1973-75; social worker Ky. Cabinet for Human Resources, Louisville, 1975-79; asst. commonwealth atty. Commonwealth Atty., 46th Jud. Dist., Brandenburg, Ky., 1982-86; asst. county atty. Meade County Atty., 1985-88; atty., assoc. Stone & Darnall, Attys.-at-Law, 1982-83; ptnr. Wade & Darnall, Attys.-at-Law, 1983-92; pvt. practice Jeffrey L. Wade, Atty.-at-Law, 1992-98, Louisville, 1997—. Master commr. Meade Cir. Ct., 1993-97; bd. dirs. Communicare, Inc., Elizabethtown, Ky., chmn., 1996-97. Mem. staff Jour. Family Law, 1980-82; Brandeis brief editor (newspaper) The Louisville Law Examiner, 1980-82. Trustee, tchr. Brandenburg United Meth. Ch., 1985-95; coach Meade County Soccer, Brandenburg, 1987-89, Meade County Little League, Brandenburg, 1982-86; pres. Brandenburg PTO, 1984-86. Recipient fellowship NIMH, 1971, scholarship U. Ky. Med. Sch., 1968, Epidemiol. Rsch. Tng. fellowship U. Ky. Med. Sch., 1968, Trustee scholarship U. Ky., 1964. Mem. ATLA, Louisville Bar Assn., Ky. Acad. Trial Attys. Democrat. Avocations: running, guitar, writing fiction and poetry. Home: 537 S 3rd St #1603 Louisville KY 40202 Office: 623 W Main St Ste 100 Louisville KY 40202-2978 E-mail: wadelaw@bellsouth.net.

WADE, KENNETH ALAN, physician assistant; b. Salt Lake City, Oct. 22, 1948; s. Lester Heber and Carol (Braby) W.; m. Denice Stratford, Dec. 17, 1970; children: Kenneth Andrew, Dennis Curtis, Christopher Aaron. BS, Okla. Univ., 1981, U. Utah, 1973; AS, Weber State Coll., 1971. Staff acct. Elwood & Barnes, CPAs, Salt Lake City, 1973-79; physician asst. U.S. Army, 1979-81, Utah Army Nat. Guard, Salt Lake City, 1981—; affiliate faculty Idaho State U., Pocatello, 1997—. Mgr. Logan (Utah) Med. Ctr., 1983—; adj. instr. U. Utah, Salt Lake City, 1982-87; physician's asst. Logan Woman's Clinic, 1981—. Co-author: Prenatal Development. Bd. dirs. Cache County Sch. Bd., North Logan, 1992-97, Cache Edn. Found., North Logan, 1992—; bd. mem. Cache Valley Boys and Girls Club, 1999—; mem. mgmt. com. Coche Valley Ind. Physicians Assn., 1999—. Fellow Am. Acad. Physician Assts., Utah Acad. Physician Assts.; mem. Assn. Mil. Surgeons U.S. Mem. Ch. Jesus Christ Latter Day Saints. Office: Logan Women's Clinic 550 E 1400 N Ste K Logan UT 84341-2450 Home: 1696 E 2700 S Salt Lake City UT 84106-3661

WADE, MICHAEL ROBERT ALEXANDER, marketing specialist; b. N.Y.C., June 29, 1945; s. Burton Jean and Celia (Handleman) W.; m. Carole Kay West, Aug. 25, 1974. AB, U. Chgo., 1967; postgrad. in pub. adminstrn., Am. U., 1967-71; MBA in Fin., NYU, 1975. Program analyst, mgmt. intern HUD, 1967-71; dep. dir. Mgmt. Comm. and Briefing Ctr. U.S. Price Commn., 1972; asst. exec. sec. policy coordination U.S. Cost of Living Coun., 1973-74; assoc. dir. U.S. Indochina Refugee Program, 1975-76; pres. China Trade Devel. Corp. Chgo., 1977—. Participant with W.R. Grace & Co. in Okla. oil and gas prodn. Recipient Meritorious Svc. award Exec. Office of Pres., 1972, Disting. Svc. award U.S. Cost of Living Coun., 1974. Mem. Soc. Contemporary Art, Internat. Bus. Coun. MidAm. (bd. dirs.). Office: China Trade Devel Corp 2049 Century Park E Ste 480 Los Angeles CA 90067-3117 E-mail: CHINA-TRADE@worldnet.att.net.

WADE, NIGEL, former editor in chief; b. New Zealand; Editor in chief Chgo. Times, 1996—2000. Recipient Ethics in Journ. award, 1999; grantee Nieman Fell., Harvard U. Office: Chgo Sun Times 401 N Wabash Ave Chicago IL 60611-5642*

WADE, REBA, music teacher, pianist; b. Dresden, Tenn., Apr. 30, 1938; d. John Buford and Willie Ruth (Todd) Tilley; m. Ronald Lee Wade, July 22, 1956; children: Tony Lee, Randy Neal. Student, U. Tenn., Martin, 1976-80. Tchr. pvt. studio, Martin, 1962-70, 76—, Sharon (Tenn.) Sch., 1968, Westview H.S., Martin, 1976--79, Greenfield (Tenn.) Sch., 1984-86; mgr., dir. Wade Bros., Martin, 1965-71, High Variety Show Mems., Martin, 1994—. Tchr., accompanist for students, shows, groups, auditions and on radio and TV; profl. pianist; judge Music Festival U. Tenn., Martin, Tenn., 2000, 2001. Prodr. Wade Bros. Rec., 1969, student recs., 1988-90, 97-2002; author lyrics, music original compositions including Little Cowboy, 1963, I Love My Jesus, 1963, Christmas Time, 1964, Happy Happy Day, 1964, Love, 1964, Oh How I Love You, 1965, Dear Mis-Fortune, 1965, Red Lace, 1965, Crazy Little Feeling, 1967, All Because of Christmas Day, 1968, Mean Mean Mama, 1968, God is Like This, 1979, Little Dreams, 1992, also tnr., prodr., 1988-90, 97-2001; performer Christmas music The White House, 1997-98, Pentagon Party, 1998; performer World Wide Air Show RAF, Fairford, Eng., London, 1999; recorded 3CDs (total 32 songs and pieces on piano), Nasville, Tenn., 2000, 2001; recorded 18 songs and pieces on piano, Hilltop Recording Studio, Nashville, Tenn., 2000, 12 others, 2001; prodr. five recording sessions Hilltop Recording Studio, Nashville, tenn., 2000; tnr. students Cerebral Palsy Telethon WBBJ TV, Jackson, Tenn., 1995-2002. Active in civic affairs, 1947--; judge music festival U. Tenn., Martin, 2000-01, fall performance, 2000-01, Kiwanis Club Talent Show, 2000-01; active Martin Elem. Chorus, 2001; fundraiser Big Cypress Tree State Park, 2000-01, Dickson (Tenn.) Police Dept., 2000, Relay for Life, 1992--; planner, tnr. fund raiser program local fire dept. to buy new fire truck, 2000, entertainment fund raiser local town to install new lights in town, 2000. Recipient Vol. Svc. award State of Tenn. Recreation and Parks Assn., 2001; selected for the crowning of ABI World Laureate; nominated for Am. medal of Honor, 2002; recipient Companion of Honor award, 2002. Mem. SAI (life, social chmn. 1979), Songwriters Guild Am., Music Tchrs. Nat. Assn., Philharm. Music Club (v.p. 1983-84, pres. 1985), Am. Coll. Musicians, Dem. Women. Baptist. Avocations: music writing, interior decorating and designing, travel, church and charity work, political and military entertaining. Home: 208 Melody Dr Martin TN 38237-5535 Fax: 731-588-0860. E-mail: ronniewade@citlink.net.

WADE, REYNOLDS, artist; b. Jasper, Ny, June 5, 1929; Instr. Acad. of Art Coll., San Francisco, 1996—98, Art Inst. of So. Calif., Laguna, Calif., 1997—. One-man shows include Palace of The Legion of Honor, Copenhagen Gallery, Santa Barbara Museum, Palm Springs Gallery, Zachary Waller Gallery, exhibitions include Louis Newman Gallery, Louis Newman Gallary, Haggin Museum; Wade Reynolds Retrospective Louis Newman Gallery, Gallery Henoch, Oklahoma Art Center Museum; Selections from the Ellen And Jerome Westheimer Collection, Gallery Henoch, Louis Newman Gallery, Louis Newman Gallery; Gallery Henoch; Leslie Levy Gallery, Opening Statements: A Group Exhibition, A Survey of Figurative Painting in Los Angeles; Let The Games Begin; Art and The Athlete, Body Language: Current Figurative Painters, Academy of Art Faculty Exhibition, Art Faculty; Passion and Patronage: The Robert A Rowan Collection, Drawings & Paintings, Representing Representation; Faculty Show, Fourth Annual Realism Invitational, Santa Barbara Museum, James Corcoran Gallery, Official Portrait of Governor Deukmejian, Cleveland Museum of Art, Times Mirror Corporation, Miami Institute of Fine Art, Art Institute of Southern California, Pate Gallery of Male Form, numerous private collections.

WADE, ROBERT ALAN, lawyer; b. Coronado, Calif., July 10, 1955; s. John William and Betty Lou (Schrader) W.; m. Barbara Louise Waters, June 18, 1977 (div.); children: John Robert, Matthew Waters; m. Eileen L. Guest, Sept. 24, 1990; stepchildren: Nathaniel Craig, Adrian Louise. BA, Coll. William and Mary, 1977; JD magna cum laude, Harvard U., 1980. Bar: Pa. 1980, U.S. Dist. Ct. (ea. dist.) Pa. 1980. Assoc. Schnader, Harrison, Segal & Lewis, Phila., 1980-85, Kalogredis Law Assocs., Ltd., Wayne, Pa., 1985; ptnr. Kalogredis & Wade Law Assocs., 1986-89, Beck & Anders Law Assocs., Plymouth Meeting, Pa., 1989-93, Wade, Goldstein, Landau & Abruzzo, PC, Berwyn, 1993—. Lectr., cons. and spkr. in field. Contbr. articles to profl. jours. Spkr. to various civic, local, and nat. groups. Mem. ABA, Pa. Bar Assn. (com. on profl. responsibility and legal ethics 1987-96), Phila. Bar Assn. (mem. sect. on probate trust law, office practices com. 1981-86). Democrat. Presbyterian. Home: 4020 Prospect Hill Ln Pottstown PA 19464-2245 Office: Wade Goldstein Landau & Abruzzo PC 61 Cassatt Ave Berwyn PA 19312-1325

WADE, ROBERT GLENN, engineering executive; b. Sturgeon, Mo., Nov. 21, 1933; s. Robert Clifford and Mildred Guinn (Bartee) W.; m. Geraldine Harris, Dec. 27, 1959; 1 child, Carolyn Ruth. BSCE, U. Mo., 1955. Registered profl. engr., Mo., Kans. Structural engr. Carter-Waters Corp., Kansas City, Mo., 1958-62; project mgr. Pfuhl & Stevson, 1962-76; prin. Stevson-Hall & Wade, Inc., 1976-82; pres. Structural Engring. Assocs., Inc., 1982-85, chmn., CEO, 1985-98. Mem. Mo. Bd. Architects, Engrs. and Land Surveyors, 1992-2000; mem. Midwest Concrete Industry Bd., pres., 1975-76. Co-author: Quality Assurance for Consulting Engineers, 1986. Com. mem. Downtown Coun., Kansas City, 1990. 1st lt. USAF, 1956-58. Recipient 1st Merit award Midwest Concrete Industry Bd., 1976, award of excellence Am. Inst. Steel Constrn., 1982, Excellence in Design award Prestressed Concrete Inst., 1988, Disting. Svc. award Nat. Coun. of Examiners for Engring. and Surveying, 2001. Fellow ASCE (pres. Kansas City sect. 1986-87, Leadership award 1987); mem. Am. Cons. Engrs. Coun. (firm rep., bd. dirs. 1987-88), Cons. Engrs. Coun. Mo. (firm rep., pres. 1986-87, Svc. award 1987). Avocation: golf. Office: Structural Engring Assocs 101 W 11th St Kansas City MO 64105-1803 E-mail: rwade4@kc.rr.com.

WADE, RODGER GRANT, information technology consultant, greenhouse owner; b. Littlefield, Tex., June 25, 1945; s. George and Jimmie Frank (Grant) W.; m. Karla Kay Morrison, Dec. 18, 1966 (div. 1974); children: Eric Shawn, Shannon Annelle, Shelby Elaine; m. Carol Ruth Manning, Mar. 28, 1981. BA in Sociology, Tex. Tech. U., 1971. Programmer First Nat. Bank, Lubbock, Tex., 1971-73, Nat. Sharedata Corp., Odessa, 1973; asst. dir. computing ctr. Odessa Community Coll., 1973-74; programmer/analyst Med. Sci. Ctr., Tex. Tech U., Lubbock, 1974-76; sys. mgr. Hosp. Info. Sys., Addison, Tex., 1976-78; programmer, analyst Harris Corp., Grapevine, 1978-80, Joy Petroleum, Waxahachie, 1980-82; owner R&C Bus. Sys./Requerdos de Santa Fe, N.Mex., 1982-84; fin. sys. analyst Los Alamos (N.Mex.) Tech. Assocs., 1984-95; cons. mngr. Unidata Corp., Denver, 1995-98; cons. Interlink Group, 1998-99; owner/cons. R.G. Wade Cons., 2000—; owner/mgr. Bear Paws Farm Greenhouse, 2002—. Owner El Rancho Herbs, Santa Fe, 1988-91, Wade Gallery, Santa Fe, 1990-91, R.G. Wade Cons., Westminster, Colo., 1998—, Bear Paws Farm Greenhouse, 2002--. Vol. programmer Los Alamos Arts Coun., 1987-88; mem. regulations task force N.Mex. Gov.'s Health Policy Adv. Com.; vol. systems support Amigos Unidos of Taos, 1990-95. Democrat. Avocation: photography. Home and Office: 6060 N Schumaker Rd Bennett CO 80102-9150 E-mail: rodger@rgwade.com.

WADE, SUZANNE, principal consultant; b. Chgo., Dec. 29, 1938; d. Edward Peter and Dorothy Rose Traxel; m. Robert Gerald Wade (dec.); children: Peter John, Robert Gerald Jr., Suzette Marie, Francesca Louise Felde, Elizabeth Rose Quigley. AA, Orange Coast Coll., 1980; BA, Calif. State U., Fullerton, 1985. Data analyst Motorola, Mesa, Ariz., 1972-75; prodn. planner Ford Aerospace, Newport Beach, Calif., 1975-79; supr. prodn. control Shiley, Inc., Irvine, 1979-81; mgr. bus. systems Hughes Aircraft Co., Fullerton, 1981-85; systems adminstr. Long Beach, Calif., 1985-89; cons. IBM, Gaithersburg, Md., 1989-94; computer assoc. project mgr., U.S. Mint IFMS project mgr. Bur. Engraving and Printing; mng. prin. cons. Oracle Corp., 1996-2000; prin. CSC Consulting, Atlanta, 2000—. Lectr. Calif. State U., Fullerton, 1984-85; speaker in field. Author: Data Services, 1985; columnist, 1984-85. Mem. Am. Prodn. and Inventory Control Soc. (editor Digest 1990-91), L.A. Aerospace and Def. Spl. Interest Group (editor Digest 1987-90), Toastmasters (treas. Long Beach 1986). Roman Catholic. Avocations: photography, acting, interior decorating, crafts, quilting. Home: Apt 103 1861 Old Meadow Rd Mc Lean VA 22102-1993 Office: CSC 3170 Fairview Park Dr Falls Church VA 22042

WADE, THOMAS EDWARD, electrical engineering educator, university research administrator; b. Jacksonville, Fla., Sept. 14, 1943; s. Wilton Fred and Alice Lucyle (Hedge) W.; m. Ann Elizabeth Chitty, Aug. 6, 1966; children: Amy Renee, Nathan Thomas, Laura Ann. BSEE, U. Fla., Gainesville, 1966, MSEE, 1968, PhD, 1974. Cert. rsch. adminstr., 1992. Interim asst. prof. U. Fla., Gainesville, 1974-76; prof. elec. engring. Miss. State U., Starkville, 1976-85; state-wide dir. microelectronics rsch. lab. Miss., 1978-85; assoc. dean, prof. elec. engring. U. South Fla., Tampa, 1985—. Dir. Engring. Indsl. Experiment Sta., 1986-93, exec. dir. Ctrs. for Engring. R&D, 1985-90, mem. presdl. faculty adv. com. for rsch. and tech. devel., 1986-88, mem. fed. demonstration project com. for contracts and grants, 1986-88; mem. adv. bd. USF Exec. Fellows Program, 1987-91; chmn. evaluation task force applied rsch. grants program High Tech. and Industry Coun. State of Fla., 1988-90, vice chmn. microelectronics and materials subcoms. 1987-93, mem. telecom. subcom., 1988-89, chmn. legis. report com. FHTIC, 1989-90, chmn. U. sabbatical com., 1997-98; vice chmn. subcom. on microelectronics and materials Enterprise Fla. Innovation Partnership, 1993-94, chmn. univ. sabbatical com., 1997-98; mem. Tampa Bay Internat. Super Task Force, 1986-92, vice chmn. edn. com. 1988; dir. Fla. Ctr. for Microelectronics Design and Test, 1986-88; bd. dirs. NASA Ctr. Comml. Devel. of Space Comm. Ctr., Fla., 1990-93; bd. trustees Trinity Coll. Fla., 1997—, exec. com. 1998—, chmn. strategic planning com., 2001-; bd. trustees Toccoa Falls Coll., 2002; bd. dirs. New Tampa YMCA; rev. panel govt.-univ.-industry rsch. round table for fed. demonstration project NAS, 1988; solid state circuit specialist Applied Micro-circuits Corp., San Diego, 1981-82; sr. scientist NASA Marshall Space Flight Ctr., Huntsville, Ala., 1983; scientist Trilogy Semiconductor Corp., Santa Clara, Calif., 1984; organizer, chmn. Very Large Scale Integrated/Ultra Large Scale Integrated Multilevel Interconnection Conf., Seminar and Exhbn., editor procs., 1991—; organizer, gen. chmn. Dielectrics for Ultra Large Scale Integrated Multilevel Interconnection Conf., 1995—, Chem.-Mech.-Polish Planarization for Ultra Large Scale Integration, 1996—, Conductors for Ultra Large Scale Integrated Multilevel Interconnection Conf., 2000—; cons. in field. Author: Polyimides for Very Large Scale Integrated Applications, 1984, (U.S. Army handbook) Modern Very Large Scale Integrated Circuit Fabrication Processes, 1984, Photosensitive Polyimides for Very Large Scale Integrated Applications, 1986, Very Large Scale Multilevel Interconnection Advanced Metals Tutorial, 1996—, Very Large Scale Multilevel Interconnection Tutorial, 1987—; contr. chpts. on electronics to World Book encys., 1997; contbr. over 125 articles to profl. jours. Active First Bapt. Ch., Temple Terrace, Fla., vice-chmn. bd. deacons 1989-90, chmn. bd. deacons, 1990-91, 93-94, chmn. pastor search com., 1990-91, vice-chmn. long range planning com., 1989-91, vice-chmn. pastor search com., 1994-95, dir. adult coed III Sunday sch. dept., 1993-94, ch. coun., 1994-95, ch. trustee, 1999—, mem. constn. and bylaws com., 1997-99, trustee, 1999—; treas. Tampa Palms Owners Assn., 1994-95, chmn. home decorating com., 1997; vol., United Fund, Miss. State U., 1983-85. Recipient Outstanding Engrng. Tchg. award Coll. Engrng. U. Fla., 1976, Outstanding Tchg. Incentive program award State of Fla., 1998, Cert. of Recognition NASA (5 times), 1981-88, Outstanding Rsch. award Sigma Xi, 1984, Outstanding Contbn. to Sci. and Tech. award Fla. Gov., 1989, 90, Outstanding Undergrad. Tchg. award U. South Fla., 1999. Mem. AAAS, NSPE, IEEE (sr. mem., guest editor periodical 1982, gen. chmn. Internat. Very Large Scale Integrated Multilevel Interconnection Conf. annually 1984-90, editor conf. procs., 1984-90, chmn. acad. affairs com. CHMT Soc., 1984-86, gen. chmn. univ./govt./industry microelectronics symposium, 1981, tech. program commn., 1991, bd. dirs. workshop on tungsten and other refractory metals 1987-90), Am. Soc. Engrng. Edn. (gen. chmn. engrng. rsch. coun. ann. meeting 1987, chmn. engrng. rsch. coun. adminstrv. com. 1987-90, chmn. coun., 1990-92, session chmn. ann. meeting 1990, 92, bd. dirs. 1990-92, mem. nominations com. 1992-94, mem. long range planning com. 1992-95, Centennial Cert. 1992, 2d Century Cert. 1993), World Future Soc. Internat. Soc. Hybrid Microelectronics, Assn. U.S. Army (bd. dir. Suncoast chpt. 1991-93), Soc. Photo Optical Instrumentation Engrng., Univ. Faculty Senate Assn. of Miss. (organizer 1985), Am. Vacuum Soc., Am. Phs. Soc., Am. Electronics Assn., Am. Inst. Physics, Nat. Coun. Univ. Rsch. Adminstrn., Soc. Rsch. Adminstrs (external rels. com. for SRA 1988-91), Fla. Engrng. Soc. (v.p. edn. com. 1987-92, pres. 1989-90, bd. dirs. 1989-90, Fla. engrng. found. trustee 1989-90, ann. meeting steering com. 1989-90, Outstanding Svc. to the Profession award 1992), Soc. Am. Mil. Engrng., Order of Engrs., 1991, Sigma Xi (v.p. 1985), Tau Beta Pi (Fla. Alpha chpt. pres. 1969, 71, faculty advisor Miss. Alpha chpt. 1977-85, faculty advisor Fla. Gamma chpt. 1986—, Outstanding hon. soc. advisor award 1994), Eta Kappa Nu (pres. U. Fla. chpt. 1968, Org. Charter Chpt. U. South Fla. 1998, faculty adv. Kappa Xi chpt. 1998—, Outstanding Honor Soc. Adv. award 1998-99), Sigma Tau, Omicron Delta Kappa, Soc. Am. Inventors, Fla. Blue Key (v.p. 1972, sec. 1971), Epsilon Lambda Chi (founder 1970, pres. 1971). Club: Downtown Tampa Rotary (Paul Harris fellow 1987,94, 2000, perfect attendance award 1986—, chmn. com. on environ. issues 1990), Rotary Club New Tampa (organizer, charter mem., pres. 1995-96, v.p. 1996-97, mem. exec. com. 1996—, dir. internat. svc. 1997-98, sr. dir. 1998-99, 99-2001). Avocations: collecting antique furniture, carpentry, restoring antique sports cars, basketball. Home: 5316 Witham Ct E Tampa FL 33647-1026

WADE, WILLIAM ALLEN, trust company-private bank executive; b. Ft. Wayne, Ind., Feb. 3, 1953; s. Edward G. and Melva (O'Shaughnessey) W.; m. Ruth Ann Lachot, Sept. 25, 1976; children: Phillip, Jonathan. BS in BA, Ind. U., Ft. Wayne, 1975. Cert. fin. planner. Asst. v.p. investments Lincoln Nat. Bank & Trust, Ft. Wayne, 1975-78; v.p. portfolio mgmt. Huntington Nat. Bank, Columbus, Ohio, 1978; v.p., reg. mgr. investments Banc Ohio Nat. Bank, Akron, 1979-83; v.p. investments Fla. Nat. Bank, Palm Beach, Fla., 1983-87; sr. v.p., city mgr. C&S/Sovran Trust Co., Sarasota, 1987-91; sr. v.p., region trust mgr. NationsBank Trust, Raleigh, N.C., 1992-93; sr. v.p., region mgr. Barnett Banks Trust Co., Sarasota, 1993-97; pres. Marshall & Ilsley Trust Co. Fla., Naples, 1998—. Bd. dirs. Fellowship Christian Athletes, Palm Beach, 1985-87; mem. adv. bd. Sarasota Meml. Hosp. Found., 1988-96; trustee Sarasota Cmty. Found., 1989-92. Mem. Internat. Assn. Fin. Planning, Inst. Cert. Fin. Planners, Kiwanis. Republican. Presbyterian. Home: 308 Wentworth Ct Naples FL 34104-6535 Office: Marshall & Ilsley Trust Co Fla 800 Laurel Oak Dr Ste 101 Naples FL 34108-2737

WADIBIA, EMMANUEL CHUMA, medicine and pharmacy educator; b. Aba, Nigeria, Mar. 21, 1959; s. Frederick Wambu and Gladys Wadibia; m. Carol Jean Wadibia; children: Ashely, Jason, Christopher. BS in Pharmacy, Creighton U., 1983, MBA, 1986, DPharm, 1994. Fellow in cardiology Creighton U., Omaha, 1995; prof. medicine and pharmacy Auburn (Ala.) U., 1996, U. South Ala. Coll. Medicine, Mobile, 1996—; pres., CEO Wadibia Network Cos., Inc. Mem. editl. bd. So. Med. Jour.; contbr. articles to sci. and profl. jours. Mem. Am. Coll. Clin. Pharmacy, Am. Soc. Hosp. Pharmacists, So. Med. Assn., Beta Gamma Sigma. Avocations: tennis, classical music, golf, swimming, fishing. Office: PO Box 266 Mobile AL 36601

WADLER, ARNOLD L. lawyer, retired; b. Bklyn., Aug. 15, 1943; s. Samuel and Anne (Lowenthal) W.; m. Elissa I. Devor, Sept. 17, 1967; children: Craig A., Todd J. BA, Bklyn. Coll., 1964; JD, NYU, 1967. Bar: N.Y. 1968, N.J. 1974. Asst. gen. counsel Metromedia, Inc., N.Y.C., 1968-82, assoc. gen. counsel L.A., 1982-85, v.p., gen. counsel Secaucus, N.J., 1985-86, sr. v.p., gen. counsel, sec. East Rutherford, 1986—2000, ret., 2000. Pres., S&A Restaurant Corp., East Rutherford, 1992; exec. v.p., gen. counsel, sec. Metromedia Internat. Group, Inc., 1995; exec. v.p., gen. counsel, sec. Micromedia Fiber Network Inc., 1997, Big City Radio, Inc., also bd. dirs. Mem. Zoning Bd. Adjustment, Marlboro Twp., N.J., 1980-82; exec. v.p. Marlboro Jewish Ctr., 1980-82. Mem. ABA, N.Y. Bar Assn., KP (asst. sec. 1961-63). Office: Metromedia Co Met Exec Towers 1 Meadowlands Plz Fl 6 East Rutherford NJ 07073-2100

WADLER, GARY I. physician, consultant; b. N.Y.C., Jan. 12, 1939; s. Samuel and Anne (Lowenthal) W.; m. Nancy Royce, Mar. 15, 1947; children: David, Erika. MD, Cornell U., 1964. Pvt. practice, Manhasset, 1979—; attending physician North Shore U. Hosp., 1997-2001. Med. advisor Office Nat. Drug Control Policy, Washington, 2000--; mem. health medicine and rsch. com. World Anti-Doping Agy., 2000--; mem. sci. com. U.S. Anti-Doping Agy., 2000-01. Author: (textbook) Drugs and the Athlete, 1989 (Internat. Olympic Com. Pres.'s prize 1993). Chmn. Nassau County Sports Commn., 1991--. Capt. USAR, 1965-68. Recipient Pres.'s prize Women's Sports Found., 1993. Fellow ACP, Am. Coll. Clin. Pharmacology, Am. Coll. Preventive Medicine, Am. Coll. Sports Medicine (chmn. health and sci. policy com. 1994-2000). Avocations: tennis, travel. Office: 1380 Northern Blvd Manhasset NY 11030 Fax: 516-365-4427. E-mail: wosportgiw@aol.com.

WADLEY, M. RICHARD, consumer products executive; b. Lehi, Utah; s. Merlyn R. and Verla Ann (Ball) W.; m. Nancy Zwiers; children: Lisa Kathleen, Staci Lin, Eric Richard, Nicole Marie. BS, Brigham Young U., 1967; MBA, Northwestern U., 1968. Brand asst. packaged soap and detergent divsn. Procter & Gamble Co., Cin., 1968-69, asst. brand mgr. packaged soap and detergent divsn., 1970-71, brand mgr. Dawn detergent, 1972-73, copy supr. packaged soap and detergent divsn., 1974-75, brand mgr. Tide detergent, 1975-77, assoc. advt. mgr. packaged soap and detergent divsn., 1977-81; corp. product dir. Hallmark Cards, Inc., Kansas City, Mo., 1982-83; corp. product dir. Ambassador Cards divsn. Hallmark Cards, Inc., 1983-85; v.p., gen. mgr. feminine protection divsn. Tambrands Inc., Lake Success, N.Y., 1986-88; sr. v.p. Bongrain, Inc., N.Y.C., 1988-89; pres., CEO Alta-Dena Inc., Divsn. of Bongrain, Inc., 1989-91; pres. The Summit Group, 1991-93; chmn., CEO, bd. dirs. T-Chem Products Inc., 1993-99; CEO The Bayshore Group, 1999—. Bd. dirs. Legacy Interactive, Funosophy, Inc. Bd. dirs. Long Beach Opera, 1991-95, L.I. Friends of the Arts, 1986-88; mem. adv. bd. Bus. Sch. Calif. State U., Long Beach, 1991-93. Avocations: Civil War history, tennis, travel. E-mail: rwbayshore@aol.com.

WADLEY, SUSAN SNOW, anthropologist; b. Balt., Nov. 18, 1943; d. Chester Page and Ellen Snow (Foster) W.; m. Bruce Woods Derr, Dec. 28, 1971 (div. July 1989); children: Shona Snow, Laura Woods; m. Richard Olanoff, July 4, 1992. BA, Carleton Coll., Northfield, 1965; MA, U. Chgo., 1967, PhD, 1973. Instr. Syracuse U., 1970-73, asst. prof., 1973-76, dir. fgn. and comparative studies program, 1978-83, prof., 1982, dir. So. Asia Ctr., 1985—, Ford-Maxwell prof. South Asian Studies, 1996—, chair anthropology dept., 1990-95. Trustee Am. Inst. Indian Studies, Chgo., 1984—, exec. com., 1991-94; mem. joint com. South Asia Social Sci. Rsch. Coun., 1982-89. Author: Shakti: Power in the Conceptual Struture of Krimpur Women, 1975, Women in India: Two Perspectives, 1978, revised, 1989, 95, Struggling with Destiny in Karimpur, 1925-84, 1994; editor: Power of Tamil Women, 1980, Oral Epics in India, 1989, Media and the Transformation of Religion in South Asia, 1995. Pres. Edward Smith Parent Tchr. Orgn., Syracuse, 1988-89; pres. bd. dirs. Open Hand Internat. Mask and Puppet Mus., 2000—. Grantee NSF, 1967-69, U.S. Dept. Edn., 1983-84, Smithsonian Instn., 1983-84, Am. Inst. Indian Studies, 1989, Social Scis. Rsch. Coun., 1989, NEH, 1995, 98. Mem. Am. Anthropological Soc., Am. Folklore Soc., Assn. for Asian Studies. Home: 302 Carlton Dr Syracuse NY 13214-1906 Office: Syracuse U Maxwell Sch Syracuse NY 13244-0001 Business E-Mail: sswadley@maxwell.syr.edu.

WADLEY, W(ILLIAM) THOMAS, lawyer; b. Tampa, Fla., Aug. 3, 1957; s. William Morrill Wadley and Allison Ray. BA, Auburn U., 1979; JD, Stetson U., 1981. Bar: Fla. 1982, U.S. Dist. Ct. (mid. dist.) Fla. 1982, U.S. Ct. Appeals (11th cir.) 1988; bd. cert. criminal trial lawyer Fla. Bar, 1994—; bd. cert. criminal trial adv. Nat. Bd. Trial Advocacy, 1998—. Lawyer Myron J. Mensh P.A., St. Petersburg, Fla., 1982-84, Yanchuck, Thompson, Young & Berman, St. Petersburg, 1984-90, Rahdert & Anderson, St. Petersburg, 1990-91; pvt. practice law, 1991-95, Yanchuck, Berman, Wadley & Zervos, 1995—. Pres. Pinellas County Criminal Def. Lawyers Assn., 1996. Mem. ATLA, Nat. Assn. Criminal Def. Lawyers, Fla. Assn. Criminal Def. Lawyers. Avocation: private pilot. Home: 231 8th Ave N Saint Petersburg FL 33701-2405 Office: Yanchuck Berman Wadley and Zervos 5453 Ctrl Ave Saint Petersburg FL 33710-

WADLINGTON, W. M. retired commodity futures trader; b. Madisonville, Ky., Oct. 28, 1944; s. W. Milton and Ellen Christine (Bryan) W.; m. Anne R. Lewis, Apr. 29, 1979; children: Andrew Stephen, Michael Edward, Thomas Scott. BA, Vanderbilt U., 1967. Commd. 2d lt. U.S. Army, 1967, advanced through grades to capt., 1970, field artillery officer, 1967-78, resigned, 1978; chmn. ChartBook.com, Ltd., San Diego, 1994-98; commodity futures trader, 1978-98; ret., 1998. Pres. Scripps Ranch Villages, 1998—; trustee LaJolla Country Day Sch., 2000—. Decorated Silver Star. Republican. Avocations: ancient languages, computer programming, opera, weightlifting, running. Home: 10981 Twinleaf Ct San Diego CA 92131-3643 E-mail: jack.wadlington@worldnet.att.net.

WADLINGTON, WALTER JAMES, law educator; b. Biloxi, Miss., Jan. 17, 1931; s. Walter and Bernice (Taylor) Wadlington; m. Ruth Miller Hardie, Aug. 20, 1955; children: Claire, Charlotte, Ian, Susan, Derek Alan. AB, Duke U., 1951; LLB, Tulane U., 1954. Bar: La. 1954, Va. 1965. Pvt. practice, New Orleans, 1954—55, 1958—59; asst. prof. Tulane U., 1960—62; mem. faculty U. Va., 1962—, prof law, 1964—, James Madison prof., 1970—2002, James Madison prof. emeritus, 2002—; prof. legal medicine U. Va. Med. Sch., 1979—2002; Harrison Found. rsch. prof. U. Va., 1990—92. Tutor civil law U. Edinburgh, Scotland, 1959—60; vis. Tazewell Taylor prof. law Coll. William and Mary, 1986; program dir. Robert Wood Johnson Med. Malpractice Program, 1985—91; mem. adv. com. Robert Wood Johnson clin. scholars program, 1989—97; chmn. nat. adv. bd. Improving Malpractice Prevention and Compensation Sys., 1994—98; Disting. Health Law Tchr. Am. Soc. Law, Medicine and Ethics; trustee-at-large Edn. Commn. Fgn. Med. Grads., 1998—. Author (with O. Brien): Cases and Materials on Domestic Relations, 1970, 5th edit., 2002, Family Law in Perspective, 2001; author: (with Waltz and Dworkin) Cases and Materials on Law and Medicine, 1980; editor-in-chief: Tulane U. Law Rev., 1953—54; author (Davis, Scott, and Whitebread): Children in the Legal System, 2d edit., 1997. Scholar Fulbright scholar, U. Edinburgh, 1959—60. Mem.: Am. Law Inst., Inst. of Medicine of NAS, Found. Advancement Internat. Med. Edn. and Rsch. (bd. mem., sec. 2001—). Home: 1620 Keith Valley Rd Charlottesville VA 22901-3018 Office: U Va Sch Law 580 Massie Rd Charlottesville VA 22903-1738 E-mail: wjw@virginia.edu.

WADLINGTON, WARWICK PAUL, English language educator; BS, U.S. Mil. Acad., 1961; MA, Tulane U., 1966, PhD, 1967. Asst. prof. English U. Tex., Austin, 1967-72, assoc. prof., 1972-78, prof., 1978—, Joan Negley Kelleher Centennial prof., 1987—2001, emeritus, 2002—. Author: The Confidence Game in American Literature, 1975, Reading Faulknerian Tragedy, 1987, As I Lay Dying: Stories Out of Stories, 1992; contbr. articles to profl. jours. With U.S. Army, 1961-64. Decorated Air medal. Office: U Tex Dept English Austin TX 78712

WADLOW, JOAN KRUEGER, academic administrator; b. LeMars, Iowa, Aug. 21, 1932; d. R. John and Norma I. (IhLe) Krueger; m. Richard R. Wadlow, July 27, 1958; children: Dawn, Kit. BA, U. Nebr., Lincoln, 1953; MA (Seacrest Journalism fellow 1953-54), Fletcher Sch. Law and Diplomacy, 1956; PhD (Rotary fellow 1956-57), U. Nebr., Lincoln, 1963; cert., Grad. Inst. Internat. Studies, Geneva, 1957. Mem. faculty U. Nebr., Lincoln, 1966-79, prof. polit. scis., 1964-79, assoc. dean Coll. Arts and Scis., 1972-79; prof. polit. scis., dean Coll. Arts and Scis., U. Wyo., Laramie, 1979-84, v.p. acad. affairs, 1984-86; prof. polit. sci., provost U. Okla., Norman, 1986-91; chancellor U. Alaska, Fairbanks, 1991-99. Cons. on fed. grants; bd. dirs. Alaska Sea Life Center, Key Bank Alaska; mem. Commn. Colls. N.W. Assn.; pres. Lan Constrn., Inc., 1999—; bd. dirs. Sanitary Dist. Author articles in field. Bd. dirs. Nat. Merit Scholarship Corp., 1988-97, Lincoln United Way, 1976-77, Bryan Hosp., Lincoln, 1978-79, Washington Ctr., 1986-99, Key Bank of Alaska, Alaska SeaLife Ctr.; v.p., exec. commr. North Cen. Assn., pres., 1991; univ. pres. mission to Isreal, 1998; pres. adv. bd. Lincoln YWCA, 1970-71; mem. def. adv. com. Women in the Svcs., 1987-89; mem. community adv. bd. Alaska Airlines; mem. Univ. Pres.'s Mission to Israel, 1998; mem. bd. commrs. San. Dist., 2002--. Recipient Mortar Board Teaching award, 1976, Disting. Teaching award U. Nebr., Lincoln, 1979, Rotary Internat. Alumni Scholar Achievement award, 1998; fellow Conf. Coop. Man, Lund, Sweden, 1956 Mem. NCAA (divsn. II pres. coun. 1997-99), Internat. Studies Assn. (co-editor Internat. Studies Notes 1978-91), Nat. Assn. State Univs. and Land-Grant Colls. (exec. com. coun. acad. affairs 1989-91, chair internat. affairs counsel 1996-97), Western Assn. Africanists (pres. 1980-82), Assn. Western Univs. (pres. 1993), Coun. Colls. Arts and Scis. (pres. 1983-84), Greater Fairbanks C. of C., Gamma Phi Beta. Republican. Congregationalist. E-mail: wadlow.oregon.vos.edu. Address: Chancellor Emerita PO Box 246 Oceanside OR 97134-0246

WADMAN, WILLIAM WOOD, III, educational director, technical research executive, consulting company executive; b. Oakland, Calif., Nov. 13, 1936; s. William Wood, Jr., and Lula Fay (Raisner) W.; children: Roxanne Alyce Wadman Hubbling, Raymond Alan (dec.), Theresa Hope Wadman Boudreaux; m. Barbara Jean Wadman; stepchildren: Denise Ellen Varine Skrypkar, Brian Ronald Varine. M.A., U. Calif., Irvine, 1978. Cert. program mgr. tng. Radiation safety specialist, accelerator health physicist U. Calif. Lawrence Berkeley Lab., 1957-68; campus radiation safety officer U. Calif., Irvine, 1968-79; dir. ops., radiation safety officer Radiation Sterilizers, Inc., Tustin, Calif., 1979-80; prin., pres. Wm. Wadman & Assocs. Inc., 1980—; mem. operational review team Princeton U. Rsch. Campus TOKOMAK Fusion Test Facility, 1993-94; technical project mgr. for upgrades projects Los Alamos Nat. Lab. 1994-96, tech. project mgr. for 3 projects, 1995—; mem. team No. 1, health physics appraisal program NRC, 1980—, operational readiness review team to Princeton U. Rsch. Campus TOKOMAK Fusion Test Facility, 1993-94; cons. health physicist to industry; lectr. sch. social ecology, 1974-79, dept. community and environ. medicine U. Calif., Irvine, 1979-80, instr. in environ. health and safety, 1968-79, Orange Coast Coll., in radiation exposure reduction design engrng. Iowa Electric Light & Power; trainer Mason & Hanger-Silas Mason Co., Los Alamos Nat. Lab.; instr. in medium energy cyclotron radiation safety UCLBL, lectr. in accelerator health physics, 1966, 67; curriculum developer in field; subject matter expert Los Alamos Nat. Lab., Earth and Environ. Scis., Tech. Support Office. Active Cub Scouts; chief umpire Mission Viejo Little League, 1973. Served with USNR, 1955-63. Recipient award for profl. achievement U. Calif. Alumni Assn., 1972, Outstanding Performance award U. Calif., Irvine, 1973. Mem. Health Physics Soc. (treas. 1979-81, editor proc. 11th symposium, pres. So. Calif. chpt. 1977, Professionalism award 1975), Internat. Radiation Protection Assn. (U.S. del. 4th Congress 1977, 8th Congress 1992), Am. Nuclear Soc., Am. Public Health Assn. (chmn. program 1978, chmn. radiol. health sect. 1979-80), Campus Radiation Safety Officers (chmn. 1975, editor proc. 5th conf. 1975), ASTM, Project Mgmt. Inst. Club: UCI Univ. (dir. 1976, sec. 1977, treas. 1978). Contbr. articles to tech. jours. Achievements include research in radiation protection and environmental sciences; Avocations: sailing, Tae Kwon Do, wood working, numesmantics. Home: 3687 Red Cedar Way Lake Oswego OR 97035-3525 Office: 675 Fairview Dr Ste 246 Carson City NV 89701-5428 *Personal philosophy: The continuous practice of patience, openmindedness, and open communication provide the essential ingredients for a full, satisfying personal and professional life. The timing of major decisions is not a matter of heart, but the culmination of the effective use of the practices above.*

WADSWORTH, DEBORAH, foundation administrator; b. New York, Dec. 25, 1938; d. Aaron Samuel and Lillian Cohn Yohalem; m. Robert Belsky (div.); children: Adam, Lisa, Joshua; m. Frank Wadsworth, Dec. 22, 1980. BA, Wellesley Coll., 1960; MA, Columbia U., 1965. Adminstrv. asst. Am. Assn. UN, N.Y.C., 1958; rsch. asst. Senator John F. Kennedy, Washington, 1959; social scis. tchr. Annapolis (Md.) H.S., 1960-62; co-founder, counselor Ednl. Assistance Ctr. Urban League of Westchester, Mount Vernon, N.Y., 1968-70; admissions counselor SUNY, Purchase, 1972-74, dir. admissions; program officer Markle Found., N.Y.C., 1980-84; exec. dir. Smart Family Found., 1984-86; pres. Public Agenda, 1986—. Cons. Ford Found. Divsn. Edn. and Pub. Policy, N.Y.C., 1979—80, Annenberg/Corp. Pub. Broadcasting Math and Sci. Project, Washington, 1992—93; adv. bd. Alliance for Redesigning Govt. Nat. Acad. Pub. Adminstrn., Washington, 1993—96; adv. com. on pub. issues Advt. Coun., N.Y.C., 1995—2000; bd. dirs. Ednl. Devel. Ctr., Newton, Mass., Pub. Edn. Network, Washington, Pub. Agenda, N.Y.C.; chmn. bd. trustees Bennington (Vt.) Coll., 1999—. Contbr. articles to profl. jours., chpts. to books. Bd. dirs. Learning Found. of Putnam/Northern Westchester, Yorktown Heights, N.Y., 1993-2000; corp. and found. liaison Wellesley Coll., Wellesley, Mass., 1985-92; v.p. New Rochelle Coun. PTAs, New Rochelle, N.Y., 1969-72. Recipient Silver Bell award for Disting. Svc. Advt. Coun., 1996. Avocations: sailing, gardening. Office: Pub Agenda 6 E 39th St New York NY 10016 Fax: 212-889-3461. E-mail: dwadsworth@publicagenda.org.

WADSWORTH, DOROTHY BUCKNAM, retired civic worker; b. Geneseo, N.Y., July 23, 1920; d. Roland Franklin and Julia Anne (Krotts) Bucknam; m. Robert Hume Wadsworth, Oct. 17, 1943; children— Ann Hunter, Barbara Jane. B.A. in Econs., Mt. Holyoke Coll., 1941. Dir. devel. Rochester Inst. Tech., N.Y., 1972-75; commr. N.Y. State Spl. Commn. on Attica, 1971-72; bd. dirs. Rochester Telephone Corp., 1972-76; commr. N.Y. State Moreland Act Commn. on Nursing Homes, N.Y.C., 1975-76, N.Y. State Commn. of Correction, Albany, 1975-79; Western N.Y. Rep., N.Y. State Senate Select Com. of Crime, Rochester and Albany, 1979-82. Active Jr. Guild for Crippled Children, Rochester Philharm. Orch. Study, 1959-60, Rochester Regional Research Library Council, 1968-72; vice chmn. N.Y. State del. White House Conf. on Libraries, 1977-79; rep. 7th Jud. Dist. Grievance Com., 1979-84; mem. Planned Parenthood Rochester and Monroe Counties, 1982-84; chmn. Monroe County Citizens for Family Planning, 1983; pres. Planned Parenthood-Monroe County, 1953-55, Meml. Art Gallery Women's Council, U. Rochester, 1957-59, Genesee Valley Mt. Holyoke Club, 1950-52, Rochester Jr. League, 1954-55; trustee Rochester Inst. Tech., 1960-72, Sta. WXXI-Pub. TV, 1968-72; founder Neighborhood Health Ctr. Rochester and Monroe Counties, 1968-72; bd. dirs. Blue Cross, 1968-75, Arts Council Monroe County, 1971-72, York State Craftsman, 1960-63, Community Chest-United Way, 1970-72; spl. asst. to chmn. Monroe County Republican Com., 1983-84; Rep. candidate for N.Y. Senate, 1984; bd. dirs. Monroe County Red Cross, 1987—, Nat. Warplane Mus., Genesco, N.Y., 1987—, GeVa Theatre, 1987—; founder, chair Athenaeum, Rochester Inst. Tech., 1986—. Recipient Helen Stone Jones award, 1968; B. Forman Flair award, 1969; Mt. Holyoke Coll. Medal of Honor, 1970; Rochester C. of C. Civic medal, 1971; Alpha Phi Omega Outstanding Service award, 1972; Anthony Jordan Health Ctr. award, 1973; UN Internat. Women's Yr. citation Rochester Assn. for UN, 1974; N.Y. State Sheriff's Assn. Friend of Law Enforcement award, 1979. Mem. Mt. Holyoke Coll. Alumni Assn. Presbyterian. Home: 147 Chelmsford Rd Rochester NY 14618-1709

WADSWORTH, DYER SEYMOUR, lawyer; b. N.Y.C., June 16, 1936; s. Seymour and Phoebe Armistead (Helmer) W.; m. Beverley Allen Dunn Barringer, Feb. 2, 1963; children: Sophia, Jennifer. BA, Yale U., 1959; JD, Harvard U., 1962. Bar: N.Y. 1963, Pa. 1979. Assoc. Humes, Andrews & Botzow, N.Y.C., 1962-64; with Inco Ltd. and subs., 1964-96; asst. gen. counsel Inco Ltd., 1982-96; pres. Inco U.S., Inc., 1993-96. Chmn., bd. dirs. Barringer Crater Co., Flagstaff, Ariz., 1996—; chmn., CEO, treas., dir. Cass County Iron Co., Linden, Tex., 1992— Gen. counsel Baseline Fin. Svcs., Inc., N.Y.C., 1997-2000, The Sailors Snug Harbor, Sea Level, N.C., 1987-2000; chmn., bd. dirs. Amsterdam Nursing Home Corp., N.Y.C., 1986-2000; trustee Isaac Tuttle Fund for the Aged, N.Y.C., 1968-96; bd. dirs. Frenchman Bay Conservancy, Hancock, Maine, 1997—. Named Trustee of Yr. N.Y. Assn. Homes and Svcs. for the Aging, 1995. Mem. Meteoritical Soc., Univ. Club, Ivy League Club, Union Club, (N.Y.C.), Pilgrims Soc. (N.Y.C.), Yale Club Suncoast (dir. 2001—, pres. 2002—). Home: 8466 Lockwood Ridge Rd PMB 304 Sarasota FL 34243-2951

WADSWORTH, FRANK WHITTEMORE, foundation executive, literature educator; b. N.Y.C., June 14, 1919; s. Prescott Kingsley and Elizabeth (Whittemore) W.; m. Roxalene Harriet Nevin, Oct. 22, 1943 (dec. 1979); Susan, Roxalene; m. Deborah Yohalem, Dec. 22, 1980. AB, Princeton U., 1946, PhD, 1951. Instr. English Princeton (N.J.) U., 1949-50; instr. to assoc. prof. English UCLA, 1950-61; prof. English, dean div. humanities U. Pitts., 1962-67; acad. v.p. SUNY-Purchase, 1967-78, prof. lit., 1967-89, emeritus, 1989—; nat. rep. Woodrow Wilson Nat. Fellowship Found., 1958-61, trustee, 1973—; vice-chmn. bd. trustees, 1992—; trustee Wenner-Gren Found., N.Y.C., 1970—, chmn. bd. trustees, 1977-87, vice-chmn. bd. trustees, 1992—. Author: The Poacher from Stratford, 1958; contbr. articles to publs. Served to lt. (j.g.) USNR, 1942-45. Woodrow Wilson fellow, 1946-47; Scribner fellow, 1948-49; Folger Shakespeare Library fellow, 1961; Guggenheim fellow, 1961-62 Mem. MLA, Am. Soc. Theatre Research, Malone Soc., Phi Beta Kappa Clubs: Princeton. Home: 430 Sterling Rd Harrison NY 10528-1316

WADSWORTH, JACQUELINE DORÈT, private investor; b. San Diego, June 15, 1928; d. Benjamin H. Dilley and Georgia E. (Elliott) Dilley Waters; m. Charles Desmond Wadsworth Jr., June 16, 1954 (dec. 1963); 1 child, Georgia Duncan Wadsworth Barber. BS, U. Oreg., 1950; MA, San Diego State U., 1952. Cert. tchr. Calif., Oreg. Dir. Jr. Red Cross, San Diego County chpt. ARC, 1952-59, asst. dir. leadership ctrs. for 8 western states Calif., 1954-59; pvt. investor, comml. real estate and property devel., 1974—. Interior designer J. Wadsworth Interiors, La Jolla, Calif., 1990—2002. Vol. chair nat. conv. ARC, San Diego, 1966; vol., fundraiser San Diego Symphony Orch. Orgn., 1974-83; mem. Gold Ribbon Patron com. San Diego Symphony, 1995-99; friends mem., vol. San Diego Mus. Art, 1958—, Asian Arts Com., 1996—; mem. Scripps Found. for Medicine and Sci., 1990—; life mem., fund raiser, bd. dirs., chmn. Scripps Mercy Hosp. Aux., 1965—; life mem., chair, bd. dirs. Social Svc. Aux., 1968—. Recipient Svc. award Mercy Hosp. Aux., 1967-70. Mem. Japanese Garden Soc. of San Diego, Globe Gilders Theatre Aux. (activity chairperson 1966-85), San Diego Zool. Soc. (curator 1976—), Mingei Internat., Palladian Soc. (San Diego County chpt.), Mus. Contemporary Art San Diego, San Diego Natural History Mus. Republican.

WADSWORTH, ROBERT DAVID, advertising agency executive; b. Prestbury, Cheshire, Eng., May 20, 1942; came to U.S., 1978; s. Eric and Irene (Thorpe) W.; m. Kathleen O'Meara, Dec. 13, 1968; children: Tracey, Charles Robert. BA, U. Natal, S. Africa, 1963. With Lever Bros. S. Africa, 1960-66, sr. brand mgr., 1964-66, Gen. Foods S. Africa, 1967; account exec. London

Press Exch., S. Africa, 1968, Grant Advt., S. Africa, 1969; dir., then mng. dir. Cen. Advt., Johannesburg, S. Africa, 1970-73; dir. new bus. coord. McCann-Erickson, South Africa, 1973-78; sr. v.p., mng. rep., new bus. coord. McCann-Erickson, Inc., N.Y.C., 1978-82; client dir., exec. v.p. Lintas, 1983-90; dir. corp. strategy, regional dir. So. Africa Lintas Worldwide, 1991-97; cons. Midlothian, Va., 1998—. Home and Office: 14018 Bayport Landing Ter Midlothian VA 23112-2038

WADZINSKI, MARY BETH, administrative assistant; b. Wausau, Wis., Apr. 26, 1953; d. Erwin Fredrick Hackbart and Selma Ruth Margaret Krueger; m. William R. Wadzinski, June 20, 1987 (div. June 1997); children: Bethany Dawn, Andrew William. AS, Northcentral Tech. Coll., 1973. Typist Wausau (Wis.) Abstract and Title Co., 1973-76; adminstrv. asst. Marathon County Dept. Social Svcs., Wausau, 1977—. Author poems, songs. Recipient Poet Merit award, Am. Poetry Assn., 1989, Editors Choice awards, Nat. Libr. Poetry, 1996—98, 2001, Honorable Mention award, Iliad Press, 1996—98. Mem.: Famous Poets Soc. (Shakespeare Trophy of Excellence 2002, Poet of Yr. medallion 2002, Recognition award 1998, Poet of Yr. medallion 1999, Diamond Homer trophy 1996, 1999, Recognition award 2001, Shakespear trophy 2002, Poet of Yr. 2002), Internat. Poetry Hall of Fame, Internat. Soc. Poets. Democrat. Lutheran. Avocations: shopping, garage sales, writing, singing. Home: 1113 N 6th Ave Wausau WI 54401-2747

WAEGER, ROBERT WRIGHT, insurance executive, lawyer; b. N.Y.C., Aug. 30, 1946; s. Robert Werner and ELizabeth (Nostrand) W.; m. Cicily Altenburg, Aug. 23, 1969 (div.); children: Cindy, Patrice, Holly, Bobby, Danny. BS in Acctg., St. Francis Coll., 1968; JD, Duquesne U., 1976. House counsel, regional claims atty. Nationwide Ins. Co., Columbus, Ohio, 1971-81; ptnr. Skarlatos, Zonarich and Waeger, Pa., 1981-85; v.p. claims Pa. Hosp. Ins. Co., Mechanicsburg, 1985—; dep. dir. Pa. Med. Malpractice Catastrophe Loss Fund, 1995—. Adj. prof. Millersville (Pa.) U., 1988—. Bd. dirs. Allendale Civic Assn., Camp Hill, Pa., 1984-85, St. Francis Alumni Bd., Loretto, Pa., 1975—; chmn. United Way, Mechanicsburg, 1988—. Mem. Hosp. Ins. Forum (chmn. claims com. 1989—), Pa. Trial Lawyers Assn., Pa. Def. Inst., Dauphin County Bar Assn., Pa. Bar Assn., Aircraft Owners and Pilots Assn. (Eagle Pilot award 1984). Avocation: flying. Home: PO Box 234 Harrisburg PA 17108-0234 Office: PA Med Malpractice CAT Fudn PO Box 85 Harrisburg PA 17108

WAELDE, LAWRENCE RICHARD, chemist; b. Teaneck, N.J., Dec. 27, 1951; s. Clinton Brewster and Eileen Florence (Kennedy) W.; m. Soledad Nélita Acedillo, May 24, 1975; children: Christine Ann, Richard Adams. BS, Fairleigh Dickinson U., 1976; postgrad., Syracuse U., 1969-72. Project leader Muralo Paints, Bayonne, N.J., 1974-79; lab. mgr. Lazon Paints, Fair Lawn, 1979-84; plant mgr. Stevens Paint Co., Yonkers, N.Y., 1984-86; mgr. powder coatings Troy Chem. Corp., Newark, 1986—. Mem. N.Y. Soc. Coating Tech. (tech. chmn. 1990-93, symposium chmn. 1993, 95, treas. 1995-96, sec. 1996-97, v.p., pres. elect 1997-98, pres. 1998-99, Roy H. Kienle award 1994), Powder Coating Inst. (tech. mem.). Office: Troy Chem Corp 1 Avenue L Newark NJ 07105-3805

WAETJEN, DANIEL G. bank executive; b. Washington, Dec. 18, 1950; s. Walter Bernhard and Betty (Wells) Waetjen; m. Cynthia Lake, May 22, 1976; children: Courtney, Lauren, Erin. BA, Guilford Coll., 1973; MBA, Cleve. State U., 1978. V.p. comml. banking Soc. Nat. Bank, Cleve., 1973-83; sr. v.p. comml. banking Signet Banking, Washington, 1983-97; COO, CFO Decision Support Sys., Inc., Ashburn, Va., 1998-99; sr. v.p. corp. banking Wachovia Bank, McLean, 1999—2001; sr. v.p. Wachovia Securities, Inc.; exec. v.p. SunTrust Bank, Fla., 2002—. Mem. adv. bd. Montgomery County Tech. Enterprise Ctr., Rockville, Md., 1995—. Bd. dirs. Alzheimer's Assn. Greater Washington, 1993—96. Named Outstanding Young Citizen, Cleve. Jaycees, 1979. Republican. Presbyterian. Avocations: reading, archery, hunting. Home: 13213 Locksley Ln Silver Spring MD 20904-6338 Office: SunTrust Bank SW Fla 12751 New Brittany Blvd Fort Myers FL 33907 E-mail: daniel.waetjen@suntrust.com.

WAETZMAN, LARRY SAMUEL, planning company executive; b. Reading, Pa., Dec. 11, 1945; s. Joseph and Lilyan B. (Berliner) W.; m. Bonnie Lynn Samuels, July 27, 1969; children: Ross, Evan, Melissa. BA, Franklin & Marshall Coll., 1967; MA, U. Wis., 1968; postgrad., Nova U., Temple U., Harvard U. Lic. profl. planner, N.J. Dir. of planning Borough of Norristown, Pa., 1972-74; dir. cmty. devel. Twp. of Haverford, Havertown, 1974-80; sr. planning cons. Govt. Studies & Systems, Phila., 1980-81; ptnr. Tredinnick/Waetzman Assocs., Havertown, 1981-87; prin. The Waetzman Planning Group, Ardmore, Pa., 1987-2001; pres. Waetleman Planning Group Inc., 2001—. Pres. Congregation Ner Tamid, Springfield, Pa., 1989-91. Served to 1st lt. U.S. Army, 1969-72. Mem. Am. Soc. Consulting Planners (pres. 1998-2000), Am. Planning Assn. (pres. eastern Pa. chpt. 1981-85), AICP, Pa. Planning Assn. (bd. dirs. 1981-85), N.J. Assn. Cons. Planners. Avocations: snow skiing. Home: 2725 Pine Valley Ln Ardmore PA 19003-1718 E-mail: lsw@waetzmanplanning.com.

WAGAMAN, JAMES BRIAN, environmentalist, educator; b. Waynesboro, Pa., Oct. 23, 1963; s. Elvin C. and Margaret Madeline (Peiffer) W.; m. Cheri Louise Ross, Jan. 28, 1994. AA, Pa. State U., Mont Alto, 1994; BHumanities, Pa. State U., Harrisburg, 1997, MA in Am. Studies, 2000. Lic. water purification, Pa. Operator, asst. supt., acting supt. Waynesboro (Pa.) Water Treatment Plant, 1980-91; pub. housing restoration coord. Franklin County Housing Authority, Chambersburg, 1992; coord. new constrn. Borough of Mont Alto (Pa.) Water Dept., 1994—. Instr. Pa. State U. Continuing Edn., 1997—; adj. prof. Ctrl. Pa. Coll., Summerdale, 2001—. Mem. MLA, Am. Water Resources Assn., Am. Water Works Assn., Popular Culture Assn (Dan Walden award 1994), N.E. MLA (panel chair, nominating com. 1998—), Mid-Atlantic Popular Culture Assn. (mem. exec. bd., area chair culture and the environment, program dir. conf. 1999). Democrat. Home: 2076 Lexington Ave Middletown PA 17057-3412 Office: Borough of Mont Alto Water Dept Mont Alto PA 17057

WAGANHEIM, ARTHUR BRIAN, marketing executive; b. Jan. 27, 1959; s. Gilbert and Edythe (Peck) W. BS, U. Md., 1981, MBA, 1984. Mgr. sales, product Warner-Lambert, Morris Plains, N.J., 1981-83; pres. Univ. Town, Inc., Greenbelt, Md., 1984-85; mktg. mgr. Greater Balt. Med. Ctr., ., 1985-87; dir. mktg. Union Meml. Hosp., Balt., 1987-88; pres. Stir Freeze, Inc., Ft. Lauderdale, Fla., 1988-93; ceo Star Bus. Sys. Inc., Miami, 1993—. Advisor Jr. Achievement, Washington, 1982-83; mktg. instr. U. Md., 1983-84, Towson State U., 1986-87. Pres. SW Broward Republican Orgn., 2001—. Republican. Jewish. Avocations: golf, hiking. Home: 10530 Buenos Aires St Hollywood FL 33026-4564

WAGAR, WARREN (WALTER WAGAR), historian, educator; b. Balt., June 5, 1932; s. Walter (Warren) and Laura Stoner Wagar; m. Dorothy Bowers, Dec. 19, 1953; children: John, Bruce, Steven, Jennifer. AB, Franklin & Marshall Coll., 1953; MA, Ind. U., 1954; PhD, Yale U., 1959; DHL (hon.), U. Maine, 1996. From instr. to assoc. prof. Wellesley (Mass.) Coll., 1958-66; assoc. prof., then prof. U. N.Mex., Albuquerque, 1966-71; prof., disting. tchg. prof. SUNY, Binghamton, 1971—2002, prof. emeritus, 2002—. Author: H.G. Wells and the World State, 1961, The City of Man, 1963, Building the City of Man, 1971, Good Tidings: The Belief in Progress from Darwin to Marcuse, 1972, Books in World History, 1973, World Views: A Study in Comparative History, 1977, Terminal visions: The Literature of Last Things, 1982, A Short History of the Future, 1989, 3d rev. edit., 1999, The Next Three Futures, 1991, Memoirs of the Future, 2001; editor: H.G. Wells: Journalism and Prophecy, 1964, European Intellectual History Since Darwin and Marx, 1967, Science, Faith, an Man: European Thought Since 1914, 1968, The Idea of Progress Since the Renaissance, 1969, History and the Idea of Mankind, 1971, The Open Conspiracy: H.G. Wells on World Revolution, 2002; mem. editl. bd. Futures Rsch. Quar. Fulbright scholar, London, 1957-58; fellow Am. Coun. Learned Socs., London, 1963-64, NEH, 1974-75. Mem. World Future Soc., N.Y. State Assn. European Historians (pres. 1977-78), H.G. Wells Soc. (v.p. 1988—), Soc. for Utopian Studies. Home: 724 Pickwick Dr Vestal NY 13850 E-mail: wwagar@stny.rr.com.

WAGEMAN, LYNETTE MENA, librarian; b. Trinidad, West Indies, Aug. 18, 1934; came to U.S., 1955. d. Hubert and Alma (Sampath) Jagbandhansingh. BA in Modern Fgn. Langs., Park Coll., Parkville, Mo., 1959; MLS, U. Hawaii, 1966, MA in Asian Studies, 1976. Serials asst. East-West Ctr. Libr., Honolulu, 1962-66; catalog libr. U. Hawaii, 1966-71, South Asia specialist, 1971-93, acting head Asia collection, 1991-93, head, 1993—, collection devel. mgr. Asia collection, pub. svc. head rep., 1991—. Exec. com. Ctr. South Asian Studies, 1973-75, 77-79, 81-83, 85-86, 87-90, acting dir., 1988, 90, 92. Mem. Hawaii Libr. Assn. (mem. bd. 1990-92, co-editor newsletter 1990-92), Assn. Asian Studies (exec. bd. com. on South Asian Librs. and Documentation 1983-85, 90—, chairperson 1992—, exec. com. Asian Libr. Liaison com. 1991—, adv. com. Bibliography Asian Studies 1992—), Internat. Assn. Orientalist Librs., South Asian Lit. Assn., Com. on Women in Asian Studies. Avocation: cultivating Bromeliads and other exotic plants. Office: U Hawaii Asia Collection Hamilton Libr 2550 The Mall Honolulu HI 96822-2233

WAGEMAN, VIRGINIA FARLEY, editor, writer; b. Jersey City, Feb. 18, 1941; d. James Christopher and Charlotte Carter (Stebbins) Farley; m. Steven Lipson, Dec. 26, 1962 (div. 1964); 1 child, Melissa; m. James Carter Wageman, Apr. 22, 1968; children: Robinson Michael, Sarah Carter. BA, Bard Coll., 1964. Book editor, prodn. asst. AICPA, N.Y.C., 1964-67; prodn. mgr. U. Hawaii Press, 1967-68; asst. dir. office univ. rels. U. Md., Balt., 1968-70; dir. publs. art mus. Princeton U., 1971-81; writer, editor Hirshhorn Mus. and Sculpture Garden, Washington, 1982-86; freelance editor, 1986—; sr. editor Hudson Hills (N.Y.) Press, 1988-89; mgr. publs. Coll. Art Assn., N.Y.C., 1989-96; editor, writer various publications, 1996—. Art critic Honolulu Advertiser, 1999-2002. Recipient Smithsonian Commendation for Exceptional Svc. Mem. Art Table, Assn. Freelance Art Editors (pres. 1984-86), Princeton Rsch. Forum, Coll. Art Assn. Home: 2015 Round Top Dr Honolulu HI 96822-2058 Fax: 808-949-8930. E-mail: vwageman@hawaii.rr.com.

WAGENAAR, ALEXANDER CLARENCE, educator; b. Grand Rapids, Mich., May 27, 1955; s. Henry and Alice (Bouwens) W.; m. Kelli Ann Komro, Jan. 31, 1998; children from previous marriage: Nathaniel Reid, Bradley Hendrik. BA, Calvin Coll., 1977; MSW, U. Mich., 1978, PhD, 1980. Asst. rsch. scientist U. Mich., Ann Arbor, 1980-85, assoc. rsch. scientist, 1985-89; assoc. prof. U. Minn., Mpls., 1990-95, prof., 1995—. Vis. scholar Marin Inst. Prevention Alcohol and Other Drug Problems, San Rafael, Calif., 1989-90; chmn. Nat. Coalition to Prevent Impaired Driving, Washington, 1989-91. Author: Alcohol, Young Drivers and Traffic Accidents, 1983; contbr. articles to profl. jours. Recipient Jellinek Meml. award for contbn. to alcohol policy and cmty. intervention rsch., 1999. Mem. Am. Pub. Health Assn. (governing coun. 1985-89, Exceptional Leadership award 1987), AAUP, Am. Evaluation Assn., Policy Studies Orgn., Nat. Assn. Pub. Health Policy, Rsch. Soc. on Alcoholism, Soc. for Prevention Rsch. Avocations: hiking, reading, travel. Office: U Minn Sch Pub Health Divsn Epidemiology 1300 S 2nd St Ste 300 Minneapolis MN 55454-1015 E-mail: wagenaar@epi.umn.edu.

WAGENAAR, THEODORE CLARENCE, sociology educator; b. Heerhugowaard, The Netherlands, July 19, 1948; came to U.S., 1951, naturalized, 1961; 1 child, Keri. AB, Calvin Coll., Grand Rapids, Mich., 1970; MA, Ohio State U., 1971, PhD, 1975. Cert. elem. sch. tchr., Ohio. Asst. prof. sociology Miami U. of Ohio, Oxford, 1975-78, assoc. prof., 1978-82, prof., 1982—, chmn. dept. sociology and anthropology, 1986-92. Program analyst Nat. Ctr. Edn. Stats., Washington, 1980. Author: Readings for Social Research, 1980, Review Guide-Sociology, 1997, Practicing Social Research, 2000; editor Teaching Sociology, 1986-91. Rsch. fellow Am. Statis. Assn./NSF, 1995—; Nat. Ctr. Edn.-Stats. grantee, 1981-85; recipient Mauksch award Disting. Contbns. to Undergrad. Sociology, 1984; Carnegie scholar, 1999-2000. Mem. Am. Sociol. Assn. (Disting. Contbn. to Undergrad. Edn. award 1992), North Ctrl. Sociol. Assn. (Disting. Contbn. to Undergrad. Edn. award 1992), Midwest Sociol. Soc. Home: 6120 Stephenson Rd Oxford OH 45056-9010 Office: Miami U Dept Sociology Oxford OH 45056 E-mail: wagenate@muohio.edu.

WAGENER, HOBART D. retired architect; b. Sioux Falls, S.D., May 10, 1921; s. Frank Samuel and Beatrice (Hobart) W.; m. Violet LaVaughn, Dec. 16, 1944; children: Diane Kay Wagener, Jeffrey Scott, Shaw Bradley. BArch, U. Mich., 1944. Registered architect, Colo. Draftsman Eggers & Higgins, Architects, N.Y.C., 1946-47, Pietro Belluschi, Architect, Portland, Oreg., 1947-50; designer James Hunter, Architect, Boulder, Colo., 1950-53; prin. Hobart D. Wagener Assocs., 1953-77; prin. ptnr. Wagener VanderVorste, Architects, 1977-86; ret., 1986. Mem. selection com. Colo. Supreme Ct., Denver, 1968-72. Co-author: The School Library, 1962; work pub. in Archtl. Record, Sunset mag., N.Y. Times, House Beautiful, 25 Years of Record Houses. Chmn. Boulder Planning Commn., 1966; pres. Boulder C. of C., 1971. Lt. (j.g.) USN, 1944-46, PTO. Named Outstanding Designer for past 50 yrs. Hist. Boulder, 1983; also numerous nat. and regional design awards. Fellow AIA (pres. Colo. 1973, Colo. Architect of Yr. award 1985, pres. awar N. chpt. 1998), Lions (pres. Boulder 1965). Avocations: travel, golf. Address: 1730 Avenida Del Mundo Coronado CA 92118-3021 E-mail: arclib@msn.com.

WAGER, CARL JOSEPH, music educator; s. William Joseph and Levina Elizabeth Wager; m. Pamela Jane Wilson, Aug. 18, 1973; children: Christopher Clement, Kristen Joy, Jonathan Joseph, Timothy Carl, Bethany Leely. BS music edu., Roberts Wesleyan Coll., Rochester, New York, 1967—71; master equivalence, U. Buffalo, Buffalo, New York, 1971—75. Vocal music tchr. Starpoint Ctrl. schools, Lockport, NY, 1972—76, Olympia H.S., Rochester, 1976—87; elemetary band tchr. Norton Shores schools, Muskegon, Mich., 1998—98; vocal music tchr. Athena Mid. Sch., Rochester, NY, 1988—. Bd. mem. Roberst Wesleyan Coll. cmty. orch., Rochester, NY, 1988—94. Dir.: Over 60 Musicals. Choir dir. Greece schools, Rochester, NY, 1996—2002. Mem.: NY State Sch. Music Assn. Conservative-R. Pentacostal Christian. Home: 5 Stoney Path Lane Rochester NY 14626-1713 Office: Greece Athena Middle School 800 Long Pond Road Rochester NY 14612 Home Fax: 585-227-5856. Personal E-mail: wagerfam@frontiernet.net.

WAGER, ELIZABETH, writer; b. London, July 16, 1962; d. John and Janet Elizabeth Aimers (Eason) C.; m. Timothy David Healing, 1985 (div. 1993); m. Jim Wager, May 20, 1995. MA in Zool. with hons., Oxford (Eng.) U., 1983. Editor Blackwell Sci., Oxford, 1985-89, Oxford Analytica, 1990-92; med. writer Janssen-Cilag, Bucks, Eng., 1992-99; head U.K. med. publs. Glaxo-SmithKline, 1999—. Mem. Brit. Ethics Jour. Ethics Com. Nat. chairperson Amnesty Internat. U.K. Sect., 1989-91; sec. Thame Amnesty Group, Oxfordshire, Eng., 1996—. Mem. European Assn. Sci. Editors, Coun. Biology Editors, European Med. Writers Assn. (editor 1994-95), Locknet. Avocations: choral singing, opera. Home: Sideview Cottage Station Rd Buckinghamshire HP27 9DE England E-mail: ew33645@glaxowellcome.co.uk.

WAGER, PAULA JEAN, artist; b. Lansing, Mich., Dec. 19, 1929; d. Mervin Elihu and Cora Della (Raymer) Fowler; m. William Douglas Wager, May 4, 1952; children: Pamela Ann, Scott Alan. Student, Mich. State U., 1949-52. Music tchr., Toledo, 1968-72, Union Lake, Mich., 1972-76; tchr. art, artist Paula Wager's Art Studio, Commerce Twp., 1984—. Hostess Artistic Touch with Paula, Media Network of Waterford, 1999—, (Cable Comcast channel 44), Waterford, Mich., 1991-94, 96—, AT&T (formerly called TCI West Oakland), Walled Lake, Mich., Channel 10, 1991-94, Channel 14, 1996—. Exhibited in group shows including Village Art Supplies, 1982-88, Pontiac Oakland Soc. Artists, 1983—, Pontiac Galleria, 1983, 99, Oakland C.C., Commerce Twp., 1985, Red Piano Gallery, Hilton Head, S.C., 1985-89, Mich. State U., East Lansing, 1986, Silver Pencil Gallery, Pontiac, 1987-89, Wooden Sleight, Vestaburg, Mich., 1988-93, Art Pad, Keego Harbor, Mich., 1990-93, Local Color Gallery, Union Pier, Mich., 1992-94, Mich. Assn. Artists, Southfield Civ. Ctr. Mich. 1995, 97, 98, Swann Gallery, Detroit, 1995—, Kiva Gallery, Waterford, 1999, Southfield Ctr. arts, 1999; solo exhbns. include Waterford Pub. Lib., 1996, Waterland Pub. Libr., 1996—, Millers Artist Supplies, Ferndale, Mich., 1996, Waterford Twp. Hall, 1996, 99, Masonic Lodge, Milford, 1997, 98, 99, Livonia Libr., 1999; represented in pvt. collections; juror Village of Fine Arts Assn., 1996. Recipient Outstanding Achievement award in instructional programming Comcast Cable TV, Waterford, 1992, 1st place, Waterford Friends of the Arts Art Show, 1988, Pontiac Oakland Soc. Artists Cmty. Rm., 1990, Am. Biog. Inst. Woman of Yr. Commemorative medal, 1995; Waterford Cable Commn. grantee, 1991, 93, Charter Twp. of Waterford grantee, 1991-94, 98. Mem. Nat. Assn. Female Exec. Pontiac Oakland Soc. Artists, Waterford Friends of the Arts, Mich. Watercolor Soc., Birmingham Bloomfield Art Assn., Colored Pencil Soc. Am., Colored Pencil Soc. Detroit, Village Fine Arts Assn., Paint Creek Ctr. for the Arts. Avocations: music, art. Home: 3316 Greenlawn Ave Commerce Township MI 48382-4629

WAGER, WALTER HERMAN, author, communications director; b. N.Y.C., Sept. 4, 1924; s. Max Louis and Jessie (Smith) W.; m. Sylvia Liebowitz Leonard, May 6, 1951 (div. May 1975); 1 child, Lisa Wendy; m. Winifred McIvor, June 4, 1975. BA, Columbia U., 1943; LLB, Harvard U., 1946; LLM, Northwestern U., 1949. Bar: N.Y. 1946. Spl. asst. to Israel dir. Civil Aviation, 1951-52; freelance writer N.Y.C., 1952-54; editor UN, 1954-56; freelance TV and mag. writer, 1956-63; editor-in-chief Playbill mag., 1963-66; editor Show mag., 1965; cons. pub. rels. and editorial dept. ASCAP, 1966-72, dir. pub. relations, 1972-78; cons. pub. relations Nat. Music Pub. Assn., 1978-84; dir. communications Juilliard Sch., 1985-86; counsel pub. relations Mann Music Ctr., Phila., 1986-87, Eugene O'Neill Theater Ctr., N.Y.C., 1987-89; dir. pub. info. U. Bridgeport, 1991-93. Tchr. Northwestern U., 1949, Columbia U., 1955-56, U. Bridgeport, 1994; spl. asst. to atty. gen. N.Y. State investigation hate lit. in elections, 1962; bd. dirs. Jazz Hall of Fame, 1975-77. Author: Death Hits the Jackpot, 1954, Operation Intrigue, 1956, I Spy, 1965, Masterstroke, 1966, Superkill, 1966, Wipeout, 1967, Countertrap, 1967, Death Twist, 1968, The Girl Who Split, 1969, Sledgehammer, 1970, Viper Three, 1971 (filmed as Twilights's Last Gleaming 1977), Swap, 1972, Telefon, 1975 (filmed in 1977), My Side-By King Kong, 1976, Time of Reckoning, 1977, Blue Leader, 1979, Blue Moon, 1980, Blue Murder, 1981, Designated Hitter, 1982, The Caribbeans, 1983, Otto's Boy, 1984, 58 The Wildcatters, 1986, Minutes, 1987 (filmed as Die Hard 2, 1990), The Spirit Team, 1996, Tunnel, 2000, Kelly's People, 2002; (non-fiction) Camp Century, 1962, Playwrights Speak, 1967, (with Mel Tillis) Stutterin' Boy, 1984. Pres. Columbia Coll., class 1944. Fulbright fellow Sorbonne, Paris, 1949-50, Northwestern U. Law Sch. fellow, 1948-49. Mem.: Mystery Writers Am. (bd. dirs. 1988—94, 1997—2000, 2002—), Writers Guild Am. Democrat. Jewish. Avocation: traveling. Home and Office: 200 W 79th St New York NY 10024-6212 Fax: (212) 769-2725. E-mail: WPotogold2000@aol.com.

WAGES, ROBERT COLEMAN, equity investor; b. Casablanca, Morocco, Aug. 28, 1963; came to U.S., 1963; s. Dan Sims and Sara Mae (Miller) W.; m. Tara Shamattee Sarwan, July 18, 1992; children: John Coleman, Thomas Sims; 1 stepchild, Jason Anthony Squillace. AB in Chemistry with honors, Princeton U., 1985. Cons. Oliver, Wyman & Co., N.Y.C., 1985—87; from assoc. to mng. dir. Castle Harlan, Inc., 1987—2001, mng. dir., 2001—. Bd. dirs. Dearborn Risk Mgmt., Inc., N.J., Gravograph New Hermes LLC, Atlanta, Stackteck Sys., Inc., Toronto, Ont., Can., CBO Mgmt. Ltd., Bermuda. Sponsor Student/Sponsor Partnership, N.Y.C., 1987-91, All Saints Episcopal Ch., vestry 1994-95, treas. 1995. Republican. Episcopalian. Avocations: sailing, travel, photography, scuba diving. Office: Castle Harlan Inc 150 E 58th St New York NY 10155-0002 E-mail: rwages@castleharlan.com

WAGGENER, MELISSA, public relations executive; b. 1954; BA Eng., Lewis & Clark Coll. With Tektronix Inc., Beaverton, Oreg., 1975-80, Regis McKenna, Portland, 1980-83, Waggener Edstrom, Inc., 1983—, now pres. and CEO. Office: Waggener Edstrom Inc 3 Centerpointe Dr Ste 300 Lake Oswego OR 97035-8663*

WAGGENER, THERYN LEE, retired law enforcement professional; b. Cedar Rapids, Iowa, Sept. 7, 1941; s. Hollis Angisa (Fowler) W.; m. Zoetta Jean Hamilton, May 30, 1967; 1 child, Drugh Kincade. BBA, Nat. U., 1977, MBA, 1979; JD, Western State Coll. Law, 1980. Traffic officer Calif. Hwy. Patrol, San Diego, 1966-72; owner, operator Am. Nat. Chem., 1972-82; chief investigator N.Mex. Real Estate Commn., Albuquerque, 1983-86, Nev. Real Estate Div., Carson City, 1986-89; lt., shift comdr. Nev. Dept. Prisons, Ely, 1989-2000. Prof., Sierra Nev. Coll., Incline Village, 1988-89, Western Nev. Community Coll., Carson City, 1987-89; No. Nev. C.C., 1992—. Mem. Washoe County (Nev.) Rep. Cen. Com., 1989. With USN, 1960-65. Mem. Nat. Assn. Real Estate Lic. Law Ofcls. (enforcement and investigative com. 1987-89), Toastmasters, Rotary, Lions, Masons, Shriners, Nu Beta Epsilon. Avocations: skiing, golf, horses, flying. E-mail: bigdaddy@netxxpress.net.

WAGGENER, THOMAS BARROW, research bioengineer; b. Alvin, Tex., Apr. 15, 1951; m. Nancy Lou Day, 1980 (div. 1989); children: Mary Allison, Hartley Barrow. BS in Aerospace Engring., U. Va., 1973; SM in Engring., Harvard U., 1974, PhD in Bioengineering, 1979. Rsch. fellow respiratory physiology Cardiovascular Rsch. Inst. U. Calif., San Francisco, 1979-81; instr. pediat. Harvard Med. Sch., Boston, 1981-85; lectr. MIT divsn. health scis. and tech. Harvard U., Cambridge, Mass., 1984-86; asst. prof. pediat. New Eng. Med. Ctr., Boston, 1985-91, dir. program rsch. tng., 1987-91; dir. Pediat. Diagnostic Svcs., Newton, Mass., 1992-94; pres. Physio Analytics, 1994—. Patentee inverted toriod toy; reviewer profl. jours.; contbr. articles to profl. jours. Bd. dirs. Newton Youth Soccer. Grantee Nat. Inst. Child Health & Human Devel.; Acad. fellow Harvard U., 1973-74; DuPont Regional scholar U. Va., 1969-73. Mem. IEEE, Am. Physiol. Soc. Office: 24 Wyoming Rd Newton MA 02460-1235

WAGGONER, DAVID KENT, government official; b. Lubbock, Tex., May 2, 1960; s. Kelley Dean and Bene (Cash) W. BS, Tex. Tech. U., 1983; MS, Va. Tech. U., 1987; MBA, George Washington U., 1991; profl. cert., Georgetown U., 1990, Carnegie Mellon U., 1991. Legis. asst. to U.S. Congressman Byron Dorgan, Washington, 1985-86; rsch. analyst Nat. Commn. on Dairy Policy, 1987-88; project dir. Bd. on Agr. NAS, 1988-89; spl. asst. Office of Sec. USDA, 1989—. Contbr. articles to profl. jours. Mem. Ag Reps., 1989-91. Recipient Hon. Am. Farmer degree FFA Orgn., Kansas City, Mo., 1990. Mem. AAAS, Am. Soc. Animal Sci., Am. Registry Profl. Animal Scientists, Masons, Alpha Zeta (Washington chpt.), Kappa Alpha (pres. Nat. Capitol alumni chpt. 1990-91, Disting. Svc. award 1990). Baptist. Avocations: showing and exhibiting livestock, water skiing, snow skiing. Home: 412 1st St SE Washington DC 20003-1804 Office: USDA 14th & Independence Ave SW Washington DC 20250-0001

WAGGONER, PAUL EDWARD, agricultural scientist; b. Appanoose County, Iowa, Mar. 29, 1923; s. Walter Loyal and Kathryn (Maring) W.; m. Barbara Ann Lockerbie, Nov. 3, 1945; children— Von Lockerbie, Daniel Maring S.B., U. Chgo., 1946; MS, Iowa State Coll., 1949, PhD, 1951. From asst. to chief scientist Conn. Agrl. Expt. Sta., New Haven, 1951-71, vice dir., 1969-71, dir., 1972-87, disting. scientist, 1987—. Lectr. Yale Forestry Sch., New Haven, 1962—; mem. panels on policy implications of global warming NAS, 1989-91. Contbr. articles to profl. jours. Served to capt. USAAF, 1943-46 Guggenheim fellow, 1963 Fellow AAAS (chmn. climate changes and water resources com. 1986-89), Am. Phytopath. Soc.; mem. NAS, Am. Meteorol. Soc. (Outstanding Achievement in Biometerology award 1967), Conn. Acad. Sci. and Engring., Recipient of the Anton-de- Bary Medal, 1996, Grads Club. Achievements include rsch. in mathematical simulation of plant disease epidemics, hydrologic role of foliar pores, climate change on agriculture and water resources, how much ten billion can spare for nature. Home: 314 Vineyard Point Rd Guilford CT 06437-3255 Office: Conn Agrl Expt Sta PO Box 1106 New Haven CT 06504-1106 E-mail: paul.waggoner@po.state.ct.us.

WAGGONER, ROBERT, chef; Studied with Michael Roberts, Trumps, 1981—83; studied with Jacques Lameloise, Charles Barrier, Pierre Gagnaire, Gerard Boyer, Mark Meneau, France; studied with Jean Paul Coupal, Caracas, Venezuela. Owner restaurant Le Monte Cristo, France; chef with Jean Pierre Silva Le Vieux Moulin , Beaune, 1991; chef Turnberry Isle, Fla., 1993, The Wild Boar , Nashville, Charleston Grill, 2002—. Guest appearances fine dining establishments James Beard Ho., N.Y.C. Appeared (TV series) Gourmet Getaways with Robin Leach, Great Chefs of the South , Nashville's Talk of the Town, Ralph Emery Show, The Food Network's In Food Today , appearances with food reporter Burt Wolf (TV series) The Travel Channel, CNN, PBS Stas. nationwide, host Salute to Southern Chefs. Supporter nat. relief hunger charity Share our Strength. Office: Charleston Grill Charleston Pl Hotel 244 King St Charleston SC 29401*

WAGGONER, SUSAN MARIE, electronics engineer; b. East Chicago, Ind., Sept. 1, 1952; d. Joseph John and Elizabeth Vasilak; m. Steven Richard Waggoner, July 31, 1976; children: Kenneth David, Michael Christopher. AS, Ind. U., 1975, BA in Journalism, 1976, BS in Physics, 1982, M in Pub. Affairs,

1991. Engring. technician Naval Surface Warfare Ctr., Crane, Ind., 1978-82, electronics engr. test and measurement equipment, 1982-91, electronics engr. batteries, 1991—. Recipient Value Engring. Spl. award Dept. of Def., 2000. Mem. AIAA, Am. Soc. Naval Engrs., Fed. Mgrs. Assn., Federally Employed Women, Am. Rose Soc., Am. Hort. Soc., Mensa, Theatre Circle Ind. U., Sigma Pi Sigma. Home: RR 5 Box 387 Loogootee IN 47553-9337 Office: Naval Surface Warfare Ctr 300 Highway 361 Crane IN 47522-5001

WAGGONER, WILLIAM JOHNSON, lawyer; b. Salisbury, N.C., Oct. 13, 1928; s. James Martin and Julia (Johnson) W.; m. Martha Anne Garwood, Aug. 8, 1953; children: William Johnson, Ellen Christine, David Garwood. Student, Catawba Coll., 1945-46, 48; AB, U. N.C., 1951, LLB, 1954. Bar: N.C. 1954. Ptnr. Weinstein, Mullenburg, Waggoner & Bledsoe, Charlotte, N.C., 1954-57; asst. U.S. atty. Western Dist. N.C., 1957-59; ptnr. Weinstein, Waggoner & Sturgess, 1959-70, Waggoner, Hasty & Kratt, Charlotte, 1970-84, Waggoner, Hamrick, Hasty, Montieth, Kratt, Cobb & McDonnell, Charlotte, 1985-88, Waggoner, Hamrick, Hasty, Montieth & Kratt PLLC, Charlotte, 1989—. Gen. counsel Mecklenburg Rep. Exec. Com., 1963-73; deacon Luth. Ch.; chmn. Charlotte Bd. Adjustment, 1970-72; mem. N.C. Bd. Elections, 1973-77. With AUS, 1946-47. Recipient Disting. Alumni award Catawba Coll. Mem. ABA, FBA, Am. Judicature Soc., N.C. Bar Assn., Toastmasters (past pres.), Kappa Alpha. Office: Waggoner Hamrick Hasty Monteith & Kratt PLLC Two First Union Ctr Ste 2750 Charlotte NC 28282 E-mail: wjwaggoner@yahoo.com.

WAGGY, CORRINA JEANNE, insurance agent; b. Ypsilanti, MI, June 4, 1966; d. Paggy Lou Kerr, James Edward Kerr; m. Steven Fitzgerald Waggy; children: Nicholas, Dylan. Bachelor's of Science in Biology, Heidelberg College, Tiffin, Ohio, 1999—2001. Insurance Agent Sunshine Insurance Agency, Upper Sandusky, OH, 1999—pres; Head Laboratory Technician Horizon Animal Hospital, Galion, 1987—96; Medical Laboratory Technician Wyandot Memorial Hospital, Upper Sandusky, 1996—99. Speaker at Elemntary Schools Horizon Animal Hospital, Galion, OH, 1987—96; Organized Teddy Bear Fair for Children Wyandot Memorial Hospital, Upper Sandusky, OH, 1997. President Parent Team of South Elementary School, Upper Sandusky, OH. Mem.: Am. Soc. Clinical Pathologists, Beta Beta Beta, Alpha Sigma Lambda, Kappa Delta Pi. Home: 506 S. Warpole St. Upper Sandusky OH 43351 Personal E-mail: cori@buzz-kill.zzn.com.

WAGMAN, GERALD HOWARD, retired biochemist; b. Mar. 4, 1926; s. David and Sophie (Milinsky) W.; m. Rhoda Kirschner, Dec. 9, 1948; children: Jan Donald, Neil Mark. BS, Lehigh U., 1946; MS, Va. Poly. Inst. and State U., 1947. Tech. rsch. asst. Squibb Inst. for Med. Rsch., New Brunswick, N.J., 1947-49, 54-57; mgr. Yankee Radio Corp., N.Y.C., 1950-54; assoc. biochemist Schering Corp. (now Schering-Plough Rsch. Inst.), Kenilworth, N.J., 1957-58, biochemist, 1958-68, sect. leader, 1969-70, from mgr. antiobiotics dept. to prin. scientist, 1970-89, mgr. libr. info. ctr., 1989-93; ret., 1993. Freelance tech. writer, editor, cons., 1993—; mem. adv. bd. Nat. Cert. Commn. in Chemistry and Chem. Engring., 1985-88. Author: Chromatography of Antiobiotics, 1973, rev. edit., 1984, The Handy HamBook, 1994; mem. editl. bd. Antimicrobial Agents and Chemotherapy, 1971-74; co-editor: Isolation, Separation and Purification of Antibiotics, 1978, Natural Products Isolation, 1989; contbr. chpts. in books and articles to profl. jours.; patentee in field. Coun. mem. Troop 23 Boy Scouts Am., 1964-66; comm. officer East Brunswick Civil Def. and Disaster Control, 1966-71; mem. sci. adv. com. East Brunswick Bd. Edn., 1960-68; bd. dirs. Tamarack N. Homeowners Assn., pres., 1989-93, treas., 1994—. Recipient Pub. Svc. award Am. Radio Relay League, 1965. Chartered chemist, Gt. Britain; fellow Am. Inst. Chemists; mem. AAAS, ALA, Spl. Librs. Assn., Am. Chem. Soc., Am. Soc. Microbiology, Am. Inst. Biol. Scis., Soc. Indsl. Microbiology, Soc. Applied Microbiology (Gt. Britain), Royal Soc. Chemistry, Sigma Xi, Tau Delta Phi. Home and Office: 17 Crommelin Ct East Brunswick NJ 08816-2406

WAGMAN, RICHARD JAY, internist, educator; b. N.Y.C., May 8, 1932; s. Morris and Thelma (Freedman) W.; m. Elizabeth Mary Plotz, June 18, 1961; children: Anne Elizabeth Kenyon, Victoria Rose, James David. AB, Harvard U., 1953, MD, 1957. Intern, resident in medicine Peter Bent Brigham Hosp., Boston, 1957-59, rsch. fellow in cardiology, 1959-61; surgeon USPHS, Washington, 1961-62, Naples, Italy, 1962-63; chief resident in medicine Kings County Hosp. Ctr., Bklyn., 1963-64; pvt. practice internal medicine, 1964—; assoc. prof. clin. medicine SUNY Health Sci. Ctr., 1964—. Cons. internal medicine Kings County Hosp. Ctr., Bklyn., 1964—; cons. cardiology Kingsboro Psychiat. Hosp., Bklyn., 1964—; cons. internal medicine and cardiology Social Security Adminstrn., N.Y.C., 1964—. Editor: Encyclopedia of Family Health and Fitness, 1980, New Complete Medical and Health Encyclopedia, 1987. Active Brooklyn Heights Assn., Bklyn., 1963—. Lt. commdr. USPHS, 1961-63. Fellow ACP, N.Y. Acad. Medicine; mem. Kings County Med. Soc., Harvard Club N.Y.C. Avocations: music, photography, wine. Home: 1 Grace Ct Brooklyn NY 11201-4195 Office: 15 Monroe Pl Brooklyn NY 11201-2602

WAGMAN, ROBERT JOHN, journalist, author; b. Chgo., Nov. 11, 1942; s. Albert Alan and Rosamond (Horner) W.; m. Carol Ann Mueller, Jan. 30, 1965; children: Jennifer, Robert, Patricia, Marilyn. AB, St. Louis U., 1966, MA, 1968, JD, 1971. Analyst Dun & Bradstreet, 1965-67; with CBS News, 1967-71, 74-77; asst. to dean St. Louis U. Sch. Law, 1971-74; Washington bur. chief N.Am. Newspaper Alliance, 1977-80, Ind. News Alliance, 1980-82; columnist Newspaper Enterprise Assn., 1980-95; pres. Fed. Real Estate Info. Svc., 1995—. Sr. corr. Soccertimes; v.p. prodn. Strategic Media All. Author, co-author: Hubert Humphrey, The Man and His Dream, 1978, Citizens Guide to the Tax Revolt, 1979, Asbestos: The Silent Killer, 1982, Lord's Justice, 1985, Instant Millionaires, 1986, The Nazi Hunters, 1988, The First Amendment Book, 1991, 2d edit., 1996, World Almanac Guide to the Supreme Court, 1993, Blood Oath, 1994, Hong Kong, 1997, And Beyond, 1997, Instant Millionaires II, 2000; editor: World Almanac of U.S. Politics, 1988—, Sm. Bus. Computing & Comm. Mag. Recipient Thomas Stokes award in journalism.

WAGNER, ALAN CYRIL, television and film producer, consultant; b. N.Y.C., Oct. 1, 1931; s. Joseph and Isabelle (Chanson) W.; m. Martha Celia Dreyfus, Mar. 11, 1956; children: David Mark, Susan Jill, Elizabeth Celia. BA, Columbia U., 1951, MA in English, 1952. Mgr. network programs Benton & Bowles, Inc., N.Y.C., 1957-61; dir. program devel. CBS, 1961-68, v.p. program devel. Hollywood, Calif., 1968-73, v.p. program planning and devel. N.Y.C., 1973-75, v.p. nighttime programs, 1975-78, v.p. programs, 1978-82; pres., chief exec. officer The Disney Channel, 1982-83; pres., CEO Alan Wagner Prodns., Inc., 1983—; exec. v.p. feature and TV devel. and prodn. Grosso-Jacobson Entertainment Corp., 1985-90; pres. Boardwalk Entertainment, 1990-97, chmn., 1997—. Sr. program cons. Todays Cath. Cable Network, 1999--; adj. assoc. prof. visual arts NYU, 1993-98; mem. adv. bd. Showondemand.com. Prodr., dir., host program Living Opera, Stas. WNYC-WNYC-FM, N.Y.C., 1958-68; host radio broadcasts N.Y.C. Opera Co., 1978-80; panelist, commentator Met. Opera broadcasts, 1996—; contbr., Opera News, 2001—; exec. prodr. film Reunion at Fairborough, 1985; prodr. TV pilot We're Puttin' on the Ritz, 1986; author: Prima Donnas and other Wild Beasts, 1961; exec. con. The Gunfighters, Diamonds; supervising prodr. Cop Talk: Behind the Shield, 1988, 89, True Blue, TV movie and series, 1989, A Family for Joe, TV movie and series, 1989-90, TV series Counterstrike, 1990-93, Top Cops, 1989-94; exec. prodr. TV movies Spenser: Ceremony, Spenser: Pale Kings and Princes, 1993, Spenser: The Judas Goat, Spenser: A Savage Place, 1994, Wounded Heart, 1995, Hearts Adrift, Reasons of the Heart, 1996, TV series The Marriage Counselor, 1994. Lt. (j.g.) USNR, 1953-57. Recipient Evelyn Burkey Meml. award Writers Guild Am., 1983, Silver Circle award NATAS, 1999. Mem. NATAS, Internat. Radio and TV Soc., Brit. Acad. Film and TV Arts, Columbia U. Alumni Assn. Avocations: opera, other music, sound reproduction, baseball, other sports. Office: Boardwalk Entertainment 210 E 39th St New York NY 10016-2754 E-mail: aw.boardwalk@infohouse.com. *A decent and abiding respect for the opinions and talents of the creative community on one hand, and the consuming community on the other, has always served as the necessary framework for any decision making in both my professional and personal life. The doers and the thinkers are crucially important, but no more so than those for whom they do and think. If I can serve as an effective middle man, a good part of my life's objective is realizable.*

WAGNER, ANDREW JAMES, meteorologist, elder, educator; b. Greenwich, Conn., Apr. 12, 1934; s. Andrew and Ruth (Machette) Wagner; m. Betty Christina Ritenour, Aug. 9, 1969; children: Jonathan, Nathaniel, Carmen, Manuel. BA, Wesleyan U., 1956; MS, MIT, 1958. Ordained elder Congregational Ch, 1968. Meteorologist Nat. Weather Svc., NOAA, 1965—, sr. forecaster, 1990—; elder, tchr. Sunday sch. Garden Meml. Presbyn. Ch., Washington, 1966-68; elder Ch. No. Va., Oakton, 1969—, treas., 1969-75, tchr. adult Sunday sch., 1990—. Adj prof N T Greek Whole Word Sem, Oakton, 1981—82. Pres Beverly Forest Civic Asn, Springfield, Va., 1976—77, vpres, 1977—78. Mem.: Nat Weather Asn, Am Sci Affiliation, Am Geophysical Union, Am Meteorol Soc. Republican. Avocations: photography, music. Home: 7568 Cloud Ct Springfield VA 22153-1804 Office: Climate Prediction Ctr NOAA Sci Ctr Rm 604 Camp Springs MD 20746 E-mail: James.Wagner@noaa.gov. *As a scientist and Christian layman, I see increasing evidence that scientific advances alone can better life in only a limited way. Only when we individually and as a nation return to the "faith of our fathers" and put Jesus Christ in His rightful position as Lord of all, will we find true meaning and purpose in life.*

WAGNER, ANN, political organization executive; m. Ray Wagner; children: Raymond III, Stephen, Mary Ruth. BSBA, U. Mo., 1984. Dir. ho. and senate redistricting commn. Mo. Reps., 1991, vice chmn., chmn., 1999—; Mo. state exec. dir. Bush/Quayle Campaign, 1992; advisor Ashcroft for Senate Campaign, 1994; 2nd congl. dist. chair Dole for Pres. Campaign, 1996. Chair Mo. Rep. Party. Vocal Music scholar U. Mo. Office: Mo Rep Party 204 East Dunklin Jefferson City MO 65101*

WAGNER, ANN LOUISE, management consultant, public relations executive; b. Omaha, Sept. 19, 1926; d. Valentine and Lois (Rickard) Capetillo; m. Clarence Hubert Wagner, July 23, 1945; children: Ann Anderson, Clarence H. Jr., Evalynne Lindberg. Mgr., owner C.H. Wagner & Co., Boston, 1972-76; mgmt. cons. Bridges for Peace, Tulsa, 1987—. Columnist Wellesley Newspaper, 1972. Mem. task force Tulsa Airport Chaplet, Adopt a Nursing Home Patient; bd. dirs. United Meth. Women, Tulsa, Okla., 1996—. Recipient State Hon. Mother of Yr. Am. Mothers, Inc., 1978, Parents of Yr. Oral Roberts U., 1977. Mem. Nat. Assn. Securities Dealers, Assn. Children with Learning Disabilities (pres.). Avocations: volunteer work in Israel with Bridges for Peace, organize activities between Christian and Jewish communities. Home: 5505 S Quincy Ave Tulsa OK 74105-6945 Office: Bridges for Peace PO Box 33145 Tulsa OK 74153-1145 E-mail: awagner@bfpusa.org.

WAGNER, ANN PRENTICE, art historian; b. Washington, Aug. 17, 1961; d. John Prentice and Polly (Sweet) W. AA in Studio Art, Montgomery Coll., 1982; BA in Art History, George Washington U., 1985; MA in Art History, Boston U., 1987. Mus. asst., docent Phillips Collection, Washington, 1987-94; art historian Nat. Portrait Gallery, 1989-91, curatorial asst., 1991-2000, asst. curator prints & drawings, 2000-2001; teaching asst. U. Md., 2001—02. Co-author: The Cultivation of Artists in Nineteenth-Century America, 1997, Eye Contact: Modern American Portrait Drawings from the National Portrait Gallery, 2002; contbr. articles to profl. publs. Grad. scholar Boston U., 1985-86; grad. alumni fellow Boston U., 1985-86. Mem.: Assn. Historians of Am. Art, Modernist Studies Assn., Internat. Coun. Mus., Am. Assn. Mus., Internat. Coun. Mus., Coll. Art Assn., Historians of 19th Century Art, Washington Print Club (bd. dirs. 1993—95). Democrat. E-mail: apwagner@starpower.net.

WAGNER, ANNICE MCBRYDE, judge; BA, law degree, Wayne State U. With Houston and Gardner; gen. counsel Nat. Capital Housing Authority; people's counsel D.C.; assoc. judge Superior Court D.C., 1977-90, D.C. Ct. Appeals, 1990—, now chief judge. Mem. teaching team, trial advocacy workshop Harvard U. Office: Dist of Columbia Court of Appeals 500 Indiana Ave NW Ste 6000 Washington DC 20001-2131*

WAGNER, ARTHUR WARD, JR. lawyer; b. Birmingham, Ala., Aug. 13, 1930; s. Arthur Ward and Lucille (Lockheart) W.; m. Ruth Shingler, May 11, 1957; children: Celia Wagner Minter, Julia Wagner Dolce, Helen Wagner McAfee. BSBA, U. Fla., 1954, JD, 1957. Bar: Fla. 1957, U.S. Dist. Ct. (so. dist.) Fla. 1957, U.S. Dist. Ct. (mid. dist.) Fla. 1975. Ptnr. Wagner & McAfee, P.A., West Palm Beach, Fla., 1959-2000; ret., 2000—. Lectr. in field. Author: Art of Advocacy: Jury Selection, 1981; co-author: Anatomy of Personal Injury Lawsuit I & II, 1968 and 1981. Mem. 15th Jud. Nominating Com., Palm Beach City, 1979—82, 4th Dist. Nominating Commn., Palm Beach City, 1982—86; mem. pres.'s coun. U. Fla.; vestry Holy Trinity Parish, v.p., 2002—; bd. dirs., pres.-elect U. Fla. Found., 1996—. Fellow Internat. Acad. Trial Lawyers, Am. Coll. Trial Lawyers, Internat. Soc. Barristers, Am. Bd. Trial Advs.; mem. Assn. Trial Lawyers Am. (pres. 1975-76, hon. life trustee Roscoe Pound Found.), So. Trial Lawyers Assn. (pres. 1991), U. Fla. Law Coll. Alumni (mem. bd. govs.). Democrat. Episcopalian.

WAGNER, BARBARA, lawyer; b. Amherst, Mass., Aug. 10, 1951; d. Robert Wanner and Sally (Marsh) W.; m. William C. Partin, Sept. 10, 1977; children: Sally Marsh Wagner Partin, William Robert Wagner Partin. BA, Yale U., 1973; MSBA, Boston U., 1977; JD, Columbia U., 1981. Bar: N.Y. 1982, Ohio 1988. Tchg. asst. ESL Albert-Einstein-Oberschule and Walter Gropius Gesamtschule, Berlin, Germany, 1974-76; translator German-English Brigade Map Supply Ctr. U.S. Army, 1976-77; lectr. English phonology Tchr.'s Coll., 1976-77; lectr. bus. fin. U. Md., Rota, Spain, 1978; assoc. Shearman & Sterling, N.Y.C., 1981-83, Haythe & Curley, N.Y.C., 1983-85, Skadden, Arps, Slate, Meagher & Flom, N.Y.C., 1985-87, Smith & Schnacke, Dayton, Ohio, 1987-88, Frost & Jacobs, Cin., 1988-91; sr. counsel Chiquita Brands Internat., Inc., 1991-92, asst. gen. counsel, 1992-98, assoc. gen. counsel, 1998—. Adj. prof. Coll. Law U. Cin.; spkr. in field. Mem. ABA, Ohio Bar Assn., Cin. Bar Assn., Cin. Yale Club (dir. alumni schs. com. 1990—, pres. 1998-99), Assn. Yale Alumni (bd. govs. 2001—). Avocations: gardening, photography. Office: Chiquita Brands International Inc 250 E 5th St Cincinnati OH 45202-5190

WAGNER, BILLY, baseball player; b. Tannersville, Va. , July 25, 1971; Student, Ferrum Coll. Baseball player Houston Astros, 1995—. Named 1st Houston pitcher to win Rolaids Relief Man award. Achievements include holds the single-season NCAA record for most strikeouts per nine innings (19.1 in 1992); Division III mark for most career K's (327 in 182.1 innings); fewest hits allowed per game (1.58 in 1992). Office: Houston Astros Po Box 288 Houston TX 77001-0288*

WAGNER, BRUCE STANLEY, marketing professional; b. San Diego, Aug. 1, 1943; s. Robert Sheldon and Janet (Lowther) Wagner; m. Elizabeth Pearsall Winslow, Oct. 4, 1975; children: Sage Elizabeth, Alexander Winslow. BA, Dartmouth Coll., 1965; MBA, U. Pa., 1984. Sr. v.p. Grey Advt., Inc., N.Y.C., 1967-81; exec. v.p., chief oper. officer Campaign '76 Media Comm., Inc., Washington, 1975-76; exec. v.p., bd. dirs. Ross Roy, Inc., Bloomfield Hills, Mich., 1981-91, Ross Roy Group, Inc., Bloomfield Hills, 1991-94; v.p. mktg. and comms. ITT Automotive Inc., Auburn Hills, 1995-99; pres. Wagner & Co., Ltd., Birmingham, 1999—; v.p. mktg. and corp. comms. MSX Internat. Inc., Southfield, 2001—. Mem. parents bd. Bucknell U., pres. parents bd., 1999—2000. Mem.: Am. Assn. Advt. Agys. (bd. govs. ctrl. region 1988—94, chmn., bd. govs. Mich. coun. 1985—86), Wharton Alumni Assn. (chmn. 1983—85), Birmingham Athletic Club, Orchard Lake Country Club, Detroit Athletic Club, Wharton Club Mich. (bd. dirs. 1985—). Home: 975 Arlington Rd Birmingham MI 48009-1684 Office: MSX Internat Inc 22355 W Eleven Mile Rd Southfield MI 48034-4735

WAGNER, BURTON ALLAN, lawyer; b. Milw., June 13, 1941; s. Irwin and Jennie (Oxman) W.; m. Georgia Olchoff, Aug. 29, 1964; children: Andrew, Laura. BBA in Acctg, U. Wis., 1963, JD, 1966, MA in Health Services Adminstrn, 1976. Bar: Wis. 1966. Assoc. legal counsel U. Wis., 1968-74; asst. to vice chancellor, legal counsel U. Wis. Hosps., 1974-77; asst. sec. Wis. Dept. Health and Social Services, 1977-83, adminstr. div. community services, 1979-83; clin. assoc. prof. health adminstrn. U. Wis.; ptnr. Thomas Harnisch & Wagner, Madison, 1983-85, Whyte & Hirschboeck, Madison, 1985-90; ptnr. (of counsel) Katten Muchin and Zavis, 1990-93; ptnr. Reinhart Boerner Van Deuren Norris & Rieselbach, 1993—. Served with USAR, 1966-68, Vietnam. Decorated Bronze Star. Mem. Soc. Law and Medicine, Wis. Bar Assn., Dane County Bar Assn. Jewish. Office: PO Box 2018 Madison WI 53701-2018 E-mail: bwagner@reinhartlaw.com.

WAGNER, CARRUTH JOHN, physician; b. Omaha, Sept. 4, 1916; s. Emil Conrad and Mabel May (Knapp) W. AB, Omaha U., 1938; B.Sc., U. Nebr., 1938, MD, 1941, D.Sc., 1966. Diplomate: Am. Bd. Sugery, Am. Bd. Orthopaedic Surgery. Intern U.S. Marine Hosp., Seattle, 1941-42; resident gen. surgery and orthopaedic surgery USPHS hosps., Shriners Hosp., Phila., 1943-46; med. dir. USPHS, 1952-62; chief orthopaedic service USPHS Hosp., San Francisco, 1946-51, S.I., N.Y., 1951-55, health mblzn., 1959-62; asst. surgeon gen. dep. chief div. hosps. UPHS, 1957-59; chief div. USPHS, 1962-65, USPHS (Indian Health), 1962-65; dir. Bur. Health Services, 1965-68; Washington rep. AMA, 1968-72; health services cons., 1972-79; dept. health services State of Calif., 1979—. Contbr. articles to med. jours. Served with USCGR, World War II. Recipient Pfizer award, 1962; Meritorious award Am. Acad. Gen. Practice, 1965; Disting. Svc. medal, 1968, Calif. Dept. Health Svcs. Pub. Health Recognition award, 1995. Fellow A.C.S. (bd. govs.), Am. Soc. Surgery Hand, Am. Assn. Surgery Trauma, Am. Geriatrics Soc., Am. Acad. Orthopaedic Surgeons; mem. Nat. Assn. Sanitarians, Am. Pub. Health Assn. Sanitarians, Am. Pub. Health Assn., Washington Orthopaedic Club, Am. Legion, Alpha Omega Alpha. Clubs: Mason (Shriner). Lutheran. Home: 6234 Silverton Way Carmichael CA 95608-0757 Office: 6234 Silverton Way Carmichael CA 95608-0757 *My success can best be summarized as the result of efforts of other people. First my family, particularly my mother, then my teachers and preceptors, and finally my associates. Throughout my life there has been a key individual who created an environment where I could exercise my maximum capabilities. Later in life when it became possible for me to provide similar opportunities for associates I found the benefits I derived far exceeded anything I could have achieved on my own. In summary, success means getting things done, getting planned things done, and getting planned things done largely through other people.*

WAGNER, CHARLENE BROOK, publishing consultant; b. L.A. d. Edward J. and Eva (Anderson) Brook; children: Gordon, Brook, John. BS, Tex. Christian U., 1952; MEd, Sam Houston U., 1973; postgrad., U. Tex., Austin, 1975, Tex. A&M U., 1977. Sci. educator Spring Branch Ind. Sch. Dist., Houston, 1970-98; ret., 2000; dir. CompuKidZ, Houston, 1998—2000; cons. Scott Foresman, Addison Wesley, Ginn. Cons. Scott Foresman Pub. Co., Houston, 2000-01; owner Sci. Instrnl. Sys. Co., 1988—; dir. Compukidz. Mem. Houston Symphony League, 1992, Mus. Fine Arts, Mus. of Art of Am. West, Houston, 1989, Mus. Natural Scis., Women's Christian Home, Houston, 1991; mem. Houston Grand Opera Guild, mem. exec. bd. 1999-2000, rec./corr. sec.; social chmn. Encore, 1988; mem. Magic Circle Rep. Women's Club. Mem.: AAUW, NAFE, NEA, Internat. Platform Assn., Spring Branch Edn. Assn., Tex. State Tchrs. Assn., Heather and Thistle Soc., Wellington Soc. for Arts (Houston chpt.), Clan Anderson Soc., Art League Houston, Shepherd Soc., Watercolor Arts Soc. (Houston), Houston Highland Games Assn., Space City Ski Club. Episcopalian. Avocations: painting, watercolor media. Home: B54 2670 Marilee Ln Apt B54 Houston TX 77057-4264 Office: 2301 Fountain View Dr Apt 85 Houston TX 77057-4620 E-mail: wagner2670@aol.com.

WAGNER, CHARLES ALAN, librarian; b. Elkhart, Ind., Apr. 27, 1948; s. Arthur and Lydia M. (Stump) W.; m. Marilynn B. Dray, Aug. 17, 1971; children: Sarah, Wendy. BA, Manchester (Ind.) Coll., 1970, MLA, Ind. U., 1973. Libr. dir. Peru (Ind.) Pub. Libr., 1973—. Contbr. articles in field; cartoons appear in comic books, newspapers, mags. With USAR, ret. Mem. Ind. Library Assn., Plymouth Club Am., Rotary. Address: 102 E Main St Peru IN 46970-2338

WAGNER, CHERI J. business owner; b. Mar. 9, 1963; Owner, mgr. Wagner Constrn., Lake Arrowhead, Calif., 1980-94, Blind Ambitions, Skyforest, 1994—. Mem. C. of C., Soroptimists, Nat. Fedn. Ind. Bus., Humane Soc., Arrowhead Bldg. Contractors Assn., Mountain Women's Assn. Office: PO Box 885 Skyforest CA 92385-0885 E-mail: poker4me247@msn.com.

WAGNER, CHRISTIAN NIKOLAUS JOHANN, materials engineering educator; b. Saarbrucken-Dudweiler, Germany, Mar. 6, 1927; came to U.S., 1959, naturalized, 1969; s. Christian Jakob and Regina (Bungert) W.; m. Rosemarie Anna Mayer, Apr. 5, 1952; children— Thomas Martin, Karla Regine, Petra Susanne. Student, U. Poitiers, France, 1948-49; Licence es Sci., U. Saar, Ger., 1951, Diplom-Ingenieur, 1954, Dr.rer.nat., 1957. Research asst. Inst. fur Metallforschung, Saarbrucken, 1953-54; vis. fellow M.I.T., 1955-56; research asso. Inst. fur Metallforschung, 1957-58; teaching, research asst. U. Saarbrucken, 1959; asst. prof. Yale U., New Haven, 1959-62, assoc. prof., 1962-70; prof. dept. materials engring. UCLA, 1970-91, prof. emeritus, 1991—, chmn. dept., 1974-79, asst. dean undergrad. studies Sch. Engring. and Applied Sci., 1982-85, acting chmn., 1990-91. Vis. prof. Tech. U., Berlin, 1969, U. Saarbrücken, 1979-80 Contbr. articles to profl. jours. Recipient U.S. Sci. Humboldt award U. Saarbrucken, 1989-90, 92. Fellow Am. Soc. Metals Internat.; mem. Am. Crystallographic Assn., Minerals, Metals and Materials Soc. Home: 37621 Golden Pebble Ave Palm Desert CA 92211-1430 Office: UCLA 6532 Boelter Hl Los Angeles CA 90095-0001 E-mail: cwagner@de.rr.com.

WAGNER, CLARENCE H., JR. charitable organization administrator; b. 1953; BSc in Mktg./BSc in Investments, Babson Coll., Wellesley, Mass., 1975; MBA with high distinction, Oral Roberts U., 1976. Adminstr. Spafford Children's Ctr., Jerusalem, 1977-80; pres., internat. dir. Bridges for Peace, 1980—. Mem. adv. bd., mem. faculty Jerusalem Univ. Coll. Author: Lessons from the Land of the Bible, 1998, 2d edit., 2000, 365 Fascinating Facts about the Holy Land, 1999, Israel Teaching Letter; editl. bd. Christians and Israel; exec. prodr. TV program Jerusalem Mosaic; editor Dispatch from Jerusalem; co-editor Israel Current News Update; contbr. articles to profl. jours. Exec. bd. Interreligious Coord. Coun., Israel; mem. Ecumenical theol. rsch. Fraternity, Israel; editl. adv. com. Internat. Forum for United Jerusalem. Named Alumnus of Yr., Oral Roberts U., 2000. Mem. Rotary. Office: PO Box 33145 Tulsa OK 74153-1145

WAGNER, CURTIS LEE, JR. judge; b. Nov. 8, 1928; m. Jeanne E. Allen (dec.); children: Curtis L. III, Rex A. Student, Tenn. Poly. Inst., 1947-49; LLB, U. Tenn., 1951. Bar: Tenn. 1952. Assoc. Kramer, Dye, McNabb and Greenwood, Knoxville, Tenn., 1951-54; atty.-adv. gen. crimes and fraud sect. Criminal Divsn. Dept. Justice, Washington, 1954-56; trial atty. Dept. Justice, 1954-60; assigned to Ct. of Claims sect. Civil Divsn., 1956-60; spl. asst. comms., transp. and utilities JAG Dept. Army, 1960-64; chief Regulatory Law Divsn., 1964-74; adminstrv. law judge FERC, 1974-79, chief adminstrv. law judge, 1979—. Mem. civilian lawyer career com., 1960-74; chmn. JAG incentive awards com. 1960-74; mem. Army Staff Awards Bd., 1964-74, Army Environ. Policy Council, 1972-74. Dist. commr. Nat. Capital Area coun. Boy Scouts Am., 1967-69; mem. bd. Govts. Watergate of Alexandria Condo, 1996—; commr. Alexandria Redevel. and Pub. Housing Commn., 1996-2000. Decorated Meritorious Civilian Svc. award, Exceptional Civilian Svc. award; recipient citation for outstanding performance Dept. Army, 1961-74, Scouter's Tng. award Boy Scouts Am., 1965, Scoutmaster's Key, 1966, Commr.'s Key, 1968, Commr.'s Arrowhead Honor, 1966, Silver Beaver award 1969. Mem. Order of Arrow, Soc. Profls. in Dispute Resolution, Annapolis Yacht (parliamentarian) Club. Methodist. Office: Fed Energy Regulatory Commn 888 1st St NE Washington DC 20426-0002 E-mail: curtis.wagner@ferc.fed.us.

WAGNER, CYNTHIA GAIL, editor, writer; b. Bethesda, Md., Oct. 3, 1956; d. Robert Cheney and Marjory Jane (Kletzing) W. BA in English, Grinnell Coll., 1978; MA in Comms., Syracuse U., 1981. Editl. asst. The Futurist/World Future Soc., Bethesda, Md., 1981-82, staff editor, 1982-85, asst. editor, 1985-91, sr. editor, 1991-92, mng. editor, 1992—. Editor: (newsletter) Futurist Update, 2000—; columnist: 3-2-1 Contact, 1994; contbr. Encyclopedia of the Future, 1995, The 21st Century, 1999. Mem. Theatre Comm. Group, Washington Shakespeare Reading Group. Avocation: theater. Office: The Futurist World Future Soc 7910 Woodmont Ave Ste 450 Bethesda MD 20814-3066 E-mail: cwagner@wfs.org.

WAGNER, DARLA L. librarian; b. Pottstown, Pa., May 9, 1951; d. Gerald L. and Ruth B. (Bittenbender) W.; m. William B. Lucas, Nov. 11, 1979 (div. May 1982). BS in Libr. Sci., Kutztown U., 1973; MLS, Drexel U., 1982. Asst. libr. Pennwalt Corp., King of Prussia, Pa., 1974-78; tech. libr. Certain Teed Corp., Blue Bell, 1978-80; libr. asst. Phila. Elec. Co., 1980-81; supr. libr. svcs. Bethlehem (Pa.) Steel Corp., 1981-86; info. reference profl. AT&T Bell Labs., Allentown, Pa., 1986-90; libr. IEEE, Piscataway, N.J., 1990—. Mem. Spl. Librs. Assn. (archivist engring. divsn. 1982-85, archivist Princeton-Trenton

1996—), Cat Fanciers Assn. (treas. local club 1995—, clk., master clk.). Avocations; breeding, raise and show Sable and Dilute Burmese kittens and cats, travel. Home: 2732 Diane Blvd Allentown PA 18109-3058 Office: IEEE 445 Hoes Ln Piscataway NJ 08854-4150

WAGNER, DARRYL WILLIAM, lawyer; b. Dixon, Ill., Jan. 14, 1943; s. Earl L. and Lois Mae W.; m. Susan A. Aldrich; children: Peter Alan, Nicholas William. BA, Northwestern U., 1965, JD, 1968. Bar: Ill. 1968, U.S. Dist. Ct. (no. dist.) Ill. 1969, U.S. Ct. Appeals (7th cir.) 1971, Calif. 1982. Sr. counsel Sidley Austin Brown & Wood, Chgo., 1969—. Dir. Housing Options for People to Excell, Inc., 1992-94, 96—. Co-author: Illinois Municipal Law: Subdivisions and Subdivisions in Controls, 1978, 81. Mem. ABA, Internat. Assn. Attys. and Execs. in Corp. Real Estate, Ill. State Bar Assn., Chgo. Bar Assn. Presbyterian. Home: 526 A San Ysdidro Rd Santa Barbara CA 93108 Office: Sidley Austin Brown & Wood 555 W 5th St Ste 4000 Los Angeles CA 90013-3000 E-mail: dwagneresq@sidley.com., wwagneresq@springmail.com.

WAGNER, DAVID JAMES, lawyer; b. Cleve., Feb. 7, 1946; m. Martha Wilson, June 22, 1979; 1 child, Diana Jane. BS, USAF Acad., 1969; JD, Georgetown U., 1973. Bar: Colo. 1973, U.S. Supreme Ct. 1975, U.S. Dist. Ct. of Colo. 1973, U.S. Tax Ct. 1974. Asst. assoc. gen. counsel Presdl. Clemency Bd., Washington, 1974-75; sec., gen. counsel Cablecomm-Gen. Inc., Denver, 1975-77; adj. prof. law Metro. State Coll., 1975-80; atty., mng. prin. Wagner & Waller, P.C., 1977-84; chmn. bd. GILA Comm., Inc., 1987; pvt. practice David Wagner & Assocs., P.C., Englewood, Colo., 1984—. Dir. Colo. Sch. of Mines Found., 1999, pres., 2002. Editor Am. Criminal Law Rev., Georgetown U. Law Sch., 1972-73. Trustee Kent Denver Sch., Cherry Hills Village, Colo., 1990-96, treas., 1992, pres., 1992-96; treas., dir. Denver Chamber Orch., 1979-81; dir. Leadership Denver Assn., 1978-80; trustee Colo. Sch. Mines, 1999. Capt. USAF, 1973-75. Republican. Episcopalian. Office: David Wagner & Assocs PC Penthouse 8400 E Prentice Ave Ph Englewood CO 80111-2927

WAGNER, DIANA MAE, English language educator; b. Neenah, Wis., Oct. 2, 1965; d. Gerald Anthony and Elaine Mary (Safford) W. BA, Alverno Coll., 1988; MA, Beaver Coll., 1993. Tchr. St. Laurentius Sc., Phila., 1989-92; adj. prof. English Beaver Coll., Glenside, 1991—99; dir. Beaver Coll. Literacy Corps, 1993-94; dir. edn. enhancement Beaver Coll., 1994-99; advising coord. Salisbury (Md.) U., 1999—. Collegiate fellow Pa. Campus Compact, Harrisburg, 1994-95, master trainer, Pa. Literacy Corps, Harrisburg, 1994. Mem. MLA, Acad. Am. Poets, Emily Dickinson Soc. Avocations: guitar, camping, fishing. E-mail: dmwagner@salisbury.edu.

WAGNER, DONALD BERT, health care consultant; b. York, Pa., July 27, 1930; s. Bert Daniel and Mary Elizabeth (Roelke) W.; m. Janet Louise Bankert, July 12, 1952; children: Kimberly, Susan, David, John. Student, Franklin & Marshall, 1948-50; BS in Phys. Therapy, Columbia U., 1952; MHA, Baylor U., 1960. Commd. 2d lt. USAF, 1952, advanced through grades to brig. gen., 1982; physical therapist Randolph AFB, San Antonio, 1952-55; asst. adminstr. USAF/RAF S. Ruislip, London; adminstr. USAF/RAF Bentwaters, Ipswich, Eng., 1955-58; various adminstrv. roles USAF Hosps. and Commands, Europe and U.S., 1958-73; dep. comdr. USAF Sch. Health Care Sci., Wichita Falls, Tex., 1973-75; adminstr. Wilford Hall Med. Ctr., San Antonio, 1975-79; chief med. svc. corps Office Surgeon Gen. USAF, 1979-82; dep. surgeon gen. USAF Med. Svc. Ctr., 1981-82, ret., 1982; adminstr., assoc. v.p. M. D. Anderson/U. Tex. Cancer Ctr., Houston, 1982-85; chief exec. officer Meml. Southwest Hosp., 1985-91; v.p. Meml. Hosp. System, 1985-91, interim hosp. chief, 1991—; mem. adv. bd. Grad. Program in Healthcare Adminstrn. Texas Women's U. Adj. prof. Baylor and Trinity U., San Antonio, 1975-82; assoc. prof. U. Houston, St. Louis U., 1982-88; exec. officer Woodlands Hosp., Angleton-Danbury Hosp., Prevention and Recovery Ctr. Bd. dirs. Hospice at the Med. Ctr., 1982-2001, Child Advocates, Houston, 1985-89, Kidney Found., Houston, 1985-88, Westland YMCA, Houston, 1985-88, 90-94, Greater Houston Hosp. Coun., 1983-87, Sam Houston area Alzheimer's Assn. 1990-94; mem.n. external adv. bd. Sch. Allied Health, U. Tex. Med. Br.; mem. adv. bd. gradrogram healthcare adminstrn. Tex. Women's U., Houston. Named Disting. Alumnus Baylor U. Program in Healthcare Adminstrn., 1993. Fellow Am. Coll. Healthcare Execs. (edn. com., ethics com., comm. com.), Royal Soc. Health; mem. Am. Hosp. Assn. (bd. dirs. hosp. rsch. and edn. found. 1990—), Tex. Hosp. Assn., Assn. Mil. Surgeons U.S. (Ray E. Brown award 1982, Outstanding Sr. Level Healthcare Exec. Ache Regents award 1991), Am. Mgmt. Soc. Republican. Methodist. Avocation: music. Home: 1746 Carriage Way Sugar Land TX 77478-4201 Office: Meml Healthcare System 9401 Southwest Fwy Houston TX 77074-1807 E-mail: don_wagner@mhhs.org.

WAGNER, DORIS WALKLING, volunteer, director; b. near Gamber, Md., Feb. 16, 1926; d. John Earl and Pearl Elizabeth (Flora) Walkling; m. William Edward McGrath, Jan. 22, 1947 (div. 1974); children: Ellen, Jane, Ann, Kevin, Mary, Timothy, Thomas, Brigid; m. George Everett Wagner, Oct. 20, 1979. Diploma, St. Agnes Hosp. Sch. Nursing, Balt., 1946. Lic. underwriter life and health ins. Md.; RN Md., 1947. Nurse, Westminster, Md., 1946—96; nurse case mgr. Home Call, Inc., 1979—89; asst. adminstr., nurse S. Carroll Adult Day Care, Eldersburg, 1989—94, Eldersburg Adult Day Care, 1994—96; field ops. asst. Green Thumb, Inc., Westminster, Md., 2001—. Show sec. Columbia (Md.) Horse Show, 1968. Author: (Poetry) Lyrical Heritage, 1996 (Editor's Choice, 1996), The Best Poems of 1997, 1997 (Editor's Choice, 1997), (Anthology) Along the Way, 1999 (Best Poem of 1999). Pres., bd. dirs. Humane Soc. of Carroll County, Md., 1987—; mem. Sr. Provider Info. Network, Westminster, 2001—. Fellow: Westminster Sr. Ctr. Republican. Roman Catholic. Avocations: bridge, gardening, painting, reading, writing. Home: 2360 Braddock Rd Mount Airy MD 21771

WAGNER, DOROTHY MARIE, retired senior creative designer, artist; b. Chgo., Jan. 12, 1926; d. William Christopher and Margaret Frances (Rowell) W. Student, Kalamazoo Coll., 1943-45; BS, Western Mich. U., 1947; BFA, Art Ctr. Coll. Design, L.A., 1962. Dir. electroencephalography lab. Bronson Hosp., Kalamazoo, 1945-51; dir. EEG lab. Terr. Hosp., Kaneohe, Hawaii, 1951-55, UCLA Med. Ctr., 1955-60; sr. creative designer GM Tech. Ctr. Styling, Warren, Mich., 1962-82. Cons. in EEG, Army Hosp., Honolulu, 1950-55; dir. sales and rental gallery Pt. Huron (Mich.) Mus., 1989-93, art and painting instr., 1992-96. Recipient Best of Show award Ea. Mich. Internat. Art Show, 1992, 1st pl. award, 1988, 89, 94. Mem. Blue Water Art Assn. (pres. 1990-96), Orion Art Ctr. Episcopalian. Avocations: horseback riding, showing in dressage, breeding and raising racing greyhounds, water color and acrylic painting, stained glass design and fabrication. Home: 14841 Pine Knoll Rd Capac MI 48014-1913 E-mail: dot@glis.net.

WAGNER, DOUGLAS ALAN, secondary school educator; b. Washington, June 20, 1957; s. Robert Earl and Bernice (Bittner) W.; m. Linda Sue Tinsley, July 18, 1981; children: John Robert, James Alan. BS in Indsl. Mgmt., Ga. Inst. Tech., 1980; student, N.C. State U., 1975-76; MEd in Math., Ga. State U., 1987, EdS, 1991, PhD in Math. Edn., 1994. Cert. spl. edn. tchr., Ga. Mfrs. rep. Hitachi Corp., Atlanta, 1981; tchr. math., football coach Gwinnett Bd. Edn., Lawrenceville, Ga., 1981-84, 85—, chmn. math. dept., 1995—; prodn. supr. Campbell Soup Co., Maxton, N.C., 1984-85. Asst. varsity football coach Parkview H.S., Lilburn, Ga., 1981-90, head jr. varsity football coach, 1983-88; grad. rsch. asst. Atlanta Math. Project/NSF, 1990-94; steering com. Coll. Mgmt., Ga. Inst. Tech., Atlanta, 1983-84, cons., U.S. Dept. Edn., 1997, Cisco Sys., 2001—. Author curriculum materials; spkr. in field. Tchr. ch. sch. St. Andrews Presbyn. Ch., Tucker, Ga., 1977-80, ordained elder, 1979—, clk. pro-tem, 2001; pres. Westminister Presbyn. Ch. Choir, Snellville, Ga., 1989-90, elem. sch. coord., 1995-96. Recipient, Parkview High Sch. Tchr. of the Yr. Runner-up, 1989-90, Parkview H.S. Tchr. of the Yr. 1992-93, Gwinnett Co. Tchr. of the Yr. Finalist, 1992-93. Mem. NEA, Ga. Assn. Educators, Nat. Coun. Tchrs. Math., Ga. Coun. Tchrs. Math., So. Assn. Colls. and Schs. (steering com. Parkview High Sch. 1988-89, peer rev. team), mem. Gwinnett Co. Curriculum Revision, 1991-94, Gwinnett Co. Textbook Adoption Com., 1999-2000). Republican. Avocations: golf, fishing, hunting, flying. Home: 1995 Pinella Dr Grayson GA 30017-1705 Office: Parkview High Sch 998 Cole Rd SW Lilburn GA 30047-5499

WAGNER, DURRETT, former publisher, picture service executive; b. El Paso, Tex., Feb. 27, 1929; s. Francis and Florence (Durrett) W.; m. Betty Jane Brown, June 7, 1951; children— Gordon, Velma, Kendra. BA, Baylor U., 1950; M.Div., Yale, 1954; postgrad., U. Chgo., 1954-59. Chmn. social sci. div. Kendall Coll., Evanston, Ill., 1959-63, dean, 1963-67; partner v.p.; Swallow Press Inc., Chgo., 1967-92; owner, partner, pres. Hist. Pictures Service, Inc., 1975-92; pres. Bookworks, Inc., 1990—2001. Home: Evanston, Ill. Died Nov. 21, 2001.

WAGNER, EDWARD KURT, publishing company executive; b. N.Y.C., Sept. 29, 1936; s. Kurt Henry and Julia Marie (Selesky) W.; m. Ann Marie Philbin, Jan. 31, 1959; children: Denise, Steven, Kenneth, Jeanne. BBA, St. Francis Coll., 1961. With Pitman Pub. Corp., N.Y.C., 1952-75, v.p., treas., 1968-71, exec. v.p., 1971-75; financial mgr. Dun-Donnelley Pub. Corp., 1975-76, contr. gen. book div., 1976-77; sr. mgr. contr.'s dept. Dun & Bradstreet, Inc., 1977-78, asst. contr., 1978-83, contr., 1983-88, v.p., contr., 1989-96; ret., 1996—. Home: 55 Shoal Rd Jackson NJ 08527

WAGNER, ELLYN S(ANTI), mathematics educator; BS, No. Ariz. U., 1971, MA, 1974; postgrad., George Mason U., 1980-82. Cert. tchr., Va. Tchr. math. Flagstaff (Ariz.) Pub. Schs., 1972-76, head math. dept., 1974-76; asst. prof. math. No. Va. C.C., Annandale, Va., 1976—. Participant Writing Across the Curriculum Workshops, Annandale, 1992-93. Recipient recognition for outstanding contbns. to edn. No. Va. C.C. Alumni Fedn., 1993. Mem. Am. Math. Assn. Two-Yr. Colls., Va. Math. Assn. Two-Yr. Colls. (regional v.p. 1989-91, coord. spring conf. 1992), Phi Kappa Phi. Avocations: classical piano, ballroom dancing. E-mail: ewagner@nv.cc.va.us.

WAGNER, ERIC ARMIN, sociology educator; b. Cleve., May 31, 1941; s. Armin Erich and Florence (Edwards) W. AB, Ohio State U., 1964; MA, U. Fla., 1968, PhD, 1973. Instr. sociology Ohio U., Athens, 1968-73, asst. prof., 1973-75, assoc. prof., 1975-83, prof., 1983-97, chmn. sociology and anthropology, 1974—78, 1986—91, vice chmn. faculty senate, 1982—84, prof. emeritus, 1997, chmn. sociology and anthropology, 1994—97. Contbr. articles on internat. sports and soc. to books and profl. jours. Dir. Planned Parenthood of Southeast Ohio, 1990-96, pres. 1992-94. Mem. Internat. Sociol. Assn., Midwest Assn. Latin Am. Studies (pres. 1979-80), U.S. Orienteering Fedn. (dir. 1976-82, sec.-treas. 1976-79, v.p. 1979-80, sec. 1980-82), Delta Sigma Phi. Presbyterian. Home: 2615 NW 82d St Gainesville FL 32606-8638

WAGNER, FLORENCE ZELEZNIK, telecommunications executive; b. McKeesport, Pa., Sept. 23, 1926; d. George and Sophia (Petros) Zeleznik; m. Francis Xavier Wagner, June, 18, 1946; children: Deborah Elaine Wagner Franke, Rebecca Susan Wagner Schroettinger, Melissa Catherine Wagner Good, Francis Xavier, Robert Francis. BA magna cum laude, U. Pitts., 1977, MPA, 1981. Sec. to pres. Tube City Iron & Metal Co., Glassport, Pa., 1944-50; cons. Raw Materials, Inc., Pitts., 1955; gen. mgr. Carson Compressed Steel Products, 1967-69; ptnr. Universal Steel Products, 1970-71; gen. mgr. Josh Steel Co., Braddock, Pa., 1971-78; owner Wagner's Candy Box, Mt. Lebanon, 1979-80; borough sec./treas. Borough of Pennsbury Village, Allegheny County, 1980-88; ptnr. Tele-Communications of Am., Burgettstown, 1984-86; trustee Profit-Sharing Trust, Pension Trust Josh Steel Co., 1986-88, Consol, Inc., Upper St. Clair, 1989—. Mem. Foster Parents, Jefferson Twp. Planning Commn., Washington County, Pa.; mem. sch. bd. St. Bernard Cath. Elem. Sch., Mt. Lebanon, Pa., sec., 1995-98; GED literacy vol. Pitts.-Carlow, 1997-98. Mem. AAUW, Pitts. Symphony Soc., Pitts. Ballet Theater Guild, Soc. Pub. Adminstrn. (founder U. Pitts. br.), Acad. Polit. Sci., U.S. Strategic Inst., Southwestern Pa. Sec. Assn., Alpha Sigma Lambda (past treas., sec., pres.). Republican. Home: 1611 Upper Saint Clair Dr Pittsburgh PA 15241-2648 E-mail: fw@libcom.com.

WAGNER, FREDERICK REESE, language professional; b. Phila., Apr. 15, 1928; m. Barbara Alexander Brady, May 9, 1959 (div. 1968); 1 child, Christopher A. BA summa cum laude, Duke U., 1948, MA, 1949, PhD, 1971. Advt mgr. Prentice-Hall, Inc., N.Y.C., 1955-57; promotion mgr. Harper & Row, 1957-65; instr. English Duke U., Durham, N.C., 1967-69; asst. prof. Hamilton Coll, Clinton, N.Y., 1969-73, assoc. prof., 1973-78, prof. English, chmn. dept., 1978-90, prof. English, 1990-95. Author: Famous Underwater Adventurers, 1962; Submarine Fighter of the American Revolution, 1963; Patriot's Choice: The Story of John Hancock, 1964; Robert Morris, Audacious Patriot, 1976. Mem. Thoreau Soc. (pres. 1984-86), Hawthorne Soc., Phi Beta Kappa. Home: 2160 Bleecker St Apt A-215 Utica NY 13501

WAGNER, FREDERICK WILLIAM (BILL WAGNER), lawyer; b. Daytona Beach, Fla., Apr. 13, 1933; s. Adam A. and Nella (Schroeder) W.; m. Ruth Whetstone; children: Alan Frederick, Darryl William, Thomas Adam. BA, U. Fla., 1955, LLB with honors, 1960. Bar: Fla. 1960, U.S. Supreme Ct. 1967, D.C. 1989; cert. civil trial lawyer, Fla. Bar; cert. aviation lawyer, Fla. Bar. Pvt. practice law, Miami, Fla., 1960-63, Orlando, 1963-65, Tampa, 1965—; ptnr. Nichols, Gaither, Beckham, Colson, Spence & Hicks, 1965-67; ptnr. shareholder Wagner, Vaughan & McLaughlin (P.A. and predecessor names), 1967—. Mem. Gov.'s Judicial Nominations Commn., 1971-72, Constnl. Judicial Nominations Commn., 1972-75; mem. Fla. Bd. Bar Examiners, 1974-77, emeritus mem., 1995—; chmn. Civil Procedure Rules Com. Fla. Bar, 1977-78; bd. govs. Fla. Bar, 1978-83; trustee Roscoe Pound Inst., 1984-92; mem. civil jury instrn. com. Fla. Supreme Ct. Contbr. articles to profl. jours. 1st lt. USAF, 1955-57. Fellow Am. Bar Found., Am. Coll. Trial Lawyers, Internat. Acad. Trial Lawyers, Am. Bd. Trial Advs.; mem. Assn. Trial Lawyers Am. (bd. govs. 1973-80, 84-89, chmn. pub. affairs dept. 1984-89, treas. 1982-84, v.p. 1986-87, pres.-elect 1987-88, pres. 1988-89), Am. Inns of Ct. Found. (bd. trustees), Acad. Fla. Trial Lawyers (bd. dirs. 1965-84, pres. 1972-73), Bay Area Trial Lawyers Assn. (v.p. 1966-68), Am. Law Inst. (coun. 1993—), Lawyer-Pilots Bar Assn., Fla. Bar Found., U. Fla. Alumni Assn., Nat. Bd. Trial Advocacy (cert. civil), Assn. Personal Injury Lawyers, Australian Plaintiff Laywers Assn., Pan European Orgn. Personal Injury Lawyers, So. Trial Lawyers Assn., Nat. Transp. Safety Bd. Bar Assn. Democrat. Methodist. Home: 901 Mariner Way Tampa FL 33602-5759 Office: Wagner Vaughan & McLaughlin 601 Bayshore Blvd Ste 910 Tampa FL 33606-2786 E-mail: wagnerfla@aol.com., Bill@WagnerLaw.com.

WAGNER, GERALDINE MARIE, nursing educator; b. Renton, Wash., Apr. 12, 1948; d. Ernest F. and Vera P. (Temiraeff) W. AA, Pasadena City Coll., 1970; BA cum laude, Calif. State U., Northridge, 1977; BSN, Calif. State U., L.A., 1982; MEd, Azusa Pacific U., 1993. Cert. pub. health nurse, Calif. Dept. Health Svcs. In utilization mgmt. Blue Cross, Woodland Hills, Calif., 1987-88, Healthmarc, Pasadena, 1988-90; nursing educator, asst. dir. vocat. nursing program Casa Loma Coll., L.A., 1991-92, dir. program planning and devel., and coord. continuing edn. Lake View Terrace, 1992-93; dir. vocal. nursing program Glendale (Calif.) Career Coll., 1994-95; with patient care rev. svcs. U. So. Calif. U. Hosp., L.A., 1996—; med.-legal nurse cons., 2000—. Capt. Nurse Corp, U.S. Army, 1979-84. Mem. Am. Nursing Informatics Assn., Soc. Bioethics and Medicine, Computer Using Educators, Order of Preachers, Pi Lambda Theta, Sigma Theta Tau. Roman Catholic. E-mail: srgmwagnerop@earthlink.net.

WAGNER, GÜNTER PAUL, biologist educator; b. Vienna, Austria, May 28, 1954; came to U.S., 1991; s. Otto Karl and Käthe Auguste (Birke) W.; m. Herta Ruttner Brinkmann, Dec. 31, 1978 (div. 1985); 1 child, Susanne Karoline; m. Michaela Sabine Hauser, July 19, 1985; children: Veronika Eszter, Nikolas Frederik. PhD, U. Vienna, Austria, 1979; MA (hon.), Yale U., 1992. Asst. prof. U. Vienna, 1985-90, assoc. prof., 1990-91; prof. biology Yale U., New Haven, 1991—, chmn. dept. ecology and evolutionary biology, 1996—2001. Bd. dirs. Konrad Lorenz Inst. for Evolution and Cognition Rsch.; vis. prof. Northwestern U., Evanston, Ill., 1987-88, U. Basel. Switzerland, 1991, U. Leiden, The Netherlands, 1995; Gompertz lectr. U. Calif., Berkeley, 1993; disting. lectr. Internat. Inst. for Applied Sys. Analysis, 1995; Sewell Wright lectr. U. Chgo., 1996. Mem. editl. bd.: Theory in the Bioscis., 1998—, mem. editl. bd.: Jour. of Theoretical Biology, 1999—2001, mem. editl. bd.: Evolution and Devel., 1999—, mem. editl. bd.: Biology and Philosophy, 2001—, mem. editl. bd.: Am. Naturalist, 2001—, chief editor: Molecular and Devel. Evolution, 1999—, mem. publ. com.: Yale U. Press, 1992—95; contbr. articles to profl. jours. Recipient MacArthur prize MacArthur Found., 1992. Fellow AAAS; mem. European Soc. Evolutionary Biology (editl. bd. 1988-92), Austrian Acad. Scis. (corr.), Soc. for Study of Evolution (assoc. editor 1994-97), Soc. Systematic Biology, Soc. for Integrative and Comparative Biology (chair divsn. evolutionary devel. biology 2000—). Lutheran. Avocations: sailing, canoeing, horseback riding, literature, music. Office: Yale Univ 165 Prospect St New Haven CT 06511-8106 E-mail: guntur.wagner@yale.edu.

WAGNER, HAROLD A. industrial gas and chemical company executive; b. Oakland, Calif., Nov. 12, 1935; s. Harold A. and Lurline Frances (Madsen) W.; m. Marcia Kenaston, July 14, 1956; children: Sandra Wagner Boyce, Kristi Wagner, Schwiering, Tracey, Erik. BS in Mech. Engring., Stanford U., 1958, SEP, 1982; MBA, Harvard U., 1963. Regional sales mgr. ind. gases U.S. Air Products & Chems., Allentown, Pa., 1963-70; mgr. GM ind. gases U.K.Air Products & Chems., 1970-76; regional sales mgr. GM Ind. Gases Continental Europe, 1976-80, GM Ind. Gases U.S., 1980-81; v.p. sales ind. gases div. FM, 1981-82; v.p. corp. planning Air Products & Chems., 1982-87, v.p. bus. div. chems., 1987-88; pres. AP Europe, 1988-90, exec. v.p., 1990-91, pres., COO, 1991-92, past chmn. pres., CEO; chmn., pres., CEO, dir. Air Products and Chems., 1992—2001, chmn., CEO, dir. 1st Lt. USAF, 1958-61. Avocations: squash, photography. Home: 1306 Prospect Ave Bethlehem PA 18018-4917 Office: Air Prods & Chems Inc 7201 Hamilton Blvd Allentown PA 18195-1501

WAGNER, HARVEY ARTHUR, nuclear engineer, consultant; b. Ann Arbor, Mich., Jan. 2, 1905; s. Emanuel M. and Emma (Kiebler) W.; m. Eleanor Mary Bond, July 6, 1929. BS in Mech. Engring., U. Mich., 1927; D.Eng., Lawrence Inst. Tech., 1969. With Proctor & Gamble Co., 1927-28; with Detroit Edison Co., 1928-70, exec. v.p., 1969-70; cons. engr., 1970-96; chmn., dir. Overseas Adv. Assocs., Inc., 1974-96. Mem. Detroit Bd. Water Commrs., 1952-60; Trustee Nat. Sanitation Found., 1965-82 Author papers in field. Recipient Disting. Alumnus award U. Mich. Coll. Engring., 1953, Outstanding Alumni Achievement award, 1989; Sesquicentennial award as outstanding exec. and nuclear power cons. U. Mich., 1967; cert. pub. service Fed. Power Commn., 1964 Fellow ASME, Am. Nuclear Soc. (Cisler Award, 1994), Engring. Soc. Detroit (pres. 1968-69); mem. Nat. Acad. Engring., Tau Beta Pi, Phi Kappa Phi. Home: 15191 Ford Rd Apt 205 Dearborn MI 48126-4654

WAGNER, JAMES PEYTON, lawyer; b. McKinney, Tex., July 22, 1939; s. Otto James and Jane Peyton (Adams) W.; m. Patricia Anne Squires, June 16, 1962; children: Jarrod Shannon, Anne Paige, Leslie Lauren, James Russell. BA, Tex. Tech. U., Lubbock, 1961; LLB, So. Meth. U., 1964. Bar: Tex. 1964, U.S. Dist. Ct. (no. dist.) Tex. 1965, U.S. Ct. Appeals (3rd and 5th cirs.) 1996, U.S. Supreme Ct. 1996. Atty. United American Ins. Co., Dallas, 1969-70, Employer's Ins. of Wausau, Dallas, 1970-73, Crumley Murphy and Shrull, Ft. Worth, 1973-77, Fillmore & Camp, Ft. Worth, 1977-78, Penner, Jones, Keith & Wagner, Ft. Worth, 1978-80, The Wagner Law Firm, Ft. Worth, Dallas, 1964-69, 80-85;, 1997—; prin. Keith and Wagner, P.C., Ft. Worth, 1985-89; assoc. Brockermeyer & Assocs., 1989-90; ptnr. Fielding, Barrett & Taylor, 1990-97. Author, contbr. course book: State Bar of Texas Personal Injury and Workers Compensation Practice Skills, 1987, 89. Mem. ATLA, State Bar Tex., Tarrant County Bar Assn., Coll. of State Bar Tex., Brain Injury Assn. Baha'i World Faith. Avocations: oenology, music. Home: 4240 Sudith Ln Midlothian TX 76065-6332 Office: Ste 1160 3232 McKinney Ave Dallas TX 75204 E-mail: jpw@jpwagnerlaw.com.

WAGNER, JAMES WARREN, engineering educator; b. Washington, July 12, 1953; s. Robert Earl and Bernice (Bittner) W.; m. Debbie Kelley, July 31, 1976; children: Kimberly Renee, Christine Kelley. BSEE, U. Del., 1975; MS, Johns Hopkins U., 1978, PhD, 1984. Electronics engr. U.S. FDA, Washington, 1975-84; asst. prof. Johns Hopkins U., Balt., 1984-88, assoc. prof., 1988-93, prof., 1993-97, chmn. dept. materials scis. and engring., 1993-97; dean Case Sch. Engring. Case Western Res. U., Cleve., 1998-2000, prof. materials sci. and engring., dean Case Sch. Engring., 1998—, provost, 2000-01, interim pres., 2001—. Contbr. articles to profl. jours. Regional v.p. Chesapeake Bay Yacht Racing Assn., Annapolis, Md., 1982; elder Presbyterian Ch. U.S.A. Mem. IEEE, Optical Soc. Am., Materials Rsch. Soc., Laser & Electro-Optics Soc., Biomed. Engring., Am. Soc. for Nondestructive Evaluation, Soc. Exptl. Mechanics (Peterson award 1988), Nat. Materials Adv. Bd. Presbyterian. Achievements include contributions to the field of optical metrology applied to materials characterization, especially advanced holographic and laser-based ultrasonic methods. Office: Case Western Res U 10900 Euclid Ave Cleveland OH 44106-7001

WAGNER, JOHN LEO, lawyer, former magistrate judge; b. Ithaca, N.Y., Mar. 12, 1954; s. Paul Francis and Doris Elizabeth (Hoffschneider) W.; m. Marilyn Modin, June 18, 1987. Student, U. Nebr., 1973-74; BA, U. Okla., 1976, JD, 1979. Bar: Okla. 1980, Calif. 1999, U.S. Dist. Ct. (we. dist.) Okla. 1980, U.S. Dist. Ct. (no. and ea. dists.) Okla. 1981, U.S. Dist. Ct. (mid. dist.) Calif. 2000, U.S. Ct. Appeals (10th cir.) 1982. Assoc. Franklin, Harmon & Satterfield Inc., Oklahoma City, 1980-82; ptnr. Franklin, Harmon & Satterfield, Inc., 1982; assoc. Kornfeld, Franklin & Phillips, 1982-85, ptnr., 1985; magistrate judge U.S. Dist. Ct. No. Dist. Okla., Tulsa, 1985-97; dir. Irell & Manella LLP Alt. Dispute Resolution Ctr., Newport Beach, Calif., 1997—. Pres. U. Okla. Coll. Law Assn., 1991-92. Fellow Am. Coll. Civil Trial Mediators, ABA, Internat. Acad. Mediators, Fed. Magistrate Judge's Assn. (dir. 10th cir. 1987-89); mem. 10th Cir. Edn. Com., Okla. Bar Assn., Council Oak Am. Inn of Cts. (pres. 1992-93), Jud. Conf. U.S. (com. ct. adminstrn. and case mgmt. 1992-97), CPR-Georgetown Commn. Ethics and Standards in ADR. Republican. Office: Irell & Manella LLP Alt Dispute Resolution Ctr 840 Newport Center Dr Ste 450 Newport Beach CA 92660-6321 E-mail: jwagner@irell.com., usmag1@cox.net.

WAGNER, JOHN PHILIP, safety engineering educator, science researcher; b. Trenton, N.J., Feb. 29, 1940; s. Joseph and Anna Wagner; m. Carol Anne Hammond, June 14, 1969; children: John Joseph (Jay), Timothy Andrew. BS in Chemistry, St. Joseph's U., 1961; MSChemE, Johns Hopkins U., 1964, PhDChemE, 1966. Registered prof. engr., Tex. Rsch. asst. chemistry Johns Hopkins U., Balt., 1961-62, rsch. fellow chem. engring., 1962-66, assoc. chemist Applied Physics Lab. Silver Spring, Md., summer 1962, sr. engr. Applied Physics, 1966-72; sr. rsch. scientist Factor Mut. Rsch. Corp., Norwood, Mass., 1972-73; rsch. supr. Gillette Rsch. Inst., 1973-78; staff engr., sr. staff engr. EXXON Rsch. and Engring. Co., 1978-83; assoc. prof. indsl. engring. Tex. A&M U., 1985-89, assoc. prof. nuclear engring., 1989—; assoc. dir. and rsch. engr. Food Protein Rsch. Devel. Ctr. Tex. Engring. Expt. Station., 1983-90; assoc. dir., rsch. engr. Engring. Bioscis. Rsch. Ctr Tex. A&M U., College Station, 1990—. Cons. O'Melveny & Myers, L.A., 1987-88, Mithoff & Jacks, Austin, Tex., 1996-97, Mills, Shirley, et. al., Galveston, Tex., 1997-98, Bricklin & Gendler, Seattle, 1998-99, Lawrence Livermore Nat. Lab., Exxon Co.-USA, Englehard Industries, Gillette Rsch. Inst., Liberty Mut., Champion Internat, John Deere. Mem. editl. adv. bd. Jour. Polymer-Plastics Tech. and Engring., 1987—, Indsl. Crops and Products, 1991-95; co-guest editor Jour. Bioresources Tech., 1991; contbr. chpts. to books, articles to profl. jours.; patentee in field. Grantee USDA/DOD, 1984-93. Mem. AICE, Am. Chem. Soc., Am. Soc. Safety Engrs., Cath. Alumni Club Balt. (pres. 1968), Sigma Xi, Phi Lambda Upsilon. Avocations: philatelics, numismatics, sports. Office: Tex A&M U Dept Nuclear Engring College Station TX 77843-3133 E-mail: wagner@txcyber.com., johnpwagner@hotmail.com.

WAGNER, JUDITH BUCK, investment firm executive; b. Altoona, Pa., Sept. 25, 1943; d. Harry Bud and Mary Elizabeth (Rhodes) B.; m. Joseph E. Wagner, Mar. 15, 1980; 1 child, Elizabeth. BA in History, U. Wash., 1965; grad., N.Y. Inst. Fin., 1968. Registered Am. Stock Exch., N.Y. Stock Exch., investment advisor. Security analyst Morgan, olmstead, Kennedy & Gardner, L.A., 1968-71, Boettcher & Co., Denver, 1972-75; pres. Wagner Investment Mgmt., 1975—. Chmn. The Women's Bank, N.A., Denver, 1977-94, organizational group pres., 1975-77; chmn. Equitable Bankshares Colo., Inc., Denver, 1980-94; pres. Equitable Bank of Littleton, Colo., 1985; lectr. Denver U., Metro State, 1975-80. Author: Woman and Money series Colo. Woman Mag., 1976, moderator "Catch 2' Sta. KWGN-TV, 1978-79. Pres. Bit Sisters Colo., Denver, 1977-82, bd. dirs., 1972-83; bd. fellows U. Denver, 1985-90; bd. dirs. Red Cross, 1980, Assn. Children's Hosp., 1985, Colo. Health Facilities Authority, 1978-84, Jr. League Cmty. ADv. Com., 1979-82, Bros. Redevel., Inc., 1979-80; mem. agy. rels. com. Mile High United Way, 1978-81, chmn. United Way Venture Way, 1978-81, chmn. United Way Venture Grant com., 1980-81; bd. dirs. Downtown Dener, Inc., 1988-95; bd. dirs., v.p., treas. The Women's Found. Colo., 1987-91; treas., trustee, v.p., Graland Country Day Sch., 1990-97, pres., 1994-97; trustee Denver Rotary Found., 1990-95; trustee Hunt Alternatives Fund, 1992-97, The Colo. Trust, 1998—. Recipient Making It award Cosmopolitan Mag., 1977, Women on the Go award, Savvy Mag., 1983, Minouri Yasoui award, 1986, Salute Spl. Honoree award, Big Sisters, 1987; named one of the Outstanding Young Women Am., 1979;

recipient Woman Who Makes A Difference award Internat. Women's Forum, 1987. Fellow Assn. Investment Mgmt. & Rsch.; mem. Women's Forum Colo. (pres. 1979), Women's Found. Colo., Inc. (bd. dirs. 1986-91), Denver Soc. Security Analysts (bd. dirs. 1976-83, v.p. 1980-81, pres. 1981-82), Colo. Investment Advisors assn., Rotary (treas. Denver chpt. found., pres. 1993-94), Leadership Denver (Outstanding Alumna award 1987), Pi Beta Phi (pres. U. Wash. chpt. 1964-65). Office: Wagner Investment Mgmt Inc Ste 240 3200 Cherry Creek South Dr Denver CO 80209-3245

WAGNER, JULIA A(NNE), retired editor; b. Alexandria, Va., Feb. 15, 1924; d. Luigi and Domenica (Di Giammarino) Coppa; widowed. BA, George Washington U., 1948, MA, 1950. With U.S. Govt., Washington, 1941-55, publs. editor, 1951-55; editl. asst. Dell Pub. Co., N.Y.C., 1956-59, mng. editor, 1959-72, editor-in-chief, 1973-87; ret., 1987.

WAGNER, KENNETH LYNN, lawyer; b. McPherson, Kans., Oct. 13, 1956; s. Francis D. and Mary V. (Van Buren) W.; m. Lida Jane McNearney, Oct. 22, 1983; 1 child, Elizabeth Ann. BS in Journalism, U. Kans., 1979, JD, 1983; LLM, Georgetown U., 1987. Bar: Mo. 1983, Ill. 1984, D.C. 1985. Atty. div. corp. fin. SEC, Washington, 1984-86, spl. counsel, 1986-88; assoc. Schlafly, Griesedieck, Ferrell & Toft, St. Louis, 1983-84, Stinson, Mag & Fizzell, Kansas City, Mo., 1988-89, Arent, Fox, Kintner, Plotkin & Kahn, Washington, 1989-94; assoc. counsel Banc One Corp., 1994-98; asst. gen. counsel Coltec Industries Inc., 1998-99; sr. counsel Goodrich Corp., 1999—. Mem. ABA, Am. Soc. Corp. Secs., Mo. Bar Assn. Republican. Office: Goodrich Corp 2730 W Tyvola Rd Ste 600 Charlotte NC 28217-4578

WAGNER, KIMBERLY A. floral designer; b. Hoisington, Kans., Sept. 22, 1962; d. Harold Elton and Norma Jean (Hartman) W. Student, Barton County C.C., 1980-82. Floral designer Floral Expressions, Great Bend, Kans., 1982-90, Great Bend Floral, 1990—. Instr. Barton County C.C., Great Bend, 1990—, Great Bend Recreation Commn., 1990—. Community devel. Great Bend Jaycees, 1988-90, pres., 1990-91, dir. human svcs., springboard and degrees dir.; dist. dir. Kans. Jaycees, 1991-92, program mgr. St. Jude Children's Hosp., Kans. Jaycees. Named Officer of Yr. Great Bend Jaycees, 1988-90, Pres. of Yr. Region C., Kans. Jaycees, 1990-91, 10th Degree Jaycee, 1991. Lutheran. Avocations: white water rafting, photography, doll collecting. Home: 1720 Harrison St Great Bend KS 67530-2117

WAGNER, LEANA MOREE, computer executive, graphic designer, fine artist; b. San Diego, Nov. 19, 1957; d. Alan Daniel and Shirley Moree (Wright) W. Lab. asst. Kearney Field Sta., Parlier, Calif., 1975-76; forms processing equipment operator IRS, Fresno, 1983-87, data comms. technician, 1994, major sys. operator, 1987—. Portrait artist, Fresno, 1979—. Featured artist in article Artist's Mag., 2002. Recipient 2d pl. ribbon Fresno Fair Fine Art's Exhibit, 1989, People's Choice award, 1994. Avocations: ceramics, horticulture.

WAGNER, LINDLEY HEATH, physician, medical educator; b. Marion, Ind., Mar. 31, 1934; s. William August and Dorothy Gladys (Bird) W.; m. Anabel Lee Ratcliff, May 15, 1957 (div.); m. Janet Rae McLuckie, Nov. 27, 1970; children: Mary Elizabeth Geerdes, Warren Lee, Marta Joan Reeves. AB, Ind. U., 1956; MD, Ind. U., Indpls., 1959. Diplomate Am. Bd. Internal Medicine. Pvt. practice internal medicine, Lafayette, Ind., 1963-74; dir. med. edn. Lafayette (Ind.) Home Hosp., Inc., 1969-97, St. Elizabeth Hosp. Med. Ctr., Lafayette, 1969-97; asst. dean Ind. U. Sch. Medicine, Indpls., 1970—98; asst. dean, dir. Ind. U. Lafayette Ctr. Med. Edn., West Lafayette, 1970-88; dir. med. edn. Purdue U., 1971—98. Med. dir. Ind. Vets. Home, Lafayette, 1963-66, mem. adv. bd., 1968-98; mem. adv. bd. Ind. Vocat. State Coll. Nursing, Lafayette, 1973-98, Purdue U. Sch. Nursing, West Lafayette, 1973-98; cons. internal medicine/gastroenterology Lafayette, 1974-98; coord. Lafayette Med. Edn. Found., Inc., 1973-97. Med. dir. Tippecanoe County Civil Def., Lafayette, 1967-89; bd. mem., v.p. Ctrl. Ind. Health Sys. Agy., Indpls., 1975-83. Maj. U.S. Army, 1960-69. Continuing med. edn. grantee State of Ind., Indpls., 1969-97; grantee various pharm. cos., 1970-97. Fellow ACP (Laureate award Ind. chpt. 2001); mem. AMA (Physician Recognition awards 1971-93), Ind. State Med. Soc. (pres. 1967-69), Assn. Ind. Dirs. of Med. Edn. (alt. trustee 1969-71, sect. on dirs. med. edn. chmn. 1973-75, commn. on med. licensure and med. edn. 1960-98, Honors award 1995), Am. Soc. Internal Medicine. Methodist. Avocations: percussionist, reading, travel, walking, church activities. Home: 1816 Ann Ave Lafayette IN 47905 also: 4953 E Farmdale Ave Mesa AZ 85206-2821

WAGNER, LYNN EDWARD, lawyer; b. Mt. Holly, N.J., Feb. 10, 1941; s. Edward John and Alma Elizabeth (Mason) W.; m. Maureen Elizabeth Bach, May 25, 1973; children: Daniel Preston, Matthew Evan. BS, Drexel U., 1965; JD, Duke U., 1968. Bar: Mass. 1968, U.S. Dist. Ct. Mass. 1968, Fla. 1972, U.S. Ct. Appeals (5th cir.) 1972, U.S. Supreme Ct. 1972, U.S. Dist. Ct. (mid. dist.) Fla. 1974, Pa. 1975, U.S. Dist. Ct. (we. dist.) Pa. 1975, U.S. Ct. Appeals (4th cir.) 1977, U.S. Ct. Appeals (11th cir.) 1978, U.S. Ct. Appeals (D.C. cir.) 1980, U.S. Ct. Appeals (3d cir.) 1985, U.S. Dist. Ct. (so. dist.) Fla. 1991, U.S. Dist. Ct. (no. dist.) Fla. 1992; cert. arbitrator and mediator; cert. Fla. Dept. Ins., U.S. Dept. Labor, U.S. EEOC, Fed. Mediation and Conciliation Svc. Assoc. Foley, Hoag & Elliot, Boston, 1968-70; asst. prof. law U. Fla., Gainesville, 1971-73; sr. trial atty. U.S. EEOC, Washington, 1973-74; ptnr. Berkman, Ruslander, Pohl, Lieber & Engel, Pitts., 1975-84, Kirkpatrick & Lockhart, Pitts., 1985-86, Rumberger, Kirk, Caldwell, Cabaniss, Burke & Wechsler, Orlando, 1986-91, Cabaniss, Burke & Wagner, Orlando, 1991-94, Baker & Hostetler, Orlando, 1995-97, Wagner & Solomon PA, Winter Park, Fla., 1997—; gen. counsel North Star Media, Inc., 1997—99; pres. Litigation Alternatives, Inc., Winter Park, 2000—. Gen. counsel Impact Comm., Inc., 1989-95; bd. dirs. Fla. Legal Svcs., Inc., 1998—. With USAR, 1960-61. Scholarship recipient Sch. Law, Duke U., Durham, N.C., 1965-68. Mem.: ABA (litig. sect., employment law sect., dispute resolution sect.), ATLA, Million Dollar Advocates Forum, Assn. for Conflict Resolution, Leading Am. Attys., Am. Judicature Soc., Fla. Acad. Trial Lawyers, Fla. Acad. Profl. Mediators, Nat. Assn. Securities Dealers (arbitration and mediation panels for securities and employment), Nat. Arbitration Forum, Am. Arbitration Assn. (arbitration & mediation panels for employment, securities and comml.), Fla. Bar Assn. (labor sect., fed. ct. practice sect., dispute resolution sect.), Pa. Bar Assn. (labor sect., dispute resolution sect.), Mass. Bar Assn. Avocations: fishing, boating, travel. Home: 526 Alokee Ct Lake Mary FL 32746-2218 Office: Wagner & Solomon 2180 N Park Ave Ste 318 Winter Park FL 32789 E-mail: lynnewagner@mindspring.com.

WAGNER, MARILYN FAITH, retired elementary school educator; b. Salinas, Calif. d. Clay Chester and Gladys Edna (Wiley) W. AA, Hartnell Coll., Salinas, 1956; BA, San Jose (Calif.) State U., 1958; MA in Computer Edn., U.S. Internat. U., San Diego, 1987; diploma, Inst. Children's Lit., Redding Ridge, Conn., 1981. Cert. elem. tchr., cross-cultural lang. acad. devel., tech. in edn., Calif. Tchr. Hollister (Calif.) Elem. Sch., Greenfield (Calif.) Schs., Alum Roc, Union Sch. Dist., San Jose; ret., 2000. Mem. Calif. Ret. Tchrs. Assn., Spartan Found., Monterey Bay Aquarium.

WAGNER, MARION KATHRYN, social work educator; b. Oil City, Pa., June 14, 1943; d. Harry Clifford and Reba Estella (Tobin) W. BA in Govt., Calif. State U., L.A., 1965; MSW, San Diego State U., 1969; PhD in Social Work, U. Ill., 1992. LCSW, Ind. Social worker Orange County Welfare Dept., Santa Ana, Calif., 1965-70, San Diego County Welfare Dept., 1970-71; employment counselor, social worker Children's Svcs. Divsn. State of Oreg., La Grande, 1971-75; supr. Children's Bur. Indpls., 1975-82; tchr. Ind. U. Sch. Social Work, Indpls., 1982-83, vis. asst. prof., 1984-86, dir. weekend/work study program, 1986-91, dir. MSW programs, 1991-96, 99—. Polit. asst. to pres. NOW, Washington, 1983; mem. Ind. State Domestic Violence Prevention and Treatment Coun., Indpls., 1991-99, chair, 1998-99; chair social/psychol. svcs. subcom. Indpls Commn. on Domestic Violence, 1992-98; pres. sojourner commn. Julian Ctr., Indpls., 1980-82. Mem. Coun. on Social Work Edn., Commn. on Women, 1997—; chair Ind. PACE, 1999-2002, NASW del. assembly, 1999, 2002. Mem. NASW (Social Worker of Yr. 1984), Coun. on Social Work Edn., Ind. Assn. Social Work Educators, Assn. for Women in Social Work, NOW (regional dir. Gt. Lakes region 1994-96, 98-2000, nat. bd. dirs. 1992-96, 98-2002), Ind. NOW (pres. 1991-94, state coord. 1978-81, Woman of Yr. 1981), NAACP. Avocations: reading, snorkeling, birdwatching, motorhome, politics. Office: Ind U Sch Social Work 902 W New York St # 4138J Indianapolis IN 46202-5156

WAGNER, MARK ALAN, lawyer; b. Papua New Guinea, Feb. 9, 1966; s. Merlyn Dean and Janet Bertha W.; m. Cheryl Rae Varoz, June 29, 1989. BS, U. Utah, 1988, JD, 1992. Bar: Utah. Jud. clk. U.S. Dist. Ct. Utah, Salt Lake City, 1993; from assoc. to shareholder Parr Waddoups Brown Gee & Loveless, 1994-2000; shareholder Van Cott, Bagley, Corwall & McCarthy, 2000—. Staff atty. Freedom of Info. Hotline Soc. Profl. Journalists, Salt Lake City, 1994-2000. Mng. editor Utah Law Rev., Salt Lake City, 1991-92. Com. Salt Lake City Mayor's Task Force on Access, 1997-00; vol. Am. Cancer Soc., 1987, 95—. Mem. ABA, ATLA, Fed. Bar Assn., Utah Trial Lawyers Assn., Fed. Bar Assn., AIA, Order of Coif. Office: Van Cott Bagley Cornwall & McCarthy 50 S Main St Ste 1600 Salt Lake City UT 84144

WAGNER, MARK ANTHONY, videotape editor; b. Bethlehem, Pa., Mar. 15, 1958; s. Harry Paul and Theresa Marie (Spadaccia) W.; m. Nancy Susan Davis, Sept. 8, 1984. BA in Comm., Temple U., 1980. Videotape operator Swell Pictures, Chgo., 1983-85; asst. editor Post Pro Video, 1985-88; sr. editor Ave. Edit, 1988-91; editor/post-prodn. supr. WMX Techs., 1992-97; owner Spark Prodns., 1997. Recipient R.L. Jacobs Meml. award Boys' Clubs Am., 1976. Mem. Nat. Amusement Park Hist. Assn., Soc. Comml. Archaeology. Avocations: table tennis, film studies.

WAGNER, MARTIN G. chemical engineer, researcher; b. Bklyn., Mar. 19, 1942; s. Joseph Bernard and Anne Bleifer Wagner; m. Aylene Parker, Apr. 15, 1965; children: Gaylia, Aaron. B in Chem. Engring., The Cooper Union, 1962; MS in Chem. Engring., Northwestern U., 1964, PhD in Chem. Engring., 1967. Sr. tech. assoc. DuPont Co. Ctrl. Sci. and Engring., Wilmington, Del., 1966—. Dir. Welcome House Adoption Agy., Doylestown, Pa., 1983-88. Mem. AIChE, Soc. Rheology, Sigma Xi. Achievements include 8 patents in field. Avocations: sailing, reading, woodworking. Home: 1013 Overbrook Rd Wilmington DE 19807-2235 Office: DuPont Ctrl Sci & Engring PO Box 80323 Wilmington DE 19880-0323 E-mail: martin.g.wagner@usa.dupont.com.

WAGNER, MARVIN, general and vascular surgeon, educator; b. Milw., Feb. 20, 1919; s. Benjamin and Ella (Drotman) W.; m. Shirley Semon; children: Terry, Jeffrey, Penny. MD, Marquette U., 1944, MS, 1951. Diplomate Am. Bd. Surgery. Intern Mt. Sinai Med. Ctr., Milw., 1944-45, jr. and sr. resident in surgery, 1945-46, 47-50; pvt. practice, 1950—. Mem. staff Columbia, Milw. Children's, Milwaukee County Gen., St. Joseph's, VA, Froedtery Meml. Luth. hosps., Good Samaritan Med. Ctr., Sinai-Samaritan Ctr.; chmn., chief dept. surgery St. Michael's Hosp., 1965-69, pres. med. staff, 1981-82; vascular cons. Trinity Meml. Hosp., Waukesha (Wis.) Meml. Hosp.; clin. prof. surgery, adj. prof. anatomy Med. Coll. Wis., Milw.; mem. occupational adv. com. Milw. Area Tech. Coll., 1982-83; lectr., condr. workshops, site visitor in field; also others. Author: (with T. Lawson) Segmental Anatomy: Applications to Clinical Medicine, 1982 (Most Outstanding Book in Health Scis. award Assn. Am. Pubs. 1982), Atlas of Chest Imaging; contbr. over 85 articles to med. jours. including Surgery, Wis. Med. Jour., Am. Jour. Obstet. Surg. Gynecology, Modern Medicine, AMA Archives Surgery, Marquette Med. Rev., Am. Jour. Gastroenterology, Surg. Gynecology and Obstetrics, Sci., Transplantation Bull., Angiology, Abdominal Surgery, Am. Jour. Surgery, Archives Surgery, Jour. AMA. Mem. United Way Corp., 1975-78; chmn. physicians div. United Fund, 1972, bd. dirs., 1973-76, chmn. profl. div., 1973, co-chmn. doctor's div., 1977; mem. agy. facilities rev. com. and steering com. Southeastern Wis. Health Systems Agy., 1976-77; mem. adlumni fund raising com. Marquette U., 1971-72; mem. fund rasing com. project 75, Med. Coll. Wis., 1975-76. Recipient Disting. Svc. award Med. Coll. Wis., 1980, Alumnus of Yr. award, 1985, citation Milw. County Bd. Supervisors, 1988; Marvin Wagner endowed chair in anatomy and cellular biology named in his honor, 1988-91; grantee Am. Heart Assn., 1957-59, Milw. Cancer Soc., 1959-60, Wis. Heart Assn., 1960, USPHS, 1960-62, 86-89, NIH, 1960-62, Taitel, 1961, 62, 64, 65, 66, 3M Corp., 1968, Med. Coll. Wis., 1972, Winters Rsch. Found., 1976-80, McMillan Pub. Co., 1979-82, Tisshberg Found., 1985. Fellow ACS (sci. exhibit award 1957, 70); mem. AAUP, AMA (Physician's recognition award 1980-85, 89), Am. Assn. Anatomists, Cen. Surg. Soc., Collegium Internat. Chirurglae Digestivae, Soc. for Surgery Alimentary Tract, Am. Assn. Clin. Anatomists, Milw. Acad. Medicine, Milw. Acad. Surgery (coun. 1973-76), N.Y. Acad. Scis., Western Surg. Assn., Wis. Heart Assn., Wis. Surg. Soc. (coun. 1973-76), Med. Soc. Milwaukee County (pres. 1975, President's citation 1975), Alpha Omega Alpha. Achievements include patent for spandex sutures and prosthesis patches. Office: Med Coll Wis Anatomy and Cellular Biology 8701 W Watertown Plank Rd Milwaukee WI 53226-3548 also: 2350 W Villard Ave Ste 203 Milwaukee WI 53209-5082

WAGNER, MARY ANN, human resources executive; b. St. Louis, May 24, 1947; d. John Gerard and Carmela Lucy (Cozza) Blethroad; 1 child, John Patrick. BA, Webster U., St. Louis, 1979, MA, 1982. Tchr. Our Lady of Fatima, St. Louis, Wetterau, St. Louis; personnel mgr. Venture, 1979-81, customer svc. coord. O'Fallon, Mo., 1981-84, personnel mgr., 1984-86; regional personnel mgr., 1986-88; dir. tng. and devel., 1988-92; divsn. v.p. dir. of assoc. rels. May Merchandising, St. Louis, 1995-98; sr. v.p. human resources Meier & Frank, Portland, Oreg., 1998-2001; sr. v.p. May Mdse. Co., St. Louis, 2001—. Adj. prof. Webster U., 1990-95, divisional v.p. tng. and devel., 1992—. Chmn. United Way, O'Fallon, 1985, bd. dirs. Mem. AAIM Mgmt. Assn., Am. Soc. Tng. and Devel., Am. Mgmt. Assn. Roman Catholic. Avocations: antiques, music, sports. Home: 325 Perceval Dr Saint Charles MO 63304-5708

WAGNER, MARY KATHRYN, sociology educator, former state legislator; b. Madison, S.D., June 19, 1932; d. Irving Macaulay and Mary Browning (Wines) Mumford; m. Robert Todd Wagner, June 23, 1954; children: Christopher John, Andrea Browning. BA, U. S.D., 1954; MEd, S.D. State U., 1974, PhD, 1978. Sec. R.A. Burleigh & Assocs., Evanston, Ill., 1954-57; dir. resource ctr. Watertown (S.D.) Sr. High Sch., 1969-71, Brookings (S.D.) High Sch., 1971-74; asst. dir. S.D. Com. on the Humanities, Brookings, 1976-90; asst. prof. rural sociology S.D. State U., 1990-96; mem. S.D. Ho. of Reps., 1981-88, S.D. Senate, 1988-92. Mem., pres. Brookings Sch. Bd., 1975-81; chair fund dr. Brookings United Way, 1985; bd. dirs. Brookings Chamber music Soc., 1981-98, Advance and Career Learning Ctr. Named Woman of Yr., Bus. and Profl. Women, 1981, Legislator Conservationist of Yr., Nat. and S.D. Wildlife Fedn., 1988. Mem. Population Assn. Am., Midwest Sociol. Soc., Rural Sociol. Soc., Brookings C. of C. (mem. indsl. devel. com. 1988-98), PEO, Rotary. Republican. Episcopalian. Avocations: reading, gardening, music, golf, bridge. Home: 24497 N Playhouse Rd Keystone SD 57751-6653 E-mail: drswagnerrtmk@aol.com.

WAGNER, MARY MARGARET, library and information science educator; b. Mpls., Feb. 4, 1946; d. Harvey F.J. and Yvonne M. (Brettner) W.; m. William Moore, June 16, 1988; children: Lebohang Y.C., Nora M. BA, Coll. St. Catherine, St. Paul, 1969; MLS, U. Wash., 1973. Asst. libr. St. Margarets Acad., Mpls., 1969-70; libr. Derham Hall High Sch., St. Paul, 1970-71; youth worker The Bridge for Runaways, Mpls., 1971-72; libr. Guthrie Theater Reference and Rsch. Libr., 1973-75; asst. br. libr. St. Paul Pub. Libr., 1975; assoc. prof. dept. info. mgmt. Coll. St. Catherine, St. Paul, 1975—. Del. Minn. Gov.'s Pre-White House Conf. on Librs. and Info. Svcs., 1990; mem. Minn. Pre-White House Program Com., 1989-90, Continuing Libr. Info. and Media Edn. Com. Minn. Dept. Edn., Libr. Devel. and Svcs., 1980-83, 87—; mem. cmty. faculty Met. State U., St. Paul, 1980—; mem. core revision com. Coll. St. Catherine, 1992-93, faculty budget adv. com., 1992-95, faculty pers. com., 1989-92, 2001—, acad. computing com. 1991-96, ednl. policies com., 1998-01; chair curriculum subcom. Minn. Vol. Cert. Com., 1993—. Contbr. articles to profl. jours. Bd. dirs. Christian Sharing Fund, 1976-80, chair, 1977-78. Grantee: U.S. Embassy, Maseru, Lesotho, Africa, Brit. Consulate, Maseru, various founds.; Upper Midwest Assn. for Intercultural Edn. travel grantee Assoc. Colls. Twin Cities. Fellow: Higher Edn Consortia for Urban Affairs (bd. dirs. 1998—); mem.: ALISE (chair internat. rels. com. 2001—), ALA (libr. book fellows program 1990—91), Twin Cities Women in Computing, Minn. Ednl. Media Orgn., Minn. Libr. Assn. (pres. 1981—82, chair continuing edn. com. 1987—90, steering com. Readers Adv. Roundtable 1989—91), Spl. Libr. Assn., Am. Soc. Indexers, Am. Soc. Info. Sci. Office: Coll St Catherine Dept Info Mgmt 2004 Randolph Ave Saint Paul MN 55105-1750 E-mail: mmwagner@stkate.edu.

WAGNER, MICHAEL DUANE, lawyer; b. Shiner, Tex., July 4, 1948; s. Martin Matthew and Mary Margaret (Prasek) W.; m. Patricia Ann Miller, July 1, 1972; children: Matthew Miller, Michael Patrick. BA, Tex. Christian U., 1970; JD, St. Mary's Sch. Law, San Antonio, 1973. Bar: Tex. 1973, U.S. Supreme Ct. 1977. Assoc. counsel United Svcs. Automobile Assn., San Antonio, 1973-78, asst. v.p., counsel, 1978-80; v.p., counsel United Scvs. Automobile Assn., 1980-98, sr. v.p., gen. counsel, 1999—. Counsel investment mgmt. co. United Services Automobile Assn., San Antonio, 1980—, pres., chmn. bd. dirs. fed. credit union, 1981-84. Counsel United San Antonio Found., 1982; rep. Target 90/Goals for San Antonio, 1985; chmn. bd. advisors Daus. Charity Svcs. San Antonio; trustee Boysville, 1988; bd. dirs. De Paul Family Ctr., San Antonio, 1985, Cancer Therapy and Rsch. Ctr., Friends of McNay, ARC, San Francisco, Archdiocese of San Antonio. Named one of Outstanding Young Men in Am., U.S. Jr. C. of C., 1984. Mem. ABA, Fed. Bar Assn., State Bar of Tex. (ethics and grievance com.) San Antonio Bar Assn., Phi Delta Theta, Phi Alpha Delta. Roman Catholic. Avocations: running, home renovation.

WAGNER, MICHAEL GRAFTON, investor, corporation executive, resources advisor, business consultant; b. Greenville, Ohio, May 31, 1935; BA, Vanderbilt U., 1957. With Henny Penny Corp., Eaton, Ohio, 1957-76, sales rep., 1957-60, dir. advt., 1960-63, dir. mktg., 1963-68, pres., CEO, 1968-76, Henny Penny Ltd., Toronto, Ont., Can.; pvt. investor, 1976—. Pres. schaefer Corp., Madison, Ala., 1979-81; cons., pvt. investor Rair Systems, Inc., Nashville, 1985-87; nat. accounts mgr. spl. products and projects Vulcan Hart Corp. divsn. Premark Corp., 1987-89, Wagner Investments, 1989—, Projects by Michael Wagner, 1993—. Area chmn. Vanderbilt U. Endowment Fund, Nashville, 1961-66, 70-74; fin. chmn. Tenn. Rep. Com., 1977-78. Mem. Nat. Commadore Club, Alpha Tau Omega. Episcopalian (sec.-treas., warden 1969-71). Home: 1602 Hillmeade Dr Nashville TN 37221-5210 E-mail: sixdad6@home.com.

WAGNER, MURIEL GINSBERG, nutrition therapist; d. Irving A. and Anna Ginsberg; divorced; 1 child, Emily Lucinda Faith. BA, MS, Wayne State U.; PhD, U. Mich., 1982. Registered dietitian. Nutritionist Merrill-Palmer Inst., Detroit; pvt. practice, nutritional therapist Southfield, 1976—. Cons. select com. on nutrition U.S. Senate, 1973-74, Ford Motor Co., Dearborn, Mich., 1975-78, Detroit Dept. Consumer Affairs, 1979—; adj. faculty mem. Wayne State U., Detroit, 1970-80, U. Mich., Dearborn, 1974-79. Author: (cookbook) Tun...ahhh, 1993; contbr. articles to profl. publs.; writer, publisher (newsletter) Eating Younger. Vol. Am. Heart Assn. of Mich.; also various local and nat. govtl. groups Recipient Outstanding Cmty. Svc. award Am. Heart Assn., 1990; named Outstanding Profl., Mich. Dietetic Assn., 1974. Fellow Am. Dietetic Assn. (organizer Dial-A-Dietitian); mem. Am. Diabetes Assn. Avocations: cooking, recipe development, gardening. Office: 4000 Town Ctr Ste 8 Southfield MI 48075-1401 E-mail: eatingyounger@ameritech.net.

WAGNER, NANCY HUGHES, secondary school educator, state legislator; b. Raleigh, N.C., Sept. 27, 1943; d. Eugene Anderson and Miriam St. Clair (Morgan) Hughes; m. Clarence Cobaugh Wagner II, Sept. 12, 1970; children: Morgan Anderson, Cobaugh Wagner III. BA, Salem Coll., Winston-Salem, N.C., 1965; MS, Wilmington (Del.) Coll., 1989. Tchr. Milford (Del.) Sch. Dist., 1965-66, Capital Sch. Dist., Dover, Del., 1966-70, 89—; job specialist Jobs for Del. Grads., 1987-89; rep. Del. Ho. of Reps., 1992—, former chair small bus., chair judiciary com., sch. to work coord., 1998—. Mem. parents bd. U. Del., Newark, 1991-93; bd. visitors Del. State U., Dover, 1995—; bd. dirs. Modern Maturity Ctr., Dover, 1995—, 801 House Aid in Dover, 1995—, Because We Care, Dover, 1995—; mem. Kent County Parks and Recreation Commn., Dover, 1990-92; pres. South Run Crossing Civic Assn., Springfield, Va., 1982-85, PTA Dover H.S., 1987-89; mem. Rep. State Com., Kent County Rep. Women's Club; bd. dirs. Murphy Sch., 1991—. Mem. AAUW, C. of C., Nat. Coun. State Legislators, Coun. of State Govts., Capital Edn. Assn., Del. Edn. Assn., Delta Kappa Gamma Soc. Internat. Republican. Presbyterian. Avocations: reading, politics, travel. Home: 283 Troon Rd Dover DE 19904-2370 Office: House of Representatives Legislatvie Hall Rm 117 PO Box 1401 Dover DE 19903-1401

WAGNER, NORMAN ERNEST, corporate education executive; b. Edenwold, Sask., Can., Mar. 29, 1935; s. Robert Eric and Gertrude Margaret (Brandt) W.; m. Catherine Hack, May 16, 1957; children: Marjorie Dianne, Richard Roger, Janet Marie. BA, MDiv, U. Sask., 1958; MA, U. Toronto, 1960, PhD in Near Eastern Studies, 1965; LLD, Wilfrid Laurier U., 1984. Asst. prof. Near Eastern studies Wilfrid Laurier U., Waterloo, Ont., 1962-65, assoc. prof., 1965-69, prof., 1970-78, dean grad. studies and rsch., 1974-78; pres. U. Calgary, Alta., Can., 1978-88; chmn. bd. Alta. Natural Gas Co., Ltd., 1988—; pres. emeritus U. Calgary, Can., 1988-95; chmn. Knowledge at Work Found., 1995—. Bd. dirs., chmn. Terry Fox Humanitarian Award Program; pres. The Corp. Higher Edn. Forum, 1996-2000. Author: From Chaos to Wisdom: A Framework for Understanding, 1998, (with others) The Moyer Site: A Prehistoric Village in Waterloo County, 1974. Mem. Adv. Coun. on Adjustment, OCO '88, Alta. Heritage Found. for Med. Rsch., Nat. Adv. Bd. Sci. and Tech., Internat. Trade Adv. Com. Decorated officer Order of Can. Mem. Can. Soc. Bibl. Studies. Lutheran. Home: 1320 720 13th Ave SW Calgary AB Canada T2R 1M5 Office: Knowledge@work 207 525 11th Ave SW Calgary AB Canada T2P 0C9 E-mail: newal1@aol.com.

WAGNER, PAUL ANTHONY, JR. education educator; b. Pitts., Aug. 28, 1947; s. Paul A. and Mary K. Wagner; children: Nicole S., Eric P., Jason G. BS, N.E. Mo. State U., 1969; MEd, U. Mo., 1972; MA in Philosophy, 1976, PhD in Philosophy of Edn., 1978. Internal expeditor electromotive div. GM, La Grange, Ill., 1970-71; instr. Moberly (Mo.) Jr. Coll., 1972-73, U. Mo., Columbia, 1973-78, acting dir. instl. rsch. and planning, 1990-92, dir. univ. self study, 1991-92; instr. Mo. Mil. Acad., 1978-79; prof. edn. and philosophy U. Houston-Clear Lake, Atrium Ctr. Disting. Rsch. Prof., 1980, Chancellor's Disting. Svc. Prof., 1985; dir. Inst. Logical and Cognitive Studies, 1980—; dir. Project in Profl. Ethics; chmn. dept. edn. U. Houston-Clear Lake, 1989-92; adj. prof. bus. mgmt. U. Houston-Victoria. Judge Sears Intercollegiate Ethics Bowl, Dallas, 1998; pres. Wagner & Assocs. Ednl. Consulting, 1988-93; dir. Tex. Ctr. for Study Profl. Ethics in Tchg., 1988-95; rsch. assoc. Ctr. for Moral Devel., Harvard U., 1985-86; vis. scholar Stanford U., Palo Alto, Calif., 1981; cons. total quality mgmt. Golden Gate U., 1992-93, M.D. Anderson Cancer Ctr. and Hosp., 1992-93, U. Houston-Victoria, 1993; cons. strategic planning Houston ChronicleNewspaper, 1997; chair So. Accreditation of Colls. and Schs. steering com. U. Houston, Clear Lake, 1990-93, pres. faculty senate, 1999-2001; chair planning and budgeting com. Houston Tenneco Marathon, 1992-94; steering com. Trilateral Conf. and Supershow Greater Human Partnership, 1994-95; cons., ethics trainer Am. Leadership Forum, 1995-98; planning com. Tex. Ethics in Govt. Ann. Conf., 1995-98; ; adj. prof. ethical theory U. Houston, 2000—; faculty exec. com. U. Houston Sys., 1999-2001; cons. in field. Author: (with F. Kierstead) The Ethical Legal and Multicultural Founds. of Teaching, 1992, Understanding Professional Ethics, 1996; contbr. articles to profl. jours. on sci. edn., mgmt. theory and philosophy of edn.; Mem. editl. bd. Jour. of Thought, 19815, Focus on Learning, 1982-85; editorial cons. Instrnl. Scis., 1981-83; editorial assoc. Brain and Behavioral Scis., 19865. Vice-chmn. Human Rights Commn., Columbia, Mo., 1978-79; Sunday sch. tchr. Mary Queen Cath. Ch., Friendswood, Tex., 1979-85; founding bd. dirs. Bay Area Symphony Soc., 1983-85; capital campaign com. Soc. Prevention Cruelty to Animals, 1989-91; publicity com. Am. Cancer Soc., Houston chpt., 1989-92; cons. in strategic planning M.D. Anderson Cancer Ctr. vol. divsn.; steering com. City of Houston Emerging Bus. Conf., 1994-95, Trilateral Conf., Greater Houston Partnership, 1994-95; active Houston Bus. Promise; chair strategic planning com. Leadership Houston, 1996-98; bd. dirs. Houston Vol. Ctr., Leanna Saprianno Dance Co., Baker Inst., 1998-2001, chair, 1999-2001; ann. leadership briefing com. Rice U., 2001; active Linda Lorelle Scholarship Com., 1995—, Project Grad Coordinating Coun., 1995-96; emcee, expert commentator for pub. TV, Channel 8, Houston, 1989-2002. Sgt. Mo. NG, 1970-76. Recipient Cert. of Appreciation, City of Columbia, 1978; K.E. Graessle scholar, 1968, Mo. Peace Studies Inst. grantee, 1971. Mem. AAUP, Assn. Applied and Profl. Ethics, Am. Assn. Pub. Adminstrs. (ethics com.), Am. Philos. Assn., Assn. Philosophers in Edn. (exec. bd., v.p.), Philosophy of Edn. Soc. (exec. sec.-treas., hospitality chair 1995-96), Am. Ednl. Studies Assn., Philosophy Sci. Assn., S.W. Philosophy Edn. Soc., Tex. Network for Tchr. Tng. in Philosophy for Children (bd. dirs. 1983-90), Tex. Ctr. for Ethics in Edn. (bd. dirs. 1990-98), Tex. Ednl. Found. Soc. (pres.

1995—), Tex. Assn. Coll. Tchrs., So. Assn. Colls. Coord., Houston Bar Assn. (steering com. NAFTA Conf. 1993-94), Informal Logic Assn., Leadership Houston, Friends Hermann Pk., Clearlake Cir. (chair 1979-85), Phi Delta Kappa, Kappa Delta Pi. Roman Catholic. Avocations: running, racquetball, reading, opera, ballet. Address: RR 4 Box 217 Navasota TX 77868-9413 Office: U Houston 2700 Bay Area Blvd Rm 338 Houston TX 77058-1002

WAGNER, PAUL DEAN, oral and maxillofacial surgeon; b. Mankato, Kans., Dec. 24, 1937; s. Oral Harlan and Mary Belle (Amis) W.; m. Sharon Kay, July 17, 1960; children: Anne, Mary Beth, Paul Jr. BS in Pharmacy, Kans. U., 1961; DDS, U. Tenn., 1968. Diplomate Am. Bd. Oral and Maxillofacial Surgery. Resident in oral and maxillofacial surgery Harrisburg (Pa.) Hosp., 1968-71; practice dentistry specializing in oral and maxillofacial surgery Hershey, Pa., 1971-75, Hays, Kans., 1975—. Chief of staff Hays Med. Ctr., 1991—. Pres. Hays Area Rd. Runners, 1975-85. Mem. ADA (life), Kans. Dental Assn. (life), Am. Soc. Oral and Maxillofacial Surgery, Kans. Soc. Oral and Maxillofacial Surgery (pres. 1984-85), Oil Belt Dental Soc. (pres. 1977-78), Kans. Dental Specialty Bd. (examiner), Hays Area C. of C., Kans. C. of C., Sierra Club. Republican. Unitarian Universalist. Avocations: running, biking, hiking. Home: 2746 Thunderbird Cir Hays KS 67601-1425 Office: 2501 Canterbury Rd Hays KS 67601-2233

WAGNER, PETER EWING, physics and electrical engineering educator; b. Ann Arbor, Mich., July 4, 1929; s. Paul Clark and Charlotta Josephine (Ewing) W.; m. Caryl Jean Veon, June 23, 1951; children: Ann Frances, Stephen Charles. Student, Occidental Coll., 1946-48; AB with honors, U. Calif., Berkeley, 1950, PhD, 1956. Teaching rsch. asst. U. Calif., 1950-56; rsch. physicist Westinghouse Rsch. Labs., Pitts., 1956-59; assoc. prof. elec. engring. Johns Hopkins, 1960-65, prof., 1965-73; dir. Ctr. for Environ. and Estuarine Studies U. Md., 1973-80, prof., 1973-81. Vis. prof. physics U. Ala., Huntsville, 1980-81, prof., 1981; vice chancellor for acad. affairs, prof. physics U. Miss., 1981-84; provost, prof. physics and elec. engring. Utah State U., 1984-89; v.p. acad. affars and provost SUNY, Binghamton, 1989-92, prof. physics and elec. engring., 1989-99, prof. emeritus, 1999—; spl. projects engr. State of Md., 1971-72; mem. Gov.'s Sci. Adv. Coun., 1973-77, Md. Power Plant Siting Adv. Com., 1972-80; cons. in field. Contbr. articles to profl. jours.; patentee in field. Trustee Chesapeake Rsch. Consortium, 1974-80, chmn. bd. trustees, 1979-80. Guggenheim fellow Oxford U., 1966-67 Mem. Nat. Assn. State Univs. and Land Grant Colls. (mem. coun. acad. affairs, mem. affirmative action com. 1986-89, chmn. nominating com. 1988-89, chmn. libr. commn. 1989-92), Ctr. Rsch. Librs. (bd. dirs. 1991-97, mem. budget and fin. com. 1991-93, vice chairperson 1992-93, chairperson 1993-94, chair nominating com. 1994-95), Blue Key, Gold Key, Phi Beta Kappa, Phi Beta Kappa Fellows (life, bd. dirs. 1995-2001), Sigma Xi (life), Phi Kappa Phi, Eta Kappa Nu. Home: 2650 Maple Ave Morro Bay CA 93442-1726 E-mail: cpwags@charter.net.

WAGNER, RAYMOND THOMAS, JR. lawyer, corporation executive; b. St. Louis, June 8, 1959; s. Raymond T. and Loretto (Muenster) W.; m. Ann L. Trousdale, Feb. 20, 1987. BA, St. Louis U., 1981, MBA, 1984; JD, U. Mo., Kansas City, 1985; LLM in Taxation, Washington U., St. Louis, 1993. Bar: Mo. 1985, Ill. 1986, U.S. Supreme Ct. 1989, U.S. Tax Ct. 1989. Legal rsch. and writing instr. U. Mo., Kansas City, 1983-84; law clk. to chief justice Mo. Supreme Ct., Jefferson City, 1985-86; assoc. Gilmore & Bell, St. Louis, 1986-87, Suelthaus & Kaplan P.C., St. Louis, 1987-89; gen. counsel Mo. Dept Revenue, 1989-90; counsel to gov. State of Mo., Jefferson City, 1990-91; dir. revenue Mo. Dept. Revenue, 1991-93; counsel Armstrong Teasdale Schlafly & Davis, St. Louis, 1993; dir. revenue Ill. Dept Revenue, Springfield, 1993-95; legal and legis. v.p. Enterprise Rent-A-Car, St. Louis, 1995—; mcpl. judge City of Ballwin, 1999—. Adj. prof. law LLM taxation program sch. law Washington U., St. Louis, 1993-; adj. prof. tax law Fontbonne U., St. Louis, 2002-; chmn. Gov.'s Ethics Com., 1991-92, Mo. Hwy. Reciprocity Commn., 1991-93; commr. Multistate Tax. Commn., 1991-93, Mo. Mil. Adv. Commn., 1991-93. Precinct capt. Gravois Twp., Webster Groves, 1988; bd. dirs. Shelter the Children, St. Louis, 1988-95; bd. dirs. Foster Care Coalition St. Louis, 1995-2002, pres. 1998-2000; chmn. platform com. Mo. Rep. Conv., 1992; exec. bd. dirs. St. Louis U. Sch. Bus.; mem. chancellor's coun. U. Mo., St. Louis, 1998—. Mem. ABA, Ill. Bar Assn., Mo. Bar Assn., Bar Assn. Met. St. Louis (chmn. law student svcs. com. 1986-87, chmn. social com. 1987-88, mem. exec. com. young lawyers assn. 1988-89, co-chmn. administrv. law com., govt. liaison com. young lawyers sect. 1989-90, chmn. legis. com. 1991—, legal svcs. oversight commn. 2001-), Regional Commerce and Growth Assn. (vice chair pub. policy coun. 1996, chair pub. policy coun. 1998-2000, vice chair govt. affairs exec. com. 2000-02), Associated Industries Mo. (bd. dirs. 1996—), Mo. C.of C. (bd. dirs. 1998—). Republican. Roman Catholic. Home: 313 Saint Andrews Ct Ballwin MO 63011-2504 Office: Enterprise Rent-A-Car 600 Corporate Park Dr Saint Louis MO 63105-4204 E-mail: rwagner@erac.com.

WAGNER, RICHARD, athletics consultant, former baseball team executive; b. Central City, Nebr., Oct. 19, 1927; s. John Howard and Esther Marie (Wolken) W.; m. Gloria Jean Larsen, May 10, 1950; children— Randolph G., Cynthia Kaye. Student, pub. schs., Central City. Gen. mgr. Lincoln (Nebr.) Baseball Club, 1955-58; mgr. Pershing Mcpl. Auditorium, Lincoln, 1958-61; exec. staff Ice Capades, Inc., Hollywood, Calif., 1961-63; gen. mgr. Sta. KSAL, Salina, Kans., 1963-65; dir. promotion and sales St. Louis Nat. Baseball Club, 1965-66; gen. mgr. Forum, Inglewood, Calif., 1966-67; asst. to exec. v.p. Cin. Reds, 1967-70, asst. to pres., 1970-74, v.p. adminstrn., 1975, exec. v.p., 1975-78, gen. mgr., 1977-83, pres., 1978-83, Houston Astros Baseball Club, 1985-87; spl. asst. Office of Baseball Commr., 1988-93; asst. to chmn. Major League Exec. Coun., 1993-94. Pres. RGW Enterprises, Inc., Phoenix, 1978-97. Served with USNR, 1945-47, 50-52. Named Exec. of Yr., Minor League Baseball, Sporting News, 1958. Republican. Methodist.

WAGNER, RICHARD E. economist, educator; b. Jamestown, N.D., Apr. 28, 1941; s. Herbert and Dorothy Mae King; m. Barbara Helen (Westgate) W., June 9, 1962; children: Stephanie Wagner Tice, Valerie Wagner Smith. AA, Fullerton (Calif.) Jr. Coll., 1961; BS, U. So. Calif., 1963; PhD, U. Va., 1966. Asst. prof. econs. U. Calif., Irvine, 1966-68, Tulane U., New Orleans, 1968-73; prof. econs. Va. Poly. Inst. and State U., Blacksburg, 1973-79, Auburn (Ala.) U., 1979-81, Fla. State U., Talahassee, 1981-88; Holbert L. Harris prof. econs. George Mason U., Fairfax, Va., 1988—. Sr. fellow, chmn. acad. adv. bd. Pub. Interest Inst., Mt. Pleasant, Iowa, 1995—. Author: Democracy in Deficit, 1977, To Promote the General Welfare, 1989, The Economics of Smoking, 1991, Trade Protection in the United States, 1995; editor: Public Choice and Constitutional Economics, 1988, Charging for Government, 1991, Limiting Leviathan, 1999, Federalist Government in Principle and Practice, 2001. Mem. Am. Econ. Assn., So. Econ. Assn. (exec. com. 1987-88), Internat. Inst. Pub. Fin., Internat. Soc. New Indtl. Econs., Pub. Choice Soc. Home: 11845 Clara Way Fairfax Station VA 22039 Office: George Mason U Dept Econs Fairfax VA 22030 Home Fax: (703) 503-9769; Office Fax: (703) 993-1133. E-mail: r.e.wagner@worldnet.att.net, rwagner@gmu.edu.

WAGNER, ROBERT EARL, retired agronomist; b. Garden City, Kans., Mar. 6, 1921; s. Fay Arthur and Margaret (Longbottom) W.; m. Bernice Bittner, Aug. 7, 1948; children— Robert Earl, James Warren, Douglas Alan. BS, Kans. State Coll., 1942; MS, U. Wis., 1943, PhD, 1950. Forage crops specialist Ft. Hays Expt. Sta., Hays, Kans., 1943-45; asso. agronomist Plant Industry Sta., U.S. Dept. Agr., Beltsville, Md., 1945-48, research agronomist, asst. project leader pasture and range project, 1951-54, research agronomist, project leader western pasture and range project, 1954-56; prof., head dept. agronomy U. Md., 1956-59; regional dir. American Potash Inst., 1959-66, also Found. for Internat. Potash Research, v.p. both orgns., 1966-67; dir. Coop. Extension Service, U. Md., 1967-75; pres., bd. dirs. Potash Inst., 1975-77, Potash and Phosphate Inst., 1977-88, pres. emeritus, 1988—; chmn., bd. dirs. Potash & Phosphate Inst. Can., 1975-88; pres., bd. dirs. Found. for Agronomic Rsch., 1980-87; owner Wagner Performance Cattle, Stone Mountain, Ga., 1985—. Bd. dirs., mem. exec. com. Internat. Fertilizer Devel. Ctr., 1975-98; bd. dirs. African Ctr. for Fertilizer Devel., 1988-98; chmn. Nat. Ext. Com. on Orgn. and Policy; mem. U.S. del. 7th Internat. Grassland Congress, New Zealand. Author tech., popular publs.; Editor: Proc. Sixth Internat. Grassland Congress. Recipient Medallion award Am. Forage and Grassland Coun., Disting. Grasslander award, 1994; award Md. Farm Bur.; Disting. Svc. award in agr. Kansas State U., 1985, Disting. Alumnus award, 1990; Cert. of Disting. Citizenship, State of Md.; Robert E. Wagner Efficient Agr. award established in his honor; Disting. Grasslander award Am. Forage and Grassland Coun., 1994. Fellow AAAS, Am. Soc. Agronomy (chmn. grassland com., mem. exec. com., bd. dirs., pres. N.E. br.), Crops Sci. Soc. Am., Soil Sci. Soc. Am.; mem. Grassland Coun. (pres.), Am. Soc. Range Mgmt., Cosmos Club (Washington), Atlanta Athletic Club, Sigma Xi, Alpha Zeta, Gamma Sigma Delta, Phi Kappa Phi. Presbyterian. Home: 1934 Mountain Creek Dr Stone Mountain GA 30087-1016 Office: 655 Engineering Dr Norcross GA 30092-2822

WAGNER, ROBERT PHILIP, zoologist, educator; b. Bronx, N.Y., May 11, 1918; s. Philip Joseph and Annette Victoria (Pavelka) Wagner; m. Margaret Lillian Campbell, June 12, 1947 (dec. Sept. 1987); children: Philip Campbell, James Robert, Ruth Annette. BSc, City Coll. N.Y., 1940; PhD, U. Tex., 1943. Tchg. fellow zoology U. Tex., 1940—43, instr. zoology, 1944, asst. prof. zoology, 1945—50, assoc. prof. zoology, 1950—56, prof. zoology, 1956—77, prof. emeritus zoology, 1977—99, emeritus prof. molecular genetics and microbiology, 1999—. Vis. prof. zoology dept. Ind. U., 1962; rsch. assoc. Calif. Inst. Tech., 1948, 51, 53, Nat. Cotton Coun., 1944—45; occasional lectr., vis. prof. U. Tex. Med. Br., 1977—82; vis. scientist Los Alamos Nat. Lab., 1975—76, cons. life scis. divsn., 1977—99; lectr. in field. Author: (novels) Genes and Proteins, 1975; author: (with HK Mitchell) Genetics and Metabolism, 1955, 1964; author: (with B. Judd, B. Sanders, and R. Richardson) An Introduction to Modern Genetics, 1980; author: (with H.E. Sutton) Genetics, A Human Concern, 1985; author: (with M. Maguire and R. Stallings) Chromosomes: A Synthesis, 1993; co-editor: (jours.) Biochem. Genetics, 1969—79; contbr. articles to profl. jours. Mem. panel on genetic biology NSF, 1961—64; mem. pre and post doctoral com. Nat. Rsch. Coun., 1962—63. Recipient Career award, NIH, 1962—77; fellow Nat. Rsch. Coun. fellow, Calif. Inst. Tech., 1946—47, Guggenheim fellow, U. Calif. Dept. Biochemistry, 1957—58. Fellow: AAAS; mem.: Tex. Genetics Soc. (Disting. Svc. award 1984), Am. Genetics Assn., Am. Soc. Biochemistry and Molecular Biology, Am. Soc. Naturalists, Soc. Study of Evolution, Genetics Soc. Am. (mem. Mendel centennial com. 1965, sec. 1965—67, v.p. 1970, pres. 1971, organizer, chmn. standing com. for maintenance of genetic stocks 1958—64). Achievements include research in in linkage conservation in vertebrates; in vertebrate evolution; in genome and chromosome structure, function, and evolution. Home: 313 Los Arboles Dr Santa Fe NM 87501-1242

WAGNER, ROBERT WALTER, photography, cinema and communications educator, media producer, consultant; b. Newport News, Va., Nov. 16, 1918; s. Walter George and Barbara Anne Wagner; m. Betty Jane Wiles, Nov. 21, 1948; children: Jonathan R., Jeffrey A., Jennifer J. BSc, Ohio State U., 1940, MA, 1941, PhD, 1953. Motion picture writer-dir. Office War Info., N.Y.C. and Washington, 1942-43; writer-dir. Office Coord. Interam. Affairs for South and Ctrl. Am., 1943-44; chief info. Divsn. Mental Hygiene, Ohio Dept. Pub. Welfare, 1944-46; dir. divsn. motion pictures Ohio State U., Columbus, 1946-58, prof. comms., photography and cinema, 1960—, chmn. dept. photo-cinema, 1966-74. Pres. Univ. Film Found., 1979-85; writer, dir. James Thurber's Columbus Town, 1990, Images of the Depression, 1990; internat. cons. comms.; bd. dirs. Am. Film Inst., 1974-81; mem. faculty U. So. Calif., 1958-59, U. P.R., 1961, 66, 68, San Jose State U., 1967, Ariz. State U., 1971, Concordia U., Montreal, 1980, 81, Danish Nat. Film Sch., 1983, 94, Emerson Coll., Boston, 1987. Author film series: Series of Motion Picture Documents on Communication Theory and New Educational Media, 1966; co-author: The American Tintype, 1999; editor: Education of Film Maker, 1975; co-producer: Cognizant Media, Studio City, Calif., 1997, The View from Malabar, 2000. Recipient Disting. Svc. award Columbus Cmty. Film Coun., 1986, Disting. Svc. award Ohio State U., 1988, Ohiana Pegasus award, 1985; Ency. Brit. fellow, 1953; Sr. Fulbright fellow, Peru, 1976. Fellow Soc. Motion Picture and TV Engrs. (Eastman Gold Medal award 1981); mem. Acad. TV Arts and Scis. (Disting. Svc. award 1966), Univ. Film/Video Assn. (bd. editors jour. 1975-85, editor jour. 1956-75), Internat. Congress Schs. Cinema and TV (v.p. 1964-82), Assn Ednl. Comm. and Tech. (bd. editors jour. 1976—), Torch Club (Columbus, pres. 1996), curator, The Art of humane Propaganda, Columbus Mus. of Art, 2001. Home: 1353 Zollinger Rd Columbus OH 43221-2939

WAGNER, ROD, library director; b. Oakland, Nebr., Sept. 14, 1948; s. Francis Lynn and Doris Jean (Egbers) W.; m. M. Diane Kennedy, June 14, 1969; children: Jennifer, Brian, James. BA Social Sci. Edn., Wayne (Nebr.) State Coll., 1970; MA Polit. Sci., U. Nebr. Lincoln, 1971; MA Libr. Sci., U. Mo., 1981. Rsch. coord. Nebr. Libr. Commn., Lincoln, 1972, planning, evaluation, rsch. coord., 1972-73, adminstrv. asst., 1973-74, dep. dir., 1974-87, dir., 1988—. Bd. dirs. Nebr. Ctr. for the Book, Nebr. Devel. Network. Mem. state govt. coun. Nebr. Info. Tech. Commn., 1999—. With U.S. Army N.G., 1970-77. Mem. ALA (contbr. yearbook 1981-84), Assn. Specialized and Cooperative Libr. Agys. (bd. dirs. 1998-2000), Nebr. Libr. Assn. (pres.-elect 1993-94, pres. 1994-95), Chief Officers State Libr. Agys., Western Coun. State Librs. (pres. 1992-93). Presbyterian. Home: 3205 W Pershing Rd Lincoln NE 68502-4844 Office: NE Libr Commn 1200 N St Ste 120 Lincoln NE 68508-2023 E-mail: rwagner@nlc.state.ne.us.

WAGNER, ROSE MARY, librarian; b. Stuttgart, Germany, Sept. 20, 1941; came to the U.S., 1948; d. Alfred Ferdinand and Lina (Hemminger) Bauer; m. Robert John Wagner, Aug. 27, 1966. BA with distinction, U. Mich., 1963, MA, 1966; MA in Libr. and Info. Sci., Rosary Coll., 1985. Head translation dept. Hill, Steadman and Simpson, Chgo., 1975-85; asst. chief libr. Sargent & Lundy Engrs., 1985-87; law libr. Goldberg, Kohn et al, Ltd., 1987-88; cons. libr. Chgo. Pub. Libr., 1988-89, cons. libr., project dir., 1989-90, reference libr., 1990-95, head fgn. lang. info. ctr., 1995—. Mem. ALA, MLA. Avocations: skiing, tennis, swimming, painting, drawing. Home: 9640 S Longwood Dr Chicago IL 60643-1608

WAGNER, ROY, anthropology educator, researcher; b. Cleve., Oct. 2, 1938; s. Richard Robert and Florence Helen (Mueller) W.; m. Brenda Sue Geilhausen, June 14, 1968 (div. Dec. 1994); children: Erika Susan, Jonathan Richard. AB, Harvard U., 1961; AM, U. Chgo., 1962, PhD, 1966. Asst. prof. anthropology So. Ill. U., Carbondale, 1966-68; assoc. prof. Northwestern U., Evanston, Ill., 1969-74; prof. U. Va., Charlottesville, 1974—, chmn. dept., 1974-79. Mem. cultural anthropology panel NSF, Washington, 1981-82. Author: (novels) Habu, 1972, The Invention fo Culture, 1975, Lethal Speech, 1978, Symbols That Stand for Themselves, 1986, An Anthropology of the Subject, 2000. Social Sci. Research Council faculty research grantee, 1968; NSF postdoctoral research grantee, 1979. Fellow Am. Anthropol. Assn. Avocation: student hot-air balloon pilot. Home: 726 Cargil Ln Charlottesville VA 22902-4302 Office: U Va Dept Anthropology University Station Charlottesville VA 22906

WAGNER, SAMUEL, V, secondary school English language educator, college counselor; b. West Chester, Pa., Dec. 28, 1965; s. Samuel and Mary Ann (Baker) Wagner; m. Allison Lee Lewis, May 25, 1991; children: Samuel Jackson, Spencer Lee. BS in English Lit., Haverford Coll., 1988; MEd, U. New Orleans, 1995. Intern in English, asst. coach Westtown (Pa.) Sch., spring 1989; tchr. upper sch. English Metairie (La.) Pk. Country Day Sch., 1989-97; head upper sch. Hutchison Sch., Memphis, 1997—99; dir. coll. counseling The Miami Valley Sch., Dayton, Ohio, 1999—. Asst. varsity soccer coach Metairie Pk. Country Day Sch., 1989—94; advisor to student senate Metairie Country Day Sch., 1990—95, chairperson headmaster adv. com., 1994—97, coll. counselor, 1995—97; interim upper sch. prin. Miami Valley Sch., 2000—01; presenter ann. conf. Ind. Sch. Assn. of the South, New Orleans, 1992, New Orleans, 96. Mem.: NACAL, Nat. Coun. Tchrs. of English, So. Assn. for Coll. Admissions Counseling, NASSP, NASAA, Kappa Delta Pi, Phi Delta Kappa, Alpha Theta Epsilon. Republican. Mem. Soc. Of Friends. Home: 5209 Mallet Club Dr Dayton OH 45439-3278 Office: The Miami Valley Sch 5151 Denise Dr Dayton OH 45429

WAGNER, SAMUEL ALBIN MAR, records management executive, educator; b. Brighton, Colo., Feb. 23, 1942; s. Jacob Doer and Leota Garnet (Wilson) W.; m. Donna Dee Person, Mar. 20, 1987; children: Kurt, Andrea, Autumn, Jan, Arthur. BA in History, U. Colo., 1964, MA in History, 1965; STB (MTS) in History of World Religions, Harvard U., 1968; cert. in archival adminstrn., U. Denver, 1978. cert. records mgr.; cert. archivist. Archival asst. Harvard U. & Harvard Bus. Sch., 1965-68; asst. curator we. hist. collections U. Colo., 1968-70; sr. asst. archivist Cornell U., Ithaca, N.Y., 1971-73; editor Brighton Blade, Ft. Lupton Press, Colo., 1973-77; city archivist City of Providence, 1978-80; state records analyst Wyo. State Archives, Cheyenne, 1979-83; pres. Records Mgmt. Cons. Internat., 1983—; records mgr. Ft. Collins (Colo.) Police Dept., 1984-87; pub. records adminstr. State R.I., Providence, 1987-90; asst. prof. master archival studies program U. B.C., Vancouver, Can., 1990-93; editor Mo. State Archives, Jefferson City, 1994-96; prodr. community access Sta. JCTV, 1994-96; chief N.J. Bur. Records Mgmt., Trenton, 1996—; pres. Historic Rsch. Svcs., Jefferson City, Trenton, 1994—. Instr. Chapman, U., 1981-87, Colo. State U., 1985-87, Lincoln U., 1995-96, U. B.C., 1990-93; speaker in field. Author: Brighton Reflections, 1976, Adams County: Crossroads of the West, 1977, Directory of Automated Records Management Systems, 1985-91, Crossroads of the West: A History of Brighton and the Platte Valley, 1977; editor The Fort Lupton Story, 1977, Adams County Colorado:A Cetennial History, 2002; contbr. articles to profl. jours. Officer, bd. dirs. Adams County Hist. Soc., 1973-77; county historian Adams County, Brighton, 1976-77; mem. Brighton Human Rels. Commn., 1977-78; bd. dirs. Brighton Bicentennial Com., 1975-76, Ft. Lupton Bicentennial Com., 1975-76, R.I. RSVP, 1978-80, R.I. Pub. Records Adv. Coun., 1987-90, R.I. Hist. Records Adv. Bd., 1987-90; chmn. info. profls. legis. task force Freedom of Info. and Privacy Assn., 1991-93; chmn. oral history project Cole County Hist. Soc., 1996. Recipient Hist. Preservation award Adams County Hist. Soc., 1978, award Freedom of Info. and Privacy Assn., 1993; grantee Ethnic Heritage Project Colo. Humanities Coun., 1977, Humanities and Social Scis. U. B.C., 1993, Nat. Historic Pub. & Records Commn., 1988-92; Ford Found. fellow, 1964-65. Mem. Assn. Records Mgrs. and Adminstrs. (pres. No. Colo. chpt. 1984-85, v.p. Ocean State chpt. 1987-90, bd. dirs., editor Vancouver chpt. 1991, bd. dirs. Ctrl. N.J. chpt. 2000—, pres. 2002—), mem. records mgmt. standards and glossary task forces, Mem. Yr. 1985, microcomputer/PC industry action com., chmn. 1984-86, editor Software Dir. 1985-91, co-chmn. tech. applications com. 1989-90, chmn. Archives ISG 1997-99, ISG mid-year seminar program com. 1998—, mgr. edn. sector 1999-2002), Inst. Cert. Records Mgrs. (regional coord., exam proctor, grader 1982—, cert. records mgr. 1983), Soc. Am. Archivists (com. automated records and techniques 1990-94, select com. task force on automated records and techniques 1994—, chmn. MicroMARC users group 1994-96, rep. joint SAA-ARMA Com. 1995-97), Nat. Assn. Govt. Archivists an Records Adminstrs., Archives Assn. B.C. (freedom of info. and privacy legis. com. 1990-93), Assn. Can. Archivists (electronic records select com. 1991-93, Acad. Cert. Archivists (outreach com. 1996-98, mem. commn. on future of archival enterprise 1999—), Am. Hist. Soc. of Germans from Russia (charter mem.), Mid-Atlantic Regional Archives Conf. (program com. 1999-2000, 2002—). Democrat. Unitarian Universalist. Avocations: local history, art, photography, film and TV production. Home: 387 N 6th Ave Brighton CO 80601 E-mail: ALBIN.WAGNER@SOS.STATE.NJ.US.

WAGNER, SUSAN JANE, sales and marketing consulting company executive; b. Englewood, N.J., Aug. 11; d. Jules A. and Florence I. (Froeba) W.; m. Mark E. McKenna, May 4, 1984. MusB with honors, Syracuse U., 1974; MPA with honors, Fairleigh Dickinson U., 1983. Dir. music, theater dependant sch. U.S. Dept. Def., Fed. Republic Germany, 1976-82; grad. asst. Fairleigh Dickinson U., Rutherford, N.J., 1982-83; account exec. Katz Radio/Katz Communications, Inc., N.Y.C., 1983-85; account mgr. network Katz Radio Group, 1985-87, v.p., dir. mktg., 1987-90, sr. v.p. dir.mktg., 1990-91; v.p. corp. mktg. Katz Comm., Inc., 1992-93; owner Exec. Dynamics Inc., Mahwah, N.J., 1993—. Mem. Am. Women in Radio and TV, Electronic Media Mktg. Assn., Am. Mktg. Assn., Promotion Mktg. Assn. Am., Broadcast Promotion Mktg. Execs., Sigma Alpha Iota, Gamma Phi Beta. Avocations: sailing, skiing, singing. Office: Exec Dynamics 2 James Brite Cir Mahwah NJ 07430-2527 E-mail: edi1@iglide.net.

WAGNER, SUSAN JILL, producer; b. N.Y.C., Nov. 8, 1960; d. Alan C. and Martha (Dreyfus) W. BA cum laude, Princeton U., 1982. Summer intern Lorimar Prodns., N.Y.C., 1978, Martin Bregman Prodns., N.Y.C., 1979, 80; assoc. producer Alan Wagner Prodns., 1982-85; dir. programs Grosso Jacobson Entertainment, 1985-90; v.p. programs Boardwalk Entertainment, 1990-95, exec. v.p., 1995-97, pres., 1997—. Exec. cons. (television films) Spenser: Ceremony, 1993, Spenser: Pale Kings and Princes, 1993, Spenser: The Judas Goat, 1994, Spenser: A Savage Place, 1994; asst. producer (television film) Reunion at Fairborough, 1985, (television pilot) We're Puttin' on the Ritz, 1986; asst. supr. producer (television series) True Blue, 1989, Cop Talk: Behind the Shield, 1989. Mem. Brit. Acad. Film and TV Arts East Coast (bd. dirs.), N.Y. Women in Film and TV. Office: Boardwalk Entertainment 210 E 39th St New York NY 10016-2754 E-mail: swlw.boardwalk@infohouse.com.

WAGNER, TANYA SUZANNE LINEBERRY, health facility administrator; b. Pitts., Jan. 12, 1936; d. Graydon Holmes and Anna Fedorovna (Donics) Lineberry; children: Lynn Holmes, Stephen Francis. RN, Bryn Mawr Hosp. Sch. Nursing, 1957; BS in Nursing, Lebanon Valley Coll., 1972; MEd, Providence Coll., 1989. RN, Mass, Pa., R.I.; cert. nurse adminstr. Dir. nursing Harrisburg (Pa.) Hosp.; v.p. nursing Med. Ctr. Beaver (Pa.) County, Newport (R.I.) Hosp., Faulkner Hosp., Boston; dir. mktg. and pub. rels. Med. Eye Care Assocs., P.C.; adminstr. Oakwood Ctr. Radiation Oncology, Harrisburg, Pa. Condr. seminars on nursing and mgmt.; mgmt. cons. to healthcare facilities and other providers. Recipient award Hosp. Assn. Pa., 1982. Mem. Health Care Educators S. Cen. Pa. (chmn.), Pa. Nurse's Assn. (dist. 15 pres.), R.I. Orgn. Nurse Execs. (chmn.), Am. Nurse's Assn. Home: 5007 Apache Dr Mechanicsburg PA 17050-2564 E-mail: tsw11236@aol.com.

WAGNER, WENCESLAS JOSEPH, law educator; b. Warsaw, Poland, Dec. 12, 1917; came to U.S., 1948; s. Joseph W. Wagner and Margaret M. de Ferrein; m. Dianne A. Moc, July 23, 1950 (div. Aug. 1970); children: Joseph V., Alexandra D., Margaret E.; m. Magdalena M. Niezychowska, Sept. 21, 1979 (dec. 1989); m. Janina Daniela Morgiewicz, Feb. 14, 1994. LLM, U. Warsaw, 1939; D in Law, U. Paris, 1947; LLM, Northwestern U., 1950, JD, 1953, D of Jud. Sci., 1957; D h.c., Nicolas Copernicus U., Torun, Poland, 1992. Bar: Ind. 1965. Asst. to full prof. law Notre Dame (Ind.) U., 1953-62; prof. law Ind. U., Bloomington, 1962-71, U. Detroit, 1971-89; disting. vis. prof. law U. Seton Hall, Newark, 1969-70; vis. prof. law various univs., various cities, Poland, 1970-71, 90-93; chmn. coun. European Faculty of Law, Warsaw, 1997—. Vis. prof. law U. Paris, U. Rennes, 1969-70; internat. invited spkr. and lectr., numerous univs. and other instns. Author over 250 publs. in English, French, Polish, German and Portuguese; bd. editors Am. Jour. Comparative Law, 1963-89. Pres. Am. Coun. Polish Culture, 1958-60; v.p. Polish Home Army Vets., Chgo., 1990—. Capt. Polish Secret Army during German Occupation, 1941-45, Warsaw. Fulbright grantee, Commn. Internat. Exchs. Scholars, 4 times; Knight Comdr. Order of St. John of Jerusalem (Malta), 1990—. Mem. Am. Fgn. Law Assn. (v.p. 1964-66), Internat. Movement of Cath. Lawyers (v.p. 1972-89), Assn. Am. Law Schs. (chmn. internat. meetings com. 1966-89), numerous other orgns. Roman Catholic. Avocations: philately, tennis, skiing, musi. Home: 3365 Sandleheath The Meadows Sarasota FL 34235

WAGNER, WILLIAM BURDETTE, business educator; b. Oswego, N.Y., Apr. 27, 1941; s. Guy Wesley and Gladys M. (Redlinger) W.; divorced; 1 child, Geoffrey D. BA with highest honors, Mich. State U., 1963; MBA, Ohio State U., 1965, PhD, 1967. Research and teaching asst. Ohio State U., Columbus, 1966-68; prof. mktg. and logistics U. Mo., Columbia, 1969-2000, prof. emeritus, 2000—. Guest prof. mktg. U. Nanjing, China, 1985-87, Prince of Songla U., Hat Yai, Thailand, 1990, 92, 98, 99, Assumption U., Bangkok, 1998-99, U. of Thai C. of C., Bangkok, 1998; vis. prof. bus. Chulalongkorn U., Bangkok, 2000, 2001; expert witness petroleum industry, 1989—; adv. dir. Mo. State Bank, St. Louis, 1981-93. Contbr. articles to profl. jours. Univ. coordinator book procurement program for minorities McDonnell Douglas, St. Louis, 1972—; mem. St. Louis-Nanjing Sister City Com., 1985—; faculty ambassador U. Mo. Alumni Assn., 1987—; mem. speakers bur., high sch. liaison team U. Mo., 1987—; Mizzou Outreach prof., 1987—; bd. dirs. Cen. Mo. Sheltered Enterprises for Handicapped, Columbia, 1985-92. Recipient Civic Svc. award McDonnell Douglas, 1977, Educator of Yr. award Jr. C. of C., 1983, Prof. of Yr. award Coll. of Bus. and Pub. Adminstrn., 1987, Golden Key Honor Soc. Faculty Mem. of Yr. award, 1987, Faculty Mem. of Yr. award Beta Theta Pi, 1990, Prof. of Yr. award Kans. City Alumni Assn., 1990; named Mktg. Prof. of Yr., U. Mo., 1987-88, 89-91; rsch. grantee SBC, Econ. Devel. Adminstrn., U. Mo.; NDEA fellow Ohio State U., 1963-66, William T. Kemper Teaching fellow, 1991, Wakonse Teaching fellow, 1995; Fulbright scholar, Korea, 1992. Mem. Nat. Assn. Purchasing Mgmt., St. Louis Purchasing Mgmt. Assn., Coun. Logistics Mgmt., Nat. Fulbright Assn., Nat. Eagle Scout Assn., Am. Soc. Transp. and Logistics (pres. Mo. chpt. 1974-75, bd. govs. 1970-74, 75-82), Delta Sigma Pi, Beta Gamma Sigma, Omicron Delta Epsilon, Rotary Internat. (Paul Harris fellow), Mo. Athletic Club (St. Louis), Country Club of Mo. (Columbia), Univ. Club (Columbia), Jefferson Club. Methodist. Avocations: bridge, golf, stamp and coin collecting, reading historical novels, jogging. Home: 2401 Bluff Blvd Columbia MO 65201-8613 Office: Univ Mo 214 Middlebush Hall Columbia MO 65211-6100 E-mail: wagnerw@missouri.edu.

WAGNER, WILLIAM GERARD, university dean, physicist, consultant, information scientist, investment manager; b. St. Cloud, Minn., Aug. 22, 1936; s. Gerard C. and Mary V. (Cloone) W.; m. Janet Agatha Rowe, Jan. 30, 1968 (div. 1978); children: Mary, Robert, David, Anne; m. Christiane LeGuen, Feb. 21, 1985 (div. 1989); m. Yvonne Naomi Moussette, Dec. 4, 1995. BS, Calif. Inst. Tech., 1958, PhD (NSF fellow, Howard Hughes fellow), 1962. Cons. Rand Corp., Santa Monica, Calif., 1960-65; sr. staff physicist Hughes Research Lab., Malibu, 1960-69; lectr. physics Calif. Inst. Tech., Pasadena, 1963-65; asst. prof. physics U. Calif. at Irvine, 1965-66; assoc. prof. physics and elec. engring. U. So. Calif., L.A., 1966-69, prof. depts. physics and elec. engring., 1969—, dean div. natural scis. and math. Coll. Letters, Arts and Scis., 1973-87, dean interdisciplinary studies and developmental activities, 1987-89, spl. asst. automated record services, 1975-81; founder program in neural, informational & behavioral scis., 1982—. Chmn. bd. Malibu Securities Corp., L.A., 1971—; cons. Janus Mgmt. Corp., L.A., 1970-71, Croesus Capital Corp., L.A., 1971-74, Fin. Horizons Inc., Beverly Hills, Calif., 1971—; allied mem. Pacific Stock Exch., 1974-82; fin. and computer cons. Hollywood Reporter, 1979-81; mem. adv. coun. for emerging engring. techs. NSF, 1987-89. Contbr. articles on physics to sci. publs. Richard Chase Tolman postdoctoral fellow, 1962-65 Mem. Am. Phys. Soc., Nat. Assn. Security Dealers, Sigma Xi. Home: 2828 Patricia Ave Los Angeles CA 90064-4425 Office: U So Calif Hedco Neurosci Bldg Los Angeles CA 90089-0001

WAGNER, WILLIAM MICHAEL, academic administrator; b. Saratoga Springs, N.Y., May 6, 1949; s. Harold Wilbur and Alice Frieda (Stauffacher) W.; m. Barbara Lee Galarneault, Jan. 25, 1980; 1 child, Harold Galarneault Wagner. BA, Bradley U., 1971; MA, U. Tex., 1973. Tchr. Happy Grove HS, Hector's River, Jamaica, 1974-75; specialist software sys. U. Tex., Austin, 1977-88, asst. dir., 1988-93; 2nd v.p. TIAA-CREF, N.Y.C., 1993-98, v.p. technol. integration, 1998—2002; dir. info. tech. svcs. Stephen F. Austin State U., Nacogdoches, Tex., 2002—. Dir. Tex. Giga POP, 2002—. Contbr. articles to profl. jours. Mem. Software AG User Group Internat. (ADABAS product rep. 1986-87, v.p. 1987-88, pres. 1989-91, adv. bd. 1990-93), Computer Measurement Group, Littlefield Soc., Chancellor's Coun., Tex. Leadership Soc., Soc. for Info. Mgmt., Mensa, Phi Eta Sigma, Phi Kappa Phi, Omicron Delta Kappa, Sigma Pi Sigma, Kappa Delta Rho. Republican. Avocations: cycling, skiing, physics and cosmology, naval history, railroads. Office: Stephen F Austin State U Box 13012 SFA Sta Nacogdoches TX 75962

WAGNER-WESTBROOK, BONNIE JOAN, management professional; b. Watertown, N.Y., July 18, 1953; d. Elmer Ethan and Joan Eleanor (Niedermeier) Wagner; m. John Drewry Westbrook Jr., Aug. 21, 1982. BS, SUNY, Geneseo, 1975, MS, 1981; EdD, Rutgers U., 1989. Tchr. elem. Rochester (N.Y.) Sch. for the Deaf, 1975-80; instr. adult basic edn. Rochester City Sch. Dist., 1981-82; profl. interpreter Nat. Tech. Inst. for the Deaf, Rochester, 1981-83; instr., interpreter Henrietta (N.Y.) Ctrl. Sch. Dist., 1983-84; intern Middlesex County Vocat. Tech. Schs., New Brunswick, N.J., 1985; adminstr. Pub. Svc. Electric and Gas Co., Newark, 1990-91; cons. on urban initiative for N.J. Dept. Edn. Rutgers U., New Brunswick, 1985-86, program specialist, 1987-88, rsch. assoc. for N.J. Commn. on Employment and Tng., 1988-89, also senator Grad. Sch. Edn., 1985-87, program dir. New Brunswick, 1991—, dir. leadership devel. program. Cons. Blueprint Project, Hudson County C.C., 1992-93. Pub. Svc. Electric and Gas Co., Newark, 1986-89. Vol. Rochester Sch. for the Deaf, 1977; mem. Rochester Oratorio Soc., 1978-81, SUNY Geneseo Chamber Singers, 1971-75. Rutgers U. scholar, 1986; Rutgers U. fellow, 1987. Mem. Am. Coun. on Edn. of Deaf, Nat. Registry Interpreters for Deaf, Rochester Amateur Radio Assn., Rutgers U. Alumni Assn., Omicron Tau Theta. Republican. Avocations: photography, gardening, computers, music, hiking. Home: 327 Becker St Highland Park NJ 08904-2522 Office: Rutgers U Sch Mgmt & Labor Rels Ctr Mgmt Devel 94 Rockafeller Rd Ste 215 Piscataway NJ 08854-8054 E-mail: westbroo@cmd.rutgers.edu.

WAGONER, DAVID EVERETT, lawyer; b. Pottstown, Pa., May 16, 1928; s. Claude Brower and Mary Kathryn (Groff) W.; children: Paul R., Colin H., Elon D., Peter B., Dana F.; m. Jean Morton Saunders; children: Constance A., Jennifer L., Melissa J. BA, Yale U., 1950; LLB, U. Pa., 1953. Bar: D.C. 1953, Pa. 1953, Wash. 1953. Law clk. U.S. Ct. Appeals (3d cir.), Pa., 1955-56; law clk. U.S. Supreme Ct., Washington, 1956-57; ptnr. Perkins & Coie, Seattle, 1957-96. Panel mem. of arbitration forum worldwide including People's Republic of China, B.C. Internat. Comml. Arbitration Ctr., Hong Kong Internat. Arbitration Centre, Asian/Pacific Ctr. for Resolution of Internat. Bus. Disputes and the Ctr. for Internat. Dispute Resolution for Asian/Pacific Region. Mem. sch. com. Mcpl. League Seattle and King County, 1958— , chmn., 1962-65; mem. Seattle schs. citizens com. on equal ednl. opportunity and adult vocat. edn., 1963-64; mem. Nat. Com. Support Pub. Schs.; mem. adv. com. on community colls., to 1965, legislature interim com. on edn., 1964-65; mem. community coll. adv. com. to state supt. pub. instrn., 1965; chmn. edn. com. Forward Thrust, 1968; mem. Univ. Congl. Ch. Council Seattle, 1968-70; bd. dirs. Met. YMCA Seattle, 1968; bd. dirs. Seattle Pub. Schs., 1965-73, v.p., 1966-67, 72-73, pres., 1968, 73; trustee Evergreen State Coll. Found., chmn. 1986-87, capitol campaign planning chmn.; trustee Pacific NW Ballet, v.p. 1986. Served to 1st lt. M.C., AUS, 1953-55 Fellow Am. Coll. Trial Lawyers (mem. ethics com., legal ethics com.), Chartered Inst. Arbitrators, Singapore Inst. Arbitrators; mem. ABA (chmn. standing com. fed. jud. imprisonment, chmn. appellate advocacy com., mem. commn. on separation of powers and jud. independence), Wash. State Bar Assn., Seattle-King County Bar Assn., Acad. Experts, Swiss Arbitration Assn., Comml. Bar Assn. London, Nat. Sch. Bds. Assn. (bd. dirs., chmn. coun. Big City bds. edn. 1971-72), English-Speaking Union (v.p. Seattle chpt. 1961-62), Chi Phi. Office: Internat Arbitration Chambers US BankCtr 1420 5th Ave Fl 22 Seattle WA 98101-4087 Home: 3916 E Pine St Seattle WA 98122-3517

WAGONER, DAVID RUSSELL, writer, educator; b. Massillon, Ohio, June 5, 1926; s. Walter Siffert and Ruth (Banyard) W.; m. Patricia Lee Parrott, July 8, 1961 (div. June 1982); m. Robin Heather Seyfried, July 24, 1982; children: Alexandra Dawn, Adrienne Campbell. BA in English, Pa. State U., 1947; MA in English, Ind. U., 1949. Instr. English DePauw U., 1949-50; instr. Pa. State U., 1950-53; asst. prof. U. Wash., 1954-57, assoc. prof., 1958-66, prof., 1966-2000, prof. emeritus, 2000—. Elliston lectr. U. Cin., 1968; editor Poetry NW, 1966— ; poetry editor Princeton U. Press, 1977-81, Mo. Press, 1983— Author: (poetry books) Dry Sun, Dry Wind, 1953, A Place to Stand, 1958, The Nesting Ground, 1963, Staying Alive, 1966, New and Selected Poems, 1969, Working Against Time, 1970, Riverbed, 1972, Sleeping in the Woods, 1974, Collected Poems, 1976, Who Shall Be the Sun?, 1978, In Broken Country, 1979, Landfall, 1981, First Light, 1983, Through the Forest, 1987, Walt Whitman Bathing, 1996, Traveling Light: Collected and New Poems, 1999, The House of Song, 2002; (novels) The Man in the Middle, 1954, Money, Money, Money, 1955, Rock, 1958, The Escape Artist (also film 1982), 1965, Baby, Come on Inside, 1968, Where is My Wandering Boy Tonight?, 1970, The Road to Many a Wonder, 1974, Tracker, 1975, Whole Hog, 1976, The Hanging Garden, 1980; editor: Straw for the Fire: From the Notebooks of Theodore Roethke, 1943-63, 1972. Recipient Morton Dauwen Zabel prize Poetry mag., 1967, Blumenthal-Leviton-Blonder prize, 1974, 2 Fels prizes Coordinating Coun. Lit. Mags., 1975, Tietjens prize, 1977, English-Speaking Union prize, 1980, Sherwood Anderson award, 1980, Ruth Lilly Poetry prize, 1991, Levinson prize, 1994; Union League Prize, 1987, Pacific N.W. Booksellers award, 2000; Guggenheim fellow, 1956, Ford fellow, 1964, Nat. Inst. Arts and Letters grantee, 1967, Nat. Endowment for Arts grantee, 1969 Mem. Acad. Am. Poets (chancellor 1978—2000), Soc. Am. Magicians, Nat. Assn. Blackfeet Indians (asso.) Home: 5416 154th Pl SW Edmonds WA 98026-4348 Office: U Wash PO Box 354330 Seattle WA 98195-4330 E-mail: renogawd@aol.com.

WAGONER, G. RICHARD, JR. automotive company executive; b. Wilmington, Del., Feb. 9, 1953; BS in Econs., Duke U., 1975; MBA, Harvard U., 1977. Analyst in treas.'s office, mgr. Latin Am. financing, dir. Can. and overseas borrowing, dir. capital analysis and investment GM, N.Y., 1977-81, treas. Sao Paulo, Brazil, 1981-84, exec. dir. fin. Brazil, 1984-87, v.p., fin. mgr. Can., 1987-88, group dir. strategic bus. planning Can., 1988-89, v.p. fin. Switzerland, 1989-91, pres. Brazil, 1992-93, head Worldwide Purchasing Group, 1993-94, exec. v.p., pres. North Am. ops., 1994-98, pres., COO, 1998—2000, pres., CEO, 2000—, also bd. dirs. Chmn. bd. visitors Fuqua Sch. Bus. Duke U.; trustee Detroit County Day Sch. Mem. Soc. Automotive Engrs. (mem. VISION 2000 exec. com.). Office: GM Corp 300 Renaissance Ctr Detroit MI 48265-0001*

WAGONER, GERALDINE VANDER POL, music educator; b. Kankakee, Ill., Sept. 16, 1931; d. Ralph and Josie (Mieras) VanderPol; children: Joel Timothy, Stephanie Anne. BA, Central U. Of Iowa, 1954; MA, Montclair State Coll., 1968; postgrad., Juilliard Sch. Music, 1955-56, 66-67, NYU, Royal Conservatory, Toronto, 1971, Mozarteum, Salzburg, Austria, 1972. Music coach, piano pedagog Bd. Edn., Edison, NJ, 1954—74; music specialist Ridgewood, 1975-95; dir. Musical Spheres Co., 1995—. Mem. Amb. to Amb. program Russian Conservatories, 1998. Composer creative tonal and rhythm curriculum for children and assessing beginning instrumental music instructional strategies. Trustee, Hudson Symphony Orch., 1965-71; mem. Met. Mus. of Art, Teaching fellow NYU, 1990-91; adj. prof. music William Paterson Coll., Wayne, N.J. Mem. Profl. Music Tchrs. Guild (cert. for highest goals and achievements 1966), Nat. Music Tchrs. Assn., N.J. Music Tchrs. Assn., Am. Orff Schulwerk Assn., NEA, Music Educators Assn., Bergen County Music Educators Assn., Theater Devel. Found., Met. Opera Guild, Netherland-American Found., Collegiate Chorale N.Y.C. 1995—, Lyceum Soc. of N.Y. Acad. Scis., Netherland Club, Overseas Yacht Club, Coll. Club. E-mail: wagoner.g@mindspring.com.

WAGONER, ROBERT VERNON, astrophysicist, educator; b. Teaneck, N.J., Aug. 6, 1938; s. Robert Vernon and Marie Theresa (Clifford) W.; m. Lynne Ray Moses, Sept. 2, 1963 (div. Feb. 1986); children: Alexa Frances, Shannon Stephanie; m. Stephanie Brewster, June 27, 1987. BME, Cornell U., 1961; MS, Stanford U., 1962, PhD, 1965. Rsch. fellow in physics Calif. Inst. Tech., 1965-68, Sherman Fairchild Disting. scholar, 1976; asst. prof. astronomy Cornell U., 1968-71, assoc. prof., 1971-73; assoc. prof. physics Stanford U., 1973-77, prof., 1977—. George Ellery Hale disting. vis. prof. U. Chgo., 1978; mem. Com. on Space Astronomy and Astrophysics, 1979-82, theory study panel Space Sci. Bd., 1980-82, physics survey com. NRC, 1983-84; grant selection com. NSERC (Can.), 1990-93; active Laser Interferometer Gravitational-Wave Obs. Sci. Collaboration. Contbr. articles on theoretical astrophysics and gravitation to profl. jours., mags.; co-author Cosmic Horizons, 1982; patentee in field. Sloan Found. rsch. fellow, 1969-71; Guggenheim Meml. fellow, 1979; grantee NSF, 1973-90, 2000—, NASA, 1982-99. Fellow Am. Phys. Soc.; mem. Am. Astron. Soc., Internat. Astron. Union, Tau Beta Pi, Phi Kappa Phi Office: Stanford U Dept Physics Stanford CA 94305-4060 E-mail: wagoner@stanford.edu.

WAGONER, WILLIAM DOUGLAS, public administrator, urban/regional planner; b. Detroit, Jan. 20, 1947; s. Bernard Leo and Ruby (Duckett) W.; Terry Ann Tolaro, Dec. 17, 1971; children: Melissa Ann, Emily Marie. BS in Edn., Wayne State U., 1971, MA in Urban Planning and Pub. Adminstrn., 1980; D in Pub. Adminstrn., Nova U., 1982; AA in Liberal Arts, U. State of N.Y., 1987, BA in Liberal Studies, 1988; BS in Emergency Disaster Mgmt./Human Svc, Thomas A. Edison State Coll., 1993. Instr. Clarkston (Mich.) Pub. Sch. Dist., 1972-74; city planner City of Berkley, Mich., 1974-80, dir. community devel., planning and rsch., 1980-92, asst. city mgr., 1978-92; cons. community mgmt. Wagoner and Assocs., Royal Oak, Mich., 1985—; dir. planning and emergency mgmt. Livingston County, 1992—. Adj. prof. Cen. Mich. U., Mt. Pleasant, 1985—, Mich. State Police div. Emergency Mgmt., 1989—; bd. registration Profl. Emergency Mgrs., 1990—; bd. dirs., treas. Berkley-LaSalette Credit Union, Oakland Family Svcs.; chair, bd. visitors Emergency Mgmt. Inst., FEMA; mem. coord. coun. Livingston County Human Svcs., 1992—; chair Cert. Emerg. Mgr. Commn., 1999—; mem. Mich. Hazard Mitigation Coord. Council, 1999—. Editorial auditor jour. Transp. and Distbn., 1987-92; bd. editors jour. World Safety Orgn., 1987-92; contbr. articles to profl. jours. Tech. chmn. Northwestern Hwy. Impact Study Com., Oakland County, Mich., 1975-77, tech. advisor Traffic Engring. Coordination Group, Oakland County, 1976-88, mem. adv. coun. Community Devel., Oakland County, 1985—; apptd. ofcl. S.E. Mich. Coun. Govts.; coun. on Environ. Strategy, Detroit, 1975-92; mem. Nat. Def. Exec. Res., Washington, 1986—; resource rep. Oakland County Cultural coun., 1975-92; mem. Task Force on Land Use Guidelines, 1992—. With U.S. Army, 1964-66. Recipient Sir John Hodsoll Pub. Works award, British Inst. of Civil Def. and Disaster Studies. Fellow Brit. Inst. Mgmt., Inst. Transp. Engrs.; mem. ASPA (pres. 1988-90), Am. Arbitration Assn. (arbitrator 1983—), Southeastern Emergency Mgrs. Assn. (pres. 1986-88), Southeastern Oakland County Water Authority (chmn. 1988-90), Can. Inst. Mgmt., U.S. Jaycees (hon.), Wayne State U. Alumni Assn. (pres. 1987-88), Am. Legion, KC (Columbian award 1984), Lions (pres. 1983-85), Shrine Dad's Club. Roman Catholic. Avocations: photography, camping, travel. Home: 2332 Hawkins Ave Royal Oak MI 48073-4803 Office: Livingston County 304 E Grand River Ave Howell MI 48843-2323

WAGUESPACK, GERALD EDWARD, music educator; b. New Orleans, Sept. 26, 1949; s. Vernon Gerald and Elaine Naquin Waguespack; m. Aimee Audrey Hebert, Aug. 11, 1972. BM, Nicholls State U, Thibodaux, LA, 1967—71; MM, U Southwestern La., Lafayette, LA, 1974—77; PhD, U So. Miss., Hattiesburg, MS, 1991—92. Band dir. Vinton H.S., Vinton, La., 1971—73, Rayne H.S., Rayne, 1973—79, Acadiana H.S., Lafayette, 1979—. Recipient Citation of Excellence, Nat. Band Assn, 1988, Cert. Of Appreciation, Acadiana Chpt. of the Vietnam Veterans of Am., 1987, La. Music Educators Assn, 1983, outstanding band dir. in La., Phi Beta Mu, 1981, Cert. Of Appreciation, Acadia Spl. Olympics, 1979; fellow Joe Barry Mullins Fellowship, U So. Miss., 1991. Mem.: Internat. Assn of Jazz Educators, Coll. Band Directors Assn, Nat. Band Assn (state chmn. 1998—2000), SW La. Band Directors Assn (v.p. 1993—95), Am. Sch. Band Directors Assn, La. Band Masters Assn, La. Music Educators Assn (bd. of directors 1978—83), Music Educators Nat. Assn, Phi Beta Mu (president-epsilon chpt. 1997—99). Avocations: gardening, cooking, collecting baseball cards, collecting baseball cards. Home: 204 Denette St Duson LA 70529 Office: Acadiana High School 15 Rue de Belier Lafayette LA 70506 Office Fax: 337-981-1726.

WAHAAB, JAY, entrepreneur; b. Arima, Trinidad, West Indies, Jan. 31, 1961; arrived in Can., 1976; came to U.S., 1981; s. A. Wahaab and Maria Sankar. AA, Westchester Bus. Inst., 1990. Prin. MJ Mktg., White Plains, N.Y., 1986—. Sgt. USMC, 1984-94. Mem. Beneath the Sea (ad dir. 1987—, Disting. Svc. award 1989), Marine Corps League (chmn. Toys for Tots 1990—, Disting. Svc. award 1992). Avocations: scuba diving, outdoor activities, sports, camping, hiking. Office: MJ Mktg PO Box 1734 White Plains NY 10602-1734 E-mail: MJMKTG@aol.com.

WAHID, ZIA UDDIN, psychiatrist; b. Sargodha, Punjab, Pakistan, Aug. 14, 1958; came to U.S., 1985; s. Mian Abdul Wahid; m. Maimoona Zia, Dec. 9, 1990; 1 child, Iqra Zia. BSc, U. Punjab, Lahore, Pakistan, 1980; MB BS, King Edward Med. Coll., 1984. Diplomate Am. Bd. Psychiatry and Neurology, Am. Bd. Adult Psychiatry, Am. Bd. Addiction Psychiatry, Am. Bd. Geriatric Psychiatry, Am. Bd. Forensic Psychiatry. Intern, resident McHarry Med. Coll., Nashville, 1988-92; staff psychiatrist Dede Wallace Ctr., 1992-95; asst. prof. Meharry Med. Coll., 1995—, dir. residency tng. in psychiatry, 1995—; med. dir. Elam Mental Health Ctr., 1995—. Examiner Am. Bd. Psychiatry & Neurology, 2001—. Author: Psychiatric Pearls, 1998, Medtex Board Review, 1998; editor Jour. Nat. Med. Assocs., 1999; reviewer Jour. Clin. Psychiatry, 2001-. Treas. Islamic Ctr., Nashville, 1992-95, mem. exec. bd., 1999—. Fellow Am. Coll. Internat. Physicians (v.p. Tenn. chpt. 1999); mem. Am. Psychiat. Assocs. Avocations: fishing, hunting, reading. Office: Meharry Med Coll 1005 D B Todd Blvd Nashville TN 37208

WAHL, ARTHUR CHARLES, retired chemistry educator; b. Des Moines, Sept. 8, 1917; s. Arthur C. and Mabel (Mussetter) W.; m. Mary Elizabeth McCauley, Dec. 1, 1943; 1 child, Nancy Wahl Miegel. BS, Iowa State Coll., 1939; PhD, U. Calif., Berkeley, 1942. Group leader Los Alamos (N.Mex.) Nat. Lab., 1943-46; assoc. prof. chemistry Washington U., St. Louis, 1946-53, Farr prof. of radiochemistry, 1953-83, prof. emeritus, 1983—. Cons. Los Alamos Nat. Lab., 1950—. Author, editor: Radioactivity Applied to Chemistry, 1951; contbr. articles to profl. jours. NSF fellow, 1967; recipient Sr. Vis. Scientist Humboldt award Humboldt Found., 1977. Mem. Am. Chem. Soc. Office: Los Alamos Nat Lab Ms # 514 Los Alamos NM 87545-0001 E-mail: awahl@lanl.gov.

WAHL, BERNT RAINER, mathematician, writer, software engineer; b. Santa Monica, Calif., June 24, 1960; s. Bruno W. and Ursula (Nunn) W. BA in Math., U. Calif., Santa Cruz, 1984, BS in Physics, 1986; MBA, U. Calif., Davis, 1999; cert. mgmt. tech., U. Calif., Berkeley, 2000; MA in Multimedia, Calif. State U., Hayward, 2001; Knowledge Revolution cert., Stanford U., 2000. Founding mem. Berkeley (Calif.) Macintosh User Group, Berkeley, 1984—; CEO Dynamic Software, Calif., 1986—; mem. Bootstrap Inst., Fremont, 1996—; chief creative officer Yellow Giant, Oakland; CEO Datahunt, Inc., 2001, Infoseek Corp., 2000—01. Tech. advisor Reliacom, Reston, Va., Quantal, Berkeley, Calif., Jhane Barnes, Inc., NY, Disney, Sunnyvale, Calif., 1995—; lectr. U. Calif., Berkeley, Davis, Santa Cruz, 1995—99; adj. prof. bus. Golden Gate U., San Francisco; prof. bus./multimedia Calif. State U., Hayward; vis. prof. U. Malaya, Malaysia, 2002—, Multimedia U., Malaysia, 2002—. Author: Chaos, 1988, Exploring Fractals, 1995; co-author: Virtual Playhouse, 1994; host (video series) Fractals, 1995, Info. Tech., 1996; film dir./ prodr.: Swing City, 1999. Fellow Fulbright fellow, 2002. Mem.: AAAS, Internat. Radio Engrs. and Elec. Engrs., IEEE Computer Soc., Urban Land Inst., Assn. Computing Machinery, Nat. Ednl. Film and Video Festival (jury chair). Avocations: Olympic photography, America Cup Heart of Am. Office: Dynamic Software PO Box 13991 Berkeley CA 94712-4991 also: Quantal 1936 University Ave Ste 355 Berkeley CA 94704-1071 E-mail: berntww@wahl.org.

WAHL, FLOYD MICHAEL, geologist; b. Hebron, Ind., July 7, 1931; s. Floyd Milford and Ann Pearl (DeCook) W.; m. Dorothy W. Daniel, July 4, 1953; children: Timothy, David, Jeffrey, Kathryn. AB, DePauw U., 1953; MS, U. Ill., 1957, PhD, 1958. Cert. profl. geologist. Prof. geology U. Fla., Gainesville, 1969-82, assoc. dean Grad. Sch., 1974-80, acting dean, 1980-81; exec. dir. Geol Soc Am., Boulder, Colo., 1982-94; ret., 1994. Contbr. articles to profl. jours. Served to cpl. U.S. Army, 1953-55. Recipient Outstanding Tchr. award U. Ill., 1967 Fellow Geol. Soc. Am. (Outstanding Svc. award 1994); mem. Am. Inst. Profl. Geologists (chpt. pres.), Sigma Xi

WAHL, HOWARD WAYNE, retired construction company executive, engineer; b. Hitterdal, Minn., Jan. 17, 1935; s. Milo Ormenzo and Esther Marie (Sorenson) W.; m. Carroll May Pollock, Aug. 16, 1958; children: Jeffrey David, Michael Edward, Nancy Elizabeth. BCE, U. Washington, 1957. Registered engr., Calif., N.Y., Mich., Ohio, Md. Structural engr. Bechtel Corp., San Francisco, 1956-69, project engr. Gaithersburg, Md., 1969-72; chief civil engr. Bechter Power Corp., San Francisco, 1972-74, mgr. engring. and constrn., 1975-78; v.p., mgr. Ann Arbor Power Div.-Bechtel, Mich., 1978-84; dir. Bechtel Group, Inc., 1982-91; pres. Bechtel Ea. Power Corp., Gaithersburg, 1984-88; mng. dir. Bechtel Power Corp., San Francisco, 1988-89; pres. European region Bechtel Corp., Paris, 1989-91; ret., 1991; pres. Pacific Voice Track, Las Vegas, 1996—2002. Dir. Ann Arbor Bank-1st Am., 1978-84. Contbr. articles to profl. jours. Campaign chmn. Washtenaw County United Way, Ann Arbor, 1982; chmn. Turkish-U.S. Bus. Coun., Washington, 1988-90; mem. exec. coun. Boy Scouts Am., Ann Arbor, 1978-84; mem. devel. coun. U Wash. Coll. Engring.; trustee emeritus Desert Rsch. Inst. U. Nev., Reno. Mem. ASCE (life), Am. Concrete Inst., U. Mich. Pres. Club and Victors Club, U. Washington Pres. Club. Republican. Presbyterian. Avocations: woodworking, gardening, cooking, antique cars, hiking. Home: 170 Canyon Dr Napa CA 94558-1255

WAHL, RICHARD LEO, radiologist, educator, nuclear medicine researcher; b. Iowa, July 13, 1952; s. Max Henry and Josephine Elizabeth (Hogan) Wahl; m. Sandra K. Moeller, June 28, 1975; children: Daniel, Matthew, Peter, Katherine. BA in Chemistry, Wartburg Coll., 1974; MD, Washington U., St. Louis, 1978. Diplomate Am. Bd. Nuc. Medicine (pres. 1998-), Am. Bd. Radiology. Intern U. Calif., San Diego, 1978—79; resident in radiology Mallinckrodt Inst. Washington U., 1979—82, fellow in nuc. medicine and immunology, 1982—83; asst. prof. U. Mich. Med. Ctr., Ann Arbor, 1983—87, assoc. prof., 1987—90, prof., 1990—2000; dir. gen. nuc. imaging, dir. radiopharm. program U. Mich. Cancer Ctr., 1999—2002; prof., dir. nuc. medicine, vice chair tech. and new bus. devel. Johns Hopkins U., Balt., 2002—. Mem. exptl. immunology study sect. NIH, Bethesda, Md., 1990—94; sec. Am. Bd. Nuc. Medicine, 1997, chmn., 98. Editor: 2 textbooks; contbr. 200 articles to profl. jours., chpts. to textbooks; holder (10 patents). Named Eugene Prendegreer New Horizon lectr., RSNA, 1999; recipient Disting. Scientist award, Acad. Molecular Imaging, 2001, Jerome W. Conn rsch. award, U. Mich., 1989; grantee rsch. grantee, NIH, ACS, Dept. of Army. Fellow: Am. Coll. Radiology, Am. Coll. Nuc. Physicians; mem.: AMA, Inst. for Clin. Positron Emission Tomography (bd. dirs., pres. 1996), Am. Assn. for Cancer Rsch., Am. Soc. for Clin. Investigation, Radiol. Soc. N.Am., Soc. Nuc. Medicine (Marc Tetalman award 1986, Berson and Yalow rsch. award 1992, Hounsfield rsch. award 1992). Avocations: reading, sports. Office: Johns Hopkins Outpatient Ctr Divsn Nuclear Medicine 601 N Caroline St Rm 3223 Baltimore MD 21287

WAHL, RICHARD ALAN, pediatrician, educator; b. N.Y.C., Mar. 24, 1952; s. Robert and Elaine (Arnow) W.; m. Margaret Wolf, May 28, 1978; 1 child, Rachel Lee. BA, U. Rochester, 1973; MD, George Washington U., 1978. Diplomate, Nat. Bd. Med. Examiners, Am. Bd. Pediatrics. Intern, then resident U. Mich., Ann Arbor, 1978-81; med. officer U.S. Pub. Health Svc., Peekskill, N.Y., 1981-84; asst. prof. N.Y. Med. Coll., Valhalla, 1984-85; clin. lectr. U. Ariz. Med. Ctr., Tucson, 1985—; clinic chief staff CIGNA Health Plan, 1987-89. Contbr. articles to profl. jours. Fellow Am. Acad. Pediatrics; mem. Am. Coll. Physician Execs., Pima County Pediatric Soc. (pres. 1991-92). Office: CIGNA Health Plan of Ariz 535 N Wilmot Rd Tucson AZ 85711-2600

WAHL, WILLIAM BRYAN, marketing professional, real estate officer; b. Aurora, Colo., Dec. 17, 1963; s. Harold Edward Wahl and Dianne (Fowler) Armstrong. BBA in Mgmt., St. Edward's U., 1987; MBA in Gen. Bus., Kent Coll., 1991; PhD in Bus., U. San Moritz, 1999. Asst. store mgr. Handy Dan, Austin, Tex., 1981-88; real estate broker Powell/Armstrong Realty, 1985—88, S&W Realty, Austin, 1988—; nat. mktg. dir. Am. Home Products, 1988—; pres. Wahl Success Systems, 1989—, project mgr. applied materials, 1995—98; procurement mgr. Dell Computer Corp., 2000—; pres. O.H.S. Prodns., 2000—. Bd. dirs. Pahl Enterprises, Austin, 1988—. Named Outstanding Citizen, Berkeley Davis, Inc., Berkeley, Calif., 1988. Mem. Austin Assn. Life Underwriters, Austin Bd. Realtors, Tex. Assn. Realtors, Nat. Assn. Realtors, Nat. Assn. Life Underwiters, Mktg. and Distributive Edn. Roman Catholic. Avocations: black belt in taekwondoe, golf, weight lifting. Home: 1206 Greenlawn Blvd Round Rock TX 78664-6918

WAHL, WILLIAM JOSEPH, JR. information systems specialist; b. Pottsville, Pa., Jan. 19, 1947; s. William Joseph and Edith (Adams) W.; m. Mary Ellen Trautman, Oct. 17, 1964; children: Patricia Marie, William Joseph III, Monica Marie, Michael Anthony. MS in Bus. Policy, Columbia U., 1983. Dir. info. sys. IBM Corp., White Plains, N.Y., 1979-84, group dir. mgmt. control sys., 1985-87, group dir. info. sys. and telecom., 1988-92; chief info. officer IBM Personal Sys. Group, Somers, 1992-94; dir. worldwide fullfillment sys.ecommunications IBM, 1995-98; v.p., mem. svc. tech. Am. OnLine, Inc., Dulles, Va., 1999, exec. v.p. internal computing, 2000—. Rsch. affiliate NYU Stern Sch. Bus., N.Y.C., 1991—; ops. mgmt. advisor Columbia Grad. Sch. Bus., N.Y.C., 1988—. Mem. Beta Gamma Sigma. Avocations: fishing, philately, music. Home: 43426 Turnberry Isle Ct Leesburg VA 20176 Office: Am OnLine Inc 22260 Pacific Blvd Dulles VA 20166

WAHLBECK, PAUL J. political science educator, lawyer; b. Ill., Sept. 11, 1961; s. Phillip and Donna Wahlbeck; m. Janice Wahlbeck, Sept. 1, 1990; children: Matthew, Katherine, Kristen. BA, Wheaton (Ill.) Coll., 1983; JD, U. Ill., 1986; PhD, Washington U., St. Louis, 1993. Bar: Ill. 1986. Staff atty. joint com. on adminstrv. rules Ill. Gen. Assembly, Springfield, 1986-88; asst. prof. polit. sci. George Washington U., Washington, 1993-99, assoc. prof., 1999—. Dir. law and social sci. program NSF, 2001—. Author: Crafting Law on the

Supreme Court: The Collegial Game, 2000; contbr. articles to profl. jours., including Am. Polit. Sci. Rev., Am. Jour. Polit. Sci., Jour. Politics. Grantee NSF, 1995, 99. Mem. Am. Polit. Sci. Assn. (exec. com. law and cts. sect. 1997-99), Midwest Polit. Sci. Assn., So. Polit. Sci. Assn., Western Polit. Sci. Assn. Presbyterian. Office: George Washington U 2201 G St NW Washington DC 20052-0001 Fax: 202-994-7743. E-mail: wahlbeck@gwu.edu.

WAHLBERG, PHILIP LAWRENCE, former bishop; b. Houston, Jan. 18, 1924; s. Philip Lawrence and Ella Alieda (Swenson) W.; m. Rachel Conrad, June 1, 1946; children: David, Christopher, Pauli, Sharon AA, Tex. Luth. Coll., 1942, DD (hon.), 1963; BA, Lenoir Rhyne Coll., Hickory, N.C., 1944; MDiv, Luth. Theol. Sem., Columbia, S.C., 1946. Ordained to ministry United Luth. Ch. in Am., 1946. Pastor St. Luke Luth. Ch., Thunderbolt, Ga., 1946-50, Redeemer Luth. Ch., Wilmington Island, 1946-50, St. Mark Luth. Ch., Corpus Christi, Tex., 1950-59; pres. Tex.-La. Synod, United Luth. Ch. Am., Austin, 1959-62; bishop Tex.-La. Synod, Luth. Ch. Am., 1963-87; acting dir. devel. Lutheran Outdoor and Retreat Ministries Southwest, 1987-88; legis. liaison Tex. Impact, Austin, 1989-91; interim coord. Regional Ctr. for Mission Evang. Luth. Ch. in Am., Dallas, 1991-92; mem. devel. staff Luth. Sem. Program of Southwest, 1992—; mem. com. on appeals, also chmn. Evang. Luth. Ch. in Am., 1988-95, hearing officer, 1995-98. Also mem. exec. coun. Luth. Ch. in Am., N.Y.C., 1980-87, chmn. com. on legal matters, 1984-87; mem. mgmt. com. Div. for Mission in N.Am., N.Y.C., 1972-80, chmn., 1972-76; bd. dirs. Bd. Am. Missions, N.Y.C., 1963-72, chmn., 1968-72; bd. dirs. Luth. Sch. Theology, Chgo., 1967-87. Author articles in religious jours., sermons; author theol. cassette, 1973 Named Disting. churchman Tex. Luth. Coll., 1978; Disting. Alumnus, Lenoir Rhyne Coll., 1962; named Man of Year, Thunderbolt, Ga. C. of C., 1950 Democrat. Avocations: winemaking, golf, choral singing. Office: 5804 Cary Dr Austin TX 78757-3108

WAHLEN, EDWIN ALFRED, lawyer; b. Gary, Ind., Mar. 12, 1919; s. Alfred and Ethel (Pearson) W.; m. Alice Elizabeth Condit, Apr. 24, 1943 (div. 1983); children: Edwin Alfred, Virginia Elizabeth, Martha Anne; m. Elizabeth L. Corey, Nov. 23, 1984. Student, U. Ala., 1936-38; AB, U. Chgo., 1942, JD, 1948. Bar: Ill. 1948. Practiced in, Chgo., 1948—; mem. firm Haight, Goldstein & Haight, 1948-55; ptnr. Goldstein & Wahlen, 1956-59, Arvey, Hodes, Costello & Burman (and predecessor), 1959-91, Wildman, Harrold, Allen & Dixon, 1992—. Author: Soldiers and Sailors Wills: A Proposal For Federal Legislation, 1948. Served to 2d lt. AUS, 1942-46. Decorated Silver Star medal, Bronze Star medal. Mem. ABA, Ill. Bar Assn., Chgo. Bar Assn., Order of Coif, Phi Beta Kappa, Phi Alpha Delta. Home: 1250 Breckenridge Ct Lake Forest IL 60045-3875 Office: 225 W Wacker Dr Chicago IL 60606-1224

WAHLERS, LINDA ANN FORD, writer; b. Great Barrington, Mass., June 20, 1948; d. George Edward and Eugenie Evelyn (Peck) Ford; m. Herman Frederick Wahlers; children: Heather. AA, Bay Path Coll., 1968. Co-founder, cons., mgr. Poetry Cir., Copake, NY, 1997—99; co-founder, web prodr. Poets Internat., 1999—. Named one of Phenomenal Women of the Net, 1998—. Mem.: Rossendale Writers, Lancashire Authors' Assn. (hon.). Avocation: genealogy, music. Home: 3132 County Rte 7 Copake NY 12516

WAHLKE, JOHN CHARLES, political science educator; b. Cin., Oct. 29, 1917; s. Albert B.C. and Clara J. (Ernst) W.; m. Virginia Joan Higgins, Dec. 1, 1943; children: Janet Parmely, Dale. AB, Harvard U., 1939, MA, 1947, PhD, 1952. Instr., asst. prof. polit. sci. Amherst (Mass.) Coll., 1949-53; assoc. prof. polit. sci. Vanderbilt U., Nashville, 1953-63; prof. polit. sci. SUNY, Buffalo, 1963-66, U. Iowa, 1966-71, SUNY, Stony Brook, 1971-72, U. Iowa, Iowa City, 1972-79, U. Ariz., Tucson, 1979-87, prof. emeritus, 1988—, retired. Author: (with others) The Legislative System, 1962, Government and Politics, 1966, The Politics of Representation, 1978; co-author: Introduction to Political Science—Reason, Reflection, and Analysis, 1997 Served to capt., F.A. AUS, 1942-46. Decorated Air medal with 2 oak leaf clusters, ETO Ribbon, 6 Battle Stars. Mem. AAAS, Am. Polit. Sci. Assn. (past pres.), Internat. Polit. Sci. Assn., So. Polit. Sci. Assn., Midwest Polit. Sci. Assn. (past pres.), Western Polit. Sci. Assn., Southwestern Polit. Sci. Assn., Assn. Politics and the Life Scis. (Founders award 1997), Internat. Soc. of Polit. Psychology. Home: 5462 N Entrada Catorce Tucson AZ 85718-4851 Office: U Ariz Social Sci Bldg Rm 315 Dept Polit Sci Tucson AZ 85721 E-mail: wahlke@email.arizona.edu.

WAHLS, HARVEY EDWARD, civil engineer, educator; b. Evanston, Ill., Aug. 8, 1931; s. Albert C. and Lydia E. (Kutz) W.; m. Margaret B. Waggoner, Sept. 3, 1960; children: Richard A., Nancy K. BSCE, Northwestern U., Evanston, Ill., 1954, MS, 1955, PhD, 1961. Registered profl. engr., N.C. Instr. civil engring. Worcester (Mass.) Poly. Inst., 1955-57, asst. prof., 1957-60; instr. Northwestern U., 1957-59; asst. prof. N.C. State U., Raleigh, 1960-63, assoc. prof., 1963-69, prof. civil engring., 1969-97, assoc. dept. head, 1983-97, prof. emeritus, 1997—. Cons. in field. Fellow ASCE (chair geotech. divsn. 1982-83); mem. ASTM, Am. Soc. Engring. Edn., Internat. Soc. Soil Mechanics and Geotech. Engring., U.S. Nat. Soc. for Soil Mechanics and Found. Engring. (sec. 1985—). Office: NC State U PO Box 7908 Raleigh NC 27695-7908

WAHLSTEEN, HERBERT GUNNAR, music publisher, writer; b. Bklyn., July 31, 1931; s. Herbert Wahlsteen and Maria Mercedes Ortiz-de la Renta; children from previous marriage: Herbert III, William Joseph3 children from previous marriage. Student, N.Y. Inst. Fin., N.Y.C. Cert. top secret clearance code-breaker, Russian lang. cryptanalysis, Washington. Opers. mgr. N.Y. Stock Exch. brokerage firms, N.Y.C. Composer: (song lyrics) all 14 songs in off Broadway revue "OFANT", 1967, (songs) (lyrics) various, including Colors of My Love, Snowgirl, Thoughts of a Wooden Soldier, others; author: (plays) There's No Business, 1989, (songs) (various lyrics, concepts) for several children's projects and radio singing comml. for Tony Roma Restaurants. Airman 1st class USAF, 1951—54. Mem.: Broadcast Music, Inc., Dramatist Guild.

WAHOSKE, MICHAEL JAMES, lawyer; b. Ripon, Wis., June 4, 1953; children: Jennifer, John. BA with highest honors, U. Notre Dame, 1975, JD summa cum laude, 1978. Bar: Minn. 1978, U.S. Dist. Ct. Minn. 1979, U.S. Ct. Appeals (7th cir.) 1979, U.S. Ct. Appeals (8th and 9th cirs.) 1980, U.S. Ct. Appeals (10th cir.) 1982, U.S. Supreme Ct. 1982, U.S. Ct. Appeals (6th cir.) 1988, U.S. Ct. Appeals (fed. cir.) 1989, U.S. Ct. Appeals (D.C. cir.) 1992, U.S. Ct. Appeals (4th cir.) 1994, U.S. Ct. Appeals (11th cir.) 1996, Supreme Ct. of Winnebago Tribe of Nebr., 1996. Law clk. to judge Luther M. Swygert U.S. Ct. Appeals (7th cir.), Chgo., 1978-79; law clk. to chief justice Warren E. Burger U.S. Supreme Ct., Washington, 1979-80; assoc. Dorsey & Whitney, Mpls., 1980-85, ptnr., 1986—. Adj. prof. law U. Minn., Mpls., 1981-83. Exec. editor U. Notre Dame Law Rev., 1977-78; co-editor: Freedom & Education: Pierce v. Society of Sisters Reconsidered, 1978. Recipient Vol. Recognition award Nat. Assn. Attys. Gen., 1993, Supreme Ct. Reception hons. State and Local Legal Ctr., 1991, 92, 93, 95. Fellow Am. Acad. Appellate Lawyers; mem. ABA (standing com. on Amicus Briefs 1997-2002), FBA, Minn. Bar Assn., Hennepin County Bar Assn., Phi Beta Kappa. Office: Dorsey & Whitney LLP Ste 1500 50 S Sixth St Minneapolis MN 55402-1498

WAIDELICH, DONALD LONG, electrical engineer, consultant; b. Allentown, Pa., May 3, 1915; s. John A. Sr. and Maisie Hamilton (Long) W.; m. Florence Emma Bennethum, June 6, 1939; 1 child, Ann Louise. BEE, Lehigh U., 1936, MS, 1938; PhD, Iowa State U., 1946. Registered profl. engr., Mo. Instr., asst. prof. electrical engring. U. Mo., Columbia, 1938-44, assoc. prof., prof., 1946-85, prof. emeritus, 1985—, assoc. head engring. experiment sta., 1955-60, chair dept., 1960-61; electrical engr. Naval Ordnance Lab., Silver Spring, Md., 1944-46. Cons. Naval Electronics Lab., San Diego, 1948-50, Argonne (Ill.) Nat. Lab., 1950-60, Nat. Aeronautics & Space, Green Belt, Md., 1961-70, Hughes Aircraft Co., Santa Monica and El Segundo, Calif., 1970-88; Fulbright prof. Cairo U., 1950-52, U. New South Wales, Sydney, Australia, 1960-62. Author: (with G. Lago) Transients in Electrical Circuits, 1958. Com. mem. Civic and U. Retirees, Columbia, Mo., 1985-95. Recipient Rsch. award Sigma Xi, 1977, Missouri Honor award, Distinguished Service, 1986. Fellow IEEE (life, Excellence award 1985), AIEE, Inst. Radio Engrs., 1961; mem. Am. Assn. Univ. Profs. (life), Am. Soc. Engring. Edn. (life), Nat. Soc. Profl. Engrs. (life). Episcopal. Achievements include research on rectifiers, electromagnetic testing of materials, steady-state transforms, microwave antennas, electrostatics, and electromagnetic fields; worked on magnetic and electric fields in space; involved with design of international communication satellites. Home: 104 E Ridgeley Rd Columbia MO 65203-3530 Office: U Mo Dept Elec & Comp Engrng 7 W Engineering Bldg Columbia MO 65211

WAILAND, GEORGE, lawyer; b. Munich, Fed. Republic Germany, Mar. 14, 1947; came to U.S., 1951; s. Max and Bella (Grylak) W.; m. Adele M. Rosen, Aug. 20, 1972; children: J. Zachary, William J. BS, NYU, 1969, JD, 1972. Bar: N.Y. 1973, U.S. Supreme Ct. 1976, U.S. Dist. Ct. (so., ea. dists.) N.Y. 1973, U.S. Dist. Ct. (no. dist.) N.Y. 1981, U.S. Claims Ct. 1979, U.S. Tax Ct., 1979, U.S. Ct. Appeals (2d cir.) 1973, U.S. Ct. Appeals (fed. cir.) 1982, U.S. Ct. Appeals (4th cir. and 9th cir.) 1986, U.S. Ct. Appeals (7th cir.) 1987. Assoc. Cahill Gordon & Reindel, N.Y.C., 1972-80, ptnr., 1980—. John Norton Pomeroy scholar NYU, 1970. Home: 1050 Park Ave New York NY 10028-1031 Office: Cahill Gordon & Reindel 80 Pine St Fl 17 New York NY 10005-1790

WAIN, CHRISTOPHER HENRY FAIRFAX MORESBY, actuary, insurance and investment consultant; b. Toronto, Ont., Can., Nov. 21, 1918; came to U.S., 1923; s. Andrew Martin and Eve Margaret (Fairbain) W.; m. Jeane Crawford Thomas, June 26, 1948; children: Christopher H. Jr., Margot Crawford. BA, UCLA, 1940. CLU. Actuarial student Occidental Life of Calif., L.A., 1946-48; various positions including v.p., actuary Prudential Ins. Co. Am., Newark and L.A., 1948-83; ins. and investment cons. L.A., 1984—. Mem. various coms. Am. Coun. Life Ins., Washington, 1965-83. Capt. U.S. Army, 1941-45. Regents scholar UCLA, 1938-39. Fellow Soc. Actuaries; mem. Am. Acad. Actuaries, The Fairfax Soc.

WAINIO, MARK ERNEST, insurance company consultant; b. Virginia, Minn., Apr. 18, 1953; BA, Gustavus Adolphus Coll., 1975. Cert. safety profl., assoc. loss control mgmt., assoc. risk mgmt., assoc. claims, CPCU. Carpenter ABI Contracting Inc., Virginia, 1975-77; co-owner Mesabi Builders, Albuquerque and Eveleth, Minn., 1977-79; sr. engring. rep. Aetna Life & Casualty, Albuquerque, 1979-86; loss control specialist CNA Ins. Cos., 1986-91, loss control cons., 1991-94, mgr. loss control svcs., 1994-95, dir. loss control svcs., 1995-97, asst. v.p. loss control svcs., 1997-98, RSKCo a bus. unit, CNA Risk Mgmt., Albuquerque, 1998—; asst. v.p. client svcs. RSKCo Cons. Svcs., 1999—. Owner MEW Safety and Risk Mgmt., 1989—; pres. MW Enterprises, 1990—. Mem. Am. Soc. Safety Engrs., CPCU. Avocations: golf, fishing, hunting, swimming, Karate. Office: RSKCo 8500 Menaul Blvd NE Ste B560 Albuquerque NM 87112-1273

WAINSCOTT, JAMES LAWRENCE, accountant; b. LaPorte, Ind., Mar. 31, 1957; s. James J. and Frances J. (Cunningham) W. BS magna cum laude, Ball State U., 1979; MBA U. Notre Dame, 1987. CPA, Ind.; cert. mgmt. acct.; cert. internal auditor; cert. info. systems auditor; chartered fin. analyst. Sr. auditor Geo. S. Olive & Co., CPAs, Indpls. and Valparaiso, Ind., 1979-82; fin. mgr. Midwest div. Nat. Steel Corp., Portage, Ind., 1982-88, mgr. pension investments, Pitts., 1988-90, asst. treas., asst. sec., Pitts., 1991-92; treas., asst. sec., Mishawaka. Ind., 1993-95, v.p. & treas., AK Steel Holding Corp., Middletown, OH, 1995—, CFO, AK Steel Holding Corp., 1998—, sr. v.p., CFO, 1999—; cons. Edward J. Wainscott, CPA, LaPorte, Ind., 1982—; instr. acctg. Purdue U.-Westville, 1980-82, Valparaiso U., 1980-84. Advisor Jr. Achievement, 1984; vol. Am. Cancer Soc., Valparaiso Income Tax Assistance Program, Valparaiso Community/Univ. Campaign; pres., treas. Midwest Steel Employees Fed. Credit Union; pres. Midwest Steel Employees Assn.; mem. Ball State U. Cardinal Connection; mem. N.W. Ind. Open Housing Council; chmn. dean's adv. council Valparaiso U.; bd. dirs. Youth Svc. Bur. St. Joseph County; chmn. fin. com. Good Shepherd Parish, Cin., 1999-2001. Mem. Ind. CPA Soc. (chmn. chpt. activities com. 1985-86, chpt. bd. dirs. 1983-86, chpt. pres. 1984-85, chmn. chpt. task force, Pres. award 1994, state bd. dirs. 1987-90), Nat. Assn. Accts. (chpt. bd. dirs. 1982-86, chpt. pres. 1983-84; Past Pres. award 1984), Am. Inst. CPA's, Inst. Mgmt. Acctg., Inst. Internal Auditors, Inst. Chartered Fin. Analysts, Assn. for Investment Mgmt. and Rsch., Chgo. Soc. Fin. Analysts, U. Notre Dame Exec. MBA Alumni Assn., Mensa, Blue Key, Golden Key, Intertel, Delta Sigma Pi. Roman Catholic. Avocations: music, chess, coin collecting, sports, travel. Home: 11990 Millstone Ct Loveland OH 45140-6220 Office: AK Steel Holding Corp 703 Curtis St Middletown OH 45043

WAINSTEIN, KENNETH L. prosecutor; b. Alexandria, Va. BA in Govt. and Internat. Rels., U. Va., 1984; JD, U. Calif., Berkeley, 1988. Corr., caseworker Office Congressman Carl D. Perkins, Washington, 1984; paralegal securities sect. Cleary, Gottlieb, Steen & Hamilton, 1984—85; summer assoc. for litigation, environ., tax and labor teams Hunton & Williams, 1986; summer assoc. for litigation, corp. and labor depts. Gibson, Dunn & Crutcher, 1987; law clk. for judge Thomas Penfield Jackson U.S. Dist. Ct. D.C., 1988—89; asst. U.S. atty. Office U.S. Atty. so. dist. N.Y., 1989—92; line prosecutor, dep. chief homicide sect. Office U.S. Atty. D.C., Washington, 1994—99, prin. asst. U.S. atty., 1999—2000, interim U.S. atty., 2000—. Mem.: Phi Beta Kappa. Home: 219 S Lee St Alexandria VA 22314

WAINWRIGHT, CARROLL LIVINGSTON, JR. lawyer; b. N.Y.C., Dec. 28, 1925; s. Carroll Livingston and Edith Katherine (Gould) W.; m. Nina Walker, July 2, 1948; children: Delos Walker, Mark Livingston. AB, Yale U., 1949; LL.B., Harvard U., 1952. Bar: N.Y. 1953. With Milbank, Tweed, Hadley & McCloy (and predecessor), N.Y.C., 1952-58, 60-62, ptnr., 1963—. Asst. counsel Gov. N.Y., 1959-60; mem. State Commn. Jud. Conduct, 1974-83; hon. dir. U.S. Trust Corp.; hon. trustee U.S. Trust Co. N.Y.; adj. prof. law Washington and Lee U. Sch. Law, 1991-97; mem. governing bd. N.Y. Community Trust, 1991—. Hon. trustee Am. Mus. Natural History; trustee Edward John Noble Found.; trustee Boys' Club N.Y., 1966—, pres., 1986-94, hon. trustee, 1999; vice-chmn. Cooper Union Advancement Sci. and Art, 1988-95, hon. trustee; trustee Ch. Pension Fund and Affiliates, 1974-91, treas. 1974-78; mem. univ. coun. Yale U., 1978-81; mem. vestry Trinity Ch., N.Y.C., 1983-90; dir. Greater Yellowstone Coalition, 1992-98, 99—. Served with USMCR, 1943-46. Mem. ABA, N.Y. State Bar Assn., Assn. Bar City N.Y. (treas. 1970-73, v.p. 1975-76), Union Club, Down Town Assn. (pres. 1985-92), Maidstone Club (pres. 1970-73). Home: 57 Dunemere Ln East Hampton NY 11937-2705 Office: Milbank Tweed Hadley & McCloy 1 Chase Manhattan Plz Fl 46 New York NY 10005-1401

WAINWRIGHT, DAVID STANLEY, intellectual property professional; b. New Haven, May 23, 1955; s. Stanley Dunstan and Lillian (Karelitz) W.;m. Catherine Demetra Kefalas, Aug. 11, 1984; children: Maxwell Stanley Hector, Eric George Alexander. BSc with 1st class honors in Physics, Dalhousie U., Halifax, N.S., 1976; MSc in Physics, U. B.C., Vancouver, 1979. Registered patent agt., U.S., Can. Model plant supr., scientist, technician Moli Energy Ltd., Maple Ridge, B.C., Can., 1978-84, project leader cell devel. Can., 1984-88, cell devel. mgr. Can., 1988-90, Moli Energy (1990) Ltd., Maple Ridge, 1990-92, mgr. intellectual property, 1992-98; patent agt. Ballard Power Sys., Burnaby, B.C., Canada, 1998—. Contbr. articles to profl. jours. Mem. Patent and Trademark Inst. Can. Home: 2585 W 1st Ave Vancouver BC Canada V6K 1G8 Office: Ballard Power Sys Inc 9000 Glenlyon Pky Burnaby BC Canada V5J 5J9 E-mail: davwai@ballard.com.

WAINWRIGHT, PAUL EDWARD BLECH, construction company executive; b. Annapolis, Md., Jan. 28, 1917; s. Richard and Alice Sorrel (Blech) W.; m. Helen Mae Rogers, July 10, 1941; children— Richard, Paul Edward Blech, John. BS in Civil Engring, Va. Mil. Inst., 1938. Cost engr. Turner Constrn. Co., N.Y.C., 1938-40, cost engr., asst. supt., 1945-46; cost. engr. for contractors Pacific Naval Air Bases, Honolulu, 1940-42; with Dillingham Corp., 1946-82, asst. v.p., then v.p., 1961-69, group v.p. constrn., 1969-82; cons. constrn. Honolulu, 1982—. Bd. dirs. Hawaii Visitors Bur., 1967, Goodwill Industries Hawaii, 1965-70; pres. Citizens Adminstrn. of Justice Found., 1968, Hawaii Epilepsy Soc., 1975. Served with AUS, 1942-45. Decorated Legion of Merit, Bronze Star, Air medal. Mem. Am. Soc. Mil. Engrs., Beavers, Gen. Contractors Assn. Hawaii (pres. 1966), Hawaii C. of C. (dir. 1964-65) Clubs: Waikiki Yacht, Outrigger Canoe. Republican. Episcopalian. Home: 4301 Providence Point Pl SE Issaquah WA 98029-6270

WAISANEN, CHRISTINE M. lawyer, writer; b. Hancock, Mich., May 27, 1949; d. Frederick B. and Helen M. (Hill) W.; m. Robert John Katzenstein, Apr. 21, 1979; children: Jeffrey Hunt, Erick Hill. BA with honors, U. Mich., 1971; JD, U. Denver, 1975. Bar: Colo. 1975, D.C. 1978. Labor rels. atty. U.S. C. of C., Washington, 1976-79; govt. rels. specialist ICI Americas, Inc., Wilmington, Del., 1979-87; dir. cultural affairs City of Wilmington, 1987; founder, chief writer Hill, Katzenstein & Waisanen, 1988—. Chmn. Delaware State Coastal Zone Indsl. Control Bd., 1993—. Mem. Fed. Bar Assn., Jr. League of Wilmington (v.p. 1985-86), Women's Rep. Club of Wilmington (bd. dirs. 1988-93), U. Mich. Club of Del. (pres. 1999—). Republican. Presbyterian. Home: 1609 Mt Salem Ln Wilmington DE 19806-1134

WAISMAN, JERRY, pathologist, educator; b. Borger, Tex., Sept. 14, 1934; s. Sammie and Lillie W.; m. Jane B. Atkins, June 15, 1958 (div. 1985); children: Eric A., Nina A. A., John C.; m. Lenore V. Gale, Mar. 24, 1990. BA, U. Tex., 1956, MD, U. Tex., Galveston, 1960. Diplomate Am. Bd. Pathology. Intern medicine SUNY, Bklyn., 1960-61; resident pathology U. Utah, Salt Lake City, 1961-62, fellow pathology, 1964-66, instr. pathology, 1967-68; asst. prof. to prof. pathology UCLA, 1968-81; prof. pathology NYU, N.Y.C., 1981—. Contbr. chpts. to books and articles to profl. jours. Capt. USAF, 1962-64. Mem. Am. Soc. Clin. Pathology, Am. Assn. Investigative Pathology, Am. Soc. Cytology, Electron Microscopy Soc. Am., N.Y. Pathol. Soc. (v.p. 1991), N.Y. State Bd. Profl. Med. Conduct, Coll. Anat. Pathology, N.Y. Pathol. Soc. (pres. 1993-95). Office: NYU Med Ctr Dept Pathology 560 1st Ave New York NY 10016-6402

WAISMAN, WARNER, retired pharmacist; b. N.Y.C., Apr. 22, 1931; s. Abraham Herbert and Pearl (Brand) W. BS in biochemistry, BS in sociology, Queens Coll., 1955; BS in pharmacy, Bklyn. Coll. Pharmacy, 1958. Registered pharmacist, N.Y., La. Pharmacist Schreir Pharmacy, N.Y.C., 1962-63; pharmacist Dew Drug, 1963-66, Raysol Pharmacy, N.Y.C., 1966-70, 72-75, Bellevue Hosp., N.Y.C., 1970-72, Bronx State Hosp., N.Y.C., 1975-78, Coler Hosp., N.Y.C., 1978-95; ret. Democrat. Jewish. Home: 132-15 Rico Pl Jamaica NY 11417-2017

WAIT, CHARLES VALENTINE, banker; b. Albany, N.Y., May 28, 1951; s. Newman Edward Jr. and Jane Caroline (Adams) W.; m. Candace Ellin Hollar, May 27, 1978; children: Charles Valentine Jr., Christopher David, Alexandra Dallas Wait. BA, Cornell U., 1973; cert. in banking, Rutgers U., 1981; LHD (hon.) , SUNY Empire State Coll., 2001. Asst. v.p. The Adirondack Trust Co., Saratoga Springs, N.Y., 1974, treas., 1978-81, sec., treas., 1981-84, pres., 1984—. Bd. trustees N.Y. Bus. Devel., 1997; mem., Saratoga County Indsl. Development Agency, 1998—, chmn. nom. com. Fed. Reserve Bank N.Y.; mem. Yaddo Corp., Saratoga Springs, 1996—, corp. sec. and asst. treas., 1997—, asst. treas., 1998—. Trustee Skidmore Coll., Saratoga Springs, 1984-2002, Nat. Mus. Dance, Saratoga Springs, 1987—, N.Y. Racing Assn., Nat. Mus. Racing, 1988-91, v.p., 1989-91; trustee Charles R. Wood Found., 1991-98; chmn. Saratoga Springs City Ctr. Authority, 1983-89; treas. Saratoga Performing Arts Ctr., 1987, chmn., 1989-97, chmn. Saratoga Care, Inc., Face of the Future Capital Campaign. Named Outstanding New Yorker, N.Y. State Jaycees, 1984; recipient Pvt. Sector Initiative award Pres. Ronald Reagan, Commitment to Community award, N.Y. State Bus. Coun., 1983, Liberty Bell award Saratoga County Bar Assn. for cmty. svc., Good Scout award Twin Rivers Coun., 1997, Exec. of Yr. award Capital Dist. Bus. Rev., 1999; Paul Harris fellow Dist. 7190, 1997, Sam Walton Bus. Leader Awd., 1997. Mem. Ind. Bankers Assn. of N.Y. State (bd. dirs., sec. 1986-87), N.Y. Bankers Assn. (bd. dirs. 1987, treas. 1995—, chmn. 1997-99), N.Y. State Bankers Retirement System (trustee 1987-95, vice chmn., chmn. 1992-94), Am. Inst. Banking (Counsel of Yr. 1976), Greater Saratoga C. of C., Pillar Soc. Republican. Home: 658 N Broadway Saratoga Springs NY 12866-1624 Office: The Adirondack Trust Co 473 Broadway Saratoga Springs NY 12866-2262

WAIT, EUGENE MEREDITH, historian, writer; b. Longview, Tex., July 13, 1936; s. Eugene and Virginia Rice Wait. AA, Schreiner Coll., 1956; BA, U. Tex., 1958, MA, 1962. Author: The March of the Teutons, 1972, America and the War of 1812, 1999, Opening of the Civil War, 1999, America and the Monroe Years, 2000, Jackson Years, 2000, Bull Run and Beyond, 2001, Explorers and the New World, 2001, Great Challenges of Reformation Europe, 2001, The Civil War, 2001, Adams vs. Jackson, 2001, The Zenith of Imperialsim, 1896-1906, 2001. Pres., treas. Kerrville Geneal. Soc.; treas., auctioneer Bluebonnet Stamp Club. With U.S. Army, 1954-62. Methodist.

WAIT, GEORGE WILLIAM, sales executive; b. Balt., Oct. 23, 1958; s. Frank H. Jr. and Betty (Cartwright) W.; m. Susan Erwin, Oct. 16, 1982; children: J. Stokes, Hannah S., C. Sam, Addy M. BSBA, Western Carolina U., 1982. From sales rep. to regional sales asst. Gen. Mills Inc., Kinston, N.C., 1982-85, dist. sales mgr. Charlotte, 1985-87, product sales mgr. Mpls., 1987-89, mgr. promotions and merchandising Raleigh, N.C., 1989-90, regional merchandising mgr., 1990—, regional tri healthway dir., 1992—, mgr. bus. devel., 1993—, corp. ops. mgr. Cary, 1995—. Author: The Job Plan, 1991. Pres. A.V. Baucom Elem. Sch. PTO, Apex, N.C., 1991-93, chmn. Wake County Fun Festival; head coach '84 Explorers Soccer Team, 1990—; mem. YMCA Indian Guides, 1991—; mem. YMCA Youth Com., 1995—; asst. scout master Boy Scouts Am., 1996—; mem. adv. com. Wake County Bd. Edn., 1996—; chmn. Apex Adv. Coun. Bd. Edn., 1997-99; pres. Davis Dr. Mid. Sch., 1997-98, 98-99; area v.p. Wake County PTA Coun., 1998-99; chmn. sch. bd. adv. coun. Wake County, 1997-99; pres. PTA Davis Drive Mid. Sch., 1997-99; selected Order of the Arrow Boy Scouts Am., 1999. Mem. Grocery Mfrs. Retail Assn., KC (3d degree, outside guard 1982-83, inside guard 1983-84), Lambda Chi Alpha. Republican. Roman Catholic. Avocations: golf, weight lifting, reading, swimming, children. Office: Gen Mills Inc PO Box 4349 Cary NC 27519-4349

WAIT, SAMUEL CHARLES, JR. academic administrator, educator; b. Albany, N.Y., Jan. 26, 1932; s. Samuel C. and Isabel M. (Cassedy) W.; m. Carol D. Petrie, June 6, 1957; children: Robert J., Alison R. BS in Chemistry, Rensselaer Polytechnic Inst., 1953, MS in Physical Chemistry, 1955, PhD in Physical Chemistry, 1956. Postdoc. teaching fellow U. Minn., 1958-59; visiting asst. prof. Carnegie Inst. Tech., 1959-60; rsch. sci. Nat. Bur. Standards, 1960-61; from asst. prof. to prof. of chemistry Rensselaer Poly. Inst., Troy, N.Y., 1961—, from asst. dean of sci. to assoc. dean of sci., 1974—, acting dean of sci., 1978-80, 88-89. Dir. Cooperative Coll. Sci. Improvement Program, Troy, 1972-73, Rsch. Participation for High Sch. Tchrs., Troy, 1962-67; asst. dir., prof. M of Sci. in Natural Scis. Program, Troy, 1962-74. Author: Scattering of Laser Radiation, 1971; contbr. articles to profl. jours. Pres. dist. 2 Niskayuna (N.Y.) Fire Co., 1970-72; mem. Niskayuna Bd. Fire Commrs., 1978-83; trustee Dudley Obs., 1978—, v.p., 1980-91, pres., 1991-2001, trustee, 2000—; mem. math., sci. and tech. adv. com. Schenectady County C.C., 1976—, chmn., 1977-78; vice chmn. Schenectady County Fire Adv. Bd., 1978-79; mem. Schenectady County Hazardous Materials Team, 1991—. Recipient Disting Faculty award Rensselaer Alumni Assn., 1988, Alumni Key award, 1994, Rensselaer Alumni Admission award of excellence, 1993, Rensseleer Alumni Assn. Albert Fox Demers medal, 1997; named fellow Rsch. Corp., 1954-55, Eastman Kodak Co., 1955-56; Fulbright scholar, 1956-58. Mem. Am. Chem. Soc., Optical Soc. Am., Coblentz Soc., Rensselaer Premed. Soc., Sigma Xi, Alpha Epsilon Delta, Phi Theta Alpha. Office: Rensselaer Poly Inst 1C 05 Sci Ctr 110 8th St Troy NY 12180-3522 E-mail: waitsc@rpi.edu.

WAITE, CHARLES MORRISON, food company executive; b. Chgo., Oct. 1, 1932; s. Norman and Lavinia M. (Fyke) W.; m. Barbara Chowning Wham, Aug. 21, 1954; children: Susan R., Charles M., John B., David T. BA, Yale, 1954; MBA, Harvard, 1958. Mgr. planning and analysis Standard Fruit & Steamship Co., New Orleans, 1958-62, v.p., exec. v.p., 1969-72, dir., 1972-76; div. mgr. Standard Fruit Co., La Ceiba, Honduras, 1962-69; dir. Standard Fruit Tropical Charities, Inc., 1970-76; sr. v.p. Castle & Cooke, Inc., Honolulu, 1972-76; exec. v.p. Castle & Cooke Foods, San Francisco, 1974-76; pres. United Fruit Co., Boston, 1976-77; sr. v.p. United Brands Co., 1976-77; pres. Genoa Packing Co., 1977-78, Catelli Foods, Inc., 1979-90, Howard Foods Inc., Danvers, Mass., 1990—, also bd. dirs. Bd. dirs. Rock of Ages Corp., Barre, Vt., Swenson Granite Co., Concord, N.H. Served to 1st lt. USAF, 1955-57. Mem. Zeta Psi. Clubs: Harvard (Boston). Republican. Episcopalian. Home: 520 Cherry Valley Rd Gilford NH 03249-7841 Office: Howard Foods Inc 5 Ray St Danvers MA 01923-3531

WAITE, DAVID ALLEN, software development executive; b. Canton, N.Y., June 7, 1947; s. Kelsey Arden and Helen Gladys (Pollock) W.; m. Dorretta Carlyle Richardson, Aug. 28, 1971; 1 child, Rebecca. BA, SUNY, Potsdam, 1969; MBA, Columbia U., 1992. Assoc. programmer IBM Corp., Poughkeepsie, N.Y., 1969-73, staff programmer Burlington, Mass., 1973-76, Vt.,

1976-79, devel. programmer, mgr. Lexington, Ky., 1979-84, IBM corp., Poughkeepsie, 1985-92; total quality mgr. ILX Systems, N.Y.C., 1992-97, mgr. product devel. coordination, 1997-99, v.p. product devel. coord., 1999—. Contbr. articles to profl. jours. Mem. Assn. for Computing Machinery, Am. Soc.for Quality, Columbia U. Bus. Sch. EMBA Alumni Assn. (pres. 1994-96), Columbia U. Bus. Sch. Alumni Club of N.Y. (sec. 1996-98, pres. 1998-2000). Avocations: sailing, cooking, golf, gardening. Home: 6 Candlewood Dr New Providence NJ 07974-1615 Office: ILX Systems 111 Fulton St New York NY 10038-2776 E-mail: dwaite92@alumni.gsb.columbia.edu.

WAITE, DONALD EUGENE, medical educator, consultant; b. Columbus, Ohio, Aug. 25, 1925; s. Sidney B. and Louise Alice (Lipsey) W.; children: David L., Larry R., James A., Steve C., Debra J., Julie A., Craig D., Tracy E., Christopher R. DO in Osteopathic Medicine, U. Osteo. Medicine and Health Scis., 1955; MPH, U. Calif., Berkeley, 1989. Intern Doctors Hosp., Columbus, Ohio, 1955-56; pvt. practice, 1956-72; prof. family medicine Mich. State U., East Lansing, 1972-90, prof. emeritus, 1990—. Cons. Environ. Health Conss., Columbus, East Lansing, 1990—; mem. occupl. health del. to Poland, Hungary and Czechoslovakia, 1992; mem. Aerospace Med. Assn. del. to People's Republic of China, 1993. Author: Your Environment, Your Health and You, 1991, Environmental Health Hazards, 1994. Med. examiner FAA, East Lansing, 1964-90; asst. scoutmaster Boy Scouts Am., East Lansing, 1980-83. With USN, 1943-45. Mem. Am. Osteo. Assn., Am. Coll. Occupl. Medicine, Aerospace Med. Assn., Ohio Osteo. Assn., Mich. Assn. Osteo. Physicians. Avocations: skiing, fishing, hunting. Home: 117 Agate Way Williamston MI 48895-9434 Office: Mich State U Dept Family Medicine East Lansing MI 48824 E-mail: waited@msu.edu.

WAITE, FRANCES W. librarian, professional genealogist; b. Newberry-town, Pa., Jan. 7, 1944; d. Jacob Kister and Mary Fisher (Conley) Wise; m. Arthur Owen Waite, May 22, 1937; children: Catherine Ann, Douglas Arthur, Mary Virginia. BS in Edn., Shippensburg U., 1964; MS, Kutztown U. Elem. sch. tchr. Cen. Bucks Sch. Dist., Doylestown, Pa., 1964-65, 67-68; receptionist Bucks County Hist. Soc., 1981-86, libr., 1987—. Lectr., tchr. family history rsch.; verifying genealogist for Nat. Soc. Colonial Dames of Am. Com. of Pa. Co-author: (books) Bucks County Tax Records 1693-1778, 1982, Bucks County Declarations and Naturalizations 1802-1906, 1985; author: (books) Descendants of Thomas Connelly, 1980, Descendants of Hans Detweiler, 1976, expanded and updated edit., 1995, Desendants of Johannes Weiss of Dover, Pa., 1997, White Families of Lower Bucks, 1999, Anderson Families of Upper York County, Pa., 1999, Connelly-Conley Descendants of Thomas Connelly of Rapho Township Lancaster County PA, 2002; editor numerous geneal. reference books, 1980-99. Charter mem. Bucks County Choral Soc., Doylestown, 1972-99. Mem. Nat. Geneal Soc. (award of merit 1997), Geneal. Soc. of Pa. (past co-chair program com. 1991-97, publs. com. 1990-99), Bucks County Geneal. Soc. (founder, v.p., pres., newsletter editor 1981-90). Avocations: choral singing, travel, crocheting, gardening. Home: 649 S Chubb Dr Doylestown PA 18901-4547

WAITE, GERALD PHILLIP, English language educator; b. Fond du Lac, Wis., July 25, 1942; s. Phillip Henry and Genevieve (Hoffman) W.; m. Susan Eckenrod; children: Bridget Appleberry, Matthew, Gregory, Michael, Nora. BA, U. Notre Dame, Ind., 1966; MA, U. Wis., Milw., 1970, PhD, 1972. Wire editor Mishawaka (Ind.) Times, 1965-66; copy editor Milw. Sentinel, 1966-72; asst. prof. journalism Slippery Rock (Pa.) State Coll., 1972-76; from assoc. to full prof. No. Mich. U., Marquette, 1976-2001, ret., 2001—. Contbr. articles, stories to profl. jours. Mem. Am. Assn. Univ. Profs., Soc. Profl. Journalists. Roman Catholic. E-mail: gwaite@nmu.edu.

WAITE, HELEN ELEANOR, funeral director; b. Richmond, Va., Aug. 7, 1947; d. Julia F. (Braxton) Candia; m. Malcolm L. Waite, July 24, 1982. AB, Va. State U., 1968, MA, 1977; degree in funeral svc., Northampton C.C., Bethlehem, Pa., 1994. Cert. tchr., Pa., N.J. Tchr. Westmoreland County Schs., Montross, Va.; tchr. English Rittenhouse Acad., Phila.; owner Helen E. Waite Funeral Service. Mem. Nat. Coun. Tchrs. English, Pa. Coun. Tchrs. English, Nat. Funeral Dirrs. Assn., Pa. Funeral Dirs. Assn. Home: 820 N 65th St Philadelphia PA 19151-3303 E-mail: waitefuneralsvc.@msn.com.

WAITE, JOY ELIZABETH, interior decorator; b. Boynton Beach, Fla., Aug. 29, 1964; d. John Henry and June (Thompson) W. AS in Interior Design, Art Inst. Ft. Lauderdale, 1984. Interior designer J.J. Chalk, West Palm Beach, Fla., 1984-88; supr. foreman Waite Painting Corp., Lake Worth, 1988-91; pres./owner J.E. Waite Corp., 1991—. Mem. Am. Soc. Interior Designers (allied practioner), The Associated General Contractors of Am. (assoc.). Avocations: faux finishing, water color painting, reading. Office: J E Waite Corp 3010A Broward Ave Lake Worth FL 33463-2006

WAITE, LAWRENCE WESLEY, osteopathic physician, educator; b. Chgo., June 27, 1951; s. Paul J. and Margaret E. (Cresson) W.; m. Courtnay M. Snyder, Nov. 1, 1974; children: Colleen Alexis, Rebecca Maureen, Alexander Quin. BA, Drake U., 1972; DO, Coll. Osteo Medicine and Surgery, Des Moines, 1975; MPH, U. Mich., 1981. Diplomate Nat. Bd. Osteo. Med. Examiners. Intern Garden City Osteo Hosp., Mich., 1975-76; practice gen. osteo. medicine Garden City, 1979-82, Battle Creek, 1982-96, La Crosse, Wis., 1996—; sect. head Onalaska Family Practice, 1999—, coord. rsch., chmn. dept., 1996-99. Cons. Nat. Bd. Examiners Osteo. Physicians and Surgeons, 1981—88, 1998—; chief med. examiner Calhoun County, 1991—93; preceptor U. Wis. Med. Sch., 1997—2000, assoc. clin. prof., 2000—, Mich. State U. Coll. Osteo. Medicine, East Lansing, 1979—97, Lakeview Gen. Osteo. Hosp., Battle Creek, Mich., 1983—87, Des Moines U. Osteo. Med. Ctr., 2001—; mem. profl. adv. coun. Good Samaritan Hosp., Battle Creek, 1982—83; exec. bd. Primary Care Network, 1994—96. Writer TV program Cross Currents Ecology, 1971; editor radio series Friendship Hour, 1971-72 Bd. dirs., La Crosse YMCA, 2000—; bd. dirs., instr. Hospice Support Services, Inc., Westland, Mich., 1981-86; exec. bd. officer Battle Creek Area Urban League, 1987-91; trustee Clearwater Farms Found., Inc., 1999—; vestryman St. Thomas Episcopal Ch., 1990-93; leader Boy Scouts Am. Served to lt. comdr. USN, 1976-79; bd. dirs. Internat. Log Rolling Assn., 2000—. State of Iowa scholar, 1969. Mem. AMA, Population Inst. (population action coun. 1984-99, Am. Pub. Health Assn., Population Inst., Aerospace Med. Assn., Natl. Eagle Scounts Assn. (life), Am. Osteo. Assn., S. Cen. Osteo. Assn. (officer, state del. 1983-96), Am. Acad. Osteopathy, Bermuda Hist. Soc. (life), Wis. Ctr., Academically Talented Youth, Brotherhood St. Andrews (life). Avocations: Geography, medieval history, genealogy. Home: 2110 Evenson Dr Onalaska WI 54650-8772 Office: Gundersen Lutheran 3100 S Kinney Coulee Rd Onalaska WI 54650-8512 E-mail: lwaite@gundluth.org.

WAITE, LEMUEL WARREN, library director; b. Ashland, Ky., July 13, 1955; s. Lemuel Crenshaw and Polly Jane (Davidson) W. BS, U. Ky., 1980, MLS, 1988. Bookkeeper Ky. Geol. Survey, Lexington, 1981-84; libr. asst. Ky. Christian Coll., Grayson, 1986-88, libr., 1988-89, dir. libr., 1989—. Minister Blue Bank Christian Ch., Flemingsburg, Ky., 1988—, Moore's Ferry Christian Ch., Salt Lick, Ky., 1986-88. Author various poems and essays. Mem. ALA, APA, ACD, Am. Theol. Libr. Assn., Disciples of Christ Hist. Soc., Ind. Hist. Soc., Ky. Libr. Assn., Beta Phi Mu. Democrat. Avocations: sculpture, poetry, sketching. Home: 501 Snodgrass Ln Grayson KY 41143-2112 Office: Ky Christian Coll Coll Libr 100 Academic Pkwy Grayson KY 41143-2205

WAITE, STEPHEN HOLDEN, lawyer; b. Rochester, N.Y., Dec. 5, 1936; s. Richard Holden and Judith H. (Lapp) Waite; m. Sarah T. Caswell, Aug. 20, 1960 (dec. Mar. 1996); m. Martha Gay Stewart, Jan. 4, 1997; children: Sarah T., Richard H. BA, Amherst Coll., 1958; JD, Yale U., 1961. Bar: N.Y. 1961. Mem. firm Nixon, Hargrave, Devans & Doyle, Rochester, NY, 1961-69; v.p., counsel Lincoln First Banks Inc., 1969-73, sr. v.p., 1973-77, exec. v.p., 1978-81, CFO, 1973-81; sr. v.p. Schlegel Corp., 1981-82; mem. firm Harris, Beach, Wilcox, Rubin & Levey, Rochester, 1982-88, Underberg & Kessler, Rochester, 1988—. Past chmn. Rochester Area Hosp. Assn.; mem. strategic planning commn. Monroe Cmty. Hosp.; past bd. dirs., treas. Hosp. Trustees N.Y. State; past bd. dirs., past chmn. Ctr. Govtl. Rsch.; bd. dirs. Planned Parenthood Rochester/Syracuse region; past bd. dirs. Mercy Flight Ctrl., Inc., Highland Hosp., Monroe County Long Term Care, Inc., Rochester Regional Rsch. Libr. Coun., Hosp. Assn. N.Y. State, Health Futures for Rochester, Harley Sch., Hearing and Speech Ctr. Rochester. With U.S. Army, 1962. Mem.: Monroe County Bar Assn., N.Y. State Bar Assn., Country Club Rochester. Home: 7 Woodcliff Ter Fairport NY 14450-4209 Office: 1800 Chase Sq Rochester NY 14604-1910

WAITE, VERNER STUART, surgeon, retired; b. Lindsay, Calif., Aug. 16, 1928; s. Albert Crew Waite and Helen Fowle; m. Elizabeth Southchick, Nov. 5, 1955; children: Peter Stuart, Elizabeth Ruth, Eva Anna, Amelia Catherine, Susan marie, Alexander Crew. AA, Compton Jr. Coll., 1948; BA, U. Calif., Berkeley, 1950; MD, U. Chgo., 1954. Intern L.A. VA Hosp., 1954-55; resident in surgery St. Louis City Hosp., 1958-61; fellow in surgery Ellis Fischel Cancer Ctr., Colulmbia, Mo., 1961-63; pvt. practice surgery Lynwood and Downey, Calif., 1963-97. Bd. dirs. Downey Hosp., 1994; mem. Lynwood Sch. Bd., 1967-75; mem. med. exec. com. St. Francis Hosp.; pres. Family Support Ctr. of Downey, 1999-2000. Fellow ACS; mem. Semmelweis Soc. (founder, pres. 1986-97), Lynwood Exch. Club, Downey Exch. Club. Republican. Avocation: stamp collecting. Home: 5243 Vista Del Sol Cypress CA 90630

WAITE-FRANZEN, ELLEN JANE, academic administrator; b. Oshkosh, Wis., Feb. 17, 1951; d. Earl Vincent and Margaret (Luft) W.; m. Thomas H. Dollar, Aug. 19, 1977 (div. July 1984); m. Kent Hendrickson, Mar. 26, 1994 (div. Dec. 1995); m. Scott Franzen, Apr. 4, 1998. BA, U. Wis., Oshkosh, 1973; MLS, U. Wis., Milw., 1977. Head of cataloging Marquette U., Milw., 1977-82; head catalog libr. U. Ariz., Tucson, 1983-85; assoc. dir. libr. Loyola U., Chgo., 1985-86, acting dir. libr., 1986-87, dir. libr., 1987-94, v.p. acad. svcs., 1994-97; assoc. provost for info. svcs. U. Richmond, 1997-99, v.p. for info. svcs., 1999—2002; v.p. for computing and info. svcs. Brown U., Providence, 2002—. Cons. Loyola U., Chgo., 1984, Boston Coll., 1986, U. San Francisco, 1989; bd. trustees Online Computer Lib. Ctr., Dublin, Ohio, 1994-2000. Contbg. author: Research Libraries and Their Implementation of AACR2, 1985; author: (with others) Women in LC's Terms: A Thesaurus of Subject Headings Related to Women, 1988. Mem. ALA. Avocation: photography. Office: Brown U Computing and Info Svcs Box 1885 Providence RI 02912-1885 E-mail: ewaite@richmond.edu.

WAITES, CANDY YAGHJIAN, former state official; b. N.Y.C., Feb. 21, 1943; d. Edmund Kirken and Dorothy Joanne (Candy) Yaghjian; children: Jennider Lisa, Robin Shelley. BA, Wheaton Coll., Mass., 1965; MPA, U. S.C., 1997. County councilwoman, Richland County, S.C., 1976-88; mem. S.C. Ho. of Reps., 1988-94; lectr. polit. sci., assoc. dean Leadership Inst. Columbia Coll., 1993-99; dir. divsn. children's svcs. Gov.'s Office, 1999—. Vice chmn. Adv. Commn. on Intergovtl. Rels., S.C., 1977-87; bd. dirs. Interagy. Council on Pub. Transp., S.C., 1977-85, Central Midlands Regional Planning Council, Columbia, S.C., 1977-84; dir. Wachovia Bank. V.p. bd. dirs. United Way of Midlands, 1977-89; trustee Columbia Mus. Art, 1982-88; bd. dirs. Rape Crisis Network, 1984-87, Nat. ATHENA Found., 1999-2001; chmn. County Coun. Coalition; mem. C. of C. Leadership Forum, S.C. Fedn. of Blind; mem. adv. bd. U. S.C. Humanities and Social Scis. Coll., Family Shelter, Nuturing Ctr.; pres. Trinity Housing Corp.; found. bd. palmetto Richland Meml. Hosp., 1995-2000; mem. Columbia Housing Authority Bd., 1997-2000. Named Outstanding Young Career Woman, Columbia YWCA, 1980, YWCA Hall of Fame, 1993, Columbia Housing Authority Bd., Outstanding Young Woman of Yr., Columbia Jaycees, 1975, Pub. Citizen of Yr. NASW; recipient Ann. Legis. award Common Cause S.C., 1990, 91. Mem. S.C. Women in Govt. (vice chmn. 1984-86), S.C. Assn. Counties (bd. dirs. 1982-88, Pres.'s award 1983, Legislator of Yr. award 1992), Columbia C. of C. (Athena award 1998), Network Female Execs., LWV (pres. 1973-76), Unic. Assocs. Club, Mortar Bd. (hon.), Omicron Delta Kappa. Democrat. Episcopalian. Avocations: exercising, drawing, gardening, walking. Home: 3419 Duncan St Columbia SC 29205-2705 Office: 1205 Pendleton St Columbia SC 29201-3731

WAITES, WILLIAM ERNEST, advertising executive; b. Detroit, Dec. 14, 1934; s. William Ernest and Jean (Bryant) W.; m. Susanne Pinkett, Jan. 5, 1957; children: Bryant Andrew, Randel Schumann. BA, Mich. State U., 1956. Sr. v.p., creative dir. Young & Rubicam, Detroit, 1973-77, mng. dir. Adelaide, Australia, 1977-79, sr. v.p., dir. creative svcs. Chgo., 1979-81; vice chmn., chief creative officer Stone & Adler, 1981-83; sr. v.p., group creative dir. Ogilvy & Mather, 1983-89; pres. Huryup & Waites Creative Cons., Ft. Myers, Fla., 1989-94. Chmn. The Spiro Group, Inc., 1994-2001, Double W. Ltd., Taos, N.Mex., The Waites Group; co-owner Aboriginals: Art of the First Person, Sanibel, Fla. Bd. trustees Calusa Nature Ctr. and Planetarium; bd. dirs. Lee County Alliance of Arts. Capt. USAF, 1957-60. Mem. Advt. Fedn. S.W. Fla. (pres.), Fla. Direct Mktg. Assn., Southwest Fla. Attractions Assn., Lee County Hotel Motel Assn., Cape Coral C. of C., S.W. Fla. C. of C., Greater Fort. Myers C. of C., Alliance for the Arts (bd. dirs.), Sanibel-Captiva Islands C. of C., Ft. Myers Mus. Found., Lambda Chi Alpha. Office: 6296 Corporate Ct Ste B202 Fort Myers FL 33919-3535 E-mail: sanibelart@earthlink.net.

WAITHE, MARY REBECCA, personnel director, dance instructor; b. N.Y.C., Oct. 10, 1934; arrived in Barbados, 1982; d. Edward A. and Beryl Margaret (Roberts) Waithe. BSc in Bus. and Pub. Adminstrn., NYU, 1973, MBA, 1975. Adj. asst. prof. Bronx (N.Y.) Community Coll., 1970-76; adminstr., chief personnel officer NYU Sch. Law, N.Y.C., 1977-81; purchasing agt., office mgr. South Bronx Devel. Orgn. Inc., 1982-86; human resource mgr. Intel Barbados Ltd., 1982-86; personnel officer Barbados Mut. Life Assurance Soc., St. Michael, 1987-91; dir. human resources Cunard Paradise Village Beach Club, 1991-92; human resource mgr. Barbados Hilton Hotel Internat., 1993-99, Cobblers Cove Hutch, 1999—. Personnel cons. Bonhus Ltd., Barbados, 1989—; tutor Barbados C.C. Hospitality Sch., pers. mgmt., supervisory mgmt., 1997, 98; part-time tutor Ctr. Mgmt. Devel. U. West Indies exec. diploma mgmt., 1999. Choreographer: Black Franchise Dance, 1989 (cert 1989), Flight of the Bird, 1989 (Gold Cup 1989). Mem. Phi Chi Theta, Mau Gamma Tau. Avocations: modern-Afro-Caribbean dance instructing, community activities, travel. Home: 22 10th Ave Newton Terr Christ Church Barbados E-mail: hunloures@cobblerscove.com.

WAITLEY, DOUGLAS D. writer; b. U.S.A., Nov. 28, 1927; 1 child. BSBA, Northwestern U., 1949, MA in History, 1955. Owner, mgr. Dale Employment Agy., Evanston, 1945-74, Dale Bldg. Maintenance Specialists, Evanston, 1975-84, Search Realty, Evanston, 1985-89, Dale Cert. Fin. Planners, Evanston, 1990-92; freelance writer, 1992—. Author: Portrait of the Midwest, 1963, The War Makers, 1971, Age of the Mad Dragons, 1981, The Last Paradise, 1993, Roadside History of Florida, 1997, The Best Back Roads of Florida: Volume I, 2000, 9 other books. Mem. Vintage Tennis Assn. (bd. dirs. 1994—).

WAITS, JOHN A. lawyer; b. Greenville, Miss., June 6, 1947; BA summa cum laude, U. Miss., 1969; MA with honors, U. Va., 1973; JD, NYU, 1977. Bar: N.Y. 1978, U.S. Dist. Ct. (ea. and so. dists.) N.Y. 1978, D.C. 1988. Counsel to Ho. Agrl. Subcom. U.S. Ho. of Reps., Washington, 1979-80, adminstrv. asst. to Congressman David R. Bowen, 1980-82; ptnr. Winston & Strawn, 1992. Fulbright scholar. Mem. Assn. Bar City N.Y. Office: Winston & Strawn 1400 L St NW Ste 800 Washington DC 20005-3508

WAITS, THOMAS ALAN, composer, actor, singer; b. Pomona, Calif., Dec. 7, 1949; s. Frank W. and Alma (Johnson) McMurray; m. Kathleen Patricia Brennan, Aug. 10, 1980; children: Kellesimone Wylder, Casey Xavier, Sullivan Blake. Composer 18 albums including Closing Time, 1973, The Heart of Saturday Nite, 1974, Nighthawks at the Diner, 1975, Small Change, 1976, Foreign Affairs, 1978, Blue Valentine, 1979, Heart Attack and Vine, 1980, One From the Heart, 1981, Swordfishtrombones, 1983, Rain Dogs, 1985, Anthology, 1985, Frank's Wild Years, 1987, Big Time, 1988, Bone Machine, 1992, Night on Earth, 1992, The Black Rider, 1993, Beautiful Maladies, 1998, Mule Variations, 1999 (Grammy Award, 1999), Alice, 2002, Blood Money, 2002; composer (film scores) One from the Heart, 1983, Streetwise, 1985, Night on Earth, 1991; co-author music and songs (with Kathleen Brennan) for Night on Earth, 1991, End of Violence, 1997, Bunny, 1999, Dead Man Walking, film American Heart; composer songs and music for The Black Rider opera, Hamburg, Germany, 1990; composer songs and music, writer (with Kathleen Brennan) Alice Avant Garde opera, Hamburg, 1992, opera Woyzeck, Copenhagen, 2000; actor (musical) Frank's Wild Years, 1986, (stage play) Demon Wine, 1989; appeared in films Paradise Alley, 1978, The Outsiders, 1983, Rumble Fish, 1983, The Cotton Club, 1984, Down by Law, 1986, Ironweed, 1987, Candy Mountain, 1987, Big Time, 1988, Cold Feet, 1989, The Bearskin, 1991, Queen's Logic, 1991, At Play in the Fields of the Lord, 1991, Bram Stoker's Dracula, 1992, Short Cuts, 1993, Mystery Men, 1999. Recipient Acad. Award nomination Best Song Score for One from the Heart, 1983; Grammy award for best alternative album Bone Machine, 1992, Grammy award for Mule Variations as best contemporary folk music, 2000, Dramalogue award for actor Demon Wine, Danish Theater award for Woyzeck as best musical, 2001. Mem. ASCAP (Founders award for career achievement in songwriting 2001), Musicians Union Local 47, SAG, AFTRA, Motion Picture Acad. Office: care Howard Grossman 10960 Wilshire Blvd Ste 2150 Los Angeles CA 90024-3807

WAITT, NORMAN W. recording industry executive; 1 child. Student, U. S.D., 1972—74; student acctg., Omaha, Nebr.; degree in bus., Morningside Coll., Sioux City, Iowa, 1984, degree in econs., 1986. Worked with his father in cattle brokerage bus., 1978—84; acct.; salesman Tex. Instruments PC's, 1986—88; asst. fin. opers. mgr.; co-founder Gateway 2000, Inc., 1985; founder Gold Circle Entertainment, Inc., Omaha, 1996, chmn., CEO. Office: Gold Circle and Samson Music 13906 Gold Circle Dr Ste 201 Omaha NE 68144*

WAITT, TED W. computer company executive; b. Sioux City, Iowa, Jan. 18, 1963; Attended, U. Iowa. CEO Gateway, San Diego, former chmn., pres., chmn., CEO, chmn., chmn., CEO, 1985—. Office: 14303 Gateway Pl Poway CA 92064-*

WAITTS, JAMES ROBERT, marketing professional; b. Glen Ridge, N.J., Nov. 16, 1964; s. Robert Rocco and Joan Lee Waitts; m. Annette Waitts, Oct. 17, 1992; children: Carla Rose, Julia Marie. BA, Hartwick Coll., 1987. Telemarketer Crown Roll Leaf Inc., Paterson, NJ, 1987-88, 1989-92, mgr. telesales, 1993-95, new product devel. staff, 1996-99, COO/mktg., 2000—. Mem. Tag and Label Mfrs. Inst., Document Mgmt. Industries Assn., Internat. Sign Assn. Republican. Avocations: guitar, music. Office: Crown Roll Leaf Inc 91 Robert Waitts Ave Paterson NJ 07503

WAITZKIN, HOWARD BRUCE, internist, sociologist, educator; b. Akron, Ohio, Sept. 6, 1945; s. Edward and Dorothy (Lederman) W.; m. Stephany Borges, Mar. 13, 1983 (div.); 1 stepchild, Daren; 1 child, Sofia. BA summa cum laude, Harvard U., 1966, MA, 1969, MD, PhD, 1972. Diplomate Am. Bd. Internal Medicine, Am. Bd. Geriatric Medicine. Resident in medicine Stanford (Calif.) U. Med. Ctr., 1972-75, Robert Wood Johnson clin. scholar depts. sociology-medicine, 1973-75; sr. resident in medicine Mass. Gen. Hosp., Boston, 1977-78; assoc. prof. sociology, clin. asst. prof. medicine U. Vt., Burlington, 1975-77; vis. assoc. prof. health and med. scis. U. Calif., Berkeley, 1978-82, clin. asst. prof. medicine San Francisco, 1978-82; internist La Clínica de la Raza, Oakland, 1978-82; prof. medicine and social scis. U. Calif., Irvine, 1982-96, chief div. gen. internal medicine and primary care, 1982-90; med. dir. U. Calif.-Irvine-North Orange County Community Clinic, Anaheim, 1982-90; prof. medicine, sociology, and Latin Am. studies U. N.Mex., Albuquerque, 1997—. Regional rep., nat. sec. bd. dirs. Physicians for Nat. Health Program, Cambridge, Mass., 1989-91; cons. documentary Health Care Across the Border, Nat. Pub. TV, N.Y.C., 1989-90, documentary on U.S. health care system Nat. TV Austria, 1991; cons. BBC, 1992, Pew Health Professions Commn., 1992-94, Assn. Am. Med. Colls., 1992-93, Robert Wood Johnson Found., 1992, Rsch. and Tng. Group in Social Medicine, Santiago, Chile, 1990—, Eisenhower Rural Health Ctrs., Idyllwild, Calif., 1995-96; lectr. med. sociology U. Amsterdam, The Netherlands, 1977; vis. prof. Northwestern U., 1994, U. Ill., Chgo., 1994, U. Wash., 1996, U. N.Mex., 1996, U. Ky., 1996, U. Guadalajara, 1997, Simon Fraser U., 1997, U. Campinas, Brazil, 1999, Cornell Med. Coll., 1999, U. Utah, 2002; mem. expert panel on comm. with elderly patients Nat. Inst. Aging, 1997; prin. investigator U.S. Agy. for Healthcare, Rsch. and Quality, NIMH, 2001. Co-author: The Exploitation of Illness in Capitalist Society, 1974; author: The Second Sickness: Contradictions of Capitalist Health Care, 1983, paperback edit., 1986, revised edit., 2000, The Politics of Medical Encounters: How Patients and Doctors Deal with Social Problems, 1991, paperback edit., 1993, At the Front Lines of Medicine: How the Health Care System Alienates Doctors and Mistreats patients...and What We Can Do About It, 2001; mem. editl. bd. Internat. Jour. Health Svcs., Social Problems, Western Jour. Medicine, Cambio y Salud (Chile), Investigacion en Salud (Mex.). Cons. on health policy Jesse Jackson Presdl. Campaign, 1988; bd. dirs., mem. com. on litigation Orange County Pub. Law Ctr., 1990-96. Fellow in ind. study & rsch. NEH, 1984-85, Fulbright fellow, 1983, 88-90, 93-94, sr. fellow NIA, 1989-91, Fogarty Internat. Ctr., NIH, 1994-98, Fulbright New Century Scholar, 2001-02, John Simon Guggenheim Meml. Found. fellow, 2002-. Fellow ACP, Am. Acad. Physician and Patient; mem. APHA, Am. Sociol. Assn. (nat. coun.-at-large med. sociology sect. 1989-92, coord. resolution process concerning nat. health program 1990-91, Leo G. Reeder award for disting. career in medicine and social scis. 1997), Soc. Gen. Internal Medicine, Phi Beta Kappa. Avocations: music, athletics, gardening, mountain hiking. Office: U NMex Sch Medicine Divsn Cmty Med 2400 Tucker NE Albuquerque NM 87131-0001 E-mail: waitzkin@unm.edu.

WAJDA, SHIRLEY TERESA, historian; b. Warren, Ohio, May 28, 1958; d. Henry Walter Wajda and Erna Emilie Boenning. BA, Boston U., 1982; AM, U. Pa., 1989, PhD, 1992. Mem. coll.-level exam. program test devel. com. Am. History (I and II) Ednl. Testing Svc., Princeton, NJ, 1998—2001. Mem. editl. bd.: American Studies, 1997—;exhibitions include Designing Domesticity: Decorating the American Home Since 1876, 2001; contbr. Recipient Disting. Achievement award, Ednl. Press Am., 1990; fellow, NEH, 1994. Mem.: Orgn. Am. Historians, Am. Studies Assn., Soc. for Historians of Early Am. Republic. Office: Kent State U Dept History 305 Bowman Hall 44242-0001

WAJDA, TADEUSZ, engineer; b. Korczyna, Poland, July 12, 1939; came to U.S., 1989; s. Wladyslaw and Janina (Kudla) W.; m. Krystyna Zawada, July 12, 1970; children: Martin, Anna. MS and Engirng., Tech. U., 1966, PhD in Engring., 1976. Asst. Inst. Soil Mechanics, Kracow, Poland, 1967-70, sr. asst. Poland, 1970-77; adj. Tech. U., 1977; researcher, inventor, writer pvt. practice, Yorktown Heights, N.Y., 1989—. Author: Na Rezydencji, 1993; freelance writer Polish Daily News; inventor, patentee in field. Recipient award Polish Assn. Higher Learning. Home: 1360 Croton Lake Rd Yorktown Heights NY 10598-6214

WAJENBERG, ARNOLD SHERMAN, retired librarian, educator; b. Indpls., Apr. 11, 1929; s. Henry and Hazel L. (Johnson) W.; m. Joyce E. Dunham, Sept. 6, 1952; 1 child, Earl S. BA, Butler U., Indpls., 1951, MA, 1953, U. Chgo., 1955. Cataloger U. Chgo. Library, 1953-69; catalog librarian U. Ill., Chgo., 1969-74, asst. catalog librarian Champaign-Urbana, 1974-78, prin. cataloguer, 1979-94; retired, 1994; prof. library adminstrn. U. Ill., Champaign-Urbana. Prin. educator, Ill. Tng. Program for Implementation of Anglo-Am. Cataloguing Rules, 2d edit., 1979-80; mem. editorial policy com. Dewey Decimal, 1981-92; Ill. rep. cataloging adv. com., Online Computer Libr. Ctr. 1979-82, cataloging and database svcs. adv. com., 1989-92. Author: FLC FEDLINK AACR 2 Cataloging Manual for Federal Libraries, 1981; contbr. articles to profl. jours. Mem. ALA (com. on cataloging: description and access 1981-86, mem.-at-large exec. com. cataloging and classification sect. 1982-86) Avocations: walking, science fiction. Home: 240 Donald Dr Goffstown NH 03045-6214

WAJER, RONALD EDWARD, management consultant; b. Chgo., Aug. 31, 1943; s. Edward Joseph and Gertrude Catherine (Rytelny) W.; m. Mary Earlene Hagan, July 5, 1969; children: Catherine, Michael. BSIE, Northwestern U., 1966; MBA, Loyola U., Chgo., 1970. Cert. mgmt. cons. Inst. Mgmt. Cons. Project engrng. mgr. Procter & Gamble, Chgo., 1966-67; indsl. engring. mgr. Johnson & Johnson, Bedford Park, Ill., 1967-71; project mgr. Jewel Cos., Franklin Park, 1971-73; divsn. engring. mgr. Abbott Labs., North Chicago, 1973-79; pres. bus. engring. divsn. R.E. Wajer & Assocs., Northbrook, 1979—. Contbr. articles to profl. jours. Sec. Downtown Redevel. Commn., Mt. Prospect, Ill., 1977-78; fundraising vol. Maryville Acad., Des Plaines, 1985—; bd. dirs. Lattof YMCA, Des Plaines, 1994-96; profl. advisor Sch. for New Learning, DePaul U., 1994—; mem. indsl. sector com. Lincoln Found. for Bus. Excellence, 1997-99. Recipient Cmty. Svc. award Chgo. Lighthouse for the Blind, 1989, Cert. of Merit, Village of Mt. Prospect, 1978. Mem. Inst. Indsl. Engrs. (cmty. svc. chmn. 1984), Inst. Mgmt. Cons. (exec. v.p., bd. dirs.

1987-94), Assn. Mgmt. Cons. (ctrl. regional v.p. 1985-87), Midwest Soc. Profl. Cons., Northwestern Club Chgo. Roman Catholic. Office: Bus Engring 5 Revere Dr Ste 200 Northbrook IL 60062-8000 E-mail: rewajer@busnengg.com.

WAKASHIGE, BENJAMIN TAKA, librarian; b. Paia, Hawaii, Sept. 3, 1947; s. Akio and Asayo (Tagawa) W.; m. Diane Marie, Dec. 29, 1969; children: David B.A., Kristen J.A. B.A. with honors, Western N.Mex. U., 1969; M. in Librarianship, Emporia State U., 1970. Reference librarian Birmingham-So. Coll., Ala., 1972-74; regional librarian for blind and physically handicapped Maine State Library, 1974-75, N.Mex. State Library, Santa Fe., 1975-77; project dir. Am. Indian Library Cultural Ctr. Project, U. N.Mex., Albuquerque, 1979-80; dist. library media coordinator Zuni Pub. Schs., N.Mex., 1980-82; library dir. U. Albuquerque, 1982-85; library dir. Albuquerque Acad., from 1985; state librarian N.Mex. State Libr., 1998-. Editor: (with others) Haiku and Haiga, 1970. Served with U.S. Army, 1970-72. Emporia State U. HEA Title II fellow, 1970. Mem. N.Mex. Library Assn. (pres. 1982-83), ALA, N.Mex. Book League, Greater Albuquerque Library Assn., N.Mex. Adv. Council Libraries. Democrat. United Ch. Christ. Office: State Library 1209 Camino Carlos Rey Santa Fe NM 87505*

WAKE, DAVID BURTON, biology educator; b. Webster, S.D., June 8, 1936; s. Thomas B. and Ina H. (Solem) W.; m. Marvalee Hendricks, June 23, 1962; 1 child, Thomas Andrew BA, Pacific Luth. U., 1958; MS, U. So. Calif., 1960, PhD, 1964. Instr. anatomy and biology U. Chgo., 1964-66, asst. prof. anatomy and biology, 1966-69; assoc. prof. zoology U. Calif., Berkeley, 1969-72, prof., 1972-89, prof. integrative biology, 1989—, John and Margaret Gompertz prof., 1991-97. Dir. Mus. Vertebrate Zoology U. Calif., Berkeley, 1971-98; curator Herpetology Mus. Vertebrate Zoology, U. Calif., 1969—; vis. Alexander Agassiz prof. Mus. Comparative Zoology, Harvard U., 2002. Author: Biology, 1979; co-editor: Functional Vertebrate Morphology, 1985, Complex Organismal Functions: Integration and Evolution in the Vertebrates, 1989. Recipient Quantrell Teaching award U. Chgo., 1967, Outstanding Alumnus award Pacific Luth. U., 1979, Joseph Grinnell medal Mus. Vertebrate Zoology, 1998, Henry S. Fitch award Am. Soc. Ichthyologists and Herpetologists, 1999; grantee NSF, 1965—; Guggenheim fellow, 1982. Fellow AAAS, Am. Acad. Arts and Scis.; mem. NAS, NRC (bd. biology 1986-92), Am. Philos. Soc., Internat. Union for Conservation of Nature and Natural Resources (chair task force on declining amphibian populations 1990-92), Am. Soc. Zoologists (pres. 1992), Am. Soc. Naturalists (pres. 1989), Am. Soc. Ichthyologists and Herpetologists (bd. govs.), Soc. Study Evolution (pres. 1983, editor 1979-81), Soc. Systematic Biology (coun. 1980-84), Herpetologist's League (Disting. Herpetologist 1984). Home: 999 Middlefield Rd Berkeley CA 94708-1509 E-mail: wakelab@uclink4.berkeley.edu.

WAKE, MADELINE MUSANTE, academic administrator, nursing educator; Diploma, St. Francis Hosp. Sch. Nursing, 1963; BS in Nursing, Marquette U., 1968, MS in Nursing, 1971; PhD, U. Wis., Milw., 1986. Clin. nurse specialist St. Mary's Hosp., Milw., 1971-74, asst. dir. nursing, 1974-77; from dir. continuing nursing edn. to provost Marquette U., 1977—2002, provost, 2002—. Mem. devel. team Internat. Classification for Nursing Practice, Geneva, 1991-99. Chmn. bd. dirs. Trinity Meml. Hosp., Cudahy, Wis., 1991-96. Recipient Profl. Svc. award Am. Diabetes Assn.-Wis. affiliate, 1978, Excellence in Nursing Edn. award Wis. Nurses Assn., 1989; named Disting. Lectr. Sigma Theta Tau Internat., 1991. Fellow Am. Acad. Nursing; mem. ANA, AACN, Am. Orgn. Nurse Execs., Am. Assn. Coll. Nursing (bd. dirs. 1999-2002), Vis. Nurs Assn. wis. (bd. dirs.). Office: Marquette Univ O'Hara Hall Milwaukee WI 53201-1881

WAKE, MARVALEE HENDRICKS, biology educator; b. Orange, Calif., July 31, 1939; d. Marvin Carlton and Velvalee (Borter) H.; m. David B. Wake, June 23, 1962; 1 child, Thomas A. BA, U. So. Calif., 1961, MS, 1964, PhD, 1968. 1968Teaching asst./instr. U. Ill., Chgo., 1964, asst. prof., 1968—69; lectr. U. Calif., Berkeley, 1969—73, asst. prof., 1973—76, assoc. prof., 1976—80, prof. zoology, 1980—89, chmn. dept. zoology, 1985—89, chmn. dept. integrative biology, 1989—91, 1999—2002, assoc. dean Coll. Letters and Sci., 1975—78, prof. integrative biology, 1989—, Chancellor's prof., 1997—2000. Mem. NAS/NRC Bd. on Sustainable Devel., 1995-99, NSF Bio Adv. Commn., 1997—; Smithsonian Sci. Commn., 2001-. Editor, co-editor: Hyman's Comparative Vertebrate Anatomy, 1979, The Origin and Evolution of Larval Forms, 1999; co-author: Biology, 1978; contbr. articles to profl. jours. NSF grantee, 1978—; Guggenheim fellow, 1988-89. Fellow: AAAS (chair Biology Sect. G 1998), Calif. Acad. Sci. (trustee 1992—98, hon. trustee 1998—); mem.: World Congress of Herpetology (sec. gen. 1994—97), Internat. Union Biol. Scis. (U.S. nat. com. 1986—, chair 1992—95, sec. gen. 1994—2000, pres. 2000—), Soc. Integrative Comparative Biol. (pres. 2001—), Am. Soc. Ichthyologists and Herpetologists (pres. 1984, bd. govs. 1978—). Office: U Calif Dept Integrative Biology Berkeley CA 94720

WAKE, ROBERT ALAN, lawyer; b. Ft. Belvoir, Va., Oct. 7, 1952; s. Robert Warner and Esther Jeannette (Schreiber) W.; m. Marcia Greenbaum, July 17, 1977; children: Benjamin Ehren, Koren Alison. BS, MIT, 1974; PhD, Brown U., 1979; JD, Harvard U., 1988. Bar: Maine 1988. Lectr. U. Wis., Milw., 1979-81; asst. prof. U. Maine, Orono, 1981-82, U. Calif., Santa Cruz, 1982-85; law clk. to chief justice Vincent L. McKusick Portland, Maine, 1988-89; asst. atty. gen. State of Maine, Augusta, 1989-93; fin. surveillance counsel Maine Bur. Ins., 1993—. Author poems. Mem. Common Cause, 1980—; chair Maine Dem. Party Rules Com.; pres. Gorham-Sebago Lake Regional Land Trust. Mem. ABA, Maine Bar Assn., Am. Math. Soc., ACLU, Am. Contract Bridge League, Ins. Regulatory Examiners Soc. Democrat. Jewish. Avocations: basketball, hiking, tennis, writing. Home: 40 Covered Bridge Rd Windham ME 04062-4608 Office: Maine Bureau of Insurance 34 State House Sta Augusta ME 04333-0001 E-mail: robert.a.wake@state.me.us.

WAKEFIELD, DAWN LEE, communications consultant; b. San Antonio, July 4, 1957; d. Harold Dawson Jr. and Marguerite Isabel (Fitzgerald) W. BSChemE, Tex. A&M U., 1979, MS in Chemistry, 1982, PhD in Chemistry, 1985, MEd in Ednl. Adminstrn., 1987. Coord. physics chem. labs. Tex. A&M U., College Station, 1986-87, coord. coop. edn., 1987; rsch. assoc. Thermodynamics Rsch. Ctr., 1986-88; process engr. ARCO Chem. Co., Channelview, Tex., 1988-90; dir. devel. Coll. Sci. Tex. A&M U. Found., College Station, 1990-93; pres. West Comms. Group, 1993—. Adv. mem. edn. com. Allen Acad., Bryan, Tex., 1998-2000. Trustee Keystone Sch., San Antonio, 1985-90; bd. dirs. Brazos County divsn. Am. Heart Assn., College Station, 1994-98; vol. fundraiser, grant writer for various cultural and ednl. orgns., 1990—; freelance polit. cons., Bryan, 1994—; mem. Leadership Brazos, 1990-91, Bryan Leadership award, 2002, Bryan Leadership Acad., 2002. Recipient Outstanding Vol. award Am. Guild Organists, 1992, Paul R. Ellis Comm. award Am. Heart Assn., 1995. Mem. Jr. League of Bryan-College Station, Phi Delta Kappa, Phi Lambda Upsilon. Methodist. Avocations: golf, tennis, swimming, walking.

WAKEFIELD, MARIE ANNETTE, librarian; b. Urbana, Ill., Dec. 23, 1953; d. William and Margaret (Frailey) Wakefield; m. Mark M. Oliver, July 4, 1983 (dec. Mar. 1991); m. George M. Coston, June 25, 1997. AA, U. Md., Munich, Germany, 1975; BS, So. Ill. U., 1978; MS in Libr./Info. Sci., U. Ill., 1979. Tech. svc. dir. Harry-Stowe Libr., St. Louis, 1981-82, pub. svc. coord., 1982-85; cataloging libr. Air Weather Svc. Lib./USAF, Scott AFB, Ill., 1975-76; engring. libr. Army Aviation Sys. Command, St. Louis, 1986-87; tech. svc. libr. U.S. Mil. Cmty., Libr. Svc. Office, Nuernberg, Germany, 1987, program mgr. libr. Germany, 1987-88, adminstrv. libr. Heilbronn, Germany, 1988-91; libr. svc. dir. 543 Area Support Group, U.S. Army, Bremerhaven, Germany, 1991-93; libr. br. chief 234 Base Support Battalion, U.S. Army, Giessen, Germany, 1993-95; engring. libr. U.S. Army C.E. Constrn. Engring. Rsch. Lab., Champaign, Ill., 1995-98; libr. sys. dir. Giessen (Germany) 284th Base Support Bn., 1998-99, Vilseck (Germany) 409th Base Support Bn., 1999—. Mem. ALA (mil. divsn.). Avocations: reading, painting. E-mail: wakefieldm. Office: 409th BSB Vilseck Library Unit 28038 APO AE 09112 E-mail: wakefieldm_200@yahoo.com.

WAKEFIELD, MARIE CYNTHIA, performing arts educator, playwright, poet; b. Chgo., Feb. 11, 1945; d. Daniel Jesse Armstrong and Margaret M. Jenkins; m. Donald Wakefield; children: Adolphus Beal III, Donald Wakefield II, Walter McIntyre Jr., Michele McIntyre, Reyna, Candace. Student, Cortez W. Peters Bus. Coll., Chgo., 1962—63. Owner Creative Works, Etc., Inglewood, Calif. Poet/playwright: Quiet Storm, 1994. Named Poet of Yr., Famous Poets Soc., 1995, 1998, 2000. Avocations: writing, singing, producing plays. Office: Creative Works Etc PO Box 10103 Inglewood CA 90304 Personal E-mail: mwake9717@aol.com.

WAKEFIELD, PHILIP MARK, obstetrician/gynecologist; b. Cuiaba Mato Grosso, Brazil, 1950; MD, U. Tenn., 1982. Diplomate Am. Bd. Ob-Gyn. Rotating intern various hosps., Memphis, 1982-83; resident Regional Med. Ctr.; chief staff Eliza Coffe Meml. Hosp., Florence, Ala., 1994-95; pvt. practice. Mem. AMA, ACOG, Am. Fertility Soc. Office: Ob-Gyn Assocs NW Ala PO Box 10000 Florence AL 35631-2000

WAKEFIELD, ROBERT, lawyer, retired marine corps officer; b. Oakland, Calif., Nov. 24, 1936; s. Hal Wesley and Elizabeth Luella Wakefield; m. Lysbeth Brooks, June 6, 1960 (div. Sept. 1978); m. Dorothy Irene Liston, Sept. 23, 1978 (div. Jan. 2001); children: Victoria A. Conway, Gregory Scott. BA, U. Calif., Berkeley, 1959; grad., USMC Command-Gen. Staff Coll., 1974; grad. with highest distinction, U.S. Naval War Coll., 1982; MA with honors, Ctrl. Mich. U., 1983; JD cum laude, U. Idaho, 1992. Bar: Idaho 1992, U.S. Dist. Ct. Idaho 1992, Colo. 1993, Wash. 2002, also Nez Perce and Coeur d'Alene tribal cts. Commd. 2d lt. USMC, 1959, advanced through grades to col., 1982; ret., 1989; law clk. 2d Dist. Ct., Moscow, 1992-93, N.Mex. Ct. Appeals, Las Cruces, 1996-97; ptnr. Liston, Wakefield & Dwelle, Moscow, 1993-96, 97—. Prof. clin. studies Indian program law U. Idaho Coll. Law, Nez Perce and Coeur d'Alene Reservations, 1992-96. Contbr. articles to mil. publs. Decorated Legion of Merit, Purple Heart, 13 Air medals, Vietnamese Cross of Gallantry. Mem. 2d Dist. Bar Assn., Marine Corps Assn., Am. Inns. Ct. Republican. Episcopalian. Avocations: scuba diving, hunting, fishing. Office: Wakefield & Dwelle 609 S Washington St Ste 206 Moscow ID 83843-3064

WAKEFIELD, STEPHEN ALAN, lawyer; b. Olney, Ill., Oct. 18, 1940; s. George William and Blanche Lucille (Sheesley) W.; children from previous marriage: Melissa Hawley, Tracy Wakefield, Stephen Alan Jr.; m. Patricia Ann McGuire, Nov. 29, 1980; 1 child, Mark. LLB, U. Tex., Austin, 1965. Bar: Tex. 1965. Assoc. Baker & Botts, Houston, 1965-70, ptnr., 1974-84, sr. ptnr., chmn. energy dept., 1986-89; atty. Federal Power Commn., Washington, 1970-72; dep. asst. sec. energy programs Dept. Interior, 1972-73, asst. sec. energy and minerals, 1973-74; asst. adminstr. Fed. Energy Office, 1973-74; vice chmn., gen. counsel United Energy Resources, Inc., Houston, 1985-86; pres. United Gas Pipe Line Co., 1985-86; exec. v.p. MidCon Corp., 1985-86; gen. coun. Dept. Energy, Washington, 1989-91; ptnr. Akin, Gump, Strauss, Hauer & Feld, L.L.P., 1991-97; sr. v.p., gen. coun. Southern Co., 1997-2001; sr. counsel Southern Co. , 2001—. Bd. visitors M.D. Anderson Cancer Ctr.; bd. govs. Robert Packard Ctr. ALS Rsch. Johns Hopkins U. Mem. Tex. Bar Assn., Capital City Club (Atlanta). Home: 201 Blackland Dr NW Atlanta GA 30342-4405 Office: Southern Company Ste 1400 270 Peachtree St NW Atlanta GA 30303-1263 E-mail: sawakefield@mindspring.com., sawakefi@southernco.com.

WAKEMAN, FREDERIC EVANS, JR. historian, educator; b. Kansas City, Kans., Dec. 12, 1937; s. Frederic Evans and Margaret Ruth (Keyes) W.; married He Lea Liang; children: Frederic Evans III, Matthew Clark, Sarah Elizabeth. BA, Harvard Coll., 1959; postgrad., Institut d'Etudes Politiques, U. Paris, 1959-60; MA, U. Calif., Berkeley, 1962, PhD, 1965. Asst. prof. history U. Calif., Berkeley, 1965-67, assoc. prof., 1968-70, prof., 1970-89, Haas prof. Asian Studies, 1989—, dir. Ctr. Chinese Studies, 1972-79; humanities research prof., vis. scholar Corpus Christi Coll., U. Cambridge, Eng., 1976-77, Beijing U., 1980-81, 85. Acad. adviser U.S. Ednl. Del. for Study in China; chmn. Joint Com. Chinese Studies Am. Coun. Learned Socs./Social Sci. Rsch. Coun.; sr. adviser Beijing office NAS; pres. Social Sci. Rsch. Coun., 1986-89, chmn. com. on scholarly comm. with China, 1995-2000; dir. Inst. East Asian Studies, Berkeley, 1990-2001; vis. prof. U. Heidelberg, Germany, 2000. Author: Strangers at the Gate, 1966, History and Will, 1973, The Fall of Imperial China, 1975, Conflict and Control in Late Imperial China, 1976, Ming and Qing Historical Studies in the People's Republic of China, 1981, The Great Enterprise, 1986, Shanghai Sojourners, 1992, Policing Shanghai, 1995, Shanghai Badlands, 1996, China's Quest for Modernization, 1997, Reappraising Republican China, 2000. Harvard Nat. scholar, 1955-59; Tower fellow, 1959-60; Fgn. Area fellow, 1963-65; Am. Coun. Learned Socs. fellow, 1967-68; Guggenheim fellow, 1973-74; NRC fellow, 1985. Mem. Am. Acad. Arts and Scis., Coun. on Fgn. Rels., Am. Hist. Assn. (pres.), Am. Philos. Soc. Home: 501 Delancey St Apt 409 San Francisco CA 94107-1432 Office: U Calif Inst East Asian Studies Berkeley CA 94720-0001 E-mail: jingcha@socrates.berkeley.edu.

WAKEMAN, MARTHA JANE, artist, educator; b. Bridgeport, Conn., Jan. 8, 1948; d. Norman Burr and Muriel (Evitts) Wakeman; m. Robert E. Proctor, Mar. 15, 1980; children: Rebecca Anne Proctor, Andrew Wakeman Proctor. BS, Skidmore Coll., 1970; MA, Villa Schifaroia-Rosary Coll., Florence, Italy, 1972, MFA, 1978. Cert. art tchr. K-12, Conn. Instr. art Gonzaga U. Jr. Yr. Abroad Program, Florence, 1974-79, Conn. Coll., 1980-81, instr. art Return to Coll. program, 1984—; instr. painting Umbra Inst., Pengra, Italy, 2002. Exhibited in one-woman shows in Milan, Florence, N.Y.C. and Conn., 1972-96; group shows include Alan Stone Gallery, N.Y.C., Skidmore Coll., Vangarde Gallery, New London, Conn., MS Gallery, Hartford, Conn., No-Ho Gallery, N.Y.C., Conn. Women Artists, New Haven; paintings included in more than 100 pvt. collections in Europe, U.S. and Can.; subject of articles. Class coord. St. Joseph Sch., New London, 1998-99, Pine Point Sch., Stonington, Conn., 1995-97; mem. parish coun. St. Joseph Ch., New London, 1993-96, lector, 1995—/ Democrat. Roman Catholic. Avocations: swimming, travel, studying foreign languages, reading. Home: 105 Oneco Ave New London CT 06320-4120 Office: Conn Coll Box 5573 New London CT 06320

WAKEMAN, THOMAS HERBERT, III, civil engineer, regional administrator; b. Apr. 20, 1946; BS, Calif. Polytech. U., 1970; MA, San Francisco State U., 1975; postgrad. studies, U. Calif., Berkeley, Davis, 1976-84; postgrad. studies DESc, Columbia U., 1997—. Pres. Earth Doctors, Davis, Calif., 1982-85; dir. bay model U.S. Army Engrs., Sausalito, 1985-89, spl. projects mgr. San Francisco, 1990-94; gen. mgr. waterways devel. Port Authority N.Y., N.Y.C., 1994—. E-mail: twakeman@panynj.gov.

WAKID, SHUKRI ABU, information technology director; b. Kfarshima, Lebanon, Dec. 20, 1945; came to U.S., 1967; s. Edward Bou and Renee Bou Wakid; m. Jane Abraham, May 29, 1978; children: Edward, Jacob. BS, Am. U. Beirut, 1967; postgrad., U. Pitts., 1967; PhD, La. State U., 1971. Chmn. dept. physics, math, CS Haigazian Coll., Beirut, 1972-76; postdoctoral fellow La. State U., 1976-77; asst. prof. computer sci. U. Pitts., Johnstown, 1977-78; sr. rsch. assoc. NASA/Goddard Space Flight Ctr., Greenbelt, Md., 1978-79; sr. mem. tech. staff Computer Scis. Corp., Seabrook, 1980; mem. tech. staff Bell Labs., Holmdel, N.J., 1981-84; group mgr. then chief adv. sys. divsn. Nat. Inst. Stds. and Tech., Gaithersburg, Md., 1988-95, dir. info. tech. lab., 1995-99, CIO, 1999—. Adj. prof. Lebanese U., Beirut, 1973-76. Founder: The North American Integrated Svcs. Digital Network Forum (Top 25 Comm. Leaders 1989, Newsmaker 1988); contbr. articles to profl. jours. Recipient Fed. 100 award Fed. Computer Week, 1991, Silver medal U.S. Dept. Commerce, 1992, Presdl. Rank award for meritorous exec. U.S. Govt., 1993; Fulbright-Hays exch. fellow U.S. Govt., 1967. Mem. IEEE (sr., vice-chair tech. adv. bd. Computer Soc. 1997—), Instnrl. Mgmt. Sys. Bd. Achievements include standardization of Intergrated Svcs. Digital Network technology, measurement techniques for high speed networks; theoretical prediction of positronium formation in hydrogen at low energy positron-hydrogen collisions; inelastic resonances in helium and lithium. Home: 12526 Hialeah Way Gaithersburg MD 20878-3784 Office: NIST MS 3207 100 Bureau Dr Bldg 222 Gaithersburg MD 20899-0003

WAKIL, SALIH JAWAD, biochemistry educator; b. Kerballa, Iraq, Aug. 16, 1927; s. Jawad and Milook (Attraqchi) W.; m. Fawzia Bahrani, Nov. 30, 1952; children: Sonya, Aida, Adil, Youssef. B.Sc., Am. U., Beirut, 1948; PhD, U. Wash., 1952. Research fellow U. Wash., 1949-52, U. Wis., Madison, 1952-56, asst. prof., 1956-59, Duke U., 1959-60, assoc. prof., 1960-65, prof., 1965-71; prof. biochemistry, chmn. dept. Baylor Coll. Medicine, Houston, 1971—, Lodwick T. Bolin prof., chmn. dept. biochemistry, 1984—, prof. biotechnology, 1986-95, Disting. Svc. prof., 1990—. Recipient Paul Lewis award in enzyme chemistry Am. Chem. Soc., 1967, Disting. Duke Med. Alumnus award, 1973, Chilton award U. Tex. Southwestern Med. Ctr., Dallas, 1985, Kuwait prize Kuwait Found. Advancement Sci., 1988, Disting. Svc. award Arab Am. Med. Assn., 1990, Supelco Rsch. award Am. Oil Chemists Soc., 1993; John Simon Guggenheim fellow, 1968-69. Fellow Am. Acad. Microbiology, Third World Acad. of Scis. (assoc.); mem. NAS, Assn. Med. and Grad. Depts. Biochemistry (pres. 1988-89). Office: Baylor Coll Medicine Dept Biochem & Mol Biology 1 Baylor Plz Houston TX 77030-3411

WAKIM, FAHD GEORGE, physicist, educator; b. Mieh-Mieh, Lebanon, Aug. 6, 1933; s. George Hanna and Marriam (Semaan) W.; m. Bertha Villarreal. BSc in Physics, Am. U. Beirut, 1956; MA in Solid State Physics, U. Tex., 1960, PhD in Solid State Physics, 1964. Rsch. physicist Itek Corp., Lexington, Mass., 1965-70; investigator Tex. Christian U., Ft. Worth, 1970-71; assoc. prof. Am. U. Cairo, 1971-73; prof. physics Kuwait U., Kuwait, 1973-84; assoc. prof. dept. elec. engring U. Mass., Lowell, 1984—, coord. for EET program, 1996—. Presenter numerous seminars. Patentee process for producing images with photosensitive materials and their products; contbr. articles to profl. jours. Grantee Kuwait Inst. for Sci. Rsch., 1978, 79, 91, Kuwait U., 1979. Mem. IEEE, Am. Phys. Soc., Materials Rsch. Soc. Office: U Mass-Lowell 1 University Ave Lowell MA 01854-5009 E-mail: fahd_wakim@uml.edu.

WAKIM, JUDITH, nursing educator; b. Cin., June 5, 1938; d. John William and Madelon Patricia Henderson; m. Jubran M. Wakim, June 8, 1963 (dec. Mar. 1999); children: Mary Ellen, Patricia Ann, James Jubran. BSN, Coll. Mt. St. Joseph, 1960; MS in Nursing Edn., Ind. U., 1961, EdD, 1976. Instr. DePauw U., 1961-63; evening charge nurse Bloomington (Ind.) Hosp., 1963-64, Obion County Gen. Hosp., Union City, Tenn., 1969-70; dir. dept. nursing U. Tenn., Martin, 1970-79; prof., chair Austin Peay State U., Clarksville, Tenn., 1980-87; chair dept. nursing, then dir. Sch. Nursing Mid. Tenn. State U., Murfreesboro, 1987-98; prof. Sch. Nursing U. Tenn., Chattanooga, 1999—. Cons. in field. Mem.: ANA, Nat. League Nursing, Am. Assn. Higher Edn., Sigma Theta Tau, Phi Kappa Phi, Sigma Xi. Avocations: tennis, gardening, reading. Home: 9 Prentice Ln Signal Mountain TN 37377-2081 E-mail: jwakim@bellsouth.net., judith-wakim@utc.edu.

WAKKER, BART P. astronomer; b. Badhoevedorp, The Netherlands, Oct. 12, 1959; came to U.S., 1990; m. Ingrid S. Kallick; children: Petra, Bart. PhD, Rijksuniversiteit, Groningen, The Netherlands, 1990. Astronomy rschr. U. Ill., Urbana, 1990-95; asst. scientist U. Wis., Madison, 1995-98, assoc. scientist, 1998—. Contbr. articles to profl. jours. Mem. Am. Astron. Soc., Internat. Astron. Union. Office: 475 N Charter St Madison WI 53706-1507 E-mail: wakker@astro.wisc.edu.

WAKOSKI, DIANE, poet, educator; b. Whittier, Calif., Aug. 3, 1937; d. John Joseph and Marie Elvira (Mengel) W. BA in English, U. Calif., Berkeley, 1960. Writer-in-residence Mich. State U., East Lansing, 1976—, Univ. disting. prof., 1990—. Vis. writer Calif. Inst. Tech., 1972, U. Va., 1972-73, Wilamette U., 1973, Lake Forest Coll., 1974, Colo. Coll., 1974, U. Calif., Irvine, 1974, Macalester Coll., 1975, U. Wis., 1975, Hollins Coll., 1974, U. Wash., 1977, Whitman Coll., 1976, Emory U., 1980-81, U. Hawaii, 1978. Author: books Coins and Coffins, 1962, Discrepancies and Apparitions, 1966, Inside The Blood Factory, 1968, The George Washington Poems, 1967, The Magellanic Clouds, 1969, The Motorcycle Betrayal Poems, 1971, Smudging, 1972, Dancing On The Grave of A Son Of A Bitch, 1973, Trilogy, 1974, Virtuoso Literature For Two and Four Hands, 1976, Waiting For the King of Spain, 1977, The Man Who Shook Hands, 1978, Cap of Darkness, 1980, The Magician's Feastletters, 1982, The Collected Greed: Parts I-XIII, 1984, The Rings of Saturn, 1986, Emerald Ice: Selected Poems 1962-87, 1988 (William Carlos Williams prize 1989), Medea The Sorceress, 1991, Jason the Sailor, 1993, The Emerald City of Las Vegas, 1995, Argonaut Rose, 1998, The Butcher's Apron: New & Selected Poems, 2000. Cassandra Found. grantee, 1970; N.Y. State Cultural Council grantee, 1971-72; Nat. Endowment for Arts grantee, 1973-74; Guggenheim grantee, 1972-73; Fulbright grantee, 1984; Mich. Arts Coun. grantee, 1988; recipient Mich. Arts Found. award, 1989, Disting. Faculty award Mich. State U., 1989, Univ. Disting. Prof., 1990. Office: Mich State U 207 Morrill Hall East Lansing MI 48824-1036 E-mail: dwakoski@aol.com., wakoski@pilot.msu.edu.

WAKS, JAY WARREN, lawyer; b. Newark, Dec. 6, 1946; s. Isadore and Miriam Waks; m. Harriet, July 27, 1969; children: Jonathan Warren, Allison Lindsay. BS, Cornell U., 1968, JD, 1971. Bar: N.Y. 1972, U.S. Ct. Appeals (2d cir.) 1972, U.S. Dist. Ct. (no. dist.) N.Y. 1972, U.S. Dist. Ct. (so. & ea. dists.) N.Y. 1973, U.S. Ct. Appeals (3d cir.) 1983, U.S. Dist. Ct. D.C. 1985, U.S. Supreme Ct. 1991. Law clk. to Hon. Inzer B. Wyatt U.S. Dist. Ct. So. Dist. N.Y., 1971-72; assoc. Kaye, Scholer, Fierman, Hays & Handler, N.Y.C., 1972-80; ptnr. Kaye Scholer LLP, 1981—, chmn. employment and labor law practice/litigation, chmn. ADR practice group, mem. E-commerce practice group and internat. practice group. Mem exec. com., bd. dirs., sec. to bd. dirs. Work in Am. Inst., Inc., Scarsdale, N.Y., 1989—; mem., chair faculty numerous employment and labor law confs., 1982—; co-chair Glasser Legal Works Inst. on Litigation/Resolution of Complex Employment Discrimination Class Actions, 2000; chair Ann. Employment Law and Litigation Conf., 1992-96; spkr. law jour. seminars Gen. Coun. Conf., 1988—, winter conf. Fed. Bar Coun., 1999; conf. spkr. Am. Employment Law Coun., Law Edn. Inst./Bur. Nat. Affairs Books Nat. Continuing Legal Edn. Conf., Vail, 1998—. Bus. Watch columnist Nat. Law Jour., 1990—; contbg. author numerous articles to profl. jours. Mem. employment disputes com. CPR Inst. for Dispute Resolution, 1988—, chair, 1991—; mem. coun. Cornell U., 2000—, exec. com. coun., chair admissions com., 2002—, nat. chmn. Cornell Law Sch. ann. fund, 2001—; chmn. 20th, 25th and 30th reunion campaigns Cornell Law Sch., former nat. co-chair Cornell Law Sch. dean's spl. leadership commn. Class of '68, major gifts com. 1998, chair devel. exec. com., 2002—; mem. law sch. adv. coun. Cornell Law Sch. Named among nation's best litigators in employment law, The Nat. Law Jour., 1992; named among best lawyers in N.Y. and among 7 best corporate side labor/employment lawyers, N.Y. Mag., 1995. Mem. ABA (spkr. ann. meetings sect. labor and employment), State Bar Calif., N.Y. State Bar Assn. (co-chair employment alternative dispute resolution com., labor and employment law sect., exec. com. 1995-99), Assn. Bar of City of N.Y. (chmn. labor and employment law com. 1990-93). Avocations: swimming, tennis, skiing, bicycling. Office: Kaye Scholer LLP 425 Park Ave New York NY 10022-3506 E-mail: jwaks@kayescholer.com.

WAKSMAN, BYRON HALSTED, neuroimmunologist, experimental pathologist, educator, medical association administrator; b. N.Y.C., Sept. 15, 1919; s. Selman A. and Bertha (Mitnik) W.; m. Joyce Ann Robertroy, Aug. 11, 1944; children: Nan, Peter. BS, Swarthmore Coll., 1940; MD, U. Pa., 1943. Intern Michael Reese Hosp., Chgo., 1944; fellow Mayo Found., 1946-48; NIH fellow Columbia U. Med. Sch., 1948-49; assoc., then asst. prof. bacteriology and immunology Harvard Med. Sch., 1949-63; research fellow, then assoc. bacteriologist (neurology) Mass. Gen. Hosp., 1949-63; prof. microbiology Yale U., 1963-74, prof. pathology, 1974-78, chmn. dept., 1964-70, 72-74, prof. pathology and biology, 1979-89; v.p. rsch. programs Nat. Multiple Sclerosis Soc., N.Y.C., 1979-87, v.p. research and med. programs, 1987-89; adj. prof. pathology NYU, 1979—, rsch. prof. biomedicine and sci. edn., 2002—, dir. (ad interim) programs for prep. edn. sci. and medicine, 2002; vis. scientist in neurology Harvard U., 1990—. Mem. expert panel immunology WHO, 1963—83; microbiology fellowships panel and study sect. mem. NIH, 1961—69; bd. trustees Found. for Microbiology, 1968—, pres., 1970—2000, chmn. bd. trustes, 2001—; bd. trustees Biosis, 1988—91; dir. sci. writing fellowships program Marine Biol. Lab., Woods Hole, Mass., 1990—95; Humboldt profl. Mac Planck Inst., Munich, 1991—92; dir. European Initiative for Communicators Sci., 1992—95. Contbr. articles to profl. jours.; editor: Progress in Allergy/Chemical Immunology, 1962—; mem. editl. adv. bd.: Cellular Immunology, 1970—95, mem. editl. adv. bd.: Immunol. Comms., 1970—95, mem. editl. adv. bd.: Inflamation, 1975—90, assoc. editor: Bacteriol. Revs., 1963—67, assoc. editor: Jour. Immunology, 1962—66, assoc. editor: Internat. Archives Allergy and Applied Immunology, 1962—95. Served as psychiatrist AUS, 1944-46. Mem. Am. Assn. Immunologists (councillor 1965-70, pres. 1970-71), British Soc. Immunology, Am. Soc. Microbiology (councillor 1967-69) Home: 300 E 54th St New York NY 10022-5018 Office: NYU Sch Medicine Dept Pathology 550 1st Ave New York NY 10016-6402 E-mail: bhw1@nyu.edu.

WAKUMOTO, YOSHIHIKO, electronics company executive, grants executive; b. Bunkyo-Ku, Tokyo, June 4, 1931; s. Yoshitaro and Fumie (Oka) W.; m. Reiko Tanaka, Mar. 28, 1959; children: Yoshiaki, Yoshiyuki. BA, Tokyo U., 1955; postgrad., Columbia U., 1960-61. Dep. mgr. license negotiation Toshiba Corp., Tokyo, 1964-67, mgr. overseas mfg. ops., 1967-72, mgr. fin. divsn., 1972-74, gen. mgr. internat. fin. divsn., 1974-81, gen. mgr. internat. affairs divsn., 1981-88, v.p., dep. group exec.-internat. staff group, 1988-91, exec. v.p. for corp. planning, info. sys. and group cos., 1991-95, exec. v.p. for internat. rels., 1995-96, bd. dirs., advisor, 1996—2001; exec. dir. Japan Found. Ctr. for Global Partnership, 1996—2002; spl. asst. to the pres. The Japan Found., 2002—. Bd. dirs. Schlumberger Ltd.; mem. Japan nat. com. United World Colls., 1996-2002. Co-author: Foreign Exchange Risk and International Financial Strategy, 1973, The Run-up of 21st Century, 1991; translator: Management By Exception, 1968. Mem. Internat. House of Japan, Am.-Japan Soc., Fgn. Corr. Club Japan (assoc.), Bus. Rsch. Inst., Inc. (trustee). Home: 3-43-18 Hongo Bunkyo-ku Tokyo 113-0033 Japan Office: Japan Found Ctr Global Ptnr 1-12-32 Akasaka Mori Bldg Minato-ku Tokyo 107-6021 Japan E-mail: yoshihiko_wakumoto@jpf.go.jp.

WALASEK, OTTO FRANK, chemical engineer, biochemist, photographer; b. Park Falls, Wis., Mar. 11, 1919; s. Frank Otto and Mary (Swoboda) W.; m. Annie May Stockton (div. Nov. 1959); 1 child, Richard A.; m. Joan Constance Ashton, Sept. 18, 1965; children: Arthur, Carl. BS in Chem. Engring., U. Wis., 1946; MS in Biochemistry, U. Ill., 1968; postgrad., Loyola U., 1968-72. Penicillin processing product engr. I Abbott Labs., North Chgo., Ill., 1946-49, antibiotic process rsch. and devel., 1950-55, biochemical rsch., 1956-68, sr. biochemist, 1968-77, staff Leukemia project, 1978-80; pvt. photographer Sonora, Calif., 1981—. Patentee in field; contbr. articles to profl. jours. Recipient Excellence award Fedn. Internat. of Art Photographic, Switzerland, 1972; named Hon. Master of Profl. Photography, Profl. Photographic Assns., Taiwan, 1990. Mem. Photographic Soc. Am. (associateship), Royal Photographic Soc., Nat. Stereoscopic Soc., Internat. Stereoscopic Union. Democrat. Avocations: nature, wilderness, canoeing adventures, travel.

WALBAUM, ROBERT C. lawyer; b. Springfield, Ill., Nov. 13, 1933; s. George Crum and Mary Emma (Taylor) W.; m. Anita P. Walbaum, Aug. 6, 1960; children: John Taylor, Charles Robert. Student, Bradley U., Peoria, Ill., 1951-53; BS in Commerce, U. Ill., Urbana, 1955; JD, Washington, St. Louis, 1960. Bar: Ill. 1961, U.S. Dist. Ct. (so. dist.) Ill. 1964, U.S. Ct. Appeals (7th cir.) 1973, U.S. Supreme Ct. 1989. With Chgo. Title and Trust Co., 1960-61; asst. states atty. County of Sangamon, Springfield, Ill., 1961-63; pvt. practice, 1963—. Atty. City Springfield, 1964-69, Village Pleasant Plains, Ill., 1970-93; tech. advisor Ill. Dept. Law Enforcement, 1969-73; counsel Springfield Park Dist., 1984—; dir. Pleasant Plains State Bank, 1982-95. Mem. Sangamon County Bd. Suprs., 1962-75, chmn., 1974; bd. dirs. Washington St. Mission, Springfield, 1966-90, pres. 1983-86. Served with U.S. Army, 1955-57. Mem. ABA, Ill. State Bar Assn., Sangamon County Bar Assn., Illini Country Club, Sangamo Club, Am. Bus. Club (Springfield). Republican. Episcopalian. Address: 1049 W Woodland Ave Springfield IL 62704-2863 E-mail: walbaumlaw@aol.com.

WALBERG, HERBERT JOHN, psychologist, educator, consultant; b. Chgo., Dec. 27, 1937; s. Herbert J. and Helen (Bauer) W.; m. Madoka Bessho, Aug. 20, 1965; 1 child, Herbert J. III. BE in Edn. and Psychology, Chgo. State U., 1959; ME in Counseling, U. Ill., 1960; PhD in Ednl. Psychology, U. Chgo., 1964. Instr. psychology Chgo. State U., 1962-63, asst. prof., 1964-65; lectr. edn. Rutgers U., New Brunswick, N.J., 1965-66; asst. prof. edn. Harvard U., Cambridge, Mass., 1966-69; assoc. prof. edn. U. Ill., Chgo., 1970-71, prof., 1971-84, rsch. prof., 1984—, external examiner, 1981. External examiner, 1981; ednl. cons. numerous orgns.; external examiner Monash U., 1974, 76, Australian Nat. U., 1977; speaker in field; former coord. worldwide radio broadcasts on Am. Edn. Voice of Am., USIA, Office Pres. U.S., cons. Ctr. for Disease Control U.S. Pub. Health Svcs., 1985-90. Author, editor 49 books; chmn. editl. bd. Internat. Jour. Ednl. Rsch., 1985—; contbr. over 350 articles to profl. jours., chpts. to books. Mem. Chgo. United Edn. Com., also other civic groups, 1971-86; bd. dirs. Family Study Inst., 1987; chmn. bd. dirs. Heartland Inst., 1995. Nat. Inst. Edn. rsch. grantee, 1973, NSF rsch. grantee, 1974, March of Dimes rsch. grantee, 1976, numerous others. Fellow AAAS, Am. Psychol. Assn., Royal Statis. Soc.; mem. Internat. Acad. Edn. (founding), Am. Ednl. Rsch. Assn., Assn. for Supervision and Curriculum Devel., Brit. Ednl. Rsch. Assn., Nat. Soc. for Study Edn., Evaluation Rsch. Soc., Internat. Acad. Scis., Phi Delta Kappa (Disting. Rsch. award U. Chgo. chpt. 1971, cert. of recognition 1985), Phi Kappa Phi (hon.). Lutheran. Avocation: travel. Home: 180 E Pearson St Apt 3607 Chicago IL 60611-2135 Office: U Ill 1040 W Harrison St Chicago IL 60607-7129

WALBESSER, HENRY HERMAN, computer science educator; b. Buffalo, May 9, 1935; s. Henry Herman and Florence (Schoenl) W.; m. Diane L. Walker, Aug. 16, 1958; children: Henry, Kathleen, James. BS, SUNY, Buffalo, 1958; MA, U. Md., 1960, PhD, 1965; DSc, U. of the Republic, Uruguay, 1976. Asst. prof. U. Tex., Austin, 1961-63; assoc. dir. AAAS, Washington, 1963-68; assoc. prof. U. Md., College Park, 1968-76, assoc. dean/assoc. provost, 1971-76, prof., chair Catonsville, 1976-92, prof. emeritus, 1992—; prof. Baylor U., Waco, Tex., 1992—, dean, 1992-96. Author: Evaluation Model, 1965, Integrity and Higher Education, 2001, A Brief Primer on Teaching, 2002; co-author: Descriptive Data Analysis, 1991, Inferential Data Analysis, 1994; contbr. articles to profl. jours. Active adv. bd. Gov.'s Econ. Devel. Office, Annapolis, Md., 1988-91, Strecker Mus., Waco, 1992—, Lyric Opera of Waco, 1997—; worker Habitat for Humanity, Waco, 1996—. Fulbright-Hays fellow, 1967, 68, SEAMEO fellow, 1981, 82, OECD fellow, 1988. Fellow AAAS; mem. Nat. Hist. Soc. Democrat. Baptist. Avocations: bioinformatics, history of university presidents, gardening. E-mail: henry. Home: 400 Shadow Mt Waco TX 76712 Office: Baylor U PO Box 97356 Waco TX 76798-7356 E-mail: walbesser@baylor.edu.

WALBORSKY, HARRY M. chemistry educator, consultant; b. Lodz, Poland, Dec. 25, 1923; came to U.S., 1929; s. Israel and Sarah (Miedowicz) Wolborski; m. Paula Levitt, Nov. 28, 1970; children: Edwin, Eric, Lisa, Irene. BS, CCNY, 1945; PhD, Ohio State U., 1949. Rsch. assoc. Calif. Inst. Tech., Pasadena, 1948, UCLA Med. Sch., 1949-50, rsch. assoc. chemistry dept. UCLA, 1950; instr. Fla. State U., Tallahassee, 1950-51, asst. prof. chemistry, 1951-54, assoc. prof., 1954-59, prof., 1959—, Disting. prof., 1980—. Cons. Dow Chem. Co., Midland, Mich., 1956-72. Contbr. over 150 articles to profl. jours., 1949—. Recipient Sr. Scientist award von Humboldt Soc., Federal Republic of Germany, 1987; USPH fellow, 1951, Japanese Soc. for Promotion Sci. fellow, 1977. Mem. Am. Chem. Soc. (award Fla. chpt. 1978), N.Y. Acad. Sci., Chem. Soc. London, Sigma Xi, Phi Lambda Upsilon. Avocations: tennis, bridge. Office: Fla State U Dept Chemistry Tallahassee FL 32306

WALBRIDGE, WILLARD EUGENE, broadcasting executive; b. Republic, Pa., Mar. 11, 1913; s. Peter D. and Anna (Higbee) W.; m. Marietta H. Arner, Nov. 15, 1941; 1 child, Peter F. AB, U. Mich., 1936. Salesman, Sta. WWJ, Detroit, 1939-43; mgr. Sta. WWJ-TV, 1946-53; exec. v.p., gen. mgr. Sta. WJIM AM-TV, Lansing, Mich., 1953-54, Sta. KTRK-TV, Houston, 1954-70; sr. v.p. corp. affairs Capital Cities Communications, Inc., 1970-78, cons., 1978-81; sr. cons. Hill & Knowlton, Inc., Houston, 1987—. Dir. Houston Lighting & Power Co., Houston Industries, Inc., 1975-83, Internat. Systems & Controls, Inc., Tex. Commerce Med. Bank. Pres., Greater Houston Community Found.; bd. dirs. Salvation Army, Houston Area council Boy Scouts Am., Houston Grand Opera Assn.; mem. nat. bd. govs. ARC, 1974-80, also bd. dirs. Houston chpt., 1965-83, chmn. Houston chpt., 1972-75; chmn. bd. TV Info. Office, N.Y.C., 1965-70; trustee Mus. Broadcasting, 1978-82. Served from ensign to lt. USNR, 1943-46. Decorated Silver Star. Mem. Maximum Service Telecasters (dir. 1971-81), Houston Assn. Community TV (dir. 1972-82), Internat. Radio and TV Fedn. (dir. 1969-76), Nat. Assn. Broadcasters (dir. 1965-70, chmn. bd. 1970-71), U.S. C. of C. (dir. 1975-81), Houston C. of C. (dir. 1971-83, chmn. bd. 1975-76), Houston Council Fgn. Relations (chmn. 1977-78) Home and Office: Apt 207 2828 Bammel Ln Houston TX 77098-1129 Office: Hill & Knowlton Inc Niels Esperson Bldg 808 Travis St Fl 21 Houston TX 77002-5706

WALBURN, JOHN CLIFFORD, mental health services professional; b. Marion, Ind., Apr. 6, 1945; s. Rex Raymond and Norma Jane (Clifford) W.; m. Linda Sue Spall, Sept. 21, 1968 (div. Dec. 1987); 1 child, Geoffrey Jacob; m. Mitzi Lynn Johnson, June 20, 1992; 1 child, Abigail Rae. BS, Ball State U., 1969, MA, 1975; JD, I.U., Indpls., 1991. Bar: Ind. 1992. Planner Metro. Planning Commn., Muncie, Ind., 1970-72; dir. adult svcs. Del. County Assn. for Retarded, 1972-76; exec. dir. Fayette-Union Assn. for Retarded, Connersville, 1976-83; cons. Ind. Protection and Advocacy, Indpls., 1984-86; case mgr. Ind. Dept. Mental Health, 1986-87; exec. dir. Cardinal Svc. Mgmt., New Castle, 1987-2000; founding ptnr. Creative Human Resource Solutions, 1998—; exec. dir., adminstr. cmty. alternative Southeast Divsn. of Rescare, Jeffersonville, 2000—. Ofcl. Ind. Spl. Olympics, 1973—; chmn. Ind. Residential Mgmt. Com., 1991—; cons. DLG Cons. and Mktg. Svc., Ind., 1992; treas. Cmty. Action, So. Ind. Co-author: Feldman/Walburn Habilitation System, 1988; photo, drawing artist, 1978—. With USN, 1965-67. Named Ky. Col., Commonwealth of Ky., 1978. Mem. Am. Assn. Mental Retardation (bd. dirs. 1991-98), Ind. Assn. Rehab. Facilities (bd. dirs. 1996—, Pres.'s award 1998). Avocations: sports, playing/listening to music, movies, art, reading fiction. Home: 2559 So College Hill Dr Hanover IN 47243-9177 Office: RES-CARE Twenty-Five-O-One Pl 6200 E Hwy 62 Ste 675 Jeffersonville IN 47130

WALCH, TIMOTHY GEORGE, library administrator; b. Detroit, Dec. 6, 1947; s. George Louis Walch and Margaret Mary (Shields) DeSchryver; m. Victoria Irons, June 24, 1978; children: Thomas Emmet, Brian Edward. BA, U. Notre Dame, 1970; PhD, Northwestern U., 1975. Assoc. dir. Soc. Am. Archivists, Chgo., 1975-79; grants analyst Nat. Hist. Publ. Commn., Washington, 1979-81; budget analyst Nat. Archives, 1981-82, editor Prologue, 1982-88; asst. dir. Hoover Presdl. Libr., West Branch, Iowa, 1988-93, dir., 1993—. Author: Catholicism in America, 1989, Pope John Paul II, 1989, Parish School, 1996, others; editor: Herbert Hoover & Harry S Truman, 1992, Immigrant America, 1994, At the President's Side, 1997, Herbert Hoover & Franklin D. Roosevelt, 1998, and others; assoc. editor: U.S. Cath. Historian, 1983—; guest columnist Cedar Rapids Gazette, 1996—. Recipient Journalism award U.S. Cath. Press Assn., 1986, 1st place publ. award Nat. Assn. Govt. Communicators, 1988, U.S. Archivist's award Nat. Archives, 1993, Iowa Gov.'s Vol. award, 1995, 97, Dominican Veritas Forum award, 1996, Rogus Lecture, U. Dayton, 1999. Mem. Orgn. Am. Historians, U.S. Cath. Hist. Soc., Rotary Internat. Home: 65 N Westminster St Iowa City IA 52245-3833 Office: Hoover Presdl Libr PO Box 488 West Branch IA 52358-0488 E-mail: timothy.walch@nara.gov., Twalch47@aol.com.

WALCHER, ALAN ERNEST, lawyer; b. Chgo., Oct. 2, 1949; s. Chester R. and Dorothy E. (Kullgren) W.; children: Dustin Alan, Michael Alan, Christopher Ray. BS, U. Utah, 1971, cert. in internat. rels., 1971, JD, 1974. Bar: Utah 1974, U.S. Dist. Ct. Utah 1974, U.S. Ct. Appeals (10th cir.) 1977, Calif. 1979, U.S. Dist. Ct. (cen. dist.) Calif. 1979, U.S. Ct. Appeals (9th cir.) 1983, U.S. Dist. Ct. (ea., no., and so. dists.) Calif. 1994. Sole practice, Salt Lake City, 1974-79; ptnr. Costello & Walcher, L.A., 1979-85, Walcher & Scheuer, 1985-88, Ford & Harrison, 1988-91, Epstein Becker & Green, 1991—; judge pro tem Los Angeles Mcpl. Ct., 1986-91; dir. Citronia, Inc., Los Angeles, 1979-81. Trial counsel Utah chpt. Common Cause, Salt Lake City, 1978-79. Robert Mukai scholar U. Utah, 1971. Mem. Soc. Bar and Gavel (v.p. 1975-77), ABA, Fed. Bar Assn., Los Angeles County Bar Assn., Century City Bar Assn., Assn. Bus. Trial Lawyers, Phi Delta Phi, Owl and Key. Home: 17933 Sunburst St Northridge CA 91325-2848 Office: Epstein Becker & Green Ste 1650 Two Embarcadero Ctr San Francisco CA 94111-5994 E-mail: awalcher@ebglaw.com., alan1002@earthlink.net.

WALCOTT, CHARLES, neurobiology and behavior educator; b. Boston, July 19, 1934; s. Charles Folsom and Susan (Cabot) W.; m. Jane Clayton Taylor, Aug. 14, 1976; children: Thomas Stewart, Samuel Cabot. AB, Harvard U., 1956; PhD, Cornell U., 1959. Asst. prof. div. engring. and applied physics Harvard U., Cambridge, Mass., 1961-65; asst. prof. biology Tufts U., Medford, 1965-67; assoc. prof. dept. biology SUNY, Stony Brook, 1967-74, prof. dept. biology, 1974-81; prof., exec. dir. Cornell Lab. of Ornithology, Ithaca, N.Y., 1981-93, Louis Agassiz Fuertes dir., 1992-95; prof. neurobiology and behavior Cornell U., 1995—, dir. divsn. biol. scis., 1998-99, assoc. dean of the univ. faculty, 2000—. Cons., dir. Elem. Sci. Study, Watertown, Mass., 1961-67; dir. 3-2-1- Contact, Children's TV Workshop, N.Y.C., 1978—; dir. L.A. Fuertes. Contbr. many rsch. papers to sci. jours. Dir. sci. TV, Mass. Audubon, Lincoln, 1959-61. Avocations: gardening, sailing, photography. Home: 84 Besemer Hill Rd Ithaca NY 14850-9636 Office: Cornell U Dept Neurobiology Behavior W255 Seeley Mudd Hall Ithaca NY 14853 E-mail: cw38@cornell.edu.

WALCOTT, CHARLES ELIOT, political science educator; b. Pasadena, Calif., Apr. 19, 1943; s. Stuart and Mary (Eliot) W.; m. Anne Stillman, June 8, 1963 (div. Feb. 1990); children: Stuart S., Donald A.; m. Karen Marie Hult, June 16, 1990. AB, Occidental Coll., 1964; MA, U. Calif., Santa Barbara, 1965, PhD, 1971. Teaching asst. U. Calif., Santa Barbara, 1967-68; asst. prof. U. Minn., Mpls., 1968-78, assoc. prof., 1978-89; prof. Va. Tech. , Blacksburg, 1989—. Author: Simple Simulations, 1976; co-author: Governing Public Organizations, 1990, Governing the White House, 1995; editor: Simple Simulations II, 1980; assoc. editor Tchg. Polit. Sci., 1970-78; co-editor: Congress and the Presidency, 2001—; contbr. articles to profl. jours. Mem. Ramsey County Local Govt. Study Commn., St. Paul, 1973-74; treas. Linwood Booster Club, St. Paul, 1979-80; dir. St. Peter (Minn.) Soccer Assn., 1983-85. Recipient Morse Alumni award U. Minn., 1988. Mem. Am. Polit. Sci. Assn. (exec. com. undergrad. edn. sect. 1995-96), So. Polit. Sci. Assn. Episcopalian. Avocations: reading, golf, racquetball. Home: 2507 Manchester St Blacksburg VA 24060-8225 Office: Va Tech Inst Dept Polit Sci Blacksburg VA 24061 E-mail: cwalcott@vt.edu.

WALCOTT, DEXTER WINN, allergist; b. Greenville, Miss., Dec. 20, 1954; s. Charles DeWitt and Ruth LaFon (Stillions) W.; m. Virginia Shackelford, Sept. 20, 1980; children: Arrington, Winn. BA cum laude, U. Miss., 1977; postgrad., U. Miss. Sch. Medicine, 1978-82. Diplomate Am. Bd. Pediatrics, Am. Bd. Allergy and Immunology; lic. physician, Miss. Intern U. Miss. Med. Ctr., Jackson, 1982-83, resident in pediatrics, 1983-85; pvt. practice Oxford, Miss., 1985-91; with Miss. Asthma and Allergy Clinic, Jackson, 1993—, chief allergy and immunology, 1996—. Pres. house staff U. Med. Ctr., 1984-85, U. Med. Ctr. del. to Miss. State Med. Soc., 1985; ethics com. mem. North Miss. Retardation Ctr.; rev. physician Miss. Found. for Med. Care; participant vis. clinician program LeBonheur Children's Hosp.; mem. staff Miss. Bapt. Med. Ctr., Meth. Med. Ctr., River Oaks Hosp., St. Dominic's Med. Ctr., U. Med. Ctr. dept. pediatrics divsn. allergy/immunology; spkr. in field. Allergy/Immunology fellow La. State U. Med. Ctr., 1991-93. Fellow Am. Bd. Allergy and Immunology, Am. Bd. Pediatrics; mem. AMA, Am. Coll. Allergy/Immunology, Am. Acad. Allergy and Immunology, Am. Acad. Pediatrics, Miss. State Med. Assn., Miss. State Acad. Pediatrics, Cen. Miss. Med. Soc. (exec. com. 1994-95, 98-99), Ctrl. Miss. Pediatric Soc. (pres. 1996), Alpha Epsilon Delta, Order of Omega, Eta Sigma Phi, Beta Beta Beta, Sigma Alpha Epsilon (pres. 1976-77). Office: Miss Asthma & Allergy Clin 1600 N State St Jackson MS 39202-1689 E-mail: wvaw@aol.com., winn@aslancorp.com.

WALCOTT, ROBERT, healthcare executive, priest; b. Boston, July 31, 1942; s. Robert and Rosamond (Pratt) W.; m. Diane Palmer, Sept. 3, 1966; 1 child, Sara. BA, Coll. of Wooster, 1964; MDiv, Ch. Div. Sch., Berkeley, Calif., 1967; M Healthcare Adminstrn., Ohio State U., 1972. Ordained Episc. priest, 1968. Planning specialist Health Planning and Devel. Coun., Wooster, Ohio, 1972-73, asst. dir., 1974-75, St. Joseph Hosp., Lorain, 1975-78, assoc. dir., 1978-81; CEO, Lakeside Meml. Hosp., Brockport, N.Y., 1981-85; adminstr. Dent Neurologic Inst., Buffalo, 1986-87, Oak Hills Nursing Ctr., Lorain, 1994; pastor Ch. of Transfiguration, Buffalo, 1988-91, St. Michael and All Angels Ch., Uniontown, Ohio, 1991-93; adminstr.-in-tng. Chapel Hill Cmty., Canal Fulton, 1993; interim adminstr. Regina Health Ctr., Richfield, 1994-95; adminstr. Ohio Pythian Sisters Home, Sophia Huntington Parker Home, Medina, 1995-2001, Homestead I and II Nursing Homes, Painesville, Ohio, 2001—; longterm care ombudsman Luth. Met. Ministries, Cleve., 2002—. Housing com. Tremont Devel. Corp., Cleve., 1994—, bd. dirs., 1997—; steering com. Habitat for Humanity, Cleve., 1994-97; chair trustees Tremont West Devel. Corp., 2000-02 Fellow Am. Coll. Healthcare Execs. Democrat. Avocations: travel, reading. Home: 2173 W 7th St Cleveland OH 44113-3621 Office: Luth Met Ministries 2800 Euclid Ave Ste 200 Cleveland OH 44115 E-mail: bobwal31@aol.com.

WALCZAK, JOANNE CAROL, accountant; b. Buffalo, Feb. 8, 1959; d. Joseph Charles and Carol Dolores (Nicklas) Moorhouse; m. John T. Walczak, Aug. 2, 1980; 1 child, Bryan. BS in Acctg., SUNY, Geneseo, 1986; MBA in Fin. and Corp. Acctg., U. Rochester, 1991. CPA, N.Y. Staff acct. Genesee C.C., Batavia, N.Y., 1986-87; sr. acct. Strong Meml. Hosp., Rochester, 1987-88; ptnr. J&L Assocs., Batavia, 1988-93, Landers & Walczak, Batavia, 1993—. Adj. faculty Genesee C.C., 1988—. Bd. dirs. YWCA Genesee County, Inc., Batavia, 1989-90; mem. bus. devel. com. Genesee County C. of C., 1992—; v.p. Zonta Club of Batavia-Genesee, 1994-95, pres. 1996-97. Mem. N.Y. State Soc. CPAs. Roman Catholic. Avocations: golf, tennis, bowling, reading, crafts. Home: 16 Linwood Ave Batavia NY 14020-3714 Office: Landers & Walczak 12 Center St Batavia NY 14020-3204

WALD, ARNOLD, gastroenterologist; b. N.Y.C., June 10, 1942; s. Jack and Ruth (Fox) W.; m. Ellen Faith Rashkow, June 26, 1966; children: Elissa Karen, Eric Lawrence. BA, Colgate U., 1964; MD, SUNY, N.Y.C., 1968. Diplomate Am. Bd. Internal Medicine, Am. Bd. Gastroenterology; lic. physician, Pa. Intern Kings County Hosp., Bklyn., 1968-69, resident, chief resident, 1969-71; fellow in medicine Johns Hopkins Hosp., Balt., 1973-75; asst. prof. medicine U. Pitts. Sch. Medicine, 1978-83, assoc. prof., 1983-91, prof., 1991—; chief gastroenterology divsn. Montefiore U. Hosp., Pitts., 1991-95; assoc. chief divsn. gastroenterology and hepatology U. Pitts. Med. Ctr., 1993—2000, dir. fellowship tng. and edn. divsn. gastroenterology, hematology and nutrition, 1999—. Head gastroenterology unit Montefiore Hosp., Pitts., 1985-91; mem. adv. bd. Internat. Found. Bowel Dysfunction, 1992—; bd. dirs. Pitts. chpt. Nat. Found. Ileitis and Colitis, Inc., 1980-84. Contbr. articles to profl. jours and books. Maj. U.S. Army, 1971-73. Fellow ACP, Am. Coll. Gastroenterology (bd. trustees 1991-98, gov. western Pa. 1988-90, chmn. internat. rels. com. 1993); mem. Am. Gastroent. Assn., Ctrl. Soc. Clin. Rsch. (councillor 1985-90, chmn. gastroent. sect. 1989-90), Am. Motility Soc., Midwest Gut Club, Gastroenterology Rsch. Group, Pa. Soc. Gastroenterology. Democrat. Jewish. Avocations: tennis, reading, hiking. Home: 1143 Shady Ave Pittsburgh PA 15232-2809 Office: U Pitts Med Ctr 200 Lothrop St Pittsburgh PA 15213-2546

WALD, BARBARA ANN, software consultant, retired; b. Council Bluffs, Iowa, Mar. 9, 1935; d. Leon Shevah and Mildred Meyerson Frankel; m. Martin Wald, Aug. 3, 1958; children: Leah Wald Zollman, Marcie Sue, Adam David. AB, U. Chgo., 1957. Advt. copywriter Brandeis Dept. Store, Omaha, 1953; tchr. White Plains (N.Y.) Pub. Sch. System, 1957-58, West Allyce (Wis.) Pub. Sch. System, 1958-59, Akiba Jewish Day Sch., Chgo., 1961-64; writing tchr. Drexel U., Phila., 1971-72; owner, cons. Software Supporters, Merion, Pa., 1983-89. Author: Achieving Patient Power: One Family Masters the Medical Maze, 1992; contbr. articles to profl. pubs. Com. chmn. Religious Sch. Main Line Reform Temple, Wynnewood, Pa., 1974-77; active patroller Lower Merion Cmty. Watch, Ardmore, Pa., 1978-87; del. Fedn. Civic Assn., Lower Merion, 1984-91; v.p. Merion Civic Assn., 1981-84; bd. dirs. Smart Family Found., Inc., 1991-94, Auerbach Ctrl. Agy. for Jewish Edn., 1995-96. Mem. Ind. Computer Cons., Main Line Women's Bus. Network (charter), Home Based Bus. Profls. (pres. 1987-88), Nat. Better Bus. Bur. (arbitrator 1988-90). Avocations: computers, reading, theater, swimming.

WALD, BERNARD JOSEPH, lawyer; b. Bklyn., Sept. 14, 1932; s. Max and Ruth (Mencher) W.; m. Francine Joy Weintraub, Feb. 2, 1964; children—David Evan, Kevin Mitchell. B.B.A. magna cum laude, CCNY; J.D. cum laude, NYU, 1955. Bar: N.Y. 1955, U.S. Dist. Ct. (so. dist.) N.Y. 1960, U.S. Dist. Ct. (ea. dist.) N.Y. 1960, U.S. Ct. Appeals (2d cir.) 1960, U.S. Supreme Ct. 1971. Mem. Herzfeld & Rubin, P.C. and predecessor firms, N.Y.C., 1955—. Mem. ABA, N.Y. State Bar Assn., Assn. Bar City N.Y., N.Y. County Lawyers Assn. Office: Herzfeld & Rubin PC 40 Wall St Ste 5400 New York NY 10005-2301

WALD, FRANCINE JOY WEINTRAUB (MRS. BERNARD J. WALD), physicist, academic administrator; b. Bklyn., Jan. 13, 1938; d. Irving and Minnie (Reisig) Weintraub; m. Bernard J. Wald, FEb. 2, 1964; children: David Evan, Kevin Mitchell. Student, Bklyn. Coll., 1955-57; BEE, CCNY, 1960; MS, Poly. Inst. Bklyn., 1962, PhD, 1969. Engr. Remington Rand Univac divsn. Sperry Rand Corp., Phila., 1960; instr. Poly. Inst. Bklyn., 1962-64, adj. rsch. assoc., 1969-70; lectr. N.Y. C.C., Bklyn., 1969, 70; instr. sci. Friends Sem., N.Y.C., 1975-76, chmn. dept. sci., 1976-94; instr. sci., chmn. dept. sci. Nightingale-Bamford Sch., 1994-99. Adj. asst. prof. NYU. NDEA fellow, 1962-64. Mem. AAAS, Am. Phys. Soc., Am. Assn. Physics Tchrs., Assn. Tchrs. in Ind. Schs., N.Y. Acad. Scis., Nat. Sci. Tchrs. Assn., Sigma Xi, Tau Beta Pi, Eta Kappa Nu.

WALD, FRANCIS JOHN, state legislator; b. N.D., Apr. 8, 1935; s. Anton S. and Magdelena (Bosch) W.; m. Sharon Kay Mischel, 1961; children: Kirk James, Mark Allen, Jo Lynn, Laura, Cara, Maria, Michael, Joe. BSBA, U. N.D., 1959. Pres., ins. broker Wald Agy. Inc., Dickinson, N.D., 1973—; mem. from dist. 37 N.D. State Ho. of Reps., Bismarck, 1979-83, 85—, chmn. appropriations, edn. and environ. coms.; speaker of the ho. N.D. State Ho of Reps. Commr. Midwestern Higher Education Commission, 2001—. Mem. exec. com. Conf. of Ins. Legislators. Recipient Korean Occupation award. Mem. Dickenson C. of C. (past pres.), N.D. Profl. Ins. Agts., Am. Legion, Rotary, KC, Elks, Alpha Tau Omega. Address: 433 7th St E Dickinson ND 58601-4525*

WALD, FRITZ VEIT, solar energy corporation executive; b. Dieringhausen, Germany, Apr. 28, 1933; came to U.S., 1963; s. Eugen and Elli (Veit) W.; m. Doris Herberg, Mar. 21, 1959; children: Kristin Dorothea, Andrea Elisabeth, Katja Frederike. BS, Coll. Tech. Chemistry, Cologne, Germany, 1955. Chemist Ed. Dörrenberg Steelworks, Ründeroth, Fed. Republic Germany, 1955-57; research asst. Philips Cen. Lab., Aachen, Fed. Republic Germany, 1957-61; research metallurgist Frigistors Ltd., Montreal, Que., Can., 1961-63; sr. scientist, head materials sci. dept. Tyco Labs., Inc., Waltham, Mass., 1963-74; dir. research Mobil Solar Energy Corp., 1974-87, sr. sci. advisor, head advanced rsch. group, 1988-93; sr. sci. advisor ASE Ams. Inc., Billerica, 1994—, mgr. U.S. Office Space Products divsn., 1996—. Bd. dirs. Radiation Monitoring Devices Inc., Watertown, Mass.; past mem. bd. visitors Duke U. Sch. Engring. Contbr. over 85 sci. and tech. articles to profl. jours.; patentee in field. Pres. Luth. Ch., Waltham; del. Am. Luth. Ch. Peace Congregation, Wayland, Mass. Recipient IR100 award, Indsl. Research Mag., 1970. Mem. AIME (mem. Metals and Materials Soc.). Avocations: travel, especially to historic sites, stamp and letter collecting. Home: 4 Blossom Ln Wayland MA 01778-2802 E-mail: fvw@attbi.net.

WALD, MARLENA MALMSTEDT, health science librarian; b. Elkhorn, Wis., Feb. 7, 1950; d. Philip John and Evelyn Jean (Romeril) Malmstedt; m. Michael Leonard Wald, June 10, 1972. BA in Psychology, George Washington U., 1980; MLS, U. Md., 1986; MPH, Emory U., 1996. Program asst. NSF, Washington, 1980; reference asst. Johns Hopkins U., Balt., 1981-86; sci. reference libr. U. Ga., Athens, 1986-90, coord. collection devel., 1990-93; mem. mgmt. intern coun. on libr. resources reference dept. U. Ga. Sci. Libr., 1988-89; rsch. dir. dept. emergency medicine Emory U., Atlanta, 1996—. Video reviewer ABC-Clio publs., 1989-93; lectr. internet applications, resources for health scis. issues, and evidence-based medicine. Book reviewer health sci. materials. V.p. Clarke County Dem. Women, 1988-89. Mem. ALA (mem. com. 1986-88), APHA, Nat. Rural Health Assn., Am. Soc. Info. Sci., Phi Kappa Phi, Phi Mu. Democrat. Lutheran. Avocations: gardening, photography, graphic arts, politics. Home: 5015 Fawn Valley Dr Loganville GA 30052-3879

WALD, MARY S. retired risk management and personal finance educator; b. Baker, Oreg., June 17, 1943; d. Paul H. and Mary Elsie (Bartshe) Stoner; m. Lance Albert Wald, June 22, 1968. BA in English, Albertson Coll. of Idaho, Caldwell, 1966; MBA in Fin., Temple U., 1984. Tchr. Salt Lake City Bd. Edn., 1967-74; office mgr. Montgomery County Homemaker-Home Health Aide Svc., Inc., Blue Bell, Pa., 1975-82; adj. instr. risk mgmt. and personal fin. Temple U., Phila., 1984-99, ret., 1999. Co-author: Controlling Your Money, Step By Step, 1987. Named Outstanding Tchr. of Yr., Salt Lake City Bd. Edn., 1973-74. Mem. Am. Risk and Ins. Assn., Gamma Iota Sigma, Golden Key Nat. Honor Soc. (hon. mem.). Republican. E-mail: mwald2@juno.com.

WALD, MICHAEL LEONARD, economist; b. Balt., Jan. 5, 1951; s. Leonard Marvin and Frances (Kosinski) W.; m. Marlena Malmstedt, June 10, 1972. BA, Am. U., 1972. Mgr. Woodward and Lothrop Dept. Store, Washington, 1972-75, Hecht Co., Washington, 1975-76; store mgr. W.J. Sloane & Co., 1976-77; economist U.S. Bur. of Labor Stats., Balt., 1977-85, Washington, 1985-86, Atlanta, 1986-96, S.E. regional economist, 1996—. Lectr. on fed. compensation issues. Editl. bd. HR Atlanta, 1993-95; contbr. articles on compensation issues to profl. publs.; reviewer Monthly Labor Rev., 1992—; peer reviewer ACA Jour., 1995-99. Bd. dirs. Athens (Ga.) Habitat for Humanity, 1990-93; venue mktg. liaison mgr. 1996 Centennial Olympic Games. Recipient Commr.'s award for outstanding mgmt. performance, 2000, Sec.'s Exceptional Achievement award, 2001. Mem. World At Work (cert. compensation profl.), Atlanta Compensation Assn. (v.p. 1992, 93, 94, pres. 1996), Atlanta Econs. Club, Nat. Assn. Bus. Econs. (treas. 2002), Alpha Tau Omega. Avocations: reading, home improvement, travel, computers. Home: 5015 Fawn Valley Dr Loganville GA 30052-3879 Office: US Bur Labor Stats 61 Forsyth St SW Ste 7t50 Atlanta GA 30303-8817 E-mail: wald_m@bls.gov.

WALD, NIEL, public health educator; b. N.Y.C., Oct. 1, 1925; s. Albert and Rose (Fischel) W.; m. Lucienne Hill, May 24, 1953; children: David, Phillip. AB, Columbia U., 1945; MD, NYU, 1948. Sr. hematologist Atomic Bomb Casualty Commn., Hiroshima, Japan, 1954-57; head biologist health physics div. Oak Ridge Nat. Lab., 1957-58; med. rsch. and teaching specializing in radiation medicine and cytogenetics Pitts., 1958—; mem. faculty U. Pitts. Grad. Sch. Pub. Health and Med. Sch., 1958—, prof. radiation health, 1962-91, prof. environ. and occupational health, 1991—, prof. radiology, 1965—; prof. human genetics U. Pitts., 1991—; chmn. dept. radiation health U. Pitts. Grad. Sch. Pub. Health and Med. Sch., 1969-76, 77-89, chmn. dept. occupational health, 1975-76, chmn. dept. indsl. environ. health scis., 1976-77. Dir. radiation medicine dept. Presbyn.-Univ. Hosp., 1966—; med. dir. Clin. Cytogenetics Lab., U. Pitts., 1982-99, radiation cytogenetics cons., 1999—; dir. U.S. Dept. Energy postdoctoral fellowship program in radiation scis., 1997--; cons. U.S. Nuclear Regulatory Commn. Office of Nuclear Materials Safety and Safeguards, mem. adv. panel for decontamination of Three Mile Island Nuclear Power Sta. Unit 2, 1981-93, cons. adv. com. on reactor safeguards, 1989-94; mem. U.S. working group on health effects, U.S.-USSR Joint Coordinating Com. for Civilian Nuclear Reactor Safety, 1989-92; cons. USN, nuclear industries and utilities; chmn. radiol. health study sect. USPHS, 1967-71; mem. Nat. Coun. Radiation Protection and Measurements, 1969-81, consociate mem., 1981—; mem. Gov. Pa. Adv. Com. Atomic Energy Devel. and Radiation Control, 1966-84, chmn., 1974-76; mem. Pa. Dept. Environ. Protection adv. com. on low level radioactive waste disposal, 1985—. Contbr. numerous articles to sci. and med. publs. Served to capt. M.C. USAF, 1952-54. Recipient Health Physics Faculty Rsch. award U.S. Dept. Energy, 1992-95. Mem. Health Physics Soc. (pres. 1973-74), Am. Pub. Health Assn. (governing council 1971-73, program devel. bd. 1973-74), Radiation Rsch. Soc. (assoc. editor jour. 1965-68), Soc. Nuclear Medicine (assoc. editor jour. 1959-69), Am. Soc. Human Genetics, Am. Coll. Occupational & Environ Medicine, AAAS, AMA, Internat. Soc. Hematology. Achievements include research in the diagnosis and treatment of accidental human radiation injury, in human radiation dosimetry by automatic image analysis of radiation-induced chromosome aberrations, in the cytogenetics of murine radiation-induced leukemia and in health studies of irradiated human populations in U.S., Japan and Russia. Office: U Pitts Grad Sch Pub Health A-744 Crabtree Hl Pittsburgh PA 15261-0001 E-mail: wald@pitt.edu.

WALD, PATRICIA MCGOWAN, retired federal judge; b. Torrington, Conn., Sept. 16, 1928; d. Joseph F. and Margaret (O'Keefe) McGowan; m. Robert L. Wald, June 22, 1952; children: Sarah, Douglas, Johanna, Frederica, Thomas. BA, Conn. Coll., 1948; LLB, Yale U., 1951; HHD (hon.) , Mt. Vernon Jr. Coll., 1980; LLD (hon.) , George Washington Law Sch., 1983, CUNY, 1984; LLD (hon.) , Notre Dame U., John Jay Sch. Criminal Justice, Mt. Holyoke Coll., 1985, Georgetown U., 1987, Villanova U., Amherst Coll., N.Y. Law Sch., 1988, Colgate U., 1989, Hofstra U., 1991; LLD (hon.) , Hoffstra U., 1991; LLD (hon.) , New Eng. Coll., 1991, Vermont Law Sch., 1995, Yale U., 2001. Bar: D.C. 1952. Clk. to Hon. Jerome Frank U.S. Ct. Appeals, 1951—52; assoc. Arnold, Fortas & Porter, Washington, 1952—53; mem. D.C. Crime Commn., 1964—65; atty. Office of Criminal Justice, 1967—68, Neighborhood Legal Svc., Washington, 1968—70; co-dir. Ford Found. Project on Drug Abuse, 1970, Ctr. for Law and Social Policy, 1971—72, Mental Health Law Project, 1972—77; asst. atty. gen. for legis. affairs U.S. Dept. Justice, Washington, 1977—79; judge U.S. Ct. Appeals (D.C. cir.), 1979—99, chief judge, 1986—91; judge Internat. Criminal Tribunal for Former Yugoslavia, The Hague, Netherlands, 1999—2001. Author: Law and Poverty, 1965; co-author: Bail in the United States, 1964, Dealing with Drug Abuse, 1973; contbr. articles to profl. jours.; bd. editors: ABA Jour., 1978—86. Trustee Ford Found., 1972—77, Phillips Exeter Acad., 1975—77, Agnes Meyer Found., 1976—77, Conn. Coll., 1976—77; active Carnegie Council on Children, 1972—77. Mem.: ABA-Ctrl. and Ea. European Law Inst. (exec. bd. 1994—), Am. Acad. Arts and Scis., Am. Law Inst. (coun. mem. 1979—, exec. com. 1985—99, 2d v.p. 1988—93, 1st v.p. 1993—98), Phi Beta Kappa. Office: 2101 Connecticut Ave NW Washington DC 20008

WALD, QUENTIN ROOSEVELT, research aerodynamics and hydrodynamics engineer; b. Freeport, N.Y., June 4, 1920; s. Charles and Elizabeth (Kegel) W.; m. Eloise Muchmore, Jan. 24, 1953; children: Ansel, Brandon, Sabrina. SB, MIT, 1941, SM, 1960. Aeronautical engr. rsch. divsn. United Aircraft Cor., East Hartford, Conn., 1941-52; project engr. Dynametrics Corp., Burlington, Mass., 1954-60; chief hydrodynamicist elec. boat divsn. Gen. Dynamics corp., Groton, Conn., 1961-72; sr. hydrodynamicist Rohr Marine Inc., Chula Vista, Calif., 1975-79; prin. engr. elec. boat divsn. Gen. Dynamics Corp., Groton, Conn., 1979-85, ret., 1985. Cons. The Wright Experience, Warrenton, Va., 1997—. Author: The Wright Brothers As Engineers, An Appraisal, 2000; contbr. articles to sci. and profl. jours.; patentee in field. Avocations: reading, writing, sailing, aerodynamics research. Home: 102 Cape George Rd Port Townsend WA 98368 E-mail: grwld@Olypen.com.

WALD, RICHARD CHARLES, broadcasting executive; b. N.Y.C. s. Joseph S. and Lily (Forstate) W.; m. Edith May Leslie; children: Matthew Leslie, Elizabeth Tole, Jonathan Simon. BA, MA, Columbia U.; AB, Clare Coll., Cambridge. From reporter to mng. editor N.Y. Herald Tribune, 1955-66; asst. mng. editor Washington Post, 1967; exec. v.p. Whitney Communications Corp., N.Y.C., 1968; pres. NBC News, 1968-77; sr. v.p. ABC News, 1978; prof. Columbia U., 1999. Chmn. bd. Columbia Daily Spectator. Annotator: (with James Bellows) The World of Jimmy Breslin, 1967. Office: ABC News 47 W 66th St New York NY 10023-6290 E-mail: richard.c.wald@abc.com.

WALD, SHERRI SUNDEM, lawyer; b. Sioux Falls, S.D., Jan. 17, 1957; d. Richard and Carol Marie Sundem; m. James Michael Wald, Sept. 17, 1988; 1 child, Sigrid Sundem Wald. BA, U. S.D., 1979, JD, 1983. Bar: S.D. 1983, U.S. Dist. Ct. S.D. 1983, U.S. Ct. Appeals (8th cir.) 1983. Law clerk S.D. Cir. Ct. (6th cir.), Pierre, S.D., 1983-84; asst. atty. gen. Office of Atty. Gen., 1984—. Mem. S.D. State Criminal Law Com. Co-chair LWV, Pierre, 1989-90; edn. com. Luth. Meml. Ch., Pierre, 1997, 2000; bd. dirs. Short Grass Arts Coun., 2000-02, Capital City Childrens Choir, 2000-02. Mem. State Bar S.D. (criminal law com. 1984-2002), AAUW, Nat. Assn. State Medicaid Fraud Control Units (exec. com. 1988-90), Nat. Assn. State Bd. Accountancy (chair legal com. 1997). Home: 512 N Grand Ave Pierre SD 57501-2116 Office: Office Atty Gen 500 E Capitol Ave Pierre SD 57501-5070 E-mail: sherri.wald@state.sd.us.

WALD, SYLVIA, artist; b. Phila., Oct. 30, 1915; Ed., Moore Inst. Art, Sci. and Industry. One-woman shows include U. Louisville, 1945, 49, Kent State Coll., 1945, Nat. Serigraph Soc., 1946, Grand Central Moderns, N.Y.C., 1957, Devorah Sherman Gallery, Chgo., 1960, New Sch., 1967, Book Gallery, White Plains, N.Y., 1968, Benson Gallery, Bridgehampton, L.I., 1977, Knoll Internat., Munich, 1979, Amerika Havs, Munich, 1979, Aaron Berman Gallery, N.Y.C., 1981, Hirschltadler Gallery, 1994, New Britain (Conn.) Mus., 1994, Dongah Art Gallery, Seoul, Korea, 1995, Hanlim Art Gallery, Daejun, 1995-96, Kwanju City Art Mus, Pusanm Korea, Dong Shin U., Kwangju, 1996, Chosun U. Mus., Kwanju City, 2001, Chosun Univ. Mus. Art, Kwangsu, Korea, 2002; exhibited in group shows at Nat. Sculpture Soc., 1940, Sculpture Internat., Phila., 1940, Chgo. Art Inst., 1941, Bklyn. Mus., 1975, Library of Congress, 1943, 52, 58, Smithsonian Instn., 1954, Internat. Print Exhbn., Salzburg and Vienna, 1952, 2d Sao Paulo Biennial, 1953, N.Y. Cultural Center, 1973, Mus. Modern Art, N.Y.C., 1975, Benson Gallery, Bridgehampton, L.I., 1982, Dumon-Landis Gallery, New Brunswick, N.J., 1982-83, Suzuki Gallery, N.Y.C., 1982, Sid Deutch Gallery, N.Y.C., 1983, Aaron Berman Gallery, N.Y.C., 1983, Full House Gallery, Kingston, N.J., 1984, Nabi Gallery, Sag Harbor, N.Y., 1989, Worcester Mus., 1991, Boston Mus. Fine Arts, 1991, Hirschl & Adler Gallery, N.Y.C., 1993, Parrish Mus., Louthampton, 2002, others; represented in permanent collections Aetna Oil Co., Am. Assn. U. Women, Ball State Tchrs. Coll., Bibliotheque Nat., Paris, Bklyn. Mus., Howard U., State U. Iowa, Library of Congress, U. Louisville, Nat. Gallery, Mus. Modern Art, Phila. Mus., N.C. Mus., Rose Mus. Art at Brandeis U., Whitney Mus., N.Y.C., Finch Coll. Mus., N.Y.C., U. Nebr., Ohio U., U. Okla., Princeton, Victoria and Albert Mus., Walker Gallery, Worcester (Mass.) Art Mus., Guggenheim Mus., N.Y.C., Grunewald Mus., UCLA, Rutgers Mus., N.J., Aschenbach Collection Mus., San Francisco, Grunewald Coll. Mus. UCLA; acquisitions Yale U. Art Gallery, 1998, Cleve. Mus., 1998; Contbr. articles to profl. jours. Address: 417 Lafayette St New York NY 10003-7005

WALDAUER, CHARLES, economics educator; b. N.Y.C., July 7, 1935; s. Sidney and Fredericka (Levinsky) W.;m. Karen Gordon, May 8, 1958; children: Jan, Kim. BS in Econs. cum laude, CCNY, 1957; PhD in Econs., Syracuse U., 1969. Prof. econs. Sch. Mgmt. Widener U., Chester, Pa., 1968—, head dept., 1987-95, chmn. social sci., 1972-75. Pres. lectr. Widener U., Chester, Pa., 1983-94. Assoc. editor The Am. Economist, 1980-83; contbr. articles to profl. jours. Treas. Media (Pa.) Upper Providence Free Library, 1985-94. Maxwell fellow, univ. fellow Syracuse U., 1960, 61-63, Ford Found. fellow, 1963-64. Mem. Am. Econs. Assn., Nat. Tax Assn., Midwest Econs. Assn., Assn. for Study Grants Economy, Taxation with Representation, Omicron Delta Epsilon, Pi Gamma Mu. Office: Widener U Sch Mgmt Dept Econs Chester PA 19013

WALDBAUER, GILBERT PETER, entomologist, educator; b. Bridgeport, Conn., Apr. 18, 1928; s. George Henry and Hedwig Martha (Gribisch) W.; m. Stephanie Margot Stiefel, Jan. 2, 1955; children: Gwen Ruth, Susan Martha. Student, U. Conn., 1949-50; BS, U. Mass., 1953; MS, U. Ill., Urbana, 1956, PhD, 1960. Instr. entomology U. Ill., Urbana, 1958-60, asst. prof., 1960-65, assoc. prof., 1965-71, prof., 1971—, prof. agrl. entomology Coll. Agr., 1971—, prof. emeritus, 1995—. Sr. scientist Ill. Natural History Survey; vis. scientist ICA, Palmira, Colombia, 1971; vis. sr. scientist Internat. Rice Rsch. Inst., 1978-79; cons. AID, 1985; vis. prof. U. Philippines, 1978-79. Author: Insects Through the Seasons, 1996, The Handy Bug Answer Book, 1998, The Birder's Bug Book, 1998, Millions of Monarchs, Bunches of Beetles, 2000; contbg. author: Insect and Mite Nutrition, 1972, Introduction to Insect Pest Management, 1975, Evolution of Insect Migration and Diapause, 1978, Sampling Methods in Soybean Entomology, 1980, Mimicry and the Evolutionary Process, 1988, Ann. Rev. Entomology, 1991; contbr. numerous articles to profl. jours. Served with AUS, 1946-47, PTO. Grantee Agrl. Rsch. Svc. USDA, 1966-71, 83-90, Nat. Geog. Soc., 1972-74, NSF, 1976-79, 82-90. Mem. AAAS, Sigma Xi, Phi Kappa Phi. Home: 807A Ramblewood Ct Savoy IL 61874-9568 Office: U Ill Dept Entomology 320 Morrill Hall Urbana IL 61801

WALDBAUM, ALAN G. lawyer; b. Seattle, Dec. 31, 1968; s. Kenneth W. and Susan G. Waldbaum. BBA, U. Wash., 1991; JD, U. Mich., 1994. Bar: Wash. 1994. Assoc. Davis Wright Tremaine, Seattle, 1994-98; assoc. counsel Teledesic, 1999-2001; in-house counsel Microsoft Corp., 2001—. Bd. dirs. Jewish Family Svc., Seattle, 1996-2001; bd. trustees Alpha Mu chpt. of Zeta Beta Tau, 2000—. Mem. Wash. State Bar Assn., King County Bar Assn. Avocations: screenwriting, basketball, skiing, swimming, drums. Office: 1010 Microsoft Way Redmond WA 98052

WALDBAUM, JANE COHN, art history educator; b. Jan. 28, 1940; d. Max Arthur and Sarah (Waldstein) Cohn. BA, Brandeis U., 1962; MA, Harvard U., 1964, PhD, 1968. Rsch. fellow in classical archaeology Harvard U., Cambridge, Mass., 1968-70, 72-73; from asst. prof. to assoc. prof. U. Wis., Milw., 1973-84, prof. art history, 1984—2002, chmn. dept., 1982-85, 86-89, 91-92, adj. prof. anthropology, 2002—. Dorot rsch. prof. W.F. Albright Inst. Archaeol. Rsch., Jerusalem, 1990-91; vis. scholar Hebrew U. Jerusalem, 1989-91. Author: From Bronze to Iron, 1978, Metalwork from Sardis, 1983; author (with others), co-editor: Sardis Report I, 1975; mem. editl. bd. Bull. Am. Schs. Oriental Rsch., 1994-98, Near Eastern Archaeology, 2000—; contbr. numerous articles to profl. jours. Woodrow Wilson Found. fellow, dissertation fellow, 1962-63, 65-66, NEH postdoctoral rsch., Jerusalem, 1989-90; grantee Am. Philos. Soc., 1972, NEH, summer 1975, U. Wis.-Milw. Found., 1983. Mem. Am. Schs. Oriental Rsch., Soc. for Archaeol. Sci., Israel Exploration Soc., Archaeol. Inst. Am. (exec. com. 1975-77, chmn. com. on membership programs 1977-81, nominating com. 1984, chmn. com. on lecture program 1985-87, acad. trustee 1993-98, 1st v.p. 1999—2002, pres. 2003-, com. profl. responsibilities 1993—, fellowships com. 1993-99, gold medal com. 1993-99, chair 1996-97, Near East Archaeology com. 1993—, chair ann. meeting com. 1999—2002, chair regional meetings com. 1999—2002, pers. com., governance com., devel. com., fin. com.), W.F. Albright Inst. Archaeol. Rsch. (trustee 1996—, mem. governance com. 1996—), Wis. Soc. Jewish Learning (trustee 1993-99), Milw. Soc. Archaeol. Inst. (bd. dirs., pres. 1983-85, 91-95, 97-99), Phi Beta Kappa. Office: U Wis Dept Anthropology PO Box 413 Milwaukee WI 53201-0413 E-mail: JCW@uwm.edu.

WALDECK, JOHN WALTER, JR. lawyer; b. Cleve., May 3, 1949; s. John Walter Sr. and Marjorie Ruth (Palenschat) W.; m. Cheryl Gene Cutter, Sept. 10, 1977; children: John III, Mathew, Rebecca. BS, John Carroll U., 1973; JD, Cleve. State U., 1977. Bar: Ohio 1977. Product applications chemist Synthetic Products Co., Cleve., 1969-76; assoc. Arter & Hadden, 1977-85, ptnr., 1986-88, Porter, Wright, Morris and Arthur, Cleve., 1988-90, ptnr. in charge, 1990-96; ptnr. Walter & Haverfield, 1996—. Bd. advisors Litigation Mgmt., Inc., 2000—. Chmn. Bainbridge Twp. Bd. Zoning Appeals, Chagrin Falls, Ohio, 1984-94; trustee Greater Cleve. chpt. Lupus Found. Am., 1978-91, sec., 1979-86; trustee LeBlond Housing Corp., Cleve., 1990-96, sec., 1996, Univ. Circle, Inc., 1993-97, Fairmount Ctr. for Performing and Fine Arts, Novelty, Ohio, 1993-96, sect., 1994-95; bd. dirs. Geauga County Mental Health Alcohol and Drug Addiction Svc. Bd., Chardon, Ohio, 1988-97, treas., 1991-93, vice-chmn., 1993-95, chmn., 1995-97; mem. bd. advisors Palliative Care Svcs., Cleve. Clinic Cancer Ctr., 1989-91. Mem. Ohio State Bar Assn. (real property sect. bd. govs. 1992), Greater Cleve. Bar Assn. (real property, corp. banking sect, co-chair real estate law inst. 1990, 95, 96). Roman Catholic. Avocations: beekeeping, gardening, jogging. Home: 18814 Rivers Edge Dr W Chagrin Falls OH 44023-4968 Office: Walter & Haverfield 50 Public Square 1300 Terminal Tower Cleveland OH 44113 E-mail: jwaldeck@walterhav.com.

WALDEGRAVE, LORD (LORD WALDEGRAVE OF NORTH HILL), financial services company executive; b. Aug. 15, 1946; s. Earl Waldegrave; m. Caroline Burrows, 1977; 4 children. Grad., Corpus Christi Coll., U. Oxford, Eng. Fellow All Souls Coll., U. Oxford, Eng., 1971-86; mem. ctrl. policy rev. staff Cabinet Office, 1971-73; mem. polit. staff Office of Prime Min., London, 1973-74; head Office Leader of Opposition, 1974-75; justice of peace Inner London Juvenile Ct., 1975-79; M.P. for Bristol West Ho. of Commons, London, 1979-97; parliamentary under sec. state Brit. Dept. Edn. and Sci., 1981-83, Brit. Dept. Environ., 1983-85, min. state for environ. and countryside, 1985-87, min. state for planning, 1986-88, min. state for housing, 1987-88; min. state Fgn. and Commonwealth Office, 1988-90; sec. state for health, 1990-92; chancellor Duchy of Lancaster, 1992-94; min. agr., fisheries and food London, 1994-95; chief sec. to treasury, 1995-97; exec. dir. Dresdner Kleinwort Benson, 1998—. Dir. Bristol & West, p.l.c., FLIT plc, Waldegrave Farms Ltd.; chrmn. The Rhode4s Trust, Henry Sotheran Ltd. Author: The Binding of Leviathan, 1977. Kennedy Fellow Harvard U., U.S.A., Disting. Fellow Austria Coll. Mem. Beefsteak Club, Pratt's Club, Clifton Club (Bristol). Office: Dresdner Kleinwort Wasserstein 20 Fenchurch St London EC3 P3DB England

WALDEN, ALICE, artist, educator; b. Billings, Mont., June 14, 1943; d. George John and Lilly (Sevick) Martin; m. Dee Edward Walden, June 23, 1962; children: San Dee Walden Russell, Kevin. BA, Mont. State U., 1980. Cert. art tchr., Mont. Bookkeeper 1st State Bank, Livingston, Mont., 1961-62, Gallatin Farmers Co., Bozeman, 1966-71; acctg. asst. Rowland Thomas & Co., Miles City, 1972-78, Don Winslow & Assocs., Miles City, 1979-80; home bound tchr. Sch. Dist. # 1, 1980-81, gifted edn. tchr., 1981-86, art tchr., 1986—; profl. artist, 1991—; owner, mgr. Wool House Gallery, 1994—. Executed various steel sculptures in pvt. collections, N.D., Wyo., Mont., Wash., Calif. Home: 419 N 7th St Miles City MT 59301-3117

WALDEN, CATHERINE JANE, not-for-profit developer, social worker, consultant; b. Fayetteville, Ark., Mar. 9, 1955; d. Betty Louise and Richard Marshall Walden. B in Social Work, U. Ark., Little Rock, 2000, MPA, 2002; cert. in life care planning, U. Fla./Intelicus, 2002. Mdse. buyer Campbell-Bell Dept. Stores, Fayetteville, Ark., 1979—81; asst. store mgr. M.M. Cohn's Dept. Store, Memphis, 1981—85; inventory shortage control mgr. Goldsmith's Dept. Stores, 1985—90; assoc. dir. Am. Amputee Found., Inc., Little Rock, 1991—2001, exec. dir., 2001—, life care planner, 2002. Vice-chair Ark. Coalition Choice, Little Rock, 1993—95; chair Com. Women's Concerns, 1999; treas. Rape Crisis, Inc., 2001—02, adv., 1997—2002; treas. Ark. Liberty Alliance, 1995—95; project bus. leader Jr. Acheivement/Memphis City Sch. Sys., 1987—89; oncology ward vol. Meth. Hosp., 1985—86. Mem.: ASPA, NASW, Pi Alpha Alpha. Office: Am Amputee Found Inc 700 S Pine St Little Rock AR 72205 Office Fax: 501-666-8367.

WALDEN, DANIEL, humanities and social sciences educator; b. Phila., Aug. 1, 1922; s. Benjamin and Reba (Freedman) Weinroth; m. Beatrice Schulman, Oct. 12, 1957; children: Moss Carl, Ruth E. Walden Turek. BA, CCNY, 1959; MA, Columbia U., 1961; PhD, NYU, 1964. Lectr. Queens Coll., N.Y.C., 1960-63; asst. prof. Mich. State U., East Lansing, 1963-66; prof. Pa. State U., University Park, 1966—. Co-editor: On Being Black, 1970, W.E.B. DuBois, The Crisis Writings, 1972, On Being Jewish, 1974, Twentieth Century American Jewish Fiction Writers, 1984, The World of Chaim Potok, 1985, The World of Cynthia Ozick, 1987, Bernard Malamud: in Memoriam, 1988, American Jewish Poets: The Roots and the Stems, 1990, Herbert Gold and Beyond, 1991, Jewish Identity: From Midrash to Modernity, 1991, American Jewish Women Writers, 1992, The Changing Mosaic: Cahan to Malamud and Ozick, 1993, New Voices in an Old Tradition, 1994, Bernard Malamud's Literary Imagination: A New Look, 1995, The Tragedy of Joy, 1996, A Significant Pattern, 1997 (ALA Disting. award 1997, 98), The Resonance of Twoness, 1998, The Ties that Bind, 1999, The Silver Mosaic, 2000, Conversations with Chaim Potok, 2001. Mem. ALA, MLA (MELUS pres. 1977-78, Disting. MELUS award 1993), N.E. MLA (pres. 1991-92, Disting. Svc. award 1994), Soc. Am. Jewish Lit., Am. Studies Assn., Am. Culture Assn., Soc. for Utopian Studies. Democrat. Jewish. Avocations: reading, music, photography. Office: Dept English/Am Studies Pa State U University Park PA 16802 E-mail: dxw8@psu.edu.

WALDEN, DAVID MICHAEL, historian, consultant; b. Omaha, Nov. 6, 1947; s. Blake Chester and Charlotte Walden. BS, Iowa State U., 1969; MA, U. Guam, Mangilao, 1979, Brigham Young U., 1989. Cert. tchr., Utah. Tchr. biology and history pvt. and pub. schs., Guam, 1974-79; historian, writer, 1982—. Adj. instr. U.S. history Salt Lake C.C., Salt Lake City, 1993—; bd. editors Assn. for History of Chiropractic, 1989-93; mem. history com. Utah Med. Assn., Salt Lake city, 1989-91; rschr. KUTV documentary A Century of Smog, 1991. Author: 7 oral biographies, (100 hist. profiles) International Directory of Company Histories, 1991—, Protestant and Catholic Churches of Provo, 1986, A Guide to Utah Medical History, 2001; co-author: Miles Goodyear and His Historic Cabin, 1995, (50 co. profiles) Centennial Utah, 1995, St. Mark's Hospital, 1872-1997, 1999; editor: As a Rose, 1982, Out of Obscurity, 1985; contbr. articles to profl. publs. Sec. West Liberty Neighborhood Assn., Salt Lake City, 1996-99; voting dist. chair, county and state del. Utah Rep. Party, Provo and Salt Lake City, 1984—. Grantee Charles Redd Ctr. for Western Studies, 1987, Brigham Young U. Ctr. for Family and Cmty. History, 1988; Folklore scholar Utah Arts Coun., 1983. Mem. League Utah Writers, Utah State Hist. Soc., History of Medicine in Utah, Inc. (founder, sec.), Oral History Assn., Beehive Intermountain Naval Acad. (sec. alumni chpt. 1994-96), Chi Omicron Gamma. Mem. Lds Ch. Avocations: chess, photography, collecting shells, swimming, collecting jokes. Home and Office: 4981 S 1645 E Salt Lake City UT 84117-5972 E-mail: davidmwalden@aol.com.

WALDEN, GREG, congressman; b. The Dalles, Oreg., Jan. 10, 1957; m. Mylene Walden; 1 child. BS in Journalism, U. Oreg., 1981. Owner Columbia Gorge Broadcasters, Inc., The Dalles, 1986—; mem. Oreg. Ho. of Reps., 1989-95, house majority leader, 1991-93; mem. Oreg. Senate, 1995-97, asst. majority leader, 1995-97; press sec., chief of staff Congressman Denny Smith, Washington, 1981-86; mem. U.S. Congress from 2d Oreg. dist., 1999—, mem. com. on energy and commerce, com. on resources. Dir. Columbia Bancorp. Bd. dirs., exec. com. Assoc. Oreg. Industires; bd. dirs. Oreg. Health Scis. Found.; former dir. Hood River Meml. Hosp. Named Outstanding Young Oregonian, Oreg. Jaycees, 1991, Legislator of the Yr., Nat. Rep. Legislators Assn., 1993. Mem. Hood River C. of C., Nat. Fedn. Ind. Bus., Elks, Rotary. Republican. Office: US Ho Reps 1404 Longworth HOB Washington DC 20515 also: 843 E Main St Ste 400 Medford OR 97504-7137 E-mail: greg.walden@mail.house.gov.*

WALDEN, JAMES WILLIAM, accountant, educator; b. Jellico, Tenn., Mar. 5, 1936; s. William Evert and Bertha L. (Faulkner) W.; m. Eva June Selvia, Jan. 16, 1957 (dec. Aug. 1988); 1 child, James William; m. Hattie Nan Lamb, Jan. 6, 1990 (div. June 1992); m. Janet Faulkner, Aug. 12, 1993 (div. May 2001). BS, Miami U., Oxford, Ohio, 1963; MBA, Xavier U., Cin., 1966. CPA, Ohio. Tchr. math. Middletown (Ohio) City Sch. Dist., 1963-67, Fairfield (Ohio) High Sch., 1967-69; instr. accounting Sinclair Community Coll., Dayton, Ohio, 1969-72, asst. prof., 1972-75, assoc. prof., 1975-78, prof., 1978-89, prof. emeritus, 1991—. Cons., public acct.; mem. adj. faculty in acctg. Capital U., 1980—. Group comdr., fin. officer, chief staff Ohio Wing, CAP. Served with USAF, 1954-59. Mem. Butler County Torch Club, Pub. Accts. Soc. Ohio (pres. S.W. chpt. 1985-86), Inst. Mgmt. Accts., Nat. Soc. Pub. Accts., Greater Hamilton Estate Planning Coun., Ohio Soc. CPAs, Springboro C. of C. (bd. dirs., treas.), Am. Legion (life), Rotary Club, Lions Club, Beta Alpha Psi. Home: PO Box 469 Springboro OH 45066-0469 Office: Sinclair C C 265 N Main St Springboro OH 45066-9255

WALDEN, JOSEPH LAWRENCE, career officer; b. Paducah, Ky., Oct. 2, 1956; s. Thomas Lorenzo and Betty Jo (Miller) W.; m. Julia Kay Johnson, Oct. 9, 1982; children: Amber Marie, Bobbi Michelle. BS in Rural Sociology, N.C. State U., 1978; MBA, Fla. Inst. Tech., Melbourne, 1988; MS in Sys. Mgmt., Fla. Inst. Tech., 1989; grad., USAF Command and Staff Coll., 1990, U.S. Army/Command Gen. Staff Coll., 2001. Commd. U.S. Army, 1978, advanced through grades col., to date, supply platoon leader 25th Inf. divsn. Hawaii, 1979-81, supply control officer, 1981-82, installation supply officer Signal Sch. Ga., 1983, brigade logistics officer 2d Signal Brigade, 1983-84; co. comdr. Co. B, 3rd Batallion, 2d Signal Brigade, 1984-86; logistics plans officer Combat Devel., Quartermaster Sch., Ft. Lee, Va., 1988-89; chief gen. support U.S. Army Quartermaster Sch., 1989-91; assigned to U.S. Army Command and Gen. Staff Coll., Ft. Leavenworth, Kans., 1991-92; exec. officer 19th Corps Materiel Mgmt. Ctr., Wiesbaden, Germany, 1992-94; chief supply mgmt. 3D Corps Support Command, 1994-95; comdr. Materiel Mgmt. Ctr., Ft. Irwin, Calif., 1995-97; program mgr. Logistics Reengring., Ft. Lee, Va., 1997-99; sr. fellow adv. operational art Ft. Leavenworth, Kans., 1999-2000; mem. faculty U.S. Army Sch. Advanced Mil. Studies, 2000-2001; comdr. nat. tng. Ctr. Theater Support Command, Fort Irwin, Calif., 2001—. Mem. adj. faculty St. Leo Coll., Ft. Lee, 1988-91; mem. faculty City Coll. of Chgo., 1994-95; pres. Walden Fitness Systems, Ft. Leavenworth, 1984-92. Contbr. articles to profl. jours. Mem. Bldg. Code Appeals Bd., City of Hopewell, 1988-91; vol. staff Negro Leagues Baseball Mus., Kansas City, Mo., 2001. Armed Forces Powerlifting Champion, 1983, Va. State Powerlifting Champion, 1990, Kans. State Powerlifting Champion, 1992, Nat. Powerlifting Champion, 1992, European Armed Forces Powerlifting Champion, 1993, 94. Mem. APICS, Internat. Soc. of Logistics, Warehousing Edn. and Rsch. Coun. (mem. edn. com.), Va. Assn. of U.S. Powerlifting Fedn. (pres. 1989-91), U.S. Golf Assn., Am. Sunbathing Assn., Fellowship Christian Athletes, Fla. Sheriffs Assn., San Diego Zool. Soc., Assn. Quartermasters, Mus. Tolerance, Save the Manatee Club. Republican. Methodist. Avocations: powerlifting (1992 Nat. Champion), naturist, golfing. E-mail: joewalden@aol.com.

WALDEN, PHILIP MICHAEL, recording company executive, publishing company executive; b. Greenville, S.C., Jan. 11, 1940; s. Clemiel Barton and Carolyn Hayes (McClendon) W.; m. Peggy Hackett, Sept. 13, 1969; children: Philip Michael, Amantha Starr. AB in Econs., Mercer U., 1962. Pres. Phil Walden & Assocs., 1961, Capricorn Records, Inc., 1969—. Campaign chmn. Macon Muscular Dystrophy Assn., 1975; chmn. Macon Heritage Found.; mem. In-Town Macon Neighborhood Assn.; Mem. nat. finance com. Jimmy Carter for Pres.; mem. Com. for Preservation of the White House; mem. nat. adv. bd. NORML; bd. dirs. Brandywine Conservancy; mem. Presdl. Inaugural Com., 1977; trustee Ga. Trust for Historic Preservation., Mercer Univ. Press, Otis Redding Meml. Found.; founder Otis Redding Scholarship Fund, Mercer U., Phil Walden scholarship; bd. dirs. Atlanta Preservation Ctr., Otis Redding Found. Served to 1st lt. Adj. Gen. Corps AUS, 1963-65. Recipient Gold and Platinum Record awards, pub. awards; Big Bear award Mercer U., 1975; Martin Luther King, Jr. Humanitarian award, 1977; Human Relations award Am. Jewish Com., 1978 Mem. Common Cause, Middle Ga. Hist. Soc., Nat. Assn. Rec. Arts and Scis., Rec. Industry Assn. Am. (dir.), Nat. Assn. Rec. Merchandisers, Phi Delta Theta Alumni Assn.; Atlanta Coll. of Art, Camp Sunshine, Ga. Trust for Historic Preservation, Capitol City Club. Home: 2740 Habersham Rd NW Atlanta GA 30305-2938

WALDER, DEBBY JEAN, program director, quality manager, nursing service administrator, nurse, educator; b. Watertown, S.D., Nov. 25, 1947; d. James Russell and Gladys Elizabeth (Owen) W. BSN with honors, S.D. State U., 1970; MSN, U. Minn., 1977. Staff nurse VAMC, Mpls., 1970-71, instr., 1971-75, coord., 1976-77, trainee-assoc. chief nursing svc. for edn., 1977, assoc. chief nursing svc. for edn. Wilmington, Del., 1977-80, Richmond, Va., 1980-83, chief nurse svc. Huntington, W.Va., 1983-85, Cin., 1985-87; quality mgmt. coord. VA Hosp., Madison, Wis., 1987-91; clin. program mgr., dir. risk mgmt. VA Hdqrs., Washington, 1991-96, dir. risk mgmt., program dir. ext. peer rev. program, 1995—. Adj. faculty Med. Coll. Va., Richmond, 1980-82; basic cardiac life support instr.-trainer Am. Heart Assn., Richmond, 1980-83; clin. prof. Marshall U. Sch. Nursing, Huntington, 1983-85. Mem. task force Richmond Area chpt. Am. Heart Assn. Recipient Outstanding Cardiopulmonary Resuscitation Instr. award Richmond Area chpt. Am. Heart Assn., 1982, Achievement award VAMC, Richmond, 1983, Recognition award for excellence in mgmt., VAMC, Huntington, 1983, Spl. Contbn. award, 1992-95, 98, 99, Unsung Heroes award, 1994; Bush Found. fellow, 1975-76. Mem. Nat. Assn. Quality Assurance Profls., Phi Kappa Phi, Sigma Theta Tau (Phi chpt. scholar 1969-70), Nat. Assn. Quality Assurance Profls., Pi Lambda Theta. Roman Catholic. Office: VA Cen Office Office Quality Mgmt 810 Vermont Ave NW Washington DC 20420-0001

WALDER, NOELEEN GWYNAETH, lawyer; b. Easton, Conn., June 8, 1970; d. Eugene and Loretta W. BA with distinction, Stanford U., 1992; JD cum laude, Harvard U., 1995. Bar: N.Y. Policy advisor N.Y. State Assembly, Rochester, 1995; assoc. Winthrop, Stimson, Putnam & Roberts, N.Y.C., 1996-98, Skadden, Arps, Slate, Meagher & Flom, LLP, N.Y.C., 1998-99, Moses & Singer, LLP, N.Y.C., 1999-2000, Morrison, Cohen, Singer & Weinstein LLP, N.Y.C., 2001—02. Mem. Phi Beta Kappa. Avocations: Italian, modern dance, photography, film, anthropology. Home: 34 W 86 th St Apt 2D New York NY 10024 Office: Morrison Cohen Singer & Weinstein LLP 750 Lexington Ave New York NY 10022

WALDERA, WAYNE EUGENE, crisis management specialist; b. Cayuga, N.D., Mar. 23, 1930; s. Bernard Cyril and Eleanor Nee (Kugler) W.; m. Eva Jenzene Personius, Jan. 13, 1958; children: Anthony, Lori, Mia, Shauna. BSBA, N.D. State U., 1952. With Gamble-Skogmo, 1954-88; pres. Gamble div. Gamble-Skogmo, Mpls., 1972-88; pres., CEO Retail Resource Co., 1988-89, Amdura Corp., Denver, 1989-92, also bd. dirs.; chmn. Sullivan Waldera, Inc., Mpls., 1992-93; prin., CEO Waldera & Co. Inc., 1993—. 1st lt. USAF, 1952-54. Home: 12125 62nd St Waconia MN 55387-9411 Office: Waldera & Co Inc 15500 Wayzata Blvd Ste 604-208 Wayzata MN 55391-1435 E-mail: wwaldera@uswest.net.

WALDHAUSEN, JOHN ANTON, surgeon, editor, retired; b. N.Y.C., May 22, 1929; s. Max. H. and Agnes H. (Stettner) W.; m. Marian Trescher, June 4, 1957; children: John H., Robert Rodney, Anthony Gordon Scarlett. BS magna cum laude, Coll. Great Falls, 1950; MD, St. Louis U., 1954. Diplomate Am. Bd. Surgery (bd. dirs. 1985-88), Am. Bd. Thoracic Surgery (bd. dirs. 1989-95). Intern Johns Hopkins Hosp., 1954-55, resident, 1955-57; clin. asst. Nat. Heart and Lung Inst., NIH, 1957-59; resident Hosp. U. Pa., 1959, Ind. U. Med. Center, 1960-62; practice medicine specializing in cardiothoracic surgery Indpls., 1962-66, Phila., 1966-70; mem. staff Milton S. Hershey (Pa.) Med. Ctr., 1969-96. From instr. to asst. prof. Ind. U. Med. Ctr., 1962—66; assoc. prof. surgery U. Pa., Phila., 1966—70; prof. surgery Pa. State U. Coll. Medicine/Milton S. Hershey Med. Ctr, Hershey, 1966—83, Hershey, 1994—99, J.W. Oswald prof., 1983—94, J.W. Oswald prof. emeritus, 1999, assoc. dean and dir. Univ. Physicians, 1993—96, sr. mem. grad. faculty, 1970—94, chmn. dept. surgery, 1969—94, interim provost, dean, 1972—73, assoc. dean health care, 1973—75; trustee U. Great Falls, Mont., 2001—. Mem. editl. bd. Jour. Cardiovascular Surgery, 1985-93, Jour. Pediatric Surgery, 1972-78, Jour. Thoracic and Cardiovascular Surgery, 1982, editor, 1994-2000; cons. editor Archives of Surgery, 1972-74; contbr. chpts. to books and articles to med. jours. Served with USPHS, 1957-59. Recipient Career Devel. award USPHS, 1964 Mem. AMA, AAAS, ACS (chpt. pres. 1974-75, gov. 1979-85, chmn. adv. coun. cardiothoracic surgery 1992-97), Am. Acad. Pediatrics, Am. Assn. Surgery of Trauma, Am. Coll. Cardiology (sec. 1981-82, trustee 1984-89, mem. editorial bd. jour. 1983, assoc. editor 1986-89), Am. Fedn. Clin. Rsch., Am. Heart Assn., Am. Physiol. Soc., Am. Soc. Artificial Internal Organs, Am. Assn. Thoracic Surgery (1st v.p. 1990-91, pres., 1991-92), Am. Surg. Assn. (1st v.p. 1984-85), Central Surg. Assn., Internat. Cardiovascular Soc. (chpt. recorder 1969-74), Pa. Assn. Thoracic Surgery (pres. 1977-78), Thoracic Surgery Dirs. Assn. (pres. 1977-79), Societe International de Chirurgie (membership chmn. 1987-92, treas. 1992-94), Soc. Clin. Surgery (treas. 1971-80, v.p. 1981-82, Pres. 1982-83), Soc. Surg. Chairmen, Soc. Thoracic Surgeons, Soc. Univ. Surgeons, Soc. Vascular Surgery, So. Surg. Assn., Sigma Xi, Alpha Omega Alpha. Home: 2149 Brandt Rd Annville PA 17003-8820 Office: Pa State U Coll Med MS Hershey Med Ctr PO Box 850 Hershey PA 17033-0850 E-mail: jwaldhausen@psu.edu.

WALDMAN, ALAN I. (ALAWANA), songwriter, composer, lyricist, computer programmer, emergency medicine provider; b. Elkins Park, Pa., Jan. 20, 1955; s. Harry and Anna Waldman; m. Deborah Anne Fulkerson, Dec. 9, 1998; 1 child, Penelope Anne. Student, U. Okla., 1973-76, U. Oreg., 1978, 79; BS in Econs., U. Wis., 1979; MS in Stats., U. Iowa, 1985. Performing songwriter, composer, lyricist, Deerfield Beach, Fla., 1986—; ind. computer programmer. Cons. Internet and World Wide Web; cardiopulmonary resuscitation and emergency cardiovascular care provider. Author: Poetic Universe Collection, How to Form Your Own Publishing Entity and Operating it Thereafter; lyricist, composer (song collections) Hit The Market, Down to Home, Sphere of Influence, Next Galaxy, Quality Rainbow, Predicaments of Life, Great Guidelines for Living, Collection of Alawana, Vol. I, 1993, The Artist Dimension Song Collection, Vols. II, III, Artsist Dimension Collection. Charter mem. Rep. Presdl. Task Force, Washington, 1984-92. Mem. U. Iowa Alumni Assn. Republican. Avocations: music clubs, book clubs, audio book clubs, computer books training and improvement. Home: 1830 NE 48th St Apt 317 Pompano Beach FL 33064-6532

WALDMAN, BEN, information technology executive; AB summa cum laude in Computer Sci., Harvard U., 1989. From devel. mgr. to corp. v.p. Microsoft, Redmond, Wash., 1989—2000, corp. v.p. mobile devices divsn., 2000—. Mem.: Phi Beta Kappa. Office: One Microsoft Way Redmond WA 98052-6399*

WALDMAN, MICHAEL, economist, educator; b. Paterson, N.J., May 12, 1955; s. Henry and Nettie Waldman; m. Karen Voris, July 9, 1982 (div. Jan. 1992); m. Lisa Berki, July 18, 1999; 1 child David Henry. BS in Econs., MIT, 1977; PhD in Econs., U. Pa., 1982. From asst. prof. to prof. econs. UCLA, 1983-93; prof. econs. Cornell U., Ithaca, N.Y., 1991-97, Charles H. Dyson prof. in mgmt., 1997—. Vis. prof. econs. Yale U. Sch. Orgn. and Mgmt., New Heaven, 1989—90, U. Chgo. Grad. Sch. Bus., 1997—99. Co-editor: Jour. Econ. Perspectives, 2000—; assoc. editor: Quar. Jour. Econs., 2000—; contbr. articles to profl. jours. Mem.: Western Econ. Assn., Soc. Labor Economists, Royal Econ. Soc., Econometric Soc., Am. Econ. Assn. Office: Cornell U Johnson Grad Sch Mgmt Sage Hall Ithaca NY 14853 E-mail: mw46@cornell.edu.

WALDMAN, SEYMOUR MORTON, lawyer; b. N.Y.C., Aug. 6, 1926; s. Louis and Bella B. Waldman; m. Lois Citrin, Aug. 5, 1951; children: David, Daniel, Michael, Ellen. BA, Columbia U., 1948, LLB, 1950. Bar: N.Y. 1950, U.S. Ct. Appeals (1st, 2d, 3d, 4th, 5th, 6th and D.C. cirs.), U.S. Dist. Ct. (so. dist.) N.Y., U.S. Dist. Ct. (ea. dist.) N.Y., U.S. Supreme Ct. 1956. From assoc. to ptnr. Waldman & Waldman, N.Y.C., 1950-82; ptnr., of counsel Vladeck, Waldman, Elias & Engelhard, P.C., 1982—; atty. Village of Croton-Hudson, N.Y., 1972—, chair zoning bd. appeals, 1963-72, trustee hosp. for Joint Diseases Orthopaedic Inst., 1968-93. With USN, 1944-46. Mem. ABA, N.Y. State Bar Assn., Assn. of the Bar of the City of N.Y., Phi Beta Kappa. Avocation: tennis. Office: Vladeck Waldman Elias & Engelhard PC 1501 Broadway Ste 800 New York NY 10036-5560

WALDMANN, KATHARINE SPRENG, public health physician; b. Cleve., Nov. 22, 1927; d. Dwight Sinclair and Elizabeth Partridge (Dial) Spreng; m. Thomas Alexander Waldmann, Mar. 29, 1958; children: Richard Allen, Robert James, Carol Ann. AB, Oberlin Coll., 1950; MD, Case-Western Res. U., 1954. Diplomate Am. Bd. Internal Medicine. Intern, then resident in internal medicine Mass. Gen. Hosp., Boston, 1954-57; fellow, instr. in psychiatry U. Md. Hosp., Balt., 1957-58; instr. internal medicine Georgetown U., Washington, 1958-62; sch. health physician Montgomery County Health Dept., Rockville, Md., 1961-88, disease control physician, 1985—, chief physician, 1985—. Med. cons. Green Acres Sch., Rockville, 1962-80, Georgetown Day Sch., Washington, 1974-84; satellite prin. investigator Washington Regional AIDS program, 1993-99; satellite prin. investigator Women's Interagy. HIV Study Georgetown U., 1993—. Trustee Am. Heart Assn., Bethesda, Md., 1967-69, Montgomery Hospice Soc. Med. Leadership Group, Health and Human Svcs. Ethics Com. Fellow ACP; mem. Am. Acad. HIV Medicine, Greater Washington Infectious Disease Soc., Silver Spring Garden Club, Alpha Omega Alpha, Phi Beta Kappa. Congregationalist. Home: 3910 Rickover Rd Silver Spring MD 20902-2329 Office: Montgomery Cty Hlth Hum Svcs 2000 Dennis Ave Silver Spring MD 20902-4136 Office Fax: 240-777-1754. E-mail: da5353@aol.com., waldmk@co.mo.md.us.

WALDMANN, THOMAS ALEXANDER, medical research scientist, physician; b. N.Y.C., Sept. 21, 1930; s. Charles Elizabeth (Sipos) Waldmann; m. Katharine Emory Spreng, Mar. 29, 1958; children: Richard Allen, Robert James, Carol Ann. AB, U. Chgo., 1951; MD, Harvard U., 1955; PhD (hon.) , U. Med. Sch., Debrecin, Hungary, 1991. Diplomate Am. Bd. Allergy and Immunology. Intern Mass. Gen. Hosp., Boston, 1955—56; clin. assoc. Nat. Cancer Inst. NIH, Bethesda, Md., 1956—58, sr. investigator, 1958—68, head immunophysiology sect., 1968—73, chief metabolism br., 1971—. Cons. WHO, 1975, 78; bd. dirs., v.p. Found. for Advanced Edn. in Scis., Bethesda, 1980—, treas., 1988—90, v.p., 1990—92; William Dameshek vis. prof. U. Calif., Irvine, 1984; mem. med. adv. bd. Howard Hughes Med. Inst., 1987—93; vis. com. mem. Harvard Med. Sch., Boston, 1988—94; mem. sci. adv. com., chmn. Mass. Gen. Hosp., 1992—96; chmn. sci. adv. bd. HealthCare Investment Corp., Princeton, NJ, 1986—. Author: Plasma Protein Metabolism, 1970; contbr. articles to profl. jours. With USPHS, 1956—58, 1959—63, 1975—94. Named Man of Yr., Am. Leukemia Soc., 1980; recipient Henry M. Stratton medal, Am. Hematology Soc., 1977, G. Burroughs Mider award, NIH, 1980, Disting. Svc. medal, Dept. Health and Human Svcs., 1983. Fellow: Am. Acad. Allergy (Bela Schick award 1974, John M. Shelton award 1984, Lila Gruber prize 1986, Simon Shubitz prize 1987, CIBA-GEIGY Drew award 1987, Milken Family Med. Found. Disting. Basic Scientist prize 1991, Artois Latour Internat. Rsch. prize 1991, Bristol-Myers Cancer prize 1992, Paul Ehrlich medal 1997); mem.: NAS (chmn. 1985—), Clin. Immunology Soc. (pres. 1988), Am. Soc. Clin. Investigation (mem. editl. bd. 1978—80, 1983—88), Assn. Am. Physicians, Hungarian Acad. Scis. (hon.), Inst. Medicine, Am. Acad. Arts and Scis. Achievements include the defining of structure of multisubunit IL-2 receptor; identifying novel cytokine IL-15; introduction of different forms of IL-2R-directed therapy using alpha and beta-emitting radionuclide chelate versions of humanized monoclonal antibodies (Zenapax) for treatment of cancer; introduction of analysis of immunoglobulin gene rearrangements to define clonality and classifying human lymphoid neoplasia; discovered intestinal lymphagesctasia and allergic gastroenteropathy. Office: Nat Inst Health 10 Center Dr Bethesda MD 20892-1374 E-mail: tawald@helix.nih.gov.

WALDMEIR, PETER NIELSEN, journalist; b. Detroit, Jan. 16, 1931; s. Joseph John and Helen Sarah (Nielsen) W.; m. Marilyn C. Choma; children—Peter William, Patti Ann, Lindsey Marilyn, Christopher Norman. Student, Wayne State U., 1949-58. With Detroit News, 1949—, sports columnist, 1962-72, gen. columnist, 1972—. Pres. Old Newsboys Goodfellow Fund, Detroit, 1988. With USMC, 1951-53. Recipient Headliners award Nat. Headliners Club, 1971, SDX Lifetime Achievement award, 2000; named Mich. Sports Writer of Yr., Nat. Sportscasters and Sportswriters, 1967, 69, 71; Heart award Variety Club Internat., 1985; inducted Mich. Journalism Hall of Fame, 2000. Mem. Sigma Delta Chi. Roman Catholic. Office: Detroit News 615 W Lafayette Blvd Detroit MI 48226-3197 E-mail: pwalmeir@aol.com.

WALDO, ANNA LEE, retired science educator, writer; b. Great Falls, Mont., Feb. 16, 1925; d. Lee William Van Artsdale and Cecelia Anna Prayzek; m. Willis Henry Waldo; children: Judith Ann, Sara Kendall, Dale Frederick, Patricia Gwyn, Richard Kird. BS in Chemistry, Mont. State Coll., 1946; MS in Organic Chemistry, U. Md., 1949. Biochemistry instr. U. Dayton, Ohio, 1950—55, Mercy Coll., Frontenac, Mo., 1964—73; sci. instr. St. Louis C.C.-Meramec, Kirkwood, 1975—85, Calif. Polu. Inst., San Luis Obispo, 1995—97. Author: Sacajawea, 1979, rev. edit., 1984, Prairie, 1986, Circle of Stones, 1999, Circle of Stars, 2001; contbr. articles to profl. jours. Recipient L. White Quest award for writing, Women of the Globe Dem. newspaper, 1980, Woman of Distinction award, AAUW, 2001. Mem.: Authors Guild, Alpha Chi Sigma. Republican. Home: 49 Los Palos Dr San Luis Obispo CA 93401-7725

WALDO, ROBERT LELAND, retired insurance company executive; b. Pittsville, Wis., Sept. 1, 1923; s. Elmer Harley and Edith Viola (Senter) W.; m. Elaine Anne Jossie, June 4, 1947; children: Daniel Robert, Thomas Parker, Susan Jeanne. BA, U. Wis., 1949, JD, 1951. Assoc. atty. Foley & Lardner, Milw., 1951-59; asst. sec., asst. gen. counsel Wis. Gas Co., 1959-69; v.p., gen. counsel Verex Corp. and Subss., Madison, Wis., 1969-72; exec. v.p., sec. Verex Corp. and subs., 1972-78, pres., chief operating officer, 1978-82, pres., chief exec. officer, 1982-85, chmn., chief exec. officer, 1985-86. Served as sgt. U.S. Army, 1943-46, ETO. Mem. Wis. Bar Assn., Dane County Bar Assn., Mortgage Ins. Co.'s Am. (pres. 1980-82), Maple Bluff Country Club. Republican. Methodist. Avocations: travel, golf. Home: 818 Charing Cross Rd Madison WI 53704-6010

WALDOCK, WILLIAM DAVID, aeronautical science and aviation safety educator; b. Ft. Worth, Aug. 4, 1952; s. Wallace Gordon and Annabelle (Wolfe) W.; m. Barbara A. Wisler, Sept. 14, 1974; children: Andrew, Kathleen. BA in History, U. Fla., 1975; student, Miami-Dade Coll., Miami, Fla., 1977-78; M of Aero. Sci. with honors, Embry-Riddle Aero. U., 1982; postgrad., Kennedy-Western U. Prof. aero. sci. Embry-Riddle Aero. U., Prescott, Ariz., 1982—, chief investigator aircraft accidents, 1991—, assoc. dir. Ctr. Aerospace Safety Edn., 1986—, dir. Robertson Aviation Safety Ctr., 1995—. Pres., chief cons. Sys. Safety, Inc., Prescott, 1990—; cons. Am. West Airlines, Phoenix, 1996-99; presenter numerous safety confs. Contbr. articles to profl. publs.; guest various T.V. shows. Lt. commdr. USCG, 1975-96, ret. Mem. SAFE Assn. (Gen. Spruance award for Outstanding Contbns. to Safety Through Edn. 1990), Aircraft Owners and Pilots Assn., Aircraft Rescue and Firefighting Working Group, Am. Soc. Safety Engrs., World Safety Orgn. (cert.), Internat. Soc. Air Safety Investigators (pres. Ariz. chpt. 1987—). Achievements include over 150 field investigations; research in accident history. Avocations: flying, hiking, boating, history. Office: Embry-Riddle Aero U Bldg 21 3200 Willow Creek Rd Prescott AZ 86301-3721 E-mail: wwaldock@msn.com.

WALDON, ALTON RONALD, JR. judge; b. Lakeland, Fla., Dec. 21, 1936; s. Alton Ronald and Rupert Juanita (Wallace) W.; m. Barbara De Costa, June 3, 1961; children: Alton III, Dana Olive, Ian Patrick. BS, John Jay Coll., 1968; JD, N.Y. Law Sch., 1973. Capt. N.Y.C. Housing Authority Police Dept., 1962-75; dep. commr. N.Y. State Divsn. Human Rights, 1975-82; assemblyman N.Y. State Assembly, 1983-86; congressman U.S. Ho. Reps., Washington, 1986-87; commr. N.Y. State Commn. Investigation, 1987-90; senator N.Y. State, 1991-00; judge Ct. of Claims State of N.Y., 2000—. Bd. dirs. USO Met. N.Y. Recipient Thurgood Marshall fellow, N.Y. State Trial Lawyers Assn., 1970-73. Mem. Met. Black Bar Assn., Macon B. Allen Bar Assn., Comus Club N.Y., Alumni Assn. N.Y. Law Sch., Alumni Assn. John Jay Coll., F&AM, Sigma Pi Phi. Democrat. Roman Catholic. Avocation: sports. E-mail: awaldon@courts.state.ny.us.

WALDON, MARJA PARKER, mental health nurse; b. Cedar Rapids, Iowa, Nov. 19, 1939; d. James N. and Mary Louise (Mussell) Parker; m. Max Eugene Waldon, Nov. 7, 1964; children: Garry, Jim, Jeff, Bill. AA, Graceland Coll., 1961; diploma, Independence Sanitarium and Hosp., 1961; postgrad., Case Western Res. U., 1962, U. Mo., Kansas City, 1963-64, Drake U., 1977-79. RN, Iowa; cert. psychiat./mental health nurse. Staff nurse oper. rm. Iowa Meth. Hosp., Des Moines, 1962-63; staff nurse emergency dept. Broadlawns Polk County Hosp., 1968-70; DON Midland Manor Nursing Home, Nampa, Idaho, 1972-73; dir. staff devel., primary care nurse med./surg. dept. Mercy Med. Ctr., 1973-75; primary care nurse mental health Charter Cmty. Hosp., Des Moines, 1983-85; primary care nurse adolescent mental health & chem. dependcy Waukesha (Wis.) Meml. Hosp., 1985-87; primary care nurse emergency dept. St. Elizabeth Hosp., Baker, Oreg., 1987-89; mental health, admission discharge nurse Broadlawns Med. Ctr., Des Moines, 1989-91; nurse clinician, staff educator Orchard Pl. Pediat. Mental Health Long-Term Residential Care, 1991-98; freelance writer, 1998—. Health supr. Freedom Bible Camp, Chariton, Iowa, Camp Prairie Schooner, Kansas City, Mo., 1963-65; nursing instr. Independence (Mo.) Sanitarium and Hosp., Boise, Idaho, 1974, U. Idaho, Iowa Meth. Sch. Nursing, Des Moines, 1975-79, Des Moines Area Community Coll., 1977-82. Author: Balloons Across America, 2000, Balloons Around the World, 2001. Missions dir. Grace Ch., 1994-98; dir. Lake Ozark Creative Ministries; moderator E-Prayer Conf. Mem. ANA. Avocations: painting, chalk art, freelance writing, calligraphy, public speaking. Home and Office: RR 1 Box 360 Linn Creek MO 65052-9750 E-mail: marjawaldon@xc.org., Marja_l_n@hotmail.com.

WALDORF, GERALDINE POLACK, lawyer; b. N.Y.C., Jan. 10, 1942; d. Marcel and Pauline (Kornbluh) Polack; m. Donald S. Waldorf, June 22, 1963; children: Heidi A., Lawrence W., Mahlon R. AB magna cum laude, Vassar Coll., 1963; MA, Sarah Lawrence Coll., 1969; JD, Columbia U., 1979; LLM in Taxation, NYU, 1986. Bar: N.Y. 1979. Assoc. Kelley, Drye & Warren, N.Y.C., 1979-84; pvt. practice, Nanuet, N.Y., 1984-88, 92—; of counsel Davidson, Dawson & Clark, N.Y.C., 1988-92. Co-author: New York Practice Guide: Probate and Estate Administration, 1985. Bd. dirs. Am. Cancer Soc., Rockland County, N.Y., 1971-77, 85-91; adv. com. Georgetown U. Child Devel. Ctr., Washington, 1991—. Harlan Fiske Stone scholar Columbia U. Sch. Law, N.Y.C., 1976-78. Mem. ABA, Women's Bar Assn. of State of N.Y., N.Y. State Bar Assn., Assn. of Bar of City of N.Y., Rockland County Bar Assn., Rockland County Tax and Estate Planning Coun. (bd. dirs. 1986-91). Office: 57 N Middletown Rd Nanuet NY 10954-2312

WALDREP, ALVIS KENT, JR. fundraising executive; b. Austin, Tex., Mar. 2, 1954; s. alvis Kent and Denise Carol Luste; m. Lynne M. Burgland, Dec. 6, 1980; children: Trey, charles. BS, Kennedy-Western U., 1993. Asst. sports info. dir. Tex. Christian U., Ft. Worth, 1977-79; founder, pres., CEO Kent Waldrep Internat. Spinal Cord Rsch. Found., 1979-81; exec. v.p. Am. Paralysis Assn., 1982, pres., CEO, 1982-85; founder, pres., CEO Kent Waldrep Nat. Paralysis Found., 1985—; chmn. Turbo Resins Internat., 1991—. Pub. spkr. numerous TV and radio shows including The Today Show, Good Morning America, NBC Nightly News; bd. dirs. Southwestern Med. Found., Dallas, Tex. Rehab. Commn., Austin; mem. adv. bd. Greater Dallas Injury Prevention Ctr., 1998—, Plano Jr. League, 1999—. Contbr. articles to profl. jours. Republican. Methodist. Home: 135 Shawnee Tr Celina TX 75009 Office: Ste 550 16415 Addison Rd Addison TX 75001-3234

WALDREP, CHARLIE DAVID, lawyer; b. Gainesville, Ga., Nov. 13, 1948; s. Robert Ernest and Bonnie Lou (Black) W.; m. Suzanne Elizabeth, Aug. 12, 1972 (div. 1997); children: Stacy, Megan, Brittany. BA, Jacksonville State U., 1971; JD cum laude, Samford U., 1976. Bar: Ala. 1976, U.S. Dist. Ct. (no. and mid. dist.) 1976, U.S. Ct. Appeals (5th and 11th cir.) 1984. Atty. Forstman & Waldrep, Birmingham, Ala., 1976-78, Gorham & Waldrep, P.C., Birmingham, 1978—. Mem. State Dem. Exec. Com., 1986-90; chmn. Gov. Folsom's Task Force on Edn. Reform, 1993; acting chief of staff Gov. Jim Folsom, 1993-94; chief of transition Gov. Jim Folsom, 1993; bd. dirs. John Croyle's Big Oak Ranch Inc., 1982-91, Positive Maturity, 1988-93; trustee Leukemia Soc. Am., 1989-94; pres. Birmingham Downtown Dem. Club, 1983-84, founding mem. City of Birmingham Park and Recreation, 1985-93, Parkway Christian Acad. Parents and Tchrs. Fellowship, 1987-89; mem. Ala. Mfg. Housing Commn., So. Regional Edn. Bd., Edn. Commn. States. With Ala. Air N.G., 1971-77. Mem. ABA, ATLA, Fed. Energy Bar Assn., Ala. State Bar Assn., Ala. Trial Lawyers Assn., Christian Legal Soc., Jacksonville State U. Nat. Alumni Assn. (pres. 1983-85), Kiwanis (pres. 1986-87). Baptist. Office: Gorham & Waldrep PC 2101 6th Ave N Ste 700 Birmingham AL 35203-2761

WALDRON, JONATHAN KENT, lawyer; b. Washington, Feb. 11, 1949; s. Russell Lee and Ruth Magdalena Waldron; m. Janet Amy Roltsch, Dec. 8, 1973; children: Nathan Jay, Nicole Lee. BS in English, USCG Acad., 1971; JD, U. Miami, 1981. Bar: Fla. 1981, D.C. 1990. Comdr. USCG, 1971-91; sr. counsel Marine Spill Response Corp., Washington, 1991-95; ptnr. Dyer Ellis & Joseph, 1996—. Recipient Schneider award Dept. Transp., 1990. Mem. Maritime Law Assn. Avocation: tennis. Home: 3302 Lauren Oaks Ct Oak Hill VA 20171-1742 Office: Dyer Ellis & Joseph Ste 1100 600 New Hampshire Ave NW Washington DC 20037-2485

WALDRON, KENNETH LYNN, lawyer; b. Cape Girardeau, Mo., Oct. 18, 1941; s. Leonard Vernal and Edna Marion (Baskerville) W.; children: Leonard, Matthew, Charles. Student, Westminster Coll., 1959-61; BS, U. Mo., 1963, JD, 1966. Bar: Mo. 1966, U.S. Dist. Ct. (ea. dist.) Mo. 1968, U.S. Ct. Appeals (8th cir.) 1971, U.S. Supreme Ct. 1975. Salesman Nat. Biscuit Co., various locations, 1963-66; assoc. Buerkle & Lowes, Jackson, Mo., 1966-71; ptnr. Waldron & Assocs., 1971-91. Pres., CEO Eagle Environ. Products, Inc.; pres. Quail Springs Farm and Kennels, Inc., Stonewall Enterprises, Inc. Served to capt. U.S. Army, 1966-68. Decorated 2 Legions of Merit; named one of Outstanding Young Men in Am., 1972, 74, 76. Mem. Mo. Bar Assn., Assn. Trial Lawyers Am., Mo. Assn. Trial Attys., Am. Soc. Law and Medicine, Nat. Inst. Mcpl. Law Officers, Jackson Jaycees (Mo. legal counsel 1972-74, disting. service award 1968, 74), Am. Legion, Rotary. Republican. Baptist. Avocations: tennis, golf, hunting, bird dog field trials, music (vocal & guitar), songwriting. Home: PO Box 270 Jackson MO 63755-0270 Office: Waldron & Assocs PO Box 270 Jackson MO 63755-0270

WALDROP, FRANCIS NEIL, physician; b. Asheville, N.C., Oct. 5, 1926; s. Troy Lester and Emma Louise (Ballard) W.; m. Eleanor Dorothy Wickes, June 10, 1950; children— Mark Lester, Barbara Louise. AB, U. Minn., 1946; MD, George Washington U., 1950. Intern George Washington U. Hosp., Washington, 1950-51; resident St. Elizabeth's Hosp., 1951-54, med. officer, 1951-71; dir. manpower and tng. programs NIMH, Rockville, Md., 1972-75; dep. adminstr. Alcohol, Drug Abuse and Mental Health Adminstrn., HEW, 1975-79; ret., 1979. Clin. prof. psychiatry George Washington U. Recipient Superior Service award HEW, 1962, Disting. Service award, 1964 Fellow Am. Psychiat. Assn. (Vestermark award 1980). Achievements include research, publs. in field. Home: 1775 Elton Rd Silver Spring MD 20903-1726

WALDROP, NORMAN ERSKINE, JR. lawyer; b. Gadsden, Ala., Feb. 27, 1946; s. Norman E. Sr. and Margaret Alice Waldrop; m. Margaret Ann Waldrop, Sept. 13, 1969; children: Margaret Carson, Norman Erskine III. BS, Auburn U., 1968; JD, U. Ala., 1971. Bar: Ala. 1971. Trial atty., ptnr. Armbrecht, Jackson LLP, Mobile, Ala., 1971—. Mem. code commn., Ala. Judicial Inquiry Commn., Montgomery, 1994-99; chmn. so. dist. Ala. adv. bd., Mobile, 1992-96; mem. Ala. Permanent Code Commn. Capt. USAR Transp. Svc., 1971-77, Mobile. Mem. Nat. Assn. Railroad Trial Counsel, Am. Bd. Trial Advocates, Maritime Law Assn., Fedn. Ins. & Corp. Counsel, Order of Coif, Omicron Delta Kappa. Avocations: tennis, golf. Office: Armbrecht Jackson LLP PO Box 290 Mobile AL 36601-0290

WALDRUM, KEITH L. furniture company executive; b. Texarkana, Tex., Aug. 28; Student, Texarkana C.C., 1979-80; BFA, U. North Tex., 1985. With Nat. Furniture Retailer, Tex., 1986—, visual presentations mgr., 1987-94, visual presentations tng. mgr. Arlington, 1987-96, visual presentations mgr. Plano, 1996—. Fine arts photographer Visions Beyond, Dallas, 1985—. Contbr. articles, photographs to profl. jours.; exhbns. include Gracy Tune Prodns., Ft. Worth, 1993, Neikrug Photographica's, N.Y.C., 1994, Stage Door Charlie, FairPark Music Hall, Dallas., 1995, L.A. Photography Gallery, 1992, Dallas Dance Coun., 1992, Irving Arts Ctr., 1993, N.W. Internat. Exhbn. of Photography, Puyallup, Wash., 1993, 500X Gallery, Dallas, 1992, Union Art Gallery, Denton, Tex., 1984, Amarillo Art Ctr., 1983, others. Recipient Grand Prize winner Today's Photographer Internat. Mag., 1994. Mem. Internat. Freelance Photographers. Avocations: autograph collecting, bodybuilding, meditation. Home: Apt 733 9702 W Ferris Branch Blvd Dallas TX 75243-8721

WALDT, RISA, therapist, artist, educator; b. Tucson, Dec. 29, 1951; d. Carl J. W. and Jane D. S.. BA in Fine Arts, U. Ariz., 1973. Cert. Am. Soc. Experiential Therapists. Art therapist Miraflores ADL Facility, Tucson, 1993-94, Sierra Tucson Art Therapist, 1993-94; cons. and presenter in field. Author, artist: A Story of Being, Grand Canyon, A River Trip; featured in Artists of Arizona, Vol. I and II; one-woman shows include Rancho Linda Vista Gallery, others, 1973—; group shows include Tucson Mus. of Art, Rosequist Gallery, Tucson's Mountain Oyster Club. Facilitator Cir. of Friends--Job Corps, Tucson Mem.: Santa Cruz Valley Art Assn., So. Ariz. Watercolor Guild, Ariz. Watercolor Soc., Nat. League Am. Pen Women, Nat. Watercolor Soc., Nat. Mus. Women in Arts, Am. Watercolor Soc. Episcopalian. Sweat Lodge. Home: PO Box 41625 Tucson AZ 85717-1625

WALEN, HARRY LEONARD, historian, lecturer, author; b. Winchester, Mass., June 26, 1915; s. Harry Leonard and Alice (Garland) W.; m. Elizabeth Rowe Benson, June 26, 1939; children: Harry Benson, Kimball Frederick, Robert Leonard. AB cum laude, Harvard U., 1937, AM, 1942. Tchr. Los Alamos (N.M.) Ranch Sch., 1937-42, head English dept., 1939-42; tchr. English Groton (Mass.) Sch., 1942-46; instr. English, faculty marshal Newton Jr. Coll., 1946-51; tchr. English and journalism Newton High Sch., Newtonville, Mass., 1946-51, adminstr., 1951-55; directing editor secondary sch. English textbooks Ginn and Co., Boston, 1955-61; prin. Needham (Mass.) High Sch., 1961-72, career and post secondary guidance counselor, 1972-79. Mem. Regional Interviewing Com. for Overseas Grants and Fellowships, 1961-84; mem. planning com. Task Force on High Sch. Graduation Requirements, Mass Dept. Edn., 1976-80. Author: (books) The Family Travel-Camper, 1955, (with E. Gordon and others) Types of Literature, American Literature, English Literature, 1964, The Memory Book of the New England Association of Teachers of English, 1981, The Sons of the American Revolution 1962-82: An Historical Anthology, 1984; (monographs) English Learning Environments, 1972, History of the Order of Founders and Patriots of America, 1982, Centennial History, 1996; co-author Alluring Rockport, rev. edit. 1986, The Little Old Meeting House and How It Grew; (poetry) Images and Perceptions, 1996; editor The English Leaflet, 1947-54; cons. editor on career edn. New Voices Series, 1978; poet laureate, Rockport, 1998, 99; contbr. chpts., articles, poems to books, profl. jours. and periodicals. Alderman City of Newton, Mass., 1961-72; corp. mem. USS Mass. Meml. Com., Inc., 1972—, bd. dirs., 1984-91, honorary dir., 1995—; chmn. edn. com. N.E. Conf. NCCJ, 1972-82, mem. study mission to Israel, 1974; vice chmn. New Eng. Conf. on Quality of Life, Boston, 1973; mem. Newton Regional Adv. Manpower Planning Bd., 1973-77; pres. counseling svcs. YMCA, Greater Boston, 1976-7; chmn. Newton Highlands Bd. Christian Edn., 1974-75; pres. bd. trustees weekday ch. sch.; 1st Congl. Ch., Rockport, Mass., ch. historian, 1982—; del. Mass. Conf. United Ch. Christ, 1989-96. John Hay fellow, 1965; Mass. Dept. Edn. Commonwealth fellow, 1971; recipient citation U.S. Commr. Edn., 1971, citation New Eng. Assn. Schs. and Colls., 1984, cert. of Appreciation, City of Newton, 1971, Service award, YMCA, 1978. Mem. Nat. Council Tchrs. English (assoc. chmn. nat. conv. 1965, chmn., co-founder Emeritus Assembly 1979-83, various other coms. and offices, Citation 1969), Nat. Assn. Secondary Sch. Prins., Headmasters Assn. (life), New Eng. Assn. Tchrs. English (life, past pres., chmn. ann. C. S. Thomas award com. 1975-96, historian 1978—, Thomas award 1978), Mass. Secondary Sch. Prins. Assn. (diploma standards com. 1973-78, Bronze plaque 1974), Mass. Council Tchrs. English (co-founder), Mass. Schoolmasters Club (past pres., hon. life), MENSA, Friends of Jackson Homestead, Newton Hist. Soc. (life, past pres.), Los Alamos (N.Mex.) Hist. Soc. (life), Sandy Bay Hist. Soc. (pres. 1983-86), Greater Boston Guidance Club (hon.), Nat. Gavel Soc., New Eng. Hist. and Geneal. Soc., SAR (pres. state 1979-81, nat. trustee 1981-83, historian gen. 1983-86, sec. Mus. Bd. 1982-88, Minuteman award 1985), Gen. Soc. Mayflower Descs. (mem. nat. exec. com. 1990-93), Mass. Soc. Mayflower Descs. (gov. 1985-88, dep. gov. gen. 1988-93), Pilgrim John Howland Soc. (pres. 1987-99, pres. emeritus 1999—, led pilgrimage to Eng., 1989), Mass. Huguenot Soc. (pres. 1990-92, nat. del. 1983-92), Descs. Colonial Clergy, Soc. Colonial Wars, Navy League U.S. (life), Sons and Daus. of 1st Settlers of Newbury (pres. 1982-84), Piscataqua Pioneers (pres. 1990-91), Order of Crown of Charlemagne, Order Founders and Patriots (nat. treas. 1978-81, dep. gov. gen. 1981-84, exec. com. 1992-2000, councillor gen. Mass. 1984—, N.H., 1987-90, 93—, gov. 1992-95, councillor gen. 1993—, Nat. Disting. Svc. award 1996), Boston Athenaeum, Harvard Club, Boston Authors Club (pres. 1995-96), English Lunch Club (pres. 1975-82), Friday Evening Club (most venerable 1979-86), Sandy Bay Yacht Club, Masons (32d degree, 50-Yr. award). Home: Penzance Rd Rockport MA 01966

WALEN, JOANNE MICHELE, secondary education educator, consultant; b. Reno, July 8, 1942; d. John Baptista and Helen Hattie (Laakonen) Pollastro; m. Wallace Donald Walen, Feb. 20, 1961; children: Lisa M. Mays, Kevin M. Walen. BA, U. Nev., Reno, 1965, MA, 1974. Cert. secondary sch. tchr., curriculum supr., Nev. Tchr. Washoe County Sch. Dist., Reno, 1965-85, English program coord., 1985-95; dir. WCSD Shakespeare in the Schs., 1985-95; cons. Shakespeare Express, 1995—, McDougal Littell, 1998—. Head reader, trainer Nev. State Dept. Edn., Carson City, 1980-2002; co-dir. Lit. Inst. U. Nev., Reno, 1986-90; essay reader ETS, Princeton, N.J., 1990-94; cons. IBEU, Rio de Janiero, Brazil, 1996, 98; cons. in field. Sr. editor (book) Secondary Writing Guide, 1995; author: (booklet) Handbook for Writing Traits, 1993; contbr. articles to profl. jours. Founder, dir. Shakespeare Performance Festival, Reno, 1986-95; co-dir. Washoe K-16 Coun. Lang. Consortium, Reno, 1995-96. Recipient Humanities award Nev. Humanities Com. State of Nev., 1991; grantee Summer Seminar NEH, Stratford Upon Avon, UK, 1994. Mem. NEA, Nat. Coun. Tchrs. of English (liaison officer 1994-2002, chair CEE commn 1996-98, chair writing awards adv. com. 1999-2002), No. Nev. Writing Project, Alpha Delta Kappa (pres. 1982-84). Lutheran. Avocations: reading, theater, travel. Home: 11500 Pickens Dr Reno NV 89511-9445 E-mail: shaxpur@aol.com.

WALENDOWSKI, GEORGE JERRY, accounting and business educator; b. Han-Minden, Germany, Mar. 25, 1947; came to U.S., 1949; s. Stefan (dec.) and Eugenia (Lewandowska) W. AA, L.A. City Coll., 1968; BS, Calif. State U., L.A., 1970, MBA, 1972; cert. completion, Inst. Mgmt. Accts., 2000—. Cert. community coll. instr. acctg. and mgmt., Calif. Acct. Unocal (formerly Union Oil Co. Calif.), L.A., 1972-76, data control supr., 1976-78, acctg. analyst, 1978-79; sr. fin. analyst Hughes Aircraft Co., El Segundo, Calif., 1979-83, fin. planning specialist, 1983-84, program controls specialist, 1984-86, bus. mgmt. specialist, 1986-92, bus. analyst, 1993-95. Adj. instr. bus. math. L.A. City Coll., 1976-80, adj. instr. acctg., 1980-97, 99—, substitute instr. acctg., 1998, mem. acctg. adv. com., 1984, 87, 89, 99; adj. instr. acctg. and bus. Pasadena City Coll., 1996—; reviewer conf. papers Western Acad. Mgmt., 1996, 97, Inst. Behavior and Applied Mgmt., 1997, So. Mgmt. Assn., 1999. Contbr. articles to profl. jours. Mem. commn. Rep. Pres. Task Force, 1986. Recipient Medal of Merit, Rep. Presdl. Task Force, 1984, cert. of merit, named registered life mem. commn., 1986, named Honor Roll life mem., 1989; recipient Vice-Presdl. Cert. of Commendation, Rep. Nat. Hall of Honor, 1992, Rep. Congl. cert. of Appreciation, 1993, Rep. Congl. Order of Freedom award Nat. Rep. Congl. Com., 1995, Recognition award L.A. chpt. Strategic Leadership Forum, 1983. Mem.: Ea. Fin. Assn. (program com. 2000), Soc. Advancement Mgmt. (selection com. mem. Internat. Conf. 2000, editl. bd. Advanced Mgmt. Jour. 1999—), Fin. Mgmt. Assn., Nat. Bus. Edn. Assn., Am. Acctg. Assn. (competitive manuscript com. 1997—98, reviewer tchg. curr. sect. 1998, tchg. and curriculum sect. two-yr. coll. issues com. 1998—99), Inst. Mgmt. Accts. (author's cir. L.A. chpt. 1980, Robert Half author's trophy 1980, cert. of appreciation 1980, 1983), Acad. Mgmt. (reviewer social issues in mgmt. divsn. 1991, mgmt. edn. and devel. disvsn. program rev. com. 1998, 1999, reviewer bus. policy and strategy divsn. 2002), U.S. Chess Fedn., Delta Pi Epsilon, Beta Gamma Sigma. Republican. Roman Catholic. Home: 426 N Citrus Ave Los Angeles CA 90036-2632 Office: LA City Coll 855 N Vermont Ave Los Angeles CA 90029 E-mail: geowalen@msn.com.

WALENGA, JEANINE MARIE, medical educator, researcher; b. Evergreen Park, Ill., Nov. 21, 1955; d. Eugene Adam and Therese Marie Walenga. BS, U. Ill., Chgo., 1978; Diplome d'Etudes Approfondies, U. Paris VI, 1984, PhD, 1987; postgrad., Loyola U., Maywood, Ill., 1981-84. Cert. med. technologist. Med. technologist MacNeal Hosp., Berwyn, Ill., 1978-79; rsch. asst. Loyola U. Med. Ctr., Maywood, 1979-80, hemostasis rsch. lab. supr., 1980-87, co-dir. hemostasis rsch. lab., 1987—, asst. prof. thoracic/cardiovascular surgery/pathology, 1988-94, assoc. prof., 1994-2000, prof., 2000—. Mem. Cardiovascular Inst., Loyola U., 1995—; cons. in field; lectr. in field; observer Nat. Com. for Clin. Lab. Stds., 1988—; del. US Pharmacopeia, 1990—. Contbr. articles to profl. jours. Named Alumnus of Yr., U. Ill., 1990; NHLBI rsch. grantee, 1989—; recipient Investigator Recognition award, 1993. Fellow Am. Coll. Angiology; mem. Internat. Inst. for Thrombosis and Vascular (sec. 1989—), Am. Assn. Pathologists, Am. Soc. Hematology, Internat. Soc. Thrombosis and Hemostasis (sci. and standardization subcoms. control anticoagulation 1990—), Am. Soc. Clin. Pathologists, Am. Heart Assn., Am. Soc. Med. Tech. Avocations: photography, archeology, gardening, birding, travel.

WALENTIK, CORINNE ANNE, pediatrician; b. Rockville Centre, N.Y., Nov. 24, 1949; d. Edward Robert and Evelyn Mary (Brinskele) Finno; m. David Stephen Walentik, June 24, 1972; children: Anne, Stephen, Kristine. AB with honors, St. Louis U., 1970, MD, 1974, MPH, 1992. Diplomate Am. Bd. Pediat., Am. Bd. Neonatal and Perinatal Medicine, cert. cert. physician exec. Certifying Commn. on Med. Mgmt., Am. Coll. Physician Execs. Resident in pediat. St. Louis U. Group Hosps., 1974-76, fellow in neonatology, 1976-78; neonatalogist St. Mary's Health Ctr., St. Louis, 1978-79; from co-dir. to dir. neonatal unit St. Louis City Hosps., 1979-85; dir. neonatology St. Louis Regional Med. Ctr., 1985-96; asst. prof. pediat. St. Louis U., 1980-94, assoc. clin. prof., 1994-98, assoc. prof. pediat., 1998—2001, prof. pediat., 2001—. Supr. nursery follow up program Cardinal Glennon Children's Hosp., St. Louis, 1979—, neonatologist, physician exec. for managed care and pub. policy, 1997—. Contbr. articles to profl. jours. Mem. adv. com. Mo. Perinatal Program., 1983-86. Fellow Am. Acad. Pediats.; mem. APHA, Mo. Pub. Health Assn. (pres. St. Louis chpt. 1995-96), Mo. Perinatal Assn. (pres. 1983), Nat. Perinatal Assn. (coun. 1984-87), Mo. State Med. Assn., St. Louis Met. Med. Soc. Roman Catholic. Avocations: bridge, baseball, sports. Home: 7234 Princeton Ave Saint Louis MO 63130-3027 Office: Cardinal Glennon Children's Hosp 1465 S Grand Blvd Saint Louis MO 63104-1003 E-mail: walentca@slu.edu.

WALES, GWYNNE HUNTINGTON, retired lawyer; b. Evanston, Ill., Apr. 18, 1933; s. Robert Willett and Solace (Huntington) W.; m. Janet McCobb, Feb. 8, 1957; children— Thomas Gwynne, Catherine Anne, Louise Carrie. AB, Princeton U., 1954; JD, Harvard U., 1961. Bar: N.Y. 1962. Assoc. White & Case, N.Y.C., 1961-69, ptnr., 1969-2000, resident ptnr. Brussels, 1969-75, Ankara, Turkey, 1998-2000. Served with USN, 1954-58. Mem.: Am. Law Inst. (life), Round Hill (Greenwich, Conn.), Mountain Lake Colony House (Lake Wales, Fla.). Home: 25 Mountain Lake Lake Wales FL 33898

WALES, ROSS ELLIOT, lawyer; b. Youngstown, Ohio, Oct. 17, 1947; s. Craig C. and Beverly (Bromley) W.; m. Juliana Fraser, Sept. 16, 1972; children: Dod Elliot, James Craig. AB, Princeton U., 1969; JD, U. Va., 1974. Bar: Ohio 1974, U.S. Dist. Ct. (so. dist.) Ohio 1974, U.S. Ct. Appeals (5th cir.) 1979. Assoc. Taft, Stettinius & Hollister, Cin., 1974-81, ptnr., 1981—. Pres. U.S. Swimming, Inc., Colorado Springs, 1979-84, U.S. Aquatic Sports, Inc., Colorado Springs, 1984-88, 94-98. Pres. Cin. Active to Support Edn., 1987-88; chmn. sch. tax levy campaign, Cin., 1987; trustee The Childrens Home Cin., 1987—, v.p., 1995-98, pres., 1998-2002; bd. sec. Cin. State Tech. and C.C., 1995-98, vice-chmn., 1998-2000, chair 2000-02; pres. Cin. Arts Sch., Inc., 2000-01; sec. Greater Cin. Arts and Edn. Ctr., 1996—; mem. U.S. Anti-Doping Agy., Colo. Springs. Mem. ABA, Ohio Bar Assn., Cin. Bar Assn., Internat. Swimming Fedn. of Lausanne, Switzerland (sec. 1988-92, v.p. 1992-2000). Presbyterian. Office: 1800 Firstar Twr 425 Walnut St Cincinnati OH 45202-3923 E-mail: wales@taftlaw.com.

WALES, WALTER D. physicist, educator; b. Oneonta, N.Y., Aug. 2, 1933; s. Walter D. and Anna Laura (Brockway) W.; m. Margaret Irene Keiter, June 19, 1955; children: Stephen Dirk, Carolyn Sue. BA, Carleton Coll., 1954; MS, Calif. Inst. Tech., 1955, PhD, 1960. Instr. physics U. Pa., Phila., 1959-62, asst. prof., 1962-64, assoc. prof., 1964-72, prof., 1972—, chmn. dept. physics, 1973-82, assoc. dean, 1982-87, acting dean, 1987-88, assoc. dean. 1988-92, dep. provost, 1992-95, interim dean, 1996-98, ombudsman, 1999-2001; assoc. dir. Princeton (N.J.)-Pa. Accelerator, 1968-71; staff physicist AEC, 1972-73. Fellow Am. Phys. Soc.; mem. Am. Assn. Physics Tchrs. Achievements include research in exptl. particle physics. Home: 404 Drew Ave Swarthmore PA 19081-2406 Office: 209 S 33rd St Philadelphia PA 19104-6317

WALETZKY, LUCY R. psychiatrist; b. N.Y.C., Mar. 9, 1941; d. Laurance Spelman and Mary Billings (French) Rockefeller; m. Jeremy Peter Waletzky (div. 1984); children: Jacob Peter, Naomi French. BA, Wellesley Coll., 1963; MD, Columbia U., 1968. Cert. Am. Bd. Psychiatry and Neurology. Pvt. practice, Chevy Chase, Md., 1975-81, 2002—; co-dir., co-founder Med. Illness Counseling Ctr., 1982-95; asst. dir. Stress Medicine Group, Pleasantville, NY, 1995—2002. Founder, pres. DateABLE, Chevy Chase, 1987—. Fellow Am. Psychiat. Assn. (Significant Achievement award 1993), Am. Holistic Med. Assn., Am. Soc. Psycho-oncology/AIDS. Episcopalian. Avocations: golf, hiking, birdwatching. Office: 358 N Broadway Ste 201 Tarrytown NY 10591

WALEY-COHEN, JOANNA, humanities educator; b. London, England, June 10, 1952; d. Bernard Nathaniel and Joyce Constance Ira Waley-Cohen; m. Keith Bradoc Gallant, May 30, 1977; children: Christopher Gallant, Isabel Gallant. BA, Cambridge U., Cambridge, UK, 1974, MA, 1977; PhD, Yale U., New Haven, CT, 1987. Fellow Columbia Soc. of Fellows, Columbia U., New York, NY, 1988—90; asst. prof. Columbia U., 1992—98; assoc. prof., history & eas NYU, 1998—2002, prof. history & asian studies, 2002—. China and inner asia com. mem. Assn. for Asian Studies, 1998—2001. Author: (book) The Sextants of Beijing: Global Currents in Chinese History, Exile in Mid-Qing China. Fellow Internat. Postdoctoral Fellowship, ACLS, 1999-2000, Postdoctoral Fellowship, NYU, 1994, Fellowship Mil. Strategic History, Yale U., 1990-1991. Mem.: Royal Asiatic Soc., Assn. for Asian Studies, Am. Hist. Assn. Avocations: reading, swimming, classical music, classical music. Office: New York University Dept of History 53 Washington Square South New York NY 10012

WALHEIM, REX J. astronaut, military officer; b. Redwood City, Calif., Oct. 10, 1962; s. Lawrence M. Jr. and Avis Walheim; m. Margie Dotson; 2 children. BS in Mech. Engring., U. Calif., Berkeley, 1984; MS in Indsl. Engring., U. Houston, 1989. Commd. 2d lt. USAF, 1984, advanced through grades to lt. col.; missile warning ops. crew cmmdr. USAF Cavalier (N.D.) Air Force Sta., 1984—86; mech. systems flight engr. , lead ops. engr. for Space Shuttle landing gear, brakes and emergency runway barrier. NASA, Houston, 1986—89; mgr. upgrading missile warning radar USAF Hdqtrs. Air Force Space Command, Colo. Springs, Colo., 1989—91; student test pilot sch. USAF, Edwards AFB, Calif., 1992; project mgr. to cmmdr. avionics and armament flight F-16 Combined Test Force, 1993—96; astronaut NASA Johnson Space Ctr., Houston, 1996—. Named Disting. grad and top flight engr., USAF Test Pilot Sch. 92A. Avocations: football, hiking, skiing, softball. Office: Astronaut Office/CB Johnson Space Ctr Houston TX 77058

WALHOUT, JUSTINE SIMON, chemistry educator; b. Aberdeen, S.D., Dec. 11, 1930; d. Otto August and Mabel Ida (Tews) S.; m. Donald Walhout, Feb. 1, 1958; children: Mark, Timothy, Lynne, Peter. BS, Wheaton Coll., 1952; PhD, Northwestern U., 1956. Instr. Wright City Community Coll., Chgo., 1955-56; asst. prof. Rockford (Ill.) Coll., 1956-59, assoc. prof., 1959-66, 81-89, prof., 1989-96, prof. emeritus, 1996—, dept. chmn., 1987-95; cons. Pierce Chem. Co., Rockford, 1968-69; trustee Rockford (Ill.) Coll., 1987-91. Contbr. articles to profl. jours. Mem. Ill. Bd. Edn., 1974-81. Mem. AAUW (Ill. bd. mem. 1985-87), Am. Chem. Soc. (councilor 1993-99), Rockford LWV (bd. dirs. 1983-85, 2002--), Sigma Xi. Presbyterian. Home: 320 N Rockford Ave Rockford IL 61107-4547 Office: Rockford Coll 5050 E State St Rockford IL 61108-2311

WALI, MOHAN KISHEN, environmental science and natural resources educator; b. Kashmir, India, Mar. 1, 1937; came to U.S., 1969, naturalized, 1975; s. Jagan Nath and Somavati (Wattal) W.; m. Sarla Safaya, Sept. 25, 1960; children: Pamela, Promod. BS, U. Jammu and Kashmir, 1957; MS, U. Allahabad, India, 1960; PhD, U. B.C., Can., 1970. Lectr. S.P. Coll., Srinagar, Kashmir, 1963-65; rsch. fellow U. Copenhagen, 1965-66; grad. fellow U. B.C., 1967-69; asst. prof. biology U. N.D., Grand Forks, 1969-73, assoc. prof., 1973-79, prof., 1979-83, Hill rsch. prof., 1973; dir. Forest River Biology Area Field Sta., 1970-79, Project Reclamation, 1975-83; spl. asst. to univ. pres., 1977-82; staff ecologist Grand Forks Energy Rsch. Lab. U.S. Dept. Interior, 1974-75; prof. Coll. Environ. Sci. and Forestry SUNY, Syracuse, 1983-89, dir. grad. program environ. sci., 1983-85, prof. Sch. Natural Resources, 1990—, dir. Sch. Natural Resources, assoc. dean Coll. Agr., 1990-93; dir. Environ. Sci. Grad. program Ohio State U. , Columbus, 2001—. Vice chmn. N.D. Air Pollution Adv. Coun., 1981-83; co-chair IV Internat. Congress on Ecology, 1986. Editor: Some Environmental Aspects of Strip-Mining in North Dakota, 1973, Prairie: A Multiple View, 1975, Practices and Problems of Land Reclamation in Western North America, 1975, Ecology and Coal Resource Development, 1979, Ecosystem Rehabilitation-Preamble to Sustainable Development, 1992; co-editor Agriculture and the Environment, 1993; sr. editor Reclamation Rev., 1976-80, chief editor, 1980-81; chief editor Reclamation and Revegetation Rsch., 1982-87; contbr. articles to profl. jours. Recipient B.C. Gamble Disting. Tchg. and Svc. award, 1977. Fellow AAAS, Nat. Acad. Scis. India; mem. Ecol. Soc. Am. (chmn. sect. internat. activities 1980-84), Bot. Ecol. Soc., Can. Bot. Assn. (dir. ecology sect. 1976-79, v.p. 1982-83), Am. Soc. Agronomy, Am. Inst. Biol. Sci. (gen. chmn. 34th ann. meeting), Internat. Assn. Ecolog (co-chmn. IV Internat. Congress Ecology), Internat. Soc. Soil Sci., N.D. Acad. Sci. (chmn. editl. com. 1979-81), Sigma Xi (nat. lectr. 1983-85, pres. Ohio State chpt. 1993-94, pres. Syracuse chpt. 1984-85, Outstanding Rsch. award U. N.D. chpt. 1975). Office: Ohio State U Sch Natural Resources 2021 Coffey Rd Columbus OH 43210-1044

WALI, SIMA, foundation administrator; b. Kandahar, Afghanistan, Apr. 7, 1951; came to U.S., 1978; d. Mohammad and Shafiqa (Sharifi) W. BA, Kabul U., Afghanistan, 1970; MA, Am. U., 1984; PhD honoris causa, Smith Coll., MA, 2002. Asst. to consular officer Am. Embassy, Kabul, 1970-71; asst. to program tech. rep. U.S. Peace Corps, 1971-78; communications officer New Trans Century Fedn., Washington, 1978-82; asst. to dir. Refugee Women in Devel., Project of OEF Internat., 1982-83, dir., 1983-86; exec. dir. Refugee Women in Devel. Inc., 1986-96, pres., 1996—; del. His Majesty the Former Kinf of Afghanistan UN Peace Talks, Bonn, 2001; chief organizer Afghan Women's Summit Democracy, Brussels, 2001. Mem. adv. com. Global Fund for Women, 1992—. Contbr. articles to profl. publs., chpt. to book. Bd. dirs. Refugee Trauma Ctr., Harvard U., 1987-89; bd. dirs. Mem. expert's com. Women's Commn. for Refugee Women and Children, 1990-94; mem. adv. com. Refugee Policy Group; rep. refugee women and devel., human rights of uprooted people at nat. and internat. confs.; bd. dirs., chair Fund for the Future of Our Children, 1995—; dir. gender, human rights, forced migration Creative Assocs. Internat., Inc., 1996; pres. Rufugee Women in Devel., Inc., 1996; advisor Women for Women Internat., 1997—. Recipient N.Y. Assn. New Ams. Outstanding Contbn. award, 1988, Gloria Steinem: Women of Vision award, 1989, Women in Leadership award Women's Commn. for Refugee Women and Children, 1992, Resourceful Women award, 1995, Amnesty Internat. Ginetta Sagan Human Rights award, 1999; named finalist Ortho 21st Centruy Woman, NOW and Ortho Pharm. Co., Women of Distinction George Washington U., 1992. Office: Refugee Women in Devel Inc 5225 Wisconsin Ave NW Ste 502 Washington DC 20015-2034 E-mail: refwid@erols.com.

WÅLINDER, MAGNUS ERIK, educator; b. Uppsala, Sweden, Feb. 9, 1965; s. Per-Eirk Karl and Birgitta Agnes W.; m. Tina Maria Helgostam, Mar. 7, 2000. MS, KTH Royal Inst. Tech., Stockholm, 1992, PhD, 2000. Rsch. assoc. U. Maine, Orono, 2000—. Mem. Soc. Wood Sci. & Tech. Avocations: sports, cars. Office: KTH Royal Inst Tech SE-10044 Stockholm Sweden Home: Gavlegatan 3 SE-11330 Stockholm Sweden Fax: 46 8 21 81 81. E-mail: magnusw@woodtech.kth.se.

WALINSKY, PAUL, cardiology educator; b. Phila., June 21, 1940; s. Aaron and Bess (Kleiman) W.; m. Stephanie Sosenko, Nov. 27, 1971; children: Shira, Daniel. BA, Temple U., 1961; MD, U. Pa., 1965. Cert. Nat. Bd. Med. Examiners, Am. Bd. Internal Medicine Cardiovascular. Instr. medicine Thomas Jefferson U., Phila., 1973-75, asst. prof. medicine, 1975-79, assoc. prof. medicine, 1979-82, prof. medicine, 1982—. Cons. EP Technologies, Mountain View, Calif., 1991-93, Baxter Edwards, Irvine, Calif.,1 988-91, C.R. Bard, Billerica, Mass., 1994. Contbr. articles to profl. jours.; reviewer profl. jours.; inventor method for high frequency ablation, percutaneous microwave catheter angioplasty. Capt. USAF, 1967-69. Fellow Am. Coll. Cardiology, ACP; mem. AMA, Pa. Med. Soc., Phila. County Med. Assn. Achievements include 14 U.S. patents in field of perfusion balloon catheter, microwave aided balloon angioplasty with lumen measurement, intravascular ultrasonic imaging catheter and method for making same, and acoustic catheter with rotary drive. Office: Thomas Jefferson U 111 S 11th St Philadelphia PA 19107-5084 E-mail: Paul.Walinsky@mail.tju.edu.

WALISH, GERALYN ROSE, business consultant, analyst; b. Bryn Mawr, Pa., Jan. 9, 1956; d. George Martin and Carolyn Rose (O'Neill) W.; m. John Francis Aigeltinger, June 24, 1978 (div. 1983); m. Robert Kenneth Cole, June 25, 1989. BA in Orgnl. Mgmt., Eastern Coll., 1994. Systems mgr. Nat. Liberty Corp., Frazer, Pa., 1978-85; project mgr. Reliance Life Cos., Phila., 1985-86; cons. Fidelity Mut. Life Ins. Co., Radnor, Pa., 1986-89; sr. bus. analyst Aon, Trevose, 1989-93, sys. dir., 1993-95; v.p. Tenic, Inc., Hartford, Conn., 1995-96; pres. Lineage, Inc., Glenmoore, Pa., 1996—; bus. cons. Neverdahl-Loft, Inc., Lincoln, Nebr., 1997—. Chmn. Moonlighting Soc., Multiple Sclerosis Soc., Phila., 1986-88; mem. Super Cities Walk Adv. Com., Devel. Com., Multiple Sclerosis Soc., Phila., 1989; trustee Greater Del. Valley Multiple Sclerosis Soc., 1990—. Mem. Life Office Mgmt. Assn., Am. Bus. Women's Assn. (treas. Frazer, Pa. 1980-82). Home and Office: 632 Greenridge Rd Glenmoore PA 19343-9500

WALIZE, REUBEN THOMPSON, III, health research administrator; b. Williamsport, Pa., May 28, 1950; s. Reuben Thompson Jr. and Marion Marie (Smith) W.; m. Kathleen Anne Smith, Aug. 13, 1979; children: Heather, Amanda, Reuben IV. BS, Pa. State U., 1972; MPH magna cum laude, U. Tenn., 1975; cert. exec. mgmt., Boston U., 1978. Manpower planner North Ctrl. Pa. Area Health Edn. Sys. The Inst. for Med. Edn. and Rsch. Geisinger Med. Ctr., Danville, Pa., 1975-76; asst. dir. Northcentral Pa. Area Health Edn. System, 1976, exec. dir., 1976-78; health mgr. Seda-Cog, Timberhaven, Pa., 1978; exec. asst. VA Med. Ctr., Erie, 1978-81, trainee Little Rock, 1981, adminstrv. officer rsch. svc. White River Junction, Vt., 1981-88, mgmt. analyst Roseburg, Oreg., 1988-90, health systems specialist, 1990-92, adminstrv. officer rsch. American Lake, Wash., 1992-95; EEO investigator Dept. Vet. Affairs, Washington, 1995—; adminstrv. officer rsch. dept. vets. affairs Am. Lake divsn. VA Puget Sound Health Care System, Tacoma, 1995-98; exec. dir. American Lake Biomed. Rsch. Inst., 1996-98; adminstrv. officer rsch. VA Med. Ctr., Lexington, Ky., 1998—. Mem. Pa. Coun. Health Profls., 1975-77, Ctrl. Pa. Health Sys. Agy. Manpower Com., 1975-77; mem. Interagy. Coun. Geisinger Med. Ctr., Danville, 1976-78; liaison for rsch. Dartmouth Med. Sch., Hanover, N.H., 1981-88; mem. instnl. rev. bd. Madigan Army Med. Ctr., 1994-98, U. Ky., 1998—, pres. Gov. Divsn. Soc. Rsch. Adminstr., 1999-2000; cons. in field. All-star mgr. Gardenside Little League, Lexington, Ky., 2000—02. Recipient Man of Achievement award Queens Coll., Eng., 1978, Student Am. Med. Assn. Found. award, 1975; 1st pl. Douglas County Lamb Cooking Contest, 1992. Mem. APHA, AAAS, N.Y. Acad. Scis., Assn. Hosps., Pa. State Alumni Assn., Nat. Audubon Soc., Steamboaters, Nat. Wildlife Fedn., Record Catch Club, VIP Club. Avocations: fly fishing, fly tying, gardening, photography, gourmet cooking. Office: VA Med Ctr 2250 Leestown Rd Lexington KY 40511-1052 E-mail: reuben.walize@med.va.gov.

WALJI, JABIR MOHAMED, management consultant, commercial analyst; b. Kampala, Uganda, Mar. 2, 1959; s. Razahusein Virji and Kubra (Mauji) W.; m. Ahlam Jaffer Ali, Nov. 8, 1989. BS with honors, John Moores U. Liverpool, Eng., 1982; DMS, U. North London, 1986; MBA, Manchester Bus. Sch., Eng., 1996. Mktg. officer Tara Arts Group, Eng., 1985-86; internat. cons. Indus Textile Mills Ltd., Pakistan, 1987-94; dir. Indus Marines, Pakistan, 1988-92; cons. Shell Oils, Eng., 1996-98, svc. team England, 1998—, strategy advisor Svc. Team Ltd. Eng., 1999—. Mem. Royal Soc. Arts, Chartered Inst. Mktg., Inst. Mgmt. Consultants, Strategy and Planning Soc., Dubai Soc., Inst. Leisure and Amenity Mgmt., Assn. MBA, Tourism Soc. Avocations: jet skiing, squash, cinema, cuisine. Home: 6 Penshurst Ct Penshurst Gardens Edgware Middlesex HA8 9TL England Home Fax: 020 8958-7593; Office Fax: 020 7346-0746. E-mail: jabirwalji@hotmail.com., jabir.walji@serviceteam.ltd.uk.

WALKER, ALAN C. anthropologist, educator; b. Leicester, Eng., Aug. 23, 1938; arrived in U.S., 1973; s. Cyril and Edith Walker; m. Patty L. Shipman, Apr. 20, 1976; 1 child Simon B. BA with honors, U. Cambridge, Eng., 1962; PhD, U. London, 1967; DSc (hon.) , U. Chgo., 2000. Lectr. Makerere U. Coll., Kampala, Uganda, 1965—69; sr. lectr. Nairobi U., Kenya, 1969—73; assoc. prof. Harvard U., Cambridge, Mass., 1973—78; prof. Johns Hopkins U., Balt., 1978—95; prof. anthropology Pa. State U., University Park, 1995—96, Disting. prof., 1996—2002, Evan Pugh prof., 2002—. Author: over 170 articles to profl. jours.; editor: several books. With Royal Air Force, 1957—59. Recipient Internat.Fyssen prize, Paris, Rhone Poulenc prize, London; fellow, Guggenheim Found., MacArthur Found. Fellow: Royal Soc.; mem.: Am. Acad. Arts and Scis. Achievements include discovery of and analysis of fossil primates and humans in East Africa. Avocations: goldsmithing, jewelry. Office: Pennsylvania State Univ Dept Anthropology 409 Carpenter Bldg University Park PA 16802

WALKER, ALICE, author; b. Eatonton, Ga., Feb. 9, 1944; d. Willie Lee and Minnie (Grant) W.; m. Melvyn R. Leventhal, Mar. 17, 1967 (div. 1976); 1 dau., Rebecca Walker Leventhal. BA, Sarah Lawrence Coll., 1966; PhD (hon.), Russell Sage U., 1972; DHL (hon.), U. Mass., 1983. Co-founder, pub. Wild Trees Pr., Navarro, Calif., 1984-88. Writer in residence, tchr. black studies Jackson State Coll., 1968-69, Tougaloo Coll., 1970-71; lectr. literature Wellesley Coll., 1972-73, U. Mass., Boston, 1972-73; disting. writer Afro-American studies dept. U. Calif., Berkeley, 1982; Fannie Hurst Prof. of Literature Brandeis U., Waltham, Mass., 1982; cons. Friends of the Children of Miss., 1967. Author: Once, 1968, The Third Life of Grange Copeland, 1970, Five Poems, 1972, Revolutionary Petunias and Other Poems, 1973 (Nat. Book award nomination 1973, Lillian Smith award So. Regional Coun. 1973), In Love and Trouble, 1973 (Richard and Hinda Rosenthal Found. award Am. Acad. and Inst. of Arts and Letters 1974) Langston Hughes: American Poet, 1973, Meridian, 1976, Goodnight, Willie Lee, I'll See You in the Morning, 1979, You Can't Keep a Good Woman Down, 1981, The Color Purple, 1982 (Nat. Book Critics Circle award nomination 1982, Pulitzer Prize for fiction 1983, Am. Book award 1983), In Search of Our Mothers' Gardens, 1983, Horses Make a Landscape Look More Beautiful, 1984, To Hell With Dying, 1988, Living By the Word: Selected Writings, 1973-1987, 1988, The Temple of My Familiar, 1989, Her Blue Body Everything We Know: Earthling Poems, 1965-1990, 1991, Finding the Green Stone, 1991, Possessing the Secret of Joy, 1992, (with Pratibha Parmar) Warrior Marks, 1993, (with others) Double Stitch: Black Women Write About Mothers & Daughters, 1993, Everyday Use, 1994, Alice Walker Banned: The Banned Works, 1996, Everything We Love Can Be Saved: A Writer's Activism: Essays, Speeches, Statements and Letters, 1997, The Same River Twice, 1997; editor: I Love Myself When I'm Laughing... And Then Again When I'm Looking Mean and Impressive, 1979, By The Light of My Father's Smile, 1998, The Way Forward is With a Broken Heart, 2000. Recipient first prize Am. Scholar essay contest, 1967, O. Henry award for "Kindred Spirits", 1986, Nora Astorga Leadership award, 1989, Fred Cody award for lifetime achievement Bay Area Book Reviewers Assn., 1990, Freedom to Write award PEN Ctr. USA West, 1990; Bread Loaf Writer's Conf. scholar, 1966; Merrill writing fellowship, 1967; McDowell Colony fellowship, 1967, 77-78; National Endowment for the Arts grantee, 1969, 77; Radcliffe Inst. fellowship, 1971-73; Guggenheim fellow, 1977-78. Address: care Random House 299 Park Ave New York NY 10171*

WALKER, ALLEN LYON, logistics analyst; b. Wellsboro, Pa., Jan. 30, 1943; s. Joseph Dewitt and Louise (Thompson) W.; m. Jean Barbara Hickson, Aug. 11, 1979 (div. Jan. 1985); 1 child, Iain Lyon Walker; m. Mary Ann Knowlton Walker, Jan. 30, 1987. A in Engring. Mech., Williamsport (Pa.) Tech. Inst., 1963; Grad., U.S. Army Aviation Sch., 1970, U.S. Army Test Pilots Sch., 1970, U.S. Army Comd./Gen. Staff. Coll., Ft. Leavensworth, Kans., 1991. Lic. comml. pilot, FAA. Exptl. lab. tech. Ille Electric Corp., Williamsport, 1963-65; commd. 2nd lt. U.S. Army, 1965, advanced through grades to maj., 1966, ret., 1995; tool engr. Ingersoli Rand Corp., Painted Post, N.Y., 1965-66; aviator, test pilot U.S. Army, Vietnam, 1966-68, aircraft maintenance officer Europe, Germany, 1969-72, co. comdr. Europe, Germany, 1969-72; maintenance engr. Ingersoll Rand Corp., Painted Post, N.Y., 1972-75; logistics mgr. Bell Helicopter, Internat., Isfahan, Iran, 1975-77; base supply mgr. Gen. Devices/Grumman, 1977-79; field engr. Northrop Grumman Corp., Phila., 1980—. Adv. Army of the Rep. of Vietnam, Anh-Khe, 1967, English instr., 1967. Author treatise, 1990. Founding warden Internat. Order of St. Vincent, Holy Nativity, Rockledge, Pa., 1992-98, life mem. ; dist. commr. Cradle of Liberty Coun. Boy Scouts of Am., Phila., 1994-99, coun. commr., 1999—. Maj. U.S. Army, 1966-72, Vietnam, Europe. Decorated Bronze Star, Air medal, Meritorious Svc. medal; recipient Silver Beaver award, award of merit, Cradle of Liberty coun. Boy Scouts Am., Disting. Commr. award, Daniel C. Beard Masonic Scouter's award; fellow, James E. West Found. Master: Friendship Williams Lodge; mem.: SAR, Soc. Logistics Engrs. (vice-chmn. 1982—85), Mil. Order of Loyal Legion of U.S., Lyons Family Assn. (v.p. 1972—75), Brit. Officers Club of Phila. (sec. 1990—93), Knight Masons, Nat. Sojourners, Knights Templar, York Rite Sovereign Coll., Shriners (comdr. Legion of Honor 2000), Scottish Rite (32d degree). Republican. Episcopalian. Avocations: genealogy, scouting, astronomy. Home: 419 Huntingdon Pike Rockledge PA 19046-4449 Office: Naval Inventory Control Pnt 700 Robbins Ave Philadelphia PA 19111-5008

WALKER, ANNETTE, retired counseling administrator; b. Birmingham, Ala., Sept. 20, 1953; d. Jesse and Luegene (Wright) W. BS in Edn., Huntingdon Coll., 1974; MS in Adminstrn. and Supervision, Troy State U., 1977, 78, MS in Sch. Counseling, 1990, AA in Sch. Adminstrn., 1992; diploma, World Travel Sch., 1990; diploma in Cosmetology, John Patterson Coll., 1992; MEd in higher Edn. Adminstrn., Auburn (Ala.) U., 1995. Cert. tchr., adminstr., Ala.; lic. cosmetologist, Ala.; lic. funeral dir., Ala. Tchr. Montgomery (Ala.) Pub. Sch. System, 1976-89, sch. counselor, 1989—2000; lit. tchr. Fed. Bur. of Justice, 1997—2000; ret., 2000. Tchr. Fed. Govt., 1997—, U.S. Bur. Justice, 1997—; gymnastics tchr. Cleveland Ave. YMCA, 1971-76; girls coach Montgomery Parks and Recreation, 1973-76; summer sch. sci. tchr. grades 7-9, 1977-88; chmn. dept. sci. Bellingrath Sch., 1987-90, courtesy com., 1987-88, sch. discipline com., 1977-84; recreation asst. Gunter AFB, Ala., 1981-83; calligraphy tchr. Gunter Youth Ctr., 1982; program dir. Maxwell AFB, Ala., 1983-89, vol. tchr. Internat. Officer Sch., 1985—, Adult Laubach Reading Prog., Ala. Goodwill Amb., 1985—, day camp dir., 1987, calligraphy tchr., 1988; trainer internat. law for sec. students, Ala., 1995—; leader of workshops in field; evening computer tchr. high sch. diploma program, 1995—; sales rep. Ala. World Travel, 1990—; behavior aid Brantwood Children's Home, 1996—; computer tchr. h.s. diploma program Montgomery County Sch., 1995—; behavior aide Brantwood Children's Home, 1995—; hotel auditor, 1995—; Am. del. to China, People to People Internat., 1998. Mem. CAP; tchr. Sunday sch. Beulah Bapt. Ch., Montgomery; vol. zoo activities Tech. Scholarship Program for Ala. Tchrs. Computer Courses, Montgomery, Ala.; bd. dirs. Cleveland Ave. YMCA, 1976-80; sponsor Bell-Howe chpt. Young Astronauts, 1986-90, Pate Howe chpt. Young Astronauts, 1991-92; judge Montgomery County Children Festival Elem. Sci. Fair, 1988-90; bd. dirs. Troy State U. Drug Free Schs., 1992—; chmn. Maxwell AFB Red Cross-Youth, 1986-88; goodwill amb. sponsor to various families (award 1989, 95); State of Ala. rep. P.A.T.C.H.-Internat. Law Inst., 1995; bd. dirs. People to People Internat., 2000. Recipient Outstanding high Sch. Sci./Math. Tchr. award Sigma Xi, 1989, Most Outstanding Youth Coun. Leader award Maxwell AFB youth Ctr., 1987, Outstanding Ala. Goodwill Amb. award, 1989, 95; named Tchr. of the Week, WCOV-TV, 1992, Ala. Tchr. in Space Program , summer 1989, Local Coodr. Young Astronaut Program, 1988, Tchr. of Yr. award Paterson Sch., 1990, Career Infusion Award (Most Appreciated Tchr. award 1987), Montgomery Pub. Sch., 1982, 84, Earthwatch Ednl. award, Israel, 1997; Fulbright scholar, Japan, 1999; selected Citizen Amb. to China, People to People Internat., 1999, 20 Class award Maxwell AFB Internat. Fgn. Officer Program. Mem. NEA, Internat. Platform Assn., People to People Internat. (founder, bd. trustees, organizer, pres. Ala. chpt. 1998), Nat. Sci. Tchrs. Assn., Ala. Sch. Counselors, Montgomery Sch. Counselors Assn., Montgomery County Ednl. Assn., Space Camp Amb., Huntingdon Alumni Assn. (sec.-treas.), Ala. Goodwill Amb., Montgomery Capital City Club, Young Astronauts, Ea. Star, Japan Friends of Fulbright Meml. Fund Tchr. Prog., Water Watch, Montgomery, AL, Zeta Phi Beta, Chi Delta Phi, Kappa Pi. Avocations: international travel, calligraphy, international food, cruising. Home: 2501 Westwood Dr Montgomery AL 36108 E-mail: awalker2001@yahoo.com.

WALKER, ANTOINE DEVON, professional basketball player; b. Chgo., Aug. 12, 1976; 1 child, Crystal. Student, U. Ky., 1996. Forward Boston Celtics, 1996—. Named to 1996-97 NBA All Rookie First Team. Avocations: dancing, bowling, video games. Office: c/o Boston Celtics 151 Merrimac St Ste 5 Boston MA 02114-4714*

WALKER, BETSY ELLEN, consulting and systems integration company executive; b. Atlanta, Sept. 14, 1953; d. John Franklin and Betty Louise (Brown) W.; children: William Franklin, Samuel Elliott, m. M. Michael Egan. BA summa cum laude, Duke U., 1974; MBA, Harvard U., 1978. Mgmt. trainee First Atlanta, 1974, officer, 1975-76; analyst Coca Cola, Atlanta, 1977; bus. analyst Am. Mgmt. Systems Inc., N.Y.C., 1978-80, prin., 1981, v.p., 1982-99, dir. fin. svcs. group, 1982-90, IBM Svcs. sector group, 1990-92, fin. strategic initiatives group, 1993; dir. fin. industry Strategic Alliance Group, 1994-96, area dep. dir. fin. industry groups, 1996-97; COO, bd. dirs. Security First Network Bank, Atlanta, 1999—. Mem. mgmt. policy com. Am. Mgmt. Systems, 1988-98, mem. corporate operating group, 1994-97; COO, bd. dirs. Security First Network Bank, 1999; pres. B.E. Walker Assoc., Inc., 1999—. J. Spencer Love fellow Harvard U., 1976-78. Mem. Alexandria North Ridge Citizens Assn. (exec. bd.), Phi Beta Kappa, Pi Mu Epsilon (bd. mgrs. Madison Green 1990-91, treas.), Harvard Bus. Sch. Club. Office: SFNB 3475 Piedmont Rd NE Ste 300 Atlanta GA 30305-2988 E-mail: bewalker@mindspring.com.

WALKER, BILLY KENNETH, computer science educator, academic administrator; b. Canyon, Tex., June 17, 1946; m. Anita Marie Ransdell, Mar. 8, 1980. BS in Math., West Tex. State U., 1968, postgrad., 1974, 77, U. Utah, 1969; MS in Math., Tex. Tech U., 1970, PhD in Math., 1974. Teaching fellow in math. U. Utah, Salt Lake City, 1968-69; teaching asst. in math. Tex. Tech U., Lubbock, 1969-70, part-time instr. math., 1970-74, adj. prof. elec. engring., 1979-83; instr. sci., physics and math. Carver Learning Ctr., Amarillo, Tex., 1974-76; instr. computer info. systems West Tex. State U., Canyon, 1976-77, acting head dept. computer info. system, 1977; asst. prof. computer info. system Amarillo Coll., 1977-79; asst. prof. elec. engring. and computer sci. U. Okla., Norman, 1979-83; assoc. prof. computer sci. East Okla. State U., Ada, 1983-87; prof. and chmn. dept. computer sci. East Cen. U., 1983—; mem. engring. computer network user's com. computer sci. U. Okla., chmn. convocation com. Coll. Engring. Cons. Amstar Corp., Dimmit, Tex., Silverman and Silverman, Attys. at Law, Hutchinson County Mus., City of Amarillo, City of Cushing, Okla., Southwestern Bell Telephone Co., U.S. Armu Corps Engrs.; researcher in field. Author: A Structured Approach to Pascal, 1983, Essentials of Pascal, 1984, Modula-2 Programming with Data Structures, 1986; editorial reviewer Math. Revs., Ann ARbor, Mich., Apple Edn. Found., Cupertino, Calif., Dept. Army; contbr. numerous articles to profl. jours. NSF fellow U. Utah, 1969. Mem. IEEE (sr.), Am. Math. Soc., Assn. for Computing Machinery, Math. Assn. Am., Am. Indian Sci. and Engring. Soc., Okla. Acad. Sci. (vice-chmn. computer sci. section 1987, 89, chmn. computer sci. section 1988, mem. exec. com. 1987-89), Am. Radio Relay League, Comanche War Dance Soc., Comanche Gourd Clan, Lone Star War Dance Soc., Masons, Order Eastern Star, Pi Mu Epsilon, Kappa Mu Epsilon, Alpha Chi. Home: PO Box 2107 Ada OK 74821-2107 Office: East Cen U Dept Computer Sci Ada OK 74820-6899

WALKER, BRIGITTE MARIA, translator, linguistic consultant; b. Stolp, Germany, Sept. 20, 1934; came to U.S., 1957; d. Joseph Karl and Ursula Maria Margot Ehrler; m. John V. Kelley (div.); 1 child, John V. Jr.; m. Edward D. Walker, July 3, 1977. Grad., Erlangen Translator's Sch., Germany, 1956; grad. fgn. corres., Berlitz Sch., Germany, 1956. Bilingual sec., translator Spencer Patent Law Office, Washington, 1959-62; office mgr., translator I. William Millen, Millen and White, Patent Law, 1962-67; prin. Tech. Translating Bur., 1967-68, St. Petersburg Beach, Fla., 1968—. Cons. for patent law offices, Washington, 1962—; ofcl. expert for ct. Paul M. Craig, Patent Atty., Rockford, Ill., 1981; cons. to sci. editor Merriam-Webster, Inc., Springfield, Mass., 1987—. Author: German-English/English-German Last-Resort Dictionary for Technical Translators, 1991, (poetry) The Other Side of the Mirror, 1992 (Poetry award Nat. League Am. Pen Women 1994); co-translator: The Many Faces of Research, 1980; holder of trademark in field. Evaluator fgn. textbooks Pinellas County Sch. Bd., St. Petersburg, 1987, German judge, 1988. Recipient Recoginition award Pinellas County Sch. Bd., 1988, Meritorious Pub. Svc. award City of St. Petersburg Beach, 1987, poetry award Nat. League Am. Pen Women, 1994, 99, 2000, essay award, 1996, short story award, 1997, Grand prize for poem DDDD Publs., 1998. Mem. Mensa (Winner Nat. award Best Fiction 1996). Democrat. Lutheran. Avocations: swimming, aerobics, piano, painting. Home: 1885 Shore Dr S Apt 428 Saint Petersburg FL 33707-4746

WALKER, BRUCE EDWARD, anatomy educator; b. Montreal, Que., Can., June 17, 1926; s. Robinson Clarence and Dorothea Winston (Brown) W.; m. Lois Catherine McCuaig, June 26, 1948; children: Brian Ross, Dianne Heather, Donald Robert, Susan Lois. BS, McGill U., 1947, MS, 1952, PhD, 1954; MD, U. Tex. at Galveston, 1966. Instr. anatomy McGill U., 1955-57; asst. prof. anatomy U. Tex. Med. Br., 1957-61, assoc. prof. anatomy, 1961-67; prof. Mich. State U., East Lansing, 1967—, chmn. dept., 1967-75. Contbr. articles to profl. jours. Mem. Am. Assn. Anatomists, Teratology Soc., Am. Assn. for Cancer Research. Office: Mich State U Dept Radiology East Lansing MI 48824

WALKER, BURTON LEITH, psychotherapist, engineering writer; b. Mt. Morris Twp., Mich., Oct. 23, 1927; s. Dalton Hugh and Muriel Joyce (Black) W.; m. Norva Jean Trochman, June 28, 1949; children: Paul, Cynthia Halverson, Mark; m. Carol Jean D'Andrea, July 31, 1981. AA, Alan Hancock Coll., 1971; BA, Chapman Coll., 1974, MA, 1975. Cert. psychology tchr.; lic. psychotherapist, hypnotherapist, Calif. Contract estimator Ryan Aeronautics, San Diego, 1949-59; logistics rep. GD/A, 1960-62; sys. engr. cons. fgn. svc. Ralph M. Parsons, L.A., 1962-68; lead engring. writer, sr. analyst Fed. Electric, Vandenberg AFB, Calif., 1969-86; psychotherapist Family Guidance Svc. Santa Ynez; Access, Vandenberg Village, 1978—; clin. dir. Valley Cmty. Counseling, Los Olivos, 1999—. Part-time prof. Allan Hancock Coll., Santa Maria, Calif., 1974-92, ret.; small bus. owner 1974-86. Active Santa Ynez Valley Presbyn. Ch. Mem. Am. Assn. Christian Counselors, Nat. Mgmt. Assn. (Outstanding Svc. award 1982), Calif. Assn. Marriage and Family Therapists, Assn. for Advancement Ret. People. Republican. Home: 3149 E Highway 246 Santa Ynez CA 93460-9634

WALKER, CAROL L. retired mathematics educator; b. Martinez, Calif., Aug. 19, 1935; d. Fred. Waldo and Alice DeVinny Hardy; m. Richard Roth Peercy, Aug. 30, 1953 (dec. Sept. 1956; m. Elbert A. Walker, Dec. 28, 1962; children: Diana, David, Daniel, Elaine. B Music Edn., U. Colo., 1957; MS in Math., N.Mex. State U., 1961, PhD in Math., 1963. Elem. and jr. high sch. music tchr., Olathe, Colo., 1955-56; mem. Inst. for Advanced Study, Princeton, N.J., 1963-64; from asst. prof. to prof. N.Mex. State U., Las Cruces, 1964-96, head math. scis., 1979-93, assoc. dean arts and scis., 1993-96, assoc. dean emeritus, 1996—. Co-author: Mathematics for Liberal Arts Students, 1967, 3d edit., 1999, Doing Mathematics with Scientific Work Place, 1995, 4th edit., 2001, Doing Calculus with Scientific Notebook, 1997. Mem. Am. Math. Soc. (com. on agenda 1985-91), Assn. for Women in Math. Office: NMex State U Dept Math Scis Las Cruces NM 88003

WALKER, CAROLYN MAE, secondary school educator; b. Neptune, N.J., Apr. 29, 1941; d. Frank and Estella (Matutis) W. BA in Sci., Montclair State Coll., 1963; MA in Edn., Newark State Coll., 1970. Cert. tchr., N.J. Elem. tchr. Howell (N.J.) Twp. Bd. Edn., 1963-65, Englishtown (N.J.)-Manalapan Regional Schs., 1965-67, Freehold (N.J.) Borough Schs., 1967-70, Freehold Regional H.S., 1970-73, North Brunswick (N.J.) Twp. Bd. Edn., 1975—. Mem. NSTA, N.J. Sci. Tchrs. Assn., N.J. Schoolwomen's Club, Alpha Delta Kappa (chair pres. 1972-74, state sec. 1974-76, state v.p. 1976-78). Roman Catholic. Avocations: cruising, dressmaking, needlework, gardening, classical/popular music. Office: North Brunswick Twp HS Raider Rd North Brunswick NJ 08902 E-mail: caramwalker@juno.com.

WALKER, CAROLYN PEYTON, English language educator; b. Charlottesville, Va., Sept. 15, 1942; d. Clay M. and Ruth Peyton. BA with distinction in Am. History/Lit., Sweet Briar Coll., 1965; cert. in French, Alliance Francaise, Paris, 1966; EdM, Tufts U., 1970; MA in Englisn and Am. Lit, Stanford U., 1974, PhD in English Edn., 1977. Tchr. elem. and jr. high schs., Switzerland, 1967-69; tchr. elem. grades Boston Sch. System, 1966-67, 69-70, Newark (Calif) Unified Sch. System, 1970-72; instr. divsn. Humanities Canada Coll., Redwood City, Calif., 1973, 76-78; instr. Sch. Bus. U. San Francisco, 1973-74; evaluation cons. Inst. Profl. Devel., San Jose, Calif., 1975-76; asst. dir. Stanford U. Learning Assistance Ctr., 1972-77, supr. counselors, tutors and tchrs., 1972-84, dir. Calif., 1977-84; lectr., dept. English Stanford U., 1977-84, lectr., Sch. Edn., 1975-84; pvt. practice corp. tng., 1983—; mem. faculty U. Calif., Santa Cruz, Berkeley, 1995—; prof. dept. English San Jose State U., 1984-93, dir. The Writing Ctr. dept. English, 1986—93, dir. Steinbeck Rsch. Ctr., 1986—87. Cons. Advanced Micro Devices, Calif., 1996, CellNet Data Sys., 1996-98, Fujitsu, Calif., 1997, Proxim, Inc., 1997-98, AMP, 1997-98, Tech. for Comm. Internat., 1997—, VISA Internat., 1999—, Inovant, Inc., 2000—; lectr. Sch. Edn., Stanford U., 1975-84, lectr. dept. English, 1977-84; supr. counselors, tutors and tchrs., Stanford U., 1972-84; head cons. to pres. to evaluate Coll.'s writing program, San Jose City Coll., 1985-87; cons. U. Tex., Dallas, 1984, Stanford U., 1984, 1977-78, CCNY, 1979, U. Wis., 1980; numerous testing programs; cons. to pres. San Diego State U. 1982, Ednl. Testing Svc., 1985-88, also to numeous univs. and colls.; condr. reading and writing workshops, 1972—; review Random House Books, 1978-95, Rsch. in the Teaching of English, 1983-95, Course Tech., Inc., 1990; cons. Basic Skills Task Force, U.S. Office Edn., 1977-79, Right to Read, Calif. State Dept. Edn., 1977-85, Program for Gifted and Talented, Fremont (Calif). Unified Sch. Dist., 1981-82; bd. dirs. The Tech Mus. of Innovation, San Jose, 1983-84; dir. Steinback Rsch. Carter, 1986-87, English dept. Writing Ctr., 1986-93; ednl. cons. Sun Microsystems, 2002--; spkr. numerous profl. confs. Author: Handbook for Teaching Assistants at Stanford University, 1977, Learning Center Courses for Faculty and Staff: Reading, Writing, and Time Management, 1981, How to Succeed as a New Teacher: A Handbook for Teaching Assistants, 1978, ESL Courses for Faculty & Staff: An Additional Opportunity to Serve the Campus Community, 1983, (with Karen Wilson) Tutor Handbook for the Writing Center at San Jose State University, 1989, (with others) Academic tutoring at the Learning Assistance Center, 1980, Writing Conference talk: Factors Associated with HIgh and Low Rated Writing Conferences, 1987, Lifeline Mac: A Handbok for Instructors in the Macintosh Computer Classrooms, 1989, Communications with the Faculty: Vital Links for the Success of Writing Centers, 1991, Coming to America, 1993, Teacher Dominance in the Writing Conference, 1992, Instant Curriculum: Just Add Tutors and Students, 1993; editor newsletter Environ. Vols. Inc., Palo Alto, Calif., 1999—; contbr. chpts. to Black American Literature Forum, 1991; contbr. articles to profl. jours. Vol. fundraiser Peninsula Ctr. for the Blind, Palo Alto, Calif., 1982—, The Resource Ctr. for Women, Palo Alto, 1975—76, Pathways Hospice, 2002—; vol. Gamble Garden, 1989—. Recipient Award for Outstanding Contbns., U.S. HEW, 1979, award ASPPIRE (federally funded program), 1985, two awards Student Affirmative Action, 1986, award Western Coll. Reading & Leanring Assn., 1984; numerous other awards and grants. Home: 2350 Waverley St Palo Alto CA 94301-4143 E-mail: wavedd@pacbell.net.

WALKER, CAROLYN SMITH, college services administrator, counselor; b. Atlanta, May 9, 1946; d. George Taft and Lonnie Bell (Bates) Smith; 1 child from previous marriage, Gary Sherard Walker II. BA in Psychology, Clark Coll., Atlanta, 1970; MS in Counseling & Guidance, U. Nebr., Omaha, 1975. Lic. and cert. profl. counselor, Ga. Adult basic edn. instr. Atlanta Pub. Schs., 1970-71, adult basic edn. site coord., 1971; adult basic edn. instr. Omaha-Nebr. Tech. C.C., Omaha, 1971-74, dir. adult basic edn., 1974; guidance counselor Omaha Pub. Schs., 1974-76; recruitment counselor Minority Women Employment Program, Atlanta, 1976-77; career planning and employment preparation instr. Discovery Learning Inc., Job Tng. and Pntrship Act, 1985-86; dir. counseling and testing svcs. Atlanta Met. Coll., 1977—, assoc. v.p. for student affairs, 1998—. Test supr. Ednl. Testing Svc., Princeton, N.J., 1980—, Psychology Corp., San Antonio, 1991-99, Law Sch. Admissions Test, Newtown, Pa., 1991-99; cons. Commn. on Colls., So. Assn. Colls. and Schs., Atlanta, 1978—; jr. c.c. rep. Placement & Coop. Edn., Atlanta, 1987-90. Editor newsletters Romar On-Line, 1997, The Brief, 1984, 85, Guided Studies News, 1974; contbg. author: (manual) AJC Self-Study, 1981, 2000; author: (manual) Policies and Procedures for Coordinated Counseling, 1981, 3d edit., 1999, Policies and Procedures for Learning Disability Services, 1997, 2d edit., 1999, Women's Coalition for Habitat for Humanity in Atlanta, 1993-95, 97. Pres. Atlanta Barristers Wives Inc., 1984, 85; mem. steering com. Atlanta Mayor's Masked Ball, 1987; mem. memberships sales com. Atlanta Arts Festival, 1986, Neighborhood Arts Ctr., 1986; state host Dem. Nat. Conv., Atlanta, 1988; mem. Heritage Valley Cmty. Neighborhood Assn., 1982—. Recipient Outstanding Svc. award Nat. Orientation Dirs. Assn., 1985, 86, Literacy Action, Inc., 1978, Atlanta Met. Coll., 1987, others. Mem. Ga. Coll. Personnel Assn., Ga. Mental Health Counselors Assn., Nat. Coun. Student Devel., Univ. System Counseling Dirs., 100 Women Internat. Inc. (charter mem.), Am. Assn. Community and Jr. Colls., The Links Inc., Ga. Assn. Women Deans, Counselors and Adminstrs., Ga. Coll. Conselors Assn. Democrat. Methodist. Avocations: tennis, travel, horticulture. Home: 3511 Toll House Ln SW Atlanta GA 30331-2330 Office: Atlanta Metro Coll 1630 Metropolitan Pkwy SW Atlanta GA 30310-4448

WALKER, CHARLES D. astronaut; b. Bedford, Ind., Aug. 29, 1948; s. Donna Lake Walker; m. Susan Y. Flowers; 1 child. BS in Aero. and Astronautical Engring., Purdue U., 1971; DSc (hon.) , St. Louis Coll. Pharmacy, 1985. Civil engring. technician, land acquisition specialist, forest firefighter U.S. Forest Svc.; design engr. Bendix Aerospace Co.; project engr. Naval Sea Systems Command; test engr., Aft Propulsion Subsys. for Space Shuttle orbiters McDonnell Douglas Corp., 1977, original mem. Space Mfg. Team (laster Electrophoresis Ops. in Space, EOS), chief test engr., payload specialist, EOS commercialization project, 1979—86, spl. asst. to pres. Space Systems Co., 1986; sr. mgr., space programs bus. devel. and mktg. Boeing Co. Ops., Washington. Industry mem. numerous NASA task forces; mem. NRC Space Applications Bd.; faculty course advisor, lectr. Internat. Space U., 1988; nat. panel mem. NASA/Industry Manned Flight Awareness Program, NASA/Industry Edn. Initiative; bd. dirs. Challenger Ctr. Space Sci. Edn.; trainer various NASA astronaut crews; astronaut Space Shuttle missions 41-D, 51-D and 61-B; chmn. organizing com. World Space Congress, 1992. Contbr. articles to profl. jours. and mags., chapters to books. Bd. mem. Astronauts Meml. Found.; vol. chmn., bd. dirs. Spacecause. Named Ky. Col., Commonwealth of Ky., 1990; recipient Space Flight medals, NASA, 1984—85, Aerospace Laurels award, Aviation Week and Space Tech. Mag., 1985, Engring. Astronaut Alumnus award, Purdue U. Schs. Engring., Lindbergh award, AIAA, St. Louis sect., 1986. Mem.: Assn. Space Explorers (bd. dirs.), Nat. Space Soc. (bd. dirs., past pres.). Achievements include patents for electrophoresis apparatus with flow control. Office: Astronaut Office/CB NASA Johnson Space Ctr. Houston TX 77058*

WALKER, CHARLES DODSLEY, conductor, organist; b. N.Y.C., Mar. 16, 1920; s. Marshall Starr and Maude Graham (Marriott) W.; m. Janet Elizabeth Hayes, May 30, 1949 (dec. Feb. 1997); children: Peter Hayes, Susan Starr; m. Elizabeth Ann Phillips, Jan. 14. 2001. BS, Trinity Coll., 1940; AM, Harvard U., 1947. Organist, choirmaster Am. Cathedral, Paris, 1948-50, Ch. of the Heavenly Rest, N.Y.C., 1951-88; music dir. Blue Hill Troupe, Ltd., 1955-90, The Chapin Sch., N.Y.C., 1961-85; mem. organ faculty Union Theol. Sem., 1962-73, NYU, 1968-80; dean, music dir. Berkshire Choral Inst., Sheffield,

Mass., 1982-91; organist, choirmaster Trinity Episcopal Ch., Southport, Conn., 1988—. Contbr. articles to profl. jours. Lt. comdr. USNR, 1942-46. Recipient Disting. Alumnus award Cathedral Choir Sch., 1988. Fellow Am. Guild of Organists (nat. pres. 1971-75); mem. Am. Fedn. of Musicians, Canterbury Choral Soc. (founder, conductor 1952—), Saint Wilfrid Club, The Bohemians. Avocations: travel, photography. Home: 160 W 96th St Apt 15N New York NY 10025-9212 Office: Trinity Episcopal Ch 651 Pequot Ave Southport CT 06490-1416 E-mail: dodsley@aol.com.

WALKER, CHARLES NORMAN, retired insurance company executive; b. Buchanan, Mich., Mar. 8, 1923; s. Leland Seymour and Beatrice (Fairchild) W.; m. Rosemary McElwee, Aug. 21, 1919 (dec.); children: James Charles, Christopher Hugh. Student, Western Mich. U., 1939-41; BS, U. Mich., 1945, MA, 1947. With Lincoln Nat. Life Ins. Co., Ft. Wayne, Ind., 1947-75, asst. v.p., mgr. accident and sickness, 1957-60, 2d v.p., 1960-64, v.p., 1964-75; v.p. selection and issue New Eng. Mut. Life Ins. Co., Boston, 1975-83. Served to 1st lt. USAF, 1943-46. Fellow Soc. Actuaries; mem. Am. Acad. Actuaries. Episcopalian. Home: 506 Mill Rd Woodstock VA 22664-2308

WALKER, CHARLES URMSTON, retired university president; b. Bolivar, Pa., June 20, 1931; s. Charles William and Frances May (Urmston) W.; m. Cherie Hall Duckworth, Aug. 7, 1959; children: Douglas Leland, Christy Lynn. BA, U. Pitts., 1953; MA, Columbia U., 1958; PhD, Stanford U., 1964; LLD (hon.), Kanto Gakuin U., 1979; LHD (hon.), Linfield Coll., 1992. Asst. prof. English Rockford (Ill.) Coll., 1958-61; dept. head, residence dir. Menlo Coll., Menlo Park, Calif., 1961-64; v.p., dean Hamline U., St. Paul, 1964-70; pres. Russell Sage Coll., Troy, N.Y., 1970-75, Linfield Coll., McMinnville, Oreg., 1975-92, pres. emeritus, 1992—; ednl. cons., 1992—; dir. managed programs Ford Family Found., Roseburg, Oreg., 1993-98. Chmn. bd. dirs. 1st Fed. Savs. & Loan, McMinnville; bd. dirs. Wespro Ins. Co., Oreg. Mut. Ins. Co.; mem. Univ. Pres. Initiative, IIE/USIA/NATO, Brussels, 1991. Bd. dirs. South Tillamook County Libr., 1994; pres. Neskowin (Oreg.) Chamber Music; co-chair bldg. com. First Bapt. Ch., McMinnville; bd. dirs., mem. exec. com., dir. Oreg. Coun. Humanities; trustee, vice chair Ford Family Found.; mem. Oreg. Gov.'s Task Force on Cultural Devel.; mem. adv. bd. Habitat for Humanity, McMinnville; chair Joint Interim Task Force on Cultural Devel.; vice chair Oreg. Cultural Trust. Warg scholar U. Pitts., 1949-51; Univ. fellow Stanford U., 1963-64; Hill Found. grantee, St. Paul, 1970; Paul Harris fellow Rotary Internat., 1987; recipient Community Svc. award Troy, N.Y. Troy C. of C., 1975, First Citizen award McMinnville, Oreg., 1989; named Man of Yr., Troy C. of C., 1975.. Mem. Univ. Club (Portland), Rotary (past pres. McMinnville). Home: 1324 SW Gilorr St Mcminnville OR 97128-6617 E-mail: cwalkc@oregoncoast.com.

WALKER, CHARLS EDWARD, economist, consultant; b. Graham, Tex., Dec. 24, 1923; s. Pinkney Clay and Sammye D. (McCombs) W.; m. Harmolyn Hart, June 24, 1949; children: Carolyn, Charls Edward. BBA, U. Tex., 1947, MBA, 1948; PhD in Econs., U. Pa., 1955. Instr. fin. U. Tex., 1947-48, asst. prof., then assoc. prof., 1950-54; instr. fin. U. Pa. Wharton Sch., 1948-50; fin. economist Fed. Res. Bank Phila., 1953; with Fed. Res. Bank Dallas, 1954-61, v.p., econ. adviser, 1958-61; economist Republic Nat. Bank Dallas, 1955-56; asst. to sec. treasury, 1959-61; exec. v.p. Am. Bankers Assn., N.Y.C., 1961-69; under sec. treasury, 1969-72; dep. sec., 1972-73. Adj. prof. U. Tex., Austin, 1986—, Tex. A&M U., 2000—; bd. dirs. Washington Campus, Nat. Coun. Econ. Edn.; chmn., CEO Charls E. Walker Assocs., Inc., 1973-96; disting. vis. prof. Emory U., 2000—. Co-editor: The Bankers Handbook, New Directions in Federal Tax Policy, The Consumption Tax: A Better Alternative, 1987, Intellectual Property Rights and Capital Formation, 1988, The U.S. Savings Challenge, 1990; contbr. articles to profl. jours. and newspapers, chpts. to books. Founder, chmn. Am. Coun. for Capital Formation; co-founder Com. on the Present Danger, 1976, chmn. Pres.'s adv. coun. on minority enterprise, 1973-75; co-chmn. Presdl. Debates, 1976; founder, chmn. Bretton Woods Com.; chmn. Ronald Reagan's Task Force on Tax Policy, 1980; sr. advisor Ctr. for Deliberative Polling, U. Tex., 1996—; chmn. The Nafta Inst. Recipient Alexander Hamilton award U.S. Dept. Treasury, Urban League award, Baker award for Exemplary Svc. to Econ. Edn.; named Disting. Alumnus, U. Tex., 1994. Mem.: Coun. Fgn. Rels., Sea Island (Ga.) Club, Congl. Club (Bethesda, Md.), Burning Tree Club. Home: 10120 Chapel Rd Potomac MD 20854-4143 Home (Winter): 105 Biltmore Saint Simons GA 31522 E-mail: charlswalk@aol.com. *What's good for the public interest ultimately is good for every person, business, or other group in the nation. This, combined with modern application of the Golden Rule, about sums it up.*

WALKER, CHRISTINE, mechanical engineer, educator; b. Chgo., Sept. 8, 1976; d. Robert H. Walker and Catherine M. MacLeod. BS Arch., U. Ill., 1998, MS Mech. Engring., 2001. Rsch. engr. Energy Resources Ctr., Chgo., 1998—. Consulting PERC, Batavia, 1999. Grantee Presdl. Fellowship, MIT, 2001—02. Mem.: Sidney and Pacific Leadership Group (chmn. of the halls 2002—), Architecture Student Coun. (bldg. tech. rep. 2001—02), AIAS, Alpha Rho Chi (rush chair /social chair 1995—96). Office: Energy Resources Ctr 851 South Morgan St Chicago IL 60607 Office Fax: 312-996-5620. E-mail: cwalker@uic.edu.

WALKER, CHRISTOPHER T. newswriter, commentator; b. N.Y.C., Nov. 27, 1964; s. Herbert and Ruth Walker; m. Dilara B. Walker, Nov. 26, 1999. BA, SUNY Binghamton, 1986; M Internat. Affairs, Columbia U., 2001. Mgr. programs European Journalism Network, Prague, 1995—98; freelance analyst Radio Free Europe/Radio Liberty, N.Y.C., 1999—2000; head rapid response unit East West Inst., 2001—. Mem. exec. bd. Transitions Online, Prague, 1999—. Editor (sr. editor): (jours.) Jour. Internat. Affairs, Columbia U., 2000—01; contbr. articles to profl. jours. Fellow Fgn. Lang. Area Studies fellowship, U.S. Dept. Edn., 2000—01, Pepsico Rsch. fellowship, Harriman Inst., 2001. Avocation: foreign languages including German, Czech, and Serbo-Croatian. Home: Apt 5B 328 W 101st St New York NY 10025-4944 Office: East West Inst 700 Broadway New York NY 10003

WALKER, CLARENCE EDWARD, financial analyst; b. John Ben, W.Va., Sept. 27, 1950; s. Harold and Vrginia Walker; m. Yvette Boykin, June 5, 1987 (div. July 10, 1988); children: Zarree, Lamarr, Erika Hoyt. BS, Merrimac Coll., N. Andover, Mass., 1973; MBA, Syracuse (N.Y.) U., 1976. Sales analyst Ford Motor Co., Milw., 1978—80; mgmt. analyst City of Atlanta, 1981—. Author: (book) Booker T. Washington Family Relations from 1859 to 1920. Strategist, campaigner Andrew Young for Mayor, Atlanta, 1981, Maynard Jackson for Mayor, Atlanta, 1991, Shirley Franklin for Mayor, Atlanta, 2001. Avocations: politics, research, travel, writing. Office: PO Box 10673 Atlanta GA 30310

WALKER, CLARENCE WESLEY, lawyer; b. Durham, N.C., July 19, 1931; s. Ernie Franklin and Mollie Elizabeth (Cole) W.; m. Ann-Heath Harris, June 5, 1954; children: Clare Ann, Wesley Gregg. AB, Duke U., 1953, LL.B., 1955. Bar: N.C. 1955. Assoc. Mudge Stern Baldwin & Todd, 1955-59; ptnr. Kennedy, Covington, Loddell & Hickman, Charlotte, N.C., 1961—. Bd. dirs. Lawyers Mut. Liability Ins. Co., Legal Services Corp. N.C., Oakwood Homes Corp. Glendale Group, Ltd.; lectr. N.C. Bar Found. Continuing Legal Edn. Insts., N.C. Jud. Planning Com., 1978-79; pres. Pvt. Adjudication Found. Chmn. bd. mgrs. Charlotte Meml. Hosp. and Med. Ctr., 1981-87; trustee N.C. Ctrl. U., 1979-83; vice-chmn. Charlotte-Mecklenburg Hosp. Authority, 1988-99; adv. bd. Ctrl. Piedmont Paralegal Sch.; trustee Carolinas Healthcare Found., Charlotte Country Day Sch., 1977-81; state chmn. Nat. Found. March of Dimes, 1968-70; chmn. Charlotte Park and Recreation Commn., 1970-73; bd. dirs. Charlotte Symphony, 1965-71, Bethlehem Ctr., 1975-77, N.C. Recreators Found., 1973-75; adv. bd. Charlotte Children's Theatre, 1972; bd. dirs. Charlotte C. of C., 1970-72; bd. visitors Duke U. Law Sch.; dir., gen. campaign chmn. United Way Ctrl. Carolinas, 1985. Fellow Am. Bar Found.; mem. N.C. Bar Assn. (pres. 1978-79, gov. 1971-75), ABA (state del. 1980-89, assembly del., bd. govs. 1997-2000, chair audit com., 2000—) 26th Jud. Dist. Bar Assn., Mecklenburg Bar Found. (trustee), Am. Law Inst., Order of Coif, Phi Eta Sigma, Phi Beta Kappa. Democrat. Methodist. Home: 1047 Ardsley Rd Charlotte NC 28207-1815 Office: Kennedy Covington Lobdell & Hickman Bank of Am Corp Ctr 100 N Tryon St Ste 4200 Charlotte NC 28202-4006

WALKER, CRAIG MICHAEL, lawyer; b. Vt., 1947; m. Patricia A. Magruder; two children. BA, Williams Coll., 1969; JD, Cornell U., 1972. Bar: N.Y. 1973, U.S. Dist. Ct. (so. dist.) N.Y. 1975, U.S. Ct. Appeals (2d cir) 1975, U.S. Supreme Ct 1976. Assoc. Alexander & Green, N.Y.C., 1972-80, ptnr., 1980-86, chmn. litigation dept., 1985-86; ptnr. Walter, Conston, Alexander & Green P.C., 1987-89, Rogers & Wells LLP, N.Y.C., 1990-99, Clifford Chance Rogers & Wells LLP, N.Y.C., 2000—. Contbr. author: New York Forms of Jury Instruction, 1992; contbr. articles to profl. jours. Fellow Am. Bar Found.; mem. ABA, N.Y. State Bar Assn., Def. Rsch. Inst., Fed. Bar Coun. Democrat.

WALKER, DALE MAXWELL, city official; b. Big Rapids, Mich., Dec. 18, 1947; s. Lewis M. and Hilma I. (Windquist) W.; m. Joanne Kay Richmond, June 22, 1968; children: Christina Elizabeth, Heather Marie. BS, Ferris State Coll., 1970; MBA, Ctrl. Mich. U., 1981. Cert. govt. fin. mgr. Dir. fin. City of Owosso, Mich., 1970-74; corp. treas. Mich. Bapt. Homes, Detroit, 1976-77; dir. fin. City of Cadillac, Mich., 1977—. Pres. Gospel Bookstore, Inc., Cadillac, 1983-98. Bd. dirs. Wexford County United Way, 1980-82, Shiawassee County United Way, 1971-72; sec.-treas. Cadillac Police and Fire Retirement System, 1977-87, bd. dirs. 1987—; chmn. Mcpl. Employees Retirement System, Mich., 1997—. Fellow Govtl. Fin. Officers Assn. U.S. and Can. (Profl. Achievement award 1984-2000); mem. Mich. Mcpl. Fin. Officers Assn. (bd. dirs. 1983-85), Internat. City Mgrs. Assn., Mich. Mcpl. Treas. Assn., Mcpl. Treas. Assn. U.S. and Can. (bd. dirs. 1982-84), McGuires Golf Club. Republican. Baptist. Avocations: golf, swimming, reading. Home: 901 Lincoln St Cadillac MI 49601-2035 Office: 200 N Lake St Cadillac MI 49601-1829

WALKER, DAN, mayor, business consultant; Mem. Torrance City Coun., 1978—92, 1994—2002; mayor City of Torrance, Calif., 2002—. Del. South Bay Cities Coun. Govts., L.A. County Sanitation Dist., South Bay Econ. Devel. Partnership; mem. Planning Commn., 1975—77. Mem. L.A. Regional Quality Control Bd.; bd. dirs. Friends of Child Advs. Office: 3031 Torrance Blvd Torrance CA 90503 E-mail: dwalker@tornet.com.*

WALKER, DAVID A(LAN), finance educator, educator; b. York, Pa., Jan. 5, 1941; s. Arthur Benjamin and Alva (Strasbougher) Walker; m. Audrey Thayer, Aug. 21, 1982; children: Matthew Billett, Elizabeth Penniman Bilhartz. BA, Pa. State U., 1962; MS, Iowa State U., 1964, PhD, 1968. Asst. prof. Pa. State U., 1968-70; economist FDIC, 1970-76, 78-80; vis. assoc. prof. Northwestern U., 1976-77; dir. rsch. Office Comptroller of Currency, 1977-78; assoc. prof. fin. Georgetown U., 1980-82, prof., 1982-92, assoc. dean, 1985-87, John A. Largay prof., 1992—. Chair governing bd. Credit Rsch. Ctr., 1997—; dir. Capital Mkts. Rsch. Ctr., 1989—; hon. com. mem. Wall St. Inst., 2002–; advisor U.S. Dept. Treas., U.S. SBA; cons. in field. Co-author textbooks; editor Jour. Fin. Rsch., 1981-87; co-editor Jour. Small Bus. Fin., 1992-95; mem. editl. bd. Jour. Fin. Rsch., Fin. Mgmt., J.F.Q.A., Fin. Rev., Quar. Rev. Econs. and Fin., Jour. Small Bus. Fin.; contbr. articles to profl. jours. NDEA fellow, 1962-64. Mem. Am. Econ. Assn., So. Fin. Assn. (bd. dirs.), Ea. Fin. Assn. (bd. dirs.), Fin. Mgmt. Assn. (v.p. 1990-91, pres. 1994-95, trustee 1995—, chair bd. trustees 1999—), Beta Gamma Sigma. Republican. Home: 4416 Que St NW Washington DC 20007 Office: Georgetown U Sch Bus Washington DC 20057-0001 E-mail: walkerd@msb.edu.

WALKER, DAVID ELLIS, JR. educator, minister, consultant; b. Richmond, Va., Oct. 5, 1938; s. David Ellis and Laura Eloise (Vaughan) W.; m. Sandra Suzanne Barnes, Feb. 3, 1964; children: David Ellis III, Virginia Suzanne Walker Frizzell, Cindy Poole Key, Michelle Poole Clark. BA, David Lipscomb U., 1960; MA, U. Fla., 1961, PhD, 1969. Ordained to ministry Ch. Christ, 1954. Instr. Jacksonville (Fla.) U., 1963-65; min. Ch. of Christ, 1954-99; prof. Middle Tenn. State U., Murfreesboro, 1965—. Cons. 1981—; acting chmn. dept. speech Middle Tenn. State U., summer 1984, fall 1990, dir. debate, 1965-70, pres. faculty senate, 1983-84; coord. comm. studies,1969-81, 97-99. Editor Jour. of NonTraditional Education, 1992-96; contbr. articles to profl. jours. and Ency. U.S.A. Grad. fellow U. Fla., 1961-63; grantee Mid. Tenn. State U., 1967, 72, 77, 78, 88, 89, 90, 92, 93, 94, David Walker scholarship Mid. Tenn. State U., 1993—. Mem. NEA, Tenn. Comm. Assn. (v.p. 1973-74, pres. 1974-75, editor Jour. Tenn. Comm. Assn. 1977-85), Tenn. Intercollegiate Forensic Assn. (pres. 1966-67, exec. sec. 1967-68), So. States Comm. Assn., Popular Culture Assn. of the South, Tenn. Edn. Assn., Pi Kappa Delta (gov. province of S.E. 1966-68), Phi Kappa Phi (chpt. treas. 1989-90). Avocations: reading, walking. Home: 2644 E Compton Rd Murfreesboro TN 37130-6848 Office: Mid Tenn State U Dept Of Speech And Theatre Murfreesboro TN 37132-0001 E-mail: dwalker@mtsu.edu.

WALKER, DAVID MICHAEL, federal official; b. Birmingham, Ala., Oct. 2, 1951; s. David Sellers and Dorothy Ann (West) W.; m. Mary Carmel Etheredge, June 12, 1971; children: Carol Marie, James Andrew. BS in Acctg., Jacksonville U., 1973; Sr. Exec. Govt. Cert., Harvard U., 1986. CPA, Fla., Tex., Ga. Sr. auditor Price Waterhouse & Co. and Coopers & Lybrand, Jacksonville, Fla., 1973-76; dir. personnel Coopers & Lybrand, Atlanta and Houston, 1976-79; Ea. regional mgr. Source Services Corp., Washington, 1979-83; acting exec. dir. and dep. exec. dir. Pension Benefit Guaranty Corp., 1983-85; dep. asst. sec. U.S. Dept. of Labor, 1985-87, asst. sec., 1987-89; ptnr., global mng. dir. human capital svcs. practice Arthur Andersen LLP, Atlanta, 1989-98; U.S. comptroller gen. U.S. Gen. Acctg. Office, Washington, 1998—. Author: Retirement Security-Understanding and Planning Your Financial Future, 1996; co-author: Delivering on the Promise: How to Attract, Manage and Retain Muman Capital, 1998; contbr. articles, editorial adv. bd. several profl. jours. Gov. bd. Internat. Orgn. Supreme Audit Instns. and numerous other not-for-profit bds. and adv. coms.; mem. fin. acctg. standards adv. com.; chmn. U.S. Intergovtl. Audit Forum; chmn. U.S. Joint Fin. Mgmt. Improvement Program. Recipient numerous industry and achievement awards for outstanding svc. and contbns. Mem. AICPA (past chmn. employee benefit plans com.), Nat. Acad. Pub. Adminstrn., Nat. Acad. Social Ins., Coun. for Excellence in Govt, Concord Coalition. Roman Catholic. Home: 9061 Tower House Pl Alexandria VA 22308-2758 Office: US Gen Acctg Office 441 G St NW Washington DC 20548-0001 E-mail: walkerd@gao.gov.

WALKER, DEBORAH LYNNE, nurse practitioner; b. Louisville, Jan. 2, 1968; d. M. Wayne and Patricia Irene (Hornbeek) Downs; m. Patrick Samuel Walker, Aug. 8, 1992. BSN with honors, U. Fla., 1992, MN, 1996. Cert. family nurse practitioner ANCC. Staff nurse pediatrics Shands Hosp., Gainesville, Fla., 1992; staff nurse in intermediate care St. Lukes Luth. Hosp., San Antonio, 1992-93; case mgr. Olsten Kimberly Quality Care, Gainesville, Fla., 1994-95, field nurse, 1995-96; nurse practitioner Gainesville Family Physicians, 1996-98, nursing coord., 1997-98; nurse practitioner Westlakes Health Ctr., San Antonio, 1998-2000, Med. Assocs. of No. Ga., Canton, 2000—. Spkr. Am. Heart Assn., 1996. Mem. ANA, Am. Acad. of Nurse Practitioners, Gainesville Nurse Practitioner Orgn., Fla. Nurses Assn. (dist. 10 bd. dirs., sec., del.), Fla. Nurses Assn., Tex. Nurses Assn., Sigma Theta Tau. Avocations: reading, hiking, cycling, aerobics, weight training. Office: Med Assocs of North Ga 320 Hospital Rd Canton GA 30114

WALKER, DEBRA, artist; b. Omaha, Apr. 23, 1953; d. Lowell Lampert and Margaret Mary (Ball) W. Student fine arts, Riverside City Coll., 1972-74, UCLA, 1974-75; student painting, Skyline Coll., 1981-83; student, Visual Arts Access, 1993-94; student intaglio etching, U. Calif., 1995. Represented by George Krevsky Fine Art, San Francisco. Designer United Artists Records, 1975-76; asst. art dir. L.A. Times, 1976-78; owner Comml. Design Advtsg. Agy., 1978-81; art cons. Bowles-Hopkins Gallery, 1981-82; print cons., 1985-91; bus., prodn. mgr. Redgate Comms., 1991-92. One-woman exhbns. include Riverside Art Mus., 1974, Cowell Theater, San Francisco, 1995, George Krevsky Fine Art, San Francisco, 1995, 96, 99, CSK. Inc., Denver, 1997; group exhbns. Riverside Press Enterprise, 1974 (Purchase prize 1974), Shenendoah Gallery, Plymouth, 1987. Studio Show, San Francisco, 1990, Riverside Art Mus., 1993, George Krevsky Fine Art, 1993, 94, Nat. Assn. Women Artists, Athens, Greece, 1996, San Francisco Mus. Modern Art, 1996, Triton Mus., San Jose, 1998, George Krevsky Fine Art, San Francisco, 1998, 99, 2000, 01; permanent collections Twentieth Century Fox, numerous pvt. collections; pub. in Visualize. Pres. Harvey Milk Lexbian, Gay, Bisexual Transgender Dem. Club; mem. San Francisco Dem. County Ctrl. Com.; founding mem. Coalition for Jobs, Arts and Housing; bd. v.p. Soundsafe; v.p. pol. action com. Harvey Nuble Dem. Club. Mem. Nat. Assn. Women Artists. Democrat. Avocations: writing, community activism, travel. E-mail: dw@debrawalker.com.

WALKER, DEWARD EDGAR, JR. anthropologist, educator; b. Johnson City, Tenn., Aug. 3, 1935; s. Deward Edgar and Matilda Jane (Clark) W.; m. Candace J. Arroyo; children: Alice, Deward Edgar III, Mary Jane, Sarah, Daniel, Joseph Benjamin. Student, Ea. Oreg. Coll., 1953-54, 56-58, Univ. of the Americas, 1958-59; BA in Anthropology with honors, U. Oreg., 1960-61, PhD in Anthropology, 1964; postgrad., Wash. State U., 1962. Asst. prof. anthropology George Washington U., Washington, 1964-65, Wash. State U., Pullman, 1965-67, research collaborator, 1967-69; assoc. prof., chmn. dept. Sociology/Anthropology, lab. dir. U. Idaho, Moscow, 1967-69; prof. U. Colo., Boulder, 1969—, research assoc. in population processes program of inst. behavioral sci., 1969-73, assoc. dean Grad. Sch., 1973-76. Founder, v.p. Walker Rsch. Group, Ltd., Boulder, Colo., 1995. Founder, co-editor Northwest Anthropol. Rsch. Notes, 1966—; editor, Plateau Vol.: Handbook of North American Indians, 1971-98; author, co-author 150 books, reports, articles and papers. Mem. tech. steering panel Hanford Environ. Dose Reconstrn. Project, 1988-95, Basalt Waste Isolation Project, Hanford, 1986-88; advisor on Native Am. affairs. With U.S. Army, 1954-62. Fellow NSF, 1961, NDEA, 1961-64. Fellow Am. Anthropol. Assn. (assoc. editor Am. Anthropologist 1973-74), Soc. Applied Anthropology (hon. life, exec. com. 1970-79, treas. 1976-79, chmn. 1960-2000, cons., expert witness western tribes, editor Human Orgn. 1970-76, rschr. over 65 projects with 150 monographs, articles, reports, and papers, editor High Plains Applied Anthropologist); mem. AAAS, Am. Acad. Polit. and Social Scis., N.W. Anthropol. Conf. Avocations: geology, mining, ranching. Home: PO Box 4147 Boulder CO 80306-4147 Office: U Colo PO Box 233 Boulder CO 80309-0233 E-mail: walkerde@spot.colorado.edu. *I have been both lucky and happy to have had the opportunities to do so many wonderful things in my life as an anthropologist.*

WALKER, DIANE RUTH, communications executive; b. Kansas City, Mo. m. R. Wayne Walker; children: Molly, Joshua. BA, U. Mo., 1978. Cert. bus. communicator. Reporter, asst. city editor Kansas City (Kans.) Kansan, 1978-84; asst. mgr. comm. Greater Kansas City C. of C., Kansas City, 1984-87; pub. rels. dir. Penn Valley C.C., 1987; comm. specialist Peoples Natural Gas, Omaha, 1988-90; comm. adminstr. Mo. Pub. Svc., Raytown, 1991-97; corp. comm. Aquila, Inc., Kansas City, 1997—. Asst. coach softball and soccer Liberty Parks and Recreation, Liberty, Mo., 1996-2002; vol. Youth Friends, Kansas City, Mo., 1996—; bd. dirs. Caring for Kids, Kansas City; mentor William Jewell Coll., Liberty, 1999-2000; pres. PTA Lewis & Clark Elem. Sch., Liberty, 1999-2001, chmn. newsletter 1999—; PTA Life Membership award, 2002; mem. Liberty, Mo. Mid. sch. Redistricting committee, 2001; mem. key messages com. Liberty Sch. Bond Election, 2000. Recipient Excellence award Liberty Sch. Dist. Mem. Internat. Assn. Bus. Comm. (co-chmn. conf. materials com. regional conf., 1997, Bronze Quill award 1994, 1998). Office: Aquila Inc 20 W 9th St # 2-133 Kansas City MO 64105-1704 Fax: 816-467-9686. E-mail: diane.walker@aquila.com.

WALKER, DONALD EDWIN, history educator; b. Hammond, Ind., Feb. 6, 1941; s. Carl Thurston and Verla Irene (Cutler) W.; m. Julie Ann Woerpel, Dec. 20, 1960; children: Theodore R., Susan J. Walker. BA, Ind. U., 1963; MA, U. S.D., 1964; postgrad., U. Wyo., 1964-65; PhD, Mich. State U., 1982. Asst. prof. Olivet (Mich.) Coll., 1965-74, assoc. prof., 1974-82, prof., 1982—. Cons. Score Cards, Westport, Conn., 1991. Co-author: Baseball and American Culture, 1995; contbr. articles to profl. jours. City coun. mem. Olivet City Coun., 1977—; police commr. Olivet Police Dept., 1984—; mayor pro tempore City of Olivet, 1983—. Mem. Orgn. of Am. Historians, Western History Assn., Phi Alpha Theta, Phi Kappa Phi, Omicron Delta Kappa, Phi Mu Alpha. Methodist. Avocations: gardening, music, reading, traveling, walking. Home: PO 516 407 Washington Olivet MI 49076-9601 Office: Olivet Coll Dept History Mott Bldg Olivet MI 49076

WALKER, DONALD ANTHONY, economist, educator; b. Mar. 6, 1934; s. Timothy Anthony and Helen (Walker) W.; m. Patricia Ann McKeage, Feb. 14, 1961; 1 dau., Valerie Alana. AB, S.W. Tex. State U., 1952; MA, U. Tex., 1956; PhD, Harvard U., 1961. Asst. prof. econs. Miami U., Oxford, Ohio, 1961-67, assoc. prof. econs., 1967-69; prof. econs. Indiana U. Pa., 1969-88, chmn. dept., 1969-98, Univ. prof., 1988-98, Univ. prof., prof. econs. emeritus, 1999—. Author: Walras's Market Models, 1996, Advances in General Equilibrium Theory, 1997; editor: William Jaffé's Essays on Walras, 1983, Money and Markets: Essays by Robert W. Clower, 1984, Perspectives on the History of Economic Thought, 1989, Welfare Economics and the Theory of Economic Policy, 1995, Jour. of the History of Econ. Thought, 1989—98, Economics, Welfare Policy and the History of Economic Thought, 1999, Equilibrium, 2000, The Legacy of Léon Walras, 2001. Recipient Commonwealth of Pa. Distinguished Acad. Service award, 1974, Ind. U.-Pa. Disting. Research Award, 1984; Harvard fellow, 1956-57, 57-58; Henry Lee Meml. fellow, 1957-58 Mem. History of Econs. Soc. (pres. 1987-88), Walras Soc. (pres. 1997-2000). Home: 48 Shady Dr Indiana PA 15701-3245

WALKER, DONALD EZZELL, retired academic administrator; b. Springfield, Mo., July 13, 1921; s. Edward Everett and Cecilia (Ezzell) W.; m. Ann Lathrop, Dec. 17, 1943; 1 son, Craig Lathrop. AB, U. So. Calif., 1943, M.Th., 1947; PhD, Stanford U., 1954; L.H.D. (hon.), Southeastern Mass. U., 1973. Recreational dir. club work All Nations Found., Los Angeles, 1941-42, Wilshire Meth. Ch., Los Angeles, 1942-43; asst. minister Vincent Meth. Ch., 1943-44; minister Encinitas Meth. Ch., 1945-47; teaching asst. Stanford U., 1947-49; instr. sociology San Diego State Coll., 1949-51, asst. prof. sociology, 1951-54, assoc. dean students, counseling, 1954-56, dean counseling, 1956-58, v.p. acad. affairs, 1968-71, acting pres., 1971-72; dean of students San Fernando Valley State Coll., Northridge, Calif., 1958-60; pres. Idaho State U., 1960-64; dean of students Sonoma State Coll., Rohnert Park, Calif., 1964-66; vice chancellor student affairs U. Calif., Irvine, 1966-68, sr. lectr. Grad. Sch. Adminstrn., 1967-68, fellow Univ. Coll., 1967-68; pres. Southeastern Mass. State U., N. Dartmouth, 1972-83; chancellor Grossmont-Cuyamaca Community Coll. Dist., El Cajon, Calif., 1983-92; ret., 1992. Author: (with others) Readings in American Public Opinion; The Effective Administrator: A Practical Approach to Problem-Solving, Decision-Making, and Campus Leadership, 1979; Never Try to Teach a Pig to Sing: Wit and Wisdom for Leaders, 1996; contbr. (with others) articles to profl. jours. Home: 8661 Lake Murray Blvd Apt 19 San Diego CA 92119-2842

WALKER, DONALD J. automotive systems company executive; b. London, Can., Aug. 29, 1956; s. Cyril Reginald and Margaret Marilyn (Wallace) W. BSc, U. Waterloo, Ont., 1980. Sr. engr., supt. GM; asst. to chair Magna Internat. Inc., Markham, Ont., 1987-88, dir. corp. mtkg. and strategic planning, 1988-89, v.p. product devel., 1989-90, exec. v.p., COO, 1990-92, pres., CEO, 1992-2001, Intier Automotive Inc., Newmarket, 2001—. Bd. dirs. Covisint. Bd. dirs. Yves Landry Tech. Endowment Fund; co-chmn. Automotive Adv. Com. Fed. Govt. Can., 1997—. Mem.: Assn. Profl. Engrs. Ont. (Gold medal 1999), Automotive Parts Mfrs. Assn. (bd. dirs. 2000—). Office: Intier Automotive Inc 521 Newpark Blvd Newmarket ON Canada L3Y 4X7 E-mail: don_walker@intier.com.

WALKER, DONALD MURRAY, minister; b. Lansing, Mich., Oct. 10, 1938; s. Paul H. and Margaret V. (Holloway) W.; m. Jacquelyn Touchstone, June 7, 1958; children: Donalyn Renee Scoggins, S. Denise Walker. BS, Lee U., 1977; MA, Ashland U., 1978; MDiv, Ch. of God Theol. Sem., 1980; EdD, Southeastern Nova U., 1983. Ordained to ministry Ch. of God, 1968. Evangelist Ch. of God, Minot, N.D., 1958-60, state dir. youth and Christian edn. Indpls., 1960-64, pastor S.C., 1964-70, state dir. youth and Christian edn. Mich., 1970-74, Ohio, 1974-78, Tenn., 1978-82; pres. Northwest Bible Coll., Minot, 1982-86; state overseer Ch. of God, N.D., S.D., 1984-86, asst. dir. gen. edn. dept. Tenn., 1986-88, state overseer Ind., 1988-93, Tenn., 1993-98, mem. exec. com., 1994-98; pres. Ch. of God Theol. Sem., Cleveland, Tenn., 1998—. Chmn. Ch. of God Chaplains Commn., Cleveland, 1990-94. Bd. dirs., chmn. bldg. com. Lee U., 1994-98. Home: 1845 Partridge Rd NW Cleveland TN 37312-2128 Office: 900 Walker St NE Cleveland TN 37311-5234 *While there are many issues and crises in life that we often do not understand our attitude toward our faith in God and His mercy can never be dictated by our circumstances.*

WALKER, DONALD ROBERT, JR. minister; b. Leavenworth, Kans., Oct. 24, 1955; s. Donald Robert and Norma Elizabeth (Wagner) W.; m. June Marie Chinn, Jan. 1, 1976; children: Heather Renee, Eric David, Michelle Renee, Meagan Renee. Student, Kans. City Kans. Community Coll., 1973-75, Full Faith Bible Coll., 1977-79. Ordained minister, 1979. Sr. pastor Abundant Life Fellowship, Leavenworth, 1978-82; assoc. pastor Full Faith Ch. of Love, Shawnee, Kans., 1982-84; sr. pastor Full Faith Ch. of Love East, Kans. City,

Mo., 1984-94; pastor Christ Covenant Ch., Kansas City, 1995—. Exec. coun. Nat. Leadership Conf., Montreat, N.C., 1988-90, bd. dirs., 1990—; mem. adv. bd. World Indigenous Missions, New Braunfels, Tex., 1990-95; mem. gen. coun. Fellowship of Christian Leaders, chmn. theol. coun.; instr. New Cambridge Inst., Santa Rosa, Calif., 1999—. Pres. Found. for the Family, Overland Park, Kans., 1989—. Mem. Internat. Churchill Soc.

WALKER, DORIS ANN, education educator; b. Oxford, Miss., Aug. 6, 1950; d. Earnest Jr. and Mildred (Blackmon) McEwen; m. Grady Walker Jr., June 19, 1971 (div. Aug. 1990); children: Maleika Rene, Cheo Da'Mu. BS, No. Mich. U., 1971; MS, Mich. State U., 1975, PhD, 1981. Cert. tchr. 7-12, secondary adminstr. 5-12, supt. endorsement, Mich.; tchr., adminstr., Nev.; secondary adminstr., supt., Ind., Wash. Tchr. Flint (Mich.) Sch. Dist., 1972; tchr., sch. adminstr. Lansing (Mich.) Sch. Dist., 1973-86; prof. U. Nev., Reno, 1986-88, 96—; asst. prin. Waverly H.S., Lansing, 1988-91; prin. East Lansing (Mich.) H.S., 1991-94; assoc. prof. Ind. U., South Bend, 1994-96; asst. supt. Edmonds Sch. Dist. 15, Lynnwood, Wash., 1996—; supt. Clover Pk. Sch. Dist., Lakewood. Edn. cons. Nev. State Dept. Edn., Carson City, 1986-88 Contbr. articles to profl. jours. Bd. dirs. Lansing Art Gallery, Neutral Zone, Wash., YWCA Pathways for Women, South Bend (Ind.) Meml. Hosp., Spice of Life, Ind.; past advisor Boy Scouts Am.; cadette leader Mich. Capitol Girl Scouts; mem. nominating bd. YWCA; trustee meml. Hosp.; mem. urban youth adv. bd. YMCA. Mem. ASCD, NAACP, Nat. Assn. Secondary Sch. Prins., Nat. Alliance Black Sch. Educators, Am. Assn. Sch. Adminstrs., Mich. Assn. Secondary Sch. Prins., Ind. Assn. Secondary Sch. Prins., Optimist Club, Phi Delta Kappa, Delta Sigma Theta. Avocations: reading, computers, multimedia. Home: 12775 Gravelly Lake Dr SW Lakewood WA 98499-1459

WALKER, DORIS ISAAK, writer, historian, educator; b. Cleve. d. Alphonse Charles and Rose Emma (Gibbons) Isaak; children: Brent Evan Walker, Blair Dana Walker; m. Jack Pierson Smith, 2001. AB, Case Western Reserve U.; postgrad., Northwestern U., U. Calif., Irvine. Publs. editor Brunswick Corp., Chgo.; pub. rels. mgr. Dana Point (Calif.) Harbor, 1970-84; field rsch. writer Kessler Exch., L.A., Calif., 1984-89. Instr. Calif. history South Orange County C.C. Dist.; lectr. in field. Author: Sections of Orange, 1989, Dana Point Harbor/Capistrano Bay: Home Port for Romance, 1981, 4th edit., 1995, Coastal Reflections, 2001, Orange County Adventures With Children, 1997, The Whales of Capistrano Bay, 1982, The Heritage of San Clemente, 2000, A Guide Book of Philatelic-Numismatic Covers, 1970; contbr., editor, photographer newspapers, mags. Commr. Orange County Hist. Commn., 1994—; founder, coord. Dana Point Festival of Whales, 1975-84. Recipient over 100 awards including Am. History award DAR, Clarion award, Unique Coverage award Women in Comm., Woman of Distinction award Capistrano Bay Area, Soroptimist Internat., Crisis Comm. Award Internat. Coun. Indsl. Editors, cert. of recognition Calif. State Senate; named Orange County Woman of Achievement in Comm., YWCA. Mem. AAUW (pres. San Clemente-Capistrano Bay br.), Nat. Fedn. Press Women (Nat. first place book award history), Calif. Media Profls., Calif. Press Women (pres. Orange County dist., state sec.), Dana Point Hist. Soc. (hon. life, co-founder, dir.), San Juan Capistrano Hist. Soc. (dir.), Orange County Hist. Soc. (dir.). Avocations: travel, photography. Office: PO Box 546 Dana Point CA 92629-0546 E-mail: homeports@aol.com.

WALKER, DOUGLAS BAYNARD, science educator; b. Knoxville, Tenn., June 26, 1941; s. Hazen Aurin and Ria Robert Walker; m. Margie Russell Ihrig, Jan. 6, 1964 (div. Mar. 12, 1966); 1 child Timothy Douglas. BA, Tex. Christian U., 1964; MA, So. Meth. U., 1972. Instr. biology Bryan Adams H.S., Dallas, 1966—68, St. Mary's Hall, San Antonio, 1969—71; tchg. asst. U. Tex. Med. Sch., 1972—76; instr. biology Highland Park H.S., Dallas, 1977—78; instr. anatomy Westminster Coll., New Wilmington, Pa., 1978—79; instr. biology Cistercian Prep. Sch., Irving, Tex., 1980—81; instr. anatomy and physiology Wharton (Tex.) County Jr. Coll., 1982—. Grantee, Meadows Found., 1989. Mem.: Tex. C.C. Tchrs. Assn. Democrat. Episcopalian. Avocations: restoring old cars, photography. Home: 414 Lazy Ln Wharton TX 77488 Office: Wharton County Jr Coll 911 Boling Hwy Wharton TX 77488

WALKER, DUARD LEE, medical educator; b. Bishop, Calif., June 2, 1921; s. Fred H. and Anna Lee (Shumate) Walker; m. Dorothea Virginia McHenry, Aug. 11, 1945; children: Douglas Keith, Donna Judith, David Cameron, Diane Susan. AB, U. Calif. - Berkeley, 1943, MA, 1947; MD, U. Calif. - San Francisco, 1945. Diplomate Am. Bd. Microbiology. Intern, U.S. Naval Hosp., Shoemaker, Calif., 1945—46; asst. resident internal medicine Stanford U. Service San Francisco Hosp., 1950—52; asso. prof. med. microbiology and preventive medicine U. Wis., Madison, 1952—59, prof. med. microbiology, 1959—88, prof., chmn. med. microbiology, 1970—76, Paul F. Clark prof. med. microbiology, 1977—88, prof. emeritus, 1988—, prof., chmn. med. microbiology, 1981—88. Cons. Naval Med. Rsch. Unit, Gt. Lakes, Ill., 1958—74; mem. microbiology tng. com. Nat. Inst. Gen. Med. Scis., 1966—70; mem. nat. adv. Allergy and Infectious Diseases Coun., 1970—74; mem. adv. com. on blood program rsch. ARC, 1978—79; mem. study group on papovaviridae Internat. Com. on Taxonomy of Viruses, 1976—90; mem. vaccines and related biol. products adv. com. FDA, 1985—89; mem. rev. panel postdoct. rsch. fellowships for physicians Howard Hughes Med Inst., 1990—93. Served to lt. (j.g.) USNR, 1943—46, served to lt. comdr. USNR, 1953—55. Fellow NRC postdoctoral virology, Rockefeller Inst. Med. Rsch., N.Y.C., 1947—49, USPHS immunology, George Williams Hooper Found., U. Calif., San Francisco, 1949—50. Fellow: Infectious Diseases Soc. Am., Am. Acad. Microbiology, Am. Pub. Health Assn.; mem.: Arts and Letters, Wis. Acad. Sics., Am. Soc. Virology, AAUP, Reticulendothelial Soc., Soc. Exptl. Biology and Medicine, AAAS, Am. Soc. Microbiology, Am. Assn. Immunologists, NAS. Home: 618 Odell St Madison WI 53711-1435 Office: U Wis Med Sch 1300 University Ave Madison WI 53706-1510 E-mail: dlwalkel@facstaff.wisc.edu.

WALKER, EDWARD KEITH, JR. business executive, retired naval officer; b. Annapolis, Md., Jan. 23, 1933; s. Edward Keith and Miriam (Whitmore) W.; m. Carol Ann Turner, June 12, 1954 (dec. June 14, 2002); children: Lynn Walker Streett, Wendy Louise. BS, U.S. Naval Acad., 1954; postgrad., Armed Forces Staff Coll., 1966; MBA in Fin. Mgmt., George Washington U., 1970. Commd. ensign U.S. Navy, 1954, advanced through grades to rear admiral, 1981; force supply officer COMSUBLANT Norfolk, Va., 1975-78; exec. officer SPCC Mechanicsburg, Pa., 1978-80; comdr. Naval Supply Ctr., Puget Sound, Bremerton, Wash., 1980-81; Atlantic Fleet supply officer CINCLANTFLT Norfolk, 1981-83; asst. comptroller Navy Dept., Washington, 1983-84; comdr. Naval Supply Systems Command and 35th chief supply corps, 1984-88; v.p. adminstrn. and corp. strategy Resource Cons. Inc., Vienna, 1989-2000, v.p. emeritus, 2000—. Bd. dirs. Herley Industries. Decorated D.S.M., Legion of Merit (3 awards); recipient Def. Superior Service medal, 1983 Mem. Vinson Hall Corp. (bd. dirs.), Naval Acad. Found. (trustee), U.S. Navy Meml. Found. (bd. dirs., treas.), Supply Corps Found. (past pres.), Supply Corps Assn. (past pres.), U.S. Naval Inst., Am. Soc. Naval Engrs., Naval Submarine League, Naval Order U.S., Surface Navy Assn., Navy League U.S., Naval Acad. Alumni Assn. (life), Ret. Officers Assn. (life), N.Y. Yacht Club, Chesapeake Yacht Club. Republican. Episcopalian. Home: 3520 Saylor Pl Alexandria VA 22304-1831 Office: Resource Cons Inc 2650 Park Tower Dr Ste 800 Vienna VA 22180-3862 *There is no greater satisfaction than to see your people succeed, and then to insure they get the credit.*

WALKER, ELJANA M. DU VALL, civic worker; b. France, Jan. 18, 1924; came to U.S., 1948; naturalized, 1954; m. John S. Walker, Jr., Dec. 31, 1947; children: John, Peter, Barbara. Pres. Loyola Sch. PTA, 1959-59; bd. dirs. Santa Claus Shop, 1959-73; treas. Archdiocese Denver Catholic Women, 1962-64; rep. Cath. Parent-Tchr. League, 1962-65; pres. Aux. Denver Gen. Hosp., 1966-69; precinct committeewoman Arapahoe County Women's Com., 1973-74; mem. re-election com. Arapahoe County Rep. Party, 1973-78, Reagan election com., 1980. Block worker Arapahoe County March of Dimes, Heart Assn., Hemophilia Drive, Muscular Dystrophy and Multiple Sclerosis Drive, 1979-81, cen. city asst. Guild Debutante Charities, Inc. Recipient Dist. Svc. award Am.-by-choice, 1966; nmaed to Honor Roll, ARC, 1971. Mem. Cherry Hills Symphony, Lyric Opera Guild, Alliance Franciase (life mem.), ARC, Civic Ballet Guild (life mem.), Needlework Guild Am. (v.p. 1980-82), Kidney Found. (life), Denver Art Mus., U. Denver Art and Conservation Assns. (chmn. 1980-82), U. Denver Women's Lib. Assn., Chancellors Soc., Passage Inc., Friends of the Fine Arts Found. (life), Children's Diabetes Found. (life), Littleton Pub. Sch. Pioneers, Union (Chgo.), Denver Athletic, 26 (Denver), Welcome to Colo. Internat. Roman Catholic. Address: 2301 Green Oaks Dr Littleton CO 80121

WALKER, FORREST A., JR. historian, educator; b. Pittsburg, Kans., Oct. 8, 1929; s. Forrest Anderson Walker, Neita Irene Hawthorne; m. Mary Jo Duck, Oct. 22, 1956; 1 child David F. BA, Tex. A&I Coll., 1951, MA, 1952; PhD, U. Okla., 1962. Tchr. Lamorque Jr. H.S., Tex., 1956—57; prof. Florence State Coll., Ala., 1961—63; prof. history Ea. N.Mex. U., Portales, N.Mex., 1963—91, prof. emeritus, 1991—. Edn. instr. U.S. Army, Dochau, Germany, 1954—55. Contbr. With USAF, 1952—56. Mem.: Kiwanis (chpt. pres. 1991—92). Avocations: reading, travel. Home: 237 Kansas Dr Portales NM 88130

WALKER, FRANCIS ROACH, rehabilitation consultant; b. Dallas, Mar. 1, 1944; s. Anan Orville and Vonda Mae (Roach) W.; m. Sherry Lynn Robins (div. Dec. 1977); children: John, Christian, Lorri; m. Karen Sue Newhouse, Aug. 2, 1980. BGS in Psychology, Chaminade U. of Honolulu, 1980; MA in Psychology, U. No. Colo., 1982. Cert. tchr., Hawaii; cert. rehab. counselor. Br. mgr. Internat. Savs. & Loan, Honolulu, 1982-83; ops. mgr. C.M. Assocs., Inc., Kaneohe, Hawaii, 1983-84; instr. adult div. St. Louis High Sch., Honolulu, 1984-87; owner Commonwealth Distbrs., Norfolk, Va., 1987-88; dir. edn. Gulf Coast Marine Inst., Inc., Sarasota, Fla., 1989-91; vocat. evaluator vets. svcs. Goodwill Industries-Suncoast, Inc., St. Petersburg, 1991-97; vocat. rehab. cons., 1997—. Adj. prof. City Colls. of Chgo., 1984-87, Ctrl. Tex. Coll., 1988-89; fellow Am. Bd. Disability Analysts. Capt. USMC, 1962-82. Mem. Internat. Assn. Rehab. Profls., Am. Legion Nat. Sojourners (chpt. pres.), Marine Corps Mustang Assn., Fla. Mustangs (co-founder, pres.), Shriners. Republican. Avocations: fishing, boating, reading, cooking. Home: 340 Colony Point Rd S Saint Petersburg FL 33705-6227 E-mail: fwalker1@tampabay.rr.com.

WALKER, FRANCIS JOSEPH, lawyer; b. Aug. 5, 1922; s. John McSweeney and Sarah Veronica (Meechan) W.; m. Julia Corinne O'Brien, Jan. 27, 1951; children: Vincent Paul, Monica Irene Hylton, Jill Marie Nudell, John Michael, Michael Joseph, Thomas More. BA, St. Martin's Coll., 1947; JD, U. Wash., 1950. Bar: Wash. Asst. atty. gen. State of Wash., 1950-51; pvt. practice Olympia, Wash., 1951—. Gen. counsel Wash. Cath. Conf., 1967-76. Lt. (j.g.) USNR, 1943-46; PTO. Home and Office: 2723 Hillside Dr SE Olympia WA 98501-3460 E-mail: fjwalker1@msn.com.

WALKER, FRED ELMER, broadcasting executive; b. Trenton, N.J., May 31, 1931; s. Elmer and Adele F. (Decker) W.; m. Catharine Middleton Sullivan, Nov. 26, 1952; children: Catharine Walker Bergstrom, Elizabeth Walker Phillips, Frederick Christopher. Student, Trenton State Coll., 1952, NYU, 1953. Dir. pub. relations Sta. WPTZ-TV, Phila., 1953; v.p., gen. mgr. Sta. WTTM-AM, Trenton, 1956-59; gen. sales mgr. Sta. KYW-AM, Cleve., 1959-62; v.p., gen. mgr. Sta. KDKA-AM, Pitts., 1962-65, Sta. KYW-TV, Phila., 1965-67, Sta. KPIX-TV, San Francisco, 1967-69, Sta. WLWT-TV, Cin., 1969-71; pres. Broad St. Communications Corp., New Haven, 1971-85; v.p. radio group Westinghouse Broadcasting, N.Y.C., 1985-88; exec. v.p. Broad St. Ventures, 1988—. Pres. Broad St. TV Corp., 1988-96, Broad St. Mgmt. Corp., 1988-96; bd. dirs. Broadcast Music, Inc., 1984-87, Call for Action, Washington, 1993-2000. Bd. dirs. Long Wharf Theatre, New Haven, WXEL-TV, 1998—; chmn. Long Wharf Theatre Future Fund campaign, 1983-85, chmn. devel., 1986-90, chmn. and pres., 1990-97; mem. Pres.'s Coun. Albertus Magnus Coll.; trustee Hamden Hall Country Day Sch., chmn. devel. com.; chmn. 250th fund dr. United Ch. Christ, 1987-89; chmn. Call For Action, Washington, 1994-2000; trustee Fla. Stage. Recipient Alfred P. Sloan award, 1954, Ohio State Ednl. award, 1953; fellow Berkeley Coll. Yale U., 1976. Mem. Radio Advt. Bur. (dir.), TV Bur. Advt., Nat. Assn. Broadcasters, New Haven Lawn Club. Democrat. Office: PO Box 148 Delray Beach FL 33447-0148 E-mail: fredewalk1@aol.com.

WALKER, GAIL FLANAGAN, pediatrics nurse, women's health nurse, nursing administrator; b. N.Y.C., Sept. 26, 1946; d. Matthew Garrett and Edith Alexandria (Russell) Flanagan; m. Bruce Lee Walker, Apr. 8, 1972; children: Erin Edria, Kendra Leigh. Diploma in nursing, Mt. Sinai Med. Ctr., N.Y.C., 1966; BS, Adelphi U., 1971; MS, U. N.H., 1990. RN. Staff nurse neonatal dept. Mt. Sinai Med. Ctr., 1966-69, head nurse neonatal dept., 1969-71, head nurse pediatrics dept., 1971-72; instr. Cen. Maine Med. Ctr., Lewiston, 1972-78; instr. staff devel. St. Mary's Hosp., 1978-80; nurse recruiter Family Hosp., Milw., 1981-82; instr. staff devel. Waukesha (Wis.) Meml. Hosp., 1982-83, Holy Family Hosp., Methuen, Mass., 1984-86; dir. maternal-child health and IV therapy Cath. Med. Ctr., Manchester, N.H., 1986-95; program dir. Women's and Children's Health Optima Health, 1996-97; perinatal mgr. St. Vincents Hosp., Worcester, Mass., 1997-99; dir. maternal child health Lowell (Mass.) Gen. Hosp., 1999—2001, Lawrence (Mass.) Gen. Hosp., 2001—. Mem. Mayor's com. on prenatal care, N.H. State Task Force on Prenatal Care; bd. incorporators Optima Health, 1994-97. Bd. dirs. Vis. Nurse Home Health and Hospice of So. N.H., 1990-94, Nat. SIDS Alliance NHA Affiliate, 1992—; bd. incorporators Optima Health, 1994-97. Mem. AWHONN, Nat. SIDS Alliance (bd. dirs. N.H. chpt.), Sigma Theta Tau. Avocations: skating, cross stitch, reading. Home: 41 Gordon Dr Londonderry NH 03053-2921 Office: Lawrence Gen Hosp 1 General St Lawrence MA 01892

WALKER, GARLAND WAYNE, aircraft inspector; b. Bixby, Okla., Dec. 16, 1935; s. Haskell and Bonnie Edith (Shores) W.; m. M. Ellen Metzger, Dec. 31, 1964; children: Teresa Joellen, Garland Wayne II. Student, Okla. A&M, 1954-55, Northeastern State U., Tahlequah, Okla., 1955—, Tulsa U., 1955-56, 62-63. Salesperson W.C. Norris Mfg. Co., Tulsa, 1955-59; aircraft mechanic Am. Airlines Maintenance and Engring., 1959-86; aircraft inspector Am. Airlines' Maintenance and Engring., 1986. Mayor City of Bixby, 1969-70. Avocations: amateur radio, woodworking, hunting, fishing, street rods.

WALKER, GEORGE KONTZ, law educator; b. Tuscaloosa, Ala., July 8, 1938; s. Joseph Henry and Catherine Louise (Indorf) W.; m. Phyllis Ann Sherman, July 30, 1966; children: Charles Edward, Mary Neel. BA, U. Ala., 1959; LLB, Vanderbilt U., 1966; AM, Duke U., 1968; LLM, U. Va., 1972; postgrad. (Sterling fellow), Law Sch. Yale U., 1975-76. Bar: Va. 1967, N.C. 1976. Law clk. U.S. Dist. Ct., Richmond, Va., 1966-67; assoc. Hunton, Williams, Gay, Powell & Gibson, 1967-70; pvt. practice Charlottesville, Va., 1970-71; asst. prof. Law Sch. Wake Forest U., Winston-Salem, N.C., 1972-73, assoc. prof. Law Sch., 1974-77, prof. Law Sch., 1977—, mem. bd. advisors Divinity Sch., 1991-94; Charles H. Stockton prof. internat. law U.S. Naval War Coll., 1992-93. Vis. prof. Marshall-Wythe Sch. Law, Coll. William and Mary, Williamsburg, Va., 1979-80, U. Ala. Law Sch., 1985; cons. Naval War Coll., 1976—, Nat. Def. Exec. Res., 1991—, Naval War Coll., Internat. Law Dept. Adv. Bd., 1993—. Author: The Tanker War, 1980-88, 2000; contbr. articles to profl. jours. With USN, 1959-62, capt. USNR, ret. Woodrow Wilson fellow, 1962-63; decorated Order of the long Leaf Pine; recipient Joseph Branch Alumni Svc. award, Wake Forest, 1988, Moritorious Unit Commendation, 1992-93; named Hon. Atty. Gen. N.C., 1986. Mem.: ABA, Maritime Law Assn., Am. Law Inst., Am. Judicature Soc., Internat. Law Assn. (exec. com. 2001—), Am. Soc. Internat. Law (exec. coun. 1988—91), N.C. Bar Assn. (v.p. 1997—98), Va. Bar Assn., Order of Barristers (hon.), Piedmont Club, Phi Delta Phi, Sigma Alpha Epsilon, Phi Beta Kappa, Order of the Coif (hon.). Democrat. Episcopalian. Home: 3321 Pennington Ln Winston Salem NC 27106-5439 Office: Wake Forest U Sch Law PO Box 7206 Winston Salem NC 27109-7206

WALKER, GEORGE THEOPHILUS, JR. composer, pianist, music educator; b. Washington, June 27, 1922; s. George Theophilus Sr. and Rosa (King) W.; children: Gregory, Ian. MusB, Oberlin Coll., 1941; student of, Rudolf Serkin, Rosario Scalero; Artist Diploma, Curtis Inst. music, 1945; D of Mus. Arts, U. Rochester, 1957; DFA (hon.), Lafayette Coll., 1982; MusD (hon.), Oberlin Coll., 1983; student of, Nadia Boulanger; MusD (hon.), Curtis Inst. Music, 1997; DHL (hon.), Montclair State U., 1997; MusD (hon.), Bloomfield Coll., 1997; DFA (hon.) , Spelman Coll., 2001. Instr. Dillard U., New Orleans, 1953-54; instr. Dalcroze Sch. Music, N.Y.C., 1960-61, New Sch. Social Research, N.Y.C., 1961; instr. to assoc. prof. Smith Coll., Northampton, Mass., 1961-68; assoc. prof. U. Colo., Boulder, 1968-69; disting. prof. Rutgers U., Newark, 1976-92, prof. emeritus, 1992. Concert pianist Nat. Concert Artists, N.Y.C., 1950-53, Columbia Artists, N.Y.C., 1959-60; adj. prof. Peabody Inst. Johns Hopkins U., Balt., 1975-78; disting. prof. U. Del., Newark, 1975-76. Composer: Sonata for 2 Pianos (Harvey Gaul prize 1963), numerous sonatas, cantatas and concertos, Concerto for Cello and Orch., 1982, Sinfonias for Orch. Bd. dirs. Am. Bach Found., 1988; mem. Mary Flagler Cary Trust Commn., 1998. Recipient award Am. Acad. and Inst. Arts and Letter, 1982, Koussevitsky award, 1988, Pulitzer prize, 1996, L.J. Govs. award 1997, Koussevitsky award 1998, Mary Flagler Cary Charitable Trust award, 1998, Dorothy Maynor Arts Citizens award, 2000; grantee Smith Coll., U. Colo., Rutger U. Rsch. Coun., NEA, N.J. State Coun. for Arts; Fulbright fellow, 1957, John Hay Whitney fellow, 1958, Guggenheim fellow, 1969, 88, Rockefeller fellow, 1971, 74; Disting. scholar U. Rochester, 1996; commd. N.Y. Philharm., Kennedy Ctr., Cleve. Orch., Boston Symphony, N.J. Symphony, Am. Guild of Organists; inducted Am. Classical Music Hall of Fame, 2000. Mem. ASCAP, Am. Acad. Arts and Letters (mem.-elect), Am. Bach Found. (bd. dirs. 1988), Am. Symphony League, Coll. Band Dirs. Nat. Assn. Democrat. Avocations: tennis, photography, audio. Home: 323 Grove St Montclair NJ 07042-4223

WALKER, GLADYS LORRAINE, author; b. Bridgeport, Conn., Dec. 11, 1927; d. Gabriel and Adele Mary (Howie) Hawie; m. Daniel Robert Walker, Apr. 16, 1950; children: Kathleen, Susan, Daniel Jr. BA in Journalism, Syracuse U., 1949. Author: I Don't Do Potholes, 1986 (Conn. Press Club award 1986), Molly Meets Mona and Friends, A Magical Day In the Museum, 1997; contbr. numerous articles to mags. and newspapers; contbr. to textbooks and reference books. Mem. Am. Soc. Journalists and Authors, Editl. Freelancers Assn., Nat. League of Am. Pen Women (pres.), Conn. Press Club. Avocation: photography. Home and Office: 618A Erie Ln Stratford CT 06614-8229

WALKER, GORDON BEVERLEY MOORE, JR. business educator; b. N.Y.C., Oct. 10, 1944; s. Gordon Beverley Moore and Nancy Holton Walker; m. Jane Edwards, June 15, 1977 (div. Sept. 1983); 1 child, Emma; m. Nancy Niebuhr, Mar. 22, 1984; children: Hugh Curran, Ian Moore. BA, Yale U., 1966; MBA, U. Pa., 1976, PhD, 1982. Assoc. prof. Sloan Sch. Mgmt., MIT, Cambridge, Mass., 1981-86, Wharton Sch., U. Pa., Phila., 1986-91, Sch. of Orgn. and Mgmt., Yale U., New Haven, 1991-93; prof., chair Cox Sch. of Bus., So. Meth. U., Dallas, 1993—. Cons. numerous orgns., 1990—. Contbr. articles to profl. jours. 1st lt. USMC, 1967-70. Decorated Bronze star; recipient numerous grants including NSF, 1987-89, 95-97. Mem. Acad. of Mgmt., Am. Sociol. Assn., Yale Club of Dallas (pres. 2001—). Home: 331 Ridgebriar Dr Richardson TX 75080-1920 Office: Cox Sch of Bus So Meth U Dallas TX 75275-0335 E-mail: gwalker@mail.cox.smu.edu.

WALKER, GORDON DAVIES, former government official, writer, lecturer, consultant; b. Logan, Utah, July 10, 1944; s. Rudger Harper and Fawn Lucile (Davies) W.; m. Carlene Martin, June 5, 1968; children— Kimberly Anne, Kelly Anne, Gordon Davies Jr., Bradford Martin AB, Brigham Young U., 1968; MBA, Harvard U., 1971. Project dir. Becker Research Co., Boston, 1969-71; dir. mktg. Am. Nat. Enterprises, Salt Lake City, 1971-72; v.p., dir. Sweetwater Properties, 1972-76; gen. ptnr. Covecrest Properties, 1976—; spl. asst. to sec. HUD, Washington, 1981-82, dep. under sec., 1983-86; cons. real estate, fin. Commerce Cons., Washington, 1986-87; pres., chief exec. officer Deseret Fed. Savs. and Loan, Salt Lake City, 1987-88; pres. U.S. Resources, Inc., Phoenix, 1988-92, also bd. dirs.; pres. Energy Lock Inc., Salt Lake City, 1992—. Author: Finance Your Own Way to Success, 1980; Develop Your Way to Success, 1981; Hottest New Ideas of the 1980's, 1982. Rep. state del., Salt Lake City, 1974; del. Rep. Nat. Conv., 1988 Mem. Nat. Assn. Realtors Mem. Lds Ch.

WALKER, HAROLD BLAKE, minister, writer; b. Denver, May 7, 1904; s. Herbert R. and Ethel G. (Blake) W.; m. Mary Alice Corder, Feb. 1, 1930; children— Herbert Elwood, Howard Deane, Timothy Blake. AB, U. Denver, 1925, DD, 1952; AM, Boston U., 1927; BD, McCormick Theol. Sem., 1932; postgrad., U. Chgo., 1933-34; DD, Emporia Coll., 1944, Hamilton Coll., 1949, U. Denver, 1952, Rocky Mountain Coll., 1971; LHD, Lake Forest U., 1959, Nat. Coll. Edn., 1970; STD, Northwestern U., 1970. Editor, writer A.P., Kansas City, 1927-30; ordained to ministry Presbyn. Ch., 1932; minister Fullerton-Covenant Ch., Chgo., 1932-36, First Ch., Utica, N.Y., 1936-42, Oklahoma City, 1942-47, 1st Presbyn. Ch., Evanston, Ill., 1947-69; columnist Splty. Salesman mag., 1954-67, Chgo. Tribune-N.Y. News syndicated columnist, 1954-81. Lectr. homiletics McCormick Theol. Sem.; lectr., bd. dirs. Harold Blake Walker chair pastoral theology; cons. W. Clement Stone Enterprises, 1970-74; sem. v.p. Bd. Fgn. Missions Presbyn. Ch. U.S.A.; Nat. Commn. Evangelism, 1946-47; dir. Presbyn. Tribune, 1943-55; mem. Presbyn. Commn. on Consolidation, 1957-58, Commn. on Ecumenical Mission Relations, 1958-61. Author: Going God's Way, 1946, Ladder of Light, 1951, Upper Room on Main Street, 1954, Power to Manage Yourself, 1955, (with wife) Venture of Faith, 1959, Heart of the Christian Year, 1962, Faith for Times of Tension, 1963, Thoughts to Live By, 1965, To Conquer Loneliness, 1966, Prayers to Live By, 1966, Memories to Live By, 1968, Inspirational Thoughts for Everyday, 1970, Days Demanding Courage, 1978, History of St. John's of Red Cross of Constantine, 1985, Caring Community, 1986; contbr. to religious publs. Bd. dirs. Nat. Presbyn. Ch. and Ctr., Washington; bd. dirs. McCormick Theol. Sem., pres., 1953-55, 57-71; bd. dirs. Ill. Masonic Med. Center, Chgo., Lake Forest Coll.; trustee Maryville Coll. Recipient DeMolay Legion of Honor; Freedoms Found. sermon prize, 1950, 55, 77; citations Protestant Fund. Greater Chgo., 1970; Chgo. Inst. Medicine Citizens fellow, 1987; citations Chgo. Friends of Lit., 1971, 79; Disting. Alumnus award McCormick Theol. Sem., 1979. Mem. Utica Council Chs. (pres. 1940), Am. Theol. Soc. Chgo. Cleric, Pi Kappa Alpha. Clubs: Univ. (Chgo.). Lodges: Masons (Chgo., Evanston) (Shriner, 33 deg., grand chaplain N.Y. 1940-41). Home: 422 Davis St Evanston IL 60201-4610

WALKER, HARVEY CAPERS, urologist; b. Eatonton, Ga., Aug. 25, 1931; s. Frank Anderson and Julia Belle (Dennis) W.; m. Caroline Griffith, Aug. 24, 1954 (div. 1961); children: Harvey Capers Jr., John Griffith; m. Henrietta Clement, Aug. 21, 1968; 1 child, Valerie Anderson. BS, U. Ga., 1957; MD, Med. Coll. Ga., 1961. Diplomate Am. Bd. Urology. Intern Univ. Hosp., Augusta, Ga., 1961-62; resident in gen. surgery and pathology Med. Coll. Ga. Hosps., 1962-63, resident in urology, 1963-66; pvt. practice, Anderson, S.C., 1967—. Active med. staff Anderson Meml. Hosp., 1967—, Greenvillle (S.C.) Meml. Hosp., 1987—, St. Francis Hosp., Greenville, 1989— Staff sgt. USAF, 1951-54. Fellow ACS; mem. Am. Urol. Assn. Home: 1001 Cobbs Glen Dr Anderson SC 29621-4215 Office: 801 E Greenville St Anderson SC 29621-4070

WALKER, HELEN SMITH, retired real estate broker; b. Grovania, Ga., Jan. 29, 1917; d. George Washington and Mattie (Ellis) Smith; m. James Lee Walker, Apr. 21, 1946; 1 child, James Kenneth. Student, Ga. Wesleyan Coll., 1934-35, U. Ga., 1935-36, Wesleyan Conservatory, 1936-37. Sales rep. Thornton Realty Co., Macon, Ga., 1959-68; owner, operator Klondike Farms, Houston County, 1960—; co-owner, v.p. Warno Corp., Macon, 1964-69; v.p. O'Neal-Willingham Realty, 1968-71; assoc. broker Fickling & Walker Realty, 1971-77; pres., co-owner Hibble, Walker & Douglas, 1977-82; assoc. broker Fickling & Walker, 1982-91; ret. Tchr. primary tng. Union Bapt. Ch., 1950-65; mem. Make Am. Better Commn., 1971; group capt. Am. Cancer Crusale, 1978; active Ga. Trust for Hist. Preservation, Macon Hist. Soc., Macon Symphony. Mem. Am. Forestry Assn., Wesleyan Alumnae Club (awards com. 1988-89, 91—), Civic Woman's Club Macon. Democrat. Avocations: reading, writing poetry, gardening, music.

WALKER, HOWARD ERNEST, lawyer; b. Mobile, Ala., Mar. 3, 1944; s. Ernest W. and Denise (Kearney) W.; m. Michelle Ann Pinsonneault, June 20, 1992. BA, U. Ill., 1966; JD, Boston U., 1974. Bar: R.I. 1974. Assoc. Hinckley, Allen & Snyder, Providence, 1974-80, ptnr., 1980—. Trustee Providence Pub. Libr., 1978-2000, pres., 2002—; trustee R.I. Wild Plant Soc., 1995-97—; trustee R.I. Civic Chorale & Orchestra, 1988-95; dir. South Shore Mental Health Ctr., 1997—, v.p. 2000—; trustee and sec. Hopkinton Land Trust, 2000—; mem. Hopkinton Planning Bd., 2002—. Lt. USNR, 1967-71. Mem. ABA, R.I. Bar Assn. (chmn. superior ct. bench/bar com. 1990-93, 94-95), Maritime Law Assn. of U.S., Nat. Assn. R.R. Trial Counsel, Phi Kappa Phi,

Phi Beta Kappa. Avocations: Western Americana, nat. hist. Home: 39A Berrie Ln PO Box 118 Rockville RI 02873-0118 Office: Hinckley Allen & Snyder 1500 Fleet Ctr Providence RI 02903-2319 E-mail: hwalker@haslaw.com.

WALKER, IRVING EDWARD, lawyer; b. Balt., Jan. 31, 1952; s. Bertram and Mildred (Shapiro) W.; children: Brandon Harris, Aaron Seth, Emily Celeste. BA, Duke U., 1973; JD, U. Md., 1978. Bar: Md. 1978, U.S. Dist. Ct. Md. 1978, U.S. Ct. Appeals (4th cir.) 1980, U.S. Supreme Ct. 1995, U.S. Ct. Appeals (3d cir.) 2001. Assoc. Frank, Bernstein, Conaway & Goldman, Balt., 1978-85, ptnr., 1986-91; prin. Miles & Stockbridge, 1991-2001; spl. counsel Saul Ewing LLP, 2001—. Chair Bankruptcy & Creditors Rights Group, 1991-2000. Contbg. author: Bankruptcy Deskbook, 1986. Bd. dirs. Jewish Community Ctr. Greater Balt., 1986-88, Temple Emanuel of Balt., Inc., 1996—. Mem. ABA, Md. Bar Assn., Bar Assn. Balt. City (chmn. bankruptcy and bus. law com. 1989-90), Am. Bankruptcy Inst., Bankruptcy Assn. Dist. Md. (pres. 1992-93, chmn. Balt. chpt. 1989-91), Order of Coif. Avocations: soccer, weightlifting. Office: Saul Ewing LLP 100 S Charles St 15th Fl Baltimore MD 21201 E-mail: iwalker@saul.com.

WALKER, J. SAMUEL, historian; b. Bradford, Pa., June 8, 1946; s. Joseph Erdman and Rachael Viola (Smith) W.; m. Patricia Ann Cattell, July 28, 1973; children: Mary Beth, Daniel Joseph. BA, U. Del., 1968; MA, U. Md., 1971, PhD, 1974. Instr. No. Va. C.C., Woodbridge, 1977-82; archivist Office Presdl. Librs. Nat. Archives, Washington, 1975-77, edn. specialist Office Ednl. Programs, 1977-79; instr. evening divsn. Univ. Coll., U. Md., 1974-76, 85-92; assoc. historian U.S. Nuclear Regulatory Commn., Washington, 1979-86, historian, 1986—. Vis. prof. U. Md., College Park, 1990, 92; adj. prof. Georgetown U., 1992; reviewer grant proposals NEH, Nat. Hist. Publs. and Records Commn., NSF, U.S. Dept. Energy History Divsn.; mem. presdl. materials rev. bd. Nat. Archives and Records Adminstrn., 1998—; cons. documentary films, 1990, 94, 95. Author: Henry A. Wallace and American Foreign Policy, 1976, Containing the Atom: Nuclear Regulation in a Changing Environment, 1963-1971, 1992, Prompt and Utter Destruction: Truman and the Use of Atomic Bombs Against Japan, 1997, 98, 99, 2001, Permissible Dose: A History of Radiation Protection in the 20th Century, 2000; co-editor: (with Gerald K. Haines) American Foreign Relations: A Historiographical Review, 1981; co-author: (with George T. Mazuzan) Controlling the Atom: The Beginnings of Nuclear Regulation, 1946-1962, 1984, 86; contbr. articles, revs. and essays to profl. jours.; reviewer manuscripts various jours.; mem. editl. bd. Diplomatic History, 1984-86. Recipient rsch. grant Harry S. Truman Libr. Inst., 1996, William Best Hesseltine award Wis. Mag. History, 1982. Mem. Soc. Historians Am. Fgn. Rels. (exec. coun. 1989-91), Soc. History in Fed. Govt. (exec. coun. 1993-95, James Madison prize 1991), Soc. History of Tech. (IEEE life mem. prize com. 1993-95, chair 1994, life mem. prize 1990). Home: 6502 43rd Ave University Park MD 20782-2120 E-mail: jsw@nrc.gov.

WALKER, JACKSON VENUS, systems analyst, consultant; b. Port Angeles, Wash., Jan. 2, 1957; s. James Venus and Betty Jean (Kilgore) W.; m. Shawn Marshall, June 13, 1981 (div. Oct. 1982). BSEE, Tenn. Technol. U., 1981. Engr. Ga. Power Co., Augusta and Columbus, 1977-84; mfg. engr. Phillips Consumer Electronics, Knoxville, Tenn., 1984; tech. engr. Dynage Controls, Hartford, Conn., 1985; tech. sales rep. CBM Computer Sys., Oak Ridge, Tenn., 1986; programmer/analyst Scitek, Inc., 1987-90; project control engr. EBASCO, Inc., Watts Bar/Spring City, Tenn., 1990; mem. tech. staff Micah Sys., Inc., Knoxville, 1990-92; pres., owner Softwalk Cons. Group, 1993—. Author: (computer manuals) Operation of PC Modeling Software, 1987, Fortran Modeling Software, 1987. Student organizer Bob Clement campaign, Cookeville, Tenn., 1979. Democrat. Avocations: golf, collecting Star Trek memorabilia. Office: Softwalk Cons Group 7509 Kingston Pike Ste 267 Knoxville TN 37919-5625

WALKER, JAMES ELLIOT CABOT, physician; b. Bryn Mawr, Pa., Sept. 28, 1926; s. Arthur Meeker and Sylvia (Cabot) W.; m. Audrey Crowder Wakeman, July 11, 1965; children— Holly Barnwell, James Elliot Cabot. BA, Williams Coll., 1949; MD, U. Pa., 1953; MS in Hygiene, Harvard U., 1966. Intern and resident in medicine U. Wis., 1953, U. Mich., 1954-55, Peter Bent Brigham Hosp., 1958-60, assoc. dir., sr. assoc. dept. medicine; also research asst., lectr. Harvard U. Med. Sch., 1959-65, prof. medicine and soc. and clin. planner, 1965-68, chmn. dept. clin. medicine, 1968-72; chmn. dept. community medicine U. Conn. Med. Sch., Farmington, 1972-86, prof. medicine, 1968-92, prof. medicine emeritus, 1992—. Vis. prof. St. Thomas' Hosp., London, 1975-76, Harvard Med. Sch., Cambridge, Mass., 1986-87; pres. Northeast Can./Am. Health Coun., 1978-87; dir. Ctr. for Internat. Cmty. Health Studies, 1981-86; assoc. dir. Traveler's Ctr. on Aging, 1987-98; chmn. Alzheimers Coalition of Conn., 1992-94; med. dir. Avery Heights Retirement Cmty., 1992-98; warden St. John's Ch., West Hartford, Conn., 1994-00; chmn. bd. Conn. Cmty. Care Inc., 1998-2001; chmn. bd. Duncaster Inc., 2000-02. Author articles, monograph in field. Served with Am. Field Service, 1945; to capt. M.C. U.S. Army, 1955-58. Fellow ACP, AGS. Home: 79 Bayberry Hill Rd Avon CT 06001-2800 Office: U Conn Health Ctr Farmington CT 06032 E-mail: jecwalker@home.com.

WALKER, JAMES ROY, microbiologist; b. Chestnut, La., Nov. 8, 1937; s. Clint Cortez and Annie Mae (Holland) W.; m. Barbara Ann Fess, Aug. 8, 1959; children: James Bryan, Melinda Lee. BS, Northwestern State U., 1960; PhD, U. Tex., 1963. Asst. prof. U. Tex., Austin, 1967-71, assoc. prof., 1971-78, prof., 1978—, chmn. dept. microbiology, 1981-93. Mem. sci. adv. com. U. Tex. Health Science Ctr., Science Park Cancer Ctr., 1984-88. Contbr. articles to profl. jours. Served to capt. U.S. Army, 1963-65. Fellow NIH, 1965-67, Rosalie B. Hite U. Tex., 1960-63; grantee NIH, 1967-91, NSF, 1978-84, 91-95, Am. Cancer Soc., 1976-91, Welch Found., 1982-91, 97—, Tex. Adv. Rsch. Program, 1992-93, Am. Heart Assn., 1995, Coun. for Tobacco Rsch., 1996-99. Mem. Am. Soc. Microbiology (vis. prof. Fed. U. Rio de Janeiro 1977). Home: 8504 Greenflint Ln Austin TX 78759-8131 Office: U Tex Dept Microbiology Austin TX 78712-1095 E-mail: jrw@mail.utexas.edu.

WALKER, JAMES STEVEN, osteopath, emergency physician; b. Hobart, Okla., Feb. 4, 1951; BS in Zoology, Okla. State U., 1973, MS in Zoology, 1975, DO, 1978. Diplomate Am. Bd. Emergency Medicine. Intern Osteo. Hosp., South Bend, Ind., 1978-79; resident in emergency medicine Darnall Army Cmty. Hosp., Ft. Hood, Tex., 1983-85; mem. staff Univ. Hosp., Oklahoma City, 1985-88; prof. emergency medicine U. Okla. Health Scis. Ctr., 1988-2001, clin. prof. surgery, 2001—. Mem. Am. Osteo. Assn., Am. Acad. Emergency Medicine, Am. Coll. Emergency Physicians, Am. Coll. Osteo. Emergency Physicians, Soc. of Acad. Emergency Medicine, Wilderness Med. Soc.

WALKER, JANE BECK, civic worker; b. Monroe, Mich., May 25, 1933; d. Elmer William and Rose B. (Corner) Beck; m. Thomas J. Walker, May 2, 1959; children: Rose Ann, William Thomas. BA, Marietta (Ohio) Coll., 1955; MSc, U. Fla., 1957. Vol., Suwannee River coord. Fla. Defenders Environ.; mem. Alachua County Commn., 1982-86, chmn., 1985-86; chmn. North Cen. Fla. Regional Planning Coun., 1986-87. Recipient Community Svc. award Gainesville (Fla.) Sun, 1980, Woman of Yr. award Gainesville Area Women's Network, 1986. Mem. Gainesville Women's Forum, LWV (pres. Alachua County-Gainesville 1987-89, bd. dirs. Fla. 1989—). Democrat. Avocations: riding and driving horses. Home: 10601 NW 23rd Ave Gainesville FL 32606-5143

WALKER, JEANNE MURRAY, English educator; b. Parkers Prairie, Minn., May 27, 1944; d. John Gerald Murray and Erna Aderhold Kelley; m. Kent F. Walker, Aug. 27, 1966 (div. 1981); 1 child, Molly; m. E. Daniel Larkin, July 16, 1983; 1 child, Jack. BA, Wheaton Coll., 1966; MA, Loyola U., Chgo., 1969; PhD, U. Pa., 1974. Lectr. Haverford (Pa.) Coll., 1974-79; prof. English U. Del., Newark, 1975—. Author: (books of poetry) Nailing Up the Home Sweet Home, 1980, Fugitive Angels, 1985, Coming into History, 1990, Stranger Than Fiction, 1993, Gaining Time, 1997; (drama) Stories from the National Enquirer (Washington Nat. Theatre Festival award 1990), The Chosen Daughter, 1992, Rowing into Light on Lake Adley, 1994, Inventing Montana, 1997, The Queen's 2 Bodies, 2002, Tillie, 2002. NEA grantee, Pa. Coun. on Arts grantee, 1983, 85, 87, 90, 94, 2001; Del. Humanities Forum fellow, 1980, Del. Coun. on Arts fellow, 1978, Atlantic Mo. fellow in poetry and fiction, 1965, NEA fellow, 1994, Pew fellow in arts, 1998; recipient Prairie Schooner Strousse award for sequence of poems, 1989, Colladay award, 1993, Lewis prize, 1994, 96. Mem. PEN, Am. Poetry Ctr., Theater Assn. Pa., Poets and Writers, The Dramatists Guild. Democrat. Episcopalian. Home: 742 S Latches Ln Merion Station PA 19066-1614 Office: Univ of Del 131 Memorial Hall Newark DE 19711 E-mail: jwalker@udel.edu.

WALKER, JEROME ROBERT, physician; b. Chgo., Oct. 14, 1936; s. Harry A. and Gladys (Lysogorski) W.; m. Mary Ellen Fogarty, June 3, 1961; children: Kathleen Jerome, Jeanne, Sherri, Mary Ann, Timothy Michael, Christine. BS, U. Notre Dame, 1958; MD, Loyola U., Chgo., 1962. Diplomate Am. Bd. Family Physicians. Intern Resurrection Hosp., Chgo., 1962-63; family physician Family Physicians Mt. Prospect, Ill., 1965-89, Clin. Assocs., Arlington Heights, 1989—. Capt. U.S. Army, 1963-65. Fellow Am. Acad. Family Physicians; mem. AMA. Roman Catholic. Avocations: collecting, gardening, tennis, shelling, travel. Home: 1410 W Pheasant Trl Palatine IL 60067-4616 Office: Clin Assocs 125 S Wilke Rd Arlington Heights IL 60005

WALKER, JEWETT LYNIUS, clergyman, church official; b. Beaumont, Tex., Apr. 7, 1930; s. Elijah Harvey and Ella Jane (Wilson) W.; m. Dorothy Mae Croom, Apr. 11, 1965; children: Cassandra Lynn, Jewett L., Kevin, Michelle, Ella, Betty Renne, Kent, Elijah H. BA, Calif. Western U., 1957; MA, Kingdom Bible Inst., 1960; B Religious Edn., St. Stephens Coll., 1966, DD, 1968; LLD, Union Bapt. Sem., 1971; postgrad., St. Paul Sch. Theology, 1979, Southwestern Bapt. Theol. Sem., 1985-86; grad., Nat. Planned Giving Inst., 1981, Philanthropy Tax Inst., 1982; DD, Clinton Jr. Coll., 1992. Ordained to ministry African Methodist Episcopal Zion Ch., 1957. Pastor Shiloh A.M.E. Zion Ch., Monrovia, Calif., 1961-64, Martin Temple A.M.E. Zion Ch., L.A., 1964-65, 1st A.M.E. Zion Ch., Compton, Calif., 1965-66, Met. A.M.E. Zion Ch., L.A., 1966-73, Logan Temple A.M.E. Zion Ch., San Diego, 1973-74, Rock Hill A.M.E. Zion Ch., Indian Trail, NC, 1974-79, Bennettsville A.M.E. Zion Ch., Norwood, 1979-86, Price Meml. A.M.E. Zion Ch., Concord, 1986-89, Mt. Zion A.M.E. Zion Ch., Hickory Grove, SC, 1989-91, Lancaster, 1993—2001, Mt. Moriah A.M.E. Zion Ch., Richburg, 2001—. Sec.-treas. dept. home missions, brotherhood pensions and relief African Methodist Episcopal Zion Ch., Charlotte, N.C., 1974-92; mem. exec. bd. Prophetic Justice Unit Com. Nat. Coun. Chs., co-chairperson pers. com.; mem. World Meth. Coun., del. 14th World Conf. Author: Is There a Man in the House, 1975, Lets Get Serious about Missions, 1991, The Denominational Dollar, 1992, also articles. Chmn. Minority Affairs Adv. Com., Mecklenburg County; trustee Clinton Coll., dir. planned giving, 1992; trustee Rock Hill, Lomax-Hannon Coll., Greenville, Ala., Union Bapt. Theol. Sem., Birmingham, Ala.; bd. mgrs. McCrorey br. YMCA; pres. Am. Ch. Fin. Svc. Corp., Carolina Home Health Svc. Inc., Meth. Life Ins. Soc. Inc., bd. trustees State N.C. Coll. Found., Inc., 1987, del. Presbyn. Ptnrs. in Ecumenism Nat. Coun. Chs. Christ, 1986, pres., 1988—; pres. Walker Funeral Home Inc. (formerly The House of Irma Funeral Home), Concord, Am. Ch. Econ. Devel. Corp.; del. Presbyn. Ch. U.S. Gen. Assembly, 1985; mem. citizens parole accountability com. Mecklenburg County, Charlotte, 1993; mem. planned giving adv. bd. Livingston Coll., Salisbury, N.C.; pres. Jewett L. Walker & Assocs.; chmn. minority affairs adv. com. Mecklenburg County; com. mem. Charlotte Mecklenburg Citizen Parole Accountability Com., 1994, vice chmn., 1998; pres. Pardue St. Apts. Inc., Lancaster, S.C., 1997—, Am. Ch. Econ. Devel. Corp., 1999. Fellow Nat. Assn. Ch. Bus. Adminstrs., Ch. Bus. Adminstrn., Presbyn. Ch. Bus. Adminstrn. Assn.; mem. NAACP (life), Nat. Soc. Fund Raising Execs., Am. Bible Soc. (state dir. vols., N.C. and S.C. dir. vol.), Nat. Spkrs. Bur., Christian Ministries Mgmt. Assn., Am. Soc. Assn. Execs., Funeral and Cremation Soc. South, Inc. (founding mem. 1998), Shriners, Masons (33 deg.), Prince Hall Affiliation. Republican. Home: 910 Bridlepath Ln Charlotte NC 28211-2022 Office: 4501 Walker Rd Charlotte NC 28211-2047

WALKER, JILL MARIE, writer, consultant; b. Olympia, Wash., June 4, 1955; d. Francis Joseph and Julia Corrine (O'Brien) W.; m. Franklin Dean Hobbs, June 21, 1975 (div. Dec. 1982); m. Bruce Mitchell Nudell, Sept. 15, 1985; children: Matthew Phillip, Jamie Alexandra. Student, Scripps Coll., Claremont, Calif., 1973-75; grad. gemologist, Gemological Inst. Am., Santa Monica, Calif., 1977; BA, UCLA, 1980. Continuing edn. course designer/internat. instr., alumni dir. Gemological Inst. Am., Santa Monica, Calif., 1983-85; course designer, instr. Safeco Ins. Cos., Seattle, 1986-89, tng. needs cons., 1990; co-author bilingual children's video Boulder, Colo., 1991—. Keynote gemology speaker Am. Gemology Soc. Nat. Conv., Washington, 1979; TV gemology guest Hour Mag. and News on Channel 9, L.A., 1984; resident instr. colored stones and gem identification Gemological Inst. Am., Santa Monica, Calif., 1977-81, asst. mgr. home study dept., 1981-83. Author: (book chpt. with others) Jade 1991; contbr. Gems and Gemology mag. (article of the year award 1981, 82, Gems and Gemology mag.). Community dir. Jr. League of L.A. Bd., 1982-85; mgr. trainer nonprofit bds. United Way of L.A., 1982-84, United Way of Seattle, 1986-87; commr. Planning Policy Commn., Issaquah, Wash., 1987-91. Mem. ASTD, Nat. Soc. Performance and Instrn. Avocations: running, community volunteer. Home: 318 Lincoln Ave Ridgewood NJ 07450-4823

WALKER, JOHN LOWELL, music educator; b. Newton, Iowa, Nov. 9, 1956; s. Jack Carl and Carol Jean Walker; m. Catalina del Pilar Andrango; m. Magdalen Elizabeth Fotovich (div. Nov. 6, 2000); children: Natalie. BMus, Drake U., 1979; MMus, Temple U., 1982; D in Musical Arts, U. Nebr., 1995. Prin. oboe Orquesta Sinfónica de Guadalajara, Guadalajara, Mexico, 1983—84, USAF Heritage of Am. Band, Langley AFB, 1991—95, Orquesta Sinfónica Nacional del Ecuador, Quito, Ecuador, 1995—99; band dir. Osage County R-1 Sch., Chamois, Mo., 2000—02, Cooper County R-4 Sch., Bunceton, 2002—. Prof. oboe Conservatorio Nacional del Ecuador, Quito, 1995—99. Contbr. articles. Sr. airman USAF, 1991—95. Mem.: Mo. Music Educators Assn.

WALKER, JOHN MERCER, JR. federal judge; b. N.Y.C., Dec. 26, 1940; s. John Mercer and Louise (Mead) W.; m. Cristy West, June 20, 1980 (div. Apr. 1983); m. Katharine Kirkland, Feb. 14, 1987. BA, Yale U., 1962; JD, U. Mich., 1966. Bar: N.Y. 1969, U.S. Dist. Ct. (so. dist.) N.Y. 1971, U.S. Ct. Appeals (2d cir.) 1972, U.S. Supreme Ct. 1977, U.S. Ct. Appeals (D.C. cir.) 1982. Maxwell Sch. Pub. Adminstrn. fellow, state counsel Republic of Botswana, Africa, 1966-68; assoc. Davis, Polk and Warwell, N.Y.C., 1969-70; asst. U.S. atty. U.S. Dist. Ct. (so. dist.) N.Y., 1971-75; assoc. to ptnr. Carter, Ledyard and Milburn, 1975-81; asst. sec. enforcement ops. Dept. Treasury, Washington, 1981-85; judge U.S. Dist. Ct. (so. dist.) N.Y., 1985-89, U.S. Ct. Appeals (2nd cir.), 1989—, chief judge, 2000—. Adj. prof. NYU Law Sch., 1995—; gen. counsel Nat. Coun. on Crime and Deliquency, N.Y.C., 1977-81; chmn. Fed. Law Enforcement Tng. Ctr., Washington, 1981-85; spl. counsel Adminstrv. Conf. U.S., Washington, 1986-92; mem. budget com. jud. conf. Inst. Jud. Adminstrn., 1992—, dir., 1992—. Del. Rep. Nat. Conv., Detroit, 1980. With USMCR, 1963-67. Recipient Alexander Hamilton award Sec. of Treas., Washington, 1985, Secret Service Honor award, 1985. Mem. ABA, D.C. Bar Assn., Assn. Bar City of N.Y., Fed. Judges Assn. (pres. 1993-95). Republican. Episcopalian. Office: US Cir Ct 157 Church St New Haven CT 06510-2100

WALKER, JOHN SAMUEL, retired pediatrician; b. Brevard, N.C., June 25, 1921; s. Hugh Raven and Mary Jane (King) W.; m. Jean Lane Davis, June 9, 1945 (div. Mar. 1986); children: Virginia Davis, Hugh Raven, Samuel Vivian, Joseph Andrew, Jean Lane; m. Chieko Akahori, May 31, 1986; 1 child, Mary Jane Haruko Walker. BS, Wake Forest U., 1943; MD, Jefferson Med. Coll., 1946. Diplomate Am. Bd. Pediatrics. Resident in pediatrics Crawford W. Long Meml. Hosp., Atlanta, 1950-51, Children's Hosp., Cin., 1951-52; pvt. practice pediatrics Children's Med. Group, Atlanta, 1952-61; mgr. clin. rsch. Upjohn Co., Kalamazoo, 1961-67; v.p. med. affairs Riker Labs., Northridge, Calif., 1967-69; dir., sr. dir. clin. rsch. Merck Rsch. Labs., West Point, Pa., 1969-77, sr. dir. regulatory affairs, 1977-92; ret., 1992. Lt. (j.g.) Med. Corps USN, 1946-49. Fellow Am. Acad. Pediatrics, Am. soc. for Clin. Pharmacology and Therapeutics, Royal Soc. Medicine; mem. AMA. Republican. Episcopalian. Avocations: study of Japanese language, collecting models of turtles and tortoises, walking. Home: 1408 Ridgemere Ln Winston Salem NC 27106-4483 E-mail: taisho10@aol.com.

WALKER, JOHN SEIBELS, artist; b. Columbia, S.C., Nov. 12, 1960; s. George Rivers Pinckney and Harriet Moore Walker; m. Karen Louise Dyndivk, Nov. 21, 0985. BA in Fine Arts, U. of the South. Instr. Charles Cecil Studios, Florence, Italy; artist, portraitist U.S. and Italy. Mem.: Am. Soc. Portrait Artists (finalist). E-mail: jseibelswalker@hotmail.com.

WALKER, JOHN SUMPTER , JR. lawyer; b. Richmond, Ark., Oct. 13, 1921; s. John Sumpter and Martha (Wilson) W.; m. Eljana M. duVall, Dec. 31, 1947; children: John Stephen, Barbara Monika Ann, Peter Mark Gregory. BA , Tulane U., 1942; MS, U. Denver, 1952, JD, 1960; diploma, Nat. Def. U., 1981. Bar: Colo. 1960, U.S. Dist. Ct. Colo. 1960, U.S. Supreme Ct. 1968, U.S. Ct. Appeals (10th cir.) 1960, U.S. Tax Ct. 1981. With Denver & Rio Grande Western R.R. Co., 1951-61, gen. solicitor, 1961-89; pres. Denver Union Terminal Rlwy. Co. Apptd. gen. counsel Moffat Tunnel Commn., 1991; life mem. Children's Diabetes Fund. With U.S. Army, 1942-46. Decorated Bronze Star. Mem.: Cath. Lawyers Guild, U. Denver Chancellor's Soc., Order of St. Ives, Arapahoe County Bar Assn., Colo. Bar Assn., Alliance Francaise (life). Republican. Roman Catholic.

WALKER, JONATHAN LEE, lawyer; b. Kalamazoo, Mar. 8, 1948; s. Harvey E. and Olivia M. (Estrada) W. BA, U. Mich., 1969; JD, Wayne State U., 1977. Bar: Mich. 1977, U.S. Dist. Ct. (we. dist.) Mich. 1989, U.S. Dist. Ct. (no. dist.) Ill. 1991, U.S. Dist. Ct. (ea. dist.) Mich. 1983, Colo. 1996, U.S. Dist. Ct. Colo. 1996, U.S. Ct. Appeals (10th cir.) 1996. Assoc. Moore, Barr & Kerwin, Detroit, 1977-79; ptnr. firm Barr & Walker, 1979-82; assoc. firm Richard M. Goodman, P.C., 1983-87; hearing officer Mich. Civil Rights Commn., 1983-86; pvt. practice, 1988-89, Birmingham, 1990—95; dep. pub. defender Office of State Pub. Defender, Colorado Springs, Colo., 1998—. Participant Detroit Bar Assn. Vol. Lawyer Program. Bd. dirs. Cmty. Treatment Ctr.-Project Rehab., Detroit, 1983-89, Colorado Springs chpt. ACLU, 2002--; bd. trustees A.R.C. of Pikes Peak region; mem. scholarship com. Latino en Marcha Scholarship Fund, Detroit, 1984; treas. youth assistance program Citizens Adv. Coun., 1987; mem. State Domestic Violence Offenders' Mgmt. Bd., 2001—. Mem. ATLA, State Bar Mich. Found., Wayne County Mediation Tribunal (mediator), Am. Arbitration Assn. (arbitrator), Nat. Lawyers Guild (exec. bd. Detroit chpt. 1988-92, pres. Detroit chpt. 1988-90), Mich. Trial Lawyers Assn. (co-chair coalition com. 1988-90, exec. bd. 1988-96, co-chair pro bono com. 1991-96), State Bar Mich. (com. on underrepresented groups in law 1980-92, chmn. 1983-85, mem. com. jud. qualifications 1985-86, Latin Am. affairs coun. 1978-96), Colo. Criminal Def. Bar, Legal Aid and Def. Assn. (bd. dirs. 1990-95), Hispanic Bar Assn., Trial Lawyers for Pub. Justice (founder 1981, mem. amicus com. 1985-86, state capt. 1991-95), Ctr. for Auto Safety. Office: 415 S Sahwatch Colorado Springs CO 80903 E-mail: jonathan.walker@state.co.us.

WALKER, JOY, visual artist; b. Tacoma, July 17, 1942; d. Louis Lisle and Muriel Pool (McKay) W.; m. Jeremy Roth, Sept. 17, 1967 (div. May 1983); 1 child, Owen Walker Roth. BA with honors, U. Oreg., 1964; MS, N.Y. Studio Sch., 1967, Adelphi U., 1988. One-woman shows include 55 Mercer Gallery and Andre Zarre Gallery, 1970—2001, Women Artists Series, Rutgers U., 1998, more than 80 group shows, Represented in permanent collections Mint Mus., Art Gallery of Toronto, Art Gallery of Hamilton, Can., Robert McLaughlin Art Gallery, Glenbow Mus., Calgary. Grantee Adolph and Esther Gottlieb Found., 1991, Yaddo Art Colony, 1997, MacDowell Art Colony, 1979, Can. Coun. Arts, 1975, Pouch Cove Artists Colony, Newfoundland, 1998. Democrat. Home: 341 13th St Brooklyn NY 11215-5003

WALKER, JOYCE MARIE, secondary school educator; b. Kansas City, Kans., Jan. 24, 1948; d. Frank Cornelius and Inez (Pennington) W.; divorced; 1 child, Kevin Cornelius. BS, U. Ark., Pine Bluff, 1972. Cert. ch. adminstr. Bus. tchr. U.S. Trade Sch., Kansas City, 1972-74; exec. sec. Kansas City Mo. Sch. Dist., 1974-77; tchr. vocat. bus. Aurora (Colo.) Pub. Sch., 1977—. Vocat. bus. tchr. Pioneer C.C., 1975—77; amb. Aurora Pub. Schs., 1999—. Mem. Aurora Human Rels. Martin Luther King Jr. Com., 1986—; sec., supt. Sunday sch. Macedonia Bapt. Ch., 1985—, evangelism counselor, 1992—; 2d v.p. E.L. Witchfield Missionary Soc., 1989; chmn. We. States Fgn. Mission, 1990. Mem. Nat. Coun. Negro Women, Nat. Assn. Bus. Educators, NAACP (Aurora br. 1990—), Delta Sigma Theta (v.p. Denver chpt. 1998-2002, pres. 2002—). Avocations: tennis, bowling, sewing. Home: 12948 E 48th Ave Denver CO 80239-4408 Office: Aurora Pub Schs 11700 E 11th Ave Aurora CO 80010-3758

WALKER, JOYE A. secondary school educator; b. Albert Lea, Minn., May 28, 1955; d. Dale Arlen and Dorothy Sophie (Rohner) Plunkett; children: Natasha Sue, Erica Ann. BA, U. Iowa, 1991. Cert. tchr., Iowa. Math. tutorial lab. mgr. U. Iowa, Iowa City, 1992-98; h.s. math. tchr. Iowa City Cmty. Sch. Dist., 1998—; Nat. Hon. Soc. sponsor, math club coach West H.S., 1999—. Bd. dirs. West Br. (Iowa) Cmty. Schs. Bd. Edn., 1993-96. Avocations: gardening, piano, golf, cooking, staying fit. Home: 1241 Esther Ct Iowa City IA 52240 Office: West HS 2901 Melrose Ave Iowa City IA 52246 E-mail: walker.joye@iccsd.k12.ia.us.

WALKER, JUANITA MOFFETT, retired elementary school educator; b. Edwards, Miss., Jan. 31, 1939; d. Fred Douglas and Matlean Allen Moffett; m. Tommy Lewis, June 11, 1962; children: Tommy Jr., Edward, Roland. AA, Utica (Miss.) Jr. Coll., 1959; BA, Jackson State U., 1961; MA, Purdue U., 1995; postgrad., Black Hills State U., Spearfish, S.D., Ind. U. Cert. tchr. Miss., S.D., counselor Ind. Tchr. Burgland H.S., McComb, Miss., 1961, Oglala Cmty. H.S., Pine Ridge, SD, 1962—69, Wirt H.S., Gary, Ind., 1969—71, West Side H.S., Gary, 1971—78; counselor Pulaski Mid. Sch., 1978—82, Bailly Mid. Sch., Gary, 1982—91, Edison Mid. Sch., Gary, 1991—2001. Testing coord. Bailly and Edison Mid. Schs., 1982—95; dept. chmn. Edison Mid. Sch., 1991—2001; chmn. guidance career day Bailly Mid. Sch., 1982—90. Author: Church Folk, 2001. Historian Gary Civic Chorale, 1980—; founder, pres. Gary Writers Workshop, 2001—; pres. Friends of Libr., Gary, 2000—. Mem.: Lake County Ret. Tchrs. Assn., Alpha Kappa Alpha. Avocations: singing, playing keyboards, travel, public speaking, reading. Home: PO Box 4286 Gary IN 46404

WALKER, KAREN DENISE, social worker; b. Columbia, S.C., Sept. 8, 1967; d. Shirley Tena (Earle) W. BSW, Winthrop Coll., 1990. Clin. social worker II Dept. Mental Health, Columbia, S.C., 1990; After Sch. Day Care counselor Rock Hill (S.C.) YMCA, 1990—. Mem. NASW, Zeta Phi Beta (mem. pub. svc. com.). Methodist. Avocations: reading, writing, walking. Home: 429 Gardners Terrace Rd West Columbia SC 29172-2629

WALKER, KAY S. geropsychiatric nurse; b. Plainwell, Mich., July 15, 1950; d. Milo Charles and Helen (Schreuder) Keith; m. William James Walker, Apr. 8, 1972; children: Charles, Bethany, John, Catherine. Diploma, Bronson Meth. Sch. Nursing, Kalamazoo, Mich., 1971. Cert. psychiat. mental health nurse Am. Nurses Credentialing Ctr. Staff nurse Borgess Hosp, Kalamazoo, 1971-74; home care nurse, 1979—83; staff nurse Lakeview Cmty. Hosp., Paw Paw, 1987—2002; dir. nursing svcs.. Sparrow's Haven, Inc., Kalamazoo, 2002—. Summer camp nurse Anchor Point Camp, Hopkins, Mich., 1972—83. Leader Girl Scouts Glowing Embers coun., Kalamazoo, 1991—. Mem.: Mich. Home Health Assn. (mem. psychiat. subcom. 2001). Avocations: reading, gardening. Office: Sparrows Haven Inc Kalamazoo MI 49001

WALKER, KENNETH ADLEY, aluminum fabricating company executive; b. Hartford, Conn., May 16, 1949; s. George Gould and Elizabeth Mae (Parcher) W.; m. Ruth Ann Danowski; children: Kenneth, Gregory, Daniel. BSME with honors, Cornell U., 1971; M in Adminstrv. Sci., Johns Hopkins U., 1978; M in Fin., Loyola Coll., Balt., 1981; postgrad., U. Md., 1990—. Test engr. Koppers Co. Inc., Balt., 1971-72, project engr., 1973; mgr. accessory equipment Environ. Elements Corp., 1974-76, mgr. scrubber/ filter products, 1976-82, gen. mgr. water treatment systems, 1983-88; v.p. ops. Washington Aluminum Co., 1988-94, pres., 1994—, also bd. dirs.; pres. TriFab, Inc., 1994—. Bd. dirs. Md. Healthcorp, Inc., 1992-94, Dovco Indsl. Fabricators, Inc., TriFab, Inc.; pvt. industry rep. Gov.'s Com. Study Anticipated Sewage Treatment Needs, State of Md., 1986-88. Patentee method and system cleansing a filter bed; patent issued for Modular Bd. dirs. Greater Balt. Med. Ctr., 1986-94, sec. 1992-94, mem. fin. and bldg. coms., 1986-94, mem. credentials com., 1998—; bd. dirs. Towson (Md.) Presbyn. Kindergarten, 1986-89, v.p. 1987-89; asst. scoutmaster, scoutmaster Boy Scouts Am., 1990—. Mem. Am. Welding Soc., Cornell Soc. Engrs., Quill and Dagger Soc., Autocrossers, Inc., UMBC Coll. of Engrg. (indsl. adv. bd.), 1999—, Adirondack Mountain Club, Porsche Club Am., Adirondack 46ers, U.S. Orienteering Fedn., Appalachian Mtn. Club, Quantico Orienteering Club, Aluminum Assn.

(mem. engring. task force 1993—), Am. Alpine Club, Tau Beta Pi, Delta Chi. Republican. Avocations: skiing, golf, winter mountaineering, autocrossing, orienteering. Office: Washington Aluminum Co Knecht Ave Baltimore MD 21229

WALKER, LARRY KENNETH ROBERT, professional baseball player; b. Maple Ridge, B.C., Dec. 1, 1966; Grad. high sch., B.C., Can. With Montreal Expos, 1989-94; outfielder Colo. Rockies, 1995—. Named "The Sporting News" Nat. League All-Star Team, 1992, "The Sporting News" NAt. League Silver Slugger Team, 1992; recipient Gold Glove as outfielder, 1992-93. Office: Colo Rockies Coors Field 2001 Blake St Denver CO 80205-2008*

WALKER, LARS, writer; b. Faribault, Minn., July 31, 1950; s. Jordan Lawrence Walker and Gladys Karen Jensen. AA, Waldorf Coll., 1968; BA, Augsburg Coll., 1974. Lic. gen. radiotel. operator. Administrv. asst. Peace Luth. Ch., Palm Bay, Fla., 1984—95, Assn. Free Luth. Congregations, Mpls., 1995—. Author: (novels) Erling's Word, 1997, Wolf Time, 1998, The Year Of the Warrior, 2000. Mem.: Sci. Fiction and Fantasy Writers Am., Sons of Norway, Viking Age Club. Lutheran. Personal E-mail: lars@larswalker.com.

WALKER, LAURENCE GORDON, technology company executive; b. New Haven, Dec. 11, 1948; s. Charles Allen and Bernice Rolf W.; m. Katharine Alcott Adams, Dec. 27, 1970; children: Nancy Karin, Courtney Alcott. BSEE, Princeton U., 1970; MSEE, MIT, 1973, PhD, 1975. Design engr., group mgr. Hewlett-Packard, Palo Alto, Calif., 1975-81; group mgr. Digital Equipment, Maynard, Mass., 1981-91, v.p. mfg. tech., 1991-92, v.p., gen. mgr. network products, 1992-96; CEO CertCo, N.Y.C., 1996-97, C-Port, North Andover, Mass., 1997—. Dir. Mass Tech Pk. Corp., Westboro, 1989—, Mass. Telecom Coun., Boston, 1994—, McData Corp., Broomfield, Colo., 1997—, The Hopkins Sch., 1999—. Contbr. articles to profl. jours.; patentee in field. Chair Fin. Com., Dover, Mass., 1990-92; mem. camp com. Two-State YMCA, Becket, Mass., 1992—. With USAR, 1970-76. Mem. IEEE. Democrat. Congregationalist. Avocations: music, swimming, skiing. Home: 22 Normandie Rd Dover MA 02030-2511 Office: C-Port Corp 120 Water St North Andover MA 01845-2648 E-mail: walkerl@mediaone.net.

WALKER, LELAND JASPER, civil engineer; b. Fallon, Nev., Apr. 18, 1923; s. Albert Willard and Grayce (Wilkinson) W.; m. Margaret Frances Noble, Jan. 21, 1946; children: Thomas, Margaret, Timothy. BS in Civil Engring, Iowa State U., 1944; D. Eng. (hon.), Mont. State U., 1983. Engr. with various govtl. depts., 1946-51, 53-55; v.p. Wenzel & Co. (cons. engrs.), Great Falls, Mont., 1955-58; pres., chmn. bd. No. Engring. and Testing, Inc., 1958-88. Pres. Ind. Labs. Assurance Co., 1977-79; bd. dirs. Mont. Power Co., Entech Inc., 1982-92, Lewis and Clark Biologicals, Inc., 1989-92, Applied Tech., Inc. Pres., trustee Endowment and Rsch. Found. Mont. State U., 1969-82, Mont. Deaconess Hosp., Great Falls, 1959-67. McLaughlin Rsch. Inst. Biol. Scis., 1989-92, Mont. Sch. Deaf and Blind Found., 1984—; trustee Rocky Mountain Coll., 1977-80, Dufresne Found., 1979-87; chmn., bd. dirs. Mont. Tech. Svcs. Adv. Coun. adv. coun. Engring. Coll. Mont. State U.; bd. dirs. Mont. State Fair, Engring. Socs. Commn. on Energy, 1977-79, Mont. Bd. Sci. and Tech., 1983-88, Great Falls Chamber Found., 1989-91, trustee Great Falls Public Libr. Found., 1995-2001. Fellow ASCE (pres. 1976-77), AAAS, Cons. Engrs. Coun. (pres. Mont. 1971), Accrediting Bd. Engring. and Tech. (v.p. 1978-79, pres. 1980-83); mem. Nat. Acad. Engring., Am. Coun. Ind. Labs. (hon., sec. 1973-76), Meadowlark Country Club, Pachyderm Club (bd. dirs., v.p. 1992-94), Chi Epsilon (nat. hon.), Tau Beta Pi (hon.). Republican. Methodist. Home: 1200 32nd St S Apt 9 Great Falls MT 59405-5333

WALKER, LEROY TASHREAU, university chancellor, coach; b. Atlanta, June 14, 1918; s. Willie and Mary Elizabeth (Thomas) W.; m. Katherine McDowell, Dec. 31, 1938 (dec.); children— LeRoy, Carolyn BS, Benedict Coll., 1940, PhD (hon.); MA, Columbia U., 1941; PhD, NYU, 1957; PhD (hon.), Defiance Coll.; D of Sports Sci., U.S. Sports Acad.; LLD (hon.), Ea. Ky. U. and N.C. Cen. U., Wake Forest U., 1993, Morehouse U., 1993; DHL (hon.), Tuskegee U., 1993, Duke U., 1995; LHD (hon.), U. N.C., 1995, Queens Coll., 1995; Dr.Humanities, Princeton U., 1996. Chmn. dept. phys. edn., coach basketball, football, track and field Benedict Coll., Columbia, S.C., 1941-42; chmn. dept. phys. edn., coach basketball, football, track and field Bishop Coll., Marshall, Tex., 1942-43, Prairie View State U., 1943-45; chmn. dept. phys. edn. and recreation, coach basketball, football, track and field N.C. Cen. U., Durham, 1945-73, vice-chancellor for univ. relations, 1974-83, chancellor, 1983-86, chancellor emeritus, 1986—. Ednl. specialist Cultural Exchange Program, Dept. State, 1959, 60, 62,; dir. program, planning and tng. Peace Corps, Africa, 1966-68; coach Ethiopian and Israeli teams Olympic Games, Rome, 1960; adviser track and field teams throughout world; mem. U.S. Collegiate Sports Coun., 1971; chmn. Coll. Commrs. Assn., 1971-74; chmn. track and field com. Athletic Union U.S.A., 1973-75; head coach U.S. track and field team Olympic Games, Montreal, 1976; chmn. bd. U.S. Olympic Festival, 1987—; mem. exec. bd., treas. U.S. Olympic Com., pres., 1992—; chef de mission for 1992 Barcelona Olympic Games, 1991—; sr. v.p. sports Atlanta Com. for the Olympic Games 1996, 1991—. Author: Manual of Adapted Physical Education, 1960; Physical Education for the Exceptional Student, 1965; Championship Techniques in Track and Field, 1969, Track and Field for Boys and Girls, 1983; also articles Bd. dirs. U.S.A.-China Rels. Com.; bd. trustees U.S. Olympic Com.; pres. Athletic Congress, U.S. Olympic Com., 1992—; pres. Spl. Olympics World championship Bd. Recipient James E. Shepard Outstanding Tchr. award Hamilton Watch Co., 1964, U. N.C. Systems Bd. Govs. award, 1989; Achievement award Cen. Intercollegiate Athletic Assn., 1967; Disting. Alumnus award Benedict Coll., 1968, Disting. Service award Kiwanis Internat., 1971, City of Durham, 1971, Durham C. of C., 1973, Gov.'s Ambassador of Goodwill award, 1974; O. Max Gardner award, 1976; N.C. Disting. Citizen award, 1977; Achievement in Life award Ency. Brit., 1977, Achievement award Sertoma; Heritage award YMCA, 1988, Robert Giegengack award The Athletics Congress, 1990, Amb. award Pres.' Coun. on Phys. Fitness and Sports, 1991, Disting. Alumni award NYU, 1993, Jim Corbett award Nat. Assn. Coll. Athletic Dirs., 1993; named to N.C. Hall of Fame, 1975, S.C. Hall of Fame, 1977, Nat. Assn. Sport and Phys. Edn. Hall of Fame, 1977, N.C. Cen. U. Hall of Fame, 1984, U.S. Olympic Hall of Fame, 1987, Ga. Hall of Fame, 1988, Benedict Coll. Hall of Fame, N.C. Soc. award The Olympic Order by Internat. Olympic Com., 1995, Toastmasters Golden Camel award, 1996, 100 Blackmen Disting. Leadership award, 1996. Mem. Am. Alliance Health, Phys. Edn., Recreation, and Dance (nat. pres.; Honor award 1972, Gulick award), NEA, U.S. Track Coaches Assn. (Nat. Track Coach of Yr. 1972), N.C. Assn. Health, Phys. Edn., Recreation and Dance (Honor award 1971; v.p. div., dir.), Internat. Assn. Athletic Fedns. (U.S. rep. 1976—), Sigma Delta Psi, Alpha Phi Omega, Omega Psi Phi Episcopalian.

WALKER, LINDA ANN, financial planner; b. Denver, May 10, 1956; d. John Bruce Elmer and Ruth Evelyn (Rogers) Metsker; m. Sidney Carr Walker III, Feb. 9, 1992; 1 child. BA, U. Colo., 1978. CFP. Account exec. E.F. Hutton, Boulder, 1980-84; with Fin. Planning and Mgmt., 1984-91, pres., 1989-91, Premier Planning Assocs., Boulder, 1991-95; pvt. practice, 1995—. Actress (play) Shadow of a Gunman, 1991, La Ronde, 1992 (dancer) Who's There, 1991. Bd. dirs. Nancy Spanier Dance Theatre, Boulder, 1986-91; mem. Win/Win, Boulder, 1989-91. Mem. Fin. Planners Assn., C. of C. Democrat. Avocations: reading, writing, meditating, horseback riding. Office: CFP Linsco/Pvt Ledger 5150 E Pch Ste 520 Long Beach CA 90804-3326

WALKER, LINDA LEE, lawyer; b. Phila., Jan. 24, 1954; d. M. Lorenzo and Romaine Yvonne (Smith) W.;children: Jessica Marie McIntyre, Nicole Yvonne McIntyre. BA with honors, U. Pa., 1975; JD, Yale U., 1978. Bar: N.Y. 1979, U.S. Dist. Ct. (so. and ea. dists.) N.Y. 1982, U.S. Ct. Appeals (1st cir.) 1982; NASD series 7 and 24. Asst. regional atty. HHS, N.Y.C., 1978-82; assoc. Shea & Gould, 1982-85; v.p., sr. assoc. counsel Chase Manhattan Bank, N.A., 1985-89; v.p., assoc. gen. counsel Citicorp Credit Svcs., 1989-97; asst. gen. counsel Prudential Ins. Co. Am., Newark, 1997-2000, v.p., chief compliance officer for ret. svcs. and guaranteed products, 2000—. Mem. Phi Beta Kappa. Office: Prudential Ins Co of Am 3 Gateway Ctr 12th Fl Newark NJ 07102-4077 E-mail: linda_walker@prudential.com.

WALKER, LOREN HAINES, electrical engineer; b. Bartow, Fla., Sept. 25, 1936; s. Robert Ellsworth and Vera May (Williams) W.; m. Barbara Gray Doss, Aug. 26, 1961; children: Linda Gray, Katherine Leigh, Virginia Kent. BEE, U. Fla., 1958; SM, MIT, 1961. Registered profl. engr., Va. Program engr. GE Corp., 1958-59, sr. design engr. specialty control dept. Va., 1959-70, elec. engr. R & D Schenectady, N.Y., 1972-76, cons. engr. drive systems Salem, Va., 1976-96; sr. devel. engr. Exide Power Systems div. ESB, Raleigh, N.C., 1970-72. Inventor 65 patents in field. Active Presbyn. Ch. Recipient IR-100 award Indsl. Rsch., 1974. Fellow IEEE (1st prize conf. papers 1979, 2d prize 1989).

WALKER, LORENZO GILES, surgeon, educator; b. Phila., June 29, 1957; s. Manuel Lorenzo and Romaine Yvonne (Smith) W.; m. Yvonne Ruiz; children: Zachary Giles, Benjamin Lee. BA cum laude, U. Pa., 1978; MD, Harvard U., 1982. Diplomate Am. Bd. Orthopaedic Surgery, Nat. Bd. Med. Examiners; lic. surgeon, Mass., Calif.; cert. added qualification hand surgery, 1993. Intern in surgery New England Deaconess-Harvard Surg. Svc., Boston, 1982-83, asst. resident in surgery, 1983-84; resident in orthopaedic surgery Harvard U., 1985-88; fellow in hand surgery UCLA Med. Sch., 1988-89, asst. clin. prof. orthopaedic surgery, 1988—, attending physician dept. orthopedics Hand Clinic, 1996-98; ptnr. Ventura (Calif.) Orthopaedic Hand and Sports Med. Group, 1994-98; solo practice hand surgery, 1998—. Staff physician St. John's Plasant Valley Hosp., Camarillo, Calif., St. John's Regional Med. Ctr., Oxnard, Calif., Cmty. Meml. Hosp., Ventura, Calif.; attending physician, cons. Sepulveda, Calif. VA Hosp.; presenter in field. Cons. reviewer Clin. Orthopaedics and related Rsch., 1990-92; contbr. numerous articles to profl. jours. Vol. Spl. Olympics, Ventura, 1994-96, Direct Relief Internat., Santa Barbara, Calif., 1994-96, Ventura County Rescue Mission, 1994-98. Recipient Cert. of Appreciation, Am. Heart Assn., 1994; UCLA faculty fellow, 1988-89. Mem. Am. Soc. for Surgery of the Hand, Am. Assn. for Hand Surgery, AMA, Calif. Med. Assn., Calif. Orthopaedic Assn., Calif. Ringside Physician, Ventura County Med. Soc., Internat. Soc. Aquatic Medicine, Western Orthopaedic Assn., Orthopaedic Overseas, UCLA Hand Club, Arthroscopy Assn. N.Am., Alpha Epsilon Delta, Onyx Honor Soc., Philomathean Soc. Avocations: photography, scuba diving, sports memorabilia, fishing, travel. Home: 3041 Shadow Mesa Cir Thousand Oaks CA 91360-1061

WALKER, LOU ANN, writer; b. Hartford City, Ind., Dec. 9, 1952; d. Gale Freeman and Doris Jean (Wells) W.; m. Speed Vogel, Sept. 8, 1986; 1 child, Katherine Walker Vogel. Student, Ball Student U., 1971—73; degree in French lang. and lit., U. Besançon, France, 1975; BA in Comparative Lit., Harvard U., France, 1976. Reporter Indpls. News, 1975-76; asst. to exec. editor N.Y. Mag., N.Y.C., 1976; asst. editor Esquire, 1977-78; features editor Diversion, 1979-80; editor-in-chief Direct, 1980-82; writer, screenwriter, lectr. Sag Harbor, N.Y., 1980—; contbg. editor N.Y. Woman, N.Y.C., 1990-92; prof. Southampton Coll., 1996—. Cons. Mus. Modern Art, N.Y.C., 1980-85, Theatre Devel. Fund, N.Y.C., 1984—; cons. Southampton (N.Y.) Coll., 1996--, vis. prof. MFA program 2002--; lectr. deafness, 1980—. Author: A Loss for Words, 1986 (Christopher award 1987), Amy, 1985 (Nat. Children's Social Studies Book Coun. award 1985), Hand, Heart & Mind, 1994, Roy Lichtenstein, 1994; contbr. articles to mags. and newspapers. Recipient Marguerite Higgins Reporting award, 2000; Rotary fellow, 1975-76; Rockefeller Found Humanities grant, 1982-83, Creative Writing grant NEA, 1988. Mem. Writers' Guild Am., Authors' Guild, Registry Interpreters Deaf. Home and Office: Box 2131 Sag Harbor NY 11963 Office Fax: 631-725-4788. E-mail: lwalker8@optonline.net.

WALKER, LUCY DORIS, secondary school educator, writer; b. Ridgeway, N.C., May 6, 1951; d. Edgerton Verl and Mary Ellen (Williams) Plummer; m. William A. Walker Jr., June 21, 1969 (div. Aug. 1974); 1 child, Lucretia Marie. BA in English Edn., Fairleigh Dickinson U., 1975; MA in Theater Arts, Montclair State U., 1977. Cert. English and theater arts tchr., N.J. Tchr., dir., actor, writer Ctr. Modern Dance Edn., Hackensack, N.J., 1978; writer, dir. Am. Theater Actors, N.Y.C., 1978-79; tchr. multicultural hub Ctr. Internat. Studies, Cultural Events, Teaneck (N.J.) H.S., 1979—. Artistic dir. Teaneck H.S. dance ensemble, 1989—; program coord. African & African-Am. Studies Resource Ctr., 1990—. Writer and choreographer various plays, 1979-95. Recipient Acad. Achievement award Fairleigh Dickinson U. Opportunities Program, 1974, Black Heritage award Nat. Assn. Negro Bus. & Profl. Women's Clubs, 1991. Mem. NEA, N.J. Edn. Assn. Democrat. Baptist. Avocations: sewing, gardening, hiking, painting, music. Home: 363 Washington Pl Englewood NJ 07631-3232 Office: Teaneck HS 100 Elizabeth Ave Teaneck NJ 07666-4713 E-mail: walkplum@aol.com.

WALKER, MACK, historian, educator; b. Springfield, Mass., June 6, 1929; s. Gilbert Creighton and Lavinia Pillsbury (Mack) W.; m. Irma Julianne Wiesinger, 1954; children: Barbara B., Gilbert C., Benjamin F. AB, Bowdoin Coll., 1950; PhD, Harvard U., 1959. Instr. RISD, Providence, 1957-59; instr., asst. prof. Harvard U., Cambridge, Mass., 1959-66; assoc. prof., prof. Cornell U., Ithaca, N.Y., 1966-74; prof. Johns Hopkins U., Balt., 1974-99, dept. chmn., 1979-82, prof. emeritus, 1999—. Author: Germany and the Emigration, 1964, German Home Towns, 1971, 2d edit., 1998, Johann Jakob Moser, 1981, The Salzburg Transaction, 1993, Der Salzburger Handel, 1997; editor: Metternich's Europe, 1968, Plombières, 1968. Sgt. USAR, 1951—53. Fellow Inst. for Advanced Study, Princeton, 1977, Wissenschaftskolleg zu Berlin, 1982-83, Max-Planck-Inst. für Geschichte, Göttingen, 1987-88; recipient Forschungspreis Alexander von Humboldt Found., 1989; Guggenheim fellow, 2000. Fellow: Am. Acad. Arts and Scis. Office: Johns Hopkins U Dept of History Baltimore MD 21218

WALKER, MALVIN EARLY, musician, educator; b. Indpls., Oct. 24, 1920; s. Howard John and Anne Loraine (Moran) W.; m. Joan Louise Leatherman, Oct. 19, 1951 (div. June 1967); children: Sara Louise, Julia Lee. BM, Butler U./Jordan Conservatory, 1942, MM, 1947; postgrad., Ind. U., Purdue U., Ariz. U., 1953-63. Tchr. Jordan Conservatory, Indpls., 1946-47, Shenandoah (Iowa) Schs., 1948-49, South Bend (Ind.) Schs., 1947-48, Indpls. Schs., 1948-82; performer South Bend Symphony, 1947-48, Indpls. Philharm., 1948-56. Author: Chronological Encyclopedia of Adolf Hitler and the Third Reich, 1979; contbr. articles to profl. jours. Amb. Estes Park (Colo.) Chamber, 1984-96; mem. ensemble music bd. dirs. Ensemble Music Soc., Indpls., 1949-82, emeritus dir.; trustee Rocky Ridge Music Ctr., Estes Park, 1985-98, Estes Park Music Festival, 1984-2001, AARP, Estes Park, 1982-88. Capt. U.S. Army, 1942-56, ETO. Decorated Purple Heart (2), Bronze Star. Named Rotarian of Yr. Estes Park Rotary, 1995. Mem. Mu Phi Alpha. Avocations: reading, military research, bridge.

WALKER, MANUEL LORENZO, physician; b. Battle Creek, Mich., Mar. 22, 1930; s. Charles Sumner and Manuella (Beck) W.; m. Romaine Yvonne Smith, Sept. 26, 1951 (dec. May 1978); children: Linda Lee, Lorenzo Giles; m. Joan Lucille Parks, May 8, 1980; 1 child, Gregory Parks. BS, Howard U., 1951, MD, 1955. Intern Phila. Gen. Hosp., 1955-56; pvt. practice Phila., 1958-95; clin. assoc. U. Pa. Health System, 1995—. Adv. bd. Episcopal Cmty. Svcs. Home Health Care, Phila., 1984-88; subcom. provider rels. Healthpass, Phila., 1989-97. Editor MSEPulse, 1970—; contbr. articles to mags. Pres. Yeadon (Pa.) Bd. Edn., 1968-71, v.p., 1966-68; v.p. Howard U. Med. Alumni Assn., Washington, 1970-75. Lt. comdr. USNR. Named Practitioner of Yr. Phila. County Med. Soc., 1979, Nat. Med. Assn., 1986; recipient Pres. award NAACP, Phila., 1990, Legion of Honor, Chapel of Four Chaplains, 1978. Fellow Am. Acad. Family Physicians; mem. Phila. Acad. Family Physicians (pres. 1982-83), Keystone State Med. Soc. (pres. 1971-73), Med. Soc. Ea. Pa. (pres. 1968-70), Howard U. Coll. Medicine Class 1955 (pres. 1954—), Sigma Pi Phi, Alpha Omega Alpha. Baptist. Avocations: golf, gardening, grandchildren. Home: 425 Jamaica Dr Cherry Hill NJ 08002-1920 Office: Clin Care Assoc 5740 W Girard Ave Philadelphia PA 19131-4812

WALKER, MARION LAVELLE, neurosurgeon; b. Columbia, Miss., Aug. 13, 1942; s. Elmo Lavelle and Myrna Wynema (Cochran) W.; m. Sue Ann Stromberg Walker, May 29, 1964; children: Carrie Jean, Katie Louise Richman, Christopher David, Cory Lavelle, Charles Jon. BS, Brigham Young U. Miss. Coll., 1961, 64, 66; MD, U. Tenn. Coll. Medicine, Memphis, 1969. Diplomate Am. Bd. Neurol. Surgery, Am. Bd. Pediatric Neurol. Surgery. Residency gen. surgery St. Joseph's Hosp., Phoenix, 1970-71; residency-neurosurgery Barrow Neurol. Inst., 1972-73; clin. asst. prof. surgery U. Utah Med. Ctr., Salt Lake City, 1976-81; asst. prof. surgery U. Utah Coll. Medicine, 1981-85; chief divsn. pediatric neurosurgery U. Utah Sch. Medicine, 1981—, adjunct asst. prof. pediatrics, 1983-85, assoc. prof. neurosurgery, 1985-93, prof. neurosurgery, 1993—, adjunct prof. pediatrics, 1994—. Sec. 1978-80, pres. 1981-83 Utah State Neurosurgical Soc.; mem., pres.-elect 1986-88, pres. 1988-89 Laser Assn. Neurol. Surgeons Internat.; treas. 1986-90, mem. exec. coun. 1986—, sec. 1990-92, v.p. 1992-94, mem., pres. 1994-96, past pres. 1996-98 Am. Soc. of Pediatric Neurosurgeons; mem. exec. coun. 1984-88, Am. Assn. of Neurol. Surgeons; chmn. Am. Soc. for Laser Medicine and Surgery, 1984; pres.-elect 1989, pres. 1990, Primary Children's Med. Ctr.; profl. adv. coun. Spina Bifida Assn. Am., 1995-2000. Contbr. articles to profl. jours. Chmn. Trauma Com. Primary Children's Med. Ctr., 1979-82; scientific program chmn. pediat. sect. Am. Assn. Neurol. Surgeons, 1984, Rocky Mountain Neurol. Soc., 1991, Am. Soc. Pediatric Neurosurgeons, 1992; chmn. edn. com. Internat. Soc. for Pediatric Neurosurgery, 1993-95; mem. neurosurgery subcom. Neurology sect. Am. Acad. pediatrics, 1995; chmn. liaison com. Internat. Soc. for Pediatric Neurosurgery, 1996-97. Mem. Am. Soc. Neurol. Surgeons, Am. Assn. Neurol. Surgeons (chmn. joint sect. pediat. neurol. surgery 1997-99), Am. Soc. Pediatric Neurosurgeons, Am. Acad. Pediatric Neurosurgery, Internat. Soc. for Pediatric Neurosurgery, Congress of Neurol. Surgeons, Neurosurg. Soc. Am., Am. Acad. Pediatrics (chmn. sect. on neurol. surgery 1999-2003), Am. Coll. Surgeons, Am. Soc. for Laser Medicine and Surgery, Laser Assn. of Neurol. Surgeons Internat., Am. Bd. Pediat. Neurol. Surgery (sec., treas. 1995-97, chmn. 1997—), Am .Soc. of Evoked Potential Monitoring, AMA, Rocky Mountain Neurosurg. Soc., Utah State Neurosurg. Soc., Utah State Med. Assn., Salt Lake County Med. Soc., Am. Acad. Cerebral Palsy and Developmental Medicine, Spina Bifida Assn. Am., Acad. Pediatric Neurosurgeons. Avocations: golf, travel, photography. Office: Primary Children's Med Ctr 100 N Medical Dr # 2400 Salt Lake City UT 84113-1103 E-mail: marion.walker@hsc.utah.edu.

WALKER, MARK A. lawyer; b. N.Y.C., June 24, 1941; s. Joseph and Eleanor (Junger) W.; m. Tania Khodjamirian; children: Marie, Andrew. BA, Stanford U., 1963; LLB, Yale U., 1966. Bar: N.Y. 1967, U.S. Dist. Ct. (so. dist.) N.Y. 1977. Assoc. Cleary, Gottlieb, Steen & Hamilton, Paris, Brussels and N.Y., 1966-75, ptnr. N.Y.C., 1975—. Mem. Assn. Bar City N.Y. E-mail: mwalker@cgsh.com.

WALKER, MARY ERLINE, critical care nurse; b. Newport, R.I., June 4, 1951; d. Edgar Hergor and Doris Elizabeth (Allen) Sherman; m. Michael Robert Walker, Dec. 22, 1970; 1 child, Michael Robert II. AS in Nursing, Lake City (Fla.) Community Coll., 1971; AA, Santa Fe C.C., Gainesville, Fla., 1974; BS in Profl. Arts, St. Joseph's Coll., North Windham, Maine, 1980; BSN cum laude, Regent's Coll., Albany, N.Y., 1996; MSN, U. Tex. Health Sci. Ctr., San Antonio, 2000. RN; cert. critical care nurse, med./surg. nurse. Staff nurse Cape Fear Valley Hosp., Fayetteville, N.C., 1971-72, surg. staff nurse, 1975-76; staff nurse Alachua Gen. Hosp., Gainesville, 1972-74; staff nurse male medicine Womack Army Community Hosp., Ft. Bragg, N.C., 1976-81, staff nurse, 1986-87, inservice coordinator, 1987; staff nurse Reynolds Army Community Hosp., Ft. Sill, Okla., 1981-83, evening supr., 1983-84; staff nurse cardiology Lettermen Army Med. Ctr., San Francisco, 1984-85, clin. nurse specialist recovery room, 1985-86, charge nurse cardiac rehab., 1985; staff nurse, insvc. coord. Bayne Jones Army Hosp., Ft. Polk, La., 1988-90; staff nurse MICU, ACLS instr. Brooke Army Med. Ctr., Fort Sam Houston, Tex., 1990-98, staff nurse progressive care unit, 1998—2001; clin. nurse U.S. Army Surg. Rsch.-Burn Ctr., 2001—. Pres. Bay Bandits Volksmarch, San Francisco, 1985-86; cub scout den leader Boy Scouts Am., 1993-96, com. mem., 1996—, merit badge counselor, 1997—. Mem. Am. Assn. Critical Care Nurses (North Cen. Fla. chpt. pres. 1974, publs. co-chair San Antonio chpt. 1997, 98, treas.-elect San Antonio chpt. 2001), Am. Heart Assn., Nat. League Nursing, Nat. Assn. Clin. Nurse Specialists, Phi Theta Kappa, Sigma Theta Tau. Republican. Methodist. Avocation: cross stitch. Home: 9719 Fortune Ridge Dr Converse TX 78109-2752 Office: Brooke Army Med Ctr San Antonio TX 78234 E-mail: threemws@worldnet.att.net.

WALKER, MARY L. federal agency administrator, lawyer; b. Dayton, Ohio, Dec. 1, 1948; d. William Willard and Lady D. Walker; 1 child, Winston Samuel. Student, U. Calif., Irvine, 1966-68; BA in Biology/Ecology, U. Calif., Berkeley, 1970; postgrad., UCLA, 1972-73; JD, Boston U., 1973. Bar: Calif. 1973, U.S. Supreme Ct. 1979. Atty. So. Pacific Co., San Francisco, 1973-76; assoc. Richards, Watson & Gershon, L.A., 1976-78, ptnr., 1979-82; dep. asst. atty. gen. lands div. U.S. Dept. Justice, Washington, 1982-84; dep. solicitor U.S. Dept. Interior, 1984-85; asst. sec. for environment, safety and health U.S. Dept. Energy, 1985-88; spl. cons. to chmn. bd. Law Engring., Atlanta, 1988-89; v.p., West Coast and the Pacific Law Environ., Inc., San Francisco, 1989; ptnr., head environ. law dept. Richards, Watson & Gershon, 1989-91; ptnr. Luce, Forward, Hamilton & Scripps, San Diego, 1991-94; ptnr. and head San Diego Environ. Practice Group Brobeck, Phleger & Harrison, LLP, 1994—2001; gen. counsel air force U.S. Dept. Defense, Washington, 2001—. U.S. commr. InterAm. Tropical Tuna Commn., 1989—95; mem. adv. bd. Floresta, Inc. Bd. dirs. Endowment for Cmty. Leadership, 1987—2000, Global Involvement Through Edn., 1998—2001. Mem. Calif. Bar Assn., San Diego Bar Assn., BIOCOM (bd. dirs. 1991-2001, pres. 1994), Profl. Women's Fellowship-San Diego (co-founder, bd. dirs. 1996-2001, pres. 1996-97), World Affairs Coun., Renaissance Women. Republican. Office: US Dept Defense Gen Counsel 1740 Air Force Pentagon Washington DC 20330-1740 Office Fax: 703-693-9355.*

WALKER, MATTHEW See MEWHINNEY, BRUCE HARRISON NICHOLAS

WALKER, MICHAEL CHARLES, SR. retirement services executive; b. Rochester, N.Y., Mar. 4, 1940; s. Charles Boyle and Evelyn Esther (Young) W.; m. Patricia Ann Camelio, Feb. 2, 1963; children: Michael Charles Jr., Lyn, Lea, Matthew. BA, U. Colo., 1962; MBA, Columbia Pacific U., 1982, DBA, 1984. Adminstrv. trainee Lincoln Rochester (N.Y.) Trust Co., 1962-64, mktg. officer, 1964-68; asst. v.p. Lincoln First Bank of Rochester, 1968-72, v.p., 1972-77; pres. M.C. Walker Co., Inc., Spencerport, N.Y., 1977-80; exec. dir. The Valley Manor, Rochester, 1980-85; pres., CEO Presbyn. Homes & Svcs. Genesee Valley, Inc., 1999—. Lectr. SUNY, Brockport, 1982—89; v.p., dir. Kilian and Caroline Schmitt Found., Rochester, 1985—; mem. adv. bd. Chase Manhattan 1st Bank, Rochester, 1989—92; trustee Rochester Hearing and Speech Ctr., 1989—95, chmn., 1993—94; bd. dirs. Genesee Region HOme Care Assn., Rochester, 1990—2000; trustee Greater Rochester C. of C., 1981—89. Author: Introduction to Bank Marketing Research, 1969, rev. edit., 1972, Practical Handbook of Marketing Definitions, 1970; contbr. articles to profl. jours. Leader task force Spencerport Ctrl. Schs. Bd. Edn., 1977, 80-81, 85; chmn. Monroe County Svs. Bond Com., Rochester, 1972-97; mem. United Way Evaluation Team, 1990-94; bus. adv. bd. SUNY, Brockport, 1993—; mem. N.Y. State Bd. Profl. Med. Conduct, 1993—; profl. adv. com. Self Help for Hard of Hearing, 1994-96. Recipient Pres.'s Geneseekers award, Rochester Area C. of C., 1979, Innovation of Yr. award, NYAHSA, 1989, Cmty. Svc. award, Self Help for Hard of Hearing, 1997, Patriotic Svc. award, U.S. Treasury, 1997. Mem. Am. Assn. Homes for Aging (various coms.), Am. Mktg. Assn. (pres. Rochester chpt. 1969-70), N.Y. State Bankers Assn. (pres. residential mortgage com. 1975-76), N.Y. Assn. Homes and Svcs. for Aging (various coms.), Ridgemont Country Club, Rochester Rotary, Am. Legion. Episcopalian. Avocations: golf, reading, travel, physical fitness. Office: Homes & Svcs Genesee Valley Inc 1570 East Ave Rochester NY 14610-1610

WALKER, MICHAEL JAMES, surgeon; b. Phila., Sept. 16, 1962; s. James Michael and Ernesta Anna (Kapourelos) W.; m. Kelly Meri Clark, Aug. 31, 1997. BS, Muhlenberg Coll., 1984; MD, Jefferson Med. Coll., 1988. Resident Thomas Jefferson U. Hosp., Phila., 1988-93, U. Wash., Seattle, 1993-95; attending thoracic/vascular surgeon Danbury (Conn.) Hosp., 1995—. Contbr. articles to profl. jours. Fellow Am. Coll. Surgeons; mem. AMA, Soc. Thoracic Surgeons, Conn. State Med. Soc., Fairfield County Med. Assn. Gen. Thoracic Surg. Club, Phi Beta Kappa, Alpha Omega Alpha. Avocations: birdwatching, reading. Office: 27 Hospital Ave Ste 405 Danbury CT 06810-5954

WALKER, MICHAEL LEON, education educator; b. Cin., May 17, 1942; s. Degree and Annie (Wynn) W. BA, Wayne State U., 1970, EdD, 1991; MA, U. Detroit, 1978. Asst. prof. La. State U., Shreveport, 1991-92, U. Nebr., Lincoln, 1992-94, SUNY, Plattsburgh, 1994-95, Ea. Mich. U., 1995—. Mem. Martin Luther King Club, Plattsburgh, 1994. Recipient award for Svc. to Children, Salvation Army, Lincoln, 1993, 1994. Mem. Nat. Coun. Tchrs. of English, Internat. Reading Assn., Nat. Reading Conf., Phi Delta Kappa. Democrat. Baptist. Avocations: reading, organ, piano. also: # 468 51 W Hancock St Detroit MI 48201-1303

WALKER, MILDRED LIIVIA, manufacturing executive; b. Centrailia, Ill., Sept. 30, 1954; d. Bobby Jack and Liivia Walker. BS, U. Ark., Arkansas, 1977; MA, U. No. Colo., Colorado, 1981. Camp dir. Camp Allegro, Pittsfield, Mass., 1977—79; phys. edn. tchr. Widefield #3, Widefield, Colo., 1981—85; sales rep. corp. accounts Hallmark, Kansas City, Mo., 1985—93; gen. mgr. Kenyon Consumer Products, West Kingston, RI, 1993—2001; owner, operator Walker Wear Inc., Colorado Springs, Colo., 2001—. Coach Spl. Olympics, Fayetteville, Ark., 1972—74, Organized Pk. Recreation, Colorado Springs, Colo., 1980—84, Spl. Olympics, Colorado Springs, 1984—87; umpire Organized Pk. Recreation, 1988—89; mem. Colo. Springs Chamber Commerce. Mem.: Pike's Peak Women's Golf Orgn., Roundtable Com. (chamber of commerce 2001—02). Achievements include Wisconsin State Junior Girls Golf Champion (1969); Wisconsin Senior Girls Golf Champion (1971); Arkansas State Women's Golf Champion (1974). Avocations: golf, woodworking, gardening. Office: Walker Wear Incorporated 2845 Janitell Road Colorado Springs CO 80906

WALKER, MORT, cartoonist; b. El Dorado, Kans., Sept. 3, 1923; s. Robin A. and Carolyn (Richards) W.; m. Catherine Prentice, Aug. 24, 1985; children: Greg, Brian, Polly, Morgan, Marjorie, Neal, Roger, Whitney, Cathy, Jr., Priscilla Student, Kansas City Jr. Coll., 1941-42, Washington U., St. Louis, 1943-44; BA, U. Mo., 1948; LL.D., William Penn Coll., 1981. Designer Hallmark Greeting Cards, 1941; editor Dell Pub. Co., 1948-49; free lance cartoonist Saturday Evening Post, other popular mags., 1948-50. Scholar in residence Mo. U., 1992. Comic strip artist King Features, 1950— ; creator Beetle Bailey, 1950, Hi and Lois, 1954, Sam's Strip, 1961, Boner's Ark, 1968, Sam and Silo, 1977, The Evermores, 1982, Betty Boop and Felix, 1984, (for United Features) Gamin and Patches, 1987; author: Most, 1971, Land of Lost Things, 1973, Backstage at the Strips, 1975, The Lexicon of Comicana, 1981, The Best of Beetle Bailey, 1984, The Coconut Crew, 1997, (autobiography) Mort Walker's Private Scrapbook, 2001; contbr. to numerous anthologies and textbooks. Mem. Pres.'s Com. to Hire Handicapped, People to People Com. Exhbn. touring group show Met. Mus. Art, N.Y.C., 1951; chmn. Internat. Mus. Cartoon Art. Served to 1st lt. AUS, 1943-46, ETO. Decorated chevalier Order Arts and Letters (France), 2000; recipient Outstanding Cartoonist award The Banshees, 1955, Il Secolo XIX award (Italy), 1972, Adamson award (Sweden), 1975, 88, Segar award, 1977, 4th Estate award Am. Legion, The Jester, 1979, Power of Printing, 1977, NCS Golden T-Square award, 1999, Disting. Civilian Svc. award U.S. Army; named Man of Yr. NCCJ, 1988. Mem. Nat. Cartoonists Soc. (pres. 1959-60, Reuben award 1953, award for best humor strip of 1966, 69, Mus. Cartoon Art Hall of Fame 1989), Artists and Writers, Newspaper Features Coun. Authors Guild, Soc. Illustrators, Nat. Press Club, Silvermine Club (Norwalk, Conn.), Greenwich Country Club, Quechee Club (Vt.), Boca Raton Resort and Club (Fla.), Kappa Sigma (Man of Yr. 1988). Office: care King Features Syndicate 888 7th Ave New York NY 10019 *If I enjoy my own life that's one life enjoyed. But if I can help others enjoy their lives more, many lives are made more enjoyable.*

WALKER, NANCY ANNE, antiques importer; b. Palo Alto, Calif., May 27, 1942; d. John Clarence and Dorothy May (Mole) Cheney; 1 child, Shelley Marie. BS, U. Oreg., 1964; MA, San Fernando State U., 1968; PhD, U. Colo., 1975. Lic. real estate broker, Calif. Instr. U. Md., Fed. Republic Germany, 1970-74; instr. history Modesto Jr. Coll., Calif., 1977-80, 88-93; owner, pres. Lockeford Clock Co., Inc., Stockton, 1978—; lectr. Calif. State U., Stanislaus, 1992; art and history docent Haggin Mus., 2002—. Owner Lockeford Angiques, 1974—, Nancy Walker Rentals. Contbr. articles to jours. including The Pioneer, Lockeford-Clements News, East European Quar., among others. Mem. Mayor's Task Force on Affirmative Action, Stockton, 1984—; pres. San Joaquin chpt. Nat. Orgn. for Women, 1988; mem. Del Tor Excavation, Israel, summer 1985; area rep. Youth for Understanding, 1987, 88; art and history docent Haggin Mus., 2002; activities chmn. 6th Ward Ch. of Jesus Christ of Latter-day Saints, 1984; mem. Stockton Opera Guild; bd. dirs. Stockton Beautiful, 2002. Austrian Govt. grantee, 1970. Mem. DAR, Daus. Am. Colonists, Soc. Mayflower Descendants, Am. Hist. Assn., Clements-Lockeford C. of C. (dir. 1977-79), Kappa Alpha Theta, Kiwanis. Avocations: writing local history, travel. Address: 18540 N Highway 88 Lockeford CA 95237-9514

WALKER, NATHAN BELT, trade association administrator; b. Macon, Mo., Apr. 18, 1952; s. Wendell K. and Azalea B. (Belt) W.; children: Madison, Samuel. BS in Agrl. Journalism, U. Mo., 1974, MS in Cmty. Devel., 1995. Owner, pub., editor La Plata (Mo.) Home Press, 1978-82; state rep. dist. 12 State of Mo., Anabel, 1981-85; dir. Mo. Divsn. Hwy. Safety, Jefferson City, 1985-91; dir. adminstrn. Mo. Office Atty. Gen., 1991-93; exec. dir. Mo. Head Injury Assn., 1993-94; dir. econ. devel. City of Boonville, Mo., 1994-96; dir. devel. Kemper Mil. Sch. and Coll., Boonville, 1996-98; dir. ops. Mo. Automobile Dealers Assn., Jefferson City, 1998—. Republican. Home: 3709B Struemph Ct Jefferson City MO 65109-4992 Office: Mo Automobile Dealers Assn 3322 American Ave Jefferson City MO 65109-1079 Fax: 573-636-5834.

WALKER, OLENE S. lieutenant governor; b. Ogden, Utah, Nov. 15, 1930; d. Thomas Ole and Nina Hadley (Smith) W.; m. J. Myron Walker, 1957; children: Stephen Brett, David Walden, Bryan Jesse, Lori, Mylene, Nina, Thomas Myron. BA, Brigham Young U., 1954; MA, Stanford U., 1954; PhD, U. Utah, 1986; HHD (hon.), Weber State U., 1997. V.p. Country Crisp Foods, 1969-92; mem. Utah Ho. of Reps. Dist. 24; lt. gov. State of Utah, 1993—. Mem. Salt Lake Edn. Found. bd. dirs. 1983-90; dir. community econ. devel.; mem. Ballet West, Sch. Vol., United Way, Commn. on Youth, Girls Village, Salt Lake Conv. and Tourism Bd.; mem. adv. coun. Weber State U. Mem. Nat. Assn. Secs. of State (Western chmn., nat. lt. gov.'s conf., pres. 1997-98). Mem. Lds Ch. Office: Lt Gov 203 State Capitol Building Salt Lake City UT 84114-1202*

WALKER, PATRICIA D. critical care nurse; b. Glenwood Springs, Colo., Aug. 30, 1948; d. O. Dale and Lucy D. (MacKenzie) St. John; m. Dennis A. Walker; children: Stephanie Ann, Steven Charles. ADN, Indian Hills Community Coll., Ottumwa, Iowa, 1986; BS in Bus. Mgmt., Fla. Gulf Coast U., 2000. Cert. emergency nurse, emergency nurse pediat. course; advanced cardiac life support, trauma nurse core course. Emergency rm. nurse N. Collier Hosp., 1986-92, 94-01; nurse chem. dependency treatment program New Beginnings, Ft. Collins, Colo., 1992-94; emergency rm. nurse Ft. Sanders Parkwest Med. Ctr., Knoxville, 2001—. Home: 729 Southview Cir Kodak TN 37764-1879 E-mail: pdwalke@attglobal.net.

WALKER, PAUL HOWARD, lawyer; b. Baldwyn, Miss., Feb. 10, 1923; s. Howard Earl and Frances Caroline (McElroy) W.; m. Gwendolyn Yvonne Loomis, June 17, 1950; children: Michael D., Melinda K. Student, E. Miss. Jr. Coll., 1940-41, La. State U., 1941-43, U. Mo., 1943-44; JD with honors, George Washington U., 1948; BA, George Washington U, 2000; LL.M., George Washington U., 1949; postgrad., Harvard U., 1975-82. Bar: D.C. 1948, Md. 1959, Mass. 1969. Atty.-editor U.S. Tax Ct., Washington, 1950-53; asst. gen. counsel Life Ins. Assn. Am. (now Am. Coun. of Life Ins.), 1953-68; tax counsel New Eng. Mut. Life Ins. Co., Boston, 1968-86. Mem. tax policy adv. bd. Taxation with Representation Fund, Washington, 1975; adv. coun. Hartford Inst. on Ins. Taxation, Conn., 1981-83.$D Contbr. articles to profl. jours.; mem. adv. bd. Estate Planning Mag., 1973-86, Compensation Planning Jour., 1973-86. Trustee New Eng. Coll., Henniker, N.H., 1978-90, trustee emeritus, 1990—; chancellor New Eng. Diocese Anglican Ch. in Am., 1981—. Served with AUS, 1943-45; to capt. USAFR, 1951-63. Decorated Silver Star, EAME Ribbon with 2 battle stars. Mem.: SAR (pres. Mass. Soc. 1981—83, nat. trustee 1983—85, chancellor gen. 1986—88, pres. gen. 1992—93), ABA, Sons of Confederate Vets., Hon. Order of Ky. Cols., Soc. of the War of 1812 in Mass. (state pres. 1996—97), Masons, Knights Templar (comdr. Boston Commandery No. 2 1997—98, named Knight Comdr. of Temple of Grand Encampment 1997, Knight York Cross of Honor 2001). Republican. Home and Office: 85A Seminary Ave Apt 347 Newton MA 02466-2648 E-mail: pwalker@lasell.edu.

WALKER, PEGGY JEAN, retired social work agency administrator; b. Carbondale, Ill., Aug. 9, 1940; d. George William and Lola Almeda (Black) Robinson; children: Edith Nell, Keith Alan. BA, So. Ill. U., 1962, PhD, 1986; MSW, Washington U., St. Louis, 1967. Lic. clin. social worker. Caseworker, casework supr. Ill. Dept. Pub. Aid, 1964-71; child welfare adminstr. Ill. Dept. Children and Family Svc., 1971-75; mem. faculty social work program So. Ill. U., 1975-79; exec. dir. Western divsn. Children's Home Soc. Fla., Pensacola, 1979-2000; ret., 2000; program and acreditation cons., 2000—. Apptd. to Fla. State Coord. Coun. for Early Childhood Devel., 1994-99, corp. programs and accreditation coord.., 1999-2000; adj. adv. bd. dept. social work U. West Fla., 1982—; appt. by Fla. Dept. Edn. to task force Edn. for Children of the Homeless, 1989-99, Dept. Children and Families, Dist. Task Force on Family Preservation and Support Svcs., 1985-99, chmn. 1988, 89; mem. steering com. Fla. Healthy Mothers/Healthy Babies, 1990-99; peer reviewer, team leader Coun. on Accreditatin of Svcs. for Families and Children, 1990—; program and accreditation cons. 2000. Co-chair chief judge Children's Coun., 1984-99; mem. Juvenile Justice Coun., 1994-99, chmn., 1996. Recipient Disting. Cmty. Svc. award United Way Escambia County, 1995. Home: 613 Silverthorn Rd Gulf Breeze FL 32561-4625 E-mail: pwalker080940@cs.com.

WALKER, PHILIP CHAMBERLAIN, II, health care executive; b. Big Spring, Tex., July 7, 1944; s. Philip Chamberlain and Mary Catherine (St. John) W.; m. Linda Jane Holsclaw, Jan. 21, 1978; children: Shannon M., Meghan M. BA, Cen. Wash. State Coll., 1970; MS, U. Idaho, 1971. Exec. dir. Multnomah Found. for Med. Care, Portland, Oreg., 1972-81; chief exec. officer Peer Rev. Orgn. for Wash. State, Seattle, 1981-84; dir. Preferred Provider Orgn. devel. Provident Life and Accident, Chattanooga, 1984-88; v.p. Maxicare Health Plans, L.A., 1988-91; v.p., gen. mgr. Maxicare Health Plans Midwest, Chgo., 1991-92; pres. Health Plus, Peoria, Ill., 1992—; CEO, chmn. bd. HCH Adminstrn., 1992-98; sr. v.p. Health Care Horizons, Albuquerque, 1992-98; exec. v.p. Proctor Health Sys., 1998—. Bd. dirs. RMR Group, HCH Adminstrn., Health Care Horizons; cons. to numerous orgns. Contbr. articles to profl. jours. Chmn., bd. dirs. Hult Health Edn. Ctr.; bd. dirs. Cancer Ctr. for Health Living, 2001—. With USAF, 1961—66, Vietnam. Mem.: Creve Coeur Club (bd. govs., sr. v.p.). Office: 5409 N Knoxville Ave Peoria IL 61614

WALKER, RADFORD, computer system architect; b. Pueblo, Colo., Apr. 12, 1957; s. Frank M. and Marian F. Walker; m. Sharon L. Stevens, Dec. 27, 1980; children: Rader Steele, Tova Sidnee Ann, Nyssa Radell Turney, Tacita Wynn Tansey. BS, Wichita State U., 1979; MS, U. Colo., 1992, MEWSE, 2001. Lab. asst. Dr. Paul Tasch, Wichita, Kans., 1978; asst. staff mgr. Southwestern Bell, St. Louis, 1979-82; sys. analyst Mountain Bell, Denver, 1983-87; mem. tech. staff U S WEST, 1988-92, sr. mem. tech. staff, 1994-97; mem. tech. staff U S WEST Advanced Tech., Boulder, Colo., 1993; sr. info. tech. architect Qwest, Thornton, 1998—. Editor newspaper Above The Line, 1989-96; exec. editor newspaper The Walker Squaker, 1994—; contbr. articles to profl. jours. Bd. dirs. Metro Wastewater Reclamation Dist., Denver, 1997—; commr. Thornton Devel. Authority, 1997—; mem. city coun. City of Thornton, 1997—; fair dir. Denver Metro Region Sci. Fair, Eastlake, Colo., 1997-2000; bd. dirs. Thornton Arts Scis. Hist. Cultural Orgn., 1997—; mem. North Front Range Trnasp. Alternatives Feasibility Study, Denver, 1999—; bd. dirs., judge Colo. Sci. and Engring. Fair, 1985—. NSF grantee, 1978; recipient Outstanding Young Man of Am. award V.I.P. Awards Ltd., 1985. Mem. IEEE Computer Soc., Am. Assn. Artificial Intelligence, Assn. Computing Machinery (chair Denver chpt. 1990-92), Platte Valley Model R.R. Club (pres. 1984—, past sec., Logo Design award 1989). Avocations: model railroading, lapidary, paleontology, NASCAR auto racing. Office: Qwest 1005 17th St Rm 1300 Denver CO 80202 E-mail: radford@qwest.net.

WALKER, RALPH CLIFFORD, lawyer; b. Bradenton, Fla., Apr. 30, 1938; s. Julius Clifford and Dorothy (Hefner) W.; m. Katherine Marie Christensen, Oct. 10, 1971; children: Laura Elizabeth, Mark Clifford, Tyler Lanier. BA cum laude, Vanderbilt U., 1959; LLB, U. Calif., Berkeley, 1965. Bar: Calif. Ptnr. Orrick Herrington & Sutcliffe, San Francisco, 1965—. Town councilman Town of Ross, Calif., 1970-72.Lt. (j.g.) USN, 1959-62. Mem. ABA, State Bar Calif., San Francisco Bar Assn., University Club (San Francisco, dir. 1986-88, counsel 1983—), Meadow Club (Fairfax, Calif.), Order of Coif. Republican. Presbyterian. Avocations: golf, wine, youth sports. Office: Orrick Herrington & Sutcliffe 400 Sansome St San Francisco CA 94111-3143

WALKER, RANDALL H. air transportation executive; b. Boulder City, Nev. m. Terry Walker; 6 children. BS in Acctg. magna cum laude, Brigham Young U. Budget analyst Clark County (Nev.) Mgr.'s Office; bus. mgr. Las Vegas Met. Police Dept.; dep. city mgr. City of Las Vegas; Las Vegas rep. to Nev. State Legislature; asst. county mgr. Clark County, dir. dept. fin.; dep. dir. Clark County Dept. Aviation, now dir. Office: c/o McCarran Internat Airport PO Box 11005 Las Vegas NV 89111-1005*

WALKER, RAYMOND FRANCIS, business and financial consulting company executive; b. Medicine Lake, Mont., Nov. 9, 1914; s. Dennis Owen and Rose (Long) W.; m. Patricia K. Blakey, May 15, 1951; children: Richard A., Mark D., Maxie R. Forest, Victoria L. Le Huray, Suzanne J. Walker, Tracy A. Marshall. Grad. pub. schs.; student, Edison Vocat. Sch., 1935-39. Truck mgr. Pacific Food Products, Seattle, 1939-42; machinist Todd Shipyard, 1943-45; owner Delbridge Auto Sales, 1945-48; pres. Pacific Coast Acceptance Corp., 1949-60; v.p. West Coast Mortgage, Seattle, 1960-67, United Equities Corp., Seattle, 1965-69; pres. Income Mgmt. Corp., 1970-90; v.p. Internat. Mint and Foundry, Redmond, Wash., 1983-87; pvt. practice bus. and fin. cons. Sequim, 1987—. Cons. Life Ins. Co. Am., Bellevue, Wash., 1982-87, Consumer Loan Svc., Lynwood Wash., 1980-92; dir., cons., v.p. fin. Am. Campgrounds, Bellevue, 1971-79; cons., bd. dirs. Straits Forest Products, Inc. , Port Angeles, Wash.; dir., cons. Synergy Techs., Inc., Sequim, 1990-97, co-founder, dir. Sequim Tech., Inc., 1994-97. Mem. Nat. Assn. Security Dealers. Lodges: Elks. Methodist. Home: 3347 W Sequim Bay Rd Sequim WA 98382-8430 E-mail: raypatrickew@prodigy.net.

WALKER, RICHARD BRIAN, chemistry educator; b. Quincy, Mass., May 14, 1948; s. George Edgar and Eva Mary (Taylor) W. BS in Biochemistry, U. So. Calif., 1970; PhD in Pharm. Chemistry, U. Calif., San Francisco, 1975. Rsch. assoc. Oreg. State U., Corvallis, 1975-76, U. Wash., Seattle, 1976-78; lectr. U.S. Internat. U., San Diego, 1978-81, Hamdard Sch. Pharmacy, New Delhi, India, 1981-82; rsch. scientist Biophysica Found., San Diego, 1982-83; assoc. prof. chemistry U. Ozarks, Clarksville, Ark., 1983-84; asst. to assoc. prof. chemistry U. Ark., Pine Bluff, 1984-96, prof. chemistry, 1996—. Prin. investigator minority biomed. rsch. support program NIH, Bethesda, Md., 1986—; project dir. Ark. Systemic Sci. Initiative. Contbr. articles to profl. jours. Coord. home Bible fellowship The Way Internat., Pine Bluff, 1984-99; judge Ctrl. Ark. Sci. Fair, Little Rock, 1986—. NIH rsch. grantee, 1986, 89, 93. Mem. Am. Chem. Soc., Ark. Acad. Scis., Am. Assn. Pharm. Scientists, Sigma Xi. Avocations: fishing, golf, skiing. Office: 1200 University Dr Pine Bluff AR 71601-2799 E-mail: walker_r@vx4500.uapb.edu.

WALKER, RICHARD BRUCE, judge; b. Newton, Kans., July 20, 1948; s. Thomas Franklin and Norma M. (Doell) W.; m. Martha Mangelsdorf, Nov. 26, 1977 (div. 1988); children: Jacob, Benjamin; m. Ann Jordan Lobo, July 28, 1990. BA, Bethel Coll., 1970; JD, U. Kans., 1973. Bar: Kans. 1973, U.S. Dist. Ct. Kans. 1973, U.S. Supreme Ct. 1977, U.S. Ct. Appeals (10th cir.) 1982. Ptnr. Adrian & Walker, Newton, 1973-77, Ice, Turner & Ice, Newton, 1982-84; chief legis. asst. to Senator James Pearson, Washington, 1977-78; mem. Kans. Parole Bd., Topeka, 1979-82; dist. judge Harvey County Ct., Newton, 1984—2002; chief judge Ninth Jud. Dist., 2002—. Mem. Kans. Sentencing Commn., 1989-2000, chmn., 1997-2000. State rep. Kans. Legislature, Topeka, 1972-77; bd. dirs. Bethel Coll., No. Newton, Kans., 1971-83, Kans. State Hist. Soc., 1999—. Mem. ABA, Kans. Bar Assn., Harvey County Bar Assn. (pres. 1991-92). Republican. Methodist. Home: 209 E 1st St Newton KS 67114-3702 Office: Harvey County Dist Ct PO Box 665 Newton KS 67114-0665

WALKER, RICHARD DAVID, civil engineer, educator; b. Washington, Feb. 19, 1931; s. Stanton and Amelia (Ramseyer) W.; m. Alice Patricia Davis, June 6, 1953; children: Patricia Vawn, Jean Brianne, Sharyl Elise. B.C.E., U. Md., 1953; M.C.E., Purdue U., 1955, PhD, 1961. Instr., Purdue U., 1957-61; asst. prof. Va. Poly. Inst., 1961-62, asso. prof., 1962-68, prof., 1968-96, head dept. civil engring., 1970-83; prof. emeritus, 1996. Author: (with R.D. Krebs) Highway Materials, 1971. Mem. Montgomery County Republican Com. Served to lt. USAF, 1955-57. Fellow ASCE; mem. ASTM (sec. com. C-9 on concrete and concrete aggregates 1970-76), Transp. Research Bd., Am. Soc. for Engring. Edn., Sigma Xi, Chi Epsilon. Presbyterian (elder 1973—). Home: 701 Broce Dr Blacksburg VA 24060-2803 *Have respect for others, their opinions and beliefs. At the same time, stand firm for what you believe. Remember, even a firmly rooted tree stands because it is flexible and can bend with the wind. Concerning goals, avoid rigidity; include service to others, then set goals sufficiently general to embrace the total purpose God has for you in this life.*

WALKER, RICHARD HAROLD, pathologist, educator; b. Cleve., Dec. 2, 1928; s. Harold Deford and Bernice Margaret (Wright) W.; m. Carolyn Franklin, Sept. 28, 1954; children: Bruce, Lynn, Cara, Leah. BS, Emory U., 1950, MD, 1953. Intern City of Memphis Hosps., 1953-54; resident in pathology Coll. Medicine U. Tenn., Memphis, 1954-55, 57-59, prof. pathology, 1966-70; Am. Cancer Soc. clin. fellow U. Tenn. Coll. Medicine, 1957-59; med. dir. blood bank and transfusion svc. City of Memphis Hosps., Memphis, 1961-70; chief of blood bank and transfusion service William Beaumont Hosp., Royal Oak, Mich., 1970-95, med. dir. Sch. Med. Tech., 1970-91. Clin. prof. pathology Sch. Medicine Wayne State U., Detroit, 1982-95. Contbr. articles on blood transfusion, blood group genetics and transfusion medicine to med. jours. Capt. USNR ret. Recipient Murray Thelin Humanitarian award Memphis chpt. Nat. Hemophilia Found., 1968 Mem. AMA, Coll. Am. Pathologists, Am. Soc. Clin. Pathologists (Disting. Svc. award 1977, Ward Burdick award 1992), Am. Assn. Blood Banks (pres. 1976-77, John Elliott Meml. award 1986), Tenn. Assn. Blood Banks (L.W. Diggs award 1986), Internat. Soc. Blood Transfusion, Am. Soc. for Histocompatibility and Immunogenetics. Republican. Presbyterian. Home: 4204 Fleet Landing Blvd Atlantic Beach FL 32233-4590

WALKER, RICHARD HUGH, orthopaedic surgeon; b. Elgin, Ill., Jan. 29, 1951; m. Wendy Allen; children: Ashley Elizabeth, Blake Allen, Emily Paige. AB cum laude, Occidental Coll., 1973; MD, U. Chgo., 1977. Diplomate Nat. Bd. Med. Examiners, Am. Bd. Orthopaedic Surgery. Jr. resident in surgery UCLA, 1977-79; jr. resident in orthopaedic surgery Stanford (Calif.) U., 1979-81, sr. resident, 1981-82, chief resident, 1982-83; clin. mem. divsn. orthop. surgery, sect. lower extremity reconstructive surgery Scripps Clinic, La Jolla, Calif., 1983—; co-dir. lower extremity reconstructive surgery fellowship, divsn. orthopaedic surgery Scripps Clinic , 1989—, assoc. head. divsn. orthopaedic surgery, 1990-97, chmn. dept. surgery, 1998—2001, v.p. surg. svcs., 2001—. Staff physician dept. surgery Green Hosp. of Scripps Clinic, La Jolla, 1983—, mem. exec. com., 1994—2001, chief of staff, 1995—97; team physician San Diego Padres, 1983—86, 1995—99; clin. instr. dept. orthopaedics and rehab. U. Calif., San Diego, 1983—92, asst. clin. prof., 1992—, chmn. dept. surgery, 1998—; mem. bd. dirs. Scripps Clinic Med. Group, La Jolla, 1992—, mem. exec. com., 1998—, med. dir. surg. specialties, 1998—2001, chmn. dept. surgery, 1998—, mem. joint exec. bd., 1992—93. Cons. reviewer Clin. Orthopaedics and Related Rsch., 1989—, Jour. Bone and Joint Surgery, 1994—; contbr. articles to profl. jours. Mem. AMA, ACS, Am. Acad. Orthopaedic Surgeons, We. Orthopaedic Assn. (program chmn. San Diego chpt. 1994-95, treas. 1995-96, v.p. 1996-97, pres. 1997-98, Resident Paper award 1983), Calif. Orthopaedic Assn., Assn. Arthritic Hip and Knee Surgery (charter mem. 1991), Am. Assn. Hip and Knee Surgeons, Assn. Bone and Joint Surgeons (Nicholas Andry Rsch. award 1997). Office: Scripps Clinic Divsn Orthop Surgery 10666 N Torrey Pines Rd La Jolla CA 92037-1092

WALKER, RICHARD K. lawyer; b. Knoxville, Tenn., Oct. 21, 1948; BA with honors, U. Kans., 1970, JD, 1975; student, U. Bonn, Germany; grad. student, U Tübingen, Germany. Bar: Ariz. 1975, D.C. 1977, U.S. Supreme Ct. 1977. Asst. prof. law U. S.C., 1977-81, assoc. prof. law, 1981-82; ptnr. Bishop, Cook, Purcell & Reynolds, Washington, 1981-90, Winston & Strawn, Washington, 1990-93; dir. Streich Lang, Phoenix, 1993-2000; ptnr. Quarles & Brady Streich Lang, 2000—. Bd. trustees Ariz. Theatre Co., 1995-2001; bd. dirs. Phoenix Cmty. Alliance, 2001—. Fulbright Direct Exchange scholar. Mem. ABA, Labor and Employment Law Sec. (mem. equal employment opportunity law com. and devel. of the law under the NLRA com., 1979—), Litigation Sec. (mem. class actions and derivitive suits com. and trial pratice com., 1998—, mem. employment rels. and labor law com., 1979—), Ariz. Assn. Def. Counsel (bd. dirs. 1997-2000), Phoenix Cmty. Alliance (bd. dirs. 2001—). Office: Quarles & Brady Streich Lang Renaissance One 2 N Central Ave Phoenix AZ 85004-2345 E-mail: rwalker@quarles.com.

WALKER, RICHARD LOUIS, former ambassador, educator, author; b. Bellefonte, Pa., Apr. 13, 1922; s. Robert Shortlidge and Genevieve (Bible) W.; m. Celeno Claypole Kenly, Mar. 29, 1945; children: Geoffrey Kenly, Dorothy Anne, Stephen Bradley. BA, Drew U., 1944; cert. Chinese lang. and area, U. Pa., 1944; MA, Yale U., 1947, PhD, 1950; LLD (hon.), Coll. of Charleston, 1985, Drew U., 1986, The Citadel, 1990; D of Polit. Sci. (hon.), Seoul Nat. U., 1982; D. Pub. Svc., U. S.C., 1991. Asst. prof. history Yale U., 1950-57; prof. internat. studies U. S.C., 1957—, James F. Byrnes prof. internat. relations, 1959—, prof. emeritus, 1992—; U.S. amb. to Republic of Korea, 1981-86; amb.-in-residence U. S.C., 1986—. Vis. assoc. prof. Nat. Taiwan U., Taipei, China, 1954-55; vis. prof. U. Wash., 1959, 65; prof. polit. affairs Nat. War Coll., 1960-61; spl. rsch. internat. rels., Far East; lectr., cons. U.S. Govt., 1953—, Dept. Def., 1969—; rep. U.S. Dept. State, USIS, 1973-74; lectr. numerous confs., major U.S. govt. svc. schs. and univs. in Asia, Australia and Europe. Author: Western Language Periodicals on China, 1949, Multi-State System of Ancient China, 1953, China Under Communism, 1955, China and the West, 1956, The Continuing Struggle, 1958, Democracy Confronts Communism in World Affairs, 1965, Edward R. Stettmius, Jr., 1965, The China Danger, 1966, Ancient China, 1969, Prospects in the Pacific, 1972, Asia in Perspective, 1974, Ancient Japan, 1975, Korean Remembrances, 1998; contbr. articles to various symposium vols., learned jours. Bd. dirs. Nat. Com. U.S.-China Rels., 1968-94, U.S. Strategic Inst., 1977—, U. S.C. Ednl. Found., 1958—, Conf. on European Problems, 1967—. With AUS, 1942-46, PTO. Recipient Alumni Achievement award in arts Drew U., 1958; Disting. Service award Air U., 1970; Fgn. Service Inst. award, 1971; Armed Forces Staff Coll. award, 1978; Fulbright-Social Sci. Research Council research scholar Academia Sinica Republic China, 1965-66. Mem. Assn. Asian Studies, Am. Assn. for China Studies (v.p. 1994-95, nat. pres. 1995-97), Aurelian Honor Soc., Korea Soc., Forest Lake Club, Torch Club, Pi Gamma Mu, Omicron Delta Kappa. Episcopalian. Home: 700 Spring Lake Rd Columbia SC 29206-2111

WALKER, ROBERT HARRIS, historian, writer, editor; b. Cin., Mar. 15, 1924; m. Grace Burtt; children: Amy, Rachel, Matthew. BS, Northwestern U., 1945; MA, Columbia U., 1950; PhD, U. Pa., 1955. Edn. specialist U.S. Mil. Govt., Japan, 1946-47; instr. Carnegie Inst. Tech., 1950-51, U. Pa., 1953-54; asst. prof., dir. Am. studies U. Wyo., 1955-59; asso. prof. George Washington U., 1959-63, prof. Am. civilization, 1963-94, dir. Am. studies program, 1959-66, 68-70. First dir. edn. and pub. programs NEH, 1966-68; fellow Woodrow Wilson Internat. Ctr., 1972-73, Rockefeller Rsch. Ctr., 1979, Hoover Instn., Huntington Libr., 1980; specialist grants to Japan, Germany, Thailand, Iran, Greece, Israel, Brazil, China, People's Republic of Korea, Hong Kong, 1964-91; Fulbright lectr., Australia, New Zealand, Philippines, 1971, Sweden, France, West Germany, Norway, all 1987; Am. Coun. Learned Socs. alt. del. UNESCO Gen. Info. Program, 1978—; co-founder Algonquin Books, 1982. Author: Poet and Gilded Age, 1963, Life in the Age of Enterprise, 1967, American Society, 1981, 2d edit., 1995, Reform in America (nominated for Pulitzer prize in history), 1985, (with R.H. Gabriel) Course of American Democratic Thought, 3d edit., 1986, Cincinnati and the Big Red Machine, 1988, Everyday Life in Victorian America, 1994; editor, compiler: American Studies in the U.S., 1958, American Studies Abroad, 1975, Reform Spirit in America, 1976, 85, American Studies: Topics and Sources, 1976, Frieds of Raoul Wallenberg, 1987-1997, 1998; editor: Am. Quar., 1953-54; sr. editor: Am. Studies Internat., 1970-80, Am. studies series for Greenwood Press, 1972—, over 100 vols. Founding mem. Japan-U.S. Friendship Commn., 1977-80; founding pres. Friends of Raoul Wallenberg Found., 1987-99. With USNR, 1943-46, 50. Mem. Am. Studies Assn. (nat. pres. 1970-71), Cosmos Club, Phi Beta Kappa. Office: 200 Riverside Blvd #4J New York NY 10069

WALKER, ROBERT KIRK, lawyer; m. Joy Holt; children: R. Kirk Jr., Marilyn Joy Walker Fisher, James Holt. Student. U. South, Sewanee; LLB, U. Va., 1948, JD, 1970; D in Civil Law (hon.), U. South, Sewanee, 2000. Bar: Va. 1948, Tenn. 1948. Assoc. Strang, Fletcher & Carriger, Chattanooga, 1949-55; ptnr. Strang, Fletcher, Carriger, Walker, Hodge & Smith, 1955-71; mayor City of Chattanooga, 1971-75; mng. ptnr. Strang, Fletcher, Carriger, Walker, Hodge & Smith, Chattanooga, 1975-97, of counsel, 1998. Life mem. U.S. Jud. Conf. 6th cir., 1966—; hearing officer Bd. Profl. Responsibility of Supreme Ct. of Tenn., 1976-84. Chmn. Chattanooga-Hamilton County Com. on Bicentennial of U.S. Constn., 1987-90, chmn. Miller Park Bd., 1974—, Tenn. Temple U. Pres.'s Forum, 1999—; chmn. bd. Ctr. City Corp. (Miller Park Plz.), 1986-89; founding chmn. Leadership Chattanooga, 1983-85; chmn. Soldiers & Sailors Meml. Auditorium Redevel. com., 1988-92; chmn. Tivoli Theatre Renovation and Restoration study com., 1979-82, mem. Chattanooga Venture Tivoli Bldg. com. 1986-89, mem. Ovation! Campaign exec. com., 1986-89; gen. campaign chmn. United Way Chattanooga, 1991, bd. dirs., 1990-96, vice chmn., 1991, exec. com., 1990-92; trustee U. Chattanooga Found., 1989—, exec. com., 1994—; mem. U. Tenn. Chattanooga Chancellors Roundtable, 1981-84; mem. Tonya Pub. Affairs adv. com., U. South, 1980—; mem. Chattanooga Sch. Consolidation Referendum coms., 1994, 96, Chattanooga Sales Tax Referendum com., 1996; mem. nat. coun. Boy Scouts of Am., 1966-76, exec. bd. Cherokee Area Coun. 1958—, v.p., 1967-69; vice chmn. adv. bd. U. Tenn. Govt.-Industry-Law Ctr., 1965-66; exec. bd. Chattanooga Area Heart Assn., 1966-75; exec. bd. Hamilton County Law Enforcement Commn., 1962-67; mem. Chattanooga-Hamilton County Health Dept. adv. com., 1966-71; mem. Tenn. Law Revision Commn., 1970-71; v.p. Tenn. Mcpl. League, 1971-75; chmn. Tenn. Local Govt. study commn., 1973-74; bd. dirs. Nat. Human Svcs. Inst. Families and Children, treas., 1974-76; mem. Nat. Conf. Social Welfare & U.S. Dept. HEW Task Force on Orgn. & Delivery of Human Svcs. in U.S., 1976-77; bd. dirs. Siskin Hosp. for Phys. Rehab., 2002–; numerous other civic offices and activities. Lt., USN, World War II and Korea. Honored by Tenn. Gen. Assembly for Svc. Contbns. to Perpetuate Pub. Good, 1998; recipient Dorothy Patten Love of Chattanooga award, 1991, award for disting. contbns. on 30th anniversary Chattanooga State Tech. C.C., 1996, numerous medals and awards Freedoms Found., including 9 George Washington honor medals for pub. address, 1966-97, Ctrl. H.S. Disting. Alumni award, 1993, Univ. Tenn. Disting. Alumni award, 1998, Dr. John. E. Huckaba City Beautiful award 1996 presented to Robert Kirk and Joy Walker, Scenic Cities Beautiful com., Crusader award Tenn. Temple U., 2000; hon. mem. Am. Women in Radio & TV; numerous other awards. Fellow Am. Bar Found., Tennessee Bar Found. (charter), Chattanooga Bar Found. (charter; chmn. 1991-97); Tenn. Bar Assn. (pres. 1965-66), Chattanooga Bar Assn. (pres. 1962-63, Ralph H. Kelley Humanitarian award 1994); mem. Chattanooga Audubon Soc. (exec. bd. 1981-84), Rotary Club of Chattanooga (bd. dirs. 1987-88, 89-90, 96-97, 1st v.p. 1989-90, pres.-elect 1994-95, pres. 1995-96, Paul Harris fellow 1990—), Kiwanis (hon., Disting. Svc. award 1992), Greater Chattanooga Area C. of C. (edn. com. 1962-71, chmn. spl. 4-yr. state coll. com. 1966-71, chmn. ednl. task force 1967-71, dir. 1969-75, 81-82, v.p. 1982), Optimist Club of Chattanooga (pres. 1958-59), Optimist Internat. (past lt. gov., Man of Yr. 1956), Mountain City Club of Chattanooga, Alpha Hon. Scholastic Soc. Office: Strang Fletcher Carriger Walker Hodge & Smith 1 Union Sq Chattanooga TN 37402-2505

WALKER, ROBERT MARTIN, writer, minister; b. Fairbanks, Alaska, Aug. 18, 1954; s. Robert Lee and Helen Eileen (Palmer) W.; m. Donna Lee Henry, May 20, 1977; children: Robert Brandon, Matthew Lee. BA, So. Meth. U., 1975, MTh, 1978, MBA, 1979; STM, Yale Y., 1985. Ordained to ministry United Meth. Ch., 1977. Assoc. pastor Oak Lawn United Meth. Ch., Dallas, 1978-79; editor United Meth. Reporter North Tex. Ann. Conf., 1979-81; sr. pastor Richland United Meth. Ch., Richardson, Tex., 1982-84, Darien (Conn.) United Meth. Ch., 1985-93, 1st Ch. of Round Hill, Greenwich, Conn., 1999—. Chair pastoral adv. com. Stamford (Conn.) Hosp., 1989-91. Author: The Jesus I Knew, 1996, Politically Correct Parables, 1996, Politically Correct Old Testament Stories, 1997, You Might Be a United Methodist If, 1998, Encounters with the Living God, 2000. Pres. Darien Clergy Assn., 1991-93; v.p. Interfaith Hospitality Network, Darien, 1992-94; mem. adv. bd. Kids in Crisis, Greenwich, Conn., 1995-97. Avocations: rowing, tennis, squash. Home: 9 McCrea Ln Darien CT 06820-5902 Office: 464 Round Hill Rd Greenwich CT 06831

WALKER, ROBERT MOWBRAY, physicist, educator; b. Phila., Feb. 6, 1929; s. Robert and Margaret (Seivwright) W.; m. Alice J. Agedal, Sept. 2, 1951 (div. 1973); children: Eric, Mark; m. Ghislaine Crozaz, Aug. 24, 1973. BS in Physics, Union Coll., 1950, D.Sc., 1967; MS, Yale U., 1951, PhD, 1954; Dr honoris causa, Université de Clermont-Ferrand, 1975. Physicist Gen. Electric Research Lab., Schenectady, 1954-62, 63-66; McDonnell prof. physics Washington U., St. Louis, 1966—; dir. McDonnell Center for Space Scis., 1975-99. Vis. prof. U. Paris, 1962—63; adj. prof. metallurgy Rensselaer Poly. Inst., 1958, adj. prof. physics, 1965—66; vis. prof. physics and geology Calif. Inst. Tech., 1972, Phys. Research Lab., Ahmedabad, India, 1981, Institut d'Astrophysique, Paris, 1981, Univ. Libre, Brussels, 2001—; nat. lectr. Sigma Xi, 1984—85; pres. Vols. for Internat. Tech. Assistance, 1960—62, 1965—66, founder, 1960; mem. Lunar Sample Analysis Planning Team, 1968—70; bd. dirs. Univs. Space Rsch. Assn., 1969—71; mem. Lunar Sample Rev. Bd., 1970—72; adv. com. Lunar Sci. Inst., 1972—75; mem. temporary nominating group in planetary scis. Nat. Acad. Scis., 1973—75, bd. on sci. and tech. for internat. devel., 1974—76, com. planetary and lunar exploration, 1977—80, mem. space sci. bd., 1979—82; mem. organizing com. Com. on Space Research-Internat. Astron. Union, Marseille, France, 1984; mem. task force on sci. uses of space sta. Solar System Exploration Com., 1985—86; mem. Antarctic Meteorite Working Group, 1985—92, NASA Planetary Geosci. Strategy Com., 1986—88, European Sci. Found. Sci. Orgn. Com., Workshop on Analysis of Samples from Solar System Bodies, 1990; chmn. Antarctic Meteorite Working Group, 1990—92; mem. cosmic dust allocation com. NASA, 1998; vis. com. dept. terrestrial magnetism Carnegie Instn., 1998; vis. com. Max Planck fur Chemie, Mainz, Germany, 1998. Decorated officer de l'Ordre des Palmes Academiques (France); recipient Disting. Svc. award Am. Nuclear Soc., 1964, Yale Engring. Assn. award for contbn. to basic and applied sci., 1966, Indsl. Rsch. awards, 1964, 65; Exceptional Sci. Achievement award NASA, 1970; E.O. Lawrence award AEC, 1971; Antarctic Svc. medal NSF, 1985; NSF fellow, 1962-63; Asteroid 1985 JWI named in his honor, 1999. Fellow AAAS, Am. Phys. Soc., Meteoritical Soc. (Leonard medal 1993), Am. Geophys. Union, Indian Inst. of Astrophysics (hon.); mem. NAS (mem. polar rsch. bd. com. 1995, J. Lawrence Smith medal 1991), Am. Astron. Soc., St. Louis Acad. Scis. (Peter Raven Lifetime Scientific Achievement award 1997). Achievements include research and publs. on cosmic rays, nuclear physics, geophysics, radiation effects in solids, particularly devel. solid state track detectors and their application to geophysics and nuclear physics problems; discovery of fossil particle tracks in terrestrial and extra-terrestrial materials and fission track method of dating; application of phys. scis. to art and archaeology; lab. studies of interplanetary dust and interstellar grains in primitive meteorites. Home: 3 Romany Park Ln Saint Louis MO 63132-4211

WALKER, ROBERT ROSS, social worker; b. Haverhill, Mass., May 26, 1954; s. Bertram Ross and Ann Elizabeth (Glass) W.; m. Jean Marie Webster, June 16, 1979; children: Jennifer Elizabeth, Heather Jean. BS in Human Devel., U. Mass., Amherst, 1976; MEd, Tufts U., 1980. Diplomate Nat. Assn. Forensic Counselors; lic. social worker, Mass.; cert. domestic violence counselor. Field instr. Salem State Coll., Fitchburg State Coll., Haverhill, 1976; continuing edn. instr. No. Essex C.C., Mass., 1976; res. police officer City of Haverhill, 1978—; counselor Hampstead (N.H.) Hosp., Haverhill, 1979-81; social worker Mass. Dept. Social Svcs., 1980-91, supr. Lawrence, 1991—. Spl. edn. cons. to area office, rep. Haverhill/Newburyport area interdeptl. human svc. team; spkr. burs., acct. exec. Merrimack Valley United Fund, Dept. Social Svcs., Merrimack Valley Sexual Assault Com. Bd. dirs. ARC, Haverhill, 1976-91, water safety, first aid and CPR instr., sec., 1984-89, co-chmn. Youth Red. Cross and Disaster Com., chmn. Haverhill chpt., 1989-91, Merrimac Valley chpt., 1991—, vice-chmn., 1991-93, sec. 1993-96; fire responder; steering com. Haverhill/Newburyport Human Svcs. Coalition; bd. dirs. Haverhill Youth Commn., 1971-72; vestry mem. Trinity Episcopal Ch. Recipient Boy Scouts Am. award, ARC award, Clara Barton award ARC, Vol. award Merrimack Valley United Fund, Commonwealth Mass. Pride in Performance Recognition award, Pub. Safety award Elks, Jewish Am. War Vets. award. Mem. Am. Personnel and Guidance Assn., Svc. Employees Internat. Union, Am. Fedn. Musicians, Nat. Honor Soc., Nat. Eagle Scout Assn., Alpha Phi Omega, Kappa Kappa Psi. Home: 1 Twelve Rod Way Haverhill MA 01830-1840 Office: Dept Social Svcs 1 Twelve Rod Way Haverhill MA 01830

WALKER, ROBERT S. government agency administrator; BS in Edn., Millersville U., Pa.; MA in Polit. Sci., U. Del.; LLD (hon.) , Franklin and Marshall Coll. Tchr. H.S., 1967-77. Rep. congressman 16th dist. Pa. Ho. of Reps., Washington; chmn., CEO Wexler & Walker Pub. Policy Assocs. Chief dep. whip, chmn. leadership, spkr. pro tempore, chmn. sci. com., vice chmn. budget com. Ho. of Reps. Recipient Disting. Svc. medal, NASA, 1996. Office: Aerospace Commn Ste 940 Crystal Gateway One 1235 Jefferson Davis Hwy Arlington VA 22202-3283*

WALKER, ROBERT SMITH, former congressman; b. Bradford, Pa., Dec. 23, 1942; s. Joseph Erdman and Rachael Viola (Smith) W.; m. Sue Ellen Albertson, Apr. 13, 1968. BS, Millersville (Pa.) U., 1964; MA in Polit. Sci, U. Del., 1968; LLD (hon.), Franklin & Marshall Coll., 1998. Tchr. Penn Manor High Sch., Lancaster, Pa., 1964-67; legis. asst. to Congressman Edwin D. Eshleman, 1967-74, adminstrv. asst., 1974-76; mem. 95th-104th Congresses from 16th Pa. dist., Washington, 1977-96, chmn. House Com. Sci.; vice chmn. house budget com., chmn. house Rep. leadership, 1995-97; chief dep. minority whip, 1989-95; spkr. pro tempore, 1996; chmn. Wexler & Walker Pub. Policy Assocs., Washington, 1997—; vice chmn. Hill & Knowlton Worldwide Pub. Affairs, 2002—. Adv. bd. Imax Corp., 1998—, Innerlink, 2001; chmn., bd. dirs. DCH Corp. Tech.; chmn. Commn. on the Future of the U.S. Aerospace Industry, 2001—02. Co-author: Congress-The Pennsylvania Dutch Representatives, 1774-1974, Can You Afford This House, 1978, House of Ill Repute, 1987; columnist: UPI, 2001; contbr. articles to profl. jours. Trustee Aerospace Corp., 1997—, U.S. Space Found., 1997—, Susquehana Valley Ctr. Pub. Policy, 1998—; bd. dirs. U.S. Capitol Hist. Soc. With Pa. NG, 1967-73. Recipient NASA Disting. Svc. medal, 1996; fellow Millersville U., 1996-2001, Franklin & Marshall Coll., 1997-2001. Mem. Am. League of Lobbyists (bd. dirs. 2000—). Republican. Presbyterian. Office: Wexler & Walker Pub Policy Assocs 1317 F St NW Ste 600 Washington DC 20004-1157 *The revolution sweeping politics, economics, culture and technology will produce new opportunities but at the same time will demand a new way of thinking about our economy and our society. The wealth of information available to each individual means that government and business must think in terms of individualized approaches.*

WALKER, ROGER GEOFFREY, geology educator, consultant; b. London, Mar. 26, 1939; s. Reginald Noel and Edith Annie (Wells) W.; m. Gay Parsons, Sept. 18, 1965; children: David John, Susan Elizabeth. BA, Oxford U., Eng., 1961, DPhil in Geology, 1964. Prof. emeritus McMaster U., Hamilton, Ont., Can., 1998—; NATO postdoctoral fellow in geology Johns Hopkins U., Balt., 1964-66; from asst. to assoc. prof. McMaster U., Hamilton, Ont., Can., 1966-73, prof. geology Can., 1973-98; vis. scientist Denver Rsch. Ctr., Marathon Oil Co., Littleton, Colo., 1973-74, Amoco Can. Petrol Co., Calgary, Alta., Can., 1982; vis. fellow Australian Nat. U., Canberra, 1981. Tchr. 80 profl. short courses on various aspects of oil exploration in clastic reservoirs, Can., U.S., Brazil, Australia, Japan, Italy, Venezuela, Norway; mem. grant selection com. earth scis. sect. Nat. Scis. and Engring. Rsch. Coun. Can., 1981-84; Judd A. & Cynthia S. Oualline Centennial lectr. U. Tex., Austin, 1986; vis. prof. Fed. U. Ouro Preto, Brazil, 1987, 89, 90, 91, Fed. U. Rio Grande do Sul, Brazil, 1992; adj. prof. U. Regina, 1997—; pres. Roger Walker Cons., Inc., 1997—. Editor: Facies Models, 1979, 3d edit., 1992; contbr. over 140 articles to profl. jours. Recipient operating and strategic grants Nat. Scis. and Engring. Rsch. Coun. Can., 1966—. Fellow: Royal Soc. Can.; mem.: Internat. Assn. Sedimentologists (Henry Clifton Sorby medal 2002), Can. Assn. Univ. Tchrs., Soc. Sedimentary Geology (Francis J. Pettijohn medal 1997), Soc. Econ. Paleontologists and Mineralogists (pres. eastern sect. 1975—76, coun. for mineralogy 1979—80, hon. mem. 1991, assoc. editor 1970—78), Am. Assn. Petroleum Geologists (Disting. lectr. 1979—80, Disting. Educator award 1999), Can. Soc. Petroleum Geologists (Link award 1983, R.J.W. Douglas Meml. medal 1990), Geol. Assn. Can. (assoc. editor 1977—80, Past Pres.'s medal 1975, Disting. Svc. award 1994, Logan medal 1999). Achievements include research in sedimentary facies analysis, sedimentology of turbidites, quantitative basin analysis, sedimentology of Western Canadian Cretaceous clastic wedge. Avocations: skiing, classical music, photography, model railroading. Home and Office: Roger Walker Cons 83 Scimitar View NW Calgary AB Canada T3L 2B4 E-mail: walkerrg@cadvsion.com.

WALKER, RONALD EDWARD, psychologist, educator; b. East St. Louis, Ill., Jan. 23, 1935; s. George Edward and Marnella (Altmeyer) W.; m. Aldona M. Mogenis, Oct. 4, 1958; children: Regina, Mark, Paula, Alexis. BS, St. Louis U., 1957; MA, Northwestern U., 1959, PhD, 1961. Lectr. psychology Northwestern U., 1959-61; faculty dept. psychology Loyola U., Chgo., 1961—, asst., then asso. prof., 1961-68, prof., chmn. dept., 1965—; acting dean Loyola U. (Coll. Arts and Scis.), 1973-74, dean, 1974-80, academic v.p., 1980-81, sr. v.p., dean faculties, 1981-89, exec. v.p., 1989-99. Cons. VA, Chgo., 1965-74; Am. Psychol. Assn.-NIMH; vis. cons., 1969; vis. scientist Am. Psychol. Assn. NSF, 1968; Cook County (Ill.) rep. from Ill. Psychol. Assn., 1969-72; cons.-evaluator North Cen. Assn., 1986-99. Contbr. articles to profl. jours. Bd. trustees St. Francis Hosp., Evanston, Ill., 1986—92, Chgo. Archdiocesan Sems., 1985—97, Loyola Acad., Wilmette, Ill., 1987—93, St. Louis U., 1988—97; bd. dirs. Holy Family Villa Nursing Home, Lemont, Ill. Recipient Disting. Psychologist of Yr. award Ill. Psychol. Assn., 1986. Mem. APA (coun. rep. 1970-72), Ill. Psychol. Assn. (chmn. student devel. com. 1965-67, chmn. acad. sec. 1966-67, disting. psychologist of yr. award 1986), Psi Chi, Phi Beta Kappa. Home: Unit 5I 1630 Sheridan Rd Wilmette IL 60091-1835

WALKER, RONALD HUGH, management consultant; b. Bryan, Tex., July 25, 1937; s. Walter Hugh and Maxine (Tarver) W.; m. Anne Lucille Collins, Aug. 8, 1959; children: Lisa, Marjorie, Lynne. BA, U. Ariz., 1960. With Allstate Ins. Co., Pasadena, Calif., 1964-67, Hudson Co., 1967-69; asst. to sec. interior, 1969-70; founder, 1st dir., staff asst. to Pres. U.S. White House Advance Office, 1970-72; spl. asst. to Pres., 1972-73; dir. Nat. Park Service, Washington, 1973-75; cons. Saudi Arabia, 1975; assoc. dir. World Championship Tennis, 1975-77; pres. Ron Walker & Assocs., Inc., Dallas, 1977-79; sr. ptnr., mng. dir. Korn/Ferry Internat., Washington, 1979-2000. Bd. dirs., chmn. Guest Svcs. Inc., Mullins Consulting, Inc., Vinson & Dimitrius; chmn. NOVAVAX. Founder, chmn. emeritus Order of Raft, 1972; spl. presdl. del. to Prime Min. Indira Gandhi's funeral New Delhi, 1984; spl. presdl. del. to Games of XXIV Olympiad Seoul, 1988; trustee Nat. Outdoor Leadership Sch., Nat. Fitness Found., Pres.'s Coun. on Phys. Fitness and Sports, 1981—85; bd. dirs., exec. com. NCAA Found.; bd. dirs. Meridian Internat.; mem. Ctr. for Study of Presidency, 1988—; chmn. Freedom Found. at Valley Forge, 1989—; trustee Ford's Theater, Washington; men's chair Project Hope Ann. Ball, 1989, 1990, 1991; chmn. ann. dinner Boys and Girls Clubs Am., 1993; chmn. 50th Presdl. Inauguration, Dedication Richard Nixon Libr., Birthplace, 1990; bd. dirs., 1990—; nat. chair Celebrities and Sports for Bush-Quayle; mem. over-site com. U.S. Rowing, 1993; active Com. for Preservation of White House, 1973—75; mem. Nat. Pk. Adv. Bd., 1973—75, Nat. Pk. Found., 1973—75, John F. Kennedy Ctr. for Performing Arts, 1973—75, Friends of Nancy Hanks Ctr.; bd. trustees Mridian House Internat., 1992—; mem.USA Gymnasium Found., 1993—; trustee U. Ariz. Found.; vol. Nixon/Agnew Campaign, 1968, transition and inauguration team, 1969; vice chmn., mem. Pres.'s Commn. on Bicentennial U.S. Constn., 1985—; mem/ Coun. for Excellence in Govt., 1988—; mgr. Rep. Nat. Conv., 1984, sr. advisor, 1988, 1992, 1996, 2000, Bush/Quayle Presdl. Campaign, 1988, Bush/Cheney Presdl. Campaign, 2000, Bush/Cheney Inauguration; hon. chmn. Cheney Inaugural Activities. Recipient Disting. Citizen award U. Ariz., 1973, Outstanding Svc. award Dept. Interior, 1975, Centennial Medallion award U. Ariz., 1989, Ellis Island Congl. medal of honor, 1992, Lincoln medal Ford's Theater, 2002. Mem. NCAA (bd. dirs. 1992—, exec. com. 1992—), Econs. Club of Washington, Met. Club of Washington, Congl. Country Club, Georgetown Club, City Club of Washington, Univ. Club. of N.Y., Burning Tree Club, Phi Delta Theta (named to Hall of Fame, 1991). Republican. Methodist. Home (Winter): 13535 Placita Montanas de Oro Tucson AZ 85737 E-mail: roadrunnerrhw@aol.com.

WALKER, RONALD R. writer, editor, educator; b. Newport News, Va., Sept. 2, 1934; s. William R. and Jean Marie (King) W.; m. O. Diane Mawson, Apr. 16, 1961; children: Mark Jonathan, Steven Christopher. BS, Pa. State U., 1956; postgrad., Harvard U., 1970-71. Reporter, news editor, sr. editor, editorial page editor, mng. editor San Juan Star (P.R.), 1962-73, Washington columnist, 1982-84, city editor, 1984-87; instr. journalism Pa. State U., State College, 1973-74; asst. prof. Columbia U. Grad. Sch. Journalism, N.Y.C., 1974-76; editor The Daily News, V.I., 1976-77; press sec. Gov. V.I., 1978-79; spl. asst., chief of staff Rep. James H. Scheuer, U.S. Congress, 1980-82, Resident Commr. Jaime B. Fuster, U.S. Congress, 1987-92; spl. asst., press sec. Resident Commr. Antonio J. Colorado, 1992-93; ind. profl. writer, weekly columnist editl. page San Juan Star, 1993—; regular columnist St. John Times, 1997—. Contbr. articles to nat. mags. and jours. including The Nation, The N.Y. Times, The Washington Post, and others. Served with U.S. Army, 1957-59. Nieman fellow in journalism Harvard U., 1970-71. Mem. Soc. Nieman Fellows, Leica Hist. Soc. Am. Address: PO Box 1358 Saint John VI 00831-1358 E-mail: ronwalker@viacess.net.

WALKER, ROSLYN ADELE, museum director; b. Memphis, July 26, 1944; Student Gen. Studies, U. Poitiers, France, 1965; BS in Art Edn. with high honors, Hampton U., 1966; MA in History of Art, Indiana U., 1969, PhD in History of Art, 1991. Registrar Mus. African Art, Washington, 1968-69; coord. Univ. Art Gallery U. Mass., Amherst, 1969-70; temporary registrar Fed. Dept Antiquities Nat. Mus., Lagos, Nigeria, 1970; curator of collections Inst. African Studies U. Idaban, Nigeria, 1973-75; curator ethnographic art collection Univ. Mus. Ill. State U., Normal, 1975-81, interim adminstr., 1975, adminstr., 1975-77, dir., 1977-81; curator Nat. Mus. African Art Smithsonian Instn., Washington, 1981-93, sr. curator, 1993-97, dir., 1997—2002. Rsch. asst. Mus. Modern Art, N.Y.C., 1971-72, guest curator African Women/African Art, The African-Am. Inst., N.Y.C., 1976, Lakeview Mus. Arts and Scis., Peoria, Ill., 1981; instr. in primitive art U. Mass., Amherst, 1969-70, in African decorative art USDA Grad. Sch., Washington, 1984. in Art in Africa, Dept. Art History, U. Md., College Park, 1990; vis. lectr. Afro-Am. Art, Ind. U., Bloomington, 1970-71, lectr. 1971-72, summer program, U. Idaban, Nigeria, 1974; asst. prof. Art Dept., Ill. State U., Normal, 1975-81. Author: (with Roy Sieber) African Art in the Cycle of Life, 1987, Olowe of Ise: A Yoruba Sculptor to Kings, 1998; contbr. catalogs for exhibitions of African Art to Royal Acad. of Arts, London, 1995, Guggenheim Mus. N.Y. and Afro-Am. Hist. and Cultural Mus., Phila., 1996; contbr., reviews, essays and articles to profl. jours. and mags. Mem. visual arts and crafts adv. panel Washington Commn. on the Arts. Recipient Ford Found. Fgn. Study grant, 1965, Faculty Rsch. grant, U. Mass., 1970, Fgn. Lang. fellowship Ind. U., Bloomington, 1971, Grant in Aid, Ind. U., 1972, Rsch. Fund grant (collections-based), Smithsonian Instn., Washington, 1994; named Twenty Yr. Student, Hampton U., 1986. Mem. Arts Coun. African Studies Assn. (past bd. dirs.), ArTable, Assn. Art Mus. Dirs.*

WALKER, SALLY BARBARA, retired glass company executive; b. Bellerose, N.Y., Nov. 21, 1921; d. Lambert Roger and Edith Demerest (Parkhouse) W. Diploma, Cathedral Sch. St. Mary, 1939; AA, Finch Jr. Coll., 1941. Tchr. interior design Finch Coll., 1941-42; draftsman AT&T, 1942-43; with Steuben Glass Co., N.Y.C., 1943—, exec. v.p., 1959-62, exec. v.p. ops., 1962-78, exec. v.p. ops. and sales, 1978-83, exec. v.p., 1983-88, ret., 1988. Pres. 116 E. 66th St. Corp. Mem. Fifth Ave. Assn., Rockaway Hunting Club, Lawrence Beach Club, Colony Club, English-Speaking Union, Garden Club of Lawrence, City Garden Club of N.Y.C. Republican. Episcopalian. Home: 116 E 66th St New York NY 10021-6547

WALKER, SALLY C. fundraising consultant; BA cum laude with honors, Stetson U., Deland, Fla., 1971; grad., Grantsmanship Ctr. Tng. Program, 1980, Mgmt. Fund Raisers Program, 1987. Devel. dir. Direct Relief Found., Santa Barbara, Calif., 1977-82; prin., cons. Walker & Assocs. Fundraising Counsel, 1982—; endowment dir. United Way Santa Barbara, 1982-96. Mem. steering com., del. Nat. Conf. Planned Giving, 1987-88, Nat. Editorial Bur. chief, 1989, bd. dirs.; faculty mem. Nat. Acad. Voluntarism, Washington. Contbg. editor: The Endowment Builder. Co-founder, pres. Planned Giving Roundtable Santa Barbara County, Calif., 1986-88, v.p., 1984-86. Mem. Nat. Soc. Fund-Raising Execs. (chair endowment com. 1989-90, Santa Barbara and Ventura counties chpts., awarded, Profl. Fundraiser Yr. 1998), Santa Barbara Audubon Soc. (bd. dirs. 1989-98, pres. 1992-93, v.p. 1993-96). Office: 1423 W Valerio St Santa Barbara CA 93101-4954 E-mail: walker160@cox.net.

WALKER, SALLY Y. educational association administrator; b. Joliet, Ill., Dec. 2, 1942; d. Elmer William and Evelyn (Bailey) Yahnke; m. Bob R. Walker, Mar. 30, 1985; children: Elizabeth, Sarah, Amy. BS, Cornell Coll., 1965; MS, No. Ill. U., 1969; PhD, LaSalle Coll., 1995. Tchr. Lin-Mar Schs., Marion, Iowa, 1966-68; instr. No. Ill. U. Lab Sch., Dekalb, 1969-71; tchr. gifted, cons. Rockford (Ill.) Sch. Dist. 205, 1980-86; cons. Regional Office Edn., Loves Park, Ill., 1986-97; exec. dir. Ill. Assn. for Gifted Children, 1997—. Adj. prof. Rockford Coll., 1989—. Author: Teaching Young Gifted Children, 1997, Making Memories, Parent Portfolio, 1996, The Survival Guide for Parents of Gifted Kids, 1991; contbr. articles to profl. jours. Named Master Tchr. Ill. State Bd. Edn., 1984. Mem. Nat. Assn. Gifted. Home: 7186 Warblers Way Roscoe IL 61073-9068 Office: Ill Assn for Gifted Children 800 E Northwest Hyw Ste 610 Palatine IL 60074-6512

WALKER, SARAH HARRIET, English educator, administrator; b. Coral Gables, Fla., Dec. 16, 1955; d. Edward Taylor and Josephine Groves (Oemler) W. BA, Fla. State U., 1977; MEd, N. Ga. Coll., 1992. Tchr. lang. arts Union County Bd. Edn., Blairsville, Ga., 1992-93; adj. instr. English, Truett-McConnell Coll., Cleveland, 1994-95, instr. English, dir. instrn. Epworth, 1995-2001. Editor: St. Luke's Sampler., 1990, St. Luke's Sensations, 1997. Bd. dirs. Friends of Libr., Inc., Blue Ridge, 1996—, pres., 1997-99. Republican. Episcopalian. Avocations: Egyptology, creative writing, reading. Home: 24 River Ridge Ct Blue Ridge GA 30513-5106 E-mail: swalker@sotol.com.

WALKER, SAVANNAH T. retired executive assistant, legislative assistant; b. Lubbock, Tex., Nov. 23, 1930; d. John Hansford and Lenore Belle (Muecke) Tunnell; m. Julius Waring Walker, Jr., July 29, 1956; children: Savannah Waring, Lucile Lenore, George Julius Stewart. BA, Tex. Tech. U., 1951; student, Radcliffe Coll., 1951. Cert. secondary sch. tchr., Tex. Tchr., English and journalism Phillips (Tex.) Ind. Sch. Dist., 1951-52; asst. to congressman Mahon U.S. Congress, Washington, 1952-54, adminstrv., exec. asst., 1954-58, 63-66; legis. asst. to chmn. House Appropriations U.S. Ho. of Reps., 1973-78; exec. asst. to v.p. Nat. Assn. Mfrs., 1985-89; exec. asst. to pres. Ogilvy Pub. Rels. Worldwide, 1990-99; sr. mgr. Pres. of the Americas, Ogilvy Pub. Rels. Worldwide, 2000—01. Vol., fundraiser for charitable orgns., Chad and Eng., 1966-73; pres. Am. Women in London, 1971-72, Am. Women in Liberia, Monrovia, 1979-80. Mem. AAUW, PEO, Am. Women in the Arts Mus., DAR, Internat. Women's Club (founder pres.) (Ouagadougou, Burkina Faso), Delta Delta Delta. Avocations: church work, bridge, reading, needlework, writing. Home: 3801 Jenifer St NW Washington DC 20015-1917 E-mail: julwalk@aol.com.

WALKER, SCOTT A. organist, choir director, educator; b. Dorchester, Mass., May 6, 1966; s. Albert Leonard and Gloria Joan (Counter) W. BA in Music, Bridgewater State Coll., 1996. Cert. elem. tchr., Mass., draftsman, Mass. Church organist, choir dir. Trinity Episcopal Ch., Rockland, Mass., 1983-85, 88-90, Ch. Good Shepherd, Barre, Vt., 1986, Quincy Cmty. United Meth. Ch., Wollaston, Mass., 1992-93, Hingham (Mass.) Congl. Ch., 1993-95, St. Luke's Episcopal Ch., Scituate, Mass., 1995—; draftsperson Eastern Engring. & Sales Corp., Quincy, 1985, Tadd Tech., South Burlington, Vt., 1986; piano, organ accompanist Harbour Choral Arts Soc., Hanover, Mass., 1992-94, 97—; accompanist choral arts ensembles Fitchburg (Mass.) State Coll., 1995-96. Pianist Main St. Studios, Plymouth, 1995-96; music dir., pianist for musicals Whitman (Mass.) Regional H.S., 1994-97, East Bridgewater (Mass.) H.S., 1994—, Valley Players, Waitsfield, Vt., 1986-87, West Bridgewater H.S., 1996—. Composer Gypsy Songs, 1992, The Elixir, 1994, I Have Labored Sore, 1994, Death and Love, 1996, A Question of Faith, 1996; co-composer A Christmas Scene, 1992. Mem. Am. Choral Dirs. Assn., Mass. Mus. Educators Assn., Mass. Soc. Mayflower Descendants (Historians Three Generations award 1988), New Eng. Hist. Geneal. Soc., Am. Guild of Organists, South Shore Geneal. Soc., Soc. Descendants William and Joanna (Blessing) Towne, Kappa Delta Pi. Home: 17 Walnut St Abington MA 02351-2508

WALKER, THOMAS H. federal agency administrator; b. Hattiesburg, Miss., Nov. 11, 1950; s. Thomas Ray and Mary Ella (Bennett) W.; m. Cynthia Kay Sherer, June 5, 1993; children: Ty, Kelly, Rachel, Stacey. BS in Engring., Miss. State U., 1972; MBA, U. West Fla., 1982; postgrad., Nat. Def. U., 1987-88, Harvard U., 1990, Fed. Exec. Inst., 1992. Registered profl. engr., Va. Indsl. engr. Navy Pub. Works Ctr., Norfolk, Va., 1973-75, Atlantic Divsn. Naval Facility Engring. Commn., Norfolk, 1975-76; supervisory gen. engr. Naval Comm. Sta., Exmouth, Australia, 1976-78; indsl. engr. Western Divsn. Naval

Facility Engring. Commn., San Bruno, Calif., 1978-79; head facilities mgmt. Navy Pub. Works Ctr., Pensacola, Fla., 1979-82, Subic Bay, The Philippines, 1982-85; dep. dir. facilities mgmt. USMC, Washington, 1985-89; asst. commr. GSA, 1989-92, dep. asst. regional adminstr., 1992-93, asst. regional adminstr. pub. bldgs. Kansas City, Mo., 1993-99; asst. regional adminstr. Pub. Bldgs. Svc., Atlanta, 1999—. Bd. dirs. Kansas City BOMA. Coach Little League Baseball, Fairfax, Va., 1986-92, Girls Softball Team, Lees Summit, Va., 1995. cub scout den father Boy Scouts Am., Fairfax, 1987-88. Miss. State U. Disting. Engring. fellow, 1992; recipient Arthur S. Fleming award Washington Jaycees, 1989, Presdl. rank award, 1996, v.p. Hammer award, 1996. Mem. NSPE, Va. Soc. Profl. Engrs., Bldg. Owners and Mgrs. Assn. (mem. govt. bldgs. com. 1991—, chmn. 1993—, mem. corp. facilities com. 1991—, nat. adv. coun. 1995—, Nat. Mem. of Yr. 1997, Atlanta Svc. award 2000), Internat. Facilities Mgmt. Assn. (mem. pub. sector com. 1991—, Golden Cir. award 1994), Sr. Execs. Assn., Phi Kappa Phi, Alpha Pi Mu, Gamma Beta Phi. Methodist. Avocation: golf. Home: 595 Kings Grant Walk Roswell GA 30075-5528 Office: 77 Forsyth St SW Ste 400 Atlanta GA 30303-3427 Fax: 404 331 0465. E-mail: thomas.walker@gsa.gov.

WALKER, THOMAS RAY, city aviation commissioner; AB in Art, Dartmouth Coll., 1970; BArch, Ill. Inst. Tech., 1977. Project mgr. Lohan Assocs., 1977-86; v.p. design and constrn. The Chgo. Dock and Canal Trust, 1986-91; exec. dir. Pub. Bldg. Commn. of Chgo., 1991-95; commr. dept. transp. City of Chgo., 1995-99; commr. Chgo. Dept. of Aviation, City of Chgo., 2000—. Prin. works include Soldier Field World Cup renovation, Chgo., Wright Coll. Addition, Chgo. Pub. Schs. capital improvement program, Cityfront Ctr., Chgo., MarketTower Officer Bldg., Indpls., Episcopal Sch. of Dallas Libr./Fine Arts addition, Frito-Lay Nat. Hdqs., Plano, Tex. Vice chmn. Chgo. Area Transp. Study; commr. State St. Commn.; mem. com. Newhouse arch. fellowship program Chgo. Arch. Found.; mem. Chgo. Planning Commn.; mem. selection com. cmty. svc. fellowship Chgo. Cmty. Trust; mem. TRB steering com. Conf. Transp. Issue in Large U.S. Cities; mem. Conf. Minority Transp. Officials; trustee Chgo. Music and Dance Theater; chmn. leadership coun. Met. Open Cmtys.; co-chmn. adv. bd./housing com. Met. Planning Coun. 1st lt. USAF, 1970-72. Mem. Intelligent Transp. Soc. of Am. (bd. dirs.), Nat. Assn. City Transp. Ofcls. (chmn.), Nat. Orgn. Minority Architects, Urban Land Inst., Lambda Alpha Internat. Office: O'Hare Internat Airport Dept of Aviation PO Box 66142 AMF Ohare IL 60666-0142*

WALKER, TIMOTHY CRAIG, transportation executive; b. Huntington, W.Va., Jan. 16, 1945; s. John Paul and Marjorie Frances (Withers) W. BA, Northwestern U., 1967; B of Fgn. Trade, Am. Grad. Sch. Internat. Mgmt., 1968. Mgmt. trainee to dir. OIM/internat. mktg. ops. NCR Corp., Dayton, Ohio, 1968-79; v.p. mktg. Do-Ray Lamp Co., Inc., Colorado City, Colo., 1979-87; v.p. sales and mktg. Truck-Lite Co., Inc., Jamestown, N.Y., 1984—; pres., COO Truck-Lite Internat., Inc., 1990—; also bd. dirs. Recruiter Am. Grad. Sch. Internat. Mgmt., 1971—. Bd. dirs. Valley Human Resources, United Way Agy., 1980-84, Goodwill Industries of Pueblo, Colo., 1983-84; mem. Working Group for U.S. Dept. Commerce MOSS Talks. Recipient Pres.'s award 1st alumnus Am. Grad. Sch. Internat. Mgmt., 1976, award for excellence in internat. advt., 1968; named to Automotive Hall of Fame. Mem. Transp. Safety Equipment Inst. N.Am. (chmn. mktg. and statis. com. 1980-82), European Transport Maintenance Coun. (bd. dirs. 1991-93), Heavy Duty Bus. Forum (bd. dirs.), Heavy Duty Mfrs. Assn. (bd. govs. 1987-95, sec. 1990-91, 95-96, vice chmn. 1997, chmn. 1998), Overseas Automotive Coun. (bd. dirs.), Pueblo Area C. of C. (transp. com. 1981-84), Coun. Fleet Specialists (mfrs. liaison com. 1989-91), 500 Automotive Execs. Club. Republican. Presbyterian. Home: PO Box 1263 Jamestown NY 14702-1263 Office: Truck-Lite Co PO Box 387 Jamestown NY 14702-0387 E-mail: tcwbhx@aol.com., twalker@truck-lite.com.

WALKER, TIMOTHY LEE, lawyer; b. Whittier, Calif., Sept. 25, 1947; s. Maurice Samuel and Esther (Scoleri) W.; m. Claire M. Duarte, Aug. 16, 1969; children: Kristen, Matthew, Megan, Kendra. BS, U. Calif., Santa Barbara, 1969; JD, Loyola U., 1972. Bar: Calif. 1972, U.S. Dist. Ct. (cen. dist.) Calif. 1973; diplomate Am. Bd. of Trial Advocates. Assoc. Shield & Smith, L.A., 1972-76, ptnr., 1976-91, Walker Haggerty & Behar, 1991—. Bd. dirs. Assn. Southern Calif. Defense Counsel, L.A., pres. 1986. Fellow Am. Coll. Trial Lawyers, Internat. Soc. Barristers; mem. Internat. Assn. Defense Counsel, Def. Rsch. Inst. (bd. dirs. 1992-98), Arbitration L.A. Superior Ct. Avocation: sports. Office: Ford Walker Haggerty & Behar 1 World Trade Ctr Fl 27 Long Beach CA 90831-0002 E-mail: walker@FWHB.com.

WALKER, VALAIDA SMITH, university administrator; b. Phila., Dec. 22, 1932; d. Samuel and Rosa (Lee) Smith. BS in Math. and Phys. Edn., Howard U., Washington, 1954; MEd in Spl. Edn., Temple U., 1970, EdD in Spl. Edn., 1973. Jr. H.S. math. tchr., Balt., 1955-58, Albuquerque, 1964-65; tchr. emotionaly disturbed and socially maladjusted children Phila., 1965-66; demonstration tchr., 1968-70; tchg. assoc., coord./supr. resource rm. tchr. tng. program Temple U., 1970-72; commr. mental retardation Southeastern region Dept. Pub. Welfare, Commonwealth Pa., 1973-74; program dir. Woodhaven Ctr. Mentally Retarded Temple U., Phila., 1974-76, chairperson dept. spl. edn., 1980-83, assoc. dean Coll. Edn., 1983-84, assoc. vice provost undergrad. programs, 1984-90, interim vice provost adminstrn., 1987-90, acting v.p. student affairs, 1990-92, prof. dept. spl. edn., 1974—, v.p. student affairs, 1992—. Past mem. steering com., chairperson cmty. svcs. task force subcom. Pres. Com. on Mental Retardation; exec. advisor Caribbean Assn. Mental Retardation, 1982-89; mem. adv. panel on spl. edn. Commonwealth Pa., 1985-93; hearing office Pa. Dept. Edn., 1978-91; gov.'s apointee Profl. Stds. and Practices Commn., 1980-83; field reader U.S. Office Edn., Bur. Handicapped, 1980-93; expert witness Pennhurst State Instn. Ct. Case, 1973-74. Bd. dirs. Elwyn Insts., 1983—, chairperson edn. and tng. com., 1984-86; chair curriculum and nominations com. William Penn Adult Cmty. Sch. Adv. Bd., 1976; bd. mem. Rebecca Gratz Assn., Phila. Recipient svc. award Chapel of Four Chaplains, cert. of honor Alumni Assn. Temple U., Phila., 1990, Svc. award Kappa Alpha Phi, Phila., 1995; named Spl. Educator Yr., Sigma Pi Epsilon Delta, 1983, Tchr. of Yr. Sigma Pi Epsilon Delta, Phila., 1995. Fellow Am. Assn. Mental Retardation (pres.-elect, program chair 1986-87, pres. 1987-88). Baptist. Office: Temple U 1801 N Broad St Philadelphia PA 19122-6003

WALKER, VAUGHN R. federal judge; b. Watseka, Ill., Feb. 27, 1944; s. Vaughn Rosenworth and Catharine (Miles) W. AB, U. Mich., 1966; JD, Stanford U., 1970. Intern economist SEC, Washington, 1966, 68; law clk. to the Hon. Robert J. Kelleher U.S. Dist. Ct. Calif., L.A., 1971-72; assoc. atty. Pillsbury Madison & Sutro, San Francisco, 1972-77, ptnr., 1978-90; judge U.S. Dist. Ct. (no. dist.) Calif., 1990—. Mem. Calif. Law Revision Commn., Palo Alto, 1986-89; bd. advisors Law and Econs. Ctr., George Mason U., 1999—. Dir. Jr. Achievement of Bay Area, San Francisco, 1979-83, St. Francis Found., San Francisco, 1991-97, 98—. Woodrow Wilson Found. fellow U. Calif., Berkeley, 1966-67. Fellow Am. Bar Found.; mem. ABA (jud. rep., antitrust sect. 1991-95), Lawyers' Club of San Francisco (pres. 1985-86), Assn. Bus. Trial Lawyers (dir. 1996-98), Am. Law Inst., Am. Saddlebred Horse Assn., San Francisco Mus. Modern Art, Bohemian Club, Olympic Club, Pacific-Union Club. Office: US Dist Ct 450 Golden Gate Ave San Francisco CA 94102-3482

WALKER, W. JACK, retired small business owner; b. Sept. 30, 1919; s. John Wesley Walker, Mattie Alma (Gilbert) Walker; m. Loraine Walker; 1 child Gayle Walker Street. BBA, U. Tenn., 1940; DHL (hon.) , Knoxville Coll., 1988. Owner W.Jack Walker Rolling Store, 1946—51, Walker Market, Knoxville, Tenn., 1954—78; cons. Ernest Youngblood Assocs., 1978—. Bd. govs. Club LeConte, 1977—; bd. dirs. St. Mary's Health Sys., Inc., Cmty. Found. East Tenn., Wellness Cmty. Knoxville, Child & Family Svcs., Salvation Army, Presbyn. Homes of Tenn., Inc., Tenn. Valley Agrl. & Indsl. Fair, v.p. exec. com., 1984—; chmn. investment com. Monday Found., 1990—; bd. dirs. Sr. Citizens Home Assistance Svcs., Pellissippi State C.C. Found., Union Planters Bank, 1990—, Blount Hearing and Speech Found.; deacon Ctrl. Bapt. Ch. Bearden; chmn. bd. First Tenn. Bank , Knoxville, Tenn., 1977—86. With U.S. Coast Guard. Named Retailer of Yr., Tenn. Retail Merchants Assn., 1977, Salesman of Yr., 1978; recipient Outstanding Leadership award, ARC, 1968, Outstanding Svc. award, Castle Heights Mil. Acad., 1980, Pres.'s award, Knoxville Area Urban League, 1987, Disting. Svc. award, Arthritis Found., 1988, Book of Golden Deeds award, Knoxville Exch. Club, 1985, Brotherhood-Sisterhood award, Nat. Conf. Christians and Jews, 1987. Mem.: Masons (32d degree), YMCA Knoxville (Red Triangle award, Man of Yr. 1968), U. Tenn. Pres.'s Club, Rotary Club Knoxville. Home: 719 Clubhouse Way Knoxville TN 37909 Office: Ernest Youngblood Assocs 1810 Ailor Ave Ste E Knoxville TN 37921

WALKER, W. LAWRENCE, JR. newspaper publishing executive; Exec. v.p. & bus. mgr. Newspaper Agency, 1987—90; pres., CEO, San Antonio Express-News, 1990—. Office: San Antonio Express-News PO Box 2171 San Antonio TX 78297-2171 also: San Antonio Express News Ave E and Third Street San Antonio TX 78205*

WALKER, WALDO SYLVESTER, biology educator, academic administrator; b. Fayette, Iowa, June 12, 1931; s. Waldo S. and Mildred (Littelle) W.; m. Marie J. Olsen, July 27, 1952 (div.); children: Martha Lynn, Gayle Ann; m. Rita K. White, June 16, 1984. BS cum laude, Upper Iowa U., Fayette, 1953; MS, U. Iowa, 1957, PhD, 1959. Mem. faculty Grinnell (Iowa) Coll., 1958, assoc. dean coll., 1963-65, chmn. div. Natl. Scis., 1968-69, dean of adminstrn., 1969-73, exec. v.p., 1973-77, dean coll., 1973-80, provost, 1977-80, exec. v.p., 1980-90, exec. v.p. and treas., 1988-90, v.p. for coll. svcs., 1990-95, prof. biology, 1968-2001, prof. emeritus, 2001—. Research assoc. U. B.C. Dept. of Botany, 1966-67. Author articles on plant physiology, ultrastructural cytology. Served with U.S. Army, 1953-55. Fellow NSF Sci. Faculty, 1966-67; recipient NSF research grants, 1960-63, 68. Mem. Am. Assn. Colls., Am. Conf. Acad. Deans (nat. chmn. 1977-78), Am. Assn. Higher Edn., Sigma Xi. Home: 1920 Country Club Dr Grinnell IA 50112-1130 Address: Grinnell Coll PO Box H2 Grinnell IA 50112-0805 E-mail: walkerws@pcpartner.net.

WALKER, WALTER FREDERICK, professional basketball team executive; b. Bradford, Pa., July 18, 1954; m. Linda Walker. Diploma, U. Va.; MBA, Stanford U., 1987; BA, U. Va., 1976. Chartered Fin. Analyst. Player Portland (Oreg.) Trail Blazers, 1976-77, Seattle SuperSonics, 1977-82, pres., CEO, 1994—; player Houston Rockets, 1982-84; with Goldman Sachs and Co., San Francisco, 1987-94; prin. Walker Capital, Inc., 1994. Mem. USA gold medal World Univ. Games basketball team, 1973; broadcaster basketball Raycom Network, 1989-94; cons. Seattle SuperSonics, 1994. Bd. dirs. Red Hook Ale Brewery; bd. dirs. Advanced Digital Info. Corp., Drexler Tech. Corp. Named 1st team Acad. All-Am. U. Va.; named to Pa. State Sports Hall of Fame. Nat. trustee Boys and Girls Clubs of Am. Office: Seattle SuperSonics 351 Elliott Ave W Seattle WA 98119-4101 E-mail: wwalker@sonics-storm.com.

WALKER, WALTER HERBERT, III, lawyer, writer; b. Quincy, Mass., Sept. 12, 1949; s. Walter H. Jr. and Irene M. (Horn) W.; m. Anne M. DiScuillo, June 17, 1982; children: Brett Daniel, Jeffrey St. John. BA, U. Pa., 1971; JD, U. Calif., San Francisco, 1974. Bar: Calif. 1974, Mass. 1981. Appellate atty. ICC, Washington, 1975-77; trial atty. Handler, Baker, Greene & Taylor, San Francisco, 1977-80; ptnr. Sterns and Walker and predecessor firm Sterns, Smith, Walker & Grell, 1981-88; ptnr. firm Walker & Durham, 1988—99, Walker & Hamilton, San Francisco, 2000—. Author: A Dime to Dance By, 1983 (Best 1st Novel by Calif. Author), The Two Dude Defense, 1985, Rules of The Knife Fight, 1986, The Immediate Prospect of Being Hanged, 1989, The Appearance of Impropriety, 1992. Mem. ATLA, Consumer Attys. of Calif., San Francisco Trial Lawyers Assn., Mystery Writers Am. Clubs: Hastings Rugby. Democrat. Home: 604 Seminary Dr Mill Valley CA 94941-3169 Office: 50 Francisco St Ste 160 San Francisco CA 94133-2108

WALKER, WALTER WILLARD, real estate and investments executive; b. Mpls., Dec. 4, 1911; s. Archie Dean and Bertha Willard (Hudson) W.; BA, Princeton U., 1935; MD, Harvard U., 1940; postgrad. U. Minn., 1942-48; m. Elva Mae Dawson, Dec. 16, 1939 (div. Oct. 1969); m. Elaine Barbatsis, Mar. 17, 1972; stepchildren: Nicholas K. Barbatsis, Marianna Barbatsis Priest, Becka Barbatsis Mourmouras, Christian Barbatsis Dayton. Teaching fellow pathology U. Minn., 1942-48; left medicine, went into bus., 1948; dir. Shasta Forest Co., Redding, Calif., 1951-71, treas., 1954-66, v.p., 1966-71; sec., dir. Barlow Realty Co., Mpls., 1954-67, pres., 1967-77, chmn., 1977-80, sec., 1980-83, v.p., 1983-88; ptnr. Barlow Assocs., 1988—; sec., bd. dir. Walker Pence Co., 1950-72; sec. Penwalk Investment Co., 1958-72, bd. dir., 1943-72; bd. dir. Craig-Hallum Corp., Mpls., 1954-92; adv. bd. Lincoln office Northwestern Nat. Bank, Mpls., 1957-74. Bd. dirs. T.B. Walker Found., 1953-76, v.p., 1954-76; bd. dirs. Minn. Opera Co., 1968-73, Archie D. and Bertha H. Walker Found., 1953— , Mpls. Found., 1962-79, Walker Art Ctr, 1954-76, United Fund, 1966-72; trustee Abbott-Northwestern Hosp., 1969-77; trustee Children's Health Ctr., Inc., 1968-73, treas., 1969-73; pres. Found. Services, 1967-73; bd. dirs., exec. com. Minn. Charities Review Council, 1965-74; mem. Hennepin County Capital Budgeting Task Force, 1973-74. Mem. Sigma Xi, Nu Sigma Nu, Mpls. Club, Princeton Club (N.Y.C.), U. Minn. Alumni Club. Methodist. Home: Minneapolis, Minn. Deceased.

WALKER, WARREN CHRISTOPHER, systems analyst; b. N.Y.C., June 9, 1965; s. Warren Christopher and Sandra Ellen (Singleton) W.; 1 child, Kyle. Student, Poly. U., 1983-86, Chgo. State U., 1992—. Cons., N.Y.C., 1986-88; analyst Hartmarx Corp., Chgo., 1988-91; systems analyst Wesley Jessen Corp., 1992—. Contbr. articles to profl. jours. Mem. Coun. on Fgn. Rels., Chgo., 1991, NAACP, 1991, Young Dems. Mem. Nat. Soc. Black Engrs., Nat. Black Data Processing Assn., Assn. for Computing Machinery, Network Users Internat. Avocations: chess, flying, horseback riding, scuba diving, handball. Home: 40 E 9th St Chicago IL 60605-2138

WALKER, WARREN STANLEY, English educator; b. Bklyn., Mar. 19, 1921; s. Harold Stanley and Althea (Luscher) W.; m. Barbara Jeanne Kerlin, Dec. 9, 1943; children— Brian, Theresa. BA, SUNY-Albany, 1947, MA, 1948; PhD, Cornell U., 1951; LittD (hon.), Selcuk U., 1989. Prof., chmn. dept. English Blackburn Coll., Carlinville, Ill., 1951-59; prof., dean arts and scis. Parsons Coll., Fairfield, Iowa, 1959-64; Fulbright lectr. Am. lit. Ankara (Turkey) U., 1961-62; prof. English Tex. Tech U., Lubbock, 1964-86, Horn prof., 1972-86. Dir. Archive Turkish Oral Narrative, 1971; adv. council Tex. Cultural Alliance, 1975 Author: Nigerian Folktales, 1961, Twentieth-Century Short Story Explication, 14 vols., 1961-93, James Fenimore Cooper, 1962, Leatherstocking and the Critics, 1965, Tales Alive in Turkey, 1966, Archive of Turkish Oral Narrative: Catalogue 1, 1975, Catalogue 2, 1988, Catalogue 3, 1994, Catalogue 4, 1998, Plots and Characters in the Fiction of J.F. Cooper, 1978, A Bibliography of American Scholarship on Turkish Folklore and Ethnography, 1982, Turkish Games for Health and Recreation, 1983, The Book of Dede Korkut-A Turkish Epic, 1991, More Tales Alive in Turkey, 1992, A Turkish Folktale: The Art of Behçet Mahir, 1996; mem. editorial bd. Definitive Edit. Works of James Fenimore Cooper, 1968; bibliographer Studies in Short Fiction, 1973. Served with USAAF, 1943-45. Recipient Tex. Writers award, 1967; citation Turkish Ministry Edn., 1967, Turkish Ministry State, 1973; research grantee Am. Council Learned Socs., 1973, 79; Am. Philos. Soc., 1974, Tex. Tech U., 1971-74, 76, 83, Republic of Turkey, 1983, Inst. Turkish Studies, 1984 Mem. MLA, Am. Folklore Soc., Nat. Coun. Tchrs. English, Internat. Soc. Folk Narrative Rsch., Middle East Studies Assn., Tex. Assn. Middle East Scholars (exec. coun.), Turkish Studies Assn., Atatürk Supreme Coun. on Turkish Culture (hon.). Home: 3703 66th St Lubbock TX 79413-5325 Office: Tex Tech U Archive Turkish Oral N Lubbock TX 79409

WALKER, WELMON, JR. (RUSTY WALKER), publisher, consultant; b. Chgo., Dec. 28, 1947; s. Welmon Sr. and Mary Ann (Befford) W.; m. Nedra Kay Carlson, Dec. 30, 1972; children: Welmon III, Whitney O. Student, U. Alaska, 1970-74; AA, Tanana Valley Community Coll., 1984; BS, U. of the State of N.Y., 1985; MBA, U. Phoenix, 1996; student, The Grad. Sch. Am., 1998-99. Gen. mgr. Sta. KMPS (name now Sta. KSUA-FM), Fairbanks, Alaska, 1971-74; duty dir. Sta. KUAC-TV, 1973-74; staff photographer Sta. KFAR-TV, 1974-75; bus. mgr. Nat. Painting Corp., 1975-76; instr. Fairbanks Native Assn., 1975-76; asst. mgr. Wometco-Lathrop Co., Fairbanks, 1978-79; pres. That New Pub. Co., 1977-93, Honolulu, 1993—. Instr. U. Alaska, Fairbanks, 1979-80, Commonwealth Internat. U., 1998-99; internat. bus. instr. Edn. Am., Inc., Honolulu, 1999—, acad. dean, 1999— Author: Alaska Corp Manual, 1977, Publishing Manual, 1987, Finding The Lowest Quality Print Bid For Your Short Run Book Project, 1997, Hawaii Corp Manual, 1997; contbr. articles to profl. jours. Dir. Lost Lake Camp, Midnight Sun Coun. Boys Scouts Am., 1986-87, bd. dirs., 1978—; pres., bd. dirs. Fairbanks Youth Svcs., Inc., 1979—; dir. Bapt. Tng. Union, St. John Bapt. Ch., Fairbanks, 1969; pres. Luth. Ch. Honolulu, 1994-95, bd. dirs., 1993-2000; student affairs chmn. univ. assembly U. Alaska, 1971-74. With U.S. Army, 1968-70. Mem. Small Pubs. Assn. N.Am. (charter), Pubs. Mktg. Assn., Star Fleet Club (lt. comdr. 1983-86), Rotary. Avocations: computer programming, chess. Office: That New Pub Co PO Box 621 Aiea HI 96701-0621

WALKER, WENDY K. healthcare risk consultant; b. Elizabeth, N.J., Nov. 11, 1961; d. William Henry Jr. and Catherine Lillian (Fulton) Knight; 1 child, Faith Corinne. Student, U. Warwick, Eng., 1981-82; BA, Duke U., 1983; postgrad., U. N.C. Cert. ins. counselor, assoc. in risk mgmt.; CPCU. Asst. v.p., risk ins. broker Aon Risk Svc., Inc. of the Carolinas, 1994—. Former bd. dirs. Human Rels. Commn., City of Winston-Salem; chmn. New Horizons Fair Housing Com., Winston-Salem, 1999-2000. Mem. CPCU Soc., Am. Coll. Healthcare Execs., Soc. Cert. Ins. Counselors. Democrat. Episcopalian. Avocations: camping, tennis. Home: 4660 Duffer Ct Pfafftown NC 27040-9722 E-mail: wendyinwinston@earthlink.net.

WALKER, WILBUR GORDON, physician, educator; b. Lena, La., Sept. 18, 1926; s. Daniel Clark and Ettie (Hodnett) W.; m. Betty Couch, Aug. 23, 1947; children: Wilbur Gordon, Martha Jane, Joseph Marshall, Carla Frances. Student, La. State U., 1942-44, 46-47, La. Coll., 1947; MD, Tulane U., 1951. Intern Johns Hopkins Hosp., Balt., 1951-52; resident Charity Hosp., New Orleans, 1952-53; asst. resident Johns Hopkins Hosp., 1953-54, fellow in medicine, 1954-56, resident physician, 1956-57, physician, 1957—, dir. Clin. Research Center, 1960-88; faculty Johns Hopkins U. Sch. Medicine, 1956—, prof. medicine, 1968—, prof. internat. health, 1990—, chmn. com. on clin. investigation, 1964-71; prof. internat. health Johns Hopkins U. Sch. Med., 1990—; ednl. policy com. Johns Hopkins U. Sch. Medicine, 1976-80; exec. com., dept. med., 1973-79; admissions com. Johns Hopkins U. Sch. Med., 1988-92; dir. renal div. Johns Hopkins U. Sch. Medicine, 1958-88, admissions com., 1988-92. Attending physician Balt. City Hosp., 1960-88; established investigator Am. Heart Assn., 1957-60; dir. dept. rsch. medicine Good Samaritan Hosp., Balt., 1968—; chmn. med. bd., 1972-74; vis. prof. Guys Hosp. Med. Sch., London, 1980; clin., rsch. ctrs. com. NIH, 1970-76, renal disease and urology grants com., 1968-76, chmn. clin. rsch. ctrs. com., 1975-76; McIlrath prof., hon. cons. physician Royal Prince Alfred Hosp., Sydney, Australia, 1968—; chmn. Coun. on Rsch. Md. Heart Assn., 1963-64; chmn. med. adv. bd. Md. Kidney Found., 1966-68; mem. Md. Gov.'s Commn. on Kidney Disease, 1970-80, 83-88; chmn. Md. Kidney Commn., 1975-80; chmn. computer com. div. rsch. resources NIH, 1973-75, hypertension and chronic renal failure working group, 1988-90. Editl. adv. bd. Am. Jour. Medicine, 1975-85; editl. bd. Kidney Internat., 1978-82; sec. editor: Principles and Practices of Medicine, 17th-21st edits.; co-editor: Potassium in Cardiovascular and Renal Medicine; contbr. articles to profl. jours. Trustee Md. Heart Assn., Good Samaritan Hosp., 1998—. Served with USNR, 1944-45. Fellow ACP; mem. Am. Physiol. Soc. Am. Fdn. Clin. Research, Am. Soc. Clin. Investigation, Am. Soc. Nephrology, Council High Blood Pressure Research, Am. Clin. and Climatol. Assn., Interurban Clin. Club (sec. 1977-81, pres. 1981-82) Clubs: Peripatetic. Home: 3812 Fenchurch Rd Baltimore MD 21218-1824 E-mail: wgordonwalkersr@msn.com.

WALKER, WILLIAM BOND, painter, retired librarian; b. Brownsville, Tenn., Apr. 15, 1930; s. Marshall Francis and Mary Louise (Taylor) W. BA, State U. Iowa, 1953; M.L.S., Rutgers U., 1958. Librarian-trainee Donnell br. N.Y. Public Library, N.Y.C., 1955-57; reference librarian/cataloger Met. Mus. Art, 1957-59; chief librarian Bklyn. Mus., 1959-64; supervisory librarian Library of Nat. Collection Fine Arts and Nat. Portrait Gallery, Smithsonian Instn., Washington, 1964-80; Arthur K. Watson chief librarian Thomas J. Watson Library, Met. Mus. Art, N.Y.C., 1980-94; ret., 1994. Adj. lectr. Columbia U. Sch. Library Service, 1987-88. Author: annotated bibliography American Sculpture, 18th-20th Century, 1979; retrospective exhbn. paintings, 1954-96, Pittsfield, Mass., 1996-97. Mem. ALA, Art Librs. Soc. N.Am (pres. 1975, Disting. Svc. award, 1992), Geneal. and Biog. Soc. (corr.), Phi Beta Kappa. Home: 54 Queechy Lake Dr PO Box 237 Canaan NY 12029-0237 E-mail: lakequeechy@taconic.net.

WALKER, WILLIAM D. physicist, educator, researcher; b. Nov. 23, 1923; s. William D. and Mildred Ramsey Walker; m. Suzanne Porter, Dec. 23, 1946 (div. Oct. 1975); m. Constance Kalbach, Oct. 16, 1975; children: Nancy Walker Davis, Elizabeth Walker Schenkel, Samuel. BA, Rice U., 1944; PhD in Physics, Cornell U., 1949. Asst. prof. Rice U., Houston, 1949-51; lectr. U. Calif., Berkeley, 1951-52; asst. prof. U. Rochester, N.Y., 1952-54; from asst. prof. to prof. U. Wis., Madison, 1954-71; prof. physics Duke U., Durham, N.C., 1971-98; chmn. dept. physics U. Wis., Madison, 1964-66, Max Mason disting. prof., 1969-71; J.B. Duke disting. prof. Duke U., Durham, N.C., 1990-94, chmn. dept. physics, 1975-81, prof. emeritus, 1993—. Chmn. users com. Argonne Nat. Lab., Lemont, Ill., 1960-63; mem. users com. Fermi Nat. Accelerator Lab., Aurora, Ill., 1971-74, chmn., 1973; mem. physics adv. bd. NSF, Washington, 1962-65. Contbr. 200 articles to profl. jours.; discovered several elementary particles. Deacon Episc. Ch., 1964-71; elder Presbyn. Ch., 1993—. Fellow Am. Phys. Soc. Avocation: tennis. Home: 907 Green St Durham NC 27701-1507 Office: Duke U Physics Dept Durham NC 27708 E-mail: walker@phy.duke.edu. *My life was renewed and rebuilt at age 35 by Jesus Christ. Any success I may have had is due to him.*

WALKER, WILLIAM EASTON, surgeon, educator, lawyer; b. Glasgow, Scotland, Aug. 7, 1945; came to U.S., 1969; s. William Telfer and Josephine Blair (Easton) W.; m. Mary Fraley Cooley, June 23, 1973; children— Sarah Cooley, Blair Easton, Denton Arthur Cooley, William Easton, II MD, Glasgow U., Scotland, 1968; PhD, Johns Hopkins U., 1975; JD, South Tex. Coll Law, 1993. Diplomate Am. Bd. Surgery, Am. Bd. Thoracic Surgery, Am. Bd. Vascular Surgery. Intern, resident Johns Hopkins U., Balt., 1969-75; resident Vanderbilt U., Nashville, 1975-79; assoc. prof., dir. div. thoracic and cardiovascular surgery U. Tex. Med. Sch., Houston, 1979-94. Cons. M.D. Anderson Hosp., Houston, 1979—. Recipient Harwell Wilson award Vanderbilt U., Nashville, 1979 Fellow ACS, So. Surg. Assn., Royal Coll. Surgeons, Am. Coll. Cardiology; mem. Am. Assn. Thoracic Surgery, Coun. Fgn. Rels., Houston Country Club, Belle Meade Country Club, Cosmos Club (Washington), Krewe of Endymion (New Orleans), Phi Beta Kappa, Sigma Xi. Republican. Presbyterian. Avocations: law, bridge, Wagner, World War I, cooking. Home and Office: 2831 Sackett St Houston TX 77098-1125 E-mail: wew2001@swbell.net.

WALKER, WILLIAM HAMILTON, civil engineering educator; b. Brookline, Mass., Dec. 28, 1934; s. William A. and Ingeborg (Thorkilsen) W.; m. Shirley Ann Ackerman, Nov. 3, 1962; children: William Franklin, John Hamilton. BS, U. Mass., 1956; MS, U. Ill., 1958, PhD, 1963. Rsch. asst. U. Ill., Urbana, 1956-61, instr. civil engring., 1961-63, asst. prof., 1963-68, assoc. prof., 1968-90, prof., 1990—, assoc. head dept., 1985—. Cons. to various govt. agys. and industry, 1965—. Contbr. articles to profl. jours. Trustee Windsor Park Fire Protection Dist., Champaign, Ill., 1972—. Mem. ASCE (pres. cen. Ill. sect. 1984); mem. Am. Soc. for Engring. Edn., Sigma Xi, Tau Beta Pi, Phi Kappa Phi. Presbyterian. Avocations: photography, videography, travel, bird watching. Home: 2402 Melrose Dr Champaign IL 61820-7607 Office: U Ill 205 N Mathews Ave Urbana IL 61801-2350

WALKER, WILLIAM JOHN, JR. ceramic engineer; b. Syracuse, N.Y., May 25, 1959; s. William John Walker and Barbara Irene Watt. BFA, Syracuse U., 1981; BS in Ceramic Engring., Alfred U., 1989, PhD in Ceramics, 1996. Modeler Hall China Co., E. Liverpool, Ohio, 1982-85; ceramic engr. Shenango China div. Syracuse China Corp., New Castle, Pa., 1989-90; post-doctoral rsch. fellow N.Y. State Coll. Ceramics Alfred (N.Y.) U., 1996-97, rsch. assoc. Ctr. Advanced Ceramic Tech., 1997-2001; asst. dir. Ctr. Advanced Ceramic Tech., 2001—. Patentee in field; contbr. articles to profl. jours. Mem. Am. Ceramic Soc. (chair Western N.Y. sect. 2000-02), Ceramic Assn. N.Y., Materials Rsch. Soc., Soc. Rheology, Keramos, Phi Kappa Phi. Office: Ctr Advanced Ceramic Tech 2 Pine St Alfred NY 14802-1214 Fax: 607-871-3469. E-mail: walkerw@alfred.edu.

WALKER, WILLIAM THOMAS, transportation engineer; b. East Stroudsburg, Pa., Sept. 4, 1946; s. Bian Blackwell and Jeanette Mable W.; m. Alison Leslie Edwards, Nov. 8, 1970 (div. June 27, 1974); m. Patricia Mary Guz Walker, Aug. 8, 1976; children: Daniel Bian, Annalisa. BS in Engring., U. Pa., Phila., 1969, M in City & Reg. Planning, Transp. Engr., 1970, PhD in City and Regional Planning, 1991. Profl. engr., Pa. Mgr. office sys. corridor planning Del. Valley Regional Planning Commn., Phila., 1971—. Affiliate Hwy. Rsch. Bd., Washington. Contbr. articles to profl. jours. Fellow Ford Found., 1969-71.

Mem. Aircraft Owners and Pilot's Assn., Philly Flyers. Democrat. Avocations: private pilot, acrobatics, model aviation, sailing. E-mail address. Office: Del Valley Regional Planning Commn The Bourse Bldg 111 S Independence Mall E Philadelphia PA 19106-2515 Fax: 215-592-9125. E-mail: twalker@dvrpc.org.

WALKER, WILLIAM TIDD, JR. investment banker; b. Detroit, Sept. 5, 1931; s. William Tidd and Irene (Rhode) W.; m. Patricia Louise Frazier, Sept. 10, 1953; children— Donna Louise, Carol Ann, Sally Lynn, Alyssa Jane. Student, Stanford, 1950. Stockbroker William R. Staats & Co., Los Angeles, 1952-57, sales mgr., 1957-58, syndicate partner, 1958-65; sr. v.p. Glore Forgan, William R. Staats Inc., N.Y.C., 1965-68; partner, exec. com. Lester, Ryons & Co., Los Angeles, 1968; exec. v.p. Bateman Eichler, Hill Richards Inc., 1969-85. Pres., CEO, WTW Inc.; chmn., CEO Walker Assocs., bd. dirs. Digid, Inc., King-Thomason Group, Aviation Distbrs., Inc., Supralife Internat., Stone Mountain Data Ctrs. Inc., Desert Health Products Inc., King Thomason Group, Inc.; adv. mem. Am. Stock Exch., 1981—. With USAF, 1949-52. Mem. Securities Industry Assn. (dir. nat. syndicate com., chmn. Calif. Dist. 10), Pacific Coast Stock Exch. (bd. govs. 1971-72), Investment Bankers Assn. (nat. pub. rels. com. 1966—), Bond Club L.A. (pres. 1973), Calif. Yacht Club, Newport Harbor Yacht Club. Office: Walker Assocs PO Box 10684 Beverly Hills CA 90213-3684

WALKER, WILLIAM WOODARD, JR. management consultant, telecommunications technology; b. Montevideo, Uruguay, Aug. 2, 1950; s. William Woodard and Jane (Wootton) W. BA in Polit. Sci., U. N.C., Chapel Hill, 1973; MBA, Coll. of William & Mary, 1978. Acct. mgr. Jarvis Corp., Alexandria, Va., 1978-80; mgmt. cons. Daniel Penn Assocs., Schuykill Haven, Pa., 1981-82; mktg. exec. Sprint Corp., McLean, Va., 1982-84; pres. Woodard Walker Assocs., Inc., Vienna, 1984—. Dir. bd. of dirs. coun. of co-owners The Colonies Condominium, McLean, 1992-94. Mem. Am. Soc. Assn. Execs. (lectr. telecomms. 1990—), Soc. Telecomms. Cons., Capitol Telecomms. Profls., Friends Assisting the Natl. Symphony Orchestra, Washington, (exec. comm. 1996-97), Metropolitan Club of Washington. Republican. Episcopalian. Avocations: tennis, bicycling, jogging. Home: 1156 N Pitt St Alexandria VA 22314-1456

WALKER, WOODROW WILSON, retired lawyer, cattle and timber farmer; b. Greenville, Mich., Feb. 19, 1919; s. Craig Walker and Mildred Chase; m. Janet K. Keiter, Oct. 7, 1950; children: Jonathan Woodrow, William Craig, Elaine Virginia. BA, U. Mich., 1943; LLB, Cath. U., 1950. Bar: D.C. 1950, U.S. Supreme Ct. 1958, Va. 1959. Operator family farm, 1937-39; dir. Libr. of Congress Fed. Credit Union, 1957-60; atty. Am. law div. legis. reference Libr. Congress, Washington, 1951-60; pvt. practice, Arlington, Va., 1960-2000. Counsel Calvary Found., Arlington, 1970-85, first pres., 1972; judge moot ct. George Mason Law Sch., 1986; owner-operator Walker Farm Front Royal, Va., 1972—. Co-author rsch. publs. for U.S. Govt.; featured in Washington Post. V.p. Jefferson Civic Assn., Arlington, 1955-61; pres. Nellie Custis PTA, Arlington, 1960-61; sec. Arlington County Bd. Equalization Real Estate Assessment, 1962, chmn. 1963; com. chmn. Arlington Troop 108 Boy Scouts Am., 1964-69; mem. Arlington County Pub. Utilities Commn., 1964-66, vice chmn., 1965-66; pres. Betschler Class Adult Sunday Sch., Calvary United Meth. Ch., Arlington, 1965. Served with U.S. Army, 1943-45, PTO. Cited for notable deed in conduct of his legal duties Washington Post, 1996. Mem. ABA, Arlington County Bar Assn., Va. Farm Bur., Va. Cattleman's Assn. Methodist. Democrat. Home and Office: 2822 Ft Scott Dr Arlington VA 22202-2307

WALKER-RICKS, GLORIA DELOISE, secondary education educator; b. Eudora, Ark., July 31, 1944; d. Edward Lee Sr. and Ella (Farris) Edwards; m. Walter Edward Ricks, May 21, 1979; children: Adrienne, Eunice, Byron. BS, U. Ark., Pine Bluff, 1964; MA, Chgo. State U., 1989. Cert. secondary tchr., Calif., Ill., adminstr., Ill. Tchr. Ctrl. H.S., Lake Village, Ark., 1964-65, Roosevelt Jr. H.S., Compton, Calif., 1966-71, Bowen H.S., Chgo., 1971-91, prin., 1991-95; tchr. Curie H.S., 1996-99, ret., 1999. Math. coach Chgo. Urban League, 1982-91; coord. Chgo. Citywide Math. League, 1982-91. Pres. 123rd and LaSalle Block Club, Skyway Tchrs. Bowling League; past chairperson Kenridge Neighborhood Girl Scouts U.S. Recipient Educator of Yr. award Phi Delta Kappa. Mem. Ill. Coun. Tchrs. of Math. (mem. contest com. 1987-96), So. Chgo. C. of C. (Educator of Yr. 1989). Home: 12316 S La Salle St Chicago IL 60628-6841

WALKER SCHLAGECK, KATHRINE L. museum educational administrator, educator; b. San Jose, Calif., Mar. 12, 1962; d. Paul D. and Barbara (White) W.; m. John L. Schlageck, Jan. 10, 1998; 1 child, Benjamin David. BA with honors, Stanford U., 1984; MA, Coll. William and Mary, 1986; cert. mus. mgmt., U. Colo., 1996. Archaeologist Va. Rsch. Ctr. for Archaeology, Newport, 1984-85; curatorial asst. Colonial Williamsburg Found., Va., 1985-86; asst. curator, coord. edn. Nantucket (Mass.) Historical Assn., 1986-88; dir. edn. Webb-Deane-Stevens Mus., Wethersfield, Conn., 1988-91, Lyman Allyn Art Mus., New London, 1991-94, Beach Mus. Art, Kans. State U., Manhattan, 1994—. Mem. Mass. Arts Lottery Coun., Nantucket, 1988-89; chair diversity subcom. Regional Adv. Com. on Edn. Reform, 1994; adv. bd. Manhattan Arts Coun., 1995-96; panelist Kans. Arts Commn., 1995; steering com. Take a Stand Ednl. Collaborative; grant reviewer Inst. Mus. and Libr. Svcs., 1995, 97, 99. Author: (curriculum) The Outsiders, 1990, The Face in Art, 1994, (gallery guide) From Distaff Side, 1992, Sunflower State Quilts: A guide to publicly held quilt collections in Kansas, 1999; author: (with others) Cultural Diversity in Literature, Art and Music, 1992, The American Collection 1620-1920: Guide to the Palmer Gallery, 1994; author, editor: (curriculum) The Prairie Through New Eyes, 2001; author and curator: Beyond Oz: Children's Book Illustration from the Region, 2002. Vol. tchr. Nantucket Learning & Resource Ctr., 1988; mem. New London Culture and Tourism Alliance, 1991—; Manhattan C. of C. Edn. com., 1996; Big Brothers, Big Sisters, 1996; fundraiser United Way, 1997. Grantee Inst. Mus. Svcs., Nantucket, 1987, 88, Rockefellor Found./Conn. Humanities Coun., New London, 1991-92; scholar Conn. Humanities Coun., 1989—, Mid Am. Arts Alliance, 1999, Kans. Arts Commn., 2001. Mem. Am. Assn. Mus. (rep. bd. 1990-93, 95—, edn. com. 1988—, Excellence and Equity award) Nat. Art Edn. Assn. (Mus. Educator of Yr. Western divsn. 2000), New Eng. Mus. Assn. (edn. com. 1988-94, chair 1991-94), Mountain Plains Mus. Assn. (chair edn. com. 1995—, sec. 1997—, program chair 2002), Conn. Art Docents Network (bd. dirs. 1991—), Alliance of Cultural Educators of Hartford, Nat. Art Edn. Assn. (Mus. Educator of the Yr. western divsn.), Kans. Art Edn. Assn. (Mus. Educator of the Yr. 1999-2000), Manhattan C. of C. (edn. com. 1996), W.a. White cmty. Partnership (bd. dirs.). Avocations: the arts, multicultural education, skiing, writing. Office: Beach Mus Art 701 Beach Ln Manhattan KS 66506-0600 E-mail: klwalk@ksu.edu.

WALKER-STOKES, BRIDGET LEUREEN, research scientist; b. Fort Lauderdale, Fla., May 27, 1955; d. Arthur Lee and Jessie Mae (Davis) Walker; m. Kenneth Wayne Stokes, Mar. 11, 2000. BS in Agriculture, U. Fla., 1978, MS in Agriculture, 1992. Lab. technologist U. Fla., Gainesville, 1978-80, chemist, 1980-97, sr. tchg. lab. specialist, 1997—. Contbr. articles to profl. jours. and chpts. to books. Mem. Inst. Food Technologists. Avocations: singing, sewing. Office: U Fla PO Box 110370 Gainesville FL 32611-0370 E-mail: bwalker@mail.ifas.ufl.edu.

WALKER-WILLIAMS, HOPE DENISE, administrator, business consultant; b. Chgo., Dec. 24, 1952; d. Welmon and Mary Ann (Brefford) Walker; children: Albert Lee, Ebony Emani Denise. Student, Ill. State U., 1971-72; BA in Psychology, St. Ambrose Coll., 1985, postgrad., 1985-87, Harvard U. Grad. Sch. Design, summer 1981, Nat. Assn. Collegiate Women Athletic Adminstrs./Higher Edn. Resources Inst., 1995, No. Ill. U., 1998—2000. Social svc. dir. Friendly House, Davenport, Iowa, 1977-78; data collector, cons., 1978; supr. summer youth employment program Cmty. Employment Tng. Act, Davenport, 1978; lead organizer Central and Western Neighborhood Devel. Corp., 1978-79; exec. dir. Inner City Devel. Corp., 1980-83; owner Midwestern Internat. Mktg. Assocs., San Francisco, 1983; ops. mgr. Dramatic Mktg. Assn., 1983-85; adminstrv. asst. Parker Ross Assocs., 1984-85; crisis intervention counselor Cath. Social Svcs., 1985-86; adminstrv. intern Scott County Iowa, 1985-86; from counselor to dir. advising Marycrest Coll., Davenport, 1986-90; dir. spl. svcs. Augustana Coll., Rock Island, Ill., 1990-97, asst. dean of student svcs., 1991-97. Cons. Dramatic Mktg. Assocs., San Francisco, 1997—; coord. student athlete support svcs. No. Ill. U., Dekalb, 1999—2001; acad. coord. football and women's basketball, athletic dept. U. Iowa, Iowa City, 2001—; bus. cons., incorporator, sec. bd. dirs. United Neighbors Inc., 1980; bd. dirs. Cmty. Health Care, 1978—80; v.p., treas. Athletes Say More Edn., 1980; treas., exec. com. F&A Cmty. Warehouse, 1982—; bd. dirs. HELP Legal Aid, v.p., 1990, pres., 91; allocations panel United Way, 1987—. Author narrative and final report for oral history project, 1979. Recipient Cert. of Appreciation Palmer Jr. Coll., Davenport, 1979, Personal Dedication plaque Jr. Achievement, 1988-90; cert. of merit Ch. Women United, 1983; grantee NEH, 1979, Presdl. grant Palmer Jr. Coll., 1978. Mem. NAFE, Assn. Black Women Higher Edn., Nat. Assn. Women Edn. (nat. treas. 1993, Dorothy Truex award for Emerging Profls. 1994), Nat. Assn. Acad. Advisors for Athletics (membership com. 2000—, minority concerns com., liaison to legis. affairs com. Region III 2001—), Quad Cities Career Womens Network (treas., exec. com.), Assn. Acad. Affairs Adminstrs. (bd. dirs. 1989-96, award for new profls. 1989, treas. 1992-96), Nat. Assn. for Blacks at Predominately White Instns. (v.p. fin.), Nat. Acad. Advisors Assn., Nat. Assn. Acad. Advisors (bd. dirs. 1988), Quad Cities Assn. Black Sch. Educators (founding, charter, treas. 1993), Quad City Negro Heritage Soc., Assn. Black Profls. (chair), Nat. Assn. Black MBAs, Alpha Kappa Alpha (chair connection com. Xi Eta Omega chpt. 1989, pres. 1990-96, internat. stds. com. 1994-98), Quad Cities Strivers Inc. (bd. dirs.). E-mail: takeball@aol.com.

WALKINGSTICK, KAY, artist, art educator; b. Syracuse, N.Y. d. Simon Ralph and Margaret Emma (McKaig) W.S. BFA, Beaver Coll., 1959; MFA, Pratt Inst., Bklyn., 1975. Asst. prof. art SUNY, Stony Brook, 1990-92; assoc. prof. art Cornell U., Ithaca, N.Y., 1988-90, prof. art NY, 1992—. Solo exhbns. include Bertha Urdang Gallery, N.Y.C., 1978, 81, 84, M-13 Gallery, N.Y.C., 1987, 90, Wenger Gallery, L.A., 1979, 84, 88, Galerie Calumet, Heidelberg, Germany, 1993, June Kelly Gallery, N.Y.C., 1994, 99, 2002; solo mus. exhbns. include N.J. State Mus. (2-person exhibit), Trenton, 1975, Heard Mus., Phoenix, 1991, Hillwood Art Mus. L.I. Univ., Brookville, N.Y., 1991, Jersey City (N.J.) Mus., 1992, Morris Mus., Morristown, N.J., 1992; group exhbns. include New Mus., N.Y.C., 1990, Security Pacific Gallery, Seattle, 1991, Nat. Gallery Can., Ottawa, 1992, U. B.C. Mus. Anthropology, Vancouver, 1993-94, Cairo Biennial USA Exhibit, 1994-95, Jan Cicero Gallery, Chgo., 1995, Currier Gallery Art, Manchester, N.Y., 1996, Rose Art Mus., Brandeis U., Boston, 1996, Katonah (N.Y.) Mus. Art, 1996, Venice Biennale "Celebration", Venice, Italy, 1999; represented in permanent mus. and univ. collections Albright-Knox Mus., Buffalo, N.Y., Israel Mus., Jerusalem, Met. Mus. Art, N.Y.C., Nat. Gallery Can., Newark Mus.; guest curator Heard Mus., Phoenix, 2002. Recipient Nat. Honor award for Achievement in the Arts, Women's Caucus for Art, Boston, 1996, Joan Mitchell Found. award in painting, 1995-96, Rockefeller Found. residency, Bellagio, Italy, 1992, Richard A. Florsheim Art Fund award, Tampa, 1991; NEA fellow, 1983-84; N.Y. Found. Arts grantee, N.Y.C., 1992.

WALKLET, JOHN JAMES, JR. publishing executive; b. Trenton, N.J., June 14, 1922; s. John James and Katherine Helen (Slamin) W.; m. Gretchen Crowell, Aug. 21, 1948; children: John III, Philip, Deborah, Preston, Richard, Colin, Keith, Christopher, Megan. BL in Journalism, Rutgers U., 1943. Reporter Montclair (N.J.) Times, 1943; prodn. editor Macmillan Pub. Co., N.Y.C., 1946-52, dir. mfg. sch. div., 1969-88, asst. v.p., 1982, v.p., 1983-88, cons., 1989, ret.; tech. writer Shell Chem. Corp., 1952-54; dir. publs. Colonial Williamsburg, Williamsburg, Va., 1954-69. Cons. book prodn. U. Press of Va., Charlottesville, 1963-69. Author, designer: Adventure in Williamsburg, 1960 (So. Books Competition award), A Window on Williamsburg, 1966 (So. Books Competition award); designer: The Journal of John Harrower, 1963 (One of 50 Books of Yr. award Am. Inst. Graphic Arts). Pres. Kiwanis Club of Williamsburg, 1969; bd. dirs. Edenton-Chowan Kiwanis Club, 1996-97, v.p., 1998; cons. Va. Travel Coun., Richmond, 1960-69. Sgt. U.S. Army, 1943-46. Mem. Assn. Am. Pubs. (mfg. com. rep. Adv. Commn. Textbook Specifications 1980-84, vice chmn. mfg. com. 1984-86, chmn. mfg. com. 1986-88), Williamsburg Stirrup Club (bd. dirs. 1965-69), James Iredell Assn. (bd. dirs. Edenton soc. 1989-97). Republican. Roman Catholic. Avocations: reading, piano and organ, golf, fishing, spectator sports. Home: 1222 Sound Shore Dr Edenton NC 27932-8916 *In one's career, success is augmented by the willingness of dedicated professionals to share their knowledge and experience and teach those individuals whose desire to learn and contribute is beyond measure.*

WALKOWIAK, ROBERT G. retired obstetrician and gynecologist; b. Detroit, Feb. 18, 1921; s. Simon Aloysius and Helen Pauline (Gryka) Walkowiak; m. Mary Jane Millard, June 29, 1945; children: Robert G. Walkowiak Jr., David J.(dec.) , James R.(dec.) , Rebecca J., Peter J., Jeffrey P.(dec.). BS, Wayne State U., 1941, MD, 1944. Diplomate Am. Bd. Ob-Gyn. Intern Grace Hosp., Detroit, 1944-45; resident in ob-gyn. St. Joseph Mercy Hosp., 1945-46, 50-52; ret. Cons. Tribunal Archdiocese Detroit, 1958—84; from clin. instr. to clin. asst. prof. ob-gyn Wayne State U., 1962—83. Lt. j.g. M.C. USNR, 1946—48. Fellow: Am. Coll. Ob-Gyn, ACS; mem.: Mich. Soc. Ob-Gyn (sec. 1972—77, pres. 1977—78), AMA, Phi Beta Pi (pres. Detroit alumni 1967—68). Roman Catholic.

WALKOWIAK, VINCENT STEVEN, lawyer; b. Apr. 22, 1946; s. Vincent Albert and Elizabeth (Modla) W.; m. Linda Kae Schweigert, Aug., 1968; children: Jenifer, Steven. BA, U. Ill., 1968, JD, 1971. Bar: Ill. 1971, Tex. 1981, U.S. Ct. Appeals (8th cir.) 1971, (5th cir.) 1982, U.S. Dist. Ct. (ea., we., so., and no. dists.) Tex. 1982. Assoc. Dorsey, Marquart, Windhorst, West & Halladay, Mpls., 1971-74; ptnr. Fulbright & Jaworski LLP, Houston, 1982—. Prof. Fla. State U., Tallahassee, 1974-76, So. Meth. U., Dallas, 1976-84. Editor: Uniform Product Liability Act, 1980, Trial of a Product Liability Case, vol. 1, 1981, vol. 2, 1982, Preparation and Presentation of Product Liability, 1983, Attorney Client Privilege in Civil Litigation, 1997. Office: Fulbright & Jaworski LLP 2200 Ross Ave Ste 2800 Dallas TX 75201-2784 E-mail: vwalkowiak@fulbright.com.

WALKUP, CHARLOTTE LLOYD, lawyer; b. N.Y.C., Apr. 28, 1910; d. Charles Henry and Helene Louise (Wheeler) Tuttle; m. David D. Lloyd, Oct. 19, 1940 (dec. Dec. 1962); children: Andrew M. Lloyd, Louisa Lloyd Hurley; m. Homer Allen Walkup, Feb. 4, 1967. AB, Vassar Coll., 1931; LLB, Columbia U., 1934. Bar: N.Y. 1935, U.S. Supreme Ct. 1939, U.S. Dist. Ct. D.C. 1953, Va. 1954. Asst. solicitor Dept. Interior, Washington, 1934-45; asst. gen. counsel UNRRA, Washington and London, 1945-48; assoc. and cons. firms Washington, 1953, 55, 60; atty., spl. asst. Office Treasury, 1961-65, asst. gen. counsel, 1965-73. Cons. Rogers & Wells, Washington, 1975-86. Editor Columbia Law Rev., 1933-34. Pres. Alexandria Cmty. Welfare Coun., 1950-52; bd. dirs. Alexandria Coun. Human Rels., 1958-60, New Hope Found., 1977. Recipient Meritorious Svc. award Dept. Treasury, 1970, Exceptional Svc. award, 1973, Career Svc. award Nat. Civil Svc. League, 1973; named Hon. fellow Harry S. Truman Libr. Inst. Mem. Columbia U. Alumni Assn., Phi Beta Kappa. Democrat. Episcopalian. Home: 4800 Fillmore Ave Apt 1251 Alexandria VA 22311-5077 E-mail: walkup@comcast.net.

WALKUP, HOMER ALLEN, lawyer, writer; b. Dunloup, W.Va., Jan. 28, 1917; s. Homer Allen and Lillie Belle (Harris) W.; m. Edna Mae Tucker, Nov. 19, 1941 (dec. 1966); m. Charlotte M. Tuttle Lloyd, Feb. 4, 1967; children: Homer Allen, Randolph Michael, Pamela Susan. AB, W.Va. U., 1935, LLB, 1938; LLM, Georgetown U., 1947. Bar: W.Va. 1938, U.S. Supreme Ct. 1946, U.S. Ct. Fed. Claims 1978, U.S. Ct. Appeals (fed. cir.) 1982, U.S. Ct. Claims 1982, U.S. Ct. Appeals Armed Forces 1984. Sole practice, W.Va., 1938-42; complaint atty. W.Va. Office OPA, Charleston, 1942; commd. ensign USNR, 1942, advanced through grades to capt., 1963; appellate judge Navy Ct. Mil. Rev., 1966-68; dep. asst., JAG of Navy, 1968-73; ret., 1973; sole practice, Summersville, W.Va., 1974-90. Mem. governing bd. Alexandria (Va.) Mental Health Ctr., 1988-92; bd. dirs. United Way Nat. Capital Area, 1990—. Mem. ABA, ATLA, Fed. Bar Assn., W.Va. State Bar, W.Va. Bar Assn., Bar Assn. D.C., Fed. Cir. Bar Assn., Judge Advs. Assn., Navy-MarCorps Retired Judge Advs. Assn., Am. Judicature Soc., Mil. Order World Wars, Res. Officers Assn., Ret. Officers Assn., Order of Coif. Democrat. Presbyterian. Club: Mil. Dist. Washington Officers. Contbr. in field. Office: Ste 1251 4800 Fillmore Ave Alexandria VA 22311-5077

WALKUP, MARSHA ANN, interior designer; b. Rolla, Mo., June 13, 1955; d. Wilbur Cline and Doris Ann (Harmon) Batson; m. Eugene Davis Carney, July 8, 1973 (div. 1976); m. Grant William Walkup, Mar. 20, 1982; stepchildren— Teresa Ann, Gregory Wayne, Barton William. B.S. in Interior Design, S.W. Mo. State U., 1979; postgrad. in design, Kans. U., 1985— . Interior designer VA, Leavenworth, Kans., 1980— . Active St. Mary's Coll. Community Cultural Club, Leavenworth, 1983— . Recipient Dir.'s commendation award VA, 1981, Performance award, 1984, 85. Affiliate mem. Inst. Bus. Designers. Democrat. Club: Pilot Internat. (treas. 1984-85). Office: VA 4th St Trafficway VA 4th St Trafficway Leavenworth KS 66048

WALKUP, ROBERT E. mayor; b. Ames, Iowa, Nov. 14, 1936; m. Beth Walkup; 3 children; 2 stepchildren. BS in Indsl. Engring., Iowa State U. Exec. Rockwell Internat., Fairchild Republic; sr. exec. Hughes Aircraft Co.; mayor Tucson, 1999—. Chmn. Greater Tucson Econ. Coun.; founder, first chmn. Ariz. Space Commn.; vol. Tucson Cmty. Food Bank; co-founder Pima-Santa Cruz County Sch.-to-Work Program; co-founder El Centro Cultural de las Americas. Capt. U.S. Army. Republican. Avocations: playing guitar, sketching, studying astronomy, restoring antique cars and motorcycles. Office: City Hall 255 W Alameda St Tucson AZ 85701-1362 Fax: 520-791-4213.

WALL, BETTY JANE, real estate consultant; b. Wichita Falls, Tex., Mar. 23, 1936; d. Albert Willis and Winnie Belle (Goodloe) Beard; m. Richard Lee Wall, Feb. 21, 1959; 1 child, Cynthia Lynn. BS, Vocat.Home Econs. Edn, U. Okla., 1958; MEd, Midwestern U., 1959. Lic. real estate salesperson, Tex. Tchr. San Diego County Schs., 1959-60, Long Beach (Calif.) City Schs., 1960-61, Norman (Okla.) Kindergarten Assn., 1961-65; real estate salesperson WestMark Realtors, Lubbock, Tex., 1983-85; now ind. real estate salesperson, 1985—. Coll. adviser Nat. Panhellenic Conf., Tex., 1979-91; judge talent and beauty pageants, Tex. N.Mex., Okla., 1984—. Treas. Lubbock Symphony Guild, 1985-87, v.p. ways and means com., 1987-88, chmn. ball, 1990, pres. elect, 1993-94, pres., 1994-95; bd. dirs. Tex. Assn. of Symphony Orchs., 1994-95, Ballet Lubbock, 1996-98, 2000—; bd. dirs. Miss Lubbock Pageant, 1992—; co-chmn. Performance Lubbock' 96, 1996; mem. Lubbock Arts Festival Com., 1997-98. Recipient Tex. Tech. U. Outstanding Greek Alumni award, 1994, Tex. Tech. Chancellor's Coun. Mem. Tex. Real Estate Assn., Jr. League Lubbock (treas. 1976-78, sustaining advisor fin. com. 1979-83, hdqrs. commn. advisor 1989-94), Mus. Tex. Tech. Univ. (chmn. planetarium com. 1996, trustee 1997—, bd. dirs., mus. league 1992—, pres. 2002), Lubbock C. of C., Lubbock Women's Club (bd. dirs. 1996-2000, pres. 1999-2000, pres. hist. found. 1999-2000), Tex. Tech. U. Faculty Women's Club (v.p. and pres. 1967-69, Lubbock chpt. Achievement Rewards for Coll. Sci. bd. 1995-96), Alpha Chi Omega (nat. coun., nat. panhellenic del. 1978-83, 88-90, nat. v.p. membership 1985-88, nat. v.p. collegians 1990-92). Avocations: needlepoint, travel, music. Home and Office: 3610 63rd Dr Lubbock TX 79413-5308

WALL, BRIAN ARTHUR, sculptor; b. London, Sept. 5, 1931; s. Arthur Francis and Dorothy (Seymour) W.; m. Sylvia Brown, Oct. 27, 1973; children— Nathaniel, Gideon. Student, Luton (Eng.) Coll. Art, 1951. First asst. to Dame Barbara Hepworth, St. Ives, Cornwall, Eng., 1954-59; instr. Ealing Coll. Art, Middlesex, Eng., 1961-62; prin. lectr. Central Sch. Art and Design, London, 1962-72, head dept. sculpture, 1962-72; vis. lectr. U. Calif., Berkeley, 1969-73, lectr., 1973-75, asst. prof., 1975-77, asso. prof. art, 1977-81, prof., 1981-93; prof. emeritus, 1993—. One-man shows U. Nev., Las Vegas, 1976, Braunstein Gallery, San Francisco, 1974, 76, 78, Sculpture Now, N.Y.C., 1977, 78, Max Hutchinson Gallery, Houston, 1979, May Hutchinson Gallery, N.Y.C., 1981, Seattle Art Mus., 1982, San Francisco Mus. Modern Art, 1983, John Berggruen Gallery, San Francisco, 1983, Lowinsky Gallery, N.Y.C., 1987, 98, Francis Graham-Dixon Gallery, London, 1992, Jernigan Wicker Fine Arts, San Francisco, 1995, 99, Sheldon Meml. Art Gallery, U. Nebr., 1995, Flowers East, London, 1999, Flowers West, L.A., 2002; exhibited in group shows, including Mus. Modern Art, Paris, 1961, U. Tex., Dallas, 1976, Crocker Art Mus., Sacramento, 1979, Tate Gallery, London, 1985, Navy Pier, Chgo., 1998; works represented in permanent collections Tate Gallery, Mus. Art, Dublin, Art Gallery NSW, Australia, Univ. Art Mus., Berkeley, U. Houston, Sheldon Meml. Art Gallery, Seattle Art Mus., Towson State U., Balt., Oakland Mus., Triton Mus., Santa Clara, Calif.; works include Thornaby, 1968, Ali, 1978. Mem. Arts Council Gt. Brit., 1969-72; trustee San Francisco Art Inst., 1974-77; mem. San Francisco Twin Bicentennial Arts Com., 1975-76. Served with RAF, 1950-52. U. Calif. at Berkeley Humanities Rsch. Fellowship Program grantee, 1978-79; recipient prize BART Sculpture Competition, 1975. Achievements include being subject of numerous profl. articles. Home: 306 Lombard St San Francisco CA 94133-2415

WALL, BRIAN RAYMOND, forest economist, business consultant, researcher; b. Jan. 26, 1940; s. Raymond Perry and Mildred Beryl (Pickert) W.; m. Joan Marie Nero, Sept. 1, 1962 (div. Aug. 1990); children: Torden Erik, Kirsten Noel. BS, U. Wash., 1962; MF, Yale U., 1964. Forestry asst. Weyerhaeuser Timber Co., Klamath Falls, Oreg., 1960; inventory forester West Tacoma Newsprint, 1961-62; timber sale compliance forester Dept. Nat. Resources, Kelso, Wash., 1963; rsch. forest economist Pacific N.W. Rsch. Sta., USDA Forest Svc., Portland, Oreg., 1964-88; cons., 1989—. Co-founder, bd. dirs. Cordero Youth Care Ctr., 1970-81; owner Brian R. Wall Images and Communications; Nikken ind. distbr. Sage Mentor Lifestyles; owner Sage Mentors Bus. Consultancy; cons. to govt. agys., Congress univs., industry, small bus.; freelance photographer. Co-author: An Analysis of the Timber Situation in the United States, 1982; contbr. articles, reports to profl. publs., newspapers. Interviewed and cited by nat. and regional news media. Recipient Cert. of Merit U.S. Dept. Agr. Forest Svc., 1982. Mem. ACLU, Soc. Am. Foresters (chmn. Portland chpt. 1973, Forester of Yr. 1975), Conf. of Western Forest Economists Inc. (founder, bd. dirs. 1988-91, treas. 1982-87), Portland Photographic Forum, Common Cause, Oregon Economists Assn., Nat. Audubon Soc., Amnesty Internat., Zeta Psi. Home: 6160 SW Alice Ln # 204 B Beaverton OR 97008 Office: Sage Mentors Consultancy PMB 1162 10117 SE Sunnyside Rd Ste F Clackamas OR 97015-7708 E-mail: brwall01@cs.com.

WALL, CLARENCE VINSON, state legislator; b. Athens, Ga., Oct. 17, 1947; s. Clarence Jacob and Fannie Lucile (Clark) W.; m. Linda Gail Mason, Dec. 6, 1969 (div. 1980); 1 child, Jeffrey Vinson. Grad. high sch., Lawrenceville, Ga., 1965. Rep. Ga. Ho. of Reps., Lawrenceville, 1973-82, 85-96. Staff sgt. Ga. ANG, 1967-73. Republican. Baptist. Home: 458 Springlake Rd Lawrenceville GA 30045-5090

WALL, CURTISS EDWIN, mathematician, educator; b. Chgo., Mar. 31, 1943; m. Nancy Marie Eure; children: Thomas. PhD, Mich. State U., 1972. Assoc. prof. of edn. Old Dominion U., Norfolk, Va., 1973—89; cons. in sci & math IBM Corp, Washington, 1989—96; prof. of math Norfolk State U., Norfolk, 1991—. Pres. faculty senate Norfolk State U., 2002—; dir. ednl. computing Norfolk Pub. Sch., 1983—89. Editor: Graph Theory with Applications to Algorithms and Computer Science, 1985. Mem.: Tidewater Coun. of Teachers of Math. (pres. 2000—02), Va. Coun. Teachers of Math. (William C. Lowry Outstanding Math. Tchr. award 1984), Am. Math. Soc., Nat. Coun. of Teachers of Math. Home: 708 Pinecliffe Dr Chesapeake VA 23322 Office: Dept of Mathematics Norfolk State Univ 700 Park Ave Norfolk VA 23504 Home Fax: 757-823-8427; Office Fax: 757-823-8427. Personal E-mail: cewall@attglobal.net. E-mail: cewall@nsu.edu.

WALL, DIANE EVE, political science educator; b. Detroit, Nov. 17, 1944; d. Albert George and Jean Carol Bradley. BA in History and Edn., Mich. State U., 1966, MA in History, 1969, MA in Polit. Sci., 1979, PhD in Polit. Sci., 1983. Cert. permanent secondary tchr., Mich. Secondary tchr. Corunna (Mich.) Pub. Schs., 1966-67, N.W. Pub. Schs., Rives Junction, Mich., 1967-73; lectr. Tidewater C.C., Chesapeake, Va., 1974-77; instr. Wayne State U., Detroit, fall 1980, Lansing (Mich.) C.C., 1981-83, Ctrl. Mich. U., Mt. Pleasant, 1982; prof. dept. polit. sci. Miss. State U., 1983—, undergrad. coord., 1993—. Pre-law advisor Miss. State U., 1990—93, chair, 1993—. Co-editor spl. issue Southea. Polit. Rev.; contbr. articles, revs. to profl. jours., chpt. to book. Evaluator Citizen's Task Force, Chesapeake, Va., 1977; panelist flag burning program Ednl. TV, Mississippi State, 1990, prayer in pub. sch., Starkville Cmty. TV, 1995. Recipient Paideia award Miss. State U. Coll. Arts and Scis., 1988, Miss. State U. Outstanding Woman Tchg. Faculty award Pres.'s Commn. on Status of Women, 1994, Acad. Advising award Miss. State U., 1994, Outstanding Advisor award Nat. Acad. Advising Assn. and ACT, 1995, Miss. State U. Upper Level Undergrad. Tchg. award Miss. State U. Alumni Assn., 2000;

Grad. Office fellow Mich. State U., 1980; Miss. State U. rsch. grantee, 1984. Mem. ASPA (exec. bd. Sect. for Women 1987-90, Miss. chpt. pres. 1992-93), LWV (Chesapeake charter pres. 1976-77), Miss. Polit. Sci. Assn. (exec. dir. 1991-93), Miss. State U. Soc. Scholars (pres. 1992-93), Miss. State U. Faculty Women's Assn. (v.p. 1985-86, pres. 1986-88, scholar 1987-89), Phi Kappa Phi (v.p. 1985-86, pres. 1986-88), Pi Sigma Alpha (Ann. Chpt. Activities award 1991). Democrat. Methodist. Avocations: dog obedience training, Corvette activities, gardening. Office: Miss State U PO Drawer PC Mississippi State MS 39762 E-mail: dew1@ps.msstate.edu .

WALL, DONALD ARTHUR, lawyer; b. Lafayette, Ind., Mar. 17, 1946; s. Dwight Arthur and Myra Virginia (Peavey) W.; m. Cheryn Lynn Heinen, Aug. 29, 1970; children: Sarah Lynn, Michael Donald. BA, Butler U., 1968; JD, Northwestern U., 1971. Bar: Ohio 1971, U.S. Dist. Ct. (no. dist.) Ohio 1973, U.S. Supreme Ct. 1980, Ariz. 1982, U.S. Dist. Ct. (no. dist.) W.Va. 1982, U.S. Ct. Appeals (6th cir.) 1982, U.S. Dist. Ct. Ariz. 1983, U.S. Ct. Appeals (9th and 10th cirs.) 1984, U.S. Ct. Appeals (5th cir.) 1988. Assoc. Squire, Sanders & Dempsey, Cleve., 1971-80, ptnr., 1980-82, Phoenix, 1983—. Spkr. at profl. meetings; program moderator. Contbr. articles to profl. jours. Trustee Ch. of the Saviour Day Ctr., Cleveland Heights, 1979-82; mem. adminstrv. bd. Ch. of Saviour, Cleveland Heights, 1980-83; fin. com. Paradise Valley (Ariz.) United Meth. Ch., 1986-87; bd. dirs., divsn. commr. North Scottsdale (Ariz.) Little League, 1983-92; bd. dirs. Epilepsy Found. N.E. Ohio, 1976-82, pres., 1981-82; bd. dirs. N.E. Cmty. Basketball Assn., 1993-99; bd. visitors U. Ariz. Law Sch., 1996—; bd. mgrs. Scottsdale-Paradise Valley YMCA, 1999—. Mem. ABA (torts and ins. practice and litigation sect., past chmn. r.r. law com., litigation sect.), Def. Rsch. Inst., Ariz. Bar Assn. (labor and trial practice sects.), Maricopa County Bar Assn., Ariz. Assn. Def. Counsel. Methodist. Office: Squire Sanders & Dempsey LLP 40 N Central Ave Ste 2700 Phoenix AZ 85004-4498 E-mail: dwall@ssd.com.

WALL, EDWARD MILLARD, environmental consulting executive; b. Newburyport, Mass., Dec. 17, 1929; s. Millard Edward and Edith Noyes (Carter) W.; m. Jean Titus, Jan. 27, 1951 (dec. 1989); children: Karen, Kenneth, Kathryn; m. Gertrude Knott, Nov. 18, 1992. BSME, Tufts U., 1951; MBA, Xavier U., 1962. Cert. hazardous materials mgr. Tech. service engr. Goodyear Tire, Akron, Ohio, 1951-53; mgr. engine test facilities Gen. Electric, Cin., 1956-62; mgr. mfg. Williams Mfg., Portsmouth, Ohio, 1962-74; sr. project mgr. N-Ren Corp., Cin., 1975-78; v.p. mfg. Nelson Electric, Tulsa, 1979-88; v.p. Techrad Environ. Svcs., Oklahoma City, 1988-92, pres., 1992-97; retired, 1997. Mem. Vo-Tech Edn. Adv. Com., Tulsa, 1982-88. Lt.(j.g.) USNR, 1953-56. Mem. ASME, NSPE, Am. Prodn. and Inventory Control Soc. (cert.), Am. Mgmt. Assn. Lodges: Rotary, Masons. Republican. Presbyterian. Avocations: golf, swimming. Home: 165 Francis Dr NE Port Charlotte FL 33952

WALL, FREDERICK THEODORE, retired chemistry educator; b. Chisholm, Minn., Dec. 14, 1912; s. Peter and Fanny Maria (Rauhala) W.; m. Clara Elizabeth Vivian, June 5, 1940; children: Elizabeth Wall Ralston, Jane Vivian Wall. B.Chemistry, U. Minn., 1933, PhD, 1937. Mem. faculty chemistry dept. U. Ill., 1937-64, dean grad. coll., 1955-63; prof., chmn. dept. chemistry U. Calif., Santa Barbara, 1964-66, vice chancellor rsch., 1965-66; vice chancellor grad. studies and research, prof. chemistry U. Calif. at San Diego, 1966-69; exec. dir. Am. Chem. Soc., Washington, 1969-72; prof. chemistry Rice U., Houston, 1972-78. Pres. Assn. Grad. Schs., 1961; trustee Inst. Def. Analyses, 1962-64; mem. governing bd. Nat. Acad. Scis.-NRC, 1963- 67. Author: Chemical Thermodynamics, 1958; editor Jour. Phys. Chemistry, 1965-69. Mem. Am. Chem. Soc. (Pure Chemistry award 1945, dir. 1962-64), Finnish Chem. Soc. (corr.), Am. Acad. Arts and Scis., Nat. Acad. Scis. Achievements include early work on Monte Carlo computer simulation of macromolecular configurations and of basic reaction probabilities. E-mail: ftwall@worldnet.att.net.

WALL, JAMES MCKENDREE, minister, editor; b. Monroe, Ga., Oct. 27, 1928; s. Louie David and Lida (Day) W.; m. Mary Eleanor Kidder, Sept. 11, 1953; children: David McKendree, Robert Kidder, Richard James. Student, Ga. Inst. Tech., 1945-47; BA, Emory U., 1949, BD, 1955, LHD (hon.), 1985; MA, U. Chgo., 1960; LittD (hon.), Ohio No. U., 1969; DHL (hon.), Willamette Coll., 1978; DD (hon.), MacMurray, 1981; DHL (hon.), Coe Coll., 1987. Ordained to ministry United Meth. Ch., 1954. Staff writer, sports dept. Atlanta Jour., 1948-50; asst. minister East Lake Meth. Ch., Atlanta, 1953; asst. to dean students Emory U., 1954-55; pastor North Ga. Conf. Moreland, Luthersville Meth. Chs., Ga., 1955-57, Bethel United Meth. Ch., Chgo., 1957-59; mng. editor Christian Adv. mag., Park Ridge, Ill., 1959-63, editor, 1963-72, Christian Century mag., Chgo., 1972-99, sr. contbg. editor, 1999—. Author: Church and Cinema, 1971, Three European Directors, 1973, Winning the War, Losing Our Soul, 1991, Hidden Treasures: Searching for God in Modern Culture, 1997; author, editor: Theologians in Transition, 1981, A Century of the Century, 1987, How My Mind Has Changed, 1991. Del. Dem. Nat. Conv., 1972, 76, 80, 92, 96, 2000; mem. Dem. Nat. Com., 1976-80, Dem. State Cen. Com., 1974-86, Pres. Commn. White House Fellowships, 1976-80. Served to 1st lt. USAF, 1950-52. Mem. Alpha Tau Omega, Omicron Delta Kappa, Sigma Delta Chi. Home: 451 S Kenilworth Ave Elmhurst IL 60126-3928 Office: Christian Century 104 S Michigan Ave Ste 700 Chicago IL 60603-5905 E-mail: jimwal165@aol.com.

WALL, JANET E. assessment, testing, evaluation, and career development professional; b. Chgo., Dec. 15, 1946; d. Al Evans and Josephine (Evinskas) Simpson; m. Robert G. Gard Jr., July 26, 1984. BS, No. Ill. U., 1968; MEd, Tex. A&M U., 1970; EdS, U. Ga., 1973; EdD, Nova U., 1979. State specialist testing and evaluation Del. Dept. Pub. Instrn., Dover, 1975-79; coord. rsch. and evaluation Dept of Defense Dependents Schs., Alexandria, Va., 1979-81; dir. rsch. adminstrn. Naval Postgrad. Sch., Monterey, Calif., 1981-84; vis. prof. Johns Hopkins U., Sch. Adv. Internat. Studies, Bologna, Italy, 1984-87; dep. div. dir. Sci. Applications Internat. Corp., Monterey, 1987-89; mgr. Dept. of Def. student testing program Def. Manpower Data Ctr., 1989-97; dep. dir. Ctr. for Exec. Edn., 1997-98; asst. v.p., exec. dir. ACT Ednl. Tech. Ctr., Hunt Valley, Md., 1998-2001; pres., CEO, Sage Solutions, 1997—. Developer: (assessment program) Delaware Objective Referenced Testing Program, 1979, (career guidance program) Armed Svcs. Vocat. Aptitude Battery Career Exploration Program, 1992, ASVAB Career Exploration System, 1995, The Interest Finder, 1995; co-editor: Measuring Cup: Assessment Issues for Teachers, Counselors and Administrators, 2002. Bd. dirs. Americorps, Nat. Civilian Cmty. Corps, 1995—; bd. advisors Youth Connect, 2000—. Mem. ACA, Assn. for Assessment in Counseling (com. chair, mem. exec. coun., pres.-elect 2001-2002), Am. Vocat. Assn. (sch. to work ptnrs. 1995-98, DOD rep. to mil. liason, 1997-98), Nat. Career Devel. Assn., Sch. Sci. and Math. (officer), Phi Delta Kappa (officer, co-chair joint com. testing practices). Avocations: travel, jogging, walking, skiing. Home: 3053 Forest Way Pebble Beach CA 93953-2904 Office: 300 King Farm Blvd Ste 300 Rockville MD 20850-5920 E-mail: jwall@miis.edu.

WALL, KENNETH E., JR. lawyer; b. Beaumont, Tex., Apr. 6, 1944; s. Kenneth E. and W. Geraldine (Peoples) W.; m. Marjorie Lee Hughes, Dec. 21, 1968; children— Barbara, Elizabeth, Kenneth. Grad. Lamar U., 1966, U. Tex.-Austin, 1969. Bar: Tex. 1969, U.S. Supreme Ct. 1979. Asst. city atty., Beaumont, 1969-73, city atty., 1973-84; with firm Olson & Olson, Houston, 1984— ; dir. Tex. Mcpl. League Ins. Trust, 1979-84, vice chmn., 1983-84; counsel S.E. Tex. Regional Planning Commn., 1974, 76. Active Boy Scouts Am., Girl Scouts U.S.A. Mem. Nat. Inst. Mcpl. Law Officers (chmn. com. on local govt. pers. 1979-81, 82-84), State Bar Tex., Tex. City Attys. Assn. (pres. 1982-83), Jefferson County Bar Assn. (dir. 1975-77), Houston Bar Assn., Phi Delta Phi. Methodist. E-mail: kwall@olson-and-olson.com Office: 333 Clay St Houston TX 77002-4000

WALL, LARRY D. financial economist; b. Grand Forks, N.D., Sept. 6, 1956; s. Robert C. and Doreen A. (Roy) W.; m. Kim M. Bryngleson, June 30, 1979. BSBA, U. N.D., 1978; PhD, U. N.C., 1983. CPA, Ga. Staff economist Fed. Res. Bank Atlanta, 1982-89, rsch. officer, 1989—. Adj. asst. prof. econs. Emory U., Atlanta, 1985-87, adj. prof. fin., 1989—. Contbr. articles to profl. jours. Mem. Am. Econ. Assn., Am. Fin. Assn., Fin. Mgmt. Assn. Office: Fed Res Bank Atlanta 104 Marietta St NW Atlanta GA 30303-2702

WALL, LLOYD L. geological engineer; b. Jerome, Idaho, Feb. 2, 1936; s. Lloyd and Ola (Buck) W.; m. Myrna Bradshaw, Aug. 25, 1954; children: Jeffrey B., Julie, Neil S., Charlene, Gail, Matthew W., Suzzane, Michael L., Connie. AS in Chemistry, Coll. Eastern Utah, 1956; BS in Geology, Brigham Young U., 1958. Pres., owner Cons. Geologist, Salt Lake City and Brigham City, 1958—; plant mgr. Thiokol, Brigham City, Utah, 1958-66; mgr. ops. Sealcraft, Salt Lake City, 1966-68; mgr. programs Eaton-Kenway, Bountiful, Utah, 1968-76; pres., owner HydraPak, Inc., Salt Lake City, 1976-86; pres. Kolt Mining Co., 1979—; owner Lloyd L. Wall & Assocs., 1986—. Author: Seal Technology, 1993; developer largest rocket motor vacuum casting system in free world, only high pressure water reclaimation system for solid propellant rocket motors in free world, only acceptable seal mfg. process for NASA Space Shuttle rocket motor. Vol. tchr. Alta Acad., Salt Lake City, 1983—. Served as sgt. N.G., 1954-62. Mem. Geol. Soc. Am., Utah Geol. Assn. Republican. Mem. Lds Ch. Avocations: hunting, fishing, mountain climbing, photography, flying. Home: PO Box 841739 Hildale UT 84784-1739 Office: PO Box 841739 Hildale UT 84784-1739

WALL, M. DANNY, financial services company executive; BArch, N.D. State U., 1963. Exec. dir. Urban Renewal Agy., Fargo, N.D., 1964-71, Salt Lake City Redevel. Agy., 1971-75; dir. legis. Office U.S. Senator Jake Garn, Washington, 1975-78; minority staff dir. Senate Com. for Banking, Housing and Urban Affairs, 1979-80, staff dir., 1980-86, Rep. staff dir., 1987; chmn. Fed. Home Loan Bank Bd./Fed. Home Loan Mortgage Corp., 1987-89; dir. Office Thrift Supervision (formerly Fed. Home Loan Bank Bd.), 1989-90; fin. svcs. cons., 1990—; sr. v.p. Dougherty Funding LLC, 1997—. Bd. dirs. Escrow Bank USA. E-mail: dwall@dfg-companies.com.

WALL, MARK EMANUEL, banker, engineer, consultant; b. N.Y.C., Mar. 12, 1937; s. Jacob Bernard and Eva (Goldstein) W.; m. Diane Nachbar, Dec. 5, 1962; children: Michael Edward, Stephen Philip. BEE cum laude, CCNY, 1957; M in Engring., Moore Sch., 1962; postgrad., N.Y.U., 1962-68. Registered profl. engr., N.J., N.Y. With tech. staff RCA Labs., Astro Elec. Div., Princeton, N.J., 1957-62; dir. R&D Computer Scis. Corp., Paramus, N.J., 1962-75; pres. Tech. Fin. Svcs., Fair Lawn, 1975-80; dir. digital sys. Western Union Telegraph co., Upper Saddle River, 1977-81; v.p. Chase Manhattan Bank N.a., N.Y.C., 1981-87, NYNEX Corp., White Plains, N.Y., 1987-94; v.p. engring. NYNEX Allink Co.; v.p., chief tech. The Data Group; dir. network mgmt. engring. Info. Sys. Group; prin. ALLMARK Internat., Ltd., 1994—. Vis. assoc. prof. Stevens Inst. Tech., Hoboken, N.J., 1979-81; adv. bd. Bramson ORT Inst., N.Y.C., 1980-84. Trustee Radburn Assn., Fair Lawn, 1981-85, pres. bd. trustees, 1985. Mem. IEEE, Eta Kappa Nu. Office: ALLMARK Internat Ltd PO Box 773 Fair Lawn NJ 07410-0773 E-mail: allmarkint@hotmail.com.

WALL, MATTHEW J., JR. surgeon, scientist; b. June 22, 1958; s. Matthew J. and Anne V. W.; m. Barbara M. Wall; children: Christopher Matthew, Patrick Joseph. BS, Rice U., Houston, 1980; MD, Baylor Coll. Medicine, Houston, 1984. Diplomate Am. Bd. Surgery, Am. Bd. Thoracic Surgeons, Am. Bd. Surg. Critical Care. Resident gen. surgery Baylor Affiliated Hosp., Houston, 1984-89, resident cardiothoracic surgery, 1989-91; asst. prof. surgery Baylor Coll. Medicine, 1991-95, assoc. prof. surgery, 1995—, dep. program dir. thoracic surgery residency, 1999—; dir. trauma and critical care svcs. Ben Taub Gen. Hosp., 1993-99; program dir. surg. critical care residency Baylor Coll. Medicine, 1999—; dep. chief surgery Ben Taub Gen. Hosp., 1993—, exec. dir. trauma and critical care, 2000—; chief thoracic surgery Ben Taub Gen. Hosp. , 2000—. Contbr. chpts. to books, articles to jours. Fellow ACS ACS COT (chair south Tex. 1994-2001), Am. Assn. Surgery Trauma, Soc. Thoracic Surgeons; mem. AAAS, Assn. Advancement Med. Instrumentation, Assn. Academic Surgeons, Tex. Surg. Soc., Harris County Med. Soc. Office: Baylor Coll Medicine One Baylor Plz Houston TX 77030

WALL, ROBERT ANTHONY, JR. lawyer; b. Hartford, Conn., Mar. 3, 1945; s. Robert Anthony and Eileen (Fitzgerald) W.; children: Andrea, Melanie, Victoria, Robert, Natalie; m. Diana M. Wall. BA, Georgetown U., Washington, 1968; JD, Am. U., Washington, 1973. Bar: Conn. 1974, U.S. Ct. Appeals (D.C. cir.) 1974, U.S. Dist. Ct. Conn. 1974, U.S. Supreme Ct. 1977. Ptnr. Wall, Wall & Frauenhofer, Torrington, Conn., 1974-87; pvt. practice, 1987—. Mem. State of Conn. Rep. Ctrl. Com., 1976-79. Mem. Conn. Trial Lawyers Assn. (bd. govs. 1984-86), Ct. Washington #67 Foresters of Am. (trustee 1988—). Roman Catholic. Home: 55 Quail Run Torrington CT 06790-2550 Office: 8 Church St Torrington CT 06790-5247 Fax: 860-496-0128. E-mail: wallgawrych@yahoo.com.

WALL, ROBERT J. writer, researcher; b. N.Y.C., June 1, 1936; s. Joseph L. and Kathleen W. BA, CCNY, 1978; diploma, N.Y. Sch. Interior Design, 1995. Archtl. renderer ann. announcement circulars N.Y. Soc. Archs., 1960s. With U.S. Army, 1955-57, ret. Mem. Disable Am. Vets. (life). Roman Catholic. Avocations: reading, writing, collecting books, collecting art work. Home: 12401 Davis Blvd Fort Myers FL 33905-1701

WALL, ROBERT THOMPSON, secondary school educator; b. Luray, Va., May 31, 1943; s. Robert Alexander and Mary Ann (Coffman) W.; m. Sarah S. Wall, Aug. 19, 1967; children: Melissa Coffman, Jennifer Grey. BA, Va. Poly. Inst. and State U., 1966; MA, Radford (Va.) U., 1971; postgrad., U. Fla., 1978. Tchr. instrumental and choral music Halifax County Schs., Halifax, Va.; tchr. instrumental music Montgomery County Schs., Christiansburg; chmn. fine arts dept. Christiansburg Middle Sch., 1991-99; fine arts supr. Montgomery County Sch. Dist., 1999—. Judge, clinician and adjudicator for marching and concert bands; curriculum and instrn. clin. affiliate Va. Poly. Inst. and State U., Blacksburg, Radford (Va.) U.; clinician, guest condr. for mid-Atlantic band camps Ferrum Coll., Va.; guest condr. all-dist. bands in Va., N.C., S.C. Composer: Published Windsor Portrait, 1990, Adagio for horn and piano, 1982, Nocturne for flute and piano, 1987, Royal Brigade, 1988, Prelude and tarantelle, 1991, An American Tattoo, 1994; compositions commd. by Va. State Symphony Orch., Charlotte (N.C.) Mecklenburg County Schs., Rural Retreat (Va.) H.S., Va. Dist. VI and Dist. V Band Dirs. Assn.; music performed at Va. Music Educators Conf., 1990, 95, 97, Midwest Band Conv., Chgo., 1990, Finland Radio, 1993, Great Britain, 1993, 94, France, 1995. Recipient Young composers award Va. Music Clubs, 1960, Va. Govs. Sch. Presdl. citation, 1990, 92, Teaching award Halifax County Schs., 1972. Mem. ASCAP, Music Educators Nat. Conf., Nat. Band Assn., Va. Music Educators Assn. (exec. bd.), Va. Band and Orch. Dirs. Assn. (instrumental chmn. dist. VI), Modern Music Masters (life, past adv. coun., exec. bd.), Phi Beta Mu, Phi Delta Kappa. Home: 2810 Mt Vernon Ln Blacksburg VA 24060-8121 E-mail: r.wall4@mail.mcps.org.

WALL, SONJA ELOISE, nurse administrator; b. Santa Cruz, Calif., Mar. 28, 1938; d. Ray Theothornton and Reva Mattie (Wingo) W.; m. Edward Gleason Holmes, Aug. 1959 (div. Jan. 1968); children: Deborah Lynn, Lance Edward; m. John Aspesi, Sept. 1969 (div. 1977); children: Sabrina Jean, Daniel John; m. Kenneth Talbot LaBoube, Nov. 1, 1978 (div. 1989); 1 child, Tiffany Amber; m. Charles Borsic, July 2002. BA, San Jose Jr. Coll., 1959; BS, Madonna Coll., 1967; student, U. Mich., 1968-70; postgrad., Wayne State U., 1967-68. RN, Calif., Mich., Colo. Staff nurse Santa Clara Valley Med. Ctr., San Jose, Calif., 1959-67, U. Mich. Hosp., Ann Arbor, 1967-73, Porter and Swedish Med. Hosp., Denver, 1973-77, Laurel Grove Hosp., Castro Valley, Calif., 1977-79, Advent Hosp., Ukiah, 1984-86; motel owner LaBoube Enterprises, Fairfield, Point Arena, Willits, 1979—; staff nurse Northridge Hosp., L.A., 1986-87, Folsom State Prison, Calif., 1987; co-owner, mgr. nursing registry Around the Clock Nursing Svc., Ukiah, 1985—; critical care staff nurse Kaiser Permanente Hosp., Sacramento, 1986-89; nurse Snowline Hospice, 1989-92; carepoint home care and travel nurse Hosp. Staffing Svcs. Inc., Placerville, Calif., 1992-94, interim home health nurse, 1994-95; nurse Finders Home Health Care, 1996; owner Sunshine Manor Resdl. Care Home, Placerville, Calif., 1995—, Rainbow Manor Residential Care Home, 2000. Owner Royal Plantation Petites Miniature Horse Farm. Contbr. articles to profl. jours. Leader Coloma 4-H, 1987-91; mem. mounted divsn. El Dorado County Search and Rescue, 1991-93; docent Calif. Marshall Gold Discovery State Hist. Park, Coloma, Calif. Mem. AACN, NAFE, Oncology Nurses Assn., Soc. Critical Care Medicine, Am. Heart Assn. (CPR trainer, recipient awards), Calif. Bd. RNs, Calif. Nursing Rev., Calif. Critical Care Nurses, Soc. Critical Care Nurses, Alzheimers Aid Soc. No. Calif., Am. Motel Assn. (beautification and remodeling award 1985), Nat. Hospice Nurses Assn., Cmty. Residential Care Assn. Calif., Soroptimist Internat. Calif., Am. Miniature Horse Assn. (winner nat. grand championship 1981-83, 85, 89), DAR (Jobs Daus. hon. mem.), C. of C. of El Dorado County, Kiwanis, Cameron Park Country Club. Republican. Episcopalian. Avocations: pinto, paint and miniature horses, real estate development, swimming. Home and Office: Sunshine Manor Residental Care Home & Around Clock Nursing 3112 Washington St Placerville CA 95667-5825 Fax: (530) 6222233. E-mail: sunshinemanor@directcon.net.

WALL, SUSAN LEE, artist; b. Cleve., Feb. 18, 1950; d. Jim and Florence (Strobl) W. BFA, Ohio U., 1972, MFA, 1974; fine arts degree (hon.), Cleve. Inst. Art, 1988. One-woman shows include Bonfoey, Cleve., 1975, 77, 79, 81, 83, 85, 87, 89, 91, Gallery 200, Columbus, Ohio, 1975, 77, 84, 86, Sandusky (Ohio) Cultural Ctr., 1978, 90, 93, Foster Harmon Gallery, Sarasota, Fla., 1982, 84, 86, 89, 91, 93, Gallery Madison 90, N.Y.C., 1974, 76, 78, 80, 84, 86, 88, 90, 92, Zanesville (Ohio) Art Ctr., 1975, 86, 89, 95, Cleve. Art Inst., 1995, Holden Arboretum, Mentor, Ohio, 1993, 97, 2000, Cleve. Bot. Garden, 1989, 99, Duncan Gallery, Hudson, Ohio, 1993, 99, The Loring Gallery, Sheffield, Mass., 1994, 96, Uptown Gallery, N.Y.C., 1995, Trisolini Gallery Ohio U., Athen, 1996, Ziegenfuss Gallery of Fine Art, Sarasota, Fla., 1996, 97, Gallery East, East Hampton, N.Y., 1997, Capricorn Gallery, Bethesda, Md., 1997, Southwest Mus., L.A., 1998, 1st Ch. Gallery, Springfield, Mass., 1998, Mondak Art Ctr., Sidney, Mont., 1999, Gallery One, Cleve., 2001; represented in permanent collections Cleve. Mus. Art, Butler Inst. Am. Art, Canton Art Inst. Mus., U. Iowa Mus. Art, Cleve. Art Assn., Zanesville (Ohio) Art Mus., Marie Selby Bot. Gardens, Kennedy Mus. Am. Art, S.W. Mus., George Streeter Circulating Collection, Nat. Arts Club, Aurora Nat. Bank Collection, The Hague, The Netherlands, Mondak Hist. and Art Soc., Sidney, Kenneth Deck Ctr. for Cultural Arts, Trisolini Gallery, Southwest Mus., Mondak Heritage Ctr., others. Recipient Grumbacher Cash award, 1975, 77, Spl. Mention award Nova Print Exhbn., 1975, spl. Mention Cleve. Art Mus., 1975, 1st Pl. award Am. Nat. Miniature Show, 1975, S.J. Wallace Truman award Nat. Acad., 1975, Am. Nat. Miniature Show 1st Place award Laramie Art Guild, 1976, Alice J. Melrose Meml. award Nat. Arts Club, 1981, 1st Place Representational award City of Atlanta, 1984, Recognition award City of Atlanta, 1984, Cash award Two Flags Festival Show, 1984, Dr. Maury Leibovitz Art award, 1986, 15th Ann. Juried Show 1st Place award Mondak Heritage Ctr., 1989, Medal of Merit award Ohio U. Alumni Assn., 1993, Lenore Mills Meml. award North Platte Valley Arts Guild, 1994, H.K. Holbein award 12th ann. Nat. Miniature Exhbn., 1995, award Da Vinci Paint Co., cert. of achievement Art Gallery of Fell's Point, Balt., 1st Pl. award, Best of Show award Zanesville Art Ctr., 1997, award of excellence Chambersburg Area Coun. for Arts, 1997, 3d pl. award Miniature Painters, Sculptors and Engravers Soc., 1997, 1st pl. award Acrylic Painging, Colorado Springs, Colo., 1998, Peoples Choice award, Roswell, N.Mex., 1998, 1st pl. award, Simons Island, Ga., 1998, 2d pl. award & 2 hon. mention awards, Sidney, Mont., 1998, 1st prize award, Omaha, 1998, Spl. Mention award, Casper, Wyo., 1999, 1st place award, Mondak Heritage Nat. Miniature Exhbn, 1999, Gallery One, Mentor, Ohio, 2000, El Dorado Gallery 18th Ann. juried show, 2001, Best in Show award Trinidad Area Arts Coun., 2000, many others. Mem. Nat. Soc. Painters in Casein and Acrylic (Grumbacher award 1977), Nat. Historic Preservation, Am. Artists Profl. League, Inc., Am. Craft Coun., Allied Artists of Am., Inc., Victorian Soc. Am., New Orgn. Visual Arts, Knickerbocker Artists, Catharine Lorillard Wolfe Art Club, The Minature Painters, Gravers, Sculptors Soc. of Washington, D.C., The Minature Art Soc. of Fla.Audubon Trust, Garrison Art Ctr., The Cider Painters of Am. Home and Office: 11 Riverside Dr Apt 8je New York NY 10023-2519

WALLA, CATHERINE ANNE, nursing administrator, educator; b. Chgo., Oct. 18, 1948; d. Louis Bernard and Mary Louise W.; m. Robert Joseph Murphy, July 2, 1972 (div. Oct. 1979); 1 child, Meghan Anne. BS, Loyola U., 1971, BSN, MA, 1978; M of Nursing, UCLA, 1988. RN Calif. Staff nurse Wadsworth VA Hosp., L.A., 1978-79; charge, staff nurse UCLA Med. Ctr., 1979-81; clin. rsch. nurse specialist L.A. County & U. So. Calif. Med. Ctr., 1981-84; asst. prof. Bethune-Cookman Coll., Daytona Beach, Fla., 1984-86; dir. perinatal rsch. L.A. County & U. Soc. Calif., 1986-90; coord. ob-gyn. rsch. Cedars-Sinai Med. Ctr., L.A., 1990—; asst. clin. prof. UCLA Sch. Nursing, 1990—. Cons. in field. Co-author: (chpts.) Maternity Nursing, 1991, 97, Diagnostic Medical Sonography, 1992, 97, Protocols for High Risk Pregnancy, 1996, Genetic Disorders and Pregnancy Outcome, 1997; Fetal Therapy, 1999; contbr. articles to profl. jours. Rsch. grantee Bethune Cookman Coll., 1985. Mem. APHA, Am. Inst. Ultrasound Medicine, Monterey Bay Aquarium, Long Beach Aquarium. Avocations: herptology, salt water aquariums, hiking, fictional writing, multi-cultural cooking. Home: 29044 Lake Dr Agoura Hills CA 91301-2947 Office: Cedars-Sinai Med Ctr Dept Ob-Gyn 8700 Beverly Blvd Los Angeles CA 90048-1865

WALLACE, ALICEANNE, civic worker; b. Chgo., Sept. 28, 1925; d. Alexander and Mary (Zurek) Zalac; m. Henry Clay Wallace, Jr., Apr. 10, 1948; children: Laura Lillian Wallace Bergin, Christine Claire Wallace Stockwell. Student, St. Teresa Coll., Winona, Minn., 1944-45, DePaul U., 1946-48, North Tex. State U., 1971, 72. City sec. City of Southlake, Tex., 1969-77; pres. AZW, Inc., real estate sales, Roanoke, 1977-84. Mem. Trinity Valley Mental Health-Mental Retardation, Ft. Worth, 1971-72; chmn. ways and means Tex. Silver-Haired Legis., Austin, 1986-90, parliamentarian, 1991-94; treas. TSHL Found., 1990-92, pres., 1992-96; sec., bd. dirs. Sr. Citizens Activities, Inc., Temple, Tex., 1989-90; sec. CTCOG Area Agy. on Aging, Citizens Adv. Comm. Bd., Belton, Tex., 1991; bd. dirs. Tex. Dept. on Aging, Austin, 1991-97; chmn. collaborative com. Tex. Dept. on Aging and Am. Assn. Ret. Persons, 1997098; congl. sr. intern U.S. Ho. of Reps., Washington, 1991; pres. Tri-County Tex. Dem. Women, 1990-94; congl. del. White House Conf. on Aging, 1995; del. Nat. Silver Haired Congress, Inaugural Convention, 1997; mem. Tex. Dem. Exec. Com. Senatorial Dist. 24, 1994-98; chair SDEC Grassroots Organizing com., 1996-98; adv. com. chair Ctrl. Tex. Coun. of Govt. Area Agy. on Aging Citizens, 1998-2000; vice chmn. Bell County Dem. Party, 1999-; pub. rels. ofcl. Tex. Dem. Women, 1999-. Mem. Am. Assn. Ret. Persons (legis. chmn. Temple chpt. 1990-94, regional coord. VOTE 1991-96, assoc. state coord. 1996-2001, co-state coord., 2001-02), Tex. Fedn. Women's Clubs (state legis. chmn. 1990-92, resolutions chmn. 1992-94, parliamentarian Capitol dist. 1990-92), North Ctrl. Tex. Secy. Assn. (pres. 1976), City Fedn. Women's Clubs (corr. sec. 1991-92, records custodian 1991-98), Triangle Forum (pres. 1992-94), Daus. Republic Tex. (assoc.), Internat. Inst. Mcpl. Clks. (state cert.), Epsilon Eta Phi. Home: 5596 W FM 436 Belton TX 76513

WALLACE, ANDREW GROVER, physician, educator, medical school dean; b. Columbus, Ohio, Mar. 22, 1935; s. Richard Homes and Eleanor Bradley (Grover) W.; m. Kathleen Barrick Altvater, June 22, 1957; children: Stephen Andrew, Michael Bradley, Kathleen Claude. BS, Duke U., 1958, MD, 1959. Diplomate Am. Bd. Internal Medicine. Intern medicine Duke U. Hosp., Durham, N.C., 1959-60, asst. resident, 1960-61; fellow NIH, Bethesda, Md., 1961-63; chief resident medicine Duke U., Durham, 1963-64, asst. prof., 1965-67, assoc. prof., 1967-71, chief, divsn. cardiology, 1970-81, prof. medicine, 1971—, Walter Kempner prof. medicine, 1973; vice chancellor health affairs, chief exec. officer Duke U. Hosp., 1981-87; v.p. health affairs Duke U., 1987-90; dean Dartmouth Med. Sch., Hanover, N.H., 1990-98. V.p. for health affairs Dartmouth Coll., 1990-98; cons. program project com., cardiology adv. com. and pharmacology study sect. Nat. Heart and Lung Inst., cardiovascular merit rev. bd. VA. Co-author: (with R.S. Williams) Biological Effects of Physical Activity, 1989; mem. editl. bd. Am. Jour. of Physiology, 1965-70, Jour. of Pharmacology and Exptl. Therapeutics, 1966-71, Jour. of Molecular and Cellular Cardiology, 1970-75, Jour. of Clin. Investigation, 1973-78. Pres. Durham YMCA Swim Assn., 1975-77; bd. dirs. Durham C. of C.; co-chmn. Nat. Jr. Olympics, 1976. Markle scholar, 1965-70 Mem. AAAS, AAMC, NAS, Inst. of Medicine, Am. Fedn. for Clin. Rsch. (coun.), Am. Soc. Internal Medicine, Am. Soc. Clin. Investigation, Am. Heart Assn. (coun. on clin. cardiology), Am. Physiol. Soc., Biomed. Engring. Soc., Soc. Med. Adminstrs., Assn. Am. Med. Colls. (adv. com. electronic residency 1992-94, generalist initiative 1993-95, mission and orgn. 1994-2000, exec. coun. 1996-98), N.H. Med. Soc., So. Soc. Clin. Investigation. Home: 2112 Faucette Mill Rd Hillsborough NC 27278-7553

WALLACE, ANTHONY FRANCIS CLARKE, anthropologist, educator; b. Toronto, Ont., Can., Apr. 15, 1923; s. Paul A.W. and Dorothy Eleanor (Clarke) W.; m. Betty Louise Shillott, Dec. 1, 1942; children: Anthony, Daniel, Sun Ai, Samuel, Cheryl, Joseph. BA, U. Pa., 1948, MA, 1949, PhD, 1950; L.H.D. (hon.), U. Chgo., 1983. Instr. anthropology Bryn Mawr Coll., 1948-50; asst.

instr. anthropology U. Pa., research sec. Behavioral Research Council, 1951-55; research asst. prof. U. Pa., 1952-55, vis. assoc. prof., 1955-61, prof., 1961—, chmn. dept., 1961-71, Geraldine R. Segal prof. Am. social thought, 1980-83, Univ. prof. anthropology, 1983-88, prof. emeritus, 1988—. Sr. research assoc. anthropology Eastern Pa. Psychiat. Inst., 1955-60, dir. clin. research, 1960-61, med. research scientist, III, 1961-80; mem. tech. adv. com. N.J. Psychiat. Inst., 1958; cons. disaster studies NRC, 1956-57; cons. Phila. Housing Authority, 1952; mem. research adv. com. Commonwealth Mental Health Research Found., 1960-61, U.S. Office Edn., 1965-68; mem. behavioral scis. study sect. NIMH, 1964-68; mem. NRC, 1963-66; mem. various adv. coms. NIMH, 1962— ; mem. social sci. adv. council NSF, 1969-72 Author: King of the Delawares: Teedyuscung, 1700-1763, 1949, Culture and Personality, 1961, rev. edit., 1970, Religion: An Anthropological View, 1966, Death and Rebirth of the Seneca, 1970, Rockdale: The Growth of an American Village in the Early Industrial Revolution, 1978, Social Context of Innovation, 1983, St. Clair, 1987, The Long, Bitter Trail, 1993, Jefferson and the Indians, 1999. Bd. mgrs. Founds. Fund for Research in Psychiatry, 1969-71. Served AUS, 1942-45. Recipient Bancroft prize in Am. History, 1979, Dexter prize in History of Technology, 1989, Caroline Bancroft prize in history, 2000; Guggenheim fellow, 1978-79 Fellow Am. Anthrop. Assn. (pres. 1971-72),; mem. Nat. Acad. Scis., Am. Philos. Soc., Am. Acad. Arts and Scis. Home: 614 Convent Rd Aston PA 19014-1208 Office: Univ PA Dept Anthropology 33rd and Spruce Sts Philadelphia PA 19104

WALLACE, ARTHUR, JR. retired college dean; b. Muskogee, Okla., June 12, 1939; s. Arthur and Edna (Collins) W.; m. Claudina Young, Oct. 4, 1969; children: Dwayne, Jon, Charles. BS, Langston U., 1960; MS, Okla. State U., Stillwater, 1962, PhD, 1964. Dir. commodity rsch. Gen. Foods Corp., White Plains, N.Y., 1964-67; v.p., sr. economist Merrill Lynch & Lionel D. Edie & Co., N.Y.C., 1968-71; econ. cons. Wall St. fin. instns. Group IV Econs., 1972-76; mgr. U.S. and Can. econs. Internat. Paper Co., 1976-78, chief economist, 1978-82, dir. corp. affairs and policy analysis, 1982-83, corp. sec. Purchase, N.Y., 1983-87, v.p., corp. sec., 1987-93; pres. Internat. Paper Co. Found., 1983-93; dean coll. bus. San Francisco State U., 1993-98; ret. Home: 80 E Hartsdale Ave Apt 617 Hartsdale NY 10530-2829

WALLACE, BARBARA BROOKS, writer; b. Soochow, China, Dec. 3, 1922; came to U.S., 1938; d. Otis Frank and Nicia Brooks; m. James Wallace Jr., Feb. 27, 1954; 1 child, James V. BA, UCLA, 1945. Script sec. Foote, Cone & Belding, Hollywood, Calif., 1946-49; tchr. Wright MacMahon Secretarial Sch., Beverly Hills, 1949-50; head fund drive Commerce and Industry Divsn. ARC, San Francisco, 1950-52. Author: Claudia, 1969 (Nat. League of Am. Pen Women Juvenile Book award 1970), Andrew the Big Deal, 1970, The Trouble with Miss Switch, 1971, Victoria, 1973, Can Do, Missy Charlie, 1974, The Secret Summer of L.E.B. (Nat. League of Am. Pen Women Juvenile Book award 1974), Julia and the Third Bad Thing, 1975, Palmer Patch, 1976, Hawkins, 1977, Peppermints in the Parlor, 1980 (William Allen White award 1983), The Contest Kid Strikes Again, 1980, Hawkins and the Soccer Solution, 1981, Miss Switch to the Rescue, 1981, Hello, Claudia, 1982, Claudia and Duffy, 1982, The Barrel in the Basement, 1985, Argyle, 1987, 92, Perfect Acres, Inc., 1988, The Twin in the Tavern, 1993 (Edgar award Mystery Writers Am. 1994), Cousins in the Castle, 1996, Sparrows in the Scullery, 1997 (Edgar award 1998), Ghosts in the Gallery, 2000, Secret in St. Something, 2001, Miss Switch Online, 2002. Mem. Children's Book Guild of Washington, Alpha Phi. Episcopalian. Home and Office: 2708 George Mason Pl Alexandria VA 22305-1620 E-mail: jimbob4@comcast.net.

WALLACE, BARBARA LYNN, writer, vocalist; b. Milledgeville, Ga., Oct. 14, 1964; d. Nathaniel Wallace Sr. and Annie Ruth Wallace. Grad., Barton Coll., 1995. Vocalist In the Heat of the Night (TV program), Conyers, Ga., 1987—89. Author: (children's book) Kids-The Life!, 1999; composer: numerous songs. With U.S. Army, 1992—95. Mem.: Assn. for Musicians, Song Writers Assn. Avocations: writing sitcoms, writing music, writing movies, acting, singing.

WALLACE, BECKY WHITLEY, protective services official; BA in Criminal Justice, Montgomery C.C. Police officer City of Troy (N.C.), 1974-75; deputy sheriff Montgomery County (N.C.), 1975-78, 82-94; alcohol law enforcement agt. N.C. Dept. Crime Control & Pub. Safety, Greensboro, 1978-82; U.S. marshal N.C., 1994—. Recipient Leadership N.C. Stanley Frank award, Breaking the Glass Ceiling award Nat. Ctr. Women in Policing; named Disting. Woman of N.c., Coun. Women. Mem. Fed. Law Enforcement Officers' Assn., N.C. Women's Law Enforcement Assn., Nat. Sheriffs Assn., N.C. Sheriff's Assn., Montgomery County Law Enforcement Assn., Profl. Women's Assn. Office: US Post Office 324 W Market St Greensboro NC 27401-2544

WALLACE, BETTY JEAN, elementary school educator, lay minister; b. Denison, Tex., Dec. 5, 1927; d. Claude Herman and Pearl Victoria (Freels) Moore; m. Billy Dean McKneely, Sept. 2, 1950 (div. Nov. 1964); children: Rebecca Lynn, Paul King, David Freels, John Walker, Philip Andrew McKneely. Student, Tulane U., 1947; BA, Baylor U., 1949; postgrad., U. Houston, 1949-50, 74, 81, Rocky Mountain Bible Inst., 1959, U. Colo., 1969-70, U. No. Colo., 1965, 68, 72, U. St. Thomas, 1992, Autonomous U. Guadalajara, summer 1993; MEd, Houston Bapt. U., 1985. Cert. life profl. elem., high sch., life profl. reading specialist, secondary field ESL tchr., Tex. Tchr. Galena Park (Tex.) Ind. Sch. Dist., 1949-50, 52-53, 72-98, Corpus Christi (Tex.) Independent Sch. Dist., 1950-51, Denver Pub. Schs., 1953-54, 63-72, Wackenhut Cleveland (Tex.) Correctional Ctr., 1999—. Author: The Holy Spirit Today, 1989, Our God of Infinite Variety, 1991, God Speaks in a Variety of Ways, 1991. Sunday sch. tchr. So. Bapt. Conv. chs., Tex., 1946-50, Denver, 1952-56; tchr. kindergarten Emmanuel Bapt. Ch., Denver, 1956-59, 60-63; missionary, Queretaro, Mex., 1977, 78; mem. Rep. Senatorial Inner Circle, Washington, 1989-91, The Pres.'s Club, 2002, Round Table for Ronald Reagan, Washington, 1989-90; helper Feed the Poor, Houston, 1983-85; active Suicide Prevention, Houston, 1973-76, Literacy, Houston, 1978-81; rep. NEA, Denver, 1966-72; mem. Retirement Com., Denver, 1970-72; bd. advisors Oliver North, 1994. Recipient Rep. Senatorial medal of freedom, 1994, Rep. Senatorial medal of Victory, Justice, Freedom and Liberty, 2002; grantee NSF, 1969-70. Mem. Tex. Classroom Tchrs. Assn. (officer rep., pres. Galena Park chpt. 1988-91), Delta Alpha Pi (pres. Waco chpt. 1948-49), Alpha Epsilon Delta. Republican. Avocations: writing, archeology, gardening, reading, gem/jewelry collecting and designing. Home: 14831 Anoka Dr Channelview TX 77530-3201 *The love of God is spread abroad through us. We need to let our lights shine before men so they will glorify the Father.*

WALLACE, C. ELIZABETH MCFARLAND, retired association director; b. Cumberland, Md., Apr. 2, 1914; d. Frank Russel and Maude Sabine (McFarland) McFarland; m. David Henry Wallace, Aug. 17, 1938; children: David Henry Jr., Stephen McFarland, Douglas Cecil; m. Charles F. Pratt, Oct. 12, 1991 (dec. Dec. 1996). BS summa cum laude, U. Md., 1936, MA, 1937. Cert. tchr., Md. Tchr. math. and sci. Annapolis (Md.) Jr. and Sr. H.S., 1952-59; exec. dir. Shellfish Inst. N.Am., Annapolis and Sayville, N.Y., 1960-72; account exec. Manna Fin. Assn., Fairfax, Va., 1972-74; exec. dir. Marine Tech. Soc., Washington, 1974-75; sr. program analyst NSF, 1975-85. Rschr. Chesapeake Biol. Lab., Solomons Island, Md., 1931-41. Editor: (biweekly newspaper) Shellfish Soundings, 1959-71. Co-founder LWV, Annapolis, 1940—, recorder Leisure World, Silver Spring, Md., 1995—; dir. Mut. 16, Leisure World, 1986-88, treas.; rep. Mut. 16 to Leisure World Comty. Coun.; life mem. Md. PTA; active Meals on Wheels; lobbyist LWV, Anne Arundel County Tchrs. Assn., shellfish industry. Fellow U. Md., 1936. Mem. Am. Fisheries Soc. Democrat. Methodist. Avocations: reading, dancing, traveling. Home: Leisure World 15501 Prince Frederick Way Silver Spring MD 20906-1318

WALLACE, CATHERINE MILES, writer; b. Chgo., Feb. 8, 1950; d. John A. and Mary J. Miles; m. Warren H. Wallace; children: Mark, Carolyn, Timothy. BA, U. Detroit, 1972; MA, Northwestern U., 1973; PhD, U. Mich., 1977. Asst. prof. Northwestern U., Evanston, Ill., 1976-82; freelance writer, 1982—; writer in residence Seabury-Western Theol. Sem., Evanston, 2001—. Author: The Design of Biographia Literaria, 1982, For Fidelity, 1998, Dance Lessons, 1999, Motherhood in the Balance, 2000. Office: Seabury Western Sem 2122 N Sheridan Evanston IL 60201

WALLACE, DON, JR. law educator; b. Vienna, Austria, Apr. 23, 1932; s. Don and Julie (Baer) Wallace; m. Daphne Mary Wickham, 1963; children: Alexandra Creed, Sarah Anne, Benjamin James. BA with high honors, Yale U., 1953; LL.B. cum laude, Harvard U., 1957. Bar: N.Y. 1957, D.C. 1978. Assoc. Fleischmann, Jaeckle, Stokes and Hitchcock, N.Y.C., 1959-60, Paul, Weiss, Rifkind, Wharton and Garrison, N.Y.C., 1957-58, 60-62; rsch. asst. to faculty mem. Harvard Law Sch., Cambridge, Mass., 1958-59; regional legal adv. Middle East AID, Dept. State, 1963-65, dep. asst. gen. counsel, 1965-66; assoc. prof. law Georgetown U. Law Ctr., Washington, 1966-71, prof., 1971—; chmn. Internat. Law Inst., 1969—. Cons. AID, 1966-70, UN Centre on Transnat. Corps., 1977-78; counsel Wald, Harkrader & Ross, Washington, 1978-86, Arnold & Porter, 1986-89, Shearman & Sterling, 1989-98, Morgan, Lewis & Bockius, 1998—; legal advisor State of Qatar, 1979-82; chmn. adv. com. on tech. and world trade Office of Tech. Assessment, U.S. Congress, 1976-79; mem. Sec. of State's Adv. Com. on Pvt. Internat. Law, 1979—; mem. U.S. del. UN Conf. on State Succession in Respect of Treaties, Vienna, 1978; mem. U.S. del. new internat. econ. order working group UN Commn. Internat. Trade Law, Vienna, 1981—; vis. com. Harvard Law Sch., 1996-97; mem. panel of judges World Trade Orgn., 1996-2000. Co-author: Internat. Business and Economics: Law and Policy; author: International Regulation of Multinational Corporations, 1976, Dear Mr. President: The Needed Turnaround in America's International Economic Affairs, 1984; editor: A Lawyer's Guide to International Business Transactions, 1977-87; contbr. numerous articles on internat. trade and law to profl. jours., books revs. on law and bus. to profl. jours. Coord. Anne Arundel County (Md.) Dem. Nat. Com., 1972-79; sec. Chesapeake Found., 1972-73; nat. chmn. Law Profs. for Bush and Quayle, 1988, 92, for Dole and Kemp, 1996; v.p., bd. govs. UNIDROIT Found., Rome, 1997—.$Dat. co-chmn. Law Profs. for Fulbright fellow, 1967, Eisenhower Exch. fellow, 1976. Mem. ABA (chmn. sect. internat. law 1978-79), Ho. of Dels. 1982-84), Am. Law Inst., Internat. Law Assn., Shaybani Soc. of Internat. Law (v.p.), Ctrl. and Ea. European Law Initiative (mem. adv. bd.), Cosmos Club, Met. Club. Home: 2800 35th St NW Washington DC 20007-1411 Office: Georgetown U Law Ctr 600 New Jersey Ave NW Washington DC 20001-2022

WALLACE, DONALD JOHN, III, rancher, former pest control company executive; b. Houston, May 17, 1941; s. D.J. Jr. and Doris Jill (Gano) W.; m. Patricia Anne McShane, Sept. 3, 1964 (div. 1984); children: Donald John IV, Megan; m. Nena Jo Isenhower, June 1, 1985 (div. 1989); 1 child, Andrew; m. Kay Fulkerson, May 31, 1997. BBA in Mktg., Texas A&M U., 1963. Regional sales dir. Orkin Exterminating Co., Inc., Dallas, 1977-79, br. mgr., 1979-80, dist. mgr., 1980-83, comml. region mgr., 1983-85, regional sales dir., 1985-86; owner Omega Telex, 1986-88; rancher Valley View, Tex., 1988—. Mem. Tex. Structural Pest Control Bd., Austin, 1983-84; leader Big Mineral Trail Riders Club, Boy Scouts Am.; bd. dirs. Frank Buck Zoo, Gainesville, Tex., 1997—; pres. Frank Buck Zool. Soc. Mem. Nat. Pest Control Assn., Tex. Pest Control Assn., Dallas Pest Control Assn. Republican. Roman Catholic. Avocations: hiking, fishing, hunting, skiing, horse riding. Home: 1034 Trails End Valley View TX 76272-6114

WALLACE, DOROTHY ALENE, special education administrator; b. Wright County, Mo., Sept. 11, 1942; d. Stephen Foster and Lois Alene (Breman) Dudley; widowed; children: Michael Dean Huckaby, David Lee. BS in Edn., Drury Coll., 1975, MS in Edn., 1978; Specialist in Ednl. Adminstrn., Southwest Mo. State U., 1988. Cert. tchr. and adminstr., Mo. Tchr. 3rd grade Mansfield (Mo.) R-IV Schs., 1975-78, tchr. 1st grade, 1978-85, tchr. learning disabled, 1985-89, adminstr. spl. edn., 1989-92, adminstr. spl. svcs., 1992—. Active sch. coms. on curriculum and nutrition Mansfield R-IV Schs., mem. sch./cmty. adv. coun., 1992—. Mem. Am. Salers Assn., Mo. State Tchrs. Assn., Mo. Coun. Adminstrs. of Spl. Edn., Coun. for Exceptional Children, Coun. Adminstrs. of Spl. Edn., Local Adminstrs. of Spl. Edn., Cmty. Tchrs. Assn. Avocations: raising beef cattle, writing, collecting antiques. Home: 3489 Jerico Rd Seymour MO 65746-9784

WALLACE, EDNA MARIE, paralegal; b. Indpls., July 22, 1945; d. William T. and Agnes L. (Pierce) Branson; m. James Michael Wallace; children: Penny Sue Wallace-Steele, Brandi Michael Wallace-Coffin. Paralegal Cert., Am. Inst. Paralegal Studies, Oak Brook Terrace, Ill., 1988. Paralegal, office adminstr. Baldwin & Baldwin, Danville, Ind., 1985—90; paralegal Tucker, Surface, Fehribach, Indpls., 1990—92; paralegal, office adminstr. Hebenstreit & Moberly, 1992—96; paralegal Kroger, Gardis & Regas, 1996—2002, Whitham, Hebenstreit & Zubek, LLP, 2002—. Presenter in field. Paralegal adv. bd. St. Mary of the Woods Coll., 1999—. Mem. ABA (assoc.), Nat. Fedn. Paralegal Assns. (registered paralegal), Indpls. Bar Assn. (chair paralegal exec. com. 1998-2000, 2002-, Legal Awareness com., Placement com., CLE comm., Paralegal of Yr. 1999), Ind. State Bar Assn., Ind. Paralegal Assn. (bd. dirs. legis. sect. chair, 1999—, chair ethics sect. , 2000—, Lifetime Achievement award 2002), Bus./Profl. Women, Order Eastern Star, Job's Daus. (adult leader 1986-2000, bd. dirs. ednl. found. 1997-2000), Epsilon Sigma Alpha (pres. chpt. 1988-90). Republican. Baptist. Office: Whitham Hebenstreit & Zubek LLP 151 N Delaware St # 2000 Indianapolis IN 46204 E-mail: emw@whzlaw.com.

WALLACE, EDWIN RUTHVEN, IV, psychiatrist, neuropsychiatrist psychotherapist; b. Portsmouth, Va., Mar. 10, 1950; s. Edwin Ruthven III and Laura Essie (Catron) W.; m. Laura Martin Elmore, May 13, 1972; children: Laura Martin, Edwin Ruthven V. BS cum laude, U. S.C., 1970, BA magna cum laude, 1976; MD, Med. U. S.C., 1973; MA summa cum laude, Johns Hopkins U., 1978. Diplomate Am. Bd. Psychiatry and Neurology. Intern in neurology Richland Meml. Hosp., Columbia, S.C.; resident in psychiatry and neurology William S. Hall Psychiat. Inst., 1973-75, chief resident, 1975-76; postdoctoral fellow in neuropsychiatry and hosp. psychiatry Yale U. Sch. Medicine, New Haven, 1977; postdoctoral fellow in history of science and medicine Sch. Medicine Johns Hopkins U., Balt., 1978; asst. prof. neuropsychiatry Sch. Medicine U. S.C., Columbia, 1978-80; asst. prof. psychiatry Yale U. Sch. Medicine, New Haven, 1980-82; assoc. prof., vice chmn. dept. psychiatry & health behavior Med. Coll. Ga., Augusta, 1982-87, prof. psychiatry and health behavior, 1987-95, acting chmn. Dept. Psychiatry, 1987-90; prof. social work U. Ga. Grad. Sch., Athens, 1988—; clin. prof. psychiatry and health behavior Med. Coll. Ga., 1995—; rsch. prof. bioethics and med. humanities U. S.C., 1995—, adj. prof. history, philosophy & religious studies, 1996—. Instr. in neuropsychiatry U. S.C. Sch. Medicine, 1975-76; cons. Army Health Svc. Command, U.S. Army Med. Corps, 1986-94, VA Hosps. Augusta, 1988-94; mem. history and libr. com., Am. Psychiat. Assn., Washington, 1986-89; vis. scholar Com. on Conceptual Foundations of Sci., U. Chgo., 1990. Author: Dynamic Psychiatry in Theory and Practice, 1983, Spanish edit., 1991, Freud and Anthropology: a History and Reappraisal, 1983 Japanese edit., 1993, Historiography and Causation in Psychoanalysis, 1985, Italian edit., 1991, 140 articles and chpts. in scholarly and profl. jours. and edited books and encyclopedias; sr. editor: Essays in the History of Psychiatry, 1980; mem. editl. bd. Bull. of History of Medicine, Balt., 1980-88, Second Opinion: Jour. Health, Faith and Ethics, Chgo., 1987-95, Rev. of Psychoanalytic Books, 1995-97; sr. edit. bd. Philosophy, Psychiatry and Psychology, 1993—. Trustee J.B. White Nat. Charitable Found., Augusta, 1988-98; co-capt. Inner City Soup Kitchens, Augusta, 1984-87. Recipient NEH fellowship, 1990. Mem. AAAS, AMA, Am. Hist. Assn., Am. Assn. for the History of Medicine, Am. Coll. Psychiatrists, Assn. for Advancement of Philosphy and Psychiatry (co-founder, exec. com.), Group for the Advancement of Psychiatry, Phi Beta Kappa, Alpha Epsilon Delta. Episcopalian. Home: 1829 Senate St Apt 3E Columbia SC 29201-3837 Fax: 803-777-4575.

WALLACE, ELIZABETH A. music educator; b. Crane, Tex., June 13, 1949; d. Charles Ray and Annie Lea Ellis; m. Alan Craig Wallace, Aug. 22, 1970; children: Elisa Annette West, Jesse Alan. B of Music Edn., Howard Payne U., 1971; MusM, Southwestern Bapt. Theol. Sem., 1977; PhD, Tex. Tech. U., 1990. Tchr., owner pvt. studio, Brownwood, Tex., 1972-90, Ft. Worth, 1972—90; prof. music Howard Payne U., Brownwood, 1991—. Accompanist Howard Payne U., Tex. Tech. U., Lubbock Christian U., Bapt. chs., 1971—, Tex. Bapt. Women's Choir, 1995, Tex. Bapt. All State Youth Choir, 1997; tchg. asst., adj. tchr. Tex. Tech. U., Lubbock, 1983-89; adj. tchr. Lubbock Christian U., 1986-90. Soloist, accompanist numerous recitals and concerts. Mem. Music Tchrs. Nat. Assn., Nat. Guild Piano Tchrs., Tex. Music Tchrs. Nat. Assn. (student affiliate bd. 1997-99), Creative Motion Alliance (pres. 1998-2000). Southern Baptist. Home: 3412 3d St Brownwood TX 76801 Office: Howard Payne U Sch Music 1000 Main St Brownwood TX 76801 E-mail: ewallace@hputx.edu.

WALLACE, F. BLAKE, aerospace executive, mechanical engineer; b. Phoenix, Jan. 10, 1933; BMechE, Calif. Inst. Tech., 1955; MS in Engring., Ariz. State U., 1963, PhD in Engring., 1967. Preliminary design engr. Pratt & Whitney, East Hartford, Conn., 1955-59; chief engr. advanced tech. Garrett Corp., Phoenix, 1959-80; mgr. advanced plans and programs Aircraft Engine Group GE, Evendale, Ohio, 1981-83; gen. mgr. Allison div. GM, Indpls., 1983-93, v.p., 1987-93; chmn. & CEO Allison Engine Co., Indpls., 1993-95; retired, 1995. Author numerous tech. papers. Fellow AIAA (chmn. air breathing propulsion tech. com. 1977-78, Air Breathing Propulsion award 1991), U.S. Advanced Ceramic Assn. (chmn. 1987-89).

WALLACE, FRANKLIN SHERWOOD, lawyer, director; b. Bklyn., Nov. 24, 1927; s. Abraham Charles and Jennie (Etkin) Wolowitz; m. Eleanor Ruth Pope, Aug. 23, 1953; children: Julia Diane, Charles Andrew. Student, U. Wis., 1943-45; BS cum laude, U.S. Mcht. Marine Acad., 1950; LLB, JD, U. Mich., 1953. Bar: Ill. 1954. Practice law, Rock Island, Ill.; ptnr. Winstein, Kavensky & Wallace. Asst. state's atty. Rock Island County, 1967-68; local counsel UAW at John Deere-J.I. Case Plants. Former bd. dirs. Tri City Jewish Ctr.; former trustee United Jewish Charities of Quad Cities; former bd. dirs. Blackhawk Coll. Found. Mem. ABA, Ill. Bar Assn. (chmn. jud. adv. polls com. 1979-84), Rock Island County Bar Assn., Am. Trial Lawyers Assn., Ill. Trial Lawyers Assn., Nat. Assn. Criminal Def. Lawyers, Ill. Appellate Lawyers Assn., Am. Judicature Soc., Blackhawk Coll. Found. Democrat. Jewish. Home: 3405 20th Street Ct Rock Island IL 61201-6201 Office: Rock Island Bank Bldg Rock Island IL 61201 Home: 36571 Tallowood Dr Palm Desert CA 92211 E-mail: fnewallace@aol.com.

WALLACE, GEORGE, poet, journalist; b. Hempstead, N.Y., Mar. 22, 1949; s. Theodore and Molly Wallace; m. Margaret Elizabeth Sloggatt; children: Theodore; m. Barbara Paula Tepper (div. Jan. 1, 1988); children: Jennifer, Karen, Grace. BA, Syracuse U., 1971; Masters Degree, U. N.C., 1979. Health care outreach U.S. Peace Corps, Suncheon, Republic of Korea, 1975—77; dir., cmty. organizer Goshen Med. Ctr., Faison, NC, 1979—81; health care adminstr. USAF, Sacramento, 1981—84, Lakenheath, England, 1984—87; journalist, arts critic Long Islander Newspapers, Huntington, NY, 1988—99; exec. editor Anton Publs., Mineola, 1990—92; editor, pub. Birnham Wood Graphics, Northport, 1990—; curator Northport Hist. Soc., 1999—. Dir. Big Sur Marathon Reading, N.Y.C., San Francisco, 2001; co-dir. Westhampton Writers Festival, Westhampton Beach. Author: (poetry) The Milking Jug, 1988, Tales of a Yuppie Dropout, 1993, The Poems of Augie Prime, 1999, Sesquicentennial Suite, 2001; editor: New Covenant: Poems for the Clinton Presidency, 1992, In Autumn: An Anthology of Long Island Poetry, 1994. Bd. mem. Huntington C. of C., 1998—2001; v.p. Long Island Poetry Collective, 2001—; vol. organizer Com. To Save Pea Ridge Road, Chapel Hill, 1978—79. Capt. USAF, 1981—87. Nominee N.Y. Press Assn. Writer of the Yr., Long Islander Newspapers, 1995, N.Y. Press Assn. Writer of Yr., 1996, 1997, 1998, Pushcart prize, Writers Ink Press, 1999; recipient Key to the City, Town of Faison, N.C., 1981; scholar Regents scholar, N.Y. State Bd. Regents, 1967—71. Mem.: Poets and Writers, Acad. Am. Poets, Returned Peace Corps Vols. Avocation: travel. Office: Birnham Wood Graphics PO Box 114 Northport NY 11768 Personal E-mail: poetrybay@aol.com. Business E-Mail: poetrybay@aol.com.

WALLACE, GLADYS BALDWIN, librarian; b. Macon, Ga., June 5, 1923; d. Carter Shepherd and Dorothy (Richard) Baldwin; m. Hugh Loring Wallace Jr., Oct. 14, 1941 (div. Sept. 1968); children: Dorothy, Hugh Loring III. BS in Edn., Oglethorpe U., 1961; MLS, Emory U., 1966; EdS, Ga. State U., 1980. Libr. pub. elem. schs., Atlanta, 1956-66; libr. Northside High Sch., 1966-87, Episc. Cathedral St. Philip. Author: The Time of My Life, 1994. Mem. High Mus. Art, Madison-Morgan Cultural Ctr. Recipient Poet of Merit award, 1999; Ga. Dept. Edn. grantee, 1950, NDEA grantee, 1963, 65. Mem.: Ga. Women of Achievement, Atlanta Hist. Soc., Ga. Geneal. Soc., Am. Assn. Ret. Persons, Atlanta Bot. Garden. Home: NC 6 136 Peachtree Memorial Dr NW Atlanta GA 30309-1096

WALLACE, GUY WILLIAM, management consultant; b. Harvey, Ill., Aug. 22, 1952; s. Willis James and Orpah Linda (Rademacher) W.; m. Karen Margaret Bakke Kennedy, Feb. 20, 1981 (div. July 1996); m. Margaret Ann Johnson, Feb. 8, 1997 B Radio/TV/Film, U. Kans., 1979. Inside salesperson Wickes Lumber, Lawrence, Kans., 1976-79, program devel. Saginaw, Mich., 1979-81; tng. project supr. Motorola, Schamburg, Ill., 1981-82; ptnr. Svenson & Wallace, Inc., Naperville, 1982-97; ptnr., pres. Curriculum Architecture Design & Devel. Inst., Inc., 1998—. Dir. Internat. Soc. for Performance Improvement, Washington, 1999-2000. Author: T&D Systems View, Lean-ISD, 2000; co-author: Quality Roadmap, 1994; developer (tng. program) Product Management Process Training, 1987 (finalist Best Instrnl. Product 1989). With USN, 1972-75. Mem.: ASTD, Internat. Soc. for Performance Improvement (bd. dirs. 1999—2001, pres.-elect 2002—). Office: CADDI Inc 175 W Jackson Ave Ste 215 Naperville IL 60540-4618 E-mail: guy.wallace@caddi.com.

WALLACE, HANK, seminar speaker, lawyer; b. Jersey City, June 7, 1946; s. Irving S. and Florence (Schneider) W. BA, Rutgers U., 1967; JD, Columbia U., 1970. Bar: N.J. 1971, U.S. Dist. Ct. D.C. 1973. Writer Legal Svcs. Tng. Project, N.Y.C., 1972-74; asst. dir. law sch. pub. Matthew Bender, 1975-77; pvt. practice writing cons., 1977-80; atty. FCC, Washington, 1980-81; seminar spkr. Write & Speak Like the News, 1981—. Law reporter for cable TV, N.Y.C., 1977-79; adj. faculty George Washington U., Washington, 1991—; media trainer ambassadorial seminar U.S. State Dept., Washington, 1993-94; moderator Internet Legal-Writing Seminar Counsel Connect, 1997—. Contbr. articles to profl. publs. Spkr. Dunbar H.S., Washington, 1991—. Named Outstanding Spkr., Am. Assn. Clin. Chemistry, 1995. Mem.: Columbia U. Club of Washington (bd. dirs. 1993—2000). Avocations: doo-wop singing, satire, swimming. Home and Office: Write & Speak Like the News 3001 Veazey Ter NW Washington DC 20008-5454

WALLACE, HARRY LELAND, lawyer; b. San Francisco, June 26, 1927; s. Leon Harry and Anna Ruth (Haworth) W.; 1 child, Mary Ann Wallace Frantz. AB in Govt.; BS in Bus, Ind. U., 1949; JD, Harvard U., 1952. Bar: Wis. 1953. Law clk. U.S. Supreme Ct. Justice Sherman Minton, Washington, 1952-53; assoc. firm Foley & Lardner, Milw., 1953-61, partner, 1961-96, retired, 1996; officer and/or dir. various corps. Treas. Mequon-Thiensville Sch. Bds., 1966-67, 71-73, pres., 1965-66, 67-71, 73-75; bd. dirs. Milw. County Assn. for Mental Health, 1970-76, Milw. Mental Health Found., 1983-94; chmn. financing policies com. Gov.'s Commn. on Edn., 1969-70; mem. Gov.'s Task Force on Sch. Financing and Property Tax Reform, 1972-73; chmn. Gov.'s Commn. on State-Local Rels. and Fin. Policies, 1975-76; trustee Pub. Policy Forum, 1976-92, sec., 1984-86, pres., 1986-88. With USN, 1945-46. Mem. Wis. Bar Assn., Am. Law Inst., Phi Beta Kappa, Beta Gamma Sigma, Delta Tau Delta. Clubs: Milwaukee. Methodist. Home: 1913 Somerset Ln Northbrook IL 60062-6067

WALLACE, HELEN MARGARET, physician, educator; b. Hoosick Falls, N.Y., Feb. 18, 1913; d. Jonas and Ray (Schweizer) W. AB, Wellesley Coll., 1933; MD, Columbia U., 1937; MPH cum laude, Harvard U., 1943. Diplomate Am. Bd. Pediatrics, Am. Bd. Preventive Medicine. Intern Bellevue Hosp., N.Y.C., 1938-40; child hygiene physician Conn. Health Dept., 1941-42; successively jr. health officer, health officer, chief maternity and new born div., dir. bur. for handicapped children N.Y.C. Health Dept., 1943-55; prof., dir. dept. pub. health N.Y. Med. Coll., 1955-56; prof. maternal and child health U. Minn. Sch. Pub. Health, 1956-59; chief profl. tng. U.S. Children's Bur., 1959-60, chief child health studies, 1961-62; prof. maternal and child health U. Calif. Sch. Pub. Health, Berkeley, 1962-80, 99; prof., head divsn. maternal and child health Sch. Pub. Health San Diego State U., 1980—; Univ. Research lectr. San Diego State U., 1985—. Cons. WHO numerous locations, including Uganda, The Philippines, Turkey, India, Geneva, Iran, Burma, Sri Lanka, East Africa, Australia, Indonesia, China, Taiwan, 1961—, traveling fellow, 1989—; cons. Hahnemann U., Phila., 1993, Ford Found., Colombia, 1971; UN cons. to Health Bur., Beijing, China, 1987; fellow Aiiku Inst. on Maternal and Child Health, Tokyo, and NIH Inst. Child Health and Human Devel., 1994; dir.

Family Planning Project, Zimbabwe, 1984-87; vis. prof. U. Calif., Berkeley, 1999, 00, prof. emeritus, 2000—; mem. adv. com., faculty APHA Com. on Continuing Edn. Author, editor: 17 textbooks; editor (sr.): Health and Welfare for Families in the 21st Century, 1999 (award Am. Coll.Nursing, Am. Jour. Nursing), 2d edit., 2002, Health & Social Reform for Families for the 21st Century, 2002; contbr. 335 articles to profl. jours. Mem. coun. on Disabled Children to Media, 1991; dir. San Diego County Infant Mortality Study, 1989—, San Diego Study of Prenatal Care, 1991. Recipient Alumnae Achievement award Wellesley Coll., 1982, U. Minn. award, 1985; Ford Found. study grantee, 1986, 87, 88; fellow World Rehab. Fund, India, 1991-92, Fulbright Found., 1992—, NIH Inst. Child Health and Human Devel., 1994, Aiiku Inst. of Maternal-Child Health, Tokyo, 1994. Fellow: APHA (officer sect., chmn. com. on internat. maternal and child health, mem. faculty and adv. com. maternal and child health program 2000, Martha May Eliot award 1978, award in Internat. Maternal and Child Health 2001), Am. Acad. Pediatrics (Job Smith award 1980); mem.: AMA, Am. Sch. Preventive Medicine, Ambulatory Pediatric Assn., Am. Acad. Cerebral Palsy, Assn. Tchrs. Maternal and Child Health. Home: 850 State St San Diego CA 92101-6046

WALLACE, HERBERT NORMAN, lawyer; b. Syracuse, N.Y., Oct. 19, 1937; s. Louis H. and Betty (Wagner) W.; m. Frances Adele Groobman, June 1, 1963 (div. Sept. 1976); children: Craig, Julie; m. Frances Mae Souza, Nov. 12, 1977; 1 child, John. BA, Davis & Elkins Coll., 1959; JD, Syracuse U., 1962. Bar: N.Y. 1962, U.S. Dist. Ct. (no. dist.) N.Y. 1962. Asst. atty. gen. State of N.Y., Albany, 1963-66, asst. atty. gen in charge of Poughkeepsie (N.Y.) office Poughkeepsie, 1966-79; counsel to banking com. N.Y. State Senate, Albany, 1979-84, counsel to Senator Rolison, asst. majority leader, 1984-88; sole practice Poughkeepsie, N.Y., 1979-86, 94—; ptnr. Wallace & Moore, 1986-94, Wallace and Wallace, 2000—. Mem. Poughkeepsie Rep. Com., 1977-91. Recipient Ellis Island medal of hon. NECO, 1997. Mem. N.Y. State Bar Assn., Dutchess County Bar Assn. Jewish. Home: 65 Cardinal Dr Poughkeepsie NY 12601-5703 Office: 299 Main St Poughkeepsie NY 12601-3144

WALLACE, J. CLIFFORD, federal judge; b. San Diego, Dec. 11, 1928; s. John Franklin and Lillie Isabel (Overing) Wallace; m. Virginia Lee Schlosser, 1957 (dec.); m. Elaine J. Barnes, Apr. 8, 1996 (dec.); m. Dixie Jenee Robison Zenger, Apr. 2, 2001. BA, San Diego State U., 1952; LLB, U. Calif., Berkeley, 1955. Bar: Calif. 1955. With Gray, Cary, Ames & Frye, San Diego, 1955—70; judge U.S. Dist. Ct. (so. dist.), 1970—72, U.S. Ct. Appeals (9th cir.), San Diego, 1972—96, chief judge, 1991—96, sr. judge, 1996—. Contbr. articles to profl. jours. Stake pres. San Diego East LDS Ch. , 1962—67, regional rep., 1967—74, 1977—79. With USN, 1946—49. Mem.: Inst. Jud. Adminstrn., Am. Bd. Trial Advocates. Mem. Lds Ch. Office: US Ct Appeals 9th Cir 940 Front St Ste 4192 San Diego CA 92101-8918 *My principles, ideals and goals and my standard of conduct are embodied in the Gospel of Jesus Christ. They come to fruition in family life, service, industry and integrity and in an attempt, in some small way, to make my community a better place within which to live.*

WALLACE, JACK HAROLD, employee development specialist, educator; b. Pleasant Ridge, Mich., Dec. 3, 1950; s. Jack Alfred and Mary Hilda (Hemming) W.; m. Laura Jeannine Placer, May 20, 1978. AA, Oakland Community Coll., 1972; BA, Oakland U., 1974; postgrad., Cen. Mich. U., 1984; MeD, Wayne State U., 1986, postgrad., 1988—. Cert. secondary tchr., Mich. Supply systems analyst TACOM, Warren, Mich., 1979-84; employee devel. specialist Army Tank Automotive Command, Tng. and Dev. Div., 1985—; site coord. TA COM long distance learning program Nat. Tech. U., 1993—; v.p. acad. affairs Virtual U., Bloomfield Hills, Mich., 1994—. Instr. Ferndale (Mich.) Bd. of Edn., 1976-86; instr., cons. Jordan Coll., Detroit, 1986—, Detroit Coll. Bus., Dearborn, Mich., 1986—; trainer, instr. govt. agys. Co-author: (book) Balancing the Scales of Justice, 1986, (cable TV prodn.) A Course in Law and Application in Everyday Living, 1989. Mem. Am. Soc. for Tng. and Devel., Assn. for Ednl. Comm. and Tech., Fed. Mgrs. Assn., Mich. Soc. Instructional Tech., Phi Delta Kappa. Lutheran. Avocations: reading, camping, fishing, public speaking, travel. Home: 3005 Kenmore Rd Berkley MI 48072-1684 Office: TACOM AMSTA-RM-PRT Warren MI 48397-5000

WALLACE, JAMES HAROLD, JR. lawyer; b. Atlanta, Feb. 8, 1941; s. James Harold Sr. and Ruth (Cocking) W. BSEE, U. S.C., 1963; JD, Georgetown U., 1966. Bar: D.C. 1967. Patent examiner U.S. Patent & Trademark Office, Washington, 1966-67; trial atty. antitrust div. U.S. Dept. Justice, 1967-70; from assoc. to ptnr. Kirkland & Ellis, 1970-83; ptnr. Wiley, Rein & Fielding, 1983—. Mem. adv. bd. BNA Patent, Trademark & Copyright Jour., Washington, 1971—. Contbr. articles to profl. jours. Mem. ABA. Home: 3029 Cambridge Pl NW Washington DC 20007-2914 Office: Wiley Rein & Fielding 1776 K St NW Washington DC 20006-2304

WALLACE, JAMES OLDHAM, retired librarian; b. San Antonio, Sept. 22, 1917; s. James Vance and Violet Edyth (Oldham) W.; m. Lillie Ruth Franklin, July 23, 1948; children: Carolyn Denning, Edith Frances Peterson, Thelma Ruth Pittman. AA, San Antonio Coll., 1936; BA, St. Mary's U., 1938, MA, 1940; BLS, Our Lady of the Lake U., 1950. Tchr. Natalia (Tex.) Ind. Sch. Dist., 1940-41; tchr. L.A. Heights Ind. Sch. Dist., San Antonio, 1941-42; clk. USAAF, Kelly AFB, Tex., 1942-43, payroll chief, certifying officer Randolph AFB, 1943-49; tchr., libr. Lanier High Sch., San Antonio, 1949-50; asst. libr. San Antonio Coll., 1950-51, libr., prof., dir. learning resources, 1951-85, dir. emeritus, 1985—; libr. dir. Hispanic Bapt. Theol. Sem., San Antonio, 1986-94. Pres. Friends of San Antonio Pub. Libr., 1986-88; cons. U.S. Office Edn., Washington, 1967-68. Contbr. articles to profl. jours. Trustee Bapt. Meml. Hosp., San Antonio, 1965-67, Mexican Bapt. Bible Inst., San Antonio, 1975-83; pres. adv. com. Hispanic Bapt. Theol. Sem., 1983-90. Named Libr. of Yr. Tex. Libr. Assn., 1968; recipient Disting. Svc. citation Assn. Coll. and Rsch. Librs., 1989, Disting. Svc. award Tex. Libr. Assn., 1991, Outstanding Svc. award, Assn. Coll. and Rsch. Librs., 1991. Mem. ALA (life), Tex. Libr. Assn. (life, pres. 1983-84), Bexar Libr. Assn. (life, pres. 1951-52). Avocations: reading, genealogy, computers. Home: PO Box 13041 San Antonio TX 78213-0041 E-mail: joldham@stic.net.

WALLACE, JAMES WENDELL, lawyer; b. Clinton, Tenn., July 13, 1930; s. John Nelson and Rose Ella (Carden) W.; m. Jeanne Mary Ellen Newlin; children: Karen Wallace Young, Michael James. Student, Syracuse U., 1952-53; BS, U. Tenn., Knoxville, 1959; JD, U. Tenn., 1958. Bar: Calif. 1959, U.S. Dist. Ct. (ctrl. dist.) Calif. 1959, U.S. Ct. Appeals (9th cir.) 1977, U.S. Supreme Ct. 1964. Sec., legal counsel Guidance Tech., Inc., Santa Monica, Calif., 1958-65; sr. atty., asst. sec. Varian Assocs., Palo Alto, 1965-67; gen. counsel, asst. sec. Electronic Splty. Co., Pasadena, 1967-69; asst. gen. counsel, asst. sec. The Times Mirror Co., L.A., 1969-75, assoc. gen. counsel, asst. sec., 1976-85, assoc. gen. counsel, sec., 1985-89; dir., v.p., sec. Flintridge Asset Mgmt. Co., San Marino, Calif., 1990—. Mem. editl. bd. Tenn. Law Rev., 1956-58. Served with USAF, 1951-55. Mem. Jonathan Club, Phi Delta Phi, Phi Kappa Phi. Home: 5822 Briartree Dr La Canada Flintridge CA 91011-1825

WALLACE, JANE HOUSE, retired geologist; b. Ft. Worth, Aug. 12, 1926; d. Fred Leroy and Helen Gould (Kixmiller) Wallace. AB, Smith Coll., 1947, MA, 1949; postgrad., Bryn Mawr Coll., 1949-52. Geologist U.S. Geol. Survey, 1952-97; chief Pub. Inquiries Offices, Washington, 1964-72, spl. asst. to dir., 1974-97, dep. bur. ethics counselor, 1975-97, Washington liaison Office of Dir., 1978-97; ret., 1997. Recipient Meritorious Service award Dept. Interior, 1971, Disting. Svc. award, 1976, Sec.'s Commendation, 1988, Smith Coll. medal, 1992. Fellow Geol. Socs. Am., Washington (treas. 1963-67); mem. Sigma Xi (asso.)

WALLACE, JEANNETTE OWENS, state legislator; b. Scottsdale, Ariz., Jan. 16, 1934; d. Albert and Velma (Whinery) Owens; m. Terry Charles Wallace Sr., May 21, 1955; children: Terry C. Jr., Randall J., Timothy A., Sheryl L., Janice M. BS, Ariz. State U., 1955. Mem. Los Alamos (N.Mex.) County Coun., 1981-82; cons. County of Los Alamos, 1983-84; chmn., vice chmn. Los Alamos County Coun., 1985-88; cons. County of Los Alamos, Los Alamos Schs., 1989-90; rep. N.Mex. State Legislature, 1991—. Mem. appropriations and fin. govt. and urban affairs, N.Mex., 1991—, legis. fin. com., Indian affairs, radioactive and hazardous materials, co-chmn. Los Alamos County's dept. energy negotiating com., 1987-88; mem. legis. policy com. Mcpl. League, N.Mex., 1986-88; mem. legis. fin. com. Info. Tech. and Energy Coun., radioactive & hazardous materials com., medicaid oversight com. Bd. dirs. Tri-Area Econ. Devel., 1988-94, 96—, Crime Stoppers, Los Alamos, 1988-92, Los Alamos Citizens Against Substance Abuse, 1989-94; mem. N.Mex. First, Albuquerque, 1989-96; legis. chmn. LWV, 1990; mem. Los Alamos Rep. Women, pres., 1989-90. Mem. Los Alamos Bus. & Profl. Women (legis. chmn. 1990), Los Alamos C. of C., Mana del Norte, Kiwanis. Methodist. Avocations: tennis, needlework, reading. Home: 1913 Spruce Los Alamos NM 87544-3041 E-mail: wallace@losalamos.com.

WALLACE, JESSE WYATT, pharmaceutical scientist; b. Canton, Ga., Jan. 24, 1925; s. Jesse Washington and Lula (Wyatt) W.; m. Myra Brown, Jan. 2, 1949; children: Karin, Kimberly, Stephen, David. BBA magna cum laude, U. Ga., 1954; MS, Ga. Inst. Tech., 1960. Chmn. svc. groups Ga. Tech, Atlanta, 1953-57; adminstrv. mgr. Am. Viscose Corp., Marcus Hook, Pa., 1957-61; various exec. positions FMC Corp., Phila., 1961-85; pres., dir. Wallco Internat. Corp., Wilmington, Del., 1985-89, 96—; v.p., sec. Pharm. Svc. and Tech., Inc., Woodbury, N.J., 1989-95. Adv. bd. Pharm. Tech. Conf. , 1986—. Editor: Controlled Release Systems, 1988; contbr. Encyclopedia, 1989; contbr. articles to profl. jours; author (manual) Problem Solver, 1980. Vice chmn. Ch. Deacons, Wilmington; v.p., pres. Wilmington Gideons, 1969-71; v.p., bd. dirs. ACA Acad., 1971-73; vice chmn. Del. Family Found., 1990—. Lt. USN, 1943-46, 50-53. Recipient Publ. award Pharm. Technology, 1989. Fellow Acad. Pharm. Scis., Am. Asnsn. of Pharm. Scientists; mem. Internat. Platform Assn., La. Fedn. Internat. Pharm., Am. Assn. Pharm. Scientists, Mensa, Delta Sigma Pi (life), Delta Mu Delta. Republican. Baptist. Avocations: family, reading, golf, racquet ball, travel. Office: Wallco Internat Corp 1106 Grinnell Rd Wilmington DE 19803-5126

WALLACE, JOHN LOYS, aviation services executive; b. Decatur, Tex., July 31, 1941; s. John K. and Flora Viola (Lumsden) Montgomery W.; m. Linda M. Jackson, May 18, 1962; children— John, Amy Lynn, Katherine Lea, Elizabeth D'Ann Student, U. Tex.-Arlington, 1961-65, North Tex. State U., Denton, 1960-61. V.p. acctg. svcs. Cooper Airmotive, Dallas, 1975-77, v.p. fin., 1977-80, exec. v.p., gen. mgr. Gen. Aviation div., 1980-82; exec. v.p. fin., adminstrn. Aviall, 1982-85; exec. v.p., chief oper. officer Aviall, Inc., 1985-89, pres. Gen. Aviation Svcs. div., 1989-93; pres. Ryder Aviall Inc., ret. 1993. Mem. Fin. Execs. Inst., North. Dallas C. of C., U.S./Mex. C. of C. (bd. dirs.), Chif Exec.'s Round Table, Cotton Creek Club, Delta Sigma Phi. Republican. Presbyterian. Avocation: gardening, fishing, golf. Home: 3651 Pinehurst Cir Gulf Shores AL 36542-9052

WALLACE, JOHN MITCHELL MAVER See DUFFY-KING, JAN

WALLACE, JON ROBERT, mortgage company executive, marketing professional; b. Phila., Feb. 24, 1963; s. Arthur Edward Wallace and Carol Jean (Haedtler) Sawyer; m. Kristen Elizabeth Smith, Sept. 10, 1988; children: Joshua David Wallace, Samuel Jacob Wallace, Andrew Joseph Wallace. Creative talent various broadcasting stas., Grand Rapids, Mich., 1980-88; pub. svc. dir. Sta. WCUZ, 1988-90; mktg. cons. Sta. WBCT, 1990-92; mktg. dir. Kellogg Arena, Battle Creek, Mich., 1992-93; mktg. cons. Wincom Comm., Benton Harbor, 1994-96, Consumer Mktg. Assn., 1988—; v.p., owner Carter-Wallace Mortgage, St. Joseph, Mich., 1999—. Mktg. bd. dirs. Project Rehab, Grand Rapids, Mich., 1990-94; dir. Media All Stars, Grand Rapids, 1991; tchr. Jr. Achievement, 1997—. V.p. Brookview Montessori Sch., Benton Harbor, Mich., 1994-97; bd. dirs. Blossomtime, Inc., St. Joseph, 1994-98, vice chair allocations, 1999, 2000, vice chair resource deployment, 2001--; active United Way S.W. Mich., Berrien County, 1996—, certification com., 1995—; mem. certification com. United Way S.W. Mich., 1995-98, panel leader, 1996-98, chair fund distbn., bd. dirs., 1999; amb. Cornerstone Chamber Svcs., 1998—, bd. dirs., 1999, cornerstone steward, 1999—; mem. Greenleaf Ctr. for Student Leadership; co-chair svc. orgn. caucus Coun. for a World Class Cmty. Named Smithsonian Instn. Artist in Residence, Washington, 1981; performing arts scholar Grand Valley State U., Allendale, Mich., 1980-81. Mem. Acad. of Mgmt., (Lakeshore chpt., bd. dirs., editarian, 1995-98, club svc. dir., 1996-97, treas. 1998, sec. 1999, v.p. 2000, pres. 2001, Rotarian of Yr. 1997), S.W. Mich. Assn. Realtors. Mem. First Ch. of God. Avocations: strategic planning, community development, poetry, Shakespeare, volunteering. Office: Carter-Wallace Mortgage 421 Main St Saint Joseph MI 49085-1235 E-mail: wallace@parrett.net.

WALLACE, JOYCE IRENE MALAKOFF, internist; b. Phila., Nov. 25, 1940; d. Samuel Leonard and Henrietta (Hameroff) Malakoff; m. Lance Arthur Wallace, Aug. 30, 1964 (div. 1974); 1 dau. Julia Ruth; m. Arthur H. Kahn, Oct. 7, 1979 (div. 1986); 1 son, Aryeh N. Kahn. AB, Queens Coll., CUNY, 1961; postgrad., Columbia U., 1962-64; MD, SUNY, 1968. Diplomate Am. Bd. Internal Medicine. Intern St. Vincent's Hosp. Med. Ctr., N.Y.C., 1968-70; practice medicine, 1970-71; resident Manhattan VA Hosp., 1972, Nassau County Med. Ctr., East Meadow, N.Y., 1972-73; practice medicine North Conway, NH, 1973—74; practice medicine specializing in internal medicine N.Y.C., 1976—; med. dir. Frost'd Primary Care, 1999—. Mem. attending staff Nassau County Med. Center, 1974, St. Vincent's Hosp. and Med. Center, N.Y.C., 1977— ; asst. prof. medicine Mt. Sinai Med. Sch., N.Y.C.; pres. Found. for Research on Sexually Transmitted Diseases, Inc., 1986-89, exec. and med. dir., 1989—. Fellow ACP, N.Y. Acad. Medicine; mem. Am. Med. Women's Assn., N.Y. County, N.Y. State Med. Socs. Office: 369 8th Ave New York NY 10001-4852

WALLACE, JULIA DIANE, newspaper editor; b. Davenport, Iowa, Dec. 3, 1956; d. Franklin Sherwood and Eleanor Ruth (Pope) W.; m. Doniver Dean Campbell, Aug. 23, 1986; children: Emmaline Livingston Campbell, Eden Jennifer Campbell. BS in Journalism, Northwestern U., 1978. Reporter Norfolk (Va.) Ledger-Star, 1978-80, Dallas Times Herald, 1980-82; reporter, editor News sect. USA Today, Arlington, Va., 1982-89, mng. editor spl. projects, 1989-92; mng. editor Chgo. Sun-Times, 1992-1996; exec. editor Statesman Jour., 1996—98; mng. editor Arizona Republic, Phoenix, 1998—2000, Atlanta Journal and Constitution, Atlanta, 2001—02, editor, 2002—. Mem. Am. Soc. Newspaper Editors. Mailing: The Atlanta Journal Constitution P O Box 4689 Atlanta GA 30302 Office: Atlanta Journal Constitution 72 Marietta St NW Atlanta GA 30303*

WALLACE, KEITH M. lawyer; b. Evansville, Ind., Apr. 2, 1956; s. B. Joe and M. Joyce (Nicolaides) W.; 1 child, Elizabeth Anne. BA in Psychology, Ind. U., 1978; JD, Valparaiso U., 1983. Bar: Ky. 1984, Ind. 1983, U.S. Dist. Ct. (so. dist.) Ind. 1983, U.S. Ct. Appeals (7th cir.) 1985, U.S. Supreme Ct., 1997. Comml. credit analyst Old Nat. Bank, Evansville, 1978-79; assoc. Cubbage & Thomason, Henderson, Ky., 1983-84, Perdue & Stigger, Evansville, 1984-86; ptnr. Jones & Wallace, 1987-90; fgn. expert Peking U. Law Dept., People's Republic China, 1990-91; ptnr. Wright, Evans & Daly, Evansville, 1991-95, Jones & Wallace, Evansville, 1996-2001; of counsel Bowers Harrison, 2001—. Asst. city atty., Evansville, 1984-90; hearing officer City of Evansville Dept. Code Enforcement, 1992-99. Steward Christian Fellowship Ch., Evansville, 1988-90; vol. Evansville Rescue Mission, 1987-92, Habitat for Humanity, 1992—; bd. dirs. Impact Ministries, 1992—; exec. dir. Families Thru Internat. Adoptions, Inc., 1995—. Recipient Sagamore of the Wabash award Gov. Frank O'Bannon, 1999, Disting. Hoosier award Gov. Evan Bayh, 1996. Mem. Am. Acad. Adoption Attys., Nat. Assn. of Counsel for Children, Ind. Bar Assn., Ky. Bar Assn., Evansville Bar Assn., Christian Legal Soc., Evansville Runners Club. Office: PO Box 1287 Evansville IN 47706-1287 Fax: (812) 464-3676. E-mail: kwallace@ftia.org.

WALLACE, KENNETH DONALD, lawyer; b. Spokane, Wash., Oct. 2, 1918; s. Donald and Adillah (Mason) W.; m. Ida H. Harvey, June 6, 1946 (div. 1965); children: Ann H., Jane B.; m. Betty Casey Major, July 31, 1965. AB summa cum laude, Wash. State U., 1940; LLB, Columbia U., 1946. Bar: N.Y. 1947, Conn. 1971. Pvt. practice law, N.Y.C. and Conn., 1947—; with Cahill, Gordon, Reindel & Ohl, 1946-60; gen. counsel, sec. Bigelow-Sanford, Inc., 1960-70; v.p., dir. Oconee Realty Corp.; dir. JAI Press, Inc., 1984—; of counsel Philip E. Silberberg, N.Y.C. Gen. counsel Johnson Assocs., Inc., JAI Press, Inc., Alpen Pantry, Inc. Editor: Columbia Law Review, 1946. Trustee Bigelow-Charitable Trust. Served to 1st lt. USAAF, 1942-46. Decorated D.F.C. with oak leaf cluster, Air medal with oak leaf cluster; recipient Presdl. citation medal, pilot's wings, Republic of China. Mem. ABA, Am. Acad. Polit. Sci. (life), Conn. Bar Assn., Am. Soc. Corp. Secs., Hump Pilor's Assn. (life), Phi Beta Kappa, Phi Sigma Kappa. Home and Office: PO Box 843 947 Ridge Rd New Canaan CT 06840-0843 E-mail: KDWallace@aol.com.

WALLACE, LOUISE MARGARET, nurse; b. Norwich, Conn., June 15, 1942; d. Irving Clifford and Helen Lucille (Fain) Hayden; m. R.D. Wallace, Dec. 2, 1967; 1 child, Donald Orville. Grad., Joseph Lawrence Sch. Nursing, Conn., 1963; student, Miami-Dade (Fla.) Jr. Coll., 1966-67, Yavapai Coll., 1970. RN, Ariz., Mo., D.C., Fla., Conn., New Zealand; cert. ACLS, Advanced Burn Life Support, Pediatric Advanced Life Support, trauma nurse course. Nurse ICU and ob-gyn. dept. George Washington U. Hosp., Washington, 1964-65; nurse pediatrics dept. Jackson Meml. Hosp., Miami, Fla., 1965-66; nurse ICU Bapt. Hosp., 1966-67; nurse ICU and CCU N. Shore Hosp., 1967-71, VA Med. Ctr., Prescott, Ariz., 1971-84, Poplar Bluff, Mo., 1984-93, relief clin. coord., 1991-92, clin. coord., 1993-97, ret., 1997; ICU nurse Doctor's Regional Med. Ctr., 1997; emergency rm. nurse Ripley County Meml. Hosp., Doniphan, Mo., 1997-2000, surgery dir., supr., 2000—. Instr. nursing Miami-Dade Jr. Coll., 1968-69; instr. basic CPR, Prescott, 1975-81. Mem.: AACCN, Am. Hosp. Assn. Avocations: needlework, knitting, travel, dogs. Home: HC 1 Box 76 Grandin MO 63943-9602 E-mail: lwallace@pbmo.net.

WALLACE, MARK, professional sports team executive; BS in Indsl. Mgmt., Ga. Inst. Tech., 1977. Team owner, CFO Jasper Motorsports, Mooresville, NC, 1993—; svc. rep. Fed.-Mogul; founder Jasper Fleet Sales, 1978, Jasper Engines and Transmissions distributorship, 1980. Office: Jasper Motorsports 110 Knob Hill Rd Mooresville NC 28117

WALLACE, MARY ELAINE, opera director, author; m. Robert House. BFA cum laude, U. Nebr., Kearney, 1940; MusM, U. Ill., 1954; postgrad., Music Acad. West, Santa Barbara, Calif., 1955, Eastman Sch. Music, 1960, Fla. State U., 1962. Prof. voice, dir. opera La. Tech. U., Ruston, 1954-62, SUNY-Fredonia, 1962-69, So. Ill. U.-Carbondale, 1969-79; dir. Marjorie Lawrence Opera Theatre, Opera on Wheels; adminstrv. adviser Summer Playhouse, Carbondale; stage mgr. Chautauqua Opera Co., N.Y., 1963; asst. mus. dir., condr. Asolo Festival, Sarasota, Fla., 1961; music editor, critic The Chautauquan Daily; adjudicator Met. Opera auditions; exec. sec. Nat. Opera Assn., 1981-91. Co-author: Opera Scenes for Class and Stage, 1979, (with Robert Wallace) More Operas Scenes for Class and Stage, 1990, Upstage Downstage, 1992. Founding mem. bd. dirs. Rockwall Alliance for the Arts, 2001; founding bd. dirs. Rockwall Musicfest, 2002. Recipient Lifetime Achievement award Nat. Opera Assn., 1998, disting. alumni award U. Nebr., 1998. Mem. Nat. Opera Assn. (pres. 1974, 75), Music Tchrs. Nat. Assn., Nat. Assn. Tchrs. Singing, AAUP, AAUW, Met. Opera Guild, Mortar Bd., Sigma Tau Delta, Pi Kappa Lambda, Phi Beta, Alpha Psi Omega, Delta Kappa Gamma Address: 3106 Lakeside Dr Rockwall TX 75087-5319 E-mail: mehouse@flash.net.

WALLACE, MARY MONAHAN, elementary and secondary schools educator; b. Teaneck, N.J., Nov. 22, 1943; d. Thomas Gabriel and Louise Grace (Monaco) Monahan; m. James Anthony Wallace, Nov. 22, 1978; (dec. May, 1992); 1 child, Meg. BS, Fordham U., 1967; MA, 1971; postgrad. in Supervision, Montclair U., 1978; postgrad. in Edn., various colls. Cert. tchr. language arts, supr., N.Y. 1st and 4th grades tchr. Holy Rosary Sch., Harlem, N.Y., 1963-65; 7th grade tchr. Immaculate Conception Sch., Bronx, 1965-66; 8th grade tchr. St. Finbar Sch., Bklyn., 1966-68, St. Patrick Mil. Acad., Harriman, N.Y., 1968-69; English tchr. St. Stephen H.S., Bklyn., 1969-70, Holy Rosary Acad., Union City, N.J., 1970-71, Harriman (N.Y.) Coll., 1971-72, Montclair (N.J.) Coll., 1981-82; English tchr. elem. and secondary schs. Fairlawn (N.J.) Schs., 1972—; clin. faculty mem. Montclair (N.J.) U., 1999—. Advisor Fair Lawn H.S. Yearbook, 1977-80, Nat. Lang. Arts Olympiad, Fair Lawn, 1987-89; mem. Mid. Sch. Task Force Fair Lawn Schs., 1991-93, dist. wide steering com. Edn. Recognition Day, Fair Lawn, 1992, 93, mem. steering com. Fair Lawn Mid. Schs., 1994-97; exec. bd. Profl. Devel. Schs., Montclair Univ., 2000—; presenter in field. Editor (newsletter) Concern, 1970-72; mem. editorial staff (newsletter) Flea Bytes, 1988, 89, 90. Participant Summer in the City U.S. Antipoverty Program, Staten Island, N.Y., 1965; pres. Bear Pond Improvement Assn., 1996—; chairperson spl. events com. marathon '99. Named Meml. Sch. Tchr. of Yr. N.J. Gov.'s Recognition Program, 1993. Mem.: NEA, Nat. Mid. Sch. Assn., Fair Lawn Edn. Assn. (treas. 1990—93, pres. 1993—), N.J. Middle Sch. Assn., Bergen County Edn. Assn., N.J. Edn. Assn. Roman Catholic. Avocations: reading, swimming, boating, travel. Home: 20-18 Saddle River Rd Fair Lawn NJ 07410-5933 Office: Fair Lawn Edn Assn 3-13 4th St Fair Lawn NJ 07410 E-mail: fairlawn@aol.com.

WALLACE, MATTHEW WALKER, retired entrepreneur; b. Salt Lake City, Jan. 7, 1924; s. John McChrystal and Glenn (Walker) W.; m. Constance Cone, June 22, 1954 (dec. May 1980); children: Matthew, Anne; m. Susan Struggles, July 11, 1981. BA, Stanford U., 1947; MCP, MIT, 1950. Prin. planner Boston City Planning Bd., 1950-53; v.p. Nat. Planning and Rsch., Inc., Boston, 1953-55; pres. Wallace-McConaughy Corp., Salt Lake City, 1955-69, Ariz. Ranch & Metals Co., Scottsdale, 1969-84, Idaho TV Corp., Channel 6, ABC, Boise, 1976-78; chmn. Wallace Assocs., Inc., Salt Lake City, 1969-98, Dir. 1st Interstate Bank, Salt Lake City, 1956—90, Wells Fargo Bank Cmty. Bd., 2000, Arnold Machinery Co., 1988—, Roosevelt Hot Springs Corp., 1978—; mem. adv. bd. Mountain Bell Tel. Co., Salt Lake City, 1975—85. Pres. Downtown Planning Assn., Salt Lake City, 1970; chmn. Utah State Arts Coun., Salt Lake City, 1977; chmn. hon. bd. Planned Parenthood; mem. Humanities and Scis. Coun., Stanford U., also mem. athletics bd., mem. alumni assn. exec. bd., bd. vis. sch. law; mem. nat. adv. bd. Coll. Bus., U. Utah; lifetime dir. Utah Symphony Orch.; chmn. arts, adv. coun. and Capital Campaign Westminster Coll. Lt. (j.g.) USN, 1944-46, PTO. Recipient Contbn. award Downtown Planning Assn., 1977, Gov.'s award in the Arts, 1991, Utah Nat. Guard Minuteman award, 1994. Mem. Am. Inst. Cert. Planners (charter), Am. Arts Alliance (bd. dirs. 1991), Alta Club (dir.), Cottonwood Club (pres. 1959-63), Salt Lake Country Club (dir.), Desert Island Golf and Country Club (Rancho Mirage, Calif.), Flat Rock Club (Island Park., Idaho pres. 1994-98), Phi Kappa Phi (hon., life). Home: 2510 Walker Ln Salt Lake City UT 84117-7729

WALLACE, MICHELE, writer, educator; b. N.Y.C., Jan. 4, 1952; d. Robert Earl Wallace and Faith Ringgold; m. Eugene Nesmith, Dec. 22, 1989. BA, CCNY, 1974, MA in English, 1990; PhD Cinema Studies, NYU, 1998. Asst. prof. English CUNY, 1989—91; assoc. prof. English, women's studies and film CUNY and CUNY Grad. Ctr., 1991—97, prof., 1998. Pres. Art Without Walls, 1974. Author: Black Macho and the Myth of the Superwoman, 1979, Invisibility Blues: Pop to Theory, 1990, Black Popular Culture, 1992; columnist: The Village Voice, 1996; contbr. to newspapers and popular mags. including; editor: Women in Art, 1971; mem. editl. bd.: Social Identities, Women and Therapy. Founding mem. Nat. Black Feminist Orgn., 1974; pres. Women Students and Artists for Black Art Liberation, 1970—76. Mem.: PEN, MLA, Oscar Micheaux Soc., Soc. Cinema Studies, Am. Studies Assn., Phi Beta Kappa.

WALLACE, MIKE, television interviewer and reporter; b. Brookline, Mass., May 9, 1918; s. Frank and Zina (Sharfman) W.; m. Lorraine Perigord (dec.); children: Peter (dec.), Christopher, Pauline; m. Mary Yates, June 28, 1986. AB, U. Mich., 1935-39, hon. degree, 1987, U. Mass., 1978, U. Pa., 1989. Associated with radio, 1939—, TV, 1946—; commentator, CBS-TV, 1951-54, TV interviewer, reporter, 1951—. CBS news corr., 1963—; co-editor: 60 Minutes, CBS; Author: Mike Wallace Asks, 1958, Close Encounters, 1984 Recipient Robert Sherwood award, 19 ATVAS Emmy awards, George Foster Peabody awards, 1963-71, 98, DuPont Columbia Journalism award, 1972, 83, Carr Van Anda award, 1977, Thomas Hart Benton award, 1978. Mem. Century Assocs., Sigma Delta Chi. Office: CBS News 60 Minutes 524 W 57th St New York NY 10019-2924

WALLACE, MIKE, race car driver; Race car driver Biagi Brothers. Recipient Champion, Winston Racing Series Mid-Am. Region, 1990, Busch Series/Indpls. Raceway Park, 1994. Office: Mike Wallace Fan Club PO Box 4450 Mooresville NC 28117*

WALLACE, NORA ANN, lawyer; b. Phila., May 24, 1951; AB, Vassar Coll., 1973; JD cum laude, Harvard U., 1976. Bar: N.Y. 1977. Mem. Willkie Farr & Gallagher, N.Y.C. Trustee Bklyn. Acad. Music, BAM Endowment Trust; bd. dirs. Joseph Collins Found.; pres. Harvard Law Sch. Assn. of N.Y.C. Office: Willkie Farr & Gallagher 787 7th Ave New York NY 10019-6099

WALLACE, PATRICIA JEAN, artist, educator, writer; b. Sacramento, Jan. 3, 1945; d. Millard Edward Rogers and Katherine Lottie (Crabtree) Briggs; m. Feb. 23, 1964 (div. July 1992); children: Raabe, Brian, Marni. Student, Calif. Bapt. Coll., 1962-63, Am. River Coll., 1976-77, Tahoe Community Coll., 1991-92. Art, music tchr. Sunrise Elem. Sch., Citrus Heights, Calif., 1977-80; art restorer Arcade Antiques, North Sacramento, 1977-79; artist P.J.'s Illustration, 1982—; instr. adult arts and crafts Community of Fair Oaks, Calif., 1982-84; instr., artist Laughing Cir. Gallery, Colo., Tex., N.Mex., 1984-92; writer On the Wing mag., No. Calif., 1988-90; artist ArtWorks Gallery, Fair Oaks, 1989—, Sacramento, 1988-91, S.W. Gallery, Fair Oaks and San Antonio, 1988—. Set artist Fair Oaks Shakespeare Theatre, 1990. Illustrator numerous books, 1982—; contbr. articles to profl. mags. Pres. Sacramento Women's Club, 1984-85; city coun. rep. South Lake Tahoe Women's Ctr., 1978-79; amb. C. of C., Citrus Heights, 1985-89; rep. Historic Assn., Citrus Heights, 1987-88; adv. Bus. and the Arts, Sacramento County, 1987-89, C. of C., Sacramento, 1987-89; mem., guest artist KVIE-Channel 6, Sacramento, 1986-88; contbr. AIDS Found., Sacramento, 1990. Recipient award Citrus Heights C. of C., 1989, U. Nev., 1990, Process Theatre Prodns., 1988. Mem. Tallac Historic Assn., Citrus Heights Art Assn. (pres., bd. dirs. 1985-89), Crocker Art Mus. Avocations: photography, cultural events, poetry, hiking, travel. Address: c/o M Gates 3313 Eisenhower Dr Sacramento CA 95826-4510

WALLACE, PAUL EDWARD, JR. health services management; b. Balt. s. Paul E. and Frances (Tindal) W.; children from previous marriage: Gregory, Demetria, Denise, Eli. BS, Morgan State U., 1974; MA, U. Pitts., 1976, PhD, 1979, MPH, 1981. Adminstrv. fellow Mercy Hosp., Pitts., 1980-81; asst. adminstr. Norfolk (Va.) Gen. Hosp., 1981-85; v.p. profl. svc. Forsyth Meml. Hosp., Winston, N.C., 1985-88; chmn., assoc. prof. Howard U., Washington, 1988—. Cons. OAS, Washington, 1989-91. Bd. dirs. Am. Heart Assn., Washington, 1991-95, Franciscan Health Sys., Aston, Pa., 1994. Recipient Recognition award Area Health Edn. Ctr., 1985, J.B. Johnson award Am. Heart Assn., 1992. Fellow Am. Coll. Healthcare Execs. (regent 1994). Presbyterian. Avocations: golf, reading, racquetball. Home: 9 E Lake Ave Baltimore MD 21212-2429 Office: Urban Med Inst 2600 Liberty Heights Ave Baltimore MD 21215-7804

WALLACE, PAUL HARVEY, lawyer, educator; b. Fresno, Calif., Oct. 27, 1944; s. Samuel Dunn and Naomi (Hickman) W.; m. Randa Fay Steckler, Mar. 20, 1987; children: Tim, Laura, Christy. BS in Criminology, Calif. State U., Fresno, 1966; JD, U.S. Internat. U., 1974; MPA, Golden Gate U., 1989. Bar: Calif. 1974, U.S. Dist. Ct. (so. dist.) Calif. 1974, U.S. Dist. Ct. (no. dist.) Calif. 1982, U.S. Ct. Appeals (9th cir.) 1985. Dep. dist. atty. San Diego Dist. Atty.'s Office, 1975-79; assoc. Harrison and Watson, San Diego, 1979-81; dep. county counsel Butte County Counsel's Office, Oroville, Calif., 1981-85, county counsel, 1985-87; city atty. City of Fresno, 1987-92; assoc. prof. Calif. State U., Fresno, 1992-96, prof., 1996—. Adj. prof. Nat. U., Fresno, 1987—; bd. dirs. Ctrl. Calaif. Legal Svcs. Corp., 1993-95. Lead author: Fundamentals of Police Administration, 1995, Principles of Criminal Law, 1996; author: Family Violence: Legal, Medical and Social Perspectives, 1996. Asst. coord. San Diego County for U.S. Senator Alan Cranston, 1974. Lt. USMCR, 1967-70, col. Res. Decorated Silver Star, Purple Heart with oak leaf cluster. Mem. State Bar Assn. Calif., Butte County Bar Assn., San Diego Dep. Dist. Attys. Assn. (sec.-treas. 1976-77, v.p. 1977-78, pres. 1978-79), Am. Legion, VFW, Masons, Shriners. Avocations: photography, jogging. Office: Calif State U Fresno CA 93740-0001

WALLACE, PAULA KATHLEEN, microcomputer consultant; b. San Diego, June 3, 1951; d. Paul W. and Betty J. (Moore) W. Auditor Stinson Beach (Calif.) Water Dist., 1978-83; mgr. support and tng. McClure Mgmt. Systems, Larkspur, Calif., 1984-86; owner Wallace & Assocs., Novato, 1986—; fin. analyst Fireman's Fund, 1992—. Instr. Calif. CPA Soc., Palo Alto, 1985-88. Mem. NAFE, Internat. Platform Assn. Office: Wallace & Assocs 8 Los Cedros Dr Novato CA 94947-3754

WALLACE, RASHEED, professional basketball player, marketing professional; b. Sept. 17, 1974; s. Jackie Wallace; m. Fatima Sanders, July 18; 3 children. Attended, U. N.C. Prof. basketball player Washington Wizards, 1995—96, Portland Trailblazers, 1996—; CEO Dir. Hit Studios, Phila., 2002—. Founder Rasheed A. Wallace Found., Phila., 1997. Address: Rasheed A Wallace Found 2207 Chesnut St 2nd Fl Philadelphia PA 19103 Office Fax: 215-563-4803.*

WALLACE, RICHARD, editor, writer; b. Bronxville, N.Y., May 25, 1947; m. Elisabeth Beeftink, May 24, 1969; 1 child, Eric B. BA, Columbia U., 1974. Reporter, editor, contbr. various industry and bus. pubs., Electronic News, EE Times, 1976-92; editor-in-chief Electronic Engring. Times, Manhasset, NY, 1992—98; editor, dir. EE Times, 1998—. Office: CMP Media LLC Electronic Engring Times 600 Community Dr Ste 1 Manhasset NY 11030-3875

WALLACE, ROANNE, hosiery company executive; b. Greenwood, Miss., Dec. 18, 1949; d. Robert Carter and Lois Anne (Vick) W. BM, U. Tenn., 1971; MA, U. N.C., 1976; MBA, Wake Forest U., 1982. Exec. dir. Am. Bd. Clin. Chemistry, Winston-Salem, N.C., 1977-78; administrv. officer Winston-Salem/Forsyth County Office Emergency Mgmt., 1978-79, sr. asst. dir., 1979-82; with Sara Lee, Winston-Salem, 1982—; mktg. dir. Sara Lee Hosiery/Just My Size, 1988—; product mgr. L'eggs Products, Inc., 1986-88. Mem. adv. coun. Winston-Salem/Forsyth County Office Piedmont Emergency Mgmt.; v.p. audience devel., bd. dirs. Piedmont Opera Theatre, Inc. Miss U. Tenn., 1970. Home: 803 Devon Ct Winston Salem NC 27104-1263 Office: Sara Lee Hosiery 5650 University Pkwy Winston Salem NC 27105-1312

WALLACE, ROBERT B. medical educator; BSM Medicine, Northwestern U., 1964, MD, 1967; MSc Epidemiology, SUNY, 1972. Intern internal medicine Cornell U. , N.Y., 1967—68, resident internal medicine, 1968—69; instr. dept. medicine Emory U. Medicine, 1969—70; instr. dept. social and preventive medicine SUNY, Buffalo, 1970—72; asst. prof. preventive medicine and internal medicine Coll. Medicine U. Iowa , 1972—75; assoc. prof. preventive medicine and internal medicine Coll. Medicine U. Iowa, 1975—79, head epidemiology sect. dept. preventive medicine Coll. Medicine, 1976—85, prof. preventive medicine and internal medicine Coll. Medicine, 1979—99, head dept. preventive medicine Col. Medicine, 1986—94, dir. cancer ctr., 1994—98, prof. epidemiology Coll. Pub. Health, 1999—. Mem.: Nat. Acad. Scis., Inst. Medicine (bd. health promotion and disease prevention 1994—), Nat. Inst. Aging (nat. adv. coun. 1994—98), U.S. Preventive Svs. Task Force (sec. office assistance DHHS 1990—95), Alpha Omega Alpha. Office: U Iowa Coll Pub Health 5190 Westlawn Iowa City IA 52242*

WALLACE, ROBERT BRUCE, surgeon, retired; b. Washington, Apr. 12, 1931; s. William B. and Anne E. W.; m. Betty Jean Newel, Aug. 28, 1955; children: Robert B., Anne E., Barbara N. BA, Columbia U., 1953, MD, 1957. Diplomate: Am. Bd. Surgery, Am. Bd. Thoracic Surgery. Chmn., prof. dept. surgery Mayo Clinic and Mayo Med. Sch., Rochester, Minn.; bd. govs. Mayo Clinic, 1968-79; prof. dept. surgery Georgetown U. Sch. Medicine, 1980—, chmn. dept. surgery, 1980-95, surgeon and chief univ. hosp., 1980-95; retired, 1995. Trustee Mayo Found., 1970-78. Mem. ACS (bd. govs. 1975-79), Am. Surg. Assn., Soc. Clin. Surgery, Am. Assn. Thoracic Surgery (pres. 1994-95), Internat. Cardiovascular Soc., Soc. Vascular Surgery, Thoracic Surgery Found. Rsch. & Edn. (bd. dirs. 1993-2001, pres. 1998-2001). Home: 1322 Darnall Dr Mc Lean VA 22101-3009 E-mail: rbwallace@erols.com.

WALLACE, ROBERT CARLSON, real estate investor; b. St. Louis, Oct. 17, 1945; s. M. Marvin and Mildred O. Wallace; m. Joan S. Russell, Sept. 16, 1966; children: Kevin R., Kimberly Anne. BA, Seattle Pacific U., 1969. Lic. broker, Wash. CEO Wallace Properties, Inc., Bellevue, Wash., 1975—. Dir. First Mut. Bank, Bellevue; chmn. Bellevue Conv. Ctr. Authority, 1993-2002. Contbr. articles to profl. jours. Chmn. Bellevue Downtown Assn., 1979-80, Bellevue C. of C., 1980-81, King County Domed Stadium Adv. Bd., 1988-90, Puget Sound Air Transp. Com., Seattle, 1994-97, Seattle C. of C., 1997-98; dir., treas. Wash. State Conv. and Trade Ctr. Corp., 1984-97; dir., pres. Bellevue Rotary Club, 1988-89; dir., chmn. Wash. State Major League Baseball Stadium Pub. Facilities Dist., Seattle, 1995-2002. With USAR, 1965-71. Named Citizen of Yr., Advance Bellevue, 1998, Alumnus of Yr., Seattle Pacific U., 1999; recipient Vocat. Svc. award Bellevue Rotary Club, 1999. Republican. Presbyterian. Avocations: running, reading, dogs. Fax: 425-646-3374. E-mail: rwallace@wallaceproperties.com.

WALLACE, ROBERT EARL, geologist; b. N.Y.C., July 16, 1916; s. Clarence Earl and Harriet (Wheeler) W.; m. Gertrude Kivela, Mar. 19, 1945; 1 child: Alan R. BS, Northwestern U., 1938; MS, Calif. Inst. Tech., 1940, PhD, 1946. Geologist U.S. Geol. Survey, various locations, 1942-98, regional geologist Menlo Park, Calif., 1970-74, chief scientist Office of Earthquakes, Volcanoes and Engring., 1974-87, emeritus, 1987-98; asst. and assoc. prof. Wash. State Coll., Pullman, 1946-51; prof. emeritus U. Nev., Reno, 1998-2000. Mem. adv. panel Nat. Earthquake Prediction Evaluation Coun., 1980-90; mem. adv. com. Stanford U. Sch. Earth Sci., 1972-82; mem. engring. criteria rev. bd. San Francisco Bay Conservation and Devel. Commn., chmn. 1981-92. Contbr. articles to profl. jours. Recipient Alfred E. Alquist award Calif. Earthquake Safety Found., 1995. Fellow AAAS, Geol. Soc. Am. (chair cordillidan sect. 1967-68), Earthquake Engring. Rsch. Inst. (hon. 1999), Calif. Acad. Scis. (hon. 1991); mem. Seismol. Soc. Am. (medalist 1989) Avocations: birding, ham radio, water color painting.

WALLACE, ROBERT LUTHER, II, engineer; b. Ronceverte, W.Va., Jan. 27, 1949; s. Robert Luther and Eloise Virginia (Houck) W.; m. Dorothy James, May 1970 (div. 1979); m. Lucy Alice Frazier, June 13, 1981; children: Sheena Rene, Lacey Christina. BS in Aerospace Engring., W.Va. U., 1970, MS in Indsl. Engring., 1973. Project engr. Naval Air Systems Commd., Washington, 1972-78, Air Force Logistics Command, Wright Patterson AFB, Ohio, 1978-81, engring. work leader, 1981-84; logistics mgmt. specialist Mil. Airlift Commd., Scott AFB, Ill., 1984-86; program mgr. Air Force Logistics Commd., Wright-Patterson AFB, 1986-91; chief mission requirements unit Edn. and Tng. Flight 88th Mission Support Group, Ohio, 1991-95; chief ops. edn. and tng. office Mission Support Squadron, 1995-96, dir. edn. and tng. flight 88th Mission Support Group, 1996-97; logistics mgmt. specialist Inventory Mgmt. divsn. Hdqrs. Air Force Material Command, 1997-98; human resource engr. Directorate of Engring. and Tech. Mgmt. Hdqs. Air Force Material Command, 1998—. Trustee Idle Hour Swim Club, Beavercreek, Ohio, 1990-98, v.p. 1996-97; mem. Beavercreek Schs. Strategic Planning Com., 1990; asst. lay minister Peace Evang. Luth. Ch., Beavercreek, 1987—, asst. dir. evang., 1987-89, v.p. for ministries, 1992-96, Hall of Servants, 1999; elected. mem. Beavercreek City Schs. Bd. Edn., 1998-2001, v.p., 2000, pres., 2001. Mem.: AIAA. Republican. Avocations: swimming, skywatching. Home: 3755 Olde Willow Dr Beavercreek OH 45431-2469 Office: HQ AFMC/ENRM 4375 Chidlaw Rd Wright Patterson AFB OH 45433-5006

WALLACE, SCOTT MICHAEL, financial services executive, investment banker; b. Toledo, Mar. 13, 1963; s. Robert Leonard and Marilynn Ann (Sartor) W.; m. Marta Lee Dotson, Jan. 29, 1994. Gen. mgr. 1776 Inc., Houston, 1986-92, Pour la France!, Houston, 1992-94; investment banker F.N. Wolf & Co., 1994, Josephthal Lyon & Ross, Houston, 1994—. Arbitration mem. Nat. Assn. Security Dealers, Houston, 1996—. Mem. Internat. Assn. Fin. Planning (v.p. fin. 1996—). Republican. Roman Catholic. Avocation: golf, snow skiing. Home: 1223 Sandy Plains Ln Houston TX 77062-2010 Office: Barrington Financial Advisors 9800 Richmond Ave Ste 250 Houston TX 77042-4517

WALLACE, SEAN DANIEL, lawyer; b. Walnut Creek, Calif., June 17, 1960; s. Daniel M. and Patricia Marie (Coyne) W.; m. Eileen Marie Lynch, May 29, 1999. BA, Hampden-Sydney Coll., 1982; JD, U. Md., 1985. Bar: Md. 1985, U.S. Dist. Ct. Md. 1986 (co-chmn. so. divsn. joint adv. com.), D.C. 1986, U.S. Dist. Ct. D.C. 1986, U.S. Ct. Appeals (4th, D.C. and Fed. cirs.) 1986. Spl. asst. to U.S. rep. Steny H. Hoyer, Washington, 1982; assoc. Knight, Manzi, Brennan & Ostrom, Upper Marlboro, Md., 1985-88; assoc. county atty. Prince George's County, 1988-95, dep. county atty., chief litig., 1995-98, county atty., 1999—2002; cir. ct. judge 7th Judicial Cir., 2002—. Bd. dirs. moot ct. U. Md. Law Sch., Balt., 1983-85. Mem. youth adv. com. City of Bowie, Md., 1976-78, security ops. staff Dem. Nat. Convention, N.Y.C., 1980, inquiry com. Md. Atty. Grievance Commn., 1986—; chmn. convention Young Dems. of Md., 1982; bd. dirs. Associated Cath. Charities Archdiocese Washington, 1994-99, chmn. fin. com., 1996-98, bd. vice chair, 1999, fundraising gala chair, 2001; bd. dirs. SHARE, 2002—. Named one of Outstanding Young Men in Am. U.S. Jaycees, 1982, 84. Mem. ABA, Md. Assn. of Counties (co-chmn. govt. liability workgroup 1995-96), Prince George's County Bar Assn., Md. Bar Assn. (bd. dirs. 1997-99, sec. 1999-2000, treas. 2000-01, pres.-elect 2001—), J. Dudley Digges Inn of Ct., Nat. Eagle Scout Assn. Democrat. Roman Catholic. Home: 2701 Lyn Pl Bowie MD 20715-2362 Office: Prince George's Co Cir Ct Courthouse Main St Upper Marlboro MD 20772

WALLACE, STEVEN CHARLES, judge; b. Lubbock, Tex., Jan. 19, 1953; s. Charles Andrew Wallace and Alice Hillene (McMillin) Stone; m. Kathleen Louise Merrill, Apr. 3, 1976; children: Christine Merrill, Zachary Charles, Steven Kyle. BA, Tex. Tech U., 1975, JD, 1979. Bar: Tex. 1979, U.S. Dist. Ct. (no. dist.) Tex. 1980, U.S. Ct. Appeals (5th cir.) 1981. Asst. county atty. Parker County, Weatherford, Tex., 1979-80; asst. dist. atty. Tarrant County, Ft. Worth, 1980-83; pvt. practice, 1983-90; judge Tarrant County Ct. at Law # 2, 1991—. Chmn. prosecution and adjudication subcom. Tarrant 2000 Task Force, 1987—. Trustee Am. Judges Found. Recipient Am. Jurisprudence award Bancroft Whitney Co., 1979. Fellow Coll. State Bar of Tex.; mem. Am. Judges Assn. (bd. govs.), State Bar Tex., Tarrant County Bar Assn., Ridotto Club, Ridglea Country Club, Phi Alpha Delta, Phi Alpha Theta. Avocations: golf, fishing, music, traveling, astronomy. Office: Tarrant County Ct at Law # 2 Tarrant County Courthouse 100 W Weatherford St 240-A Fort Worth TX 76196-0234

WALLACE, TERRY CHARLES, SR. retired technical administrator, researcher; b. Phoenix, May 18, 1933; s. Terry Milton Wallace and Fair June (Hartman) Wallace Timberlake; m. Yvonne Jeannette Owens, May 21, 1955; children: Terry Charles, Randall James, Timothy Alan, Sheryl Lynn, Janice Marie. BS, Ariz. State U., 1955; PhD, Iowa State U., 1958. Staff Los Alamos Nat. Lab., 1958-71, dep. group leader, 1971-80, group leader, 1980-83, assoc. divsn. leader, 1983-89, tech. program coord., 1989-91, ret., 1991. Sr. tech. adv. SAIC, Inc., 1994-95; ptnr. Stonewall Enterprises, Los Alamos, 1966-71. Contbr. chpts., articles to profl. jours.; patentee in field. Fundraiser Los Alamos County Republican Party, N.Mex., 1983-84. Served to 1st lt. Chem. Corps, U.S. Army, 1959-61. Mem. Am. Chem. Soc., AAAS, Lab. Retiree Group, Inc. (Los Alamos, treas., bd. dirs. 1995-98), Los Alamos Ret. and Sr. Orgn. (pres., bd. dirs. 1999-2002), Mil. Order World Wars (MG Franklin E. Miles chpt. adj. 1997-99, treas. 2000-02). Methodist. Home and Office: 1913 Spruce St Los Alamos NM 87544-3041

WALLACE, THOMAS C(HRISTOPHER), editor, literary agent; b. Vienna, Austria, Dec. 13, 1933; came to U.S., 1938; s. Don and Julia (Baer) W.; m. Lois Kahn, July 19, 1962 (div. May 2000); 1 son, George Baer; m. Barbara Shortt, Nov. 12, 2000. Grad., Peddie Sch., 1951; BA, Yale U., 1955, MA in History, 1957. Editor G.P. Putnam Sons, N.Y.C., 1959-63; with Holt, Rinehart & Winston, 1963-81, editor-in-chief gen. books div., 1968-81; v.p., sr. editor Simon and Schuster, 1981; editor W.W. Norton, 1982-87; v.p. Wallace Lit. Agy., 1987-98; pres. T. C. Wallace, Ltd., 1998—. Bd. dirs. Roger Klein Found. Mem. PEN, Yale Club, Century Assn. (N.Y.C.). Office: Ste 1001 425 Madison Ave Rm 1001 New York NY 10017-1110 E-mail: tcwallace@mindspring.com.

WALLACE, VICTOR LEW, computer science educator; b. Bklyn., Mar. 20, 1933; s. Frank Hobart and Victoria (Schwerthoffer) W.; m. Mary E. Jamieson, June 23, 1962; children: Robert Joseph, Andrew Gilbert. BEE, Poly. Inst. N.Y., 1955, MEE, 1957; PhD in Elec. Engring., Computer Sci., U. Mich., 1967. Mem. tech. staff Bell Telephone Labs., N.Y.C., 1954-55; mathematician-programmer IBM Corp., 1955-57; instr. elec. engring. U. Mich., Ann Arbor, 1957-61, research scientist, 1959-69; assoc. prof. computer sci. U. N.C., Chapel Hill, 1969-76; prof. computer sci. U. Kans., Lawrence, 1976—2001, chmn. dept. computer sci., 1976-84, prof. emeritus, 2001—. Acad. vis. U. London, Eng., 1970; cons. Los Alamos (N.Mex.) Nat. Lab., 1975-78, Honeywell Corp., Phoenix, 1982-87; cons. in field., 1962—. Co-author: To Compute Numerically--Concepts and Strategies, 1983; contbr. articles to profl. jours. Mem. IEEE (life), AAUP, Assn. Computing Machinery, Inst. Ops. Rsch. & Mgmt. Scis. , Sigma Xi. Democrat. Congregationalist. Home: 1509 Massachusetts St Lawrence KS 66044-4253 Office: U Kans ITTC Nicholls Hall Lawrence KS 66045 E-mail: wallace@ukans.edu.

WALLACE, VIRGINIA BARTON, retired lawyer; b. Butler, PA, Sept. 14, 1908; d. James Lowrie and Olive Louise (Roberts) Barton; m. Sillman Eugene Wallace, Aug. 23, 1947 (div. Feb. 1979). BA, Wellesley Coll., Mass., 1930; postgrad., U. Wyo., 1946-48; JD, U. Penn., 1950. Bar: Pa. 1950. Editor Bulletin Index Mag., Pitts., 1931-34; freelance journalist Pitts./Gettysburg, 1934-42; assoc. White and Williams, LLP, Phila., 1950-61, ptnr., 1961-80; ret., 1980. 1st Lt. WAC, 1942-45, PTO. Decorated three Bronze stars, U.S. Army Mem. ABA, Pa. Bar Assn., Phila. Bar Assn., AAUW, LWV, VFW. Episcopalian. Avocations: music, bridge, travel, history. Home: 255 Crosslands Dr Kennett Square PA 19348-2324 E-mail: vbwallace@mymailstation.com.

WALLACE, WALTER C. lawyer, government official; b. N.Y.C., Mar. 25, 1924; m. Frances Helm, Apr. 5, 1963; 1 dau., Laura. BA magna cum laude, St. John's U., Hillsdale, N.Y., 1948; LLB with distinction, Cornell U., 1951. Bar: N.Y. 1952, Calif. 1954, D.C. 1975, U.S. Dist. Ct. (no. dist.) Calif. 1954, U.S. Ct. Appeals (9th cir.) 1954, D.C. 1975, U.S. Dist. Ct. D.C. 1975, U.S. Ct. Appeals (D.C. cir.) 1975. Assoc. Cahill, Gordan & Reindel, N.Y.C., 1951-54; exec. asst. sec. of labor Dept. of Labor, Washington, 1955-60, asst. sec. of labor, 1960-61; gen. counsel Presdl. R.R. Commn., 1961; v.p. labor rels. Hudson Pulp & Paper Corp., N.Y.C., 1963-73; pres. Bituminous Coal Operators Assoc., Washington, 1974-75; ptnr. Ables & Wallace, 1977-80; prin. Law Offices Walter C. Wallace, N.Y.C., 1981-82; mem. Nat. Mediation Bd., Washington, 1982—, chmn., 1983, 85, 88. U.S. del. Internat. Labor Orgn. Conf. on Labor Rels. in Timber Industry, Geneva, 1958. Mem. bd. editors Cornell Law Quar., 1950-51. Bd. dirs. Nat. Safety Coun., Washington, 1974-75; asst. to chmn. United Givers Fund, Washington, 1956, mem. admission and allocations com., 1957-58. Staff sgt. U.S. Army, 1943-45, ETO. Decorated Bronze Star; recipient Presdl. commendation Pres. Eisenhower, Washington, 1961, Disting. Svc. award United Givers Fund, 1956, Disting. Svc. award Nat. Mediation Bd., 1990. Mem. Calif. Bar Assn., N.Y. State Bar Assn., D.C. Bar Assn., Order of Coif. Republican. Roman Catholic. Home: 55 Central Park W New York NY 10023-6003

WALLACE, WILLIAM, III, engineering executive; b. Bklyn., June 7, 1926; s. William and Ruth (Fitch) W.; m. Dorothy Ann Reimann, Aug. 2, 1969 (dec.); 1 child, Andrew William. B.E.E., Union Coll., 1947. Registered prof. engr., 22 states. Test engr. Gen. Electric Co., Schenectady, 1947; engr. Ebasco Services Inc., N.Y.C., 1948-67, chief elec. engr., 1967-70, mgr. projects, 1970-73, v.p. Atlanta office Norcross, Ga., 1973-76, exec. v.p. N.Y.C., 1976-80, dir., pres., chief exec. officer, 1980-82, chmn., chief exec. officer, 1982-86, also bd. dirs.; cons., 1986—. Bd. dirs. McNab Corp. Chmn. bd. advisors Sch. engring., N.C. State U., 1986-89; mem. adv. bd. trustees Union Coll.; trustee Poly. Prep. Country Day Sch.; trustee Saddle River Day Sch.; deacon West Side Presbyn. Ch., Ridgewood, N.J., 1988-90, 96-2000, elder, 1990-93, trustee, 2000-2003. Mem. IEEE (sr.), NSPE, N.J. State Soc. Profl. Engrs., World Rehab. Fund (bd. dirs. 1986-96), N.Y.C. C. of C. and Industry (bd. dirs. 1980-88), Delta Upsilon (vice chmn. Ednl. Found. 1986-95). Republican. Home and Office: 84 Buckhaven Hl Upper Saddle River NJ 07458 E-mail: wwallaceiii@mindspring.com.

WALLACE, WILLIAM AUGUSTINE, philosophy and history educator; b. N.Y.C., May 11, 1918; s. William Augustine and Louise Cecilia (Teufel) W. BEE, Manhattan Coll., 1940, LHD (hon.), 1975; MS in Physics, Cath. U. Am., 1952; PhD in Philosophy, U. Freiburg, Switzerland, 1959, STD, 1962; Lector of Sacred Theology, Dominican House of Studies, Washington, 1954, M of Sacred Theology, 1967; DSc (hon.), Providence Coll., 1973; DLitt (hon.), Molloy Coll., 1974; LHD (hon.), Fairfield U., 1986. Entered Dominican Order, 1946; ordained priest Roman Cath. Ch., 1953. Elec. engr. Consol. Edison, N.Y.C., 1940-41; rsch. engr. Naval Ordnance Lab., Washington, 1941-43; lector philosophy Dominican House of Philosophy, Dover, Mass., 1954-62; philosophy editor New Cath. Ency., Washington, 1962-65; rsch. assoc. Harvard U., Cambridge, Mass., 1965-67; regent of studies Dominican House of Studies, Washington, 1967-70; prof. philosophy and history Cath. U. Am., 1970-88, prof. emeritus, 1988—; prof. philosophy U. Md., College Park, 1988—. Mem. Inst. for Advanced Study, Princeton, 1976-77; fellow Woodrow Wilson Ctr. for Scholars, Washington, 1983-84; dir. gen. Leonine Commn., Washington, 1976-87. Author: The Scientific Methodology of Theodoric of Freiberg, 1959, The Role of Demonstration in Moral Theology, 1963, Causality and Scientific Explanation, vol. 1, 1972, vol. 2, 1974, The Elements of Philosophy, 1977, From a Realist Point of View, 1979 2d edit. 1983, Prelude to Galileo, 1981, Galileo and His Sources, 1984, Galileo, the Jesuits, and the Medieval Aristotle, 1991, Galileo's Logic of Discovery and Proof, 1992, The Modeling of Nature, 1996; editor, translator: Thomas Aquinas: Cosmogony, 1967, Galileo's Early Notebooks: the Physical Questions, 1977, Galileo's Logical Treatises, 1992; editor: Reinterpreting Galileo, 1986, Albertus Magnus, 1996; co-editor: Galileo Galilei: De praecognitionibus and De demonstratione, 1988; assoc. editor for sci. and philosophy Encyclopedia of the Renaissance, 1999; mem. editl. bd. Rev. of Metaphysics, The Thomist; contbr. over 350 articles to jours., encys. and books. Lt. Comdr. USN, 1941-46, PTO. Decorated Legion of Merit; recipient Alumni Achievement award Manhattan Coll., 1967, Alumni Achievement award Cath. U. Am., 1986; grantee NSF, 1965-84, NEH, 1981-89. Mem. Am. Cath. Philos. Assn. (pres. 1969-70, Aquinas medal 1983), History of Sci. Soc. (mem. coun. 1974-77, 88-91), Philosophy of Sci. Assn., Phi Beta Kappa, Sigma Xi. Democrat. E-mail: wallacew@wam.umd.edu.

WALLACE, WILLIAM HALL, economic and financial consultant; b. Senatobia, Miss., Aug. 8, 1933; s. Woodard Harvey and Cellie (Carter) W.; m. Margaret Jaeger, Mar. 7, 1964 (dec. 1978); children— Amy Margaret, William Douglas, John Richard Bruce; m. Virginia Wilson, Aug. 25, 1979 BBA, U. Miss., 1955, MBA, 1956; PhD, U. Ill., 1962. Asst. prof. econs. Duke U., Durham, N.C., 1962-67; v.p. Fed. Res. Bank Richmond, Va., 1967-73; prof. econs. N.C. State U., Raleigh, 1973-74; staff dir. Fed. Res. Bd., Washington, 1974-80; 1st v.p., chief oper. officer Fed. Res. Bank Dallas, 1981-91; prof. fin., dean Coll. Bus. and Pub. Adminstrn. Old Dominion U., Norfolk, Va., 1991-94; ret., 1994; pres. Wallace Cons., Inc., 1994—. Co-dir. Eurasia Found. Program in Banking & Fin. Markets for Russia and CIS, 1994-95; tchr. Israel Coll., Tel Aviv, 1998-2000; adj. prof. econs. U. North Tex., Denton, Tex., 2001—. Trustee Dallas Hist. Soc.; mem. Dallas Com. Fgn. Rels. Served to 1st lt. U.S. Army, 1956-58 Mem. Am. Econs. Assn., Am. Statis. Assn., Cen. Dallas Assn. (exec. com.), Greater Dallas C. of C. (edn. com. 1984-88, chmn. edn. com. 1989-90), Rotary. Methodist. Home: 3945 Evesham Dr Plano TX 75025-3820 Office: U North Tex Dept Econs Wooten Hall 353 Denton TX 76203 E-mail: whw2511@aol.com.

WALLACE DOUGLAS, JEAN, conservationist; b. Des Moines, June 30, 1920; d. Henry A. and Ilo Wallace; m. Wallace Leslie Douglas, Oct. 12, 1946; children: David, Joan, Ann. BA, Connecticut Coll., 1943. Pres. Wallace Genetic Found., Washington, 1965—. Bd. dirs. America, The Beautiful, Am. Bird Conservancy, Cornell Lab. of Ornithology, The Land Inst., Wallace House Birthplae; past mem. bd. dirs. The Accokeek Found., Am. Farmland Trust, Concern, Henry A. Wallace Inst. for Alternative Agr. Office: Wallace Genetic Found Ste 220 4900 Massachusetts Ave NW Washington DC 20016-4358

WALLACH, ALAN, art historian, educator; b. Bklyn., June 8, 1942; s. Israel and Vivian (Esner) W.; m. Phyllis Rosenzweig, Jan. 3, 1988. BA, Columbia U., 1963, MA, 1965, PhD, 1973. Assoc. prof. Kean Coll., Union, N.J., 1974-89; Ralph H. Wark prof. art and art history, prof. Am. studies Coll. William and Mary, Williamsburg, Va., 1989—. Vis. prof. UCLA, 1982-83, Stanford (Calif.) U., 1987, CUNY, 1988, U. Mich., 1989; co-curator Nat. Mus. Am. Art, Washington, 1991-94. Author: (with William Truettner) Thomas Cole: Landscape into History, 1994; Exhibiting Contradiction: Essays on the Art Museum in the United States, 1998; contbr. articles to profl. jours. Sr. Postdoctorate Rsch. award Smithsonian Inst., 1985-86. Mem. Am. Studies Assn., Coll. Art Assn. (bd. dirs. 1996-2000), Assn. Art Historians, editorial bd. Am. Quarterly. Home: 2009 Belmont Rd NW Washington DC 20009-5449 Office: Coll William and Mary Dept Art and Art History Williamsburg VA 23187-8795 E-mail: axwall@wm.edn.

WALLACH, ANNE JACKSON See JACKSON, ANNE

WALLACH, BARBARA PRICE, classicist, educator; b. Roanoke, Va., Aug. 31, 1946; d. Benjamin Thomas and Geneva Mae (Bittinger) Price; m. Luitpold Wallach, Aug. 22, 1970 (dec. Nov. 1986). BA in Latin, Mary Washington

Coll., 1968; MA in Classics, U. Ill., 1970, PhD in Classical Philology, 1974. Summer vis. lectr. U. Ill., Urbana, 1977; vis. asst. prof. U. Pitts., 1979-80; asst. prof. U. Mo., Columbia, 1980-85, assoc. prof., 1985—. Author: Lucretius and the Diatribe, 1976; contbr. articles to profl. jours. Mem. Am. Philol. Assn., Classical Assn. Middle West and South, Internat. Soc. for the History of Rhetoric, Vergilian Soc., Phi Beta Kappa. Democrat. Avocations: music, flute, reading, sports. Office: U Mo Dept Classical Studies Columbia MO 65211-0001

WALLACH, DAVID MICHAEL, lawyer; b. Ft. Worth, Nov. 13, 1954; s. David Edward and Zelma Jane (Gilbreath) W.; m. Susan Danell Hailey, Aug. 16, 1975; children: Landon James, Tyler Field, Carter Hailey. BA, Tex. Christian U., 1975; JD, U. Houston, 1979. Bar: Tex. 1979, U.S. Dist. Ct. (no. dist.) Tex. 1979, U.S. Ct. Appeals (5th and 11th cirs.) 1979, U.S. Dist. Ct. (so. dist.) Tex. 1986, U.S. Dist. Ct. (we. dist.) Tex. 1992. Assoc. Shannon, Gracey, Ratliff & Miller, Ft. Worth, 1979-83, ptnr., 1983-91; shareholder Wallach & Moore PC, 1991—. Contbr. articles to profl. jours. Named Boss of Yr. Fort Worth Legal Secs. Assn., 1991. Fellow Tex. Bar Found.; mem. Tex. Assn. Def. Counsel (v.p. programs 1993-96, bd. dirs. 1989-96, 97—, v.p. North Tex. region 1997-98, exec. v.p. 1999-00, pres.'s award 1992), Def. Rsch. Inst., Tarrant County Civil Trial Lawyers Assn. (pres. 1988-89, exec. v.p. 1987-88), State Bar Tex., Tarrant County Bar Assn., North Tex. Soc. for Health Care Risk Mgmt., Health Industry Coun. Dallas-Ft. Worth Region, Shriners, Masons. Republican. Methodist. Avocations: golf, snow skiing, racquetball. Office: Wallach & Moore PC 1300 Summit Ave Ste 300 Fort Worth TX 76102-4417 E-mail: mwallach@wallachmoore.com.

WALLACH, EDWARD ELIOT, physician, educator; b. N.Y.C., Oct. 8, 1933; s. David Abraham and Madeleine (Spiro) W.; m. Joanne Levey, June 24, 1956; children: Paul, Julie. BA, Swarthmore Coll., 1954; MD, Cornell U., 1958; MA (hon.), U. Pa., 1970. Diplomate Am. Bd. Ob-Gyn. (bd. dirs. 1989-97, dir. divsn. reproductive endocrinology 1989-96), Am. Bd. Reproductive Endocrinology. Intern 2d med. div. Bellevue Hosp., N.Y.C., 1958-59; resident obstetrics and gynecology Kings County Hosp., Bklyn., 1959-63; asst. instr. State U. N.Y. Downstate Med. Center, 1962-63; mem. faculty U. Pa. Sch. Medicine, 1965-84, prof. obstetrics and gynecology, 1971-84, chief endocrinology sect., div. human reprodn., dept. obstetrics and gynecology, 1968-71, mem. admissions com., 1970-73, mem. community health com., 1966-71, mem. student adv. com., 1966-84, mem. com. for appointments and promotions, 1972-77, chmn., 1974-77; dir. dept. obstetrics and gynecology Pa. Hosp., 1971-84, sec., treas. profl. staff, 1972-75; prof., chmn. dept. ob-gyn. Johns Hopkins U. Sch. Medicine, 1984-94, chmn. med. staff, 1991-94, prof., 1984-94. Vis. prof. ob-gyn. U. Kyoto Sch. Medicine, 1981; vis. prof. Keio U. Sch. Medicine, 1987; mem. fertility and maternal health drugs adv. com. FDA, 1992-96; bd. dirs. Am. Bd. Emergency Medicine, 1998—. Assoc. editor: Fertility and Sterility, 1974—; co-editor: Modern Trends in Infertility and Conception Control; editor-in-chief Postgrad. Ob-Gyn., 1980—; mem. editl. bd. Fertility and Sterility, 1970—, Ob-Gyn., 1976-79, Contemporary Ob-Gyn., 1976—, Biology of Reprodn., 1978-84; editor-in-chief Current Opinion in Ob-Gyn., 1989-93; contbr. to med. jours. Trustee Marriage Council Phila., 1970-78; chmn. finance com. Phila. Coordinating Council for Family Planning, 1972-73, chmn. med. adv. com., 1973-76; trustee Balt. Chamber Orch., 1989-97. Served as surgeon USPHS, 1963-65. Trainee NIH, 1961-62; recipient Lindback Found. Disting. Teaching award U. Pa., 1971 Fellow Am. Coll. Ob-Gyn., Am. Fertility Soc. (dir. 1977-81, pres. 1985-86); mem. Am. Gynecol. and Obstet. Soc. (v.p. 1983-84), Soc. Gynecol. Investigation (pres. 1986-87), Am. Bd. Ob-Gyn. (bd. dirs. 1989-97, dir. divsn. reproductive endocrinology 1989-96), Phila. Endocrine Soc., Obstet. Soc. Phila. (program chmn. 1969-70, 70-71, 71-72, mem. coun. 1972-83, v.p. 1976-77, pres. 1979-80), Soc. Study Reprodn., Inst. Medicine/NAS, Am. Fertility Soc. (pres. 1985-86), Soc. Gynecol. Investigation (pres. 1986-87), Am. Gynecol. and Obstet. Soc. (v.p. 1984), Phila. Obstet. Soc. (pres. 1980), Inst. of Medicine, Alpha Omega Alpha. Office: Johns Hopkins Med Instn 600 N Wolfe St Baltimore MD 21287-0005

WALLACH, ELI, actor; b. Bklyn., Dec. 7, 1915; s. Abraham and Bertha (Schorr) W.; m. Anne Jackson, Mar. 5, 1948; children: Peter Douglas, Roberta Lee, Katherine Beatrice. AB, U. Tex., 1936; MS in Edn, CCNY, 1938; student, Neighborhood Playhouse Sch. of Theatre, 1940; hon. doctorate, Emerson Coll., Boston, Sch. for Visual Arts, 1991. Corp. mem., dir. Neighborhood Playhouse Sch. Theatre. Actor, 1945—; Broadway plays include Antony and Cleopatra, 1948, Mr. Roberts, 1949-50, Rose Tatoo, 1950-52, Camino Real, 1953, Mademoiselle Colombe, 1953, Teahouse of the August Moon, 1954-55, London prodn., 1954, Major Barbara, 1956, Rhinoceros, 1961, Luv, 1964, Promenade All, 1972, Twice Around the Park, 1983, Opera Comique, Kennedy Ctr. Performing Arts, 1987, The Flowering Peach, Fla., 1987, Broadway, 1994, Cafe Crown, 1989; appeared off-Broadway prodn. Typists and the Tiger, 1962-63, London prodn., 1964, Saturday, Sunday, Monday, 1974, (with wife and 2 daus.) Diary of Anne Frank, 1977-78, Visiting Mr. Green, 1997; off-Broadway in Tennessee Williams Remembered, 1999; on tour Down the Garden Paths, 1998-99; appeared in: nat. tour co. Waltz of the Toreadors, 1973-74; appeared in TV film Murder By Reason of Insanity, 1985, TV series Our Family Honor, 1985, TV miniseries Christopher Columbus, 1985, Executioner's Song, 1986, Monday Night Mayhem, 2000, The Education of Max Bickford, 2002; motion pictures include Baby Doll, 1955, The Misfits, 1960, The Victors, 1962, Lord Jim, 1964, How To Steal a Million, The Good, the Bad and the Ugly, The Tiger Makes Out, Band of Gold, Zig-Zag, Cinderella Liberty, 1973, Crazy Joe, 1973, Movie, Movie, 1976, Sam's Son, 1985, Tough Guys, 1986, Rocket to the Moon,1986, Nuts, 1987, The Impossible Spy, 1987, Godfather III, 1990, The Two Jakes, 1990, Article 99, Mistress, 1991, Night and the City, 1991, Honey, Sweet Love, 1993, Two Much, 1995, The Associate, 1996, Keeping the Faith, 1999, (TV movie) Monday Night Mahem. Served to capt. Med. Adminstrn. Corps AUS, World War II. Recipient Donaldson, Theatre World, Variety, Antoinette Perry, Drama League awards, Brit. Film Acad. award, 1956, Disting. Alumnus award U. Tex., 1989. Original mem. Actors Studio.

WALLACH, ERIC JEAN, lawyer; b. N.Y.C., June 11, 1947; s. Milton Harold and Jacqueline (Goldschmidt) W.; m. Miriam Grunberger, Mar. 21, 1976; children: Katherine, Emily, Peter. BA, Harvard U., 1968, JD, 1972. Bar: N.Y. 1973, U.S. Dist. Ct. (so. and ea. dists.) N.Y. 1973, U.S. Dist. Ct. (no. dist.) N.Y. 1989, U.S. Ct. Appeals (2nd cir.) 1973, (3d cir.) 1996, U.S. Tax Ct. 1976. Assoc. Webster & Sheffield, N.Y.C., 1972-77, Rosenman & Colin, N.Y.C., 1977-80, ptnr., 1981-96, mem. mgmt. com., 1993-96, chmn. employment practice group, 1985-96; ptnr., chmn. employment practice group Kasowitz, Benson, Torres & Friedman LLP, 1996—. Presenter, chmn. CLE programs, Practising Law Inst., Cambridge Inst., others. Mem. editl. bd. You and the Law, 1992-96; contbr. articles to profl. jours. Sec.-treas. Art Dealers Assn. Am., Inc., N.Y.C., 1985-96; trustee C.G. Jung Found. for Analytical Psychology; trustee Am. Jewish World Svc., Inc., N.Y.C., 1989-97, chmn., 1995-97; dir. N.Y. Jr. Tennis League. Mem. Harvard Club N.Y.C. (admissions com. 1992-94), Sunningdale Country Club, Poughkeepsie Tennis Club. Democrat. Avocations: sports, travel, reading. Home: 940 Park Ave New York NY 10028 also: 16 Buttonwood Ln Rhinebeck NY 12572-3510 Office: Kasowitz Benson Torres & Friedman LLP 1633 Broadway New York NY 10019 E-mail: ewallach@kasowitz.com.

WALLACH, HAROLD CHARLES, health policy and health services research administrator, educator; b. N.Y.C., Oct. 25, 1935; s. Albert and Sarah Wallach; m. Anita Deanna Gambone, May 7, 1967; children: Jason, Noah. BA, U. Bridgeport, 1957; MS, U. Mich., 1958. Rsch. psychologist Human Factors Lab., Aberdeen, Md., 1960-62; statistician Bur. Census, Suitland, 1962-64, chief social rsch. staff, 1975-80; supr. statistician HUD, Washington, 1964-66; sr. social scientist Booz Allen, Bethesda, Md., 1966-70; prin. statistician U.S. Gen. Acctg. Office, Washington, 1981—. Cons., adj. prof. U. Md., College Park, 1970-75, adj. prof. Dept. Social/Med. Sci., 1995—; adj. prof. Georgetown Med. Sch., Washington. Contbr. articles to profl. jours. Adj. minister Washington Ethical Soc., Washington, 1990—, v.p., bd. trustee, 1988-89; pres. Civic Assn., 1972-80, PTA, Montgomery County, Md., 1972-80; bd. dirs. United Way Metro Area, Washington, 1975-79; chair health com. Am. Ethical Union, 2000—; mem. Aging Commn., Montgomery County, 2001—; chmn. Md. State Coalition for Health Care Accountability, 2001—. Named Ky. Col. Gov. Ky., Frankfurt, 1977. Mem. Am. Sociol. Assn. (com. mem. 1985-87, 96—), Am. Stat. Assn. (com. chmn. 1984-85), Am. Pub. Health Assn. (com. sect. 1977), Nat. Coun. Family Relations (v.p. 1987-91, Svc. award 1987-91), Nat. Assn. Retired Fed. Employees (legis. v.p. 2000—). Home: 5205 Myer Ct Rockville MD 20853-2349

WALLACH, HOWARD FREDERIC, psychiatrist; b. Chgo., Sept. 4, 1923; s. Leo and Mildred (Ebert) W.; m. Laurie Rochelle Gettleman, Sept. 15, 1945 (div. July 1968); children: Joan, John, Richard; m. Gloria Bunny Jackman, July 14, 1968; children: Rand, Steve, Beth. MD, U. Ill., Chgo., 1946; M.Social Psychiatry, UCLA, 1969. Diplomate Am. Bd. Psychiatry and Neurology. Intern Cook County Hosp., Chgo., 1946—47, resident internal medicine, 1947—49; pres. Mount Sinai Hosp. Med. Rsch. Found., 1952—64; asst. clin. prof. psychiatry UCLA, 1968—80, assoc. clin. prof., 1980—; chief allied mental health Brentwood VA Hosp., 1970—72; chief psychiatry Sepulveda VA Hosp., 1972—74; pvt. practice. Bd. govs. Cedars-Sinai Med. Ctr., L.A., 1985—, mem. exec. com., 2000—; cons. VA Med. Ctr., L.A., 1982-90; developer maj. high rise apts., Chgo., 1951-64. Contbr. articles to profl. jours. Sec. Am. Psychiat. Found., Washington, 1990-99; bd. dirs. Nat. Mus. Health and Medicine, Washington, 1989-99; v.p. Jewish Family Svc. of L.A., 1997-98; bd. dirs., pres. Young Men's Jewish Charities, Chgo., 1951-62; mem. Cook County Blue Ribbon Commn., 1959-63. 1st lt. U.S. Army, 1943-46. Recipient Bronze award Boys Clubs of Am., 1962, Pres.'s Spl. Achievement award So. Calif. Psychiat. Soc., 1991. Fellow Am. Coll. Psychoanalysts, Am. Psychiat. Assn. (exec. com. 1982-88), Am. Acad. Psychoanalysis; mem. Calif. Psychiat. Assn. (pres. 1986-88), So. Calif. Psychiat. Soc. (pres. 1979-80, mem. coun. 1975-83), Alpha Omega Alpha. Avocations: photography, computers, golf, walking, presidential manuscript collecting. Office: 2080 Century Park E Los Angeles CA 90067-2001 E-mail: hfwallach@yahoo.com.

WALLACH, IRA DAVID, lawyer, business executive; b. N.Y.C., June 3, 1909; s. Joseph and Della (Kahn) W.; m. Miriam Gottesman, Dec. 25, 1938. BA, Columbia U., 1929, JD, 1931, LLD (hon.), 1983, U. Maine, 1983. Bar: N.Y. 1932. Practiced in, N.Y.C., 1932-45; exec. v.p. Gottesman & Co., Inc. (name changed to Central Nat.-Gottesman Inc. 1984), 1952-56, pres., CEO, 1956-74, chmn., CEO, 1974-79, chmn., 1979-2001, sr. vice chmn., 2001—, also bd. dirs. Exec. v.p. Ctrl. Nat. Corp., N.Y.C., 1952-56, pres., CEO, 1956-74, chmn., CEO, 1974-79, chmn., 1979—; exec. v.p. Eastern Corp., Bangor, Maine, 1951-52; dir., pres. Sejak Corp., N.Y.C., dir., exec. v.p. Cenro Corp., N.Y.C. Pres. D.S. and R.H. Gottesman Found., 1956—, bd. dirs., 1941—; chmn., dir. Miriam and Ira D. Wallach Found., 1956—; co-founder, chmn. emeritus East West Inst., 1981—; bd. dirs. Internat. Peace Acad., People for the Am. Way Found. Lt. USNR, 1943-46. Mem. Am. Bar Assn., Assn. of Bar of City of N.Y., N.Y. Co. Lawyers Assn. Home: 5 Sherbrooke Rd Scarsdale NY 10583-4429 Office: 3 Manhattanville Rd Purchase NY 10577-2116

WALLACH, JACQUES BURTON, pathologist, educator; b. N.Y.C., Jan. 25, 1926; s. Joseph Irving and Rose Gertrude (Bernstein) W.; m. Doris Foss, Sept. 5, 1953; children: Kim, Lisa, Tracy. Student, NYU, 1941-43; MD, L.I. Coll. Medicine, SUNY, 1947. Diplomate Am. Bd. Pathology. Instr. pathology Albert Einstein Coll. Medicine, Bronx, N.Y., 1954-55, asst. prof. pathology, 1955-59, vis. asst. prof. pathology, 1959-69; clin. assoc. prof. pathology Rutgers Med. Sch., Piscataway, N.J., 1971—; clin. prof. pathology SUNY, Bklyn., 1979—. Cons. in clin. pathology N.Y. Zool. Soc., Bronx (N.Y.) Zoo, 1954-84. Author: Rheumatic Heart Disease, 1962, Interpretation of Diagnostic Tests, 1970, 7th edit., 2000 (translated into Spanish, Italian, Portuguese, Greek, Russian, Romanian, Hungarian, Turkish, Chinese and Japanese), Interpretation of Pediatric Tests, 1983. With USNR, 1944-45. Named Hon. Prof. of Pathology, Univ. Ica, Peru, 1981. Fellow Am. Coll. Physicians, Am. Soc. Clin. Pathologists, Coll. Am. Pathologists, N.Y. Acad. Medicine. Achievements include patents in apparatus and method for processing flexible medical slides. Home and Office: 10 Ashbourne Dr Monroe Township NJ 08831-4655

WALLACH, KENNETH L. paper company executive; b. N.Y.C., 1946; BA, Harvard Coll., 1968, JD, 1972. Chmn., pres., CEO Ctrl. Nat.-Gottesman Inc., Purchase, N.Y., 1998—. Trustee Am. Mus. Natural History; dir. 92d St. Y, Syracuse Pulp and Paper Found. Office: Ctrl Nat-Gottesman Inc 3 Manhattanville Rd Purchase NY 10577-2110

WALLACH, LESLIE ROTHAUS, architect; b. Pitts., Feb. 4, 1944; s. Albert and Sara F. (Rothaus) W.; m. Susan Rose Berger, June 15, 1969; 1 child, Aaron. BS in Mining Engring., U. Ariz., 1967, BArch, 1974. Registered architect, Ariz.; registered contractor, Ariz. Prin. Line and Space LLC, Tucson, 1978—. Mem. awards jury Sunset mag., 1997, Ariz. Homes of Yr., 1997, L.A. AIA; keynote spkr. various confs.; chair Coll. of Arch. Design Coun., U. Ariz., 1998. Representative projects include Ariz. Sonora Desert Mus. Restaurant Complex, Tucson, Elgin Elem. Sch., Ariz., Hillel Student Ctr. U. Ariz., Tucson, Boyce Thompson Southwestern Arborteum Vis. Ctr., Superior, Ariz., San Pedro Riparian Ctr., Sierra Vista, Ariz., Nat. Hist. Trails Ctr., Casper, Wyo., 2002, Vis. Ctr. and Arborteum, Flagstaff, Ariz., 2001, Regional Libr., Phoenix, 2002; contbr. Sunset Mag., Architecture Mag. and Fine Homebuilding; pub.: Space and Society (Italy), Hinge (Hong Kong), Wallpaper (London); exhibited at U. Ariz., AIA Nat. Conv., Washington. Bd. dirs Tucson Regional Plan, Inc.; pres. Civitas Sonoran (The Environ. Design Coun. of the U. of Ariz. Coll. of Arch.). Recipient Roy P. Drachman Design award, 1982, 85, 93, 2001, Electric League Ariz. Design award, 1987, 88, Gov. Solar Energy award, 1989, Desert Living awards citation, 1991, Ariz. Architect's medal, 1989, Disting. Alumni award U. Ariz., 1998, also 35 additional design awards, including 4 received in 1995, winner $25,000 prize, nat. Endowment of the Arts, 2002, Coll. of Architecture Alumni of Yr., U. Az., 2001. Fellow AIA (Ariz. Honor award 1989, 92, 96, AIA/ACSA Nat. Design award 1991, Western Mountain region Design award 1992, 96, CA AIA/Phoenix Homes and Gardens Home of the Yr. Honor award 1992, 96, Western Region Silver medal 1996); mem. SAC AIA (past pres., Design award 1985, 88, 90), Mountain Region AIA (named Firm of Yr. 1999). Office: Line and Space 627 E Speedway Blvd Tucson AZ 85705-7433 E-mail: studio627@lineandspace.com.

WALLACH, MAGDALENA FALKENBERG (CARLA WALLACH), writer; b. Brussels; d. Carl Albert and Renee Antoinette (Meunier) Falkenberg; m. Philip Charles Wallach, Mar. 5, 1950. Student, Columbia U., Hunter Coll., New Sch. for Social Rsch. Ptnr. Williams-Falkenberg Advt. Assocs., Inc., N.Y.C., 1951-55. Author: Reluctant Weekend Gardener, 1971, Interior Decorating with Plants, 1976, Gardening in the City, 1976, Garden in a Teacup, 1978; contbr. articles to N.Y. Times, Glamour, Working Woman, Greenwich Time, Stamford Adv, others. Former bd. dirs. ARC, N.Y.C.; active Bruce Mus., 1987—, chmn. spl. events 75th anniversary gala, chmn. Renaissance Ball, bd. dirs., also other fundraising activities; former bd. dirs., v.p. Greenwich Adult Day Ctr. Mem. Nat. League Am. PEN Women (pres. Greenwich br. 1987-92, Owl award 1996), Authors Guild, Garden Writers Assn., English-Speaking Union (past bd. dirs. Greenwich br.), Alliance Francaise, Nat. Inst. Social Scis. Roman Catholic. Avocations: gardening, reading, travel, music, theater. Home: 126 W Lyon Farm Dr Greenwich CT 06831-4352

WALLACH, MARK IRWIN, lawyer; b. May 19, 1949; s. Ivan A. and Janice (Grossman) W.; m. Karla L. Wallach, 1996; children: Kerry Melissa, Philip Alexander; stepchildren: Daniel Kanter, Rachel Kanter, Adam Kanger BA magna cum laude, Wesleyan U., 1971; JD cum laude, Harvard U., 1974. Bar: Ohio 1974, U.S. Dist. Ct. (no. dist.) Ohio, 1974, U.S. Ct. Appeals (6th cir.) 1985, U.S. Supreme Ct. 1985. Law clk. U.S. Dist. Ct., Cleve., 1974-75; assoc. Baker & Hostetler, 1975-79; chief trial counsel City of Cleve., 1979-81; assoc. Calfee, Halter & Griswold, Cleve., 1981-82, ptnr., 1982—, exec. com., 1997-99. Mem. fed. ct. adv. com. U.S. Dist. Ct. (no. dist.) Ohio, 1991-95; chmn. bd. trustees Ohio Group Against Smoking Pollution, 1986-90; trustee Cleve. chpt. Am. Jewish Com., 1986—, sec. 1989-91, v.p., 1991-95, pres., 1995-97; bd. trustees Citizens League of Greater Cleve., 1978-79, 87-92. Author: Christopher Morley, 1976. Pres. Wesleyan Alumni Club, Cleve., 1983-87, 92—; trustee Lyric Opera, Cleve., 1995—, pres., 1996-98, Ratner Schs., 1994-96; pres. Performing Arts Together, 1997-2001; trustee The Sculpture Ctr.. 2001,pres., 2001—; trustee Bellefaire Jewish Children's Bur., 2001—. Mem. ABA, Ohio Bar Assn., Fed. Bar Assn., Cuyahoga County Law Dirs. Assn., The Cleve. Racquet Club, Greater Cleve. Bar Assn., The Club at Soc. Ctr. Avocations: reading, bicycling, space exploration, politics. Home: 2758 Claythorne Rd Shaker Heights OH 44122-1938 Office: Calfee Halter & Griswold 1400 McDonald Investment Ctr 800 Superior Ave E Ste 1800 Cleveland OH 44114-2688 E-mail: mwallach@calfee.com.

WALLACH, PHILIP C(HARLES), financial, public relations consultant; b. N.Y.C., Nov. 17, 1912; s. Edgar Smith and Rix Wallach; m. Magdalena Charlotta Falkenberg, Mar. 5, 1950. Student, NYU, 1930-33. Editor, writer Hearst Publs., N.Y.C., 1933-42; editor Shell Oil Co., 1943-46; editor, dir. pub. relations W.R. Grace & Co., 1946-54; dir. pub. relations and advt. H.K. Porter & Co., 1954-58; pres. Wallach Assocs., Inc., 1958-85; officer and v.p. investor rels. Occidental Petroleum Co., L.A., 1985-91; v.p. Occidental Internat. Corp., N.Y.C., 1987-91, cons., 1991-92. Pres. St. Paul Guild, N.Y.C., 1959-68, bd. dirs., 1964-72; pres. Cath. Inst. Press, N.Y.C., 1959-75; co-founder Air Force Assn., Washington, 1946; nat. committeeman Rep. Party, N.Y., 1945-60; mem. Rep. Nat. Com., Greenwich, Conn., 1982-91; bd. dirs., mem. exec. com. U.S. Pakistan Econ. Coun. With USAF, 1942-43. Mem. Overseas Press Club. Home: Greenwich, Conn. Died Oct. 28, 1992.

WALLACH, STEVEN ERNST, lawyer, pilot; b. N.Y.C., Mar. 21, 1944; s. Eduard Herbert Wallach and Karin (Wassermann) Grunebaum; m. Stefany Gay Rosehill (div. Oct. 1990); children: Shelby Karin, Shawna Beth; m. Geri Joan Grieco, Nov. 21, 1992. BS, USAF Acad., 1965; MS summa cum laude, U. So. Calif., 1971; JD magna cum laude, Nova U., 1986. Bar: Fla. 1986, D.C. 1988, U.S. Dist. Ct. (so. dist.) Fla. 1987, U.S. Dist. Ct. (mid. dist.) Fla. 1989, U.S. Dist. Ct. Ariz. 1989; cert. airline transport pilot, 1969; bd. cert. aviation law, 1998. Systems analyst Hughes Aircraft Co., L.A., 1971-72; airline capt. Eastern Air Lines, Miami, 1972-91; atty. Barwick, Dillian & Lambert P.A., Miami Shores, Fla., 1987-96; atty., ptnr. Thornton Davis & Murray, P.A., Miami, 1996-98. Aviation mgmt. cons. PRC Speas, Lake Success, N.Y., 1977-83, TRAMCO, Cambridge, Mass., 1972-77, A.V. lawyer, 1997, Steven Wallach Assoc., 1998—. Trustee Karin Grunebaum Cancer Found., Cambridge, 1979—. Capt. USAF, 1965-70. Decorated DFC, 5 air medals. Avocation: flying. Home: 2600 S Ocean Blvd Apt 21-E Boca Raton FL 33432

WALLACH-LEVY, WENDEE ESTHER, astrophotographer; b. N.Y.C., Dec. 29, 1948; d. Leonard Morris and Annette (Cohen) W.; m. David H. Levy, Mar. 23, 1997; 1 child, Nanette R. Vigil. BS in Edn., SUNY, Cortland, 1970; MA in Teaching, N.Mex. State U., 1975. Cert. tchr., N.Mex. Ret. tchr. phys. edn. Las Cruces (N.Mex.) Pub. Schs., 1970-96; mem. Shoemaker-Levy Observing Team, 1996—; mgr. Jarnac Obs., Vail, Ariz., 1997—; mem. Jarnac Sky Survey Team, 2001—. Intramural and athletic coord. White Sands Sch., 1970—93; instr. swimming N.Mex. State U. Weekend Coll., Las Cruces, 1986—96; dir., coord. learn to swim program ARC, Las Cruces, 1970—96; instr. phys. edn., coach volleyball and track, athletic coord. Sierra Mid. Sch., 1993—96. Co-author: Making Friends with the Stars, Cosmic Discoveries, 2001; co-host (local radio show) Let's Talk Stars. Instr. trainer water safety ARC, 1973-98, CPR, 1974-98; instr. life guard, trainer, health and safety specialist, 1988-96, instr., trainer standard first aid, 1991-98; chair com. health and safety svcs. Dona Ana County Red Cross. Named Water Safety Instr. of Yr. ARC, Las Cruces, 1986, 89, 25 Yr. Svc. award, 1992., 30 Yr. Svc. award, 1997; Asteroid 6485 named in her honor, 1997. Mem.: AAHPERD, Nat. Intramural-Recreational Sports Assn., N.Mex. Alliance Health, Phys. Edn. Recreation and Dance (spkr., aquatic chmn. 1990—92), Internat. Dark Sky Assn. (life). Democrat. Jewish. Avocations: skywatching, swimming, needlework, astro photography. Home and Office: 2500 E Wetstones Rd Vail AZ 85641-9754 E-mail: wendee@jarnac.org.

WALLA-MURPHY, MEGHAN ANNE, foundation administrator; b. Evanston, Ill., Feb. 8, 1975; d. Robert Joseph Murphy and Catherine Anne Walla. BA in Asian History with honors, BA in Molecular Biology, U. Calif., Santa Cruz, 1997. Co-founder, program dir. Wilderness Outdoor Leadership Found., Malibu, Calif. Vol. San Fernando Vol. Ctr., Panorama City, 1998—. Mem. Assn. Experiential Edn. Avocations: hiking, reading, rock climbing. Office: Wilderness Outdoor Leadership Found PO Box 2854 Malibu CA 09265

WALLANCE, GREGORY J. lawyer; b. Washington, Oct. 24, 1948; s. Donald Aaron Wallance and Shula Cohen; m. Elizabeth Van Veen, Jan. 4, 1981; children: Daniel, Carina, Lisanne. BA, Grinnell Coll., 1970; JD, Bklyn. Law Sch., 1976. Bar: N.Y. 1977, U.S. Dist. Ct. (ea. dist.) N.Y. 1977, U.S. Dist. Ct. (so. dist.) N.Y. 1978, U.S. Ct. Appeals (2d cir.) 1980, U.S. Dist. Ct. (no. dist.) 1989. Clk. to Hon. Jacob Mishler, N.Y.C., 1976-77; assoc. Paul, Weiss, Rifkind, Wharton & Garrison, 1977-79; asst. U.S. atty., U.S. Atty's. Office, 1979-85; assoc. Kaye Scholer Fierman Hays & Handler, 1985-88; ptnr. Kaye, Scholer, Fierman, Hays & Handler, 1988—; chief litigation counsel Kidder Peabody & Co., Inc., 1995—. Author: Papa's Game, 1981; assoc. prodr. (HBO) Sakharov, 1981; co-host The Law Show, (BBC), 1998; columnist Nat. Law Jour., 1993-98; contbr. articles to profl. jours. Vol. VISTA, N.Y.C., 1970-72. Mem. ABA, Assn. for Bar of City of N.Y. Office: Kaye Scholer Fierman Hays & Handler 425 Park Ave New York NY 10022-3506

WALLEM, PAUL SIGURD, financial planner; b. Ottawa, Ill., Mar. 14, 1934; s. Sigurd and Bertha Elene W.; m. Joan B. Wallem, Aug. 12, 1956; children: Jeffery, Linda, Stephen. BS, U. Ill., 1956. CFP. Terr. and sales mgr. Internat. Harvester Co., Chgo., 1958-66, export mgr., 1966-68; pres. Wallem Internat., Belvidere, Ill., 1969-86; owner Wallem Assocs., Rockford, 1986—. Chmn., bd. trustees Highland Hosp., Belvidere, 1977-79; founding dir. Vintage Wings and Wheels Mus., Poplar Grove, Ill., 1996—. 1st lt. U.S. Army, 1956-58. Republican. Methodist. Avocation: aviation. Office: Wallem Assocs 6068 Palo Verde Dr Rockford IL 61114

WALLEN, CARL JOSEPH, JR. education educator; b. Glendale, Calif., Dec. 12, 1931; s. Carl Joseph and Winifred (Batten) W.; m. LaDonna Leigh Stanley, Nov. 29, 1959; children: Erik Stanley, Todd Alan, Michael Carl. BA, U. Calif., Santa Barbara, 1956; MA, San Francisco State U., 1960; EdD, Stanford U., 1962. Tchr. 5th grade Mt. Eden Sch. Dist., Hayward, Calif., 1956-58; tchr. 3d and 6th grades Pacifica (Calif.) Sch. Dist., 1958-60; grad. asst. Stanford U., Palo Alto, Calif., 1960-62; asst. prof. Oreg. State U., Corvallis, 1962-65; assoc. prof. tchg. rsch. Oreg. Sys. Higher Edn., Monmouth, 1965-67; assoc. prof. U. Oreg., Eugene, 1967-73, dir. of U.S. Office of Edn. fellowship program, 1972-73; prof., chmn. dept. elem. edn. Ariz. State U., Tempe, 1973-78, prof., 1978-97, prof. emeritus, 1997—. Cons. to schs., dists. and state depts. edn. in Oreg. and Ariz., 1962—. Author: Competency in Teaching Reading, 1973, 82, Cognition and Effective Instruction, 1993, 94, 95, 96; co-author: Effective Classroom Management, 1978, Fraud Recognition: Claims Adjustors, 1993; also monographs and jour. articles. Mem. com. Am. Friends Svc. Com., Oreg. and Ariz., 1963—; co-founder, pres. Ariz. Ctr. to Reverse Arms Race, Phoenix, 1978-82; rep. Ariz. Ecumenical Coun., 1978—, pres., 1990-93, prison visitation and support, 1997—. With U.S. Army, 1952-54. U.S. OfficeEdn. fellow, 1972-73. Mem. Am. Ednl. Rsch. Assn., Phi Delta Kappa. Democrat. Mem. Soc. Of Friends. Avocations: woodworking, stained glass making, gardening. Home: 525 E Alameda Dr Tempe AZ 85282-3822 E-mail: clwallen@aol.com.

WALLENDER, MICHAEL TODD, lawyer; b. Schenectady, N.Y., Apr. 8, 1950; s. Kenneth Clark and Martha Lee (Getty) W.; m. Joyce Ann Mushaw, June 3, 1978; children: Kristina Lee, Michael David. BA, Colgate U., 1972; JD, Harvard U., 1975. Law asst. N.Y. State Supreme Ct. Appellate Div., Albany, 1975-76; assoc. DeGraff, Foy, Conway, Holt-Harris & Mealey, 1976-80, ptnr., 1981-90. Counsel N.Y. State Assn. Realtors, Albany, 1981—, Albany County Bd. Realtors, 1985-92, Capital Regional Multiple Listing Svc., Albany, 1986—, Greater Capitol Assn. Realtors, 1992—. Author: Realtors and the Law of Agency, 1988. Mem. ATLA, ABA, Lawyers for Justice in Ireland, N.Y. State Bar Assn., Albany County Bar Assn., Ft. Orange Club, Mohawk Golf Club, Colgate Club (capital dist. chpt., Albany), Saratoga Reading Rm. Avocation: thoroughbred horse racing. Home: 209 Agostino Ave Niskayuna NY 12309-1331 Office: 90 State St Ste 1501 Albany NY 12207-1714

WALLENGREN, ERNEST FERRIN, television producer, writer; b. Midway, Utah, Dec. 15, 1952; s. Delbert Ernest and Orma Claire W.; m. Cheryl Ann Alexis, Oct. 11, 1981; children: Alexis Claire, Katherine Louise, Seth Michael Ferrin, Brian Joseph, Daniel Evan. BA, Loyola Marymount U., Los Angeles, 1977. Story editor The Waltons Lorimar Prodns., Culver City, Calif., 1980-81, story editor, exec. story cons., supr. producer Falcon Crest, 1981-87, producer Our House, 1987-88; supervising producer Murphy's Law, 1988-89; exec. producer Baywatch, 1989-90; creative cons. Life Goes On, 1991-93;

exec. producer The New Flipper, 1994-96; co-exec. producer Promised Land, 1996-98. Mem. Writers Guild Am. (West chpt. bd. dirs. 1989-96). Mem. Lds Ch. Avocations: basketball, computers.

WALLENMEYER, WILLIAM ANTON, retired physicist; b. Evansville, Ind., Feb. 3, 1926; s. William Anton and Mindie (Madden) W.; m. Diane Mae Hankins, June 1, 1952; children: Wendy, Jon, Ann, Timothy. BS, Purdue U., 1950, MS, 1954, PhD, 1957. Jr. rsch. assoc. Brookhaven Nat. Lab., L.I., NY, 1954—55; asst. prof. physics Wabash Coll., Crawfordsville, Ind., 1955-56; dir. accelerator divsn. Midwestern U. Rsch. Assn., Madison, Wis., 1957-62; dir. divsn. high energy physics U.S. Dept. Energy, Germantown, Md., 1962-87; pres. Southeastern Univs. Rsch. Assn., Washington, 1987-92; spl. asst. to pres. Univs. Rsch. Assn., 1993-94. With Air Corps U.S. Army, 1944—46. Fellow AAAS, Am. Phys. Soc. Home: 1204 Azalea Dr Rockville MD 20850-2024

WALLENSTEIN, BARRY, literature and creative writing educator, poet; b. N.Y.C., Feb. 13, 1940; s. Maxwell and Pearl (Squires) W.; m. Lorna Harbus; children: Daniel, Jessica. BA, N.Y. U., 1962, MA, 1964, PhD, 1972. Instr. Stern Coll., N.Y.C., 1963-64, City Coll., N.Y.C., 1964-71, prof., 1971-2001, dir. Poetry Outreach Ctr., 1972-2001. Lectr. Cooper Union, N.Y.C., 1964-96. Editor: (poetry) Am. Book Review, 1982-2001; author: (poetry) Beast is a Wolf, 1977, Love and Crush, 1991, Short Life, 1993, A Measure of Conduct, 1999; recs. of poetry with jazz accompaniment: Benst is, 1978, Taking Off, 1982, In Case you MIssed It, 1995, Tony's Blues, 2001. Residency fellow MacDowell Colony, 1995, Hawthorndon Castle, Scotland, 1999. Mem. Acad. Am. Poet, Poets House. Home: 340 Riverside Dr New York NY 10025 Office: City Coll 138th St at Convent Ave New York NY 10031

WALLER, ANN, charitable organization executive; b. Augsburg, Fed. Republic Germany, Nov. 2, 1946; came to U.S., 1951; d. Anton and Eva (Makowsky) Iwanciwsky; m. George Anthony Waller, Apr. 22, 1967 (div. 1975); children: Elizabeth Jane, Jennifer Eve Rebecca. BA in English, U. Conn., 1971; MA in Communications, U. Hartford, 1987. Mgr. internal communications Hartford (Conn.) Nat. Bank, 1979-81; publs. editor Indsl. Risk Insurers, Hartford, 1981—89; v.p. mktg. and communications United Way Capital Area, 1989—90; dir. Comm. HSB Group, Inc., 1990—. Recipient Excellence in Communications Program award United Way Capital Region, 1980; lst place award Conn. Soc. Tech. Communication, 1981, award of merit, 1988; award of merit Editors Workshop, 1981. Mem. Internat. Assn. Bus. Communicators (pres. Conn. chpt. 1987-88, dist. dir. 1994-96), Women in Communications (pres. Conn. chpt. 1985-86), Hartford C. of C. Home: 405 E Chimney Sweep Hill Rd Glastonbury CT 06033-3944 Office: HSB Group Inc One State St Hartford CT 06102-5024

WALLER, ANNE ENGLISH, pediatrician; b. Jan. 12, 1954; BA, Agnes Scott Coll., Atlanta, 1976; MD, U. N.C., 1980. Resident Vanderbilt Children's Hosp., Nashville, 1981-83; pediatrician Walker Pediat. Clinic, Charlotte, N.C., 1983-88, Providence Pediats., Charlotte, 1989—; clin. asst. prof. pediats. U. N.C., Chapel Hill, 1989—. Ordained elder Presbyn. Ch., Charlotte, 1986—; chief peds. dept., Carolina Med. Ctr., 1992-93; bd. dirs. Metrolina AIDS Project, 1990-93. Office: Providence Pediatrics 427 N Wendover Rd Charlotte NC 28211-1064

WALLER, DELORIS AMY, musician, educator; b. Fergus Falls, Minn., Aug. 2, 1928; d. Albin and Amy Adeline (Peterson) Bloomquist; m. John Thomas Waller, July 30, 1955; children: Anita Jean, Bruce Robert. AB in Music Theory, N.W. Nazarene Coll., 1950; M in Music Edn., U. Idaho, 1955; postgrad., U. Oreg., 1956; AAGO Am. Guild of Organists, SUNY, Albany, 1963. Tchr. N.W. Nazarene Coll., Nampa, Idaho, 1954-76. Organist First United Meth. Ch., Nampa, 1963—, music dir., 1996—; music specialist Zion Luth. Sch., Nampa, 1971-82. Mem.: Am. Guild Organists (Les Bois chpt. treas. 1996—2001), Idaho Music Tchrs. Assn. (state v.p. 1978—80, pres. 1980—84, Idaho Stae Found. chair 1996—2000), Music Tchrs. Nat. Assn. (cert. organ and piano tchr.). Avocations: language study, gardening, flower arranging. Home: 2330 S Wildrye Way Nampa ID 83686-4920

WALLER, EDWARD MARTIN, JR. lawyer; b. Memphis, July 2, 1942; s. Edward Martin and Freda (Lazarov) W.; m. Laura Jayne Rhodes, June 18, 1982; children: Lauren, Jonathan, Melissa. BA, Columbia U., 1964; JD, U. Chgo., 1967. Bar: Fla. 1967. Assoc. Fowler, White, Gillen, Boggs, Villareal & Banker, P.A., Tampa, Fla., 1967-72, ptnr., 1972—. Mem. ABA (standing com. professionalism chmn. 1995-97, banking and fin. transactions com., litigation sect. 1978-82, co-chmn. 1983-87, coun. 1990-92, budget officer 1996-2000, litigation sect.), Fla. Bar Assn., Hillsborough County Bar Assn., Bay Area Legal Svcs. (bd. dirs. 1996-2002). Democrat. Jewish. Office: Fowler White Boggs Banker PO Box 1438 Tampa FL 33601-1438

WALLER, EPHRAIM EVERETT, retired professional association executive; b. Sioux City, Iowa, Aug. 10, 1928; s. Everett and Ruth Emma (Little) W.; m. Virginia Louise Harper, Oct. 3, 1959. BA, U. Iowa, 1951, MA, 1959; grad., Strategic Intelligence Sch., 1955, Army Security Agy. Sch., 1962, Nat. Cryptologic Sch., 1966, Comd. and Gen. Staff Coll., 1966; grad. with honors, State Dept. Fgn. Svc. Inst., 1967, Turkish Lang. Sch., 1968; grad., Indsl. Coll. Armed Forces, 1972; EdD with honors, U. S.D., 1981. Cert. fgn. area specialist, cryptologist. Commd. 2d lt. U.S. Army, 1951, advanced through grades to lt. col., 1967, retired, 1979; exec. dir. Midwest Agrl. Chems. Assn., Sioux City, Iowa, 1981-95; cons., 1996—. Mem. sci. and regulatory oversight coun. Am. Crop Protection Assn., Washington, 1990-95; mem. interregional coord. coun. Joint Body U.S. Regional Agrl. Assns., Dawson, Ga., 1991-95. Contbr. numerous articles to profl. jours. Mem. coms. 1st Congrl. Ch., Sioux City, 1937—. Decorated Bronze Star, Cross of Gallantry with Silver Star, Legion of Merit with oak leaf cluster, Chinese and Vietnamese Honor medals, Meritorious Svc. medal with oak leaf cluster, Joint Svc. Commendation medal with oak leaf cluster, Army Commendation medal with oak leaf cluster, Army Gen. Staff badge, Vietnamese Combat Merit medal; recipient Outstanding Leadership in the Industry award Am. Crop Protection Assn., Leadership in Cmty. and Pub. Edn. award Chem. Prodrs. and Distbrs. Assn., Dedication and Svc. to Agrl. Industry award Ill. Fertilizer and Chems. Assn., Dean Roy Exceptional Svc. award Midwest Agrl. Chems. Assn., Industry Vision award Mid Am. Crop Protection Assn., Significant Svc. to Agr. and Agrl. Chems. Industry award So. Crop Protection Assn., Outstanding Leadership in the Industry award Am. Crop Protection Assn., Leadership award Chem. Prodrs. and Distbrs. Assn., Dean Roy Exceptional Svc. award Midwest Agrl. Chems. Assn., others. Mem. Ret. Officers Assn., Siouxland C. of C. (com. mem. 1981-95), Interprofl. Inst., Scottish Rite, Masons, Eastern Star, Phi Delta Kappa, Delta Sigma Rho. Avocations: swimming, hiking, travel, stamp collecting, writing. Home: 2847 Valley Dr Sioux City IA 51104-4071

WALLER, GARY FREDRIC, English language educator, administrator, poet; b. Auckland, N.Z., Jan. 3, 1944; came to U.S., 1983; s. Fred and Joan Elsie (Smythe) W.; m. Jennifer Robyn Denham, July 2, 1966 (div. 1980); children: Michael, Andrew; m. Kathleen Ann McCormick, Nov. 12, 1988; one child, Philip. BA, U. Auckland, 1965, MA, 1966; PhD, Cambridge U., Eng., 1970. Donaldson Bye fellow Magdalene Coll., Cambridge, Eng., 1967-69; assoc. prof. English U. Auckland, New Zealand, 1969-72, Dalhousie U., N.S., Can., 1972-78; head, prof. English Wilfrid Laurier U., Waterloo, Can., 1978-83; head, prof. lit. and cultural studies Carnegie Mellon U., Pitts., 1983-92; dean arts and scis., prof. lit. and cultural studies U. Hartford, West Hartford, Conn., 1992-95; provost, v.p. acad. affairs, prof. lit. and cultural studies Purchase (N.Y.) Coll., SUNY, 1995—. Author: The Strong Necessity of Time, 1976, The Triumph of Death, 1977, Pamphilia to Amphilanthus, 1977, Dreaming America, 1979, Mary Sidney Countess of Pembroke, 1979, Sir Philip Sidney and the Interpretation of Renaissance Culture, 1984, Sixteenth Century Poetry, 1986, 2d edit., 1993, Reading Texts, 1986, Lexington Introduction to Literature, 1987, Shakespeare's Comedies, 1991, Reading Mary Wroth, 1991, The Sidney Family Romance, 1993, Edmund Spenser: A Literary Life, 1994, Lady Mary Sidney's Antonie and a Discourse of Life and Death, 1996; (poems) Other Flights, Always, 1991, Impossible Futures Indelible Pasts, 1983 Office: Purchase Coll Acad Affairs Purchase NY 10577

WALLER, HAROLD MYRON, political science educator; b. Detroit, Oct. 12, 1940; s. Allan L. and Lillian R. (LeVine) W.; m. Diane Carol Goodman, June 28, 1966; children: Sharon, Dahvi, Jeffrey. SB, MIT, 1962; MS, Northwestern U., 1966; PhD, Georgetown U., 1968. Asst. prof. McGill U., Montreal, 1967-71, assoc. prof., 1971-93, prof., 1993—, chmn. polit. sci. dept., 1969-74, 89-90, acting chmn., 1980-81, 86-87, assoc. dean (acad.) faculty arts, 1991-94, acting dean faculty arts, 1994-95. Pres. McGill Assn. Univ. Tchrs., Montreal, 1978-79; fellow Jerusalem Ctr. Pub. Affairs, 1980—; dir. Can. Ctr. Jewish Community Studies, Montreal, 1980—. Co-author: Maintaining Consensus: The Canadian Jewish Polity in the Postwar World, 1990; co-editor: Canadian Federalism: From Crisis to Constitution; contbg. editor: Middle East Focus; mem. editorial bd. Jewish Political Studies, Patterns of Prejudice; chmn. editorial bd. Viewpoints; contbr. numerous articles to profl. jours. and books in field. Com. chmn. Can. Jewish Congress, Montreal, 1971-74; chair, nat. exec. Can. Profs. for Peace in Middle East, Toronto, 1975-85; pres. Akiva Sch., Montreal, 1984-85; com. chmn. Jewish Edn. Council, Montreal, 1986-88. Recipient Nat. Jewish Book award Jewish Book Coun., N.Y.C., 1991; Grad. fellow NSF, Washington, 1965-66, Leave fellow Social Sci. Humanities Rsch. Coun., Ottawa, 1981-82. Mem. Am. Polit. Sci. Assn., Can. Polit. Sci. Assn., Assn. Jewish Studies, Assn. Sociol. Study of Jewry, Assn. Israel Studies, Faculty Club, Sigma Xi, Pi Sigma Alpha. Jewish. Avocations: travel, athletics, reading, politics. Office: McGill U Dept Polit Sci 855 Sherbrooke St W Montreal QC Canada H3A 2T7 E-mail: harold.waller@mcgill.ca.

WALLER, JOHN HENRY, author; b. Paw Paw, Mich., May 8, 1923; s. George and Marguerite (Rowland) W.; m. Barbara Steuart Hans, Sept. 2, 1947; children: Stephanie Robinson, Gregory, Maria. BA, U. Mich., 1946. Vice consul U.S. Fgn. Svc., Iran, 1947-53, 2d sec. Sudan, 1960-62, spl. asst. to ambassador New Delhi, India, 1955-57, 68-71; polit. analyst State Dept., Washington, 1962-68; insp. gen. CIA, 1976-80; free-lance author, 1968—. Bd. dirs. internat. affairs dept. Va. Mil. Inst. Author: (pen name John Rowland) Hostile Co-existance, history of Sino-Indian Relations, 1988, Gordon of Khartoum: The Saga of a Victorian Hero, (pen name John McGregor) Tibet, A Chronicle of Exploration, 1970, Beyond the Khyber Pass, 1990, The Unseen War in Europe, 1996, The Devil's Doctor, 2002; contbr. articles to popular history to profl. jours. Recipient Career Svcs. award Nat. Civil Svc. League, 1979, 80, Disting. Intelligence medal CIA, 1980. Mem. Washington Inst. Fgn. Affairs (bd. dirs.), Cosmos Club (Washington), Office of Strategic Svcs. Soc. (chmn. bd. dirs.).

WALLER, JOHN HENRY, JR. state supreme court justice; b. Mullins, S.C., Oct. 31, 1937; s. John Henry and Elnita (Rabon) Waller; m. Jane McLaurin Cooper, Nov. 16, 1963 (div.); children: John Henry III, Melissa McLaurin; m. Debra Ann Meares, May 9, 1981; children: Ryan Meares, Rand Ellis. AB in Psychology, Wofford Coll., 1959; LLB, JD, U. S.C., 1963. Mem. S.C. Ho. of Reps., 1967—77, S.C. Senate, 1977—80; judge S.C. Cir. Ct., 1980—94; assoc. justice S.C. Supreme Ct., 1994—. Capt. U.S. Army, 1959—60. Mem.: Millins Rotary Club (1st pres.), Shriners, Masons. Avocations: woodworking, golf, water sports, snow skiing. Office: SC Supreme Ct 103 Main St PO Box 1059 Marion SC 29571-1059 also: SC Supreme Ct Supreme Court PO Box 11330 Columbia SC 29211-1330*

WALLER, JOHN LOUIS, anesthesiology educator; b. Loma Linda, Calif., Dec. 1, 1944; s. Louis Clinton and Sue (Bruce) W.; m. Jo Lynn Marie Haas, Aug. 4, 1968; children: Kristina, Karla, David. BA, So. Coll., Collegedale, Tenn., 1967; MD, Loma Linda U., 1971. Diplomate Am. Bd. Anesthesiology. Intern Hartford (Conn.) Hosp., 1971—72; resident in anesthesiology Harvard U. Med. Sch.-Mass. Gen. Hosp., Boston, 1972—74, fellow, 1974—75; asst. prof. anesthesiology Emory U. Sch. Medicine, Atlanta, 1977—80, assoc. prof., 1980—86, prof., 1986—2001; chmn. dept. anesthesiology Emory U. Sch. Med., 1986—2000; chief anesthesiology Emory U. Hosp., 1986-94, med. dir., 1993-95; assoc. v.p. info. svcs. Woodruff Health Scis. Ctr., 1995-97; chief info. officer Emory U. System Healthcare, Atlanta, 1995-97; prof. anesthesiology Med. U. S.C., Charleston, 2002—, chmn. dept. anesthesia and perioperative medicine, 2002—, prof. anesthesiology, 2002—, chmn. dept. anesthesia and perioperative medicine, 2002—. Cons. Arrow Internat., Inc., Reading, Pa., 1988—; mem. adv. com. on anesthetic and life support drugs FDA, Washington, 1986—92; numerous vis. professorships and lectures. Contbr. articles to med. jours. Maj. M.C., USAF, 1975-77. Recipient cert. of appreciation Office Sec. Def., 1983. Fellow: Am. Coll. Chest Physicians, Am. Coll. Anesthesiologists; mem.: AMA, Assn. Cardiac Anesthesiologists, Soc. Acad. Anesthesia Chmn. (councillor 1989—), Assn. Univ. Anesthesiologists, Internat. Anesthesia Rsch. Soc. (trustee 1984—2002, sec. 1996—98, chair 1998—2000), Soc. Cardiovascular Anesthesiologists (pres. 1991—93), Am. Soc. Anesthesiologists. Avocations: tennis, sailing, swimming. Office: Med U SC Dept Anes and Perioperative Medicine 165 Ashley Ave Ste 525 Charleston SC 29425

WALLER, MARILYN JEAN, podiatric surgeon, educator; b. Mpls., Nov. 30, 1950; m. John w. Niewold, Aug. 19, 1995; children: Skot Waller, Richard Waller, Khrystofer Waller, Daniel Waller, Rebekah Waller. Student, Bethel Coll., 1969-71; BS, U. Minn., 1975; postgrad., Calif. Poly., 1983-86; DPM, Calif. Coll Podiatric Medicine, 1990. Cert. foot and ankle surgeon Calif. Bd. Podiatric Medicine. Instr. h.s., Minn., 1975-78, Arroyo Grande, Calif., 1980-83; resident in surgery VA Med. Ctr., San Francisco, 1990-92; rsch. fellow VA Med. Ctr./Travis AFB, 1992-93; pvt. practice Hayward, Calif., 1993—. Wound advisor St. Rose Hosp. Phys. Rehab., Hayward, 1994—. Mem. Am. Podiatric Med. Soc., Am. Diabetes Assn., Am. Assn. Women Podiatrists, Calif. Podiatric Med. Soc., Alameda-Contra Costa Podiatric Med. Soc., Omicron Nu. Avocations: ice skating, needlework. Office: 27001 Calaroga Ave Ste 1 Hayward CA 94545

WALLER, MARTHA S. retired English educator, writer; b. Beijing, June 27, 1920; came to U.S., 1923; d. William Warren and Susan Reed Stifler; m. George MacGregor Waller, Oct. 16, 1943; children: Susan, Marguerite, Elizabeth, Donald, Richard. BA, Mt. Holyoke Coll., 1941; MA, Columbia U., 1942; PhD, Ind. U., 1973. Rsch. analyst U.S. Army Signal Corps, Arlington, Va., 1942-44; tchr. Orchard Country Day Sch., Indpls., 1959-61; asst. prof. English Ind. Ctrl. Coll., 1962-71, assoc. prof. English, 1971-74, Butler U., Indpls., 1974-79, prof. English, 1979-81, Demia Butler Prof., 1981-89, prof. emerita, 1989—. Linguistics cons., bus. and law firms, Indpls., 1960-89; lectr., local groups, Indpls. and Rushville, Ind.; presenter Internat. Medieval Studies Congress, Kalamazoo, 1991; mem. grad. fellowships com. Mt. Holyoke Coll., 1974-77. Co-author: Cloak and Cipher, 1962; contbr. articles to profl. jours., including Speculum, Chaucer Newsletter, Ind. Social Studies Quar., others. Fellow, Counl Internat. Exch. Scholars, 1983; Mary Woolley fellow, Mt. Holyoke Coll., 1971; English Spkg. Union fellow, U. Kent, Canterbury, Eng., 1978. Mem. MLA, Medieval Acad. Am., New Chaucer Soc. (asst. bibliographer 1977—, presenter Phila. 1986), Mt. Holyoke Alumnae Assn., Indpls. Woman's Club, Phi Beta Kappa (exec. com. Ind. Alpha Assn.). Presbyterian.

WALLER, MARY BELLIS, psychotherapist, education educator, consultant; b. Milw., May 18, 1940; d. Ernest Anthony and Hazel Mary (Addie) Bellis; m. Michael I. Waller, May 9, 1987 (dec. Nov. 1996); children: Eric B. Griswold, Andrew D. Griswold, Megan E. Griswold Simone BS, U. Wis., Milw., 1969, MS, 1971, PhD, 1992. Coord. Wis. Coalition for Ednl. Reform, Milw., 1971-74; instr. U. Wis., 1974-77; exec. dir. Worker Rights Inst., 1977-87; adj. prof. Nat. Coll. Edn., Evanston, Ill., 1981-96; preceptor, clin. program coord. U. Wis.-Parkside, Kenosha, 1987-96; Wis. lead cons. Emprise Designs, 1993-97; psychotherapist, dir. outreach programs Achievement Assocs., Ltd., 1998—; clin. assoc. prof. U. Wis., Milw., 2002—. Cons. on drug-affected children; ctr. scientist Ctr. for Addiction and Behavioral Health Rsch., 1996—; pres. Program Devel. and Evaluation, 1993—, Priority Group, Inc., 1998—. Author: Crack-Affected Children: A Teacher's Guide, 1993, Lady of the Manor: Medieval Cooking with Herbs, 1994; author numerous articles on drug-affected children. Mem. ASCD, NAEYC, Am. Ednl. Rsch. Assn., Assn. Tchr. Educators, Phi Delta Kappa (Disting. Svc. award 1992). Home: 8316 N Regent Rd Milwaukee WI 53217-2736 E-mail: mwaller@execpc.com

WALLER, MICHAEL E. publishing executive; Grad, Milliken U., Decatur, Illinois, 1963. Editor Hartford (Conn.) Courant, 1990-94, pub., CEO, 1994-97, Baltimore Sun, Md., 1997—. Office: Baltimore Sun 501 N Calvert St Baltimore MD 21278-0001*

WALLER, PATRICIA FOSSUM, transportation executive, researcher, psychologist; b. Winnipeg, Man., Can., Oct. 12, 1932; d. Magnus Samuel and Diana Isabel (Briggs) Fossum; m. Marcus Bishop Waller, Dec. 27, 1957; children: Anna Estelle, Justin Magnus, Martha Wilkinson, Benjamin Earl. AB in Psychology cum laude, U. Miami, Coral Gables, 1953, MS in Psychology, 1955; PhD in Psychology, U. N.C., 1959. Lic. psychologist, N.C. Psychology intern VA Hosp., Salem, Va., 1956; psychology instr. Med. Sch. U. N.C., Chapel Hill, 1957; USPHS postdoctoral fellow R.B. Jackson Lab., Bar Harbor, Maine, 1958-60; psychologist VA Hosp., Brockton, Mass., 1961-62; psychology lectr. U. N.C., Chapel Hill, Greensboro, 1962-67, assoc. dir. driver studies Hwy. Safety Rsch. Ctr. Chapel Hill, 1967-89, founding dir. Injury Prevention Rsch. Ctr., 1987-89; dir. Transp. Rsch. Inst. U. Mich., Ann Arbor, 1989-99, sr. rsch. scientist emerita, prof. emerita, 1999—; sr. rsch. scientist Ctr. for Transp. Safety, Tex. Transp. Inst. Tex. A&M U., 2002—. Bd. dirs. Intelligent Transp. Soc. Am., Washington, 1991—99, Traffic Safety Assn. Mich., Lansing, 1991—99; bd. advisors Eno Transp. Found., Inc., Lndnsdowne, Va., 1994—97; chair group 5 coun. Transp. Rsch. Bd. of NRC, Washington, 1992—95; chmn. Task Force Operation Regulations, 1974—76, mem. study com. devel. ranking rail safety R&D projects, 1980—82, chmn. group 3 coun. operation, safety and maintenance transp. facilities, 1980—83, mem. IVHS-IDEA tech. rev. panel, 1993—2000, chair workshop human factors rsch. in hwy. safety, 1992, chair ad hoc com. environ. activies, 92, mem. task force on elderly drivers, 1990—93, mem. com. vehicle user characteristics, 1983—86, mem. com. planning and adminstrn. of transp. safety, 1986—92, mem. com. alcohol, other drugs and transp., 1986—98, numerous other coms., mem. spl. coms. including Inst. Medicine Dana Award com., 1986—90, com. of 55MPH nat. maximum speed limit, 1983—84; mem. motor vehicle safety rsch. adv. com. Dept. Transp., Washington, 1991—94; reviewer JAMA, Jour. Studies on Alcohol, Jour. of Gerontology, Am. Jour. Pub. Health; apptd. Pres. Coun. Spinal Cord Injury, 1981; apptd. advisor Nat. Hwy. Safety Adv. Com. to Sec. U.S. Dept. Transp., 1979—80, 1980—83, chair nat. motor carrier adv. com., 1997—98; author numerous reports on transp. to govtl. coms. and univs. Author: (with Paul G. Shinkman) Instructor's Manual for Mogan and King: Introduction to Psychology, 1971; author: (with others) Psychological Concepts in the Classroom, 1974, Drinking: Alcohol in American Society—Issues and Current Research, 1978, The American Handbook of Alcoholism, 1982, The Role of the Civil Engineer in Highway Safety, 1983, Aging and Public Health, 1985, Young Driver Accidents: In Search of Solutions, 1985, Alcohol, Accidents and Injuries, 1986, Transportation in an Aging Society: Improving the Mobility and Safety for Older Persons, 1988, Young Drivers Impaired by Alcohol and Drugs, 1988; mem. editorial bd. Jour. Safety Rsch., 1979—; assoc. guest editor Health Edn. Quar., 1989; assoc. editor Accident, Analysis, and Prevention, 1978-84, mem. editorial bd., 1976-87; contbr. articles to profl. jours. Grantee HHS, 1982, 92-97, NIH; named Widmark laureate Internat. Coun. Alcohol, Drugs and Traffic Safety, 1995; Dist. Alumnus Awd., Dept. Psych., UNC Chapel Hill, 1997; recipient James J. Howard Trailblazer award Nat. Assn. of Govs. Hwy. Safety Reps., 1998, Svc. Awd., Intelligent Transportation Soc. of Amer., 1999; World Traffic Soc. Awd., 1999, World Safety Symposium, 1999; Lifetime Acheivement Awd., Mich. Traffic Safety Summit, 1999. Mem. AAAS, APA (Harold M. Hildreth award 1993), APHA (injury control and emergency health svcs. sect., Disting. Career award 1994, transp. rsch. bd., 1995, Roy W. Crum award for rsch. contbns. 1995), Assn. for the Advancement of Automotive Medicine (chmn. human factors sect. 1978-80, bd. dirs. 1979-82, pres. 1981-82), Coun. Univ. Transp. Ctrs. (exec. com. 1991-93), Transp. Rsch. Bd., Ea. Psychol. Assn., Sigma Xi. Democrat. Avocations: gardening, reading. Office: 1779 Crawford Dairy Rd Chapel Hill NC 27516 E-mail: pwaller@umich.edu.

WALLER, PETER WILLIAM, public affairs executive; b. Kewanee, Ill., Oct. 1, 1926; s. Ellis Julian and Barodel (Gould) W.; m. Anne-Marie Appelius van Hoboken, Nov. 10, 1950; children: Catherine, Hans. BA with hons., Princeton U., 1949; MA with hons., San Jose State U., 1978. Bur. chief Fairchild Publs., San Francisco, 1953-55; freelance writer Mountain View, Calif., 1956-57; pub. relations coord. Lockheed Missiles and Space, Sunnyvale, 1957-64; info. mgr. for 1st missions to Jupiter, Saturn, Venus NASA Ames Rsch. Ctr., Mountain View, 1964-83, mgr. pub. info., 1983-95; cons. NASA-Ames Galileo, Lunar Prospector, 1996-97; prodr. space films PacPAW Assoc., 1998—. Speechwriter for pres. Lockheed Missiles and Space, 1960-64. Producer (documentary) Jupiter Odyssey, 1974 (Golden Eagle, 1974); producer, writer NASA Aero. program, 1984; contbr. articles to profl. jours, encyclopedias. Cons. on preservation of Lake Tahoe, Calif. Resources Agy., Sacramento, 1984. Mem. No. Calif. Sci. Writers Assn., Sierra Club. Democrat. Congregationalist. Avocations: skiing, travel, architecture, construction, hiking. Home: 3655 La Calle Ct Palo Alto CA 94306-2619

WALLER, RAY ALBERT, statistician; b. Grenola, Kans., Mar. 4, 1937; s. Clarence Freeman and Dorothea Mae (Wilson) W.; m. Carolyn Ann McCoy, July 23, 1960; children: Lance Allyn, Jay Andrew. BA, Southwestern Coll., 1959; MS, Kans. State U., 1963; PhD, The Johns Hopkins U., 1967. Tchr. St. John's Sch., Santurce, P.R., 1960-61; grad. teaching asst. Kans. State U., Manhattan, 1961-63, from asst. to assoc. prof., 1967-74; NDEA fellow The Johns Hopkins U., Balt., 1963-66; asst.prof. Towson (Md.) State Coll., 1966-67; mem. staff, from asst. to group leader Los Alamos (N.Mex.) Nat. Lab., 1974-80, dep. div. leader, 1980-87, staff asst., 1987-92, directorate office leader, 1992-93; retired, 1993. Instr. Johns Hopkins U., Balt., 1964—67; tech. staff mem. Ewing Tech. Design, Inc., 1994—95, Los Alamos Nat. Lab., 1995; vis. prof. dept. stats. Kans. State U., 1995; vis. prof. dept. math. and stats. Williams Coll., 2002; exec. dir. Am. Statis. Assn., 1995—2001. Author: Statistics: An Introduction to Numerical Reasoning, 1979; co-author: Stastical Applications in the Feed Industry, 1972, Bayesian Reliability Analysis, 1982; co-editor: Proceedings for Workshop on Low Probability/High Consequence Risk Analysis, 1984; assoc. editor Jour. Statis. Computation and Simulation, 1978-80; contbr. articles to profl. jours. Mem. Los Alamos br. adv. bd. U. N.Mex., 1993, chmn. bd., 1995; tchr. Sunday sch. Bush Hill Presbyn. Session. With USAR, 1959-65. Recipient NSF summer fellow, 1962, NDEA fellow, 1963-66. Mem. IEEE, Am. Statis. Assn. (chair sect. on phys. and engring. scis. 1994), Soc. for Risk Analysis. Avocations: woodworking, golf.

WALLER, ROBERT REX, ophthalmologist, educator, foundation executive; b. N.Y.C., Feb. 19, 1937; s. Madison Rex and Sally Elizabeth (Pearce) W.; m. Sarah Elizabeth Pickens, Dec. 27, 1963; children: Elizabeth, Katherine, Robert Jr. BA, Duke U., 1958; MD, U. Tenn., 1963. Diplomate Am. Bd. Ophthalmology (dir. 1982—, vice chmn. 1988-89, chmn. 1989—). Intern City of Memphis Hosps., 1963-64; resident in internal medicine Mayo Grad. Sch. Medicine, Rochester, Minn., 1966-67, resident in ophthalmology, 1967-70, faculty, 1970—; assoc. prof. ophthalmology Mayo Clinic, 1974-78, prof., 1978—; chmn. dept. ophthalmology Mayo Med. Sch., 1974-84, cons., 1970—, bd. govs., 1978-93, chmn., 1988-93; trustee Mayo Found., 1978—, pres., CEO, 1988-98, pres. emeritus, 1999—. Chmn. bd. trustees Healthcare Leadership Coun., Washington, 1999-2001. Contbr. chpts. to books, articles to profl. jours. Elder 1st Presbyn. Ch., Rochester, 1975-78; mem. Rochester Task Force on Pub. Assembly Facilities, 1983-84. Ocuplastic Surgery fellow U. Calif. San Francisco, 1973. Mem. AMA, Minn. State Med. Assn., Zumbro Valley Med. Assn., Am. Acad. Ophthalmology, Am. Ophthalmol. Soc., Orbital Soc., Am. Soc. Ophthalmic Plastic and Reconstructive Surgery, Minn. Acad. Ophthalmology and Otolaryngology, Memphis Country Club, Old Baldy Golf Club, Augusta Nat. Golf Club, Alpha Omega Alpha, Delta Tau Delta. Presbyterian. Avocations: golf, travel, photography, dogs. Home: 199 Greenbriar Dr Memphis TN 38117-3238 E-mail: RWaller@mayo.edu.

WALLER, WILHELMINE KIRBY (MRS. THOMAS MERCER WALLER), civic worker, organization official; b. N.Y.C., Jan. 19, 1914; d. Gustavus Town and Wilhelmine (Claflin) Kirby; m. Thomas Mercer Waller, Apr. 7, 1942. Ed., Chapin Sch., N.Y.C. Conservation chmn. Garden Club Am., 1959-61, pres., 1965-68, chmn. nat. affairs, 1968-74, dir., 1969-71; mem. adv. com. N.Y. State Conservation Commn., 1959-70; mem. Nat. Adv. Com. Hwy. Beautification, 1965-68; trustee Mianus River Gorge Conservation Com. of Nature Conservancy, 1955—, Arthur W. Butler Meml. Sanctuary, 1955-79; dir. Westchester County Soil and Water Conservation Dist., 1967-74; adviser N.Y. Gov.'s Study Commn. Future of Adirondacks, 1968-70; adv. com. N.Y. State Parks and Recreation Commn., 1971-72; adv. com. to sec. state UN Conf. Human Environment, 1971-72; mem. Pres.'s Citizens Adv. Com. on Environ. Quality, 1974-78. Mem. planning bd., Bedford, 1953-57; mem. Conservation adv. coun., Bedford, N.Y., 1968-70, Westchester County Planning Bd., 1970-88; bd. govs. Nature Conservancy, 1970-78; Mem. Lyndhurst council Nat. Trust for Historic Preservation, 1965-74; bd. dirs. Scenic Hudson, Inc., 1985-88. Recipient Frances K. Hutchinson medal Garden Club Am., 1971,

Holiday mag. award for beautiful Am., 1971, Conservation award Am. Motors Corp., 1975, Oak Leaf award Nature Conservancy, 1988. Mem. Nat. Soc. Colonial Dames, Huguenot Soc. Am., Daus. of Cincinnati Address: Tanrackin Farm Bedford Hills NY 10507

WALLER, WILMA RUTH, retired secondary school educator and librarian; b. Jacksonville, Tex., Nov. 15, 1921; d. William Wesley and Myrtle (Nesbitt) W. BA with honors, Tex. Woman's U., 1954, MA with honors, 1963, MLS with honors, 1976. Tchr. English Dell (Ark.) High Sch., 1953-54, Jefferson (Tex.) Ind. Schs., 1954-56, Tyler (Tex.) Ind. Schs., 1956-68; librarian Wise County Schs., Decatur, Tex., 1969-71, Thomas K. Gorman High Sch., Tyler, 1971-74, Sweetwater (Tex.) Ind. Sch. Dist., 1974-86; ret. Lectr., book reviewer for various clubs. Active in past as vol. for ARC, U. Tex. Health Ctr. Ford Found. fellow, 1959; recipient Delta Kappa Gamma Achievement award, 1992. Mem. UDC, Smith County Ret. Sch. Pers., Bible Study Group, Delta Kappa Gamma. Republican. Baptist. Avocations: reading, gourmet cooking, piano, writing letters. Home: 1117 N Azalea Dr Tyler TX 75701-5206

WALLERSTEIN, IMMANUEL, sociologist; b. N.Y.C., Sept. 28, 1930; a. Lazar and Sally (Guensberg) W.; m. Beatrice Friedman, Sept. 28, 1930; children: Katharine Ellen; stepchildren: Susan E. Morgenstern, Robert S. Morgenstern. BA, Columbia U., 1951, MA, 1954, PhD, 1959; D (hon.), U. Paris, 1976; DLitt, York U., Toronto, Can., 1995; D (hon.), Free U. Brussels, 1996, U. Nat. Autonoma Mex., Mexico City, 1998, Inst. Superior Ciencas, Lisbon, 1999, U. Autonoma, Puebla, Mex., 1999, U. Bucharest, 2001, U. Alicante, 2002. With Columbia U., N.Y.C., 1958-71; prof. McGill U., Montreal, Que., Can., 1971-76; disting. prof. Binghamton (N.Y.) U., 1976-99; dir. Fernand Braudel Ctr. Study of Econs., 1976—; sr. rsch. scholar Yale U., New Haven, 2000—. Dir. d'etudes associé Ecole des Hautes Etudes en Scis. Sociales, Paris, 1975-76, 80-95; chair Gulbenkian Com. on Restructuring of Social Scis., 1993-95; mem. sci. com. Inst. Internat. di Storia Econ. "F. Datini", Prato, 1977—; Wei Lun vis. prof. Chinese U. of Hong Kong, 1991; Tripartite lectr. Royal Geog. Soc., Geog. Assn., Inst. Brit. Geographers, London, 1988. Author: The Modern World-System, I: Capitalist Agriculture and the Origins of the European World-Economy in the Sixteenth Century, 1974, The Capitalist World-Economy, 1979, The Modern World-System, II: Mercantilism and the Consolidation of the European World-Economy, 1600-1750, 1980, The Modern World-System III: The Second Great Expansion of the Capitalist World-Economy, 1730-1840's, 1989, Geopolitics and Geoculture: Essays on the Changing World-System, 1991, Unthinking Social Science: The Limits of Nineteenth Century Paradigms, 1991, Historical Capitalism, with Capitalist Civilization, 1995, Utopistics or Historical Choices of the Twenty-First Century, 1998, The End of the World As We Know It: Social Science for the 21st Century, 1999, The Essential Wallerstein, 2000; co-author: (with others) Open the Social Sciences: Report of the Gulbenkian Commission on the Restructuring of the Social Sciences, 1996; (with T.K. Hopkins) The Age of Transition: Trajectory of the World-System, 1945-2025, 1996. With U.S. Army, 1951-53. Recipient medal U. Helsinki, 1992; named Officer of Ordre des Arts et des Lettres, France, 1984. Fellow Am. Acad. of Arts and Scis.; mem. Internat. Sociol. Assn. (pres. 1994-98), African Studies Assn. (pres. 1973-74). Democrat. Jewish. Office: Yale U Dept Sociology PO Box 208625 New Haven CT 06520 E-mail: immanuel.wallerstein@yale.edu.

WALLERSTEIN, JUDITH SARETSKY, psychologist, researcher; b. N.Y.C., Dec. 27, 1921; d. Samuel Saretsky and Augusta (Tucker) Weinberger; m. Robert S. Wallerstein, Jan. 27, 1949; children: Michael, Nina, Amy. BA, CUNY, 1943; MS, Columbia U., 1946; PhD in Psychology, Lund (Sweden) U., 1978. Sr. lectr. U. Calif., Berkeley, 1966-91, sr. lectr. emeritus, 1991—; dir. Calif. Children of Divorce Project, Marin County, 1971—. Founder, former exec. dir. Judith Wallerstein Ctr. Family in Transition, Corte Madera, Calif., 1980—93. Author: (book) Surviving the Breakup, 1980, Second Chances, 1989, The Good Marriage, 1995, The Unexpected Legacy of Divorce, 2000; contbr. articles to profl. jours. Mem. adv. com. on family law Calif. Senate Subcom. Adminstrn. of Justice, 1977—79; mem. task force family equity Calif. State Senate, 1986. Recipient Koshland award in social welfare, San Francisco Found., 1975, Renè Spitz award, Denver Psychoanalytic Soc., 1991, Geri Taylor Meml. award, No. Calif. Psychiat. Soc., 1993, Presdl. citation, APA Divsn. Family Psychology, 1995, Dale Richmond award, Am. Acad. Pediat., 1996, award, ABA Section on Family Law, 2001, Presdl. citation, APA, 2001; fellow, Ctr. Advanced Study in the Behavioral Scis., Stanford, Calif., 1979—80, Rockefeller Found. Study Ctr., Bellagio, Italy, 1992. Mem.: NASW, Assn. Family Conciliation Cts., Assn. Child Psychoanalysis (mem. exec. coun. 1977—80), Am. Orthopsychiat. Assn., San Francisco Psychoanalytic Soc. (interdisciplinary mem.), N.Y. Freudian Soc. (hon.), Am. Psychoanalytic Assn. (hon.), Phi Beta Kappa. Achievements include principal investigator follow-up study effects of divorce on children and their parents; principal investigator study of good marriages.

WALLERSTEIN, LAURA WERNER, volunteer, social worker; b. N.Y.C., May 17, 1914; d. Hymen and Helen Werner; m. Leon Wallerstein Jr., June 28, 1937; children: Lynn W. Huber, Larry H. Student, Smith Coll.; BA, Barnard Coll., 1936; MSW, SUNY, Buffalo, 1969. Social worker St. Vincent Health/Rehab. Ctr., 1967-69, chief social worker in rehab., 1969-76; chief social svc. rehab. div. St. Vincent Health Ctr., Erie, Pa., 1969-76; vol. social worker Mercy Ctr. for Aging, 1978—. Co-founder, pres. Stairways, Erie, 1958-64; founder, pres. Erie Independence House, 1971—; vol. Meals on Wheels, Erie, 1978—. Recipient de Toqueville award United Way, 1998, Ed Doll award Erie Cmty. Found., 1992, Benjamin Rush award Erie County Med. Soc., 1995. Mem. NASW (Social Worker of the Yr., Lifetime Achievement award).

WALLERSTEIN, LEIBERT BENET, economist; b. Bklyn., July 5, 1922; s. William Mark and Ray Leah (Goldberg) W.; m. Alice Stehle, Oct. 10, 1929; stepchildren: Nora Odendahl, Steven Odendahl. BA in Econs., U. N.Mex., 1950; MA in Econs., U. Minn., 1951; PhD in Econs., Social Scis., Columbia Pacific U., 1988; AA in Creative Writing, Montgomery Jr. Coll., 1998. With U.S. Corps of Engrs. and Army Air Corps Matl. Command, Washington, 1943-46; Merchant Marine; with AUS, 1945-47, U.S. Navy Bur. ORD, 1954-55, U.S. Dept. Labor, 1956-67, HUD, 1967-69, U.S. DOT, 1961-80. With U.S. Merchant Marine Acad., Kings Point, 1977; faculty U. Minn., U. Md., U. N. Mex., Pentagon, Georgetown U., Ben Franklin U., Montgomery Coll., La Salle U., Montgomery County Adult Edn. Ctr.; cons. economist, 1980—; v.p. Reano Co., L.A. Contbr. articles to profl. jours. Vol. Shepard's Table, Washington, 1985—, Jewish Community Ctr. D.C. Area, Chevy Chase (Md.) grade schs., 1986, polit. pres. campaigns, 1980, 84, 92; v.p. Univ. Young Dems., U. N.Mex., Albuquerque, 1947-50, NAACP, 1947-50. Mem. Atlantic Econ. Soc., Am. Econ. Assn., Economists Club Washington (charter), Soc. Govt. Economists, Sr. Club (chmn. 1983), Disabled Am. Vets., Am. Legion, Mensa, Phi Delta Kappa, Fossils. Jewish. Avocations: fishing, hiking, reading, swimming, fgn. travel. Home and Office: 3505 Thornapple St Chevy Chase MD 20815-4014

WALLERSTEIN, RALPH OLIVER, physician; b. Dusseldorf, Germany, Mar. 7, 1922; arrived in U.S., 1938, naturalized, 1944; s. Otto R. and Ilse (Hollander) Wallerstein; m. Betty Ane Christensen, June 21, 1952; children: Ralph Oliver, Richard, Ann. AB, U. Calif., Berkeley, 1943; MD, U. Calif., San Francisco, 1945. Diplomate Am. Bd. Internal Medicine. Intern San Francisco Hosp., 1945—46, resident, 1948—49, U. Calif. Hosp., San Francisco, 1949—50; research fellow Thorndike Meml. Lab., Boston City Hosp., 1950—52; chief clin. hematology San Francisco Gen. Hosp., 1953—87; mem. faculty U. Calif., San Francisco, 1952—, clin. prof. medicine, 1969—, prof. emeritus of medicine. Bd. govs. Am. Bd. Internal Medicine, 1975—83, chmn., 1982—83. Capt. M.C. U.S. Army, 1946—48. Mem.: ACP (gov. 1977—87, chmn. bd. govs. 1980—81, regent 1981—87, pres. 1988—89), AMA, Western Assn. Physicians, Western Soc. Clin. Rsch., Internat. Soc. Hematology, Calif. Acad. Medicine, Inst. Medicine, Am. Assn. Blood Banks, Am. Soc. Internal Medicine, Am. Fedn. Clin. Rsch., Am. Clin. and Climatol. Assn., San Francisco Med. Soc., Am. Soc. Hematology (pres. 1978), Gold Headed Cane Soc. Republican. Home: 3447 Clay St San Francisco CA 94118-2008 E-mail: rowmdsf@aol.com.

WALLERSTEIN, ROBERT SOLOMON, psychiatrist; b. Berlin, Jan. 28, 1921; s. Lazar and Sarah (Guensberg) W.; m. Judith Hannah Saretsky, Jan. 26, 1947; children: Michael Jonathan, Nina Beth, Amy Lisa. BA, Columbia U., 1941, MD, 1944; postgrad., Topeka Inst. Psychoanalysis, 1951-58. Assoc. dir., then dir. rsch. Menninger Found., Topeka, 1954-66; chief psychiatry Mt. Zion Hosp., San Francisco, 1966-78; tng. and supervising analyst San Francisco Psychoanalytic Inst., 1966—; clin. prof. U. Calif. Sch. Medicine, Langley-Porter Neuropsychiat. Inst., 1967-75, prof., chmn. dept. psychiatry, also dir. inst., 1975-85, prof. dept. psychiatry, 1985-91, prof. emeritus, 1991—. Vis. prof. psychiatry La. State U. Sch. Medicine, also New Orleans Psychoanalytic Inst., 1972-73, Pahlavi U., Shiraz, Iran, 1977, Fed. U. Rio Grande do Sul, Porto Alegre, Brasil, 1980; mem., chmn. rsch. scientist career devel. com. NIMH, 1966-70; fellow Ctr. Advanced Study Behavioral Scis., Stanford, Calif., 1964-65, 81-82, Rockefeller Found. Study Ctr., Bellagio, Italy, 1992. Author: 19 books ; mem. editl. bd. : numerous profl. jours.; contbr. over 315 articles to profl. jours. With AUS, 1946-48. Recipient Heinz Hartmann award N.Y. Psychoanalytic Inst., 1968, Disting. Alumnus award Menninger Sch. Psychiatry, 1972, J. Elliott Royer award U. Calif., San Francisco, 1973, Outstanding Achievement award No. Calif. Psychiat. Soc., 1987, Mt. Airy gold medal, 1990, Mary Singleton Sigourney award, 1991, Outstanding Contbn. to Psychoanalytic Edn. award Internat. Fedn. Psychoanalytic Edn., 1999. Fellow ACP, Am. Coll. Psychoanalysts, Am. Psychiat. Assn., Am. Orthopsychiat. Assn.; mem. Am. Psychoanlytic Assn. (pres. 1971-72), Internat. Psychoanalytic Assn. (v.p. 1977-85, pres. 1985-89, hon. v.p. 1999—), Group for Advancement Psychiatry, Mexican Psychoanalytic Assn. (hon.), Brit. Psycho-Analytical Soc. (hon.), Phi Beta Kappa, Alpha Omega Alpha. Home: 290 Beach Rd Belvedere CA 94920-2472

WALLEY, JAMES MARVIN, JR. engineering and real estate executive, management consultant; b. Orange, Calif., Oct. 25, 1947; s. James Marvin Sr. and Edna Amelia (Rohr) W.; m. Marynelle Lorimer Walley, Apr. 28, 1990; children: Charlotte, Elizabeth, Edward, Joseph. BSCE, Tulane U., 1970; MSCE, George Washington U., 1974; MBA in Fin., U. So. Miss., 1980. Registered profl. engr., Tex., Va.; cert. property mgr., lic. broker. Commd. ensign USN, 1970, advanced through grades to lt. comdr. Civil Engr. Corps, served in Vietnam, 1970-71, resigned, 1981; exec. v.p. SPW, Inc., Dallas, 1981-84; chief ops. officer, ptnr. Montgomery Cos., Inc., 1984-87; sr. v.p. Law Engring., Inc., 1988-94; pres., COO Cura, Inc., 1995. Pres., CEO Geo. Marine, Inc., 1996; v.p. Archon Group, 1997—. Vice chmn., chmn. ARC, 1985, sec.; councilman University Park City, 1998-2002. Rear Admiral Civil Engr. Corps, USN Res. Fellow: ASCE; mem.: Soc. Am. Mil. Engrs., Seabee Meml. Scholarship Assn. (pres. 2001—), Leadership Dallas Alumni (pres. 1986), Tulane Alumni Coun. Assn. (pres. 1989), Salesmanship Club Dallas, Masons (32d Degree, KCCH). Republican. Roman Catholic. Avocations: golf, skiing. Address: RADM CEC USNR 600 E Las Colinas Blvd Ste 400 Irving TX 75039 E-mail: james.walley@archongroup.com.

WALLFESH, HENRY MAURICE, business communications company executive, editor, writer; b. N.Y.C., June 15, 1937; s. David Shibe and Rose (Silk) W.; m. Suzanne Krakowitch, Dec. 26, 1960; children: Saundra Kay, Gerald Bruce. Grad. indsl. and labor rels., Cornell U., 1958. Editor, co-pub. Indsl. Rels. News, N.Y.C. and Stamford, Conn., 1960-67; pres., chief exec. officer RAI div. Hearst Bus. Communications, N.Y.C., 1968-91, sr. v.p., editor at large, 1991; pres. Whale Communications, Inc., Stamford, Conn., 1992—. Pres. Indsl. Rels. Inst., Stamford, 1964-67; founder, bd. dirs. Internat. Soc. Pre-Retirement Planners, 1975-88; bd. dirs. VSOP Mktg., Boston. Author: Implications of the Age Discrimination in Employment, 1977, When a CEO Retires, 1978. Bd. dirs. Aging in Am., N.Y.C., 1985-90, N.Y.C. Anti-Defamation League, 1987-89; mem. alumni bd. dirs. Cornell Inst. Labor Rels., 1995—. Capt. inf. USAR, 19658-67. Recipient Corp. Achievement award Nat. Assn. for Sr. Living Industries, 1990; inducted into Internat. Soc. Pre-Retirement Planners Hall of Fame, 1988. Mem. Roxbury Swim and Tennis Club (bd. dirs. 1975-78), Cornell Club. Jewish. Avocations: tennis, theatre, writing. Home and Office: 1616 Long Ridge Rd Stamford CT 06903-3902

WALLHAUSEN, MILDRED CAROLYN, publisher; b. N.Y.C., Apr. 3, 1914; d. James Meroe and Frances (Bronson) Savell; m. Arthur Louis Wallhausen Sr., Sept. 25, 1936 (dec. Nov. 1969); children: Art L. Jr., Elizabeth Gail. Grad., Brown Bus. Coll., 1932. Proofreader Daily Am. Rep., Poplar Bluff, 1933-36; co-owner Enterprise-Courier, Charleston, 1936-69, pub., 1969—. Illustrator: (children's book) Bobby Butterfly, 1986; watercolor artist. Mem. Mo. Gov.'s Adv. Coun., Comprehensive Health Planning Coun., 1969-73; mem. Bootheel CHP Coun,. 1971-72, Charleston Park and Recreation Bd., 1972-77, Sr. Citizens Housing Project, 1973, Miss. County TB Assn., 1945-53, S.E. Mo. Regional Coun. Alcoholism and Drug Abuse, 1976-78, Miss. County Child Welfare Coun., 1974-77; bd. dirs. Miss. County Child Devel. Ctr., 1974-77; pres. Eugene Field Elem. Sch. PTA, 1948, Charleston H.S. PTA, 1935; chpt. mother FHA, 1955, 62; mem. Miss. County Cmty. Chs.; commr. East Prairie Housing Authority, 1992—; SEMO State U. Copper Dome Soc.(pres. coun.), mem. citizens adv. bd. S.E. U., Cape Girardeau KRCU-Public Radio, 1996-1999. Inducted Mo. Press Assn. Hall of Fame, 2000. Mem. NAACP, S.E. Mo. Press Assn (pres. 1981, historian 1982-), Miss. County Sheltered Workshops (bd. mem. 1985-), Am. Legion Aux, Citzens' Adv. Bd. 1997-99. Republican. Episcopalian. Office: Enterprise-Courier 206 S Main Charleston MO 63834

WALLIN, JAMES PETER, lawyer; b. Huntington, N.Y., May 9, 1958; s. Jerome Peter and Margaret Mary (Gilvarry) W.; m. Julia Katherine Springen, Aug. 11, 1984; children: James Peter Jr., Thomas George, Katherine Grace, Sarah Elizabeth. BA in Econs., SUNY, Stony Brook, 1980; JD, N.Y. Law Sch., 1983. Bar: N.Y. 1984. Counsel Alliance Capital Mgmt., N.Y.C., 1982-86; assoc. Cole & Dietz (now Winston & Strawn), 1986-87; counsel The Dreyfus Corp., 1987-88; gen. counsel Yamaichi Capital Mgmt. Inc., 1988-92, Yamaichi Internat. (Am.) Inc., N.Y.C., 1992-94, Evergreen Asset Mgmt. Corp., 1994-97; dir. risk mgmt. Morgan Stanley Investment Mgmt., N.Y.C., 1997—. Faculty Practicing Law Inst., N.Y.C., 1992—. Author: (seminar materials) Broker Dealer Regulation, 1992. Avocations: aviation, skiing.

WALLIN, LELAND DEAN, artist, educator; b. Sioux Falls, S.D., Oct. 14, 1942; s. Clarence Forrest and Leona Mae (McInnis) W.; m. Meredith Maria Hawkins, Mar. 26, 1977; 1 child, Jessica Hawkins. Student, Columbus Coll. Art and Design, 1961-62; BFA in Painting, Kansas City (Mo.) Art Inst., 1965; MFA in Painting, U. Cin. with Cin. Art Acad., 1967. Prof. drawing, painting, sculpture St. Cloud (Minn.) State U., 1967-86; prof. Queens Coll., CUNY, Flushing, 1983-84; prof., coord. MFA painting Marywood U., Scranton, Pa., 1985-90; prof. painting and drawing East Carolina U., Greenville, N.C., 1992—. Lectr. Carnegie-Mellon U., Pitts., 1988; juror Belin Arts Grant Com., Waverly, Pa., 1989; curator Philip Pearlstein Retrospective Exhibit, Scranton, 1988; vis. prof. painting East Carolina U., Greenville, 1992-93; judge/juror No. Nat. Art Competition, 1993. One-man shows include include Mpls. Coll. Art and Design, 1978, Harold Reed Gallery, 1983, Gallery henoch, N.Y.C., 1991, others, exhibited in group shows at include The Bklyn. Mus., 1983, Greenville County Mus. of Art, S.C., 1983, The Mus. of Modern Art, Fla., 1993, huntsville Mus. Art, 1994, San Bernardino County Mus. Internat., Calif., 1995, Contemporary Realism,'96, Internat., '98 , '98 Internat., Phila., Sacramento Fine Arts Ctr. Internat., 1999, 2000, Laredo Ctr. for Arts, Tex. (Internat. 1st prize oil awards 1997, 2000), Downey (Calif.) Mus. Art, 1998, Palm Springs Desert Mus., 1999, Bellevue Art Mus., Wash., 2001, Morris Mus. of Art, Ga., 2001, Huntsville Mus. Art, Ala., 2002, Miss. Mus. Art, 2002, Represented in permanent collections represented in various collections; contbr. articles. Named Outstanding Tchr., East Carolina U., 1994, 95; recipient numerous rsch. awards East Carolina U., 1994—. Mem. Coll. Art Assn. Am., Pa. Soc. Watercolor Painters. Home: 218 York Rd Greenville NC 27858-5601

WALLIN, LORI ANN, English language educator; b. Moscow, Oct. 14, 1961; d. John Neal and Agnes Ann Wallin; m. Sam Joe Taylor, Nov. 14, 1981. BA in English, U. Idaho, Moscow, 1988; MFA in Creative Writing, Ea. Wash. U., Cheney, Wash., 1996. Editor, graphic artist S&L Enterprises, Hayden, Idaho, 1990-95; tchg. asst. Ea. Wash. U., Cheney, 1994-96; instr. English North Idaho Coll., Coeur d'Alene, 1996—; tchg. cons., adv. bd. N.W. Inland Writing Project, Moscow, 1999—. Mem.: So. Poverty Law Ctr., Nat. Coun. Tchrs. English, Inland N.W. Coun. Tchrs. English, Rocky Mt. Elk Found., Sigma Tau Delta. Avocations: writing, reading, hot springs, camping, cooking. Office: North Idaho Coll Dept English 1000 W Garden Ave Coeur D Alene ID 83814

WALLIN, SUSAN MARIE, secondary school counselor; b. Berkeley, Calif., Mar. 16, 1967; d. Richard William and Marilyn Diane (Moxness) Duerst; m. Matthew Oscar Wallin, May 7, 1993. BA in Music and Math., St. Olaf Coll., 1989; MS in Profl. Sch. Counseling, Minn. State U., Mankato, 1996. Cert. mid. secondary sch. counselor. Accompanist, asst. music dir. Valley View Mid. Sch., Edina, Minn., 1992-94; early incentive program tutor Minn. State U., Mankato, 1994-95, grad. asst., 1995-96; counselor intern Hayfield (Minn.) Pub. Schs., 1995-96; counselor Triton Pub. Schs., Dodge Center, Minn., 1996—; music dir. Mantorville (Minn.) Theater Co., 1994—. Mem. S.E. Minn. Career Curriculum Com., Owatonna, Minn., 1995-96; participant Dodge County Child Protection Team, Mantorville, 1995—. Concerto Contest winner Chippewa Symphony Orchestra, Chippewa Falls, 1985. Mem. ACA, Am. Sch. Counseling Assn., S.E. Minn. Sch. Counseling Assn. (newsletter editor, comms. chair 1998—), Nat. Music Tchrs. Assn., Minn. Music Tchrs. Assn., Minn. Sch. Counseling Assn., Pi Kappa Lambda. Democrat. Avocations: gardening, arts and crafts, tennis, singing, composing songs. Home: 303 4th St NE Kasson MN 55944-1523 Office: Triton Pub Schs PO Box 40 Dodge Center MN 55927-0040

WALLING, DONOVAN ROBERT, educational book editor; b. Kansas City, Mo., Jan. 9, 1948; s. Donovan Ernest and Dorothy Jane (Goyette) W.; m. Diana Lynn Eveland, Oct. 19, 1968 (dec. 1991); children: Katherine Anne, Donovan David, Alexander James. BS in Edn., Kans. State Tchrs. Coll., 1970; MS, U. Wis., Milw., 1975. Cert. tchr., adminstr., Wis., Ind. Tchr. Sheboygan (Wis.) Area Sch. Dist., 1970-81, 83-86, coord. lang. arts and reading, 1986-91; tchr. Dept. Def. Dependents Schs., Zweibruecken, Germany, 1981-83; dir. instrnl. svcs. Carmel (Ind.)-Clay Schs., 1991-93; dir. publs. and rsch. Phi Delta Kappa Internat., Bloomington, Ind., 1993—. Mem. adj. faculty U. Wis., Oshkosh, 1986-91, Silver Lake Coll., Manitowoc, Wis., 1987-91. Author: Complete Book of School Public Relations, 1982, How To Build Staff Involvement in School Management, 1984, Teachers as Leaders, 1994, Rethinking How Art Is Taught, 2000; also numerous articles. Mem. ASCD, Nat. Coun. Tchrs. English, Internat. Reading Assn., Phi Delta Kappa (v.p. Cen. Ind. chpt. 1992-93). Avocations: writing, painting. Office: Phi Delta Kappa PO Box 789 Bloomington IN 47402-0789 E-mail: dwalling@pdkintl.org.

WALLING, LINDA LUCAS, librarian, educator; b. Creston, Iowa, Nov. 5, 1939; d. Arthur Eugene and Florence Faye (Francis) Lucas; m. William Orin Walling, Apr. 25, 1991. BA, U. No. Iowa, 1961; MLS, U. Wash., 1966; PhD, U. Ill., 1980. Libr. Sidney (Mont.) High Sch., 1961-62; asst. libr. Minot (N.D.) High Sch., 1962-65; instr., reference libr. Iowa State U., Ames, 1966-69, asst. prof., reference libr., 1969-71, head gifts and exch., 1971-74; asst. prof. coll. libr. info. sci. U. S.C., Columbia, 1977-83, assoc. prof., 1983-87, prof., 1987—. Co-author: Disabled Child in the Library, 1983, Disabilities, Children and Libraries, 1993; editor: Library Service to Developmentally Disabled Children and Adults, 1982; co-editor: Information Services for People with Developmental Disabilities, 1995; editor: Hidden Abilities in Higher Education, 1996; contr. articles to profl. jours. Mem. ALA, Assn. Specialized and Coop. Libr. Agys. (bd. dirs. 1984-86, 89-91), Librs. Serving Spl. Populations (chair 1984-86), Assn. Libr. Info. Sci. Edn., S.C. Libr. Assn., Beta Phi Mu. Office: U SC Coll Libr Info Sci Columbia SC 29208-0001

WALLINGER, JOHN D(AVID) A(RNOLD), investment banker; b. Buenos Aires, May 1, 1940; (parents Brit. citizens); s. Sir Geoffrey Arnold Wallinger and Diana (Peel-Nelson) Clarabut; m. Rosamund Elizabeth Clifford-Wolff, Feb. 22, 1966; 1 child, Mark Robert Arnold. BA in French, German and History, Cambridge (Eng.) U., 1962. Various positions to gen. ptnr. Panmure Gordon, London, 1963-75; gen. ptnr. Rowe and Pitman, 1975-87; dir. S.G. Warburg Securities, 1987-93; vice chmn. S.G. Warburg Internat., 1993-96; exec. dir. Swiss Bank Corp. Warburg, 1996-99; cons. UBS A.G., 1999—. Chmn. Gen. and Oriental Ltd., 1999—. Mem. Inst. Investment Mgmt. and Rsch. Anglican. Avocations: golf, fishing. Office: UBS AG 1 Curzon St London W1Y 7FN England

WALLINGFORD, ANNE, writer, editor, project developer; b. Chgo., June 29, 1949; d. Lester Arlyn and Roseanne (Jones) W. BS in Edn., Chgo. State U., 1975. Cert. elem. and mid. sch. tchr., Ill. Profl. dressmaker Annie's Original's, Chgo., 1968-72; instr., asst. prin., St. Bonaventure Sch., 1972-81; instr., chair sci. dept. Our Lady of Lourdes Sch., 1981-87; product designer, catalog mgr. FSC Ednl., Inc., Mansfield, Ohio, 1988-91; interim dir. pub. rels. Shelby Meml. Hosp., 1991-92; founder, dir. Anne Wallingford WordSmith, Chgo., 1992—. Instr. English lit. and bus. writing North Ctrl. Tech. Coll., 1991-92. Editor/writer: Steck-Vaughn, editor/writer: ZCI Edn., editor/writer: Gale Rsch., editor/writer: WCTS/McGraw-Hill, editor/writer: Quarasan Group, editor/writer: Proof Positive/Farrowlyne, editor/writer: McGraw Hill Higher Edn., editor/writer: Lucas Mfg., editor/writer: Kemtec, editor/writer: Sci. First, editor/writer: Ctrl. Sci., editor/writer: Fisher Sci., 1992—94, catalog/project developer: ETA, 1992—95, catalog/project developer: Sargent-Welch, 1993—; catalog cons. WGBH of Boston, 2001—02; contbr. Active The Vol. Ctr., Mansfield, 1992-93, steering com. Wright Community Ctr., 1991; treas. Wolfram St. Block Club, Chgo., 1975-78. Recipient Gold award Adler Planetarium, Chgo., 1985. Mem. Nat. Writers's Union, Chgo., Women in Pub. (Individual Excellence in Prodn., 1994, 95), Soc. Tech. Communicators, Profl. Freelance Assn. (founder, pres., 1991-92), Mensa. Avocations: telecommunications, reading, theater , museums. Office: 6155 N Moody Ave Chicago IL 60646-3806

WALLINGTON, TIMOTHY J. atmospheric chemist; b. Northampton, Eng., Nov. 4, 1958; came to U.S., 1984; s. John Allen and Valarie Margaret (Green) W. BA, Oxford U., Eng., 1981, MA, PhD, 1983. Postgrad. chemist Statewide Air Pollution Research Ctr., Riverside, Calif., 1984, asst. research chemist, 1984-86; fgn. guest worker Nat. Bur. Standards, Boulder, Colo., 1986—. Mem. Royal Soc. Chemistry (grad.), Sigma Xi. Clubs: Athletic Express Track (Riverside). Anglican. Home: 9218 Warfield Rd Gaithersburg MD 20882-4220

WALLIS, BEN ALTON, JR. lawyer; b. Llano County, Tex., Apr. 27, 1936; s. Ben A. and Jessie Ella (Longbotham) W.; children from previous marriage: Ben a. III, M. Jessica; m. Joan Mery, 1987. BBA, U. Tex., 1961, JD, 1971; postgrad., Law Sch. So. Meth. U. Bar: Tex. 1966, U.S. Dist. Ct. (no. dist.) Tex. 1971, U.S. Ct. Appeals D.C. 1974, U.S. Dist. Ct. D.C. 1975, U.S. Dist. Ct. (we. dist.) Tex. 1975, U.S. Dist. Ct. (no. dist.) Calif. 1983, U.S. Ct. Appeals (5th cir.) 1975, U.S. Ct. Appeals (8th cir.) 1980, U.S. Ct. Appeals (11th cir.) 1981, U.S. Dist. Ct. (ea. dist.) Wis. 1983, U.S. Supreme Ct. 1974. Pvt. practice, Llano, 1966-67, Dallas, 1971-73; investigator, prosecutor State Securities Bd. Tex., 1967-71; v.p. of devel. Club Corp. Am., Dallas, 1973; assoc. counsel impeachment task force U.S. Ho. of Reps. Com. on Judiciary, Washington, 1974; prin. Law Offices of Ben Wallis, P.C., San Antonio, 1974—. Chmn. Nat. Land Use Conf., 1979-81; mem. Gov.'s Areawide Planning Adv. Com., 1975-78; pres. Inst. Human Rights Rsch., 1979-2000. Mem. ATLA, FBA, Coll. of State Bar of Tex., State Bar Tex. (former chmn. agr. tax com.), D.C. Bar Assn., San Antonio Bar Assn., Delta Theta Phi, Delta Sigma Pi. Republican. Baptist. Office: GPM South Tower 800 NW Loop 410 Ste 350 San Antonio TX 78216-5619 E-mail: wallis@txdirect.net.

WALLIS, CARLTON LAMAR, librarian; b. Blue Springs, Miss., Oct. 15, 1915; s. William Ralph and Tellie (Jones) W.; m. Mary Elizabeth Cooper, Feb. 22, 1944; 1 child, Carlton Lamar. BA with spl. distinction, Miss. Coll., 1936; MA, Tulane U., 1946; B.L.S., U. Chgo., 1947; L.H.D., Rhodes Coll., Memphis, 1980. English tchr., coach Miss. Pub. Schs., 1936-41; teaching fellow Miss. Coll. and Tulane U., 1941-42; chief librarian Rosenberg Library, Galveston, Tex., 1947-55; city librarian Richmond, Va., 1955-58; dir. Memphis Pub. Library, 1958-80, ret., 1980. Author: Libraries in the Golden Triangle, 1966; contbr. articles to library jours. Trustee Belhaven Coll., 1978-82, Nat. Ornamental Metal Mus., 1989—. Served as chief warrant officer AUS, 1942-46. Decorated Bronze Star. Mem. ALA (chmn. library mgmt. sect. 1969-71), Pub. Library Assn. (dir. 1973-77), Tex. Library Assn. (pres. 1952-53), Va. Library Assn., Southwestern Library Assn. (exec. bd. 1950-55), Southeastern Library Assn. (chmn. pub. library sect. 1960-62), Tenn. Library Assn. (pres. 1969-70, Distinguished Service award 1979, Intellectual Freedom award 1998). Presbyterian (elder). Club: Egyptian (pres. 1973-74). Home: 365 Kenilworth Pl Memphis TN 38112-5405

WALLIS, DIANA LYNN, artistic director; b. Windsor, Eng., Dec. 11, 1946; d. Dennis Blackwell and Joan Williamson (Gatcombe) W. Grad., Royal Ballet Sch., Eng., 1962-65. Dancer Royal Ballet Touring Co., London, 1965-68;

ballet mistress Royal Ballet Sch., 1969-81, dep. ballet prin., 1981-84; artistic coord. Nat. Ballet of Can., Toronto, 1984-86, assoc. artistic dir., 1986-87, co-artistic dir., 1987-89; free-lance prod., tchr. London; dep. artistic dir. English Nat. Ballet, 1990-94; artistic dir. Royal Acad. Dance, 1994—. Fellow Imperial Soc. Tchrs. Dancing. E-mail: lwallis@rad.org.uk.

WALLIS, DONALD WILLS, lawyer; b. Wilkes-Barre, Pa., Aug. 22, 1950; s. Donald and Hazel (Jansen) W.; m. Kathryn Macon Waggoner, Aug. 28, 1971; children: Neill Jansen, Kathryn Spencer. AB, Duke U., 1971, JD, 1974. Bar: Fla. 1974, U.S. Tax Ct. 1975, U.S. Dist. Ct. (mid. dist.) Fla. 1977, U.S. Ct. Appeals (5th cir.) 1978, U.S. Claims Ct. 1978, U.S. Supreme Ct. 1979. Assoc. Mahoney, Hadlow, Chambers & Adams, Jacksonville, Fla., 1974-78; mem. firm Fisher, Tousey & Wallis, P.A., 1978-89; ptnr. Holland & Knight LLP, 1989—; treas. Holland & Knight Consulting LLC, 2001—, also bd. dirs. Co-author: Bank Holding Companies: A Practical Guide to Bank Acquisitions and Mergers, 1978; tax notes editor: The Florida Probate System, 1977; contbg. editor Jour. Partnership Taxation, 1989-95. Chmn. Duke U. Alumni Admissions Adv. Com., Jacksonville, 1986-2000; pres. Beaches Fine Arts Series, Inc., Jacksonville Beach, Fla., 1990-2000. Recipient Charles A. Dukes award Outstanding Vol. Svc., 2000, Vol. of the Yr. award Vol. Jacksonville, Inc., 2000. Mem. ABA (taxation sect.), Fla. Bar (tax sect., bd. cert. tax atty.), Jacksonville Bar Assn. (tax sect.), Duke U. Alumni assn. (admissions com. 1986-2000), Selva Marina Country Club, Inc. (bd. govs. 1987-89). Episcopalian. Avocations: Jacksonville symphony chorus, sailing, scuba diving, backpacking, cycling. Office: Holland & Knight LLP 50 N Laura St Ste 3900 Jacksonville FL 32202-3622 E-mail: dwallis@hklaw.com.

WALLIS, JOHN JAMES (JIMMY WALLIS), comedian, impressionist, ventriloquist, comedy writer, Internet site designer; b. Searcy, Ark., Mar. 21, 1939; s. Prentiss Bascom and Maxine (James) W.; children: Lori Diana Wallis Bledsoe, Shauna Kathleen. Grad., Okla. U., 1960. Advisor Am. Acad. for Entertainment at U.S. Vets. Hosps., N.Y.C., 1988-97. Nat. TV debut Art Linkletter's Hollywood Talent Scouts, 1966; entertained troops in S.E. Asia, 1967-70; performed with Ann Murray, Lou Rawls, Lola Falana, Ben Vereen, Al Hirt, Debbie Reynolds, Rip Taylor, Suzanne Somers, others; performed in numerous clubs including Tropicana, Las Vegas, The Sahara, Las Vegas, The Flamingo, Las Vegas, Chauteau Champlain, Montreal, The Cave, Vancouver, The Paradise Island Casino, The Bahamas, The Superstar Theater, Atlantic City, Riviera, Las Vegas, Harrah's, Reno, The Reno Hilton, Las Vegas Hilton, Flamingo Hilton, Disneyland, L.A.; featured in Royal Caribbean Cruise Lines, Premier's Disney Theme Cruises, Norwegian Cruise Lines, Holland Am. and Celebrity Cruise Lines, Night of the Stars, Las Vegas; featured in Distinguished Oklahomans (Victoria Lee). Named Okla.'s Top Comedian, Okla. Ho. of Reps.; recipient Am. Legion medal. Mem.: NRA. Presbyterian. Avocations: photography, scuba diving, computers, tennis, target shooting.

WALLIS, MARY CAMILLA, civic leader; b. Albany, N.Y., Nov. 3, 1923; d. Huntington and Mary Camilla (McKim) Williams; m. Richard Fisher Wallis, Aug. 20, 1955; children: Maria Fisher, Sylvia Camilla. BA, Bryn Mawr Coll., 1946. Research asst. Cryogenic Lab Johns Hopkins U., Balt., 1946-52, research assoc. Applied Physics Lab. Silver Spring, Md., 1952-55; pres. Natural History Found. Orange County, Newport Beach, Calif., 1978. Docent Newport-Mesa Unified Sch. Dist., 1972—, Smithsonian Inst., Washington, 1956-64. Contbr. articles profl. jours. Vol. curator Natural History Found. Orange County, 1980—; pres. Carderuck Springs (Md.) PTA, 1967; v.p. Newport Beach Parent Faculty Orgn., 1971; pres. U. Calif. Irvine Town and Gown, 1976-77. Mem. Geol. Soc. Am. Clubs: University (Irvine); Newport Beach Tennis. Republican. Episcopalian. Avocations: fossil collecting, photography. Home: 2635 Alta Vista Dr Newport Beach CA 92660-4102 Office: Natural History Mus Orange County 2627 Vista Del Oro Newport Beach CA 92660-3548

WALLIS, OLNEY GRAY, lawyer; b. Llano, Tex., July 27, 1940; s. Ben Alton and Jessie Ella (Longbotham) W.; m. Linda Lee Johnson, June 29, 1963; children: Anne, Brett. BA, U. Tex., 1962, JD, 1965. Bar: Tex. 1965, U.S. Dist. Ct. (so. dist.) Tex. 1966, U.S. Ct. Mil. Appeals 1968, U.S. Surpeme Ct. 1970, U.S. dist. Ct. (we. dist.) Tex. 1976, U.S. Ct. Appeals (5th cir.) 1977, U.S. Tax Ct. 1980, U.S. Ct. Appeals (10th cir.) 1981, U.S. Ct. Appeals (11th cir.) 1983, U.S. Dist. Ct. (no. dist.) Tex. 1985, U.S. Dist. Ct. (ea. and we. dists.) Ark. 1985, U.S. Ct. Appeals (8th cir.) 1985. Assoc. Brown & Cecil, Houston, 1965-66; asst. U.S. atty. Dept. Justice, 1971-74; mem. Jefferson, Wallis & Sherman, 1975-81, Wallis & Pruitt, Houston, 1981-87, Wallis and Short, Houston, 1987—. Instr. U. Md., Keflauik, Iceland, 1968-69; mem. faculty continuing legal edn. U. Houston, 1981-84. Capt. USAF, 1969-70. Decorated Air Force Commendation medal. Mem. Assn. Trial Lawyers Am., Am. Judicature Soc., Tex. Trial Lawyers Assn., Houston Bar Found., Phi Delta Phi, Phi Kappa Tau. Office: Wallis & Short 4300 Scotland St Houston TX 77007-7328 E-mail: ogwlawyer@earthlink.net.

WALLIS, RICHARD FISHER, physicist, educator; b. Washington, May 14, 1924; s. William F. and Alberta (Sigelen) W.; m. Mary Camilla Williams, Aug. 20, 1955; children: Maria Fisher, Sylvia Camilla. BS, George Washington U., 1945, MS, 1948; PhD, Cath. U. Am., 1952. Postdoctoral fellow (U. Md.), College Park, 1951-53; chemist Applied Physics Lab. Johns Hopkins U., Silver Spring, Md., 1953-56; physicist Naval Rsch. Lab., Washington, 1956-66, 67-69, head semiconductors br., 1958-66, 67-69; prof. physics U. Calif., Irvine, 1966-67, 69—; prof. emeritus, 1993—; chmn. dept. physics U. Calif., Irvine, 1972-75, 80-83. Vis. prof. U. Paris, 1975-76, 79, 85. Author: (with Maradudin and Dobrzynski) Handbook of Surfaces and Interfaces, 1980, (with Balkanski) Many-Body Aspects of Solid State Spectroscopy, 1986; editor: Lattice Dynamics, 1965, Localized Excitations in Solids, 1968 (with Stegeman) Electromagnetic Surface Excitations, 1986, (with Birman and Sebenne) Elementary Excitations in Solids, 1992; contbr. articles to profl. jours. Served with U.S. Army, 1945-46. Recipient Pure Sci. award Naval Rsch. Lab., 1964, Disting. Alumni Achievement award George Washington U., 1991. Fellow Am. Phys. Soc., AAAS; mem. Philos. Soc. Washington, Phi Beta Kappa, Sigma Xi Home: 2635 Alta Vista Dr Newport Beach CA 92660-4102 Office: U Calif Dept Physics Irvine CA 92697-0001

WALLIS, ROBERT RAY, psychologist; b. Hardwood, Okla., Sept. 1, 1927; s. Walter William and Osie Oma (Luckett) W.; m. Joan Elaine Martino, Sept. 10, 1955; children: Rosalie, Glenn, Damon, Gina, Darren. Student, Southwestern Inst. Tech., 1945; BA, U. Okla., 1951, Ed.M., 1960, PhD, 1963. Lic. psychologist, Pa., N.J. From psychology intern to dir. div. psychology Greater Kansas City Mental Health Found., 1962-71; from fellow to chief psychologist Western Mo. Mental Health Center, Kansas City, 1965-71; from program dir. to exec. dir. Horizon House Inc., Phila., 1971-79; chief exec. officer Ancora Psychiat. Hosp., Hammonton, N.J., 1979-81; individual practice clin. and cons. psychology, Medford, 1981-97; propr. Wallis Printing Ctr., Phila., 1985-91; clin. supr. Alcoholism and Psychotherapy Assocs., Medford, N.J., 1985-98, Middlesex Counseling Assocs., Cranbury, 1985-89. From asst. prof. to chmn. div. psychology dept. psychiatry, U. Mo., Kansas City Sch. Medicine, 1965-71. Contbr. articles to profl. jours. Served with USNR, 1945-46. Mem. Am. Psychol. Assn. Home and Office: 2839 Chelsea Dr Norman OK 73072-2235 *Treat each person with respect and dignity, without regard to rank or power.*

WALLISCH, CAROLYN E. principal; b. Denver, Aug. 23, 1939; d. Morgan Franklin and Margaret C. (Kopf) White; m. Darrell Dean Wallisch, June 9, 1963; children: Michael Dean, Kerri Elise. BA in Elem. Edn., U. No. Colo., 1961, MA in Elem. Edn., 1965; postgrad., Denver U., 1989. Cert. tchr. grades K-8, adminstrn. grades K-12. Tchr. grade 1 San Jose Unified Sch. Dist., 1961-62, Greeley (Colo.) Pub. Schs., 1962-69; tchr. grades 2-8, dean of students Jefferson County Schs., Lakewood, Colo., 1984-94; prin. grades K-5 Littleton (Colo.) Pub. Schs., 1994—2001; ret., 2001. Adj. prof. dept. edn. Colo. Christian U., Lakewood, Colo. Contbr. articles to profl. jours. Leader 4-H Clubs of Am., Littleton, 1982-84, Girl Scouts U.S.A., Littleton, 1979-82; den leader Boy Scouts Am., Littleton, 1976-78; precinct committeewoman Littleton, 1984-90. Named one of Outstanding Young Women of Am., 1965, Model Tchr., ABC News Peter Jennings Who's Happening in Edn., 1993, Instr. Mag., 1993. Mem. ASCD, Internat. Reading Assn. (Colo. coun. 1989—), Colo. Coun. Tchrs. Math. (conf. presenter), Colo. Assn. Sch. Execs. (conf. presenter), PTO (v.p. 1994—), Kiwanis, Kappa Delta Pi (bd. dirs.), Sigma Sigma Sigma (bd. dirs.), Alpha Delta Kappa (bd. dirs.), Phi Delta Kappa (bd. dirs., rsch. chmn. 1987—). Republican. Avocations: tennis, golf. Home: 5549 W Hinsdale Ave Littleton CO 80128-7021 Office: Colo Christian U Sch Edn 180 South Garrison St Lakewood CO 80226

WALL-LIEVSAY, BONNIE LEE, human resources specialist, educator; b. Chicago, Ill., Feb. 13, 1949; d. Harry Joseph Burgess, Lois Elizabeth Burgess; m. David Ray Lievsay; children: Diana Lievsay. BA, Antioch Coll., 1970; MPA, San Jose State U., 1979; MA, Fielding Inst., 1995, PhD, 1998. Internal orgnl. develop. cons. Portland Gen. Electric, Portland, Oreg., 1985—91; prin. cons. West Slope Cons., 1991—99; tng. coord. R.R. Donnelley & Sons Co., Salem, Va., 2000—01; sr. instrnl. designer The Performance Edge Inc., Hardy, 2001—. Recipient The Golden Penguin for Orgnl. Innovation award, Am. Soc. Tng. and Develop., Portland chpt., 1987; fellow Donna Bushnell Meml. fellow, Fielding Inst., 1997. Mem.: Soc. Human Resources Mgmt., Orgnl. Develop. Network, Acad. Mgmt. Home: 5586 Highfields Rd Roanoke VA 24018 Personal E-mail: westslope@att.net.

WALLMAN, STEVEN MARK HARTE, financial computer services provider; b. N.Y.C., Nov. 14, 1953; s. Eugene and Doris (Lee) W.; m. Kathleen M. Harte, May 5, 1985. BS, MIT, 1975, MS, 1976; postgrad., Harvard U., 1976-77; JD, Columbia U., 1978. Bar: D.C. 1978, Va. 1986. Assoc. Covington & Burling, Washington, 1978-86, ptnr., 1986-94; commr. SEC, 1994-97; sr. fellow The Brooking Instn., 1997—; founder, CEO FOLIOfn, Inc., Vienna, 1998—. Office: FOLIOfn Inc 8000 Towers Crescent Dr Vienna VA 22182

WALLMANN, JEFFREY MINER, author; b. Seattle, Dec. 5, 1941; s. George Rudolph and Elizabeth (Biggs) W. BS, Portland State U., 1962; PhD, U. Nev., 1998. Pvt. investigator Dale Sys., N.Y.C., 1962-63; asst. buyer, mgr., pub. money bidder Dohrmann Co., San Francisco, 1966-69; dir. pub. rels. London Films, Cinelux-Universal, Trans-European Publs., 1970-75; editor-in-chief Riviera Life mag., 1975-77; instr. U. Nev., Reno, 1990—, Las Vegas, 1998—, U. Phoenix, 2001—. Author: The Spiral Web, 1969, Judas Cross, 1974, Clean Sweep, 1976, Jamaica, 1977, Deathtrek, 1980, Blood and Passion, 1980, Brand of the Damned, 1981, The Manipulator, 1982, Return to Conta Lupe, 1983, The Celluloid Kid, 1984, Business Basic for Bunglers, 1984, Guide to Applications Basic, 1984, The Western: Parables of the American Dream, 1999, (under pseudonym Leon DaSilva) Green Hell, 1976, Breakout in Angola, 1977, (under pseudonym Nick Carger) Hour of the Wolf, 1973, Ice Trap Terror, 1974, (under pseudonym Margaret Maitland) The Trial, 1974, Come Slowly, Eden, 1974, How Deep My Cup, 1975, (under pseudonym Amanda Hart Douglass) First Rapture, 1972, Jamaica!, 1978, (under pseudonym Grant Roberts) The Reluctant Couple, 1969, Wayward Wives, 1970, (under pseudonym Gregory St. Germain) Resistance # 1: Night and Fog, 1982, Resistance #2: Magyar Massacre, 1983, (pseudonym Wesley Ellis) Lonestar on the Treachery Trail, 1982, numerous others, (pseudonym Tabor Evans) Longarm and the Lonestar Showdown, 1986, (pseudonym Jon Sharpe) Trailsman 58: Slaughter Express, 1986, numerous others in Trailsman series, also others under pseudonyms; co-author, under pseudonym William Jeffrey) Duel at Gold Buttes, 1980, Border Fever, 1982, Day of the Moon, 1983, The Western: Parables of the American Dream, 1999; contbr. articles and short stories to Argosy, Ellery Queen's Mystery Mag., Alfred Hitchcock's Mystery Mag., Zane Grey Western, Venture, Oui, TV Guide. Mem. Mystery Writers Am., Sci. fiction Writers Am., We. Writers Am., Nat. Coun. tchrs. English, Crime Writers Am., Nev. state Coun. Tchrs. English, Esperanto League N.Am., We. Lit. Assn., Internacia Soc. Amikeco Kaj Bonvolo, Sci. Fiction Rsch. Assn., Internat. Assn. Fantastic in the Arts, We. Lit. Assn. Office: care of Barry Malzberg PO Box 61 Teaneck NJ 07666-0061

WALLMARK, JOHN TORKEL, scientist, educator; b. Stockholm, June 4, 1919; s. Gunnar and Vivi (Osterlund) W.; m. Madeline Mihelyi, Apr. 18, 1949; children: John Sigurd, John Torbjorn; m. Gunnel Alsen, Aug. 20, 1975. D Tech., Royal Inst. Tech., Stockholm, 1953. Engr. Standard Radio AB, Stockholm, 1944-45; rsch. asst. Royal Inst. tech., 1945-53; staff mem. RCA Labs., Princeton, N.J., 1947-48, 53-64, 66-68; prof. elec. engring. Chalmers U., Gothenburg, Sweden, 1964-66, 68-83, prof. innovations Sweden, 1983-91. Mem. invention com. Fed. Bd. Tech. Devel., 1968-78; rsch. adv. com. Perstorp AB, 1977-85, Fed. Bd. Tech. Devel., 1979-87, Ericsson AB, 1982-85, SKF AB, 1986-89, Frico AB, 1985-90; bd. dirs. Chemtronics AB, 1984-87, Gothenburg Product Devel. Ctr., Inst. Opt. Res.; chmn. idea stipend com. Job Security Coun. SAF-PTK, 1988-92. Author: (with others) Integrated Electronics, 1963, Field-Effect Transistors, 1966, Field-Effect Transistors in Integrated Circuits, 1974, 100 Major Swedish Innovations, 1988. Recipient Polhem award Swedish Engrs. Assn., 1982; H.T. Cedergren medal Royal Inst. Tech., 1984, KTH grand prize, 1989, John Ericsson award Am. Soc. Swedish Engrs., 1994, Chalmers medal Chalmers U. Tech., 1989. Fellow IEEE, AAAS; mem. Royal Swedish Acad. Sci. (L.J. Wallmark award 1954), Royal Swedish Acad. Engring. Sci. (IVA Large Gold medal 1989), Royal Soc. Arts and Sci. Home: Sjoallen 5 43431 Kungsbacka Sweden Office: Chalmers U 41296 Gothenburg Sweden

WALLNER, LUDWIG JOHN, principal; b. N.Y.C., Sept. 14, 1941; s. Ludwig and Antoinette (Maier) W.; m. Carolyn Elizabeth Holzer, Dec. 19, 1964; children: Heidi Elizabeth, Kurt Andrew. AAS, Orange County Community Coll., Middletown, N.Y., 1961; BS, SUNY, Oswego, 1964, MS, 1967; cert. advanced study, SUNY, Cortland, 1977; EdD, Highland U., 1982. Tchr. North Syracuse Ctrl. Schs., Clay, N.Y., 1964-66, sch. counselor, 1966-70, head sch. counselor, 1970-73, middle sch. asst. prin., 1973-80, house prin., 1980-86; middle sch. prin. Schalmont Ctrl. Schs., Schenectady, 1986-89, high sch. prin., 1989-95, mid. sch. prin., 1995-96; ret., 1999. Trainer Nat. Crisis Prevention Inst., Inc., Brookfield, Wis., 1994-95. Author, editor: (video) Testing Activity, 1969. Dist. chmn. Boy Scouts Am., Schenectady, 1989 (recipient arrowhead award 1986). Recipient St. George award Episcopal Ch. (nat.), Syracuse, N.Y., 1989. Mem. Sch. Adminstrs. Assn. N.Y., Schalmont Prins. Assn. (pres. 1989-96), North Syracuse Prins. Assn. (pres. 1978), N.Am. Assn. Deacons, Epsilon Pi Tau, Inc., Phi Delta Kappa. Republican. Episcopalian. Avocations: traveling, cross-country skiing, cycling, walking, woodworking. Home: 12 Killarney Ct Saratoga Springs NY 12866-7502

WALLOT, JEAN-PIERRE, archivist, historian; b. Valleyfield, Que., Can., May 22, 1935; s. Albert and Adrienne (Thibodeau) W.; m. Denyse Caron; children: Normand, Robert, Sylvie. BA, Coll. Valleyfield, 1954; lic. es lettres, MA in History, U. Montreal, 1957, PhD in History, 1965; D (hon.), U. Rennes, France, 1987, U. Ottawa, Can., 1996. Reporter Le Progres de Valleyfield, 1954-61; from lectr. to prof. dept. history U. Montreal, 1961-85, dept. chmn., 1973-75, vice-dean studies faculty arts and scis., 1975-78, vice-dean research Faculty Arts and Scis, 1979-82, academic v.p., 1982-85. Nat. archivist, Can., 1985-97; historian Nat. Mus. Man, Ottawa, Ont., 1966-69, assoc. prof. U. Toronto, 1969-71; prof. Concordia U., Montreal, Que., 1971-73; vis. prof. U. Ottawa, 1997—, dir. Ctr. de Rsch. en Civilisation Canadienne-Francaise, 2000—; dir. Etude Assn. Ecole Pratique des Hautes Etudes en Scis. Sociales, Paris, 1975, 79, 81, 83, 85, 87, 89, 94. Author: Intrigues françaises et americaines au Canada, 1965, (with John Hare) Les Imprimés dans le Bas-Canada, 1967, Confrontations, 1971, (with G. Paquet) Patronage et Pouvoir dans le Bas-Canada, 1973; Un Quebec qui bougeait, 1973; Editor: (with R. Girard) Memoires de J.E. McComber, bourgeois de Montréal, 1981; (with J. Goy) Evolution et eclatement du monde rural, 1986, Constructions identitaires et pratiques sociales, 2002. Pres. internat. adv. com. on memory of the world, UNESCO, 1993-98. Decorated officer Order Arts et Lettres (France); officer Order of Can.; recipient Marie Tremaine medal, 1973, Tyrrell medal, 1982, Royal Soc. Centenary medal, 1994, Jacques Ducharme prize, 1997. Fellow Royal Soc. Can. (sect. pres. 1985-87, pres. 1997-99); mem. Am. Antiquarian Soc., Acad. des Lettres du Quebec, Inst. d'Histoire l'Amerique Francaise (pres. 1973-77), Can. Hist. Assn. (pres. 1982), Assn. Can.-Francaise l'Avancement Scis. (pres. 1981-83, emeritus mem.), Assn. Archivists Que., Assn. Can. Archivists, Internat. Coun. on Archives (v.p. 1988-92, pres. 1992-96, pres. emeritus). Roman Catholic. Office: U Ottawa CDtr Rsch PO Box 450 Sta A Ottawa ON Canada K1N 6N5

WALLS, CARL EDWARD, JR. food service executive; b. Sept. 9, 1948; s. Carl E. and Melba Rene W.; m. Doris Duhart, Aug. 1, 1970; children: Carl Edward, Forrest Allen. Student, San Antonio Coll., 1966-68. Divsn. mgr. Sears Roebuck & Co., San Antonio, 1967-73, area sales mgr., 1973-78; svc. cons. Southwestern Bell, 1978-79, acct. exec., 1979-82; acct. exec., industry cons. AT&T Info. Sys., 1983-88, acct. mgr., 1988-89; solutions gen. mgr. AT&T; gen. mgr. Tex. State Govt., 1989-95, group sales mgr., 1998-99; solutions gen. mgr. AT&T, 1999—; v.p. Louie LeDeaux Restaurant. Mem. citizens adv. com. Tex. Senate, 1975-81; legis. aide Tex. Ho. of Reps., 1981-85; commr. Alamo Area cou. boy Scouts Am., 1970-79, Capitol Area coun., 1980—, nat. jamboree staff, 1973, 77, 81, 85, 89, 93; mem. Rep. Nat. Com., 1980—, Rep. Presdl. Task Force, 1980—, Rep. Senatorial Club, 1981—. Recipient Patriotic Svc. award U.S. Treasury Dept., 1975-76, Scouters Key and Commrs. award Boy Scouts Am., Disting. Merit award Boy Scouts Am., 1978. Mem. Scouting Collectors Assn. (pres. South Ctrl. region 1979-80, v.p. region 1980-81, sec. 1983-86), U. Ark. Alumni Assn. (life), Am. Legion. Home: 11712 D K Ranch Rd Austin TX 78759-3770

WALLS, CARMAGE LEE, JR. newspaper publisher/executive, consultant; b. Cleveland, Tenn., May 4, 1962; s. Carmage Lee Walls Sr. and Sarah (Smith) Bailey; m. Jeanne Marie Waller, June 4, 1989; children: Courtney Marie, Kathryn Jessica. BA in Journalism and English, U. Ala., Birmingham, 1988. Writer Birmingham News, 1987; exec. v.p. Cleveland Newspapers Inc., Birmingham, 1989—; pres., creative dir. Walls New Media, Inc., 1997—. Mem. bd. visitors Sch. Comm. and Info. Scis., U. Ala.; bd. trustees Magic City Art Connection, Birmingham, 2001—; bd. visitors U. Ala. Sch. Comm., Tuscaloosa, 2001—. Republican. United Methodist.

WALLS, JAMES DOUGLAS, minister; b. Washington, Aug. 1, 1931; s. George Washington and Emma (Benson) W.; m. Donna Marie Payne, June 16, 1962; children: Quentin Douglas, Janice Marie. Student, Washington Bible Inst., 1957-61; DD, Faith Evangelistic Christian Coll., Detroit, 1990, So. Calif. Sch. Ministry, Inglewood, 1991; HHD (hon.), Faith Evang. Christian Schs., Detroit, 1991. Ordained to ministry Ch. of God, 1960. Pastor Ch. of God, Xenia, Ohio, 1968—; mem. program and planning com., nominating com. Nat. Assn. Ch. of God, West Middlesex, Pa., 1983-89, coord. nat. preachers clinic, 1986—2000, mem. mass comm. bd., 1988-92, mem. ch. rels. bd., 1989-93, chief ops. officer, 2000—. Chair. bd. dirs. Women's Abuse of Substance Intervention Tactics, 1990-94 Editor Words of Truth, 1972-84, Xenia Herald, 1988-2000. Mem. Cumberland Ridge Civic Assn., Columbus, Ohio, 1971—. With U.S. Army, 1952-54. Mem. Urban Christian Leadership Assn., Xenia Area Assn. Chs., African Am. Ministerial Alliance, Ohio State Ch. of God Missionary Bd. Home: 3032 Pine Valley Rd Columbus OH 43219-1643

WALLS, MARTHA ANN WILLIAMS (MRS. B. CARMAGE WALLS), newspaper executive; b. Gadsden, Ala., Apr. 21, 1927; d. Aubrey Joseph and Inez (Cooper) Williams; m. B. Carmage Walls, Jan. 2, 1954; children: Byrd Cooper, Lissa Walls Vahldiek. Student pub. schs., Gadsden. Pres., dir. Walls Newspapers, Inc., 1969-70; sec., treas., dir. Summer Camps, Inc., Guntersville, Ala., 1954-69; CEO, pres., dir. So. Newspapers, Inc., Houston, 1970—; pres., dir. So. Newspapers of Ala., Inc., Scottsboro. V.p., dir. Ft. Payne (Ala.) Newspapers, Inc. Bay City (Tex.) Newspapers, Inc., Galveston Newspapers, Inc.; dir. Monroe (Ga.) Newspapers, Inc.; bd. dirs. Jefferson Pilot Corp., Greensboro, N.C., 1990-98, Jefferson-Pilot Life Ins. Co., 1990-98, Jefferson Pilot Comm., 1990-98. Bd. dirs. Montgomery Acad., 1970-74. Mem. Soc. Profl. Journalists, The Houstonian. Episcopalian. Office: So Newspapers Inc 1050 Wilcrest Dr Houston TX 77042-1608

WALLS, THOMAS FRANCIS, professional services administrator; b. Phila., June 4, 1947; s. Thomas Francis and Margaret Mary (Whalen) W.; m. Kathleen Cecilia Lyons, Dec. 7, 1968; children: Thomas, James, Eleanor. ABA in Econs., U. Pa., 1974, BBA in Mgmt., 1977. Programmer Gen. Elec. Re-entry Sys., King of Prussia, Pa., 1965-69; mgr. Keane Assocs., Paoli, 1969-73, Alco Std. Corp., Valley Forge, 1973-80, Comserv Corp., Mendota Heights, Minn., 1980-88, Andersen Cons., Chgo., 1988-89, Phila., 1989-95, dir. SAP tng. St. Charles, Ill., 1995-97; with JGI, Inc., Exton, Pa., 1997-99, dir. profl. svcs., 1998-99; project mgr. Intentia, 1999—. Contbg. author: APICS Dictionary. With USNR, 1967-68, Vietnam. Mem. Am. Prodn. and Inventory Control Soc. (cert. practitioner inventory mgmt.). Roman Catholic. Avocations: family, rowing, soccer, reading. Office: # 217 1442 Pottstown Pike West Chester PA 19380

WALLS, WESLEY (CHARLES WESLEY WALLS), football player; b. Pontotoc, Miss. m. Christy; children: Alexandria Bailey, Wesley Colton. Student, U. Miss. Tight end, long snapper, backup holder on punts San Francisco 49ers, 1989-93; winner Super Bowl XXIV, 1989; tight end New Orleans Saints, 1994-96, Carolina Panthers, 1996—. Named to Pro Bowl, 1996, 97, 98, 99; named second-team All-Pro, AP, Coll. and Pro Football Newsweekly, 1996, 99, second-team All-Pro, Football Digest, first-team All-NFC, Football News, United Press Internat., 1996, All-NFC selection Pro Football Weekly, Football News, 1999; recipient first-team All-NFC honors Football News, United Press Internat., 1997. Office: Carolina Panthers 800 S Mint St Ste 2 Charlotte NC 28202-1502*

WALLS, WILLIAM WALTON, JR. management consultant; b. Phila., Oct. 3, 1932; s. William Walton and Mary Crown (Elliott) W.; m. Nina Catherine deAngeli, July 1, 1961; 1 child, Deborah. BSME, Swarthmore Coll., 1959. With Boeing Helicopters, Phila., 1959-96, v.p. light helicopter joint venture, 1988-91, v.p. devel. programs, 1991-92, v.p. rsch. and engring., 1992-96; small high-tech. bus. cons. Ridley Park, Pa., 1996—. Cons. in field. Chmn. aerospace adv. coun. Pa. State Coll., 1974-79; mem. NATO Indsl. Advisors Group, 1988-93; mem. bd. advisors Rotocraft Ctr. Excellence, Rensselaer Polytech. Inst., 1982-84 Mem. Am. Helicopter Soc. (pres. 1988-89, chmn. 1989-90). Republican. Avocations: skiing, jogging, personal computer applications, classical music, golf. Home: 502 Harrison St Ridley Park PA 19078-3208

WALLSCHLAEGER, JOSEPHINE INGEBORG, mental health nurse; b. Montevideo, Minn., Nov. 20, 1942; d. Carl J. and Gertrude G. (Qualley) Nerison; m. Joseph F. Wallschlaeger, Aug. 6, 1967; children: Joseph, Melanie. BSN, Augustana Coll., Sioux Falls, S.D., 1965. Cert. psychiat.-mental health nurse, ANA. Staff nurse U.S. Army Nurse Corps, Washington, 1965, asst. head nurse Vung Tau, Vietnam, 1966, recruiter Indpls., 1967; dir. nursing Granite Falls (Minn.) Hosp., 1968; staff nurse Mankato (Minn.) House Nursing Home, 1973; staff nurse, access Immanuel-St. Joseph's Hosp., Mankato, 1974-92; supr. St. Peter (Minn.) Regional Treatment Ctr., 1992—. Instr. Mankato State U., 1991—2000. Leader Cub Scouts Boy Scouts Am., Mankato, 1975—86, Girl Scouts U.S.A., 1977—80; vol. PTA, Washington Sch., Mankato, 1975—78; vol. ARC, 1971—; mem. State Adv. Coun. for Mental Health, 1992—96; bd. mem. YWCA, Mankato, 1996—2001. Recipient Amb. award City of Mankato, 1991. Mem. Mid. Mgmt. Assn., Sigma Theta Tau. Lutheran. Avocations: walking, music.

WALLSKOG, JOYCE MARIE, nursing educator, psychologist; b. Melrose Park, Ill., Apr. 20, 1942; BSN, Alverno Coll., 1977; MSN, U. Wis., Milw., 1982; PhD, Marquette U., 1992. RN, Wis.; lic. psychologist; diplomate Am. Coll. Forensic Examiners. Staff nurse St. Mary's Hill Hosp., Milw., 1977-78, Waukesha (Wis.) Meml. Hosp., 1978-80, clin. nurse specialist, 1980-87; asst. prof. nursing Marquette U., Milw., 1986—; psychotherapist Psychiat. Assocs. Comprehensive Services, Ltd., 1982-85; nurse psychotherapist Counseling and Wellness Ctr., Waukesha, 1982—; adv. practice nurse prescriber, 1995—. Cons. Alverno Coll., Milw., 1983-84, Health Care Cons., Sussex, Wis., 1985—; coord. Waukesha Premenstrual Syndrome Program, 1980—; nurse psychotherapist Stress Mgmt. and Mental Health Svcs., Waukesha, 1991-94; co-founder Turning Point Mental Health and Cons. Svcs., Waukesha, 1994—; advanced practice nurse prescriber, 1995—. Contbr. articles to profl. jours. Bd. dirs. Waukesha County Mental Health Assn., 1982; mem. Waukesha County Unified Svcs., 1984; adv. bd. Northwest Rehab. Ctr., 1992-94; advisor Resolve Through Sharing, 1986-2001, Women's Health Svcs., 1987-2001; advisor Parish Nurse Program. Mem. ANA (coun. psychiat. and mental health nursing), Wis. Nurses Assn. (rep. Wis. Coalition on Sexual Misconduct by Psychotherapists and Counselors 1988-93), Delta Upsilon Sigma, Phi Lambda Delta. Office: Ctr for Behavioral Health 721 American Ave Ste 501 Waukesha WI 53188-5071 E-mail: wallskogj@aol.com.

WALLWORK, WILLIAM WILSON, III, automobile executive; b. Fargo, N.D., Mar. 8, 1961; s. William Wilson Jr.; m. Shannon Wallwork, July 12, 1991. AA in Automotive Mktg., Northwood Inst., 1981; student, San Diego State U., Moorhead State U. Lease rep. Wallwork Lease and Rental, 1984-86; sales mgr. W.W. Wallwork, Inc., Fargo, N.D., 1986-87, v.p., 1987-91, pres.,

1991—; v.p. Valley Imports Inc, 1986-91; pres. Valley Imports Inc., 1991—. Vice chmn. Kenworth 20 Group, 1992-93, chmn., 1994-96; mem. PACCAR Chmn.'s Meeting, 1993; mem. Rockwell Internat. Dealer Adv. Bd., 1995-98. Mem. adv. bd. N.D. State U. Coll. Bus. Adminstrn., 1995-2001; mem. Civic Opera Bd., 1999—. Mem. Fargo-Moorhead Automobile Dealers Assn. (v.p. 1986-88, pres. 1988-90, share house bd. 1998—). Avocation: skiing. Office: W W Wallwork Inc PO Box 1819 Fargo ND 58107-1819

WALMAN, A. TERRY, physician, lawyer; b. Norfolk, Va., June 21, 1951; s. Philip and Miriam (Siegel) W.; m. Linda Mary Elliott, Sept. 7, 1980; children: Whitney Anne E., Catharine Marie E. BA, U. Va., 1973, MD, 1977; JD, U. Md., 1990. Bar: Md. 1990; diplomate Am. Bd. Legal Medicine; diplomate in anesthesiology and critical care medicine Am. Bd. Anesthesiology. Asst. prof. Johns Hopkins U., Balt., 1982—; of counsel Richard E. McAlee P.A., Annapolis, Md., 1995—. Sr. examiner Am. Bd. Anesthesiology, 1991—. Editor: Anesthesiology Malpractice Protector, 1989-95, Anesthesiology Malpractice Prevention, 1996—, Anesthesiology Alert, 1996—. Fellow Am. Coll. Legal Medicine. Avocations: sailing, bicycling, running, music. Office: care Richard G McAlee PA PO Box 2968 Annapolis MD 21404-2968

WALMER, EDWIN FITCH, lawyer; b. Chgo., Mar. 24, 1930; s. Hillard Wentz and Anna C. (Fitch) W.; m. Florence Poling, June 17, 1952; children: Linda Diane Walmer Dennis, Fred Fitch. BS with distinction, Ind. U., 1952, JD with high distinction, 1957. Bar: Wis. 1957, U.S. Dist. Ct. (ea. dist.) Wis. 1957. Assoc. Foley & Lardner, Milw., 1957-65, ptnr., 1965-90, ret., 1990. Served to 1st lt. U.S. Army, 1952-54. Recipient Cal. C. Chambers award Culver (Ind.) Mil. Acad., 1948. Fellow Am. Coll. Trust and Estate Counsel; mem. Order of Coif, Dairymen's Country Club (Boulder Junction, Wis.), Vineyards Country Club (Naples, Fla.), Phi Eta Sigma, Beta Gamma Sigma. Republican. Congregationalist. Avocations: golf, fishing. Office: Foley & Lardner 777 E Wisconsin Ave Ste 3800 Milwaukee WI 53202-5367

WALMER, JAMES L. lawyer; b. Wabash, Ind., Oct. 18, 1948; s. Warren D. and Josephine (Clupper) W.; m. Carolyn Gwen Lackey, Apr. 23, 1977; children: Ryan, Christian, Jonathan, Geoffrey. BS, Ball State U., 1971; JD, U. Tulsa, 1973. Bar: Okla. 1974, Ind. 1974, U.S. Dist. Ct. (no. and ea. dists.) Okla. 1974, U.S. Dist. Ct. (so. dist.) Ind. 1974, U.S. Dist. Ct. (no. dist.) Ind. 1975. Sole practice, Warsaw, 1974—; dep. prosecutor Kosciusko County, 1976-96. Town atty. Winona Lake, Ind., 1976—, Pierceton, Ind., 1980—. Chmn. bd. dirs. Cardinal Ctr. Inc., Warsaw, 1978-84; mem. philanthropy com. Ball State U., Muncie, Ind., 1986—; pres. Lincoln PTO, 1989-90; co-pres. Harrison PTO, 1993-94; trustee First United Meth. Ch., 1992-94; dir. Ind. Prosecutors Child Support Alliance, 1994-96; bd. dirs. Warsaw Little League, 1994-98, coach, 1990-96, 98. Mem. ABA, Ind. Bar Assn. (chmn. surrogacy com. family law sect. 1987-88), Kosciusko County Bar Assn. (treas. 1979—), Okla. Bar Assn., Ind. Mcpl. Lawyers Assn. Lodges: Optimists (v.p. 1979-80), Shriners, Masons. Republican. Methodist. Home: 1705 E Springhill Rd Warsaw IN 46580-1805 Office: PO Box 1056 Warsaw IN 46581-1056 E-mail: walmer@kconline.com.

WALMER, VIRGINIA RUTH NICHOLS, retired accountant, writer; b. Vinland, Kans., Oct. 26, 1926; d. Clyde Eugene Nichols and Minnie Sarah Hoskinson; m. Robert Gene Walmer, April 3, 1949; children: Daphne Rose, Colette Elaine, David Paul. Grad. h.s., Vinland, Kans., 1944. Accountant Evans Auto Supply, Lawrence, Kans., 1944-52, Squire Pubs., Leawood, 1973-83, ret., 1983. Author: For Better, For Worse, 1987, A Grand Old Couple, 1993, From Voss to Vinland, 1997; contbr. articles to profl. jours., chpts. to book. Vol. Johnson County Libr., Overland Park, Kans., 1982-99; campfire girls leader, dist. officer Campfire Girls, Wichita, Kans., 1965-73. Democrat. Methodist. Avocations: genealogy, reading, writing, sewing.

WALMSLEY, JAMES NAYLOR, hydroponic farming executive; b. Rockford, Ill., Sept. 6, 1929; s. James A. and Louella H. (Gage) W.; m. Ann Walmsley (divorced); children: Dana, Lauren, Michael, Daryl Lynn; m. Helga Walmsley (div.); children: Kristen V., Tanya J. Student, George Washington, 1950-52, Loyola U., 1953-55, Northwestern U., 1955. Investment banker Hornblower & Weeks, Chgo., 1955-61; pres. Manin Internat. Inc., 1961-72, Jinga Hydroponic Farms Ltd., Chgo., 1972—, Bahedeshar Ltd., tech. R & D, 1995—; mng. dir. Manin Internat., Inc., Las Vegas, Nev., 2000—. Mem. Points of Light Found., Children Def. Fund; rep. W.Va. Rep. Presdl. Roundtable, 2001. With USN, 1949-53. Recipient Internat. Am. award, 1987. Mem. Royal Horticulture Soc., Am. Horticulture Soc., N.Y. Acad. Scis., The Heritage Found. Republican. Avocations: travel, art, reading. Office: Bahedeshar Ltd 736 Locust Ave Clarksburg WV 26301-3600 Fax: 304-623-4745.

WALNER, ROBERT JOEL, lawyer; b. Chgo., Dec. 22, 1946; s. Wallace and Elsie W.; m. Charlene Walner; children: Marci, Lisa. BA, U. Ill., 1968; JD, De Paul U., 1972; MBA with distinction, Northwestern U., 1991. Bar: Ill. 1972, U.S. Dist. Ct. (no. dist.) Ill. 1972, U.S. Ct. Appeals (7th cir.) 1972, Fla. 1973. Atty. SEC, Chgo., 1972-73; pvt. practice, 1973—; adminstrv. law judge Ill. Commerce Comm., 1973-76; atty. Allied Van Lines, Inc., Broadview, 1976-79; sr. v.p., gen. counsel, corp. sec. The Balcor Co., Skokie, 1979-92; prin. fin. ops. Balcor Securities divsn. The Balcor Co., 1984-92, pres., 1989-92; of counsel Lawrence, Walner & Assocs., Ltd., Chgo., 1992-93; sr. v.p., gen. counsel, corp. sec. Grubb & Ellis Co., Northbrook, 1994—2001, exec. v.p., chief adminstrv. and legal officer, corp. sec., 2001—. Mem. securities adv. com. to Ill. Sec. of State, 1984-94; mem. editl. bd. Real Estate Securities Jour., Real Estate Securities and Capital Markets; program chmn. Regulators and You seminar. Contbr. chpts. to books, articles on real estate and securities law to profl. jours.; assoc. editor De Paul U. Law Rev. Mem. Kellogg Career Devel. Com., 1992-94, Kellogg Bus. Adv. Com., 1992-2001; mem. enterprise forum MIT, 1992—, mem. exec. com., 1993-94. With USAR, 1968-73. Mem. ABA, Ill. Bar Assn., Chgo. Bar Assn., Am. Real Estate Com. (pres. com. 1985-90), Real Estate Syndication Com. (chmn. 1982-85), Ill. Inst. Continuing Legal Edn., N.Am. Securities Adminstrs. Assn. Inc. (industry adv. com. to real estate com., 1987-89), Real Estate Securities and Syndication Inst. of Nat. Assn. Realtors (chmn. regulatory and legis. com., 1984, 87, group v.p. 1987, exec. com. 1987-90, specialist, real estate investment, counselor of real estate), Nat. Real Estate Investment Forum (chmn. 1985, 88), Real Estate Investment Assn. (founder, exec. com. 1990-92), Kellogg Alumni Club (bd. dirs., event chmn. 1996-98, v.p., exec. com. 1998-99), Beta G amma Sigma.

WALPIN, GERALD, lawyer; b. N.Y.C., Sept. 1, 1931; s. Michael and Mary (Gordon) W.; m. Sheila Kainer, Apr. 13, 1957; children: Amanda Eve, Edward Andrew, Jennifer Hope BA, CCNY, 1952; LLB cum laude, Yale Law Sch., 1955. Bar: N.Y. 1955, U.S. Supreme Ct. 1965, U.S. Ct. Appeals (2d cir.) 1960, (6th cir.) 1969, (3d cir.) 1976, (8th cir.) 1982, (9th cir.) 1983, (llth cir.) 1983, (7th cir.) 1984, U.S. Ct. Claims 1984. Law clk. to Hon. E.J. Dimock U.S. Dist. Ct. (so. dist.) N.Y., N.Y.C.; law clk. to Hon. F.P. Bryan U.S. Dist. Judge (so. dist.) N.Y., 1955-57; asst. U.S. atty., chief spl. prosecutions U.S. Atty. Office, 1960-65; sr. ptnr. Rosenman & Colin and predecessor firm, 1965—, chmn. litigation dept., 1985-96. Adv. com. Fed. Ct. So. Dist. N.Y., 1991—; co-chmn. lawyers divsn. Anti-Defamation League, N.Y., 1994-97; bd. dirs. Ctr. for Individual Rights, 1997—. Editor Yale Law Jour., 1953-54, mng. editor, 1954-55; contbr. articles to profl. jours. Pres. Parker Jewish Inst. for Health Care and Rehab., New Hyde Park, N.Y., 1987-90, trustee, 1979—; bd. dirs. Fund for Modern Cts., N.Y.C., 1985-91; mem. law com. Am. Jewish Com., 1980—; mem. Com. for Free World, N.Y.C., 1983-91; trustee, mem. exec. com. United Jewish Appeal-Fedn. Jewish Philanthropies, N.Y.C., 1984-96; mem. Nassau County Crime Commn., 1970; pres. Kensington Civic Orgn., Gt. Neck, N.Y., 1972-73. Recipient Quality of Life award United Jewish Appeal Fedn., 1978, Human Rels. award Am. Jewish Com., 1982, Gift of Life award Jewish Inst. Geriatric Care, 1987, Learned Hand award Am. Jewish Com., 1990, Human Rels. award Anti-Defamation League, 1998. Mem. ABA, Assn. Bar City N.Y., Fed. Bar Coun. (chmn. modern cts. com. 1989, v.p. 1991-95, chmn. bench and bar liaison com. 1994-95, vice chmn. 1995-97, chmn. bd. dirs. 1997-99, pres.-elect 2000—), Federalist Soc. (chmn. litigation sect. 1996-99, mem. bd. visitors 1999—), Univ. Club, Yale Club. Republican. Jewish. Home: 875 Park Ave New York NY 10021-0341 Office: Rosenman & Colin 575 Madison Ave Fl 20 New York NY 10022-2511 E-mail: GWalpin@Rosenman.com. *My life should be an appropriate response to God and this country for providing me with the opportunities I have had: Contribution to our society and strengthening of our country's steadfast opposition to discrimination for or against anyone based on race, religion or sex.*

WALRATH, HARRY RIENZI, retired minister; b. Alameda, Calif., Mar. 7, 1926; s. Frank Rienzi and Cathren (Michlar) W.; m. Dorothy M. Baxter, June 24, 1961; 1 son, Gregory Rienzi. AA, City Coll., San Francisco, 1950; BA, U. Calif., Berkeley, 1952; MDiv, Ch. Div. Sch. of Pacific, 1959. Ordained deacon Epsicopal Ch., 1959, priest, 1960. Dist. exec. San Mateo area Boy Scouts Am., 1952-55; curate All Souls Parish, Berkeley, Calif., 1959-61; vicar St. Luke's, Atascadero, 1961-63, St. Andrew's, Garberville, 1963-64; assoc. rector St. Luke's Ch., Los Gatos, 1964-65, Holy Spirit Parish, Missoula, Mont., 1965-67; vicar St. Peter's Ch., Litchfield Park, Ariz., 1967-69; also headmaster St. Peter's Schs., 1967-69; chaplain U. Mont., 1965-67; asst. rector Trinity Parish, Reno, 1969-72; coord. counciling svcs. Washoe County Coun. Alcholism, 1972-74; adminstr. Cons. Assistance Svcs., Inc., 1974-76; pastoral counselor, contract chaplain Nev. Mental Health Inst., 1976-78; contract mental health chaplain VA Hosp., Reno, 1976-78; mental health chaplain VA Med. Ctr., 1978-83, staff chaplain, 1983-85, chief chaplain svc., 1985-91, triage coord. mental health, ret., 1991. Per diem chaplain Washoe Med. Ctr., Reno, 1993; assoc. priest Trinity Epsicopal Ch., Reno, 1995; assoc. Mountain Ministries, Susanville, Calif., 1995—. Author: God Rides the Rails-Chapel Cars on American Railroads at the Turn of the Century, 1994. Dir. youth Paso Robles Presbytery; chmn. Diocesan Commn. on Alcoholism; cons. teen-age problems Berkeley Presbytery; mem. clergy team Epsicopal Marriage Encounter; chaplain Make A Wish Found., 1998-2000; mem. at-large Washoe dist. Nev. area coun. Boy Scouts Am., scoutmaster troop 73, 1976, troop 585, 1979-82, asst. scoutmaster troop 35, 1982-92, assoc. adviser area 3 Western region, 1987-89, regional com. Western Region, 1989-90; lodge adviser Tannu Lodge 346, Order of Arrow, 1982-87; docent coun. Nev. Hist. Sch., 1992; South Humboldt County chmn. Am. Cancer Soc.; trustee Cmty. Youth Ctr., Reno. With USNR, 1944-46. Decorated Pacific Theatre medal with star, Am. Theatre medal, Victory medal, Fleet Unit Commendation medal; recipient dist. award of merit Boy Scouts Am., St. George award Episc. Ch.-Boy Scouts Am., Silver Beaver award Boy Scouts Am., 1986, Founders' award Order of the Arrow, Boy Scouts Am., 1995; performance awards VA-VA Med. Ctr., 1983, 84; named Arrowman of Yr., Order of Arrow, Boy Scouts Am. Cert. substance abuse counselor, Nev. Mem. Ch. Hist. Soc., U. Calif. Alumni Assn., Nat. Model R.R. Assn. (life), Sierra Club Calif., Missoula Coun. Chs. (pres.), Rotary, Alpha Phi Omega. Democrat. Home: 4822 Ramcreek Trl Reno NV 89509-8029

WALRATH, MICHELLE TAYLOR, accountant; b. Knobnoster, Mo., July 22, 1970; d. John Thomas Taylor and Ellen Louise Hinton; m. Douglas Scott Walrath, Apr. 19, 1997; 1 child, Madison Grae. BS in Acctg., Clemson U., 1991. CPA, S.C. Pub. acct. Deloitte & Touche, Greenville, S.C., 1992-94; fin. analyst AT&T Global Info., Liberty, 1994-96; acctg. supr. HydroChem. Indsl. Svc., Deer Park, Tex., 1996—. Vol. instr. karate Am. Black Belt Acad., Houston, 1996—. Recipient Silver medal Internat. Amateur Sport Karate Assn., World Karate Championships, 1997, Gold medal Vienna Open Karate Tournament, 1998; named Woman Fighter of Yr., Profl. Karate League. Mem. AICPA, S.C. Assn. CPAs. Republican. Lutheran. Avocations: karate, bowling, billiards, softball. Office: HydroChem Indsl Svc 900 Georgia Ave Deer Park TX 77536-2518 E-mail: shellwalrath@pdq.net.

WALRATH, PATRICIA A. state legislator; b. Brainerd, Minn., Aug. 11, 1941; d. Joseph James and Pansy Patricia (Drake) McCarvill; m. Robert Eugene Walrath, Sept. 1, 1961; children: Karen, Susan, David, Julie. BS, Bemidji State U., 1962; MS, SUNY, Oswego, 1975. Cert. secondary math. tchr., N.Y., Mass. Programmer analyst Control Data Corp., Mpls., 1962-65; crewleader dept. commerce U.S. Census, Middlesex County, Mass., 1979-80; selectman Town of Stow, 1980-85; tchr. math. Hale Jr. High Sch., Stow, 1981-82; instr. math. Johnson & Wale Coll. Hanscom AFB, Bedford, Mass., 1983-84, test examiner, 1983-84; state rep. 3d Middlesex dist. State of Mass., Boston, 1985—. Mem. ways and means com. Mass. Ho. of Reps., 1987—92, 1996, mem. joint coms. on local affairs, 1993—95, mem. pub. svc. com., 1993—96, mem. election law com., 1985—86, 1995—96, mem. sci. and tech. com., 1995—96, mem. commerce and labor com., 1996, mem. govt. regulations com., 96, chmn. com. long term debt and capital expenditures, 1997—2001, asst. whip, floor chair, 2001—. Chmn. Mass. Indoor Air Pollution Commn., Boston, 1987-88; mem. Stow Dem. Com., 1988—; merit badge counselor Boy Scouts Am., Stow and Hudson, Mass., 1990—. Recipient Disting. Svc. award Auburn N.Y. Jaycees, 1976. Mem. LWV (pres. 1973-76, dir. fin. 1977-78), Mass. Legislators' Assn., Mass. Dem. Leadership Coun. (v.p. 1991-92, co-chmn. 1993-94, treas. 1995—), Mass. Women's Legis. Caucus (chair 1986). Roman Catholic. Avocations: gardening, stamp collecting, travel. Home: 20 Middlemost Way Stow MA 01775-1363 Office: State Capital RM480 Boston MA 02133 E-mail: Rep.PatriciaWalrath@hou.state.ma.us.

WALROD, PAUL ANTHONY, music educator; b. Fort Scott, Kans., Oct. 20, 1969; s. Dwight (Tony) Anthony and Joyce Elaine Walrod; m. Cherri Ann Cable; children: Loryn, Landon, Loryn, Landon, Jamison. AS in Music, Ft. Scott (Kans.) C.C., 1991; MusB in Edn., Pittsburg State U., 1993, postgrad., 2000—. Cert. music tchr. grades K-12. K-12 music instr. Marmaton Valley Schs., Moran, Kans., 1993—95; dir. bands Ft. Scott Mid. and H.S., 1995—2001; dir. bands grades 9-12 Labette County H.S., Altamont, 2001—; band instr. grades 5-8 Altamont (Kans.) Grade Sch. , 2001—, Edna (Kans.) Grade Sch., 2001—. Mid. sch. and h.s. band co-chair S.E. KMEA Dist., 1999—2001. Dir.: (concert band performance) Nat. Ajudicators Invitational, 1997; singer (Boys of the Fort): (cd) In Search of a Song, 1998. Program chair Lions Club, Fort Scott, 1995—98; bd. mem. Bourbon County Arts Coun., 1995—2001; mem. Praise Band Cmty. Christian Ch., 1990. Named one of, Outstanding Young Men of Am., 1998. Mem.: Am. Educators Assn., Kans. Music Educators Assn., Music Educators Nat. Conf., Kans. Bandmaster's Assn., Ft. Scott Alumni Assn., Pittsburg State U. Alumni Assn., Omicron Delta Kappa, Phi Kappa Phi, Phi Theta Kappa. Republican. Avocation: sports. Home: 901 E 2nd St Altamont KS 67330 Office: Labette County High School PO Box 407 601 S High School St Altamont KS 67330 Office Fax: 620-784-5326. Personal E-mail: pcwalrod@altamontks.com. Business E-Mail: pwalrod@usd506.k12.ks.us.

WALSER, CLARKE L. management consultant; b. Feb. 18, 1937; Student, U. Chgo., 1954-55. Investment analyst, 1955-70; dir. rsch., 1970-72; gen. ptnr. Bacon, Whipple & Co., Chgo., 1972-84; sr. v.p. The Chgo. Corp., 1984-91, Hamilton Investments, Inc., Chgo., 1991-94; prin. Walser & Assocs., Arlington Heights, Ill., 1995—.

WALSER, MACKENZIE, physician, educator; b. N.Y.C., Sept. 19, 1924; s. Kenneth Eastwood and Jean (Mackenzie) W.; m. Elizabeth C. Gearon, Sept. 17, 1988; children from previous marriage: Karen D., Jennifer McK., Cameron M., Eric H. Grad., Phillips Exeter Acad., 1941; AB, Yale, 1944; MD, Columbia, 1948. Diplomate: Am. Bd. Internal Medicine. Intern Mass. Gen. Hosp., Boston, 1948-49, asst. resident in medicine, 1949-50; resident Parkland Hosp., Dallas, 1950-52; staff mem. Johns Hopkins Hosp., Balt., 1957—; instr. U. Tex. at Dallas, 1950-51, asst. prof., 1951-52; investigator Nat. Heart Inst., Bethesda, Md., 1954-57; asst. prof. pharmacology Johns Hopkins Med. Sch., 1957-61, assoc. prof., 1961-70, prof., 1970—, asst. prof. medicine, 1957-64, assoc. prof., 1964-74, prof., 1974—. Med. dir. USPHS, 1970— , pharmacology study sect., 1968-72 Co-author: Mineral Metabolism, 2d edit., 1969, Handbook of Physiology, 1973, The Kidney, 1976, 5th edit., 1996, also articles; co-editor: Branched-Chain Amino and Ketoacids, 1981, Nutritional Management, 1984. Served with USNR, 1942-45; to lt. M.C. USNR, 1952-54. Recipient Research Career Devel. award USPHS, 1959-69, lifetime achievement award Nat. Kidney Found., 2000. Mem. AAAS, AAUP (pres. Johns Hopkins 1970), Am. Soc. Clin. Investigation, Assn. Am. Physicians, Am. Fedn. Clin. Rsch., Am. Physiol. Soc., Biophys. Soc., Am. Soc. Pharmacology and Exptl. Therapeutics (Exptl. Therapeutics award 1975), Am. Soc. Nephrology, Am. Inst. Nutrition, Am. Soc. Clin. Nutrition (Hermann award 1988), Internat. Soc. Nutrition and Metabolism in Renal Disease (Addis award 1994). Century Assn. Club. Home: 7513 Club Rd Baltimore MD 21204-6418 Office: Johns Hopkins U Sch Medicine Baltimore MD 21205

WALSER, SANDRA TERESA JOHNSON, rehabilitation nurse, preceptor; b. Lexington, N.C., Dec. 9, 1951; d. Thomas Victory and Mary Johnson; m. Ellis Kent Walser, Nov. 14, 1970; children: Andrea Elise, Joshua Kent, Jonathan Patrick. ADN, Forsyth Tech. Community Coll., Winston-Salem, N.C., 1989. RN, N.C. Nurse physical neuro brain injury rehab. unit Forsyth Meml. Hosp., Winston-Salem, 1989—. Mem. Assn. Rehab. Nurses (cert. rehab. RN), Christian Nurses Fellowship. Home: 497 Baileys Chapel Rd Advance NC 27006-7141

WALSH, ANNMARIE HAUCK, research firm executive; b. N.Y.C., May 5, 1938; d. James Smith and Ann-Marie (Kennedy) Hauck; m. John F. Walsh, Jr., Aug. 20, 1960; children: Peter Hauck, John David. BA, Barnard Coll., 1961; MA, Columbia U., 1969, PhD, 1971. Sr. staff mem. Inst. Pub. Adminstrn., N.Y.C., 1961-72, pres., 1982-89, trustee, Gulick scholar, 1989—, dir. programs in Ctrl. Europe and NIS, 1991—; dir. Ctr. for Urban and Policy Studies, CUNY Grad. Ctr., 1972-79, Govs.' Task Force on Regional Planning, N.Y., Conn., N.J., 1979-81. Disting. vis. prof. Bklyn. Coll., CUNY, 1991-93; cons. pub. enterprise, civil svc., urban and regional mgmt., tng., pub. fin. adminstrn. reform UN, China, Indonesia, Bangladesh, Czech Republic and Slovakia, Poland, Macedonia, Uzbekistan, Kazakstan, state and local govts., U.S. Postal Svc., U.S. Dept. Transp., Senate com. govt. ops. Author: Urban Government for Zagreb, Yugoslavia, 1968, Urban Government for Lagos, Nigeria, 1968, Urban Government for the Paris Region, 1968, The Urban Challenge to Government: An International Comparisons of Thirteen Cities, 1969, The Public's Business: Politics and Practices of Government Corporations, 1978, 2d edit., 1980, Designing and Managing the Procurement Process, 1989, Privatization-Implications for Public Management, 1996; editor: Agenda for a City, 1970. Project dir. 20th Century Fund, Pub. Enterprise, 1972-76, pub.-pvt. partnerships, 1989-93; bd. dirs. Ralph Bunche Inst., UN, 1978-82, Regional Plan Assn., 1987-91. Herbert Lehmann fellow, 1966-69 Fellow, Nat. Acad. Pub. Adminstrn. (bd. dirs. 1996—); mem. Phi Beta Kappa. Office: Inst Pub Admistrn 411 Lafayette St Ste 303 New York NY 10003-7032

WALSH, ARTHUR CAMPBELL, psychiatrist; b. Vancouver, B.C., Can., Dec. 21, 1919; came to U.S., 1964; s. William Charles and Kathleen (Patterson) W.; m. Bernice Martha Hessom, Dec. 26, 1944; children: Kathleen, David, Thomas. MD, U. Alta., Edmonton, 1943. Intern Vancouver Gen. Hosp., B.C., 1943; pvt. practice Vancouver, 1964-67; resident psychiatry U. Pitts., 1967-99, clin. asst. prof. psychiatry, 1967-99; semi-ret., 1999; pvt. practice Pitts., 1969-2000; pres. Alzheimer Treatment Rsch. Ctr., 1969-98. Psychiat. cons. VA, Pitts., 1969-89, Woodville State Hosp., Pitts., 1969-86. Author: Conquering Senility; co-author: Mental Capacity: Legal and Medical Aspects of Assessment and Treatment, 2nd edit., 1999; contbr. med. articles to profl. jours. With Royal Can. Army Med. Corps, 1943-45. Mem. Am. Psychiat. Assn. Achievements include development of anticoagulant therapy for dementia due to impaired brain circulation with arrest of dementia in 50% diagnosed as Alzheimers Disease and complete reversal in 15% of people tested. Home and Office: 279 Norman Dr Cranberry Township PA 16066-4235

WALSH, CHARLES RICHARD, retired banker; b. Bklyn., Jan. 30, 1939; s. Charles John and Anna Ellen Walsh; m. Marie Anne Goulden, June 24, 1961; children: Kevin C., Brian R., Gregory M. BS, Fordham U., 1960; MBA, St. John's U., 1966, D of Comml. Scis. (hon.), 1985. V.p. Mfrs. Hanover Trust Co., Hicksville, N.Y., 1974-80, sr. v.p., 1980-86, exec. v.p., 1986-90, group exec., mem. mgmt. com., 1990-92; exec. v.p., group exec. Chem. Banking Corp., 1992-95, The Chase Manhattan Corp., 1995-97; ret., 1997. Bd. dirs. Mastercard Internat.; bd. dirs., former chmn. Eastern States Monetary Svcs., Lake Success, N.Y., 1978-88; former pres., CEO, bd. dirs. The Bankcard Assn., Hicksville, 1988-91. Sustaining mem. Rep. Nat. Com., 1978—; vice chmn. adv. bd. St. John's U., 1982—. With USAR, 1960, 61-62. Mem. N.Y. State Bankers Assn. (former bd. dirs., mem. gov. coun., chmn. consumer banking divsn.), Am. Bankers Assn. (mem. govt. rels. coun., chmn. bank card divsn., mem. exec. com., former mem. comms. coun. and chmn. edn. com.), Am. Mgmt. Assn., N.Y. Credit and Fin. Mgmt. Assn., Soc. Cert. Consumer Credit Execs. (cert.), Beta Gamma Sigma, Omicron Delta Epsilon, North Hempstead Country Club, Gov.'s Club Kiawah Island (S.C.), Kiawah Island Club. Republican. Home: 9 Blueberry Ln Oyster Bay NY 11771-3901 also: 107 Goldeneye Dr Kiawah Island SC 29455-5773 E-mail: crwalsh@aol.com.

WALSH, CHRISTINE ANN, pediatric cardiologist; b. Bklyn., Dec. 31, 1947; d. Martin and Loretta (Lesniewski) Kull; m. Sean Michael Walsh, June 10, 1978; children: Kathleen, Sean, Stephen. BS, Fordham U., 1969; MD, Yale U., 1973. Diplomate Am. Bd. Pediat., Am. Bd. Crit. Care Medicine, Am. Bd. Pediatric Cardiology. Intern, then resident Babies Hosp., N.Y., Columbia-Presbyn. Med. Ctr.; fellow in pediatric cardiology Columbia U., asst. prof. Coll. Physicians and Surgeons, 1980-84; asst. prof. Albert Einstein Coll. of Medicine, 1984-91; asst. attending physician N.C. Bronx Hosp., 1984—; asst. attending pediatrician Jacobi Med. Ctr., Bronx, 1984—; dir. Pediat. Dysrhythmia Ctr. Montefiore Med. Ctr., 1984—, from asst. to assoc. attending pediatrician, 1984-98, attending pediatrician, 1998—; assoc. prof. pediat. Albert Einstein Coll. of Medicine, 1991-98, prof., 1998—, co-chairperson admissions com., 1998—. Cons. Adult Arrhythmia Svc., Montefiore Med. Ctr., cons. Pacemaker Ctr., epilepsy unit, also Cranio-facial Ctr.; postdoctorate in cardiac electrophysiology and pharmacology, Columbia U. Coll. Physicians and Surgeons, N.Y., 1978-80. Editor Adolescent Medicine, State of the Art Revs., Adolescent Cardiology; contbr. articles to profl. jours. Bd. dirs. Velo-Cardio-Facial Syndrome Ednl. Found., N.Y.C., 1995—. Grantee Albert Einstein Interdivisional, 1995, 99. Fellow Am. Coll. Cardiology, Am. Acad. Pediatrics; mem. N.Am. Soc. for Pacing and Electrophysiology, Pediatric Cardiology Soc. (pres. 1990-91, v.p. 1989-90, sec. 1988-89, treas. 1987-88), Pediat. Electrophysiology Soc., Am. Heart Assn., N.Y. Soc. of Pediatric Critical Care, Assn. Yale Alumni in Medicine (exec. com.), Phi Beta Kappa. Avocations: gardening, skiing, scuba diving, piano, camping. Home: PO Box 238 Flushing NY 11363-0238 Office: Montefiore Med Ctr 111 E 210th St Bronx NY 10467-2401

WALSH, DANIEL FRANCIS, bishop; b. San Francisco, Oct. 2, 1937; Grad., St. Joseph Sem., St. Patrick Sem., Catholic U. Am. Ordained priest, Roman Catholic Ch., 1963. Ordained titular bishop of Tigia, 1981; aux. bishop of San Francisco, 1981-87; bishop of Reno-Las Vegas, 1987—2002; bishop of Santa Rosa Calif., 2002—. Address: Bishop of Santa Rosa PO Box 1297 Santa Rosa CA 95402

WALSH, DAVID GRAVES, lawyer; b. Madison, Wis., Jan. 7, 1943; s. John J. and Audrey B. Walsh; married; children: Michael, Katherine, Molly, John. BBA, U. Wis., 1965; JD, Harvard U., 1970. Bar: Wis. Law clk. Wis. Supreme Ct., Madison, 1970-71; ptnr. Walsh, Walsh, Sweeney & Whitney, 1971-86; ptnr.-in-charge Foley & Lardner, 1986—. Bd. dirs. Nat. Guardian Life, Madison, 1981—; lectr. U. Wis., Madison, 1974-75, 77-78. Chmn. State of Wis. Elections Bd., Madison, 1978. Lt. USN, 1965-67, Vietnam. Recipient Disting. Bus. Alumnus award U. Wis. Sch. Bus., 1997. Maple Bluff Country Club (Madison) (pres. 1987). Roman Catholic. Avocations: tennis, golf, fishing. Home: 41 Fuller Dr Madison WI 53704-5962 Office: Foley & Lardner PO Box 1497 Madison WI 53701-1497

WALSH, DENNY JAY, reporter; b. Omaha, Nov. 23, 1935; s. Gerald Jerome and Muriel (Morton) W.; m. Peggy Marie Moore, Feb. 12, 1966; children by previous marriage— Catherine Camille, Colleen Cecile; 1 son, Sean Joseph. B.J., U. Mo., 1962. Staff writer St. Louis Globe-Democrat, 1961-68; asst. editor Life mag., N.Y.C., 1968-70, assoc. editor, 1970-73; reporter N.Y. Times, 1973-74, Sacramento Bee, 1974—. Served with USMC, 1954-58. Recipient Con Lee Kelliher award St. Louis chpt. Sigma Delta Chi, 1962; award Am. Polit. Sci. Assn., 1963; award Sigma Delta Chi, 1968; Pulitzer prize spl. local reporting, 1969; 1st prize San Francisco Press Club, 1977 Office: Sacramento Bee 21st & Q Sts Sacramento CA 95816 E-mail: dwalsh@sacbee.com.

WALSH, DIANA CHAPMAN, academic administrator, social and behavioral sciences educator; b. Phila., July 30, 1944; d. Robert Francis and Gwen (Jenkins) Chapman; m. Christopher Thomas Walsh, June 18, 1966; 1 child, Allison Chapman Walsh. BA, Wellesley Coll., 1966; MS, Boston U. Sch. of Pub. Comm., 1971; PhD, Boston U., 1983; LHD (hon.), Boston U, 1994, Amer. Coll. of Greece, Athens, 1995; LHD (hon.) , U. Mass., Amherst, 1999. Dir. info., edn. Planned Parenthood League, Newton, Mass., 1971-74; sr. program assoc. Dept Pub. Health, Boston, 1974-76; assoc. dir. Boston U. Health Policy Inst., 1985-90; prof. Sch. Pub. Health, Sch. Medicine, Boston

U., 1987-90, adj. prof. pub. health, 1990—; chair Harvard Sch. Pub. Health, 1990—93, adj. prof., 1993—; pres. Wellesley Coll., 1993—. Author: (book) Corporate Physicians, 1987; editor: Women, Work and Health: Challenges to Corporate Policy, 1980, (book series) Industry and Health Care, 1977—80; co-author: Payer, Provider, Consumer, 1977; contbr. Bd. dirs. Planned Parenthood League of Mass., 1974—79, 1981—85, bd. overseers, 1993—94; trustee Occupl. Physicians Scholarship Fund, 1987—94, WGBH Ednl. Found., 1993—2000. Recipient Book of the Yr. award, Am. Jour. Nursing, 1980; fellow, Kellogg Nat. fellow, 1987—90. Mem.: AHA, AAAS, Asian Univ. for Women, Consortium on Financiang Higher Edn., Mass. Pub. Health Assn., Soc. for the Study of Social Problems, Am. Sociol. Assn. Avocations: gender and health, leadership studies, social policy, the craft of writing, skiing. Office: Wellesley Coll Office of the Pres 106 Central St Wellesley MA 02481-8268

WALSH, DIANE, pianist; b. Washington, Aug. 16, 1950; d. William Donald and Estelle Louise (Stokes) W.; m. Henry Forbes, 1969 (div. 1979); m. Richard Pollak, 1982. MusB, Juilliard Sch. Music, 1971; MusM, Mannes Coll., 1982. N.Y.C. debut Young Concert Artists Series, 1974; founding mem. Mannes Trio, 1983-94; solo appearances include: Kennedy Ctr. for Performing Arts, Washington, 1976, Met. Mus., N.Y.C., 1976, Wigmore Hall, London, 1980, Merkin Concert Hall, 1989, Miller Theatre, 1994, 96; with Mannes Trio: Lincoln Ctr.'s Alice Tully Hall, Libr. of Congress, 1987; appeared with maj. orchs. worldwide, including St. Louis Symphony, Indpls. Symphony, San Francisco Symphony, Am. Symphony, Bavarian Radio Symphony of Munich, Berlin Radio Symphony, Radio Symphony Frankfurt, Radio Symphony Stuttgart; has toured Europe, N.Am., S.Am., C.Am., former Soviet Union, Marlboro Festival, 1982, Bard Festival, 1990-99, Chopin Festival, Marianske Lazne, Czech Republic; recs. for Nonesuch Records, 1980, 82, Book-of-Month Records, 1985, Music and Arts, 1990, CRI, 1991, Koch, 1995, Biddulph Records, 1998, Stereophile, 1998, Newport Classic, 1998, Sony, 2000, Arabesque, 2003; artistic dir. Skaneateles Festival, 1999—; mem. piano and chamber music faculty Mannes Coll. Music, 1982—. Recipient 3d prize Busoni Internat. Piano Competition, Italy, 1974, 2nd prize Mozart Internat. Piano Competition, Salzburg, Austria, 1975, 1st prize Munich Internat. Piano Competition, 1975, Naumburg Chamber Music award, 1986; NEA grantee, 1981.

WALSH, DOLORES ANN GONCZO (LORRY WALSH), special education educator; b. Detroit, Sept. 3, 1933; d. Joseph John and Dolores (Carey) Gonczo; m. Bernard Waldrup, Aug. 23, 1958 (div. 1980, dec. 2000); children: Elizabeth, Carey, Leslie, Bernard III; m. Deleon Walsh, Sept. 3, 1982 (dec. 1990). Student, Barat Coll., 1951-52; PhB, U. Detroit, 1955; MPS, Manhattanville Coll., 1978. Tchr. 2d grade East Detroit (Mich.) Pub. Schs., 1955-58; tchr. 4th grade Birmingham (Ala.) Schs., 1958-59, St. Franics Xavier Sch., Birmingham, 1959-62; homebound tchr. Greenburg Ctrl. 7, Hartsdale, NY, 1969-73, tchr. spl. edn., 1973-91; ret., 1998. Tchr. English, China, summer 1998; mem. team of evaluators, mid. state schs., 1988-91. Dist. leader Dem. Party Greenburgh, 1981-91; sec. Greenburgh Health Cen. Bd., Greenburgh, N.Y., 1986-91; leader Girl Scouts U.S., 1968-69; CCD tchr. Convent of Sacred Heart, Greenwich, Conn.; vol. West Valley Art Mus., 1992-2001. Mem. Ariz. Alumnae of Sacred Heart, Delta Zeta. E-mail: lorry2@quik.com.

WALSH, DON, marine consultant, executive; b. Berkeley, Calif., Nov. 2, 1931; s. J. Don and Marguerite Grace (Van Auker) W.; m. Joan A. Betzmer, Aug. 18, 1962; children— Kelly Drennan, Elizabeth McDonough BS, U.S. Naval Acad., 1954; MS, Tex. A&M U., 1967, PhD, 1968; MA, San Diego State U., 1968. Commd. ensign USN, 1954, advanced through grades to capt., 1974, officer-in-charge Bathyscaph Trieste, 1959-62, comdr. in USS Bashaw, 1968-69; dir. Inst. Marine and Coastal Studies, prof. ocean engring. U. So. Calif., L.A., 1975-83; pres., CEO Internat. Maritime, Inc., 1976—; mng. dir. Deep Ocean Engring., Inc., 1990—2000, also bd. dirs. Dir. Ctr. for Marine Transp. Studies, U. So. Calif., 1980-83, Coastal Resources Ctr., 1990-94; trustee USN Mus. Found., 1989—; mem. Nat. Adv. Com. on Oceans and Atmosphere, 1979-85; bd. govs. Calif. Maritime Acad., 1985-95; pres. Parker Diving, 1989-94. Editor, contbr.: Law of the Sea: Issues in Ocean Resource Management, 1977, Energy and Resources Development of Continental Margins, 1980, Energy and Sea Power: Challenge for the Decade, 1981, Waste Disposal in the Oceans: Minimizing Impact, Maximizing Benefits, 1983; editor Jour. Marine Tech. Soc., 1975-80; mem. editorial bd. U.S. Naval Inst., 1974-75. Bd. dirs. Charles and Anne Lindbergh Found., 1996—. Decorated Legion of Merit (2); Woodrow Wilson Internat. Ctr. for Scholars fellow, 1973-74. Fellow Marine Tech. Soc., Acad. Underwater Arts and Scis., Explorers Club (hon. life, bd. dirs. 1994-2000, Explorers Medal, 2001), Royal Geog. Soc. (Eng.); mem. AAAS, Soc. Naval Archs. and Marine Engrs., Am. Soc. Naval Engrs., Navy League, Navy Inst., Adventurers Club (hon. life), Am. Geog. Soc. (hon. life), Nat. Acad. Engring. Home and Office: Internat Maritime Inc 14758 Sitkum Ln Myrtle Point OR 97458-9726 E-mail: imiwalsh@worldnet.att.net.

WALSH, EDWARD JOSEPH, toiletries and food company executive; b. Mt. Vernon, N.Y., Mar. 18, 1932; s. Edward Aloysius and Charlotte Cecilia (Borup) W.; m. Patricia Ann Farrell, Sept. 16, 1961; children: Edward Joseph, Megan Simpson, John, Robert. BBA, Iona Coll., 1953; MBA, NYU, 1958. Sales rep. M & R Dietetic Labs., Columbus, Ohio, 1955-60; with Armour & Co., 1961-71, Greyhound Corp., 1971-87; v.p. toiletries div. Armour Dial Co., Phoenix, 1973-74, exec. v.p., 1975-77; pres. Armour Internat. Co., Phoenix, 1978-84, The Dial Corp. (formerly Armour-Dial Co.), Phoenix, 1984-87, chief exec. officer, 1984-87; pres., chief exec. officer Purex Corp., 1985; chmn., chief exec. officer The Sparta Group Ltd., Scottsdale, Ariz., 1988—. Bd. dirs. Guest Supply Inc., New Brunswick, NJ, 1988—2001, WD-40 Co., San Diego, Nortrust Holding Corp., Phoenix, No. Trust Bank of Ariz., N.A., Inc., Matrixx Initiatives, Inc., Phoenix; mem. bd. advisors Universal Tech. Inst., Phoenix. Trustee Scottsdale Meml. Health Found., 1995-98; pres. Mt. Vernon Fire Dept. Mems. Assn., 1960-61. Served with U.S. Army, 1953-55, Germany. Mem. Am. Mgmt. Assn., Nat. Meat Canner Assn. (pres. 1971-72), Cosmetic, Toiletries and Fragrance Assn. (bd. dirs. 1985—87), Nat. Food Processors Assn. (bd. dirs.). Republican. Roman Catholic. Office: The Sparta Group Ltd 6623 N Scottsdale Rd Scottsdale AZ 85250-4421

WALSH, ELIZABETH JAMESON, musician; b. Panhandle, Tex., Oct. 23, 1913; d. Edwin Reece and Lela (Blackshear) Jameson; m. Thomas Norris Walsh, Nov. 1, 1951 (dec. May 5, 1990); children: Thomas Edwin, Richard Malcolm, Lela Elizabeth. MusB, U. North Tex., 1941, MusM, 1942. Cert. tchr. music. Piano tchr. U. North Tex., Denton, 1940-42; music tchr. Perryton (Tex.) H.S., 1942-43, Plainview (Tex.) H.S., 1943-45; choir dir. Presbyn. and Disciples Ch., Plainview, 1943-45; music tchr. Dallas Pub. Schs., 1945-53; organist, choir dir. Midway Hills Ch., Dallas, 1954-60; piano tchr. Hockaday Pvt. Sch., 1960-70; music tchr. Dallas Pub. Schs., 1970-82; organist, choir dir. Greenville Ave. Christian Ch., Dallas, 1975-82, Grace Meth. Ch., Dallas, 1982-91, St. Andrews Episcopal Ch., Farmers Branch, Tex., 1991—, Christ United Meth. Ch., 2001—. Composer (operetta) Day in Mexico, 1971, various titles for choir, 1996—; author: The Echo Tower, 1987, The House on the Hill, 1989; appeared as Cleopatra as Caesar and Cleopatra, Dallas Little Theatre, 1933, Jane in Jane Eyre, Amarillo Little Theatre, 1935, Anna in Anna and the King of Siam, Northway Ch. Players, 1971. Mem. Dallas Civic Chorus, 1960-65, Dallas Symphony Chorus, 1970-75, Farmer's Br. Women's Club, 1995—. Recipient 2nd prize in Nat. Recording Contest, Nat. Piano Guild, 1973. Mem. Dallas Music Tchrs. Assn., Dallas chpt. Am. Guild Organists, Musical Arts Club (sec. 2001—), Daus. of Republic of Tex. (chaplain 1993-95, pres. James Butler Bonham chpt. 1997—, Mamie Wynne Cox award 1995, sec. 1995-97, chmn. yearbook), Pro Musica (pres. 1976-77, 85-86, 2001—, treas. 1980-81, 96-97), Pi Beta Phi, Mu Phi Epsilon. Avocations: reading, travel. Home: 14339 Tanglewood Dr Farmers Branch TX 75234-3855

WALSH, FRANCIS RICHARD, law educator, lawyer, arbitrator; b. Newark, Jan. 1, 1924; s. Francis R. Sr. and Loretta Anne (Norton) W.; m. Ethel Anne Walsh, Mar. 12, 1944; 1 child, Jeffrey R. BSBA, Seton Hall U., 1943; JD, Georgetown U., 1948. Prof. Law Sch. Georgetown U., Washington, 1949-51; law clk. to presiding justice U.S. Ct. Appeals (9th cir.), San Francisco, 1948-49; chief broadcast bur. FCC, Washington, 1970-71; pvt. practice San Francisco, 1954-70; prof. law U. San Francisco, 1951-54, 71-74, dean, prof. law, 1957-70; prof. law Hastings Coll. of Law, U. Calif., San Francisco, 1974—. Lt. USNR, 1943-46, PTO. Avocations: golf, travel. Home: 28 Spring Rd Kentfield CA 94904 Office: Hastings Coll Law 200 Mcallister St San Francisco CA 94102

WALSH, FRANCIS R. law educator; b. Newark; s. Francis Richard and Loretta Marie Walsh; m. Ethel A Nerney, Mar. 12, 1944; 1 child, Jeffrey R. BSBA, Seton Hall U., 1944; JD, Georgetown U., 1948. Bar: Calif. 1949, U.S. Supreme Ct. 1957. Law clk. to Judge Healy U.S. Ct. Appeals (9th cir.), 1948-49; prof. law Georgetown U., 1949-51, U. San Francisco, 1951-54; pvt. practice, San Francisco, 1954-57; prof. law U. San Francisco, 1957-74, dean, 1957-70; chief Broadcast Bur., FCC, Washington, 1970-71; prof. law U. Calif. Hastings Coll. Law, San Francisco, 1974—. Lt. USNR, 1943-46, PTO. Mem. Meadow Club. Roman Catholic. Avocations: golf, travel. Home: 28 Spring Rd Kentfield CA 94904-2625 Office: U Calif Hastings Coll Law 200 Mcallister St San Francisco CA 94102-4707

WALSH, GEORGE WILLIAM, publishing company executive, editor, author; b. N.Y.C., Jan. 16, 1931; s. William Francis and Madeline (Maass) W.; m. Joan Mary Dunn, May 20, 1961; children— Grail, Simon. BS, Fordham U., 1952; MS, Columbia U. Sch. Journalism, 1953. Copy editor, reporter Cape Cod Standard-Times, Hyannis, Mass., 1955; communications specialist IBM, N.Y.C., 1955-58; editorial trainee Time, Inc., 1958-59; writer-reporter Sports Illus., N.Y.C., 1959-62; book editor Cosmopolitan, 1962-65, mng. editor, 1965-74; editor-in-chief, v.p. Ballantine Books div. Random House, N.Y.C., 1974-79, Macmillan Pub. Co., N.Y.C., 1979-85; pub. cons., 1985—. Author: Gentleman Jimmy Walker, 1974, Public Enemies, 1980, Damage Them All You Can--Robert E. Lee's Army of Northern Virginia, 2002. Served with AUS, 1953-55. Mem. Assn. Am. Pubs. Clubs: Univ. (N.Y.C.); Pamet Harbor Yacht and Tennis (Truro, Mass.). Roman Catholic. Home: 35 Prospect Park W Brooklyn NY 11215-2370 E-mail: edchief@aol.com.

WALSH, GEORGE WILLIAM, engineering executive; b. Teton County, Idaho, Mar. 22, 1923; s. Raymond Eugene and Maude Ethel (Brack) W.; m. Catherine Mary Yunker, July 1, 1950; children: Dwight, Maureen, John. BSEE, U. Idaho, 1947; MEE, Rensselaer Poly. Inst., 1960. Registered profl. engr., N.Y. With GE, 1947-94, test engr., 1947-49, design engr. Pittsfield, Mass., 1949-50, power system engr. Schenectady, 1950-66, mgr. power system engring., 1966-85, mgr. power system cons. engring., 1985-93, cons., 1993-94; profl. cons. engr., 1994—. Contbr. numerous papers and articles relating to electric power system engring. to profl. publs. Recipient GE Power Systems Engring. awards for Outstanding Tech. Contbn., 1986, and Outstanding Profl. and Social Svcs., 1991. Fellow IEEE (life, Centennial medal 1984, Richard Harold Kaufmann field award for outstanding contbn. to indsl. engring. 1993); mem. IEEE Industry Applications Soc. (pres., mem. exec. bd., adminstrv. and tech. coms., Power Systems Achievement award 1980, Outstanding Achievement award 1990), IEEE Power Engring. Soc., Sigma Xi, Sigma Tau. Home and Office: 26 St Stephens Ln E Schenectady NY 12302-4221

WALSH, GERALDINE FRANCES, nursing administrator; b. Phila., July 3, 1946; d. Raymond S. and Marie Ruth (Lipsett) Lore; m. Harry G. Walsh, Jan. 29, 1966; children: Michael, Gregory. AA, No. Va. Community Coll., 1979; BS, St. Joseph's Coll., Windham, Maine, 1987, postgrad. Cert. in nursing adminstrn.; cert. dir. nursing adminstrn. long term care; lic. nursing home adminstr. Charge nurse, asst. head nurse Parkview Hosp., Phila., 1968-73; staff nurse JFK Med. Ctr., Edison, 1973-76; clin. nursing supr., charge nurse med.-surg. Loudoun Hosp. Ctr., Leesburg, Va., 1976-88; asst. dir. nursing Loudoun Long Term Care Ctr., 1988-95; dir. nursing Inova Cameron Glen Care Ctr., Reston, Va., 1995-99, Integrated Health Svcs. No. Va., 1999—. Recipient Nursing Achievement award. Fellow Nat. Assn. Dirs. Nursing; mem. ANA, NAFE, Nat. League Nursing, Va. League Nursing, Va. Nurses Assn., Am. Coll. Healthcare Execs. (student assoc. mem.), Assn. Healthcare Adminstrs. of Nat. Capitol Area, Va. Orgn. Nurse Execs. Address: 20380 Harmony Ct Ashburn VA 20147-3300 E-mail: walshge@attglobal.net.

WALSH, GREGORY SHEEHAN, optical systems professional; b. Buffalo, Dec. 24, 1955; s. John Kevin and Ruth (Murphy) W.; m. Patricia DelGiudice, Apr. 8, 1976; children: James, Kevin, Patrick. BBA, U. North Fla., 1989; cert. in submarine periscope design, Dept. of Navy, 1992. Optical systems specialist Naval Aviation Depot, Jacksonville, Fla., 1984-91, Trident Refit Facility, Kings Bay, Ga., 1991—. Tech. adv. Naval Tech. Tng., Pensacola, Fla., 1992; bd. dirs. Strategic Bus. Plan Naval Aviation Depot, Jacksonville, 1989; cons. Small Bus. Adminstrn., Jacksonville, 1989. Coach Orange Park (Fla.) Soccer Assn., 1989—; com. mem. Olympic devel. Fla. Youth Soccer Assn. With USN, 1974-78. Achievements include performed the first retrofit to the trident submarine periscope system at an IMA; design of submarine periscope stadimeter sling, submarine optical periscope bushing, submarine optical periscope torque sleeve, submarine optical quick evacuation plug puller, aircraft optical hot mock-up; performed the first article acceptance test on the FA-18 aircraft optical systems. Home: 450 Sigsbee Ct Orange Park FL 32073-3409 Address: PO Box 1017 Orange Park FL 32067-1017

WALSH, JAMES ANTHONY (TONY WALSH), theater and film educator; b. Bklyn., Aug. 21, 1947; s. Henry Michael and Clara (Nappi) W. BA in Theater, Hofstra U., 1968; MA in Theater, Adelphi U., 1976. Tchr., dir. theater N.C. Sch. of Arts, Winston-Salem, 1976-81; artistic dir. Cross and Sword/State Play of Fla., St. Augustine, 1982-91; dean Fla. Sch. of Arts, Palatka, 1982-91; dir. Inst. of Entertainment Technologies Valencia C.C., Orlando, Fla., 1992-93, dir. Ctr. Profl. Devel., 1993-96; producing dir. TV and video prodn. Valencia Coll., 1996-2001; mng. dir. The Thrasher-Horn Ctr. for Arts St. Johns River C.C., Orange Park, Fla., 2000—, mng. dir. The Performing and Visual Arts Ctr., 01—. Freelance theater dir., acting coach, N.Y.C., 1973-76; cons. Network of Performing and Visual Arts Schs., Washington, 1980—, Inst. Outdoor Drama, Chapel Hill, N.C., 1989—, Univ. Film and Video Assn., Sarasota, Fla., 1992, Internat. Film Workshops, Rockport, Maine, 1992, Dir. Guild Am. Educators Workshop, L.A., 1993, Dir.'s Workshop, 1996, Acad. TV Arts and Scis. Educators Seminar, L.A., 1995; writer, dir. LifeMap, PBS Teleconf., 2000. Writer PBS documentary World of Family, NCCJ, 1995; exptl. theater playwright; lyricist (off-Broadway mus.) Sugar Hill, 1990. Bd. dirs. Enzian Film Theatre, Concert on the Green, Maitland Art Ctr.; mem. adv. coun. Fla. Film Festival. NEH grantee, 1978; recipient playwriting fellowships Atlantic Ctr. for Arts, 1983, Fla. Divsn. Cultural Affairs, 1983; named Winner Fla. Playwrite Competition, 1994, Winner Best Video, Fla. Assn. C.C., 1996. Mem. Assn. Theater in Higher Edn., Fla. Motion Picture and TV Assn. (bd. dirs., v.p.), Ctrl. Fla. Film Commn. (bd. dirs.), Fla. Inst. for Film Edn. (bd. dirs.) Actors Equity Assn., Dramatists Guild N.Y.C., Players Club (N.Y.C.). Home: 2375 Coleen Lane Green Cove Springs FL 32043 Office: St Johns River CC 283 College Dr Orange Park FL 32065 E-mail: TWalshWPK@aol.com.

WALSH, JAMES FRANCIS, JR. financial services executive; b. Easton, Pa., Aug. 28, 1949; s. James F. Sr. and Jean N. W.; m. Teresa Di Giorgio, Mar. 20, 1971; children: Russell, Ryan, Jamie. BA in Econs., Rutgers Coll., 1971; MBA, U. Bridgeport, 1978. With GE Capital/GE, 1971-93; sr. v.p., CFO GE Capital Aviation Svcs., Stamford, Conn., 1993-96; v.p., CFO Global Ptnr. Ventures, Richmond, Va., 1997-98; sr. v.p., CFO C-S Aviation Svcs., Inc., N.Y.C., 1998-2000, pres., 2000—. Mem. Fin. Exec. Inst. Avocations: golf, running, music, reading, home repair. Home: 208 Brookschase Ln Richmond VA 23229-8432 Office: C-S Aviation Svcs Inc 900 3rd Ave Ste 401 New York NY 10022 E-mail: j.walsh@csaviation.com.

WALSH, JAMES HAMILTON, lawyer; b. N.Y.C., N.Y., May 20, 1947; s. Edward James and Helen Smith (Hamilton) W.; m. Janice Ausherman, Aug. 3, 1967; children: Tracy, Courtney, Eric. BA in Psychology, Bridgewater Coll., 1968; JD, U. Va., 1975. Bar: Va. 1975, U.S. Dist. Ct. (ea. and we. dists.) Va. 1975, U.S. Ct. Appeals (4thc ir.) 1976, U.S. Supreme Ct. 1982. Assoc. McGuire, Woods LLPms), Richmond, Va., 1975-82; ptnr. McGuire, Woods, Battle & Boothe (and predecessor firms), 1982—. Instr. Nat. Inst. Trial Adv.; adj. prof. U. Richmond, 1992, 93; spl. prosecutor U.S. Dist. Ct. (ea. dist.) Va., 1979, 84. Contbr. articles to profl. jours. Mem. bd. trustees Bridgewater (Va.) Coll., mem. exec. com.; mem. staff Va. Law Rev. With U.S. Army, 1969-72. Mem. ABA (mem. antitrust sect. health care com., litigation sect.), Va. State Bar (bd. govs. antitrust sect. 1984-90, chmn. 1986), Va. Bar Assn. (chmn. criminal law sect. 1997, 98), Richmond Bar Assn., Willow Oaks, Order Coif, Phi Delta Phi. Episcopalian. Home: 113 Adingham Ct Richmond VA 23229-7761 Office: McGuire Woods LLP 1 James Ctr 910 E Cary St Richmond VA 23219-4004 E-mail: jwalsh@mcguirewoods.com.

WALSH, JAMES J. priest; b. Cin., Dec. 11, 1941; s. Joseph George Walsh and Frances Gies. BA in Philosophy, Athenaeum of Ohio, 1963, MA in Philosophy, 1964; licentiate in sacred theology, Gregorian U., Rome, 1969; M in Religious Edn., Loyola U., Chgo., 1976. Religion tchr., guidance counselor Fenwick HS, Middletown, Ohio, 1969—72, McNicholas HS, Cin., 1972—74; cons. adult edn. Office Religious Edn. Archdiocese of Cin., 0174—1980, dir. dept. pastoral svcs., 1980—84, pastor St. Dominic Ch., 2000—; pres., rector Athenaeum of Ohio Mt. St. Mary's Sem. of West, 1984—90; cons. Internat. Office of Renew, Plainfield, NJ, 1990—93; exec. dir. sem. dept. Nat. Cath. Edn. Assn., Washington, 1993—2000. Cons. on priestly formation U.S. Bishop's Com., Washington, 1993—2000; evaluator Lilly Endowment Religion Divsn., Indpls., 1995—2000; mem. priest's coun. Archdiocese of Cin., 2000—. Author: Grace Under Pressure: What Gives Life to American Priests, 1995; editor (exec.): Sem. Jour., 1995—. Avocations: skiing, travel. Office: St Dominic Parish 4551 Delhi Rd Cincinnati OH 45238

WALSH, JAMES JEROME, philosophy educator; b. Seattle, May 23, 1924; s. John Jerome and Agnes (Counihan) W.; m. Carol Jean Paton, Sept. 16, 1946; children— John Jerome II, James Paton. BA, Reed Coll., 1949, Oxford (Eng.) U., 1951, MA, 1956; PhD, Columbia U., 1960. Mem. faculty Columbia U., 1954-90, prof. philosophy, 1966-90, prof. emeritus, 1990—, dir. grad. studies philosophy dept., 1963-66, 73-88, chmn. dept., 1967-73, acting chmn. dept., 1982-83. Vis. instr. U. Calif.-Berkeley, 1958; cons. TV series G.E. Coll. Bowl, 1965-70 Author: Aristotle's Conception of Moral Weakness, 1963, Philosophy in the Middle Ages, 1967, 2d edit., 1983; Editor Jour. Philosophy, 1965-90. Mem. Rockland County Democratic Com., 1960-63. Served with AUS, 1943-45. Decorated Purple Heart.; Rhodes scholar, 1949; Ford Found. fellow, 1958; Am. Coun. Learned Socs. fellow, 1962; Guggenheim fellow, 1966 Mem. Soc. Medieval and Renaissance Philosophy. Home: 300 Haverstraw Rd Suffern NY 10901-3137

WALSH, JAMES JOSEPH, lawyer; b. New Orleans, June 21, 1948; s. Francis Michael and Violet (Young) W.; m. Priscilla Robson Ferris, Oct. 12, 1972; children: Caitlin Marian, Alison Robson. BA, La. State U., 1970, JD, 1975. Bar: La. 1975, Mich. 1977, U.S. Ct. Appeals (6th cir.) 1981, U.S. Supreme Ct. 1991. Law clk. Mich. Ct. Appeals, Detroit, 1975-77; assoc. Bodman, Longley & Dahling, 1977-84, ptnr., 1984—. Counsel Outdoor Advt. Assn. Mich. Editor: La. Law Rev., 1975. Named to Hall of Fame, La. State U. Law Sch., 1988. Mem. ABA, State Bar Mich., Washtenaw County Bar Assn., Ann Arbor Club, Detroit Athletic Club, Mich. C. of C., Jefferson City Buzzards. Avocations: fishing, gardening, carpentry. Home: 8025 Mast Rd Dexter MI 48130-9301 Office: Bodman Longley & Dahling 110 Miller Ave Ste 300 Ann Arbor MI 48104-1339 E-mail: jwalsh@bodmanlongley.com.

WALSH, JAMES THOMAS, congressman; b. Syracuse, N.Y., June 19, 1947; BA, St. Bonaventure U., 1970. Agrl. extension agt. Peace Corps, 1970-72; mktg. exec. telecommunications co., 1974-88; exec.-in-residence telecommunications inst. Coll. Tech. SUNY, Utica, Rome, N.Y., 1986-87; common councilor City of Syracuse, 1977-85, pres. common coun., 1986-88; mem. U.S. Congress from 25th N.Y. dist., Washington, 1989—; mem. appropriations com., military constrn. subcom., chmn. VA, HUD and Ind. Agys. subcom. Republican. Office: US House of Reps 2351 Rayburn Hob Washington DC 20515-0001 also: PO Box 7306 Syracuse NY 13261-7306 also: 21 Lincoln St Auburn NY 13021-3831*

WALSH, JANICE MAUREEN, counselor, educator; b. Monroe, Ga., June 17, 1948; d. Herschel Thomas and Joan (Williford) Scott; m. Dennis Warner Anderson, June 24, 1967 (div. Sept. 1988); children: Jeffrey, Timothy; m. Francis Raymond Walsh, July 6, 1993 (dec. Sept. 1998). AA, Windward C.C., 1988; BA, U. Hawaii, 1990; MBA, Chaminade U., Honolulu, 1991, advanced profl. cert., 1992. Cert. clin. hypnotherapist Hawaii. Instr. Windward C.C., Kaneohe, Hawaii, 1991-92; prof. Chaminade U., Honolulu, 1993; instr., counselor Kapiolani C.C., 1993-99, asst. prof., 1999—. Cons. Changing Me, Kailua, Hawaii, 1993-99. Mem. disaster action team Hawaii Red Cross. Mem. ACA, Hawaii Counseling Assn. (treas., pres., past pres. 1990-97), Nat. Career Devel. Assn., Guild of Hypnotists, Hawaii Career Devel. Assn. (treas. 1995-97), Soroptimist Internat. of Windward Oahu. Avocations: bridge, movies, crossword puzzles. Office: Kapiolani C C 4303 Diamond Head Rd Honolulu HI 96816-4421

WALSH, JOANNE ELIZABETH, retired educator, librarian; b. Chgo., Nov. 25, 1942; d. Joseph Frank and Elizabeth Margaret (Gretz) Fiali; m. John Kerwin Walsh, July 17, 1976; 1 child, Kevin Joseph. BA in English, Mundelein Coll., Chgo., 1965; MEd Ednl. Adminstrn. and Supervision, Loyola U., Chgo., 1969. Tchr. Chgo. Pub. Schs., 1965-83, prin., 1983-89; tchr. libr. Burbank (Ill.) Dist III, 1990-93; tchr. art Tate Sch. of Discovery, Knoxville, Tenn., 1994-95. Vol. Palos Cmty. Hosp., Palos Park, Ill., 1990, Palos Heights Libr., 1993; Rainbow facilitator, 1992, 93; mem. St. John Neumann Cath. Ch.; mem. Knoxville Symphony League; mem. decorating com. City of Farragut. Recipient Tchr. of Yr. award McCord Sch., 1992-93. Mem.: Fox Den Woman's Club, Knoxville Newcomers Club (pres. 2002—), Knoxville Welcome Wagon Club (pres. 1999—2000). Avocations: reading, gardening, crafts, painting, golf. Home: 609 Augusta National Way Knoxville TN 37922-2536 E-mail: NDISGR8@aol.com.

WALSH, JOHN, museum director; b. Mason City, Wash., Dec. 9, 1937; s. John J. and Eleanor (Wilson) W.; m. Virginia Alys Galston, Feb. 17, 1962; children: Peter Wilson, Anne Galston, Frederick Matthiessen. BA, Yale U., 1961; postgrad., U. Leyden, Netherlands, 1965-66; MA, Columbia U., 1965, PhD, 1971; LHD (hon.), Wheaton Coll., 2000. Lectr., rsch. asst. Frick Collection, N.Y.C., 1966-68; assoc. higher edn. Met. Mus. Art, 1968-71, assoc. curator European paintings, 1970-72, curator dept. European paintings, 1972-74, vice-chmn., 1974-75; adj. asso. prof. art history Columbia U., N.Y.C., 1969-72, adj. prof., 1972-75; prof. art history Barnard Coll., Columbia U., N.Y.C., 1975-77; Mrs. Russell W. Baker curator paintings Mus. Fine Arts, Boston, 1977-83; dir. J. Paul Getty Mus., Malibu, Calif., 1983-2000, dir. emeritus, 2000—. Vis. prof. fine arts Harvard U., 1979; mem. governing bd. Yale U. Art Gallery, 1975—, Smithsonian Coun., 1990—; mem. Inst. for Advanced Study, Princeton, 2000; trustee Burlington Mag. Found., 1999-. Contbr. articles to profl. jours. Mem. Dem. County Com., N.Y.C., 1968-71; mem. vis. com. Fogg Mus., Harvard U., 1982-87; bd. fellows Claremont U. Ctr. and Grad. Sch., 1988-2000. With USNR, 1957-63. Fulbright grad. fellow The Netherlands, 1965-66 Mem. Am. Acad. Arts and Scis., Coll. Art Assn., Am. Assn. Mus., Archaeol. Inst. Am., Am. Antiquarian Soc., Assn. Art Mus. Dirs. (trustee 1986-90, pres. 1989-90), Century Assn. N.Y.C. Office: J Paul Getty Mus 1200 Getty Center Dr Ste 1000 Los Angeles CA 90049-1687

WALSH, JOHN ALRED, retired social worker; b. N.Y.C., N.Y., June 4, 1927; s. Joseph Thomas and May Catherine (Moran) Walsh; m. Gwendolyn Ann Stockton, Apr. 13, 1952; children: Ralph, Carl, Nils. BA cum laude, St. Mary's U., Balt., 1949; M in Social Svc., Fordham U., 1954. Lic. clin. social worker, nursing home adminstr., marriage/family therapist. Social worker Cath. Charities, Bklyn., 1949—56; supr. after care clinics Ancora (N.J.) Psychiat. Hosp., 1956—57; dir. social svc. Trenton (N.J.) Psychiat. Hosp., 1958—68; asst. supt. Hunterdon Devel. Ctr., Clinton, 1968—91; ret. Author: (pamphlet) Fabulous Rosts, 1982. V.p. Warren County Hist. Soc., Belvidere, NJ, 1990—, Assn. Hunterdon Devel. Ctr., Clinton, 1991—; mem. bd. edn. Belvidere Sch. Dist., 1991—2001. Capt. U.S. Army, 1953—56, Korea. Avocation: collecting stamps and post cards. Home: 703 Oxford St Belvidere NJ 07823

WALSH, JOHN BREFFNI, aerospace consultant; b. Bklyn., Aug. 20, 1927; s. George and Margaret Mary (Rigney) W.; m. Marie Louise Leclerc, June 18, 1955; children: George Breffni, John Leclerc, Darina Louise. BEE, Manhattan Coll., 1948; MS, Columbia U., 1950; postgrad., NYU, 1954-62. Asst., instr. Columbia U., N.Y.C., 1948-51, asst. prof., assoc. dir. Electronics Rsch. Labs., 1953-66; various positions through tech. dir. Intelligence and Reconnaissance Div., Rome Air Devel. Center, N.Y., 1951-53; dep. for rsch. to asst. sec. Air Force, 1966-71; sr. staff mem. Nat. Security Council, 1971-72, asst. to Pres.'s sci. advisor, 1971-72; dep. dir. Def. Research and Engring., 1972-77; asst. sec. gen. for def. support NATO, 1977-80; holder chair in systems acquisition mgmt., dean exec. inst. Def. Systems Mgmt. Coll., Ft. Belvoir, Va., 1981-82, prof. emeritus, 1982—; v.p., chief scientist Boeing Mil. Airplane Co., Wichita, Kans., 1982-89; v.p. rsch. and engring. programs Boeing Aerospace and Electronics div., Seattle, 1990-92; v.p. strategic analysis Boeing Defense and Space Group, 1992-93; prin. John B. Walsh Assocs., 1993—. Mem. aeros. adv. com. NASA; mem. Congl. Adv. Com. on Aeros., 1984-85; assoc. Def. Sci. Bd.; mem. indsl. adv. bd. Wichita State U. Coll. Engring., adj. prof. elec. engring., 1989-90; chmn. tech. working group Def. Trade Adv. Group Dept. State, 1992-95; chmn. com. on adv. group on aeronautics R & D, NATO, 1981-82. Author: Electromagnetic Theory and Engineering Applications, 1960, (with K.S. Miller) Introductory Electric Circuits, 1960, Elementary and Advanced Trigonometry, 1977; contbr. tech. papers to publs.; patentee in field. Mem. planning bd., Cresskill, N.J., 1964-66; commr. Kans. Advanced Tech. Commn., 1985-86; bd. dirs. Kans. Inc., 1986-90; mem. math. scis. edn. bd. NRC, 1989-92. Served with U.S. Army, 1946-47, USAR, 1947-52. Recipient Air Force Exceptional Civilian Service award, 1969; recipient Dept. Def. Meritorious Civilian Service award, 1971, Disting. Civilian Service award, 1977, Air Force Assn. citation of honor as outstanding Air Force civilian employee of year, 1971, Theodore von Karman award Air Force Assn., 1977. Fellow IEEE (life), AIAA (v.p. tech. 1987-89); mem. Internat. Inst. for Strategic Studies, N.Y. Acad. Scis., GPS Internat. Assn., Electromagnetics Acad., Sigma Xi, Eta Kappa Nu. Roman Catholic. Office: 8800 Prestwould Pl Mc Lean VA 22102-2231

WALSH, J(OHN) B(RONSON), lawyer; b. Buffalo, Feb. 20, 1927; s. John A. and Alice (Condon) W.; m. Barbara Ashford, May 20, 1966 (dec. Feb. 2001); 1 child, Martha. AB, Canisius Coll., 1950; JD, Georgetown U., 1952. Bar: N.Y. 1953, U.S. Supreme Ct. 1958, U.S. Ct. Internat. Trade 1969, U.S. Ct. Customs and Patent Appeals 1973. Trial atty. Garvey & Conway, N.Y.C., 1953-54; vol. atty. Nativity Mission, 1953-54; ptnr. Jaeckle, Fleischmann, Kelly, Swart & Augspurger, Buffalo, 1955-60; pvt. practice, 1961-75; ptnr. Jaeckle, Fleischmann & Mugel, 1976-80; with Walsh & Cleary, P.C., 1980-84; pvt. practice, 1984—; spl. counsel Ecology and Environment, Inc., Lancaster, N.Y., 1989—. Trial counsel antitrust div. Dept. Justice, Washington, 1960-61; spl. counsel on disciplinary procedures N.Y. Supreme Ct., 1960-76; appointee legal disciplinary coordinating com. State of N.Y., 1971; legis. counsel, spl. counsel to mayor Buffalo, 1995—; counsel to sheriff Erie County, 1969-72; legis counsel Niagara Frontier Transp. Authority; cons. Norfolk So. R.R., Ecology and Environment on Govtl. Affairs; guest lectr. univs. and profl. groups. Author: (TV series) The Law and You (Freedom Found. award, ABA award, Internat. Police Assn. award). Past pres. Ashford Hollow Found. Visual and Performing Arts; past trustee Dollar Bills, Inc.; past co-producer Grand Island Playhouse and Players. With U.S. Army, 1945-46. Recipient Gold Key Buffalo Jr. C. of C., 1962, award Freedom Found., 1966. Fellow Am. Bar Found.; mem. ABA (del. internat. conf. Brussels 1963, Mexico City 1964, Lausanne, Switzerland 1964, Award of Merit com. 1961-70, sec., vice chair, chmn. sect. bar activities 1965-69, mem. ho. of dels. 1969-70, mem. crime prevention and control com. 1968-70, vice chair sr. lawyers divsn., com. legislation and adminstrn. regulations 1992—, vice chair sr. lawyers divsn. membership com. 1993-94), N.Y. Trial Lawyers Assn., Am. Immigration Lawyers Assn., Am. Judicature Soc., N.Y. State Bar Assn. (past exec. sec.), Erie County Bar Assn., Buffalo Bar Assn., Nat. Pub. Employer Labor Relations Assn., Capital Hill Club of Buffalo, Am. Assn. Airport Execs., N.Y. State Bus. Coun. (environ. law subcom., chmn. subcom.), Buffalo Irish Club (bd. dirs.), Buffalo Athletic Club (past bd. dirs., past v.p.), Buffalo Canoe Club, Buffalo Club, Ft. Orange of Albany Club, KC, Knights of Equity, Leoknights, Phi Delta Phi, Delta Gamma. Roman Catholic. Office: 368 Pleasant View Dr Lancaster NY 14086-1316 also: 210 Ellicott Sq Bldg Buffalo NY 14203-2402 Home: Apt 302 1217 Delaware Ave Buffalo NY 14209-1432 E-mail: jbwalsh@ene.com.

WALSH, JOHN CHARLES, metallurgical company executive; b. Indpls., Sept. 8, 1924; s. John Charles and Nell (O'Neil) W.; m. Mary Louise Dreiss, Feb. 5, 1949; children: Michael S., Carolyn Ann, Anne D. BS, Notre Dame U., 1949. Auditor Herdrich Boggs & Co., Indpls., 1949-50; with P.R. Mallory & Co., Inc., 1949-80; pres. Walgang Co. Inc., Indpls., 1980—. V.p., treas. P.R. Mallory & Co., 1971. Served with USMCR, 1943-45. Mem. Fin. Execs. Inst., Indpls. C. of C., Ind. Hist. Soc., Econ. Club, Notre Dame Club, Rotary. Home: 4974 Shadow Rock Cir Carmel IN 46033-9500 Office: Ste B2 598 W Carmel Dr Carmel IN 46032-2667

WALSH, JOHN E., JR. business educator, consultant; b. St. Louis, Apr. 28, 1927; s. John E. and Ann M. (Narkewicz) W. BS, U.S. Naval Acad., 1950; MBA, Washington U., St. Louis, 1957; DBA, Harvard U., 1960. Asst. prof. Washington U., St. Louis, 1959-60, assoc. prof., 1960-68, prof., 1968-2001, prof. emeritus, 2001—; vis. assoc. prof. Stanford U., 1964-65; vis. prof. INSEAD, Fontainebleau, France, 1970. Mem. exec. com. Econ. Strategy Inst. Author: Preparing Feasibility Studies in Asia, 1971, Guidelines for Management Consultants in Asia, 1973, Planning New Ventures in International Business, 1976, (with others) Strategies in Business, 1978, Management Tactics, 1980, International Business Case Studies: For the Multicultural Market Place, 1994, Joint Authoring: Managing Cultural Differences, 1994. Mem. State of Mo. leadership initiative to former Soviet Union, Poland, Hungary, 1990; mem. coun. Kearny Found., Internat. Ho., Washington U. 1st lt. USAF, 1950-54. Zurn Found. fellow, 1958; Presdl. fellow Am. Grad. Sch. Internat. Mgmt. Mem. Harvard Club N.Y.C. Home: 2301 Gulf of Mexico Dr Apt 24N Longboat Key FL 34228 E-mail: walsh@olin.wustl.edu.

WALSH, JOHN FRANCIS, lawyer; b. N.Y.C., May 28, 1961; s. John Francis Walsh, Jr. and Grace S. Walsh; m. Lisa Astrid Christian; children: Madeline, Maren, John. BA, Williams Coll., 1983; JD, Stanford U., 1986. Bar: Colo., Calif. Law clk. to Judge Skelly Wright U.S. Ct. Appeals (D.C. cir.), Washington, 1986—87; asst. U.S. atty. U.S. Atty.'s Office Cen. Dist. Calif., L.A., 1987—95, chief maj. frauds sect., 1993—95; ptnr. Holland & Hart, Denver, 1995—99, Hill & Robbins, PC, Denver, 1999—. Legal cons., commentator CBS News, N.Y.C., 1996—98. Author: (book chpt.) Federal Grand Jury Procedure, Federal Criminal Litigation, 1994. Co-chair bd. Invest in Kids, Inc., Denver, 1996—; bd. dirs. Colo. Lawyer's Com., 1997—. Mem.: ABA, Colo. Bar Assn., Denver Bar Assn. Democrat. Avocations: mountaineering, skiing. Office: Hill & Robbins PC 1441 18th St Denver CO 80202

WALSH, JOSEPH BRENNAN, ophthalmologist; b. Troy, N.Y., Mar. 6, 1941; s. Joseph Edward and Edna Margaret (Molloy) W. BS in Biology, Georgetown U., 1962, MD, 1966. Diplomate Am. Bd. Ophthalmology. Intern SUNY Upstate Med. Ctr., Syracuse, 1966-67; resident in medicine Univ. Hosp., Boston, 1968—69; resident in ophthalmology The N.Y. Eye and Ear Infirmary, N.Y.C., 1970-73; retina fellow Montefiore Hosp. and Med. Ctr./Albert Einstein Coll. Medicine, Bronx, 1973-74; from instr. to assoc. prof. dept. ophthalmology Montefiore Med. Ctr./Albert Einstein Coll. of Medicine, N.Y., 1973-88; chmn., prof. dept. ophthalmology N.Y. Eye and Ear Infirmary/N.Y. Med. Coll., N.Y.C., 1988—. Lectr. in field. Capt. M.C. USAF, 1968—70. Decorated Knight Hospitaller U.S. Priory of the Most Venerable Order of Hosp. St. John Jerusalem. Fellow N.Y. Acad. Medicine (Charles H. May Meml. lectr. 1998—), N.Y. Acad. Scis., Royal Coll. Ophthalmologists, Am. Acad. Ophthalmology; mem. Assn. for Rsch. in Vision and Ophthalmology, Ophthalmic Laser Surg. Soc. (pres. 1992-94), Macula Soc., Retina Soc., N.Y. Soc. for Clin. Ophthalmology (pres. 1984-85, Schoenberg lectr. 1993—). Office: NY Eye and Ear Infirmary 310 E 14th St New York NY 10003-4201 Fax: 212-979-4268. E-mail: jwalsh@nyee.edu.

WALSH, JOSEPH LEO, III, lawyer; b. St. Louis, Dec. 7, 1954; s. Joseph Leo and Joan Marie (Bocklage) W.; m. Eileen Rose Boland, June 11, 1982; children: Katie Rose, Joseph L. IV, Brian James, John Patrick, Mary Elizabeth. BS cum laude, Loras Coll., 1977; JD, St. Mary's U., 1984. Bar: Tex. 1984, U.S. Dist. Ct. (so. dist.) Tex. 1985, Mo. 1986, U.S. Dist. Ct. (ea. dist.) Mo. 1989, U.S. Ct. Appeals (8th cir.) 1989, U.S. Supreme Ct. 1991. Assoc. Chamberlain, Hrdlicka, White, Johnson & Williams, Houston, 1984-86; atty. Haley, Fredrickson & Walsh, St. Louis, 1986-88; assoc. Gray & Ritter, 1988-95; pvt. practice, 1995—; mcpl. judge 21st Jud. Cir. Ct., Frontenac, 2000—01. Pro bono legal clinic St. Patrick Ctr., 1991—, Holy Guardian Angel Settlement, 1995—; jud. clk. U.S. Dist. Ct. (we. dist.) Tex., 1984. Co-author: Missouri Bar CLE Treatise on Torts, 2d edit., 1990; sr. assoc. editor St. Mary's U. Sch. Law Jour., 1983-84. Active Holly Hills Neighborhood Assn., 1991-93; v.p. Our Lady of Pillar Men's Club, 1998, pres., 1999-2000. Recipient Torts and Evidence award Lawyers' Co-op Pub. Co., 1982; named to Nat. Order Barristers, 1984. Mem. Assn. Trial Lawyers Am., Mo. Assn. Trial Attys., Bar Assn. Met. St. Louis, Lawyers Assn. St. Louis, Phi Delta Phi (pres. 1984). Roman Catholic. Home and Office: 10469 White Bridge Ln Saint Louis MO 63141-8415 Office: 720 Olive St Ste 750 Saint Louis MO 63101-2330

WALSH, JOSEPH THOMAS, state supreme court justice; b. Wilmington, Del., May 18, 1930; s. Joseph Patrick and Mary Agnes (Bolton) W.; m. Madeline Maria Lamb, Oct. 6, 1955; children: Kevin, Lois, Patrick, Daniel, Thomas, Nancy. BA, LaSalle Coll., 1952; LLB, Georgetown U., 1955. Bar: D.C. 1955, Del. 1955. Atty. Ho. of Reps., Dover, Del., 1961-62; chief counsel Pub. Svc. Commn., 1964-72; judge Del. Superior Ct., Wilmington, 1972-84; vice chancellor Ct. of Chancery, 1984-85; justice Del. Supreme Ct., 1985—. Capt. U.S. Army, 1955-58. Democrat. Roman Catholic. Office: Del Supreme Ct Carvel State Bldg Wilmington DE 19801-3509*

WALSH, JUANITA MARIE, theatre educator, actress; b. Milw., May 03; d. Melvin John and Evelyn Dorothy (Heinrich) W.; m. Mark Jeffrey Rowen, Sept. 14, 1980. BFA, Stephens Coll., 1972; cert. speech, U. Wis., Milw., 1981. Mem. faculty NYU, 1985-89, Marymount Manhattan Coll., 1989-92, Temple U., Phila., 1991, Rutgers U., New Brunswick, N.J., 1992-93, HB Studio, N.Y.C., 1985-2000; prof. NYU, 1997-2000. Founder, artistic dir. Actors Alliance Inc,. N.Y.C., 1986-90. Off-Broadway performances include Grandma Sylvia's Funeral, 1997-98, Tribute to Uta Hagen, 1995; regional performance in Glass Menagerie, 2001, Baker's Wife, 2002; co-star TV show Ed, 2002, TV miniseries War of China's Fate, 1999; starred in films The Two Henrys, Fresh Cut Grass. Mem. Actors Equity Assn., SAG, AFTRA. Avocation: gardening. E-mail: jwract@yahoo.com.

WALSH, KENNETH ANDREW, biochemist; b. Sherbrooke, Que., Can., Aug. 7, 1931; s. George Stanley and Dorothy Maud (Sangster) W.; m. Deirdre Anne Clarke, Aug. 22, 1953; children: Andrew, Michael, Erin. BSc in Agr., McGill U., 1951; MS, Purdue U., 1953; PhD, U. Toronto, 1959. Postdoctoral fellow U. Wash., Seattle, 1959-62, from asst. prof. to assoc. prof. Biochemistry, 1962-69, prof. Biochemistry, 1969—, chair, 1990-2000. Author (book) Methods in Protein Sequence Analysis, 1986. Mem. The Protein Soc. (sec.-treas. 1987-90), Am. So. Biochemistry/Molecular Biology. Office: U Wash PO Box 357350 Seattle WA 98195-7350

WALSH, LAWRENCE EDWARD, lawyer; b. Port Maitland, N.S., Can., Jan. 8, 1912; came to U.S., 1914, naturalized, 1922; s. Cornelius Edward and Lila May (Sanders) W.; m. Mary Alma Porter; children: Barbara Marie, Janet Maxine (Mrs. Alan Larson), Sara Porter, Dale Edward, Elizabeth Porter (Mrs. Joseph Wells). AB, Columbia, 1932, LL.B., 1935; LL.D., Union U., 1959, St. John's U., 1975, Suffolk U., 1975, Waynesburg Coll., 1976, Vt. Law Sch., 1976. Bar: N.Y. 1936, D.C. 1981, Okla. 1981, U.S. Supreme Ct. 1951. Spl. asst. atty. gen. Drukman Investigation, 1936-38; dep. asst. dist. atty. N.Y. County, 1938-41; assoc. Davis Polk Wardwell Sunderland & Kiendl, 1941-43; asst. counsel to gov. N.Y., 1943-49; counsel to gov., 1950-51; counsel Pub. Service Commn., 1951-53; gen. counsel, exec. dir. Waterfront Commn. of N.Y. Harbor, 1953-54; U.S. judge So. Dist. N.Y., 1954-57; U.S. dep. atty. gen., 1957-60; partner firm Davis, Polk & Wardwell, 1961-81; counsel firm Crowe & Dunlevy, Oklahoma City, 1981—. Ind. counsel Iran/Contra investigation, 1986-93; chmn. N.Y. State Moreland Commn. Alcoholic Beverage Control Law, 1963-64; pres. Columbia Alumni Fedn., 1968-69; dep. head with rank of amb. U.S. del. meetings on Vietnam, Paris, 1969; counsel to N.Y. State Ct. on Judiciary, 1971-72; 2d crct. mem. U.S. Crct. Judge Nominating Commn., 1978-80. Author: Firewall The Iran-Contra Conspiracy and Cover-Up, 1997. Trustee emeritus Columbia U., Mut. Life Ins. Co., N.Y. Recipient medal for excellence Columbia U., 1959, Law Sch., Columbia U., 1980, John Jay award Columbia Coll., 1989. Fellow Am. Bar Found., Am. Coll. Trial Lawyers; mem. Am. Law Inst., ABA (pres. 1975-76), N.Y. State Bar Assn. (pres. 1966-67), Oklahoma County Bar Assn., Okla. State Bar Assn., Internat. Bar Assn., Assn. of Bar of City of New York, N.Y. County Lawyers Assn., Fed. Bar Coun.; hon. mem. Law Soc. Eng. and Wales, Can. Bar Assn., Mexican Bar Assn., N.Y. Club, The Century Club, Oklahoma City Golf and Country Club, Petroleum Club (Oklahoma City), Beacon Club (Oklahoma City), Beta Theta Pi. Presbyterian. Home: 1902 Bedford Dr Oklahoma City OK 73116-5306 Office: 1800 Mid Am Towers Oklahoma City OK 73102

WALSH, M. EMMET, actor; b. Ogdensburg, N.Y., Mar. 22, 1935; BBA, Clarkson Coll., 1958; student, Am. Acad. Dramatic Arts, 1959-61. Appeared in films, including Raising Arizona, Ordinary People, The Milagro Beanfield War, Romeo and Juliet, Winterdance, My Best Friend's Wedding, Twilight, A Time To Kill, Albino Alligator, Free Willy II, Snow Dogs, Music of Chance, White Sands, Narrow Margin, The Mighty Quinn, Clean and Sober, Harry and The Hendersons, Fletch, Missing in Action, Back to School, Blood Simple, Blade Runner, Silkwood, Sundown, Brubaker, Raise the Titanic, Fast Walking, Reds, The Jerk, Straight Time, At Long Last Long, Serpico, What's Up Doc?, They Might Be Giants, Midnight Cowboy, End of the Road, Cannery Row, Straight Time, Slap Shot, Cold Turkey, The Traveling Exceuctioner, Alice's Restaurant, Airport '77, Wild Wild West; TV shows include Sandy Duncan Show, Bonanza, Mind of the Married Man, The Rockford Files, All in the Family, Bob Newhart Show, The Waltons, Little House on the Prairie, Early Edition, Tales from the Crypt, Home Improvement, The Outer Limits, X Files, The Abduction of Kari Swenson, Resting Place, The Woman Who Willed a Miracle, HBO series The Mind of the Married Man; Broadway shows include That Championship Season, Does the Tiger Wear a Necktie?, The Beauty Part; Off-Broadway shows include Death of a Well-Loved Boy, 1967, Shepherds of the Shelf, 1961, Are You Now Or Have You Ever Been?; also appeared in regional theatre and summer stock.

WALSH, MARIE LECLERC, nurse; b. Providence, Sept. 11, 1928; d. Walter Normand and Anna Mary (Ryan) Leclerc; m. John Breffni Walsh, June 18, 1955; children: George Breffni, John Leclerc, Darina Louise. Grad., Waterbury Hosp. Sch. Nursing, Conn., 1951; BS, Columbia U., 1954, MA, 1955. Team leader Hartford (Conn.) Hosp., 1951-53; pvt. duty nurse St. Luke's Hosp., N.Y.C., 1953-57; sch. nurse tchr. Agnes Russel Ctr., Tchrs. Coll. Columbia U., 1955-56; clin. nursing instr. St. Luke's Hosp., 1957-58; chmn. disaster nursing ARC Fairfax County, Va., 1975; course coord. occupational health nursing U. Va. Sch. Continuing Edn., Falls Church, 1975-77; mem. disaster steering com. No. Va. C.C., Annandale, 1976; adj. faculty U. Va. Sch. Continuing Edn., Falls Church, 1981; disaster svcs. nurse ARC, Wichita, Kans., 1985-90, disaster svcs. nurse Seattle-King County chpt. Seattle, 1990-96; ret. Rsch. and statis. analyst U. Va. Sch. Continuing Edn. Nursing, Falls Church, 1975; rsch. libr. Olive Garvey Ctr. for Improvement Human Functioning, Inc., Wichita, 1985. Sec. Dem. party, Cresskill, N.J., 1964-66; county committeewoman, Bergen County, N.J., 1965-66; pres., v.p., Internat. Staff Wives, NATO, Brussels, Belgium, 1978-80; election officer, supr. Election Bd., Wichita, 1987, 88; v.p. McLean Newcomers, 1997-99, pres., 1999-2000. Mem. AAAS, AAUW, N.Y. Acad. Sci., Pi Lambda Theta, Sigma Theta Tau. Avocation: travel, gardening. Home: 8800 Prestwould Pl Mc Lean VA 22102-2231

WALSH, MARY D. FLEMING, civic worker; b. Whitewright, Tex., Oct. 29, 1913; d. William Fleming and Anna Maud (Lewis) Fleming; B.A., So. Meth. U., 1934; LL.D. (hon.), Tex. Christian U., 1979; m. F. Howard Walsh, Mar. 13, 1937; children: Richard, Howard, D'Ann Walsh Bonnell, Maudi Walsh Roe, William Lloyd. Pres. Fleming Found.; v.p. Walsh Found.; partner Walsh Co.; charter mem. Lloyd Shaw Found., Colorado Springs; mem. Big Bros. Tarrant County; guarantor Fort Worth Arts Council, Scholar Cantorum, Fort Worth Opera, Fort Worth Ballet, Fort Worth Theater, Tex. Boys Choir; hon. mem. bd. dirs. Van Cliburn Internat. Piano Competition; co-founder Am. Field Service in Ft. Worth; mem. Tex. Commn. for Arts and Humanities, 1968-72, mem. adv. council, 1972-84; bd. dirs. Wm. Edrington Scott Theatre, 1977-83, Colorado Springs Day Nursery, Colorado Springs Symphony, Ft. Worth Symphony, 1974-81; hon. chmn. Opera Ball, 1975, Opera Guild Internat. Conf., 1976; co-presenter (with husband) through Walsh Found., Tex. Boys Choir and Dorothy Shaw Bell Choir ann. presentation of The Littlest Wiseman to City of Ft. Worth; granted with husband land and bldgs. to Tex. Boys Choir for permanent home, 1971, Walsh-Lloyd organ to Casa Manana, 1972. Sem. Recipient numerous awards, including Altrusa Civic award as 1st Lady of Ft. Worth, 1968; (with husband) Disting. Service award So. Bapt. Radio and Television Commn., 1972; Opera award Girl Scouts, 1977-79; award Streams and Valleys, 1976-80; named (with husband) Patron of Arts in Ft. Worth, 1970, 91, Edna Gladney Internat. Grandparents of 1972, (with husband) Sr. Citizens of Yr, 1985; Mary D. and Howard Walsh Meml. Organ dedicated by Bapt. Radio and TV Commn., 1967, tng. ctr. named for the Walshes, 1976; Mary D. and Howard Walsh Med. Bldg., Southwestern Bapt. Theol. Sem.; library at Tarrant County Jr. Coll. N.W. Campus dedicated to her and husband, 1978; Brotherhood citation Tarrant County chpt. NCCJ, 1978; Spl. Recognition award Ft. Worth Ballet Assn.; Royal Purple award Tex. Christian U., 1979; Friends of Tex. Boys Choir award, 1981; appreciation award Southwestern Bapt. Theol. Sem., 1981, B. H. Carroll Founders award, 1982, (with husband) Patrons of the Arts award, 1991; Outstanding Women of Fort Worth award City of Fort Worth, 1994, numerous other award for civic activities. Mem. Ft. Worth Boys Club, Ft. Worth Children's Hosp., Jewel Charity Ball, Ft. Worth Pan Hellenic (pres. 1940), Opera Guild, Fine Arts Found. Guild of Tex. Christian U., Girl's Service League (hon. life, hon. chmn. Fine Arts Guild Spring Ballet, 1985), AAUW, Goodwill Industries Aux., Child Study Center, Tarrant County Aux. of Edna Gladney Home, YWCA (life), Ft. Worth Art Assn., Ft. Worth Ballet Assn., Tex. Boys Choir Aux., Friends of Tex. Boys Choir, Round Table, Colorado Springs Fine Art Center, Am. Automobile Assn., Nat. Assn. Cowbelles, Ft. Worth Arts Council (hon. bd. mem.), Am. Guild Organists (hon., Ft. Worth chpt.), Rae Reimers Bible Study Class (pres. 1968), Tex. League Composers (hon. life), Children's Hosp. Woman's Bd. (hon. 1991), Chi Omega (pres. 1935-36, hon. chmn. 1986), others. Baptist. Clubs: The Woman's (Club Fidelite), Colorado Springs Country, Garden of Gods, Colonial Country, Ridglea Country, Shady Oaks Country, Chi Omega Mothers, Chi Omega Carousel, TCU Woman's. Home: 2425 Stadium Dr Fort Worth TX 76109-1055 also: 1801 Culebra Ave Colorado Springs CO 80907-7328

WALSH, MICHAEL J. lawyer; b. Portland, Oreg., Sept. 4, 1932; s. Frank M.J. and Elisemary (Derbes) W.; m. June Griffin, Nov. 28, 1959; children: Molly, Erin, Kathryn (dec.), Anne. BA, U. Portland, 1954; JD, Georgetown U., 1959. Bar: D.C. 1959, Oreg. 1959, U.S. Ct. Appeals (fed. and 9th cirs.) 1959, U.S. Tax Ct. 1959, U.S. Supreme Ct. 1968. Law ck. to presiding justice Oreg. Supreme Ct., Salem, 1959-60; mng. ptnr. Rankin, Walsh, Ragen and Roberts, Portland, 1960-75; sole practice, 1976-81; ptnr. Walsh and Conolly, 1982-83; of counsel McEwen, Hanna, Gisvold and Rankin, 1983-85, Bullivant, Houser, Bailey, Pendergrass, & Hoffman, Washington, 1985—; chmn. Employees Compensation Appeals Bd. U.S. Dept. Labor, 1985—. Legal counsel to Reagan-Bush '84, Nat. Hdqtrs., Washington, 1983-84. Chmn. legal dev. March of Dimes, 1967; chmn. admissions Georgetown U., Oreg., 1972-83; trustee Christie Sch., 1974-78; trustee Cath. Charities Oreg., 1966-72, pres. 1971; trustee Parry Ctr. for Children, 1967-73, v.p. 1970-71; trustee Portland Tennis Ctr. Assn., 1972-83, pres. 1976-82; bd. dirs. Portland Traffic Safety Commn., 1981-83. Served with JAGC, USAF, capt. res. Mem. Am. Judicature Soc., Am. Trial Lawyers Assn., Nat. Assn. Coll. and Uiv. Attys., Am. Arbitration Assn., D.C. Bar Assn., Oreg. Bar Assn. (mem. various coms.), Multnomah County Bar Assn., Portland C. of C. (bd. dirs. 1975-78, chmn. legis. coun. 1975), John Carroll Soc., Thomas More Soc. Clubs: Georgetown Univ. (Oreg.) (pres. 1966). Home: 3273 Sutton Pl NW # B Washington DC 20016-3537

WALSH, MICHAEL JOSEPH, special operations and maritime security consulting company executive; b. Boston, Aug. 19, 1947; s. James Patrick and Margaret Mary (Watson) W.; m. Linda Susan Newton, Dec. 29, 1971 (div. Oct. 1987); m. Esperanza Gonzales, June 1, 1991 (div. June 1996). AA in Spanish, AS in Bus. Mgmt., Southwestern C.C., Chula Vista, Calif., 1975; BS in Edn., So. Ill. U., 1978. With USN, 1966-93, commd. ensign, 1978, advanced through grades to lt. comdr., 1989; mem. Seal Team One, Coronado, Calif., 1968-73; platoon comdr. Seal Team Two, Norfolk, Va., 1978-80; combat craft officer in charge Spl. Boat Unit Twenty, 1980-82; command tng. officer, platoon comdr. Seal Team Four, 1982-84; comdr. Naval Spl. Warfare Task Unit, Grenada and Lebanon, 1983-84; chief exercise divsn. U.S. naval forces So. Command, Panama, 1984-87; chief navy rep. counter terror work group Panama, 1985-87; dir. logistics Naval Spl. Warfare Group Two, Norfolk, 1987-89; dep. dir. intelligence Spl. Ops. Command Atlantic, 1989-93; ret. USN, 1993; dir. security Symmetry By Design, Inc., Castle Rock, Colo., 1996-97; pres. Seafarer Internat., Quinebaug, Conn., 2001—. Author: SEAL!, 1995; contbg. editor Behind the Lines mag., 1993-95. Decorated 3 Bronze Star with combat V, Purple Heart, Def. Meritorious Svc. medal, 2 Navy Commendation medal with combat V, Navy Achievement with combat V, 24 others. Mem. Am. Soc. Indsl. Security, Spl. Ops. Assn., UDT/SEAL Assn. (life, pres. 1992-93). Fax: 860-935-5176. E-mail: seawolfman@hotmail.com., seafarer@alienlaw.com.

WALSH, MILTON O'NEAL, lawyer; b. Memphis, June 17, 1941; BS, La. State U., 1964, JD, 1971. Bar: La. 1971. Salesman Met. Ins. Co., Baton Rouge, 1963-65; claims adjustor Safeco Ins. Co., 1965-68; law clk. Franklin, Moore, Beychok & Cooper, 1968-71, assoc., 1971-73; ptnr. Franklin, Moore, Cooper & Walsh, 1973-74, Franklin, Moore & Walsh, Baton Rouge, 1974-90; prin. O'Neal Walsh and Assocs., 1990—. Chmn. rules com. Baton Rouge City Ct., 1975-76, liaison com. 19th Jud. Dist. Ct., 1977; instr. in bus. law La. State U., 1974. Mem. ABA (mem. products liability com. 1978-79), Baton Rouge Bar Assn., La. Bar Assn., La. Assn. Def. Counsel (bd. dirs. 1982-84, 96-97), Internat. Assn. Def. Counsel (mem. casualty ins. com. 1980-81, mem. faculty 14th ann. counsel trial acad. 1986), Def. Rsch. Inst. (state chmn. 1980-82, regional v.p. 1983-86, bd. dirs. 1986-89, 96-98, mem. arbitration com., mem. nat. nominating com. 2000, Scroll of Merit award 1981, 82), Am. Bd. Trial Advocates (L.A. chpt., treas. 2000-01, v.p. 2001—, faculty mem. Masters in Trail 2000, pres. 2002), Assn. Def. Trial Attys. (state chmn. 1984—, S.W. mem. chmn. 1985-95, v.p./pres.-elect 1995-96, pres. 1996-97, mem. exec. coun. 1990-93), Sherwood Forest Country Club (bd. dirs. 1977-79, pres. 1979), Phi Delta Phi. Office: O'Neal Walsh & Assocs 501 Louisiana Ave Baton Rouge LA 70802-5921 E-mail: onealwalsh@onealwalsh.com.

WALSH, NAN, fine artist, painter, sculptor, consultant; b. N.Y.C., Nov. 4, 1932; d. Joseph Edward and Mary Ellen (White) Heinl; m. Albert Anthony Walsh, July 10, 1954; children: Maryellen, Nanette, Mark, Gregg (dec.). BS in Elem. Edn., Fordham U., 1954; postgrad., Nat. Acad. Sch. Fine Arts, Art Life Studio Inc., White Plains and Portchester, N.Y., 1984-94, V.K. Jonynas, L.I., N.Y., 1968-88, Art Ctr. No. N.J., 1996—2002. Fashion model Martha Clyde, N.Y.C., 1951-54; tchr. Yonkers (N.Y.) Pub. Schs., 1953-55; gallery dir. Mamaroneck Artists Guild, Larchmont, N.Y., 1988-95; fine artist, art juror, cons., 1995—. Membership juror Mamaroneck Artists Guild, Larchmont, 1982-84, membership juror chair, 1996-98, mem. adv. bd., 1996-98; mem. Ctr. for Contemporary Printmaking, 1998—. One-woman shows and juried exhbns. Westchester and N.Y.C., 1976—; works represented in corp. and pvt. collecitons. Hostess chairperson Citizens for John Lindsay, Gracie Mansion, N.Y., 1970; mem. Studio Twelve, pres., show chair, 1972-80; mem. Katonah Mus. Art. Recipient numerous 1st place awards for art. Mem. Nat. League Am. Penwomen, Nat. Mus. Women in the Arts, N.Y. Soc. Women Artists, Guild Creative Art, N.Y. Artists Equity, Mamaroneck Artists Guild (v.p. 1982, 83, membership chair 1992-95 Fordham U. Art Club (show chair 1965-80). Avocations: gardening, bridge, tennis, swimming, travel.

WALSH, NICOLAS EUGENE, rehabilitation medicine physician, educator; b. Mpls., July 1, 1947; s. Leonard Cyril and June Alice Walsh; m. Wendy Sarah Allnutt, June 1, 1973; children: Meghan, Rorey, Katlin, Alaine. BS, USAF Acad., 1969; MS, Marquette U., 1974; MD, U. Colo., 1979. Asst. prof. naval sci. Marquette U., Milw., 1972—74; from asst. prof. to assoc. prof. rehab. medicine U. Tex. Health Sci. Ctr., San Antonio, 1982—89, prof., chmn. rehab. medicine, 1989—, exec. assoc. dean Sch. Medicine, 1999—2000, disting. prof., 2001—. Dir. Am. Bd. Phys. Medicine and Rehab., Rochester, Minn., 1994—, sec., Minn., 1996—98, chmn., Minn., 1998—; pres., CEO Univ. Physician Group, 1998—2001. Author book chpts.; editor: Rehabilitation of Chronic Pain, 1991; editor-in-chief Archibes of Phys. Medicine and Rehab., Chgo., 1994—2000. Named Health Care Profl. of Yr., Gov.'s Com. for Disabled Persons, 1989; recipient Excellence in Rsch. award, Am. Jour. Phys. Medicine and Rehab., 1991. Fellow: Am. Acad. Phys. Medicine and Rehab. (Richard and Hinda Rosenthal Found. award 1991), Am. Bd. Pain Medicine (v.p. 1993—94, sec. 1994—96); mem.: Phys. Medicine and Rehab. Edn. and Rsch. Found. (pres. 1993—2000, Excellence in Rsch. award 1991), Assn. Acad. Physiatrists (v.p. 1993—95, pres. 1996—98). Office: U Tex Health Sci Ctr Mail Code 7872 7703 Floyd Curl Dr San Antonio TX 78229-3900 E-mail: walshn@uthscsa.edu.

WALSH, PATRICIA MAACK, special education educator; b. Yokohama, Japan, Sept. 10, 1950; d. Johan Gustof and Dorothy Maack; m. Frederic Peterson Walsh, Sept. 10, 1971; children: Audra Louise Walsh Lexin, Frederic Maack. AA in Art, Weber State U., 1972, BS in Child Devel., 1973; BS in Elem. Edn., Peru State Coll., 1988; MS in Psychology, U. La Verne, 1991; MS in Spl. Edn., Calif. State U., Northridge, 1996. Clear credential in spl. edn., Calif. Tchr. spl. edn. Papillion (Nebr.)-LaVista Sch. Dist., 1988-89, Eastside Union Sch. Dist., Lancaster, Calif., 1989-96, Antelope Valley Union H.S. Dist., Lancaster. Advisor H.S. Stds. Com., Lancaster, 1997—. Exit pole worker Rep. Women's Club, Palmdale, Calif., 1996. Mem. Coun. for Exceptional Children, Calif. Assn. Resource Specialists (cert.), Assistance League, Delta Kappa Gamma. Methodist. Avocations: art, travel, ministry with children. Office: Lancaster H S 44701 32nd St W Lancaster CA 93536-7023

WALSH, PATRICIA REGINA, trauma nurse, coordinator, educator; b. Phila., Nov. 16, 1955; d. William Aloysius and Patricia Delores (Smith) W.; 1 child, William. BSN, West Chester U., 1977; MSN, Widener U., 1987. RN, Pa.; cert. ACLS, BCLS Am. Heart Assn. Staff nurse Hosp. of U. Pa., Phila., 1977-80, asst. head nurse, head nurse neuro-med. unit, 1980-82, advanced clin. staff nurse neuro-med. unit, 1982-84, staff nurse oper. rm., 1984-87; coord. trauma edn. Thomas Jefferson U. Hosp., 1987—, coord. trauma program, 1996. Adj. faculty Widener U., 1988, Thomas Jefferson U., 1990—; presenter at profl. confs. Contbr. to profl. publs. Mem. Am. Trauma Soc. (Pub. Svc. award 1990, Disting. Svc. award 1993), Delaware Valley Trauma Nurses Consortium, Sigma Theta Tau. Avocations: competitive swimming, reading, sports. Home: 800 Gainsboro Rd Drexel Hill PA 19026-1614 Office: Jefferson U Hosp Trauma Ctr 118 S 11th St Philadelphia PA 19107-4801 E-mail: Patricia.R.Walsh@mail.tju.edu.

WALSH, PATRICIA TALLON, fundraiser; b. Perth Amboy, N.J., May 14, 1951; d. Thomas Lawrence Tallon and Nancie Wight; m. Gary R. Walsh, Sept. 12, 1981; children: Colleen, Amanda. BA, Moravian Coll., 1973. Cert. fundraising exec. Am. Fundraisers. Sr. v.p. Muhlenberg Found., Plainfield, N.J., 1974-94; dir. devel. Plainfield Health Ctr., 1994-98, Georgian Ct. Coll., Lakewood, N.J., 1998—. Mem. Bd. Edn., Manasquan, N.J., 1997—, Planning Bd., Manasquan, 1989-97; officer PTO, Manasquan, 1998—. Recipient Pres.'s award Vol. Hosps. Am., 1990 Mem. Nat. Soc. Fund Raising Execs. (chair newsletter 2001), N.J. Hosp. Mktg. Assn. (pres. 1983-85), Monmouth/Ocean Devel. Coun., Plainfield C. of C. (pres. 1993-94), Coun. for Advancement Secondary Edn. Avocations: sking, tennis, needlepoint. Office: Georgian Ct Coll 900 Lakewood Ave Lakewood NJ 08701-2697 E-mail: walshp@georgian.edu.

WALSH, PETER JOSEPH, physics educator; b. N.Y.C., Aug. 21, 1929; s. Peter and Mary Ellen (Kelly) W.; m. Rosemarie Imundo, May 13, 1952; children: Kathleen, Mary Ellen, Susan, Carole, Karen. BS, Fordham U., 1951; MS, N.Y.U., 1953, PhD, 1960. Research physicist Westinghouse Elec. Co., Bloomfield, N.J., 1951-60; supervisory physicist Am. Standard, Piscattaway, 1960-62; prof. Fairleigh Dickinson U., 1962-93; prof. emeritus, 1993—. Vis. rsch. scientist MIT, 1977; vis. prof. electronics and elec. engring. U. Sheffield, 1978-79; NASA fellow U. Santa Clara, 1980; Am. Soc. Engring. Edn. Navy fellow Naval Rsch. Labs., 1981, 82, 86, NASA Langley, 1987, Air Force fellow Hanscom AFB, 1988, Kirtland AFB, 1990; vis. prof. U. Genoa, 1984; vis. scholar Stanford U., 1984-85, cons. physics to 20 labs., 1963—; chmn. bd. trustees EMS Ednl. Corp., 1982—. Author: Dark Side of Knowledge, articles in field; patentee in field. Mem. Am. Phys. Soc., AAAS, N.J. Acad. Sci., Sigma Xi (sec. 1969) Home: 40 Saint Josephs Dr Stirling NJ 07980-1224 E-mail: peterj@gowebway.com.

WALSH, PETER JOSEPH, multimedia marketing professional; b. Newport, R.I., Jan. 22, 1948; s. Alexander Ronald and Mary (O'Connell) W.; m. Virginia Diana Santore, May 11, 1978 (div. May 1992); children: Bridget, Peter, Lara, Elizabeth, Vanessa. BA, Santa Clara U., 1970; MA, Johns Hopkins U., 1978. V.p. Noblemet Internat., N.Y.C., 1978-80; mktg. dir. Multi-Arc Scientific Coatings, St. Paul, 1980-88; sr. v.p. Projects Devel., Inc., N.Y.C., 1988-91; pres. Kiser Rsch., Inc., Washington, 1990-93; v.p. Sonalysts, Inc., Waterford, Conn., 1993—. Bd. dirs. Conn. Tech. Coun., 2002—. Bd. dirs. Portsmouth Abbey Sch. Alumni, Portsmouth, RI, 1996—2000. Roman Catholic. Avocations: tennis, golf, running. Home: 108 Catherine St Newport RI 02840-3150 Office: Sonalysts Inc 215 Parkway N Waterford CT 06385-1209 E-mail: walsh@sonalysts.com.

WALSH, PETER L. arts administrator, writer, consultant, researcher, critic; b. N.Y.C., Jan. 14, 1951; s. Dwight Rolfe and Jane Rae Walsh. AB, Oberlin Coll., 1973; M in Liberal Arts, Harvard U., 1985. Asst. dir. pub. programs Mus. Cmparative Zoology, Harvard U., Cambridge, Mass., 1974-78, dir. publs. and info. art museums, 1979-92; dir. campaign and devel. comms. Mus. Fine Arts, Boston, 1992-94, cons., writer, 1994—; dir. info. and instnl. rels. Davis Mus. and Cultural Ctr., Wellesley (Mass.) Coll., 1994-99; chmn. Mass. Art Commn., Boston, 1996—. Cons., writer Met. Mus. Art, N.Y.C., 1999—2001; founding organizer Art Mus. Image Consortium, Pitts., 1996—99, cons., 2000—01; cons., rschr. writer Jemison Inst. Dartmouth Coll., Hanover, NH, 2000—01, cons. writer pub. affairs, 2002—, cons. writer Com. on Race in the Acad., 2002; art critic WBUR-NPR, Boston, 2001—; cons. Jan Krukowski & Co., N.Y.C., 2002—. Contbg. author: A Cloud on Sand, 1990, contbg. author: The Great Image Debate, 1996, contbg. author: Computing and Visual Culture, 1999, contbg. author: Democracy and New Media, 2002; author: (exhbn. guide) van Gogh, 1998, Gauguin, 2002, Egypt Exhbn., 2002; contbr. articles to profl. jours. including Jour. Am. Assn. Info. Sci., Archives and Mus. Informatics. Mem.: Coll. Art Assn. (chmn. com. on intellectual property 2001—02). Office: Mass Art Commn State House Rm 61-G Boston MA 02133 Fax: 617-727-5400. E-mail: plwalsh@mindspring.com.

WALSH, PHILIP CORNELIUS, retired mining executive; b. Harrison, N.J., May 23, 1921; s. Philip Cornelius and Frances Walsh (Prendergast) Walsh; m. Alexandra Somerville Tuck, May 19, 1945 (dec. Sept. 1993); children: Eugenie Philbin Flaherty, Alexander Tuck, Nicholas Holladay, Elizabeth Lovering, Philip C.C., Francis Cummings; m. Peggy Flanigan McDonnell, Oct. 13, 1996. BA, Yale U., 1943; member of the Class of 1944. With W.R. Grace & Co., Lima, Peru and N.Y.C., 1946-71; v.p. parent co., chief operating officer Latin Am. group, 1961-71, group exec. corp. adminstrv. group, 1970-71; v.p. Cerro Corp., 1972-74, Newmont Mining Corp., 1974-80; chmn. bd. Foote Mineral Co., Exton, Pa., 1979-80; vice chmn. St. Joe Minerals Corp., 1980-85; chmn. bd. Chilean Lithium Co. Ltd., 1980-94, T. Rowe Price Assocs., Inc., 1986—2000. Dir. So. Peru Copper Co., 1973—80, Cyprus Minerals Co., 1985—93, Piedmont Mining Co., 1985—94; bd. advisors Fond Elec.; mem. Nat. Strategic Minerals and Metals Program Adv. Commn. Mem. Harding Twp. Bd. Edn., NJ, 1960—66, Harding Twp. Com., 1966—72, police commr., 1966—72; trustee Morristown Meml. Hosp., 1969—79; vis. com. Colo. Sch. Mines, Global Sys. and Cultures. Lst lt. U.S. Army. Decorated Silver Star, Purple Heart. Mem.: AIME (Saunders gold medal 1992, Disting. Mem. award 1993), Am. Soc. (hon. dir.), Pan Am. Soc. U.S. (past vice chmn.), Fed. Assn. Order of Malta, Edgartown Golf Club, Essex Hunt Club, Edgartown Yacht Club (commodore 1993—95), Racquet and Tennis Club, Somerset Hills Country Club, Sigma Xi, Phi Beta Kappa. Republican. Roman Catholic. Home: Pleasant Valley Peapack NJ 07977

WALSH, RICHARD A. medical educator; b. Trenton, N.J. m. Donna Carol Parsons; children: Sean Patrick, Ryan Robert. BS in Biology cum laude, Georgetown U., 1968, MD magna cum laude, 1972. Intern U. N.C., Chapel Hill, 1972-73, resident, 1973-75; asst. prof. medicine divsn. cardiology U. Tex. Health Sci. Ctr., San Antonio, 1977-82, assoc. prof. medicine divsn. cardiology, 1982-87, prof. medicine divsn. cardiology, 1987-89; prof. medicine, pharm. & cell biophys. U. Cin. Med. Ctr., 1990-98, Mabel S. Stonehill prof. medicine, 1992-98; John J. Hord prof. medicine, prof. physiology Case Western Res. U., Cleve., 1998—. Pfizer vis. prof. George Washington U., 1995; assoc. found. scientist Southwest Found. Biomed. Rsch., San Antonio, 1979-87, found. scientist, 1987-92; chair dept. medicine Case Western Res. U., 1998—; physician-in-chief Univ. Hosps., Cleve., 1998—; cons. in field; invited lectr. numerous locations. Editor-in-chief Jour. Molecular and Cellular Cardiology, 1999—; mem. editl. bd. Am. Heart Jour., 1989—, Am. Jour. Cardiology, 1985—, Am. Jour. Physiology: Heart and Circulatory Physiology, 1989-93, Circulation Rsch., 1992-99, Circulation, 1993—, Am. Jour. Physiology, 1995-99, Cardiology Jour. Club Jour., 1995—, Congestive Heart Failure, 1995—; contbr. articles to profl. jours. Recipient Disting. Alumnu award Georgetown U. Med. Sch., 1997. Fellow Am. Physiol. Soc., Am. Coll. Cardiology, Am. Heart Assn. (San Antonio chpt. v.p., bd. dirs., pres. elect, program chmn., pres., coun. circulation, coun. clin. cardiology), Soc. Cardiac Angiography; mem. AAAS, Am. Fedn. Clin. Rsch., Am. Soc. Clin. Investigation, Assn. Am. Physicians, Am. Soc. Hypertension, Assn. Profs. Cardiology (counselor 1997-99), Assn. Univ. Cardiologists, Cardiac Muscle Soc., Ctr. Soc. clin. Rsch. (counselor 1997—), Heart Failure Soc. Am. (founder, exec. com.), Internat. Acad. Cardiovascular Scis. (bd. trustees), Internat. Soc. Heart Rsch. (program com. N.Am. sect. ann. meeting 1991), N.Y. Acad. Scis., San Antonio Cardiovascular Soc. (co-founder), Soc. Cardiac Angiography & Intervention (program com. 1987-89, nat. meeting scientific program chmn. 1989-90), So. Soc. Clin. Investigation, Sigma Xi. Office: U Hosps Cleve Dept Medicine 11100 Euclid Ave Cleveland OH 44106-1736

WALSH, ROBERT ANTHONY, lawyer; b. Boston, Aug. 26, 1938; s. Frank and Emily Angelica (Bissitt) W.; m. Angela Rosalie Barile, Aug. 3, 1966; children: Maria, Robert II, Amy. SB, MIT, 1960; MS, Fla. Inst. Tech., 1967; JD, Suffolk U., 1971. Bar: Mass. 1971, U.S. Dist. Ct. Mass. 1972, U.S. Patent Office 1972, Can. Patent Office 1973, Ill. 1976, U.S. Supreme Ct. 1976, U.S. Ct. Appeals (Fed. cir.) 1982, U.S. Ct. Mil. Appeals 1983, Vt. 1996; registered profl. engr., Mass. Engr. Saturn Boeing, Michaud, La., 1964-65; program analyst RCA, Cape Canaveral, Fla., 1965-68; patent trainee, engr. Avco Research Lab., Everett, Mass., 1968-72; patent atty. GTE Labs., Waltham, 1972-73; group patent counsel Bell & Howell Co., Chgo., 1973-78; patent counsel ITT E. Coast Patents, Nutley, N.J., 1978-80, patent counsel internat., 1980-82, sr. patent counsel internat., 1982-86; dir. internat. patents ITT Corp., N.Y.C., 1986-87; gen. patent counsel ITT Def. Tech. Corp., Nutley, 1987-89; chief patent counsel Allied-Signal Aerospace Co., Phoenix, 1989-94; atty. IBM Corp., Essex Junction, Vt., 1994—. Ednl. counselor admissions MIT, No. N.J., 1978-89, Ariz., 1989-94; with Office of Judge Adv. Gen., Washington. Col. USAF, 1960-92. (ret.) Mem. ABA (co-chmn. subcom. PTC sect. 105), Tri-State USAFR Lawyers Assn. (Meritorious Achievement award 1980), KC (fin. sec. Scottsdale, Ariz. 1993-95), Internat. Patent Club (pres. 1988-89), Am. Intellectual Property Law Assn., Aerospace Industry Assn. (chmn. Intellectual Property com.), Chgo. Patent Law Assn., N.J. Patent Law Assn., Ariz. Patent Law Assn. (bd. dirs.), Sigma Xi. Roman Catholic. Home: 171 Yacht Haven Dr Shelburne VT 05482-7776 Office: Intellectual Property Law Dept 915 1000 River St Essex Junction VT 05452-4201

WALSH, ROBERT JOSEPH, psychotherapist; b. Chgo., Sept. 16, 1948; s. Robert Paul Walsh and Louise Tirado; children: Brigid, Justin, Clare. BA, Loyola U., 1970; MA, Governors State U., 1974. Cert. counselor. Family svc. facilitator LaGrange (Ill.) Area Spl. Edn., 1996-99; social worker Sch. Dist. 107, Burr Ridge, Ill., 1998—; therapist R.J. Walsh and Assocs., Western Springs, 1979—. Author: The Complete Guide to Private Practice, 2000. Parent edn. vol. YMCA, LaGrange, 1996-99; advisor Lyons Twp. Youth Com. Bd., LaGrange, 1979-80. Named Vol. of Yr. Young Mens Christian Assn., 1997, Counselor of Yr. Am. Mental Health Counselors, 1999. Mem.: ACA (pub. policy and legis. com. 2001—, chair 2002—), Ill. Mental Health Counselors Assn. (chair managed care task force 1993—, bd. dirs. 1994—), Jackson Park Yacht Club (sec. exec. bd. 1999—). Democrat. Roman Catholic. Avocations: sailing, scuba diving. Home: 234 S Madison La Grange IL 60525 Office: RJ Walsh & Assocs 822 W Hillgrove Western Springs IL 60558 E-mail: Walshgasp@aol.com.

WALSH, ROGER N. humanities educator; b. Brisbane, Australia, July 3, 1946; arrived in U.S., 1972; s. Nugent William and Patricia Walsh; m. Frances Elizabeth Vaughan, June 30, 1985. B in Med. Sci., U. Queensland, Australia, 1968; diploma in psychology, U. Queensland, 1969, MD, 1970, PhD, 1972. Diplomate Am. Bd. Psychiatry and Neurology, lic. physician Calif. Rsch. fellow U. Queensland, Brisbane, 1969; intern Repatriation Hosp., 1971; resident in psychiatry Stanford (Calif.) U., 1972—75, Foundations Fund fellow, 1975—77; prof. psychiatry U. Calif., Irvine, 1978—, prof. philosophy, 1986—, prof. anthropology, 1991—. Mem. internat. adv. com. Internat. Sch. Psychotherapy, St. Petersburg, 1996—, The Peace U., Berlin, 1996—; mem. internat. sci. adv. com. European Transpersonal Assn., Rome, 1996—. Editor: Meditation, 1984 (Outstanding Acad. Book of Yr., 1985), Beyond Ego, 1993 (named one of 100 Great Psychol. Books of the Century, 1999); author: Essential Spirituality, 1999; sr. editor: Revision Jour., 1980—85. Mem. adv. bd. Dzogchen Found., Cambridge, 1996—. Mem.: Internat. Transpersonal Assn. (bd. dirs. 1992—95), Physicians for Human Rights. Achievements include discovery of plasticity of geriatric brain; seven common practices in the world religions; enhanced perceptual sensitivity induced by meditation.

WALSH, SARAH FEENEY (SALLY WALSH), elementary education educator; b. Somerset, Pa., Jan. 13, 1961; d. William Joseph and Catherine O'Bryn (Feeney) W. BS, Duquesne U., 1983, MS in Edn., 1985; postgrad., Tex. Women's U., 1987. Cert. reading specialist/elem. edn. Resident asst. Duquesne U., Pitts., 1981-82, grad. asst., 1984-85; tchr. St. Canice Sch., 1982-83, William Brown Miller, Dallas, 1985-86, J.P. Starks Elem. Sch., Dallas, 1986-89, W.W. Bushman Elem. Sch., Dallas, 1989—, Preston Hollow Sch., Dallas, 1994—. Tchr. Sunday sch. Holy Trinity Parish, Dallas, 1987-93, mem. Edn. Coun., mem. Singles Group, 1987—; mem. St. Thomas Aquinas Coun./Edn.; mem. 500 Inc., Dallas Mus. Art. Mem. Tchrs. Applying Whole Lang., Internat. Reading Assn. (mem. Dallas coun., membership chair 1992-94, historian 1994-95, recording sec. 1995-96), Kappa Delta Epsilon (pres. 1983). Roman Catholic. Avocations: reading, swimming. Home: 6630 Vanderbilt Ave Dallas TX 75214-3423

WALSH, SEAN M. lawyer, audio-video computer forensics consultant; b. N.Y.C., Dec. 26, 1947; s. John W. and Catherine M. Walsh; m. Christine Ann Kull, June 10, 1978; children: Kathleen, Sean, Stephen. BS, Fordham U., 1970, JD, 1973. Bar: N.Y. 1974. Chief, asst. dist. atty. Dist. Atty.'s Office, N.Y.C., 1973-96; pres. Walsh Assocs. Forensic Cons., Douglaston, N.Y., 1997—. Officer/dir. Law Enforcement Video Assocs., Ft. Worth, 1989-95; counsel Office Inspector Gen., N.Y.C., 1996-. Author: Video and the Law, 1979; inventor non-linear video wire tapping rec. sys. Vice-chmn. N.Y.C. Cmty. Planning Bd., 1986-98; pres. Queens (N.Y.) Civic Congress, 1996—, past pres./dir. Douglaston Civic Assn. Recipient Outstanding Cmty. Bd. Work, N.Y.C., 1973, Outstanding Svc. to N.Y. State Police, 1992, Van Zandt Cmty. Svc. award, 1999; named Marshall to Little Neck Douglaston Meml. Day Parade, 1990. Mem. Assn. Bar City N.Y. (Comm. com. 1983-85, Computer com. 1997-2000), High Tech. Crime Investigation Assn. (pres. local chpt. 1994-96, internat. pres. 2000-2001). Avocations: sailing, skiing, scuba diving. Home: PO Box 238 Douglaston NY 11363-0238

WALSH, THOMAS CHARLES, lawyer; b. Mpls., July 6, 1940; s. William G. and Kathryne M. Walsh; m. Joyce Williams, Sept. 7, 1968; children: Brian Christopher, Timothy Daniel, Laura Elizabeth Smith. BS in Commerce magna cum laude, St. Louis U., 1962, LLB cum laude, 1964. Bar: Mo. 1964, U.S. Dist. Ct. (ea. dist.) Mo. 1964, U.S. Ct. Appeals (8th cir.) 1968, U.S. Supreme Ct. 1971, U.S. Ct. Appeals (6th cir.) 1972, U.S. Ct. Appeals (5th cir.) 1974, U.S. Ct. Appeals (D.C. cir.) 1980, U.S. Ct. Appeals (7th cir.) 1982, U.S. Ct. Appeals (9th cir.) 1987, U.S. Ct. Appeals (4th cir.) 1989, U.S. Ct. Appeals (11th and fed. cirs.) 1992, U.S. Ct. Appeals (2d and 10th cirs.) 1993. Jr. ptnr. Bryan, Cave, McPheeters & McRoberts, St. Louis, 1964-73; ptnr. Bryan Cave LLP, 1974—; mem. exec. com. Bryan Cave LLP, 1980-96. Mem. 8th Cir. Adv. Com., 1983-86. Bd. dirs. St. Louis Symphony Soc., 1983-95. With U.S. Army, 1965-66; lt. USNR, 1966-71. Fellow Am. Coll. Trial Lawyers, Am. Acad. Appellate Lawyers; mem. Mo. Bar Assn., St. Louis Bar Assn., Am. Law Inst., Mo. Athletic Club, Bellerive Country Club. Roman Catholic. Office: Bryan Cave LLP 1 Metropolitan Sq 211 N Broadway Saint Louis MO 63102-2733 E-mail: tcwalsh@bryancave.com.

WALSH, THOMAS FRANCIS, JR. producer, writer, director; b. N.Y.C., Aug. 15, 1956; s. Thomas Francis and Catherine Alice (May) W.; m. Adriana Mia Stastny, Oct. 19, 1996; children: Barron, Arielle, Thomas III. BFA, NYU, 1977. Pres. Tom Walsh Prodns. Inc., N.Y.C. and Del., 1977-89; chmn., CEO I.D.L. Inc., N.Y.C. and Calif., 1989-91, Wonderland Dream Factory Inc., Calif. and Del., 1991-93, Enteraktion Inc. and Enteraktion Studios, Inc., Miramar, Fla., 1993—, also prodr., dir. 8 new entertainment web series, prodr., dir. Kidsline (TV), 2002—. Prodr.: (feature film) Denial, 1991; (CD-ROM) The Arrival, 1996; exec. prodr.: (TV) We Dare You!, 1982, House to House, 1982, Mismatch, 1979; prodr., dir.: The Whole Truth, 1977, (TV) Global Trade with Toms Travis, 2002; prodr., dir., writer (TV) 14 Stories, 2002; created and developed more than 175 creatures and characters for TV, movies and animation. Scholar Helena Rubenstein Co., N.Y.C., 1976-77; recipient 1st prize for best TV show Conn. Assn. Profl. Communicators, 1974, Bronze and Silver awards Nat. Forensic League, 1977, Kate Garland award NYU/Columbia Pictures, 1976. Mem. Psi Upsilon (Delta chpt.), Alpha Epsilon Rho. Avocations: boating, diving, trains. Office: Enteraktion Inc/NBC Studios 15000 Peacock Plz Miramar FL 33027 E-mail: tomwalsh@enteraktion.com.

WALSH, THOMAS GEORGE, information services industry executive; b. Carroll, Iowa, Aug. 28, 1945; s. Raphael Edward and Helen Esther (Lawler) W.; m. Barbara Ellen Stoffel, Aug. 16, 1969; children: Meghan M., Molly A., Michaela E., Thomas P., Timothy R., Mary Colleen, Michael F., Brighid C., Daniel X., Emily M. BSBA, Creighton U., 1967. Customer svc. mgr. Mid-Am. Bankcard Assn., Omaha, 1969-71; customer svc. dir. First Data Resources, 1971-74, customer svc. dir. SE region Atlanta, 1975-77, v.p. mktg. Omaha, 1978-88; v.p. client svcs. Am. Express Integrated Payment Sys., Englewood, Colo., 1989-91, sr. v.p. mktg., 1991-92; exec. v.p. integrated svcs. divsn. First Data Corp., 1992—. Mem. exec. com. FDC Colo. Open Golf Tournament, Englewood, 1992—. Sec., treas., bd. dirs. Travis Hukil Fund, Englewood, 1989—; mem. Boys Hope-Denver, St. Louis, 1994—; pres. bd. dirs. Boys Town Booster Club, 1984-92; trustee Am. Irish Youth Found., 1995—. With U.S. Army, 1967-68. Mem. KC (Family of Yr. award 1988), Ducks Unltd., N.Am. Fishing Club (life), Douglas County Soccer Assn. (bd. dirs. 1991-93), Am. Legion. Roman Catholic. Avocations: kids activities, golf, fishing, hunting, boating. Office: First Data Corp 6200 S Quebec St Englewood CO 80111-4729

WALSH, THOMAS J., JR. lawyer; b. Newark, Jan. 23, 1961; s. Thomas J. and Ellen M. Walsh; m. Catherine M. Twomey, Nov. 19, 1988; children: Christopher, Claire. BA, U. Conn., 1983, JD, 1986. Ptnr. Marsh, Day & Calhoun, Southport, Conn., 1986-98; town atty. Town of Fairfield, 1993-97, asst. town atty., 1999—2001; prin. Brody, Wilkinson and Ober, P.C., Southport, 1999—. Dir. Bridgeport Neighborhood Fund, 1999—. Mem. ABA, Conn. Bar Assn., Bridgeport Bar Assn., Rotary. Avocations: tennis, politics. Office: Brody Wilkinson and Ober PC 2507 Post Rd Southport CT 06490-1259 E-mail: twalsh@brodywilk.com.

WALSH, THOMAS JAMES, JR. lawyer; b. Memphis, Oct. 22, 1947; s. Thomas James and Lois Rhine (Gibson) w.; m. Jean Clay McKee, May 31, 1969; children: Courtney Michelle Walsh Marsh, Meredith McKee. BA, Yale Coll., 1969; JD, U. Va., 1975. Bar: Tenn. 1975, U.S. Dist. Ct. (we. dist.) Tenn. 1976, U.S. Ct. Appeals (5th cir.) 1982, U.S. Ct. Appeals (6th cir.) 1985, U.S. Ct. Appeals (11th cir.) 1986, U.S. Supreme Ct. 1986, U.S. Ct. Appeals (10th cir.) 1991, U.S. Ct. Appeals (8th cir.) 1992, U.S. Ct. Appeals (3d cir.) 1998, U.S. Ct. Appeals (7th cir.) 1999. Assoc. Canada, Russell & Turner, Memphis, 1975-78, Wildman, Harrold, Allen, Dixon & McDonnell, Memphis, 1978-80, ptnr., 1981-89, McDonnell, Boyd, Smith & Solmson, Memphis, 1989-90, McDonnell Boyd, Memphis, 1990-94; atty. Wolff Ardis, P.C., 1995-97; sr. counsel McKnight, Hudson, Lewis, Ford & Harrison, 1997-99, Ford & Harrison LLP (formerly McKnight Hudson Lewis et al), Memphis, 1999—. Hearing officer Bd. of Profl. Responsibility Supreme Ct. Tenn., 1988-95. Chmn. bd. dirs. Multiple Sclerosis Soc. mid-south chpt., Memphis, 1978, World Affairs Coun. Memphis, 1985—; vol. atty. pro bono panel for sr. citizens, Memphis, 1982—; v.p. Bapt. Peace Fellowship of N.Am., Memphis, 1984-89; coun. chmn. Prescott Meml. Bapt. Ch., Memphis, 1993-95. Mem. Class award Leadership Memphis, 1985, Community Class award Unitarian Universalist Fellowship, Memphis, 1989. Mem. ABA, Tenn. Bar Assn., Memphis Bar Assn. Democrat. Avocations: photography, baseball. Office: 6750 PoplarAve Ste 600 Memphis TN 38138 E-mail: twalsh@fordharrison.com.

WALSH, THOMAS JOHN, infectious disease physician, oncologist, researcher, educator; b. Hartford, Conn., May 5, 1952; s. John Thomas and Frances Walsh; m. Sherril Ross, Apr. 8, 1989; children: Laura, Emma. BA in Biology/Chemistry, Assumption Coll., Worcester, Mass., 1974; MD, The Johns Hopkins U., 1978. Diplomate Am. Bd. Internal Medicine, Am. Bd. Infectious Diseases, Am. Bd. Med. Oncology. Resident in medicine Michael Reese Hosp., U. Chgo., 1978-82; fellow pathology Johns Hopkins Hosp. and Univ., Balt., 1979-80; fellow infectious diseases U. Md., 1982-85, fellow med. oncology, 1985-86, Nat. Cancer Inst., Bethesda, Md., 1986-87, sr. staff fellow, 1987-88, med. officer, 1988-93, sr. investigator, 1993—, head mycology unit, 1993—, chief immunocompromised host sect., 1996—; assoc. prof. U. Md. Sch. Medicine, Balt., 1992-98, prof., 1998—. Lectr. The Johns Hopkins U. Sch. Medicine, Balt., 1985—. Contbr. chpts. to Management of Infections in Patients with Cancer, 1985, Critical Problems in Trauma Care, Vol. II Medical Management, Current Therapy in Hematology/Oncology, 1987, Tenth Congress of the International Society for Human and Animal Mycology-ISHAM Proceedings, 1988, Diagnosis and Therapy of Systemic Mycoses, 1989, Respiratory Diseases in the Immunosuppressed Host, 1990, Hematology: Basic Principles and Practice, 3d edit., 1999, Medical Microbiology, 3d edit., 1991, Pediatric AIDS, 1990, Current Therapy in Critical Care Medicine, 1990, Emerging Targets in Antibacterial and Antifungal Chemotherapy, 1991, The Principles and Practice of Medical Intensive Care, 1993, Aspergillus: The Biology and Industrial Applications, 1991, New Strategies in Fungal Disease, 1992, Oral Fungal Infections in Immunocompromised Patients, 1991, Current Therapy in Pediatric Infectious Diseases, 3d edit., 1993, Hematopoietic Growth Factors and Mononuclear Phagocytes, 1993, Fungal Diseases of the Lung, 2d edit., 1993, Manual of Clinical Microbiology, 7th edit., 1994, Infectious Diseases, 1994, Infectious Complications of Cancer, 1995, Principles and Practice of Pediatric Oncology, 2d edit., 1996, Current Therapy in Adult Medicine, 4th edit., 1997, Cutaneous Infection and Therapy, 1997, Manual of Bone Marrow Transplantation, 1997, Adrenomedullin, 1998, Transplant Infections, 1998, Hunter's Tropical Medicine, 1999, Cancer: Principles and Practice of Oncology, 2001, others; contbr. more than 300 publications to profl. jours. and 200 rsch. abstracts. Comdr. USPHS, 1991—, NIH. Recipient Med. Mycology Fellow award Nat. Found. for Infectious Diseases, 1984, Young Investigator award ICAAC and Am. Soc. Microbiology, USPHS Commendation medal, 1993, 01, Outstanding Svc. medal, USPHS, 1996. Fellow ACP, Am. Acad. Microbiology, Infectious Diseases Soc. Am., Am. Coll. Chest Physicians. Achievements include development of exptl. and clin. found. for new approaches to diagnosis, treatment and prevention of invasive candidiasis and aspergillosis in immunocompromised patients; devel. of new understanding of pathogenesis, diagnosis, and treatment of emerging mycoses; devel. new approaches to augmentation of host defenses in neutropenic hosts against invasive mycoses. Office: NIH 9000 Rockville Pike Bethesda MD 20892-0003

WALSH, THOMAS JOSEPH, neuro-ophthalmologist; b. N.Y.C., Sept. 18, 1931; s. Thomas Joseph and Virginia (Hughes) W.; m. Sally Ann Maust, June 21, 1958; children: Thomas Raymond, Sara Ann, Mary Kelly, Kathleen Meghan. BA, Coll. Fordham, 1954; MD, Bowman Gray Med. Sch., 1958. Intern St. Vincent's Hosp., N.Y.C., 1958-59; resident ophthalmology Bowman Gray Med. Sch., Winston-Salem, N.C., 1961-64; fellow neuro-ophthalmology Bascom Palmer Eye Inst., Miami, Fla., 1964-65; practice medicine specializing in neuro-ophthalmology Stamford, Conn., 1965—; dir. neuro-ophthalmology service, asst. prof. ophthalmology and neurology Yale Sch. Medicine, New Haven, 1965-74, assoc. prof., 1974-79, prof., 1979—, also bd. permanent officers; dir. ophthalmology Stamford Hosp., 1978-83; mem. staff St. Joseph Hosp., Yale New Haven Hosp.; fellow Yale Sch. Mgmt., 1999. Cons. to surgeon gen. army in neuro-ophthalmology Walter Reed Hosp., Washington, 1966—, VA Hosp., West Haven, 1965—, Silver Hill Found., New Canaan, Conn., 1974—; adj. prof. Dartmouth Med. Sch.; frequent lectr. various univs. Contbr. articles to various publs. Mem. adv. bd. Stamford Salvation Army, 1972-92; mem. med. bd. Darien Nurses Assn., Conn., 1972—; surgeon Darien Fire Dept., 1969—. With AUS, 1959-61. Decorated Knight of Malta, 1983; Centennial fellow Johns Hopkins, 1976 Mem. AMA, Conn., Fairfield County med. socs., Acad. Ophthalmology, Oxford Ophthal. Congress, Acad. Neurology, Am. Assn. Neurol. Surgeons, Internat. Neuro-

Ophthalmology Soc., Soc. Med. Cons. to Armed Forces, Cosmos Club (Washington), Darien County Club, Yale Club (N.Y.C), Lions, Army-Navy Club. Office: 1250 Summer St Ste 205 Stamford CT 06905-5318

WALSH, THOMAS JOSEPH, lawyer; b. Kansas City, Mo., Oct. 3, 1932; s. Thomas E. and Clare E. (O'Leary) W.; m. Ellen B. Butler; children: Carolyn, David, Kathy. AB, U. Mo., 1953; JD, Georgetown U., 1958. Bar: D.C. 1958, Mo. 1958. Sole practice, Lee's Summit, Mo., 1958—. Mem. 4th Congl. Dist. Youth Coun., 1985-92; vice chmn. Mo. Coun. on Criminal Justice, 1977-80; sec. Jackson County Bd. Election Commrs., 1993-96, chmn. 1997-2001. Served to 1st lt. U.S. Army, 1953-55. Mem. Mo. Bar Assn., Assn. Trial Lawyers Am., Met. Kansas City Bar Assn., Knights of Columbus. Lodges: Optimists (lt. gov. 1963-64, pres. 1960-61). Democrat. Roman Catholic. Home: 210 NW Hillcrest Ln Lees Summit MO 64063-2103 Office: 528 W 3rd St Lees Summit MO 64063-2248

WALSH, TRUDY CATHERINE, journalist; b. Washington, June 1, 1959; d. William Francis and Rosalie Elizabeth (Borengasser) W. AB, St. Joseph's U., Phila., 1981; MA, U. Md., 1985. Instr. English, teaching fellow U. Md., College Park, 1982-85, part-time instr. Univ. Coll., 1992-94; copy editor Govt. Computer News, Silver Spring, Md., 1988-91, chief copy editor, 1991-95; writer-editor AMTI, Washington, 1995-96; tech. writer-editor PRC Inc., McLean, Va., 1996-97; sr. editor Post-Newsweek Tech Media, Washington, 1997—. Roman Catholic. Home: Apt 204 7500 Woodmont Ave Bethesda MD 20814-5362 E-mail: twalsh@postnewsweektech.com.

WALSH, VIRGINIA, artist, educator; b. Newark; d. James T. and Virginia M. Walsh; children: Victoria, Alexander. Student, Ridgewood Art Inst., 1996-2000, Art Students League, N.Y.C., 1975-81; BA, SUNY Empire. Dir., part owner J.P. Garutin Gallery & Printmaking Studio, N.Y.C., 1973-80; pres., owner Artisans w/Colour, Chester, N.Y., 1984-91; coord., instr. Rockland Conservatory of Music, 1989—. Advt. designer Shop-Rite Corp., Fla. and NY, 1995—98; designer, sculptor costum Armour, Cornwall, NY, 1999—; instr. Star Gallery, Middletown, NY, 1998—; pvt. rpactice, Bergen County, NJ, 1998—. Recipient Pres. award Salmagundi Club, 1981, Ernest Wiemann award Internat. Metal Smith Conv., 1996, Gold Medal award NOMMA Assn., 1998. Mem. Pen & Brush N.Y.C. (Adele Le Leeuw award 1999, Margaret Sussmann award 2000), Pastel Plus N.J.,Conn. Pastel Soc., Ridgewood Art Inst. Home and Office: 103 Hamilton Ave Hasbrouck Heights NJ 07604 E-mail: muffin4fun@aol.com.

WALSH, W. TERENCE, lawyer; b. Toledo, Nov. 18, 1943; s. Walter James and Ann (Gifford) W.; m. Patricia Jane Walker, Dec. 17, 1966; children: Christopher O'Brien, Ryan Kerrick, Ann Elisabeth. AB, Brown U., 1965; JD, Emory U., 1970. Bar: Ga., 1971, U.S. Dist. Ct. (no. dist.) Ga., 1971, U.S. Ct. Appeals (11th cir.), 1971. Assoc. Alston, Miller & Gaines, Atlanta, 1970-76, ptnr., 1976-83, Alston & Bird, Atlanta, 1983—. Lectr. various seminars on bus. litig., appellate procedure, juvenile law, ethics, and professionalism. Contbr. articles to profl. jours. Co-founder Truancy Intervention Project, 1991—; chmn. Kids In Need of Dreams, Inc., 1993--; bd. dirs. Georgians for Children, 1993—, The Bridge, 1994-99, Ga. Justice Project, 1987-97, Fulton County Juvenile Justice Fund, 2000—, Ga. Acad., 2000—, Family Connection Partnership, 2001--; mem. Atlanta Legal Aid Soc., Inc., 1976-98, pres., 1987; chmn. Capital Area Mosaic, 1994-96; chmn. sch. bd. Christ the King Sch., 1982-84; alumni trustee Brown U., 1994—; chmn. State Bar Com. on Children and the Cts., 1996—; bd. dirs. The Truancy Intervention Project, 1991—, Ga. Acad., 2000—, Fulton County Juvenile Justice Fund, 2000—, Child Placement Project Adv. Bd. Supreme Ct. Ga., 2000—. Recipient cmty. svc. award Martin Luther King, Jr. Ctr. for Nonviolent Social Change, 1995. Fellow Ga. Bar Found.; mem. ABA, State Bar Ga. (bd. govs. 1979-99, pres. young lawyers sect. 1980-81, H. Sol Clark award 1987, Chief Justice's award for cmty. svc. 1998), Atlanta Bar Assn. (bd. dirs. 1987-93, pres. 1991-92, Charles E. Watkins award 1994, S. Phillip Heiner award 1994, David Pollard award 1995), Gate City Bar Assn., Emory Law Alumni Assn. (exec. com. 1990-98, Disting. Law Alumnus award 2000). Avocations: sports, gardening, reading. Office: Alston & Bird 1201 W Peachtree St NW Ste 4200 Atlanta GA 30309-3449 E-mail: t.walsh@alston.com.

WALSH, WILLIAM DESMOND, investor; b. N.Y.C., Aug. 4, 1930; s. William J. and Catherine Grace (Desmond) W.; m. Mary Jane Gordon, Apr. 5, 1951; children: Deborah, Caroline, Michael, Suzanne, Tara Jane, Peter. BA, Fordham U., 1951; JD, Harvard U., 1955. Bar: N.Y. 1955. Asst. U.S. atty. So. dist. N.Y., N.Y.C., 1955-58; counsel N.Y. Commn. Investigation, 1958-61; mgmt. cons. McKinsey & Co., 1961-67; sr. v.p. Arcata Corp., Menlo Park, Calif., 1967-82; chmn. Sequoia Assocs. LLC, 1982—; pres., CEO Atacra Liquidating Trust, 1982-88. Chmn. bd. dirs. Consol. Freightways Corp., Vancouver, Wash., Neuroscis. Inst./Scripps, Ameriscape, Inc., North Salem, NY, Bemiss Jason Corp., Newark; bd. dirs. URS Corp., San Francisco, UNOVA, Woodland Hills, Calif., Am. Ireland Fund. Bd. overseers Hoover Inst. Mem. N.Y. State Bar Assn., Harvard Club (N.Y.C. and San Francisco), Fordham Club No. Calif., Knights of Malta (amb. to Bolivia). Home: 279 Park Ln Atherton CA 94027-5448 Office: 1550 El Camino Real Ste 220 Menlo Park CA 94025 E-mail: bill@sequoiaassociates.com.

WALSH, WILLIAM ALBERT, management consultant, former naval officer; b. Gilman, Ill., Aug. 15, 1933; s. Lawrence Eugene and Myrtle R. (Mulder) W.; m. Joan Elizabeth Kennedy, Dec. 28, 1957; children: Kathryn, Michael, Julie. BS in Commerce, U. Notre Dame, 1955; MS in Mgmt. with distinction, U.S. Naval Postgrad. Sch., Monterey, Calif., 1962; MS in Internat. Affairs with honors, George Washington U., 1972. Commd. ensign U.S. Navy, 1955, advanced through grades to rear adm., 1981; exec. asst. to dep. chief naval ops. (Surface Warfare), Washington, 1974-76; comdg. officer USS Juneau, San Diego, 1976-78; comdr. Amphibious Squadron Three, 1978-79; head plans and policy div., comdr. rapid deployment naval forces Comdr. in Chief U.S. Pacific Fleet, Honolulu, 1979-81; comdr. Amphibious Group Eastern Pacific, San Diego, 1981-82; dir. surface warfare div. Office Chief Naval Ops., Pentagon, Washington, 1983-85; ret., 1985; pres. Air/Space Am., San Diego, 1986-89, W.A. Walsh Enterprises, 1990—. Decorated Legion of Merit with 2 gold stars, Bronze Star, Navy Commendation medal U.S.; Disting. Service Order 2d Class Vietnam

WALSH, WILLIAM ARTHUR, JR. lawyer; b. Washington, Mar. 17, 1949; children: Jesse Creighton, Patrick McKay. BS in Econs. and Fin., U. Md., 1972; JD, U. Richmond, 1977. Bar: Va. Ptnr., head real estate, fin. and devel. team Hunton & Williams, Richmond, Va., 1977—. Mem. adv. bd. for law rev. U. Richmond. Trustee, bd. dirs. Va. Commonwealth U. Real Estate Found.; mem. Va. Commonwealth U. Real Estate Circle of Excellence. Mem. ABA, Va. Bar Assn., Richmond Bar Assn., Am. Coll. Real Estate Lawyers. Home: 4705 Leonard Pky Richmond VA 23226-1337 Office: Hunton & Williams Riverfront Pla East Tower 951 E Byrd St Richmond VA 23219-4074

WALSH, WILLIAM JOSEPH, business educator, labor arbitrator; b. Passaic, N.J., May 26, 1944; s. David Michael and Catherine Elizabeth Walsh; m. Paula Ruth Walsh, June 5, 1968; children: Brent W., Shannon C. (deceased). BS, USAF Acad., 1968; MA, Ind. U., 1974, PhD, 1986. Profl. cert. pilot. Commd. 2d lt. USAF, 1968, advanced through grades to lt. col., 1985, ret., 1990; assoc. prof. USAF Acad., Colo., 1984-86; dir. ops., tng. Tech. Tng. Group, Rantoul, Ill., 1986-87; inspector gen. Chanute Tech. Tng. Ctr., 1987-90; assoc. prof. bus. Ill. Wesleyan U., Bloomington, 1990—. Cons. McLean County Hist. Soc., Bloomington, 1991-96; mem. adv. bd. W.M. Putnam Co., Bloomington, 1994-97. Co-author: Collective-Bargaining & Impasse Resolution, 1988. Vice chmn., treas. OSF/St. Joseph's Med. Ctr. Found., Bloomington, 1995— Recipient Disting. Paper award Midwest Acad. Legal Studies, 1997. Mem. Midwest Soc. for Human Resources/Indsl. Rels. (pres. 1999-2000, Disting. Paper award 1998), Rotary (pres. Paxton chpt. 1985-86). Roman Catholic. Avocations: flying, acting. Office: Ill Wesleyan U PO Box 2900 Bloomington IL 61702-2900

WALSH, WILLIAM KERSHAW, retired textile engineering educator; b. Columbus, Ohio, Sept. 29, 1932; s. Merrick Kershaw and Genevieve (McCaw) W.; m. Josie Shearin; 1 child, Genevieve S. BSChemE, U. S.C., 1954; PhD in Chem. Engring., N.C. State U., 1967. Asst. prof. Coll. Textiles N.C. State U., Raleigh, 1967-72, assoc. prof., 1972-77, prof. textiles, 1977—, assoc. dean Coll. Textiles, 1980-89; dept. head textile engring. Auburn (Ala.) U., 1989-2000; ret., 2000. Contbr. over 100 articles to profl. publs.; patentee in field. Capt. USAF, 1954-57. Mem. Am. Chem. Soc., Am. Assn. Textile Chemists and Colorists, Fiber Soc., Sigma Xi. Episcopalian. Avocations: gardening, reading. Home: 572 Cross Creek Rd Auburn AL 36832-3417

WALSHAM, BRUCE TAYLOR, mining company executive; b. Grimsby, England, Feb. 28, 1936; s. Arthur and Phyllis Elsie (Stokes) W.; m. Denise Cox, 1961; m. Ann Barry; children: Alexandra, Nicola; m. Carole Moore, Jan. 3, 1998. BS in Geology with honors, Birmingham (Eng.) U., 1958. Profl. soccer player, 1958-65; provincial and rep. Cricketer, 1955-70; geologist Union Corp. Ltd., Johannesburg, Republic of South Africa, 1958-62, geologist in charge London, 1964-71; geologist MacKay and Schnellmann Ltd., 1962-64; dir. MacKay and Schnellmann P.L., Brisbane, Queensland, Australia, 1971-72; exploration mgr. Bond Corp., Perth, West Australia, 1971; v.p. Freeport of Australia Inc., Melbourne, Victoria, Australia, 1972-76, pres. Australia, 1979-89; v.p. Freeport Explorn Co., Reno, Tucson, Nev., Ariz, 1976-79, Freeport Minerals Co., New Orleans, 1986-89; pres. Pittston Mineral Ventures Internat. Ltd., Melbourne, 1989-93. Exec. chmn. Panorama Resources Australia, 1993-98; chmn., pres., CEO Diamond Works Ltd, Vancouver, 1997—; dir. Aurora Gold Ltd, Perth, 1994-98, Tonganyika Gold, Perth, 1998—. Contbr. articles to profl. jours. Fellow Inst. Mining and Metallurgy, Australasian Inst. Mining and Metallurgy; mem. Am. Inst. Mining Engrs., Soc. Econ. Geologists, Soc. for Geology Applied to Mineral Deposits (v.p. 1986-90), Geol. Soc. South Africa, Australian Club, Carlton Club. Avocations: philately, photography, various sports, theatre, films.

WALSHOK, MARY LINDENSTEIN, academic administrator, sociology educator; b. Sept. 10, 1942; BA, Pomona Coll., 1964; MA in Sociology, Ind. U., 1966, PhD in Sociology, 1969. Asst. prof. sociology Calif. State U., Fullerton, 1972-75; dir. women's programs, assoc. dean U. Ext. U. Calif., San Diego, 1975-80, dean, 1981-87; assoc. prof. sociology U. Calif., 1981-87, assoc. vice-chancellor pub. programs, adj. prof. sociology, 1990—. Adj. prof. Stockholm Sch. Econ.; bd. dirs. Calif. Coun. Humanities, San Diego Cmty. Found., Girard Found., Eureka Communities. Author: Blue Collar Women, 1982, Knowledge Without Boundaries, 1995; contbr. over 50 articles to profl. jours. Address: 150 12th St Del Mar CA 92014-2315 E-mail: mwalshok@ucsd.edu.

WALSKE, M(AX) CARL, JR. physicist; b. Seattle, June 2, 1922; s. Max Carl and Margaret Ella (Fowler) W.; m. Elsa Marjorie Nelson, Dec. 28, 1946; children: C. Susan, Steven C., Carol A. BS in Math. cum laude, U. Wash., 1944; PhD in Theoretical Physics, Cornell U., 1951. Staff, asst. theoretical divsn. leader Los Alamos Sci. Lab., 1951-56; dep. rsch. dir. Atomics Internat., Canoga Park, Calif., 1956-59; sci. rep. AEC in U.K., London, 1961-62; theoretical physicist RAND Corp., 1962-63; sci. attache U.S. missions to NATO and OECD, Paris, 1963-65; staff mem. Los Alamos Sci. Lab., 1965-66; asst. to sec. def. atomic energy, 1966-73; pres., COO Atomic Indsl. Forum, Inc., Washington, 1973-87. Chmn. Dept. Def. Mil. Liaison Com. to U.S. AEC, 1966-73; mem. U.S. del. Conf. Suspension Nuclear Tests, Geneva, 1959-61; chair reunion com. U. Wash., 1994-95; mem. fin. com. Ctrl. Kitsap Sch. Dist., 1994-96. Chmn. Upper Hood Canal Watershed Mgmt. Com., 1994-2000; budget steering com. Kitsap County, 1996, budget com., 1997-99, participant strategic planning, 1997, planning commn., 1998-2000. Lt. (j.g.) USNR, 1943-51. Recipient Disting. Civilian Service medal Dept. Def. Fellow Explorers Club, Am. Phys. Soc.; mem. Am. Nuclear Soc., U.S. Power Squadrons (comdr. Agate Pass squadron 1995-96), Poulsbo Yacht Club (trustee 1996-98), Phi Beta Kappa, Sigma Xi. Home: PO Box 370 Silverdale WA 98383-0370 E-mail: cwalske@home.com. *To seek out positions which appeared the most challenging and personally satisfying; to gain my reward through self-respect rather than public recognition; to expend extra effort as an offset to my limitations.*

WALSS, RODOLFO J. obstetrician-gynecologist, hypnotherapist, artist; b. Monclova, Coahuila, Mex., June 13, 1945; came to U.S., 1992; s. Rodolfo and Maria Consuelo W.; m. Maria Eugenia Aurioles, Dec. 17, 1967; children: Eugenia, Consuelo, Rodolfo, Patricia, Leonardo. MD, U. Coahuila (Mex.), Torreón, 1970; PhD in Hypnotherapy, LaSalle U., 2001. Diplomate Am. Bd. Ob-Gyn., Am. Bd. Med. Hypnosis. Intern Ohio Valley Med. Ctr., Wheeling, W.Va., 1973-74; resident U. W.Va. Ohio Valley Med. Ctr., 1974-77; prof. obstetrics faculty of medicine U. Coahuila (Mex.), Torrón, 1978-92, prof. gynecology faculty of medicine, 1982-92; chief ob-gyn svc. Mexican Social Security Inst., Torrón, 1986-90, chief divsn. ob-gyn., 1990-92; ob-gyn. Women Healthcare Group, Brownsville, Tex., 1992; chief ob-gyn. Columbia Valley Regional Med. Ctr., 1994-97, mem. edn. com., 1997—; pvt. practice, 1997—. Contbr. 22 articles to profl. jours. Fellow Am. Coll. Ob-Gyn., ACS; mem. Am. Soc. Reproductive Medicine, AMA, Tex. Med. Assn. Avocation: painting. Home: 24 Summit Dr Brownsville TX 78521-3610 Office: Alton Bloor Blvd Ste 260 Brownsville TX 78523

WALSTON, LOLA INGE, dietitian; b. Chgo., Jan. 26, 1943; d. Willy and Ingeborg (Smith) Neumann; m. Steven Ward Walston, Aug. 5, 1967; children: Bradley, Scott. BS, No. Ill. U., 1965; MS, U. Iowa, 1967. Registered, lic. dietitian. Asst. dietary dir. Alaska Hosp. Med. Ctr., Anchorage, 1973-76; cons. dietitian Mercer County Hosp., Coldwater, Ohio, 1979; profl. svc. cons. Health Care and Retirement Corp. Am., Lima, 1981-84; dietary dir. Estes Health Care Ctr., Montgomery, Ala., 1979-80, Mercy Meml. Hosp., Urbana, Ohio, 1984-86, Dairy & Nutrition Coun. Mid East, Dayton, 1987-89. Cons. Sharonview Nursing Home, South Vienna, Ohio, Columbia House, 1987—; Miami Health Care Ctr., Troy, Ohio, SCOPE Nutrition Program for the elderly, Fairborn, Ohio, CLS Nutrition Program, Bellefontaine, Ohio, 1987-90, Westview Acres Care Ctr., Eaton, Ohio, 1988-97, St. John's Nursing Home, Springfield, 1989-95, Oakwood Village, Springfield, 1989-97, Villa Springfield, Springfield, Ohio, 1988—, Covington (Ohio) Care Ctr., 1990-91, Champaign Nursing Home, 1993-97, Covenant House, 1993, Toward Independence, Inc., 1995—, Hospitality Homes, 1999—. Mem. com. Tecumseh coun. Boy Scouts Am., 1984—. Mem.: AAUW, Dayton Dietetic Assn. (treas. 1995—96, nominating com. chair 1997—98, mktg. com. chair 1998—2000, mem. com. 2000—02, nominating com. chair 2002—), Ohio Cons. Dietitians Health Care Facilities (chmn. 1982—84, treas.-elect 1996—97, treas. 1997—98, chmn. elect 2001—02, chmn. 2002—), Ohio Dietetic Assn., Am. Dietetic Assn., Hilltoppers Club (pres. 1982—83, Fairborn, Ohio). Avocations: camping, sewing, knitting, crocheting, cooking.

WALSTON, RODERICK EUGENE, federal official; b. Gooding, Idaho, Dec. 15, 1935; s. Loren R. and Iva M. (Boyer) W.; m. Margaret D. Grandey; children: Gregory Scott W., Valerie Lynne W. AA, Boise Jr. Coll., 1956; BA cum laude, Columbia Coll., 1958; LL.B. scholar, Stanford U., 1961. Bar: Calif. 1961, U.S. Supreme Ct. 1973. Law clk to judge U.S. Ct. Appeals 9th Cir., 1961-62; dep. atty. gen State of Calif., San Francisco, 1963-91, head natural resources sect, 1969-91, chief asst. atty. gen. pub. rights div., 1991-99; spl. dep counsel Kings County, 1975-76; gen. counsel Metropolitan Water Dist. So. Calif., 2000—02; dep. solicitor U.S. Dept. Interior, 2002—. Mem. environ. and natural resources adv. coun. Stanford (Calif.) Law Sch. Contbr. articles to profl. jours.; bd. editors: Stanford Law Rev., 1959-61, Western Natural Resources Litigation Digest, Calif. Water Law and Policy Reporter; spl. editor Jour. of the West. Co-chmn. Idaho campaign against Right-to-Work initiative, 1958; Calif. rep. Western States Water Coun., 1986—; environ. and natural resources adv. coun., Stanford Law Sch. Nat. Essay Contest winner Nat. Assn. Internat. Rels. Clubs, 1956, Stanford Law Rev. prize, 1961; recipient Best Brief award Nat. Assn. Attys. Gen., 1997; Astor Found. scholar, 1956-58. Mem. ABA (chmn. water resources com. 1988-90, vice chmn. and conf. chmn. 1985-88, 90—), Contra Costa County Bar Assn., U.S. Supreme Ct., Hist. Soc., Federalist Soc., World Affairs Coun. No. Calif. Office: Office of the Solicitor U.S. Dept. of the Interior 1849 C St. ,N.W. Washington DC 20240

WALT, HAROLD LOUIS, music educator; b. Queens, Ny, Sept. 1, 1959; s. Donald Daniel and Helen C. Walt; m. Rita C. Walt; children: Daniel. BS Music Ed., Ind. State Univ., Terre Haute, IN, 1981, M. Ed., 1985. Band dir. Vigo County Schools, Terre Haute, Ind., 1981—84; grad. tchg. asst. Ind. State Univ. Lab Sch., 1984—85; band dir. Western Boone Sch. Corp., Thorntown, 1985—89, Hamilton Heights Sch. Corp., Acadia, 1989—91, Quincy Pub. Schools, Quincy, 1991—. Percussionist Quincy Cmty. Theater, Quincy, Ill., 1998—, Quincy Symphony Orch., Quincy, Ill., 1992—. Mem.: Phi Mu Alpha Sinfonia, Music Educators Nat. Conf., Ill. Music Educators Assn., Sunriser's Drum & Bugle Corp., Tri-M Music Honor Soc. (sponsor 1991). Baptist. Achievements include guest conductor, jazz festival, Illinois Music Educators Assn., junior high school 2000, high school 2002. Avocations: tennis, fishing, miniature golf, miniature golf. Office: Quincy Public Schools 1444 Maine St Quincy IL 62301

WALT, MARTIN, physicist, consulting educator; b. West Plains, Mo., June 1, 1926; s. Martin and Dorothy (Mantz) W.; m. Mary Estelle Thompson, Aug. 16, 1950; children: Susan Mary, Stephen Martin, Anne Elizabeth, Patricia Ruth. BS, Calif. Inst. Tech., 1950; MS, U. Wis., 1951, PhD, 1953. Staff mem. Los Alamos Sci. Lab., 1953-56; research scientist, mgr. physics Lockheed Missiles and Space Co., Palo Alto (Calif.) Rsch. Lab., 1956-71, dir. phys. scis., 1971-86, dir. research, 1986-93; cons. prof. Stanford U., 1986—. Mem. adv. com. NRC, NASA, Dept. Def., U. Calif. Lawrence Berkeley Lab. Author 2 books; contbr. articles to sci. jours. Served with USNR, 1944-46. Wis. Research Found. fellow, 1950-51; AEC fellow, 1951-53 Fellow Am. Geophys. Union, Am. Phys. Soc.; mem. Am. Inst. Physics (bd. govs.), Fremont Hills Country Club. Home: 12650 Viscaino Ct Los Altos Hills CA 94022-2517 Office: Stanford U Starlab Packard 352 Stanford CA 94305 E-mail: walt@nova.stanford.edu.

WALTER, CAROLYN AMBLER, clinical social worker, educator; b. Phila., Jan. 29, 1945; d. Joseph Penrose and Betty (Alles) Ambler; m. John Wallace Walter, Aug. 19, 1967 (dec. 1993); children: Kimberly, Brian. BA, Juniata Coll., Huntingdon, Pa., 1966; MSS, Bryn Mawr (Pa.) Coll., 1968, PhD, 1984. Lic. social worker, Pa. Family counselor Family Svc. Phila., 1968-69; psychiat. social worker Cen. Montgomery County Mental Health Ctr., Norristown, Pa., 1969-71; clin. social worker, field instr. Crozer Chester (Pa.) Community Mental Health Ctr., 1974-75; program dir., family counselor Family Svc. Montgomery County, 1975-84; asst. prof. sch. social work U. Md., Balt., 1984-86; vis. lectr. grad. sch. social work Bryn Mawr Coll., 1986-87; assoc. prof. Widener U. Ctr. for Social Work Edn., Chester, 1987—; dir. baccalaureate social work program Widener U., 1991-97. Adj. instr. Great Lakes Coll. Assn., Phila., 1983-84; pvt. practice, Wallingford, Pa., 1982—. Author: The Timing of Motherhood, 1986; co-author: Breast Cancer in the Life Course, 1991; cons. editor: Jour. Social Work Edn., 1994—; contbr. articles to profl. jours. Bd. dirs. Sr. Cmty. Svcs., Folsom, Pa., 1990-96, Youth Advocates, Media, Pa., 1973-75. Grantee Widener U., 1989-90, 90-91, 92—, Tirlawyn Bd. Dirs., 1989. Mem. Am. Evaluation Assn., Coun. Social Work Edn., Pa. Assn. Undergrad. Social Work Educators (sec. 1988-90), Pa. Soc. for Clin. Social Work, NASW, ACSW, Coun. Social Work Edn., Nat. Registry Health Care Providers in Clin. Social Work (diplomate 1988). Home: 22 Mallard Mill Run Wallingford PA 19086-6670 Office: Widener U Ctr for Social Work Edn Chester PA 19013

WALTER, CHARLES SEBASTIAN, Roman Catholic priest; b. Grafton, W.Va., Aug. 19, 1940; s. Sebastian Julius Walter and Mary Elizabeth Macdonald. BA, U. San Diego, 1962; B in Sacred Theology, Pontifical Urban U., Rome, 1964, Licentiate in Sacred Theology, 1966; DMin, Cath. Theol. Union, 1999. Ordained priest Roman Cath. Ch., 1966. Prin. Sacred Heart Seminary, Cin., 1966-68; missionary Diocese of Witbank, South Africa, 1968-74; asst. gen. Comboni Missionaries, Rome, 1975-79, provincial superior Cin., 1980-86; missionary Archdiocese of Lima, Peru, 1987-90; prof. theology Faculty of Theology, Lima, 1991-95; assoc. dir., adj. prof. Cath. Theol. Union, Chgo., 1999—. Bd. dirs. Peru Peace Network, Jefferson City, Mo. Trustee Cath. Theol. Union, Chgo., 1995-99. Mem. Am. Soc. Missiology (editl. bd. 1997), Assn. Profs. of Mission. Home and Office: Chgo Ctr Global Ministries 5401 S Cornell Ave Chicago IL 60615-5664

WALTER, EUGENE VICTOR, writer; b. N.Y.C., Mar. 16, 1925; s. Abraham and Jean Sklar Walter; m. Ruth Ice, Sept. 20, 1957; children: Lacey, Claudia, Ian, Natasha, Jenia, Alexandra. BA, U. Miami, 1947; MA, Duke U., 1949; PhD, U. Minn., 1953. Assoc. prof. polit. sci. Ohio Wesleyan U., Delaware, 1954-57; assoc. prof. sociology Brandeis U., Waltham, Mass., 1958-65; lectr. sociology, dept. psychiatry Harvard Med. Sch., Boston, 1969-73; Simon Sr. rsch. fellow U. Manchester, Eng., 1974-76; prof. sociology Boston U., 1967-83; novelist, 1983—. Author: Terror and Resistance, 1969, Placeways, 1988, The Voice of Manush, 1996, The Craftsmen, 2001; contbr. short stories to various mags. Lt. (j.g.) USNR, 1944-46. Rockefeller Found. fellow, 1957-58. Home: 204 Aspinwall Ave Brookline MA 02446-6960 E-mail: manush@bu.edu.

WALTER, GEORGE ANTHONY, elementary education educator; b. Cin., July 16, 1948; s. George Winton and Yvonne Iola (Rivard) W. AA, Brevard C.C., 1968; BA in Edn., U. Fla., 1970; MEd, Stetson U., 1978. Tchr. Brevard County Sch. Sys., Vierra, Fla., 1971—. V.p. Rockledge Little League, 1991—; v.p. bd. dirs. Fla. Miss Softball, 1988; pres. bd. dirs. Rockledge Miss Softball, 1988-89; mem. Rep. Nat. Party. With U.S. Army, 1970-76, USAR. Recipient Newspapers in Edn. cert. Fla. Today, 1997. Mem. Brevard Fedn. Tchrs., Am. Legion. Republican. Avocations: photography, softball. Home: 155 Becora Ave Merritt Island FL 32953-3141

WALTER, GLENN RICHARD, lawyer; b. Lancaster, Pa., May 16, 1962; s. Richard Kupp and Gayle Marie Walter; m. Nancy Donita Messer, Jan. 11, 1992; children: Jessica Morgan, Kyle Reed, Sydney Paige. BSBA, U. Pa., Bloomsburg, 1984; JD, U. Tenn., 1987. Bar: Tenn., U.S. Dist. Ct. (ea. dist.) Tenn., U.S. Ct. Appeals (6th cir.). Atty. Kramer Rayson Leake Rodgers & Morgan, Knoxville, 1987-96, Lewis King Krieg & Waldrop, Knoxville, 1996—. Mem. ABA (spl. projects coord. young lawyers divsn. 1997-98), Tenn. Bar Assn. (bd. govs. 1997-99, pres. young lawyers divsn. 1998-99), Knoxville Bar Assn. Office: Lewis King Krieg & Waldrop 620 Market St Knoxville TN 37902-2231

WALTER, HUGO GÜNTHER, humanities educator, poet; b. Phila., Mar. 12, 1959; s. Paul and Elli R. Walter. BA, Princeton U., 1981; PhD in Lit., Yale U., 1985; MA in Humanities, Old Dominion U., 1989; PhD in Interdisciplinary Humanities, Drew U., 1996. Adj. instr. Yale U., New Haven, 1981-85, Old Dominion U., Norfolk, Va., 1988-89; asst. prof. Washington and Jefferson Coll., Washington, 1989-92, Fairleigh Dickinson U., Madison, N.J., 1992-96, Kettering U., Flint, Mich., 1996-99, Berkeley Coll., White Plains, N.Y., 1999—. Vis. asst. prof. Rhodes Coll., Memphis, 1986-87, U. Mo., Columbia, 1987-88. Author: (poetry) The Fragile Edge, 1988, Velvet Rhythms, 1989, Amber Blossoms and Evening Shadows, 1990, Golden Thorns of Light and Sterling Silhouettes, 1991, Waiting for Babel Prophesies of Sunflower Dreams, 1992, Along the Maroon-Prismed Threshold of Bronze-Pealing Eternity, 1992, The Light of the Dance Is the Music of Eternity, 1993, Dusk-Gloaming Mirrors and Castle-Winding Dreams, 1994, Amaranth-Sage Epiphanies of Dusk-Weaving Paradise, 1995, 2d edit., 1996, A Purple-Golden Renascence of Eden-Exalting Rainbows, 2001, (monographs) The Apostrophic Moment in 19th and 20th Century Lyric Poetry, 1988, Space and Time on the Magic Mountain: Studies in the 19th and 20th Century European Literature, 1999. Mem. Acad. Am. Poets, Internat. Soc. Poets. Avocations: music, painting. Home: 157 Loomis Ct Princeton NJ 08540-3438

WALTER, INGO, economics educator; b. Kiel, Fed. Republic of Germany, Apr. 11, 1940; s. Hellmuth and Ingeborg (Moeller) W.; m. Jutta Ragnhild Dobernecker, June 28, 1963; children: Carsten Erik, Inga Maria. AB summa cum laude, Lehigh U., 1962, MS, 1963; PhD, NYU, 1966. Asst. prof. econs. U. Mo., St. Louis, 1965-67, assoc. prof., chmn. dept., 1967-70; prof. econs. and fin. Stern Sch. Bus. Adminstrn. NYU, N.Y.C., 1970—, assoc. dean academic affairs, 1970-79, chmn. internat. bus. and fin. depts., 1980-85, Dean Abraham L. Gitlow chair, 1987-90; Charles Simon chair, dir. NYU Salomon Ctr., 1990—. Prof. internat. mgmt. (joint appointment) INSEAD, Fontainebleau, France, 1985—; cons. in field. Author. editor 28 books including Secret Money, 1985, 2d edit., 1990, Global Banking, 3d edit., 2003, Universal Banking in the United States, 1994, Street Smarts, 1997. High Finance in the Euro-Zone, 2000, Financial Takeovers, 2003; contbr. articles to profl. jours. Recipient Bernhard Harms medal, 1992; Ford Found. fellow, 1974-76, Rockefeller Found. fellow, 1977-78. Mem. Am. Econ. Assn., Am. Fin. Assn., Acad. Internat. Bus., Royal Econ. Soc., So. Econ. Assn., Phi Beta Kappa, Beta Gamma Sigma, Omicron Delta Epsilon. Home: 77 Club Rd Montclair NJ 07043-2528 Office: NYU Stern Sch Bus 44 W 4th St New York NY 10012-1106 E-mail: iwalter@stern.nyu.edu.

WALTER, J. JACKSON, consultant; b. Abington, Pa., Nov. 6, 1940; s. Joseph Horace and Edith Wilson (Jackson) W.; m. Susan Draude, Feb. 3, 1978; 1 child, Allison K. Vann. AB, Amherst Coll., Mass., 1962; LLB, Yale U., New Haven, 1966. Sec. Fla. Dept. Bus. Regulation, Tallahassee, 1976-79; dir. U.S. Office Govt. Ethics, Washington, 1979-82; pres. Nat. Acad. Pub. Adminstrn., 1982-84, Nat. Trust Historic Preservation, Washington, 1984-92; exec. dir. Waterford (Va.) Found., 1996-98. Cons. in field. Co-author: America's Unelected Government, 1983. Contbr. articles to profl. jours. Bd. dirs. Sabre Found., Boston, 1983—. Mem. Nat. Acad. Pub. Adminstrn., Met. (Washington) Club.

WALTER, JOHN FREDERICK, historical researcher, genealogist; b. Bklyn., Sept. 27, 1939; s. William O. and Madeline (Dittrich) W.; m. Margaret Killeen, Feb. 9, 1963; children: Mark, Michael, Robin, Brian. Student, St. John's U., 1955-61. Records mgr. Ladenburg Thalmann & Co., N.Y.C., 1961-76, W.R. Family Assocs., N.Y.C., 1976-94; dir., owner Inst. for Civil War Rsch., Middle Village, N.Y., 1994—. Merit badge counselor Boy Scouts Am., Middle Village, 1990—. Sgt. U.S. Army Res., 1961-65. Mem. Nat. Geneal. Soc., Co. Mil. Historians, Assn. Profl. Genealogists, Cartophilic Soc. Great Britain. Roman Catholic. Avocations: walking, volleyball, racquetball, cigarette card collecting. Home and Office: 79-13 67 Dr Middle Village NY 11379 E-mail: icwrjohn@aol.com.

WALTER, KENNETH GAINES, library director; b. Atlanta, Mar. 14, 1932; s. Gaines Winningham and Freddie Lou (Thigpen) W.; m. Eva Lou McClelland, June 10, 1965; children: Regina Eileen, Kevin Michael. BA, Emory U., 1954, MS, 1958; postgrad., U. Vienna, Austria, 1962; MSLS, U. N.C., Chapel Hill, 1966; EdD, U. Ga., 1995. Asst. cataloging libr. Ohio U., Athens, 1961-65, head cataloging libr., 1965-68, faculty rep. Bapt. Student Union New Haven, 1965-68; asst. dir. librs. U. S.C., Columbia, 1968-75; dir. librs. Ga. So. U., Statesboro, 1975-84; dir. libr. svcs. So. Conn. State U., New Haven, 1985-97, dir. libr. svcs. emeritus, 1997—. Cons. libr. strategic planning, budgeting, evaluation of book collections; faculty advisor Delta Tau Delta, Statesboro, 1976-83; book reviewer Libr. Jour., 1970-78. Contbr. articles to profl. jours. Mem. Conn. State U. Sys. Lib. Autom. RFP com., 1991-93, lib. dirs. com., 1985-97, Conn. Coun. Acad. Lib. Dirs., 1989-97 (emeritus mem. 1997—), Interagy. Libr. Planning Com., Hartford, Conn., 1986-89; mem. com. in-state svc. Conn. Acad. Libr. Dirs., 1985-89; mem. cataloging bd. New Haven Colony Hist. Soc., 1987-89; mem. Statesboro-Ga. So. Community Chorus, 1980-84; chmn. bd. suprs. CORE Credit Union, Statesboro, 1978-81. Staff sgt. U.S. Army, 1956-57. Recipient scholarship Emory U., 1950-53; Fulbright scholar, 1961-62; grantee Austrian Govt., 1961-62. Mem. ALA (life), Ga. Acad. Libr. Dirs., Ga. regents com. 1975-83 (sub com. coop. purchasing, 1978-1980, autom., 1980-1983, a/v 1975-1978), Assn. Coll. and Rsch. Librs., Libr. Adminstrn. and Mgmt. Assn., Reference and User Svcs. Assn., Southeastern Libr. Assn., Ga. Libr. Assn., Conn. Libr. Assn., Cen. Ga. Assoc. Librs. (pres. 1980-82), East. Ga. Libr. Triangle (pres. 1976-83), Ga. Acad. Sci., Ga. Assn. Coll. and Rsch. Librs. (pres. 1983), Rotary (New Haven), Sigma Gamma Epsilon, Beta Phi Mu, Phi Delta Kappa, Delta Tau Delta. Baptist. Avocations: camping, rock collecting, philately, woodworking. Home: 512 Wallingford Rd Cheshire CT 06410-2844

WALTER, LESLIE, nephrologist; b. London, June 20, 1944; came to U.S., 1949; BA, Yeshiva U., 1965; MD, SUNY Downstate, N.Y.C., 1969. Diplomate Am. Bd. Internal Medicine, Am. Bd. Nephrology. Fellow in nephrology Beth Israel Hosp., Boston, 1972-74; clin. instr. medicine Harvard Med. Sch., 1972-74; med. dir. hemodialysis unit Montefiore Hosp., N.Y.c., 1975-84; pvt. practice Bronx, N.Y., 1984—; med. dir. Riverdale Nursing Home, 1986-99. Office: 75 E Gun Hill Rd Bronx NY 10467-2103

WALTER, MELINDA KAY, health department evaluator; b. Taylorville, Ill., Aug. 6, 1957; d. Ray and Betty (Jones) W.; m. Laurence M. Nakrin, Dec. 21, 1983. BA, Millikin U., 1979; MPA, Sangamon State U., 1981. Acctg. intern Archer Daniels Midland, Decatur, Ill., 1978; econ. devel. intern City of Decatur, 1979; resident dir. Millikin U., Decatur, 1978-79; classification analyst Ill. Dept. Personnel, Springfield, 1979-81; rules analyst Ill. Gen. Assembly, 1981-84; regulatory cons. Ill. Dept. Pub. Health, Chgo., 1984-85, asst. to div. chief, 1985-88; health planner Lake County Health Dept., Waukegan, Ill., 1988-89, program evaluator, 1989—. Cons., Waukegan St. People Task Force, 1990-91; mem. pub. health com., Lake County Coalition for Homeless, Grayslake, Ill., 1990-91; legis. com. mem., Ill Pub. Health Assn., Springfield, 1989-90. Named Student Marshall, Sangamon State U., 1981, Outstanding Young Women Am., 1983. Mem. AAUW, Am. Soc. Pub. Adminstrn. (exec. bd. Springfield, Chgo. 1983-84), Am. Evaluation Assn., Ill. Pub. Health Assn., Ill. Farmers Union, Chgo. Area Health Planning Mktg. Assn. Avocations: bicycling, travel, museums, art galleries, cooking. Home: 61 Jansen Ln Vernon Hills IL 60061-3264 Office: Lake County Health Dept 3010 Grand Ave Waukegan IL 60085-2321

WALTER, PAUL HERMANN LAWRENCE, chemistry educator; b. Jersey City, Sept. 22, 1934; s. Helmuth Justus and Adelaide C. J. (Twardy) W.; m. Grace Louise Carpenter, Aug. 25, 1956; children: Katherine Elizabeth Walter Bousquet, Marjorie Allison Walter Moran. BS, MIT, 1956; PhD, U. Kans., 1960. Rsch. scientist DuPont Cen. Rsch. Dept., Wilmington, Del., 1960-67; prof. chemistry Skidmore Coll., Saratoga Springs, N.Y., 1967-96, chair chemistry and physics, 1975-85, prof. emeritus, 1996—. Translator: (book) Foundations of Crystal Chemistry, 1968; contbr. articles to sci. publs. Fellow Chem. Inst. Can.; mem. AAAS, AAUP (pres. 1984-86), Am. Chem. Soc. (bd. dirs. 1991-99, chmn. 1993-95, pres.-elect 1997, pres. 1998), Sociedad Quimica de Mexico (hon.). Presbyterian. Achievements include patents in field. Home: 3 Benedictine Retreat Savannah GA 31411-1624 E-mail: phlw@alum.mit.edu.

WALTER, REBECCA A. academic administrator; b. Altoona, Pa., Apr. 21, 1967; BA speech communication, George Mason U., Fairfax, VA, 1994, MA communication and gender studies, 1998. Admissions rep. Office of Admissions and Fin. Aid, Pittsburgh, Pa., 1986—89; fin. aid adminstr. Semester at Sea, 1989—92; mgr. Calvert and Co., Fairfax, Va., 1992—93; sales rep. Leeco Computers, Falls Church, 1993—95; adminstrv. asst. Inst. of Pub. Policy, George Mason U., Fairfax, 1996—98; adj. faculty No. Va. CC, 1998—99; program mgr. Contract Tng., OCPE, George Mason U., Fairfax, VI, 1998—2000; adj. faculty George Mason U., Va., 1995—; assoc. dir. Women's Studies Rsch. & Resource Ctr., GMU, 2000—. Founding mem. Staff Senate, George Mason U., Fairfax, Va.; vol. disc jockey Wpts, 98.5, Pittsburgh, Pa., 1989—92, Wyep, 91.3 Fm, 1991—91. Contbr. articles to profl. jours. Coun. mem. Sexual Assault Services Multicultural Adv., Fairfax, Va.; moderator Women's Studies Panels (local & nat.), 2002—02. Recipient Lambda Pi Eta, Nat. Communication Honor Soc., Dean's List, U. of Pitts., 1990-1992, George Mason U., 1990-1992. Mem.: Staff Senate (founderr, ad hoc com. classified employees), Coll. Arts and Scis. (mem. staff adv. bd.), Eating Disorders and Body Image Concerns Task Force, Golden Key, Lamda Pi Eta. Office: George Mason University 4400 University Drive Fairfax VA 22030 Office Fax: 703-993-1808. E-mail: rwalter@gmu.edu.

WALTER, RICHARD LAWRENCE, physicist, educator; b. Chgo., Nov. 1, 1933; s. Lawrence Barnabas and Marie Ann (Boehmer) Walter; m. Carol Elizabeth Goethals, Dec. 27, 1958; children: Timothy, Susan, Matthew. BS, St. Procopius Coll., 1955; PhD, Notre Dame U., 1960. Teaching asst., research asst. Notre Dame U., 1955-59; research asso. dept. physics U. Wis., 1960-61, instr., 1961-62; asst. prof. physics Duke U., Durham, N.C., 1962-67, asso. prof., 1967-74, prof., 1974—. Vis. staff mem. Los Alamos Sci Lab., 1964, 70, 75; vis. prof. Max Planck Inst fur Kernphysik, Heidelberg, Germany, 1970—71, Fudan Univ, Shanghai and Tsinghua Univ., Beijing, 1985, Fudan Univ., Shanghai and Tsinghua Uni., Beijing, 1991, Fudan Univ., Shanghai and Tsinghua Univ. , Beijing, 1994—96, Fudan Univ., Shanghai and Tsinghua Univ., Beijing, 1998; staff Triangle Univs Nuclear Lab, 1970—, assoc. dir., 1998—2001; vis. scientist China Inst. Atomic Energy, Beijing, 1985, Beijing, 91, Beijing, 1994—96, Beijing, 1998. Contbr. articles to profl jours. Scholar Fulbright, 1970—71. Mem.: Environ Metals Group (coun 1973—76), Am Physical Soc, Sigma Pi Sigma (nat coun 1964—68), Sigma Xi. Home: 2818 Mc Dowell Rd Durham NC 27705-5621 Office: Duke Univ Dept Physics PO Box 90305 Durham NC 27708-0305 E-mail: walter@tunl.duke.edu.

WALTER, ROBERT IRVING, chemistry educator, chemist; b. Johnstown, Pa., Mar. 12, 1920; s. Charles Weller and Frances (Riethmiller) W.; m. Farideh Asghari, Oct. 17, 1973. AB, Swarthmore Coll., 1941; MA, Johns Hopkins U., 1942; PhD, U. Chgo., 1949. Instr. U. Colo., 1949-51, U. Conn., 1953-55; rsch. assoc. Rutgers U., 1951-53; assoc. physicist Brookhaven Nat. Lab., 1955-56; mem. faculty Haverford Coll., 1956-68, prof. chemistry, 1963-68; prof. U. Ill., Chgo., 1968—, prof. emeritus, 1990—. Vis. lectr. Stanford (Calif.) U., winter 1967; acad. guest U. Zurich, 1976; U.S. NAS exch. visitor to Romania, 1982, 88. Mem. Adv. Council Coll. Chemistry, 1966-70. Served with USNR, 1944-46. Grantee U.S. Army Signal Research and Devel. Lab., NIH, NSF, Dept. Energy; NSF fellow, 1960-61 Fellow AAAS; mem. Am. Chem. Soc. (vis. scientist div. chem. edn. 1964-73), Sigma Xi. Achievements include special research preparation, proof of structure, chemical and physical properties of stable aromatic free radicals, C1 reactions and mechanisms in heterogeneous catalysis, reactions of porphyrin bases. Home: 2951 Central St Unit 308 Evanston IL 60201-1284 E-mail: mhry@aol.com.

WALTER, ROBERT D. wholesale pharmaceutical distribution executive; b. 1945; BMechE, Ohio U., 1967; MBA, Harvard U., 1970. Founder Cardinal Foods Inc. (acquired by Roundy's Inc. 1988), Dublin, 1971-88; CEO, chmn. bd. Cardinal Health, Inc., 1971—. Bd. dirs. Bank One Corp., Viacom Inc. Trustee Battelle Meml. Inst., Ohio U. Office: Cardinal Health Inc 7000 Cardinal Pl Dublin OH 43017-1092*

WALTER, VIRGINIA LEE, psychologist, educator; b. Temple, Tex., Oct. 30, 1937; d. Luther Patterson and Virginia Lafayette (Wilkins) W.; m. Glen Ellis, 1958 (div.); children: Glen Edward, David Walter; m. Robert Reinehr, 1963 (div.); 1 son, Charles Allen; m. Robert Bruininks, 1975 (div.). BS, U. Tex.-Austin, 1959, M.Edn., 1967; postgrad. internship program in spl. Edn. Adminstrn., 1970; Ed.D., U. Houston, 1973. Prof. ednl. psychology dept. ednl. psychology U. Minn., Mpls., 1973-85; pres. Sch. Resource Ctr., Austin, Tex., 1985-90; tchr. Llano Pub. Schs., 1988-97; dir. Walter Resources, 1998—. Chmn. State Adv. Council for Inservice Tng. Regular Classroom Tchrs., 1977-79; cons. spl. ednl. various sch. dists., state depts. and agys. Editorial cons.: Jour. Ednl. Psychology, 1979, Reading Research Quar., 1982; assoc. editor: Exceptional Children, 1979-84; assoc. editor Teaching Exceptional Children, 1985-89; contbr. articles to profl. jours., papers to profl. confs. Named Minn. Spl. Educator of Yr., 1978; recipient Service award Internat. Council Exceptional Children, 1978; HEW Office of Human Devel. Services grantee, 1976-80; Dept. Edn. contractee, 1980-83 Mem. Council for Exceptional Children, Nat. Assn. Children with Learning Disabilities (dir. Minn. chpt. 1978-80), Nat. Assn. Retarded Citizens, AAUP, Assn. Supervision and Curriculum Devel. Home and Office: 3212 Meredith St Austin TX 78703

WALTER JR. BURL LEROY, retired music educator; b. Lawrence, Kans., Aug. 15, 1933; s. Burl Leroy and Ruth Christian Walter; m. Evelyn Ruth Shuline, Mar. 26, 1956; children: Burl Leroy Walter III, Ellen Ruth Walter. BS, NW Mo. State U., Maryville, MO, 1951—56. Music educator Hopkins Pub. Schools, Hopkins, Mo., 1955—56; army bandsman 22nd Army Band, San Francisco, 1956—58; music educator Macksberg H.S., Macksburg, Iowa, 1958—60, Schleswig H.S., Schleswig, 1960—63; musician Glenn Houpt Trio and Symphony Orch., Sioux City, 1963—64; music educator Kings Canyon Unified Sch. Dist., Reedley, Calif., 1964—2000; lectr. Calif. State U., Fresno, 1974—75. Mem. Kings Canyon Edn. Assn., 1965; treas. Fresno-Madera Music Edn. Assn., Calif., 1965; v.p. Calif. Band Directors Assn., Calif., 1968; mem. Calif. Teachers Assn., Calif., 1965, Fresno Dixieland Soc., Calif., 1985, Percusive Arts Soc., Calif., 1965, Local 210 Musicians Union, Calif., 1965. Pfc U.S. Army, 1956—58, San Francisco. Recipient Outstanding Music Educator, Fresno-Madera Music Edn. Assn., 1996-1997, Outstanding Band Dir., 1997, Disting. Svc. Award, Calif. Band Directors Assn., 1968, Outstanding Music Educator, Calif. Music Educators Assn., 1988, 1996, State of Calif., 1996, Man Of The Yr., Reedley Chamber of Commerce, 1997, Hall Of Fame, 1999, Lifetime Svc. Award, Calif. Band Directors, 2001. Home: 1425 E Street Reedley CA 93654

WALTER-ROBINSON, CAROL SUE, investment executive; b. Joliet, Ill., Dec. 24, 1942; d. Loren John Sr. and Myrtle F. (Sistler) Walter; adopted d. Lillian M. Winnett; m. Patrick Allen Robinson, Apr. 17, 1991; adopted children: Teresa, Christopher, Ellen, Melissa, Catrina, Elizabeth, Sherlene. Student, Waubonsee Jr. Coll., Aurora, Ill., 1963-65, Aurora Coll., 1967-71, Hypnosis Motivation Inst., 1992, U. Metaphysics, 1992. Lic., cosmetologist, paralegal; cert. hypnotherapist. Office mgr., bookkeeper Edward M. Kyser Appraiser, Aurora, 1961-66; legal sec., aide Hon. Paul Schnake, 1961-66; pers. mgr. H.W. Gossard Co., Batavia, Ill., 1966-68; pers. recruiter Dresser Industries, Franklin Park, 1968-71; exec. sec., pres. Am. Picture Co., Anaheim, Calif., 1972-75; contract mgr. state operators incorp. divsn. Mobil Oil Corp., Orange County, 1975-81; owner Inland Tele-Sec., Riverside, 1982-84; pvt. practice investment mgr., 1984—. Sec. Legal Sec.-Fox Valley, Aurora, 1964-66. Author: Capital Punishment—Pro and Con, 1970; editor (newsletter) Humane News, 1964-68. Pres./founder The Fosterkids Alliance, Riverside, 1988-91; exec. sec. Fox Valley Animal Welfare, Aurora, 1963-68; historian Am. Cancer Soc., Aurora, 1964; exec. sec. pub. rels. Humane Soc. U.S., Garden Grove, Calif., 1972; community liaison El Centro Hispano Americano, Aurora, 1970; coord. No. Ill. Pers. Assn., Chgo., 1966-68; com. chair-advisor Employee Personnel Testing, Melrose Park, Ill., 1965; arbitration moderator I.G.W.U., Chgo., 1969. Democrat. Unity. Avocations: researching para-normal psychology, genealogy, music, metaphysics. Office: TFA PO Box 52092 Riverside CA 92517-3092 Home: PO Box 987 Klamath CA 95548-0987

WALTERS, ALAN WAYNE, judge; b. Georgetown, S.C., Feb. 8, 1963; s. Burl T. and Emily W. Walters; m. Susan Welch, May 13, 1989; children: Robert Alan, Jason Scott. AS in Criminal Justice, Horry-Georgetown Tech. Coll., Conway, S.C., 1996; BS in Edn., So. Ill. U., Carbondale, 1999. Mem. investigations divsn. Georgetown County Sheriff's Dept., 1985-93; law enforcement ofcl. Andrews (S.C.) Police Dept., 1993-94; mem. investigations/crime prevention divsn. Georgetown Police Dept., 1994—2002; summary ct. judge Georgetown County Summary Ct., 2002—. Chmn. Georgetown County Rep. Com., 1997-99, Black River Dist. coun. Boy Scouts Am., 2000—; vice chmn. Georgetown County Easter Seals, 1997—; elder Georgetown Presbyn. Ch., 1998-00; bd. dirs. Horry-Georgetown Tech. Alumni Assn., 1998-2001, Coastal Carolina coun. Boy Scouts Am., 2000—. Named State Dep. Sheriff of Yr., S.C. Sheriff's Assn., 1992. Mem. S.C. Law Enforcement Officers Assn. (State Law Enforcement Officer of Yr. 1996), Rotary (pres. Georgetown chpt. 1999-00, asst. dir. gov. 2002-, Pub. Safety Officer of Yr. award 1992). Home: 306 Kaufman St Georgetown SC 29440-3814 E-mail: alnwltrs@aol.com.

WALTERS, ARTHUR SCOTT, neurologist, educator, clinical research scientist; b. Balt., Feb. 20, 1943; s. Charles Henry and Jean Vivian (Scott) W.; m. Bokyun Kim, May 18, 1985 (div. Oct. 1992); m. Lesley J. Gill, Dec. 19, 1992. BA, Kalamazoo Coll., 1965; MS, Northwestern U., 1967; MD, Wayne State U., 1972. Diplomate Am. Bd. Psychiatry and Neurology; diplomate Am. Bd. Sleep Medicine. Intern Oakwood Hosp., Dearborn, Mich., 1972-73; resident in neurology SUNY Downstate Med. Ctr., Bklyn., 1976-79; movement disorder fellow Neurol. Inst., N.Y.C., 1982-84; asst. prof. neurology Robert Wood Johnson Med. Sch., U. Medicine & Dentistry N.J., New Brunswick, 1984-91, assoc. prof. neurology, 1991-99, clin. prof. neurology, 1999—; asst. chief divsn. neurology Lyons (N.J.) VA Med. ctr., 1985-89; neurology cons. Lyons (N.J.) VA Med. Ctr., 1984-99; prof. neurosci. Seton Hall U. Sch. Grad. Med. Edn., South Orange, N.J., 1999—, N.J. Neurosci. Inst., Edison, 1999—. Nat. chmn. med. adv. bd. Restless Legs Syndrome Found., 1992-98; organizer Internat. Restless Legs Study Group, 1992—; head Restless Legs Syndrome and Periodic Limb Movement Coun. for the Nat. Sleep Found., 1994-96; neurology cons. Coney Island Hosp., Bklyn., Bklyn. Jewish Hosp., 1980-81; presenter in field. Contbr. articles to profl. publs., chpts. to books; organizer symposia. Grantee UMDNJ, 1984-86, VA RAG, 1985-86, Sandoz Corp., 1985-88, VA Merit Rev., 1989-98, Clemente Found., 1994-95, Purdue Pharma, 2000—, NIH, 2002. Fellow Am. Acad. Neurology, Am. Sleep Disorders Assn.; mem. AAAS, Sleep Rsch. Soc., Movement Disorder Soc., N.Y. Acad. Scis., N.J. Sleep Soc. (sec. 1995-96, treas. 1996-97, v.p. 1998-99). Home: 207 S Adelaide Ave Highland Park NJ 08904-1605 Office: 65 James St Edison NJ 08820-3947 E-mail: artumdnj@aol.com.

WALTERS, BARBARA, television journalist; b. Sept. 25, 1931; d. Lou and Dena (Selett) W.; 1 child, Jacqueline. Grad., Sarah Lawrence Coll., 1953; LHD (hon.), Ohio State U., Marymount Coll., Tarrytown, N.Y., 1975, Wheaton Coll., 1983. Former writer-producer WNBC-TV; then with Stas. WPIX and CBS-TV; joined Today Show, 1961, regular panel mem., 1964-74, co-host, 1974-76; moderator syndicated program Not For Women Only, 1974-76; newscaster ABC Evening News (now ABC World News Tonight), 1976-78; host The Barbara Walters Spls., 1976—; co-host ABC TV news show 20/20, 1979—; co-exec. prodr., co-owner, co-host The View, ABC, N.Y.C., 1997—. Contbr. to ABC programs Issues and Answers. Author: How To Talk With Practically Anybody About Practically Anything, 1970; contbr. to Reader's Digest, Good Housekeeping, Family Weekly. Recipient award of yr. Nat. Assn. TV Program Execs., 1975, Emmy award Nat. Acad. TV Arts and Scis., 1975, Mass Media award Am. Jewish Com. Inst. Human Relations, 1975, Hubert H. Humphrey Freedom prize Anti-Defamation League-B'nai B'rith, 1978, Matrix award N.Y. Women in Communications, 1977, Barbara Walters' Coll. Scholarship in Broadcast Journalism established in her honor Ill. Broadcasters Assn., 1975, Pres.'s award Overseas Press Club, 1988, Lowell Thomas award Marist Coll., 1990, Lifetime Achievement award Internat. Women's Media Found., 1992, Lifetime Achievement award Daytime Emmy Awards, 2000; named to 100 Women Accomplishment Harper's Bazaar, 1967, 71, One of Am.'s 75 Most Important Women Ladies' Home Jour., 1970, One of 10 Women of Decade Ladies' Home Jour., 1979, One of Am.'s 100 Most Important Women Ladies' Home Jour., 1983, Woman of Year in Communications, 1974, Woman of Year Theta Sigma Phi, Broadcaster of Yr. Internat. Radio and TV Soc., 1975, One of 200 Leaders of Future Time Mag., 1974, One of Most Important Women of 1979 Roper Report, One of Women Most Admired by Am. People Gallup Poll, 1982, 84, to Hall of Fame Acad. TV Arts and Scis., 1990 Office: 20/20 147 Columbus Ave Fl 10 New York NY 10023-5900*

WALTERS, BILL, state senator, lawyer; b. Paris, Apr. 17, 1943; s. Peter Louis and Elizabeth Cecelia (Wilhelm) W.; m. Joyce Leslie Garrett Moore, Jan. 9, 1964 (div. 1970); children: Jamie, Sherry Ann; m. Shirley Ann Dixon, Aug. 20, 1971; 1 child, Sandra. BS, U. Ark., 1966, JD, 1971. Bar: Ark. 1971, U.S. Dist. Ct. Ark. 1971. Asst. prosecuting atty. 12th Jud. Dist. Ark., Ft. Smith, 1971-74; pvt. practice Greenwood, Ark., 1975—; mem. Ark. Senate, Little Rock, 1982-2000. Bd. dirs., sec.-treas. Mineral Owners Collective Assn. Inc., Greenwood; v.p., bd. dirs. Sebastian County Abstract & Title Ins. Co., Greenwood and Ft. Smith, Ark.; mem. Ark. Real Estate Commn., Ark. Abstract and Title Commn. Committeeman Rep. Ctrl. Com. Ark., Ft. Smith, 1980; search pilot CAP, Ft. Smith. Decorated Silver Medal of Valor; recipient Cert. of Honor Justice for Crime's Victims, 1983. Mem. Ark. Bar Assn., South Sebastian County Bar Assn. (pres. 1991-94), Profl. Landmen's Assn. Roman Catholic. Home: PO Box 280 Greenwood AR 72936-0280 Office: 1405 W Center Greenwood AR 72936-3200 E-mail: walters@waltlaw.net.

WALTERS, BRANDY S. writer; b. Reading, Pa., Nov. 23, 1973; d. Karen E. DeWitte and Bruce H. Walters, Mark H. De Witte (Stepfather). BA, La Salle U., Phila., 1995. Writer/editor Shared Med. Systems, Malvern, Pa., 1995—99; writer Med. Broadcasting Co., Phila., 1999—2002; sr. writer Insight Interactive Group, 2002—02, content mgr., 2002—. Editor: (book) Lyrical Ballads: The Complete Works of William Wordsworth, 1999. Mem. Phila. Ethical Soc., 2002. Recipient Robert L. Dean award for Excellence in Writing, Robert L. Dean Scholarship Fund, 1998. Mem.: Am. Med. Writers Assn., Phila. Art Dirs. Club. D-Liberal. Avocations: acoustic guitar, cooking, exercise, reading. Office: Insight Interactive Group 121 N Broad St 6th Fl Philadelphia PA 19107 Personal E-mail: bwalters@insight-interactive.com. E-mail: bwalters@insight-interactive.com.

WALTERS, CARRIE LOU, neurosurgeon; b. Salem, Oreg., Sept. 28, 1945; d. Eugene F. and Thelma L. Walters. BA in Chemistry, Willamette U., Salem, 1967; MD, Northwestern U., Chgo., 1971. Neurosurg. resident U. Chgo., 1977; neurosurg. fellow NIH, Bethesda, Md., 1977-79; asst. prof. neurosurgery U. Vt., Burlington, 1980-87; pvt. practice neurosurgery Neurol. Surgeons, P.C., Phoenix, 1988—. Vis. prof. Dartmouth Coll., Hanover, N.H., 1982, U. Nev., Reno, 1983; co-capt. Spinal Cord Injury Team, U. Vt. Contbr. articles to profl. jours., chpts. to books. Lt. comdr. nat. Health Svc., 1977-79. Recipient award Ariz. Humane Soc., Phoenix, 1999. Mem. AMA, Rsch. Soc. Neurol. Surgeons, New Eng. Neurol. Soc., Am. Assn. Neurol. Surgeons, Congress Neurol. Surgeons, Am. Spinal Injury Assn., Maricopa County Med. Soc. Avocations: scuba diving, travel, animal rights. Office: Neurol Surgeons PC 345 E Virginia Phoenix AZ 85004

WALTERS, CHARLES JOSEPH, real estate developer; b. Phila., Mar. 11, 1945; s. Vincent William and Gertrude Clare Walters; children: Charles J., Timothy M., Kristen A., Kathleen M., Lindsay E., Ryan M.; m. Sharleen Sandler, Dec. 1, 1984. BS, Drexel U., 1968; MBA, U. Pa., 1972. Project mgr. Griffith Services, Inc., Jacksonville, Fla., 1967-69; asst. to pres. Valley Forge (Pa.) Corp., 1972-74; v.p. Pureland Indsl. Complex, Bridgeport, Pa., 1976—. Bd. dirs. Ctr. Sq. Real Estate Devel. Co., Inc., Ctr. Sq. Builders. Bd. dirs. South Jersey Devel. Coun., South Jersey Tech. Consortium, Gloucester County Coll. Human Resource Devel., So. N.J. C. of C. Decorated Silver Star with oak leaf cluster, Bronze Star with Valor device, Purple Heart with oak leaf cluster, Air medal. Mem. Nat. Assn. Office and Indsl. Parks, Soc. Indsl. Realtors, Soc. for Advancement Mgmt., Raquet Club, Wharton Club. Home: Frog Spring Farm PO Box 544 Chadds Ford PA 19317-0544 Office: Pureland Indsl Complex 510 Heron Dr Bridgeport NJ 08014

WALTERS, CLAUDIA M. management consultant; b. Detroit, Mar. 3, 1950; d. Leonard Angelo and Mary Castiglione; m. Russell John Collins, July 24, 1970 (div. Feb. 1974); m. Grant Robert Walters, Mar. 20, 1979; stepchildren: Grant Robert III, Josh William. Student, U. Detroit. Dental hygienist Office Dr. Felix Abaldo, Harper Woods, Mich., 1970-76, Office Dr. Grant R. Walters, St. Clair Shores, 1970-87; profl. mgmt. cons. Paul Goldman & Assocs., Southfield, 1987-96. Artist, ceramics, 1985-88. Sponsor Cops for Kids, St. Clair Shores, 1987-89. Republican. Methodist. Avocations: tennis, private pilot, SCUBA diver. Home: 4495 Philbrook Sq San Diego CA 92130

WALTERS, DAVID, musician; b. Evanston, Ill., Apr. 4, 1962; s. Harold L. and Dolores Miller Walters. BFA in Music Performance-Music Edn., Fla. Atlantic U., 1986; MusM in Music Industry-Entertainment Bus., U. Miami, Coral Gables, Fla., 1990. Music cons. Promusic, Inc., Boca Raton, 1989—99; artist-in-residence Broward Band Instruments & Music, Ft. Lauderdale, 1999—. Assoc. prodr. Global Solutions Network, Deerfield Beach, 1999—2001; music exec. Ind. Music Assocs. (IMA), Ft. Lauderdale; music educator, music cons. Broward County Pub. Schs., Ft. Lauderdale. Recipient 1st. place award winds divsn., Nat. Fedn. Music Clubs Student Auditions, Fla., 1983, 1st pl. award winds divsn., Nat. Fedn. Music Clubs Student Auditions, S.E. region, 1985, nat. finalist winds divsn., Nat. Fedn. Music Clubs Student Auditions, 1985, Gold Coast Trio, Nat. Chamber Music award, Nat. Fedn. Music Clubs, 1998, award, Aspen Music Festival, Colo., 1985, Victoria Internat. Music Festival, B.C., 1986, 1st pl. award winds divsn., Nat. Fedn. Music Clubs Student Auditions, Fla., 1985; scholar Dorothy Schmidt Music scholar, Fla. Atlantic U., 1983—86. Mem.: Nat. Flute Assn., Fla. State Music Tchrs. Assn., Fla. Fedn. Music Clubs, Alpha Lambda Delta, Phi Mu Alpha. Personal E-mail: VirtuosoFL@aol.com.

WALTERS, DONALD BENJAMIN, JR. civil engineer; b. Newark, June 4, 1950; s. Donald B. and Helen M. (Rickerhauser) W.; m. Kathleen R. Vogel; children: Allison S., Sara N., Brian D. MS, Cornell U., 1974; MBA, Fla. Inst. Tech., 1987. Registered profl. engr., N.J., Pa., Fla. Resident asst. Elson T. Killam Assocs., Millburn, N.J., 1972-74; mgr. S.E. ops. Burns & Roe, Oradell, 1974-89; mgr. new generation Gilbert/Commonwealth, Inc., Reading, Pa., 1989—98; v.p. BD Constellation Power, 1998—2001. v.p. project devel., 2001—. Bd. dirs. Suntree United Meth. Ch., Melbourne, Fla., 1986. Mem. ASCE, ASME, Internat. Soc. Pharm. Engrs., Tech. Assn. Pulp and Paper Industries, Tau Beta Pi, Chi Epsilon. Republican. Home: 78 Palomino Dr North Andover MA 01845-3377

WALTERS, DONALD LEE, education educator; b. Roachdale, Ind., Feb. 13, 1937; s. Lee and Beryl (Douglas) W.; m. Nina Walters, June 10, 1972; 1 child, Mark R. BS, Ind. U., 1959, MS, 1960; EdD, U. Miami, 1966. Tchr. math. Kokomo (Ind.)-Ctr. Twp. Schs., 1961-63; asst. to bus. mgr. Dade County Sch. Dist., Miami, Fla., 1964-65; prof. edn. Temple U., Phila., 1966—, Charles

Erny prof. edn., chair dept. ednl. leadership and policy studies, pres. faculty senate, univ. marshal, prof. emeritus, 2002—. Cons. on sch. fiscal adminstrn.; speaker in field. Author: Financial Analysis for Academic Units, 1981, (with James J. Jones) Human Resource Management in Education, 1994; contbr. articles to profl. jours. Cert. lay speaker, United Meth. Ch. Capt. USAR, 1959-66. Mem. Am. Fedn. Tchrs., Assn. Sch. Bus. Ofcls. Internat. (panel of rev. for cert. of excellence in fin. reporting), NEA, Univ. Coun. for Ednl. Adminstrn., Phi Eta Sigma, Phi Kappa Phi, Phi Delta Kappa. E-mail: dwalters@temple.edu.

WALTERS, DORIS LAVONNE, pastoral counselor, counseling services facility administrator; b. Peachland, N.C., Feb. 24, 1931; d. H. Lloyd and Mary Lou (Helms) W. AA, Gardner Webb U., 1959; BA cum laude, Carson-Newman Coll., 1961; MRE, Southwestern Bapt. Theol. Sem., 1963; MA in Pastoral Counseling, Wake Forest U., 1982; DMIn in Pastoral Counseling, Southeastern Bapt. Theol. Sem., 1988. Min. of edn. and youth First Bapt. Ch., Orange, Tex., 1963-66; assoc. prof. Seinan Jo Gakuin Jr. Coll., Japan, 1968-72; dir. Fukuoka (Japan) Friendship House, 1972-88, pastoral counselor, chaplain, 1983-86; Tokyo lifeline referral counselor (in English) Hiroshima-South, Fukuoka, 1983-86; supr. Japanese and Am. staff Fukuoka Friendship House, 1972-86; with chaplaincy Med. Coll. Va., Richmond, 1976; resident chaplain N.C. Bapt. Hosp., Winston-Salem, 1981-82, counselor-in-tng. pastoral care dept., 1986-88; dir. missionary counseling and support svcs. Pastoral Care Found. N.C. Bapt. Hosp., 1989-93; dir. Missionary Family Counseling Svcs., Inc., 1993—. Mem. Japan Bapt. Mission Exec. Com., Tokyo, 1973-76. Author: An Assessment of the Reentry Issues of the Children of Missionaries, 1991, 2d printing with title Missionary Children: Caught between Cultures, 1996; translator: The Story of the Craft Dogs, 1983. Trustee Gardner Webb U., 1999—. Named Alumnus of Yr., Gardner Webb U., 1993; J.M. Price scholar Southwestern Bapt. Theol. Sem., 1962; First Bapt. Ch. Blackwell grantee Southeastern Sem., 1986-88. Mem. Am. Assn. Pastoral Counselors, Am. Psychotherapy Assn. (diplomate). Democrat. Avocations: photography, travel, reading, classical music, concerts. Home: 208 Oakwood Sq Winston Salem NC 27103 Office: Missionary Family Counseling Svcs Inc 514 S Stratford Rd Winston Salem NC 27103-1823 E-mail: mfcs@juno.com.

WALTERS, GEORGE JOHN, oral and maxillofacial surgeon; b. Balt., June 16, 1956; s. George John Sr. and Henrietta Jean (Parker) W.; m. Melanie Ann Goodreau, June 23, 1989. BS, Loyola Coll., 1978; DDS, U. Md., 1983; postgrad., John Hopkins, 1991, U. Pa., 1992, postgrad., 1993. Cert. argon laser. Rsch. asst. dept. otolaryngology The Johns Hopkins Sch. Medicine, Balt., 1978-79; ind. learning ctr. technician Balt. Coll. Dental Surgery, Dental Sch., U. Md., 1980-81; audio-visual technician U. Md. Law Sch., Balt., 1981-82, res. material circulation asst., 1982-83; resident gen. practice residency York (Pa.) Hosp., 1983-84; resident dept. anesthesia The Med. Coll. of Pa. and Hosp., Phila., 1984-85; resident dept. dentistry div. oral and maxillofacial surgery U. Md. Med. System, Balt., 1985-89, chief adminstrv. resident dept. dentistry, 1988-89; assoc. in oral and maxillofacial surgery Miller Oral Surgery and Pa. Jaw Treatment Ctr., Harrisburg, Pa., 1989-91; ptrn. Oral and Maxillofacial Surgery, Panama City, Fla., 1991-95; individual practice oral and maxillofacial surgery, 1995—. Explorer advisor for health career explorer post Balt. Coll. Dental Surgery, Dental Sch., U. Md., 1981, dental rsch. student com., 1982, vol. for recruitment of minority students, 1983; testifier Sen. House Com. on Medicaid Funding, State House, Annapolis, Md., 1987-88; lectr. Gulf Coast C.C., 1991—. Copntbr. to profl. jours. Health vol. overseas Nepal Mission for Cleft Lip and Palate, 1989; vol. Guatemala Med. Mission Cleft Lip and Palate, 1994; bd. dirs. Am. Cancer Soc. Bay County, 1996-97; chmn. Cath. sharing appeal St. Bernadette's Ch., Panama City, 1996-98, eucharistic min.; lectr. St. Romalotto's Parish. John Hopkins fellow 1989. Mem. ADA, Am. Assn. Oral and Maxillofacial Surgery, Mid. Atlantic Soc. Oral and Maxillofacial Surgery, Bay County Dental Soc. (sec./treas. 1997-98, v.p. 1998-99), Fla. Dental Soc., N.W. Dental Soc. Fla., Fla. Soc. Oral and Maxillofacial Surgery, Gorgas Odontological Soc., Rotary, Bay County Civil War Roundtable, Gamma Pi Delta. Roman Catholic. Avocations: golf, boating, baseball, travel, reading. Office: 2202 State Ave Ste 200 Panama City FL 32405-4582 Home: 1906 Dewitt St Panama City FL 32401-4049

WALTERS, GLEN ROBERT, banker; b. Mpls., Sept. 11, 1943; s. Sterling Thomas and Mildred Eunice (Parkinson) W.; m. Gail Elvira Engelsen, June 11, 1966; children— Nicole Marie, Brent Aaron, Hillary Renee. BA, U. Minn., Mpls., 1965, postgrad., 1965-67; banking degree, Stonier Grad. Sch. Banking, Rutgers U., New Brunswick, N.J., 1982. Comml. banker 1st Nat. Bank, Mpls., 1967-83, sr. v.p. human resources, 1983-90; sr. v.p. Firstar Bank Minn., 1990-2001, US Bank, Mpls., 2001—. Served to sgt. USNG, 1967-73 Republican. Presbyterian. Office: US Bank 9633 Lyndale Ave S Minneapolis MN 55420

WALTERS, JEFFERSON BROOKS, musician, retired real estate broker; b. Dayton, Ohio, Jan. 20, 1922; s. Jefferson Brooks and Mildred Frances (Smith) W.; m. Mary Elizabeth Espey, Apr. 6, 1963 (dec. July 22, 1983); children: Dinah Christine Basson, Jefferson Brooks; m. Carol Elaine Clayton Gillette, Feb. 19, 1984. Student, U. Dayton, 1947. Composer, cornetist, Dayton, 1934—; real estate broker, 1948-88; ret., 1988. Condr., composer choral, solo voice settings of psalms and poetry Alfred Lord Tennyson; composer Crossing the Bar (meml. performances U.S. Navy band), 1961; composer The Yorktown Grand March (Good Citizenship medal SAR, 1988). Founder Am. Psalm Choir, 1965; apptd. deferred giving officer Kettering (Ohio) Med. Ctr., 1982-85. Served with USCGR, 1942-45, PTO, ETO. Mem. SAR (life), Greater Dayton Antique Study Club (past pres.), Dayton Art Inst., Montgomery County Hist. Soc., Masons (32d deg.). Brethren Ch. Home: 4113 Roman Dr Dayton OH 45415-2423

WALTERS, SISTER JOANNE-THERESA, social worker; b. Bklyn., Jan. 28, 1942; d. Joseph Vincent and Mary Cecilia (Jacobs) W. BA, St. Francis Coll., Bklyn., 1972; MA in Teaching, St. Michael U., Winooski, Vt., 1976; cert., Postgrad. Inst. Mental Health, 1981; MSW, Yeshiva U., 1986. Cert. sch. social worker, pastoral counselor, English tchr., N.Y. With Sisters St. Dominic, N.Y., 1960—; elem. tchr. Cath. schs. Diocese of Bklyn., 1962-72, dir. religious edn. Cath. chs., 1972-80; co-dir. Samaria Prayer Ctr., Hicksville, N.Y., 1980-86; sch. social worker United Cerebral Palsy, Bklyn., 1986-89, Martin DePorres Sch., Springfield Gardens, N.Y., 1989—; psychotherapist Ecumenical Consultation Ctr., Hicksville, 1984-99. Rite of Christian Initiation of Adults team mem., choir AIDS Ministry, st. Helen's Parish, Howard Beach, N.Y. Mem. NASW (diplomate, cert.).

WALTERS, JOHN P. federal agency administrator; BA, Mich. State U.; MA, U. Toronto. Acting asst. dir. and program officer div. edn. programs NEH, 1982—85; asst. to sec. U.S. Dept. Edn., 1985—88; dep. dir. supply reduction Office Nat. Drug Control Policy, Washington, 1991—93; dir. exec. office of pres. Office Nat Drug Control Policy, 2001—. Vis. fellow Hudson Inst., 1993; instr. polit. sci. Mich. State U., Boston Coll. Co-author: (book) How to Win America's War Against Crime and Drugs. Pres. New Citizenship Program. Mem.: Philanthropy Roundtable (pres. 1996—2001). Office: Exec Office of Pres Office Nat Drug Control Policy 750 17th St NW Washington DC 20503*

WALTERS, JOHN SHERWOOD, retired newspaperman; b. Junction City, Ark., May 15, 1917; s. John Thomas and Cora (McBride) W.; m. Claire Dailey, June 1, 1941; children: Elizabeth Claire, Mary Dailey (dec.). BA, La. Tech. Inst., 1939; MA, La. State U., 1941. Editor Ruston (La.) Daily Leader, 1940; reporter Baton Rouge Morning Adv., 1941; rating examiner Jacksonville Naval Air Sta., 1941-42; reporter Fla. Times-Union, Jacksonville, 1943, 44-53, city editor, 1953-60; exec. editor Times-Union and Jacksonville Jour., 1960-78, asso. pub., 1978-82, ret., 1982. Asst. prof. journalism La. Tech. Inst., 1943-44; mem. jud. Nominating Commn., 1st Dist. Ct. Appeals of Fla. Bd. dirs. Duval County chpt. A.R.C., chmn., 1966-67; charter trustee U. North Fla. Found., Inc., pres., 1973-75; chmn. council advisers U. North Fla., 1975; bd. dirs. Health Planning Council, N.E. Fla. Cancer Program, Jacksonville Blood Bank. Mem. Am. Soc. Newspaper Editors, Fla. Soc. Newspaper Editors (pres. 1971-72), Alpha Lambda Tau, Sigma Delta Chi. Clubs: Rotarian (Jacksonville) (sec. 1970-71, pres. 1971-72); Timuquana Country. Democrat. Methodist. Home: 1750 Dogwood Pl Jacksonville FL 32210-2202

WALTERS, JOHNNIE MCKEIVER, lawyer; b. Hartsville, S.C., Dec. 20, 1919; s. Tommie Ellis and Lizzie Dee (Grantham) W.; m. Donna Lucile Hall, Sept. 1, 1947; children: Donna Dianne Walters Gent, Lizbeth Kathern Walters Kukorowski, Hilton Horace, John Roy. AB, Furman U., 1942, LLD, 1973; LLB, U. Mich., 1948. Bar: Mich. 1948, N.Y. 1955, S.C. 1961, D.C. 1973. Atty. office chief counsel IRS, Washington, 1949-53; asst. mgr. tax div. law dept. Texaco, Inc., N.Y.C., 1953-61; ptnr. firm Geer, Walters & Demo, Greenville, SC, 1961-69; asst. atty. gen. tax div. Dept. Justice, Washington, 1969-71; commr. IRS, 1971-73; ptnr. firm Hunton & Williams, Washington, 1973-79, Leatherwood Walker Todd & Mann, P.C., Greenville, 1979-95; exec. v.p., gen. counsel Colonial Trust Co., 1996—. Bd. dirs. Textile Hall Corp., Greenville, Santee Cooper. Mem. S.C. Coun. on Competitiveness, 1987-91; bd. dirs. Greenville Hosp. System Found., S.C. State Mus. Found. With USAF, 1942—45. Fellow Am. Coll. Tax Counsel (founding regent), Am. Coll. Trust and Estate Counsel, Am. Bar Found., S.C. Bar Found. (bd. dirs. 1988-92); mem. ABA (taxation sect.), S.C. Bar (chmn. taxation sect. 1983-84), Rotary (pres. local club 1968-69). Republican. Baptist. Office: Colonial Trust Co PO Box 2817 Greenville SC 29602-2817 Home: 1804 N Main St Greenville SC 29609-4729

WALTERS, KENNETH C. retired educator; b. Constantine, Mich., Apr. 2, 1913; s. Roy Irvin and Pearl Valentine (Ashbaugh) Walters. Student, Western Mich. U., 1931-35; MA in Math., MA in Edn., U. Mich., 1948; PhD in Math., U. Fla., 1952. Tchr. coll. level, 1936-52. One-man shows include , Thousand Oaks, Calif; author: (novels) Gone with the Winter, 1980, I, the President, 1980, (plays) Irene, the Nurse's Aide, 1980, (instructional) Begineers Play Piano in 60 Minutes, 1996, numerous poems, performer (standup comedian) ; composer: songs for comms, Broadway musicals; musician: Hollywood Quints. Advisor to Bill Clinton; mem steering comt Al Gore's Campaign. Scholar 4-yr, Western Mich Univ, 1931—35. Mem.: Burbank Catalina Art Asn (pres), San Fernando Art Club. Home: 2233 N Catalina St Burbank CA 91504-3246

WALTERS, LINDA JANE, marine biologist, educator, researcher; b. Easton, Pa., Aug. 2, 1961; d. Lee Rudyard and Evelyn (Hood) W.; m. Paul Eric Sacks, Aug. 2, 1992; children: Joshua. BS, Bates Coll., 1983; MS, U. S.C., 1986, PhD, 1991. Project leader Operation Raleigh, Chile, Australia, N.Z., Alaska, 1985-87; rschr. U. Hawaii-Manoa, Honolulu, 1992—; coord. UCF/SeaWorld Whale Watch Program. Asst. prof. U. Ctrl. Fla., Orlando, 1997--; dir. U. Ctrl. Fla., Fellers House Field Sta., 1997--. Contbr. articles to profl. jours. Recipient Lerner-Gray award Am. Mus. Natural History, 1986, 90, Excellence in Undergrad. Tchg. award UCF Coll. Arts and Scis., 1999-2000; Fulbright Indo-Am. fellow, 1993; NOAA grantee, 2000-01.. Mem. AAUW (America fellowship 1990-91), Assn. for Women in Sci. (mentor 1992—), Am. Soc. Zoologists, Ecol. Soc. Am., Internat. Bryozoan Assn., Western Soc. Naturalists, Soc. Comparative and Integrative Biology (sec. ecology and evolution divsn. 1999-2001), Sigma Xi (outstanding grad. award 1992). Home: 556 Whipporwill Ln Oviedo FL 32765 Office: Dept Biology U Ctrl Fla Orlando FL 32816

WALTERS, MATTHEW PAUL, recreational facility executive, consultant; b. Columbus, Ohio, Aug. 3, 1977; s. Thomas Edward and Kathy Ann Walters. BA, Ottawa U., 2002. Mktg., and pub. rels. Artist Direct, Encino, Calif., 1998—2000; owner Adventure Ventures, Tempe, Ariz., 1998—. Vol. plan creator Good Samaritan Hosp., Phoenix, 2001. Mem.: IndUS Entrepreneur. R-Liberal. Roman Catholic. Avocations: running, basketball. Home: 1544 Compromise Line Glendora CA 91741 Personal E-mail: matt.walters@ptk.org.

WALTERS, MILTON JAMES, investment banker; b. Hornell, N.Y., May 21, 1942; s. James Henry and Frances Eleanor (Simmons) W.; m. Caroline Houck, May 24, 1963; children: Melissa Ann, Gregory Thomas, Timothy Allen. BA, Hamilton Coll., 1964. Trainee Mfrs. Hanover, 1964-65; with A.G. Becker Paribas Inc., N.Y.C., 1965-84, v.p., 1969-78; mng. dir. Smith Barney, 1984-88, Prudential Securities, N.Y.C., 1997-99; pres. Tri-River Capital, 1988—; dir. Sun Healthcare Group, Inc., 2001—. Dir. Murray Discount AutoStores SunHealthcare Group and Quest Products. Trustee Hamilton Coll., Clinton, N.Y., 1983-88, Friends Acad., Locust Valley, N.Y., 1981-91; pres. 16 Sutton Pl. Apt. Corp. Mem. Econ. Club N.Y., Mill River Club. Republican. Presbyterian. Office: Tri-River Capital PO Box 128 New York NY 10150-0128 E-mail: mwalters@tri-rivercapital.com.

WALTERS, PAUL HENRY, music educator, musician; b. Steeleville, Ill., 1932; s. August Karl and Anna Maria Walters; m. Marianna Henrietta Dirks Walters; children: David, Paul, KristeAnna, Kimberly, Maray Beth. BME, SIU, Carbondale, ILL, 1957; M.M., SIU, Carbondale, IL, 1958. Band dir. Webber Twp H.S., Bluford, Ill., 1958—60; orchestra Rantoul City Schools, Rantoul, 1960—62, music supr. Rantouls, 1962—87; organist Our Savior Lutherans Ch., Carbondale, 1951—58; organist choir dir. Peace Luth. Ch., Thomasbora, 1960—73; organist St.Paul's Luth. Church, Rantoul, 1973. Bd. menber IL, elementry Sch., Bloomington, Ill., 1956—70; pres. IL, Music Edn. Assn, Bloomington, Ill., 1980—83, Rantoul City Schools Edn. Ass, Rantoul, Ill., 1971—72. Bd. mem. Randoul Exch. Club, Randoul, Ill., 1998—2001, pres., 2001—02. Sp 3 U.S. Army, 1956—58, Japan. Recipient Who's who in Midwest, Marquis, 1999 to 2000. Mem.: MFNC (assoc.), Phi Beha Mu (assoc.; bd. mem. 1999—2000). Lutheran. Avocations: fishing, photography, taraveling. Home: 609 Eden Park Drive Rantoul IL 61866 Personal E-mail: pwol250098@aol.com.

WALTERS, PHILIP RAYMOND, foundation executive; b. Frankfort, Ind., Jan. 26, 1938; s. Raymond and Ruth Edna (Grimes) W.; m. Sharon Pearl Wilfong, May 31, 1958 (div. Nov. 1992); children: Raymond (dec.), Robert, Sharon Ruth; m. Candace Gina Oden, Jan. 29, 1994. BSBA, Olivet Nazarene Coll., 1959; JD, Ind. U., Indpls., 1969; postgrad., NYU, 1969-70. Bar: Ind. 1969, U.S. Dist. Ct. (so. dist.) Ind. 1969. Co-corp. counsel Ind. Farm Bur. Ins., Indpls., 1975-79; dir. gift and estate planning Orlando (Fla.) Regional Healthcare Found., 1991-96; assoc. v.p. planned giving Arthritis Found., Atlanta, 1996—. Dep. atty. gen. State of Ind., Indpls.; planned giving officer Wheaton (Ill.) Coll.; campaign dir. Ketchum, Inc., Pitts.,; dir. planned giving Presbyn. Sch. Christian Edn., Richmond, Va.; presenter in field. Contbr. articles to profl. jours. Mem.: Assn. Fundraising Profls., Nat. Com. on Planned Giving. Republican. Presbyterian. Avocation: golf, auto racing, reading. Home: 897 Cutler Rd Longwood FL 32779-3525

WALTERS, RAYMOND, JR. newspaper editor, author; b. Bethlehem, Pa., Aug. 23, 1912; s. Raymond and Elsie (Rosenberg) W. AB, Swarthmore Coll., 1933; postgrad., Princeton U., 1933-35; MA, Columbia U., 1937, PhD, 1942. Editorial staff Current History mag., 1937-39; editorial staff Saturday Rev., 1946-58, book rev. editor, 1948-58; editor Encore mag., 1946-48; editor, columnist N.Y. Times Book Rev., 1958-82. Mem. fiction jury Pulitzer Prize adv. bd., 1968 Author: Alexander James Dallas: Lawyer, Politician, Financier, 1943, Albert Gallatin: Jeffersonian Financier and Diplomat, 1957 (named One of Notable Books of Year, ALA), The Virginia Dynasty, 1965, Paperback Talk, 1985; Contbr. articles to profl. jours. Served with USAAF, 1942-46; hist. office hdqrs. USAAF, 1943-46. Mem. Am. Hist. Assn., Soc. Am. Historians. Episcopalian. Home: 1800 Riverside Dr Apt 305 Columbus OH 43212

WALTERS, RICHARD FRANCIS, computer science educator; b. Teleajen, Romania, Aug. 30, 1930; s. Ray Pearce and Gertrude (Gravett) W.; m. Shipley Newlin, Aug. 30, 1952; children: Leslie Walters Tuomi, David Todd. BA magna cum laude, Williams Coll., 1952; MA, U. Wyo., 1953; Diplome superieur en scis. naturalles, U. Bordeaux, France, 1955; PhD, Stanford U., 1957. Geologist Humble Oil and Refining Co., Los Angeles, 1956-60, subsurface geologist Chico, Calif., 1960-63, sr. subsurface geologist New Orleans, 1963-66; sr. research geologist Esso Prodn. Research Co., Houston, 1966-67; lectr. computer sci. U. Calif., Davis, 1967-68, asst. prof. med. edn. and biomed. engirng., 1968-73, assoc. prof. med. edn. and biomed. engring., 1973-78, assoc. prof. community health, 1978-79, prof. community health, 1979-83, prof. elec. and computer engring., 1980-83, prof., chair div. computer sci., 1983—, prof. family practice, 1984-96, prof. med. informatics, 1996—. Editorial cons. Soc. for Computer Simulations, 1970-76; editorial rev. bd. mem. Jour. of Computer Basted Instrn., 1975-89, Med. Informatics, 1977—, MUMPS Users' Group Quarterly, 1981—, Computers in Biology and Medicine, 1982—, MD Computing, 1985-93; contbr. articles to profl. jours. Fellow Am. Geol. Soc., Am. Coll. Med. Informatics; mem. Am. Arbitration Assn. Assn. Computing Machinery (mem. spl. interest group on programming langs. 1980—, 1974—, mem. spl. interest group on mgmt. data base, 1981), MUMPS Users' Group (vice chmn. 1974-75, chmn. 1975-77, 81-83, devel. com. chmn. 1977-79, 80-82, hon. life mem. Europe and Japan), Am. Assn. Med. Systems and Informatics, IEEE (sr.). Democrat. Episcopalian. Avocation: music. Home: 647 Elmwood Dr Davis CA 95616-3514 Office: U Calif Computer Sci Dv Davis CA 95616-8562

WALTERS, ROBERT ANCIL, physicist, mathematician; b. Russell Springs, Ky., Mar. 12, 1915; s. Robert Edmund Lee and Talitha Margaret (Wilson) W.; m. Etha Jane McKinley, Feb. 2, 1943; 1 child, Robert Ancil II; m. Sandra Faye Roy, June 29, 1969; 1 child, Forrest Wayne. BS, Western Ky. U., 1941; postgrad., George Washington U., 1943-45, Agrl. Grad. Sch., 1947-48, Am. U., 1951-52. H.S. asst. prin. Russell County Bd. Edn., 1941-42; physicist, head exterior ballistics U.S. Naval Weapons Lab., Dahlgren, Va., 1942-59; pres. Walters Ins. and Investment Counselor, 1948-80; engr., head systems planning U.S. Naval Space Surveillance, Va., 1959-69; R&D specialist, physicist interdisplinary math. cons. U.S. Naval Warfare Lab., 1969-75. Pres. Navel Weapons Lab. Fed. Credit Union, Dahlgren, 1968-74; bd. examiners Potomac River Naval Com., Washington, 1953-56; biology lab. instr. Western Ky. U., Bowling Green, 1935-36. Chmn. Old Dominion Eye Bank, Richmond, Va., 1975-76; co-chair Dem. Party, Ky., 1937-42; pres. Nat. Fedn. Fed. Employees, Washington, 1963-69. Recipient Nat. Quality award Nat. Assn. Life Underwriters, 1976; named Ky. Col., gov. of Ky., 1976, Outstanding Citizen of Yr., VFW, 1981, Guest of Honor King George County Fall Festival, 1994. Mem. Lions Internat. (dep. dist. gov. 1976-77, Disting. Svc. award 1975, Melvin Jones Fellow 2001). Baptist. Home: 5460 Potomac Dr PO Box 877 Dahlgren VA 22448-0877

WALTERS, RONALD OGDEN, mortgage banker; b. Holcombe, Wis., July 13, 1939; s. Ogden Eugene and Josephine Ann (Hennekens) W.; m. Margaret Ellen Weisheipl, July 14, 1962; children— Laurie, Cheryl, Michael, Patrick Student, U. Wis., 1959-62. Mgr. Thorp Fin., LaCrosse, Wis., 1962-65, regional mgr. Milw., 1965-69, ITT Consumer Fin. Corp., Milw., 1969-74, sr. v.p. Brookfield, Wis., 1974-90, exec. v.p. adminstrn., 1990-92; CEO Ideal Fin. Corp., 1993—, USA Funding Corp., Brookfield, Wis., 1993—. Mem. Wis. Fin. Services Assn. (pres. 1980) Republican. Roman Catholic. Avocations: boating, fishing, hunting. Home: 808 Back Bay Rd Delafield WI 53018-1528 also: 17035 W Wisconsin Ave Brookfield WI 53005-5734 E-mail: rowmew@earthlink.net.

WALTERS, ROSS A. federal judge; Magistrate judge U.S. Dist. Ct. (so. dist.) Iowa, 1994—. Office: US Courthouse Rm 440 123 E Walnut St Des Moines IA 50309-2035

WALTERS, SHERWOOD GEORGE, finance educator, consultant; b. Detroit, May 9, 1926; s. George Henry and Helen (Parker) Walters; m. Alexandra Sielcken, Sept. 4, 1952; children: Margaret Taylor Clifford, Karen Chapin, George Alexander, Virginia Sherwood McFee. BA cum laude, W. Maryland Coll., 1949; MS, Columbia U., 1950; MBA with distinction, Columbia U., Grad. Sch. Bus., 1953; PhD hons. scholar, NYU, 1960. Assoc. prof. econ. sociology Coll. Bus. Econ., Lehigh U., Bethlehem, Pa., 1950-60; exec. v.p., dir. ctrs., retail planning mgr. Mobil Oil, N.Y.C., 1960-65; exec. officer, mktg. dir. Gen. Tire & Rubber Internat. Plastics Co., Chem. Plastics Divsn., Akron, Ohio, 1965-70; prof. Rutgers U., Newark, 1970-93, prof. emeritus mgmt. studies, 1993—, founding dir. interfunctional mgmt. program, 1970-88. Cons. in field. Co-author: (book) Marketing Management Veiwpoints, 2d edit., 1970, Mandatory Housing Finance Programs, 1975, Managing the Industry University Cooperative Research Centers: A Guide for Directors and Other Stakeholders, 1998. Adv. nat. rep. congl. com. on tax reform, 2001; chmn. N.J. Gov. Pub. Utility Commn. Task Force, 1973—75, U./Indsl. Partnerships, John Von Neumann Ctr., Princeton, 1986. 1st lt. Inf./Quatermater Corps U.S. Army, 1944—47. Mem.: Newcomen Soc. Presbyterian. Avocation: deep sea fishing. Home: 110 Topsail Watch Ln Hampstead NC 28443-2728 E-mail: s.george.walters@worldnet.att.net.

WALTERS, SUE FOX, business executive, accountant; b. Louisville, June 9, 1941; d. Thomas Burke and Reva Crick Fox; m. Hugh Alexander Walters (dec. Feb. 2001); children: Thomas Wade Walters, Alexandra Walters Ebling. Student, N.C. State U., Ky. Wesleyan Coll. Acct., paralegal for fin. instns. and firms; ct. adminstr. 45th Jud. Cir. Ct., Ky.; v.p., treas. Alexander and Assocs., CATV cons. firm, Greenville; corp. adminstr., pub. corp. Bellevue, Wash.; sr. acctg. specialist Japanese/Am. automotive mfg. co., Bowling Green, Ky.; land developer. Pres., Jr. Woman's Club Greenville, 1964-65, Woman's Club of Greenville, 76-78; vice gov. 2nd dist. Ky. Fedn. Women's Clubs, 1980. Avocations: historical restoration, design, antiques, dogs, flying. Home: 151 N Main St Greenville KY 42345-1503

WALTERS, TOM FREDERICK, manufacturing company official; b. Des Moines, Oct. 18, 1931; s. Basil Leon and Reah E. (Handy) W.; m. Mary Katherine Russell, Dec. 8, 1956; children: Karen E., Juliet M., Thomas R., Alexandra K., Suzanne C. BA, Beloit Coll., 1953; postgrad., Northwestern U., 1962-66. Sales and advt. staff Eaton, Yale and Towne, Chgo., 1956-62, prodn. mgr., 1962-65; sr. cons. Cresap, McCormick & Paget, 1965-67; materials mgr. Joy Mfg. Co., Michigan City, Ind., 1967-73, gen. mgr. Elk Grove Village, Ill., 1973-87; mktg. mgr. Cooper Industries, 1987—. Contbr. articles to profl. jours. Pres. LaPorte County Young Reps., Ind., 1970-71; dist. chmn. Boy Scouts Am., 1972; elder, trustee 1st Presbyn. Ch., Libertyville, Ill., 1980-83; mem. village bd. Village of Long Beach, Ind., 1969. Lt. (j.g.) USNR, 1953-56, Far East. Mem.Indsl. Compressor Distbrs. Assn. (chmn. com. 1979-84), Constrn. Industry Mfrs. Assn. (bd. dirs., com. chmn. 1975-82), Am. Prodn. and Invenory Control Soc. (chpt. pres. 1970-71), Greater O'Hare Assn. Commerce and Industry, Quincy Hist. Soc., U.S. Power Squadrons, Abbey Yacht Club, Michigan City Yacht Club, Spring Lake Country Club, Phi Kappa Psi, Omicron Delta Kappa. Republican. Presbyterian. Avocations: boating, fishing, skiing, swimming. Home: 419 Spring Lake Dr Quincy IL 62305-1051 Office: 1800 Gardner Expy Quincy IL 62305-9364

WALTERS, WILLIAM BEN, chemistry educator; b. Highland, Kans., Apr. 26, 1938; s. Ben Guthrie and Dolly Varden (Shaw) W.; m. Barbara Lulu Sternaman, Aug. 5, 1962; children: Katharine, David. AS, Highland Coll., 1957; BS, Kans. State U., 1960; PhD, U. Ill., 1964. Asst. prof. MIT, Cambridge, 1965-70; assoc. prof. chemistry U. Md., College Park, 1970-77, prof., 1977—, assoc. chmn. dept., 1982-86. Vis. prof. U. Louvain, Belgium, 1978; chair U. Senate, 1999-00. Recipient Nuclear Chemistry award Am. Chemical Soc., 2001; Guggenheim fellow Oxford U., 1986-87, Von Humboldt fellow Univ. Mainz, 2001-02. Mem. Am. Phys. Soc., European Phys. Soc., Am. Chem. Soc. (chmn. div. nuclear chemistry 1986), Rotary (bd. dirs. College Park 1990-91, 2000—). Office: U Md Dept Chemistry College Park MD 20742-0001 E-mail: ww3@umail.umd.edu.

WALTERS, WILLIAM LEE, accountant; b. New Orleans, Feb. 26, 1946; s. Elton E. and Helen (England) W.; m. Wanda Lovorn, Aug. 24, 1968; 1 child, Jack. BS in Acctg., Miss. State U., 1969. CPA, Miss. Acct. Ellis & Hirsberg, CPA's, Clarksdale, Miss., 1969-75; prin. W.L. Walters, CPA's, 1975—. Founding dir. Found. for N.Am. Wild Sheep, Cody, Wyo., 1978-82, ofcl. measurer Boone and Crockett Club, 1997—; com. man U.S. Golf Assn., Far Hills, N.J., 1986-97; panel mem. Golf Digest 100 Greatest Courses, 1985—; bd. dirs. Lula-Rich Ednl. Found., Clarksdale, 1995-98, pres., 1997-98. Mem. AICPA, Miss. Soc. CPAs, Miss State U. Alumni Assn. (pres. Coahoma County chpt. 1996), Clarksdale Country Club (pres. 1980, 85), Bulldog Club (bd. dirs. 1986—), Old Waverly Golf Club. Methodist. Avocations: golf, hunting, bodybuilding, competitive water skiing. Home and Office: PO Box 896 Clarksdale MS 38614-0896

WALTERS-LUCY, JEAN MARIE, personal growth educator, consultant; b. St. Louis, Feb. 7, 1941; d. James Blaine Davenport and Helen Elizabeth (Vosbrink) Davenport; m. John E. Walters, Sept. 26, 1959 (div. Oct. 1975); m. Marvin Lucy, Aug. 13, 1988; children: Steven John, Debra Jean, Jeffrey Scott, Cynthia Leigh. D of Metaphys., Coll. of Metaphys., 1977; cert. reality therapist, Inst. Reality Therapy, 1982; DDiv, Ch. of Metaphys., 1977, Universal Life Ch., 1980. Personal growth cons., St. Louis, 1978—; tchr. personal growth Maryville U., 1988—, St. Louis C.C., 1992—. Co-host McKenna-Walters Psychotherapy radio show, Sta. KXOK, 1985; pres., sr. cons. Psi Bus. Cons., St. Louis, 1980-85; founder, pres. Mind Dynamics, St.

Louis, 1980-83; cons. Ctr. for Aging Studies, U. Mo., Kansas City, 1979-80. Author: (novels) Game of Life, Dreams & Symbology of Life, Look, Ma, I'm Flying, Choosing Health, Set Yourself Free, Evolution: The Master Plan; columnist: St. Louis Globe Dem., 1983—84, columnist: St. Louis Home Mag., 1985, columnist: St. Louis Fax Daily; prodr.: Transformation Radio; host: Transformation Radio, host: www.success-talk.com; prodr.: www.success-talk.com; columnist: Yes You Can, 1999—, host radio show: Positive Moments, 2000—01. Avocations: travel, writing, decorating, creative activities.

WALTH, BRENT DAVID, journalist, writer; b. Portland, OR, Nov. 8, 1961; s. Conrad Donald Walth, Megan David Walth; m. Shannon Leigh Buono. BS, University of Oregon, Eugene, Oregon, 1980—84. Senior reporter The Oregonian, Portland, OR, 1994—; Political reporter The Register-Guard, Eugene, 1990—94; Staff writer Willamette Week, Portland, 1986—90. Author: (Book) Fire at Eden's Gate: Tom McCall and the Oregon Story, 1994 (Award of Commendation, American Society of State and Local History, 1995). Recipient Gerald Loeb award for Distinguished Business and Financial Journalism, 1987, Bruce Baer award, 1999, Finalist, Pulitzer Prize for Explanatory Journalism, 2000, Finalist, Edward Meeman award for Environ. Reporting, 2000, Finalist, John B. Oakes award for Disting. Environ. Reporting, 2000, C.B. Blethen Meml. award for Disting. Newspaper Reporting, 2000, 2001, Pulitzer Prize for Pub. Svc., 2001, Unity awards in media, investigative reporting, 2001, Bruce Baer award, 2001, Young Alumnus award, U. Oreg., 2002. Office: The Oregonian 1320 S.W. Broadway Portland OR 97202

WALTHER, JOSEPH EDWARD, health facility administrator, retired physician; b. Indpls., Nov. 24, 1912; s. Joseph Edward and Winona (McCampbell) W.; m. Mary Margaret Ruddell, July 11, 1945 (dec. July 1983); children: Mary Ann Margolis, Karl, Joanne Landman, Suzanne Conran, Diane Paczesny, Kurt. BS, MD, Ind. U., 1936; postgrad., U. Chgo., Harvard U., U. Minn., 1945-47; DSc (hon.) , Ind. U., 1997, Purdue U., 1998. Diplomate Nat. Bd. Med. Examiners, Am. Bd. Internal Medicine, Am. Bd. Gastroenterology. Intern Meth. Hosp. and St. Vincent Hosp. of Indpls., 1936-37; physician, surgeon U.S. Engrs./Pan Am. Airways, Midway Island, 1937-38; chief resident, med. dir. Wilcox Meml. Hosp., Lihue, Kauai, 1938-39; internist, gastroenterologist Meml. Clinic Indpls., 1947-83, med. dir., pres., chief exec. officer, 1947—; founder, pres. Doctors' Offices Inc., Indpls., 1947—; founder, pres., chief exec. officer Winona Meml. Found. and Hosp. (now Walther Cancer Inst.), 1956—. Clinical asst. prof. medicine Ind. U. Sch. Medicine, Indpls., 1948-93, clin. asst. prof. emeritus, 1993—. Author: (with others) Current Therapy, 1965; mem. edit. rsch. bd. Postgrad. Medicine, 1982-83; contbr. articles to profl. jours. Bd. dirs. March of Dimes, Marion County div., 1962-66, Am. Cancer Soc., Ind. div., 1983-92. Col. USAAF, 1941-47, PTO. Decorated Bronze Star, Silver Star, Air medal; named to Pres.'s Cir., Ind. U., 1999; recipient Disting. Alumni Svc. award, 2001, Sing the Heroes award, Ind. U. Sch. Medicine, 2001, Healthcare Heroes Award for Corp. Achievement in healthcare, 2002. Mem.: AMA (del. 1970—76), Hoosier Hundred, Marion County Med. Assn., Ind. Med. Assn., Soc. Cons. to Armed Forces, Am. Coll. Gastroenterology (pres. 1970—71, master and charter, Weiss award 1988), Ind. U. Alumni Assn. (life), 702 Club, Indpls. Athletic Club, Waikoloa Golf and Country Club (Hawaii), Highland Golf and Country Club (hon.). Republican. Home: 3266 N Meridian St Ste 104 Indianapolis IN 46208-5846 Office: Walther Cancer Inst 3202 N Meridian St Indianapolis IN 46208-4646

WALTHER, RICHARD ERNEST, psychology educator, library administrator; b. Des Moines, Nov. 12, 1921; s. Rudolph Herman and Ruth Viola (Leekley) W.; m. Viola Eugenia Godwin, May 4, 1951; children: Mark Edward, Diane Elaine. Student, U. Ill., 1941-42; BA, Tex. Christian U., 1949-50, MA, 1950-52; EdD, North Tex. State U., Denton, 1954-62. Cert. Lifetime Teaching Credentials, Tex. Supt. Dallas Juvenile Home, 1951-61; v.p. rsch and devel. U.S. Industries, Ednl., N.Y.C., 1961-69; pres. Walther & Assoc., Silver Springs, Md., 1969-72; dir. of libr. Ambassador U., Pasadena, Calif., 1972-90, dir., instl. rsch. Big Sandy, Tex., 1990-92, assoc. dir. Coll. Libr., prof. psychology, 1992-96; prof. emeritus, 1996—. V.p. rsch. Humane Soc. of the U.S., Washington, 1968-70; tng. cons. Bell Telephone Labs., Piscataway, N.J., 1968-72. Author: Handling Behavior Problems, 1959. Mem. APA, Am. Ednl. Rsch. Assn. Avocations: photography, writing, research. Home: PO Box 211332 Bedford TX 76095-8332 Office: 2428 Spring Valley Dr Bedford TX 76021-4352 E-mail: richrew@earthlink.net.

WALTHER, ZERITA ESPERANCE, paralegal; b. N.Y.C., Nov. 22, 1927; d. James Alexander and Sarah Rebecca (Esperance) Potter; m. George P. Walther II; children: Joseph, Leona. BS in Edn., Met. Inst., London, 1973; cert. in labor studies, Cornell U., 1979; paralegal cert., Manhattanville Coll., 1984. Tchr. OEO, L.I. City, N.Y., 1966-69, Washington Bus. Inst., N.Y.C., 1969-70; editorial asst., feature writer N.Y. Times, 1973-85; legal asst. Marcus, Rippa & Gould, White Plains, N.Y., 1985-88; corp. legal asst. Kim Taylor Profls., 1988-92. Casting cons., 1962-63; bd. dirs., cons. Rockingchair Press News Svc., Elmsford, N.Y., 1978-93. Soprano Westfair Chamber Singers, Westchester, Fairfield Counties, 1991-94, White Plains Coalition Singers, 1993—, Our Lady of Mt. Carmel Adult Choir, Elmsford, 1989-94, St. Christopher's Adult Choir, Buchanan, 1994—. Sec. Women of Westchester, 1978-80; mem. Westchester Black Women's Polit. Caucus, 1989-91; coord. Elmsford chpt. Women in Self Help, 1982-84; mediator, vol. BBB, White Plains, 1983-85, Westchester Mediation Ctr., Yonkers, N.Y., 1988-91; legis. asst. to 12th dist. Westchester County legislator, White Plains, 1984-92; cert. ombudsman N.Y. State Office for the Aging, 1994—, VITA/TCE, AARP tax aide, Peekskill, 1995—; chaplain Chaplain program Hudson Valley Hosp. Ctr., Peekskill, Cortlandt, N.Y., 1998—. Lily Endowment Found. and Smithsonian Inst. scholar Sarah Lawrence Coll., summer 1979. Democrat. Roman Catholic. Avocations: singing (opera, classical, show tunes, gospel), numerology and astrology. Office: PO Box 431 Crugers NY 10521-0431

WALTHERS, BRUCE JULIUS, hobby industry executive; b. Plymouth, Wis., Sept. 9, 1919; s. William Kearney and Annette Esther (Peterson) W.; m. Barbara Anne Banach, Dec. 27, 1941 (dec. May 1991); children: Bruce J., Joanne B., J. Philip, Peter M., Judith L., Thomas W.; m. Marcia T. Obloy, Mar. 1, 1997. Diploma in meteorol. engring., UCLA, 1944; BPH in Bus., U. Wis., 1943. Treas. William K. Walthers, Inc., Milw., 1946-58, pres., 1958-84, chmn. bd. dirs., treas., 1984—. Bd. dirs. St. Anthony Hosp., Milw., 1978-84, pres., 1980-82; trustee Cardinal Stritch Coll., Milw., 1984-86; autoline arbitrator Better Bus. Bur., Milw., 1982-85. With USNR, 1943-46. Mem. Hobby Industry Am. (life, bd. dirs. 1971-86, pres. 1977-78, Meritorious Award Honor 1983), Model RR Industry Assn. (bd. dirs. 1967-73, pres. 1969-71, Hall Fame award 1996), Coun. Ind. Mgrs. (life, bd. dirs. 1962-84, pres. 1965-66). Home: 330 E Beaumont Ave Milwaukee WI 53217-4867 Office: 5601 W Florist Ave Milwaukee WI 53218-1622

WALTMAN, JEROLD LLOYD, political scientist, educator; b. Monroe, La., July 26, 1945; s. Otho Lloyd and Carlotta Waltman; m. Alta Faye Harrison, May 5, 1962 (div. Aug. 1984); children: Timothy, Amy; m. Linda Diane Waltman, June 12,1986. BA, La. Tech. U., Ruston, 1967; MA, U. Denver, 1969; PhD, Ind. U., Bloomington, 1976. Instr. Kankakee (Ill.) C.C., 1969-72; prof. La. Coll., Pineville, 1976-78, U. So. Miss., Hattiesburg, 1978—. Author: Copying Other Nations Policies, 1980, Political Origins of the Income Tax, 1985, American Government: Politics and Citizenship, 1993, 2d rev. edit., 1999, The Politics of the Minimum Wage, 2000. Mem. So. Polit. Sci. Assn., Miss. Polit. Sci. Assn., Am. Soc. Appraisers (bus. valuation sect.). Democrat. Lutheran. Avocations: hiking, fishing. Office: U So Miss Hardy St Hattiesburg MS 39402 E-mail: jerold.waltman@usm.edu.

WALTON, ALAN GEORGE, venture capitalist; b. Birmingham, Eng., Apr. 3, 1936; s. Thomas George and Hilda (Glover) W.; m. Jasmin Yvonne Christensen, Sept. 1, 1958 (dec. Nov. 1970); children: Kimm A., Keir D.A.; m. Elenor Jean McElliott, Aug. 6, 1977; children: Kristin M., Sherri L. PhD, U. Nottingham, Eng., 1960, DSc, 1973. Rsch. assoc. Ind. U., Bloomington, 1960-62; asst. prof. chemistry Case Western Res. U., Cleve., 1962-66, assoc. prof., 1966-69, assoc. prof. macromolecular sci., 1969-71, prof., 1971-81, dir. lab. for biol. macromolecules, 1972-81; pres., CEO Univ. Genetics Co., 1981-86, chmn., 1986-87; ptnr. Oxford Ptnrs., Westport, Conn., 1987—; chmn. Oxford Biosci. Corp., 1992—. Vis. lectr. biol. chemistry Harvard Med. Sch., 1971; mem. Pres. Carter's Task Force on Sci. and Tech.; U.S. project officer Rudjer Boskovic Inst., Zagreb, Yugoslavia, 1967—75; bd. dirs. Physiome Scis., Alexandria R.E.I.T., Rsch. Am.; chmn. Psychiat. Genomics Inc., Asterand Inc., Avalon Therapeutics, Cell Logic. Author: Formation and Properties of Precipitates, 1967, Biopolymers, 1973, Structure and Properties of Amorphous Polymers, 1980, Polypeptide and Protein Structure, 1981, Recombinant DNA, 1981, Yearbook of Genetic Engineering and Biotechnology, 1983, 85, 88, (biography) Beneath This Gruff Exterior There Beats a Heart of Plastic, 2000. Bd. dirs. Friends of Nottingham U. Recipient Israel State medal, 1972, Case Inst. Centennial Scholar medal, 1981. Mem. Nat. Venture Capital Assn., Sigma Xi (Research award 1973), Pi Kappa Alpha. Home: 11 Beachside Common Westport CT 06880 Office: Oxford Biosci Corp 315 Post Rd W Westport CT 06880-4739 E-mail: awalton@oxbio.com.

WALTON, ALICE L. bank executive; b. Newport, Ark., Oct. 7, 1949; d. Sam and Helen (Robson) W. BBA, Trinity U., 1971; D. of Bus. Adminstrn. (hon.), S.W. Bapt. U., 1988. Investment analyst First Commerce Corp., New Orleans, 1972-75; dir., v.p. investments Walton Enterprises, Bentonville, Ark., 1975—; retail & investment broker E.F. Hutton Co., New Orleans, 1975-79; vice chair, investment dir. Walton Bank Group, Bentonville, Ark., 1982-88; pres., chair, CEO Llama Co./Llama Asset Mgmt. Co., Fayetteville, 1988—. Dean's adv. coun. U. Ark. Coll. Bus. Adminstrn., Fayetteville, 1989-90; internat. judge Students in Free Enterprise, Springfield, Mo., 1990; bd. trustees The Asia Soc., N.Y.C., 1991. Chairperson N.W. Ark. Coun., Fayetteville, 1990—; bd. dirs. Pillar's Club-United Way, Easter Seals Soc.-Arkansas of Yr., Walton Arts Ctr. Coun., Fayetteville, Ark. Named Disting. Bus. Lectr. Cen. State U., Edmond, Okla., 1989. Office: Llama Company PO Box 2189 Bentonville AR 72712-2189*

WALTON, ANTHONY JOHN (TONY WALTON), theater and film designer, book illustrator; b. Walton on Thames, Eng., Oct. 24, 1934; s. Lancelot Henry Frederick and Hilda Betty (Drew) W.; m. Julie Andrews, May 10, 1959 (div. 1968); 1 child, Emma Kate; m. Genevieve LeRoy, Sept. 12, 1991; 1 stepchild, Bridget. Student, Oxford Sch. Tech. Art and Commerce, 1949-52, Slade Sch. Fine Art, London, 1954-55. Designer settings, costumes for theater prodns., London, off-Broadway, 1957-60, Broadway, 1961—; Broadway prodns. include Pippin, 1972 (Tony award 1972-73, Drama Desk award 1972-73), Shelter, 1973 (Drama Desk award 1972-73), Chicago, 1975, Sophisticated Ladies, 1981, The Real Thing, 1984, Hurlyburly, 1984, I'm Not Rappaport, 1985, House of Blue Leaves, 1986 (Tony award 1985-86), Drama Desk award 1985-86), Front Page, 1986, Social Security, 1986 (Drama Desk award 1985-86), Anything Goes, 1987, Grand Hotel, 1989, Six Degrees of Separation, 1990, The Will Rogers Follies, 1991, Death and the Maiden, 1992, Conversations with My Father, 1992, Four Baboons Adoring the Sun, 1992, Guys and Dolls, 1992 (Tony award 1991-92, Drama Desk award 1991-92), Tommy Tune Tonight, 1992, She Loves Me, 1993, A Grand Night for Singing, 1993, Laughter on the 23rd Floor, 1993, Picnic, 1994, A Christmas Carol, N.Y.C., 1994, Company, 1995, Moonlight, 1995, A Fair Country, 1996, A Funny Thing Happened on the Way to the Forum, 1996, The Shawl, 1996, Make Someone Happy, Bay St. Theater Festival, 1997, Not Waving, 1997, Steel Pier, 1997, King David, 1997, 1776, 1997; The Cripple of Inishman, 1998; Noel & Gertie, 1998; House, 1998; Ashes to Ashes, 1999; Annie Get Your Gun, 1999; On Raferty's Hill, 2000 (Dublin and London); If Love Were All, 1999; Taller Than a Dwarf, 2000, Uncle Vanya, 2000, The Man Who Came To Dinner, 2000; dir., designer The Importance of Being Earnest, 1996, Major Barbara, 1997; dir. NoelCoward in Two Keys Bay St. Theatre Festival, 1996; dir. Missing Footage, 1999; dir., co-writer, costume designer Oops! The Big Apple Circus Stage Show, 1999; ballets, principally San Francisco Ballet Co., Am. Ballet Theatre; films include Mary Poppins, A Funny Thing Happened on the Way to the Forum, Murder on the Orient Express, The Wiz, All That Jazz (Acad. award with Philip Rosenberg 1980), Prince of the City, Star 80, The Glass Menagerie, 1987, Regarding Henry, 1991; operas in London, 1963-68, Spoleto, Italy, 1965, Santa Fe, 1975, San Francisco, 1992, Chgo., 1993; author: Adelie Penguin in Wonders, 1981; illustrator (books) Wonders, 1981, The Importance of Being Earnest, 1973, Lady Windemere's Fan, 1973, Popcorn, 1972, God Is a Good friend, 1969, Witches Holiday, 1971, Dumpy the Dump Truck, 2000, Dumpy at School, 2000, others. Served with RAF, 1952-54. Recipient Emmy award Death of a Salesman, 1986; named to Theatre Hall of Fame, 1991; elected to Interior Design Hall of Fame, 1993. Mem. United Scenic Artists, Costume Designers Guild Calif., Acad. Motion Picture Arts and Scis. Office: care Martino ICM 40 W 57th St New York NY 10019-4001

WALTON, CARMELITA NOREEN, retired nurse; b. Chgo., Nov. 15, 1926; d. Elmo Augusta and Evelyn Mae (Terry) Desobrey; 1 child by previous marriage: Michael Jerome. Student, St. Marys Coll., U. Notre Dame, 1943-45; grad., Cook County Sch. Nursing, Chgo., 1949; BA in Behavioral Social Sci., DePaul U., 1993. Cert. nursing adminstr. ANCC; cert. correctional health profl. Head nurse, supr., nurse clinician Cook County Hosp., Chgo., 1951-71; supr. U. Chgo. Hosps. and Clinics, 1963-68; DON, Woodlawn Child Health Ctr., Chgo., 1968-69; DON prison health care Cermak Health Svcs., Cook County Jail, 1973-93; ret., 1993. Nurse cons. Quality Mgmt., In-Svc. Edn.; med.-surg. staff nurse; cons., surveyor Nat. Commn. on Correctional Health Care, speaker 13th ann. conv., 1989, apptd. to bd. certification correctional health, 1991—. Contbr. articles to profl. jours. Recipient Superior Pub. Svc. award City of Chgo., 1984. Mem. APHA, ANA (coun. nursing adminstrn.), Ill. Nurses Assn., Nat. League Nursing, Am. Assn. Diabetes Educators. Democrat. Roman Catholic. Home: 5050 S Lake Shore Dr Chicago IL 60615-3200

WALTON, CAROLE LORRAINE, clinical social worker; b. Harrison, Ark., Oct. 20, 1949; d. Leo Woodrow Walton and Arlette Alegra (Cohen) Armstrong. BA, Lambuth Coll., Jackson, Tenn., 1971; MA, U. Chgo., 1974. Diplomate Clin. Social Work, Acad. Cert. Social Workers; bd. cert. diplomate; lic. clin. social worker. Social worker Community Mental Health, Flint, Mich., 1971-72, clin. social worker Westchester, Ill., 1974-76; dir. self-travel program Chgo. Assn. Retarded Citizens, 1973; coord. family svcs. Inner Harbors Psych. Hosp., Douglasville, Ga., 1976-83; sr. mental health clinician Northside Mental Health Ctr., Atlanta, 1983—; pvt. practice clin. social work, 1997—2001. Mem. NASW, Ga. Soc. for Clin. Work (pres. 1981-82, pres. 1993-95). Avocation: tennis. Office: Northside Mental Health Ctr 5825 Glenridge Dr NE Bldg 4 Atlanta GA 30328-7145

WALTON, CHARLES MICHAEL, civil engineering educator; b. Hickory, N.C., July 28, 1941; s. Charles O. and Virginia Ruth (Hart) W.; m. Betty Grey Hughes; children: Susan, Camila, Michael, Gantt. BS, Va. Mil. Inst., 1963; MCE, N.C. State U., 1969, PhD, 1971. Research asst. N.C. State U., Raleigh, 1967-71; transp. planning engr. N.C. Hwy. Commn., 1970-71; asst. prof. civil engring. U. Tex., Austin, 1971-76, assoc. prof., 1976-83, prof., 1983—, Bess Harris Jones Centennial prof. natural resource policy studies, 1987-91, Paul D. and Betty Robertson Meek Centennial prof. engring., 1991-93, Ernest H. Cockrell Centennial chair engring., 1993—, chmn. dept. civil engring., 1988-96. Transp. cons., 1970—; assoc. dir. Ctr. for Transp. Rsch. U. Tex., 1980-88; chmn., exec. com. Transp. Rsch. Bd., NRC, 1991, Disting. Lectr., 1994. Contbr. articles to profl. jours. Past chmn. Urban Transp. Commn., Austin. Recipient Disting. Engring. award N.C. State U., 1995, Joe J. King Profl. Engring. Achievement award U. Tex. at Austin, 1995-96, W.N. Carey Jr. Disting. Svc. award Transp. Rsch. Bd., 1998, George S. Bartlett award AASHTO, Transp. Rsch. Bd., ARTBA, 2000 Fellow ASCE (Harland Bartholomew urban planning award 1987, Frank M. Masters transp. engring. award 1987, James Laurie prize 1992, Francis C. Turner lectr. 1999), Inst. Transp. Engrs.; mem. NSPE, NAE, Intelligent Transp. Soc. Am. (tech. coord. coun., chair bd. dirs., past chair tech. coord. coun.), Am. Rd. and Transp. Assn. (western v.p., past pres. edn. divsn.), Soc. Automotive Engrs., Urban Land Inst., Inst. for Ops. Rsch. and Mgmt. Scis., Soc. Am. Mil. Engrs., Internat. Rd. Fedn. (bd. dirs.), Internat. Rd. Ednl. Found. (bd. dirs.), Austin C. of C. (Leadership Austin program). Democrat. Methodist. Home: 3404 River Rd Austin TX 78703-1031 Office: U Tex Dept Civil Engring Dept Civil Engring ECJ Hall Ste 6.3 Austin TX 78712 E-mail: cmwalton@mail.utexas.edu.

WALTON, CONRAD GORDON , SR. architect; b. Houston, June 18, 1928; s. John Edward and Evelyn Lucile (Gordon) W.; m. Rilda Ellen Akin, Dec. 10, 1954; children: Conrad Gordon, Evelyn Coleman, Roberta Agnes. BS (Walsh scholar), Rice U., 1951; postgrad., U. Houston, 1955. Registered architect, Tex., NCARB. Pres. DCW Architects, Inc. *As founding principal of his firm, Conrad G. Walton, Sr. A.I.A. has 42 years of design experience on hundreds of projects for institutions, corporations and government agencies. Representative projects in Texas include University of Houston Old Science Building, Texas Southern University Library, Blinn College Gymnasium, and Houston Heights World War II Memorial. Land planning and real estate developments include Forest Hills Subdivision Section II, Polk County, Texas, and Holiday Oaks Subdivision, Section I and II, Washington County, Texas.* Mem. AIA. Home: 9014 Springview Ln Houston TX 77080-1755 Office: 2425 Fountain View Dr Ste 225 Houston TX 77057-4834

WALTON, DAN GIBSON, lawyer; b. Houston, Mar. 26, 1950; s. Dan Edward and Lucy Frances (Gibson) W.; m. Martha Sandlin, June 24, 1972; children: Cole Gibson, Emily Wyatt. BA with honors, U. Va., 1972; JD with honors, U. Tex., 1975. Bar: Tex. 1975, U.S. Dist. Ct. (so. dist.) Tex. 1977, U.S. Ct. Appeals (D.C. cir.) 1975, U.S. Ct. Appeals (5th cir.) 1981, U.S. Supreme Ct. 2001; bd. cert. in civil trial law. Law clk. to hon. Malcolm R. Wilkey D.C. Ct. Appeals (D.C. cir.), 1975-76; assoc. Vinson & Elkins, Houston, 1976-82, ptnr., 1982—. Bd. dirs. The Meth. Hosp., Houston. Bd. dirs. Tex. Equal Access to Justice Found., 2000—, State Bar of Tex., 1999—, South Tex. Coll. Law, Houston, 1994—, Briarwood Sch./Brookwood Cmty., Houston, 1991—; trustee St. John's Sch., Houston, 1997—, Good Samaritan Found., 1998—, Cullen Trust for Health Care, 2002—; co-chancellor Tex. Ann. Conf., United Meth. Ch., Houston, 1996—; mem. admission commn. U.S. Dist. Cts. for So. Dist. Tex. Fellow Am. Bar Found., Tex. Bar Found., Houston Bar Found. (chair 1994), Houston Bar Assn. (pres. 1998-99), Garland Walker Am. Inn of Ct. (master), Am. Bd. Trial Advocates (assoc.), Internat. Soc. Barristers, Internat. Assn. Def. Counsel, Tex. Assn. Def. Counsel. Avocations: golf, skiing. Office: Vinson & Elkins LLP 2300 First City Tower 1001 Fannin St Ste 3201 Houston TX 77002-6706

WALTON, DAVID P. utility company executive; b. Phila., Jan. 12, 1953; s. Paul Roberts and June Mary (Omen) W.; m. Julie Gurtcheff, Apr. 4, 1977; children: Michael, Andrew, Steven. BS, Kings Coll., 1976; MBA, Lehigh U., 1981. Programmer Pa. Power & Light, Allentown, 1976-78, sr. programmer, 1978-81, supr. application programming, 1981-85, supr. computer applications, 1985-93, mgr. continuous improvement, 1993-96, mgr. bus. planning, 1997, mgr. info. solutions, 1998-2000, dir. info. technology, 2000—; pres. Push the Rock, 1998—. Pres. Upper Milford (Pa.) Youth, 1989-94, v.p., 1985-89; mem. allocation com. United Way, Allentown, 1996-99; mem. alumni exec. com. Kings Coll., Briarcliff, N.YU., 1980-87; soccer coach Western Lehigh Soccer Club, Emmaus, Pa., 1985-2002; basketball coach Lower Macungie Youth, Trexlertown, 1990-99, Amateur Athletic Assn. (Lehigh Valley), 2000—; elder Faith Evang. Free Ch., 1996—; bd. dirs. PPL Credit Union, 2002—. Recipient West Chester Alumni award Kings Coll., 1975, Cmty. Svc. award Upper Milford Twp., 1994. Home: 4940 Gwen Cir Zionsville PA 18092-2015 Office: Pa Power and Light 2 N 9th St Allentown PA 18101-1139

WALTON, DEWITT TALMAGE, JR. dentist; b. Macon, Ga., May 25, 1937; s. DeWitt T. Sr. and Jimmie (Braswell) W.; m. Joan Robinson, June 11, 1960; children: Jimmie Walton Paschall, Gwen N., Gayle N., Joy A. BS, Howard U., 1960, DDS, 1961. Pvt. practice, Macon, 1963—. Chmn. dental adv. com. Ga. Dept. Med. Assistance; dental svcs. adv. com. Dept. Physical Health, Ga. Dept. Human Resources; adv. bd. dirs. Wachovia Bank, Macon-Warner Robins area; bd. dirs. The Ga. Dept. Cmty. Affairs. Fin. chmn. Boy Scouts Am., Piedmont/Creek Dist., 1978-80, exec. bd., 1978-82, v.p. exec. com., 1983-84; apptd. Bibb County Bd. Edn., 1969-73; vice chmn. Macon-Bibb County Transit Authority, 1981-87; dir. exec. com. Devel. Corp. Mid. Ga., 1984-91; sec.-treas. Urban Devel. Authority, Macon-Bibb County, 1984-87; trustee Macon Heritage Found., 1983-87; bd. dirs. Ctrl. Ga. Speech and Hearing Ctr., 1984-87, Boys' Club Macon, Inc., 1986, 87, 88, The Grand Opera House, 1988, 89, 90, Booker T. Washington Ctr., 1993, Pub. Edn. Found., 1995—, Douglass Theater, 1995—; mem. oversight com. Minority Bus. Assistance Program, 1984-91; active Bibb County Commn. on Excellence in Edn., 1984; trustee United Way Macon-Bibb County, 1985, 86, 87; deacon, elder, treas. Washington Ave. Presbyn. Ch.; active Downtown Coun., Coalition for Polit. Awareness, So. Poverty Law Ctr., NAACP; mem. "Cmty. Hero"-torchbearer Olympic Torch Relay for 1996 Olympic games, Atlanta; advisory bd. Wachovia Bank, Macon, Warner-Robins, 1999—; apptd. bd. dirs. Ga. Dept. Cmty. Affairs, 1999—, Cmty. Found. Ctrl. Ga., 2001—. With U.S. Army, 1961-63. Recipient Cert. of Appreciation State Bar of Ga., Citizenship award Bibb County Voter's Registration League, Inc., 1977, Cmty. Svc. award NAACP, 1982, Cmty. Svc. award Alpha Kappa Alpha Sorority, 1982, Meritorious Svc. award United Negro Coll. Fund, 1983, Comml. Bldg. of Yr. award Macon Heritage Found., 1983, Faithful Svc. award Bibb County Dept. Family and Children's Svcs., 1983-90, Lifetime Achievement award for cmty. svc., Boys' and Girls' Clubs, 2002, citation Macon-Bibb County Beautification Clean Cmty. Comm., 1983-84, Cert. appreciation Macon-Bibb County Econ. Opportunity Coun., 1984, Outstanding Svc. award So. Poverty Law Ctr., 1984, Proclamation Mayor George Israel Svc. on Macon-Bibb County Transit Authority, 1984, Outstanding Alumni award Coll. Dentistry Howard U., 1985, award for Outstanding Svc. Macon-Bibb County Urban Devel. Authority, 1987, award for Outstanding Svc. Macon-Bibb County Transit Authority, 1987, cert. Appreciation Close-Up Found., 1988, cert. Appreciation Ga. Dental Edn. Found., 1988, Cmty. Svc. award United Way Macon-Bibb County, 1988, cert. Disting. Svc. Devel. Corp. Middle Ga., 1990, Continuous Corp. Support award Entrepreneurship and Black Youth Program U. Ga., 1990, cert. Recognition Outstanding Svc. So. Poverty Law Ctr., 1990, cert. Appreciation Keep Macon-Bibb Beautiful Commn. and Cherry Blossom Festival, 1990, James E. Carter award Ga. Dental Soc., 1993; named Olympic Torchbearer, 1996. Fellow Acad. Gen. Dentistry (Membership award 1983-85), Acad. Dentistry Internat., Am. Coll. Dentists, Ga. Dental Assn. (hon.), Internat. Coll. Dentists, Pierre Fauchard Acad.; mem. AAAS, ADA (alt. del. Ga. 1986-91, life mem.), Am. Analgesic Soc., Am. Endodontic Soc., Am. Fund Dental Health, Am. Sch. Health Assn., Am. Soc. Dentistry for Children, Nat. Dental Assn. (life), Nat. Rehab. Assn., Ga. Dental Soc. (pres., 1978, Citizenship award 1979-80, Humanitarian award 1981-82, James E. Carter Jr. award 1993), North Ga. Dental Soc. (pres. 1978-79), Cen. Dist. Dental Soc. (peer rev. com., legis. com., alt. del. to Ga. Dental Assn. 1982, 83, 84, del. 1984, 85, 86, 87), Bibb County Dental Soc. (charter), Acad. Continuing Edn., Fed. Dentaire Internat. (life), Pres'. Club Howard U. (life), Am. Running and Fitness Assn. (life), Greater Macon C. of C. (bd. dirs. 1995-97), Macon Tracks, Sigma Pi Phi, Omega Psi Phi (life). Presbyterian. Avocations: walking, jogging, aerobics, coin collecting, real estate. Home: 2988 Malibu Dr Macon GA 31211-2609 Office: DeWitt T Walton Jr DDS 591 DT Walton Sr Way Macon GA 31201-7504

WALTON, DONALD CAMERON, JR. retired obstetrician, gynecologist; b. Providence, Apr. 11, 1934; s. Donald Cameron and Ebba Louise (Anderson) W.; m. Mary Jane Gibbons, Sept. 17, 1960; children: Kathleen Ann, Kyle Marie, Donald Cameron III, James Joseph, Diane Jeanne. BA, Bowdoin Coll., 1955; MD, Tufts U., 1959. Diplomate Am. Bd. Obstetrics and Gynecology. Intern Maine Med. Ctr., Portland, 1959-60, resident in gen. surgery, 1960-61; residency in ob/gyn Tufts-New England Med. Ctr./Carney and St. Margaret's Hosps., Boston, 1963-66; pvt. practice North Andover, Andover, Mass., 1966-73; physician Montgomery County Health Dept., Rockville, Md., 1973-95; pvt. practice, 1995-98; ret., 1998. Capt. U.S. Army, 1961-63, Germany. Fellow Am. Coll. Obstetricians and Gynecologists; mem. Mass. Med. Soc., Am. Soc. for Reproductive Medicine. Republican. Roman Catholic. Avocation: tennis.

WALTON, EDMUND LEWIS, JR. lawyer; b. Salisbury, Md., Sept. 4, 1936; s. Edmund Lewis and Iris Tull (White) W.; m. Barbara Post, Sept. 18, 1965; children: Southy E., Kristen P. BA, Coll. William and Mary, 1961, JD (Godwin scholar), 1963. Bar: Va. 1963, U.S. Dist. Ct. (ea. dist.) Va. 1964, U.S. Supreme Ct. 1971, U.S. Dist Ct. (we. dist.) Va. 1972, U.S. Ct. Appeals (4th cir.) 1980. Grad. asst. Coll. William and Mary, 1961-62; assoc. Simmonds, Coleburn, Towner & Carman, Arlington, Fairfax, Va., 1963-68, ptnr., 1968-74, Putbrese and Walton, McLean, Va., 1975; pvt. practice, 1976-82; sr. ptnr. Walton and Adams P.C., 1983—. Judge pro tem Fairfax County Cir. Ct., 1977—; commr. in chancery, 1990-97, legis. com. Va. State Bar, 1974-76; bus. law sect. exec. com. 1983-88, sec. 1984-85, vice chmn. 1985-86, chmn. 1986-87. Editor William and Mary Law Sch. Rev. 1961-63. Bd. dirs. Home Run Acres Civic Assn. 1968-70, v.p. 1969-70; bd. dirs. McLean Citizens Assn., 1976-79, 1st v.p. 1977-78; bd. dirs., pres. Rocky Run Citizens Assn.,

1973-74; bd. dirs. Langley Sch. Inc., 1975-77, treas. 1976-77; mem. Fairfax County Rep. Com., 1966-82, chmn. 1970-72; del. Rep. Nat. Conv. 1972; mem Va. Rep. Ctrl. Com. 1974-77, exec. com. 1976-77; chmn. Providence Dist. Rep. Com., 1968-70; mem. 10th Congl. Dist. Rep. Com. 1970-77, vice chmn. 1974-76, chmn. 1976-77, mem. 8th Congl. Dist. Rep. Com. 1967-70; v.p. Arlington County Young Reps., 1965-66, counsel Arlington County Rep. Com. 1965-66; bd. dirs. McLean Planning Com. 1975-79, chmn. 1976-77; bd. dirs. McLean Office Sq. Condominium Assn., 1979-83, pres. 1979-82; chmn. Tysons Corner Citizens Task Force 1977-78; mem. Fairfax County Coun. on Arts; bd. dirs. Fairfax YMCA 1974-75; bd. dirs. Friends of Turkey Run Farm, 1981—, counsel 1981—, mem. exec. com. 1981-83. With U.S. Army 1956-59. Named McLean (Va.) Bus. Citizen of Yr. 1996. Fellow ABA Found. (life), Va. Law Found. (dir. 1991-97, mem. com. on continuing legal edn. 1990-91, chmn. 1992-93); mem. ABA, Am. Law Inst., Va. Bar Assn. (spl. com. to study rules of ethics 1981-84, membership com. 1981-84, exec. com. 1982-88, chmn. 1984-85, pres.-elect 1985-86, pres. 1986-87), Va. Continuing Legal Edn. Bd. (chmn. 1995-98), Arlington County Bar Assn., Fairfax County Bar Assn. (cts. com. 1975-77, dir. 1976-77), McLean Bar Assn. (dir. 1978-79, 80-83, sec. 1978-79, pres. 1980-82), Va. Trial Lawyers Assn., Am. Judicature Soc., William and Mary Law Sch. Assn. (dir. 1970-76), Fairfax County C. of C. (dir. ex officio 1981-83), McLean C. of C. (bd. dirs. 1995-96), McLean Bus. and Profl. Assn. (dir. 1976-85, 89-90, pres. 1981-83), Washington Golf and Country Club, Daufuskie Island Club, Lowes Island Club, Phi Alpha Delta. Episcopalian. Home: 2032 Mayfair Mclean Ct Falls Church VA 22043-1760 Office: PO Drawer EE 6862 Elm St Ste 400 Mc Lean VA 22101-3869 E-mail: ewalton@walton-adams.com.

WALTON, G. CLIFFORD, family practice physician; b. Richmond, Va., Jan. 5, 1968; s. Eugene Marion and Mary Ann (McNabb) W.; m. Tami Marie Daniel, June 26, 1998. BS summa cum laude, Hampden-Sydney Coll., 1990; MD, Med. Coll. Va., 1994. Intern Med. Coll. Va., Richmond, 1994-95; resident Blackstone (Va.) Family Practice, 1995-97; pvt. practice, Kenbridge, Va., 1997-99, Richmond, 1996—. Med. examiner Va. Dept. Health, Powhatan, 1996—; mem. housestaff coun. Med. Coll. Va., 1995-97. Sci. fair judge Southside Va. H.S., Farmville, 1988-97. Mem. AMA, Am. Acad. Family Physicians, Med. Soc. Va., Phi Beta Kappa, Sigma Xi, Omicron Delta Kappa. Avocations: baseball card collecting, gardening, photography. Home: 1640 Jeter Rd Powhatan VA 23139-6907 Office: Patient First 8110 Midlothian Tpke Richmond VA 23235-5100

WALTON, GERALD WAYNE, retired university official; b. Union, Miss., Sept. 11, 1934; s. Willie Jay and Ruby Elizabeth (Williamson) W.; m. Juliet Katherine Hart, Aug. 26, 1960; children: Katherine Hart, Dorothy Elizabeth, Margaret Stevens. AA, East Central Jr. Coll., 1954; BS, U. So. Miss., 1956; MA, U. Miss., 1959, PhD, 1967. Tchr. asst. U. Miss., 1956-59, instr. English, 1959-62, asst. prof., 1962-67, assoc. prof., 1967-70, prof., 1970-99, assoc. dean Coll. Liberal Arts, 1970-76, dean, 1976-82, assoc. vice chancellor for acad. affairs, 1982-94, interim vice chancellor for acad. affairs, 1994-96, provost, 1996-99. Contbr. articles to profl. jours. Vice-pres. Oxford Human Rels. Coun., 1968; mem. adminstrv. bd. Oxford U. Meth. Ch., chmn. bd. trustees, 1971-72, lay leader, 1999-2001; bd. dirs. Yoknapatawpha Arts Coun., 1980-81; sec.-treas. So. Lit. Festival, 1965; sec. U. Miss. Friends of Libr.; v.p. U. Miss. Friends Mus. Tri-Univ. fellow in linguistics U. Nebr., 1969-70. Mem. MLA, Am. Dialect Soc., Miss. Folklore Soc., Friends of Arts in Miss., Miss. Assn. English Tchrs. (sec. 1968), Miss. Inst. Arts and Letters (sec. 1979-80), Nat. Coun. Tchrs. English, William Faulkner Soc., Miss. Hist. Soc., Oxford-Lafayette County Heritage Soc., So. Studies Adv. Coun., Rotary, Golden Key, Phi Kappa Phi, Sigma Tau Delta, Omicron Delta Kappa. Home: 106 Ole Miss Dr Oxford MS 38655-2615 E-mail: gww@olemiss.edu.

WALTON, HAROLD VINCENT, former agricultural engineering educator, academic administrator; b. Christiana, Pa., June 17, 1921; s. Howard King and Alice Lauretta (Kirk) W.; m. Velma Purvis Braun, June 24, 1946; children: H. Richard, Marilyn J. Walton Friedersdorf, Carol A. BS in Agrl. Engring., Pa. State U., 1942, MS in Agrl. Engring., 1950; PhD in Agrl. Engring., Purdue U., 1961. Test engr. Gen. Electric Co., Schenectady, 1943-45; instr. Pa. State U., 1947-50, asst. prof. agrl. engring., 1950-52, assoc. prof., 1952-61, prof., 1961, 76-85, head dept. agrl. engring., 1976-85, ret., 1985; prof., chmn. dept. agrl. engring. U. Mo.-Columbia, 1962-69, chief of party India, 1969-71, prof., 1971-76. Cons. OAS, Trinidad and Tobago, 1980, Ptnrs. of Ams., Brazil, 1984. Served with U.S. Army, 1945-46. Fulbright scholar, Cyprus, 1989-90 Fellow Am. Soc. Agrl. Engrs. (bd. dirs. 1967-69, 85-87). Republican. E-mail: hvw2@psu.edu.

WALTON, JAMES MELLON, investment company executive; b. Pitts., Dec. 18, 1930; m. Ellen Carroll; 4 children. BA, Yale U.; MBA, Harvard U. With Gulf Oil Corp., Phila., Houston, Pitts., Tokyo, Rome, 1958-67; pres. Carnegie Inst., Pitts., 1968-84, Carnegie Mus. Natural History and Mus. of Art, Pitts., 1968-84, Carnegie Library, Pitts., 1968-84; life trustee, pres. emeritus Carnegie Inst. and Carnegie Library, 1984—. Vice chmn. bd. dirs. MMC Group Inc.; bd. dirs. Irish Investment Fund, Inc. Mem. sponsoring com. Penn's Southwest Assn.; trustee emeritus Carnegie-Mellon U.; treas. Carnegie Hero Fund Commn.; dir. World Affairs Coun. of Pitts., One Hundred Friends of Pitts. Art; trustee Sarah Scaife Found. Inc., Extra Mile Found.; chmn. Vira I. Heinz Endowment; mem. Cultural Dist. Devel. Com. Lt. U.S. Army, 1954-56. Office: 525 William Penn Way Ste 3902 Pittsburgh PA 15219-1710 E-mail: jmwa@earthlink.net.

WALTON, JON DAVID, lawyer; b. Clairton, Pa., Sept. 18, 1942; s. Thomas Edward and Matilda Lucy (Sunday) W.; m. Carol Jeanne Rowland, Sept. 15, 1964; children: David Edward, Diane Elizabeth. BS, Purdue U., 1964; JD, Valparaiso U., 1969. Bar: Pa. 1969. Atty. U.S. Steel Corp. (now USX Corp.), Pitts., 1969-73; asst. gen. counsel Harbison-Walker Refractories, 1973-75, gen. counsel, 1975-81, v.p., gen. counsel, 1981-83; regional gen. counsel Dresser Industries, Inc., 1983-86; gen. counsel, sec. Allegheny Ludlum Corp., 1986-90, v.p., gen. counsel, sec., 1990-96, Allegheny Techs. Inc., Pitts., 1996—, sr. v.p., gen. counsel, sec., 1997—. Trustee Westminster Coll., 1997—; pres., bd. dirs. Music for Mt. Lebanon, 1996—; bd. dirs. Pitts. Youth Golf Found., 1991--; clk. of session Southminster Presbyn. Ch., 1998-2001. Mem. ABA, Pa. Bar Assn., Allegheny County Bar Assn., Am. Soc. Corp. Secs. (former pres. regional group), Am. Corp. Counsel Assn., Am. Arbitration Assn. (panel arbitrators), Duquesne Club, Valley Brook Country Club, Rolling Rock Club. Home: 137 Hoodridge Dr Pittsburgh PA 15228-1803 Office: Allegheny Technologies Inc 1000 Six PPG Pl Pittsburgh PA 15222-5479 E-mail: jwalton@alleghenytechnologies.com.

WALTON, JOSEPH CARROLL, investor; b. Frankfurt, Fed. Republic Germany, Nov. 23, 1955; (parents Am. citizens); s. James Mellon and Ellen Marie (Carroll) W.; m. Molly Erwin, Mar. 23, 1985; 3 children. BA in Eng. Lit., Williams Coll., 1979; MBA, U. Tex., 1983. Pvt. investor, Pitts. Dir. Amy's Ice Creams Inc., Austin, Tex., Physicians Data Corp., Atlanta; trustee Scaife Family Found., Pitts. Trustee Children's Hosp. Pitts. Recipient Outstanding Advisor award Jr. Achievement, 1984. Mem.: Rolling Rock (Ligonier, Pa.); Beaumaris Yacht (bd. dirs., Ont., Can.). Office: 525 William Penn Way Ste 3902 Pittsburgh PA 15219-1707

WALTON, MATT SAVAGE, retired geologist, educator; b. Lexington, Ky., Sept. 16, 1915; m. Kathryn Ralston, Dec. 6, 1940 (div.); m. Nalda Robison, May 22, 1969 (dec.); m. Kay Ann Thorson, June 21, 1970; children: Matt Savage III, Kate Johns, Lisa Baar, Anne Elizabeth, Owen Hardwick. BA, U. Chgo., 1936; MA (James Furman Kemp fellow), Columbia U., 1947, PhD, 1951. Geologist U.S. Geol. Survey, 1942-46; assoc. prof. Yale U., New Haven, 1948-65; geologist N.Y. State Geol. Survey, 1947-57; regents lectr. environ. sci. and engring. UCLA, 1970-71; dir. Minn. Geol. Survey, U. Minn., 1973-86, prof. geology and geophysics, 1973-86, prof. emeritus, 1986—; cons. on geologic conditions affecting excavation and underground constrn., 1995—. Dir. Deep Observation and Sampling of the Earth's Continental Crust, Inc., 1984-86; exec. com. Great Lakes Internat. Project; cons. in field. Contbr. articles to profl. jours. Pres. Old Town Restorations, Inc., St. Paul, 1974-79; bd. dirs. Summit Hill Assn., 1974-79. Fellow Geol. Soc. Am.; mem. Assn. Am. State Geologists. Avocations: writing, consulting. Home: 30 Crocus Pl Saint Paul MN 55102-2810

WALTON, MORGAN LAUCK, III, lawyer; b. Woodstock, Va., July 30, 1932; s. Morgan Lauck Jr. and Frances (Allen) W.; m. Jeannette Freeman Minor, Mar. 4, 1961; children: Morgan Lauck IV, Charles Lancelot Minor, Christopher Allen, Laura Cathlyn Hirschfeld. BA, Randolph-Macon Coll., 1953; LLB, U. Va., 1959. Bar: Va. 1959, N.Y. 1959, U.S. Ct. Appeals (2d cir.) 1959, U.S. Dist. Ct. (ea. and so. dists.) N.Y. 1960, U.S. Dist. Ct. (we. dist.) Va. 1988. Assoc. Donovan Leisure Newton & Irvine, N.Y.C., 1959-68, ptnr., 1968-84; counsel FDIC, Washington, 1989-90, asst. gen. counsel, 1990-97; mem. editl. adv. bd. Free Advice, San Francisco, 1997—. Contbr. articles to legal jours. Trustee Randolph-Macon Acad., Front Royal, Va., 1987-92, trustee emeritus, 2002—; trustee Unitarian Ch. Shenandoah Valley, Stephens City, Va., 1987—; mem. coun. Law Sch. U. Va., 1989-92; treas. Shenandoah Valley Music Festival, Woodstock, 1986-87; chmn. bd. All Souls Ch., N.Y.C., 1974-76; mem. Shenandoah County Dem. Com., 1999—. With U.S. Army, 1953-56. Mem. Univ. Club (N.Y.C.), Collectors Club, Order of Coif, Phi Beta Kappa. Democrat. Home: 908 Kern Springs Rd Woodstock VA 22664-3216

WALTON, R. KEITH, academic administrator, lawyer; b. Birmingham, Ala. s. Reginald Jr. and Cynthia (Williams) W.; m. Aubria D. Corbitt; three children. BA, Yale U., 1986; JD, Harvard U., 1990. Bar: Ga. Assoc. King & Spaulding, Atlanta, 1991-93; law clk. for Judge. U.W. Clemon U.S. Dist. Ct. (no. dist.) Ala., Birmingham, 1990-91; chief of staff Office Enforcement Dept. Treas., Washington, 1993-96; sec. of univ. Columbia U., N.Y.C., 1996—, polit. sci. lectr., 1997. Del. Young Leaders Conf., 1998. Del. Interpol, Rome, 1994, Beijing, 1995; treas. Yale Coll. Class of 1986, 1985-96; dep. dir. White House Security Rev., Washington, 1994-95; sr. advisor Good Ol' Boy Round Up Rev., Washington, 1995-96; U.S. Del., UN Crime Commn., Vienna, 1996; mem. adv. bd. Human Rights Watch, 1997—; bd. dirs. Apollo Theatre Found., Orch. St. Luke's; vice chair The Riverside Ch.. Mem. Am. Law Inst., Coun. for U.S. and Italy, Coun. Fgn. Rels. (adv. bd. 1997—), Am. Coun. on Germany (steering com. 1999-2000), Enterprise Found. (N.Y. adv. bd. 1997—), Century Assn., Alpha Phi Alpha, Sigma Pi Phi. Office: Columbia U Office of Sec 211 Low Meml Libr 535 W 116th St New York NY 10027-7030

WALTON, RALPH GERALD, psychiatrist, educator; b. Darlington, Eng., Aug. 18, 1942; came to U.S., 1950; s. Kenneth and Paula (Weissman) W.; m. Ellen Paula Liebling, Feb. 15, 1970 (div. 1980); children: Deborah, Rachel; m. Mary Elaine Hultburg, Sept. 27, 1981; children: Lisa, Jonathan. AB, U. Rochester, 1963; MD, SUNY, Syracuse, 1967. Diplomate Am. Bd. Psychiatry and Neurology. Intern Strong Meml. Hosp., Rochester, N.Y., 1967-68, resident in psychiatry, 1968-71; asst. prof. psychiatry Sch. Medicine U. Rochester, 1973-76; chief psychiatry Jamestown (N.Y.) Gen. Hosp., 1976-88; commr. mental health Chautauqua County, Jamestown, 1985-88; chmn. dept. psychiatry Western Res. Care System, Youngstown, Ohio, 1988-98; prof., chmn. dept. psychiatry N.E. Ohio Univs. Coll. of Medicine, Rootstown, 1998—. Med. dir. Profl. Recovery Plus Alcoholic Clinic, Youngstown, 1992—. Contbr. chpt. to: Dietary Phenylalanine and Brain Function, 1988; contbr. foreword to: Katherine It's Time, 1989; contbr. articles to profl. jours., 1972—. Maj. U.S. Army, 1971-73, Panama. Fellow Am. Psychiat. Assn. Jewish. Office: 725 Boardman Canfield Rd Youngstown OH 44512-4380 E-mail: rwalton193@aol.com.

WALTON, ROBERT PRENTISS, lawyer; b. Cleve., Jan. 11, 1938; s. Robert Clark and Elizabeth (Bowman) W.; m. Rosalie S., May 29, 1965; children—Jenifer S., Robert D. B.A., Yale U., 1959; LL.B., U. Va., 1962. Bar: N.Y. 1963, Conn. 1962, Va. 1962, U.S. Supreme Ct. 1967. Assoc. gen. counsel NYU, 1977-83, sr. assoc. counsel, 1983— ; asst. U.S. atty. So. Dist. N.Y., 1970-75; mem. McGarrahan & Heard, N.Y.C., 1975-77. Recipient Am. Jurisprudence prize Bancroft Whitney Co., 1962. Mem. N.Y. State Bar Assn. Home: 69 Midland St Cold Spring Harbor NY 11724-1805

WALTON, RODNEY EARL, lawyer; b. Corvallis, Oreg., Apr. 28, 1947; s. Ray Daniel Jr. and Carolyn Jane (Smith) W. BA, Coll. of Wooster, 1969; JD, Cornell U., 1976; MA in History, Fla. Internat. U., Miami, 2001. Bar: Fla. 1976, U.S. Dist. Ct. (so. dist.) Fla. 1976, U.S. Dist. Ct. (mid. dist.) Fla. 1977, U.S. Supreme Ct. 1980, U.S. Ct. Appeals (11th cir.) 1981. Assoc. to jr. ptnr. Smathers & Thompson, Miami, Fla., 1976-87; ptnr. Kelley, Drye and Warren, 1987-93; atty. Heinrich Gordon Hargrove Weihe & James, P.A., Ft. Lauderdale, 1994-97. Adj. instr. U.S. mil. history Fla. Internat. U., 2001. Sec. bd. dirs. Kings Creek Condominium Assn., Miami, 1984-89, treas., 1984, pres., 1990-91. 1st lt. U.S. Army, 1969-73, Vietnam. Decorated Bronze Star. Mem. ABA, Fla. Bar. Republican. Methodist. Avocations: travel, reading, tennis, history. Home: 7985 SW 86th St Apt 430 Miami FL 33143-7014 E-mail: RodneyEarlWalton@aol.com.

WALTON, ROGER ALAN, public relations executive, mediator, writer; b. Denver, June 25, 1941; s. Lyle R. and Velda V. (Nicholson) W.; m. Helen Anderson. Attended, U. Colo., 1960-63. Govt. rep. Continental Airlines, Denver, 1964-72; dir. pub. affairs Regional Transp. Dist., 1972-77; pub. affairs cons., 1977—; res. pub. info. officer Fed. Emergency Mgmt. Agy., 1995-96; pres. Colo. Times Pub. Co., 1999-2000; internet mediator for Square Trade, 2000—. Pres. Colo. Times Pub. Co. Author: Colorado-A Practical Guide to its Government and Politics, 1973-92, 6th rev. edit., 1990, Colorado Gambling - A Guide, 1991; columnist The Denver Post newspaper, 1983—, The Rocky Mountain Jour., 1977-81. Mem. U.S. Presdl. Electoral Coll., Washington, 1968; commr. U.S. Bicentennial Revolution Commn., Colo., 1972-76, U.S. Commn. on Bicentennial of U.S. Constn., Denver, 1985-90, pres.; trustee Arapahoe County (Colo.) Libr. Bd., 1982-86; chmn. lobbyist ethics com. Colo. Gen. Assembly, 1990-91. Republican. Avocations: reading, fishing, photography. Home and Office: 12550 W 2d Dr Lakewood CO 80228-5012

WALTON, STANLEY ANTHONY, III, lawyer; b. Chgo., Dec. 10, 1939; s. Stanley Anthony and Emily Ann (Pouzar) W.; m. Karen Kayser, Aug. 10, 1963; children: Katherine, Anne, Alex. BA, Washington and Lee U., 1962, LLB, 1965. Bar: Ill. 1965, U.S. Dist. Ct. (no. dist.) Ill. 1966, U.S. Ct. Appeals (7th cir.) 1966. Ptnr. Winston & Strawn, Chgo., 1965-89, Sayfarth Shaw Fairweather, Chgo., 1989-96. Trustee Village of Hinsdale (Ill.), 1985-89; bd. dirs. Washington and Lee Law Sch., Lexington, Va., 1975-78, bd. dirs. univ. alumni, 1983-87, pres., 1986-87; bd. dirs. UNICEF, Chgo., 1983; pres. Hinsdale Hist. Soc., 1979-81, 2001—, St. Isaac Jogues PTA, 1980; sec. Hinsdale Cmty. Svc., 2000—; bd. dirs. Hinsdale Ctrl. Found., 2000—. Mem. Ill. State Bar Assn., Phi Alpha Delta, Hinsdale Golf Club. Republican. Roman Catholic. Home and Office: 6679 Snug Harbor Dr Willowbrook IL 60527

WALTON, TRACY MATTHEW, JR. radiologist; b. Columbia, S.C., Nov. 12, 1930; MD, Howard U., 1961. Diplomate Am. Bd. Radiology. Intern Freedmans Hosp., Washington, 1961-62, resident in radiology, 1962-66; pvt. practice. Mem. AMA, Am. Coll. Radiology, Nat. Med. Assn. (pres. 1994-95). Address: 4118 Grant St NE Washington DC 20019-3550

WALTON, WILLIAM ROBERT, academic administrator; b. Macon, Ga., Aug. 28, 1949; s. Swift Jessie and LouVenia Mattie (Helms) W.; m. Cynthia Bonell Pollock, Dec. 14, 1969; children: David Anthony, Kelly Melissa. Student, Marsh-Draughon Bus. Coll., 1968; BBA, Ga. State U., 1972, M Pub. Adminstrn., 1977. Acct. K.L. Kemp, Atlanta, 1968-72, Berman Mills & Co., Atlanta, 1972; internal auditor U. Ga. System, 1972-74, asst. dir. budgets, 1974-78; dir. bus. and fin. Ft. Valley (Ga.) State Coll., 1978-82; v.p. bus. affairs Roanoke Coll., Salem, Va., 1982-92; adminstr. Joseph W. Jones Ecol. Rsch. Ctr., Newton, Ga., 1992—. Treas. bd. trustees Roanoke Coll, Salem, 1983-92; trustee June Cheelsman Unitrust, Salem, 1984-92, Lois C. Fisher Unitrust, Salem, 1984-92, Harold W. Harris Unitrust, Salem, 1983-92, James W. Sieg Annuity Trust, Salem, 1984-92, T.B. & R.E. Meador Annuity Trust, Salem, 1985-92, Pendleton Hogan Unitrust, Salem, 1989-92, Francis T. West Annuity Trust, Salem, 1988-92. Pres. West Salem PTA, 1985-87; bd. dirs. Am. Lung Assn. Va., 1991-93, Baker Co. Sch.; bd. dirs. (pres. bd. dirs. 1998—), treas. Albany Area Primary Health Care, 1993—; commr. Keep Albany-Dougherty Beautiful Commn., 1993—. vestryman St. Patrick's Episcopal Ch.; mem. Workforce Investment Bd., 2000—; mem. coun. Baker County Scho., 2001—. Mem. Nat. Assn. Coll. and Univ. Bus. Officers, Nat. Coun. Rsch. Adminstrs., Luth. Coll. Bus. Officers, Coll. and Univ. Pers. Assn., Assn. Phys. Plant Adminstrs., Salem-Roanoke County C. of C., Rotary Internat. (bd. dirs. Salem 1985-89, pres. 1987-88), South Ga. C. of C. (bd. dirs.), Baker County Collaborative (bd. dirs.), Albany C. of C., Rotary. Home: 2718 Somerset Dr Albany GA 31707-8100 Office: Joseph W Jones Ecol Rsch Ce RR 2 Box 2324 Newton GA 31770-9640 E-mail: wwalton@jonesctr.org.

WALTZ, ALAN KENT, clergyman, denominational executive; b. Normal, Ill., Oct. 10, 1931; s. James Edwin Sr. and Ethel Leona (Hawkins) W.; m. Mary Joyce Horton, June 5, 1966; children: Sharon Kay, Reid Alan. BA, Ill. Wesleyan U., 1953; MDiv, Garrett Theol. Sem., Evanston, Ill., 1957; MA, Northwestern U., 1958, PhD, 1961. Ordained to ministry United Methodist Ch., 1957. Pastor Braceville Meth. Ch., Ill., 1954-56; denominational exec. United Meth. Ch., 1960-98; asst. dir. Bd. Missions, Phila., 1960-64; asst. gen. sec. Coun. on Fin., Evanston, 1964-68; assoc. gen. sec. Gen. Coun. on Ministries, Dayton, Ohio, 1969-84, Gen. Bd. Discipleship, Nashville, 1984-98. Author: Images of the Future, 1980, To Proclaim the Fair, 1983, Facts and Possibilities, 1987, A Dictionary for United Methodists, 1991; editor book series Into Our Third Century, 1981-84. Trustee Ill. Wesleyan U., Bloomington, 1984-93.

WALTZ, JAMES RICHARD, physician; b. Massillon, Ohio, June 30, 1935; AB, Ohio U., 1957; MD, Ohio State U., 1962. Intern Milw. County Hosp., 1962-63; resident U. Ill. Rsch. Edn. Hosps., 1963-67; gen. surgeon Liberty Hosp. Mem. ACS. Office: 15724 Oakmont Dr Kearney MO 64060-9251

WALTZ, JOSEPH MCKENDREE, neurosurgeon, educator; b. Detroit, July 23, 1931; s. Ralph McKinley and Bertha (Seelye) W.; m. Janet Maureen Journey, June 26, 1954; children: Jeffrey McKinley, Mary Elaine, David Seelye, Stephen McKendree; m. Marilyn Liska, June 5, 1967; 1 child, Tristana McKendree. Student, U. Mich., 1950; BS, U. Oreg., 1954, MD, 1956. Diplomate Am. Bd. Neurol. Surgery. Surg. intern U. Mich. Hosp., 1956-57, gen. surg. resident, 1957-58, clin. instr. neurosurgery, 1960-63; neurosurg. assoc. St. Barnabas Hosp., N.Y.C., 1963—; assoc. dir. Inst. Neurosci., 1974—, dir. dept. neurol. surgery, 1977—. Assoc. cons. in neurosurgery Englewood (N.J.) Hosp., 1964—; assoc. prof. neurosurgery NYU Med. Str., 1974—; asst. prof. dept. surgery (neurosurgery) N.Y. Coll. Osteo. Medicine, 1989—; bd. dirs. Neurol. Surgery Rsch. Found., 1978; mem. alumni bd. U. Mich. Med. Ctr., 1995, Attending Neuroscience Inst.-Our Lady Mercy Hosp.; dir. Med. Court Graphics. Author: (chpt.) Cryogenic Surgery, Neurology, 1982, Advances in Neurology, 1983, Textbook of Stereotactic and Functional Neurosurgery, 1997; contbr. articles to profl. jours.; patentee in field. Mem. sci. adv. bd. Dystonia Med. Research Found., 1980—; trustee St. Barnabas Hosp., 1980—. Served to capt. M.C. AUS, 1958-60. Recipient Bronze award Am. Congress Rehab. Medicine, 1967, World Cmty. Svc. award Rotary, Disting. Trustee award United Hosp. Fund, 1995. Mem. AMA, Am. Paralysis Assn., World Soc. Stereotactic and Functional Neurosurgery, Congress Neurol. Surgeons, Math. Assn. Am., Internat. Neural Network Soc., Soc. for Cryobiology, N.Y. State Med. Soc., Bronx County Med. Soc., N.Y. State Neurosurg Soc., Nat. Ski Patrol, Phi Beta Pi. Achievements include spl. rsch. on neurophysiology and treatment of epilepsy, basal ganglia disorders, abnormal movement disorders, cerebral palsy, also neurosurg. application stereotactic thalamic surgery and spinal cord stimulation. Home: Four B Island South 720 Milton Rd Rye NY 10580-3258 Office: St Barnabas Hosp Dept Neurosurgery Bronx NY 10457

WALTZ, KATHLEEN M. publishing executive; b. Mar. 6, 1954; BA, DePaul U.; postgrad., Northwestern U. Telemarketers Chgo. Tribune, dir. customer satisfaction, classified advt. dir., v.p./dir. of developing bus.; gen. chief exec. Daily Press, Newport News, Va.; pub., chief exec., pres. Orlando Sentinel, 2000—. Bd. dirs. United Way of Va. Peninsula, Peninsula Allice for Econ. Devel. WHRO Found. and Greater Peninsula Now; bd. dirs., exec. com. Hampton Roads Partnership; ABC/NAA liaison com., sr. exec. resource corps. Coll. of William and Mary. Mem. So. Newspapers Pub. Assn. (diversity com.). Avocations: travel, golf, gardening. Office: Orlando Sentinel 1000 N Garland Ave Orlando FL 32801*

WALTZ, KENNETH NEAL, political science educator; b. Ann Arbor, Mich., June 8, 1924; s. Christian Benjamin and Luella (Braun) W.; m. Helen Elizabeth Lindsley, June 4, 1949; children: Kenneth L., Thomas E. (dec.), Daniel E. AB, Oberlin Coll., 1948, LLD, 2002; MA, Columbia U., 1950, PhD, 1954; D honoris causa, Copenhagen U., 1995. Instr., then asst. prof. Columbia U., 1953-57; from assoc. prof. to prof. politics Swarthmore Coll., 1957-66; research assoc. Center Internat. Affairs, Harvard, 1963-64, 68-69, 72; prof. politics Brandeis U., Waltham, Mass., 1966-71, Adlai E. Stevenson prof. internat. politics, 1967-71; Ford prof. polit. sci. U. Calif., Berkeley, 1971-94, Ford prof. emeritus, 1994—; vis. sr. rsch. assoc. King's Coll., U. London, 1986-87; adj. prof., rsch. assoc. Inst. War and Peace Studies Columbia U., 1997—. Cons. govt. agys. Author: Man, The State and War, 1959, Foreign Policy and Democratic Politics, 1967, Theory of International Politics, 1979, The Spread of Nuclear Weapons, 1981; co-author: The Spread of Nuclear Weapons: A Debate, 1995, The Spread of Nuclear Weapons: A Debate Renewed, 2002; co-author, co-editor: Conflict in World Politics, 1971, The Use of Force, 1971, 5th edit., 1999; mem. edtl. bd. Jour. Strategic Studies, Jour. Chinese Polit. Sci. Served to 1st lt. AUS, 1944-46, 51-52. Recipient Heinz Eulau award for best article, Am. Polit. Sci. Rev., 1990, James Madison award disting. scholarly contbn. to polit. sci., 1999; grantee, NSF, 1968—71, Guggenheim, 1976—77, Woodrow Wilson Ctr., Inernat. Ctr. Scholars, 1979—80; scholar vis. scholar philosophy, London Sch. Econs., 1976—77, vis. scholar, Rsch. Sch. Pacific Studies, Australian Nat. U., 1978, U. Peking Dept. Internat. Politics, 1982, 1991, 1996, Fudan U., Shanghai, 1991, 2001, USAF Acad., 1991—92. Fellow Am. Acad. Arts and Scis.; mem. Am. Polit. Sci. Assn. (sec. 1966-67, pres. 1987-88), Internat. Studies Assn. (pres. New Eng. sect. 1966-67), Coun. Fgn. Rels., Phi Beta Kappa.

WALTZ, MARCUS ERNEST, retired prosthodontist; b. Brownsville, Oreg., July 29, 1921; s. Roswell Starr and Eva Ione (Cherrington) W.; m. Constance Jean Elwood, May 31, 1952 (div. Nov. 1973); children: Melody Ann, Martha Louise, Kathryn Jean, Holly Jay, Joy Evalyn, Ross Elwood; m. Shelby Annette Schwab, June 10, 1975. AB, Willamette U., 1942; DMD, U. Oreg., 1945. Cert. Nev. State Bd. Dental Examiners. Practice dentistry, Forest Grove, Oreg., 1946-52; practice dentistry specializing in prosthodontics Reno, 1954-95; ret., 1995. Councillor Pacific Coast Dental Conf., bd. dirs., 1979-84; pres. Pacific Coast Soc. of Prosthodontics, 1983; mem. Nev. State Bd. Dental Examiners, 1960-66, pres., 1964. Contbr. essays to dentistry jours. Mem. State of Nev. Selective Svc. Appeals Bd., 1970-76, pres., 1974-76. Lt. USN, 1945-46, 52-54, Korea. Decorated Combat Medics award, Battle Stars (oak leaf cluster), Fellow Internat. Coll. Dentistry, Acad. Dentistry Internat.; mem. ADA, Northern Nev. Dental Soc. (pres. 1959), Nev. Dental Assn., Nev. Acad. Gen. Dentistry (pres. 1974), Sigma Chi, Omicron Kappa Upsilon. Clubs: Reno Exec. (dir. 1960-66, pres. 1964-65). Lodges: Sigma Tau (pres. 1941-42), Masons (32 degree), Shriners. Democrat. Methodist. Avocations: outdoor activities, arranging choral music. Home: 715 Manor Dr Reno NV 89509-1944

WALUK, STANLEY PETER, corporate engineering official; b. Palmer, Mass., July 29, 1943; s. Stanley John and Bertha Rose (Mozden) W.; A.S. in E.E., Northeast Inst., 1963; B.S. in Indsl. Engring., Western New Eng. Coll., 1973; postgrad. in forensic engring. and patent law Brown U., 1983; postgrad. in product liability law Providence Coll., 1981; m. Mary Ann Mechonski, June 6, 1964; 1 dau., Angela Kim. Quality control mgr., chief engr. Gavitt Wire and Cable Co., Brookfield, Mass., 1963-71; spl. project engr. TRW-Holyoke Wire and Cable Co., South Hadley, Mass., 1971-74; plant mgr. Standard Wire and Cable Co., Attleboro, Mass., 1974-75; v.p., gen. mgr. Lyall Electric, Kendallville, Ind., 1975; tech. dir. Miller Electric Co. (Carol Cable Co.), Woonsocket, R.I., 1976-83; engring. mgr. Judd Wire Inc. div. High Voltage Engring., 1983-90; corp. mgr. quality and standards Judd Wire, Inc., 1990-92; cons. wire and cable engring., 1975—; owner, mgr., W Ma Assocs., Deerfield, Mass., 1992—; dir. engring. and quality Am. Electric Cable Co., Holyoke, Mass., 1994—. mem. tech. adv. panel Underwriters Lab., also rep. Industry Adv. Conf. Aux. staff officer USCG; mfg. insp. rep. FAA, 1985—. Mem. ASTM, Nat. Fire Protection Assn., Stat. Process Control Soc., Internat. Electrotech. Comm. (mem. com.), Am. Inst. Indsl. Engrs., Wire Assn., Am. Soc. Quality Control, Soc. Automotive Engrs., Am. Mgmt. Soc. (affiliate), Providence Engring. Soc. (affiliate), U.S. Coast Guard Aux. (staff officer), U.S. Yacht Racing Union. Expert in elec. engring. and consumer elec. products. Home and Office: 3 Oak Knoll Dr South Deerfield MA 01373-9672

WALUSIS, ERIC MICHAEL, product developer, consultant; b. Dayton, Ohio, Dec. 3, 1966; s. John M. and Donna L. (Urban) W.; m. Maria L. Czeiszperger, Dec. 13, 1986; children: Hannah, Madeline. BFA, Ohio State U.,

1991. Prodr., dir. Searchlight Comms., Dayton, Ohio, 1991-97; product developer Lion Apparel, 1995-97; pres., CEO, founder Searchlight eBook Tng. Inc., 1999—. Prodr. Dayton (Ohio) Access TV, 1983-87. Prodr. documentary film stories From Old North Dayton, 1995 (Bronze plaque Columbus Film Festival, 1995). Bd. dirs. Old North Dayton Devel. Corp., 1998-99. Recipient 2000 Impact 30 award, eSchoolNews mag.; Kettering grantee Kettering Found., 1984, grantee Montgomery County Regional Arts Cultural Dist., 1994. Mem. Ohio State U. photography cinema alumni. Avocations: cinema, lit. Home: 7618 Little Richmond Rd Dayton OH 45427-1308 E-mail: denarista@earthlink.net.

WALWORTH, ARTHUR, author; b. Newton, Mass., July 9, 1903; s. Arthur Clarence and Ruth Richardson (Lippincott) W. Grad., Phillips Andover Acad., 1921; BA, Yale U., 1925. Ednl. dept. Houghton Mifflin Co., 1927-43; staff OWI, 1943; Staff Medomak Camp, Washington, summers 1943-63. Author: School Histories at War, 1938, Black Ships Off Japan, 1946, Cape Breton, 1948, The Medomak Way, 1953, Woodrow Wilson, 2 vols, 1958, 1 vol., 1967, 78, America's Moment: 1918, 1977, Wilson and His Peacemakers, 1986 Recipient Pulitzer prize in biography, 1958 Mem.: Cosmos Club. Home: North Hill 865 Central Ave Apt D506 Needham MA 02492-1338

WALZ, GREGORY STEPHEN, lawyer; b. St. Cloud, Minn., Mar. 8, 1957; s. Wendelin George and Ilse Marie Walz; m. Sandra Jean Theis, Nov. 17, 1987; children: Nicole, Joseph, Jacob, Jessica, Alexandra. BA, St. Johns U., Collegeville, Minn., 1981; JD, William Mitchell Coll. Law, St. Paul, 1987. Bar: Minn. 1987, U.S. Dist. Ct. Minn. 1987. Atty. Walz Law Office, St. Cloud, 1990—. Office: Walz Law Office PO Box 1794 Saint Cloud MN 56302-1794 E-mail: info@walzlaw.com.

WALZ, JONATHAN RICHARD, archaeologist; b. Greensboro, N.C., Nov. 26, 1971; s. David Henry and Ruth Todd Walz; m. Joella Ann Wilson, May 11, 1996. BA, U. N.C., 1994; MA, U. Fla., 1997, postgrad., 1999—, U. Dar es Salaam, Tanzania, 1997—98. Archaeologist Louis Berger and Assocs., East Orange, NJ, 1994—95; instr./tchg. asst. U. Fla., Gainesville, 1999—2001. Archaeol. and paleontol. rschr. Co-founder Student Peace Initiative, Chapel Hill, NC, 1992. Fellow Title VI Fgn. Lang. and Area Studies fellowship, U.S. Dept. Edn., 1995—98, 1999, Fulbright Hays Doctoral Dissertation Rsch. Abroad fellow, 2001—02; grantee Predissertation Field grantee, Found. for African Prehistory and Archaeology, 1996, 1999. Master: Order of the Bell Tower; mem.: World Archaeol. Congress, African Studies Assn., Am. Anthrop. Assn., Phi Kappa Phi, Phi Beta Kappa. Home: 7200 SW 8th Ave B8 Gainesville FL 32607

WALZ, KENNETH GORDON, communications executive; b. Holland, Mich., Apr. 29; s. Chester S. and Graye (Vick) W.; m. Joan VanderVeen, June, 1966 (div. 1970); 1 child, Bryan Christopher. BA, Hope Coll., 1966. Asst. account exec. Foote, Cone and Belding, N.Y.C., 1969-70; account exec. Ogilvy and Mather, 1971-72; pres. Ken Walz Prodns., Inc., 1972—. Prodr.: (ABC-TV documentary) Bengal Tiger in Nepal, 1981, (Nickelodeon) Adventures of Pete and Pete, Wildside, TV commls. and corp. films, 1980—, (cable TV spls.) Ron Reagan, Carol Leifer, Adam West, Julie Brown, (music videos) Cyndi Lauper, Dionne Warwick, Huey Lewis, AC/DC, The Oak Ridge Boys, Carly Simon, others, 1972—; exec. prodr. (TV movie) Like Father, Like Santa, 1998. Recipient Grand Prize Internat. Film and TV Festival of N.Y., 1985, Best Pop Video award Am. Music Awards, 1985, Gold award Houston Internat. Film Festival, 1987, CableAce award, 1995. Office: 3000 Olympic Blvd Santa Monica CA 90404-5073

WALZ, KENT, publishing executive; Editor Albuquerque Jour. Office: Albuquerque Jour Albuquerque Jour Newsroom 7777 Jefferson St NE Albuquerque NM 87109-4360*

WALZER, JAMES HARVEY, lawyer, author; b. Neptune, N.J., Jan. 24, 1949; s. Elwood John and Mary Elizabeth (Harvey) W.; m. Gloria Jean Demkowski, May 29, 1971; children: Sara, Emily, Amanda, Adam. BA, Bowdoin Coll., 1972; JD, Cleve. State U., 1975. Bar: N.J. 1975, U.S. Dist. Ct. N.J. 1975. Pvt. practice, Newark, 1975-78, Livingston, N.J., 1978-81, Boonton, 1981—. Legal forms editor All-State Legal, a div. of All-State Internat., Inc., Cranford, N.J., 1978—96. Author: Employment, Agency, Service Agreements, 1986, Motor Vehicle Law and Practice--Forms, 1988, 2 vols., 2000, Civil Practice Forms, 5 vols., 1990, 8 vols., 5th edit., 1998; editor, author: Legal Forms, 7 vols., 1995-96. Mem. Manville (N.J.) Bd. Adjustment, 1976; bd. dirs. Somerset-Sussex Legal Svcs. Mem. ABA, N.J. Bar Assn., Morris County Bar Assn. Democrat. E-mai. Home: 18 Magda Ln Hillsborough NJ 08844-4217 Office: 103 William St PO Box 675 Boonton NJ 07005-0675 E-mail: jhwalzer@aol.com.

WALZER, JUDITH BORODOVKO, academic administrator, educator; b. N.Y.C., May 27, 1935; d. Isidore and Ida (Gins) Borodovko; m. Michael L. Walzer, June 17, 1956; children— Sarah, Rebecca BA, Brandeis U., 1958, MA, 1960, PhD, 1967. Dir. office women's edn. Radcliffe Coll., Cambridge, Mass., 1974-77, assoc. dean., 1976-77; Allston Burr sr. tutor, asst. dean for co-edn. Harvard Coll., 1977-80; asst. to the pres. Princeton U., N.J., 1980-85; provost New Sch. U., N.Y.C., 1985-98, prof. lit., 1998—. Mem. adv. com. Overseas Sch., Hebrew U. in Jerusalem, 1989—. Democrat. Jewish. Office: New Sch U 65 W 11th St New York NY 10011 E-mail: walzer@newschool.edu.

WALZER, MICHAEL, political science educator; b. N.Y.C., Mar. 3, 1935; s. Joseph P. and Sally (Hochman) W.; m. Judith Borodovko, June 17, 1956; children: Sarah, Rebecca. BA, Brandeis U., 1956; PhD, Harvard U., 1961. Fulbright fellow Cambridge (Eng.) U., 1956-57; asst. prof. Princeton U., 1962-66; faculty Harvard U., 1966-80, prof. govt., 1968-80; prof. Sch. Social Scis., Inst. Advanced Study, Princeton, N.J., 1980—. Author: The Revolution of the Saints, 1965, Obligations: Essays on Disobedience, War and Citizenship, 1970, Political Action, 1971, Regicide and Revolution, 1974, Just and Unjust Wars, 1977, Radical Principles: Reflections of an Unreconstructed Democrat, 1980, Spheres of Justice: A Defense of Pluralism and Equality, 1983, Exodus and Revolution, 1985, Interpretation and Social Criticism, 1987, The Company of Critics: Social Criticism and Political Commitment in the Twentieth Century, 1988, What It Means To Be an American, 1993, Thick and Thin: Moral Argument at Home and Abroad, 1994, (with David Miller) Pluralism, Justice, and Equality, 1995, On Toleration, 1997; editor: (with others) The Jewish Political Tradition, 2000; mem. editl. bd. Dissent mag., 1960—; contbg. editor New Republic, 1976—. Bd. govs. Hebrew U., Jerusalem, 1975— ; trustee Brandeis U., 1983-88 ; chmn. faculty adv. cabinet United Jewish Appeal, 1977-81. Home: 103 Linwood Cir Princeton NJ 08540-3625

WALZER, NORMAN CHARLES, economics educator; b. Mendota, Ill., Mar. 17, 1943; s. Elmer J. and Anna L. Walzer; m. Dona Lee Maurer, Aug. 22, 1970; children: Steven, Mark. BS, Ill. State U., Normal, 1966; MA, U. Ill., 1969, PhD, 1970. Rsch. dir. Cities and Villages Mcpl. Problems Com., Springfield, Ill., 1974-84; vis. prof. U. Ill., Urbana, 1977-78; prof. econs. Western Ill. U., Macomb, 1978—, chmn. dept. econs., 1980-89, dir. Ill. Inst. Rural Affairs, 1988—, interim dean coll. bus. and tech., 1993-95. Author: Cities, Suburbs and Property Tax, 1981, Government Structure and Public Finance, 1984; editor: Financing State and Local Governments, 1981, Rural Community Economic Development, 1991; co-editor: Financing Local Infrastructure in Non Metro Areas, 1986, Financing Economic Development in The 1980s, 1986, Financing Rural Health Care, 1988, Rural Health Care, 1992, Rural Community Economic Development, 1992, Local Economic Development: International Trends and Issues, 1995, Community Visioning Programs: Practice and Principles, 1996, Public-Private Partnerships for Local Economic Development, 1998, Cooperative Approach to Community Economic Development, 2000, Local Government Innovations, 2000, American Midwest: Managing Change in Rural Transition, 2002. Mem. Am. Econs. Assn., Ill. Econs. Assn. (pres. 1979-80), Mid-Continent Regional Sci. Assn. (pres. 1985-86). Office: Western Ill U Ill Inst Rural Affairs 518 Stipes Hall Macomb IL 61455

WAMP, ZACH, congressman; b. Ft. Benning, Ga., Oct. 28, 1957; m. Kim Wamp; 2 children. Student, U. N.C., U. Tenn. Chmn. Hamilton County Rep. Party, 1987; regional dir. Tenn. Rep. Party, 1989; v.p. Charter Real Estate Corp., 1989-92; comml. and indsl. real estate broker Fletcher Bright Co., 1992-94; mem. U.S. Congress from 3d Tenn. dist., 1995—, mem. sci. com., transp. and infrastructure com., small bus. com., vice chmn. water resources and environment subcom. Office: US House Reps 423 Cannon Ho Office Bldg Washington DC 20515-4203*

WAMPLER, LLOYD CHARLES, retired lawyer; b. Spencer, Ind., Nov. 4, 1920; s. Charles and Vivian (Hawkins) W.; m. Joyce Ann Hoppenrath, Sept. 28, 1950 (dec. 1954); 1 child, Natalie Gay (dec.); m. Mary E. Shumaker, Sept. 16, 1982 AB, Ind. U., 1942, JD, 1947. Bar: Ind. 1947, U.S. Supreme Ct. 1971. Instr. bus. law U. Kans., 1947-49; dep. atty. gen. Ind., 1949-50; mem. legal com. Interstate Oil Compact Commn., 1950; asst. pub. counselor Ind., 1950-53; mem. Stevens, Wampler, Travis & Fortin, Plymouth, 1953-83; claim counsel Am. Family Ins. Group, Indpls., 1983-88; ret., 1988. Mem. Ind. Rehab. Services Bd., 1978-86; Dem. nominee for judge Ind. Supreme Ct., 1956. With USNR, 1942-46 Mem. ABA, Am. Judicature Soc., Ind. Bar Assn. (bd. mgrs. 1975-77), Indpls. Bar Assn., Ind. Acad. Sci., Ind. Def. Lawyers Assn. (bd. dirs. 1967-72, v.p. 1970, pres. 1971-72), Ind. Hist. Soc., Marshall County Hist. Soc. (bd. dirs. 1969-75), Sagamore of the Wabash, Am. Legion, Phi Delta Phi. Home: 4000 N Meridian St Indianapolis IN 46208-4034

WAMPLER, ROBERT JOSEPH, lawyer; b. Greensboro, Ind., Mar. 3, 1936; s. Cruden V. and Mary L. (James) W.; m. Karen A. Wiggins, Feb. 19, 1977; children: Eric J., Kelly L., Michael J. AB, Yale U., 1959; JD, Ind. U., 1963. Bar: Ind. 1963, U.S. Dist. Ct. (so. dist.) Ind. 1963, U.S. Supreme Ct. 1966, U.S. Ct. Appeals (7th cir.) 1972. Assoc. Kightlinger & Gray, Indpls., 1963—, ptnr., 1968—, sr. ptnr., 1971—. Author handbook on product liability; co-author: Trial Advocacy in Indiana, 1989. Sec., bd. dirs. Ivy Ridge Civic Assn., Indpls., 1975—. Fellow Indpls. Bar Found.; mem. Indpls. Bar Assn. (chmn. litigation sect. 1987), Ind. Bar Assn., Def. Trial Counsel Ind., Masons, Order of Coif, Phi Delta Phi. Republican. Episcopalian. Home: 5939 Cape Cod Ct Indianapolis IN 46250-1845 Office: Kightlinger & Gray LLP 151 N Delaware St Ste 660 Indianapolis IN 46204-2574 E-mail: rwampler@k-glaw.com.

WAMPLER, STEPHEN GEORGE, music educator; b. Wichita, Kans., Apr. 26, 1954; s. Harry George Wampler, Ruth (Lee) Wampler; m. Barbara Jean Wampler, Sept. 10, 1989; children: Spencer Freed, Jason Freed, Sarah Tiffany Little, Molly, Emily. AA, Bellevue C.C., Bellevue, Wash., 1975; BMus, We. Wash. U., 1981; MMus, U. Wash., 1991, D of Musical Arts, 1998. Cert. Continuing tchg. cert. Wash. Freelance musician, tchr. Greater Seattle Area, 1982—93; dir. jazz ensemble and chorus Edmonds Sch. Dist., Lynnwood, Wash., 1993—94; dir. band, tchr. strings Ctrl. Kitsap Sch. Dist., Silverdale, 1994—95; dir. band, tchr. music Darrington Sch. Dist., Darrington, 1995—. Musician Bellevue Philharm. Orch., Seattle Choral Co., Roadside Attraction Jazz Ensemble, Bob Hope Show, Sammy Davis Jr., Chrystal Gayle, Bobby Shaw, Diane Schures, Seattle Music Hall; instr. trumpet and trombone pvt. lessons, 1982—93. Recipient Eagle Scout award, Boy Scouts Am., 1971. Mem.: NEA, Coll. Music Soc., Darrington Edn. Assn., Musicians Assn. Local 76-493. Avocations: cooking, hiking, camping, fishing, electric bass playing in rock band. Home: PO Box 528 Darrington WA 98241-0528 Office: Darrington High Sch PO Box 27 Darrington WA 98241-0027

WAMPOLD, BABETTE LEVY, civic volunteer; b. Birmingham, Ala., May 19, 1934; d. Jerome Milton and Emma Marie (Ullman) Levy; m. Charles Henry Wampold, Jr., Mar. 14, 1954; children: Jerre Lynn Waters, Carolyn Beller, Charles Henry III. Student, Tulane U., 1952-54. Contbg. editor R.C.D.A. quar. (formerly Religion in Communist Dominated Areas), 1980-92. Pres. Ala. Coun. to Save Soviet Jews, Montgomery, 1976-89; mem. nat. bd. dirs. Union of Couns. for Soviet Jews, Washington, 1978-89, Rsch. Ctr. for Religion and Human Rights in Closed Socs., N.Y.C., 1979-93; mem., past pres. Sisterhood, Temple Beth Or. Mem. Nat. Coun. Jewish Women (past v.p. Montgomery sect.), Hadassah (past bd. dirs.). Avocations: travel, reading, history. Home: 3113 Jasmine Rd Montgomery AL 36111-1114

WAN, JULIA CHANG, retired science educator; b. Hong Kong, Oct. 13, 1937; d. Charles S.Y. and Lucy (Wong) Chang; m. Frederic Y.M. Wan, Sept 10, 1960. BA, Wellesley Coll., 1960, MA, 1970; EdD, Boston Coll., 1978. Mem. staff Bio Rsch. Inst., Cambridge, Mass., 1960-64; physics tchr. Watertown (Mass.) H.S., 1970-73; sci. dir. Watertown Pub. Schs., 1973-79; curriculum dir. Fed. Way Sch. Dist., Fed. Way, Wash., 1979-83; asst. supt. Bainbridge Island (Wash.) Sch. Dist., 1983-93; program dir. NSF, Washington, 1993-95; dir. Ctr. for Excellence in Sci. and Math. Edn. Calif. State U., Fullerton, 1995-2000. Mem. accreditation com. N.W. Assn. Schs. and Colls., Boise, Idaho, 1981-95; mem. edn. opportunity coun. AAAS, Washington, 1995-99; bd. dirs. Challenger Ctr., Alexandria, Va., 1997-2000. Author: Designing School Health Education Curricula, 1992, 2d edit. 1995; contbr. articles and revs. to sci. mags. Bd. dirs. NOW, 1985-88; mem. Commn. on Asian-Am. Affairs, Olympia, Wash., 1990-93; bd. trustees Girls, Inc., Orange County, Calif., 1995-2000. Recipient award profl. excellence We. Wash. U., Bellingham, 1988, exemplary program award Met. Life Found., N.Y.C., 1989; grantee: NSF (numerous), Arlington, Va., 1989-2000, Beckman Found., Irvine, Calif., 1998-2000. Mem. ASCD, Am. Edml. Rsch. Assn., Nat. Sci. Tchrs. Assn., Phi Delta Kappa. Office: Calif State U Fullerton PO Box 6850 Fullerton CA 92834-4565 E-mail: Jwan@fullerton.edu.

WAN, KAI-TAK, university educator; b. Hong Kong, Hong Kong, Oct. 23, 1964; s. Lun Wan and Chuen-Chu Woo; m. Gwen Wing-Fong Siu. BSc, U. New South Wales, 1987; PhD, U. Md., 1992. Assoc. prof. Nanyang Tech. U., Singapore, 1996—2001; vis. prof. ESM, Va. Tech, Blacksburg, 2001—02; asst. prof. mechanical engr. U. Missouri-Rolla, 2002—. Mem.: Adhesion Soc. Home: 1315E Henry St Blacksburg VA 24060 Office: U Missouri-Rolla ME Building 1870 Miner Circle Rolla MO 65409 Office Fax: 540-231-9187 . Personal E-mail: kaitakw@yahoo.com. Business E-Mail: kwan@vt.edu.

WANDEN, STIG, economist, researcher; b. Stockholm, Aug. 25, 1940; s. Johan and Ingegerd (Bergh) W.; m. Elena Wanden, 1997. PhD, Lund (Sweden) U., Lund, Sweden, 1963, M in Polit. Scis., 1968. Head of sect. Ministry of Fin., Stockholm, 1969-75; economist Swedish Adminstrn., 1975-77, IMF, Washington, 1977-80; researcher Swedish Adminstrn., Stockholm, 1980—. Lectr. in field. Author: Economic Thinking, 1981, Economics In A Philosophical Light, 1986, Ethics and Environment, 1992, Ideological Controversies in Environment Policy, 1993, Environment and Responsibility, 1996, Environment, Lifestyle, and Society, 1997, Goal Conflicts and Policy Instruments, 1997; co-author: Understanding Biodiversity, 1997, Goals and Sectors-Issues in Environmental Policies, 2000. Harvard fellow Am. Coun. Learned Soc., 1964-65. Home: G Ekmans V 10 129 35 Stockholm Sweden E-mail: stig.wanden@swipnet.se., stig.wanden@environ.se.

WANDER, HERBERT STANTON, lawyer; b. Cin., Mar. 17, 1935; s. Louis Marvin and Pauline (Schuster) W.; m. Ruth Cele Fell, Aug. 7, 1960; children: Daniel Jerome, Susan Gail, Lois Marlene. AB, U. Mich., 1957; LLB, Yale U., 1960. Bar: Ohio 1960, Ill. 1960. Law clk. to judge U.S. Dist. Ct. (no. dist.) Ill., 1960—61; ptnr. Pope Ballard Shepard & Fowle, Chgo., 1961—78, Katten Muchin Zavis Rosenman, Chgo., 1978—. Trustee Michael Reese Found., 1991—; bd. dirs. Tel. & Data Systems, Chgo.; mem. legal adv. com. to the bd. govs. N.Y. Stock Exch., 1989-92; mem. legal adv. bd. Nat. Assn. Securities Dealers, Inc., 1996-99. Editor: (jour.) Bus. Law Today, 1992-93; editor-in-chief: (jour.) The Bus. Lawyer, 1993-94; contbr. numerous articles to profl. jours. Bd. dirs. Jewish Fedn. Met. Chgo., 1972—, pres., 1981-83; bd. dirs. Jewish United Fund, 1972—, pres., 1981-83, chmn. pub. affairs com., 1984-87, gen. campaign chmn., 1993; former regional chmn. nat. young leadership cabinet United Jewish Appeal; vice-chmn. large city budgeting conf. Coun. Jewish Fedns., 1979-82, bd. dirs., 1980—, exec. com., 1983-84. Mem. ABA (sec. bus. law sect. 1992-93, vice-chair 1993-94, chair-elect 1994-95, chair 1995-96, apptd. to commn. on multidisciplinary practice 1998), Ill. State Bar Assn., Chgo. Bar Assn., Yale Law Sch. Assn. (exec. com. 1982-86), Std. Club, Econ. Club, Northmoor Country Club, Phi Beta Kappa. Home: 70 Prospect Ave Highland Park IL 60035-3329 Office: Katten Muchin Zavis Rosenman 525 W Monroe St Ste 1600 Chicago IL 60661-3693 E-mail: hwander@kmzr.com.

WANDERMAN, MIRIAM, library studies educator; b. Bklyn. m. Jay S. Wanderman, 1973; children: Adam, Joshua, Daniel. BA, Herbert Lehman Coll., 1970; MLS, Pratt Inst., Bklyn., 1972; MA, Herbert Lehman Coll., 1975. Adj. asst. prof. Libr. Svcs. Medgar Evers Coll., Bklyn., 1972-88; adj. asst. prof. Libr. Svcs. Adelphi U., Garden City, N.Y., 1988-95, Hofstra U., Hempstead, 1995—. Pres. Lakeside Elem. Sch. PTA, Merrick, N.Y., 1995-97, Merrick Ave. Mid. Sch. PTA, Merrick, 1998-99, John F. Kennedy H.S. PTA, Bellmore, N.Y., 2000-02; pres. Bellmore-Merrick Ctrl. HS Dist. Coun. of PTAs, 2002—; historian Nassau Dist. PTA, 1997-2000; bd. trustees Merrick Libr. Bd., 2001—. Recipient N.Y. State PTA Hon. Life Membership award, 1990, N.Y. State PTA Disting. Svc. award, 1997, Merrick Union Free Sch. Dist. Disting. Svc. award, 1997, Nat. PTA Hon. Life Membership award, 1999, Golden Cir. of Leadership award N.Y. State PTA, 1998, 99, Bellmore-Merrick Ctrl. High Sch. Dist. United Tchrs. PTA svc. award, 2001. Mem. ALA, Nassau County Libr. Assn., Assn. of Coll. and Rsch. Librs./N.Y., N.Y. Libr. Assn. Home: 3039 Whaleneck Dr Merrick NY 11566-5324

WANDERMAN, SUSAN MAE, lawyer; b. Mar. 12, 1947; d. Leo and Muriel D. Wanderman. AB, Wheaton Coll., Norton, Mass., 1967; JD, St. John's U., 1970; LLM, NYU, 1976. Bar: N.Y. 1971, U.S. Dist. Ct. (ea. and so. dists.) N.Y. 1972, U.S. Ct. Appeals (2d cir.) 1973, U.S. Supreme Ct. 1974. Asst. legal officer, legal dept. Chem. Bank, N.Y.C., 1972—75; 2d v.p. legal dept. Chase Manhattan Bank N.A., 1975—82; asst. gen. counsel Citicorp Svcs., Inc., 1982—84; v.p. Citibank, N.A., 1984—. Instr. bus. law and law for the layman LaGuardia C.C., 1976—77; law day spkr. Queens County Supreme Ct., 1979—83; mem. Cmty. Bd. 6, Queens County, N.Y.C., 1987—. Contbr. articles to legal publs. Past vol. N.Y. State Bar Assn. Lawyers in the Classroom. Mem.: ABA, Queens County Bar Assn., N.Y. State Bar Assn. Office: Citibank NA One Court Sq Long Island City NY 11120

WANDERS, HANS WALTER, banker; b. Aachen, Germany, Apr. 3, 1925; came to U.S., 1929, naturalized, 1943; s. Herbert and Anna Maria (Kusters) W.; m. Elizabeth Knox Kimball, Apr. 2, 1949; children: Crayton Kimball, David Gillette. BS, Yale U., 1947; postgrad. Grad. Sch. Banking, Rutgers U., 1961-64. With GE, 1947-48, Libbey-Owens-Ford Glass Co., 1948-53, Allied Chem. Co., 1953-55, McKinsey & Co., Inc., 1955-57; from asst. cashier to v.p. No. Trust Co., Chgo., 1957-65; v.p. Nat. Blvd. Bank, 1965-66, pres., 1966-70; exec. v.p. Wachovia Bank & Trust Co., N.A., Winston-Salem, N.C., 1970-74, chmn., 1977-85, vice chmn., 1985-88, also bd. dirs.; pres. Wachovia Corp., 1974-76, 85-87, chmn., 1977-85, vice chmn., 1987-88, also bd. dirs.; pres., chief exec. officer 1st Wachovia Corp. Services, Inc., 1986-88, ret., 1988; dir. Exxon Supply Co., 1989-94, Goody's Pharmaceuticals, 1989-94; dir. Gulf USA, Inc., 1989-92; dir. Turnpike Properties, Inc., 2001—. Chmn. Winston-Salem Found. Com., 1981-82; bd. dirs. N.C. Textile Found., N.C. Engring. Found., Inc., 1971-88; trustee, mem. exec. com. Salem Coll. and Acad., 1986-91, Tax Found., 1982—, vice chmn., 1984-86, chmn., 1986-88, chmn. exec. com., 1989; mem. bd. visitors Fuqua Sch. Bus., Duke U., 1978-89, N.C. Japan Ctr., 1982—; mem. nat. corps. com. United Negro Coll. Fund; mem., chmn. N.C. Bd. Econ. Devel., 1989-93; corporator Belmont Hill Sch., 1996—. Lt. USNR, 1943-46, 51-53. Mem. Am. Bankers Assn. (chmn. mktg. divsn. 1979-80, dir. 1971-73), Assn. Res. City Bankers, Conf. Bd. (So. regional adv. coun.), Assn. Bank Holding Cos. (bd. dirs., exec. com. 1981-83), Chgo. Club, Commonwealth Club Chgo., Twin-City Club Winston Salem, Old Town Club Winston-Salem, Roaring Gap Club N.C. Home: 10 Graylyn Pl Winston Salem NC 27106 Office: Wachovia Corp 420 W 4th St Ste 202-A Winston Salem NC 27101-2837

WANDYCZ, PIOTR STEFAN, history educator; b. Krakow, Poland, Sept. 20, 1923; s. Damian Stanislaw and Stefania (Dunikowska) W.; m. Maria Teresa Chrzaszcz, Aug. 13, 1963; children: Anna, Joanna, Antoni. BA, Cambridge U., 1948, MA, 1952; PhD, London U., 1951; MA (hon.), Yale U., 1968; PhD (hon.), Wroclaw U., Poland, 1993; DHC, Sorbonne U., Paris, 1997, Jagiellonian U., 2000. Instr. to assoc. prof. history Ind. U., 1954-66; fellow Harvard's Russian Rsch. Ctr., 1963-65; assoc. prof. history Yale U., 1966-68, prof., 1968-89, chmn. Russian and East European coun., 1974-76, 81-83, Bradford Durfee prof., 1989-97, prof. emeritus, 1997—. Vis. prof. history Columbia U., 1967, 69, 74 Author: Czechoslovak-Polish Confederation and Great Powers, 1956, France and Her Eastern Allies, 1962, Soviet-Polish Relations, 1969, The Lands of Partitioned Poland, 1974, United States and Poland, 1980, August Zaleski, 1980, Polska i Zagranica, 1986, The Twilight of French Eastern Alliances, 1988, Z Dziejow dyplomacji, 1988, Polish Diplomacy 1914-1945, 1988, The Price of Freedom, 1992, 2nd edit., 2001, Die Freiheit und ihr Preis, 1993, Pod zaborami, 1994, Cena wolnosci, 1995, Laisves Kaina, 1997, Stredni Evropa v Dejinach, 1998, Tsenata na svobodata, 1999, Z Pilsudskim i Sikorskim, 1999, Il prezzo della liberta, 2001; co-author: Historia Europy Srodkowo-Wschodniej, 2000; contbr. articles to profl. jours.; mem. editl. bd. Slavic Rev., Internat. History Rev., Polish Rev., Polin., East European Politics and Soc. Served as 2d lt. Polish Army, 1942-45. Decorated Comdr.'s Cross of Polonia Restituta; recipient Alfred Jurzykowski Found. award in history, 1977; fellow Guggenheim Found., Ford Found., Rockefeller Found., Am. Philos. Soc., Am. Coun. Learned Socs., Social Sci. Rsch. Coun., Internat. Rsch. and Exchs. Bd. Mem. AAAS (Wayne Vucinich prize 1989), Am. Hist. Assn. (George Louis Beer prize 1962, 89), Polish Hist. Assn. (hon.), Polish Acad. Arts and Scis., Polish Acad. Scis., Polish Inst. Arts and Scis. (pres. 1999—), Polish Soc. Abroad (A. Lenkszewicz prize 1991, Oscar Halecki History award 1997), Czechoslovak Acad. of Scis. (Hlavka medal 1992), Czechoslovak Soc. Arts and Scis. Home: 27 Spring Garden St Hamden CT 06517-1913 Office: Yale U Dept History New Haven CT 06520-8324

WANEBO, HAROLD J. surgeon, educator; b. Denver, Feb. 12, 1935; s. Clifford P. and JoAnn (Curtin) W.; m. Claire Anne Wanebo, Oct. 27, 1964; children: John Eric, Michael David, Jacqueline Elise. BS, Regis Coll., 1957; MD, U. Colo., 1961. Intern Cornell Med. divsn. Bellevue Hosp., N.Y., 1961-62, resident, 1962-63; surg. resident U. Calif. Med. Ctr., San Francisco, 1963-65, 67-69; fellow in tumor immunology Meml. Sloan-Kettering Cancer Ctr., N.Y., 1965-67, sr. surg. fellow, 1971-73, clin. asst. attending surgeon, 1973-74, assoc., 1973-77, asst. attending surgeon, 1974-77, assoc. scientist, 1977-83, cons. clin. immunology svc., 1977-90; instr. surgery Cornell U.-N.Y. Hosp. Med. Ctr., 1973-75, asst. prof. surgery, 1975-77; chief divsn. surg. oncology Med. Ctr., prof. surgery U. Va., Charlottesville, 1977-87; prof. surgery, dir. surg. oncology Brown U., Providence, 1987—; chief surgery Roger Williams Med. Ctr., 1987—. Editor: Hepatic and Biliary Cancer, 1987, Common Problems in Cancer Surgery, 1990, Colorectal Cancer, 1993, Surgery for Gastrointestinal Cancer, 1996; contbr. numerous chpts. to books and articles to profl. jours. Maj. U.S. Army, 1969-71, Vietnam. Decorated Bronze star; recipient Commendation medal V device. Mem. ACS, Am. Assn. Cancer Edn., Am. Assn. Cancer Rsch., Am. Assn. Immunologists, Am. Cancer Soc. (Jr. Faculty Clin. Fellowship award 1974-77), Am. Surg. Assn., Am. Soc. Clin. Oncology, Assn. Am. Vol. Physicians, Med. Soc. State of N.Y., Med. Soc. R.I., Med. Soc. Va., Nafziggter Surg. Soc., New Eng. Surg. Soc., N.Y. Acad. Scis., N.Y. Surg. Soc., Soc. Surgery of Alimentary Tract, Soc. Surg. Oncology, Soc. Univ. Surgeons, Southeastern Surg. Congress, So. Surg. Assn., Soc. Head and Neck Surgery, Albemarle County Med. Soc. Office: Roger Williams Med Ctr 825 Chalkstone Ave Providence RI 02908-4728 E-mail: haroldjwanebo@juno.com.

WANEK, RONALD MELVIN, orthodontist; b. Richland Center, Wis., Nov. 3, 1938; s. Melvin Leo and Mary Esther (Picha) W.; m. Janet Eleanor Lundquist, June 22, 1974; children: Lynn Ann, Mark Ronald. Student, U. Wis., 1956-60; DDS, Marquette U., 1964, MS, 1969. Practice dentistry specializing in orthodontics, Madison, Wis., 1969—. Served to lt. USNR, 1964-67, Vietnam. Mem. ADA, Wis. Dental Assn., Dane County Dental Assn., Am. Assn. Orthodontists, Wis. Soc. Orthodontists, Midwest Soc. Orthodontists, Omicron Kappa Upsilon. Republican. Methodist. Avocations: organ, piano, directing handbell choir. Office: 4915 Monona Dr Madison WI 53716-2665

WANEK, WILLIAM CHARLES, public relations executive; b. Ridgewood, N.Y., Oct. 21, 1932; s. William John and Anna (Benes) W.; m. Robbie Gene Fairbanks, Feb. 14, 1974; children: William Robert, Jennifer Leigh. BA in English, CCNY, 1954; MA in Psychology, The New Sch. Social Rsch., N.Y.C., 1982. Asst. editor Soap Chem. Spltys. Mag., N.Y.C., 1956-58; editor in chief Maintenance Supplies Mag., 1958-60; acct. exec. O.S. Tyson & Co. Inc., 1960-62; dir. advt. and pub. rels. Pa. Glass Sand Corp., 1962-64; sr. acct. exec. McCann-Erickson Inc., 1964-66; acct. supr. Burson-Marsteller Assocs., 1966-71; exec. v.p. Gibbs & Soell Inc., 1971—. With U.S. Army, 1954-56. Mem.

Am. Agrl. Editors Assn., Nat. Agri-Mktg. Assn. (bd. dirs. ea. chpt. 1974-76), Nat. Assn. Farm Broadcasters. Presbyterian. Avocations: horticulture, classical music, theater, reading, swimming. Office: Gibbs & Soell Inc 600 3rd Ave Fl 6 New York NY 10016-1903

WANG, ALBERT HUAI-EN, lawyer; b. Tainan, Taiwan, Feb. 21, 1967; s. Tien-Yu Wang and Shiu-Yin Chen. BA magna cum laude, MA magna cum laude, UCLA, 1990; JD, Cornell U., 1994. Bar: N.Y. 1995. Tax specialist KPMG Peat Marwick, L.A., 1990-91; tchr. asst. Cornell Law Sch., 1993; assoc. Willkie Farr & Gallagher, N.Y.C., 1994-99, Schulte Roth & Zabel LLP, N.Y.C., 1999—2001; legal counsel, mem. adv. coun. Asian Am. Bus. Devel. Ctr., 1999—. Legal counsel, adv. coun. Asian Am. Bus. Devel. ctr., N.Y.C., 1999—2002. U. Calif. regent scholar, 1986-90, Alumni scholar UCLA, 1986, Departmental scholar, 1989. Mem. ABA, N.Y. State Bar Assn., Chinese Fin. Soc. (dir., legal counsel 2000-02), Taiwan Merchant Assn. N.Y., China Inst., Asia Soc., Chinese Am. Voters Assn. of Queens (dir. N.Y. chpt. 1999-), U.S.-China Lawyers Soc. (bd. dirs. 2002-), Phi Beta Kappa, Phi Delta Phi, Omicron Delta Epsilon. Democrat. Home: 138-10 Franklin Ave Apt 5N Flushing NY 11355-3305 Office: Phillips Nizer LLP 666 Fifth Ave New York NY 10103-0084 Office Fax: 212-262-5152. Business E-Mail: awang@phillipsnizer.com.

WANG, ALBERT JAMES, violinist, educator; b. Ann Arbor, Mich., Nov. 19, 1958; s. James and Lydia (Ebenhoch) Wang; m. Bridget Renee Becker, June 30, 1987 (div. 2000); children: Ona Lenore, Kevin Lewis. MusB, Ind. U., 1979; MusM, U. Mich., 1981; DMA, Am. Conservatory, 1993. Prin. second violin Baton Rouge Symphony Orch., 1981-82; first violin Valcour String Quartet, Baton Rouge, 1981-82, Loyola String Quartet, 1982-83; mem. Lyric Opera Chgo. Orch., 1982—; mem. Orch. Ill., Chgo., 1982-88; prin. 2d violin Internat. Symphony Orch., Port Huron, Mich., 1984; 1st violin Internat. String Quartet, 1984; concertmaster, soloist Chgo. Chamber Orch., 1985-88, Chgo. Philharm., 1985—; mem. Grant Park Symphony Orch., Chgo., 1986-87; concertmaster, soloist Birch Creek Music Festival, Wis., Woodstock (Ill.) Mozart Festival Orch., 1988-90; concertmaster Rockford (Ill.) Symphony Orch., 1990-91, Northwestern Music Festival Orch., 1990—; soloist, concertmaster Pro Musica Orch. of Mauritius, 1992-93; soloist, concertmaster China tour Classical Symphony Orch., 1994, 95; soloist, concertmaster Midwest Symphony Orch., 1995-96; music dir. Baroque Masterplayers, 1994—; soloist, concertmaster Met. Arts Orch., 1995-98. Artist-in-residence St. Clair Coll., Port Huron, 1984, Elgin C.C., 1994—97; lectr. Am. Conservatory Music, Chgo., 1989—92; Fulbright lectr. Francois Mitterand Conservatory of Music, Quatre Bornes, Mauritius, 1992—93; asst. prof. violin Roosevelt U., 1993—2002; adj. prof. violin Wheaton (Ill.) Coll., 1997—2000; adj. asst. prof. violin Moody Bible Inst., Chgo., 1997—2000; v.p. sales and mktg. Music Edn. Publs., Inc., Coral Springs, Fla., 1997—98. Numerous solo, recital and chamber music appearances and master classes throughout U.S., Can., France, Mauritius and China; recs. and broadcasts by Mauritian Nat. Radio and WFMT Chgo. Fine Arts Sta., PBS, Nat. Pub. Radio, and Chinese Nat. Radio and TV; numerous world premiers; recs. on New World Records and with Slavic Projection Ensemble; N.Y. recital debut at Carnegie Hall, 1998; adjudicator for state and nat. music competitions; contbr. articles and revs. to profl. jours. Vol. ARC, Literacy Vols. Am., Chgo. Pub. Librs., United Way; bd. advisors Prism Music Festival, 1984—, Am. Chamber Symphony, 1985, Symphony II, 1993-94. Fulbright grantee, 1992-93; recipient 1st prize Ann Arbor (Mich.) Symphony Competition, 1976, Soc. Am. Musicians Competition, Chgo., 1984, Internat. Concerts Atlantique Competition, N.Y.C., 1989, Chgo. Park Dist. Competition, 1991, 2nd prize Biennial Adult Artist Competition, 1992, Helmuth Fuchs Performance award 1998; selected to Arts Am. Touring Artist Roster, 1993; finalist Lilly Fellows Program in Humanities and the Arts, Valparaiso U., 1994, Harry and Sarah Zelzer Fellowship and prize; recipient Leo Sowerby medal, 1994; Christian Performing Artists' fellow. Mem. ASCAP, Am. Fedn. Musicians, Am. String Tchrs. Assn., Coll. Music Soc., Chamber Music Am., Am. Music Ctr., Music Tchrs. Nat. Assn., Christian Performing Artists' Fellowship. Avocations: powerlifting, fishing, travel, woodworking. Home: 6110 N Glenwood Ave Chicago IL 60660-1804 Office: Lyric Opera Chgo 20 N Wacker Dr Chicago IL 60606-2806 also: Baroque Masterplayers 5528 S Hyde Park Blvd Ste 1102 Chicago IL 60637-2091 E-mail: embrown1@earthlink.net.

WANG, ANDREW HSING-JEN, information marketing executive, journalist, librarian; b. Tainan, Taiwan, June 12, 1939; came to U.S., 1966. s. John Chin-Yuan and Ping Huang W. m. Miaw-Jen Lin Wang, Nov. 21, 1979; children: Sherry, Stanley, Jeffrey, Justina. BA in Journalism, Nat. Cheng-Chi U., Taipei, Taiwan, 1962; MLS, Atlanta U., 1967; MBA, Ohio State U., 1984. News reporter and internat. news wire translator China Times, Taipei, Taiwan, 1964-66; head cataloging dept. St. Mary's (Md.) Coll., 1967-69; asst. univ. libr. Denison U., Granville, Ohio, 1969-76; exec. dir. OCLC Asia Pacific, Dublin, 1976—. Advisor Natl. Ctrl. Libr., Taiwan, 1995—. Contbr. numerous articles to profl. jours. Beta Phi Mu, Internatl. Hon. Soc. of Libr. Sci., 1967. Office: OCLC Online Computer Libr Ctr 6565 Frantz Rd Dublin OH 43017-3395

WANG, AN-MING, composer; b. Shanghai, China, Nov. 7, 1926; Came to U.S., 1948; d. Cheng Hsu and Eling (Tong) W.; children: Elise, Darrell. BE, Central China U., 1947; MusB, Wesleyan Conservatory, Macon, Ga., 1950; MA in Music Edn., Columbia U., 1951. Freelance composer, 1951—. Composer: Songs for All Seasons, 1982, Requiem for chorus and orch. and organ, 1982, The Song of Endless Sorrow, 1985, Piano Concerto, 1990, Gloria for Chorus and Orch., 1991, The Christmas Gift for Chorus and Keyboard/Orch., 1993, Lan Ying (opera in 3 acts), 1995, East Wind for Flute and Piano, 1997, Fantasy for Solo Organ, 2001. Mem. ASCAP, Internat. Alliance for Women in Music, Southeastern Composers League, Soc. of Composers, League Am. Pen Women, Nat. Fedn. Music Clubs, Am. Music Ctr., Friday Morning Music Club (Washington). Republican. Episcopalian. Home and Office: 11920 Canfield Rd Potomac MD 20854-2816

WANG, ARTHUR CHING-LI, administrative law judge, law educator; b. Boston, Feb. 4, 1949; s. Kung Shou and Lucy (Chow) W.; m. Wendy F. Hamai, May 22, 1976 (div. 1981). m. Nancy J. Norton, Sept. 1, 1985; children: Alexander Xinglin, Sierra Xinan. BA, Franconia Coll., 1970; JD, U. Puget Sound, 1984. Bar: Wash. 1984. Printer Carmel Valley (Calif.) Outlook, 1970-73; project coord. Tacoma (Wash.) Cmty. House, 1973-76; rsch. analyst Wash. Ho. of Reps., Olympia, Wash., 1977-80, mem., 1981-94; of counsel Davies Pearson, P.C., Tacoma, 1984-94. Adj. prof. U. Puget Sound Law Sch., Tacoma, 1987-93, Seattle U. Law Sch., Tacoma, 1995-98; chmn House Capital Budget Com., 1993-94, Revenue Com., 1989-92, Commerce and Labor Com., 1985-88; mem. Wash. Pers. Appeals Bd., Olympia, 1994-96; chief adminstrv. law judge Washington Office Adminstrv. Hearings, 1997—; judge Wash. Ct. Appeals, 2000. Assoc. editor U. Puget Sound Law Review, 1983-84. Vista vol. Tacoma Urban League, 1973-74; del. Dem. Nat. Conv., 1976. Named Chinese Am. Man of Yr., Seattle Chinese Post, 1991, Legislator of Yr., Wash. Health Care Assn., 1992, Alumni of Yr., U. Puget Sound Law Sch. Alumni Assn., 1993. Democrat. Avocation: birding. Home: 3319 N Union Ave Tacoma WA 98407-6043 E-mail: awang@oah.wa.gov.

WANG, ARTHUR WOODS, retired publisher; b. Port Chester, N.Y., Oct. 7, 1918; s. Israel and Madolin (Woods) W.; m. Mary Ellen Mackay, Aug. 13, 1955; 1 son, Michael Anthony. BS, Bowdoin Coll., 1940; postgrad., Columbia U., 1949-52. Advt. rsch. McCann-Erickson, Inc., 1940-41; editor Doubleday & Co., 1942-43, Alfred A. Knopf, Inc., 1943, T.Y. Crowell (Pub.), 1943-47; with E.M. Hale & Co., Eau Claire, Wis., 1947-52; editor A.A. Wyn, Inc., 1952-55; co-founder, pres., editor-in-chief Hill & Wang, Inc., 1956-71; pub., editor-in-chief Hill & Wang divsn. Farrar, Straus & Giroux, Inc., N.Y.C., 1971-87; sr. editor Hill and Wang divsn. Farrar, Straus & Giroux, Inc., 1988-98, ret., 1998. Exhibitions include Beinecke Rare Book and Manuscript Libr., Yale U., 2002. Home: 150 E 69th St Apt 17-L New York NY 10021-5704

WANG, BAOLIANG (BOB WANG), applications scientist, researcher; b. Xinji, Hebei, China, Jan. 9, 1963; came to U.S., 1988; s. Yuzhuang and Shuyin (Yang) W.; m. Haiying Li, May 15, 1987; children: George, May. BS, Nankai U., Tianjin, China, 1978-82; PhD, U. Ill., Chgo., 1993. Lectr. Hebei Tchrs. U., 1985-88; postdoctoral rschr. U. Ill., Chgo., 1993-94; sr. applications scientist Hinds Instrument, Inc., Hillsboro, Oreg., 1995—. Achievements include research in polarization modulation instrumentation; investigation of vibrational Zeeman effect using magnetic vibrational circular dichroism; Fourier transform infrared-vibrational circular dichroism spectroscopy; invention of a highly sensitive birefringence measurement system known as EXICOR; measurement of optical rotation. Avocations: Tai chi, table tennis. Home: 16254 NW Joscelyn St Beaverton OR 97006-7258 E-mail: bwang@hindspem.com.

WANG, BUQIAN, materials research scientist; b. Nantong, China, Sept. 8, 1938; came to U.S., 1984, citizen, 1999; s. Jizhou Wang and Shujun Zhu; m. Zheng-Rong Shui, July 1, 1962; children: Xiao-Dan, Jue. BS, Xian Jiaotong U., China, 1961, PhD, 1979. Teaching asst., lectr., assoc. prof. Xian Hwy. U., China, 1961-84, prof., dir. Tribology Rsch. Inst. China, 1987-88; sr. rsch. scientist, cons. Metalspray Internat., Inc., Richmond, Va., 1992—. Vis. scientist, staff scientist Lawrence Berkeley Lab., U. Calif., 1985-87, 88-92; cons. in field. Author: Corrosion and Particle Erosion, 1989; contbr. over 100 articles to profl. jours. V.p. Chinese Student & Vis. Scholar Assn., Berkeley, 1986-87. Recipient Sci. & Tech. award, Xian Hwy. U., 1976, Xian City, 1978, Heat Treatment award, Chinese Sci. & Tech. Assn., 1980; vis. scholar SUNY, Mat. Sci. & Engring. Dept., Stony Brook, 1984-85. Mem. Nat. Assn. Corrosions Engrs., Am. Soc. Materials Internat. Avocations: photography, folk songs, stamp collecting, hiking. Home: 408 Whitaker Rd Richmond VA 23235-4056 Office: FBE Tech Ctr Metalspray United 2713 Oak Lake Blvd Midlothian VA 23112 E-mail: BQ.Wang@metalspray.com.

WANG, CHAO-CHENG, mathematician, engineer; b. Peoples Republic of China, July 20, 1938; came to U.S., 1961; s. N.S. and V.T. Wang; m. Sophia C.L. Wang; children: Ferdinand, Edward. BS, Nat. Taiwan U., 1959; PhD, Johns Hopkins U., 1965. Registered profl. engr., Tex. Asst. prof. Johns Hopkins U., Balt., 1966-68, assoc. prof., 1968-69; prof. Rice U., Houston, 1968-79, Noah Harding prof., 1979—, chmn. math. sci. dept., 1983-89, chmn. mech. engring. and materials sci., 1991-94. Author numerous books in field; contbr. articles to profl. jours. Named Disting. Young Scientist Md. Acad. Sci., 1968. Mem. ASME, Soc. Natural Philosophy (treas. 1985-86), Am. Acad. Mechs. Office: Rice Univ Dept Mech Engring Materials Sci Houston TX 77251

WANG, CHARLES B. computer software company executive, professional sports team executice; b. Shanghai, Rep. China, Aug. 19, 1944; came to U.S., 1952; BS in Math., Queens Coll., 1967. Programming trainee Riverside Rsch. Inst. Columbia U., Islandia, N.Y., 1976—; v.p. sales Standard Data Corp.; chmn., CEO Computer Assocs., Islandia, N.Y., 1976—; owner, CEO N.Y. Islanders, Uniondale, 1999—. Author: Techno Vision, 1994, Techno Vision II: Every Executive's Guide to Understanding and Mastering Technology and the Internet, 1997 (transl. 7 langs.). Founder The Smile Train; contbr. Nat. Ctr. for Missing and Exploited Children, Make-A-Wish Found.; bd. dirs. several pub. and pvt. orgns. Avocations: cooking, basketball. Office: Computer Assocs Internat Inc 1 Computer Associates Plz Farmingville NY 11749-7000 Address: NY Islanders Nassau Veterans Memorial Coliseum Uniondale NY 11553*

WANG, CHARLES PING, engineering executive; b. Shanghai, Republic of China, Apr. 25, 1937; came to U.S., 1962; s. Kuan-Ying and Ping-Lu (Ming) W.; m. Lily L. Lee, June 29, 1963. BS, Taiwan U., Republic of China, 1959; MS, Tsinghua U., Singchu, Republic of China, 1961; PhD, Calif. Inst. Tech., 1967. Mem. tech. staff Bellcomm, Washington, 1967-69; research engr. U. San Diego, 1969-74; sr. scientist Aerspace Corp., Los Angeles, 1976-86; pres. Optodyne, Inc., Compton, Calif., 1986—. Adj. prof. U. Calif., San Diego, 1979-90; pres. Chinese-Am. Engr. and Scientists Assn. So. Calif., Los Angeles, 1979-81; program chmn. Internation Conf. of Lasers, Shanghai, 1979-80; organizer and session chmn. Lasers Conf., Los Angeles, 1981-84, program chmn., Las Vegas, 1985. Editor in chief Series in Laser Tech., 1983-91; contbr. articles to profl. jours.; inventor discharge excimer laser. Calif. Inst. Tech. scholar, 1965. Fellow Am. Optical Soc., AIAA (assoc., jour. editor 1981-83). Office: Optodyne Inc 1180 W Mahalo Pl Compton CA 90220-5443 E-mail: optodyne@aol.com.

WANG, CHEN CHI, electronics company, real estate, finance company, investment services, and international trade executive; b. Taipei, Taiwan, Aug. 10, 1932; came to U.S., 1959, naturalized, 1970; s. Chin-Ting and Chen-Kim Wang; m. Victoria Rebisoff, Mar. 5, 1965; children: Katherine Kim, Gregory Chen, John Christopher, Michael Edward. BA in Econs., Nat. Taiwan U., 1955; BSEE, San Jose State U., 1965; MBA, U. Calif., Berkeley, 1961. With IBM Corp., San Jose, Calif., 1965-72; founder, CEO Electronics Internat. Co., Santa Clara, 1968-72, owner, gen. mgr., 1972-81; reorganized as EIC Group, 1981-2000; chmn. bd., CEO EIC Investment Corp., 1982—; dir. Systek Electronics Corp., Santa Clara, 1970-73; founder, sr. ptnr. Wang Enterprises (name changed to Chen Kim Enterprises 1982), 1974-75, Hanson & Wang Devel. Co., Woodside, Calif., 1977-85; chmn. bd. Golden Alpha Enterprises, San Mateo, 1979-99; mng. ptnr. Woodside Acres-Las Pulgas Estate, Woodside, 1980-85; founder, sr. ptnr. DeVine & Wang, Oakland, Calif., 1977-83, Van Heal & Wang, West Village, 1981-82; founder, chmn. bd. EIC Fin. Corp. (now EIC Investment Corp.), Redwood City, 1985-90; chmn. bd. Maritek Corp., Corpus Christi, Tex., 1988-89; chmn. EIC Internat. Trade Corp., Lancaster, Calif., 1989-90, EIC Capital Corp., Redwood City, 1990-91. Mng. mem. Sixtieth West, LLC, 1997—, Land Investment Co. Calif., LLC, 1998—, Aceh Capital, LLC, 1998—. Author: Monetary and Banking System of Taiwan, 1955, The Small Car Market in the U.S., 1961. Served to 2d lt., Nationalist Chinese Army, 1955-56. Mem. Internat. Platform Assn., Tau Beta Pi. Mem. Christian Ch. Home: 195 Brookwood Rd Woodside CA 94062-2302 Office: ACE Group Head Office Bldg 2055-2075 Woodside Rd Redwood City CA 94061-3355 E-mail: chenwang@acecap.net.

WANG, CHENG JULIUS, reliability specialist; b. Taipei, Taiwan, Republic China, July 18, 1959; m. Jane-Ling Elsa Soong, Mar. 30, 1990. BS, Cheng-Kung U., Tainan, Taiwan, 1981; MS, U. Mich., 1984; postgrad., Wayne State U., 1987-89. Cert. reliability and quality engr. Lt. instr. Chinese Army Communication Inst., Taiwan, 1982-83; rsch. assoc. GrandTec Cons., Inc., 1984-85, Mech. Industry Rsch. Lab., Indsl. Tech. Rsch. Inst., Taiwan, 1985-86; product and computer application engr. GM Inland Div., Warren, Mich., 1987-88; rsch. and teacing asst. indsl. engring/ops. rsch. dept. Wayne State U., Detroit, 1987-88; product and computer application engr. Ford Motor Casting Div., Dearborn, Mich., 1988; product assurance specialist Chrysler Corp., Highland Park, 1988-92; reliability specialist Hill-Rom Co., Batesville, Ind., 1992—. Co-author: (with D. G. Raheja) Design Optimization for Robustness: Taguchi Approach section, Assurance Technologies: Principles and Practices, 1991, Automotive Engineering and Litigation, vol. 5, 1993; contbr. articles to profl. jours. Mem. Am. Soc. for Quality Control (sr. mem., cert reliability and quality engr., exec. bd. dirs., asst. vice chair edn. com. 1989-92, Craig award 1990), Internat. Soc. Reliability Engrs. (founding pres. S.E. Mich. chpt. 1990-92), Am. Statis. Assn., Am. Supplier Inst., Inc. (Taguchi Recognition award 1990). Address: 1691 Spring Creek Dr Rochester MI 48306-3255 Office: Hill-Rom 1069 State Route 46 E # M20 Batesville IN 47006-9167

WANG, CHEN-KU, retired library director; b. Peiping, China, July 18, 1924; s. Bing-fong Wang and Fong-gen Hsia; m. Shuo-fen Wang, Aug. 15, 1946; children: Pei-chi, Sheng-shiang, Sheng-Wen. MA, Peabody Coll. Tchrs., 1959; LLD (hon.), Ohio U., 1988. Prof. Nat. Taiwan Normal U., Teipei, 1960-94; dir. Nat. Ctrl. Libr., China, 1977-89; ret., 1994. Dir. Ctr. for Chinese Studies, 1977-89. Author: Selection and Acquisition of Library Materials, 1978; hon. editor Jour. Libr. and Info. Sci., 1975—. Decorated knight comdr. Silvestri, Vatican; recipient Disting. Svc. award Chinese-Am. Libr. Assn., 1987. Mem. Libr. Assn. China (pres. 1992-97).

WANG, CHIA PING, physicist, educator; b. The Philippines; came to U.S., 1963, naturalized; (parents Chinese citizens). s. Guan Can and Tah (Lin) W. *Born in the Philippines, Chinese by birth. Grandparents and parents were business proprietors. Received basic training in nuclear electron physics and theoretical physics from Professor Sir Norman Alexander, student of Lord Rutherford, and Professor Otto Frisch, University of Cambridge, and closely associated with Otto Frisch for more than 20 years.* BS, U. London, 1950; MS, U. Malaya (now U. Singapore), 1951; PhD in Physics, U. Malaya (now U. Singapore) and U. Cambridge, 1953; DSc in Physics, U. Singapore, 1972. Asst. lectr. U. Malaya, 1951-53; mem. faculty Nankai U., Tientsin, 1954-58, prof. physics, 1956-58, head electron physics divsn., 1955-58; head electron physics Lanchow Atomic Project, 1958; faculty Hong Kong U., Chinese U., Hong Kong, 1958, prof. physics, 1959-63, acting head physics, math. depts., 1959; rsch. assoc. lab. nuclear studies Cornell U., Ithaca, N.Y., 1963-64; assoc. prof. space sci. and applied physics Cath. U. Am., Washington, 1964-68; assoc. prof. physics Case Inst. Tech. Case Western Res. U., Cleve., 1966-70; vis. scientist, vis. prof. Cavendish Lab. U. Cambridge (Eng.), Inst. Theoretical Physics, U. Leuven (Belgium), Cosmic Ray Lab., U.S. Naval Rsch. Labs., U. Md., MIT, 1970-75; rsch. physicist radiation lab. U.S. Army Natick (Mass.) R & D Command, 1975—. Steering com. sci. and tech. directorate U.S. Army Natick R & D Command, 1993—; steering com. nuclear physics divsn. Nankai U., Tientsin, 1956-58; vis. scientist, vis. prof. U. Cambridge (Eng.), U. Leuven, Belgium, U.S. Naval Rsch. Labs., U. Md., MIT, 1970-75. *Initiated extensive air shower project in China; first to convert in 1963 picosecond pulses to pulse-heights; discovered in 1965-1968 from more than 50 experiments the many-subunit (parton) structure of the nucleon and other hadrons, opening up the field of multiparticle production in high-energy physics; and the 3-quark-qq-bar (later known as Valence quarks- sea quarks) structure of the nucleon from electron-, neutrino-, meson, and nucleon-nucleon high-energy scattering experiments at the Cavendish Laboratory in 1970-72; performed one of the first experiments at the Fermi National Laboratory's (then) 200 GeV accelerator in 1972; and work on laser interferometry (with Otto Frisch), thermal Physics, microwaves, Laser, quantum fields,and Superstrings.* Co-author: Atomic Structure and Interactions of Ionizing Radiations with Matter in Preservation of Food by Ionizing Radiation, 1982; contbr. more than 80 articles to profl. jours. and reports. Recipient Outstanding Performance award Dept. Army, 1980, Quality Increase award, 1980, Sustained Superior Performance awards, 1990, 96.. Mem. AAAS, Am. Nuclear Soc., Am. Phys. Soc., Inst. Physics London, N.Y. Acad. Scis., Sigma Xi. Achievements include pioneering research in nuclear sub-structure (now often referred to as parton), establishing the 3-quark-many-qq-bar nucleor sub-unit structure, multiparticle production, cosmic radiation, picosecond time to pulse-height conversion, thermal physics, power law of laser steel melting, microwaves absorption and scattering, initiating cosmic-ray extensive air shower research in China; visualizing with Otto Frisch the sinusoidal interference laser light waves in Frisch's laser interferometer at the Cavendish Lavoratory. Office: US Army Natick 28 Hallett Hill Rd Weston MA 02493-1753

WANG, CHIN-HUA, rehabilitation service professional; b. Shanghai, China, Feb. 10, 1935; came to U.S., 1985; m. Yi-Ling Wang, July 3, 1963; children: Ying, Tong. MD, Shanghai Med. U., 1957; postgrad., Chinese Traditional Med. Coll., Shanghai, 1972-73, Mich. State U., 1985-86. Lic. acupuncturist, D.C., Md., Vt. Resident in gen. surgery Shanghai First Peoples Hosp., 1957-58; anesthesiologist, physician chest surgery Shanghai First Tuberculosis Hosp., 1958-62, chest surgeon, 1962-66; chief sanesthesiologist, vis. surgeon Shanghai Seamens Hosp., 1966-84; acupuncture instr. Coll. Osteo. Medicine/Mich. State U., Lansing, 1985-86; rsch. fellow lab. thoracic surgery Henry Ford Hosp., Detroit, 1986-89; West-Eastern med. specialist Washington Pain and Rehabilitation, Inc., 1990-91; West-Eastern med. specialist pain & relaxation program Neurodiagnostic and Pain Therapy, Inc., Washington, 1991-94; alternative medicine specialist Am. Therapeutic Svcs., Inc., 1994; acupuncturist Nat. Rehab. Hosp., Bethesda, Md., 1994—. Dir. Chinese sect. Womens Internat. Pub. Health Network, Bethesda, 1989-91. Contbr. articles to profl. jours. Mem. Nat. Commn. for Cert. Acupuncturists, Chinese Med. Assn., Chinese Nat. Microcirculation Com., Henry Ford Med. Assn., Am. Pub. Health Certifies. Home: 2354 Deckman Ln Silver Spring MD 20906-2266 Office: 6410 Rockledge Dr Bethesda MD 20817-1809 E-mail: wang2354@aol.com.

WANG, CHUAN-BAO, chemist, researcher; b. Huaining, Peoples Republic China, Jan. 1, 1964; s. Guojia and Nan (He) Wang; m. Xiaojing Zhang, Sept. 24, 1988; children: Derek S., Janet Z. BS, Anyhui Normal U., Wuhu, China, 1985; MS, U. Sci. and Tech., Hefei, China, 1988; PhD, Peking U., Beijing, 1991. From asst. to prof. Peking U., Beijing, 1991—94; rsch. scientist Lehigh U., Bethlehem, Pa., 1994—98; devel. chemist, project mgr. Indsl. Sci. Corp., Oakdale, 1998—. Contbr. articles to profl. jours.; patentee formaldehyde production. Fellow, Japan Soc. for Promotion of Sci., 1994. Mem.: Am. Assn. for Advanced Soc., N.Am. Catalysis Soc., Am. Chem. Soc., Pitts.-Cleve. Catalysis Soc. (treas. 1999—). Avocations: jogging, reading, music. Home: 505 Jonathan Ct Oakdale PA 15071 Office: Indsl Sci Corp 1001 Oakdale Rd Oakdale PA 15071 E-mail: cwang8@yahoo.com.

WANG, CHUNG SHAN, physicist; b. Fukien, China, Dec. 16, 1937; came to U.S., 1964; s. Pey-jen and I-jen (Liu) W.; m. Kaiwen K. Mao, June 2, 1969 (div. Sept. 1988); children: Alicia K., Jason K. BS, Nat. Cheng Kung U., 1962; MS, U. Idaho, 1966, PhD, 1969. Asst. prof. SUNY, Albany, 1969-77; staff scientist Systems and Applied Sci. Corp., College Park, Md., 1977-78; rsch. staff Tech. Svc. Corp., Silver Spring, 1978-79; tech. staff Tex. Instruments, Inc., Suitland, 1979-81; sr. physicist Vitro Corp., Rockville, 1981-99, BAE Sys., Rockville, 2000—. Contbr. articles to profl. jours. Mem. Am. Geophys. Union. Avocation: ballroom dancing. Home: 12 Sebastiani Blvd Gaithersburg MD 20878-4120 Office: BAE Systems 1601 Research Blvd Rockville MD 20850-3173 E-mail: chung.wang@baesystems.com.

WANG, COLLEEN IONA, medical association administrator, writer; b. Mpls., Oct. 23, 1953; d. Dillard Wayne and Nova Bardeen (Vaught) Greenwood; m. Hansen Stephen Wang, Aug. 22, 1976; children: Hansen Jeremiah, Nathaniel Stephen. AS in Nursing, Loma Linda U., 1974. Registered nurse, Calif. Staff nurse cardio-thoracic ICU Loma Linda (Calif.) U. Med. Ctr., 1975-77, staff nurse pediats. ICU, 1978-80; staff nurse med.-surg. cardiothoracic ICU St. Bernardine's Hosp., San Bernardino, Calif., 1977-78; nurse medically fragile, high risk infants, foster care San Bernardino County, Alta Loma, 1980-87; coord. support group So. Calif. chpt. San Bernardino-Riverside County Tourette Syndrome Assn., Loma Linda, 1987-97; med. liaison So. Calif. chpt. Tourette Syndrome Assn., Redlands, 1991-99, nursing educator, 1993—, bd. dirs. med. liaison Encino, 1993-99, chmn. western regional med. conf. Pasadena, 1994, bd. dirs., pres. Encino, 1996, host chmn. with Tourette Syndrome Assn. N.Y. Burbank, 1996, chmn. educators conf. San Diego, 1998; chair western regional med. conf. Tourette Spectrum Disorder Assn., Ontario, Calif., 1999, med. v.p., bd. dirs., 1999—. Co-author, editor: Tourette Syndrome: A Continuing Education Program for Nurses, 1993, updated, 1996 (Outstanding Chpt. Achievement award Nat. Tourette Syndrome Assn. Inc. 1994); co-author: National Curriculum on Educating & Managing of Children with Neurobiological Disorders; contbr. articles to profl. jours. Founding officer, sec. Challenging Kids, Inc., Atlanta; vol. instr. gifted and talented math Mariposa Elem. Redlands (Calif.) Sch. Dist., 1990-91; mem. PTA Mariposa Elem., Redlands, Calif., 1992-95, vol. instr. first aid Flash Class, 1990-92; presenter-in-svc. edn. Multiple Schs. San Bernardino County, Riverside County, L.A. County, 1992—; mem. PTA Moore Middle Sch., Redlands, 1995-97, Redlands H.S., 1994—. Mem. Ams. for Nonsmoker's Rights, Tourette Spectrum Disorder Assn., Tourette Syndrome Assn. (nat. membership Bayside, N.Y. emm. com. underserved area conf. 1986-97). Avocations: computers, snorkeling, travel. Office: Tourette Syndrome Assn So Calif 30733 E Sunset Dr S Redlands CA 92373-7350 E-mail: wangci@earthlink.net.

WANG, CONGYING, physiologist, researcher; b. Xi'an, Shaanxi, China, Feb. 1, 1968; d. Zhigong Pang and Baoqi Wang; m. Guangwen Li; children: Kunqian Li. PhD, Xi'an Med. U., China, 1997. Instr. Xi'an Med. U., 1993—97; asst. prof. Shanghai Inst. Physiology, Chinese Acad. of Sci., Shanghai, 1997—2000; postdoctor U. Tex. Med. Br., Galveston, Tex., 2000—. Contbr. articles. Mem.: Am. Soc. Neurosci. Home: 928 Post Office St Apt 8 Galveston TX 77550 Office: Univ Tex Med Br 301 University Blvd Galveston TX 77555 Home Fax: 409-762-9382; Office Fax: 409-762-9382. Personal E-mail: conwang@utmb.edu.

WANG, DEXIN, engineer; b. Wuhu, Anhui Province, China, Nov. 14, 1962; s. Mingfu Wang and Sanjiu Li; m. Xiuhong Wu; 1 child Tina. PhD, U. Ariz., 1999. Asst. rsch. fellow China Acad. Ry. Scis., Beijing, 1985—93; rsch. asst. U. Ariz., Tucson, 1995—99; prodn. devel. engr. Ford Motor Co., Dearborn, 1999—. Author: (rsch.) Effect of Rail Irregularities on Vehicle Derailment , 1987 (Ry. Sci. and Tech. Progress award, 1987). Recipient award for excellence in tchg., Nat. Edn. Promotion Com., 1987. Mem.: Soc. Automotive Engrs. Home: 9129 Stonehouse Ave Livonia MI 48150 Office: Ford Motor Co 20400 Oakwood Blvd Dearborn MI 48121 Personal E-mail: dexinwang@peoplepc.com.

WANG, DONNA HUI, investigative medicine director; b. Guangdong, China, Aug. 20, 1961; d. Xuanwu and Huijuan (Ouyang) W.; m. Eugene J. Yu, June 8, 1985; 1 child, Eunice Yu. MD, Sun Yat-Sen Med. U., Guangzhou, China, 1984; postdoc. fellow, Eastern Va. Med. Sch., Norfolk, 1990. Resident Sun Yat-Sen Ophthalmic Ctr., Sun Yat-Sen Med. U., Guangzhou, China, 1984-85; vis. scholar dept. surgery and physiology Bowman Gray Sch. Medicine, Winston-Salem, N.C., 1985-87; rsch. assoc. dept. physiology Eastern Va. Med. Sch., Norfolk, 1987-90, asst. prof. dept. physiology, 1990-93; asst. prof. dept. internal medicine U. Tex. Med. Branch, Galveston, Tex., 1993-97, assoc. prof. dept. internal medicine, 1997-99; scientist, dir. histochemical core Sealy Ctr. for Molecular Cardiology, U. Tex. Med. Sch., 1994-99; prof. dept. medicine Michigan State U., East Lansing, 1999—. Dir. Investigative medicine, Dept. Medicine, Mich. State U., East Lansing, 1999—; mem. Pub. Com. Am. Heart Assn. Coun. for High Blood Pressure, Dallas, 1999-02. Editor: Angiotensin Protocol, Methods in Molecular Medicine, 2000; contbr. articles to profl. jours. Chair The Session of Physiology and Genetics of Angiotensin I and II Receptors, The 68th Scientific Sessions of Am. Heart Assn., Anaham, Calif., 1995, The Session of Hypertension, Am. Physiol. Soc., San Francisco, 1998; peer reviewer Am. Heart Assn-Western State Affiliates Peer Review, San Francisco, 1998-99; mem. prof. com. The Microcirculatory Soc. Inc., San Diego, 1997-01. Recipient First Ind. Rsch. Support Transition award, Nat. Inst. Health, 1993, 98, 1997 Outstanding Young Investigator Travel award, The Microcirculatory Soc., Inc., Hoechst Marion Roussel 1998 Young Scholar award, The Am. Soc. Hypertension, 1998, Established Investigator award Am. Heart Assn., 1999-03. Fellow Am. Heart Assn. Coun. for High Blood Pressure Rsxh. Pub. com. mem., 1995—, Cardiovascular sect., Am. Physiol. Soc. Woman in Physiology com. mem., 1999—; mem. The Microcirculatory Soc. Inc. Office: Dept Medicine B316 Clinical Center East Lansing MI 48824 Fax: 517-432-1326. E-mail: donna.wang@ht.msu.edu.

WANG, FRANCIS WEI-YU, biomedical materials scientist, researcher; b. Pei-Kang, Yun-Lin, Taiwan, July 21, 1936; came to U.S., 1956; s. Yin-Kwei and Tsai-Wei Wang; m. Susan Shu-Huei Liao, June 18, 1966; children: Anthony, Andrea, Edwin. BSChemE, Calif. Inst. Tech., 1961, MSChemE, 1962; PhD in Chemistry, U. Calif., San Diego, 1971. Chemist Pacific Soap Co., San Diego, 1962-66; rsch. asst. U. Calif.-San Diego, La Jolla, 1966-71; USPHS postdoctoral fellow Polytechnic U., Bklyn., 1971-72; project leader biomaterials Nat. Inst. Stds. and Tech., Gaithersburg, Md., 1972—. Rep. Dept. Commerce Accredited Stds. Comm. MD156, Dental Materials, Instruments, and Equipment, Chgo., 1997—. Contbr. numerous articles to profl. jours. Recipient W.P. Slichter award Dept. Commerce, 1997, Bronze medal, 1985. Mem. Internat. Assn. for Dental Rsch., Soc. for Biomaterials, Am. Chem. Soc., Am. Phys. Soc. Achievements include patents on non-destructive method for fluorescence monitoring of polymerization and solidification of thermoplastic polymer, fluorescence monitoring of polymer injection molding, and fluorescence monitoring of polymer viscosity and orientation. Office: Nat Inst Stds and Tech 100 Bureau Dr Stop 8545 Gaithersburg MD 20899-8545 E-mail: francis.wang@nist.gov.

WANG, FREDERICK MARK, pediatric ophthalmologist, medical educator; b. N.Y.C., Feb. 17, 1948; Student, Northwestern U., 1968; MD, Yeshiva U., 1972. Diplomate Am. Bd. Ophthalmology, Am. Bd. Pediats., Nat. Bd. Med. Examiners. Intern in pediats. H.C. Moffitt-U. Calif. San Francisco Hosps., 1972-73; resident in pediats. Bronx Mcpl. Hosp. Ctr.-Albert Einstein Coll. Medicine, 1973-74, resident in ophthalmology, 1976-79; Heed fellow in ophthalmology and strabismus Children's Hosp. Nat. Med. Ctr., Washington, 1979-80; asst. prof. ophthalmology Albert Einstein Coll. Medicine, Bronx, 1980-82, asst. clin. prof., 1982-85, assoc. clin. prof., 1985-95, clin. prof., 1995—, asst. prof. pediats., 1980-82, asst. clin. prof. pediats., 1982-92; dir. pediat. ophthalmology and strabismus svc. Montefiore Med. Ctr., 1980-90. Cons. ophthalmologist Children's Evaluation & Rehab. Ctr., Rose Kennedy Ctr. for Rsch. in Mental Retardation and Human Devel., Bronx, 1980—, Craniofacial Ctr., Montefiore Med. Ctr., Bronx, 1980—; attending physician in ophthalmology Bronx Mcpl. Hosp./Montefiore Med. Ctr., 1980—; asst. attending physician in ophthalmology North Ctrl. Bronx Hosp., 1980-98; attending physician Strabismus Svc., N.Y. Eye & Ear Infirmary, N.Y.C., 1982-99, attending surgeon, 1999—; mem. dept. ophthalmology Lenox Hill Hosp., N.Y.C., 1988—; sci. reviewer Jour. Am. Acad. Ophthalmology, 1980-86; mem. profl. adv. bd. Found. for Children with Learning Disabilities, N.Y.C., 1983-89; mem. sci. adv. bd. The Glaucoma Found., N.Y.C., 1986-92; mem. profl. adv. bd. Nat. Assn. for Visually Handicapped, N.Y.C., 1988—; coord. pediat. sect. Greater N.Y. Ophthalmology Clin. Lectr. Series, 1990-93; mem. Velo-Cardio-Facial Syndrome Ednl. Found., 1994—, nominating com., 1995—. Mem. editl. bd. Jour. Pediat. Ophthalmology and Strabismus, 1998—; contbr. articles to profl. jours., chpts. to books. Maj. med. officer USAF, 1974-76. Mem. Am. Acad. Pediats., Am. Acad. Ophthalmology, Am. Assn. for Pediat. Ophthalmology and Strabismus, N.Y. Soc. for Pediat. Ophthalmology and Strabismus (program chmn. 1987-89, pres. 1990-92), N.Y. Soc. for Clin. Ophthalmology (corr. sec. 1988-90, membership chmn. 1990-91, program chmn. 1991-92, pres. 1992-93), N.Y. Acad. Medicine (sec. sect. on ophthalmology 1993-94, sect. chmn. 1995-96), Alpha Omega Alpha. Avocations: fishing, chess, swimming. Office: Pediat Ophthalmology of NY 30 E 40th St New York NY 10016-1201

WANG, FU-KUO ALBERT, finance educator; b. Taipei, Taiwan, Dec. 15, 1959; s. Fan Wang and Yeu-Er Jiang; m. Lih-Jen Joyce Kang, Aug. 27, 1986; children: Annie, David. BA in Econs., Nat. Taiwan U., Taipei, 1982; MBA, U. NC, 1989, PhD in Fin., 1994. Asst. prof. Columbia U., N.Y.C., 1994—98, Rice U., Houston, 1998—. 2d lt. ROC USAF, 1982—84, Taiwan. Office: Rice U Jones Grad Sch Mgmt 6100 Main St Houston TX 77005

WANG, FU-ZHANG, medical researcher; b. Dali, Shaanxi, China, Mar. 23, 1964; p. Zeng-Suo Wang and Jun-Fang Yang; m. Jing Hou, Aug. 15, 1996. MB, Xian (China) Med. U., 1985; M in Medicine, Beijing Med. U., 1988, Karolinska Inst., Stockholm, 1995, PhD in Med. Scis., 1999. Clin. physician Beijing Med. U., 1988-89, rsch. assoc., 1990-92; vis. scientist Karolinska Inst., Stockholm, 1992-93; rsch. assoc. Swedish Inst. for Infectious Disease Control, 1995-99; rsch. fellow U. Kans. Med. Ctr., Kansas City, 2000—. Contbr. articles to profl. jours. Mem. European Soc. for Clin. Virology, Swedish Soc. for Med. Microbiology, Internat. Immunocompromised Host Soc. Avocations: swimming, tennis. Home: 3900 Booth St Apt 9 Kansas City KS 66103-2840 Office: Dept Microbiol/Molec Gen 3901 Rainbow Blvd Kansas City KS 66160-0001 Fax: 913-588-7295.

WANG, GENE-JACK, physician, educator, scientist; b. Tainan, Taiwan, Aug. 20, 1954; came to the U.S., 1982; s. Chen and Chin-Chuan (Hu) W.; m. Michelle Fang, June 27, 1987; children: Ja-Rei, Ja-Ann, Ja-Hon, Ja-Way. MD, Kaohsiung Med. Coll., 1980; M in Health Scis., Johns Hopkins U., 1984. Cert. Am. Bd. Nuclear Medicine. Resident in nuclear medicine U. Mo., Columbia, 1984-86; fellow in hematology Albany (N.Y.) Med. Coll., 1986-88; fellow in nuclear radiology SUNY, Stony Brook, 1988-90; asst. scientist Brookhaven Nat. Lab., Upton, N.Y., 1990-92, assoc. scientist, 1992-95, scientist, 1995—, assoc. chief of staff clin. rsch. ctr., 1996-98, chief of staff clin. rsch. ctr., 1998-99, interim chmn. med. dept., 1999-2000. Asst. prof. radiology SUNY, Stony Brook, 1992-98, rsch. assoc. prof. radiology, 1999—. Contbr. articles to profl. jours. Deacon Chinese Christian Gospel Ch., Stony Brook, 1990-93. Recipient Rsch. grant Brookhaven Nat. Lab., Upton, 1993. Mem. AMA, Am. Coll. Nuclear Physics, Soc. Nuclear Medicine, Radiology Soc. N.Am. Avocations: swimming, jogging, tennis. Office: Brookhaven Nat Lab Med Dept Bldg 490 Upton NY 11973 E-mail: gjwang@bnl.gov.

WANG, GEORGE K.F. international lawyer; b. Nanking, China, Jan. 2, 1927; m. Lei Lei, Jan. 10, 2000. LLB, Soochow U., Taipei, Taiwan, 1957; LLM, Golden State U., 1982, PhD, 1984. Internat. lawyer, Taiwan, U.S., 1976—; prof. law Nat. Taiwan U., 1977-80, Golden State U., L.A., 1984-86. Advisor, Yunnan Province, China, 1997—, legal advisor, Wego Chiang, Comr. in Chief Taiwan, 1992-94; def. atty., USAF, 327 Divsn., Taiwan, 1978-80; legal advisor ex-premier Taiwan, 1978-80. Author: Domestic Relation, 1961, Jade Warrior, 2000. Chmn. Dr. Sun Yat-Sen Internat. Found., L.A., 1990; sr. Rep., U.S. Reps. Abroad, Taiwan, 1980. Mem. Internat. Bar Assn., Am. Immigration Lawyer Assn., Taiwan Bar Assn., Chinese Am. Assn. (chmn.). Avocations: writing, reading, travel. E-mail: georgekf28@hotmail.com.

WANG, GUANGMIAO, business executive, consultant; b. Ninghai, China, Jan. 19, 1947; came to U.S., 1992; s. Yuegnan and Hehua (Zhou) W.; m. Guiyan Xu, May 1, 1973; children: Haixiang, Haijia. BA, Hangzhou Coll. Fgn. Lang., China, 1969; grad., Shanghai Jiaotong U., China, 1985, U. N.D., 1993; postgrad., Heriot-Watt U., Edinburgh, U.K., 1997—. Supr. Heiman Ship Co., China, 1971-74; lectr. Zhejiang U. Tech., Hangzhou, 1974-91; exec. Kin Lin Corp., Kansas City, Mo., 1997—, Jia Xiang Inc., Springfield, 1997—. Cons. Heimen Bus. Assn., 1972-74. Contbr. articles to profl. jours. U. N.D. grantee, 1992. Mem. Zhejiang Lang. Assn. (advisor 1980-91), N.Am. Chinese Restaurant Assn. (dir. 1997—), Phi Beta Delta. Avocations: golf, boating, photography, collecting stamps and coins. Office: 2118 S Campbell Ave Springfield MO 65807-2853

WANG, GUANG-ZHEN, sociologist; b. Tianjin, China; arrived in U.S., 1989; BA in English Lit., Hopei U., Tianjin, 1966; MS in Adult Edn., U. Wis., Platteville, 1992; PhD in Sociology, U. North Tex., Denton, 1996. Asst. prof. Sage Colls., Troy, NY, 1996, U. Ark., Little Rock, 1997, assoc. prof., 2002. Guest prof. U. Graz, Austria, 1998; vis. prof. U. Dubuque, Iowa, 1989—90; gender studies coord. U. Ark., Little Rock, 1997—; faculty advisor Ark. Children's Hosp. Rsch. Inst. Survey, Little Rock, 2000. Author: (book) Women's Reproductive Rights in Developing Countries, 1999; contbr. Named Hon. Citizen of City of Dubuque, 1990; grantee Women in Pub. Svc. Project grantee, Ctr. for Am. Women and Politics, 1999, 2000. Mem.: Nat. Women's Assn., Am. Sociol. Assn., Alpha Kappa Delta. Office: U Ark Little Rock 2801 S University Little Rock AR 72204 Fax: 501-569-8458. E-mail: gxwang@ualr.edu.

WANG, GUIYUN, biologist, researcher; b. Fujin, Heilongjiang, China, Feb. 4, 1964; d. Yuzhong Wang and Enrong Xie; m. Dequan Song; children: Hong Song, Hui Song. PhD, Iwate University, Iwate, Japan, 1995—98. Postdoctoral fellow Nat. Inst. of Agrobiol. Resources, Tsukuba, Japan, 1999—2000, Univ. of Tex. Med. Br., Galveston, Tex., 2000—. Lecturer Heilongjiang Univ. of Traditional Chinese Medicine, Harbin, Heilongjiang Province, China, 1988—94. Editor textbooks. Mem.: Sigma. Avocation: travel. Home: 918 Winnie St. Apt.101 Galveston TX 77550 Office: Univ of Tex Med Branch 301 University Blvd Galveston TX 77555 Home Fax: 409-770-0877; Office Fax: 409-770-0877. Personal E-mail: guwang@utmb.edu.

WANG, GWO JAW, orthopaedic surgery educator; Lillian T. Pratt prof. and chmn. orthopedic surgery U. Va. Sch. Medicine, Charlottesville; pres. Kaohsiung (Taiwan) Med. U., 2000—. Recipient U. Va. Pres.'s Report award, 1992, Otto Aufranc award, Hip Soc. and Am. Acad. Orthop. Surgeons, 1992, 1997, Stinchfield award, 1986, Nicholas Andry award, 1998. Office: Kaohsiung Med Univ 100 Shih Chuan 1st Rd Kaohsiung Taiwan Office Fax: 886-7-3212062. E-mail: gwojaw@cc.kmu.edu.tw.

WANG, HAN, developmental biologist; b. Yingshang, Anhui, People's Republic of China, July 12, 1963; came to U.S., 1991; s. ChaoLong Wang and Zeming Lu. BS in Botany, Anhui U., Hefei, 1984; MS in Ecology, Chinese Acad. Scis., 1987; PhD in Evolutionary Biology, Wayne State U., 1996. Rsch. asst. Wayne State U., Detroit, 1991-96; postdoctoral fellow Med. Coll. of Ga., Augusta, 1996-98; rsch. assoc. U. Oreg., Eugene, 1998—2001; asst. prof. U. Okla., Norman, 2001—. Thomas C. Rumbe fellowship Wayne State U., 1991. Mem. AAAS, Soc. for the Study of Evolution, Soc. for Developmental Biology, Soc. for Rsch. on Biol. Rhythms, Sigma Xi (grant 1994). Office: U Okla Dept Zoology Norman OK 73019 Office Fax: 405-325-9324. E-mail: hwang@ou.edu.

WANG, HONG, engineer, researcher; b. Qianjiang, Hubei, China, June 27, 1963; s. Chuanzhong Wang, Qiande Liu; m. Lili Yu; children: Yu. PhD, Michigan Technological University, Michigan, United States, 1996—2001; D.E., Wuhan University of Hydraulic and Electric Engineering, Hubei, China, 1988—91; M.E., Wuhan University of Hydraulic and Electric Engineering, Hubai, China, 1983—86; B.E., Wuhan University of Hydraulic and Electric Engineering, Hubei, China, 1979—83. Post-Doc Researcher Dept. of ME, The Johns Hopkins University, Baltimore, MD, 2001—02; Research Assistant Depts. of MEEM/Min. Eng., Michigan Technological University, Houghton, MI, 1996—2001; Visiting Scholar Dept. of MGE, The University of Arizona, Tucson, 1995—96; Associate Professor Wuhan University of Hydraulic and Electric Engineering, Wuhan, China, 1992—95, Lecturer China, 1986—92. Visiting Engineer Geo-Eng Australia PTY LTD, Morwell, Victoria, Australia, 1994—94; Field Engineer The 9th Hydroelectric Constructional Bureau, Qinzheng, Guizhou, China, 1990—90. Author: (journal) Wear, 2002, Journal of the Mechanics and Physics of Solids, 2002, Wear, 2001, (Ph.D. Dissertation) Mechanics of Material Removal during the Formation of Single-Grit Rotating Scratch with a Conical Tool, 2001, (journal) International Journal of Rock Mechanics and Mining Science, 1997, (book) Properties of Fissured Rock Mass and Constructional Mechanics of Tunnel System, 1993 (The First Class Award of Science and Technology Progress, Wuhan Univ. of Hydr. and Elec. Eng. , 1995), Mechanics of Jointed and Fractured Rock, 1992 (The First Class Award of Science and Technology Progress, Wuhan Univ. of Hydr. and Elec. Eng., 1994), (journal) Journal of Wuhan University of Hydr. and Elec. Eng., 1994, Chinese Journal of Hydraulic Engineering, 1993, (D.E. Dissertation) Statistical Fracture Mechanical Analysis and Joint Network Simulation Technique of Rocks, 1991, (journal) Sichuan Water Power, 1991 (The Third Class Award of Science and Technology Progress, The Ministry of Electric Industry, China, 1992), Site Investigation Science and Technique, 1990, (journal) Journal of Yangtze Institute of Science Research, 1990 (The Third Class Award of Science and Technology Award, The Ministry of Water Conservancy, China, 1994), (journal) Journal of Wuhan Univerity of Hydr. and Elec. Eng., 1989, Chinese Journal of Rock Mechanics, 1988, Fracture and Strength of Rock and Concrete, 1986. Mem.: Society of Experimental Mechanics, American Society of Mechanical Engineers, Sigma Xi, The Scientific Research Society. Home: 235 Rodgers Forge Rd Apt A Baltimore MD 21212 Office: Dept. of ME, The Johns Hopkins Univ. 26 Latrobe Hall/ 3400 N. Charles Str. Baltimore MD 21218 Office Fax: 410-516-4316. Business E-Mail: hwang@pegasus.me.jhu.edu.

WANG, HUAI-LIANG WILLIAM, mechanical engineer; b. Hsinchu, Taiwan, Republic of China, Apr. 4, 1959; came to U.S., 1984; s. Feng-Chi and Hu-Mei (Chou) W.; m. Wen-Pei Chen, June 28, 1986; children: James, Edward. BSME, Tatung Inst. of Tech., Taipei, Taiwan, 1981; MSME, Okla. State U., 1985. Asst. engr. Teco Electric and Machinery Corp., Taipei, Taiwan, 1984; electro-mech. engr. Microsci. Internat. Corp., Sunnyvale, Calif., 1987-89; engr. Lockheed Engring. and Scis. Co., Houston, 1989-91, sr. engr., 1991-92; mgr. mech. engring. Orbiter Tech. Co., Fremont, Calif., 1992; sr. engr. Avatar Sys. Corp., Milpitas, 1993, Quantum Corp., Milpitas, 1994-2000; sr. opto-mech. engr. Phaethon Comms., Fremont, Calif., 2000-01; sr. mech. engr. Paracer Inc., Santa Clara, 2001—. Mem. IEEE, ASME. Office: Paracer 3303 Octavius Dr Ste 100 Santa Clara CA 95054 E-mail: williamwang@yahoo.com., william@paracer.com.

WANG, I-TUNG, atmospheric scientist; b. Peking, People's Republic of China, Feb. 16, 1933; came to U.S., 1958; s. Shen and Wei-Yun (Wen) W.; m. Amy Hung Kong; children: Cynthia P., Clifford T. BS in Physics, Nat. Taiwan U., 1955; MA in Physics, U. Toronto, 1957; PhD in Physics, Columbia U., 1965. Rsch. physicist Carnegie-Mellon U., Pitts., 1965-67, asst. prof., 1967-70; environ. systems engr. Argonne (Ill.) Nat. Lab., 1970-76; mem. tech. staff Environ. Monitoring and Svcs. Ctr. Rockwell Internat., Creve Coeur, Mo., 1976-80, Newbury Park, Calif., 1980-84; sr. scientist, combustion engr. Environ. Monitoring and Svcs. Inc., Newbury Park, Camarillo, 1984-88; sr. scientist ENSR Corp (formerly ERT), 1988; pres. EMA Co., Thosand Oaks, Calif., 1989—. Tech. advisor Bur. of Environ. Protection, Republic of China, 1985; environ. cons. ABB Environ, 1989-92, ARCO, 1990-91, Du Pont (SAFER Sys. Divsn.), 1992-93, So. Calif. Edison, 1993-95, So. Coast Air Quality Mgmt. Dist., 1995-96, Tetra Tech., 1996—. Contbr. papers to profl jours. Grantee Bureau of Environ. Protection, Taiwan, 1985. Mem. N.Y. Acad. of Scis., Air and Waste Mgmt. Assn., Sigma Xi. Avocations: violin and chamber music. Office: EMA Co Ste 435 2219 E Thousand Oaks Blvd Thousand Oaks CA 91362-2930 *Personal philosophy: The pursuit of science is much like the pursuit of art. It requires one's complete involvement and devotion.*

WANG, JAMES HONGXUE, polymer scientist; b. Tongbei, Heilongjiang, China, June 28, 1962; came to U.S., 1984; s. Xiuyi and Shuzen W.; m. Lisha Yu, Oct. 12, 1985; children: Eric K., Jacob C. BS, Northeastern Forestry U., Harbin, China, 1982; MS, Virginia Tech., 1986; PhD, Case Western Reserve U., 1991. Product devel. chemist Chevron Corp., Orange, Tex., 1991-93; sr. rsch. scientist Kimberly-Clark Corp., Neenah, Wis., 1994-95, assoc. rsch. fellow, 1996—. Inventor reactive extrusion process for making improved polymer materials, novel material microstructures, synthesized new polymer compositions and structures, developed novel polymer blends with engineered phys. and mech. properties, tailored comml. polymers for various applications, elucidated polymerization mechanism of anion-radical polymerization in producing polyphenylene ethers, investigated kinetics of copolymerization, synthesized maromonomers; contbr. numerous articles to profl. jours. Nat. scholar Ministry of Edn. of China, Beijing, 1984. Mem. Am. Chem. Soc., Soc. Plastics Engrs., N.E. Wis. Chinese Assn. (pres. 1997-98, v.p. 1996-97), Phi Kappa Phi. Avocations: travel, history, music, hiking, art appreciation. Office: Kimberly-Clark Corp 2100 Winchester Rd Neenah WI 54956-9317 E-mail: jhwang@kcc.com.

WANG, JAMES K. internist, medical administrator; m. Jennifer C.; children: Katherine, Karoline. BS, U. Mich., 1973, MD, 1977. Diplomate Am. Bd. Internal Medicine. Resident in internal medicine U. Mich., 1980; physician Blue Care Network, Lansing, Mich., 1980-89, chief of internal medicine, 1985-89; physician Cigna Healthcare of So. Calif., Fullerton, 1989-94, dept. head internal medicine, 1989-92, chief of staff, 1992-94, med. dir. Glendale, Calif., 1994—2000; regional med. dir., v.p. west coat Cigna Healthcare, 2000—. Mem. ACP. Office: Cigna Healthcare of So Calif 400 N Brand Blvd Ste 400 Glendale CA 91203-2311

WANG, JAMES Z. computer scientist, educator; s. Yuan Wang and B.W. Guo; m. Jia Li, Nov. 5, 1997. MS in Computer Sci., MS, PhD, Stanford U. Prof. Pa. State U., Univ. Pk., Pa., 2000—. Office: School of Info Sci and Tech The Penn State University University Park PA 16802

WANG, JAW-KAI, agricultural engineering educator; b. Nanjing, Jiangsu, People's Republic of China, Mar. 4, 1932; came to U.S., 1955; s. Shuling and Hsi-Ying (Lo) W.; m. Kwang Mei Chow, Sept. 7, 1957 (div. Oct. 1989); children: Angela C.C., Dora C.C., Lawrence C.Y.; m. Bichuan Li, Sept. 25, 1999. BS, Nat. Taiwan U., 1953; MS in Agrl. Engring., Mich. State U., 1956, PhD, 1958. Registered profl. engr., Hawaii. Faculty agrl. engring. dept. U. Hawaii, Honolulu, 1959-93, assoc. prof., chmn. dept. agrl. engring., 1964-68, prof., chmn. dept. agrl. engring., 1968-75, dir. Aquaculture Program, 1990-96; prof. biosystems engring. dept. U. Hawaii-Manoa, Honolulu, 1994—; spl. asst., Internat. Rsch. Dept., Office of Internat. Cooperation and Devel. U.S. Dept. Agr., 1988; pres. Aquaculture Tech., Inc., 1990—. Co-dir. internat. sci. and edn. coun. USDA; vis. assoc. dir. internat. programs and studies office Nat. Assn. State Univs. and Land-Grant Colls., 1979; vis. prof. Nat. Taiwan U., 1964-65, U. Calif., Davis, 1980; cons. U.S. Army Civilian Adminstrn., Ryukus, Okinawa, 1965, Internat. Rice Rsch. Inst., The Philippines, 1971, Pacific Concrete and Rock Co. Ltd., 1974, AID, 1974, Universe Tankships, Del., 1980-81, World Bank, 1981, 82, ABA Internat., 1981-85, Internat. Found. for Agrl. Devel./World Bank, 1981, Rockefeller Found., 1980, Orizaba, Inc., 1983, Agrisys./FAO, 1983, Info. Processing Assocs., 1984, County of Maui, 1984, 85, Dept. of State, 1985, Alexander and Baldwin, 1986; mem. expert panel on agrl. mechanization FAO/UN, 1984-90; sr. fellow East-West Ctr. Food Inst., 1973-74; dir. Info. Sys. and Svcs. Internat., Inc., 1986-90. Author: Irrigated Rice Production Systems, 1980; editor: Taro-A Review of Colocasia Esculenta and its Potentials, 1983; mem. editl. bd. Aquacultural Engring., 1982—. Recipient Exemplary State Employee award State of Hawaii, 1986, State of Hawaii Disting. Svc. award Office of Gov., 1990. Fellow Am. Soc. Agrl. Engrs. (chmn. Hawaii sect. 1962-63, chmn. grad. instrn. com. 1971-73, various coms., Engr. of Yr. 1976, Tech. Paper award 1978, Kishida Internat. award 1991), Am. Inst. Med. and Biol. Engring.; mem. Nat. Acad. Engring., Aquaculture Engring. Soc. (pres. 1993-95), Sigma Xi, Gamma Sigma Delta (pres. Hawaii chpt. 1974-75), Pi Mu Epsilon. Office: U Hawaii MBBE Dept 1955 East West Rd Honolulu HI 96822 *To be allowed a continuing search for truth even when you are doubting its existence, is to be blessed.*

WANG, JENNIE, literature educator; b. Shanghai, China, Mar. 19, 1952; came to U.S., 1979; BA in English and Am. Lit., San Francisco State U., 1983; MA in English and Am. Lit., Stanford U., 1984; PhD in English and Am. Lit., SUNY, Buffalo, 1992. Instr. Shanghai Jiao-Tong U., 1977-79; preceptor Harvard U., Cambridge, Mass., 1992-93; asst. prof. Eng. U. No. Iowa, Cedar Falls, 1993—97, assoc. prof. Eng., 1998—. Vis. scholar U. Calif. English dept., Berkeley, 2000-2001. Author: Novelistic Love in the Platonic Tradition: Fielding, Faulkner and the Postmodernists, 1997, ; Chinese translator: Smiles on Washington Square: A Love Story of Sorts (Raymond Federman), 1999; contbr. articles to profl. jours. Office: U No Iowa Dept English Cedar Falls IA 50614-0502

WANG, JIA, educator; b. Wenzhou, Zhejiang, China, Dec. 25, 1968; came to the U.S., 1990; p. KeQiang Wang and DanPing Cai. BA, Wenzhou Tchrs.' U., 1988; MS, Ft. Valley State U., 1992; PhD, UCLA, 1996. Sr. statistician Applied Mgmt. and Planning Group, L.A., 1995-97; asst. dir., sr. rsch. assoc. Ctr. for Pacific Rim Studies UCLA, 1997—. Cons. The World Bank, Washington, 1997-99, WHO, Geneva, Switzerland, 1999—. 1st author: (book) Measuring Country Performance on Health: Selected Indicators for 115 Countries, 1999; contbr. articles to profl. jours. Univ. fellow UCLA, 1992-96. Mem. AAAS, Am. Ednl. Rsch. Assn., Comparative and Internat. Edn. Soc. Avocations: reading, hiking, traveling. Office: UCLA Program Global Health & Edn 11288 Bunche Hl Los Angeles CA 90095-0001 E-mail: jiawang@ucla.edu.

WANG, JIAN, physical chemist, researcher; b. Weiyuan, Sichuan , China, Mar. 3, 1971; s. Fengyan Wang and Shufen Deng; m. Lingyun Zhu, Apr. 16, 1974. BS, Peking U., Beijing, China, 1992, PhD, 1998. Postdoctoral fellow U. Tex., Austin, 1999—2001; rsch. assoc. Boston U., 2001—. Contbr. articles to profl jours. including:, (DuPont Prize, 1997), (Star of Photoelectronics, 1997). Co-founder and v.p. Austin Peking U. Alumni Assn., 2000—01. Mem.: AAAS, N.Y. Acad. Scis., Am. Chem. Soc. Avocations: photography, reading, travel, sports. Home: 7 Eric Rd Allston MA 02134 Office: 590 Commonwealth Ave Boston MA 02215 Office Fax: 617-353-6466. Business E-Mail: jianwang@chem.bu.edu.

WANG, JIAN CHUAN-QIU, artist; b. Dalian, China, Sept. 26, 1958; came to U.S., 1986; s. Shoulun and Jing (Xu) W.; m. Xiutao Zhu, Oct. 2, 1983; 1 child, Shuya. BS in Engring., Dalian (China) Railway Inst., 1982; MA in Fine Art, Calif. State U., Sacramento, 1994. Chmn. Dalian (China) Coll. Student Arts Assn., 1979-82; bd. dirs. Dalian (China) Painting and Calligraphy Assn., 1982-86; artist self-employed Carmichael, Calif., 1986—. Exhibited in one-man shows at Aaron Gallery, 1994, Artists Contemporary Gallery, 1988-94, Gump's Gallery, 1992-94, Karl Walburg Gallery, 1993-94, Ray and Joyce Witt Galery, 1992-94, Sunbird Gallery, 1994; works represented in Owl-57 Gallery, N.Y., Kurtz Bingham Gallery, Memphis, Fay Gold Gallery, Atlanta, Contemporary Realist Gallery, San Francisco, Winfield Gallery, Carmel, Watezman Gallery, London; represented in pvt. and pub. institutions. Recipient Roberson fellowship Calif. State U. Sacramento, 1992. Home and Office: 2641 Riverpine Ct Carmichael CA 95608-5321

WANG, JIAN-MING, research scientist; b. Zhaozhou, China, May 23, 1963; came to U.S., 1989; s. Xuchen and Shuqin (Zhang) W.; m. Shu-Yu Wang, Nov. 20, 1987; 1 child, Seraphina T. MS, Inst. Optics, Changchun, China, 1985; PhD with very high honors, U. Paris-Sud, 1989. Rsch. asst. scientist Inst. Optics, 1985; rsch. asst. U. Paris-Sud, 1986-89; rsch. assoc. U. So. Calif., L.A., 1989-92; rsch. scientist InterDigital Telecom., Great Neck, N.Y., 1992-96; sr. systems engr. Sierra Semiconductor, San Jose, Calif., 1996-97; sr. staff engr. Rockwell Semiconductor, Newport Beach, 1997-98; mgr. systems engring. Xirlink, Inc., Santa Anna, 1998—. Contbr. articles to Applied Optics, Photonic Switching Proc. Mem. IEEE, Optical Soc. Am., Optical Soc. France. Home: 11 Trieste Irvine CA 92606-8944 Office: Xirlink Inc 505 N Tustin Ave Santa Ana CA 92705-3735

WANG, JICHUAN, sociologist, consultant, researcher; b. Chengdu, Peoples Republic of China, Apr. 1, 1947; came to U.S., 1984; s. Xi and Yufan W.; m. Li Wang, May 15, 1975; 1 child, Xiaojing. BA, Sichuan U., Chengdu, 1982; MA, Cornell U., Ithaca, N.Y., 1986, PhD, 1990. Vis. scientist sociology dept. U. Washington, Seattle, 1988-89; adjunct asst. prof. U. Mich., Ann Arbor, Mich., 1991; postdoc. Pop Studies Ctr. U. Mich., 1989-91; project rsch. dir. SOM Wright State U., Dayton, Ohio, 1991—, asst. prof., 1993-96, assoc. prof., 1996—. Contbr. articles tor profl. jours. Recipient Travel award Grad. Sch., Cornell U., 1987. Fellow UN, Hewlett Found.; mem. APHA. Avocations: reading, swimming, table tennis, fishing. Office: Sch Medicine Wright State U 3640 Colonel Glenn Hwy Dayton OH 45435-0001

WANG, JIE, computer science educator; b. Guangzhou, Guangdong, China, Aug. 28, 1961; s. Yeu-Yun and Lian-Fang (Hu) W.; m. Helen Hong Zhao, Dec. 26, 1986; 1 child, Jesse. BS, Zhongshan U., Guangzhou, 1982, ME, 1984; PhD, Boston U., 1990. Asst. prof. Wilkes U., Wilkes-Barre, Pa., 1990-93; asst. prof. math. dept. U. N.C., Greensboro, 1993-96, assoc. prof. Director Network and Systems Security Laboratory, Lowell, MA, 2001—. Contbr. articles to profl. confs.; referee jours. Boston U. Presdl. fellow 1989-90; grantee NSF, 1991—. Mem. IEEE Computer Soc., Assn. Computing Machinery (spl. interest group on algorithms and computation theory 1988—), European Assn. Theoretical Computer Sci. Avocation: painting. Office: U NC Dept Math Scis Greensboro NC 27412-0001

WANG, JIE, research scientist, science administrator; b. Linhai, Zhejiang, China, May 3, 1956; came to U.S., 1992; s. Youyuan and Xianglian (Xu) W.; m. Wei Li, Jan. 25, 1984; children: Jing, Lisa. BS, Zhejiang U., Hangzhou, 1982, MS, 1984; PhD, SUNY, Syracuse, 1996. Tchr. Linhai County 2nd Mid. Sch., 1974-78; instr., then asst. prof. China Textile U., Shanghai, 1984-88; asst. prof. Shanghai Inst. Elec. Power, 1988-92; postdoctoral rschr. Iowa State U., Ames, 1996-98; sr. scientist, exec. PolymTech, Inc., 1999-2000; sr. scientist R&D Graphic Scis., Inc., Portland, 2000—, gen. mgr. graphic digital divsn., 2001—. Rsch. asst. Coll. Environ. Sci. and Forestry, SUNY, Syracuse, 1992-96; postdoctoral fellow Ames lab. U.S. Dept. Energy, 1997. Contbr. articles to sci. publs. Recipient Young Prof. award China Dept. Energy, Shanghai, 1991. Mem. Am. Chem. Soc., China Chem. and Engring. Soc. Achievements include patents for 3-(p-substituted benzoyl)-2, 5-dichlorothiophenes; for 3 novel soluble organic electrooptical polythiophene derivatives possessing high molecular weight and high thermal stability, patents for water-base pigmented inkjet inks and dispersions; research in mechanical breaking theory and mechanism of polymeric materials and high-performance inks and coatings. Avocations: fishing, swimming, reading, travel. Home: 1915 Arena Ct West Linn OR 97068 Office: Graphic Scis Inc Ste G 4252 International Way Milwaukie OR 97222 E-mail: jwang@graphicsciences.com., jiewang898@yahoo.com.

WANG, JIN, economics educator; b. Taiyuan, Peoples Republic of China, July 18, 1955; came to U.S., 1982; m. Yijun Miao, Nov. 9, 1982; children: Xiaoyin, Xiaoyu. BA, Zhongshan U., China, 1982; MA, Ohio U., 1984; PhD, Kans. State U., 1989. Asst. prof. Eureka (Ill.) Coll., 1989-92, U. Wis., Stevens Point, 1992—. Contbr. articles to profl. jours. Mem. Am. Econ. Assn., Midwest Econ. Assn., Wis. Econ. Assn. Home: 2408 Simonis St Stevens Point WI 54481-3168

WANG, JIN-CHEN CAMILLA, physician, geneticist; b. Lan-Chon, China, Oct. 28, 1945; MD, Nat. Taiwan U., 1970; MS, Purdue U., 1972. Diplomate Am. Bd. Pediatrics, Am. Bd. Med. Genetics in Clin. Genetics and Clin. Cytogenetics. Postdoctoral rsch. assoc. Cornell U., Ithaca, NY, 1973—74; resident North Shore U. Hosp./Cornell U. Med. Ctr., 1974—79; staff physician E.K. Kennedy-Schriver Ctr., Waltham, Mass., 1979-81; fellow in pediatric, instr. Mass. Gen. Hosp./Harvard U., Boston, 1981-84; clin. cytogeneticist The Genetics Inst., Pasadena, Calif., 1985-89; clin. dir., asst. prof. Harbor/UCLA, Torrance, 1989-91; lab. co-dir. Prenatal Diagnostic Ctr., Lexington, Mass., 1991-94; med. dir., lab. dir. Alfigen/The Genetics Inst., 1995—. Contbr. chpts. to books and articles to profl. jours. Fellow Am. Coll. of Med. Genetics. Office: Alfigen/The Genetics Inst 11 W Del Mar Blvd Pasadena CA 91105-2505

WANG, JOHN CHENG HWAI, communications engineer, researcher; b. Beijing, Feb. 12, 1934; s. Hwa Lung and Shu Shiang (Shia) W.; m. Rosa Jenny Chu, Sept. 9, 1967; children: Sophia, Maria, Nina, Amy. BS, U. Md., 1959; MS, U. Pitts., 1968. Engr. Chesapeake Instrument Corp., Shadyside, Md., 1959-64; rsch. scientist Rsch. Ctr. U.S. Steel Corp., Monroeville, Pa., 1964-67; asst. prof. Pa. State U., New Kensington, 1967-69; rsch. engr. FCC, Washington, 1969—. Cmn. working party ionospheric propogation, Internat. Telecom. Union (ITU), Geneva, 1983-. Contbr. articles to profl. jours. Fellow IEEE. Avocations: astronomy, bridge, Chinese history. Office: FCC 445 12 St SW Washington DC 20554-0001

WANG, JOHN XIAOWU, software company executive; b. Hefei, Anhui, China, July 6, 1958; came to US, 1982; s. Zhi Dao Wang and Xian Zhen Fang; m. Lin Hu, Aug. 24, 1985; children: Fanny, Kathy, Bill. B in Physics, U. Sci. and Tech. China, Hefei, 1982; MS, NYU, 1984, PhD in Physics, 1990. Sr. engr. Micromath, Salt Lake City, 1990-92; chmn., chief engr. Poly Software Internat. Ltd., 1992-95, pres., CEO, 1995—, software engr. Pearl River, N.Y., 2000—. Contbr. articles to profl. jours. James Arthur fellow NYU, 1990. Home: 7 Kerry Ct Pearl River NY 10965-3034 E-mail: Wang@polysoftware.com.

WANG, JOSEPH, scientist, educator; b. Haifa, Israel, Jan. 8, 1948; came to U.S., 1978; s. Moshe and Elka Wang; m. Ruth Wang, Mar. 2, 1976; 1 child, Sharon. BSc, Technion, Israel, 1972, MS, 1974, DSc, 1978. Rsch. assoc. U. Wis., Madison, 1978-80; asst. prof. N.Mex. State U., Las Cruces, 1980-84, assoc. prof., 1984-88, prof., 1988—2001, regents prof., 2002—. Author 5 books and 570 papers in field; chief editor Electroanalysis, 1988—; mem. editl. bd. 6 jours. Recipient Heyrovsky medal, 1994. Office: NMex State U Dept Chem Las Cruces NM 88003

WANG, JUI HSIN, biochemistry educator; b. Beijing, Mar. 16, 1921; s. Lieh and Sun Li (Sun) W.; m. Yen Chan Yang, Apr. 2, 1949 (dec. 1993); children: Jane, Nancy. BS, Nat. S.W. Assoc. U., Kunming, China, 1945; PhD, Washington U., St. Louis, 1949; MA (hon.), Yale U., 1960. Postdoctoral fellow radiochemistry Washington U., 1949-51; mem. faculty Yale U., New Haven, 1951-72, prof. chemistry, 1960-62, Eugene Higgins prof. chemistry, 1962-65, Eugene Higgins prof. chemistry and molecular biophysics, 1965-72; Einstein prof. sci. SUNY, Buffalo, 1972—. Rschr. molecular structure and biochem. activity, superconductivity. Contbr. articles to profl. jours., chapters in books. Guggenheim fellow Cambridge U., 1960-61. Fellow AAAS, Am. Acad. Arts and Scis.; mem. Am. Chem. Soc., Am. Soc. Microbiology, Yale Chemists Assn., Am. Soc. for Biochemistry and Molecular Biology, Am. Phys. Soc., Biophys. Soc., Academia Sinica, Materials Rsch. Soc., Sigma Xi. Home: 755 Renaissance Dr Apt 206 Williamsville NY 14221-8046 Office: SUNY Dept Chemistry Buffalo NY 14260-0001 E-mail: juiwang@acsu.buffalo.edu., dac@acsu.buffalo.edu.

WANG, KEGANG, physicist, researcher, materials scientist; b. Lianhua, Jiangxi, People's Republic of China, Mar. 23, 1963; s. Jinqian and Sanmei (Li) W.; m. Li Song, Jan. 28, 1992; children: David Shuo, Gabriel Qi. BS, Jiang Xi Ednl. Inst., Nanchung, 1984; MS, Sichuan U., Chengdu, People's Republic of China, 1988; PhD, Chinese Acad. of Scis., Shenyang, People's Republic of China, 1992. Postdoctoral rschr. Bejing U. of Sci. and Tech., 1992-94, assoc. prof., 1997—2000; postdoctoral fellow U. Barcelona, Spain, 1994-95; postdoctoral assoc. U. Minn., 1995-96; vis. scientist Tohwa U., Japan, 1998-99; vis. scholar Rensselaer Polytech. Inst., 1999—. Contbr. articles to profl. pubs. Postdoctoral fellowship Ministry Edn. and Sci. of Spain, 1994. Mem. Am. Phys. Soc., Materials Rsch. Soc., Minerals, Metals and Materials Soc., Scientific Rsch. Soc., Sigma Xi. Avocation: swimming. Office: Rensselaer Polytech Inst CII Rm 4219 110 8th St Troy NY 12180-3522 E-mail: wangk2@rpi.edu.

WANG, KUNG-LEE, economics consultant; b. Pei Tai-Ho, Hopei, China, Aug. 12, 1925; came to U.S., 1947; s. Cheng-Fu Wang and Funghin Liu; m. Christine Wen, Aug. 15, 1959 (div.); 1 child, Christopher Ching-Yu. BA, Yenching U., 1947; MA, Brown U., 1950; MBA, Columbia U., 1958; MPA, Harvard U., 1965. Acct. in charge fiscal mgmt. Bushwick Hosp., Bklyn., 1952-55; economist, civilian and mil. ops. analyst, internat affairs C-E-I-R., Inc., Washington, 1955-60; cons., 1960-61; chief qualitative econs. analysis, Bur. Mines U.S. Dept. Interior, Washington, 1960-82; pres. KLW Internat., Inc., 1982—, Chi Am Metals & Energy, Inc., 1983-86. Vice chmn. Chinatown Devel. Corp., 1983-96, chmn., 1996-99; pres. The Truth Coun. for Second World War in Aisa, 2000—; vice chmn. MLS Inc., 1986-87, AmerAsia Inc., 1988-89, pres., 1989; dir. Internat. Data Applications Inc., 1969-71; dir. Yenching Grad. Inst., 1994—; L.P. mng. dir. North Gallery Place Assoc., L.P., 1995-99, econ. ops. advisor to ministry econs. affairs Republic of China, 1969-71; cons. ops. rsch. office John Hopkins, Bethesda, Md., 1960-61; trustee OCA Endowment Fund, 1988—; pres. U.S.-China Coun. Internat. Exchange Inc., 1988—; founding chmn. Chinese Heritage Ctr., Inc., 1991-94; ethnic advisor U.S. OEO, 1972-75; dir. Com. of 100, 1990—, exec. dir., 1993-95; pres. Civic League of Brookmont, 1963-64; coord. Chinese-Am. Leadership Council, 1971-73, pres. Rho Psi Found., Inc., 1966-97; nat. v.p. Asian-Pacific Am. C. of C., 1983-84; co-founder, dir. Asian Pacific Am. Heritage Coun., Inc., 1979-97, pres., 1982-83; co-founder and nat. dir. Asian Am. Voters Coalition, 1985-91; co-founder and bd. dir. Nat. Chinese Am. Voters League, 1984-91; founder, nat. pres. Orgn. Chinese Ams. Inc., 1973-77, nat. treas., v.p. fin., 1979-81, hon. mem., 1982; chmn. U.S.-China Capital Cities Friendship Council, 1984-94; dir. Md. Civil Rights Coalition, 1990-92; v.p.-U.S. ea. states The Global Alliance for Preserving the History of World War II in Asia, Inc., 2001—. Contbr. articles to encys. and profl. jours. Recipient Engr. of Yr. award Am. Inst. Mining, Metall. and Petroleum Engrs., 1976, Mineral Economist of Yr. award, 1984, award Asian and Pacific Am. Civil Rights Alliance, 1983, Ellis Island medal Honor Nat. Ethnic Coalition Found., 1993; Nat. Inst. Pub. Affairs fellow, 1965. Mem. Am. Soc. Pub. Adminstrn., Kennedy Sch. Govt. Alumni Assn. of Harvard U. (bd. dirs. 1978-82), Asian-Am. Bus. Roundtable (pres. 1989-95), Am. Econs. Assn., Rho Psi. Mem. Chinese Christian Ch. Home: 1940 Dundee Rd Rockville MD 20850-3137 Office: 11228 Georgia Ave Ste 9 Silver Spring MD 20902-4694 Fax: 301-946-4517. E-mail: uscc@uschinacouncil.org.

WANG, KUO-KING, manufacturing engineer, educator; BSME, Nat. Ctrl. U., China, 1947; MSME, U. Wis., 1962, PhD in Mech. Engring., 1968. Sibley prof. emeritus mech. engring. Cornell U., Ithaca, N.Y. Founder, dir. Cornell Injection Molding Program, 1974—; cofounder Cornell Mfg. Engring. and Productivity Program, Advanced CAE Tech., Inc. Recipient Disting. Svc. citation U. Wis., 1990. Fellow ASME (Blackall Machine Tool and Gage award 1968, William T. Ennor Mfg. Tech. award 1991), Soc. Mfg. Engrs. (Frederick W. Taylor Rsch. medal 1987); mem. CIRP, ASM Internat., Nat. Acad. Engring., Am. Welding Soc. (Adams Meml. Membership award 1976), Soc. Plastic Engrs., Polymer Processing Soc. Achievements include pioneering research in injection molding, friction welding and applications of solid modeling to CAD/CAM. Office: Cornell Univ Dept Mech/Aero Engring Upson Hall Ithaca NY 14853

WANG, LAWRENCE KONGPU, educator; b. China, Nov. 20, 1940; s. Pu-Chen and Shu-Yu W.; m. Mu-Hao, June 8, 1968; children: John, Norman, Betty. BS, Nat. Cheng Kung U., Taiwan, 1962; M of Engring., U. Mo., 1965; MS, U. R.I., 1967; PhD, Rutgers U., 1972. Environ. engr. Arvin Corp., Buffalo, 1970-73; asst. prof. Rensselaer Polytech. Inst., Troy, N.Y., 1973-77; assoc. prof. Stevens Inst. Tech., Hoboken, N.J., 1977-80; dir. Lenox (Mass.) Inst. Water Tech., 1980-89, dean., prof., 1999—; v.p. Zerox Corp., Newtonville, N.Y., 1989-95, 96-99; prof. U. Ulll., Urbana, 1993-95; sr. advisor UN, Vienna, 1995-96. Mem. adv. bd. U.S. EPA, Washington, 1977—, N.Y. State Dept. Environ. Conservation, 1973-78; adj. prof. Nat. Cheng Kung U., Taiwan, 1973-80; examiner Nat. Profl. Engrs., Bd., 1973-89. Author 5 books; contbr. articles to profl. jous.; inventor/patentee in field. Recipient Kenenth Rsch. award N.Y. Water Pollution Control Assn., N.Y.C., 1978. Mem. AIChE (treas. 1977-79), Am. Water Works Assn. (chmn. 1986-88), Water Environ. Fedn. (ann. rev. 1997-99), Assn. Environ. Engring. Profs., Overseas Chinese Environ. Engrs. & Scientists Assn. Republican. Home: 1 Dawn Dr Latham NY 12110-5305 Office: Lenox Inst Water Tech 107 Yokun Ave Lenox MA 01240-2032

WANG, LEON RU-LIANG, civil engineer, educator; b. Canton, China, June 15, 1932; came to U.S., 1959; s. Huai-Kao and Yuen-Chin (Ho) W.; m. Joyce Chieh-Chun Tien, July 22, 1961; children: Frank Yu-Heng, Mark Yu-Da, Cindy Chi-Wen. BSC.E., Cheng-Kung U., Tainan, Republic of China, 1957; MSC.E., U. Ill., 1961; ScD, MIT, 1965. Asst. prof. civil engring. Rensselaer Poly. Inst., Troy, N.Y., 1965-69, assoc. prof. civil engring., 1969-80; prof. civil engring. U. Okla., Norman, 1980-84, Old Dominion U., Norfolk, Va., 1984-95, chair civil engring. dept., 1984-90, prof. emeritus civil engring. dept., 1995—. Adj. prof. civil and structural engring. dept. Hong Kong U. Sci. and Tech., 1993-95; tech. cons. Watervliet (N.Y.) Arsenal, 1966-80. Editor: Research for Multiple Hazard Mitigations, 1983, Seismic Evaluation of Lifeline Systems-Case Studies, 1986. Founding mem. Chinese Community Ctr., Albany, 1973. Recipient rsch. awards NSF, 1976—. Fellow ASCE (br. pres. 1987-88), Hong Kong Inst. of Engrs.; mem. Earthquake Engr. Rsch. Inst., Am. Soc. Engring. Edn., Chinese-Am. Assn. Nat. Hazard Mitigation Rsch. (founding mem.).

WANG, LIANG-GUO, research scientist; b. Foochow, People's Republic of China, Apr. 23, 1945; parents Chi-hsi Wang and Yunqing Chen; m. Shu-fen Zhang, Sept. 27, 1977; children: Zhijing, Zhijian. BS in Physics, Peking U., Beijing, 1969; MS in Physics, Ohio State U., 1983, PhD in Physics, 1986. Tech. mgr. and electronics engr. various cos., People's Republic of China, 1971-78; rsch. asst. Inst. of Academia Sinica, Beijing, 1978-80, U. Ky., Lexington, 1981, Ohio State U., Columbus, 1981-86, U. Va., Charlottesville, 1987-89; rsch. scientist Coll. of William and Mary, Williamsburg, Va., 1989-97. Cons. NASA Langley Rsch. Ctr., Hampton, Va., 1989-97; mem. tech. staff Applied Materials, Sunnyvale, Calif., 1997—. Contbr. articles to profl. jours. Recipient Pub. Svc. medal NASA, 1992. Mem. Optical Soc. Am., Internat. Soc. for Optical Engring, Photonics Soc. of Chinese-Ams. Achievements include patents in field; research and development of highly sensitive frequency modulation laser spectrometers, advanced laser and passive radiometer instruments for airborne and spaceborne applications. Home: PO Box 2337 Santa Clara CA 95055-2337 E-mail: lwang818@aol.com.

WANG, LIN, physicist, computer science educator, computer software consultant; b. Dandong, China, June 11, 1929; came to U.S., 1961, naturalized, 1972; s. Lu-Ting and Shou-Jean (Sun) W.; m. Ingrid Ling-Fen Tsow, July 8 1961; children: W. Larry, Ben. BS in Physics, Taiwan U., 1956; MS in Physics, Okla. State U., 1965, PhD in Physics, 1972. Mem. physics faculty Cheng Kung U., Tainan, China, 1957-61; asst. prof. physics Southwestern Okla. State U., Weatherford, 1965-72; prof., chmn. physics dept. N.E. Coll. Arts and Sci., Maiduguri, Nigeria, 1973-75; mem. tech. staff Pacific Engring. Corp., Bellevue, Wash., 1976-78; sr. software engr., Far East cons. Electro-Sci. Industries, Inc., Portland, Oreg., 1979-82; mem. sr. computer sci. faculty South Seattle C.C., 1983—. Mem. Assn. for Computing Machinery, Am. Phys. Soc., AAUP. Avocations: classical music, world travel. Home: 9214 181st Ave E Bonney Lake WA 98390-7187 Germany

WANG, MING DE, engineer; b. Yibin, Sichuan, Peoples Republic of China, July 04; came to U.S., 1994; d. Xisheng and Shoumai (Wu) W.; m. Guoxian Zhang, Oct. 4, 1970; 1 child, Ying. BSc in Chemistry, Nankai U., Tianjin, China, 1978, MSc in Organic Chemistry, 1981; PhD in Chemistry, U. Ottawa, Ont., Can., 1993. Rsch. asst. Nankai U., Tianjin, 1978-81, lectr., 1981-87; rsch. asst. in chemistry U. Ottawa, Can., 1987-89, rsch. asst. Can., 1989-93; postdoctoral fellow in chemistry SUNY, Albany, 1994-95, U. Ottawa, 1995-96; process engr. Hadco Santa Clara, Calif., 1996-98, Carolina Circuits, C-MAC of Am., Inc., Greenville, S.C., 1998—. Co-author 3 chpts. to books; contbr. 16 articles to profl. jours. Cert. instr. CPR, ARC, SUNY, Albany, 1994—. Recipient scholarship Ont. Min. Edn. and Tng., 1992, Sci. and Tech. award Nat. Edn. Com. Peoples Republic of China, 1990. Mem. Am. Chem. Soc., Chem. Inst. Can., China Chem. Soc. Avocations: gospel music, classic movies, travel. Home: 107 Raleigh Ct Simpsonville SC 29681-1981 Office: Carolina Circuits C-MAC of Am Inc 200 Fairforest Way Greenville SC 29607-4609 E-mail: mwang@carolina.cmac.com., Inchrist-1@excite.com.

WANG, NANZE PATRICK, engineer; b. Shishi, Fujian, China, May 28, 1963; came to U.S., 1988; s. Zhiyan Wang and Xiuque Shi; m. Yurjour Lily Pay, Dec. 23, 1991; 1 child, Jerry Zhengxu. BS in Chemistry, Xiamen U., Fujian, China, 1983; MS in Chemistry, U. Ala., Huntsville, 1991, PhD in Materials Sci., 1995. Chemist Inst. Synthetic Materials, Guangzhou, China, 1983-87; asst. mgr. Shenzhen Petrochem. Co., China, 1987-88; postdoctoral mem. tech. staff Bell Labs. Lucent Techs., Murray Hill, N.J., 1995-97; sr. R&D engr. Fiberguide Industries, Stirling, 1998-2000; sr. rsch. engr. SpectraSwitch, Inc., Santa Rosa, Calif., 2000—. Contbr. articles to profl. jours. Mem. IEEE Lasers and Electro Optics Soc., Am. Chem. Soc. (demonstrator in chemistry week N.J. sect. 1996, 97), Internat. Soc. for Optical Engring., Materials Rsch. Soc., Phi Kappa Phi. Home: 93 Airport Blvd E Santa Rosa CA 95403-8008 Office: SpectraSwitch Inc 445 Tesconi Cir Santa Rosa CA 95401 E-mail: patrick@spectraswitch.com., npwang@prodigy.net.

WANG, N(IAN) T(ZU), economist, educator; Student, U. London; AB in Econs., Columbia U.; AM in Econs., PhD in Econs., Harvard U. Adj. prof., dir. China-Internat. Bus. Project Grad. Sch. Bus. & Sch. Internat. & Pub. Affairs Columbia U., N.Y.C.; sr. rsch. scholar East Asian Inst., Columbia U. Mem. disting. scholar exch. program, com. on scholarly comm. with Peoples Republic of China, Chinese Acad. Social Scis.; dir. info. analysis divsn. UN Ctr. on Transnat. Corps.; chief econ. survey sect. UN Secretariat; vis. prof. Pitts. U., Nankai U., Nat. Chengchi U., CUNY, Chinese U. Hong Kong; assoc. project on Chinese Studies Harvard U.; instr. Columbia Coll., Columbia U.; cons. World Bank, UN, Internat. Fin. Corp., major cos.; lectr. univs. and ednl. instns. N.Am., S.Am., Asia and Africa. Editor: Taxation and Development, 1976, Business With China: An International Assessment, 1980, Taiwan's Enterprises in Global Perspective, 1992; author: China's Modernization and Transnational Corporations, 1984, Chinese Legal Framework for Foreign Investment and Its Implications, 1986; (with Teng Weizao) Transnational Corporations and China's Open Door Policy, 1988; How to Penetrate the World Market by Chinese Enterprises, 1995; dir., prin. author Multinational Corporations in World Development, 1973, A Reexamination, 1978; contbr. articles to profl. jours. Univ. fellow Harvard U.; Austin scholar; recipient N.Y. Gov. Outstanding Asian-Am. award; named Hon. Prof. Shanghai U. Fin. and Econs., U. Internat. Bus. and Econs., Beijing, Beijing Inst. Chem. Engring. Mgmt., East China U. Chem. Tech., Shanghai, Guangzhou U., Guangdong Inst. Commerce, Nankai U., Shandong Inst. Econs., Hefei U. Tech., Yunnen Inst. of Fin. and Econs. Fellow Internat. Acad. Mgmt., Phi Beta Kappa. Office: Columbia U East Asian Inst New York NY 10027

WANG, PAO-KUAN, meteorologist, educator; b. Tainan, Taiwan, Dec. 1, 1949; came to U.S., 1973; s. Shou and Luan-Chao (Chiu) W.; m. Li-Bi Tseng, Aug. 28, 1926; children: Lawrence, Victor. BS in Atmospheric Scis., Nat. Taiwan U., Taipei, 1971; MS, UCLA, 1975, PhD, 1978. Rsch. meteorologist UCLA, 1978-80, adj. asst. prof., 1980; from asst. to assoc. prof. U. Wis., Madison, 1980-88, prof., 1988—, chmn. Atmospheric and Oceanic Sci., 1994-97, mem. Air Resources Mgmt., Program, 1998—. Cons. Nelson Industries, Stoughton, Wis., 1985—; vis. prof. UCLA, 1988, Nat. Taiwan U., 1993, U. Mainz, Germany, 1993, MIT, Cambridge, 1997, U. Ferrara, Italy, 2001. Author: Heaven and Earth, 1996 (10 Best Books), Cloud Physics, 1997, Insight, 2001. Recipient Humboldt award Alexander V. Humboldt Found., Mainz, 1993; S.C. JohnsonDisting. fellow Johnson Wax Co., Racine, Wis., 1993. Mem. Am. Meteorol. Soc. (chmn. Cloud Physics Com. 1990-93). E-mial. Office: U Wis Dept Atmospheric Oceanic Sci 1225 W Dayton St Madison WI 53706-1612 E-mail: pao@windy.meteor.wisc.edu.

WANG, PAUL WEILY, materials science and physics educator; b. Kao-Hsiung, Taiwan, Republic of China, Nov. 4, 1951; came to U.S., 1979; s. Yao Wen Wang and Yue Hua Lo; m. Diana Chung-Chung Chow, June 9, 1979; children: Agnes J., Carol H., Alfred Z. PhD, SUNY, Albany, 1986. Rsch. asst. prof. Vanderbilt U., Nashville, 1986-90; asst. prof. U. Tex., El Paso, 1990-96, assoc. prof., 1996—. Hon. prof. Dalian Inst. Light Industry, 1995—; cons. EOTec Inc., 1987-88, Midtex Comm. Instruments Inc., 1996—. Contbr. articles to Jour. Applied Physics, Nuclear Instru. and Math., Springer Series in Surface Scis., Applied Surface Sci., Applied Optics, Jour. of Am. Ceramic Soc., Jour. Materials Sci., Jour. Luminescence, Jour. Non-cyrs. Solids, Lasers, Surface and Interface Analysis, Thin Solid Films, Jour. Materials Chemistry and Physics. Fellow Inst. for Study of Defects in Solids; mem. Am. Ceramic Soc., Am. Phys. Soc., Materials Rsch. Soc., Am. Vacuum Soc. Achievements include iron in silicon gettered by thermally grown silicon dioxide thin film, dopants effects on the structure of fluoride glasses, surface modification of heavy metal doped glasses under x-ray and electron irradiations, luminescence centers in silica stimulated by particle bombardments, defects introducted by gamma-ray radiation enhance the luminescence in silica, development of defects creation mechanism in silica by 5 and 50 eV photons, investigation of silver diffuses and precipitates thermally on the surface in ion exchange sodium calcium silicate glass, investigate the radiation effects on lead silicate glasses, electron beam processing on trimethylsilane covered Si(100) surface, aluminum nitride/aluminum oxide composite films grown by plasma, conduct and manage numerous research projects in materials research. Office: U Tex Dept Physics And Materials R El Paso TX 79968-0001 Home: 1718 W Teton Dr Peoria IL 61614-2638

WANG, PETER ZHENMING, physicist; b. Quanzhou, Fujian, People's Republic of China, Nov. 30, 1940; came to U.S., 1983; s. Guohua and Shunhua (Chen) W.; m. Grace Ruhui Xu, Mar. 14, 1967; children: Yili, Yile. MS, Qinghua U., Peking, People's Republic of China, 1964; postgrad., U. Tex., Dallas, 1983-84. Sr. engr. Particle Accelerator Inst., Shanghai, 1964-83; electronic engr. Benchmark Media Systems, Inc., Syracuse, N.Y., 1984-87; project engr. McGaw Inc., Carrollton, Tex., 1988—. Physicist High Energy Physics Inst., Peking, 1978-79. Co-author: (book) Vacuum World, 1984. Tchr. Bible study, Plano, Tex., 1990. Baptist. Achievements include research and design of a variety of proton and electron accelerators for low energy nuclear physics experiments, industries and hospitals; design of 50 GEV proton synchrotron, design of audio distribution amplifiers and consoles for BBC, ABC, and other TV and radio stations; development and design of air bubble detector, pressure transducer and noise reduction solution for the microprocessor based infusion therapy instrument used in hospitals. Home: 1510 Chesterfield Dr Carrollton TX 75007-2847 Office: McGaw Inc 1601 Wallace Dr Carrollton TX 75006-6666

WANG, PETER ZUGUANG, telecommunication executive; b. Shanghai, Sept. 7, 1954; came to the U.S., 1979; s. Shizhuo and Wentao (Yu) W.; m. Ellie Zhang, Jan. 6, 1977 (div. 1990); m. Jennifer Wang; children: John, Raymond. BS in Computer Sci., U. Ill., Chgo., 1983, MSEE, 1984; MBA, Nova U., 1988. Sr. engr. Racal-Milgo, Inc., Sunrise, Fla., 1984-88; mem. tech. staff AT&T Bell Labs., Holmdel, N.J., 1988-91; pres. ATD Corp., 1991-92; exec. v.p. Unitech Telcom, Inc., Oakland, Calif., 1992-95; pres., CEO World Communication Group Inc., Hazlet, N.J., 1995—, also bd. dirs. Chmn. World Mobile Communications Co., Ltd., Hangzhou, China; bd. dirs. World PCS, Inc., Princeton, N.J., SynCom Inc., Hazlet, United Med. Industries, Inc., North Bergen, N.J. Avocations: tennis, skiing. Home: 5 Remington Ct Holmdel NJ 07733-1864 Office: World Communication Group Inc 1 Bethany Rd Ste 76 Hazlet NJ 07730-1668

WANG, PING, biomedical investigator; b. Qingzhou, China, Feb. 5, 1959; came to U.S., 1987, naturalized, 1998; s. Tangbang Wang and Xiuzheng Quan; m. Mian Zhou, May 14, 1986; children: Stephanie M., Christie M. MD, Changwei Med. Coll., Weifong, China, 1982; MS, 3d Med. U., Chongqing, China, 1985; MA, Brown U., 1998. Rsch. assoc. U. Wash., Seattle, 1987-88, Mich. State U., East Lansing, 1988-92, asst. prof. surgery, 1992-96, Brown U. Sch. Medicine, Providence, 1996-97, assoc. prof. surgery, 1997-2000; prof. depts. surgery, pathology, physiology and biophysics U. Ala. Sch. Medicine, Birmingham, 2000—, assoc. dir. Ctr. for Surg. Rsch., 2000—, sr. scientist Ctr. for Metabolic Bone Disease, 2001—; sr. scientist Clin. Nutrition Rsch. Ctr., 2001—. Recipient NIH individual rsch. project awards, 1998—, ind. scientist award NIH, 1996-2001, 1st ind. rsch. support and transition award NIH, 1995-2001, grant-in-Aid award Am. Heart Assn., Dallas, 1994-98. Mem. AAAS, Am. Physiol. Soc., Shock Soc., Surg. Infection Soc., Assn. for Acad. Surgery, Soc. Critical Care Medicine, Am. Heart Assn. (cardiopulmonary and critical care coun.), N.Y. Acad. Scis. Office: U Ala Dept Surgery Volker Hall Rm G094P 1670 University Blvd Birmingham AL 35294-0019 Fax: 205-975-9715. E-mail: ping.wang@ccc.uab.edu.

WANG, QIGUI, materials engineer, researcher; b. Funing, Jiangsu, China, Nov. 23, 1960; s. Chengchao and Yun (Guo) Wang; m. Jiaping Zhang, Mar. 3, 1961; 1 child Weike. Bachelor in Sci. and Engring., Nanjing Inst. of Tech., Nanjing, Jiangsu, China, 1982; MSc in Sci. and Engring., SE U., Nanjing, Jiangsu, China, 1987; PhD, U. Queensland, Brisbane, Australia, 1997. Lectr. Nanjing (Jiangzu) Inst. of Tech., China, 1982—87; asst. prof. SE U., Nanjing, China, 1988—92; vis. rsch. scientist Dederal U. of Rio Grande do Sol(U-FRGS), Porto Alegre, Brazil, 1992—94; rsch. scholar Australian Government's Coop. Rsch. Ctr. (CAST), Brisbane, Australia, 1994—97; postdoctoral rsch. scientist Worcester (Mass.) Poly. Inst., 1997—99; sr. rsch. engr. Aerotek, Saginaw, Mich., 1999—2000; sr. materials engr. Gen. Motors Corp, 2000—. Consulting engr. Nthe Metall. Machinery Plant of Jiangsu Province, Nanjing, China, 1982—87; sr. consulting engr. Nanjing (Jiangzu) Non-Ferrous Metals Corp, China, 1987—89, Nanjing Motors Corp., Nanjing, Jiangsu, China, 1989—92. Contbr. articles to profl. jours. Named for The Best Rsch. Work, The Sci. and Tech. Com. of Jiangsu Province, China, 1991; recipient OPRS Scholarship, Australian Edn. Dept., 1994-1997, CAST Rsch. Scholarship, The U. of Queensland, Australia, 1994-1997, Rsch. Fellowship, Brazilian Rsch. Coun. (CNPq), 1992-1994, Rsch. Found. of Rio Grande do Sul (FAPERGS), Brazil, 1992-1994, The Best Undergraduate Thesis award, The State Edn. Com. of China, 1982. Mem.: Am. Foundrymen's Soc., ASM Internat. (chpt. sec. 2001), The Minerals, Metals & Materials Soc. Achievements include Chinese patent. Avocations: coin collecting, stamp collecting, travel.

WANG, QIN, computer engineer, researcher; b. Lishui, Zhejiang, China, Jan. 15, 1973; d. Jixu Wang and Xuewen Chen; m. Ying Hu. PhD, Iowa State U., 1998—2001. Rsch. asst. Iowa State U., Ames, Iowa, 1998—2001; sr. hardware engr. EMC , Hopkinton, Mass., 2001—. Contbr. articles (Best Thesis Award, 1998). Recipient PACE, Iowa State U., 1998, ABD, 2001, Best Grad. award, Zhejiang Province, 1995, Best Grad award, 1998, Best Thesis award, 1995, 1998, Siemens prize, Siemens Inc., 1996, Nari award, Chinese State Power, 1997, Outstanding Student award, Zhejiang Univ., 1991—94; scholar Grad. Coll. scholar, Iowa State U., 1998—2001, First Level Outstanding Student Scholarship, Zhejiang Univ., 1991—94. Mem.: SWE, IEEE, Nat. Scholars Honor Soc., Delta Epsilon Iota, Tau Beta Pi, Sigma Xi. Personal E-mail: qwanghz@yahoo.com.

WANG, QIONG, research scientist, pharmaceutical executive; b. Jiu Jiang, Jiang Xi, China, Aug. 17, 1960; arrived in U.S., 1999; d. Xiue Qun Wang and Din Mei Hung; m. Wei He Chen, Jan. 10, 1985 (div. Aug. 11, 1993); m. Claude Lavallée, Nov. 20, 1993; children: Cheng Chen, Muriel Lavallée. MD, Jiu Jiang Med. Coll., 1984; cert., Hunan (China) Med. Coll., 1988; MSc, Montreal (Can.) U., 1995. Physician, surgeon Lu Shan Hosp., Jiu Jiang, 1984—87; libr. Libr. Jin Jiang Med. Coll., 1987—89; rsch. asst. dept. microbiology and immunology U. Montreal, 1991—94; rsch. asst. Royal Victoria Hosp. Montreal, 1994—95, Montreal Neurol. Inst. and Hosp., 1995—99; scientist Novartis Pharm. Corp., Summit, NJ, 1999—. Contbr. articles to profl. jours. Chmn. Chinese Student Assn., Montreal U., 1993—95. Mem.: Am. Chem. Soc. Office: Novartis Pharm 556 Morris Ave Summit NJ 07901

WANG, RICHARD Y. emergency physician, osteopath; b. Taiwan, 1961; DO, N.Y. Coll., 1986. Diplomate Am. Bd. Emergency Medicine, Am. Coll. Med. Toxicology. Intern Metro Hosp., Phila., 1986-87; resident in emergency medicine Sparrow Hosp./Ingham Med. Ctr., East Lansing, Mich., 1987-90; fellow in clin. toxicology N.Y.C. Poison Control/Bellev, 1990-92; mem. staff R.I. Hosp., Providence; assoc. prof. Brown Univ., 1992—2001; mem. staff Grady Health Sys., Atlanta, 2001—. Mem. Am. Coll. Emergency Physicians, Am. Acad. Clin. Toxicology, Am. Coll. Med. Toxicology, Soc. Acad. Emergency Medicine. Office: Nat Ctr Environ Health Ctrs Disease Control and Prevention 4770 Buford Hwy MS F-17 Atlanta GA 30341

WANG, SAM SHU-YI, hydraulic and mechanical engineer, educator; b. Chungking, Szechuan, China, Sept. 21, 1936; came to U.S., 1963; s. San-chuan and Mayhsun (Chen) W.; m. Jine Yang, Aug. 27, 1966. BSME, Nat. Cheng Kung U., Tainan, Taiwan, 1959; MS in Mech. and Aerospace Sci., U. Rochester, 1965, PhD in Computational Hydrodynamics, 1968. Registered profl. engr., Miss. Asst. design engr. Yue Loong Motors Corp., Taipei, Taiwan, 1960-61; rsch. asst. Nat. Chengking U., Tainan, 1961-63; teaching and rsch. asst. U. Rochester, N.Y., 1963-67; asst. prof. mech. engring. U. Miss., University, 1967-72, assoc. prof., 1972-81, prof., 1981—, Barnard disting. prof., 1988—, acting chmn. dept., 1982-83, dir. Nat. Ctr. for Computational Hydrosci. and Engring., 1983—. Pres., prin. rsch. engr. Computational Engring. Rsch. Inst., Inc., Oxford, Miss., 1983—; UN expert UN Devel. Program, 1987; gen. chmn. Internat. Conf. on Hydro-Sci. and Engring., 1993; gen. chmn. Internat. Symposium on Sediment Transport Modeling, 1989, Internat. Conf. on Finite Elements in Water Resources, 1980. Prin. editor: Finite Element in Water Resources, 1980, River Sedimentation, 1986, Developments in Theoretical and Applied Mechanics, 1988; editor: Sediment Transport Modeling, 1989, Advances in Hydro-Science and Engineering, Vol. I, parts A and B, 1993. Recipient Ralph R. Teetor award Soc. Automotive Engrs., 1975, Outstanding Engring. educator award U. Miss., 1977, Outstanding Faculty award Miss. Legislature, 1989. Mem. AIAA (spl. award 1979, Space Shuttle Flag plaque 1984), ASCE (Hydraulic Engring. Achievement award 1988), Chinese Soc. Theoretical and Applied Mechancis (hon.). Avocations: travel, chess, stamp and coin collecting. Office: U Miss NaCtr Computational Hydrosci and Engring University MS 38677

WANG, SHENG-WEI, geophysicist; b. Taichung, Taiwan, July 13, 1970; s. Kuang-Wu Wang, Chin-Kwan Tseng; m. Pei-Ling Chu. PhD, Rutgers U., New Brunswick, N.J., 1998. Vis. scientist Atmospheric & Oceanic Scis., Princeton, NJ, 1998—2000; sr. scientist Environ. and Occupl. Health Scv., Piscataway, 2000—. Contbr. articles. Mem.: Am. Chem. Soc., Am. Geophys. Union. Office: Environ and Occupl Health Sc 356 170 Frelinghuysen Rd. Piscataway NJ 08854 Office Fax: 732-445-0915. Business E-Mail: shengwei@fidelio.rutgers.edu.

WANG, SHIH-HO, electrical engineer, educator; b. Kiangsu, China, June 29, 1944; came to U.S., 1968; s. C.C. Wang and Man Shih. BEE, Nat. Taiwan U., Taipei, 1967; MEE, U. Calif., Berkeley, 1970, PhD in Elec. Engring., 1971. Asst. prof. elec. engring. U. Colo., Colo. Springs, 1973-76, Boulder, 1976-77; asst. prof. electrical engring. U. Md., College Park, 1977-78, assoc. prof., 1978-84; prof. U. Calif., Davis, 1984—. Cons. Lawrence Livermore (Calif.) Nat. Lab., 1986-88; scientific officer Office Naval Research, Arlington, Va., 1983-84. Assoc. editor Internat. Jour. Robotics and Automation, 1986-90. Served to 2d lt. China Air Force, Taiwan, 1967-68. Mem. IEEE (hon. mention award control systems soc. 1975). Office: Univ Calif Dept Elec Computer Engring Davis CA 95616 E-mail: wang@ece.ucdavis.edu.

WANG, SHOUHONG, business educator; b. Anhui, China, Oct. 5, 1946; arrived in U.S., 1998; s. Yujun and Wenying (Zhang) W.; m. Zhengjun Su, Oct. 1, 1972; 1 child, Hai. B in Engring., Tsinghua U., Beijing, China, 1970, MBA, 1981; PhD, McMaster U., Hamilton, Can., 1990. Chief prodn. mgr. Handan Iron & Steel Co., China, 1976-79; lectr. Tsinghua U., China, 1981-86; asst. prof. U. New Brunswick, Can., 1990-92, assoc. prof. Can., 1992-96, prof. Can., 1996-98; assoc. prof. U. Mass., Dartmouth, 1998-2001, prof., 2001—. Co-author: (in Chinese) Management Information Systems, 1988, (in Taiwan Chinese), 1992, Problem Solving and Programming: Essentials of Computer Languages for Commerce, 2000; author: Analyzing Business Information Systems: An Object-Oriented Approach, 1999; contbr. numerous articles to profl. pubs. Grantee Nat. Scis. and Engring. Rsch. Coun. of Can., 1992-96, 96-2000, Social Scis. and Humanities Rsch. Coun. of Can., 1993-96, 96-2000. Mem. Adminstrv. Sci. Assn. of Can. Avocations: classical music, piano. Home: 40 Idlewood Ave Dartmouth MA 02747 Office: U Mass Dartmouth Dept Marketing/Bus Info 285 Old Westport Rd Dartmouth MA 02747-2300

WANG, SUWEN, physicist, consultant; b. Yangzhou, China, May 14, 1959; came to U.S., 1982; s. Changrong Wang and Yun Zhang; m. Xiao Shuang Fu, Apr. 3, 1994; children: Oliver Shizi Wang, Alice Fuzi Wang. BS, Nanjing (China) U., 1982; MS, La. State U., 1983; PhD, Duke U., 1988. Postdoctoral fellow Duke U., Durham, N.C., 1988-89; postdoctoral rsch. assoc. Manchester (Eng.) U., 1989-90; rsch. assoc. U. Mass., Amherst, 1990-92; sr. rsch. scientist Stanford (Calif.) U., 1992—. Cons. Simplex Solutions, Inc., Sunnyvale, Calif., 1996—. Contbr. articles to sci. jours.; inventor in field. Mem. Am. Phys. Soc., Sigma Xi. Achievements include being one of the first to discover non wetting of superfluid helium on cesium substrate with the third sound technique; contributions to the field of crit. phenomena by studying properties of liquid helium; contributions to studying of gravitational physics. Office: Stanford Univ GP-B HEPL Stanford CA 94305

WANG, TSILI, research scientist; b. Hexian, Anhui, China, Jan. 15, 1964; s. Xinya Wang, Xianyin Wang; m. Saijin Huang, Aug. 8, 1988; children: Haven, Max. BS, Hefei (China) Inst. Tech., 1984; MSc, Chinese Acad. Scis., Beijing, 1988; PhD, U. Utah, 1993. Postdoctoral rschr. U. Utah, Salt Lake City, 1993—94, Schlumberger, Ridgefield, Conn., 1994—95; sr. scientist Baker Hughes Inc., Houston, 1996—2000, staff scientist, 2000—01, sr. staff scientist, 2001—. Contbr. articles to profl. jours. Mem.: IEEE, Soc. Petroleum Engrs., Soc. Exploration Geophysicists. Office: Baker Hughes Inc 2001 Rankin Rd Houston TX 77073 Business E-Mail: tsili.wang@bakeratlas.com.

WANG, TSUEY TANG, science educator, venture capitalist; b. Tainan, Taiwan, Nov. 12, 1932; came to U.S., 1958; s. Shih-Neng and Tsun (Chen) W.; m. Margaret Mei-Tieh Lin, June 12, 1965; children: David, Marjorie, Vanessa. BS, Cheng Kung U., Tainan, 1955; PhD, Brown U., 1965. Asst. prof. Poly. U. N.Y., Bklyn., 1965-67; disting. mem. tech. staff AT&T Bell Labs., Murray Hill, N.J., 1967-88; vis. prof. Rutgers U., New Brunswick, 1988—; pres., chmn. bd. dirs. Transpac Capital Corp., Springfield, 1988—. Vis. prof. Tokyo U. Agr. and Tech., 1984; mem. indsl. adv. bd. Nat. Ctr. Composite Materials, U. Del., 1986-89; bd. dirs. Internat. Power Devices, Inc., Boston, 1989-99; spl. invited vis. prof. Japan Ministry Edn., Tokyo, 1992; bd. dirs. Nat. Assn. Investment Cos., Washington, 1990-94. Author: (chpt.) Polymer Blends, 1978, (chpt.) Optical Telecommunications, 1979; editor: The Applications of Ferroelectric Polymers, 1988; patentee in field. Recipient Borden Corina Keen fellow Brown U., 1961. Fellow Am. Phys. Soc.; mem. ASME, Soc. Advancement Material and Process Engring., Materials Rsch. Soc., N.Y. Acad. Scis. Achievements include research in spinodal decomposition in polymer blends; melting point depression in compatible polymer blends. Office: Rutgers Univ Chem and Biochem Engring Piscataway NJ 08854 E-mail: tsuey@rci.rutgers.edu.

WANG, WANLONG, engineer, researcher; b. Yingshang, China; s. Hechang Wang and Hongying Cai; m. Chunlin Lou, Oct. 7, 1992; 1 child, Taiyu. BSc, Northwestern Polytech. U., Xi'an, China, 1986; MSc, Beijing U. Aeronautics & Astro, 1992; PhD, Tsinghua U., Beijing, 1995. Assoc. engr. Shaanxi Aircraft Co., Chenggu, China, 1986-89; postdoctoral fellow Nat. U. Singapore, 1995-96; tech. support engr. Parametric Tech. Corp. Singapore, 1996-97; rsch. engr. Northwestern U., Evanston, Ill., 1997—2000; v.p. Castingtrade.com, 2000—01; engr. Mitutoyo Am. Corp., City of Industry, Calif., 2001—. Author: Rapid Tooling Guidelines for Sand Casting, 2000. Recipient cert. state sci. and tech. project accomplishment State Sci. and Tech. Commn. China, 1996.

WANG, WEI, chemist, researcher; b. Dongtai, Jiangsu, China, Oct. 27, 1966; s. Changgui Wang and Yulin Fu; m. Hjijuan Zhang, Sept. 12, 1994. BS in Sci., Nanjing (China) Normal U., 1988; MS, Shanghai Inst. Material Medica, 1993; PhD in Sci., N.C. State U., 2000. Tchr. chemistry Sizao H.S., Dongtai, 1988-90; rsch. scientist East China U. Sci. and Tech., Shanghai, 1993-94; rsch. assoc. U. Okla. Health Scis. Ctr., Oklahoma City, 1994-96; rsch. scientist dept. chemistry U. Ariz., Tucson, 2000—. Contbg. author: Methods in Molecular Medicine, 1998, Peptide and Protein Drug Delivery, 1998; contbr. articles to sci. jours., including Current Medicinal Chemistry, Chem. Comm., Jour. Peptide Rsch. Univ. scholar Nanjing Normal U., 1985-87; Glaxo fellow N.C. State U., 1998-99. Mem. AAAS, Am. Chem. Soc., Am. Peptide Soc., Phi Lambda Upsilon. Office: U Ariz Dept Chemistry 1306 E University Blvd Tucson AZ 85721

WANG, WEI, research scientist; BS in Physics, Tsinghua U., Beijing, 1993; MS in Physics, U. Miami, 1996; PhD in Biophysics, U. Calif., San Francisco, 2000. Rsch. assoc. Stanford (Calif.) U., 2001—. Recipient Intelligent Sys. for Molecular Biology Travel award, The Internat. Soc. for Computational Biology, 2000, NASA Travel award, 2001, NCSA Small Allocation award, Nat. Ctr. for Supercomputing, 2001—. Mem.: AAAS, Am. Chem. Soc. (Nat. Chem. Computing Group Excellence award 2000), Sigma Xi.

WANG, WENLI, finance educator; b. Tianjin, China, Dec. 1, 1971; d. ZongZhi and GuiRu Wang. PhD, U. Tex., 2000. Asst. prof. Goizueta Bus. Sch. Emory U., 2000—. Vis. scholar Ctr. for Rsch. in Electronic Commerce U. Tex., Austin, 2000—. Fellow, Motorola, 1992, Ctr. for Rsch. in Electronic Commerce, 1998, 1999, 2000; scholar, Hua Wei, 1991, 1993. Mem.: Assn. Info. Systems. Avocation: travel, dance. Office: Goizueta Bus Sch Emory U 1300 Clifton Rd Atlanta GA 30322

WANG, WILLIAM KAI-SHENG, law educator; b. N.Y.C., Feb. 28, 1946; s. Yuan-Chao and Julia Ying-Ru (Li) W.; m. Kwan Kwan Tan, July 29, 1972; 1 child, Karen You-Chuan. BA, Amherst Coll., 1967; JD, Yale U., 1971. Bar: Calif. 1972. Asst. to mng. partner Gruss & Co., N.Y.C., 1971-72; asst. prof. law U. San Diego, 1972-74, asso. prof., 1974-77, prof., 1977-81, Hastings Coll. Law, U. Calif., San Francisco, 1981—. Vis. prof. law U. Calif., Davis, 1975-76, Hastings Coll. Law, U. Calif., 1980, U. Calif., L.A., 1990; Reuschlein vis. prof. law Villanova U., 1999; vis. prof. Bklyn. Law Sch., fall 2000; cons. to White House Domestic Policy Staff, Washington, 1979; participant with bd., chair investment policy oversight group Law Sch. Admissions Coun.; mem. steering com. Legal Svcs. for Entrepreneurs; mem editl. bd. Internat. and Comparative Corp. Law Jour. Co-author: Insider Trading, 1996, supplement, 2002; contbr. articles to newspapers, mags., scholarly jours.; , editor. Mem. State Bar Calif., Am. Law Inst., Assn. of Am. Law Schs. (mem., then chair com. on audit and assn. investment policy 1995-98). Home: 455 39th Ave San Francisco CA 94121-1507 Office: U Calif Hastings Coll Law 200 McAllister St San Francisco CA 94102-4707 E-mail: wangw@uchastings.edu.

WANG, WILLIAM WEIQI, physician; b. Shanghai, China, June 3, 1962; MD, Shanghai Med. U., 1985; PhD, U Medicine and Dentistry N.J., Newark, 1995. Fellow NIMH, Bethesda, Md., 1995-96; rsch. assoc. Baylor Coll. Medicine, Houston, 1997-98; resident in psychiatry Washington U., St. Louis, 1998—2002; attending psychiatrist SSM Healthcare, 2002—. Author: Psychiatry Pearls of Wisdom, 1999, Psychiatry for the Boards, 2002; contbr. articles to profl. jours. Recipient Clin. Rec. awrad Shanghai Bur. Pub. Health, 1988. Mem. AMA, Am. Psychiat. Assn., Am. Acad. Neurology, Am. Soc. for Biochemistry and Molecular Biology, So. Med. Assn. Avocations: poetry, history, fine arts, martial arts, ethnic cuisine. Office: 330 First Capital Dr Ste 410 Saint Charles MO 63301 E-mail: wwwang@rocketmail.com.

WANG, XIANG, cardiologist, researcher; b. Nanchang, Jiangxi, China, May 29, 1956; came to U.S., 1998; s. Fengpo Wang and Derong Liu; m. Dandan Zhao, Jan. 24, 1984; 1 child, Jingyu. BS in Medicine, Jiangxi Med. Coll., Nanchang, 1982; assoc. level, Okayama (Japan) U., 1998; MS, Ball State U., Muncie, Ind., 2001. Resident in medicine Jiangxi Provincial People's Hosp., Nanchang, 1982-87, attending physician, 1988-92, assoc. prof. dept. cardiology medicine, 1993-96; rsch. scientist dept. cardiology medicine Okayama U. Med. Sch., 1996-98; bioinformatics specialist dept. molecular genetics and microbiology U. Medicine and Dentistry of N.J., 2001—. Contbr. articles to med. jours., including Chinese Jour. Internal Medicine, Chinese Jour. Cardiovasc. Medicine, Med. Jour. China, Acta Med. Okayama. Mem. Chinese Med. Assn., Japanese Circulation Soc. Home: 574 Auten Rd Apt 4H Hillsborough NJ 08844

WANG, XIAODONG, mechanical engineer, educator; b. Changzhou, Jiangsu, China, Jan. 6, 1966; arrived in U.S., 1990; s. Changyou Wang and Youxong Chen; m. Jinghua Qian, Dec. 22, 1994. BS in Naval Arch., Shanghai Jiao Tong U., 1988, postgrad., 1988—90, Tufts U., 1990—91; MS in Ocean Engring., MIT, 1993, PhD in Applied Mechanics, 1995. Aast. prof. Inst. Paper Sci. and Tech., Atlanta, 1995—99; asst. prof. Poly. U., Bklyn., 1999—. Mem. sci. adv. bd. MIT Conf. on Computational Fluid and Solid Mechanics. Author (with K.J. Bathe): Fundamentals of Fluid-Solid Systems, 2001; mem. editl. bd.: Computer Modeling in Engring. and Scis., 1999—2001, mem. editl. bd.: Computer and Structures, 2000—; contbr. articles to profl. jours. Mem.: ASME (mem. dynamics and control of structures and sys. tech. com.), Internat. Soc. for Computational Engring. and Scis. (founder), Soc. for Indsl.. and Applied Math., U.S. Assn. for Computational Mechanics. Achievements include research in linear and nonlinear fluid-structure interaction analyses; mathematical theory of computational methods; vibration, nonlinear dynamics, and instability theory; applied numerical methods for solids, fluids, heat and mass transfer problems; hybrid computation with molecular dynamics and continum mechanics. Office: Dept Mech Engring Six Metro Tech Ctr Brooklyn NY 11201

WANG, XIAODU, engineering educator; b. Beijing, Oct. 3, 1954; came to U.S. 1991; p. Yu Miao and Fang He; m. Yuhong Liu, May 1, 1984; 1 child, Grace. BS, Beijing Inst. Aeronautics and Astronautics, 1982, MS, 1985; D in Engring., Yokohama (Japan) Nat. U., 1990. Asst. lectr. Beijing Inst. Aeronautics and Astronautics, 1985-86; rsch. engr. NKK Corp., Kawasaki, Japan, 1990-91; postdoctoral rsch. asst. U. Tex. Health Sci. Ctr., San Antonio, 1992-94, asst. instr., 1995-97, asst. prof., 1997-99, U. Tex., San Antonio, 1999—. Faculty advisor Chinese Student and Scholars Assn., San Antonio, 1996-99. Contbr. chpt. to book and articles to profl. jours. Recipient Fgn. Rsch. Studentship, Ministry Edn. Japan, Yokohama, 1986-90, Biomed. Rsch. award The Whitaker Found., 1998; Japan Overseas Tech. Tng. scholar Japan Overseas Tech. Exch. Assn., Kawasaki, 1991; rsch. grantee NIH, 1999. Mem. ASME, Orthopaedic Rsch. Soc., Biomed. Engring. Soc. Avocations: reading, traveling, ancient history. Home: 7810 Parsley San Antonio TX 78240-2275 Office: Univ Tex 6900 N Loop 1604 W San Antonio TX 78249-1130 Fax: 210-458-5589. E-mail: xwang@utsa.edu.

WANG, XIAOZHI, structural engineer; b. Jiangsu, China, Nov. 19, 1967; arrived in U.S., 2000; d. Helin and Jianmei (Zhou) W. BSc, Shanghai Jiaotong U., 1989; MSc, Norwegian Inst. Tech., Trondheim, 1991, PhD, 1995. Structural specialist engr. Kvaerner Maritime, Oslo, Norway, 1995-96, sr. project engr. Norway, 1996; sr. engr. Norsk Hydro, 1996, Am. Bur. Shipping, Houston, 2000—. Contbr. articles to profl. jours. Mem.: Soc. Naval Archs. and Marine Engrs. Home: 1311 Belham Ridge Ct Spring TX 77379- Office: Am Bur Shipping 16855 Northchase Dr 77060 E-mail: cwang@eagle.org.

WANG, XING, power systems engineer; b. Haerbin, Heilongjiang, China, June 25, 1970; arrived in U.S., 2001; s. Shaohu Wang and Jianshan Mao; m. Ying Xiao. PhD, Brunel U., London, 2001. Power systems engr., rschr. Electric Power Rsch. Inst., Beijing, 1991—96, team leader energy mgmt. sys., 1997—98; power systems engr. Alstom Esca Corp., Bellevue, 2001—. Recipient China Nat. award sci. and tech., 1997. Mem.: IEEE Power Engring. Soc. (sr.). Home: # 7205 4331 Lake Washington Blvd NE Kirkland WA 98033 Office: Alstom Esca Corp 11120 NE 33rd Pl Bellevue WA 98004 Personal E-mail: xingwang@yahoo.com. Business E-Mail: xing.wang@tde.alstom.com.

WANG, XINGWU, physics educator; b. Hangzhou, China, Feb. 19, 1953; came to U.S., 1982; s. Jinguang and Xiuying (Lin) W. BS, Harbin N. Eng. Inst., 1978; MS, Hangzhou U., 1981; PhD, SUNY, Buffalo, 1987. Tchr., technician Hangzhou N. Sch., China, 1978-81; tchr. physics Hangzhou U., 1981-84; rsch. asst. SUNY, Buffalo, 1984-87, rsch. assoc., 1987-88; asst. prof. elec. engring. Alfred U., 1988-93, assoc. prof., 1993-97, prof., 1997—. Physics educator; b. Hangzhou, China, Feb. 19, 1953; came to U.S., 1982; s. Jinguang and Xiuying (Lin) W. BS, Harbin N. Eng. Inst., 1978; MS, Hangzhou U., 1981; PhD SUNY, Buffalo, 1987. Tchr., technician Hangzhou N. Sch., China, 1978-81; tchr. physics Hangzhou U., 1981-84; rsch. asst. SUNY, Buffalo, 1984-87, rsch. assoc., 1987-88; asst. prof. elec. engring. Alfred U., 1988-93, assoc. prof., 1993-97, prof., 1997—. Mem. Am. Phys. Soc. Mem. Am. Phys. Soc. Home: PO Box 1133 Alfred NY 14802-0133 Office: Alfred U Dept Elec Engring Alfred NY 14802 E-mail: fwangx@alfred.edu.

WANG, X.T. (XIAOTIAN WANG), educator; b. Beijing, China, Oct. 10, 1957; arrived in U.S., 1987; s. Zhong Wang, Nancy Zilin Tian; m. Ying Shi, May 19, 1957; children: Geng. M in Patho-physiology, Jinan U., China, 1985; MA in Physiol. Psychology, Beijing Med. U., 1991; PhD, N.Mex. State U., 1993. Lectr. Jinan U. Med. Sch., Guangzhou, China, 1986—87; grad. ass. N.Mex. State U., 1987—93; asst. prof. U. S.D., Vermillion, 1993—98, assoc. prof., 1998—. Vis. scientist Max Planck Inst., Berlin, 1998—99; vis. prof. Hong Kong U. Sci. and Tech. Sch. Bus. and Mgmt., Hong Kong, 2000—01; prin. investigator U. S.D., Vermillion, 1999—. Mem. editl. bd.: Jour. Behavioral Decision Making, 2002—, guest editor: Jour. Bioeconomics, 2001—02; contbr. chapters to books, articles to profl. jours. Grantee, NSF, 1999, James McDonnell Found., 2000; scholar Nat. Grad. scholar, Dept. Edn. China, 1982. Mem.: Human Behavior and Evolution Soc. (Young Investigator award 1992), Soc. for Judgement and Decision Making, Psychonomic Soc., Acad. Mgmt., Behavioral and Brain Scis. (assoc.). Home: 849 Valley View Dr Vermillion SD 57069 Office: Univ SD 414 East Clark St Vermillion SD 57069 Home Fax: 605-677-6604; Office Fax: 605-677-6604. Personal E-mail: xtwang@usd.edu. Business E-Mail: xtwang@usd.edu.

WANG, YANXIN, research scientist; b. Dandong, Liaoning, China, June 19, 1962; arrived in United States, 1995; d. Dianlu Wang and Guiying Chen; m. Wanmin Xin, July 2, 1988; 1 child, Xin. BS, Shenyang (China) Agr. U., 1985, MS, 1988; MS, PhD, Rutgers U., 1999. Sr. lectr. Shenyang Agr. U., 1988-94; postdoc. assoc. U. Tenn., Knoxville, 1999-2000; rsch. assoc. Rutgers U., New Brunswick, N.J., 2000—. Grad. asst. Rutgers U., New Brunswick, 1995-99. Author: Nutrient Gene Interactions in Health & Disease, 2001; contbr. articles to profl. jours. Recipient Rsch. award Agr. Dept. Liaoning, 1992. Mem. AAAS, Am. Soc. Animal Sci., Soc. Exptl. Medicine Biology, N.Am. Assn. Study Obesity. Home: 615 Benner St Highland Park NJ 08904 Office: Rutgers U 96 Lipman Dr New Brunswick NJ 08901 E-mail: wyx@rci.rutgers.edu.

WANG, YAOYU, electrical engineer; b. Shandong, China, July 30, 1965; m. Chunyan Xie, Sept. 20, 1971. PhD, Tianjin U., China, 1994. 199rsch. fellow U. Hawaii, Honolulu, 2009; sr. rsch. assoc. Inst. Tech., Chgo., 1999—. Guest scientist Alexander von Humboldt Found., U. Dortmund, Germany, 1997-98. Co-author: Electric Power Systems Communications and Control Rsch. fellow U. Hawaii, Honolulu, 1999, Tsinghua U., Beijing, 1994-97. Mem. IEEE (sr.). Office: Inst Tech Siegel Hall Ste 136 3301 S Dearborn St Chicago IL 60616 Fax: 312-567-8976. E-mail: wangy@iit.edu.

WANG, YEN, nuclear medicine physician, radiologist; b. 1928; MD, Nat. Taiwan U., 1953. Diplomate Am. Bd. Nuclear Medicine, Am. Bd. Radiology. Intern Holy Cross Hosp., Salt Lake City, 1953-54; resident Mercy Hosp., Pitts., 1955-58; with Thomas Jefferson U. Hosp., Phila. Prof. radiology Thomas Jefferson U. Mem. AMA, NMS, Am. Coll. Radiology, Am. Roentgen Ray Soc., Radiol. Soc. N.Am. Office: Thomas Jefferson U Hosp Philadelphia PA 19107-5084 also: VA Med Ctr Philadelphia PA 19104

WANG, YI-FENG, polymer scientist, consultant; b. Nanbu, Sichuan, China, Oct. 10, 1963; came to U.S., 1996; s. Zhi Jin Wang and Rong Fang Lei; m. Dong Xiao Yang, June 26, 1992; 1 child, Jeffery Jia-Hua. BSc, S.W. Petroleum U., Sichuan, 1985; PhD, U. Manchester Inst. Sci./Tech., Eng., 1992. Postdoctoral rsch. fellow McGill U., Montreal, Que., Can., 1993-95; product devel. chemist GE Silicones, Waterford, N.Y., 1996-2000; polymer scientist, co-founder Cyclics Corp., Rensselaer, 2000—. Patentee in field; contbr. articles to profl. jours. Mem. Am. Chem. Soc. Home: 6 Anchor Dr Waterford NY 12188-1149 E-mail: yfwang66@yahoo.com.

WANG, YONG, science educator; b. Lianyungang, China, Feb. 13, 1967; p. Deyou Wang and Shuhua Li; m. Jing Huang, Jan. 8, 1992; 1 child, Henry. BS, U. Sci. and Tech., Chengdu, China, 1989; PhD, Sichuan U., Chengdu, 1995. Postdoctoral fellow Chinese Acad. Scis., Beijing, 1995-97, assoc. prof., 1997—; sr. rsch. assoc. U. Mass., Amherst, 1997-98; sr. rsch. fellow U. Mo., Kansas City, 1998-2000, asst. prof., 2000—. Advisor Inst. Chemistry, Chinese Acad. Scis.; chmn. internat. symposium on molecular condensed state Internat. Union Pure Applied Chemistry, Beijing, 1996. Mem. editl bd. Polymer-Plastics Tech. and Engring., 2001—; contbr. numerous articles to profl. jours. Postdoctoral fellow Chinese Acad. Scis., 1996; sr. rsch. fellow 3M co., 1997. Mem. AAAS, ADA, Am. Phys. Soc., Internat. Assn. Dental Rsch., Sigma Xi. Office: U Mo-Kansas City Sch Dentistry 650 E 25th St Kansas City MO 64108 Fax: (816) 235-5524. E-mail: wangyo@umkc.edu.

WANG, YUAN, pharmacist, researcher; b. Shanghai, China, July 24, 1975; d. Wan-Chao Wang and Chuan-Zheng Yan. BS in Biochemistry, BS in Pharmaceutics, SUNY, Buffalo, 1998, BS in Pharmacy, 1999, Pharm D, 2000. Cert. pharmacist, N.Y. Pharmacist Omicare Long-term Care Pharmacy of Western N.Y., West Seneca, N.Y., 1997-2000, Pfizer Inc., Morris Plains, N.J., 2000—. Rsch. asst. dept. pharmaceutics SUNY, Buffalo, 1996; cons. pharmacist McGuire Pharmacy, Williamsville, NY. Scholar Top's Edn. Safety and

Culture, 1994-97, CVS Pharmacy, 1998. Mem. N.Y. State coun. Health Sysm. Pharmacists. Avocations: tennis, violin, travel, singing. Office: Pfizer Inc Med Info 201 Tabor Rd Morris Plains NJ 07950 E-mail: yuanguo75@hotmail.com.

WANG, YUNHUA, biomedical engineer; b. Xianjin, China, Dec. 7, 1965; s. Ruxin Wang and Jinying Dun; Liying Shi, Dec. 26, 1995; 1 child, Yinhuo. BE, Tsinghua U., China, 1988, PhD, 1992. Lectr. Tsinghua U., 1992-94, assoc. prof., 1994—, vice dir. Biomed. Engring. Divsn., 1993-95; rsch. assoc. Max-Planck Inst., Germany, 1999-2000; rsch. scientist MNI, McGill U. & Stellate Systems, 2000—. Vis. scholar U. Ill., 1995-96 Pres. Union Grad. Students, 1990. Rsch. fellow Humboldt Found., Germany, 1997—. Mem. IEEE, China Instrument Soc. Home: 5055 Bourret Ave Apt 19 Montreal QC Canada H3W 1L3 Office: MNI Rm 028 3081 U Str Montreal QC Canada H3A 2B4 E-mail: yunhuaw@hotmail.com.

WANG, YUWEN, chemist, researcher; b. Yangyuan, Hebei, China, Aug. 28, 1954; came to U.S., 1987; s. Ji Wang and Guiying Ma; m. Zengjuan Li, Jan. 6, 1981; children: Lei, Julie. B, Hebei U., 1977; PhD, Va. Poly. and U., 1997. Asst. rsch. fellow Hebei Acad. Scis., Shijiazhuang, China, 1978-81, assoc. dir., 1982-86, assoc. rsch. fellow, 1989-91; rsch. assoc. Iowa State U., Ames, 1987-88; rsch. scientist Va. Poly. and State U., Blacksburg, 1992-2000; sr. scientist Boehringer Ingelheim Pharms. Inc., Ridgefield, Conn., 2000—. Cons. Cultor Inc., Groton, Conn., 1995, Pfizer Inc., Groton, 1996. Contbr. articles to profl. jours.; mem. editl. bd. Internat. Jour. Information, 1999—. Recipient Chinese Nat. Sci. Progress award Nat. Sci. Com., 1985, Hebei Sci. Progress award Hebei Sci. Com., 1979, 83, 91. Mem. AAAS, Am. Chem. Soc., Assn. Students in Va. Tech. (v.p.), Phi Lambda Upsilon, Sigma Xi. Achievements include research on gas chromatography mass spectrometry, liquid chromatography, capillary zone electrophoresis and atomic absorption spectroscopy, development of explosive simulants, invention of electrogenerated chemiluminescence detector for HPLC, development of parts per trillion levels of cancerogenic compound detection technologies. Avocations: tennis, racquet ball, jogging, singing. Home: 9 Ashley Ct Danbury CT 06810 Office: Boehringer Ingelheim Pharms Inc PO Box 368 900 Ridgebury Rd Ridgefield CT 06877-1058 E-mail: ywang3@rdg.boehringer-ingelheim.com.

WANGAARD, FREDERICK F, science educator, consultant; b. Minneapolis, Minn., Mar. 3, 1902; s. Christian Wanfeerd and Hanna Marie Wangaard. BS, Univearsity of Minn., St. Paul, MN, 1933; MS, State Univeresity of NY, Syracuse, NY, 1935; PhD, SUNY, Syracuse, NY, 1939. Instr. U. of Wash., Saettle, Wash., 1936—39, asst. prof. Seattle, 1939—42; technologist Forest Products Laboretory, Madison, Wis., 1942—45; asst. to assoc. prof. Yale U., New Haven, 1945—52, prof., 1952—67; dept head for w.d. sci. Colo. State U., Fort Collins, Colo., 1967—76, prof. emeritus, 1976. Fao(un) advisor Forest Products Rsch. Int, Los Banos, Philippines, 1957; fulbright rsch. scholar Norsk Trefeknisk Institutt, Norway, 1958; cooedinator clark heritage workshop Forest Products Lab., Madison, Wis., 1979. Author: (textbook) Mechanical Properties and Wood. Recipient Borden Chem. Award, Forest Products Rsch. Soc., 1973, Outstanding Achievemant Award, Regents U. of Moraesala, 1917, Hon. Alummus Award, Coll. of For. Resources, U., 1999. Mem.: Internat. Acad. of wood sci. (assoc.; pres. 1968—72), Soc. of wood sci. & tech. (assoc.; pres. 1964—65, Distring Svc. 1983), Forest Products Soc. (assoc.; pres. 1975—76, Distring Svc. 1976). Presbyterian. Home: 900 Worthington CirApt324 Fort Collins CO 80526

WANGER, OLIVER WINSTON, federal judge; b. L.A., Nov. 27, 1940; m. Lorrie A. Reinhart; children: Guy A., Christopher L., Andrew G., W. Derek, Oliver Winston II. Student, Colo. Sch. Mines, 1958-60; BS, U. So. Calif., 1963; LLB, U. Calif., Berkeley, 1966. Bar: Calif. 1967, U.S. Dist. Ct. (ea. dist.) Calif. 1969, U.S. Tax Ct. 1969, U.S. Dist. Ct. (cen. dist.) Calif. 1975, U.S. Dist. Ct. (so. dist.) Calif. 1977, U.S. Dist. Ct. (no. dist.) Calif. 1989, U.S. Ct. Appeals (9th cir.) 1989. Dep. dist. atty. Fresno (Calif.) County Dist. Atty., 1967-69; ptnr. Gallagher, Baker & Manock, Fresno, 1969-74; sr. ptnr. McCormick, Barstow, Sheppard, Wayte & Carruth, 1974-91; judge U.S. Dist. Ct. (ea. dist.) Calif., 1991—. Adj. prof. law Humphreys Coll. Law, Fresno, 1968-70. Fellow Am. Coll. Trial Lawyers, Internat. Acad. Trial Lawyers; mem. Am. Bd. Trial Advs. (pres. San Joaquin Valley chpt. 1987-89, nat. bd. dirs. 1989-91), Am. Bd. Profl. Liability Attys. (founder, diplomate), Calif. State Bar (mem. exec. com. litigation sect. 1989-92, mem. com. on fed. cts. 1989-90), San Joaquin Valley Am. Inn of Ct. (pres. 1992-93), Beta Gamma Sigma. Office: US Dist Ct 5104 US Courthouse 1130 O St Fresno CA 93721-2201

WANGLER, MARK ADRIAN, anesthesiologist; b. Coldwater, Ohio, Sept. 29, 1955; s. William Henry and Rita Francis (Vielkind) W.; m. Kathleen Sara Schlarman, May 6, 1977; children: Nathan, Aaron. BS in Biology, Wright State U., 1977; MD, Ohio State U., 1981. Diplomate Am. Bd. Anesthesiology. Intern Ohio State U., Columbus, 1981-82, resident, 1982-84, chief resident, 1983-84; asst. prof. anesthesiology Northeastern Ohio Coll. Medicine, Canton, 1984-86; dir. anesthesiology Mercer County Joint Twp. Community Hosp., Coldwater, 1987-90; ptnr. Anesthesia Assocs. of Lima, Inc., 1990-2000. Dir. rsch. Northeastern Ohio Coll. Medicine, Canton, 1985-86, dir. pain clinic, 1985-86; dir. pain clinic Mercer County Cmty. Hosp., Coldwater, 1986-90, St. Rita's Med. Ctr., 1994-2000; dir. anesthesiology Orthopaedic Inst. Ohio, 2000—. Contbr. articles to numerous profl. jours. Mem. Mercer County Hist. Soc., Celina, Ohio, 1988; patron Lighthouse Ministries, Celina, 1988. Grantee, NIH, Bethesda, Md., 1978. Mem. AMA, Internat. Anesthesia Rsch. Soc., Am. Soc. Anesthesiologists, Ohio Med. Assn., Ohio Soc. Anesthesiologists, Allen County Acad. of Medicine. Republican. Avocations: biking, camping, reading. Home: 860 Yorkshire Dr Lima OH 45804-3300 Office: 1103 Bank One Twr Lima OH 45801

WANGLER, WILLIAM CLARENCE, retired insurance company executive; b. Buffalo, Dec. 7, 1929; s. Emil A. and Viola M. (Roesser) W.; m. Carol B. Sullivan, Aug. 17, 1957; children: Jeffrey W., Eric J. BS, SUNY, Cortland, 1951. Claims adjuster Liberty Mut. Ins. Co., Buffalo, 1954-60, claims supr. Miami, Fla., 1960-65, home office examiner Boston, 1965-68, asst. claims mgr. Cleve., 1966-69, claims mgr. Cleve, 1969-73, div. claims service mgr. Pitts., 1973-79, div. claims mgr., 1979-86, v.p. asst. gen. claims mgr. adminstrn. Boston, 1986-94; ret., 1994. Pres. Claims Mgrs. Counsel, Cleve., 1970; chmn. Nationwide Intercompany Arbitration, Cleve., 1969-70. Loaned exec. Mass. Bay United Way, Boston, 1964; account exec. Pitts. United Way, 1985-86. Served to capt. USMC, 1951-54. Republican. Roman Catholic. Home: 64 Trout Farm Ln Duxbury MA 02332-4609

WANGSNESS, WAYNE ROGER, economics educator; b. Decorah, Iowa, June 20, 1941; s. Elmer Melvin and Hazel Orleans (Lee) WW..; m. Cheryl Ann Lee, Feb. 9, 1974; children: Amy, Ryan, Karin, Philip. Degree in tech. agriculture, Iowa State U., 1965; BA in Econs., Luther Coll., 1968; MA in Econs., U. Iowa, 1971. Teaching asst. U. Iowa, Iowa City, 1970-71; instr. agriculture N.E. Iowa C.C., Calmar, 1972-78, instr. computers, 1982-84, instr. econs., 1990-91, 95—; vis. asst. prof. econs. Luther Coll., Decorah, Iowa, 1986-91; econs. faculty Upper Iowa U., 1996—. Cons. Small Bus. Devel. Corp., Dubuque, Iowa, 1988-97; pres. Ostrick Producers Co-op. of the Midwest, 1997—. Contbr. articles to profl. jours. Bd. dirs. N.E. Iowa Rsch. Ctr., Nashua, 1980-83. With U.S. Army, 1961-64. Mem. Nat. Corn Growers Assn. (bd. dirs. Washington and St. Louis 1980-83), Northeast Iowa Organics Assn. (pres. 1996—), Rotary (bd. dirs. Decorah 1986-89). Republican. Lutheran. Avocations: trees, reading, riding. Home: 1869 Middle Ossian Rd Decorah IA 52101-7542

WANIEK, MARILYN NELSON See NELSON, MARILYN

WANJOHI, ELSIE WAIRIMU, communications educator; b. Nyeri, Kenya, Nov. 17, 1949; came to U.S., 1990; d. David Kinyua and Martha Nyawira Githiru; 1 child, Anne W. BS in Comm., Okla. State U., 1992, MS in Mass Comm., 1994, D in Comm., 1996. Dir. Wambugu, Embu, Thika Inc., Kenya, 1973-87; info. officer Kabete Info. Ctr., Nairobi, Kenya, 1988-90; publs. editor Okla. State U., Stillwater, 1992-96, tchg. asst., 1995-96; asst. prof. Bethune-Cookman Coll., Daytona Beach, Fla., 1996—. Internat. fellow AAUW, 1993-94. Mem. Fla. Pub. Rels. Assn., Phi Kappa Phi. Avocations: tennis, jogging, reading, TV documentaries. Home: 3537 Forest Branch Dr Apt A Port Orange FL 32129-8952 Office: Bethune-Cookman Coll 640 Mary McLeod Bethune Blvd Daytona Beach FL 32114 E-mail: wanjohie@cookman.edu.

WANK, GERALD SIDNEY, periodontist, educator; b. Bklyn., Jan. 20, 1925; s. Joseph and Sadie (Ikowitz) W.; m. Gloria Baum, June 4, 1949; children: David, Stephen, Daniel. BA, NYU, 1945, DDS, 1949; cert. in orthodontia, Columbia U., 1951, cert. in periodontia, 1956. Intern Bellevue Hosp., 1949-50; pvt. practice N.Y.C., Great Neck, N.Y., 1949—; instr. dept. periodontia, oral medicine NYU Dental Sch., 1956-63, asst. clin. prof. dept. periodontia, 1963-67, asst. prof. periodontia, oral medicine, former postgrad. dir. periodontal-prosthesis dept. fixed partial prosthesis, 1970—, clin. assoc. prof. periodontia and oral medicine, 1970-77, clin. prof., 1977—, postgrad. dir. periodontia, 1968-71; lectr. periodontology Harvard U. Sch. Dental Medicine, 1973-74; vis. lectr. N.Y.C. C.C. Sch. Dental Hygiene, 1960-65, Albert Einstein Coll. Medicine, 1967-96; sr. asst. attending staff North Shore U. Hosp., 1974-77, sr. asst. attending divsn. surgery, 1977—. Cons. orthodontic panel N.Y. State, N.Y.C. depts. health, 1953-80; cons. periodontal prosthesis, Goldwater Meml. Hosp., N.Y.C.; former postgrad. instr. 1st Dist. Dental Soc. Postgrad. Sch., dist. claims com.; lectr. in field; mem. com. admissions N.Y. U. Coll. Dentistry, 1975-86, chmn. fund raising, 1976-77; cons. N.Y. VA Hosp., 1996—. Contbr. to: Practice of Periodontia, 1960, Dental Clinics of North America, 1972, 81, Manual of Clinical Periodontics, 1973; contbr. articles to profl. jours. Capt. USAF, 1953-55. Recipient Alumni Meritorious Service award NYU, 1981, Coll. Dentistry Alumni Achievement award NYU, 1983. Fellow Acad. Gen. Dentistry, N.Y. Acad. Dentistry (life), Internat. Coll. Dentists (life), Am. Coll. Dentistry (life), Am. Acad. Oral Medicine (pres. N.Y. sect. 1971-72), Am. Pub. Health Assn.; mem. N.Y. Coll. Dentists (dir.), ADA, Dental Soc. N.Y.C. (dir. 1st dist., chmn. ethics com. 1985-86), Fedn. Dentaire Internat., Am. Assn. Dental Schs., N.Y. State Pub. Health Assn., AAUP, Pan Am. Med. Assn. (life), AAAS, ADA, Am. Acad. Periodontology, Sci. Rsch. Soc. Am., Northeastern Soc. Periodontia (life), Am. Acad. Dental Medicine, Acad. Gen. Dentistry, Internat. Acad. Orthodontia, Am. Assn. Endodontists (life), Am. Acad. Periodontia (life), Am. Acad. Oral Medicine (life), NYU Coll. Dentistry Alumni Assn. (dir., sec. 1973-74, v.p. 1974-75, pres. 1976-77), Am. Assn. Endodontists, NYU Coll. Dentistry Dental Assocs. (charter), Acad. Oral Rehab. (hon.), First Dist. Dental Soc. (program chmn. 1984, chmn. continuing edn. 1983, sec., 1985, v.p. Eastern Dental Soc. br. 1986, pres.-elect 1987, pres. br. 1988, bd. dirs. 1989—, Meritorious Svc. award 1997), Am. Acad. Osseointegration (life), NYU Gallatin Assocs., Alumni Fedn. NYU (dir. 1976-81), N.Y. County Dental Soc. (Dist. Claims Com.), Soc. of the Torch, Masons, Century Club, NYU Club, Fresh Meadow Country Club, Omicron Kappa Upsilon (life), Alpha Omega. Jewish. Home and Office: 40 Bayview Ave Great Neck NY 11021-2819 Office: 30 E 40th St New York NY 10016-1201

WANKAT, PHILLIP CHARLES, chemical engineering educator; b. Oak Park, Ill., July 11, 1944; s. Charles and Grace Leona (Pryor) W.; m. Dorothy Nel Richardson, Dec. 13, 1980; children: Charles, Jennifer. BS in Chem. Engring., Purdue U., 1966, MS in Edn., 1982; PhD, Princeton U., 1970. From asst. prof. to C.L. Lovell disting. prof. chem. engring Purdue U., West Lafayette, Ind., 1970—, head freshman engring., 1987-95, interim dir. continuing engring. edn., 1996, head interdisciplinary engring., 2000—. Cons. pharm. firm, 1985-94. Author: Large Scale Ads and Chromatog, 1986, Equil Staged Separations, 1988, Rate Controlled Separations, 1990, Teaching Engineering, 1993, The Effective, Efficient Professor, 2002; patentee in field. With AUS, 1962-64. Recipient award in Separations Sci. and Tech., Am. Chem. Soc., 1994. Mem. AIChE, Am. Soc. Engring. Edn. (Union Carbide Lectr. award 1997), Am. Chem. Soc. Avocations: fishing, canoeing, camping. Office: Purdue U Dept Interdisciplinary Engring West Lafayette IN 47907-1292 E-mail: wankat@ecn.purdue.edu.

WANKE, RONALD LEE, lawyer, educator; b. Chgo., June 22, 1941; s. William F. and Lucille (Kleinwachter) W.; m. Rose Klonowski, Oct. 23, 1987. BSEE, Northwestern U., 1964; JD, DePaul U., 1968. Bar: Ill. 1968. Assoc. Wood, Dalton, Phillips, Mason & Rowe, Chgo., 1968-71, ptnr., 1971-84, Jenner & Block, Chgo., 1984--. Lectr. John Marshall Law Sch., Chgo., 1985-94; mem. adv. com. intellectual property program, U. Fla. Coll. Law. Co-author: (book chpt.) International Intellectual Property Law, 1997; contbr. articles to Software Law Jour., 1987, Internat. Legal Strategy, 1995. Mem.: ABA, Intellectual Property Law Assn. Chgo. (chmn. inventor svcs. com. 1976, chmn. fed. rules com. 1981). Home: 1806 N Sedgwick St Chicago IL 60614-5306 Office: Jenner & Block 1 E Ibm Plz Fl 4000 Chicago IL 60611-7603

WANKO, MICHAEL ANDREW, school system administrator; b. Bayonne, N.J., May 19, 1947; s. Andrew A. and Lydia (Perhach) W.; m. Justine Maria Dworzanski, July 24, 1971; 1 child, Jason. BA, N.J. City U., 1969, MA, 1971, Seton Hall U., 1974; PhD, Walden U., 1977. Cert. tchr., supr., prin., sch. administr., student personnel svcs. and assoc. ednl. media specialist, N.J. Coach Bayonne (N.J.) Bd. Edn., 1969-72, elem. tchr., 1969-72, secondary tchr., 1972-75, dist. media coord., 1975-76, house dir., 1976-77, v.p., 1977-81, prin. Piscataway (N.J.) H.S., 1981—. Pres. Wanko Cons. Svcs., 1989—. Author: Safe Schools Crisis Preparation and Response, 2001. Chmn. Nat. Conf. Cmty. and Justice, Bayonne, 1988; co-chmn. Edn. Component/Mayor's Com. on Holocaust/Genocide, 1987; pres. St. Peter & Paul Russian Orthodox Ch., Bayonne, 1982; exec. bd. Boy Scouts Am., 1984; co-coord. Bayonne Youth Hockey Assn., 1987-89; co-chmn. Holocaust Dedication Com., 1988-89; exec. bd. Dr. Herbert E. Cassidy Found., 1986—; mem. YWCA Community Adv. Coun., 1985-90; trustee Found. for Ednl. Adminstrn. Recipient Silver medallion Nat. Conf. Cmty. and Justice, Bayonne, 1989, Golden Lamp award for excellence in ednl. leadership N.J. Prins. and Suprs. Assn., 1994; named State Prin. of Yr., N.J. Nat. Assn. Secondary Sch. Prins., 1995, Prin. of Yr. N.J. State Dept. Edn. and Dodge Found., 2001. Mem. Nat. Assn. Secondary Sch. Prins. (nat. chair larger secondary schs. com. 1997), N.J. Prin. and Supr. Assn. (v.p., pres. 2001—), Hudson County Pub. H.S. Prins. Assn. (pres. 1990-91), Bayonne Pub. Schs. Adminstrs. Assn. (v.p. 1988-89), Carpathian Club. Avocations: skiing, swimming, karate (8th degree black belt). Home: 6 Library Ct Bayonne NJ 07002-3716 Office: Bayonne Bd Edn 29 Avenue A Bayonne NJ 07002-5218

WANN, LAYMOND DOYLE, retired petroleum research scientist; b. Magazine, Ark., Apr. 25, 1924; s. Vernon Cecil and Emma (McCrary) W.; m. Betty Lou Brown, Nov. 6, 1948; children: Jacqueline, Lyndall Doyle. BS in Physics (Phi Eta Sigma scholar), Okla. State U., 1949, MS, 1950. With Conoco Inc., Ponca City, Okla., 1951-84, sr. rsch. scientist, 1957-60, rsch. group leader, 1960-81, assoc. rsch. dir., 1981-84, staff scientist, 1984-85, ret., 1985. Cons. in disciplines of phys. Contbr. articles on elec. and radioactive well-logging, elec. design to profl. jours. Patentee in field. Mem. Mcpl. Airport Bd., Ponca City. Served with AUS, 1942-46; ETO. Decorated Bronze Star. Mem. Am. Petroleum Inst. (chmn. well logging subcom.), IEEE, Aircraft Owners and Pilots Assn., Seaplane Pilots Assn., VFW, Am. Legion, Phi Kappa Phi, Pi Mu Epsilon, Sigma Pi Sigma. Republican. Episcopalian (vestryman). Home: 1501 Monument Rd Ponca City OK 74604-3522 Office: 1000 S Pine St Ponca City OK 74601-7509

WANNAMAKER, MARY RUTH, music educator; b. Ft. Collins, Colo., July 29, 1922; d. Jerry Albert and Daisy B. (Burington) Lyman; m. William H. Anderson, June 14, 1944 (dec. 1944); m. John S. Wannamaker, Sept. 7, 1946; children: Lois Wannamaker, Daisy Wannamaker Van Valkenburg. MusB, Colo. State U., 1944; M in Musicology, U. Minn., 1949, M in Ednl. Psychology, 1969. Piano tchr. U. Minn., Mpls., 1945-46; piano tchr. Drake U., Des Moines, 1945-47; prof. piano Kletzing Coll., University Park, Iowa, 1948-49; ednl. cons. Des Moines, 1975-85. Pvt. piano tchr. Des Moines, 1950—. Composer Easter ch. svc., 1965. Vol. Iowa State Hist. Libr., Des Moines, 1990—; pres. Delta Omicron Alumnae, Des Moines, 1946-50, Profl. Women's League, Des Moines, 1974-75, Iowa Pers. & Guidance Assn., Des Moines, 1978-79; violist Des Moines Symphony Orch., 1946-65; mem. Altrusa, 1970-75. Mem. Music Techs. Nat. Assn., PEO, Phi Kappa Phi (scholarship 1944). Avocations: reading, travel, concerts. Home: 200 Buffalo Hills Ln E # 107 Brainerd MN 56401-4555

WANNER, ERIC, foundation executive; b. Wilmington, Del., Mar. 14, 1942; s. Edwin and Isabel Smith (Speakman) W.; m. Patricia Attix, June 13, 1964 (div. 1976); children: Noel Edwin, Erin Cole; m. Carla Francesca Seal, June 18, 1983; children: Lindzay Elizabeth. BA, Amherst Coll., 1963; PhD, Harvard U., 1969. Asst. to assoc. prof. Harvard U., Cambridge, Mass., 1968-76; behavioral sci. editor Harvard U. Press, 1976-82; program officer Alfred P. Sloan Found., N.Y.C., 1982-84, v.p., 1984-86; pres. Russell Sage Found, 1986—. Mem. adv. bd. Malcolm Weiner Ctr. for Social Policy, Harvard U., 1988—; trustee Ctr. for Advanced Study in Behavioral Scis., 1993-99; bd. dirs. Life Trends Inc. Author: Remembering, Forgetting and Understanding Sentences, 1974; editor: Language Acquisition: the State of the Art, 1982; contbr. articles to profl. jours. Fulbright fellow Sussex U., Brighton, Eng., 1979, fellow N.Y. Inst. for Humanities, NYU, 1985-93, Am. Acad. Arts and Scis., 1994—. Mem. APA, Cognitive Sci. Soc., N.Y. Acad. Scis., Century Club, Sigma Xi. Office: Russell Sage Found 112 E 64th St New York NY 10021-7383 E-mail: ew@rsage.org.

WANSTREET, BRENT LEE, company executive; b. Clarksburg, W.Va., Apr. 13, 1954; s. Paul and Mary (Hurley) M.; m. Juli (Vargo), Apr. 20, 1974; children: Matthew, Amanda, Jessica. Student, Vol. State C.C., Gallatin, Tenn., 1979-81, County Coll. Morris, Flanders, N.J., 1988-91. Gen. mgr. Rickel Home Ctr., N.J., 1981-87; ops. mgr. Hoboken Wood Floors, Hoboken, NJ, 1987-89; area dir. of stores Toys R Us, Paramus, N.J., 1989-94; dist. mgr. Michaels Stores, Dallas, 1994-96, metro mgr., 1996; v.p. ops. Aaron Bros. (Divsn. Michaels Stores), Commerce, Calif., 1996—. With USAF, 1972-73. Named one of Outstanding Young Men of Am., 1976. Republican. Roman Catholic. Home: 26 Laurelwood Irvine CA 92620-1299 Office: Aaron Bros 1270 Goodrich Blvd Los Angeles CA 90022-5107

WANTLAND, WILLIAM CHARLES, retired bishop, lawyer; b. Edmond, Okla., Apr. 14, 1934; s. William Lindsay and Edna Louise (Yost) W. BA, U. Hawaii, 1957; JD, Okla. City U., 1967; D in Religion, Geneva Theol. Coll., Knoxville, Tenn., 1976; DD (hon.), Nashotah House, Wis., 1983, Seabury-Western Sem., Evanston, Ill., 1983. With FBI, various locations, 1954-59, Ins. Co. of N.Am., Oklahoma City, 1960-62; law clk.-atty. Bishop & Wantland, Seminole, 1962-77; vicar St. Mark's Ch., 1963-77, St. Paul's Ch., Holdenville, Okla., 1974-77; presiding judge Seminole Mcpl. Ct., 1970-77; atty. gen. Seminole Nation of Okla., 1969-72, 75-77; exec. dir. Okla. Indian Rights Assn., Norman, 1972-73; rector St. John's Ch., Oklahoma City, 1977-80; bishop Episcopal Diocese of Eau Claire, Wis., 1980-99; interim bishop of Navajoland, 1993-94; ret., 1999; assisting bishop Episcopal Diocese of Dallas, 2002—. Adj. prof. Law Sch. U. Okla., Norman, 1970-78; instr. canon law Nashotah House, 1983-97; mem. nat. coun. Evang. & Cath. Mission, Chgo., 1977-90; mem. Episcopal Commn. on Racism, 1990-92, Episcopal Coun. Indian Ministries, 1990-95, Standing Commn. on Constn. and Canons, 1992-95. Author: Foundations of the Faith, 1982, Canon Law of the Episcopal Church, 1984, The Prayer Book and the Catholic Faith, 1994; The Catholic Faith, The Episcopal Church and the Ordination of Women, 1997; co-author: Oklahoma Probate Forms, 1971; contbr. articles to profl. jours. Pres. Okla. Conf. Mcpl. Judges, 1973; v.p. South African Ch. Union, 1985-95; trustee Nashotah House, Wis., 1981-2000, chmn., 1992-98; bd. dirs. SPEAK, Eureka Springs, Ark., 1983-89; mem. Wis. adv. com. U.S. Civil Rights Commn., 1990-91; mem. support com. Native Am. Rights Fund, 1990—; co-chmn. Luth.-Anglican-Roman Cath. Commn. of Wis., 1989-95; pres. Wis. Episc. Conf., 1995-97. Recipient Most Outstanding Contbn. to Law and Order award Okla. Supreme Ct., 1975, Outstanding Alumnus award Okla. City U., 1980, Wis. Equal Rights Coun. award, 1986, Manitou Ikwe award Indian Alcoholism Coun., 1988, Episcopal Synod Pres.'s award, 1995. Mem. Okla. Bar Assn., Okla. Indian Bar Assn., Living Ch. Found., Oklahoma City Law Sch. Alumni Assn. (pres. 1968), Wis. Coun. Chs. (pres. 1985-86). Democrat. Avocations: canoeing, skin-diving, cross-country skiing. E-mail: puca382@nbo.net. *If we truly believe that God reigns, we will so order our lives that such a belief is clearly reflected in all that we do and say; further, such a belief will shape our relations, not only with all other people, but all of God's created order.*

WANZER, MARY KATHRYN, computer company executive, consultant; b. South Bend, Ind., Sept. 12, 1942; d. Cyril Joseph and Kathryn Alice (Dumke) Tlusty; m. Boyd Eugene Wanzer, May 30, 1964; children: Adam James, Christopher James. BS, Northland Coll., 1964; student, Am. U., Washington, 1972-75. Tchr. Montgomery Co. Md. Schs., Rockville, 1964-66; mathematician Johns Hopkins U., Silver Spring, Md., 1966-68; systems analyst ITT Fed. Elec. Corp., Kennedy Space Ctr., Fla., 1968-69; computer programmer Atlantic City (N.J.) Hosp., 1969-71; project leader Fairfax Hosp. Assn., Falls Church, Va., 1971-73; sr. systems analyst Xerox Corp., Leesburg, 1973-76; software engr. E-Systems, Falls Church, 1982-85; pres. Atlantic Office Svcs., Ltd., Bethany Beach, Del., 1988-99. Cons. Chesapeake Utilities, Dover, Del., 1990, Intervet, Millsboro, Del., 1990—92; MIS mgr. Thompson Pub. Group, Salisbury, Md., 1992—93; sys. analyst Mountaire, Selbyville, Del., 1993—96; fin. analyst Peninsula Regional Med. Ctr., Salisbury, 1996—2002; realtor Island Palms Real estate, Vero beach, 2002—. Leader LaLeche League, Annandale, Va., 1980—83; v.p. No. Va. Hockey Club, Fairfax County, 1986—87. Roman Catholic. Avocation: Avocations: boating, swimming. Home: The Atrium on the Ocean 2900 N AIA Unit 9C Hutchinson Island FL 34949- E-mail: MaryWanzer@cs.com.

WAPIENNIK, CARL FRANCIS, manufacturing firm executive, planetarium and science institute executive; b. Donora, Pa., Oct. 10, 1926; s. Karl and Rose (Kidzinski) W.; m. Elva Louise Bartron, Nov. 27, 1953; children: Carl Eric, Ellen Louise. BS, U. Pitts., 1953. Prodn. supr. RCA, Canonsburg, Pa., 1953-54; staff physicist Buhl Planetarium and Inst. Popular Sci., Pitts., 1954-64, exec. dir., 1964-82; owner, operator Work-o-Art Miniatures (small mfg. firm), 1983—. Patentee means for controlling liquid flow. Mem. Rostraver Twp. Planning Commn., 1965-67; mem. adv. bd. Allegheny C. of C. (formerly North Side Pitts. C. of C.), 1966-67, dir., 1968-73, pres., 1970; mem. adv. coun. Salvation Army, 1978-82; bd. dirs. Bapt. Homes, Pitts., 1982-94; chmn. Rostraver Twp. Mcpl. Water Authority, 1990-94. With USNR, 1945-46. Recipient Man of Yr. award in sci. Pitts. Jaycees, 1969 Mem. Service Core Ret. Execs., Pitts. Bapt. Assn. (bd. dirs. 1976-82), Phi Beta Kappa, Sigma Pi Sigma. Home and Office: Work-o-Art Miniatures 602 Salem Church Rd Belle Vernon PA 15012-2906

WAPNER, ALAN DEAN, security professional, mayor pro tem; b. Newark, May 26, 1956; s. Gerald Harold and Sandra Linda Wapner; m. Karen Dian Vaughn, Aug. 14, 1977 (div. May 1986); children: Robyn, Jennifer, Bryan, Amber; m. Judith Ann Vasquez, Aug. 29, 1993; 1 child, Sarah. BA in Polit. Sci./Pub. Rels., U. So. Calif., 1978; JD, Whittier Coll., 1981. Police sgt. City of Ontario, Calif., 1982-98, city councilman, 1994-98, mayor pro tem, 1998—; v.p. Ontario-Montclair Elem. Sch. Dist., 1991-94; prin. Alan D. Wapner & Assocs., Ontario, 1994—. Trustee Temple Sholom Ontario, 1994—; vice chmn. bd. dirs. City of Ontario Redevelopment Agy., 1994—, City of Ontario Housing Authority, 1994—; bd dirs. Inland Empire Econ. Partnership, San Bernardino, Calif., 1998—; mem. Calif.-Nev. Super Speed Train Commn., Las Vegas, 1998—. Mem. Pi Kappa Phi (housing corp. pres. 1996—). Republican. Jewish. Avocations: youth sports, baseball, travel. Home: 2733 S Monterey Pl Ontario CA 91761-8703 Office: City of Ontario 303 E B St Ontario CA 91764-4196 Fax: 909-988-8807.

WAPNER, MYRNA, retired principal; b. Bklyn., Sept. 17, 1936; d. Nathan and Sylvia (Bromstein) Honig; divorced. BA, Bklyn. Coll., 1958, MA, 1962; postgrad., NYU, 1980. Tchr. Pub. Sch. 7, Bklyn., 1958-66, Pub. Sch. 58, Bklyn., 1966-67; asst. prin. Pub. Sch. 272, 1967-71, Pub. Sch. 233, Bklyn., 1971-84; prin. Pub. Sch. 135, 1984-98; ret. N.Y.C. Bd. Edn., 1998. Adj. lectr. Baruch Coll. Sch. Pub. Affairs, 1997—, Touro Coll., 2000—. Recipient Reliance award for excellence in edn. Elem. Sch. Prin. of Yr., Borough of Bklyn., 1991, Nat. Recognition award for outstanding sch. chpt. I math. program, 1993; named Outstanding Prin. N.Y.C., 1991. Mem. ASCD, Am. Fedn. Suprs., N.Y.C. Adminstrv. Women in Edn., N.Y. City Prin.'s Assn., Coun. Supr. Assns. (mem. dist. coun. CSA sec., mem. exec. bd. 1971-95). Avocations: reading, sewing, painting, theatre, opera. Home: 142 Amherst St Brooklyn NY 11235-4115

WAPNER, SEYMOUR, psychologist, educator, administrator; b. Bklyn., Nov. 20, 1917; s. Hyman and Rose S. (Liese) W.; m. Lorraine E. Gallant, June 4, 1946; children: Jeffrey Gallant, Amy Beth. AB, NYU, 1939; A.M., U. Mich., 1940, PhD, 1943. Instr., dir. U. Rochester Office Com. Selection and Tng. Aircraft Pilots, NRC, N.Y., 1943-46, 45-46; asst. prof. Bklyn. Coll., 1946-48, acting chmn. psychology dept., 1947-48; assoc. prof. dept. psychology Clark U., Worcester, Mass., 1948-56, prof., 1956-63, chmn. dept., 1960-86, G. Stanley Hall prof. genetic psychology, 1963-88, prof. emeritus,

1988—; chmn. exec. com. H. Werner Inst. Devel. Analysis, 1957—; mem. exec. bd. Council Grad. Depts. of Psychology, 1981-84; mem. U.S. Nat. Com. for Man and the Biosphere Directorate, 1975-86. Author: (with H.A. Witkin, et al), Personality Through Perception, 1954, (with H. Werner) Perceptual Development, 1957; editor: The Body Percept, 1965, (with W.A. Koelsch) Freud In Our Time, 1988, (with S.B. Cohen, B. Kaplan) Experiencing the Environment, 1976, (with B. Kaplan) Toward a Holistic Developmental Psychology, 1983, Perspectives in Psychological Theory, 1960, (with M. Bertini and L. Pizzamiglio) Field Dependence in Psychological Theory, Research and Application, 1986, (with L. Cirillo) Value Presuppositions in Theories of Human Development, 1986, (with L. Cirillo and B. Kaplan) Emotions in Ideal Human Development, 1989, (with J. Demick) Field Dependence-Independence, 1991, (with T. Yamamoto) Developmental Psychology of Life Transitions, 1992, Relations Between Psychology and Allied Fields, 1995, (with J. Demick, T. Yamamoto, T. Takahashi) Handbook of Japan-US Environment-behavior research: Towards a transactional approach, 1997, (with J. Demick, et. al.) Theoretical Perspectives in Environment-Behavior Research: Underlying Assumptions, Research Problems and Methodologies, 2000. Fellow APA, AAAS; mem. AAUP, Internat. Assn. Applied Psychology, Soc. Rsch. in Child Devel., Eastern Psychol. Assn. (dir. 1968-70, 71-74, 85-88, 93—, pres. 1979-80), New Eng. Psychol. Assn. (pres. 1979-80), Mass. Psychol. Assn., Phi Beta Kappa, Sigma Xi. Office: Clark U Werner Inst for Devel Analysis 950 Main St Worcester MA 01610-1477 E-mail: swapner@clarku.edu.

WARACH, MARIE, artist; b. N.Y.C., Feb. 19, 1922; d. Jacob and Diena (Friedlander) Sieff; m. Sam Norkin, Feb. 19, 1941 (div. June 1968); children: Richard Norkin, Laura De Sena; m. Bernard Warach, May 30, 1976; stepchildren: Joshua, Jonathan, Beth. Postgrad., Art Students League, 1956—60; BS in Studio Art, Hunter Coll., CUNY, 1980; cert. in art therapy, New Sch., 1982. Registered art therapist, Am. Art Therapy Assn. Sr. photographer Internat. Paper Co., N.Y.c., 1964-72; freelance photographer Jewish Assn. Svcs. for Aged, 1974-82; art therapist Fedn. Employment and Guidance, 1982-86; artist East Hampton, N.Y. Exhibited in solo and group shows, L.I. Mem. Artists Alliance of East Hampton (pres. 1996—). Avocations: family, reading, museums, classical music, film.

WARAKOMSKI, ALPHONSE WALTER JOSEPH, JR. sales and marketing executive; b. N.Y.C., Apr. 1, 1943; s. Alphonse Walter and Mary (Dupnock) W. BS in Chemistry, St. Bonaventure, Allegheny, N.Y., 1968; MBA in Mktg., Keller Grad. Sch., Chgo., 1981. Chemist, lab. mgr. Purification Scis., Geneva, 1968-73; applications engr. Pollution Control Industries, Stamford, Conn., 1973; sales mgr. Kopper's Environ. Elements, Balt., 1974; mktg. specialist, regional mgr. Union Carbide Linde, Chgo., 1975-79; sales engr. Dorr Oliver, 1980-81; dir. mktg. and sales Linde AG Lotepro, Valhalla, N.Y., 1981—. Contbr. articles to profl. jours. Contbr. articles to profl. jours. Mem.: AIChE, Water Environment Fedn., Internat. Ozone Assn. (dir. internat. bd.), Am. Water Works Assn. Home: 15 Brevoort Dr Apt 1C Pomona NY 10970-3077 Office: Linde AG Lotepro 115 E Stevens Ave Valhalla NY 10595-1252 E-mail: awarakomski@msn.com., dawarkomski@loteproesq.com.

WARBERG, WILLETTA, concert pianist, writer, piano educator; b. Twin Falls, Idaho, June 2, 1932; d. George William Warberg and Ethel Margaret (Sargent) Warberg-Chandler; m. David Jacob Bar-Illan, Sept. 3, 1954 (div.); children: Daniela, Jeremy Oscar. Student, Colo. Women's Coll., 1950-51, Aspen Music Camp, 1951; studied with, Rudolph Firkusny, 1951-53; BS, Mannes Coll. Music, N.Y.C., 1954. Assoc. food editor Look mag., N.Y.C., 1956-61; food editor Status mag., 1961-62, Ladie's Home Jour., N.Y.C., 1964-66; photog. stylist Gourmet mag., 1961-64, freelance writer, photog. stylist, 1965-75; pres., owner Willetta Enterprises, advt. agy., Twin Falls, 1976-84; food columinst, music and arts critic Times News, 1978-87; duo-piano ptnr. with Robert Starer, N.Y.C., Woodstock, N.Y., 1991—; pvt. piano tchr., Saugerties, 1991—. Made feasibility study of restaurant situation in Israel, U.S. Dept. State ICA Point 4 Program, Washington and Israel, 1960; artist-in-residence Holy Cross Concert Series, Kingston, N.Y., 1994—. Concert pianist, Idaho, Oreg., Utah, Wash., Colo., N.Y.C., N.Y. State, 1940—; author: Cooking from Scratch, 1976, Space Age Cookery, 1977; syndicated food columnist Willetta Says, 1978-87; contbr. food and sci. articles to Cosmopolitan, Modern Maturity, Esquire, Sun Valley, Sci. Diegest, also other mags. Bd. dirs. N.W. Opera Assn., 1984-87; pres. bd. dirs. Woodstock Lyric Theatre, 1994—; v.p. bd. dirs. Woodstock Chamber Orch., 1993—; chmn. Friends of the Maverick Concerts Inc., Woodstock, N.Y., 1999—. Winner Rocky Mountain talent search contest Salt Lake Tribune and Salt Lake Telegram, 1949. Mem. Nat. Fedn. Music Clubs, Music Tchrs. Nat. Assn. (cert.), Kingston Music Soc.. Avocations: designing and sewing clothes, painting still lifes, swimming, developing recipes, writing science fiction book.

WARBURTON, MINNIE, writer, artist; b. Beverly, Mass., July 12, 1949; d. Barclay Harding and Margarett McKean (Vernon) W.; 1 child, Samantha. BA, MA in Theology, U. of South, 1994. Writer Procter & Gamble, Cin., 1980-81, ABC, L.A., 1991-82; owner Sargent Gallery, Sewanee, Tenn., 1996-99; owner/tchr. Pink Flamingo Studio, 1999—. Author: Mykonos, 1979; author poetry. Fund raising vol. Sewanee Elem. Sch., 1997; vol. Hospitalty Shop, 1999, Thurmond Libr., 1999—. Mem. NAACP, World Jewish Congress, Writers Guild Am. Office: Pink Flamingo Studios 201 Kentucky Ave Sewanee TN 37375-2101

WARBURTON, RALPH JOSEPH, architect, engineer, planner, educator; b. Kansas City, Mo., Sept. 5, 1935; s. Ralph Gray and Emma Frieda (Niemann) W.; m. Carol Ruth Hychka, June 14, 1958; children: John Geoffrey, Joy Frances W. Tracey. B.Arch., MIT, 1958; M.Arch., Yale U., 1959, M.C.P., 1960. Registered architect, Colo., Conn., Fla., Ill., La., Md., N.J., N.Y., Va., D.C.; registered profl. engr., Conn., Fla., N.J., N.Y.; registered cmty. planner, Mich., N.J.; lic. interior designer, Fla. With various archtl. planning and engring. firms, Kansas City, Mo., 1952-55, Boston, 1956-58, N.Y.C., 1959-62, Chgo., 1962-64; chief planning Skidmore, Owings & Merrill, 1964-66; spl. asst. for urban design HUD, Washington, 1966-72, cons., 1972-77; prof. architecture, archtl. engring. and planning U. Miami, Coral Gables, Fla., 1972-2000, chmn. dept. architecture, archtl. engring. and planning, 1972-75, assoc. dean engring. and environ. design, 1973-74, dir. grad. urban and regional planning program, 1973-75, 81, 87-93, prof. emeritus, 2000—. Advisor govt. Iran, 1970; advisor govt. France, 1973, govt. Ecuador, 1974, govt. Saudi Arabia, 1985; cons. in field, 1972—, lectr., critic design juror in field, 1965—; mem./chmn. Coral Gables Bd. Archs., 1980-82. Assoc. author: Man-Made America: Chaos or Control, 1963; editor: New Concepts in Urban Transportation, 1968, Housing Systems Proposals for Operation Breakthrough, 1970, Focus on Furniture, 1971, National Community Art Competition, 1971, Defining Critical Environmental Areas, 1974; contbg. editor: Progressive Architecture, 1974-84; editl. adv. bd.: Jour. Am. Planning Assn., 1983-88, Planning for Higher Edn., 1986-94, Urban Design and Preservation Quar., 1987-94; contbr. over 130 articles to profl. jours.; mem. adv. panel Industrialization Forum Quar., 1969-79, archtl. portfolio jury Am. Sch. and Univ., 1993. Mem. Met. Housing and Planning Coun., Chgo., 1965-67; mem. exec. com. Yale U. Arts Assn., 1965-70; pres. Yale U. Planning Alumni Assn., 1983-89—; mem. ednl. adv.com. Fla. Bd. Architecture, 1975; mem. grievance com. The Fla. Bar, 1996-99. Recipient W.E. Parsons medal Yale U., 1960; recipient Spl. Achievement award HUD, 1972, commendation Fla. Bd. Architecture, 1974, Fla. Trust Historic Preservation award, 1983, Group Achievement award NASA, 1976; Skidmore, Owings & Merrill traveling fellow MIT, 1958; vis. fellow Inst. Architecture and Urban Studies, N.Y.C., 1972-74; NSF grantee, 1980-82 Fellow AIA (nat. housing com. 1968-72, nat. regional devel. and natural resources com. 1974-75, nat. sys. devel. com. 1972-73, nat. urban design com. 1968-73, bd. dirs. Fla. S. chpt. 1974-75, Edn. Leadership award Miami chpt. 2000, Test of Time award Fla. Assn. 2002), ASCE, Fla. Engring. Soc. (bd. dirs. 1984-85, Miami chpt. bd. dirs. 1982-83, 84-85), Nat. Acad. Forensic Engrs. NSPE; mem. Am. Inst. Cert. Planners (exec. com. dept. environ. planning 1973-74), Am. Soc. Engring. Edn. (chmn. archtl. engring. divsn. 1975-76), Dade Heritage Trust (Cmty. Svc. award 2002), Nat. Sculpture Soc. (allied profl.), Nat. Soc. Arch. Engrs. (founding), Nat. Trust Hist. Preservation (principles and guidelines com. 1967), Am. Soc. Landscape Architects (hon., chmn. design awards jury 1971, 72), Am. Planning Assn. (Fla. chpt. award excellence 1983), Am. Soc. Interior Designers (hon.), Omicron Delta Kappa, Sigma Xi, Tau Beta Pi. Home: 6600 SW 54th Ln South Miami FL 33155-6413 Office: 420 S Dixie Hwy Coral Gables FL 33146-2222 E-mail: ProfRJWarc@aol.com. *My contribution to society is made through comprehensive determination, design and development activity leading to habitats most suited to the optimum continuing progress of mankind.*

WARCH, RICHARD, academic administrator; b. Hackensack, N.J., Aug. 4, 1939; s. George William and Helen Anna (Hansen) W.; m. Margot Lynn Moses, Sept. 8, 1962; children: Stephen Knud, David Preston, Karin Joy. BA, Williams Coll., 1961; B.D., Yale Div. Sch., 1964; PhD, Yale U., 1969; postgrad., U. Edinburgh, 1962-63; H.H.D., Ripon Coll., 1980. Asst. prof. history and Am. studies Yale U., 1968-73, asso. prof., 1973-77; asso. dean Yale Coll.; dir. summer plans Yale U., 1976-77; asso. dir. Nat. Humanities Inst., New Haven, 1975-76; v.p. acad. affairs Lawrence U., Appleton, Wis., 1977-79, pres., 1979—. Cons. Nat. Humanities Faculty; ordained to ministry United Presbyn. Ch. in U.S.A., 1968; dir. Bank One of Appleton. Author: School of the Prophets, Yale College, 1701-1740, 1973; editor: John Brown, 1973. Rockefeller Bros. Theol. fellow, 1961-62 Mem. Am. Studies Assn., Soc. for Values in Higher Edn., Winnebago Presbytery. Clubs: Rotary. Home: 229 North Park Ave Appleton WI 54911 Office: Lawrence U PO Box 599 Appleton WI 54912-0599

WARD, AILEEN, retired humanities educator; b. Apr. 1, 1919; BA, Smith Coll., 1940; MA, Radcliffe Coll., 1942; PhD, Harvard U., 1953. Prof. English lit. Wellesley Coll., 1946-47, Barnard Coll., 1947-49, Vassar Coll., 1954-58, Sarah Lawrence Coll., 1960-64, Brandeis U., 1964-75; Schweitzer prof. humanities NYU, 1975-91, prof. emeritus, 1991—. Author: John Keats: The Making of a Poet, 1963 (Nat. Book award in arts and letters Nat. Book Found., 1964), The Unfurling of Entity, 1985. Fellow Am. Acad. Arts and Scis. Home: 201 E 69th St Apt 6O New York NY 10021-5409

WARD, ALBERT EUGENE, archaeologist, ethnohistorian, research center executive; b. Carlinville, Ill., Aug. 20, 1940; s. Albert Alan and Ellen (Boston) W.; m. Gladys Anena Lea, Apr. 26, 1961 (div. Apr. 1974); children: Scott Bradley, Brian Todd; m. Stefanie Helen Tschaikowsky, Apr. 24, 1982. AA, Bethany Luth. Jr. Coll., Mankato, Minn., 1961; BS, No. Ariz. U., 1968; MA, U. Ariz., 1972. Lab. asst., asst., archaeologist Mus. No. Ariz., Flagstaff, 1965-67; rsch. archaeologist Desert Rsch. Inst. U. Nev., Las Vegas, 1968; rsch. archaeologist Archaeol. Survey Prescott Coll., Ariz., 1969-71, rsch. assoc., 1971-73; rsch. archaeologist Ariz. Archaeol. Ctr. Nat. Park Svc., Tucson, 1972-73; rsch. collaborator Chaco Ctr., Albuquerque, 1975; founder, dir. archaeol., rsch. program Mus. Albuquerque, 1975-76; founder, dir., 1976-79; pres. bd. dirs. Ctr. Anthrop. Studies, Albuquerque, 1976—. Lectr. U. N.Mex. C.C., 1974-77, others; contract archaeol. salvage and rsch. projects in N.Mex. and Ariz. Mem. editl. adv. bd. Hist. Archeaology, 1978-80; editor: publs. Ctr. Anthrop. Studies, 1978—; contbr. articles to scholarly jours. Grantee Mus. No. Ariz., 1972, S.W. Monuments Assn., 1973, CETA, 1975-79, Nat. Park Svc., 1978-79. Mem. Am. Soc. Conservation, Am. Anthrop. Assn., Soc. Am. Archaeology, Soc. Hist. Archaeology, No. Ariz. Soc. Sci. and Art, Ariz. Archaeol. and Hist. Soc., Archaeol. Soc. N.Mex., Albuquerque Archaeol. Soc., S.W. Mission Rsch. Ctr., Soc. Archaeol. Scis., Southwestern Anthrop. Assn., N.Mex. Archaeol. Coun., Living Hist. Farms and Agrl. Mus. Assn. Republican. Lutheran.

WARD, ANTHONY G. stock, options and futures exchange consultant; b. Bloomington, Ill., July 16, 1938; s. William V. and Leone J. (Costigan) W.; m. Diane J. Anstett, Jan. 9, 1965; children: Joseph M., Daniel S., Kevin P., Christopher B. BS in Polit. Sci., Loyola U., Chgo., 1961; postgrad., U. Chgo., 1967-68. Cert. mgmt. cons. Mktg. mgr./trainee Ill. Bell Telephone, Chgo., 1965-69; cons. Fry Cons., 1969-72; mng. assoc. Booz, Allen & Hamilton, Chgo. and N.Y.C., 1972-78; v.p. Space/Mgmt. Programs, Chgo., 1978-83; sr. v.p. ops. Chgo. Merc. Exch., 1983-88; sr. v.p. Tellefsen Cons. Group, N.Y.C. and Chgo., 1988-91; dir. info. tech. Swiss Bank Corp., Chgo., 1991-93; exec. v.p., COO, Phila. Stock Exch., 1993-98; stock, options and futures exch. cons. Internat. Trading Places, Inc., 1998—. With U.S. Army, 1962-65. Mem. Univ. Club Chgo. Roman Catholic. Avocations: military history, walking, gardening.

WARD, BARRY LEE, music educator, musician; b. Richmond, Va., Oct. 20, 1952; s. Robert Lee and Virginia Alice Ward; m. Cheryl Lynn Fox, May 31, 1975; children: Nicholas Taylor. MusB Edn., U. of So. Miss., Hattiesburg, MS, 1974, Masters of Music, 1975; MA, The Cath. U. of Am., Washington, DC, 1977. Band instr. Music for Am., Washington, 1977—78; band dir. Garwood Whaley Music, Va., 1978—. Bishop Ireton H.S., Alexandria, 1981—; clarinetist Arlington Symphonic Orch., Arlington, 2001—. Guest condr. All Dist. Bands, Alexandria, Va., 1992—; judge All Dist. Festivals, Va., 1992—. Contbr. articles to profl. jours.; composer: of various school band compositions. Swim referee North Va. Swim League, Va., 1998—92. Recipient Barry L. Ward Hall, All St. Sch., 2002. Mem.: Musicians Union, Music Educators Nat. Conf. Home: 9202 Lake Braddock Drive Burke VA 22015 Home Fax: 703-764-2823.

WARD, BART JAMES, investment executive; b. Mpls., Jan. 7, 1955; s. James E. and Johann (Zenz) W.; m. Ellen M. Ward, June 11, 1997. AA, Anoka-Ramsey Coll., 1975; BS, MS, UCLA, 1982. Pres. Leer, Pfeiffer, Ward, L.A., 1982-85; CEO, sr. portfolio mgr. Ward & Co., Mpls., 1985—. Dir. Starcom, Inc., 1992—. Contbr. column to newspaper The Corner, 1991—. Chmn. capital contbn. com. Anoka County Hist. Soc.; mem. Anoka Anti-Crime Commn. Mem. Mpls. Club. Office: Ward & Co 1918 1st Ave Anoka MN 55303-2437 E-mail: ward@wardcompany.com.

WARD, BENNIE FRANKLIN LEON, physics educator; b. Millen, Ga., Oct. 19, 1948; s. Enoch and Irene (Clark) W. BS in Physics, Math., MIT, 1970; MA in Physics, Princeton U., 1971, PhD in Physics, 1973. Asst. prof. physics Purdue U., West Lafayette, Ind., 1975-78; rsch. assoc. Stanford (Calif.) Linear Accelerator Ctr., 1978; staff scientist Intel Corp., Santa Clara, Calif., 1979-80, LMSC, Sunnyvale, 1980-84; assoc. prof. physics U. Tenn., Knoxville, 1986-90, prof. physics, 1990—. Contbr. articles to profl. jours. Grantee Dept. Energy, Washington, 1987-2000, Tex. Nat. Lab. Commn., 1991, 92, 93. Fellow Am. Phys. Soc.; mem. N.Y. Acad. Scis., AAAS, AAUP, Sigma Xi. Democrat. Baptist. Achievements include computation of MD/MPsi/J from renormalized field theory; computation of rho-pi pi in lattice QCD; development of renormalization group improved Yennie-Frautschi-Suura theory; development and implementation of multiple photon Monte Carlo simulations of high precision higher order radiative corrections to the SU2LxU1 theory for Z physics; research on violation of dimensional analysis in perturbation theory; quantitative predictions for CP violation phenomena in rare B decays. Office: U Tenn Dept Physics Knoxville TN 37996-1200 E-mail: bflw@slac.stanford.edu.

WARD, BONNIE J. insurance company executive; b. Boston, Feb. 16, 1957; d. Marcia M. and Russell A. Ward; children: Creighton A. A., Reilly X. X. BA in Polic. Sci., U. Mass., 1978. Telecomm. mgr. City of Boston/Boston City Hall, 1979—84; sr. telecomm. analyst WANG Lab., Lowell, 1984—86; sys. integration mgr. Shawmut Nat. Corp., Boston, 1986—91; v.p. telecomm. First Data Corp., Medford, 1991—95; gen. dir. tech. ops. support John Hancock Mut. Life Co., Boston, 1995—98; v.p. telecomm. Liberty Mut. Group, Portsmouth, NH, 1998—. Vol. Yankee Homecoming, Newburyport, 1985—99. Recipient Dist. svc. award, Newburyport Lions Club, 1990. Mem.: BPOE Lodge #909. Roman Catholic. Home: 19 Basinfront Dr Newburyport MA 01951 Office: Liberty Mutual Group 225 Borthwick Ave Portsmouth NH 03801 Business E-Mail: bonnie.ward@libertymutual.com.

WARD, CARL EDWARD, research chemist; b. Albuquerque, Oct. 16, 1948; s. Joe E. and Loris E. (Wenk) W.; m. Bertha R. Schloer, June 9, 1970. BS in Chemistry, N.Mex. Inst. Mining and Tech., 1970; MS in Chemistry, Oreg. Grad. Ctr., 1972; PhD in Chemistry, Stanford U., 1977. Research chemist Union Carbide Corp., Charleston, W.Va., 1977-79, Dynapol Corp., Palo Alto, Calif., 1979-80, Chevron Chem. Co., Richmond, 1980-85, sr. research chemist, 1986-88, apptd. supr. chemical synthesis, 1988-90; sr. rsch. assoc. Chevron Rsch. & Tech. Co., 1990-91, staff scientist, 1991—, ChevronTexaco Products Co.-Global Lubricants, Richmond, 1997—, sr. staff scientist, 2000—. Referee Jour. Organic Chemistry, 1983—; patentee in field; contbr. articles to profl. jours. Recipient NSF traineeship, Stanford U., 1972-73; Upjohn fellow, Stanford U., 1976-77, NLGI fellow, 1998; recipient Clarence E. Earle Meml. award, 1995. Mem. Soc. Tribologists and Lubrication Engrs., Nat. Lubricating Grease Inst. (Clarence E. Earle Meml. award 1995), Am. Chem. Soc., Calif. Acad. Sci., N.Mex. Inst. Mining and Tech. Pres. Club, Stanford U. Alumni Assn. Avocations: gardening, camping, fishing. Home: 1355 Nisich Dr San Jose CA 95122-3061 Office: Chevron Products Co PO Box 1627 Richmond CA 94802-1796 E-mail: caew@ChevronTexaco.com.

WARD, CAROL BUHNER, textile artist, educator; b. Sullivan, Ind., Apr. 13, 1947; d. John Colin and Betty (Bevis) Buhner; m. Charles Wesley Ward, Aug. 22, 1969. Student, U. Bologna, 1967-68, Ind. U., 1969-70, BA, 1970. Lectr. Herron sch. art Ind. U., Indpls., 1970-72, 78-81, 87; artist-in-residence Indpls. Parks Dept., 1975-77; instr. Indpls. Arts League, 1976-78, 82-85; artist-in-residence St. Mary-of-the-Woods Coll., Terre Haute, Ind., 1977; artist-in-service Met. Arts Council, Indpls., 1978-79; owner Carol Ward Tours, 1980—; pvt. practice textile artist, 1981—. Participating artist Ind. Arts Commn., Indpls., 1975-85; curator craft exhbn. Indpls. Art League, 1979, 81, 83, 85; rschr., art historian legal firm, Indpls., 1980-87; judge art exhbns. throughout Midwest, 1978—; lectr. art history Franklin (Ind.) Coll., 1990—; artist in residence Sprillmill Sch., Indpls., 1992; acad. escort Guatemala study tour San Jose (Calif.) State U., 1992, Cote d'Azur Study Tour, 1995, Women's Issues in China 4th UN Conf. on Women, Bejing; NGO participant San Jose State U., 1995. Exhbns. include 1st Glass Biennale Tour for San Jose Mus. of Art, Venice, Italy, 1996 V.p. edn. Indpls. Art League, 1978-80; pres. bd. dirs. visual arts orgn. Art Net, Indpls., 1985-86; sec. bd. dirs. Arts Insight, 1979-82; bd. dirs. Friends of Planned Parenthood, Indpls. Mem. Nat. Soc. Colonial Dames, Mayflower Soc., Indpls. Women's Club, Rotary Club (Scholarship 1967). Avocation: raising orchids. Home and Office: 21 W 59th St Indianapolis IN 46208-1512 E-mail: cwt@in.net.

WARD, CHARLES RAYMOND, systems engineer; b. Lansing, Mich., Oct. 23, 1949; s. George Merrill and Dorothy Irene (Hupp) W.; m. Sarah Hopkins Eddy, June 23, 1979; children: Katherine Emily, Rachel Elizabeth. BS in Math., Purdue U., 1971; MSEE, Naval Postgrad. Sch., 1977. Commd. ensign USN, 1971, advanced through grades to lt. commdr., served on USS Barbel, 1972-75, served on USS James Madison, 1978-81, served on USS Alabama, 1983-85; strategic navigation project mgr. Strategic Systems Programs, Arlington, Va., 1985-91; surveillance towed array sensor sys., mgr. sys. engring. Govt. Info. Sys. divsn. TRW, McLean, 1991-95; integrated undersea surveillance sys., mgr. internat. programs TRW, San Diego, 1995-2000; integrated undersea surveillance, mgr. fixed surveillance command, control and Command, Control and Intelligence divsn. TRW, 2000—. Editor: Trident Navigation Standard Operating Procedures, 1991, Acoustic Warfare Operating Doctrine, 1992, Surveillance Towed Array Sensor Passive User's Guide, 1994. Chmn. grounds com. Burke (Va.) United Meth. Ch., 1989-97, chmn. worship com., 1993-94; chmn. Camp Va. site adv. com., 2001—. Mem. IEEE, Eta Kappa Nu, Sigma Xi. Republican. Achievements include research in automatic depth and pitch control for a near surface submarine. Office: TRW 1843 Hotel Circle S San Diego CA 92108-3320 E-mail: chuck.ward@trw.com.

WARD, CHESTER LAWRENCE, physician, retired county health official, retired military officer; b. Woodland, Yolo, Calif., June 8, 1932; s. Benjamin Briggs and Nora Elizabeth (Cash) W.; m. Sally Diane McCloud, Dec. 10, 1960; children: Katharine, Lynda. BA, U. Calif., Santa Barbara, 1955; MD, U. So. Calif., 1962; MPH, U. Calif., Berkeley, 1966; grad., Indsl. Coll. Armed Forces, 1978. Commd. 2d lt., inf. U.S. Army, 1954; advanced through grades to brig. gen., 1980; surgeon 5th Spl. Forces, Ft. Bragg, N.C. and Vietnam, 1963-64; chief aviation medicine, preventive medicine and aeromed. consultation service Ft. Rucker, Ala., 1967-68; surgeon Aviation Brigade and USA Vietnam Aviation Medicine Cons., 1968-69; flight surgeon Office of U.S. Army Surgeon Gen., 1970-71; physician The White House, Washington, 1971-75, 76; dir. environ. quality research U.S. Army Med. Research and Devel. Commd., 1975-76; comdr. Womack Community Hosp.; surgeon XVIII Airborne Corps, Ft. Bragg, N.C., 1978-80; comdr. William Beaumont Army Med. Center, El Paso, Tex., 1980-82; med. dir. Union Oil Co., Schaumburg, Ill., 1982-83, dir. domestic medicine Los Angeles, 1983-84; exec. dir. continuing med. edn. and clin. prof. emergency medicine U. So. Calif. Sch. Medicine, 1984-85; dir., health officer Dept. Health, Butte County, Calif., 1985-95; cons., contractor, pvt. med. practice, 1996—; med. dir. NorCal EMS, 2001—. Apptd. by Gov. Wilson Calif. Commn. Emergency Med. Svcs., past commr.; elected trustee, pres. Oroville Union H.S. Dist., 1998-2002. Decorated D.S.M., Legion of Merit (2), Bronze Star, Air medal (5). Fellow Am. Coll. Preventive Medicine (past regent), Aerospace Med. Assn., Butte-Glenn County Med. Soc. (past pres.), Calif. Med. Assn. (past del., interim med. dir.), No. Calif. Emergency Med. Svcs., Inc. (dir., governing bd.), Ret. Officers Assn. (past chpt. pres.). Home: 4 Lemon Hill Ct Oroville CA 95966-3700 Office: Enloe Outpatient Ctr 888 Lakeside Vlg Commons Chico CA 95928-3979

WARD, CRANLEY THOMAS, computer software specialist; b. Atlanta, Oct. 24, 1966; s. Henry H. and Laurel (Dalton) W.; m. Joy McNeal. BBA cum laude, Piedmont Coll., 1989. Loan officer Habersham Bank, Cornelia, Ga. Mem. Banks County Hist. Soc. (publicity chmn. 1988), Bank County C. of C., Computer Club (v.p. 1988-89), Alpha Chi (v.p. 1988-89). Democrat. Baptist. Avocations; racquetball, softball, motorcycling, boating, miniature golf. Home: RR 1 Homer GA 30547-9801

WARD, CURTIS WILLIAM, process engineer; b. Rochester, N.Y., Aug. 14, 1972; s. Joseph Wells and Jo Ann Ward. BS, Rensselaer Poly. Inst., 1993; MS, Cornell U., 1996, PhD, 1998. Rsch. asst. Clarkson U., Potsdam, N.Y., 1988-89; physicist Xerox Corp., Webster, 1992-93; rsch. asst. Rensselaer Poly. Inst., Troy, 1992-93, Cornell U., Ithaca, 1993-98; sr. process engr. Intel Corp., Hillsboro, Oreg., 1998—. Contbr. articles to profl. jours. Rsch. fellow NSF, 1993. Mem. Am. Inst. Physics/Soc. Physics Students, Soc. Automotive Engrs., Sports Car Club Am. Avocations: auto racing, electronics. Home: 309 NE Edison St Hillsboro OR 97124-3133 Office: Intel Corp 5200 NE Elam Young Pkwy Hillsboro OR 97124-6497 Fax: (503-613-8963. E-mail: Curtis.W.Ward@intel.com.

WARD, DAVID, academic administrator, educator; b. Manchester, Eng., July 8, 1938; came to U.S., 1960; s. Horace and Alice (Harwood) W.; m. Judith B. Freifeld, June 11, 1964; children: Michael J.H., Peter F.B. BA, U. Leeds, Eng., 1959; MA, U. Leeds, 1961; MS, U. Wis., 1961, PhD, 1963; LittD, U. Leeds, 1992. Lectr. Carleton U., Ottawa, Ont., Can., 1963-64; asst. prof. Univ. B.C., Vancouver, Can., 1964-66, U. Wis., Madison, 1966-67, assoc. prof., 1967-70, prof., 1970—, chmn. geography dept., 1974-77, assoc. dean Grad. Sch., 1980-88, provost and vice chancellor acad. affairs, Andrew Clark prof. geography, 1989—; chancellor U. Wis. Madison, 1994-2000; pres. Am. Coun. on Edn., 2001—. Mem. exec. com. Argonne (Ill.) Nat. Lab., 1990-93; dir.-at-large Social Sci. Rsch. Coun., 1991-93; mem. Kellogg Commn. on Future of Land Grant Univs.; chair Internet 2, Univ. Consortium on Advanced Network Devel. Author: Cities and Immigrants, 1970, Geographic Perspectives on Americas Past, 1978, Poverty Ethnicity and the American City, 1989, Landscape of Modernity, 1992; contbr. articles to profl. jours. Guggenheim fellow, 1970, Einstein fellow Hebrew U., 1980, Fulbright fellow, Australian Nat. U., 1979. Fellow Am. Acad. Arts and Scis.; mem. Assn. Am. Geographers (pres. 1989). Office: One Dupont Circle NW Washington DC 20036-1193 E-mail: david_ward@ace.nche.edu.

WARD, DAVID ALLEN, sociology educator; b. Dedham, Mass., June 21, 1933; s. Theodore Allen and Jessie Miller (Ketchum) W.; m. Carol Jane Barton, June 10, 1957 (div. 1964); children: Douglas Allen, Andrew Barton; m. Reneé Ellen Light, Mar. 10, 1967. BA, Colby Coll., 1955; PhD, U. Ill., 1960. Asst. prof. Wash. State U., Pullman, 1960-61; asst. research sociologist UCLA, 1961-64; assoc. prof. U. Minn., Mpls., 1965-68, prof., 1968—, chmn. dept. sociology, 1984-88, 92-95. Chmn. Salzburg (Austria) Seminar in Am. Studies, 1977; cons. jud. com. U.S. Ho. Reps., Washington, 1984. Co-author: Women's Prison, 1965, Prison Treatment, 1971; co-editor: Delinquency, Crime and Social Process, 1969, Confinement in Maximum Custody, 1981; editorial cons. Jour. Criminal Law and Criminology, 1968-97. Mem. Mpls. Civilan Police Rev. Bd., 1991-94. Liberal Arts fellow Harvard U. Law Sch., 1968-69; Fulbright research fellow, 1971-72; research fellow Norwegian Fgn. Office, Oslo, 1976. Mem.: Am. Soc. Criminology, Am. Sociol. Assn. (chmn. sect. criminology 1976—77). Office: Univ of Minn Dept of Sociology 909 Social Sci Bldg Minneapolis MN 55455

WARD, DAVID HENRY (DAVE WARD), television news reporter, anchorman; b. Dallas, May 6, 1939; s. H.M. and Mary Ward; m. Glenda Lois Odom, Nov. 10, 1959 (div.); children: Linda Ann, David H.; m. Debra Rene Holland, Apr. 25, 1976 (div.); children: Jonathan H., Christopher H. Student, Tyler Jr. Coll., Tex., 1957—59. Announcer Sta. KGKB, Tyler, 1958—60; program dir. Sta. WACO (Tex.), 1960—62; news dir. Sta. KNUZ, Houston, 1962—66; news reporter, photographer, writer, prodr. Sta. KTRK-TV, 1966—. Freelance writer, prodr., cons. Chmn. pub. affairs adv. bd. Houston Bus. Coun.; pub. info. com. Am. Cancer Soc.; pres. bd. dirs. Easter Seal Soc., Harris, Ft. Bend counties; committeeman Houston Livestock Show and Rodeo, 1997—98. Named Man of Yr., Houston Sertoma Club, 1973, TV Personality of Yr., Am. Women in Radio and TV, 1983, Best TV Anchor, Houston Press, 1995, 1996, 2001; recipient Best TV Newscast award, Tex. UPI, 1968, 1972, 1973—80, TV Svc. award, Houston Jaycees, 1982. Mem.: Houston Press Club, Sigma Delta Chi. Baptist. Office: Channel 13 PO Box 13 3310 Bissonnet St Houston TX 77005-2195

WARD, DAVID SCHAD, screenwriter, film director; b. Providence, Oct. 24, 1947; s. Robert McCollum and Miriam (Schad) W.; children: Joaquin Atwood, Sylvana Soto. BA, Pomona Coll., 1967; M.F.A., UCLA, 1970. Scriptwriter: films include Steelyard Blues, 1971, The Sting, 1973 (Acad. award best original screenplay 1973), The Milagro Beanfield War, 1988, (with Nora Ephron and Jeff Arch) Sleepless in Seattle, 1993 (Academy award nominee Best Original Screenplay 1993), (with John Eskow, Ted Elliott and Terry Rossio) The Mask of Zorro; writer, dir. films include Cannery Row, 1981, Major League, 1989, King Ralph, 1991, The Program, 1993, Major League II, 1995, Down Periscope, 1996. Mem. Dirs. Guild Am., Acad. Motion Picture Arts and Scis. Office: c/o CAA Ken Stovitz 9830 Wilshire Blvd Beverly Hills CA 90212-1804

WARD, DAVID WAYNE, chiropractor; b. Oak Pk., Ill., Nov. 22, 1951; s. Harold Helen Alice Ward; m. Thelma Jean Smith, July 4, 1982 (div. Jan. 1997); m. Tyeann Dillon, May 29, 1999. BA, Knox Coll., 1973; BS, Nat. Coll. Chiropractic, Lombard, Ill., 1983, D in Chiropractic, 1984. Diplomate Am. Chiropractic Bd. Sports Physicians. Intern Brookfield (Ill.) Chiropractice Clinic Nat. Coll. Chiropractic, 1984, asst. prof., 1988-95; chiropractic physician 375th Med. Group, Scott AFB, Ill., 1995—. Cons. First Health, Downers Grove, Ill., 1989-95. Mem. Am. Chiropractic Assn., Ill. Chiropractic Soc. Lutheran. Avocations: running, bicycling, marksmanship, scuba. Home: 512 Windrift Dr Belleville IL 62221-5844 Office: 375th Med Group SGCPC 310 W Losey St Stop 49 Scott Air Force Base IL 62225-5250 Fax: 618-355-5703.

WARD, DEAN MORRIS, appliance manufacturing executive; b. Ladora, Iowa, Dec. 30, 1925; s. Andrew Morris and Bess (Balmer) W.; m. Elizabeth Slings, July 22, 1948; children: Mary Elizabeth Ward Ahrenholz, Mark Dean. Student, Drake U., 1962-70. Optician B.C. Jensen, Optometrist, Newton, Iowa, 1942-44, 46-54; with Maytag Corp., 1954—, asst. dir. purchases, 1977, dir. purchases, 1977-90; pvt. practice purchasing cons., 1991—. Mem. Svc. Corps of Ret. Execs., chair Des Moines chpt.; adj. instr. Des Moines Area C.C.-Newton Campus, 1993-98; chair Progress Industries, 1994-95, Progress Industries Found., 1996-99; dist. mgr. Svc. Corps. of Retired Execs. (SCORE), Des Moines, 1999-2000, dist. dir., 2000-02; cons. in field. Assoc. editor: Purchasing Handbook, 1st edit. Precinct chmn. Rep. Party, Newton, 1960-68; industry chmn. United Way, Newton, 1962; chmn. Key 73 Evangelistic Program, Newton, 1973; mem. denominational bd. Christian Reformed Ch., 1985-90, del. Nat. Synod, 1991, 93, 2001; mem. Jasper County Compensation Bd., 1998—, Newton Pub. Libr. Bd., 2000—. Sgt. U.S. Army, 1944-46, PTO, 1950-51. Recipient 4-Way Test award Newton Rotary, 1996. Mem. Nat. Assn. Purchasing Mgmt. (pres. 1980, sec.-treas. exec. steel buyers sect. 1989, cert. purchasing mgr., Joseph P. Stagg award for purchasing excellence 1990), Nat. Mgmt. Assn., Am. Prodn. and Inventory Control Soc. (pres. 1966-67). Avocations: golf, gardening. Home: 308 E 28th St S Newton IA 50208-2714

WARD, DEBORA ELLIOTT, psychologist; b. Malone, N.Y., Mar. 24, 1954; d. Donald Joseph and Marion Pearl (Briggs) Elliott; m. Bernard Daniel Ward, Sept. 26, 1987; 1 child, Daniel Elliott. BA in Psychology, Binghamton U., 1976; MS in Clin. Psychology, Syracuse U., 1978, PhD in Clin. Psychology, 1983. Lic. in psychology, Maine. Psychol. asst. Neuropsychology Lab., Hutchings Psychiatric Ctr., Syracuse, N.Y., 1978-79, Syracuse U. Counseling Ctr., 1979-80; psychology assoc. West Haven (Conn.) VA Med. Ctr., 1980-81; rsch. asst. Syracuse U., 1981-82; psychology trainee Syracuse VA Med. Ctr., 1982; staff psychologist Bangor (Maine) Mental Health Inst., 1983-91; psychiat. clinician Acadia Hosp., Bangor, Maine, 1992-98, staff psychologist, 1998—. Cons. psychologist Greater Bangor Area Crisis Stabilization Svcs., 1995-98. Contbr. articles to profl. jours. USPHS fellow, 1976-78. Mem. APA, Maine Psychol. Assn., Phi Beta Kappa. Avocations: seashell collecting, flower gardening, painting. Home: RR 2 Box 3355 Carmel ME 04419-9622 Office: Acadia Hosp 268 Stillwater Ave Bangor ME 04401-3980

WARD, DOUGLAS ANDREW, Spanish and special education educator; b. Elgin, Ill., Mar. 24, 1958; s. Joseph James Ward and Agnes Jane Krecioch. BA, Rockford Coll., 1994, MAT, 1997. Cert. Spanish educator, Ill.; cert. bilingual spel. edn. resource tchr., fgn. lang. tchr., Ill. Cook, bartender, asst. mgr. Nordic Steak Ho., W. Dundee, Ill., 1976-80; tel. operator Ill. Bell, Elgin, 1980-82; long distance tel. operator AT&T, Rockford, Ill., 1987-94; distn. clk. U.S. Post Office, 1994-99; bilingual LD resource tchr. Barbour Two-Way Lang., 1999, Nashold Sch., Rockford, 1999—. With USN, 1982-86. Mem. Phi Sigma Iota. Democrat. Roman Catholic. Avocations: singing, gardening, reading, soccer, piano. Home: 316 Dawn Ave Rockford IL 61107-5009 Office: Nashold Sch 3303 20th St Rockford IL 61109-2398

WARD, EDWARD NORTON, retired application developer, artist; b. L.A., Oct. 26, 1928; s. Lawrence Edward Norton and Cynthia May (Brooks) Ward; m. Johanna Mary Van Pareen, Apr. 22, 1950; children: Mary Jane, Cynthia. BA, UCLA, 1952. Computer programmer Ramo-Wooldridge Corp., L.A., 1954—59; mathematician, computer software developer U.S. Naval Post Grad. Sch., Monterey, 1959—90; ret., 1990. Author: First Impressions, Sketching Nature in Watercolor, 1990. St lt. USAF, 1952—54. Mem.: Carmel Art Assn. (pres. 1978—80, 1995—96). Republican. Avocations: fly fishing, mountaineering, traveling.

WARD, ELAINE, artist; b. Boston, June 4, 1927; d. Robert and Gertrude (Toibb) Winston; m. William Ward (dec.); 1 child, Heather; m. Arthur Lee Dann. BA, Ecole des Beaux Arts, Paris, 1958; student, Art Students League, N.Y.C.; hon. degree, Ecole des Beaux Arts, Cannes, France. Mem. Phoenix Gallery, N.Y.C., 8 yrs. Tchr. watercolor class, San Miguel de allende, Mexico, 2002. Solo show at Phoenix Gallery, 1989, East End Art Coun., Riverhead, N.Y., 1997, Viewpoint Gallery, 1998; juried shows include Shelter Rock Art Gallery, Manhasset, N.Y., 1999; group shows include Lever House, N.Y.C., 1987-89, 93, 95, Guild Hall, Easthampton, N.Y., 1988, 95, Phoenix Gallery, N.Y.C., 1992-94, Elaine Benson Gallery, Bridgehampton, N.Y., 1992, Palmas Del Mar, P.R., 1993, C.W. Post Coll., 1993, Agora Gallery, N.Y.C., 1994, Meadowlands Ctr. for Arts, N.J., 1995, Marcella Geltman Gallery, N.J., 1995, East End Art Coun., N.Y.C., 1995 (winner), 2002, Focus on Art, Livingston, N.J., 1995 (prize), Banana Factory, Pottstown, Pa., 2002; represented in collections at Coastal Steel Co., Carteret, N.H., Pandora and Co., Conway, N.H., Ardan Assocs., Ltd., N.Y.C., Zeckendorf Twrs., N.Y.C.; subject of articles. Winner Juried Show, East End Arts Coun., 1995. Mem. Nat. Arts Club, Nat. Assn. Women Artists (Juried Show winner 1997, Dorothy Seligman Meml. award 1999), Guild Hall Mus., Parrish Mus. Studio: 41 Union Sq W New York NY 10003-3208

WARD, FREDERICK CHAMPION, retired educational educator; b. New Brunswick, N.J., Dec. 29, 1910; s. Clarence and Helen (Eshbaugh) W.; m. Rachel Buira Baldinger, June 13, 1936; children: Geoffrey, Andrew, Helen. BA, Oberlin (Ohio) Coll., 1932, MA, 1934; PhD, Yale U., 1937. From asst. prof. to assoc. prof. Denison U., Granville, Ohio, 1938-45, U. Chgo., 1945-58, assoc. dean coll., 1946-47, dean, 1947-54, William Rainey Harper prof. humanities, 1955-56; ednl. cons. Govt. India Ford Found., N.Y.C., 1954-58, dir. Mid. East and Africa, 1958-63, dep. v.p. internat. programs, 1963-66, v.p. edn. and rsch., 1966-71, sr. advisor edn. internat. divsn., 1971-76; ret. Mem. UNESCO's Internat. Commn. on Devel. Edn.; cons. World Bank and various founds. Editor: The Idea and Practice of General Education, Education and Development Reconsidered, 1974; contbr.: The Knowledge Most Worth Having, 1964, General Education in the Social Sciences, 1992. Mem., v.p. Greenwich (Conn.) Bd. Edn., 1974-82; trustee Oberlin Coll., 1970—; chmn. bd. dirs. Ctr. for Effective Philanthropy, Cambridge, Mass., 1986-87; chancellor New Sch. Social Rsch., N.Y.C.; chmn. White House Task Force on Edn. Gifted Persons, 1968. Democrat. Avocations: tennis, trail-blazing, volunteering in soup cellar, writing casuals. Home: 88 Notch Hill Rd Apt 336 North Branford CT 06471-1864

WARD, GEOFFREY CHAMPION, author, editor; b. Newark, Nov. 30, 1940; s. Frederick Champion and Duira Rachel (Baldinger) W.; m. Diane Raines; children— Nathan, Kelly; 1 stepchild, Garrett. BA, Oberlin Coll., 1962; DHL (hon.), Wilkes U., 1995. Sr. picture editor Ency. Britannica, Chgo., 1964-68; co-founder, editor Audience mag., Boston, 1969-73; mng. editor Am. Heritage Mag., N.Y.C., 1976-78, editor, 1978-82. Author: Lincoln's Thought and the Present, 1978, Treasures of the Maharajas, 1983, Before the Trumpet: Young Franklin Roosevelt, 1882-1905, 1985, A First-Class Temperament: The Emergence of Franklin Roosevelt, 1989 (Nat. Book Critics Cir. award, Francis Parkman prize Soc. Am. Historians, L.A. Times biography prize, Ohioana award), The Civil War: An Illustrated History, 1990, American Originals: The Private Worlds of Some Singular Men and Women, 1991; (with Diane Raines Ward) Tiger Wallahs, Encounters with the Men Who Tried to Save the Greatest of the Great Cats, 1993, Baseball: An Illustrated History, 1994, Closest Companion: The Unknown Story of the Intimate Friendship between Franklin Roosevelt and Margaret Suckley, 1995, The West: An Illustrated History, 1996, (with Michael Nichols) The Year of the Tiger, 1998, Not for Ourselves Alone: Elizabeth Cady Stanton and Susan B. Anthony, 1999, Jazz: A History of America's Music, 2000, (with Dayton Duncan) Mark Twain, 2001; editor: The Best American Essays of 1996; (TV documentaries) Huey Long, 1985, Thomas Hart Benton, 1989, Lindbergh, 1990, Nixon, 1990 (Writer's Guild Am. award), The Civil War, 1990 (Emmy award), Reminiscing in Tempo, 1991, Empire of the Air, 1992, The Kennedys, 1992 (Emmy award), George Marshall and the American Century, 1993, Baseball, 1994 (Emmy award), Daley: The Last Boss, 1995, The West, 1996, Theodore Roosevelt, 1996 (Emmy award), Thomas Jefferson, 1997, Frank Lloyd Wright, 1998, Not for Ourselves Alone, 1999, Jazz, 2000, (with Dayton Duncan) Mark Twain, 2001; contbr. articles to mags., jours. Recipient Christopher awards for The Statue of Liberty, Theodore Roosevelt, Not For Ourselves Alone, Mark Twain, The Christophers, The Civil War, New Eng. Booksellers Assn. award, Am. Booksellers award, Lila Acheson Wallace Readers Digest writers award. Mem. Soc. Am. Historians, Writers Guild Am., East Inc., Century Assn. Home: 17 C 290 W End Ave New York NY 10023-8106 Office: Brandt &Hochman care Carl Brandt 1501 Broadway Ste 2310 New York NY 10036-5689

WARD, GEORGE, JR. music educator, musician; b. Binghamton, N.Y., June 27, 1932; s. George and Melanie Quma (Rowley) W.; m. Sandra Kay Gorham, Oct. 15, 1960 (div. Sept. 1979); children: Bradley Lawrence, Tamara Susan; m. Marion A. McDermott, Nov. 19, 1997. BA magna cum laude, Syracuse U., 1954, M of Music Edn., 1960. Cert. music tchr., N.Y. Music tchr. Marcellus (N.Y.) Ctrl. Sch., 1960-62, West Genesoe Ctrl. Sch., Camillus, N.Y., 1963-91; percussion instr. Onondaga C.C., Syracuse, 1962-71, Syracuse U., 1965-75; percussionist and tympany Syracuse Symphony, 1964-69; percussionist Syracuse Concert Band, 1975-85, Utica (N.Y.) Symphony, 1950-55, No. Chgo. Symphony, 1955-58, Syracuse New Music Soc., 1960-85. Pvt. percussion instr., Syracuse, 1958-93. With USN, 1954-58. Recipient assistantship Syracuse U., 1959-60, 2d place award at Ed Sullivan Show, All-Navy Talent Show and Tour, 1957. Mem. N.Y. State Tchrs. Assn., Music Educators Nat. Conf., Percussive Arts Soc., Syracuse Musicians Union. Democrat. Unitarian Universalist. Home: 4482 Frank Gay Rd Marcellus NY 13108-9709

WARD, GEORGE FRANK , JR. ambassador; b. Jamaica, N.Y., Apr. 9, 1945; s. George Frank and Hildegard Louisa (Evans) W.; m. Peggy Elizabeth Coote, June 12, 1965; 1 child, Pamela Ward Priester. BA, U. Rochester, 1965; MPA, Harvard U., 1980. U.S. vice consul Am. Consulate, Hamburg, Germany, 1970-72; ops. officer Office Sec. State, Washington, 1972-74; U.S. consul Am. Consulate Gen., Genoa, Italy, 1974-76; polit. officer Am. Embassy, Rome, 1976-77, exec. asst., 1977-79, polit. officer Bonn, Germany, 1984-85, dep. chief mission Germany, 1989-92; polit.-mil. officer U.S. Dept. State, Washington, 1980-84, dep. dir. European Security and Polit. Affairs, 1985-88, prin. dep. asst. sec. Bur. Internat. Orgns., 1992-96, U.S. ambassador to Namibia, 1996-99; dir. tng. program U.S. Inst. Peace, Washington, 1999—. Capt. USMC, 1965-69. Decorated Vietnamese Cross Gallantry , Naval Commendation medal with combat V; recipient Presdl. Meritorious Svc. awards, 1992, 1994, Disting. Honor award, U.S. State Dept., 1992. Mem.: Am. Fgn. Svc. Assn., Washington Inst. Fgn. Affairs, Fellows of Phi Beta Kappa. Episcopalian. Home: 3404 Walnut Hill Ct Falls Church VA 22042-3546 E-mail: gward@usip.org.

WARD, GEORGE TRUMAN, architect; b. Washington, July 24, 1927; s. Truman and Gladys Anna (Nutt) W.; m. Margaret Ann Hall, Sept. 10, 1949; children: Carol Ann Ward Dickson, Donna Lynne Ward Solomon, George Truman, Robert Stephen. BS, Va. Poly. Inst., 1951, MS, 1952; postgrad., George Washington U., 1966. Registered profl. arch., Va., Md., D.C., W.Va., Ohio, N.J., Del., N.C. Archtl. draftsman Charles A. Pearson, Radford, Va., 1950; head archtl. sect. Hayes, Seay, Mattern & Mattern, Radford and Roanoke, 1951-52; with Joseph Saunders & Assocs., Alexandria, Va., 1952-57, assoc. arch., 1955-57; ptnr. Vosbeck-Ward & Assocs., 1957-64, Ward/Hall Assocs., Fairfax, 1964—. Dir. Crestar Bank/Greater Washington Region, 1967-99. Pres. PTA Burke (Va.) Sch., 1970-71; mem. bd. mgrs. Fairfax (Va.) County YMCA, 1964-76; chmn. adv. com. Coll. Arch., Va. Poly. Inst., 1984-90; bd. dirs., mem. investment com. Va. Tech. Found., Inc., 1986-91, 93-98; pres. Springfield Rotary Found.. 1978-79; chmn. county adv. bd. Salvation Army, 1978-79, 89-95, co-chmn. Fairfax County Salvation Army Capital Campaign, 1991-95; mem. Gen. Bd. Va. Bapts., deacon, moderator; mem. bd. vis. Va. Poly. Inst. & State U., 1984-87; trustee Fairfax County Pub. Schs. Edn. Found., Inc. With AUS, 1946-47. Paul Harris fellow; recipient Disting. Svc. award Va. Tech. Alumni Assn., 1988; recipient William H. Ruffner medal Va. Tech., 1996, VSAIA William C. Noland award, 1998, Va. Tech. Coll. Arch. and Urban Studies Lifetime Contbn. award, 1998. Fellow Coll. AIA; mem. AIA (corp., charter Octagon Soc.), No. Va. Soc. AIA (chmn. polit. action com. 1991-93, Disting. Svc. award 1990, treas. Va. soc. 1994-98, Outstanding Achievement award 1996), Rowe Fellowship (charter mem. 1988), Alumni Assn. Va. Poly. Inst. & State U. (bd. dirs., v.p. 1992, pres. 1994), Interfaith Forum on Religion, Art and Arch., Va. Found. for Arch. (trustee), Va. Assn. Professions, Va. C. of C., No. Va. Angus Assn. (pres. 1987-88), Va. Tech. Alumni Assn. (hon., life, bd. dirs. Disting. Svc. award 1988), Masons, Shriners, KT, Rotary (charter mem., pres. Springfield 1973-74, Disting. Svc. award dist. 7610 1995), Tau Sigma Delta, Omicron Delta Kappa, Phi Kappa Phi, Pi Delta Epsilon, Ut Prosim. Baptist. Office: Ward Hall Assoc AIA Ste 300 12011 Lee Jackson Memorial Hwy Fairfax VA 22033-3310 E-mail: gtward@wardhall.com.

WARD, HAROLD WILLIAM COWPER, oncologist, educator; b. Southend-On-Sea, Essex, Eng., Nov. 24, 1925; came to U.S., 1976; s. William Samuel and Winifred (Marjorie) W.; m. Barbara Mary Sanderson, Oct. 6, 1962; children: Belinda Mary Jane Morris, Rosemary Sylvia, Timothy Harold. MB BS, U. London, 1953; diploma in med. radiation therapy, Royal Coll. Physicians London, 1957. Cert. therapeutic radiology Am. Bd. Radiology, cert. basic cardiopulmonary resuscitation Am. Heart Assn. Intern Charing Cross Hosp., London, 1953, resident in radiotherapy, 1955-56; intern Royal Postgrad. Med. Sch., 1954-55; intern in surgery The Bolinbroke Hosp., 1954; sr. resident in radiotherapy Edinburgh (Scotland) Royal Infirmary, 1958-59; rsch. fellow in radiotherapy St. Bartholomew's Hosp., London, 1959-65; cons. radiotherapist Queen Elizabeth Hosp., Birmingham, Eng., 1965-75; clin. lectr. U. Birmingham, 1965-75; dir. radiation oncology Parkland Meml. Hosp., Dallas, 1976-78; prof. radiology U. Tex. Southwestern Med. Sch., 1976-78; clin. prof. radiology divsn. radiation oncology U. Cin., 1978-82, assoc. prof. medicine divsn. hematology, 1980-82; dir. radiation oncology Meml. Med. Ctr., Corpus Christi, Tex., 1982-95; clin. assoc. prof. radiation oncology U. Tex. Med. Br., Galveston, 1984-90. Mem. Oncology Assocs., Inc., Cin., 1978-82; travelling fellow in radiotherapy Meml. Hosp. for Cancer and Allied Diseases, N.Y.C., M.D. Anderson Hosp., Houston, U. Calif. Med. Sch., San Francisco, 1965; mem. U.K. Med. Rsch. Coun. Working Party for study of embryonal tumors of childhood, 1967-75; mem. steering com. U.K. Nat. Ovarian Cancer Clin. Survey, 1967-75; site vis. team NCI, 1984-87; physician advisor Tex. Med. Found. Peer Rev. Orgn., 1985—; mem. regional quality rev. com., 1989—. Bd. dirs. Symphony Orch., Corpus Christi, 1992-95. Fellow Royal Coll. Radiology; mem. AMA,Royal Coll. Surgeons Eng., Royal Coll. Physicians, Soc. Apthecaries, Am. Soc. Therapeutic Radiologists, Am. Soc. Clin. Oncology, Am. Coll. Radiology, Am. Cancer Soc. (Nueces County br. 1984-88), Brit. Inst. Radiology, Brit. Med. Assn., Tex. Med. Assn., Nueces County Med. Soc. (pub. rels., environ. pollution control, Cancer adv. com. 1984-98, consultative fee rev. com. 1988-98). Episcopalian. Avocations: music, gardening. Home: 131 Naples St Corpus Christi TX 78404-1828 Fax: (361) 883-7126.

WARD, HARRY MERRILL, history educator; b. West Lafayette, Ind., July 30, 1929; s. Hiley L. and Agnes Ward. Student, U. Ill., 1947-49; BA, William Jewell Coll., 1951; MA, Columbia U., 1954, PhD, 1960. Social investigator N.Y.C. Dept. Welfare, 1958-59; asst. prof. Georgetown (Ky.) Coll., 1959-61; from asst. to assoc. prof. Morehead (Ky.) State U., 1961-65; vis. assoc. prof. So. Ill. U., 1967-68; assoc. prof. history U. Richmond, Va., 1965-77, prof. history, 1977—, William Binford Vest prof. history, 1993-99, William Binford Vest prof. history emeritus, 1999—. Cons. in field. Author: The United Colonies of New England, 1643-1690, 1961, Department of War, 1781-95, 1962, 81, Unite or Die: Intercolony Relations, 1690-1763, 1971, Statism in Plymouth Colony, 1973, Duty, Honor or Country: General George Weedon and the American Revolution, 1979, Richmond: An Illustrated History, 1985, 88, Charles Scott and the Spirit of '76, 1988, Major General Adam Stephen and the Cause of American Liberty, 1989, Colonial America, 1607-1763, 1990, American Revolution: Nationhood Achieved, 1763-1788, 1994, General William Maxwell and the New Jersey Continentals, 1997, The War for Independence and the Transformation of American Society, 1999, Between the Lines: Banditti of the American Revolution, 2002; co-author: Richmond During the Revolution, 1775-1783, 1977; contbr. articles to prof. publs. With USMC, 1951—53. Recipient Fraunces Tavern Mus. Book award, 1990; Scholar award in history Va. Social Sci. Assn., 1992. Fellow Pilgrim Soc.; mem. Am. Hist. Assn., Orgn. Am. Historians, So. Hist. Assn. Office: U Richmond Dept History Richmond VA 23173-0180

WARD, HARRY PFEFFER, physician, retired university chancellor; b. Pueblo, Colo., June 6, 1933; s. Lester L. and Alysmai (Pfeffer) W.; m. Betty Jo Stewart, Aug. 20, 1955; children— Stewart, Leslie, Elizabeth, Mary Alice, Amy. AB, Princeton U., 1955; MD, U. Colo., 1959; MS, U. Minn., 1963. Intern Bellevue Hosp., N.Y.C., 1959; resident Mayo Clinic, Rochester, Minn., 1960-63; practice medicine specializing in hematology; chief medicine Denver VA hosp., 1968-72; dean, asso. v.p. U. Colo. Sch. Medicine, 1972-78, prof. medicine, 1972; chancellor U. Ark. Med. Sci., Little Rock, 1979-2000, chancellor emeritus, 2000—. Clin. investigator VA, 1964-67 Chmn. Assn. Acad. Health Ctr., 1993-94. Mem. ACP, AMA, Am. Fedn. Clin. Research, Central Soc. Clin. Investigation, Am. Soc. Hematology, Internat. Soc. Hematology, Western Soc. Clin. Research. Home: 369 Valley Club Cir Little Rock AR 72212-2900 Office: U Ark Med Scis 4301 W Markham St Little Rock AR 72205-7101 E-mail: hpward1@msn.com.

WARD, HILEY HENRY, journalist, educator; b. Lafayette, Ind., July 30, 1929; s. Hiley Lemen and Agnes (Fuller) W.; m. Charlotte Burns, May 28, 1951 (div. 1971); children: Dianne, Carolee, Marceline, Laurel; m. Joan Bastel, Aug. 20, 1977. BA, William Jewell Coll., 1951; MA, Berkeley Bapt. Div. Sch., 1953; MDiv, McCormick Theol. Sem., Chgo., 1955; student, Northwestern U., 1948, 54, 56-57; PhD, U. Minn., 1977. News asst. Christian Advocate, 1953-55; editor jr. publs. David C. Cook Pub. Co., 1956-59; editor Record, Buchanan, Mich., 1960; religion editor Detroit Free Press, 1960-73; asst. prof. journalism Mankato (Minn.) State U., 1974-76; assoc. prof. journalism Wichita (Kans.) State U., 1976; prof. journalism Temple U., Phila., 1977-96, prof. emeritus, 1997—, dir. news-editorial sequence, journalism dept., 1977-80, chmn. dept., 1978-80. Instr. journalism Oakland U., Rochester, Mich., evenings 1963-66. Author: Creative Giving, 1958, Space-age Sunday, 1960, Documents of Dialogue, 1966, God and Marx Today, 1968, Ecumania, 1968, Rock 2000, 1969, Prophet of the Black Nation, 1969, The Far-out Saints of the Jesus Communes, 1972, Religion 2101 A.D., 1975, Feeling Good About Myself, 1983, Professional Newswriting, 1985, My Friend's Beliefs: A Young Reader's Guide to World Religions, 1988, Reporting in Depth, 1991, Magazine and Feature Writing, 1993, Mainstreams of American Media History, 1997; editor: Media History Digest, 1979-94; exec. editor: Kidbits, 1981-82; book editor: Editor and Publisher, 1989-98; contbr. articles to profl. jours., feature articles to newspapers and mags.; also short stories and poems. Religious Pub. Rels. Coun. fellow, 1970; recipient citation Religious Heritage Am., 1962, Leidt award Epsic. Ch., 1969, citation U.S. Am. Revolution Bicentennial Adminstrn., 1976, Text and Acad. Authors citation, 1997. Mem. Religion Newswriters Assn. (pres. 1970-72), Am. Soc. Journalists and Authors, Am. Journalism Historians Assn. (bd. dirs. 1994-96, Kobre lifetime achievement award 1999), Overseas Press Club. Home: PO Box 399 1263 Folly Rd Warrington PA 18976-1422 E-mail: bastel@voicenet.com.

WARD, HORACE TALIAFERRO, federal judge; b. LaGrange, Ga., July 29, 1927; m. Ruth LeFlore (dec.); 1 son (dec.). AB, Morehouse Coll., 1949; MA, Atlanta U., 1950; JD, Northwestern U., 1959. Bar: Ga. 1960. Instr. polit. sci. Ark. A.M. and N. Coll., 1950-51, Ala. State Coll., 1951-53, 55-56; claims authorizer U.S. Social Security Adminstrn., 1959-60; assoc. firm Hollowell Ward Moore & Alexander (and successors), Atlanta, 1960-69; individual practice law, 1971-74; judge Civil Ct. of Fulton County, 1974-77, Fulton Superior Ct., 1977-79; U.S. Dist. Ct. judge No. Dist. Ga., Atlanta, 1979-93; sr. judge U.S. Dist. Ct. No. Dist. Ga., 1993—. Lectr. bus. and sch. law Atlanta U., 1965-70; dep. city atty., Atlanta, 1969-70, asst. county atty., Fulton County, 1971-74 Former Trustee Friendship Baptist Ch., Atlanta; mem. Ga. adv. com. U.S. Civil Rights Commn., 1963-65; assisting lawyer NAACP Legal Def. and Edn. Fund, Inc., 1960-70; mem. Jud. Selection Commn., Atlanta, 1972-74, Charter Commn., 1971-72; mem. Ga. Senate, 1964-74, jud. com., rules com., county and urban affairs com.; mem. State Democratic Exec. com., 1966-74; former bd. dirs. Atlanta Legal Aid Soc.; bd. dirs. Atlanta Urban League, Fed. Defender Program, No. Dist. Ga.; trustee Met. Atlanta Commn. on Crime and Delinquency, Atlanta U., Fledgling Found. Mem. Am. Bar Assn., Nat. Bar Assn. (chmn. jud. council 1978-79), State Bar Ga., Atlanta Bar Assn., Gate City Bar Assn. (pres. 1972-74), Atlanta Lawyers Club, Phi Beta Kappa, Alpha Phi Alpha, Phi Alpha Delta, Sigma Pi Phi. Office: US Dist Court 2388 US Courthouse 75 Spring St SW Atlanta GA 30303-3309

WARD, JACQUELINE ANN BEAS, nurse, healthcare administrator; b. Somerset, Pa., Oct. 23, 1945; d. Donald C. and Thelma R. (Wable) Beas; divorced; children: Charles L. Jr., Shawn M. BS in Nursing, U. Pitts., 1966; MA in Counseling and Guidance, W.Va. Coll. Grad. Studies, 1976; AS Hlth. Svcs. Mgmt./Nursing Home Admin., St. Petersburg Jr. Coll., 1997; MBA, Columbus Coll., 1983. Cert. in advanced nursing adminstrn.; cert. adult living facility adminstr. Staff nurse W.Va. U. Hosp., Morgantown, 1966-67; staff nurse, head nurse Meml. Hosp, Charleston, W.Va., 1967-69; staff nurse Santa Rosa Hosp., San Antonio, 1969; staff nurse, supr. Bexar County Hosp., 1970; charge and staff nurse Rocky Mountain Osteo. Hosp., Denver, 1971; staff nurse Charleston Area Med. Ctr., 1971-74, asst. dir. nursing, 1974-82; dir. nursing H.D. Cobb Meml. Hosp., Phenix City, Ala., 1982-84; v.p. nursing Venice (Fla.) Hosp., 1984—90, v.p. ops., 1990—94; exec. dir., v.p. Life Counseling Ctr., Osprey, Fla., 1994—95; dir. skilled unit and spl. projects Bon Secours/Venice Hosp., 1995—97; adj. clin. nursing faculty Manatee C.C., Bradenton, Fla., 1998—99; interim adminstr. DON contracting, 1999—2000; adminstr. Ctrs. for Long Term Care Venice Beach, Venice , 2000—01, Lake Towers/Sun Terrace Health Care Ctr., Sun City Center, 2002—. Clin. instr. Chattahoochie Valley C.C., Phenix City, 1982—84; support svcs. cons. Bon Secours Healthcare, Venice, Fla., 1996—97, Long Term Care, 1997—98. Office: Sun Terrace Health Care Ctr 105 Trinity Lakers Dr Sun City Center FL 33573 Fax: 813-634-0729.

WARD, JAMES D. government educator, writer; b. Nettleton, Miss., Feb. 3, 1959; s. Alice Harper Marion. BA, U. Miss., 1980; MPA, U. Cin., 1983, PhD, 1988. Newspaper reporter Knoxville (Tenn.) News-Sentinel, 1980; TV news reporter WCBI-TV, Columbus, Miss., 1980-81; asst. prof. U. New Orleans, 1990-94; vis. asst. prof. U. N.Mex., Albuquerque, 1995-98; assoc. prof. N.Mex. State U., Las Cruces, 1998—. Author: The Fuhrer's Heart, 1997; contbg. author: International Encyclopedia of Public Policy and Administration, 1998; contbr. articles to profl. jours. Mem. Am. Soc. for Pub. Adminstrn., Am. Polit. Sci. Assn., Conf. Minority Pub. Adminstrs. Baptist. Avocations: running, tennis, travel. Office: NMex State U PO Box 4042 Las Cruces NM 88003-4042

WARD, JAMES GORDON, education administration educator; b. Auburn, N.Y., June 28, 1944; s. Gordon J. and Alice A. Ward; m. Lynn Elizabeth Harmon, Jan. 19, 1981; children: Heather Anne Davis, James Thomas, Audrey Lynn. BA, SUNY, Albany, 1966, MPA, 1975, MA, 1968; EdD, Va. Poltechnic Inst., 1984. Tchr. social studies Waterloo (N.Y.) Central Schs., 1967-72; policy analyst N.Y. State United Tchrs., Albany, 1972-77; dir. rsch. Am. Fedn. Tchrs., Washington, 1977-85; asst. prof. U. Ill., Champaign, 1985-89, assoc. prof. edn. adminstrn., 1989-93, prof. ednl. adminstrn., 1993—, assoc. dean edn., 1990-95. Cons. in field; mem. Urbana Bd. Edn., 1991-96. Contbr. over 80 chpts. to books and articles to profl. jours. Mem. Am. Soc. Pub. Adminstrn., Am. Edn. Fin. Assn. (bd. dirs. 1980-86, pres. 1986-87), Am. Ednl. Rsch. Assn. Home: 703 W Iowa St Urbana IL 61801-4037 Office: Univ Ill 1310 S 6th St Champaign IL 61820-6925

WARD, JAMES OTTICE, JR. civil engineer; b. Jackson, Miss., Jan. 19, 1951; s. James Ottice and Isobel Grace (Riley) W. BS in Civil Engring., Miss. State U., 1973; MS in Civil Engring., Va. Tech., 1989; grad., Army Mgmt. Staff Coll., 1994. Registered profl. engr., Miss. Hydraulic engr. U.S. Army Engr. Waterways Experiment Sta., Vicksburg, Miss., 1973-75, U.S. Army Engr. Dist. Vicksburg Hydraulics Br., 1978-82, spl. asst. chief, 1982-87, project mgr., 1987-92; project action officer U.S. Army Corps of Engrs. Lower Miss. Valley Divsn., Vicksburg, 1992-93, program coord. Miss. River Channel improvement, 1993-96, chief tech. engring. br., 1996—. Chmn. Interagy. Erosion Task Force, Vicksburg, 1986-89. Dean's scholar Miss. State U., 1972-73. Mem. ASCE, Soc. Am. Mil. Engrs., Chi Epsilon. Clubs: Miss. State U. Alumni Assn., Va. Tech. Alumni Assn., Army Mgmt. Staff Coll. Alumni Assn. Home: 112 Fairways Pl Vicksburg MS 39183-8323 Office: USACE Miss Valley Divsn CEMVO-ET-ET PO Box 80 Vicksburg MS 39181-0080

WARD, JEANNETTE POOLE, retired psychologist, educator; b. Honolulu, June 19, 1932; d. Russell Masterton and Bessie Naomi (Hammett) Poole; children: John Russell Ward, Lisa Joy Ward. BA, Birmingham (Ala.) So. Coll., 1963; PhD in Psychology, Vanderbilt U., 1969. NSF summer rsch. asst. U. Iowa, Iowa City, 1962, Vanderbilt U., Nashville, 1963, NASA fellow, 1963-66, NIH postdoctoral fellow, 1966-67; spl. rsch. fellow Duke U., Durham, N.C., 1970-71; asst. prof. psychology U. Memphis, 1967-72, assoc. prof., 1972-77, prof., 1977-2000; ret., 2001. Editor: Current Research in Primate Laterality, 1990, Primate Laterality, 1992; mem. editl. bd. Jour. Comparative Psychology, 1988-95, Internat. Jour. of Comparative Psychology, 1995—; contbr. chpts. to books and articles to profl. jours. Fellow APA; mem. Psychonomic Soc., Animal Behavior Soc., Am. Primatology Soc., Southeastern Psychol. Assn., Soc. for Neuroscis., Internat. Soc. for Comparative Psychology (treas. 1989-90, pres.-elect 1996-98, pres. 1998-2000), Sigma Xi (pres. Memphis State U. chpt. 1989-90, rsch. award 1985). Democrat. Avocations: dogs, reading, art, music. E-mail: jeannetteward@cs.com.

WARD, JERRY WASHINGTON, English language educator; b. Washington, July 31, 1943; s. Jerry Washington Ward Sr. and Mary Theriot. BS, Tougaloo Coll., 1964; MS, Ill. Inst. Tech., 1966; PhD, U. Va., 1978. From asst. prof. to assoc. prof. Tougaloo (Miss.) Coll., 1970-84; lectr. U. Va., Charlottesville, 1976-77; prof. English Tougaloo Coll., 1984—, Lawrence Durgin prof., 1988—. Program officer NEH, Washington, 1985; United Negro Coll. Fund scholar-in-residence Talladega (Ala.) Coll., 1987-88. Editor: (books) Black Southern Voices, 1992, Trouble the Water: 250 Years of African-American Poetry, 1997; contbr. articles to revs. Mem. Miss. Adv. Com. to U.S. Commn. on Civil Rights, 1988-98, Miss. Humanities Coun., Jackson, 1984-87. With U.S. Army, 1968-70. Kent fellow Danforth Found., 1975-77; Outstanding Rsch. scholar Tougaloo Coll., 1995, Pub. Humanities scholar Miss. Humanities Coun., 1997. Fellow Nat. Humanities Ctr.; mem. MLA, VFW, The Authors Guild, Coll. Lang. Assn., St. George Tucker Soc., Alpha Phi Alpha. Democrat. Roman Catholic. Avocations: photography, running. Office: Tougaloo Coll 500 W County Line Rd Tougaloo MS 39174-9700 E-mail: jerryward31@hotmail.com.

WARD, JOANN BOETTNER, convention and tourist bureau administrator; BS, U. Wis. Publicity and spl. events dir. Carson, Pirie, Scott & Co., Chgo., 1958-69; mktg. cons. Masonic Med. Ctr. Bd. Trustees, 1969-76; exec. dir. Fond du Lac (Wis.) Conv. and Visitor's Bur., 1976-99; ret., 1999. Mktg. cons. Am. Invesco Shopping Ctrs, Chances R. Systems, Rand McNally, Carson, Pirie, Scott and Co.; Wis. rep. Great Lake Delegation to Tokyo; appointed Sesquicentnnial Commn. by Gov. Thompson, 1996-98. Bd. dirs. United Fund; pres., bd. dirs., pres. East Wis. Waters Region, Service League (pres.); trustee 1st Presbyn Ch.; developer Walleye Weekend Festival, developer, 1st breakfast with Santa for 5000, Chgo., Lakeside Winter Celebration, Fond du Lac Fall Flyway; mem. adv. bd. Fond du Lac Jazz Festival, Windhover Ctr. for the Arts; host Internat. Aerobatic Competition, Fond du Lac, 1979-99. Named Woman of Yr. Fond du Lac Bus. and Profl. Women's Club, 1981; recipient award for outstanding contbns. Wis. Tourism Fedn., Pres.' award Internat. Aerobatic Club, 1981, corp. award Chgo. Publicity Club, gold award Nat. Retail Merchants Assn., best spl. event., U.S., Lifetime Achievement award Upper Midwest Conf. and Visitors Bur., 1999, Comm. and Leadership award Toastmasters Internat., 1999, Wisconsin Trailblazer award for lifetime achievement, 1999; inducted into Internat. Festival and Events Assn. Hall of Fame, 1997; honored in Congl. Record, 1999. Mem. Internat. Festivl and Events Assn. (bd. dirs), Wis. Festival and Events Assn. (founder), Wis. Conv. and Visitors Bur. (founding mem., pres., bd. dirs.), Rotary (Paul Harris fellow), Sigma Beta Delta.

WARD, JOE HENRY, JR. retired lawyer; b. Childress, Tex., Apr. 18, 1930; s. Joe Henry and Helen Ida (Chastain) W.; m. Carlotta Agnes Abreu, Feb. 7, 1959; children: James, Robert, William, John. BS in Acctg., Tex. Christian U., 1952; JD, So. Meth. U., 1964. Bar: Tex. 1964, Va. 1972, D.C. 1974; CPA, Tex. Mgr. Alexander Grant & Co. CPA's, Dallas, 1956-64; atty. U.S. Treasury, 1965-68; tax counsel U.S. Senate Fin. Com., 1968-72; pvt. practice Washington, 1972-83; asst. gen. counsel, tax mgr. Epic Holdings, Ltd. and Crysopt Corp., 1983-87; pvt. practice Washington and Va., 1987-95; ret., 1995. Lt. USNR, 1952-56. Mem. ABA, AICPA, Am. Assn. Atty.-CPA's, Univ. Club. Home: 2639 Mann Ct Falls Church VA 22046-2721

WARD, JOHN ROBERT, physician, educator; b. Salt Lake City, Nov. 23, 1923; s. John I. and Clara (Elzi) W.; m. Norma Harris, Nov. 5, 1948; children: John Harris, Pamela Lyn, Robert Scott, James Alan. BS, U. Utah, 1944, MD, 1946; MPH, U. Calif., Berkeley, 1967; Masters, Am. Coll. of Rheumatology, 1990. Diplomate Am. Bd. Internal Medicine. Intern Salt Lake County Gen. Hosp., 1947-48, asst. resident, 1949-50, resident physician internal medicine, 1950-51, asst. physician, 1957-58, assoc. physician, 1958-69; clin. fellow medicine Harvard U., Boston, 1955-57; instr. medicine U. Utah Med. Sch., Salt Lake City, 1954-58, asst. prof., 1958-63, assoc. prof., 1963, prof., 1966-93, chmn. dept. preventive medicine, 1966-70, emeritus prof. internal medicine, 1993—, chief div. rheumatology, 1957-88; prof. internal medicine emeritus U. Utah. Med. Sch., 1994—; attending physician internal medicine Salt Lake City VA Hosp., 1957-70. Nora Eccles Harrison prof. medicine. Served as capt. M.C. AUS, 1951-53. Master Am. Coll. Rheumatology; fellow ACP; mem. Am. Coll. Rheumatology (Disting. rheumatologist award 1994), Utah State Med. Assn. (hon. pres. 1994-95), U. Utah Sch. Medicine Alumni Assn. (Disting. Alumnus 1996). Home: 1249 E 3770 S Salt Lake City UT 84106-2446 Office: U Utah Health Scis Ctr 50 N Medical Dr Salt Lake City UT 84132-0001

WARD, JOHN WESLEY, retired pharmacologist; b. Martin, Tenn., Apr. 8, 1925; s. Charles Wesley and Sara Elizabeth (Little) W.; m. Martha Isabelle Hendley, Dec. 7, 1947; children: Judith Carol, Charles Wesley, Richard Little. AA, George Washington U., 1948, BS, 1950, MS, 1955; PhD, Georgetown U., 1959. Research assoc. in pharmacology Hazleton Labs., Falls Church, Va., 1950-55, head dept. pharmacology, 1955-58, chief depts. biochemistry and pharmacology, 1958-59; with A. H. Robins Co., Richmond, Va., 1959-90, dir. biol. research, 1978-80, dir. research, 1980-82, v.p. research, 1982-89, v.p., gen. mgr. R & D div., 1989-90; ret., 1990. Lectr. in pharmacology Med. Coll. Va., 1960-64, adj. assoc. prof. pharmacology, 1982-90; guest lectr. Seminar on Good Lab. Practices, FDA, Washington, 1979, Chgo., 1979, San Francisco, 1979; apptd. expert pharmacologue toxicologue, France, 1986. Contbr. articles on pharmacology, toxicology and medicinal chemistry to profl. publs. Served with USMC, 1943; Served with USN, 1944-46; Served with U.S. Army, 1944. Mem. AAAS, N.Y. Acad. Sci., Va. Acad. Sci., Am. Chem. Soc., Soc. Toxicology (charter), Am. Soc. Pharmacology and Exptl. Therapeutics, Internat. Soc. Regulatory Toxicology and Pharmacology (charter), Pharm. Mfrs. Assn. (chmn. animal care and use com. 1971-88), Am. Assn. for Accreditation Lab. Animal Care (chmn. bd. trustees 1976-80), Sigma Xi. Clubs: Willow Oaks (Richmond); Cosmos (Washington), Masons (Washington). Achievements include patents in field. Home: 10275 Cherokee Rd Richmond VA 23235-1107 *An appreciation of the responsibility we have to society has set the standards by which I live. These responsibilities are as important as the rights to be gained from society. Those who are unwilling to assume responsibility should have no rights.*

WARD, JON DAVID, insurance company executive; b. Marshalltown, Iowa, Nov. 30, 1944; s. Wiley Granger and Maxine Lucille (Culbertson) W.; children: Wendy, Stacey, Christine. BS in Acctg., U. No. Iowa, 1969; MBA, Ill. State U., 1973. Cert. internal auditor; CLU. Audit dir. State Farm Ins. Cos., Bloomington, Ill., 1969—. Contbr. articles to profl. jours. and chpts. to books. Ct.-apptd. spl. advocate Child Protection Network and Children's Advocacy Ctr., Bloomington, 1997—; sec. Bloomington-Normal Sister Cities Commn., 1989-95. Fellow Life Mgmt. Inst.; mem. Inst. Internal Auditors (bd. dirs. 1984-97). Methodist. Avocations: racquetball, running, skiing, travel, reading. Home: 19319 Great Crane Rd Bloomington IL 61704-5231 Office: State Farm Ins Cos 112 E Washington St Bloomington IL 61701-1001

WARD, JONATHAN P. communications executive; BSChemE, U. N.H., 1976; grad. advanced mgmt. program, Harvard Bus. Sch. With R.R. Donnelley, 1977—, pres. Merchandise Media and Fin. Svcs. bus. units, mgr. comml. printing operation, v.p., dir. Spartanburg, S.C., mfg. divsn., pres., COO, 1997—. Dir. Metromail Corp., Siegwerk, Inc. USA, Direct Mktg. Assn., Nat. Assn. Mfrs. Trustee Goodman Theatre, Chgo.; dir. Chgo. Youth Ctrs. Office: RR Donnelley & Sons Co Corp Hdqs 77 W Wacker Dr Ste 1900 Chicago IL 60601-1649*

WARD, JOSEPH WANIS, computer engineer; b. Boston, June 1, 1959; BA in Math., Boston U., 1984. Mgr., promoter, producer rock band The Runes, Boston, 1980-85; ind. record producer N.Y.C., 1986—; musician, 1976—; pres., chief engr. Studio 4B, Bklyn., 1987—; microcomputer specialist United Way of Tri-State, N.Y.C., 1991—. Ind. software cons., N.Y.C., 1986-90. Vol. phys. therapist Waltham (Mass.) Hosp., 1985. Mem. Sierra Club. Avocations: hiking, ice skating, political history. Home: 329 3rd St Apt 4B Brooklyn NY 11215-7409

WARD, KATHERINE MARIE, retired school system administrator; b. Raton, N.Mex., Oct. 31, 1936; d. Robert Lee and Lucille (Gasperetti) Davis; m. Leonard Carlin Ward, Aug. 30, 1953; children: Kathy Ann, Ronnie, Tonia, Jess. BS, Ea. N.Mex. U., 1972, MEd, 1977; edn. specialist, U. N.Mex., 1981. Data reduction tech. phys. sci. lab. N.Mex. State U., Las Cruces, 1955-61; 3d and 4th grade tchr. Clayton Pub. Schs., Amistad, N.Mex., 1972-74; 4th grade tchr. Grants/Cibola County (N.Mex.) Schs., 1974-76, Title I reading tchr., 1976-77, Title I coord., 1977-82, Chpt. I coord., 1982-89, coord. Chpt. I and drug free schs. and cmtys., 1989-90, coord. Chpt. I, drug free, DARE and Title II, 1990-92, coord. Chpt. I, Title I, drug free and Title II, 1992-96, fed. program coord., 1996-98; ret., 1999. Leader Girl Scouts U.S., Las Cruces, 1966-67, 4-H, Grants, 1977-80; mem., sec. Fighting Back Robert Wood Johnson Found. Prevent Drug and Alcohol Use Grants, 1991-96. Recipient Adminstrn. award N.Mex. Study and Rsch. Coun., 1986, Chpt. I Exemplary award U.S. Dept. Edn., 1988, Merit award DARE program Grants Police Dept., 1991. Mem. Internat. Reading Assn., Malpais Internat. Reading Assn. (pres. 1977-79, Literacy award 1979), N.Mex. Internat. Reading Assn. (Land of Enchantment Book award com. 1983-86). Avocations: grandchildren, travel, writing children's literature, recreational reading. Home: PO Box 11161 112117 Emperor NE Albuquerque NM 87192-0161

WARD, KELLY, social worker, educator; b. Cleve., July 20, 1962; d. Francis Davis and Patricia Doris Hughes; m. Robert Chris Ward, Aug. 5, 1995. BS, Ea. Mich. U., Ypsilanti, 1984; MSW, Rutgers, New Brunswick, N.J., 1988; PhD, Fordham U., New York, 2001. Cert. Alcohol and Drug Counselor; lic. clin. social worker. Child care worker Ohio Boy's Town, Berea, 1985-87, 88-89, Somerset Youth Shelter, Bridgewater, N.J., 1987-88; program dir. Integrity House, Newark, 1987-88, 89-93; psychiatric social worker Kimball Med. Ctr., Toms River, N.J., 1993-97; pvt. practice Colts Neck Cons. Group, 1997—; asst. prof. Monmouth U., W. Long Branch, 1995—. Adv. bd. Hyacinth Essex Co., Newark, N.J., 1989-92. Author: HIV Affected and Vulnerable Youth, 1999, Bridges to Recovery, 2000. Vol. coord. Names Project, 1990. Contbr. author: (book) Bridges to Recovery, 2000. Office: Monmouth U Social Work Dept Cedar Ave West Long Branch NJ 07764 E-mail: kward@monmouth.edu.

WARD, KENNETH G. agricultural products executive; b. Bath, N.Y., Mar. 30, 1946; s. Kenneth Duel and Katherine E. (Gray) W.; m. Sharon Fowler, Apr. 22, 1966; children: Scott Manley, Wendy Jo, Erica. AAS in Agrl. Bus., Alfred State Coll., 1966; BSA in Agrl. Econ., U. Ga., 1968. V.p. M.J. Ward & Son Inc., Bath, 1966-76, pres., 1976—. Chmn. bd. Village of Bath, 1978—; commr. Bath Electric Gas & Water, 1994—; pres. Bath Ctrl. Sch., 1986-96. Mem. Cooperative Feed Dealers (bd. dirs. 1976—, pres. 1991-99), Elks (exauted ruler). Republican. Avocations: hunting, fishing. Office: MJ Ward & Son Inc PO Box 747 Bath NY 14810-0747

WARD, LARRY THOMAS, social program administrator; b. Abington, Va., Sept. 10, 1951; s. Manuel Thomas and Virginia June (Meade) W.; m. Jacqueline June Moore, Aug. 7, 1982 (div. June 1995); 1 child, Nicholas Lawrence; m. Kathleen Denise McCaslin, July 14, 1998. BSW cum laude, U. Md., 1983, MSW, 1984; PhD in Counseling Psychology, Columbia State U., 1997. Lic. social worker. Legis. lobbyist Citizen Action Coalition, Balt., 1982-83; mgmt. cons. United Way Md., 1983-84; program adminstr. Adams County Office Aging, Gettysburg, Pa., 1985-86; dir. social work Margaret E. Moul Home, York, 1986-87; coord. employee assistance program, family svc. supr. Family and Children's Svcs., Harrisburg, 1987-92, cons. drug & alcohol Gettysburg, 1984-86; pres., CEO Impact Sems., Guffey, Colo., 1988-97; pub. Guffey Co., 1992-97; pres., CEO Family Adv., Guffey, 1997—2001; CEO Internat. Child Advocacy Resource Enterprise, Inc., 2002—. Author: Meditatinos on Descartes, 1979, A Philosophical Perspective, 1979, Heracles Reborn, 1983, Protective Services for the Elerly, 1984, Why A Psychiatrist, 1985, The blue ridge Summit Project, 1986, The Effects of Office Design on the Delivery of Therapeutic Social Work Services, 1987, Emotional Disorders of the Chronically Disabled Adolscent, 1987, Resistance to School-based EAPs, 1989, 2d edit., 1993, What Healthy Couples Seem to Know, 1990, Good Relationships Have Certain Traits, 1991; exec. prodr. film on courtroom survival techniques, 1996. Ex-officio bd. dirs. Grass Roots, Inc., Columbia, Md., 1984; del. Gov.'s Youth Adv. Coun., Annapolis, Md., 1970-72; mem. consumer adv. coun. Met. Edison Co., Harrisburg, 1986-87. Recipient Original Art award Md. Pub. Broadcasting, 1969. Democrat. Avocations: tennis, baseball. Home: 365 Eagles Nest Trl Guffey CO 80820-9624 Office: PO Box 324 Guffey CO 80820-0324

WARD, LESTER LOWE, JR. arts executive, lawyer; b. Pueblo, Colo., Dec. 21, 1930; s. Lester Lowe and Alysmai (Pfeffer) W.; m. Rosalind H. Felps, Apr. 18, 1964; children: Ann Marie, Alison, Lester Lowe. AB cum laude, Harvard U., 1952, LLB, 1955. Bar: Colo. 1955. Pvt. practice, Pueblo, 1957-89; ptnr. Predovich, Ward & Banner, 1974-89; pres., COO Denver Ctr. for Performing Arts, 1989—. Trustee, Thatcher Found., Frank I. Lamb Found., Helen G. Bonfils Found.; pres. bd. trustees Pueblo Pub. Library, 1960-66; trustee St. Mary-Corwin Hosp., 1972-80, pres., 1979-80. With U.S. Army, 1955-57 Named Outstanding Young Man of Yr., Pueblo Jaycees, 1964 Fellow Am. Coll. Trust and Estate Counsel; mem. ABA (ho. of dels. 1986-88), Colo. Bar Assn. (bd. govs. 1977-79, 82-88, pres. 1983-84), Pueblo County Bar Assn. (Outstanding Young Lawyer award 1965, 67, pres. 1976-77), Denver Metro C. of C. (bd. dirs.), Denver Civic Ventures, Harvard Law Sch. Assn. Colo. (pres. 1972), Kiwanis (pres. 1969). Democrat. Roman Catholic. Home: 1551 Larimer St Apt 2601 Denver CO 80202-1638 Office: Denver Ctr Performing Arts 1050 13th St Denver CO 80204-2157 E-mail: lward@dcpa.org.

WARD, LILLIAN HAZEL, music educator; b. Hastings, Colo., Sept. 19, 1920; d. Frank Joseph and Jane (Shields) Baker; m. Peter Joseph Ward, Sept. 12, 1942; children: Mary Jane Eickhoff, Michael George. Student, Western State Coll., 1938-42. Piano tchr., San Francisco, 1951-54, Los Altos, Calif., 1955—. Author: (composition for piano) Girl Scout Song Book, 1957. Leader brownies Girl Scouts USA, San Francisco, 1952-54, Los Altos, Calif., 1955-59; guardian coun. Jobs Daus., Los Altos, 1959-68; tchr., dir. United Meth. Ch., Los Altos, 1955-73. Mem. Nat. Music Tchrs. Assn., Calif. Assn. Profl. Music Tchrs. Avocations: gardening, reading, working with the blind, spending time with grandchildren, watercolor and oil painting. Home: 246 Alicia Way Los Altos CA 94022-2346

WARD, LINDA V. nursing administrator; b. Oxford, N.C., May 3, 1948; d. Caspair and Annie Louise (Hicks) Cooper; m. Alan C. Ward, May 4, 1968; children: Alan, Lenore. Diploma, Sharon Gen. Hosp. Sch. Nursing, 1981; BSN, Pa. State U., 1994; MSN, Youngstown (Ohio) State U., 2001. Cert. for insertion of peripheral indwelling cen. catheters; cert. neonatal resuscitation instr., pediat. advanced life support instr., cert. high risk neonatal nursing, Resolve Through Sharing bereavement counselor, clin. nurse III clin. ladder program; cert. basic life support instr. Gen. staff nurse med. (renal) fl. Western Res. Care System, Youngstown, Ohio, 1981-82, gen. staff nurse neonatal ICU, 1982-87, acting clin. nurse mgr., 1991, asst. clin. nurse mgr. neonatal ICU, 1987-97, acting clin. nurse mgr., 1991, clin. nurse mgr., 1997—. Mem. Nat. Assn. Neonatal Nurses, Ohio Nurses Assn., Pa. State U. Alumna Assn., Alpha Sigma Lambda, Sigma Theta Tau. Democrat. Baptist. Office: Western Res Care Systems 500 Gypsy Ln Youngstown OH 44504-1315

WARD, LLEWELLYN ORCUTT, III, oil company executive; b. Oklahoma City, July 24, 1930; s. Llewellyn Orcutt II and Addie (Reisdorph) W.; m. Myra Beth Gungoll, Oct. 29, 1955; children: Casidy Ann, William Carlton. Student, Okla. Mil. Acad. Jr. Coll., 1948-50; BS, Okla. U., 1953; postgrad., Harvard U., 1986. Registered profl. engr., Okla. Dist. engr. Delhi-Taylor Oil Corp., Tulsa, 1955-56; ptnr. Ward-Gungoll Oil Investments, Enid, Okla., 1956—; owner L.O. Ward Oil Ops., 1963—; chmn., CEO Ward Petroleum Corp. Mem. Okla. Gov.'s Adv. Coun. on Energy; rep. to Interstate Oil Compact Commn.; dir. Hydril Corp; chmn., CEO Ward Petroleum Corp. Chmn. Indsl. Devel. Commn., Enid, 1968—; active YMCA; mem. bd. visitors Coll. Engring., U. Okla.; mem. adv. coun. Sch. Bus., trustee Phillips U., Enid, Univ. Bd., Pepperdine, Calif.; Okla. chmn. U.S. Olympic Com., 1986—; Rep. nat. committeeman from Okla., 1982-88; mem. Pres.'s adv. com. on arts Kennedy Ctr. Served with C.E., U.S. Army, 1953-55. Recipient Chief Roughneck of Yr., Lone Star Steel, 1999. Mem. Ind. Petroleum Assn. Am. (chmn. 1996-98), Okla. Ind. Petroleum Assn. Am. (pres., bd. dirs.), Nat. Petroleum Coun., Enid C. of C., Am. Bus. Club (pres. 1964), Masons, Shriners, Rotary (pres. Enid 1990-91), Alpha Tau Omega. Methodist. Home: 900 Brookside Dr Enid OK 73703-6941 Office: 502 S Fillmore St Enid OK 73703-5703

WARD, LOUIS EMMERSON, retired physician; b. Mt. Vernon, Ill., Jan. 19, 1918; s. Henry Ben (Pope) and Aline (Emmerson) Ward; m. Nan Talbot, June 5, 1942; children: Nancy, Louis, Robert, Mark; m. Marian Mansfield, Jan. 27, 1979. AB, U. Ill., 1939; MD, Harvard, 1943; MS in Medicine, U. Minn., 1949. Intern Ill. Research and Ednl. Hosp., Chgo., 1943; fellow medicine Mayo Found., 1946—49; cons. medicine, rheumatology Mayo Clinic, 1950—83, chmn. bd. govs., 1964—75. Contbr. articles. Vice chmn. bd. trustees Mayo Found., 1964—76; past bd. dirs. Fund for Republic, Ctr. for Study Dem. Instns., Arthritis Found.; mem. Nat. Coun. Health Planning and Devel., 1976—83. With M.C. U.S. Army, 1944—46. Recipient Achievement award, U. Ill., 1968, Disting. Alumnus award, Mayo Found., 1983. Master: Am. Coll. Rheumatology; mem.: So. Minn. Med. Assn., Zumbro Valley Med. Soc., Minn. Med. Soc., Ctrl. Soc. Clin. Rsch., Nat. Soc. Clin. Rheumatologists, AAAS, AMA, Phi Delta Theta, Alpha Omega Alpha, Sigma Xi, Phi Beta Kappa. Home: Apt 916 211 2nd St NW Rochester MN 55901-2820

WARD, MARGARET CHARLOTTE, literature educator, interpreter; b. Miami Beach, Fla., Apr. 10, 1946; d. Charles Gaylor and Margaret Reddoch Ward; m. Stephen Ellis Gersh, Aug. 1, 1975; children: Alcuin Immanuel, Camilla Naomi. BA with spl. honors, Wellesley Coll., 1968; MA, Harvard U., 1971, PhD, 1981. Cert. Profl. Assn. Translators and Interpreters P.R. English tchr. Gewerbeschule der Stadt Zurich, Switzerland, 1969; tchr. fellow, resident tutor history and lit. honors program Harvard Coll., Cambridge, Mass., 1971—72, 1976—78; supr. English and Welsh Cambridge (Eng.) U., 1974—76; instr. English U. Conn., Storrs, 1978—82; asst. prof. English Ohio U., Athens, 1982—83, U. Minn., Mpls., 1983—89; full prof. grad. program in translation U. P.R. Coll. Humanities, San Juan, PR, 1989—. French interpreter Dept. State, Agt. for Internat. Devel., Washington, 1967; instr. first aid Cruz Roja Uruguaya, Montevideo, Uruguay, 1970; presenter in field. Editor: Ezra Pound, Forked Branches, 1985; contbr. chapters to books, articles to profl. jours.; (commentator): Pound's Translations of Arnaut Daniel, 1991. Recipient Mary Sibley Fellowship French, Phi Beta Kappa, Poitiers, France, 1972—73, Summer stipend, NEH, Binghamton, N.Y., 1988, NEH, Aberystwyth, Wales, 1989; grantee Faculty Devel. grant, Andrew W. Mellon, Aberystwyth, 1989. Mem.: MLA, Celtic Studies Assn. N.Am., Internat. Comparative Lit. Assn., Am. Comparative Lit. Assn., Wellesley Alumnae Club (book reviewer 1995—), Harvard Alumni Club (interviewer 2000—). Avocations: art history, theater , opera, travel. Home: 49 Copsewood Way Northwood NA6 2TZ England Office: U PR Grad Program in Translation PO Box 22613 San Juan PR 00931-2613

WARD, MARVIN MARTIN, retired state senator; b. Newport News, Va., Feb. 10, 1914; s. Charles Tilden and Nora Belle (Martin) W.; m. Mary June Darden, Aug. 23, 1941; children: Elizabeth Darden Ward Cone, Marvin Thomas. BS, Appalachian U., 1934; MA, U. N.C., 1940. Tchr. Bethel Sch., Midland, N.C., 1934-37, Reynolds High Sch., Winston-Salem, 1937-46; prin. Granville Elem. Sch., 1946-49; asst. supt. Winston-Salem City Schs., 1949-62, supt., 1962-63, Winston-Salem/Forsyth County Schs., 1963-76; mem. N.C. State Senate, Raleigh, 1979-94; ret., 1994. Mem. exec. com. N.C. Pub. Sch. Forum, Raleigh, 1986—; mem. edn. com. Nat. Cong. State Legis., Denver, 1985—. Sunday sch. tchr. Centenary Meth. Ch., Winston-Salem, 1941—; mem. Forsyth County Emergency Planning Com., Winston-Salem, 1987—. Recipient Valand award Mental Health Assocs. Inc., Raleigh, 1982, Leadership award N.C. Assn. Educators, 1985; named Disting. Alumni Appalachian State U., 1986, The Educator A. Phillip Randolph Inst., 1989, Legis. of Yr. N.C. Nurses Assn., 1989. Mem. Winston-Salem C. of C., Lions, Ardmore Community Club (pres. 1950). Democrat. Avocations: golf, fishing, travel, photography, wood carving. Home: 641 Yorkshire Rd Winston Salem NC 27106-5541

WARD, MICHAEL W. lawyer; b. Chgo., Aug. 16, 1950; s. John Francis and Mary Frances (Brophy) W.; m. Amy Louise Alsopiedy, June 29, 1974; children: Daniel Joseph, James Patrick. BA, U. Notre Dame, 1972; JD, Ill. Inst. Tech., 1976. Bar: Ill. 1976, U.S. Dist. Ct. (no. dist.) Ill. 1976, U.S. Ct. Appeals (7th cir.) 1976, U.S. Supreme Ct. 1980, U.S. Dist. Ct. (no. dist.) Ill. 1982, U.S. Ct. Appeals (6th cir.) 1985. Asst. state's atty. Cook County, Chgo., 1976-80; assoc. O'Keefe, Ashenden, Lyons & Ward, 1980-85, ptnr., 1986—. V.p. Northshore Fellowship League, Evanston, Ill., 1982-84; mem. St. Nicholas Sch. Bd., Evanston, 1984-86; bd. dirs. New Horizons Youth Group, Evanston, 1979-85; mem. adv. bd. Cath. Charities, 1989—; mem. fin. coun. St. Nicholas Ch., Evanston, 1988—. Mem. Ill. State Bar Assn. (pub. utilities section council 1988-90, Chgo. Bar Assn., Fed. Comm. Bar Assn. (charter mem. midwest coordinating com.). Roman Catholic. Home: 1012 Mulford St Evanston IL 60202-3317 Office: Michael W Ward PC 1608 Barclay Blvd Buffalo Grove IL 60089-4523

WARD, MILTON HAWKINS, former mining company executive; b. Bessemer, Ala., Aug. 1, 1932; s. William Howard and Mae Ivy (Smith) W.; m. Sylvia Adele Randle, June 30, 1951; children: Jeffrey Randle, Lisa Adele. BS in Mining Engring., U. Ala., 1955, MS in Engring., 1981; MBA, U. N.Mex., 1974; DEng (hon.), Colo. Sch. of Mines, 1994; PhD, U. London, 1995. Registered profl. engr., Tex., Ala. Supr., engr. San Manuel (Ariz.) Copper Corp., 1955-60; gen. supt. of mines Kerr-McGee Corp., Oklahoma City, 1960-66; gen. mgr. Homestake Mining Co., Grants, 1966-70; v.p. ops. Ranchers Exploration & Devel. Corp., Albuquerque, 1970-74; pres., COO Freeport-McMoRan, Inc., New Orleans, 1974-92, also bd. dirs.; chmn., pres. CEO Cyprus Amax Minerals Co., Englewood, Colo., 1992-99; dir. Kinross

Gold (formerly Amax Gold Inc.), 1993-99. Bd. dirs. Mineral Info. Inst., Inc., Internat. Copper Assn.; mem. Geoscience and Environment Ctr's. adv. bd. Sandia Nat. Labs., 1998—. Bd. trustees Western Regional Coun.; bd. dirs. Smithsonian Nat. Mus. Natural History, Nat. Mining Hall of Fame and Mus.; disting. engring. fellow U. Ala., mem. Pres.'s cabinet. Recipient Daniel C. Jackling award and Saunders gold medal Soc. Mining, Metallurgy and Exploration, 1992; inductee Am. Mining Hall of Fame, State of Ala. Engring. Hall of Fame, 1996; Honoree of Yr. Achievement Rewards Coll. Scientists, 1998-99. Fellow Inst. Mining and Metallurgy (London); mem. NAE, AIME (former sect. chmn., Disting. Mem. award), Am. Mining Congress, Nat. Mining Assn. (dir.), Am. Australian Assn., Mining and Metall. Soc. Am. (pres., exec. com.), Can. Inst. Mining and Metall., Nat. Rsch. Coun. (com. on earth and scis.), NAM (natural resources com.), Internat. Copper Assn. (bd. dirs.), Copper Club, Met. Club (Washington), Met. Club (Englewood), Las Campanas Country Club (Santa Fe, N.M.), Ventana Canyon Country Club (Tucson, Ariz.). Republican. Presbyterian. Office: Cyprus Amax Minerals Co Kinross Gold Corp 40 King St W 57th Fl Toronto ON 85004-3012 Canada M5H 3Y2

WARD, NEIL ANTHONY, corporate communications specialist; b. Oakland, Calif., May 20, 1954; s. Wilfred Hamlin and Alice Ruth (Collings) W.; children: Camilo, Andrea. BA, Brown U., 1976; MFA, Carnegie-Mellon U., 1980. Sec. Am. Pulpwood Assn., Washington, 1982-85, adminstrv. asst., 1985-87, publs. mgr., 1987-89, comm. mgr. Washington & Rockville, Md., 1989-96, dir. comm. Rockville, 1996-99, Forest Resources Assn., Inc., Rockville, 1999—. Editor (newsletters) Enfoprensa USA, 1983-88, Pulpwood Highlights, 1984-99, FRA Bull., 1999—, Forest Ops. Rev., 1999—; contbr. articles to profl. jours. Shubert fellow Shubert Found., Pitts., 1980. Mem. Am. Soc. Assn. Execs. Avocations: philology, theater history, cooking, literature. Home: 1420 T St NW Washington DC 20009-3906 Office: Forest Resources Assn Inc #350 600 Jefferson Plaza Rockville MD 20852 E-mail: nward@forestresources.org.

WARD, NINA GILLSON, jewelry store executive; b. Boston, Dec. 19, 1950; d. Rev. John Robert and Patricia (Gillson) Baker; m. Jorge Alberto Lievanos, June 6, 1981 (div.); children: Jeremy John Baker, Wendy Mara Baker, Raoul Salvador Baker-Lievanos; m. David Ward, July 24, 1998; stepchildren: Johnna Ward, Tavi Sterling. Student, Mills Coll., 1969-70; grad. course in diamond grading, Gemology Inst. Am., 1983; student in diamondtology designation, Diamond Coun. Am., 1986—. Cert. store mgr., Jewelers Cert. Coun., Jewelers Am. Artist, tchr., Claremont, Calif., 1973-78; escrow officer Bank of Am., 1978-81; retail salesman William Pitt Jewelers, Puente Hills, Montclair, Calif., 1981-83, asst. mgr., 1983, mgr. Santa Maria, 1983-91, corp. sales trainer, 1988-89; sales and design specialist Merksamer Jewelers, 1991, mgr. San Luis Obispo, Calif., 1991-92, Santa Maria, 1992-94, diamond specialist cons., 1994-96; pres., ops. mgr. Dancer House Designs, Calif., 1996; pres. primary jewelry designer Dancer House Design Fine Jewelry, Inc., Kennebunk, Maine, 1997—. Artist tapestry hanging Laguna Beach Mus. Art, 1974; exhibited in Nat. Jeweler's Design Competition, 1999. Mem. Cen. Coast Pla. Adv. Bd., 1992; mem. Rep. Bus. Majority Coun. Recipient Cert. Merit Art Bank Am., 1968, 1st pl. Best of show award for jewelry design Maine Jeweler's Assn., 1998, design award, 2000, Rep. of Yr. Award Maine, 2000, 1st place award crystal divsn. nat. design competition Mfg. Jewelers and Suppliers of Am., 2001. Mem. NAFE, Internat. Platform Assn., Maine Jewelers Assn. (bd. dirs. 1999—), Speaker's Bur., Santa Maria C. of C., Compassion Internat. Republican. Avocations: tapestry weaving, creative writing. Office: Dancer House Design Fine Jewelry 36 B Main St Kennebunk ME 04043-7154

WARD, PAMELA LYNN, business executive, consultant; b. Jamaica, N.Y., Nov. 11; d. Jessee Williams and Mary (Bailey) Ward. Student, Audrey Cohen Coll., 1998. Youth min. Mt. Pisgah A.M.E. Ch., Harlem, N.Y., 1994—; founder, CEO Redeemed Internat., Rosedale, 1993—; pub. Redeemed, 1993—. Cons. Kerri Edge Cultural Dance Ensemble!, Jamaica, N.Y., 1993-94; asst. to pres. CUNY, Jamaica, 1995-96; freelance writer Hampton Rd. Happenings, Portsmouth, Va., 1997—.

WARD, PATRICIA SCOTT, secondary special education educator; b. Atlanta, Feb. 2, 1937; d. Daniel M. and Susie (Ramsey) Scott; m. Albert Ray Ward, Jan. 6, 1956; children: Albert Ray Jr., Felicia Gail. BA, Spelman Coll., Atlanta, 1963; MA, Atlanta U., 1974, EdS, 1979; cert. in computer literacy, Dartmouth Coll., 1986. Cert. learning disabilities, computer literacy, info. processing, ga. Tchr. handicapped Atlanta Pub. Schs. Adj. prof. Atlanta U. Computer literacy fellow, 1986; computer grantee, 1988. Mem. ASCD, Nat. Coun. Tchrs. Math., ASPEW.

WARD, PETER ALLAN, pathologist, educator; b. Winsted, Conn., Nov. 1, 1934; s. Parker J. and Mary Alice (McEvoy) Ward. BS, U. Mich., Ann Arbor, 1958, MD, 1960. Diplomate Am. Bd. Anat. Pathology, Am. Bd. Immunopathology. Intern Bellevue Hosp., 1960—61; resident U. Mich. Hosp., Ann Arbor, 1961—63; postdoctoral fellow Scripps Clinic, La Jolla, Calif., 1963—65; chief immunobiology br. Armed Forces Inst. Pathology, Washington, 1967—71; prof. dept. pathology, chmn. dept. U. Conn. Health Center, Farmington, 1971—80; prof., chmn. dept. pathology U. Mich., Ann Arbor, 1980—; interim dean U. Mich. Med. Sch., 1982—85, 1st Godfrey D. Stobbe prof. pathology, 1987; Disting. faculty lectr. U. Mich. Biomed. Rsch. Coun., 1989. Cons. VA Hosp., 1980—; mem. rsch. rev. com. NHLBI, NIH, Bethesda, Md., 1978—82, Inst. Medicine/NAS, 1990—; trustee Am. Bd. Pathology, 1988—97, pres., 1996; bd. dirs. Univs. Assoc. for Rsch. and Edn. in Pathology, Inc., 1978—, pres. bd. dirs., 1988—90; chmn., mem. sch. adv. bd. Armed Forces Inst. Pathology, Washington, 1981—83; mem. pathology A study sect. NIH, 1972—76, chmn., 1976—78; pres.-elect U.S./Can. Acad. Pathology, 1991—92, pres., 1992—93; bd. dirs. Inst. Lab. Resources, NRC. Capt. M.C. U.S. Army, 1965—67. Recipient Borden Rsch. award, U. Mich. Med. Sch., Ann Arbor, 1960, R&D and Devel. award, U.S. Army, 1969, Meritorious Civilian Svc. award, Dept. Army, 1970, Parke-Davis award, Am. Soc. Exptl. Pathology, 1971, Rous-Whipple award, Am. Soc. Investigative Pathology, 1996, Gold Headed Cane award, 2000. Fellow: AAAS; mem.: Mich. Soc. Pathologists, Assn. Am. Physicians, Assn. Pathology Chmn., U.S. and Can. Acad. Pathologists (pres. 1993—94), Am. Assn. Immunologists, Am. Soc. Clin. Investigation, Am. Assn. Pathologists (pres. 1978—79). Office: 1301 Catherine St Rm M5240 PO Box 602 Ann Arbor MI 48106-0602

WARD, RICHARD HURLEY, university dean, writer; b. N.Y.C., Sept. 2, 1939; s. Hurley and Anna C. (Mittasch) W.; children from a previous marriage: Jeanne M., Jonathan B.; m. Michelle Pierczynski, June 15, 1987. BS, John Jay Coll., CUNY, 1968; M in Criminology, U. Calif., Berkeley, 1969, D in Criminology, 1971. Detective N.Y.C. Police Dept., 1962-70; coord. student activities John Jay Coll., N.Y.C., 1970-71, dean students, 1971-75, v.p., 1975-77, vice chancellor, 1977-93; assoc. chancellor and prof. internat. criminology U. Ill., Chgo., 1993-98; exec. dir. Office Internat. Criminal Justice, 1985-99; exec. v.p. MBF Edn. Group, Malaysia, 1996-97; dean Coll. Criminal Justice, Sam Houston State U., Huntsville, Tex., 1999—. Vis. prof. Zagazig U., Egypt, Egyptian Police Acad., 1986, East China Inst. Politics and Law, Shanghai, 1990-91; lectr., various confs. in China, Egypt, Russia, Italy, Eng., Peru, Germany, Vietnam and U.S., 1983—. Author: (with others) Police Robbery Control Manual, 1975; Introduction to Criminal Investigation, 1975, An Anti-Corruption Manual for Administrators in Law Enforcement; (with Robert McCormack) Quest for Quality, 1984; gen. editor Foundations of Criminal Justice, 46 vols., 1972-75; editor: (with Austin Fowler) Police and Law Enforcement, Vol. I, 1972; Police and Law Enforcement, Vol. II, 1975; (with Harold Smith) International Terrorism: The Domestic Response, 1982, International Terrorism: Operational Issues, 1988; co-author: (with James Osterburg) Criminal Investigation: A Method for Reconstructing the Past, 1992, 3d edit., 1999. Mem. Mayor of Chgo.'s Blue Ribbon Pannel on Police Promotion; varsity baseball coach U. Ill., Chgo., 1980-82, John Jay Coll. Criminal Justice, N.U.C., 1971-72; chief investigator Mayor's Commn. Police Integrity, 1998. Cpl. USMC, 1957-61. Recipient Leonard Reisman award John Jay Coll. Criminal Justice, 1968, Alumni Achievement award, 1978, Richard McGee award U. Calif., Berkeley Sch. Criminology, 1971, Friendship medal Peoples Republic of China, 1994, Hans Mattick award Ill. Acad. Criminology, 1999; Justice Dept. fellow U. Calif., Berkeley, 1971. Mem. ASPA, Acad. Criminal Justice Scis. (pres. 1977-78, Founder's award 1985), Internat. Assn. Chiefs of Police (chmn. edn. and tng. sect. 1974-75), Sigma Delta Chi. Office: Sam Houston State U Coll Criminal Justice Huntsville TX 77341 E-mail: on2ward@aol.com.

WARD, RICHARD JOSEPH, university dean, educator, author; b. Beverly, Mass., Nov. 7, 1921; s. Ralph Woodbury and Margaret (Lyons) W.; m. Cecilia Butler, Sept. 1, 1951; children: Timothy, Mary, Richard, Christopher. BS, Harvard U., 1946; MA, U. Mich., 1948, PhD, 1958. Dir. planning AID Mission to Jordan, 1961-63; chmn. econ. dept. C.W. Post Coll., L.I. U., 1960-61, 63-65; chief planning Bur. for Near East and South Asia, AID, 1965-69; mgr. internat. cons. Peat, Marwick, Mitchell & Co., Washington, 1969-75; dean U. Mass. Coll. Bus., Dartmouth, 1975-87, dean, dir. rsch., prof., 1990-96, Chancellor prof. emeritus, 1996; dir. U.S. Internat. U. Sch. Bus., London, 1988-89; cons. in field. Author: Principles of Economics, 1967, Development Problems, 1973, The Palestine State, 1978, Development Horizon '80, 1980; editor: The Challenge of Development, 1967, Grampas Are For All Seasons, 2001; contbr. articles to profl. jours. Bd. dirs. Indsl. Found., 1976-82, New Bedford Symphony, 1982—; bd. dirs. Jr. Achievement, 1977-99, also past pres.; mem. exec. com. World Congress on Violence and Human Co-existence. Lt. USN, 1943-46, PTO. Recipient Disting. Svc. award AID, Jordan Mission, 1963, Univ. Svc. award U. Mass. Alumni Assn., 1983; fellow Ford Found., 1957. Mem. Assn. Social Econs. (pres. 1970-71), Ea. Econ. Assn. (exec. com.), Am. Econ. Assn., Harvard Club (pres. 1984-87, regional bd. dirs. Mass. and R.I. 1989-92), U.S. Signatory/Found. for Human Co-Existence. Home: 20 Pleasant St South Dartmouth MA 02748-3813 E-mail: wardjrichard@attbi.com.

WARD, RICHARD VANCE, JR. management executive; b. Montreal, Que., Can., June 19, 1929; s. Richard Vance Ward and Isobel Eugene Mosley; m. Elizabeth Anne Gareau, Aug. 15, 1953; children: Carolyn, Jennifer, Philip, Karen, Katherine. BSc, McGill U., Montreal, 1951; diploma in bus. adminstrn., U. Western Ont., London, Can., 1952. Indsl. engr. CIL Inc., Montreal, 1952-63, prodn. mgr., 1963-65; prodn. dir. ICI Am. Inc., Stamford, 1965-73, CIL Inc., Montreal, 1973-76, v.p., 1976-84; pres. CIL Corp. of Am., Stamford, Conn., 1984-89, Ward Assocs. Mgmt. Cons., 1989—. Chmn., pres., dir. Friends of McGill, Inc., N.Y.C.; bd. dirs. Chlorine Inst. Washington, mem. exec. com., 1984—86; bd. dirs. Cornwall Chems. Inc., CIL Corp. Am., Cansco Chems. Inc., Canada. Mem. Chem. Mfrs. Assn., Sr. Men's Club (dir., pres.), SCORE (vice chmn.), Exchange Club (dir.). Avocations: sailing, hiking, curling, skiing. Home: 45 Brushy Ridge Rd New Canaan CT 06840-4207 E-mail: wardllc@aol.com.

WARD, ROBERT, composer, conductor, educator; b. Cleve., Sept. 13, 1917; s. Albert E. and Carrie (Mollenkopf) W.; m. Mary Raymond Benedict, June 19, 1944; children: Melinda, Johanna, Jonathon, Mark, Timothy. B.Mus., Eastman Sch. Music, 1939; cert., Juilliard Grad. Sch. Music, 1946; student composition with, Bernard Rogers, Howard Hanson, Frederick Jacobi, Aaron Copland; conducting with, Albert Stoessel, Edgar Schenkman; D.F.A., Duke, 1972; Mus.D., Peabody Inst., 1975; D.F.A., U. N.C., Greensboro, 1992. Tchr. Juilliard Sch. Music, 1946-56; mng. editor, exec. v.p. Galaxy Music Corp., until 1967, dir., 1967—; exec. v.p. Highgate Press, 1967; pres. N.C. Sch. Arts, Winston-Salem, 1967-74, tchr. composition, 1974-79; prof. composition Duke U., Durham, N.C., 1978-87, Mary Duke Biddle prof. music, 1978-87; composer Mus. Natural Sci., 1999—. Chmn. bd. Triangle Music Theater Assocs. Composer: 1st Symphony, 1942, Hush'd Be the Camps Today, 1943, Second Symphony, 1947, Third Symphony, 1951, Fourth Symphony, 1958, Divertimento for Orchestra, 1961, Earth Shall Be Fair, 1960, He Who Gets Slapped (Pantaloon) (opera in 3 acts); opera in 4 acts The Crucible, 1962 (Pulitzer Prize in music); Hymn and Celebration (for orch.), 1962; for orch. Invocation and Toccata, 1963; opera in 2 acts The Lady From Colorado, 1964; Let the Word Go Forth, 1965; cantata Sweet Freedom's Song, 1965, Hymn To The Night, 1966; First String Quartet, 1966, Concerto for Piano and Orchestra, 1968; opera Claudia Legare, 1974; Fifth Symphony-Canticles for America, 1976, Sonic Structure (for orch.), 1980; opera Abelard and Heloise, 1981, Minutes Till Midnight, 1982, Dialogues for Violin, Cello and Orchestra, 1983, Concerto for Saxophone and Orchestra, 1984, Raleigh Divertimento for Wind Quintet, 1986, Festival Triptych, 1987, Sixth Symphony, 1988, First Symphonic Set for the New South, 1988, Fanfare, 1988, Second Symphonic Set, 1988, Appalachian Ditties and Dances, 1988, 5x5, 1989, Images of God, 1989, Ballet Music on The Scarlet Letter, 1990, Second Sonata for Violin and Piano, 1990, Bath County Rhapsody, 1991, Serenade for Mallarmé, 1991, By The Way of Memories for Orchestra, 1997, one act opera Roman Fever, 1993, Love's Seasons, 1994, song cycle Sacred Carticles, 1994, The Hill Song, 1996, Brass Ablaze for British Brass Band, 1996, Night Under the Big Sky for Wind Quintet and Piano, 1997, Echoes of America, Trio for Clarinet, Cello and Piano, 1997, Cherish Your Land-Chorus, 2000, Bayou Rhapsody, 2001, Dialogues: A Triple Concerto for Violin, Cello and Piano and Orch., 2002. Bd. dirs. Martha Baird Rockefeller Fund for Music, 1971-82, Am. Symphony Orch. League, 1977-89, Nat. Inst. Music Theatre, 1977-85; mem. music com. Henry St. Settlement; bd. dirs. Durham Arts Coun. Served with AUS, 1942-46. Decorated Bronze Star; MacDowell Colony fellow, 1938; recipient Juilliard Pub. award, 1942, Fine Arts award State of N.C., 1975, Gold Baton award Am. Symphony Orch. League, 1991, Disting. Faculty Alumnus award U. N.C., 1992, A.I. DuPont award of Del. Symphony, 1995; Alice M. Ditson fellow Columbia U., 1944, Guggenheim fellow, 1950, 52, 66-67; Am. Acad. Arts and Letters grantee, 1946. Mem. Nat. Acad. Arts and Letters. Home: The Forest at Duke 2701 Pickett Rd # 4022 Durham NC 27705-5688

WARD, ROBERT ALLEN, JR. advertising executive; b. Summit, N.J., Sept. 25, 1937; s. Robert Allen and Edith Allen (Edith) Seiberling; m. Nancy Prescott, Oct. 3, 1964; children: Victoria, Jennifer, Robert. BA, Yale U., 1959. Electronics analyst and account exec. U.S. Trust Co., N.Y.C., 1959-62; v.p., dir. Progressive Mktg. Svcs., 1962-63, Coin Depot Corp., Elizabeth, N.J., 1963-68; pres. J.S. Riley Co., Wayne, 1964-70; pres., dir. C.G.W. Enterprises, Butler, Carelli, Glynn & Ward Advt. Co., 1969-95, All Hours Answering Svc., Pompton Lakes, N.J., 1969-93; v.p., dir. N.J. Exch., 1969-93; v.p. direct Anserve Inc., 1993—. Pres., dir. B.E.K., Inc., real estate mgmt. co., Wayne, N.J., Litho Four Printers, 1970-88, Healthserve, 1996—; dir. Devon Pubs., Butler, N.J., 1977-78; owner 1250 Rt # 23 LLC, 817 Ringwood Ave. LLC. Pres. Kinnelon PTA, N.J., 1972-73; councilman Kinnelon Borough Coun., 1978-83; police commr., Kinnelon, 1978-83; mem. Kinnelon Drug Adv. Coun., 1978-83; vestry St. David Episc. Ch., Kinnelon, 1969-72, 78-87, 90-93, sr. warden, 1978-87; bd. dirs. Morris Area Coun. Girl Scouts U.S.A., 1977-80, Morris Land Conservancy, 2002, Inner City Ensemble, 1983-90; bd. dirs. Willing Hands, 1989—, chmn., 2000—; mem. sports awards dinner com. North Jersey March of Dimes, 1986-90; chmn. Yale Alumni Schs. Commn., 1984—; dir. Morris Land Conservancy, 2002—; mem. Christman Cove Improvement Assn. With USMC, 1959-60, served to capt. USAR, 1960-72. With USANG. Mem. No. N.J. Advt. Club (bd. dirs. 1970-72), Commerce and Industry Assn. of N.J. (Penpac bd. dirs. 1982-90), N.J. Home Builder Assoc. (bd. dirs. 1967-70), Bank Mktg. Assn., Hugueuot Soc., S.A.R., Inner City Ensemble/NJ.J. Dance Troupe (bd. dirs. 1983-89), Yale Club (trustee, v.p. 1981—, pres. 1993-96, Montclair), Smoke Rise Club (Kinnelon), Smoke Rise Paddle Tennis Club (pres. 1988—). Republican. Home: 393 Ski Trl Kinnelon NJ 07405-2247 Office: Anserve 1250 State Rt 23 Butler NJ 07405-2002 E-mail: medserve@intac.com.

WARD, ROBERT EDWARD, retired political science educator and university administrator; b. San Francisco, Jan. 29, 1916; s. Edward Butler and Claire Catherine (Unger) W.; m. Constance Regina Barnett, Oct. 31, 1942; children: Erica Anne, Katherine Elizabeth. BA, Stanford U., 1936; MA, U. Calif.-Berkeley, 1938, PhD, 1948. Instr. in polit. sci. U. Mich., 1948-50, asst. prof. polit. sci., 1950-54, assoc. prof., 1954-58, prof., 1958-73, Stanford U., 1973-87, dir. Center for Research in Internat. Studies, 1973-87. Cons. in field; advisor Center for Strategic and Internat. Studies, Washington, 1968-87 Author: Modern Political Systems: Asia, 1963, Political Modernization in Japan and Turkey, 1964. Mem. nat. council Nat. Endowment for Humanities, Washington, 1968-73; mem. Pres.'s Commn. on Fgn. Lang.-Internat. Studies, 1978-79; chmn. Japan-U.S. Friendship Commn., 1980-83; mem. Dept. Def. Univ. Forum, 1982-87. Served to lt. (j.g.) USN, 1942-45. Decorated Legion of MErit, 1945; recipient Japan Found. award Tokyo, 1976, Order of Sacred Treasure (Japan), 1983 Fellow Am. Acad. Arts and Scis.; mem. Am. Polit. Sci. Assn. (pres. 1972-73), Assn. Asian Studies (pres. 1972-73), Social Sci. Research Council (chmn. 1969-71), Am. Philos. Soc. Home: Box 8129 501 Portola Rd Portola Valley CA 94028

WARD, ROBERT JOSEPH, federal judge; b. N.Y.C., Jan. 31, 1926; s. Joseph G. and Honor V. (Hess) W.; m. Florence C. Maisel, Apr. 15, 1951 (dec. Mar. 1994); children: Laura Alice, Carolyn; m. Renée J. Sokolow, May 28, 1995. SB, Harvard Coll., 1945, LLB, 1949. Bar: N.Y. 1949. Practiced in, N.Y.C., 1949-51, 61-72; asst. dist. atty. N.Y. County, 1951-55; asst. U.S. atty. So. Dist. N.Y., 1956-61; judge U.S. Dist. Ct. (so. dist.) N.Y., 1972-91, sr. judge, 1991—. With USNR, 1944-46. Mem. N.Y. State Bar Assn., Assn. of Bar of City of N.Y., Fed. Bar Coun. Office: US Dist Ct US Courthouse Foley Sq New York NY 10007-1501

WARD, RODMAN, JR. lawyer, director; b. Wilmington, Del., Apr. 8, 1934; s. Rodman and Dorcas (Andrews) W.; m. Susan Speakman Hill, Oct. 10, 1959; children: Margery Ward Garnett, Emily Ward Neilson, Rodman III, Jennifer Ward Oppenheimer. BA, Williams Coll., 1956; LLB, Harvard U., 1959. Bar: Del. 1959, D.C. 1959. Partner Prickett, Ward, Burt & Sanders, Wilmington, 1967-79, Skadden, Arps, Slate, Meagher & Flom, Wilmington, 1979—. Bd. dirs. WMB Holdings, Inc. Author: (with Folk and Welch) Folk on the Delaware General Corporation Law, 1987; contbr. articles to profl. jours. Trustee Christiana Care Corp.; trustee, mem. fin. com. Winterthur Mus. Gardens and Libr. Capt. USAF, 1960—63. Fellow Am. Coll. Trial Lawyers, Am. Bar Found.; mem. ABA, Am. Law Inst., Del. State Bar Assn. (pres. 1989-90), D.C. Bar Assn., Assn. of Bar of City of N.Y., Am. Judicature Soc., Wilmington Club, Wilmington Country Club, Vicmead Hunt Club. Home: 52 Selborne Dr Wilmington DE 19807-1216 Office: PO Box 636 Wilmington DE 19899-0636 E-mail: rward@skadden.com.

WARD, ROGER COURSEN, lawyer; b. Newark, June 19, 1922; s. Waldron Merry and Aline Toppin (Coursen) W.; m. Katharine More Stevens, Oct. 22, 1949; children: James Olney, Alexander More. Grad., Phillips Exeter Acad., 1940; AB, Princeton U., 1943; LL.B., Columbia U., 1949. Bar: N.J. 1949. Law clk. to justice N.J. Supreme Ct., 1951; since practiced in Newark, Morristown, Montclair, N.J.; ptnr. Pitney, Hardin, Kipp & Szuch, 1959-91, counsel, 1991-92, Schwartz, Tobia & Stanziale, 1993—. Bd. advisors Am. Inst. Law Tng. Within Office, Phila. 1986-88, Law Hiring and Tng. Report, Chgo., 1983-88. Bd. dirs. United Hosps. Newark, 1965-78, pres., 1973; trustee, v.p. Newark Mus. Assn., 1969-92; bd. dirs. Better Bus. Bur. Greater Newark, 1970-84; mem. Summit Zoning Bd. Adjustment, 1966-70; trustee Eye Inst. N.J., 1973, Pingry Sch., 1966-68, Summit YMCA, 1960-62, Newark Council Social Agys., 1956-60; vice chmn. Newark Mayor's Commn. on Youth, 1958-60. Served to lt. (j.g.) USNR, 1943-46, PTO, ETO. Harlan Fiske Stone scholar Columbia U., 1949. Mem. N.J. State Bar Assn., Essex County Bar Assn., Princeton Club N.Y., Short Hills (N.J.) Club, Phi Beta Kappa. Office: Schwartz Tobia Stanziale Rosensweig & Sedita 22 Crestmont Rd Montclair NJ 07042 E-mail: wardr@kipslaw.com.

WARD, ROSCOE FREDRICK, engineering educator; b. Boise, Idaho, Dec. 5, 1930; s. Roscoe C. W. and Alice E. (Ward); m. Julia Duffy, June 8, 1963; children: Eric R., David C. Student, U. Oreg., 1949-50; BA, Coll. of Idaho, 1953; postgrad., U. Wash., 1955-57; BS, Oreg. State U., 1959; MS, Wash. State U., 1961; Sc.D., Washington U., St. Louis, 1964. Registered profl. engr., Ohio. Asst. prof. civil engring. U. Mo., Columbia, 1963-65, Robert Coll., Istanbul, Turkey, 1965-67; assoc. prof. civil engring. Asian Inst. Tech., Bangkok, Thailand, 1967-68; assoc. prof. civil engring., assoc. dean Sch. Engring. U. Mass., Amherst, 1968-75; prof. Bogazici U., Istanbul, 1974-75; br. chief biomass energy Dept. Energy, Washington, 1975-79; interregional advisor UN/World Bank, N.Y.C., 1979-83; dean Sch. Applied Scis. Miami U., Oxford, Ohio, 1983-88; prof. paper sci. and engring. Sch. Engring. and Applied Scis. Miami U., 1983—. Vis. scientist Csir, Republic of South Africa, 1990-91. Contbr. chpts. to books, articles to profl. jours. Fellow ASCE Home: 4818 Bonham Rd Oxford OH 45056-1423 E-mail: WARDRF@MUOHIO.EDU.

WARD, SELA, actress; b. Meridian, Miss. d. Granberry Holland and Annie Kate Ward. BA, U. Ala. Appearances include: (TV series) Emerald Point, N.A.S., 1983-84, Sisters, 1991— (Emmy award for Lead Actress in Drama Series 1994), Once and Again, 1999-2002 (winner lead actress in a drama series, Emmy award 2000, winner lead actress in a drama series, Golden Globe award 2001), The Rescuers: Two Women, 1997, (TV movies) Rainbow Drive, 1990, Double Jeopardy, 1993, Almost Golden: The Jessica Savitch Story, 1995 (winner lead actress in drama movie Cableace award 1996), (films) Rustler's Rhapsody, 1985, Nothing in Common, 1986, Hello Again, 1987, The Fugitive, 1993, My Fellow Americans, 1996, The Reef, 1997, 54, 1998, Rescuers: Stories of Courage, Two Women, 1997, 54, 1998; lead actress (TV series) Once and Again, 1999-00; prodr. (Lifetime cable network) documentary Changing Face of Beauty, 2000, Lifetime "Intimate Portrait", 2001. Office: 289 S Robertson Blvd Ste 469 Beverly Hills CA 90211-2834

WARD, SUSAN ANNETTE, music teacher; b. Frederick, Md., Aug. 18, 1962; d. Harold Edwin and Raetta Mildred Stotelmyer; m. James Arthur Ward, May 16, 1982; children: Cody, Lindsay. Student, Shenandoah Coll./Conservatory, Winchester, Va., 1980-81; cert., Inst. Children's Lit., West Redding, Conn., 1986; cert. in Web design, P.C. technician cert. Owner Simply Music, Jefferson, Md.; co-owner The Homeowner's Helper, 1997—; owner Personally Yours. Vol., Valley Elem. Sch., Jefferson, 1992—, Brunswick (Md.) Mid. Sch., 1997—. Jordan Kitt grantee, 1998. Mem.: Frederick County Music Tchrs. Assn. (sec. 1998—99, pres. 2000—01, v.p. 2001—), Md. State Music Tchrs. Assn., Music Tchrs. Nat. Assn. Lutheran. Avocations: reading, collectibles. Home: 5916 Broad Run Rd Jefferson MD 21755-9113 Office: Simply Music 5916 Broad Run Rd Jefferson MD 21755-9113

WARD, SYLVIA A. humanities educator; b. Detroit, July 31, 1949; d. Munsie Lee and Frances Gertrude Ward. AA, Forest Pk. CC, St. Louis, MO, 1973. Educator Dept. of Recreation, St. Louis, 1976—77; cashier Friends Bookstore, 1977—83; educator VISTA/ Vietnam Leadership Program, 1988—89; caretaker live-in, 1989—94; cashier U. of Mo., 1996—99. Vol. Divsn. of Family Svc., St.Louis, Mo., Kinloch Multi Svc. Ctr., Kinloch; educator VISTA, St. Louis, 1988—88. Avocations: writing, teaching, crochet, drawing, volleyball. Home: 8368 Delmar Blvd Apt3N Saint Louis MO 63124

WARD, THOMAS JEROME, lawyer; b. New Kensington, Pa., May 6, 1936; s. Richard Thomas and Renatha Ann (Hruscienski) W.; m. Lindley Ann Bennett, Aug. 20, 1960; children: Christine Lester, Janice Nolte, Thomas, James, Jeffrey, Matthew. BS, Duquesne U., 1958; JD, Villanova U., 1961. Tax atty. Westinghouse Electric Corp., Pitts., 1961-65; successively atty., sr. atty., asst. gen. atty. Rockwell Mfg. Co., 1965-71, mgr. corp. devel., 1971-73; v.p., gen. counsel, sec. Disston Inc., 1973-78; ptnr. Meyer, Darragh, Buckler, Bebenek & Eck, 1978-84; v.p. fin. and law, gen. counsel, sec. Dravo Corp., 1984-87, sr. v.p. fin. and adminstrn., 1987-88, exec. v.p., 1988-90; sr. atty. Buchanan Ingersoll. PC; dir. Buchanan Ingersoll (Europa), Frankfurt, Germany, 1990-91; sr. v.p., gen. counsel Federated Svcs. Co., Pitts., 1991-99; spl. counsel Pietragallo, Bosick & Gordon, 1999—. Editor Villanova Law Rev., 1960-61. Past bd. dirs., past pres. Cath. Charities of Pitts.; past bd. advisors Duquesne U. Sch. Bus. and Adminstrn., Pitts.; past bd. dirs., past pres. Bethel Park Cmty. Found. Mem. ABA, Pa. Bar Assn., Allegheny County Bar Assn., Century Club Disting. Alumni Duquesne U. Clubs: Duquesne. Democrat. Roman Catholic. Office: 38th Fl 1 Oxford Ct Fl 38 Pittsburgh PA 15219-1407 E-mail: tjw@pbandg.com.

WARD, THOMAS JOSEPH, association executive, lecturer, researcher, writer; b. Pitts., Oct. 18, 1948; s. Thomas James and Mary (Conroy) W.; m. Julia Alexandra Fish, July 1, 1982; children: Alexander, Masjo Hamilton, Rebecca, Roosevelt Fish. BA, U. Notre Dame, 1970; MA, Calif. State U., Dominguez Hills, 1985; doctorate, De La Salle U., Manila, Phillipines, 1988. With internat. dept. Equibank, Pitts., 1970-71, Bank of Am., Lyons, France, 1972-73; dir. Internat. One World Crusade, U.S., Japan, Korea, 1973-76; dir. Spanish lang. ministries Unification Ch. of N.Y., 1977-79; exec. v.p. Causa Internat., U.S., Latin Am., 1980-86; exec. dir. Am. Leadership Conf., U.S., Latin Am., Ea. Asia, Ea. Europe, 1986-95, pres. Ea. Europe, 1995—. Field faculty advisor Vt. Coll. of Norwich U., 1994-96, U. Bridgeport, Conn., 1997—, v.p. internat. programs, 2000—, dean of Internat. Coll. Co-author: Cause Lecture Manual, 1985; translator: A Guide to Pension, in the EEC, 1991; editor: The 104th Congress and the UN: Understanding the Issues, 1996; editl. bd. Universario Jour., Montevideo, Uruguay. Advisor Am. Constn. Com., Washington, 1987-92; mem. adv. bd. World Conference Preservation &

Sustainable Devel. of the Pantanal; v.p. World Devel. Inst., Washington; pres. the Causa Found. Mem. Phi Beta Kappa. Office: U Bridgeport Wahlstrom Libr Internat Coll Bridgeport CT 06601 E-mail: ward@bridgeport.edu.

WARD, VERNETTA LAVERN, foundation administrator, lay organization official; b. Detroit, Sept. 29, 1948; d. Henry Hilery and Arnetta Melvyn (Williams) Brown; m. Santonius R.L. Ward; children: Lawrence, Terrence, Kimberley, Shinese, Racquel, Tiffany. BA, U. Detroit, 1980; postgrad., Wayne State U., 1981. LPN, Mich. LPN various hosps., Detroit, 1971-77; sch. health worker Detroit Bd. Edn., 1977-80; med. tech. instr. Detroit Inst. Commerce, 1980-82; tchr., adminstrv. asst. Greater Grace Acad., Detroit, 1982-84; instr. med. sci. Cambridge Bus. Sch., 1984-86; prog. dir. YWCA of Greater Milw., 1986—. Pastoral minister St. Elizabeth/St. Gall Ch., Milw., 1987—. Author: (plays) Family Affair, 1987, Working at the Y, 1988. Pres. Parents Against Violence Emerge, Milw., 1987—; coordinator Students Against Violence Emerge; presenter Women to Women, Inc., Milw., 1987; sponsor St. Elizabeth/St. Gall Youth Club, 1987—, Little Sis. Club, 1987—; producer, dir. Vel-Phillips Talent Ensemble, 1987—; sponsor, group ldr. Explorers Boy Scouts Am.; coach girls basketball YWCA, 1987; co-dir. God Is For Teens; facilitator local Christian leadership inst., 1988. Recipient Appreciation awards St. Gall Youth Group, 1988, Shade Tree Women's Ctr., 1987. Mem. Nat. Assn. Female Execs., Nat. Black Ministers. Clubs: Photo, Ebony, Women. Democrat. Roman Catholic. Avocations: sewing, acting, writing, theatre. Office: St Elizabeth/St Gall YWCA 128 W Burleigh 3940 N 21st St Milwaukee WI 53206-1969

WARD, VERNON GRAVES, internist; b. Palisade, Nebr., Mar. 5, 1928; s. Charles Bennett and Mildred Belle (Graves) W.; m. Eleanore Mae Farstveet, Aug. 28, 1952; children: Margo, Alison, Barry. BA, Nebr. Wesleyan U., 1948; MD cum laude, U. Nebr., Omaha, 1954. Diplomate Am. Bd. Internal Medicine. Instr. in anatomy Columbia U., N.Y.C., 1948-50; intern U. Wis., Madison, 1954-55, resident internal medicine, 1955-58, chief resident, physician, 1957-58; fellow in neurophysiology and psychosomatic medicine U. Okla., Oklahoma City, 1960-61; asst. clin. prof. medicine U. Wis., Madison, 1961-62; pvt. practice internal medicine Kearney, Nebr., 1962-67; asst. prof. U. Nebr. Coll. Medicine, Omaha, 1967-69; assoc. clin. prof. medicine U. Nebr., 1969—; pvt. practice internal medicine, 1969—. Chmn. dept. internal medicine Clarkson Hosp., Omaha, 1976-78, 96-98. Contbr. articles to profl. jours. including JAMA, Nebr. State Med. Jour., Wis. State Med. Jour., Am. Heart Jour., Postgrad. Medicine. Pres. Nebr. chpt. Arthritis Found., 1969-71. Lt. Commdr. USNR, 1958-60. Recipient Cmty. Based Tchg. award ACP-ASIM, 2000; named Hutton Traveling Scholar Coll. of Physicians, 1965. Fellow ACP, Am. Coll. Rheumatology; mem. AMA, Nebr. State Med. Soc., Omaha Med. Soc., Am. Soc. Internal Medicine (Cmty.-Based Tchg. award 2000), Am. Psychosomatic Soc., Nebr. Soc. Internal Medicine (pres. 1980-82, Disting. Internist award 1990), Phi Kappa Phi, Alpha Omega Alpha (pres. Nebr. chpt. 1984-85), Phi Chi (grand sec.-treas. 1986—, co-chmn. nat. conv. Omaha 1953), Phi Kappa Tau. Republican. Lutheran. Home: 302 N 54th St Omaha NE 68132-2813 Office: 201 S Doctor's Bldg Omaha NE 68131

WARD, VICKI DAWNE, family nurse practitioner, rural health specialist; b. Concord, Mass., Sept. 19, 1954; d. John A. and Bonnie C. (Pyles) Harrison; m. Rob Llana, Nov. 15, 1986 (div. 1994); m. Michael Ward, Jan. 20, 1996; 1 child, Skye Nelson Ward. BSN, Simmons Coll., 1985; postgrad., NYU, 1994; MSN, SUNY, Binghamton, 1997. RN Vt., Mass.; cert. FNP, ANCC; lic. family nurse practitioner, Vt., Mass. Pub. health nurse Rensselaer County Health Dept., Hoosick Falls, N.Y., 1986-89; hospice home care nurse St. Peter's Hospice, Troy, 1988-94; clin. supr. CompCare, Adams, Mass., 1989-91; home care cons., 1992; MCH clin. supr. CompCare, Adams, Mass., 1992-93; per diem home care nurse Seton Home Health Care, Troy, N.Y., 1991-98; home care nurse Dominican Sisters, Amagansett, NY, 1996; part-time family nurse practitioner Bennington (Vt.) Surgeons, 1997-98; family nurse practitioner vascular surgery Fletcher Allen Health Care, Burlington, Vt., 1999; part-time family nurse practitioner Dr. Michael Corrigan, Swanton, 1999—2001; family nurse practitioner inpatient psychiatry Ctrl. Vt. Hosp., 2000—01; family nurse practitioner O'Neil/Duffy Health Clinic, Hyannis, Mass., 2001—. Co-owner organic vegetable crop bird and sheep farm, 1986—98. Mem. Inst. Noetic Scis., Nat. Health Svc. Corp., Sigma Theta Tau.

WARD, WES, race car driver; Race car driver NASCAR, Hickory, NC, 1985—88; mem. Busch Series Crew, 1989—92, Dale Jarret's Busch Series Op., 1992—96; crew chief BGN Gary Bechtel, dirver Jeff Green, 1997—99; crew chief Sawyer driver Akins Motor Sports, Concord, NC, 1999—2000; crew chief BGN-Jarrett, 2000—01; crew chief=Elder driver Akins Motor Sports, Concord, NC, 2001—. Office: Akins MotorSports 400 Akins Dr Concord NC 28027

WARD, WILLIAM E. mayor; b. Lunenburg County, VA, 1933; BA, Virginia State Coll., Petersburg, Va., 1957, MA, 1960; PhD, Clark Univ., Worchester, Mass., 1972; studied, Hampton, African History Inst., 1963, Norfolk State Coll., Am. History Inst., 1967, Carnegie-Mellon Univ., Afro-Am. History Inst., 1969, Am. Forum Internat. Study, Ghana, West Africa, 1972, Univ. West Indies, Kingston, Jamaica, 1977. Mayor City of Chesapeake, Chesapeake, VA., 1990—; tchr. I.C. Norcom H.S., Portsmouth, Va., 1958—62, P.S. 181, Baltimore, Md., 1962—63; asst. prof. Norfolk State Coll., 1968—70; TTT fellow Clark Univ.; assoc. prof. Norfolk State Coll., 1973—79; prof. Norfolk State Univ., 1980—98, chair, history dept., 1997—2000; ret., 2000; part-time tchr., 2000—. Course instr. Clark Univ., 1972; co-dir. In-Svc. Workshop , 1971; cons. Norfolk State Coll., 1971—72, Norfolk Com., 1970—78; participated Econ. Trade Cultural Missions to Japan, Brazil, Taiwan, Israel, Europe, Japan, 1990—99; former host PRIDE, WAVY-TV; chmn., insurance com. Norfolk State Univ., chmn., faculty senate Va. benefits com., chmn., senate grievance com. , chmn., black history com. , mem., coll. wide coun. tchr. ed., coll. exe. coun., 1971—82, pres. faculty senate, 1975—77. Bd. dir. Norfolk Chesapeake Va. Beach United Way, Tidewater Va. Urban League; mem. Chesapeake City Coun., 1978—, mayor, 1990—; mem. U.S. Conf. Mayors, Chesapeake Forward Civic Orgn.; past pres. Chesapeake Men Progress Civic Orgn., Fernwood Farms Civic League; mem. Hampton Rds. Military Diplomats; chmn. Fourth Congl. Voters League; mem. Va. State Dem. Ctr. Com., WAVY-TV Minority Adv. Bd.; delegate Nat. Dem. Conv. , N.Y.C., 1976, San Francisco, 1984; chmn. Hampton Rds. Mayors Chair Caucus, 1995—96; elected to joint subcom. study use of incentives for joint activities by localities appointed by Va. Senate Com. Privileges , 1996; appointed Va. Municipal League Legislative Com., 1997; exe. bd. Tidewater Coun. Boy Scouts Am., 1997—2000; delegate 17th Ann. Jerusalm Conf. Mayors, 1997; 2nd vice chmn. Hampton Rds. Partnership, 1997; bd. dirs. Hampton Rds. Econ. Alliance, 1997; appointed Internat. Task Force, Nat. League Cities, 1998, U.S. Conf. Mayors Task Force Electronic Commerce Internet Tech., 1999. Recipient cmty. svc. award, Kappa Alpha Psi Fraternity, 1970, three yr. acad. fellowship award, Clark Univ., brotherhood award, Christians and Jews, outstanding alumni award, Va. State Univ., 1993, chamber of commerce commendation award, 1994, various cmty. awards, Martin Luther King, Jr. memorial award, Old Dominion Univ., 1995; grantee study in Africa, Clark Univ., 1972. Mem.: Va. Soc. Sci. Assn., Am. Historical Assn., Southern Historical Assn., Assn. Study Negro Life History, Va. Soc. History Tchrs., Nat. Fatherhood Initiative (co-chair mayor 2001—02), Great Bridge Battlefield Waterways History Found. (pres.), Tidewater Regional Health Coun., Va. World Tech. Fair Commn., Internat. Torch Club, Kappa Alpha Psi. Office: Office of Mayor 306 Cedar Rd Chesapeake VA 23322 E-mail: wward@council.chesapeakeva.net.

WARD, WILLIAM EDWARD, museum exhibition designer; b. Apr. 4, 1922; s. Edward and Lura Dell (Eckelberry) W.; m. Evelyn Svec, Nov. 12, 1952; 1 child, Pamela. BS, Western Res. U., 1947, MA, 1948; diploma, Cleve. Inst. Art, 1947; postgrad., Columbia U., 1950. Mem. staff edn. Oriental depts. Cleve. Mus. Art, 1947—, designer, 1957—, ret. chief designer; prof. calligraphy and watercolor Cleve. Inst. Art, 1960—; prof., cons. graphic and installation exhbn., design cons. Egyptian Mus., Cairo, 1995—. Exhibited in numerous exhbns. including (with Evelyn Svec Ward) Oaxacan Inspirations: An Exhibition of Collage and Watercolor, 1986, Valley of Oaxaca: Exhibition of Watercolors and Photographs, Folk Art Gallery, Cleve., 1992, Cleve. Playhouse Gallery, 1984, Butler Inst. Am. Art, Salem Ohio Br., 2000; designer George Gund Collection of Western Art Mus., 1972, Firemen's Meml., Cleve., sculpture design, 1968; designer ofcl. seals Case Western Res. U., also Sch. Medicine, 1969; curator Culcon exhbn. Masterpieces of World Art from Am. Museums, Tokyo and Kyoto, Japan, 1976; co-author (catalogue, exhbn.) Folk Art of Oaxaca: The Ward Colection, Cleve Inst. Art, 1987; textile designs in Cleve. Artists Found. collection; represented in permanent collections of Cleve. Mus. of Art, Akron Art Mus., Art Assn. of Cleve. Inst. of Art, Artists Archives Western Res., Cleve. Mem. Internat. Design Conf., Aspen, 1959—; mem. Tridecca Soc. (trustee 1995-98); mem. Fine Arts Adv. Com. City Cleve., 1966-90; mem. mayor's com. for selection of ofcl. seal City of Cleve., 1973, mem. design rev. com., 1991-92. Served with Terrain Intelligence, AUS, 1942-45, S.E. Asia Command. Recipient commn. award City Canvas competition Cleve. Area Arts Coun., 1975, No. Ohio LIVE Achievement award Cleve. Mus. Art, 1987, Hall of Fame award West Tech. Alumni Assn., 1995. Mem. Cleve. Soc. Contemporary Art, Artists Archives of the Western Reserve, Print Club Cleve., Cleve. Artist Found. (exhibiting mem. Beck Ctr. Gallery, Cleve. 1999), Rowfant Club, Women's City Club Cleve. (Arts Prize Spl. citation 1988). Home: 27045 Solon Rd Solon OH 44139-3452

WARD, WILLIAM FRANCIS, JR. real estate investment banker; b. Everett, Mass., Aug. 23, 1928; s. William Francis and Helen (Schriber) W.; m. Elaine L. Wilson, June 11, 1950 (dec. Oct. 1993); children: Jeffrey W., Gary T., Michelle A., Gregory W., Suzanne M.; m. Marie-Louise Buchheit, Nov. 5, 1994. BS, U.S. Mil. Acad., 1950; MBA, Harvard U., 1956; LLB, La Salle U., 1966; LLD (hon.), So. Vermont U., 1996. Commd. 2d lt. U.S. Army, 1950; resigned, 1956; econ. analyst E.I. duPont de Nemours & Co., Inc., Wilmington, Del., 1956-58; sec. N.Y. State Bridge Authority, Poughkeepsie, 1958-60; div. contr., dir. mktg. svcs. GAF Corp., N.Y.C., 1960-63; asst. to pres. Grosset & Dunlap, Inc., 1963-65, v.p., 1965-67; contr. Dun & Bradstreet, 1967-71, v.p., 1968-71; chmn. bd., pres. Dun-Donnelley Pub. Corp., 1971-77; from v.p., treas. to pres. Gestam, Inc., 1981-86; chief Army Res., 1986-91; chmn., pres. Realicam, 1985—. Bd. dirs. Quotron Electronics, Inc., Empire Nat. Bank, Eastern Savs. Bank, Apple Bank for Savs., Greater N.Y. Bank for Savs.; trustee All-City Funds; mem. adv. bd. Astoria Fin. Bank; mem. faculty NYU Sch. Commerce, 1960-64. Pres. Ramapo Central Sch. Dist., 1966-72, 1982-87; mem. facilities and planning bd. Good Samaritan Hosp., 1980-85; chmn. United Way, Rockland County, 1992-94; county chmn. Citizen for Kennedy and Johnson, 1960; Dem. candidate for Ho. of Reps., 1962; chmn. Young Citizens for Johnson and Humphrey, 55 counties N.Y., 1964; exec. v.p. Am. Cancer Soc., 1976-81; bd. dirs. N.Y.C. div. Aerospace Edn. Found., U.S. Army War Coll. Found., West Point Fund, 1979, Franciscan Sisters of the Poor Found., 1980-92; trustee N.Y. Mil. Acad., 1982-86, 91-96, trustee emeritus, 1996—; trustee Assn. Grads. U.S. Mil. Acad., 1993—, exec. com., 1996—, chmn. audit com., 1996—; trustee Hist. Soc. Rockland County, 1993-95, N.Y. Coll. Podiatric Medicine, 2000. Served to capt. AUS, 1950-54; to maj. gen. USAR 1978-91. Decorated D.S.M. with 1 oak leaf cluster, Legion of Merit, Meritorious Svc. medal with oak leaf cluster, Air medal with 3 oak leaf clusters, Army Commendation medal with oak leaf cluster, Purple Heart, Army Achievement medal. Mem. West Point Soc. (Washington chpt., Space Coast chpt., N.Y. chpt., pres. 1974-76), Antrim Players, Soc. Harvard Engrs. and Scientists, Fin. Execs. Inst., Newcomen Soc., Res. Officers Assn., Am. Friends of Viet Nam (nat. chmn.), VFW, Am. Legion, Disabled Am. Vets., Pilgrim Soc., Army and Navy Club, Squadron "A" Club, Univ. Club (N.Y.), Harvard Club (Washington), Nat. Press Club. Roman Catholic. Home: Summit View Farm RJ17A PO Box 150 Goshen NY 10924-0150 also: PO Box 150 Goshen NY 10924-0150 E-mail: wfwjr77@warwick.net., wfwjr77@webtv.net.

WARD, WILLIAM WEAVER, electrical engineer; b. Dallas, Feb. 19, 1924; s. Carroll Ross Ward and Dorothy Jane (Weaver) O'Rourke; m. Lydia Maeve McPeek, June 4, 1955; children: Geoffrey William, Christopher Andrew. BSEE, Tex. A & M Coll., 1948; MSEE, Calif. Inst. Tech., 1949, PhD in Elec. Engring., 1952. Registered profl. elec. engr., Mass. Engr. Texaco Geophys. Lab., Bellaire, Tex., summer 1948, Hughes Aircraft Co., Culver City, Calif., summer 1949, 50; teaching asst. Calif. Inst. Tech., Pasadena, 1949-52; staff mem. to group leader to mgr. satellite ops. Lincoln Lab., MIT, Lexington, 1952-94. Cons. on various tech. matters U.S., Can., British, and Australian govts.; presenter, lectr. in field. Vestryman, treas. local ch., Newton Highlands, Mass. With U.S. Army, 1943-46, PTO. Mem. IEEE (reviewer, named regional outstanding lectr. 1974, disting. lectr. 1995—), AIAA (disting. lectr. 1986-87), Nat. Soc. Profl. Engrs., Mass. Soc. Profl. Engrs., Order of the Engr., Dalhousie Lodge, Masons, Sigma Xi, Tau Beta Pi. Democrat. Episcopalian. Achievements include research and development on UHF airborne-early-warning radar; development of worldwide tracking range for Project Mercury, ballistic-missile testing, UHF and EHF satellites for military communication. Home: 22 Carver Rd Newton MA 02461-1008 E-mail: w.ward@ieee.org.

WARD, YOLANDA JEAN, communications executive; b. Washington, Feb. 17, 1957; d. Harold Wayne and Wilma LaVonne (Taylor) Tyner; m. George Wilmont Ward, Apr. 3, 1976; children: Jessica Jean, Edward Wayne. Dept. mgr. Howerter Appliance, Parsons, Kans., 1980-82; disc jockey, sales mgr. Community Broadcast Co. dba KLKC Radio, 1982-87; account exec., sales mgr. Am. TV and Communication, Parsons and Independence (Kans.), 1987-89, Kans. area group sales mgr. Emporia, Kans., 1989—. Founding mem. Kans. Cable Network dba KCN, 1990—. Dir. Emporia Downtown Assn., 1990; bd. dirs. Emporia Mainstreet, Inc.; commr. Parsons City Commn.; fundraiser Emporia State U. Athletic Assn., 1990; mem. chmn. club. Emporia C. of C., 1989—; mem. exec. bd. The Farm, Inc. boys home. Recipient Golden Quill award Kans. Nat. Edn. Assn., 1987. Mem. Nat. Fedn. Rep. Women., Kiwanis (bd. dirs. 1989—). Republican. Baptist. Avocations: organizing fundraising drives, canning, writing poetry, foster parenting. Home: 12232 Palm Springs Ave NE Albuquerque NM 87111-5422 Office: Time Warner Inc 120 Southmont Blvd Johnstown PA 15905-4236

WARDELL, J(AMES) THOMAS, civil and environment engineer; b. Glens Falls, N.Y., May 1, 1957; s. Frank Stanley and Pauline Anita (Lawlor) W.; m. Elizabeth Renée O'Bryan, June 21, 1980. BS in Forest Engring., SUNY, Syracuse, 1979; M Engring., Rensselaer Poly. Inst., 1980. Registered profl. engr., N.Y. Jr. engr. N.Y. State Dept. Environ. Conservation, Albany, 1981-82, asst. san. engr., 1982-85, sr. san. engr., 1985-90; dir. engring. Lake George (N.Y.) Park Commn., 1990—. Mem. water quality adv. com. Washington County, Ft. Edward, N.Y., 1991—, Warren County, Lake George, N.Y., 1991—; mem. nonpoint source subcom. of Lake Champlain Mgmt. Conf., 1991—. Co-contbr. articles to profl. jours. Mem. ASCE, Water Pollution Control Fedn. Office: Lake George Park Commn PO Box 749 Lake George NY 12845-0749

WARDELL, LINDY CONSTANCE, nonprofit organization administrator; b. Potsdam, N.Y., Apr. 28, 1928; d. Stewart A. and Mabel A. Henderson; m. David F. Constance, Sept. 6, 1947 (dec. Apr. 1984); children: John, Kathryn, Marie, Thomas, Richard; m. Frank M. Wardell, 1989. Student, Powellson Jr. Coll., Syracuse, N.Y., 1946-47, Ctrl. City Bus. Inst., Syracuse, 1946-47. Lic. realtor. V.p. Bicentennial Bus Co., Phila., 1974-77; assoc. cons. Constance & Wallace, 1976-84; v.p. Trade Devel. Corp., 1977-84; realtor assoc. Louis Gaev Realtors, Haverford, Pa., 1985-87; pres., chmn. bd. dirs. Darby (Pa.) Cmty. Forum, 1997—; pres., chmn. bd. Darby Borough Hist. Soc., Darby, 1998—. Chmn. Friends of Darby Meth. Meeting Cemetery, 1996—; mem. adv. bd. Delaware County Daily Times, Primos, Pa., 1998-99; bd. dirs. Darby Cmty. Project, 1991—. Author newspaper articles. Pres., Coun. Rep. Women, Newtown Square, Pa., 1977-85; charter mem. Hist. Soc. Recipient Outstanding Individual Achievement award Delaware County Heritage Commn., 1999; Golden Rule Found. grantee, 1997. Mem Darby Hist. Soc. (founding mem. 1998), Delaware County Hist. Soc., Coun. of Presidents. Republican. Avocations: genealogical research, arts and crafts, historical research. Home: 16 Winthrop Rd Darby PA 19023-1116

WARDEN, JACK RAY, restaurant executive; b. Charleston, W.Va., July 25, 1942; s. Thomas Jefferson Warden and Ersel Marie (Litton) Copen; stepfather, William R. Coper; m. Ruth Elaine Redinger, June 11, 1966; 1 child, Randal Joe. AA, St. Leo (Fla.) Coll., 1977; BS, So. Ill. U., 1986. Enlisted USN, 1962, commd. chief warrant officer, 1976, advanced through grades to chief warrant officer 3, 1982, resigned, 1982; sr. prin. engr., ops. mgr. SYSCON Corp., Mt. Laurel, N.J., 1982-95; owner McDonald's Restaurants, Roanoke and Ashland, Ala., 1995—. Chmn. Gov.'s Com. Employment People with Disabilities, Randolph County, Ala., 1996, 97; mem. steering com. for funding and establishing, bd. dirs. Boys & Girls Club Funding, Roanoke, 1997. Mem. Internat. Rotary Found. (v.p. Roanoke br. 1998), Fleet Res. Assn. Avocations: golf, tennis, basketball. Office: JRW Enterprises Inc 367 Cauthen Cir Roanoke AL 36274-5354

WARDEN, JOHN L. lawyer; b. Evansville, Ind., Sept. 22, 1941; s. Walter Wilson and Juanita (Veatch) W.; m. Phillis Ann Rodgers, Oct. 27, 1960; children: Anne W. Clark, John L., W. Carson. AB, Harvard U., 1962; LLB, U. Va., 1965. Bar: N.Y. 1966, U.S. Ct. Appeals (2d cir.) 1966, U.S. Dist. Ct. (so. and ea. dists.) N.Y. 1967, U.S. Ct. Appeals (10th cir.) 1971, U.S. Supreme Ct. 1972, U.S. Ct. Appeals (D.C. cir.) 1980. Assoc. Sullivan & Cromwell, N.Y.C., 1965-73, ptnr., 1973—. Pres. U. Va. Law Sch. Found.; trustee Am. Ballet Theatre. Editor-in-chief: Va. Law Rev., 1964-65. Fellow Am. Coll. Trial Lawyers; mem. ABA, Am. Law Inst., N.Y. State Bar Assn., Assn. Bar City N.Y., N.Y. County Lawyers Assn., Knickerbocker Club, Down Town Assn. Club, Doubles Club, Bedford Golf and Tennis Club, Lyford Cay Club. Republican. Episcopalian. Office: Sullivan & Cromwell 125 Broad St Fl 28 New York NY 10004-2489 E-mail: wardenj@sullcrom.com.

WARDEN, RICHARD DANA, government labor union official; b. Great Falls, Mont., Dec. 10, 1931; s. Robert Dickinson and Helen (Leach) W.; m. Barbara Freeman; children: Denise, Michael, Joseph, Jerome. BA, Mont. State U., 1957, MA, 1958. Reporter, then state editor Gt. Falls (Mont.) Tribune, 1959-61; legis. asst. to U.S. Senator Lee Metcalf of Mont., 1962-63; adminstrv. asst. to U.S. Congressman James G. O'Hara of Mich., 1963-67; dep. dir. Office Civil Rights, HEW, 1967-68; legis. rep. AFL-CIO, 1969-70; dir. Washington Research Project Action Council, 1970-72; legis. rep. UAW, 1972-75, legis. dir., 1975-77, 79-91, ret., 1991. Asst. sec. legis. HEW, 1977-79 Served with USN, 1951-54. Congressional fellow, 1961-62; recipient Pub. Affairs Reporting award Am. Polit. Sci. Assn., 1960 Home: 211 Marina Dr Lewes DE 19958

WARDE-NORBURY, WILLIAM GEORGE ANTONY, financial executive; b. Doncaster, Eng., Mar. 13, 1936; s. Harold George Warde-Norbury and Mary Betty Warde-Aldam; m. Philippa Marjorie Davies-Cooke, Oct. 15, 1938; children: Mark William Antony, Alastair George. Capt. Coldstream Guards, 1956-63; with Allied-Domec (then Allied-Lyons), 1964-66, dir. subs. companies, 1966-76; dir. Allied Breweries, 1976-82; main bd. dirs. Allied-Lyons and other cos., London, 1982-86; non-exec. chmn. Skol Internat. & Oldham Claudgen, Ind Coope African Invests., 1986-94. Non-exec. dir. Provident Fin. plc, Bradford, 1988-97, chmn., 1995-96; non-exec. dir. Gallup Orgn., Weybridge, 1986-98, Yorkshire Regional Con. Prince's Trust; trustee Hardman Trust. Dep. lt., South Yorkshire, 1990—, high sheriff, 1996. Avocations: field sports, travelling, music. Home: Hooton Pagnell Hall Doncaster DN5 7BW England

WARDER, MICHAEL YOUNG, think tank executive; b. Buffalo, June 29, 1946; s. Thomas Grayston and Norma A. (Young) W.; m. Cheryl Lynn Gilkerson, Feb. 8, 1975; children: Maureen, Amy, Michael Jr. BA, Stanford U., 1968. Tchr. Drew Sch., San Francisco, 1968—69; pres. Internat. Re-edn. Found., 1970—73; sec.-gen. Internat. Conf. on the Unity of Scis., N.Y.C., 1974—79; pres., pub. Newsworld Comm., 1976—79; dir. adminstrn. Heritage Found., Washington, 1980—83; exec. v.p. Ethics and Pub. Policy Ctr., 1983—84, The Rockford (Ill.) Inst., 1985—95; v.p. devel. The Claremont (Calif.) Inst., 1995—2001; exec. dir. L.A. Children's Scholarship Fund, 2001—. Radio commentator (bi-weekly) Sta. WNIJ-FM NPR Affiliate, DeKalb, Ill., 1991—95; del. leader People to People, USSR, 1991, Rockford Inst., Lithuania, Latvia, Estonia, 1994; del. leader to London Claremont Inst., 1996, del. leader to Hong Kong, 97, del. leader to Israel, 98, del leader to Rome, 2000; guest TV programs Politically Incorrect/ABC, Fox News Channel, MSNBC, others; spkr. in field ; polit. analyst in field. Op-ed columnist The Wall Street Jour., USA Today, L.A. Times, The Chgo. Tribune, Chgo. Sun Times, San Francisco Chronicle, San Diego Union Tribune, St. Louis Post Dispatch, Indpls. Star, 1985—; host/prodr. (TV weekly public affairs show) Stateline-Newsmakers, 1990-92; columnist (weekly) Rockford Register Star, 1991-92. Recipient Silver Dome award Ill. Broadcasters Assn., 1993, 95, 96; grantee Earhart Found., 1988. Mem.: L.A. World Affairs Coun., Phila. Soc., Town Hall L.A. Republican. Avocations: travel abroad, history, geography. Office: LA Children's Scholarship Fund 1650 Ximeno Ave Ste 245 Long Beach CA 90804 E-mail: mwarder@lacsf.org.

WARDER, RICHARD CURREY , JR. dean, mechanical aerospace engineering educator; b. Nitro, W.Va., Sept. 30, 1936; s. Richard Currey and Edith Irene (Moser) W.; m. Carolyn Strickler, Mar. 7, 1964 (div. Dec. 1978); children: Jennifer, Jeffrey W.; m. Marjorie Dianne Forney, Jan. 10, 1981. BS, S.D. Sch. Mines, 1958; MS, Northwestern U., 1959, PhD, 1963. Registered profl. engr., Mo., Tenn. Asst. prof. Northwestern U., Evanston, Ill., 1963-65; mgr. energy processes research Litton Industries, Beverly Hills, Calif., 1965-68; assoc. prof. mech. and aerospace engring. U. Mo., Columbia, 1968-72, prof., 1972-94, James C. Dowell prof., 1989-94, chmn. mech. aerospace engring., 1988-94; dean U. Memphis Herff Coll. Engring., 1994—. Program mgr., head resources sect. NSF, Washington, 1974-76; cons. to industry U.S. govt. Bd. dirs. Columbia Montessori Sch., 1971-73; bd. dirs. Columbia Soccer Club, 1976-80, pres., 1978-80; referee Maj. Indoor Soccer League, 1979-83. Fellow: ASME, AIAA (assoc.); mem.: AAAS, Am. Assn. Aerosol Rsch., Am. Soc. Engring. Edn., Am. Phys. Soc. Methodist.

WARDLAW, KIM A.M. federal judge; b. San Francisco, July 2, 1954; m. William M. Wardlaw Sr., Sept. 8, 1984. Student, Santa Clara U., 1972—73, Foothill C.C., Los Altos Hills, Calif., 1973—74; AB in Comm. summa cum laude, UCLA, 1976, JD with honors, 1979. Bar: Calif., U.S. Dist. Ct. (ctrl. dist.) Calif. 1979, U.S. Dist. Ct. (so. dist.) Calif. 1982, U.S. Dist. Ct. Nev. 1985, U.S. Dist. Ct. (no. dist.) Calif. 1992, U.S. Dist. Ct. Mont. 1993, U.S. Dist. Ct. Minn. 1994, U.S. Dist. Ct. (no. dist.) Ala. 1994, U.S. Dist. Ct. (so. dist.) Miss. 1995, U.S. Supreme Ct. Law clk. U.S. Dist. Ct. Ctrl. Dist. Calif., 1979—80; assoc. O'Melveny and Myers, 1980—87, ptnr., 1987—95; cir. judge U.S. Dist. Ct. Calif., LA, 1995—98, U.S. Ct. Appeals (9th cir.), 1998—. Presdl. transition team Dept. Justice, Washington, 1993; mayoral transition team City of LA, 1995—; bd. govs. UCLA Ctr. for Comm. Policy, 1994—, vice-chair, 1994—; cons. in field. Co-author: The Encyclopedia of the American Constitution, 1986; contbr. articles to profl. jours. Pres. Women Lawyers Pub. Action Grant Found., 1986—87; founding mem. LA Chamber Orch., 1992—; active Legal Def. and Edn. Fund Calif. Leadership Coun., 1993—; active Blue Ribbon of LA Music Ctr., 1993—; del. Dem. Nat. Conv., 1992. Named one of Most Prominent Bus. Attys. in LA County, LA Bus. Jour., 1995; recipient Buddy award, NOW, 1995. Mem.: NOW, ABA, Orgn. Women Execs., Assn. Bus. Trial Lawyers (gov. 1988—), LA County Bar Assn. (trustee 1993—94), Women Lawyers Assn. LA, Calif. Women Lawyers, Mex.-Am. Bar Assn. LA County, Hollywood Womens Polit. Com., Downtown Women Ptnrs., City Club Bunker Hill, Breakfast Club, Chancery Club, Phi Beta Kappa. Mailing: US Court of Appeals 9th Circuit PO Box 193939 San Francisco CA 94119-3939 Office: US Court of Appeals 9th Circuit 95 Seventh St San Francisco CA 94119*

WARDLAW, WILLIAM PATTERSON, mathematician, educator; b. L.A., Mar. 3, 1936; s. Andrew Bowie Wardlaw, Marie Virginia Benjamin; m. Hansi Edith Wharton, Aug. 24, 1963; children: Kenneth Patterson, Heidi Marie, Kathleen Eliza, William Andrew. BA in Physics, Rice Inst., Houston, 1958; PhD in Math., UCLA, 1967. Electronics engr. Douglas Aircraft Co., Santa Monica, Calif., 1960—62; prof. math. U. Ga., Athens, 1967—72, U.S. Naval Acad., Annapolis, Md., 1972—. Leader Boy Scouts Am. Lt. USNR. Avocations: canoeing, kayaking. Home: 798 MacSherry Dr Arnold MD 21012 Office: US Naval Acad Dept Math Annapolis MD 21402

WARDLOW, BILL, record industry consultant, entertainer; b. Columbus, Ohio, Jan. 2, 1921; s. Clayton Jesse and Angeline Naomi (Peckham) W. BBA, Ohio State U., 1942; cert., Am. Mgmt. Assn., N.Y.C., 1964. Vice pres. Capitol Records, Los Angeles, 1947-56; gen. mgr. Columbia Record Club, N.Y.C., 1957-61; exec. v.p. Hammond Industries, 1961-64; assoc. pub. Billboard Mag., 1964-83; pres. Bill Wardlow & Assocs., Los Angeles, 1983—; ptnr. Dealmakers Connection, Inc., 1983—; cons. to disco industry, worldwide, 1974-83. Author: (preface) This Business of Disco, 1976, (biography) Against All Odds, 1999; TV appearances include 60 Minutes, Merv Griffin Show, Mike Douglas Show, Ted Turner Network, Good Morning America. Named Father of Disco, Rec. Industry Am., 1976; reipient numerous Gold and

Platinum records, 1974-83 Mem. Regines Club (N.Y.C. and Paris). Episcopalian. Home and Office: 2212 Laurel Canyon Blvd Los Angeles CA 90046-1503 *Always be interested in the careers of those around you; i.e., recording artists. Discover them, help in every way possible for them to achieve stardom. And by helping others reach their goals, you have automatically reached yours.*

WARDROPPER, IAN BRUCE, museum curator, educator; b. Balt., May 11, 1951; s. Bruce Wear and Joyce (Vaz) W.; stepmother: Nancy Hélène (Palmer) W.; m. Laurel Ellen Bradley, May 22, 1982 (div. 1996); 1 child, Chloe Bradley; m. Sarah Anne McNear, June 21, 1997. BA, Brown U., 1973; MA, NYU, 1976, PhD, 1985. Asst. curator European sculpture Art Inst. Chgo., 1982-85, assoc. curator European decorative arts and sculpture, 1985-89, Eloise W. Martin curator European decorative arts and sculpture, and classical art, 1989-2001; Iris and B. Gerald Cantor curator in charge dept. European sculpture and decorative arts Met. Mus. Art, N.Y.C., 2001—. Adj. instr. Drew U., NJ, 1982; vis. asst. prof. Northwestern U., Evanston, Ill., 1986, Sch. of Art Inst. Chgo., 1988; guest scholar J. Paul Getty Mus., Malibu, Calif., 1995; Rhoades lectr. U. Chgo., 1997; exhbns. panelist NEA, 1993, creation and presentation panelist, 98, indemnity panelist, 1998—2001. Co-author: European Decorative Arts in the Art Institute of Chicago, 1991, Austrian Architecture and Design beyond Tradition in the 1990s, 1991, News from a Radiant Future: Soviet Porcelain from the Collection of Craig H. and Kay A. Tuber, 1992, Chiseled with a Brush: Italian Sculpture, 1860-1925, from The Gilgore Collections, 1994, From the Sculptor's Hand: Italian Baroque Terracottas from the State Hermitage Museum, 1998; contbr. articles to profl. jours. NEA fellow, 1976-77, Chester Dale fellow Met. Mus. Art, 1978-79; Kress Found. rsch. grantee, Paris, 1979-81, Am. Philos. Soc. grantee, 1991; named Chicagoan of the Yr. in Arts Chicago Tribune, 1994. Mem. Phi Beta Kappa. Office: Met Mus Art 1000 Fifth Ave New York NY 10028-0198 Business E-Mail: Ian.wardropper@Metmuseum.org.

WARD-STEINMAN, DAVID, composer, music educator, pianist; b. Alexandria, La., Nov. 6, 1936; s. Irving Steinman and Daisy Leila (Ward) W.-S.; m. Susan Diana Lucas, Dec. 28, 1956 (div. 1993); children: Jenna, Matthew; m. Patrice Dawn Madura, May 28, 2001. MusB cum laude, Fla. State U., 1957; MusM, U. Ill., 1958, DMA, 1961; studies with Nadia Boulanger, Paris, 1958-59; postdoctoral vis. fellow, Princeton U., 1970. Grad. instr. U. Ill., 1957-58; mem. faculty San Diego State U., 1961—, prof. music, 1968—, dir. comprehensive musicianship program, 1972—, composer in residence, 1961—, univ. research lectr., 1986-87. Mem. summer faculty Eastman Sch. Music Workshop, 1969; Ford Found. composer in residence Tampa Bay (Fla.) Area, 1970-72, Brevard Music Ctr., N.C., summer 1986; acad. cons. U. North Sumatra (Indonesia), 1982; concert and lecture tour U.S. Info. Agy., Indonesia, 1982; mem. faculty Coll. Music Soc. Nat. Inst. for Music in Gen. Studies, U. Colo., 1983, 84, Calif. State Summer Sch. for the Arts, Loyola Marymount U., 1988; master tchr. in residence Atlantic Ctr. for the Arts, New Smyrna Beach, Fla., summer 1996; vis. artist in residence Victorian Ctr. for the Arts, Melbourne, Australia, summer 1997. Composer: Symphony, 1959, Prelude & Toccata for orch., 1962, Concerto No. 2 for chamber orch., 1962, ballet Western Orpheus, 1964, Cello Concerto, 1966, These Three ballet, 1966, The Tale of Issoumbochi chamber opera, 1968, Rituals for Dancers and Musicians, 1971, Antares, 1971, Arcturus, 1972, The Tracker, 1976, Brancusi's Brass Beds, 1977; oratorio Song of Moses, 1964; Jazz Tangents, 1967, Childs Play, 1968; 3-act opera Tamar, 1977; Golden Apples, 1981; choral suite Of Wind and Water, 1982; Christmas cantata And In These Times, 1982; Moiré for piano and chamber ensemble, 1983, And Waken Green, song cycle on poems by Douglas Worth, 1983, Olympics Overture for orchestra, 1984, Children's Corner Revisited, song cycle, 1984, Summer Suite for oboe and piano, 1984, Quintessence for double quintet and percussion, 1985, Chroma concerto for multiple keyboards, percussion and chamber orch., 1985, Winging It for chamber orchestra, 1986, Elegy for Astronauts, for orchestra, 1986, What's Left for piano, 1987, Gemini for 2 guitars, 1988, Intersections II: Borobudur, Under Capricorn, 1989, Voices from the Gallery, 1990, Cinnabar for viola and piano, 1991, Seasons Fantastic for chorus and harp, 1992, Cinnabar Concerto for Viola and Chamber Orchestra, 1993, Night Winds Quintet # 2 for woodwinds, 1993, Double Concerto for Two Violins and Orchestra, 1995, Prisms and Reflections (3rd Piano Sonata), 1996, Millenium Fanfare for Symph. Orch., 2000, Millenium Dances for Symph. Orch., 2001, FIESTA! for Symph. Orch., 2002, I Am the Wind for voice and chamber ensemble, 2002; recs. include Fragments from Sappho, 1969; Duo for cello and piano, 1974, Childs Play for bassoon and piano, 1974, The Tracker, 1989, Brancusi's Brass Beds, 1984, concert suite from Western Orpheus, 1987, Sonata for Piano Fortified, 1987, Moiré, 1987, 3 Songs for Clarinet and Piano, 1987, Concerto #2 for Chamber Orchestra, 1990, Prisms and Reflections, 1999, Cinnabar, 1999, Sonata for Piano Fortified, 1999, Night Winds, 1999, Borobudur, 1999, Cello Concerto, 2000, Cinnabar Concerto, 2000, Chroma Concerto, 2000, Millenium Dances, 2001; commd. by Chgo. Symphony, Joffrey Ballet, San Diego Symphony, numerous others; author: (with Susan L. Ward-Steinman) Comparative Anthology of Musical Forms, 2 vols, 1976, Toward a Comparative Structural Theory of the Arts, 1989. Recipient Joseph H. Bearns prize in Music Columbia U., 1961, SAI Am. Music award, 1962, Dohnanyi award Fla. State U., 1965, ann. BMI awards, 1970—, Broadcast Music prize, 1954, 55, 60, 61; named Outstanding Prof., Calif. State Univs. and Colls., 1968, Outstanding Alumnus of Yr., Fla. State U., 1976; Fulbright sr. scholar La Trobe U. and Victorian Coll. Arts, Victorian Arts Ctr., Melbourne, Australia, 1989-90. Mem. Coll. Music Soc. (nat. bd. for composition 1991-93), Broadcast Music, Inc., Soc. of Composers, inc., Nat. Assn. of Composers U.S.A., Golden State Flying Club. Presbyterian. Office: San Diego State U Dept Music San Diego CA 92182 E-mail: dwardste@mail.sdsu.edu.

WARE, ALBERTA, minister, educator; b. Chgo., Mar. 23, 1943; d. Lucille and Lamar, Jr. Coleman(Stepfather); children: Paula Marie West. BS, San Diego State, 1966. Prin. Cabrini-Green Alternative H.S., Chicago, Ill., 1973—77; min., tchr., outreach min., dir. of youth dept. (full & part-time) Christ Universal Temple, 1982—93; program coord., instr. & student affairs asst. City Colleges of Chgo. - Olive/Harvey Coll., 1988—98; asst. pastor South Side Ctr. of Christianity, 1995—97, pastor, 1997—2001; dir. ch. & cmty. moblzn./tng. The Balm In Gilead, N.Y., NY, 1999—. Program dir./ctr. assoc. Nat. Coll. Edn. Ctr. Prog. Devel. in Equal Edn. Opportunity, Evanston, Ill., 1978—81. Mem.: The Coun. Religious AIDS Networks, Nat. HIV Vaccine Comm. Steering Group. Avocations: travel, reading, dancing, art, sewing. Office: The Balm In Gilead 130 West 42nd Street New York NY 10036 Personal E-mail: alware@balmingilead.org.*

WARE, BENNIE, university administrator; b. Ponca City, Okla., Sept. 21, 1946; s. Clyde Elmer and Lois Aliene (Smith) W.; m. Sheridan Lee Welch, May 28, 1967 (div. 1976); 1 child, Winston Arthur; m. Claudia Borman, Dec. 21, 1979 (div. 1998); children: Jeffrey Bright, Amelia Marie; m. Eleanor Gallagher, Mar. 7, 1998. BS in Chemistry, Okla. State U., 1968; PhD in Biophys. Chemistry, U. Ill., 1972. Asst. prof. chemistry Harvard U., Cambridge, Mass., 1972-75, assoc. prof., 1975-79; prof., chmn. dept. chemistry Syracuse U., 1979-84, Kenan prof. sci., 1984-91, v.p. rsch., 1989-92, v.p. rsch., computing, 1992—. Contbr. articles to profl. jours. Grantee NIH, 1972, 74, 77, 80, 83, 86, 89, NIH, 1972, 74, 76, 77, 79, 81, 84, 86; Alfred P. Sloan fellow, 1976-80. Fellow AAAS; mem. Phi Beta Kappa, Phi Kappa Phi. Achievements include invention of electrophoretic light scattering; first to combine laser light scattering and fluorescence photobleaching recovery to distinguish mutual and tracer diffusion; first to apply laser Doppler velocimetry to protoplasmic streaming. Home: 333 Berkeley Dr Syracuse NY 13210-3041 Office: Syracuse Univ 3-014D Ctr Sci And Tech Syracuse NY 13244-0001 E-mail: bware@syr.edu.

WARE, BRENDAN JOHN, retired electrical engineer and utility executive; b. Dublin, Ireland, Aug. 27, 1932; came to U.S., 1959, naturalized, 1967; s. Michael and Rose Anna (Ryan) W.; m. Jane Mills Orth, Oct. 7, 1961; children— Michael, Henry, Frieda B.E. with honors, Nat. U. Ireland, Dublin, 1954; MSE.E., Newark Coll. Engring., 1967. Various engring. positions Am. Elec. Power Service Corp., N.Y.C., 1960-76, mgr. elec. research and tech. svcs. Columbus, Ohio, 1976-96. Contbr. articles to profl. jours. Fellow IEEE; mem. Conf. Internat. de Grand Reseau Roman Catholic. Home: 2478 Bryden Rd Columbus OH 43209-2132 E-mail: bware@columbus.rr.com.

WARE, D. CLIFTON, singer, educator; b. Newton, Miss., Mar. 15, 1937; s. Durward Clifton and Emma Edna (Blount) W.; m. Elizabeth Jean Oldham, June 20, 1958; children: Jon Clifton, David Michael, Stephen Alan. BA, Millsaps Coll., 1959; MusM, U. So. Miss., 1962; MusD, Northwestern U., 1970. Voice instr. U. So. Miss., Hattiesburg, 1964-69; prof. voice and pedagogy U. Minn., Mpls., 1970—, chmn. Roy A. Schuessler Vocal Arts Ctr., 1970—. Clinician, cons., adjudicator. Author: (book, song collection and video) Voice Adventures, 1988, (text, song collection, audio cassette, CD) Adventures in Singing, 1995, 2d edit., 1998, Basics of Vocal Pedagogy, 1998; made recs. St. Nicolas, 1977, Paul Bunyan, 1988; tenor soloist opera, oratorio, recitals. Mem. Nat. Assn. Tchrs. Singing (pres. Minn. chpt. 1972-73, 81-82, found.d. 1995—), Nat. Opera Assn. (pres. 1978-79), Music Tchrs. Nat. Assn., Pi Kappa Lambda, Phi Kappa Delta, Phi Mu Alpha Sinfonia, Pi Kappa Alha. Avocations: travel, hiking, reading. Home: 1923 3d St NW New Brighton MN 55112-7254 Office: U Minn Sch Music 100 Ferguson Minneapolis MN 55455 E-mail: warex001@tc.umn.edu.

WARE, DAVID JOSEPH, financial consultant; b. Oberlin, Ohio, Dec. 1, 1928; s. Elmer Edwin and Jessie VanStone (Potter) W.; m. Diane Sue Adams, Sept. 12, 1958 (dec. July 1980); m. Mary Ann Spadafora, Aug. 15, 1981; children: Stacey Whitman, Joel Potter. BA, DePauw U., 1950; postgrad., Miami U., 1950—51, postgrad., 1954—55. CFP. Grain trader Glidden Co., Chgo., 1955-57; dept. mgr. Merrill Lynch, San Francisco, 1958-59; br. and regional mgmt. Dean Witter Reynolds, 1969-92; prin. Experts Co., Mill Valley, Calif., 1992—. Panelist, guest lectr. U. Calif., Berkeley, 1970-71; instr. Golden Gate U., San Francisco, 1987-89; adj. prof. Coll. Fin. Planning, Denver, 1986-87. Counselor Jr. Achievement, San Francisco, 1963; bd. dirs. Jr. C. of C., Mill Valley, 1964, Joint Powers Authority, Marin County, Calif., 1992-96, Marin County Local Agy. Formation Commn., 1995-2000, chmn., 1998-99; com. chmn. San Francisco C. of C., 1975-78; v.p. Marin County Spl. Dists. Assn., 1995; bd. chmn. Strawberry Dist., Marin County, 1996; mem. exec. bd. Calif. Local Agy. Formation Commn., 1998—2000. Recipient Achievement award Chgo. Bd. of Trade, 1956. Mem. Nat. Assn. SEC Dealers (panelist), Assn. Cert. Fin. Planners, Nat. Futures Assn. (panelist), N.Y. Stock Exch. (panelist, disciplinary com. 1975-92), Olympic Club (chmn. house com. 1987), Phi Beta Kappa, Alpha Delta Sigma. Republican. Avocations: tennis, handball, sailing, bridge, reading. Home and Office: 248 E Strawberry Dr Mill Valley CA 94941-2507

WARE, GEORGE HENRY, botanist; b. Avery, Okla., Apr. 27, 1924; s. Charles and Mildred (Eshelman) W.; m. June Marie Gleason, Dec. 21, 1955; children: David, Daniel, Patrick, John. BS, U. Okla., 1945, MS, 1948; PhD, U. Wis., 1955. Asst. prof. Northwestern State U. of La., Natchitoches, 1948-56, assoc. prof., 1956-62, prof., 1962-67; dir. Conservation Sect., No. La. Supplementary Edn. Ctr., 1967-68; dendrologist Morton Arboretum, Lisle, Ill., 1968-92; adminstr. Urban Vegetation Lab., 1986-92, rsch. fellow in dendrology, 1992-94, dendrologist emeritus, rsch. assoc., 1995—. Vis. prof. U. Okla., Norman, summers, 1957, 61, 63, 64; adj. prof. Western Ill. U., 1972-85; mem. extension faculty George Williams Coll., Downers Grove, Ill., 1969-76, Nat. Coll. Edn., Evanston, Ill., 1972-76. Trustee nomination caucus Coll. of DuPage, Glen Ellyn, Ill., 1974-78; bd. dirs. Kane-DuPage Soil and Water Conservation Dist., 1969-81, DuPage Environ. Commn., 1992—, Openlands Project, 1996—; pres. La. Acad. Scis., 1966-67; dir. La. State Sci. Fair, 1966. With USN, 1942-46. Recipient Gold Seal award, Nat. Coun. State Garden Clubs, 1991, Am. Forests Urban Forestry Rsch. medal, 1994, Lifetime Svc. award, Nat. Urban and Cmty. Forestry Adv. Coun., 1995, Hutchinson medal, Chgo. Botanic Garden, 1997, Norman J. Colman award, Am. Nursery and Landscape Assn., 1998, award of merit, Am. Assn. Botanic Gardens and Arboreta, 2000, Liberty Hyde Bailey award, Am. Horticultural Soc., 2002. Mem.: Am. Forests, Nature Conservancy, Ill. Arborist Assn. (pres. 1987—88), Am. Assn. Bot. Gardens and Arboreta, Internat. Soc. Arboriculture (Pres. Commendation award 2000), Southwestern Assn. Naturalists (treas. 1963—69). Home: 573 59th St Lisle IL 60532-3102 Office: Morton Arboretum Lisle IL 60532-1293 E-mail: gware@mortonarb.org.

WARE, JAMES LATANÉ, plastic surgeon; b. Richmond, Va., Mar. 31, 1934; s. Harry Hudnall Jr. and Mary Warren (Williams) W.; m. Betsy Schaeffer Jones, June 7, 1958; children: James Latané Jr., Elizabeth Schaeffer. BA, U. Va., 1955; MD, Med. Coll. Va., 1959. Surg. intern Duke Hosp., Durham, N.C., 1959-60, jr. asst. resident in surgery, 1960-61; asst. resident, resident in surgery Grady Hosp., 1961-64; asst. resident, resident plastic surgery Duke Hosp., 1964-67; plastic surgeon USN, Bethesda, Md., 1967-69, Drs. Smith and Ware, Richmond, 1969-77, Plastic Surg. Ctr. Richmond, Va., 1977-99; retired. Clin. prof. surgery Va. Commonwealth U. Comdr. USNR, 1967-69. Fellow ACS; mem. AMA, Am. Soc. Plastic and Reconstructive Surgeons, Southeastern Soc. Plastic and Reconstructive Surgeons, Va. Soc. Plastic and Reconstructive Surgeons (pres.), Am. Soc. Aesthetic Plastic Surgery, Med. Soc. Va., Richmond Acad. Medicine (pres.).

WARE, JENNIFER PEYTON, communications professional; b. White Plains, N.Y., Dec. 15, 1955; d. John Peyton and Mary Page (Blanchard) W.; m. Stephen Ellis, May 30, 1992. BA in English, Ohio Wesleyan U., 1977; MS in Journalism, Boston U., 1980. Supr. Times Mirror Books, N.Y.C., 1978-79; copywriter Addison-Wesley Pub. Co., Reading, Mass., 1980-83; account exec., copywriter Clarke, Goward, Fitts Advt., Boston, 1983-84; communications mgr. Cahners Pub. Co., Newton, 1984-88; dir. mktg. and communications Act III Pub. Co., N.Y.C., 1988-90; promotion dir. Daily & Weekly Variety/Cahners Pub. Co., 1990-93; corp. promotion dir. Cowles Bus. Media, Stamford, Conn., 1993—94; mgr. mktg. & promotion Cruising World and Sailing World/N.Y. Times Co. Mag. Group, N.Y.C., 1995—96; dir. mktg. and promotion Golf Digest/The N.Y. Times Co. Mag. Group, 1996—2000; dir. mktg. Reed Exhbns., 2000—. Freelance copywriter Houghton Mifflin Co., Boston, 1983-84. Thomas Fleming Day scholar Boston U., Nat. Marine Mfgs. Assn., 1980. Democrat. Presbyterian. Avocations: sailing, skiing, platform tennis. Home: 7 Dancing Bear Rd Norwalk CT 06853-1125 Office: Reed Exhbns 383 Main Ave Norwalk CT 06851

WARE, J(OE) ANTHONY, cardiologist; b. Topeka, Dec. 12, 1952; s. Joe F. and Jane C. (Casper) Ware; children: Gabriel, Rachel, Emily. BS summa cum laude, Washburn U., 1974; MD, Kans. U., 1977. Diplomate Am. Bd. Internal Medicine, Am. Bd. Cardiovasc. Disease. Intern, resident Baylor Coll. Medicine, Houston, 1977-81, chief resident, 1981, clin. fellow in cardiovasc. disease, 1981-84; rsch. fellow Beth Israel Hosp., Med. Sch. Harvard U., Boston, 1984-86, assoc. prof. medicine, 1986-97; Sidney L. & Miriam K. Olson prof. cardiology Albert Einstein Coll. Medicine and Montefiore Med. Ctr., N.Y.C., 1997-2001, chief cardiovasc. divsn., 1997-2001; v.p. cardiovasc. rsch. and clin. investigation Eli Lilly and Co., Indpls., 2001—. Dir. CCU Beth Israel Hosp., Med. Sch. Harvard U., 1992—93, dir. vascular biol. unit, 1992—97. Author, editor: book Angiogenesis in Cardiovascular Disease, 1999; contbr. articles to profl. jours. Fellow: Am. Coll. Cardiology; mem.: Molecular Medicine Soc., Assn. Profs. Cariology, Assn. Univ. Cardiologists, Am. Soc. Clin. Investigation, Am. Heart Assn., Am. Soc. Cell Biology, Am. Soc. Hematology, Assn. Am. Physicians, Interurban Clin. Club. Office: Eli Lilly Corp Ctr DC 0520 Indianapolis IN 46285 E-mail: jaware@lilly.com.

WARE, JOHN DAVID, valve and hydrant company executive; b. Beaumont, Tex., Feb. 2, 1947; s. Clarence David Ware and Lois Pearl (Coffey) Hardy; m. Dorothy Ann Jones, Mar. 27, 1986. Cert. in mgmt., James Madison U. Announcer Stas. KAYC and KAYD-FM, Beaumont, 1966-71, 1971-77; asst. supr. Am. Valve & Hydrant, Beaumont. Mem. Am. Soc. for Quality Control (chmn. SE Tex. 1989-90), Nat. Mgmt. Assn., Inst. Cert. Profl. Mgrs. (cert. mgr.). Baptist. Avocations: coin collecting, oil painting. Home: PO Box 1390 Mauriceville TX 77626-1390 Office: Am Valve & Hydrant 3350 Hollywood St Beaumont TX 77701-3820

WARE, RICHARD ANDERSON, foundation executive; b. N.Y.C., Nov. 7, 1919; s. John Sayers and Mabelle (Anderson) W.; m. Lucille Henney, Mar. 20, 1942 (div. 1972); children: Alexander W., Janet M., Bradley J., Patricia E.; m. Beverly G. Mytinger, Dec. 22, 1972. BA, Lehigh U., 1941; M in Pub. Adminstrn., Wayne State U., 1943; D in Social Sci. (honoris causa), Francisco Marroquin U., Guatemala, 1988. Research asst. Detroit Bur. Govt. Research, 1941-42; personnel technician Lend-Lease Adminstrn., Washington, 1942-43; research asso. to asst. dir. Citizens Research Council, Detroit, 1946-56; sec. Earhart and Relm Founds., Ann Arbor, Mich., 1951-70, trustee, pres., 1970-84, trustee, pres. emeritus, 1985—. Prin. dep. asst. sec. def. for internat. security affairs, Washington, 1969-70; cons. Office Asst. Sec. Def., 1970-73; dir. Citizens Trust Co., 1970-87. Vice pres. Ann Arbor United Fund and Community Svcs., 1968, pres., 1969; asst. dir. Mich. Joint Legis. Com. on State Reorgn., 1950-52; sec. Gov.'s Com. to Study Prisons, 1952-53; com. to chmn. Ann Arbor City Planning Commn., 1958-67; mem. Detroit Com. on Fgn. Rels., 1971-87; mem. coun. Woodrow Wilson Internat. Center for Scholars, 1977-85; vis. com. div. social scis. U. Chgo., 1977-85; mem. adv. com. The Citadel, 1977-85; mem. adv. coun. internat. studies program Fletcher Sch., Tufts U., 1979-85; trustee Greenhills Sch., 1973-80, Ann Arbor Area Found., 1977-83, Inst. Fgn. Policy Analysis, 1985—, Inst. Polit. Economy, 1985—, Ctr. for Study Social and Polit. Change Smith Coll., 1988—, Pequawket Found., 1989—, Intercollegiate Studies Inst., 1996—; polit. analyst Republican Nat. Com., Washington, 1964; bd. dirs. The Liberty Fund, Inc., Indpls., 1980—, Bd. Fgn. Scholarships, 1984-90, chmn., 1987-89. With USAAF, 1943-46. Recipient Civilian Meritorious Service medal Dept. Def., 1970; Paul Harris fellow Rotary, 1997. Fellow Mont Pelerin Soc.; mem. Govtl. Research Assoc. (trustee, v.p. 1955-56), Am. Polit. Sci. Assn., Ann Arbor Club, North Conway Country Club, Cosmos Club (Washington), Phi Beta Kappa, Phi Alpha Theta Congregationalist. Home: PO Box 310 Intervale NH 03845-0310 Office: 2200 Green Rd Ste H Ann Arbor MI 48105-1569

WARE, THADDEUS VAN, government official; b. High Point, N.C., Mar. 31, 1935; s. Elsec and Irene (Myers) W.; m. Doretha Ardella Lee, June 18, 1960; children— Kimberly Melissa, Chrystal Lynn. BA cum laude, Va. Union U., 1957; JD, Howard U., 1960. Bar: Va. bar 1961, D.C. bar 1970, U.S. Supreme Ct. bar 1970. Gen. atty. Office of Solicitor, Dept. Labor, 1961-66; trial counsel Chief Counsel's Office, Fed. Hwy. Adminstrn., 1966-69; staff asst. to Pres. Richard M. Nixon, 1969-70; chief adminstrv. judge, chmn. Bd. Contract Appeals, Dept. Transp., 1987—. Served with AUS, 1960-61. Mem. Va., D.C., U.S. Supreme Ct., Fed. Bar Assns., Urban League, NAACP, Bd. Contract Appeals Judges Assn. (pres. 1988-89), Alpha Phi Alpha, Sigma Delta Tau, Alpha Kappa Mu Home: 2213 Parallel Ln Silver Spring MD 20904-5446 Office: 400 7th St SW Washington DC 20590-0001

WARE, THOMAS EARLE, building consultant; b. Cleve., Apr. 13, 1931; s. Orval Bertele and Dorothy Lillian (Brammar) W.; m. Ann Sanborn Gilkey, Dec. 21, 1955 (div. Dec. 1960); 1 child, Thomas Earle Jr.; m. Gillian May Arnold, June 8, 1968 (div. Dec. 1983); 1 child, Elizabeth; m. Mary Erin Chandler, Apr. 19, 1994. BArch, Cornell U., 1955. Assoc. ptnr. Kelly and Kress and Assocs., Architects and Planners, Cleve., 1955-59; project architect J. Gordon Lorimer, F.A.I.A., N.Y.C., 1959; gen. mgr., ptnr. Project Design, Inc., Cleve., 1960-64; project architect, mgr. Cleve. dist. and hdqrs. The Austin Co., 1961-68; project architect, mgr., asst. and acting chief bldg. systems sect., bldg. rsch. divsn. Inst. Applied Tech., Nat. Bur. Standards U.S. Dept. Commerce, Washington, 1968-71, sr. program specialist, Office of the Sec., Office of Asst. Sec. for Sci. and Tech., Office of Dep. Asst. Sec. for Environ. Affairs, 1971-72; with Bldg. Cons., Reston, Va., 1972-73; v.p., dir. Bldg. Tech., Inc., Silver Spring, Md., 1973-99, TCSB, Inc., Silver Spring, Tehran and Shiraz, Iran, 1974-82; with Ware Devel. Cons., Alexandria, 2000—. Instr. continuing engring. edn. program, Sch. Engring. and Applied Sci., George Washington U., 1969-71; lectr. dept. architecture The Cath. U. Am., 1969-71; lectr., discussion leader U. Wis.-Ext., 1980-83; presenter in field. Contbr. articles to profl. jours. Named Architect of Yr., D.C. Coun. Engring. and Archtl. Socs., 1971; recipient Sci. and Tech. fellowship U.S. Dept. Commerce, 1971. Home: 11478 Links Dr Reston VA 20190-4814 Office: Ware Devel Cons 220 S Alfred St Alexandria VA 22314 E-mail: wdcthomasware@aol.com.

WARE, WILLIAM LEVI, physical education educator, researcher; b. Greenwood, Miss., May 15, 1934; s. Leslie and Catherine (Bowden) W.; m. Lottie Herger, Apr. 26, 1958; children: Felicia Rogene, Trevor Lesleo, Melvinia Simone. BS, Mississippi Valley State U., 1957; MA, Calif. State U., L.A., 1969; PhD, U. So. Calif., 1978. Tchr., coach Greenwood Pub. Schs., 1957-63, Bellflower (Calif.) Unified Sch. Dist., 1963-72; teaching asst. U. So. Calif., L.A., 1972-73; asst. prof. Calif. State U., Northridge, 1973-79; assoc. prof. Miss. State U., Starkville, 1979-90; prof. phys. edn., chmn. dept. Mississippi Valley State U., Itta Bena, 1990—, asst. to pres., 1995-98, cmty. outreach specialist, exec. dir. svc. learning, 1998—. Presenter in field; chmn. Delta Algebra Project Planning & Coordinating Group, 1991-93. Advisor Affirmative Action Adv. Coun., Whittier, Calif., 1977-78; bd. dirs. United Way, Starkville, 1983-86. Recipient Outstanding Svc. award Kiwanis Internat., 1985, Outstanding Educator award Greenwood Cultural Club, 1986, Presdl. citation Nat. Assn. for Equal Opportunity in Higher Edn., 1989; Inducted into Southwestern Athletic Conf. Hall of Fame, 1993; Faculty fellow Found. for Mid-South, 1994. Mem. Phi Delta Kappa (svc. award 1989), Greenwood/Leflore C. of C. (chmn. Leadership Tomorrow 1992-93). Avocations: racquetball, jogging. Office: Miss Valley State U PO Box 620 Itta Bena MS 38941-0620

WARE, WILLIS HOWARD, computer scientist; b. Atlantic City, Aug. 31, 1920; s. Willis and Ethel (Rosswork) W.; m. Floy Hoffer, Oct. 10, 1943; children— Deborah Susanne Ware Pinson, David Willis, Alison Floy Ware Manoli. BSEE, U. Pa., 1941; MSEE, MIT, 1942; PhD in Elec. Engring, Princeton U., 1951. Research engr. Hazeltine Electronics Corp., Little Neck, N.Y., 1942-46; mem. research staff Inst. Advanced Study, Princeton, N.J., 1946-51, North Am. Aviation, Downey, Calif., 1951-52; mem. corp. research staff, research engr. Rand Corp., Santa Monica, 1952—. Adj. prof. UCLA Extension Service, 1955-68; first chmn. Am. Fedn. Info. Processing Socs., 1961, 62; chmn. HEW sec.'s Adv. Com. on Automated Personal Data Systems, 1971-73; mem. Privacy Protection Study Commn., 1975-77, vice chmn., 1975-77; mem. numerous other adv. groups, spl. coms. for fed. govt., 1959— Author: Digital Computer Technology and Design, vols. I and II, 1963. Recipient Computers Scis. Man of Yr. award Data Processing Mgmt. Assn., 1975, Exceptional Civilian Svc. medal USAF, 1979, Disting. Svc. award Am. Fedn. Info. Processing Socs., 1986, Nat. Computer Sys. Security award Nat. Computer Sys. Lab./Nat. Computer Security Ctr., 1989, Computer Pioneer award IEEE Computer Soc., 1993, Pioneer award Electronic Frontier Found., 1995, Kristain Beckman award Internat. Fedn. Info. Processing, 1999; named one of Fed. 100 of 1994, Fed. Computer Week. Fellow IEEE (Centennial medal 1984), AAAS, Assn. for Computing Machinery; mem. NAE, AIAA, Sigma Xi, Eta Kappa Nu, Pi Mu Epsilon, Tau Beta Pi. Office: 1700 Main St Santa Monica CA 90401-3208 E-mail: willis@rand.org.

WAREHAM, RAYMOND NOBLE, investment professional; b. Rochester, N.Y., Nov. 20, 1948; s. Simon Harold and Barbara (Snell) W.; m. Cornelia Lee Clifford, June 28, 1975; children: Ellinor Park, Laura Stewart, Cornelia Ashley. BS in Indsl. Engring., Northwestern U., 1970; MBA, Harvard U., 1975. With J.P. Morgan & Co., N.Y., 1975-80, head-corp. fin., 1980-85; exec. dir. J.P. Morgan Securities Ltd., London, 1986-87; mngr. dir., head banking industry group J.P. Morgan & Co., N.Y., 1988-92; mng. dir. corp. fin. dept. J.P. Morgan Securities, N.Y.C., 1992-98; sr. portfolio mgr., mng. dir. Sanford C. Bernstein Alliance Capital, 1999—. Trustee Am. Sch., Tokyo, 1982-85; elder Brick Presbyn. Ch., N.Y.C., 1989-92; bd. dirs. Brick Ch. Day Sch., 1989-92, Juvenile Diabetes Found., 1997-98; pres. bd. trustees Spence Sch., N.Y.C., 1995—. Lt. Supply Corps, USN, 1970-73. Mem. DERU (Northwestern hon.), Union Club (N.Y.), Duxbury (Mass.) Yacht Club, Century Club (Harvard Bus. hon.). Republican. Avocations: athletics, Japanese antique furniture, secondary school education. Home: 1148 5th Ave New York NY 10128-0807 Office: Alliance Capital/Sanford C Bernstein 17th Fl 1345 Ave of Americas New York NY 10105-0096

WAREN, ALLAN DAVID, computer information scientist, educator; b. Toronto, Ontario, Can., Nov. 23, 1935; s. David and Sirkka Siiri (Kahara) W.; m. Marion Veronica Halligan, Jan. 25, 1962; children: David, Melissa, Melanie, Jessica. BASc, U. Toronto, 1960; MSEE, Case Inst. Tech., Cleve., 1962, PhD, 1964. Profl. engr., Ontario. Staff engr. Clevite Electronics Research Divsn., Cleve., 1963-66; assoc. prof. Cleve. State U., 1966-69, prof., 1971-93, prof. emeritus, 1993—, interim dean Coll. Bus. Adminstrn., 1990-91, interim assoc. dean, 1997-98, interim dean, 1998-2000; chair of info. tech. Kapalan Coll., 2002—. Pres. Com-Share Ltd., Toronto, 1969-71; cons. Gould, Cleve., 1974-84, Texaco, Houston, 1987-88, PPG Industries, Cleve., 1988-92, LTV Steel, 1993-96, Transat Corp., Cleve., 1996-99; v.p. Optimal Methods, Austin, Tex., 1993—; expert witness Rose Law Firm, 1993-95, Calfee, Halter & Griswold, 1999-2000, others. Co-author: Modeling and Optimization with

Gino, 1986, Optimization with the IBM Optimization Subroutine Library, 1994, Handbook for IBM OSL, 1994; co-developer computer software GRG2, 1973, What-If-Solver, 1988, Excel Solver, 1991, Borland Quatro Pro Solver, 1991, Lotus1-2-3 Solver, 1997; co-author case study, 1985 (runner-up best case 1985); contbr. articles to profl. jours., chpts. to many books. Recipient Disting. Faculty Rsch. award, Cleve. State U., 1979, First Annual Faculty Rsch. award, Nance Coll. of Bus. Adminstrn., 1993, grant in Ohio Rsch. Challenge Program, State of Ohio, 1988, various other rsch. grants, 1973-84. Mem. IEEE (sr.), Assn. Computing Machinery, Ops. Rsch. Soc. Am., Math. Programming Soc. Avocations: Oriental objects of art, philately. Home: 9155 Woods Way Dr Willoughby OH 44094-9370 Office: Cleve State U E 24th and Euclid Ave Cleveland OH 44115

WAREN, STANLEY ARNOLD, university administrator, theatre and arts center administrator, director; b. N.Y.C., Mar. 22, 1919; s. Maurice and Minnie (Rosen) W.; m. Florence Rigal, Nov. 21, 1949; 1 child, Mark BSS., CCNY, 1938; MA, Columbia U., 1939, PhD, 1953. Exec. producer, dir. theatre, U.S. and abroad, 1953-70; prof., chmn. dept. speech and theatre CCNY, 1967-72; prof., exec. officer Ph.D. program theatre CUNY, 1972-81, v.p., provost, dep. pres. Grad. Sch., 1981-84; dir. Ctr. for Advanced Study in Theatre Arts, N.Y.C., 1979-82, 84-86. Reviewer NEH, 1978-91; advisor humanities com. Bklyn. Acad. Music, N.Y.C., 1980-81; spl. edn. cons. Double Image Theatre, N.Y.C., 1982-90; mem. adv. council Roundabout Theatre, N.Y.C., 1985-93; Fulbright-Hayes vis. prof. Nat. Taiwan U., 1986-87; vis. prof. Shanghai Drama Inst., 1988; USIS grant, lectr., Hong Kong, 1988, Ctr. for Living and Learning, Marymount Manhattan, 1998-2001, New Sch. U., 2000-2002. Dir. musical The Chess King (Taiwan) 1987, Old B Hanging on the Wall (Shanghai), 1988, Judas, Mexico (N.Y.), 1989. Bd. dirs. Women's Inter. Art Ctr., N.Y.C., 1978-82; mem. grants panel N.Y.C. Dept. Cultural Affairs, 1979; bd. dirs. Frank Silvera Workshops for Writers, N.Y.C., 1979-81. Served to capt. USAF, 1942-46 Grantee Herman Goldman Found., 1980-82, NEH, 1980-81, N.Y. Coun. Humanities, USIA/Arts Am., Singapore, 1990. Mem. AAUP, Assn. for Theatre in Higher Edn., Soc. Stage Dirs. and Choreographers, Profl. Staff Congress CUNY, The Drama League (mem. awards nominating com. 1997—). Clubs: The Century Assn. (resident 1984—). Democrat. Avocations: arts; tennis; swimming. Home: 465 W End Ave #110 New York NY 10024-4926 Office: Theatre PhD Program Grad Sch 365 5th Ave New York NY 10016-4309

WARFIELD, GERALD ALEXANDER, composer, writer; b. Ft. Worth, Feb. 23, 1940; s. George Alexander and Geraldine (Spencer) W. Student, Tex. Christian U., 1958-61; BA, North Tex. State U., 1963, M.Mus., 1965; M.F.A., Princeton U., 1967; postgrad., Tanglewood, summers 1963-64. Instr. Princeton, 1968-71; asso. dir. Index of New Mus. Notation, N.Y.C., 1971-75. Lectr. contemporary music notation. Mem. conf. com. Internat. Conf. on New Mus. Notation, Belgium, 1974; chmn. program com. 2d Nat. Conf. Music Theory, 1977 Author: A Beginner's Manual of Music 4B, 1967, Layer Analysis: a Primer of Elementary Tonal Structures, 1976, Writings on Contemporary Music Notations, 1977, How to Write Music Manuscript, 1977, (with others) Layer Dictation, 1978, The Investor's Guide to Stock Quotations, 1982, How To Buy Foreign Stocks and Bonds, 1984, How to Read the Financial News, 1986; (with others) Export-Import Financing, 1986; No Nonsense Guides to the Stock Market, Mutual Funds, Tax-Free Bonds, 1991, Managing Your Stock Portfolio, Money Market Funds, 1993, (with others) Feng Shui Revealed, 1997; composer: Variations and Metamorphoses, 1973 (1st prize Ariz. Cello Soc.); filmstrip Introduction to Musical Notation, 1976; Fantasy Quintet, 1978 (2d prize New Music for Young Ensembles); contbr.: Grove's Dictionary of Music and Musicians, 1976; editor: Longman Music Series, 1976-85; contbr. articles to profl. jours. Mem. Soc. Composers, Inc. (chmn. exec. com. 1972-74, conf. chmn. 9th Ann. Conf., 1974, founding editor Jour. of Music Scores, gen. mgr. 1977—), Am. Composers Alliance (treas. 1979-96), Coll. Music Soc. (coun., conf. chmn. 1981), Broadcast Music Inc. E-mail: gerald. Home: 410 SW 4th Ave # 4 Mineral Wells TX 76067-5840

WARFIELD, JOHN NELSON, retired engineering educator, consultant; b. Sullivan, Mo., Nov. 21, 1925; s. John Daniel and Flora Alice (Land) W.; m. Rosamond Arline Howe, Feb. 2, 1948; children: Daniel, Nancy, Thomas. BA, BSEE, U. Mo., 1948, MSEE, 1949; PhD, Purdue U., 1952. Assoc. prof. Pa. State U., University Park, 1949-55, U. Ill.-Urbana, 1955-57, Purdue U., West Lafayette, Ind., 1957-58; prof. elec. engring U. Kans., Lawrence, 1958-66; sr. research leader Battelle Meml. Inst., Columbus, Ohio, 1966-74; prof. elec. engring U. Va., Charlottesville, 1974-83; sr. mgr. Burroughs Corp., 1983-84; dir. Inst. for Info. Tech. George Mason U., Fairfax, Va., 1984-87, dir. Inst. for Advanced Study in Integrative Scis., 1987-98; prof. emeritus, 2000—. Cons. IBM, Armonk, N.Y., 1979-82, Saudi Arabian Nat. Ctr. Sci. and Tech., Riyadh, 1978-82, Ghana Coun. for Sci. and Indsl. Rsch., Accra, 1989—, Niagara-Mohawk Power Co., 89, Ford Motor Co., 1990—, Defense Systems Mgmt. Coll., 1990—. Author: Societal Systems, 1976, A Science of Generic Design, 1990, A Handbook of Interactive Management, 1994, Understanding Complexity: Thought and Behavior, 2002; inventor interpretive structural modeling, 1973; editor: IEEE Transactions on Systems, Man, and Cybernetics, 1968-73, Systems Research, 1981-90. Recipient Excellence in Instrn. award Western Electric Co., 1966, Peace Pipe award Ams. for Indian Opportunity, 1987, Best Paper award European Conf. Cybernetics and Systems, 1988, Mayour's cert. City of Austin, 1993, Plaque of Recognition, Mex. Ministry of Social Devel., 1994, Spl. Recognition award Internat. Soc. Design and Process Sci., 1995, Laureate award George Mason U., 2002. Fellow IEEE (life, outstanding contbn. award 1977, Centennial medal 1984, Third Millennium medal 2000), Soc. for Design and Process Sci. (fellow award, 1996); mem. Internat. Soc. Panetics, Assn. for Integrative Studies. Home: 2673 Westcott Cir Palm Harbor FL 34684-1746 E-mail: jnwarfield@aol.com.

WARG, PAULINE, artist, educator; b. Detroit, Oct. 15, 1951; d. Clifford Rudolf and Marguerite Evelyn (Kaiser) W.; m. Gary Dean Snider, Apr. 14, 1990. Student, Bowling Green State U., 1969-72, diploma, 1972-75; BA summa cum laude, U. So. Maine, 1999. Cert. Spl. Needs Vocat. Instr. Maine. Owner, pres. Warg Designs Inc., Scarborough, Maine, 1975—; instr. The Jewelry Inst., Providence, 1983-87; resident instr. Lexington Arts & Crafts Ctr., Lexington, Mass., 1987; asst. mgr. cons. J.S. Ritter Jewelers Tool & Supply Co., Portland, Maine, 1991-92; instr. Maine Coll. of Art, 1992—; owner, dir. metalsmithing program Future Builders, Inc., Scarborough, Maine, 1992-2001. Lectr. Paul Revere House Mus., Boston, 1981, juror League of N.H. Craftsmen, Concord, N.H., 1985-87, stds. com. juror League of N.H. Craftsman, Concord, 1985-87, exhbn. juror Boston Mus. Sch., Boston, 1992. Contbr. articles to profl. jours. Founding mem. Portsmouth Artisans, Portsmouth, N.H., 1975-77, founding owners, treas. Sail Loft Cmty. Arts Program, Portsmouth, 1977-79. Recipient Svc. award, Maine Coll. Art, Portland, 1997, 10 Yr. Svc. award, 2001. Mem. Soc. Am. Silversmiths (artisan mem. 1992—), Maine Crafts Assn. Democratic. Avocations: bicycling, canoeing, photography, gardening, travel. Office: Warg Designs Inc Pine Point Business Park 15 Holly St Ste 210 Scarborough ME 04074-8867 E-mail: wargine@sacoriver.net.

WARGA, JACK, mathematician, educator; b. Warsaw, Poland, Dec. 5, 1922; came to U.S., 1943, naturalized, 1944; s. Herman and Czarna (Lichtenstein) W.; m. Faye Kleinman, Feb. 27, 1949; children— Charna Ruth, Arthur David. Student, Brussels (Belgium) U., 1939-40; BA, Carleton Coll., 1944; PhD, NYU, 1950. Assoc. mathematician Reeves Instrument Corp., N.Y.C., 1951-52; Chief engring. computing sect. Republic Aviation Corp., Farmingdale, N.Y., 1952-53; head math dept. Burroughs Corp., Pasadena, Cal., 1954-56; mgr., math dept. Avco Research and Devel., Wilmington, Mass., 1957-66; prof. math. Northeastern U., Boston, 1966-93, prof. emeritus, 1993—. Author: Optimal Control of Differential and Functional Equations, 1972, expanded Russian transl., 1977; contbr. articles to profl. jours. Served with AUS, 1944-46. Weizmann Meml. fellow, 1956-57 Fellow AAAS; mem. Am. Math. Soc., Soc. Indsl. and Applied Math. (editor Jour. on Control and Optimization 1963-89). Home: 233 Clark Rd Brookline MA 02445-5847 Office: Northeastern U Dept Math Boston MA 02115 E-mail: warga@neu.edu.

WARGO, ANDREA ANN, retired public health official, commissioned officer; b. Pottsville, Pa., Dec. 27, 1941; d. John Andrew and Anna Mary (Blischok) W.; m. Roger Fredrick Sies, Mar. 31, 1981. BS in Biology, Chestnut Hill Coll., 1972; PhD in Biology, Georgetown U., 1978. Educator, adminstr. Cath. Archdiocese Phila., 1961-74; tchg. asst. Georgetown U., Washington, 1974-78, postdoctoral fellow, 1978-80; acting br. chief FDA, Silver Spring, Md., 1980-86, acting chief gen. hosp. and personal use devices, 1986-88; assoc. adminstr. Agy. for Toxic Substances and Disease Registry, Washington, 1988-2001; ret., 2001. Mem. Surgeon Gen.'s Policy Adv. Coun., 1996—. Contbr. articles to sci. publs. Grantee NSF, 1972, 73, Kidney Found., 19790-80. Mem. Assn. Women in Sci. (treas. Washington-Balt. chpt. 1979-80), Commd. Officers Assn., Georgetown U. Alumni Assn., Toastmistress Club (pres. Bethesda chpt. 1978-79), Pub. Health Svc. (scientist profl. adv. com., exec. sec. 1984-86, vice chmn. 1986-87), Sigma Xi. Avocations: gardening, computers, financial planning, handwriting analysis. Home: 17604 N Stone Haven Dr Surprise AZ 85374

WARGOWSKY, ROBIN KAY, nurse; b. Columbus, Ohio, Apr. 30, 1954; d. Eugene Burgess Morgan and Charlotte Ann (Renner) Schall; m. Paul George Wargowsky, June 7, 1975; 1 child, Amy Nicole. BA summa cum laude, Ohio U., 1976; BS magna cum laude, U. Alaska, 1984. RN, Ohio, Fla., Ill.; cert. inpatient obs. nurse, high risk perinatal nurse. Staff nurse Providence Hosp., Anchorage, 1984, Cmty. Hosp., New Port Richey, Fla., 1985, Humana Women's Hosp., Tampa, 1985-87, Anderson Hosp., Maryville, Ill., 1988-92, Lake Mead Hosp., Las Vegas, 1993-99; patient educator Healthdyne/Matria, 1993-97. Mem. Assn. Women's Health, Obs. & Neonatal Nurses. Sigma Theta Tau, Phi Kappa Phi. Republican. Lutheran.

WARHEIT, PETER S. anesthesiologist; b. N.Y.C., Feb. 19, 1952; MD, U. Autonoma, Guadalajara, 1979. Diplomate Am. Bd. Anesthesiology. Intern SUNY, Stony Brook, 1980-81, resident in surgery, 1981-82; resident in anesthesia Mt. Sinai Med. Ctr., N.Y.C., 1982-84, mem. staff, 1984-88, Delray Med. Ctr., Delray Beach, Fla., 1989—, West Boca Med. Ctr., Boca Raton, 1989—, chief of staff, 1999—2002, chief of anesthesiology, 1996—. Mem. Am. Soc. Anesthesia, Internat. Anesthesia Rsch. Assn., Fla. Soc. Anesthesia. Fax: 561-995-8096. E-mail: docpsw@aol.com.

WARICK, LAWRENCE HERBERT, psychiatrist; b. Warsaw, Poland, May 2, 1936; came to U.S., 1949, naturalized, 1954; s. Joseph and Marsha (Beck) W.; m. Elaine Ruth Christensen, Feb. 24, 1963; children: Catherine Ann, David Mark. BS, CCNY, 1956; MD, Albert Einstein Coll. Medicine, 1960; PhD, So. Calif. Psychoanalytic Inst, 1980. Diplomate Am. Bd. Psychiatry and Neurology. Rotating intern L.A. County Gen. Hosp., 1960-61; resident neurology U. So. Calif. Sch. Medicine, L.A. County Gen. Hosp., 1961-62, resident psychiatry, 1962-65; clin. assoc. So. Calif. Psychoanalytic Inst., L.A., 1973-80, instr., 1981—; pvt. practice, 1980—; asst. clin. prof. psychiatry UCLA Sch. Medicine, 1967-97, assoc. clin. prof. psychiatry, 1997—; instr. faculty Psychoanalytic Inst. So. Calif., L.A., 1980—, 1980—. Contbr. chpts. to books and articles to profl. jours. Capt. USAF, 1962-68. Mem. Am. Psychiat. Assn., Am. Acad. Psychiatry and Law, So. Calif. Psychiatry Soc., So. Calif. Psychoanalytic Soc., Phi Beta Kappa. Avocations: swimming, music, hiking, tennis, racketball, reading. Office: 2444 Wilshire Blvd Ste 418 Santa Monica CA 90403-5811

WARING, MARY LOUISE, retired social worker; b. Pitts., Feb. 15, 1928; d. Harold R. and Edith (McCallum) W. AB, Duke U., 1949; MSS, Smith Coll., 1951; PhD, Brandeis U., 1974. Lic. clin. social worker, Tenn. Sr. supervising social worker Judge Baker Guidance Ctr., Boston, 1955-65; dir. social svc. Cambridge (Mass.) Mental Health Ctr., 1965-70; assoc. prof. Sch. Social Work Fla. State U., Tallahassee, 1974-77; prof. Grad. Sch. Social Svc. Fordham U., N.Y.C., 1977-82; cons. Dept. Human Svc., N.J., 1983-84; cons., sr. staff mem. Family Counseling Svc. Bergen County, Hackensack, 1984-86; dir. Step One Employee Assistance Program Fortwood Ctr., Inc., Chattanooga, 1986-96; part-time psychotherapist Greenleaf Svcs., 1996, pvt. practice, 1997-98; ret., 1999. Mem. ethics com. Chattanooga Rehab. Hosp., 1995. Contbr. articles to profl. jours. Mem. Citizen Amb. Program Human Resource Mgmt. Delegation to Russia, 1993; active Nat. Trust for Hist. Preservation, Hunter Mus. Am. Art, Chattanooga Symphony and Opera Assn., Friends of Hamilton County Bicentennial Libr. Recipient Career Tchr. award Nat. Inst. Alchohol and Alchohol Abuse, 1972-74; traineeship NIMH, 1949-51. Mem. NASW (charter), Acad. Cert. Social Workers, Nat. Mus. Women in Arts (charter), Smithsonian Assocs., Cmty. Svcs. Club Greater Chattanooga (pres. 1995, 96, v.p. 1994, 97, membership chair 1998—).

WARING, WILLIAM WINBURN, pediatric pulmonologist, educator; b. Savannah, Ga., July 20, 1923; s. Antonio Johnston and Sue Cole (Winburn) W.; m. Nell Pape Williams, July 19, 1952; children— William Winburn, Benjamin Joseph, Antonio Johnston, Peter Ayraud, Patrick Houstoun Grad., Hotchkiss Sch., Lakeville, Conn., 1942; student, Yale U., 1942-43; MD, Harvard U., 1947. Diplomate Am. Bd. Pediatrics (subbd. of pediatric pulmonology 1985-89). Intern Children's Hosp., Boston, 1947-48; intern, then resident Johns Hopkins Hosp., Balt., 1948-52; practice medicine specializing in pediatrics Jacksonville, Fla., 1955-57; instr. dept. pediatrics Sch. Medicine, Tulane U., New Orleans, 1957-58, asst. prof., 1958-61, assoc. prof., 1961-66, prof. emeritus, 1966—, Jane B. Aron Prof. Pediatrics, 1987-96. Dir. Pediat. Pulmonary Ctr., New Orleans, 1969-88, Cystic Fibrosis Ctr., Tulane U., New Orleans, 1963-88; chmn. profl. tng. com. Cystic Fibrosis Found., 1978-86; cons. La. State Handicapped Children's Assn., 1963-88; mem. pulmonary diseases adv. com. NIH, 1978-80. Co-author, editor: Practical Manual of Pediatrics, 1975, 2d edit., 1982; editor: Harriet Lane Handbook: A Manual for Pediatric House Officers, 1952, Hospital Pediatric Manual, 1958; contbg. author books on pediatric pulmonary disease, also articles in field; assoc. editor Am. Jour. Diseases of Children, 1989-91; mem. editl. bd. Pediatric Pulmonology, 1985-94. Served to capt. M.C., U.S. Army, 1952-54. Recipient Research Career Devel. award NIH, 1970-72 Fellow Am. Acad. Pediatrics (exec. com. 1966-71), Am. Coll. Chest Physicians; mem. Am. Pediatric Soc., Am. Thoracic Soc. (v.p. 1977). Clubs: Boston, So. Yacht, Wyvern (New Orleans). Republican. Roman Catholic. Avocations: fly fishing; running; computing. Home: 123 Walnut St Apt 905 New Orleans LA 70118-4846 Office: Tulane U Sch of Medicine Dept of Pediatrics 1430 Tulane Ave New Orleans LA 70112-2699

WARITZ, RICHARD STEFAN, toxicologist, researcher; b. Portland, Oreg., Apr. 1, 1929; s. Anton John and Theresa (Stegelmaier) W.; m. Ruth Evelyn White, June 7, 1950; children: Joyce E., Gary S., Sharon J., Carol L. BA, Reed Coll., 1951; PhD, Stanford U., 1957. Diplomate Am. Bd. Toxicology, Acad. Toxicological Scis. Sr. rsch. scientist E.I. DuPont de Nemours & Co., Wilmington, Del., 1957-64, mgr. inhalation toxicology, 1964-72, mgr. biosciences, 1972-75; sr. toxicologist Hercules Inc., 1975-80, mgr. toxicology, 1980-92; pres. BioSante Internat., Inc., 1992—. Grad. toxicology edn. adv. bd. Rutgers U., Piscataway, N.J., 1980—; life scis. adv. bd. U.S. Army, Aberdeen, Md., 1982-92; toxicology peer rev. bd. U.S. Army Ctr. for Health Promotion and Preventive Medicine, 1992—; vis. prof. toxicology Rutgers U., 1993—. Contbr. articles to profl. jours. Mem.: Am. Chem. Soc., Am. Conf. Govtl. Indsl. Hygienists, Am. Indsl. Hygiene Assn., Internat. Union Toxicol. Socs. (councillor 1983—88), Soc. Toxicology (treas. 1981-85, pres. Mid-Atlantic chpt. 1989). Roman Catholic. Avocations: golf, surf fishing. Home and Office: 2613 Turnstone Dr Wilmington DE 19808-1638 E-mail: waritz.bio@att.net.

WARKULWIZ, VICTOR PHILIP, priest, physicist, educator; b. Phila., Nov. 24, 1940; s. Victor and Emily Frances (Strudwick) Warkulwiz. BS in Electronic Physics, LaSalle Coll., 1967; PhD in Physics, Temple U., 1974; MDiv, Mt. St. Mary's Sem., 1986; MA in Theology, Holy Apostles Sem., 1990. Ordained priest Roman Cath. Ch. 91. Guest physicist Nat. Bur. Stds., Gaithersburg, Md., 1970—73; intelligence officer, phys. scientist CIA, Langley, Va., 1974—76; math., sci. tutor Magdalen Coll., Bedford, NH, 1976—79; physicist, cons. Analytic Svcs. Corp., Arlington, Va., 1981—84; local superior, tchr. Franciscan Friars of Mary Immaculate, Hartford, Conn., 1987—91; seminarian, faculty Holy Apostles Sem., Cromwell, 1990—91; missionary priest, nat. dir. Apostolate for Perpetual Eucharistic Adoration, Mt. Clemens, Mich., 1991—. Theol. reviewer Kolbe Ctr. for Study of Creation, Woodstock, Va., 2001—. Contbr. articles to profl. jours. 2d class petty officer Air Res. USN, 1962—70. Home and Office: Missionaries Blessed Sacrament 2933 Street Rd Bensalem PA 19020 E-mail: vpw@webtv.net.

WARLTIER, DAVID CHARLES, anesthesiologist, medical researcher; b. Hartford, Conn., Mar. 28, 1947; s. Benjamin Charles and Arline M. (Brown) W.; children: Candice, Charles, Kristin, Karin; m. Marilyn A Warltier, May 27, 1989. BS, Carroll Coll., Waukesha, Wis., 1969; PhD, Med. Coll. Wis., Milw., 1976, MD, 1982; DSc (hon.), Carroll Coll., 1991. Intern Med. Coll. Wis., Milw., 1985-86; resident dept. anesthesiology Med. Coll. Wis. Affiliated Hosps., 1986-88; from asst. prof. to assoc. prof. Med. Coll. Wis., 1979-90, vice-chmn. anesthesiology, 1989—, prof., 1990—, dir. med. scientist tng. program, 2000—. Staff anesthesiologist Zablocki VA Med. Ctr., Milw., 1989—; adj. prof. Marquette U., Milw., 1995—. Editor: Ventricular Function, 1995; editor Jour. Anesthesiology, 1992—, Am. Jour. Physiology, 1999—; contbr. articles to med. jours. Bd. dirs. Milw. Kickers Soccer Club, 1983-88. Am. Heart Assn. postdoctoral fellow, 1976-78; recipient grant NIH Heart & Lung, 1985—. Fellow Am. Coll. Cardiology; mem. Assn. Univ. Anesthesiologists, Am. Soc. Anesthesiologists (rsch. com. 1994-98, Excellence in Rsch. award 2001), Soc. Cardiovasc. Anesthesiologists (chmn. publs. com. 1993-97), Am. Physiol. Soc., Am. Soc. Pharmacology and Exptl. Therapeutics, Alpha Omega Alpha. Avocations: photography, painting, metal sculpture. Office: Medical College of Wis 8701 W Watertown Plank Rd Milwaukee WI 53226-4801

WARLUM, MICHAEL FRANK, training, consulting and writing company executive; b. Neillsville, Wis., Nov. 28, 1940; s. Elliot Clarence and Mida Quinlan Warlum. BS, U. Wis., 1962, MS, 1964, PhD, 1967. Asst. prof. U. Wis., Madison, 1966-69; exec.dir. Ind. Arts Commn., Indpls., 1969-72; dir. cmty. svc. Mich. Coun. for Arts, Detroit, 1974-76; devel. dir. Seattle Repertory Theatre, 1976-78; mem. faculty Shoreline Cmty. Coll., Seattle, 1978-85; sr. instr. The Boeing Co., 1986-92; instnl. assoc. Ctr. for Performance Tech., Phoenix, 1994-97; pres. Warlum Inc., Seattle, 1993—. Author: (poetry) Meridian Maiden, 1977, (novels) The Hank Bradford Series, 1980, The Keating Dynasty, 1986; co-author: The Arts in the Small Community, 1969, Business Mathematics, A Positive Approach, 1988. Nat. Endowment for Arts scholar, 1972; NDEA fellow, 1962-67. Home: 4412 50th Ave SW Seattle WA 98116-4024

WARMBROD, CATHARINE PHELPS, educational researcher, consultant; b. Lost Nation, Iowa, July 2, 1929; d. Paul Edward and Ruth Dorthea (Langhorst) Phelps; m. J. Robert Warmbrod, Jan. 30, 1965. BA, U. Iowa, 1952; MS, U. Ill., 1965, advanced cert. in edn., 1967. Head supr. student tchrs. in bus. edn. U. Ill., Urbana, 1966-67; chmn. office adminstrn. Columbus (Ohio) State Community Coll., 1970-77; rsch. specialist NCRVE Ohio State U., Columbus, 1977-88, rsch. specialist emeritus, 1988—; prin. Warmbrod Ednl. Svcs., 1988-2001. Bd. dirs. Nat. Assn. Industry/Edn. Cooperation, Buffalo, 1980-88. Author: Retraining and Upgrading Workers, 1983; contbr. to profl. publs.; editor: VocEd Insider for Tech. Edn., 1981. Bd. dirs. Ohio Women, Inc., Columbus, 1986-92, Friendship Village, Dublin, Columbus, 1990—. Mem. Am. Vocat. Assn. (policy com. 1980-83), Assn. Faculty and Profl. Women Ohio State U. (pres. 1984-85), Am. Assn. Cmty. Colls., Am. Tech. Edn. Assn., Delta Pi Epsilon. United Methodist. Office: Warmbrod Ednl Svcs 3853 Surrey Hill Pl Columbus OH 43220-4778 E-mail: warmbrod.2@osu.edu.

WARMBROD, JAMES ROBERT, agriculture educator, university administrator; b. Belvidere, Tenn., Dec. 13, 1929; s. George Victor and Anna Sophia (Zimmerman) W.; m. Catharine P. Phelps, Jan. 30, 1965. BS, U. Tenn., 1952, MS, 1954; Ed.D. (Univ. fellow), U. Ill., 1962. Instr. edn. U. Tenn., Knoxville, 1956-57; tchr. high sch. Winchester, Tenn., 1957-59; asst. prof. U. Ill., Urbana, 1961-66, assoc. prof., 1966-67; prof. agrl. edn. Ohio State U., Columbus, 1968-95; ret.; Presdl. prof. Ohio State U., Columbus, 1989, Presdl. prof. emeritus, 1995, Disting. univ. prof. emeritus, 1995—, chmn. dept., 1978-86, acting assoc. dean Coll. Agr., 1989, acting v.p. agrl. adminstrn., dean Coll. Agr., 1989-91. Vis. prof. Pa. State U., 1970, U. Minn., 1971, Iowa State U., 1974, La. State U., 1986; vis. scholar Va. Poly. Inst. and State U., 1976, Univ. Coun. Vocat. Edn., 1988-89; mem. com. on agr. in secondary schs. Nat. Acad. Scis., 1985-87 Author: Review and Synthesis of Research on the Economics of Vocational Education, 1968, The Liberalization of Vocat. Education, 1974, (with others) Methods of Teaching Agriculture, 1986, 2d edit. 1993; editor: Agrl. Edn. mag., 1968-71. Served with USAF, 1954-56. Recipient Tchg. award Gamma Sigma Delta, 1977. Fellow Am. Assn. Agrl. Edn.; mem. Am. Vocat. Assn. (v.p. 1976-79, Outstanding Svc. award 1987), Am. Ednl. Rsch. Assn., Am. Vocat. Edn. Rsch. Assn. (pres. 1976), Am. Assn. Tchr. Educators in Agr. (Disting. Svc. award 1974, Disting. lectr. 1974). Home: 3853 Surrey Hill Pl Columbus OH 43220-4778 Office: 2120 Fyffe Rd Columbus OH 43210-1010

WARMER, RICHARD CRAIG, lawyer; b. Los Angeles, Aug. 12, 1936; s. George A. and Marian L. (Paine) W.; children: Craig McEchron, Alexander Richard. AB, Occidental Coll., 1958; MA, Tufts U., 1959; LLB, NYU, 1962. Bar: Calif. 1963, D.C. 1976. Assoc. O'Melveny & Myers, LLP, Los Angeles, 1962-69, ptnr., 1970-75, mng. ptnr. Washington, 1976-92, mem. mgmt. com., 1986-92, with San Francisco, 1994—. Speaker in field. Contbr. articles to profl. jours. Trustee Law Ctr. Found. NYU, 1981-94; dir. Headland Ctr. for Arts, San Francisco Jazz Orgn. Mem. ABA, D.C. Bar, State Bar Calif., Order of Coif, Phi Beta Kappa, Cosmos Club. Office: O'Melveny & Myers LLP Embarcadero Ctr W 275 Battery St San Francisco CA 94111-3305 E-mail: rwarmer@omm.com.

WARMKA, ELIZABETH FRANCES, journalist; b. Wells, Minn., Aug. 23, 1976; BS, Marquette U., 1999. Court reporter Gloucester Co. Times, Woodbury, NJ, 1999—2001, The Express Times, Easton, Pa., 2001—. Office: The Expres-Times Fourth St Easton PA 18042

WARNE, WILLIAM ROBERT, economist; b. Washington, Nov. 30, 1937; BA, Princeton U., 1960; MA, Johns Hopkins U., 1974. Provincial advisor U.S. Mission, Vinh Binh, Vinh Long, Vietnam, 1962-64; officer in charge trade, devel. and fin. policy U.S. Mission to European Communities, Brussels, 1974-77; dep. dir. East Asian Econ. Policy, 1977-79; dir. Caribbean affairs U.S. Dept. State, Kingston, Jamaica, 1979-81, charge d'affaires, dep. chief mission Jamaica, 1981-84, dir. Latin Am. Econ. Policy Washington, 1984-86; counselor for trade, energy, social affairs and agr. U.S. Delegation OECD, Paris, 1986-88; v.p. Midwest Ctr. Exec. Coun. on Fgn. Diplomats, Indpls., 1988-89; pres. Korea Econ. Inst. Am., Washington, 1990-99; instr. Fgn. Svc. Inst., U.S. Dept. State, 2000—; prof. internat. studies Ewha Woman's U., Seoul, Korea, 2000-2001; instr. Fgn. Svc. Inst. U.S. Dept. State, Washington, 2001—. With U.S. Army, 1960-62.

WARNER, ADOLPHE JOSEPH, economist, financial analyst; b. Frankfurt, Germany, May 22, 1917; came to U.S., 1936; s. Moritz and Ella (Plaut) W.; m. Ursula Wolter; children: Joan, Theodore M. MA in Econs., U. Ill., 1945. V.p., ptnr. Model Roland & Co., N.Y.C., 1954-68; v.p. Smith Barney & Co., Inc., 1968-73; sr. v.p. Warburg Paribas Becker, 1974-77; v.p. Salomon Bros., Inc., 1978-80; chmn. Global Asset Mgmt. Assocs., Inc., 1981-92; sr. advisor Deutsche Bank Capital Corp., 1984-92. Spl. advisor The Germany Fund, Inc., N.Y.C., 1988-92, The New Germany Fund, 1989-92, The Future Germany Fund, 1990-92, U.S. Dept. Def., Washington, 1961-62, UN Environ. Program, N.Y.C., Nairobi, 1981-82. Assoc. editor Fin. Analysts Jour., 1967-87; contbr. articles to profl. jours. Capt. U.S. Army, 1943-46, USAR, ETO. Mem. Am. Econ. Assn., U.S. Coun. on Germany, Assn. for Investment Mgmt. and Rsch. (chmn. internat. analysts rels. com. 1967-77), N.Y. Soc. Security Analysts (program com.), Analysts Club (chmn. N.Y.C. 1985-86).

WARNER, ANDREW MARK, economist; b. Rome, Mar. 27, 1959; s. Dwight Patrick and Marjorie Ruth Warner; m. Benilda Velandia, May 27, 1999; 1 child Patrick. AB, Georgetown U., 1981; PhD, Harvard U ., 1991. Economist Bd. Govs. Fed. Reserve, Washington, 1991—92, World Bank, Washington, 1992—93; rsch. fellow Harvard U. Ctr. for Internat. Devel., Cambridge, Mass., 1993—. Office: Ctr Internat Devel Harvard U 79 JFK St E403 Cambridge MA 02138-5801 Office Fax: 617-495-0712.

WARNER, BARRY GREGORY, geographer, educator; b. Cambridge, Ont., Can., July 20, 1955; s. Gregory O. and Alma (Jansen) W. B in Environ. Studies, U. Waterloo, 1978, MS, 1980; PhD, Simon Fraser U., Burnaby, Can., 1984. Rsch. asst. prof. U. Waterloo, Ont., 1985-89, rsch. assoc. prof., 1989-91, assoc. prof. geography, 1991-96, prof. biology, earth sci. and geography, 1996—; dir. Wetlands Rsch. Inst., 1991—; U. Neuchatel. Vis. prof. U. Neuchatel, 1993; chair Can. Nat. Wetlands Working Group, 1993—; bd. dirs. Internat. Mire Conservation Group. Editor: Methods in Quaternary Ecology, 1990; co-editor: Wetlands: Envigradients, Boundaries and Buffers, 1996; contbr. articles to profl. jours. Postdoctoral fellow Natural Scis. and Engring. Rsch. Coun. of Can., 1984-85, rsch. fellow, 1985-90; fellow Suisse

Nat. Res. Fond, 1993. Fellow Geol. Assn. Can., Soc. Wetland Sicentists (pres., v.p. 2000-2002). Office: U of Waterloo Wetlands Rsch Ctr Waterloo ON Canada N2L 3G1 E-mail: bwarner@uwaterloo.ca.

WARNER, CHARLES COLLINS, lawyer; b. Cambridge, Mass., June 19, 1942; s. Hoyt Landon and Charlotte (Collins) W.; m. Elizabeth Denny, Aug. 24, 1964; children: Peter, Andrew, Elizabeth. BA, Yale U., 1964; JD cum laude, Ohio State U., 1970. Bar: Ohio 1970. Assoc. Porter, Wright, Morris & Arthur and predecessor, Columbus, 1970-76, ptnr., 1976—, also mgr. labor and employment law dept., 1988-92. Pres. Peace Corps Svc. Coun., Columbus, 1974—76, Old Worthington (Ohio) Assn., 1976—78, Worthington Ednl. Found., 1994—96, Opera Columbus, 1999—2001; chmn. lawyers sect. United Way, 1983—84; mem. alumni adv. coun. Ohio State U.; pres. Alliance for Quality Edn., Worthington, 1987—89. Fellow Am. Bar Found., Ohio Bar Found., Columbus Bar Found., Coll. Labor and Employment Lawyers; mem. ABA (subcom. chmn. EEO com. 1986-89, co-chair 2000-02, exec. com. Met. Bar Caucus 1992-94, chmn. state & local bar ADR com. 1995-98), Ohio State Bar Assn. (coun. of dels. 1993—, chmn. fed. cts. com. 1992-94), Ohio Met. Bar Assn. (pres. 1991-92), Columbus Bar Assn. (pres. 1991-92, bd. govs. 1982-87, 88-93), FBA, Ohio Assn. Civil Trial Attys. (exec. bd. 1988-97), Ohio State U. Law Alumni Assn. (pres. 1996-97), Nat. Coun. Ohio State U. Coll. Law (pres. 2002—), Capital Club, Yale Club (pres. 1979-81). Avocations: clarinet, singing, tennis. Home: 145 E South St Columbus OH 43085-4129 Office: Porter Wright Morris & Arthur 41 S High St Ste 2800 Columbus OH 43215-6194 E-mail: cwarner@porterwright.com.

WARNER, CHARLES DAVID, III, academic administrator; b. Hagerstown, Md., Feb. 2, 1957; s. Charles David Jr. and Ivy Ella Warner; m. Debra Jean Teter, May 25, 1985; children: Betsy, Molly, Charles. B in Music Edn., Shepherd Coll., 1980; M in Music Edn., Towson U., 1985; EdD, Va. Poly. Inst. and State U., 1999. Prof. music Hagerstown (Md.) C.C., 1989-2001, chair humanities divsn., 2000—. Author: Opinions of Administrators, Faculty, and Students Regarding Academic Freedom and Student Artistic Expression, 2001. Mem. NEA, Phi Kappa Phi. Republican. Lutheran. Avocations: sailing, reading. Home: 17729 Bluebell Dr Hagerstown MD 21740 Office: Hagerstown CC 11400 Robinwood Dr Hagerstown MD 21742 Fax: 301-393-3680. E-mail: warnerd@hcc.cc.md.us.

WARNER, CURT, retired professional football player; b. Wyoming, Vt., Mar. 18, 1961; Student, Pa. State U. With Seattle Seahawks, 1983—; player NFL Pro Bowl, 1984; mem. NFL Pro Bowl Team, 1987, 88.*

WARNER, DAVID COOK, public affairs educator; b. Boston, Apr. 22, 1940; s. Roger Lewis and Dorothy Flora (Cook) W.; m. Phyllis Gail Erman, July 9, 1967; children: Ann Fitch, Michael Beers. BA, Princeton U., 1963; MPA, Syracuse U., 1965, PhD in Econs., 1969. Rsch. assoc. Ctr. Urban Studies Wayne State U., Detroit, 1969, asst. prof. econs., 1969-71; dep. dir. program analysis and budget N.Y.C. Health and Hosp. Corp., 1971-72; postdoctoral fellow Yale U., New Haven, 1972-73, lectr., 1973-75; assoc. prof. L.B.J. Sch. Pub. Affairs U. Tex., Austin, 1975-81, prof. pub. affairs, 1981—, Wilbur Cohen prof. pub. affairs, 1989—. Vis. prof. pub. health, 1983—; bd. dirs. Brackenridge Hosp., Austin, 1976—83; mem. Tex. Diabetes Coun., 1983—88, chmn., 1985—88; mem. adv. bd. Hogg Found. for Mental Health, 1990—93; vice chair quality methods tech. adv. com. Health Care Info. Coun., 1999—. Author: Health of Mexican Americans in South Texas, 1979, Developing Programs to Prevent and Control Diabetes, 1982, Maternal and Child Health on the U.S.-Mexico Border, 1987, Health Care Across the Border, 1993, NAFTA and Trade in Health Services, 1997, Cost of Diabetes in Texas in 1992, 1996, Getting What You Paid For: Extending Medicare Coverage to Retirees in Mexico, 1999; co-author: Cost of Cancer in Texas, 2001; editor: Toward New Human Rights, 1977, Public Affairs Comment, 1978—; mem. editl. bd. Jour. Health, Politics, Policy and Law, 1975-93; contbr. numerous articles to profl. jours. Mem. U.S.-Mex. Border Health Assn. (chmn. rsch., edn., tng. com. 1982-84), Am. Pub. Health Assn., Tex. Philosophical Soc. Democrat. Congregationalist. Home: 5701 Trailridge Dr Austin TX 78731-4226 Office: U Tex LBJ Sch Pub Affairs Austin TX 78713 E-mail: david.warner@mail.utexas.edu.

WARNER, DAVID SAMUEL, anesthesiologist, educator; b. Evanston, Ill., July 20, 1953; s. James Daniel and Marcella Anne Warner; m. Rosanne T. Warner, June 14, 1980; children: Lindsay, Seth. BA, U. Wis., 1976, MD, 1980. Diplomate Am. Bd. Anesthesiology. Resident U. Iowa, Iowa City, 1980-84; rsch. assoc. U. Lund, Sweden, 1984-85; asst. prof. U. Iowa, Iowa City, 1985-89, assoc. prof., 1989-94; prof. anesthesiology Duke U., Durham, N.C., 1994—. Mem. editl. bd. Jour. Neurosurg. Anesthesia, 1989—, Anesthesia and Analgesia, 1995—; contbr. over 130 articles to profl. jours. NIH grantee, 1987—. Mem. Soc. for Neurosurg. Anesthesia and Critical Care (pres. 1994-95), Soc. for Neurosci., Am. Soc. Anesthesiologists, Internat. Anesthesia Rsch. Soc. Episcopalian. Home: 1006 Camden Ln Chapel Hill NC 27516-7756 Office: Duke Univ Med Ctr Dept Anesthesiology PO Box 3094 Durham NC 27710-0001

WARNER, DENNIS ALLAN, psychology educator; b. Idaho Falls, Idaho, Apr. 27, 1940; s. Perry and Marcia E. (Finlayson) W.; m. Charyl Ann DeHart, Dec. 12, 1962; children: Lisa Rae, Sara Michelle, David Perry, Matthew Arie. BS, Brigham Young U., 1964; MS with honors, U. Oreg., 1966, PhD, 1968. Asst. prof. edn. Wash. State U., Pullman, 1968-72, assoc. prof. edn., 1972-78, prof. edn., 1978-85, dir. tchr. edn., 1983-85, prof., chmn. ednl. counseling psychology, 1985-93, interim dir. Partnership Ctr., 1993-94, prof. edn. leadership and counseling psychology Pulman, 1994—, assoc. dean Coll. Edn., 1999—. Vis. asst. prof. psychology U. Idaho, Moscow, 1971. Author: Interpreting and Improving Student Test Performance, 1982; contbr. articles to profl. jours. Postdoctoral research assoc. U. Kans., 1976-77. Fellow APA; mem. Delta Kappa. Mem. Lds Ch. Home: 645 SW Mies St Pullman WA 99163-2057 Office: Wash State Univ Dept Ednl & Counsel Psych Cleveland Hl Rm 160B Pullman WA 99164-0001 E-mail: dawarner@wsu.edu.

WARNER, DON LEE, dean emeritus; b. Norfolk, N.B., Jan. 4, 1934; s. Donald A. and Cleo V. (Slagel) W.; m. Patricia Ann Walker, Feb. 24, 1957; children: Mark J., Scott Lee. BS in Geol. Engring., Colo. Sch. Mines, 1956, MSc in Geol. Engring., 1961; PhD in Engring. Sci., U. Calif., Berkeley, 1964. Registered profl. engr., Mo., geologist, Mo., Miss. Geol. engr. Gulf Oil Corp., Casper, Wyo., 1956, Calif. Exploration Co., Guatemala, 1957-58; civil engr. U.S. Forest Svc., Gunnison, Colo., 1958-59; teaching asst. Colo. Sch. Mines, Golden, 1959-61; rsch. asst. U. Calif., Berkeley, 1962-64; rsch. geologist and engr. U.S. Pub. Health Svc., Cin., 1964-67; chief, earth scis. Ohio Basin Region Fed. Water Pollution Control Adminstrn., 1967-69; prof. geol. engring. U. Mo., Rolla, 1969-92, prof. emeritus geol. engring., 1992—, dean emeritus Sch. Mines and Metallurgy, 1992—, chmn., geol. engring., 1980-81, dean Sch. Mines and Metallurgy, 1981-93. Bd. dirs. Underground Injection Practices Coun., 1985-89; mem. adv. com. to Sec. of Interior for Mineral Resources Rsch., 1985-92. Author: Subsurface Wastewater Injection, 1977. Special award scholarship Colo. Sch. Mines, 1951-56, grad. fellowship Colo. Sch. Mines, 1959-51, rsch. fellowship U. Calif., 1962-64; recipient Best Paper award Am. Water Works Assn., 1971. Fellow Geol. Soc. Am.; mem. Am. Inst. Profl. Geologists (cert.), Am. Assn. Petroleum Geologists, Geol. Soc. Am., Nat. Ground Water Assn. (sci. award 1984, disting. lectr. 1986), Ground Water Protection Coun., Blue Key, Soc. Petroleum Engrs., Scabbard and Blade, Theta Tau, Tau Beta Pi. Avocations: fishing, boating, tennis, golf. Office: U Mo-Rolla Sch Mines and Metallurgy 1870 Miner Cir Rolla MO 65409-0001

WARNER, FRANK WILSON, III, mathematics educator; b. Pittsfield, Mass., Mar. 2, 1938; s. Frank Wilson Jr. and Charlotte (Walton) W.; m. Ada Woodward, June 6, 1958; children: Bruce Woodward, Clifford Powell. BS, Pa. State U., 1959; PhD, MIT, 1963. Instr. MIT, Cambridge, 1963-64; acting asst. prof. U. Calif., Berkeley, 1964-65, asst. prof., 1965-68; assoc. prof. U. Pa., Phila., 1968-73, prof. math., 1973-2000, assoc. dean Sch. Arts and Scis., 1992-95, dep. dean Sch. Arts and Scis., 1995-97, prof. emeritus, 2000—. Author: Foundations of Differentiable Manifolds and Lie Groups, 1971; contbr. articles to scholarly jours. Fellow Guggenheim Found., 1976. Fellow AAAS; mem. Am. Math. Soc., Math. Assn. Am., Sigma Xi. Achievements include research on the conjugate locus of a Riemannian manifold, on existence and conformal deformation of metrics with prescribed gaussian and scalar curvatures, on great circle fibrations of spheres. Office: U Pa 209 S 33d St Philadelphia PA 19104-6395

WARNER, FRANK SHRAKE, lawyer; b. Ogden, Utah, Dec. 14, 1940; s. Frank D. and Emma (Sorensen) W.; 1 child, Sheri; m. Sherry Lynn Clary. JD, U. Utah, 1964. Bar: Utah 1964. Assoc. Young, Thatcher, Glasmann & Warner, and predecessor, Ogden, 1964-67, ptnr., 1967-72; chmn. Pub. Svc. Comn. Utah, Salt Lake City, 1972-76; ptnr. Warner & Wikstrom, Ogden, 1976-79, Warner, Marquardt & Hasenyager, Ogden, 1979-82; pvt. practice, 1982-89, Warner & Phillips, 1989-96, Warner Law Firm, 1996—. Mem. Utah Gov.'s Com. on Exec. Reorgn., 1978-80. Mem. Utah Bar Assn. (ethics and discipline com. 1981-90), Am. Inns of Ct, Am. Trial Lawyers Assn., Ogden Gun Club (past pres.). Office: Lincoln Pl 3544 Lincoln Ave # F Ogden UT 84401

WARNER, HAROLD CLAY, JR. banker, investment management executive; b. Knoxville, Tenn., Feb. 24, 1939; s. Harold Clay and Mary Frances (Waters) W.; m. Patricia Alice Rethorst, Sept. 1, 1961; children— Martha Lee, Carol Frances. BS in Econs, U. Tenn., 1961, PhD, 1965. Asst. to pres. First Fed. Savs., Savannah, Ga., 1965-67; v.p. and economist No. Trust Co., Chgo., 1967-73; sr. v.p. and chief economist Crocker Nat. Bank, San Francisco, 1974-79, sr. v.p. liability mgmt., 1979-82; exec. v.p., dir. fixed income mgmt. BA Investment Mgmt. Corp., 1982-84, dir., pres., chief operating officer, 1984-86; dir., pres. Montgomery St. Income Securities, Inc., 1984-86; sr. v.p. Bank of Am., San Francisco, 1982-86; chmn. BA Investment Mgmt. Internat., Ltd., 1985-86; pres. Arthur D. Gimbel, Inc., San Mateo, Calif., 1986-87; exec. v.p., chief investment officer Riggs Nat. Bank Washington, 1987-88; chmn. Riggs Investment Mgmt. Corp., 1988-89; sr. v.p., chief economist Bank of Calif., San Francisco, 1989-93; pres., chief investment officer MERUS Capital Mgmt., 1989-93; pres. Govett Asset Mgmt. Co., 1993-95, Govett Fin. Svcs. Ltd., 1993-95; pres., COO Fisher Investments, Inc., Woodside, Calif., 1996; pres. Warner Fiduciary Counsel, LLC, San Francisco, 1997; sr. v.p. Mellon Pvt. Asset Mgmt., San Francisco, 1998—. Lectr. dept. econs. U. Tenn., 1962-63, Grad. Sch. Bus., Loyola U., Chgo., 1969-73; lectr. Pacific Coast Banking Sch., U. Wash., 1978-79. Bd. trustees Children's Hosp., Oakland, Calif. NDEA fellow, 1961-64 Mem. Burlingame Country Club, Phi Gamma Delta, Phi Eta Sigma, Beta Gamma Sigma, Omicron Delta Kappa, Phi Kappa Phi. Home: PO Box 2449 Yountville CA 94599-2449 Office: 1 Embarcadero Ctr Ste 2200 San Francisco CA 94111-3711 E-mail: warnerfc@msn.com., warner.hc@mellon.com.

WARNER, HARRY BACKER, JR. retired journalist, freelance writer; b. Chambersburg, Pa., Dec. 19, 1922; s. Harry Backer, Sr. and Margaret Caroline (Klipp) W. Student, Hagerstown, Md. Reporter, editor, columnist Herald-Mail Co., Hagerstown, 1942-82; ret., 1982. Author: All Our Yesterdays, 1969, A Wealth of Fable, 1976; editor, author (amateur jour.) Horizons, 1939—. Com. mem. Community Action Coun., Hagerstown, Civic Music Assn., Hagerstown, Washington County Adult Edn., Hagerstown; mem. publicity com. Washington County United Fund, Hagerstown. Recipient Hugo award World Sci. Fiction Convs., 1968, 72, 93, Hist. Preservation award Washington County Commrs., 1980, First Fandom Hall of Fame award, 1995. Mem. Spectator Amateur Press Soc. (v.p. 1982-97), So. Fandom Pubs. Alliance. Republican. Lutheran. Avocations: science fiction fandom, classical music. Home: 423 Summit Ave Hagerstown MD 21740-6229

WARNER, HEIDI CELESTE, clinical trials consultant; b. Thomasville, N.C. BSN, N.C. U., Charlotte, 1985. RN N.C. Clin. rsch. assoc. tng. The Blethen Group, Research Triangle Park, N.C. Walter C. Teagle Found. nursing scholar, Exxon Co. USA. Mem.: Assn. Clin. Rsch. Profls., Soc. Clin. Rsch. Assocs. (cert. clin. rsch. profl.), Phi Eta Sigma.

WARNER, IRVING R. fundraising executive, consultant; b. N.Y.C., Oct. 25, 1924; s. Samuel Winogradsky and Sarah Hellman; m. Phala Ann Fuller, July 29, 1972; 1 child, Seth philip. Cert., NYU, 1949. City mgr. State of Israel Bonds, various cities, 1950-58; pres. Irving R. Warner Co., L.A., 1959—. Cons. to more than 150 not-for-profit agys.; mem. faculty UCLA, 1977-87. Author: Art of Fund Raising, 1975; columnist Chronicle of Philanthropy, 1995—. Mem. bd. advisors NYU, 1999—. Sgt. Air Corps, 1943-46. Home: 3235 Berry Dr Studio City CA 91604 E-mail: irwarner@earthlink.net.

WARNER, JAMES JOHN, small business owner; b. Paw Paw, Mich., Feb. 22, 1942; s. James Kelley and Arleta Alice (Turner) W.; m. Lynne Ann McGuire, June 19, 1965 (div. Apr. 4, 1994); children: Todd M., Kirk T., Beth K. BA, Mich. State U., 1965; postgrad., Western Mich. U., 1968-72. Sales rep. Warner Vineyards, Paw Paw, 1965-70, gen. mgr., 1970-73, v.p., 1973-75, pres., 1976—, also bd. dirs. Chmn. Lakeview Found., Paw Paw, Mich., 1978, Van Buren County Econ. Devel. Corp., Paw Paw, 1977; dir. Van Buren Emergency Med. Svcs., Paw Paw, 1982; sec. Hospice Care of S.W. Mich., 1988. With U.S. Army, 1966-68, Vietnam. Decorated Bronze Star. Mem. Am. Mktg. Assn. (Man of Yr. 1978), Am. Assn. Vintners (dir. 1981—), Young Pres.' Orgn. (chmn. 1982-83), Mich. Grape and Wine Industry Coun. Episcopalian. Avocations: reading, walking, sailing, gardening, swimming. Home: 304 S Kalamazoo St Paw Paw MI 49079-1528 Office: Warner Vineyards 706 S Kalamazoo St Paw Paw MI 49079-1558

WARNER, JANET CLAIRE, software design engineer; b. Portland, Oreg., May 2, 1964; d. W. J. and Wendelyn A. (Twombly) W. Student, Clackamas Community Coll., 1982-85; BS in Computer Sci., U. Portland, 1987, MSEE, 1992. Systems asst. U. Portland, 1986-87, programmer Applied Rsch. Ctr., 1987; software design engr. Photon Kinetics, Inc., Beaverton, Oreg., 1987-92; software engr. FLIR Sys., Inc., Portland, 1993; software cons., 1993-97; sr. software engr. Flight Dynamics, Portland, 1998—. Mem. IEEE, Assn. Computing Machinery (chmn. U. Portland chpt. 1986-87), Soc. Women Engrs. (treas. Oreg. sect. 1988-89), U. Portland Alumni Assn. (Portland programming bd. 1993—), Portland Rose Soc., Eta Kappa Nu (treas. chpt. 1991-92). Avocations: drawing, photography, sailing, swimming, downhill skiing, gardening.

WARNER, JEAN LOLLICH, poet; b. Clinton, Iowa, June 22, 1916; d. Jens George Christenson and Dibga (Allen) L.; m. Charles Howard Warner, Mar. 26, 1959 (dec.); stepchildren: Judith, Leonard. BA in Elem. Edn., Cornell Coll., Mt. Vernon, Iowa, 1938; MA in Early Childhood Edn., Columbia U., 1945. Tchr. grades 4-6 Mt. Vernon Pub. Sch., 1938-39; tchr. kindergarten-1st grade Lyons Pub. Schs., Clinton, 1939-44; tchr. kindergarten Clinton Pub. Schs., 1945-59. Iowa state rep. Early Childhood Edn. Conf., Washington, 1958, Study Conf. of Childhood in Edn., St. Louis, 1959. Contbr. poetry to American Poetry Anthology, 1984, I Have Need of the Poets, 1984, Hearts on Fire, 1985, Impressions, 1986, Best New Poets of 1989, 1989, Best Poems of the 90's, 1990, Expressions, 1991 (award of merit), Awaken to a Dream, 1991, Poetic Voices of America, 1991, Windows of the World, 1991, Down Peaceful Paths, 1991, Language of the Soul, 1992, Best Poems of 1995, 1995 (Editor's Choice award); contbr. poetry to mags. Sponsor Foster Parents Plan, Warwick, R.I., 1986-92, Children Internat., 1987-92. Summer sch. scholar Rockefeller Found., Duke U., Durham, N.C., 1955. Mem. AAUW (charter), NEA (life), PEO (internat. chpt. sisterhood), Internat. Soc. Poets, Delta Kappa Gamma (charter). Presbyterian. Avocations: reading, china painting, playing organ, knitting, travel. Home: Sarah Harding Retirement Home 308 S Bluff Blvd Room 502 Clinton IA 52732

WARNER, JEAN SHUMWAY, state agency administrator; b. Bronxville, N.Y., Feb. 24, 1946; d. Floyd Mallory Shumway and Margaret Rabling McAvoy; m. Larkin B. Warner. BA, Roosevelt U., Chgo., 1968; PhD, U. Okla., 1995. Project dir. Policy Scis. Rsch. Ctr. Okla. State U., Stillwater, Ala., 1982—86; dir. NEW Leadership Okla. U. Okla., Norman, 2001—02. Pres. LWV of Oklahoma County, Oklahoma City, 1999—2002; mem. tutoring/mentoring adv. com. Oklahoma City Pub. Sch. Dist., 1999—2002; co-chair edn. reform study task force Citizens League of Cen. Okla., 1998—2000; mem. after sch. adv. com. Okla. Inst. for Child Advocacy, 2000—02; chair adminstrv. coun. Nichols Hills United Meth. Ch., 2000; bd. dirs. Payne Edn. Ctr., 1999—2001. Methodist. Office: U Okla Rm 101 630 Parrington Oval Norman OK 73019-4031 Business E-Mail: jeanwarner@ou.edu.

WARNER, JO F. mathematics educator; b. Kansas City, Kans., Nov. 22, 1949; d. William Halpin and Anna Lorene Fitzsimmons; m. Allen Robert Warner, July 22, 1978; children: Robin William, Gilbert Nathaniel, Lee Alexander. BS, Ea. Mich. U., 1971, MA, 1990; EdD, Grambling State U., 2001. Math. tchr. Ann Arbor (Mich.) Pub. Schs., 1983-86; vis. lectr. math. Washtenaw C.C., Ann Arbor, 1987—; instr. tchr., placement specialist Ea. Mich. U., Ypsilanti, 1989—. Author: Math Concepts for Algebra Prep, 1998, 3d edit., 2000. Mem.: AAUW, Mich. Devel. Edn. Consortium (pres.), Math. Assn. Am., Nat. Assn. for Devel. Edn. Avocations: reading, walking, cross country skiing. Office: Ea Mich Univ 515 Pray-Harrold Ypsilanti MI 48197

WARNER, JOHN ANDREW, foundry executive; b. Kansas City, Mo., Jan. 1, 1924; s. Richard G. and Margaret (Falconer) W.; m. Patricia Pooley, Feb. 25, 1950; children: Katherine, Amanda. Sec. Warner Oil Co., Oklahoma City, 1948-50; pres., chief exec. officer Tyler Pipe Industries, Tex., 1950-89; ret., 1989. Mem. adv. bd. Tex. Utilities Electric Co. Past chmn. East Tex. Hosp. Found.; trustee Tex. Chest Found.; former mem. Tex. Gov.'s Commn. on Phys. Fitness. Served with USCGR, 1942-46. Named Tyler's Most Outstanding Citizen, 1973 Mem. Tyler C. of C. (dir., past pres.), Cast Iron Soil Pipe Inst. (dir., past pres.), Am. Foundrymen's Soc., Tex. Assn. Bus. (dir., past state chmn.), Country Club of the Rockies, Willow Brook Country Club (dir., past pres. Tyler), Masons, Shriners, Sigma Alpha Epsilon. Presbyterian. Home: 608 Rosemont Pl Tyler TX 75701-8664

WARNER, JOHN EDWARD, advertising executive; b. Troy, N.Y., Mar. 26, 1936; s. George Edward and Ann Frances (Teson) W.; m. Anne Elizabeth Hibbard, Sept. 19, 1959; children: Matthew J., Barbara A., Peter J., Christopher J. BS in Chemistry and Philosophy, Coll. Holy Cross, 1957. Promotion mgr. Union Carbide Corp., N.Y.C., 1957-62; acct. exec. McCann-Erickson, Inc., 1962-64; pres. Warner, Bicking & Fenwick, Inc., 1964-84; chmn. Warner, Bicking, Morris & Ptnrs. Inc., 1984-97; pres. Transworld Advt. Agy. network, 1987-97, Quatrefoil, Inc., 1998—. Bd. dirs. Thomas Pub. Co., N.Y.C. Author: (novels) Decorating Time Savers by Jack Warner, 2001. Home: 706 Hillcrest Rd Ridgewood NJ 07450-1110 E-mail: jwaw706@aol.com.

WARNER, JOHN HILLIARD, JR. technical services, military and commercial systems and software company executive; b. Santa Monica, Calif., Mar. 2, 1941; s. John Hilliard and Irene Anne (Oliva) W.; m. Helga Magdalena Farrington, Sept. 4, 1961; children: Tania Renee, James Michael. BS in Engring. with honors, UCLA, 1963, MS in Engring., 1965, PhD in Engring., 1967. Mem. staff Marquardt Corp., Van Nuys, Calif., 1963; mem. faculty West Coast U., Los Angeles, 1969-72; mem. staff TRW Systems Group, Redondo Beach, Calif., 1967-70, sect. mgr., 1970-73; mem. staff Sci. Applications Internat. Corp., San Diego, 1973-75, asst. v.p., 1975-77, v.p., 1977-80, corp. v.p., 1980-81, sr. v.p., 1981-87, sector v.p., 1987-89; exec. v.p. Sci. Applications Internat Corp., 1989-96, bd. dirs., 1988—; corp. exec. v.p. Sci. Applications Internat. Corp., 1996—. Cons. Rand Corp., Santa Monica, 1964-66; bd. dirs. AMSEC LLC, BSC LLC. Contbr. articles to profl. jours. Trustee Scripps Health, 2001—; bd. dirs. Corp. Dirs. Forum, 2001—. AEC fellow, 1963, 66, NSF fellow, 1964, 65. Mem. AIAA, Healthcare Info. and Mgmt. Sys. Soc., Assn. U.S. Army, Air Force Assn., NDIA, Armed Forces Communications and Electronics Assn., Navy League U.S., La Jolla Chamber Music Soc. (bd. dirs. 1990-97, adv. bd. 1998-2001), San Diego C. of C. (bd. dirs. 2000—), Calif. C. of C. (bd. dirs. 2000—), Calif. Bus. Roundtable, Sigma Nu, Tau Beta Pi. Methodist. Avocations: bicycling, fishing, music. Office: SAIC 10260 Campus Point Dr San Diego CA 92121-1522

WARNER, JOHN WILLIAM, senator; b. Washington, Feb. 18, 1927; s. John William and Martha Stuart (Budd) W.; children: Mary Conover, Virginia Stuart, John William IV. BS Engring., Washington and Lee U., 1949; LL.B., U. Va., 1953. Law clk. to U.S. judge, 1953-54; spl. asst. to U.S. atty., 1956-57; asst. U.S. atty. Dept. Justice, 1957-60; ptnr. Hogan & Hartson, 1960-68; owner, operator Cattle Farm, 1961—; undersec. of navy, 1969-72; sec. of navy, 1972-74; adminstr. Am. Revolution Bicentennial Adminstrn., 1974-76; U.S. senator from Va., 1979—. Mem. environment and pub. works com., rules and adminstrn. com., nat. Rep. senatorial com. Served with USNR, 1944-46; to capt. USMCR, 1949-52. Mem. Bar Assn. D.C. Clubs: Metropolitan. Republican. Episcopalian. Office: US Senate 225 Russell Senate Bldg Washington DC 20510-0001*

WARNER, KATHY JOANNE, marketing professional; b. York, Pa., May 8, 1964; d. Leonard Edward and M. Agnes Cooke Warner. BSBA, U. Tenn., 1991; MA in Internat. Affairs, Ohio U., 1995. Paid staff mem. Clinton/Gore Presdl. Campaign, Nashville, 1992; constituent svcs. caseworker Office of the Mayor, 1992-94; cons. Satyam Computer Svcs. Ltd., Secunderabad, India, 1994; asst. v.p. Strategic Rsch. Inst., N.Y.C., 1998-99; product devel. specialist ASME Internat., 2000—02. Mem. Fgn. Policy Assn., N.Y.C., 1998—. Contbr. poetry to anthologies (Editor's award, 1994); actor(performing artist, singer): The Most Happy Fella, 2000; (plays) Manhattan Towers, 2001, A Day in the Life of New York City, 2001; musician: An Evening in the Spotlight, 2000, (cabaret showcases) Old Friends, New Beginnings, 2000, Cabaret 13, 2002, (Carnegie Hall performance) St. Cecilia Chorus, 1998; actor: (plays) Don Giovanni, 1994; musician: Duets, 2002. Vol. New York Cares. Herbert Walters scholar U. Tenn., 1990, scholar Ohio U., 1994-95. E-mail: kathyjo4261@yahoo.com.

WARNER, KENNETH E. public health educator, consultant; b. Washington, Jan. 25, 1947; s. Edgar W. Jr. and Betty (Strasburger) W.; m. Patricia A. Hilty, Oct. 1, 1977; children— Peter, Andrew AB, Dartmouth Coll., 1968; MPhil, Yale U., 1970, PhD, 1974. Lectr. dept. health mgmt. and policy Sch. Pub. Health, U. Mich., Ann Arbor, 1972—74, asst. prof., 1974—77, assoc. prof., 1977—83, prof., 1983—, chmn., 1982—88, 1992—95, Richard D. Remington Collegiate prof. pub. health, 1995—2001, dir. Tobacco Rsch. Network, Avedis Donabedian Disting. prof. pub. health, 2001—. Cons., Washington, 1976—95, Office on Smoking and Health, USPHS, Rockville, Md., 1978—, Inst. Medicine, Nat. Acad. Scis., Washington, 1984—, numerous additional pub. and pvt. orgns.; mem. bd. sci. counselors divsn. cancer prevention and control Nat. Cancer Inst., Bethesda, Md., 1985—89. Author: (with Bryan Luce) Cost-Benefit & Cost Effectiveness Analysis in Health Care, 1982; contbr. articles to profl. jours. Trustee Am. Lung Assn., Mich., Lansing, 1982; mem. subcom. on smoking Am. Heart Assn., Dallas, 1983-87; mem. com. on tobacco and cancer Am. Cancer Soc., N.Y.C., 1984-92; bd. dirs. Am. Legacy Found., 1999—. Hon. Woodrow Wilson fellow, 1968; W.K. Kellog Found. fellow, 1980-83; vis. scholar Nat. Bur. Econ. Research, Stanford, Calif., 1975-76; recipient Surgeon Gen.'s medallion Dr. C. Everett Koop, 1989. Fellow Assn. Health Svcs. Rsch.; mem. APHA (leadership award 1990), Am. Econ. Assn., Inst. Medicine, Nat. Assn. Pub. Health Policy, Phi Beta Kappa. Office: U Michigan Dept Health Sch Pub Health Mgmt Policy 109 Observatory St Ann Arbor MI 48109-2029 E-mail: kwarner@umich.edu.

WARNER, KENNETH WILSON, JR. editor, association and publications executive; b. Chgo., Dec. 22, 1928; s. Kenneth Wilson and Ann S. (Knapp) W.; m. Deborah Ann Bollo, Dec. 28, 1982 (div. Apr. 1995); 1 child, Joseph; children by previous marriages: Sara, Seth, Katharin. BS Ed., No. Ill. U., 1950. Staff editor Bldg. Supply News, Chgo., 1953-56; staff editor Elec. Merchandising, 1956-60; free-lance writer Sarasota, Fla., 1960-66; editor Gunsport Mag., Alexandria and Falls Church, Va., 1966-67, Gunfacts Mag., Arlington, 1968-70, pub., 1968-70; exec. editor Am. Rifleman, Nat. Rifle Assn., Washington, 1971-78, asst. dir. publs. div., 1972-78; editor Am. Hunter, 1973-78, Am. Rifleman, 1976-78; dir. publs. NRA, Washington, 1977-78; editor in chief Gun Digest, Knives Annual-Krause Publs., Inc., Greenville, W.Va., 1979-99; editor, pub. Knives Digest Two Knife Guys Pub., Inc., Chattanooga, 2000—; pres. Knifeware, Inc., Greenville, W.Va. Cons. firearms and cutlery cos.; co-founder Am. Knife and Tool Inst., 1997. Author: The Practical Book of Knives. 1976; The Practical Book of Guns, 1978. Editor: The Bolt Action, 1976. Contbr. articles to profl. jours. Cpl. U.S. Army. 1951-53. Recipient Cutlery Hall of Fame; inducted into Am. Bladesmith Soc. Hall of Fame, 1999. Mem. NRA (life), Knifemaker's Guild. Am. (assoc.). Office: Prin Editorial Office PO Box 52 Greenville WV 24945-0052 E-mail: knifeware@inetone.com.

WARNER, KRIS, state official; Chmn. Republican Party W.Va., 2002—. Republican. Achievements include raising more than $100,000 for the Republican party; getting 94 Republican candidates to file to run for the House of Delegates and the State Senate. Office: 1620 Kanawha Blvd E Ste 4B Charleston WV 25311*

WARNER, LAVERNE, education educator; b. Huntsville, Tex., Aug. 14, 1941; d. Clifton Partney and Velma Oneta (Steely) W. BS, Sam Houston State U., 1962, MEd, 1969; PhD, East Tex. State U., 1977. Cert. elem. sch. tchr., Tex. First grade tchr. Port Arthur (Tex.) Ind. Sch. Dist., 1962-64; kindergarten tchr. Burlington (Vt.) Cmty. Schs., 1964-66; first grade tchr. Aldine Sch. Dist., Houston, 1967-68; music tchr. Crawfordsville (Ind.) Cmty. Schs., 1968-71; prof. early childhood edn. Sam Houston State U., Huntsville, 1975—, chmn. faculty senate, 1988-89. Chair faculty senate Sam Houston State U., 1990-91, chair-elect, 1989-90; educator preparation Improvement Initiative, 1996-97. Author: (with P. Berry) Tunes for Tots, 1982; (with K. Craycraft) Fun with Familiar Tunes, 1987, Language in Centers: Kids Communicating, 1991, Theme Escapades, 1992, What If...Themes, 1993; contbg. editor Good Apple, Inc., 1986-88, 91-93; contbr. over 90 articles to profl. jours. Mem. Huntsville Leadership Inst., 1986-88, chmn. adv. bd. 1987-88, chmn. 1987-88; Community Child Care Assn., Huntsville, 1988-90. Recipient Sam Houston State U. Excellence in Teaching award, 1992, Tchr. Educator of Yr. award Tex. Assn. for Edn. Young Children, 1992, Sammy award Divsn. of Student Life, 1996, Millennium Counselor's award Kappa Delta Pi; grantee Am. Assn. Higher Edn., Tex. Mem. Nat. Assn. Edn. Young Children (life, co-editor Young Children), So. Early Childhood Assn. (chair publs. adv. bd. 1998-2000, bd. dirs. 2002-), Tex. Assn. Coll. Tchrs. (life, past pres.), Tex. Elementary-Kindergarten Nursery Educators (state pres. 1982-84), Tex. Assn. for Edn. Young Children (v.p. 1988-89, newsletter editor, 1991-93, Tchr. Educator of Yr. 1992, pres.-elect 1993-95, pres. 1995-97, so. early childhood rep. 2002-), Huntsville Leadership Inst. Alumni Assn. (pres. 1988-89), Phi Delta Kappa (area 3H coord. 1986-92, Svc. Key 1987), Sam Houston Assn. for Edn. Young Children (charter, pres-elect, 1991-92, pres. 1992-93), Sam Houston Univ. Women (pres. 1985-86), Huntsville High Sch. Ex-Students Assn. (charter, pres. 1989-91), Sam Houston Alumni Assn. (bd. dirs. 1996-99). Mem. Ch. of Christ. Avocations: music, reading, shopping. Office: Sam Houston State U Coll Edn and Applied Sci Huntsville TX 77341 E-mail: edu_lxw@shsu.edu.

WARNER, MARK A. anesthesiologist; b. Greenville, Ohio, Oct. 7, 1953; s. Paul C. Jr. and Mildred G. Warner; m. Mary Ellen Bunch, Oct. 14, 1978; children: Paul, Mark, Matthew, Daniel. AB in Chemistry, Miami U., Oxford, Ohio, 1976; MD, Med. Coll. Ohio, 1979. Diplomate Am. Bd. Anesthesiology. Intern, resident Mayo Clinic, Rochester, 1979-82, prof. and chmn. dept. anes. Minn., 1999—, dir. hosp. ops., 1995-99. Bd. dirs. Am. Bd. Anesthesiology, Raleigh, N.C., 1999—, bd. dirs. Anesthesia Patient Safety Found., Boston, 1996—. Bd. dirs. Rochester Family YMCA, Rochester, 1998—, Rochester Airport Co., 1992—, Mayo Med. Transp. Sys., Rochester, 1995—, Gold Cross Ambulance, Rochester, 1995—. Mem. Am. Soc. Anesthesiologists (bd. dirs. 1996—). Office: Mayo Clinic 200 1st St SW Rochester MN 55905-0001 E-mail: warner.mark@mayo.edu.

WARNER, MICHAEL P. application developer; b. Middletown, Pa., Apr. 22, 1965; s. Russell L and Diana M. Warner, Diana M Warner; m. Kristen K Kidwell; children: Matthew, Jonathan. AS in Elec. Engring. Tech., Pa. Inst. Tech., Media, 1987; BS in Engring., Widener U., Chester, Pa., 1995. Tech. asst. PECO Energy, Limerck, Pa., 1988—93, sr. programmer analyst, 1996, systems ubtegratir orub, Wayne, 1998; project mgr. Venator Group, Camp Hill, 1998—2000, application devel. mgr., 2000—. Republican. Baptist. Avocation: Gardening, Automobiles, Kids Activities. Home: 5325 Joshua Rd Mechanicsburg PA 17050 Office: Venator Group 3543 Simpson Ferry Rd Camp Hill PA 17011 Home Fax: 717-972-3570; Office Fax: 717-972-3750. Personal E-mail: mwarner@panetwork.com. Business E-Mail: mwarner@venatorgroup.com.

WARNER, MINER HILL, investment banker; b. N.Y.C., Aug. 13, 1942; s. Bradford Arnold and Nancy (Hill) W.; m. Ellen C. Murphy, Mar. 18, 1972; children— Alix Mallet-Prevost, Lily Wolcott. AB, Harvard U., 1964; C.E.P., Institut d'Etudes Politiques, Paris, 1963; M.Sc. in Econs., London Sch. Econs., 1965; LL.B., U. Pa., 1968; postgrad., NYU. Grad. Sch. Bus. Adminstrn., 1971-73. Bar: N.Y. 1969. Assoc. Shearman & Sterling, N.Y.C., 1968-71; assoc. Salomon Bros. Inc., 1971-73; v.p. Salomon Bros. Internat. Ltd., London, 1974-78; v.p., mgr. Salomon Bros. Inc., N.Y.C., 1979-87; dir. Merrill Lynch & Co., 1988-92; pres. Pub. Resources Internat., 1992-95, chmn., 1996—. Advisory dir. Council of the Americas, 1991-93, former dir. Woodwin Mgmt. Inc. Mem. Pres.'s Pvt. Sector Survey on Cost Control, Washington, 1982-83; mem. coun. Grad. Theol. Union, Berkeley, Calif.; vestryman St. John's Ch., Fishers Island, N.Y., 1980-99, sr. warden, 1994-99; regent Cathedral of St. John the Divine, N.Y., 1995-97, trustee, 1997—; mem. task force Gen. Theol. Sem., N.Y.; mem. exec. com. Pilgrims, N.Y.C.; trustee N.Y. Hist. Soc. 1985—, chmn. 1994-99, chmn. emeritus, 1999—, Econ. Club, N.Y. Decorated Order of St. John of Jerusalem. Mem. Pub. Securities Assn. (guaranteed loan com. 1980-86), Mayflower Soc. (gov.), Brook Club (sec.), Links Club, River Club, Met. Club (Washington), Fishers Island Club, Hay Harbor Club (Fishers Island) (former dir.). Republican. Episcopalian. Home: 148 E End Ave New York NY 10028-7503 Office: Pub Resources Internat 780 3d Ave Ste 2805 New York NY 10017-2024

WARNER, NEARI FRANCOIS, university president; b. New Orleans , July 20, 1945; d. Cornelius and Enell (Brimmer) Francois; m. Jimmie Duel Warner Sr., June 6, 1970 (div. Sept. 1983); 1 child, Jimmie Duel Jr. BS, Grambling (La.) State U., 1967; MA, Atlanta U., 1968; PhD, La. State U., 1992. Dir. Upward Bound So. U., New Orleans, 1976-89, dean jr. divsn., 1989-94; asst. v.p. acad. affairs Grambling State U., 1994-96, v.p. student affairs, 1996-97, v.p. devel., 1997-99, acting v.p. acad. affairs, 1999, provost, v.p. acad. affairs, 1999—. Sec. Conf. La. Colls./Univs., 1999—; mem. State Funding Task Force, State of La., 1998-99; bd. dirs. La. Endowment for Humanities, 1998—; pres. La. Assn. Student Asst. Program, 1986-88. Preface writer: Interdisciplinary Approach, 1998. Mem. adv. bd. Pupil Progression Commn., New Orleans, 1989-93; mem. task force Gov.'s Tech. Prep., Baton Rouge, 1991-93, Mayor's Task Force for Edn., New Orleans, 1992, Monroe (La.) City Sch., 1995. Named Role model YWCA, New Orleans, 1992, Disting. Alumnae Nat. Assn. Equal Opportunity, Washington, 1996. Mem. AAUW, NAACP, The Links, Inc. (treas. 1999—, Unsung Hero 1993), Alpha Kappa Alpha, Kappa Delta Pi, Pi Gamma Mu Democrat. Baptist. Avocations: reading, bowling. Home: PO Box 989 Grambling LA 71245-0989 Office: Grambling State U PO Box 1170 Grambling LA 71245-1170 E-mail: nfwarner@martin.gram.edu.

WARNER, NELSON ALFRED, dermatologist; b. Detroit, July 31, 1940; s. Stanley Lester and Dorothy Blanch (Nelson) W.; m. Sheryl Lee Pearson, Feb., 1966 (div. Oct. 1976); children: Christine Berea, Jennifer Lee, Pamela Suzanne; m. Kathleen Ann Dailey, Nov. 23, 1976 (div. Oct. 1986); 1 child, Andrew James; m. Jacqueline Patricia Hanks, Sept. 21, 1992 (div. Jan. 1999). AB, Albion Coll., 1962; MD, U. Mich., 1966. Diplomate Am. Bd. Dermatology. Flight surgeon USAF, San Antonio and Nakhon Phanom, Thailand, 1967-69; resident in dermatology Meml. Hosp., U. N.C., Chapel Hill, 1970-73; dermatologist Winter Haven, Fla., 1973—. Author: (with others) Manual for Nurse Practitioners, 1975. Pres. Rotary Club of Cypress Gardens, Winter Haven, Fla., 1981-82; bd. dirs. Theatre of Winter Haven, 1985-87. Capt. USAF, 1967-69. Recipient Alfred P. Sloan scholarship, 1958, U. Mich. Regents Alumni scholarship, 1962, Commendation medal USAF, 1969. Fellow Am. Acad. Dermatology; mem. AMA, Fla. Med. Assn., Fla. Soc. Dermatology, Polk County Med. Assn., Air Force Assn. Avocations: antique and custom automobiles, cooking, guitar playing, motorcycles, garden railroading. Home: 1245 Lake Elbert Dr NE Winter Haven FL 33881-4380 Office: 429 2nd St NW Winter Haven FL 33881-4168 E-mail: naw4skin@aol.com, naw1skin@aol.com.

WARNER, PATRICIA ANN, secondary school educator; b. Wooster, Ohio, Dec. 21, 1949; d. Kent Branson and Irene Mae (Graves) W. BA in English, Coll. of Wooster, 1972, MAT in English, 1973. Cert. tchr., Ohio; nat. bd. cert. tchr. adolescence and young adulthood English lang. arts. Instr. in English Orrville (Ohio) H.S., 1974—, Wayne Col., Orrville, Ohio, 1988-91. Named Orrville (Ohio) City Schs. Tchr. of Yr., 1987-88, Jennings Scholar Jennings Found., 1994-95. Mem. NEA, NCTE, Ohio Council of Tchrs. of English and Language Arts. Office: Orrville HS 841 N Ella St Orrville OH 44667-1154

WARNER, PETER DAVID, publishing executive; b. Phila., Aug. 15, 1942; s. Robert and Myra (Spector) W.; m. Ruth Bluestein (div. 1982); m. Jill Sansone, 1983; children: Emily, Cynthia, Nicholas. BA, NYU, 1964. Asst. dir. membership and devel. Mus. Modern Art, N.Y.C., 1973-76; editor, promotion dir. Book-of-the-Month Club, 1976-79; pres. Thames and Hudson, 1979—. Author: Loose Ends, 1972, Lifestyle, 1986. Mem. The Writers Room (bd. dirs.), The Century Assn. Office: Thames & Hudson Inc 500 5th Ave New York NY 10110-0002

WARNER, RAWLEIGH, JR. oil company executive; b. Chgo., Feb. 13, 1921; s. Rawleigh and Dorothy (Haskins) W.; m. Mary Ann deClairmont, Nov. 2, 1946; children: Alison W. Pyne, Suzanne W. Parsons. Grad., Lawrenceville (N.J.) Sch., 1940; AB cum laude, Princeton U., 1943. Sec., treas. Warner Bard Co., Chgo., 1946-48; with Continental Oil Co., 1948-53, asst. treas., 1952-53; treas. Socony-Vacuum Overseas Supply Co., 1953-55; asst. treas. Mobil Overseas Oil Co., 1955-56; mgr. econs. dept., then mgr. Middle East dept. Socony Mobil Oil Co. Inc., 1956-59; regional v.p. Mobil Internat. Oil Co., 1959-60, exec. v.p., 1960-63, pres., 1963-64; exec. v.p., dir. Mobil Oil Corp. (formerly Socony Mobil Oil Co., Inc.), 1964, pres., 1965-69, chmn. bd., chief exec. officer, 1969-86; chmn. Mobil Corp., 1976-86. Served to capt. F.A., AUS, 1943-45. Decorated Purple Heart, Bronze Star, Silver Star. Mem. Am. Petroleum Inst. Clubs: Augusta (Ga.) Nat. Golf; Links (N.Y.C.) ; New Canaan Country; Blind Brook (Rye Brook, N.Y.); Jupiter Island (Hobe Sound, Fla.); Seminole (North Palm Beach, Fla.). Republican. Presbyterian. Office: Mobil Corp 375 Park Ave Ste 2901 New York NY 10152-2999

WARNER, ROBERT EDSON, physics educator; b. Gallipolis, Ohio, Apr. 11, 1931; s. Robert and Ada Florence (Roush) W.; m. Mary Lou Clark, June 26, 1954 (div. May 1977); children: Ruth Berlow, Margaret Bushee, Deborah Blackburn, Elizabeth Seth; m. Mary Ann Stepka, Jan. 4, 1986. BS, Antioch Coll., 1954; PhD, U. Rochester, 1959. Asst. prof. physics U. Rochester, 1959-61, Antioch Coll., Yellow Springs, Ohio, 1961-63; asst. to assoc. prof. physics U. Manitoba, Winnipeg, 1963-65; assoc. to full prof. physics Oberlin (Ohio) Coll., 1965—2002, physics dept. chair, 1990-93, Longman prof. natural sci., 1995—2002. Vis. prof. of physics, master tchr. U. Mich., Ann Arbor, 1993-94; users exec. com. Nat. Superconducting Cyclotron Lab., East Lansing, Mich., 1995-98; reviewer NSF; vis. fellowship Japan Soc. for Promotion of Sci., 1995. Contbr. numerous articles to profl. jours.; referee Am. Jour. of Physics and Phys. Rev. Mem. Cleve. Orch. Chorus. Rsch. grantee NSF, 1965-99; postdoctoral fellowship NSF, 1971-72, predoctoral fellowship, 1957-59. Mem. AAUP, Am. Phys. Soc. (faculty mem. for rsch. in undergrad. inst. prize 1999), Audubon Soc. Democrat. Baptist. Avocations: singing, hiking, cross country skiing, reading, conservation activities. Office: Oberlin Coll Physics Dept Oberlin OH 44074 E-mail: robert.warner@oberlin.edu.

WARNER, ROBERT MARK, university dean, archivist, historian; b. Montrose, Colo., June 28, 1927; s. Mark Thomas and Bertha Margaret (Rich) W.; m. Eleanor Jane Bullock, Aug. 21, 1954; children: Mark Steven, Jennifer Jane. Student, U. Denver, 1945; BA, Muskingum Coll., 1949, LL.D. (hon.), 1981; MA, U. Mich., 1953, PhD, 1958; H.H.D. (hon.), Westminster (Pa.) Coll., 1981; L.H.D. (hon.), DePaul U., 1983. Tchr. high sch., Montrose, Colo., 1949-50; lectr. dept. history U. Mich., 1958-66, assoc. prof., 1966-71, prof., 1971-97, prof. emeritus, 1997—, prof. Sch. Info., 1974-97, emeritus, 1997—, dean Sch. Info. and Library Studies, 1985-92, univ. historian, 1992—, interim dir. Univ. Libraries, 1988-90; asst. in rsch. Bentley Hist. Libr., 1953-57, asst. curator, 1957-61, asst. dir., 1961-66, dir., 1966-80; archivist of U.S., 1980-85. Mem. exec. com. Bentley Hist. Libr., 1988—; bd. visitors Sch. Libr. Sci., Case Western Res. U., 1976-80, chmn., 1980-84, Maxwell Sch. Govt., Syracuse U., 1982-87; chmn. Gerald R. Ford Presdl. Libr. Bldg. Com., 1977-79; bd. dirs., sec. Gerald R. Ford Found., 1987—; trustee Woodrow Wilson Internat. Ctr. for Scholars, 1980-85, chmn. fellowship com., 1983-85; chmn. Nat. Hist. Publs. and Records Commn., 1980-85; mem. exec. com. Internat. Coun. on Archives, 1984-88; pres. 2d European Conf. on Archives, 1989; comptroller gen. U.S. Rsch. and Edn. Adv. Com., 1988-2000; rsch. adv. com. Online Computer Libr. Ctr., 1990-93; bd. govs. Clements Libr., 1988-90, 93—, Clark Hist. Libr. Ctrl. Mich. U., 1987—; vis. prof. UCLA, 1993. Author: Chase S. Osborn, 1860-1949, 1960, Profile of a Profession, 1964, (with R. Bordin) The Modern Manuscript Library, 1966, (with C.W. Vanderhill) A Michigan Reader: 1865 to the Present, 1974, (with F. Blouin) Sources for the Study of Migration and Ethnicity, 1979, Diary of a Dream: A History of the National Archives Independence Movement, 1980-1985, 1995. Served with U.S. Army, 1950-52. Recipient Disting. Svc. award Muskingum Coll., 1990, Disting. Svc. award Nat. Hist. Pub. and Records Commn., 1992. Fellow Soc. Am. Archivists; mem. Am. Hist. Assn. (council 1981-85), Orgn. Am. Historians, ALA (council 1986-91), Assn. for Library and Info. Sci. Edn., Presbyn. Hist. Soc. (bd. dirs. 1981-87), Am. Assn. State and Local History, Hist. Soc. Mich. (trustee 1960-66, v.p. 1972-73, pres. 1973-74), Soc. Am. Archivists (mem. council 1967-71, sec., exec. dir. 1971-73, v.p. 1974-75, pres. 1976-77), Am. Antiquarian Soc., Phi Alpha Theta, Beta Phi Mu. Clubs: U. Mich. Research. Lodges: Rotary. Presbyterian. Home: 1821 Coronada St Ann Arbor MI 48103-5066 Office: U Mich Sch Info 550 E University Ave Ann Arbor MI 48109-1092 E-mail: archlib@umich.edu.

WARNER, ROBERTA ARLENE, accountant, financial services executive; b. Binghamton, N.Y., Dec. 31, 1938; d. Murrilan Earl and Ethel Margaret (Bell) W. BA, SUNY, Binghamton, 1960; MBA, Ind. U., 1962, MHA with highest distinction, 1973. C.P.A., N.Y. State; lic. nursing home adminstr., N.Y. State. Sr. acct. Arthur Young & Co., C.P.A.s, Buffalo, 1962-66; acctg. supr. Children's Hosp., 1966-68; controller King Manor Nursing Homes-Ave. Bldg. Corp., 1968-71; asst. dir. health fin. Hosp. Assn. N.Y. State, Albany, 1973-80, dir. health fin., 1980-93, Healthcare Assn. N.Y. State, Albany, 1994-97, dir. data analysis and standards, 1997-98; pres. Roberta A. Warner Co., 1999—. Author articles in field. Trustee Ednl. Found. of Am. Women's Soc. C.P.A.s/Am. Soc. Women Accts., 1985-87. Fellow Healthcare Fin. Mgmt. Assn.; mem. Am. Inst. C.P.A.s, Am. Acctg. Assn., Am. Soc. Women Accts. (pres. Buffalo chpt. 1967-68), Am. Women's Soc. CPAs, N.Y. State Soc. C.P.A.s, Ind. U. Alumni Assn. (life), SUNY Binghamton Alumni Assn. (life), Grange. Methodist. Home and Office: 569 NY Rte 79 Windsor NY 13865-2714

WARNER, ROLLIN MILES, JR. economics educator, real estate broker; b. Evanston, Ill., Dec. 25, 1930; s. Rollin Miles Warner Sr. and Julia Herndon (Polk) Clarkson. BA, Yale U., 1953; cert. in law, Harvard U., 1956; MBA, Stanford U., 1960; cert. in edn. adminstrn., U. San Francisco, 1974. Lic. real estate broker Calif. Asst. to v.p. fin. Stanford U., 1960-63; instr. history Town Sch., San Francisco, 1963-70, instr. econs. and history, dean, 1975—; prin. Mt. Tamalpais, Ross, Calif., 1972-74; dir. devel. Katharine Branson Sch., 1974-75, instr. econs., history, math. and outdoor edn. Author: America, 1986, Europe, 1986, Africa, Asia, Russia, 1986, Greece, Rome, 1981, Free Enterprise at Work, 1986. From scoutmaster to assistant camp commr. Boy Scouts Am., San Francisco, 1956—. Served to lt. USNR, 1953—55, Korea, Pacific, Vietnam. Recipient Silver Beaver award Boy Scouts Am., 1986, Town Sch. medal Town Sch. for Boys Alumni Coun., 1995. Mem.: Math. Assn. Am., Marines Meml. ASsn., San Francisco Yacht Club (Belvedere, Calif.), Grolier Club NY. Office: Town Sch 2750 Jackson St San Francisco CA 94115-1195 E-mail: warnerrollinm1960@alumni-gsb.stanford.edu.

WARNER, SCOTT DENNIS, investment banker; b. York, Pa., July 13, 1963; s. Earl Dennis and Sandra Glee (Barnhart) W. SB in Elec. Engring., SB in Computer Sci. and Engring., SM in Elec. Engring. and Computer Sci., MIT, 1986; MBA in Fin., U. Chgo., 1990. Rschr., teaching asst. MIT Lab. for Computer Sci., Cambridge, Mass., 1982-86; intern IBM Corp., Yorktown Heights, N.Y., 1983-86; fin. analyst Merrill Lynch & Co., N.Y.C., 1986-88, assoc., 1990-94, v.p., 1994-95; summer assoc. Goldman, Sachs & Co., 1989; v.p. Lipper & Co., L.P., 1995-98, Gerard Klauer Mattison & Co., Inc., N.Y.C., 1998—. Nat. Merit scholar, 1981, ROTC scholar, 1981, teaching asst. scholar MIT, 1985, 86; Leon C. Marshall scholar U. Chgo., 1988. Mem. Nat. Eagle Scout Assn., Delta Upsilon Frat. Republican. Presbyterian. Home: 235 E 95th St Apt 34J New York NY 10128-4025 Office: Gerard Klauer Mattison & Co Inc 529 5th Ave New York NY 10017-4608 E-mail: swarner@gkm.com.

WARNER, SHAUNA RUTH, city official; b. Mesa, Ariz., Dec. 27, 1973; BA, NYU, 1996; MPA, Ariz. State U., 1998. Mgmt. asst. City of Tempe, Ariz., 1998-99, neighborhood specialist, 1999—. Vol. Child Crisis Ctr., Mesa, 1996—. Martin Luther King Jr. scholar NYU, 1992-96. Mem. ASPA, Nat. Civic League, Internat. City and Country Mgrs. Assn., Neighborhoods USA.

WARNER, SUSAN, federal agency administrator; b. Rochester, N.Y., July 20, 1956; d. Harold J. and Jeannette (Nichols) Warner; divorced; children: Jennifer Lynn, Kathryn Alice. BA, Miami U., Oxford, Ohio, 1978; postgrad., Xavier U. Loan specialist HUD, Columbus, Ohio, 1978-79, Cin., 1979-83; fin. planner IDS Fin. Services, Inc., 1983-86, Manufacturer's Hanover Mortgage Corp., 1986, Shawmut Mortgage Corp., 1986-87, U.S. Dept. HUD, St. Louis, 1987—. Housing cons., Cin., 1985—. Author: Community Land Coop. Residents' Handbook, 1986. Adv. Cin. Tech. Coll., 1984—; mem. fin. com. Community Land Coop., Cin., 1985—; exhibits chair Conf. Cin. Women, 1985, corp. patrons chair, 1986, conf. coordinator, 1987—; vol. Am. Cancer soc., 1981-84, March of Dimes, 1996-99; leader Girl Scouts. Recipient profl. awards; Mercury awards IDS, Cin., 1984, award for superior performance U.S. Inspector Gen. HUD, 1990. Republican. Roman Catholic. Avocations: reading, costume designing, making teddy bears, softball, theater. Home: 771 Seven Hills Ln Saint Charles MO 63304-1436 Office: US Dept HUD 1222 Spruce St Saint Louis MO 63103-2818

WARNER, THEODORE KUGLER , JR. lawyer; b. Phila., Sept. 13, 1909; s. Theodore Kugler and Anna (Allen) W.; m. Dorothy Wark Hoehler, Nov. 23, 1935 (dec. 1985); children: Betsy Ann, Peter Joyce; m. Lynn Howell, May 20, 1995. AB, U. Pa., 1931, LL.B. cum laude, 1934. Bar: Pa. 1934. With Pa. R.R., Phila., 1934-70, chief tax counsel, 1952-58, dir. taxation, 1958-68; v.p. taxes Penn Central, 1968, v.p. accounting and taxes, 1968-69, v.p. corp. adminstrn., 1969-70; pres. Can. So. Ry., 1968-70; v.p. Pitts. & Lake Eric R.R., 1968-70; officer, dir. other Penn Central cos., 1968-70; counsel Duane, Morris & Heckscher, Phila., 1970-71, Harper & Driver, 1975—. Lectr. on consol. returns various tax forums. *The Independence Foundation, a Philadelphia-based private foundation, which specializes in funding for nurse-managed primary healthcare, culture and the arts, and public interest legal services, endowed the Warner Professorship in 1998 at the University of PA Law School to honor Theodore "Ted" K. Warner, Jr., C'31, L'34 cum laude. The gift recognizes his service to the foundation. Mr. Warner was president of his law class of 1934 from 1933-1956. The Warner Professorship will be designated for the area of business law, and a search for the chair holders is being completed.* Bd. suprs. Easttown Twp., Pa., 1962-70, chmn., 1966-70; bd. dirs. Independence Found., 1991—, sec. 1993, pres., 1993-95, sec.-treas., 1996— Mem. ABA, Nat. Tax Assn. (pres. 1965-66), Am. Law Inst. (life mem.), Pa. Bar Assn., Order of Coif, Union League, Masons (33 deg., com. on masonic homes 1970-84, chmn. 1975-77, 81-83, Franklin medal 1983, bd. dirs., treas. Masonic libr. and mus. 1991-99), Tau Kappa Epsilon. Republican. Lutheran. Home: 607 Benson House 930 W Montgomery Ave Bryn Mawr PA 19010 Office: 200 S Broad St Ste 1101 Philadelphia PA 19102

WARNER, WALTER DUKE, corporate executive; b. Davenport, Iowa, Feb. 26, 1952; s. Robert Martin and Opal Louise (Gibbons) W.; m. Susan Dee Hafferkamp, Nov. 15, 1975 (div. 1982); 1 child, Natalie. BS, Drake U., 1975. Ops. officer Iowa-Des Moines Nat. Bank, 1975-78; from v.p. ops. to v.p. mktg. and pub. rels. Cen. Savs. and Loan Assn., San Diego, 1978-84; pres. The Lomas Santa Fe Cos., Solana Beach, 1985-91; pres., co-founder Ebert Composites Corp., San Diego, 1991—, also bd. dirs.; pres., CEO Strongwell Ebert LLC, 1998-01, also bd. dirs.; CEO Pacific Environ. Sys. LLC, 2001—. Bd. dirs. Torrey Pines Bank, Solana Beach, Lomas Group Inc., Del Mar, Calif., Madison Valley Properties, Inc., La Jolla, Calif., Nature Preserved of Am. Inc., San Clemente, Calif.; pres., bd. dirs. Regents Park Comml. Assn., La Jolla, Strongwell Ebert. Bd. dirs. Inst. of the Ams., La Jolla, 1986-90, mem. internat. coun., 1986-90; chmn. bd. dirs., pres. San Diego chpt. Arthritis Found., 1985-87; dir., pres. Gildred Found., Solana Beach, 1986-90; founding dir., treas. Golden Triangle Arts Found. Mem. Calif. League of Savs. and Loans (mktg. and ops. com. 1982-84), Internat. Forum for Corp. Dirs., Iowa Club San Diego (founding dir. 1984-85). Republican. Protestant. Avocations: tennis, piano.

WARNER, WILLIAM HAMER, applied mathematician; b. Pitts., Oct. 6, 1929; s. John Christian and Louise (Hamer) W.; m. Janet Louise West, June 29, 1957; 1 dau., Katherine Patricia. Student, Haverford Coll., 1946-48; BS, Carnegie Inst. Tech., 1950, MS, 1951, PhD, 1953. Research asso. grad. div. applied math. Brown U., Providence, 1953-55; asst. prof. dept. aerospace engring. and mechanics U. Minn., Mpls., 1955-58, asso. prof., 1958-68, prof., 1968-95, prof. emeritus, 1995—. Author: (with L.E. Goodman) Statics, 1963, Dynamics, 1964; contbr. articles to profl. jours. Mem.: Soc. Natural Philosophy, Math. Assn. Am., Soc. Indsl. and Applied Math., Am. Math. Soc. Office: Univ Minn 107 Akerman Hall 110 Union St SE Minneapolis MN 55455-0153 E-mail: warner@aem.umn.edu.

WARNER-MILLS, SUSAN, organizational and community development consultant; b. Columbus, Ohio, Jan. 1, 1958; d. Robert Lawrence and Elise (Ackley) Mills; m. Thomas Everett Warner, Sept. 14, 1980; 1 child, Robert. BA, Bucknell U., 1979; MPA, Pa. State U., 1991. Office mgr. Tech. Edn. Resource Ctrs., Cambridge, Mass., 1980-81; editl. asst. Daedalus Jour., 1981-82; mng. ptnr. The Lewisburg (Pa.) Inn, 1982—; project dir., Cmty. Connection Project LWV of Pa. Citizen Edn. Fund, Harrisburg, 1995-98; program devel. specialist Cmty. Connection of Pa., 1999—; ptnr. Groupworks Cons., 1998—. Contbr. articles to profl. jours. Pres. LWV Lewisburg Area, 1991-94; citizens jury rev. com., LWV of Pa., 1993, budget com. mem., 1992, bd. dirs. 1997-99; founder Indsl. Roundtable Environ. Mgmt. Ctr. Pa., 1994; bd. dirs. Merrill Linn Land and Waterways Conservancy, 1993-96; Slifer House Mus., 1992-97; sec., Union County appointee Mid-State Resource Conservation and Devel. Coun., 1992-97; elected mem. Union County Dem. Com., 1984-86; co-founder, dir. Citizens for Social Responsibility, 1982-84. Avocations: swimming, skiing, music, running. Office: 202 S 3rd St Lewisburg PA 17837-1912 E-mail: swm@groupworksconsulting.com.

WARNEX, PAUL DAVID, music educator; b. Lexington, Mo., Oct. 4, 1954; s. John David and Barbara Ann Warnex; m. Deborah Lynn Kallenbach, Aug. 6, 1977; children: David Paul. BM, Ctrl. Mo. State U., Warrensburg, MO, 1976, MA, 1981. Teachers Certificate K-12 Mo., Iowa. Band dir. Holden Sch. Dist., Holden, Mo., 1977—79, LeMars Cmty. Schools, LeMars, Iowa, 1980—89, dir. of music, 1988—99; band dir. Liberty Pub. Schools, Liberty, Mo., 1989—. Contbr. articles to profl. jours. Recipient outstanding young band dir. for Iowa, ASBDA/Stanbury, 1984, Outstanding Tchr., Nat. Assn. of Music Edn., 2000, Outstanding Band Dir., Lamda Chapter-Phi Beta Mu, 2002. Mem.: Music Educators Nat. Conf., Mo. Music Educators Assn. (band v.p. 2000—02), Mo. Bandmasters Assoc. Achievements include Liberty Symphonic Band-Grand Champions of Dixie Classic Festival, 1994; performed at MMEA convention, 1994 & 1998; sweepstakes winner of Worlds of Fun Band Festival, 1999. Avocations: home improvement, home improvement, home improvement. Home: 631 Cosby St Liberty MO 64068 Office: Liberty Public Schools 200 Blue Jay Dr Liberty MO 64068 E-mail: pwarnex@mail.liberty.k12.mo.us.

WARNICK, PATRICIA ANN, healthcare consultant, nurse ethicist; b. Shenandoah, Pa., Sept. 30, 1948; d. Alfred Samuel and Anna Patricia (Knapp) W. Diploma in nursing, Coatesville (Pa.) Hosp., 1972; BS in Sociology, St. Joseph's U., 1980, MS in Health Adminstrn., 1982; postgrad., Villanova U., 1996, cert. palliative nursing; cert. life care nursing curriculum, UPHS; cert. mgmt. skills for practicing mgr., Villanova U. RN, cert. emergency nurse, pediatric advanced life support, emergency nursing pediatric curriculum, ACLS. Clin. nurse IV, Presbyn. Hosp.-U. Pa. Med. Ctr., Phila., 1972-75, 87—, asst. nurse mgr. ICU, 1975-76, staff nurse emergency dept., 1976-78, hospice nurse, 1978-80, asst. nurse mgr. emergency room, 1981-82, clin. specialist emergency dept. and ambulatory care, 1982-83, dir. hospice services and asst. dir. Presbyn. Home Health, 1983-87, nurse emergency dept., 1987—. Clin. preceptor Villanova (Pa.) U., 1985-86; mem. hosp.-wide ethics com., mem. faculty Decisions Near End of Life, Presbyn. Hosp.-U. Pa. Health Systems; trustee Phila. Gospel Sems., Inc., 1995-98. Vol. nurse ARC; chmn. svc. and rehab. com. Am. Cancer Soc., Phila., 1987—, hosp. ethics com.; mem. Del. Valley Ethics Com. Network; mem. Phila. Gospel Seminar Choir, 1990—. Mem. Nat. Hospice Orgn., Nat. Assn. for Advancement of Fat Acceptance, Pa. Hospice Orgn. (ethics com.), Emergency Nurses Assn. (cert. emergency nurse), Alpha Sigma Lambda. Democrat. Roman Catholic. Avocations: reading, music. Home: Park Heights Apt 501 5555 Wissahickon Ave Philadelphia PA 19144-4555 Office: Presbyn U Pa Med Ctr 51 N 39th St Philadelphia PA 19104-2640 E-mail: patricia.warnick@uphs.upenn.edu.

WARNOCK, JOHN EDWARD, computer company executive; b. Salt Lake City, Oct. 6, 1940; BS in Math. and Philosophy, U. Utah, 1961, MS in Math., 1964, PhD in Elec. Engring. and Computer Sci., 1969. With Evans & Sutherland Computer Corp., Computer Scis. Corp., IBM; prin. scientist Xerox Palo Alto Rsch. Ctr., Calif., 1978-81; co-founder, chmn. Adobe Sys., Inc., San Jose, Calif., 1982—, CEO, 1982—2000. Bd. dirs. Netscape Comm. Corp.,

Red Brick Sys., Evans & Sutherland Computer Corp. Patentee in field; contbr. articles to profl. jours. and industry mags.; spkr. in field. Chmn. Tech Mus. Innovation; mem. entrepreneurial bd. adv. com. Am. Film Inst. Recipient Computer Achievement award Assn. for Computing Machinery SIGGRAPH, 1989, Tech. Excellence award Nat. Graphics Assn., 1989, ACM Software Sys. award, 1989, Lifetime Achievement award for tech. excellence, PC Mag., 1989, J. Anderson Disting. Achievement award, 1991, Disting. Alumnus award U. Utah, 1995, Cary award Rochester Inst. Tech., 1995; named Entrepreneur of Yr. Ernst & Young, Merril Lynch, Inc., 1991. Mem. NAE. Office: Adobe Sys Inc 345 Park Ave San Jose CA 95110-2704*

WARNOCK, MICHAEL DAVID, music educator; b. Dallas, Mar. 21, 1973; s. David Ronald Warnock, Adoria (Martin) Warnock; m. Vicki Lynn Smith, Aug. 7, 1999. B in Music Edn., Va. State U., 2001; postgrad., George Washington U. Tchr., dir. band Prince George County Schs., Prince George, Va., 2001—. Specialist, percussionist U.S. Army, 1993—97. Recipient Commendation medal, U.S. Army, 1997. Mem.: Va. Edn. Assn., Music Educators Nat. Conf. Home: 408 Rivers Bend Ct Chester VA 23836 Office: Prince George County Schs 7801 Laurel Spring Rd Prince George VA 23873

WARNOCK, WILLIAM REID, lawyer; b. Detroit, July 25, 1939; s. William G. and Margery E. (Ford) W.; m. Sandra L. Klarich, Dec. 27, 1961; children: Cheryl Lynn, Laura Ellen. BBA, U. Mich., 1961, JD with distinction, 1964. Bar: Ill. 1964, U.S. Dist. Ct. (no. dist.) Ill. 1965, U.S. Supreme Ct. 1972, Mich. 1995. With Ross & Hardies, Chgo., 1964-70; regional counsel U.S. Dept. HUD, 1970-73; ptnr. Roan & Grossman, 1973-82; sole practice, 1982-85; ptnr. Siegel & Warnock, 1985-91; of counsel Donovan & Olsen, 1991; pres. William R. Warnock P.C., LaGrange, 1992—2002, Three Rivers, Mich., 2002—. Cons. Ill. Dept. Bus. and Econ. Devel., Chgo., 1977-78, Ill. Housing Devel. Authority, Chgo., 1973-78, Council State Housing Financing Agys., Washington, 1975-78; past pres., chmn. Atty.'s Title Guaranty Fund, Inc., Chgo., 1986-88, also bd. dirs., 1976—. Author: (legal references) Land Use and Zoning, 1974-88, Ward on Title Examination, 1975, Illinois Real Property Service: Real Estate Exchanges, 1988, Environmental Law and the Real Estate Lawyer, 1989-90. Mem. Ill. State Bar Assn., Am. Coll. Real Estate Lawyers. Republican. Methodist. Avocations: boating, woodworking. Home: 13556 Pleasant View Rd Three Rivers MI 49093-8406 Fax: 616-244-8580.

WARNSTADT, STEVEN H. state legislator; b. Sioux City, Iowa, Aug. 2, 1967; s. Steven B. and Jackie R. (Harshfield) W.; m. Mary S. Green, Aug. 16, 1997; 1 child. BA magna cum laude, Drake U., 1989; MA, Temple U., 1992. Package handler UPS, Phila., 1993; optical engr. TKC Optical, Sioux City, 1994; state rep. Iowa Ho. of Reps., 1995—. Instr. Western Iowa Tech. C.C., Sioux City, 1998—. Mem. Woodbury County Dem. Ctrl. Com., 1996-98; bd. dirs. Sioux Trails coun. Girl Scouts U.S., 1994-2000. With U.S. Army, 1989-92, Pa. N.G. 1993, Iowa N.G., 1993—. Decorated Army Commendation medal. Mem. VFW, Officers of the First Divsn., Am. Legion. Democrat.

WARPINSKI, TERRI L. academic administrator, artist; b. Green Bay, Wis., June 2, 1955; d. Robert J. and Lucille J. (Kehoe) W. BA, U. Wis., 1979; MA, U. Iowa, 1982, MFA, 1983. Vis. instr. Sch. Art, U. Fla., Gainesville, 1983-84; prof. dept. arts U. Oreg., Eugene, 1984—, dir. Malheur Photography Workshop, 1984—, assoc. prof. art, 1990—2001, prof., 2001—, assoc. dean Sch. Architecture and Allied Arts, 1997—. Mem. vis. faculty Arrowmont Sch. Arts and Crafts, Gatlinburg, Tenn., 1990-2000; vis. artist Linfield Coll., Coll. St. Catherine, U. Arts, Phila. One person show at Internat. PhotoFest, Houston, 1996; exhibited in group show at Woodstock (N.Y.) Ctr. for Photography, 1998; pub. art commns., Port of Portland, Oreg. State U., Ctrl. Oreg. C.C. Active Oreg. Natural Desert Assn., 1991—. Artist residence Ucross Found., Wyo., 2000; Fulbright fellow rsch. Arava Inst. Environ. Studies, Israel, 2000, 01; Rsch. grantee Ctr. for the Study of Women in Soc., 1996. Mem. Internat. Coun. Fine Arts Deans, Coll. Art Assn., Soc. Photographic Edn. (regional dir. 1987-92, nat. bd. dirs. 2001—). Avocations: backpacking, sailing, skiing, gardening. Office: U Oreg 5249 Sch Architecture & Allied Arts Eugene OR 97403-5249 Fax: 541-346-3626. E-mail: warpinsk@darkwing.uoregon.edu.

WARREN, ALBERT, publishing executive; b. Warren, Ohio, May 18, 1920; s. David and Clara Warren; m. Margaret Virginia Yeomans, Jan. 9, 1947; children: Ellen, Paul, Claire, Daniel, Thomas, Joan. BA in Journalism, Ohio State U., 1942. Assoc. editor TV Digest, Washington, 1945-50, sr. editor, 1950-58, chief Washington Bur., 1958-61; chmn., editor, pub. Warren Comm. News, Inc., 1961—. Lectr Columbia Grad Sch Journalism, New York, NY, 1962—75; mem alumni adv coun Ohio State Univ, Columbus, 1982—88. Pub: 15 periodicals in communications area; contbr. articles to profl jours. Mem adv coun Sch Journalism, Ohio State Univ, 1982—. With USNR, 1942—45, PTO. Mem.: Soc. Profl. Journalists (Hall of Fame 1991), U.S. Congress Periodical Gallery, Internat. Radio and TV Soc. Pubs., Cable TV Pioneers, Broadcast Pioneers (Annual Recognition Award 1982, Hall of Fame 1995), Newsletter Pubs. Assn. (Hall of Fame 1985), Ind. Newsletter Assn. (co-founder 1963, pres 1965—66), Cosmos Club. Home: 26 W Kirke St Chevy Chase MD 20815-4261 Office: Warren Comm News Inc 2115 Ward Ct NW Washington DC 20037-1209

WARREN, ALICE LOUISE, artist; b. Springfield, Mass., May 7, 1927; d. Roland D. and Ella May (McGrath) Eaton Von Der Lancken; m. John Homer Warren, June 5, 1948 (dec. Jan. 1988); children: John David, Daniel Wayne. Student, N.Y. Sch. Writing, 1952-55, Mansion House Art Sch., 1969, 70, 71; grad., Nat. Landscape Inst., 1960, Famous Writers Sch., 1965; Cert., United UMA Sch., 1967. Home nursing cert.; cert. home health aide paramedical. Nurses aide ARC, Springfield, 1942-45; hot-line councilor Check Line, West Springfield, Mass., 1945-46; freelance columnist New England Homestead, Springfield, 1960-63; freelance columnist, editor Garden Page Woman's Circle, Horticulture mags. Author, photographer: (booklet) Evergreen Shrubs, 1964. solo art exhbns. Mercy Hosp., Arts Unltd. Gallery, 1997, Bay State Med., Springfield, Mass., 1999; featured artist Barnes and Noble Bookstore, Oct. 1999, Westfield Antheneum, 2000; on-line exhbns. MindsIsland.com, 2002. Recipient Bill Curtin award for watercolor, 1983. Mem. Amherst Writers & Artists Inst., Springfield Art League, Scriptures Writers, Mass. Writers Guild (treas. 1963), Tobacco Valley Artists Assn. Avocations: painting, travel, photography, reading. Home: 40 Midway St Indian Orchard MA 01151-1325

WARREN, BRADFORD LLOYD, lawyer; b. Indpls., Oct. 2, 1948; s. Claude Marion and Nina Jean (Davidson) W. AB, Ind. U., Bloomington, 1970; JD, Ind. U., Indpls., 1973. Bar: Ind. 1973, U.S. Dist. Ct. (so. dist.) Ind. 1973, U.S. Supreme Ct. 1983. Tax staffman Arthur Andersen & Co., Indpls., 1972-74; ptnr. Warren, Snider & Warren, 1974-77; sole practice, 1977—. Active Libertarian Party Ind. 1976—, candidate U.S. Ho. Reps., 1984, candidate U.S. Senate, 1986. Mem. Ind. U. Alumni Assn., Delta Tau Delta (bd. dirs., sec., treas. Beta Alpha Shelter 1976-94). Lodges: Order of Demolay, Chevalier citation. Home: 5204 N Winthrop Ave Indianapolis IN 46220-3259 Office: 926 E 52nd St Indianapolis IN 46205-1124

WARREN, CHARLES DAVID, library administrator; b. Martin, Tenn., June 12, 1944; s. Charles Aulton and Evelyn (Bell) W.; children: Aaron David, Meredith Hild, Julia Myers. BS, U. Tenn., 1967; MS, U. Ill., Urbana, 1969. cert. pub. library adminstr. Dir. Shiloh Regional Library, Jackson, Tenn., 1969-72, Cumberland County Pub. Library, Fayetteville, N.C., 1973-79; exec. dir. Richland County Pub. Library, Columbia, S.C., 1979—; v.p. LHW Creations, Inc., 1979—. Bd. dirs. Civic Music Assn., Fayetteville, N.C., 1973-79, Fayetteville Symphony, 1973-78, Fayetteville Arts Commn., 1975; v.p. Friends of Librs. U.S.A., 1994—; mem. Columbia Coord. Coun., 1987-88; chmn. Richland County History Commn., 1987-93; mem. John Cotton Dana Awards Commn., 1994-99. Recipient Lucy Hampton Bostick award, 1993, S.C. Pub. Adminstr. Yr. award, 1993; named Young Man of Yr., Fayetteville Jaycees, 1977, S.C. Libr. of Yr., 1991, Internat. Fedn. Librs., 1997-2001, Order of Silver Crescent, 1999. Mem. ALA (pres. Jr. Member Roundtable 1977, chmn. awards com. 1984), Southeastern Libr. Assn. (pres. pub. libr. sect. 1978), S.C. Libr. Assn. (bd. dirs. 1980), Spring Valley Country Club, Rotary, Kiwanis, Beta Phi Mu. Democrat. Episcopalian. Home: 619 King St #806 Columbia SC 29205 Office: Richland County Pub Libr 1431 Assembly St Columbia SC 29201-3101

WARREN, CHRISTOPHER CHARLES, electronics executive; b. Helena, Mont., July 27, 1949; s. William Louis and Myrtle Estelle (Moren) W.; m. Danette Marie Geordge, Apr. 21, 1972; 1 child, Jeffrey Scott. Grad. high sch., Helena, 1967. Electrician Supreme Electronics, Helena, 1972-81; v.p., svc. technician Capital Music Inc., 1981—. State exec. Amusement & Music Operators Assn. Coun. of Affiliated States, Chgo., 1990-92. Sgt. USAF, 1968-72, Vietnam. Mem.: Amusement and Music Operators Assn. (bd. dirs. 1992—95, v.p. 1995—2000, sec. 2000—01, treas. 2001—), Rocky Mountain Elk Found., Valley Nat. 8-Ball Assn. (charter), Ducks Unltd., Mont. Coin Machine Operators State 8-Ball (chmn.), Internat. Flipper Pinball Assn. (sec./treas. 1991—92, pres. 1993—94), Mont. Coin Machine Operators Assn. (pres. 1989—91, 1997—99, treas. 2000), Eagles, Moose, VFW (life). Avocations: photography, restoring old cars and trucks, hunting, fishing. Home: 8473 Green Meadow Dr Helena MT 59602-8312 Office: Capital Music Inc PO Box 5416 Helena MT 59604-5416 E-mail: ccwar@aol.com.

WARREN, CINDY MICHELLE, author; b. Warren, Mich., Jan. 3, 1962; d William Henry and Margaret Helen (Cooper) W. Writer/journalist, Detroit, 1982—; bus. mgr. Detroit Writers Project, 1987—; founder, pres. Detroit Performance Army United, 1990—; asst. chair Women's Studies, Wayne State U., Detroit, 1991-92; poetry editor The Word Enamel, 1995-96, fiction editor, 1992-93. Mgr. various poetry reading series, Detroit, 1987—; pub. Manque Mag., Detroit, 1980-83, Four Points of Love mag., Detroit, 1983-85. Author: Wayne Literary Review, 1990, 91, 92, Triage, 1991-94, Babyfish Lost Its Momma, 1989-94; contbr. articles to profl. jours. Fundraiser Detroit Writers Project, 1987—, Adrian (Mich.) Four, 1991, Poetry Resource Ctr., Detroit, 1989-94; mem. Detroit Zool. Soc., 1993—. Avocations: filmmaking, photography, dancing, vocalist, performance artist.

WARREN, CLAY, communication educator; b. Lexington Park, Md., Aug. 11, 1946; s. Cassius Clay and Dorothy Dean Warren; m. Gitte Bonde Kolind, May 1, 1985; children: Laura Kolind, Daniel Clay Kolind. BS, U.S. Naval Acad., 1968; MA, U. Colo., 1973, PhD, 1976. Instr. U. Colo., Boulder, 1973-76; asst. prof. semester-at-sea program Inst. Shipbd. Edn., Laguna Hills, Calif., 1977; vis. asst. prof. U. Coll. Cape Breton, Sydney, N.S., Can., 1978, assoc. prof. Can., 1984-90; asst. prof. Shepherd Coll., Shepherdstown, W.Va., 1978-79, U. Hawaii at Manoa, Honolulu, 1979-82; sr. lectr. Internat. People's Coll., Elsinore, Denmark, 1982-84; assoc. prof. George Washington U., Washington, 1990-91, Chauncey M. Depew prof., 1991—. Assoc. cons. M J Solutions, Westport, Conn., 1986—; dir. comm. program George Washington U., Washington, 1990—, Warren Consulting, Washington, 1990—. Author: Coming Around, 1986; editor: Inner Visions, Outer Voices, 1988, Democracy Is Born in Conversations, 1998; contbr. articles to scholarly jours. Mem. site team Mil. Installation Vol. Edn. Rev. Project Office of Asst. Sec. of Def., 1992—; nat. coord. CREDIT, Am. Coun. Edn., 1996—. Lt. USN, 1968-71. Latin Am. Teaching fellow Tufts U., 1977, Tompkins Inst. Rsch. fellow, 1987-89; Rudolf Dreikurs Meml. scholar Internat. Com. for Adlerian Summer Schs. and Inst., 1988; named Princeton Seminarian Acad. Consciousness Studies, Princeton U., 1994. Mem. AAUP (v.p. George Washington U. chpt. 1994-98), Nat. Comm. Assn., N.Am. Soc. Adlerian Psychology, Folk Edn. Assn. Am. (exec. coun. 1992-96). Avocations: certified scuba diver, sport parachutist, pvt. pilot, pianist, creative writer. Office: George Washington U 2130 H St NW Ste 707 Washington DC 20052-0001

WARREN, DANIEL CHURCHMAN, health facility administrator; b. Washington, Sept. 23, 1939; s. Walter Thomas and Laura Katherine W.; m. C. Frederica Lescure, June 5, 1958; 1 child, Christopher C. BS, Roanoke Coll., 1960; MD, Med. Coll. Va., 1964; MPH, U. N.C., 1971; MMAS, U.S. Army Command & Gen. Coll., 1974. Diplomate Nat. Bd. Med. Examiners, Am. Bd. Preventive Medicine, lic. physician VA. Intern Georgetown U. Hosp., 1964-65; resident in surgery Med. Coll. Va., 1967-68, William Beaumont Gen. Hosp., 1968-69; resident in preventive medicine Walter Reed Army Inst. Rsch., 1971-73; commd. 2d lt. U.S. Army, 1965, advanced through grades to col., 1986; asst. med. dir. HealthAm. Va., 1986; pvt. practice travel, 1987-89; dir. Peninsula Health Dist., Newport News, Va., 1990—2001; warden Holyrood Sem., 2001—. Clin. asst. prof. family and cmty. medicine Ea. Va. Med. Sch., Norfolk; cons. Riverside Regional Med Ctr., Newport News. Active Gloucester County Rep. Com., 1987-96, chmn. 1992-95, Gloucester County Redistricting Adv. Com., 1991, 2001; hon. chmn. Combined Va. Campaign United Way the Va. Peninsula, 1992. Fellow Am. Coll. Preventive Medicine, Royal Soc. Medicine; mem. Med. Soc. Va., Mid-Tidewater Med. Soc., Ret. Officers Assn., Cremona Fiddlers, Kiwanis. Republican. Anglican. Avocations: English and Virginia history. Office: Peninsula Health Dist 416 J Clyde Morris Blvd Newport News VA 23601-1927

WARREN, DANIEL YEOMANS, publishing executive; b. Washington, Dec. 30, 1953; s. Albert and Margaret (Yeomans) W.; m. Kerry Ann Foley, June 20, 1981; children: David F., Stuart F., Helen F. BA summa cum laude, Boston U., 1975; PhD, Cornell U., 1984. Mng. editor Warren Publ., Washington, 1981-85, sr. v.p., 1985-2000, vice chmn., 2000—. Chmn., bd. trustees Sheridan Sch., Washington, 1999—, Folger Shakespeare Libr. Corp. (mem. adv. com.), Newsletter Pub. Assn. (1993-98, pres. Wash. chpt. 1988). Mem. Newsletter Publ. Found. (bd. dirs. 1996—), Soc. Profl. Journalists, Phi Beta Kappa, Sigma Delta Chi (treas. 1994-2000). Avocations: woodworking, reading, skiing, basketball, weightlifting. Office: Warren Comm News Inc. 2115 Ward Ct NW Washington DC 20037-1209 E-mail: dwarren@warren-news.com.

WARREN, DAVID LILES, educational association executive; b. Goldsboro, N.C., Sept. 15, 1943; s. James Hubert and Katherine (Liles) W.; m. Ellen Elizabeth LeGendre, Mar. 1, 1969; children— Jamison, Mackenzie, Katrin BA in English, Wash. State U., 1965; M. Urban Studies, M.Div., Yale U., 1970; PhD, U. Mich., 1976; LittD, Elmhurst Coll., 1994, Moravian Coll., 1994; LLD, Rider U., 1996, Mt. Union Coll., 1997, Centre Coll., 1997, Mercer U., 1998, Franklin and Marshall Coll, 1999; Doctor of Public Service, Rocky Mountain Coll., 1999; LLD, Ky. Wesleyan Coll., 2000; LHD, U. of New Haven, 2001; LittD, Middlebury Coll., 2001. Gen. sec. Dwight Hall, Yale U., New Haven, 1969-76, bd. dirs., 1976—; assoc. dir. community relations Yale U., 1976-78; sr. v.p., provost Antioch U., N.Y.C. and Yellow Springs, Ohio, 1978-82; chief adminstrv. officer City of New Haven, 1982-84; pres. Ohio Wesleyan U., Delaware, 1984-93, Nat. Assn. Indep. Colls. and Univs., Washington, 1993—; with Franklin and Marshall Coll., 1999. Cons. to hosps., sch. systems, colls., univs.; bd. dirs. Delaware County Bank; chmn. NCAA Pres. Commn., Div. III, 1990-92. Contbr. chpts. to books, articles to Yale Alumni Mag. Mem. NEw Haven Bd. Alderman, 1973-75; vice chmn. New Haven Commn. on Poverty, 1981-82; pres. North Coast Athletic Conf., 1988-90; justice of peace New Haven Dem. Party, 1974-76; state chmn. People to People, 1987; chmn. Gov.'s Task Force on Dep. Registrar, 1987; chmn. Ohio Five Coll. Commn., 1985-95, Campus Compact Nat. Exec. Com., 1987-88; bd. dirs. U.S. Health Corp., Coun. Ethics and Econs.; exec. com. Great Lakes Colls. Assn., Ctrl. Ohio Symphony Orch.; chmn. Ohio Ethics commn. Fulbright scholar Wash. State U., 1965-66; Rockefeller fellow Yale U., 1966; disting. Centennial Alumnus Wash. State U. Mem. Am. Assn. Higher Edn., Assn. Ind. Colls. Univs. (sec. 1987-88), Phi Beta Kappa Clubs: University (Columbus, Ohio); Graduate (New Haven). Democrat. Methodist. Avocations: jogging; writing; tennis. Office: Nat Assn Ind Colls & Univs 1025 Connecticut Ave NW Ste 700 Washington DC 20036-5409

WARREN, DEAN STUART, artist; b. Mpls., June 30, 1949; s. Jefferson Trowbridge and Dorothy Ann (Edin) W.; m. Betty Sharon Poe, Aug. 14, 1971; children: Jeremy, Adam. BFA, Fla. Atlantic U., 1973; MA, Northwestern State U., 1975; MFA, Stephen F. Austin State U., 1980. Instr. art Cisco (Tex.) Jr. Coll., 1976-78; staff craftsworker Walt E. Disney Show Prodn. Walt Disney World, Lake Buena Vista, Fla., 1981-83, staff craftsworker staff shop, 1983, property craftsworker, 1983-87, artist preparator animation dept., 1987—; lead prodn. artist Marvac, Inc., Seminole County, 1983. Founder Dean S. Warren Studio, 1991—; cons. Mt. Dora (Fla.) Ctr. for Arts Children's Edn. Program; instr. Bok Tower Gardens Edn. Ctr. Workshop, Lake Wales, Fla., 1996. Author: Runemaster, 1991; project artist Youth Art Symposium, U. Ctrl. Fla., 1993, Children's Art program, Atlantic Ctr. for arts, 1993, 95, Children's Art Program Mount Dora Ctr. for Arts, 1995, Edn. Ctr., 1996; one-man shows include Ormond Beach (Fla.) Meml. Art Gallery and Gardens, 1987, U. Ctrl. Fla. Art Gallery, Orlando, 1991, Harris House Atlantic Ctr. for Arts, New Smyrna Beach, Fla., 1993, Dars Studio, Gallery Agy., Milan, 2000; exhibited in group shows at U. Miami (Fla.) Sculpture Invitational, 1982, Valencia C.C. Fine Arts Gallery, Orlando, 1989, Polk C.C. Fine Arts Gallery, Winter Haven, Fla., 1990, U. Ga., Athens, 1990, U. Tampa (Fla.) Scarfone Gallery, 1991, World Cup Soccer, Valencia C.C., 1994, Mt. Dora Ctr. of Arts, 1996, Crealdé Sch. of Art Sculpture Garden, Winter Park, Fla., 1997, 2000, 621 Gallery, Tallahassee, Fla., 1998, Barbara Gillman Gallery, Miami Beach, Fla., 1999, D'Ars Gallery Agy., Milan, Italy, 1999, 2000, 01, 02, Warehouse Gallery, Orlando, 1999, 2000, Leonardo DaVinci Mus. of Sci. and Tech., Milan, 1999, Walt Disney World Art Exhbn., 2000, Alice and William Jenkins Gallery, Crealde Sch. Art, 2001, Banca Popolare di Milano, Bergano, Italy, 2001, Postart Gallery, Milan, 2002, Galleria Blanchaert, Milan, 2002.. Recipient Artist in the Schs. grant Tex. Commn. on the Arts, 1980, awards U. Ga. Bot. Gardens, Athens, 1980, Valencia C.C., East Campus, Orlando, 1983, Arts on The Park, Lakeland, Fla., 1995. Home: 8069 Wellsmere Cir Orlando FL 32835-5361

WARREN, DONALD JOHN, retired surgeon, educator; b. New Haven, Jan. 23, 1924; s. John Walls and Jane Margaret (Pendorf) W.; m. Muriel Celia Beach, June 24, 1944 (div. 1980); children: Douglas, Mark, Barbara; m. Betty V. Jones, Apr. 3, 1982. BA, SUNY, Syracuse, 1945, MD, 1947. Cert. surgery. Intern Syracuse U. Hosp., 1947-48; resident in surgery Millard Fillmore Hosp., Buffalo, 1952-56; gen. surgeon USAF, 1956-66, 80-84, ret., 1984; pvt. practice, 1966-75, 1985-88; ret., 1988. Gen. surgeon VA, 1975-80; asst. prof. surgery U. Calif., Davis, 1973-75; asst. clin. prof. surgery, U.S.D., 1977-80. Fellow ACS. Home: 1616 79th Pl Lubbock TX 79423-2402 E-mail: wbettyvan@aol.com.

WARREN, DONALD WILLIAM, physiology educator, dentistry educator; b. Bklyn., Mar. 22, 1935; s. Sol B. and Frances (Plotkin) W.; m. Priscilla Girardi, June 10, 1956; children: Donald W. Jr., Michael C. BS, U. N.C., 1956, DDS, 1959; MS, U. Pa., 1961, PhD, 1963; D in Odontology (hon.), U. Kuopio, Finland, 1991. Asst. prof. dentistry U. N.C., Chapel Hill, 1963-65, dir. Craniofacial Ctr., 1963-2000, assoc. prof., 1965-69, prof., 1969-80, chmn. dept. dental ecology, 1970-85, Kenan prof., 1980—, rsch. prof. otolaryngology, 1985—. Cons. NIH, Bethesda, Md., 1967—, R. J. Reynolds-Nabisco, Winston-Salem, N.C., 1986-99. Contbr. articles to profl. jours. Recipient Honor award Am. Cleft Palate Assn./Craniofacial Assn., 1992, O. Max Garner award U. N.C. Bd. Govs., 1993, honors award Angle Orthodontic Soc., 1998. Fellow AAAS, Internat. Coll. Dentists, Am. Speech and Hearing Lang. Assn. (Editors award 1998), Internat. Assn. Dental Rsch., Acoustical Soc. Am., Am. Cleft Palate Assn. (pres. 1981-82, Disting. Svc. award 1984), Am. Cleft Palate Edn. Found. (pres. 1976-77). Avocations: horse related activities, running, farming. Home: PO Box 1356 Southern Pines NC 28388-1356 Office: U NC Sch Dentistry Cb 7450 Chapel Hill NC 27599-0001 E-mail: don_warren@dentistry.unc.edu.

WARREN, ELLEN, writer; b. Warrensburg, Mo., June 13, 1969; d. George and Katherine Azar; m. David Warren; children: Alicia, Ethan. Author: Midst the Shadow of Love, 2000, Spitting Images, 2002. Baptist. Home: 7525 Blue Bird Rd Versailles MO 65084 Personal E-mail: lemay@access2k1.net.

WARREN, EMILY P. retired secondary and adult school educator; b. Dayton, Ky., Oct. 6, 1928; d. Morris C. and Kathleen (B.) Parker; m. Richard E. Warren (dec.); children: Richard Warren Jr., George Michael. BS in Home Econs., U. Ky., 1950; MS in Edn., Barry U., 1968; postgrad., Fla. State U. Cert. tchr., Fla. Tchr. home econs., Vevay, Ind., 1950-52, Ludlow, Ky., 1952-53, Cin., 1953-54; part-time adult home econs. tchr. Sch. Practical Nursing Mt. Sinai Hosp., Miami Beach, Fla., 1955-57; elem. tchr. Dade County, 1957-59; tchr. home econs., 1960-66; coord. vocat. home econs. Dade County Pub. Schs., 1966-91. Group leader home econs. tchrs., Russia, 1993, China, 1994, Russia/Hungary, 1995; cons. in field. Named Fla. Tchr. of Yr., 1965. Mem. Am. Assn. Family and Consumer Scis., Am. Vocat. Assn., Dade County Adminstrs. Assn., Dade County Home and Family Edn. Assn., Fla. Adult Edn. Assn., Fla. Assn. for Supervision and Curriculum Devel., Fla. Assn. Family and Consumer Scis., Nat. Assn. Local Suprs. Home Econs. Econs. Assn. (pres.), Internat. Furnishings and Design Assn. (Fla. chpt. v.p, and sec.), Ret. Educators Assn. (pres. Dade County 1994-98, Delta Kappa Gamma. Home: 165 NE 162nd St Miami FL 33162-4226

WARREN, FAN LEE, artist, educator; b. Birmingham, Ala., Dec. 31, 1957; d. Hattie May W. BFA, Ill. State U., 1982; MFA, Sch. of Art Inst., Chgo., 1985. Dir. Bobl Art Cultural Ctr., Chgo., 1986-89; instr. art Urban Gateways, 1990-93, Mexican Mus., San Francisco, 1994-98, Chabot C.C., Hayward, Calif., 1995-99, Las Positas Coll., Livermore, 1997-99. Active So. Exposure Gallery, 1998—, Berkeley Arts Ctr., 1997—, Pro Arts, 1997—. Regional fellow for visual arts WESTAF/NEA, Calif., 1994, Creative Artist fellow Cultural Arts divsn., City of Oakland, Calif., 1998; Cmty. Arts grantee Dept. Cultural Affairs, Chgo., 1989, 91, Artist in Residence grantee Calif. Arts Coun., 1995. Mem. Coll. Art Assn. Home: 3607 Maple Ave Oakland CA 94602-3338

WARREN, GARRY WILBUR, engineering educator; BS in Metall. Engring., U. Tex., El Paso, 1970, MS in Metall. Engring., 1973; PhD in Metallurgy, U. Utah, 1978. Process and quality control metallurgist Armco Steel Corp., Houston, 1970-72; grad. rsch. asst. dept. metall. engring. U. Tex., El Paso, 1973; grad. rsch. asst. dept. metallurgy and metall. engring. U. Utah, Salt Lake City, 1974-78; asst. prof. metall. engring./materials sci. Carnegie Mellon U., Pitts., 1978-84, assoc. prof., 1984-86; assoc. prof. metall./materials engring. U. Ala., Tuscaloosa, 1986-92, prof., 1992—. Rschr. in field of materials/metall. engring.; cons. in field. Co-editor: Hydrometallurgical Reactor Design and Kinetics, 1986, Innovations in Materials Processing Using Aqueous Colloid and Surface Chemistry, 1989, Hydrometallurgy Fundamentals, Technology and Innovation, 1993, Techniques for Corrosion Measurement, 1992; editor: Proc. of the Extraction and Processing Division Congress, TMS, 1994, 95, 96; contbr. numerous articles to profl. jours., chpts. to books. Mem. Minerals, Metals and Materials Soc. of AIME (bd. dirs. 1999-2002, mem. James Douglas Gold Medal Award com. 1995-98, mem. rev. bd. Metall. Transactions B 1985—, adv. bd. Jour. Metals 1989-90, mem. process fundamentals com. 1978—, numerous others comms., Disting. Svc. award 1998), Soc. Mining, Metallurgy and Exploration (mem. rev. bd. Minerals and Metall. Processing 1984—), Nat. Assn. Corrosion Engrs., Magnetics Soc. of IEEE, Electrochem. Soc. Office: Univ of Ala A129J Bevill Bldg PO Box 870202 Tuscaloosa AL 35487-0154 E-mail: gwarren@coe.eng.ua.edu.

WARREN, GRAHAM BARRY, cell biology educator; b. London, Feb. 25, 1948; s. Charles Graham and Joyce Thelma (Roberts) W.; m. Philippa Mary Temple-Cole, June 18, 1966; children: Joanna, Eleanor, Katya, Alexandra. MA, Cambridge U., 1969, PhD, 1972. Group leader EMBL, Heidelberg, Germany, 1977-85; prof., chair dept. biochemistry U. Dundee, Scotland, 1985-88; prin. scientist ICRF, London, 1988-99; prof. cell biology Yale U. Med. Sch., New Haven, 1999—. Mem. editl. bd. Jour. Cell Biology, 1985-88, 95—. Fellow Royal Soc. (London); mem. Biochem. Soc., Am. Soc. Cell Biology, Academia Europaea, European Molecular Biology Orgn. Office: 333 Cedar St New Haven CT 06510-3206 Fax: 203-785-4301. E-mail: graham.warren@yale.edu.

WARREN, J. BENEDICT, retired history educator; b. Waterflow, N.Mex., June 30, 1930; s. Benedict Alfred and Mary Ursula (Clark) W.; m. Patricia Susan Hyde, June 15, 1968. BA, Duns Scotus Coll., 1953; postgrad., Holy Family Sch. Theology, 1953-57, Cath. U. of Am., 1957-58; MA, U. N.Mex., 1960, PhD, 1963. Franciscan priest various chs., 1957-67; asst. prof. history U. Md., Coll. Park, 1968-70, assoc. prof. hist., 1970-77, prof. history, 1977-93; ret., 1993; rsch. prof. Colegio de Michoacán, Zamora, Mex., 1994—. Cons. Library of Congress, Washington, 1967-77. Author: (hist. studies) Vasco de Quiroga and His Pueblo-Hospitals of Santa Fe, 1963 (rev. Spanish edits. 1977, 90, 97), Hans P. Kraus Collection of Hispanic American Manuscripts, a Guide, 1974, La conquista de Michoacán, 1521-1530, 1977 (rev. edit, 1989, rev. English version, 1985); editor: (novels) Michoacan en la decada de 1580; Relaciones del obispo Juan de Medina Rincon, O.S.A. (1582) y de fray Diego Muñoz (1585) , 2000, Ordenanzas de Santa Fe de Vasco de Quiroga, 1999, Vasco de Quiroga en Africa, 1998, Testamento de Vasco de Quiroga: edícíon facsimilar con otros documentos, 1997, Diego Basalenque, Arte, 1994, Gonzalo Gómez primer poblador espanol de Guayangareo (Morelia), 1991, Diccionario grande de la lengua de Michoacan (2 vol.), 1991, Maturino Gilberti, Arte, 1987, Vocabulario, 1989, Juan Baptista de Lagunas, Arte y dictionario, 1983, Latin America: a Guide to the Historical Literature, 1971, (jours.) The Americas: A Quarterly Rev. of Inter-Am. Cultural History, 1963—66. Decorated Orden del Aguila Azteca Mex. Govt.; recipient Testimonial, State Michoacán, 2001, Presea José Tocavén, Voz de Michoacán, 2001, Presea Vasco de Quiroga of the City of Pátzcuaro, Mex., 2000; fellow John Carter Brown Libr. fellow, 1965, Fulbright fellow, 1981—82. Mem. Conf. on Latin Am. History, Acad. Mexicana de la Historia (corr.). Democrat. Avocation: gardening. Office: Lic J Ma Mendoza Pardo 99 Col Nueva Chapultepec 58280 Morelia Michoacan Mexico E-mail: bpwarren@unimedia.net.mx .

WARREN, JACK HAMILTON, former diplomat and trade policy adviser; b. Apr. 10, 1921; m. Hilary J. Titterington; children: Hilary Warren Nicolson, Martin, Jennifer Warren Part, Ian. Student, Queens U., Kingston, Ont., Can., 1938-41. Joined Dept. External Affairs, 1945; assigned London, 1948-51; fin. counsellor Washington, 1954-57; asst. dep. minister trade and commerce, 1958-64; dep. minister, trade and commerce, 1964-68; dep minister industry, trade & commerce, 1968-71; high commr. to U.K., 1971-75; ambassador to U.S., 1975-77; Can. coordinator for multilateral trade negotiations, 1977-79; vice-chmn. Bank of Montreal, Que., Can., 1979-86; prin. trade policy advisor Govt. Que., 1986-94. Served with Royal Canadian Navy, 1941-45; officer Order of Can., 1982. Recipient Pub. Svc. Outstanding Achievement award, 1976. Home: 37 Chemin Larrimac Chelsea QC Canada J9B 2C4

WARREN, JAMES RONALD, retired museum director, writer, columnist; b. Goldendale, Wash., May 25, 1925; stepson H.S. W.; m. Gwen Davis, June 25, 1949; children: Gail, Jeffrey. BA, Wash. State U., 1949; MA, U. Wash., 1953, PhD, 1963. Adminstrv. v.p. Seattle Community Coll., 1965-69; pres. Edmonds Community Coll., Lynnwood, Wash., 1969-79; dir. Mus. of History and Industry, Seattle, 1979-89. Lectr. in field. Author history books; columnist Seattle Post Intelligencer, 1979-92, Seattle Times, 1992-96. Served with U.S. Army, 1943-45, ETO, prisoner-of-war, Germany. Mem. VFW, Am. Ex-POW Assn., 42d (Rainbow) Div. Vets., Rotary, also others. Home and Office: 3235 99th Ave NE Bellevue WA 98004-1803

WARREN, JANET ELAINE, librarian; b. Lindsborg, Kans., Sept. 19, 1951; d. Jack Edward and Mildred Louise (Ahlstedt) Beebe; m. Perry DeLong Warren, July 6, 1974; children: Emily Louise, Britta Elizabeth. Student Stephens Women's Coll., 1969-70; BS in Edn., U. Kans., 1973; MLS, Emporia State U., 1974. Asst. dir. Goodland Pub. Library (Kans.), 1974-75, libr. dir., 1975—. Bd. dirs. Sherman County Jr. Miss Program, 1979; mem. exec. com. N.W. Kans. Library System, 1988—; pres. Chpt. Philantropic Edn. Orgn., 1992-94, 97; mem. bd. Goodland Arts Coun., 1997—, pres., 1999; mem. bd. Sherman County Leadership Program, 1997-98. Mem. ALA, Kans. Libr. Assn., Mountain Plains Libr. Assn., Thalia Women's Club (pres. 1982-83, 90-91). Republican. Home: PO Box 185 Goodland KS 67735-0185 Office: Goodland Pub Libr 812 Broadway Goodland KS 67735-3037

WARREN, JARED SCOTT, psychologist; b. Provo, Utah, May 21, 1972; s. Daniel Jerry and Aleta Ann W.; m. Melissa Marie Griggs, June 10, 1995; children: Janae, Daniel, Tyler. BS in Psychology, Brigham Young U., 1996; MA in Clin. Child Psychology, U. Kans., 1999. Tchr. Portuguese Missionary Tng. Ctr., Brigham Young U., Provo, Utah, 1993-95; rsch. asst. U. Kans., Lawrence, 1998—2002; child and family therapist Bert Nash Cmty. Mental Health Ctr., 1999—2001; tchr. supr. Missionary Tng. Ctr., Brigham Young U., 1995-97; program instr. ADHD Lifeline, Lawrence, 1997-98; resident in psychology U. Wash. Sch. Medicine, Seattle, 2002—. Adj. prof. Avila Coll., Kansas City, 1999-2000; instr. psychology U. Kans., 1999; clin. assoc. KU Child and Family Svcs. Clinic, Lawrence, 1997-2000. Vol. missionary LDS Ch., Belo Horizonte, Brazil, 1991-93; scoutmaster Boy Scouts Am., Lawrence, 2000-02. Mem. APA, Soc. Sci. Clin. Psychology. Avocations: softball, bicycling, reading. Home: 15700 44th Ave W Apt D105 Lynnwood WA 98037 Office: U Wash Sch Medicine Dept Psychiatry and Behavioral Scis 1959 NE Pacific St BB 1627 HSB Seattle WA 98195-6560 Fax: 206-685-8952. E-mail: jsw@ku.edu.

WARREN, JENNIFER ELIZABETH, family nurse practitioner; b. Clovis, N.Mex., Nov. 13, 1964; d. Ronald Dwayne and Lillian Ann (Reed) Carter; m. Johnny Lynn Warren Jr., May 18, 1991. BSN, West Tex. State U., 1988; MSN-FNP, West Tex. A&M U., 1998. RN, Tex.; cert. family nurse practitioner. Clin. asst. Northwest Tex. Hosp., Amarillo, 1987-88; neonatal ICU nurse Meth. Children's Hosp., Lubbock, Tex., 1988-98, Covenant Med. Ctr., Lubbock, 1999-2000; FNP Covenant Family Health Care Ctr., 2000—. Mem. Am. Acad. Nurse Practitioners, Tex. Nursing Assn., Endometriosis Assn. (organizer/contact, Lubbock leader 1993—), South Plains Nurse Practitioners Assn. Democrat. Methodist. Avocations: gardening, cross-stitch, latch hook, swimming. Home: 1002 W 10th St Post TX 79356-2450 Office: Covenant Family Healthcare Ctr 608 W 6th St Post TX 79356 Fax: (806) 495-3576.

WARREN, JOAN LEIGH, pediatrician; b. St. Louis, Oct. 15, 1957; d. Harold Lee and Lorraine Jeanette (Hurley) W.; m. Paul J. Malkin; children: Mallory, Celeste. BA, U. Mo., Kansas City, 1980, MD, 1982. Diplomate Am. Bd. Pediatrics. Resident in pediatrics Sacred Heart Children's Hosp., Pensacola, Fla., 1982-85; pvt. practice, St. Louis, 1985-87; dir. pediatric svcs. Barnes St. Peters (Mo.) Hosp., 1987-94; pvt. practice St. Charles, Mo., 1994-99, St. Louis, 1999—; locum tenens pediatrics, 1999—; phlebologist performing laser vein reitonal and sclerotherapy Vein Doctor, Palm Desert, Calif., 1999—. Fellow Am. Acad. Pediatrics; mem. St. Louis Pediatric Soc. Avocations: tennis, softball, camping. Office: Vein Doctor 44-300 Monterey Ste B Palm Desert CA 92010-1659

WARREN, JOHN COOLIDGE, private school dean, history educator; b. Boston, May 16, 1956; s. William Bradford and Mary-Elizabeth (Coolidge) W.; m. Laura Parker Appell, June 18, 1983; children: Ethan Reynolds Appell, Amanda Pfaltzgraff Appell. BA, Stanford U., 1978, MA, 1980; MEd, Harvard U., 1991, EdD, 1994. Tchr. history Robert Louis Stevenson Sch., Pebble Beach, Calif., 1979-81, Milton (Mass.) Acad., 1981—, chmn. dept. history, 1992-95, acad. dean, 1995—2001, spl. asst. to head of sch., 2001—. Faculty cons. Ednl. Testing Svc., Princeton, 1990—, William Joiner Ctr., Boston, 1992—; editl. cons. Longman Inc., White Plains, N.Y., 1991—. Editor: America's Intervention in Vietnam, 1987. NEH fellow, 1985, advanced doctoral fellow, Harvard U., 1993. Mem. Am. Hist. Assn., Orgn. Am. Historians, Assn. Asian Studies, World History Assn., Boston Athaneum, Colonial Soc. Mass., Mass. Hist. Soc., Phi Beta Kappa. Avocations: canoeing, fishing. Home and Office: Milton Acad 170 Centre St Milton MA 02186-3338

WARREN, JOHN FLOYD, music educator; b. Louisville, July 14, 1965; s. Jerry Lee and Dorothy Floyd Warren; m. Jennifer Kolb Lees, June 21, 1997; children: Hannah Elizabeth. BM, Furman U., Greenville, SC, 1987; MM, U. Cin., Cincinnati, OH, 1989; Dr. Musical Arts, U. Miami, Miami, FL, 1999. Music dir. Crievewood United Meth. Ch., Nashville, 1990—96; asst. dir. Nashville Children's Choir, 1992—96; tchg. asst. U. Miami, Miami, Fla., 1996—99; dir. choral activities Erskine Coll., Due West, SC, 1999—. Mem.: Nat. Assn. Teachers Singing, Music Educators Nat. Conf., Am. Choral Directors Assn. Presbyterian. Avocations: golf, reading, exercise. Home: 706 Britton St Anderson SC 29621 Office: Erskine College Music Department 2 Washington St Due West SC 29639 Office Fax: 864-379-2167. E-mail: warren@erskine.edu.

WARREN, JOHN WILLIAM, professional society administrator; b. Clarksville, Ark., June 27, 1927; s. Frederick H. and Fannie Emily (Casey) W.; m. Marguerette Christine Cohoon, Oct. 9, 1948 (dec. Dec. 1987); children: Catherine Gail, Carolyn Anne, Eve Colette; m. Anna Jane Taylor, Feb. 10, 1990. BA, Abilene Christian U., 1949; MA, U. Ark., 1951; PhD, U. Tenn., 1961. Instr. U. Tenn., Knoxville, 1954-61; assoc. prof. David Lipscomb Coll., Nashville, 1961-62; prof., chmn. English Tenn. Tech. U., Cookeville, 1962-88; assoc. exec. dir. Phi Kappa Phi, Baton Rouge, 1988-92, exec. dir., 1992-99, exec. dir. emeritus, 1999—; v.p. Assn. Coll. Honor Socs., 1999-2001, pres., 2001—. Author Ofcl. Lit. Map of Tenn., 1976; author: Tennessee Belles-Lettres-Guide to Tennessee Literature, 1976. Mem. Rotary (Cookeville pres. 1972-73), Phi Kappa Phi (Tenn. Tech. U. chpt. pres. 1980, SE region v.p. 1982-88, nat. bd. dirs. 1982-88). Republican. Mem. Ch. of Christ. Avocations: gardening, travel. E-mail: pkpjwarren@aol.com.

WARREN, JOSEPH ADDISON, III, law and history educator; b. Ft. Pierce, Fla., July 23, 1944; s. Joseph Addison and Donna Belle (Fenstermacher) W. BA, Mich. State U., 1966, MA, 1967, PhD, 1976; JD, Thomas M. Cooley Law Sch., 1980. Bar: Mich., 1981, U.S. Supreme Ct. 1985. Prof. history and humanities Lansing (Mich.) C.C., 1969—; pvt. practice law Lansing, 1981—; owner Center Point Press, 1998—. Lectr. continuing edn. Mich. State U., East Lansing, 1995—; pub., editor Faculty Advocate Mag., Lansing, 1981-98; dir. Ctr. for Inner Awareness, Inc., Lansing, 1992—; rschr. Ralph Nader's Task Force on Congress, Lansing, 1971-74; forensic photographer Forensic Photographic Svcs., Lansing, 1977—; mem. Gov.'s Adv. Com. on Mich. Meat Stds., Lansing, 1974; co-counsel Wygant V. Jackson vs. Bd. of Edn., 1985; mem. com. on legal edn. State Bar of Mich., Lansing, 1987-89, U.S. Supreme Ct. Author: The Origins of the American Presidency, 1976; contbr. numerous articles to profl. publs. Mem. Mich. Fed. Bar Assn., Mich. State Bar Assn., Am. Acad. of Religion Studies, World Assn. Vedic Studies, Ctr. for Study of the Presidency, Internat. Vedanta Scholars in Indian Civilization, Am. Legal Studies Assn. Avocations: mentoring students and beginning professionals, international travel. Home: 1012 N Washington Ave Lansing MI 48906-4839 Office: 1016 N Washington Lansing MI 48906-4839

WARREN, LARRY MICHAEL, clergyman; b. Bonne Terre, Mo., Nov. 25, 1946; s. Orson Wesley and Ruth Margaret (Stine) W.; m. Bonnie Jean Monk Chandler, Apr. 9, 1983; children: Samantha Chandler, John, Abigail Chandler, Anne, Meredith. BA cum laude, Lincoln U., 1969; MDiv with honors, St. Paul Sch. Theology, Kansas City, Mo., 1976; D of Ministry, San Francisco Theol. Sem., 1987. Ordained elder United Meth. Ch., 1978. Pastor Cainsville (Mo.) United Meth. Ch., 1975-76, Lakelands Parish, Rathdrum, Idaho, 1976-78; assoc. pastor Audubon Park United Meth. Ch., Spokane, Wash., 1978-83; pastor Faith United Meth. Ch., Everett, 1983-90, Tacoma First United Meth. Ch., 1990-95; co-pastor Renton First United Meth. Ch., 1995—. Adviser Kairos Prison Ministry Wash., Monroe, 1984-92; conf. rep. grad. bd. St. Paul Sch. Theology, Kansas City, 1984, 94-96. Contbr. to col. Dialogue Everett Herald, 1984-88. Adviser DeMolay, Spokane, 1979-81; team mem. Night-Walk, inner-city ministry, Spokane, 1979-82; coord. Ch. Relief Overseas Project Hunger Walk, Spokane and Everett, 1981, 85; vol. chaplain Gen. Hosp. Everett, 1983-90; trustee Deaconess Children's Svcs., Everett, 1983-88. Recipient Legion of Honor DeMolay Internat., 1982. Mem. Fellowship of Reconciliation, North Snohomish County Assn. Chs. (v.p. 1985-89), Pacific N.W. Ann. Conf. Bd. Global Ministries (sec. 1988-92, pres. 1993-97), Renton Ecumenical Assn. Chs. (pres. 1996-98). Democrat. Avocations: reading, traveling, stamps and coins, woodworking. Home: 121 Monterey Pl NE Renton WA 98056-4032 Office: Renton First United Meth Ch 2201 NE 4th St Renton WA 98056-4073 E-mail: revlmw@aol.com. *Personal philosophy: To seek peace and reconciliation among all people and nations, and with the creation given to us as stewards.*

WARREN, MARK EDWARD, lawyer; b. Rochester, Minn., Nov. 26, 1951; s. Edward Joseph and Eunice (Golberg) W.; m. Jasmine Margaret Syracuse, Feb. 18, 1984; children: Natalie, Stephanie. Cert., Instituto de Estudios Europeos, Madrid, 1972; BA, Gustavus Adolphus Coll., St. Peter, Minn., 1974; JD, U. Minn., 1977. Bar: Calif. 1977, U.S. Dist. Ct. (no. and cen. dists.) Calif. 1978, U.S. Ct. Appeals (9th cir.) 1985, U.S. Dist. Ct. (ea. dist.) Calif. 1986, U.S. Dist. Ct. (so. dist.) Calif. 1987, D.C. 1989, U.S. Supreme Ct. 1989, U.S. Ct. Appeals (D.C. cir.) 1989, U.S. Dist. Ct. (D.C. dist.) 1989, U.S. Dist. Ct. Md. 1991, Va. 1992. Assoc. Gibson, Dunn & Crutcher, L.A., 1977-78; spl. asst. to V.P. Walter Mondale Washington, 1979-80; assoc. Gibson, Dunn & Crutcher, L.A., 1980-84, ptnr. L.A. and Washington, 1985-93; sr. v.p., gen. counsel Princess Cruises, L.A., 1993-96; pres. The Gt. Am. Sta. Found., Washington, 1997-99. Mem. U. Minn. Law Alumni Assn. (bd. dirs. 1990-98).

WARREN, PETER, advertising executive; b. Iran, Sept. 9, 1943; s. Paul and Heda (Adler) W.; m. Carla Ringler, Aug. 26, 1967; children: Jill, Paul. BS, NYU, 1965; MBA, Pace U., 1968. Promotion rsch. analyst Look Mag., N.Y.C., 1965; from media planner to account supr. Ogilvy & Mather, 1966-72; exec. v.p. Tromson Monroe, 1972-74; founder, pres. Warren/Kremer Advt., Inc., 1974—. Mem. Marlboro (N.J.) Twp. Zoning Bd. Adjustment; pres. bd. edn. Freehold Regional H.S.; advisor United Jewish Appeal, Marlboro Bd. Edn., Monmouth County Dem. and Rep. Coms., Marlboro Econ. Devel. Bd.; chmn. Gateway Am. Courtesy and Tng. Com.; exec. com., chair Hospitality Sales and Mktg. Assn. Internat.; exec. bd. mem. NYU Sch. Hospitality, Travel and Tourism. Recipient Effie award Am. Mktg. Assn., 1978. Mem. Hospitality Sales and Mktg. Assn. (co-chmn. mktg. adv. com, numerous platinum, gold, silver and bronze awards 1976-92), Travel and Tourism Rsch. Assn., Caribbean Tourism Orgn. (treas. N.Y.C. chpt., 3 Best of Show awards internat. competition 1982, 83, 85), Advt. Club N.Y. (Addy awards 1982, 83), Alpha Delta Sigma (pres. NYU). Jewish. Avocations: reading, golfing, softball, traveling, coin collecting. Office: Warren/Kremer/Paino Advt Inc 2 Park Ave Rm 1400 New York NY 10016-5701

WARREN, RALPH LOUNSBURY, surgery educator; b. Orange, N.J., Sept. 28, 1954; AB, Harvard Coll.; MD, Harvard U., Boston, 1981. Diplomate Am. Bd. Surgery, Am. Bd. Surg. Critical Care. Resident in surgery Mass. Gen. Hosp., Boston, 1981-87, fellow in cardiothoracic surgery, 1987-89, assoc. vis. surgeon, 1994—, asst. chief, clin. dir. trauma svc., 1992—. Lt. col. Air NAt. Guard. Fellow ACS, Internat. Coll. Surgeons, Assn. Mil. Surgeons U.S., Ea. Assn. for Soc. of Trauma, Alliance Air Nat. Guard Flight Surgeons; mem. AMA, Soc. Critical Care Medicine, Aerospace Med. Assn., Soc. Air Force Flight Surgeons, Mass. Med. Soc. Office: Mass Gen Hosp Dept Surgery Trauma Fruit St Boston MA 02114

WARREN, RICHARD ERNEST, advertising executive; b. Managua, Nicaragua, Jan. 27, 1942; came to U.S., 1948; s. Ernest R. and Marina E. (Echeverria) W.; m. Betty Lou Murray (dec. Apr. 1980); 1 child, Deborah Marie; m. Cynthia Ann Welch, Sept. 13, 1975; 1 child, James Lymon Kendrick III. Degree in bus. adminstrn., Loyola U., New Orleans, 1968, B in Comml. Sci., 1971; Cert. Master degree, Cruise Lines Internat. Assn., 1995; graduate, Fletcher Real Estate Sch., 2001, WAR Acad., 2002. Sales office mgr. Avoncraft div. Avondale Shipyards, Inc., New Orleans, 1964-68; exec. dir. Info. Council Ams., 1968-73; account supr. Ladas Advt. Agy., 1973-76; pres., gen. mgr. Warren Advt. Agy., 1976-77; regional account exec. Mace Advt., Inc., 1977-79; nat. account supr. J. Walter Thompson USA, Chgo., 1979-83; v.p., dir. advt. Snapper Power Equipment, McDonough, Ga., 1983-89; pres., gen. mgr. Henco Advt., Inc., 1983-89; owner Confectionately Yours, Inc., Atlanta, 1985-2000; pres. Dick Warren Advt. Agy., Marietta, 1989—; owner Dick Warren Worldwide Travel, 1989—2001, AABA Cruise Super Store, 1997-2000. Cons. Fuqua Industries, Inc., Atlanta, 1984-89; nat. adv. bd. Internat. Care Exploration Soc., 1989, Merehurst Press, Ltd., London, 1989, Nicholas Lodge Brand Products; chmn. adv. com. WFOM-AM; nat. spkr. on effective advt. to travel industry; nat. advisor Holland Am. Cruise Lines, 1996—; bd. dirs. Consortium of N.Y., Cobb Bd. Realtors, mem. RPAC com., 2002. Editor: (newspapers) Singles Critique, 1972-79, Metairie/Fat City News, 1974-75; producer: Jerry Lewis Muscular Dystrophy Telethon, New Orleans, 1970-73, (TV shows) Spirit '76, New Orleans, 1976, Sportsmen's Paradise, New Orleans, 1976. Served with USAF, 1960-64. Chmn. bus. and fin. com. World Outreach Missionary Ch., 1992—; bd. dirs. Internat. New Testament Ch., 1992-94; sec. Cobb County Rep. Party; adv. bd. The Consortium. Mem. Am. Film Inst., Nat. Assn. Cruise Only Travel Agy., Joseph's Investment Group, Internat. Confectioner Exploration Soc. (mem. adv. bd. nat. cake decorating and candy supply shops), Young Men's Bus. Club (chmn. 1970), Cruise Line Internat. Assn., Assn. Retail Travel Agts., Nat. Assn. Cruise Only Agencies, Nat. Bd. Realtors, Ga. Bd. Realtors, Metro Brokers. Republican. E-mails. Fax: 770-425-0046. E-mail: dick@dickwarren.com., dick@cruisesale.com.

WARREN, RICHARD M. experimental psychologist, educator; b. N.Y.C., Apr. 8, 1925; s. Morris and Rae (Greenberg) W.; m. Roslyn Pauker, Mar. 31, 1950. BS in Chemistry, CCNY, 1946; PhD in Organic Chemistry, NYU, 1951. Flavor chemist Gen. Foods Co., Hoboken, N.J., 1951-53; rsch. assoc. psychology Brown U., Providence, 1954-56; Carnegie sr. rsch. fellow NYU Coll. Medicine, 1956-57, Cambridge (Eng.) U., 1957-58, rsch. psychologist applied psychology rsch. unit, 1958-59; rsch. psychologist NIMH, Bethesda, Md., 1959-61; chmn. psychology Shimer Coll., Mt. Carroll, Ill., 1961-64; assoc. prof. psychology U. Wis., Milw., 1964-66, prof., 1966-73, rsch. prof., 1973-75, disting. prof., 1975-95, adj. disting. prof., 1995—. Vis. scientist Inst. Exptl. Psychology, Oxford (Eng.) U., 1969-70, 77-78. Author: (with Roslyn Warren) Helmholtz on Perception: Its Physiology and Development, 1968, Auditory Perception: A New Analysis and Synthesis, 1999; contbr. articles to profl. jours. Fellow APA, Am. Psychol. Soc., Acoustical Soc. Am.; mem. AAAS, Am. Chem. Soc., Am. Speech and Hearing Assn., Sigma Xi. Office: U Wis Dept Psychology Milwaukee WI 53201

WARREN, RICHARD WAYNE, obstetrician, gynecologist; b. Puxico, Mo., Nov. 26, 1935; s. Martin R. and Sarah E. (Crump) W.; m. Rosalie J. Franzoia, Aug. 16, 1959; children: Lani Marie, Richard W., Paul D. BA, U. Calif., Berkeley, 1957; MD, Stanford U., 1961. Diplomate Am. Bd. Ob-Gyn. Intern Oakland (Calif.) Naval Hosp., 1961-62; resident on ob-gyn. Stanford (Calif.) Med. Ctr., 1964-67; pvt. practice specializing in ob-gyn. Mountain View, Calif., 1967—. Mem. staff Stanford Hosp., El Camino Hosp.; pres. Warren Medical Corp.; assoc. clin. prof. ob-gyn Stanford Sch. Medicine. Contbr. articles to profl. jours. With USN, 1961-64. Fellow Am. Coll. Ob-Gyn.; mem. AMA, Am. Fertility Soc., Am. Assn. Gynecologic Laparoscopists, Calif. Med. Assn., San Francisco Gynecol. soc., Peninsula Gynecol. Soc., Assn. Profs. Gynecology and Obstetrics, Royal Soc. Medicine, Shufelt Gynecol. Soc. Santa Clara Valley. Home: 102 Atherton Ave Menlo Park CA 94027-4021 Office: 2500 Hospital Dr Mountain View CA 94040-4106

WARREN, RITA SIMPSON, manufacturing company executive; b. Borger, Tex., Jan. 17, 1949; d. William D. and Bobbie J. (Hindman) S.; m. Harry E. Warren, jr., June 10, 1978. BA in Sociology, U. Tex., 1977; MBA, North Tex. State U., 1982. V.p. comms. Tetra Pak, Inc., Dallas, 1977-85; v.p. mktg. Devex, Inc., 1986-87; v.p. Neotech Industries, Inc., Irving, Tex., 1987-88; sales mgr. worldwide Optek Tech., Inc., 1989-2001; key account mgr. Alcatel Optronics Inc., 2001—. Bd. dirs. Dallas Women's Found.; mem. women's resource ctr. adv. com. YWCA of Dallas, 1993-2001. Recipient various awards Dairy and Food Industries Supply Assn., 1979-84, Soc. Visual Comm., 1979, Dallas Ad League TOPS, 1984. Mem. Sportscar Vintage Racing Assn., Hist. Sportscar Racing Assn., Pub. Rels. Soc., Jaguar Owner's Assn. S.W. (co-pres. 1979-83), The Women's Ctr. of Dallas (bd. dirs. WISER 1991-92, Women in Leadership 1993, pres.-elect 1994, pres. 1995, past pres. 1996), Imagine Dallas (pres. 1997-98, bd. dirs. 1995-98). Avocations: classic European automobiles, driving vintage race car, Golden Retrievers, sailing. Office: Ste 200 3601 E Plano Pkwy Plano TX 75074

WARREN, ROSANNA, poet; b. Fairfield, Conn., July 27, 1953; d. Robert Penn Warren and Eleanor Clark; m. Stephen Scully, 1981; children: Katherine, Chiara; stepson, Benjamin. BA summa cum laude, Yale U., 1976; MA, Johns Hopkins U., 1980. Private art tchr., 1977-78; clerical worker St. Martin's Pr., N.Y.C., 1977-78; asst. prof. English Vanderbilt U., Nashville, 1981-82; vis. asst. prof. Boston U., 1982-88, asst. prof. English and modern fgn. langs., 1989-95, assoc. prof. English, 1995—. Poetry cons., contbg. editor Partisan Rev., 1985-98; poet-in-residence Robert Frost Farm, 1990. Author: The Joey Story, 1963, Snow Day, 1981, Each Leaf Shines Separate, 1984, Stained Glass, 1993; editor, contbr.: The Art of Translation: Voices from the Field, 1989; editor: Eugenio Montale's Cuttlefish Bones, 1993, Satura, 1998; translator (with Stephen Scully) Euripides' Suppliant Women, 1995, poetry anthologies include In Time, 1995, From This Distance, 1996, Springshine, 1998; contbr. to periodicals including Agni Rev., Am. Poetry Rev., Antioch Rev., Atlantic Monthly, Chelsea, Chgo. Rev., Georgia Rev., Nation, New Republic, New Yorker, N.Y. Times, Paris Rev., Threepenny Rev., Partisan Rev., Ploughshares, Southern Rev., Washington Post. Recipient McLaughlin English prize Yale U., 1973, Charles E. Clark award Yale U., 1976, Nat. Discovery award in poetry 92nd St. YMHA-YWCA, 1980, Newton Arts Coun. award, 1983, Lavan Younger Poets prize Acad. Am. Poets, 1992, Lamont Poetry prize Acad. Am. Poets, 1993, Lila Wallace Writers' Fund award, 1994, Witter Bynner prize in poetry Acad. Arts and Letters, 1994, May Sarton award New Eng. and Poetry Club, 1995; named Scholar of House Yale U., 1975-76; Yaddo fellow, 1980; Ingram Merrill grantee, 1983, 93; Guggenheim fellow, 1985-86; Am. Coun. Learned Societies grantee, 1989-90. Mem.: PEN, ALTA, MLA, Am. Acad. Poets (chancellor 2000), Assn. Literary Scholars and Critics. Home: 28 Tappan St Roslindale MA 02131-1621 Office: Univ Professors Program Boston Univ 745 Commonwealth Ave Boston MA 02215-1401

WARREN, RUSSELL GLEN, academic administrator; b. Balt., Apr. 29, 1942; s. Clarence N. and Kathryn (Butler) W. BBA, U. Richmond, 1964; PhD, Tulane U., 1968. Asst. prof., then assoc. prof. U. Richmond (Va.), 1971-74, dean of Richmond Coll., 1974-76, asst. to univ. v.p., then. asst. to univ. pres., 1976-78; v.p. for acad. affairs U. Montevallo, Ala., 1978-84, James Madison U., Harrisonburg, Va., 1984-90, acting pres., 1986-87; pres. N.E. Mo. State U., Kirksville, 1990-95; Disting. prof. econs. and mgmt. Hardin-Simmons U., Abilene, Tex., 1995-97, dir. Ctr. for Rsch. on Teaching and Learning, 1995-97; exec. v.p., provost Mercer U., Macon, Ga., 1997—2002; sr. fellow Nat Assn. Ind. Colls. and Univs., Kiawah Island, SC, 2001—. Author: Antitrust in Theory and Practice, 1976, Carpe Diem, 1995. Bd. dirs. Va. Rural Devel. Corp., Richmond, 1988-90. Capt. U.S. Army, 1969-71. Named One of Outstanding Young Men of Va., Va. Jaycees, 1976. Mem.: Am. Coun. on Edn. (coun. of fellows), Am. Assn. Colls. and Univs. (bd. dirs. 1994—95). Methodist. Avocations: golf, collecting cars. Home and Office: 175 Marsh Island Dr Kiawah Island SC 29455

WARREN, RUSSELL JAMES, investment banker, consultant; b. Cleve., July 28, 1938; s. Harold Fulton and Agnes Elmenah (Hawkswell) Warren; m. Doris Helen Kenyeres, June 6, 1964. BS, Case Western Res. U., 1960; MBA, Harvard U., 1962. CPA Ohio. With Ernst & Whinney, Cleve., 1962-87, ptnr. in charge merger and acquisition svcs., 1976—87, pres. TransAction Group, 1987—. Bd. dirs. Seneca Capital Mgmt., Inc. Co-author: (book) Implementing Mergers and Acquisitions in the Financial and Service Industry, 1985; assoc. editor: Jour. Corp. Growth, 1986—87, mem. editl. bd.: , 1988; contbg. editor: Jour. Buyouts and Acquisitions, 1984—86; contbg. author: venture capital financing study conducted in five countries for Asian Devel. Bank, 1986. Trustee Case Western Res. U., 1980—, chmn. audit com., 1991—; trustee Cleve. Bot. Garden, 1995—2001, Western Res. Hist. Soc., 1996—, chmn. investments com., 1999—; trustee Cmty. Improvement Corp. Summit, Medina and Portage Counties, 1992—2000, Cascade CDC, 1992—2000, Brit.-Am. C. of C., Great Lakes Region, 2001—; dir. Univ. Tech., Inc., 1986—88; adv. bd. Shaker Investments, 1992—; v.p. M&A Internat. Inc., 1990—91, pres., 1992; bd. zoning appeals City of Lyndhurst, 1978—, chmn., 1980—82, 1991—93, 2000—; mem. vis. com. Case Sch. Engrng., Weatherhead Sch. Mgmt., 1998—; trustee Fairmont Presbyn. Ch., 1987—93, elder, 1991—93. Mem.: AICPA, Cleve. World Trade Assn., Cleve. Com. Fgn. Rels., Assn. Corp. Growth, Ohio Soc. CPAs, Harvard Club N.Y.C., Catawba Island Club, Mayfield Country Club, Union Club, Jesters. Office: The TransAction Group 500 Hanna Bldg Cleveland OH 44115

WARREN, THOMAS LYNN, mechanical engineer; b. Cortland, NY, May 5, 1961; s. William Ernst and Barbara Mary Warren. BS, U. N.Mex., 1986; MS, Northwestern U., 1989; PhD, Ariz. State U., 1995. EIT N.Mex. Staff engr. Applied Rsch. Assocs. Inc., Tyndall AFB, Fla., 1989—91; post doctoral appointee Sandia Nat. Labs., Albuquerque, 1995—96, sr. mem. tech. staff, 1996—. Mem.: ASME, Am. Acad. Mechanics (prof.), Pi Tau Sigma, Tau Beta Pi, Sigma Xi. Office: Sandia Nat Labs PO Box 5800 Albuquerque NM 87185-1174 Business E-Mail: tlwarre@sandia.gov.

WARREN, THOMAS PAUL, consulting executive; b. Atlanta, Oct. 2, 1952; s. Thomas J. and Irma Louise (Denson) W.; m. Cheryl M. Barringer, Apr. 8, 1978; 1 child, Thomas Peyton. BS, BA, St. Andrews Coll., Laurinburg, N.C., 1974; BS, Ga. Tech., 1975; MBA, Ga. State U., 1977. V.p. investment banking Merrill Lynch White Weld, N.Y.C., 1977-82; mng. dir. Brooks Internat., Montvale, N.J., 1982-85; sr. v.p. C4 practice Gemini Consulting, Paris, 1985-94; mng. ptnr. comm. and media practice Perot Systems Corp., Dallas, 1994—. Bd. dirs. Mancon Inc., Anderson, S.C., 1982-85. Bd. dirs. Juvenile Diabetes Found., Atlanta, 1989-92, Camp Twin Lakes, Atlanta. Rsch. fellow NSF, 1975. Mem. Golf Club Ga. (charter). Avocations: golf, tennis, photography. Office: Perot Systems Corp 12377 Merit Dr Dallas TX 75251-2224

WARREN, WILLIAM BRADFORD, lawyer; b. Boston, July 25, 1934; s. Minton Machado and Sarah Ripley (Robbins) W.; children: John Coolidge, Sarah W. Jaffe; m. Arete B. Swartz, Sept. 20, 1985. AB magna cum laude, Harvard U., 1956, LLB cum laude, 1959. Bar: N.Y. 1960. Assoc. Dewey Ballantine, N.Y.C., 1959-68; ptnr. Dewey Ballantine, LLP, 1968—. Lectr. Inst. Fed. Taxation, N.Y. U., So. Fed. Tax Inst., Practicing Law Inst. Pres. Cintas

Found., N.Y.C.; bd. dirs. emeritus John Carter Brown Libr., Providence, R.I.; adv. bd. dirs. Met. Opera Assn., N.Y.C.; mem. coun. fellows Morgan Lebrury, N.Y.C. Mem. Am. Law Inst., Am. Coll. Trust and Estate Counsel (former regent), Acad. Am. Poets (bd. dirs., treas.), Internat. Acad. Estate and Trust Law (former exec. com.), N.Y. State Bar Assn. (chmn. com. taxation of trust and estates sect. 1980-83), Assn. Bar City N.Y., Soc. Mayflower Descs., Harvard Club, Knickerbocker Club, Century Club, Grolier Club (past pres.). Home: 520 E 86th St New York NY 10028-7534 Office: Dewey Ballantine LLP 1301 Avenue Of The Americas New York NY 10019-6022

WARREN, WILLIAM FRAMPTON, JR. religion educator; b. Shelbyville, Tenn., Nov. 16, 1954; s. William Frampton Sr. and Miriam (O'Quinn) W.; m. Katie Cutrer, Dec. 22, 1979; children: William Frampton III, Benjamin Isaac. AA, Okaloosa Walton Jr. Coll., 1974; BS, Miss. Coll., 1976; MDiv, New Orleans Bapt. Theol. Sem., 1979, ThD, 1983. Asst. pastor Istrouma Bapt. Ch., Baton Rouge, 1978-80; pastor Plank Road Bapt. Ch., Slaughter, La., 1980-83; missionary prof. Seminario Teologico Bautista Internat., Cali, Colombia, 1983-89; Landrum P. Leavell disting. prof. New Testament Studies New Orleans Bapt. Theol. Sem., 1990—, dir. Ctr. for New Testament Textual Studies, 1998—; pastor New Henleyfield Bapt. Ch., 1994-2000. Coord., advisor, missionary Buenaventura, Colombia, 1985-89, coord. hunger relief program, 1987-89; mem. exec. com. Colombian Bapt. Mission Bogota, Colombia, 1988-89; collator, supr. collations Internat. Greek New Testament Project. Author: Luke: A Study Guide; editor: La Teologia De La Liberacion: Una Respuesta Evangelica, 1990; contbr. articles to profl. jours. Mem. Nat. Assn. Bapt. Prof. Religion, Am. Acad. Religion, Soc. Bibl. Lit., Coll. Theology Soc., Christians for Bibl. Equality. Democrat. Office: New Orleans Bapt Theol Sem 3939 Gentilly Blvd # 60 New Orleans LA 70126-4858 E-mail: wfwarren@aol.com. *The context for doing theology consists of the doing of the will of God in the midst of a hurting world. One cannot claim to know God while at the same time refusing to participate in what God is doing in this world.*

WARREN, WILLIAM KERMIT, retired media company executive; b. Harlem, Ga., May 27, 1941; s. William Kermit and Willie Garnell (Thaxton) Warren; m. Nancy Carolyn Andrews, Sept. 5, 1964; children: Wendy Karen, William Kermit. BA in Journalism, U. Ga., 1964. Reporter Augusta Ga. Chronicle, Ga., 1964-65; reporter Chattanooga Times, Tenn., 1965-66, reporter, city editor, 1971-80; mng. editor Roanoke (Va.) Times & World News, 1980-95; electronic pub. cons., 1995-98; prin. New City Media, Blacksburg, Va., 1998-99. Served to capt USAF, 1966—70. Recipient Best Feature Story Award, Ga AP, 1964. Mem.: AP Managing Eds Asn, Sigma Delta Chi. Episcopalian. Avocation: reading. Home: 3355 Dawn Cir Roanoke VA 24018-3837 E-mail: bwarren33@cox.net.

WARRES, MARGIE BLACK, social work administrator emerita; b. Phila., Feb. 17, 1918; d. Harry M. and Eva (Stulbaum) Black; m. H. Leonard Warres, June 11, 1939; children: Stephen Elliot, Neil Eric. Student, Goucher Coll., 1936-38; BA magna cum laude, Bklyn. Coll., 1941; MSW, U. Pa., 1944. Cert. ACSW, LCSW. Past caseworker Pub. Welfare Office, Kent County, Del.; exec. sec. pub. welfare com. Md. Conf. Social Concern, 1948-50; exec. dir. Cen. Scholarship Bur., 1952-88. Condr. workshops for pub. sch. counselors Balt. Dept. Edn., 1967. Author: The Birth and Blossoming of a Bureau: CSB 1924-88, 1991; contbr. articles to profl. jours. Vol. Care-Medico, Afghanistan, 1973; Past mem. Jewish Bd. Edn.; nat. chair internat. health com., past bd. dirs. AMA Alliance; bd. electors Balt. Hebrew Congregation; active Parents Coun. of Balt., Bd. Md. Higher Edn. Loan Corp., 1986—96; past pres. Child Study Assn. of Balt. and Md., Balt. City Med. Aux., Aux. to the Med. and Chirurgical Faculty Md.; v.p. Balt. Hebrew Congregation Sisterhood, 1997—2002; chair Uniongram Luncheon, 2002, Bernice Kramer Meml., Balt., 2002; chair Ann. Interfaith Inst., 1996; steering com. cir. of giving Assoc. Jewish Cmty. Fedn., Balt.; bd. dirs. Ctl. Scholarship Bur. for Life, Med. Chi Alliance, STEP, Inc., Balt. Hebrew Congregation Sisterhood. Recipient Harry Greenstein award; Disting. Mem. honoree Child Study's 75th Anniversary Gala, 1999. Mem. Child Study Assn. Md. (adv. bd.). Jewish. Avocations: travel, theler, art, music, swimming.

WARRICK, PETER, football player; b. Bradenton, Fla., June 19, 1977; Postgrad in political sci., Fla. State Univ. Wide receiver Cin. Bengals, 2001—. Achievements include club record for rushing yards in a season by a wide receiver. Office: Cin Bengals 1 Paul Brown Stadium Cincinnati OH 45202*

WARRICK, RUTH, actress; b. St. Joseph, Mo., June 29, 1916; d. Frederick R. Jr. and Annie L. (Scott) W.; m. Erik Rolf (div.); m. Carl Neubert (div.); m. Robert McNamara, (div.); m. L. Jarvis Cushing Jr. (div.). Student, U. Mo.; studies with Antoinette Perry, Brock Pemberton. Cons. High Sch. Drop-out Program, U.S. Dept. Labor, 1962, Job Tng. Corps., 1964-66. Actress: (stage prodns.) Bury the Dead, 1937, Dial M for Murder, 1955, The Thorntons, 1956, Miss Lonelyhearts, 1957, Anna in The King & I, 1957-58, Single Man at a Party, 1959, Take Me Along, 1960, Who's Afraid of Virginia Woolf?, 1965, Long Day's Journey into Night, 1966, The Secret Life of Walter Mitty, 1966, Any Resemblance to Persons Living or Dead, 1971, Misalliance, 1972, Conditions of Agreement, 1972, Irene, 1973-74, Roberta, 1976, Legends, 1987 Butterflies Are Free, 1988, (broadway) Irene, 1971-72, Roberta, 1980, The King and I, 1958-59; (feature films) 34 films including The Corsican Brothers, 1941, Citizen Kane, 1942, Journey into Fear, 1942, The Iron Major, 1943, Forever and a Day, 1943, The Iron Major, 1943, Guest in the House, 1944, Mr. Winkle Goes to War, 1944, China Sky, 1945, Song of the South, 1946, Daisy Kenyon, 1947, Perilous Holiday, 1947, Let's Dance, 1947, The Great Dan Patch, 1949,, Three Husbands, 1950, Ride Beyond Vengeance, 1966, How to Steal the World, 1968, The Great Bank Robbery, 1969, (TV series) Father of the Bride, 1961-62, Peyton Place, 1965-67, As The World Turns, All My Children (2 Emmy award nominations); rec. artist Phoebe Tyler Regrets; author: (autobiography) The Confessions of Phoebe Tyler, 1980. Del. Global Forum for Human Survival, Moscow, 1990; bd. dirs. Bus. and Industry for Arts in Edn.; sponsor Learning to Read Through the Arts; co-founder Operation Bootstrap Watts, Calif., 1949-52, 64; regent of Cathedral St. John the Divine, N.Y.C. Recipient Humanitarian award Midland Empire Arthritis Found. given each year in her name, 1976, Arts in Edn. award given each year in her name, 1983, Arts in Edn. award Bus. and Industry for Arts in Edn., 1983, Medal N.Y. Arts Assn., 1996; Emmy Silver Circle, 1997; named Tchr. Cities in Schs., N.Y.C. Schs., 1976, TV-Hall of Fame, 1998. Mem. Bus. and Industry for Arts in Edn. (bd. dirs.), English-Speaking Union (bd. dirs.), Juvenille Diabetes Assn. (chair). Avocations: swimming, walking, music, metaphysics. Office: 250 W 57th St Ste 1308-9 New York NY 10107-0001 also: ABC Press Rels 77 W 66th St Fl 5 New York NY 10023-6201

WARRING, JEROME THOMAS, management consultant; b. Bloomington, Ind., Feb. 2, 1941; s. Thomas Edward Warring and Ellen Chase Hanna Murphy; 1 child, Frank Anthony. AB in Polit. Sci., Ind. U., 1962, MBA in Fin., 1972. Sr. cons. KMPG/Peat Marwick & Co., L.A., 1969-70; v.p. Korn/Ferry Internat., 1971-78; pres. Warring & Assocs., Anaheim Hills, Calif., 1978—, Warring Internat. Ins. Adv. Svcs., Ltd., Anaheim Hills, 1987—. Retained sr. advisor Asia-Pacific bus. devel. strategy, negotiation, and fgn. regulatory affairs Citicorp Global Ins. Ops., N.Y.C., 1989-93; internat. spkr. in field. Founder, pres. nonprofit Sonshine Youth Svcs. Inc., Bell Gardens, Cudahy, Commerce, Calif., 1976—; pres. Rio Hondo Boys & Girls Club, Bell Gardens, 1978-80; mem. nat. task force com. Boys & Girls Clubs Am., Inc., N.Y.C., 1980-82. Named Man of Yr., Federated Vol. Orgns., Downey, Calif., 1981, Bd. Vol. of Yr., United Way Greater L.A., 1995. Mem. Rotary (chmn. youth com.). Republican. Reformed Ch. of Am. Avocations: volunteer public service, mountain biking, running, boating, global travel. Office: Warring Internat Adv Svcs Ltd Ste 150 5241 E Santa Ana Canyon Rd Anaheim CA 92807-3741

WARRINGTON, WILLARD GLADE, former university official; b. Macomb, Ill., Oct. 24, 1920; s. Henry K. and Farie V. (Prather) W.; m. A. Irene Windser, Aug. 9, 1945 (dec. 1969); m. Janette Moffatt Cooper, Apr. 26, 1972; children: David, Steven, Douglas, Jane Ann, Stephen Cooper. B.Ed., Western Ill. State Tchrs. Coll., 1941; MS, U. Ill., 1949, MS, 1950, Ed.D., 1952. Tchr. public high schs., Ill., 1941-42, 45-48; mem. faculty Mich. State U., 1952-58, dir. office evaluation services, 1958-74, asso. dean Univ. Coll., 1974-78, acting dean Univ. Coll., 1978-80, dir. undergrad. univ. div., 1980-85, dir., prof. emeritus, 1986—. Cons. edn.; Ford Found. cons. U. Philippines. Contbr. articles on ednl. measurement to profl. publs.; editorial bd.: Ednl. and Psychol. Measurement, 1968-85. Active Boy Scouts Am., 1957-68. Served to lt. col. USAAF, 1942-45. Mem. Nat. Council on Measurement in Edn. (pres. 1973-74), Am. Ednl. Research Assn., Assn. for Gen. and Liberal Studies (sec.-treas. 1973-79) Methodist. Home: 1211 Ascot Pl Haslett MI 48840

WARSAWER, HAROLD NEWTON, real estate appraiser and consultant; b. N.Y.C. s. Sidney L. and Alice W.; m. Sally Kingsbury; children: Alice Cooper, Nancy Arkuss, Carole Greenblatt. BA, U. Mo.; MBA, Harvard. Property mgr. and real estate broker Sidney L. Warsawer & Son, N.Y.C., 1950—; pres., dir. Consol. Capital, 1962-68; pres. Atlantic Appraisal Co., Inc., 1960—96; pres., dir. Contemporary Enterprises, 1974-76. Mem. editl. bd. The Appraisal Jour., 1970-85. Candidate Teaneck (N.J.) Sch. Bd., Town Coun.; chmn. bldg. com. Temple Emeth, Teaneck, 1954-64; bd. dirs. Friends Teaneck Libr. Capt. Army Air Corp., 1942-46. Mem. Appraisal Inst. (pres. N.Y. chpt. 1977, bd. dirs. 1970-80, 90-92, gov. counselor 1978), Nat. Assn. Rev. Appraisers, Real Estate Bd. N.Y. (chair com.), Nat. Realty Club (pres. 1992, bd. dirs.), Am. Arbitration Assn., Haworth Golf Club. Avocations: golf, clocks, library. Home: 430 Rutland Ave Teaneck NJ 07666-2823 Office: Ste 1446 60 E 42nd St Rm 1446 New York NY 10165-1499

WARSH, LEWIS DAVID, poet, educator; b. Bronx, N.Y., Nov. 9, 1944; s. Harry and Ray (Bienhacker) W.; m. Bernadette Mayer, Nov. 1, 1975 (div. Aug. 1985); children: Marie, Sophia, Max. BA, CCNY, 1966, MA, 1975. Instr. New England Coll., Henniker, N.H., 1979-80, Queens (N.Y.) Coll., 1985-87, Yeshiva U., N.Y.C., 1986-87, Fairleigh Dickinson U., Teaneck, N.J., 1987-89, La Guardia Community Coll., Queens, 1989-90. Adj. assoc. prof. L.I. U., Bklyn., 1985—, instr. The Poetry Project, 1991—; publ., editor Angel Hair Books, N.Y.C., 1966-75, United Artists Books, N.Y.C., 1977—. Author: Dreaming as One, 1971, Blue Heaven, 1977, Agnes and Sally, 1984, Information From the Surface of Venus, 1987, The Corset, 1987, A Free Man, 1991, Avenue of Escape, 1995, Private Agenda, 1996, Money Under the Table, 1997; editor: Boston Eagle, 1972-74, United Artists mag., 1977-83, The World, 1991-94. Grantee CAPS Found., 1977, Coord. Coun. on Lit. Mags., 1982, N.Y. Found. Arts, 1988, Fund for Poetry, 1994; NEA fellow, 1980. Home: 701 President St Brooklyn NY 11215-1270

WARSHAUER, IRENE C. lawyer; b. N.Y.C., May 4, 1942; m. Alan M. Warshauer, Nov. 27, 1966; 1 child, Susan. BA with distinction, U. Mich., 1963; LLB cum laude, Columbia U., 1966. Bar: N.Y. 1966, U.S. Dsit. Ct. (so. and ea. dist.) N.Y. 1969, U.S. Ct. Appeals (2d cir.) 1969, U.S. Dist. Ct. (no. dist.) N.Y. 1980, U.S. Supreme Ct. 1972. With 1st Jud. Dept., N.Y. State Mental Health Info. Svc., 1966-68; assoc. Chadbourne Parke Whiteside & Wolff, 1968-75; mem. Anderson Kill & Olick, P.C., N.Y.C., 1975-99, Fried & Epstein, N.Y.C., 2000—. Mediator U.S. Dist. Ct. (so. dist.) N.Y., N.Y. State Supreme Ct.; lectr. Columbia Law Sch., Def. Rsch. Inst., Aspen Inst. Humanistic Studies, ABA, Rocky Mountain Mineral Law Found., CPR Inst. Dispute Resolution; arbitrator NASD EEOC, NYSE, Am. Arbitration Assn. Contbr. chpts. to books, articles to profl. jours. Mem. County Dem. Com., 1968—. Named to Hon. Order Ky. Cols. Mem.: ABA, N.Y. State Bar Assn. (chmn. subcom. mentally disabled and cmty. 1978—82), Assn. Bar City N.Y. (judiciary com. 1982—84, mem. alternative dispute resolution com. 2000—). Avocations: gardening, cooking, birding, theatre. Office: Fried & Epstein 1350 Broadway New York NY 10018-7702

WARSHAW, ALLEN CHARLES, lawyer; b. Harrisburg, Pa., Aug. 27, 1948; s. Julius and Miriam (Nepove) W.; m. Shirley Anne Nes, Aug. 23, 1970; children: Christopher James, Andrew Charles, William Robert. BA, U. Pa., 1970; JD, Villanova U., 1973. Bar: Pa. 1973, U.S. Dist. Ct. (ea. and mid. dists.) Pa. 1974, U.S. Ct. Appeals (3d cir.) 1975, U.S. Supreme Ct. 1977, Calif. 1978. Staff atty. Office Atty. Gen., State of Pa., Harrisburg, 1973-79, chief civil litigation, 1979-85, dir. civil law, 1985-86; ptnr., head appellate practice group Duane, Morris & Heckscher, 1986—2002; shareholder Klett, Rooney, Lieber & Schorling, 2002—. Past pres. Mechanicsburg Soccer Assn.; Dem. committeeperson, area leader Cumberland County; mem. exec. com. Cumberland County Dem. Party; bd. dirs. Mechanicsburg Area Sch. Dist. Fellow Am. Bar Found.; mem. ABA, Fed. Bar Assn., Am. Bankruptcy Inst., Pa. Bar Assn., Dauphin County Bar Assn., Turnabout Mgmt. Assn. Home: 1035 Mccormick Rd Mechanicsburg PA 17055-5970 Office: Klett Rooney Lieber & Schorling 240 N 3d St Harrisburg PA 17101 E-mail: acwarshaw@KlettRooney.com.

WARSHAW, JOSEPH BENNETT, dean, pediatrician; b. Miami Beach, Fla., July 17, 1936; s. Phillip Robert and Mona (Monashefsky) Warshaw; m. Cynthia Ann Stober, June 6, 1961; children: Deborah, Kathryn, Lawrence. BS, U. Fla., 1957; MD, Duke U., 1961; MS (hon.) , Yale U., 1976; MD (hon.) , Catholic U., Santiago, Chile; Josiah Macy Jr. faculty scholar, U. Oxford, 1979—80. Diplomate Am. Bd. Pediat., subsplty bd. in neonatal-perinatal medicine. Intern, resident in pediat. Strong Meml. Hosp., Rochester, NY, 1961—63; resident in pediat. Duke Hosp., Durham, NC, 1963—64; research assoc. NIH, 1964—66, Retina Found., Boston, 1966—68; assoc. in pediat. Harvard U., 1968—71, asst. prof. pediat., 1971—72, assoc. prof., 1972—73; assoc. prof. pediat. and ob-gyn Yale U. Sch. Medicine, New Haven, 1973—76, prof. pediat. and ob-gyn, 1976—82; prof., chmn. dept. pediat. U. Tex. Health Sci. Ctr., Dallas, 1982—87; chief staff Children's Med. Ctr., 1982—87; chief pediat. Parkland Meml. Hosp., 1982—87; prof., chmn. dept. pediat. Yale U. Sch. Medicine, New Haven, 1987—2000, dep. dean for clin. affairs, 1995—2000; dean Coll. Medicine U. Vt., Burlington, 2000—; dep. dean clin. affairs Sch. Medicine Yale U., New Haven. Physician-in-chief Children's Hosp. at Yale-New Haven Hosp., 1987—2000; mem. human embryology and devel. study sect. NIH, 1974—78; nat. adv. con. Nat. Inst. Child Health and Human Devel., 1987—91. Clin. rsch. adv. com. Nat. Found. March of Dimes, 1978—92; mem. rsch. com. United Cerebral Palsy, 1987—2000. Served USPHS, 1964—66. Fellow: Am. Acad. Pediat.; mem.: Conn. Acad. Sci. and Engring., Conn. Acad. Arts and Scis., Internat. Pediatric Rsch. Found. (chmn. bd. 1989—93), Assn. Am. Physicians, Soc. Pediatric Rsch. (pres. 1981—82), Soc. Devel. Biology, Am. Soc. Cell Biology, Am. Soc. Biol. Chemistry, Am. Soc. Clin. Investigation, Am. Pediatric Soc. (coun. mem. 1988—94), Inst. Medicine NAS. Home: 120 Crescent Rd Burlington VT 05401 Office: U Vt Coll Medicine Dean's Office Burlington VT 05405 E-mail: joseph.warshaw@uvm.edu.

WARSHAW, MICHAEL THOMAS, lawyer; b. Jersey City, June 29, 1950; s. Thomas T. and June C. (Lancaster) W.; m. Mary Jane Egidio, July 12, 1986. BA in Sociology, Coll. of the Holy Cross, 1972; JD, Bklyn. Law Sch., 1975. Bar: N.J. 1976, U.S. Dist. Ct. N.J. 1976, U.S. Ct. Appeals (3d cir.) 1982, N.Y. Ct. of Appeals 1987, U.S. Supreme Ct. 1982. Law sec. to judge N.J. Superior Ct., 1975-76; assoc. Drazin & Warshaw PC, Red Bank, N.J., 1976-88, Magee & Graham, Wall, 1988-90; pres. Michael T. Warshaw, PC, Red Bank, 1990-95, 2001—; shareholder Warshaw & Barnes, PC, 1995-2001; adj. prof. bus. law Brookdale C.C., Lincroft. Speaker Mock Trial Sem., Young Lawyers div. N.J. Bar Assn., 1984, Discovery Sem., 1986; mem. com. on mcpl. cts. N.J. Supreme Ct., 1984-88; master Hadyn Proctor Inns of Ct., 1999—. Chmn. Red Bank Cath. H.S. Devel. Adv. Coun., 1994—, elder law seminar Trenton Diocese, 1996; trustee Brookdale C.C. Found., 1995—. Mem. ABA, N.J. Bar Assn. (young lawyers divsn., exec. com. 1983-86), N.J. Bar Found. (spkrs. bur.), Monmouth County Bar Assn. (civil practice com. 1985—, chair alternative dispute resolution com.), Christian Bros. Acad. Alumni Assn. (pres. 1993-95), Phi Delta Phi. Roman Catholic. Avocation: golf. Home: 18 Quaker Rd Middletown NJ 07748-3193 Office: 10 W Bergen Pl Ste 202 Red Bank NJ 07701-1500 E-mail: mtwarshaw2000@yahoo.com.

WARSHAW, ROBERTA SUE, lawyer, financial specialist; b. Chgo., July 10, 1934; d. Charles and Frieda (Feldman) Weiner; m. Lawrence Warshaw, July 5, 1959 (div. June 1978); children: Nan R., Adam; m. Paul A. Heise, Apr. 2, 1994. Student, U. Ill., 1952-55; BFA, U. So. Calif., 1956; JD, Northwestern U., 1980. Bar: Ill. 1980. Atty., fin. specialist Housing Svcs. Ctr., Chgo., 1980-84, Chgo. Rehab. Network, 1985-91, 92-95; dir. housing State Treas., State of Ill., Chgo., 1991; sole practitioner, 1995—. Legal worker Sch. of Law, Northwestern U. Legal Clinic, Chgo., 1977-80; real estate developer, mgr., marketer, Chgo., 1961-77; bd. dirs. Single Room Housing Assistance Corp., Lebanon County Mediation Svcs., mediator, sec., 2001; asst. dir. Lebanon Valley Coll. Program, Hania, Crete, 1998. Co-author: (manual) The Cook County Scavenger Sale Program and The City of Chicago Reactivation Program, 1991, (booklet) Fix the Worst First, 1989; co-editor: The Caring Contract, Voices of American Leaders, 1996. Alderman 9th ward City of Evanston, Ill., 1985-93, mem. planning and devel., rules com., unified budget com., chair flood and pollution control com.; pres. Sister Cities Found.; mem. cmty. and econ. devel. policy Nat. League Cities, 1990-93; mem. Dem. Nat. Com.; bd. dirs. Dem. Ctrl. Com. Evanston, 1973—; elected committeeman Evanston Twp. Dem. Com., 1994-98, dem. committeeman Mt. Gretna Borough, 2000—; del. Dem. Nat. Conv., 1996; Dem. committeeman Mt. Gretna Borough, 2000—; vol. tax preparer; tax counseling for elderly, 2000—; bd. dirs., mediator Lebanon County Mediation Svcs., 2000—, sec., 2001—. Mem. ABA (affordable housing com.), Ill. State Bar Assn., Chgo. Bar Assn. (real estate coms.), Decalogue Soc. Lawyers, Chgo. Coun. Lawyers (housing com.), IRS Tax Counseling for the Elderly (vol. tax preparer). Avocations: politics, travel, hiking, camping, athletic activities. Home: 104 Brown Ave PO Box 537 Mount Gretna PA 17064-0537

WARSHAW, STANLEY IRVING, policy advisor; b. Boston, Nov. 5, 1931; s. Alec and Sarah (Laserson) W.; m. Wanda Faye Capino, Feb., 12, 1992; 1 child from previous marriage, Karen Beth. BS in Ceramic Engring, Ga. Tech. Inst., 1957; Sc.D. in Ceramics, M.I.T., 1961; grad., Advanced Mgmt. Program, Harvard Bus. Sch., 1978. Sr. scientist research div. Raytheon Co., Waltham, Mass., 1961-64; with Am. Standard, Inc., New Brunswick, N.J., 1964-75, gen. mgr. engring. and devel., 1972-75; dir. Ctr. for Consumer Product Tech., Nat. Inst. Stds. and Tech. (formerly Nat. Bur. Stds.), Washington, 1975-80, dir. Office Product Standards Policy, 1981-86, assoc. dir., 1987-89, dir. Office Standards Svcs. Gaithersburg, Md., 1989-93; sr. policy advisor for stds. and tech. U.S. Dept. Commerce, 1994-99. Served to capt. U.S. Army, 1951-53. Fellow N.Y. Acad. Scis., Washington Acad. Scis. Home: 9730 Washingtonian Blvd Gaithersburg MD 20878-7302 also: 555 SE 6th Ave Apt 5B Delray Beach FL 33483-5250 E-mail: s.warshaw@att.net.

WARSHAWSKY, ISIDORE, physicist, consultant; b. N.Y.C., May 27, 1911; s. Morris and Esther (Sherman) W. BS cum laude, CCNY, 1930. Physicist Nat. Adv. Com. Aeronautics, Langley Field, Va., 1930-42, chief instrumentation sect. Cleve., 1942-50; chief instrument rsch. br. Nat. Adv. Com. Aeronautics/ NASA, 1950-72; instrumentation cons. NASA, 1972-90, ret., 1990, disting. rsch. cons. (unsalaried), 1990-95. *Some historically more notable inventions are: for studies of an airplane's acrobatic flight, the first mechanical gauge that could record the time history of structural stress in the wing (1935), the first panel plane-accelaration-indicator for the pilot (1937) and the first electrical-signal-recorder that was rugged enough to withstand the plane's vibration (1939); novel circuits that permitted flight use of the new electric strain gauges (1940); precise calibration system for meters used to measure the flow of liquid hydrogen to rocket engines (1961); precise calibration system for determining true pressure indicated by vacuum gauges used in space and in nuclear particle accelerators (1972).* Author: (textbook) Foundations of Measurement and Instrumentation, 1990; author 10 NACA/NASA tech. reports; contbr. 20 articles to sci. jours. and books. Fellow Instrument Soc. Am.; mem. Am. Phys. Soc., Combustion Inst., Am. Vacuum Soc, Phi Beta Kappa.

WARSHAWSKY, STANFORD SEYMOUR, investment banker; b. Asbury Park, N.J., Oct. 14, 1937; s. Harry and Eva (Holland) W.; m. Sandra Faith Weinstein, Aug. 14, 1960; children: Susan Abrams, Deborah Farfel, Cynthia, Mark. BBA, U. Mich., 1959; LLB, U. Va., 1962. Lawyer Shearman & Sterling, N.Y.C., 1962-71; v.p. Arnhold and S. Bleichroeder, Inc., 1972-77, mng. dir., 1978-86, vice-chmn., 1986-94, co-pres., co-CEO, 1994—, also bd. dirs. Bd. dirs. Arnhold and S. Bleichroeder Advisers, Inc., N.Y.C.; chmn. Arnhold and S. Bleichroeder U.K. Ltd., London, 1998—, First Eagle Funds, N.Y.C., 1994—; chmn. nominating com., mem. N.Y. area firms adv. com. N.Y. Stock Exch., N.Y.C., 1998—; exch. ofcl. Am. Stock Exch., N.Y.C., 1994-97. Bd. dirs. Gen. Ceramics, Inc., N.Y., 1975-89, Leybold Inficon, Inc., N.Y., 1976-89, Mt. Sinai Ctr. Aux., N.Y.C., 1986-96. Mem. N.Y. State Bar Assn., Va. State Bar Assn., Hebrew Free Loan Soc. of N.Y. (bd. dirs. 1989—), German-Am. C. of C. (bd. dirs. 1980—), Met. Club, Harmonie Club, Doubles, India House. Office: Arnhold and S Bleichroeder Inc 1345 Avenue Of The Americas New York NY 10105-0302

WARTELLA, ELLEN ANN, communications educator, consultant; b. Kingston, Pa., Oct. 16, 1949; d. Nicholas and Margaret (Lipko) W.; m. D. Charles Whitney, Aug. 1, 1976; children: David Charles, Stephen Wright. BA, U. Pitts., 1971; MA, U. Minn., 1974, PhD, 1977. Asst. prof. Ohio State U., Columbus, 1976-79; rsch. asst. prof. communications U. Ill., Champaign, 1979-83, rsch. assoc. prof., 1983-89, rsch. prof., 1989-93; dean Coll. Comm., Walter Cronkite Regents Chair in Comm. U. Tex., Austin, 1993—. Vis. prof. U. Calif., Santa Barbara, 1992-93; cons. Children's TV Workshop, N.Y.C., 1988-89, FTC, Washington, 1978, 1991-92, FCC, Washington, 1979. Coauthor National Television Violence Study, 1994-98, The Audience and Its Landscape, 1996, The American Communication Research: The Remembered History, 1996. Mem. bd. advisors Am. Children's TV Festival, Chgo., 1988; bd. trustees Children's TV Workshop, 1996—; bd. dirs. Headliners Found., Austin, Sta. KLRU-TV (ex officio), Austin. Recipient Krieghbaum award Assn. for Edn. in Journalism and Mass Communication, 1984; Univ. scholar U. Ill., 1989-93; Gannett Ctr. for Media Studies fellow, 1985-86. Fellow Internat. Comm. Assn. (pres. 1992-93), Broadcast Edn. Assn. (bd. dirs. 1990-94), Speech Comm. Assn., Soc. for Rsch. in Child Devel.

WARTH, JAMES ARTHUR, physician, researcher; b. N.Y.C., Apr. 30, 1942; s. Peter and Anne Warth; m. Maria Archer Russell, May 3, 1969; children: David M., Andrew A. BS, Tufts U., 1963, MD, 1967. Diplomate Am. Bd. Internal Medicine, Am. Bd. Hematology, Am. Bd. Oncology. Hematologist Harvard Health Svcs. Harvard U., Cambridge, Mass., 1976-77, Officer, 1976-77; Lectr. on medicine Harvard Med. Sch., Boston, 2000—; attending hematologist Harper-Grace Hosps., Detroit, 1977-84; asst. prof. medicine Wayne State U., 1977-84; rsch. scientist New Eng. Med. Ctr., Boston, 1984-86; attending hematologist-oncologist Faulkner Hosp., 1986—; asst. prof. medicine Tufts U. Sch. Medicine, 1986—, assoc. course dir. phys. diagnosis, 1996—; course dir. phys. diagnosis Faulkner Hosp., 1992—, dir. dept. medicine-physician asst. program, 1996-97. Cons. in hematology NIH, Bethesda , Md., 1980—83, 1987, Mass. Profl. Rev. Orgn., Waltham, 1991—93, Medfield State Hosp., Mass., 1993—; vis. prof. Yale U., New Haven, 1986; Max Millman Meml. Lectr. in Medicine Baystate Med. Ctr., Tufts U., Springfield, Mass., 2000; invited lectr. Columbia U., 1982, Harvard U., 1984, SUNY, Syracuse, 1991, New Eng. Med. Ctr., Tufts U., 1992; invited spkr. Dana Farber Cancer Inst., 1999; Med. Grand Rounds spkr. Faulkner Hosp., Boston, 1986, 88, 92, 96; mem. pharmacy and therapeutics com. Faulkner Hosp., Boston, 1991—; chmn. subcom. on anticoagulation of pharmacy and therapeutics Faulkner Hosp. , Boston, 1994—; mem. case devel. com., problem based learning Tufts U. Sch. Medicine, 1994—95, faculty advisor , 1991—; rsch. lectr. NIH, Tarrytown, NY, 1986; bd. dirs. Faulkner Physicians Assn., Inc., Boston, 1994—; mem. melanoma adv. bd. N.E. region Schering-Plough Co., Kenilworth, NJ, 1995; guest appearance NBC affiliate NBC News, Detroit, 1980; physician med. grand rounds Shattuck Hosp., Boston, 1999. Author (contbg. author): (textbook) Hematologic Disorders in Maternal-Fetal Medicine, 1990; reviewer: Am. Jour. Hematology, 1986, reviewer: Jour. Andrology, 1990—92; contbr. articles to profl. jours. Preceptor Nat. Youth Forum, 1996—98. Maj. U.S. Army, 1969—71. Recipient Mark Aisner M.D. award for Excellence in Tchg. Physical Diagnosis, Tufts U. Sch. Medicine, 2001; grantee Spl. Fellowship, NIH, 1974—76, grantee Rsch., 1980—83, 1983—86. Fellow: ACP; mem.: Biomembranes Sickle Cell Rsch. Group, Am. Fedn. Med. Rsch., Am. Soc. Hematology. Achievements include discovery of new red blood cell, sequestrocyte accepted into Am. Soc. Hematology slide bank, 1995. Avocations: art, music, architecture, tennis. Office: Faulkner Hosp 1153 Centre St Rm 5950 Boston MA 02130-3446

WARTH, ROBERT DOUGLAS, history educator; b. Houston, Dec. 16, 1921; s. Robert Douglas and Virginia (Adams) W.; m. Lillian Eleanor Terry, Sept. 18, 1945. BS, U. Ky., 1943; MA, U. Chgo., 1945, PhD, 1949. Instr. history U. Tenn., Knoxville, 1950-51; instr. Rutgers U., Newark, 1951-54, asst. prof., 1954-58; vis. prof. Paine Coll., Augusta, Ga., 1960; asso. editor Grolier, Inc., N.Y.C., 1960-62, 63-64; lectr. Hunter Coll., part time, 1962-63; asso. prof. S.I. C.C., 1964-68; prof. history U. Ky., Lexington, 1968-92, prof. emeritus history, 1992—. Pres. So. Conf. Slavic Studies, 1982-83 Author: The Allies and the Russian Revolution, 1954, Soviet Russia in World Politics, 1963, Joseph Stalin, 1969, Lenin, 1973, Leon Trotsky, 1977, Nicholas II: The

Life and Reign of Russia's Last Monarch, 1997. Served with AUS, 1943-44. Sr. scholar award So. Conf. Slavic Studies, 1992. Mem. Am. Hist. Assn., Am. Assn. Advancement Slavic Studies, AAUP Home: 640 Cooper Dr Lexington KY 40502-2277 Office: U Ky Dept History Lexington KY 40506-0001

WARTHEN, HARRY JUSTICE, III, lawyer; b. Richmond, Va., July 8, 1939; s. Harry Justice Jr. and Martha Winston (Alsop) W.; m. Sally Berkeley Trapnell, Sept. 7, 1968; children: Martha Alsop, William Trapnell. BA, U. Va., 1961, LLB, 1967. Bar: Va. 1967, U.S. Ct. Appeals (4th cir.) 1967, U.S. Dist. Ct. (ea. dist.) Va. 1969. Law clk. to judge U.S. Ct. Appeals (4th cir.), Richmond, Va., 1967-68; assoc. Hunton & Williams, 1968—. Lectr. U. Va. Law Sch., Charlottesville, 1975-77, in field. Trustee exec. com. Hist. Richmond Found., 1986-95, 96—, pres., 2000-02; trustee Woodrow Wilson Birthplace and Mus., 1997—; dir. exec. com. Preservation Alliance of Va., 1991-97, pres., 1994-96; elder, trustee endowment fund Grace Covenant Presbyn. Ch.; moderator Hanover Presbytery, Presbyn. Ch. (USA), 1988. Lt. U.S. Army, 1962-64. Fellow Am. Coll. Trust and Estate Counsel, Va. Law Found.; mem. ABA, Richmond Bar Assn., Va. Bar Assn. (chmn. sect. on wills, trusts and estates 1981-89), Antiquarian Soc. Richmond (pres. 1977-78, 98-99), Country Club Va., Deep Run Hunt Club. Republican. Home: 1319 Shallow Well Rd Manakin-Sabot VA 23103-2305 Office: Hunton & Williams Riverfront Plz E Tower 951 E Byrd St Richmond VA 23219 E-mail: hwarthen@hunton.com.

WARTLUFT, DAVID JONATHAN, librarian, clergyman; b. Stouchsburg, Pa., Sept. 22, 1938; s. Cleaver Milvard and Dorothy (Stump) W.; m. Joyce Claudia Dittmer, June 15, 1963 (div. Sept. 1988); children: Elizabeth Marie, Deborah Joy, Rebecca Janet, Andrew Jonathan. AB (Trexler scholar), Muhlenberg Coll., 1960; Div.M. (Danforth scholar), Luth. Theol. Sem., Phila., 1964; A.M. (scholar), U. Pa., 1964; MS (Lilly Found. scholar), Drexel U., 1968. Asst. chaplain, instr. religion Springfield (Mass.) Coll., 1962-63; ordained minister Luth. Ch., 1964; pastor Jerusalem Luth. Ch., Allentown, Pa., 1964-66; cataloger, reference librarian Luth. Sem. Phila., 1966-68, asst. librarian, 1968-77, dir. library, 1977—2002, chaplain, 1978-79, dir. 1st yr. field edn., 1979-81, 82-83, faculty sec., 1985—2002. Archivist Northeastern Pa. Synod, Luth. Ch. Am., 1970-87, mem. comms. com., 1967-78, sec., 1975-78, mem. conv. com., 1976; archivist Northeastern Pa. Synod, Evang. Luth. Ch. Am., 1988-91, 2001—; v.p. Luth. Archives Ctr. at Phila., 1979-85, 97—, bd. dirs., 1979—; libr. cons. Gurkul Luth. Ch., Madras, India, 1989, Huria Kristen Batak Protestant Sem., Pematang Siantar, Sumatra, Indonesia, 1989, Luther Sem., Adelaide, Australia, 1996; mem. archives adv. bd. Evang. Luth. Ch. Am., 2000—. Editor: Teamwork, 1970-84, The Periodical, 1979-84, Luth. Hist. Soc. Eastern Pa.; author: (index) Luther in Mid-Career (H. Bornkamm), 1983, Theodicy in the Old Testament (J. Crenshaw), 1983, The Roots of Anti-Semitism (H. Obermann), 1984, The Book of Revelation: Justice and Judgment (E.S. Fiorenza), 1985, Rediscovering Paul (N.R. Peterson), 1985, The Opponents of Paul in Second Corinthians (D. Georgi), 1986, Psychological Aspects of Pauline Theology (G. Theissen), 1986, Ethics of the New Testament (W. Schragg), 1987, Israel's Praise (W. Brueggemann), 1987, Commitment to Unity (W.K. Gilbert), 1988, Paul and His Letters (L. Keck), 2d rev. edit., 1988, Finally Comes the Poet (W. Bruggemann), 1989, Community and Commitment (G. Rupp), 1989, Protest and Praise (J.M. Spenser), 1990, After the Absolute (L. Swidler), 1990, Greeks, Romans and Christians, 1990, The New Era in Religious Education (P. Babin), 1991, A Commentary on the Book of Amos (S.M. Paul), 1992, The Book of Revelation (J. Roloff), 1993, What is Scripture? (W.C. Smith), 1993, Jesus in the Gospels (R. Schnackenburg), 1995, Amos (Jeremias), 1998, World Religions in America (J. Neusner), 1999, Luth. Hist. Conf. publs., 1998—, Revolution and Renewal (Campolo), 2000, Nicholas Lyra: The Senses of Scripture (Krey and Smith), 2000, Beleagured Rulers, 2001, Practical Theology for Black Churches; contbr. articles to profl. jours. Active Boy Scouts Am., 1964-66. Mem. Am. Theol. Libr. Assn. (exec. sec. 1971-81, editor procs. 1971-81, bd. dirs. 1991-94, sec. 1992-94, recording sec. 1995-97, devel. officer, 1998-99), Southeastern Pa. Theol. Librs. Assn. (sec. 1970-73, chair 1982-85, chair planning com. 1986-89), Coun. Nat. Libr. and Info. Assn. (counselor 1978-81), Coun. on Study Religion (liaison com. 1974-77, 81-82, nominating com. 1978-80), Luth. Hist. Conf. (com. on scholarly rsch. and pub. 1981—, constl. revision com. 1984-86, bd. dirs. 1988-94, 96-2002, treas. 1988-94, 96-2002, membership chair 1994-96, editor essays and reports 1996-2000), Assn. Theol. Schs. in U.S. and Can. (selection panel for libr. grants), Paradise Falls Luth. Assn. (bd. dirs. 1985-87, chmn. religious activities 1985-86), Assn. Uniting Religion and Art (chmn. membership com., treas. 1995—), Mid. States Assn. (accreditation visitor), Luth. Hist. Soc. Ea. Pa. (life, bd. dirs. 1991-94, v.p. 1994-96), Drexel U. Grad. Sch. Libr. and Info. Sci. Alumni Assn. (bd. dirs. 1978-80), Eta Sigma Phi, Phi Sigma Tau, Beta Phi Mu. Democrat. E-mail: dwartluft@ltsp.edu. *By God's grace I am freed to live a life of joyful service in gratitude.*

WARTMAN, STEVEN, dean, educator; Grad., Cornell U. , 1966; MD, Johns Hopkins U. , 1970, PhD Sociology, 1979. Diplomate Am. Bd. Internal Medicine. Dir. med. svcs., chmn. medicine Mount Sinai Med. Ctr. , Miami Beach; prof. medicine U. Miami; sr. residency in internal medicine Baltimore City Hosp.; intern in internal medicine Stanford U. Med. Ctr.; resident in internal medicine Yale-New Haven Hosp.; prof. medicine Albert Einstein Coll. Medicine; physician-in-chief L.I. Jewish Med. Ctr.; with Edward Meilman Disting. Chair Medicine; dir. Ctr. Quality Rsch. North Shore-L.I. Jewish Health Sys.; dean U. Tex. Med. Sch. San Antonio , 2000—. Contbr. more than 120 peer-reviewed jour. articles, abstracts, chapters to books. Recipient Leadership and Achievement award, Soc. Gen. Internal Medicine, 1997, Excellence award, U.S. Health Resources and Svcs. Adminstrn., 1999; fellow Internat. in Health Care, Yugoslavia, 1969, Primary Care Policy, USPHS, 1991; scholar Henry Luce, Indonesia, 1975—76, Robert Wood Johnson Clin., Johns Hopkins U., 1976—78. Fellow: ACP; mem.: Alpha Omega Alpha, Phi Beta Kappa. Office: 7703 Floyd Curl Dr San Antonio TX 78229*

WARTOFSKY, LEONARD, medical educator; b. N.Y.C., July 14, 1937; s. Harry and Sadie (Gondelman) W.; m. Donna L. Brodsky, Dec. 18, 1959; 1 child, Michael. BS, George Washington U., 1959, MS, 1961, MD, 1964, MPH, 1995. Diplomate Am. Bd. Internal Medicine, Am. Bd. Endocrinology. Intern Washington U., St. Louis, 1964-65, resident, 1965-66, Albert Einstein Coll., Bronx, N.Y., 1966-67; fellow Harvard U., Boston, 1967-69; chief dept. medicine Walter Reed Med. Ctr., Washington, 1990-93; prof. medicine Uniformed Svcs. U.; chmn. dept. medicine Washington Hosp. Ctr., 1993—. Clinical prof. Georgetown U., Howard U., George Washington Univ., U. Md. Editor: Thyroid Cancer, 2000; assoc. editor: Principles and Practice of Endocrinology, 2001; contbr. 200 articles to profl. jours. Mem. ACP (master), Am. Thyroid Assn. (bd. dirs. 1986-89, nat. sec. 1988-93, pres. 1995), Am. Fedn. Clin. Rsch., Endocrine Soc., Am. Soc. Clin. Invstigation, Assn. Am. Physicians, Assn. Profs. Medicine. Democrat. Jewish. Office: Washington Hosp Ctr 110 Irving St NW Washington DC 20010-2975

WARTOFSKY, WILLIAM VICTOR, writer, consultant; b. N.Y.C., June 15, 1931; s. Harry and Sadie (Gondelman) W.; m. Tamar Chachik, Feb. 8, 1957; children: Leora, Alona, Ariel. BA in Journalism, Am. U., 1963. Corr. UPI, Washington, 1954-60; writer NIH, Bethesda, Md., 1960-85, NASW, Washington, 1985-88; cons. Editl. Experts., Alexandria, Va., 1989-97. Author: Mr. Double, 1967, Meeting the Pieman, 1971, 2d edit., 2000, Year of the Yahoo, 1972, The Passage, 1980, Prescription for Justice, 1988, Terminal Justice, 1989. Corp. U.S. Army, 1952-54, Korea. Jewish. Avocations: jogging, reading, playgoing. Home: 8507 Wild Olive Dr Potomac MD 20854-3437 E-mail: vwarto@hotmail.com.

WASAN, DARSH TILAKCHAND, university official, chemical engineer educator; b. Sarai, Salah, West Pakistan, July 15, 1938; came to U.S., 1957, naturalized, 1974; s. Tilakchand Gokalchand and Ishari Devi (Obhan) W.; m. Usha Kapur, Aug. 21, 1966; children: Ajay, Kern. BSChemE, U. Ill., 1960; PhD, U. Calif., Berkeley, 1965. Asst. prof. chem. engring. Ill. Inst. Tech., Chgo., 1964-67, assoc. prof., 1967-70, prof., 1970—, chmn. dept., 1971-77, 78-87, acting dean, 1977-78, 87-88, v.p. rsch. and tech., 1988-91, provost, 1991—, provost and sr. v.p., 1995-96, v.p., internat. and Motorola chair, 1996—. Cons. Inst. Gas Tech., 1965-70, Chgo. Bridge & Iron Co., 1967-71, Ill. EPA, 1971-72, NSF, 1971, 78-79, 87-89, Nelson Industries, 1976—, B.F. Goodrich Chem. Co., 1976-78, Exxon Rsch. & Engring. Co., 1977-89, Stauffer Chem. Co., 1980-88, ICI Ams., 1988-92; Procter & Gamble lectr. U. Cin. Editor-in-chief Jour. colloid and Interface sci.; mem. publs. bd. Chem. Engring. Edn. Jour.; mem. adv. bd. Jour. Separations Tech., Current Opinion in Colloid and Interface Sci., Jour. of Dispersion Sci. and Tech.; contbr. articles to profl. jours. Recipient Donald Gage Stevens Disting. Lectureship award Syracuse U., 1991, Jakob J. Bikerman Lectureship award Case Western U., 1994, Robert Gilpin Lectr. award Clarkson U., 1995, MacMoran Disting. Lectureship award Tulane U., 1996, Sidney Ross lectr. award, 1996, Bonnet Dodge Disting. Lectureship award Yale U., 1998, Spl. citation U.S. FDA, 2000. Fellow AIChE (Ernest Thiele award 1989, Thmas Baron awrd in fluid-particle systems 2002); mem. AAAS, Am. Chem. Soc. (award in colloid chemistry 2000), Soc. Rheology, Am. Soc. Engring. Edn. (Western Electric award 1972, 3M Lectureship award chem. engring. divsn. 1991), Am. Physics Inst., Fine Particles Soc. (pres. 1976-77, Hausner award 1982), Sigma Xi. Home: 8705 Royal Swan Ln Darien IL 60561-8433 Office: Ill Inst Tech 3300 S Federal St Chicago IL 60616-3793 E-mail: wasan@iit.edu.

WASCH, WILLIAM KARL, gerontologist, contractor; b. Mt. Vernon, N.Y., May 11, 1931; s. Karl F. and Lina M. (Krauth) W.; m. Susan Beck Wasch, Aug. 23, 1958; children: Christina, William K. Jr., Heidi, Frederick. BA with honors, Wesleyan U., 1952; MS in Bus., Columbia U., 1953. Fin. analyst Std. Oil of N.J., N.Y.C., 1956-59; mktg. rep. Esso Std., 1959-61; mktg. economist Sinclair Refining Co., 1961-64; dir. devel. and alumni rels. Wesleyan U., Middletown, Conn., 1965-84; pres. William K. Wasch Assocs., 1985—. Builder accessible housing. Author: Home Planning for Your Later Years, 1996. Trustee Wesleyan U., Middletown, 1997-2000, Nat. Coun. on the Aging, Inc., Washington, 1994-96, 98—, Seabury Retirement Cmty., Bloomfield, Conn., 1990—; chair Middletown Sr. Affairs Commn., 1996—. Lt. j.g. USNR, 1953-56. Mem. Hartford Club, Adelphic Ednl. Fund (sec., treas.), Am. Assn. for Support of Ecological Initiatives (sec., treas.), Phi Beta Kappa. Republican. Episcopalian. Avocation: squash. Home and Office: 150 Coleman Rd Middletown CT 06457-5065

WASFI, SADIQ HASSAN, chemistry educator; b. Basrah, Iraq, July 1, 1936; established residency in the U.S., 1978; s. Hassan Mohammed and Seniye (Omar) W.; m. Ellen Olivia Schwarz, Nov. 15, 1968; children: Yasmine, Dahlia, Ammar. BS in Chemistry Edn., Baghdad (Iraq) U., 1961; MS in Analytical Chemistry, Georgetown U., 1966, PhD in Inorganic Chemistry, 1971. Lectr. chemistry Basrah U., 1971-77; rsch. assoc. U. Hawaii, Honolulu, 1975-76, Georgetown U., Washington, 1977-78; assoc. prof. Montgomery Coll., Takoma Park, Md., 1978-79; prof. chemistry Del. State U., Dover, 1979—. Vis. assoc. prof. Georgetown U., 1980, 81. Contbr. articles to profl. jours; patent in antimony oxometalate complexes having anti-viral activity, 1991. Mem. Am.-Arab Anti-Discrimination Com. Mem. Am. Chem. Soc., Sigma Xi. Moslem. Home: 286 Pine Valley Rd Dover DE 19904-7111 Office: Del State Univ Dept Chemistry 1200 N Dupont Hwy Dover DE 19901-2202 E-mail: swasfi@dsc.edu.

WASFIE, TARIK JAWAD, surgeon, educator; b. Baghdad, Iraq, July 1, 1946; m. Barina Y. Wasfie, Mar. 11, 1975; children: Giselle, Nissan. BS, Central U., Iraq, 1964; MD, Baghdad Med. Sch., 1970. Cert. gen. surgeon. Surg. rsch. assoc. Sinai Hosp. of Detroit/Wayne State U., 1981-85; clin. fellow Coll. Phys. & Surg., Columbia U., N.Y.C., 1985-91, postdoctoral rsch. scientist, 1987-91; attending surgeon Mich. State U./McLaren Hosp., Flint, 1991—. Contbr. articles to profl. jours. NIH grantee, 1984. Fellow ACS, Internat. Coll. Surgeons; mem. AMA, Mich. State Med. Soc., Flint Acad. Surgeons, Am. Soc. Artificial Internal Organs, Internat. Soc. Artificial Organs, Soc. Am. Gast. Endoscopic Surgeons. Achievements include production of antiidiotypic antibodies and their role in transplant immunology; development of percutenous access device. Home: 1125 Kings Carriage Rd Grand Blanc MI 48439-8715

WASHBURN, ABBOTT MCCONNELL, government official; b. Duluth, Minn., Mar. 1, 1915; s. Abbott McConnell and Ruby Leslie (Frisk) W.; m. Mary Brennan, May 12, 1939 (div. 1959); children: Abbott Michael, Daniel Norton; m. Wanda Allender, Aug. 3, 1963; 1 dau., Julie. BA, Harvard, 1937. Mgr. dept. pub. services Gen. Mills, Inc., Mpls., 1937-52; exec. vice chmn. Crusade for Freedom, Inc. (nat. hdqrs.), N.Y.C., 1950-52; dir. orgn. Nat. Hdqrs. Citizens for Eisenhower, 1952; corr. sec., mem. personal staff Gen. Eisenhower, Denver, N.Y.C., 1952; exec. sec. Pres.'s Com. on Internat. Information Activities., Washington, 1953; dep. to spl. asst. to Pres., 1953; dep. dir. USIA, 1954-61; v.p. internat. operations Carl Byoir & Assos., 1961-62; pres. Washburn, Stringer Assocs., Inc., Washington, Mexico City, 1962-69; dep. chmn. U.S. delegation Conf. on Definitive Arrangements for Internat. Telecommunications Satellite Orgn., 1969-70, chmn. with rank ambassador, 1970-71; cons. to dir. Office Telecommunications Policy, Exec. Office Pres., 1972-74; mem. Bd. for Internat. Broadcasting, 1974; commr. Fed. Communications Commn., 1974-82; chmn. U.S. del. with rank ambassador Internat. Telecommunication Union Radio Conf. on Direct-to-Home Satellite Broadcasting Western Hemisphere, 1982-83. Cons. Dept. State, 1984-88; dir. Metro Mobile Cellular Telephone Service, Inc., 1985-92, Lorimar-Telepictures, Inc., 1984-88; mem. bd. George Foster Peabody Awards, 1984-88; mem. Pres.' Task Force on U.S. Govt. Internat. Broadcasting, 1991; bd. dirs. Eisenhower World Affairs Inst., 1988—. Active World Freedom Bell project, Berlin, 1950. Served from ensign to lt. USNR, 1942-45. Recipient Distinguished Service medal USIA, 1960 Mem. Council on Fgn. Relations, Washington Inst. Fgn. Affairs. Clubs: National Press, DACOR (Washington). Home: 4622 Broad Branch Rd NW Washington DC 20008-1007

WASHBURN, BARBARA POLK, cartographer, researcher, explorer; b. Boston, Nov. 10, 1914; m. Bradford Washburn, Apr. 27, 1940; children: Dorothy, Edward, Elizabeth. Grad., Smith Coll., 1935; DSc (hon.) , U. Alaska, 1995, Boston U., 1996, Simmons Coll., 2001. Sec. Harvard Biol. Labs., 1936-38; exec. sec. Mus. of Sci., 1939-40; remedial reading tchr. Shady Hill Sch., Cambridge, Mass.; asst. to Henry Bradford Washburn Jr. First ascent of Mt. Bertha, Alaska, 1940, Mt. Hayes, Alaska, 1941; first woman to climb Mt. McKinley, Alaska, 1947; worked with husband on numerous sci. expdns., including Mt. McKinley, the Grand Canyon, Bangkok, London, Nepal, China, Alaska, Zurich, Milan, 1945—; participated in remapping the Grand Canyon for Nat. Geographic/Mus. of Sci., 1971-76; cons. to Govt. of Alaska State Parks Recreational Area in Tokositna Valley, 1980. Editor new chart of Squam Lake, 1977, new map of Presdl. Range, Squam Lake, N.H., 1989; contbr. articles to Anchorage Daily News, 1987. Bd. dirs. Boston Children's Svc. Assn.; overseer Brigham & Women's Hosp., Boston; mem. corp. Fernald Sch., 1976; mem. Cambridge LWV, 1945-50, Mt. Auburn Hosp. Aux., Cambridge, 1945-60; pres. Women's Travel Club of Boston, 1949-51; pres. Cambridge Smith Coll. Club, 1952-54; bd. svc. league Mus. of Sci., 1959-62, sec., 1961-62; chmn. personal interview program for Smith, Alumnae Fund in Boston, 1964-65. Recipient Achievement award 100th Ann. Dinner of the Girl's Latin Sch. Alumni Assn., 1978; honored by Mus. of Sci. with plaque for yrs. of work, 1974, gold medal Royal Scottish Geog. Soc. for Outstanding Contbns. to Cartographic Rsch., 1979, Smith medal for Lifetime Exploration and Mapmaking, 1980, 1st Alexander Graham Bell award of Nat. Geog. Soc., 1980, Centennial award, 1988, award of Yukon Ter. Commr., 1997. Home: 1010 Waltham St Lexington MA 02421-8044

WASHBURN, BRADFORD (HENRY B. WASHBURN JR.), museum administrator, cartographer, photographer; b. Cambridge, Mass., June 7, 1910; s. Henry Bradford and Edith (Hall) W.; m. Barbara Teel Polk, Apr. 27, 1940; children: Dorothy Polk, Edward Hall, Elizabeth Bradford. Grad., Groton Sch., 1929; AB, Harvard U., 1933, A.M., 1960, D.H.L. (hon.), 1975; postgrad., Inst. Geog. Exploration, 1934-35; postgrad. hon. degrees; PhD, U. Alaska, 1951; DSc, Tufts U., 1957, Colby Coll., 1957, Northeastern U., 1958; D.Sc., U. Mass., 1972; DSc, Curry Coll., 1982; DFA, Suffolk U., 1965; DHL, Boston Coll., 1974; LLD, Babson Coll., 1980. Instr. Inst. Geog. Exploration, Harvard U., 1935-42; dir. Mus. Sci., Boston, 1939-80, chmn. of the corp., 1980-85, hon. dir., 1985—. Dir. Mountaineer in Alps, 1926-31; explorer Alaska Coast Range, 1930-40; served as leader numerous mountain, subarctic area explorations; cons. various govtl. agys. on Alaska and cold climate equipment; leader in spl. expdns. investigating high altitude cosmic rays, Alaska, 1947; rep. Nat. Geog. Soc., 17th Internat. Geog. Congress, 1952; leader Nat. Geog. mapping expdns. to, Grand Canyon, 1971-75; chmn. Mass. Com. Rhodes Scholars, 1959-64; chmn. arts and scis. com. UNESCO conf., Boston, 1961; mem. adv. com. John F. Kennedy Library, 1977; mem. vis. com. Internat. Mus. Photography, 1978; mem. U.S. Nat. Commn. for UNESCO, 1978; lectr. work of Yukon Expdn., Royal Geog. Soc., London, 1936-37, on mapping Grand Canyon, 1976; lectr. Mus. Imaging Tech., Bangkok, 1989, Royal Geog. Soc., London, on mapping Mt. Everest, 1990; lectr. Antarctica, 1994. Contbr. articles, photographs on Alaska, Alps, glaciers, and mountains to mags., books.; editor, pub. 1st large-scale map Mt. McKinley, Am. Acad. Arts and Scis.-Swiss Found. Alpine Rsch., Bern, 1960; mapped Mt. Kennedy for Nat. Geog. Soc., 1965, Grand Canyon, 1971-74, Muldrow Glacier (Mt. McKinley), 1977; editor new chart, Squam Lake, N.H., 1968, new Grand Canyon map for Nat. Geog. Soc., 1978, Bright Angel Trail map, 1981; photo-mapped Mt. Everest for Nat. Geog. Soc., 1984; dir., pub. large-scale map of Mt. Everest for Nat. Geog. Soc., 1984-88; project chief new 1:50,000 map of Mt. Everest for Nat. Geog. Soc. and Boston Sci. Mus., 1988; pub. Tourist Guide to Mt. McKinley, 1971, new map of Presdl. Range, N.H, 1989; completed new large-scale relief model Mt. Everest, 1990; one-man photographic shows Whyte Art Mus., Banff, Can., Internat. Mus. Photography, N.Y.C., Rochester, N.Y. Bd. overseers Harvard, 1955-61; trustee Smith Coll., 1962-68, Richard E. Byrd Found., 1979-84, Mt. Washington Obs., 1979—; mem. Task Force on Future Financing of Arts in Mass., 1978; hon. bd. dirs. Swiss Found. Alpine Research, 1984—. Recipient Royal Geog. Soc. Cuthbert Peek award for Alaska Exploration and Glacier Studies, 1938, Burr prize Nat. Geog. Soc., 1940, 65, Stratton prize Friends of Switzerland, 1970, Lantern award Rotary Club, Boston, 1978, New Englander of Yr. award New Eng. Coun., 1974, Gold Research medal Royal Scottish Geog. Soc. (with wife), 1979, Alexander Graham Bell award Nat. Geog. Soc., 1980, Disting. Grotonian award Groton Sch., 1979, Explorers medal Explorers Club, 1984, award for lifelong contbns. to cartography and surveying Engring. Socs. New Eng., 1985, King Albert medal of merit, 1994, Commonwealth award State of Mass., 1999; named Bus. Statesman of Yr. Harvard Bus. Sch. Assn., Boston, 1970; named to Acad. Disting. Bostonians Boston C. of C., 1983; one of nine Photographic Masters, Boston U., prize for outstanding contbn. to pub. understanding of geology Am. Geol. inst., 1996, Discovery Lifetime award Royal Geog. Soc., 2000. Fellow Royal Geog. Soc. London (hon., Commonwealth award State of Mass. 1999), Harvard Travelers Club (Gold medal 1959), Nat. Geog. Soc. (with wife, Centennial award 1988), AAAS, Am. Acad. Arts and Scis., Am. Geog. Soc. (hon., major photographic exhibit for ann. conv. 1993—), Commercial Club, Harvard Varsity Club, St. Botolph Club (hon. life), Aero Club of New Eng. Club (hon.), Harvard Mountaineering Club (Cambridge, hon., past pres.), Am. Alpine Club (N.Y.C., hon.), Alpine Club (London, hon.), Sierra Club of San Francisco (hon.), Mountaineers Club (Seattle, hon.), Mountaineering of Alaska Club (hon.); hon. mem. several clubs. Achievements include leading 1st ascent Mt. Crillon, Alaska, 1934, Nat. Geog. Soc. Yukon Expdn., 1935; leading 1st aerial photog. exploration Mt. McKinley, 1936, ascending its summit, 1942, 47, 51; leading 1st aerial exploration St. Elias range, 1938; 1st ascents Mount Sanford and Mount Marcus Baker in Alaska, 1938, Mt. Lucania, Yukon, 1937, Mt. Bertha, Alaska, 1940, Mt. Hayes, Alaska, 1941; 1st ascent West side Mt. McKinley 1951; leader Nat. Geog. Soc. Mt. Everest mapping project, 1981-88; expdn. to S.E. Asia, guest Chinese Acad. Scis., met with King of Nepal, 1988; leader expdn. to Nepal, 1992; 1st laser-distance observation to summit of Mt. Everest, 1992; 50th trip to Alaska to open exhibit of own photos Anchorage Art Mus., 1993; 57th Alaska-Yukon trip on occasion of 60th anniversary of Lucania ascent, 1997. Home: 1010 Waltham St Lexington MA 02421-8044 Office: Science Park Boston MA 02114

WASHBURN, CARYL ANNE, occupational therapist; b. Los Cruces, N.Mex., May 3, 1943; d. Peyton Randolph Walmsley and Eleanor (Kellar) Walmsley Davis; m. Arlon Craig Washburn, Dec. 19, 1981. BS, Tex. Woman's U., 1983, MA, 1991. Registered occupational therapist. Flight attendant Am. Flyers Airline, Ardmore, Okla., 1969; libr. asst. Douglas County Libr., Roseburg, Oreg., 1970-71; clk. Forrest Industries, 1971-73; adminstrv. asst. pers. Alaska Hosp., Anchorage, 1974-77; psychiat. occupational therapist Harris-H.E.B. Hosp., Bedford, Tex., 1983-84; self-contractor Multiple Home Health Agys., Dallas, 1984-87; prin. Caryls Clinic Occupational Therapy, Denton, 1987—99; co-owner, operator Applied Therapeutic Scis., South Lake, 1994—2000; co-owner Corp. Therapeutic Svc., Inc., Lewisville, 2000; prin., CEO Corp. Therapeutic Svcs., Inc.; co-owner, operator clinic Anchorage; pvt. practice Caryl's Clinic Occupl. Therapy. Mentor O.T. students; condr. seminars for reversal of carpal tunnel syndrome without surgery (Washburn Technique); designer, prodr. wrist exerciser to resolve carpal tunnel syndrome; devel. and filmed video for therapists on how to resolve carpal tunnel syndrome; appointed to editl. bd. Advance O.T. News, 1998; counselor SPEDY Program Coll. Siski-yous, Weed, Calif., 1978—. Contbr. articles to profl. jours.; patentee in field. Vol. horseback therapy for handicapped Freedom Ride, 1983. Mem.: Tex. Occupl. Thearapy Assn. (Clin. Excellence award 1995, Critical Selection for Best Practice award 1998). Achievements include patents in field. Avocations: gardening, mountain hiking, remodeling, swimming, camping.

WASHBURN, DAVID THACHER, lawyer; b. Claremont, N.H., May 2, 1930; s. Walter Henry and Josephine Emmeline (Dana) W.; m. Joycemarie Springer, June 10, 1957 (div. Dec. 1975); children: Margaret Dana, David Thacher Jr., Robert Springer, John Putnam. BA, U. Vt., 1952; JD, NYU, 1955. Bar: N.Y. 1956, D.C. 1970, U.S. Supreme Ct 1970. From assoc. to ptnr. Paul, Weiss, Rifkind, Wharton & Garrison, N.Y.C., 1955-95, of counsel, 1996—. Adj. prof. CUNY Law Sch., 1997-98. Trustee Rye Neck Bd. Edn., Mamaroneck, N.Y., 1971-73, Cambridge (Mass.) Coll., 1980-88, The Yard, N.Y.C., 1986-95, ARIA Found., Inc., Williston, Vt., 1991—; trustee, mem. exec. com. Rare Ctr. for Tropical Conservation, Phila., 1979-80; dir. Sanctuary for Families, Inc., N.Y.C., 1994—, mem. exec. com., treas. 1995-2000. Mem. ABA, N.Y. State Bar Assn., Assn. of Bar of City of N.Y., The Coffee House, Doubles, Westchester Country Club. Home: 10 W 66th St New York NY 10023-6206 Office: Paul Weiss Rifkind Wharton & Garrison Fl 2 1285 Avenue of the Americas New York NY 10019-6064 E-mail: dwashburn@paulweiss.com.

WASHBURN, DEBORAH FIELD, publishing executive; b. Boston, Oct. 14, 1941; d. Donald Timberlake and Adelaide Anderson (Cummings) Field; m. John Lawrence Washburn, Sept. 27, 1969; children: Susannah, Jonathan. AB , MA, Harvard/Radcliffe Coll., 1963; MPhil, George Washington U., 1982. Asst. editor Charles Scribner's Sons, N.Y.C., 1965—68; asst. lit. editor The New Republic, Washington, 1969; assoc. book rev. editor Sci. Mag., 1986—88; sr./exec. editor Asia Soc., N.Y.C., 1989—95; editor Random House, 1995—97; dir. publ. Carnegie Coun. on Ethics and Internat. Affairs, 1997—. Reading and writing tutor Lit. Ptnrs., N.Y.C., 2000—01; English-lang. tutor Internat. Ctr., 1998—99. Grantee Psychol. rsch Jakarta, Indonesia, Sigma Xi, 1981—82, Psychol. rsch., NIH, 1979—80. Democrat. Unitarian Universalist. Avocation: Avocations: snorkeling, hiking, travel, languages. Home: 111 E 30th St New York NY 10016 Office: Carnegia Council 170 E 64th St New York NY 10021

WASHBURN, DONALD ARTHUR, business executive, private investor; b. Mankato, Minn., Sept. 24, 1944; s. Donald and Geraldine Helen (Pint) W.; m. Christine Carvell, Aug. 24, 1968; children: Timothy, Abigail. BBA with high honors, Loyola U., Chgo., 1971; MBA, Northwestern U., 1973, JD cum laude, 1978. Bar: Ill. 1978. With prodn. mgmt. dept. J.T. Ryerson/Inland Steel, Chgo., 1963-68; asst. to the pres. G.B. Frank, Inc., 1969-70; cons. Intec, Inc., 1970-72; mktg. mgmt., atty. Quaker Oats, Co., 1972-79; sr. cons. Booz, Allen & Hamilton, 1979-80; from corp. v.p. to sr. v.p. Marriott Corp., Washington, 1980-90; sr. v.p. N.W. Airlines, Mpls., 1990-94, exec. v.p., 1994-98; investor, 1998—. Bd. dirs. LaSalle Hotel Properties, Princess House, Inc.; law bd. Northwestern U., alumni adv. bd. Kellogg Grad. Sch.; adv. bd. Spell Capital Partners Fund II, LP, Bank pf Am.-Twin Cities. Contbr. articles to profl. jours. Bd. dir. Hearing & Speech Inst. Mem. ABA, Ill. Bar Assn., Chgo. Bar Assn., Alpha Sigma Nu, Beta Gamma Sigma. Unitarian Universalist.

WASHBURN, DOROTHY A. entrepreneur; b. Detroit, Oct. 28, 1934; d. Dajad and Mary (Pevrenkjian) Katchadoorian; m. Floyd Donald Washburn, June 23, 1956; children: Mary Susan, Dorothy Ann, Sherry Lynn, Tina Marie. Addressograph and graphotype instr. Burrough's Corp., Detroit, 1952-54; sec. to wire divsn. mgr. Mich. Oven Co., 1954-58; exec. sec. to pres. Walch Metal Products, 1961-62; sec. and treas. Record Distbrs. Corp., 1963-65; fundraiser and trip coord. Edison High Sch., Huntington Beach, Calif., 1972-90; pres. Sunset Sales, 1977—. Editor: Annual Assembly Booklet of Ladies Society of the Armenian Church of North America Western Diocese, 1993-96. Campaign com. Gov. George Deukmejian, Doris Allen Campaign com.; chair band boosters Edison High Sch., 1975-77, chair choir boosters, 1988-90; vice chair parish coun. St. Mary Armenian Apostolic Ch., 1994, treas., social and entertainment com., 1993, advisor Ladies Soc., 1994-96, advisor cultural com., 1993-96, tchr. Sunday sch., 1992-96; corr. sec. Armenian Ch. N.Am., Western Diocese, Ladies Ctrl. Coun., 1985-89. Recipient Hon. Svc. award Calif. Congress of Parents, Tchrs. and Students, 1990. Armenian Orthodox. Avocations: creative cooking, music, folk dancing, swimming, travel.

WASHBURN, JERRY MARTIN, accountant, corporate executive; b. Powell, Wyo., Dec. 31, 1943; s. Roland and Lavon (Martin) W.; divorced; children: Garth, Gavin, Kristina; m. Mary Scatterday. BS in Acctg., Brigham Young U., 1969. CPA, Wash., Idaho, Oreg. Staff acct. Arthur Andersen & Co., Seattle, 1969-70, sr. auditor Boise, Idaho, 1971-73, audit mgr., 1974-75, Arthur Anderson & Co., Boise and Portland, Oreg., 1976-79; v.p. contr. Washburn Musicland, Inc., Phoenix, 1980-82; mgr., ptnr. Washburn Enterprises, 1977-90; pres. Total Info. Systems, Inc., 1984-90; v.p. KJ Mktg., Inc., 1990-91; dir. mktg. IPRO, Inc., 1991-94; assoc. Perfect Strategies, Inc., 1994—. V.p., CFO Global Indsl. Products, Inc., Scottsdale, Ariz., 1995-96; pres./CEO OneSource Techs., Inc., Scottsdale, 1996—, dir., chmn. 1999; founding dir. Internat. and Commerce Bank, Phoenix, 1985-86. Mem. Inst. Internat. Auditors (pres. Boise chpt. 1974, bd. dirs. Boise and Portland chpts. 1975-77), Am. Mgmt. Soc., Am. Inst. CPAs, Wash. Soc. CPAs, Idaho Soc. CPAs. Republican. Office: OneSource 7419 E Helm Dr Scottsdale AZ 85260-2470 E-mail: jwashburn@1sourcetech.com.

WASHBURN, JOAN THOMAS, business owner, art gallery director; b. N.Y.C., Dec. 26, 1929; d. Frank B. and Josephine (Hartman) Thomas; m. Alan Lindsay Washburn, Sept. 26, 1953; children: Brian, Susan. BA, Middlebury (Vt.) Coll., 1951. Asst. Kraushaar Gallery, N.Y.C., 1951-53; dir. pub. rels. Wadsworth Atheneum, Hartford, Conn., 1953-55; dir. contemporary art Graham Gallery, N.Y.C., 1955-67; asst. Cordier-Ekstrom Gallery, 1967-69; dir. Am. painting dept. Sotheby Parke-Bernet, 1973-75; pres., dir. Washburn Gallery, 1971—. Mem. Art Dealers Assn. (bd. dirs. 1989—, v.p. 1991—). Gallery: 20 W 57th St New York NY 10019-3917

WASHBURN, JOHN LEE, music educator; b. Reidsville, NC, Aug. 20, 1967; s. Tricilla Jan Roberston and Joyner D. Washburn, Philip J. Robertson (Stepfather); m. Lisa Grimm, June 27, 1992; children: Claire. MusB, U. NC, Greensboro, 1990. Cert. tchr. NC. Band dir. Seventy-First Classical Mid. Sch., Fayetteville, NC, 1997; dir. of bands Terry Sanford H.S., 1998—. Performer Fayetteville Symphony Orch., 1998—2000. Mem.: Southeastern Dist. Bandmasters Assn. (parliamentarian 1992—2002). Republican. Avocations: woodworking, music. Office: Terry Sanford High School 2301 Ft Bragg Rd Fayetteville NC 28303 Office Fax: 910-484-7203. Personal E-mail: johnwashburn@ccs.k12.nc.us. E-mail: johnwashburn@ccs.k12.nc.us.

WASHBURN, JOHN ROSSER, entrepreneur; b. Hopewell, Va., July 24, 1943; s. Winthrop Doane and Mary Virginia (Overstreet) W.; m. Rebecca m. Wells, Sept. 1991; 1 child, Amanda Ashley Washburn; stepchildren: Eric Joseph Harrison, Leo M. Cicone, Suzann R. Weldon. Student, Louisburg Jr. Coll., 1963-64, U. Richmond Ext., 1967-69, Williams Coll., 1985, Stanford U., 1986-87. Asst. mgr. Liberty Loan Corp., Richmond, Va., 1965-67; loan interviewer Ctrl. Fidelity Bank, 1967-69; regional credit/sales supr. Moores Bldg Supplies, Inc., Roanoke, 1969-74; corp. credit mgt. Owens & Minor, Inc., Richmond, 1974-88; fin., investment cons. JA-GO Enterprises, 1982-98; prin. agt., owner Washburn Ins. and Fin. Svcs. Group, 1996—. Instr., lectr. investment fin., credit mgmt. Washburn Enterprises, 1970—; sec.-treas. Multi-Enterprises, Inc., Richmond, 1988-98; ind. agt. N.Y. Life Ins. Co., Richmond, 1994-98; dir., v.p. Forbes Clin. Rsch. Group, Richmond, 1995—; sr. v.p. E-Com Cons., Inc., Richmond, 1998—; charter mem., ptnr. Nations Bus. Cons. Group, Tysons Corner, Va., 1998—. Active Nat. Rep. Congl. Com., 1980—, YMCA, 1979—, Am. Mus. Nat. history, 1982—, U.S. Def. Com., 1981—; mem. Credit Rsch. Found. Mem. Internat. Platform Assn., Nat. Assn. Credit Mgmt. (Appreciation cert. for outstanding svc. 1980-81, pres. ctrl. Va. sect. 1979-80, chmn. legis. com. 1977-79, dir. 1983—), Am. Mgmt. Assn., Nat. Wildlife Fedn., Nat. Assn. Life underwriters (Nat. Quality award 1996, 97), Va. Assn. Life Underwriters, Congressional Club, Hopewell Yacht Club. Episcopalian. Office: Washburn Enterprises PO Box 6826 Richmond VA 23230 E-mail: washjr@erols.com.

WASHBURN, KATHRYN HAZEL, government agency executive; b. L.A., May 22, 1944; d. S. Edward and Hazel Irene Lafler; m. Wilcomb Edward Washburn, Jan. 2, 1985 (Feb. 1997); m. William A. Niskanen, Apr. 23, 2000. BA, UCLA, 1966; MA, George Washington U., 1974. Planner Orange County, Santa Ana, Calif., 1966-70; urban planner So. Calif. Assn. Govt., L.A., 1970-71; planner U.S. Dept. Transp., Washington, 1971, U.S. EPA, Washington, 1972, Hwy. Users Fedn., Washington, 1972-73; regional mgr. North Atlantic NOAA, U.S. Dept. Commerce, 1974-89; dir. internat. affairs U.S. Dept. Interior, 1989—. Bd. dirs. Am. Inst. Cert. Planners, Washington, 1977-79, Preservation Md., Balt., 1997—, Salisbury U. Found., 1997—; bd. dirs. Rsch. Ctr. Delmarva History and Culture, Salisbury (Md.) U., 1996—; mem. Chesapeake Bay Found. Mem. Nat. Audubon Soc., African Wildlife Found., Nature Conservancy, Sierra Club. Home: 638 A St SE Washington DC 20003 Office: US Dept Interior Dept Internat Affairs 1849 C St NW # Ms4426 Washington DC 20240-0001 E-mail: kwashburn@ios.doi.gov.

WASHBURN, LAWRENCE ROBERT, manufacturing executive; b. Jackson, Mich., Aug. 5, 1941; s. Lawrence Merton and Elvina Marie W.; m. Kay Frances Wieczerzak, Nov. 21, 1970; children: Lawrence Robert II, Alexa Kay. BA in History, Govt., So. Calif. Coll., 1974. Supr., engr. Tool Rsch. & Engring., Inc., Santa Ana, Calif., 1968-77; ops. mgr. Knudsen Systems, Inc., Anaheim, 1977-86; plant mgr. Flourcarbon, 1986-88; dir. engring. Ricoh Electronics, Inc., Tustin, 1988-92; chmn., CEO TEQCOM Industries, Santa Ana, 1992—. Dist. commr. Boy Scouts Am., Orange County, Calif., 1982-90; exec. dir. Immanuel Luth. Ch. & Sch., 1987-92; bd. dirs. Luth. High Sch. Orange County, 1990-96. With USN, 1966-68. Decorated Navy Achievement medal; recipient Scouter medal Boy Scouts Am., 1986, Award of Merit, 1988. Mem. ASME, Soc. Mfg. Engrs., Air Traffic Control Assn., Balboa Bay Club, Ctr. Club. Republican. Avocations: golf, body surfing, backpacking. Office: TEQCOM Industries 1712 Newport Cir Ste O Santa Ana CA 92705-5118 E-mail: teqcom@pacbell.net.

WASHBURN, STAN, artist; b. N.Y.C., Jan. 2, 1943; s. Sherwood Larned and Henrietta (Pease) W.; m. Andrea Aall Stub, Mar. 5, 1966; children: Anne Elizabeth, John Larned. MFA, Calif. Coll. Arts and Crafts, 1968. Founding ptnr. The Griffin Co., Oakland, Calif., 1968-70. Author: George's Dragon, 1974, A Moral Alphabet of Vice and Folly, 1986, Intent to Harm, 1994, Into Thin Air, 1996; one-man shows include Achenbach Found., San Francisco, 1977, St. Botolph Club, Boston, 1977, Pucker/Safrai, Boston, 1975, 77, 80, 85, Ames, Berkeley, Calif., 1974, 78, 81, 84, Thackrey & Robertson, San Francisco, 1981, 86, Charles Campbell, San Francisco, 1983, 86, 88, 90, 91, Bannatyne, Santa Monica, 1990, North Point, San Francisco, 1993, 96, Frye Mus., Seattle, 1998; represented in permanent collections at Bklyn. Mus., Achenbach Found., Chgo. Art Inst., Libr. of Congress, Houghton Libr., Phila. Mus. Art, Boston Mus. Fine Arts. Mem. Berkeley Police Res., 1973-78; mem. Berkeley Police Rev. Commn., 1979-83; trustee The Coll. Prep. Sch., Oakland, 1986-98. Address: 2010 Virginia St Berkeley CA 94709-2138

WASHBURN, STEWART ALEXANDER, management consultant; b. Boston, June 14, 1923; s. Charles Parker and Mary Ethel (Stewart) W. AB, St. John's Coll., Annapolis, Md., 1951. Cert. mgmt. cons. Sr. engr. to asst. dir. indsl. hygiene Nat. Safety Council, Chgo., 1951-54; mng. dir. Stewart A. Washburn & Co., Inc., N.Y.C., 1954-62; ptnr. Porter Henry & Co., Inc., 1962-77; pvt. practice cons. Lakeville, Mass., 1977—. Dir. Southeastern Mass. Venture Forum; econ. devel. advisor Southeastern Mass. Legis. Caucus and two govs., Commonwealth of Mass. Author: Measuring Sales Effectiveness and Productivity, 1983, Successful Pricing, 1985, Finding and Launching Successful New Products, 1985, Managing the Market Functions, 1988; editor: Powering your Check in E-commerce; co-founder, assoc. editor and practice devel. editor Jour. Mgmtm. Cons., 1982—. Pres. Alvin Ailey Am. Dance Theater Found., N.Y.C., 1970-74; Alumni rep. bd. visitors and govs. St. John's Coll., Annapolis and Santa Fe, 1994-98; active various mcpl. offices and coms.; pub. mem. Seed Corp. With U.S. Army, 1943-46. Recipient Silver medal Internat. Film Festival, 1968, 69. Fellow Inst. Mgmt. Consultants, mem. (cert.) Inst. Mgmt. Cons. (founding mem., chpt. pres. 1984-87), Am. Arbitration Assn. (mem. comml. panel), Inst. Mgmt. Cons. (China, hon. mem.), Solidarity. Home and Office: 46 Old Main St Lakeville MA 02347-1601 E-mail: washburn@tmlp.com.

WASHBURN, STEWART PUTNAM, management consultant; b. Claremont, N.H., Apr. 6, 1929; s. Walter Henry and Josephine (Dana) W.; m. Josephine F. Foster, Aug. 20, 1960 (dec. 1980); children: Patricia, Alice. BS in Commerce and Econs., U. Vt., 1951; MBA, Harvard U., 1953. Cert. comml. lender. V.p. Worcester County Nat. Bank, Worcester, Mass., 1955-74; v.p., sr. loan officer First Nat. Bank, New Bedford, 1974-77; sr. v.p., sr. loan officer Durfee Attleboro Bank, Fall River, 1977-90; mgmt. cons. in comml. lending, 1990—. Dir. Bristol Workforce Investment Bd., Fall River, 1982—, chmn., 1987-99; dir. Southeastern Econ. Devel. Corp., Taunton, Mass., 1983—, treas., v.p., pres., 1995-98; dir. Jobs for Fall River 1981—, chair loan com. 1997—; mem. coun., mem. loan com. New Bedford Econ. Devel. Coun.; mem. town mtg., mem. fin. com. Dartmouth, Mass. With U.S. Army, 1953-55. Mem. Inst. Mgmt. Cons. (treas. New Eng. chpt. 1997-2001), Robert Morris Assocs. (life, bd. govs. N.E. chpt. 1973-75, chmn. credit policy roundtable 1989, Spl. Svc. award 1989). Avocations: bowling, gardening, fishing. Home: 5 Middle St Dartmouth MA 02748-3427 Office: PO Box 643 Fall River MA 02722-0643 E-mail: stewartp@stewartwashburn.com.

WASHINGTON, ALICE HESTER, human services professional; b. Durham, N.C., Oct. 28, 1960; d. Melvin and Martha Elizabeth (Bridges) Hester; m. Melvin Preston Washington Sr., Aug. 13, 1988; 1 child, Melvin Preston Washington II. BS in Home Econs., N.C. Agrl. and Tech. State U., 1983; grad. cert. in gerontology, Fla. Internat. U., 1995, MSW, 1999. Dietetic technician N.C. divsn. mental health Mental Retardation and Substance Abuse Svcs., Butner, 1984-85; dietary supr. Svcs. Systems, Marriott Corp., Boca Raton, Fla., 1985; dietetic technician HBA Mgmt. Corp., Ft. Lauderdale, 1986-87; registered dietetic technician Boca Raton (Fla.) Community Hosp., 1987-89; pub. assistance specialist II Fla. Dept. of Children and Families, Lauderhill, 1989-91, human svcs. counselor III, 1993—; case worker Fla. Fin. Assistance Specialists, Inc., Ft. Lauderdale, 1991-93. Mem. Mount Bethel Bapt. Ch. Social Svc. Ministry, Ft. Lauderdale, 1993, Presch. Ministry, 1993—; pres. Saint Luke Primitive Bapt. Ch. Young Matrons Aux., Hollywood, Fla., 1989. Mem. NASW, Phi Alpha Nat. Social Work Honor Soc. Baptist. Avocations: reading, badminton, traveling. Office: Fla Dept Children and Families 1400 W Commercial Blvd Ste 115 Fort Lauderdale FL 33309-3782

WASHINGTON, ANTHONY NATHANIEL, mechanical engineer; b. L.A., Jan. 19, 1969; s. Ralph Anthony and Naomi (Jemison) W. BSME, A&M U. Prairie View, 1992; postgrad., U. Phoenix, 1999—. Engr. Detroit Edison Co., 1992-95, GMC, Dayton, Ohio, 1995-96; area supr. Chrysler Corp., Detroit, 1997-99; product engr. Daimler Chrysler Corp., 1999—. Mem. Nat. Black MBA Assn., Nat. Soc. Black Engrs., Metro Detroit Optimist Club, Kappa Alpha Psi Fraternity Inc., Pi Tau Sigma. Avocations: sports, music, travel, reading. Home: 26678 E Carnegie Park Dr Southfield MI 48034-6151

WASHINGTON, BRIAN KEITH, secondary school educator, music educator; b. New Orleans, May 27, 1966; s. Carl Washington, Sr. and Janice Alcorn Washington; m. Kimberly Michelle Johnson; children: Derek, Devon, Dustin. BA in Instrumental Music Edn., So. U. New Orleans, 1998. Cert. instrumental music La. Dept. Edn. Music instr. New Orleans Children's Advocacy Program, 1996—96; dir. bands McMain Secondary Sch., New Orleans Pub. Schs., 1998—. Mem.: Dist. VI Band Dirs. Assn., La. Music Educators Assn., Music Educators Nat. Conf. Democrat. Baptist. Avocations: reading, travel, movies, music, cooking. Home: 3538 Timber Bluff Ln New Orleans LA 70131 Office: McMain Secondary Sch 5712 S Claiborne Ave New Orleans LA 70125 Office Fax: 504-862-5123.

WASHINGTON, CHARLES HENDERSON, laser systems designer, consultant; b. Little Rock, Apr. 8, 1953; s. John David and Antoinette LaVerne (Henderson) W. BA in Comm., U. Ill., 1979; PhD in Comm., Columbia State U. Lineman apprentice IBEW, Springfield, Ill., 1976-80; data comms. specialist State of Ill., 1980-85; v.p. engring. NATAC, 1983—. Cons. North Am. Tec-Hec, Springfield, Ill., 1991-93. Author: Datacom Systems Operation Manual, 1984, Datacom Systems Configuration Manual, 1985. Mem. A. Philip Randolph Inst., Springfield, 1994. With U.S. Navy, 1970-75. Named to Outstanding Young Men of Am., 1984. Mem. AAAS, Internat. Soc. Photo-Optical Engrs., N.Y. Acad. Sci., Omega Psi Phi, Phi Theta Kappa. Methodist.

WASHINGTON, CLARENCE EDWARD, JR. insurance company executive; b. New Orleans, Nov. 20, 1953; s. Clarence Edward and Alice Mildred (Jones) W.; m. Denise Sandra Agard, June 29, 1985. BS cum laude, Xavier U., 1983. Mgr. Time Saver, Inc., New Orleans, 1972-79; budget, fin. analyst Equitable Life Assurance, N.Y.C., 1983-84; actuarial asst. Prudential Life Assurance, Newark, 1984-87; pension mgr. Am. Internat. Life, N.Y.C., 1987—. Mem. Am. Mus. Natural History (assoc.). Democrat. Roman Catholic. Office: Am Internat Life 80 Pine St Fl 13 New York NY 10005-1702

WASHINGTON, DENNIS, construction executive; CEO Washington Corp., Missoula, Mont. Office: Washington Corp 101 International Way Missoula MT 59808-1549

WASHINGTON, DENZEL, actor; b. Mt. Vernon, N.Y., Dec. 28, 1954; m. Pauletta Pearson; children: John David, Katia, Malcolm and Olivia (twins). BA in Journalism, Fordham U.; student, Am. Conservatory Theatre, San Francisco. With N.Y. Shakespeare Festival, Manhattan Theatre Club, New Fed. Theatre. Actor: (stage prodns.) Coriolanus, 1979, Spell No. 7, The Mighty Gents, Richard III, One Tiger to a Hill, Ceremonies in Old Dark Men, When the Chicken Comes Home to Roost (Audelco award), A Soldier's Play (Obie award 1981), Checkmates, 1988, Split Second, (feature films) Carbon Copy, 1981, A Soldier's Story, 1981, Power, 1986, Cry Freedom, 1987, For Queen and Country, 1988, The Mighty Quinn, 1989, Glory, 1989 (Golden Globe award 1989, Acad. award 1990, NAACP Image award 1990), Heart Condition, 1990, Mo' Better Blues, 1990, Ricochet, 1991, Mississippi Masala, 1992, Malcolm X, 1992, Much Ado About Nothing, 1993, Philadelphia, 1993, The Pelican Brief, 1993, Crimson Tide, 1995, Virtuosity, 1995, Devil in a Blue Dress, 1995, Courage Under Fire, 1996 (NAACP Image award 1997), The Preacher's Wife, 1996, Fallen, 1998, He Got Game, 1998, The Siege, 1998, The Bone Collector, 1999, The Hurricane, 2000 (nominee Best Actor Acad. award 2000, Best Performance by Actor in Motion Picture Drama Golden Globe 2000), Remember the Titans, 2000, Training, Day, 2001 (Best Actor Acad. award 2002, nominee Best Performance by Actor in Motion Picture Drama Golden Globe 2002), John Q, 2002, actor, dir. prodr. The Antwone Fisher Story, 2002; (TV Movies) Wilma, 1977, License to Kill, 1984, The George McKenna Story, 1986, (TV miniseries) Flesh and Blood, 1979; regular (TV series) St. Elsewhere, 1982-88. Recipient Harvard Found. award, 1996; Am. Conservatory Theater scholar. Avocations: basketball, reading, cooking.*

WASHINGTON, EARLINE, healthcare executive; b. Balt., Dec. 6, 1947; d. Clifton Lee Cox and Dorothy Mae (Cooper) Ford; m. Curtis Washington, June 6, 1964; children: Curtis Jr., Kimberly. Student, Essex (Md.) C.C., 1978, Towson State U., Balt., 1985, Balt. City C.C., 1997. Nursing asst. Md. Gen. Hosp., Balt., 1965-66; optical asst. Greater Balt. Med. Ctr., optician; enrollment coord. Cmty. Family Health Ctr., Balt.; admissions dir. Elder Health Inc., 1996—. Sec. Empowerment Zone, East Harbor Village Ctr., Balt., 1994-96; mem. F.O.F. Family Support Adv., Balt., 1995-96, flaghouse Cts. Adv. Bd., Balt., 1994-96; cmty. activist Greater Balt. Med. Ctr., 1989-96; mem. Provider Network Group, Balt., 1996—; chmn. bldg. fund New Antioch Bapt. Ch., 1993-95, pres. Flower Cir., 1990-96; mentor Women Entrepreneur Bus., balt., 1993-95. Named Outstanding Cmty. Liaison, Flag House Cts., 1993; recipient Outstanding Vol. award City Springs Elem. Sch., 1993; T. Rowe Price Corp. Acad. scholar, 1994. Democrat. Baptist. Avocations: flora design, cooking, travel. Office: 1154 Sherwood Ave Baltimore MD 21239-2230

WASHINGTON, JAMES MACKNIGHT, former chemical engineer; b. Hackensack, N.J., Dec. 1, 1938; s. Everett Gladstone and Josephine Alice (MacKnight) W.; m. Anne LeBaron Allen, Aug. 18, 1956 (dec. Sept. 1987); children: Jean LeBaron Hall, James MacKnight Jr., John Allen, David Emory; m. Laura Elizabeth Jenison, Feb. 14, 1988 (div. Dec. 1993); 1 child, George Trowbridge. BSChemE, Clemson U., 1961; MSChemE, Va. Polytech. Inst., 1964, PhD, 1969. Asst. prof. U. New Brunswick, Fredericton, Can., 1965-66; rsch. engr. DuPont, Martinsville, Va., 1966-68; scientist Allied Chem. Corp., Petersburg, 1968-72; rsch. engr. Philip Morris Rsch. Ctr., Richmond, 1972-79, assoc. sr. engr., 1979-93; ret., 1993. With U.S. Army, 1956-59. Mem. AIChE, Sigma Xi. Episcopalian. Achievements include ten patents in field. Home: 2400 Stuts Ln Richmond VA 23236-1638

WASHINGTON, JAMES WINSTON, JR. artist, sculptor; b. Gloster, Miss., Nov. 10, 1909; s. James and Lizie (Howard) W.; m. Janie R. Miller, Mar. 29, 1943. Student, Nat. Landscape Inst., 1944-47; D.F.A., Center Urban-Black Studies, 1975. Tchr. summer class N.W. Theol. Union Seattle U., 1988. One man shows U.S.O. Gallery, Little Rock, 1943, Foster-White Gallery, Seattle, 1974, 78, 80, 83, 89 (also at Bellevue Art Mus., 89), Charles and Emma Frye Art Mus., Seattle, 1980, 95, Mus. History and Industry, Seattle, 1981; exhibited in group shows Willard Gallery, N.Y.C., 1960-64, Feingarten Galleries, San Francisco, 1958-59, Grosvenor Gallery, London, Eng., 1964, Lee Nordness Gallery, N.Y.C, 1962 Woodside Gallery, Seattle, 1962-65, Foster-White Gallery, Seattle, 1974, 76, 89, 92, Smithsonian Instn., 1974, San Diego, 1977, others; retrospective exhbn. Bellevue Art Mus., Washington, 1989; represented in permanent collections Seattle, San Francisco, Oakland art museums, Seattle First Nat. Bank, Seattle Pub. Libr. YWCA, Seattle, Meany Jr. H.S., Seattle World's Fair, Expo 70 Osaka, Japan, Whitney Mus. Am. Art, N.Y.C.; commd. sculpture: Bird With Covey, Wash. State Capitol Mus., Olympia, 1983, Obelisk with Phoenix and Esoteric Symbols of Nature in granite, Sheraton Hotel Seattle, 1982, Life Surrounding the Astral Alter, In Matrix, owner T.M. Rosenblume, Charles Z. Smith & Assocs., Seattle, 1986, The Oracle of Truth (6 1/2 ton sculpture) Mt. Zion Bapt. Ch., Seattle, 1987, commd. sculptures King County Arts Commn., 1989, Bailey Gatzent Elem. Sch., Seattle, 1991, Twin Eaglets of the Cosmic Cycle (Quincy Jones), 1993, Fountain of Triumph (Bangasser Assocs. Inc.), 1992-93, Seattle, 1993-94, 94-95, Child in Matrix, 1995, Blunt Tail Owl, 1996, Bunny Rabbit and Robbin, 1996; author book of poetry Poems of Life, 1997 (Internat. Hall of Fame Nat. Soc. Poets). Passover leader Mt. Zion Baptist Ch., Seattle, 1974-87; founder James W. Washington, Jr. and Mrs. Janie Rogella Washington Found. Recipient Spl. Commendation award for many contbns. to artistic heritage of state Gov., 1973, plaque City of Seattle, 1973, plaque Benefit Guild, Inc., 1973, arts service award King County Arts Commn., 1984, cert. of recognition Gov. of Wash., 1984, Editor's Choice award Outstanding Achievement in Poetry Nat. Libr. Poetry, 1993; named to Wash. State Centennial Hall of Honor, Wash. State Hist. Soc., 1984; home and studio designated historic landmark (city and state), 1991; Dr. James W. Washington Jr. and Mrs. Janie Rosella Washington Found. established, 1997. Mem. Internat. Platform Assn., Internat. Soc. Poets (life, awards 1993), Profl. Artists Phila., Masons (33d degree). Home: 1816 26th Ave Seattle WA 98122-3110

WASHINGTON, JOHN AUGUSTINE, retired physician, pathologist; b. Istanbul, Turkey, May 29, 1936; (parents Am. citizens); s. Samuel Walter and Simone (Fleisher) Washington; m. Maaja Harms, July 11, 1959; children: Stephen L., Richard R., Mikaela A. BA with honors, U. Va., 1957; MD, Johns Hopkins U., 1961. Diplomate Am. Bd. Pathology, (Clin. Pathology, Med. Microbiology). Intern Duke U. Med. Ctr., Durham, N.C., 1961-62, resident in surgery, 1962-63; clin. assoc. surg. br. Nat. Cancer Inst. NIH, Bethesda, Md., 1963-65, resident in clin. pathology, 1965-67, asst. chief microbiology svc., 1966-67; assoc. cons. microbiology Mayo Clinic, Rochester, Minn., 1967-68, dir. bacteriology lab., 1968-86, head sect. clin. microbiology, 1971-86; chmn. dept. microbiology Cleve. Clinic Found., 1986-92, vice chmn. divsn. pathology and lab. medicine, 1992-96, chmn. dept. clin. pathology, 1992-96, head microbiology sect., 1992-97. Trustee Am. Bd. Pathology, Tampa, Fla., 1989-94. Former editor Jour. Clin. Microbiology, Antimicrobial Agts. and Chemotherapy; mem. edit. bd. European Jour. Clin. Microbiology and Infectious Diseases, Jour. Clin. Microbiology, Antimicrobial Agts. and Chemotherapy, Jour. Infectious Diseases; sect. editor Infectious Diseases in Clin. Practice; contbr. more than 400 articles to profl. jours.; author numerous chapters in books. Lt. comdr. USPHS, 1963-67. Fellow ACP, Coll. Am. Pathologists, Am. Soc. Clin. Pathologists, Am. Coll. Chest Physicians, Infectious Diseases Soc. Am., Am. Acad. Microbiology. Independent. Avocations: gardening, swimming. Office: Cleve Clin Found 9500 Euclid Ave Cleveland OH 44195-5140

WASHINGTON, KAREN ROBERTS, lawyer; b. Dallas, Mar. 29, 1960; d. Thomas Edwin and Mary Lee Roberts; m. Bruce Edward Washington, Aug. 16, 1986. BA in Spanish, Tex. Tech U., 1981; JD, U. Tex., 1984. Bar: Tex. 1984, U.D. Dist. Ct. (no. dist.) Tex. 1985, U.S. Dist. Ct. (so. and we. dists.) Tex. 1988, U.S. Supreme Ct. 1989, U.S. Ct. Appeals (5th cir.) 1989, U.S. Dist. Ct. (ea. dist.) Tex. 1996. Briefing atty. 5th Ct. Appeals Tex., Dallas, 1984-85; asst. city atty. City of Dallas, 1985-86; assoc. Godwin, Carlton & Maxwell, Dallas, 1986-89, mem. firm, 1990-93, Thorpe Hatcher & Washington, L.L.P., Dallas, 1994—. V.p. gen. counsel Theatre 3. Mem. Nat. Employment Lawyers Assn., Dallas Bar Assn., Assn. Atty. Mediators, Patrick E. Higginbotham Am. Inn of Ct., State Bar Coll., Altrusa Club Downtown Dallas, Alpha Phi. Episcopalian. Office: Thorpe Hatcher & Washington LLP 2929 Carlisle St Ste 250 Dallas TX 75204-1017 E-mail: karenwl@airmail.net.

WASHINGTON, KEITH DONALD, military officer, social worker; b. Slidell, La., Nov. 21, 1966; s. Isaac Randolph Washington Jr. and Mary Ann (Selmon) Washington. BA, Dillard U., 1988; MSW, Tulane U., 1990, MPH, 1993. Lic. social worker Mass., cert. addiction therapist, marriage and family therapist, cognitive behavioral therapist. Commd. 2d lt. USN, 1994, advanced through grades to lt. Adj. field placement prof. Howard U., DC, Salve Regina U., Newport, RI, R.I. Coll., Providence, Roger Williams U., Bristol, RI. Founding adv. bd. Safe Harbour Battered Womens Shelter, Slidelll, 1992—95; adv. bd., program chmn. ARC, 1996—2000; coach Spl. Olympics , Fall River, Mass., 1997—2001; youth adv. Notre Dame Ch. Youth Group, 2000—02. Mem.: NASW, Am. Acad. Med. Adminstrn., KC, Masons, Kappa Alpha Psi. Republican. Roman Catholic. Avocations: reading, travel, music. Home: 24 Keene St 2WF Fall River MA 02723-3812

WASHINGTON, LANTZ H. small business owner; b. Port Huron, Mich., Dec. 13, 1961; s. Felix and Jacqueline Washington; m. Sharline Dobson, Jan. 3, 1991 (div.); 1 child, Lantz Tarvon. Student, Redford H.S., Detroit, 1977-79. CEO Washington Bros. Carpet and Upholstery Cleaning, Detroit. Home: 15509 Ardmore Detroit MI 48227

WASHINGTON, REGINALD LOUIS, pediatric cardiologist; b. Colorado Springs, Colo., Dec. 31, 1949; s. Lucius Louis and Brenette Y. (Wheeler) W.; m. Billye Faye Ned, Aug. 18, 1973; children: Danielle Larae, Reginald Quinn. BS in Zoology, Colo. State U., 1971; MD, U. Colo., 1975. Diplomate Nat. Bd. Med. Examiners, Am. Bd. Pediatrics, Pediatric Cardiology. Intern in pediatrics U. Colo. Med. Ctr., Denver, 1975-76, resident in pediatrics, 1976-78, chief resident, instr., 1978-79, fellow in pediatric cardiology, 1979-81, asst. prof. pediatrics, 1981-1988, assoc. prof. pediatrics, 1988-90, assoc. clin. prof. pediatrics, 1990—; staff cardiologist Children's Hosp., 1981-90; v.p. Rocky Mountain Pediatric Cardiology, 1990—; chief of staff Presbyn./St. Lukes Med. Ctr., 1999-2001. Mem. admissions com. U. Colo. Sch. Medicine, Denver, 1985-89; chmn., bd. dirs. Coop. Health Care Agreements, 1994-98; chmn. dept. pediatrics Presbyn./St. Lukes Med. Ctr, Denver, 1996-99, pres.-elect med. staff, 1997-99; adv. coun. Nat. Heart Lung Blood Inst., NIH, 1996-98. Cons. editor Your Patient and Fitness, 1989-92. Chmn. Coop. Health Care Agreements Bd., State of Colo., 1994-98; adv. bd. dirs. Equitable Bank of Littleton, Colo., 1984-86; bd. dirs. Ctrl. City Opera, 1989-95, Cleo Parker Robinson Dance Co., 1992-94, Rocky Mountain Heart Fund for Children, 1984-89, Rainbo Ironkids, 1989-95; nat. bd. dirs. Am. Heart Assn., 1992-96; bd. dirs. Nat. Coun. Patient Info. and Edn., 1992-98, Children's Heart Alliance, 1993-94, Colo. State U. Devel. Coun., 1994—, Caring for Colo. Found., 1999-2001; trustee Denver Ctr. Performing Arts, 1994—, Regis U., 1994-99; mem. Gov.'s Coun. Phys. Fitness, 1990-91; mem. Bd. Govs. of Co. State U., 1996—, pres., 2001—. trustee The Colorado Trust, 2002-. Named Salute Vol. of Yr. Big Sisters of Colo., 1990; honoree NCCJ, 1994, Physician of Yr., Nat. Am. Heart Assn., 1995. Fellow Am. Acad. Pediatrics (cardiology subsect., chmn. sports medicine and fitness com. 2000—), Am. Coll. Cardiology, Am. Heart Assn. (coun. on cardiovascular disease in the young, exec. com. 1988-91, nat. devel. program com. 1990-94, vol. of yr. 1989, pres. Colo. chpt. 1989-90, Torch of Hope 1987, Gold Heart award Colo. chpt. 1990, bd. dirs. Colo. chpt., exec. com. Colo. chpt. 1987-2000, grantee Colo. chpt.

1983-84, mem. editorial bd. Pediatric Exercise Scis. 1988-2002), Soc. Critical Care Medicine; mem. Am. Acad. Pediatrics/Perinatology, , Am. Acad. Pediatrics/Pediatric Cardiology (exec. com. 1996—), N.Am. Soc. Pediatric Exercise Medicine (pres. 1986-87), Colo. Med. Soc. (chmn. sports medicine coun. 1993-94), Leadership Denver 1990, Denver Athletic Club, Met. Club, Glenmoor Golf Club. Democrat. Roman Catholic. Avocations: golf, fishing. Office: Rocky Mountain Pediatric Cardiology 1601 E 19th Ave Ste 5600 Denver CO 80218-1255 E-mail: rlwash@aol.com.

WASHINGTON, VALORA, non-profit administrator; b. Columbus, Ohio, Dec. 16, 1953; d. Timothy Washington and Elizabeth (Jackson) Barbour; children: Omari, Kamilah. BA in Social Sci. with honors, Mich. State U., 1974; PhD, Ind. U., 1978; PhD (hon.), Bennett Coll., 1992. Assoc. instr. sch. edn. Ind. U., Bloomington, 1975-77; dir., cons. Urban League Ind., Indpls., 1977-78; substitute tchr. Indpl. Pub. Schs., 1978; dir. U. N.C., Chapel Hill, 1980-82; congrl. sci. fellow Soc. for Rsch. in Child Devel., Washington, 1981-82; prof. edn. U. N.C., Chapel Hill, 1978-83; asst. dean, assoc. prof. Howard U., Washington, 1983-86, Am. U., Washington, 1986-87; prof., v.p. Antioch Coll., Yellow Springs, Ohio, 1987-90; v.p. Kellogg Found., Battle Creek, Mich., 1990-99; exec. dir. Unitarian Universalist Svc. Com., 1999—. Cons. Ford Found., N.Y.C., 1990; project evaluator Carnegie Corp., N.Y.C., 1989-90, Ohio Bd. Regents, Columbus, 1990—. Author: (with others) Creating New Linkages for the Adoption of Black Children, 1984, Project Head Start: Past, Present and Future Trends in the Context of Family Needs, 1987, Black Children and American Institutions: An Ecological Review and Resource Guide, 1988, Affirmative Rhetoric, Negative Action: The Status of Black and Hispanic Faculty in Higher Education, 1989; contbr. articles to profl. jours; contbr. chapters to numerous books. Recipient Capitol U. award, 1990, award Springfield Alliance Black Educators, 1989; named one of Ten Outstanding Young Women Am., 1980, Outstanding Young Woman N.C., 1980, one of 100 Young Women of Promise Good Housekeeping Mag., 1985, one of 25 Most Influential Working Mothers, Working Mothers Mag., 1997. Mem. Nat. Coun. Negro Women (chmn. 1982-83), Am. Assn. for Higher Edn. (sec. black caucus 1989), Soc. for Rsch. in Child Devel. (pres. black caucus 1987-89), Nat. Assn. for the Edn. of Young Children (sec. of bd. dir. 1990—), Phi Delta Kappa, Delta Kappa Gamma.

WASHINGTON, WARREN MORTON, meteorologist; b. Portland, Oreg., Aug. 28, 1936; s. Edwin and Dorothy Grace (Morton) W.; m. LaRae Herring, July 30, 1959 (div. Aug. 1975); children: Teri, Kim, Marc (dec.), Tracy; m. Jona Ann, July 3, 1978 (dec. Jan. 1987); m. Mary Elizabeth Washington, Apr., 1995. BS in Physics, Ore. State U., 1958, MS in Meteorology, 1960; PhD in Meteorology, Pa. State U., 1964. Dir. of climate and global dynamics div. Nat. Center Atmospheric Research, Boulder, Colo., 1978-95; affiliate prof. meteorology oceanography U. Mich. at Ann Arbor, 1968-71; mem. Nat. Adv. Com. for Oceans and Atmospheres, 1978-84. Mem. sec. of energy adv. bd. U.S. Dept. Energy, 1990-93. Contbr. articles to meteorol. jours. Mem. Boulder Human Relations Commn., 1969-71; mem. Gov.'s Sci. Adv. Com., 1975-78. Recipient Disting. Alumni award Oreg. State U., 1991, E.B. Lemon Disting. Alumni award Pa. State U., 1991, Le Verrier medal Soc. Meteorol. France, 1995, Bonfils-Stanton Found. award, 2000; inductee NAS portrait collection African Am. in Sci., Engring., and Medicine, 1997; named Sigma Xi Disting. lectr., 1998-99. Fellow AAAS (bd. dirs.), Am. Meteorol. Soc. (pres. 1994, Anderson award 2000); mem. NAE, Am. Geog. Union, Nat. Sci. Bd. (1994-2006, chair 2002-04). Home: 725 Pinehurst Ct Louisville CO 80027-3285 Office: PO Box 3000 Boulder CO 80307-3000

WASHINGTON, WILLIAM NICOLAI, government official; b. Kansas City, Mo., Aug. 12, 1948; s. Lawrence Bassett and Lillian Rose (Rod) W. BS in Psychology, Kans. State U., 1970; MS in Psychology, Trinity U., San Antonio, 1974; postgrad., Mich. State U., 1979, U. Tex., 1995. Indsl. rsch. psychologist USAF Human Resources Lab., Brooks AFB, Tex., 1980-81; ops. rsch. analyst HQ CECOM, Ft. Monmouth, N.J., 1981—. Contbr. articles to profl. jours. and symposium. Sgt. USAF, 1970-74. Recipient Outstanding Achievement award Sec. of Army, 1993, medal for Civilian Svc., Dept. of Army, 1998, Commdrs. award Dept. Army, 2000; named Asst. Sec. of Army (Fin. Mgmt. & Comptroller) Author of Yr., 1997, 98, 99. Mem. Army Acquisition Corps, Soc. Mayflower Descendants. Episcopalian. Avocation: genealogy. Home: 33 Mill Pond Rd Jackson NJ 08527-4888 E-mail: squire-by-the-sea@iname.com.

WASHOW, PAULA BURNETTE, security company and investigation agency executive; b. Milw., Feb. 14, 1948; d. John W. and Darlene A. (Johnson) Hudson; children: Kimberly Anderson, Paul Washow. Student, Alverno Coll. Cert. detective agy. owner, Wis.; cert. in advanced criminal interrogations and investigations, audio and CCTV surveillance and counter-measures. Owner, pres. Alpha Omega Security, Milw., 1976—, Always Freight Inc., Franklin, 1980-85, Amrac Trucking, Franklin, Wis., 1985-91; pres. Amrac Distbrs., Inc., 1985—, Angé, Ltd., 1994—. Mem. adv. bd. Wis. Dept. Regulation and Licensing, 1992—; profl. nat. spkr. in field. Vol., corp. sponsor, bd. dirs. Make-a-Wish Found. of Wis., 1989— corp sponser Milw. Women's Ctr.; security chair Am. Cancer Soc. Ball, Milw., 1989; vol. Spl. Olympics Torch Run; bd. dirs. Milw. Women's Ctr., Joint cert. Program, City of Milw.; mem. firearms subcom. State of Wis., 1992—. Recipient Nat. Women of Enterprise award, 1995, Judges award in ceramics, 1999. Mem. Am. Soc. Indsl. Security, Internat. Chiefs Police Assn., Wis. Chiefs Police Assn. (pvt. security liaison 1988—), Inter County Assn. Crime Prevention Practioners, World Assn. Detectives, Internat. Assn. Credit Card Investigators (past v.p.), Am. Assn. Handwriting Analysts, Wis. Narcotics Officers Assn., Hispanic C. of C. (corp. sponsor, bd. dirs.), Wis. Juvenile Officers, Wis. Fire and Burglar Alarm Assn. (legis. com.), Wis. Women Entrepreneurs, Wis. Bus. Initiative Corp. Mentor Program., Internat. Credit Assn. (bd. dirs.), Wisc Burglar and Fire Alarm Assoc., Women's Ctr. of Milw., Nat. Spkrs. Assn., Wis. Spkrs. Assn. Avocations: scuba diving, paper making artist, pottery, graphologist, artist.

WASILKOWSKI, GRZEGORZ W. computer scientist; b. Legnica, Poland, Apr. 20, 1952; s. Roman Wasilkowska and Jadwiga Wasilkowski; m. Anna Maria Szczekowska; children: Bart, Jacob. MS, U. Warsaw, 1977, PhD, 1980. Vis. scholar Carnegie-Mellon U., Pitts., 1978—79; asst. prof. U. Warsaw, Warsaw, 1980—82, Columbia U., N.Y.C., 1982—85, assoc. prof., 1985—87, U. of Ky., Lexington, 1987—90, prof., 1990—. Dir. of grad. program computer sci. dept. U. Ky., Lexington, 1993—; vis. rsch. scholar Hong Kong Bapt. U., 2002. Author: (rsch. monograph) Information, Uncertainty, Complexity, 1983, Information-Based Complexity, 1988; contbr. articles to profl. jours. Grantee Info. and Complexity, NSF, 1982—85, Average Case and Probabilistic Settings for Information-based Complexity, 1986—89, Average Case and Average Case and Probabilistic Settings for Information-based Complexity, 1989—91, Average Case and Probabilistic Settings for Information-based Complexity, 1991—94, 1995—98, Information-based Complexity of Multivariate Problems, 1998—2001, 2001—04, Information-Based Complexity Prize for 2001, 2001. Mem.: SIAM. Office: U Ky Dept Computer Sci Lexington KY 40506-0046 Office Fax: 859-323-1971. Personal E-mail: greg@cs.uky.edu. Business E-mail: greg@cs.uky.edu.

WASIOLEK, EDWARD, literary critic, language and literature educator; b. Camden, N.J., Apr. 27, 1924; s. Ignac and Mary (Szczesniewska) W.; m. Emma Jones Thomson, 1948; children: Mark Allan, Karen Lee, Eric Wade. BA, Rutgers U., 1949; MA, Harvard, 1950, PhD, 1955; postgrad., U. Bordeaux, France, 1950-51. Teaching fellow Harvard U., Cambridge, Mass., 1953-54, research fellow Russian Research Ctr., 1952-54; instr. English Ohio Wesleyan U., 1954-55; asst. prof. U. Chgo., 1955-60, assoc. prof. English and Russian, 1960-64, prof. Russian and comparative lit., 1964-69, Avalon prof. comparative lit. and Russian, 1969-76, Disting. Services prof. of English, comparative lit., and Slavic studies, 1976—, chmn. comparative lit. program, 1965-83, chmn. dept. Slavic langs. and lit., 1971-77. Vis. prof. Slavic and comparative lit. Harvard, 1966-67 Author: (with R. Bauer) Nine Soviet Portraits, 1955, Crime and Punishment and the Critics, 1961, Dostoevsky: The Major Fiction, 1964, The Notebooks for Crime and Punishment, 1967, The Brothers Karamazov and the Critics, 1967, The Notebooks for the Idiot, 1968, The Notebooks for the Possessed, 1968, The Notebooks for A Raw Youth, 1969, The Notebooks for the Brothers Karamazov, 1970, The Gambler, with Paulina Suslova's Diary, 1972, Tolstoy's Major Fiction, 1978, Critical Essays on Tolstoy, 1986, Fathers and Sons: Russia at the Crossroads, 1993. Addressed UN on Tolstoy, 1988. With USNR, 1943-46. Recipient Quantrell teaching prize U. Chgo., 1961; Laing Press prize, 1972; Research fellow USSR, 1963; Guggenheim fellow, 1983-84 Mem. Modern Lang. Assn., Phi Beta Kappa, Lambda Chi Alpha. Home: 1832 Butterfield Ln Flossmoor IL 60422-2107 Office: Univ Chicago Dept English Chicago IL 60637 E-mail: e_wasiolek@uchicago.edu. *I believe in the life of the mind and I believe with Albert Camus that man's dignity lies in his lucidity: in seeing his fate clearly and in having the courage to accept it. Man is capable of sensitivity, courage, love, and compassion, and all of these are more human because he can think. He is also capable of cruelty, hatred, and destruction, and these are more tolerable because he can reason. Man is not man without reason.*

WASKA, RONALD JEROME, lawyer; b. Helena, Mont., Aug. 18, 1942; s. Charles Daniel and Mildred (Jablonski) W.; m. Elizabeth Ann Helten, Dec. 3, 1973; children: Amber Ann, Autumn Ann. BA, U. Tex., 1964; JD in Law, U. Houston, 1969. Bar: Tex. 1969, U.S. Supreme Ct. 1975, U.S. Dist. Ct. (no., so., we., and ea. dists.) Tex., U.S. Tax Ct., U.S. Ct. Appeals (5th, 8th and 11th cirs.). Asst. U.S. atty. Civil and Criminal Div., chief Criminal Div. So. Dist. of Tex., Houston, 1970-75; pvt. practice law, 1976—. Recipient Outstanding Performance Rating Dept. of Justice, Washington, 1970-75, AV Rating Martindale-Hubbell, 1974. Fellow Tex. Bar Found., Houston Fed. Bar; mem. ABA, Houston Bar Assn., Tex. Trial Lawyers Assn., Assn. Trial Lawyers Am., Fed. Bar Assn. (Outstanding svc. 1974, Younger Fed. Lawyer award 1974), Assn. of Criminal Attys., Bar Assn. of 5th Fed. Cir., Tex. Assn. of Criminal Attys., Harris County Assn. Criminal Attys., Phi Alpha Delta, Pi Kappa Alpha. Republican. Roman Catholic. Avocations: writing, music, sports. Office: 952 Echo Ln Ste 180 Houston TX 77024-2753

WASKO, STEVEN E. lawyer; b. Chgo., May 10, 1954; s. Theodore J. and Beverly W.; m. Elaine L. Enger, Oct. 3, 1981 (div. Aug. 1996); 1 child, Christine; m. Deborah Wasko; stepchildren: Tara, Raef, Brooke and Christopher. B in Spl. Studies cum laude, Cornell Coll., 1976; JD cum laude, Kent U., 1979. Bar: Ill. 1979, U.S. Dist. Ct. (no. dist.) Ill. 1979. Assoc. atty. Blanshan & Summerfield, Park Ridge, Ill., 1979-81; ptnr. Summerfield & Wasko, 1981-86; sole practitioner Steven Wasko and Assocs., 1986-90, mng. ptnr., 1992-95; ptnr. Wasko & Michaels, 1990-91, Steponate & Wasko Ltd., Park Ridge and Chgo., 1995—. Dir. Kolan Corp., Park Ridge, 1988—. Great Books leader Field Sch. Dist., Park Ridge, 1997—. Avocations: weight training, watercolors, fine art. Office: 1580 N Northwest Hwy Park Ridge IL 60068-1444

WASKO-FLOOD, SANDRA JEAN, artist, educator; b. N.Y.C., Mar. 12, 1943; d. Peter Edmund and Margaret Dalores (Kubek) Wasko; m. Michael Timothy Flood, June 28, 1969. BA, UCLA, 1965, postgrad., 1968-69, Calif. State U., Northridge, summer 1968; student, Otis Art Inst., L.A., 1969, Marie Kaufman, Rio de Janeiro, 1970-72, Museo de Arte Moderno, 1970-73, Foothill Coll., Los Altos, Calif., 1973-74, Claremont (Calif.) Coll., 1975, U. Wis., Janesville, 1977, Beloit (Wis.) Coll., 1977-78, U. Wis., 1977-78; grad. etching student, Warrington Colescott. Instr. printmaking Washington Women's Arts Ctr., 1983; artist-in-residence U. Md., College Park, 1985; instr. printmaking Arlington (Va.) Arts Ctr., 1984-85; prof. St. Mary's (Md.) Coll., 1985; instr. printmaking Arlington County Lee Arts Ctr., 1989-97; workshop coord. cultural affairs div. Arlington County Cultural Affairs, 1989-97; printmaking instr. Home Studio, Alexandria, Va., 1987—. One woman shows include Wisconsin Women in the Arts Gallery, Madison, 1977, Mbari Art, Washington, 1981, Miya Gallery, Washington, 1981, Slavin Gallery, Washington, 1982, Stuart Mott House, Washington, 1983, Washington Printmakers Gallery, 1986, 88, 91, St. Peter's Ch., N.Y.C., 1989, Montana Gallery, Alexandria, Va., 1991, Montpelier Cultural Arts Ctr., Laurel, Md., 1992, Gallery 10, Washington, 1994, 96, Sch. 33, Balt., 1996; mus. and internat. shows include Boston Printmakers: The 39th North Am. Print Exhbn., Framingham, Mass., Jan.-Mar., 1986, Internat. Graphic Arts Found. and Silvermine Guild Arts Ctr., New Canaan, Conn., Feb., 1988, prints: Washington, The Phillips Collection, Washington, Sept.-Oct., 1988, Contemporary Am. Graphics, Book Chamber Internat., Moscow, 1990, Gallery 10 Artists of Washington D.C. Vartai Gallery, Lithuania, 1994, Peninsula Fine Arts Ctr., Newport News, Va., 1995-96, Riva Sinistra Arte, Florence, Italy, 1997, Contemporary Art Ctr. Va., Virginia Beach, 1998, numerous others; juried shows include Washington Women's Arts Ctr.: Printmakers VII show, 1985, Washington Women's Arts Ctr., 1981, 82, Seventh Ann. Faber Birren Color Show Nat. Juried Open Exhibit, Stamford, Conn., 1987, Acad. of the Arts 25th Ann. Juried Exhbn., 1989, Fla. Printmakers Nat., 1994, S.W. Tex. State U., 1995, Peninsula Fivie Arts Ctr., Newport News, Va., 1998, Rockville Art Place, Md., 2002, and numerous others; invitational shows include Office of the Mayor, Mini Art Gallery, Washington, "Glimpses: Women Printmakers", 1981, Pyramid Paperworks, Balt., 1984, Gallery 10 "Nightmare Show", Washington, D.C., 1987, The Intaglio Process, The Benedicta Art Ctr. Gallery, St. Joseph, Minn., 1988, Women's Caucus for Art, Washington Artists in Perspective, Westbeth Gallery, N.Y.C., 1990, 91, Wesley Theol. Sem., 1992, Balt. City Hall, N.Am. Print Alliance, 1993, The Five Elements Women's Caucus For Art, 1994, WPA/Corcoran Auction, 1999, Washington Theological Union, Washington, 1999, Cannon Rotunda, U.S. House of Reps., Washington, 2000, Charles Sumner Sch. Mus., Washington, 2001, Washington Women Artists Marching into the Millennium, Women's Caucus for Art, 2001 and numerous others; galleries: Slavin Gallery, Washington, D.C., 1981-83, Washington Printmakers Gallery, Washington, 1985-96, White Light Collaborative, Inc., N.Y.C., 1988-89, Montana Gallery, Alexandria, Va., 1989-91, Gallery 10, Washington, 1992-97, Charleuoix Gallery, Albuquerque, NM, 1999, and numerous others; collections include Nat. Mus. of Women in the Arts, Washington, Corcoran Gallery of Art, Washington, Museo de Arte Moderno, Buenos Aires, Cultural Found., USSR, Coll. Notre Dame, Balt., Potomac Hosp., Woodbridge, Md.; dir. Labyringhs for Peace 2000, U.S. Capitol, 2002; featured artist Kali Guide: A Directory of Resources for Women, 2d reprint, 2002. Pres. Washington Area Printmakers, Washington, D.C., 1985-86; pub. rels. dir. Washington Women's Arts Ctr., 1980; bd. dirs. Washington Women's Arts Ctr., 1981-82; program chair D.C. chpt. Women's Caucus for Art, 1998—; founding mem. the Labyrinth Soc., 1999-2000; special projects dir. Labryinth Soc., 2000; cons. Labyrinth Making and Products. Recipient Award of Honorable Mention Nat. Gallery of Art, 1989, Best of Show, Artists Equity Exhibit, Gallery 901, Washington, 1997; grantee Friends of the Torpedo Factory Art Ctr., Alexandria, Va., 1989, Va. Commn. for the Arts, D.C. Commn. on the Arts and Humanities Summer Edn. and Sports Program, 2000, 01; individual artists fellow Va. Commn. for Arts, 1994. Mem.: Washington Sculpture Group, Am. Print Alliance, Md. Printmakers, Women's Caucus for Art, So. Graphics Coun., Pyramic Atlantic, Nat. Print Orgn., Corcoran Gallery/Washington Project for the Arts. Avocations: classical music, hiking, reading. Home: 8106 Norwood Dr Alexandria VA 22309-1331 Studio: 57 N St NW Washington DC 20001-1254

WASKOW, JOYCE ANN, school administrator; b. Meriden, Iowa, Aug. 15, 1941; d. Clarence Emory and Lucille Dorothy (Horstman) Smith; m. James R. Waskow, July 6, 1963; children: Susan, Brent. BS, Iowa State U., 1963; MA, U. Mo., St. Louis, 1992. Cert. edn. specialist, Mo. Home econs./sci. tchr. Collins (Iowa) H.S., 1963-64; home economist Met. Sewer Dist., Omaha, 1964-65; home econs. tchr. Westbrook Jr. H.S., 1965-67; home economist The Merchandising Group, N.Y.C., 1970-76; home econs. tchr. Pattonville H.S., St. Louis, 1976-79, Maplewood-Richmond Hts. H.S., St. Louis, 1979-80, Webster Groves H.S., St. Louis, 1980-93; dir. Tchr.'s Acad. Network for Ednl. Devel., 1989-92; asst. prin. Lafayette H.S., 1993—. Spkr./workshop leader Network for Edn. Devel., 1987—. SASSP Assistant Principal of Year, 1998; recipient Eddy award Mo. Pub. Sch. Edn., 1999. Mem. ASCD, Nat. Assn. Secondary Sch. Prins., Am. Home Econs. Assn. (nominating com.), Suburban Home Econs. Assn. (pres. 1986-87), Nat. Assn. Vocat. Home Econs. Tchrs. (Disting. Svc. award 1989), Mo. Home Econs. Tchrs. Assn. (Tchr. of the Yr. 1987, nominating com. 1987-88), Mo. Assn. Secondary Sch. Prins. (sec.-treas. 1997—, asst. prin. of yr. 1999, pres. 2000-01), St. Louis Area Secondary Sch. Prin. Assn. (Mo. asst. prin. of yr. 1999, v.p.). Avocations: reading, whitewater rafting, hiking, antiquing, orienteering. Office: Lafayette High School 17050 Clayton Rd Ballwin MO 63011-1794

WASNAK, LYNN, publishing executive, writer; b. Canton, Ohio, July 21, 1944; d. George Henry and Iverne (Golloway) Koehler; m. Richard Dale Wasnak, Mar. 22, 1961 (div. 1977); children: Diane M., James R. Publ., owner Many Voices Press, Cin., 1989—. Editor: MPD From the Inside Out, 1991 (Media award, 1991), Mending Ourselves, 1993. Reader Cin. Assn. for the Blind, 1989—. Recipient 1st pl. fiction, Midwest Writers Conf., 1976, Excellence in Journalism award, Cleve. Press Club, 1989. Mem.: Am. Soc. Journalists & Authors, Nat. Writers Union, Internat. Soc. for the Study of Multiple Personality and Dissociation (bd. dirs. 1991—93, Pres. award 1993). Office: Many Voices Press PO Box 2639 Cincinnati OH 45201 E-mail: lynnw@manyvoicespress.com.

WASS, C(HARLES) THOMAS, anesthesiologist; b. Glendale, Calif., Apr. 11, 1961; s. Charles Wallace and Janice Lane (Buchanan) W.; m. Sharon Lorraine, June 13, 1987; children: Luke Thomas, Claire Elizabeth, Grant Taylor, Kate Lorraine. BA in Chemistry, W.Va. U., 1984, MD, 1989. Diplomate Am. Bd. Anesthesiology. Intern W.Va. Univ. Hosp., Morgantown, 1989—90, resident, 1990—93; fellow in neurosurg. anesthesia Mayo Clinic, Rochester, Minn., 1993—95, sr. assoc. cons., 1995—97, instr. in anesthesiology, 1994—97, cons., asst. prof. anesthesiology, 1997—2002, assoc. prof. anesthesiology, 2002—. Mem. Mayo Rsch. and Human Studies Com., 1995—; mem. Mayo Exec. Edn. Com., Rochester, 1996—; mentor Mayo Neurosurg. Anesthesia Rsch., Rochester, 1996—; neuroanesthesia coord. Mayo Didactic Edn. Com., Rochester, 1996—. Author: (with others) Anesthesia Clinic North America, 1995; contbg. editor: Anesthesiology: A Comprehensive Review, 1997; contbr. articles to profl. jours.; assoc. editor: Anesthesiology Review, 1994, 2002. Recipient Tchr. of Yr. award Mayo found., 1995, 96, 97, 98, 99; NIH rsch. tng. grantee, 1993-95; Am. Heart Assn. grantee, 1994-95. Mem. Am. Soc. of Anesthesiologists, Internat. Anesthesia Rsch. Soc. (Tchg. award 2000), Soc. of Neurol. Anesthesia and Critical Care, Minn. Soc. of Anesthesiologists, Soc. for Edn. in Anesthesia. Avocations: bicycling, fishing, snow skiing, camping. Office: Mayo Clinic 200 1st St SW Rochester MN 55905-0002 E-mail: wass.thomas@mayo.edu.

WASS, HANNELORE LINA, educational psychology educator; b. Heidelberg, Germany, Sept. 12, 1926; came to U.S., 1957, naturalized, 1963; d. Hermann and Mina (Lasch) Kraft; m. Irvin R. Wass, Nov. 24, 1959 (dec.); 1 child, Brian C.; m. Harry H. Sisler, Apr. 13, 1978. BA, Tchrs. Coll., Heidelberg, 1951; MA, U. Mich., 1960, PhD, 1968. Tchr. W. Ger. Univ. Lab. Schs., 1958-60; mem. faculty U. Mich., Ann Arbor, 1958-60, U. Chgo. Lab. Sch., 1960-61, U. Mich., 1963-64, Eastern Mich. U., 1965-69; prof. ednl. psychology U. Fla., Gainesville, 1969-92; prof. emeritus, 1992—; faculty assoc. Ctr. for Gerontol. Studies U. Fla., Gainesville. Cons., lectr. in thanatology. Author: The Professional Education of Teachers, 1974, Dying-Facing the Facts, 1979, 2d edit., 1988, 3d edit., 1995, Death Education: An Annotated Resource Guide, 1980, vol. 2, 1985, Helping Children Cope With Death, 1982, 2d edit., 1984, Childhood and Death, 1984; founding editor (jour.) Death Studies, 1977-92; cons. editor: Ednl. Gerontology, 1977-92, (book series) Death Education, Aging and Health Care, 1980-96; contbr. approximately 200 articles to profl. jours. and chpts. in books. Mem. Am. Psychol. Assn., Gerontol. Soc., Internat. Work Group Dying, Death and Bereavement (bd. dirs.), Assn. Death Edn. and Counseling. Home: 6014 NW 54th Way Gainesville FL 32653-3265 Office: U Fla 346 Norman Hall Gainesville FL 32611-2053 E-mail: hannelore@telocity.com., wass@nersp.nerdc.ufl.edu .

WASSEL, THOMAS SHELLY, engineering executive; b. Springville, N.Y., Sept. 29, 1952; s. Robert Montgomery and Allie (Watson) W.; m. Jean Marie Brooks, July 28, 1953; children: Michelle Lee, Gregory Thomas. AAS, SUNY, Alfred, 1972, BS, 1974. Profl. engr., Ohio. Product mgr., sales engr. North Am. Mfg., Cleve., 1974-79; mgr. studies Bricmont & Assocs., Pitts., 1979-86; from chief engr. to gen. mgr. Konus Energy Sys., Atlanta, Marietta, Ga., 1986-93; project mgr. ESI of Tenn., Inc., Kennesaw, 1993-2000, Von Rull Inc., 2000—. Vice chmn. Rep. Party, Cobb County, Ga., 1996; elder Grace Brethren Ch., 1991—. Home: 4515 Blackwater Trl Marietta GA 30066-6715 E-mail: twassel@earthlink.net.

WASSELL, LOREN W. public affairs professional, writer; b. Chgo., July 15, 1948; s. H. W. and Bernice (Kramer) W.; m. Rhonda Rothballer, Sept. 29, 1979; 1 daughter, Courtney C. BA, Lakeland Coll., 1969; postgrad., Ill. Cen. Coll., 1981-83. Reporter, anchorman Stas. WXCL and WZRO, Peoria, Ill., 1970-73; reporter Journal Star, 1973-82; publs. editor Cen. Ill. Light co., 1982-84; exec. comm. writer Caterpillar Tractor Co., 1984-85; mgr. editl. svcs. Monsanto Co., St. Louis, 1985-90; pub. affairs dir. Monsanto Chem. Co., 1990-95; dir. pub. affairs, agrl. biotech. Monsanto Co., 1995-97; dir. pub. affairs Solutia Inc., 1997-99, chmn. comm. coun., 1999-2000; dir. pub. affairs Monsanto Co., St. Louis, 2000—. Mem. Peoria Pub. Bldg. Commn., 1982-85; trustee Orchard Lakes Subdiv., 1988-2000. Recipient Enterprise Reporting award Ill. Valley Press Club, 1974, Spot News Reporting award Ill. Valley Press Club, 1974. Mem. Internat. Assn. Bus. Communicators, Pub. Rels. Soc. Am., Coun. Communication Mgmt. Avocations: bicycle touring, reading, computer programming. Home: 12017 Lake Meade Dr Saint Louis MO 63146-4828 E-mail: loren_w_wassell@hotmail.com.

WASSELL, STEPHEN ROBERT, mathematics educator, researcher; b. Santa Monica, Calif., Jan. 17, 1963; s. Desmond Anthony and Catherine Ann (Stephens) W. BS in Arch., U. Va., Charlottesville, 1984, PhD in Math., 1990, M in Computer Sci., 1999. Programmer, analyst UNISYS, McLean, Va., 1984-85, graphics artist, 1986; tutor summer transition program U. Va., Charlottesville, 1987-88, tchg. asst., 1986-90; asst. prof. math. Sweet Briar (Va.) Coll., 1990-96, assoc. prof. math., 1996—2002, prof. math., 2002—, dept. chmn., 1996—97, 1999—2002. Prof. of record Ctr. for the Liberal Arts, U. Va., 1991; vis. asst. prof. math., U. Va., Charlottesville, 1992, vis. assoc. prof. computer sci., 1998-99; doctoral cons., Charlottesville, 1989-90. Author: (with Kim Williams) On Ratio and Proportion, 2001; author: Nexus 2: Architecture and Mathematics, 1998, Nexus 3: Architecture and Mathematics, 2000; contbr. chpt. to book. Recipient Grad. assistantship award U. Va., 1986-90; Gordon T. Whyburn fellow, 1985-86. Mem. AAUP (Sweet Briar chpt. sec.-treas. 1993-99), Am. Math. Soc., Math. Assn. Am., Am. Solar Energy Soc., Sigma Nu (Beta chpt. treas. 1985-86). Achievements include patents for solar powered lawnmover, for solar shed, for ear muffs. Home: 4500 Monacan Trail Rd North Garden VA 22959-2215 Office: Sweet Briar Coll Dept Math Scis Sweet Briar VA 24595 E-mail: wassell@sbc.edu.

WASSENBERG, EVELYN M. medical and surgical nurse, nursing educator; b. Oct. 8, 1933; d. Patrick A. and Mary A. (Kieffer) L'Ecuyer; m. Maurice P. Wassenberg, Oct. 29, 1955; children: Sherry Ann Gaines, Laura Marie O'Neil. Diploma in nursing, Marymount Sch. Nursing, Salina, Kans., 1955; BS in Nursing, Marymount Coll. of Salina, 1982; MN, Wichita State U., 1987. Cert. nurse specialist. Dir. nursing svc. Community Meml. Hosp. Inc., Marysville, Kans., 1962-79; house supr. Luth. Hosp., Beatrice, Nebr., 1980-82; instr. Ft. Scott (Kans.) C.C., 1983-2001; primary nurse Beatrice Cmty. Hosp., 2001; nurse Girard (Kans.) Hosp., 2001—; ICU nurse Nevada (Mo.) Regional Med. Ctr., 2001—. Mem. Mary Queen of Angels Cath. Ch. Named Nurse of Yr. Bourbon County Kans., 1992. Mem. Am. Nursing Assn., Kans. State Nursing Assn., Sigma Theta Tau. Address: 216 S Crawford St Fort Scott KS 66701-3231 Office: Nev Regional Med Ctr 800 S Ash St Nevada MO 64772

WASSENICH, LINDA PILCHER, retired health policy analyst, fund raiser; b. Washington, Aug. 27, 1943; d. Mason Johnson and Vera Bell (Stephenson) Pilcher; m. Mark Wassenich, May 14, 1965; children: Paul Mason, David Mark. BA magna cum laude, Tex. Christian U., 1965; MSW, U. N.C., 1970. Licensed advanced practitioner, cert. social worker, Tex. Counselor family ct. Dallas County Juvenile Dept., Dallas, 1970-73, 75-76; dir. govt. rels. Vis. Nurse Assn., 1980-84, exec. officer of hospice, 1984-85; exec. dir. Incest Recovery Assn., 1985-86; assoc. exec. dir. Lone Star Coun. Camp Fire, 1986-89; exec. v.p. Vis. Nurse Assn. Found., 1989-91; dir. policy & resource devel. Vis. Nurse Assn. Tex., 1992-99; ret. Field instr. U. Tex. Arlington Sch. Social Work, 1993-99. Contbr. articles to profl. publs. Bd. dirs. Women's Coun. Dallas County, 1986-95, 99-2001, pres., 1992-93; chmn. Dallas County Welfare Adv. Bd., 1991-95; bd. dirs. United Way of Met. Dallas, 1992-94, Youth Impact Ctrs., Dallas, 1993-94; mem. adv. bd. Maternal Health and Family Planning Dallas, 1990-94; mem. Leadership Dallas, 1988-89. Recipient Laurel award AAUW, Dallas, 1995; named Field Inst. of Yr., U. Tex. Arlington Sch. Social Work, 1999, Golden Rule award finalist JC Penney, 2000. Mem.: LWV (bd. dirs. Dallas 1974—80, pres. 1985—89, bd. dirs. Tex. 1999—, Tex. v.p. pub. rels. 2001—, Myrtle Bales Bulkley award 2000), NASW (co-chmn. Dallas unit 1981—82, nominating com. 1990—92, Tex. bd.

dirs., Social Worker of Yr. award 1988, Lifetime Achievement in Social Work award 2002), Nat. Soc. Fundraising Execs. (bd. dirs. Dallas chpt. 1994—97, v.p. governance 1995—96, cert., Outstanding Fund Raising Exec. of Yr. 1999), Acad. Cert. Social Workers. Home: 5221 Pebblebrook Dallas TX 75229-5504

WASSER, HENRY, retired American literature and sociology educator; b. Pitts., Apr. 13, 1919; s. Nathan and Mollie (Mendelson) W.; m. Solidelle Felicité Fortier, Aug. 20, 1942; children: Michael Frederick (dec.), Eric Anthony (dec.), Frederick Anthony, Felicity Louise. BA, MA, Ohio State U., 1940; PhD, Columbia U., 1951. Teaching fellow George Washington U., 1940-42; analyst USAAF intelligence, 1941-43; chemist Goodyear Synthetic Rubber Co., 1943-45; from tutor to assoc. prof. City Coll., CUNY, 1946-66; prof. English, dean faculties Richmond Coll., CUNY, 1966-73; v.p. for acad. affairs Calif. State U., Sacramento, 1973-74; prof. English Coll. S.I., CUNY, 1974-89; dir. Center for European Studies, Grad. Sch. CUNY, 1979-93, prof. emeritus of sociology and English, 1989—. Fulbright prof. U. Salonika, Greece, 1955-56; Higher Edn. Seminar assoc. Columbia U., 1961—, co-chair, 1982-87, chair, 1987-89; mem. Colloquium on Higher Edn., Yale U., 1974-75; Fulbright prof. Am. Lit. U. Oslo, 1962-64, dir., prof. Am. Inst., 1963-64; vis. prof. U. Sussex, Eng., 1972, U. Salonika, 1955-56; lectr. in field, Sweden, Norway, Eng., Germany, Poland, Yugoslavia, Italy, Turkey, Greece, Bulgaria; Fulbright prof. Am. Lit. and Civilization U. Bergen, Norway, 1989-90, U. Aveiro, Portugal, 1993; rsch. scholar comparative higher edn. CUNY, 1989—. Author: The Scientific Thought of Henry Adams, 1956, (with others) Higher Education in Western Europe and North America: A Selected and Annotated Bibliography, 1979, American Literature and Language: A Selected and Annotated Bibliography, 1980; editor: (with Sigmund Skard) Americana Norvegica; Norwegian Contributions to American Studies, 1968, (with others) The Compleat University, 1983, Problems of the Urban University: A Comparative Perspective, 1984, Impact of Changing Labor Force on Higher Education, 1987; editor (with Ulrich Teichler) German and American Universities: Mutual Influences, 1992, Diversification in Higher Education: A Comparative View, 1999; mem. bd. editors History of European Ideas, 1986—, guest editor, summer, 1987; guest editor Higher Edn. Policy, spring, 1994, contbr. articles to newspapers and profl. jours. Faculty trustee CUNY, 1981-86, trustee emeritus, 1986—; bd. dirs. Scandinavian Seminar, 1978-86, sec., 1980-83, vice chmn., 1983-86. Recipient Am. Scandinavian Found. award, 1969, 71, German Acad. Exchange Service award, 1973, 80, Swedish Info. Service award, 1979, Norwegian Ministry of Culture award, 1983, NEH award, 1984, Foscolo medal U. Pavia, Italy, 1986, German Marshall Fund award, 1985, 87, Atheneum medal U. Pavia, Italy, 1988, Disting. Senator award CUNY Faculty Senate, 1994. Mem. Am. Studies Assn. (pres. Met. N.Y. chpt. 1961-62, mem. nat. exec. council 1968-74), Melville Soc. Am. (historian 1969-74), MLA, Am. Scandinavian Found. (fellow 1971), Internat. Assn. Univ. Profs. English, Assn. Upper Level Colls. and Univs. (2d v.p. 1971-72), Assn. for World Edn. (internat. council), Phi Beta Kappa (sec. City Coll. chpt. 1957-62, 64-67, pres. CUNY Acad. for Humanities and Scis. 1991—), Internat. Conf. Higher Edn. (steering com. 1989—), Henry Adams Soc. (exec. coun. 1994—, pres. 1996—), Mass. Hist. Soc. (fellow 2001). Home: 333 E 34th St Apt 16C New York NY 10016-4950 also: 5517 Fieldston Rd Bronx NY 10471-2503 Office: CUNY Academy Grad Sch 365 Fifth Ave New York NY 10016-4309 E-mail: hwasser@gccuny.edu.

WASSER, LARRY PAUL, retired hematologist, oncologist; b. Moline, Ill., July 27, 1943; s. Paul Ernest and Harriet Lenore (Swan) W.; m. Mary Elizabeth Hannaford, 1983. BA, Baylor U., 1965, MD, 1969. Diplomate Am. Bd. Internal Medicine, Am. Bd. Hematology, Am. Bd. Oncology. Intern Presbyn.-St. Luke's Hosp., Chgo., 1969-70, resident in medicine, 1970-71; fellow in hematology Baylor U. Med. Sch., Houston, 1971-72; fellow in oncology U. Va. Hosp., Charlottesville, 1974-75; mem. staff Riverside Med. Ctr., Kankakee, Ill., 1984—2001; med. dir. Hematology-Oncology Clinic St. Mary's Hosp., 1993—2001, chief of staff, 1997—2001; pvt. practice; med. dir. St. Mary's Cancer Ctr., 1993—2001; ret., 2001. Mem. Am. Soc. Hematology, Am. Soc. Clin. Oncology. Home: 1680 N Rd 3750 W Kankakee IL 60901 E-mail: bona.parte137@aol.com.

WASSERBURG, GERALD JOSEPH, geology and geophysics educator; b. New Brunswick, N.J., Mar. 25, 1927; s. Charles and Sarah (Levine) W.; m. Naomi Z. Orlick, Dec. 21, 1951; children: Charles David, Daniel Morris. Student, Rutgers U.; BS in Physics, U. Chgo., 1951, MSc in Geology, 1952, PhD, 1954, DSc (hon.), 1992; Dr. Hon. Causa, Brussels U., 1985, U. Paris, 1986; DSc (hon.), Ariz. State U., 1987; Dr. (hon.), U. Rennes, 1998; DSc (hon.), U. Turin (Italy), 2000. Research assoc. Inst. Nuclear Studies, U. Chgo., 1954-55; asst. prof. Calif. Inst. Tech., Pasadena, 1955-59, assoc. prof., 1959-62, prof. geology and geophysics, 1962-82, John D. MacArthur prof. geology and geophysics, 1982—2001, prof. emeritus, 2001—. Served on Juneau Ice Field Rsch. Project, 1950; cons. Argonne Nat. Lab., Lamont, Ill., 1952-55; former mem. U.S. Nat. Com. for Geochem., com. for Planetary Exploration Study, NRC, adv. coun. Petroleum Rsch. Fund, Am. Chem. Soc.; me. lunar sample analysis planning team (LSAPT) manned Spacecraft Ctr., NASA, Houston, 1968-71, chmn., 1970; lunar sample rev. bd., 1970-72; mem. Facilities Working Group LSAPT, Johnson Space Ctr., 1972-82; mem. sci. working panel for Apollo missions, Johnson Space Ctr., 1971-73; advisor NASA, 1968-88, phys. scis. com., 1971-75, mem. lunar base steering com., 1984; chmn. com. for planetary and lunar exploration, mem. space sci. bd. NAS, 1975-78; chmn. divsn. Geol. and Planetary Scis., Calif. Inst. Tech., 1987-89; vis. prof. U. Kiel, Fed. Republic of Germany, 1960, Harvard U., 1962, U. Bern, Switzerland, 1966, Swiss Fed. Tech. Inst., 1967, Max Planck Inst., Mainz and Heidelberg, Fed. Republic of Germany, 1985, and others; invited lectr., Vinton Hayes Sr. fellow Harvard U., 1980, Jaeger-Hales lectr. Australian Nat. U., 1980, Harold Jeffreys lectr. Royal Astron. Soc., 1981, Ernst Cloos lectr. Johns Hopkins U., 1984, H.L. Welsh Disting. lectr. U. Toronto, Can., 1986, Danz lectr. U. Washington, 1989, Goldschmidt Centennial lectr. Norwegian Acad. Sci. and Letters, 1989, Lindsay lectr. Goddard Space Flight Ctr., 1996, others; plenary spkr. 125th Anniversary Geol. Soc. Sweden, 1996; 60th Anniversary Symposium spkr. Hebrew U., Jerusalem, 1985, 75th Anniversary Symposium spkr., 2000; 300th Anniversary Silliman lectr. Uale U., 2001. Served with U.S. Army, 1944-46. Decorated Combat Inf. badge. Recipient Group Achievement award NASA, 1969, Exceptional Sci. Achievement award NASA, 1970, Disting. Pub. Svc. medal NASA, 1973, J.F. Kemp medal Columbia U., 1973, Profl. Achievement award U. Chgo. Alumni Assn., 1978, Goldschmidt medal Geochem. Soc., 1978, Disting. Pub. Svc. medal with cluster NASA, 1978, Wollaston medal Geol. Soc. London, 1985, Sr. Scientist award Alexander von Humboldt-Stiftung, 1985, Crafoord prize Royal Swedish Acad. Scis., 1986, Holmes medal, 1987, Regents fellow Smithsonian Inst., Gold medal Royal Astron. Soc., 1991; named Hon. Fgn. fellow European Union Geoscis., 1983. Fellow Am. Acad. Arts and Scis., Geol. Soc. London (hon.), Am. Geophys. Union (planetology sect., Harry H. Hess medal 1985), Geol. Soc. Am. (life, Arthur L. Day medal 1970), Meteoritical Soc. (pres. 1987-88, Leonard medal 1975), Geochemical Society and the European Assn. for Geochemistry, 1996; mem. Nat. Acad. Scis. (Arthur L. Day prize and lectureship 1981, J. Lawrence Smith medal 1985), Norwegian Acad. Sci. and Letters, Am. Phil. Soc. Achievements include research in geochemistry and geophysics and the application of the methods of chemical physics to problems in the earth scis. Major researches have been the determination of the time scales of nucleosynthesis, connections between the interstellar medium and solar material, the time of the formation of the solar system, the chronology and evolution of the earth, moon and meteorites, the establishment of dating methods using long-lived natural radio-activities, the study of geologic and cosmic processes using nuclear and isotopic effects as a tracer in nature, the origin of natural gases, and the application of thermodynamic methods to geologic systems. Office: Calif Inst Tech Divsn Geol & Planetary Scis Pasadena CA 91125-2500 E-mail: isotopes@gps.caltech.edu.

WASSERMAN, ALBERT, film producer, writer, director; b. N.Y.C., Feb. 9, 1921; s. Martin S. and Beatrice (Schaffer) W.; m. Della Newmark, Aug. 5, 1943 (div. Mar. 1965); children— Paul, Vicki; m. Barbara Alson, June 19, 1968. BS, CCNY, 1941. Pres. Wasserman Prodns., Inc., N.Y.C., 1968-75. Writer documentary, ednl. and indsl. films, 1946-53; freelance writer, dir. TV documentary films, 1953-55; staff writer, dir., prodr., CBS-TV, 1955-60; prodr., dir., writer: NBC News, 1960-67; prodr.: 60 Minutes, 1976-86; writer, prodr., dir.: Out of Darkness; writer film: First Steps; writer, dir. films for: CBS Pub. Affairs Series The Search; prodr., writer dir.: NBC White Paper programs, films for CBS News series The Twentieth Century and CBS Reports; prodr., dir.: TV Spl. The Making of the President, 1972; still photographer and collagist, N.Y.C., 1987—; exhibited works at Cortland Jessup Gallery, Provincetown, Mass., 1990-97, Provincetown Art Assn. and Mus., Atlantic Gallery, N.Y.C., 1995-98, Cast Iron Gallery, N.Y.C., 1995, Cortland Jessup Gallery, N.Y.C., 1997, eyeonart.com, N.Y.C., 2000. Recipient Sylvania TV award, Robert Flaherty film award, Acad. award, 1947, Peabody award for CBS pub. affairs series, Lasker med. journalism awards (2); Edinburgh Film Festival silver medal, 1948, George Polk award, 1960, Journalism award Ohio State U., 1961. Mem. Writers Guild Am. East (treas. 1965-66), Dirs. Guild Am. (eastern regional council 1965-66, 69-70) Home: 259 W 11th St New York NY 10014-2412

WASSERMAN, BARRY L(EE), architect; b. Cambridge, Mass., May 25, 1935; s. Theodore and Adelaide (Levin) W.; m. Wilma Louise Greenfield, June 21, 1957 (div. 1971); children: Tim Andrew, Andrew Glenn; m. Judith Ella Michalowski, Apr. 22, 1979. BA, Harvard U., 1957, M. Arch., 1960. Registered architect, Calif. Assoc. John S. Bolles Assocs., San Francisco, 1960-69; prin. Wasserman-Herman Assocs., 1969-72; prin., dir. Office Lawrence Halprin U Assocs., 1972-76; dep. state architect State of Calif., Sacramento, 1976-78, state architect, 1978-83; prof. dept. architecture, dir. Inst. Environ. Design, Sch. Environ. Design Calif. State Poly. U., Pomona, 1983-87, chair dept. architecture, Coll. Environ. Design, 1988-96, prof. emeritus, 1997—; cons. architecture, Sacramento, 1983—; program advisor Fla. A&M U., Tallahassee, 1981-83. Architect Wasserman House, San Rafael, Calif., 1963 (AIA-Sunset Mag. award of Merit 1965-66), Anna Waden Library, San Francisco, 1969 (AIA award of Merit 1970), Capitol Area Plan, Sacramento, 1977 (Central Valley chpt. AIA Honor award 1979), co-author: Ethics and the Practice of Architecture, 2000. Recipient Awards citation Progressive Architecture 26th awards Program, 1979, Octavius Morgan award Calif. Architects Bd., 2000. Fellow AIA chmn. architecture in govt. com. (1979) Democrat. Jewish. Home: 6456 Fordham Way Sacramento CA 95831-2218 E-mail: blw2@mindspring.com.

WASSERMAN, BRIAN ALAN, investment banker; b. Freeport, N.Y., Sept. 6, 1965; s. Arnold and Linda K. (Rosen) W.; m. Andrea Goodman, June 21, 1992. BS in Acctg., Lehigh U., 1987. CPA. Acct. Coopers & Lybrand, N.Y.C., 1987-93; chief fin. officer D.H. Blair Investment Banking, 1993—; treas. Engex, Inc., 1993—. Bd. dirs. 399 E 72 St. Assocs., N.Y.C. Mem. AICPA, N.Y. State Soc. CPAs. Office: D H Blair Investment Banking Corp 44 Wall St New York NY 10005-2401

WASSERMAN, DONALD EUGENE, human vibration and ergonomics consultant; b. New Haven, Apr. 1, 1939; s. Arthur and Eva Helen (Berkowitz) W.; m. Helen Ann Schwartz, July 15, 1967; children: Melissa, Sherri. BA in Physics/Biophysics, U. Conn., 1962; MSEE in Elec. Engring./Bioengring., NYU, 1971; MBA in Mgmt., Xavier U., Cin., 1984. Biomed. engr. depts. cardiovascular surgery Yale U. Med. Sch., New Haven, 1957-62; biomed. project engr. Mnemotron divsn., Tech. Measurements Corp., North Haven, Conn., 1962-63; sr. biomed. engr. Cambridge Instruments Co., Ossining, N.Y., 1964; sr. biomed. project, rsch. engr. Perkin-Elmer Corp., Norwalk, Conn., 1965-71; chief bioacoustics and occupational vibration group USPHS, Nat. Inst. Occupational Safety and Health, Cin., 1971-84; dir. engring. and ops., sr. rsch. investigator Nat. Ctr. Rehab. Engring., Wright State U., Dayton, Ohio, 1984-86; dir. human vibration engring. Anatrol Corp., Cin., 1986-88; pvt. cons. to industry, state and fed. govt., legal, 1988—; human vibration and biomed. engring. cons. Author: Human Aspects of Occupational Vibration; mem. editorial bd., contbg. editor Sound and Vibration; biomed. patent reviewer Jour. Acoustical Soc. Am.; manuscript reviewer Jour. Occupational Medicine; contbr. numerous articles to profl. jours. Avocation: electronics. Home and Office: 7910 Mitchell Farm Ln Cincinnati OH 45242-6437

WASSERMAN, EDWARD ARNOLD, psychology educator; b. L.A., Apr. 2, 1946; s. Albert Leonard and May (Sabin) W. BA, UCLA, 1968; PhD, Ind. U., 1972. Postdoctoral fellow U. Sussex, Brighton, Eng., 1972; from asst. prof. to prof. psychology U. Iowa, Iowa City, 1972-83, prof., 1983—, Stuit prof. exptl. psychology, 1997—. Pres. faculty senate U. Iowa, 1997-98; vis. scientist CNRS, Marseille, France, 1999. Contbr. articles to profl. jours., chpts. to books; assoc. editor several jours. Bd. dirs. Big Bros., Big Sisters, Johnson County, Iowa, 1982-85 Ind. U. fellow, 1968, U. Iowa fellow, 1975, 82, NAS fellow, former USSR, 1976, James Van Allen Natural Scis. fellow, 1994-95. Fellow APA, Am. Psychol. Soc.; mem. Psychonomic Soc. (governing bd.), Midwestern Psychol. Assn., Phi Beta Kappa. Office: U Iowa Dept Psychology Iowa City IA 52242

WASSERMAN, GARY B. political scientist, writer, consultant; b. Washington, Dec. 1, 1944; s. Samuel and Helen Disman Wasserman; m. Ann Stewart, Apr. 5, 1984; children: Daniel, Laura. BS, Georgetown U., 1966; PhD, Columbia U., 1973. Asst. prof. Medgar Evans Coll., N.Y.C., 1973-75; legis. asst. U.S. Ho. Reps., Washington, 1976-77; asst. prof. Columbia U., N.Y.C., 1977-78; spl. asst. U.S. Agy. Internat. Devel., 1979-81; ptnr. Bob Beckel & Assocs., 1984-92; sr. v.p. Bozell Sawyer Miller, Washington, 1992-95; prin. Wasserman & Assocs., 1995—. Author: Politics of Decolonization, 1976, America's Government, 1990; author: Basics of American Politics, 10th edit., 2001, The Founding Family, 2001; contbr. articles to profl. jours. Nat. issues coord. Fred Harris for Pres., Washington, 1975-76. Fulbright scholar, 1969. Mem. Coun. Excellence Govt. Democrat. Jewish. Avocations: meditation, tennis. Home and Office: 3626 Van Ness St NW Washington DC 20008

WASSERMAN, HELENE WALTMAN, art dealer, artist; b. Phila., Jan. 29, 1929; d. William T. and Bertha (Brener) Waltman; m. Richard M. Wasserman, June 23, 1950 (div. 1972); children: Ann Zelver, Ellen Rubinfeld, Stephen; m. Mark C. Cooper, Jan. 22, 1988. BFA, U. Pa., 1951. Pvt. practice art dealer, 1972—. Apptd. appraiser Supreme Ct., State of N.Y., 1978. One-woman shows at Philmont Gallery, Phila., 1964, Roko Gallery, N.Y., 1965; exhibited in group shows at Phila. Mus. Art, Pa. Acad. Fine Arts, Philbrook Mus., Tulsa, Woodmere Gallery, Roko Gallery, 1953-68. Active Nassau County Art Commn., 1968-72; trustee, Sculpture Ctr., N.Y.C., bd. dirs., 1991. Mem. Pvt. Art Dealers Assn., Cosmopolitan Club, Nature Conservancy. Avocations: painting, sculpting, garden design.

WASSERMAN, IRENE, research scientist, educator; b. Uman, Ukraine, Russia, June 1, 1965; arrived in Israel, 1990; d. Avram and Ludmila (Khazin) W. MSc, Inst. Chem. and Chem. Engring., Dnjepropetrovsk, Russia, 1987; DSc, Technion, Haifa, Israel, 1994. R&D engr. Perlite Industries Ltd., Moshav Habonim, Israel, 1990-91; rschr. Golan Devel. Co., Katzrin, Israel, 1992-94; head concrete dept. Galilee Lab., Kiryat Shmonah, Israel, 1994-95; scientist Inst. for Bldg. Materials TU Munchen, Munich, Germany, 1996-97; lectr. Tel-Hi Coll., Israel, 1994-95, 97—; rsch. scientist Nat. Bldg. Rsch. Inst. Technion, Haifa, Israel, 1997—. Cons. Nat. Bldg. Rsch. Inst., Haifa, 1995-96, coord. implementation dept., 1998—. Contbr. articles to profl. jours. Recipient Minerva fellow, 1996-97, fellow Hebrew Immigrant Aid Soc., 1991. Avocations: reading, art. Office: Nat Bldg Rsch Inst Kiryat Technion 32000 Haifa Israel

WASSERMAN, JACK F. corporate executive, educator; b. Dayton, Ohio, July 29, 1941; s. Lee Simond and Louise (Cockerill) W.; m. Susan Ainsworth, June 5, 1965 (div. May 1975); children: Ric, Andrea; m. Betty M. McClain, July 29, 1978; 1 child, Michel. BS, Purdue U., 1964; MS, U. Cin., 1971, PhD, 1975; cert. physician asst., Cin. Tech. Coll., 1977. Registered profl. engr., Ohio. Assoc. prof. U. Tenn., Knoxville, 1979—, cons. Meml. Rsch. Ctr. Hosp., 1979—, adj. assoc. prof. Inst. Agr., 1983—, prof. biomed. engring., 1986, adj. prof. exercise sci., 1996—; pres. ops., sr. v.p. R&D product integration Hydro Force Corp. Adj. assoc. prof. U. Cin., 1975-79, rsch. assoc., 1975-79; vis. prof. U.S. Army Aeromed. Rsch. Lab., Ft. Rucker, Ala., summer 1984. Inventor acoustic aneurysm detector and associated method, exercise and/or therapy apparatus having an impeller for use in a pool of liquid. Mem. Am. Acad. Physician's Asst., Am. Soc. Biomechanics, ASME, Aquatic Exercise Assn. (bd. advisors), Acoustic Soc. Am., Orthopedic Rsch. Soc., Tenn. Acad. Scis. Avocations: mountain biking, aerobics, water aerobics. Home: 4512 Westover Ter Knoxville TN 37914-5055 Office: 10512 Lexington Dr Ste 500 Knoxville TN 37932-3247

WASSERMAN, KAREN BOLING, clinical psychologist, nursing consultant; b. Olney, Ill., July 29, 1944; d. Kenneth G. and Betty Jean (Varner) Boling; m. James M. Wasserman, Apr. 14, 1965; children: Nicole C., Michael B. RN, Barnes Hosp. Sch. Nursing, St. Louis, 1965; BA, Antioch Coll., 1977; Dr. of Psychology, Wright State U., 1986. Lic. psychologist, Ohio, Ind.; RN, Mo., Ohio. Staff nurse various med. facilities, 1965-76; instr. practical nurse program Ind. Vocat. Tech. Coll., Richmond, 1976-77; staff, float nurse Good Samaritan Hosp., Dayton, Ohio, 1977-78; pub. health nurse coord. Bur. Alcoholism Svcs., 1978-79, alcoholism counselor IV Ohio, 1979-82; practicum student Wright State U. Sch. Profl. Psychology, 1983-85; psychology intern Balt. VAMC Consortium, 1985-86; clin. psychologist Dayton VAMC, 1987-89; founder, ptnr., dir. clin. svcs. Fairhaven Clinic, P.A., Biloxi, Miss., 1989-98; clin. psychologist Gulf Oaks Hosp., 1989-98, Sand Hill Hosp., Gulfport, Miss., 1993-98, chief psychol. svcs., 1998; cons. psychologist Sr. Life Cons., Dublin, 2000; exec. dir. The Ridge Counseling Ctr., Hilliard, 2001—. Psychiat. nursing cons. Mercy Hosp., Omaha, Council Bluffs, Iowa, 1987; instr. William Carey Coll. on the Coast, 1993; owner/propr. Angel Garden, Ocean Springs, 1996-98; founder, co-owner Ebenezer's Antiques, Springfield, Ohio, 1999—. Chmn. cmty. svcs. Altrusa Internat., Biloxi, 1990—94, treas., 1993—94; Friend of the Rainbow Warrior, Greenpeace, 1986—93; mem. adminstrv. bd. Gulf Coast Ctr. for Nonviolence, 1996—98; mem. adv. bd. Ohio Coalition for Suicide Prevention, 2002; mem. evangelism com. First United Meth. Ch., Gulfport, Miss., 1991—93, mem. coun. on ministries, 1994—95; mem. libr. com., ch. and soc. com. Worthington (Ohio) United Meth. Ch., 1999—2001; mem. Internat. Order of St. Luke the Physician, 1997—. Recipient Alumnae award in Acads., Barnes Hosp. Sch. Nursing, 1965, Career Woman of Yr. award, Lighthouse of Biloxi chpt., Bus. and Profl. Women, 1994. Fellow Am. Acad. Psychologists Treating Addiction; mem. Ohio Psychol. Assn. (legis. com. 1998-), Miss. Psychol. Assn. (region IV rep. exec. coun., continuing edn. com. 1990-95, chair 1994-95, chair membership com. 1997-98). Avocations: architecture, gardening, travel, movies. Fax: 614-876-5132. E-mail: theridgecc@aol.com.

WASSERMAN, KRYSTYNA, librarian, art historian; b. Lodz, Poland, Aug. 10, 1937; came to U.S., 1971; d. Henryk and Polina (Volk) Ostrowski; m. Paul Wasserman, Apr. 14, 1972. M in Journalism, U. Warsaw, Poland, 1963; MLS, Pratt Inst., 1972; MA, U. Md., 1981. Reporter Ekran-The Screen Mag., Warsaw, 1960-62; sec. edn. com. Inst. Sci., Tech. and Econ. Info., Poland and Internat. Fedn. for Documentation, The Hague, Netherlands, 1962-71; ind. editor reference books College Park, Md., 1972-82; libr. Nat. Mus. Women Arts, Washington, 1982—2002, curator book arts, 2002—. Curator numerous art exhbns. Contbr. articles to profl. jours.; editor: A Guide to the World Training Facilities in Documentation and Information Work, 1965, 2nd edit., 1969. ASTEF fellow Govt. of France, 1967. Avocations: photography, walking, travel, collecting socks, collecting masks. Office: Nat Mus Women in Arts 1250 New York Ave NW Washington DC 20005-3970

WASSERMAN, PAUL, library and information science educator; b. Newark, Jan. 8, 1924; s. Joseph and Sadie (Ringelescu) W.; m. Krystyna Ostrowska, 1973; children: Jacqueline R., Steven R. BBA, Coll. City N.Y., 1948; MS in L.S., Columbia, 1949, MS, 1950; PhD, U. Mich., 1960; postgrad., Western Res. U., 1963-64. Advt. mgr. Zuckerberg Co., N.Y.C., 1946-48; asst. to bus. libr. Bklyn. Pub. Library, 1949-51, chief sci. and industry div., 1951-53; librarian, asst. prof. Grad. Sch. Bus. and Pub. Adminstrn., Cornell U., 1953-56, libr., assoc. prof., 1956-62, librarian, prof., 1962-65; dean U. Md. Coll. Library and Info. Scis., 1965-70, prof., 1970-97, prof. emeritus, 1997—. Vis. prof. U. Mich., summers 1960, 63, 64, Asian Inst. Tech., U. Hawaii, U. Hong Kong, summer 1988, Chulalongkorn U., Bangkok, 1990, U. Wash., summer 1991, U. Wis., summer 1991, U. Wis., summer 1992, C.W. Post Coll., L.I. U., 1993, Inst. Sci. and Tech. China, Beijing, 1996; Isabel Nichol lectr. Denver U. Libr. Sch., 1968; market rsch. cons. Laux Advt., Inc., 1955-59, Gale Rsch. Co., Detroit, 1959-60, 63-64; rsch. planning cons. Ind. U. Sch. Bus., 1961-62; cons. to USPHS as mem. manpower tng. rev. com. Nat. Libr. Medicine, 1966-69, Ohio Bd. Regents, 1969, Omngraphics Inc., 1988-91, VITA, summer 1987; dir. Documentation Abstracts, Inc., 1970-73, v.p., 1971-73; Fulbright prof. Warsaw U., 1993-94; rsch. project dir. Kellogg Study, 1996-98. Author: Information for Adminstrators, 1956, (with Fred Silander) Decision Making, 1958, Measurement and Evaluation of Organization Performance, 1959, Sources of Commodity Prices, 1960, 2d edit., 1974, Sources for Hospital Administrators, 1961, Decision Making: An Annotated Bibliography, supplement, 1958-63, 1964, Librarian and the Machine, 1965; Book rev. editor: Adminstrv. Sci. Quar, 1956-61; editor: Service to Business, 1952-53, Directory of University Research Bureaus and Institutes, 1960, Health Organizations of the U.S. and Canada, 1961, and 2d to 4th edit., 1977, Statistics Sources, 1962 and 4th to 8th edits., 1984, (with Bundy) Reader in Library Adminstration, 1968, Reader in Research Methods in Librarianship, 1969; mng. editor: Mgmt. Information Guide Series, 1963-83, Consultants and Consulting Organizations, 1966, 4th edit., 1979, 5th edit., 1982, Who's Who in Consulting, 1968, 2d edit., 1974, Awards, Honors and Prizes: A Sourcebook and Directory, 1969, 2d edit., 1972, 4th edit. Vol. 1, 1978, International and Foreign Awards, 1975, New Consultants, 1973-74, 76-77, 78-79, Readers in Librarianship and Information Science, 1968-78, Ency. Bus. Information Sources, 1971, 3d edit., 1976, 4th edit., 1980, 5th edit., 1983, Library and Information Services Today, 1971-75, Consumer Sourcebook, 1974, 2d edit., 1978, 3d edit., 1980, 4th edit., 1983; series editor: Contributions in Librarianship and Information Science, 1969-99; coordinating mgmt. editor: Information Guide Library, 1971-83, The New Librarianship-A Challenge for Change, 1972; mng. editor: Museum Media, 1973, Library Bibliographies and Indexes, 1975, Ethnic Groups in the United States, 1976, 2d edit., 1982, Training and Development Organizations, 1978, 2d edit., 1983, Speakers and Lecturers: How to Find Them, 1979, 2d edit., 1982, Learning Independently, 1979, 2d edit., 1983, Recreation and Outdoor Life Directory, 1979, Law and Legal Information Directory, 1980, 2d edit., 1982, Ency. Health Info. Sources, 1986, Ency. Sr. Citizen Info. Sources, 1987, Ency. Pub. Affairs Info. Sources, 1987, Ency. Legal Info. Sources, 1987; mem. editorial bd. Social Scis. Citation Index, Inst. Scientific Info., 1972-95, Jour. Library Adminstrn., 1979-89, Social Sci. Info. Studies, 1979— , 1991 Education for Info.: The Internat. Rev. of Education and Tng. in Library and Info. Sci., 1983-88, The Best of Times: A Personal and Occupational Odyssey, 2000. Active U.S. Com. on Edn. and Tng. for Internat. Fedn. for Info. and Documentation, 1993-94. Served with U.S. Army, 1943-46. Decorated Purple Heart, Bronze Star; recipient ALA Ref. Svcs. Divsn./Gale Rsch. Bus. Libr. award, 1997; Fulbright scholar, Sri Lanka, 1986-87. Mem. AAUP, ALA, Am. Soc. Info. Sci., Spl. Librs. Assn. (editor, chmn. publ. project., Disting. Mem. award bus. divsn. 1996—). Home: 4940 Sentinel Dr Apt 203 Bethesda MD 20816-3552 Office: U Md Coll Info Studies College Park MD 20742-0001 E-mail: pw11@umail.umd.edu.

WASSERMAN, RICHARD LEO, lawyer; b. Balt., Aug. 6, 1948; s. Jack B. and Claire (Gutman) W.; m. Manuele Delbourgo, May 13, 1973; children: Alexander E., Lauren E. AB, Princeton U., 1970; JD, Columbia U., 1973. Bar: N.Y. 1975, Md. 1978, U.S. Dist. Ct. (so. and ea. dists.) N.Y. 1975, U.S. Dist. Ct. Md. 1978, U.S. Ct. Appeals (2d cir.) 1975, U.S. Ct. Appeals (4th cir.) 1979, U.S. Supreme Ct. 1982. Law clk. to hon. Roszel C. Thomsen U.S. Dist. Ct. Md., Balt., 1973-74; assoc. Proskauer Rose Goetz & Mendelsohn, N.Y.C., 1974-78, Venable, Baetjer & Howard, Balt., 1978-81, ptnr., 1982—, also bd. dirs. Fellow Am. Coll. Bankruptcy, Md. Bar Found.; mem. ABA (bus. bankruptcy com.), Md. Bar Assn. (sec. coun. bus. law sect. 1989-92), Bar Assn. Balt. City (chmn. banking, bankruptcy and bus. law com. 1987-88), Bankruptcy Bar Assn. Dist. Md. (bd. dirs. 1988—, pres. 1990-91), Assn. Bar City N.Y., Am. Bankruptcy Inst., Princeton U. Alumni Assn. Md. (bd. dirs. 1980-98, pres. 1985-87), Suburban Club Baltimore County (bd. govs. 1982-89, 94-98, 2d v.p. 1986-87, sec. 1987-88, pres.-elect 1994-95, pres. 1995-97). Democrat. Jewish. Avocations: tennis, golf, bridge. Office: Venable Baetjer & Howard LLP 1800 Mercantile Bank Bldg Baltimore MD 21201 E-mail: rlwasserman@venable.com.

WASSERMAN, ROBERT HAROLD, biology educator; b. Schenectady, Feb. 11, 1926; s. Joseph and Sylvia (Rosenberg) W.; m. Marilyn Mintz, June 11, 1950; children: Diane Jean, Arlene Lee, Judith Rose. BS, Cornell U., 1949, PhD, 1953; MS, Mich. State U., 1951. Research assoc. AEC project U. Tenn., Oak Ridge, 1953-55; sr. scientist med. div. Oak Ridge Inst. Nuclear Studies, 1955-57; assoc. prof. dept. phys. biology N.Y. State Vet. Coll., Cornell U., 1957-63, prof., 1963—, James Law prof. physiology, 1989-97, James Law prof. emeritus, 1998—, acting head phys. biology dept., 1963-64, 71, 75-76, chmn. dept. /sect. physiology, 1983-87, mem. exec. com. div. biol. sci., 1983-87. Vis. fellow Inst. Biol. Chemistry, Copenhagen, 1964-65; chmn. Conf. on Calcium Transport, 1962; co-chmn. Conf. on Cell Mechanisms for Calcium Transfer and Homeostasis, 1970; mem. adv. bd. Vitamin D Symposia, 1976—; mem. adv. bd. Symposia Calcium-Binding Proteins, 1977-2001, chmn., 1977; mem. food and nutrition bd. NRC; cons. NIH, Oak Ridge Inst. Nuclear Studies; mem. pub. affairs com. Fedn. Am. Socs. Exptl. Biology, 1974-77 ; chmn. com. MPI, NRC Bd. editors: Calcified Tissue Research, 1977-80, Procs. Soc. Exptl. Biol. Medicine, 1970-76, Cornell Veterinarian, Jour. Nutrition; contbr.: articles to profl. jours. Served with U.S. Army, 1944-45. Recipient Mead Johnson award, 1969, Andre Lichtwitz prize INSERM, 1982, W.F. Neuman award Am. Soc. Bone and Mineral Rsch., 1990, merit award NIH, 1993-96; Guggenheim fellow, 1964-65, 72, fellow NSF-OECD, 1964-65. Fellow Am. Inst. Nutrition, mem. Am. Physiol. Soc., Soc. Exptl. Biology and Medicine, AAAS, Nat. Acad. Scis., Sigma Xi, Phi Kappa Phi, Phi Zeta Home: 207 Texas Ln Ithaca NY 14850-1758 E-mail: RHW2@cornell.edu.

WASSERMAN, STANLEY, statistician, educator; b. Louisville, Aug. 29, 1951; s. Irvin Levitch and Jeanne (Plattus) W.; m. Sarah Wilson, Feb. 3, 1974; children: Andrew Joseph, Eliot Miles. BS in Econs., U. Pa., 1973; PhD in Stats., Harvard U., 1977. Asst. prof. U. Minn., Mpls., 1977-82; assoc. prof. U. Ill., Urbana, 1982-88, prof. psychology, stats., sociology, 1988—; prof. Beckman Inst., 1993—. Vis. rschr. Columbia Univ., N.Y.C., 1978; cons., expert witness EEOC, Cleve., 1979-81; cons. V.A. Med. Ctr., Mpls., 1980-82, AT&T Communications, Basking Ridge, N.J., 1988-90. Author: Social Network Analysis, 1994; assoc. editor: Sociological Methodology, 1978-81, Jour. Am. Statis. Assn., 1987—, Psychometrika, 1988-2000, Am. Statistician, 1993-96, Structural Analysis, 1997-2000; guest editor: Sociol. Methods and Rsch., 1992; book review editor: Chance, 1993—; consulting editor Am. Jour. Sociology, 2000—. Treas. Montessori Sch. of Champaign-Urbana, Savoy, Ill., 1990-92. Grantee NSF, Washington, 1979-81, 84-89, 93—, NIH, 1995-98; postdoctoral fellow Social Sci. Rsch. Coun., N.Y.C., 1978. Fellow AAAS, Am. Statis. Assn.; mem. Psychometric Soc., Royal Statis. Soc., Classification Soc. N.Am. (sec., treas. 1993-95, bd. dirs. 1996-98. 99-2000), Internat. Network for Social Network Analysis (bd. dirs. 1997). Achievements include reseach in applied statistics, categorical data analysis, social network analysis. Home: 2066 County Road 125 E Mahomet IL 61853-8907 Office: U Ill 603 E Daniel St Champaign IL 61820-6232 E-mail: stanwass@uiuc.edu.

WASSERMAN, STEPHEN ALAN, lawyer; b. Cleve., Apr. 7, 1948; s. Myron Earl and Eve Ruth (Milstein) W.; m. Sandra Shulamith Moltz, Oct. 20, 1978. BA, U. Wis., 1970; JD, Northeastern U., Boston, 1978. Bar: Mass. 1978, U.S. Dist. Ct. Mass. 1978. Housing atty. Neighborhood Legal Svcs., Lynn, Mass., 1978-83; ptnr. Barmack, Boggs and Wasserman, 1983-91; pvt. practice Salem, Mass., 1991-97, 98—, Boston, 1997-98. Bd. dirs. North Shore Cmty. Action Program, Peabody, Mass., 1995—. Avocations: reading, baseball, jogging. Office: 32 Church St Salem MA 01970-3737 E-mail: S.A.Wasserman@verizon.net.

WASSERMAN, STEPHEN IRA, physician, educator; b. Los Angeles, Dec. 17, 1942; m. Linda Morgan; children: Matthew, Zachary. BA, Stanford U., 1964; MD, UCLA, 1968. Diplomate Am. Bd. Internal Medicine, Am. Bd. Allergy and Immunology. Intern, resident Peter B. Brigham Hosp., Boston, 1968-70; fellow in allergy, immunology Robert B. Brigham Hosp., 1972-75; asst. prof. medicine Harvard U., 1975-79, assoc. prof., 1979, U. Calif.-San Diego, La Jolla, 1979-85, prof., 1985—, chief allergy tng. program Sch. Medicine, 1979-85, chief allergy div. Sch. Medicine, 1985-93, acting chmn. dept. medicine, 1986-88, chmn. dept. medicine, 1988-2000, Helen M. Ranney prof., 1992—. Co-dir. allergy sect. Robert B. and Peter B. Brigham Hosps., 1977-79; dir. Am. Bd. Allergy and Immunology; dir. Am. Bd. Internal Medicine., chair, 1999-2000. Contbr. articles to profl. jours. Served to lt. comdr. USPHS, 1970-72, San Francisco. Fellow Am. Acad. Allergy and Immunology (pres. 1997-98); mem. Am. Soc. Clin. Investigation, Assn. Am. Physicians, Am. Assn. Immunologists, Collegium Internationale Allergologicum, Phi Beta Kappa, Alpha Omega Alpha. Office: U Calif San Diego Stein Clin Rsch Bldg Rm 244 9500 Gilman Dr MC 0637 San Diego CA 92093-0637

WASSERMAN, STEPHEN MILES, communications director; b. Chgo., Apr. 26, 1945; s. Samuel Isreal and Rayna (Krassner) W.; m. Faye Rita Samuelson, Oct. 17, 1971; children: Rayna, Alyssa. BA in Journalism, Bradley U., 1968. Mgr. corp. comm. Underwriters Labs., Inc., Northbrook, Ill., 1991-98, corp. mgr. global comm. svcs., 1997-98, dir. global comm. svcs., 1998-2001, mem. steering com. home fire sprinkler coalition, 1998-2001; dir. comms. group Am. Optometric Assn., Creve Coeur, Mo., 2001—. Mem. pub. rels. and fundraising com. Ill. Math. and Sci. Acad., Aurora, 1992-96; comms. chair Nat. Electric Safety Found., Washington, 1994-96; mem. steering com. Home Fire Sprinkler Corp. Campaign chmn. United Way, Buffalo Grove, Ill., 1991-93, pres., 1994-95. Mem. Nat. Press Club. Office: Am Optometric Assn 243 N Lindbergh Blvd Creve Coeur MO 63141 E-mail: smwasserman@theaoa.org.

WASSERMAN, SUSAN VALESKY, accountant, artist, yoga instructor; b. St. Petersburg, Fla., June 5, 1956; d. Charles B. Valesky and Jeanne I. (Schulz) Morgan; m. Fred Wasserman III, May 19, 1990; 1 child, Sara Elisabeth. BS in Merchandising, Fla. State U., 1978; BA in Acctg., U. South Fla., 1983; ChFC, Am. Coll., 1991. CPA Fla.; ChFC, cert. yoga tchr. Fla. Inst. for Integrated Yoga Studies, 2002. Mgmt. trainee Burdines Dept. Stores, Miami, Fla., 1978-79; store mgr. Levi Straus Inc., San Francisco, 1979; pvt. practice St. Petersburg, Fla., 1980—; internet practice, 1996—; acct., tax and fin. planning specialist Barber, Stowe & Co., St. Petersburg, 1997-98; owner While Egret Yoga Studio, South Pasadena, Fla., 2002—. Paintings shown at Longboat Key (Fla.) Art Ctr. Watercolor 10 Art Show, 1993, Fla. Suncoast Watercolor Soc. Aqueous Show, Sarasota, 1994, South Pasadena Artspring, 1998-2000; quoted in The Tax Advisor (nat. syndicated column); developer 1st worldwide Internet discussion group on fin. planning. Recipient Judges award South Pasadena Artspring, 1998. Mem.: AICPA (personal fin. specialist), Yoga Alliance, Fla. Inst. CPAs. Home and Studio: 7015 Grevilla Ave S Saint Petersburg FL 33707-2050 Office: 5800 4th St N Saint Petersburg FL 33703-1402 E-mail: yogisue@prodigy.net.

WASSERMAN, SYLVIA KATZ, lawyer; b. Milw., Mar. 30, 1916; d. Abraham and Anna Esther Katz; m. Eugene Wasserman (dec. Mar. 1970); children: Barbara Wasserman Vinson, Louis. BA, U. Ill., 1937; B of Law, Northwestern U., 1939, JD, 1970. Lawyer Office of Daniel D. Carmell, Chgo., Legal Br. N.Y. Ordnance Dist., N.Y.C.; lawyer, brief editor Bala Cynwyd, Pa.; lawyer Sheboygan, Wis., 1951—. Commr. Sheboygan Police and Fire Commn., 1980-93; bd. dirs. Friendship House, Sheboygan, 1974-96. Recipient Commendation award Friendship House, 1986. Mem. ABA, Ill. Bar Assn., Wis. Bar Assn., Sheboygan Bar Assn. Democrat. Jewish. Home: 215 Superior Ave Sheboygan WI 53081-2957 Office: 2808 Kohler Memorial Dr Sheboygan WI 53081-3166

WASSERSTEIN, WENDY, playwright; b. Bklyn., Oct. 18, 1950; d. Morris and Lola W. BA, Mt. Holyoke Coll., 1971; MA, CCNY, 1973; MFA, Yale Drama Sch., 1976. Author: (plays) Any Woman Can't, 1973, Happy Birthday, Montpelier Pizz-zazz, 1974, (with Christopher Durang) When Dinah Shore Ruled the Earth, 1975, Uncommon Women and Others, 1975, Isn't It Romantic, 1981, Tender Offer, 1983, The Man in a Case, 1986, Miami, 1986, The Heidi Chronicles, 1988 (Pulitzer prize for drama 1989, Outer Critics Cir. award for best play 1989, N.Y. Drama Critics Cir. award 1989, Susan Smith Blackburn prize 1989), The Sisters Rosensweig, 1991 (Outer Critics Cir. award 1993); (essays) Bachelor Girls, 1990; (screenplays) Uncommon Women and Others, 1978, The Sorrows of Gin, 1979, (with Durang) House of Husbands, Isn't It Romantic, The Heidi Chronicles; (children's book) Pamela's First Musical, 1995; actress in play An American Daughter, Life with Mikey. Bd. dirs. Channel Thirteen MacDowell Colony, British Am. Arts. Assn. Am. Playwrights Project grantee, 1988, Brit.-Am. Arts Assn. grantee, Hale Matthews Found. award, Commissioning Program Phoenix Theater grantee, Guggenheim fellow, 1983. Mem. Coun. Dramatists Guild.*

WASSERSTROM, EVELYN YAFFE (MRS. DEXTER JEROME WASSERSTROM), civic worker; b. Boston, Sept. 11, 1927; d. Joseph Harry and Tena (Drew) Yaffe; m. Dexter Jerome Wasserstrom, Dec. 25, 1948; children— Tena Lynn (dec.), Bruce Alan. Student Kansas City Art Inst., 1946-47, Kansas City Jr. Coll., 1946-47. Project dir. Housing Survey for Retarded, Kansas City Assn. for Retarded, 1969; pres. YWCA, Kansas City, Mo., 1964-65; co-chmn. Met. Action, 1969-80; mem. Kansas City Commn. Human Relations, 1979— ; bd. dirs. Kansas City region NCCJ, 1963— , exec. dir., 1980— , Jewish chmn., 1973-76; bd. dirs. Jewish Community Relations Bur., 1969— , United Community Services, Inc., 1981-84; bd. dirs. Jewish Ednl. Council, 1970— , chmn., 1973-77; mem. adv. group Met. Jr. Coll., 1967-69; co-chmn. High Sch. Jewish Studies of Greater Kansas City, 1971-73; mem. Panel of Am. Women, 1966— ; v.p. woman's div. Jewish Fedn. and Council of Greater Kansas City, pres. 1984-86, bd. govs., 1974— ; bd. dirs. Vol. Action Center, 1974-84, Jewish Community Center, 1977— , pres., 1986— ; chmn. Kansas City Mayor's Commn. Human Relations, 1982— ; mem. Social Studies Adv. Com. Shawnee Mission Sch. Dist. Recipient Citation and Brotherhood award Kansas City sect. NCCJ, 1971, Disting. Missourian award Kansas City, 1980, Disting. Alumnus award BBG, 1977, Matrix award Kansas City chpt. Women in Communication, 1979, Woman of Achievement award Mid-Continent Council Girl Scouts, 1983, Commn. Status of Women award, 1984, Crisis Mgmt. award Am. Soc. Pub. Adminstrn. (Kansas City Chpt.) mem. Central Exchange. Mem. B'nai B'rith Women (internat. pres. 1978-80, counselor 1980-82). Home: 449 W Dartmouth Rd Kansas City MO 64113-2026

WASSERSUG, STEPHEN ROBERT, environmental consultant; b. Nov. 4, 1943; BS, U. Mass., 1965, MS, 1968. Environ. dir., Worcester, Mass., 1965-68; divsn. dir. air, water and waste EPA, Phila., 1968-90, dep. asst. adminstr. Washington, 1988, mgr. Regional Environ. Ctr. for Ctrl. and Ea. Europe, Budapest, Hungary, 1990-94; pres., COO, Global Environ. and Tech. Found., Annandale, Va., 1995-98; founder, prin. FLW Enterprises Inc., Ft. Myers, Fla., 1998—. Adj. prof. Temple U., Phila., 1982-87; ptnr. Greenports Ent Inc.; rsch. assoc. Ctr. Sustainable Devel. Fla. Gulf Coast U. Bd. dirs. U.S. Ctrl. and Eastern European Found. Office: 14620 Fair Havens Rd Fort Myers FL 33908 E-mail: steve.wassersug@getf.org.

WASSHAUSEN, DIETER CARL, systematic botanist; b. Jena, Germany, Apr. 15, 1938; came to U.S., 1950, naturalized, 1957; s. Heinz P. and Elizabeth A. (Mueller) W.; m. Merrilee M. Locklin, Dec. 23, 1961; children— Lisa A., David B. BS, George Washington U., 1962, MS, 1965, PhD, 1972. Assoc. curator dept. botany Smithsonian Instn., Washington, 1969-76; chmn., curator dept. botany Nat. Mus. Natural History, 1976—. Recipient Smithsonian Research Found. awards, 1974, 75, Willdenow medal, 1979 Mem. Am. Soc. Plant Taxonomists, Internat. Assn. Plant Taxonomy, Neotropical Field Botanists Assn., Am. Inst. Biol. Scis., AAAS, Assn. Tropical Biology, Sigma Xi. Presbyterian. Achievements include research on systematics of neotropical Acanthaceae, floristic studies in Graminea of Brazil, floristic studies in Begoniaceae, revision of Nat. List Sci. Plant Names. Home: 9406 Chatteroy Pl Gaithersburg MD 20886-1424 Office: Nat Mus Natural History 10th St And Constitution Ave N Washington DC 20560-0001 E-mail: wasshausen.dieter@nmnh.si.edu.

WASSMAN, E. ROBERT, JR. geneticist, medical educator, management consultant; b. New Rochelle, N.Y., Oct. 2, 1951; s. Edward Robert and Eleanor Elizabeth (Humphrey) W.; m. Susan Louise Woody; children: Edward Robert III, Anna Cecelia. BS in Biology cum laude, Yale U., 1973; MD, Albany (N.Y.) Med. Coll., 1977. Med. lic. N.Y. and Calif.; COQ cert. N.Y. State Lab Dir.; lic. cytogeneticist and clin. molecular biologist, Calif. Resident N.Y. Hosp./Cornell U. Med. Ctr., N.Y.C., 1977-79; fellow med. genetics Harbor-UCLA Med. Ctr., Torrance, 1979-83, clin. asst. prof. pediatrics, 1983—; med. dir., rsch. dir. Alfigen, The Genetics Inst., Pasadena, Calif., 1983-89; v.p. corp. devel. Genetrix, Inc., Scottsdale, Ariz., 1990-94; chief So. Calif. Regional Offices Dept. Health Svcs., Childrens Med. Svcs., L.A., 1995-96; pres., CEO Perinatal Alliance Med. Group, Inc.; assoc. med. dir. Prometheus Labs. Inc., 1998—; med. dir. Ambry Genetics, 2000—; v.p. clin. and oncology svcs. Alfigen, Inc., 2001—. Pres. and CEO ACCME, Internat., Seal Beach, Calif., 1990—; trustee Billy Barty Found. Burbank, Calif., 1983—; v.p. corp. devel. and strategic alliances perinatal practice holdings Alfigen, Inc.; dir. bus. devel./genetics specialty labs., Santa Monica, Calif., 1996-97. Contbr. chpt. to Obstetrics and Gynecology Clinics of North America, 1993; contbr. articles to profl. jours.; presenter in field. Bd. dirs. med. adv. So. Calif. March of Dimes, L.A., 1987-90, Long Beach March of Dimes, chmn., 1984-89; mem. alumni schs. com. Yale U. Alumni Assn., Orange County, Calif., 1987—. Recipient Humanitarian award Found. for Children's Health Care, Long Beach, 1986; Giannini Found. fellow Bank of America, L.A., 1981-83; recipient Unsung Heroes award Harbor UCLA Med. Ctr., 1997. Fellow Am. Coll. of Med. Genetics founding, Am. Acad. of Pediat.; mem. AMA, NIH Alumni Assn. (life), Am. Soc. of Human Genetics, N.Y. Acad. Sci. Achievements include findings on causes of morbidity and mortality in short statured persons and inactivation of human X-chromosome, methods for growth of fetal cells in maternal bloodstream, Co-developer of first private genetic testing firm; developer of strategies for technology rationalization and deployment in managed care enviornments. Avocations: skiing, surfing, ice hockey, golf, tai chi. Home: 107 Ocean Ave Seal Beach CA 90740 Office: 31 W Del Mar Pasadena CA 91105 E-mail: accme@aol.com., bobw@alfigen.com.

WASSMER, DANIEL SCOTT, lawyer; b. Mineola, NY, Aug. 9, 1960; s. Rudolph Otto and Marjorie Ann Wassmer; m. Miriam Gomez, Aug. 8, 1987; children: Christopher, Michael. BA, Adelphi U., 1983, MBA, 1986; JD, NY Law Sch., 1989. Bar: N.Y. 1990, Conn. 1990, Pa. 1991, N.J. 1999. Trust adminstr. Nat. Westminster Bank, N.Y.C., 1983—86; assoc. Hayt, Hayt & Landau, Great Neck, 1991—94; atty. Law Office of Daniel S. Wassmer, Chalfont, 1994—2001; ptnr. Dommel Hill & Wassmer, LLP, Doylestown, Pa., 2001—. Commr. Del. River Joint Toll Bridge Commn., Morrisville, Pa., 2000—; dir. Bucks County Housing Corp., Doylestown, Pa., 2001—; asst. county solicitor Bucks County Pa., Doylestown, Pa., 2001—. County presdl. campaign coord. - Bush campaign Bucks County Rep. Com., Doylestown, Pa., 2000—00. Mem.: Pa. Bar Assn., John Zenger Law Soc., Federalist Soc., Lion Club Internat., F&AM #245. Lutheran. Avocations: outdoors, reading. Office: Dommel Hill & Wassmer LLP 123 N Broad St Doylestown PA 18901 Office Fax: 215-348-8060.

WASSMER, ROBERT WILLIAM, economics educator; b. Detroit, Sept. 15, 1961; s. Robert Oscar and Sandra Jean (Evely) E.; m. Dana I-Tan Wu, Feb. 10, 1990. BS in Econs., Oakland U., 1983; MA in Econs., SUNY, Binghamton, 1985; PhD in Econs., Mich. State U., 1989. Asst. prof. Wayne State U., Detroit, 1989—; assoc. prof. grad. program in pub. policy and adminstrn. Calif. State U., Sacramento, 1997—. Recipient Student Achievement award Wall St. Jour., 1983; rsch. grantee Upjohn Inst., 1996, Pub. Policy Inst. Calif., 1997. Mem. Am. Econ. Assn., Nat. Tax Assn. (mem. property taxation com., Hon. Mention doctoral dissertation, 1990), Am. Real Estate and Urban Econs. Assn., Western Econs. Assn., Soc. Govt. Econs. Democrat. Avocations: running, hiking, skiing, biking. Home: 933 Sonoma Way Sacramento CA 95819-3421 Office: Calif State U Grad Program in Pub Policy Sacramento CA 95819-6081

WASSMER, THEODORE MILTON, artist; b. Salt Lake City, Feb. 23, 1910; s. Theodore James and Hester Sadie (Hall) W.; m. Julia Farnsworth Lund, Dec. 8, 1945 (dec. May 1996). Student, Art Students League, N.Y.C., 1947-51; student under Raphael Soyer, Am. Art Sch., N.Y.C., 1949-51. Employed by engraving and wholesale hardware cos., Salt Lake City, 1925-42; artist N.Y.C., 1946-52, Woodstock, N.Y., 1952-85, Salt Lake City, 1985—. Apprentice to Florence E. Ware painting murals for the WPA, 1934-39. More than 2,000 works are in museums, colls., schs. and pvt. collections in U.S., Europe and Japan; with wife donated more than 900 works to Springville Mus. of Art, Snow Coll., Brigham City Mus.-Gallery, Fairview Mus. of History and Art and Nora Eccles Harrison Mus. Art, Utah; solo show at Albany (N.Y.) Inst. History and Art, 1974; other solo shows in Alaska, Ariz., Tex., Utah, Fla., N.Y. and Calif.; in Art Access Gallery traveling show (Utah), exhibited with 4 other artists over 80, 1994; solo show of 50 recent works at Myra Powell Gallery, Ogden, Utah, 1997; works reproduced in various publs. Sgt. U.S. Army Air Force, 1942-45. Springville Mus. Art honored his 80th yr. with reception and 60-yr. retrospective show, 1930-90, showing 100 of his works and issuing a 24-page catalog. Avocation: collecting art. Home: 130 S 1300 E Apt 501 Salt Lake City UT 84102-1779

WASSNER, STEVEN JOEL, pediatric nephrologist, educator; b. N.Y.C., Dec. 16, 1946; s. Abraham and Clara (Weitzner) W.; m. Enid K. Kling, June 11, 1972; children: Adam Jacob, Nancy Shane. BS, CCNY, 1968; MD, NYU, 1972. Diplomate Am. Bd. Pediatrics , Am. Bd. Pediatrics Nephrology. Intern, resident Children's Hosp. L.A., 1972-74, fellow in pediatric nephrology, 1974-75; rsch. fellow in pediatric nephrology UCLA, 1975-77; asst. prof. pediat. Pa. State U. M.S. Hershey Med. Ctr., Hershey, 1978-83, assoc. prof., 1983-91, prof., 1991—, vice chmn. dept., 1989-99, chief divsn. pediat. nephrology and hypertension, 1978—, chief divsn. pediatric nephrology and diabetes, 1991-99, vice-chmn. edn., 2000—. Vis. prof. human biochemistry Hebrew U., Hadassah Hosp., 1985-86; dir. Pediatric Diabetes Svc., 1998-99. Contbr. articles to med. jours. Mem. adv. bd. Kidney Found. South Ctrl. Pa., Harrisburg, 1980-90, sci. adv. coun. for pediatric nephrology/urology Nat. Kidney Found., 1986-92, Harrisburg com. for Hebrew U.; bd. dirs. Jewish Family Svc., Harrisburg, 1979-85, pres., 1983-85; bd. dirs. United Jewish Fedn., 1983-85, 94-97, Yeshiva Acad., 1987-90. Recipient Rsch. Career Devel. award NIH, 1983; Musclar Dystrophy Assn. grantee, 1979-81; Sr. Internat. fellow Fogarty Internat. Ctr. NIH, 1985. Fellow Am. Acad. Pediatrics (exec. com. sect. on nephrology, chair program subcom. 1998-2002, chmn. exec. com. sect. on nephrology 2002—), Am. Bd. Pediatrics; mem. Am. Pediatrics Soc., Soc. Pediatric Rsch., Am. Soc. Nephrology, Internat. Soc. Nephrology, Am. Soc. Pediatr, Nephrology, Internat. Soc. Pediatric Nephrology, Internat. Pediatric Nephrology Assn. (counsellor 1989-95). Office: MS Hershey Med Ctr PO Box 850 Hershey PA 17033-0850

WASSOM, JOHN CLARK, economics educator; b. Nov. 13, 1939; s. Samuel Jesse and Jane Deloras (Becknell) Wassom; m. Sharon Mae Ferneau, Sept. 2, 1961; 1 child Gregory Scott. BA in Econs., Grinell Coll., 1961; MA, Ind. U., 1963, PHD, 1970. Asst. prof. fin. U. Fla., Gainesville, 1966—71; assoc. prof. econs. Western Ky. U., Bowling Green, 1971—77, prof., 1977—, interim dean Coll. Bus. Adminstrn, 1987—, head dept. econs., 1978—, developer, coord. 2 yr. banking program, 1974—78. Rschr., contbr.: articles to profl. jours. Mem.: So. Econ. Assn., Am. Econ. Assn. Office: Western Ky U Econs Dept Big Red Way Bowling Green KY 42101 E-mail: john.wassom.@wku.edu.

WASSON, BARBARA HICKAM, music educator; b. Spencer, Ind., Feb. 12, 1918; Student, DePauw U., 1937-38; BA, Vassar Coll., 1939; MusM, Chgo. Mus. Coll., 1944; postgrad., Ind. U., 1962-63. Founder, co-dir. Wasson Piano Studios, Dayton, 1946—; instr. Cedarville (Ohio) Coll., 1970-72; adj. prof. Wright State U., 1973-78; asst. prof. U. Cin., 1982-87. Named Cert. Tchr. of Yr., Western Dist. of Ohio, 1998, 2001; recipient Family of Yr. award Ohio Fedn. Music Clubs, 2002. Mem. Ohio Music Tchrs. Assn. (pres. 1980-82, chmn. western dist. 1976-78), Dayton Music Club (pres. 1989-91), Mu Phi Epsilon (pres. Dayton alumnae chpt. 1986-88). Home: 5797 Paddington Rd Dayton OH 45459-1749 E-mail: wassonpno@aol.com.

WASSON, ELEANOR WALSH, volunteer; b. Salt Lake City, Feb. 28, 1908; d. John William and Mary Ann (Dalrymple) Walsh; m. George F. Wasson; children: E. Dianne Wright, Joan Smith. Student, Nat. Pk. Sem., Washington, 1926-27, U. Utah, 1927-28, UCLA, 1929-30. Coord. vol. svcs. UCLA Ctr. for Health Sciences. Founder, pres. Internat. Assn. Vol. Effort; pres. Am. Soc. Dirs. Vol. Svcs., Am. Hosp. Assn. Co-prodr.: (exhibit) Contiuum, the Imortality Principle. Mem. adv. com. status women UCLA Med. Ctr. Aux.; mem. com. Beyond War; bd. dirs. French Found. Alzheimer's Rsch., Am. Women Internat. Understanding; chmn. planning com. Our Common Future, Healing the Planet Symposium, 1989; bd. dirs. Santa Cruz Environ. Coun., U. Calif.-Santa Cruz Found., EarthSave Found.; exec. bd. Santa Cruz Environ. Coun., 2002. Recipient Merit award, Com. Adv. Sci. Tng., 1974, City of L.A. award for advancement status of women, 1974, Women's Achievement award, L.A. Times, 1975, Vol. Spirit award, King, Drew Med. Ctr. Aux., 1980, Disting. Svc. award, UCLA Alumni, award, Physicians Social Responsibility, 1989, Lifetime Achievement award, 2000, Eleanor's cir., Natural Step, 2002. Democrat. Episcopalian. Home: 660 Escalona Dr Santa Cruz CA 95060-2639 E-mail: elwwasson@aol.com.

WASSON, JAMES WALTER, aircraft electronics manufacturing company executive; b. Pitts., Dec. 9, 1951; s. George Fredrick and Dolores Helen (Wuerl) W.; m. Evelyn Fay Gonzales, Dec. 28, 1974; children: Robert, Brian. AST, Pitts. Inst. Aeronautics, 1972; BSET, Northrop U., Inglewood, Calif., 1981; MBA, U. Phoenix, Mesa, 1988, govt. contracts mgmt. cert., 1989. Avionics technician various cos., 1972-74; electronics prodn. mgr. Ostgaard Industries, Gardena, Calif., 1974-75; sr. avionics design engr. Allied Signal Garrett Airesearch Aviation Co., L.A., 1975-81; v.p. engring., co-founder Avionics Engring. Svcs., Inc., Tucson, 1980-81; sr. tech. specialist Northrop Aircraft Div., Hawthorne, Calif., 1981-84; prog. mgr. McDonnell Douglas Helicopter Co., Mesa, Ariz., 1984-93; exec. v.p., co-founder Leading Edge Technologies, Inc., 1991-95; mgr. bus. devel. McDonnell Douglas Helicopter Sys., 1993-95; dir. advanced tech. devel. Smiths Aerospace, Inc., Grand Rapids, Mich., 1995—. Adj. prof. ops. mgmt., contract mgmt., program mgmt., proposal devel., strategic mgmt., mktg., tech. mgmt., rsch. projects U. Phoenix, 1990—, chair Grad. Bus. and Mgmt. Coll., U. Phoenix, W. Mich. Campus, 2000—, acad. cabinet, 2001—; cons. in field. Author: Avionics Systems Operation and Maintenance, 1993, Business Opportunities in Artificial Intelligence, 1988; contbr. articles to profl. jours. Inventor in field. Com. chmn. industry adv. bd. Northrop U., 1981; chmn. bd. dirs., pres. Alta Mesa Community Assn., 1989; organizer Boy Scouts Am., Mesa, 1988. Named Engr. of Yr., Northrop U., 1980; recipient Disting. Alumnus award Pitts. Inst. Aeronautics, 1981, U. Phoenix, 1996; named to Hall of Fame, Career Colls. Assn., 1991. Mem. IEEE, NSPE, Soc. Automotive Engrs., Army Aviation Assn. (chpt. sr. v.p. 1988-91, treas. 1993-95), Nat. Def. Indsl. Assn., Assn. U.S. Army, Am. Helicopter Soc. (chmn. avionics com. 1990), Assn. Avionics Educators, Rotorcraft Industry Tech. Assn. (bd. dirs. 1998-99), Crystal Springs Country Club (fin. com. 2000-01). Republican. Roman Catholic. Avocations: flying, scuba diving, hiking, golf, camping. E-mail: wasson_jim@si.com.

WASSON, JEFFREY, music educator; b. Evanston, Ill., Aug. 24, 1948; s. Newton Oliver and Hilda Crowell Wasson. MusB, Northwestern U., 1970, MusM, 1973, PhD, 1987. Instr. music Northwestern U., Evanston, Ill., 1980-85; asst. prof. music Barat Coll., Lake Forest, 1986-92; dir. music St. Mary of the Angels, Chgo., 1992-97, Barat Coll., 1987—, assoc. prof. music, 1992-99, prof. music, 1999-2001, Barat Coll. DePaul U., 2001—. Vis. prof. music, Northwestern U., 1990, 93; bd. mem. New Music Chgo., 1987, 92-94, v.p., 1987-88, pres., 1988-92; NEH summer seminar participant, Brandeis U., 1995, Boston U., 2000; lectr. Yale U., U. Mich., Ann Arbor, U. Minn., Mich. State U., Loyola U. of Chgo., U. Nebr. Editor: A Commpendium of American Musicology, 2000; contbr. articles to profl. jours., chpts. to books. Summer seminar grantee NEH, U. Rochester (declined). Mem. NARAS, Am. Musicol. Soc., Am. Guild Organists, Internat. Musicol. Soc., Coll. Music Soc., Club Internationale, Phi Kappa Lambda. Episcopalian. Avocations: fine art collecting, Lionel trains. Office: Barat College 700 E Westleigh Rd Lake Forest IL 60045-3297

WASSON, JEROME M. social worker; b. Chewelah, Wash., Mar. 15, 1939; s. Merle Edward and Catherine Marie Wasson; m. Marilyn T. Wasson, June 10, 1961; children: Christopher, Timothy, Kevin, Gregory, John. BA in Sociology, Gonzaga U., 1961; MSW, U. Wash., 1969. LCSW Wash. Juvenile parole counselor II State of Wash., Bremerton, 1963—64; supr. Woodinville (Wash.) Group Home, 1964—67; instn. group life supr. Cascadia Juvenile Diagnostic Ctr., Tacoma, 1967—72; instn. asst. supt. Maple Lane Sch. Wash. State Dept. Social and Health Svcs., Centralia, 1972—76, instn. supt. Green Hill Sch. Chehalis, 1976—78, asst. dir. juvenile rehab. Olympia, 1978—80, dir. juvenile rehab., 1980—94; lic. ind. social worker Centralia, 1994—. Panel therapist Comprehensive Mental Health Ctr., Tacoma, 1969—72; mgmt. cons. Performance Resources, Inc., Austin, Tex., 1986—96. Mem. sch. bd. Centralia Sch. Dist., 1986—92. Recipient Successful Projects Initiative award, Am. Pub. Welfare Assn., 1989, cert. of appreciation, Wash. State Coun. on Crime and Delinquency, 1992, recognition, King County Coun., 1992. Mem.: NASW, Am. Coun. Social Workers, Wash. Coun. for Prevention of Child Abuse and Neglect, Rotary. Democrat. Roman Catholic. Avocations: golf, fishing, hunting, travel, sports. Home: 921 E Manzanita Dr Union WA 98592 Fax: 360-736-4867. E-mail: wasson@hctc.com.

WASSON, LILA ELIZABETH, educational consultant; b. Bradenton, Fla., Jan. 6, 1924; d. Lawyer and Margaret Jane (Moore) Jenkins; m. Robert Paul Wasson, June 14, 1951; children: Robert Paul, Sandra Wasson Brown, Kathy Elizabeth. BS, Fla. A&M U., 1945, MS, 1968. Tchr. sci. Union Acad., Bartow, Fla., 1946; tchr. phys. edn. Rosenwald High Sch., Panama City, 1946-51; subs. tchr. Sunflower and Wilson Village Schs., Anchorage, 1960-63; elem. tchr. Hanscom Primary Sch., Hanscom AFB, Mass., 1965-87; ednl. cons. J.B. Enterprises, Bedford, 1990-91. Master tchr. MA in Teaching program Harvard U., Cambridge, Mass., 1968-71 Author: The Classroom Teacher's Guide: For the Beginning Years and Beyond, 1998. Mem. AAUW (rec. sec. 1990-91), LWV, Mass. Ret. Tchrs. Assn. Democrat. Baptist. Avocations: travel, reading, teaching and promoting children's literature. Home: 26 Gould Rd Bedford MA 01730-1248

WASSON, ROY D. lawyer; b. Kingsville, Tex., Dec. 4, 1950; s. Virgil Dale and Magdalina Isabella (Flowers) W.; m. Carol Ann Fenello, May 23, 1987. BA, Ea. Ky. U., Richmond, 1975; JD with distinction, U. Ky., 1981. Bar: Fla. 1981, U.S Supreme Ct. 1987, U.S. Ct. Appeals (11th cir.) 1982, U.S. Dist. Ct. (so. dist.) Fla., 1981, U.S. Dist. Ct. (mid. dist.) 1983. Assoc. Kimbrell & Hamann, Miami, Fla., 1981-87; pvt. practice, 1987—. Mem. Assn. Trial Lawyers Am., Acad. Fla. Trial Lawyers (bd. dirs., past chmn. amicus curiae com., past chmn. appellate practice sect.), Fla. Bar (appellate rules com. 1988-97, chmn. appellate practice sect. 1994-97), Dade County Trial Lawyers Assn. (bd. dirs. 1992-), Dade County Bar Assn. (appellate cts. com., past vice-chmn.), Order of Coif. Democrat. Avocations: sailing, scuba diving. Office: 1320 S Dixie Hwy Miami FL 33146-2926

WASSON-SHAW, CAROL R. music teacher; b. Dayton, Ohio, Feb. 8, 1951; d. Audley Jackson and Barbara (Hickam) Wasson; m. Stephen D. Shaw, Feb. 21, 1981 (div. Apr. 1998); children: Tiffany Elise, Tia Nicole. BMusic in Piano Performance, Wright State U., Fairborn, Ohio, 1978. Pvt. tchr. piano, 1965—; pvt. tchr. violin and viola, 1980—; owner, mentor to music tchrs. Shaw's Music Ctr., Centerville, Ohio, 1993—. Lectr., tcht. piano to preschoolers. Chmn. jr. philharm. Dayton Philharm. Women's Assn., 1979-80; chmn. fundraiser South Dayton Montessori, Kettering, Ohio, 1987-88. Mem. Nat. Guild Piano Tchrs. (chmn. Dayton-Wasson Audition Ctr. 1998—), Music Tchrs. Nat. Assn., Dayton Music Club (chmn. judges Dist. IIIB Jr. Festival 1994—, co-chmn. 1999-2002, chmn. 2001—), Mu Phi Epsilon, Centerville Noon Optimists. Office: Shaw's Music Ctr 35 Marco Ln Centerville OH 45458-3818

WASTBERG, OLLE M. diplomat; b. Stockholm, May 6, 1945; s. Erik and Greta (Hirsch) W.; m. Inger Claesson, Feb. 21, 1968; children: David, Elias. BA, U. Stockholm, 1972. Tchr. polit. sci. U. Stockholm, 1967-68; journalist polit. dept. Expressen, 1968-71; editor-in-chief, 1994-95; rsch. fellow Bus. and Soc. Rsch. Ctr., 1971-76; pres. Aktieframjandet, 1976-82; mem. Parliament, 1976-82; pres. Swedish Newspaper Promotion Assn., 1983-91; under-sec. of state for fin. affairs Ministry of Fin., Stockholm, 1991-93; pres. bd. Nordic Investment Bank, 1992-94, Swedish Broadcasting Corp., 1996-99; consul gen. for Sweden in N.Y., 1999—. Dir. Stockholm Stock Exchange, 1977-82, 88-92;group of 10 deputies IMF, 1991-93; Swedish del. meeting of ministries of fin., 1992; mem. govt. coms. on S. Africa consumer politics and stock market; pres. Bertil Ohlin Inst., 1996-2000. Author books on African problems, immigration politics and econ. topics; contbr. articles to profl. jours. Polit. sec. Liberal Youth Sweden, 1966, v.p., 1996-71; bd. Liberal Party, 1972-93, 97-2000, pres. exec. com., 1982-83; bd. dirs. Friends of Hebrew U. of Jerusalem. Recipient Gold medal Swedish Mktg. Group, 1982. Home: 600 Park Ave New York NY 10021-7010 Office: Consolate Gen of Sweden One Dag Hammarskjold Plz 885 2d Ave 45th Fl New York NY 10017-2201 E-mail: olle@wastberg.nu.

WASTERLAIN, CLAUDE GUY, neurologist; b. Courcelles, Belgium, Apr. 15, 1935; s. Desire and Simone (De Taeye) W.; m. Anne Marguerite Thomsin, Feb. 28, 1967; 1 child, Jean Michel. Cand. Sci., U. Liege, 1957, MD, 1961; LS in Molecular Biology, U. Brussels, 1969. Resident Cornell U. Med. Coll., N.Y.C., 1964-67, instr. neurology, 1969-70, asst. prof., 1970-75, assoc. prof., 1975-76, UCLA Sch. Medicine, 1976-79, prof., 1979—, vice chair dept. neurology, 1976—; chief neurology svc. VA Med. Ctr., Sepulveda, Calif., 1976—; cons. neurologist Olive View Med. Ctr., Sylmar, 1976—. Attending neurologist UCLA Ctr. Health Scis., 1976—; chief neurology Greater L.A. VA Health Care System, 1998—. Author, editor: Status Epilepticus, 1984, Neonatal Seizures, 1990, Molecular Neurobiology and Epilepsy, 1992, Progressive Nature of Epileptogenesis, 1996; contbr. articles to med. jours. William Evans fellow, U. Auckland, New Zealand, 1984; recipient N.Y. Neurol. Soc. Young Investigator award, 1965, Rsch. Career Devel. award NIH, 1973-76, Worldwide AES award, 1992, Golden Hammer Teaching award, 1996. Fellow Am. Acad. Neurology; mem. Am. Neurol. Assn., Am. Soc. Neurochemsitry (coun. mem. 1991-97), Internat. Neurochemistry, Am. Epilepsy Soc., Royal Soc. Medicine . Avocations: tennis, skiing, jazz, theatre. Office: West LA VA Med Ctr 11301 Wilshire Blvd Los Angeles CA 90073 Fax: 818-895-5801.

WATABE, NORIMITSU, biology and marine science educator; b. Kure, Hiroshima, Japan, Nov. 29, 1922; came to U.S., 1957; s. Isamu and Matsuko (Takamatsu) W.; m. Sakuko Kobayashi, Dec. 12, 1952; children: Shoichi, Sachiko. BS, 1st Nat. High Sch., Tokyo, 1945; MS, Tohoku U., Sendai, Japan, 1948, DSc, 1960. Rsch. investigator Fuji Pearl Co., Mie-ken, Japan, 1948-52; instr. Prefect U. Mie, Tsu, Mie-ken, 1952-55, asst. prof., 1955-59; rsch. assoc. Duke U., Durham, N.C., 1957-70; assoc. prof. U. S.C., Columbia, 1970-72, prof. biology and marine sci., 1972-93, disting. prof., 1993-94, disting. prof. emeritus, 1994—. Cons. Ford Found., 1968; vis. prof. U. Bonn, Germany, 1976-77; dir. Electron Microscipy Ctr., 19770-95; cons. in field. Author: Studies on Pearls, 1959; editor: Mechanisms of Mineralization, 1976, Mechanisms of Biomineralization, 1980, Hard Tissue Mineralization and Demineralization, 1991; contbr. numerous sci. articles to profl. jours. Recipient Pearl Rsch. award Elmer W. Ellsworth, 1952, alexander Von Humboldt award Govt. of Germany, Russel award U. S.C., 1981; grantee NIH, 1971-76, NSF, 1973-95. Fellow AAAS, Royal Micros. Soc., Gt. Britain; mem. Am. Micros. Soc. (rev. bd.), Am. Malacological Union (rev. bd.), Am. Soc. Zoologists, Micros. Soc. Am. Avocations: music, piano playing. Home: 3510 Greenway Dr Columbia SC 29206-3416 Office: Dept Biol Sci Univ S Carolina Columbia SC 29208-0001

WATANABE, AUGUST MASARU, physician, scientist, medical educator, corporate executive; b. Portland, Oreg., Aug. 17, 1941; s. Frank H. and Mary Y. W.; m. Margaret Whildin Reese, Mar. 14, 1964; children: Nan Reiko, Todd Franklin, Scott Masaru. BS, Wheaton (Ill.) Coll., 1963; MD, Ind. U., 1967. Diplomate Am. Bd. Internal Medicine. Intern Ind. U. Med. Center, Indpls., 1967-68, resident, 1968-69, 71-72, fellow in cardiology, 1972-74; clin. asso. NIH, 1969-71; clin. instr. medicine Georgetown U. Med. Sch., Washington, 1970-71; mem. faculty Ind. U. Sch. Medicine, Indpls., 1972—, prof. medicine and pharmacology, 1978—, chmn. dept. medicine, 1983-90; dir. Regenstrief Inst. for Health Care Ind. U. Sch. of Medicine, 1984-90; from v.p. to group v.p. rsch. labs. Eli Lilly & Co., 1990-94, v.p., pres. labs, 1994-95; exec. v.p. sci. and tech. Eli Lilly and Co., 1996—, also bd. dirs., 1994—; dir. Guidant Corp. Mem. pharmacology study sect. NIH, 1979-81, chmn., 1981-83; mem. cardiovasc.-renal adv. com. FDA, 1982-85; mem. com. A, Nat. Heart, Lung and Blood Inst., 1984-88, chmn., 1986-88; cons. to fed. govt. and industry. Contbr. articles to profl. jours.; editorial bds. sci. jours. Dir. Ind. U. Found., 1989—, Indpls. Symphony Orch., 1994—, Regenstrief Found., 1995—, Riley Meml. Assn. NIH grantee, 1972-92. Fellow ACP, Am. Coll. Cardiology, Am. Heart Assn. (councils on clin. cardiology and circulation, research rev. com. Ind. affiliate 1978-82, research and adv. com. North Central region 1978-82, adv. com. cardiovascular drugs 1976-79, chmn. com. 1979-81, chmn. program com. council on basic sci. 1982-84, chmn. com. on sci. sessions programs 1985-88, bd. dirs. 1985-88), Am. Coll. Cardiology (govt. relations com. 1979-81, trustee 1982-87); mem. Am. Fedn. Clin. Research (councilor Midwest sect. 1976-77, chmn.-elect Midwest sect. 1977-78, chmn. sect. 1978-79, chmn. sect. nominating com. 1979-80), Am. Soc. Clin. Investigation, Am. Soc. Clin. Pharmacology and Therapeutics, Am. Soc. Pharmacology and Exptl. Therapeutics (exec. com. div. clin. pharmacology 1978-81), Cardiac Muscle Soc., Central Soc. Clin. Research (councillor 1983-86, pres.-elect 1989, pres. 1990), Internat. Soc. Heart Research, Assn. Am. Physicians, Assn. Profs. of Medicine, Sigma Xi. Office: Eli Lilly & Co Drop Code 1209 Lilly Corp Ctr Indianapolis IN 46285-0001

WATANABE, KYOICHI A(LOYSIUS), chemist, researcher, pharmacology educator; b. Amagasaki, Hyogo, Japan, Feb. 28, 1935; s. Yujiro Paul and Yoshiko Francisca (Hashimoto) W.; m. Krystyna Lesiak; children: Kanna, Kay, Kenneth, Kim, Kelly, Katherine. BA, Hokkaido U., 1958, PhD, 1963. Lectr. Sophia U., Tokyo, 1963; rsch. assoc. Sloan-Kettering Inst., N.Y.C., 1963-66, assoc., 1968-72, 1972-81, prof., 1981-95; rsch. fellow U. Alta., Edmonton, Can., 1966-68; assoc. prof. Cornell U. Med. Coll., N.Y.C., 1972-81, prof. pharmacology, 1981-98; dir. organic chemistry Codon Pharm., Inc., Gaithersburg, Md., 1996-98; v.p. R&D Pharmasset Inc., Tucker, Ga., 1998—. Study sect. NIH, Washington, 1981-84. Mem. Polish Chem. Soc. (hon.), Russian Acad. Sci. (bd. sci. cons. Engelhardt Inst. Molecular Biology 1994-97). Achievements include rsch. in total synthesis of nucleoside antibiotics, novel heterocycle ring transformation, C-nucleoside chemistry, antiviral and anticancer nucleosides, intercalating agents, modified oligonucleotides, triplex DNA for gene repair.

WATANABE, MAMORU, former university dean, physician, researcher; b. Vancouver, B.C., Can., Mar. 15, 1933; s. Takazo and Nao (Suginobu) W.; m. Marie Katie Bryndzak, June 1, 1974; 1 child, David. MD, McGill U., 1957, PhD, 1963. Intern Royal Victoria Hosp., Montreal, 1957—58, resident in medicine, 1958—63; prof. medicine U. Alta., Edmonton, 1967—74, U. Calgary, 1974—97, head internal medicine, 1974—76, assoc. dean edn., 1976—80, assoc. dean research, 1980—81, acting dean medicine, 1981—82, dean faculty medicine, 1982—92, prof. emeritus, 1997—. Fellow Royal Coll. Physicians and Surgeons (Can.); mem. Endocrine Soc., Can. soc. Clin. Investigation, Can. Soc. Endocrinology and Metabolism, Can. Hypertension Soc. Home: 162 Pumpridge Place SW Calgary AB Canada T2V 5E6 Office: U Calgary 3330 Hospital Dr NW Calgary AB Canada T2N 1N4 E-mail: watanabe@ucalgary.ca.

WATANABE, MARK DAVID, pharmacist, educator; b. Santa Monica, Calif., Dec. 7, 1955; s. Jack Shigeru and Rose Nobuko (Iida) W. BA in Chemistry, U. Calif., Irvine, 1977, BS in Biol. Sci., 1978; PharmD, U. Calif., San Francisco, 1982, PhD in Pharm. Chemistry, 1990. Lic. pharmacist Calif., Oreg. Pharmacy intern various locations, San Francisco, 1979-82; pharmacist Kaiser Permanente, 1981-87; clin. scis. rsch. fellow in psychiat. pharmacy U. Tex., Austin, 1987-89; clin. asst. prof. pharmacy practice U. Ill., Chgo., 1989-98. Rsch. asst. U. Calif., San Francisco, 1980-87; clin. pharmacy cons. Ill. Dept. Mental Health & Devel. Disabilities, 1994-98; med. sci. mgr. Bristol-Myers Squibb, 1998-99; clin. pharmacy specialist, Alameda Co., Calif., 1999—; asst. cli. prof. clin. pharmacy, U. Calif., San Francisco, 1999—. Regents scholar U. Calif., San Francisco, 1979-82; recipient Excellence in Teaching award Long Found., San Francisco, 1984. Mem.: Am. Pharm. Assn., Am. Soc. Health-Sys. Pharmacists, Am. Coll. Clin. Pharmacy, Mensa, Rho Chi. Unitarian Universalist. Avocations: individual and fitness sports, reading, travel, music. Home: PO Box 193162 San Francisco CA 94119-3162 Office: Alameda County BHCS 2000 Embarcadero Ste 400 Oakland CA 94606-5300

WATANABE, PAUL YASHIHIKO, political scientist, educator; b. Murray, Utah, Mar. 14, 1951; s. Hikomune and Ida (Hiraga) W.; m. Gloria Gustafson, Aug. 25, 1975; children: Benjamin Gustafson, Joanna Stahr. BS, U. Utah, 1972; MA, Harvard U., 1975, PhD, 1980. Asst. prof. dept. polit. sci. U. Mass., Boston, 1980-85, assoc. prof., 1985—, chair dept. polit. sci., 1985-90, dir. hons. program, 1990-93, co-dir. inst. Asian Am. studies, 1993—, co-dir., acting dir. pub. policiy PhD program, 1995-96. Author: Ethnic Groups, Congress and American Foreign Policy, 1984. Mem. South Shore area bd. Dept. Social Svc. Com. Mass., Quincy, 1983-89; bd. Overseers Harvard Cmty. Health Plan, Brookline, Mass., 1985-91; mem. acad. adv. com. John. F. Kennedy Libr., Boston, 1991—; bd. dirs. Mass. Immigrant Refugee Advocacy Coalition, Boston, 1992—, Asian Pacific Am. Agenda Coalition, Boston, 1995—; mem. nat. acad. bd. Asian Am. Policy Rev., Cambridge, 1994—. Mem. Phi Beta Kappa. Home: 65 Torrey St South Weymouth MA 02190-2533 Office: Inst Asian Am Studies U Mass 100 Morrissey Blvd Boston MA 02125-3300 E-mail: paul.watanabe@umb.edu.

WATANABE, ROY NOBORU, lawyer; b. Honolulu, July 23, 1947; s. Tadao I. and Clara Y. W. AB, Columbia Coll., 1969; JD, Columbia U., 1973. Bar: N.Y. 1974, U.S. Dist. Ct. (so. and ea. dists.) N.Y. 1976, U.S. Ct. Appeals (2d cir.) 1976. Honors program atty. Office of Labor Rels., Office of Mayor, N.Y.C., 1973-76; assoc. Frankle & Greenwald, 1976, Cohn, Glickstein, Lurie, Ostrin, Lubell & Lubell, N.Y.C., 1976-79; ptnr. Cohn, Glickstein & Lurie (formerly Cohn, Glickstein, Lurie, Ostrin, Lubell & Lubell, 1979-88, Spivak, Lipton, Watanabe, Spivak & Moss, 1989—. Guest lectr. labor law Boston Coll., 1982, Union U., 1983, 85, Mercer U., 1997—2001, NYU Law Sch., 1998; mem. faculty Practicing Law Inst., N.Y.C., 1987; panelist, lectr. regional conf. NY State Bar Assn. and NLRB, N.Y.C., 1986; mem. adv. bd. Ctr. for Labor and Employment Law, NYU Sch. Law, 2000—; author, commentator 50th ann. labor conf. NYU, 1997. Contbg. author: NLRA Law and Practice, 1991. Cooperating atty. Asian Am. Legal Def. & Edn. Fund., N.Y.C., 1982—; mem. bd. dirs. lawyers coordinating com. AFL-CIO, 2000—. Nat. Def. Fgn. Language fellow, Columbia U., 1967. Mem. Assn. of Bar of City of N.Y. (labor and employment law com. 1980-83, 86-89, legal and edn. and admission to bar com. 1984-85), N.Y. State Bar Assn. (exec. com., co-chair practice before N.Y. State Labor Rels. Bd. and Nat. Labor Rels. Bd. com. 1989-93, labor arbitration com. 1983—, entertainment, arts and sports law sect. 1989—). Office: Spivak Lipton Et Al 1700 Broadway Fl 21 New York NY 10019-5905

WATANABE, SATOSHI PATTEN, economist, researcher; b. Koriyama, Fukushima, Japan, Oct. 19, 1966; s. Keiki Watanabe, Mieko Watanabe; m. Nicole Michelle Patten; children: Daichi Joseph. BA, cert. in gerontology, Weber State U., 1990; MA in Econ., Columbia U., 1993, MEd, 1997, MA in Stats., 1999, MPhil, PhD, Columbia U., 2000. Lectr. Manhattan Coll., Riverdale, NY, 1998; stat. data analyst City of N.Y., 1998—99; rsch. assoc. Am. Inst. Rsch., Arlington, Va., 1999—2000, rsch. scientist, 2000—01, sr. rsch. scientist, 2001—. Bd. dirs. Policy Rsch. and Analysis Network for Japan, Washington, 1999—; cons. World Bank, Washington, 2000—01. Contbr. articles. Mem.: Soc. Labor Economists, Am. Econ. Assn., Phi Kappa Phi. Unitarian Universalist. Avocations: travel, guitar, marathons. Office: Am Inst for Rsch 1815 N Fort Myer Dr Arlington VA 22209-1805 Office Fax: 703-527-4661. Personal E-mail: sw259@columbia.edu.

WATANABE, WADE OSAMU, marine biologist; b. Honolulu, Sept. 19, 1951; s. Charles Shujiro and Clara Mieko (Hasegawa) W.; m. Colleen Aiko Sasaki, June 26, 1976; children: Skye, Laine, Landon. BS in Zoology, Oreg. State U., 1973; MS in Zoology, U. Hawaii, 1975, PhD in Zoology, 1982. Lab. technician Fish Physiology Lab., Oceanic Inst., Hawaii, 1976-77, rsch. asst., 1977-81; marine biologist Internat. Ctr. for Living Aquatic Resources Mgmt., Manila, Philippines, 1982-84; chief scientist Caribbean Marine Rsch. Ctr., Vero Beach, Fla., 1986-95, Sea Change Found., Vero Beach, 1996-97; assoc. rsch. scientist U. N.C., Wilmington, 1997-99, rsch. scientist, assoc. prof., 1999—, rsch. prof., 2000—. Adj. grad. faculty mem. Dept. Biol. Scis., Fla. Inst. Tech., 1991-97; cons. in fie ld; lectr. in field; grant reviewer NSF, Nat. Coastal Resources Rsch. and Devel. Inst., Nat. Sea Grant Coll. Program, Nat. Marine Fisheries Svc., USDA. Co-editor: Aquaculture of the Milkfish, 1986; assoc. editor: Journal World Aquaculture Society; reviewer Aquaculture Jour., Jour. World Aquaculture Soc., Aquaculture Engrng., Can. Jour. Zoology, Jour. Fish Biology, Aquatic Living Resources, Jour. Applied Aquaculture, Asian Fisheries Soc., Gulf and Caribbean Fisheries Inst., Jour. Aquaculture in the Tropics; contbr. articles to profl. jours. Grad. rsch. assistantship Hawaii Inst. Marine Biology, 1975; Jessie Smith Noyes Found. pre-doctoral fellow, 1977-81, Rockfeller Found. postdoctoral rsch. fellow, 1982-84; grantee Caribbean Marine Rsch. Ctr., 1987-91, 92, Oceanic Inst. Hawaii, 1993, 94, George F. Baker Trust, 1993, 94, 95, Marine Scis. and Tech. Ctr./U. Conn., 1995, 96, N.C. Sea Grant Coll. Program, 1998, William Kenan Found., 1999, U.S. Dept. Agr. Cooperative State Rsch. Edn. Extensive Svc., 1998-99, S.E. Regional Agr. Ctr., 1999. Mem. Am. Tilapia Assn. (bd. dirs. 1991-92), Fla. Foodfish, Gamefish and Aquatic Bait Farmers Assn. (bd. dirs. 1992), Internat. Ctr. for Living Aquatic Resources Mgmt. (affiliate scientist 1984-88), World Aquaculture Soc. (assoc. editor Jour World Aquaculture Soc.), Asian Fisheries Soc., Caribbean Aquaculture Assn. (bd. dirs. 1993-96), Fla. Aquaculture Assn., Network of Tropical Aquaculture Scientists., Wrightsville Beach Longboard Assn. Avocation: youth baseball coach. Home: 5128 Treybrooke Dr Wilmington NC 28409-2738 Office: U NC at Wilmington Ctr Marine Sci 7205 Wrightsville Ave Wilmington NC 28403-7224 E-mail: watanabew@uncwil.edu.

WATANABE, YOICHI, nuclear engineer, researcher; b. Kakuda, Miyagi, Japan, June 1, 1954; came to U.S., 1980; s. Etsuro and Rikiko (Haneda) W.; m. Mariko Tsutsumi, May 8, 1962; 1 child, Shin. BS, U. Tokyo, 1978; MS, U. Tsukuba, 1980, U. Wis., 1982, PhD, 1984. Rsch. assoc. U. Wis., 1984-86; assoc. devel. engr. U. Calif., L.A., 1987-89; rsch. scientist U. Fla., Gainesville, 1989-93; fellow Meml. Sloan-Kettering Cancer Ctr., N.Y.C., 1994—. Vis. researcher Japan Atomic Energy Rsch. Inst., 1987; industry cons., 1989—. Mem. IEEE, AAAS, Am. Assn. of Physicists in Medicine, Am. Nuclear Soc., Soc. for Indsl. and Applied Math, Sigma Xi. Buddism. Achievements include research on nuclear fission and fusion systems for terrestrial and space applications, nonequilibrium statistical mechanics. Office: MSKCC Dept Med Physics 1275 York Ave Dept Med New York NY 10021-6007

WATCHORN, WILLIAM ERNEST, venture capitalist; b. Toronto, Ont., Can., Aug. 8, 1943; s. Roy Elgin and Josephine (Swyrida) W.; m. Maureen Emmett, Dec. 28, 1967; 1 child, Meghan. Chartered Acct., Toronto, 1967. Mgr. fin. planning Found. Group of Cos., Toronto, 1968-70; cons. Regional Master Planning Study, Malaysia, 1970-72; controller Selkirk Holdings, Ltd., Toronto, 1972-75; corp. contr. Torstar Corp., 1975-78; v.p. fin. Canwest Capital Corp., Winnipeg, Man., 1978-82; exec. v.p. Kaiser Resources Ltd., Vancouver, B.C., 1982; sr. v.p., CFO, Fed. Industries Ltd., Winnipeg, 1982-88; pres., CEO, Fed. Industries Indsl. Group, 1989-91, Ensis Corp., Inc., Winnipeg, 1991-97; founder, pres., CEO, Ensis Growth Fund Inc., Ensis Mgmt. Inc., 1997—. Bd. dirs. Ensis Mgmt. Inc., Ensis Growth Fund Inc., Winnipeg Airports Authority Inc. Bd. dirs. C.D. Howe Inst., Toronto; dir. Can. Stds. Assn. (CSA); past chmn. Assocs.; faculty mgmt. U. Manitoba. Mem. Can. Inst. Chartered Accts., Fellowship Inst. of Chartered Accts., Man. Inst., Chartered Accts., Ont. Inst. Chartered Accts., Winter Club, St. Charles Country Club. Avocations: squash, golf, tennis. Home: 6453 Southboine Dr Winnipeg MB Canada R3R 0B7 Office: Ensis Growth Fund Inc 200 Graham Ave Ste 1120 Winnipeg MB Canada R3C 4L5

WATERBURY, JACKSON DEWITT, retired marketing executive; b. Evanston, Ill., Feb. 4, 1937; s. Jackson D. and Eleanor (Barrows) W.; m. Suzanne Butler, Aug. 27, 1958 (div. Jan. 1970); children: JAckson D. III, Arthur Barrows; m. Lynn Hardin, Mar. 17, 1971 (div. July 1984); 1 child, Timothy Bradford; m. Carolyn Jenkins, Sept. 20, 1986; children: Kathryn Britt, Daniel Jenkins. AB, Brown U., 1959. Acct. exec. D'Arcy Advt. Co., St. Louis, 1958-63, Batz-Hodgson-Neuwohner, Inc., St. Louis, 1963-66; exec. v.p., sec. Lynch, Philips & Waterbury, Inc., 1966-68; pres. Jackson Waterbury & Co., 1968-73; v.p., ptnr. Vinyard & Lee & Ptnrs., 1973-74; pres. Waterbury, Inc., 1975-80, Bright Ideas, Inc., St. Louis, 1977-80; v.p., group supr. Batz-Hodgson-Neuwoehner, 1980-81; sr. v.p. Fawcett McDermott Cavanagh, Honolulu, 1981-82; prin. Waterbury Cons., 1982-88; sr. v.p. planning & rsch. Kenrick Advt., Inc., St. Louis, 1984-86; chmn. Pocket Guide Publs., Inc., Denver, 1986-97, Mountain Sports Sales, Inc., Denver, 1986-89; v.p., group supr. Kerlick Switzer & Johnson, Inc., St. Louis, 1987-88; chmn., CEO Keystone Group, 1988-92; v.p. mktg. Cambridge Engring., Chesterfield, Mo., 1997-2000; ret., 2000. Chmn. publicity U.S. Golf assn. Open Championship, 1964. Bd. dirs. Alice Blake Realtors, 1971-79, Children's Christmas Found., 1966-79; football coach Mo. High Sch. All-Stars, 1966-67, St. Louis U., 1968-70; vice chmn. bd. dirs. Hawaii Soccer Assn., 1981-83. Mem. Ducks Unltd., St. Louis Advt. Producers Assn. (steering com., neogtiating com. 1977-80), Beta Theta Pi. Episcopalian. Home: 118 N Bemiston Ave Saint Louis MO 63105-3811

WATERBURY, LARRY, physician, educator; b. Ft. Worth, May 30, 1937; m. Marcia Winkelman, 1968. Student, Princeton U., 1955-57, S.W. Tex. Coll., 1957-58; MD, U. Tex., Galveston, 1962. Diplomate Am. Bd. Internal Medicine, Am. Bd. Hematology, Am. Bd. Oncology. Intern U. Okla. Hosps., Oklahoma City, 1962-63; resident internal medicine parkland Meml. Hosp., Dallas, 1965-67; instr. dpet. Medicine U. Tex., 1969-70; from instr. to assoc. prof. sch. medicine Johns Hopskins U., Balt., 1970-82, assoc. prof. medicine, 1982—, assoc. prof. oncology, 1986—. Asst. chief physician Balt. City Hosps., 1970—, dir. blood bank, 1970-73; chief divsn. hematology, oncology Francis Scott Key Med. Ctr., Balt., 1978—; mem. adv. com. Johns Hopkins Home Health Care Hospice, 1995—. Author: Hematology for the House Officer, 1981, 4th edit., 1996, (chpt.) Clinical Pathology, 1973, Complications of Neoplastic Disorders, 1979, Guide to Hematologic Disorders, 1980; co-author: (chpt.) Clinical Anesthesia, Vol. 3, 1968; author, co-author: (chpt.) Principles and Practice of Medicine, 19th edit., 1976, Principles of Ambulatory Medicine, 3d edit., 1991; contbr. articles to profl. jours. With U.S. Army Spl. Forces, 1963-65, Vietnam. Mem. Am. Soc. Hematology, Am. Soc. Clin. Oncology. Home: 5713 Visitation Way Baltimore MD 21210-1348 Office: Johns Hopkins Bayview Med Ctr Bayview Campus Divsn Hematology Oncology 4940 Eastern Ave Baltimore MD 21224-2735 E-mail: lawaterbur@aol.com.

WATERER, BONNIE CLAUSING, retired high school educator; b. Toledo, Sept. 25, 1940; d. Kermit Henry and Helen Ethel (Waggoner) Clausing; m. Louis P. Waterer, June 17, 1961; children: Ryan, Reid. BS in Home Econs. Edn., Ohio State U., 1962; MA in Home Econs. Edn., San Jose State U., 1966. Cert. family and consumer scis. Tchr. James Lick H.S., San Jose, 1963-67, 1973-76; adult edn. instr. Met. Adult Edn. Program, 1968-75; home econs. instr. Independence H.S., 1976-99, home econs. dept. chair, 1976-80; home econs. coord. East Side Union H.S. Dist., 1980-99, coord. coll. and career resource ctrs., 1995-99. Child care occupations instr. Ctrl. County Occupl. Ctr., San Jose, 1989-99; child devel. instr. Evergreen Valley Coll., San Jose, 1995 Bd. dirs. NAMI Yavapai County, Ariz., 2001-02; docent Highlands Ctr. for Natural History, 2000-. Mem.: AAUW, Home Econs. Tchrs. Assn. Calif. (pres. 1989—91, Outstanding Tchr. award 1987), Calif. Assn. Family and Consumer Sci. (Tchr. of Yr. award 1994), Am. Assn. Family and Consumer Sci., Phi Upsilon Omicron, Delta Kappa Gamma, Omicron Nu. Democrat. Methodist. Avocations: travel, computing, cooking, sewing. Home: 1052 Vantage Pt Cir Prescott AZ 86301 E-mail: bh2oer@aol.com.

WATERFORD, GWEN ANTIONETTE, poet; b. Indpls., May 24, 1963; d. Charlie (Junior) and Omega Waterford. Poet, songwriter.: Recipient Copyright award, U.S. Copyright, 1997, Editor's Choice award, Nat. Libr. Poetry, 1997.

WATERHOUSE, RACHEL L. lawyer; b. Orlando, Fla., Oct. 17, 1962; d. Linton S. and Louise J. Waterhouse; m. James B. Selleh; 1 child, Sarah Louise. BA, U. S.C., 1984; JD cum laude, Stetson U., 1988. Bar: Fla. 1988, Tenn. 1989, U.S. Dist. Ct. (mid. dist.) Tenn. 1989, U.S. Dist. Ct. (we. dist.) Tenn. 1994, U.S. Ct. Appeals (6th cir.) 1994, U.S. Supreme Ct. 1994, U.S. Dist. Ct. (ea. dist.) Tenn. 1995. Jud. law clk. hon. Thomas A. Higgins U.S. Dist. Ct., Nashville, 1989-91; atty. King & Ballow, 1991-94; asst. atty. gen. Tenn. Atty. Gens. Office, 1994-95; asst. U.S. atty. U.S. Dept. Justice, 1995—. Co-author: Americans With Disabilities Act, 1994; notes editor Stetson Law Rev., 1987. Stephen ministry Episcopal Ch., Nashville, 1989-91; bd. dirs. Focus, Nashville, 1991-94. Named to Outstanding Young Women of Am., 1988. Mem. ABA, Fla. Bar Assn., Nashville Bar Assn. (various coms.), Fed. Bar Assn. (pres.-elect Nashville chpt.), Lawyers Assn. for Women (various coms.). Avocations: running, reading, hiking. Office: US Attys Office Dept Justice 110 9th Ave S Ste A961 Nashville TN 37203-3870

WATERHOUSE, RICHARD VALENTINE, retired science educator, consultant; b. London, England, Feb. 28, 1924; s. Percival Waterhouse and Josephine Margaret Williams; m. Janet Marie Becker, June 20, 2001; m. Jean Sylvia Tooke, Jan. 6, 1951 (div. Apr. 24, 1981); children: Sarah J, Jennifer A, Elizabeth J, Geoffrey V. BA, Oxford U., Oxford, England, 1945, MA, 1949, DSc, 1984. Physicist Nat. Bur. of Standards, Washington, 1951—59; physics prof. Am. U., 1960—85; consultant-usn David Taylor Model Basion, Corderock, Md., 1960—86. Vis. prof. U. California-Berkeley, Berkeley, Calif.,

1968—70, U., U. Delft, Netherlands, 1979—80. Contbr. articles to profl. jour. Recipient Sabine Medal, Acoustical Soc. of Am., 1990. Home: 2190 Washington St #906 San Francisco CA 94109 Personal E-mail: odino@earthlink.net.

WATERHOUSE, STEPHEN LEE, management consultant; b. Sanford, Maine, Mar. 31, 1943; s. James William and Evelyn Anita Waterhouse; m. Linda S. Lenge, July 3, 1967; children: Melinda Harwood, James Stephen. AB in Chemistry, Dartmouth Coll., 1965, MBA in Mktg., 1967. Mfg. exec. Procter and Gamble, Boston, Chgo., N.Y.C., 1967-73; cons. to pres. Avon Products, N.Y.C., 1973-75; head European ops. London, 1976-77; sr. exec. officer jewelry div. N.Y.C., 1978-80; v.p. European ops. Revlon, Paris, 1981-82; v.p. U.S. div. Thomas Tilling Ltd., N.Y.C. and London, 1983; chmn., sr. ptnr. Hanover Ptnrs. Ltd., N.Y.C., London, Zurich and Lugano, Switzerland, 1983—; ptnr. Occom Ptnrs. LLC, Boston, 1995—. Alumni coun. mem. Dartmouth Coll., Hanover, N.H., 1979-82, pres. class 1975-80; pres. Dartmouth Coll. Treas. Assn., 1993-95; trustee Hartwick Coll., Oneonta, N.Y., 1995—; bd. dirs. Internat. Festival Statue of Liberty Celebration, N.Y.C., 1986-87. With USAR, 1967-73. Recipient Dartmouth Alumni award, 1992. Mem. Global Exec. Search Profl. Assn., U.K. Inst. Dirs., Friends of Templeton Coll., Oxford U., London Sch. Econs. Club., Yale Club, London Capital Club. Avocations: skiing, travel. Office: 50 E 42nd St Ste 507 New York NY 10017-5405

WATERHOUSE, TRENTON DEAN, marketing director; b. Phoenix, Oct. 28, 1968; s. Larry D. and Judith A. (Timmer) W. BSBA, Georgetown U., 1990. Mktg. asst. NYNEX, Washington, 1987-90, syst. engr., 1990-92, Cabletron Sys., Washington, 1992-93; program mktg. mgr. Cabletron Systems Federal, Rochester, N.H., 1993-97, program mktg. dir., 1997-2000; dir. mktg. Aprisma, Portsmouth, NH, 2000—. Contbr. articles to profl. jours. Avocations: reading, fine arts, plays, Broadway shows, dining. Office: Aprisma 273 Corporate Dr Portsmouth NH 03801 E-mail: trent@aprisma.com.

WATERMAN, CHARLES ALBERT, actor, director, retired sales executive; b. New Rochelle, N.Y., June 15, 1935; s. Burleigh R. and Mabel O. (Thompson) W. BS in Speech, Northwestern U., 1957. Sales rep. The Wall St. Jour., N.Y.C., 1964-66, McCalls Mag., N.Y.C., 1966-67, Holiday Mag., N.Y.C., 1967-69, Time Mag., N.Y.C., 1969-71, Travel & Leisure Mag., N.Y.C., 1971-73; sales mgr. Gambler's World Mag., 1973-74; travel mgr. Bon Apetit Mag., 1974-76. Author: The Snappy Poems; dir. Gallery Theatre Round Top Ctr. for the Arts, Damariscotta, Maine, 1991-94; dir. Lincoln County Cmty. Theatre and Orch., Damariscotta, 1997—. Capt. USMCR, 1957-60. Mem. Am. Fedn. Radio and TV Artists, SAG (N.Y.C., L.A.). Home: 22 River Rd Apt A Newcastle ME 04553

WATERMAN, DIANNE CORRINE, artist, educator, writer; b. Bklyn., Feb. 9, 1949; d. Beverly D. and Bernice Iona (Dowling) Waterman; children: Christopher, Tutankhamon, Joy, Derrick, Idiah, Kia. BA, Hunter Coll., 1984; postgrad., L.I. U., 1984-86. Cert. leisure profl., N.Y. Art instr./adminstr. Afro-Am. Experience, Hempstead, N.Y., 1968-73; art specialist/adminstr. MLK Youth Ctr., Westbury, 1968-71; substance abuse counselor 5 Town Cmty. Ctr., Lawrence, 1969-71; adminstr., counselor UJAMAA Acad., Hempstead, 1971-75; adminstr. asst. Inservice Learning Program Hunter Coll., 1981-84; unit mgr., youth divsn. counselor N.Y. State Divsn. for Youth, Bklyn., 1986-89; dean of women Claflin Coll., Orangeburg, S.C., 1989-90; dir. recreation and art therapy Dept. Homeless Svcs., N.Y.C., 1984-95; adj. prof. Touro Coll., Bklyn., 1995—; corrections officer Haynesville (Va.) Correctional Ctr., 1998-99; program dir. Hempstead Cmty. Action Program, 1999—; spiritual leader Loving Spirit Ministries Internat., 1999—, Women 2 Women, 2000—; asst. mgr. GAP, Inc., 2001—. Founder Renaissance Woman Cons. Internat., N.Y.C., 1984—; pres., founder Better Living Gen. Svc., N.Y.C., 1988—; designer Ethnic Wear, Empress Fashions, N.Y.C., 1993—; founder Artist in Focus, N.Y.C., 1991-94. Mem. PTA (pres. Bklyn. 1985), Citizens Com. N.Y.C., 1986, Dynamics of Leadership, Bklyn., 1995; program dir. ednl. alliance Lillian Wald Cmty. Ctr., 2001—. Recipient Outstanding Cooperation award Dept. Homeless Svcs., 1994, Outstanding Svc. award N.Y.C. Tech. Coll., 1987, Cert. of Appreciation Edwin Gould Svcs. for Children, 1984. Mem. Dress for Success Profl. Women's Group, Lioness Club, Zeta Iota Phi (sec. 1968—). Mem. Working Families Party. Avocations: art, writing, dancing, jogging, public advocacy. Home and Office: PO Box 466 Westbury NY 11590-0151

WATERMAN, GERALD SCOTT, psychiatrist, physician educator; b. Grand Rapids, Mich., June 22, 1956; s. Donald Frederick and Jerrie Ann (Rosenbaum) W.; m. Sandra Steingard, Aug. 2, 1986; children: Martha, Donna. AB, Harvard U., 1978; MD, U. Mich., 1982. Diplomate in psychiatry and in child and adolescent psychiatry Am. Bd. Psychiatry and Neurology. Resident in psychiatry Beth Israel Hosp., Boston, 1984-86; chief resident in psychopharmacology Mass. Mental Health Ctr., 1986-87; fellow in child and adolescent psychiatry Western Psychiat. Inst. and Clinic, U. Pitts. Med. Ctr., 1988-90, fellow in clin. rsch., 1989-91; co-dir. child & adolescent mood program, 1990-93; asst. prof. psychiatry U. Pitts. Sch. Med., 1990-93; dir. psychiatry cons. svc. U. Vt. Coll. Medicine, Burlington, 1994-96, asst. prof. psychiatry, 1994-98, dir. psychopharmacology, 1997—, dir. child and adolescent psychiatric svcs., 1997-2000, assoc. prof. psychiatry, 1998—, dir. med. student edn. in psychiatry, 2000—, assoc. dir. clin. neurosci. rsch. unit, 2001—. Contbr. articles to profl. publs. Mem. Am. Psychiat. Assn., Am. Acad. Child and Adolescent Psychiatry, Vt. Med. Soc., Am. Soc. Clin. Psychopharmacology, Assn. Dirs. of Med. Student Edn. in Psychiatry, Assn. Advancement of Philosophy and Psychiatry, Alpha Omega Alpha Honor Med. Soc. Avocations: history, politics, philosophy, boating. Office: U Vt Coll Medicine Dept Psychiatry 1 S Prospect St Burlington VT 05401-3456

WATERMAN, MICHAEL SPENCER, mathematics educator, biology educator; b. Coquille, Oreg., 1942; s. Ray S. and Bessie E. Waterman; m. Vicki Lynn Buss, 1962 (div. 1977); 1 child, Tracey Lynn BS, Oreg. State U., 1964, MS, 1966; MA, Mich. State U., 1968, PhD, 1969. Assoc. prof. Idaho State U., Pocatello, 1969-75; mem. staff Los Alamos Nat. Lab., 1975-82, cons., 1982—; prof. math. and biology U. So. Calif., L.A., 1982—, U. So. Calif. Assocs. Endowed Chair, 1991—. Vis. prof. math. U. Hawaii, Honolulu, 1979-80; vis. prof. structural biology U. Calif.-San Francisco, 1982; vis. prof. Mt. Sinai Med. Sch., N.Y.C., 1988; 150th anniversary vis. prof. Chalmers U., 2000; Aisenstadt chair U. Montreal, 2001. Author: Introduction to Computational Biology, 1995; editor: Mathematical Methods for DNA Sequences, Calculating the Secrets of Life, 1995, Genetic Mapping and DNA Sequencing, 1996, Mathematical Support for Molecular Biology, 1999; mem. editl. bd. Jour. Advances in Applied Math. Jour., Annals of Combinatories, Methodology and Computing in Applied Probability, Genomics, Soc. for Indsl. and Applied Math. Jour. Applied Math.; editor-in-chief: Jour. Computational Biology; contbr. numerous articles on math. stats., biology to profl. jours. Grantee NSF, 1971, 72, 75, 88—, Los Alamos Nat. Lab, 1976, 81, Sys. Devel. Found., 1982-87, NIH, 1986-99, Sloan Found., 1990-91; Guggenheim Found. fellow, 1995. Fellow AAAS, Am. Acad. Arts and Scis., Celera Genomics, Inst. Math. Stats.; mem. NAS, Am. Statis. Assn., Soc. Math. Biology, Soc. Indsl. and Applied Math. Office: U So Calif Dept Math Los Angeles CA 90007

WATERMAN, WILLIAM, JR. lawyer; b. Chgo., July 17, 1937; AB, Harvard U., 1959, LLB, 1962. Bar: Ill. 1962, N.Y. 1966, U.S. Ct. Dist. Ct. (so. and ea. dists.) 1968, U.S. Ct. Appeals (2nd cir.) 1975, U.S. Supreme Ct. 1976. Legal advisor Ministry Fin. No. Nigeria, Kaduna, 1963; asst. lectr. U. Lagos, Nigeria, 1963-64; assoc. Spear and Hill, N.Y.C., 1965-68; pvt. practice, 1969—. Co-author: Immigration Law and Defense, 1977, 4th rev. edit. 1986; contbr. articles to profl. jours. Mem. Am. Immigration Lawyers Assn., Nat. Lawyers Guild, N.Y. State Bar Assn., Assn. of Bar of City of N.Y. Address: 305 Broadway Fl 7 New York NY 10007-1109

WATERS, ALICE, executive chef, restaurant owner, writer; b. Chatham, N.J., Apr. 28, 1944; 1 child. Grad. in French Cultural Studies, U. Calif., Berkeley, 1967; postgrad., Montessori Sch., London; degree (hon.) , Mills Coll., Oakland, Calif., 1994. Exec. chef, owner Chez Panisse, Berkeley, Calif., 1971—, Chez Panisse Cafe, Berkeley, 1980—, Cafe Fanny, Berkeley, 1984—. Mem. adv. bd. U. Calif., Berkeley; active The Garden Project, San Francisco; spkr. in field of food safety and health. Author: Chez Panisse Menu Cookbook, Chez Panisse Vegetables, (storybook and cookbook for children) Fanny at Chez Panisse. Developer Martin Luther King Jr. Mid. Sch. Edible Schoolyard, Berkeley. Named Best Chef in Am., James Beard Found., 1992, Best Restaurant in Am., 1992, Humanitarian of Yr., 1997, Mother of Am. Cooking, N.Y. Times; named one of 10 Best Chefs in the World, Cuisine et Vins du France, 1986; recipient Spl. Achievement award, James Beard Found., 1985, Restaurant and Bus. Leadership award, Restaurants and Instns. Mag., 1987, Barbar Boxer Top Ten Women award, 1991, Le Tour du Monde en 80 Toques, Metziner & Varaut, 1991, Nat. Edn. Diplomate award, 1996. Office: Chez Panisse 1517 Shattuck Ave Berkeley CA 94709-1598

WATERS, BETTY LOU, newspaper reporter, writer; b. Texarkana, Tex., June 13, 1943; d. Chester Hinton and Una Erby (Walls) W. AA, Texarkana Jr. Coll., 1963; BA, East Tex. State U., 1965. Gen. assignment reporter Galveston County Pub. Co., Galveston and Texas City, 1965-68; news and feature writer Ind. and Daily Mail, Anderson, S.C., 1968-69; reporter Citizen-Times newspaper, Asheville, N.C., 1969-74; edn. and med. reporter News Star World Pub. Co., Monroe, La., 1974-79; reporter, writer Delta Democrat Times, Greenville, Miss., 1980-89; staff writer Tyler (Tex.) Morning Telegraph, 1990—. Named Citizen of Yr., Sigma Sigma chpt. Omega Psi Phi, 2001; recipient 1st place award for articles, La. Press Women's Contest, 1978, 1st place for interview, 1979, news media award, N.C. Easter Seal Soc., 1973, 3d place award for feature writing, Miss. Press Assn., 1984, for gen. news, 1983, for investigative reporting, 1988, 1st place for best series of articles, 1990, award for outstanding edn. series, Tex. State Tchrs. Assn., 1998, Sch. Bell award for outstanding series, 1997, Tex. Coll. Women Changing the World award, 2000, hon. mentions, Tex. AP, 1966. Mem. Sigma Delta Chi.

WATERS, CHERYL DIANE, accountant; b. Kalamazoo, May 24, 1966; d. Milton Oneal and Delores Roberta (Holloway) W. BA, U. Mich., Dearborn, 1989; postgrad., U. Phoenix, 1996—. Valuation specialist, Mich., 1993. Loan counselor Source One Mortgage, Farmington Hills, Mich., 1989-91; substitute tchr. Detroit Pub. Schs., 1991; Student Employee In Tng. program Mich. Dept. Transp., Lansing, 1993-94; lead worker, prin. clerk City of Lansing, 1994-96; accountant Holland Sys. Corp., Lansing, 1996—. Mem. Mich. Assn. CPAs, Inst. Mgmt. Accts., U. Mich. Alumni Assn., Delta Sigma Theta (asst. leader minerva circle 1990-91). Avocations: horseback riding, reading, swimming, bicycle riding. Office: Holland Sys Corp 120 N Washington Sq Ste 1000 Lansing MI 48933-1631

WATERS, DONALD EUGENE, academic administrator; b. Muncie, Ind., Mar. 28, 1941; s. William James and Mary Harriet (Peare) W.; m. Kathryn Elaine Small, Aug. 17, 1963; children: Jill Maras, Janet Schulenburg. BS in Social Studies and English, Ball State U., 1963, MS in Guidance, 1964; EdD in Adminstrn. and Higher Edn., U. Mo., 1973. Dir. residence hall Ball State U., Muncie, 1964-66; asst. dean of students U. No. Iowa, Cedar Falls, 1966-70; with U. Mo., Columbia, 1970-73; dir. community edn. Muscatine (Iowa) Community Coll., 1973-75, dean arts and scis., 1975-77; asst. to pres. Elgin (Ill.) Community Coll., 1977-88, v.p. corp. devel., 1988-96; counselor W. Aurora H.S., 2002; ret., 2002. Councilman City of Elgin, 1980-87; mem. policy steering com. Nat. League of Cities, Washington, 1986-87; v.p., bd. dirs. United Way of Elgin, 1986-94, chair, bd. dirs. Golden Corridor Steering Com., Ill., 1986-90. Mem. Nat. Coun. Resource Devel. (pres. 1993, treas., bd. dirs. 1986-90, Lifetime Svc. award 1994), Ill. Resource Devel. Commn. (pres. 1986-87), Kiwanis (dist. pres. 1983-84). Methodist. Avocations: reading, model trains, exercise, boating. E-mail: trinkadonwaters@msn.com.

WATERS, DONALD JOSEPH, information services administrator; b. Balt., Sept. 16, 1952; s. Richard Hunter and Annette Catharine (Hannan) W.; m. Beverly Ann Brent, Apr. 5, 1974; children: Laura Elizabeth, Sarah Elizabeth. BA, U. Md., 1973; M Phil, Yale U., 1976, PhD, 1982. Resource specialist Yale Computer Ctr., New Haven, 1982-84; dir. computer services Yale Sch. Mgmt., 1984-87; head, systems office Yale U. Library, 1987-92, dir., libr. and adminstrv. systems, 1992-93, assoc. univ. librarian, 1993-97; dir. Digital Libr. Fedn., Coun. Libr. & Info. Resources, 1997-99; program officer Andrew W. Mellon Found., N.Y., 1999—. Author: Strange Ways and Sweet Dreams: Afro-American Folklore From the Hampton Institute, 1983. Mem. AAAS, ALA, Am. Soc. Info. Sci. Roman Catholic. Avocations: jazz, rowing, cabinet making. Home: 40 Overbrook Rd Madison CT 06443-1834 Office: 140 E 62nd St New York NY 10021-8124

WATERS, ED (EDWARD SARSFIELD WATERS), screenwriter, television producer, writer; b. N.Y.C., Sept. 23, 1930; s. Edward Sarsfield and Winifred Cunningham (O'Brien) W.; m. Diane Ernestene Garrett, Oct. 23, 1965; 1 child, Peter Gregory. BA magna cum laude, U. Notre Dame, 1952. Freelance film and TV writer various studios, Los Angeles, 1956-73, 78-83; exec. story editor Kung Fu Warner Bros., Burbank, Calif., 1973-75, producer The Mississippi, 1983-84; exec. story cons. Police Story Columbia, 1975-77; supervising producer Baretta Universal, Universal City, Calif., 1977-78, supervising producer Miami Vice, 1985-86, co-exec. producer The Equalizer, 1986-88; exec. producer Jake and the Fat Man, 1988-89; ind. screenwriter, TV series creator Calif., 1989—. Writer numerous films, dramatic episodes, TV films and pilots; frequently cited in Tom Stempel's "Storytellers to the Nation" - A History of American Television Writing. Recipient Golden Reel award Miami Vice TV episode, 1985, Emmy award for Police Story, Acad. TV Arts and Scis., 1977. Mem. Writers Guild Am. West. Roman Catholic.

WATERS, GEORGE BAUSCH, newspaper publisher; b. Syracuse, N.Y., July 4, 1920; s. Louis Addison and Mildred Elaine (Bausch) W.; m. Shirley Kessinger Barnard, Sept. 23, 1943; children: Peter, Stephen, Nancy, Kristin, Dean. BA, Syracuse U., 1943. With Rome (N.Y.) Sentinel Co. Pub., 1947—, asst. gen. mgr., 1954-60, gen. mgr., 1960-66, pub., 1966-93, pres., 1993—. Bd. dirs. N.Y. State Photonics Devel. Corp. Chmn. Rome Art and Community Ctr., 1967-85; trustee Stevens Kingsley Found., N.Y.C., 1966—, Kirkland Coll., Clinton, N.Y., 1973-79, Utica Coll. Syracuse U., Utica, 1963-78; past mem. Rome Bd. Edn., Rome Hosp.; bd. dirs. Cen. Assn. Blind. Capt. inf. U.S. Army, 1943-47, ETO. Mem. Am. Newspaper Pubs. Assn., N.Y. State Newspaper Pubs. Assn., N.Y. State Associated Dailies (pres. 1974), Am. Soc. Newspaper Editors, Jervis Libr. Assn. (pres. 1959-65), Soc. Profl. Journalists, Rotary, Ft. Schuyler Club, Yale Club, Washington Press Club, Delta Kappa Epsilon. Republican. Presbyterian. Office: Rome Sentinel Co 333 W Dominick St Rome NY 13440-5791 E-mail: sentinel@rng.com.

WATERS, H. FRANKLIN, federal judge; b. Hackett, Ark., July 20, 1932; s. William A. and Wilma W.; m. Janie C. Waters, May 31, 1958; children—Carolyn Denise, Melanie Jane, Melissa Ann BS, U. Ark., 1955; LL.B., St. Louis U., 1964. Engr., atty. Ralston-Purina Co., St. Louis, 1958-66; ptnr. Crouch, Blair, Cypert & Waters, 1967-81; judge U.S. Dist. Ct. (we. dist.) Ark., from 1981, chief judge, sr. judge, 1997—. Former bd. dirs. Springdale Schs.; former bd. govs. Washington Regional Med. Ctr. Mem. ABA, Ark. Bar Assn., Springdale C. of C. (past bd. dirs.) Office: US Dist Ct PO Box 1908 Fayetteville AR 72702-1908

WATERS, JENNIFER NASH, lawyer; b. Bridgeport, Conn., Dec. 21, 1951; d. Lewis William and Patricia (Cousins) W.; m. Todd David Peterson, Sept. 19, 1981; children: Elizabeth, Andrew. BA, Radcliffe, 1972; JD, Harvard, 1976. Bar: D.C. 1977, U.S. Supreme Ct. 1980. Clk. U.S. Ct. Appeals (D.C. cir.), Washington, 1976-77; assoc. Jones, Day, Reavis & Poque, 1977-79, Crowell & Moring, Washington, 1979-83, ptnr., 1983—. Mem. ABA (ho. of dels. 1997-99), Fed. Energy Bar Assn. (bd. dirs. 1988-99, v.p. 1994-95, pres. 1996-97). Office: Crowell & Moring LLP 1001 Pennsylvania Ave NW Fl 10 Washington DC 20004-2505

WATERS, JOHN, film director, writer, actor; b. Balt., Apr. 22, 1946; s. John Samuel and Patricia Ann (Whitaker) W. Student, NYU, 1966. Speaker various colls., comedy clubs, U.S., Europe, Australia, 1968—. Writer, dir. films Roman Candles, 1966, Eat Your Makeup, 1968, Mondo Trasho, 1969, Multiple Maniacs, 1970, Pink Flamingos, 1972, Female Trouble, 1974, Desperate Living, 1977, Polyester, 1981, Cry-Baby, 1990, Serial Mom, 1994, Pecker, 1998, Cecil B. DeMented, 2000; writer, dir., actor film Hairspray, 1987; actor Something Wild, 1988, Homer and Eddie, 1990, Sweet and Lowdown, 1999, 21 Jump Street, 1990, Divine Trash, In Bad Taste, 1999; author: Shock Value, 1981, Crackpot, 1986, Trash Trio, 1988, Director's Cut, 1997; contbr. articles to N.Y. Times, Am. Film, other mags. Fund raiser AIDS Action Balt.; spokesperson Anti-Violence Campaign, N.Y.C., 1991. John Waters Day named in his honor State of Md., 1985; John Waters Week named in his honor City of Balt., 1988. Mem. AFTRA, SAG, Dirs. Guild Am., Writers Guild Am., Acad. Motion Picture Arts and Scis. Avocation: study of extreme Catholic behavior before the Reformation. Address: care CAA 9830 Wilshire Blvd Beverly Hills CA 90210 Office Fax: 310-288-4800.

WATERS, JOHN B. lawyer; b. Sevierville, Tenn., July 15, 1929; s. J. B. and Myrtle (Paine) W.; m. Patsy Temple, Apr. 8, 1953; children: John B., Cynthia Beth. BS, U. Tenn., 1952, JD, 1961; D in Environ. Sci. (hon.), Milligan Coll., 1993. Bar: Tenn. 1961, U.S. Dist. Ct. (ea. dist.) Tenn. 1961, U.S. Supreme Ct. 1969, U.S. Dist. Ct. D.C. 1970. Of counsel Long, Ragsdale & Waters, P.C., Knoxville, Tenn. Mem. hearing com. Bd. Profl. Responsibility Supreme Ct., 1974—80, 1995—2001, Fed. co-chmn. Appalachian Regional Commn., 1696—1971; chmn. Sevier County Indsl. Bd., Sevierville Libr. Found.; mem. Gov.'s Com. Econ. Devel.; Tenn. rep. to So. Growth Policies Bd., 1970—74; appointed dir. by Pres. Reagan, TVA, Knoxville, 1984, appointed chmn. bd. dirs. by Pres. Bush, 92; bd. dirs. Inst. Nuclear Power Ops., 1985—93; trustee East Tenn. Bapt. Hosp., Knoxville; mem. Tenn.-Tombigbee Waterway Authority, 1993—2000; bd. dirs. East Tenn. Found.; chmn. Leadership Sevier, 1996—2001. Dir. Friends of Great Smoky Mountain Nat. Pk. Lt. USN, 1952—55. Fellow Am. Bar Found.; mem. Tenn. Bar Assn. (pres. 1983-84), Sevier County Bar Assn. (past pres.). Republican. Baptist. Home: Waters Edge 405 Burridge Dr Sevierville TN 37862-3202 also: 119 Commerce St Sevierville TN 37862-3524

WATERS, JOHN W. minister, educator; b. Atlanta, Feb. 5, 1936; s. Henry and Mary Annie (Randall) W. Cert., U. Geneva, Switzerland, 1962; BA, Fisk U., 1957; STB, Boston U., 1967, PhD, 1970. Ordained to ministry Bapt. Ch., 1967. Min. religious edn. Ebenezer Bapt. Ch., Boston, 1965-67, assoc. min., 1967-69; min. Myrtle Bapt. Ch., West Newton, Mass., 1969, Greater Solid Rock Bapt. Ch., Atlanta, 1980—. Prof. Interdenominational Theol. Ctr. , Atlanta, 1976-86, trustee, 1980-83; bd. dirs. Habitat for Humanities, Atlanta, 1984-90; chmn. South Atlanta Joint Urban Ministries, 1983-93; chairperson Coun. Overseers New Era Bapt. Conv. Ctr., 1996-2001; pres. Clayton County Ministers Conf., 2000. Contbr. articles to profl. jours. Mem. Va. Highlands Neighborhood Assn., Atlanta, 1977-87, Butler St. YMCA, 1980-86, South Atlanta Civic League, 1983, others; treas. Prison Ministries with Women, Inc.; v.p. South Met. Ministries Fellowahip, Atlanta, 1990-94. Fund for Theol. Edn. fellow, 1965-67, Nat. Fellowship Fund fellow, 1968-70, Rockefeller doctoral fellow, 1969. Mem. AAUP (chpt. pres. 1971-72), Am. Acad. Religion, Soc. Bibl. Lit., Blacks in Bibl. Studies, New Era Missionary Bapt. Conf. Ga., So. Bapt. Conv. Home: 1516 Niskey Lake Trl SW Atlanta GA 30331-6318 Office: The Greater Solid Rock Bapt Ch 6280 Camp Rd Riverdale GA 30296-2803 *In life, each of us faces a variety of choices. The choices made determine our destiny, fate. When more of us assume responsibility and accountability for the choices made, the world in which we live will be decisively better.*

WATERS, M. BRUCE, engineering technician; b. Houston, Apr. 17, 1950; s. Wayland O. and Snellah G. (Holt) W.; m. Jean H. Sudduth, June 26, 1971 (div. Apr. 2002); 1 child, Tegan Joy . Student, La. State U., 1968-69, 70-74, U. Houston, 1969, San Jacinto Jr. Coll., Deer Park, Tex., 1969. Engring. aide I La. Dept. Highways, Baton Rouge, 1971-73, engring. aide II, 1973-74; sta. mgr. Cliff Brice Gas Stas., Boulder, Colo., 1975; mill worker Red Dale Coach, Longmont, 1975; engring. aide B Colo. Dept. Highways, Boulder, 1975-76, engring. aide C, 1976-91, engring tech. I, 1991—. Blood donor Belle Bonfils, Boulder, Colo., 1975—; mem. Vols. for Outdoor Colo.; sec. Libertarian Party of Boulder County, 1991-93, 95-96, 2000-01; appointed to 20th Judicial Dist. Domestic Violence Treament Providers Cert. Bd., 1998-2000. Eagle Scout, 1967. Mem. Nat. Inst. Cert. Engring. Techs., Colo. Freewheelers (sec. 1993-95, 98-99, 2001, Rider of Yr. 1998), Am. Motorcyclist Assn., Am. Hist. Racing Motorcycle Assn. Avocations: collecting antique motorcycles, skiing, reading, music. Office: Colo Dept Transp 1050 Lee Hill Dr Boulder CO 80302-9404 E-mail: bruce.waters@dot.state.co.us.

WATERS, MARY BRICE KIRTLEY, federal agency administrator; B, U. Ill.; JD, George Mason U. Bar: D.C. Sr. dir., legis. counsel ConAgra Foods, 1986—2001; asst. sec. congl. rels. USDA, Washington, 2001—; legis. asst. Rep. Larry Hopkins, Ky., 1982—86; dir. agrl. task force Rep. Rsch. Com., 1981—82. Past chair Washington Agrl. Roundtable; mem. Trade Policy Forum. Office: USDA Congl Rels 1400 Independence Ave SW Washington DC 20250 Office Fax: 202-720-8077.*

WATERS, MAXINE, congresswoman; b. St. Louis, Aug. 15, 1938; d. Remus and Velma (Moore) Carr; m. Sidney Williams, July 23, 1977; children: Edward, Karen. Grad. in sociology, Calif. State U., L.A.; hon. doctorates, Spelman Coll., N.C. Agrl. &, Tech. State U., Morgan State U. Former tchr. Head Start. Mem. Calif. Assembly from dist. 48, 1976-91, Dem. caucus chair, 1984; mem. U.S.Congress from 35th Calif. dist., 1991—; mem. Banking, Fin., Urban Affairs com., Ho. subcom. on banking, capitol subcom. on banking, employment and tng. subcom. on vets., veterans affairs com., banking and fin. svcs. com., ranking house subcom. on gen. oversight and investigations; chair Congl. Black Caucus. Mem. Dem. Nat. Com., Dem. Congrl. Campaign com.; del. Dem. Nat. Conv., 1972, 76, 80, 84, 88, 92, mem. rules com. 1984; mem. Nat. Adv. Com. for Women, 1978—; bd. dirs. TransAfrica Found., Nat. Women's Polit. Caucus, Ctr. Nat. Policy, Clara Elizabeth Jackson Carter Found. Spelman Coll., Nat. Minority AIDS Project, Women for a Meaningful Summit, Nat. Coun. Negro Women, Black Women's Agenda; founder Black Women's Forum. Office: US Ho Reps 2344 Rayburn HOB Washington DC 20515-0001*

WATERS, RICHARD, retired publishing company executive; b. Sterling, Mass., May 13, 1926; s. Sherman Hoar and Viola (Arnold) W.; m. June Hollweg Dorer, Aug. 27, 1949; children: Karl (dec.), Kurt, Kris. BA, Hobart Coll., 1950, LLD hon., 1970; MBA, Harvard U., 1951. Assoc. acct. Hunter & Weldon, N.Y.C., 1953-55; exec. v.p., CFO Reader's Digest Assn., Pleasantville, N.Y., 1955-77; assoc. dean Harvard U. Bus. Sch., Boston, 1977-81; pres., CEO Sporting News, St. Louis, 1981-90, ret., 1990. Bd. dirs. Republic Nat. Bank, N.Y.C. Trustee Hobart Coll., 1971-91, William Smith Coll., 1971-91; regional v.p. Associated Industries N.Y. State, Albany, 1965-79; chmn. bd. Westchester Heart Assn., Port Chester, N.Y., 1975-76; bd. dirs., vice-chmn. Gateway chpt. Nat. Multiple Sclerosis Soc., 1991-95, chmn., 1996-98, chair emeritus 1999—; mem. St. Louis Sports Commn., 1985—; hon. trustee Hobart and William Smith Colls., 1992—. With USN, 1944-46, PTO; 1st lt. USAF, 1951-53. Mem. Baseball Writers Assn. Am. Clubs: Old Warson Country, St. Louis Club, Sky (N.Y.C.). Republican. Home: 20 Somerset Downs Saint Louis MO 63124-1007 E-mail: somersetdw@aol.com.

WATERS, ROGER ALLEN, music educator; b. Atlanta, June 12, 1949; s. John Clarence Waters, Virginia Elizabeth Waters; m. Sandra Lynn Smith, Aug. 12, 1978; children: Michael Allen, Melody Elizabeth. BMus, Ga. State U., 1973, MMus, 1981. Lic. min. Salem Bapt. Ch. Dir. choral activities Southwest DeKalb H.S., Decatur, Ga., 1976—82; min. music High Point Bapt. Ch., Covington, 1982—89, Salem Bapt. Ch., McDonough, 1989—. Instr. voice Ga. Perimeter Coll., Clarkston, Ga., 1998—; dir./condr. music Covington/Conyers Choral Guild, Covington, Ga., 1985—. Bd. dirs. Covington/Conyers Choral Guild, Covington; deputized sheriff DeKalb County Sheriff's Dept., Decatur, 1970—. Staff sgt. USAF, 1967—73. Mem.: Am. Choral Dirs. Assn. (state pres. 1991—93), Music Educators Nat. Conf., Nat. Assn. Tchrs. Singing. Republican. Avocations: golf, tennis, mint collectibles, scale trains. Home: 1996 Gibralter Way Conyers GA 30012

WATERS, ROLLIE O. management consultant; b. Charleston, S.C., Oct. 14, 1942; s. Rollie Robert and Mary Olivia (Brown) W.; m. Stacy Layton Waters, Dec. 31, 1998; children: Wendie Kay, Lauren Olivia. AA, Spartanburg Coll., 1968; BS, U. S.C., 1969; MBA, Pepperdine U., 1980. Cert. mgmt. cons. Supr. comms. and spl. activities Owens-Corning Fiberglas, Aiken, S.C., 1970-71, asst. pers. dir. Fairburn, Ga., 1971-72; pers. dir. Meisel Photochrome Corp., Atlanta, 1972-73, dir. corp. pers. Dallas, 1973-76, asst. v.p., dir. human resources, after 1976; co-founder, sr. ptnr., CEO Waters, Trego & Davis, 1976-98; pres., CEO The Waters Cons. Group Inc. Publicity dir., program dir. 35th and 36th North Tex. Pers. Confs.; guest lectr. Lorch Found., London, Calif. Inst. Tech., U. Md., Am. Mgmt. Assn. So. Meth. U.; spkr. in field. Author: (tng. sys.) The Manager, Skill-based Pay for Cities, HRNavigator Software for Compensation and Performance Management, others; contbr. articles to profl. jours. With USAF, 1962-66. Mem. ASTD, Internat. Pers. Mgmt. Assn., Inst. Mgmt. Cons. (bd. dirs. Texoma chpt.), Soc. Human Resource Mgmt. (nat. compensation and benefits com.), Dallas Pers. Assn.

(v.p. membership 1977-78), Am. Compensation Assn., Mensa, Psi Chi, Phi Theta Kappa, Omicron Delta Kappa, Beta Phi Gamma. Office: 2695 Villa Creek Dr Ste 104 Dallas TX 75234-7310 E-mail: rwaters@watersconsulting.com.

WATERS, RONALD W. educator, church executive, pastor; b. Kokomo, Ind., July 23, 1951; s. Ronald Lee and Carolyn Elizabeth (Myers) W.; m. Norma Lee Grumbling Waters, June 16, 1973; 1 child, Melinda Ronee Waters. BA magna cum laude, Ashland (Ohio) Coll., 1973; MA in Comms. with high honors, Wheaton (Ill.) Coll., 1975; MDiv with high honors, Ashland (Ohio) Theol. Seminary, 1985; postgrad., Asbury Theol. Seminary, 1993—2002. Ordained elder Brethren Ch., 1986; lic. minister, 1985-86. Asst. to dir. Bd. of Christian Edn. The Brethren Ch., Ashland, Ohio, 1971-74; mng. editor of publs. Brethren Pub. Co., 1975-78, asst. to dir. and gen. mgr., 1978-80, exec. dir., 1980-82; dir. of Denom. Bus. The Brethren Ch. Nat. Office, 1982-84; cons. in mgmt. and computer applications, 1984-85; pastor Mt. Olive Brethren Ch., McGaheysville, Va., 1985-89; dir. Brethren Ch. Ministries The Brethren Ch. Nat. Office, Ashland, Ohio, 1989-95; asst. prof. evangelism Ashland Theol. Sem., 1996-2001; cons. for evangelism and ch. growth The Brethren Ch. Nat. Office, Ashland, 1996—2001; pastor Hammond Ave. Brethren Ch., Waterloo, Iowa, 2002—. Bd. dirs. corp. sec. Brethern Printing Co., Ashland, 1989-96; mem. mission bd. Brethren Ch. Southeastern Dist., 1987-89; mem., sec. exec. bd. Ctrl. Dist., The Brethren Ch., 2002—; mem. statement of faith task force Gen. Conf. Brethern Ch., 1981-84, polity com. 1986-91, bd. ref. congl. adv. The Andrew Ctr., Elgin, Ill., 1994-97; founder, tchr. Young Adult Sunday Sch. class Park St Brethern Ch., Ashland, 1990-93; adv. com. Ashland Theol. Sem., 1990-95; mem. evangelism mgmt. team New Life Ministries, Mt. Joy, Pa., 1992-2001; spkr. in field. Author: Promise for the Future, 1993, Leader's Manual for Inviting and Welcoming New People, 1995; editor: The Brethren Evangelist mag., 1975-78, New Beginnings mag., 1995-97; contbg. editor LIFE process, 1998-99; contbr. numerous articles to religious jours.; webmaster, www.newlifeministries-nlm.org, 2000—. Mem. adv. coun. World Relief Corp., Wheaton, Ill., 1990-92; dir. vol. ministries Park St. Brethren Ch., 1998-99; sec.-treas. Ohio dist. Mission Bd., 1996-2001. Mem. Am. Soc. Ch. Growth, Nat. Assn. Brethern Ch. Elders. Avocation: gardening. Office: Hammond Ave Brethren Ch 1604 Hammond Ave Waterloo IA 50702 E-mail: ron@hammondavenuebrethren.com.

WATERS, RUTH VON JAHNKE, artist, art administrator; b. Seattle, Oct. 30, 1933; d. William Frank and Lucile Irene (Hagerty) Jahnke; m. Philip Lyman Waters, Sept. 10, 1954; children: Richard Ian, Sharon Deirdre, Kirk Jonathan. AB, Stanford U., 1955. Journalism instr. St. Clair County C.C., Port Huron, Mich., 1970-72; tech. editor Vega Inc., Vienna, 1973-74; dept. editor Port Huron Herald, 1973; tech. editor, graphics mgr. Tensor Industries, Vienna, 1974-76; founder, dir. Twin Pines Art Ctr., Belmont, Calif., 1977-85, 1870 Art Ctr., Belmont, 1985—. Founder, past pres. Peninsula Sculptors' Guild, Belmont, 1979—; founder, pres. Peninsula Ch. Women's Caucus for Art, Belmont, 1991—; founding bd. Redwood City (Calif.) Art Ctr., 1993—; bd. dirs. San Mateo County ARTshare, San Mateo, Calif., 1996-2002; founder, chair Silicon Valley Art Mus., Belmont, Calif., 1998—; lectr. in field. One-woman shows include Barrios Gallery, Sacramento, annually 1964-70, Placerville (Calif.) Gallery, annually 1965-70, Pandora's Box Gallery, Victoria, B.C., Can., 1968, 69, Art League No. Va., Alexandria, 1974, John Pence Gallery, San Francisco, 1977, Gallery House, Palo Alto, Calif., 1978, 82, Manor Gallery, Belmont, 1979, PARTA Gallery, San Mateo, 1984, 1870 Gallery, Belmont, 1987, John Gualbert Gallery, San Francisco, 1988, Coastal Arts League Mus., Half Moon Bay, Calif., 1988, Creative Arts Ctr., Sunnyvale, Calif., 1989, SOMAR Gallery, San Francisco, 1994, Seipp Gallery, Palo Alto, 1994-95, The Gallery, Burlingame, Calif., 1995; works exhibited in group shows Grace Cathedral, San Francisco, 1992, Skyline Coll., San Bruno, Calif., 1992, The New Art Pl., San Francisco, 1992, Hayward State U., 1993, Bedford Gallery, Walnut Creek, Calif., 1993, Cork Gallery, Avery Fisher Hall, Lincoln Ctr., N.Y., 1994, Syntex Gallery, Palo Alto, 1994, City of Santa Clara, 1994-95, Bay Arts '94, Belmont, Pacific Rim Sculptors Group, Syntex, Palo Alto, 1994, Ave. of the Arts, Belmont, 1995-97, others; represented in permanent collections Provident Ctrl. Credit Union, Redwood City, McCracken & Byers, Burlingame, Calif., Robert Lyon Assocs., Redwood City, Paul Barulich, Esq., Redwood City, and pvt. collections. Avocations: long-distance running, tennis. Office: 1870 Art Ctr 1870 Ralston Ave Belmont CA 94002-1859 E-mail: rjwaters@mindspring.com.

WATERS, TERRANCE J, architect; b. El Centro, Calif., Nov. 6, 1920; s. John and Grace May (Cox) W.; m. Beatrice Ecker, Sept. 15, 1944; 1 child, Michael Terrance. Student, L.A. City Coll., 1940, U. So. Calif., 1941, UCLA, 1948. Registered arch., Calif. Apprentice draftsman John Lautner Arch., L.A., 1949-51; prin. Arch. Terrance Waters, Malibu, Calif., 1956—. Spkr. Internat. Conf. Low Cost Housing for Devel. Countries, Roorkee, India, 1985; presenter in field. Author: The Tungsten Conspiracy, 1968. Chmn., exec. sec. Malibu Citizens for Conservation, 1963-67. With USAAC, 1941-45, ETO. Recipient Svc. medal with 4 bronze stars. Mem. Am. Astonautical Soc. (sr.), Planetary Soc., Earthquake Engring. Rsch. Soc., Space Frontier Found. Achievements include patents for hyperboloid buildings, hyperboloidal deployable antennas and spacecraft.

WATERS, WILLIAM CARTER, III, retired internist, educator; b. Atlanta, Dec. 12, 1929; s. William Carter and Nannie Ellen (Starr) W.; m. Sarah Ann Bankston; children: William Carter IV, Sarah Walker Waters McEntire. AB, Emory U., 1950, MD, 1958. Diplomate in internal medicine and nephrology Am. Bd. Internal Medicine. Resident in internal medicine Grady Meml. Hosp./Emory U., Atlanta, 1958-60, 61-62; fellow in nephrology New Eng. Med. Ctr., 1960-61; practice medicine specializing in internal medicine and nephrology, Atlanta, 1962—2002; from instr. to assoc. prof. Emory U. Sch. Medicine, 1962-70, clin. assoc. prof., 1970-85, clin. prof., 1985—. Chief staff internal medicine Piedmont Hosp., Atlanta, chmn. bd., 1991-94; 1st chmn. bd Promina Health Sys., Atlanta, 1994-96. Contbr. articles to med. jours. Served with USAF, 1951-52. Fellow ACP (master: gov. for Ga.); mem. AMA, Med. Assn. Ga., Med. Assn. Met. Atlanta, Am. Soc. Nephrology, S.E. Clin. Club, Atlanta Country Club, Piedmont Driving Club, Big Canoe Club. Methodist. E-mail: drwaters@mindspring.com.

WATERS, WILLIAM ERNEST, microelectronics executive; b. Toronto, Aug. 18, 1928; s. Charles Lacy and Margaret Waters; m. Evelyn Elizabeth Phillips, Jan. 18, 1952; children: Kenneth Geoffrey, Brian Gregory, Kimberly William. BASc, U. Toronto, 1950. Gen. mgr. Hoskins Alloys of Can. Ltd., Toronto, 1953-59; pres. Waters Metal Products Ltd., 1960—, Waters Metal Products, Inc., Buffalo, 1960-69, Watmet Inc., Niagara Falls, N.Y., 1968—, Microtectonics, Inc., Buffalo, 1968-71. Served with RCAF, 1946-52. Mem. Engring. Inst. Can., Ont. Assn. Profl. Engrs., Can. Soc. for Elec. Engring., Internat. Soc. Hybrid Microelectronics, Mfrs. Agts. Nat. Assn. (dir. 1973-77), Niagara Falls Golf and Country Club, Port Colborne Club, Rotary, Beta Theta Pi. Home: 554 Mountain View Dr Lewiston NY 14092

WATFORD, PAUL STEPHEN, finance analyst; b. Bklyn., Mar. 26, 1959; s. Paul and Evelyn J. Watford; m. Brenda A. Darrell, Oct. 16, 1993; 1 child, Everett A. BA in History, U. Rochester, 1980; BS in Mech. Engring., Howard U., 1982; MM in Fin., Northwestern U., 1989. Sr. prin. engr. Commonwealth Edison, Chgo., 1982-91; bus. analyst FMC Corp., 1991-92; strategic planner United Airlines, Elk Grove Township, 1992-95; dir. fin. WTTW Ch. 11, Chgo., 1995-99; dir. fin. planning and analysis Sears Roebuck & Co., Hoffman Estates, 1999—2002. Trustee St. Mark's Sch., Southborough, Mass., 1993—; young leader Chgo. Cmty. Trust, 1995—. Mem. Nat. Black MBA Assn. (pres. Chgo. chpt. 1999-2002). Home: 4254 N Hermitage Ave Chicago IL 60613-1104

WATHEN, DANIEL EVERETT, state supreme court chief justice; b. Easton, Maine, Nov. 4, 1939; s. Joseph Jackson and Wilda Persis (Dow) W.; m. Judith Carol Foren, July 14, 1960; children: Julanne Carol, Daniel Arthur. AB, Ricker Coll., 1962; JD, U. Maine, 1965; LLM (hon.), U. Va. Law Sch., 1988. Bar: Maine 1965. Atty. Wathen & Wathen, Augusta, Maine, 1965-77; trial judge Superior Ct. Maine, 1977-81; appellate judge Supreme Jud. Ct. Maine, 1981-92, state chief justice, 1992—. E-mail: Daniel.Wathen@state.me.us.

WATKINS, BIRGE SWIFT, government contractor; b. Grand Rapids, Mich., May 2, 1949; s. Robert Goodell and Betty Jane (Swift) W.; m. Elizabeth Beverly Price, Nov. 28, 1985; children: Elizabeth Porter, Benjamin Thorne Swift, Robert William MacIntosh. BA, Alma Coll., 1971; MBA, London Bus. Sch., 1981; MPA, Harvard U., 1989. Staff asst. to Pres. of U.S., Washington, 1974-77; congl. press sec. U.S. Ho. of Reps., 1977; v.p. Arbor Internat. Inc., McLean, Va., 1980-81; asst. office dir. AID, Washington, 1982-88; asst. dir. Pres.'s Task Force on Internal Pvt. Enterprise, 1983-85; dep. asst. sec. USDA, 1989-90; dir. investor outreach Resolution Trust Corp., 1991-94; ptnr. Benton Resources, 1994-95; cons. Com Mac, 1995; mng. dir. Thornfalcon Internat., 1996-99; sr. v.p. Lifecare Mgmt. Ptnrs., 1999—. Bd. dirs. Corp. Healthcare Svcs. Inc., Springfield, Va., pres., dir.; bd. dirs. Asia Forum - Japan; cons. Washington Campus Inc., 1977, Va. Med. Assocs. Inc., Springfield, 1988, U.S. C. of C. Mem. campaign staff Reagan-Bush campaign, Washington, 1980, Bush for President, 1988; mem. transition team office of Pres.-elect Bush, 1988; chmn. bd. trustees Partnership Warrenton Found.; bd. dirs. Voice Internat.; bd. dirs., founder John Singleton Mosby Found. and Mus., Land Trust of Va. Mem. Urban Land Inst., Harvard Club (Washington). Avocations: skiing, running, contemporary art. Home: 832 Blackwell Rd Warrenton VA 20186-2216 Office: 6601 Little River Tpke Ste 300 Alexandria VA 22312-1303

WATKINS, CHARLES REYNOLDS, medical equipment company executive; b. San Diego, Oct. 28, 1951; s. Charles R. and Edith A. (Muff) W.; children: Charles Devin, Gregory Michael, Joshua Tomas. BS, Lewis and Clark Coll., 1974; postgrad., U. Portland, 1976. Internat. salesman Hyster Co., Portland, Oreg., 1975-80, Hinds Internat. Corp., Portland, 1980-83; mgr. internat. sales Wade Mfg. Co., Tualatin, Oreg., 1983-84; regional sales mgr. U.S. Surg., Inc., Norwalk, Conn., 1984-86; nat. sales mgr. NeuroCom Internat., Inc., Clackamas, Oreg., 1986-87; pres. Wave Form Systems, Inc., Portland, 1987-98; pres., dir. Wave Form Mfg., Inc., 1998—; prin. Wave Form Lithotripsy LLC, 1998—; pres. Wave Form Mfg., Inc., 1998—. Bd. dirs. Portland World Affairs Coun., 1980. Mem. Am. Soc. Laser Medicine and Surgery, Am. Assn. Gynecol. Laparoscopists, Ind. Med. Distbrs. Assn., Portland City Club. Republican. Avocations: flying, photography, travel. Office: Wave Form Sys Inc PO Box 3195 Portland OR 97208-3195

WATKINS, CURTIS WINTHROP, artist; b. Pontiac, Mich., Apr. 9, 1946; s. Robert James and Arvella Marquitta (Chenoweth) W.; m. Gayle Lynn Blom, Dec. 19, 1975; 1 dau., Darcy Ann. Student, Ann Arbor Art Ctr., 1964-66, Kendall Sch. Design, 1966-68, Kraus Hypnosis Ctr., 1966, 70, Arons Ethical Hypnosis Tng. Ctr., 1977. Illustrator, instr. Ann Arbor Art Ctr., 1969-71; owner, dir. Hypno-Art Rsch. Ctr. and Studio, Howell, Mich., 1971—. Research on visualization process of subconscious by doing art work under hypnosis; lectr. hypnosis convs. and schs. One-man shows include LeVern's Gallery, 1969, Rackham Gallery, 1973, Hartland Gallery, 1974, Platt Gallery, 1975, Detroit Artists Guild Gallery, 1975, Golden Gallery, 1977, Cromaine Gallery, 1982, Driggett Gallery, 1982, Mill Gallery, 1983, Walnut Street Gallerya, 1983, Merrill Gallery, 1986, Corbino Gallery, 1986, VanAntwerp, 1991; group shows include Mich. All-State Show, 1980, Mich. State Fine Arts Exhibit, 1980, Washington Internat., 1981, Lansing (Mich.) Art Gallery, 1981, Capitol City Arts Show, 1981, Mich. Ann., 1981, Mich. Ann., 1982-83; illustrator: Handbook of Hypnotic Techniques, 1988. Bd. dirs. 9th Ann. Hartland Art Show, 1975, Livingston Arts and Crafts Assn., 1977-79, Hartland Art Coun., 1974-78. Recipient Dr. Garland H. Fross award, 1989, numerous awards of excellence in art. Mem. Internat. Soc. Artists, Assn. Advance Ethical Hypnosis, Am. Assn. Profl. Hypnologists, Internat. Soc. Profl. Hypnosis, Internat. Platform Assn. Presbyterian. Home: 1749 Pinckney Rd Howell MI 48843-7874

WATKINS, DANIEL ANTHONY, emergency nurse practitioner, paramedic; b. Chester, Pa., Mar. 23, 1961; s. Nevil Charles and Mary Ann Watkins; m. George Ann Watkins, Apr. 14, 1984; children: Amanda, Jessica, Alexis. MS Parapsychic Sci., Am. Inst. of Holistic Theology, Youngstown, OH, 1999, BS Parapsychic Sci., 1996; AA Nursing, Del. County CC, Marple, PA, 1993. Emergency nurse Meth. Hosp., Philadelphia, Pa., 2001—; dir. emergency ctr. Med. Coll. of Pa, 1998—2001; dir. emergency med. services Del. County Govt., Media, 1994—98; paramedic Riddle Meml. Hosp., 1984—; paramedic supr. Crozer Health Systems, Chester, 1980—98. Safety officer Trainer Fire Co., Trainer, Pa., 1985—; pres., dep. fire chief Aston-Beechwood Fire Co., Aston, Pa., 1977—98. Maj. Marines, 1976—81, United States. Mem.: Marine Corp Assn., Pa, Assn. of Notary. Roman Catholic. Avocations: reading, chess, bike riding. Home: 2449 Weir Road Chester PA 19014-1601 Personal E-mail: docwattrn@aol.com.

WATKINS, DEAN ALLEN, electronics executive, educator; b. Omaha, Oct. 23, 1922; s. Ernest E. and Pauline (Simpson) W.; m. Bessie Ena Hansen, June 28, 1944; children— Clark Lynn, Alan Scott, Eric Ross. BS, Iowa State Coll., 1944; MS, Calif. Inst. Tech., 1947; PhD, Stanford, 1951. Engr. Collins Radio Co., 1947-48; mem. staff Los Alamos Lab., 1948-49; tech. staff Hughes Research Labs., 1951-53; asso. prof. elec. engring. Stanford, 1953-56; prof., dir. Electron Devices Lab., 1956-64, lectr. elec. engring., 1964-70; co-founder, pres., chief exec. officer, dir. Watkins Johnson Co., Palo Alto, Calif., 1957-67, chmn., chief exec. officer, dir., 1967-80, chmn., dir., 1980-2000. Cons. Dept. Def., 1956-66; mem. White House Sci. Coun., 1988-89. Patentee in field; contbr. articles to profl. jours. Legis. chmn., dir. San Meteo County Sch. Bds. Assn., 1959-69; gov. San Francisco Bay Area Coun., 1966-75; Rep. precinct capt. Portola Valley, 1964; vice chmn. San Mateo County Fin. Com., 1967-69; mem. Calif. Rep. Ctrl. Com., 1964-68; trustee Stanford, 1966-69; regent U. Calif., 1969-96, chmn., 1972-74; mem. governing bd. Sequoia Union H.S. Dist., 1964-68, chmn., 1967-68; mem. governing bd. Portola Valley Sch. Dist., 1958-66; mem. bd. overseers Hoover Instn. on War, Revolution and Peace, Stanford, 1969—, chmn., 1971-73, 85-86; adv. policy commn. Santa Clara County Jr. Achievement; trustee Nat. Security Indsl. Assn., 1965-78. Served from pvt. to 1st lt. C.E., O.R.C. AUS, 1943-46. Fellow IEEE (7th region Achievement award 1957, Frederik Philips award 1981), AAAS; mem. Am. Phys. Soc., Am. Mgmt. Assn., Western Electronic Mfrs. Assn. (chmn. San Francisco coun. 1967, v.p., dir.), Calif. C. of C. (dir. 1965-92, treas. 1978, pres. 1981), Nat. Acad. Engring., Mounted Patrol San Mateo County (spl. dep. sheriff 1960-70), San Mateo County Horseman's Assn., San Benito County Farm Bur., Calif. Cattlemen's Assn., Delta Upsilon. Clubs: Palo Alto (Palo Alto), University (Palo Alto); Shack Riders (San Mateo County); Commonwealth (San Francisco); Rancheros Visitadores.

WATKINS, EUGENE LEONARD, surgeon, educator; b. Worcester, Mass., Jan. 4, 1918; s. George Joseph and Marcella Katherine (Akels) W.; A.B. with honors in biology, Clark U., 1940; M.D. (Hood scholar), Harvard U., 1943; m. Victoria Peake, Sept. 23, 1944; children: Roswell Peake, Priscilla Avery. Intern, Roosevelt Hosp., N.Y.C., 1944; resident in surgery, 1944-46, 49-50, asst. resident in surgery, 1948-49; fellow in surgery, clin. rsch. fellow Mass. Gen. Hosp., Boston, 1947-48; practice medicine specializing in surgery, N.Y.C., 1950-56, Morristown, N.J., 1950-90, Denville, N.J., 1956-85, Boonton, N.J., 1961-85; mem. staff Morristown Meml. Hosp., 1950, vice chmn. dept. surgery, 1974-77, chmn., 1959-61, mem. corp.; cons. surgeon St. Clare's Hosp., Denville, N.J., Riverside Hosp., Boonton, N.J., Community Med. Center, Morristown; courtesy surg. staff St. Luke's-Roosevelt Hosp. Center, N.Y.C.; asst. clin. prof. surgery Rutgers U. Coll. Medicine and Dentistry, New Brunswick, N.J., 1972-85; asst. clin. prof. surgery Columbia U. Coll. Phys. and Surg., 1985-90; v.p. chmn. fin. com. Morristown Bd. Health, 1954-56. Served to 1st lt., AUS, 1946. Diplomate Am. Bd. Surgery. Fellow ACS (chmn. N.J. Adv. Com. 1965-77, chmn. N.J. State com. Trauma, 1960); mem. N.J., Morris County med. socs., AMA, Soc. Surgeons N.J. (1st v.p. 1982, pres. 1983), Am. Thoracic Soc., AAAS, Harvard Med. Soc. N.Y. (pres. 1960-61), West Side Med. Soc., Roosevelt Hosp. Alumni Assn. Republican. Presbyterian. Clubs: Harvard (N.Y.C.), Morristown, Morristown Field. Achievements include development of spring-loop surgical suture holder. Home: Unit 419 7501 E Thompson Peak Pkwy Scottsdale AZ 85255-4537

WATKINS, FELIX SCOTT, printing company executive; b. Sutton, W.Va., Nov. 27, 1946; s. Felix Sutton and Helena Sara (Cogar) W.; m. Vivian L. Watkins, June 20, 1970; children: Jeffrey Scott, Jamie Leigh. Student, W. Va. Inst. Tech. Salesman Kingsport (Tenn.) Press, 1971-73; sales mgr. George Banta Co., N.Y.C., 1973-74; prodn. mgr. Fuller Typesetting, Phila., 1974-78; acct. exec. Rocappi, Pennsauken, NJ, 1978—78; pres. Photo Data, Inc., Washington, 1978—90, Signature Printing, Inc., Chantilly, Va., 1991—. Founding mem. Print Polit. Action Com. Mem. Washington Club Printing House Craftsmen, Washington Printing Guild (dir. masters printers divsn.), Printing Industries Met. Washington (chmn. govt. affairs com.), Printing Industries Am. (Chmn.'s Club). Home: 9521 Orion Ct Burke VA 22015-3241 Office: Signature Printing Inc 14310 Sullyfield Cir Ste 200 Chantilly VA 20151-1629

WATKINS, GEORGE DANIELS, physics educator; b. Evanston, Ill., Apr. 28, 1924; s. Paul F. and Lois V. (Daniels) W.; m. Carolyn Lenore Nevin, June 19, 1949; children: Lois Roberta, Paul Brent, Ann Romaine. BS, Randolph-Macon Coll., 1943; D.Sc. (hon.), 1976; MA, Harvard U., 1947, PhD, 1952. Research physicist Gen. Electric Research Lab., Schenectady, 1952-75; adj. prof. Rensselaer Poly. Inst., 1962-65, SUNY-Albany, 1969-72; Sherman Fairchild prof. physics Lehigh U., Bethlehem, Pa., 1975-95, prof. emeritus, 1995—; chmn. Gordon Research Conf. on Defects in Semiconductors, 1981; mem. solid state adv. com. Oak Ridge Nat. Lab., 1980-85. Mem. editorial bd. Phys. Rev. B, 1978-82; contbr. articles to profl. jours. Served to lt. (j.g.) USNR, 1943-46. NSF fellow, 1966-67; named Virginian of Yr. Va. Press Assn., 1980; recipient Alexander von Humboldt sr. U.S. Scientist award, 1983, 91. Fellow Am. Phys. Soc. (Oliver E. Buckley award 1978), AAAS, Nat. Acad. Scis. Democrat. Unitarian Universalist. Office: Lehigh U Dept Physics Bethlehem PA 18015

WATKINS, HAROLD ROBERT, minister; b. Wauseon, Ohio, July 30, 1928; s. Orra Lynn and Florence Margaret (Bruner) W.; m. Evelyn Norma Earlywine, June 18, 1950; children: Mark Edwin, Nancy Jo Watkins. AB, Bethany Coll., 1950; MDiv, Lexington Theol. Sem., 1997; DD, Phillips U., 1985, Christian Theol. Sem., Indpls., 1995; BD, Coll. of Bible, 1953. Ordained minister Disciples of Christ, 1950. Min. Park Ave. Christian Ch., Tucson, 1953-56, First Christian Ch., Tuscaloosa, Ala., 1956-57; gen. ch. adminstr. Bd. Ch. Extension of Disciples of Christ, Indpls., 1958-95, pres., 1980-95; mem. faculty Lexington Theol. Sem., 1996-97, 98-99, interim pres., 2001. Chmn. bd. dirs. Discipledata, Inc., Indpls., 1980—94. Trustee Bethany (W.Va.) Coll., 1976—, Nat. City Christian Ch. Corp., Washington, 1981—; bd. dirs. Ecumenical Ch. Loan Fund, Geneva; pres. World Conv. Chs. of Christ, Nashville, 1988-92; bd. dirs. United Ch. of Christ Ins. Bd., 1997—. Recipient Outstanding Alumnus award Bethany Coll., 1975. Mem. Interfaith Forum on Religion, Art and Arch. (dir. officer 1979-95, pres. 1981-82, Elbert M. Conover award 1989). Home: 7402 Somerset Bay Apt 118 Indianapolis IN 46240-3495 E-mail: hwatkins@aol.com.

WATKINS, HAYS THOMAS, retired railroad executive; b. Fern Creek, Ky., Jan. 26, 1926; s. Hays Thomas Sr. and Minnie Catherine (Whiteley) W.; m. Betty Jean Wright, Apr. 15, 1950; 1 son, Hays Thomas III. BS in Acctg., Western Ky. U., 1947; MBA, Northwestern U., 1948; LLD (hon.), Baldwin Wallace Coll., 1975, Alderson Broaddus Coll., 1980, Coll. of William and Mary, 1982, Va. Union U., 1987. CPA, Ill., Ohio. With C. & O. Ry. Cleve., 1949-80, v.p. fin., 1964-67, v.p. adminstrv. group, 1967-71, pres., chief exec. officer, 1971-73, chmn. bd., chief exec. officer, 1973-80; with B. & O. R.R., 1964-80, v.p. finance, 1964-71, pres., chief exec. officer, 1971-73, vice chmn. bd., chief exec. officer, 1973-80; chmn., chief exec. officer Chessie System, Inc., 1973-80; pres. and co-chief exec. officer CSX Corp. (merger of Chessie System, Inc. and Seaboard Coast Line Industries, Inc.), Richmond, Va., 1980-82, chmn. bd., chief exec. officer, 1982-89, chmn. bd., 1989-91; chmn. emeritus, 1991—. Vice rector bd. visitors Coll. William and mary, 1984-87, rector, 1987-93. With AUS, 1945-47. Named Man of Yr., Modern R.R. mag., 1984; recipient Excellence in Mgmt. award Industry Week mag., 1982. Mem. Nat. Assn. Accts., Am. Inst. C.P.A.'s. Clubs: Commonwealth (Richmond, Va.); Country of Va. (Richmond). Home: 22 Lower Tuckahoe Rd W Richmond VA 23233-6108 Office: CSX Corp PO Box 85629 Richmond VA 23285-5629

WATKINS, HORTENSE CATHERINE, middle school educator; b. St. Louis, Nov. 29, 1924; d. Isaiah S. and Katie M. (Phelps) W. BA, Harris-Stowe State Coll., St. Louis, 1946; MEd, U. Ill., 1953; postgrad. U. Chgo., InterAm. U., Saltillo, Coahuila, Mex.; postgrad., U. Seville, Spain, Webster U., St. Louis. Cert. life tchr., reading specialist, Mo. Coord. urban rural programs Carver-Dunbar Schs., St. Louis, 1975-76; adminstrv. asst. Shaw Visual Performing Arts Sch., 1978-82; team IV leader Woerner IGE, 1982-87; tchr., head lang. arts dept. Nottingham Mid. Sch., 1987-92. Tutor fgn.-speaking religious, presenter, lectr. numerous workshops; curriculum advisor St. Louis Pub. Schs. Active numerous comty. orgns.; bd. dirs. St. Louis Cathedral Sch., St. Louis Metro Singers, Concert Series of St. Louis Cathedral, Quartet Seraphin; bd. dirs. Cath. Family Counseling. Mem. ASCD, Nat. Coun. Tchrs. English, Mo. State Tchrs. Assn., Greater St. Louis Coun. Social Studies, Delta Sigma Theta (Golden life), Delta Kappa Gamma. Home: 5070A Enright Ave Saint Louis MO 63108-1008

WATKINS, JAMES DAVID, federal official, military officer; b. Alhambra, Calif., Mar. 7, 1927; s. Edward Francis and Louise Whipple (Ward) Watkins; m. Sheila Jo McKinney, Aug. 19, 1950 (dec. Sept. 1996); m. Janet L. McDonough, June 17, 2000; children: Katherine Marie, Laura Jo, Charles Lancaster, Susan Elizabeth, James David, Edward Francis. BS, U.S. Naval Acad., 1949; MS, Naval Postgrad. Sch., 1958; LHD (hon.) , Marymount Coll., 1982, N.Y. Med. Coll., 1988; DSc (hon.) , Dowling Coll., 1983, U. Ala., 1991; LLD (hon.) , Cath. U. Am., 1985, Mt. Sinai Sch. Medicine, 1993, Calif. U. Pa., 1994; DS (hon.) , Coll. William and Mary, 1999. Commd. ensign USN, 1949, advanced through grades to adm., 1979, comdg. officer U.S.S. Snook, 1964-66, exec. officer U.S.S. Long Beach, 1967-69; head submarine/nuclear power distbn. control br. Bur. Naval Pers., Dept. Navy, Washington, 1969-71, dir. enlisted pers. div., 1971-72, asst. chief naval pers. for enlisted pers. control, 1972-73; comdr. Cruiser-Destroyer Group 1 USN, 1973-75; dep. chief naval ops. manpower Dept. Navy, Washington, 1975-78, chief of naval pers., 1975-78, chief Bur. Naval Pers., 1975-78; comdr. U.S. Sixth Fleet USN, 1978-79; vice chief naval ops. Dept. Navy, Washington, 1979-81, comdr.-in-chief U.S. Pacific Fleet, 1981-82, chief naval ops., 1982-86; chmn. Presdl. Commn. Human Immunodeficiency Virus Epidemic, 1987-88; sec. Dept. Energy, Washington, 1989-93; pres. Joint Oceanographic Instn., 1993-2000, Consortium Oceanographic Rsch. and Edn., 1993-2001. Chmn. Presidentially Apptd. Commn. Ocean Policy, 2001—. Decorated DSM with 1 gold star, Legion of Merit with 2 gold stars, Bronze Star medal with combat v; recipient Disting. Alumni award, Naval Postgrad. Sch., 1958, Chmn.'s award, Am. Assn. Engring. Socs., 1991, Disting. Grad. award, U.S. Naval Acad., 2001. Mem.: U.S. Naval Acad. Alumni Assn., Knights of Malta. Roman Catholic.

WATKINS, JERRY WEST, retired oil company executive, lawyer; b. Vernon, Tex., Dec. 10, 1931; s. Terrell Clark and Daisy (West) W.; m. Elizabeth Jill Cole, Sept. 3, 1955. Student, Hendrix Coll., 1949-50, La. Poly. Inst., 1950-51; JD, U. Ark., 1954. Bar: Ark. 1954. Law clk. Supreme Ct. Ark., Little Rock, 1954-55; with Murphy Oil Corp., El Dorado, Ark., 1955-89, sec., gen. atty., 1966-71, sec., gen. counsel, 1971-88, v.p., dir., 1975-88, exec. v.p., 1991-92, also bd. dirs., 1975-89. CEO, bd. dirs. Ocean Drilling and Exploration Co., New Orleans, 1989-91; mem. Ark. Bd. Law Examiners, 1969-74; bd. dirs. Simmons First Bank of El Dorado, N.A., Simmons First Nat. Corp., Cross Oil Rifining & Mktg., Inc., 2001--. Mem. Barton Libr. Bd., El Dorado, 1966—89; trustee Ark. State U., 1982—87; bd. dirs. South Ark. Arts Ctr., El Dorado, 1979—82, 1985—88, Warner Brown Hosp., El Dorado, 1984—87, South Ark. Med. Sys., 1987—89, Presbyn. Found. Ark., 1998—, Union County Cmty. Found., 2001—. Mem. ABA, Ark. Bar Assn., Union County Bar Assn. Home: 111 Watkins Dr El Dorado AR 71730-2752

WATKINS, JOAN MARIE, osteopath, occupational medicine physician; b. Anderson, Ind., Mar. 9, 1943; d. Curtis David and Dorothy Ruth (Beckett) W.; m. Stanley G. Nodvik, Dec. 25, 1969 (div. Apr. 1974). BS, West Liberty State Coll., 1965; Cert. of Grad. Phy. Therapy, Ohio State U., 1966; DO, Phila. Coll. Osteo., 1972; M of Health Professions Edn., U. Ill., Chgo., 1986; MPH, U. Ill., 1989. Diplomate Osteo. Nat. Bds., Am. Bd. Preventive Medicine, Am. Bd. Occupl. and Environ. Medicine. Resident in phys. medicine and rehab. U. Pa., 1973—74; emergency osteo. physician Cooper Med. Ctr., Camden, 1974-79, Shore Meml. Hosp., Somers Point, N.J., 1979-81, St. Francis Hosp., Blue Island, Ill., 1981-82, Mercy Hosp. and Med. Ctr., Chgo., 1982-90, dir. emergency ctr., 1984-88; resident in occupational and preventive medicine U. Ill., 1988-90; corp. med. dir. occupl. health svc. Univ. Cmty. Hosp., Tampa, 1992—. Fellow Am. Coll. Occupl. and Environ. Medicine, Am. Soc. Preventive Medicine, Fla. Assn. Occupl. and Environ. Medicine (pres. 1999-2001). Avocations: sailing, needlework, swimming. Home: 4306 Harbor House Dr

Tampa FL 33615-5408 Office: U Community Hosp Occupational Health Svcs 3100 E Fletcher Ave Tampa FL 33613-4613 Office Fax: (813) 632-7711. E-mail: watkinsoccmed@worldnet.att.net., jwatkins@tampabay.com.

WATKINS, JOANNE PATRICIA, clinical social worker; b. Key West, Fla., Oct. 23, 1928; d. Joseph Nielsen and Jennie Mae (Johnson) W. BA, Winthrop Coll., 1950; MSW, U. N.C., 1955. Diplomate Am. Bd. Examiners in Clin. Social Work; cert. Acad. Cert. Social Workers; lic. social worker, marriage & family therapist. Psychiat. social worker Dept. Psychiatry Johns Hopkins Hosp., Balt., 1954-55, Dept. Psychiatry N.C. Meml. Hosp., Chapel Hill, 1957-60; sr. clin. social worker Phila. Child Guidance Clinic, 1960-65; supervising social worker Children's Hosp. of Phila., 1965-70; dir. profl. svcs. Family Svc. Assn. Bucks County, Doylestown, Pa., 1970-80; social worker, cons. pvt. practice, Southampton, 1980-84, social worker, Atlanta, 1984-93; treatment coord., family therapist Ctrs. for Psychiatry & Psychology, Smyrna, 1987-91; sr. social worker mental health unit Brunswick (Ga.) Gen. Hosp., 1993-96, Gateway Mental Health Clinic, Brunswick, 1997-99; part time social worker skilled nursing unit Gulf Health Care Ctr., Galveston, Tex., 2000—. Bd. dirs. Satir Tng. Inst. of Southeast, Chapel Hill, 1990-92. Mem. NASW, Pa. Assn. Social Workers (sec. 1970-71), Assn. for Humanistic Psychology, Audubon Soc., Sierra Club. Avocations: walking, fishing, theater, concerts. Home: 500 Tiki Dr Apt 203 Galveston TX 77554-7152

WATKINS, JOHN FRANCIS, management consultant; b. Alhambra, Calif., May 21, 1925; s. Edward F. and Louise (Ward) W.; divorced; children—Stephen, Katherine, John Francis, William. BSCE, U. Tex., Austin, 1947. With Earle M. Jorgensen Co., Lynwood, Calif., 1947-90, sr. v.p. adminstrn., 1978-90, ret.; owner John F. Watkins Assocs., Pasadena, 1990—. Pres. bd. Poly. Sch., Pasadena, 1978—80, Holy Family Sch., 1994—2002; adv. bd. mem. Serra H.S., Verbum Dei H.S., Dolores Mission Sch., 1996—; mem. dean's coun. Coll. Sci. and Engring./Loyola Marymount U.; adv. bd. Bishop Mora Salesian H.S., 1994—; mem. Edn. Found. Archdiocese L.A., 1995—; St. Gabriel pastoral region bd. dirs. Cath. Charities, 1994—; bd. dirs. Boys Republic, Chino Hills, Calif., 1970—, pres., 1977—80; bd. dirs. St. Luke Hosp., Pasadena, 1979—86, chmn. bd., 1982—86; bd. dirs. Econ. Literacy Coun. Calif., 1980—87, Pasadena Hist. Mus., 1990—99. Mem. U.S. Navy League (nat. bd. dirs. 1989—, pres. Pasadena coun. 1992-93), Calif. Club, Annandale Golf Club, Serra Club (pres. 1995-97), Valley Club (San Marino, Calif.). Republican. Roman Catholic. Home and Office: 410 California Ter Pasadena CA 91105-2419 E-mail: jwatkins@dacorworld.com.

WATKINS, JOHN CLETIS, lawyer; b. Black Oak, Ark., Mar. 26, 1917; s. Joseph Cleveland and Sylvia Ann (Hamilton) W.; m. Arna Lana Shields, Sept. 11, 1924; 1 child, Mary lana Watkins Schult. Student Ark. State U., 1939-40, 46-48; J.D., U. Ark., 1952. Practice law, West Memphis, Ark., 1951-54, Paragould, Ark., 1954-73; of counsel Joe Hollifield, Paragould; mcpl. judge City of Paragould, 1959-63. Author: (novel) With Another Mans Gold, 1986. Served to sgt. AUS, 1940-45. Mem. Greene Clay Bar Assn. (pres. 1965), Ark. Bar Assn., VFW, Am. Legion, DAV. Lodge: Masons. Home: 28 Hillcrest Dr Paragould AR 72450

WATKINS, JUDITH ANN, nurse administrator; b. Chgo., Mar. 11, 1942; d. Russell and Louise Bernadine (Aloy) Keim; m. Thomas H. Watkins III, Dec. 24, 1961; children: Tamara Sue, Randall Scott. Grad. in nursing, Knapp Coll. Nursing, Santa Barbara, Calif., 1963; BSN, PHN cert., Pacific Union Coll., 1991; MHA, U. LaVerne, 1995. Cert. CPR instr., vocat. edn. instr. Obstetrics supr. Bowling Green (Ky.) Warren County Hosp., 1963-67; clin. staff nurse Chula Vista (Calif.) Med. Clinic, 1967-69; nurse aide instr. Sawyers Coll., Ventura, Calif., 1972; ob-gyn. supr. Westlake (Calif.) Community Hosp., 1972-77; RN acute patient care Medical Personnel Pool, Bakersfield, Calif., 1984; med. asst. instr., dir. of allied health San Joaquin Valley Coll., 1984-88; dir. nurses Bakersfield Family Med. Ctr., 1988-91, dir. client svcs., 1991-94, asst. adminstr. clin. svcs., 1994-99, v.p. clin. svcs., 1998—, sr. v.p. clin. svcs., 2000-2001, sr. v.p. patient rels., 2001—; asst. prof. UCLA, 1998—. Recipient Nursing Leadership award Sigma Beta Tau, 1998; named Mother of the Yr., Frazier Pk. (Calif.) Community Ch., 1979, Instr. of the Yr., 1986. Mem. Kern County RN Soc., Kern County Trade Club, Pine Mt. Golf Club (founder Lilac Festival 1982, Lady of the Yr. 1983) Sundale Country Club, Seven Oaks Country Club, Toastmasters Internat. Avocations: swimming, golf. Home: 8004 Nairn Ct Bakersfield CA 93309-4276 Office: Bakersfield Family Med Ctr 4580 California Ave Bakersfield CA 93309-7013 *Personal philosophy: All things are possible through Christ who strengthens me.*

WATKINS, LEWIS BOONE, artist; b. Beckley, W.Va., July 24, 1945; s. Fred Boone and Margaret Theodris (Laurie) W.; m. Marinda Ann Hogan, Aug. 18, 1979; children: Mary Sheridan, Marinda Laurie. BS, W.Va. State Coll., 1978; postgrad., U. South Fla., 1979-82. Artist in residence Boxwood Gallery, Brooksville, Fla., 1978-79; instr. of gifted Hernando County, 1979-81; artist in residence Casa Serena Gallery, Brooksville, 1981—. Vis. artist W.Va. State Coll., Samford U., St. Leo Coll., U. Tampa (Fla.); works include numerous lithograph print edits., sculpture represented in permanent collections Fla. State Mus., U. Fla., Gainesville, Vatican Mus., Vatican City, Italy, W.Va. Fine Arts and Cultural Ctr., Charleston, Nat. Fine Arts Mus., Santiago, Chile, Nat. Art Gallery, Chile, St. Petersburg Fine Art Mus., Nat. Baseball Hall of Fame and Mus., Cooperstown, N.Y., Boston Sport Mus., San Diego Sport Mus., also numerous pvt. collections; sculptures include Hernando Heritage Sculpture, 1981, Crosses of Life, 1982, Youth of Today, 1983; Am. Farmer Meml. Sculpture, Bonner, Kans., 1986. Bd. advisors Hernando County YMCA (Fla.); pres. Boxwood Art Guild, 1978; treas. Hernando County Young Republicans, 1981. Recipient various awards including Amb. Artistic Achievement award State of W.Va., 1981, Amb. of Art award, 1989; Outstanding Achievement award State of Fla., 1982; proclamation declaring Lewis Watkins Day, Hernando County, Fla., 1981; Cert. of Recognition in Art, State of Ga., 1983, award for sculpture, Tampa, Fla., 1984, Pub. Svc. award City of Atlanta, 1984. Mem. Hernando Heritage Mus. Assn. (bd. dirs.), Hernando County C. of C.

WATKINS, LINDA THERESA, educational researcher; b. York, Pa., Sept. 29, 1947; d. Nathan Franklin and Madelyn Marie (Mandl) W.; m. Hugh Jerald Silverman, June 22, 1968 (div. Apr. 1983); children: Claire Christine Silverman, Hugh Christopher Silverman; m. Patrick Grim. BA, Muhlenberg Coll., 1968; MA, San Jose (Calif.) State Coll., 1970; PhD, Stanford (Calif.) U., 1977; cert., Hofstra U., 1991. Rsch. asst. prof. L.I. Rsch. Inst., Stony Brook, N.Y., 1977-79; asst. prof. NYU, 1979-85; rsch. assoc. Psychiatry dept. SUNY, Stony Brook, 1985-87; dir. of rsch., planning and grants mgmt. Bd. Coop. Ednl. Svcs. Eastern Suffolk, Patchogue, N.Y., 1987—. Adj. lectr. SUNY Sch. Soc. Welfare, 1994; cons. Dowling Coll., Oakdale, N.Y., 1991, Tele-Niger Evaluation Project, Paris, 1972; survey cons. Redbook Mag., N.Y., 1987; interviewer Am. Inst. for Rsch., Kensington, Md., 1973. Contbr. articles to profl. jours. Rsch. grant Ronald McDonald Children's Charities, 1988, Am. Broadcasting Co., 1978, Dissertation rsch. grant Nat. Assn. of Broadcasters, 1974; NDEA fellowship, 1972. Mem. ASCD, APA, Soc. for Rsch. in Child Devel., Am. Ednl. Rsch. Assn. Avocation: house restoration. Home: 99 Sweezey St Patchogue NY 11772-4160 Office: Bd Coop Ednl Svcs Suffolk 1 15 Andrea Rd Holbrook NY 11741 E-mail: twatkins@sricboces.org.

WATKINS, MICHAEL JAMES, real estate broker; b. Crawfordsville, Ind., Dec. 18, 1945; s. James H. Gordon and Mary Jane Harlson; m. Jeanne Watkins, Apr. 3, 1971; children: Patrick, christopher. BS, U. Indpls., 1968; MS, Butler U., 1972. Tchr., coach New Palestine (Ind.) High Sch., 1968-69, Franklin (Ind.) High Sch., 1969-72; admissions counselor U. Indpls., 1972-73, dir. fin. aid, 1973-76, dean of students, 1975-78; owner Michael J. Realty, Indpls., 1978-80; sales mgr. Credence Contractors, Greenwood, Ind., 1980-83; broker, assoc. Tomlin Realtors, 1983-95; pres. Mike Watkins Real Estate Group, 1995—. Mem. Pres.'s Club, U. Indpls., 1984—; trustee Marian Coll., Indpls., 1989-92, U. Indpls., 1992—. Named to Outstanding Young Men of Am., 1974, 76. Mem. Met. Bd. Realtors (named Southside Realtor of Yr. 1984), Nat. Assn. Realtors, U. Indpls. Alumni Varsity Club (Alumnus of Yr. 1986). Republican. Roman Catholic. Avocations: golf, boating, family activities. Home: 4265 Sagewood Ct Greenwood IN 46143-8455 Office: Mike Watkins Real Estate 633 Library Park Dr Ste J Greenwood IN 46142-1578

WATKINS, RONDA GAIL, interior design company executive; b. Dallas, Dec. 11, 1947; d. Alton Dee and Iva Foncell (Fields) Powell; m. Ronald D. Watkins, Sept. 24, 1966 (div. Oct. 1977); 1 child, Natalie Noelle. Degree in interior decoration and design, Internat. Corr. Sch., Scranton, Pa., 1975. Design intern Total Interiors & Gallery, Euless, Tex., 1973; interior designer, office mgr. Melinda McGill Interiors, Richland Hills, 1973-74; owner, interior designer Interior Concepts, Arlington, 1975-77; interior designer Decorative Ctr. Arlington, 1977-80; owner, interior designer Ronda Watkins's Interior Concepts, Arlington, 1980—90; interior designer Dillard's Custom Interiors, Ft. Worth, 1990—97; owner Ronda Watkins Interiors, Arlington, 1997—. Democrat. Baptist. Avocations: watercolor, pastel and pencil-sketching, guitar.

WATKINS, SHERRY LIGON, medical facility data executive, nurse; b. Richmond, Va., May 8, 1949; d. James Harold and Gladys Marie (Wright) Ligon; children: Elizabeth Watkins Hurt, James Edwin Watkins. Diploma, Grace Hosp. Sch. Nursing, Richmond, 1970; BSN, U. Va., 1972; MBA, Averett Coll., Richmond, 1996. RN, Va. Staff nurse Grace Hosp., Richmond, 1970-71; head nurse Children's Rehab Ctr. Univ. Va., Charlottesville, 1972-78; staff nurse Richmond Meml. Hosp., 1978; supr., edn. coord. Richmond Eye & Ear Hosp., 1978-85, 91-99; inservice coord. Southside Regional Med. Ctr., Petersburg, Va., 1985-90, clin. application support specialist, 1990—. Election officer Chesterfield County (Va.) Electoral Bd., 1984-91, dep. chief judge, 1992—. Mem. Healthcare Info. and Mgmt. Systems Soc., Mid-Atlantic Regional Users Group (nursing SIG chmn. 1995, membership chmn. 1996, pres. 1997-98), UDC. Baptist. Avocations: hiking, camping, reading, sewing, fishing, civil war re-enactment. Office: Southside Regional Med Ctr 801 S Adams St Petersburg VA 23803-5133

WATKINS, SHERRY LYNNE, elementary school educator; b. Bloomington, Ind., Oct. 13, 1944; d. Quentin Odell and Velma Ruth W. BSEd, Ind. U., 1966, MSEd, 1968. Tchr. 4th grade North Grove Elem. Sch., Ctr. Grove Sch. Dist., Greenwood, Ind., 1966-68; tchr. 4th and 6th grades John Strange Sch., Met. Dist. of Wash. Twp., Indpls., 1968-91; tchr. 4th grade Allisonville Sch. Met. Sch. Dist. of Wash. Twp., 1991—. Bd. dirs. ISTA Ins. Trust and Fin. Svcs. Mem. People for Ethical Treatment of Animals. Mem.: AAUW, ACLU, NEA (nat. del. 1978—), State Profl. Affairs (chair 2001—03), World Confedn. Orgn. of Tchg. Profls. (del. Costa Rica 1990), Washington Twp. Edn. Assn. (pres. 1986—89), Ind. Tchrs. Assn. (state del. 1966—), Alpha Omicron Pi, Delta Kappa Gamma (chpt. pres. 1992—94, chmn. coordinating coun. Indpls. area 1994—96, state legislature chair 1997—99, chair profl. affairs 2001—). Avocations: traveling, cultural activities. Office: Allisonville Sch 4920 E 79th St Indianapolis IN 46250-1615

WATKINS, STEPHEN EDWARD, accountant, newspaper executive; b. Oklahoma City, Sept. 1, 1922; s. Ralph Bushnell and Jane (Howell) W.; m. Suzanne Fowler, Aug. 16, 1976; children— Elizabeth Ann Watkins Racicot, Stephen Edward, Jr. BBA, U. N.Mex., 1944. C.P.A., N.Mex. With Peat, Marwick, Mitchell & Co., 1944-67; pres. The New Mexican daily newspaper, Santa Fe, 1967-78, 90—; pvt. practice pub. acctg., 1978—. Vestryman Ch. of Holy Faith; trustee St. Vincent Hosp., 1979-85, Orchestra Santa Fe, 1976-82, Hist. Santa Fe Found. (pres. 1990). Mem. AICPA, Sons of Am. Revolution, Rotary. Home: 1325 Don Gaspar Ave Santa Fe NM 87505-4627 Office: 223 E Palace Ave Santa Fe NM 87501-1947

WATKINS, SUSAN GAIL, lawyer; b. Independence, Mo., May 17, 1962; d. Floyd L. and Judy G. (Bell) W.; children: Eva, Andrea, Grant, Kyle. BA, Graceland Coll., 1983; JD, U. Mo., 1986. Bar: Mo. 1986, U.S. Dist. Ct. (we. dist.) Mo. 1986, U.S. Ct. Appeals 1990. Assoc. Les D. Wight, P.C., Independence, 1986-87; ptnr. Snoke & Watkins, 1987-90, Watkins Law Offices, 1990—; asst. prosecuting atty. Jackson County, Mo., 1991-94. Instr. Draughon Bus. Coll., Independence, 1987-90; exec. dir. Independence Youth Ct., 1988—, Ea. Jackson County Youth Ct., 2000—; judge Independence Mcpl. Ct., 1995—. Bd. dirs. Music Arts Inst., Randall Elem. Sch.; mem. Independence Jr. Svc. League. Mem. ABA, ATLA, Mo. Assn. Trial Attys., Assn. Women Lawyers, Mo. Assn. Criminal Def. Lawyers, East Jackson County Bar Assn. (bd. dirs.), Mo. Mcpl. Judges Assn., Ednl. Adv. Coun., L.E.A.D. Youth Friends Independence C. of C., Phi Alpha Delta. Mem. Reorganized Ch. of Jesus Christ of Latter-day Saints. Avocations: swimming, sailing, skiing, scuba diving, music. Office: Watkins Law Offices 17521 E 24 Hwy # 10 Independence MO 64056

WATKINS, SYDNEY LYNN, sales executive; b. Hartford, Conn., Sept. 12, 1964; s. Robert Lee and Joan (Hardy) W. BS, Howard U., 1986, MS, 1989. Cert. U.S. Olympic Acad., Sport Adminstrn. Facility Mgmt. Inst. Water safety instr. Howard U. Satellite Youth Program, Washington, 1986, D.C. Dept. Recreation, Washington, 1986-87, phys. therapeutic recreation specialist, 1987-88; account rep. AT&T, Silver Spring, Md., 1988-90; program assoc. Amateur Athletic Found., L.A., 1991-95; program mgr. L.A. Team Mentoring, 1995-96; ind. cons., 1996—; pharm. sales cons. Wyeth-Ayerst Labs., 1997-99; dist. sales mgr. Takeda Pharms. Am., 1999—. Spl. asst. to pres. Dr. LeRoy T. Walker Found., Durham, N.C., 1993. African Am. Summit fellow NAACP, L.A., 1994; Patricia Roberts Harris grantee Howard U., 1989. Mem. AAHPERD, Alpha Kappa Alpha. Home: 3675 River Summit Trail Duluth GA 30097 E-mail: Rokwest@aol.com.

WATKINS, TED ROSS, social work educator; b. Terrell, Tex., Dec. 2, 1938; s. Daniel Webster and Iva Lucy (Lowrie) W.; m. Betty Diane Dobbs, May 30, 1959; children: Evan Scott, Brett Dobbs, James David. BA in Psychology, U. North Tex., 1961; MSW, La. State U., 1963; D of Social Work, U. Pa., 1976. Staff social worker Mercer County Mental Health Ctr., Sharon, Pa., 1963-65; chief social worker, assoc. exec. Talbot Hall Treatment Ctr., Jonestown, 1965-70; chief social worker Harrisburg (Pa.) Mental Health Ctr., 1970-71; asst. prof. social work U. Tex., Arlington, 1971-76; dir. counseling svcs. Family Svcs., Inc., Ft. Worth, 1976-79; assoc. prof. social work U. Tex., 1979-85, dir. criminal justice, 1985-87, chair dept. sociology, 1987-91, assoc. prof., grad. advisor social work, 1991-99; assoc. prof., dir. Bachelor of Social Work program S.W. Tex. State U., San Marcos, 1999—. Cons. in field. Author (with James Callicutt): Mental Health Policy and Practice Today, 1997; author: (with A. Lewellen and M. Barrett) Dual Diagnosis: An Integrated Approach to Treatment, 2001. Tex. del. to Pres.'s Commn. in Mental Health, Austin, 1978. Recipient Golladay Teaching award Coll. Liberal Arts, Arlington, 1990; named Outstanding Profl. Human Svcs., 1972. Mem. NASW (state bd. dirs. 1976-78, 80-82, unit chair, vol. lobbyist 1982), Acad. Cert. Social Workers (lic. master social worker, advanced clin. practitioner), World Assn. for Psychosocial Rehab., Alliance for the Mentally Ill, Nat. Assn. for Rural Mental Health, Nat. Social Sci. Assn. Democrat. Methodist. Avocations: music, painting, camping. Office: SW Tex State U Dept Social Work 601 University Dr San Marcos TX 78666-4685 E-mail: tw11@swt.edu.

WATKINS, WESLEY WADE, congressman; b. DeQueen, Ark., Dec. 15, 1938; s. L. V. and Mary J. W.; m. Elizabeth Lou Rogers, June 9, 1963; children: Sally, Martha, Wade. BS, Okla. State U., 1960, MS, 1961. With USDA, Washington, 1961; asst. dir. admissions Okla. State U., 1963-66; exec. dir. Kiamichi Econ. Devel. Dist. of Okla., 1966-68; founder, owner constrn. and land devel. bus., 1968-76; mem. Okla. Senate, 1975-76, U.S. Congress from 3d Okla. Dist., 1977—91, 1997—; mem. ways and means com., human resources subcom., budget com.; pres. World Export Services, Stillwater, Okla., 1991—96. Pres. Higher Edn. Alumni Council of Okla.; Okla. chmn. Nat. Future Farmers Am. Found.; mem. Okla. Health Planning Council.; Pres. Ada (Okla). Growth and Devel. Assn. Served with Air N.G., 1960-66. Recipient Nat. Security Leadership award U.S. Air N.G., 1967, Okla. 4-H Alumni Recognition award, 1978, Disting. Alumnus award Okla. State U. Alumni Assn., 1978, others; named Policymaker of the Yr. Am. Vocational Assn., One of 3 Outstanding Young Men in Okla., Okla. Jaycees, 1968; named to Okla. State U. Hall of Fame, 1989. Mem. C. of C. Clubs: Masons, Lions. Republican. Presbyterian. Office: US Ho Reps 1401 Longworth Ho Office Bldg Washington DC 20515-3603*

WATKINS, WILLIAM, JR. electric power industry executive; b. Jersey City, Aug. 12, 1932; s. William James and Willie Ree (Blount) W.; m. Sylvia I. Mulzac, Oct. 16, 1955; children: Cheryl, Rene, Linda. BBA, Pace U., 1954; MBA, NYU, 1962; postgrad. advanced mgmt. program, U. Mich., 1979; postgrad. exec. program, Edison Electric Inst., 1988. Staff asst. Consol. Edison Co. N.Y., N.Y.C., 1957-64; sys. mgr. Volkswagen Am., Englewood Cliffs, N.J., 1964-71; v.p., dir. adminstrn. New Eng. Power Svc. Co., Westboro, Mass., 1972-82, v.p., dir. human resources, 1986-92; v.p., dist. mgr. Narragansett Electric Co., Providence, 1982-86, exec. v.p., 1992-97; retired. Bd. dirs. Peerless Precision Corp., Lincoln, R.I., 1982-91; mem. bd. advisors Sarasota Pvt. Bank, Fleet Fin. Group, 2001. Chmn. R.I. Urban Project, Providence, 1984, R.I. Coun. for Econ. Edn., Providence, 1984; mem. Gov.'s Commn. on Health Care Reform, 1993-94; trustee R.I. Hosp., 1995-96, Lifespan, 1996-99, Roger Williams U., Bristol, R.I., 1991-94; bd. dirs. R.I. Hosp. Fin. Corp., Providence, 1987-91, Inroads, 1993-97, Leadership R.I., 1993-95, NCCJ, 1993-97; mem. resource and devel. commn. Episcopal Diocese Mass., 1988-92; chmn. bd. trustees RISD, 1998-2000. Recipient Cmty. Svc. award Urban League R.I., 1986, Paris V. Sterett award John Hope Settlement House, 1987, Small Bus. Adminstrn. Adv. of the Yr. award, 1994; named Developer of Yr., Am. Econ. Devel. Coun., 1996. Mem. N.E. Econ. Developers Assn. (bd. dirs. 1993-97), R.I. Urban Bankers Assn., Kappa Alpha Psi, Sigma Pi Phi. Avocations: swimming, biking, hiking, traveling, golf. Home: 5114 87th Ct E Bradenton FL 34211-3743

WATKINS, WILLIAM DAVID, editor, writer, consultant, mentor; b. Sacto., Sept. 22, 1952; s. William Wallace and Martha Margaret (Combs) W.; m. Pamela Ann Norton, Sept. 30, 1972 (div. 1998); children: Krista Ann, Jared David, Shannon Marie, Hillary Elizabeth, Katie Brookem. Donna Rae Manzanares, July 6, 2002. BA in Philosophy, Calif. State U., Fresno, 1978; M of Theology in Systematic Theology, Dallas Theol. Sem., 1984. Percussionist, trombonist various musical groups, 1967-84; dir. ednl. resources Insight for Living, Fullerton, Calif., 1984-86; assoc. dir. Quest Ministries, Dallas, 1986-87; mng. editor, then sr. editor Thomas Nelson Pubs., Nashville, 1987-92; sr. acquisitions editor Moody Press, Chgo., 1992-93; v.p. pub. Liberty, Life and Family, Virginia Beach, Va., 1993-96; dir. publs. Am. Ctr. for Law and Justice, 1993-96; pres., founder William Pens, Longmont, Colo., 1986—; sr. acquisitions and devel. editor Broadman & Holman Pubs., Nashville, 1997-98. Adj. faculty Talbot Sch. Theology, La Mirada, Calif., 1986; speaker in field. Author: The New Absolutes, 1996, The Busy Christian's Guide to the Deeper Life, 1996, The Busy Christian's Guide to Experiencing God More, 1997; co-author: Worlds Apart, 1989, In Defense of Life, 1996; mem. editorial adv. bd. Culture Wars mag., 1994—, Dallas/Ft. Worth Heritage Newspaper, 1992—. Tchr. Sunday Sch., various chs., Calif., Tex., Tenn., 1974—. Mem. Evangel. Theol. Soc., Evangel. Philos. Soc. Republican. Episcopalian. Avocations: walking, listening to music, reading, attending plays, concerts and art shows. E-mail: wmpens@aol.com.

WATKISS, ERIC JOHN, career officer; b. East Point, Ga., May 17, 1964; s. George Philip Watkiss and Barbara Anne Seaman; m. Lynne Lee Novak, Nov. 25, 1989. B of Aerospace Engring., Ga. Inst. Tech., 1986; MS in Aero. Engring., Naval Postgrad. Sch., 1994; grad., U.S. Naval Test Pilot Sch., 1995. Lic. pvt. pilot FAA. Airport mgr. Aerocountry Airport, McKinney, Tex., 1981-86; advanced through grades to lt. comdr. USN, 1996, naval flight officer, 1986—, EA-6B Prowler electronic countermeasures officer, 1989—, naval flight test officer, 1995-96, naval test pilot sch. instr., 1996-98, EA-6B Prowler weapon sys. support activity mil. lead, 1998—2001, naval weapons test squadron Pt. Mugu chief test pilot, 2001; with Nat. Reconnaissance Office, Chantilly, Va., 2001—. Decorated two Navy Achievement medals, 1990, 91, one Navy Commendation medal, Meritorious Svc. medal. Mem. AIAA (winner 1st pl. aircraft design competition 1993, 94), MENSA, Aircraft Owners and Pilots Assn, Assn. Naval Aviation, Concours Owners Group, Ret. Officers Assn. Republican. Episcopalian. Avocations: flying, mountain biking, skiing. Home: 26235 Rachel Hill Dr Chantilly VA 20152-2500 E-mail: watkiss_eric@yahoo.com.

WATLINGTON, SARAH JANE, community volunteer, retired military officer; b. Denver, May 6, 1938; d. William Thomas and Margaret (Stewart) W. BS, Purdue U., 1960; MA, Naval Post Grad. Sch., 1970. Commd. ensign USN, 1960, advanced through grades to capt., 1979; social sec. Chief of Naval Operations, Washington, 1966-69; exec. officer Recruit Tng. Command, Bainbridge, Md., 1971-73; head officer student placement Bur. Naval Personnel, Washington, 1973-75; exec. officer NROTC Unit, Purdue U., West Lafayette, Ind., 1976-79; commanding officer Navy Manpower and Material Analysis Ctr., San Diego, 1979-82; dep. dir. manpower & tng. Office Chief of Naval Ops., Washington, 1982-83; ret., USN, 1984. Sec. Cmty. and Family Resource Ctr., Lafayette, Ind., 1990-91; mem. dean of liberal arts adv. coun., 1992-96. Vol. YWCA, Lafayette, 1984-2000, bd. dirs., 1985-2000, pres., 1988-90, v.p., 1994-95, sec., 1995-96; bd. dirs. YWCA Found., Lafayette, 1988-90, 94-97, Greater Lafayette Mus. Art, 1984-85; mem. Greater Lafayette Cmty. Found., 1991-2001, pres., 1995-97; pres. Ind. Coun. YWCAs, 1994-98, Cmty. Health Clinic, 1995-2000, 02--; mem. nat. nominating com. YWCA U.S.A., 1991-94; trustee, sec.-treas. Alpha Chi Omega Found., 1991-97; co-chair Census 2000 Complete Count Com. for Tippecanoe County, 1999-2000; bd. dirs. West Lafayette Village found., Lafayette Parks Found.; interim exec. dir. Cmty. Health Clinic, 2001; mem. Vision 2020 Strategic Planning Steering Com., 1997-2002. Decorated Legion of Merit with gold star; recipient Jefferson award, 1989, Disting. Alumna award Purdue Sch. Liberal Arts, 1990, Grand Marquis de Lafayette award for Cmty. Svc., 1995, Mortar Bd. nat. award of achievement, 1995, Sagamore of the Wabash award Ind. Gov., 1995, 98, Unsung Hero award Ind. U. Ctr. on Philanthropy, 1997, JC Penney Golden Rule award, 1998; named Woman of Distinction, Girl Scouts of U.S., 1992. Mem. Purdue U. Sch. Liberal Arts Alumni Assn. (pres. 1991-92), Purdue Pres. Coun., John Purdue Club, Gold Block Booster Club (sec. 1986-87), Boilermaker Network Booster Club (sec. 1991-94), Purdue Alumni Assn. (assoc., Citizenship award 1997), Rotary, Alpha Chi Omega (Disting. Alumna award 1980, Golden Gavel Woman of Distinction award 1994). Congregationalist. Avocations: gardening, golf. Home: 9 Elvernan Dr West Lafayette IN 47906-9424

WATNE, DONALD ARTHUR, accountant, educator, retired; b. Gt. Falls, Mont., Jan. 18, 1939; BA with high honors, U. Mont., 1960, MA, 1961; PhD, U. Calif., Berkeley, 1977. CPA, Oreg. Acct. Piquet & Minihan, Eugene, Oreg., 1961-65; mgr. capital investment analysis Weyerhaeuser Co., Tacoma, 1965-68; mktg. rep. IBM Corp., Portland, Oreg., 1968-70; dir. EDP Ctr. in Concejo Mcpl., Barquisimeto, Venezuela, 1971-72; prof. acctg. Portland State U., 1976-2001, prof. emeritus, 2001—. Vis. prof. Xiamen (Fujian, People's Rep. China), 1985-86, U. Otago, Dunedin, New Zealand, 1985-86, U. Newcastle, Australia, 1985-86; cons. in field; acctg. qualifications com. Oregon State Bd. Acctg., 1989-98, CPE com., 1998-2001. Author: (with Peter B.B. Turney) Auditing EDP Systems, 2d edit. 1990; contbr. chpts. to books, articles to profl. jours. Del. to Soviet Union citizen amb. program People to People Internat., 1990; active Tng. the Trainers Program, Vilnius, Lithuania, 1993; trustee First Unitarian Ch. of Portland, 2002--, mem. bd. stewards, 2002--. Mem.: AICPA, Oreg. Soc. CPAs, Mensa, Mazamas Mountain Climbing Club. Home: 2826 NE 26th Ave Portland OR 97212-3503 Office: Portland State U Sch Bus Adminstrn PO Box 751 Portland OR 97207-0751 Personal E-mail: dawatne@msn.com.

WATNICK, ROCHELLE, assistant principal; b. N.Y.C., June 3, 1948; d. Alexander and Tillie (Ziskin) Ockun; m. Philip Barry Watnick, Mar. 28, 1970; 1 child, Erica Joy. BA in Elem. Edn., Bklyn. Coll., 1970, MS in Urban Edn., 1972, MS in Reading, 1976; cert. advanced study in edn. adminstrn., Hofstra U., 1982. Cert. prin., N.Y.; cert. tchr., N.Y. Tchr. grades 1, 4 and English as a second lang. P.S. 113, N.Y.C. Bd. Edn., 1970; tchr. grade 6 P.S. 86, N.Y.C. Bd. Edn., 1977; tchr. grades 4-6 P.S. 183, N.Y.C. Bd. Edn., 1978, Astor tchr. of the gifted, 1981; curriculum leader CIMS Edn. Adminstr., N.Y.C., 1983; reading tchr. P.S. 197, N.Y.C. Bd. Edn., 1984; dir. lang. arts, reading Dist. 27, N.Y.C. Bd. Edn., 1988; asst. prin. P.S. 42, N.Y.C. Bd. Edn., 1990; schoolwide projects coord. Dist. 27, N.Y.C. Bd. Edn., 1990; asst. prin. P.S. 155, N.Y.C. Bd. Edn., 1991, P.S. 146, N.Y.C. Bd. Edn., 1992—. Tchr. Vacation Day Camp, Dist. 19, N.Y.C. Bd. of Edn., 1968-73; adminstrv. intern Dist. 27 Office of Reimbursable Funds, 1981; tchr. in charge of Vacation Day Camp 60, 1982; curriculum leader CIMS Edn. Adminstr., N.Y.C., 1983; site supr. Summer Primary Program, Dist 27, 1986, 91; instr. whole lang. in-svc. course N.Y.C. Staff Devel. Tng. Program, 1988; instr. children's lit. in-svc. course N.Y.C. Staff Devel. Tng. Program, 1989. Author: Gates to Learning Communication Arts: Enrichment Program for Promotional Center, 1982, (with others) Integrating Learning and Testing: Handbooks for Teachers of Grades Three and Six, 1984; editor, author Lang. Arts Newsletter, 1988, Dist. 27 Monthly Newsletter, 1990, Dist. 27 Parent Orientation Handbook, 1990; contbr. articles to profl. jours. Vol. Hewlett-Woodmere Pub. Sch. PTA, 1979-82; fundraiser, organizing chairperson P.S. 155Q/146Q, 1992; career trainer Bus. Kids T-shirts, P.S. 183Q, 1982; mem. supr. adv. coun. Educators for Gateway, N.Y. City Bd. Edn.

Mem. ASCD, Nat. Coun. Tchrs. Math., Queensboro Reading Coun. (exec. bd. dirs., pres.), Phi Delta Kappa. Avocations: reading, crafts. Office: PS 146 98-01 159th Ave Howard Beach NY 11414-3543

WATREL, WARREN GEORGE, pharmaceutical company executive; b. N.Y.C. s. John and Julia (Rock) W.; children: Marc, Justin, Stephen. BS, Syracuse U., 1957, MS, postgrad., Syracuse U., 1958, Columbia U. Gen. sales mgr. Pharmacia AB Sweden, Piscataway, N.J., 1964-65, dir. mktg. and sales, gen. mgr., 1965-72; v.p., gen. mgr. Damon Corp., Vineland, 1972-74; ops. and mktg. exec. Pharmachem Corp., Bethlehem, Pa., 1974-75; exec. v.p., chief operating officer Newton (N.J.) Industry Inc., 1976-79; v.p. Seton Co., Newark, 1980-84, George Warren Assocs., Hasbrouck Heights, 1984—. Bd. dirs. Newton Industries, 1976-79; cons. ITT, Paramus, N.J., 1971-72, Jay Holland-Moritz Inc., Hillside, N.Y., 1975, Xonics Inc., L.A., 1975; instr. bacteriology Syracuse (N.Y.) U., 1958. Author: Encyclopedia of Chemistry, 3d edition., 1971. Capt. U.S. Army, 1959-60. Mem. Am. Chem. Soc., AAAS, Am. Soc. Microbiology, N.Y. Acad. Scis., Inst. Chemists. Home: 506 Collins Ave Hasbrouck Heights NJ 07604-2232

WATRING, WATSON GLENN, retired gynecologic oncologist, educator; b. St. Albans, W.Va., June 2, 1936; m. Roberta Tawell. BS, Washington & Lee U., 1958; MD, W.Va. U., 1962. Diplomate Am. Bd. Ob-Gyn, Am. Bd. Gynecol. Oncology. Intern The Toledo Hosp., 1963; resident in ob-gyn Ind. U., Indpls., 1964-66, Tripler Gen. Hosp., Honolulu, 1968-70; resident in gen. and oncologic surgery City of Hope Nat. Med. Ctr., Duarte, Calif., 1970-71, assoc. dir. gynecol. oncology, sr. surgeon, 1973-77; fellow in gynecol. oncology City of Hope Nat. Med. Ctr. and UCLA Med. Ctr., 1972-74; asst. prof. ob-gyn UCLA Med. Ctr., 1972-77; assoc. prof., sr. gynecologist, sr. surgeon Tufts New Eng. Med. Ctr. Hosp., Boston, 1977-80, asst. prof. radiation therapy, 1978-80; practice medicine specializing in ob-gyn, 1980-82; assoc. prof. ob-gyn U. Mass., Worcester, 1982; regional dir. gynecol. oncology So. Calif. Permanente Med. Group, L.A., 1982-99, asst. dir. residency tng., 1985-99, ret., 1999. Dir. gynecol. oncology St. Margarets Hosp. for Women, Dorchester, Mass., 1977—80; clin. prof. ob-gyn U. Calif., Irvine, 1982—99. Contbr. Mem. ch. coun. Luth. Ch. of the Foothills, 1973—75. Lt. col. M.C. U.S. Army, 1965—71. Fellow: L.A. Obstet. and Gynecol. Soc., Am. Coll. Ob-Gyn; mem.: ACS (Calif. and Mass. chpts.), AAAS, AMA, Obstet. Soc. Boston, Boston Surg. Soc., Mass. Suffolk Dist. Med. Soc., Mass. Med. Soc., New Eng. Cancer Soc., New Eng. Obstet. and Gynecol. Soc., New Eng. Assn. Gynecol. Oncologists (chmn. charter com.), We. Assn. Gynecol. Oncologists (sec.-treas. 1976—81, program chmn. 1984, pres. 1985—), We. Soc. Gynecologists and Obstetricians, Internat. Gynecol. Cancer Soc., Soc. Study Breast Disease, Am. Radium Soc., Soc. Gynecol. Oncologists, Am. Soc. Clin. Oncology, Internat. Soc. Gynecol. Pathologists, Daniel Morton Soc., Sigma Xi. Republican. Avocation: Avocations: golf, skiing, horticulture.

WATROUS, NAOMA DICKSION, retired clinical psychologist; b. Pauls Valley, Okla. d. William M. and Almeda (Cosby) Dicksion. BS, Okla. Coll. for Women, 1940; EdD, Okla. U., 1960; MS, Okla. State U., 1950; cert. in gerontology, U. Calif., Long Beach, 1993. Lic. clin. psychologist, Washington; lic. marriage, family and child counselor, gerontologist. Clin. psychologist VA Hosp., Washington, 1961-72; supervisory clin. psychologist Washington D.C. Mental Health Svc., 1972-76, clin. psychologist, 1988-96, VA Hosp. and Med. Svcs., Long Beach, Calif., 1976-88; ret., 1996. Cons. KDH Mental Health Svc., Noble, Okla., 1996-97. Amb. Noble C. of C., Okla., 1997-98; vol. Ret. Srs. Vol. Program, 2000—. Recipient Cert. of Commendation Dept. Human Svcs., Govt. of D.C., 1990, 95. Mem. APA (group psychotherapy charter mem.). Avocations: oil painting, art therapy. Home: 201 Skyridge Trl Noble OK 73068-8111 Personal E-mail: dick4139_ou@ionet.net.

WATROUS, ROBERT THOMAS, academic director; b. Cleve., Apr. 20, 1952; s. Frank Thomas and Marie Anne (Kmeicik) W.; m. Robin Joyce Braun, Mar. 14, 1981 (div. 1993); 1 child, Michael Francis. BS, U. Dayton, 1974, MS, 1977. Dir. student ctr. for off campus cmty. rels. U. Dayton, Ohio, 1974-76, resident dir., 1976-78; dir. of housing St. Bonaventure U., Olean, N.Y., 1978-81; asst. dean of student life/housing Kutztown U. of Pa., 1981-86, dir. commuter and jud. affairs, 1986—. Faculty senate Kutztown (Pa.) U., 1986-89, 92-95; mem. Pa. Task Force on Intergroup Behavior in Higher Edn., 1991-94; trainer Pa. Interagy. Task Force on Civil Tension, Harrisburg, Pa., 1989—; exec. coun. Adult Learners Consortium, Bloomsburg, Pa., 1990-91; mem. Lehigh Valley Svc. Learning Consortium, 1994—. Bd. mgr. Tri Valley YMCA, Fleetwood, Pa., 1983-94; adv. bd. Crossroads, Kutztown, 1989-94; bd. dirs. Jr. Achievement of Berks County, Reading, Pa., 1990, Reading, Pa., 1990, Reading and Berks Coun. YMCA, 1992-96; mem. Leadership Berks, Reading, 1990; bd. dirs. Leadership Berks, 1995—, sec. 1998-99, pres., 2000—; co-founder Leading Sch. Bds., 1994—; mem. YMCA cultural diversity and internat. awareness com., 1994—; mem. Berks County Conflict Resolution Task Force, 1996—; v.p. Fleetwood Activities Booster Club, 1998—, pres., 1999-2001. Mem. Nat. Assn. Student Pers. Adminstrs. (profl. affiliate), Hawk Mt. Coun. Boy Scouts Am. (sustaining mem.), Berks County C. of C. (sch. bd. governance com. 1993—), Fleetwood Youth Soccer Club (v.p., pres. 1999), Fleetwood Youth Basketball Assn. (coach 1995-96). Avocations: golf, sports, gardening. Office: Kutztown Univ PO Box 37 Kutztown PA 19530-0037

WATSON, ALEXANDER FLETCHER, organization executive, former ambassador; b. Boston, Aug. 8, 1939; s. Fletcher G. and Alice Victoria (Hodson) W.; m. Judith Dawson Tuttle, June 23, 1962; children: David F., Caitlin H. BA, Harvard U., 1961; MA, U. Wis., 1969. Consular officer Am. Embassy, Santo Domingo, Dominican Republic, 1962-64, Madrid, 1964-66; internat. relations officer Dept. State, Washington, 1966-68, 73-75; polit. officer Am. Embassy, Brasilia, Brazil, 1969-70; prin. officer Am. Consulate, Salvador, Brazil, 1970-73; spl. asst. Dept. State, Washington, Brazil, 1975-77, dir. Office of Devel Fin. Brazil, 1978-79; dep. chief of mission Am. Embassy, La Paz, Bolivia, 1979-81, Bogota, Colombia, 1981-84, Brasilia, Brazil, 1984-86; U.S. ambassador to Lima, Peru, 1986-89; dep. U.S. permanent rep. to UN, 1989-93; asst. sec. of state for inter-Am. affairs Dept. of State, Washington, 1993-96; v.p., exec. dir. L.Am. and Caribbean region The Nature Conservancy, Arlington, Va., 1996-98; v.p., exec. dir. Internat. Conservation, The Nature Conservancy, 1998—. Pres., bd. dirs. Pan Am. Devel. Found., Caribbean/Latin Am. Action; bd. visitors Dept. Def. Ctrs. for Regional Security. Decorated Order of San Carlos (Colombia), Order of Condor (Bolivia), Labor Justice Order of Merit (Brazil), Order of Sun (Peru), Order of Rio Branco (Brazil). Mem. Am. Fgn. Svc. Assn., Coun. on Fgn. Rels., InterAm. Dialogue, Pacific Coun. Internat. Policy, Washington Inst. Fgn. Affairs., Am. Acad. Diplomacy. Office: The Nature Conservancy Internat Hdqs 4245 Fairfax Dr Ste 100 Arlington VA 22203-1650

WATSON, ARTHUR DENNIS, federal official; b. Brownsville, Pa., May 11, 1950; s. Arthur Francis Publia and Margaret Teresa Mastile; m. Kathleen Frances Zaccardo, July 16, 1983; 1 child Fiona Kathleen ;1 stepchild John Leslie. BSBA, U. Richmond, 1972; MS in Bus.-Govt. Rels., Am. U., 1977, MA in Lit., 1979; PhD in English Lang. and Lit., Cath. U., 1987. Statis. asst. U.S. Postal Svc. Hdqrs., Washington, 1972-73, economist assoc., 1973-74, staff economist, 1974-77, mktg. analyst, 1977; rate analyst U.S. Postal Rate Commn., 1977-79, dir. pub. affairs, 1979-82; pub. affairs officer ICC, 1982-89, dep. dir. pub. affairs, 1989-93, assoc. dir. congl. and pub. affairs, 1993-95; dir. media affairs surface transp. bd. Dept. Transp., 1996—. Reader Washington Ear Sta. WETA-FM, 1977; pres. Arthur D. Watson and Co., Clifton, Va., 1983—; Washington corr. Linn's Stamp News, Sidney, Ohio, 1983—84; pubs. rels. columnist Arundel Comm., Reston, Va., 1991—92. Contbr. articles to profl. jours. With USCG, 1972—78. Recipient Meritorious Svc. medal, U.S.C.G. Res., 1989, Pub. Svc. award, ICC, 1989, Spl. Achievement award, Team Achievement award, Surface Transp. Bd., 1999, Response Team award, 2000, Agy. Performance award Merger team, 2001, Internat. Plastic Modelers Soc. award, 2000, Performance award for Web site enhancements, 2002. Mem.: Assn. Transp. Law, Logistics and Policy, USS Natoma Bay Assn., E. Clairborne Robins Sch. Bus. Alumni Assn. Roman Catholic. Avocations: classical music, reading, writing, model building, travel. Home: 6521 Rockland Dr Clifton VA 20124-2415 Office: Surface Transp Bd 1925 K St NW Ste 845 Washington DC 20423-0001

WATSON, BARRY LEE, real estate and mortgage broker, investor, contractor, builder, developer; b. Morris, Minn., June 10, 1963; s. Richard Jay and Lila Richa (Goll) W. Student, Havti U., 1981-82. Metallurgist Reinheart & Assoc., Pasadena, Tex., 1982-83; realtor ISI Inc., Winter Park, Fla., 1983-84; owner First Am. Capital Corp., Orlando, 1984—. Bd. dirs. Farmbank Real Estate, Inc., Orlando; v.p. Oak Harbour Assn., Altamonte Springs, Fla., 1985-86, pres., 1986; pres. Watson Fin. Corp., Orlando, 1986-95, U.S. Devel. Corp., Orlando, 1986—, Southeastern Capital of Orlando, Inc., 1986-95, The Watson Group Inc. Bus. Mgmt.,1991—. Author: Watson Winning and Wealth, 1985, 86. Advisor Cen. Fla. Young Reps., Orlando, 1984-89, bd. dirs., 1987, 88, 89. Mem. Orlando C. of C. Lutheran. Avocations: reading, travel, writing, golf. Office: The Watson Group 219 Pasadena Pl Orlando FL 32803-3877

WATSON, BERNARD CHARLES, educator, foundation administrator; m. Lois Lathan, July 1, 1961; children: Barbra, Bernard Jr. BS, Ind. U., 1951; MEd, U. Ill., 1955; PhD, U. Chgo., 1967; postdoctoral work, Harvard U., 1968; LHD (hon.), Allen U., 1981, LaSalle U., 1987, Spring Garden Coll., Elizabethtown Coll, Beaver Coll., 1988, Harris-Stowe State Coll., Morris Brown Coll., 1989, Millersville U., 1991, N.C. Ctrl. U., 1999; LLD (hon.), Lincoln U., 1974, Fla. Meml. Coll., 1984, Temple U., 1986, Med. Coll. Pa., 1986, Tuskegee U., 1991, Lincoln U., 1992, Morgan State U., 1992, Phila. Coll. Pharmacy and Sci., 1994, Bethune-Cookman Coll., 1995; HHD (hon.), Wilberforce U., 1979; DFA, Univ. of the Arts, 1992; D of Pedagogy, Drexel U., 1992. Tchr., prin. Roosevelt Jr. and Sr. H.S., Gary, Ind., 1955-65; staff assoc. Midwest Adminstrn. Ctr. U. Chgo., 1965-67; assoc. supt. innovative programs Sch. Dist. Phila., 1967-68, dep. supt. for planning, 1968-70; prof., chmn. dept. urban edn. Temple U., Phila., 1970-75, also prof. social foundations Coll. Edn. and prof. urban studies Coll. Liberal Arts, 1970-75, v.p. acad. adminstrn., 1976-81, presdl. scholar, 1994—; pres., CEO William Penn Found, 1982-93; chmn. HMA Found., 1994-97. Bd. dirs. Comcast Corp., First Union Bancorp North, First Union Bank, Keystone AAA Club, Keystone Ins. Co., Phila. Contributionship; assoc. edn. Grad. Sch. Edn. Harvard U., 1970-72, mem. vis. com., 1981-87; mem. vis. com. dept. Afro-Am. studies Harvard Coll., 1974-78. Author: In Spite of the System: The Individual and Educational Reform, 1974; editor in chief Cross Reference: A Jour. Pub. Policy and Multi-Cultural Edn., 1976-79, Testing Its Origin, Use and Misuse, 1997, Colored, Negro, Black: Chasing the American Dream, 1997; contbr. numerous articles to profl. jours., chpts. to books. Mem. steering com., mem. exec. com. Nat. Urban Coalition, 1973-89; vice chmn. Nat. Adv. Coun. Edn. Professions Devel., 1967-70, Pa. Coun. on Arts, 1986-93; mem. Nat. Coun. Ednl. Rsch., 1980-82, William T. Grant Found. Commn. Work, Family and Citizenship, 1987-88; sr. vice chmn. bd. trustees Nat. Urban League, 1983-96; vice chmn. bd. dirs. Pa. Conv. Ctr. Authority, 1986—; trustee Thomas Jefferson U., 1993-95; sec. bd. N.J. State Aquarium, 1988-93; chmn. Ave. the Arts Inc., 1992—; mem. fed. judiciary nominating com. Pa., 1981-89; bd. dirs. Friends of the Nelson Mandela Children's Fund, 1996—, Marian Anderson Hist. Soc., 1998—; mem. adv. com. Frederick D. Patterson Rsch. Inst., 1998—; chmn. bd. dirs. Barnes Found., 1999—. Recipient numerous honors and awards for leadership in edn., the arts, and civil rights. Mem. Am. Philosophical Soc., Am. Acad. Polit. and Social Sci., Phi Delta Kappa, Kappa Delta Pi. Office: TUCC 1616 Walnut St Philadelphia PA 19103-5313

WATSON, BEVERLY HALE, writer; b. Highland Park, Mich., Aug. 30, 1940; m. Paul Harrison Watson, May 9, 1959; children: Kimberly, Kay. Legal Stenographer, U. Detroit, 1959; Dress Designer/Pattern Maker Diploma, Hennepin County Vo-Tech, Mpls., 1974; Grad. in Writing, Inst. of Children's Lit., West Redding, Conn., 1994; Minister's Cert., Lively Stone Fellowship, Charlotte, N.C., 1995. Ordained to ministry Lively Stones Fellowship, 1995. Sci., math. tchr.'s aide Oak Grove Jr. Hi., Bloomington, Minn., 1971-74; owner, designer Beverly Watson Originals, 1974-80; office mgr., adminstrv. asst. Temporary Svc., Louisville, 1980; mgr. computer, monetary donations Dept. Prayer Book Soc., 1980-82; adminstrv. asst. Minn. Fabrics/DSS, Charlotte, 1982-85; pub. rels., adminstrv. personnel The Salvation Army City Command, 1986-88; founder, dir., writer Sevenfold Peace Found., Charlotte and Double Oak, Tex., 1988—. V.p. Exec. Bd. Youth Performing Arts Sch., Louisville, 1980-82; pub. rels. liaison Cen. State Hosp., Louisville, 1981-82; sml. bus. cons. Normandale C.C., Bloomington, 1975-80; vol. chaplain's office Charlotte Meml. Hosp., 1996. Author: (books) Reflections of the Heart, 1989, Keys to the Book of Revelation, 1990, Exploring Universal Laws, 1990, Paranormal Phenomena in the Bible, 1990, Venturing Into the Unknown, 1992, Psalm 23, 1995, The Perfect Gift, 1995, Messages from the Dove, 1995, The Angel's Bride, 1993, Reincarnation: Evolutionary Path of the Soul, 1998, Death Our Portal to Live, 1998, Walk-ins-Special Spirits on Assignment, 1998, God is! You Are...Reflecting the Twelve Powers Within, 2000. Vol. women's aux. Children's Hosp., Fairview-Southdale Hosp. Minn., 1970-72. Recipient Blue Ribbon Poetry award So. Poetry Assn., Pass Christian, Miss., 1996, Vol. Svc. award Carolinas Med. Ctr., Mpls., 1996, Style/Creativity award Legions of Light Mag., Margaretville, N.Y., 1994. Office: Founder Sevenfold Peace Found 215 Lake Trail Dr Double Oak TX 75077-3003

WATSON, BRADLEY CHARLES STEPHEN, political science educator, lawyer, writer; b. Toronto, Ont., Can., Jan. 7, 1961; s. Charles William and Winnifred Nelsie Watson; m. Barbara Jean Morton, Aug. 27, 1988; children: Victoria Jean, Charles Morton, James Bradley. BA, U. B.C., 1983; LLB, Queen's U., Kingston, Ont., 1986; MA, Claremont (Calif.) U., 1992, PhD, 1996; MPhil, Cath. U. Louvain, Belgium, 1995. Bar: B.C. 1987. Articled student Campney & Murphy, Vancouver, B.C., Can., 1986-87; assoc. Palkowski & Co., 1987-89; asst. prof. Norwich U., Northfield, Vt., 1996-99, St. Vincent Coll., Latrobe, Pa., 1999—2002, assoc. prof., 2002—. Adj. faculty U. Redlands, Calif., 1994-96; vis. asst. prof. Claremont McKenna Coll., Claremont, 1995-96; adj. prof. Norwich U. Mil. Grad Program, 1997—; adj. fellow Claremont Inst. Study Statesmanship and Polit. Philosophy, 1998—, John M. Ashbrook Ctr. for Pub. Affairs, Ashland U., 1999—; fellow in politics and culture Ctr. for Econ. and Policy Edn., St. Vincent Coll., 1999—; dir. St. Vincent Coll. Govt. and Polit. Edn. Lecture Series, Culture and Policy Conf., Duquesne Club lecture series, Civitas Forum, George Washington Fellowship Program, 1999—. Author: Civil Rights and the Paradox of Liberal Democracy, 1999; contbr. Rethinking the Constitution, 1996, Microsoft Encarta Ency., 1997-2001; editor: Liberalism in the New Millennium, 2000, Citizens and Statesmen, 2001, Courts and the Culture Wars, 2002; contbr. articles to profl. jours. and other publs. Faculty fellow John M. Olin Found., 1997-98, postdoctoral fellow Social Scis. and Humanities Rsch. Coun. of Can., 1996, faculty fellowship Gould Ctr. for Humanistic Studies, Claremont McKenna Coll., 1996, Salvatori fellow Heritage Found., 1995; Freedom Project grantee, John Templeton Found., 2001. Mem. Am. Polit. Sci. Assn., Can. Polit. Sci. Assn., Nat. Assn. of Scholars, Civitas. Anglican. Avocations: foreign travel, astronomy, skiing, photography. Office: St Vincent Coll Ctr for Econ and Policy Edn Latrobe PA 15650-2690 E-mail: bwatson@email.stvincent.edu.

WATSON, BRENDA BENNETT, insurance company executive; b. Decatur, Ga., Aug. 26, 1940; d. Robert Joseph and Clarissa Mae (Weekes) Bennett; m. James H. Pair Jr., Apr. 4, 1969 (div. Aug. 1993); children: Richard S. Pair, Randall J. Pair, Ronald G. Pair; m. James Leigh Watson, Sept. 9, 1995. Student, DeKalb Coll., 1971. Lic. property and casualty agt., Fla., Ga., Okla., Tenn., Tex. Underwriter W. K. Stringer Co., Atlanta, 1961-65, Tharpe & Assocs., Atlanta, 1965-68; sr. v.p. Alexander - Howden, 1968-82; exec. v.p., ptnr. Pair Underwriting Mgrs. Inc., 1982-86; pres. Walkingstick-LaGere-Pair Underwriting Mgrs., Inc., Chandler, Okla., 1986-88; exec. v.p., dir. LaGere-Walkingstick Ins. Agy., 1988—. Exec. v.p. Nat. Am. Ins. Co., Chandler, Okla., 1987—, Austin, Tex., 1999—; exec. v.p., bd. dirs. Chandler Ins. Ltd., Cayman Islands, 1985—. Dir., past pres. Gateway to Prevention and Recovery, 1994-98. Mem. Nat. Assn. Ins. Women (pres. Atlanta chpt. 1978-79, Woman of Yr. 1979-80). Republican. Episcopalian. Home: 10002 Shinnecock Hills Dr Austin TX 78747-1315 Office: Wells Fargo Bank Bldg 2028 E Ben White Blvd Ste 200 Austin TX 78741 E-mail: bwatson@naico.com.

WATSON, BRIAN COLBATH See COLBATH, BRIAN

WATSON, CARRIE ANN, writer, artist; b. Wheatridge, Colo., July 22, 1971; d. James Linden and Florence Irene McClure; m. Christopher John Watson, June 26, 1994; children: Cassandra Aunna, Stephanie Lynne, Christopher John II. Grad. high sch., Canon City, Colo. Receptionist Morgan Refractories, Canon City, 1989; cert. nurse asst. Valley View, 1991, Progressive Care Ctr., Canon City, 1991-93; jewelry maker, 1993-95; writer, 1995—. Author: A Treasury of Famous Poems, 1997, Sketches of the Soul, 1997 (Editors' Choice award 1997), Even Then, Even Now, 1997. Vol. libr. asst. Canon City Pub. Libr., 1987-88, Canon city H.S., 1987-89; founder Sangre De Cristo Christian Acad., Westcliffe, Colo., 1995. Republican. Avocations: music, naturopathic medicine studies, painting, beauty consultant. Home: 0053 County Rd 277 Canon City CO 81212

WATSON, CHARLOTTE BUSHNELL, management consultant; b. Phila., Nov. 24, 1943; d. George Smith Watson and Helen Elise (Wilmer) Hilbert; 1 child, Edward Giulian Pecelli. BS, John Hopkins U., 1969; MPhil, Grad. Ctr. CUNY, 1980, D in Polit. Sci., 1985; cert. in internat. trade, NYU, 1989. Cert. Italian lang. tchr. Grad. asst. Bklyn. Coll., 1972-76; adj. lectr. Hunter Coll., N.Y.C., 1976-80; pres. TMS Imports, N.Y.C. and Irvington, Va., 1985-90, Bushnell Assocs., N.Y.C., 1990-94; dir. Counterpart Svc. Ctr. for Ukraine, Moldova & Belarus, Kiev, 1994-96; cons. Charles Stewart Mott Found., 1997-98; democracy officer USAID Mission, Albania, 1998-99. Adj. asst. prof. mgmt. NYU, 1990-93; cons. ind. Italian mfrs., 1982-90. Author: The Politics of Agrarian Assistance in Italy, 1985. Mem. Am. Polit. Sci. Assn. Avocations: photography, fencing, boating. Home: 88 Rockledge Ct Front Royal VA 22630-5635

WATSON, CHERYL S. cell and molecular biology educator, researcher; b. Evansville, Ind., Apr. 29, 1950; d. Casey Lee and Thelma Ruth (Meyer) W. BS, Purdue U., 1972, MS, 1974; PhD, Baylor Coll. Medicine, 1980; postgrad., Nat. Inst. Med. Rsch., London, 1980-82, Population Coun./Rockefeller, U., 1982-85. Instr. Purdue U., W. Lafayette, Ind., 1972-74; asst. prof. U. Tex. Med. Br., Galveston, 1985-93, assoc. prof., 1993—2000, prof., 2000—, assoc. dir. Ctr. for Interdisciplinary Rsch. on Women's Health, 2001—. Manuscript reviewer and grant reviewer in field. Contbr. numerous articles to profl. jours. Recipient award Assn. for Women in Sci., 1975, Nat. Student Rsch. Forum, 1977, 1978; NIH postdoctoral fellow NIH, London, 1980-82, Population Coun. postdoctoral fellow, N.Y., 1982-85; recipient numerous grants in field. Mem. AAAS, Am. Soc. Cell Biology, Endocrine Soc. Achievements include research in field of steroid receptors, membrane steroid receptors, steroid effects on reproductive systems and in cancer.

WATSON, DAVID A. biomedical researcher, educator; b. Honolulu, Apr. 27, 1960; s. Richard McClellan and Mary Suzanne (Rue) W.; m. Fay Nieves Wright, Oct. 22, 1983; children: Emily, Ross, Jonathon, Zachary. BS in Biology magna cum laude, Millikin U., 1981; MS in Marine Biology, U. Houston, 1986, PhD in Molecular Biology with honors, 1991. Chief rsch. technician, lab. mgr. VA Med. Ctr., Houston, 1986-92; postdoctoral fellow dept. microbiology/immunology Baylor Coll. Medicine, 1991-92; postdoctoral fellow Eijkman-Winkler Inst. Utrecht U., The Netherlands, 1992-93; asst. prof. dept. vet. and microbiol. scis. N.D. State U., Fargo, 1993-95; asst. prof. dept. microbiology and immunology U. Tex. Med. Br., Galveston, 1995-97; program mgr. peer rev. Nat. Space Biomed. Rsch. Inst., 1997—; sr. scientist InDyne, Inc., 1997—. Adj. assoc. prof. dept. microbiology and immunology U. Tex. Med. Br., 1998—; internet cons. Medscape.com. Inc., N.Y.C., 1996-97; sr. sci. cons. VA Med. Ctr., Houston, 1997—; dir. summer undergrad. rsch. program, U. Tex. Med. Br., 1996-97; exec. sec. industry forum, Nat. Space Biomed. Rsch. Inst., 1997-2000; grant reviewer USDA Nat. Rsch. Initiative, 1993—, U.S. Dept. VA, 1999. Co-editor: Constitutional Resistance to Infection, 1995; contbr. articles to profl. jours.; columnist Baycomber monthly newsmagazine. Bd. trustees Pearland (Tex.) Ind. Sch. Dist., 2001—; chair exec. com. Pearland Cub Scouts, 1997—2001; judge sci. competitions at various ednl. levels, 1994—; mentor 15 jr. high and h.s. sci. fair projects, 1987—. Mem. AAAS, Am. Soc. for Microbiology, Am. Soc. for Gravitational and Space Biology, Lancefield Soc., Lions (pres. local club 1988-89), Sigma Xi, Phi Kappa Phi. Avocations: parenting, gardening, reading. Office: NSBRI Program Office 18108 Point Lookout Dr Ste B Houston TX 77058-3506 E-mail: dwatson@nsbri.com.

WATSON, DAVID BRUCE, civil, structural engineer; b. Yuma, Colo., Aug. 5, 1955; s. Eldon Glen and Patricia Ruth (Hartwell) W.; m. Sheila Christine Most-Watson; children: Amber Ann, Alicia Dawn. BSCE, U. Nebr., 1980. Registered profl. engr., Kans., Nebr., Colo., Mo., Tenn., Iowa, Ohio, Oreg., Ark.; pvt. pilot. Structural engr. Howard-Needles-Tammen & Bergendoff, Overland Park, Kans., 1980-81; project engr. Butler Mfg. Inc., Kansas City, Mo., 1981-82; civil design mgr. Payless Cashways, Inc., 1982-88, design mgr., 1992—; chief engr. Oppenheimer Design/Build, 1988-90; civil/structural engr. Lutz, Daily & Brian, Overland Park, 1990; prin. Watson & Assocs., Shawnee, Kans., 1990-92; v.p. Facility Design, Inc., Overland Park, 1994—. Scholarship Bd. Regents, 1976. Mem. ASCE (program com. 1987—), Am. Concrete Inst., Aircraft Owners and Pilots Assn., Exptl. Aircraft Assn. Republican. Lutheran. Avocations: fishing, flying, water skiing, coin collecting, wood working. Home: 13706 W 47th Ter Shawnee KS 66216-1155 Office: Facility Design Inc 8500 W 110th St Ste 525 Overland Park KS 66210-4018

WATSON, DAVID COLQUITT, electrical engineer, educator; b. Linden, Tex., Feb. 9, 1936; s. Colvin Colquitt and Nelena Gertrude (Kaesler) W.; m. Flora Janet Thayn, Nov. 10, 1959; children: Flora Janeen, Melanie Beth, Morrie Gaylene, Cheralyn Gail, Nathan David, Amy Melissa, Brian Colvin. BSEE, U. Utah, 1964, PhD in Elec. Engring., 1968. Elec. tech. Hercules Pwoder Co., Magna, Utah, 1961-62; rsch. asst. microwave devices and phys. elecs. lab. U. Utah, 1964-68; sr. mem. tech. staff ESL, Inc., Sunnyvale, Calif., 1968-78, head dept. comm., 1969-70; sr. engring. specialist Probe Systems, Inc., 1978-79; sr. mem. tech. staff ARGO Systems, Inc., 1979-90, GTE Govt. Systems Corp., Mountain View, 1990-91; sr. cons. Watson Cons. Svcs., 1991-92, 94-97; sr. staff engr. ESL, Inc., 1992-94. Mem. faculty U. Santa Clara, 1978-81, 1992-94, San Jose State U., 1981-92, Coll. Notre Dame, 1992, Chapman U., 1993; sr. engring. specialist Space Sys. Loral, 1997—. Contbr. articles to IEEE Transactions, 1965-79; co-inventor cyclotron-wave rectifier; inventor gradient descrambler. With USAF, 1956-60. NASA fellow, 1968. Mem. IEEE, Phi Kappa Phi, Tau Beta Pi, Eta Kappa Nu. Mem. Lds Ch. Office: Space Sys Loral 3825 Fabian Way Palo Alto CA 94303-4604 E-mail: watson.david@ssd.loral.com. *Personal philosophy: I believe in hard work and strict honesty, in giving full value for consideration received, to God and fellow man or woman.*

WATSON, DENNIS WALLACE, microbiology educator, scientist; b. Morpeth, Ont., Can., Apr. 29, 1914; came to U.S., 1938, naturalized, 1946; s. William and Sarah (Verity) W.; m. Alicemay Whittier, June 15, 1941; children: Catherine W., William V. BSA, U. Toronto, 1934; MS, Dalhousie U., 1937; PhD, U. Wis., 1941, DSc (hon.), 1981. Rsch. assoc. U. Wis., 1942, asst. prof., 1946-49; vis. investigator Rockefeller Inst., 1942; investigator Connaught Lab. Med. Rsch. U. Toronto, 1942-44; assoc. prof. U. Minn., Mpls., 1949-52, prof., 1953-63, head dept. microbiology, 1964-84, Regents prof. microbiology, 1980-84, Regents prof. emeritus, 1984—. Vis. prof. Med. Sch. U. Wash., 1950; mem. Commn. Immunization Armed Forces Epidemiology Bd., 1946-59; mem. bd. sci. counselors, div. biol. standards NIH, 1957-59, mem. allergy and immunology study sect., 1954-58; chmn. tgn. grant com. Inst. Allergy and Infectious Diseases, 1964, mem. adv. coun., 1967-71; mem. microbiology panel Office Naval Rsch., 1963-66; vice chmn. Am. Soc. Microbiology Found., 1973; bd. dirs. Nat. Found. Infectious Diseases, 1976-81 Editorial bd. Infection and Immunity, 1971-72; editorial cons. Medcom Faculty Medicine, 1973—. With AUS, 1944-46. Recipient USPHS Research Career award, 1962-64; Spl. research fellow USPHS, 1960-61 Mem. AAAS, Am. Assn. Immunologists, Am. Chem. Soc., Am. Acad. Microbiology (vice chmn. bd. govs. 1967), Am. Soc. Microbiology (pres. 1969, v.p. Found. 1972-73), Internat. Endotoxin Soc. (hon., life), Soc. Exptl. Biology and Medicine (coun. 1977-79, pres. 1976-77), Lancefield Soc., Sigma Xi, Phi Zeta. Home: 2106 Hendon Ave Saint Paul MN 55108-1419 Office: U Minn Med Sch Dept Microbiology PO Box 196 Minneapolis MN 55440-0196 E-mail: watso006@tc.umn.edu.

WATSON, DIANE EDITH, congresswoman; b. L.A., Nov. 12, 1933; d. William Allen Louis and Dorothy Elizabeth (O'Neal) Watson. AA, L.A. City Coll., 1954; BA, UCLA, 1956; MS, Calif. State U., L.A.; PhD, Claremont Grad. Sch., 1987. Tchr., sch. psychologist L.A. Unified Sch. Dist., 1960-69, 73-74; assoc. prof. Calif. State U., L.A., 1969-71; health occupations specialist Bur. Indsl. Edn., Calif. Dept. Edn., 1971-73; mem. L.A. Unified Sch. Bd., 1975-78, Calif. Senate from dist. 26, 1978-98, chairperson health and human svcs. com.; U.S. amb. to Micronesia Dept. of State, 1999-2001; mem. U.S.

Congress from 32d Calif. dist., 2001—; mem. govt. reform com. and internat. rels. com. Legis. Black Caucus, mem. edn. com., budget and fiscal rev. com., criminal procedure com., housing and land use com.; del. Calif. Democratic Party; mem. exec. com. Nat. Conf. State Legislators; amb. to the Federated States of Micronesia, 1999. Author: Health Occupations Instructional Units-Secondary Schools, 1975, Planning Guide for Health Occupations, 1975; co-author: Introduction to Health Care, 1976. Del. Dem. Nat. Conv., 1980. Recipient Mary Church Terrell award, 1976, Brotherhood Crusade award, 1981, Black Woman of Achievement award NAACP Legal Def. Fund, 1988; named Alumnus of Yr., UCLA, 1980, 82. Mem. Calif. Assn. Sch. Psychologists, L.A. Urban League, Calif. Tchrs. Assn., Calif. Commn. on Status Women. Roman Catholic. Office: US Ho Reps 2413 Rayburn Ho Office Bldg Washington DC 20515 Fax: 202-225-2422.

WATSON, DONALD CHARLES, cardiothoracic surgeon, educator; b. Fairfield, Ohio, Mar. 15, 1945; s. Donald Charles and Pricilla H. Watson; m. Susan Robertson Prince, June 23, 1973; children: Kea Huntington, Katherine Anne, Kirsten Prince. BA in Applied Sci., BSME, Lehigh U., 1968; MSME, Stanford U., 1969; MD, Duke U., 1972. Diplomate Am. Bd. Thoracic Surgery, Am. Bd. Surgery. Intern in surgery Stanford U. Med. Ctr., Calif., 1972-73, resident in cardiovasc. surgery, 1973-74, resident in surgery, 1976-78, chief resident in heart transplant, 1978-79, chief resident in cardiovasc. and gen. surgery, 1978-80; clin. assoc. surgery br. Nat. Heart and Lung Inst., 1974-76, acting sr. surgeon, 1976; assoc. cardiovasc. surgeon dept. child health and devel. George Washington U., Washington, 1980-84, asst. prof. surgery, asst. prof. child health and devel., 1980-84, attending cardiovasc. surgeon dept. child health and devel., 1984-89, assoc. prof. surgery, 1984-89; assoc. prof. pediats. U. Tenn.-Memphis, 1984-90, prof. surgery, prof. pediats., 1990—, chmn. cardiothoracic surgery, 1984-99, assoc. chief med. officer, 1999—. Mem. staff Le Bonheur Children's Med. Ctr., Memphis, chmn. cardiothoracic surgery, 1984—; mem. staff William F. Bowld Med. Ctr., Memphis, Regional Med. Ctr. at Memphis, Bapt. Meml. Med. Ctr., Memphis; cons. in field; instr. advanced trauma life support; profl. cons., program reviewer HHS. Contbr. chpts., numerous articles, revs. to profl. publs. Bd. dirs. Internat. Children's Heart Found., Child Health Alliance of the Mid-South. Served to lt. comdr. USPHS, 1974-76. Smith Kline & French fellow Lehigh U., 1967; NSF fellow Lehigh U., 1968; univ. interdepartmental scholar and univ. scholar Lehigh U., 1968. Fellow Am. Coll. Cardiology, Am. Coll. Chest Physicians (forum cardiovasc. surgery, coun. critical care), Southeastern Surg. Congress, Am. Acad. Pediats. (surgery sect.), ACS; mem. Assn. Surg. Edn., Am. Assn. Thoracic Surgery, Soc. Thoracic Surgeons, So. Thoracic Surg. Assn., Am. Thoracic Soc., Assn. Acad. Surgery, Internat. Soc. Heart Transplantation, Am. Fedn. Clin. Rsch., Found. Advanced Edn. in Scis., Andrew G. Morrow Soc., Norman E. Shumway Soc. (multiple bd. dirs.), Coun. on Cardiovasc. Surgery Am. Heart Assn., Soc. Internat. di Chirig., AAAS, N.Y. Acad. Sci., AMA, NIH Alumni Assn., Stanford U. Med. Alumni Assn., Stanford U. Alumni Assn., Lehigh U. Alumni Assn., Smithsonian Assocs., Sierra Club, U. Tenn. Pres.'s Club, LeBonheur Pres's Club, U.S. Yacht Racing Assn., Pilots Internat. Assn., Nat. Assn. Flight Instrs., Aircraft Owners and Pilots Assn., Order Ky. Cols., Crescent Club, Phi Beta Kappa, Tau Beta Pi, Pi Tau Sigma, Phi Gamma Delta. Republican. Presbyterian. Avocations: sailing, racquet sports, flying, computers. Office: Office of the CMO 66 N Panhine Ste 334 Memphis TN 38105-5123 E-mail: dwatson@utmem.edu.

WATSON, DONALD NATHANIEL, lawyer; b. Elberton, Ga., May 1, 1953; s. Thomas Clark and Alice Roberta (Blackwell) W.; m. Paula Jean Lockett, June 16, 1984; children: Alyson, Nathaniel, Cimone. BA, Yale U., 1975; JD, U. Miami, 1980. Bar: Fla., U.S. Dist. Ct. (so. dist.) Fla., U.S. Ct. Appeals (11th cir.). Asst. state atty. Legal Svcs. Greater Miami, Inc., Fla., 1979-80, Legal Aid Svc. Broward County, 1980-84, Broward County State Atty.'s Office, 1984-88; ptnr. Gary, Williams, Parenti, Finney, Lewis, McManus, Watson & Sperando, Stuart, 1988—. Bd. dirs. Share Ctrl. Fla., 1996-97; trustee St. Mark Missionary Bapt. Ch., Ft. Pierece, Fla., 1996-97. Mem. Nat. Bar Assn., ABA, ATLA, T.J. Reddick Bar Assn., Martin County Bar Assn., Acad. Fla. Trial Lawyers, Fla. Bar Assn. (grievance com. 1994-95), Omi Psi Phi. Democrat. Avocations: bowling, skating, swimming. Home: 1556 SE Faculty Ct Port Saint Lucie FL 34952-7603 Office: Gary Williams Parenti Finney Lewis McManus Watson & Sperando 221 SE Osceola St Ste 300 Stuart FL 34994-2289

WATSON, DONALD RALPH, architect, artist, educator, author; b. Providence, Sept. 27, 1937; s. Ralph Giles W. and Ethel (Fletcher) Pastene; m. Marja Palmqvist, Sept. 8, 1966 (div. Jan. 1984); children: Petrik, Elise; m. Judith Criste, Jan. 3, 1986 (dec. Oct. 8, 2000). AB, Yale U., 1959, BArch, 1962, MEd, 1969. Lic. architect Nat. Council Archtl. Registration Bds. Architect Peace Corps, Tunisia, 1962-64; archtl. cons. Govt. of Tunisia, 1964-65; pvt. practice, Trumbull, Conn., 1969—; dean Sch. Architecture, Rensselaer Poly. Inst., Troy, N.Y., 1990-95, prof. NY, 1990—2001. Frederick C. Baker vis. prof. U. Oreg., 1995; chmn. environ. design program, Yale U., 1979-90; vis. prof. Yale U., 1995-2000. Author: Designing and Building a Solar House, 1977, Energy Conservation Through Building Design, 1979, Climatic Design, 1983, Energy Design Handbook, 1993; editor-in-chief Time Saver Standards: Architectural Design Data, 1997, Time-Saver Standards: Urban Design, 2001. Bd. dirs. Save the Children Fedn., 1979-82. Recipient Honor Design award Conn. Soc. Architects, 1974, Honor Design award region AIA, 1978, 84, 1st award Owens Corning Energy Conservation Bldg. Design Program, 1983, Excellence in housing award Energy Efficient Bldg. Assn., 1988, Lifetime Achievement award Passive and Low Energy Architecture, 1990, Best in Show Watercolors, Soc. Creative Artists, 1999, Green Bldg. Design award NESEA, 2002, Disting. Prof. award ACSA, 2002; Assn. of Collegiate Schs. of Archtecture/Am. Metals Climax rsch. fellow, 1967-69; rsch. fellow Rockefeller Found., 1978. Fellow: AIA. Home and Office: 54 Larkspur Dr Trumbull CT 06611-4652 E-mail: lakesidedj@aol.com.

WATSON, DUANE FREDERICK, religious studies educator; b. Watertown, N.Y., May 15, 1956; s. Frederick Halsted and Beverley Alice (Taylor) W.; m. JoAnn Christine Ford, June 2, 1984; 1 child, Christina Lucille. BA, Houghton (N.Y.) Coll., 1978; MDiv, Princeton Theol. Sem., 1981; PhD, Duke U., 1986. Ordained to ministry Meth. U., 1980. Asst. prof. biblical studies Ashland (Ohio) Theol. Sem., 1984-86; pastor Northwestern (N.Y.) United Meth. Ch., 1987-89; asst. prof. N.T. studies Malone Coll., Canton, Ohio, 1989-92, assoc. prof., 1992-96, prof., 1996—, chair dept. religion and philosophy, 1993-99. Owner, operator internet stoneware auction svc. Doc's Crocks. Author: Invention, Arrangement and Style, 1988, Persuasive Artistry, 1991, Rhetorical Criticism of The Bible, 1994, Commentary on Jude and 2 Peter for the New Interpreter's Bible, 1998, History of Biblical Interpretation, 2002; contbr. articles to profl. jours. and edited volumes; mem. editl. bd. Procs., Ea. Gt. Lakes and Midwest Bibl. Socs., 1993-95; co-editor: Currents in Research: Biblical Studies, 1997-2000, Rhetoric in Religious Antiquity, 1997—. Recipient Excellence in Bibl. studies award Am. Bible Soc., Houghton Coll., 1978. Mem. Studiorum Novi Testamenti Societas, Soc. Bibl. Lit. (steering com. rhetoric sect. 1990-96, program unit chair rhetoric and N.T. sect. 1997-2002), Cath. Bibl. Assn., Internat. Soc. for History of Rhetoric, Rsch., Ea. Great Lakes Bibl. Soc. Republican. Avocations: writing, weight lifting. Office: Malone Coll 515 25th St NW Canton OH 44709-3823

WATSON, EDWARD BRUCE, science educator; b. Nashua, N.H., Oct. 16, 1950; m. M. Susan Watson; 1 child, Jonah. Student, Williams Coll., 1968-69; BA in Geology, U. N.H., 1972; PhD in Geochemistry, MIT, 1976. Postdoctoral fellow Carnegie Inst., 1976-77; from asst. to full prof. Rensselaer Polytechnic Inst., Troy, N.Y., 1977—, chmn. dept. earth and environ. scis., 1990-95, Inst. prof. sci., 1995—. Vis. scientist Max Planck Inst. for Chemistry, Mainz, Germany, 1984. Assoc. editor Geochimica et Cosmochimica Acta, 1985-88; editor petrology and geochemistry Neues Jahrbuch fur Mineralogie, 1988-96; editor Chem. Geology, 1991-95; mem. editl. bd. Geochimica et Cosmochimica Acta, 1997—; contbr. articles to profl. jours., chpts. to books. Vis. rsch. fellow Macquarie U., Australia, 1981, geochemistry fellow European Assn. Geochemistry and Geochem. Soc.; named Disting. alumnus U. N.H., 1999. Fellow AAAS, Am. Geophys. Union (fellows com. 1992-95, nominating com. 1997-98, R.A. Daly lectr. 1999), Mineral. Soc. Am. (pres. 1998), Geol. Soc. Am. (Arthur L. Day medal 1998); mem. NAS, Geochem. Soc. (budget com. 1990, councilor 1991-94, F.W. Clarke medal 1983), 151 Thomsen Scientific. Office: Rensselaer Polytechnic Inst 110 8th St Troy NY 12180-3522 E-mail: watsoe@rpi.edu.

WATSON, ERIC N. corporate executive; b. Charlotte, N.C., Feb. 26, 1956; s. Climmie Newell and Lula Jane Watson; m. Susan Adele Watson; children: Jarrod, Alexandria. BA, Livingston Coll., 1978. Cert. Inst. Auditors Tools and Techniques; cert. trainer, quality facilitator, claim law assoc. Tchr. English Enderly Pk. Elem. Sch., Charlotte, 1978; claims op. rep. St. Paul Cos., Inc., 1979-82, supr., 1983-89, lead auditor/mgr., 1990-93, claim quality cons., 1994, asst. v.p. global diversity, 1995-98, v.p. global diversity, 1999-2000; exec. dir. diversity Williams, Tulsa, Okla., 2000—. Diversity cons. Guident CPI, St. Paul, Thermo King, St. Paul, Carlson Co., St. Paul, Cargill, Inc., St. Paul, Nat. United Way of Am., Minn., State of Minn., St. Paul, United Negro Coll. Fund, St. Paul, Fed. Res. Bank, St. Paul, Minn. Affirmative Action Coun., St. Paul, State Dept. Internal Revenue, St. Paul, Minn. Cultural Diversity Ctr., St. Paul; corp. rep. TC Diversity Roundtable, Mpls.-St. Paul, Mpls. NAACP, 1999-2000; mem. Def. Rsch. Inst. for Profl. Edn. of Def. Bar, Princeton, N.J., 1991-94. Mem. Multicultural Forum, St. Paul, 1992—, Gov.'s Scholar Program, St. Paul, 1995—, Workforce Diversity Coun., N.Y.C., 1996—, Black Achievers Bd., St. Paul, 1998—, Bus. Social Responsibility, Ca lif., 1998—, Minn. Urban Coalition, 1999—; mentor Minn. 100 Mentoring, St. Paul, 1994—. Mem. Kappa Alpha Psi. Avocations: reading, creative writing, coaching youth sports, mentoring and counseling. Home: 3700 N Narcissus Ave Broken Arrow OK 74012-1706 Office: Williams 1 Williams Ctr PO Box 2400 Tulsa OK 74102-2400

WATSON, EVELYN EGNER, radiation scientist; b. Corbin, Ky., Dec. 15, 1928; d. Edgar Mattison and Bertha Mae (Mayfield) Egner; m. Earl Greene Watson, Nov. 10, 1953; children: Nancy Eileen, Philip Allen. AA, Cumberland Coll., 1946; student, Lincoln Meml. U., 1947-48; BA, U. Ky., 1949; postgrad., U. Tenn., 1968. Math. and sci. tchr. Lynch (Ky.) High Sch., 1949-50; office mgr. Whitley County Sch. System, Williamsburg, Ky., 1950-53; sr. lab. tech. Radiation Internal Dose Ctr. Oak Ridge (Tenn.) Assoc. Univs., 1961-71, scientist, 1971-79, program mgr., 1979-89, program dir., 1989-94; cons. internal dosimetry Tenn., 1994—. Lectr. in field; cons. USFDA, Rockville, Md., 1983-88. Assoc. editor Jour. Nuclear Medicine, 1981-86; editor newsletter Soc. Nuclear Medicine S.E. chpt., 1988-99; co-author: MIRD Primer, 1988; contbr. articles to profl., chpts. to books. Bd. dirs. Youth Haven, Oak Ridge, Tenn., 1970-74, Clinch River Home Health, Clinton, Tenn., 1988-94. Recipient Excellence in Tech. Transfer award Fed. Lab. Consortium, 1985, Lifetime Scientific Achievement award Assn. Women in Sci., 1993. Mem. Soc. Nuclear Medicine (med. internal radiation dose com. 1980—, chmn. 1994—, Marshall Brucer award for Disting. Svc. to S.E. chpt. 1999), Health Physics Soc. (Disting. Svc. award 1981, treas. 1976-77, Lifetime Achievement award 1994), European Assn. Nuclear Medicine, Nat. Coun. on Radiation Protection and Measurements (sci. com. 1986-98), Sigma Xi. Mem. Ch. of Christ. Avocations: reading, word puzzles, handicrafts. Home: 104 New Bedford Ln Oak Ridge TN 37830-8289

WATSON, FORREST ALBERT, JR. lawyer, bank executive; b. Atlanta, May 7, 1951; s. Forrest Albert and Virginia Doris (Ritch) W.; m. Marlys Wise, Oct. 16, 1982; children: Annaliese Marie Elizabeth, Forrest Albert Watson III. AB, Emory U., 1973; JD, U. Ga., 1975; postgrad., Mercer U., 1979-80. Bar: Ga. 1975, U.S. Dist. Ct. (mid. dist.) Ga. 1976, U.S. Tax Ct. 1976, U.S. Ct. Appeals (5th cir.) 1977, U.S. Supreme Ct. 1980; cert. data processor; CFP. Assoc. Banks, Smith & Lambdin, Barnesville, Ga., 1976-78; ptnr. Watson & Lindsey, 1978-82; v.p., gen. counsel United Bank Corp., 1981-91, chief ops. officer, 1990-2000, exec. v.p., gen. counsel, 1991-2000, mem., bd. dirs., exec. v.p., 1991; pres. United Bank Mortgage; exec. v.p., sr. trust officer United Bank, Griffin, Ga., 1995-98, exec. v.p., bd. dirs. Zebulon, 1998—. Pres. United Bank Mortgage, 1993-95; gen. counsel Lamar State Bank, Barnesville, 1976-84; judge Small Claims Ct., Lamar County, Ga., 1976, City Ct. of Milner, Ga., 1977; lectr. IBM, 1984-85; atty. City of Meansville, Ga., 1976, City of Milner, 1977; bd. dirs. United Bank Corp. Assoc. editor Ga. Jour. Internat. Law, 1975. Gen. counsel Lamar County Devel. Authority, Barnesville, 1977; bd. dirs. Legaline Inc., Atlanta, 1983-85. Mem. ABA, Ga. Bar Assn., Cir. Ct. Bar Assn., Griffin Cir. Bar Assn., Ga. Rural Health Assn. (trustee 1981-82), S.E. Bank Card Assn. (operating com. 1986-91), Assn. Cert. Fin. Planners, Assn. Inst. Cert. Computer Profls., Internat. Assn. Fin. Planners. Methodist. Avocations: art, antiques, travel. Home: PO Box 347 Zebulon GA 30295-0347 Office: United Bank Corp PO Box 1337 110 Griffin St Zebulon GA 30295

WATSON, GAIL H. librarian; b. Hattiesburg, Miss., May 12, 1941; d. Robert Elkin and Virginia Lucille (Swann) Hill; m. Tommy Gene Watson, June 4, 1963; children: James Todd, Thomas Gregory. BA, U. So. Miss., 1963; M in Librarianship, U. S.C., 1975; MEd, Tenn. State U., Nashville, 1983. Tchr. Hawkins Jr. H.S., Hattiesburg, 1963-64, Seminary (Miss.) H.S., 1965-66; libr. Bush River Elem. Sch., Newberry, S.C., 1973-74, Prosperity (S.C.) Elem. Sch., 1974-76; tchr. Franklin County H.S., Winchester, Tenn., 1977-83; libr. South/J.D. Jackson Jr. H.S., Cowan, 1983—. Mem. SACS rev. teams, Tenn., 1985—. Tenn. Dept. Edn. grantee, 1995. Mem. ALA, Soc. for Promotion of Christian Knowledge, Franklin County Librs. (chair 1998—), Delta Kappa Gamma. Democrat. Episcopalian. Avocations: reading, travel. Home: 143 S Carolina Ave Sewanee TN 37375-2405 Office: JD Jackson Jr HS 601 W Cumberland St Cowan TN 37318-3108

WATSON, GEORGE HENRY, JR. journalist, broadcaster; b. Birmingham, Ala., July 27, 1936; s. George Henry and Grace Elizabeth (Carr) W.; m. Ellen Havican Bradley, July 13, 1979; children: George H., III, Ellen Havican BA, Harvard U., 1959; MS, Columbia U., 1960. Reporter Washington Post, 1960-61; corr. ABC News, 1962-75, Moscow bur. chief, 1966-69, London bur. chief, 1969-75, v.p., Washington bur. chief, 1976-80; v.p., mng. editor Cable News Network, 1980; v.p. news ABC News, N.Y.C., 1981-85, exec. in charge ABC News Viewpoint, 1981-85, v.p., Washington bur. chief, 1985-93, sr. contbg. editor, 1993-2001; freelance broadcast journalist. Served with U.S. Army, 1958. Recipient Peabody award, 1982, DuPont Columbia award, 1983, nat. news Emmy award, 1984. Mem. Radio Television News Dirs. Assn., Soc. Profl. Journalists, Nat. Press Club, Overseas Press Club (award for best television documentary 1971, citation for excellence 1974), Nat. Press Club, Com. to Protect Journalists, Fgn. Policy Assn., Cosmos Club. E-mail: ebw327@aol.com.

WATSON, GEORGE W. energy executive; BSEE, MBA in Fin. Mktg., Queen's U., Kingston, Can.; grad. advanced mgmt. program, Harvard U., 1988. With Can. Imperial Bank Commerce, Toronto; asst. gen. mgr. worldwide, oil and gas divsn. Calgary, 1981; dir. fin. Dome Petroleum, v.p. fin.; v.p., treas. Amoco Can.; pres., CEO Intensity Resources, 1988-90; chief fin. officer TransCanada, 1990-93, pres., 1993-99, CEO, 1994-99; ptnr. Northridge Can. Inc., 1999—. Pres., CEO WNS Emergent Inc.; bd. dirs. Badger Daylighting Inc., Geodyne Energy Ltd., Can. 88 Energy Inc.; chmn. Spirit Energy Fax, CODA. Bd. dirs. Queen's U.

WATSON, GEORGIANNA, librarian; b. Lock Haven, Pa., Feb. 18, 1949; d. George and Anna (Eisenhower) Rhine; children: Sharga Nicolle, George Winfield-Martin. BS in Edn., Lock Haven State U., 1971; MLS, Brigham Young U., 1978; M in Pub. Adminstrn., John Jay Coll. Criminal Justice, N.Y.C., 1986. Tchr. Mifflin County Sch. Dist., Lewistown, Pa., 1971-72; librarian Shiprock Boarding Sch. Bur. Indian Affairs, Shiprock, N.Mex., 1972-79, Ft. Sill Indian Sch. Bur. Indian Affairs, Lawton, Okla., 1979-80, U.S. Mil. Acad., West Point, N.Y., 1980-83, head pub. services, library, 1983—. Mem. Southeastern N.Y. Library Resource Council (mem. continuing edn. com., govt. documents interest group), Southeastern N.Y. Reference Library Interest Group, Am. Quarter Horse Assn., Internat. Arabian Horse Assn., Am. Paint Horse Assn., N.Y. State Horse Coun. (Mid-Hudson dir.), Pi Alpha Alpha. Republican. Home: 8 St Michaels Ln Walden NY 12586-2466 Office: US Mil Acad Dept Army West Point NY 10996-1799 E-mail: ug0202@exmail.usma.edu.

WATSON, GLENN ROBERT, lawyer; b. Okla., May 2, 1917; s. Albert Thomas and Ethel (Riddle) W.; m. Dorothy Ann Mosiman, Feb. 25, 1945; 1 dau., Carol Ann. Student, East Cen. State U., Okla., 1933-36; LL.B., Okla. U., 1939. Bar: Okla. 1939, Calif. 1946. Pvt. practice law, Okla., 1939-41; ptnr., pres. Richards, Watson & Gershon, Los Angeles, 1946—; city atty. Industry, Calif., 1958-65, 78-83, Commerce, 1960-61, Cerritos, 1956-64, Victorville, 1962-63, Carson, 1968-2000, Rosemead, 1960-76, Seal Beach, 1972-78, South El Monte, 1976-78, Avalon, 1976-80, Artesia, 1976-97. Served with USNR, 1942-46. Mem. ABA, Los Angeles County Bar Assn., Am. Judicature Soc., Lawyers Club of Los Angeles (past pres.), Los Angeles World Affairs Council, Internat. Cir., La Canada C. of C. (past pres.), Order of Coif, Phi Delta Phi, Delta Chi. Home: 522 Paulette Pl La Canada CA 91011 Office: Richards Watson & Gershon 355 S Grand Ave 40th Flr Los Angeles CA 90071-3101 E-mail: gwatson@rwglaw.com.

WATSON, GUY EDWARDS, mechanical engineer, consultant; b. Los Angeles, Nov. 1, 1923; s. Russell Allen and Sacca Mauree (Hardesty) W.; m. Margie Anne Ruffin, July 10, 1948 (dec. Nov. 2000); one child, Kimberly Anne. BS, U. Calif., Berkeley, 1950; MSME, Santa Clara (Calif.) U., 1967; Engr. in Mech. Engring., Stanford U., 1972. Registered profl. engr., Calif., Kans. Sr. svc. rep. Fed.-Mogul Corp., Detroit, 1950-54; design and research engr. Coleman Co. Inc., Wichita, Kans., 1954-60; pres. Midwest Plastics Corp., 1960-63; technical cons. Lockheed Missiles & Space Co., Sunnyvale, Calif., 1963-87; pres. Watson Mark Corp., Cupertino, 1987-94; gen. mgr. propeller divsn. Wings of History Air Mus., San Martin, 1994—. Cons. Fahlin Propellers, Cupertino, Calif., 1980-91. Patentee in field. Served to capt. USAAF, 1942-46, PTO. Mem. AIAA (sr.), Quiet Birdmen. Home: 7723 Kilmarnok Dr San Jose CA 95135-2140 E-mail: Propmaker@aol.com .

WATSON, HARLAN L(EROY), federal official, physicist, economist; b. Macomb, Ill., Dec. 17, 1944; s. Joseph Carroll and Helen Louise (Sanders) Watson; m. Sharon Ann Rinkus Diguette, Apr. 22, 1977. BA in Physics, Western Ill. U., 1967; PhD in Physics, Iowa State U., 1973; MA in Econs., Georgetown U., 1981. Postdoctoral fellow Argonne (Ill.) Nat. Lab., 1973-75; project scientist, then sr. scientist B-K Dynamics, Inc., Rockville, Md., 1975-78; tech. staff TRW Energy Systems Planning Group, Mc Lean, Va., 1978-80; profl. staff mem. subcom. on energy nuclear proliferation and govt. processes Com. on Govtl. Affairs, U.S. Senate, Washington, 1980-81; tech. and sci. cons. Com. on Sci. and Tech., U.S. Ho. of Reps., 1981-86; rep. energy and environ., coord. Com. on Sci., Space and Tech., U.S. Ho. of Reps., 1986-89; sci. adviser to sec. Dept. Interior, Washington, 1989-93, dep. asst. sec. for sci.-water and sci., 1989-90, prin. dep. asst. to sec. for water and sci., 1990-93; rep. spl. asst. subcom. energy, com. sci., space, tech. U.S. Ho. of Reps., 1993-95, staff dir. subcom. energy and environment, com. sci., 1995—2001; sr climate negotiator, spec rep US Dept State, 2001—. Contbr. articles to profl jours. Home: 6719 Tomlinson Ter Cabin John MD 20818-1328 Office: 2201 C St NW Rm 4330 Washington DC 20520-0001 E-mail: WatsonHL@state.gov.

WATSON, HELEN RICHTER, educator, ceramic artist; b. Laredo, Tex., May 10, 1926; d. Horace Edward and Helen Mary (Richter) Watson. B.A., Scripps Coll., 1947; M.F.A., Claremont Grad. Sch. and U. Ctr., 1949; postgrad. Alfred U., 1966; Swedish Govt. fellow Konstfackskolan, Stockholm, 1952-53. Mem. faculty Chaffey Coll., Ontario, Calif., 1950-52; chmn. ceramics Mt. San Antonio Coll., Walnut, Calif., 1955-57; prof., chmn. ceramics dept. Otis Art Inst., Los Angeles, 1958-81; mem. faculty Otis-Parsons Sch. Design, 1983-88, ret. 1988; studio ceramic artist, Claremont, Calif. and Laredo, Tex., 1949— ; design cons. Interpace, Glendale, Calif., 1963-64; artist-in-residence Claremont Men's Coll., 1977. Claremont Grad. Sch. fellow, 1948-49; Swedish Govt. grantee, 1952-53; recipient First Ann. Scripps Coll. Disting. Alumna award, Claremont, 1978. Address: 1906 Houston St Laredo TX 78040-7709

WATSON, JACK CROZIER, retired state supreme court justice; b. Jonesville, La., Sept. 17, 1928; s. Jesse Crozier and Gladys Lucille (Talbot) W.; m. Henrietta Sue Carter, Dec. 26, 1958; children: Carter Crozier (dec.), Wells Talbot. BA, U. Southwestern La., 1949; JD, La. State U., 1956; completed with honor, Appellate Judges Seminar, N.Y. U., 1974, Sr. Appellate Judges Seminar, 1980. Bar: La. 1956. Atty. King, Anderson & Swift, Lake Charles, La., 1956-58; prosecutor City of Lake Charles, 1960; asst. dist. atty. Calcasieu Parish, La., 1961-64; ptnr. Watson & Watson, Lake Charles, 1961-64; judge 14th Jud. Dist., La., 1964-72; judge ad hoc Ct. Appeals, 1st Circuit, Baton Rouge, 1972-73; judge Ct. Appeals, 3rd Circuit, Lake Charles, 1973-79; assoc. justice La. Supreme Ct., New Orleans, 1979-96, ret., 1996. Faculty advisor Nat. Coll. State Judiciary, Reno, 1970, 73; adj. prof. law summer sch. program in Greece, Tulane U., 1988-2000; adj. prof. law So. U., Baton Rouge, 1998-99; del. NEH Seminar, 1976; La. del to Internat. Conf. Appellate Magistrates, The Philippines, 1977; mem. La. Jud. Coun., 1986-92. 1st lt. USAF, 1950-54. Mem. ABA, La. Bar Assn., S.W. La. Bar Assn. (pres. 1973), Law Inst. State of La., La. Coun. Juvenile Ct. Judges (pres. 1969-70), Am. Judicature Soc., S.W. La. Camellia Soc. (pres. 1973-74), Am. Legion (post comdr. 1963), Lake Charles Yacht Club (commodore 1974), Blue Key, Sigma Alpha Epsilon, Phi Delta Phi, Pi Kappa Delta. Democrat. Baptist.

WATSON, JAMES DEWEY, molecular biologist, educator; b. Chgo., Apr. 6, 1928; s. James Dewey and Jean (Mitchell) W.; m. Elizabeth Lewis, 1968; children: Rufus Robert, Duncan James. BS, U. Chgo., 1947; PhD in Zoology, Ind. U., 1950; DSc (hon.) , U. Chgo., 1961, Ind. U., 1963; LLD (hon.) , U. Notre Dame, 1965; DSc (hon.) , L.I. U., 1970, Adelphi U., 1972, Brandeis U., 1973, Albert Einstein Coll. Medicine, 1979, Hofstra U., 1976, Harvard U., 1978, Rockefeller U., 1980, Clarkson Coll., 1981, SUNY, 1983; MD (hon.) , U. Buenos Aires, Argentina, 1986; DSc (hon.) , Rutgers U., 1988, Bard Coll., 1991, U. Cambridge, 1993, Fairfield U., 1993, U. Stellenbosch, 1993, U. Oxford; MD, Charles Univ., Prague, 1998; DSc (hon.) , Washington Coll., 1999, U. Judaism, 1999, U. Coll. London, 2000, Ill. Wesleyan U., 2000, Widener U., 2001, Dartmouth, 2001, Trinity Coll., Dublin, 2001. Rsch. fellow NRC, U. Copenhagen, 1950-51; Nat. Found. Infantile Paralysis fellow Cavendish Lab., Cambridge U., 1951-52, 55-56; sr. rsch. fellow biology Calif. Inst. Tech., 1953-55; asst. prof. biology Harvard U., 1955-58, assoc. prof., 1958-61, prof., 1961-76; dir. Cold Spring Harbor Lab., N.Y., 1968-93, pres., 1994—; assoc. dir. Nat. Ctr. for Human Genome Rsch., NIH, 1988-89, dir. Nat. Ctr. for Human Genome Rsch., 1989-92. Newton-Abraham vis. prof. Oxford U., 1994. Author: Molecular Biology of the Gene, 1965, 4th edit., 1986, The Double Helix, 1968, (with John Tooze) The DNA Story, 1981, (with others) The Molecular Biology of the Cell, 1983, 2d edit., 1989, 3d edit. 1994, (with John Tooze and David Kurtz) Recombinant DNA, A Short Course, 1983, 2d edit., 1992, A Passion for DNA, 2000, Genes, Girls and Gamow, 2001. Named Hon. fellow Clare Coll., Cambridge U., hon. knight of Brit. Empire, 2002; recipient (with F.H.C. Crick) John Collins Warren prize Mass. Gen. Hosp., 1959, Eli Lilly award in biochemistry Am. Chem. Soc., 1959, Albert Lasker prize Am. Pub. Health Assn., 1960, (with F.H.C. Crick) Rsch. Corp. prize, 1962, (with F.H.C. Crick and M.H.F. Wilkins) Nobel prize in medicine, 1962, Presdl. Medal of Freedom, 1977, Kaul Found. award for excellence, 1993, Nat. Biotech. Venture award, 1993, Copley Medal, 1993, Charles A. Dana award, 1994, Lomonosov medal Russian Acad. Sci., 1995, Nat. medal of Sci., 1997, Liberty medal City of Phila., 2000, Benjamin Franklin medal for disting. achievement in scis. Am. Philos. Soc., 2001. Mem. NAS (Carty medal 1971), Am. Philos. Soc., Am. Assn. Cancer Rsch., Am. Acad. Arts and Scis., Am. Soc. Biol. Chemistry, Royal Soc. (London), Acad. Scis. Russia, Danish Acad. Arts and Scis; Mendel Medal, Brno, 1998. Achievements include co-discovery of Double-Helix DNA. Office: Cold Spring Harbor Lab PO Box 100 Cold Spring Harbor NY 11724-0100

WATSON, JAMES RAY, JR. education educator; b. Anniston, Ala., Dec. 6, 1935; s. James Ray and Mary Garrity (Profumo) W.; m. Shirley Jean Lesesne, 1960 (div. 1972); children: Laura Catherine, Gregory Andrew, Jennifer Ann; m. Louise Edmonds, 1973. BS in Animal Sci., Auburn U., 1957, MS in Agronomy, 1960; PhD in Botany, Iowa State U., 1963. Rsch. asst. dept. agronomy Auburn (Ala.) U., 1958-60; rsch. asst. dept. botany Iowa State U., Ames, 1960-61, teaching asst. dept. botany, 1961-63; asst. prof. dept. botany Miss. State U., Mississipi State, 1963-68, assoc. prof. dept. botany, 1968-77, head dept. botany, 1975-78, prof. dept. botany, 1977-78, prof. dept. biol. sci., 1978-2000, prof. emeritus, 2000—. Participant Smithsonians Summer Inst. Systematics, Washington, 1968; vis. scholar U. Mich., Ann Arbor, 1964-65. Contbr. articles to profl. jours. Mem. The Nature Conservancy. With U.S. Army, 1957-58. NSF postdoctoral fellow U. Mich., 1963-64; Nat. Natural Landmarks Miss. grantee, 1973-74. Mem. Natural Areas Assn., Bot. Soc. Am. (paleobot. sect.), Miss. Native Plant Soc., Sigma Xi, Xi Sigma Pi. Republican. Roman Catholic. Avocation: pocket watch collector. Home: 217 Seville Pl Starkville MS 39759-2133 Office: Miss State U Dept Biol Sci PO Drawer GY Mississippi State MS 39762

WATSON, JERRY CARROLL, advertising executive; b. Greenville, Ala., Aug. 22, 1943; s. William J. and Georgia Katherine (Mixon) W.; m. Judith Zeigler Brooks, Sept. 16, 1988; 2 child, Theodore William, Hunter Brooks. BS, U. Ala., Tuscaloosa, 1967; MS, U. Va., 1995. Staff writer Phillips, Eindhoven, The Netherlands, 1967-68; mgr. mktg. Fuller & Dees Mktg., Montgomery, Ala., 1968-70; v.p. Univ. Programs, Washington, 1970-73; pres. Coll. & Univ. Press, 1973-80; ptnr. Direct Response Consulting Svcs., McLean, Va., 1981-96. Bd. dirs. Foxhall Corp., The Art Co., Mustique Co. Founding mem. Am. Inst. Cancer Rsch. Mem. Direct Mktg. Assn., Non-Profit Mailer Fedn., Promotional Mktg. Assn., Nature Conservancy, Sierra Club, Falls Church (Va.) C. of C. (bd. dirs.). Avocation: gardening, astronomy. Home: Apt 402 850 Dolley Madison Blvd Mc Lean VA 22101-1821 Office: Direct Response Cons Svcs 6849 Old Dominion Dr Ste 300 Mc Lean VA 22101-3791 E-mail: watson@drcs.com., watson@mouselink.net.

WATSON, JESSICA LEWIS, writer; b. Urbana, Ill., June 16, 1964; d. Jane Eileen Lewis; m. Bruce S. Watson, Aug. 9, 1986. BA in English, U. Ill., 1987; Diploma in Am. Lit., U. Liege, 1988; MA in English, Baylor U., 1994. Social worker Roundhouse, Champaign, Ill., 1988-89; cmty. liaison Krannert Ctr. for the Performing Arts, Urbana, 1989-90; freelance, writer and author Waco, 1990—; lectr. in English Baylor U., Tex., 1996-98; English instr. U. Ill., Urbana, 1988. Author: (books) Bastardy as a Gifted Status in Chaucer and Malory, 1996, Illegitimacy Empowered, 1994.; contbr. articles to nat. jours. Singer Austin Civic Chorus, Tex., 1996-2000. Recipient Literary Touring Program award Tex. Commn. on the Arts, Temple, Longview, Ft. Hood, 1994-97, Helen Chambers Poetry award Baylor U., Waco, 1994; grantee Aspen Writers Found., Colo., 1992. Avocations: modern dance, swimming, playing and singing classical music. Home: 315 Cottage Ct Champaign IL 61820

WATSON, JOANN FORD, theology educator; b. Ashland, Ohio, Apr. 11, 1956; d. Laurence Wesley and Edna Lucille (Garber) F.; m Duane Frederick Watson, June 2, 1984; 1 child, Christina Lucille. BA, DePauw U., 1978; MDiv, Princeton Theol. Sem., 1981; PhD, Northwestern U., 1984. Ordained to ministry, Presbyn. Ch. Asst. prof. hist. theology Ashland Theol. Sem., 1984-86, assoc. prof. theology, chair dept. ch. history and theology, 1989-95, H.R. Gill Prof. of theology, 1996—; chaplain Grady Meml. Hosp., Atlanta, 1986-87; co-pastor Tri-Ch. Parish United Meth. Chs. Northwestern, N.Y., 1987-89; pastor Camroden Presbyn. Ch., Rome, 1987-89. Clergy commr. del. Gen. Assembly of Presbyn. Ch., 1995. Author: Manna for Sisters in Christ, 1989, Mutuality in Christ, 1991, Meditations on Suffering, 1993, Study of Karl Barth's Doctrine of Man and Woman, 1995, Sister to Sister, 1998. Missionary vol. Mother Teresa's Missionaries of Charity, Calcutta, 1988; mem. Hospice Ashland County chpt., 1989-93; assoc. mem. Women's Symphony League, Ashland Symphony Orch., 1989-94. Doctoral fellowship Northwestern U., 1982-84. Mem. Internat. Assn. of Women Mins. (exec. bd., trustee 1990-95), Presbyn. Women in Leadership, Nat. Assn. of Presbyn. Clergywomen, Soc. of Biblical Lit., Am. Acad. of Religion, Alpha Lambda Delta, Phi Beta Kappa. Republican. Avocations: travel, music, water sports. Office: Ashland Theolog Sem 910 Center St Ashland OH 44805-4007

WATSON, JOE CRAIG, music educator; b. Gainesville, Fla., Aug. 16, 1956; s. Joseph Berton Watson Jr., Frances (Bailey) Watson; m. Rebecca Louise Gibson; children: Jennifer Claire, Lauren Bailey. BS, Auburn U., 1981. Dir. band, instr. Lyman Ward Mil. Acad., Camp Hill, Ala., 1981—. Composer (arranger music for jazz bands): Prayer for Jennie; composer: (music for marching bands) Ranger March. Councilman Town of Camp Hill, 1994—97, 2000—. Recipient Citation for Outstanding Musicianship, Nat. Assn. Jazz Educators, 1973. Mem.: Auburn Knights Alumni Assn., Ala. Bandmasters Assn., Music Educators Nat. Conf. Home: 21378 Claude Pepper Dr Camp Hill AL 36850 Office: Lyman Ward Mil Acad Ward Circle Camp Hill AL 36850

WATSON, JOHN SKELLY, retired surgeon; b. Tulsa, Aug. 3, 1935; s. James K. Watson and Marie Francis (Iovine) Cone; 1 child, Randall. MD, U. Nebr., 1967. Diplomate Am. Bd. Surgery. Asst. clin. prof. surgery U. Okla., Tulsa. Mem. Leadership Tulsa, 1994; vol. Tulsa Police Homicide. Lt. col. (ret.) USAF, 1992—2001. Fellow: ACS (hon.); mem.: AMA (hon.), Tulsa Surg. Soc. (hon.), Tulsa County Med. Soc. (hon.), Okla. State Med. Soc. (hon.). Republican. Roman Catholic. Home: 1820 S Lynn Lane Rd Tulsa OK 74108-6300 E-mail: jswatson1@aol.com.

WATSON, JOHN ALLAN, clergyman; b. Detroit, June 26, 1938; s. Roy Allan and Charlotte Luella (Piper) W.; m. Mary Louise Strawbridge, June 25, 1960; children: Paul Allan, Stephen John, Mark Andrew, Philip Scott. BA, Wheaton (Ill.) Coll., 1960; BD, Princeton Sem., 1964; MTh, U. Aberdeen, Scotland, 1971. Ordained minister Presbyn. Ch., 1964. Minister 1st Presbyn. Ch., Kentland, Ind., 1964-68, Bethel Presbyn. Ch., Columbus, Ohio, 1970—. Dean Anselm Inst., Columbus, 1986—; moderator Presbytery of Scioto Valley, 2001-02. Mem. Presbytery Scioto Valley (chmn. minister rels. 1982-85, jud. commn. 1987-96), chmn. Bills and Overtures, 1996-99, N.W. Presbyn. Urban Ministry, 1996—, Internat. Brotherhood Magicians. Democrat. Home: 46 Winthrop Rd Columbus OH 43214-3629 Office: Bethel Presbyn Ch 1735 Bethel Rd Columbus OH 43220-1870 *One of the great mistakes of our time is living by a philosophy which has amended the great affirmation that "our chief end is to glorify God and enjoy Him forever" to "our chief end is to enjoy."*.

WATSON, JOHN ALLEN, lawyer; b. Ft. Worth, Sept. 18, 1946; s. John and Mary (Barlow) W.; m. Patricia L. Clardy, Oct. 24, 1946; 1 child, Virginia E. BA, Rice U., 1968; JD, U. Tex., Austin, 1971. Bar: Tex. 1971. Assoc. Fulbright & Jaworski, Houston, 1971-78, ptnr., 1978—. Mem. ABA. Office: Fulbright & Jaworski LLP 1301 McKinney St Ste 5100 Houston TX 77010-3031 E-mail: jwatson@fulbright.com.

WATSON, JOHN LAWRENCE, III, former trade association executive; b. Rome, Jan. 14, 1932; s. John Lawrence and Mary (Cowen) W.; m. Dorothy Palmer McLanahan, Aug. 9, 1958; children: Mary Palmer Watson Gard, Valerie Catherine Watson Bilbrough, John Lawrence IV. BS, Auburn U., 1954. Trader-over the counter J.C. Bradford & Co., Atlanta, 1957-58; with Robinson Humphrey & Co., 1958-64, dept. head-over the counter, 1964-74, dir. equity trading, 1974-83, dir. capital markets, 1983-85; pres. Security Traders Assn., N.Y.C., 1985-96. Mem. bd. visitors Babcock Sch. Mgmt. Wake Forest U.; past chmn. Parent's Coun. Wofford Coll.; life trustee Pace Acad.; trustee Securities Industry Found. for Econ. Edn. Named Man of Yr., Equities mag. Mem. Nat. Assn. Securities Dealers (dist. chmn. 1982, bd. govs. 1983-85), Am. Mus. Fin. History (trustee), Capital City Club, Piedmont Driving Club (Atlanta), Ponte Vedra Club, Sawgrass Country Club (Ponte Vedra), Univ. Club (N.Y.C.). Home: 505 Ponte Vedra Blvd Ponte Vedra Beach FL 32082-2317

WATSON, JOHN MICHAEL, lawyer; b. Karnes, Tex., May 9, 1956; s. Jarvis Schooley and Edwina Louise Watson; m. Margaret Marie Blackshear; children: Maggie, John. BA, Washington and Lee U., 1979; JD, U. Houston, 1982. Bar: Tex. 1982, U.S. Dist. Ct. (so., no., ea. and we. dists.) Tex. 1994. Counsel Union Bank Houston, 1982-85; asst. gen. counsel, v.p. Allied Bank Tex., Houston, 1985-88; asst. gen. counsel, sr. v.p. First Interstate Bank Tex., N.A., 1988-96; sr. counsel Wells Fargo Bank, 1996—. Dir. The Agnes Carter Helms Sch., Camden, Tex., 1986-89, Supreme Ct. Bd. Disciplinary Appeals, Houston, 1996—2002. Mem. Tex. Assn. Bank Counsel (dir. 1989-92). Republican. Methodist. E-mail: watsonm1@wellsfargo.com.

WATSON, JOYCE LESLIE, elementary educator; b. Riverside, N.J., May 31, 1950; d. Robert Eugene and Doris Virginia (Robinson) Stockton; 1 child, Michelle Leslie. BS, Trenton State Coll., 1972, MEd, 1978. Cert. elem. tchr., N.J., Pa. Tchr. elem. Willingboro (N.J.) Sch. Dist., 1972-81, Pennsbury Sch. Dist., Fallsington, Pa., 1987—, tchr. gifted/talented, advanced math. tchr., 1987-88, 92—, elem. demonstration tchr., 1995-97, 98—. Coach Odyssey of the Mind, Penwood Mid. Sch., Yardley, Pa., 1993—94; participant 8th Ann. Capital Area Space Orientation Program, Washington, 1996, NASA Educators Workshop, Kennedy Space Center, Fla., 2000, Pa. Gov.'s Inst. on Math, College Park, 2000, Share-a-thon at Nat. Congress on Aviation and Space Edn., 2002. Mem.: CAP, NEA, AIAA, Exptl. Aircraft Assn., Nat. Coun. Tchrs. Math., Women in Aviation Internat., Nat. Aero. Assn., Airplane Owners and Pilots Assn., Pa. State Edn. Assn., Pa. Assn. for Gifted Edn., Phi Delta Kappa. Home: 2293 Seabird Dr Bristol PA 19007 Office: Makefield Elem Sch Makefield Rd Yardley PA 19067 E-mail: joy1watson@aol.com.

WATSON, JULIAN See BLAKE, BUD

WATSON, KATHY, political organization administrator; b. Skowhegan, Maine; Owner Kathy Watson Co.; mem. Pittsfield Rep. Com., 1982—, Somerset County Rep. Com., 1982—; vice chmn. Maine Rep. Party, 1986-88, 94-98, chmn., 1998—. Co-chmn. Maine women for Reagan/Bush, 1984; county chair Reagan for Pres., 1988, McKernan for Gov., 1990, Snowe for Congress, 1990, 92, Cohen for U.S. Senate, 1990, Snowe for Senate, 1994; mem. Bush adv. com., 1992; del. Rep. Nat. Conv., 1988, 92, 96; mem. rules com. Rep. Nat. Com., 1992, 96. Bd. dirs. Sr. Connections/Bridges. Mem. Assoc. Gen. Contractors Am.*

WATSON, KAY, educational consultant; b. Rotan, Tex., Feb. 5, 1942; d. C.M. and Marie (Reeder) W. BA, Baylor U., 1964; MA, Colo. State Coll., 1968; MEd, Sul Ross State U., Alpine, Tex., 1982; EdD, Tex. Tech. U., 1988. Tchr. grade 6 Dallas Ind. Sch. Dist., Dallas, 1964-67, counselor J.L. Long Jr. H.S., 1968-70, tchr. grade 7, 1970-72; tchr. grade 5 Weatherford (Tex.) Ind. Sch. Dist., 1972-73; spl. edn. counselor Parker County Coop., Weatherford, 1973-74, Monahans-Wickett-Pyote Ind. Sch. Dist., 1974-78; dir. spl. edn. Monahans (Tex.)-Wickett-Pyote Ind. Sch. Dist., 1978-85; supr. pre-sch. ctr. Ector County Ind. Sch. Dist., Odessa, Tex., 1985-86, prin. elem. Magnet Sch. at Travis, 1986-89, prin. LBJ Elem. Sch., 1989-90, assoc. dir. elem. edn., 1990-92, assoc. exec. dir., clusters I and II, 1992; asst. supt. Calhoun County Ind. Sch. Dist., Port Lavaca, 1992-96; vis. asst. prof. U. Tex. of the Permian Basin, Odessa, 1996-99; edn. cons., 1999—. Bd. dirs. West Tex. Educators Conf., 1997-2000. Bd. dirs. Am. Cancer Soc., Odessa, 1991-92; bd. mgrs. Ward Meml. Hosp., 1997-99, vice-chmn., 1998-99; mem. Odessa Symphony Guild, 1990-92, Port Lavaca Crisis Hotline Vol.; bd. dirs. United Way of Calhoun County, 1996; vol. Port Lavaca Crisis Hotline, 1995-96. Mem. Tex. Assn. Secondary Sch. Adminstrs., Tex. Assn. Profl. Educators, Delta Kappa Gamma Soc. Internat. Baptist. Home and Office: 1204 S Eric St Monahans TX 79756-5719 E-mail: kwatson@nwol.net.

WATSON, KENNETH MARSHALL, physics educator; b. Des Moines, Sept. 7, 1921; s. Louis Erwin and Irene Nellie (Marshall) W.; m. Elaine Carol Miller, Mar. 30, 1946; children: Ronald M., Mark Louis. BS, Iowa State U., 1943; PhD, U. Iowa, 1948; ScD (hon.), U. Ind., 1976. Rsch. engr. Naval Rsch. Lab., Washington, 1943-46; staff Inst. Advanced Study Princeton (N.J.) U., 1948-49; rsch. fellow Lawrence Berkeley (Calif.) Lab., 1949-52, staff, 1957-81; asst. prof. physics U. Ind., Bloomington, 1952-54; assoc. prof. physics U. Wis., Madison, 1954-57; prof. physics U. Calif., Berkeley, 1957-81, prof. oceanography, dir. marine physics lab. San Diego, 1981-93. Cons. Sci. Application Corp.; mem. U.S. Pres.'s Sci. Adv. Com. Panels, 1962-71; adviser Nat. Security Coun., 1972-75; mem. JASON Adv. Panel; sci. adv. bd. George C. Marshall Inst., 1989—. Author: (with M.L. Goldberger) Collision Theory, 1964; (with J. Welch and J. Bond) Atomic Theory of Gas Dynamics, 1966; (with J. Nutall) Topics in Several Particle Dynamics, 1970; (with Flatté, Munk, Dashen) Sound Transmission Through a Fluctuating Ocean, 1979. Mem. Nat. Acad. Scis. Home: Unit 2008 8515 Costa Verde Blvd San Diego CA 92122-1150 Office: U Calif Marine Physics Lab La Jolla CA 92093 E-mail: kmw@mpl.ucsd.edu.

WATSON, KIPP ELLIOTT, lawyer; b. L.A., Oct. 30, 1950; s. Benjamin And Irene Cohen; m. Emily Strauss; 1 child, Lisa Jo. BA, NYU, 1977; JD, Benjamin N. Cardozo Sch. Law, 1980. Bar: N.Y. Pvt. practice, N.Y.C., 1984-98; of counsel Mark B. Stumer & Assocs., 1998—. Roothbert fellow, N.Y.C., 1979. Mem. N.Y.State Bar Assn. (civil rights com.), Nat. Employment Lawyers Assn. N.Y. (bd. dirs. 1992-99, newsletter editor 1994-97), 504 Dem. Club (pres. 1993). Avocations: computer programming, chess, wheelchair basketball-forward for LI Express. Office: Mark B Stumer & Assocs 101 5th Ave Rm 10E New York NY 10003-1008

WATSON, LINDA BARBARA, special education educator; b. Phila., Sept. 27, 1951; d. Lazarus Fuller and Louise (Blackman) Conner; m. James D. Watson, Aug. 1, 1987; children: Asher, Antonio; children from previous marriage: Dana, Janine. BA, Antioch U., 1980, MEd, 1982; postgrad., U. Del., 1992-94. Cert. spl. edn. and elem. edn. tchr., Pa. Tchr. Phila. Pub. Schs. With Delaware Valley Child Care, 1984—; pres. L.& L. Day Care Ctr. Inc., 19890—. Dep. commr. for voter registration, City of Phila., 1992—. Mem. Nat. Coalition Black Women (v.p. 1992—), Coun. Exceptional Children, Delta Sigma Theta. Democrat. Baptist. Avocations: swimming, roller skating. Home: 8041 Lindbergh Blvd Philadelphia PA 19153-1109

WATSON, MARILYN KAYE, elementary education educator; b. Liberty, Ky., Nov. 30, 1950; d. Lewis Joshua and Lois Sue (Ross) W. BA, Ea. Ky. U., 1974, postgrad., 1977, 81. Tchr. Casey County Bd. of Edn., Liberty, 1977—. Mem. NEA, Ky. Edn. Assn., Order of Eastern Star (sec. Casey chpt. 1979-85, grand Esther 1981-82, worthy matron 1989-90). Republican. Methodist. Avocations: reading, basketball, needlepoint, hiking, traveling.

WATSON, MATHEW D. optical scientist; b. L.A., Feb. 9, 1958; BS in Physics, San Jose State U., 1984; MS in Optical Scis., U. Ariz., 1989, PhD in Optical Scis., 1991. Mem. tech. staff Uniphase, Inc., San Jose, Calif., 1984-86; rsch. assoc. Optical Scis. Ctr., Tucson, 1986-91; electro optical engr. ILX Lightwave, Inc., Bozeman, Mont., 1991-93; sr. optical engr. Quest Integrated, Inc., Kent, Wash., 1994-96; pres. Eclipse Optics, Inc., Bellevue, 1997—. Contbr. articles to profl. jours.; patentee in field. Grad. rsch. scholar Optical Scis. Ctr., 1989; recipient ARCS scholarship ARCS Found., 1983. Mem. Optical Soc. Am., IEEE/Laser and Electro-optic Soc., Soc. Photometric and Instrumentation Engrs. Home: 10439 NE 28th Pl Bellevue WA 98004-2043 Office: Eclipse Optics Inc 10439 NE 28th Pl Bellevue WA 98004-2043 E-mail: matw@eclipse-optics.com.

WATSON, N. CAMERON, artist, caterer; b. Putney, Vt., Jan. 24, 1955; d. Aldren Auld and Nancy (Dingman) Watson; m. William G. Keane, Nov. 26, 1987. BA, Yale U., 1980. Asst. buyer Bergdorf Goodman, N.Y.C., 1980; creative asst. Grey Advt., 1981; kitchen mgr., pastry chef Another Season Restaurant, Boston, 1981-84; owner, chef Sweet Williams Catering, Truro, Mass., 1984—; owner, artist, painter Watson Graphics, 1986—. Apprentice Gerhardt's Marionettes, Schwaebisch Hall, Germany, 1973-76; puppeteer/tchr. Truro Ctr. for the Arts at Castle Hill, 1983-86, Acad. for Performing Arts, Orleans, Mass., 1983-86. Author, illustrator: (children's books) The Little Pigs' First Cookbook, 1987, The Little Pigs' Puppet Book, 1990; illustrator: (children's books) Mister Toad, 1992, The Weeds and the Weather, 1994. Recipient awards Soc. Illustrators, 1992, 93. Mem. Provincetown Arts Assn. Avocations: gardening, cooking, animals. Home: PO Box 730 Truro MA 02666-0730

WATSON, OLIVER LEE, III, aerospace engineering manager; b. Lubbock, Tex., Sept. 18, 1938; m. Judith Valeria Horvath, June 13, 1964; 1 child, Clarke Stanford. BSEE, U. Tex., 1961; MSEE, Stanford U., 1963; MBA, Calif. State U., Fullerton, 1972; cert., U. So. Calif., 1980; cert. comm. & networks, U. Calif., Irvine, 1999. Cert. comm. & networks U. Calif., Irvine, 1999. Mgr. ballistic analysis Rockwell Internat. Autonetics Divsn., Anaheim, Calif., 1973-78, mgr. minuteman systems, 1978-83, mgr. preliminary engring., 1983-84; mgr. analysis group autonetics divsn. Rockwell Internat., 1984-85, mgr. aircraft sys. autonetics dept., 1985-93, dep. dir. integrated product devel. N.Am. aircraft aircraft modification divsn., 1993-94, dep. dir. engring. N.Am. aircraft modification divsn., 1994-96; dep. dir. engring. comm. and combat sys. divsn. Boeing N.Am., 1996-98; skills, process and metrics mgr. Comm. and Battle Mgmt., 1998-99; process, metrics and tools dir. Anaheim Site Engring., Integrated Def. Sys., Calif., 1999—, 2001—. Lectr. engring. Calif. State U., Fullerton, 1981—90, mem. indsl. adv. bd., 1994—, vice-chmn., 1995—97; spkr. welcome address Engring. & Computer Sci. Commencement, 1997; adv. com. Accreditation Bd. for Engring. and Tech., 2000; sec. Elec. Engring. Indsl. Adv. Bd., 2001—. Co-author Digital Computing Using Fortran IV, 1982; Fortran 77, A Complete Primer, 1986; contbg. author: The World's Best Shortest Stories, 2001. Bd. dirs. Olive Little League, Orange, 1980; vol. Stanford U. Engring. Fund, Orange County, Calif., 1983, regional chmn. 1984-86, So. Calif. chmn. 1986-91; mem. Stanford Assocs., 1988—. Recipient Stanford Assocs. Centennial Medallion award, 1991; fellow N.Am. Aviation Sci.-Engring., L.A., 1962-63, Inst. Advancement Engring., L.A., 1976. Mem. IEEE (sr., sec. v.p. 1974-75, sect. chmn. 1975-76), Jaycees (v.p. Orange chpt. 1973-74), Rockwell-Calif. State Univ. Alumni Club (v.p. 1993, pres. 1993-94), Lido Sailing Club. Republican. Avocations: sailing, swimming, humor writing, scriptwriting, reading. Office: Boeing NAm 031-CA92 3370 E Miraloma Ave Anaheim CA 92806-1911

WATSON, PAMELA GAHERIN, rehabilitation nurse; b. N.Y.C., Oct. 5, 1941; d. John Joseph and Rita (O'Brien) Gaherin; diploma Mass. Gen. Hosp. Sch. Nursing, 1964; BS in Nursing, Boston U., 1971, MS, 1972, Sc.D. in Rehab. Counseling, 1982; m. Barron C. Watson, May 4, 1970; 1 child, Willis Fanning. Head nurse Yale-New Haven Hosp., 1964-66, Tufts-New Eng. Med. Ctr., Boston, 1966-67; instr. Boston U. Sch. Nursing, 1973-77, asst. prof., 1977-83, assoc. prof., 1983—, chmn. dept. rehab. nursing, 1978—, chair dept. med./surg. rehab. and gerontology, 1985-86, chair MS degree program, 1986-87; prof., chmn. dept. nursing Coll. Allied Health Scis., Thomas Jefferson U., Phila., also prof. Jefferson Med. Coll. and prof. Coll. Grad. Studies. Bd. dirs. PTA, Peirce Sch., Newton, Mass., 1981-82; bd. dirs., cons. Extended Day Program, Newton, 1982-84. Mem. Am. Nurses Assn., Am. Psychol. Assn. Am. Congress Rehab. Medicine, Am. Nurses Assn., Council Nurse Researchers, Am. Pub. Health Assn., Am. Assn. Cancer Educators, Sigma Theta Tau. Club: Cambridge Boat. Editor N.E. region Internat. Assn. Enterostomal Therapy Newsletter, 1981-83; assoc. editor: Jour. Enterostomal Therapy, 1984—; book rev. editor Rehab. Nursing, 1979-83; mem. editorial bd. Cancer Nursing, 1979—, Rehab. Nursing, 1979-87; contbr. articles in field to profl. publs. Office: Thomas Jefferson U Coll Allied Health Scis 130 S 9th St Dept Nursing Philadelphia PA 19107-5233

WATSON, PATTY JO, anthropology educator; b. Superior, Nebr., Apr. 26, 1932; d. Ralph Clifton and Elaine Elizabeth (Lance) Andersen; m. Richard Allan Watson, July 30, 1955; 1 child, Anna Melissa MA, U. Chgo., 1956, PhD in Anthropology, 1959. Archaeologist-ethnographer Oriental Inst.-U. Chgo., 1959-60, research assoc., archaeologist, 1964-70; instr. anthropology U. So. Calif., Los Angeles, 1961, UCLA, 1961, L.A. State U., 1961; asst. prof. anthropology Washington U., St. Louis, 1969-70, assoc. prof., 1970-73, prof., 1973—, Edward Mallinckrodt disting. univ. prof., 1993—. Mem. rev. panel NSF, Washington, 1974-76; fellow Ctr. Advanced Study in Behavioral Scis., Stanford, Calif., 1981-82, 91-92. Author: The Prehistory of Salts Cave, Kentucky, 1969, Archaeological Ethnography in Western Iran, 1979; author: (with others) Man and Nature, 1969, Explanation in Archeology, 1971, Archeological Explanation, 1984, Girikihaciyan, A Halafian Site in Southeastern Turkey; author: (editor) Archeology of the Mammoth Cave Area, 1974, Prehistoric Archeology Along the Zagros Flanks, 1983; co-editor: The Origins of Agriculture, 1992, Of Caves and Shell Mounds, 1996. Grantee NSF, 1959-60, 68, 70, 72-74, 78-79, NEH, 1977-78, Nat. Geog. Soc., 1969-75. Fellow Am. Anthropol. Assn. (editor for archaeology 1973-77, Disting. Lectr. award 1994, Disting. Svc. award 1996), AAAS (chair sect. H 1991-92), Cave rsch. Found.; mem. NAS, Am. Acad. Arts and Scis., Am. Philos. Soc., Soc. Am. Archaeology (exec. com. 1974-76, 82-84, editor Am. Antiquity 1984-87, Fryxell medal 1990), Assn. Paleorient (sci. bd.), Nat. Speleological Soc. (hon. life, editorial bd. bull. 1979—, sci. award), Archaeol. Inst. Am. (Gold Medal for Disting. Archaeol. Achievement 1999). Office: Dept Anthropol CB #1114 Washington U Saint Louis MO 63130-4899 E-mail: pjwatson@artsci.wustl.edu.

WATSON, PAULA D. library administrator; b. N.Y.C., Mar. 6, 1945; d. Joseph Francis and Anna Julia (Miksza) De Simone; m. William Douglas Watson, Aug. 23, 1969; children— Lucia, Elizabeth AB, Barnard Coll., 1965; MA, Columbia U., 1966; MSL.S., Syracuse U., 1972. Reference librarian U. Ill., Urbana, 1972-77, city planning and landscape architecture librarian, 1977-79, head documents library, 1979-81; asst. dir. gen. services U. Ill. Library, 1981-88, acting dir. gen. svcs., 1988-93, dir. ctrl. pub. svcs., 1989-93, asst. univ. libr., 1993-95, dir. electronic info. svcs., 1995—. Contbr. articles to profl. jours. N.Y. State Regents fellow Columbia U., N.Y.C., 1965-66; Council on Library Resources profl. edn. and tng. for librarianship grantee, 1983 Mem. ALA (sec. univ. librs. sect. ALA-Assn. Coll. and Rsch. Librs. 1989-91, com. on instnl. coop., chair pub. svcs. dirs. group, 1997-99, mem. com. inst. coop./OCLC virtual electronic libr. steering com.), Ill. Library Assn. Avocation: gardening. Home: 715 W Delaware Ave Urbana IL 61801-4806 Office: U Ill 246 A Library 1408 W Gregory Dr Urbana IL 61801-3607 E-mail: pdwatson@uiuc.edu.

WATSON, PETER S. federal agency administrator; married. LLB, Auckland U.; LLM, McGill U.; MIBA, West Coast U. Pvt. practice internat. and bus. law, L.A., Washington, 1976, 78-88; spl. advisor to Pres. Overseas Pvt. Investment Corp.; dir. Asian affairs Nat. Security Coun., 1989-91; commr. U.S. Internat. Trade Commn., 1991—, vice chmn., 1992-94, chmn., 1994-96; pres. and C.E.O. overseas private investment corp. Off. of the Pres., Washington, 2001—. Adj. prof. internat. trade and investment law and internat. bus. law. Contbr. articles to profl. jours. Republican. Office: Overseas Private Investment Corp Off of the Pres 1100 New York Ave NW Washington DC 20527*

WATSON, RAYMOND COKE, JR. engineering executive, academic administrator; b. Anniston, Ala., Aug. 31, 1926; BS, Jacksonville State U.; MSE, U. Ala.; MS, U. Fla.; MBA and PhD in Engring. Sci., Calif. Coast U. Chief engr. Dixie Svc. Co., 1948-54; head dept. physics and engring. Jacksonville State U., 1954-60; v.p. engring. and rsch. Teledyne Brown Engring., 1960-70, chief engr., chief scientist, 1990—2001; dir. continuing edn., engring. and math. U. Ala., Huntsville, 1970-76; pres., prof. engring. and math. Southeastern Inst. Tech., 1976—; owner RC Watson & Assocs., 1980—; pres., CEO Vision Techs. Kinetics, 2000—. Adj. assoc. prof. U. Ala., Huntsville, 1961-70. Contbr. more than 400 articles and reports to profl. jours. Chmn. elec. engring. adv. bd. Ala. A&M U. Recipient NASA Pub. Svc. award; NSF Sci. Faculty Fellow. Mem. IEEE, AIAA, Optical Soc. Am., Ops. Rsch. Soc. Am., Inst. Mgmt. Sci., Internat. Soc. Optical Engrs., Inst. Indsl. Engrs. Achievements include research in defense systems, space systems and electro-optics. Home: 1801 Inspiration Ln SE Huntsville AL 35801-1150 Office: RC Watson & Assocs PO Box 1485 Huntsville AL 35807 E-mail: rxxwatson@aol.com., ray.watson@tbe.com.

WATSON, REBECCA ELAINE, human resources software consultant; b. Dallas, Nov. 11, 1960; d. John Cephas and Mary Magdeline (Rhea) Bishop; m. Billy Don Wilkinson, July 31, 1982 (div.); children: Eric Tyler, Kristen Rhea; m. David John Watson, June 12, 1999; 1 child, Laura Nicole. BEd, U. Dallas, 1982, MBA, 1995. Adminstrv. asst. IBM, Irving, Tex., 1982-85, equal opportunity coord., 1985-90, human resources data analyst Roanoke, Tex., 1990-94; sr. human resources/payroll application specialist Westinghouse Security Sys., Irving, 1994-97, team leader fin. and adminstrv. sys., 1996-97; sr. cons. Cambridge Tech. Ptnrs., 1997-98; sr. assoc. dir. Comp-U-Temp, USA, Tex., 1998-2000; v.p. WW Cons., 2000—. V.p. WW Cons., 2000—. Mem. NAFE, NOW, Greenpeace, Sigma Iota Epsilon. Democrat. Episcopalian. Avocations: needlework, rollerblading, reading, golfing, bowling.

WATSON, REBECCA WUNDER, Federal Agency Administrator, Lawyer; b. Chgo., Feb. 17, 1952; d. David Hart and Shirley May (Dahlin) Wunder; m. Keith C. Thomson, Oct. 6, 1979 (div. Dec. 1989); m. Gregory B. Watson, Jan. 20, 1996. BA, U. Denver, 1974, MA in LS, 1975, JD, 1978. Bar: Bar: Wyo. 1978, Colo. 1989, D.C. 1995, Mont. 1995. Law clk. U.S. Dist. Ct. for Dist. Wyo., Cheyenne, 1978-80; assoc., then ptnr. Burgess & Davis, Sheridan, Wyo., 1980-88; pvt. practice, Denver, 1988-90; asst. gen. counsel for energy policy Dept. Energy, Washington, 1990-93; of counsel Crowell & Moring, 1993-95; ptnr. Gough Shanahan Johnson & Waterman, Helena, Mont., 1995—2002; asst. secy. land mgt. U.S. Dept Interior, Washington, 2002—. Contbr. author: ABA Natural Resource Law Handbook, 1993; contbr. articles to law jours. Mem. ABA (chmn. natural resource com. sect. adminstrv. law 1994-97, chmn. pub. lands com. sect. natural resources, energy and environ. law 1997-99), Wyo. Bar Assn., Mont. Bar Assn., Phi Beta Kappa. Republican. Avocations: cooking, reading, travel, hunting. Home: Little Blackfoot River Rch 560 Dana Ln Garrison MT 59731-9741 Office: US Dept Interior Land and Materials Mgt 1849 C St NW Washington DC 20240*

WATSON, RENÉE, marketing professional, special events consultant; b. San Antonio, Apr. 1, 1962; d. Clarence and Lettye Watson. BBA, U. Tex., San Antonio, 1987; MPA, CUNY, 1989. Chief staff to Councilman George Stevens, San Diego, 1991-95; dep. chief staff for Senator Rodney Ellis, Tex. Senate, Houston, 1995-97; dir. field mktg. UniverSoul Circus, Atlanta,

1997-99; cons. Watson Consulting, 1999—; program coord. planning and resource mgmt. Bexas County Courthouse, San Antonio, 2000—; program coord. Small Minority Women Owned Bus. Enterprise. Mem. Leadership San Antonio, 1991, Leadership Calif., Pasadena, 1993, Leadership Am., N.Y.C., 1995, Leadershiop Tex., 2002; mem. China del. People to People Amb. Program, 1997. Fellow Nat. Urban Fellows, 1989; named 40 under 40 Rising Stars in San Antonio Bus. Jour. Democrat. Baptist. Avocations: reading, travel, walking, gardening, dancing. E-mail: powernae@hotmail.com.

WATSON, RICHARD ALLAN, philosophy educator, writer; b. New Market, Iowa, Feb. 23, 1931; s. Roscoe Richard and Daisy Belle (Penwell) W.; m. Patty Jo Andersen, July 30, 1955; 1 child, Anna Melissa BA, U. Iowa, 1953, MA, 1957, PhD in Philosophy, 1961; MS in Geology, U. Minn., 1959. Instr. philosophy U. Mich., Ann Arbor, 1961-64; asst. prof. Washington U., St. Louis, 1964-67, assoc. prof., 1967-74, prof., 1974—. Pres. Cave Research Found., Mammoth Cave, Ky., 1965-67; trustee Nat. Parks and Conservation Assn., Washington, 1969-81 Author: The Downfall of Cartesianism, 1966, Under Plowman's Floor, 1978, The Runner, 1981, The Philosopher's Diet, 1985, The Breakdown of Cartesian Metaphysics, 1987, The Philosopher's Joke, 1990, Writing Philosophy, 1992, Niagara, 1993, Caving, 1994, The Philosopher's Demise, 1995, Representational Ideas, 1995, Good Teaching, 1997, Cogito, Ergo Sum: The Life of René Descartes, 2002;(with others) Man and Nature, 1969, The Longest Cave, 1976; editor: Classics in Speleology, 1968-73, Speleologia, 1974-79, Cave Books, 1980—, Jour. History of Philosophy, 1983, Jour. History of Philosophy Monograph Series, 1985-95, Jour. History of Philosophy Book Series, 2001. Served to 1st lt. USAF, 1953-55 NEH grantee, 1975; fellow Ctr. Advanced Study in Behavioral Scis., Stanford, Calif., 1967-68, 81-82, 91-92, Am. Coun. Learned Socs., 1967-68, Princeton Ctr. Internat. Studies, 1975-76, Camargo Found., 1995, Bogliasco Found., 1998. Mem. Nat. Speleological Soc. (hon. life), Am. Philos. Assn., Cave Research Found; fellow AAAS. Office: Washington U Dept Philosophy Saint Louis MO 63130-4899

WATSON, RICHARD THOMAS, lawyer; b. Lakewood, Ohio, Aug. 21, 1933; s. Thomas Earl Watson and Sara Lucille (Whapham) Hadfield; m. Judith C. Briggs, Aug. 6, 1960; children: David, Andrew, Susan (dec.). AB, Harvard U., 1954, JD, 1960. Bar: Ohio 1960. Assoc. Spieth, Bell, McCurdy & Newell, Cleve., 1960, ptnr., 1965, mng. ptnr., 1987—. Bd. dirs. numerous corps. Chancellor Episcopal Diocese of Ohio, Cleve., 1986—; mem. Harvard U. com. on univ. resources, 1992—; bd. trustees Cleve. Mus. Art, 1991—; trustee Case Western Res. U., 1993—. Mem. Union Club Cleve. Office: Spieth Bell McCurdy & Newell 925 Euclid Ave Ste 2000 Cleveland OH 44115-1408 E-mail: richardtwatson@worldnet.att.net.

WATSON, ROBERT D. allergist, immunologist, pediatric rheumatologist; b. Vancouver, B.C., Can., May 19, 1947; Phd, U. B.C., 1975; MD, U. Autonoma Ciudad Juarez, Mex., 1980. Diplomate Am. Bd. Allergy & Immunology, Am. Bd. Pediatrics. Intern U. Tex. Health Scis. Ctr., San Antonio, 1980-81; resident in pediatrics U. Calif.-Davis, Sacto., 1981-83, fellow in allergy & immunology and pediatric rheumatology, 1983-86; pvt. practice. Mem. staff Mercy Gen. Hosp., Sacto. Fellow Am. Acad. Allergy and Immunology, Am. Acad. Pediatrics, Am. Coll. Rheumatology. Office: Med Clinic Sacto 3160 Folsom Blvd Sacramento CA 95816-5219 E-mail: rwatson2@chw.edu.

WATSON, ROBERT EDWARD, librarian, information specialist; b. Grand Rapids, Mich., June 16, 1951; s. Preston Keith and Leah Jane Watson; m. Judith Schmidt, July 10, 1976 (div. Dec. 1981); 1 child, Robert; m. Laurilyn Gay Kincaid, Aug. 2, 1986; children: Stuart, Alec. BA, Blackburn Coll., 1973; MLS, George Peabody Coll. Tchrs., 1975. Instnl. libr. DuPage Libr. Sys., Geneva, 1975-80; bookmobile libr. Aurora (Ill.) Pub. Libr., 1980; corp. rsch. libr. Masonite Corp., St. Charles, Ill., 1980-82; asst. dir. Franklin Park (Ill.) Pub. Libr. Dist., 1985-87, exec. dir., 1987—. Adj. prof. Coll. DuPage, Glen Ellyn, Ill., 1985-87; conf. prodr. ISP Channel, Mountain View, Calif., 1998-99; conf. host mgr. Electric Minds Virtual Cmty., Santa Barbara, 1998; conf. host, cons. Bright (London) Virtual Bus. Cmty., 1998-99; conf. host Brainstorms Virtual Cmty., 1998—, Chgo. Libr. Sys. Virtual Cmty., 2000—. Contbr. articles to profl. jours. Mem. Ill. Juvenile Mental Health LAN # 42, Franklin Park, Ill., 1995-99; pres. Cmty. Svcs. Coun. Leyden Twp., Franklin Park, 2000—. Mem. ALA, Pub. Libr. Assn., Franklin Park C. of C. (pres. 1988), Kiwanis (Franklin Park chpt.), Rotary. Avocations: reading, woodworking, remodeling, painting. Office: Franklin Park Pub Libr Dist 10311 Grand Ave Franklin Park IL 60131-2225 E-mail: bwatson@linc.lib.il.us.

WATSON, ROBERT FRANCIS, lawyer; b. Houston, Jan. 9, 1936; s. Louis Leon and Lora Elizabeth (Hodges) W.; m. Marietta Kiser, Nov. 24, 1961; children: Julia, Melissa, Rebecca. BA, Vanderbilt U., 1957; JD, U. Denver, 1959. Bar: Colo. 1959, U.S. Dist. Ct. (no. dist.) Tex. 1967, U.S. Supreme Ct. 1968, Tex. 1973, U.S. Ct. Appeals (5th cir.) 1973, U.S. Dist. Ct. (so. dist.) Tex. 1980, U.S. Ct. Appeals (11th cir.) 1981. Law clk. U.S. Dist. Ct. Colo., 1960-61; trial atty. SEC, Denver, 1961-67, asst. regional adminstr. Ft. Worth, 1967-72, regional adminstr., 1972-75; ptnr. Law, Snakard & Gambill, P.C., 1975-98, of counsel, 1998—; gen. counsel USPA&IRA (now First Command Fin. Svcs., Inc.), 1998—. Counsel City of Ft. Worth Police Investigation Commn., 1975; spl. counsel Office Atty. Gen. State Ariz., 1977-78. Contbr. articles to profl. jours. Mem. Ft. Worth Crime Commn., 1987-93. Honoree 27th Ann. Rocky Mountain State-Fed.-Provincial Securities Conf. Fellow: Coll. of State Bar Tex., U. Denver Law Sch. Alumni Coun., Tarrant County Bar Assn., Tex. Bar Found., Colo. Bar Assn. (life), Ft. Worth Club; mem.: ABA, Tex. Bus. Law Found. (bd.dirs. 1988—93), Fed. Bar Assn., State Bar Tex. (life), Shady Oak Country Club (Ft. Worth), Phi Delta Phi. Republican. Presbyterian. Office: First Command 4100 S Hulen St Fort Worth TX 76109 also: Law Snakard & Gambill PC 1600 W 7th St Ste 500 Fort Worth TX 76102-3819 E-mail: rfwatson@firstcommand.com.

WATSON, ROBERT JOE, hospital administrator, retired career officer; b. Wellington, Kans., Nov. 12, 1934; s. Charles Bruce and Marguerite B. (Scholes) W.; m. Ursula Eschenroeder, Dec. 26, 1983; children: Stephanie, Stacy Watson Bruce, Susannah Watson Gold; stepchildren: Jurgen Wanke, Claudia Beeck. MS in Edn., Kans. State Tchrs. Coll., 1963; MBA, U. Hawaii, 1969; MHA, George Washington U., 1973, EdD, 1976; student, Command-Gen. Staff Coll., 1973, U.S. Army War Coll., 1986. Commd. 2nd lt. U.S. Army, 1963, advanced through grades to col., 1989; stationed at Tripler Army Med. Ctr., Honolulu, 1967-69, USARV Surgeons Office, Long Binh, Vietnam, 1969-70, Surgeon Gen.'s Office, Washington, 1970-74, Walter Reed Med. Ctr., Washington, 1974-76, Acad. Health Svcs., Ft. Sam Houston, Tex., 1976-80, 87-89, 68th Med. Group, Ziegenberg, Germany, 1980-82, U.S. Army Hosp., Ft. Riley, Kans., 1982-84, 34th Gen. Hosp., Augsburg, Germany, 1984-87; ret., 1989; assoc. dir. Student Health Ctr. U. Fla., Gainesville, 1989—. Fellow Am. Coll. Healthcare Execs. (adv., regent 1982-84). Episcopalian. Avocations: tennis, golf, gardening. Office: U Fla Student Health Ctr Gainesville FL 32611

WATSON, ROBERT WINTHROP, poet; b. Passaic, N.J., Dec. 26, 1925; s. Winthrop and Laura Berdan (Trimble) W.; m. Elizabeth Ann Rean, Jan. 12, 1952; children: Winthrop, Caroline. BA, Williams Coll., 1946; postgrad., U. Zurich, 1947; MA, Johns Hopkins, 1950, PhD in English, 1955. Instr. English Williams Coll., 1946, 47-48, 52-53, Johns Hopkins, 1950-52; mem. faculty U. N.C., Greensboro, 1953—, prof. English, 1963-90. Vis. poet, prof. English Calif. State U., Northridge, 1968-69 Author: (poetry) A Paper Horse, 1962, Advantages of Dark, 1966, Christmas in Las Vegas, 1971, Selected Poems, 1974, Island of Bones, 1977, Night Blooming Cactus, 1980, The Pendulum: New and Selected Poems, 1995; (novels) Three Sides of the Mirror, 1966, Lily Lang, 1977, (art book) Betty Watson Paintings, 1999; co-founder The Greensboro Rev., 1966. Swiss-Am. exch. fellow, 1947; grantee Nat. Endowment for Arts, 1973; recipient Am. Scholar Poetry prize, 1959, Lit. award Am. Acad. Inst. Arts Letters, 1977. Home: 9 Fountain Manor Dr Apt D Greensboro NC 27405-8032

WATSON, ROBERTA CASPER, lawyer; b. Boise, Idaho, July 11, 1949; d. John Blaine and Joyce Lucile (Mercer) C.; m. Robert George Watson, July 22, 1972; 1 child, Rebecca Joyce. BA cum laude, U. Idaho, 1971; JD, Harvard U., 1974. Bar: Mass. 1974, U.S. Dist. Ct. Mass. 1975, U.S. Supreme Ct. 1979, U.S. Ct. Appeals (1st cir.) 1979, U.S. Tax Ct. 1979, Fla. 1985, U.S. Dist. Ct. (mid. dist.) Fla. 1985, U.S. Dist. Ct. (so. dist.) Fla. 1987. Assoc. Peabody & Brown, Boston, 1974-78, Mintz, Levin, Cohn, Ferris, Glovsky & Popeo, Boston, 1978-84; sr. dir. Wolper Ross & Co., Miami, 1983-85; assoc. Trenam, Kemker, Scharf, Barkin, Frye, O'Neill & Mullis, P.A., Tampa, Fla., 1985-87, ptnr., 1988—. Co-author: A Physician's Guide to Professional Corporations; co-editor-in-chief COBRA Adv. Newsletter, 1997-2000; contbr. articles to profl. jours. Pres. Performing Arts Ctr. Greater Framingham, Mass., 1983; bd. dirs., Northside Mental Health Ctr., 1987—, pres. 1999-2001; trustee Unitarian Universalist Found., Clearwater, Fla., 1986—; bd. dirs. dist. 6 Cmty. Health Purchasing Alliance, pers. com. chair, 1998-2000. Named Bd. Nem. of Yr., Fla. Cmty. Mental Health, 1994. Mem.: ABA (chair employee benefit com sect. taxation 1995—96, chair employee benefits interest group health law sect. 1998—2001), Fla. West Coast Employee Benefits Coun. (bd. dirs., treas. 1997—98, v.p 1998—2001, pres. 2001—02), Am. Coll. Employee Benefits Counsel (charter mem.), Tampa Club, Harvard Club (bd. dirs. West Coast Fla. chpt.), Order Ea. Star. Democrat. Avocations: music, metaphysics, Lincoln historian, genealogy. Home: 124 Adalia Ave Tampa FL 33606-3304 Office: Trenam Kemker et al 2700 Bank of Am Plz Tampa FL 33602 E-mail: rcwatson@trenam.com.

WATSON, ROYCE ANDREW, retired federal official; b. N.Y.C., Mar. 8, 1932; s. Robert Dealing and Kirsten Marie (Johansen) W.; m. Edith Christine Luik, Aug . 29, 1964; children: Paul Andrew, Gayle Ellen, Jeanne Marie. BS in Chemistry, U. Miami, Coral Gables, Fla., 1954, MS in Microbiology, BBA, 1967, MBA, 1968; PhD, Fla. State U., 1971. Lic. lab. dir., Fla.; cert. med. technologist; ordained deacon Luth. Ch., 1985. Dir. clin. anatomical and blood bank Dept. of Hosps., Miami, Fla., 1957-68; dir. health svcs. planning and state programs Gov.'s Office, Tallahassee, 1968-72; dir. health planning, project officer Nat. Ctr. Health Svcs. Rsch., Washington, 1972-78, br. chief, 1978-81; br. chief exptl. health delivery sys. HEW/HHS, 1981—82; chief advisor Office Asst. Sec. for Health and Surgeon Gen. HHS, 1982—87; pres. Watson & Assocs., Gaithersburg, 1987—. Instr.U. Miami Sch. Med. Tech., 1962—69; worldwide health cons.; U.S. del. Internat. Assn. Med. Lab. Tech., 1964—95, WHO, 1968—2001, Pan Am. Health Orgn., 1972—97; instr. pathology U. Miami Med. Sch., 1964—68. Author: Foundations in Relation to Their Partial Involvment in the Financing of the Health Field, 1971; co-author: Medical Education in Florida: Examination of the Issues, 1964, and others; contbr. articles to profl. jours. Deacon Good Shepherd Luth. Ch., Gaithersburg, 1985-2001; bd. dirs. Nat. Chamber Orch., Washington, 1986—. 1st lt. USMCR, 1952-58. Decorated Cross of Colors, Internat. Order Rainbow Girls, 1985, Royal Order of Scotland, 1995, Order of Purple Cross, 1998; recipient Outstanding Svc. award Asst. Sec. for Health/Surgeon Gen., 1982, Demolay Cross Honor, 1995, Demolay Legion of Honor, 1999, Red Cross of Constantine, 2001, Svc. award Soc. Dept. Def., 2001; inducted Hall of Fame Ft. Hamilton H.S. Fellow Royal Soc. Health; mem. Am. Soc. Med. Technologists (pres. Fla. divsn. 1970-72, numerous local, state, nat. and internat. leadership positions, Mem. of Yr. award 1972, 76), Md. Soc. Med. Technologists (pres. 1981, 86, nat. Mem. of Yr. award 1986), Am. Soc. Clin. Lab. Scis., Marine Corps League (life), Nat. Sojourners (pres. Bethesda chpt. 1991-92), Heroes of '76 (comdr. 1994), Legion of Honor (comdr. 1995-97), Montgomery County Agrl. Fair (life), Fla. End. Found. (life), Masons (active youth orgns., Top Nat. award Order De Molay and Rainbow Order for Girls, Md. Master Mason of Yr. 1984, p.m. 1984, right worshipful past master 1990, pres. Knight Masons of Md. 2000-01), Shriners (Almas, Divan 2000—), York Rite (past high priest 1994, past thrice illustrious master 1995, emminent comdr. 1998, knight of York cross of honor 1999, grand king 2001), Scottish Rite (Knight Comdr. Cross of Honor 2000), Am. Legion, VFW, Boys Scouts Am. (Lamb award 1983), Knights of Mecca (regional pres. N.E. Conf. 1998), Alpha Kappa Psi, Alpha Mu Tau. Republican. Lutheran. Avocations: scuba diving, gardening, skiing, philately. Home: 16728 Shea Ln Gaithersburg MD 20877-1230

WATSON, RUBIE, museum director; BS in archaeology and anthropology, U. Calif., Berkeley; MS in Anthropology, Rice U.; PhD in Social Anthropology, London Sch. Econs. Assoc. prof. anthropology, acting dir. Asian Studies program U. Pitts.; assoc. curator Peabody Mus. Archeology & Ethnology, sr. lectr. dept. anthropology Harvard U., Cambridge, Mass., 1992-95, assoc. dir., then Howells dir. Peabody Mus., 1995—. Author several books including Inequality Among Brothers: Class and Kinship in South China, 1985; editor: Memory, History, and Opposition under State Socialism, 1994; co-editor: Marriage and Inequality in Chinese Society, 1990, Harmony and Counterpoint: Ritual Music in Chinese Context, 1996. Office: Peabody Mus Archeology Harvard U 11 Divinity Ave Cambridge MA 02138-2019*

WATSON, S. MICHELE, school nurse; b. Selma, Ala., Apr. 21, 1965; d. Kenneth and Linda (Bishop) Wilds; m. H. Alan Watson, May 30, 1987. AAS, Cleveland State Community Coll, Tenn., 1987, AS, 1985. RN, Tenn. ICU staff Meml. Hosp., 1987-88; emergency rm. staff Cleveland (Tenn.) Cmty. Hosp., 1988; team leader Bradley Meml. Home Health, Cleveland, 1988-2001; sch. nurse Cleveland City Schs., 2001—. Home: 146 Hicks Rd NE Cleveland TN 37312-5853 : 3635 Georgetown Rd Cleveland TN 37312 E-mail: mwatson@clevelandschools.org.

WATSON, SHARON GITIN, psychologist, executive; b. N.Y.C., Oct. 21, 1943; d. Louis Leonard and Miriam (Myers) Gitin; m. Eric Watson, Oct. 31, 1969; 1 child, Carrie Dunbar BA cum laude, Cornell U., 1965; MA, U. Ill., 1968, PhD, 1971. Psychologist City N.Y. Prison Mental Health, Riker's Island, 1973-74, Youth Services Ctr., Los Angeles County Dept. Pub. Social Services, L.A., 1975-77, dir. clin. services, 1978, dir. Youth Services Ctr., 1978-80; exec. dir. Crittenton Ctr. for Young Women and Infants, 1980-89, Assn. Children's Svcs. Agys. of So. Calif., L.A., 1989-92, L.A. County Children's Planning Coun., 1992-99; cons. L.A. County Chief Adminstrv. Office, 2001—; mem. L.A. City Commn. for Children, Youth and Their Families, 2000—. L.A. County Children's Planning Coun., 2001—. Mem. L.A. delegation Pres.'s Summit for Am.'s Future, 1997. Mem. Commn. for Children's Svcs. Family Preservation and Family Support Policy Com., 1989—99, Interagy. Coun. Child Abuse and Neglect Policy Com., 1993—99, Mayor's Com. on Children, Youth and Families, 1993—95; bd. dirs. Adolescent Pregnancy Childwatch, 1985—89, L.A. Ednl. Partnership, 1999—, LISC Health Sector, 1996—99, L.A. Roundtable for Children, 1988—94; trustee L.A. Ednl. Alliance for Restructuring Now, 1992—99. Mem.: APA, Assn. Children's Svcs. Agys. So. Calif. (sec. 1981—83, pres. elect 1983—84, pres. 1984—85), Calif. Assn. Svcs. for Children (sec.-treas. 1983—84, pres. elect 1985—86, pres. 1986—87), U.S. Figure Skating Assn. (chmn. sanctions and eligibility 1993—96, membership com. 1996—99, bd. dirs., chmn. strategic planning com., regional vice chmn. competitions com., nat. competition judge), U.S. Olympics Com. (Jr. Olympics com. 1998—2000), Pasadena Figure Skating Club (pres. 1985—87, 1989—90), So. Calif. Inter-Club Assn. of Figure Skating Clubs (vice chair 1989—91, chair 1991—93). Home and Office: 4056 Camino Real Los Angeles CA 90065-3928 E-mail: sharonla12@aol.com.

WATSON, SOLOMON BROWN, IV, lawyer, business executive; b. Salem, N.J., Apr. 14, 1944; s. Solomon Brown and Denise Amelia W.; m. Bernadette Aldrich, Mar. 18, 1967 (div.); children: Katitti Madrid, Kira Pallis (twins); m. Brenda J. Wilson, Apr. 28, 1984. BA in English, Howard U., 1966; JD, Harvard U., 1971. Bar: Mass. 1972, N.Y. 1977. Assoc. Bingham, Dana & Gould, Boston, 1971-74; corp. sec., asst. gen. counsel N.Y. Times Co., N.Y.C., 1979-89, gen. counsel, 1989-90, v.p., gen. counsel, 1990-96, sr. v.p., gen. counsel, sec., 1996—. Active Vols. Legal Svc., Jobs for Youth Inc., until 1989; v.p. N.Y. Vietnam Vets. Leadership Program, Inc., until 1992, Agent Orange Assistance Fund, Vets. Adv. Bd. Lt. U.S. Army, 1966-68. Decorated Bronze Star with oak leaf cluster, Army Commendation medal with oak leaf cluster and V. Mem. ABA (com. on corp. law depts.), Nat. Bar Assn., Assn. Bar City N.Y., Mass. Bar Assn., Newspaper Assn. Am. (mem. legal affairs com.), N.Y. Stock Exch. Home: 341 W 87th St New York NY 10024-2635 Office: NY Times Co 229 W 43rd St New York NY 10036-3959

WATSON, STANLEY ELLIS, clergyman, small business owner; b. New Orleans, July 25, 1957; s. Joseph and Dorothy (Jones) W.. EdB, Jarvis Christian Coll., Hawkins, Tex., 1977; MRE, Tex. Christian U., Ft. Worth, 1979; spl. edn., So. U. A&M, Baton Rouge, 1986; grad., U.S. Acad. Pvt. Investigation, 1991; DD (hon.), Charter Ecumenical Ministries, 1994; pvt. investigation tng. cert., La. State U., 2000. Cert. tchr.; registered notary Mich.; lic. pvt. investigator, La. Asst. min. Jarvis Christian Coll., Hawkins, Tex., 1974-77; tchr. pub. sch., Daingerfield, 1977-78; asst. min. Park Manor Christian Ch., Chgo., 1980-81; asst. mgr. K Mart, Shreveport, La., 1981-82; min. United Christian Ch., Jackson, Miss., 1982-83; tchr. pub. sch., Napoleonville, La., 1986-87, Zachary, 1987-88; min. Vt. Christian Ch., Flint, Mich., 1988-90; sr. pastor, 1990—. Owner, mgr. Watson Diversified Fin. Co., 1989—, Watson Detective Agy., Donaldsonville, La., 1992—; v.p. DVY Sys., Inc., 1997—; CEO Watson and Julien Cmty. Mission, Inc., Donaldsonville, La.; clin. pastoral counseling, christian counseling, 2001.e Mem. NAACP, NEA. Recipient Presdl. citation Nat. Assn. for Equal Opportunity in Higher Edn.; Christian Women's fellow, 1975-77, St. Louis Bd. Edn. fellow, 1977-79, Tex. Christian U. Brite Div. Sch. scholar, 1977; Jarvis Christian Coll. cert. of Honor and Merit, 1974-77; named Rev. Stanley Watson Day City of Flint, Mich., 1989, Disting. Alumnus, Jarvis Christian Coll., 1995. Mem. Nat. Assn. Investigative Specialists, Am. Inst. Profl. Bookeepers, Am. Fin. Coord. Assn. (fin. coord.), Christian Counselors Assn., Nat. Assn Investigative Specialist, Nat. Assn. Federated Tax Preparers, Am. Soc. Notaries, Aircraft Owners and Pilots Assn. Coun. for Exceptional Children, Forgotten Man Ministries, Jarvis Christian Coll. Alumni Assn. (v.p.), NAACP, Urban League of Flint, Urban Coalition of Greater Flint, Flint C. of C., Internat. Reading Assn., NEA, Am. Sailing Assn., Phi Beta Sigma, Kappa Delta Pi. Democrat. Avocations: beekeeping, collecting coins, stamps, sports cards, coffees. Office: Watson's Detective Agy PO Box 668 Donaldsonville LA 70346-0668 also: Vt Christian Ch 1201 Lippincott Blvd Flint MI 48503-5849 E-mail: jarvis1977@iwon.com.

WATSON, STEWART CHARLES, construction company executive; b. Brock, Sask., Can., Sept. 17, 1922; s. Samuel Henry and Elva Jane (St. John) W.; m. Irene Lillian Ahrens, Aug. 4, 1943; children: Judith Gail (Mrs. David Stafford), Wendy Carolyn (Mrs. Rocco Amuso), Ronald James, Candyce Louise. Student, U. Buffalo. With Acme Steel & Malleable Iron Works, Buffalo, 1940-42, Acme Hwy. Products, Buffalo, 1946-69, internat. mktg. mgr., 1955-69; pres. Watson-Bowman Assocs. Inc., 1970—, Kinematics, 1984—. Chmn. bd. Air Stewart Inc.; Internat. lectr. on kinetics of civil engrng. structures; mem. U.S. Transp. Rsch. Bd.; bd. dirs. Internat. Bridge of Peace for Bering Strait Crossing. With AUS, 1943-45, ETO. Fellow Am. concrete Inst. (dir. 1984—, Delmar Bloehm award 1984, Charles S. Whitney medal 1987, hon. mem.); mem. ASTM, NAS, Internat. Jts. and Bearings Rsch. Coun. (chmn. 1988—), Internat. Activities Commn., Masons (32 degree), Shriners. Home: 3 Chicory Ln East Amherst NY 14051

WATSON, THOMAS ROGER, lawyer; b. Concord, N.H., May 14, 1951; s. Roger Edward and Mary (Hannigan) W. BA in Polit. Sci. cum laude, U. N.H., 1973; JD, Franklin Pierce Law Ctr., 1978. Bar: N.H. 1978, U.S. Dist. Ct. N.H. 1978, U.S. Ct. Appeals (1st cir.) 1978, Maine 1982, U.S. Dist. Ct. Maine 1982, U.S. Supreme Ct. 1986. Ptnr. Tybursky & Watson, Portsmouth, N.H., 1979-86, Tybursky, Watson & Harman, Portsmouth, 1987-88, Taylor, Keane, Blanchard, Lyons & Watson, P.A., Portsmouth, 1988-94, Watson, Lyons, & Bosen, P.A., Portsmouth, 1994-99, Watson & Bosen, P.A., Portsmouth, 2000—01, Watson, Bosen, Harman, Venci & Lemire, P.A., Portsmouth, 2001—. Del. N.H. Constl. Conv., Concord, 1974. Mem. Maritime Heritage Commn., 1986-95, City of Portsmouth Hist. Dist. Commn., 1992, City of Portsmouth Planning Bd., 1992-94; bd. dirs. N.H. Small Bus. Devel. Ctr., 1993-95, N.H. Main St. Ctr., 1998-2002, sec., 2001-02; mem. adv. bd. Ballet New England, 1997—; bd. advisors N.H. Small Bus. Devel. Ctr., 1992-95; bd. trustees Strawberry Banke Mus., 2000—, sec., 2001—. Named Portsmouth Citizen of Yr., 1995. Mem. ABA, ATLA (state del. 1996—, chair-elect 1997-98, chair 1998-99, exec. com. 1998-99, co-chair coordinating com. on state rels. 2000—, mem. pub. affairs com. 1999-, Outstanding State Del. 1997), N.H. Bar Assn. (bd. govs. 1985-90), N.H. Trial Lawyers Assn. (bd. govs. 1989—, sec. 1982-92, treas. 1993-94, pres. elect 1994-95, pres. 1995-96, chair legis. com. 1992-95, 96-2000, exec. com. 1992--, recipient Pres.'s award 1993, 97, Spl. Recognition award 2000), Rockingham County Bar Assn. (Profl. award 2001), Franklin Pierce Law Ctr. Alumni Assn. (pres. 1985-86), N.H. Bar Found. (bd. govs. 1987-90), Greater Portmouth C. of C. (bd. dirs. 1988-92, chmn. 1990-92), Portsmouth Hist. Soc. (trustee 1994—, pres. 1995-97), Portsmouth Atheneum (propr. 1991—). Office: Watson Bosen Harman Venci & Lemire PA PO Box 469 Portsmouth NH 03802-0469

WATSON, WILLIAM HUGHES, news service publisher, network executive; b. York, S.C., Nov. 21, 1950; s. Archie China and LaVerne (Hughes) W.; m. Virginia Thompson, Oct. 14, 1988. Student, U. S.C., 1970-76. Reporter Onion (S.C.) Daily Times, 1980-84; regional editor Soundings, Essex, Conn., 1984-85; mng. editor The Hour, Norwalk, 1985-87, Record Jour., Meriden, 1987-91; cons. editor The Hartford (Conn.) Courant, 1991-92; mng. editor Thomson Newspapers Inc., Stamford, Conn., 1992-93; publ., v.p. News USA, Inc., Falls Church, Va., 1994—; CEO, exec. prodr. Washington News Network, Washington, 2001—. Staff sgt. USAFR, 1970-76. Named Ky. Col. Gov. of Ky., 1981, Hon. Citizen Mayor of New Orleans, 1982. Mem.: AP, Soc. Profl. Journalists, Pub. Rels. Soc. Am., Radio-TV News Dirs. Assn., U. S.C. Alumni Assn., Am. Legion, Rotary, Nat. Press Club. Roman Catholic. Avocations: scuba diving, boating, sailing. Office: Washington News Network Inc 400 N Capitol St NW Ste G-50 Washington DC 20001

WATSON-BOONE, REBECCA A. library and information studies educator, researcher; b. Springfield, Ohio, Mar. 7, 1946; d. Roger S. and Elizabeth Boone; m. Dennis David Ash, 1967 (div. 1975); m. Frederick Kellogg, 1979 (div. 1988); m. Peter G. Watson, May 26, 1989. Student, Earlham Coll., 1964-67; BA, Case Western Res. U., 1968; MLS, U. N.C., 1971; PhD, U. Wis., 1995. Asst. reference libr. Princeton (N.J) U., 1970-76; head cen. reference dept. U. Ariz., Tucson, 1976-83, assoc. dean Coll. Arts and Scis., 1984-89. Loaned exec. Ariz. Bd. Regents, 1988-89; pres. Ctr. for Study of Info. Profls., 1995—2002. Author: Constancy and Change in the Worklife of Research University Librarians, 1998; contbr. articles to profl. jours. Mem. ALA (div. pres. 1985-86, councilor 1988-92), Assn. for Libr. and Info. Sci. Edn., NAFE. Mem. Soc. Of Friends. Office: 4721 W Parkview Dr Mequon WI 53092-2022 E-mail: prwb@execpc.com.

WATSULA, LINDA MARIE, social worker; b. Hartsville, S.C., Sept. 30, 1955; d. K.C. and Mary Jane (Sylvestre) Smith; children: Michael, Daniel, David. B in Social Work, Westchester U., 1977; MSW, Marywood Coll., 1978. ACSW, lic. social worker. Social worker Wiley House, Bethlehem, Pa., 1978-80; foster care worker Family and Children's Svc., Allentown, 1980-81; oncological social worker Lehigh Valley Hosp. Ctr., 1981-83; cons. Holy Family Manor, Bethlehem, Pa., 1984-85; adoption social worker Cath. Social Agy., Allentown, 1984-91; ERI trauma social worker St. Luke's Hosp., Bethlehem, Pa., 1991—. Supr. practicum Marywood Coll., Lehigh Valley Campus, Pa., 1984-85. Coord. NASW Explorer Post 520 Girl Scouts of U.S., Lehigh Valley, 1978-81. Mem. NASW (sec., treas. Lehigh Valley Div. 1980-86). Democrat. Roman Catholic. Home: 3455 Kipling Pl Bethlehem PA 18017-1511

WATT, DEAN DAY, retired biochemistry educator; b. McCammon, Idaho, Sept. 21, 1917; s. George William and Mary Amelia (Day) W.; m. Frances Elaine Murdock, Aug. 23, 1945; children: Sharon (Mrs. William E. Shull, Jr.), Nola Jean (Mrs. Thomas E. Barzee, Jr.), Barbara (Mrs. Robert Lauritzen), David, Stuart. Student, Idaho State U., 1936-37, 38-40; BS, U. Idaho, 1942; PhD, Iowa State U., 1949; postgrad., Case-Western Res. U., 1946-47. Research chemist Westvaco Chlorine Products, Newark, 1942-44; instr. Iowa State U., 1947-49; asst. prof. Purdue U., 1949-53; head dept. physiol. scis. Southeast La. Hosp., Mandeville, 1953-60; asso. prof. Tulane U., 1955-60, Ariz. State U., 1960-63; prin. biochemist Midwest Research Inst., Kansas City, Mo., 1963-69; prof. biochemistry Creighton U., 1969-88, prof. emeritus, 1988—. Fellow AAAS; mem. Internat. Soc. Toxinology (founding mem.), Sigma Xi Mem. Ch. of Jesus Christ of Latter-day Saints. Achievements include research on animal venoms, biochemistry mental diseases. Home: 618 S 130th St Omaha NE 68154-2910

WATT, DOUGLAS (BENJAMIN WATT), writer, critic; b. N.Y.C., Jan. 20, 1914; s. Benjamin Douglas and Agnes Rita (Neimann) W.; m. Ray Mantel, Nov. 5, 1937 (div.); children— Richard David, James Douglas; m. Ethel Madsen, Aug. 13, 1951; children— Patricia, Katherine. AB, Cornell U., 1934. Copy boy N.Y. News, 1936-37, radio columnist, 1937-40, drama reporter, 1940-71, sr. drama critic, 1971-87, critic-at-large, 1987-93; staff writer New Yorker mag., 1946-95; profl. song writer; columnist Small World, 1955-70. Pres. Hampton Animal Shelter, 1965-79. Served with USAAF, World War II. Mem. ASCAP, N.Y. Drama Critics Circle (pres. 1975-77) Clubs: Dutch Treat (N.Y.C.) (bd. govs.). Home: 27 W 86th St New York NY 10024-3615 *To say* *one has achieved success, except perhaps in isolated instances, is an exercise in vanity and contrary to man's experience. At best, some satisfaction can be gained in one's career, and then almost always because of intense effort.*

WATT, DWIGHT, JR. (ARTHUR DWIGHT WATT JR.), computer programming and microcomputer specialist; b. Washington, Jan. 25, 1955; s. Arthur Dwight and Myrtle Lorraine (Putnam) W.; m. Shari Elizabeth Gambrell, July 30, 1988. BA, Winthrop U., 1977, MBA, 1979; EdD, U. Ga., 1989. Cert. computer profl. and internet profl. Inst. Cert. Computer Profls., Microsoft computer profl., Microsoft Office User Specialist 97 Master; cert. Home Fire Arms Safety, NRA; A+ cert. personal computer technician, CompTIA, Microsoft cert. sys. engr.; i-net plus cert. Comptia; cert. Microsoft Office user specialist instr., Microsoft cert. sys. adminstr.; Network + cert.; Cisco cert. network adminstr. and acad. instr. Data processing instr. York Tech. Coll., Rock Hill, S.C., 1977-78; computer ctr. asst. Winthrop U., 1976-79; data processing instr. Brunswick (Ga.) Coll., 1979-80; system operator, asst. programmer Sea Island (Ga.) Co., The Cloister, 1981; pvt. practice data processing cons. Swainsboro, Ga., 1981—; computer programming/microcomputer specialist instr. Swainsboro Tech. Inst., 1981-96; sr. programmer/analyst Policy Mgmt. Sys. Corp., Columbia, S.C., 1996-97; microcomputer specialist instr. Athens Tech. Coll.-Elbert County Campus, Elberton, Ga., 1997-2001; chair IT dept. Heart of Ga. Tech. Coll., Dublin, 2001—; CIO Ga. Healthcare Sys., Atlanta, 2001. Cons., spkr. in field; chmn. exec. bd. computer curricula Ga. Dept. Tech. and Adult Edn., 1990-92, 2002-, mem. exec. bd. computer curricula, 1994-96, vice chair, 2000-02; chmn. East Ctrl. Ga. Consortium for Computer Occupations, 1990-93, 94-96; co-facilitator CIS curriculum rev. and update Ga. Tech. Colls., 2001. Author: District Revenue Potential and Teachers Salaries in Georgia, 1989, Structured COBOL for Technical Students, 1998; co-author: District Property Wealth and Teachers Salaries in Georgia, 1990, Factors Influencing Teachers Salaries: An Examination of Alternative Models, 1991, Local Wealth and Teachers Salaries in Pennsylvania, 1992, School District Wealth and Teachers' Salaries in South Carolina, 1993, Test Yourself A+ Certification Practice Exams, 1998. Chmn. Emanuel County chpt. ARC, Swainsboro, 1989-90, 92-93, bd. dirs., 1989-96; pres. United Meth. Men. Swainsboro, 1984-86; trustee Greater Swainsboro Tech. Inst. Found., Inc., 1995-96. Recipient Nat. Tech. Tchr. of Yr. finalist award Am. Tech. Edn. Assn., 1994; Olympic Cmty. Hero Torchbearer, 1996. Mem. Inst. Cert. Computing Profls., Ga. Bus. Edn. Assn. (dir. dist. 1 1986, 96, dist. sec.-treas. 1993-95, dist. 1 dir.-elect 1995-96, Dist. 1 Postsecondary Tchr. of Yr. 1985, state postsecondary tchr. of yr. 1995), Profl. Assn. Ga. Educators, Swainsboro Jaycees (Outstanding Young Citizen 1985, treas. 1984-89, pres. 1987-88, pres. S.E. Ga. Jaycee Fair 1995, treas. S.E. Ga. Jaycee Fair 1993-94), Ga. Jaycees (v.p. area C. mem. 1988-89, chaplain 1989-90, dir. region 6 1990-91, chmn. state shooting edn. 1991-92, chair Internat. BB Gun Match Championship 1999, co-chair match 2000, treas. match 2002), U.S. Jr. C. of C. (nat. rep. shooting edn. program 1992-95, Shooting Edn. State Program Mgr. of Yr. 1992), Kiwanis. Methodist. Home: PO Box 1637 206 Hereford Rd Swainsboro GA 30401 Office: 560 Pinehill Rd Dublin GA 31021-1253 Fax: 706-213-2149. E-mail: dwight-watt@att.net.

WATT, JOSEPH MICHAEL, state supreme court justice; b. Austin, Tex., Mar. 8, 1947; BA in History, Tex. Tech U., 1969; JD, U. Tex., 1972. Bar: Tex. 1972, Okla. 1974. Pvt. practice, Altus, Okla., 1972-85; judge Dist. Trial Ct., 1985-91; gen. counsel to gov. State of Okla., Oklahoma City, 1991-92; justice Okla Supreme Ct., Okahoma City, 1992—. Office: Okla State Supreme Ct State Capitol Rm 240 Oklahoma City OK 73105 Fax: 405-521-6982.

WATT, KENNETH EDMUND FERGUSON, zoology educator; b. Toronto, July 13, 1929; s. William Black Ferguson Watt and Irene Eleanor (Hubbard) Dodd; m. Genevieve Bernice Bendig, Oct. 28, 1955; children: Tanis Jocelyn, Tara Alexis. BA with honor, U. Toronto, 1951; PhD in Zoology, U. Chgo., 1954; LLD, Simon Fraser U., 1970. Biometrician Rsch. div. Dept. Lands and Forests, Ont., Canada, 1954-57; sr. biometrician Can. Dept. Agr., Ottawa, 1957-60; head, statis. rsch. and svcs. Canadian Dept. Forestry, 1960-63; from assoc. prof. to prof. Dept. Zoology, U. Calif., Davis, 1963-93. Author: Ecology and Resource Management, 1968, Principles of Environmental Sciences, 1973, Understanding the Environment, 1982, Taming the Future, 1991. Recipient Gold medal Entomol. Soc., 1969. Achievements include development of new approach to forecasting future based on exhaustive statistic testing of nonlinear math. equations to long runs of historical data; discovery that change through time in real world systems violates Markov principles. Home: 2916 Quail St Davis CA 95616-5711 Office: U Calif Dept Evolution & Ecology Davis CA 95616 *The actual causes of present events are much further back in time than most people suspect. Failure to understand this is why forecasting is such a disaster area.*

WATT, LYNN, academic administrator; Prof. elect. engring. U. Waterloo, 1966—90, prof. emeritus Canada, 1990—. Dean grad. studies U. Waterloo, 1969—70, 1972—83, 1987, acting dean rsch., 1988—89. Mem.: U. Waterloo Retirees Assn. (pres. 1997—2000). Office: Univ Waterloo 200 University Ave W Waterloo N2L 3G1 Canada*

WATT, MELVIN L. congressman, lawyer; b. Mecklenburg County, N.C., Aug. 26, 1945; m. Eulada Paysour; children: Brian, Jason. BS in Bus. Adminstrn., U. N.C., 1967; JD, Yale U., 1970. Atty. Ferguson, Stein, Watt, Wallis, Adkins, & Grensham, 1971-92; state senator N.C., 1985-86; co-owner East Towne Manor, 1989—; mem. U.S. Congress from 12th N.C. dist., Washington, 1993—; mem. fin. svcs. com.; mem. judiciary com., ranking mem. comml. and adminstrv. law subcom. Pres. Mecklenburg County Bar. Active Ctrl. Piedmont C.C. Found., Legal Aid of Southern Piedmont, N.C. NB Community Devel. Corp., Auditorium-Coliseum-Civic Ctr. Authority, United Way, Mint Mus., Family Housing Svcs., Pub. Edn. Forum, Dilworth Community Devel. Assn., Cities in Schs., Housing Authority Scholarship Bd., Morehead Scholarship Selection Com.; bd. visitors Johnson C. Smith Univ. Mem. NAACP (life), N.C. Assn. Black Lawyers, N.C. Acad. Trial Lawyers, Charlotte C. of C. (sports action coun.), West Charlotte Bus. Incubator, Inroads Inc., Phi Beta Kappa. Democrat. Presbyterian. Office: US Ho of Reps 1230 Longworth Ho Office Bldg Washington DC 20515-3312*

WATT, WILLIS MARTIN, academic administrator, communications, adult education, leadership educator; b. Ottawa, Kans., Dec. 20, 1950; s. Gerald Omri and Shirley Arlene (Tush) W.; m. Katherine Ann Young, Feb. 14, 1970; 1 child, Derek Lee. BS in Christian Edn., Manhattan Christian Coll., 1976; BS in Secondary Edn.-Speech/Drama, Kans. State U., 1976, MA in Speech/Drama, 1978, PhD in Curriculum/Instrn./Speech, 1980; postdoctoral, Flint Hills Leadership Program, 1999; continuing edn. unit tng., Franklin/Covey, 2000. Ordained to ministry Christian Ch., 1976; cert. leadership tng., 2002. Pastor Colony (Kans.) Christian Ch., 1969-71, Barnes (Kans.) Christian Ch., 1974-75, 1975-76; assoc. pastor Burlington (Kans.) Christian Ch., summers 1970-71; pastor Ogden (Kans.) Union Ch., 1979-80; elder, evangelist Hays (Kans.) Christian Ch., 1984-97; grad. tchg. asst. dept. speech, theatre and dance Kans. State U., Manhattan, 1976-78, instr., 1978-80; teaching intern speech/drama Manhattan (Kans.) Christian Coll., 1979; asst. prof. dept. speech comm. Iowa State U., Ames, 1980-84; dir. forensics dept. comm. Ft. Hays (Kans.) State U., 1984-91, chair, 1991-97; v.p. acad. affairs Manhattan (Kans.) Christian Coll., 1997-2000, dept. head adult edn., 1999-2000; pastor Clay Center (Kans.) Christian Ch., 1998-99. Interim min. South Hutchinson (Kans.) Christian Ch., 1999-2000; adj. assoc. prof. dept. speech comm., theater and dance Kans. State U., 1999-2000; dir. speech comm., assoc. prof. Meth. Coll., Fayetteville, N.C., 2000—; dir. Talking Tiger Rsch. Inst., Hays, 1985-91, Comm. Tng. Consulting Svcs., Fayetteville, N.C., 1986—; exec. dir. Chi Rho Players Religious Drama Troupe, Ames, Iowa, 1981-84; adjudicator Am. Coll. Theatre Festival, Region V, 1982-2000; mem. adv. coun. for acad. affairs Ctr. for Policy in Higher Edn.; artistic dir. Kyriou Drama Troupe, Manhattan, 1998-2000. Author: Fundamentals of Speech, 1988, Theory and Application for Effective Bus. and Profl. Presentations, 1994, Fundamentals of Oral Communication: Theory and Practice, 1995, Fundamentals of Oral Communication, 1997, Speech Communication: Theories & Practices, 2001; editor Kans. Speech Jour., 1994-2000; assoc. editor Nat. Forensic Jour., 1987-97; rev. editor The Forensic, 1989-95; mem. editl. adv. bd. Privacy on Campus. Edn. divsn. leader United Way of Ellis County, Hays, 1989, mem. allocations com. Riley County (Kans.) United Way, 1999-2002; Ft. Hays State U. chmn. leader, 1992; baseball coach Little League, Ames, Iowa and Hays, 1982-86; bd. dirs. Actors Cmty. Theatre, Ames, 1982-84; elder Fayetteville (N.C.) Christian Ch., 1999-2002. With U.S. Army, 1971-74. Recipient Bronze award Ellis County United Way, 1996, Outstanding Coll. Tchr. award Kans. Speech Comm. Assn., 1996, Editor's Choice award for poem Ode to Lost Love and Friends, Silver and Bronze awards for Poet of Merit Internat. Soc. Poets, 2002; inductee Mid-Am. Edn. Hall of Fame, J. Paul Jewell Ctr., Kansas City, 1998. Mem. Theta Alpha Phi (hon. drama), Pi Kappa Delta (gov. plains province 1986-88, 90-91, Exemplary Svc. award 1987, 91, Svc. award 1993, Order of Highest Distinction 1995), Pi Delta Kappa, Alpha Psi Omega. Avocations: racketball, chess, reading, writing, travel. Home: 5624 Watersplash Ln Fayetteville NC 28311-0221 Office: Meth Coll 5400 Ramsey St Fayetteville NC 28311-1420 E-mail: wmwatt@methodist.edu.

WATTEL, HAROLD LOUIS, economics educator; b. Bklyn., Sept. 30, 1921; s. David Max and Carolyn (Abrams) W.; m. Sara Gordon, Sept. 1, 1946; children: Karen, Jill. BA, Queens Coll., 1942, MA, Columbia U., 1947; PhD magna cum laude, New Sch. Social Research, 1954. Jr. economist WPB, 1942; economist Dept. Agr., 1946; econ. cons. Boni, Watkins & Mounteer, 1952; economist Bur. Bus. and Community Research, Hofstra U., 1954, 57, dir., 1957-58; prof. econs. Bur. Bus. and Community Rsch., Hofstra U., 1957-86, prof. emeritus, 1986—, chmn. dept. econs., 1957-61, chmn. div. bus., 1961—, dean Sch. Bus., 1965-73. Econ. cons. to consumer counsel Staff Gov. N.Y., 1956—58; cons. N.Y. State Moreland Commn. on Alcoholic Beverage Control Law, 1963—64, Legislative Refernce Bur. U. Hawaii, 1966, Schenley Industries , 1967—, Ralston Purina Co., 1967—, Am. Can Co., 1965—; econ. cons. Nat. Millinery Planning Bd., 1959—70; ednl. cons. U.S. Merchant Marine Acad., Kings Point, 1972; cons. Bulova Watch Co. , 1975—82. Author ann. publ.: The Millinery Industry; Editor: Planning in Higher Education, 1975, Chief Executive Officer Compensation, 1978, The Gross Personal Income Tax, 1981; Contbr. chpts. to books, encys., dictionaries, also reports.; Editor, contbr.: L.I. Bus, 1954-59. Mem. Comprehensive Health Planning Coun., 1970-75; bd. dirs., v. p., N.Y. State unit Am. Lung Assn.; pres. Nassau-Suffolk unit; bd. dirs. Comprehensive Health Planning Coun., Nassau-Suffolk, N.Y., N.Y. State Citizen Coun., Regional Med. Program Nassau-Suffolk, consumer rep., bd. dirs. Island Peer Rev. Orgn. , 1990; treas. Parodneck Found.; chair Pronet Citizens Advocacy Ctr., 1997—. Lt. USNR, 1942-46. Edn. fellow, 1949; Hazen Found. fellow, 1952; Ford Found. regional fellow, 1960 Mem. AAUP (chpt. pres. 1953), Middle Atlantic Assn. Colls. Bus. Adminstrn. (pres. 1970-71), Am., Met. econs. assns., N.Y. State Environ. Health Assn. (v.p.), Island Peer Rev. Orgn. (consumer/AARP rep. 1990—), Pi Gamma Mu, Omicron Chi Epsilon, Beta Gamma Sigma (hon. assoc.). Home: 181 Shepherd Ln Roslyn Heights NY 11577-2525 Office: Hofstra U Dept Econ Hempstead NY 11550 E-mail: phdhlw@juno.com.

WATTENBERG, ALBERT, physicist, educator; b. N.Y.C., Apr. 13, 1917; s. Louis and Bella (Wolff) W.; m. Alice von Neumann, May 23, 1992; children from a previous marriage: Beth, Jill, Nina Diane. BS, Coll. City N.Y., 1938; MA, Columbia, 1939; PhD, U. Chgo., 1947. Spectroscopist Schenley Distilleries, N.Y.C., 1939-42; physicist Manhattan Project, Metall. Lab., Chgo., 1942-46; group leader Argonne Nat. Lab., 1946-50; asst. prof. U. Ill., Urbana, 1950-51, prof. physics, 1958—. Research physicist Mass. Inst. Tech., 1951-58 Recipient award for 1st nuclear reactor Am. Nuclear Soc., 1962; Nuclear Pioneer award Soc. Nuclear Medicine, 1977; NSF fellow U. Rome, 1962-63 Achievements include pioneering controlled nuclear reactor.

WATTENMAKER, RICHARD JOEL, archive director, art scholar; b. Phila., Feb. 22, 1941; s. Nathan H. and Frances (Rynes) W.; m. Eva Augusta Oscarsson, June 25, 1968; children: Adrian Ezra, Barnaby Leo. BA, U. Pa., 1963; MA, NYU Inst. Fine Arts, 1965, PhD, 1972; student, The Barnes Found., 1959-66. Dir. Rutgers U. Art Gallery, New Brunswick, N.J., 1966-69; chief curator Art Gallery Ont., Toronto, Can., 1972-78; dir. Chrysler Mus., Norfolk, Va., 1979-80, Flint (Mich.) Inst. Arts, 1980-88, Archives of Am. Art, Smithsonian Instn., Washington, 1990—. Lectr. Barnes Found., 1991-92. Author: The Art of Charles Prendergast, 1968, The Art of Jean Hugo, 1973, Puvis de Chavannes and the Modern Tradition, 1975, Dr. Albert C. Barnes and The Barnes Foundation, 1993, Maurice Prendergast, 1994. Trustee Intermus. Conservation Lab., Oberlin, Ohio, 1982-88. Recipient Founders Day award NYU, 1972 Office: Smithsonian Instn Archives of Am Art Victor Bldg Ste 2200 MRC937 PO Box 37012 Washington DC 20013-7012 Fax: 202-275-1955.

WATTERS, ANNABEL, accountant, consultant; b. Texarkana, Tex., Aug. 12, 1944; d. John Robert and Elizabeth Anne (Oglesby) Greisser; m. Allen Ray Watters, June 11, 1965; children: Allen Ray Jr., William Thomas. AA, Texarkana Jr. Coll., 1964; BFA, Stephen F. Austin State U., 1975; MBA, Angelo State U., 1997. Acct. Citizens Comm., Dallas, 1997, Ctrl. & S.W. Energy, Dallas, 1998—. Precinct chmn. Taylor County Dems., Abilene, Tex., 1986-90; team Abilene, City of Abilene, 1988-95. Presbyterian. Avocations: book club, needlework, knitting, soccer.

WATTERS, CORA TULA, musician, educator; b. Portsmouth, Ohio; d. James Arthur and Nellie (Barber) W.; children: Gina Marie, Michael Earnest III, Lisa Michelle Iezzi, Patrice Annette England, Lora Diane Okwesa, James Vincent Yezzi (dec.). B in Gen. Studies cum laude, Ohio U., 1979; student, Miami U., Oxford, Ohio, LaSalle U., Rio Grande Grad. Sch., 1996. Mem. USMC Band, Quantico, Va., 1954—55; tchr. Musician Performer, 1950—; tchr. Spl. Edn. MRDD Sch., West Union, Ohio, 1983-88; dir. Shawnee Hills Sch. Fine and Performing Arts, 1983-88; tchr. Spl. Edn. West Union (Ohio) Elem. Sch., 1989-91; adjunct faculty music Southern State, Hillsboro, Ohio, 1989-92; tchr. Art West Union (Ohio) Jr. H.S., 1991-92; tchr. Music Seaman (Ohio) Elem. Sch., 1992-94; adj. faculty Am. Indian studies Antioch Coll., Yellow Springs, Ohio, 1993—; tchr. Acad. Tutor Ohio Valley Vocat. Sch., West Union, 1994-97; tchr. Ohio Valley Schs., 1999-2000; instr. vocal music North Adams H.S., Adams County, Ohio, 2000-01. Bldg. rep., state union rep., union rep., Ohio Valley Sch. Edn. Assn., 1992-96; owner Shawnee Hills Pub., 1996—; singer, dancer, profl. storyteller. Co-author: Brain Tanning-Indian Style, 1980; composer: Red, White and Blues, 1989, Watters and Daughter-At Last!, 1990, (CD) Red, White and Blues, 2000; music dir., screenwriter White Buffalo Media, Inc., 2000; author: Tales of 10 Moons, 1993, Jimmie's Place, 1996, Ohio Indians-Prehistoric to Present, 1997, Progressive Revelations of God, 1997, Progressive Revelation (Children's Workbook), 1997, Woodland Indians Children's Workbook, 1997, Digging Up Your Indian Roots, 1996, Meals from Tula's Lodge, 1997, Caproni's History and Cookbook, 1998; From the Rocking Chair, 1999; contbr. to Encyclopedia of Appalachia, 1999-2000; profl. storyteller of Appalachian & American Indian tales; performances include VA Creative Arts Festival, Constn. Hall, Washington (Gold medal vocal solo 2000, Nat. Silver medal jazz/blues solo 2000). Chair Humane Soc., Adams County, Ohio, 1980-83; bd. mem. Adams Brown Alcohol Coun., West Union, Ohio, Adams Co. Arts Coun., 1981-83; prin. chief Shawnee Nation-Ohio Blue Creek Band; minority rep., mem. exec. com. Adams County to Ohio Valley Regional Devel. Devel. Com. Cpl. USMC, 1952-55. With USMC, 1952—55. Named Outstanding Tchr. Spl. Edn. Consortium, 1987, 95, Ashland Oil Outstanding Tchr. Nominee, 1992, 95, One of 1000 Outstanding Women (Native Am.) in OYOHO, 1982, 83; recipient Holloway Human Rights award State Ohio Edn. Assn., 1993, Ohio State Commendation award for outstanding tchg., 1993, found. & chair 4 yrs. of OMEA- Music Comp. for those with spec. needs (Ohio); 5 Gold medals regional winner music/drama VA Creative Arts Competition, 2000, 1st pl., 2001, silver medal for poster art and wood sculpture, 2002; nat. gold medal for original vocal solo, silver medal for jazz solo; 1954 winner Ted Mack show N.Y.C., USMC Base, Quantico, Va.; Gold and Silver medals for vocal and jazz performance Vets. Adminstrn.. Mem. Am. Indian Inter-Tribal Alliance (leader), Ohio Shawnees Blue Creek Band (prin. chief), Am. Cancer Soc., So. Ohio Nat. Am. Substance Abuse, Native Am. Coun. of Ohio, Ohio Mental Health and Ohio Arts Coun., N.Am. Alliance Ohio, Families and Children First. Baha'i Faith. Avocations: family, religion, my tribe. Home: 696 Blacks Run Rd Lynx OH 45650-9702

WATTERS, EDWARD MCLAIN, III, lawyer; b. 1943; s. Edward McL. and Lucy F. (Disston) W.; m. Susan Secor, May 12, 1979; children: Jennifer Susan, Ann Elizabeth. BA cum laude, Yale U., 1965; JD cum laude, U. Pa., 1970. Bar: Pa. 1970. Ptnr. Pepper Hamilton LLP, Phila., 1977—. Lectr. programs on estate planning and will drafting Pa. Bar Inst. Bd. dirs. Children's Cruise and Playground Soc. Pa., Sanitarium Playgrounds of N.J., others. Lt. USNR, 1965-75; chair Decedents Estate Adv. Com. to Pa. Legislature's Joint Sate Govt. Commn. Fellow Am. Coll. Trust and Estate Counsel (com. state laws); mem. ABA, Phila. Bar Assn., Pa. Bar Assn. (past chmn. legis. com. probate sect.), Phila. Estate Planning Coun. (past pres.), Yale Club of Phila., Penn Club, Merion Golf Club. Office: Pepper Hamilton LLP 400 Berwyn Park 899 Cassatt Rd Berwyn PA 19312-1183 E-mail: watterse@pepperlaw.com.

WATTERS, RICHARD DONALD, lawyer; b. Midland, Mich., May 3, 1951; s. Donald Wayne and Madalyn Bird (Tinetti) W.; m. Ann Elizabeth Hutchison, May 24, 1975; children: Kelly E., Nathan Paul. BS in Indsl. Engring., Bradley U., 1973; JD cum laude, St. Louis U., 1976. Bar: Mo. 1976, U.S. Dist. Ct. (we. and ea. dists.) Mo. 1976, Ill. 1977, U.S. Ct. Appeals (8th cir.) 1981; cert. healthcare mediator. Assoc. Lashly & Baer, P.C., St. Louis, 1976-81, ptnr., 1981—, dept. chmn., 1989—. Instr. St. Louis U. Sch. Law, 1977-79. Chmn., pres. United Cerebral Palsy Assn. St. Louis, 1985-88; bd. dirs. Canterbury Enterprises, sheltered workshop, St. Louis, 1988-94, participant Leadershp St. Louis, 1988-89; ethics com. DePaul Health Ctr., 1990—. Mem. Am. Health Lawyers Assn., Mo. Soc. Hosp. Attys. (bd. dirs. 1988-94, pres. 1990-91), Mo. Bar Assn. (vice chmn. health and hosp. com. 1988-90), Bar Assn. Metro. St. Louis (co-chmn. med.-legal com.). Republican. Avocation: sailing. Office: Lashly & Baer PC 714 Locust St Saint Louis MO 63101-1699 E-mail: rdwatters@lashlybaer.com.

WATTERS, RICHARD JAMES, professional football player; b. Harrisburg, Pa., Apr. 7, 1969; Degree in design, U. Notre Dame. With San Francisco 49'ers, 1991-94; running back Phila. Eagles, 1995-98, Seattle Seahawks, 1998—2001; currently free agt. Selected to Pro Bowl, 1992-94. Achievements include member San Francisco 49'ers Super Bowl XXIX Champions, 1994, holds NFL postseason single game for most points (30), most touchdowns (5), Jan. 15, 1994 vs N.Y. Giants. Office: Seattle Seahawks 11220 NE 53d St Kirkland WA 98033*

WATTERS, THOMAS ROBERT, geologist, planetary scientist; b. West Chester, Pa., Feb. 1, 1955; s. Frank Edward Sr. and Beatrice Josephine (Speirs) W.; m. Nancy Rae Tracey, June 18, 1983; children: James T. Samantha E., Adam T. BS in Earth Scis., West Chester U., 1977; MA in Geology, Bryn Mawr Coll., 1979; PhD in Geology, George Washington U., 1985. Rsch. fellow Am. Mus. Natural History, 1978-80; rsch. asst. dept. terrestrial magnetism Carnegie Instn. Washington, 1980-81; rsch. geologist Ctr. for Earth and Planetary Studies Smithsonian Instn., Washington, 1981-89, chmn. Ctr. for Earth and Planetary Studies, 1989-98, sr. scientist Ctr. for Earth and Planetary Studies, 1998—. Lectr. in field. Author: Plants: A Smithsonian Guide; contbr. over 100 articles to profl. jours.; curator Earth Today, 1998—. Active Plum Point Elem. PTA, 1991-2000, mem. exec. bd. 1991-92; coach Calvert T-Ball, 1992-93; coach Babe Ruth League, 1994-96, 99-2000. William P. Phillips Meml. scholar; grantee NASA, 1985—; Exhibition award Smithsonian Inst., 1999. Mem.: AAAS, Nat. Youth Sports Coaches Assn., Am. Geophys. Union (rep. Am. Inst. Physics award for sci. writing aimed at children com. 1998—2001, Editor's citation 1998—2001), Geol. Soc. Am. (mem. editl. bd. Geology 1993—98), Kappa Delta Phi. Achievements include research in planetary and terrestrial tectonics and tectonophysics; morphological and structural comparisons of tectonic features on the terrestrial planets and analogous features on Earth. Office: Smithsonian Instn Nat Air & Space Museum Rm 3789 Ctr Earth & Planetary Studies Washington DC 20560 E-mail: twatters@nasm.si.edu.

WATTLETON, FAYE (ALYCE FAYE WATTLETON), educational association administrator; b. St. Louis, July 8, 1943; d. George and Ozie (Garrett) Wattleton; m. Franklin Gordon (div.); 1 child, Felicia. BS in Nursing, Ohio State U., 1964; MS in Maternal and Infant Health Care, Columbia U., 1967; LHD (hon.), St. Paul's Coll., 1985, Spelman Coll., 1986; LLD (hon.), Northeastern Univ. Law Sch., 1990; LHD (hon.), Long Island Univ., 1990, Univ. of Pa., 1990, Bard Coll., 1991; HHD (hon.), Oberlin Coll., 1991; LLD (hon.), Wesleyan Univ., 1991; LHD (hon.), Hofstra U., 1992, Haverford Coll., 1992; D in Pub. Svc. (hon.), Simmons Coll., 1993; LHD (hon.) , Meadville-Lombar Sem./U. Chicago. Tchr. Miami Valley Hosp. Sch. Nursing, Dayton, Ohio, 1964-66; asst. dir. Montgomery County Combined Pub. Health Dist., 1967-70; exec. dir. Planned Parenthood, 1970-78; pres. Planned Parenthood Fedn. Am., Inc., N.Y.C., 1978-92, Ctr. for Gender Equality, N.Y.C., 1995—. Bd. dirs. Estee Lauder. Author: How to Talk to Your Child About Sexuality, 1986, Life on the Line, 1996. Bd. dirs. Kaiser Family Found., Inst. for Internat. Edn., Quidel Corp., Empire Blue Cross Blue Shield, Bio-Tech. Gen. Recipient Am. Humanist award, 1986, John Gardner award, 1987, award of Excellence Am. Public Health Assn., 1989, Humanitarian award Congrl. Black Caucus Found., 1989, Claude Pepper Humanitarian award Internat. Platform Assn., 1990, Pioneer of Civil Rights and Human Rights award Nat. Conf. of Black Lawyers, 1990, Florina Lasker award N.Y. Civil Liberties Union Found., 1990, Whitney M. Young Jr. Service award Boy Scouts of Am., 1990, Ministry of Women award Unitarian Universalist Women's Fed., 1990, Spirit of Achievement award Albert Einstein Coll. of Med. Yeshiva Univ., 1991, 20th Anniversary Advocacy award Nat. Family Planning and Reproductive Health Assn., 1991, Women of Achievement award Women's Projects and Production, 1991, Margaret Sanger award, 1992, Jefferson Public Service award, 1992, Dean's Distinguished Service award Columbia Sch. of Public Health, 1992; named one of Best Mgrs. of Non-Profit Orgns. in Am., Bus. Week, Outstanding Mother Nat. Mother's Day Com., 1997; inducted to Nat. Women's Hall of Fame, 1993. Office: Ctr for Gender Equality 25 W 43d St Ste # 1014 New York NY 10036

WATTLEWORTH, ROBERTA ANN, physician, medical educator; b. Sioux City, Iowa, Dec. 26, 1955; d. Roland Joseph and Elizabeth Ann (Ahart) Eickholt; m. John Wade Wattleworth, Nov. 7, 1984; children: Adam, Ashley. BS, Morningside Coll., Sioux City, 1978; D of Osteopathy, Coll. Osteo. Medicine/Surgery, Des Moines, 1981; M.Healthcare Adminstrn., U. Osteo. Med. & Health Scis., Des Moines, 1999. Intern Richmond Heights (Ohio) Gen. Hosp., 1981-82, resident in anesthesiology, 1982-84; anesthesiologist Doctor's Gen. Hosp., Plantation, Fla., 1984-85; resident in family practice J.F. Kennedy Hosp., Stratford, N.J., 1985-87; educator family practice U. Osteo. Medicine and Health Scis., Des Moines, 1987-89; family practitioner McFarland Clinic, P.C., Jewell, Iowa, 1989-94; lectr. family practice Osteopath. Med. Ctr., Des Moines U., 1999—. Med. dir. nursing home Bethany Manor, Story City, Iowa, 1990-99, Jewell Vol. Fire and Rescue Squad, 1990-99. Bd. dirs. Heartland Sr. Svcs., 1995—99, Iowa Rural Health Assn. Named Nat. Outstanding Osteo. Educator of Yr., Nat. Student Osteo. Med. Assn., 2001—02. Fellow Am. Coll. of Osteo. Family Physicians; mem. Am. Osteo. Assn., Am. Med. Dirs. Assn. (sec.-treas. Iowa chpt. 1997-99), Am. Geriatric Assn., Am. Coll. Osteo. Family Physicians (pres. Iowa chpt. 1995-96), Iowa Osteo. Med. Assn. (trustee 1995-99, v.p. 1999—, pres.-elect, 2000-01, pres. 2001—). Lutheran. Avocations: gardening, cooking, painting. Office: 3200 Grand Ave Des Moines IA 50312-4104 E-mail: Roberta.Wattleworth@dmu.edu.

WATTS, ALICE L. nurse; b. Kremlin, Mt., Dec. 15, 1920; d. Joseph Martin and Lucia Marie (Meyr) Mangels; m. Everett Bowen Watts, Jan. 25, 1946; children: Javes Everett, Donald Elton, Sheila Ann, Sandra Elaine. LPN. Nurse/lpn Phillips Co Hosp., Malta, Mont., PCH-Home Health, Malta. Leader Brownie Scouts, Malta, 1963-64, 4-H club, 1966-68; deaconess Congregational Ch., 1989-99. Avocations: knitting, crocheting. Home: PO Box 924 Malta MT 59538-0924 Office: Phillips Co Hosp Health Malta MT 59538

WATTS, ANTHONY LEE, bank executive; b. Griffin, Ga., Jan. 24, 1947; s. Edgar Lee and Eula Mae (Benton) W.; m. Barbara Malinda Harp, Oct. 11, 1969; children: Natalie Paige, Barbara Leigh, Melanie Marie. AA, Gordon Mil. Coll., 1967; ABJ, U. Ga., 1969. Conventional loan rep. Fed. Nat. Mortgage Assn., Atlanta, from 1971, asst. regional appraiser, quality control and property mgr., to 1976; v.p., dir. ins. svcs. Ticor Mortgage Ins. Co., 1976-82; v.p., regional sales and exec. v.p. Ticor Indemnity Co., 1982-85; sr. v.p., regional mgr. Ticor Mortgage Ins. Co., Atlanta, 1984, sr. v.p., ea. divsn. mgr., 1984-85; pres. Mt. Vernon Fed. Savs. Bank, Dunwoody, Ga., 1985-95, Mt Vernon Fin. Corp., 1993-95, Banc Mortgage Fin. Corp., 1996-99, vice chmn., co-CEO, 1999—. Lectr. to trade assns. With U.S. Army, 1969-71.

Decorated Bronze Star; Paul Harris fellow, 1987. Mem. Ga. Mortgage Bankers Assn., Rotary (past pres. Dunwoody club). Office: 990 Hammond Dr NE Ste 1020 Atlanta GA 30328-5519 E-mail: twatts@bancmortgage.com.

WATTS, C. ALLEN, lawyer; b. Winter Haven, Fla., Oct. 7, 1946; s. Charles Meredith and Lois Jeanette (Thornhill) W.; m. Joyce Elaine McDeavitt DeLoach, Dec. 29, 1967 (div. Oct. 1980); m. Margaret Jean Morris, Sept. 28, 1982; children: Ashley, Kristin, Kelly, Mark, Evan, Caitlin. BA in Religion, Stetson U., 1967, JD magna cum laude, 1971. Bar: Fla. 1971, N.C. 1977, U.S. Ct. Appeals (5th and 11th cirs.) 1981, U.S. Ct. Appeals (4th cir.) 1982, U.S. Supreme Ct. 1979. Ptnr. Fogle & Watts, Deland, Fla., 1972-76; assoc. prof. law Campbell U., Buies Creek, N.C., 1976-78; ptnr. Watts & Biernacki, Deland, Fla., 1978-81; assoc. Watts & Karl, 1981-83; ptnr. Fishback Davis et al, Daytona Beach, 1983-86, Cobb Cole & Bell, Daytona Beach, 1986—. Bd. advisors Stetson U. Coll. of Arts & Scis., Deland, 1992—; bd. dirs. 1000 Friends of Fla., Tallahassee, 1993—, pres., 2001; vice chair Volusia County Bus. Devel. Corp., Daytona Beach, 1993-95, 98—; bd. counsel Volusia County Sch. Bd., Deland, 1990-97. Author: (with others) Florida Environmental & Land Use, 1996; editor-in-chief Stetson Law Rev., 1970-71; contbr. articles to profl. jours. Mem. Fla. Bar (appellate rules com. 1983-85, 94—), Deland Jaycees (pres. 1974-75, Outstanding Young Man award 1978), Fla. Jaycees (dist. pres. 1975-76), Rotary (Daytona Beach, Fla.), Lake Beresford Yacht Club. Democrat. Episcopalian. Avocations: gardening, travel. Office: Cobb Cole & Bell 150 Magnolia Ave Daytona Beach FL 32114-4346

WATTS, CLAUDIUS ELMER, III, retired air force officer; b. Bennettsville, S.C., Sept. 22, 1936; s. Claudius Elmer and Blanche Robey (Wannamaker) W.; m. Patricia Jane Sims, July 23, 1960; children: Claudius Elmer IV, Patricia Watts Heck. AB in Polit. Sci., The Citadel, 1958; postgrad. (Fulbright scholar), London Sch. Econs. and Polit. Sci., 1958-59; MBA, Stanford U., 1967. Commd. officer USAF, 1958, advanced through grades to lt. gen., 1986, comdr. 438th Mil. Airlift Group N.J., 1979-80, comdr. 63d Mil. Airlift Wing Norton AFB, Calif., 1980-82, asst. dep. chief staff plans Mil. Airlift Command Scott AFB, Ill., 1982-83, dep. chief staff plans Mil. Airlift Command, 1983-84; dir. budget Hdqrs. U.S. Air Force, Washington, 1984-85; sr. mil. asst. to dep. sec. def. U.S. Dept. Def., 1985-86; compt. USAF, 1986-89; pres. The Citadel, Charleston, S.C., 1989-96; ret. Former mem. adv. coun. grad. sch. bus. Stanford U.; former mem. bd. visitors Air U.; former mem. NCAA Coun., chmn. peer rev. teams for cert.; bd. dirs. First Cmty. Bank S.C.; bd. trustees Aerospace Edn. Found. Past trustee Palmetto Partnership; past. chmn. Marion Sq. Commn.; former bd. dirs., mem. fin. com. Air Force Aid Soc.; mem. bd. advisors Am. Leadership Found. Decorated Def. Disting. Svc. medal, USAF Disting. Svc. medal, Legion of Merit with oak leaf cluster, DFC with two oak leaf clusters, Air Medal with 10 oak leaf clusters, Gallantry Cross with Palm (Vietnam), Vietnamese Svc. medal with 2 svc. stars. Mem. Air Force Assn., Am. Soc. Mil. Comptrollers, Mil. Order World Wars, Air Force Sgts. Assn., Airlift Assn., VFW, Order of Daedalians, Am. Legion. Methodist. Avocations: golf; reading. Office: 229 Country Club Ln Charleston SC 29412-2208

WATTS, DAVID EIDE, lawyer; b. Fairfield, Iowa, June 13, 1921; BA, U. Iowa, 1941, JD, 1942; postgrad., Columbia Law Sch., 1946-47. Bar: Iowa 1942, Mass. 1950, N.Y. 1954. Instr. U. Iowa, Iowa City, 1947-48; asst. prof. U. Pa., 1948-49, Harvard Law Sch., 1949-52; ptnr. Dewey Ballantine, N.Y.C., 1958-90, of counsel, 1990—. Adj. assoc. prof. NYU, 1952-55; vis. lectr. Columbia U., 1954. Contbr. articles to legal jours. Mem. ABA, N.Y. State Bar Assn., Assn. Bar City N.Y., Am. Law Inst., Am. Coll. Tax Counsel, Am. Inst. Tax Policy. Home: 33 W 74th St New York NY 10023-2402 Office: Dewey Ballantine 1301 Avenue Of The Americas New York NY 10019-6022

WATTS, DENNIS LESTER, retired military officer; b. Rockford, Ill., Sept. 26, 1947; s. Lester George and Marjorie Doris (Kindell) W.; m. Betty Ann Homb, Oct. 9, 1970; 1 child, Kimberly. BS in Radiol. Tech., Midwestern State U., 1975; MS in Radiol., U. Colo., 1986; postgrad., Nova Southeastern U., 1996—. Lic. med. physicist, Tex. X-ray technician USAF, Wichita Falls, Tex., 1971-76, nuclear medicine technician, 1976-79; commd. capt. U.S. Army, San Antonio, 1979—. Med. physics chief Brooke Army Med. Ctr., Ft. Sam Houston, Tex.; radiation protection officer Reynolds Army Hosp., Ft. Sill, Okla.; med. physicist Berkshire Med. Ctr., Pittsfield, Mass., chmn. radiation safety com.; creator, course dir. Northeastern Conf. on Radiol. Scis.; mem. faculty Breast and Cervical Cancer Tng. Inst. Sch. Medicine Boston U.; adj. instr. Incarnate World Coll., San Antonio; mem. organizing com. World Congress on Med. Physics and Biomed. Engring, San Antonio. Author: (with others) Medical Physics, 1987; mem. editl. bd. Berkshire Med. Jour; rev. Med. Physics; contbr. articles to profl. jours. Mem. Am. Assn. Physicists in Medicine, Health Physics Soc. Mem. Am. Coll. Radiology, Am. Assn. Physicist in Medicine, Health Physics Soc. Avocations: scuba diving, tennis, photography, golf. Home: 8642 Fredericksburg Rd Apt 203 San Antonio TX 78240-1274 Office: Berkshire Med Ctr 725 North St Pittsfield MA 01201-4132 E-mail: dlwatts@vgernet.net.

WATTS, DONALD VERNEL, career officer, art educator; b. Chgo., Nov. 20, 1961; s. Lotha Alva and Mattie Pearl (Boyette) W.; m. Cristina Concepcion Feria, June 15, 1984; children: Nicole, Samantha. BS, Trinity Coll. and U., 2000. Commd. USN, 1981; advanced through grades to chief petty officer; signalman supr. USS Towers DDG 9 Yokosuka, Japan, 1981-84; signalbridge supr. USS Knox FF 1052, 1984-86; tng. leading petty officer Navy Res. Ctr. Dayton, Ohio, 1986-90; signalman leading petty officer USS Cochrane DDG 21 Yokosuka, 1990; navigation divsn. officer USS Hewitt DD 966, 1990-95; leading petty officer, 1995-98; asst. dir. personal property office, 1997; leading chief petty officer N3 divsn. comnavforjapan, 1998—2001. Vol. Girl Scouts U.S.A., Yokosuka, chmn., 1999-2000. Named Vol. of Yr. Girl Scouts U.S.A., 2000. Baptist. Avocations: art, scouting, volunteering. E-mail: don_watts@hotmail.com.

WATTS, EMILY STIPES, English language educator; b. Urbana, Ill., Mar. 16, 1936; d. Royal Arthur and Virginia Louise (Schenck) Stipes; m. Robert Allan Watts, Aug. 30, 1958; children: Benjamin, Edward, Thomas. Student, Smith Coll., 1954-56; AB, U. Ill., 1958, MA (Woodrow Wilson Nat. fellow), 1959, PhD, 1963. Instr. English U. Ill., Urbana, 1963-67, asst. prof., 1967-73, assoc. prof., 1973-77, prof., dir. grad. studies dept. English, 1977—; bd. dirs. U. Ill. Athletic Assn., chmn., 1981-83; mem. faculty adv. com. Ill. Bd. Higher Edn., 1984—, vice chmn., 1986-87, chmn., 1987-88. Author: Ernest Hemingway and The Arts, 1971, The Poetry of American Women from 1632 to 1945, 1977, The Businessman in American Literature, 1982; contbg. editor: English Women Writers from the Middle Ages to the Present, 1990; contbr. articles on Jonathan Edwards, Anne Bradstreet to lit. jours. John Simon Guggenheim Meml. Found. fellow, 1973-74 Mem. AAUP, Midwest MLA, Am. Inst. Archaeology, Assn. Lit. Scholars Critics, Authors Guild, Ill. Hist. Soc., The Phila. Soc., Phi Beta Kappa, Phi Kappa Phi. Presbyterian. Home: 1009 W University Ave Champaign IL 61821-3317 Office: U Ill 208 English Bldg 608 S Wright St Urbana IL 61801

WATTS, GINNY (VIRGINIA C. WATTS), artist; b. Chester, Pa., Jan. 24, 1931; d. Edwin Swoope Craig and Ruth Irene Tonge; m. Lynch S. Watts, Jr., July 21, 1951 (wid.); children: L. Kenneth, Karen Elizabeth Watts Kline, Monica Faye Watts Maladruccolo, Dawn Ellen Watts Eller; m. Alfred E. Meeds, May 5, 1948 (div. Nov. 1950); children: Brenda Joyce Meeds Parker, Edwin Lewis, Michael Alfred. Student, Del. Tech. and C.C., Georgetown, 1998-99. County coord. Easter Seals, Wilmington, Del., 1985-86; resident advisor Dept. Mental Retardation Kencrest Svcs., Dover, 1986-87, program mgr., 1987-90; artist Delware, 1942—; fine arts instr. Del. Tech. and C.C. , Georgetown, 1998—, 2002—. Instr. workshops, Millsboro Art League, Del., 1998-99. One person shows include Millsboro Art Gallery, 2000; exhibited in group shows at Del. Art Ctr., 1942—, Del. Tech. and C.C., 1997-99, 2000, 01, Millsboro Art League and Gallery, Del., 1997-99, 2001, Fine Arts Event, Rehoboth Beach, Del., 2000, Geyers Art Gallery, Milford, Del., 2000, 01, 2002, others; artist oil, graphite and watercolor paintings, 1942—; group mural: wall of Art Gallery/Del. Tech. C.C., 1998; mural for lobby of Presentations, 2000; contbr. articles to area newspapers. Vice-pres. Adult Art League, Del. Tech. C.C., 1997—; bd. dirs. Millsboro Art League, 1998—, pres., 2001—; mem. Sussex County Arts Coun., 1997—, Nat. Mus. Women in the Arts; bd. advisors Del. Tech. adult plus program Del. Tech. and C.C.; pres. Adult PLUS Art League, 1998—; pres. Millsboro Art League, 2001-. Recipient Excellence of Artistic Achievement award DAPA and Del. Tech. C.C. Avocations: fitness swimming, hiking, biking, camping, gardening. Home: 14106 Blanchard Rd Greenwood DE 19950-9458

WATTS, GLENN ELLIS, union official; b. Stony Point, N.C., June 4, 1920; s. George Dewey and Nellie Viola (Ellis) W.; m. Bernice Elizabeth Willett, Nov. 8, 1941; children: Glenn Ellis II (dec.), Sharon Elizabeth Ann Perlmutter, Marianne Elizabeth Watts Erickson. With Chesapeake & Potomac Telephone Co., Washington, 1941-48, Communications Workers Am., Washington, 1942-85, pres. div. 36, 1948-51, dir. dist. 2, 1951-56, asst. to pres., 1956-65, v.p., 1965-69, sec.-treas. union, 1969-74, pres., 1974-85, pres. emeritus, 1985—. V.p. exec. council AFL-CIO, 1974-85, v.p. emeritus, 1985—; v.p. indsl. union dept., 1968-85, mem. exec. bd. maritime trades dept., 1974-85; mem. Nat. Labor Com. for U.S. Savs. Bonds, 1975; nat. adv. bd. Labor Council for Latin Am. Advancement, 1975-85; mem. labor policy adv. com. for trade negotiations Dept. Labor, 1975-79; mem. industry-labor council White House Conf. on Handicapped Individuals, 1976; chmn. labor subcom. Pres.'s Com. on Employment of Handicapped, 1977; mem. sec.'s adv. council Dept. Commerce, 1976-77; mem. Pres.'s Commn. on Mental Health, 1977-78. Mem. Pres.'s Commn. on the Holocaust, 1978-79; mem. U.S. Holocaust Meml. Coun., 1979-93; past mem. D.C. Appeals and Rev. Bd., D.C. Wage and Hour Rev. Panel, Home Rule for D.C. Com.; mem. nat. advisory com. Nat. Congress Community Econ. Devel., 1974; past chmn. community chest relations com. Nat. Capital Area council Boy Scouts Am., past chmn. James E. West Dist., 1969-71; pres. Health and Welfare Council of Nat. Capital Area, 1967-69; mem. Inter-Am. adv. com. Postal Tel. and Tel. Internat., 1968-74, mem. exec. com., 1977-85, v.p., 1978-81, pres., 1981-85; gen. chmn. United Giver's Fund, 1968, pres., 1971-75; sec. United Way of Am., 1971-76; bd. dirs., treas. United Way Internat., 1974-78; mem.-at-large Dem. Nat. Com., 1974-85, mem. incomes policy study group of domestic affairs task group, 1974-76; trustee, sec.-treas. Am. Inst. Free Labor Devel., 1974-85; mem. U.S. Assn. for Club of Rome, 1978-80; trustee AFL-CIO Human Resources Devel. Inst., 1974-85, George Meany Ctr. for Labor Studies, 1976-85; trustee Ford Found., 1976-88; trustee Aspen Inst. for Humanistic Studies, 1974-89, trustee emeritus, 1989—; trustee Nat. Planning Assn., 1974-80; governing bd. Common Cause, 1974-77; sec.-treas. Ctr. for Mgmt. Services, 1974; hon. vice chmn. Am. Trade Union Council for Histadrut, 1974; mem. nat. adv. council Ariz. Heart Inst., 1974-80; bd. dirs. Am. Arbitration Assn., 1975-79, Am. Productivity Ctr., 1978-82, New Directions, 1977-80, Alliance to Save Energy, 1977-80; mem. nat. com. on coping with interdependence Aspen Program of Humanistic Studies, 1975-77; bd. dirs. Council on Fgn. Rels., 1987-90, Initiative Com. for Nat. Econ. Planning, 1975-76, Overseas Devel. Council, 1987-91; trustee, mem. exec. com. Joint Council Econ. Edn., 1976-79, Collective Bargaining Forum, 1983-92, co-chmn. 1983-87, adv. bd. Collective Bargaining Inst. George Washington U., 1987-92; mem. Commn. on a Nat. Inst. Justice, 1976-79, Trilateral Commn., 1977—, Helsinki Watch, 1978-90, commn. Future U.S.-Mex. Relations, 1987-89, exec. com. Am. Agenda, 1988. Recipient Urban Trade Unionist award Nat. Urban Coalition, 1978, Silver Beaver award, 1965 Unitarian Universalist.

WATTS, HAROLD WESLEY, economist, educator; b. Salem, Oreg., Sept. 30, 1932; s. Elton and Claire W.; m. Doris A. Roth, Sept. 28, 1951 (div. 1973); children— Michael Lee, Suzanne, Jane Marie, Kristin BA, U. Oreg., 1954; MA, Yale U., 1956, PhD, 1957. From instr. to assoc. prof. Yale U., New Haven, 1957-63; from assoc. prof. to prof. econs. U. Wis., Madison, 1963-76, dir. Inst. Research on Poverty, 1966-71; prof. econs. and pub. policy Columbia U., N.Y.C., 1976-98, prof. econs. and pub. policy emeritus, 1998—, dir. Pub. Policy Rsch. Ctr., 1988-93; sr. fellow Mathematica Policy Research Princeton, N.J., 1979-92; sr. rsch. assoc. Urban Inst., 1994-95. Recipient Paul Lazarsfeld award, 1980; Guggenheim fellow, 1975 Fellow Assn. Pub. Policy Analysis and Mgmt., Econometric Soc.; mem. Am. Econ. Assn., Am. Statis. Assn. Democrat. Home: 144 Bay Ave Greenport NY 11944-1404 Office: Ternhaven Cellars PO Box 758 Greenport NY 11944 E-mail: harold@ternhaven.com.

WATTS, HELEN CASWELL, civil engineer; b. Brunswick, Maine, July 28, 1958; d. Forrest and Frances Caswell; m. Austin Watts. BS in Civil Engring., U. N.H., 1980; cert. 5th yr. pulp and paper, U. Maine, 1983. Registered profl. engr., Maine. Constrn. engr., 1980-82, Oklahoma Dept. Transp., Okla. City, 1983-84; design engr. Structural Design Cons., Inc., Portland, Maine, 1985; facility engr. Bath (Maine) Iron Works, 1986-96; cons. engr. Watts Engring., Bowdoin, Maine, 1996, Helen Watts Engring., Bowdoin, 1997, NEWG, Brunswick, Maine, 1998—2000; structural engr. Criterium-Mooney Engrs., Portland, 2000—. Judge New Eng. Regional ASCE Concrete Canoe Race, 1994. Mem. ASCE (assoc.), Tech. Assn. Pulp and Paper Industry (assoc.), Soc. Women Engrs. (assoc.). Achievements include adapting 4500 page paper machine training manual to an electronic document, permits and construction of 300 ton transporter roadway across wetlands and mitigation site; planning and construction of a four story medical building and permits for dredge material landspreading. Office: Criterium Mooney Engineers 22 Monument Square Ste 300 Portland ME 04101

WATTS, HELENA ROSELLE, military analyst; b. East Lynne, Mo., May 29, 1921; d. Elmer Wayne and Nellie Irene (Barrington) Long; m. Henry Millard Watts, June 14, 1940; children: Helena Roselle Watts Scott, Patricia Marie Watts Foble. BA, Johns Hopkins U., 1952, postgrad., 1952-53. Assoc. engr. Westinghouse Corp., Balt., 1965-67; sr. analyst Merck, Sharp & Dohme, Westpoint, Pa., 1967-69; sr. engr. Bendix Radio divsn. Bendix Corp., Balt., 1970-72; sr. scientist Sci. Applications Internat. Corp., McLean, Va., 1975-84; mem. tech. staff The MITRE Corp., 1985-94; ret., 1994. Adj. prof. Def. Intelligence Coll., Washington, 1984-85. Contbr. articles to profl. jours. Mem. IEEE, AAAS, AIAA, Nat. Mil. Intelligence Assn., U.S. Naval Inst., Navy League U.S., Air Force Assn., Assn. Former Intelligence Officers, Assn. Old Crows, Mensa, N.Y. Acad. Sci. Republican. Roman Catholic. Avocations: photography, reading. Home: 6541 Franconia Rd # 108 Springfield VA 22150

WATTS, ILONA, geriatrics nurse; b. Bad Wildungen, Germany, Apr. 21, 1946; d. Anton Hermann and Maria (Molnar) Vargas; children: Kenneth A. White, Michelle I. Stewart. LPN, Lake of the Woods Hosp., Kenora, Ont., Can., 1973; cert. in nursing, Can. Career Centre, Surrey, B.C., Can., 1977; RN, Douglas Coll., New Westminster, B.C., Can., 1985. With shipping and billing dept. Perth's Laundry & Cleaners, Kenora; lab. asst., data entry operator pathology dept. Vancouver (B.C., Can.) Gen. Hosp., nurse; charge nurse Dallas Rehab. Inst.; staff RN, student preceptor Parkland Meml. Hosp.; staff PRN Trinity Med. Ctr. Mem. Registered Nurses Assn. of B.C. Home: 758 Meadowlark Dr Lewisville TX 75067-5850

WATTS, J. C., JR. congressman, retired football player; b. Eufaula, Okla., Nov. 8, 1957; m. Frankie Watts; 5 children. BA in Journalism, U. Okla., 1981. Profl. football player Ottawa and Toronto Teams Can. Football League, 1981-86; youth min. Sunnylane So. Bapt. Ch., Del City, 1987-94; mem. Okla. Corp. Commn., 1990—95, chmn., 1992—95; mem. U.S. Congress from 4th Okla. dist., 1995—; mem. armed svcs. com.; mem. special oversight panel on terrorism. Mem. Nat. Drinking Water Adv. Coun.; mem. electricity com. Nat. Assn. Regulatory Utility Commrs; hon. co-chmn. Rep. Nat. Conv., 2000. Bd. of rep. Fellowship of Christian Athletes, Okla. Republican. Office: US House Reps 1007 Longworth 40 B Washington DC 20515-3604*

WATTS, JERI HANEL, elementary education educator, writer; b. Lynchburg, Va., June 6, 1957; d. Robert Crowe Jr. and Dorothy Elizabeth (Bryant) Hanel; m. Charles Leo Watts, Jr., Apr. 16, 1982; children: Mary Carson Watts, Ellen Chandler Watts. BA, Coll. William & Mary, 1979; MEd, U. Va., 1991. Cert. elem. tchr., Va. Asst. dir., playground dir. recreation playground prog. Va. Beach (Va.) Recreation Dept., 1978; phys. edn. tchr. Lexington (Va.) City Schs., 1979-91, title I reading tchr., coord., 1991—. Mem. Dabney Lancaster Tchr. Adv. Bd., Clifton Forge, Va., 1997. Author: (picture book) Keepers, 1997. Avocation: reading.

WATTS, JOHN RANSFORD, university administrator; b. Boston, Feb. 9, 1930; s. Henry Fowler Ransford and Mary Marion (Macdonald) Watts; m. Joyce Lannom, Dec. 20, 1975; 1 child David Allister. AB, Boston Coll., 1950, MEd, 1965; MFA, Yale U., 1953; PhD, Union Grad. Sch., 1978. Prof., ast. dean Boston U., 1958-74; prof., dean fine arts Calif. State U., Long Beach, 1974-79; dean and artistic dir. The Theatre Sch./Goodman Sch. Drama, DePaul U., Chgo., 1979-99, prof. and dean emeritus, 1999—. Mng. dir. DePaul U. Merle Reskin Theatre, 1988-99; gen. mgr. Boston Arts Festivals, 1955-64; adminstr. Arts Programs at Tanglewood, 1966-69; producing dir. Theatre Co. of Boston, 1973-75. Chmn. Mass. Coun. on Arts and Humanities, 1968-72; bd. dirs., v.p. Long Beach Pub. Cofp. for the Arts, 1975-79; mem. theatre panel Ill. Arts Coun., 1981-90. With U.S. Army, 1953-55. Recipient Lifetime Achievement award Joseph Jefferson Com., Chgo., 2000. Mem. Mass. Ednl. Comms. Commn., Am. Theatre Asasn., Nat. Coun. on Arts in Edn., Met. Cultural Alliance, U.S. Inst. Theatre Tech., League Chgo. Theatres, Chgo. Internat. Theatre Festival, St. Botolph Club (Boston), Univ. Club (Chgo.), Phi Beta Kappa, Phi Kappa Phi.

WATTS, JUDITH-ANN WHITE, secondary school educator; b. Moline, Ill., Nov. 11, 1955; d. Harry Cameron and Jennie Elizabeth (Brockevelt) White; 1 child, Cameron Paul. BSEd, Ill. State U., 1976; MSEd, Western Ill. U., 1987; postgrad., George Mason U., 1992-96, U. So. Calif., 1996-97. English tchr. United Twp. High Sch., East Moline, Ill., 1976-77, English tchr., curriculum designer/asst. theatre dir., 1978-84; county coord. Simon for Senate Campaign, Rock Island, 1984; legis. asst. U.S. Sen. Paul Simon, Washington, 1985-89; program devel. specialist NEA, 1989-90; dir. constituent rels. Nat. Coun. Accreditation Tchr. Edn., 1990-92; exec. assoc. policy devel. Nat. Bd. Profl. Teaching Standards, 1992-93; spl. asst. to pres. Va. State U., Petersburg, 1993-96; exec. asst. ofc. of the dean U. So. Calif. Sch. of Edn., L.A., 1996-97; tchr. English, theatre, speech, choral music Hillview H.S., Tustin, Calif., 1998—. V.p. bd. dirs. Rappahannock Mediation Ctr., Fredericksburg, Va., mediator, 1989-96, trainer, 1991-96. Mem. Fredericksburg Singers, 1990-96, Fredericksburg Community Chorus, 1990-96; precinct capt. Spotsylvania County (Va.) Dem. Com., 1989-96; campaign worker various polit. campaigns, Va., Ill., Calif., 1972—; exec. com. of vestry St. George's Ch., Fredericksburg, mem. ch. choir, 1990-96; family program coord. St. Paul's Episcopal Ch., Tustin, Calif., 1998-2000. Mem. NEA, ASCD, Am. Ednl. Rsch. Assn., Am. Assn. Sch. Adminstrs., Nat. Assn. Sec. Sch. Prins., Ill. Edn. Assn. (regional vice chair 1982-84, regional pub. rels. chair 1982-84), Va. Edn. Assn., Va. Meditation Network, Calif. Tchrs. Assn. Episcopalian. Avocations: sewing, singing, crafts, community theater, exercise/fitness. Home: 1131 Triumphal Way Santa Ana CA 92705-2925 E-mail: garyjudy_watts@msn.com., jwatts@hillview.tustin.k12.ca.us., judywatts55@hotmail.com.

WATTS, KEVIN, IS supervisor; b. Houston, Nov. 30, 1965; s. Charles Watts, Barbara Goss. Mailroom, courier Med. Billing Svcs., Inc., Houston, 1992—94, IS supr., 1994—. Mem. HAL-PC, Houston, 1999—, Brainbench-.com. Musician: (musical composition) One Lonely Night, 1991, Crossfire, 1991. Office: Med Billing Svcs Inc 10700 Richmond Houston TX 77042

WATTS, MALCOLM S(TUART) M(CNEAL), physician, medical educator; b. N.Y.C., Apr. 30, 1915; s. Malcolm S.M. and Elizabeth (Forbes) W.; m. Genevieve Moffitt, July 12, 1947; children: Pauline, Elizabeth, Malcolm, James. AB, Harvard U., 1937; MD, 1941. Diplomate: Pan Am. Med. Assn. Group practice internal medicine, San Francisco, 1948-76; clin. prof. medicine U. Calif. Sch. Medicine, 1972-89, assoc. dean, 1966-89, clin. prof. medicine emeritus, 1989—, dir. Extended Programs in Med. Edn., 1973-82; dir. Calif. Statewide Area Health Edn. System, 1979-89. Chmn. bd. trustees San Francisco Consortium, 1968-74, trustee, 1974-80, exec. dir., 1981-94; dir. Soc. Med. Coll. Dirs. Continuing Med. Edn., 1975-82, pres., 1980-81; trustee Hospice of San Francisco, v.p., 1979-85; pres. Alliance Continuing Med. Edn., 1979-81. Editor Western Jour. Medicine, 1968-90, Jour. Continuing Edn. in the Health Professions, 1988-91. Served to capt. M.C. AUS, 1942-46. Recipient Outstanding Community Funds and Councils Am., 1964, U. Calif. San Francisco medal, 1983, Disting. Svc. award Alliance for Continuing Med. Edn., 1990, Disting. Svc. award soc. Med. Coll. Dirs. of Continuing Med. Edn., 1991. Master ACP; fellow Am. Coll. Hosp. Adminstrs. (hon.); mem. AMA, AAAS, Calif. Acad. Scis., Calif. Acad. Medicine, Am. Med. Writers Assn. (John T. McGovern award 1986), San Francisco Med. Soc. (pres. 1961), Am. Soc. Internal Medicine (pres. 1964-65), Calif. Med. Assn. (bd. dirs. 1962-90), Nat. Inst. Medicine, Soc. Med. Friends Wine, Acad. Mexicana Ciencias Mexicano de Cultura (corr.). Home: 1661 Pine St Apt 1146 San Francisco CA 94109-0426

WATTS, MARVIN LEE, minerals company executive, chemist, educator; b. Portales, N.Mex., Apr. 6, 1932; s. William Ellis and Jewel Reata (Holder) W.; m. Mary Myrtle Kiber, July 25, 1952; children: Marvin Lee, Mark Dwight, Wesley Lyle. BS in Chemistry and Math., Ea. N.Mex. U., 1959, MS in Chemistry, 1960; postgrad., U. Okla., 1966, U. Kans., 1967. Analytical chemistr Dow Chem. Co., Midland, Mich., 1960-62; instr. chemistry N.Mex. Mil. Inst., Roswell, 1962-65, asst. prof., 1965-67; chief chemist AMAX Chem. Corp., Carlsbad, N.Mex., 1967-78, gen. surface supt., 1978-84; pres. N.Mex. Salt and Minerals Corp., 1984—. Chem. cons. Western Woils Lab., Roswell, 1962-67; instr. chemistry N.Mex. State U., Carlsbad, 1967—; owner, operator cattle ranch, Carlsbad and Loving, N.Mex., 1969—; bd. dirs. Mountain States Mut. Casualty Co., 1981; gen. mgr. Eddy Potash, Inc., 1987—, v.p., gen. mgr., 1987-95; cons. Potash Industry, 1995—. Pres. Carlsbad Dept. Devel., 1996. N.Mex. BLM Resoource Adv. Coun., 1994; chmn. Eddy County Land USF Commn., Eddy County Labor Rels. Bd.; dir. Soil Donservation Svc.; mem. Roswell dist. adv. bd. Bur. Land Mgmt.; bd. dirs. Southeastern N.Mex. Regional Sci. Fair, 1996; mem. adv. bd. Roswell dist. Bur. Land Mgmt.; mem. Eddy County Fair Bd., 1976—, chmn., 1978, 82; mem. pub. sch. reform com.; chmn. higher edn. reform com.; mem. sponsor of N.Mex. pub. Sch. Reform Act; bd. dirs. Carlsbad Found., 1979-82; adv. bd. N.Mex. State U. at Carlsbad, 1976-80; vice chmn. bd. Guadalupe Med. Ctr.; bd. dirs. N.Mex. Legis, 1984-89; mem. Rep. State Exec. com., 1972—; Rep. chmn. Eddy County (N.MEx.), 1970-74, 78-82, dirs. Conquistador coun. Boy Scouts Am., Regional Environ. Ednl. Rsch. and Improvement Orgn. With Mil. Police Corps, AUS, 1953-55, Germany. Recipient Albert K. Mitchell award as outstanding Rep. in N.Mex., 1976; hon. state farmer N.Mex. Future Farmers Am.; hon. mem. 4-H. Fellow N.Mex. Acad. Sci.; mem. Am. Chem. Soc. (chmn. subsect.), Western States Pub. Lands Coalition, Carlsbad C. of C. (dir. 1979-83), N.Mex. Mining Assn. (dir.), AIME (chmn. Carlsbad potash sect. 1975), Carlsbad Mental Health Assn. (pres. 1994—), N.Mex. Inst. Mining and Tech. (adv. bd. mining dept.), Am. Angus Assn., Am. Quarter Horse Assn., N.Mex. Cattle Growers Assn. (bd. dirs. 1989—), Carlsbad Farm and Ranch Assn., Nat. Cattlemen's Assn., Kiwanis (Disting. lt. gov.). Baptist. Home: PO Box 56 Carlsbad NM 88221-0056 Office: PO Box 101 Carlsbad NM 88221-5603

WATTS, MARY ANN, retired elementary education educator; b. Harrisburg, Pa., Sept. 13, 1927; d. Major Allan and Ellana Susan (Robinson) Brown; m. Spencer R. Watts, June 23, 1951; children: Shelley Lynn, Allison Dee, Howard Allan. BS, Cheyney U., 1949; student, Temple U., 1965-67, Pa. State U., 1969-72. Tchr. Harrisburg Sch. Dist., 1949-51, 59-69, Balt. Sch. Dist., 1951-57, Reading (Pa.) Sch. Dist., 1969-89. Mem. sch. dist. dress and discipline code com., 1977-79. Corr. Hamburg Item, West Berks Crier. Bd. dirs. Pa. State Assn. Boroughs, mem. resolutions and policy com.; mem. Bernville Borough Coun., 1976—, v.p., 1988-93, 96-98; sec., treas. Berks County Borough Assn., 1977—. Recipient Disting. Alumna award for achievement in govt. and politics Cheyney U., 1999. Mem. NAACP, Women's Polit. Network Pa., Pa. State Edn. Assn. (life), Pa. Assn. Sch. Retirees, Bernville Woman's Club (pres. 1978-80, 86-88, Woman of Yr. 1985, Grange Cmty. Svc. award 1988), GNO Harrisburg. Democrat. Mem. United Ch. of Christ.

WATTS, MICHAEL WAYNE, economist; b. Medicine Lodge, Kans., Nov. 3, 1950; s. Victor Wayne and Lois Melba (Anthony) W.; m. Julie Ann Bolotte, May 17, 1974; children: Jonathan Wayne, Matthew Michael. BA, La. State U., 1972, MA, 1974, PhD, 1978. Prof., dir. ctr. econ. edn. Krannert Ctr. Purdue U., West Lafayette, Ind., 1981—. Cons. Nat. Coun. on Econ. Edn., N.Y.C., 1978—, USIA, 1991, Ednl. Testing Svcs., 1991, 93—, Agy. Instrn. Tech., 1984-86, IMF, 1988-89, TRW, Inc., 1993—. Assoc. editor: (jour.) Jour. Econ. Edn., 1988—. Mem. Nat. Assn. Econ. Educators (pres. 1986-87), Am. Econ. Assn. (com. on econ. edn. 1993—), Nat. Coun. for Social Studies, Soc. Econ. Educators (v.p. 1994-95), Am. Ednl. Rsch. Assn., Soc. Econ. Assn., Midwest Econ. Assn. Democrat. Home: 3930 Kensington Dr Lafayette IN 47905-4174 Office: Purdue U Krannert Ctr West Lafayette IN 47907

WATTS, OLIVER EDWARD, engineering consultancy company executive; b. Hayden, Colo., Sept. 22, 1939; s. Oliver Easton and Vera Irene (Hockett) W.; m. Charla Ann French, Aug. 12, 1962; children: Erik Sean, Oliver Eron,

Sherilyn. BS, Colo. State U., 1962. Registered profl. engr., Colo., Calif.; profl. hand surveyor, Colo. Crew chief Colo. State U. Rsch. Found., Ft. Collins, 1962; with Calif. Dept. Water Resources, Gustine and Castaic, 1964-70; land and water engr. CF&I Steel Corp., Pueblo, Colo., 1970-71; engring. dir. United Western Engrs., Colorado Springs., 1971-76; ptnr. United Planning and Engring Co., Colorado Springs, 1976-79; owner Oliver E. Watts, Cons. Engr., 1979—. Dir. edn. local Ch. of Christ, 1969-71, deacon, 1977-87, elder, 1987-96. 1st lt. C.E., AUS, 1962-64. Recipient Individual Achievement award Colo. State U. Coll. Engring., 1981 Fellow ASCE (v.p. Colorado Springs br. 1975, pres. 1978); mem. NSPE (pres. Pike's Peak chpt. 1975, sec. Colo. sect. 1976, v.p. 1977, pres. 1978-79, Young Engr. award 1976, Pres.'s award 1979), Cons. Engrs. Coun. Colo. (bd. dirs. 1981-83), Am. Cons. Engrs. Coun., Profl. Land Surveyors Colo., Colo. Engrs. Coun. (del. 1980—), Colo. State U. Alumni Assn. (v.p., dir. Pike's Peak chpt. 1972-76), Lancers, Lambda Chi Alpha. Home: 7195 Dark Horse Pl Colorado Springs CO 80919-1442 Office: 614 Elkton Dr Colorado Springs CO 80907-3514 E-mail: owatts8167@aol.com., OllieWatts@aol.com.

WATTS, ROBERT ALLAN, publisher, lawyer; b. July 4, 1936; s. Richard P. and Florence (Hooker) W.; m. Emily Stipes, Aug. 30, 1958; children: Benjamin H., Edward S., Thomas J. Student, DePauw U., 1954-55; BA, U. Ill., 1959, JD, 1961. Bar: Ill. 1961. Assoc. Stipes Pub. Co., Champaign, Ill., 1962-67, ptnr., editor, 1967—. Treas. Planned Parenthood, 1976-80; mem. Pres.'s Coun., U. Ill.; pres. Friends of Libr., U. Ill., 1980-82; bd. dirs. local United Way, 1972-81, City of Champaign Libr. Found., 1993—. Mem. Ill. Bar Assn., U. Ill. Found., Nat. Acad. Arts (bd. dirs. 1983-89), Champaign Country Club, Saugatuck Yacht Club (commodore), Lake Shore Bath & Tennis Club (pres. 1983-85). Home: 1009 W University Ave Champaign IL 61821-3317 Office: Stipes Publishing Co 204 W University Ave Champaign IL 61820-3912

WATTS, ROBERT GLENN, retired pharmaceutical executive; b. Norton, Va., Apr. 28, 1933; s. Clifford Amburgey and Stella Lee (Cornette) Watts; m. Doris Juanita Slaughter, Aug. 29, 1953 (dec. 1980); children: Cynthia L. Watts Waller, Robert Glenn, Kelly L.; m. Sara Lowry Childrey, Aug. 20, 1982; 1 child Matthew R. Alexander 1 stepchild J. Eric Alexander. BA, U. Richmond, 1959. Dir. ops. A.H. Robins Co., Inc., Richmond, Va., 1967-71, asst. v.p., 1971-73, v.p., 1973-75, sr. v.p., 1975-79, exec. v.p., 1979-92; ret., 1992. Bd. dirs. Little Oil Co., BB&T Bank, Fidelity Group. Mem. Pvt. Industry Coun., Richmond, 1983—; sec. YMCA, 1984—; bd. dirs. United Way, 1982—. With USN, 1952—56. Mem.: Met. Richmond C. of C. (chmn. 1985—86). Episcopalian. Home: 2409 Islandview Dr Richmond VA 23233-2525 E-mail: RGW433@aol.com.

WATTS, RONALD LESTER, retired military officer; b. Seneca, Mo., June 27, 1934; s. Lester N. and Naomi (Montgomery) W.; m. Anita Abelquist, Sept. 26, 1981; 1 child, Christina; children by previous marriage— Elizabeth Ann, Ronald Allen BS in Edn., Pitts. State U., 1956; MS in Polit. Sci., Auburn U., 1976. Commd. officer U.S. Army, 1956, advanced through grades to lt. gen., 1987; asst. div. comdr. 1st Inf. Div., Ft. Riley, Kans., 1981-83; comdg. gen. U.S. Army Readiness, Fort Meade, Md., 1983; dep. comdg. gen. 1st U.S. Army, 1983-84; comdg. gen. 1st Inf. Div., Ft. Riley, Kans., 1984-86; chief staff Hdqrs. Forces Command, Ft. McPherson, Ga., 1986-87; commdg. gen. VII Corps, 1987-89, ret., 1989; pres. Watts Leadership Devel. Svcs., Greensboro, Ga., 1990—. Decorated D.S.M. with oak leaf cluster, Legion of Merit with 2 oak leaf clusters, Bronze Star, Air medal with 10 oak leaf clusters, Combat Inf. badge, Def. Superior Svc. medal with cluster. Home: 1531 Lighthouse Cir Greensboro GA 30642-3489

WATTS, ROSS LESLIE, accounting educator, consultant; b. Hamilton, Australia, Nov. 10, 1942; came to U.S., 1966; s. Leslie R. and Elsie B. (Horadam) W. m. Helen Clare Firkin, Jan. 15, 1966; children: Andrew David, James Michael. B. Commerce with honors (Commonwealth Govt. scholar 1960-65), U. Newcastle (Australia), 1966; MBA (Ford Found. fellow 1967-68), U. Chgo., 1968, PhD, 1971. Audit clk. Forsythe & Co., Newcastle, Australia, 1960-64, acct. Australia, 1964-66; instr. Grad. Sch. Bus., U. Chgo., 1969-70; asst. prof. Simon Sch. Mgmt., U. Rochester (N.Y.), 1971-78, assoc. prof., 1978-84, prof., 1984-86; endowed chair Rochester Telephone Corp., 1986-98; William H. Meckling prof. U. Rochester (N.Y.), 1998—. Prof. commerce U. Newcastle, 1974-76; hon. prof. City U. Hong Kong, 1996-2001; cons. to bus. firms, 1972—; disting. lectr. Hong Kong Univ. Sci. and Tech., 1994; hon. prof. Xiamen U., China, 1999—. Contbr. articles on acctg. rsch. to profl. jours.; assoc. editor Jour. Acctg. Rsch., 1972-78, Jour. Fin. Econs., 1974-89, Australian Jour. Mgmt., 1976-81; co-editor Jour. Acctg. and Econs., 1979—; editor Jour. Acctg. Abstracts, 1995-97; dir., editor Acctg. Rsch. Network, 1997—; mem. adv. bd. Midland Corp. Fin. Jour., 1983-88, Continental Bank Jour. of Applied Corp. Fin., 1988-94, Bank Am. Jour. Applied Corp. Fin., 1994—; mem. editorial bd. Contemporary Acctg. Rsch., 1983-85; cons. editor Asia Pacific Jour. Acctg. Econs., 1998—. Recipient Notable Contbn. award AICPA, 1979, 80, award Alpha Kappa Psi Found., 1985. Mem. Am. Acctg. Assn. (Outstanding Educator award 2000), Am. Fin. Assn., Inst. Chartered Accts. in Australia. Home: 17 Burncoat Way Pittsford NY 14534-2215 Office: U Rochester Simon Sch Mgmt Wilson Blvd Rochester NY 14627-2241 E-mail: Watts@simon.rochester.edu.

WATTS, STEVEN RICHARD, lawyer; b. Toledo, Oct. 5, 1955; s. James Hupp and Lona Jane Katherine (Miller) W.; m. Marcia Ann Jackson, Mar. 6, 1982; children: Lauren Brooke, Madison Ann. BA in History, Ohio State U., 1978; JD summa cum laude, U. Dayton, 1981. Bar: Ohio 1981, U.S. Dist. Ct. (so. dist.) Ohio 1981. Assoc. Smith & Schnacke, Dayton, Ohio, 1981-84, Porter, Wright, Morris & Arthur, Dayton, 1984-89, ptnr., 1990, Chernesky, Heyman & Kress P.L.L., Dayton, 1990—. Mem. ABA, Ohio State Bar Assn., Dayton Bar Assn. Presbyterian. Avocation: golf. Home: 1101 Viewpoint Dr Dayton OH 45459-1442 Office: Chernesky Heyman & Kress PLL 1100 Courthouse Pla SW Dayton OH 45402 E-mail: srw@chklaw.com.

WATTS, TONI EILEEN, executive secretary, actress; b. Roanoke, Va., Aug. 10, 1967; d. Diane Carole Watts. B in Creative Arts, U. N.C., 1990. Sales sec. Creative Network Studios, Charlotte, N.C., 1991; sec. The Quantum Group, Davidson, 1991-92; pub. rels. sec. Arts & Sci. Coun., Charlotte, 1992-93; sales sec. Creative Temporaries, Raleigh, N.C., 1993-94; adminstrv. sec. Burroughs Wellcome, Research Triangle Park, 1994-95; adminstrv. specialist Glaxo SmithKline, 1995-2001. Recipient Nat. Speech and Drama award, 1985; former Roanoke Valley Jr. Miss and 1st runner-up at Va. Jr. Miss; Va. State Baton Twirling Champ; 1st runner-up Miss Majorette of Va. Mem. Am. Guild Variety Artists, Delta Zeta. Avocations: dancing, billiards, cooking, self-help, baton-twirling. E-mail: actrez2b@netscape.net.

WATTS, WILLIAM DAVID, corporate executive, business owner; b. Birmingham, Dec. 2, 1938; s. Edgar Reid and Ruth (Appling) W.; m. Lynda Louise Moseley, Aug. 1964 (div. Aug. 2, 1974); children: William David, Jr., Mark Chadwick; m. Lynn Saccone, June 28, 1975; children: Trudy, Paul William. BS in Indsl. Arts, Auburn U., 1963; student, Dale Carnegie, Birmingham, Ala., 1969, Ed Winner, Hagerstown, Md., 1971-72. Field erector engr. Pangborn Corp., Hagerstown, Md., 1963-64, sales svc. engr., 1964-68, dist. sales engr., 1968-71, acct. exec., 1971-76; owner, pres. Watts Equipment & Supply Co., Atlanta, 1976-89, Blastec, Inc., Alpharetta, Ga., 1989—. Holder 14 U.S. blast machine patents. Ticket chmn. Am. Foundry Soc., Birmingham, 1964-66, arrangements chmn., 1966-68, dir., 1968-69, treas., 1969-72. With USAR, 1957-63. Mem. Atlanta Athletic, Lake Arrowhead Yacht & Country, Masonic Lodge. Avocations: boating, swimming, motorcycling. Office: Blastec Inc 4965 Highway 9 N Alpharetta GA 30004-2922

WATTS, WILLIAM PARK, naval officer; b. Huntsville, Ala., Mar. 25, 1916; s. Clarence Lee and Inez Elizabeth (Looney) W.; m. Eleanor Ruth Roth, July 2, 1949; children: Deborah Clark Watts, Lauren McCrary Watts Buchner. BS, U.S. Naval Acad., 1938; grad., Naval War Coll., 1949; MBA, NYU, 1961; PHD in Bus. Adminstrn., U. Ala., 1977. Commd. ensign U.S. Navy, 1938, advanced through grades to capt., 1962; duty assignments include commdg. officer of naval supply depot, various Navy, joint, NATO staffs and in combatant ships; adminstrv. mgr. Rsch. Inst. U. Ala., Huntsville, 1963-70, mem. faculty, 1970-77, asst. prof., 1970-77, acting chmn. dept. bus. adminstrn., 1974-75; mgmt. cons. Mgmt. Sci. Applications Assocs., 1979-82. Pres., 1st v.p., sec., mem. exec. com. Huntsville-Madison County Council for Internat. Visitors, 1978-93; bd. trustees Huntsville Symphony Orch. Assn., 1983-93, sec., mem. exec. com., 1988-90, assoc. mem. bd. trustees 1993—; vestryman Episcopal Ch. of the Nativity, Huntsville, 1982-84; founding pres. Randolph Sch. Athletics and Activities Assn., Huntsville, 1966-67; mem. Huntsville-Madison County Library Devel. Council, 1985; mem. Huntsville Community Chorus, 1980-86, bd. dirs., 1981-82, mem. Huntsville Pilgrimmage Assn, 1987-93; chmn. storm water mgmt. bd. City of Huntsville, 1991-92. Decorated Asiatic-Pacific Campaign medal with three stars, WWII Victory medal, Occupation service medal, Am. Campaign, Navy Commendation medal, 1946, Nat. Defense Service medal, 1954; Paul Harris fellow. Mem. Carl Jung Soc. of Tenn. Valley, Inc. (founder and founding chmn., pres., 1993, bd. dirs. 1993—), Huntsville Rotary Club. Republican. Episcopalian. Avocations: music, photography, gardening, reading, family history. Home: 2300 Big Cove Rd SE Huntsville AL 35801-1350

WATTS-WILSON, DENISE, secondary school educator; b. Bklyn., Aug. 20, 1954; d. James and Hattie (Jowers) Watts; m. Jimmy Lee Wilson, July 30, 1983; 1 child, Gregory Alexander. BA, CUNY, 1976; MA in Christian Edn., So. Bapt. Sem., Louisville, 1978, MDiv, RE, 1982. Dir. edn. and youth Bethany Bapt. Ch., Bklyn., 1978-80; substitute tchr. Jefferson County Bd. Edn., Louisville, 1980-83; min. edn. and youth South Park Bapt. Ch., Houston, 1983-84, Greenspoint Bapt. Ch., Houston, 1986-88; tchr. Barrick Elem. Sch., Houston Ind. Sch. Dist., 1985-88; tchr. history Wells Mid. Sch., Spring Ind. Sch. Dist., Houston, 1988-93; asst. pastor and minister of edn. St. Stephen Bapt. Ch., Louisville, 1993-95; tchr. U.S. history Bruce Middle Sch. Jefferson County Schs., 1995-96, tchr. computer tech. Bruce Mid. Sch., 1996-97; proprietor Gifts from Home, 1995-99; program coord. Rites of Passage Acad., Jefferson County Schs., 1997-98; computer tech. tchr. Farnsley Mid. Sch., Jefferson County Schs., Louisville, 1998-2000, Kammerer Mid. Sch., Jefferson County Schs., Louisville, 2000—; pres. Deliverance Enterprises Internat., 1999—. Youth dir. Zion Bapt. Ch., Louisville, 1982-83. Author: Devotions for Christian Staff, 1982. Founding pastor Lighthouse Christian Fellowship, LaGrange, Ky., 1997—. Benjamin Mays fellow Fund for Theol. Edn., 1981. Mem. N.G. Assn. U.S.A., N.G. Assn. Tex. (life). Democrat. Avocations: walking, jogging, singing, crocheting, swimming. Office: 7315 Wesboro Rd Louisville KY 40222-6457 E-mail: deeww@quixnet.net.

WATZ, MARTIN CHARLES, brewery consultant; b. St. Louis, Oct. 31, 1938; s. George Michael and Caroline Theresa (Doggendorf) W.; m. Deborah Perkowski; children: Pamela, Kathlene, Karen. BS in Chemistry and Microbiology, SE Mo. State U., 1961; MBA, Washington U., 1966-67. Safety engr. McDonnell-Douglas, 1962-64; sr. brewing chemist Anheuser-Busch, Inc., St. Louis, 1965-68, asst. brewmaster Columbus, Ohio, 1968-79, sr. asst. brewmaster St. Louis, 1979-82, resident brewmaster Baldwinsville, N.Y., 1982-84, Williamsburg, Va., 1984-87; v.p. bakers yeast divsn. Anheuser-Busch Indsl. Products Corp., St. Louis, 1987-88, dir. brewing ops., 1988-89; sr. brewmaster Anheuser-Busch, Ft. Collins, Colo., 1989-99; brewing cons., 1999—. Patentee in field. With USAF, 1962-65. Mem. Master Brewers Assn. Am. (pres., nat. bd. govs.), Am. Soc. Brewing Chemists, Internat. Food Tech. Assocs., Aircraft Owners and Pilots Assn., U.S. Pilots Assn., Profl. Assn. Diving Instrs. Avocations: flying, collectible cars. Home and Office: 1417 N County Rd # 3 Fort Collins CO 80524-9312

WAUD, ROGER NEIL, economics educator; b. Detroit, Mar. 26, 1938; s. Othneil Stockwell and Mary Josephine (Gough) W.; children: Heather, Neil. BA, Harvard U., 1960; MA, U. Calif., Berkeley, 1962; PhD (Ford Found. fellow), U. Calif., Berekley, 1965. Asst. prof. bus. econs. Grad. Sch. Bus. U. Chgo., 1964-69; assoc. prof. econs. U. N.C., Chapel Hill, 1969-72, prof., 1972-97, prof. emeritus, 1997—; sr. economist, bd. govs. Fed. Res. System, Washington, 1973-75; prof., dir. grad. econs. program Va. Tech., 1997—2002. Cons. Dept. Labor; mem. adv. bd. Taxpayers Ednl. Coalition, 1981; research assoc. Nat. Bur. Econ. Research, 1982-92; mem. N.C. Energy Policy Council, 1986-92; vis. prof. Duke U., 1992-94. Author: Macroeconomics, 5th edit., 1992, Microeconomics, 5th edit., 1992; contbr. articles to profl. jours.; mem. editorial bd. So. Econ. Jour, 1970-73, Studies in Econs. & Fin., 1995-97. Mem. Am. Econ. Assn., So. Econ. Assn. (exec. com. 1977-79) Office: No Va Ctr 7054 Haycock Rd Falls Church VA 22043-2311

WAUGAMAN, RICHARD MERLE, psychiatrist, psychoanalyst, educator; b. Easton, Pa., Apr. 27, 1949; s. Charles Hoffmeier and Ruth Alviene (Melee) W.; m. Elisabeth Leone Pearson, June 20, 1970; children: Adele Marie, Garrett Dennis. AB, Princeton U., 1970; MD, Duke U., 1973. Cert. psychiatry, 1978, psychoanalysis, 1984. Resident in psychiatry Sheppard-Pratt Hosp., Towson, Md., 1973-76; mem. faculty Washington Sch. Psychiatry, 1983-96; grad. Washington Psychoanalytic Inst., 1984, tng. and supervising analyst, 1989-2001, emeritus tng. and supervising analyst, 2001—; from clin. instr. to clin. assoc. prof. Georgetown U. Sch. Medicine, Washington, 1978-92, clin. prof. psychiatry, 1992—; staff psychiatrist Chestnut Lodge, Rockville, Md., 1986-99. Cons. psychiat. residency program Nat. Naval Med. Ctr., Bethesda, Md., 1994—96; adj. prof. psychiatry Uniformed Svcs. U. of Health Scis., 1999—. Contbr. articles to profl. jours. Mem. Washington Psychoanalytic Soc., Am. Psychoanalytic Assn. (exec. coun. 1995-97, com. on certification 1998-2002), Internat. Psychoanalytic Assn., Am. Psychiat. Assn., Cosmos Club. Methodist. Home: 8109 Horseshoe Ln Potomac MD 20854-3834

WAUGAMAN, RICHARD WILLIAM, sales executive; b. Freedom, Pa., Aug. 29, 1958; s. Harry and Bonita (Reed) Waugaman. Student, Robert Morris Coll., 1984. Cert. travel agt. Purchasing coord. Integrated Supply Network, Lakeland, 1993—98; contract sales rep. The Ledger (A N.Y. Times Co.), Fla., 1998—. Avocations: travel, collecting. Home: #176 202 East Griffin Rd Lakeland FL 33805 Office: The Ledger (A N Y Times Co) 300 West Lime St Lakeland FL 33802 Personal E-mail: PandaBear1958@att.net.

WAUGH, JOHN STEWART, chemist, educator; b. Willimantic, Conn., Apr. 25, 1929; s. Albert E. and Edith (Stewart) W.; married 1983; children: Alice Collier, Frederick Pierce. AB, Dartmouth Coll., 1949; PhD, Calif. Inst. Tech., 1953; ScD (hon.), Dartmouth Coll., 1989. Rsch. fellow in physics Calif. Inst. Tech., 1952-53; mem. faculty MIT, Cambridge, 1953—, prof. chemistry, 1962—, Albert Amos Noyes prof. chemistry, 1973-88, inst. prof., 1989—, emeritus, 1996—. Vis. prof. U. Calif.-Berkeley, 1963-64; lectr. Robert Welch Found., 1968; Falk-Plaut lectr. Columbia U., 1973; DuPont lectr. U. S.C., 1974; Lucy Pickett lectr. Mt. Holyoke Coll., 1978; Reilly lectr. U. Notre Dame, 1978; Spedding lectr. Iowa State U., 1979; McElvain lectr. U. Wis., 1981; Vaughan lectr. Rocky Mountain Conf., 1981; G.N. Lewis meml. lectr. U. Calif., 1982; Dreyfus lectr. Dartmouth Coll., 1984; G.B. Kistiakowsky lectr. Harvard U., 1984; O.K. Rice lectr. U. N.C., Chapel Hill, 1986, Baker lectr. Cornell U., 1990; Smith lectr. Duke U., 1992; sr. fellow Alexander von Humboldt-Stiftung; also vis. prof. Max Planck Inst., Heidelberg, 1972; vis. scientist Harvard U., 1976; mem. chemistry adv. panel NSF, 1966-69, vice chmn., 1968-69; mem. rev. com. Argonne Nat. Lab., 1970-74; mem. sci. and edn. adv. com. Lawrence Berkeley Lab., 1980-86; exchange visitor USSR Acad. Scis., 1962, 75; mem. vis. com. Tufts U., 1966-69, Princeton, 1973-78; mem. fellowship com. Alfred P. Sloan Found., 1977-82; Joliot-Curie prof. École Supérieure de Physique et Chemie, Paris, 1985, 96. Author: New NMR Methods in Solid State Physics, 1978; editor: Advances in Magnetic Resonance, 1965-87; assoc. editor: Jour. Chem. Physics, 1965-67, Spectrochimica Acta, 1964-78; mem. editorial bd. Chem. Revs., 1978-82, Jour. Magnetic Resonance, 1989—, Applied Magnetic Resonance, 1989—. Recipient Irving Langmuir award, 1976, Gold Pick Axe award, 1976, Pitts. award Spectroscopic Soc. Pitts., 1979, Wolf prize, 1984, Pauling medal, 1985, Calif. Inst. Tech. disting. alumnus award, 1987, Killian award, 1988, ISMAR prize, 1989, Richards medal, 1992, Evans award, 1994, Ea. Analytical Symposium award 1996; Sloan fellow, 1958-62, Guggenheim fellow, 1963-64, 72; Sherman Fairchild scholar Calif. Inst. Tech., 1989. Fellow: AAAS, Am. Phys. Soc. (chmn. divsn. chemistry and physics 1983—84); mem.: NAS, Slovenian Acad. Sci. and Arts (fgn. corr.), Internat. Soc. Magnetic Resonance (mem. coun. 1989—95, mem. exec. com. 1996—, v.p. 1997—, pres. 1999—2002), Phi Beta Kappa, Sigma Xi. Office: MIT 6-231 77 Massachusetts Ave Cambridge MA 02139-4307 E-mail: jswaugh@mit.edu.

WAUGH, THEODORE ROGERS, orthopedic surgeon; b. Montreal, Sept. 21, 1926; s. Theodore Rogers and Anne Maude (Lawlor) W.; children: Susanne Rogers, Margaret Stewart, Theodore Rogers. BA, Yale U., 1949; MD, CM, McGill U., 1953; D Med.Sci., U. Goteborg, Sweden, 1968. Diplomate Am. Bd. Orthopaedic Surgery. Intern Royal Victoria Hosp., Montreal, 1953-54; asst. resident in pathology McGill U., 1954-55; asst. resident in surgery N.Y. U. Bellevue Med. Center, 1955-56; asst. resident, resident, fellow N.Y. Orthopedic Hosp., Columbia U., 1958-62, instr., clin. asst. prof. orthopedic surgery, 1962-68; asst. attending Presbyn. Hosp., N.Y.C., 1962-68; prof., chief div. orthopedic surgery U. Calif., Irvine, 1968-78; prof., chmn. dept. orthopedic surgery N.Y.U. Med. Center, 1978-96, emeritus prof., 1997—. Adj. prof. surgery, Dartmouth U. Sch. Medicine, 1998—. Contbr. numerous articles to profl. jours. Capt., M.C. USAF, 1956-58. Fellow ACS, Royal Coll. Surgeons (Can.), Am. Acad. Orthopaedic Surgeons, Scoliosis Research Soc., Assn. Bone and Joint Surgeons, Am. Orthopaedic Assn., Am. Orthopaedic Soc. for Sports Medicine.; mem. Soc. Colonial Wars, Alpha Omega Alpha. Clubs: 20th Century Orthopedic. Presbyterian. Achievements include developing designer surgical devices used in orthopaedic surgery. Office: Dartmouth-Hitchcock Med Ctr One Medical Center Dr Lebanon NH 03756 E-mail: trwmd@cyberportal.net.

WAUGH, WILLIAM HOWARD, biomedical educator; b. N.Y.C., May 13, 1925; s. Richey Laughlin and Lyda Pearl (Leamer) W.; m. Eileen Loretta Garrigan, Oct. 4, 1952; children: Mark Howard, Kathleen Cary, William Peter. Student, Boston U., 1943, W.Va. U., 1944; MD, Tufts U., 1948, postgrad., 1949-50. Cardiovascular rsch. trainee Med. Coll. Ga., Augusta, 1954-55, asst. rsch. prof. physiology, 1955-60, assoc. medicine, 1957-60; assoc. prof. medicine U. Ky., Lexington, 1960-69; Ky. Heart Assn. Chair in cardiovascular rsch. Ky. Heart Assn., 1963-71; prof. medicine U. Ky., 1969-71; prof. medicine and physiology East Carolina U., Greenville, 1971—2001, rsch. prof. physiology, 2001—, prof. emeritus, 2001—. Head renal sect. U. Ky. Coll., Lexington, 1960-68; chmn. dept. clin. scis. East Carolina U., Greenville, 1971-75, chmn. policy and rev. com. on human rsch., 1972-90. Contbr. articles to profl. jours. With AUS, 1943-46; capt. USAF, 1952-54. Fellow ACP; mem. AAAS, Am. Physiology Soc., Am. Heart Assn., Am. Soc. Nephrology, Microcirculatory Soc. Republican. Achievements include basic advances in excitation contraction coupling in vasc. smooth muscle; basic advances in autoregulation of renal blood flow and urine flow; adj. therapy in acute lung edema; noncovalent antisickling agents and amino acid nutrient in sickle cell hemoglobinopathy; oral citrulline as dietary supplement in man. Home: 119 Oxford Rd Greenville NC 27858-4954 Office: E Carolina U Sch Medicine Dept Physiology Greenville NC 27858

WAUTISCHER, HELMUT, philosopher; s. Franz and Aloisia Wautischer. PhD, Karl Franzens U., Graz, Austria. Lectr. San Diego State U., 1988—91, Calif. State U., Long Beach, 1989—92; vis. asst prof. Humboldt State U., Arcata, 1992—94; sr. lectr. Sonoma State U., Rohnert Park, 1995—. Editor: (book) Tribal Epistemologies, 1998. Mem.: Soc. for the Anthropology of Consciousness (exec. bd. 1991—99), Coun. of Philos. Socs. (exec. bd. 1997). Office: Sonoma State U 1801 E Cotati Ave Cotati CA 94928 Office Fax: 707-664-2505. E-mail: wautisch@sonoma.edu.

WAVLE, ELIZABETH MARGARET, college official; b. Homer, N.Y., Jan. 18, 1957; d. John Andrew Jr. and Louise Hayford (Estey) W. BMus, SUNY, Potsdam, 1979; AM in Libr. Sci., U. Mich., 1980; MS in Edn., Elmira Coll., 1990. Sr. libr. asst. U. Mich., Ann Arbor, 1979-80; pub. svcs. libr. Elmira (N.Y.) Coll., 1980-84, instr. music, 1981-97, head tech. svcs., 1984-97, coord. women's studies, 1992, 96-97; assoc. dir. collection svcs. Ithaca (N.Y.) Coll., 1998—. Mem. South Ctrl. Rsch. Libr. Coun. Interlibr. Loan Adv. Com., Ithaca, N.Y., 1991-93; mem. regional automation com. South Ctrl. Rsch. Libr. Coun., Ithaca, 1994-95, resource sharing com., 1996-97, pers. com., 2000—. Contbr. revs., essays to profl. publs. Mem. steering com. Unitarian Universalist Fellowship of Ithaca. Democrat. Avocations: music, reading, antiques. Home: 30 Washington St Trumansburg NY 14886-1008 Office: 1201 Gannett Ctr Ithaca Coll Ithaca NY 14850 E-mail: ewavle@ithaca.edu.

WAVLE, JAMES EDWARD, JR. pharmaceutical company executive, lawyer; b. N.Y.C., July 19, 1942; s. James Edward and Florence Marie (Kehoe) W.; children from previous marriage: James Edward, William Patrick, Robert Thomas, Stephanie Elizabeth; m. Elizabeth Edith Symons Tallett; 1 child, Christopher Andrew; stepchildren: James E. Tallett, Alexander M. Tallett. BA, Adelphi U., 1964; JD, Georgetown U., 1967; LLM, NYU, 1968. Bar: N.Y. bar 1967. With Warner-Lambert Co., Morris Plains, N.J., 1968-87, internat. counsel, 1971-74, assoc. gen. counsel, 1974-77, v.p., gen. counsel, 1977-80, sr. v.p., gen. counsel, 1980-81; corp. sr. v.p. and pres. Parke-Davis Group, 1982-87; pres., CEO Centocor Inc., Malvern, Pa., 1987-92; chmn. Dioscor Inc., Stockton, N.J., 1993-97; chmn., pres., CEO Therics, Inc., Princeton, 1997—. Mem. ABA, Lookaway golf Club, Stamford Yacht Club. Office: Therics Inc 115 Campus Dr Princeton NJ 08540-6400

WAWREJKO COCHRAN, DIANE, performing arts association administrator; BA in Classical Ballet, Mercyhurst Coll., 1978; MFA in Performance & Choreography, Ariz. State U.; student in Dance , U. Surrey. Resident, workshop artist Urban Gateways, Chgo.; prof., dance program dir. U. Tex.-Pan Am.; exec. dir. Nat. Dance Assn. Dancer Ctrl. Ballet of China, first U.S. tour, Laurie Eisenhower and Dances, Repertory Dance Theatre, PBS; contbr. articles to profl. jours. Office: NDA c/o AAHPERD 1900 Association Drive Reston VA 20191-1598*

WAWROSE, FREDERICK EUGENE, psychiatrist; b. Binghamton, N.Y., Jan. 23, 1929; s. John Joseph and Marie Johanna (Anton) W.; m. Dorothy Jean Stewart, Sept. ll, 1954; children: John, David, Susan, Stephen, Dorothy. AB cum laude, U. Colo., 1950; MD, U. Pa., 1954. Diplomate Am. Bd. Psychiatry and Neurology, Am. Bd. Child Psychiatry. Dir. pre-sch. unit Child Study Ctr., Phila., 1963-64, dir. Ctr., 1964-70; psychiatrist J.C. Blair Hosp., Huntingdon, Pa., 1970-94, dir., 1986—; intern Univ. Pa. Hosp., 1954-55; resident in adult psychiatry Inst. of the Pa. Hosp., 1958-61; resident in child psychiatry Child Study Ctr. Phila., 1961-63. Psychiatrist State Correctional Inst., Huntington, 197l—, Juniata Valley Mental Health-Mental Retardation Program, Huntington, 970—. Capt. M.C., U.S. Army, 1955-57. Fellow Am. Acad. Child Psychiatry; mem. AMA (physicians recognition award l977), Am. Psychiat. Assn., Am. Acad. Psychiatry and Law. Avocations: gardening, writing.

WAX, ARNOLD, physician; b. Bklyn., Mar. 11, 1949; s. Emanuel and Eleanor (Greenfield) W.; m. Francine Wax; children: Erin, Rachael, Adam, Benjamin. BS in Pharm. Scis., Columbia U., 1971; MD, SUNY, Buffalo, 1976. Diplomate Nat. Bd. Med. Examiners, Am. Bd. Internal Medicine, Am. Bd. Quality Assurance and Utilization Rev. Physicians, Am. Acad. Pain Mgmt.; lic. physician, Fla., Calif., N.D., Minn., N.Y., Nev., Ariz. Intern, resident Millard Fillmore Hosp., Buffalo, 1976-79; clin. asst. instr. SUNY, 1977-79; instr. medicine U. Rochester, N.Y., 1979-81; dir. internal medicine U. N.D., Grand Forks, 1982-83, clin. asst. prof., 1982-85; pvt. practice Las Vegas, Nev., 1987—. Mem. staff Sunrise Hosp., Las Vegas, Desert Springs Hosp., Las Vegas, Nathan Adelson Hospice, Las Vegas. Contbr. articles to profl. jours. Grantee So. Nev. Cancer Rsch. Found., Ea. Coop. Oncology Group, Gynecol. Oncology Group, North Ctrl. Cancer Treatment Group, S.W. Oncology Group. Fellow Am. Coll. Physicians; mem. AMA, Am. Cancer Soc. (fellow 1979), Am. Soc. Clin. Oncology, Am. Coll. Physicians (gov. State of Nev.), Nev. Oncology So. (v.p.), Nev. Med. Soc., Clark County Med. Soc. (trustee, peer rev. com., treas.), Nev. Peer Rev. Orgn., U. Nev. Las Vegas Found., Nev. Dance Theater, Nev. Opera Theater, Las Vegas Symphony, Nev. Inst. Contemporary Art, Lied Mus., Allied Arts Coun., James Platt White Soc., U. Buffalo Found., Rho Chi (Bronze medal 1971). Home: 2224 Chatsworth Ct Henderson NV 89074-5309 Office: 3730 S Eastern Ave Ste 202 Las Vegas NV 89109-3321 E-mail: arnold.wax@usoncology.com.

WAX, GEORGE LOUIS, lawyer; b. New Orleans, Dec. 6, 1928; s. John Edward and Theresa (Schaff) W.; LL.B., Loyola U. of South, 1952, B.C.S., 1960; m. Patricia Ann Delaney, Feb. 20, 1965; children: Louis Jude, Joann Olga, Therese Marie. Admitted to La. bar, 1952, practiced in New Orleans, 1954—. Served with USNR, 1952-54. Mem. La., New Orleans bar assns., Am. Legion. Roman Catholic. Kiwanian. Clubs: New Orleans Athletic, Suburban Gun and Rod, Southern Yacht. Home: 6001 Charlotte Dr New Orleans LA 70122-2731 Office: 210 Baronne St Ste 1222 New Orleans LA 70112-1714

WAX, NADINE VIRGINIA, retired banker; b. Van Horne, Iowa, Dec. 7, 1927; d. Laurel Lloyd and Viola Henrietta (Schrader) Bobzien; divorced; 1 child, Sharlyn K. Wax Munns. Student, U. Iowa, 1970-71; grad. Nat. Sch. Real Estate and Fin., Ohio State U., 1980-81. Jr. acct. McGladrey, Hansen, Dunn (now McGladrey-Pullen Co., CPAs), Cedar Rapids, Iowa, 1944-47; office mgr. Iowa Securities Co. (now Wells Fargo Mortgage Co.), 1954-55; asst. cashier

Mchts. Nat. Bank (now U.S. Bancorp.), 1956-75; asst. v.p. Mchts. Nat. Bank (now U.S. Bancorp), 1976-78, v.p., 1979-90; ret., 1990. Vol. St. Luke's Hosp. Aux., Cedar Rapids, 1981—85, SCORE, 1999—2002; bd. dirs., v.p. Kirkwood C.C. Facilities Found., 1970—2002; bd. dirs., treas. Kirkwood C.C., 1984—91; trustee Indian Creek Nature Ctr., Cedar Rapids, 1974—2002, pres., 1980—81; mem. Linn County Regional Planning Commn., 1982—92, Cedar Rapids-Marion Fine Arts Coun., 1994—97; bd. suprs. Compensation Commn. for Condemnation, 1987—92; bd. dirs. Am. Heart Assn., Cedar Rapids, 1983—94; mem. Iowa Employment and Tng. Coun., Des Moines, 1982—83. Recipient Outstanding Woman award Cedar Rapids Tribute to Women and Industry, 1984. Mem. Fin. Women Internat. (state edn. chmn. 1982-83), Am. Inst. Banking (bd. dirs. 1968-70), Soc. Real Estate Appraisers (treas. 1978-80), Linn. County Bankers Assn. (pres. 1979-80), Cedar Rapids Bd. Realtors, Cedar Rapids C. of C. (bus.-edn. com. 1986-91), Cedar Rapids Country Club. Independent. Lutheran. Avocations: travel, reading, walking. Home: 147 Ashcombe SE Cedar Rapids IA 52403-1700

WAX, PAUL MATTHEW, emergency medicine physician, educator, medical toxicologist; b. Hanover, N.H., Mar. 8, 1958; s. Sandor Harry and Edith Mae (Ellen) W.; m. Janet Ruth Reiser, Oct. 23, 1988; children: Rebecca Sasha, Sarah Elisa. BA, Dartmouth Coll., 1980; MD, Mt. Sinai Sch. Medicine, 1984. Diplomate Am. Bd. Emergency Medicine, Am. Bd. Med. Toxicology. Intern in gen. surgery U. Mich., 1984-86; resident in emergency medicine UCLA Med. Ctr., 1986-89; fellow in med. toxicology Bellevue Med. Ctr., 1989-91; instr. emergency medicine/surgery NYU, N.Y.C., 1989-91; asst. prof. emergency medicine U. Rochester, N.Y., 1991-96, assoc. prof. emergency medicine, 1996—. Asst. dir. Finger Lakes Poison Control Ctr., Rochester, 1991—; bd. dirs. Am. Bd. Emergency Medicine Subboard of Med. Toxicology, Lansing, Mich., 1997—. Contbg. author: (textbook) Goldfrank's Emergency Toxicology, 1994, revised edit. 98, Emergency Medicine, 1996; mem. editl. bd. Jour. Toxicology, Clin. Toxicology; contbr. articles to profl. jours. Fellow Am. Coll. Emergency Medicine, Am. Coll. Med. Toxicology (bd. dirs. 1998—); mem. Am. Acad. Clin. Toxicology, Soc. Acad. Emergency Medicine, Toxicology History Soc. Jewish. Avocations: photography, genealogy, jazz. Office: U Rochester Med Ctr 601 Elmwood Ave # Rochester NY 14642-0001 Home: 5431 E Cheryl Dr Paradise Valley AZ 85253-1136

WAX, WILLIAM EDWARD, photojournalist; b. Miami, Fla., Dec. 7, 1956; s. Ira and Rita (Gunshor) W. AS, Berry Coll., Rome, Ga., 1976; BS in Engring., U. Fla., 1983. With Ind. Fla. Alligator, Gainesville, Fla., 1977-79; staff photographer Gainesville (Fla.) Sun, 1979-87; photo cons. N.Y. Times regional newspapers, 1984—; freelance photographer Miami, 1987—; pres. Wax & Co. Inc., Miami Beach, Fla., 1989—, Waxcom, Miami Beach, 1996—. Owner Studio SoBe, Miami Beach, 1992—; guest lectr. various univs.; faculty So. Short Course in News Photography, 1985—. Named Photographer of Yr., NPPA/U. Mo. and Nikon, 1980, So. Photographer of Yr., 1980, Regional Photographer of Yr., 1979, 82, 85; recipient Mark of Excellence, Sigma Delta Chi, 1978, Best of Show award Atlanta Seminar on Photojournalism, 1982, Best of Show and Silver medal Hearst awards, 1978, Design Gold award Fla. Tech. Writers Assn., 1992, Design award, Gold award, Excellence award Soc. Tech. Comm. Internat. Tech. Art Competition, 1993, 94, 97, 98, 99, Best of Show, 1994, 98, 2001, Disting. Design award, 1993, 97, 99, 2000, 2001, Excellence Design award, 1993, 98, 99, 2 Design Excellence awards and award of merit, 1995, 2000, Best of Show award Ann. Report Fla. Pub. Rels., 1995, Silver and Bronze awards Fla. Mag. Assn., 1994, 96, 97, 98, 99, 2000, Gold, Silver and Bronze awards Fla. Mag. Assn., 1995-98, Merit award STC, 1995, Apex Design awards 1996-97, 98, Global award/Ann. Report Photography, 1996; nominated for Pulitzer prize, 1979, 89, STC Internat. Design, 1996-97. Mem. Nat. Press Photographers Assn., Fla. Mag. Assn., Profl. Photographers Am., Nikon Profl. Svcs., Fla. Press Photographers Assn. Office: Wax & Co 350 Lincoln Rd Ste 516 Miami FL 33139-3148

WAXBERG, JONATHAN ABEL, urologic surgeon, oncologist; b. Pensacola, Fla., Jan. 10, 1955; s. Joseph David and Carol Ita Waxberg; m. Anita Lor, Apr. 12, 1980. BA, Oberlin Coll., 1976; MD, U. Cin., 1980. Diplomate Am. Bd. Urology. Resident in urology Maimonides Hosp., Bklyn., 1980-86; attending physician in urology Stamford (Conn.) Hosp., 1986—, chief dept. urology, 1999—. Fellow ACS; mem. Stamford Med. Soc. (pres. 1998-99). Avocations: tennis, golf, travel. Address: 35 Hoyt St Stamford CT 06905-5602

WAXLER, BEVERLY JEAN, anesthesiologist, physician; b. Chgo., Apr. 11, 1949; d. Isadore and Ada Belle (Gross) Marcus; m. Richard Norman Waxler, Dec. 24, 1972; 1 child, Adam R. BS in Biology, No. Ill. U., 1971; MD, U. Ill., Chgo., 1975. Diplomate Am. Bd. Anesthesiology, Am. Bd. Pathology. Intern dept. pathology Northwestern U., Chgo., 1975-76, resident, 1976-79; instr. Rush Presbyn. St. Luke's Med. Ctr., 1979-81; asst. prof. pathology Loyola U., Maywood, Ill., 1981-84; resident dept. anesthesiology Cook County Hosp., Chgo., 1984-87, attending anesthesiologist, 1987—; clin. asst. prof. U. Ill., 1988-95; asst. prof. Rush Med. Coll., 1996—. Contbr. papers to Tissue and Cell. Recipient B.B. Sankey Anesthesia Advancement award Internat. Anesthesia Rsch. Soc., 1989; Nat. Rsch. Svc. award fellow Nat. Cancer Inst., 1980; grantee Varlen Corp., 1982. Mem. AAAS, Internat. Anesthesia Rsch. Soc., Am. Soc. Anesthesiologists, hicago Soc. of Anesthesiologists, Ill. Soc. of Anesthesiologists, Sigma Xi.C Office: Cook County Hosp Chicago IL 60612

WAXMAN, ALAN GARLETT, obstetrician/gynecologist, educator; b. Phila., 1946; MD, U. Colo., 1972; MPH, Emory U., 1989. Diplomate Am. Bd. Ob-Gyn. Intern Med. Ctr. VA Hosp., Richmond, Va., 1972-73; resident ob-gyn Colo. Affiliate Hosps.-St. Luke's Hosp., Denver, 1973-76; chief ob-gyn dept. Gallup (N.Mex.) Indian Med. Ctr., 1980-91; assoc. prof. dept. ob-gyn. U. N.Mex. Sch. of Medicine, Albuquerque, 2000—. Sr. clinician ob-gyn Indian Health Svc., 1994-2000. Fellow Am. Coll. Ob-Gyn; mem. APHA, Am. Soc. Colposcopy and Cervical Pathology (bd. dirs.), N.Mex. Breast and Cervical Cancer Program (adv. coun., chair quality assurance com.). Office: U NMex Health Scis Ctr 4-ACC 2211 Lomas Blvd NE Albuquerque NM 87131-5286

WAXMAN, CHAIM I. sociology educator, researcher; b. N.Y.C., Feb. 26, 1941; s. Nissan and Sara R. W.; m. Chaya Lifshitz, June 12, 1962; children: Ari, Shani, Dani. MA, New Sch. for Social Rsch., N.Y.C., 1965, PhD, 1974; MHL, Yeshiva U., 1966. Asst. prof. sociology Ctrl. Conn. State Coll., New Britain, 1965-72, Bklyn. Coll. CUNY, 1972-75, Rutgers U., New Brunswick, N.J., 1975-78, assoc. prof., 1978-96, prof., 1996—. Mem. adv. com. Am Jewish Com., N.Y.C., 1975—, NEH, Washington, 1975—; vis. prof. Yeshiva U.. N.Y.C., 1985—, Author: America's Jews in Transition, 1953, The Stigma of Poverty 2d edit., 1983, American Aliya, 1989, Jewish Baby Boomers, 2001; co-author: Historical Dictionary of Zionism, 2000; editor Israel Studies Bull., New Brunswick, 1993—; book rev. editor Society Mag., New Brunswick, 1975-82. Grantee Found. for Middle East Peace, Washington, 1984, Lucius Littauer Found., N.Y.C., 1987, Meml. Found. for Jewish Culture, 1989. Mem. Am. Sociol. Soc., Easter Sociol. Soc., Soc. for Sci. Study Religion, Assn. for Sociol. Study of Jewry (pres. 1979-81), Assn. for Jewish Studies, Assn. for Israel Studies. Jewish. Avocation: numismatics. Office: Rutgers U Dept Sociology 54 Joyce Kilmer Ave Piscataway NJ 08854-8045 E-mail: Waxmanci@rci.rutgers.edu.

WAXMAN, DAVID, physician, university consultant; b. Albany, N.Y., Feb. 7, 1918; s. Meyer and Fannie (Strosberg) W.; m. Jane Zabel; children: Gail, Michael, Dan, Ann, Steve, Abby. BS, Syracuse U., 1942, MD, 1950. Intern Grace Hosp., Detroit, 1950-51; resident in medicine, fellow in cardiology Kans. U. Med. Ctr., Kansas City, 1958-61, instr. internal medicine, 1961-64; asst. prof. internal medicine Kans. City Med. Ctr., 1964-69, assoc. prof., 1969-77, prof., 1977—, dir. dept. medicine outpatient service, 1970-74, asst. dean, 1970-71, assoc. dean for student affairs, 1971-72, dean of students, 1972-74, vice chancellor for students, 1974-76, vice chancellor, 1976-77, exec. vice chancellor, 1977-83, spl. cons. to chancellor for health affairs, 1983-94; ret. Nat. cons. to surgeon gen. USAF. Contbr. articles to med. jours. Mem. Kans. State Bd. Healing Arts, 1984-88. Maj. gen. USAFR ret. Decorated D.S.M., Legion of Merit with one oak leaf cluster. Fellow ACP, Alpha Omega Alpha; mem. Kans. Med. Soc., Soc. Med. Cons. to the Armed Forces. Office: Kans U Med Ctr 39th and Rainbow Blvd Kansas City KS 66103

WAXMAN, HENRY ARNOLD, congressman; b. L.A., Sept. 12, 1939; s. Louis and Esther (Silverman) W.; m. Janet Kessler, Oct. 17, 1971; children: Carol Lynn, Michael David. BA in Polit. Sci, UCLA, 1961, JD, 1964. Bar: Calif. 1965. Mem. Calif. State Assembly, 1969-74, U.S. Congress from 29th Calif. dist., 1975—; chmn. commerce subcom. on health and environment, 1979-94; ranking minority mem. govt. reform & oversight com. Pres. Calif. Fedn. Young Democrats, 1965-67. Mem. Calif. Bar Assn., Guardians Jewish Home for Aged, Am. Jewish Congress, Sierra Club, B'nai B'rith, Phi Sigma Alpha. Office: US Ho Reps 2204 Rayburn Ho Office Bldg Washington DC 20515-0001*

WAXMAN, MERLE, dean; b. Newark, Mar. 6, 1946; m. Stephen G. Waxman, June 25, 1968; children: Matthew Curtis, David Mitchell. BS, Boston U., 1968; MA, CUNY, 1972. Rsch. asst. MIT, 1977-78; coord. Peninsula French Am. Sch., Palo Alto, Calif., 1980-83; mng. editor Customer Survey, CA, 1980-82; asst. ombudsman Stanford U. Med. Ctr., 1983-86; dir. office for women in medicine Yale U., 1986—; ombuds person Yale U. Sch. Medicine, 1992—, assoc. dean acad. devel., 1993—. Cons. conflict resolution, gender and profl. devel., mentoring; presenter in field. Editor: Women in Medicine Newsletter, 1986—; contbr. articles to profl. jours. Recipient: Womens Leadership award, Amer Assoc. Med Coll., 1996, Cole award, Yale U. Physicians Assoc., 1992. Mem. Am. Arbitration Assn., Am. Med. Women's Assn., Nat. Coun. Women's Health, Calif. Caucus U. and Coll. Ombudspersons, Assn. Women Sci.(trustee, 1992-94), Coun. Concerns Women on New England Colls. and Univs., Coun. Employee Respinsibilities and Rights (mem. edit. bd. Jour. 1987), Grad. Women in Sci., Soc. Profls. Dispute Resolution, The ombudsman Assn. Office: Yale U Sch Medicine 333 Cedar St PO Box 208012 New Haven CT 06520-8012 E-mail: merle.waxman@yale.edu.

WAXMAN, RONALD, computer engineer; b. Newark, Nov. 28, 1933; s. Benjamin and Rose (Lifson) W.; m. Pearl Latterman, June 19, 1955; children: David, Roberta, Benjamin. BSEE, N.J. Inst. Tech., 1955; MEE, Syracuse U., 1963. Engr. IBM, Poughkeepsie, N.Y., 1955-56, 58-64, East Fishkill, 1964-70, Poughkeepsie and Kingston, 1970-80, sr. engr. Manassas, Va., 1980-87; prin. scientist U. Va., Charlottesville, 1987-97; cons. pvt. practice, Reston, Va., 1997—. IEEE rep. and tech. advisor to Internat. Elec. Commn. U.S. tech. activities group for internat. design automation stds., 1994-98; mem. steering com. very high speed integrated circuits hardware description lang. VHDL Users Group, 1987-91. Contbr. numerous articles to profl. jours. and tech. presentations. 1st lt. USAF, 1956-58. Fellow IEEE, IEEE Computer Soc. (bd. govs. 1989-94, 96-98, 2000-02, chmn. fellows evaluation com. 1995-96, chmn. audit com., 1997, founder, chmn. design automation stds. subcom. 1983-88, steering com. 1989—, chmn. design automation tech. com. 1988-90, steering com. 1991—, vice-chmn. tech. activities bd. 1991-92, 99, chmn. awards com. 1993, disting. visitor 1986-88, v.p. mem. activities bd. 1994, v.p. tech. activities, 1998, Meritorious Svc. cert. 1988, Disting. Svc. cert. 1994, TAB Pioneer award 1989, 3d. Millennium medal 2000), Internat. Fedn. Info. Processing Orgns. TC5 (CS rep.), Assn. for Computing Machinery (spl. interest group DA). Achievements include patents in field.

WAXMAN, SAMUEL, oncologist, researcher; b. N.Y.C., July 26, 1936; s. Leo and Sally (Berkwitz) W. BS, Cornell U., 1957; MD, SUNY Downstate Med. Ctr., 1963; Prof., Shanghai (China) 2nd Med. U., 1998. Prof. medicine Mt. Sinai Sch. Medicine, N.Y.C., 1983—, Zena and Michael Wiener prof. medicine, 1994—; co-dir. Ctr. Canter Differential Shanghai 2nd Med. U., 1998—. Bd. dirs. Israel Diaspora Inst., Jerusalem, 1986-94. 1st lt. U.S. Army, 1960-61. Recipient Magnolia award Municipality of Shanghai, 1998; inducted N.Y. Mag. Hall of Fame of Physicians, 1998. Fellow ACP, Am. Soc. Clin. Investigation; mem. Am. Soc. Hematology (counselor hepatology 1996—), Am. Assn. Cancer Rsch. (mem. internat. rels. com. 1993-96). Avocations: outdoors, golf, music, art, travel. Home: 1158 5th Ave New York NY 10029-6917 Office: Mt Sinai Med Ctr Box 1178 One Gustave Levy Pl New York NY 10029 E-mail: samuel.waxman@mssm.edu.

WAXMAN, SETH PAUL, lawyer; b. Hartford, Conn., Nov. 28, 1951; s. Felix H. and Frieda (Goodman) W.; m. Debra F. Goldberg, Mar. 20, 1977; children: Noah, Sarah, Ethan. AB summa cum laude, Harvard U., 1973; JD, Yale U., 1977. Bar: D.C. 1978, U.S. Dist. Ct. D.C., 1979, U.S. Ct. Appeals D.C Circuit, 1979, U.S. Supreme Ct. 1982, U.S. Ct. Appeals (1st cir.), 2000, (2d cir.), 1998, (3d cir.), 1983, (4th cir.), 1982, (5th cir.), 1997, (6th cir.), 1998, (7th cir.), 1998, (8th cir.), 1998, (9th cir.), 1989, (10th cir.), 1998, (11th cir.), 1989, U.S. Ct. Appeals Fed. Circuit, 1998. Law clk to Judge Gerhard A. Gesell, Washington, 1977-78; ptnr. Miller Cassidy Larroca & Lewin, 1978-94; assoc. dep. atty. gen. U.S. Dept. Justice, 1994-96, dep. solicitor gen., 1996-97, acting dep. atty. gen., 1997, solicitor gen. of the U.S., 1997-2001; partner Wilmer, Cutler & Pickering, 2001—. Disting. vis. from practice Georgetown U Law Ctr., 2001—; vis. prof. Georgetown U. Law Ctr., 2001; vis. fellow Harvard U. JFK Sch. Govt., 2001; fellow Am. Coll. Trial Lawyers, Am. Law Inst., Am. Acad. of Appellate Lawyers; dir. Supreme Ct. Inst., Georgetown U. Law Ctr.; lawyer Com. for Civil Rights Law. Prin. Coun. for Excellence in Govt.; trustee Supreme Ct. Hist. Soc.; director Nat. Found. for Jewish Culture; elected dir. Harvard Alumni Assn.; mem. com. to visit Harvard Coll. Harvard U.; trustee Bruce J. Ennis Found. Named hon. spl. agt., FBI, 2001; recipient Pro Bono Publico award, ABA, 1988, Edmund J. Randolph award, U.S. Dept. Justic, 2001, Benjamin L. Cardozo Cert. of Merit, Anti-Defamation League, 1987, Thomas Jefferson Found. medal in law, U. Va., 2002, Pursuit of Justice award, Internat. Assn. Jewish Lawyers and Jurists, 2001, Rex,Lee Advocacy Award, 2002; fellow Michael C. Rockefeller, Harvard U., 1973—74. Master: Edward Coke Appellate Inn Court; fellow: Am Acad. Appellate Attys., Am. Bar Found.; mem.: Am. Law Inst. E-mail: swaxman@wilmer.com.

WAXMAN, SHELDON ROBERT, lawyer; b. Chgo., Apr. 22, 1941; s. Henri and Ann (Sokolsky) W.; m. Katherine Slamski, Aug. 23, 1979; children: Josiah, Zoe. BA, U. Ill., 1963; JD, DePaul U., 1965. Bar: Ill. 1965, U.S. Supreme Ct. 1976, Mich. 1985. Staff atty. Argonne (Ill.) Nat. Lab., 1968-71; asst. U.S. Atty., Chgo., 1971-74; owner firm Waxman Tax & Legal Network, Chgo. and South Haven, Mich., 1976—; pres. Indecon Bus. Cons. Network, Ltd. Owner Ind. Contractor Cons. Svcs. Author: In the Teeth of the Wind, 2002; editor-in-chief New Z Letter; contbr. articles to profl. jours. Founder Freedom Lawyers of Am., People for Simplified Tax Law, Nukes to the Sun. Office: PO Box 309 South Haven MI 49090-0309

WAXSE, DAVID JOHN, judge; b. Oswego, Kans., June 29, 1945; s. I. Joseph and Mary (Poole) W.; m. Linda Schilling (div.); children: Rachel, Ryan, Rebecca; m. Judy Pfannenstiel, May 29, 1982; 1 child, Elayna. BA, U. Kans., 1967; teaching cert., Columbia U., 1968, JD, 1971. Bar: Kans. 1971, U.S. Ct. Appeals (10th cir.) 1971, U.S. Supreme Ct. 1975, U.S. Ct. Appeals (8th Cir.) 1998. Dean of students Intermediate Sch. 88, N.Y.C., 1968-70; spl. edn. tchr. Peter Cooper Sch., 1970-71; assoc. Payne & Jones, Olathe, Kans., 1971-74, ptnr., 1974-84; of counsel Shook, Hardy & Bacon, Overland Park, 1984-86, ptnr., 1986-95; shareholder Shook, Hardy & Bacon P.C., 1993-95; ptnr. Shook, Hardy & Bacon L.L.P., Kans., 1995-99; shareholder Shook, Hardy & Bacon P.C., 1993-95, v.p., asst. gen. counsel, 1995-99; U.S. magistrate judge Kansas City, 1999—. Mcpl. judge City of Shawnee, Kans., 1974-80; atty. City of DeSoto, Kans., 1972-79; adj. prof. U. Kans. Sch. Law, Lawrence, 1981-82; mem. juv. code adv. com. Kans. Jud. Coun., 1979-83, guardianship adv. com., 1982-83, atty. fees adv. com., 1986-87; mem. Civil Justice Reform Act Adv. Com., U.S. Dist. Ct. for Dist. Kans., 1991-95; mem. Kans. Commn. on Jud. Qualifications, 1992-99, vice-chmn. 1994-97, chair, 1997-99; v.p. Kans. Legal Svcs., Inc., 1980-82, pres., 1985-87; bd. advisors Kans. Coll. Advocacy, 1979-80; bd. trustees, lawyers' com. Civil Rights Under Law, 1997-99. Author: (with others) Kansas Employment Law, 1985, Litigating Employment Law Cases, 1987, Kansas Employment Law Handbook, 1991, supplements, 1992, 95, Kansas Annual Survey, 1990—. Mem. Kan. Gov.'s Adv. Com. on Criminal Justice, 1974-77; mem. Kans. Justice Commn., 1997-99; gen. counsel Western Mo. Dist. ACLU, 1976-78, 86-97, v.p., 1983-86, nat. bd. dirs., 1979-86, 91-99, chmn. children's rights com., 1980-86; mem. AIDS Pol. Network, 1987-99, med. treatment issues com., 1991-96, constn. com., 1991-99; mem. med./tech. com. AIDS Coun. Greater Kans. City, 1986-98, ethics com. consortium Midwest Bioethics Ctr., 1990—; bd. dirs. Parents Anonymous Kans., 1978-83, pres., 1979; bd. dirs., mem. fin. com. Kans. Com. for Prevention Child Abuse, 1980-83. Fellow Am. Bar Found., Kans. Bar Found.; mem. ABA (chmn. children's rights com. and family law sects. 1985-86, mem. ho. of dels. 2000—, professionalism com. 2000—), Am. Judicature Soc. (bd. dirs. 1997—, adv. com. for ctr. for judicial conduct 1997—), Kans. Bar Assn. (chmn. legal aid com. 1978-83, bd. govs. 1988—, v.p. 1996-97, pres.-elect 1997-98, pres. 1998-99, mem. ABA ho. dels. 2000—, Pres.' Outstanding Svc. award 1982), Kans. City Met. Bar Assn., Johnson County Bar Assn. (chmn. legal aid com. 1975-82, 92-96). Office: U S Courthouse 500 State Ave Rm 219 Kansas City KS 66101-2400 E-mail: judge_waxse@ksd.uscourts.gov.

WAY, BARBARA HAIGHT, dermatologist; b. Franklin, N.J., Dec. 27, 1941; d. Charles Padley and Alice Barbara (Haight) Shoemaker; m. Anthony Biden Way; children: Matthew Shoemaker Way, Sarah Shoemaker Way. AB in Music cum laude, Bryn Mawr Coll., 1962, postgrad., 1963-64; MD, U. Pa., 1968. Diplomate Am. Bd. Dermatology. Systems engr. IBM, Balt., 1962-63; mem. dean's staff Bryn Mawr (Pa.) Coll., 1963-64; med. intern U. Wis. Hosps., Madison, 1968-69, resident in dermatology, 1969-72; physician emergency rm. St. Francis Hosp., La Crosse, Wis., 1969-72, founder dept. dermatology, 1972; asst. prof. dept. dermatology Tex. Tech U. Sch. Medicine, Lubbock, 1972-73, from asst. clin. to assoc. clin. prof., 1973-74, asst. prof., assoc. chair, 1974-76, assoc. prof., chair, 1976-81, assoc. clin. prof., 1981-92; clin. prof. Tex. Tech. U. Health Scis. Ctr., 1995—, founder, dir. dermatology residency tng. program, 1978-81, pvt. practice, 1973-74, 81—; acting dir. Lubbock City Health Dept., 1982-83. Courtesy staff Covenant Hosp., Lubbock, subsect. chief, 1992, 94; courtesy staff Covenant Lakeside Hosp., Lubbock, mem. credentials com., 1990, 92, 94, 95, founding dir. phototherapy unit, 1990-91, 93, mem. exec. com., 1991, 93, 98, chief dermatology sect., 1991, 93, 98. Alumna admissions rep. Bryn Mawr Coll., 1972-75, 87-96; mem. selection com. outstanding physician Lubbock chpt. Am. Cancer Soc., 1991-94, chmn., 1991; bd. dirs. Tex. Tech. U. Med. Found., 1987-89, Double T. Connection, 1988-90. Fellow Am. Acad. Dermatology (reviewer jour.); mem. Tex. Dermatol. Soc. (chmn. roster com. 1980), Tex. Med. Assn. (mem. sexually transmitted diseases com. 1986-90, mem. coun. pub. health 1990-92, vice councillor dist. III 1992-98, councillor dist. III 1998-2000, chmn. reference com. fin. and orgnl. affairs ann. session 1992), Lubbock County-Garza County Med. Soc. (mem. various coms. 1980-2000, chmn. sch. and pub. health com. 1983, mem. bd. censors 1983-85, chair 1985, sec. 1986, v.p. 1987, liaison with Tex. Tech. U. Health Scis. Ctr. com. 1988-91, co-chmn. pub. rels. com. 1988-89, alt. Tex. Med. Assn. del. 1988-89, del. 1990-95, 98-2000, pres.-elect 1989, pres. 1990, chmn. ad hoc bylaws com. 1991-94, chmn. Hippocratic award 1991), Women's Dermatologic Soc. (founding sec.). Office: 4102 24th St Ste 201 Lubbock TX 79410-1801 Fax: 806 797-1102.

WAY, E(DWARD) LEONG, pharmacologist, toxicologist, educator; b. Watsonville, Calif., July 10, 1916; s. Leong Man and Lai Har (Shew) W.; m. Madeline Li, Aug. 11, 1944; children: Eric, Linette. BS, U. Calif., Berkeley, 1938, MS, 1940; PhD, U. Calif., San Francisco, 1942. Pharm. chemist Merck & Co., Rahway, N.J., 1942; instr. pharmacology George Washington U., 1943-46, asst. prof., 1946-48; asst. prof. pharmacology U. Calif., San Francisco, 1949-52, assoc. prof., 1952-57, prof., 1957-87, prof. emeritus, 1987—, chmn. dept. pharmacology, 1973-78. USPHS spl. rsch. fellow U. Berne, Switzerland, 1955-56, China Med. Bd.; rsch. fellow, vis. prof. U. Hong Kong, 1962-63; Sterling Sullivan disting. vis. prof. Martin Luther King U., 1982; hon. prof. pharmacology and neurosci. Guangzhou Med. Coll., 1987; mem. adv. com. Pharm. Rsch. Mfrs. Assn. Found., 1968-98; mem. coun. Am. Bur. for Med. Advancement in China, 1982; bd. dirs. Li Found., 1970—, pres., 1985-98, bd. dirs. Haight Ashbury Free Clinics, 1986-93; Tsumura prof. neuropsychopharmacology med. sch. Gunma U., Maebashi, Japan, 1989-90; sr. staff fellow Nat. Inst. on Drug Abuse, 1990-91; researcher on drug metabolism, analgetics, devel. pharmacology, drug tolerance, drug dependence and Chinese materia medica. Editor: New Concepts in Pain, 1967, (with others) Fundamentals of Drug Metabolism and Drug Disposition, 1971, Endogenous and Exogenous Opiate Agonists and Antagonists, 1979; mem. editl. bd. Clin. Pharmacology, Therapeutics, 1975-87, Drug, Alcohol Dependence, 1976-87, Progress in Neuro-Psychopharmacology, 1977-91, Research Communications in Chem. Pathology and Pharmacology, 1978-91, Alcohol and Drug Dependence, 1986-91, Asian Pacific Jour. Pharm., 1985—, Jour. Chinese Medicine, 1993—; contbr. numerous articles and revs. to profl. publs. Recipient Faculty Rsch. Lectr. award, U. Calif., San Francisco, 1974, San Francisco Chinese Hosp. award, 1976, Cultural citation and Gold medal, Ministry of Edn., Republic of China, 1978, Nathan B. Eddy award, Coll. on Problems in Drug Dependence, 1979, Chancellor's award for pub. svc., U. Calif., 1986, Disting. Alumnus award, U. Calif., San Francisco, 1990, Asian Pacific Am. Systemwide Alliance award, 1993, Lifetime Achievement award, Chinese Hist. Soc., 2001. Fellow Am. Coll. Neuropsychopharmacology (life, emeritus), Am. Coll. Clin. Pharmacology (hon.), Coll. on Problems of Drug Dependence (exec. com. 1978-92, chmn. bd. dirs. 1978-82); mem. AAAS, Am. Soc. Pharmacology, Exptl. Therapeutics (bd. editors 1957-65, pres. 1976-77, Torald Sollman award 1992), Fedn. Am. Socs. Exptl. Biology (exec. bd. 1975-79, pres. 1977-78), Am. Pharm. Assn. (life, Rsch. Achievement award 1962), AMA, Soc. Aid and Rehab. Drug Addicts (Hong Kong, life), Western Pharmacology Soc. (pres. 1963-64), Japanese Pharm. Soc. (hon.), Coun. Sci. Soc. Pres.' (exec. com. 1979-84, treas. 1980-84), Chinese Pharmacology Soc. (hon.), Academia Sinica (academician). Office: U Calif Dept Cellular and Molecular Pharmacology 1210 S San Francisco CA 94143-0001

WAY, JACOB EDSON, III, museum director; b. Chgo., May 18, 1947; s. Jacob Edson Jr. and Amelia (Evans) W.; m. Jean Ellwood Chappell, Sept. 6, 1969; children: Sarah Chappell Quiroga, Rebecca Stoddard, Jacob Edson IV. BA, Beloit Coll., 1968; MA, U. Toronto, 1971, PhD, 1978. Instr. Beloit (Wis.) Coll., 1972-73, asst. prof., 1973-80, assoc. prof., 1980-85; dir. Logan Mus. Anthropology, Beloit, 1980-85, Wheelwright Mus. Am. Indian, Santa Fe, 1985-89; interim dir. N.Mex. Mus. Natural History, Albuquerque, 1990-91; exec. dir. Space Ctr. Internat. Space Hall of Fame, Alamogordo, N.Mex., 1991-94; dir. N.Mex. Farm and Ranch Heritage Mus., 1994-99; cultural affairs officer State of N.Mex., Santa Fe, 1997—. Evaluator Nat. Park Service, Denver, 1986. Contbr. articles to profl. jours. Mem. Nuke Watch, Beloit, 1983-84; cultural affairs officer State of N.Mex., 1997—. Research grants Wis. Humanities Com., 1984, NSF, 1981; grantee Cullister Found., 1978-84; fellow U. Toronto, 1971. Mem. Am. Assn. Mus., Am. Assn. Phys. Anthropology, Can. Assn. for Phys. Anthropology, N.Mex. Assn. Mus. (pres. 1994-96), Soc. Am. Archaeology, Wis. Fedn. Mus. (adv. bd. 1982-85). Mem. Soc. Friends. Avocations: camping, skiing, fishing, reading, horseback riding. Office: Office Cultural Affairs 228 E Palace Ave Santa Fe NM 87501-2000

WAYE, JEROME D. internist, gastroenterologist; b. Sept. 22, 1932; m. Marguerite B. Waye, May 26, 1953. BS in Quantitative Biology, MIT, 1954; MD cum laude, Boston U., 1958. Diplomate Am. Bd. Internal Medicine, Am. Bd. Gastroenterology. Rotating intern Mt. Sinai Hosp., N.Y.C., 1958-59, resident in internal medicine and gastroenterology, 1959-62; clin. prof. medicine Mt. Sinai Med. Ctr., chief gastrointestinal endoscopy unit, Lenox Hill and Mt. Sinai Hosp.s, N.Y.C. Contbr. articles to profl. jours.; internat. editor Gastrointestinal Endoscopy; mem. editl. bd. Am. Jour. Gastroenterology, 1985-91, Italian Jour. Gastroenterology, 1986—, Hepato-Gastroenterology, 1988—. Fellow ACP, Am. Coll. Gastroenterology (pres. 1982-83, bd. trustees 1974-81); mem. AMA, Am. Soc. Internal Medicine, Assn. Advancement Med. Instrumentation, Am. Soc. Gastrointestinal Endoscopy (pres. 1980-81, mem. various coms., Rudolf Schindler award 1986), Am. Fedn. Clin. Rsch., others. Office: 650 Park Ave New York NY 10021-6115

WAYLAND, BRADFORD BRITTON, science educator; b. Lakewood, Ohio, Dec. 14, 1939; s. Robert Edwin and Marguerite V Wayland. AB, Case Western Res., Cleveland, OH, 1957—61; Master (hon.) , U Penn, Philadelphia, PA, 1968; PhD, U. Ill., Urbana, IL, 1961—64. Chemistry prof. U Penn, Philadelphia, Pa., 1964—. Bd. mem. and pres. U. City Hospitality Coalition, Philadelphia, Pa., 1995—2002. Recipient Phila. ACS Sect. Award, Philadelphia-American Chem. Soc., 2002. Mem.: Catalyst Soc., Am. Chem. Soc. Achievements include 130 Publications And Patents. Office: U Penn Dept Chemistry 231 S 34th St Philadelphia PA 19104 E-mail: wayland@sas.upenn.edu.

WAYLAND, RUSSELL GIBSON, JR. retired geologist, government official; b. Treadwell, Alaska, Jan. 23, 1913; s. Russell Gibson and Fanchon (Borie) W.; m. Mary Mildred Brown, 1943 (div. 1964); children: Nancy, Paul R.; m. Virginia Bradford Phillis, Dec. 24, 1965 (dec. Dec. 1995). BS, U. Wash., 1934; AM, Harvard, 1937; MS, U. Minn., 1935, PhD, 1939. Engr., geologist Homestake Mining Co., Lead, S.D., summers 1930-39; with U.S. Geol. Survey, 1939-42, 1952-80, chief conservation div., 1966-78; Washington rep. Am. Inst. Profl. Geologists, 1982-88; commr. VA Oil and Gas Conservation Bd., 1982-90. With Army-Navy Munitions Bd., 1942-45, Office Mil. Govt. and Allied High Commn., Germany, 1945-52; instr. geology U. Minn., 1937-39. Author sci. bulls. in field. Served to lt. col. AUS, 1942-46, col. CE-USAR, ret. Recipient Distinguished Service award Dept. Interior. Mem. Soc. Mining Engrs., Mineral Soc. Am., Geol. Soc. Am., Am. Inst. Profl. Geologists, Soc. Econ. Geologists, Assn. Engring. Geologists, Cosmos Club, Sigma Xi, Tau Beta Pi, Phi Gamma Delta, Sigma Gamma Epsilon, Phi Mu Alpha Sinfonia. Episcopalian. Home: 900 N Taylor St Apt 2029 Arlington VA 22203-1895

WAYLAND-SMITH, ROBERT DEAN, retired banker; b. Oneida, N.Y., July 2, 1943; s. Robert and Prudence Cragin W.-S.; m. Kathleen Anne Schultz, Aug. 24, 1968 (dec. Oct. 1999); children: Kristin, Debra. BA in Econs., U. Rochester, 1965. Mgr. equipment svc. Strong Meml. Hosp., Rochester, N.Y., 1965-67; mgmt. trainee Chase Lincoln First Bank, N.A., 1967-68, mgr. mcpl. securities, 1968-81, mgr. portfolio mgmt. depart., 1981-84, mgr. fin. and investment svc. dept., 1984-87, mgr. trust and fin. svc. dept., 1987-88; pres. and CEO Rochester region Chase Manhattan Bank, N.A., 1988-93, upstate trust and investment divsn. exec., 1993-98; ret., 1998. Mem. adv. bd. Roberts Wesleyan Coll., Rochester, 1989-99; mem. adv. coun. J.W. Jones Sch. Bus. SUNY, Geneseo, 1990-99. Trustee Ctr. for Govtl. Rsch., 1985—, Greater Rochester Visitors Assn., 1990-93, Rochester Downtown Devel. Corp., 1991-93; dir. United Neighborhood Ctrs., Greater Rochester Found., 1992—; mem. fin. execs. adv. bd. Coll. Bus. Rochester Inst. Tech., 1994—; mem. adv. bd. Help Our World Found., 1990—; mem. United Way Greater Rochester Corp., 1998—; bd. dirs. Oneida Cmty. Mansion House, 1988—, Via Health, 1999-2001; bd. govs. The Genesee Hosp., 1992-2001; chair coll. coun. SUNY Coll. Geneseo, 1999—. Fellow: Assn. for Investment Mgmt. and Rsch.; mem.: Greater Rochester Met. C. of C. (bd. dirs. 1992—95), Greater Rochester Ind. Practice Assn. (bd. dirs. 2000—), Rochester Soc. Security Analysts, Oak Hill Country Club, Genesee Valley Club. Avocations: golf, gardening, reading. Office: JP Morgan Chase One Chase Sq Rochester NY 14643 E-mail: Robert.D.Wayland-Smith@Chase.com.

WAYMAN, DAVID ANTHONY, state agency administrator; b. Feb. 8, 1950; BA in Psychology, Sangamon State U., 1980; MA in Psychology, U. Tex., 1983. Devel. dir. Travis Assn., Austin, Tex., 1980-83; market researcher Support Svcs., Springfield, Ill., 1983-85; devel. dir. Ill. Issues mag., 1985-92; exec. dir. Ill. Coalition to End Homeless, 1992-94, Ill. Coalition to End Homelessness, Springfield, 1992-94; prin. D. Anthony Wayman Consulting, 1994—. Cons. Ill. Alcoholism and Drug Dependence Assn., 1976; evaluator, expert witness various Springfield law firms, 1983-84; fundraising cons., devel. assoc. Sta. WSSU-FM Sangamon State U., Springfield, 1989-91; area rep. Aspect Found., 1991-92. Organizer presdl. campaigns of Eugene McCarthy, Springfield, 1964, George McGovern, Chgo., 1968, John Anderson, Springfield, 1980, Paul Simon, Iowa, Springfield, 1988; organizer Paul Simon for U.S. Senate campaign, 1990; organizer Ill. gubenatorial campaign for Neil Hartigan, 1990; organizer Ill. primary election campaign Rod Blagoyevich for Gov.; active Curran Twp. Dem. Ctrl. Com.; dep. voter registrar Sangamon County; coach, organizer Ill. Spl. Olympics, Springfield and Chgo., 1971-73. Democrat. Avocations: tennis, racquetball, swimming. Address: 1325 S Wabash Ave Ste 204 2 Chicago IL 60605-2500

WAYMAN, JOSEPH MCKELDEN, editor, researcher; b. Strasburg, Va., Mar. 22, 1927; s. Joseph McKelden Wayman and Cathryn Bernice Loomis. Def. contract classes, UCLA, 1964—67; BS, Va. Tech., 1952. Gen. duty assignments Am. Safety Razor Yorkville Paper Co., N.Y.C., 1952—54; statis. compiler U.S. Census Bur., Washington, 1954—56; mail distbn. U.S. Post Office, U.S. Gen. Svcs. Adminstrn., San Francisco, 1956—58; item mgr. USAF, San Bernardino, 1958—62, price analyst L.A., 1962—84; editor Grandstand Baseball Ann., Downey, Calif., 1985—. Contbr. book. With USAF, 1945—47. Mem.: Baseball Reliquary, Inc., Pacific Coast League Hist. Soc., Soc. for Am. Baseball Rsch. (pub. pitching W-L records Nat. League, 1890-1999 1996). Democrat. Methodist. Avocations: stamp collecting, walking, attending baseball functions. Office: Grandstand Baseball Ann PO Box 4203 Downey CA 90241

WAYMIRE, BONNIE GLADINE, nursing administrator; b. Williamsport, Ind., Dec. 16, 1954; d. Jackie Lee and Mary Lou (Jennings) W. LPN diploma, Danville Jr. Coll., 1978; diploma, Lakeview Sch. Nursing, 1986; BS in Bus. Mgmt., Ind. Inst. of Tech., 1996; postgrad., Lakeview Coll. Nursing. RN, Ind., Ill.; cert. vascular nurse, dir. nursing. Supr. evening shift Vermillion Manor, Danville, Ill., 1986; staff nurse, rsch. coord. VA Med. Ctr., Indpls., 1986-92; vis. nurse Vis. Nurse Svc., 1992; charge nurse Eagle Valley Health Care, 1992; dir. nursing svc. Vinewood Health Care, Plainfield, 1992-93; DON Records Autumn Care, Franklin, 1993, Bloomfield (Ind.) Health Care, 1993-94, Shakamak Good Samaritan, Jasonville, Ind., 1994-98, Provena United Samaritan Med. Ctr., 1998—2000; state long term care surveyor Ind. State Dept. Health Long Term Care Div., 2001; program dir., instr. CNA and QMA classes Nurse Aide Tng. Ctr., Indpls., 2001. Co-author: Am. Jour. Vascular Surgery, 1992. Mem.: Nat. Assn. Dirs. Nursing Adminstr. in Long Term Care, Soc. Vascular Nursing (nursing standard and practice Acte com. 1988—92), Gen. Fedn. Womens' Clubs, Plainfield Jr. Women's Club, Fedn. Women's Clubs Ind., Gen. Fedn. Women's Club Ill., Am. Legion Aux., Women of the Moose (Acad. Friendship award 1992), VFW Aux. Roman Catholic. Avocations: collecting stamps, coins and Star Trek memorabilia. Home: 6429 Atlanta Dr Indianapolis IN 46241

WAYMIRE, JOHN THOMAS, principal; b. Rensselaer, Ind., June 10, 1949; s. John Frederick and Elizabeth Ann (Pettet) W.; m. Kristi Antoinette Cerny, Oct. 4, 1975; children: John Johanson, Thomas Joseph. BS, St. Joseph's Coll., 1971; MS, Ind. U., Gary, 1976; postgrad., U. Iowa, 1978-82. Cert. tchr., adminstr., Ind., Iowa, S.D. Tchr. Kankakee Valley Schs., DeMotte, Ind., 1971-73, South Ctrl. Schs., Union Mills, 1973-78; grad. asst. U. Iowa, Iowa City, 1978-79; tchr. sci. Lincoln Community Schs., Mechanicsville, Ind., 1979-80; test editorial asst. Riverside Pub. Co., Iowa City, 1980-82; prin. elem. edn. Sully Buttes Schs., Onida, S.D., 1982-86; asst. prin. Tippecanoe Valley Schs., Mentone, Ind., 1986-90; prin. Pioneer Regional Schs., Royal Center, 1990-94, Granville Wells Sch., Jamestown, 1994—. Mem. ASCD, NAESP, S.D. Assn. Elem. Sch. Prins. (dist. rep. 1985), Ind. Assn. Sch. Prins. (charter 1992), Ind. Prin.'s Leadership Acad. (grad., exec. bd. mem. 1999—), Royal Center Lions (pres. 1992-94), Jamestown Cmty. Lions Club (pres. 1998-99), Phi Delta Kappa (pres. 1989-90). Avocations: reading, model ship building, gardening, horseback riding. Home: 425 E 500 S Lebanon IN 46052-9765 Office: 5046 S State Road 75 Jamestown IN 46147-9294

WAYNE, ALAN S. pediatric oncologist, educator; b. Dec. 8, 1958; BS in Medicine with honors, Northwestern U., 1982, MD with honors, 1984. Diplomate Am. Bd. Pediats., Am. Bd. Pediat. Hematology-Oncology. Intern in pediats. Children's Hosp., Boston, 1984-85, jr. asst. resident pediats., 1985-86, sr. asst. resident in pediats., 1986-87, chief resident in pediats., 1987-88; fellow in pediat. hematology/oncology Children's Hosp. Dana-Farber Cancer inst., 1988-91; clin. fellow in pediats. Harvard U. Sch. Medicine, Cambridge, 1984-89, rsch. fellow, 1989, instr. pediats., 1989-92; asst. prof. pediats. U. South Fla. Coll. Medicine, Tampa, 1992-95; asst. prof. clin. pathology U. Miami Sch. Medicine, 1996-98, asst. prof. clin. pediats., 1996-98, assoc. prof., 1998-99; clin. tenure track investigator pediat. oncology Nat. Cancer Inst., NIH, 1999—; clin. dir. Pediat. Oncology Br. Nat. Cancer Inst., NIH, NCI, 1999—. Mem. Sylvester Comprehensive Cancer Ctr., Miami, 1996-99; dir. pediat. bone marrow transplantation, attending physician pediat. hematology/oncology, Jackson Meml. Hosp., Miami, 1996-99. Office: Nat Cancer Inst NIH 10 Center Dr Msc 1928 Bldg 10 Bethesda MD 20892-0001 E-mail: wayne@mail.nih.gov.

WAYNE, BILL TOM, secondary school educator, coach; b. Evansville, Ind., Oct. 31, 1946; s. George William and Agnes Ledbetter W.; m. Donna Marie Agnew, Aug. 24, 1968; 1 child, Erin Marie. BS, Murray (Ky.) State U., 1971; MS, Western Ky. U., 1978. Tchr., coach Henderson County (Ky.) Sr. High Sch., 1971—. Scout Kansas City Royals, 1985—. Deacon 1st Christian Ch. Named Coach of Yr. Ky. High Sch. Big 8 Conf., 1979, 1982, 1984, 87, Baseball Coach of Yr., Ky. Coaches Assn., 2000, Coach of Yr., Ky. H.S. Baseball Coaches Assn., 2000; named to Hon. Order Ky. Cols., Ky. Baseball Hall of Fame, 1998; inducted into Ky. H.S. Baseball Coaches Assn. Baseball Hall of Fame, 1998. Mem. NEA, Ky. Edn. Assn., Ky. High Sch. Athletic Assn., Am. Baseball Coaches Assn., Ky. Baseball Coaches Assn. (pres. 1989-91, 98-99), U.S. Baseball Fedn., Nat. Hot Rod Assn., Waterfowl U.S.A, Ducks Unltd., Elks. Democrat. Avocations: deer and goose hunting, drag racing, baseball. Home: 847 Lamont Ln Henderson KY 42420-2472 Office: Henderson County Sr High Sch 2424 Zion Rd Henderson KY 42420-4713

WAYNE, EARL ANTHONY, federal agency administrator; BA, U. Calif., Berkeley; MA, Princeton U., Stanford U.; MPA, Harvard U. Joined Fgn. Svc., 1975, various positions; spl. asst. to sec. of state U.S. State Dept., 1981—83; first sec. Embassy, Paris, 1984—87; nat. security corr. Christian Sci. Monitor, 1987—89; dir. regional affairs U.S. Amb. at Large for Counter-Terrorism, 1989—91; dir. Western European affairs Nat. Security Coun., 1991—93; dep. chief mission U.S. Mission to European Union, 1993—96; dept. asst. sec. for Europe U.S. Dept. of State, 1996—97, prin. dep. asst. sec. for European affairs, 1997—2000, asst. sec. of state for econ. and bus. affairs, 2000—. Office: US Dept of State Econ and Bus Affairs Bur 2201 C St NW Washington DC 20520 Office Fax: 202-647-5713.

WAYNE, JANE O(XENHANDLER), poet, writing educator; b. St. Louis, Oct. 10, 1938; d. David Oxenhandler and Frances Rosen; m. Sam Wayne (dec. Nov. 1992); children: Ursula Claire, Justine Allegra. BA, Washington U., St. Louis, 1965, MA, 1977. Tchr. creative writing Webster U., St. Louis, 1981-88, 92-94, Washington U., 1996-99. Author: (poetry) Looking Both Ways, 1984 (Devins award 1985), A Strange Heart, 1996 (Marianne Moore award 1995). Recipient Devins award for poetry U. Mo. Press, 1985, Poetry award Soc. Midland Authors, 1996. Home: 6376 Washington Ave Saint Louis MO 63130-4705 E-mail: jowayne@inlink.com.

WAYNE, JEANETTE MARIE, auditor; b. Mt. Clemens, Mich., Apr. 17, 1965; d. Robert Thomas W. and Sharon Elaine (Mominee) Nole; m. Ronald Edward Klicki, Sept. 14, 1985 (div. Oct. 1989). Asst. mgr. Little Caesars, Mt. Clemens, Mich., 1981-83, Cheese & Co., Birmingham, 1984; courier Chevrolet, Detroit, 1984; libr. EDS Chevorlet, 1985-86, migration specialist, 1987; software support EDS Saturn, Troy, 1988-89, ops. tech., 1990-93; ops. tech. cons. EDS Tech. Architecture, Plano, Tex., 1993-2000; sr. auditor EDS Corp. Audit, 1997-2000, program mgr., 2000—. Program mgr. Bus. Process Leadership SAP Deployment. Republican. Office: EDS 5400 Legacy Dr Plano TX 75024-3199

WAYNE, KYRA PETROVSKAYA, writer; b. Crimea, USSR, Dec. 31, 1918; came to U.S., 1948, naturalized, 1951; d. Prince Vasily Sergeyevich and Baroness Zinaida Fedorovna (Fon-Haffenberg) Obolensky; m. George J. Wayne, Apr. 21, 1961; 1 child, Ronald George. BA, Leningrad Inst. Theatre Arts, 1939, MA, 1940. Actress, concert singer, USSR, 1939-46; actress U.S., 1948-59; enrichment lectr. Royal Viking Line cruises, Alaska-Can., Greek Islands-Black Sea, Russia/Europe, 1978-79, 81-82, 83-84, 86-8, 88. Author: Kyra, 1959, Kyra's Secrets of Russian Cooking, 1960, 93, The Quest for the Golden Fleece, 1962, Shurik, 1971, 92, The Awakening, 1972, The Witches of Barguzin, 1975, Max, The Dog That Refused to Die, 1979 (Best Fiction award Dog Writers Assn. Am. 1980), Rekindle the Dreams, 1979, Quest For Empire, 1986, Li'l Ol' Charlie, 1989, Quest For Bigfoot, 1996, Pepper's Ordeal, 2000. Founder, pres. Clean Air Program, L.A. County, 1971-72; mem. women's coun. KCET-Ednl. TV, Monterey County Symphony Guild, 1989-91, Monterey Bay Aquarium, Monterey Peninsula Mus. Art, Friends of La Mirada, Fresno Art Mus., Fresno Met. Mus., Valley Children's Hosp. Served to lt. Russian Army, 1941-43. Decorated Red Star, numerous other decorations USSR; recipient award Crusade for Freedom, 1955-56; award L.A. County, 1972, Merit award Am. Lung Assn. L.A. County, 1988, Award of Merit The Congress of Russian Ams., 1999. Mem. PEN, Soc. Children's Book Writers, Authors Guild, UCLA Med. Faculty Wives (pres. 1970-71, dir. 1971-75) UCLA affiliates (life), L.A. Lung Assn. (life), Friends of the Lung Assn. (pres. 1988), Carmel Music Soc. (bd. dirs. 1992-94), Idyllwild Sch. Music, Art and Theatre Assn. (trustee 1987), Los Angelenos Club (life), Fresno Philharmonic, Club 25. Home: 561 E Mariners Cir Fresno CA 93720-0848 *Personal philosophy: I believe in total loyalty. Loyalty to one's family and friends, to one's colleagues and to one's country. In my case - to my chosen country, the U.S.A.*

WAYNE, MARVIN ALAN, emergency medicine physician; b. Detroit, Dec. 11, 1943; s. Jack I. and Marian M. (Berk) W.; m. Joan A. Tobin, Dec. 30, 1971; children: Michelle, Dana. MD, U. Mich., 1968. Diplomate Am. Bd. Emergency Medicine. Fellow St. Bartholomew's Hosp., London, 1968, Virginia Mason Hosp., Seattle, 1973-74; resident in surgery U. Colo. Med. Ctr., Denver, 1968-71; pvt. practice Bellingham, Wash., 1974—; staff emergency dept. St. Joseph's Hosp. (merger St. Joseph's Hosp. and St. Luke's Hosp.), 1974—, vice chmn. dept. emergency medicine, 1980-83, chmn., 1984-86; med. dir. Emergency Med. Svcs., 1975—; assoc. clin. prof. sch. medicine U. Wash., Seattle, 1986—; asst. clin. prof. Yale U. Sch. of Medicine, New Haven. Vice chmn. emergency med. svcs. com. State of Wash., 1982-83, chmn., 1983-86; med. dir. Med-Flight Helicopter, 1980—, Inst. for Pre-Hosp. Medicine, 1980—; pres. Whatcom County Emergency Med. Svcs. Coun., 1979; med. advisor Mt. Baker Ski Patrol; spkr. nat. and internat. edn. programs; founder, owner Dr. Cookie Inc., Edmonds, Wash., 1985—. Contbr. articles to med. jours. Bd. dirs. YMCA, Bellingham, 1980-84. Maj. M.C., U.S. Army, 1971-73, Vietnam. Recipient Outstanding Achievement award Whatcom County Emergency Med. Svcs. Coun., 1980, Outstanding Ednl. Achievement award Abbott Labs., 1982, Outstanding Advanced Life Support System award State of Wash., 1983, Emergency Med. Svc. rsch. award Wash. Assn. Emergency Med. Technicians and Paramedics, 1983. Fellow Am. Coll. Emergency Physicians (bd. dirs. Wash. chpt. 1977-84, pres. 1978, sci. meetings com. 1984, Outstanding Ednl. Achievement award 1982), Royal Soc. Medicine (Eng.); mem. Wash. State Med. Soc. (emergency med. svc. adv. com. 1978--), Whatcom County Med. Soc., Univ. Assn. for Emergency Medicine, Soc. Critical Care Medicine, Am. Trauma Soc. (founding), Nat. Assn. Emergency Med. Svc. Physicians, Am. Soc. Automotive Medicine, Nat. Assn. Emergency Med. Technicians. Avocations: sailing, windsurfing, skiing, baking. Office: Emergency Med Svcs 1800 Broadway Bellingham WA 98225-3133

WAYNE, NEIL RUSSELL, investment management company executive; b. N.Y.C., May 18, 1942; s. Paul Victor and Sylvia Lynette (Benjamin) W.; m. Monica Harriet Gilbert, Oct. 7, 1984; 1 child, Brittany Megan. BA, Hofstra U., 1963, MBA, 1969. Registered investment adviser. Mng. editor Value Line Investment Survey, N.Y.C., 1966-90; chief investment officer Heine Mgmt. Group, Westport, Conn., 1990-95; pres. Sound Asset Mgmt. Inc., 1995—; mng. prin. Capital Internat., 1998—99. Mng. dir. Advisors Internat., Westport, 1997-99. Contbr. articles. Bd. dirs. Western Advs. for Gifted Edn., Weston, Conn., 1996-97; coach Weston Babe Ruth Softball, 1997-2000. Avocations: woodworking, wine, travel, gardening, photography. Home: 5 Glen Ln Weston CT 06883-2308 Office: Sound Asset Mgmt Inc 3 Sylvan Rd S Westport CT 06880-4642

WAYNE, ROBERT JONATHAN, lawyer, educator; b. Fresno, Calif., Apr. 4, 1951; s. William W. and Blanche Wayne; m. Dorothy A. Madden, Oct. 23, 1981; children: Daniel, Julia. BS, U. Oreg., 1971; JD, UCLA, 1974. Bar: Calif. 1974, Wash. 1975, U.S. Dist. Ct. (we. dist.) Wash. 1975, U.S. Ct. Appeals (9th and D.C. cirs.) 1975, U.S. Supreme Ct. 1979. Law clk. U.S. Ct. Appeals (D.C. cir.), 1974-75; assoc. Perkins, Coie, Stone, Olsen & Williams, Seattle, 1975-76; dep. prosecutor King County Prosecutor's Office, 1976-78; pvt. practice, 1978—. Instr. trial advocacy U. Wash., Seattle, 1977—; instr. trial advocacy Nat. Inst. Trial Advocacy, Seattle, 1979—, asst. team leader, 1990, team leader, 1991-2002, team leader nat. session, 1993, program dir. N.W. region, 1998—; lectr. implementing technology in trials. Mem. ATLA, NACDL (life, chmn. lawyers assistance strike force 1993-94), Wash. State Trial Lawyers Assn. (chmn. tort sect. 1983-85), Wash. State Bar Assn. (chmn. criminal law sect. 1982-83, 86-87, exec. com. 1980-88), Seattle-King County Bar Assn. (jud. screening com. 1988-91), Wash. Assn. Criminal Def. Lawyers (founder, bd. govs. 1986-89, 99-2001, chmn. lawyers assistance strike force 1986-90, 91-93, chmn. ann. meeting 1989-90, 2001), Order of Coif, Order of Barristers. Avocations: skiing, flying. Office: 2110 N Pacific St Ste 100 Seattle WA 98103-9181 E-mail: bwayne@trialsnw.com.

WAYNE, STEPHEN J. lectr., writer, educator; b. N.Y.C., Mar. 22, 1939; s. Arthur G. and Muriel Wayne; m. Cheryl Beil, May 22, 1982; children: Jared B., Jeremy B. BA with honors, U. Rochester, 1961; MA, Columbia U., 1963, PhD, 1968. Instr. polit. sci. U.S. Naval Postgrad. Sch., 1963-65; instr. politics and govt. Ohio Wesleyan U., 1966-68; asst. prof. to prof. polit. sci. and pub. affairs The George Washington U., 1968—88; prof. govt. Georgetown U., Washington, 1989—. Presenter and lectr. in field. Author: The Legislative Presidency, 1978, The Road to the White House, 1980, 6th postelection edit., 2001, (with George C. Edwards) Presidential Leadership: Politics and Policy Making, 1985, 6th edit., 2002 (with Cal MacKenzie, David O'Brien and Richard L. Cole) The Politics of American Government, 1995, 3d edit., 1999, Is This Any Way to Run a Democratic Election?, 2002; editor: Investigating the American Political System: Problems, Methods, and Projects, 1974, (with George C. Edwards) Studying the Presidency, 1983, (with Clyde Wilcox) The Quest for National Office, 1992, (with Wilcox) The Election of the Century and What It Tells Us About the Future of American Politics, 2002, (with Clyde Wilcox) The Election of the Century; appeared on 3 one-hour programs on presidency Every Four Years, sta. WHYY-TV, PBS, 1980; election night analyst ARD-German TV, 1992; adv. editor Polit. Sci. McGraw Hill Coll. Divsn., 1982—; series editor Am. Political Institutions and Pub. Policy, M. E. Sharpe, Inc., 1990—; contbr. numerous articles, chpts. and book revs. to books and profl. jours. Office: Georgetown U Dept Govt 37th And O NW Washington DC 20057-0001

WAYTE, ALAN (PAUL WAYTE), lawyer; b. Huntington Park, Calif., Dec. 30, 1936; s. Paul Henry and Helen Lucille (McCarthy) W.; m. Beverly A. Bruen, Feb. 19, 1959 (div. 1972); children: David Alan, Lawrence Andrew, Marcia Louise; m. Nancy Kelly Wayte, July 5, 1975. AB, Stanford U., 1958, JD, 1960. Bar: Calif. 1961, U.S. Dist. Ct. (so. dist.) Calif. 1961, U.S. Supreme Ct. 1984. Ptnr. Adams, Duque & Hazeltine, Los Angeles, 1966-85, Dewey Ballantine, Los Angeles, 1985—. Mem. L.A. County Bar Assn. (chmn. real property sect. 1981-82), Am. Coll. Real Estate Lawyers (bd. govs. 1989—, pres. 1994), Am. Coll. Mortgage Attys., Anglo-Am. Real Property Inst. (bd. govs. 1989-91), L.A. Philharm. Assn. (exec. com. bd. dirs. 1973—), Chancery Club, Calif. Club (L.A.), Valley Hunt Club (Pasadena). Home: 1745 Orlando Rd Pasadena CA 91106-4131 Office: Dewey Ballantine 333 S Hope St Los Angeles CA 90071-1406 E-mail: awayte@deweyballantine.com.

WAZ, JOSEPH WALTER, JR. government relations consultant, author; b. Meriden, Conn., Jan. 13, 1953; s. Joseph Walter and Rose Marie (Barillaro) W.; m. Ann Stookey, Sept. 25, 1981; 1 child, Joseph W. III. AB, Boston U., 1975; JD, U. Conn., 1978. Bar: Conn. 1978; D.C. 1979, U.S. Ct. Appeals D.C. 1980. Dep. dir. Telecommunications Research and Action Ctr., Washington, 1979-82; sr. assoc. govt. rels. Wexler, Reynolds, Harrison & Schule, Inc., 1983-86; gen. counsel Wexler, Reynolds, Fuller, Harrison & Schule, Inc., 1986-90, ptnr., 1989-90; sr. v.p. The Wexler Group, a unit of Hill and Knowlton, Inc., Washington, 1990-92, exec. v.p., 1993—; gen. counsel The Wexler Group, 1990—. Author (with S. Simon): Reverse The Charges, 1983 (Book of the Month Club pro bono selection 1983); editor Telematics jour., The Computer Lawyer; contbr. articles to communications trade publs. Polit. broadcasting advisor Californians for Recycling and Litter Clean-up, L.A., 1982, Dukakis for Pres. Campaign, Boston, 1987-88; comm. policy advisor Clinton/Gore campaign, 1992; founding trustee FCBA Found., treas., 1992-93; mem. Montgomery County Alcohol and Other Drug Abuse Adv. Commn., 1993—. Mem. ABA (steering com., electronic media div., forum com. on communications), D.C. Bar Assn., Fed. Communications Bar Assn. (chmn. CLE and legislation coms.). Democrat. Avocations: music, travel, team sports. Home: 46 Summit St Philadelphia PA 19118-2833 Office: The Wexler Group 1317 F St NW Ste 600 Washington DC 20004-1157

WAZEN, JACK JOSEPH, otolaryngologist, educator; b. Beirut, Sept. 9, 1954; BS in Biology with Distinction, Am. U. Beirut, 1974, MD, 1978. Intern Am. U. Beirut Hosp., 1977-78, resident in otolaryngology, 1978-79, resident in gen. surgery, 1979-80; resident in otolaryngology Columbia Presbyn. Med. Ctr., N.Y., 1980-83; fellow in otology, neurotology Ear Rsch. Found. Fla., Sarasota, 1983-84; asst. prof. dept. speech and lang. pathology Columbia U., N.Y.C., 1984, course dir. otolaryngology, 1984-90, asst. prof., 1984-90, assoc. prof., 1990—, assoc. dir. clin. affairs dept. otolaryngology-head & neck surgery, 1996-98, med. dir. speech & hearing dept.; assoc. prof. clin. otolaryngology/neurol. surgery Columbia Presbyn. Med. Ctr., 1995—; chief neurotology-skull base surgery Lenox Hill Hosp., 1999—; pres. Rsch. Inst. for Hearing and Balance Disorders, 1999—. Assoc. attending physician Columbia Presbyn. Med. Ctr., N.Y.C., 1990—, asst. attending physician, 1984-90, dir. divsn. neurotology, 1984-88, dir. otology-neurotology, 1988-98, pres. rsch. inst. for hearing and balance disorders, 1999—; cons. dept. otolaryngology Englewood (N.J.) Hosp., 1991—, attending physician, Lenox Hill Hosp., NYC, 1998—, chief neurotology skull base surgery, 1999—. Contbr. articles to profl. jours.; mem. editorial rev. bd. Otolaryngology: Head and Neck Surgery, 1991—, Internat. Tinnitis Jour. Rsch. grantee N.Y. Ear Found., 1990. Fellow Am. Acad. Otolaryngology Head and Neck Surgery, Am. Neurotology Soc., ACS; mem. AMA, N.Y. Acad. Sci., Deafness Rsch. Found., Assn. for Rsch. in Otolaryngology, Ear Rsch. Found., N.Y. Acad. Medicine, N.Y. Otological Soc., Soc. Univ. Otolaryngologists Head and Neck Surgeons, Am. Laryngological, Rhinological and Otological Soc, Inc., Am. Otological Soc. Office: Columbia Presbyn Med Ctr 161 Fort Washington Ave New York NY 10032-3713

WAZONTEK, STELLA CATHERINE, computer programmer, analyst, software engineer; b. Bethlehem, Pa., Feb. 17, 1961; d. Edward Walter and Stella Bernice (Stankus) W. BS in Computer Sci., Moravian Coll., 1983; MS in Computer Sci., N.J. Inst. Tech., 1989; postgrad., LaSalle U., 1991—. Software engr. RCA Aerospace GE, Moorestown, N.J., 1983-87; sr. programmer, analyst Paramax Corp., Warminster, Pa., 1987-93; sr. systems analyst Unisys Corp., Blue Bell, 1993—. Mem. IEEE, Assn. for Computing Machinery (treas. student chpt. 1982-83), Upsilon Pi Epsilon. Republican. Roman Catholic. Avocations: horseback riding, hiking, reading, softball. Home: 2126 Barley Dr Quakertown PA 18951-3875

WAZZAN, A(HMED) R(ASSEM) FRANK, engineering educator, dean; b. Lattakia, Syria, Oct. 17, 1935; married, 1959; 3 children. BS, U. Calif., Berkeley, 1959, MS, 1961, PhD in Engring. Sci., 1963. From asst. prof. to assoc. prof. engring. UCLA, 1962-69, prof. engring. and applied sci., 1974—, assoc. dean Henry Samueli Sch. Engring. and Applied Sci., 1981-86, dean Henry Samueli Sch. Engring. and Applied Sci., 1986—2001. Cons. McDonnell Douglas Corp., 1962-71, Lawrence Radiation Lab., 1965-67, Westinghouse Electric Corp., 1974-76, N.Am. Aviation, 1975-78, Rand Corp., 1975—; Honeywell Corp., 1976-78; vis. scholar Electricité de France, Paris, Office of Commr. Atomic Energy, Saclay, France, 1973-79. Reviewer Applied Mech. Rev., 1971-87. Guggenheim fellow, 1966. Fellow Am. Nuclear Soc. Achievements include research in modeling of fuel elements for fast breeder reactor, stability and transition of laminar flows, thermodynamics of solids and of dense gases, and thermal hydraulics of pressurized water reactors. Office: UCLA Henry Samueli Sch Engring Sci Box 951592 6288 Boelter Hall Los Angeles CA 90095-1592

WEADON, DONALD ALFORD, JR. lawyer; b. Brisbane, Australia, Sept. 15, 1945; arrived in U.S., 1946; s. Donald Alford and Ellen Martha (Salisbury) Weadon; m. Suzanne Hayden Cameron, Sept. 9, 1995. BA, Cornell U., 1967; JD, U. Calif., 1975; MBA, Harvard U., Iran Ctr. Mgmt. Studies, Tehran, 1976. Bar: Calif. 1976, D.C. 1988. Assoc. Hancock, Rothert & Bunshoft, San Francisco, 1977-80; ptnr. Bryan, Cave, McPheeters & McRoberts, Washington, 1980-83; ptnr., head internat. dept. Anderson Baker Kill & Olick, 1983-84; sr. ptnr. Weadon & Assocs., 1984—. Adj. prof. internat. law Golden Gate U., San Francisco, 1979—82, George Mason U., Arlington, Va., 1989—; spkr., cons. U.S. Dept. Commerce, 1980—83; cons. Internat. Mktg. Assn., 1980—, Sci. Apparatus Mfg. Assn., 1983—, Valve Mfrs. Assn., 1983—; internat. counsel Am. Electronics Assn., 1986—. Contbr. articles to profl. jours. Trustee coun. Cornell U., 2000—. Lt. comdr. USNR, 1968—72. Named Cornell U. Disting. Alumnus, 2000. Mem.: ABA (chmn. China trade law com. 1982—84, chmn. software and tech. data com. 1983—85), Press Club, Harvard Club, Savage Club, Met. Club, Olympic Club, Sovereign Mil. Order Temple Jerusalem (Grand Cross, Order Merit), Delta Kappa Epsilon (alumni pres. 1997—, nat. bd. dirs. 1998—). Episcopalian. Office: Weadon & Assocs Internat House 3338 N St NW Washington DC 20007

WEAGLEY, ROBERT OTIS, finance educator, financial planner; b. Kansas City, Mo., Apr. 18, 1952; s. Robert Jr. and Margaret (Davidson) W.; m. Pamela Norum, May 26, 1984; children: Daniel Robert, Julianne Nicole, James

Stephen. BS with honors, U. Mo., Columbia, 1974, MS, 1976; PhD, Cornell U., 1985. CFP. Lectr. Mt. St. Vincent U., Halifax, N.S., Can., 1976-78, U. Calif., Davis 1980; investment advisor Sundvold Capitol Mgmt., Columbia, Mo., 1999—; assoc. prof., chair U. Mo., 1984—, chair faculty coun., 1998-99. Author: Personal Finance Workbook, 1996, rev. edit., 2000; contbr. articles to profl. jours. including Jor. Consumer Affairs, Fin. Counseling and Planning, Home Econs. Rsch. Jour. Mem. Columbus 2000-II, Columbia, 1993-94; pres. Univ. YMCA, Columbia, 1993-2000. Grantee Divsn. Family Svcs., 1993. Mem. Am. Coun. Consumer Interests (chair fin. com. 1990-93), Am. Econs. Assn., Acad. Fin. Svcs. (v.p. mktg. 2002—), Assn. Fin. Counseling and Planning Edn. (treas. 1990-93), Resource Advisors Coun. (chair 1998-2002), Strategic Planning Advisor Coun., Rotary. Methodist. Avocations: running, fishing, whitewater canoeing, photography, skiing. Home: 1701 Oakwood Ct Columbia MO 65203 Office: U Mo 239 Stanley Hall Columbia MO 65211 E-mail: weagleyr@missouri.edu.

WEAGRAFF, PATRICK JAMES, psychology educator, writer; b. Buffalo, May 27, 1940; s. Harry Edward and Donnabelle (O'Brien) W.; children from a previous marriage: Michael, Patrick Jr., Kim Marie, Susan Lynn; m. Sandra Weagraff, Sept. 19, 1993; 1 stepchild, Nicholas Turner. BS, SUNY, Buffalo, 1963; MEd, U. Md., 1965; EdD, UCLA, 1970, PhD, 1971. Cert. psychology, post secondary edn., secondary edn., ednl. adminstrn., drug and alcohol counseling. Assoc. dir. U.S. Peace Corps, Lagos, Nigeria, 1965-68; ednl. adminstr. Calif. Dept. Edn., Sacramento, 1971-75; assoc. commr. edn. Mass. Dept. Edn., Boston, 1975-76; psychologist Sierra View Mental Health, Auburn, Calif., 1978-81; chief clin. svcs. Calif. Dept. Mental Health, Sacramento, 1981-93; clin. dir. St. Joseph's Hosp., Stockton, Calif., 1993-95; prof. psychology Profl. Sch. Psychology, Sacramento, 1993-98; assoc. prof. Nat. U., Stockton, Calif., 1983-99; mng. SP Behavioral Health LLC. Author 9 books including Careers in Focus, 1993, Communications, 1993, Public Service Occupations, 1993, Construction Occupations, 1993, Decision Making, 1995, Making Decisions Work, 1997. Trustee Crossroads Inc., Sacramento, 1982-90; bd. dirs. Golden Empire Scouts, Sacramento, 1985-91; trustee Western Inst. Therapeutic Studies, 1996—. Edn. Profession Devel. Act fellow UCLA, 1970. Mem. Phi Delta Kappa, Epsilon Pi Tau. Jewish. Avocation: classic cars. Home: PO Box 25756 Miami FL 33102-5756 E-mail: p.j.weagraff@yahoo.com.

WEAKLAND, REMBERT G. archbishop; b. Patton, Pa., Apr. 2, 1927; s. Basil and Mary (Kane) W. AB, St. Vincent Coll., Latrobe, Pa., 1948, DD (hon.), 1963, LHD (hon.), 1987; MS in Piano, Juilliard Sch. Music, 1954; grad. studies sch. music, Columbia U., 1954-56, PhD in Musicology, 2000; LHD (hon.), Duquesne U., 1964, Belmont Coll., 1964, Cath. U. Am., 1975, Xavier U., Cin., 1988, DePaul U., 1989, Loyola U., New Orleans, 1991, Villanova U., 1992, Dayton U., 1993, Marian Coll., Fond du Lac, Wis., 1995, St. Anselm Coll., Manchester, N.H., 1996, St. Norbert Coll., De Pere, Wis., 1996, U. San Francisco, 1997, Scholastica Coll., 1998; HHD (hon.), St. Ambrose U., Davenport, 1990, Aquinas Inst. Theology, St. Louis, 1991, St Mary's Coll., Notre Dame, Ind., 1994; LLD (hon.), Cardinal Stritch Coll., Milw., 1978, Marquette U., 1981, Loyola U., Chgo., 1986, U. Notre Dame, 1987, Mt. Mary Coll., Milw., 1989, John Carroll U., Cleve., 1992, Fairfield U., 1994; D of Sacred Music (hon.), St. Joseph's Coll., Rensselaer, Ind., 1979; DST (hon.), Jesuit Sch. Theology, Berkeley, Calif., 1989, St. John's U., Collegeville, Minn., 1991, Santa Clara U., 1991, Yale U., 1993; DD (hon.), Lakeland Coll., Sheboygan, 1991, Ill. Benedictine Coll., Lisle, Ill., 1992, Regis Coll., Toronto, 1993, Trinity Coll., Hartford, 1996, Trinity Lutheran Sem., Columbus, Ohio, 1998; D of Ministry (hon.), Catholic Theol. Union, Chgo., 1999. Joined Benedictines, Roman Cath. Ch., 1945, ordained priest, 1951. Mem. faculty music dept. St. Vincent Coll., 1957-63, chmn., 1961-63, chancellor chmn. of bd. of Coll., 1963-67; elected co-adjutor archabbot, 1963; abbot primate Benedictine Confederation, 1967-77; archbishop of Milw., 1997—2002. Mem. Ch. Music Assn. Am. (pres. 1964-66), Am. Guild Organists. Office: PO Box 070912 Milwaukee WI 53207-0912

WEAKLEY, CLARE GEORGE, JR. insurance executive, theologian, entrepreneur; b. Dallas, Apr. 14, 1928; s. Clare George and Louise (Cunningham) W.; children: Clare George III, Carol J., Charles E.; m. Jean C. Burrow, July 20, 1962. BBA, So. Meth. U., 1948, ThM, 1967. Ordained min. Christian Cmty., 1967. With Employers Ins., Dallas, 1948-52; owner Weakley & Co., 1952-2001. Founder, pres. Am. Svc. Found., Inc., 1967—, Small Bus. Assn., Inc., 1988—; vis. prof. western bus. theory and Christian ethics Internat. Mgmt. Inst. (formerly Leningrad Internat. Mgmt. Inst.), St. Petersburg, Russia, 1990—; founder, leader The Christian Cmty., internat. ch. on World Wide Web. Author: In God We Trust, 1997, God 101, 1998; author, editor: The Wesley Library Series for Today's Reader, The Nature of the Kingdom, 1976, The Nature of Spiritual Growth, 1977, The Nature of Revival, 1987, The Nature of Salvation, 1988, The Nature of Holiness, 1988. Republican. Home: 13731 Goldmark Dr Apt 1207 Dallas TX 75240-4220 Office: Christian Cmty PO Box 836961 Richardson TX 75083-6961

WEAKLEY-JONES, BARBARA ANN, forensic pathologist, educator; b. Louisville, June 29, 1950; d. Sam D. Weakley and Lolita N. Snodgrass; m. W. Scott Jones, May 20, 1976; 2 children. AA, Stephens Coll., Columbia, Mo., 1970; BS, U. Louisville, 1973, MD, 1977. Diplomate in anat. pathology and forensic pathology Am. Bd. Pathology. V.p. Lab. Physicians, Louisville, 1988—. Fellow Am. Acad. Forensic Scis.; mem. Nat. Acad. Med. Examiners, Jefferson County Med. Soc. (judicial counsel mem. 1996—). Democrat. Home: 1898 Tyler Ln Louisville KY 40205-2817 Office: Medical Examiners Office 810 Barret Ave Louisville KY 40204-1782

WEAMER, ALAN PHILIP, family practice physician; b. Detroit, Apr. 22, 1948; s. Philip Edwin and Margaret Elizabeth (Schrubbe) W.; m. Jean Elinor Peters, June 14, 1975; children: Elizabeth Ann, Rebecca Lynn. BA in Zoology with high distinction, U. Mich., 1970, MD, 1974. Diplomate Am. Bd. Family Practice. Resident in family practice St. Joseph Hosp., Flint, Mich., 1974-77; family physician pvt. practice, Davison, 1977—. Mem. faculty St. Joseph Hosp. Family Practice Residency Program, Flint, Mich., 1977-87, chmn. bylaws com., 1991-95; clin. prof. Mich. State U., Flint, 1980—; bd. dirs. Genesys Ind. Group Practice, Inc.; sec., treas. Wheelock Hosp., Goodrich, Mich., 1982-85. Organist: Frequent recitals in Flint, Mich. area, 1977—; contbr. articles to Genesee County Med. Bull. Asst. organist Court St. United Meth. Ch., Flint, Mich., 1975—; organist Lessons and Carols St. Paul's Episcopal Ch., Flint, 1985—; vol. Genesee Free Clinic, Flint, 1993—. Mem. AMA, Mich. State Med. Soc. (mem. bioethics com. 1993-95, 97—), Genesee County Med. Soc. (chmn. bioethics com. 1994—), Am. Acad. Family Practice, Am. Guild Organists, Phi Beta Kappa. Avocations: organist, pianist, travel, choral singing. Office: 8020 Davison Rd Davison MI 48423-2029 E-mail: aweamer@genesyspho.com.

WEAN, BLANCHE MCNEELY, accountant; b. Monroe County, Ind., Jan. 28, 1901; d. Homer Clark and Ruth Jane (Tutterrow) McNeely; m. Francis Willard Wean, June 16, 1926 (dec.); children: Jane, Doris, Ruth. BA, Ind. U., 1923, MA, 1932, postgrad., 1945-46. CPA, Ind. Tchr. Mt. Carroll (Ill.) High Sch., 1918-19, Bloomington (Ind.) High Sch., 1923-26, Jefferson High Sch., Lafayette, Ind., 1923-26; head bus. dept. Cen. Normal Coll., Danville, 1931-47; acct. Wean Acctg., 1947-80, Wean, Andrews & Co., Danville, 1980—. Author: Blanche Accountant, 1996. Mem. Danville Pub. Libr. Bd., 1969-82, treas. Recipient John F. Jenner III Citizenship award, 1972. Mem. Nat. Assn. Pub. Accts., Ind. Pub. Accts. Assn. (pres. 1977-78, 89, Hall of Fame), Danville C. of C. (sec. 1950-75), Bus. and Profl. Womens Assn., Beta Gamma Sigma. Republican. Achievements include being the first woman to be admitted to Sch. of Commerce, Ind. U., 1922. Home and Office: 395 W State Road 45 Morgantown IN 46160-8816

WEARLY, WILLIAM LEVI, business executive; b. Warren, Ind., Dec. 5, 1915; s. Purvis Gardner and Ethel Ada (Jones) W.; m. Mary Jane Riddle, Mar. 8, 1941; children: Patricia Ann, Susan, William Levi, Elizabeth. BS, Purdue U., 1937, Dr Engring. (hon.), 1959. Student career engr. C.A. Dunham Co., Michigan City, Ind., 1936; mem. elec. design staff Joy Mfg. Co., Franklin, Pa., 1937-39, v.p., gen. sales mgr., 1952-56, exec. v.p., 1956-57, pres., dir., 1957-62; v.p., dir. Ingersoll-Rand Co., 1964-66, exec. v.p., 1966-67, chmn., chief exec. officer, 1967-80, chmn. exec. com., 1981-85. Dir. ASA Ltd., Med. Care Am.; trustee LMI; speaker engring. groups. Author tech. publs. relating to mining; patentee in field. Bd. dirs. Boys Clubs Am. Mem. NAE, IEEE, AIME, Nat. Acad. of Engring., C. of C., Sky Club N.Y.C., Blind Brook Golf Club, Desert Forest Golf Club, Minikahda Club, Ariz. Club, Masons, Shriners, Eta Kappa Nu, Tau Beta Pi, Beta Theta Pi. Republican. Methodist. also: 1 Milbank Ave Apt 11F Greenwich CT 06830-5767 also: PO Box 1072 Carefree AZ 85377-1072

WEARN, WILSON CANNON, retired media executive; b. Newberry, S.C., Oct. 7, 1919; s. George F. and Mary (Cannon) W.; m. Mildred Colson, Feb. 21, 1948; children: Jean Wearn Held, Joan Wearn Gilbert, Wilson Cannon Jr. B.E.E., Clemson U., 1941. Engr. Westinghouse Electric Corp., Pitts., 1941, FCC, Washington, 1946-48; assoc. cons. electronic engr. firm Weldon & Carr, 1948-50; ptnr. Vandivere, Cohen & Wearn (cons. engrs.), 1950-53; with Multimedia Broadcasting Co., Greenville, S.C., 1953-68, organizer of corp., 1953, became corp. officer, 1960, pres., 1966-77, Multimedia, Inc., Greenville, 1977-81, chief exec. officer, 1978-84, chmn. bd., 1981-89, chmn. emeritus, 1989-95. Instr. electronic engring. Clemson U., 1946. Mem. S.C. Hosp. Adv. Council, 1969-71; bd. dirs. Family and Children Service of Greenville County, 1967-69, pres., 1969; bd. dirs. Newspaper Advt. Bur., 1981-85; trustee Greenville Symphony Assn., 1960-62, 71-77, pres., 1977; trustee Greenville Hosp. System, 1964-70, chmn., 1968-70; trustee Broadcast Rating Council, 1969-73, chmn., 1971-73; trustee Clemson U. Found., 1973-79, pres., 1979; trustee Presbyn. Coll., F.W. Symmes Found. Served to capt. Signal Corps, AUS, 1941-45, PTO. Decorated Bronze Star; recipient Outstanding Alumni award Clemson U., 1972 Mem. Nat. Assn. Broadcasters (chmn. bd. 1975-77), S.C. Broadcasters Assn. (pres. 1967), Greater Greenville C. of C. (pres. 1972), Nat. Assn. Securities Dealers (bd. govs. 1985-88), Kiwanis (Greenville), Poinsett Club (Greenville), Green Valley Country Club (Greenville), Augusta (Ga.) Nat. Golf Club. Presbyterian (elder).

WEART, SPENCER RICHARD, historian; b. Detroit, Mar. 8, 1942; s. Spencer Augustus and Janet (Streng) W.; m. Carole Ege, June 30, 1971; children: Lara Kimi, Spencer Gen. BA, Cornell U., 1963; PhD, U. Colo., 1968. Postdoctoral fellow Calif. Inst. Tech., 1968-71, U. Calif., Berkeley, 1971-74; dir. Ctr. for History Physics, Am. Inst. Physics, College Park, Md., 1974—. Author: Scientists in Power, 1979, Nuclear Fear, 1988, Never at War, 1998; contbr. articles to profl. jours. Recipient Andrew Gemant award Am. Inst. of Physics, 1994 Fellow AAAS. Home: 12 Buena Vista Dr Hastings On Hudson NY 10706-1104 Office: Am Inst Physics One Physics Ellipse College Park MD 20740-3843 E-mail: sweart@aip.org.

WEARY, PEYTON EDWIN, retired medical educator; b. Evanston, Ill., Jan. 10, 1930; s. Leslie Albert and Conway Christian (Fleming) W.; m. Janet Edsall Gregory, Aug. 23, 1952; children: Terry, Conway Christian, Carolyn Fielder. BA, Princeton U., 1970; MD, U. Va., 1955; M in Dermatology, 2000. Diplomate: Am. Bd. Dermatology (dir. 1978-88, pres. 1987-88). Intern, case Western Res. U. Hosps., Cleve., 1955-56; rotating intern Univ. Hosp. Cleve., 1955-56; asst. resident dermatology U. Va., Charlottesville, 1958-60, resident dermatology, 1960-61, instr. dept. dermatology, 1961-62, asst. prof., 1962-65, asso. prof., 1965-70, prof., chmn. dept. dermatology, 1970-93; mem. staff Univ. Hosp., mem. cancer com., 1979—98, ret., 2001, prof. emeritus, 2001—. Univ. Hosp. house staff, 1960-61, clin. staff, 1965-66, pres. clin. staff, 1966-67; co-chair Nat. Coun. on Skin Cancer Prevention, Fed. Coun. on Skin Cancer Prevention, 1997-2001, Ctr. for Disease Control, 1997-2000. Mem. editorial bd. Jour. Am. Acad. Dermatology, 1978-87; editorial adv. bd. Skin and Allergy News, 1978—; contbr. articles to profl. jours. Bd. dirs. Lupus Found. Am., 1980-84; trustee, mem. exec. com. Dermatology Found., 1975-79; pres. Albermarle County unit Am. Cancer Soc., 1967-69. Served from 1st lt. to capt., M.C. U.S. Army, 1956-58. Recipient Walter Reed Disting. Achievement award U. Va. Alumni Assn., 2001 Mem.: Coun. Med. Splty. Socs. (bd. dir. 1989—92, sec. 1992—95), Am. Bd. Med. Spltys. (v.p. 1988, pres.-elect 1989, pres. 1990—92, Disting. Svc. award 1999), Raven Soc., So. Med. Assn., Med. Soc. Va. (Cmty. Svc. award 2001), Albermarie County Med. Soc., Dermatology Found., Am. Dermatol. Assn. (bd. dir. 1987—93, pres. 1992—93), Assn. Profs. Dermatology (sec.-treas. 1976—79), Soc. Investigative Dermatology (bd. dir. 1976—81, v.p. 1985, hon. mem. 1996), Am. Acad. Dermatology (hon. bd. dir. 1973—76, pres. 1993—95, elected master in dermatology 2000, Gold medal 1990), Va. Dermatol. Soc. (sec.-treas. 1965—71), Nat. Assn. Physicians Environ. (pres. 1995—97), Boar's Head Sports Club, Alpha Omega Alpha, Sigma Xi. Presbyterian. Home: 110 Magnolia Dr Charlottesville VA 22901-2015 Office: Dept Dermatology Univ Va Hosp Charlottesville VA 22908-0001

WEATHERALL, WILLIAM BAILEY, human resources administrator; b. Port Arthur, Tex., July 2, 1949; s. Lee Thomason and Joyce (Bailey) W.; m. Marguerite Ciccosanti, Dec. 18, 1971; children: Jennifer, Benjamin, Kathryn. BS in Psychology, Lamar State Coll. of Tech., Beaumont, Tex., 1971. Employee rels. asst. Texaco, Port Arthur, Tex., 1972-74, coord. employee rels., 1974-76, asst. supr. employee rels. Lawrenceville, Ill., 1976-78; mgr. indsl. rels. Kerr-McGee, Corpus Christi, Tex., 1978-80; mgr. employee rels. Mitchell Energy and Devel., Houston, 1980-86; coord. St. Lukes Episc. Hosp., 1986-89; dir. Human Resources Internat. Drilling Fluids, 1989-90; mgr. Human Resources Foster Valve Corp., 1990-93; dir. human resources GSE Lining Tech., Inc., 1993-95, Eco Resources, Inc., Sugar Land, Tex., 1996—. Elder The Woodlands (Tex.) Cmty. Presbyn. Ch., 1987—. Mem. Soc. for Human Resource Mgmt., Inst. for Internat. Human Resources, Human Resource Systems Profls. Presbyterian. Avocations: golf, cooking. Home: 12 Sand Piper Pl The Woodlands TX 77381-3117 Office: Eco Resources Inc 12550 Emily Ct Sugar Land TX 77478-3195

WEATHERBEE, ELLEN GENE ELLIOTT, botanist, educator; b. Lansing, Mich., Sept. 16, 1939; d. Eugene Bradley and Wilma Alcott (Gardner) Elliott; m. Lee Weatherbee, Aug. 18, 1958 (dec. 1996); children: Anne Susan, Brent Robert, Julie Patricia. BA in Edn., U. Mich., 1960, postgrad., 1972-77; MA in English Lit., Eastern Mich. U., 1962. Cert. tchr. Tchr. adult edn. Schoolcraft Coll., Livonia, Mich., 1983-85; tchr. adult edn. lifelong learning program U. Mich./Wayne State U., Ann Arbor and Detroit, 1973-84; tchr. adult edn. Leelanau Schs./Sleeping Bear Nat. Lakeshore, 1982-86; tchr., nature trip leader adult edn. program Matthaei Bot. Gardens, U. Mich., Ann Arbor, 1984—, dir., founder adult edn. program, 1984—; cons. botanist U. Mich., 1977—. Cons. on plant and mushroom identification Mich. Hosps. Poison Control Ctr., 1978—; founder, dir. Weatherbee's Bot. Trips, 1990—; field worker for wetlands and threatened and endangered species Mich. Dept. Natural Resources and Army Corp of Engrs.; bot. cons. for wetlands permits, 1991—; botany instr. for in-svc. tng. Mich. Dept. Environ. Quality Wetland Regulators; botany trainer Mich. Dept. Environ. Quality Corps Engrs., USDA Soil Scientists in Wetland Tng., 1999. Co-author: Edible Wild Plants, A Guide to Collecting and Cooking, 1982; mem. editorial bd. Mich. Botanist, 1978—; contbr. articles to profl. jours. Constable Dem. party,Ann Arbor Twp., Mich. Mem. Austrian Mountain Climbing Soc., British Canoe Union, Fedn. Ont. Naturalists, Great Lakes Sea Kayaking Club, Mich. Acad. Sci., Mich. Bot. Club, Nature Conservancy, N.Am. Mycological Assn., Pipsissewa Chamber Music Soc. Avocations: new plants, backpacking, sea kayaking, playing cello, swimming. Home: 11405 Patterson Lake Dr Pinckney MI 48169-9748 Office: U Mich Matthaei Bot Gardens 1800 N Dixboro Rd Ann Arbor MI 48105-9741 E-mail: eew@umich.edu.

WEATHERBY, DONALD ALAN, telecommunications industry executive, writer; b. Columbus, Ohio, Dec. 11, 1954; s. Virgil Byron and Janet JoAnn Weatherby. Student, Columbus State C.C. UNIX sys. adminstr. Contract to Bell Labs., Columbus, 1981—86; ops. mgr. AT&T Labs., Reynoldsburg, Ohio, 1996—. Sys. developer and implementation AT&T Labs., Reynoldsburg, 1996—2002. Author: (tech. mgmt.) Geekology 101: Managing the Aliens, Your Computer Support Staff, 1999, (novels) The Star Spangled Specter, 1995; composer: (jazz rock lit.fusion) Plush Hush CD - Generation Y, 2000. Recipient Vol. award, Ohio Legal Rights Svc. - State of Ohio, 1999. Mem.: MUFON (assoc.; data specialist 1999—2002, award for creation of MUFON Web database 2001). Unitarian Universalist. Avocations: writing macabre fiction, astronomy, UFO researcher, jazz-literary music. Home: 1226 S Fountain Ave Springfield OH 45506 Personal E-mail: geekology@worldnet.att.net.

WEATHERBY, M. MADGE, retired library director; b. Guymon, Okla., June 17, 1922; d. Robert Myron and Cora Evelyn (Gideon) Moore; m. Lee M. Weatherby, Aug. 4, 1946 (div. 1968); children: Gwendolyn, Norman Lee, Paul Kevin, Rebecca Sue, Alice Gail, Robert Wayne; m. James S. Weatherby, Dec. 16, 1972. Student, Panhandle A&M Coll., 1939-40; BS in Bus., U. Colo., 1945; postgrad., Angelo State U., 1979. Income tax acct. Hinsey, Butz, and Burnham, Ft. Stockton, Tex., 1962-65; county office clk. Farmers Home Adminstrn., 1965-75; substitute tchr. Reagan County High Sch., Big Lake, Tex., 1977-80; libr. dir. Reagan County Libr., 1980-91; ret., 1991. Organist 1st Bapt. Ch., Big Lake, 1980-90; adult literacy tutor trainer. Named Outstanding Citizen of Big Lake, Big Lake C. of C., 1986, Outstanding Adult 4-H Club Leader State of Tex., Tex. Extension Svc., 1963. Mem. DAR, Tex. Libr. Assn. (Outstanding Small Community Libr. of Yr. 1988), Small Community Librs. Round Table (Austin, Tex.), Nat. Assn. Ret. Fed. Employees, Tex. Fedn. Women's Clubs (pres. 20th Century Club 1986-88), Happy Homemakers Club (pres. 1985-86), Order Ea. Star (organist 1976-91), Beta Sigma Phi (life). Avocations: music, sewing, quilting, well/fitness training, traveling. Home: PO Box 116 407 Maryland Stse Big Lake TX 76932

WEATHERFORD, GEORGE EDWARD, civil engineer; b. Oakdale, Tenn., Jan. 8, 1932; s. Walter Clyde and Kathleen (Hinds) W.; m. Martha Jeannette Beck, July 9, 1960; children: Kathleen Jeannette, Elizabeth Lynn. BSCE, Ind. Inst. Tech., Fort Wayne, 1957; BS Engr. in Constrn., U. Mich., 1959; MSBA, St. Francis U., 1975. Registered profl. engr., Ind., Ga., Ohio, Iowa, S.C., Pa., Ill., Md., La., Tenn., Mich., Kans. Plant engr. Cen. Soya Co., Inc., Decatur, Ind., 1959, civil engr., 1959-64; county hwy. engr. Allen County Ind. Govt., Ft. Wayne, 1964-66; sr. civil engr. Cen. Soya Co., Inc., Fort Wayne, 1966-69, engring. mgr., 1969-77, prin. engr., 1977-97; cons. engr. Weatherford Engring., Ft. Wayne, Ind., 1997—. Ind. cons. 1964—. Author book chpts.; contbr. articles to profl. jours. Trustee Ft. Wayne YWCA, 1973-76, North Christian Ch. and Endowment Trust. Sgt. USMC, 1950-54. Mem. ASCE (state treas. 1957), NSPE, Am. Concrete Inst., Am. Inst. Steel Constrn., Nat. Grain & Feed Assn., Nat. Fire Protection Assn., Ill. Assn. Structural Engrs., Grain Elevator and Processing Soc. (edn. programming com.). Republican. Home: 3617 Delray Dr Fort Wayne IN 46815-6012 E-mail: george.weatherford@gte.net.

WEATHERFORD, LAWRENCE ROBERT, business educator, consultant; BA, Brigham Young U., 1982; MBA, U. Va., 1990, PhD, 1991. Prof. bus. U. Wyo., Laramie, 1991—. Cons. Swissair, Lufthansa, Air New Zealand, South Africa Airways, Walt Disney World. Author: Introductory Management Science, 1998, Decision Modeling With MS Excel, 2001; contbr. numerous articles to profl. jours. Lt. USN, 1982-87. Office: U Wyo Coll Bus PO Box 3275 Laramie WY 82071-3275 Fax: 307-766-3488. E-mail: lrw@uwyo.edu.

WEATHERHEAD, ALBERT JOHN, III, business executive; b. Cleve., Feb. 17, 1925; s. Albert J. and Dorothy (Jones) W.; m. Celia Scott, Jan. 1, 1975; children: Dwight S., Michael H., Mary H. AB, Harvard U., 1950, postgrad., 1951. Prodn. mgr. Yale & Towne, Stamford, Conn., 1951-54, Blaw-Knox, Pitts., 1954-56; plant mgr. Weatherhead Co., Cleve., 1957-59, gen. mgr., 1959-61, v.p., gen. mgr., 1962-66, gen. sales mgr., 1962-63, v.p. mfg., 1964-66; v.p., dir. Weatherhead Co. of Can., Ltd., 1960-63, pres., CEO, dir., 1964-66; treas. Weatherchem Corp., 1971-82, pres., dir., 1971—; also bd. dirs., 1987—. Bd. dirs. Weatherhead Co., Protane Corp., L.P.G. Leasing Corp, Leasepac Corp., Leasepac Can., Ltd., Creative Resources, Inc. Author: The New Age of Business, 1965; patentee in field. Mem. Harvard U. com. on univ. resources, Weatherhead Ctr. Internat. Affairs, vis. com.; trustee Case Western Res. U., mem. resources com., coun. on rsch. involving human subjects, trustee Michelson-Morley Centennial Celebration; mem. Univ. Sch. alumni coun., trustee Univ. Sch., hon. trustee for life Univ. Sch., Cleve., 1988—; trustee, adv. bd. Egyptian Studies Assn., U. S.C.; mem. vis. com. Ohio U., Athens; v.p. nat. adv. com. Rollins Coll., Winter park, Fla.; adv. trustee Pinecrest Sch., Ft. Lauderdale, Fla.; mem. capital campaign steering com. Laurel Sch.; trustee Vocat. Guidance and Rehab. Svcs., Hwy. Safety Found., Arthritis Found.; v.p. Weatherhead Found., 1953-86, pres., 1987—; bd. dirs. New Directions Inc., Glenwillow, Ohio; mem. chancellor's coun. U. Tex. Sys. Col. CAF. With USAAF, 1943-46. Mem. Am. Newcomen Soc., Beta Gamma Sigma (hon.), Union (Cleve.), Country (Shaker Heights, Ohio), Ottawa Shooting (Freemont, Ohio), Ocean (Delray, Fla.), Everglades (Palm Beach, Fla.), Codrington (Oxford, Eng.). Home: 90 Falls Creek Trail Moreland Hills OH 44022 Office: 25825 Science Park Dr Beachwood OH 44122-7323

WEATHERLEY-WHITE, ROY CHRISTOPHER ANTHONY, surgeon, consultant; b. Peshawar, India, Dec. 1, 1931; S. Roy and Elfreda (Milward) Boehm, m. Dorian Jeanne Freeman Weatherley-White, Dec. 27, 1961; children: Carl Christopher, Matthew Richard, Larissa Chantal. MA, Cambridge U., 1953; MD, Harvard U., 1958. Surgeon Biomedical Cons., Denver, 1970—; pres. Plastic Surgery Group, 1992-97. Chmn. Plastic Surgery Rsch. Coun., 1975-76; pres. Rocky Mountain Assn. Plastic Surgeons, 1973-74; v.p. Am. Cleft Palate Assn. Author: Plastic Surgery of the Female Breast, 1982; contbr. over 45 articles to profl. jours. Cons. Colo. Biomedical Venture Ctr., Denver, 1993—; chmn. bd. trustees Colo. Venture Ctrs., 1999—; bd. chairperson Operation Smile, Colo., 2000—. Recipient Rsch. award Am. Soc. Plastic Surgery, 1962, 64. Mem. Harvard Club of N.Y., Oxford-Cambridge Club, Denver Country Club, Denver Athletic Club. Episcopalian. Avocations: flying, skiing, scuba diving, archaeology. Home: 2101 E Hawthorne Pl Denver CO 80206-4116 Office: 2101 E Hawthorne Pl Denver CO 80206-4116

WEATHERLY, ALVIS MORRISON, JR. retired association developer; b. Atlanta, Nov. 19, 1925; s. Alvis Morrison and Frances Louise (Stocks) W.; m. Mary Elizabeth Hyndman, Dec. 27, 1947; children: Mary Ann Weatherly Cobb, Elizabeth Louise Weatherly Williamson, Alvis Morrison III. Student, Ga. Inst. Tech., 1942-44; BBA, U. Ga., 1947; LLB, Atlanta Law Sch., 1952. Treasury cashier for Ga. So. Bell Te. Co. (now BellSouth), Atlanta, 1948-82; devel. dir. Atlanta Area Coun. Boy Scouts Am., 1984-93. Author, editor: History of Georgia Jaycees 1921-1962, 1962. Club pres., dist. pres., state chmn., state treas., state historian Ga. Jaycees, 1955-63, past asst. coun. comm., coun. adv. bd.; instr. commr. conf. Boy Scouts Am., 1982, coun. commr. sci., wood badge, asst. course dir., nat. exec. tng. inst., pres. basic training course class, coun. encampment chief, 1976; past dean Coll. of Commr. Sci., 1980-1983; past asst. coun. com., coun. adv. bd. Jr. Achievement, Atlanta, 1951, 63; loaned exec. Atlanta United Appeal, 1964, 65; mem. Selective Svc. Bd., Atlanta, 1964-74; mem. staff Atlanta Olympics, 1996; del. 17th World Meth. Conf., Rio de Janeiro, 1996; bd. dirs., pres. Ga., Nat. Meml. Day Assn. and Ave. of Flags; adminstrv. bd. mem., usher, past sec. fin. com., past tchr. adult Sunday sch., trustee, past pres., past ch. sch. membership cultivation supt., past ast. ch. sch. supt., past mem. commn. on edn., past mem. evangelism commn., past ch. sch. greeter adminstrv. bd. Peachtree Rd. United Meth. Ch. Sgt. U.S. Army Air Corps, 1946, WWII; 1st lt. USAFR, 1961. Named Jaycee of Yr. North DeKalb chpt., Jaycees, Outstanding Dist. Pres.-Ga., Key Man of Ga., Hal Salfen Outstanding State Com. Chmn., Outstanding State V.P.; recipient Silver Beaver award, Boy Scouts Am., 1974, James E. West fellow, 1996, Whitney M. Young Jr. Svc. in Urban Scouting award, 1996, Scout Show honoree, 1996, Disting. Award of Merit, Disting. Commr. award, Vigil honor, Order of the Arrow, Spirit of Op. 1st class, 2001, Willing Svc. banner, WSB Radio, Atlanta, 1974, 1976, Cert., Indian Creek Garden Club, Atlanta, Cross of Mil. Svc., United Daus. of the Confederacy, Cross and Flame award, Peachtree Rd. United Meth. Ch. Master Masons; mem. SAR- Sons Am. Revolution (past pres. Atlanta chpt., War Svc. medal), Rotary (bd. dirs., treas. Sandy Springs club, bd. dirs., sec., v.p. Smyrna-Cumberland club, sgt.-at-arms, bd. dirs., treas., sec., past pres. Buckhead club, Paul Harris fellow, Will Watt fellow, Otis Jackson scholar, Otis Jackson fellow, Cmty. Svc. award, Tom Slaughter fellow, Svc. Above Self award, Rotarian of Yr., Dist. Svc. award), Am. Legion, Tel. Pioneers of Am., Shriners, 1st Families of Ga., Sons of Confederate Vets. (War Svc. medal), Mil. Order of Stars and Bars (comdr.), Huguenot Soc. in Town of Manakin in Colony of Va. (state pres.), Jamestowne Soc. (past 1st Ga. Co. Gov.), Sons and Daus. of the Pilgrims (past 2d dep. gov.), Sons and Daus. of Antebellum Planters (founding), Order of Indian Wars of U.S., Soc. of Descendents of Washington's Army at Valley Forge, Order of Washington, Magna Charta Barons, Magna Charta Dames and Barons (past state chmn.), Sovereign Colonial Soc., Ams. of Royal Descent, Colonial Order of the Crown, Soc. Descendants of Knights of the Most Noble Order of the Garter, Plantagenet Soc., Old Guard of the Gate City Guard (commandant-elect lt. col., Hancock medal, Charles Gavin Trophy, The Dr. George Turnbull Pursley award), Sigma Nu, Beta Gamma Sigma (past pres. Atlanta chpt.), Alpha Phi Omega, Delta Sigma Pi, Omicron Delta Kappa (alumni), Scabbard and Blade, Gridiron Secret Soc., Buckhead 50 Club. Home: 710 Starlight Ln NE Atlanta GA 30342-2838

WEATHERLY, MARINA, artist, educator, writer, dancer; b. Cottonwood, Ariz., Dec. 19, 1957; d. Joseph Epes and Elenita R. Brown; m. Chris Weatherly, Aug. 5, 1984; children: Elena, Lara. BFA in Visual Arts, U. Mont., 1979; MFA in Fiber Arts, Ariz. State U., 1984. Mem. faculty tapestry and drawing Piedmont Va. C.C., Charlottesville, 1986-89; mem. faculty weaving and textile design U. Mont., Missoula, 1990-91; with artists in schs Mont. Arts Coun., Helena, 1990—; dance instr. Elenita Brown Dance Studio, Stevensville, Mont., 1990—; founding dir., instr. Learning Through the Arts, Rocky Mountain Ballet Theater Sch., Missoula, 1996—; instr. Kootenai Creek Ranch Summer Day , Stevensville. 1991—. Art cons. to pub. schs. nationwide, 1990—; script cons., editor, artistic dir. ind. films, Mont., 1991—. Exhibitions include paintings on silk, 1983—. Mem. Project Pride, Stevensville, 1998-99; mem. Ravalli County Planning Bd., 1993-98; pres. Stevensville PTA, 1993-98. James Bardley history fellow, 1989; grantee in field. Avocations: donkeys for packing in the wilderness, kayaking, gardening, riding. Home: PO Box 565 Stevensville MT 59870-0565

WEATHERLY, ROBERT STONE, JR. banker; b. Birmingham, Ala., May 12, 1929; s. Robert Stone and Gladys (Manning) W.; m. Mary Anne Burr, May 1, 1954; children: Robert Stone, III, Henry, William. AB, Princeton U., 1950; LL.B., Harvard U., 1953, grad. advanced mgmt. program, 1972. Bar: Ala. 1953. Assoc. firm Burr, McKamy Moore & Thomas, Birmingham, 1955-62; asst. gen. atty. Vulcan Materials Co., 1962-69, v.p. chems. div. Wichita, Kans., 1969-71, treas., 1971-74, v.p. and controller, 1974-77, pres. metals div. Ala., 1977-87, pres. Middle East div., 1982-87; chmn., chief exec. officer Jefferson Fed. Savings, 1987-91; dir., sec. All Seasons Travel, 1991—. Disting. lectr.-practitioner U. Ga. Served with U.S. Army, 1953-55. Mem. Nat. Assn. Accts. (cert. mgmt. acct.), Beta Gamma Sigma. Clubs: Country of Birmingham, Chattooga (Cashiers, N.C.). Presbyterian. Home: 4608 Old Leeds Rd Birmingham AL 35213-1802 Office: All Seasons Travel 120 Office Park Dr Birmingham AL 35223-2422

WEATHERLY, STEPHEN GEORGE, retired military officer, defense consultant; b. Oneonta, N.Y., Oct. 5, 1941; s. Le Roy Stephen and Luella Maryette (Wallace) W.; m. Jin Hyun Ahn, May 4, 1970 (div. Dec. 1993); 1 child, Jane Leah. BS, Syracuse U., 1963; BS in Wood Products Engring., SUNY, Syause, 1963; M in Computing Scis., Tex. A&M U., 1969. Comd. 2d lt. USAF, 1964, advanced through grades to maj., 1975, various positions, 1964—84, ret., 1984; sr. assoc. Booz Allen & Hamilton, Inc., McLean, Va., 1984—2001; ret. Data comms. analyst Def. Comms. Agy., Arlington,Va., 1977-84. Mem., leader Boy Scouts Am., DeWitt, N.Y., 1952-62. Mem. Armed Forces Comms. and Electronics Assn., Am. Legion. Republican. Episcopalian. Avocations: reading, home improvement. Home: 5743 Bent Oak Dr Sarasota FL 34232-6606 E-mail: sgwxly@aol.com.

WEATHERLY-MCWATERS, BARBARA CANNON, artist; b. Savannah, Ga., Mar. 27, 1927; d. John Respess and Irma Elizabeth (Murray) Cannon; m. William Earl Weatherly, Nov. 11, 1950 (dec. Jan. 1990); children: William Craig, Barbara Page; m. Roy McWaters, May 1, 1993. Student, U. Ga., 1946-48, High Mus. Sch. of Art, 1948-50, Continuing Art Edn. Workshops, 1960—. Mem. Gallery 209, Savannah, Ga., 1975, pres., 1986-87, 94-95. Scenery chief Cmty. Children's Theatre, Savannah, 1964-65; treas. Huntingdon Jr. Woman's Club, Savannah, 1964-65. Recipient First award Ga. Fedn. of Women's Clubs. Mem. DAR. Home: 2745 Forest Ridge Rd Dandridge TN 37725-6961

WEATHERMON, SIDNEY EARL, elementary school educator; b. Abilene, Tex., Jan. 20, 1937; s. Sidney Elliot Weathermon and Evelyn Marie (Landreth) Parker. BA, U. Colo., 1962, MA, 1968, EdD, 1976. Cert. K-12 reading tchr., elem. edn. tchr., K-12 reading specialist. Tchr. Jefferson County (Colo.) Pub. Schs., 1963-66; grades 5-6 tchr. Boulder (Colo.) Valley Pub. Schs., 1962-63, reading tchr., 1968-71, consortium dir. right-to-read project Louisville Mid. Sch., 1974-75, comm. skills program coord. Vocat.-Tech. H.S., 1976, K-12 dist. reading specialist, 1971-85, chpt. 1 tchr. grades 1-6, 1985-89, chpt. 1 kindergarten project coord., 1985-89, grade 1 tchr., 1989-95. Instr. U. Colo., Boulder, 1971-72, U. No. Colo., Greeley, 1977; adj. faculty Regis U., Denver, 1972-95, dept. edn. instr., 1982. Contbr. articles to profl. jours. Recipient Celebrate Literacy award, Boulder Coun. Internat. Reading Assn., 1986, IBM Corp. Tchr. of Yr. award, 1989, Colo./Nat. Educator, Milkin Family Found., 1990; NDEA fellow, 1966-68. Mem. NEA, Internat. Reading Assn., Colo. Edn. Assn., Boulder Valley Edn. Assn. (chair tchr. adv coun., assoc. rep., tchrs. rights and activities commn., negotiations team, profl. leave com.), Phi Delta Kappa (certs. of recognition 1987, 90), Kappa Delta Pi. Democrat. Avocation: Southwest Indian art. Home: 449 S Shore Dr Osprey FL 34229-9657 Office: 449 N Shore Dr Osprey FL 34229-9282 E-mail: drsidw@comcast.net.

WEATHERS, LAURA SUE, pediatrician; b. Atlanta, May 30, 1962; d. Robert Lewis and Gertrude Elizabeth (Richards) W.; m. William Grant Brooks Jr., May 25, 1991; children: Pearson, Ashley, Garrett. BSN, Vanderbilt U., 1984; MD, Med. Coll. Ga., 1988. Intern U. South Fla., Tampa, 1988-89, resident, 1989-91; pediatrician pvt. practice, Brandon, 1991-92; assoc. prof. pediatrics U. So. Fla., 1992—. Med. dir. newborn nursery Tampa Gen. Hosp., 1994—. Fellow Am. Acad. Pediat.; mem. So. Soc. Pediat. Rsch., Hillsborough County Pediat. Soc., Jr. League Tampa. Methodist. Office: U So Fla Dept Pediatrics 17 Davis Blvd Ste 308 Tampa FL 33606-3438 E-mail: lweather@hsc.usf.edu.

WEATHERS, MILLEDGE WRIGHT, retired economics educator; b. Augusta, Ga., May 11, 1926; s. Robert Edward Lee and Margaret Elizabeth (Johnson) W.; m. Anna-Maria Helene von Bertrab; children: Helene, Martin, Margarete, Benjamin. BA, George Washington U., 1949, MA, 1957; Dr. oec. publ., U. Munich, 1961. Rsch. analyst U.S. Dept. Air Force, Washington, 1951-57, Gen. Electric Co., Santa Barbara, Calif., 1959-62; pvt. practice cons. Munich, 1962-64; cons. Gesellschaft fuer Anlagewerte, 1964-66; sr. staff analyst Lockheed-Ga. Co., Marietta, 1966-68; prof. econs. Adrian (Mich.) Coll., 1968-91. Contbr. articles to profl. jours. With U.S. Army, 1944-46. Mem. Am. Econs. Assn., Assn. for Evolutionary Econs., Nat. Tax Assn., Economists Allied for Arms Reduction, Kappa Sigma. Avocations: music, walking. Home: 930 Lincoln Ave Adrian MI 49221-3230 E-mail: Mweathers@adrian.edu.

WEATHERSBY, CECIL JERRY, accounting and finance manager; b. Birmingham, Ala., Oct. 28, 1952; s. E.W. and Dorothy M. (Zuiderhoek) W.; m. Julia Diane Harris, Feb. 26, 1976; children: Matthew, Blake, Nathan. BBA, St. Bernard Coll., 1975; MS in Adminstrv. Sci., U. Ala., Huntsville, 1988. Acct. City of Cullman, 1977; asst. plant acct. Cullman (Ala.) Electric Coop., 1977-82, contr., 1982-88, mgr. acctg. and fin., 1988-95; chief fin. officer Hired Hand Mfg., Inc., 1995—. Bd. dirs. HessAire Products, Inc., Cullman, Hired Hand Mfg., Inc.; mem. adj. faculty Wallace State C.C., Hanceville, Ala. Bd. dirs. Cullman Regional Med. Ctr., 1994—, sec. 1997, vice chmn. 1998, chmn. bd. dirs., 2001; bd. dirs. Cullman Area C. of C., 1999-2002, Leadership Cullman County, 1999; moderator Cullman Presbytery, 2000; trustee Cullman Regional Med. Ctr. Found., 2001. Recipient Founders award Cullman Family Recreation Complex, 1990. Mem. Nat. Inst. Mgmt. Accts., North Ala. Power Accts. Assn. (chmn. 1986-87), Tenn. Valley Pub. Power Assn. (pres. acctg. sect. 1989), Kiwanis (bd. dirs. 1994-95). Presbyterian. Office: Hired Hand Mfg Inc PO Box 99 Bremen AL 35033-0099

WEATHERSBY, GEORGE BYRON, business executive; b. Albany, Calif., Dec. 9, 1944; s. Byron and Fannie A. W.; m. Linda Rose Scheirer, June 29, 1979; children: Deborah Jane, Geoffrey Byron. BS, U. Calif., Berkeley, 1965, MS, 1966, MBA, 1967; MS, Harvard U., 1968, PhD, 1970; DHL (hon.), U. San Francisco, 1987; LLD (hon.), U. So. Ind., 1992. Mem. faculty, assoc. dir. analytical studies, dir. Ford Found. rsch. program U. Calif., Berkeley, 1969-72; spl. asst. to U.S. sec. of State Washington, 1972-73; dir. rsch. Nat. Commn. on Financing Higher Edn., 1973-74; assoc. prof. mgmt. Harvard U., Cambridge, Mass., 1974-78; commr. higher edn. State of Ind., 1977-83; pres. Curtis Pub. Co., 1983-86, New UPI Inc., Washington, 1985-86; corp. v.p. fin. Ontario Corp., Muncie, Ind., 1986-88, pres., 1988-91, also bd. dirs.; ptnr. Founders Court Inc., Princeton, N.J., 1991-93; independant cons., 1975—; pres. Oxford Mgmt. Corp., 1993-98, Cambridge Parallel Processing, 1994-98, Electronic Retailing Syss. Internat., 1996-98; pres., CEO, bd. dirs. Am. Mgmt. Assn., N.Y.C., 1998-2000; chmn., CEO Genesys Corp., LLC, 2002—. CEO, bd. dirs. Quisic, Inc., 2001-02; chmn. bd. dirs. Otis Conner Cos., 1984-86, Curtis Media Corp., 1984-86, Curtis Internat. Ltd., 1985-86, Prince Gardner, Inc., 1991-93, Alma Industries, 1992-93, Hanes Holding Co., 1992-93; bd. dirs. Holnam Inc., Farm Fans Inc., Delta Consol. Industries, Cambridge Parallel Processing, Advanced Retail Mktg., ERS, Inc. Author: (books) Financing Postsecondary Education in the U.S, 1974, Colleges and Money, 1976; contbr. numerous articles to profl. jours., 1967— ; cons. editor: Jour. Higher Edn., 1974— ; exec. editor: Change mag., 1980-84. Bd. dirs. Nat. Ctr. for Higher Edn Mgmt. Sys., 1980-83, U.S.A. Group, 1989—; mem. steering com. Edn. Commn. of States, 1978-82; mem. Ind. Com. Humanities, 1981-87; trustee U. So. Ind., 1985-91, Park Tudor Sch. Indpls., 1986-91, Butler U., 1987-93; mem. adv. coun. Invest in New Zealand, 2001--. Calif. Regents scholar, 1963-65; NSF fellow, 1966-67; AEC fellow, 1966-67; Kent fellow, 1967-70; White House fellow, 1972-73; named 1 of 100 Outstanding Young Leaders in Higher Edn. Change Mag., 1978 Mem. Am. Mgmt. Assn., Am. Coun. Edn., Ops. Rsch. Soc. Am., Inst. Mgmt. Scis., Econometrica, Young Pres. Orgn. Republican. E-mail: gweathersby@rcn.com.

WEATHERSBY, JAMES ROY, lawyer; b. Pine Bluff, Ark., Aug. 28, 1935; s. Willard Alton and Francis (McCormick) W.; children: Jim, Brad; m. Lydia Huber, Jan. 20, 1990. BSCE, U. Tenn., 1958; JD, Vanderbilt U., 1964. Bar: Ala. 1965, Tenn. 1965, Ga. 1971, U.S. Dist. Ct. (no. dist.) Ala. 1966, U.S. Dist. Ct. (no. dist.) Ga. 1971, U.S. Dist. Ct. (middle dist.) Ga. 1985, U.S. Dist. Ct. (so. dist.) Ga. 1990, U.S. Dist. Ct. (ea. dist.) Tenn. 1997, U.S. Ct. Appeals (D.C., 4th, 5th, 6th, 7th, 8th and 11th cirs.), U.S. Supreme Ct. 1969. Labor counsel Rust Engring. Co., Pitts., Pa., Birmingham, Ala., 1964-70; ptnr. Wilson & Wilson, Atlanta, 1971-76; ptnr., head labor sect. Powell Goldstein Fraser & Murphy, 1976-90; mng. ptnr. Ogletree Deakins Nash Smoak & Stewart, 1991-95, Littler Mendelson, Atlanta, 1996—. Dep. atty. gen. State of Ga., Atlanta, 1974—; gen. counsel Assoc. Builders & Contractors of Ga., Atlanta, 1976—. Mem. ABA, Lawyers Club Atlanta, Ga. Bar Assn., Atlanta Bar Assn. Home: 5056 Green Pine Dr NE Atlanta GA 30342-2402 Office: Littler Mendelson 3348 Peachtree Rd NE Atlanta GA 30326-1067

WEATHERSPOON, TERESA GAYE, professional basketball player; b. Jasper, Tex., Dec. 8, 1965; Grad., La. Tech. Inst., 1988. Guard Blusto, Italy, 1988-89, 90-93, Magenta, Italy, 1989-90, Como, Italy, 1996-97, CSKA, Russia, 1993-95, WNBA - N.Y. Liberty, N.Y.C., 1997—. Recipient Gold medals World Championship, 1986, Goodwill Games, 1986, World Univ. Games, 1987, Broderick Cup, Wade Trophy; named NCAA Women's Basketball Team Decade, 1980s, La. State Player of Yr., 1988, Kodak All-Am., 1987, 88, WNBA defensive player of the year, 1997 & 1998, WNBA All-Star, 1999-2001. Office: NY Liberty 2 Penn Plz 14th Fl New York NY 10121-0101*

WEATHERUP, ROY GARFIELD, lawyer; b. Annapolis, Md., Apr. 20, 1947; s. Robert Alexander and Kathryn Crites (Hesser) W.; m. Wendy Gaines, Sept. 10, 1977; children: Jennifer, Christine. AB in Polit. Sci., Stanford U., 1968, JD, 1972. Bar: Calif. 1972, U.S. Dist. Ct. 1973, U.S. Ct. Appeals (9th cir.) 1975, U.S. Supreme Ct. 1980. Assoc. Haight, Brown & Bonesteel, L.A., Santa Ana, 1972—78, ptnr., 1979—. Judge Moot Ct. UCLA, Loyola U., Pepperdine U.; arbitrator Am. Arbitration Assn.; mem. com. Book Approved Jury Instrns. L.A. Superior Ct. Mem. ABA, Calif. Acad. Appellate Lawyers, Los Angeles County Bar Assn., Town Hall Calif. Republican. Methodist. Home: 17260 Rayen St Northridge CA 91325-2919 Office: Haight Brown & Bonesteel Ste 800 6080 Center Dr Los Angeles CA 90045 E-mail: weatherup@hbblaw.com.

WEATHERUP, WENDY GAINES, graphic designer, writer; b. Oct. 20, 1952; d. William Hughes and Janet Ruth (Neptune) Gaines; m. Roy Garfield Weatherup, Sept. 10, 1977; children: Jennifer, Christine. BA, U. So. Calif., 1974. Lic. ins. agt. Freelance graphic designer, desktop pub., Northridge, Calif. Mem. NAFE, U. So. Calif. Alumni Assn., Alpha Gamma Delta. Republican. Methodist. Avocations: photography, travel, writing novels, computers. Home: 17260 Rayen St Northridge CA 91325-2919

WEATHERWAX, LISA, newswriter; b. Ft. Knox, Ky., Sept. 2, 1960; d. Gerald Jerry and Francoise Tecla Teal; m. Lee Alan Weatherwax, Dec. 18, 1982; 1 child, Jean Marie. AA, Edmonds C.C., Lynnwood, Wash., 1994; BA in Liberal Studies summa cum laude, U. Wash., Bothell, 2000. Mgr. Cir. K Convenience Store, Moscow, 1983-85; cashier Pike Pl. Market, Seattle, 1985-88; writing cons. U. Wash., Bothell, 1996-98, editor-in-chief The Bothell Commons, 1998-2000; ind. newswriter Bothell, 2000—. Mem. adv. bd. Pub. Policy Jour., U. Wash., Bothell, 1997; mem. curriculum rev. com. Cascadia C.C., Bothell, 2000. Contbg. author Shared Memories jour., 1997, U. Wash. Bothell Pub. Policy Jour., 1997-2000. Co-founder Multicultural Women's Ctr., U. Wash., Bothell, 1997, initiator Mentoring Young Writers Program, 1997—. Recipient Matrix Table Promise of Excellence award Assn. Women in Comm., Seattle, 1999. Mem. Soc. Profl. Journalists, Golden Key. Avocations: gardening, reading, walking, drawing with daughter, visiting new places and people. Home: 16914 21st Ave SE Bothell WA 98012-6904

WEATHINGTON, BILLY CHRISTOPHER, analytical chemist; b. Bossier City, La., Dec. 3, 1951; s. Billy and Christine (Lowman) W.; m. Tamara R.A. Horman, Aug. 23, 1973 (div. May 1975); m. Gwendolyn C. Adamson, May 19, 1979; 1 child, Leia C. BA, Auburn U., 1972, BS, 1979. Chemist U.S. Dept. Agriculture, Beltsville, Md., 1978-80; sr. rsch. chemist Midwest Rsch. Inst., Riyadh, Saudi Arabia, 1980-82; quality assurance mgr. Hittman Assocs. Inc., Columbia, Md., 1982-84, dir. mktg., 1984-86, tech. dir., 1986-88; lab. dir. RMC Environ. Svcs. Inc., Pottstown, Pa., 1988-89, v.p. analytical div., 1989-93; ops. dir. Quanterra Environ. Svcs., St. Louis, 1993-98, mgr. info. tech., 1998—; divsn. mgr. TestAmerica, Dayton, Ohio, 1998—. Contbr. articles to profl. jours. Mem. ASTM, Am. Chem. Soc. Achievements include patent disclosure for destruction of simple and complex cyanides; research on the destruction of cyanide in wastewaters, on phyotoxins in Rhizoctonia Solani, on the monitoring of contaminated soil for methyl mercury, on computer automation of PCB isomer identification, and on single blind versus double blind evaluations; managed Times Beach (Mo.) Dioxin Incineration Analytical Program and Cleveland Hopkins International Airport expansion analytical program. Home: 7978 Southbury Dr Centerville OH 45458-2921 Office: TestAmerica 3601 S Dixie Dr Dayton OH 45439-2307 E-mail: chriswea@donet.com.

WEAVER, ARTHUR LAWRENCE, physician; b. Lincoln, Nebr., Sept. 3, 1936; s. Arthur J. and Harriet Elizabeth (Walt) Weaver; m. JoAnn Versemann, July 6, 1980; children: Arthur Jensen, Anne Christine. BS (Regents scholar) with distinction, U. Nebr., 1958; MD, Northwestern U., 1962; MS in Medicine, U. Minn., 1966. Diplomate Am. Bd. Internal Medicine, Am. Bd. Rheumatology. Intern U. Mich. Hosps., Ann Arbor, 1962-63; resident Mayo Grad. Sch. Medicine, Rochester, Minn., 1963-66; practice medicine specializing in rheumatology and internal Lincoln, 1968—; med. dir. Arthritis Ctr. Nebr., 1968—. Staff mem., chmn. Rheumatology Dept. Bryan Meml. Hosp., 1976—78, 1982—85, 1989—91, vice-chief staff, 1984—87; bd. dirs. Bryancarc, 1995—96, chmn. fin. com., 1995—96; courtesy staff mem. St. Elizabeths Hosp., Lincoln Gen. Hosp.; cons. staff mem. VA Hosp.; chmn. Juvenile Rheumatoid Arthritis Clinic, 1970—88; asst. prof. Internal Medicine Dept. U. Nebr., Omaha, 1976—88, assoc. prof., 1988—95, prof., 1995—; med. dir. Lincoln Benefit Life Co., 1972—90; bd. dirs. Lincoln Mutual Life Ins. Co., med. dirs., 1995—; adv. com. mem. Coop. Systematic Studies in Rheumatic Diseases III; bd. dirs. M.G.I. Pharma Inc., Internat. Rheumatology Network. Contbr. Bd. dirs. Nebr. chpt. Arthritis Found.; mem. tech. cons. panel for rheumatology Harvard Resource Based Relative Value Study; trustee U. Nebr. Found., 1974—. Capt. med. corps U.S. Army, 1966—68. Recipient Outstanding Nebraskan award, U. Nebr., 1958, C.W. Boucher award, 1958, Philip S. Hench Rheumatology award, Mayo Grad. Sch. Medicine, 1966, Founders award Nebr. chpt., Arthritis Found., 1997. Fellow: ACP (Nebr. coun. 1983—85, Laureate award Nebr. chpt. 1996), Am. Coll. Rheumatology (bd. dirs. 1985—96, planning com. 1987—96, sec. 1991—93, pres. rsch. and edn. found. 1991—93, exec. com. 1991—96, 2d v.p. 1993—94, 1st v.p., pres.-elect 1994—95, pres. 1995—96, chmn. nominating com. 1996—97, master 2001, 1st Paulding Phelps award 1989), Am. Rheumatism Assn. (pres.-elect Ctrl. region 1983—84, com. on rheumatologic practice 1983—87, pres. Ctrl. region 1984—85); mem.: AMA, Arthritis Found. (profl. del.-at-large 1987—88, 1989, 1990, 1995—96, blue ribbon rsch. com. 1995—96, bd. dirs. Nebr. chpt., Nat. Vol. Svc. citation 1988, Founder award 1997), Midwest Coop. Rheumatic Disease Study Group (chmn. exec. com. 1986—92), Nat. Soc. Clin. Rheumatology (program chairperson 1986—87, exec. com. 1987—92, program chairperson 1988), Arthritis Health Professions Assn. (com. on practice 1984—87), Lancaster County Med. Soc., Nebr. Med. Assn., Nebr. Rheumatism Assn., Nebr. Soc. Internal Medicine (Internist of Yr. 1988), Am. Soc. Internal Medicine (coord. com. phys. payment svcs. 1988—93), U. Minn. Med. Sch. Alumni Assn., U. Mich Med. Sch. Alumni Assn., Mayo Grad. Sch. Medicine Alumni Assn., Phi Rho Sigma, Pi Kappa Epsilon, Alpha Omega Alpha, Sigma Xi, Phi Beta Kappa. Republican. Presbyterian. Home: 9914 Weavers Point Rd Pequot Lakes MN 56472-6472 Office: 2121 S 56th St Lincoln NE 68506-2111

WEAVER, BARBARA FRANCES, librarian, consultant; b. Boston, Aug. 29, 1927; d. Leo Francis and Nina Margaret (Durham) Weisse; m. George B. Weaver, June 6, 1951; 1 dau., Valerie S. Clark. BA, Radcliffe Coll., 1949; MLS., U. R.I., 1968; EdM, Boston U., 1978. Head libr. Thompson (Conn.) Pub. Libr., 1961-69; dir. Conn. State Libr. Svc. Ctr., Willimantic, 1969-72; regional adminstr. Cen. Mass. Regional Libr. System, Worcester, 1972-78; asst. commr. of edn., state libr. State of N.J., Trenton, 1978-91; dir. R.I. Dept. State Libr. Svcs., Providence, 1991-96; chief info. officer State of RI, 1996—2001. Lectr. Simmons Coll., Boston, 1976-78 Mem. Conn. Libr. Assn. E-mail: barbaraw829@earthlink.net.

WEAVER, CARLTON DAVIS, retired oil company executive; b. Grantsville, W.Va., May 27, 1921; s. Arley Ezra and Grace (Davis) W.; m. Nancy Mason McIntosh, Mar. 21, 1951; 1 child, Nancy Mason. BS Engr. Mines, W.Va. U., 1948. Office engr. E.I. du Pont de Nemours & Co., 1941-42, tech. service rep., 1948-51; with Ashland (Ky.) Oil, Inc., 1951-81, exec. asst., 1960-67, v.p., 1967-72, sr. v.p., 1972-81, group operating officer, 1976-81, pres. Ashland Resources Co. div., 1970-74; chmn. bd. Ashland Coal, Inc., 1981-84, Ven-Black, Inc., 1983-86. Chmn. vis. com. Coll. Mineral and Energy Resources, W.Va. U., 1967-80. Served to maj. USMCR, 1942-46, 52-53. Home: 64 Surfsong Rd Kiawah Island SC 29455-5753 also: PO Box 578 White Sulphur Springs WV 24986-0578 Office: 1409 Winchester Ave Ashland KY 41101-7555 E-mail: buckweav@starboard.net.

WEAVER, CAROLYN LESLIE, economist, public policy researcher; b. Washington, Jan. 20, 1952; d. Kenneth Faulkner and Margaret Mae (Taylor) Weaver; m. Robert John Mackay, Aug. 12, 1980; children: Taylor Cotesworth, Bennett Faulkner. BA, Mary Washington Coll., 1973; PhD in Econs., Va. Poly. Inst. and State U., 1977; DHL (hon.), Urbana U., 1994. From instr. to asst. prof. econs. Tulane U., New Orleans., 1976-78; from asst. prof. to assoc. prof. and rsch. assoc. Ctr. for Study of Pub. Choice, Va. Poly. Inst. and State U., Blacksburg, 1978-83; chief profl. staff mem. on social security U.S. Senate Com. on Fin., Washington, 1981-84; sr. rsch. fellow Hoover Inst., Stanford U., Calif., 1984-86; resident scholar, dir. social security and pension studies Am. Enterprise Inst., Washington, 1987—. Sr. advisor Nat. Commn. on Social Security Reform, 1982-83; cons. U.S. Senate Fin. Com., 1984, Social Security Adminstrn., 1984-85, U.S. AID, 1992-93; mem. U.S. Disability Adv. Coun., 1987-88, U.S. Social Security Commrs. Disability Adv. Com., 1989, Social Security Pub. Trustees Working Group on Trust Fund Solvency, 1989-90, Congl. Study Group on Women and Retirement, 1992, U.S. Social Security Notch Commn., 1994, U.S. Social Security Adv. Coun., 1994-97, U.S. Social Security Adv. Bd., 1994-97, Acad. Bd. Advisors Ams. for Generational Equity, 1986-92, Ind. Inst., 1986—, Retirement Policy Inst., 1989—; founding mem. Nat. Acad. Social Ins., 1988-96; bd. dirs. Secure Retirement Coalition, 1996-00; nat. adv. bd. Americans Discuss Social Security, 1997-99, Ind. Womens Forum, 1997-99; del. Nat. Summit on Retirement Saving, 1998. Author: The Sources and Dimensions of Crisis in Social Security: A First Step Toward Meaningful Reform, 1981, Crisis in Social Security: Economic and Political Origins, 1982; editor: Social Security's Looming Surpluses: Prospects and Implications, 1990, Disability and Work, 1991, Regulation mag., 1986-88; sr. editor Am. Enterprise mag., 1989-94; contbr. numerous articles to profl. jours., editls. to bus. publs. Grad. fellow The Scaife Found, 1973-75, The Earhart Found., 1975-76; rsch. grantee NSF, Washington, 1979-81. Mem. Am. Econs. Assn. Episcopalian. Office: Am Enterprise Inst 1150 17th St NW Washington DC 20036-4603 E-mail: cweaver@aei.org.

WEAVER, CHARLES HORACE, educator; b. Statesville, N.C., Nov. 11, 1927; s. Lucius Stacy and Elizabeth Roderick (Hallyburton) W.; m. Nancy Jane Veale, June 24, 1955; 1 child, Charles Horace. BA, Wofford Coll., Spartanburg, S.C., 1951; MA, Columbia U., 1956; PhD, U. N.C., 1961. Tchr. English Oak Ridge Mil. Inst., N.C., 1951-54, High Point (N.C.) Cen. High Sch., 1954-56; asst. prin. Ferndale Jr. High Sch., High Point, 1956-58; prin. N.E. Jr. High Sch., 1959-60, Ferndale Jr. High Sch., High Point, 1960-62; asst. supt. Asheboro (N.C.) City Schs., 1962-65; supt. Elizabeth City (N.C.) pub. schs., 1965-69, Burke County Pub. Schs., Morganton, N.C., 1969-79; with State Dept. Pub. Instrn., Raleigh, 1979—, asst. state supt. aux. svcs., 1989-96; educator Shook Design, Charlotte, N.C., 1996—. Bd. dirs. We. Carolina Bank & Trust Co., Wilmington Food Sys., Inc., Greenville Food Sys., Inc. Contbr. articles to profl. ours. Bd. dirs. Burke County United Fund, Burke County Council on Alcoholism, We. Piedmont Mental Health Assn., We Piedmont Symphony. Mem. Am. Assn. Sch. Adminstrs., N.C. Assn. Sch. Adminstrs., Horace Mann League (pres. 1975-76), High Point Jr. C. of C. (bd. dirs.), Burke Country C. of C., Rotary, Asheboro Country Club, Raleigh Capital City Club. Democrat. Methodist. Avocations: reading, golf, antiques.

WEAVER, CHARLES LYNDELL, JR. institutional and manufacturing facilities administrator, management and marketing systems consultant; b. Canonsburg, Pa., July 5, 1945; s. Charles Lyndell and Georgia Lavelle (Gardner) W.; m. Ruth Marguerite Uxa, Feb. 27, 1982; children: Charles Lyndell III, John Francis. BArch, Pa. State U., 1969; cert. in assoc. studies, U. Florence, Italy, 1968; cert. designer, Design Biuld Inst. Am., 2002. Registered architect, Pa., Md., Mo., Va., Mass., Ky., Ga.; cert. Nat. Coun. Arch. Registration Bd. With Celento & Edson, Canonsburg, part-time 1966-71; project architect Meyers & D'Aleo, Balt., 1971-76, corp. dir., v.p., 1974-76; ptnr. Borrow Assocs.-Developers, 1976-79, Crowley/Weaver Constrn. Mgmt., Balt., 1976-79; pvt. practice arch., 1976-79; cons., project mgr. U. Md., College Park, 1979-80; corp. cons. architect Bank Bldg. & Equipment Corp., Am., St. Louis, 1980-83; dir. archtl. and engring. svcs. Ladue Bldg. and Engring. Inc., 1983-84; v.p., sec. Graphic Products Corp.; pres. CWCM Inc. Internat., 1987-2000. Dir. K-12 Edn. Market Ctr. and sr. program mgr., Sverdrup Corp., 1989-95; prin. Benham Internat. Eurasia, 1995, v.p., dir. mktg. and bus. devel. The Benham Group, St. Louis, 1995-96; v.p. Chiodini Assocs., 1997-98; asst. lectr. Washington U., 1997-2000, 2002-; cons. Stifel Cap. Start Up Venture Capital Fund; ops. mgr., generations cons. Stifel Capco Venture Capital, 1998; dir. mktg. sys. The Maiman Co., 1998-99; dir. edn. program mgmt. The Integral Group, Atlanta, 1999-2001; vis. Alpha Rho Chi lectr. Pa. State U., 1983; vis. lectr. Washington U. Lindenwood Coll., 1987, Wentworth Inst., Boston, Am. Assn. Cost Engrs., So. Fla., 1994; mem. panel Assn. Univ. Architects Conv., 1983; v.p. program mgmt. and ednl. facilities Kennedy Assoc. Inc. Project bus. cons. Jr. Achievement, 1982-85; mem. cluster com., advisor Explorer Program, 1982-85; mem. Design Build Inst. Am., 1998—, splty. contractor task force chmn., 2000-2002; presenter So. Ill. Econ. Devel. Conf., 1998. Recipient 5 brochure and graphic awards Nat. Assn. Indsl. Artists, 1973; 1st award Profl. Builder/Am. Plywood Assn., 1974; Honor award, 2 articles Balt. chpt. AIA, 1974; Better Homes and Gardens award Sensible Growth, Nat. Assn. Home Builders, 1975; winner Ridgely's Delight Competition, Balt., 1976. Mem. ASCD, BBC Credit Union (bd. dirs. 1983-85), AACE (conv. spkr. So. Fla. sect. 1994), Vitruvius Alumni Assn., Pa. State Alumni Assn., BOCA, NFPA, AIA, Constrn. Specifications Inst., Am. Assn. Sch. Adminstrs. (nat. coun., panel moderator 1994), Coun. Ednl. Facilities Planners, Assn. Sch. Bus. Ofcls. (Mehlville Mo. schs. program mgmt. 1992-94, Chelsea, Mass. 1993-95, Orange County, Fla. 1994-95, Macon, Ga. 1999-2000, Atlantic City, N.J. 2000-2001), Alpha Rho Chi (nat. treas. 1980-82, dir. nat. found. treas. 1989-97), Optimists Internat. Office: 1318 Shenandoah Ave Saint Louis MO 63104-4123

WEAVER, CHRISTOPHER E. naval officer; BS, U.S. Naval Acad., 1971; MPA, George Washington U.; Disting. Grad., Indsl. Coll. of Armed Forces. Commd. ensign USN, 1971, advanced through ranks to rear adm.; various assignments to comdg. officer USS Spruance (DD 963), U.S. Naval Sta., Norfolk, Va.; commandant Naval Dist., Washington. Decorated Legion of Merit. Office: Commandant Naval Dist Washington 1014 N St SE Ste 200 Washington DC 20374-5001 E-mail: christopher.weaver@ndw.navy.mil.

WEAVER, CRYSTAL DAWN, interior design educator; b. Baltimore, Ohio, Feb. 9, 1957; d. Richard Laurence and Dawn Lamont (Brehm) W. BS, Morehead State U., 1979; MS, U. Tenn., 1980, PhD, 1984. Asst. prof. Ball State U., Muncie, Ind., 1983-86; assoc. prof. Mankato (Minn.) State U., 1986-89; assoc. prof. interior design Western Carolina U., Cullowhee, N.C., 1989-91; prof. interior design The Savannah Coll. Art and Design, 1992—. Owner The Interiors Group, Sylva, N.C., 1989—, Mankato, Minn., 1988-89; lectr. in field. Mem. Am. Soc. Interior Designers-Allied, Nat. Trust for Historic Preservation, Phi Kappa Phi, Kappa Omicron Phi, Phi Upsilon Omicron. Avocation: travel. Office: Savannah Coll Art and Design PO Box 3146 Savannah GA 31402-3146

WEAVER, DAVID HUGH, journalism educator, communications researcher; b. Hammond, Ind., Dec. 23, 1946; s. David W. and Josephine L. Weaver; m. Gail Shriver, June 28, 1969; children: Quinn David, Lesley Jo. BA, Ind. U., Bloomington, 1968, MA, 1969; PhD, U. N.C., 1974. Copy editor The Post-Tribune, Gary, Ind., 1968; wire editor, reporter The Courier-Tribune, Bloomington, 1968; wire editor The Chapel Hill Newspaper, N.C., 1973; asst. prof. journalism Ind. U., Bloomington, 1974-78, assoc. prof., 1978-83, prof., 1983-88, Roy W. Howard prof. Ind., 1988—. Author: Videotex Journalism, 1983; co-author: Newsroom Guide to Polls and Surveys, 1980, 90, Media Agenda-Setting, 1981, The American Journalist, 1986 (award Soc. Profl. Journalists 1987), 2d edit., 1991, The Formation of Campaign Agendas, 1991, Contemporary Public Opinion, 1991, The American Journalist in the 1990's, 1996 (award Soc. Profl. Journalists 1997); co-editor: Communication and Democracy, 1997; editor: The Global Journalist, 1998. Lt. U.S. Army, 1969-71. Fellow Midwest Pub. Opinion Rsch. (pres. 1986-87), Internat. Comm. Assn.; mem. Assn. for Edn. in Journalism and Mass Comm. (pres. 1987-88, Krieghbaum award 1983), Soc. Prof. Journalists. Avocations: guitar, music. Office: Ind U Sch Journalism Ernie Pyle Hall Bloomington IN 47405-7108

WEAVER, DELBERT ALLEN, lawyer; b. Shoshone, Idaho, May 28, 1931; s. Arlo Irving and Kate Rosamond (McCarter) W.; m. Jeanne Carol Alford, June 1959; children: Tobin Elizabeth, Michael Andrew, Matthew Stewart, Edward Malcolm. BA, U. Oreg., 1953, LLB, 1956. Bar: Oreg. 1956, U.S. Dist. Ct. Oreg. 1956, U.S. Ct. Appeals (9th cir.) 1968. Ptnr. Weaver & Oram, Eugene, Oreg., 1956-59; dep. atty. City of Portland, 1959-68; assoc. Winfree, Latourette, Murphy, et al., Portland, 1968-71; stockbroker Dupont Glore Forgan, 1971-73; securities examiner corp. div. State of Oreg., Salem, 1973-75, dep. commr. corp. div., 1975-80; pvt. practice Portland, 1980-87; counsel Schwabe, Williamson & Wyatt, 1987-90, sr. ptnr., 1991-96; pvt. practice, 1996-2000; counsel Dunn, Carney, 2000—. Office: Ste 1500 851 SW 6th Ave Portland OR 97204-1001

WEAVER, DONNA RAE, company executive; b. Chgo., Oct. 15, 1945; d. Albert Louis and Gloria Elaine (Graffis) Florence; m. Clifford L. Weaver, Aug. 20, 1966; 1 child, Megan Rae. BS in Edn., No. Ill. U., 1966, EdD, 1977; MEd, De Paul U., 1974. Tchr. H.L. Richards High Sch., Oak Lawn, Ill., 1966-71, Sawyer Coll. Bus., Evanston, 1971-72; asst. prof. Oakton Community Coll., Morton Grove, 1972-75; vis. prof. U. Ill., Chgo., 1977-78; dir. devel. Mallinckrodt Coll., Wilmette, Ill., 1978-80, dean, 1980-83; campus dir. Nat.-Louis U., Chgo., 1983-90, dean div. applied behavioral scis., 1985-89; dean Coll. Mgmt. and Bus., 1989-90; pres. The Oliver Group, Inc., Kenilworth, Ill., 1993-97; mng. ptnr. Le Miccine, Gaiole-in-Chianti, Tuscany, Italy, 1996—. Cons. Nancy Lovely and Assocs., Wilmette, 1981-84, North Ctrl. Assn., Chgo., 1982-90. Contbr. articles to Am. Vocat. Jour., Ill. Bus. Edn. Assn. Monograph, Nat. Coll. Edn.'s ABS Rev., Nat. View. Mem. Ill. Quality of Work Life Coun., 1987-90, New Trier Twp. Health and Human Svcs. Adv. Bd., Winnetka, Ill., 1985-88; bd. dirs. Open Lands Project, 1985-87, Kenilworth (Ill.) Village House, 1986-87. Recipient Achievement award Women in Mgmt., 1981; Am. Bd. Master Educators charter disting. fellow, 1986. Mem. Nat. Bus. Edn. Assn., Delta Pi Epsilon (past pres.). Avocations: reading, traveling, decorating. Office: 505 N Lake Shore Dr Apt 4010 Chicago IL 60611-3619

WEAVER, ELIZABETH A. state supreme court justice; b. New Orleans; d. Louis and Mary Weaver. BA, Newcomb Coll.; JD, Tulane U. Elem. tchr. Glen Lake Cmty. Sch., Maple City, Mich.; French tchr. Leelanau Sch., Glen Arbor; pvt. practice; law clk. Civil Dist. Ct., New Orleans; atty. Coleman, Dutrey & Thomson; atty., title specialist Chevron Oil Co.; probate and juvenile judge Leelanau County, Mich., 1975—86; judge Mich. Ct. of Appeals, 1987—94; justice Mich. Supreme Ct., Lansing, 1995—. Chief justice Mich. Supreme Ct., 1999—2000; instr. edn. dept. Ctr. Mich. U.; mem. Mich. Com. on Juvenile Justice, Nat. Conv. State Adv. Groups on Juvenile Justice for U.S.; chair Gov.'s Task Force on Children's Justice, Trial Ct. Assessment Commn., Office Juvenile Justice and Delinquency Prevention; jud. adv. bd. mem. Law and Orgnl. Econs. Ctr. U. Kans.; treas. Children's Charter of Cts. of Mich. Chairperson Western Mich. U. CLE Adv. Bd.; mem. steering com. Grand Traverse/Leelanau Commn. on Youth; mem. Glen Arbor Twp. Zoning Bd.; mem. charter arts north Leelanau County; mem. citizen's adv. coun. Arnell Engstrom Children's Ctr.; mem. cmty. adv. com. Pathfinder Sch. Treaty Law Demonstration Project; active Grand Traverse/Leelanau Mental Health Found. Named Jurist of Yr., Police Officers Assn. of Mich.; named one of five Outstanding Young Women in Mich., Mich. Jaycees; recipient Eastern award, Warren Easton Hall of Fame. Fellow: Mich. State Bar Found.; mem.: ABA, Antrim County Bar Assn., Leelanau County Bar Assn., Grand Traverse County Bar Assn., La. Bar Assn., Nat. Coun. Juvenile and Family Judges, Mich. Bar Assn. (chair CLE adv. bd., chair crime prevention ctr., chair juvenile law com.), Delta Kappa Gamma (hon.). Office: Mich Supreme Ct 3300 Grandview Plz 10850 E Traverse Hwy Traverse City MI 49684-1364

WEAVER, ESTHER RUTH, medical and surgical, geriatrics and oncology nurse; b. Kansas City, Mo., Mar. 20, 1951; d. Fred Bicknell and Mary Elizabeth (Williams) Crigler; 1 child, Scott Lee McPhee; m. Charles Edward Weaver, June 10, 1995; stepchildren: Alan Bower, Ward. ADN, Eastern N.Mex. U., Roswell, 1989. RN; cert. chemotherapy nurse, cert. in basic critical care, ACLS. Staff nurse med. floor St. Mary's Hosp., Roswell, Eastern N.Mex. Med. Ctr., Roswell; night nurse Sunset Villa Care Ctr.; nurse supr. Turtle Creek Health Care Ctr., Jacksonville, Fla.; oncology staff nurse dept. corrections unit Meml. Med. Ctr.; oncology nurse Office of Dr. Harvey Sher; asst. dir. nursing Tandem of Jacksonville; DON SunBridge of North Jacksonville; nursing assessment coord. IHS, Orange Park, Fla. Mem. Merrill Rd. Bapt. Ch.; MDS Coord., IHS Orange Park. Nursing Found. scholar. Mem.: N.Mex. Nurses Assn. (publicity chmn. Dist. 5), Assn. for Profls. in Infection Control and Epidemiology, Inc., Phi Theta Kappa (v.p.). E-mail: clownrn@hotmail.com.

WEAVER, FRANCES M. health services researcher; b. Arlington, Va., Feb. 24, 1959; d. Joseph F.P. and Hedwig Weaver; m. Joseph A. Tomaszek, Oct. 10, 1987; children: Lindsay Tomaszek, Lauren Tomaszek. PhD, Loyola U., 1987. Dep. dir. Midwest Ctr. Health Svcs. and Policy Rsch. VA Hosp., Hines, Ill., 2000—. Rschr. JAMA, 2000. Mem. editl. bd. Evaluation and the Health Professions, 1996; prin. investigator Dept. Vet. Affairs, 1997-2002. Mem. Assn. Health Svcs. Rsch., Am. Evaluation Assn., Am. Paraplegia Soc. (prin. investigator). Office: Health Svcs R&D 151H VA Hosp Hines IL 60141 Fax: 708-202-2316. E-mail: weaver@research.hines.med.va.gov.

WEAVER, GLENN DAVID, minister, educator; b. Glen Ridge, Nj, July 30, 1947; s. John Vetter and Jannette Weaver; m. Linda Lee Weaver, Feb. 11, 1978; children: David Evan, Andrew Mark. PhD Psychology, Princeton U., Princeton, New Jersey, 1978, MA Psychology, 1974; M.Div., Princeton Theol. Sem., Princeton, New Jersey, 1972; BA, Wheaton Coll., Wheaton, Illinois, 1969. Psychology educator Calvin Coll., Grand Rapids, Mich., 1975—. Min. Presbyn. Ch. U.S.A., Grand Rapids, Mich., 1985—. Contbr. chapters to books on psychology and religion. Recipient Templeton Sci. and Religion Course Award, The John Templeton Found., 1998, 2001. Mem.: APA, Am. Psychol. Soc. Presbyterian. Office: Calvin College 3201 Burton South East Grand Rapids MI 49546 Office Fax: 616-957-8551. E-mail: weav@calvin.edu.

WEAVER, HENRY DAVID, retired educational administrator, consultant; b. Harrisonburg, Va., May 5, 1928; s. Henry D. and Sallie J. Weaver; m. Mary Eby, June 7, 1952; children: Sally, Judy, Debora, Donald. BS, George Washington U., 1950; PhD, U. Del., 1953. Assoc. prof. chemistry Ea. Mennonite Coll., Harrisonburg, 1951-57; prof. chemistry, provost Goshen (Ind.) Coll., 1957-79; cons. chemistry San Marcos U., Lima, Peru, 1964-65; prof. chemistry Tribhuvon U., Kathmandu, Nepal, 1969-70; interim pres. Goshen Coll., 1996; interim dean Am. U. in Bulgaria, Blageovgrad, 1995; dep. dir. edn. abroad U. Calif. Sys., Santa Barbara, 1979-91; ret. Examiner North Cen. Assn. Schs. and Colls., Chgo., 1971-79; cons. Whirlpool Corp., Benton Harbor, Mich., 1962-64, also various ednl. orgns., Santa Barbara, Calif., 1979—. Author: (book) Confronting the Big C, 1983 (Silver Angel 1987); editor: (book) Research on U.S. Students Abroad, 1989; co-author: (book) Students Abroad-Strangers at Home, 1992, (textbook) Physical Science Survey, 1958. Fellow Am. Sci. Affiliation (chair 1962); mem. AAAS, Am. Chem. Soc. (sect. chair 1969), Internat. Student Exch. Program (chair 1962), NAFSA Assn. of Internat. Educators (life, sect. chair 1984-85), Coun. on Internat. Ednl. Exch. (chair 1973-78, Svc. award 1991). Avocation: photography. Home: 1332 Pebble Ct Goshen IN 46528-5064

WEAVER, HOWARD C. newspaper executive; b. Anchorage, Oct. 15, 1950; s. Howard Gilbert and Lurlene Eloise (Gamble) W.; m. Alice Laprele Gauchay, July 16, 1970 (div. 1974); m. Barbara Lynn Hodgin, Sept. 16, 1978. BA Johns Hopkins U., 1972, MPhil Cambridge U., 1993. Reporter, staff writer Anchorage Daily News, 1972—76, columnist, 1979—80, mng. editor, 1980—83, editor, 1983—95; editor, owner Alaska Advocate, 1976—79; asst. to pres. McClatchy Newspapers, 1995—97, editor of editl. pages, 1997—2001; v.p. news The McClatchy Co., 2001—. Internat. co-chair Northern News Svc., 1989—94; disting. lectr. journalism U. Alaska, Fairbanks, 1991. Pulitzer Prize juror, 1988, 1989, 1994, 1995, 2001; bd. visitors John S. Knight Fellowship Stanford U. Recipient Pulitzer prize, 1976, 1989, Headliner award, Press Club of Atlantic City, 1976, 1989, Gold medal, Investigative Reporters and Editors, 1989, Pub. Svc. award, AP Mng. Editor's Assn., 1976, 1989. Mem.: Investigative Reporters and Editors, Am. Soc. Newspaper Editors, Upper Yukon River Press Club (pres. 1972), Alaska Press Club (bd. dirs. 1972—84), Sigma Delta Chi (Nat. award 1989). Avocations: ice hockey, foreign travel, opera .

WEAVER, JACQUELYN KUNKEL IVEY, artist, educator; b. Richmond, Ky., Mar. 14, 1931; d. Marion David and Margaret Tabitha (Brandenburg) Kunkel; m. George Thomas IveySr., 1951 (dec. 1989); children: George Thomas Ivey Jr., David Richard Ivey; m. Harrell Fuller Weaver, 1991. BFA, Wesleyan Coll., 1987. Owner J. K. Ivey Art, Macon, Ga., 1974-91, J.K. Ivey Bookkeeping and Tax Svc., Macon, 1976-84, Ivey-Weaver Art Studio, Macon, 1991—. Tchg. drawing, painting and sculpture, 1991—. Exhibited works in galleries including Mid. Ga. Art Assn. Gallery, Macon, 1980—, Mus. Arts and Scis., 1987—, 1991—, 1994—, 1996—, 1998—, Attaway Cottage, 1990—, AAPL Salmugundi Club, N.Y.C., 1992, Frames and Art Gallery, Macon, 1995—, CLWAC Nat. Arts Club, N.Y.C., 1995—, Stofko-Dixon Fine Arts, Bolingbroke, Ga., 1996—2001, Hilton Head Island (S.C.) Art League, Self Family Art Ctr., 1997—2001, Christopher Gallery, Cohasset, Mass., 1997, 1998, Parthenon (Tenn. Art League) Centennial Park, Nashville, 1998, Lowndes/Valdosta Cult. Arts Ctr., Valdosta, Ga., 1992, 1994—98. Bd. dirs., treas. Mid. Ga. Art Assn., Macon, 1981-84, 92, publicity chmn., 1988-89, chmn. nominating com., 1997, mem. fin. com., 1998-99, audit com., 1998. Mem. Nat. Mus. Women in Arts (charter mem.), Wesleyan Coll. Alumnae Assn., Mus. Arts and Scis., Catherine Lorillard Wolf Art Club, Middle Ga. Art Assn., Portrait Painters Am., Inc. Presbyterian. Avocations: ballroom dancing, reading, walking, music. Office: Ivey-Weaver Art Studio 6183 Hwy 87 Macon GA 31210 Fax: 478-744-0983. E-mail: jweave550@bellsouth.net.

WEAVER, JOEL SMITH, education educator; b. Kinshasa, Zaire, June 3, 1962; came to U.S., 1980; s. Cecil Gerald and Lillian Lee (Smith) W.; m. Michelle Yunu Lee, Dec. 29, 1990; children: Brianna Lee, Sabrina Lee. BA, Calif. Poly. State U., 1986; MA, U. Hawaii, 1988. Instr. Zaire-Am. Lang. Inst., Kinshasa, 1985; instr. English Lang. Inst. U. Hawaii, Honolulu, 1986-88, instr. new intensive courses in English, 1988-90, coord. new intensive courses in English, 1990, program coord. spl. English programs, 1990-91, learning resources coord. John Burns Sch. Medicine, 1991-92; ednl. specialist Multifunctional Resource Ctr., 1992-96; multimedia lab. coord. Intercultural Comm. Coll., 1996-98, dir., 1998—. Presenter Am. Assn. for Applied Linguistics, 1995, Pacific Region Edn. Conf., Saipan, 1993-94; cons. for lang. Pacific Math./Sci. Leadership Team, Honolulu, 1994; on-site accreditation evaluater Accrediting Coun. for Continuing Edn. and Tng. Author, presenter: (video module) Adapting Materials for Science & Math, 1993; co-author: (annotated bibliography) Methods/Strategies for Teaching Pacific Islanders, 1994 Mem. ASCD, TESOL, Nat. Assn. Fgn. Student Advisors, Fedn. Ind. Youth Travel Orgns., Hawaii Assn. Asian/Pacific-Am. Educators. Evangelical. Avocations: playing guitar, riding, motorcycles, surfing. Office: Intercultural Comm Coll Ste 1000 1601 Kapiolani Blvd Honolulu HI 96814 E-mail: weaver@jgvenglish.com.

WEAVER, KARL E. psychiatrist; b. Lakewood, Ohio, July 1, 1950; m. Christine R. Weaver. BA in Psychology, Haverford (Pa.) Coll., 1972; MD, Case Western Res. U., 1978. Bd. cert., cert. in forensic psychiatry Am. Bd. Psychiatry and Neurology; lic. physician Calif. Flexible intern Mt. Sinai Hosp., Cleve., 1978-79; psychiatry resident Univ. Hosps. of Cleve., 1979-82; pvt. practice Cleve., 1982-94; staff psychiatrist Calif. Men's Colony, San Luis Obispo, 1994-95, sr. psychiatrist, supr., 1995, chief psychiatrist, 1995—. Chmn. dept. psychiatry St. John & St. John Westshore Hosps., Cleve., 1985-90, Fairview Gen. Hosp., Cleve., 1992-94; pres., bd. dirs. St. John & St. John Westshore Profl. Corp., 1989-90; contract psychiatrist San Luis Obispo County Mental Health, 1997—, TeleCare, Santa Maria, Calif., 1998—. Address: PO Box 12826 San Luis Obispo CA 93406-2826 Office: PO Box 8101 San Luis Obispo CA 93403-8101 E-mail: karlweaver@msn.com.

WEAVER, KITRA K. sales executive; b. Tawas City, Mich., Apr. 12, 1957; d. James Elmer Jr. and Glenda Kay (Ray) Weaver; m. Mark William Goldstein, Apr. 20, 1985 (div. Mar. 1989). Grad. h.s., Houston, 1975. Contract sales rep. Gen. Office Outfitters, Dallas, 1982-85; v.p. Money Saver Advertiser, 1985-88; dir. mktg. One Hour Motophoto, 1985-88; br. mgr. Meta Gram Am., 1988-90; sales rep. Rollins Protective Svc., Atlanta, 1990-92; regional sales mgr. The Marlin Co., North Haven, Conn., 1992—. Mentor The Marlin Co., Orlando, Fla., 1993-98. Chair ticket com. SOS/Taste of the Nation, Orlando, 1991-2000; chair ticket sales UCP.Ctrl. Fla. Chili Cookoff, Orlando, 1990-93. Republican. Methodist. Avocations: cooking, reading, sports, fundraising, the arts. Office: The Marlin Co 100 Kenna Dr North Haven CT 06473-2516

WEAVER, KITTY DUNLAP, author; b. Frankfort, Ky., Sept. 24, 1910; d. Arch Robertson and Rebecca (Johnson) Dunlap; m. Henry Byrne Weaver, June 29, 1933. Student, Sorbonne, Paris, summer 1930; AB, William and Mary Coll., 1932; MA, George Washington U., 1933; BS, U. Md., 1947; postgrad., Georgetown U., U. Pa., George Washington U., 1964-67, Moscow U., 1983; studied with Alfred Adler, Vienna, 1932. Jr. H.S. tchr., 1931-32; poultry farmer, 1947-55; author, 1970—. Author: Lenin's Grandchildren, 1971, Russia's Future, 1981, Bushels of Rubles, 1992. Mem. Sulgrave (Washington) Club, Aldie Hort. Soc., Chevy Chase (Md.) Club, Met. Club (Washington), Garden Club Am., Fauquier London Garden Club. Home: 40820 John Mosby Hwy Aldie VA 20105-2820 also: 603 Pennsylvania Ave NW Apt 504 Washington DC 20004-2602

WEAVER, LEAH ANN, journalist, speech writer; b. Galion, Ohio, May 4, 1958; d. William Hiram and Virginia Louise (Reif) Weaver; m. Charles Lamont Hall, Jr., Apr. 14, 1990. BA, Malone Coll., Canton, Ohio, 1980; MA, Ohio State U., 1989. Program coord. editorial projects Ohio State U. Office of the Pres., Columbus, 1989-92, editorial coord., 1992-96, editor, 1996-99; copywriter Resource Marketing, 1999-2001, Gerbig, Snell & Weisheimer Advt., Inc., Columbus, 2001; dir. comms Big Lots, Inc., 2001—. English tutor Creative Living, Columbus, 1987, 88. Author: (plays) Wilber and Wife, 1989, Dora Dodd, 1991; contbg. writer Univ. Comms., Columbus, 1993—; spl. assignment reporter The Lantern, Columbus, 1987-88; freelance scriptwriter Ctr. for Teaching Excellence, Columbus, 1989; contbr. articles to jours. Mem. Soc. Profl. Journalists, N.Y. Dramatists Guild (playwright and assoc. mem.), Authors League Am., Coun. for Advancement and Support of Edn., Kappa Tau Alpha, Phi Kappa Phi. Avocations: playwrighting, freelance feature writing. E-mail: lweaver@biglots.com.

WEAVER, LYNN EDWARD, academic administrator, consultant, editor; b. St. Louis, Jan. 12, 1930; s. Lienous E. and Estelle F. (Laspe) W.; m. JoAnn D., 1951 (div. 1981); children: Terry Sollenberger, Gwen, Bart, Stephen, Wes; m. Anita G. Gomez, Oct. 27, 1983. BSEE, U. Mo., 1951; MSEE, So. Meth. U., 1955; PhD, Purdue U., 1958. Devel. engr. McDonnell Aircraft, St. Louis, 1952-53; aerophysics engr. Convair Corp., Ft. Worth, 1953-55; instr. elec. engring. Purdue U., Lafayette, Ind., 1955-58; assoc. prof., then prof., dept. head U. Ariz., Tucson, 1959-69; assoc. dean coll. engring. U. Okla., Norman, 1969-70; exec. asst. to pres. Argonne Univs., Chgo., 1970-72; dir. sch. nuclear engring. and health physics Ga. Inst. Tech., 1972-82; dean engring., disting. prof. Auburn (Ala.) U., 1982-87; pres. Fla. Inst. Tech., Melbourne, 1987—. Cons. Ga. Power; bd. dirs. Oak Ridge Associated Univs., 1984-87, DBA Systems, Inc., Melbourne, Fla.; chmn. pub. affairs coun. Am. Assn. Engring. Soc., Washington, 1984-87; bd. advisors Ctr. for Sci., Tech. & Media, Washington; chmn. Ind. Colls. and Univs. of Fla., 1998. Author: (textbook) Reactor Dynamics & Control, State Space Techniques, 1968; exec. editor Annals of Nuclear Energy; contbr. numerous articles to tech. jours. U.S. rep. World Fedn., Engring. Orgn. Energy Com., 1981-86. Served to lt. USAF, 1951-53. Recipient Mo. Honors award for disting. svc. in engring., 1996. Fellow Am. Nuclear Soc.; mem. IEEE (sr.), Am. Soc. Engring. Edn., Sigma Xi. Clubs: Eau Gallie Yacht. Republican. Roman Catholic. Avocations: tennis, jogging. Office: Fla Inst Tech 150 W University Blvd Melbourne FL 32901-6975

WEAVER, MARIANNE GRUHN, flutist; b. Milw., Apr. 30, 1942; d. Harold William and Helen Kathryn (Pearson) Gruhn; m. John Borland Weaver, Dec. 28, 1965; children: Jonathan Kirk, Kirianne Elizabeth. BS in Music Edn., U. Wis., Milw., 1964; MusM in Flute, Manhattan Sch. Music, 1965; studied with, Academie Internationale D'ete, Nice, France, 1969; master classes with Marcel Moyse, Brattleboro, Vt., 1980. Ind. flutist various groups, 1965—; 1st flutist Bach Cantata Orch., N.Y.C., 1968-94, Village Light Opera Group, 1970—. Adj. artist, Karen McFarlane Artists, Inc., 1967—, treas. Nat. Centennial Convention of the Am. Guild of Organists (AGO), 1996. Albums: Music For Flute and Organ, 1969, The Sounds of MAPC, 1978, The Music of John Weaver, 1986. Mu Phi Epsilon scholar, Milw., 1964. Mem. Nat. Flute Assn., Associated Musicians Greater N.Y. (local 802). Avocations: bicycling, hiking, gardening, reading, knitting. Home and Office: 921 Madison Ave New York NY 10021-3508

WEAVER, MARIE ANTOINETTE, graphic design educator; b. Wilmington, Del., Feb. 16, 1952; d. Luther Conwell and Mary Antoinette (Maucher) W.; m. Larry Leroy Sampson, Dec. 13, 1978 (div. Aug. 1983); 1 child, Ian Ezekiel; m. Stephen Craig Harvey, Jan. 3, 1987. BA, U. Vt., 1976; MFA, Syracuse U., 1989. Printmaker's asst. Tontine Press/Sabra Field, East Barnard, Vt., 1976-77; chief graphic arts U. Ala., Birmingham, 1982-85, prof. graphic design, 1990—; instr. U. Montevallo (Ala.), 1985-86. Owner Weaver Design, Birmingham, 1985—; ptnr. Weaver Miller Martin, Inc., Birmingham, 1986-88. Group exhbns., Ala., 1992-2001; design work published in books. Recipient Tchg. Excellence award U. Ala. Birmingham; grantee in field. Mem. Am. Inst. Graphic Artists (v.p. Birmingham 1987-89, pres. 1989-90, treas. 1994-99). Avocations: book arts, gardening, film/video, travel, hiking. Office: U Ala 1530 3d Ave S Birmingham AL 35294-1260

WEAVER, MARSHALL GUERINGER, lawyer; b. New Orleans, Mar. 8, 1954; s. Walter Albert and Virginia (Dove) W.; m. Maria Loo, May 23, 2000. BA, Washington and Lee U., 1977; JD, Tulane U., 1980. Bar: La. 1980. Law clk. to judge 24th Jud. Dist. Ct., Jefferson, La., 1980-81; assoc. Donovan & Lawler, Metairie, 1981-86, Henican, James & Cleveland, Metairie, 1986-88, ptnr., 1988—. Mem. New Orleans Pro Bono Project, 1988—. Mem. student editorial bd. Maritime Lawyer, 1979-80. Mem. France-Amerique La., Inc. New Orleans, 1985—, Preservation Resource Ctr., New Orleans, 1987—. Mem. ABA, La. Bar Assn., New Orleans Bar Assn., Def. Rsch. Inst., La. Mayflower Soc., New Orleans Mus. Art, La. Div. Magna Carta Barons, So. Yacht Club. Republican. Episcopalian. Avocations: tennis, golf, sailing. Home: 418 Audubon St New Orleans LA 70118-4902 Office: Ste 1520 111 Veterans Memorial Blvd Metairie LA 70005-3012 E-mail: mweaver@henja.com.

WEAVER, MICHAEL GLENN, pharmacist; b. Tuscola, Ill., Sept. 11, 1955; s. Glen H. and Margaret I. (Long) W.; m. Catherine A. (Paynic), Sept. 30, 1978; children: Jennifer L., Michelle R., Gregory M. BS, St. Louis Coll. of Pharmacy, 1978; MBA, So. Ill. U., 1989. Registered pharmacist, Ill. Clin. coordinator, staff pharmacist St. Elizabeth Med. Ctr., Granite City, Ill., 1975-87; dir. pharmacy Freeport (Ill.) Meml. Hosp. (now Freeport Health Network), 1987-92, dir. pharmacy and info. systems, 1992-97, dir. info. and telecom. svcs., 1997—; dir. Ill. Bd. Pharmacy, 1995-99, AeroComputing, Inc., 2001—. Allocations com. United Way of N.W. Ill., 2000—. Mem.: Am. Coll. Healthcare Execs., Ill. Coun. Hosp. Pharmacists (dir. ednl. affairs 1991—94), Ill. Pharm. Assn., Am. Soc. Hosp. Pharmacists, Kiwanis (bd. dirs. Lincoln-Douglas chpt. 2002—), Delta Sigma Theta, Beta Gamma Sigma, Phi Kappa Phi. Republican. Mem. United Church of Christ. Avocations: computer, music, tennis, swimming, racquetball. Home: 1346 Carriage Hill Ln Freeport IL 61032-6168 Office: Freeport Health Network 1045 W Stephenson St Freeport IL 61032-4899

WEAVER, MICHAEL JAMES, lawyer; b. Bakersfield, Calif., Feb. 11, 1946; s. Kenneth James and Elsa Hope (Rogers) W.; m. Valerie Scott, Sept. 2, 1966; children: Christopher James, Brett Michael, Karen Ashley. AB, Calif. State U., Long Beach, 1968; JD magna cum laude, U. San Diego, 1973. Bar: Calif., 1973, U.S. Dist. Ct. (so. dist.) Calif. 1973, U.S. Ct. Appeals (9th cir.) 1975, U.S. Supreme Ct. 1977. Law clk. to chief judge U.S. Dist. Ct. (so. dist.) Calif., San Diego, 1973-75; 1st v.p. Latham & Watkins. Judge pro tem San Diego Superior Ct.; master of the Bench of the Inn, Am. Inns of Ct., Louis M. Welch chpt.; lectr. Inn of Ct., San Diego, 1981—, Continuing Edn. of Bar, Calif., 1983—, Workshop for Judges U.S. Ct. Appeals (9th cir.), 1990; mem. task force on establishment of bus. cts. sys. Jud. Coun. Calif., 1996-97. Editor-in-chief: San Diego Law Rev., 1973; contbr. articles to profl. jours. Bd. dirs., pres. San Diego Kidney Found., 1985-90; bd. dirs. San Diego Aerospace Mus., 1985-97; trustee La Jolla (Calif.) Playhouse, 1990-91. lt. USNR, 1968-74. Fellow Am. Coll. Trial Lawyers; mem. San Diego Assn. Bus. Trial Lawyers (founding mem., bd. govs.), San Diego Def. Lawyers Assn. (dir.), Am. Arbitration Assn., 9th Cir. Jud. Conf. (del. 1987-90), Calif. Supreme Ct. Hist. Assn. (bd. dirs. 1998—), Safari Club Internat. (San Diego chpt.), San Diego Sportsmen's Club, Coronado Yacht Club. Republican. Presbyterian. Avocations: reading, family activities, flying, skiing. Office: Latham & Watkins 701 B St Ste 2100 San Diego CA 92101-8197 E-mail: mike.weaver@lw.com.

WEAVER, MICHELE, project director; b. Paterson, N.J., Aug. 13, 1947; d. Frederick John Croegaert and Marie Louise Nunnink; m. David Anthony Weaver, Feb. 19, 1971 (div. 1986); 1 child, Dawn Marie Hallit. Student, Immaculate Heart Acad., 1965, Montclair State, 1965-66. Directory prod. mgr. Bell Atlantic, Glen Ridge, N.J., 1992-93, project lead "pride" implementation Bethesda, Md., 1993-94, project lead billing engine implementation Arlington, Va., 1995—2001; ret., 2001. Cons. Talisman Technologies, McLean, Va., 1998-99. Home: 7 Saddleback Tr Rochester NY 14624

WEAVER, NORMAN LAZELLE, software engineer; b. Rockingham, Vt., Nov. 25, 1951; s. Frank Linn and Martha (Norris) W.; m. Lynette Darlene Norton, Aug. 5, 1975; children: Bryn, Lauren. BSME, U. Colo., 1975; MS, Stanford U., 1976. Registered profl. engr., Colo. Mem. energy ctr. staff SRI Internat., Menlo Park, Calif., 1976-77; rsch. asst. Colo. State U., Ft. Collins, 1977-80; staff engr. Regional Systems Svcs. Group, Denver, 1980-84; software engr. Solar Energy Rsch. Inst., Golden, 1984—90; v.p. engring. Environ. Rsch. Group Internat., 1990—95; pres. InterWeaver Consulting, 1995—. Mem. Am. Assn. for Artificial Intelligence, IEEE (computer soc.). Avocations: sailing, ski mountaineering.

WEAVER, PAMELA ANN, hospitality research professional; b. Little Falls, N.Y., July 7, 1947; d. Floyd Aron Weaver and Norma May (Putnam) Hoyer; m. Ken Ward McCleary, Mar. 2, 1947; children: Brian Wilson, Blake McCleary, Ryan McCleary. AA, Fulton Montgomery C.C., Amsterdam, NY, 1968; BA, SUNY, 1970; MA, U. South Fla., 1973; PhD, Mich. State U., East Lansing, 1978. Mem. math. dept. Riviera Jr. H.S., Miami, Fla., 1970-72; grad. asst. Office Med., Edn. R & D Mich. State U., East Lansing, 1973-74, grad. asst. dept. mktg., 1974-75, instr. mktg.; asst. prof. mktg., hospitality svcs. administrn. Ctrl. Mich. State U., Mt. Pleasant, 1978-79, 1982-86, chair acad. senate, 1985-86, prof. mktg., hospitality svcs. administrn., 1986-89; prof. dept. hospitality and tourism mgmt. Va. Poly. Inst. and State U., Blacksburg,

1989—. Contbr. articles to profl. jours. Mem. Coun. on Hotel, Restaurant and Instl. Edn. (John Wiley & Sons, Inc. award for Lifetime Achievement to Hospitality Industry 1994). Office: Va Poly Inst and State U Wallace Hall Blacksburg VA 24061-0429

WEAVER, PEGGY (MARGUERITE MCKINNIE WEAVER), plantation owner; b. Jackson, Tenn., June 7, 1925; d. Franklin Allen and Mary Alice (Caradine) McKinnie; children: Elizabeth Lynn, Thomas Jackson III, Franklin A. McKinnie. Student, U. Colo., 1943-45, Am. Acad. Dramatic Arts, 1945-46, S. Meisner's Profl. Classes, 1949, Oxford U., 1990, 91. Actress, 1946-52; mem. staff Mus. Modern Art, N.Y.C., 1949-50; woman's editor radio sta. WTJS-AM-FM, Jackson, Tenn., 1952-55; editor, radio/TV Jackson Sun Newspaper, 1952-55; columnist Bolivar (Tenn.) Bulletin-Times, 1986—; chmn. Ho. of Reps. of Old Line Dist., Hardeman County, Tenn., 1985-91, 94-97. Founder Paris-Henry County (Tenn.) Arts Coun., 1965; pres. Assn. Preservation of Tenn. Antiquities, Hardeman County chpt., 1991-95; charter mem. adv. bd. Tenn. Arts Commn., Nashville, 1967-74, Tenn. Performing Arts Ctr., Nashville, 1972—; chmn. Tenn. Libr. Assn., Nashville, 1973-74; regional chmn. Opera Memphis, 1979-91; mem. nat. coun. Met. Opera, N.Y.C., 1980-92, Tenn. Bicentennial Com., Hardeman County, 1993-96; sec. Memphis Brooks Mus. League, 1998-99. Mem. DAR, Nat. Soc. Colonial Dames Am. (chmn. Memphis chpt. 2002), Oxford Alumni Assn. N.Y., English Speaking Union (London chpt.), Summit (Memphis), Dilettantes (Memphis) (treas. 1997-98). Methodist. Avocations: horseback riding, travel, theatre. Office: 402 Heritage Plantation Hickory Valley TN 38042

WEAVER, RICHARD L., II, writer, speaker, educator; b. Hanover, N.H., Dec. 5, 1941; s. Richard L. and Florence B. (Grow) W.; m. Andrea A. Willis; children: R. Scott, Jacquelynn Michelle, Anthony Keith, Joanna Corinne. AB, U. Mich., 1964, MA, 1965; PhD, Ind. U., 1969. Asst. prof. U. Mass., 1968-74; assoc. prof. speech communication Bowling Green State U., 1974-79, prof., 1979-96, dir., basic speech communication course, 1974-96. Vis. prof. U. Hawaii-Manoa, 1981-82, Bond U., Queensland, Australia, 1990, St. Albans, Melbourne, Australia, 1990, Western Inst., Perth, Australia, 1990. Author: (with Saundra Hybels) Speech/Communication, 1974, 2d edit., 1979, Speech/Communication: A Reader, 1975, 2d edit., 1979, Speech/Communication: A Student Manual, 1976, 2d edit., 1979, Understanding Interpersonal Communication, 1978, 2d edit., 1981, 3d edit., 1984, 4th edit., 1987, 5th edit., 1990, 6th edit., 1993, 7th edit., 1996, (with Raymond K. Tucker, Cynthia Berryman-Fink) Research in Speech Communication, 1981, Foundations of Speech Communication: Perspectives of a Discipline, 1982, Speech Communication Skills, 1982, Understanding Public Communication, 1983, Understanding Business Communication, 1985, Understanding Speech Communication Skills, 1985, Readings in Speech Communication, 1985, (with Saundra Hybels) Communicating Effectively, 1986, 2d edit., 1989, 3d edit., 1992, 4th edit., 1995, 5th edit., 1998, 6th edit., 2001, Skills for Communicating Effectively, 1985, 2d edit., 1988, 3d edit., 1991, 4th edit., 1993, rev. edit., 1995, (with Howard W. Cotrell) Innovative Instructional Strategies, 1987, 2d edit., 1988, 3d edit., 1989, 4th edit., 1990, 5th edit., 1992, 6th edit., 1993, (with Curt Bechler) Listen to Win: A Guide to Effective Listening, 1994, Study Guide to Accompany Communicating Effectively, 1995, 2d edit., 1998, Essentials of Public Speaking, 1996, 2d edit., 2001. Mem. emeritus Nat. Comm. Assn., Ctrl. States Speech Assn., Ohio Speech Assn. Home and Office: 9583 Woodleigh Ct Perrysburg OH 43551-2669 E-mail: WeaverII@wcnet.org.

WEAVER, RICHARD LINDSAY NEWTON, financial services executive; b. Miami, Fla., Aug. 10, 1957; s. Robert Almon and Rita Margaret (Gaylord) W.; m. Christine Ann Curley, Sept. 28, 1991; children: Katherine Emory, Emily Price. BS in Econs., U. Pa., 1979; MBA, NYU, 1983. Internat. adminstr. Prudential-Bache, N.Y.C., 1979—81, instnl. bond sales, 1981—82, assoc., internat. corp. fin. London, 1982—84; assoc. v.p., risk arbitrage Prudential Securities, Inc., N.Y.C., 1984—87, v.p. managed futures, 1987—88, 1st v.p., pvt. client equity svcs., 1988—94, sr. v.p. exec. svcs., high net worth strategies/investments, 1994—2001, sr. v.p., dir., pvt. wealth mgmt., 2001—. Mem. ctr. circle com. Lincoln Ctr., N.Y.C., 1993-96; mus. chmn., treas. Frances Tavern Mus., N.Y.C., 1994-96; trustee The Browning Sch., N.Y.C., 1995—, The Episc. Sch., N.Y.C., 2000—; jr. com. Sch. of Am. Ballet, N.Y.C., 1982-91. Mem. N.Y. Soc. Security Analysts, Assn. Investment Mgmt. Profls., Investment Assn. N.Y. Office: Prudential Securities Inc One New York Plaza New York NY 10292 E-mail: richard_weaver@prusec.com.

WEAVER, SIGOURNEY (SUSAN ALEXANDRA WEAVER), actress; b. N.Y.C., Oct. 8, 1949; d. Sylvester (Pat) Weaver and Elizabeth Inglish; m. James Simpson, 1984; 1 child, Charlotte. BA in English, Stanford U., 1971; MA in Drama, Yale U., 1974. First profl. theater appearance in The Constant Wife, 1974; other roles in Beyond Therapy, Hurlyburly, 1984, The Merchant of Venice, 1987; films include: Annie Hall, 1977, Alien, 1979, Eyewitness, 1981, The Year of Living Dangerously, 1982, Deal of the Century, 1983, Ghostbusters, 1984, Aliens, 1986 (Acad. award nomination for best actress), Half Moon Street, 1986, One Woman or Two, 1987, Working Girl, 1988, Gorillas in the Mist, 1988 (Golden Globe award 1989), Ghostbusters II, 1989, Alien 3, 1992, 1492: Conquest of Paradise, 1992, Dave, 1993, Death and the Maiden, 1994, Jeffrey, 1995, Copycat, 1995, Snow White in the Black Forest, 1996, Ice Storm, 1996, Alien: Resurrection, 1997, A Map of the World, 1999, Get Bruce, 1999, Galaxy Quest, 1999, Company Man, 1999, Airframe, 1999, Speak Truth to Power, 2000, Heartbreakers, 2001, Tadpole, 2002, The Guys, 2002, Holes, 2002. Recipient Lifetime Achievement award, Chicago Internat. Film Festival, 2001. Office: ICM 8942 Wilshire Blvd Beverly Hills CA 90211-1934*

WEAVER, STEVEN M. publishing executive; Pub., pres. The Tampa Tribune, 2001—. Office: 200 S Parker St Tampa FL 33606 Address: PO Box 191 Tampa FL 33601 Business E-Mail: SWeaver@tampatrib.com.*

WEAVER, THOMAS HAROLD, health facility administrator; b. Asheville, N.C., July 21, 1943; s. Thomas Harold and Evelyn (Morris) W.; m. Marsha Va Fossen, Dec. 17, 1982; 1 child, Sallie Jayne. BA, Va. Mil. Inst., 1964; MEd, U. Ga., 1970; MAHA, George Washington U., 1973. Vol. EMS, various locations, 1965-94; mgmt. analyst VA Med. Ctr., Martinez, Calif., 1972-74; health planner VA Ctrl. Hdqs., Washington, 1974-76, sr. health sys. specialist, 1976-79; asst. dir. VA Med. Ctr., Lexington, Ky., 1979, COO, assoc. dir. Ft. Howard, Md., 1980-82, sr. exec. sys. specialist Durham, N.C., 1982-85, COO, assoc. med. dir. Pitts., 1985-89, CEO, med. ctr. dir. Martinsburg, W.Va., 1989-94, CEO, dir. Bay Pines, Fla., 1994—. V.p., bd. dirs. Berkeley County Emergency Ambulance Authority, Martinsburg, 1989—94; pres., chmn. bd. Bedington Vol. Fire and Rescue Dept., 1989—93; disting. vis. lectr. W.Va. U., 1992—94; adj. prof. U. Tampa, 1996—98; instr. dept. emergency mgmt. St. Petersburg Coll., 1997—2002. Contbr. articles to profl. jours., chpt. to book. Emergency med. svcs. instr. various locations, 1967—98, W.Va., 1990—94; bd. dirs. Pinellas County EMS MEd. Control Bd., 1995—2001, Hurricanes and Health Care Consortium, 1995—98; mem. Pinellas County Disaster Adv. Com., 1996—2002; incident comdr. Bay Pines Hazmat Decon Team , 1997—2002; chair hosp. terrorism task force Fla. Dept. Health, 2000—01; bd. dirs. Hurricanes and Health Care Consortium, 2001—02. Named Preceptor of Yr., Xavier U., 2002; recipient Nat. Cmty. Svc. award, Sec. Vet. Affairs, Washington, 1975, cert. of merit, Geico Pub. Svc., Washington, 1985, Spl. Act Commendation award, DVA and County Commn. for outstanding actions during cmty. disaster, 1993, John J. Stuvdevent Partnership award, 1998, Fla. Sch.-to-Work Gold award, 1998, award, Nat. Assn. State Dirs. of Vocat. Edn., 1999, Outstanding Achievement award, Fla. State Emergency Response Commn., 2001. Fellow Am. Coll. Healthcare Execs. (Fed. Exec. of Yr. W.Va. chpt. 1994); mem. Nat. Registry EMTs. Office: Dept VA Affairs Med Ctr PO Box 3975 Bay Pines FL 33744-3975

WEAVER, TIMOTHY ALLAN, lawyer; b. Elkhart, Ind., Nov. 30, 1948; s. Arthur and Joan Lucile (Yoder) W.; m. Catherine Anne Power, Nov. 23, 1974; children: Daniel Timothy, Christopher Matthew, David Colwell. AB, Brown U., 1971; JD, U. Ill., 1974. Bar: Ill. 1974, Wis. 1999, U.S. Dist. Ct. (no. dist.) Ill. 1975, U.S. Ct. Appeals (7th cir.) 1975, U.S. Dist. Ct. (no. dist. trial bar) Ill. 1982, U.S. Dist. Ct. (ea. dist.) Wis. 1999. Asst. pub. defender Cook County Pub. Defender, Chgo., 1974-75; trial atty. Chgo. Transit Authority, 1975-78; assoc. Philip E. Howard Ltd., Chgo., 1978, Pretzel & Stouffer, Chartered, Chgo., 1978-82, ptnr., 1982—. Editor: Medical Malpractice, 1989, 92, 96; contbr. chpts. to books. Mem. ABA, Ill. State Bar Assn., Ill. Assn. Def. Trial Counsel, State Bar of Wis., Civil Trial Counsel of Wis., The Lawyers Club of Chgo. Office: Pretzel & Stouffer One S Wacker Dr #2500 Chicago IL 60606 E-mail: tweaver@pretzel-stouffer.com.

WEAVER, VELATHER EDWARDS, small business owner; b. Va. d. Willie and Ethel Edwards; m. Ellerson Weaver; children: Frank Mattox Jr., Terence Mattox, Christopher Williams, Sharon, Shelley, Stephanie. Student, Sonoma State Coll., 1972, U. Calif., Berkeley, 1972; BA, Calif. State U., Hayward, 1973; MBA, St. Mary's Coll., Moraga, Calif., 1989. Coach, counselor Opportunities Industrialization Ctr., Oakland, Calif., 1967-69; tchr. Berkeley Headstart, 1969-70; instr., cons. external degree program Antioch Coll.-West, San Francisco, 1971-74; market analyst World Airways, Inc., Oakland, 1972-75, affirmative action adminstr., 1975-78; cons. A.C. Transit, 1982; owner, mgr. Val's Designs and Profl. Svcs., Lafayette, Calif., 1980—; mgr. adminstrn., tng. supr. North Oakland Pharmacy, Inc., 1970—, also bd. dirs. Adv. bd. The Tribune, Oakland, 1982-88. Author RAPRO Self Mgmt. Program, 1985. Program coord., mem. publicity com. Lafayette Arts and Sci. Found., 1982-83; mem. admission bd. St. Mary's Coll. Grad. Sch. Bus., 1990; bd. dirs. Acalanes H.S., Lafayette, 1980-82, Lafayette Elem. Sch., 1975-80; mem. Lafayette Econ. Devel. Task Force, 1994-95; vice chmn. Lafayette Econ. Devel. Commn., 1995—. Mem. Calif. State Pharmacists Assn. Aux. (pres. Contra Costa Aux. 1980, pres. state aux. 1986-88, recognition award 1987), Calif. Pharmacists Polit. Action Com. (appreciation award 1988), Diablo Valley Bus. and Profl. Women (pub. rels. com. 1986-87, best local orgn. award 1987, author yearbook 1987), No. Calif. Med., Dental and Pharm. Assn. Aux. (bd. dirs., com. chair 1975—, pres. elect 1991, pres. 1991-93), Internat. Platform Assn., Links, Inc. Avocations: reading, researching family businesses, travel, attending auctions. Office: North Oakland Pharmacy Inc 5705 Market St Emeryville CA 94608-2811

WEAVER, WILLIAM CLAIR, JR. (MIKE WEAVER), human resources development executive; b. Indiana, Pa., Apr. 11, 1936; s. William Clair and Zaida (Bley) W.; m. Janet Marcelle Boyd, Sept. 18, 1963 (div. 1978); 1 child, William Michael; m. Donna June Hubbuch, Feb. 10, 1984. B Aero Engring., Rensselaer Poly. Inst., 1958; MBA, Washington U., St. Louis, 1971; postgrad., Rutgers U.; grad., Armed Forces Indsl. Coll. Registered profl. engr. Engr. aerodynamics N.Am. Aviation, Los Angeles, 1959-60; engr. flight test ops. Boeing/Vertol, Phila., 1963-66; engr. flight test project Lockhead Electronics, Plainfield, N.J., 1966-69; project engr. advanced systems, sr. staff engr. Emerson Electric Co., St. Louis, 1969-72; pres. Achievement Assocs., Inc., 1972—. Founder, charter mem. Catalyst, 1978—; speaker in field. Author: Winning Selling, 1983; contbr. articles to profl. jours. Adv. com. Boy Scouts Am., Bridgeton, Mo., 1974, Mo. Athletic Club, Am. Soc. Tng. & Devel. Capt. USAF, 1960-63, USAFR. Mem. AIAA, NSPE, ASTD, Am. Soc. Tng. and Devel., Am. Soc. Bus. and Mgmt. Cons., Am. Ordnance Soc., Assn. MBA Execs., Air Force Assn., Am. Helicopter Soc., Acacia Frat., St. Louis C. of C., Mensa, Mo. Athletic Club, Beta Gamma Sigma. Republican. Lutheran. Avocations: photography, music, sports. Home and Office: 1016 Evergreen Rd Yardley PA 19067-1018

WEAVER, WILLIAM CHARLES, retired industrial executive; b. Nov. 10, 1941; s. Curtis D. and Mary (Yahres) W.; m. Karla Lee Kottas, June 13, 1964; children: Michael, Kelli. BS in Edn., Indiana U. of Pa., 1963; postgrad. in acctg., Tex. Christian U., 1964-65. CPA, Pa. With Price Waterhouse & Co., Pitts., 1965-73, audit mgr., 1970-73; corp. contr. Kennametal Inc., Latrobe, Pa., 1973-78, v.p., contr., 1978-83, v.p., treas., 1983-86, v.p., CFO, 1987-89; sr. v.p., CFO Oak Industries, Inc., Waltham, Mass., 1990-95; ret., 1995. Bd. dirs. Gemini Precision Products; chmn. bd. Weaver Enterprises, Inc., 1996—. Trustee Hampton United Presbyn. Ch., 1972-73; pres. Mountain View Parent Tchrs. Orgn., 1976-77; bd. dirs. East High Acres Civic Assn., 1976-77; treas. Greater Latrobe Hockey Club, 1982-87; chmn. bd. dirs., mem. adv. coun. Jr. Achievement, Latrobe, 1982-85; chmn. bd. trustees Latrobe United Way, 1988-89. 1st lt. U.S. Army, 1963-65. Mem.: AICPA, Fin. Execs. Inst., Pa. Inst. CPAs, Palmetto Dunes Club Inc. (pres. 1998—2001).

WEAVER, WILLIAM SCHILDECKER, electric power industry executive; b. Pitts., Jan. 15, 1944; s. Charles Henry and Louise (Schildecker) W.; m. Janet Kae Jones, Mar. 7, 1981. BA, Hamilton Coll., 1965; JD, U. Mich., 1968. Bar: Wash. 1968. Assoc. Perkins Coie, Seattle, 1968-74, ptnr., 1975-91; exec. v.p., CFO Puget Sound Power & Light Co., Bellevue, Wash., 1991-97; vice chmn., chmn. unregulated subsidiaries Puget Sound Energy, 1997—, pres., COO, 1997, pres., CEO, 1998—, also bd. dirs. Bd. dirs. Kinetic Ventures, Chevy Chase, Md., Edison Electric Inst. Bd. dirs. Wash. Rsch. Coun., Seattle, 1991-97, chmn., 1995-97; trustee Seattle Repertory Theatre, 1992-95, 99-2000, chmn., 2000—, Corp. Coun. Arts, 1995—, Pacific Sci. Ctr., 1997—. Mem. ABA, Wash. State Bar Assn., Wash. Bus. Round Table, Cmty. Devel. Round Table, Seattle Yacht Club, Rainier Club. Office: Puget Sound Energy PO Box 97034-obc- Bellevue WA 98009

WEAVER-STROH, JOANNE MATEER, education educator, consultant; b. May 21, 1930; d. Kenneth Hall and Jean (Weakley) Mateer; children: Karen, Mark, Laurie. BS in Edn., U. Pa., 1952, elem. and secondary prin. cert., 1979; MS in Psychology Reading, Temple U., 1968. Tchr. Paoli (Pa.) Sch., 1952-53, Somerville Sch., Ridgewood, N.J., 1953-55, Bryn Mawr (Pa.) Sch., 1955-57, Erdenheim Sch., Springfield, Pa., 1957-58; reading specialist Abington (Pa.) Sch. Dist., 1966-67, curriculum specialist, 1967-73, coord. human rels. programs, 1973-80; prin. Rydal Elem. Sch., Abington, 1980-88, Willow Hill Elem. Sch., 1988-96; ret., 1996. Cons., tchr. Marywood Coll., Scranton, Pa., 1972—; coord. drug and alcohol abuse program Abington Sch. Dist., 1989-96; cons. Conflict Resolution, 1996—. Chmn. Abington Human Rels. Adv. Coun., 1973-88; chmn. Cmty. Rels. Com. Abington Twp., 1978—; mem. Ea. Montgomery County Human Rels. Adv. Coun., 1981-83; chmn. No Place for Hate project Abington Twp.; leader Stephen Minstry program Abington Presbyn. Ch. Named Citizen of the Week Times Chronicle Newspaper, 1976; recipient award Four Chaplian Temple U., 1979, Disting. Citizens award Roslyn Jr. C. of C., 1981, Citizens for Progress Humanitarian award, 1982, Cmty. award Abington YMCA, 1987, Dr. Martin Luther King Jr. award Abington Twp., 1989, East Montgomery County/Pa. State Human Rels. Interfaith award, 2000. Mem. ASCD, NASEP, Internat. Coop. Learning Assn., Pa. Assn. Elem. Prins., Phi Delta Kappa, Delta Kappa Gamma. Republican. Home: 109 Durham Ct Maple Glen PA 19002-2854

WEBB, ADELE ANN, nursing administrator; b. Akron, Ohio, July 22, 1951; d. John L. and Hazel B. (Bliss) Bickett; m. Scott E. Webb, Jan. 11, 1969; children: Andrea M., Steven E., Jennifer D. BSN, U. Akron, Ohio, 1983; MS, Ohio State U., 1985; PhD, Wayne State U., Detroit, 1988. Nurse scholar Henry Ford Hosp., Detroit, 1997-99; staff nurse Children's Hosp., Akron, 1984-97; assoc. prof. nursing U. Akron, 1985-96; nurse cons. Perantinides & Nolan, 1999-2001; exec. dir. Assn. of Nurses in AIDS Care, 2001—. Mem. N.E. Ohio Task Force on Aids, 1992—97, sec., 1992—; AIDS cert. nurse, 2002—. Contbr. articles to profl. jours. Recipient Nat. Rsch. Svc. award U. Akron, 1989; fellow Ohio State U., clin. fellow Nat. Pediatric HIV Resource Ctr., 1994. Fellow: Am. Acad. Nursing; mem.: Summit Portage Health Edn. Network (steering com.), Assn. Nurses in AIDS Care (pres. 1999—2001), Ohio Nurses Assn., Sigma Theta Tau (chmn. ways and means com., bd. dirs., Excellence in Edn. award 1989). Home: 515 High Point Dr Akron OH 44321-1170 Office: Assn of Nurses in AIDS Care 80 S Summit St Ste 500 Akron OH 44308 E-mail: awebbphd@apk.net.

WEBB, ANTHONY ALLAN, banker; b. Lincoln, Nebr., May 24, 1943; s. Robert McGraw and Ruth Irene (Good) W.; m. Micheline Touchette, July 10, 1971; children— Annie, Christian BA, U. Colo., 1965; B.Internat. Mgmt., Am. Grad. Sch. Internat. Mgmt., 1970. Various positions Royal Bank Can., Montreal and London, 1970-77, assoc. mgr. Toronto, Ont., Can., 1977-80, v.p., 1980-83, sr. v.p. merchant banking, 1983-84, dir. gen. Geneva, 1984-88, sr. v.p. personal fin. svcs. Montreal, 1988-93; chmn. Royal Bank Can. Suisse, Royal Bank Can., Channel Islands; pres., CEO Royal Trust, Toronto, 1993-99; chair The Exec. Com., 2000—. Served to lt. comdr. USNR, 1965-69 Home: 90 Binscarth Rd Toronto ON Canada M4W 1Y4 Office: PO Box 7500 Sta A Toronto ON Canada M5W 1P9

WEBB, BOBBIE JAMES, insurance broker; b. Detroit, Feb. 4, 1954; arrived in Canada; s. Bobbie J. Sr. and Jennell W.; m. Lillie Webb, March 13, 1972 (div. May 1979); children: Kevin, Bobbie III. Office: Webb Casino Gambling Inc 2257 Hurlbut St Detroit MI 48214-4048

WEBB, CHARLES HAIZLIP, JR. retired university dean; b. Dallas, Feb. 14, 1933; s. Charles Haizlip and Marion (Gilker) W.; m. Kenda McGibbon, June 21, 1958; children: Mark, Kent, Malcolm, Charles Haizlip III. AB, MMus, So. Meth. U., 1955; DMus, Ind. U., 1964; DMus (hon.), Anderson Coll., 1979. Asst. to dean Sch. Music, So. Meth. U., 1957-58; mem. faculty Sch. Music, Ind. U., 1960-97, dean, 1973-97. Dir. Indpls. Symphony Choir, 1967-81; guest condr. chorus and orch. festivals throughout U.S.; duo-pianist with Wallace Hornibrook in U.S. and Australian tour, 1973; organist First Meth. Ch., Bloomington, 1961— , mem. hymnal revision com. Meth. Ch.; mem. jury Chopin competition; mem. jury internat. piano competitions in Munich, Budapest, South Africa, Paris, Chile, Warsaw, Bolzano, London, Cologne, Japan, Israel; mem. adv. bd. Classical Insites. Chmn. adv. bd. Internat. Music Festivals, Inc.; mem. Ind. Arts Commn., 1975-83, U.S.-USSR Commn. on Music Performance Edn., Am. Coun. Learned Socs./USSR Ministry of Culture; mem. adv. panel The Music Found.; mem. recommendation bd. Avery Fisher Prize Program; bd. dirs. Busoni Found.; mem. bd. advisors Van Cliburn Internat. Piano Competition; mem. nat. adv. bd. Am. Guild Organists; trustee Indpls. Symphony Orch. With U.S. Army, 1955-57. Decorated D.S.M.; recipient Disting. Alumni award So. Meth. U., 1980, Sagamore of Wabash Gov. award, 1987, 89, 97, Thomas Hart Benton medal Ind. U., 1987, Disting. Alumni award Highland Park High Sch., Dallas, 1989, Ind. Gov. award for arts, 1989, Rocking Chair award, Ind. U., 1997, Sterling Patron award Mu Phi Epsilon Internat., 1989, Ind. Gen. Assembly House Resolution # 39 for meritorious svc., 1997, Pres.'s award Ind. U., 2000; subject of tribute in U.S. Congl. Record, 1997; Rockefeller scholar Bellagio Study Ctr., 1997; named Disting. Prof. (hon.) Ind. U., 1997, Paul Harris fellow, Rotary Internat., 1997. Mem. Ind. Acad., Century Assn. of N.Y., Pi Kappa Lambda, Phi Mu Alpha, Phi Delta Theta. Home: 648 S Woodcrest Dr Bloomington IN 47401-5417

WEBB, CHARLES RICHARD, retired university president; b. Berkeley, Calif., Oct. 4, 1919; s. Charles Richard and Adele (McDaniel) W.; m. Andrée Bonno; 1 child, Charles Richard III. AB, U. Calif., Berkeley, 1942, MA, 1944, Harvard U., 1947, PhD, 1949. Faculty San Diego State Coll., 1949-64, prof., 1958-64, chmn. dept. history, 1956-58; dean acad. affairs Stanislaus State Coll., Turlock, Calif., 1964-66; prof. history San Diego State Coll., 1966-70; pres. Eastern Conn. State U., Willimantic, 1970-88; ret., 1988; former assoc. dean acad. planning Calif. State Colls., 1966-69, former dep. state coll. dean acad. planning. Author: Workbook in Western Civilization, 2 vols, 1959, Western Civilization vol. 1 (with Schaefer), vol. 2 (with Palm), 1958, (with Crosby) The Past as Prologue, 2 vols, 1973; contbr. articles to profl. jours. Mem. pers. com. Santa Rosa Symphony Assn., New Eng. Program, Windham Meml. Comty. Hosp., Sea Rsch. Found.; mem. Commn. on Conn.'s Future. With USNR, 1941-45. Mem. AAUP, Am. Hist. Assn., Am. Fedn. Musicians, Nat. Pks. and Conservation, Sonoma Land Trust, Sierra Club, Nature Conservancy, New Eng. Hist. Assn., Assn. Calif. State Coll. Profs. (v.p. 1958-60), Save the Redwoods League, Conn. Employees Assn., Am. Assn. State Colls. and Univs., Phi Alpha Theta, Kappa Delta Pi, Omicron Delta Pi, Alpha Delta Phi. Clubs: University (San Diego), Commonwealth of Calif., Willimantic Country, Saddle Club, Santa Rosa, Montecito Heights Health & Raquet Club, Santa Rosa. Home: 6495 Timber Springs Dr Santa Rosa CA 95409-5900

WEBB, CHARLES ROBERT, lawyer, police officer; b. Boston, Dec. 11, 1946; s. Charles R. Webb and Evelyn J. Levine; m. Susan Webb, July 19, 1976 (div. Aug. 1986); children: Victoria, Veronica, Charles III; children: Brendan, Leilani. BA in Polit. Sci., U. Mass., 1969; student, U. Colo., 1964-66; JD, Suffolk Law Sch., 1973. Bar: Mass. 1973, Hawaii 1982. Patrolman Boston Police Dept., 1968-75, sgt., 1975-78, lt., 1978-81, 99—; solo practice atty. Kailua, Hawaii, 1982-99, Wellesley, Mass., 1999—. Hawaiian del. Dem. Nat. Conv., N.Y.C., 1992; bd. dirs. Boston Police Relief Assn., 1971-75, 77-81; v.p. Boston Police Superior Officers Assn., 1979-81. Mem. Mensa. Home and Office: # 3 276 Paris St Boston MA 02128-3061 E-mail: bostbarr@aol.com.

WEBB, DANIEL LAWSON, real estate investor; b. Evanston, Ill., Oct. 7, 1963; s. Daniel F. and Virginia (Schneider) W. BS, U. Iowa, 1985; MS, U. Wisc., 1990. CPA. Staff auditor Continental Bank, Chgo., 1985-88; analyst State Wisc. Investment Bd., Madison, 1988-90; investment manager Kensington Realty Advisors, Inc., Chgo., 1990—. Vol. Am. Cancer Soc., Chgo., 1985-88. Mem. Nat. Assn. Office and Indsl. Parks, Chgo. Real Estate Coun., Chgo. Social Club, Midtown Tennis Club, Sigma Chi. Republican. Episcopalian. Avocations: boating, tennis, skiing, volleyball, running. Office: Kensington Realty Advs 77 W Wacker Dr Ste 3350 Chicago IL 60601-1604

WEBB, DAVID ALLEN, writer; b. Beloit, Wis. s. Charles Webb and Marion Cecelia (Doud) Michaels. BS in Agrl. Journalism, U. Wis., 1981. Asst. mgr. Nature Food Ctrs., Eau Claire, Wis., 1993-95; mgr. Gen. Nutrition Ctr., 1995-96. Cons. Tab Books, Inc., Blue Ridge Summit, Pa., 1983-85. Author: Growing Fruits & Berries, 1983, Practical Landscaping & Lawn Care, 1985, Making Potpourri, Colognes and Soaps-102 Natural Recipies, 1988, Easy Potpourri, 1992, (novel) Kong Forest, 1999, Edwardian Summer, 1999. Recipient Editor's Choice award for poems, 1998-2000; Carnegie Fund for Authors grant, 1985; named to Internat. Poetry Hall of Fame, 1998. Avocations: gardening, reading, travel.

WEBB, DONNA LOUISE, academic director, educator; b. Yakima, Wash., Aug. 12, 1929; d. Manuel Lawrence and Rena May (Sewell) Matson; (div.); children: Marlene Park, Ed Webb III. AA in Vocat. Edn., Portland (Oreg.) Community Coll., 1976; BA in Psychology, Warner Pacific Coll., 1980; MEd in Career and Vocat. Edn., Oreg. State U., Corvallis, 1980, EdD in Career and Vocat. Edn., 1983. Dir. placement Andrews U., Mich., 1969-74; dir. career edn. and coop. work experience Portland, 1976-78; coord. youth program Fed. Experiment/Chronically Unemployed Youth, Vancouver, Wash., 1979; dir. career counseling Clark Coll., 1979; tchr. coop. edn. project Multnomah County ESD, Portland, 1981; pvt. practice counselor, 1982-84; dir. career devel. & coop. edn. Walla Walla (Wash.) Coll., 1984-87; assoc. dir. Ctr. for Lifelong Learning Loma Linda (Calif.) U., 1987-91; corp. trainer Pacific Inst., Seattle, 1991-94, account mgr. consulting and rsch., 1994—. Home decorator Frederick & Nelson; payroll and computerized bookkeeper Hilo Care Ctr.; with pers. office Flour-Utah Mining; employment counselor Snelling & Snelling Employment Agy.; tchr. bus. edn. Portland Adventist Acad. Contbr. articles to profl. jours. Mem. ASTD, Assn. Pers. Adminstrs. (columnist San Bernardino Sun newspaper), Coun. for Adult and Exptl. Learning, Calif. Assn. for Counseling and Devel., Coop. Edn. Assn., Nat. Commn. for Coop. Edn., Phi Delta Kappa. Office: 4501 W Powell Blvd Apt 72 Gresham OR 97030-5070

WEBB, DORIS MCINTOSH, human resources specialist; b. Aliquippa, Pa., May 26, 1930; d. Hayward Victor and Elaine Eloise (Kiernan) McIntosh; m. Alan D. Webb Sr. JD, Aug. 15, 1953 (dec. Sept. 1979); children: Alan D. Jr., Amy E. Webb-Burke. Student, Western Coll. for Women, 1949-51; BS in Bus. Adminstrn., Geneva Coll., 1953, tchr. cert., 1968; MEd, U. Pitts., 1972. Mgr. Crestmont Home Supply Co., Aliquippa, 1953-57; real estate mgr. McIntosh Constrn. Co., 1957-62; tchr. bus. Rochester (Pa.) H.S., 1968-78; bus. tchr. adult edn. Alleghney C.C., Pitts., 1972-75, Draughon's Jr. Bus. Coll., Knoxville, Tenn., 1979—81, Hartford C.C., Bel Air, Md., 1981—85; corp. sec. McIntosh & Webb Inc., Cockeysville, 1981-88; exec. dir., CEO housing authority City of Havre de Grace, 1989-98; v.p. human resources, tng., devel. McIntosh and Webb Assocs., Charlottesville, Va., 1999—. Chmn. North Boroughs, WQED, Pitts., 1964-68; mem. fin. com. Housing Authority Risk Retention Corp. of Housing Authority Ins. Co., Cheshire, Conn., 1995-97, mem. fin. com. Housing Authority Ins. Co., 1995-97; housing cons. for pub. housing and modernization programs, 1989-97; Sect. 8 Fed. Housing insp., 1996—. Recipient Geneva coll. Alumni Disting. Svc. award, 1993. Mem.: ASTD, NAFE, AAUW, The Profl. Woman Network, Profl. Woman Spkrs. Bur., Colonial Williamsburg Found. Republican. Lutheran. Avocations: fox hunting, beagling, traveling, remodeling homes, decorating. Office: McIntosh and Webb Assocs HCR3 Box 359 Rochelle VA 22738 E-mail: dmwebb@cstone.net.

WEBB, EDSEL PHILIP, retired textile engineer; b. Birmingham, Ala., May 18, 1928; s. Evan Hall and Mary Lee (Hough) W.; m. Mary Ann Pritchett, 1954; children: Phyllis Ann, Rebecca Hough Webb Harlow, Jeffery, Richard. BS in Textiles, Ga. Inst. Tech., 1954, MS in Indsl. Mgmt., 1955. Textile mfr. Callaway Mills, Manchester and LaGrange, Ga., 1954-59; devel. engr. Firestone Tire and Rubber Co., Akron, Ohio, 1959-62, tire and process engr. radial tires, 1962-65, mgr. internat. radial tire engring., 1965-68; sales engr., mgr. water mgmt. Firestone Coated Fabrics Co., Magnolia, Ark., 1968-70, product sales mgr. fuel cells and allied products worldwide, 1970-75, developer of rubber-coated fuel tank for GM Corvette, 1973-75, sales mgr. coated fabrics northern divsn. and internat., 1975-79, sales mgr. Ea. U.S., Can. and all exports, 1979-80, staff prodn., processing, testing and R & D engr., 1980-83, Am. Fuel Cell and Coated Fabric Co., Magnolia, 1983-92, ret., 1992; exec. v.p. TFR Financial Svcs., 1990-93. Participant internat. conf. for radial tire devel. and engring. Firestone Tire & Rubber Co., London, Rome, Madrid, and Hamburg, Germany, 1965; served on team with reps. of Belgium, Sweden, Italy, Eng. and Germany for NATO, 1974. Asst. scoutmaster Troop 54 Boy Scouts Am., Anchorage, 1947-50; asst. scoutmaster and scoutmaster Troop and Post 24, Manchester, Ga., 1955-56, explorer advisor, 1956-58, explorer, scout commr., 1957-59, instl. rep., 1957-58; asst. scoutmaster, mem. troop com. Troop 50, Akron, Ohio, 1960-70; asst. scoutmaster Troop 49, Magnolia, Ark., 1971-73, scoutmaster, 1973-76, dist. chmn., dist. vice chmn., 1973-76, mem. coun. exec. bd., 1974—, dist. commr., 1976-79, 90-92, fin. chmn., 1977-78; numerous other positions Boy Scouts Am.; chmn. mfg. com. Am.'s Pub. Works Assn. 85th Congress FWPA, 1968-69; deacon Presbyn. Ch., Ohio and Ga., supt. Sunday Sch., Ohio and Ga., asst. supt. Sunday Sch., Ark.; pres. Men of Ch., Ohio, Ark. and Ga.; pres. Couples Club, Ohio; elder, trustee 1st Presbyn. Ch., Magnolia; tchr. Sunday Sch.; Stephen's min. Peachtree Presbyn. Ch., Atlanta, 1995—; mem. various chs. orgnl. coms.; mem. Vols. in Probation, Vols.-in-Drug-Abuse Edn. Program, Ohio and Ark.; mem. adv. bd. Magnolia Adult Drug Edn. Program; mem. DeSoto Area Coun. Exec. Bd., 1971-93; exec. bd. Atlanta Area coun., 1993—, v.p. camping com., 1993-96; asst. leader Boy Scouts Am. Atlanta group to 1st Russian Boy Scouts Am. Jamboree, Russia, 1994—; mem. internat. com. as ptnr. to World Scouting Program, Boy Scouts Am., Atlanta, 1990—, mem. Jamboree com. Atlanta area coun., 1997. Staff sgt. USAF, 1946-49, USAFR, 1949-52. Recipient Wood Badge award Boy Scouts Am., 1972, Scouter Trainer award and cert., 1977, Scouter Key Tng. Recognition award, 1978, Silver Beaver award, 1978, cub scout cub master and dist. cub commr., 1978-90, Man of Achievement award, 1979, 17th edit., 1996, Vigil Honor Order of Arrow award, 1980, Dist. Merit award, 1993, Heritage Soc. award, 1995, James E. West Soc. award, 1999; recognized for 57 years in scouting as a vol. Com. Nat. Jamboree Boy Scouts Am., 1996; recipient Good Neighbor award City of Magnolia, 1993, Heritage Soc. award Boy Scouts Am., 1995, James Evert West Nat. award 1997, others. Mem. Am. Assn. Textile Chemists and Colorists, Nat. Fire Protection Assn., So. Overseers Assn., Soc. Automotive Engrs. (mem. and cons. G9 and AE5 com.), Kiwanis, Jaycees, Rotary, Masons, Toastmasters Internat. (pres. club 151, dist. commr.), Scottish Rite, Akron Rubber Group, Sigma Nu, Alpha Phi Omega (pres., commr. of scouting). Avocations: camping, hiking, tennis, golf, photography. Home: 4807 Turtle Bay Ter Bradenton FL 34203-3158 Fax: (770) 926-6439. E-mail: maphwebb@cs.com.

WEBB, EMILY, retired plant morphologist; b. Charleston, S.C., Apr. 10, 1924; d. Malcolm Syfan and Emily Kirk (Moore) W.; m. John James Rosemond, Apr. 23, 1942 (div. 1953); 1 child, John Kirk; m. Julius Goldberg, Sept. 9, 1954; children: Michael, Judith. AB in Liberal Arts and Sci. with honors, U. Ill., Chgo., 1968, MS in Biol. Scis., 1972, PhD in Biol. Scis., 1985; student, Coll. Charleston, 1951—54. Undergrad. fellow in bacteriology Med. Coll. S.C., Charleston, 1952-54; teaching asst. U. Ill., Chgo., 1969-72, 77-84, rsch. asst., 1977; teaching fellow W.Va. U., Morgantown, 1974, instr., 1974-75. Rsch. in N.Am. bot. needlework art, 1986—. Author: Studies in Several North American Species of Ophioglossum, 1986; translator Nat. Transl. Ctr., Chgo., 1976; contbr. articles to profl. jours. James scholar U. Ill., 1968-69. Mem. DAR. Democrat. Episcopalian. Avocations: garden design, writing, money management. Home and Office: 1356 Mandel Ave Westchester IL 60154-3433

WEBB, GENEÁ LYNETTA, journalist; b. Pitts., Mar. 13, 1973; d. Richard Kenneth and Hannah Lynetta Webb. BA, Point Park Coll., 1997. Journalist New Pitts. Courier, 1997—; sports writer South Hills Record, 1998—; freelance writer The Lawyers Jour., 2000—01. Editor: (newsletter) Negro Ednl. Emergency Dr., 1997—98. Named Outstanding Student Journalist, Matrix, Pitts., 1996; recipient Cmty. Svc. award, All State Ins. Co., Pitts., 1997. Mem.: Am. Advt. Fedn. (named one of 25 most promising minority students 1997). Avocations: poetry, writing poetry and short stories, dancing, dining out. Home: 92 W Bruceton Rd Pittsburgh PA 15236

WEBB, GWYNETH GUILES, artist; b. Detroit, Oct. 6, 1926; d. Austin Philip and Louise E. Guiles; m. Leonard Paul Webb, Jr., Feb. 17, 1951; children: Morgaine Swann, Paul Webb III, Laurie Daniel, Susan Gregg, John Webb. BA, Smith Coll., 1948; BFA, Atlanta Coll. Art, 1987. Artist, illustrator, portrait painter. Coord., dir. art shows Ga. Bar Assn., Savannah, 983, 95; lectr. Sr. Svcs., Atlanta, 1988-89; gallery chair, dir. traveling show Atlanta Artists Club, 1979, 81; judge art shows, Atlanta, 1991-95. Illustrator: From My Window, 1965; exhibited in one-person show U. Ga., 1989; artwork featured in play Painting Churches, Woodruff Art Ctr., Atlanta. Vol. art tchr. Girls Club, Atlanta, 1965, Morris Brandon Sch., Atlanta, 1973; bd. dirs. Schenck Sch., Atlanta, 1994-95. Recipient Alpha award Smith Coll., 1948, honorarium Nat. Endowment for Arts, Yazoo City, Miss., 1982. Mem. Am. Soc. Portrait Artists, Atlanta Artists Club, Portrait Soc. Atlanta, Inc. Methodist. Avocations: study of history and theology, music, travel. Home and Office: 2525 Peachtree Rd NE Apt 16 Atlanta GA 30305-3669

WEBB, H. LAWRENCE, real estate executive; m. Janet Hadley; children: Laura, Emily. Pres. Calif. divsn. John Laing Homes; CEO, WL Homes LLC (merger John Laing Homes and Watt Homes), Irvine, Calif., 1996—. Bd. dirs. Orange County Housing Authority, Interval House. Mem. Nat. Assn. Home Builders (bd. trustees Nat. Sales and Mktg. Coun., inducted into Legends of Mktg. Hall of Fame). Office: WL Homes LLC 895 Dove St Newport Beach CA 92660

WEBB, HOWARD WILLIAM, JR. retired humanities educator, university official; b. Dayton, Ohio, June 23, 1925; s. Howard William and Martha (Brown) W.; m. Joyce Moore Cooper, Nov. 20, 1947; children: Howard William (dec.), Amy Forrest, Sarah Winship. BA, Denison U., 1947; MA, State U. Iowa, 1950, PhD, 1953. Asst. prof. English Central Mo. State Coll., 1953-56, So. Ill. U., Carbondale, 1956-62, assoc. prof., 1962-67, prof., 1967-90, dir. grad. studies in English, 1961-67, acting chmn., 1968, chmn., 1968-72, acad. affairs officer on bd. trustees staff, 1974-79, system acad. officer on chancellor's staff, 1979-85, vice chancellor for acad. affairs, 1985-90; interim dir. SIU Press, 1993. Editor: Illinois Prose Writers: An Anthology, 1968; contbr. articles to profl. jours. With USNR, 1943-46. Mem. MLA, Melville Soc. Home: 904 S Oakland Ave Carbondale IL 62901-2557

WEBB, IGOR MICHAEL, academic administrator; b. Malacky, Czechoslovakia, Nov. 8, 1941; came to U.S., 1952; s. Michael and Josephine (Nash) W.; m. Catherine Lamb (div. 1989); 1 child, Kelly Webb-Lamb; m. Marianne F. Walters, 1990; children: Rebecca Alice, Sarah Elizabeth, Benjamin Oliver, Hannah Olivia. BA, Tufts U., 1963; MA, Stanford U., 1966, PhD, 1971. Asst. prof. English Loyola U. Montreal, Can., 1968-70, U. Mass., Boston, 1971-77, assoc. prof., 1977-78; chair div. humanities Richmond Coll., London, 1979-86; spl. asst. to pres. Adelphi U., Garden City, N.Y., 1986-87, acting provost, 1987-89, provost, 1989-97, sr. v.p., 1992-97, prof. English, 1997—, acting pres., 1997. Author: From Custom to Capital, 1981, Against Capitulation, 1984. Creative Writing fellow Nat. Endowment for Arts, 1978. Mem. Phi Beta Kappa. Office: Adelphi U Garden City NY 11530 E-mail: webb@adelphi.edu.

WEBB, JACK M. lawyer; b. Monroe, La., Feb. 23, 1936; s. Sam L. and Lillian Etta (McCowen) W.; m. Diane Adele Waterman, Aug. 22, 1964; children: Julia Lillian Pogue, Kathryn Joy, Samuel Logan. BS in Geology, Centenary Coll. La., 1957; JD, Tulane U., 1960; student, JFK Sch. Govt. Harvard U., 1999. Bar: La. 1960, Tex. 1962. Atty. Standard Oil Co. Tex., Houston, 1961-66; staff atty. Trunkline Gas Co., 1966-71; sr. atty. M.W. Kellogg Co., 1971-73; sec., asst. gen. counsel Gulf Resources & Chem. Corp., 1973-78, v.p. govt. rels., adminstrv. asst. to chmn. bd., 1978-82; pres. Jack M. Webb & Assocs., 1983—; U.S. spl. amb. Bolivia, 1985, Finland, 1986, Haiti, 1991, Angola, 1992, Ghana, 1993. Bd. dirs. Bradmark, Inc., Am. Meridian Ins. Co., Scotia Pacific Holding Co., Techxas Ventures. Bd. dirs. U.S. Peace Corps, 1985-86, Nat. Park Found., 1986-92, Boy Scouts Am., 1975—. Capt. U.S. Army, 1960-61. Mem. Tex. Bar Assn., La. Bar Assn. Methodist. Home: 3434 Locke Ln Houston TX 77027-4139

WEBB, JAMES CALVIN, minister; b. Washington, Dec. 16, 1947; s. Mack Clifton and Thelma (Walker) W.; m. Lynda Sue Gravely, Mar. 18, 1967; children: Wendell Lewis, Christopher Andrew. BA, Mercer U., Atlanta, 1977; MDiv, Southwestern Bapt. Theol. Sem., Ft. Worth, Tex., 1980, DMin, 1987. Ordained to ministry So. Bapt. Conv., 1980. Pastor Abbott (Tex.) Bapt. Ch., 1978-81, Bethesda Bapt. Ch., Burleson, Tex., 1981-84, White Oak Bapt. Ch., Lilburn, Ga., 1985-98, Ardsley Park Bapt. Ch., Savannah, 1998—. Chmn. Ga. Bapt. Conv. arrangements com., 2000. Contbr. articles to profl. jours. With Army N.G. 1967-73. Home: 179 Junco Way Savannah GA 31419-8800 Office: Ardsley Park Bapt Ch 1 E 55th St Savannah GA 31405-3317 E-mail: docjcw@juno.com.

WEBB, JAMES OKRUM, JR. insurance company executive; b. Cleve., Nov. 25, 1931; s. James Okrum and Bessie Ruth (Eubanks) W.; m. Frankie L. Lowe, Feb. 19, 1954; children: Pamela Ruth, Lisa Suzanne. BA, Morehouse Coll., Atlanta, 1953; MBA in Actuarial Sci, U. Mich., 1955-57. Actuarial asst. Mut. of N.Y., N.Y.C., 1957-62; asst. to pres., actuary Supreme Life Ins. Co. Am., Chgo., 1962-64, v.p., actuary, 1964-66; asst. actuary Health Care Service Corp. (Blue Cross and Blue Shield), Chgo., 1966-68, asst. v.p. product devel., 1968-69, v.p. product and project mgmt., 1969-73, v.p. finance, asst. treas., 1973-74, v.p. finance, treas., 1974-75, v.p. corp. planning and devel., 1975-79, sr. v.p. planning and devel., 1979-85; pres., chief exec. officer Effective Data Processing, Inc., Oakbrook Terrace, Ill., 1985-94; pres. Managed Dental Care of Can., Toronto, 1987-94; chmn., pres., CEO Dental Network Am., 1985-94; pres. Village of Glencoe, Ill., 1993-2001. Dir. South Shore Nat. Bank Chgo., 1975-87, Harris Bank Glencoe/Northbrook, 1994—, Harris Bankcorp, 1995—, Harris Bankmont, 1995—, Harris Trust and Savings Bank, 1995—, Ill. Facilities Fund, 1996-2000, Highland Park Hosp. and Lakeland Health Svcs., Inc., 1999-2000, Evanston Northwestern Healthcare, 2000—, Chgo. Botanic Garden, 2000—, Nat.-Levis Univ.; Mem. Ill. Ins. Adv. Com., 1965-67; mem. Ill. Commn. Urban Area Govt., 1970-72 Mem. Glencoe (Ill.) Sch. Bd., 1970-77, pres., 1976-77; pres. Glencoe Human Relations Com., 1970-71; Bd. dirs., mem. budget and finance com. Mid-Am. chpt. ARC, 1974-75; v.p., mem. exec. com., chmn. devel. com. Chgo. Black United Fund, 1974-76; pres., bd. dirs. Chgo. Caucus; founder, past pres. bd. dirs. Home Investments Fund, 1968—; mem. Gov.'s Commn. on Health Assistance Programs; bd. dirs., v.p. Leadership Coun. for Met. Open Cmtys.; mem. City of Chgo.-Durban, South Africa Sister Cities Com., 1997—. Served with C.E. AUS, 1953-55. Mem. Am. Acad. Actuaries (dir., treas. 1975-78), Conf. Actuaries in Pub. Practice (assoc.), Alpha Phi Alpha. Clubs: Economics, Executives (Chgo.). Home: 71012 Everard Chapel Hill NC 27517

WEBB, JAMES R. finance educator, consultant; b. Granite City, Ill., Apr. 5, 1947; s. Gene and Lucille (Arney) W.; m. Anais Harding Brown, 1978; children: Clinton, Stuart, Carissa. BS in Mgmt., No. Ill. U., 1972, MBA in Fin., 1974; PhD in Fin., U. Ill., 1982. Asst. prof. fin. Kent (Ohio) State U., 1979-82; assoc. prof. U. Akron (Ohio), 1982-89; prof. fin. Cleve. State U. Coll. Bus., 1989—. Vis. prof. U. Tex., Austin, 1987-88, U. Hong Kong, 1993, 95, 96, 98. U. We. Australia, Sydney, 1993, 97, 2001; dir. Real Estate Rsch. Ctr. Cleve. State U., 1992—; CEO, Nat. Bur. Real Estate Rsch., 1989—. Contbr. over 100 articles to profl. jours. Exec. dir. Am. Real Estate Soc., 1987-2001, past pres., 1986. Fellow Am. Real Estate Soc. Found., 1988—. Mem. Avocations: Japanese cloisonne, art glass, ornamental horticulture. Office: Cleve State U Dept Fin Cleveland OH 44115

WEBB, JANET DOLORES, secondary school educator; b. Wurtzburg, Fed. Republic Germany, Sept. 30, 1954; d. Robert I. and Christine (Lewis) W. BA, Nat. Coll. Edn., Evanston, Ill., 1976, MEd, 1982. Cert. secondary gen. sci., elem. tchr., Ill. Tchr. math., chmn. dept. Haven Mid. Sch., Evanston; tchr. math. Evanston Twp. High Sch. Recipient Outstanding Vol. Svc. award Haven Mid. Sch., 1985, Fleetwood-Jourdain Outstanding Vol. Svc. award, 1987. Mem. NEA, Nat. Coun. Tchrs. Math., Ill. Edn. Assn., Ill. Coun. Tchrs. Math., Met. Coun. Tchrs. Math.

WEBB, JOHN GIBBON, III, lawyer; b. Flint, Mich., June 1, 1944; s. John Gibbon Jr. and Martha W.; m. Fain Murphy, July 6, 1968; children: Jennifer Horn, Philip, Andrew, John Matthew. AB, Davidson Coll., 1966; JD, Vanderbilt U., 1970. Bar: N.Y. 1971, N.J. 1981. Assoc. Curtis, Mallet-Prevost, Colt & Mosle, N.Y.C., 1970-80; gen. counsel, v.p. & sec. J.M. Huber Corp., Edison, N.J., 1980-95; pvt. bus. law practice Mt. Olive, 1996—. Episcopalian. Office: Ste 300 500 International Dr N Budd Lake NJ 07828 E-mail: webbgc@aol.com.

WEBB, KATHLEEN ROCHFORD, lawyer; b. Santa Ana, Calif., Apr. 30, 1956; d. Thomas Francis and Eileen (Travers) Rochford; m. William Alan Webb, May 27, 1978; children: Alan Travers, Shannon Kristin. BBA, Memphis State U., 1981, JD, 1987. Bar: Tenn. 1988. Real estate broker Rochford & Assocs., Cordova, Tenn., 1976-88; with Murphy, DeZonia & Webb, Memphis, 1987—. Instr. U. Memphis, 1985-98. Leader Girl Scouts USA, Memphis, 1993-2002. Mem. Memphis Bar Assn. (past chair real estate sect.), ABA, Tenn. Bar Assn., Real Estate Industry Trade Assn. (pres. 1996), Women's Coun. Realtors (local pres. 1983-84, Woman of Yr. 1984, state pres. 1988), Memphis Area Assn. Realtors (dir. 1986-87, trustee 1988-90, Affiliate of Yr. 1991). Republican. Roman Catholic. Avocations: fitness and exercise, outdoor activities, girl scouts. Office: Murphy DeZonia & Webb 6389 N Quail Hollow Rd Ste 102 Memphis TN 38120-1422 E-mail: kwebb@mdwlaw.com.

WEBB, KAYE LYNNE, educational foundation official; b. Texarkana, Tex., Mar. 19, 1939; d. William Bruce and Anita Ann Johnson; m. Charles Richard Webb; children: Susan Webb Lundy, Richard Bruce. BS in Edn., Pittsburg (Kans.) State U., 1964. Cert. secondary tchr., Kans. Tchr. N.E. H.S., Arma, Kans., 1966-70, St. Mary's Jr. H.S., Pittsburg, 1970-71; adminstrv. asst. to pres. Pittsburg State U., 1972-96, actor, host pub. radio talk show PSU Spotlight, 1993—; sec. Unified Sch. Dist. 250 Ednl. Found., Pittsburg, 2000—. Moivational spkr. various cmty., ednl. and profl. orgns., Pitts., 1975—. Co-chmn. cardiac arrest fund drive Am. Heart Assn., Pitts., 1993—2002; pres. Pittsburg Beautiful, 2001, Hearts and Hammers, Pittsburg, 1998—; mem. Unified Sch. Dist. 249 Ednl. Found., Frontenac, Kans., 1999—2001; mentor Sch. Dist. Reading Program, Pittsburg, 1999—; bd. dirs. United Way Crawford County, 1993—96, divsn. chmn. Pitts., 1996; bd. dirs. Safehouse, domestic abuse shelter, Pittsburg, 1995—2002, Elm Acres Youth and Family Svcs., Pitts., 1998—2001. Recipient Outstanding Fund Raiser award United Way Crawford County, 1995-98, 1st Kaye Lynne Webb Spirit award Pittsburg State U., 1996, Spirit of Pittsburg award Pittsburg Area C. of C.-Pittsburg Morning Sun, 1999. Mem. Phi Kappa Phi (sec. 1990-96, Outstanding Svc. award 1996). Roman Catholic. Avocations: cooking, walking, needlework, sports events. E-mail: klwebb@terraworld.net.

WEBB, LAMAR THAXTER, architect; b. Hapeville, Ga., Sept. 13, 1928; s. Eugene Garnette and Sara Ethel (Moore) W.; m. Bettye Jayne Jackson, Dec. 6, 1957; children: Mark Maynard, Robin Lynn. BBA in Fin., U. Ga., 1950; BS, Ga. Inst. Tech., 1959, BArch, 1960. Registered architect, Ga., Fla. Intern architect Abreu and Robeson, Inc., Brunswick, Ga., 1960-66; architect, pres. Webb & Baldwin, Inc., St. Simons Island, 1966-72; pres., owner Lamar Webb, Arch., Inc., 1972—. Lst lt. USAF, 1953-55. Mem. AIA (State bd. dirs. 1985—, v.p. Golden Isles chpt. 1988-89, pres. 1989-90), Am. Soc. Interior Designers, Am. Soc. Landscape Architects (assoc.), Audubon Soc., Nat. Hort. Soc., Humane Soc. (local bd. dirs. 1985-87), Smithsonian Assocs., Coastal Alliance for Arts, Nat. Trust for Hist. Preservation, Ga. Trust for Hist. Preservation, Coastal Ga. Hist. Assn., Met. Mus. Art, Golden Isles Gourmet Club (bd. dirs.) Chien de Rotessieurs, G.I. Chap. Avocations: cooking, drawing, painting, travel. Home: Marshoaks St Simons Saint Simons GA 31522 Office: 13 Retreat Pl Saint Simons GA 31522

WEBB, LESLIE EVERETT, III, international training executive; b. Maryville, Tenn., Jan. 21, 1947; s. Leslie Everett Jr. and Elaine (King) W.; m. Mutsuko Kuwano, Aug. 19, 1978; 1 child. BA, Eckerd Coll., 1969; MPh, Columbia U., 1975; postgrad. studies, Kyoto U., Kyoto, Japan, 1977. English tchr. U.S. Peace Corps, Seoul, Korea, 1970-71; instr. OTC, Inc., Osaka, Japan, 1978-84, Omron Corp., Kyoto, Japan, 1985-2001, mgr. internat. tng., 1990—. Named Woodrow Wilson fellow, Woodrow Wilson Found., Princeton, N.J., 1968, Fulbright fellow U.S. Govt., Washington, 1977. Mem. ASTD, Internat. Bus. Communicators. Avocations: reading, Japanese Go. Home: 2-26-5 Ono Sui Mei ShigaKen Shiga Cho 520-05 Japan Office: Omron Corp-Human Resources Dept Shiokaji Horikawa Shimogyo-ku, Kyoto 600 Japan E-mail: leslie_webb@omron.co.jp.

WEBB, LYNNE MCGOVERN, communication scholar, consultant; b. Shamokin, Pa., Mar. 20, 1951; d. Charles Ralph and Ethel Elizabeth (Harris) McGovern; m. Ronald E. Webb, Sept. 28, 1974 (div. June 1981); m. Robert Blakely Moberly, Apr. 6, 1984; children: Laura Ellen, Richard Edward, Reed JeeMinSeo (dec.). BS, Pa. State U., 1972; MS, U. Oreg., 1975, PhD, 1980. Field rep. East Ctrl. Ill. Area Agy. on Aging, Campaign, Ill., 1972-74; grad. tchg. asst. U. Oreg., Eugene, 1974-78; instr. Berea (Ky.) Coll., 1978-80; asst. prof. U. Fla., Gainesville, 1980-86, assoc. prof., 1986-90; vis. assoc. prof. U. Hawaii, Honolulu, 1990-91; assoc. prof. U. Memphis, 1991-99; prof., assoc. dept. chair U. Ark., Fayetteville, 1999—. Cons. Fla. Farm Bur., Gainesville, 1981, Clay County Electric Coop., Keystone Heights, Fla., 1987, Retirement Rsch. Found., Chgo., 1988. Mem. Am. Comm. Assn. (bd. dirs. 1999-2000), Fla. Speech Comm. Assn. (v.p. 1986-87), So. States Comm. Assn. (chair applied comm. divsn. 1989-90, chair gender studies divsn. 1992-93, chair membership 1993, v.p. 1994, pres. 1995), Nat. Comm. Assn. (chair com. on comm. and aging 1982-83, legis. coun. 1989-92, 93-96, chair applied comm. sect. 1994-95, resolutions com. 1996, chair women's caucus 1998-99, mem. affirmative action com. 2000—, nominating com. 2001). Democrat. Methodist. Avocation: gourmet cooking. Office: Univ Ark Dept Comm 417 Kimpel Hall Fayetteville AR 72701

WEBB, MARGOT, writer; b. Halle, Germany, Aug. 28, 1927; d. Egmont and Ilse Lewin; widowed; children: Robert Dave, Peter Dave, Sandy Kyte; m. Marcus Webb, May 3, 1983. B, Calif. State U., 1960, M, 1964; PhD, U. So. Calif. Tchr. 6th grade L.A. Unified Sch. Dist., 1958-88. Lectr. in field. Author: Shadows at Noon, 1992, Coping With Street Gangs. Jewish. Avocations: classical music, scrabble, walking, travel. Home: Pvt Mail Box 805 25852 Mcbean Pkwy Valencia CA 91355-2004

WEBB, MARILYN MCCOY, middle school educator; b. Oct. 19, 1938; d. Floyd Warren and Virginia Nell (Engle) McCoy; m. Derek A.R. Webb, Feb. 14, 1984; children: Ruth Beauchan, Linda Sue, Roy Derek, Naomi McCoy, Enoch Evans, Aaron Evans, Ephraim Evans. Student, U. Mich.; BS, Brigham Young U., 1961; MEd, U. Hawaii, 1969. Cert. elem. tchr., Hawaii, Idaho. Sem. tchr. 1st Ward LDS Ch., Kailua-Kona, Hawaii; 6th grade tchr. Kealakehe Intermediate Sch., tchr. aerospace sci. and whole lang., ret. 1995. Exch. tchr. Parkway Sch., Glendale, Wis., 1981-82, South Milw. Mid. Sch., 1992-93; tchr. homebound students, Rigby, Idaho; spl. edn. tchr. Rigby Jr. HS, 1994-2001; initiator alternate class Rigby Jr. H.S., Idaho; regional resource person Nat. Air and Space Mus., Smithsonian Instn. Active LDS Ch. Mission Employment Resource Ctr., Honolulu, 2002—. Fellow Hawaii Writers Program, 1990. Mem. NEA, Nat. Sci. Tchrs. Assn., Nat. Mid. Sch. Assn., Hawaii Assn. Mid. Schs., Hawaii State Tchrs. Assn. (past pres. Kona chpt.), CAP (Exceptional Svc. award, Gill Robb Wilson award, Paul E. Garber award, Grover Loening award, Chuck Yeager award), Pi Lambda Theta. Home: 3609 E Menan Lorenzo Hwy Menan ID 83434-5205 Address: 1500 S Beretania Ste 200 Honolulu HI 96826

WEBB, MARTY FOX, principal; b. Des Moines, July 15, 1942; d. Joseph John and Jean (Way) Fox; m. Andrew H. Rudolph, Aug. 17, 1963 (div. Jan. 1988); children: Kristen Ann, Kevin Andrew; m. Eugene J. Webb, Nov. 23, 1991. BS, U. Mich., 1964; MEd, Houston Bapt. U., 1982; EdD, U. San Francisco, 1993. Cert. adminstr., Tex., elem. and spl. edn. educator, Mich., Tex. Tchr. spl. edn. Hawthorn Ctr., Northville, Mich., 1964-70; tchr. Bellaire (Tex.) Sch. for Children, 1977-80; prin. Corpus Christi Sch., Houston, 1980-97; founding head The Monarch Sch., 1997—. Speaker in field. Bd. dirs. DeBusk Found.; pres. exec. bd. Monarch Sch. Recipient Elem. Sch. Recognition award U.S. Dept. Edn., 1989-90, Blue Ribbon Sch. award, 1990, Outstanding Doctoral Student award, 1994. Mem. ASCD, U. Mich. Alumni. Avocations: reading, flyfishing, camping, exercise, hiking. Home: 3531 Sun Valley Dr Houston TX 77025-4148 Office: The Monarch Sch 1231 Wirt Rd Houston TX 77055-6852 E-mail: mwebb@monarchschool.org.

WEBB, MARY CHRISTINE, special education educator; b. Ames, Iowa, Jan. 3, 1947; d. Howard Darrell and Lorena Faye (North) Webb; m. Harlen DuWayne Groe, Dec. 29, 1989 (div. Oct. 1997). BS in Elem. Edn., Iowa State U., 1969, MS in Emotional Disabilities, 1980, MEd in Learning Disabilities, 1986. Cert. tchr. K-9, learning disabilities, behavioral disabilities, multicategorical, Iowa. 1st grade tchr. Holy Spirit Sch., Carroll, Iowa, 1970; severe behavior disabilities tchr. Area Edn. Agy 7, Waterloo, 1979-85; tchg. and rsch. assistantship Iowa State U., Ames, 1985-86; multicategorical 3-8 self contained with integration tchr. Madrid Elem. and Jr. H.S., 1986-87; behavior disability self contained with integration tchr. Des Moines Pub. Schs., 1987-88, resource rm. tchr., 1988-95, multicategorical self contained with integration tchr., 1995-99, reading recovery tchr., behavior interventionist, 1999-2000, reading recovery tchr., title reading tchr., 2000—02, reading recovery tchr., reading specialist, 2002—. Mem. People to People Spl. Edn. Del. to Mainland China, 1993. Mem. ASCD, NEA, Des Moines Edn. Assn., Iowa State Edn. Assn., Coun. for Exceptional Children. Office: King Acad Math and Sci 1849 Forest Ave Des Moines IA 50314-1336

WEBB, MAURICE JAMES, surgical consultant, educator; b. Brisbane, Australia, Sept. 27, 1941; came to U.S., 1971; s. Arthur John and Violet Beatrice (Sinnamon) W.; m. Valerie Joan Skerman, Apr. 29, 1966; children: Helen Joan, Paul Maurice, Karen Diane. MB, BS, U. Queensland, Australia, 1965. Tchg. registrar Queensland (Australia) U., 1965-69; registrar St. Marys Hosp., Portsmouth, U.K., 1970-71; cons. gynecologic surgery Mayo Clinic, Rochester, Minn., 1972-81; state dir. gynecologic oncology Queensland, 1981-88; prof., chair. gynecologic surgery Mayo Clinic, Rochester, Minn., 1988—. Oncology fellow Mayo Clinic, 1971-72. Mem. ACS (bd. regents), ACOG, Royal Coll. Ob-Gyn (London), Royal Australian and New Zealand Coll. Ob-Gyn. (cert. gynecologic oncologist), Soc. Pelvic Surgeons, Sigma Xi. Methodist. Avocations: photography, travel, cooking. E-mail: webb.maurice@mayo.edu.

WEBB, O. GLENN, retired farm supplies company executive; b. 1936; married BS, U. Ill., 1957; PhD, So. Ill. U., 1973. With Growmark, Inc., Bloomington, Ill., 1965—, sec., 1968-72, v.p., 1972-80, pres., from 1980, chmn., 1980—, also dir. Trustee, chmn. Am. Inst. Coop.; dir. St. Louis Farm Credit Banks, Farmers Export Co., Nat. Coop. Refinery Assn., Ill. Agr. Leadership Found.; trustee Grad. Inst. Coop. Leadership. Home: 365 Webbtown Rd Tunnel Hill IL 62991

WEBB, O(RVILLE) LYNN, physician, pharmacologist, educator; b. Tulsa, Aug. 29, 1931; s. Rufus Aclen and Berla Ophelia (Caudle) W.; m. Joan Liebenheim, June 1, 1954 Idiv. Jan. 1980); children: Kathryn, Gilbert, Benjamin; m. Jeanne P. Heath, aug. 24, 1991. BS, Okla. State U., 1953; MS, U. Okla., 1961; PhD in Pharmacology, U. Mo., 1966, MD, 1968. Diplomate Nat. Bd. Med. Examiners, Am. Bd. Family Practice; cert. medical examiner, 1999. Rsch. assoc. in pharmacology U. Okla., 1959-61; rsch. fellow NIH, 1962-66; instr. pharmacology U. Mo., Columbia, 1966-68, asst. prof., 1968-69; intern U. Mo. Med. Ctr., 1968-69; family practice New Castle, Ind., 1969-89; med. dir. VA Clinic, Lawton, Okla., 1989-94, Comanche County Hosp., 1994-98; pvt. practice medicine, 1998—; owner Comanche County Med. Clinic, Lawton, Okla., 1998—2002, Okla. Med. Clinic, Lawton, 1999—. Clin. assoc. prof. family medicine U. Okla. Coll. Medicine, 1989—; adj. assoc. prof. pharmacology U. Okla. Coll. Medicine, 1989—; mem. U. Okla. Medicine Admissions Bd., 1995-98; mem. staff Henry County Meml. Hosp., New Castle, 1969-89; guest prof. pharmacy and pharmacology Butler U. Coll. Pharmacy, Indpls., 1970-75; owner, dir. Carthage Clinic, 1975-89; clin. assoc. prof. family medicine Ind. U. Coll. Medicine, 1986-89; county physician, jail med. dir. Henry County, Ind., 1976-89. Author: (with Blissitt and Stanaszek, Lea and Febiger) Clinical Pharmacy Practice, 1972; contbr. numerous articles to profl. jours. Bd. dirs. Lawton Philharm., 1990-95. Recipient Cert. of merit in Pharmacol. and Clin. Med. Rsch., 1970, Med. Student Rsch. Essay award

Am. Acad. Neurology, 1968. Fellow Am. Acad. Family Physicians, Am. Coll. Physician Execs.; mem. AMA (ann. award recognition 1975—), AAAS, Ind. State Med. Assn., Am. Coll. Sports Medicine, Am. Coll. Occupl. and Environ. Medicine, N.Y. Acad. Scis., Am. Soc. Contemporary Medicine and Surgery, Okla. State Med. Assn., Festival Chamber Music Soc. (bd. dirs. Indpls. 1981-87), Nat. Fraternity Eagle Scouts, Mensa, Columbia Club, Skyline Club , Country Club, Kiwanis, Elks, Sigma Xi, Phi Sigma. Home: 30 Quail Creek Dr Lawton OK 73501-9026

WEBB, PAUL, physician, researcher, consultant, educator; b. Cleve., Dec. 2, 1923; s. Monte F. and Barbara (Webb) Bourjaily; m. Eileen Whalen, Mar. 13, 1948; children: Shaun P., Paul S. Womacks. BA, U. Va., 1943, MD, 1946; MS in Physiol., U. Wash., 1951. Asst. prof. physiol. U. Okla. Sch. Medicine, Oklahoma City, 1952-54; chief environ. sect. Aeromed. Lab., Wright-Patterson AFB, Ohio, 1954-58; prin. assoc. Webb Assocs., Yellow Springs, 1959-82; vis. scientist INSERM, Paris, 1983; vis. prof. U. Limburg, Maastricht, The Netherlands, 1986, U. Uppsala, Sweden, 1988-89; clin. prof. Wright State U. Sch. Medicine, Dayton, Ohio, 1980—. Cons. aerospace and undersea medicine, energy balance and thermal physiology, Yellow Springs, 1980—. Author: Human Calorimeters, 1985; contbr. articles to profl. jours. Village councilman Village of Yellow Springs, Ohio, 1969-75; mem. Air Force Scientific Adv. Bd., Washington, 1984-88. Recipient Ely award Human Factors Soc., 1972. Fellow Aerospace Med. Assn. (Aerospace Indsl. Life Scis. Assn. award 1969), Am. Inst. Med. and Biol. Engring.; mem. Am. Physiol. Soc., Am. Soc. for Clin. Nutrition, Undersea Med. Soc. (oceaneering internat. award 1979, pres. 1980-81). Home and Office: 370 Orton Rd Yellow Springs OH 45387-1321

WEBB, RALPH LEE, mechanical engineering educator; b. Parker, Kans., 1934; m. Sylvia Apple; children: Janet, Laura. BSME (with honors), Kans. State U., 1957; MME, Rensselaer Poly. Inst., 1962; PhD, U. Minn., 1969. Registered profl. engr., Wis. Instr. mech. engring. Kans. State U., 1957; engring. maintenance officer USAF, Nellis AFB, Nev., 1957-59; engr. Knolls Atomic Power Lab., Schenectady, N.Y., 1960-62; mgr. heat transfer rsch. Trane Co., La Crosse, Wis., 1963-77; assoc. prof. mech. engring. Pa. State U., University Park, 1977-81, prof., 1981—. Lectr., cons. in field; condr. various workshops. Author: Principles of Enhanced Heat Transfer, 1994; contbr. articles to profl. jours. Recipient Hall-Thermotank gold medal Inst. Refrigeration, 1989; rsch. grantee NSF, 1978-80, 83-86, Dept. Energy, 1979-82, 90-92, Internat. Copper Assn., 1984-98, EPRI, 1988-98, Improved Radiators Studies Assn., 1988—, Wolverine, 1988-89, York Internat., 1988-89, 94—, Olin Brass Corp., 1992—, Marlow Industries, 1994-97, Showa Aluminum Corp., 1992—, Thermo King Corp., 1994—, LG Electronics, Inc., 1995—, Dell Computers, 1997-. Fellow ASME, fell. ASHRAE, (chmn. heat transfer divsn., honors and awards com. 1987-90, nat. nominating com. 1983-86, heat transfer divsn. rep. to basic engring. group 1980-86, exec. com. heat transfer divsn. 1976-81, tech. editor Jour. Heat Transfer 1972-76, nat. heat transfer conf. coordinating com. 1972-77, Outstanding Svc. award 1973-76, 82, Heat Transfer Meml. award 1987); mem. ASHRAE (Heat Transfer Engring. 1978—, Jour. Heat Recovery Sys. 1981-98, editor-in-chief Jour. Enhanced Heat Transfer 1992—, Jour. Paper award 1985). Office: PA State Univ Dept Mech Engring University Park PA 16802

WEBB, RICHARD C. engineering company executive; b. Omaha, Sept. 2, 1915; m. Virginia; 1 son. BSE.E., U. Denver, 1937, DSc (hon.), 1996; MSE.E., Purdue U., 1944, PhD, 1951; DSc (hon.), U. Denver, 1996. Registered profl. engr., Colo. Traffic engr. Mountain States Telephone and Telegraph Co., Denver, 1937-39; research engr. RCA Labs. Div., Princeton, N.J., 1945-53; pres., founder, tech. dir. Colo. Research Corp. (subs. Carrier Corp.), Syracuse, N.Y., 1956-61; pres., founder. tech. dir. Colo. Instruments, Inc., Broomfield, Colo., 1961-71; pres., gen. mgr. Colo. Instruments div. Mohawk Data Scis. Corp., Utica, N.Y.C., 1971-73; pres. Webb Engring. Co. (name changed to Data Ray Corp.). Boulder, Colo., 1973-85. Vis. lectr. U. Colo., 1962-82; prof. elec. engring. U. Denver, 1953-56, Iowa State Coll., 1950 Contbr. articles to profl. jours.; patentee in field. Recipient Disting. Engring. Alumnus award Purdue U., 1970, Profl. Achievement award U. Denver Alumni Assn., 1983, Outstanding Elec. Engr. award Purdue U., 1992. Fellow IEEE; mem. Soc. Motion Picture and TV Engrs., Acoustical Soc. Am., Inst. Aerospace Scis., Am. Ordnance Assn., Western Electronics Mfrs. Assn. (past v.p., dir.), Sigma Xi, Tau Beta Pi, Eta Kappa Nu. Home: PO Box 3078 Estes Park CO 80517-3078

WEBB, RICHARD GILBERT, financial executive, antique selling service executive; b. Tulsa, May 11, 1932; s. William Leslie and Cora (Kroshus) W.; m. Patricia S. Wagdin, Apr. 13, 1957 (div. Sept. 1974); children: Catherine, Andrea, Nicholas; m. Judith A. Burke, Jan. 12, 1980; stepchildren: Mara, Karen, Jennifer, Christopher. Student, U. Okla., 1950-52; BBA, So. Meth. U., 1954; MBA, Harvard U., 1956. CPA, Okla. Mgmt. cons. McKinsey & Co., N.Y.C., 1959-61; planning analyst Mobil Oil Co., 1961-64; sub controller, treas. ITT, 1964-66; v.p., mgr. corp. devel. Ill. Tool Works, Chgo., 1966-70; v.p. planning, treas., chief fin. officer Interstate Bakers, Kansas City, Mo., 1970-78; v.p., treas., chief fin. officer Gen. Host Corp., Stamford, Conn., 1979-81, Grolier, Inc., Danbury, 1981-89, fin. cons., 1989—2000; co-owner Antique Assocs., 2000—. Cons. to State Ill., Springfield, 1969; adj. prof. fin. dept. We. Conn. State U., 1984; adv. bd. Conn. Bank and Trust Co., Danbury, 1986-88. Fundraiser, bd. dirs. United Way, Danbury, Conn., 1982-86; bd. dirs. Danbury YMCA, 1983-89, treas., 1985-87, chmn. bd. dirs., 1987-89, chmn. bd. trustees, 1981-91, trustee, 1991-00; mem. bd. advisors dept. fin. U. Conn., 1984-88; trustee Conn. Pub. Expenditure Coun., 1986-88. 1st lt. U.S. Army, 1956-59. Mem. AICPA, Okla. Soc. CPAs, Greater Danbury C. of C. (bd. dirs. 1985-89, treas. 1986-88, chmn. bd.dirs. 1988-89, trustee 1989-2000, chmn. bd. trustees 1989-91), Universalist-Unitarian Soc. Stamford (chmn. fin. com.). Republican. Avocations: swimming, reading, antiques, golf. Home and Office: 37 Saddle Ridge Rd Pound Ridge NY 10576-1111

WEBB, RICHARD SLADE, JR. surgeon; b. Porto, Portugal, Aug. 4, 1930; came to U.S., 1944; Richard Slade and Rosanna Doreen (Wright) W.; m. Jean Rose Marshall, Apr. 16, 1955; children: Richard, Steven, James, David. BS, U. Ill., Urbana, 1952; MD, U. Ill., Chgo., 1955. Intern Rsch. and Ednl. Hosp., Chgo., 1955-56, resident in surgery, 1958-62; asst. prof. surgeon Univ. Ill. Coll. of Med., 1962-73; advisor dept. surgery Chiengmai (Thailand) Med. Sch., 1964-66; sr. assoc. Office Rsch. in Med. Edn., U. Ill., Chgo., 1966-67; assoc. prof. surgery U. Ill. Coll. Medicine, Rockford, 1973-83, clin. prof., 1984-95, prof. clin. surgery, 1990-95, emeritus prof., 1995—, chmn. surgery, 1985-95, acting chmn. surgery, 1995-2000; assoc. med. dir. Rockford Health Plan, 1996—. Bd. dirs. Rockford Cmty. Trust, 1984-90. Capt., U.S. Army Med. Corps, 1956-58. Fellow ACS; mem. Midwest Surg. Assn. (sec. 1973-76, pres. 1976-77), Warren W. Cole Soc., Assn. Surg. Edn., Phi Kappa Phi, Phi Beta Kappa, Alpha Omega Alpha. Avocations: reading, home computer, home repairs, travel. Home: 3679 Sage Dr Rockford IL 61114-7329 Office: 3401 N Perryville Rd Rockford IL 61114 E-mail: dicksw8430@aol.com.

WEBB, RICHARD STEPHEN, manufacturing executive; b. Nottingham, Eng., Aug. 3, 1944; came to U.S., 1988; s. Sydney and Kathleen Florence (Day) W.; m. Pamela Anne Fowlds, Sept. 3, 1966 (dec. July 1976); children: Jane, Simon, Elizabeth; m. Anne Hessel, Aug. 19, 1978 (div. 1997); children: Clare, Penelope. BSc, U. Sheffield, Eng., 1966, PhD, 1970. Rsch. scientist U. Sheffield, 1966-69; tech. asst. C.E. Ramsden & Co. Ltd., Stoke-on-Trent, Eng., 1969-74; mktg. exec. Magnesium Elektron Ltd., Manchester, Eng., 1974-80, mktg. mgr. Eng., 1980-84; bus. devel. mgr. Alcan Aluminium, Mont., Can., 1984-88; bus. mgr. Alanx Products Inc., Newark, 1988-91, pres., 1992-95, Lanxide Coated Products divsn. Lanxide Performance Materials, Newark, 1995-97; dir. sales and mktg. Electro-Sci. Labs., Inc., King of Prussia, Pa., 1997—. Chmn. Del. Mfg. Alliance, 1993-95. Contbr. articles to profl. jours. Fellow Inst. Materials U.K.; mem. Am. Ceramic Soc., Can. Ceramic Soc., Am. Chem. Soc. Avocations: marathon and road running. Office: Electro-Sci Labs Inc 416 E Church Rd King Of Prussia PA 19406-2625

WEBB, SAMUEL CLEMENT, economist; b. Oak Grove, Mo., Aug. 14, 1934; s. Clement Holly and Minnie Vivian (Everman) W.; m. Jane Rae Kirk, June 6, 1959; children: Bronson, Jennifer, Mark, Holly. BSC, U. Mo., 1957, MS in Bus. Adminstrn., 1959; PhD in Econs., U. Kans., 1968. Registered profl. engr., Mo. Engr., mgr. Southwestern Bell Telephone Co., St. Louis, 1959-63; asst. prof. econs. Wichita State U., Kans., 1966-70, assoc. prof., 1970-76, prof., 1976—. Cons. in field, Wichita. Author: Managerial Economics, 1976, Economica de la Empresa, 1981, Health Care Management Review, 1989; contbr. articles to profl. jours. Capt. USAR, 1957-65. Grantee U. Wis. Grad. Sch. Banking, 1991. Mem. Am. Econ. Assn., Nat. Assn. Forensic Econs., Chi Epsilon, Alpha Pi Zeta, Phi Kappa Phi. Avocation: golf. Office: Wichita State U Dept Econs Wichita KS 67208

WEBB, SARAH ANN, artist; b. Nashville, Feb. 19, 1948; d. Samuel Stone and Carolyn (Horton) Butler; m. Gary Alan Webb, Jan. 11, 1966. BA with honors, U. Tenn., 1978; postgrad., Vanderbilt U., 1979-80. Exhibited in group shows at Parthenon Gallery, Nashville, 1982, 87, Omell Gallery, London, 1984, 85, 87, Soc. Women Artists, London, 1989, 90, 91, Grand Cen. Gallery, N.Y.C., 1985; represented in numerous pvt. and corp. art cllections throught the U.S., Europe and Mid. East. Recipient First Prize, Tenn. Art League Show, Nashville, 1980, Best of Show, Cen. South Ann. Art Competition, Nashville, 1987, Athena award Cen. South Annual Art Competition, Nashville, 1992. Home: PO Box 50134 Nashville TN 37205-0134 Office: Studio 56 Lakeside Rd London N13 4PR England

WEBB, THEODORE STRATTON, JR. aerospace scientist, consultant; b. Oklahoma City, Mar. 4, 1930; s. Theodore S. and Helen (Klabzuba) W.; m. Cuba Evans, Sept. 2, 1952; children: Theodore S. III, Kelly Elizabeth. BS in Physics, Okla. U., 1951; PhD in Physics and Math., Calif. Inst. Tech., 1955. Engr. Ft. Worth div. Gen. Dynamics, 1955-62, program mgr., 1962-69, dir. aero. tech., 1969-75, v.p. rsch. and engring., 1975-80, v.p. F-16 programs, 1980-89; pvt. practice cons. Ft. Worth, 1989—. Mem. engring. adv. bd. U. Okla., Norman, 1983-87; mem. aerospace coun. Soc. Automotive Engrs., 1975-81. Bd. mem. Engring. Found. U. Tex., Austin, 1975-81, Found. for Sci. and Engring. So. Meth. U., Dallas, 1974-81, Tarrant County Day Care Assn., Ft. Worth, 1975-80, 89-96; All Saints Episcopal Hosp., 1989—, Goodwill Industries of Tarrant Country, 1989-96. Mem. AAAS, Am. Phys. Soc., Rivercrest Country Club. Home: 4901 Westridge Ave Fort Worth TX 76116-8222 Office: 6100 Southwest Blvd Ste 250 Fort Worth TX 76109-6902 E-mail: ted.webb@nationwide.net.

WEBB, THOMAS IRWIN, JR. lawyer, director; b. Toledo, Sept. 16, 1948; s. Thomas Irwin and Marcia Davis (Winters) W.; m. Polly S. DeWitt, Oct. 11, 1986; 1 child, Elisabeth Hurst. BA, Williams Coll., 1970; postgrad., Boston U., 1970-71; JD, Case Western Res. U., 1973. Bar: Ohio. Assoc. Shumaker, Loop & Kendrick, Toledo, 1973-79, ptnr., 1979—, chmn. corp. law dept., 1992-94, mgmt. com., 1994-99. Dir. Calphalon Corp., 1990-98, Yark Automotive Group, Inc. Mem. coun. Village of Ottawa Hills, Ohio, 1979-85, adviser Ohio divsn. Securities, 1979-85, commr. of taxation, Village of Ottawa Hills, Ohio, 1999—; bd. dirs. Kiwanis Youth Found. of Toledo, 1982-2002, Toledo Area Regional Transit Authority, 1989-91, Arts Commn. Greater Toledo, 1993—, exec. com., 1994-99, v.p., 1994-96, pres., 1996-97; bd. dirs. Jr. Achievement of Northwestern Ohio, Inc., 1992—, Lourdes Coll. Found., 1995-01, Toledo Orch. Assn., 1999—, Med. Coll. Ohio, 2001—, Lourdes Coll., 2001—. Mem. ABA, Ohio Bar Assn. (corp. law com. 1989—), Toledo Bar Assn., Northwestern Ohio Alumni Assn. of Williams Coll. (pres. 1974-83), Toledo-Rowing Found. (trustee 1985-2001), Toledo Area C. of C. (trustee 1991-98, exec. com. 1993-98, fin. com. 1993—), Order of Coif, Crystal Downs Country Club, Toledo Country Club, The Toledo Club (trustee 1984-90, pres. 1987-90), Williams Club N.Y., Crystal Lake Yacht Club. Republican. Episcopalian. Office: Shumaker Loop & Kendrick 1000 Jackson St Toledo OH 43624-1573

WEBB, THOMAS J. utilities executive; b. Alexandria, Va., Oct. 3, 1952; m. Donna; 3 children. B in Fin. with honors, George Mason U.; MBA. Various fin. mgmt. positions Ford Motor Co. and subs.; controller Electronics divsn., Large Front-Wheel Drive Vehicle Ctr.; CFO Visteon Corp.; chief fin. info. officer Ford Motor Co.; exec. v.p., CFO Kellogg Co., Battle Creek, Mich., 2000—02; CFO CMS Energy, Dearborn, 2002—. Bd. dirs. Conix, Can., Hall Climate Control, Korea, Halla Electronics, Korea, Samcor, South Africa, Yan Feng, China, Toledo (Ohio) Molding and Die, Climate Sys., India, others. Office: CMS Energy Fairlane Plaza S Ste 1100 330 Town Center Dr Dearborn MI 48126*

WEBB, WATTS RANKIN, surgeon; b. Columbia, Ky., Sept. 8, 1922; s. Frank Elbert and Susie Josephine (Rankin) W.; m. Frances Luella Cooke, Aug. 19, 1944; children: Andrew Michael, Paul Alan, Harvey Elbert, Gordon Lewis. BA, U. Miss., 1942; MD, Johns Hopkins U., 1945. Diplomate Am. Bd. Surgery, Am. Bd. Thoracic Surgery, Am. Bd. Surg. Critical Care. Intern Barnes Hosp., St. Louis, 1945-46; resident in surgery VA Hosp., Biloxi, Miss., 1946-48; resident in gen. and thoracic surgery Barnes Hosp., 1948-52; chief surgeon Miss. State Sanatorium, 1952-63; instr. surgery U. Miss., 1955-56, asst. prof. surgery, 1956-58, prof., 1958-63; prof., chmn. div. thoracic and cardiovascular surgery U. Tex. Southwestern Med. Sch., Dallas, 1964-70; prof., chmn. dept. surgery SUNY Upstate Med. Center, Syracuse, 1970-77; prof. surgery Tulane U., New Orleans, 1977-93, La. State U., New Orleans, 1993—; chmn. dept. Tulane U., 1977-89. Author: Pulmonary Problems in Surgery, 1974, Surgery in Acute Coronary Problems, 1974, Aneurysms, 1983, Cardiovascular Emergencies, 1986, Atlas of Pulmonary Resections, 1988, (with others) Surgical Management for Chest Injuries, Vol. VII, 1990; editorial bd.: Annals of Thoracic Surgery, 1968-79, Surg. Rounds, 1978-82, Surgery Clinics, 1980-82, Microcirculation, 1983-84, Brit. Jour. Surgery, 1981-89; contbr. over 450 articles to profl. jours. Recipient award Hadassah, 1965, Knockers Soc. Outstanding Tchr. award SUNY Upstate Med. Ctr., 1972, Owl Club Clin. Tchr. of Yr. award Tulane U. Med. Sch., 1978, 86, 88-93, Gloria P. Walsh award for best tchr. in Med. Sch., 1992, Aesculapian Tchr. of Yr. award La. State U., 1995, 96. Fellow ACS, Am. Coll. Chest Physicians; mem. AMA, Am. Assn. Thoracic Surgery, Am. Coll. Cardiology, Am. Fedn. Clin. Research, Am. Heart Assn. (Silver medal 1963), Am. Physiol. Soc., Am. Surg. Assn., Am. Thoracic Soc., Halsted Soc., La. Med. Soc., Orleans Parish Med. Soc., New Orleans Surg. Soc., Societe International de Chirurgie, Soc. Cryobiology, Soc. Thoracic Surgeons, Soc. Univ. Surgeons, Southeastern Surg. Congress, So. Med. Assn., So. Soc. Clin. Research, So. Surg. Assn. (Shipley medal 1961), So. Thoracic Soc., So. Thoracic Surg. Assn., Surg. Assn. La., Surg. Biology Club II, Internat. Soc. Heart Transplantation, Gulf Coast Vascular Soc., Sigma Xi, Alpha Omega Alpha, Pi Kappa Pi, Beta Beta Beta, Alpha Epsilon Delta. Methodist. Home: 21 Park Island Dr New Orleans LA 70122-1228 Office: La State U Dept Surgery 1542 Tulane Ave New Orleans LA 70112-2825 E-mail: wattsrwebb@yahoo.com.

WEBB, WELLINGTON E. mayor; b. Chgo., Feb. 17, 1941; BA in Edn., Colo. State Coll., 1964; MA in Edn., U. No. Colo., 1970. Tchr., 1964-76; elected Colo. Ho. of Reps., 1972, 74, 76; regional dir. HEW, 1977-81; gov.'s cabinet, 1981-87; elected auditor City of Denver, 1987-91, mayor, 1991—. Pres. U.S. Conf. of Mayors, 1993—, Nat. Conf. Black Mayors, 2000—. Named Chevalier of the Legion of Honor, Country of France, 1999; recipient Govt. Leadership in the Arts award, Ams. for the Arts, 2001, Nat. Wildlife Fedn. Achievement award, 1999, Bridge Builders award. Office: Office Mayor City & County Bldg Rm 350 1437 Bannock St Denver CO 80202-5337*

WEBB, WILLIAM DUNCAN, lawyer, mediator; b. Dayton, Ohio, Feb. 14, 1930; s. Herbert Henry and Dorothy (Chamberlain) W.; m. Nancy Helen Regester, June 12, 1953; children: Joseph Chamberlain (dec.), Mary Helen, Nancy Katherine, Sarah Elizabeth, Lucy Ellen. AB, U. Mich., 1952, JD, 1956. Bar: Mo. 1956, Kans. 1958, U.S. Supreme Ct. 1969. Assoc. Stinson, Mag, Thomson, McEvers & Fizzell, Kansas City, Mo., 1956-58; sec. Kansas City (Mo.) Power & Light Co., 1960-78, asst. treas., 1969-78, asst. v.p. communications, 1978-79, asst. v.p. fed. affairs, 1979-84; v.p. investments Paine Webber, 1984-98. Legal counsel Fellowship of Christian Athletes. Mem. city coun. Roeland Park, Kans., 1960-62; chmn. Kansas City Myasthenia Gravis Found., 1965-67; bd. dirs. Boys Club of Kansas City, Mo., 1969-74, Greater Kansas City YMCA, Greater Kansas City chpt. ARC; chmn. bd. councilors Avila Coll., 1969-70; trustee, asst. sec., 1970-89; bd. dirs. Rural Water Dist. # 7, Johnson County, Kans., 1992-94. Mem. Internat. Maine-Anjou Assn. (dir., sec.-treas. 1969-76), Theta Delta Chi, Phi Alpha Delta. Presbyterian. Home and Office: 37000 W 155th St Gardner KS 66030-9617 E-mail: webb37ooo@aol.com.

WEBB, WILLIAM H. consumer products company executive; Joined Philip Morris, Port Chester, N.Y., 1966, from various mgmt. positions to pres. Asia/Pacific region, 1966-93, COO N.Y.C., 1993—. Office: Philip Morris Internat 120 Park Ave New York NY 10017-5592

WEBB, WILLIAM LOYD, JR. army officer; b. Mineral Wells, Tex., Sept. 30, 1925; s. William Loyd and Francis (Mayer) W.; m. Muriel Emma Hinson, Dec. 27, 1947; children: George Sidney, William Loyd III, Lucinda Adrienne, Alicia Muriel. Student, Tex. A & M Coll., 1942-44; BS, U.S. Mil. Acad., 1947; MA, U. Pa., 1958. Commd. 2d lt. U.S. Army, 1947, advanced through grades to maj. gen., 1974; co. comdr. Korea, 1950, Ft. Riley, Kans., 1951-52, Germany, 1953-54; assoc. prof. English U.S. Mil. Acad. West Point, N.Y., 1958-61; regimental comdr., dep. comdt. of cadets U.S. Mil. Acad., 1969-71; squadron comdr. 14th Armored Cavalry Germany, 1963-64; mem. faculty U.S Army War Coll., 1965-68; comdr. support command 1st Inf. Div. Vietnam, 1969; dep. comdg. gen. Ft. Ord, Calif., 1971-73; ops. officer 8th Army, U.S. Forces Korea, UN Command Korea, 1973-75; sr. mem. UN Command Mil. Armistice Commn. Korea, 1975; comdr. 1st Armored Div., U.S. Army Europe W.Ger., 1975-78; dep. comdg. gen. V Corps, U.S. Army Europe W. Ger., 1978; asst. dep. chief of staff for personnel Dept. Army Washington, 1978-82. Decorated D.S.M., Legion of Merit with oak leaf cluster, D.F.C., Bronze Star medal with oak leaf cluster, Air medal with 5 oak leaf clusters, Army Commendation medal with 2 oak leaf clusters, Purple Heart. Mem. Assn. U.S. Army, Armor Assn. Episcopalian. Office: 10148 Hillington Ct Vienna VA 22182-2908

WEBB, WILLIAM TIMOTHY, mobile communications professional; b. Walton-on-Thames, U.K., May 4, 1967; s. Christopher David and Genebeth Carol W.; m. Alison Margaret Porter, June 17, 1995; children: Katherine, Hannah. B of Engring., U. Southampton, 1989, PhD, 1992; MBA, Southampton Mgmt. Sch., 1997. Chartered engr. Tech. dir. Multiple Access Technologies, Southampton, U.K., 1990-94; prin. cons. Smith System Engring., Guildford, U.K., 1994-98; dir. strategy Motorola, Schaumburg, Ill., 1998—2001; mng. cons. PA Cons., 2001—. Author: Modern Quadrature Amplitude Modultion, 1994, Introduction to Wireless Local Loop, 1998, Understanding Cellular Radio, 1998, The Complete Wireless Communications Professional, 1999, Single and Multi-Carrier QAM, 2000, Narrowband and Broadband Wireless Local Loop, 2000, The Future of Wireless Communications, 2001; contbr. articles to profl. jours. Fellow Inst. for Elec. Engrs.; mem. IEEE (sr.). E-mail: William.webb@paconsulting.com.

WEBB ANDERSON, JOANN MARIE, lawyer, community advocate; b. St. Louis, Nov. 19, 1942; d. Jeff and Nancy Mae (Harris) Webb; m. Clifton Earl Anderson, Dec. 30, 1966; children: Ronald James Anderson, Nancy Delia Anderson. Student, U. Mo., Columbia and St. Louis, 1960-62; BA in History, St. Louis U., 1967, JD, 1978; grad., Ind. U., 1974-75. Bar: Mo. 1979, U.S. Dist. Ct. U.S. V.I. 1981, U.S. Dist. Ct. (ea. dist.) Mo. 1979, U.S. Ct. Appeals (8th cir.) 1979, U.S. Ct. Appeals (3d cir.) 1982. Staff atty. Legal Svcs. Ea. Mo., St. Louis, 1979-80; staff atty., mng. atty. Legal Svcs. V.I., Christiansted, Frederiksted, 1980-81; asst. atty. gen. Govt. of V.I., St. Croix, 1981-83; supervising atty. civil divsn. Dept. of Justice, Office of Atty. Gen., 1984-85, acting chief, supervising atty., 1985-87; exec.dir. Navy Relief Soc./Japan Aux., Yokusuka, 1988-89; sole practitioner St. Louis, 1997—2002; ptnr. Anderson and Webb Anderson, LLP, 2002—. Music arranger, exec. dir. St. Croix Inspirational Singers, 1983-85. Bd. dirs. Archway Cmtys., Inc., St. Louis, 1998-2001, Child Ctr. of Our Lady, 2001—; polit. action com. Coalition of 100 Black Women, St. Louis, 1990; planning and focus group Hyde Park Neighbors/Trinity Sq., St. Louis, 1990—; cmty. adv. panel bd. Mallinkrodt Chemical Co., 1998—. Mem. Bar Assn. Met. St. Louis (econ. devel. com.), Jr. League of St. Louis, Caths. Against Capital Punishment, Blacks for Life/Mo. Right to Life, Lawyers for Life (bd. dirs. St. Louis chot.), Zeta Phi Beta. Roman Catholic. Avocations: neighborhood development, historical preservation, reading, grandparenting, international travel. Home: 1420 Bremen Ave Saint Louis MO 63107-2918 Office: 3920 Lindell Blvd Ste 207 Saint Louis MO 63108 E-mail: justmo@att.net.

WEBBER, CHARLES LEWIS, JR. physiologist, educator; b. Bay Shore, N.Y., July 26, 1947; s. Charles Lewis Sr. and Hazel Carolyn W.; m. Constance Anne Webber, June 28, 1970; children: Kevin Lewis, Stephanie Anne. BA, Taylor U., 1969; PhD, Loyola U., 1974. Asst. prof. Loyola U., Chgo., 1975-81, assoc. prof., 1981-95, prof., 1995—. Vis. scientist Max Planck Inst., Bad Nauheim, Germany, 1982, 92; vis. prof. U. Rome, 1999; course dir. med. physiology, Loyola U., Chgo, 1977-88, course dir. function of human body, 1998—, dir. biomed. electronics, 1988—. Author nonlinear software; contbr. some 60 articles to profl. jours. Sci. fair judge Ill. Jr. Acad. Sci., 1992, 93; tutor Circle Urban Ministries, Chgo., 1993-98, sci. demonstrator Am. Heart Assn., Chgo., 1995-99, h.s. sci. mentor Ill. Math and Sci. Acad., Aurora, 1988—. Recipient Gold Star award Adler Planetarium, Chgo., 1995, Pleindes Star Cluster award, 2000, Ralph P. Leischner Master Tchr. award, 2002; named Med. Tchr. of Yr., 1979, 85, 96, 99, 2000. Mem. Am. Physiol. Soc., Soc. Neurosci., Am. Sci. Affiliation, Soc. Indsl. and Applied Math. Avocations: astronomy, biblical studies, public speaking, radio essays. Office: Loyola U Med Ctr Dept Physiology 2160 S 1st Ave Maywood IL 60153-5500 E-mail: cwebber@lumc.edu.

WEBBER, CHRIS, III (MAYCE EDWARD CHRISTOPHER WEBBER), professional basketball player; b. Detroit, Mar. 1, 1973; s. Mayce and Doris Webber. Student, U. Mich., 1991-93. Drafted Orlando (Fla.) Magic, 1993; forward Golden State Warriors, San Francisco, 1993-94, Washington Bullets, 1994-98, Sacramento Kings, 1998-. Founder Timeout Found. Drafted 1st round Orlando Magic, 1993; named Nat. H.S. Player of Yr., 1990-91, Mr. Basketball State of Mich., 1991, Coca-Cola Classic NBA Player of Yr., 1994, Brut Bullets Player of Yr., 1994-95, NBA All-Rookie 1st Team, 1994. Avocations: collecting signed historical documents of prominent African-Americans. Office: Sacremento Kings One Sports Parkway Sacramento CA 95834*

WEBBER, FREDERICK NELSON, psychiatrist; b. Takoma Park, Md., July 11, 1934; s. Frederick N. Webber and Rose Mary Cockerille. BS in Chemistry, George Washington U., 1959; MD, Va. Commonwealth U., 1964; JD, Am. U., 1977. Diplomate Nat. Bd. Med. Examiners, Am. Bd. Psychiatry and Neurology. Summer extern psychiatry Perry Point (Md.) VA Hosp., 1962—63; intern Med. Coll. Va., 1964—65; resident psychiatry Northwestern U., Downey, Va., 1965—68; fellow child psychiatry Langley Porter Inst., U. Calif., San Francisco, 1968—80, U. Louisville, 1980; consulting psychiatrist adolescent unit Developmental Svcs. Ctr., Dept. Human Resources, Washington, 1976—77; psychiatrist Cts. and Corrections of San Mateo County, Redwood City, Calif., 1978; consulting child psychiatrist Seven Counties Svcs., Louisville, 1980—82; pvt. practice psychiatry, 1980—82; dir. forensic svcs. Bangor (Maine) Mental Health Inst., 1983—85; part-time child psychiatrist Cmty. Health and Counseling Svcs., 1984—86; pvt. practice psychiatrist Bangor, Bar Harbor, 1984—89; psychiat. cons. Penobscot County Jail, 1984—89; med. dir. Le Moyne Ctr. and Associated Programs, Mobile Mental Health Ctr., Mobile, Ala., 1989—97; psychiatrist Physician's Psychiat. Clinic, 1989—91; pvt. practice psychiatry Coastal Ala. Psychaitry, 1991—93; med. dir. Eufaula (Ala.) Adolescent Treatment Ctr., 1993—94; psychiatrist Pinefield Children and Youth, Affiliation of Mohawk Valley Psychiat. Ctr., Utica, NY, 1994—95, Charter Hosp., Evansville, Ind., 1996—98, River Valley Behavioral Health Ctr., Owensboro, Ky., 1998, St. Joseph Hosp., Syracuse, NY, 1998—99, Sheppard Pratt , Bel Air, Md., 1989—2000, Granite House Inc., Randallstown, 2000—01, Sheppard Pratt Hosp., Balt., 1999—, Dulaney Station INc., Balt., 2001—. Clin. instr. Northwestern U., 1966—68; instr. U. N.Mex., 1968—71, asst. prof., 1971; clin. instr. Howard U., 1971—75; clin. asst. prof. U. Louisville, 1982, U. South Ala., 1989—93; sub-contract psychiatrist Mountain View Psychiat. Hosp., Gadsden, Ala., 1995—96; part-time psychiatrist Carefirst BCBS, Mobile, 1996, Rivendell Day Treatment, Dothan, Ala., 1996; hosp. affiliation Bernalillo County Med. Ctr., Albuquerque, 1968—71, Mount Desert Island Hosp., Bar Harbor, 1983—89, Maine Coast Meml. Hosp., Ellsworth, 1984—89, St. Joseph Hosp., Bangor, 1986—89; chief psychiatry Ea. Maine Med. Ctr., Bangor, 1986—89. Mem.: Am. Psychiat. Assn. (sec. and fed. legis. rep. Maine dist. 1988—89), N.Y. Acad. Scis., Assn. for Family and Conciliation Cts., Nat. Assn. Counsel for Children, Am. Acad. Child and

Adolescent Psychiatry (del. to L.A. coun. 1991), Am. Orthopsychiat. Assn., Am. Assn. for Social Psychiatry, Am. Acad. Psychiatry and Law, Alpha Chi Sigma. Home: Apt 4 7 Stonehenge Cir Baltimore MD 21208-3230

WEBBER, HELEN, artist, designer; b. N.Y.C. d. David and Frieda (Berlin) Ross; children: Joel Benjamin (dec.), Daniel Saul, Rachel Frieda. BA, Queens Coll., 1951; postgrad., Columbia U., 1953; MA, RISD, 1963. Site specific artist/designer, product designer toys, books; tchr. in design dept. Calif. Coll. Arts and Crafts , Santa Cruz, Calif., 1982, 1984, 1987; lectr. U. Calif. Keynote spkr. ASID, San Diego and Kansas City, 1983,Nat. Home Furnishings League, San Ferancisco, 1980, Chgo., 1982; lectr., exhibitor 6th Internat. Congress Women Architects, Paris, 1983, U. Calif., Santa Cruz, 1987, Commnwealth Club, San Francisco, 1989, guest lectr. RISD Alumni Conf., 1996. Author, illustrator: Good-Night, Night, The Sea Is My Blanket, 1963, My Kite it the Magic Me, Summer Sun; prin. commissions in 5 media tapestry, clay, glass, metal and wood for 6 Carnival Cruise Line ships; Festival, Tropical Fantasy, Holiday, Celebration, Destiny, Pittsburg Calif. Civic Ctr., Metro Commerce Bank, Statendam/Holland Am. Cruise Lines, Vets. Cemetery, Riverside, Calif., East Tex. Med. Ctr., Tyler, St. Patrick's Hosp., Lake Charles, La., Gatwick Penta Hotel, London, Jewish Home for the Aged, Houston, Betty Ford Pavilion, Palm Springs, Fla., Sphohn Hosp., Corpus Christi, Tex., Chevron Corp., San Ramon, Calif., Merck & Co., Rahway, N.J., Kodak, Kingsport, Tenn., Kaiser Permanente, Sacramento and San Jose, Calif., Quail Lodge Resort, Carmel Valley, Calif., Episcopal Homes Found., San Francisco, VA Hosp., Lyons, N.J., Hyatt Regency, Phoenix, Ariz., 1st United Meth. Ch., Wichita Falls, Tex.; designer, artist textile, wallpaper, sheets, towels, children's games for Collins & Aikman, Burlington, Covington, Peerage of Eng., Edward Fields, Pastime Industries. Mem. Design Internat. (pres., co-founder San Francisco 1984-85), Women -in-Design Internat. (founder, pres. 1977-83, Outstanding Contbn. to Design award 1980), Urban Art Internat. (bd. dirs.). Studio: 12236 Marcel Lake Est Dingmans Ferry PA 18328-3043 E-mail: hwdes@pikeonline.net.

WEBBER, HOWARD RODNEY, computer company executive; b. Berlin, Oct. 20, 1933; s. Robert Alfred and Amelia (Rousseau) W.; m. Helen Margaret McCubbin, May 6, 1959; children: Benjamin James, Adam Brooks, Holly Isabella. AB, Dartmouth Coll., 1956; postgrad., Lehigh U., 1956-57. Editor in chief U. N.C. Press, Chapel Hill, 1960-63, Johns Hopkins Press, Balt., 1963-65; dir. Case Western Res. U. Press Cleve., 1965-70, MIT Press, Cambridge, 1970-74; v.p., gen. mgr., pub. Open Court Pub. Co., LaSalle, Ill., 1974-83; v.p., pub. Reference div. Houghton Mifflin Co., Boston, 1983-87; mgr. advanced devel. Groupware Systems Digital Equipment Corp., Nashua, N.H., 1987-95; chmn. FutureTense, Inc., Acton, Mass., 1995-99; cons. Open Market, Inc., Burlington, 1999—2000; info. and tech. cons., 2001—. Served with AUS, 1957-59. Mem. Phi Beta Kappa. Democrat. Episcopalian. Home and Office: 49 Wilson Rd Bedford MA 01730-1340 E-mail: h.r.webber@verizon.net.

WEBBER, JOHN BENTLEY, orthopedic surgeon; b. Morristown, N.J., Jan. 27, 1941; s. George Bentley and Gladys (Moody) W.; m. Mary Christina Thometz, Feb. 25, 1978; children: John Bentley, Edward Alan BA, Lehigh U., 1962; MD, Temple U., 1966. Intern Rochester Gen. Hosp., N.Y., 1966-67; resident Temple U. Med. Ctr., Phila., 1967-70; Stelrling Bunnell fellow in hand surgery Pacific Med. Ctr., San Francisco, 1971; practice medicine specializing in orthopedic surgery and surgery of hand Phila., 1973—; assoc. prof. orthopedic surgery and rehab. Hahnemann Med. Coll. and Hosp., 1973—, chief sect. on hand surgery, 1973—; attending surgeon St. Christopher's Hosp. for Children, 1996—. Cons. in hand surgery Mcpl. Med. Svcs., Phila., 1973-87, USPHS, Phila., 1973-76, burn ctr. St. Agnes Med. Ctr., Phila., 1973—, Phila. unit Shriners' Hosp. for Crippled Children, 1979-95. Served to maj. USAF, 1971-73. Fellow ACS (Pa. com. on trauma), Am. Acad. Orthopedic Surgeons; mem. AMA, Am. Soc. for Surgery of Hand, Bunnell Hand Club (pres. 1978-80), Assn. for Acad. Surgery, Eastern Orthopedic Soc., Pa. Med. Soc., Phila. Orthopedic Soc., Phila. Hand Soc. (pres. 1987-89), Phila. County Med. Soc., Phila. Coll. Physicians, Meigs Med. Assn., Rotary, Union Leauge, Riverside Yacht Club (fleet surgeon), Phila. Country Club, Delaware Valley Ducks Unltd. (chmn. 1983-88), U.S. Coast Guard (cert. master). Republican. Congregationalist. Home: 1139 Rock Creek Rd Gladwyne PA 19035-1439 Office: Feinstein Bldg 216-220 N Broad St Ste 200 Philadelphia PA 19102

WEBBER, JOHN ROBERT, real estate broker, musician, educator; b. Preston, Idaho, June 22, 1935; s. John Ulris and Ruth Mecham Webber; m. Mary Elizabeth Speigle, Aug. 4, 1970; children: Bobbie, Maralee. Cert. of sci., Weber State U., Ogden, Utah, 1959; MusB, U. Utah, 1961, MusM, 1967. Cert. resdl. specialist Nat. Assn. Real Estate Bds. Sales assoc. Webber Real Estate Co., Ogden, 1960—76; prin. broker Bonafide of Utah, 1976—80; assoc. broker ERA Webber Real Estate Co., 1980—. Composer: 9 polonaises for piano, 2 sonatas, overture. Served with USAF, 1958—64. Mem.: The Leschetizky Assn., Music Tchrs. Nat. Assn., Greater Ogden Area Assn. Realtors (edn. com. 1990—95), Kappa Delta Pi. Mem. Lds Ch. Avocations: skiing, hiking, painting, meteorology, tennis. Home: 1588 Apache Way Ogden UT 84403 E-mail: RWe222@aol.com.

WEBBER, LINDA JUDITH RITZ, interior designer; b. Bronx, N.Y. d. Murray and Marilyn Ritz; children: Ronald Alan, Amy Beth. BFA, Boston U., 1964; MEd, U. Hartford, 1967. Lic. interior designer, Conn. Elem. art supr., Winthrop, Mass., 1964-65; jr. high sch. art tchr. Wethersfield, Conn., 1965-66; freelance artist various bus. and industries; interior designer A. J. Skenderian, West Hartford, Conn., 1975-77, John LaFalce Inc., Canton, 1978-97; art tchr. Avon Mid. Sch., 1995-96; art curator U. Conn. Health Ctr., 2001. Art career counsellor Bloomfield (Conn.) Mid. Sch., 1979-81; lectr. in found. studies and interior design Paier Coll. of Art, 1988-89. One-woman shows include Reno Gallery, Hartford, Conn., 1971, Represented in permanent collections U. Conn. Health Ctr., Farmington. Mem. adv. com. for fine arts Bloomfield Bd. Edn., 1975-78; mem. title VII com., , 1978-81; mem. bd. for student publs. Boston U., 1962-64; curator Weyerhauser and Musser Mansions, Historic Homes on Miss., 1997; cons. art. adv. com. U. Conn. Health Ctr., 1998—. Recipient Graphic Artist award West Hartford Art League, 1975, Carriage House prize Art League of New Britain, 1996, 99, Color Explorations painting prize West Hartford Art League, 1996. Mem. Conn. Women Artists, Clinton Art Soc. (merit award 1971), Wintonbury Art League (pres. 1991-93, Leonard Waller Meml. award 1981, Pritchett prize, Freidman Floor Covering award for a watercolor 1988, Honorable Mention award Essex 1989), Conn. Watercolor Soc. Avocation: ballroom dancing. E-mail: webberbydesign@attbi.com.

WEBBER, MARY ELAINE, social worker; b. Laurel, Mont., June 17, 1950; d. Frederick Jordan and Gloria (Thaut) W. BS, Ea. Mont. Coll., 1972; MS in Social Work, U. Tenn., 1980; fellow, Karl Menninger Sch. Psychiatry, and Mental Health Scis., Topeka, Kans., 1986-87. Cert./lic. clin. social worker; cert. addictions counselor, level III; cert. educator/sch. social worker, K-12, Colo.; diplomate clin. social work Am. Bd. Examiners Clin. Social Work. Instr. spl. edn. Big Horn Basin Childrens Ctr., Thermopolis, Wyo., 1972-76; social worker, I & II Big Horn County Dept. Pub. Welfare, Hardin, Mont., 1976-79; grad. asst. Sch. of Social Work U. Tenn., Nashville, 1979-80; psychiat. social worker Capital Area Counselling Svc., Pierre, S.D., 1980-83; sch. social worker Aberdeen Area Spl. Edn. Coop. Svc. Unit, 1983-85; geriatrics social worker Mary House, Inc., 1985-86; clin. social worker Cedar Springs Hosp., Colorado Springs, 1987-89; clin. social worker/family therapist Penrose-St. Francis Healthcare Systems, 1989-91; clin. case cons. Elder Care Network, Boulder, Colo., 1991—; asst. dir. Halcyon adolescent treatment program Mental Health Ctr. Boulder (Colo.) County, 1991—. Grant cons. Sioux Vocat. Sch. for the Handicapped, Sioux Falls, S.D., 1983; social svcs. supr./cons. Rivercrest Manor (Beverly Enterprises), Pierre, 1985-86. Vol. coord. Domestic Violence Crisis Line, Pierre, 1980-82, Nashville, 1980. Recipient Profl. Writing award (2nd place) The Menninger Alumni Assn., 1987. Avocations: outdoor activities, reading, traveling, writing.

WEBBER, MICHAEL DAVID, management consultant; b. Enid, Okla., May 27, 1940; s. Mike E. and Lorine L. (Loomis) W.; BBA, U. Okla., 1962; MBA (fellow), U. Pa., 1964; m. Janet Joyce Dodson, June 30, 1962; children: Michael David, Meredith. Vice pres. A.T. Kearney, Inc., Chgo., 1967-77; pres., dir. Kearney Mgmt. Cons., Ltd., Toronto, Ont., Can., 1975-77; sr. v.p. Booz-Allen & Hamilton, Inc., N.Y.C., 1977-87, Diebold Group, N.Y.C, 1987-89; pres. MDW Ltd., Colo. 1st lt. USAF, 1964-67. Cert. mgmt. cons. Inst. Mgmt. Cons. U.S. and Ont. Mem. Inst. Mgmt. Scis., Ops. Research Soc. Am. Clubs: Greenwich Country; Milbrook Country; Internat. (Chgo.); Union League (N.Y.C.); Garden of Gods (Colorado Springs, Colo.); Boca Raton (Fla.). Contbr. articles to profl. jours. Home: 8820 Ute Rd Cascade CO 80809-1339

WEBBER, PEGGY, actress, producer, director, writer; b. Laredo, Tex., Sept. 15, 1925; d. Mathew Edward and Margaret Ann (Pierce) Weber; m. Robert Sinskey, Aug. 8, 1951 (div. 1968); children: Teresa Dickinson, Patricia Wynn, Robert Marshall Jr.; m. Sean McClory, Mar. 17, 1983. Student, U. So. Calif., L.A., 1942-44; AA, CUESTA, 1973; student, Calif. Poly. U. Founder Calif. Artists Repertory and Radio Theatre, 1972—. (Actress, writer, dir., prodr.): (TV series) Treasures of Literature (Outstanding Prodn. award Acad. TV Arts and Scis., 1948); (writer, dir., prodr.): Calif. Artists Radio Theatre Series; (Nat. Pub. Radio series) Mysteries in the Air; actor: over 8,000 network radio broadcasts, and 300 nat. TV telecasts; (films) Orson Welles' Macbeth, Hitchcock's The Wrong Man, Farrow's Submarine Command; (exec. dir. 7 theaters): (prodr., writer, dir. over 100 drama, lit., music prodns.): Nat. Pub. Radio. Pres. Calif. Artists Radio Theatre Non-profit Corp., artistic dir. Named Silver award for best drama spl., Internat. Radio Festival, 2002; recipient Outstanding Radio Personality, Time Mag., 1946, Ray Bradbury Creativity award, Woodbury U., L.A., 1998, Double Gold award, Corp. for Pub. Broadcasting, 1992, Gold and Silver award, Internat. Radio Festival, 2001, 27 nat. and internat. awards. Mem.: SAG, AFTRA, Pacific Pioneer Broadcasters (former bd. dirs.), Actors Equity Assn. Avocations: walking, history, genealogy, archaeology. Office: Calif Artists Repertory and Radio Theatre 6612 Whitley Ter Los Angeles CA 90068-3221 E-mail: info4Peggy@cs.com.

WEBBER, RICHARD JOHN, lawyer; b. Mpls., July 27, 1948; s. Richard John and Mary Lee (Moore) W.; m. Susan Barbara Listerman, Jan. 8, 1972; children: Hillary, Joanna. BA, Princeton U., 1970; JD, U. Mich., 1973. Bar: D.C. Ct. Appeals 1974, U.S. Ct. Appeals (9th and D.C. cirs.) 1980, U.S. Dist. Ct. D.C. 1980, U.S. Claims Ct. 1974, U.S. Supreme Ct. 1980. Law clk. U.S. Ct. Claims, Washington, 1973-75; trial atty. U.S. Dept. Justice, 1975-80; assoc. Arent, Fox et al, 1980-85, ptnr., 1985—. Mem. ABA (chmn. fed. contract claims and remedies com. sect. pub. contract law 1986-91), Fed. Bar Assn. (chmn. ADP procurement com. govt. contracts sect. 1992-94, chmn. govt. contracts sect. 1994-96). Office: Arent Fox Washington Sq 1050 Connecticut Ave NW Ste 500 Washington DC 20036-5303 E-mail: webberr@arentfox.com.

WEBBER, ROSS ARKELL, management educator; b. New Rochelle, N.Y., July 18, 1934; s. Richard and Muriel (Arkels) W.; m. Mary Louise Foradora, Sept. 29, 1956; children: Sarah Ruth, Judith Mary, Gregory Ross, Jennifer Louise, Stephen Andrew. BSE, Princeton U., 1956; PhD, Columbia U., 1966; MS (hon.), U. Pa., 1972. Indsl. engr. Eastman Kodak Co., Rochester, N.Y., 1959-61; instr. Columbia U., New York, 1961-64; lectr. Wharton Sch. U. Pa., Phila., 1964-65, asst. prof., 1965-70, assoc. prof., 1970-76, prof., 1976-2000; v.p. U. Pa., 1981-86; chmn. dept. mgmt. Wharton Sch. U. Pa., 1992-95, prof. emeritus, 2000—. Dir. Wharton-Industry Exec. Program, U. Pa., 1966-68, chmn. Wharton Internat. Bus. com., 1968-69, coord. Orgn. Behavior and Mgmt. Group, 1968-75, asst. dept. chmn., PhD com., 1972-75, coord. Orgnl. and Mgmt. Component, Advanced Mgmt. Program in Health Care Adminstrn., 1973-74, mem. Univ. Coun., 1975-77, adv. com. Pub. Mgmt. Unit, The Wharton Sch., 1977-81, chmn. Grad. Admissions com.; mem. editl. bd. The Wharton Mag.; bd. dirs. Arcadis N.V., Am. Water Works Co., N.J.-Am. Water Co.; owner, prin. Ross A. Webber Assocs., 1970—. Author: Organizational Behavior and the Practice of Management, 1968, 5th rev. edit., 1987; Spanish lang. edit., 1982, Culture and Management: Text and Reading in Comparative Management, 1969, Management: Basic Elements of Managing Organizations, 1979, 3rd rev. edit., 1984, Polish lang. edit., 1984, Management Pragmatics: Readings and Cases on Managing Organizations, 1979, Time is Money!: The Key to Managerial Success, 1980, Japanese lang. edit. 1983, Swedish edit. 1983, Spanish lang. edit., 1985, Portugese lang. edit., 1989, To Be a Manager, 1981, A Guide to Getting Things Done, 1984, Becoming a Courageous Manager: Overcoming Career Problems of New Managers, 1991, Breaking Your Time Barriers: Becoming a More Effective Strategic Time Manager, 1992; also over 55 articles to profl. jours. Past mem. bd. dirs. United Way Southeastern Pa.; coach youth athletics, fund raiser for church and religious educator. Lt. (jg) USN, 1956-59. Avocations: painting, tennis, skiing. Office: U Pa Wharton Sch 2000 Steinberg Hall Philadelphia PA 19104 E-mail: webber@wharton.upenn.edu.

WEBBER, WILLIAM ALEXANDER, university administrator, physician; b. Nfld., Can., Apr. 8, 1934; s. William Grant and Hester Mary (Constable) W.; m. Marilyn Joan Robson, May 17, 1958; children— Susan Joyce, Eric Michael, George David. MD, U. B.C., Can., Vancouver, 1958; LLD, U. B.C., 2000. Intern Vancouver Gen. Hosp., 1958-59; fellow Cornell U. Med. Coll., N.Y.C., 1959-61; asst. prof. medicine U. B.C., 1961-66, assoc. prof., 1966-69, prof., 1969—99, dean faculty medicine, 1977-90, assoc. v.p. acad., 1990-96, dean emeritus, 1999—. Mem. B.C. Med. Assn., Can. Assn. Anatomists, Am. Assn. Anatomists. Achievements include research on renal structure and function. Home: 2478 Crown St Vancouver BC Canada V6R 3V8 Office: U BC 2177 Westbrook Mall Vancouver BC Canada V6T 1Z3 E-mail: webber@interchange.ubc.ca.

WEBER, ADELHEID LISA, former nurse, chemist; b. Cottbus, Germany, June 1, 1934; came to the U.S., 1958; d. Johannes Gustav Paul and Johanna Katinka (Askevold) Haertwig; m. Joseph Cottrell Weber (dec. 1986), Oct. 25, 1957; children: Robert Andreas, Miriam Lisa. RN, Stadtisches Hosp., Dortmund, Germany, 1956; BS in Distributive Sci., Am. U., 1983; MBA, U. Md., 1991; postgrad., New Eng. Acupuncture Sch., 2000—. RN. Nurse Krankenhaus, Wuppertal, Germany, 1956-57; pvt. nurse Wellesley, Mass., 1969-74; lab. tech. Microbiol. Assoc., Bethesda, Md., 1979-84; switchboard operator Best Products Co., 1983-87; lab. tech. Uniformed Svcs. U. Health Scis., 1984-90; info. rsch. tech. Info. Rsch. Internat. Inc., 1987; chemist USDA, Beltsville, Md., 1990-93, ret., 1993; distbr. Morinda Health Product-Noni Juice, 1999—. Vol. Sibley Meml. Hosp., Washington, 1991. Recipient Cert. award County of Montgomery, Md., 1988, Whitman Walker Clinic, 1987. Mem. NAFE, Soc. for Rsch. Adminstrs., Am. Chem. Soc., Nat. Assn. for Amputees, Soc. for Applied Spectroscopy, Nat. Trust for Historic Preservation, Hemlock Soc. Nat. Capital Area, Nat. Mus. for Women in Arts, Wash. Performing Arts Soc. Avocations: stained glass, pottery, gardening, needlework, reading. Home: 23 Sunset Ln Osterville MA 02655-2036

WEBER, ALFONS, physicist; b. Dortmund, Germany, Oct. 8, 1927; s. Alexander and Ilona (Banda) W.; m. Jeannine K. Weber, Oct. 8, 1955; children: Karl, Louise, Paul. PhD, Ill. Inst. Tech., 1956. Instr. physics Ill. Inst. Tech., Chgo., 1953-56; from asst. prof. physics to prof. Fordham U., Bronx, N.Y., 1957-81, prof. physics and chemistry, 1976-81, chmn. dept. physics, 1964-70; rsch. physicist Nat. Inst. Stds. and Tech., Gaithersburg, Md., 1977-98, acting chief molecular spectroscopy divsn., 1980-81, chief molecular physics divsn., 1982-95, sr. scientist physics lab., 1995-98, scientist emeritus, 1999—; program mgr. condensed matter physics divsn., materials rsch NSF, 1998—2001, program dir. exptl. phys. chemistry, chemistry divsn., 2001—. With chem scis. divsn. U.S. Dept. Energy, 1991-92, chem. divsn. NSF, 1992-95. Editor: Raman Spectroscopy of Gases and Liquids, 1979; Structure and Dynamics of Weakly Bound Molecular Complexes, 1987, Spectroscopy of the Earth's Atmosphere and Interstellar Medium, 1992; mem. editorial bd. Jour. of Raman Spectroscopy, Jour. Chem. and Phys. Reference Data. V.p. Union Free Dist. # 1 Sch. Bd., Eastchester, N.Y., 1970-73. Postdoctoral fellow NRC Can., U. Toronto, 1956-57. Fellow Am. Phys. Soc. (councillor 1987-91); mem. AAAS, ASTM, Optical Soc. Am., Coblentz Soc., Soc. Applied Spectroscopy. Office: Nat Sci Found Chemistry Divsn Arlington VA 22230-0001

WEBER, ALOIS HUGHES, principal; b. Clay County, Mo., Dec. 19, 1910; d. William Swan and Nora Mildred (Elam) Hughes; m. Frank Thomas Ewing Weber, May 28, 1934 (dec. 1980); children: Patricia Katherine Weber Brusuelas, Susan Weber Mills. BA, William Jewell Coll., Liberty, Mo., 1932; MA, U. Mo., Kansas City, 1971. Elem. prin. Linden (Mo.) Sch. Dist. #72, 1931-34; elem. tchr. Eugene (Mo.) Sch. Dist., 1935-38, Sycamore Sch., Boone County, Mo., 1938-41; reserve tchr. Kansas City (Mo.) Schs., 1941-55, contract tchr., 1955-63; head tchr. Allen Sch., Kansas City, 1963-67; remedial reading tchr. Benjamin Franklin Sch., 1967-69; reading cons. Div. Urban Edn., 1969-73; coord. Title I Elem. Reading and Compensatory Edn., 1974-79; ret. Instr., trainer ARC, Am. Assn. Ret. Persons, Staying Healthy After Fifty, State of N.Mex., 1987-89, Growing Old with Health and Wisdom, 1989-95; tutor Literacy Vols. of Am., Inc., Rio Rancho, N.Mex., 1990-93; spkr. AARP Health Care Reform, Health Care Am., 1992—. Lovelace Sr. Adv. Group, 1993-98. Vol. Corrales Libr., 1980-88; bd. dirs. Read West, Literacy Vols. Am., Rio Rancho, 1989-92; bd. dirs. Adobe Comty. Theatre, Corrales, 1989-90; lectr. in field; mem. State of N.Mex. steering com. Growing Old with Health and Wisdom, 1989-95; asst. state coord. Am. Assn. Ret. Persons, Health Advocacy Svcs., N.Mex., 1995-98; pres. adv. bd. Meadowlark Sr. Ctr., Rio Rancho, 1997-2003. Recipient Area Cmty. Svc. award AARP, Nat. award for HAS Outstanding Project Achievement, 1993; Area Cmty. Svc. award State of N.Mex., 1988, Cert. of Appreciation, ARC, 1988, Cert. of Appreciation for outstanding cmty. svc. N.Mex. Legislature, State Senate, 1997, Cert. of Appreciation Rio Rancho, N.Mex. Dept. Pub. Safety Srs. and Law Enforcement Together, 1997; NSF grantee, 1973. Mem. AAUW, N.Mex. Assn. Edn. Retirees (exec. com. 1987-89), Albuquerque Assn. Edn. Retirees (exec. sec., bd. dirs. 1990-95), PEO (chpt. BD chaplain, 1990-94), West Mesa Assn. Ednl. Retirees (membership chmn. 1991, v.p. 1993, pres. 1994), Grad. Club Albuquerque. Democrat. Baptist. Avocations: bridge, reading, travel. Home: 3321 Esplanade Cir SE Rio Rancho NM 87124-2198

WEBER, ALVIN JULIAN, III, radiologist; b. Knoxville, Tenn., Apr. 3, 1936; s. Alvin Julian and Nancy Rhea (Freeman) W.; m. Judith Anne Rowe, Sept. 16, 1967; children: Alvin Julian IV, Philip Rowe. MD, U. Tenn., 1962. Cert. Am. Bd. Internal Medicine, Am. Bd. Nuclear Medicine, Am. Bd. Radiology. Chmn. credentials com. Meth. Hosps. Memphis, 1986—91, dir. dept. nuclear medicine, 1990—2000. Cons. in nuc. medicine, Va., 1976—79, Tenn., 1976—79, Tenn., 2001—02, Ala., 2001—02, Miss., 2001—. Lt. USN, 1963-66. Mem. ACP, Am. Coll. Radiology, Am. Coll. Nuclear Physicians, Radiol. Soc. N.Am. Baptist. Avocations: marksmanship, hiking, camping.

WEBER, ARNOLD I. lawyer; b. Little Cedar, Iowa, Oct. 4, 1926; divorced; children: Katherine Weber Hickle, Thomas, Margaret Weber Robertson. PhB magna cum laude, Marquette U., 1949; MA, Harvard U., 1950; JD, George Washington U., 1954, LLM, 1956. Bar: D.C. 1954, Md. 1961, Calif. 1962, U.S. Dist Ct. D.C. 1954, (no. dist.) Calif. 1962, (cen. dist.) Calif. 1992, U.S. Ct. Claims 1960, U.S. Tax Ct. 1965, U.S. Ct. Appeals (D.C. cir.) 1954, (9th cir.) 1962, (fed. cir.) 1991, U.S. Supreme Ct. 1959. Lawyer Housing and Home Fin., Washington, 1954; pvt. practice, 1954-55; lawyer Tariff Commn., 1954-55, FCC, Washington, 1955-56, IRS, Washington, 1956-61; assoc. Brobeck, Phleger & Harrison, San Francisco, 1961-64; sr. gen. atty. So. Pacific Transp., 1964-84; western tax counsel Santa Fe Pacific Corp., 1985-88; pvt. practice, 1988—. With USNR, 1944-54, PTO. Mem. ABA, Olympic Club, Bar Assn. San Francisco, State Bar of Calif. Office: 57 Post St Ste 502 San Francisco CA 94104-5020

WEBER, ARNOLD ROBERT, academic administrator; b. N.Y.C., Sept. 20, 1929; s. Jack and Lena (Smith) W.; m. Edna M. Files, Feb. 7, 1954; children: David, Paul, Robert. BA, U. Ill., 1951; MA, PhD in Econs., MIT, 1958. Instr., then asst. prof. econs. MIT, 1955-58; faculty U. Chgo. Grad. Sch. Bus., 1958-69, prof. indsl. relations, 1963-69; asst. sec. for manpower Dept. Labor, 1969-70; exec. dir. Cost of Living Council; also spl. asst. to Pres. Nixon, 1971; Gladys C. and Isidore Brown prof. urban and labor econs. U. Chgo., 1971-73; former provost Carnegie-Mellon U.; dean Carnegie-Mellon U. (Grad. Sch. Indsl. Adminstrn.), prof. labor econs. and pub. policy, 1973-80; pres. U. Colo., Boulder, 1980-85, Northwestern U., Evanston, Ill., 1985-95, chancellor, 1995-98, pres. emeritus, 1998—. Cons. union, mgmt. and govt. agys., 1960—; cons. Dept. Labor, 1965; mem. Pres.'s Adv. Com. Labor Mgmt. Policy, 1964, Orgn. Econ. Coop. and Devel., 1987; vice chmn. Sec. Labor Task Force Improving Employment Svcs., 1965; chmn. rsch. adv. com. U.S. Employment Svc., 1966; assoc. dir. OMB Exec. Office of Pres., 1970—71; chmn. Presdl. R.R. Emergency Bd., 1982; trustee Com. for Econ. Devel., Nat. Multiple Sclerosis Soc.; bd. dirs. Diamond Tech. Ptnrs. Inc.; asst. sec. manpower U.S. Dept. Labor, 1969—70. Contbr. articles to profl. jours. Trustee Aspen Inst. Laureate, Lincoln Acad. Ill.; Ford Found. Faculty Rsch. fellow, 1964-65. Mem. Am. Acad. Arts and Scis., Indsl. Rels. Rsch. Assn., Nat. Acad. Pub. Adminstrn., Comml. Club Chgo. (pres., civic com. 1995-2000), Econ. Club Chgo. (pres. 1995-97), Phi Beta Kappa. Jewish. Office: Northwestern U Office of Pres Emeritus 555 Clark St 209 Evanston IL 60208-0805 E-mail: arnold-weber@nwu.edu.

WEBER, BRUCE, publishing executive; b. Bklyn., Nov. 20, 1942; s. Paul Karl and Miriam (Goldstein) W.; m. Annette Katz, May 30, 1968; children: Allison Emma, Jonathan Russell. BS, U. Md., 1964; postgrad. study, Pace U., 1965-68. Editorial asst. Scholastic Coach Mag., N.Y.C., 1965-68, asst. editor, 1968-73, assoc. editor, 1973-81, publisher, 1981—. Author: (TV series) Scholastic Sports Academy 1981-84 (ACT award 1982); (books) Questions and Answers about Baseball, 1974, Weird Moments in Sports, 1975, The Dynamite Animal Hall of Fame, 1978, Bruce Weber's Inside Pro Football 1983, 1983, Larry Bird and Magic Johnson, 1986, Sparky Anderson, 1988, Bruce Weber's Inside Baseball 1992, 1991, numerous others. Trustee Paramus (N.J.) Bd. Edn., 1978-87; bd. dirs. Paramus Run, 1978—; pres. bd. govs. Devonshire Sch., Mahwah, N.J., 1987-90. Named Contributor to Sports in Am. Athletic Inst., North Palm Beach, Fla., 1987. Mem. Football Writers Assn. of Am., Am. Football Coaches Assn. (life). Democrat. Jewish. Avocations: sports, music, theater. Home: 511 Marion Ln Paramus NJ 07652-4721 Office: Scholastic Inc 555 Broadway New York NY 10012-3919 E-mail: bweber@scholastic.com.

WEBER, CHARLES ALFRED, II, internist, rheumatologist; b. Harrisburg, Pa., Apr. 9, 1953; s. Otto Roy and Alberta May Weber; m. Kathy Anne Shearman, June 19, 1982; children: Charles Alfred, Drew Thomas, Alexia Anne, Chad Christian. BA in Physics and Math., Franklin and Marshall Coll., 1974; MS in Physics, Lehigh U., 1976; MD with honors, Autonomous U. Guadalajara, Mex., 1981; postgrad., U. Medicine and Dentistry N.J., 1981-82. Diplomate Am. Bd. Internal Medicine, Am. Bd. Rheumatology. Tchg. asst. in physics Lehigh U., Bethlehem, Pa., 1974-76; intern in medicine Jersey Shore Med. Ctr., Neptune, N.J., 1982-83, resident in medicine, 1983-85, asst. and assoc. attending dept. medicine and rheumatology, 1987-96, attending, 1996—; pvt. practice, 1987—. Instr. medicine U. Medicine and Dentistry Robert Wood Johnson Med. Sch., Piscataway; mem. patient svcs. com. N.J. chpt. Arthritis Found., Iselin, 1994—. Contbr. articles to med. jours. Fellow Am. Coll. Rheumatology; mem. ACP, AAAS, N.J. Rheumatism Soc., Space Studies Inst., N.Y. Acad. Scis., Sigma Pi Sigma. Roman Catholic. Avocations: architecture, oil painting, cabinet making, travel, computers. Office: Shore Rheumatology Assocs 10 Neptune Blvd Ste 106 Neptune NJ 07753-4848

WEBER, CHARLES WALTER, nutrition educator; b. Harold, S.D., Nov. 30, 1931; s. Walter Earl and Vera Jean (Scott) W.; m. Marylou Merkel Adam, Feb. 3, 1961; children: Matthew, Scott. BS, Colo. State U., 1956, MS, 1958; PhD, U. Ariz., 1966. Research asst. U. Ariz., Tucson, 1963-66, asst. prof., 1966-68, assoc. prof., 1969-72, prof. nutrition, 1973-97, prof. emeritus, 1997—. Cons. Hermosillo, Mex., 1970-74, Inst. of Health, Cairo, 1981-82, U. Fortaleza, Rio de Janiero, 1986. Contbr. articles to sci. jours. Served as cpl. U.S. Army, 1952-54. Mem. Am. Assn. Cereal Chemists, Am. Inst. Nutrition, Inst. Food Technologists, N.Y. Acad. Scis., Am. Soc. Clin. Nutrition, Poultry Sci. Assn., Ariz. Referees Assn., Sigma Xi. Clubs: Randolph Soccer (Tucson) (pres. 1976-79). Avocation: stamp collection. Home: 4031 E Calle De Jardin Tucson AZ 85711-3410

WEBER, CHRISTOPHER B. music educator; b. Sea Cliff, Ny, June 23, 1954; s. Harold S. and Geraldine Weber; m. Martha Lorey. Degree? Music Ed., Ithaca Coll., Ithaca, NY, 1978. Teachers Certificate NY State. Elem. band dir. Elenville Ctrl. Schools, Ellenville, NY, 1978—79; h.s. band dir. Union-Endicott Schools, Endicott, 1979—; coll. jazz ensemble dir. Broome County Cmty. Coll., Binghamton, 1997—. Adjudicator NY State Sch. Music Assn., 1979—, all-state jazz selection com., 1988—. Editor: (book) School Music News. Recipient Educator of the Week, WBNG TV, Binghamton, NY. Mem.: Internat. Assn. of Jazz Educators, Internat. Trumpet Guild. Achievements include professional trumpet player; performs with many groups including

The Sammy Kaye Orchestra. Home: 274 Arbor Glade Road Owego NY 13827-7404 Office: Union-Endicott High School 1200 East Main Street Endicott NY 13760-5220 E-mail: cweber@uegw.stier.org.

WEBER, DANIEL E. association executive; b. Chgo., July 6, 1940; BS in Bus. Mgmt., DePaul U., 1962. Asst. to exec. dir. Am. Oil Chemists Soc., Chgo., 1962-67; administrv. mgr. Inst. Food Tech, 1967-69, dir. conv. svcs., 1969-79, dir. mktg. and meetings, 1979-91; exec. dir. Inst. Food Technologists, 1991-99, exec. v.p., CEO, 1999—. Chmn. 25th Anniversary Com. City of Rolling Meadows, 2 term ind. mem. city coun., chmn. every major com., street dedicated "Weber Drive"; officer Crusade of Mercy; bd. dirs., treas., v.p. Northwest Mental Health Assn., Disting. Svc. award. Named Meeting Planner of Yr. Assn. Conv. Ops. Mgmt., 1990. Mem. Internat. Assn. Exposition Mgrs. (charter cert. exposition mgr., v.p. 1987, pres. 1988, nat. bd. mem., chair Midwestern chpt., awards com. 1998—, chair scholarship com. 2000), Nat. Assn. Exposition Mgrs. (bd. dirs., officer, pres. 1988, v.p. 1987, cert. exposition mgr.), Am. Soc. Assn. Execs., Trade Show Bur. (bd. dirs. 1987—), Coun. Engring. and Sci. Soc. Exec. (conv. liaison coun. del. 1980-81, program chmn. meetings, expositions), Profl. Conv. Mgmt. Assn. (bd. dirs. 1992, 93), Conv. Liaison Coun. (task force on reorganization), Chgo. Soc. Assn. Execs. (chmn. directory advt., chmn. membership svcs. com., chmn. awards com.). Avocation: golf. Office: Inst of Food Techs 525 W Van Buren St Ste 1000 Chicago IL 60607-3814 E-mail: info@ift.org.

WEBER, DAVID V. physician, medical director; b. Evanston, Ill., Nov. 10, 1944; s. Warren E. Weber and Rita F. Irick; children: Julie M., Kerri A. BS, No. Ill. U., 1966; MD, Loyola U., 1971. Diplomate Am. Bd. Internal Medicine. Intern St. Joseph Hosp., Chgo., 1971-72, resident in internal medicine, 1976-78; nephrology fellow Michael Reese Med. Ctr., 1978-80; staff clinician Hines VA Med. Ctr., Maywood, Ill., 1978-80; staff physician Wheaton (Ill.) Med. Clinic, 1980-88; pvt. practice Naperville, Ill., 1988-94; med. dir. Health Chgo./Humana HMO, Lisle, 1989-93; staff physician Premier Med. Assoc., Aurora, 1994-96; med. dir. Spine and Rehab. Assn., Montgomery, 1996—. Staff nephrologist N.Am. Nephrology Assoc., Oak Park, Ill., 1981-93; clin. instr. Loyola U. Stritch Sch. of Medicine, 1978-81. Capt. USAF, 1972-74. Fellow ACP; mem. Am. Soc. of Nephrology, Renal Physicians Assn., Am. Legion. Avocations: hiking, boating, fishing, cross country skiing. Home: 302 Normandie Dr Aurora IL 60506-9304 Office: Montgomery Spine and Rehab Assn 1851 Douglas Rd Montgomery IL 60538-2159

WEBER, DONALD B. advertising and marketing executive; b. Jersey City, Nov. 6, 1932; s. John William and Rose Ann (Saroshi) W.; m. Ann McDermaid, 1955 (div. 1975); children: Martha Elizabeth, Margaret Ann; m. Jean Host, 1980. BA, Rollins Coll., 1954; MBA, Northwestern U., 1959. Account exec. Leo Burnett Co., Inc., Chgo., 1958-63; sr. v.p., mgmt. supr. Foote, Cone & Belding, 1963-76; pres. Blau Bishop Assocs., 1976-79; v.p. Russell Reynolds Assocs., Chgo., 1979-82; sr. v.p., regional mgr. MSL Internat., 1982-85; exec. v.p. Rumrill-Hoyt, Inc., Rochester, N.Y., 1985-88; sr. v.p. D'Arcy Masius Benton & Bowles, Chgo., 1988-95; sr. v.p., group mgmt. dir. Cramer-Krasselt, 1996-99; sr. v.p. mgmt. dir. Intact, Inc., 1999—. Lectr. Northwestern U. Chmn. bd. Ill. divsn. Am. Cancer Soc., Chgo., 1996-99, bd. dirs., exec. com., 1999—, chmn. comm.; bd. dirs. Am. Inst. of Wine and Food, 1995-97; chmn. Chgo. coun. Boy Scouts Am., 1991-95. Lt. comdr. USNR, 1955-58. Lt. comdr. USNR, 1955—58. Mem. Chgo. Advtg. Fedn. (bd. dirs. 1988-93), Oak Hill Country Club, Exmoor Country Club, Tavern Club. Republican. Episcopalian. E-mail: intactdbw@aol.com.

WEBER, DONNA, non-profit agency administrator; b. St. Louis, Nov. 9, 1944; d. Lee William and Alta Cornelia (Windsor) W.; m. Henry Paul Lowinger, June 3, 1971 (div. Feb. 1980); children: Jakob Lowinger, Sean Weber. BSW, Temple U., 1978, MSW, 1979, postgrad., 1981—. Research coordinator ABT Assocs., Cambridge, Mass., 1979; adminstr. Temple U., Phila., 1980-83; asst. dir. Phila. Clearinghouse, 1983-85, mng. dir., 1985-86, exec. dir., trainer, 1986—. Fundraising chair United Community Ctrs., Inc., Bklyn., 1973-75; treas. Neighbors Community Program, Phila., 1976-79. Democrat. Office: Phila Clearinghouse 419 S 15th St Philadelphia PA 19146-1637

WEBER, EICKE RICHARD, physicist; b. Muennerstadt, Germany, Oct. 28, 1949; s. Martin and Irene (Kistner) W.; m. Monika Rähse, Aug. 28, 1999. BS, U. Cologne, Fed. Republic of Germany, 1970, MS, 1973, PhD, 1976, Dr.Habil., 1983. Sci. asst. U. Koeln, 1976-82; rsch. asst. U. Lund, Sweden, 1982-83; asst. prof. Dept. Material Sci. U. Calif., Berkeley, 1983-87, assoc. prof., 1987-91, prof. materials sci., 1991—; prin. investigator Lawrence Berkeley Lab., 1984—. Vis. prof. Tohoku U., Sendai, Japan, 1990, Kyoto (Japan) U., 2000; cons. in field; internat. fellow Inst. for Study of Defects in Solids, SUNY, Albany, 1978-79; chmn. numerous confs.; mem. founding com. CAESAR Found., Bonn, 1995-97, mem. scientific coun. 1999—; lectr. in field. Editor: Defect Recognition and Image Processing in III-V Compounds, 1987, Imperfections in III-V Compounds, 1993; co-editor: Chemistry and Defects in Semiconductor Structures, 1989, others; series co-editor: Semiconductors and Semimetals, 1991—; contbr. over 450 articles to profl. jours. Pres. Alexander von Humboldt Assn. Am., 2001—. Recipient IBM Faculty award, 1984, Humboldt U.S. Sr. Scientist award, 1994; rsch. grantee Dept. of Energy, 1984—, Office Naval Rsch., 1985—, Air Force Office Sci. Rsch., 1988—, NASA, 1988-90, Nat. Renewable Energy Lab., 1992—. Fellow: Am. Phys. Soc.; mem.: Materials Rsch. Soc., IEEE. Achievements include first identification of point defects formed by dislocation motion in silicon; determination of the energy levels of antisite defects in GaAs, of 3d transition metal solubility, diffusivity, and lattice site in silicon, of mechanism of internal gettering in silicon; research in defects formed in III/V thin films and interfaces; on lattice mismatched heteroepitaxial growth; in structure and electronic properties of metal GaAs heterostructures; in nature and electronic properties of defects in GaAs, GaN, and related compounds; in MBE growth of GaN and related compounds; in low-temperature MBE growth of As-rich GaAs; in transition metal gettering in silicon; multicrystalline silicon for photovoltaic applications; scanning tunneling microscopy of semiconductor thin films and interfaces; on electron paramagnetic resonance of defects in semiconductors. Office: U Calif Dept Materials Sci & Engring 475 Evans Hall Berkeley CA 94720-1767 E-mail: weber@socrates.berkeley.edu.

WEBER, ELLEN SCHMOYER, pediatric speech pathologist; b. Allentown, Pa., Oct. 6, 1952; BS in Speech Pathology, Kutztown State Coll., 1975; MS in Speech Pathology, U. So. Fla., 1982, MEd in Ednl. Leadership, 1991. Cert. tchr., ednl. adminstr., Fla. Itinerant therapist Schuylkill County Ind. Sch. Dist., Pottsville, Pa., 1975-76, Pinellas County Sch. Dist., Largo, Fla., 1979-95; pvt. therapist Pinellas County, 1982-87, 94—; owner, dir. Children's Speech and Lang. Svcs. Staffing team coord. Pinellas County Sch. Dist., Largo, Fla., 1986-91, 93-94, mem. sch. adv. coun., 1990-93, union rep., 1989-92. Computer grantee Pinellas County Sch. Dist., 1986-87, travel grantee, 1991-92. Mem. Am. Speech-Lang.-Hearing Assn., Fla. Speech-Lang.-Hearing Assn. Avocations: travel, skiing, cycling, hiking, computer. Office: 2141 Main St Ste P Dunedin FL 34698

WEBER, EUGEN, historian, educator, writer; b. Bucharest, Romania, Apr. 24, 1925; came to U.S., 1955; s. Emanuel and Sonia (Garrett) W.; m. Jacqueline Brument-Roth, June 12, 1950. Student, Inst. d'études politiques, Paris, 1948-49, 51-52; MA, Emmanuel Coll., Cambridge U., 1954, M.Litt., 1956. History supr. Emmanuel Coll., 1953-54; lectr. U. Alta., 1954-55; asst. prof. U. Iowa, 1955-56; asst. prof. history UCLA, 1956, assoc. prof., 1959-63, prof., 1963—, Joan Palevsky prof. modern European history, 1984—, chmn. dept., 1965-68; dir. study center U. Calif., France, 1968-70; dean social scis. UCLA, 1976-77, dean Coll. Letters and Scis., 1977-82. Frum Meml. lectr. Toronto U., 1999; Ford faculty lectr. Stanford U., 1965; Patten lectr. Ind. U., 1981; vis. prof. Collège de France, Paris, 1983; dir. d'études Ecole des hautes ètudes, Paris, 1984-85; Christian Gauss lectr., Princeton U., 1990. Author: Nationalist Revival in France, 1959, The Western Tradition, 1959, Paths to the Present, 1960, Action Française, 1962, Satan Franc-Maçon, 1964, Varieties of Fascism, 1964; (with H. Rogger) The European Right, 1965, A Modern History of Europe, 1970, Europe Since 1715, 1972, Peasants into Frenchmen, 1976 (Commonwealth prize Calif. 1977), La Fin des Terroirs, 1983 (Prix de la Société des gens de lettres 1984), France Fin-de-siècle, 1986 (Commonwealth prize Calif. 1987), The Western Tradition (WGBH/PBS TV series), 1989, My France, 1990, Movements, Currents, Trends, 1991, The Hollow Years, 1994, La France des annèes trente (Prix littèraire Etats-Unis/France, 1995, Prix Maurice Baumont 1995, Prix de Jeux Floraux 1997), 1995, Apocalypses, 1999; adv. editor Jour. Contemporary History, 1966—, French History, 1985—, French Cultural Studies, 1990—, Am. Scholar, 1992-98, Nuova Storia Contemporanea, 1999—. Served as capt. inf. Brit. Army, 1943-47. Recipient Luckman Disting. Teaching award UCLA Alumnae Assn., 1992; decorated Ordre Nat. des Palmes Academiques, France; Fulbright fellow, 1952, 82-83; research fellow Am. Philos. Soc., 1959, Social Sci. Research Council, 1959-61, Am. Council Learned Socs., 1962; Guggenheim fellow, 1963-64; NEH sr. fellow, 1973-74, 82-83. Fellow Netherlands Inst. Advanced Studies, Assn. française de science politique, Am. Acad. Arts and Scis., Am. Philos. Soc.; mem. Am. Hist. Assn. (scholary distinction award 1999), Soc. d'histoire moderne, Soc. French Hist. Studies, Phi Beta Kappa (hon., Ralph Waldo Emerson prize 1977, senator 1988-2000). Office: UCLA Dept History Los Angeles CA 90095-0001

WEBER, FREDERICK EDWIN, management recruiter; b. Quincy, Ill., Aug. 9, 1924; s. Edwin Frederick and Minnie Catherine (Boschulte) W.; m. Wanda Lou Woody, Aug. 10, 1946; children: Barbara L., Marcia A. (dec. 1990), William F. BS in Indsl. Mgmt., U. Ill., 1948. Cert. personnel cons. Foreman US Rubber Co., Mishawaka, Ind., 1948-56, supt., 1956-59, plant mgr. Stoughton, Wis., 1959-65, Uniroyal Inc., Port Clinton, Ohio, 1965-67, mng. dir. Edinburgh, Scotland, 1968-70; factory mgr. Masland Duraleather, Phila., 1971-74; indsl. cons. J.L. Tunnel Co., Blue Bell, Pa., 1974-76; pres. Mgmt. Recruiters, Cedar Rapids, Iowa, 1976—. Farm mgr., 1993—; regional rep. Midwest Region Mgmt. Recruiters, 1994—. Mem. Iowa Job Svc. Adv. Coun., Des Moines, 1982-95, chmn., 1984, 87, 93; mem. Bd. Edn., Stoughton, Wis., 1962-65; pres. Iowa Assn. Pers. Cons., 1982-83. With USN, 1943-46, PTO. Mem. Am. Legion, Rotary (bd. dirs. 1980-83). Republican. Lutheran. Avocations: travel, golf, photography, poetry. Home: 360 Red Fox Rd SE Cedar Rapids IA 52403-2056 Office: Mgmt Recruiters 150 1st Ave NE Ste 400 Cedar Rapids IA 52401-1126

WEBER, FREDRIC ALAN, lawyer; b. Paterson, N.J., July 31, 1948; s. Frederick Edward and Alida (Hessels) W.; m. Mary Elizabeth Cook, June 18, 1983. BA in History, Rice U., 1970; JD, Yale U., 1976. Bar: Tex. 1976, U.S. Dist. Ct. (so. dist.) Tex. Assoc. Fulbright & Jaworski, Houston, 1976-80, participating assoc., 1980-83, ptnr., 1983—. Dir. Houston Symphony Soc., 1993—, v.p. devel., 2001—. Recipient Benjamin Scharps prize Yale Law Sch., 1976, Ambrose Gherini prize Yale Law Sch., 1976. Mem. ABA, Am. Coll. Bond Counsel, Nat. Assn. Bond Lawyers (bd. dirs. 1988-89, treas. 1989-90, pres.-elect 1991, pres. 1991-92), Houston Bar Assn. Office: Fulbright & Jaworski LLP 1301 Mckinney St Ste 5100 Houston TX 77010-3095 E-mail: fweber@fulbright.com.

WEBER, GEORG, sociologist, educator; b. Zendersch, Romania, Oct. 22, 1931; arrived in Germany, 1944; s. Georg and Sara (Bürger) W.; m. Renate Schlenther, Apr. 6, 1962; children: Cornelius, Markus, Ricarda. MTh, Wittenberg U., Springfield, Ohio, 1958; DrTheol, U. Münster, Germany, 1965, Habil in Sociology and Paedagogics, 1971; DrPhil honoris causa, U. Cluj, Romania, 1992. Ordained to ministry Lutheran Ch. Tchr. high sch., Münster, 1963-64, 68-69; rschr. U. Dortmund, Germany, 1961-62, Comenius Inst., Münster, 1965-68; asst. prof. Tchrs. Coll., 1970-72, assoc. prof., 1972-73; univ. prof., dir. inst. U. Münster, 1973—. Cons. U. Cluj, 1976—; cons. Inst. de Cercetari Socio-Umane, Sibiu, Romania, 1990—; bd. dirs. AKSL, Heidelberg, Germany, 1980—. Author: Beharrung und Einfügung, 1968, Anspruch und Wirklichkeit, 1972; co-author: Altersbilder in der professionellen Altenpflege, 1997, Die Deportation von Siebenbürger Sachsen in die Sowjetunion 1945-1949, 3d vol., 1995, Soziale Hilfe-ein Teilsystem der Gesellschaft?, 1999; editor: Zugänge zur Gemeinde, Soziologische, historische und sprachwissenschaftliche Beiträge, 2000; co-author, editor other books; editor Archiv für Siebenbürgische Landeskunde, Studia Transilvanica, Schriften zur Siebenbürgischen Landeskunde, Studien zur interdisziplinären Thanatologie; co-editor other jours. Bd. dirs. Com. for Refugees, München, 1958-78. Mem. Deutsche Gesellschaft für Soziologie, Deutsche Gesellschaft für Erziehungswissenschaften. Avocations: history, literature, sports. E-mail: weberg@uni-muenster.de.

WEBER, GEORG FRANZ, immunologist, cancer researcher; b. Erlangen, Germany, July 7, 1962; came to U.S., 1989; s. Otto and Margret (Hartung) W.; m. Chitra Edwin, Sept. 21, 1991; 1 child, Ramona Sara. BS, Ohm-Gymnasium, Erlangen, Germany, 1981; MD, PhD, Julius Maximilians U., Wuerzburg, Germany, 1988. Rsch. assoc. U. S. Ala., Mobile, 1989; rsch. fellow dept. biochemistry and Dana-Farber Cancer Inst. Harvard U., Boston, 1990-91, rsch. assoc. dept. pathology and Dana-Farber Cancer Inst., 1991-93, instr., 1993-2000; asst. prof. in radiation oncology New Eng. Med. Ctr. and Tufts U., 1999—; assoc. prof. in immunology Tufts U. Contbr. articles to profl. jours. Mem. Amnesty Internat., N.Y.C., 1991–. Deutsche Forschungsgemeinschaft fellow, 1989-91. Mem. AMA, Deutscher Aerzteverband, Oxygen Soc., Am. Assn. for Cancer Rsch., Metastasis Rsch. Soc. Achievements include research into reactive oxygen species in medicine, immunology, cancer research, theory of chess, biomechanics. Office: New England Med Ctr Divsn Radiation & Cancer Biology 750 Washington St Boston MA 02111-1526

WEBER, GEORGE, oncology and pharmacology researcher, educator; b. Budapest, Hungary, Mar. 29, 1922; came to U.S., 1959; s. Salamon and Hajnalka (Arvai) W.; m. Catherine Elizabeth Forrest, June 30, 1958; children: Elizabeth Dolly Arvai, Julie Vibert Wallace, Jefferson James. BA, Queen's U., 1950, MD, 1952; MD (hon.), U. Chieti, Italy, 1979, Med. Faculty, Budapest, 1982, U. Leipzig, Fed. Republic of Germany, 1987, Tokushima (Japan) U., 1988, Kagawa (Japan) U., 1992. Rsch. assoc. Montreal Cancer Inst., 1953-59; prof. pharmacology Ind. U. Sch. Medicine, Indpls., 1959—; dir. Lab for Exptl. Oncology Sch. Medicine, Ind. U., 1974—; Milan Panič prof. oncology Ind. U., 1994—, Wellcome prof., 1995—; prof. Lab. for Exptl. Oncology Sch. Medicine, Ind. U., 1974-90, disting. prof. Lab. for Exptl. Oncology, 1990—. Chmn. study sect. USPHS, Washington, 1976-78; sci. adv. com. Am. Cancer Soc., N.Y.C., 1972-76, 94—, Damon Runyon Fund, N.Y.C., 1971-76; mem. U.S. Nat. Com., Internat. Union Against Cancer, Washington, 1974-80, 90-94, NAS, Washington, 1974-80, 90-94, U.S. Army Med. Rsch. & Breast Cancer Rsch. Program, 1996-97; prof. Brit. cancer campaign U. Oxford, Oxford, Eng., 2001; vis. prof. U. Bologna, Italy, 2001-02. Editor: Advances in Enzyme Regulation, Vols. 1-43, 1962—; assoc. editor Jour. Cancer Rsch., 1969-80, 82-89. Recipient Alecce Prize for cancer rsch. Tiberine Acad., Rome, 1971, Best Prof. award Student AMA, Indpls., 1966, 68, G.F. Gallanti prize for enzymology Internat. Soc. Clin. Chemists, 1984, Outstanding Investigator award Nat. Cancer Inst., NIH, 1986-94, Semmelweis medal & diploma Budapest, Hungary, 2001, medal Gastroenterological Soc., Aliga, Hungary, 2001, Prestigious External Award Recognition Ind. U., Indpls., Ind., 2002. Mem. Am. Soc. for Pharmacology and Exptl. Therapeutics, Am. Assn. Cancer Rsch. (G.H.A. Clowes award 1982), Russian Acad. Sci. (hon.), Hungarian Cancer Soc. (hon.), Hungarian Acad. Scis. (hon.), Acad. Scis. Bologna (Italy) (hon.). Home: 7307 Lakeside Dr Indianapolis IN 46278-1618 Office: Ind U Sch Medicine Lab Exptl Oncology 699 West Dr Indianapolis IN 46202-5119

WEBER, GEORGE RICHARD, financial and internet marketing executive, writer; b. The Dalles, Oreg., Feb. 7, 1929; s. Richard Merle and Maud (Winchell) W.; m. Nadine Hanson, Oct. 12, 1957; children: Elizabeth Ann Weber Katooli, Karen Louise Weber Zaro, Linda Marie. BS, Oreg. State U., 1950; MBA, U. Oreg., 1962. CPA, Oreg. Sr. trainee U.S. Nat. Bank of Portland (Oreg.), 1950-51; jr. acct. Ben Musa, CPA, The Dalles, Oreg., 1954; tax and audit asst. Price Waterhouse, Portland, 1955-59; sr. acct. Burton M. Smith, CPA, 1959-62; pvt. practice, 1962-99; assoc. World Mktg. Alliance, 1996-99, Waterman and Assocs., 2000—01, Allstate Fin. Svcs., 2001—. Lectr. acctg. Portland State Coll.; expert witness fin. and tax matters. Author: Small Business Long-term Finance, 1962, A History of the Coroner and Medical Examiner Offices, 1963, CPA Litigation Service References, 1991, Letters to a Friend, 1995; contbr. to profl. publs. and poetry jours. Sec.-treas. Mt. Hood Kiwanis Camp, Inc., 1965; exec. counselor SBA; mem. fin. com., powerlifting team U.S. Powerlifting Fedn., 1984, amb. People to People, China, 1987. Arty. officer AUS, 1951-53. Decorated Bronze Star. Mem. AICPA, Internat. Platform Assn., Oreg. Hist. Soc., Oreg. City Traditional Jazz Soc., Order of the Holy Cross Jerusalem, Order St. Stephen the Martyr, Order St. Gregory the Illuminator, Knightly Assn. St. George the Martyr, World Literary Acad., Portland C.S. Lewis Soc., Beta Alpha Psi, Pi Kappa Alpha. Clubs: Kiwanis, Portland Track, City (Portland); Multnomah Athletic; Sunrise Toastmasters. Republican. Lutheran. Home and Office: 3715 NE Alberta Ct Portland OR 97211-8144 E-mail: grweber@earthlink.net. *My basic beliefs are in faith, family and freedom through limited government and personal responsibility, with personal responsibility including development and use of capabilities.*

WEBER, GERALD RICHARD, legal association administrator, educator; b. Middletown, Conn., June 2, 1964; s. Gerald Richard Sr. and Norma Jean W.; m. Stephanie Stuckey, May 27, 1996 (div. Dec. 1997). BS in Fin. and Law summa cum laude, Ill. State U., 1986; JD summa cum laude, U. Ga., 1989. Bar: Ga., 1990, U.S. Ct. Appeals (5th and 11th cirs.) U.S. Supreme Ct., 1990, U.S. Dist. Ct. (no. and mid. dists.) Ga., 1990. Jud. clk. to Hon. Thelma Wyatt Cummings Fulton Superior Ct., Atlanta, 1987; jud. clk. to Hon. Carolyn Dineen King U.S. Ct. Appeals (5th cir.), Houston, 1989-90; assoc. Dow, Lohnes & Albertson, Atlanta, 1990-91; legal dir. Am. Civil Liberties Union, 1991—. Adj. prof. Emory U. Sch. Law, Atlanta, 1997—, Ga. State U. Coll. Law, Atlanta, 1998—; chair legal com. Task Force for Homeless, 1992—; barrister Joseph Henry Lumpkin Inns of Ct., 1994-96; bd. dirs. Ga. First Amendment Found., 1994—, Ga. Ctr. Law in Pub. Interest, 1998—; mem. Atlanta steering com. Lawyers Com. Civil Rights Under Law, 1996—; panelist in field; lectr. in field. Symposium editor Ga. Law Rev.; contbr. articles to mags. and profl. jours.; appearances in numerous local and nat. TV and radio shows. Bd. trustees U. Ga. Libr., 1996-97; pres. Leadership Atlanta, 1997-98; pres. Cabbagetown Neighborhood Improvement Assn., 1998—, rep. neighborhood planning unit-N, 1998—; mem. adv. com. AID Atlanta, 1998—; mem. adv. bd. Jeanette Rankin Found., 1997—; election monitor S. African Elections, 1994; bd. dirs. Table of Elements. Recipient Cert. Appreciation, U.S. Dept. Justice, 1998; named one of 21 Young Lawyers Leading Us Into 21st Century, ABA, 1995, Forty Top Georgians Under 40, Ga. Trend Mag., 1997. Mem. FBA, State Bar Ga. (co-chair individual rights sect. 1998—, mem. various coms.), Lawyers Club Atlanta, Order of Coif. Democrat. Lutheran. Avocations: Theremin musician, tennis, biking, fossil collecting. Office: Am Civil Liberties Union Ga 142 Mitchell St SW Ste 301 Atlanta GA 30303-3428 E-mail: gweber@acluga.org.

WEBER, HANNO, architect; b. Barranquilla, Colombia, Sept. 24, 1937; came to U.S., 1952; s. Hans and Ester (Oks) W. BA magna cum laude, Princeton U., 1959, MArch, 1961. Registered architect, Ill., Fla., Mo., Pa., N.J., Va. Urban designer, research assoc. Guayana project MIT and Harvard U., Caracas, Venezuela, 1961-63; project architect Paul Schweikher Assocs., Pitts., 1963-67; asst. prof. architecture Princeton U., 1967-73; assoc. prof. architecture Washington U., St. Louis, 1973-80; sr. design architect, studio head, assoc. Skidmore, Owings & Merrill, Chgo., 1980-83; prin. Hanno Weber & Assocs., 1984—. Vis. lectr. Escuela Nacional de Arquitectura Universidad Nacional de Mex., 1975; rsch. assoc. Rsch. Ctr. Urban and Environ. Planning, Princeton, N.J., 1967-70; project dir. The Cmty. Design Workshop, Washington U. Sch. Architecture, St. Louis, 1973-78; prof. architecture U. Wis., Milw., 1983—. Contbr. articles to profl. jours. Mem. Pres.'s Commn. on Education of Women Princeton U., 1968-69. Fellow NEH, 1970, Graham Found., 1973; 1st prize winner Flagler Dr. Waterfront Master Plan design competition, West Palm Beach, Fla., 1984; 1st prize winner Mcpl. Ctr. design competition, Leesburg, Va., 1987; finalist Okla. City Meml. Internat. design competition, 1997; Chgo. AIA Disting. Bldg. award Citation of Merit, Altamira, Terrace, Highland Park, Fla., 1987. Mem. AIA (Urban Design award Mcpl. Govt. Ctr., Leesburg, Va., 1992, Chgo. AIA Interior Architecture award citation of merit, Mcpl. Govt. Ctr., Leesburg, 1992), The Arch. Assn., Phi Beta Kappa. Office: Hanno Weber & Assocs 417 S Dearborn St Chicago IL 60605-1120 E-mail: weber@hannoweber.com.

WEBER, JAMES STUART, management educator; b. Sayre, Pa., Apr. 8, 1947; s. Arthur William and Margaret (Jensen) W. BA in Math., Northwestern U., 1971; AM in Math., Loyola U., Chgo., 1973; MS in Math. Stats., U. Ill., Chgo., 1975, PhD in Policy Analysis, 1981. Teaching asst. Loyola U., Chgo., 1972-73; teaching and rsch. asst. dept. math. and polit. sci. U. Ill., 1973-75, 76-81; vis. asst. prof. Roosevelt U., 1981-82, asst. prof., 1982-88, program dir. MS degree MIS, 1982-86, grad. faculty, 1986-88. Vis. lectr. Loyola U. Chgo., 1989; vis. asst. prof. U. Wis., Milw., 1989-91, U. Ill., Chgo., 1991—. Co-editor: Business and Society, 1984-85; reviewer IEEE Software Engring.; Proc. editor Structured Devel. Forum, 1987; contbr. to profl. jours. Block capt. Waukegan (Ill.) Neighborhood Watch Program, 1982-85; mem. Waukegan Downtown Assn., 1986-88. Mem. AAUP, Ops. Rsch. Soc. Am. (full), London Math. Soc., Regional Sci. Assn., Acad. Mgmt., Am. Math. Soc., Am. Statis. Assn., Hill Sch. Alumni Assn., Northwestern U. Club, RROC (life), Informs (Chgo. chpt. treas. 1994—). Republican. Episcopalian. Office: PO Box 603 Gurnee IL 60031-0603

WEBER, JANICE ANN, library director, grant writer; b. Baytown, Tex., Aug. 28, 1952; d. James Thelmer Jr. and Doris Geraldine (Bush) Foster; m. Louis Haldane Weber, Feb. 1, 1983. BS, Tex. Women's U., Denton, 1982, MLS, 1985. Libr. dir. Dimmit County Libr., Carrilo Springs, Tex., 1985-86, Val Verde County Libr., Del Rio, 1986-89, Laredo (Tex.) Pub. Libr., 1989—. Sec., bd. dirs. Literary Vol. of Am., Laredo, 1989-95, bd. dirs. Webb County Heritage Found., Laredo, 1990-94; chmn. Webb County Hist. Commn., 1989-94; mem. Tuesday Music & Lit., Laredo, 1997—. Grantee numerous orgns., 1990—. Mem. Nonprofit Mgmt. Assn., Tex. Libr. Assn., Tex. Mcpl. Libr. Dirs. Assn. Avocations: gourmet cooking, weaving. Office: Laredo Pub Libr 1120 E Calton Rd Laredo TX 78041-7328

WEBER, JEFFREY RANDOLPH, record producer; b. L.A., Feb. 3, 1952; s. Jerome and Doris (Robbin) W.; m. Denise Esola, Mar. 31, 1979 (div.); children: Jason Ryan, Jayme Nicole, Jordan Caitlin. BA, UCLA, 1973; JD, Southwestern Law Sch., 1976. Pres. Weberworks Inc., Beverly Hills, Calif., 1979—. Specialist in high tech. rec. (digital, live 2 track); voice-over talent for commls., animation and films. Producer over 135 albums (6 Grammy nominations, 2 Grammy awards). Mem. NARAS (bd. govs. 1986-98, v.p. 1990-91, 95-96, trustee 1991-95). Avocations: films, collecting signed first edition mysteries, rare and exotic wo od. Office: Weberworks PO Box 1451 Beverly Hills CA 90213-1451 E-mail: weberworks@earthlink.net.

WEBER, JEROME CHARLES, education and human relations educator, former academic dean and vice-provost; b. Bklyn., Sept. 1, 1938; s. Meyer and Ethel (Shier) W.; m. Elizabeth Lynn Wiley, July 18, 1975; children: Amy Elizabeth, Jeffrey Glenn. BS, Bklyn. Coll., 1960; MA, Mich. State U., 1961, PhD, 1966. Mem. faculty U. Okla., Norman, 1964—, prof. edn., phys. edn., human rels. and social work, 1973—, Regents' prof. edn. and human rels., 1991—, asst. and acting dean, 1969-72, dean Univ. Coll., 1973-91, vice provost instructional svcs., 1979-91; chmn. ednl. leadership and policy studies, 1991-93. Author: (with D.R. Lamb) Statistics and Research in Physical Education, 1970, (with G. Henderson) College Survival for Student-Athletes, 1985, (with R. Cintron) Enduring Enigmas: Issues in Adult and Higher Education, 1997; contbr. articles to profl. jours. Bd. dirs. Univ. div. United Way, 1970; pres. Norman Kindergarten Assn., 1968; commr. Norman Bd. Parks, 1971-79. Fellow Am. Coun. Sports Medicine; mem. Am. Assn. Higher Edn., Coun. Sports Psychology, Am. Coun. on Edn. Democrat. Jewish. Home: 5 Pebble Creek Rd Norman OK 73072-2822 Office: 630 Parrington Oval Norman OK 73069-8813 E-mail: jcweber@ou.edu.

WEBER, JOHN BERTRAM, architect; b. Evanston, Ill., Oct. 15, 1930; s. Bertram Anton and Dorothea W.; m. Sally Ann French; children: Suzanne French Roulston, Jane Marie McCarthy, Patricia Ann Blodgett, Nancy B. AB in Architecture, Princeton U., 1953; postgrad., Ill. Inst. Tech., 1959. Lic. arch.; registered interior designer. Field engr. United Constrn. Co., Riverdale, N.D., 1952; draftsman Bertram A. Weber Arch., Chgo., 1947, 53, architect, 1958-1973; field engr. Atkinson United Constrn. Co., Greenup and Skiland, Ky., 1956-58; ptnr., proprietor Weber & Weber Arch., Winnetka, Ill., 1973—; pvt. practice, 1987—. Mem. Ill. Architecture Act Revision task force, 1982-89. Prin. works include Prestwick Country Club, the 3175 Commercial Ave. Bldg., Northbrook, med. office bldg. and additions to Bi-county hospital, Warren, Mich., additions and alterations to Detroit Osteopathic Hosp., addition to Duraclean Internat. Bldg., Deerfield, additions to The Admiral (a retirement home in Chgo.), Villa Stresov, Borovets, Bulgaria, and numerous pvt. residences, churches, comml., ednl., and recreational bldgs. Active Winnetka Cmty. Caucus, 1965, 74; mem. Mayor's adv. com. on bldg. codes, Chgo., 1975-80; chmn. bldg. com. Winnetka Cmty. House, 1977-81; mem. Winnetka

Zoning Bd. Appeals, 1983-88, chmn., 1987-88; mem. Winnetka Ad Hoc Zoning Com., 1995-96; deacon, elder Winnetka Presbyn. Ch.; mem. Winnetka Design Review Bd., 2002—. With USN, 1953-56. Fellow: Assn. Lic. Arch., Ill. Soc. Arch. (bd. dirs. 1969—84, pres. 1976—78, bd. dirs. 1991—99); mem.: AIA (health com. 1969—76), Constrn. Specifications Inst., Northbrook C. of C., Ill. Arch.-Engr. Coun. (del. 1976—87, chmn. 1981—82), Am. Legion, Dairymen's Country Club, Old Willow Club (pres. 1983), Builders Club Chgo. (bd. dirs. 1966—, pres. 1973—74), Architects Club Chgo. (bd. dirs. 1976—86, pres. 1981, bd. dirs. 1994). Office: John B Weber Architect 415 Berkeley Ave Winnetka IL 60093-2109 *Do what you should do, not what you have to do. In the end, it is only the things that we do that impact on other people's and other living being's lives that have real meaning.*

WEBER, JOHN PITMAN, artist, educator; b. Washington, Dec. 6, 1942; s. F. Palmer and Lillian Dropkin W.; m. Marguerite Munch, 1966 (div. 1969); 1 child, Pascal Richard; m. Elsa Koenig, Jan. 23, 1971; children: Daniel Abraham, Alexander Samuel, Benjamin John. BA, Harvard U., 1964; MFA, Sch. of Art Inst., Chgo., 1968. Art prof. Elmhurst (Ill.) Coll., 1968—. Founder Chgo. Pub. Art Group, 1970—; artist-in-residence Artists and Cmtys. 2000, State of Iowa, Spencer; The Gathering mosaic plaza. Co-author: Toward A People's Art, 1977, 2d edit., 1998; murals executed Urban World, Chgo., 1997, Remembered Gates New Song, Chgo., 1999, The Gathering, mosaic plaza, Spencer, Iowa, 2000. Fulbright travel fellowship, 1964-66, fellow French Govt., Paris, 1964-65. Mem. Cmty. Built Assn., Coll. Art Assn. Office: Elmhurst Coll 190 Prospect Ave Elmhurst IL 60126-3271 E-mail: johnw@elmhurst.edu.

WEBER, JOHN WALTER, insurance company executive; b. Rochester, N.Y., Jan. 10, 1959; s. Donald J. and Patricia M. (Mangon) W. BS, U. Conn., 1984. Claims supr. Hartford Ins. Group, Southington, Conn., 1986-90; regional claims mgr. Housing Authority Risk Retention Group, Cheshire, 1990—. Mem. U. Conn. Alumni Assn. Avocations: running, reading, softball, cooking. E-mail: Jweber6@earthlink.net.

WEBER, KENT, wildlife organization administrator; b. Wallace, Idaho, Mar. 9, 1959; s. Leonard Scott and Emma Louvine (Schell) W.; m. Dana Ann, May 14, 1983 (div. Nov. 1988); m. Tracy Ann Brooks, Apr. 16, 1989; 1 child, Tamas Christopher. BS, Colo. State U., 1982. Lic. wildlife refuge operator, educator. Constrn./project mgr. Pinkerton & Laws, Atlanta, Avon, Colo., 1982-87; cons., arch.-engr. Holland & Hart, Denver, 1985-88; founder, exec. dir. Mission: Wolf, Silver Cliff, Colo., 1986—. Advisor Wolf Edn. and Rsch. Ctr., Winchester, Idaho, 1999—; leader, educator Amb. Wolf Program, 1988—. Creator: (ednl. slide show) In the Eye of a Wolf, 1996. Endangered species activist, Washington, 1992, 93, 94, 96, 98. Recipient Smart Growth and Devel. award Gov. Colo., 1997. Avocations: travel, backcountry camping, skiing. Home and Office: Mission Wolf Box 211 80 Sheep Creek Rd Silver Cliff CO 81252 E-mail: kent@missionwolf.com.

WEBER, LARRY, public relations executive; Founder, pres. Weber Group, Inc., Cambridge, Mass., 1987—2000; chmn., CEO The Weber Group, Inc.; founder, chmn., CEO Weber Shandwick Worldwide, 2001—02; CEO, chmn. bd. MIMC, Advanced Mktg. Svcs., 2002—. Author, The Provocateur, 2002. Office: MIMC 43 Charles St Boston MA 02114*

WEBER, LAVERN JOHN, retired marine science administrator, educator; b. Isabel, S.D., June 7, 1933; s. Jacob and Irene Rose (Bock) W.; m. Shirley Jean Carlson, June 19, 1959 (div. 1992); children: Timothy L., Peter J., Pamela C., Elizabeth T.; m. Patricia Rae Lewis, Oct. 17, 1992. AAS, Everett Jr. Coll., 1956; BA, Pacific Luth. U., 1958; MS, U. Wash., 1962, PhD, 1964. Instr. U. Wash., Seattle, 1964-67, asst. prof., 1967-69, acting state toxicologist, 1968-69; assoc. prof. Oreg. State U., Corvallis, 1969-75, prof., 1976—, asst. dean grad. sch., 1974-77; dir. Hatfield Marine Sci. Ctr. Oregon State U., Newport, 1977—, supt. Coastal Oreg. Marine Exptl. Sta., 1989-98, assoc. dean Coll. Agrl. Sci., 1998—. Pres., trustee Newport Pub. Libr., 1991-92, Yaquina Bay Econ. Found., Newport, 1991-92; chmn. Oreg. Coast Aquarium, 1983-95. Recipient Pres. award Newport Rotary, 1984-85. Mem. South Slough Mgmt. Commn., Am. Soc. Pharm. and Exptl. Therapy, West Pharm. Soc., Soc. Toxicology, Soc. Exptl. Biol. Med. (n.w. divsn., pres. 1978, 82, 87), Pacific N.W. Assn. Toxicologists (chair 1985-86, coun. 1991-93), Nat. Assn. Marine Lab. (pres.-elect 1998-99), Western Assn. Marine Lab. (pres. 1993). Avocations: woodworking, reading, walking, scuba, gardening.

WEBER, MARGARET LAURA JANE, retired accountant; b. Fairview, Mo., Jan. 4, 1933; d. Mert James and Margaret Orr (Mortensen) Joel; m. James E. Jennings, Mar. 1953 (div.); children: James Edward Jennings, Janie Lea Franks, David Alan Jennings; m. Albert H. Weber, June 1956; children: Luhwanna Stonecipher, Margaret Anne Shadwick. AA, Crowder Coll., Mo., 1972; postgrad. Mo. So. Coll., 1988. Teller, First State Bank, Joplin, Mo., 1951-53; clk. Mo. Lic. Dept., Joplin, 1954-57, U. Mo. Ext. Dept., Neosho, 1967-68; cashier Crowder Coll., Neosho, Mo., 1968-83, acct., 1983-98m, ret., 1998. Mem., Newton County Welfare Com., 1984—. Mem. Am. Bus. Women's Assn. (Woman of Yr. 1982, Bus. Assoc. of Yr. 1987), Nat. Assn. Female Execs., Mo. Assn. Community Jr. Colls. (bd. dirs. 1978-82). Republican. Baptist. Home: 1205 Ozark Dr Neosho MO 64850-1363 Office: Crowder Coll 601 Laclede Ave Neosho MO 64850-9165

WEBER, MARK EDWARD, editor, historian; b. Portland, Oreg., Oct. 9, 1951; s. Stanley Edward and Yvonne (Bernard) W.; children: Laura Marie, Andrew Edward. BA with high honors, Portland State U., 1976; MA, Ind. U., 1978. Editor Jour. Hist. Rev., Newport Beach, Calif., 1992—2001; dir. Inst. for Hist. Rev., 1995—. Roman Catholic. Office: Inst for Hist Rev PO Box 2739 Newport Beach CA 92659-1339 E-mail: weber@ihr.org.

WEBER, MARY LINDA, preschool educator; b. Hermon, N.Y., May 21, 1947; d. Stanley Albert and Shirley Lucille (Holland) Morrill; m. John Weber, July 23, 1966 (div. Nov. 1980); children: James, Mark. AAS, Agrl. and Tech. Coll., Canton, N.Y., 1971; BA, SUNY, Potsdam, 1973; MA, U. South Fla., 1981. Cert. pre-sch., elem. and reading K-12 tchr., N.Y., Fla. Tchr. elem. Hermon-DeKalb Ctrl. Sch., DeKalb Junction, N.Y., 1974-76, Westside Elem. Sch., Spring Hill, Fla., 1976-77; tchr. kindergarten Spring Hill Elem. Sch., 1977-89; tchr. pre-kindergarten Deltona Elem. Sch., Spring Hill, 1989-99, tchr. kindergarten, 1999—. Author mini-grant Home-Sch. Partnerships, 1990, Multi-Cultural Ctr., 1992, Family Info. Ctr., 1993, Parent Partners in Literacy, 1996, Pillars of Character, 1999. Mem. NEA (Young Children sect.), Assn. Childhood Edn. Internat., Internat. Reading Assn., So. Early Childhood Assn., Fla. Reading Assn., Hernando County Reading Coun. Avocations: reading, cross-stitch, bicycling. Home: 4132 Redwing Dr Spring Hill FL 34606-2425 Office: Deltona Elem Sch 2055 Deltona Blvd Spring Hill FL 34606-3216

WEBER, MARYANN, language educator; b. Cleve., Mar. 9, 1943; d. Richard James and Charlotte (Pfahl) W. BA in English, Notre Dame Coll., Cleve., 1965; MA in French, Middlebury Coll., 1976, MA in Spanish, D of Modern Langs., Middlebury Coll., 1985. Cert. English, French, Latin, Spanish tchr., Ohio. Tchr. Regina Sch., South Euclid, Ohio, 1965-71, Notre Dame Acad., Middleburg, Va., 1971-72; instr. to assoc. prof. Notre Dame Coll., Cleve., 1972-93; assoc. prof., then prof. Mo. So. State Coll., Joplin, 1993—. Bibliographer Modern Language Jour., 1998—; contbr. articles to profl. jours. Co-recipient Cmty. Svc. award Ohio Fgn. Lang. Assn., 1990; scholar AATF, 1988, NEH, 89, 91, French Govt., 1995; grantee NEH, 1995-96, Title VI U.S. Dept. Edn., 1997-98. Mem. MLA, Am. Assn. Tchrs. French., Am. Coun. Tchg. Fgn. Langs., Mo. Fgn. Lang. Assn., Rocky Mountain MLA, Phi Sigma Iota. Roman Catholic. Avocations: reading, hiking, volunteer work. Office: Mo So State Coll Dept Comm 3950 Newman Rd Dept Comm Joplin MO 64801-1512 E-mail: weber-m@mail.mssc.edu.

WEBER, MICHAEL HOWARD, senior nuclear control operator; b. Provo, Utah, Sept. 9, 1960; s. Allen Howard and Bonnie Jilene (Hoggan) W.; m. Laura Jean Smith, May 19, 1990. AAS in Nuclear Tech., Aiken Tech. Coll., 1983; BS in Nuclear Sci., U. Md., 1995. Lic. sr. reactor operator. Aux. operator Carolina Power & Light Co., New Hill, N.C., 1983-88, control operator, 1988-92, sr. control operator, 1992-96, control rm. supr. NC, 1996-2000, supt. shift ops., 1998—2000, project mgr., 2000—01, supt. ops. support, 2001—. Recipient scholarship Aiken County Homebuilders Assn., 1982. Mem. Am. Nuclear Soc. Republican. Lutheran. Home: 3008 Brozack Dr Fuquay Varina NC 27526-8466 Office: Carolina Power & Light Co PO Box 165 New Hill NC 27562-0165

WEBER, MICHAEL JAMES, conductor, educator; b. Grand Forks, ND, Jan. 28, 1957; s. James Warren and Donna Jean (Christiansen) W. BS in Edn., U. N.D., 1980; MusM, Calif. State U., 1986; MusD, U. Ariz., 1990. Music tchr. Hillsboro (N.D.) Pub. Schs., 1980-84, Grand Forks (N.D.) Pub. Schs., 1990-92; choral conductor The Victoria (Tex.) Coll., 1992-97; organist, choir master Trinity Episcopal Ch., Victoria, Tex., 1994-97; conductor Victoria Master Chorale, 1995-97; dir. vocal studies Salisbury (Md.) State U., Salisbury, Md., 1997—, assoc. prof., 2001—. Arranger (choral music): I Wonder As I Wander, 1996; choral editor Beati Mortui, 1998. Adv. bd. Hopkins Fine Arts Sch., Victoria, Tex., 1994-97. Recipient Outstanding Faculty award Student Govt. Assn. at Salisbury State U., 1998. Mem. Am. Choral Dirs. Assn., Victoria Symphony Soc. (bd. dirs. 1993-97), Victoria Fine Arts Assn. (bd. dirs. 1992-97), Music Educators Nat. Conf. Office: Salisbury State U 1101 Camden Ave Salisbury MD 21801-6860 E-mail: mjweber@ssu.edu.

WEBER, NANCY WALKER, charitable trust administrator; b. Adrian, W.Va., Aug. 26, 1936; d. James Everett and Wanna Virginia (Alderman) Walker; m. J. Raymond Jacob, Jr., June 12, 1955 (div. 1967); children: Paul M., Sharon J. Kazdin; m. George Harry Weber, Apr. 27, 1983 (dec. Mar. 1995). Student, Peabody Prep. Mus., 1946-53. Asst. buyer cosmetics Hutzler's Dept. Store, Balt., 1967-69; exec. sec. to exec. v.p. Martin Marietta Corp., Bethesda, Md., 1969-75; asst. exec. to exec. dir. hosp. U. Utah, Salt Lake City, 1976-80; dir. program adminstrn. Lucille P. Markey Charitable Trust, Miami, Fla., 1983-97; evaluation adminstr. for Markey Programs NRC, Balt., 1997—. Pianist, organist Middle River Bapt. Ch., Balt., 1953-61; vol. Keswick Multicare Ctr. Named Mrs. Del. in Mrs. Del./Am. Pagent, 1967. Baptist. Avocations: piano, organ. Home and Office: 2345 Barrison Point Rd Baltimore MD 21221-6407 E-mail: hamletnww@aol.com.

WEBER, PHILIP JOSEPH, retired manufacturing company executive; b. Chgo., Mar. 15, 1909; s. Joseph and Theresa (Zollner); m. Esther P. White, Aug. 29, 1941; 1 child, Patricia G. BBA, Northwestern U., 1938. With Ernst & Ernst, Chgo., 1938-41; with Doall Co., Des Plaines, Ill., 1941—88, exec. v.p., 1960-69, pres., 1969-74, chmn. bd., 1974-88, ret. Mem.: Mason (Shriner), Elk, Park Ridge Country. Home: 709 N Merrill St Park Ridge IL 60068-2701 also: 4545 N Ocean Blvd Apt 9-d Boca Raton FL 33431-5342

WEBER, RALPH EDWARD, history educator; b. St. Cloud, Minn., Apr. 19, 1926; s. Andrew A. and Kathryn (Desmond) W.; m. Rosemarie Hoyt; children: Mary, Elizabeth, Ralph A., Anne, Catherine, Neil, Therese, Thomas, Andrew. AB, St. John's U., Collegeville, Minn., 1948; MS in Edn., U. Notre Dame, 1950, PhD, 1956. Instr. U. Notre Dame, South Bend, Ind., 1953-54; asst. to dean Marquette U., Milw., 1954-57, registrar, dir. admissions, 1958-61, assoc. prof. history, 1961-69, prof. history, 1969—, chmn. history dept., 1993-96, bd. dirs. Marquette U. Press, 1994—. Scholar-in-residence CIA, Washington, 1987-88, Nat. Security Agy., Ft. Meade, Md., 1991-92; bd. visitors Les Aspin Ctr., Washington, 1994—. Author: Notre Dame's John Zahm, 1961, U.S. Diplomatic Codes and Ciphers, 1979 (Best Scholarly Intelligence Book award Nat. Intelligence Study Ctr. 1980), Masked Dispatches, 1993, Spymasters: Ten CIA Officers, 1999; co-author: Admission to College, 1963; editor: From the Foreign Press, 2 vols., 1980, The Final Memoranda, 1988, Talking with Harry: Candid Conversations with President Harry S. Truman, 2001; co-editor: Voices of Revolution, 1972. With USN, 1944-46. Grantee Am. Philos. Soc., 1974, rsch. grantee Bradley Ctr., Milw., 1995, 98. Mem. Soc. for Historians Am. Fgn. Rels. (membership chmn. 1976-94), Am. Cath. Historians Assn. (exec. coun. 1972-75), Assn. Former Intelligence Officers (bd. dirs. 1994—), Am. Legion. Avocations: fishing, skiing, hunting, forestry, farming. Office: Marquette U History Dept Milwaukee WI 53233 E-mail: weber09@earthlink.net.

WEBER, RANDAL SCOTT, head and neck surgeon, educator; b. Chattanooga, Feb. 14, 1952; s. Harry Nathan and Rosemary (Munsey) W.; m. Jane Covington Edmond, Sept. 1, 1984; children: Austin Edmond, Sophia Lyon. Student, U. Tenn., 1970-71; BA in Chemistry magna cum laude, U. Tenn., Chattanooga, 1975; MD, U. Tenn. Ctr. Health Scis., 1976. Diplomate Am. Bd. Otolaryngology; lic. physician, Tex., Tenn. Intern in surgery Nat. Naval Med. Ctr., Bethesda, Md., 1977-78; resident in surgery Baylor Coll. Medicine, Houston, 1981-82, resident in otolaryngology, 1982-85; fellow in head and neck surgery U. Tex. M. D. Anderson Cancer Ctr., 1985-86, faculty assoc., 1986, asst. prof. otolaryngology, 1987, assoc. prof. surgery, 1991—, vice chmn. dept. head and neck surgery, 1994. Adj. asst. prof. otolaryngology Baylor Coll. Medicine, Houston, 1990, adj. assoc. prof., 1992; mem. med. records com. U. Tex. M. D. Anderson Cancer Clinic, Houston, 1987-88, laser com., 1987—, surg. svcs. com., 1989-92, faculty senate, 1991-94, exec. com. faculty senate, 1993, dir. clin. rsch., 1993; mem. task force for new materials Am. Acad. Otolaryngology-Head and Neck Surgery/Am. Bd. Otolaryngology, 1992-96; guest examiner Ann. Oral Qualifying Exam., Am. Bd. Otolaryngology, 1992-93; dir., chmn., coord. numerous confs.; lectr. in field. Assoc. editor: Head and Neck, 1992-93, editor, 1994; assoc. editor: Cancer, 2000; mem. editl. bd. Cancer Bull., 1992-93; reviewer Archives of Otolaryngology-Head and Neck Surgery, 1992—; contbr. articles and abstracts to profl. publs., chpts. to books. Lt. comdr. USN, 1980-81. Recipient presdl. citation Am. Head and Neck Soc., 2000, Louis Durhing Outstanding Clin. Subspecialist award U. Pa. Health Sys., 2001. Health Professions scholar USN, 1973-76. Fellow ACS; mem. AMA, Am. Soc. Head and Neck Surgery (program chmn. 33d ann. meeting 1991), Soc. Head and Neck Surgeons, Am. Acad. Otolaryngology-Head and Neck Surgery (subcom. on endocrine surgery 1988-94), Soc. Univ. Otolaryngologists, Tex. Med. Assn., Houston Otolaryngologic Soc., Harris County Med. Soc., Alpha Omega Alpha.

WEBER, RAY EVERETT, engineering executive, consultant; b. Kenton, Ohio, Dec. 11, 1946; s. Mervin Clarence and Phylis Jean Weber; m. Carolyn Antinoro, Aug. 16, 1980; children: David Charles, Stephen Ray. BS in Physics, Ohio State U., 1973. lic. real estate agent, N.Y. Project engr. Erie Lackawanna R.R., Hoboken, NJ, 1974—75; nuclear engring. adminstr. ASME, N.Y.C., 1975—78; cognizant engr. Burns & Roe Inc., Oradell, NJ, 1978—80; supervising engr. Impell Corp., Melville, NY, 1980—88; pres. Webtor Inc., Northport, 1988—; owner Weber Real Estate, 1978—. Pres. Forest Ventures Inc., Northport, N.Y., 1987—. Author nuclear plans and codes. With USN, 1966-70. Mem.: ASME (nuclear subcom.), Marco Island Yacht Club, Northport Yacht Club, Am. Legion. Avocations: boating, fishing, skiing, golf. Office: Forest Ventures Inc 115 Soundview Ter Northport NY 11768-1231 E-mail: rweber3@optonline.net.

WEBER, ROBERT CHARLES, adapted physical education educator, academic administrator; b. West Union, Iowa, Oct. 11, 1948; s. Victor Duane and Elaine I. (Johnson) W.; m. Debra Elaine Nay, Aug. 12, 1972 (div.); childrenL Heidi, Mindy Rae; m. Nancy Jo Johnson, Aug. 9, 1986; 1 child, Ryan Anthony. BS in Phys. Edn. and Health, Bemidji (Minn.) State U., 1971; MS in Phys. Edn., Ea. Ill. U., 1973; EdD in Spl. Phys. Edn. and Adminstrn., U. Utah, 1985. Dir. recreation and adult edn., coach Cass Lake (Minn.) Pub. Schs., 1971-72; tchr. elem. phys. edn., asst. coach basketball Charleston (Ill.) Pub. Schs., 1972-73; grad. asst. Ea. Ill. U., Charleston, 1972-73, asst. prof., 1987-89; instr., coach, dir. intramural sports Iowa Wesleyan Coll., Mt. Pleasant, 1973-75; tchr. driver edn., head football and track coach Virden (Ill.) High Sch., 1975-78; asst. prof. health and phys. edn., coach Dakota State Coll. Madison, S.D., 1978-80; supr. spl. phys. edn. Lubbock (Tex.) State Sch., 1981-83; asst. prof., coord. adapted phys. edn. program Tex. Tech U., Lubbock, 1996; asst. prof. phys. edn. Bemidji State U., Minn., 1996—97, Minot State U., Minot, 1998—99; phys. edn. tchr. Dakota Meml. Sch., 1999—2000; assoc. prof. phys. edn. Minn. State U., Mankato, Minn., 2000—02; coord. adapted phys. edn. U. Wis., Oshkosh, 2002—. Instr. U. Utah, Salt Lake City, 1981; lectr. U. N.C., Wilmington, 1983-84, So. Ill. U., Carbondale, 1986-87; counselor therapeutic recreation Camp Kostopulos, Salt Lake City, 1981, Salt Lake City EBD and TMR Group, 1981; counselor N.W. Juvenile Tng. Ctr. Bemidji State U., 1980, adj. prof. edn., 1985-86, 96-; cons., lectr. in field. Developer audio-visual aids. Vol. Spl. Olympics, 1987—, adv. bd. region 17, 1989—; v.p. Lubbock Ind. Sch. Dist. Swimming and Diving Booster Club, 1991-91; v.p. Lubbock H.S. Gymnastic Booster Club, 1991-92, v.p. Swimming and Diving Booster Club, 1991-92, others; cons. Lubbock Office Planning for Cruise for Disabled Program, 1990-91; co-captain His Step Stewardship Drive St. Luke's Meth. Ch., 1990; advisor South Plains Wheelchair Spokers, 1989—. Grantee numerous founds. and orgns.; recipient 15 Yr. Svc. award Spl. Plympics Internat., 1990, Spl. Svc. award Ill. H.S. Athletic Assn., 1989, Internat. Man of Yr., 1994-95, citation of Meritorious Achievement in Edn. and Habilatation, 1994; named one of Outstanding Young Men. Am. Jaycees, 1990, Hon. Coach Tex. Tech. U. Football Team, 1990, Honored Guest Can. Spl. Olympics for Summer Games, Vancouver, 1990. Mem. AAHPERD (presenter various confs.), Nat. Assn. Sports and Phys. Edn., Adapted Phys. Edn. Acad., Nat. Consrotium Phys. Edn. and Recreation Handicapped, Internat. Fedn. Adapted Phys. Activities, Leisure Spl. Populations, Therapeutic Coun., Tex. Alliance Health, Phys. Edn., Recreation and Dance (rep. region 17 1989—). Home: 1809 Marie Ln Mankato MN 56003-3410

WEBER, ROBERT CARL, lawyer; b. Chester, Pa., Dec. 18, 1950; s. Robert Francis and Lucille (Nobili) W.; m. Linda Brediger, June 30, 1972; children: Robert F., Mary Therese, David P., Joseph T. BA cum laude, Yale U., 1972; JD, Duke U., 1976. Bar: Ohio 1976, U.S. Dist. ct. (no. dist.) Ohio 1976, U.S. Ct. Claims 1980, U.S. Ct. Appeals (6th cir.) 1981, U.S. Ct. Appeals (5th cir.) 1995. Assoc. Jones, Day, Reavis & Pogue, Cleve., 1976-83, ptnr., 1983—. Bd. dirs. United Way Svcs. of Cleve., 1992—. Fellow Am. Coll. Trial Lawyers, Internat. Acad. Trial Lawyers; mem. Ohio Bar Assn., Am. Law Inst., Product Liability Adv. Coun., Cleve. Bar Assn. (chmn. jud. selection com. 1985-86, trustee 1990-93, pres.-elect 1994-95, pres. 1995-96), Jud. Conf. for 8th Jud. Dist. Ohio (life), Order of Coif. Roman Catholic. Office: Jones Day Reavis & Pogue 901 Lakeside Ave E Cleveland OH 44114-1190 E-mail: rcweber@jonesday.com.

WEBER, ROBERT MAXWELL, cartoonist; b. L.A., Apr. 22, 1924; p. Milton and Edith (Huston) W.; m. Marilyn Baum, Oct. 11, 1953 (div.); children— Peter, Lee; m. Debora Graves, Dec. 24, 1988. Student, Pratt Inst., 1945-48, Art Students League, 1948-50. Fashion illustrator, 1949-54; artist New Yorker mag., 1962—; work commd. by IBM, N.Y. Telephone, Am. Airlines, Mobil, Blue Cross/Blue Shield, U.S. Healthcare, Goodyear Co., J.C. Penney Co., Air Canada, Swissair, others; contbr. cartoons to nat. mags. Served with USCGR, 1942-45. Office: New Yorker 4 Times Sq New York NY 10036-6522

WEBER, SAMUEL, editor, retired; b. N.Y.C., July 31, 1926; s. Bernard and Gertrude (Ellenberg) W.; m. Eileen Gloria Hornstein, Mar. 5, 1950; children— Bruce Jay, Robert Matthew. BS in Elec. Engring, Va. Poly. Inst., 1947. Engr. N.Y. Bd. Transp., 1948-50, U.S. Naval Shipyard, Bklyn., 1950-52, Barlow Engring. Co., N.Y.C., 1952-54; engring. supr. Curtiss Wright Corp., Woodridge, N.J., 1954-56; electronics engr. Loral Electronics Corp., N.Y.C., 1957-58; with Electronics mag., 1958-67, assoc. mng. editor, 1968-70, exec. editor, 1970-79, editor in chief, 1979-84, exec. tech. editor, 1984-88, editor-at-large, 1988-92; editor in chief Electrotechnology mag., 1968—; pres. Samuel Weber & Assocs., 1988-91, Samuel Weber & Assocs., Inc., 1991-96; contbg. editor Asic & Eda Magazine, 1991-94; spl. projects editor Electronic Engring. Times, 1992-96, ret., 1997. Author: Modern Digital Circuits, 1964, Optoelectronic Devices and Circuits, 1968, Large and Medium Scale Integration, 1974, Circuits for Electronics Engineers, 1977, Electronic Circuits Notebook, 1981. Served with AUS, 1944-46. Mem. IEEE (life). Home and Office: 160 E 84th St #11K New York NY 10028 E-mail: samhart@aol.com.

WEBER, SCOTT LOUIS, lawyer; b. Livingston, N.J., Oct. 21, 1968; s. David Bernard and Janice Risa Weber; m. Irene Barbara Lubawy, May 24, 1992; children: Michael Harris, Alexandra Jewel. BA, Rutgers Coll., 1990; JD, Boston Coll., 1993. Bar: N.J. 1993, U.S. Dist. Ct. N.J. 1993, N.Y. 1994, Pa. 1994, U.S. Dist. Ct. (so. and ea. dists.) N.Y. 1998. Atty., assoc. Pitney, Hardin, Kipp & Szuch, Morristown, N.J., 1993-97, Latham & Watkins, Newark, 1997—. Mediator Superior Cts., Morris County, N.J., 1996-97; vol. atty., tng. coord. Jersey Battered Women's Legal Advocacy Program, Morris County, 1993-97; spl. counsel N.J. Senate Judiciary Com., 2001-02; mem. Racial Profiling and N.J. State Police Investigation. Mem. ABA, Cap and Skull Honors Soc., Pi Sigma Alpha. Avocations: fitness, bonsai, opera and blues music, golf. Office: 1 Newark Ctr Newark NJ 07102-5235

WEBER, STEPHEN LEWIS, university president; b. Boston, Mar. 17, 1942; s. Lewis F. and Catherine (Warns) W.; m. Susan M. Keim, June 27, 1965; children: Richard, Matthew. BA, Bowling Green State U., 1964; postgrad., U. Colo., 1964-66; PhD, U. Notre Dame, 1969; EdD (hon.), Capital Normal U., China, 1993. Asst. prof. philosophy U. Maine, Orono, 1969-75, assoc. prof., 1975-79, asst. to pres., 1976-79; dean arts and scis. Fairfield (Conn.) U., 1979-84; v.p. acad. affairs St. Cloud (Minn.) State U., 1984-88; pres. SUNY Oswego, 1988-95; interim provost SUNY Albany, 1995-96; pres. San Diego State U., 1996—. Participant Harvard Inst. Ednl. Mgmt., Cambridge, Mass., 1985. Contbr. numerous articles on philosophy and acad. adminstrn. to profl. jours. Mentor Am. Coun. Edn. Fellowship Program, Am. Coun. on Edn., Commn. on Internat. Edn. and Commn. on Govtl. Rels.; bd. govs. The Peres Ctr. for Peace, San Diego Found.; bd. dirs. San Diego Regional Econ. Devel. Corp.; mem. internat. adv. bd. Found. for the Children of the Californias. Named Outstanding Humanities Tchr., U. Maine, 1975; Rsch. fellow U. Notre Dame, 1968-69. Mem. Am. Philos. Assn., Am. Assn. Higher Edn. Democrat. Avocations: art, woodworking, swimming, boating. Office: San Diego State Univ Office Pres 5500 Campanile Dr San Diego CA 92182-8000 E-mail: presidents.office@sdsu.edu.

WEBER, THOMAS WILLIAM, chemical engineering educator; b. Orange, N.J., July 15, 1930; s. William A. and Dorothy (Negus) W.; m. Marianne S. Hartmann, June 4, 1966; children: Anne Louise, William Alois B.Chem. Engring., Cornell U., 1953, PhD, 1963; MS in Chem. Engring., Newark Coll. Engring., 1958. Registered profl. engr., N.Y. Chem. engr. econs. and planning Esso Research & Engring., Linden, N.J., 1955-58; instr. Cornell U., 1961-62; asst. prof. SUNY-Buffalo, 1963-66, assoc. prof. chem. engring., 1966-82, prof., 1982-2000, assoc. chmn. dept., 1980-82, chmn. dept., 1982-89, acting chmn., 1996-97, prof. emeritus, 2000—. Author: An Introduction to Process Dynamics and Control, 1973 Named Prof. of Yr., Tau Kappa Chi, 1965; recipient Chancellor's award for excellence in teaching, 1981, Tchr. of Yr. award Tau Beta Pi, 1982 Fellow AIChE (chmn. western N.Y. sect. 1969-70, Profl. Achievement award western N.Y. sect. 1978), Am. Soc. Engring. Edn. (chmn. instrumentation divsn. 1975-77, chmn. St. Lawrence sect. 1979-80, 92-94, chmn. divsn. experimentation and lab.-oriented studies 1985-86, chmn. Zone I 1999-2001, Outstanding Zone Campus Rep. award 1988, AT&T Found. award 1987-88); mem. Tech. Socs. Coun. Niagara Frontier (sec. 1973-75, pres. 1975-76, treas. 1978—), Swedish Club of Buffalo (pres. 1974-76), U.S. Masters Swimming Club, Sigma Xi, Phi Kappa Phi, Tau Beta Pi, Theta Xi. Presbyterian. Home: 52 Autumnview Rd Buffalo NY 14221-1602 E-mail: twweber@eng.buffalo.edu .

WEBER, WENDELL WILLIAM, pharmacologist; b. Maplewood, Mo., Sept. 2, 1925; s. Theodore William and Flora Ann (Holt) W.; m. La Donna Tavis, Sept. 29, 1952; children— Jane Holt, Theodore Wendell. AB, Central Coll., 1945; PhD in Phys. Chemistry, Northwestern U., 1950; MD, U. Chgo., 1959. Diplomate Am. Bd. Pediatrics; lic. Mich., N.Y., Calif. Asst. prof. chemistry U. Tenn., Knoxville, 1949-51; mem. ops. research staff U.S. Army Chem. Center, Edgewood, Md., 1951-55; successively instr., asst. prof., asso. prof., prof. pharmacology N.Y. U. Sch. Medicine, N.Y.C., 1963-74; prof. U. Mich., Ann Arbor, 1974-98, Disting. lectureship in Biomedical Rsch., 1993, emeritus prof., 1998—; Disting. lectureship Ctr. for Environ. Genetics U. Cin., 1997. Mem. pharmacology-toxicology com. NIH, 1969-73, rev. coms., 1968— Mem. editl. bd. Bioessays, 1984-91, Pharmacogenetics, 1990—; author: Pharmacogenetics, 1997, The Acetylator Genes and Drug Response, 1987. NIH spl. fellow, 1962-65; research grantee, 1967— ; recipient Career Scientist awards N.Y.C. Health Research Council, 1965-70, 70-74 Fellow N.Y. Acad. Scis.; mem. Am. Soc. Pharmacology and Therapeutics, Am. Chem. Soc., Am. Soc. Human Genetics, Soc. Toxicology (hon.), AAAS, Sigma Xi, Phi Lambda Upsilon. Achievements include research specialty in pharmacogenetics. Home: 14 Geddes Hts Ann Arbor MI 48104-1724 Office: Dept Pharmacology U Mich Ann Arbor MI 48109-0632 E-mail: wwweber@umich.edu.

WEBER, WILFORD ALEXANDER, education educator; b. Allentown, Pa., Apr. 29, 1939; s. Alexander F. and Kathryn A. (Campbell) W.; children from previous marriage: Kendra L., Brad A.; m. Cheryl Angelo. BA, Muhlenberg Coll., 1963; EdD, Temple U., 1967. Tchr., counselor New Life Boys Ranch, Harleysville, Pa., 1963-65; rsch. asst. Temple U., Phila., 1965-67; asst. prof. Syracuse (N.Y.) U., 1967-71; prof. U. Houston, 1971—, chair dept. curriculum & instrn. Author approximately 165 books, monographs, papers and articles. Grantee, Syracuse U., U. Houston. Mem. Am. Ednl. Rsch. Assn., Assn. Tchr. Educators. Avocation: sports. Home: 2015 Swift Blvd Houston TX 77030-1213

WEBER, WILLIAM WESLEY, accountant; b. Columbus, Ohio, Dec. 2, 1951; s. Richard Dick and Donna Marie (Inboden) W.; m. Kay Ruth Swope, Feb. 14, 1976; children: Kristen Marie, Richard Stewart. BS, Ohio State U., 1973; MBA, Baldwin-Wallace Coll., 1983. CPA, Tex.; cert. internal auditor, cert. fraud examiner, cert. info. tech. prol. Staff acct. Arthur Andersen, Cin., 1973-74; staff auditor Federated Dept. Stores, 1974-75, Diamond Shamrock, Cleve., 1975-77, sr. auditor, 1977-83, audit supr. San Antonio, 1983-97; acctg. mgr. Ultramar Diamond Shamrock, 1997-2000, bus. process specialist, 2000-01, mgr. fin. support, 2001—02, Valero Energy Corp., 2002—. Treas. Holy Trinity Presbyn. Ch., San Antonio, 1986-95. Mem. AICPA, Assn. Cert. Fraud Examiners, Inst. Internal Auditors (adj. faculty 1988-97, internat. seminars com. 1996-97), Tex. Soc. CPAs. Avocations: reading, watching auto racing. Home: 14307 Rowe Dr San Antonio TX 78247-3122 Office: Valero Energy Corp One Valero Pl San Antonio TX 78212-3186 E-mail: bill.w.weber@valero.com.

WEBERPAL, MICHAEL ANDREW, lawyer; b. Sycamore, Ill., Sept. 16, 1951; s. Michael Andrew Sr. and Mary Elizabeth (Egan) W.; m. Michelle Vinet, Aug. 20, 1971. BA in Econs., U. Wis., Milw., 1975; JD, U. Wis., Madison, 1978; LLM, So. Meth. U., 1992. Bar: Wis. 1978, Tex. 1980, U.S. Dist. Ct. (we. dist.) Wis. Assoc. LaRowe & Gerlach, Reedsburg, Wis., 1978-79; tax specialist Laventhol & Horwath, Dallas, 1980-81; sr. atty. Otis Engring. Corp. (subsidiary of Halliburton Co.), Dallas and London, 1983-88; sr. tax counsel Halliburton Co., Dallas, 1988-92, sr. atty., asst. sec., 1992-93; v.p., gen. counsel, sec. Highlands Ins. Co., Houston, 1993-97; gen. counsel, sec. Landmark Graphics Corp. subs. Halliburton Co., 1997—2000; asst. gen. counsel, Asia Pacific regional counsel Halliburton, Singapore, 2001—. Mem. ABA, State Bar Tex., State Bar Wis. Republican. Roman Catholic. Avocations: skiing, jogging, golf. Address: 87 Kheam Hock Road Singapore 298840 Singapore Office: 79 Anson Rd #20-01 Singapore

WEBER STERLING, LAURA, lawyer; b. Green Bay, Wis., Feb. 16, 1969; d. Jonathan N. Weber and Ruth Ann Riebe. BA, Marquette U., 1991, JD cum laude, 1994. Bar: Wis. 1994. Assoc. Clair Law Offices, S.C., Delavan, Wis., 1995—. Office: Clair Law Offices SC PO Box 445 Delavan WI 53115-0445 E-mail: clairlaw@elknet.net.

WEBSTER, ARTHUR EDWARD, lawyer; b. Hartford, Conn., Dec. 2, 1956; s. Arthur Ellsworth and Carrie Mabel (Goodrich) W. BA summa cum laude, Bradley U., 1978; JD, Georgetown U., 1982. Bar: Conn. 1982, U.S. Dist. Ct. Conn. 1983. Assoc. Halloran, Sage, Phelan & Hagarty, Hartford, 1982-85; asst. atty. gen. Office of Atty. Gen., State of Conn., 1986—. Adj. faculty U. Conn. Sch. Law, Hartford, 1991—; faculty mem. Dept. Children & Families Tng. Acad., 1989—; co-dir., instr. Conn. Bar Assn./State of Conn. Jud. Dept. CLE seminars, Hartford, 1992—, mem. faculty trial skills seminar for child protection lawyers, 1996; panelist (TV program) Child Abuse, 1992. Author: Child Protection in Connecticut Courts, 1992, rev. edit., 1996, The Art of the Deal: A Common Sense Approach to Settlement of Child Protection Cases, 1996, For the Sake of a Child's Safety: The Law of Emergency Removal Proceedings, 1997. Pres. Middletown br. Am. Heart Assn., 1989-90, v.p., 1987-89; mem. steering com. March of Dimes, WalkAmerica, 1988-90. Nyaradi Meml. fellow Bradley U. Inst. Internat. Studies, 1978; law fellow Georgetown U. Law Ctr., Washington, 1981, Beaudry fellow, 1982; recipient Order of Lincoln from Gov. of Ill., 1978. Mem. Conn. Bar Assn. (chmn. juvenile justice com. 1983—). Home: 359 Main St Cromwell CT 06416-2308 Office: Office of Atty Gen 110 Sherman St Hartford CT 06105-2267

WEBSTER, CHRISTOPHER R. chemist, physicist, research scientist; b. Anglesey, Wales, Mar. 3, 1953; s. Donald McLeod Webster, Pamela Lilian Webster; m. Julie C. Webster; children: Genevieve, Philip, Jeffrey Foster, John Foster. BSc with honors, Reading (Eng.) U., 1974; PhD, Bristol (Eng.) U., 1977. Sr. rsch. scientist Jet Propulsion Lab., Pasadena, Calif., 1981—. Contbr. articles to profl. jours. Office: Jet Propulsion Lab 4800 Oak Grove Dr Pasadena CA 91109 Business E-Mail: Chris.R.Webster@jpl.nasa.gov.

WEBSTER, CHRISTOPHER WHITE, foreign service officer; b. Boston, Oct. 30, 1953; s. Henry deForest and Marion (Havas) W. BA cum laude, Amherst Coll., 1975; MA, Johns Hopkins U., 1977. Asst. comml. attache Am. Embassy, Buenos Aires, 1977-79; econ. comml. officer Georgetown, Guyana, 1979-81; desk officer for Jamaica and Guyana Washington, 1982-84; econ. officer Office of Energy, 1984-86; fin. and devel. officer Lisbon, Portugal, 1986-89; econ. sect. chief Algiers, Algeria, 1989-92; dept. dir. Office of Pakistan, Afghanistan and Bangladesh Affairs, Washington, 1992-95; dep. chief of mission Khartoum, Sudan and Addis Ababa, Ethiopia, 1995-96; chief, developed Country Trade Divsn., Washington, 1996-98; dep. dir. Office of Ctrl. Am. and Panamanian Affairs, 1998-00; dep. chief of mission Dhaka, Bangladesh, 2000—. Recipient Superior Honor award Dept. State, 1983, 91, 98-2000. Office: Dept of State 6120 Dhaka Pl Washington DC 20521-6120 E-mail: webstercw@state.gov.

WEBSTER, DAVID ARTHUR, retired life insurance company executive; b. Downs, Ill., July 20, 1937; s. Harold Sanford and Carmen Mildred (Moore) W.; m. Anna Elizabeth Prosch, June 10, 1956; children: Theodore David, Elizabeth Anna, Arthur Lee, William Harold. BS, U. Ill., 1960. Actuarial asst. Mass. Mut. Life Ins. Co., Springfield, 1960-64; cons. actuary George Stennes & Assocs., Mpls., 1964-68; v.p., actuary Piedmont Life Ins. Co., Atlanta, 1968-72, Pacific Fidelity Life Ins. Co., Los Angeles, 1972-74; v.p., chief actuary U.S. Life Corp., N.Y.C., 1974-76, exec. v.p., 1976-78, dir., 1976-78; pres., dir. Beneficial Pension Svcs, BPS Agy., Inc.; v.p., treas., dir. Beneficial Assurance Co., 1978-82; asst. sec., dir. Beneficial Computer Svcs., Inc.; treas. Tel-Assurance Corp.; exec. v.p., dir. Beneficial Standard Life, 1978-82; pres., dir. U.S. Life Ins. Co. of Calif., 1982-84, Western World Fin. Group Inc., 1984-86; exec. v.p., COO R.W. Durham and Co., 1987-99. Fellow Soc. Actuaries; mem. Am. Acad. Actuaries. Home: 1150 Ladera Ln Paso Robles CA 93446 E-mail: SLODavidPaso@aol.com.

WEBSTER, DAVID MACPHERSON, lawyer; b. Chgo., June 22, 1950; s. Robert Fielden and Julia Orendorff (Macpherson) W.; m. Lucia Maxwell Blair, Oct. 3, 1987; 1 child, Jessie Maxwell. BA magna cum laude with hons. in History, Williams Coll., 1972; JD, U. Va., 1975; DD (hon.), Seabury-Western Theol. Sem., 2000. Bar: Ill. 1975. Assoc. Winston & Strawn, Chgo., 1975-81, ptnr., 1981-87; White House fellow Washington, 1987-88; spl. asst. to dir. FBI, 1988-89; asst. gen. counsel for multilateral negotiations U.S. Arms Control and Disarmament Agy., 1989-94; v.p., gen. counsel A.T. Kearney, Inc., Chgo., 1994—. Mem. adv. com. on Ill. Bus. Corp. Act Ill. Sec. of State, Chgo., 1982-87. Bd. dirs. WBEZ Alliance, Inc., Chgo., 1996—, Ill. Soc. for Prevention of Blindness, Chgo., 1980-87, 97-99, pres. 1999—, Better Govt. Assn., Chgo., 1997-99; chair bd. trustees Seabury-Western Theol. Sem., Evanston, Ill., 1993-96, trustee, 1988-96, 2002—; trustee Episc. Charities and Profl. Svcs., Chgo., 1980-87. Mem. Am. Hist. Assn. (assoc.), Orgn. Am. Historians (assoc.), Ill. State Hist. Soc. (life), Chgo. Hist. Soc., Manuscript Soc., Abraham Lincoln Assn., White House Fellows Assn., Mid-Day Club (Chgo.), Univ. Club Chgo., Chgo. Coun. Fgn. Rels., Law Club City of Chgo., Phi Beta Kappa Assn. Chgo. (exec. com. 1996-98). Episcopalian. Avocations: history, writing. Home: 596 Arbor Vitae Rd Winnetka IL 60093-2302 Office: AT Kearney Inc 222 W Adams St Ste 2393 Chicago IL 60606-5307 E-mail: david.webster@atkearney.com., davidmwebster@attbi.com.

WEBSTER, DEBBIE ANN, social worker; b. Jamestown, N.Y., Jan. 29, 1959; d. George Thomas and Nicolina Marie (Lupica) Shagla; m. Otis Lee Webster, Mar. 19, 1986; children: Jordan Lee, Justin Thomas, Jasmine Nichol. BA in Psychology, St. Bonaventure U., 1981. Cert. child protective svcs., S.C.; cert. mental health profl., S.C., Ga.; cert. mental retardation profl., S.C., Ga.; cert. qualified developmental disabilities profl., N.C. Telephone operator Midstate Telephone Co., Jamestown, N.Y., 1981-82; supr. Hillside Children's Ctr., Rochester, 1982-86; tchr. Family Resource Ctr., Seaside, Calif., 1986, Aliamanu Child Devel. Ctr., Honolulu, 1987-88; med. social worker Hale Nani Health Ctr., 1988-90; supr. case mgmt. svc. Bibb County Mental Health, Macon, Ga., 1991-94; supr. child protective svcs. Richland County Dept. Social Svcs., Columbia, 1994-98; quality assurance coord. Thomas S. Svcs. Cumberland County Mental Health, Fayetteville, NC, 1998—99; program coord. divsn. MH/DD/SAS NC DHHS, Raleigh, 1999—. Mem. NAFE, County Dirs. and Suprs. Assn., Nat. Assn. Devel. Disabilities. Democrat. Avocations: exercise, reading, computers. Home: 2721 Red Ruby Ln Raleigh NC 27610 Office: Mail Svc Ctr 3014 Raleigh NC 27699-3014 E-mail: debbie.webster@ncmail.net.

WEBSTER, DOUGLAS PETER, emergency physician; b. Chgo., July 4, 1957; s. David Ferguson and Margaret Webster; m. Mariruth K. Burkhart, Sept. 25, 1989. BA in Chemistry, BS in Psychology, Loyola U., Chgo., 1978; MS in Chem. Physics, Wayne State U., 1980; DO, Chgo. Coll. Osteo. Medicine, 1985. Diplomate in emergency medicine Am. Osteo. Bd. Emergency Medicine, Am. Bd. Forensic Examiners. Intern Chgo. Coll. Osteo Medicine, 1985-86; resident in gen. surgery Sinai Hosp. Detroit, 1986-87; resident in emergency medicine Chgo. Coll. Osteo Medicine, 1988-90; clin. asst. prof. emergency medicine Chgo. Coll. Osteo. Medicine, 1990-93, clin. assoc. prof., 1993-2001, assoc. chmn. dept. emergency medicine, 1995-98; assoc. dir. emergency svcs. Olympia Fields (Ill.) Osteo Med./Trauma Ctr., 1990-91; dir. emergency svcs. St. Anthony Hosp., Chgo., 1991-93; sr. ptnr. Med. Rev. Assocs., S.C., 1992-97; chmn., med. dir. emergency medicine Little Co. of Mary Hosp., Evergreen Park, Ill., 1993-95; med. dir. Trauma Ctr. Columbia Olympia Fields (Ill.) Osteo. Med. Ctr., 1996-97; pres. Emergency Med. Assocs., Ill., Ind., 1996-97; med. dir. emergency dept. St. Margaret Mercy Healthcare Ctrs., Dyer, Ind., 1997-99; v.p./regional med. dir. Em Care, Inc., Elmhurst, Ill., 1997—2001, CEO Midwest region., 2001—; med. dir. emergency dept. Grant Hosp., Chgo., 1999—. Assoc. clin. coord., cons. Crescent Counties Found. for Med. Care, 1992-97; chair dept. emergency medicine Chgo. Coll. Osteo. Medicine, 1998-2001; mem. Ill. State Med. Disciplinary Bd., 2000—; spkr. in field. Diplomate in emergency medicine Am. Osteo. Bd. Emergency Medicine, Am. Bd. Forensic Examiners, Am. Bd. Forensic Medicine. Recipient award Disting. Physicians Am., 1991, Family Medicine award Lemmon Pharm. Found., 1985, others; Univ. Grad. fellow Wayne State U., 1979. Fellow Am. Coll. Osteo. Emergency Physicians, Am. Coll. Emergency Physicians; mem. Am. Bd. Forensic Examiners, Am. Bd. Forensic Medicine, Am. Osteo. Assn., Ill. Assn. Osteo. Physicians and Surgeons, Phi Lambda Upsilon, Alpha Epsilon Delta. Avocation: flying. Home: 2020 N Lincoln Pk W #38DE Chicago IL 60614 Office: Em Care Inc 533 W North Ave Elmhurst IL 60126-2100 also: Grant Hospital 550 W Webster Chicago IL 60614

WEBSTER, EDWARD WILLIAM, physicist; b. London, Apr. 12, 1922; came to U.S., 1949, naturalized, 1957; s. Edward and Bertha Louisa (Cornish) W.; m. Irene Ruth Henry, June 4, 1950 (dec. 1958); m. Dorothea Anne Wood, June 24, 1961; children: John, Peter, Anne, Edward, Mark, Susan. BSc in Elec. Engring., U. London, 1943, PhD, 1946; postgrad., MIT, 1949-51, 65-66, Columbia U., 1966; AM (hon.), Harvard U., 1989. Diplomate in radiol. physics Am. Bd. Radiology, examiner 1958-84, chmn. physics com. 1966-76; diplomate Am. Bd. Health Physics. Research engr. English Electric Co., Stafford, Eng., 1945-49; travelling fellow lab. for nuclear sci. MIT, 1949-50, staff scientist, 1950-51; lectr. U. London, 1952-53; physicist Mass. Gen. Hosp., Boston, 1953-2000, chief radiol. scis. div., 1970-2000; prof. radiology Harvard U. Med. Sch., 1975-92, prof. emeritus, 1992—; prof. radiology div. health scis. and tech. Harvard-MIT, 1978-86. Mem. com. on dose distbns. of high energy radiation beams for cancer therapy Internat. Atomic Energy Agy., Vienna, Austria, 1960-64; mem. com. radiology NAS, 1962-68; mem. com. on planning radiotherapy facilities, WHO, Geneva, Switzerland, 1964, Radiological Health Study section, U.S. Environ. Control Adminstrn., 1969-72, biol. effects of ionizing radiation com. NAS, 1977-80, oversight com. on Radioepidemiologic Tables, NAS, 1983-84; adv. com. on environ. hazards VA, 1985-95, Med. Use of Isotopes, U.S. Nuclear Regulatory Commn., 1971-93; U.S. del. UN Sci. Com. on Effects of Atomic Radiation, 1987-97; sec.-gen. 2d Internat. Conf. Med. Physics, Boston, 1966-69; lectr. Harvard Sch. Pub. Health, 1971-86; Garland lectr. Calif. Radiol. Soc., 1980; cons. Radiation Effects Rsch. Found., Hiroshima, Japan, 1988; Adams lectr. U Okla. Med. Ctr., 1989; Langham lectr. U. Ky. Coll. Medicine, 1989; Taylor lectr. Nat. Coun. on Radiation Protection, 1992, mem., 1965-89, hon. mem., 1989—, cons. Presdl. Adv. Com. on Human Radiation Experiments, 1994-95. Author: A Basic Radioisotopes Course, 1959, Atlas of Radiation Dose Distributions, 1965, Physics in Diagnostic Radiology, 1970; co-author: Instrumentation and Monitoring Methods for Radiation Protection, 1978, Low-level Radiation Effects, 1982; co-editor: Advances in Medical Physics, 1971, Biological Risks of Medical Irradiations, 1980; inventor composite shields against low energy X-rays, 1970. Robert Blair travelling fellow London County Council, 1949; USPHS fellow, 1965-66; NIH grantee, 1958-80. Fellow Health Physics Soc. (Landauer award 1985, Failla award 1989), Am. Coll. Radiology (commn. mem. 1963-93, Gold medal 1991), Am. Assn. Physicists in Medicine (founding mem., dir. 1958-65, pres. 1963-64, Coolidge medal 1983); mem. Soc. Nuclear Medicine (trustee 1973-77), Radiol. Soc. N.Am. (v.p. 1977-78), New Eng. Roentgen Ray Soc. (hon., exec. com. 1976-77), Radiation Rsch. Soc., Sigma Xi (nat. lectr. 1988-89). Office: Mass Gen Hosp Fruit St Boston MA 02114-2620 E-mail: edwebster@mediaone.net.

WEBSTER, GORDON VISSCHER, JR. minister; b. Huntington, N.Y., Oct. 2, 1947; s. Gordon Visscher and Marion Beatrice W.; m. Gloria Marie Farwagi, May 31, 1975; children: David Gordon, Daniel Farwagi, Diana Alexandra. AB, Hamilton Coll., 1969; postgrad., St. Andrews Div. Sch., 1970-71, McCormick Theol. Sem., 1982-87; MDiv, Union Theol. Sem., 1973. Ordained to ministry Presbyn. Ch. (USA), 1973. Staff assoc. Met. Ch. Bd., Syracuse, NY, 1973-75; assoc. pastor 1st Presbyn. Ch., 1975-83; missionary Mid. East Coun. of Chs., Limassol, Cyprus, 1983-84; missionary-in-residence Presbyn. Ch. (USA), Stony Point Center, NY, 1984-86; interim pastor 1st Presbyn. Ch., Oneida, 1988-89, United Presbyn. Ch., Cortland, 1989-91; pastor Ogden Presbyn. Ch., Spencerport, 1991-2001, Downtown United Presbyn. Ch., Rochester, 2001—. Exec. dir. Am. Coalition for Mid. East Dialogue, Jamesville, N.Y., 1986-88, Common Good Planning Ctr. of the Rochester Area Cmty. Found., 1998-2001; v.p. Greater Rochester Cmty. of Chs., 1992-93, pres., 1994-97; chair Interfaith Forum of Greater Rochester, 1995, 99; pres. Interfaith Alliance of Rochester, 1998-99; mem. Mayor's Adv. Bd. for Comprehensive Planning, City of Rochester, 1996—; mem. Mayor's Task Force on Race and Ethnicity, 2000—; mem. Martin Luther King Jr. Commn. of Monroe County, 1995—; public policy commn. N.Y. State Cmty. Chs., 1996-99; mem. Presbytery Genesee Valley, 1991—; leader workshops on Mid. East, 1983-89; moderator Syracuse Mid. East Dialogue Group, 1981-83; mem. coun. Presbytery of Utica, 1988-89. Chaplain Internat. Mgmt. Assn., Liverpool, N.Y., 1982-83, Svc. Club-Oneidas Tribe, 1988-89; gen. coun. Cayuga-Syracuse Presbytery, 1975-83. Grantee George Gund Found., 1987, Presbyn. Women's Opportunity Giving, 1987, Joan and Harold Feinbloom Supporting Found. of the Rochester Area Cmty. Found., 1998-2002. Mem. Witherspoon Soc. (steering com. 1974-76), Presbyn. Peace Fellowship (bd. advisors, nat. com. 1972-83). Democrat. Office: Downtown United Presbyn Ch 121 N Fitzhugh St Rochester NY 14614 E-mail: cmngood@aol.com.

WEBSTER, HENRY DE FOREST, neuroscientist; b. N.Y.C., Apr. 22, 1927; s. Leslie Tillotson and Emily (deForest) W.; m. Marion Havas, June 12, 1951; children: Christopher, Henry, Sally, David, Steven. AB cum laude, Amherst Coll., 1948; MD, Harvard U., 1952. Intern Boston City Hosp., 1952-53, resident, 1953-54; resident in neurology Mass. Gen. Hosp., 1954-56, research fellow in neuropathology, 1956-59; prin. investigator NIH research grants for electron microscopic studies of peripheral neuropathy, 1959-69; mem. staffs Mass. Gen., Newton-Wellesley hosps.; instr. neurology Harvard Med. Sch., 1959-63, assoc. in neurology, 1963-66, asst. prof. neuropathology, 1966; assoc. prof. neurology U. Miami Sch. Medicine, 1966-69, prof., 1969; chief sect. cellular neuropathology Nat. Inst. Neurol. Diseases and Stroke, Bethesda, Md., 1969-97; chief Lab. Exptl. Neuropathology, 1984-97; scientist emeritus Nat. Insts. Health, 1997—. Disting. scientist, lectr. dept. anatomy Tulane U. Sch. Medicine, 1973; Royal Coll. lectr. Can. Assn. Neuropathologists, 1982; Saul Korey lectr. Am. Assn. Neuropathologists, 1992; chmn. Winter Conf. on Brain Rsch., 1985, 86; head neuropathology delegation to visit China in 1990, Citizen Amb. Program, People to People Internat.; mem. exec. com. rsch. group on neuromuscular disease World Fedn. Neurology, 1986-93. Author: (with A. Peters and S.L. Palay) The Fine Structure of the Nervous System, 1970, 76, 91; contbr. articles to sci. jours. Recipient Superior Svc. award USPHS, 1977, A. von Humboldt award Fed. Republic Germany, 1985, Sci. award Peripheral Neuropathy Assn., 1994; named hon. prof. Norman Bethune U. of Med. Scis., Chanchun, China, 1991. Mem. Am. Assn. Neuropathologists (v.p. 1976-77, pres. 1978-79, Weil award 1960, Meritorious Contbns. to Neuropathology award 2001), Internat. Soc. Neuropathology (councillor 1976-80, v.p. 1980-84, exec. com. 1980-84, 86-94, pres. 1986-90, hon. mem. 1999—), Internat. Congress Neuropathology (sec. gen. VIII 1978), Peripheral Nerve Study Group (exec. com. 1975-93, chmn. 1977 meeting), Japanese Soc. Neuropathology (hon.), Am. Neurol. Assn., Am. Acad. Neurology, Royal Soc. Medicine, Am. Soc. Cell Biologists, Soc. Neurosci., Rotary Internat., Ausable Club. Office: NIH Rm 4A 29 Bldg 36 Bethesda MD 20892-4123 E-mail: websterh@ninds.nih.gov.

WEBSTER, JAMES RANDOLPH, JR. physician; b. Chgo., Aug. 25, 1931; s. James Randolph and Ruth Marian (Burtis) W.; m. Joan Burchfield, Dec. 28, 1954; children: Susan, Donovan, John. BS, U. Chgo.-Northwestern U., 1953; MD, MS, Northwestern U., 1956. Diplomate: Am. Bd. Internal Medicine (sub bd. pulmonary disease and geriatrics). Intern Phila. Gen. Hosp., 1956-57; resident in medicine Northwestern U., 1957-60, NIH fellow in pulmonary disease, 1962-64; chief medicine Northwestern Meml. Hosp., Chgo., 1976—88; prof. medicine Northwestern U. Med. Sch., 1977—2002, chief gen. med. sect. Dept. Medicine, 1978-88; chief exec. officer Northwestern Med. Group Practice, 1978-88; dir. Buehler Ctr. on Aging Northwestern U. Med. Ctr., 1988-2000. Chief staff Northwestern Meml. Hosp., 1988-90. Contbr. chpts. to books, articles to med. jours. Capt. U.S. Army, 1960-62. Recipient Outstanding Clin. tchr. award Northwestern U. Med. Sch., 1974, 77, 84, 86, Alumni Merit award Northwestern U., 1979, Henry P. Russe-Inst. of Medicine award for exemplary compassion in health care, 1997, Aeschulapian award as Physician of Yr., Anti Defamation League, 1998. Master: ACP (gov. for Ill. 1988—92, chair sub-com. on aging 1993, Clayppole award 1994); mem.: Ill. Geriatrics Soc. (pres. 1992—94, chair Ill. ad hoc com. to defend health care), Am. Geriatrics Soc., Inst. Medicine Chgo. (pres. 2002—), Alpha Omega Alpha. Home: Apt 6C 227 E Delaware Pl Chicago IL 60611-7758 Office: Buehler Ctr on Aging Ste 601 750 N Lake Shore Dr Chicago IL 60611-4403 E-mail: j.webster@northwestern.edu. *Life should best be measured not by how long you live, but how well you function.*

WEBSTER, JEFFERY NORMAN, computer engineer; b. Erie, Pa., Oct. 23, 1954; s. Norman A. and Betty B. (Bessetti) W.; m. Harriet Marie McGinley, Nov. 27, 1982; 1 child, Jessica Marie. BA, Pa. State U., 1980; MPA, U. So. Calif., 1985. Sr. analyst, technologist U.S. Gen. Acctg. Office, L.A., 1981—2001; staff engr. NASA/Calif. Inst. Tech. Jet Propulsion Lab., 2001—. Author numerous technology assessment reports to the Congress, 1983—. Mem. AIAA (sr., chmn. adv. coun. San Gabriel Valley sect.). Achievements include congl. testimony on tech. risks and scientific utility of NASA's space sta. design, congl. report on tech. risks of assembling and maintaining NASA's space sta., loss of irreproduceable space sci. data due to faulty archiving practices by NASA, improvements needed in NASA's spacecraft computer technology, nuclear safety of NASA's cassini mission to Saturn, status of NASA's X-33 RLV program. Home: 1191 E Mendocino St Altadena CA 91001-2524

WEBSTER, JEFFREY LEON, graphic designer; b. Idaho Falls, Idaho, Nov. 23, 1941; s. Leon A. and Marjory M. (McAllister) W.; student Sch. Associated Arts, St. Paul, 1962; m. Judith Kess, Apr. 17, 1965; children: Eric J., Marjorie P. Sci. illustrator Mayo Clinic, Rochester, Minn., 1963-66; layout artist Brown & Bigelow, St. Paul, 1966; graphic designer U. Minn., Mpls., 1966-67, U. Calgary (Alta., Can.), 1967-68; sr. artist Control Data Corp., St. Paul, 1968-70; mem. Idaho State U. Meml. Lectureship Com.; graphic designer Idaho State U., 1970-78; owner, operator studio, Harmony, Minn.; mktg. and advt. cons. to 45 regional and nat. firms, 1978—. Mem. Idaho Civic Symphony Bd. Chairperson rub. rels. Unitarian Ch. Rochester, 1991—; bd. dirs. Gift of Life Transplant House, Rochester, Minn. 1996, Rochester Orch. and Chorale, 1996. Recipient Profl. citation Libr. Congress, 1976; 1st Pl. Best Trucking ad, Overdrive Mag., 1990. Artist pub. ednl. exhibits. Home and Office: RR 1 Harmony MN 55939-9801

WEBSTER, JOHN GOODWIN, biomedical engineering educator, researcher; b. Plainfield, N.J., May 27, 1932; s. Franklin Folger and Emily Sykes (Boody) W.; m. Nancy Egan, Dec. 27, 1954; children: Paul, Robin, Mark, Lark BEE, Cornell U., 1953; MSEE, U. Rochester, 1965, PhD, 1967. Engr. North American Aviation, Downey, Calif., 1954-55; engr. Boeing Airplane Co., Seattle, 1955-59, Radiation Inc., Melbourne, Fla., 1959-61; staff engr. Mitre Corp., Bedford, Mass., 1961-62, IBM Corp., Kingston, N.Y., 1962-63; asst. prof. elec. engring. U. Wis., Madison, 1967-70, assoc. prof. elec. engring., 1970-73, prof. elec. and computer engring., 1973-99, prof. biomed. engring., 1999—. Author: (with others) Medicine and Clinical Engineering, 1977, Sensors and Signal Conditioning, 1991, 2d edit., 2001, Analog Signal Processing, 1999; editor: Medical Instrumentation: Application and Design, 3d edit. 1978, 1998, Clinical Engineering: Principles and Practices, 1979, Design of Microcomputer-Based Medical Instrumentation, 1981, Therapeutic Medical Devices: Application and Design, 1982; Electronic Devices for Rehabilitation, 1985; Interfacing Sensors to the IBM-PC, 1988, Encyclopedia of Medical Devices and Instrumentation, 1988, Tactile Sensors for Robotics and Medicine, 1988, Electrical Impedance Tomography, 1990, Teaching Design in Electrical Engineering, 1990, Prevention of Pressure Sores, 1991, Design of Cardiac Pacemakers, 1995, Design of Pulse Oximeters, 1997, The Measurement Instrumentation, and Sensors Handbook, 1999, Encyclopedia of Electrical and Electronics Engineering, 1999, Mechanical Variables Measurement, 2000, Minimally Invasive Medical Technology, 2001. Recipient Rsch. Career Devel. award NIH, 1971-76; NIH fellow, 1963-67; recipient Western Electric Fund award Am. Soc. Engring. Edn., 1978, Best Reference Work award, 1999, Theo C. Pilkington Outstanding Educator award, 1994. Fellow IEEE (3d Millenium medal 2000, IEEE-EMBS Career achievement award 2001), Am. Inst. Med. and Biol. Engring., Inst. Physics, Instrument Soc. Am. (Donald P. Eckman Edn. award 1974), Assn. for Advancement Med. Instrumentation (Found. Laufman-Greatbatch prize 1996). Office: Univ Wis Dept Biomed Engring 1550 Engineering Dr Madison WI 53706-1609 E-mail: webster@engr.wisc.edu.

WEBSTER, JOHN KINGSLEY OHL, II, health administrator, rehabilitation manager; b. L.A., July 27, 1950; s. John Kingsley Ohl and Inez (Gilbert) W.; children: David Lilly, Jason Kingsley McKnight. AA, Pasadena (Calif.) City Coll., 1973; BS, San Jose (Calif.) State U., 1975; MS, Calif. State U., L.A., 1989. Registered occupational therapist, Calif. Supervising occupational therapy cons. San Gabriel Valley Regional Ctr., 1976-79; supr. II occupational therapy cons. San Diego Regional Ctr., 1979-83; sr. occupational therapist Mesa Vista Hosp., 1983-84; pvt. practice Vista, Calif., 1983-85; occupational therapy cons. Calif. Children Svcs., State Dept. Health Svcs., L.A., 1985-86, regional adminstrv. cons., 1986-90; dir. occupational therapy Eureka Gen. Hosp., 1990; dir. ops. and mktg. Life Dimensions Inc., Newport Beach, Calif., 1990; occupational therapy cons., licensing and cert. Calif. Dept. Health Svcs., 1990-93; program dir. rehab. svcs. Scripps Meml. Hosp., Encinitas, Calif., 1993-94; dir. rehab. Vista (Calif.) Knoll, 1994; clin. dir. occupational therapy Sundance Rehab., San Diego, 1994-95; regional dir. ops. Quest Rehab, L.A., 1995-96; area mgr. Am. Therapy Svc., 1996; western divsn. dir. of ops. Accelerated Care Plus, L.A., 1996-97; clin. svcs. mgr. Tustin Rehab. Hosp., 1998-99; supr. therapist Calif. Childrens Svcs., 1999; regional dir. ops. Healthpoint, Vista, Calif., 1999-2000; chief restorative svcs. Calif. Vets. Home, Barstow, 2000—. Cons. Hopi and Navajo Tribes, Winslow, Ariz., 1978; dir. Imperial County SPRANS grant, El Centro, Calif., 1986-88; pres., owner Ergonomix & Regs., San Diego, 1988—. Artist (sculpture) Free Form (3d pl. award 1973), (oil painting) Jamaican Woman (3d pl. award 1979). Recipient Esquire title Lady Elliott of STOBS, Edinbourgh, Scotland, 1973, spl. dept. recognition Calif. State U., 1989. Mem. Am. Occupational Therapy Assn., Inst. Profl. Health Svc. Adminstrs., Student Assn. of Am. Coll. Health Care Execs. Avocations: oil painting, sculpting, producing films, woodworking, tennis. E-mail: ergonomixjw@hotmail.com.

WEBSTER, LESLIE TILLOTSON, JR. pharmacologist, educator; b. N.Y.C., Mar. 31, 1926; s. Leslie Tillotson and Emily (de Forest) W.; m. Alice Katharine Holland, June 24, 1955; children— Katharine White, Susan Holland Webster Van Drie, Leslie Tillotson III, Romi Anne. BA, Amherst Coll., 1947, Sc.D. (hon.), 1982; student, Union Coll., 1944; MD, Harvard U., 1948. Diplomate: Am. Bd. Internal Medicine. Rotating intern Cleve. City Hosp., 1948-49, jr. asst. resident in medicine, 1949-50; asst. resident medicine Bellevue Hosp., N.Y.C., 1952-53; research fellow medicine Harvard and Boston City Hosp. Thorndike Meml. Lab., 1953-55; from demonstrator to instr. medicine Sch. of Medicine Western Res. U., 1955-60; research assoc. to sr. instr. biochemistry Case Western Res. U. Sch. Medicine, 1959-60, asst. prof. medicine, 1960-70, asst. prof: biochemistry, 1960-65, asst. prof. pharmacology, 1965-67, asso. prof., 1967-70, prof. pharmacology, 1976-92, chmn. pharmacology dept., 1976-91, prof. pharmacology dept. emeritus, 1992, prof. medicine, 1980-86. Prof., chmn. pharmacology dept. Northwestern U. Med. and Dental Sch., 1970-76; dir. med. scientist tng. program Case Western Res. U. Sch. Medicine, 1979-92. Served to lt. med. corps. USNR, 1950-52. Russell M. Wilder fellow Nat. Vitamin Found., 1956-59; Sr. USPHS Research fellow, 1959-61; Research Career Devel. awardee, 1961-69; Macy faculty scholar, 1980-81 Mem. ACP (life), Central Soc. Clin. Rsch. Coalition (emeritus), Am. Soc. Clin. Investigation, Am. Soc. Biochemistry and Molecular Biology (emeritus), Assn. Med. Sch. Pharmacology (emeritus), Am. Soc. Pharmacology and Exptl. Therapeutics (emeritus), Alpha Omega Alpha (hon.). Home: 12546 Cedar Rd No 4 Cleveland Heights OH 44106-3294 Office: Univ Hosps of Cleve Rainbow Babies and Childrens Hosp 2074 Abington Rd Cleveland OH 44106-2602 E-mail: ltwjr@aol.com.

WEBSTER, LINDA JANE, clinical social worker, consultant; b. Whitinsville, Mass., Mar. 23, 1948; d. David and Erva Viola (Chesley) Longmuir; m. Barry Ward Webster, Dec. 16, 1988; 1 child, Jeffrey. BS magna cum laude, Springfield (Mass.) Coll., 1969; MEd, U. Hartford, 1971; M. in Social Work, U. Utah, 1981, PhD, 1997. Lic. clin. social worker Utah; diplomate Am. Bd. Examiners and Nat. Assn. Social Workers. Sch. psychologist Bd. Edn., New Britain, Conn., 1969-77; dir. Project React Capital Region Edn. Coun., Bloomfield, 1977-79; coord. acute and intensive treatment Valley West Mental Health Ctr., Salt Lake City, 1981-86; program dir. Western Inst. NeuroPsychiatry, 1986-88; social worker pvt. practice Murray, Utah, 1988—. Cons. Episcopal Social and Pastoral Ministries, Salt Lake City, 1986-88; adj. faculty U. Utah, Grad. Sch. Social Work, Salt Lake City, 1986-93. Vol. Episcopalian Ch., Salt Lake City, 1980—; mentor Murray (Utah) H.S., 1997. Mem. Nat. Assn. Social Workers (sec. Utah chpt. 1986-88), Alumni Assn. U. Utah Grad Sch. Social Workers, (pres. 1986-89), Phi Kappa Phi. Avocations: skiing, tennis, basketball, teddy bears, crafts. Office: PhD LCSW 111 E 5600 S Ste 314 Murray UT 84107-8167

WEBSTER, LINDA JEAN, communications educator, media consultant; b. L.A., July 16, 1948; d. Stanley Stewart and Irene M. (Sabo) W. BS, So. Conn. State U., New Haven, 1981, MA, 1983; PhD, La. State U., Baton Rouge, 1987; BA, St. Gregory U., 2002. CEO CBE Enterprises, Inc., Baton Rouge, 1984-89; rsch. fellow La. State U., 1983-87; instr. speech Southeastern La. U., Hammond, 1984-89, Hancock Coll., Santa Maria, Calif., 1989; curator of edn. Lompoc (Calif.) Mus., 1989; asst. prof. speech U. Ark., Monticello, 1990-95, assoc. prof. speech, dir. honors program, 1995-2000, prof. speech and journalism, 2000—. Faclty advisor The Weevil student newspaper; exec. dir. Drew County Hist. Mus., Monticello, 1992-95; media dir. Oasis Resources-Homeless Shelter, Warren, Ark., 1991-99, chair bd. dirs., 1998-99; bur. chief Pine Bluff (Ark.) Comml.; 1992-94; media consulting WZXS-FM, Holly Ridge, N.C., 1995-97; apptd. State Ark. Mus. Svcs. Rev. Panel, 1997-98, re-apptd., 1999-2000, elected chmn. panel, 1999; chair Drew County Salvation Army, 1999-2000; mem. faculty U. Chgo. Exec. MBA program, 2001. Editor Jour. Comm. Studies, 1997-2000, on-line version, 2001—; assoc. editor; asst. Popular Measurement, 1998—; S.E. regional corr. Ark. Cath., 1999-2000; contbr. chpts. to books and articles to profl. jours. Vol. Boyus/Girls Club, Monticello, 1992—93; campaign dir. Gloria Wright Election, 1995, dir. re-election campaign, 2000; campaign media dir. Ken Harper Election-Dist. 82, 1996; sec. Drew County Rep. Conv., 1998—2000; vice chair St. Mark Parish Coun., 2001—02; chair Migrant Worker Ministry to S.E. Ark. Recipient Noel Ross Strader award Coll. Media Advisors, Inc., 1991, Coll. Tchr. of the Yr. award Ark. State Commn. Assn., 1993, Alpha Chi Tchr. of Yr. award, 1999, Faculty Excellence Gold award, 1999; Master fellow Ark. Distance Learning Acad., 2000-01. Mem. AAUW, AAUP, Nat. Women's Studies Assn., Am. Soc. for History of Rhetoric, Ark. Press Women (state pres. 1993-95, Communicator of Achievement award 1991), Ark. State Comm. Assn. (1st v.p.-elect 1997-98, 1st v.p. 1998-99, pres. 1999-2000, Stds. Bearer 1997—), So. State Comm. Assn. (chair honors session 1995, mem. constitutio com. 1997-2000), Internat. Comm. Assn., Oral History Assn., Speech Comm. Assn. (commn. chair 1993-96), Nat. Comm. Assn. (sec. sr. coll. and univ. sect. 1997-99), Edn. Comm. Assn. (campus Cath. minister 1999—). Roman Catholic. Avocations: historic preservation, gardening, baseball, Boston Terriers, driving. Office: U Ark-Arts & Humanities Monticello AR 71656 E-mail: webster@uamont.edu.

WEBSTER, MARC ALAN, music educator; s. J B and Ivy Mae Webster; m. Diana C Crane, May 26, 1979; children: Alaina Louise, Christa Noel, Erica Lynn. Associates, Barton County CC, Great Bend, Kansas, 1973—75; Bachelor Music Edn., U. Kans., Lawrence, Kansas, 1975—78. Music tchr. Kinsley-Offerle Sch. Dist., Kinsley, Kans., 1978—82; instrumentat music tchr. Coffeyville H.S., Coffeyville, 1982—88; instrumental vocal music tchr. Stanton county sch. dist., Johnson, 1988—94; instrumental music tchr. Ellsworth-Kanopolis schools, Ellsworth, 1994—. Chair dir. First United Methodists Ch., Ellsworth, Kans., 2001—02. Recipient Outstanding Young Bandmaster, Kans. Bandmaster Assn., 1983, Outstanding Mid. Sch. Tchr., Kans. Music Edn. Assn., 2000. Mem.: Kans. Bandmaster Assn., Kans. Music Educators Assn. Home: 510 Webb Street Ellsworth KS 67439-4248 Personal E-mail: kmsband@yahoo.com.

WEBSTER, MARK KENYON, management consultnat, educator; b. Akron, Ohio, Apr. 15, 1954; s. Thomas Forbes and Olive May Webster; m. Brenda Joy Stevens; children: Joshua, Jessica, Jillian. Student, Northwestern U., 1972-74; BBA, Cleve. State U., 1980, MBA, 1989. CPA; cert. cash mgr., cert. systems profl., cert. data processor. Res. cash teller Ctrl. Nat. Bank, Cleve., 1974-75; acctg. analyst The Cleve. Trust Co., 1975-77; asst. v.p. Women's Fed. Savs. & Loan, Cleve., 1977-81; product mgr. Mellon Bank, Pitts., 1981-82; chief info. officer, v.p. data processing Women's Fed. Savs. Bank, Cleve., 1982-90; sr. mng. cons. Coopers & Lybrand, 1990-98; ptnr. PricewaterhouseCoopers LLP, 1998—2002, Capco (The Capital Markets Co.), 2002—. Mem. rules and ops. com. Nat. Automated Clearing Ho. Assn., Herndon, Va., 1999—, mem. exec. com. affiliates coun., 1998—; mem. faculty treasury mgmt. series Haas Sch. Bus., U. Calif., Berkeley, 1991—; bd. dirs. Data Processing Mgmt. Assn., Cleve., 1985-90. Contbr. articles to profl. jours. Treas. St. Alban's Episcopal Ch., Cleveland Heights, Ohio, 1985-2001. Mem. AICPA (Elijah Watt Sells award 1987), Assn. Fin. Profls., Ohio Soc. CPAs, Beta Gamma Sigma. Republican. Avocations: golf, bicycling, woodworking. Home: 2281 Lamberton Rd Cleveland Heights OH 44118 Office: Capco 120 Broadway New York NY 10271 Office Fax: 212-932-1678. E-mail: mark.webster@capco.com.

WEBSTER, MARY HULL, artist, writer; b. Raleigh, N.C., Feb. 17, 1947; d. William Terrell Jr. and Leila (McKimmon) W. BA, Hollins U., 1969; MA, U. N.C., 1971; BFA, San Francisco Art Inst., 1981. Core faculty arts and conscious dept. Sch. Holistic Studies John F. Kennedy U., Orinda, Calif., 1984—; contbg. editor Artweek Mag., San Jose, 1991—. Exhibited in group and solo shows; organizer What Is Art For? at Oakland Mus. Calif., 1999; author of books, essays and poetry. Buddhist. Avocation: cooking. Home: PO Box 1117 Woodacre CA 94973 Office: John F Kennedy U Arts and Conscious Dept 2956 San Pablo Ave Berkeley CA 94702-2471 Fax: 415-488-0224.

WEBSTER, MERLYN HUGH, JR. manufacturing engineer, information systems consultant; b. Beaver Falls, Pa., Nov. 7, 1946; s. Merlyn Hugh and Helen Ruth (Dillon) W.; m. Linda Jeanne Gundlach, June 14, 1969; children: Matthew Jason, Nathaniel Kevin. AA, Palomar Coll., San Marcos, Calif., 1975; BA, Chapman Coll., 1978. Registered profl. engr., Calif. Mfg. analyst NCR Corp., Rancho Bernardo, Calif., 1968-72, indsl. engr., 1972-76, sr. indsl. engr., 1976-78; sr. project mgr. Tektronix, Beaverton, Oreg., 1978-83, corp. distbn. I.E. mgr., 1983-86; sr. info. systems cons. Intel Corp., Hillsboro, 1986—; pres. WEB Internat. Corp., Tualatin, 1992—. Cons. material handling Intel Mfg., Puerto rico and Ireland, 1989-92; cons. info. systems M.I.S.I., N.Y.C., 1992-93. Chmn. United Way Hillsboro, Oreg., 1986. With USMC, 1964-68, Vietnam. Mem. NSPE, Inst. Indsl. Engrs. (cert.), Shelby Car Club Am. Republican. Office: WEB Internat Corp 5200 SW Joshua St Ste 101 Tualatin OR 97062-9792 E-mail: WebWeb@aol.com.

WEBSTER, MURRAY ALEXANDER, JR. sociologist, educator; b. Manila, Philippines, Dec. 10, 1941; s. M.A. and Patricia (Morse) W. AB, Stanford U., 1963, MA, 1966, PhD, 1968. Asst. prof. social rels. Johns Hopkins U., Balt., 1968-74, assoc. prof., 1974-76; prof. sociology, adj. prof. psychology U. S.C., Columbia, 1976-86; vis. prof. sociology Stanford U., 1981-82, 85, 88-89; sr. lectr. San Jose State U., 1987-89; dir. sociology program NSF, 1989-91,99-2000; prof. sociology U. N.C., Charlotte, 1993—. Author: (with Barbara Sobieszek) Sources of Self-Evaluation, 1974, Actions and Actors, 1975, (with Martha Foschi) Status Generalization: New Theory and Research, 1988; mem. editl. bd. Am. Jour. Sociology, 1976-79, Social Psychology Quar., 1977-80, 84-87, 93—, Social Sci. Rsch., 1975—. NIH fellow, 1966-68; grantee NSF, Nat. Inst. Edn. Mem. AAAS, Am. Sociol. Assn., So. Sociol. Soc., Am. Psychol. Assn., Am. Psychol. Soc., N.Y. Acad. Scis. Presbyterian. Office: Univ NC Dept Sociology Charlotte NC 28223 E-mail: mawebste@email.uncc.edu.

WEBSTER, NANCY JOAN, employee relations administrator; b. Geneva, Ohio, Jan. 21, 1949; d. Arthur Clair and Alice Mary (Falk) Eisbrenner; m. Bruce Alan Webster, June 15, 1968; children— Teresa Lynn, Melanie Marie. B.A. in Bus. Mgmt., Hiram Coll., 1985. Placement specialist Goodwill Industries, Ashtabula, Ohio, 1973-77, Ohio Job Service, Ashtabula, 1977-80; employee relations adminstr. RMI Co., Ashtabula, 1980— ; EEO affirmative action, 1984—. Pub. relations chmn. Saybrook Elem. Sch. PTO, Ashtabula, 1976-78, carnival chmn., 1975-78, pres. 1976-78; sec. Mallory Sharon Metals Recreational Assn., Ashtabula, 1982-84; mem. job service employer com. Ashtabula County, 1986—, chairperson nominating com., 1988; mem. Youth Citizens Council Planning Com., 1987—; bd. dirs. United Way, Ashtabula County, 1976-79; vice chmn. allocations com., 1978-79, com. mem. priorities, nomination, Ohio Citizens Council, services innovations, 1977-80. Recipient Cert. of Appreciation, Goodwill Industries, 1975, Ashtabula County Vocat. Edn. Sch., 1985. Mem. Ashtabula County Personnel Assn. (v.p. 1987-88, pres. 1988—), Am. Soc. Personnel Adminstrs. Catholic. Avocations: consumer advocacy; volunteer work; home remodeling and repair. Home: 731 Park Rd Painesville OH 44077-5048 Office: RMI Co Metals Reduction Plant E 21 and State Rd PO Box 550 Ashtabula OH 44005-0550

WEBSTER, NORMAN ERIC, journalist, charitable foundation administrator; b. Summerside, P.E.I., Can., June 4, 1941; s. Eric and Elizabeth (Paterson) W.; m. Pat Roop, 1966; children: David, Andrew, Derek, Gillian, Hilary. BA, Bishop's U., Que., Can.; MA, St. John's Coll., Oxford, Eng. Corr. Globe and Mail, Que. and Ottawa, Ont., Can.; editor Globe Mag., Toronto; corr. Globe and Mail, Peking, China, 1969-71, columnist Ont. affairs Toronto, European corr. London, editor-in-chief Toronto, 1983-89, Montreal (Que.) Gazette, 1989-93; pres. R. Howard Webster Found., Montreal, 1993—. Chancellor U. P.E.I.; chmn. North-South Inst., Ottawa, 1998-2000; bd. dirs. Internat. Press Inst., Vienna, Montreal Children's Hosp. Found., McGill U. Health Ctr. Found., Can. Inst. for Advanced Rsch., Bishop's U., Michener Found. Recipient Nat. Newspaper award for Peking corr., 1971, for editl. writing, 1988; Rhodes scholar; mem. Order of Can. Office: R Howard Webster Found Ste 2912 1155 Rene Levesque Blvd W Montreal QC Canada H3B 2L5

WEBSTER, PETER DAVID, judge; b. Framingham, Mass., Feb. 12, 1949; s. Waldo John and Helen Anne (Borovek) W.; m. Michele Page Hernandez, Jan. 13, 1989; 1 stepchild, Alana Perryman. BS, Georgetown U., 1971; JD, Duke U., 1974; LLM, U. Va., 1995. Bar: Fla. 1974, U.S. Dist. Ct. (mid. dist.) Fla. 1975, U.S. Ct. Appeals (5th cir.) 1975, U.S. Dist. Ct. (so. dist.) Fla. 1977, U.S. Dist. Ct. (no. dist.) Fla. 1978, U.S. Supreme Ct. 1978, U.S. Ct. Appeals (11th cir.) 1981. Law clk. U.S. Dist. Judge, Jacksonville, Fla., 1974-75; assoc. Bedell, Bedell, Dittmar, Smith & Zehmer, 1975-78; ptnr. Bedell, Bedell, Dittmar & Zehmer, 1978-85; cir. judge State Fla., 1986-91; judge Dist. Ct. of Appeal, First Dist., State of Fla., Tallahassee, 1991—. Master of bench Chester Bedell Am. Inn of Ct., 1988-91, Tallahassee Am. Inn of Ct., 1992—; chmn. com. on standard jury instrns. in civil cases, chmn. court reporter cert. planning com.; mem. com. on trial ct. info. sys.; com. on confidentiality of records of jud. br. Fla. Supreme Ct. Contbg. author: Sanctions: Rule 11 and Other Powers, 1986, Florida Criminal Rules and Practice Manual, 1990. Bd. dirs. Jacksonville Area Legal Aid, Inc., 1978-82, River Region Human Svcs., Inc., Jacksonville, 1986-88; mem. adv. bd. P.A.C.E. Ctr. for Girls, Inc., Jacksonville, 1986-91; com. mem. Shawnee dist. North Fla. coun. Boy Scouts Am., 1974-78; mem. delinquency task force Mayor's Commn. on Children and Youth, City of Jacksonville, 1988-91; officer, mem. exec. bd. Suwanee River Area coun. Boy Scouts, 1991-96. Mem. Fla. Conf. Appellate Judges, Jacksonville Bar Assn., Tallahassee Bar Assn., Phi Beta Kappa, Phi Alpha Theta, Phi Eta Sigma. Office: 1st Dist Ct Appeal 301 Martin Luther King Blvd Tallahassee FL 32399-1850

WEBSTER, RAYMOND EARL, psychology educator, director, psychotherapist; b. Providence, Dec. 3, 1948; s. Earl Harold and Madeline (D'Antuono) W.; m. Angela Grenier, Jan. 31, 1984; children: Matthew Raymond, Patrick Gregory, Timothy Andrew. BA, R.I. Coll., 1971, MA, 1973; MS, Purdue U., 1976; PhD, U. Conn., 1978. Diplomate Am. Bd. Forenseic Med., Am. Bd. Forensic Examiners; lic. psychologist, N.C. Dir. pupil svcs. and spl. edn. Northeastern Area Regional Edn. Svcs., Wauregan, Conn., 1978-79; dir. alternative vocat. sch. Capital Region Edn. Coun., West Hartford, 1979-83; prof. psychology, dir. sch. psychology program East Carolina U., Greenville, N.C., 1983—. Rsch. assoc. ednl. psychology U. Conn., Storrs, 1976-78; cons. Bolton (Conn.) Pub. Schs., 1976-78, Columbia (Conn.) Pub. Schs., 1976-78, N.C. Dept. Instrn., Raleigh, 1983—; speaker at profl. meetings. Guest reviewer Jour. Applied Behavior Analysis, 1975, Clin. Psychology Pub. Co., 1992, Psychol. Reports, 1993—, Perceptual and Motor Skills, 1993—; mem. editl. bd. Psychology in Schs., 1987—, The Forensic Examiner, 2000—; assoc. editor The N.C. Psychologist, 2000—; contbr. numerous articles to profl. jours., chpts. to books. Trustee N.C. Ctr. for Advancement of Tchg., Cullowhee, 1990-93. Sgt. U.S. Army Spl. Forces N.G., 1969-75. Recipient spl. distinction award Conn. Assn. Sch. Psychologists, 1983. Mem. APA, Am. Coll. Forensic Examiners (cert. Forensic Examiner), Nat. Assn. Sch. Psychologists (cert., alt. del. 1985-86, spl. distinction in profl. devel. 1982, 83), Sigma Xi. Methodist. Avocations: running, karate (3d degree black belt in Goju Shorin), bicycling, flower gardening. Home: 200 Williams St Greenville NC 27858-8712 Office: East Carolina U Rawl Bldg Greenville NC 27834-4353 E-mail: senseiwebsterr@earthlink.net.

WEBSTER, ROBERT MCNAUGHT, physician, researcher; b. Yarmouth, N.S., Can., June 27, 1920; came to U.S., 1952; s. Charles Ashton and Mary Page (Murray) W.; m. Inez Katherine Dodge, May 17, 1952; children: Ann, Janie. BS, MD, Dalhousie U.; diploma in clin. pathology, U. London. Diplomate in clin. pathology and anat. pathology Am. Bd. Pathology. Intern Victoria Gen. Hosp., Halifax, N.S., Hurley Hosp., Flint, Mich.; staff physician Newport (R.I.) Hosp., Princeton (N.J.) Hosp., Holy Family Hosp., Grady Meml. Hosp., South Fulton Hosp.; exec. dir Cancer and Disease Detection and Rsch. Inc.; med. dir. Christian City Convalescent Ctr., Arrowhead Nursing Home. Contbr. articles to profl. jours. Served with RCAF, 1942-45. Tufts U. tchg. fellow. Mem.: AMA, Am. Coll. Gen. Physicians (pres., founder,), Am. Bd. Gen. Med. (pres., founder), Am. Acad. Gen. Physicians, Royal Coll. Pathologists (founder), Am. Coll. Physicians Exec., Am. Geriat. Soc., Soc. Nuc. Medicine, Am. Soc. Clin. Pathologists, Internat. Acad. Pathology, Assn. Clin. Pathologists, Allergy and Immunology Soc. Ga., Ga. Assn. Pathologists, Med. Assn. Ga., Med. Assn. Atlanta, Am. Med. Dirs. Assn. (v.p., founder), Ga. Med. Dirs. Assn. (pres., founder), Jasper Rotary Club (pres.), Masons, Pickens Star 220, Royal Arch, Scottish Rite, Shrine. Presbyterian. Home and Office: 18 Hummingbird Ln # 20826 Jasper GA 30143-7871

WEBSTER, ROBERT KENLY, lawyer; b. N.Y.C., May 16, 1933; s. Francis Kenly and Mary Louise (Rathbone) W.; m. Sally Irene Stratton, Apr. 16, 1960; children: Timothy Kenly, Kimberly Anne. AB, Princeton U., 1955; LLB, U. Va., 1960. Assoc. Cadwalader, Wickersham & Taft, N.Y.C., 1960-65; asst. U.S. atty. Dept. of Justice, Washington, 1965-68; prin. dep. gen. counsel Dept. of Army, 1968-73; ptnr. Kennedy & Webster, 1973-81, Shaw, Pittman, Potts & Trowbridge, Washington, 1981-98; sole practice, 1999—. Spl. investigator Iran FMS program Sec. of Def., Washington, 1977; advisor conflict of interest issues Watergate defendants Dept. Justice, Washington, 1977. Gen. counsel, bd. dirs. Princeton (N.J.) Project 55, Inc., 1989—. Lt. j.g. USN, 1955—57. Mem. ABA, Assn. Trial Lawyers Am., Fed. Bar Assn., Met. Club. Avocations: pottery, reading, travel, tennis. Fax: (202) 659-0084.

WEBSTER, ROBERT LEE, accounting educator, researcher; b. Little Rock, Oct. 4, 1946; s. Daniel and Mildred LaNette (Patishall) W.; m. Mary Katherine Fiske, Aug. 26, 1967; children: Elizabeth Ashley, Jessica Lee. BA, Ouachita Bapt. U., 1968; MBA, Syracuse U., 1975; MS, L.I. U., 1986; DBA, La. Tech. U., 1993. Cert. govt. fin. mgr. Commd. 2d lt. U.S. Army, 1968, advanced through grades to lt. col., 1985; dep. contr. U.S. Army Electronics R&D Command, Adelphi, Md., 1975-80; chief of ops., comms. security NATO, Mons, Belgium, 1980-83; asst. prof. acctg. and fin. U.S. Mil. Acad., West Point, N.Y., 1983-86; prof. mil. sci. Henderson State U., Arkadelphia, Ark., 1986-88; ret. U.S. Army, 1988; asst. prof. acctg. Henderson State U., 1988-91, chair dept. acctg., econs. and bus. edn., 1991-93; chair dept. acctg. Ouachita Bapt. U., Arkadelphia, 1993—, George Young chair bus., 1995—. Bd. dirs. Hospitality Care Ctr., Arkadelphia, 1992-93; speaker in field. Editor Jour. Bus. & Behavioral Scis., 1995; author articles. Army scholar Syracuse U., 1974-75; Exch. Educator to Republic of Kazakhstan, 1994-95; recipient Dean's award for acad. achievement L.I. U., 1986. Mem. Nat. Social Sci. Assn. (bd. govs. 1992—, Outstanding Conf. Paper award 1992), Am. Acctg. Assn., Assn. of Govt. Accts., Beta Gamma Sigma, Sigma Beta Delta. Avocations: coin collecting, exercising. Home: 205 Forrest Park Dr Arkadelphia AR 71923-2811 Office: Ouachita Bapt U PO Box 3689 Arkadelphia AR 71998 E-mail: websterb@obu.edu.

WEBSTER, ROBIN WELANDER, interior designer; b. Bethesda, Md., Sept. 24, 1956; d. Robert Oscar and Patricia (Benson) W.; m. Bryan Douglas Webster, Oct. 9, 1982. BA, Mary Washington Coll., Fredericksburg, Va., 1978. Design asst. Del Mar (Calif.) Designs, 1983-84; ptnr., interior designer Corp. Design, Solana Beach, Calif., 1984-86; owner, mgr. R Designs, San Diego, 1986—. Bd. dirs. Save Our Heritage Orgn., San Diego, 1986-92, pres., 1988-89; vol. San Diego Mus. Art, 1986-95; bd. dirs. Contemporaries San Diego Mus. Art, 1989-95; del. Calif. Legis. Conf. on Interior Design. Lt. USN, 1978-83. Mem. Internat. Interior Design Assn. (com. chmn. San Diego 1989—), Nat. Coun. Interior Design (cert.), Calif. Coun. Interior Design (cert.), Color Mktg. Group.

WEBSTER, RONALD B. lawyer; b. Cle Elum, Wash., June 11, 1942; s. Burnette O. and Lucille (Beck) W.; m. M. Gail Skinner, June 26, 1971; children: Noel, Michelle. BA, U. Wash., 1964; JD, Gonzaga U., 1969. Bar: Wash., U.S. Dist. Ct. (ea. and we. dists.) Wash., U.S. Ct. Appeals (9th cir.). Dep. pros. atty. Cowlitz County, Kelso, Wash., 1970-73; ptnr. Hickman, Webster, Ensley & Carpenter, Colfax, 1973-90, Hickman, Webster & Moulton, 1990-92, Hickman & Webster, P.S., 1992-95. Mem. Whitman County Bd. Mental Health, Pullman, Wash., 1973-83; chmn. civil svc. commn. Whitman County Sheriffs Office, Colfax, 1973—; pres. Colfax and Cmty. Fund, 1973-74; pres. Whitman Cmty. Concerts, 1990-93; mem. ch. coun. Peace Luth. Ch., 1996-98; chmn. bd. dirs. Whitman County Libr., 1997—, chmn. bd. trustees, 1998—. Named Rotarian of Yr., 1998, Paul Harris fellow, 1998. Mem. Whitman County Bar Assn. (pres. 1981-82), Wash. State Bar Assn. (inter profl. com. 1986-89—, disciplinary com. 1986-97). Clubs: Colfax Golf and Country. Lodges: Rotary (pres. Colfax club 1983-84). Home: 1801 N Oak St Colfax WA 99111-9705 Office: Hickman Webster Tracy PLLC 302 N Mill St Colfax WA 99111-1865

WEBSTER, RONALD D. communications company executive; b. Richwood, W.Va., Aug. 9, 1949; s. Ralph D. and Victoria M. (Cisek) W.; m. Donna M. Falkenthal, Aug. 9, 1975; 1 child, Kathryn E. BSBA with high distinction, U. Ill., Chgo., 1971; MBA, U. Chgo., 1980. CPA, Ill. Sr. auditor Arthur Andersen & Co., Chgo., 1970-75; dir. corp. reporting Trans Union Corp., Lincolnshire, Ill., 1975-77; asst. group contr. Union Tank Car Co. (subs. of Trans Union Corp.), Chgo., 1977-83; treas. Telephone and Data Systems, Inc., 1983-87, 88-97, v.p., 1992-97; v.p., CFO Ideal Sch. Supply Corp., Oak Lawn, Ill., 1987-88; sr. v.p., CFO 21st Century Telecom. Group, Inc., Chgo., 1997-2000; sr. v.p. ctrl. region RCN Corp., 2000-01; exec. v.p., CFO 02wireless Solutions, INc., Atlanta, 2001—. Bd. dirs., v.p. fin. Ivy Glen Homeowners Assn., Aurora, Ill., 1972-73. Staff sgt. USNG, 1970-76. Mem. Fin. Execs. Inst., Am. Soc. CPAs (Elijah Watt Sells nat. honorable mention 1973), Ill. CPA Soc., Beta Gamma Sigma. Home: 7637 Ridgewood Ln Burr Ridge IL 60527-8024 Office: o2wireless Solutions Inc 440 Interstate North Pkwy Atlanta GA 30339 E-mail: rdw@enteract.com.

WEBSTER, SCOTT, finance educator; b. Cleve., Mar. 12, 1958; s. Jack and Judith Webster; m. Deborah Lynn Stoller; children: Bryce, Jordan. BS, Miami U., Oxford, Ohio, 1980; PhD, Ind. U., 1990. Asst. prof. U. Wis., Madison, 1990—97; assoc. prof. Syracuse (N.Y.) U., 1997—. Contbr. articles to profl. jours. Mem.: INFORMS. Office: Syracuse U Sch Mgmt Syracuse NY 13244 Business E-Mail: stwebste@syr.edu.

WEBSTER, SHARON B. economist; b. Wildwood, Fla., Aug. 23, 1937; d. James McWilliams and Marion (Hallbrook) Boen; BA in Polit. Sci., Econs. and Psychology, U. Fla., 1959; postgrad. (vis. doctoral fellow), Princeton U., 1964-65; PhD, U. Va., 1965. . Asst. prof. No. Mich. U., Marquette, 1962-64, U. Md., 1964-66, Hollins Coll., Roanoke, Va., 1966-71; prof. Fed. Exec. Inst., Charlottesville, Va., 1971-72; internat. program mgr. Dept. Treasury, Washington, 1972-74; economist Econs., Statistics and Coop. Svc., U.S. Dept. Agr., Washington, 1974-79; mem. Presdl. Commn. for Exec. Exchange, 1979-80; dir. internat. econs. Occidental Petroleum Corp., L.A., 1980-83; investment banker, account exec. Johnston, Lemon and Co., Inc., Washington, 1983-88; fin. cons. Shearson Lehman Hutton, 1988—. Mem. adv. bd. Pres.'s Carribbean Basin Initiative, 1982; chmn. bd. dirs. NATA, Inc.; bd. dirs. GENTA, Inc., NABE; pres., chief exec. officer A.A. Global; bd. advisors Sintal Communications USA, Inc., Internat. Trade Council, Patterson Sch. Diplomacy and Internat. Commerce, U. Ky., Consumer Health and Svcs. of Am., Inc. Contbr. articles to profl. jours. Recipient Presdl. award Pvt. Sector Initiative, 1982; NDEA fellow. Mem. AAUP, Internat. Policy Inst. (v.p. 1977—), Internat. Assn. Energy Economists, Am. Assn. Agrl. Economists, Am. Polit. Sci. Assn., Nat. Assn. Bus. Economists, Internat. Studies Assn., Soc. Internat. Devel., Nat. Council Career Women, Washington Soc. Money Mgrs., Assn. Polit. Risk Analysts, Pres.'s Exec. Exchange Assn., Fed. Exec. Inst. Alumni Assn., Capital Speakers Club, Army Navy Club, Internat. Club. Home: The Winthrop # 602 1727 Massachusetts Ave NW Washington DC 20036-2153 Office: AA Global 9039 Furrow Ave Ellicott City MD 21042-1841

WEBSTER, STEPHEN BURTIS, physician, educator; b. Chgo., Dec. 3, 1935; s. James Randolph Webster and Ruth Marion (Burtis) Holmes; m. Katherine Griffith Webster, Apr. 4, 1959; children: David Randolph, Margaret Elizabeth, James Lucian. BS, Northwestern U., 1957, MD, 1960. Diplomate Am. Bd. Dermatology (bd. dirs. 1992—, v.p. 1997-98, pres.). Intern Colo. Gen. Hosp., Denver, 1960-61; resident Walter Reed Gen. Hosp., Washington, 1962-65; staff physician Henry Ford Hosp., Detroit, 1969-71, Gundersen Clinic, La Crosse, 1971—; assoc. clin. prof. U. Wis., Madison, 1976—; clin. prof. U. Minn., Mpls., 1978—. Lt. col. U.S. Army, 1962-69. Fellow Am. Acad. Dermatology (sec.-treas. 1985-88, pres. 1991); mem. AMA, Am. Dermatol. Assn. (pres. 1996-97), Am. Bd. Dermatology (v.p. 1997-98, pres. 1999-2000, assoc. exec. dir. 2001—), Wis. Med. Soc., La Crosse County Med. Soc., Soc. Investigative Dermatology, Alpha Omega Alpha. Republican. Congregationalist. Avocations: bagpipes, model R.R. Home: N2062 Wedgewood Dr E La Crosse WI 54601-7175 Office: Gundersen Clinic Ltd 1836 South Ave La Crosse WI 54601-5494

WEBSTER, THOMAS GLENN, psychiatrist, educator; b. Topeka, Jan. 23, 1924; s. Guy Welland and Iva Amanda (Keefover) W.; m. Mary Tupper Dooly, June 27, 1948; children— Warnie Louise, Guy Weyman, David Michael AB, Ft. Hays State Coll., 1946; MD, Wayne State U., 1949. Intern Los Angeles County Gen. Hosp., Calif., 1949-50; resident in psychiatry Mass. Mental Health Ctr., Boston, 1953-55, resident in child psychiatry, 1955-56, James Jackson Putnam Children's Ctr., Boston, 1956-58; dir. presch. program for retarded children Greater Boston, 1958-62; coordinator 3d yr. med. student psychiatry clerkship Harvard U. Med. Sch.-Mass. Mental Health Ctr., Boston, 1960-63; practice medicine specializing in psychiatry, 1953-62, Bethesda, Md., 1963-72, Washington, 1972—; tng. specialist psychiatry, then chief continuing edn. br. NIMH, Bethesda, Md., 1963-72; prof. psychiatry George Washington U., Washington, 1972-86, chmn. dept. psychiatry and behavioral scis., 1972-75, prof. emeritus, 1986-96. Vis. prof. Harvard U. Med. Sch., 1980-83, McLean Hosp., 1980-86; U.S.-Poland exchange health scientist, 1981 Pres. Woodhaven Citizens Assn., 1971-72. Served with AUS, 1943-46; as sr. asst. surgeon USPHS, 1951-53 Fellow Am. Coll. Psychiatrists, Am. Coll. Psychoanalysts; mem. Assn. Acad. Psychiatry (pres. 1976-78), Group Advancement Psychiatry Home: 8506 Woodhaven Blvd Bethesda MD 20817-3117 Office: 2112 F St NW Washington DC 20037-2715

WEBSTER, WILLIAM HEDGCOCK, lawyer; b. St. Louis, Mar. 6, 1924; s. Thomas M. and Katherine (Hedgcock) W.; m. Drusilla Lane, May 5, 1950 (dec. 1984); children: Drusilla Lane Busch, William Hedgcock, Katherine Hagee Roessle; m. Lynda Clugston, Oct. 20, 1990. AB, Amherst Coll., 1947, LLD, 1975; JD, Washington U., 1949, LLD, 1978; LLD (hon.), William Wood Coll., 1978, DePauw U., 1978, Drury Coll., Columbia Coll., U. Dayton, U. Notre Dame, Center Coll., Dickinson Coll., U. Miami, DePaul U., Am. U., John Jay Coll., Westminster Coll., Georgetown U., Rockhurst Coll., Pepperdine U. Bar: Mo. 1949, D.C. 1981. With Armstrong, Teasdale, Kramer and Vaughan (and predecessors), St. Louis, 1949-50, 52-59, 61-70; U.S. atty. U.S. Dist. Ct. (ea. dist.) Mo., 1960-61, judge, 1971-73; judge U.S. Ct. Appeals (8th cir.), 1973-78; dir. FBI, 1978-87, CIA, 1987-91; sr. ptnr. Milbank, Tweed, Hadley & McCloy, Washington, 1991—. Mem. Mo. Bd. Law Examiners, 1964-69, mem. adv. com. on criminal rules, 1971-78, mem. ct. adminstrs. com., 1975-78; bd. dirs. Anhauser-Busch Cos., Maritz Inc., Pinkertons Inc., T.L.C. Beatrice Internat. Holdings Inc., Nextwave, Inc. Trustee Washington U., 1974—; bd. dirs. Atlantic Coun., Nat. Legal Ctr. for Pub. Interest, Nat. Symphony Assn., Coun. on Fgn. Rels.; bd. dirs., chmn. Police Found; hon. life pres. Big Bros. Orgn. St. Louis; bd. dirs. Big Bros. Am., 1966, hon. bd. dirs., 1978—. Lt. USNR, 1943-46, 50-52. Recipient Disting. Alumnus award Washington U., 1977, Stein award Fordham U., Law award U. Va., Nat. Svc. medal Freedoms Found., Theodore Roosevelt award, Presdl. medal of Freedom, Nat. Security medal, Silver Buffalo award Boy Scouts Am., Disting. Svc. award Am. Legion; named Father of Yr., 1986, Man of Yr., St. Louis Globe Dem., 1980. Fellow Am. Bar Found.; mem. ABA (chmn. sect. on corp. banking and bus. law 1977-78), FBA, Mo. Bar Assn., St. Louis Bar Assn., Am. Law Inst. (mem. coun. 1978—), Wash. U. Alumni Fedn. (pres. 1956-57), Rotary, St. Louis Country Club, Noonday Club (St. Louis), Met. Club, Chevy Chase Club, Alfalfa Club, St. Alban's Tennis Club, Order of Coif, Psi Upsilon, Delta Sigma Rho, Phi Delta Phi. Office: Milbank Tweed Hadley & McCloy 1825 I St NW Ste 1100 Washington DC 20006-5492

WEBSTER, WILLIAM HODGES, lawyer; b. N.Y.C., Oct. 26, 1946; s. Eugene Burnett and Verna May Webster; m. Joan Leslie Strawder, Dec. 30, 1967; 1 child, Sydney Kristen. BA cum laude, NYU, 1972; JD, U. Calif., Berkeley, 1975. Bar: Calif. 1976, U.S. Dist. Ct. (no. dist.) Calif. 1976, U.S. Tax Ct. 1984. Rsch. assoc. Nat. Econ. Devel. & Law Ctr., Berkeley, 1974-76, staff atty., 1976-81, mng. atty., 1981-83; ptnr. Hunter & Anderson, Oakland, Calif., 1983-86, mng. ptnr., 1986-93, Webster & Anderson, Oakland, 1993—. Contbr. articles to profl. jours. Mem. Mayor's Com. on Responsible Investments, City of Berkeley, 1990, Mayor's Housing Task Force, City of Berkeley, 1986; bd. dirs. Ctr. for Elders Independence, Inc., 2001—. Recipient Cert. of Merit, Nat. Congress for Cmty. Econ. Devel., 1983. Mem. Nat. Assn. Bond Lawyers, Calif. Bar Assn. (bus. law sect.), Charles Houston Bar Assn., Kappa Alpha Psi. Democrat. Avocations: yoga, bicycling, swimming, chess, reading. Office: Webster and Anderson 469 9th St Ste 240 Oakland CA 94607-4068 E-mail: bwebster@websteranderson.com.

WECHMAN, ROBERT JOSEPH, economist, educator; b. Sept. 23, 1939; s. David Samuel and Blanche (Udell) W.; m. Stephanie Helene Kellman, June 18, 1967; children: Craig Samuel, Evan Mitchell, Darren Max. BA, CUNY, 1961; MA, Columbia U., 1966; PhD, Syracuse U., 1970; postdoc., U. Pa., 1974. Tchr. history and econs., N.Y.C., 1961-63, Dobbs Ferry (N.Y.) High Sch., 1963-66; instr. Elmira (N.Y.) Coll., 1966-70; asst. prof. social sci. Hartwick Coll., N.Y.C., N.Y., 1970-74; asst. v.p. Beavertown Mills, 1976-80, v.p., 1980-90; prin., owner Robert J. Wechman, Cons., 1984-90, Verdin Assocs., Inc., N.Y.C., 1982-88, Robert J. Wechman Assocs., Inc., N.Y.C., 1990-93. Vis. lectr. SUNY, Corning, summers 1967, 1970; adj. prof. New Sch. U., SUNY, Rockland Cmty. Coll., 1974-80, Empire State Coll., 1974—, Bergen Cmty. Coll., 1976-80, Berkeley Coll., 1979, 99-2001, Pace U., 1980-86, St. Thomas Aquinas Coll., 1981-94, Dominican Coll., summer 1981; adj. prof. Econs., Bus. CUNY, 1981—; adj. prof. Econs. St. Peters Coll., 1998—; adj. prof. Econs., Fin. Ramapo Coll., 1999—; cons. Choice Jour., 1972—. Author: the Eager Immigrants, 1972, The Economic Development of the Italian-American, 1983, Encountering Management, 1987, Essentials of American Business, 1990, Aspects of German Nationlism, 1994, Dictionary of Economics and Business, 1997; editor: Critical Issues in Modern American Life, 1968, The Crisis in Population, 1969, Urban America: A Guide to the Literature, 1971; reviewer for profl. jours. Mem. Oneonta Bd. Ethics, 1971-74, Oneonta Anti-Pollution commn., 1972-74, Rockland County Bd. Ethics, 1997-99; committeeman, dist. chmn. Rockalnd County Rep. com., 1978-97, Heritage Found., Hudson Inst. With U.S. Army, 1959, USAR, 1959-65. Recipient Marcus award for Excellence in Tchg. 1972, Outstanding Educators Am. award 1972, Pres. Appreciation award 1989, 90, 91, Congl. Cert. Appreciation award 1991, 93, Disting. Svc. award Rockland County, 1992, Cert. of Merit award N.Y. State Senate, 1992, Appreciation award CUNY, 1993, Excellence in Tchg. Econs. award Found. for Tchg. Econs., 1994, 95, Tchr. Recognition award Newsday, 1995. Mem. K.P. Club, Phi Alpha Theta, Delta Tau Kappa, Delta Pi Epsilon. Republican. Home: 9 Verdin Dr New City NY 10956-3707

WECHSLER, ANDREW ROBERT, international economic consultant; b. N.Y.C., Oct. 24, 1946; s. Herbert and Jennie (Epstein) W.; m. Christine Macfarlane, Sept. 21, 1991. BA cum laude, Yale U., 1969; MA, Stanford U., 1974, postgrad., 1976-79. Tchr., high schs., New Haven and Balt., 1969-72; lectr. Calif. State U., Hayward, 1973-74; guest researcher Nationalekonoiska institutionen, Uppsala, Sweden, 1974-76; lectr. econs. San Francisco State U., 1976-77, Stanford U., Calif., 1978-79; sr. econ. adviser to chairwoman U.S. Internat. Trade Commn., Washington, 1979-87; sr. economist Economists Inc., Washington., 1987-89, sr. v.p., 1989-91; prin., mng. dir. LECG, Inc., 1991—. Contbr. articles to profl. jours. Yale U. Ranking scholar, 1964-65; Social Sci. Rsch. Coun. West European fellow, 1975-76; John F. Kennedy fellow Swedish Embassy, Washington, 1974; Stanford U. fellow, 1972-74; Grumman Aircraft Engrng. scholar, 1964-68; N.Y. State Regents scholar, 1968; recipient Elks Nat. Most Valuable Student award, 1964. Mem. Am. Econ. Assn., Nat. Assn. Bus. Economists, Swedish Am. Cultural Union (U.S.-New Zealand coun.). Clubs: Nat. Econs. Yale of Washington. Avocations: photography, travel, tennis. Home: 5114 Edgemoor Ln Bethesda MD 20814-2311

WECHSLER, ARNOLD, osteopathic obstetrician and gynecologist; b. N.Y.C., June 10, 1923; s. David and Eva (Kirsch) W.; m. Marlene Esta Jurnovoy, Sept. 11, 1955 (div. Sept. 1986); children: Diane, Paul, Stewart. Grad., Rutgers U.; DO, Phila. Coll. Osteo. Medicine, 1952. Diplomate Am. Bd. Osteo. Obstetricians and Gynecologists; lic. physician, Pa., N.Y., Fla. Intern Hosps. of Phila. Coll. Osteo. Medicine, 1952-53, resident in ob-gyn. and gen. surgery, 1953-56; lectr. in ob-gyn. Nursing Sch. Phila. Coll. Osteo. Medicine; founder, mem. staff Tri County Hosp., Delaware County, Pa., from 1960, chief staff, 1960-62, chief dept. ob-gyn. surgery, 1960-77, dir. med. edn., 1968-71; attending and cons. in ob-gyn. surgery Met. Hosp., Phila., 1956-60, 71-75; chief dept. ob-gyn. Humana Hosp.-South Broward, Hollywood, Fla., 1980-84; cons. and attending in gynecol. surgery Drs. Hosp. of Hollywood, 1982-86. Insp. for intern and resident tng. programs Bur. Hosps. of Am. Osteo. Assn., 1965-66; founder, med. dir. Women's Med. Svcs., 1973-77, Nutrients Inc., Phila., 1977-79, Supplements Inc., Phila., 1979-80, Alternative Lifestyle Ctr., Fla., 1983-86; founder, dir. A.W. Profl. Consultants, Inc.; cons. Practice Mgmt. Group, Med Temps Plus, Plantation, Fla.; provider ambulatory gyn. surgery for multiple gyn ctrs. in Dade, Broward and Palm Beach Counties, Fla. Author: Dr. Wechsler's New You Diet, 1978. Staff Sgt. Signal Corps, USAF, 1942-46, PTO, Japan. Fellow Am. Coll. Osteo. Obstetricians and Gynecologists, Internat. Coll. Applied Nutrition; mem. Am. Osteo. Assn., Pa. Osteo. Med. Assn., Philadelphia County Osteo. Soc., Fla. Osteo. Med. Assn., Fla. Med. Soc., Fla. Ob-Gyn. Soc., Broward County Osteo. Med. Assn., Am. Soc. Bariatric Physicians, Assn. Maternal and Child Welfare, Internat. Acad. Preventive Medicine, Inst. Food Technologists, Coun. for Responsible Nutrition, Internat. Coll. Gynecologic Laparoscopists, Assn. Reproductive Health Profls. Avocations: photography, sculpture, woodworking.

WECHSLER, GIL, lighting designer; b. N.Y.C., Feb. 5, 1942; s. Arnold J. and Miriam (Steinberg) W. Student, Rensselaer Poly. Inst., 1958-61; BS, NYU, 1964; MFA, Yale U., 1967. Lighting designer Harkness Ballet, N.Y.C., 1967-69, Pa. Ballet, Phila., 1969-70, Stratford Shakespeare Festival, Ont., Can., 1969-78, 97, Guthrie Theatre, Mpls., 1971, Lyric Opera, Chgo., 1972-76, Met. Opera, N.Y.C., 1976-96, Equus, Stratford Sheakespeare Festival, 1997. Tchr. NYU, Rensselaer Poly. Inst., 1998; guest lectr. Teatro Colon, Buenos Aires, 1985, Yale U., New Haven, 1980, Broadway Lighting Designers, 1994—98; guest lighting designer Am. Ballet Theatre, N.Y.C., 1980, Paris Opera, 1983, Chatelet Theatre, Paris, 1991; dean's adv. coun. Rensselaer Poly. Inst., Troy, NY. Cons. editor Opera Quar., 1983-90. Recipient Emmy award nominations, Illuminating Engring. Soc., United Scenic Artists. Avocations: collecting ocean liner memorabilia, gardening, kayaking. Home: 1 Lincoln Plz New York NY 10023-7129 E-mail: gillights@aol.com.

WECHSLER, HAROLD HERBERT, surgeon; b. N.Y.C., July 30, 1931; s. David and Rebecca (Matthews) W.; m. Helene Wechsler; children: Lee, Gregg, Dale. BS cum laude, Tufts U.; MD, NYU. Diplomate Am. Bd. Surgery. Attending surgeon Kimbal Med. Ctr., Lakewood, N.J., Centra State Hosp., Freehold; breast surgeon Breast Health Care, Lakewood. Adj. staff surgeon Jersey Shore Med. Ctr., Neptune, N.J. Fellow ACS, Soc. Surgeons N.J.; mem. Am. Soc. Breast Surgeons, Am. Soc. Breast Disease, Med. Soc. N.J., Ocean County Med. Soc. Office: Kimbal Profl Bldg 101 Prospect Ave Ste 115 Lakewood NJ 08701

WECHSLER, HENRY, research psychologist; b. Warsaw, Poland, Aug. 16, 1932; came to U.S., 1941, naturalized, 1953; s. William and Lucy (Fryd) W.; m. Joan Goldstein, Oct. 16, 1955; children: Stephen Bruce, Pamela Jane, Peter Thomas. AB summa cum laude, Washington and Jefferson Coll., 1953; MA (Harvard Found. Advanced Study fellow, resident fellow), Harvard U., 1955, PhD in Social Psychology, 1957. USPHS postdoctoral rsch. fellow, 1957; rsch. assoc. Joint Commn. Mental Illness and Health, 1957-58; rsch. assoc., asst. prof. Clark U., 1958-59; rsch. social psychologist Mass. Mental Health Ctr., 1959-65; rsch. assoc. in psychology Med. Sch., Harvard U., 1960-66, Harvard Sch. Pub. Health, 1963-66, lectr. social psychology, 1966—, dir. Youth Alcohol-Drug Program, dept. health & social behavior, 1988—; dir. rsch. and community health programs Med. Found., Inc., Boston, 1965-88; vis. lectr. Boston U., 1967-68; pres. SocioTech. Systems, 1969-74; lectr. in rsch. Simmons Coll. Sch. Social Work, 1969-80; dir. coll. alcohol study Harvard Sch. Pub. Health, 1992—. Adj. prof. Simmons Coll. Sch. Social Work, 1981-84. Author, editor: The Threat of Impending Disaster; contbr. to books Psychology of Stress, 1964, Social Psychology and Mental Health, 1970, Emergency Medical Services: Behavioral and Planning Perspectives, 1973, Social Work Research in the Human Services, 1976, Handbook of Medical Specialties, 1976, The Horizons of Health, 1977, Explorations in Nursing Research, 1978, Handbook of Dental Specialties, 1979, Minimum Drinking Age Laws, 1980, The Social Context of Medical Research, 1981, Medical School Admissions, 1982; contbr. numerous articles to profl. jours. Fellow Am. Psychol. Assn., Am. Sociol. Assn., Am. Pub. Health Assn.; mem. Phi Beta Kappa. Clubs: Harvard (Boston). Home: 148 Puritan Dr Quincy MA 02169-1739 Office: Harvard Sch Pub Health Dept Health & Social Behavior 677 Huntington Ave Boston MA 02115-6096 E-mail: hwechsler@hsph.harvard.edu.

WECHSLER, MARY HEYRMAN, lawyer; b. Green Bay, Wis., Jan. 8, 1948; d. Donald Hubert and Helen (Polcyn) Heyrman; m. Roger Wechsler, Aug. 1971 (div. 1977); 1 child, Risa Heyrman; m. David Jay Sellinger, Aug. 15, 1981; 1 stepchild, Kirk Benjamin; 1 child, Michael Paul. Student, U. Chgo., 1966-67, 68-69; BA, U. Wash., 1971; JD cum laude, U. Puget Sound, 1979. Bar: Wash. 1979. Assoc. Law Offices Ann Johnson, Seattle, 1979-81; ptnr. Johnson, Wechsler, Thompson, 1981-83; pvt. practice, 1984-87; ptnr. Mussehl, Rosenberg et al, 1987-88, Wechsler, Becker, Erickson, Ross, Roubik & Edwards, Seattle, 1988—. Mem. Bd. of Ct. Edn., 1998—2002; bd. dirs. U. Wash. Law Sch. Child Advocacy Clinic, 1996—99; mem. Wash. State Commn. on Jud. Selection, 1995—96, Wash. State Commn. on Domestic Rels., 1996—97, 1999—2002; chair edn. com. Access to Justice Bd., 1996—99, mem. pub. trust and confidence com., 2000—02; presenter in field. Author: Family Law in Washington, 1987, rev. edit., 1988, Marriage and Separation, Divorce and Your Rights, 1994; contbr. articles to legal publs. Mem. Wash. State Ethics Adv. Com., 1992-95; bd. dirs. Seattle LWV, 1991-92. Fellow Am. Acad. Matrimonial Lawyers (Wash. state chpt., sec.-treas. 1996, v.p. 1997-98, pres. 1999-2000, nat. arbitration com. 1999-2000, nat. interdisciplinary com. 1999-2000, nat. admissions procedure com. 2000-02); mem. ABA (chmn. membership Wash. state 1987-88), Wash. State Bar Assn. (exec. com. family law sect. 1985-91, chair 1988-89, media project com. 2001, ct. improvement com. 1998-2000, legs. com. 1991-96, Outstanding Atty. of Yr. family law sect. 1988, comms. com. 1997-98, disciplinary hearing officer 1998—), Wash. Women Lawyers, King County Bar Assn. (legis. com. 1985-2000, vice-chair 1990-91, chair family law sect. 1986-87, chair domestic violence com. 1986-87, trustee 1988-90, policy planning com. 1991-92, 2d v.p. 1992-93, 1st v.p. 1993-94, pres. 1994-95, long-range planning com. 1998-99, awards com. 1997-99, Outstanding Atty. award 1999), Nat. Conf. of Bar Pres. (commn. com. 1994-95, long range planning com. 1998-99), King County Bar Found. (trustee 1997-2000), Am. Judicature Soc. (v.p. Washington chpt. 2000-2002). Office: Wechsler Becker Erickson Ross Roubik & Edwards Ste 4550 701 5th Ave Seattle WA 98104-7097

WECHSLER, SERGIO, automotive executive, consultant; b. Rio de Janeiro, Aug. 10, 1944; came to U.S., 1965; s. Michael and Gertrud (Putziger) W.; m. Suzana Brauer, June 26, 1969; children: Mark, Andrew. Student, Mackenzie U., 1962, Gen. Motors Inst. Engring., 1967; MBA in Internat. Bus., NYU, 1974; PhD in Internat. Bus., Kennedy-Western U., 1996. Quality supr. GM do Brasil, Sao Paulo, 1963-65, quality control supt., 1967-70; quality control mgr. Gillette Corp., Berlin, 1970-71; project mgr. GM, N.Y.C., 1971-76; plant mgr. GM de Portugal, Lisbon, 1976-79; project mgr. Adam Opel AG, Russelheim, Fed. Republic of Germany, 1979-81; quality dir. GM, Linden, N.J., 1981-85, dir. ops. and quality control Warren, Mich., 1985-93, mgr. internat. programs, 1985-95, program mgr. Cadillac Luxury Car divsn. Flint, 1995-96. Pres. Marswex Global Enterprises, St. Petersburg, Fla., 1982—, Hudson Plaza, 1984-99; chmn. Auto Exchange Club, Clearwater, Fla., 1997, 2001, MSX Internat., Detroit, 1996-99, v.p. German ops., 1999-2001. V.P. Temple Beth Jacob, Pontiac, Mich., 1986, pres., 1987-89. Mem. Am. Soc. Quality Control (cert. quality engr. 1992), Radio Club. Republican. Avocations: ham radio, travel, automobile restoration.

WECHSLER, SUSAN LINDA, research and development software manager; b. Burbank, Calif., Oct. 7, 1956; d. Robert Edward and Sharron Ilene Wechsler; m. Gary Daniel Grove, Aug. 24, 1975 (dec. Dec. 1980); m. Dane Bruce Rogers, Feb. 28, 1987; children: Shayna Marneen Rogers, Ayla Corinne Rogers. BA in Math., Calif. State U., Long Beach, 1979. R&D software design engr. Hewlett-Packard Co., Corvallis, Oreg., 1980-97, R&D project mgr. sys. integration team for laptops, 1997—. Presenter at confs. Contbr. articles to profl. publs.; co-developer nine calculators and handheld computers; patentee in field; co-designer HP 200LX Palmtop PC/Organizer, 1994; writer user interface DMI and BIOS software for laptop computers, 1994-97. Pres. Gifts for a Better World, Corvallis, Oreg., 1994, bd. dirs. 1990-1995. Democrat. Avocations: sewing, raising orchids, reading. Office: Hewlett-Packard Mail Stop 423A 1000 NE Circle Blvd Corvallis OR 97330-4291 E-mail: susan_wechsler@hp.com.

WECHTER, CLARI ANN, paint manufacturing company executive; b. Chgo., June 1, 1953; d. Norman Robert and Harriet Beverly (Golub) W.; m. Gordon Jay Siegel, Feb. 10, 1980; 1 child, Alix Jessica. BA, U. Ariz., 1975; BE, Loyola U., Chgo., 1977. Cert. tchr., Ill. Saleswoman, v.p. sales Federated Paint Mfg. Co., Chgo., 1979—. Republican. Jewish. Avocation: travel. Home: 25 E Cedar St Chicago IL 60611-1109 Office: Federated Paint and Pioneer Powder Mfg Co 1521 N 31st Ave Melrose Park IL 60160

WECHTER, IRA MARTIN, tax specialist, financial planner; b. Bkyn., June 26, 1947; s. Nathan Harris and Mollie (Bauer) W.; m. Myrna Ellen Rosenbaum, Dec. 22, 1968; 1 child, Megan Jill. BA, CCNY, 1969; MPA, Bernard Baruch Coll., 1973. CFP; cert. practitioner of taxation; accredited tax advisor; registered investment advisor; lic. gen. securities prin.; enrolled to practice before IRS; lic. gen. securities prin., life, health and disability ins., N.J., N.Y. Dir. adminstrv. svcs. N.Y.C. Dept. City Planning, 1971-77; dep. asst. budget dir. N.Y., N.Y.C. Office Mgmt. and Budget, 1977-81; dep. commr. N.Y.C. Dept. Environ. Protection, 1981-84; pres. Wechter Fin. Svcs., Inc., Parsippany, N.J., 1984—. Mem. Community Bd. No. 1 S.I., 1973-76, 1st v.p., 1976-77; treas. S.I. Coun. on Arts, 1974-75. Recipient Outstanding Citizenship award Borough Pres. of S.I., 1977. Mem. Nat. Assn. Enrolled Agts., Inst. Cert. Fin. Planners, Nat. Assn. Tax Practitioners, Nat. Soc. Tax Preparers, Nat. Soc. Pub. Accts. Republican. Jewish. Avocations: U.S. mint stamp collecting, organist. Office: Wechter Fin Svcs Inc 1719 State Rt 10 Ste 310 Parsippany NJ 07054-4507 also: 1719 Route 10 Ste 118 Parsippany NJ 07054-4507

WECHTER, VIVIENNE THAUL, artist, poet, educator; b. N.Y.C. d. Samuel Joshua and Hilda (Thaul) Rosenthal; m. Nathan Wechter; 1 dau., Robyrta Joan Wechter Rapoport. B. Pedagogy, Jamaica Tchrs. Coll.; postgrad., Columbia U., NYU, New Sch. for Social Rsch., Art Students League, Sculpture Ctr., Pratt Inst. Graphic Ctr.; PhD in Interarts and Psychology of Creativity, Union Inst. Artist in residence Fordham U., 1964—, asst. prof. art and esthetics, 1964, now prof. interdisciplinary creative arts, chmn. acquisitions and exhbns.; vis. poet-artist Kansas City Art Inst., 1975, Md. Inst. Coll. Art, 1975, New Sch., N.Y.C., 1976, Marist Coll., Poughkeepsie, N.Y., 1977; vis. prof. New Sch. for Social Rsch., spring 1986; past chmn. coll. liaison divsn. Bronx Coun. on Arts; vis. prof. creative devel. Miami (Fla.) Jewish Home and Hosp. for Aged, 1993; lect. Sch. Internat. Affairs U. Malta; sole U.S. rep. Internat. Brennale, Malta, 1995. Moderator: weekly radio broadcast Today's World, WFUV, 1951—, created 6 programs in South Pacific, 1986-87; one hour film, The Thunderbolt about Wechter by Prof. Donna, NYU Tisch Sch. of Arts, 1999; illustrator: (Alfeo Marzi) book cover Park of Jonas, 1965; author: A View from the Ark, 1973; contbr. articles to profl. jours.; one-woman shows Castellane Gallery, East Hampton Gallery, N.Y.C., Cornell U., Ithaca, N.Y., Neville Pub. Mus., Green Bay, Wis., Nashville Fine Arts Ctr., Fairleigh Dickinson U., Rutgers U., Waterloo (Iowa) Mcpl. Galleries, Bodley Gallery, Gloria Cortella Gallery, N.Y.C., Manhattan Coll., N.Y.C., Kouros Gallery, N.Y.C., Everson Mus. Art, Syracuse, N.Y., CCNY, B.R. Kornblatt Gallery, Balt., New Sch. Social Research, N.Y.C., Arts Interaction, N.Y.C., 1993, Douglass Gardens, Miami, also Paris, Rejik, Yugoslavia, multimedia show, Everson Mus. Fine Art, Syracuse, 1979, Dyansen Gallery, N.Y.C., 1981, L.I. U., 1986, Schiller-Wapner, N.Y.C., Shapolsky Gallery, N.Y.C., 1989, New England Mus. Contemporary Arts, 1991, 92, Douglas Gardens, Miami, 1992, Nassau County Mus. Art, 1994; solo shows and poetry readings New Sch., N.Y.C., Arts Interaction, N.Y.C., L.I. U., 1988, Arts Interaction Gallery 12, N.Y.C., 1988, 93, Fordham U., N.Y.C., 1994; represented in permanent collections Corcoran Gallery, Washington, Houston Mus. Fine Arts, Jewish Mus. N.Y.C., Fordham U., N.Y.C., Univ. Art Museum Berkeley, Calif., Museum Art and Sci., Norfolk, Va., NYU, Mus. of Fine Arts, Moscow, Russia, Mus. of Fine Art, Newark, Ohio State U., Phoenix Mus. Fine Arts, Fairleigh Dickinson U., Madison, N.J., UN, Internat. Culture Ctr., Jerusalem, Mus. Modern Art Warsaw, Poland, Mus. Fine Arts Moscow, N.J. State Mus., Trenton, others; monumental outdoor sculpture The Emerging Sun commd. for Manhattan Psychiat. Ctr., Ward's Island, N.Y.C.; permanent sculpture installed George Meany Internat. Ctr. Labor Studies, Washington, 1981, Simple Justice on Columbus Ave. nr. Lincoln Ctr., N.Y.C., 1989; logo sculpture Miami Jewish Home & Hosp. for Aged; developer, curator, 1st Biennial of Outdoor Sculpture, Fordham U. Rose Hill Campus, 1983. Author: Art, Where Are We Today and Why?, 1985; solo exbn. and video presentation New Sch. for Social Research, Mar. and Apr., 1986, Wagner-Schiller Galleries, Sept., 1986; solo painting, sculpture, video presentation and poetry reading, Nov. Dec., 1986; sole exhbn. and poetry reading, The Silver Dream, Provincetown Art Assn. and Mus., July, 1987; chair, moderator Influences in Art (Italian Am. Roundtable Art & Lit., 1988, video on RAI TV, Rome, 1989; panelist St. Bartholomew's, N.Y.C., 1987; rep., exhbns. Leister Fine Arts, Ltd., London; prin. speaker annual cong. Arts Interaction, N.Y.C., 1993. Bd. dirs. Urban Arts Corps; founder, trustee, past pres. Bronx Mus. Art; v.p. U.S. Com. IAA-UNESCO; trustee Bronx Soc. Arts and Letters, 1988—, New England Ctr. Contemporary Arts, 1992—. Recipient awards Am. Acad. Arts and Letters, awards Am. Soc. Contemporary Art, Sivler Malta Cross, 1996. Mem. Am. Abstract Artists, Univ. Council of Art Educators, Urban League Center Greater N.Y. (dir., mem. advisory bd. 1952—), United World Federalists (1st chmn.), Fedn. Modern Painters and Sculptors (v.p.), Alpha Mu Gamma, Kappa Pi. Home: New York, NY. *To be an artist-poet who requires solitude in order to create yet has the urgent need to be actively involved in the human community is a frightening challenge. Yet I know that to live one without the other will be for me, neither.* Died June 12, 2001.

WECK, EDWARD ALEXANDER, molecular biologist, biochemist; b. Gary, Ind., Aug. 26, 1952; s. Herman Immanuel and Barbara Dawn (Fiola) W.; m. Mary Lynn Beckwith, Oct. 2, 1980; children: Alex, Peter, Michael. BS in Biochemistry, U. Ill., 1974; PhD in Chemistry, U. Ark., 1981. Rsch. assoc. Advanced Genetic Scis., Oakland, Calif., 1983-85; rsch. biologist Stauffer Chem., Richmond, 1985-87; head dept. molecular genetics Northrup King, Stanton, Minn., 1987-91, head dept. molecular biology, 1991-92; tech. cons. Biotechnology Innovation, 1993-94; molecular biologist Joint FAO/IAEA Divsn., Vienna, Austria, 1995-97; pres. Consortium Plant Biotech. Rsch., Inc., St. Simons Island, Ga., 1997, BioTec Info., Northfield, Minn., 1998—. Tech. cons. Contbr. articles to profl. jours. Chair Unitarian-Univs. Fellowship, Northfield, Minn., 1990-91; dir. religious edn. Unitarian-Univs. Northfield, 1991-92; registrar Northfield Soccer Assn., 2001—; chair Northfield Environ. Quality Commn., 2001. Mem. AAAS, Am. Soc. Agronomy, Genetics Soc. Am., Internat. Soc. for Plant Molecular Biology, Northfield Environ. Quality Commn. Avocations: tennis, coaching soccer and baseball. E-mail: eweck@rconnect.com.

WECK, KRISTIN WILLA, bank executive; b. Elgin, Ill., Nov. 5, 1959; d. John Francis and Florence Elaine (Ebel) W. BBA, Augustana Coll., Rock Island, Ill., 1981. Lic. real estate broker, Ill., life/health ins. producer; registered securities rep. (series 7 and series 24); registered uniform investment advisor series 65. Intern with investment banking group First Chgo. Bank, London, 1980; intern Prudential-Bache Co., Ft. Lauderdale, Fla., 1981; residential appraiser Fox Valley Appraisal Counselors, Ltd., West Dundee, Ill., 1982-84; asst. real estate loan officer First Nat. Bank, Barrington, 1982-84; savs. and loan field examiner III Office of Thrift Supervision, Chgo., 1984-90; mng. agt. Resolution Trust Corp., Elk Grove Village, 1990-91; pres., treas., bd. dirs. Cardunal Savs. Bank, West Dundee, 1991—; dir. Prairie State Bank, Marengo, 1998—2002. Project Bus. cons. Jr. Achievement, 1992-96; literacy tutor Vols. of Am., 1998-99. Recipient Outstanding Achievement award Fed. Home Loan Bank Bd., 1985, Leading Us In Commerce and Industry award for fin. svcs., 1998, Sam Walton Bus. Cmty. Leader award, 1999. Mem. Nat. Assn. Securities Dealers (registered rep., registered prin.), Rotary Club Dundee Twp. (pres. 2001-02, Rotarian of Yr. 1997-98, Disting. Pres. 2002). Republican. Lutheran. Avocations: scuba diving, golfing, walking, reading. Home: PO Box 930 Dundee IL 60118-0930 Office: Cardunal Savs Bank 704 W Main St # 97 Dundee IL 60118-2028 E-mail: kweck@cardunal.net.

WECKER, WILLIAM A. preventive medicine physician, neuropsychiatrist; b. N.Y.C., Mar. 14, 1923; BA, NYU, 1943, MD, 1946; MPH in Adminstrn., Harvard U., 1950; diploma Sch. Aviation Medicine, USAF, 1953. Lic. physician, surgeon, psychiatrist, N.Y.; cert. treating physician N.Y. State Workmen's Compensation Bd.; qualified psychiatrist N.Y. State Dept. Mental Health. Intern Bellevue Hosp., N.Y.C., 1946, Bayonne Gen. Hosp., 1946-47; health officer N.Y.C. Health Dept., 1948-50; dist. health officer N.Y. State Health Dept., Albany, 1950-52; pvt. practice medicine N.Y.C., 1954-59; grad. Sch. Aviation Medicine USAF, 1953; resident in psychiatry U.S. VA Hosp., N.Y.C., 1959-62, psychiatrist, 1962-64, Riverside Hosp., N.Y.C. Hosp. Dept., 1964-65, Postgrad. Ctr. for Mental Health, N.Y.C., 1964-65; pvt. practice preventive medicine, neuropsychiatry, 1948—. Advisor Pan Am. Med. Assn., N.Y.C., 1952-55; cons. World Med. Assn., N.Y.C., 1954-61; staff physician Meml. Hosp., Queens, N.Y., 1955-64, Springfield (Mass.) Hosp., 1970-71; civil def. lectr. N.Y.C. Dept. of Health, 1955-58; advisor, chart mem. Acad. Religion and Mental Health, N.Y.C., 1959-62; psychiatrist, mgmt. cons., advisor in staff devel. program Youth House, N.Y.C., 1963-71; psychiatrist, cons. Mahoney Health Ctr., N.Y.C. Dept. Health, Bklyn., 1964-71; psychiatrist

N.Y. State Narcotic Addiction Control Commn., 1970-71; med. examining physician N.Y.C. Workers Compensation Bd., 1971-76 Author: 3rd World Economics, 1981, Psychecology for Everybody, 1983, Comprehensive Psychenomics, 1983, American Confetti, 1990, Anatomy of an Asylum, 1968, The Story of "H", 1971, The Honduran Syndrome, 1973, Devil's Den, 1978, Growing Up in Honduras, 1980. Cons. Allen Haus, Zurich, 1990-91; advisor English Gentlemen's Club, Zurich, 1982-87, Centro Cultural, Honduras, 1978-82; corr. Harry Schulz Internat. Newsletter, Switzerland and monaco, 1983-91. 2d lt. U.S. Army, 1943-45, ATO, capt. MC-USAF, 1952-54, ETO. Fellow Nat. Poliomyelitis Found., 1949-50, U.S. VA, 1960-61, NIMH fellow Postgrad. Ctr. for Mental Health, N.Y.C., 1964-65; recipient 50th Anniversary cert. NYU, 1996; decorated Nat. Def. Svc. medal, WWII Victory medal, Am. Theatre medal, Occupation medal (Germany). Mem. VFW, Am. Legion, Acad. Medicine Bklyn. (life), Nat. Inst. Mental Health, N.Y. State Med. Soc. (life, citation for 50 yrs. of svc. 1996), N.Y. Coun. Child Psychiatry, Kings County Med. Soc. (life), Royal Soc. Health (London), VFW. Avocations: medical astrology and medical psychology, writing science books, esperanto and languages. Home: 859 Chenango St Binghamton NY 13901-1745

WECKESSER, ERNEST PROSPER, JR. publisher, educator; b. Akron, Ohio, Mar. 23, 1933; s. Ernest Prosper and Sadie (Liken) W.; m. Mary B. Hunter, Jan. 12, 1959; children— Jeffrey, Franz, Kathleen, Lynne. BA, Bowling Green State U., 1955, MA, 1960; PhD, Mich. State U., 1963. Asst. prof. speech SUNY-Oneonta, 1962-63, Kent State U., 1963-64; mem. faculty Purdue U., 1964-70, assoc. prof., 1968-70; prof. speech Montclair (N.J.) Coll., 1970-71; assoc. prof. speech Pa. State U., 1971-72; dir. Ernest Weckesser Assos.; chmn. bd. dirs. Green Tree Press, Inc., Dunkirk, N.Y.; pres. Bierhaus Internat., Inc., Erie, Pa. Author: The Radio Rhetoric of John L. Lewis, 1963, How To Succeed in College, 1971, The 12,000 Housewife, 1975, Dollars in Your Mailbox, 1975, Alternatives: A Network of Small Business Opportunities, 1992; co-author: The Bradley-Cooper Smoke Cessation Program, 1995. Bd. dirs. Florerence Crittenden Home, Erie, Erie County Ct. Apptd. Spl. Advocates for children; Mem. Pres.'s Council Gannon U.; Mem. adv. bd. Villa Maria Coll. Served to capt. USAF, 1955—59, provost marshal, 1956—59, RAF Sta. Woodbridge, Eng. Named Disting. Pennsylvanian William Penn Soc., 1983

WECKESSER, SUSAN ONEACRE, lawyer; b. Akron, Ohio, July 23, 1938; d. Leland E. and Maryethel (Parsons) Oneacre; m. John V. Rhinehart, Mar. 28, 1958 (div. 1971); children: Kirk Andrew Rhinehart, Kristin Rhinehart; m. John C. Weckesser, Aug. 19, 1972 (div. 1997). BEd, Ohio U., 1959; MA, CUNY, 1974; JD, U. N.Mex., 1983. Bar: N.Mex. 1983, U.S. Dist. Ct. (N.Mex.) 1984, U.S. Ct. Appeals (10th cir.) 1987. Dir. publs. N.Mex. Mcpl. League, Santa Fe, 1972-83; assoc. Patrick A. Casey, 1983-86; pvt. practice, 1986-98; mem. legal bur. N. Mex. Risk Mgmt. Divsn., 1998—. Bd. dirs. St. Elizabeth Shelter, Santa Fe, 1996—. Mem.: N.Mex. Trial Lawyers Assn. (bd. dirs. 1996—98). Democrat. Office: PO Box 4819 Santa Fe NM 87502-4819

WECKSELL, ALAN, radiologist; b. N.Y.C., 1939; MD, N.Y. Med. Coll., 1965. Diplomate Am. Bd. Radiology. Intern L.I. Coll. Hosp., Bklyn., 1965-66, resident in radiology, 1966-69; hosp. staff radiology North Shore U. Hosp., Manhasset, 1991—; asst. clin. prof. radiology NYU. Mem. AMA, Am. Roentgen Ray Soc., Radiol. Soc. of N.Am. Office: North Shore Hosp Radiology Manhasset NY 11030 Address: Irving Goldman Family Care Ctr 865 Northern Blvd Great Neck NY 11021

WECLEW, VICTOR T. retired dentist; b. Chgo., Mar. 18, 1916; m. Gertrude David, 1945; 1 child, Victor T. III BS, U. Ill., 1939, D.D.S., 1943. Gen. practice dentistry, Chgo., 1946-86. Contbr. articles to profl. jours. Active Boy Scouts Am. Served to maj. AC, U.S. Army, 1943-46. Fellow Acad. Gen. Dentistry (co-founder 1952, bd. dirs., asst. editor jour. 21 yrs.), Acad. Continuing Edn. (co-founder 1974), Am. Coll. Dentists, Acad. of Dentistry Internat. (trustee); mem. ADA, Ill. State Dental Soc., Chgo. Dental Soc. (various coms., past. dir., pres. N.W. br. 1969-70), U. Ill. Dental Alumni Assn. (bd. dirs. 10 yrs., Disting. Alumnus award 1991), Omicron Kappa Upsilon, Psi Omega. Roman Catholic. Home: 5781 N Forest Glen Ave Chicago IL 60646-6610 E-mail: vicwec@cs.com.

WEDDERMAN, WAYNE ALLAN, elementary school educator; b. New Brunswick, N.J. s. Richard Wedderman, Emma Victoria Soukup; m. Deborah Ann Vosseller, Oct. 4, 1969 (div. Dec. 1994); children: Wayne A. Jr., Eric Jay, Tara Marie; m. Barbara Joan Posik, Dec. 28, 1994. BA, Rutgers U., New Brunswick, N.J., 1969. Cert. tchr. music K-12 N.J. Tchr. Warren Twp. Bd. of Edn., Warren, NJ, 1969—73, Jackson Twp. Bd. of Edn., Jackson, 1973—. 1st lt. U.S. Army, 1970—71. Named Tchr. of Yr., Rosenauer Elem. Sch., 1995; recipient Innovator award, Jackson Schs., 1996, Supt. Superlative award, Rosenauer Elem. Sch., 2002. Avocations: record collecting, antique phonographs, fishing, antique collecting. Home: 174 20th Ave Brick NJ 08724 Mailing: Sylvia Rosenauer Elem Sch 60 Citadel Dr Jackson NJ 08724

WEDDING, CHARLES RANDOLPH, architect; b. St. Petersburg, Fla., Nov. 16, 1934; s. Charles Reid and L. Marion (Whitaker) W.; m. Audrey Whitsel, Aug. 18, 1956 (div. Apr. 1979); children: Daryl L., Douglas R., Dorian B.; m. Vonnie Sue Hayes, June 22, 1984 (div. Dec. 1991); stepchildren: Stephanie W., Brian E.; m. June A. Free, Mar. 31, 1993; stepchildren: Gregory, Kristine. BArch, U. Fla., 1957. Registered arch., Fla., Ga., N.C., S.C., Del., Va., Tex., Ill., Ind., Kans., La., Mo., Okla., Tenn. Arch. in tng. Harvard & Jolly AIA, St. Petersburg, 1957-60; arch., prin., pres. Wedding & Assocs., 1960—. Mayor City of St. Petersburg, 1973-75; past chmn. Pinellas County Com. of 100, Bldg. Dept. Survey Team, City of St. Petersburg; trustee All Children's Hosp., 1968-70; sect. leader St. Petersburg United Fund, 1965-70; mem. city coun. Action Team for Pier Redevel., 1967-68; mem. exec. com. Goals for City of St. Petersburg, 1970-72; den leader Webelos, Boy Scouts Am., 1971-72; chmn., trustee Canterbury Sch. YMCA, 1968-72; mem. adv. com. Tomlinson Vocat. Sch., 1969-79; past trustee Mus. Fine Arts; past bd. dirs. Neighborly Ctr., Jr. Achievement Pinellas County; chair Downtown Partnership, 2001—. Served to 1st lt. U.S. Army, 1958-60. Fellow AIA (5 Silver Spike awards, Merit of Honor, Medal of Honor); mem. Am. Soc. Landscape Archs., St. Petersburg Assn. Archs. (past pres.), Fla. Assn. Archs. (8 Merit Design awards), St. Petersburg Yacht Club, Suncoasters Club. Republican. Episcopalian. Avocations: sailing, hunting, golfing, tennis. Home: 6900 10th Ave N Saint Petersburg FL 33710-6152 Office: Wedding/Stephenson/Ibargüen Archs Inc 300 1st Ave S Saint Petersburg FL 33701-4209 E-mail: randy@weddingarchitects.com.

WEDDINGTON, ELIZABETH GARDNER (LIZ GARDNER), actress, editor; b. N.Y.C., Oct. 13, 1932; d. A. Adolph and Anne Mary (Gardner) Blank; m. George Lee Weddington, Jr., Oct. 23, 1965; 1 child, Georgiana Marie. Student, Moravian Sem. for Girls. Actress TV, radio, telephone, N.Y./Calif, 1957—; editor comml. scripts N.Y., 1969—; freelance writer N.Y. City Tribune, various other publs., 1984—. Columnist polit. commentary, 1984—; appeared in over 300 TV commls., also TV and radio voice-overs. Mem. County Com., Conservative Party, N.Y.C., 1988-90, 94-96, 17th Precinct Comty. Coun., N.Y.C., 1974-96; rep. Yorkville Area Cath. Coun., N.Y.C., 1986-93. Recipient Mayor's Vol. Action Ctr. award, N.Y.C., 1981-82, Cert. Recognition N.Y.C. Dept. Police Dep. Commr. Community Affairs, 1981. Mem.: Nat. League Am. Pen Women, Am. Fedn. Radio and TV Artists, Screen Actors Guild, N.Y. State Soc. Children Am. Revolution (sr. historian 1988—90, sr. 2d v.p. 1990—92), Colonial Dames Am. (N.Y. claims com. 1993—96, chpt. XXIX N.C. 1999—, courtesy mem. parent chpt.), Daus. Colonial Wars, United Daus. of Confederacy (pres. N.Y. divsn. 1988—90, nat. chmn. revision of gen. bylaws com. 1989—91, McMath Scholar gen. com. 1991—92, nat. chmn. gen. bylaws com. 1992—96, gen. chmn. radio and TV com. 1998—2000, mem. Mrs. Simon Baruch Univ. award com. 2000—), N.Y. State Soc. Dames of Ct. of Honor (pres. 1984—88), N.Y. State Soc. Daus. 1812, Nat. Soc. U.S. Daus. of 1812 (organizing pres. Pres. James Madison chpt. 360 1988—98), Nat. Soc. Children and Am. Revolutin - Fraunces Tavern Soc. (sr. pres. 1985—89), Nat. Soc. DAR (assoc.; corr. sec. 1992—94, Washington colonial chpt. 1996—, Mary Washington Colonial chpt. 1996—, mem. Warren chpt. 1996—, chair nat. defense com. 2001—, treas. 2001—, Warren chpt., chmn. com. Mary Washington Colonial chpt.). Republican. Roman Catholic. Avocations: genealogy, military, English, constitutional and religious history, opera, antiques, porcelains. Home and Office: 316 N Main St Warrenton NC 27589-1826 E-mail: betsy1013@vance.net.

WEDDINGTON, SARAH RAGLE, lawyer, educator, speaker, writer; b. Abilene, Tex., Feb. 5, 1945; d. Herbert Doyle and Lena Catherine Ragle. BS magna cum laude, McMurry Coll., 1965, hon. doctorate, 1979; JD, U. Tex., 1967; hon. doctorate, Hamilton Coll., 1979, Southwestern U., 1989, Austin Coll., 1993, Nova Southeastern U., 1999. Bar: Tex. 1967, D.C. 1979, U.S. Dist. Ct. (we., no. and ea. dists.) Tex., U.S. Ct. Appeals (5th cir.), U.S. Supreme Ct. Pvt. practice law, Austin, 1967-77; gen. counsel Dept. Agr., Washington, 1977-78; spl. asst. to U.S. pres., 1978—79; asst. to U.S. pres., 1979—81; chmn. Interdepartmental Task Force on Women, 1978-81; mem. Pres.'s Commn. on Exec. Exchange, 1981; Carl Hatch prof. law and pub. adminstrn. U. N.Mex., Albuquerque, 1982-83; pvt. practice law Austin, Tex., 1985—; dir. Tex. Office State-Fed. Rels., Austin, Washington, 1983-85. Vis. prof. govt. Wheaton Coll., Norton, Mass., 1981-83; sr. lectr. Tex. Woman's U., Denton, 1981-90, 93, U. Tex., Austin, 1986—. Author: A Question of Choice, 1992; contbg. editor Glamour mag., 1981-83. Mem. Tex. Ho. of Reps., 1973-77. Recipient Woman of Yr. award Tex. Women's Polit. Caucus, 1973, Time Mag. Outstanding Young Am. Leaders, 1979, Leadership awards Ladies Home Jour., 1980, spl. recognition Esquire mag., 1984, Elizabeth (Betty) Boyer award Equity Action League, 1992, Woman Who Dares award Nat. Coun. Jewish Women, 1993, Woman of Distinction award Nat. Conf. for Coll. Women Student Leaders, 1993, Colby award for Pub. Svc. Sigma Kappa, 1996, Hummingbird award Leadership Am., 1998, Tallest Texan award Houston Chronicle, 2000, Speaking Out for Justice award AAUW Legal Advocacy Fund, 2001, Ally award Possible Woman Leadership Conf., 2001; named Lectr. of Yr. Nat. Assn. for Coll. Activities, 1990, Tex. Women's C. of C. Tex. Woman of Century, 1999, San Antonio Express News Face of Century, 1999, 2000; named One of the Most Influential Lawyers of the 20th Century, Tex. Lawyer, 2000; Sarah Weddington Leadership Conf. named in her honor, Tex. Woman's U., 2001. Mem. Tex. Bar Assn. Office: The Weddington Ctr 709 W 14th St Austin TX 78701-1707 E-mail: sw@weddingtoncenter.com.

WEDDINGTON, SUSAN, political party official; m. Bob Weddington; 1 child, Sean. BA in Comms. with honors, Trinity U. Tchr. photojournalism; owner three small bus.; dir. media rels. Tex. Conservative Coalition, rsch. analyst; legis. asst. Rep. state rep.; vice chmn. Rep. Party Tex., 1994, 96, state chmn., 1997—. Del. four State Rep. Convs.; Tex. del. Rep. Nat. Conv., San Diego, 1996, Tex. rep. Nat. Rules Com.; worked 76 in 96 Polit. Action Com.; RPT liaison Campaign for Rep. Leadership Polit. Action Com. Active Drug Stop, San Antonio Citizens Against Pornography, crisis pregnancy ctrs.; bd. dirs. Pray Tex.; mem. Castle Hills First Bapt. Ch., San Antonio; dir. comms., rsch. Tex. Pub. Policy Found. Mem. Nat. Coun. Women Advisors to Congress (charter), Bexar County Rep. Women's Forum, Daus. of Liberty Rep. Club, Bexar County Hispanic Rep. Women's Club. Office: 211 E 7th St Ste 620 Austin TX 78701-3218*

WEDDLE, DOUGLAS PAUL, family practice physician; b. South Bend, Ind., Jan. 28, 1943; s. Paul Emerson and Pauline (Burger) W.; children: Jodi Lynn, Julia Anne, Mark Douglas. AB, Manchester Coll., 1965; MD, Ind. U., 1969. Diplomate Am. Bd. Family Practice. Intern Meml. Hosp., South Bend, 1969-70; resident Midland (Mich.) Hosp., 1972-73; gen. practice Hosp. Castañer, P.R., 1970-72; group practic Newman-Young Clinic, Ft. Scott, Kans., 1973-85, Ft. Scott Family Physicians, 1985—. Trustee Mercy Health System Kans., Ft. Scott, 1998—; pres. med. staff Mercy Hosp., Ft. Scott, 1983-85; chief of staff Hosp. Castañer, 1971-72. Bd. dirs. Kans. divsn. Am. Cancer Soc., 1994-96, pres. Bourbon County chpt., 1986-91. Fellow Am. Acad. Family Physicians; mem. AMA, Kans. Med. Soc., Kans. Acad. Family Physicians, Bourbon County Med. Soc. Avocation: sailing. Office: Ft Scott Family Physicians 902 Horton St Fort Scott KS 66701-2438

WEDDLE, LAURA MILDRED THOMAS, retired language educator; b. Keene, Ky., June 28, 1933; d. John Wesley and Elizabeth (Munson) Thomas; m. Leo Franklin Weddle, June 15, 1955; children: Laura Lynn, Leo Jeffrey. BA, Georgetown Coll., 1955; MA, U. Ky., 1959, Morehead State U., 1977, MA, 1986. Asst. prof. Campbellsville (Ky.) Coll., 1961—65, U. Ky. C.C., Somerset, 1965—66, assoc. prof. Prestonsburg, 1966—72, prof., 1972—94; ret. Adv. bd. Nat. Coun. Staff Devel., Washington, 1975—90, David (Ky.) Alternative Sch., 1980—90. Author short stories. Dir. Children's Theater, Prestonsburg, 1970—75; mem. Prestonsburg City Coun., 1973—74. Mem.: Penwomen Am. Avocations: reading, antiques, traveling, swimming.

WEDEEN, RICHARD PETER, physician; b. Bklyn., Jan. 19, 1934; s. Marcus D. and Dorothy Mason; m. Roberta Rubien, June 28, 1957; 1 child, Timothy Douglas. AB, Harvard Coll., 1955; MD, NYU, 1959. Diplomate Am. Bd. Internal Medicine, Am. Bd. Nephrology. Intern Beth Israel Hosp., N.Y.C., 1959-60, med. resident, 1960-61, Mt. Sinai Hosp., N.Y.C., 1963-64, rsch. fellow in medicine, NIH trainee, 1961-63, rsch. asst., 1961-65, rsch. assoc., 1965-66, Polechek Found. Fellow, 1967-68; various hosp. appointments to dir., dept. medicine Jersey City Med. Ctr., 1976-78; assoc., chief of staff for rsch. and devel. VA Med. Ctr., East Orange, N.J., 1978—; staff physician Univ. Hosp., Newark, 1990—. Various univ. positions, including prof. medicine, prof. preventive medicine, 1990—, prof. of medicine, 1976—, others; vis. lectr. Harvard Med. Sch., Boston, 1968-69; vis. prof. U. Antwerp, Edegem, Belgium, 1985, others. Author: Poison in the Pot: The Legacy of Lead, 1984; co-editor: Toxic Circles: Environmental Hazards from the Workplace into the Community, 1993; contbg. editor: Am. Jour. Indsl. Medicine, 1987-92; cons. editor: Archives of Environ. Health, 1986—; asst. editor: Mt. Sinai Jour. Medicine, 1990—; contbr. articles to profl. jours. Active Operation Crossroads Africa, 1964-76, others. Recipient VA Merit Rev., 1978-88; rsch. grantee NIH, 1964-77, Nat. Inst. Environ. Health Svcs., 1993-98, others. Fellow Am. Coll. Physicians, Collegium Ramazzini, Am. Physiol. Soc., Am. Fedn. Clin. Rsch. Med. Hist. Soc. N.J. (v.p. 1986-87, pres. 1988-89); mem. Am. Soc. Clin. Investigation (emeritus). Office: VA Medical Ctr Tremont Ave East Orange NJ 07018-1095

WEDEL, CHERYL STRUM, social worker; b. Richmond, Va., Nov. 7, 1963; d. Michael David and Sylvia Marie (Arthurs) Strum; m. Stuart William Wedel, Oct. 17, 1992; children: Joshua, Matthew. BS in Social Work, Va. Commonwealth U., 1986, MSW, 1989. Social worker VA Med. Ctr., Hunter Holmes McGuire Hosp., Richmond, 1988-89, Libbie Convalescent Ctr., Richmond, 1989-90; social worker, discharger planner Riverside Tappahannock (Va.) Hosp. & Skilled Nursing Home, 1990-91; case mgr., social worker Health-south Med. Ctr. Rehab. Unit, Richmond, 1991-92; admissions coord. Marshall (Va.) Manor, 1993; case mgr./social worker Prince William Hosp., Manassas, Va., 1993—. Mem. NASW, Va. Orgn. Hosp. Social Workers, Prince William Interfaith Vol. Caregivers (bd. 1994-95). Avocations: cooking, youth soccer, gardening.

WEDEL, PAUL GEORGE, retired hospital administrator; b. Elizabeth, N.J., Jan. 1, 1927; s. Paul John and Helen (Cleary) W.; m. Jean Marie Martin, June 18, 1949; children: Dana Lyn Wedel, Laurie Ann Wedel Bouthan, Paul John II, Kurt Frederick. Grad., Peddie Sch., Hightstown, N.J., 1944; BS in Bus. Adminstrn., Am. U., 1952; MS in Hosp. Adminstrn., Northwestern U., 1955. Adminstrv. resident Harrisburg (Pa.) Polyclinic Hosp., 1953-54; asst. adminstr. Williamsport (Pa.) Hosp., 1954-59, adminstr., 1959-64; pres. Lancaster (Pa.) Gen. Hosp., 1964-89, Lancaster Gen. Hosp. Found., 1989-92, pres. emeritus, 1992—; ret., 1994. Bd. dirs. Inter-County Hospitalization Plan, Inc., 1966-84, James Buchanan Found., Preservation Wheatland, 1968-80, Linden Hall Sch., 1984-91; sr. warden St. Thomas Episcopal Ch., 1979-81; trustee Millersville U., 1991—. Served with USNR, 1944-46, 50-51. Named Outstanding Young Man, Williamsport Jr. C. of C., 1957 Fellow Am. Coll. Health Care Execs. (regent Pa. 1984-89); mem. Am. Hosp. Assn., Hosp. Assn. Pa. (bd. dirs. 1970-73, 84-89), Lancaster Assn. Commerce and Industry (bd. dirs.), Hamilton Club, Pirates Club Slubering Groonmog Lodge, Quarryville Pa, Rotary (pres. 1978-79), Masons. Home: Rock Rimmon Ridges 203 Riveredge Dr Leola PA 17540-9745 E-mail: pgwedelpax@webtv.net.

WEDEL-COWGILL, MILLIE REDMOND, secondary school educator, performing arts educator; b. Harrisburg, Pa., Aug. 18, 1939; d. Clair L. and Florence (Heiges) Aungst; m. T.S. Redmond, 1956 (div. 1967); children: T.S. Redmond II; m. Frederick L. Wedel, Jr., 1974 (div. 1986); m. Paul R. Cowgill, May 19, 2001. BA, Alaska Meth. U., 1966; MEd, U. Alaska, Anchorage, 1972; postgrad. in comm., Stanford U., 1975-76. Lic. third class broadcasting, FCC. Profl. actress Charming Models & Models Guild of Phila., 1954-61; asst. dir. devel. in charge pub. rels. Alaska Meth. U., Anchorage, 1966, part-time lectr., 1966, 73; comm. tchr. Anchorage Sch. Dist., 1967-96; owner Wedel Prodns., Anchorage, 1976-86; cons. comms., media and edn. Pub. rels. staff Alaska Purchase Centennial Exhibit, U.S. Dept. Commerce, 1967; writer gubernatorial campaign, 1971; instr. Chapman Coll., 1990-93; adj. instr. U. Alaska, Anchorage, 1972, 77-79, 89-2001; cons. Cook Inlet Native Assn., 1978, No. Inst., 1979; judge Ark. Press Women's Writing Contest, 1990-91; sec. exec. bd. Alaska Dept. Edn. Profl. Tchg. Practices Commn., 1993-94. Bd. dirs. Sta. KAKM, Alaska Pub. TV, membership chmn., 1978-80, nat. lay rep. to Pub. Broadcasting Svc. and Nat. Assn. Pub. TV Stas., 1979; bd. dirs. Ednl. Telecom. Consortium for Alaska, 1979, Mid-Hillside Cmty. Coun., Municipality of Anchorage, 1979-80, 83-88, Hillside East Cmty. Coun., 1984-88, pres., 1984-85; rsch. writer, legal asst. Vinson & Elkins, Houston, 1981; v.p., bd. dirs. Inlet View ASD Cmty. Sch., 1994-95, pres., 1995-97; mem. Valley Forge Freedoms Found., Murdoch Scholarships, Valley Forge; bd. dirs. Rev. Richard Gay Trust, Alaska and Pa., 1992—; active Anchorage Opera Guild, Anchorage Concert Assn. Recipient awards for newspapers, lit. mags.; award Nat. Scholastic Press Assn., 1981, 82, 83, 84; Alaska Coun. Econs., 1982, Merits award Alaska Dept. Edn., 1982-93, Legis. commendation State of Alaska, Nat. Blue Ribbon Outstanding Sch. award, 1993. Mem. NEA (AEA bldg. rep., state del. 70s, 80s, 94-95), Assn. Pub. Broadcasting (charter mem., nat. lay del. 1980), Indsl. TV Assn. (San Francisco and Houston 1975-81), Alaska Press Club (chmn. high sch. journalism workshops, 1968-69, 73, awards for sch. newspapers 1972, 74, 77), Alaska Fedn. Press Women (dir. 1978-86, 94-95, pres. 1995-96, h.s. journalism competition youth projects dir., award for brochures 1978, chair youth writing contest 1994-95), Internat. Platform Assn., World Affairs Coun., Chugach Electric (chair 1990, nomination com. for bd. dirs. 1988-90), Stanford U. Alumni Club (Alaska pres. 1982-84, 90-92, 99-2000, v.p. 1998-99), Petroleum Club Anchorage, Rotary, Imperial Golf Course Country Club, Club at Pelican Bay, Naples (Fla.) Philharm. League, Naples Players Theatre Guild, Pelican Bay Women's League, Delta Kappa Gamma. Presbyterian. Office: PO Box 111489 Anchorage AK 99511-1489 also: PO Box 770662 Naples FL 34107-0662

WEDEPOHL, LEONHARD MARTIN, electrical engineering educator; b. Pretoria, Republic of South Africa, Jan. 26, 1933; s. Martin Willie and Liselotte B.M. (Franz) W.; m. Sylvia A.L. St. Jean; children: Martin, Graham. B.Sc. (Eng.), Rand U., 1953; PhD, U. Manchester, Eng., 1957. Registered profl. engr., B.C. Planning engr. Escom, Johannesburg, Republic of South Africa, 1957-61; mgr. L.M. Erricson, Pretoria, Republic of South Africa, 1961-62; sect. leader Reyrolle, Newcastle, Eng., 1962-64; prof., head dept. Manchester U., 1964-74; dean engring. U. Manitoba, Winnipeg, Can., 1974-79; dean applied sci. U. B.C., Vancouver, Can., 1979-85, prof. elec. engring. Can., 1985-97, prof. emeritus Can., 1998—, dean applied sci. emeritus Can., 1998—. Mem. Sci. Rsch. Coun., London, 1968-74; dir. Manitoba Hydro, Winnipeg, 1975-79, B.C. Hydro, Vancouver, 1980-84, B.C. Sci. Coun., 1982-84; cons. Horizon Robotics, Saskatoon, 1986; chmn. implementation team Sci. Place, Can., 1985; cons. CEPEL, Rio de Janeiro; adv. Manitoba High Voltage D.C. Rsch. Ctr.; tech. advisor RTDS Techs., Inc., Winnipeg, 1994—; head protection devel. Rolls Royce Indsl. Power Group, 1995-96. Contbr. articles to sci. jours.; patentee in field Named Hon. Citizen City of Winnipeg, 1979 Fellow Instn. Elec. Engrs. (premium 1967), Engring. Inst. Can.; mem. Assn. Profl. Engrs. B.C. Avocations: music, cross-country skiing, hiking. Office: 1511 Chardonnay Pl Westbank BC Canada V4T 2P9 E-mail: wedepohl@home.com.

WEDGE, CHRIS, animation director, studio executive; Stop-motion animator; with MAGI/SynthaVision; v.p. creative devel., founder Blue Sky, Ossining, N.Y. Animator films Tron, 1992, Joe's Apt., 1996, Alien Resurrection, 1997, Bunny, 1998 (Best Animation Oscar award 1999); dir. Ice Age, 2002; creator ind. films The Daymaker, Tuber's Two Step, Balloon Guy. Office: c/o Jayson Engquist Blue Sky Studios Inc 44 S Broadway 17th Fl White Plains NY 10601 also: Blue Sky Prodns 100 Executive Blvd Ossining NY 10562-2557 Fax: (914) 259-6505. E-mail: christ@blueskystudios.com.*

WEDGE, THOMAS WILLIM, occult consultant, criminologist; b. Carey, Ohio, Oct. 16, 1943; s. Rosco Wedge and Margreat (Twining) Casper; m. Brenda Susan Krum, Oct. 6, 1966; 1 child, Gloria. BA, Cedarville Coll., 1981-84; diploma in Bible, Worthing Bible Inst., 1981; student, Central State Coll., 1984, Moody Bible Inst., 1984. Finish carpenter, Columbus, Ohio, 1967-76; sales mgr. Key Renault, 1971-76, Miley's Sporting Goods, Delaware, 1976-80; dir. Logan County Residential Treatment Ctr., Bellefontaine, 1984-89; jail adminstr. Union County Sheriff's Dept., Marysville, 1985-86; prin. Tom Wedge Co., Columbus, 1989—. Lectr. in field. Author: The Satan Hunter, 1989. With U.S. Army, 1963-66, Vietnam. Recipient Disting. Svc. award Sheriff's Office Punta Gorda, Fla., 1988, Sheriff's Office Jefferson Parish, 1990, Appreciation plaque La. State Police Acad., 1989; named for Disting. Svc., Atty. Gen. Ohio, 1992. Mem. Am. Soc. Law Enforcement Trainers, Nat. Sheriff's Assn., Internat. Assn. Asian Gangs, Ohio Crime Prevention Assn., Midwest Gang Investigation Assocs. (instr.). Republican. Baptist. Avocations: golf, fishing.

WEDGEWORTH, ANN, actress; b. Abilene, Tex., Jan. 21, 1935; m. Rip Torn (div.); 1 child, Danae; m. Ernest Martin; 1 child, Dianna. Attended, U. Tex.; BA in Drama, So. Methodist U. Broadway debut in Make A Million, 1958; other Broadway appearances Chapter Two (Tony award), Thieves, Blues for Mr. Charlie, The Last Analysis; off-Broadway appearances Line, Chapparal, The Crucible, Days and Nights of Beebee Fenstermaker, Ludlow Fair, The Honest to God Shnozzola, A Lie of the Mind, Elba, The Debutante's Ball; premier of In the Moonlight Eddie at Pasadena Playhouse; toured with nat. cos. of The Sign in Sidney Brustein's Window and Kennedy's Children; appeared: in TV series Three's Company, The Edge of Night, Another World, Somerset, Filthy Rich, Evening Shade; other TV appearances All That Glitters, The Equalizer, Roseanne, Bronk, Evening Shade, Twilight Zone, Trapper John, M.D.; TV film The War Between the Tates, Right to Kill, Cooperstown, Fight for Justice: The Nancy Conn Story, Bogie, A Stranger Waits; movies Handle With Care (Nat. Soc. Film Critics award), Thieves, Bang the Drum Slowly, Scarecrow, Catamount Killing, Law and Disorder, One Summer Love, Dragon-Fly, Birch Intervals, Soggy Bottom, USA, No Small Affair, Sweet Dreams, Mens Club, A Tiger's Tale, Made in Heaven, Far North, Miss Firecracker, Green Card, Steel Magnolias, Love and a 45, The Whole Wide World, The Hunter's Moon (aka Wolverton Mountain), My Science Project. Address: 70 Riverside Dr Apt 6E New York NY 10024-5716

WEDGWOOD, JOSIAH FRANCIS, pediatrician, immunologist; b. Boston, Feb. 1, 1950; s. Ralph Josiah and Virginia (Hunt) W.; m. Ruth Glushien, May 29, 1982; 1 child, Josiah Ruskin. AB, Harvard U., 1971, PhD, 1978; MD, George Washington U., 1980. Diplomate Am. Bd. Pediat., Am. Bd. Neonatal/Perinatal Medicine, Am. Bd. Clin. and Lab. Immunology. Intern, then resident in pediat. Cornell U. Sch. Med., N.Y.C., 1980-83; asst. prof. pediat. Schneider Children's Hosp., New Hyde Park, N.Y., 1985-89, Mt. Sinai Sch. Med., N.Y.C., 1989-98, Yale Med. Sch., New Haven, 1998—; dir. newborn svcs. Hosp. St. Raphael, 1998—. Sci. advisory bd. Jeffrey Modell Found., N.Y.C., 1991—; mem. infection control com., pharmacy/therapeutics com. Hosp. St. Raphael, New Haven, 1999—. Contbr. articles to profl. jours. including J. Biol. Chemistry, Clin. Immunology and Immunopathology, and Pediatrics. Pediat. Infectious Diseses and Immunology fellow Cornell U. Sch. Medicine, 1983-85; recipient Basil O'Connor award, March of Dimes, 1991-93. Mem. Harvey Soc., Am. Acad. Pediatrics, Am. Col. Rheumatology, New Haven Lawn Club. Avocations: gardening, pottery. Home: 240 Saint Ronan St New Haven CT 06511-2314 Office: Hosp St Raphael 1450 Chapel St New Haven CT 06511-4440 E-mail: jwedgwood@srhs.org.

WEDGWOOD, RUTH, law educator, international affairs expert; b. N.Y.C. d. Morris P. and Anne (Williams) Glushien; m. Josiah Francis Wedgwood; May 29, 1982; 1 child, Josiah Ruskin Wedgwood. BA magna cum laude, Harvard U., 1972; fellow, London Sch. Econs., 1972-73; JD, Yale U., 1976. Bar: D.C., N.Y., U.S. Supreme Ct. Law clk. to judge Henry Friendly U.S. Ct. Appeals (2d cir.), N.Y.C., 1976-77; law clk. to justice Harry Blackmun U.S. Supreme Ct., Washington, 1977-78; spl. asst. to asst. atty. gen. U.S. Dept. Justice, 1978-80; asst. U.S. atty. U.S. Dist. Ct. (so. dist.) N.Y., N.Y.C., 1980-86; prof. law Yale U., New Haven, 1986—, faculty fellow Inst. for Social and Policy Studies, 1989—; faculty fellow Berkeley Coll., Yale U., 1989—; faculty internat. security program Yale U., 1992—, faculty UN studies program, 1992—. Mem. Sec. of State's Adv. Com. Internat. Law,

1993—; dir., sr. fellow project internat orgns. and law Coun. Fgn. Rels., 1994—; Chalres Stockton prof. internat. law U.S. Naval War Coll., Newport, RI, 1998—99; mem. Hart-Rudman Commn. on Nat. Security in the 21st Century, Dept. Def. Adv. Comm., 1999—2001; mem. acad. adv. com. to spl. rep. UN Sec.-Gen. for Children and Armed Conflict, 1999—; dir. studies Am. Soc. Internat. Law, 2000—; Edward B. Burling profl internat. law and diplomacy, dir. internat. law and orgns. programs Nitze Sch. ADvances Internat. Studies, Johns Hopkins U., Washington, 2001—; guest scholar U.S. Inst. Peace, 2001—; dir. studies Hague Acad. Inernat. Law, The Netherlands, 2001—. Exec. editor Yale Law Jour., 1975-76; author: The Revolutionary Martyrdom of Jonathan Robbins, 1990, The Use of Force in International Affairs, 1992, American National Interest and the United Nations, 1996, Toward an International Criminal Court?, 1999, After Dayton: Lessons of the Bosnian Peace Process, 1999; mem. bd. editors Yale Jour. Law and Humanities, 1988-98, Am. Jour. Internat. Law, 1998—, World Policy Jour. (New Sch. Social Rsch.), 2001-; contbr. articles to profl jours. and popular publs. including N.Y. Times, Washington Post, Christian Sci. Monitor, Internat. Herald Tribune, Washington Times, Fin. Times, L.A. Times, Fgn. Affairs; commentator for CNN, Fox. Nat. Pub. Radio, Pub Broadcasting Systems. Prin. rapporteur U.S. Atty. Gen.'s Guidelines on FBI Undercover Ops., Informant Use and Racketeering and Gen. Crime Investigations, 1980; bd. dirs. Lawyers Com. for Human Rights, N.Y.C., 1988-94; mem. policy adv. com. UN Assn. U.S.A., 1998—; bd. dirs. Lawyers Alliance for World Security, 1999—. Recipient Israel Peres prize, 1976, Disting. Contbn. to Internat. Law award N.Y. State Bar Assn., 2000; Ford Found. Rsch. grantee; Rockefeller Found. fellow. Mem. ABA, Am. Law Inst., Am. Soc. Internat. Law (exec. com. 1995-98), Internat. Law Assn. (v.p. 1994—, program chmn. Am. br. 1992), Assn. Am. Law Sch. (chmn. sect. internat. law 1995-96), Assn. of the Bar of the City of N.Y. (arms control and internat. security affairs com., chmn. 1989-92, chmn. internat. affairs coun. 1992-95, exec. com. 1995-99), Union Internationale des Avocats, U.S.A. (chpt. bd. govs. 1993-98), Coun. on Fgn. Rels., Elizabethan Club, Mory's Assn., Yale Club (N.Y.C.), Lawn Club. Office: Yale U Sch Law PO Box 208215 New Haven CT 06520-8215 also: Coun on Fgn Rels 58 E 68th St New York NY 10021-5953 E-mail: ruth.wedgwood@yale.edu. *Notable cases include: U.S. vs. Kostadinov, involving a Bulgarian spy traded for 25 East Bloc detainees; U.S. vs. Kampiles, involving government employee who gave satellite secrest to the Soviet Unionl U.S. vs. Gold, Orosz, Egerhazi and Kompar, involving a million dollar racketeering/landlord arson ring in N.Y.C. that defrauded Lloyd's of London Sasse Syndicate; U.S. vs. Kazemzadeh and DeVelasco, involving pub. corruption in N.Y.C. Health and Hospitals Corporation and the fed. WIC program.*

WEDIG, REGINA SCOTTO, lawyer; b. Pensacola, Fla., July 30, 1955; d. Anthony P. and Janet (Treadway) Scotto; m. Eric M. Wedig. BA magna cum laude, Loyola U., 1977; MA, Tulane U., 1979; JD, La. State U., 1984. Bar: Tenn. 1984, U.S. Dist. Ct. (ea., mid. and we. dists.) Tenn. 1984, La. 1985, U.S. Dist. Ct. (ea., mid. and we. dists.) La. 1985, U.S. Ct. Appeals (5th cir.) 1985, U.S. Ct. Appeals (11th cir.) 1998. Assoc. Harkavy, Shainberg, Kosten, et al, Memphis, 1984-88, Bordelon, Hamlin & Theriot, New Orleans, 1988-94, ptnr., 1994—. Chmn. moot ct. bd. Paul M. Herbert Law Sch., La. State U., Baton Rouge, 1983-84. Editor: (newsletter) LSU-Coastal Law Newsletter, 1983-84; author: (law jour.) La. Bar Jour., 1996. Mem. La. Bar Assn., Tenn. Bar Assn., New Orleans Bar Assn. Office: Bordelon Hamlin & Theriot 701 S Peters St New Orleans LA 70130-1588

WEDNER, H. JAMES, physician, researcher; b. Pitts., May 12, 1941; s. Benjamin Mayer and Lucille Ruth (Jacobs) W.; m. Maureen Patricia Martin, June 18, 1978; children: Bryna Kimberly, Jason Oliver. BS, Cornell U., 1963; MD, Cornell Med. Coll., N.Y.C., 1967. Intern Barnes Hosp., St. Louis, 1967-68; resident internal medicine Washington U. Med. Sch., 1970-71, fellow allergy and immunology, 1971-73; lt. comdr. USPHS, Govenor's Island, N.Y., 1968-70; dir. tng. program allergy and immunology Washington U. Med. Sch., St. Louis, 1986-95, chief clin. allergy and immunology, 1988—, prof. medicine, 1990—, med. dir. The Asthma Ctr., 2000—, acting chief divsn. of Allergy and Clin. Immunology, 2001—. Vis. prof. Am. Coll. of Allergy and Immunology, Little Rock, 1991, U. Buffalo Med. Sch., 1999; prin. investigator psychosocial aspects of asthma, St. Louis Asthma Study Unit; chmn. steering com. Nat. Coop. Inner City Asthma Study; prin. investigator Fungal Alleries Innercity Homes. Editor: Allergy: Theory and Practice, 1984, 2d rev. edit., 1991; mem. editl. bd. Jour. Immunology, 1980-82, Jour. Allergy and Clin. Immunology, 1991-96; assoc. editor Anaphylaxis and Drug Allergy Current Allergy Reports, 2000—; sect. editor Anaplylaxis and Drug Allergy, Current Allergy and Asthma Reports Fellow Am. Acad. Allergy Asthma Immunology; mem. Internat. Soc. Immunopharmacology, Am. Coll. Allergy Asthma Immunology, Am. Assn. Immunology, Clin. Immunology Soc., European Acad. Allergology and Clin. Immunology. Achievements include initial description of Parthenium hysterophruis allergy; reearch on asthma and the psychosocial aspects of asthma, allergen, molecular characteriation of plant and fungal allergens and the role of fungi in asthma. Office: Washington U Med Sch Campus Box 8122 660 S Euclid Ave Saint Louis MO 63110-1010 E-mail: wednerj@msnotes.wustl.edu., wedners@worldnett.att.net.

WEED, EDWARD REILLY, marketing executive; b. Chgo., Jan. 25, 1940; s. Cornelius Cahill and Adelaide E. (Reilly) W.; m. Lawrie Irving Bowes, Feb. 2, 1969. Student, Fordham U., 1959-61, Loyola U., 1961-62. Account exec. Leo Burnett Co., Chgo., 1961-71; pres., corp. officer GDC Ad Inc., Miami, Fla., 1971-74; v.p., account supr D'Arcy Mac Manus & Masius, Chgo., 1975; group v.p. mktg. Hart Schaffner & Marx (Hartmarx); pres. Hart Svcs., Inc., 1975-82; v.p mktg. Tishman, 1983-86; exec. v.p. Hannah Marine, 1986-87; exec. v.p., dir. U.S. Auction, 1988-92; v.p. mktg. Telemedia, 1992-95; mng. dir. Brochure Assocs./The Consultancy, Lake Geneva, Wis., 1996—. Dir. First Nat. Bank So. Miami; seminar instr. Grad. Sch. Notre Dame U., South Bend, Ind.; guest faculty Loyola U., Chgo., Fla. Internat. U. Contbr. articles to profl. jours. Trustee Latin Sch. Found., 1976—, The Admiral, 1999—; bd. dirs. North Ave. Day Nursery, 1969-73, Santa for Poor, 1975-87, Off-the-Street, 1982-87, Chgo. Boys' and Girls' Clubs, 1983-87, Map Inc., 1988-98, Geneva Lake Conservancy, 1994—; adv. bd. Fiduciary Mgmt. Assocs., 1998—. With Ill. N.G. Recipient Chi Ad Club award. Mem. Tavern Club, Lake Geneva Country Club, Casino Club. Republican. Roman Catholic. Office: Brochure Assocs/The Consultancy 3638 Snake Rd Lake Geneva WI 53147

WEED, MAURICE JAMES, composer, retired music educator; b. Kalamazoo, Oct. 16, 1912; s. Frank Eugene and Ella May (Britton) W.; m. Berneice Laverne Pope, Aug. 23, 1937; children: Allison Gilbert (Mrs. Walter D. Herrick), Laurice Ellen (Mrs. Samuel L. Rich). BA, Western Mich. U., 1934; MusB, Eastman Sch. Music, 1940, MusM, 1952, PhD, 1954. Supr. instrumental music pub. schs., Ionia, Mich., 1934-36, Three Rivers, 1937-43; asst. prof. music, dir. instrumental music, tchr. music theory Ripon Coll., 1946-51; tchr. Eastman Sch. Music, summer 1954; prof., head dept. music No. Ill. U., 1954-61, prof. music, 1961-74; adj. prof. music Western Carolina U., 1974-75; ret., 1975. Composer in residence, MacDowell Colony, 1961; performances include: Serenity for chamber orch. Eastman-Rochester Symphony, 1953, Symphony Number 1, Nat. Symphony Orch., Washington, 1956, Symphony of the Air, Carnegie Hall, 1957, Wonder of the Starry Night, 1st ann. symposium Contemporary Am. Music, U. Kans., 1959, Serenity and Fanfare for Two Trumpets and Organ, 8th ann. symposium Univ. Composers Exchange, Valparaiso, Ind., 1959; Sept Cinquains for Soprano Voice and chamber instrumental group, No. Ill. U., 1964, 67, Symphonie Breve, 6th ann. symposium Contemporary Am. Music U. Kans., 1967, Symphonie Breve, Oklahoma City Symphony Orch.; MBS broadcast, 1965, U. Redlands, 1964, Asheville (N.C.) Symphony Orch., 1979; condr. symposium of 8 sacred choral and 2 organ works by 6 coll., univ., high sch. and ch. choirs, Atlanta, 1975; Serenity, Asheville Symphony Orch., 1977; composer: over 65 works including Ships, Witchery (songs for soprano and piano), 1937, Rain, for contralto and piano, 1940, Three Preludes for Organ, 1945, Introduction and Scherzo, symphonic band, 1948, Gratitude, for contralto with organ, 1950, An After Easter Prayer, 1950, Serenity, for chamber orch., 1953, Wonder of the Starry Night, a capella choir, 1958, Symphonie Breve, 1959, Trio for violin, cello and piano, 1961, Concertino for cello and orch, 1962, Psalm XIII (mixed choir and organ), 1964, Hopkins Park, concert march, 1966, Triptych for Voices, a cappella choir, 1966, Vestigia Nulla Retrorsum, processional march, 1968, Praise Ye the Lord (mixed choir), 1968, A Wedding Song (soprano and organ), 1969, In the Midnight Hour (soprano and organ), 1970, In Te, Domini, Speravi (mixed choir), 1970, 4 Anthems for Mixed Choir, 1973, Postlude for Organ, 1974, The Catamounts, concert march for band, 1974, Duo for Viola and C Trumpet, 1977, Choral Fanfare No. 2, 1977, An Appalachian Celebration for Choir and Band, 1978; Celebration (hymn-anthem), 1981; 3 anthems for mixed voices Let All the People Praise Thee, 1980, Sing Praises to God, 1981, Praise Ye the Lord, 1982, The 3Bs-Brass Sextet, 1982, Voices of Appalachia, 1986; numerous others. Recipient 25th Anniversary award Nat. Symphony Orch., 1956, Ostwald award, 1959, J. Fisher & Bro. Centennial award, 1964, Pedro Paz award, 1966; Eastman Sch. Music teaching fellow, 1951-54. Mem. Nat. Assn. Composers U.S.A., Am. Music Ctr., Music Edn. Nat. Conf., N.C. Music Educators, Am. Soc. Univ. Composers, Phi Mu Alpha. Methodist. Home: Asheville Manor 308 Overlook Rd Rm 55 Asheville NC 28803-3319

WEED, ROBERT CLYDE, mining executive, cattle rancher; b. Lansing, Mich., Mar. 18, 1920; s. Stanley V. and Marian Harper W.; m. Lydia Campoy, Oct. 26, 1964 (div.); children: Robert Jr., Carolyn, Ricardo, Jose, Marco A., Miriam Casavandes, Lydia Huerta, James. BS in Mining Engring., Mich. Technol. U., 1942. Various positions Cananea Consol. Copper, Sonora, Mex., 1948-71; pres., natural resources div. Anaconda Co., Tuscon, 1971-73, CEO, natural resources group, corp. sr. v.p., 1973-75; cattle rancher Mex., 1965-89; owner/operator Wahoo Ranch, Winston, N.Mex. Capt., U.S. Army, 1942-46. Deocrated Silver Star medal; recipient Bd. Control Silver medal Mich. Technol. U., 1973. Avocations: hunting, fishing, poetry, gardening. Home: 68 Wendy Rd Silver City NM 88061

WEED, ROGER OREN, rehabilitation services professional, educator; b. Bend, Oreg., Feb. 2, 1944; s. Chester Elbert and Ruth Marie (Urie) W.; m. Paula J. Keller; children: Nicholette, Andrew. BS in Sociology, U. Oreg., 1967, MS in Rehab. Counseling, 1969; PhD in Rehab. Counseling, U. Ga., 1986. Cert. rehab. counselor; cert. disability mgmt. specialist; lic. profl. counselor; cert. case mgr., cert. life care planner. Vocat. rehab. counselor State of Alaska, Anchorage, 1969-71; instr. U. Alaska, 1970-76; counselor Langdon Psychiat. Clinic, 1971-74; from asst. dir. to exec. dir. Hope Cottages, 1974-79; owner Profl. Resources Group, 1978-80; mng. ptnr. Collins, Weed & Assocs., 1980-84; assoc. dir. Ctr. for Rehab. Tech. Ga. Tech. U., Atlanta, 1986-87; catastrophic injury rehab. Weed & Assocs., 1984—; from asst. prof. to prof. Ga. State U., 1987—. Adj. faculty Ga. Inst. Tech.; courtesy faculty U. Fla., 1996—; chmn. Ga. Composite Bd. for Licensing Profl. Counselors. Co-author: Vocational Expert Handbook, 1986, Transferable Work Skills, 1988, Life Care Planning: Spinal Cord Injured, 1989, 94, Life Care Planning: Head Injured, 1994, Life Care Planning for the Amputee, 1992, Rehab Consultant Handbook, 1994, rev. edit., 2001; editor: Life Care Planning and Case Management Handbook, 1999; mem. editl. bd. Jour. of Pvt. Sector Rehab., Athens, Ga., 1986—; mem. Disting. Editl. Bd. Vanguard Series in Rehab., Athens, 1988—; contbr. articles to profl. publs. Chair Ga. Composite Bd. for Lic. Profl. Counselors, 2000-01. Recipient Gov.'s award Gov.'s Com. on Employment, Alaska, 1982, Goldpan Svc. award Gov.'s Com. on Employment, Alaska, 1978, Profl. Svcs. award Am. Rehab. Counselors Assn., 1993. Fellow Nat. Rehab. Assn. (chair legis. com., bd. dirs. met. Atlanta chpt. 1988—, pres. Pacific region 1983-85, pres.'s award Pacific region 1986), Nat. Assn. Rehab. Profls. in Pvt. Sector (chair resh. and tng. com. 1988-93, pres. 1994-95, Educator of the Yr. award 1991, 97), Nat. Brain Injury Assn., Pvt. Rehab. Suppliers Ga., Rehab. Engring. Soc. N.Am., Anchorage Amateur Radio Club. Republican. Methodist. Avocations: sailing, skiing, bicycling, flying, computers. Office: Ga State U Coll of Edn Dept Counseling/Psychol Svc 9th Fl Atlanta GA 30303

WEED, WILLIAM ALGEO, III, band director; b. Sistersville, W.Va., Nov. 28, 1960; m. Bobbi Jené Weed, Dec. 14, 1984; children: William IV, Kailena, Isaac. BS in Edn., Concord Coll., Athens, 1987. Cert. music tchr. Band and choir dir. Alleghany Highlands Schs., Covington, Va., 1987—98; band and ochestra dir. Jefferson County Schs., Rigby, Idaho, 1988—. Prin. trombonist Alleghany Highalnds Orch., Covington, Va., 1987—98, Rockbridge Symphony Orch., Buena Vista, Va., 1989—95, Yellowstone Brass Quintet, Rigby, Idaho, 2000—; pvt. trombone instr. Ricks Coll., Rexburg, Idaho, 1999—2001. Pres. PTA, Sharon, Va., 1992—96. Mem.: NEA (local rep. 1993—94), Gem-State Band Dirs. Assn. (v.p. 2001—), Alleghany Highlands Edn. Assn. (pres. 1993—94), Idaho Music Educators Conf. Office: Rigby High Sch 290 North 3800 E Rigby ID 83442 Personal E-mail: bandrhs@hotmail.com. E-mail: bandrhs@hotmail.com.

WEEDN, SONNEE D. psychologist; b. Mpls., Apr. 19, 1947; d. John E. Stallman and Delight M. Jaax; m. Robert A. Weedn, Aug. 16, 1969; children: Isaiah, Simon. BS in Social Sci., U. So. Calif., 1968, MS in Edn., 1969, MS in Counseling Psychology, 1973; PhD in Clin. Psychology, Calif. Grad. Sch. Psychology, 1988. Lic. psychologist. Pvt. practice marriage & family therapist, Novato, Petaluma, Calif., 1980—; pvt. practice psychologist, 1992—. Mem.: APA, Soc. Personality Assessment, Calif. Psychol. Assn. Democrat. Prebyterian. Office: 825 De Long Ave Novato CA 94945 Office Fax: 415-899-1376.

WEEKLEY, AUGUSTINE SMYTHE, JR. lawyer, physician; b. Tampa, Fla., Apr. 12, 1930; s. Augustine Smythe Sr. and Ruby M. (Nye) W.; children: Augustine Smythe III, Paul Marshall, Alexandra Rico. MD, Boston U., 1955; JD cum laude, Stetson U., 1989. Diplomate Am. Bd. Surgery, Am. Bd. Healthcare Risk Mgrs., Am. Bd. Risk Mgmt.-Healthcare sect.; bar: Fla. 1990, U.S. Dist. Ct. (mid. dist.) Fla. 1990. Intern Youngstown (Ohio) Hosp., 1955-56; surgery resident Mass. Meml. Hosp., Boston, 1956-59, chief surgery resident, 1960-61; fellow in surgery Lahey Clinic, 1960; chmn. dept. surgery U. Cmty. Hosp., 1979-81, Tampa Bay Cmty. Hosp., 1983-84, chief of staff, 1985; pvt. practice law, , Tampa, 1990—. Pres. Bay Area Healthcare Risk Mgmt. Soc., 1995; mem. exec. coun. health law sect. Fla. Bar, 1995—; bd. advisors CPA Edn. Soc. Mem. editl. rev. bd. Jour. Healthcare Risk Mgmt., Managed Care Medicine. Fellow Am. Coll. Legal Medicine, ACS, Internat. coll. Surgeons; mem. ABA, AMA, Fla. Bar Assn., D.C. Bar Assn., Hillsborough County Bar Assn., Assn. Trial Lawyers Am., Fla. Assn. Trial Lawyers, Nat. Health Lawyers Assn., Am. Soc. Law and Medicine, Am. Soc. Healthcare Risk Mgmt., Acad. Fla. Trial Lawyers, Am. Soc. Abdominal Surgeons, Fla. Med. Assn., Hillsborough County Med. Assn., Mass. Med. Soc. Office: Holland & Knight LLP PO Box 1288 Tampa FL 33601-1288

WEEKLEY, FREDERICK CLAY, JR. lawyer; b. San Antonio, Aug. 29, 1939; s. F. Clay and Topsy (Stevens) W.; m. Lynda Freeman; children: Amber Lee Carothers, Caroline Lee. BBA, Baylor U., 1962, JD, 1963; LLM, NYU, 1969. Bar: Tex. 1963. Ptnr. Bracewell & Patterson, Houston, 1974-90; trust counsel Bank One, Tex., N.A., 1990-98; ptnr. Shannon, Gracey, Ratliff & Miller, LLP, Ft. Worth, 1999—. Mem. coun. real property, probate and trust law sect., State Bar of Tex., 1987-90; mem. adminstrv. coun. trust divsn. Tex. Bankers Assn., 1992-95, chmn. legis. com., 1992-95. Editor: Texas Wills System, 1984. Mem. Commn. Probate Law Examiners, Tex. Bd. Legal Specialization, 1978-82. Fellow Am. Coll. Trust and Estate Counsel. Home: 1821 Mossy Oak St Arlington TX 76012-5619 Office: 777 Main St Fort Worth TX 76102

WEEKLEY, LESLIE BRUCE, veterinarian, pharmacologist; b. Palatka, Fla., Sept. 9, 1953; s. Leslie B. and Shirley (Roberts) W. BS, MS, Va. Commonwealth U., 1978; MS, Med. Coll. of Va., 1981; PhD, U. Wyo., 1985; DVM, Colo. State U., 1989. Toxicologist Va. Dept. Health, Richmond, 1989-90; rsch. scientist Va.-Md. Regional Coll. Vet. Medicine, Blacksburg, 1990-93; clin. veterinarian U. Tex. S.W. Med. Ctr., Dallas, 1993-96; sr. veterinarian Toxicology Rsch. Labs., Eli Lilly and Co., Greenfield, Ind., 1996-99; sr. rsch. veterinarian Merck Rsch. Labs., Merck and Co., Inc., West Point, Pa., 1999—. Toxicology cons. George Washington U., 1987—90; lectr. Va. Commonwealth U., Richmond, 1990—91, U. Pa., 2001; mem. expert com. on vet. drug standards U.S. Pharmacopeia, 2000—; mem. Annapolis Ctr. Workshop (to educate pub. and legislators on toxicology studies); sect. chair, organizer Internat. Coun. for Lab. Animal Sci., Can. Coun. on Animal Care, Internat. Symposium on Regulatory Testing and Animal Welfare. Mem. bd. sci. reviewers Am. Jour. Vet. Rsch.; contbr. articles to profl. jours. including Biochem. Pharmacology, Cardiovasc. Rsch., Compendium on Continuing Edn., 1995, 98; Sci., Health, and Econ. Adv. Coun. Annapolis Ctr.. Mem.: AVMA, Am. Physiol. Soc., Am. Soc. Bone Mineral Rsch., N.Y. Acad. Scis., Am. Coll. Lab. Animal Medicine (diplomate, publ. com.), Am. Assn. Lab. Animal Sci., Am. Coll. Clin. Pharmacology (publ. com.), Sigma Xi. Achievements include research in laboratory animal science and veterinary medicine to improve the welfare of animals and the scientific value of animal studies in toxicology and pharmacology. Home: 17810 Wilkinson Rd Dinwiddie VA 23841- Office: Merck Research Labs Merck and Co Inc Dept Comparative Med WP 44-201 West Point PA 19486 E-mail: Bweekley215@aol.com.

WEEKLY, JOHN WILLIAM, insurance company executive; b. Sioux City, Iowa, June 21, 1931; s. John E. Weekly and Alyce Beatrice (Preble) Nichols; children: John William Jr., Thomas Patrick, Michael Craig, James Matthew, Daniel Kevin. Grad. high sch., Omaha. V.p. First Data Resources, Inc., Omaha, 1969-74, Mut. of Omaha/United of Omaha Ins. Co., Omaha, 1974-81, sr. exec. v.p., 1981-87, pres., COO, 1987-95, vice chmn., pres., COO, 1995, vice chmn., pres., CEO, 1996-97, vice chmn., CEO, 1997, chmn., CEO, 1998—. Chmn. bd. dirs. Companiion Life Ins. Co., Mutual Omaha Investor Svcs., Inc., United World Life Ins. Co.; bd. dirs. Innowave, Inc., Kirkpatrick Pettis, Omaha Property and Casualty Ins. Co., Midwest Express Airlines, Inc., 1995—, Cabelas, Inc., 2000—. Bd. govs. Ak-Sar-Ben, 2001—; bd. dirs. Omaha Zool. Soc. , 1998, Avera St. Luke's Hosp., 1999. Mem.: Greater Omaha C. of C. (bd. dirs. 1991—96), Health Ins. Assn. Am. (bd. dirs. 1992—96, chmn. 1996), Am. Coun. Life Ins. (bd. dirs. 1995—98, 2001—). Avocations: fishing, hunting. Office: Mut Omaha Ins Co Mutual Omaha Plz Omaha NE 68175-0001

WEEKS, ALBERT LOREN, author, educator, journalist; b. Highland Park, Mich., Mar. 28, 1923; s. Albert Loren and Vera Grace (Jarvis) W. Student, U. Mich., 1942-43; MA, U. Chgo., 1949; PhD, Columbia U., 1965; cert., Russian Inst., 1960. Reporter Chgo. City News Bur., 1946; polit. analyst U.S. Dept. State, 1950-53, Free Europe Com., Inc., 1953-56; editorial asst. Newsweek mag., 1957-58; Russian tech. glossary compiler McGraw-Hill Book Co., 1960-61; prof. continuing edn. NYU, 1959-89. Lectr. U.S. diplomatic history and soviet govt. Columbia U., 1951-52; mem. adv. coun. Nat. Strategy Info. Ctr., 1979-89; instr. Ringling Sch. Art and Design, 1991—; pub. spkr. S.W. Fla. Host: A Week's View of Red Press, Sta. WNBC, 1965-68; series Myths That Rule America, NBC-TV, 1979-82; author: Reading American History, 1963, The First Bolshevik: A Political Biography of Peter Tkachev, 1968, The Other Side of Coexistence: An Analysis of Russian Foreign Policy, 1970, Richard Hofstadter's The American Political Tradition and the Age of Reform, 1973, Andrei Sakharov and the Soviet Dissidents, 1975, The Troubled Detente, 1976, Solzhenitsyn's One Day in the Life of Ivan Denisovich, 1976, Myths That Rule America, 1980, War and Peace: Soviet Russia Speaks, 1983; editor/compiler Brassey's Soviet and Communist Quotations, 1987, The Soviet Nomenklatura, 1987-1991, Stalin's Other War: Soviet Grand Strategy 1939-1941, 2002; internat. affairs editor Def. Sci. mag., 1982-85; columnist Def. Report, 1982-90; contbr. articles to N.Y. Times, New Republic, New Leader, Annals, Russian, Slavic revs., Christian Sci. Monitor, Problems of Communism, Survey, Mil. Intelligence, Strategic Rev., World War II mag., Air Univ. Rev., L.A. Times, Washington Times, Orbis, Global Affairs, Panorama, Sarasota Herald-Tribune, Bradenton Herald, Defense and Diplomacy, Am. Intelligence Jour., USA Today, Rossiiskiye Vesti, Vechernii Vladimir, CityTempo mag., Modern Age mag. Home: 4884 Kestral Park Cir Sarasota FL 34231-3369 E-mail: aweeks1@compuserve.com.

WEEKS, Mrs. ANDI EMERSON See EMERSON, ANDI

WEEKS, ANNE MACLEOD, English language eductor, education director; b. Princeton, N.J., Jan. 20, 1955; d. Donald and Norma Eliner (Harper) Macleod; m. James Otis Weeks, July 10, 1982; 1 child, Jedediah Mackenzie. BA in English and Slavic Lang., Lawrence U., 1977; MA in English, Villanova U., 1988. English tchr. Elkhart Lake (Wis.)-Glenbeulah H.S., 1978-79; English tchr., coll. guidance staff Perkiomen Sch., Pennsburg, Pa., 1979-88; dir. coll. guidance and English Oldfields Sch., Glencoe, Md., 1988—, cons. to AP program Coll. Bd., 1993—. Coord. Assn. Ind. Md. Schs. Coll. Fair, 1989, 92, 2000; pres. Assn. Ind. Md. Schs. Coll. Counselors, 1993, 2001; continuing edn. seminar tchr. Goucher Coll., Towson, Md., 1995. Author: Counseling Practitioners, Eduction Week, (column) Jour. for Coll. Admissions. Mem. Nat. Assn. Coll. Admissions Counselors, Potomac and Chesapeake Assn. Coll. Admissions Counselors. Presbyterian. Avocations: needlepoint, gardening, kayaking. Home: 1500 Glencoe Rd Glencoe MD 21152-9388 Office: Oldfields Sch 1500 Glencoe Rd Glencoe MD 21152-9321 E-mail: weeksa@oldfields.pvt.k12.md.us.

WEEKS, ARTHUR ANDREW, lawyer, law educator; b. Hanceville, Ala., Dec. 2, 1914; s. A.A. and Anna S. (Seibert) W.; m. Carol P. Weeks; children: John David, Carol Christine, Nancy Anna. AB, Samford U., 1936; LL.B., JD, U. Ala., 1939; LL.M., Duke U., 1950; LL.D. (hon.), Widener U., 1980. Bar: Ala. 1939, Tenn. 1948. Sole practice, Birmingham, Ala., 1939-41, 1946-47, 1954-61; dean, prof. law Cumberland U. Sch. Law, 1947-54; dean, prof. Samford U., 1961-72, prof. law, 1972-74, Cumberland Sch. Law, Samford U., 1984—, Del. Sch. Law of Widener U., Wilmington, 1974-82, dean, 1974-80, interim dean, 1982-83, dean emeritus, prof., 1983—. Served to capt. AUS, 1941-46. Mem. ABA, Tenn. Bar Assn., Ala. Bar Assn., Birmingham Bar Assn., Del. Bar Assn. (assoc.), Phi Alpha Delta, Phi Kappa Phi, Delta Theta Phi Home: 1105 Water Edge Ct Birmingham AL 35244-1437

WEEKS, CHARLES, JR. real estate executive, retired publishing company executive; b. Palo Alto, Calif., Apr. 25, 1919; s. Charles and Mary Alice (Johnson) W.; m. Patricia Anne Blair, Apr. 7, 1949; children: Patricia Alice, Charles Blair, Clayton Brian, Phyllis Anne. Student, U. Fla., 1936-38. Prin. Fla. Airmotive, Inc., Lantana, 1946-50; v.p., dir. Perry Publs., Inc., West Palm Beach, 1950-69; bd. dirs. Perry Oceanographics, Inc., Riveria Beach, Fla., 1969-84; dir. mgmt. bd. Flagler Nat Bank, West Palm Beach, 1992. Mem. Planning and Zoning Bd., Lantana, 1962-65; assoc. trustee John F. Kennedy Hosp., Atlantis, Fla., 1985. Served as pilot USAF, 1943-46, ETO. Decorated Air medal; recipient Pilot Safety award Nat. Bus. Aircraft Assn., 1970, 74, 78. Mem. Quiet Birdman, Handersonville (N.C.) Country Club, Sailfish of Fla. (Palm Beach) Club. Episcopalian. Democrat. Home: PO Box 3411 Lantana FL 33465-3411 Office: Palermo-Long Realty Inc 223 E Ocean Ave Lantana FL 33462-3201

WEEKS, CHRISTOPHER HENRY CLARK, writer, historian; b. Schenectady, N.Y., May 4, 1950; s. Maurice Harold and June King (Clark) W. BA, U. Va., 1972, MA, 1976. Cons. The Nat. Trust, Gloucestershire, U.K., 1973-74; writer, editor Md. Hist. Trust, Annapolis, Md., 1976-85; adj. lectr. U. Md., College Pk., 1978—; curator, cons. Centro Internazionale A. Palladio, Vicenza, Italy, 1976-80; lectr. Goucher Coll., Towson, Md., 1979. Trustee Balt. Mus. of Art, 1985-90, Friends of the Am. Wing, 1999—; v.p. Ctr. for Palladian Studies, Richmond, Va., 1980—; speakers' com. Md. Hist. Soc., Balt., 1978-84. Author: Architectural History of Westminster, 1978, Where Land and Water Intertwine, 1985, Between the Nanticoke and Choptank, 1985, AIA Guide to Washington, D.C., 1994, Alexander Smith Cochran, Modernist Pioneer in Traditional Baltimore, 1995, An Architectural History of Harford County, Maryland, 1996, Perfectly Delightful: The Life and Gardens of Harvey Ladew, 1999; co-author: W.L. Bottomley in Richmond, 1986, Clues to American Gardens, 1988; contbr. numerous articles to profl. jours. Trustee Ladew Topiary Gardens, 1999—. Named Knight of St. John., Episcopal Ch., 1989. Mem. Hist. Soc. of Harford County (dir. 1988—), Liriodendron Found. (dir. 1979—). Democrat. Episcopalian. Avocations: swimming, gardening, bridge. Home and Office: 230 Stony Run Ln Apt 4G Baltimore MD 21210-3023 E-mail: chweeks@co.ha.md.us.

WEEKS, CLIFFORD MYERS, musician, educational administrator; b. N.Y.C., Apr. 15, 1938; s. Vernal C. and Adeline (Campbell) W.; m. Ethel Lynn Fleming, Oct. 26, 1963 (dec. 1982); children: Clifford M. Jr., Michele Lynn. Diploma in Arranging and Composition, Berklee Coll. Music, 1962; MusB magna cum laude, Boston Conservatory Music, 1963, MusM, 1975; cert. in edn. adminstrn., Boston State Coll., 1977. Cert. secondary sch. adminstr. and tchr. music, Mass. Tchr. music Boston Pub. Schs., 1964-74, condr. All-City Stage Band, 1972-79, adminstrv. asst. to asst. supt., 1974-75, coordinator instrumental music, 1975-79, asst. prin., 1979, adminstrv. asst. to asst. supt., 1979-96, acting community supt., 1983, cluster coord., 1996-2001, exec. asst. to chief of staff, 2001—. Arranger, composer, trombonist, 1963—; condr. Boston Coll. Jazz and Stage Band, Chestnut Hill, Mass., 1976-78. Composer Tryptych for tuba and piano, 1971, (oratorio) The King-Life and Teachings of Dr. Martin Luther King Jr., 1976; composer, arranger various jazz compositions, 1975. Mem. Medford (Mass.) Jaycees, 1975-76; adv. bd. Roxbury

(Mass.) Boys and Girls Club, 1970—, Berklee Coll. Music, Boston, 1972. Recipient Mayor's Parkman Club award, 1999, Suskind Young at Art award Wang Ctr. Boston Theatres, 2001. Mem. Boston Assn. Sch. Adminstrs. and Suprs. (adminstrs. union 1997—), Boston Tchrs. Union, Black Educators Alliance Mass. (treas. 1972-76, award 1976), ASCAP, Adminstrv. Assts. Assn. (chmn. local chpt. 1982—), Assn. for Supervision and Curriculum Devel., Omega Psi Phi. Methodist. Office: Boston Pub Schs Office Supt. 26 Court St Boston MA 02108

WEEKS, DANIEL JAMES, writer, educator, musician; b. Neptune, N.J., Apr. 25, 1958; s. Harold James and Doris Joan W.; m. Jackie Trester, Nov. 10, 1985; 1 child, Jared. BA in Am. History, Washington & Lee U., 1980; MA in History, Monmouth U., 1995. Reporter The Herald, Allaire, N.J., 1984; mng. editor Allaire Pub. Co., 1984-86; staff writer The Jour., Freehold, N.J., 1986-87; editor Summerfield Newspapers, Asbury Park, 1987-89; editor of publs. Monmouth U., West Long Branch, 1989-98, history instr., 1999—; pres. Ratamacue Records, 1995—. Musician, drummer Jazzlamic Jihad, Long Branch, 1990—. Author: Ancestral Songs, 1992, Indignities, 1999, Thomas Osborne of Ashford, Kent, 1994, The Weeks/Wickes Families, 1999, X Poems, 1992, Les Symbolistes, 2000, Not for Filthy Lucre's Sake, 2001; musician (CD) Forbidden Expression, 1994, We're in Your Neighborhood, 1998; exec. prodr. (CD) Myrtle Strange, 1995, Tom Timko and the Horn Dogs, 1997, Skrap-Anywhere But Here, 1998, Danny Walsh Quartet, 2000, Ralph Bowen Qt. Grantee N.J. Hist. Commn., 1992, 2000. Republican. Episcopalian. Home: 15 Sandspring Dr Eatontown NJ 07724 Office: Ratamacue Records PO Box 279 West Long Branch NJ 07764 E-mail: jazzlamic@aol.com.

WEEKS, DUDLEY LEE, adult education educator; PhD in Polit. Sci., U. Hawaii, 1978. Dir. programs and planning Overseas Edn. Fund, Washington, 1980; dir. edn. Martin Luther King Ctr., Atlanta, 1981—82; prof. Am. U., Washington, 1989—95; dir. Global FutureLinks, 1983—, Partnership Life Skills Ctr., Great Cacapon, W.Va., 1995—, Ctr. for Effective Partnership, Great Cacapon, 2000—. Cons. in field; moderator, trainer, 1980—. Co-author: (book) Humatroitism, 1978, The Unsteady State, 1979; author: The Eight Essential Steps to Conflict Resolution, 1992, (poetry book) So Far to Go When We Get There, 1992, On Love and Change and Other Subversive Things, 1999, Through the Mist, 2002, (book) The Conflict Partnership Catalyst Process: An Effective Alternative to Mediation, 2002, (novels) Between Two Worlds, 2002; songwriter/performer (record) The World As People, 1970, Timechild, 1982, creator/developer (process/model) The Conflict Partnership Process for Relationship Building and Conflict Resolution, 1978. Recipient Peacebldrs. award, UN of Youth, The Hague, 1993; fellow Sr. fellow, East-West Ctr., U. Hawaii, 1975; scholar Scholar-in-residence, Inst. for Social Rsch., Rhodes U., Grahamstown, South Africa, 1988. Avocations: art, creative writing, songwriting, athletics. Home and Office: Ctr for Effective Partnership 826 Pioneer Trail Great Cacapon WV 25422-3176

WEEKS, GERALD, psychology educator; b. Morehead City, N.C., Nov. 20, 1948; s. Marion G. and Ada (Willis) W.; m. Kathleen Glass, Sept. 2, 1972. BA in Philosophy and Psychology, East Carolina U., 1971, MA in Gen. Psychology, 1973; PhD in Clin. Psychology, Ga. State U., 1979. Diplomate Am. Bd. Profl. Psychology (pres. 1987-88, bd. dirs. 1982-87), Am. Bd. Family Psychology, Am. Bd. Sexology; cert. marital and family therapist; lic. practicing psychologist, N.C., Pa.; registered Health Care Providers in Psychology. Intern in family therapy Harlem Valley Psychiatric Ctr., Wingdale, N.Y., 1978-79; assoc. prof. psychology U. N.C., Wilmington, 1979-85; dir. tng. Penn Coun. for Relationships, 1985—; clin. asst. prof. psychology Sch. Medicine U. Pa., Phila., 1985-87, clin. assoc. prof., 1988-98; chair, prof. dept. counseling U. Nev.-Las Vegas, 1999—. Pvt. practice Carolina Ob-gyn Ctr., Wilmington, 1980-85. Author: Promoting Change Through Paradoxical Therapy, 1985, Treating Couples: The Intersystem Model of the Marriage Council of Philadelphia, 1989, Promoting Change through Paradoxical Therapy, 1991, (with L. L'Abate) Paradoxical Psychotherapy: Theory and Practice with Individuals, Couples, and Families, 1982, (with R. Sauber, L. L'Abate) Family Therapy: Basic Concepts and Terms, 1985, (with L. Hof) Integrating Sex and Marital Therapy: A Clinicians Guide, 1987, (with S. Treat) Couples in Treatment, 1992, rev. edit., 2001, Integrative Solutions: Treating Common Problems in Couple's Therapy, 1995, (with L. Hof) Erectile Dysfunction, 2000, (with N. Manhescia) Focused Genograms: Intergenerational Assessment of Individuals, Couples and Families, 1999, (with Nancy Mamnescia) Hypoactive Sexual Desire, 2002; contbr. articles to profl. jours. Fellow Am. Assn. Marital and Family Therapy (clin. mem., nat. adv. bd., approved supr.); mem. APA, Acad. Family Psychology, Interpersonal and Social Skills Assn. (founding mem.), Acad. Psychologists in Marital, Sex, and Family Therapy. Office: U Nev PO Box 453007 4505 S Maryland Pkwy Las Vegas NV 89154-9900

WEEKS, JOHN ROBERT, geographer, sociology educator; b. Sacramento, June 1, 1944; s. Robert Louis and Thelma Hope (Evans) W.; m. Deanna Jean Hosea, May 16, 1965; children: John Robert, Gregory, Jennifer. AB, U. Calif., Berkeley, 1966, MA, 1969, PhD, 1972. Asst. prof. sociology Mich. State U., East Lansing, 1971-74, San Diego State U., 1974-78, assoc. prof., 1978-81, prof., 1981-92, prof. geography, 1992—, chmn. dept., 1978-85; adminstrv. dir. Internat. Population Ctr., 1985—; clin. prof. family & preventive medicine U. Calif. Sch. Medicine, San Diego, 1998—. Vis. rsch. demographer U. Calif., Berkeley, 1972; cons. Allied Home Health Assn., 1978-80, Area Agy. on Aging, San Diego, 1979-81, Los Angeles Regional Family Planning Coun., 1986—, East County Econ. Devel. Coun., 1986—. Author: Teenage Marriages, 1976, Population, 8th edit., 2002, Aging, 1984, Demography of Islamic Nations, 1988, High Fertility Among Indochinese Refuges, 1989, Demographic Dynamics of the U.S.-Mex. Border, 1992. Grantee USPHS, 1983-84, 87-88, 88-89, 90—, U.S. Administrn. on Aging, 1979-80, U.S. Bur. of Census, 1988-89, Andrew W. Mellon Found., 1998-2001, NSF, 2001—; trainee USPHS, 1967-71 Mem. Population Assn. Am., Am. Sociol. Assn., Internat. Union for Sci. Study Population, Am. Assn. Geographers. Democrat. Office: San Diego State U Dept Geography San Diego CA 92182 E-mail: john.weeks@sdsu.edu.

WEEKS, M. J. international management consultant; b. N.Y.C., June 12, 1942; d. Kenneth James and Annette Jude (Williams) Altman; m. Robert S. Weeks, June 15, 1960; children: Sean Robert, Megan Elizabeth. BA cum laude, U. S.D., 1967, MA, 1969. Tchr. high sch. Orono Schs., Long Lake, Minn., 1970-74; mem. faculty Winona (Minn.) State U., 1976-82, Sioux Falls (S.D.) Coll., 1982—, dir. Ctr. Mgmt., 1985-89; pres. M.J. Weeks Seminars, Sioux Falls, 1982—. Cons. to numerous Fortune 500 orgns.; mgmt. cons., Sioux Falls, 1982—; speaker at numerous nat. assns., seminars, workshops, and convs. throughout U.S., S.Am., Can., and Mexico. Author: Taking Control with Time Management, 4th edit., (cassette tapes) Listening: The Quiet Side of Communication, How To Deliver Unpopular Information; also videos on strategic communication. Bd. dirs. League of Women Voters, Sioux Falls, 1983-85; mem. Women's Network, S.D., 1984-86, Peace and Justice Ctr., 1984-86, Sioux Falls Leadership II; trustee Crestwood United Ch. of Christ. Mem. AAUW (bd. dirs. 1983-84), ASTD, Internat. Platform Assn., Nat. Coun. Tchrs. of English, Nat. Am. Soc. Tng., Sioux Falls Pers. Assn. Avocations: duplicate bridge, reading, writing, traveling, gourmet cooking. Home and Office: 3575 S Ocean Blvd Ste 301 Palm Beach FL 33480 E-mail: mjwseminar@aol.com.

WEEKS, MARTA JOAN, priest; b. Buenos Aires, May 24, 1930; arrived in U.S., 1932; d. Frederick Albert and Anne (Newman) Sutton; m. Lewis Austin Weeks, Aug. 17, 1951; children: Kermit Austin, Leslie Anne. BA in Polit. Sci., Stanford U., 1951; MDiv, Episcopal Theol. Sem. S.W., 1991. Ordained priest Episcopal Ch., 1992. Legal libr., sec. Mene Grande Oil Co., Caracas, Venezuela, 1948; English tchr. Centro-Venezolano Americano, 1948; sec. Household Fin. Corp., Salt Lake City, 1951; legal sec. McKelvey & McKelvey Attys., Durango, Colo., 1952; sec., dir. Weeks Air Mus., Miami, Fla., 1985—2001; chaplain Jackson Meml. Hosp., 1992-93; priest-at-large Episcopal Diocese of S.E. Fla., 2002; interim asst. St. James Episcopal Ch., Salt Lake City, 1994-95; assisting priest St. Andrew's Episcopal Ch., Miami, Fla., 1999—2002. Trustee Beloit Coll., Wis., 1980—82, U. Miami, 1983—88, 1995—, Bishop Gray Inns, Lake Worth and Davenport, Fla., 1992—2002; advisor Ctr. for Sexuality and Religion, 1997—; mem. adv. coun. U. Utah, 1998—. Mem.: Am. Soc. Order St. John of Jerusalem. Address: 7350 SW 162nd St Miami FL 33157-3820 E-mail: msweeks@attglobal.net.

WEEKS, MAURICE RICHARD, JR. educational consultant, academic administrator; b. Washington, Dec. 14, 1943; s. Maurice Richard Sr. and Etienetta Adina (Duurloo) W.; children: Maurice III, Carol-Anne, William. BS, Villanova U., 1965; MEd, Temple U., 1966; EdD, Rutgers U., 1978. Cert. elem. tchr., Pa., cert. secondary tchr., Pa.; cert. secondary prin., Pa. Tchr. Sch. Dist. Phila., 1965-74, prin., 1974-95; ednl. cons., 1995—. Bd. trustees PILOT Svcs., Inc., Voorhees, N.J., 1992—. Bd. trustees Moorestown Libr. Assn., N.J., 1978-85, Phila. Parent/Child Ctr., 1983-90; bd. dirs. YMCA Camp Ockanickon, Medford, N.J., 1995—; coach Moorestown Men's League, 1982—, Camden Over 35 League, N.J., 1982—, Willingboro Summer Leagur, N.J., 1972-73. Mem. Am. Counseling. Assn., N.J. Assn. Sch. Adminstrs., Schoolman's Club Phila (v.p.), Alpha Phi Alpha. Democrat. Roman Catholic. Avocations: basketball, tennis, pinochle, bidwhist. Home: 724 Kimberly Dr Moorestown NJ 08057-4407

WEEKS, PHILIP, historian, educator; m. Jeanette Weeks, Dec. 0, 1972; children: Michael. PhD, Case Western Res. U. History prof. Kent State U., Canton, Ohio, 1986—. Author: (books) Farewell, My Nation, 2001. Republican. Evangelical Christian. Office: Kent State U 6000 Frank Ave Canton OH 44720

WEEKS, ROBERT LEE, electronic engineer, program manager; b. Woonsocket, R.I., Mar. 8, 1957; s. Joseph Bernard and Claire Lorraine (Jolicoeur) W.; m. Christine Ann Bentley; children: Barbara Ann, Christopher Lee. BSEE, U. Ariz., 1985, postgrad., 1987; MBA, U. Phoenix, 1996. Laborer ASARCO Mine Inc., Sahuarita, Ariz., 1979-82; test engr. EMI and TEMPEST br. U.S. Army Electronic Proving Ground, Ft. Huachuca, 1985-88, chief EMI and TEMPEST br., 1988-95, chief electromagnetics br., 1995-96, mgr. R&D program, 1996-2000, chief RF test and measurements br., 2000—. Mem. MIL-STD-461 Joint Working Group, 1989-94; mem. DOD and industry E3 standards com. Dept. Def., 1994—; mem. Army E3 Bd., 2000—. Bd. dirs. Bristol Park Neighborhood Assn., Tucson, 1994—; vol. YMCA, 1994—. With USMC, 1975-79. Mem. IEEE (named Engr. of Yr. local chpt. 1994), Electromagnetic Compatibility Soc. of IEEE, Nat. Assn. Radio and Telecomms. Engrs. (cert. electromagnetic compatibility engr.). Democrat. Roman Catholic. Avocations: basketball, bowling, hiking. Office: US Army Electronic Proving Ground STEWS-EPG-TE Fort Huachuca AZ 85613

WEEKS, ROBET ANDREW, materials science researcher, educator; b. Birmingham, Ala., Aug. 23, 1924; s. William Andrew and Annie Bell (Hammond) W.; m. Jane Sutherland, Mar. 20, 1948; children: Kevin Dale, Robin Dee, Loren Hammond, Kerry Andrew. BS, Birmingham-So. Coll., 1947; MS, U. Tenn., 1951; PhD, Brown U., 1966. Sr. physicist Union Carbide Corp., Oak Ridge, Tenn., 1951-84; rsch. prof. material sci. Vanderbilt U., 1984-99, prof. emeritus, 1999—. Disting. vis. prof. Am. U. in Cairo, 1970-71; invited prof. Ecole Poly. Fed. de Lausanne, Switzerland, 1981; vis. prof. Cath. U., Leuven, Belgium, 1983; cons. numerous pvt. corps. and fed. agys.; prin. investigator lunar materials, 1968-74; co-prin. investigator expdn. Western desert of Egypt to desert glass site, 1981; CEO Oak Ridge Cons., 1993—. Co-editor: Effects of Modes of Formation on Structure of Glass, 1985, 88, Editing the Refereed Scientific Journal, 1994; assoc. editor Jour. Geophys. Rsch., 1968-74; editor Jour. Noncrystalline Solids, 1988-98; conf. editor Jour. Non-Crystalline Solids, 1998-2000; contbr. numerous articles to profl. jours. Served with U.S. Army, 1943-46. Union Carbide fellow, 1964; Fulbright lectr., 1980; research fellow Reading U., 1971, USIA Am. participant Egypt, India, Nepal and Sri Lanka, 1986. Fellow Am. Ceramic Soc. (R. A. Weeks Symposium on Sci. and Tech. Si02 and Related Materials named in his honor, Honolulu 1993, George W. Morey award for contbns. to glass ci. 1998); mem. AAAS, Am. Phys. Soc. Avocation: photography. Home and Office: 331 Southshore Dr Greenback TN 37742-2301 E-mail: E1E2E4@aol.com.

WEEKS, ROSS LEONARD, JR. museum executive; b. Jamestown, N.Y., Sept. 11, 1936; s. Ross Leonard and Cecile Forbes (Carrie) W.; m. Patricia Ann Earley, June 10, 1961 (div.); children: Susan Woodall, Ross Leonard III, William Andrew, David James. AB, Colgate U., 1958; MS, George Washington U., 1971; cert., Fed. Exec. Inst., 1988. Reporter Jamestown Post-Jour., 1958-60, Richmond (Va.) News Leader, 1960-65; dir. pub. info. Coll. William and Mary, Williamsburg, Va., 1965-71, asst. to exec. v.p., 1971-74, asst. to pres., dir. univ. comms., 1974-81; exec. dir. Jamestown (Va.)-Yorktown Found., 1981-91, Hist. Crab Orchard Mus., Inc., Tazewell, Va., 1992—2002; ret., 2002; pres. Blue Ridge Concepts, Ltd., 1999—. Grant reviewer U.S. Inst. Mus. Svcs., Va. Arts Commn. Editor William & Mary Alumni Gazette, 1966-81; author: Virginia's Tazewell County: A Last Great Place, 2000; editor: 'Cause I'm Colored-The Black Heritage of Tazewell County, 2001; columnist: Clinch Valley News, 1998—. Chmn. Williamsburg-James City Bicentennial, 1975-77; treas. Coalfield Regional Tourism Devel. Authority S.W. Va., 1993-97; Va. S.W. Blue Ridge Highlands, Inc., 1993-97, v.p., 1996-97, pres., 1997-99; sec., treas. Frontier Culture Found., 1982-86; exec. dir. Va. Independence Bicentennial Commn., 1981-83; trustee coun. Thirteen Original States, 1982-87; chair Tazewell County Tourism Devel. Commn., 1993-97; mem. regional grant panel Va. Com. on the Arts, 1998—; mem. Gov.'s Va. History Initiative, 1995—; pres. Tazewell County Preservation Alliance, 2000—; lay eucharistic min. Cluster Episc. Parishes, Tazewell. Mem. Am. Assn. Mus. (mus. assessment cons. 1988—), Am. Assn. State and Local History, Masons, Rotary (Paul Harris fellow 1987), Clan Ross Assn., SAR (pres. Clinch Mountain Militia chpt. 2001—), Sigma Delta Chi, Kappa Delta Rho (Ordo Honora 1986). Avocations: travel, landscaping, antiquities, historical research. Home: 5 Windswept Tazewell VA 24651 E-mail: bluridge@earthlink.net.

WEEKS, STANLEY BYRON, foreign and defense policy consultant; b. Oakland, Calif., Dec. 11, 1948; s. Charles Roy and Evelyn Maxcy Weeks; m. Kathleen Case, Mar. 17, 1973; children: Christine, Elizabeth, Brian, Anne. BS in Fgn. Affairs, U.S. Naval Acad., 1970; MA in Internat. Studies, Am. Univ., 1974, PhD in Internat. Studies, 1977. Commd. ensign USN, 1970, advanced through grades to comdr., 1985, ret., 1990; sr. scientist Sci. Applications Internat. Corp., McLean, Va., 1990—. Adj. prof. Naval War Coll., Newport, R.I., 1994—; mil. cons. CBS News, N.Y.C., 1990—. Author: The Armed Forces of the USA in the Asia Pacific Region, 1999. Def. and fgn. policy advisor Dole Presdl. Campaign, Washington, 1995-96, Bush Campaign, 2000. Mem. Arms Control Assn., Navy League, U.S. Naval Inst., Internat. Inst. of Strategic Studies (London), Royal Inst. of Internat. Affairs (London), U.S. Coun. for Security Coop. in Asia-Pacific (bd. dirs. 1994—). Roman Catholic. Avocations: reading, skiing, travel. Home: 6221 Rockhurst Rd Bethesda MD 20817-1755 Office: Science Applications Internat Corp MS1-6-1 1710 SAIC Dr Mc Lean VA 22102-3799

WEEKS, STEVEN WILEY, lawyer; b. Topeka, Mar. 7, 1950; s. Glen Wiley and Grace Aileen (West) W.; m. Lee Nordgren, Aug. 1, 1974 (div. 1985); 1 child, Kirstin Nordgren. BS summa cum laude, Washburn U., 1972; JD cum laude, Harvard U., 1977. Bar: Ohio. Project leader Nat. Sanitation Found., Ann Arbor, Mich., 1972; engr. Kans. Dept. Health and Environ., Topeka, 1972-74; ptnr. Taft, Stettinius & Hollister, Cin., 1977—. Dir. The Myers Y. Cooper Co., Cin.; adj. faculty Chase Coll. Law, 1987-88. Mem. adv. com. prosecuting atty., Hamilton County, Cin., 1992; mem. Hamilton County Rep. Ctrl. Com., 1994—. Mem. Ohio State Bar Assn., Cin. Bar Assn. Republican. Methodist. Avocations: computers, golf. Home: 3641 Michigan Ave Cincinnati OH 45208-1411

WEEKS, TRESI LEA, lawyer; b. Brownwood, Tex., Dec. 3, 1961; d. Dean Moore and Patsy Ruth (Evans) Adams; m. Kevin Weeks, Oct. 26, 1998. BA in Fgn. Svc., BA in French, Baylor U., 1984, JD, 1987. Bar: Tex. 1987, U.S. Dist. Ct. (no. dist.) Tex. 1988, U.S. Ct. Appeals (5th cir.) 1989. Atty. Richard Jackson & Assocs., Dallas, 1987-91, Amis, Bell & Moore, Arlington, 1992-98; business owner, 2002—. Vol. Legal Svcs. of North Tex., Dallas, 1988-97, Dallas Com. for Fgn. Visitors, 1989-92; bd. dirs. Plano Internat. Presch., 1995-96. Recipient Pro Bono Svc. award Legal Svcs. of North Tex., 1989, 90, 91. Mem. AAUW (pub. policy dir. Plano, Tex. br. 1992, 93-94, v.p. 1994-95), State Bar Tex. (mem. mentor program for lawyers com. 1994-98, mem. local bar svcs. com. 1994-96), Dallas Bar Assn., Dallas Women Lawyers Assn. (bd. dirs. 1989-90, v.p. 1992, pres. 1993). Avocations: scuba diving, reading, bicycling, hiking, growing herbs.

WEEKS, WILFORD FRANK, retired geophysics educator, glaciologist; b. Champaign, Ill., Jan. 8, 1929; married; 2 children. BS, U. Ill., 1951, MS, 1953; PhD in Geology, U. Chgo., 1956. Geologist mineral deposits br. U.S. Geol. Survey, 1952-55; glaciologist USAF Cambridge Research Ctr., 1955-57; asst. prof. Washington U., St. Louis, 1957-62; adj. prof. earth scis. Dartmouth Coll., Hanover, N.H., 1962-85; glaciologist Cold Regions Rsch. and Engring. Lab., 1962-89; chief scientist Alaska Synthetic Aperture Radar Facility, Fairbanks, 1986-93; prof. geophysics Geophys. Inst. U. Alaska, 1986-96. Cons. in field, 1996—; vis. prof. Inst. Low Temperature Sci. Hokkaido U., Sapporo, Japan, 1973; chair Arctic marine sci. USN Postgrad. Sch., Monterey, Calif., 1978-79; mem. earth sys. sci. com. NASA, Washington, 1984-87; advisor U.S. Arctic Rsch. Commn., divsn. polar programs NSF, Washington, 1987-88; chmn. NAS Com. on Cooperation with Russia in Ice Mechanics, 1991-92; mem. environ. task force MEDEA Cons. Group, 1992—. Capt. USAF, 1955-57. Recipient Emil Usibelli Prize for Rsch., 1996, U. Ill. Dept. Geology Alumni Achievment award, 1999. Fellow Arctic Inst. N.Am., Am. Geophys. Union; mem. NAE, Internat. Glaciological Soc. (v.p. 1969-72, pres. 1973-75, Seligman Crystal award 1989), Am. Polar Soc. (hon.). Avocations: skiing, diving, contrabassist. Home and Office: 6533 SW 34th Ave Portland OR 97201-1077 E-mail: w-f-weeks@attbi.com.

WEEKS, WILLIAM BRINSON, physician; b. Oklahoma City, June 14, 1963; s. Warren Brinson Weeks and Linda Adams Cutchall; m. Amy Elisabeth Wallace; children: Tanner Wallace, Atticus Wallace, Savannah Wallace, Scout Wallace, Joplin Wallace, Hoke Wallace. MD, U. Tex., Galveston , 1988; MBA, Columbia U., 1996. Sr. scholar Vets. Healthcare Adminstrn., WRJ, Vt., 1997—2002; dir. Vets. Rural Health Initiative, 1999—2002, Patient Safety Ctr. Inquiry, WRJ, 1998—2002. Contbr. to various sci. pubs. Treas. Lyme Congl. Ch., Lyme, NH, 1998—2002. Mem.: Am. Coll. Healthcare Execs., Am. Coll. Physicians Execs. Office: Vets Healthcare Adminstrn VAMC (11Q) White River Junction VT 05009 Office Fax: 802 291 6286.

WEEKS, WILLIAM RAWLE, JR. oil company executive; b. Denver, Oct. 23, 1920; s. William Rawle Sr. and Besse Elizabeth (Griffith) W.; m. June Suzanne Stephens, Jan. 22, 1944 (div. 1980); children: Stephen R., Tacy A. Weeks Hahn. BA, Stanford U., 1943. With book prodn. divsn. Stanford U. Press, 1948-49; advt. exec. Palo Alto, Calif., 1949-50; with CIA, 1951—; gen. ptnr. Weeks, Brewer & Assocs., 1971; CEO Fort Collins Consol. Royalties, Inc., Cheyenne, Wyo., 1983—. Author: Knock and Wait Awhile, 1957 (Edgar Allan Poe award 1958, Commonwealth award 1958). Nat. press and media advance man Muskie Vice Presdl. Campaign, 1968. 2nd lt. U.S. Army, 1943-46. Mem. Nat. Press Club, Denver Petroleum Club, Heather Ridge Country Club. Avocations: flying, skiing, golfing, hiking. Home: 1201 Williams St Apt 11C Denver CO 80218-2678 Office: Fort Collins Consol Royalties Inc 1508 Stillwater Ave Cheyenne WY 82009-7349

WEEKS-BROWN, RHODA LETHEA, lawyer; b. Harper City, Liberia, Apr. 3, 1967; d. Rocheforte L. Weeks and Fannie Elizabeth (Thomson) Goll; m. Lionel T. Brown. BA in Econs. summa cum laude, Howard U., 1988; JD, Harvard U., 1991. Bar: N.Y. 1992, Mass. 1992, D.C. 1992. Assoc. Skadden, Arps, Slate, Meagher & Flom, L.L.P., Washington, 1991-97; counsel IMF, 1997—2001, sr. counsel, 2001—. Contbr. articles to profl. jours. Mem.: ABA, Internat. Bar Assn. Baptist. Avocation: tennis. Office: IMF 700 19th St NW Washington DC 20431-0001

WEEMS, CARRIE MAE, photographer; BA, Calif. Inst. Arts, Valencia, 1981; MFA, U. Calif., San Diego, 1984; postgrad., U. Calif., Berkeley, 1984-87. Asst. prof. Hampshire Coll., Amherst, Mass., 1987-91, Calif. Coll. Arts and Crafts, Oakland, 1991-95; artist, prof. Harvard U., 1995—. Vis. prof. Hunter Coll., N.Y., 1988-89, Williams Coll., 2000, Harvard U., 2001. One-person shows include Inst. Contemporary Art, 1991, Trustman Gallery, Simmons Coll., Boston, 1991, The New Mus. Contemporary Art, N.Y., 1991, Matrix Gallery, Wadsworth Atheneum, Hartford, Conn., 1991, Albright Coll., Reading, Pa., 1991, Greenville County Mus. Art, S.C., 1992, San Francisco Art Inst., 1992, Linda Cathcart Gallery, Santa Monica, Calif., 1993, Rhonda Hoffman Gallery, Chgo., 1993, New Langton Arts, San Francisco, 1993, Hood Mus. Art, Dartmouth Coll., N.H., 1994, Mus. Modern Art, N.Y., 1995, The Bunting Inst., 1996, Contemporary Arts Mus., Houston, 1996, Everson Art Mus., Syracuse, N.Y., 1998, High Mus. Art, Atlanta, 2000, Internat. Ctr. Photography N.Y., 2000, Parrish Art Mus., 2001; group shows include Reframing the Family Artists Space, 1991, Whitney Mus. Am. Art, 1991, Mus. Modern Art, 1992, Randy Alexander, 1992, Artists of Conscience: 16 Years of Social and Polit. Commentary, Alt. Mus. N.Y., 1991-92, Through the Kitchen Door, NAME, 1991-92, Disclosing the Myth of Family, Art Inst. Chgo., The Betty Rymer Gallery, Chgo., 1992, The Theater of Refusal: Black Art and the Mainstream Criticism (traveling), 1993-94, States of Loss: Migration, Displacement, Colonialism and Power, Jersey City Mus., N.J., 1993-94, Gesture and Pose, Mus. Modern Art, N.Y., 1994, Bad Girls, Part 1, New Mus. Contemporary Art, N.Y., 1994, Who's Looking at the Family? Barbican Art Gallery, London, 1994, Equal Rights and Justice, High Mus. Art and Nat. Black Arts Fest, Atlanta, 1994, Imaging Families: Images and Voices, Smithsonian Instn., 1994-95, Black Male, Representations of Masculinity in Contemporary Am. Art, Whitney Mus. Am. Art, N.Y., 1994-95, Embedded Metaphor, Ringling Mus. Art, Sarasota, 1996, Alternate Cultures, Johannesberg Biennial, Africa, 1997, Changing Spaces, Detroit Inst. Art, 1998, Bearing Witness, Polk Mus. Art, 1998, Art Worlds in Dialog, Mus. Ludwig, Cologne, Germany, 1999, Paradise Now, Exit Art, N.Y., 2000, Collection in Context, Studio Mus. Harlem, N.Y., 2001. Office: c/o PPOW 476 Broome St Fl 3 New York NY 10013-2237

WEEMS, HELEN RACHEL, piano teacher, accompanist; b. Morgantown, W.Va., Dec. 12, 1962; d. David Burnola and Charys (Ford) Weems; m. Robert Raymond Provine, June 8, 1996. BA, Sch. of the Ozarks, Point Lookout, Mo., 1986; MM, Peabody Conservatory of Music, Balt., 1991; MA, U. Md. Baltimore County, Balt., 1996. Radio host Sta. KSOZ, Point Lookout, 1985-86, Sta. WJHU, Balt., 1994-96; piano tchr., pianist singer, 1975—. Contbr. articles to profl. jours. Balinese dancer UMBC Gamelan, Balt., 1993—96; pres. Harper's Glen Townhouse Assn., Columbia, 1998—99; coord. Harper's Glen Watch, 1998—; Choir dir., lay min. St. Luke's Episcopal Ch., Brookeville, Md., 1997—. Grantee neighrborhood improvement, 1999—. Mem.: Greater Columbia Music Tchrs. Assn. (v.p. 1997—2000), Howard County Music Tchrs. Assn. (pres. 1996—). Democrat. Episcopalian. Avocations: running, gardening. Office: Helen R Weems Piano Studio 5473 Green Dory Ln Columbia MD 21044-1912

WEEMS, JOHN EDWARD, writer; b. Grand Prairie, Tex., Nov. 2, 1924; s. J. Eddie and Anna Lee (Scott) W.; m. Jane Ellen Homeyer, Sept. 11, 1946; children: Donald (dec.), Carol, Mary, Barbara, Janet. BJ, U. Tex., 1948, M.Journalism, 1949; MA in Libr. Sci., Fla. State U., 1954. Tel. editor Temple (Tex.) Daily Telegram, 1950; instr. Calif. State Poly. Coll., San Dimas, 1950-51; night news editor San Angelo (Tex.) Standard-Times, 1951; copy editor Dallas Morning News, 1952-53; asst. prof., head cataloger main library Baylor U., 1954-57; asst. prof. U. Ala., also asst. mgr. Ala. Press Assn., 1957-58; asst. to dir. U. Tex. Press, 1958-68; prof. English, Baylor U., 1968-71, lectr. creative writing, fall 1979; reference librarian McLennan Community Coll., Waco, Tex., 1969-70; freelance writer, 1971—. With USNR, 1943-46, 51-52; lt. Res. (ret.). Am. Philos. Soc. grantee, 1964. Fellow Tex. State Hist. Assn., Tex. Inst. Letters; mem. PEN, Nat. Book Critics Circle, Authors Guild, Western Writers Am., Sigma Delta Chi, Beta Phi Mu. Author: A Weekend in September, 1957; The Fate of the Maine, 1958; Race for the Pole, 1960; Peary: The Explorer and the Man, 1967; Men Without Countries, 1969; Dream of Empire (Amon G. Carter award), 1971; To Conquer a Peace: The War Between the United States and Mexico (Richard Fleming award), 1974; Death Song, 1976; The Tornado, 1977; (with John Biggers and Carroll Simms) Black Art in Houston, 1978; "If You Don't Like the Weather," 1986; editor: A Texas Christmas: A Miscellany of Art, Poetry, Fiction, Vol. I, 1983, Vol. II, 1986; (San Antonio Conservation Soc. Spl. award), The Story of Texas, 1986, Austin (Texas): 1839-1989, 1989 (Tex. Inst. Letters Barbara McCombs Lon Tinkle award lifetime Writing achievement 1989). Address: 394 River Rd Waco TX 76705-5621

WEEMS, MARY ANN, art gallery owner; b. Carlsbad, N.Mex., June 12, 1948; d. Myer and Nadine Lolita (Miller) Rosenberg; div. 1993; children: Elizabeth Nadine, Brian Eli. BS in Art cum laude, William Woods Coll., 1970. Cert. tchr., Mo., Tex. Tchr. art Lubbock (Tex.) Pub. Sch., 1970-71; profl. artist Albuquerque, 1972-77; owner Weems Galleries & Framing, 1981—, Weems Artfest, Albuquerque, 1982—, Weems Gallery - Old Town, Albuquerque,

1994—. Bd. dirs. N.Mex. Arts and Crafts Fair, Albuquerque, 1972-76, Rio Grande Arts and Crafts Fair, 1974-77. Mem. Albuquerque Conv. and Visitors Bur., 1981—, bd. dirs., 1990-92; loan fund mem. West Corp., Albuquerque, 1992-95; bd. dirs. Albuquerque Mus., 1986-88; mem. N.Mex. Arts Commn., 1998—; bd. dirs. U. N.Mex. Found., 1999—, Presbyn. Healthcare, 1999—. Named one of Women on the Move YWCA, 1996, 10 Top Smart, Savvy, Successful Albuquerque Women's Mag., 1997; named #1 Fine Arts and Crafts Fair in N.Mex. Harris List, 1996. Mem. Internat. Festivals and Events Assn. (Pinnacle award 1996), S.W. Festivals and Events Assn., Albuquerque C. of C., Albuquerque Gallery Assn. (pres. 1984-86). Jewish. Avocations: tennis, performing arts. Office: Weems Galleries and Framing 2801 Eubank Blvd NE Ste M Albuquerque NM 87112-1300

WEENING, RICHARD WILLIAM, JR. banker, finance and communications executive, venture capitalist; b. San Bernardino, Calif., Dec. 24, 1945; s. Richard William and Alice Louise (Young) W.; m. Elizabeth Louise Halmbacher, June, 1965 (div. Aug. 1973); children: Elicia Louise, Mia Lynn; M. Robin Lorraine Woodard, July, 1990. Student, St. Johns U., 1963-65, U. Wis., 1966-68. Legis. asst. U.S. Congressman Henry S. Reuss, Washington, 1968-70; exec. sec., chief of staff Wis. Gov. Patrick J. Lucey, Madison, 1970-72; pres., pub., dir. Raintree Pubs., Inc., Milw., 1972-85; pres., chief exec. officer, dir. McDonald-Raintree, Inc., 1977-82, George Philip Raintree, Cartographers, Inc., 1978-82; chmn., dir. Raintree Pubs. Internat., Ltd., London, 1978-82, Raintree de Mexico Editores, SA, Mexico City, 1978-82; chief exec. officer AgriData Resources, Inc. (now known as ARI Network Svcs., Inc.), 1981-87, chmn., chief. exec. officer, 1987-89, chmn., 1989—; mng. prin. Quaestus Ltd. Ptnrs., 1990—; pres., chief exec. officer RPI Holdings, Inc., 1985—; owner Northcote Vineyards, 1979—. Bd. dirs. CONNECT, Inc., MERX, Inc., Electronic Product Info. Corp., Dynatec Systems Corp.; chmn. Lakefront Devel. Task Force, Milw., 1974, Chenequa Cable Com., 1991—; pres. Bd Harbor Commrs., Port of Milw., 1976-78; commr. Lake Area Communications System, 1990—. Bd. dirs. FFA Found., 19830-87; active Chenqua Police and Fire Commn., Lake Area Comm. System Commn. in Hartland, Wis., 1990—. Mem. Info. Industry Assn., Young Pres.'s Orgn., Milw. Athletic Club, Milw. Yacht Club. Office: 330 E Kilbourn Ave Milwaukee WI 53202-3170

WEERS, JEFFRY G. research scientist; b. Jamestown, Nd, Nov. 10, 1958; s. Harold Alvin and Gladys Laura Weer; m. Janice Weers, Mar. 26, 1988; children: Alena Nicole, Emma Adelle, Audrey Elise. PhD, U. of Calif. at Davis, Davis, California, 1985; BS, U. of Puget Sound, Tacoma, Washington. Dir. Inhale Therapeutic Systems Inc., San Carlos, Calif., 1999—; sr. scientist/dir. Alliance Pharm. Corp., San Diego, 1990—99; scientist Clorox, Pleasanton, 1985—89. Editl. bd. Elsevier Sci., Oxford, United Kingdom, 1996—2002. Contbr. chapters to books and articles to profl. jours. Mem.: Internat. Soc. for Aerosols in Medicine, Controlled Release Soc., Am. Assn. for Pharm. Scientists, Am. Chem. Soc. Achievements include patents for And Patents Pending, Respiration, Blood Substitutes, Drug Delivery; invention of FDA approved ultrasound contrast agent; Blood Substitute Formulation; Partial Liquid Ventilation. Home: 432 Corando Avenue Half Moon Bay CA 94019 Office: Inhale Therapeutic Systems Incorporated 150 Industrial Road San Carlos CA E-mail: jweers@inhale.com.

WEERTMAN, JOHANNES, materials science educator; b. Fairfield, Ala., May 11, 1925; s. Roelof and Christina (van Vlaardingen) W.; m. Julia Ann Randall, Feb. 10, 1950; children: Julia Ann, Bruce Randall. Student, Pa. State Coll., 1943-44; BS, Carnegie Inst. Tech. (now Carnegie Mellon U.), 1948, DSc, 1951; postgrad., Ecole Normale Superieure, Paris, 1951-52. Solid State physicist U.S. Naval Rsch. Lab., Washington, 1952-58, cons., 1960-67; sci. liaison officer U.S. Office Naval Rsch., Am. Embassy, London, 1958-59; faculty Northwestern U., Evanston, Ill., 1959—, prof. materials sci. dept., 1961-68, chmn. dept., 1964-68, prof. geol. scis. dept., 1963—, Walter P. Murphy prof. materials sci. and engring. emeritus, 1999—. Vis. prof. geophysics Calif. Inst. Tech., 1964, Scott Polar Rsch. Inst., Cambridge (Eng.) U., 1970-71, Swiss Fed. Inst. Reactor Rsch., 1986; cons. Cold Regions Rsch. and Engring. Lab., U.S. Army, 1960-75, Oak Ridge (Tenn.) Nat. Lab., 1963-67, Los Alamos (N.Mex.) Sci. Lab., 1967—; co-editor materials sci. books MacMillan Co., 1962-76. Author: Dislocation Based Fracture Mechanics, 1996, (with Julia Weertman) Elementary Dislocation Theory, 1964, 2d edit., 1992; mem. editorial bd. Metal. Trans., 1967-75, Jour. Glaciology, 1972—; assoc. editor Jour. Geophys. Rsch., 1973-75, 2000-01; contbr. articles to profl. jours. With USMC, 1943-46. Honored with naming of Weertman Island in Antarctica.; Fulbright fellow, 1951-52; recipient Acta Metallurgica gold medal, 1980; Guggenheim fellow, 1970-71 Fellow Am. Acad. Arts and Scis., Am. Soc. Metals, Am. Phys. Soc., Geol. Soc. Am., Am. Geophys. Union (Horton award 1972, AIME Mathewson Gold medal 1977); mem. AAAS, NAE, Am. Inst. Physics, Internat. Glaciol. Soc. (Seligman Crystal award 1983), Arctic Inst., Am. Quaternary Assn., Explorers Club, Fulbright Assn., Sigma Xi, Tau Beta Pi, Phi Kappa Phi, Alpha Sigma Mu, Pi Mu Epsilon. Home: 834 Lincoln St Evanston IL 60201-2405 Office: Northwestern U Materials Sci Dept Evanston IL 60208-0001 E-mail: j-weertman2@nwu.edu.

WEERTMAN, JULIA RANDALL, materials science and engineering educator; b. Muskegon, Mich., Feb. 10, 1926; BS in Physics, Carnegie-Mellon U., 1946, MS in Physics, 1947, DSc in Physics, 1951. Physicist U.S. Naval Rsch. Lab., Washington, 1952-58; vis. asst. prof. dept. materials sci. and engring. Northwestern U., Evanston, Ill., 1972-73, asst. prof., 1973-78, from asst. prof. to assoc. prof., 1973-82, prof., 1982-99, Walter P. Murphy prof., 1989, chmn. dept., 1987-92, asst. to dean grad. studies and rsch. Tech. Inst., 1973-76, Walter P. Murphy prof. emeritus, 1999—. Mem. various NRC coms. and panels. Co-author: Elementary Dislocation Theory, 1964, 1992, also pub. in French, Japanese and Polish; contbr. numerous articles to profl. jours. Mem. Evanston Environ. Control Bd., 1972-79. Recipient Creativity award NSF, 1981, 86; Guggenheim Found. fellow, 1986-87. Fellow Am. Soc. Metals Internat., Minerals, Metals and Materials Soc. (leadership award 1997); mem. ASTM, NAE, Am. Acad. Arts and Scis., Am. Phys. Soc., Materials Rsch. Soc., Soc. Women Engrs. (disting. engring. educator award 1989, achievement award 1991). Home: 834 Lincoln St Evanston IL 60201-2405 Office: Northwestern U Dept Material Sci & Engring 2225 N Campus Dr Evanston IL 60208-0876 E-mail: jrweertman@northwestern.edu.

WEESE, BENJAMIN HORACE, architect; b. Evanston, Ill., June 4, 1929; s. Harry Ernest and Marjorie (Mohr) W.; m. Cynthia Rogers, July 5, 1963; children: Daniel Peter, Catharine Mohr. B.Arch., Harvard U., 1951, M.Arch., 1957; cert., Ecole des Beaux Arts, Fontainebleau, France, 1956. Assoc., Harry Weese & Assocs., Architects, Chgo., 1957-77; prin. Weese Langley Weese, 1977—. Co-founder, pres. Chgo. Arch. Found., Glessner House, Chgo., 1966— Trustee Graham Found. for Advanced Studies in Fine Arts, 1988—, pres. 1995-99; mem. Commn. Chgo. Landmarks, 1998—. Fellow AIA; mem. Nat. Council Archtl. Registration Bds. Home: 2133 N Hudson Ave Chicago IL 60614-4522 Office: Weese Langley Weese Ltd 9 W Hubbard St Chicago IL 60610-4630 E-mail: bweese@wlwltd.com.

WEESE, BRUCE ERIC, pharmaceutical sales executive; b. Chewelah, Wash., Mar. 22, 1942; s. Harry M. and Roberta B. (Carman) W.; m. Elaine M. Smith, June 18, 1962 (div. July 1972); children: Sandra G., Michael D.; m. Vera B. Reed, Mar. 22, 1975; stepchildren: Kevin E. Bayron, Kelly M. Bayron. BA in Edn., Ea. Wash. State U., Cheney, 1964; MBA, Pepperdine U., 1981. Tchr. Grant Joint Union High Sch. Dist., Sacramento, 1964-70; pharm. sales McNeil Labs., San Jose, Calif., 1970-77, Adria Labs., San Francisco, 1977-83, Serono Labs., San Francisco, 1983-84, Boehringer Ingelheim, Santa Rosa, Calif., 1984-91, mgr. govt. affairs (lobbyist) for western states, 1991-97, area mgr. managed care, 1997-98; pharm. sales rep. Olympia, Wash., 2000—. Bd. dirs. Russian River Health Ctr., Guerneville, Calif., 1994-95, 98—, Redwood Empire br. Am. Lung Assn., 1998—. Mem. United Anglers, Sequoia Paddlers, Santa Rosa Sailing Club, Sierra Club. Democrat. Avocations: kayaking, sailing, fishing. Home and Office: 4013 Grove Rd NW Olympia WA 98502-3766

WEESE, MIRANDA, dancer; b. San Bernardino, Calif. Student, Sch. Am. Ballet, 1990. Apprentice N.Y.C. Ballet, 1991—93, mem. corps de ballet, 1993—94, soloist, 1994—95, prin., 1996—. Dancer (ballets) Apollo, Concerto Barocco, Divertimento No. 15, The Four Temperaments, Romeo and Juliet, Chiaroscuro, The Sleeping Beauty, others, PBS TV spl. Martins' Swan Lake Live from Lincoln Ctr. Fellow USA Dance fellow, Princess Grace Found., 1995—96. Office: NYC Ballet NY State Theatre 20 Lincoln Ctr Plz New York NY 10023-6913*

WEFLER, WILSON DANIEL, publisher, management consultant; b. Rocky River, Ohio, Feb. 27, 1927; s. Wilson Daniel and Myra (Johns) W.; m. Bonnie Kistner, Feb. 9, 1952; children: Wendy, Nancy, Bonnie, Susan, John. BS in Journalism, Northwestern U., 1950, postgrad., 1950-51. Asst. editor, writer Standard Oil Co., Chgo., 1951-55; asst. editor Keeney Pub. Co., 1955-56; pub. rep. Urban Farley & Co., 1957-61; dir. alumni relations Northwestern U., Evanston, Ill., 1961-65; pres. Com. for Middle Western Bus. Devel., Inc., Chgo., 1965-75; sr. v.p. Unimark Internat., Chgo., N.Y.C., Milan, 1975-79; pres. Wefler & Assocs., Inc., Evanston, 1979—. Past pres. Assn. Profl. Design Firms, San Francisco, 1985-88, chmn. founding com., 1984; pub. Design Firm Directory, 1979—. Editor Design Firm Mgmt., 1980-95. Bd. commrs. Lighthouse Park Dist., Evanston, 1992—, pres., 1999—. Recipient Service award Northwestern U. Alumni Assn., 1966. Mem. Soc. Typographic Arts, John Evans Club, Half Century Club (chmn. 2001). Home: 6 Milburn Park Evanston IL 60201-1744 Office: Wefler & Assocs Inc PO Box 1167 Evanston IL 60204-1167

WEG, IRA, internist, cardiologist, educator; b. Bklyn., Jan. 16, 1951; MD, SUNY, Bklyn., 1976. Diplomate Am. Bd. Internal Medicine, Am. Bd. Cardiovascular Diseases; cert. Bd. Nuclear Cardiology. Intern SUNY Kings County Hosp.-Bklyn. VA Hosp., 1976-77, resident in internal medicine, 1977-79; fellow in cardiovasc. diseases Montefiore Hosp. Med. Ctr., Bronx, N.Y., 1979-81; mem. staff L.I. Jewish Med. Ctr., New Hyde Park, North Shore Univ. Hosp., Manhasset, NY, South Nassau Cmtys. Hosp., Oceanside, Mercy Med. Ctr., Rockville Centre; pvt. practice Lynbrook, NY, 2000—. Asst. prof. medicine Albert Einstein Coll. Medicine. Fellow Am. Coll. Cardiology, Am. Coll. Chest Physicians. Office: 158 Hempstead Ave Lynbrook NY 11563-1605

WEG, JOHN GERARD, physician; b. N.Y.C., Feb. 16, 1934; s. Leonard and Pauline M. (Kanzleiter) W.; m. Mary Loretta Flynn, June 2, 1956; children: Diane Marie, Kathryn Mary, Carol Ann, Loretta Louise, Veronica Susanne, Michelle Celeste. BA cum laude, Coll. Holy Cross, Worcester, Mass., 1955; MD, N.Y. Med. Coll., 1959. Diplomate: Am. Bd. Internal Medicine. Commd. 2d lt. USAF, 1958, advanced through grades to capt., 1967; intern Walter Reed Gen. Hosp., Washington, 1959-60; resident, then chief resident in internal medicine Wilford Hall USAF Hosp., Lackland AFB, Tex., 1960-64, chief pulmonary sect., 1964-66, chief inhalation sect., 1964-66, chief pulmonary and infectious disease service, 1966-67; resigned, 1967; clin. dir. pulmonary disease div. Jefferson Davis Hosp., Houston, 1967-71; from asst. prof. to assoc. prof. medicine Baylor U. Coll. Medicine, 1967-71; assoc. prof. medicine U. Mich. Med. Sch. Univ. Hosp., Ann Arbor, 1971-74, prof., 1974—2001, prof. emeritus, 2001—. Physician-in-charge pulmonary div., 1971-81, physician-in-charge pulmonary and critical care med. div., 1981-85; cons. Ann Arbor VA, 1971—, Wayne County Gen. hosps., 1971-84; mem. adv. bd. Washtenaw County Health Dept., 1973—; mem. respiratory and nervous system panel, anesthesiology Sect. Nat. Ctr. Devices and Radiol. Health, FDA, 1983—, chmn., 1985-88. Contbr. med. jours., reviewer, mem. editorial bds. Decorated Air Force Commendation medal; travelling fellow Nat. Tb and Respiratory Disease Assn., 1971; recipient Aesculpaius award Tex. Med. Assn., 1971 Fellow Am. Coll. Chest Physicians (chmn. bd. govs. 1976-79, gov. Mich. 1975-79, chmn. membership com. 1976-79, prof.-in-residence 1972—, chmn. critical care coun. 1982-85, chmn. ethics com. 1998), Am. Coll. Chest Physicians and Internat. Acad. Chest Physicians (exec. council 1976-82, pres. 1980-81), ACP (chmn. Mich. program com. 1974); mem. AAAS, Am. Fedn. Clin. Rsch., AMA, Am. Thoracic Soc. (sec.-treas. 1974-76), Am. Assn. Inhalation Therapy, Air Force Soc. Internists and Allied Specialists, Soc. Med. Consultants to Armed Forces, Internat. Union Against Tb, Mich. Thoracic Soc. (pres. 1976-78), Mich. Lung Assn. (dir., Bruce Douglas award 1981), Am. Lung Assn., Rsch. Club U. Mich., Assn. Advancement Med. Instrumentation, Central Soc. Clin. Rsch., Am. Bd. Internal Medicine (subsplty. com. on pulmonary disease 1980-86, critical care medicine test com. 1985-87, critical care medicine policy com. 1986-87), N.Y. Med. Coll. Alumni Assn. (medal of honor 1990), Alpha Omega Alpha. Home: 3060 Exmoor Rd Ann Arbor MI 48104-4132 Office: B I H 245 Box 0026 1500 E Medical Center Dr Ann Arbor MI 48109-0005 E-mail: jweg@umich.edu.

WEGELIN, JACOB ANDREAS, statistician; b. Eugene, Oreg., Dec. 14, 1954; s. Christof Andreas and Caroline (Locke) W. BA, BS, U. Wash., 1986, MS, 1989, PhD, 2001. With Shiloh Youth Revival Ctrs., Inc., Oreg., Wash., Calif., Ariz., Alaska, 1971-76, Eugene Hotel, 1976-78; deckhand fishing industry, Alaska, 1978-79; tech. writer, editor IBM Corp., San Jose, Calif. and, N.Y., Poughkeepsie, N.Y., 1985-86; cook, deckhand, bull cook Alaska Boat Co., Wards Cove Packing Co., 1991-93; instr. MathSoft, Seattle, 1995; statistician U. Wash., 1996—. Recipient Pres.'s medal U. Wash., 1986; NSF fellow, 1986-89. Mem. Am. Statis. Assn., Phi Beta Kappa. Office: U Wash Dept Stats PO Box 354322 Seattle WA 98195-4322

WEGENER, DUANE T. social psychology educator; b. Winona, Minn., Mar. 18, 1966; s. Merlen F. and Nancy L. Wegener; m. Laura J. Wegener, June 16, 1990; children: Jonathan, Rachel. AB, U. Mo., 1989; MA, Ohio State U., 1991, PhD, 1994. Asst. prof. Yale U., New Haven; assoc. prof. Purdue U., West Lafayette, Ind., 1997—. Assoc. editor: Personality and Social Psychology Bull., 2000-2001; contbr. articles to profl. jours. Mem. APA (Disting. Sci. Early Career Contbns. to Psychology award 2001), Soc. for Exptl. Social Psychology (elected), Soc. for Personality and Social Psychology, Midwestern Psychol. Assn., Am. Psychol. Assn. Office: Purdue U Psychol Scis West Lafayette IN 47907-1364

WEGENER, MARK DOUGLAS, lawyer; b. Nov. 1, 1948; s. Virgil Albert and Jean Frances (Wilke) W.; m. Donna Chait, May 28, 1972; children: Tara, David, Marisa. BA cum laude, Cen. Coll., Pella, Iowa, 1970; JD, Rutgers U., 1973. Bar: D.C. 1974, U.S. Dist. Ct. D.C. 1974, U.S. Ct. Appeals (D.C. cir.) 1974. Assoc. Howrey & Simon, Washington, 1973-79; ptnr. Howrey Simon Arnold & White, 1979—. Mem. ABA (anti-trust sect., litigation sect.), The Metropolitan Club, Stage Harbor Yacht Club. Office: Howrey Simon Arnold & White LLP 1299 Pennsylvania Ave NW Washington DC 20004-2400

WEGENER, PETER PAUL, engineering educator, author; b. Berlin, Aug. 29, 1917; came to U.S., 1946; naturalized, 1953. m. Annette Schleiermacher, Aug. 14, 1961; children: Paul, Christopher, Philip. Dr rer. nat., U. Berlin, 1943; MA (priv.), Yale U., 1960; Dr. Ing. (E.h.) (hon.), U. Karlsruhe, Germany, 1979. Researcher supersonic wind tunnels, Kochel, Germany, 1943-45; researcher gasdynamics, hypersonic wind tunnels U.S. Naval Ordnance Lab., 1946-53, Jet Propulsion Lab. Calif. Inst. Tech., 1953-60; prof. applied sci. Yale U., New Haven, 1960-72, Harold Hodgkinson prof. engring. and applied sci., 1972—, chmn. dept. engring. applied sci., 1966-71, prof. emeritus, 1987—. Sr. Am. scientist Humboldt Found., 1979 Author: (books) The Peenemünde Wind Tunnels: A Memoir, 1996, What Makes Airplanes Fly?, 1997; researcher and contbr. articles on hypersonics, condensation metastable state, chem. kinetics, flow systems real gases, bubbles to profl. jours. Inst. Advanced Study Berlin fellow, 1986. Fellow Am. Phys. Soc., Conn. Acad. Sci. & Engring. (charter). Home: 29 Montgomery Pkwy Branford CT 06405-5128

WEGENER, ROBERT PAUL, communications educator; b. Sept. 22, 1947; BS, Okla. State U., 1969, MS, 1975. Asst. prof. Okla. State U. Sch. Journalism and Broadcasting, Stillwater, 1978-84; assoc. prof. dept. journalism Tex. A&M U., College Station, 1984-90, gen. mgr. student media, 1990—. Office: Tex A&M U 1111 TAMU College Station TX 77843-1111

WEGGE, LEON LOUIS FRANÇOIS, retired economics educator; b. Breendonk, Antwerp, Belgium, June 9, 1933; came to U.S., 1959; s. Petrus Maria and Alberta (De Maeyer) W.; m. Beate Maria Teipel, Nov. 22, 1962; children: Simone, Robert, Elizabeth. B in Thomistical Philosophy, Cath. U. Louvain, Belgium, 1957, Licentiate in Econ. Sci., 1958; PhD in Indsl. Econs., MIT, 1963. Assoc. lectr. U. New S. Wales, Kensington, Australia, 1963-66; prof. econs. U. Calif., Davis, 1966-94, retired, 1994. Vis. prof. U. Bonn, Fed. Republic Germany, 1980-81. Assoc. editor Jour. Internat. Econs., 1971-84; contbr. articles to profl. jours. Rsch. fellow Ctr. for Ops. Rsch. and Econometrics, 1972-73, fellow The Netherlands Inst. for Advanced Study, 1987-88. Mem. Econometric Soc., Am. Statistical Assn. Roman Catholic. Home: 26320 County Rd # 98 Davis CA 95616

WEGLARZ, NATALIE M. accountant, legal consultant; b. Chgo., Mar. 11, 1975; d. Marion J. and Bess A. (Kolarik) W. BS, DePaul U., 1997. CPA. Sr. II Grant Thornton, Chgo., 1997—. Legal cons. Title Svcs., Naperville, Ill., 1990—. Mem. Ill. CPA Soc. Avocations: snow skiing, piano, jet skiing, volleyball, mountain biking. Office: Grant Thornton 130 E Randolph St Ste 700 Chicago IL 60601-6144

WEGMAN, DAVID HOWE, health science educator, consultant; b. Balt., Mar. 13, 1940; s. Myron Ezra and Isabel (Howe) W.; m. Cynthia Heynen, June 18, 1962 (div. Aug. 1968); m. Peggy Nelson, June 7, 1969; children: Jesse Howe, Marya Nelson. BA, Swarthmore Coll., 1962; MD, Harvard U., 1966, MS in Physiology, 1972. Diplomate Am. Bd. Preventive Medicine. Intern Cleve. Met. Gen. Hosp., 1966-67; med. epidemiologist, N.Y.C Health Dept. Nat. Communicable Disease Ctr., USPHS, 1967-69; dir. indsl. health project Urban Planning Aid, Inc., Cambridge, Mass., 1969-71; occupational hygiene physician Mass. Dept. Labor and Industry, Boston, 1972-78; asst. prof. pub. health Harvard U., 1972-77, assoc. prof. pub. health, 1977-83; prof., dir. environ. occupational health scis. UCLA, 1983-87; prof., chair work environ. Coll. Engring. U. Mass., Lowell, Mass., 1987—. Mem. com. role of practicing physicians in occupl. and environ. health Inst. Medicine, 1987-88, mem. com. to review health consequences during Persian Gulf War, 1994-96, chair com. on health and safety implications of child labor, 1997-98, mem. com. on gender differences in susceptibility to environ. factors, 1997-98, mem. com. on musculoskeletal disorders and the workplace, 1999-2001, mem. planning meeting for study on changing dimensions of older Am. workers and their occupl. health and safety needs, 1999; chair adv. com. on elimination of pneumoconiosis among coal mine workers Mine Safety and Health Adminstrn., 1996; mem. stds. adv. com. on metal working fluids dept. labor Occupl. Safety and Health Adminstrn., 1997-99. Author, editor: Occupational Health, 1983, 4th edit., 2000; editor, manuscript reviewer various health publs.; contbr. numerous articles to profl. jours. Adv. Bd. mem. Working Women, 1981-85. Recipient Alfred L. Frechette award Mass. Pub. Health Assn., 1979, Harriet Hardy award New Eng. Coll. Occupl. and Environ. Medicine, 1994; Fulbright Sr. fellow, 1998. Fellow Am. Coll. Epidemiology, Am. Coll. Preventive Medicine; mem. APHA (panel environ. studies 1976-78, exec. bd. 1982, chmn. occupl. health and safety sect. 1976, governing coun. 1974-80, 83-85), Internat. Epidemiol. Assn. (treas. 1999—), Internat. Commn. Occupl. Health (mem. exec. bd. 1996—, chair sci. com. epidemiology in occupl. health 1993-96, sec. 1990-93), Am. Conf. Govtl. Indsl. Hygienists, Am. Occupl. Medicine Assn., Am. Coll. Epidemiology, Soc. Epidemiol. Rsch., Soc. Occupl. and Environ. Health. Avocations: hiking, swimming, camping. Home: 398 Wolcott St Auburndale MA 02466-1533 Office: U Mass Lowell Dept Work Environ Coll Engring Lowell MA 01854 E-mail: david_wegman@uml.edu.

WEGMAN, HAROLD HUGH, management consultant; b. Cin., June 29, 1916; s. Clarence H. and Lillian (de Tellem) W.; m. Ruth Ellen Volk, May 1, 1937; children— Susan Ruth (Mrs. Michael Manning), Sally Ann (Mrs. Jerry Fine). BBA, U. Cin., 1941; MBA, Xavier U., 1954. Band leader, studio mgr. Rudolph Wurlitzer Co., 1946-50; Tng. supr., then asst. to v.p. Gruen Watch Co., 1950-55; personnel dir., asst. to pres. Bavarian Brewing Co., Covington, Ky., 1955-59; dir. indsl. relations, asst. to pres. Howard Paper Co., Dayton, Ohio, 1959-62; v.p., gen. mgr. Elano Corp., Xenia, 1962-64; v.p., dir. indsl. relations Champion Papers Inc., Hamilton, 1964-67; v.p. U.S. Plywood Champion Papers, Inc., 1967-71, Champion Internat., 1971-72; pres. PEP Group, 1972—; dir. Mgmt. Center, Sacred Heart U., 1974—. Contbr. articles to profl. publs. Trustee Foreman Found., 1965-71. Served to lt. (j.g.) USNR, 1944-46. Mem. Am. Soc. Personnel Adminstrs. (bd. dirs. 1969— , treas. 1970), Am. Soc. for Tng. and Devel., NAM, Am. Paper Inst., Am. Mgmt. Assn., Conn. songwriters assn., Lambda Chi Alpha. Home: 3150 N Highway A1A Ph 3-5 Hutchinson Island FL 34949-8871 E-mail: halwegman@aol.com.

WEGMANN, MARY KATHERINE, art director; b. New Orleans, Sept. 18, 1948; d. Joseph A. and Catherine (Lyons) W. BA in English lit., Spring Hill Coll., Mobile, Ala., 1970; MA in English Lit., U. New Orleans, 1972. Asst. mgr., actor, dir. La Mise En Scene Theatre, New Orleans, 1970-72; loan processor First Homestead Savs. and Loan, 1972-74; home improvement contractor Superior Distbrs., 1974-75; adminstr. Freeman-Anacker, Inc., 1975-77; assoc. dir. Contemporary Arts Ctr., 1978-91, acting dir., 1986-88, 88-89; owner MK Arts Co., 1991—; mng. dir. Junebug Prodns., 1993-99; pres., CEO Nat. Performance Network, 2001—. Cons. Junebug Prodn., New Orleans, 1985-93, Alternate Roots, Atlanta, 1986, 92, Cultural Arts Coun. Houston, 1988-89, Seven Stages Performing Arts Ctr., Atlanta, 1989, 91, Nat. Endowment Arts, Washington, 1983-93, Assn. Performing Arts Presenters, 1994, Arts Coun. New Orleans, 1991, 92, La. Philharm. Orch., New Orleans, 1992, Melanie Beene and Assocs., 1991-93, La. Divsn. Arts, 1992—, Arts Coun. New Orleans, 1991—; mem. various panels, juries and adv. coms., 1980—. Bd. dirs. Dog & Pony Theatre Co., New Orleans, 1993—; bd. dirs., treas. Junebug Prodns., 1985—, Nat. Performance Network, 1998—, Contemporary Arts Ctr., 1999—. Office: MK Arts Co PO Box 71914 New Orleans LA 70172-1914 E-mail: mkw@npnweb.org., mkarts@earthlink.net.

WEGMILLER, DONALD CHARLES, health care corporation executive; b. Cloquet, Minn., Sept. 25, 1938; m. Janet A. Listerud, Apr. 27, 1957; children: Katherine, Mark, Dean. BA, U. Minn., 1960, MHA, 1962. Asst. adminstr. Fairview Hosp., Mpls., 1962-65, Fairview-Southdale Hosp., Mpls., 1965-66, adminstr., 1966-76; sr. v.p. Health Central System, 1976-78; pres. Health Central, Inc., 1978-80, Health Central Corp., Mpls., 1980-87; pres., CEO Health One Corp., 1987-92; pres. HealthSpan, 1992-93; pres. & CEO Clark/Bardes Consulting-Healthcare Group, 1993—2002, chmn., 2002—. Preceptor clin. faculty U. Minn., 1975—; lectr., adj. faculty U. Mich., 1980—; clin. faculty, lectr. Duke U., 1981—; cons. div. med. services U.S. Dept. State, Washington, 1975; bd. dirs. Health Providers Ins. Co., Hosp. Rsch. and Ednl. Trust, Med. Graphics Corp., HBO & Co., G.D. Searle & Co., Minn. Power, Profile Group, LifeRate; U.S. del. King's Fund Internat., 1979-85, nat. coord., 1985; U.S. Internat. Hosp. Fedn., 1987; keynote speaker Australian Pvt. Hosps. Assn. 10th Nat. Congress, 1990; mem. leadership adv. com. Am. Coll. Healthcare Execs., 1994. Mem. adv. bd. Health Mgmt. Quar. mag.; editorial bd. of Frontiers an Am. Coll. of Healthcare Execs. publ.; contbr. articles to profl. jours. Chmn. Bd. Edn., Richfield, Minn., 1971-74; staff asst. to Presidents Nixon, Ford and Reagan, 1972-89; adv. com. Sen. Durenberger's Health Care, Mpls., 1979—; trustee Nat. Adv. Coun. on Social Security, 1989—, Nat. Com. for Quality Health Care. Recipient Outstanding Pres. of Yr. award Mpls. Jaycees, 1969, Young Man of Yr. award, 1971, Nat. Healthcare award B'nai B'rith, 1987, Merit award Duke U. Program in Healthcare Adminstrn. Alumni Assn., 1990. Fellow Am. Coll. Health Care Execs. (Robert S. Hudgen's award 1969), Am. Hosp. Assn. (chmn. bd. trustees 1987), Minn. Hosp. Assn. (Disting. Svc. award 1988). Lodges: Rotary. Republican. Methodist. Home: 7871 Chesshire Ln N Maple Grove MN 55311-2207 Office: Clark/Bardes Consulting- Healthcare Group 608 2nd Ave S Ste 370 Minneapolis MN 55402-1906

WEGNER, GARY ALAN, astronomer; b. Seattle, Dec. 26, 1944; s. Herbert Edward and Melba Jean (Gardner) W.; m. Cynthia Kay Goodfellow, June 25, 1966; children: Josef, Kurt, Christian, Peter-Jürgen, Emma. Student, Wash. State U., Pullman, 1963-65; BS, U. Ariz., 1967; PhD, U. Wash., Seattle, 1971. Fulbright fellow Mount Stromlo Obs., Canberra, A.C.T., 1971-72; departmental demonstrator in astrophysics Oxford U., Eng., 1972-75; sr. sci. rsch. officer South African Astron. Obs., Capetown, Republic of South Africa, 1975-78; Annie J. Cannon fellow U. Del., Newark, 1978-79; asst. prof. Pa. State U., State College, 1979-82; asst. prof. to assoc. prof. physics and astronomy Dartmouth Coll., Hanover, N.H., 1982-88, Margaret Anne and Edward Leede Disting. prof. physics and astronomy, 1988—; dir. Mich.-Dartmouth-MIT Obs., 1991-99. Vis. astronomer Cornell U., 1992. Editor: White Dwarfs, 1989; contbr. articles to jours. in field. Keeley fellow Wadham Coll., Oxford, 1992-93, vis. fellow in astrophysics Oxford U., 1992-93; vis. prof. Astron. Inst. Ruhr U. Bochum, Germany, 1993-94; recipient rsch. prize

The Alexander von Humboldt Found., Germany, 1993-94, numerous grants NSF, NASA. Mem. Am. Astron. Soc., Internat. Astron. Union. Luthran. Office: Dartmouth Coll Dept Physics & Astronomy Wilder Lab Hanover NH 03755 E-mail: gary.wegner@dartmouth.edu.

WEGNER, JUDITH WELCH, law educator, dean; b. Hartford, Conn., Feb. 14, 1950; d. John Raymond and Ruth (Thulen) Welch; m. Warren W. Wegner, Oct. 13, 1972. BA with honors, U. Wis., 1972; JD, UCLA, 1976. Bar: Calif. 1976, D.C. 1977, N.C. 1988, U.S. Supreme Ct. 1980, U.S. Ct. Appeals. Law clk. to Judge Warren Ferguson, U.S. Dist. Ct. for So. Dist. Calif., L.A., 1976-77; atty. Office Legal Counsel and Land & Natural Resources Divsn. U.S. Dept. Justice, Washington, 1977-79; spl. asst. to sec. U.S. Dept. Edn., 1979-80; vis. assoc. prof. U. Iowa Coll. Law, Iowa City, 1981; asst. prof. U. N.C. Sch. Law, Chapel Hill, 1981-84, assoc. prof., 1984-88, prof., 1988—, assoc. dean, 1986-88, dean, 1989-99; sr. scholar Carnegie Found. for Advancement of Tchg., 1999—. Spkr. in field. Chief comment editor UCLA Law Rev., 1975-76; contbr. articles to legal publs. Mem. ABA (chmn. planning com. African Law Sch. Initiative 1994, co-chmn. planning com. 1994 mid-yr. deans meeting sect. on legal edn. and admission to bar), N.C. Assn. Women Attys. (Gweneth Davis award 1989), N.C. State Bar Assn., Assn. Am. Law Schs. (mem. exec. com. sect. on law & edn. 1985-88, mem. exec. com. sect. on local govt. law 1989-92, mem. accreditation com. 1986-88, chmn. 1989-91, program chmn. 1992 ann. meeting, program chmn. 1994 ann. meeting, mem. exec. com. 1992-96, pres. 1995), Soc. Am. Law Tchrs., Nat. League Cities (coun.-mentor program 1989-91), Women's Internat. Forum, Order of Coif (nat. exec. com. 1989-91), Phi Beta Kappa. Democrat. Office: U NC Sch Law Van Hecke Wettach Hall Campus Box 3380 Chapel Hill NC 27599-3380 E-mail: judith_wegner@unc.edu.

WEGNER, KARL HEINRICH, physician, educator; b. Pierre, S.D., Jan. 5, 1930; s. Lester Fred and Nellie (Norbeck) W.; m. Mary Josephine Waddell, June 15, 1957; children: Madeleine Jean, Peter Norbeck, Mary Nell. BA, Yale U., 1952; MD, Harvard U., 1959. Intern, resident Mass. Gen. Hosp./Harvard U., 1959-62; pathologist Sioux Valley Hosp., Sioux Falls, S.D., 1962-90; pathologist, dir. Lab. Clin. Medicine, 1962-90; prof., chmn. dept. pathology U. S.D., 1968-73, v.p. health affairs, founding dean Sch. Medicine, 1973-79, Regents Disting. prof. emeritus, 1992—; owner Meadowlark Farms, Montrose, S.D. Mem. Bd. of Regents for Higher Edn., State of S.D., pres. bd. regents, 1996-97. Bd. dirs. U. S.D. Found.; pres. bd. dirs. Sioux Valley Hosp. Found., Sioux Falls Area Cmty. Found. With USMC, 1952—54, capt. Reserves USMC, 1952—54. Karl H. Wegner Endowed Professorship, Bd. of Regents for Higher Edn., 1979; recipient Disting. Svc. award S.D. State Med. Assn., 1984, Community Svc. award, 1975; inducted to S.D. Hall of Fame, 1987; Karl and Mary Jo Wegner Health Scis. Info. Ctr. named in his honor, 1998. Fellow Coll. Am. Pathologists, Internat. Acad. Pathologists, Am. Soc. Pathologists; mem. Am. Pathology Found. (pres. 1984-85, Am. Pathologist of Yr award, 1989), Alpha Omega Alpha. Home: 5010 S Sunnymede Cir Sioux Falls SD 57108-2823

WEGNER, MARY JOSEPHINE, civic volunteer, farmer; b. Cleve., Apr. 10, 1934; d. William Wayne and Jean (Rathbun) Waddell; m. Karl Heinrich Wegner, June 15, 1957; children: Madeleine, Peter, Mary Nell. BA, Wellesley Coll., 1956. Endocrinology lab. rsch. technician Mass. Gen. Hosp., Boston, 1956-58; tchr. sci. Concord (Mass.) Acad., 1958-59; ptnr. Wegner Farms, Montrose, S.D., 1965—. Mem. cmty. bd. U.S. Bank, Sioux Falls, 1984—. Pres. S.D. Symphony, Sioux Falls, 1984-86; bd. dirs. Nature Conservancy, Sioux Falls, 1983—, Ctr. for Western Studies, Augustana Coll., Sioux Falls, 1990—, No. Plains Tribal Arts, Sioux Falls, 1988—; mem. Coun. on Cultural Affairs, Sioux Falls; co-chair Cultural Plan for Sioux Empire, 1999—. Recipient Leadership Award in the Arts, YWCA, 1983, Spl. Award for Leadership, All Saints Sch., Sioux Falls, 1976, Neighbor Helping Neighbor award Gov. of State of S.D., 1989; named (with husband) SD Philanthopist of Yr., 2002. Mem. Sioux Falls Area C. of C. (bd. dirs. 1984-87), PEO. Republican. Episcopalian. Avocations: reading, gardening, hiking, tennis, piano. Home: 5010 S Sunnymede Cir Sioux Falls SD 57108-2823

WEGNER, STEPHAN REINHARD, economist, consultant; b. Halle, Germany, Sept. 16, 1971; s. Reinhard Wegner and Edda Leopold. Diploma in econs., Martin Luther U., Halle, 1997; MA in Internat. Rels., Johns Hopkins U., 2000. Stagiaire European Commn., Brussels, 1997; cons. Multilateral Investment Guarantee Agy., World Bank Group, Washington, 1999—2001, evaluation officer, 2001—.

WEH, ALLEN EDWARD, airline executive; b. Salem, Oreg., Nov. 17, 1942; s. Edward and Harriet Ann (Hicklin) W.; m. Rebecca Ann Roberton, July 5, 1968; children: Deborah Susan, Ashley Elizabeth, Brian Roberton. BS, U. N.Mex., 1966, MA, 1973. Asst. to chief adminstrv. officer Bank N.Mex., Albuquerque, 1973; pres. N.Mex. Airways, Inc., 1974; dep. dir. N.Mex. Indochina Refugee Program, Santa Fe, 1975-76; dir. pub. affairs UNC Mining & Milling Co., Albuquerque, 1977-79; pres., CEO, CSI Aviation Svcs., Inc., 1979—. Mem. steering com. Colin McMillan for lt. gov., Albuquerque, 1982; bd. dirs. N.Mex. Symphony Orgh., Albuquerque Conv. and Visitors Bur., 1982; mem. Albuquerque Police Adv. Bd., 1977-78; co-chmn. fin. com. Rep. Heather Wilson (Rep.-N.Mex.) Re-Election Campaign, 1999—; mem. state fin. com. G.W. Bush for Pres.; co-chmn. N.Mex. Victory, 2000; mem. nat. adv. bd. U. N.Mex. Anderson Sch. Bus.; elected del. GOP Nat. Conv., 2000. Capt. USMC, 1966-71, Vietnam; col. USMCR, 1971-97, Col. USMC, 1990-91, Persian Gulf, 1992-93, Somalia. Decorated Silver Star, Legion of Merit, Bronze Star with V device, Purple Heart with two gold stars, Meritorious Svc. medal with gold star, Air medal. Mem. Marine Corps Res. Officers Assn. (life, bd. dirs. 1973, 86), Res. Officers Assn. U.S. (life), SCV (life), Mil. Order Stars and Bars (life), SAR, N.Mex. Retail Assn. (chmn. 1999-2000). Republican. Episcopalian. Home: 6722 Rio Grande Blvd NW Albuquerque NM 87107-6330 Office: CSI Aviation Svcs Inc 3700 Rio Grande Blvd NW Albuquerque NM 87107-2876

WEHAUSEN, JOHN VROOMAN, mathematician, educator; b. Duluth, Sept. 23, 1913; s. George W. and Elizabeth (Vroman) W.; m. Mary Katherine Wertime, Aug. 19, 1938 (dec. 2001); children— Sarah, Peter Vrooman, Julia, John David. BS, U. Mich., 1934, MS, 1935, PhD, 1938; Doctorate (hon.), Joseph Fourier U., Grenoble, France, 1993. Instr. math. Brown U., 1937-38, Columbia, 1938-40, U. Mo., 1940-44; cons. Ops. Rsch. Group USN, 1944-46; mathematician David Taylor Model Basin, Carderock, Md., 1946-49; acting head mechanics br. Office Naval Research, 1949-50; exec. editor Math. Revs., 1950-56; asso. research mathematician Inst. Engring. Research, U. Calif. at Berkeley, 1956-57, research mathematician, 1957—, asso. prof. engring. sci., 1958-59, prof., 1959-84, prof. emeritus, 1984—; Fulbright lectr. U. Hamburg, 1960-61. Vis. prof. Flinders U., Australia, 1967, U. de Nantes, 1973, 84, U. Grenoble, 1979, Technion, Haifa, 1982, Chalmers Inst. Tech., Gothenburg, 1982. Fellow Soc. Naval Architects and Marine Engrs. (Davidson medal 1984); mem. Am. Math. Soc., Math. Assn. Am., Nat. Acad. Engring. Home: 15 Hillside Ct Berkeley CA 94704-2530

WEHDE, ALBERT EDWARD, lawyer; b. Milw., Feb. 14, 1935; s. Albert Christian and Mary Hubbel (Dewey) W.; m. Joan M. Forney, Nov. 4, 1978; children: John C., Edward T. BS, Marquette U., 1956, JD, 1960. Bar: Wis. 1960, Calif. 1968. Atty. AEC, Albuquerque, 1963-66; counsel Lockheed Aircraft Co., Sunnyvale and Redlands, Calif., 1966-73; assoc. Schultz & Manfield, Palo Alto, 1973-74; sr. counsel FMC Corp., Santa Clara, 1974-95; atty. AEW Internat. Cons., 1995—. Bd. dirs. Tech. Fed. Credit Union, San Jose, Calif., chmn., 1994-96. Pres. Mountain View (Calif.) Babe Ruth League, 1976; trustee Mid-Peninsula Family Services Assn., Palo Alto, 1973-74. Served to capt. U.S. Army, 1960-63. Mem. ABA (chmn. region VII pub. contracts sect. 1977-81), Santa Clara County Bar Assn. (co-chmn. corp. counsel sect. 1983-84, mem. exec. com.), Am. Corp. Counsel Assn. (chpt. sec., pres. 1988, bd. dirs. 1983-93). Democrat. Roman Catholic. Avocations: gourmet cooking, music, sports. Home: 1106 Lorne Way Sunnyvale CA 94087-5157

WEHINGER, PETER AUGUSTUS, astronomer, educator; b. Goshen, N.Y., Feb. 18, 1938; s. George Edward and Elizabeth Marie (Goode) W.; m. Susan Wyckoff, July 29, 1967. BS in Physics, Union Coll., Schenectady, N.Y., 1960; MA in Astronomy, Ind. U., 1962; PhD, Case Western Reserve U., 1966. NASA predoctoral fellow Case Western Reserve U., Cleve., 1963-65; instr. U. Mich., Ann Arbor, 1965-67, asst. prof., 1967-70; assoc. prof. U. Kans., Lawrence, 1970-72; vis. assoc. prof. Tel Aviv U., Ramat-Aviv, Israel, 1972-75; prin. rsch. fellow Royal Greenwich Observatory, Herstmonceux, Sussex, Eng., 1975-78; vis. sr. scientist Max Planck Inst. for Astronomy, Heidelberg, Germany, 1978-80; vis. prof. Ariz. State U., Tempe, 1981-84, rsch. prof., 1984—. Project mgr. 1.3 meter telescope dept. astronomy U. Mich., 1966-70; tech. cons. Boller & Chivens divsn. Perkin Elmer Corp., South Pasadena, Calif., 1974-75, Photek Ltd., St. Leonard's-on-the-Sea, Sussex, Eng., 1992-94, Torus Precision Optics, Iowa City, 1997-99; mem. Ariz. Astronomy Bd., 1999-; vis. prof. Astronomy Ctr. U. Sussex, Brighton, Eng., 1975-78, sr. rsch. fellow dept. astronomy Ohio State U., Columbus, 1978-79; vis. prof. physics-astronomy dept. No. Ariz. U., Flagstaff, 1981-82; discipline specialist in spectroscopy Internat. Halley Watch, NASA/JPL, 1982-89; vis. rsch. fellow Mt. Stromlo Observatory and Siding Spring, Australian Nat. U., Canberra, 1986—; assoc. dir. Ariz./NASA Space Grant Consortium, Ariz. State U., 1990-94; adj. staff astronomer Steward Observatory U. Ariz., 1991-97, staff astronomer Dir.'s Office, 1997—; mem. Ariz. Sci. Ctr. Adv. Bd., 1995-97; vis. prof. physics and astronomy Mesa C.C., 1996-98; faculty assoc. plant biology Ariz. State U., 1997-2000. Contbr. 105 articles to profl. jours.; editor: (conf. proceedings) Observations of Recent Comets, 1990; editor electronic newsletter On Periodic Comets, 1985-90, electronic bull. bd. Halley Hotline; co-editor (CDROM Archives) Spectroscopic Observations of Comets, 1990. Grantee NASA, 1982-90, 98-99, 1983-93, 1989-94, 1995-99, GTE-Sprint, 1985-87, NSF, 1985-87, 1994-97, Ariz. Pub. Svc. Corp., 1998-2001, CEMEX Corp., 2000. Fellow Royal Astron. Soc.; mem. Am. Astron. Soc. (divsn. planetry scis.), Astron. Soc. of the Pacific, Internat. Astron. Union, Sigma Xi. Achievements include measurement of carbon isotope abundances in comets; titanium isotope abundances in red giant stars, identification of H2O+ in comets; digital imaging and spectroscopy of quasar host galaxies detected at their cosmological distances; spectroscopy of sodium torus associated with Jupiter and Io. Home: 2135 E Loma Vista Dr Tempe AZ 85282-2927 Office: U Ariz Dir Office Steward Obs 933 N Cherry Ave Tucson AZ 85721-0065 E-mail: pwehinger@as.arizona.edu.

WEHLING, FRED LOWELL, political scientist, consultant; b. Burbank, Calif., Jan. 7, 1963; s. Robert and Anna Clara (Chiodo) W. AB in Internat. Rels., U. So. Calif., 1985; MA in Polit. Sci., UCLA, 1987, PhD in Polit. Sci., 1992. Cons. Rand/UCLA Ctr. Soviet Studies, Santa Monica, Calif., 1985—. Contbr. articles, papers to profl. publs. Graham fellow UCLA, 1990. Mem. Am. Assn. Advancement of Slavic Studies, Am. Polit. Sci. Assn., Internat. Studies Assn., Sierra Club, Phi Beta Kappa. Avocations: hiking, camping, science fiction. Office: Rand UCLA Ctr Soviet Studies 1700 Main St Santa Monica CA 90401-3208

WEHMAN, ADELE See BAYNE, ADELE WEHMAN

WEHMEYER, DONALD LEE, hand surgeon; b. Bklyn., Aug. 9, 1945; s. George and Virginia (Lyder) W.; m. Patrician Ann Morrow, Aug. 24, 1968; children: Michael, Wendy, Jeffrey. BS, U. Mo., 1967, MD, 1971. Diplomate Am. Bd. Plastic Surgery, Am. Bd. Surgery, Nat. Bd. Med. Examiners. Hand surgeon Tex. Hand Ctr, Abilene, 1980—. Bd. dirs. Boy Scouts Am., Abilene. Major USAF, 1975-77. Avocations: flying, scuba diving, scouting. Home: 2109 Shoreline Dr Abilene TX 79602-6201

WEHNER, HENRY OTTO, III, pharmacist, consultant; b. Birmingham, Ala., Mar. 3, 1942; s. Henry O. Jr. and Carolyn (Kirkland) W.; m. Sammye Ruth Murphy, June 8, 1974 (div. July 1989); m. Sharron Marie Culp, Mar. 5, 1998. AA, Daytona Beach Community Coll., 1967; BS in Biology, North Ga. Coll., Dahlonega, 1971; BS in Pharmacy, U. Ga., 1978. Registered pharmacist, Fla., Ga.; cert. sci. tchr. grades 7-12, Ga. Tchr. biology Irwin County High Sch., Ocilla, Ga., 1971-75; extern Eckerd Drugs, Athens, 1977; intern/extern St. Mary's Hosp., 1977; pharmacy intern Button Gwinnett Hosp., Lawrenceville, Ga., 1978; co-owner, mgr. Hiawassee (Ga.) Pharmacy, 1978-79; staff pharmacist Dyal's Pharmacy, Daytona Beach, Fla., 1979, Little Drug Co., New Smyrna Beach, 1979-80; staff pharmacist, mgr. Super X Drugs, 1980-81; staff pharmacist Fish Meml. Hosp., 1981-92, Halifax Med. Ctr., Daytona Beach, Fla., 1992—. Oncology pharmacist Regional Oncology Ctr. Halifax Med. Ctr., 2000; staff pharmacist Halifax Keech Med. Ctr., 2000—. With USAF, 1961-65. Mem. Am. Pharm. Assn., Fla. Soc. Hosp. Pharmacists, Volusia County Pharm. Assn., Ea. Shores Soc. Hosp. Pharmacists (charter, pres. 1995-96), Eastern Shores Fla. Soc. Hosp. Pharmacists, Phi Lambda Sigma, Phi Theta Kappa. Methodist. Avocations: painting, cycling, tennis. Office: Halifax Med Ctr PO Box 1350 303 N Clyde Morris Blvd Daytona Beach FL 32114-2709

WEHR, WILLIAM JAMES, judge; b. Covington, Ky., July 13, 1950; s. Robert F. and Margaret O. (Schmaeling) W.; m. Nancy Jean Harrison, Dec. 29, 1971; children: Laura Beth, Lindsay Ann. BA, U. Ky., 1972; JD, No. Ky. U., 1976. Bar: Ky. 1976, U.S. Dist. Ct. (ea. dist.) Ky., 1976, U.S. Supreme Ct. 1980. Assoc. Kaufman, Johnson and Blau, Newport, Ky., 1976-77; ptnr. Twehues, Verst & Wehr, 1978-88; asst. county atty. Campbell County, 1978-88; judge Campbell County Cir. Ct. Divsn. I, 1988—; also chief regional cir. judge No. Ky. Region, 1996—. Guest lectr. Chase Coll. Law, 1981-90, adj. faculty, 1991—. Bd. dirs. Sr. Citizens No. Ky., Inc., Covington, 1980-87, pres., 1984-85; bd. dirs. Hosea House Soup Kitchen, 1992—. Served with USCGR, 1968-74. Recipient Disting. Prosecutor award Citizens for Decency Through Law, Inc., 1981. Mem.: No. Ky. Bar Assn. (pres. 1984), Ky. Bar Assn. (ho. of dels. 1985—88), Elks. Democrat. Roman Catholic. Office: Campbell County Courthouse Newport KY 41071

WEHRER, CHARLES SIECKE, business and education educator; b. Norfolk, Nebr., July 13, 1914; s. Charles C. and Ella (Augusta) W.; m. May Winther Hansen, Aug. 21, 1982 (dec. Oct. 27, 1991). BA, Nebr. State Tchrs. Coll., 1940; MA in Sch. Adminstrn., postgrad., U. Nebr., 1950, Columbia U., 1950, U. So. Calif., 1954-55; PhD without dissertation, Ohio State U., 1961; LHD (hon.), Sioux Empire Coll., 1967. Asst. commandant, basketball coach Black-Foxe Mil. Inst., Hollywood, Calif., 1945-46; coach, supt. local schs. Wood Lake, Nebr., 1947-49; prin. Scottsbluff (Nebr.) Jr. High Sch., 1950-51; grad. asst. in edn. U. Nebr., 1949-50, U. So. Calif., 1954-55; grad. asst. prof. elem. edn. Ohio State U., 1960; tchr. pub. schs. Paramount, Calif., 1953-54; tchr. Excelsior Adult Sch., Norwalk, 1953-57; supt. local schs. Shandon, 1956-57; assoc. prof. edn., supr. student teaching Ohio No. U., Ada, 1958-60; assoc. prof., supr. elem. student teaching Capital U., Columbus, Ohio, 1961-62; prin. Norwalk Iowa Elem. Jr. High Sch., 1962-63; prof. edn., dir. student affairs, asst. to pres. Grand View Coll., Des Moines, 1962-64; with depts. youth, TV, edn. programming City of Des Moines, 1965; cons. program Iowa Civil Def./Health Dept., 1966; prof. edn. and psychology S.W. Community Coll., Creston, Iowa, 1967; acad. dean Sioux Empire Coll., Hawarden, 1967-68; chmn. depts. edn., psychology, dir. tchr. edn. J.F. Kennedy Coll., Wahoo, Nebr., 1970-71; prodr., emcee youth radio/TV program Let's Listen to Youth, Lincoln, 1971, Des Moines, Sioux City, Iowa, 1952-74, L.A., Columbus, Ohio, 1952-74; prof. edn. Concordia Coll., Seward, Nebr., 1973; tng. coord., dir. spl. tng. programs for mgmt. State of Nebr., 1974-75; prof. bus. Metro Tech., Omaha, 1976-82; prof. mgmt. tng. Bus. Devel. Ctr. U. Nebr., 1976-82; prof. bus. Nebr. State Coll., Wayne, 1982-88, ret.; pres. Bus. Mgmt. Cons. Co., Wisner, Nebr., 1982-90. Lectr. in field. Author: Keep in Touch, My Students, 1966; contbr. articles to profl. jours. Phys. dir. YMCA, Norfolk, 1934-36, McCook, Nebr., 1937-38, L.A. Downtown Y, 1940-41; counselor, adv. Nebr. Boys' State, 1949-50; Nebr. del. White House Conf. on Children and Youth, 1950; chmn. Nebr. Com. on Juvenile Delinquency; mem. Gov.'s Com. on Youth, Calif., Nebr.; spl. youth cons. radio program Art Linkletter House Party, Calif., 1952; dir. dept. guest rels. NBC, Hollywood, Calif., 1952; dir. spl. project Iowa Dept. Health, 1965-66; contbr. to sub-com. on poverty-youth programs U.S. Congress, 1964-65; chmn. youth sect. Iowa Congress Parents & Tchrs., 1966-67; lay min. Protestant Chs., 1967—, past ch. official First Cong. United Ch. of Christ, Norfolk, Elkhorn Valley Hist. Soc. Capt. USAAF, 1941-45. Decorated Bronze Star, Soldiers medal, 3 Battle Stars, 15th AF Unit citation, Pres. Unit citation, others; recipient spl. awards/commendations for radio/TV programs State PTA and other civic and youth groups, 1960-75, numerous awards for tchg. and youth work; named Outstanding Sch. Adminstr. in Nebr. dept. sch. adminstrn. U. Nebr., Nebr. Dept. Edn., 1948-50; named to Hall of Honor, Nebr. Softball Assn., 1993, Norfolk H.S. Students honor as Sr. Citizens of Yr., 1995, Spl. Proclamation for Edn. and Youth Svcs. State of Nebr., 1994, Outstanding Noted Alumni award U. Nebr. Tchrs. Coll., 1998, Alumni Football Quarterback honor, 1998; named to Norfolk H.S. Close Up Club Unanimous Spl. Honor Selection to Wall of Fame. Mem. NEA (Spl. Commendation for tchr. edn. programs), AAUP, Am. Assn. Ret. Persons (pres. Norfolk chpt. 1997-98, Nebr. Sr. Citizen Spl. Commendation 1980-81), Assn. for Higher Edn., Nat. Assn. Sch. Adminstrs., Nat. Soc. for Study of Edn., Internat. Platform Assn. (spl. spkr. conv. 1970, spl. honors for Vets. Day, Meml. Day spkr. for 52 yrs.), Am. Legion, VFW (spl. commendation for helping veterans, sr. citizens and youth 1997), SCORE, Lions (bd. dirs., past pres.), Kiwanis (past pres.), Rotary (Norfolk Noon Rotary Club Cmty. Svc. award, Pres.'s award 1998), Delta Sigma, Phi Delta Kappa (Spl. Recognition award 1992), Sigma Tau Delta (past pres.). Address: 1000 Village Green Dr Apt 1 Norfolk NE 68701-2279 *We are living in a dangerous world of unrest, a difficult time for all of us to adjust to the emotional and mental problems of this changing environmental world. If we can be of help to those who are in need of a friendly act then let us do our best to be of help and service to young and old alike as we may not pass this way again.*

WEHRING, BERNARD WILLIAM, nuclear engineering educator; b. Monroe, Mich., Aug. 3, 1937; s. Bernard Albert and Alma Christina (Graf) W.; m. Margaret Mary Robinson, Sept. 5, 1959; children: Mary Ann, James, Susan, Barbara. BSE. in Physics, BSE. in Math, U. Mich., 1959; MS in Physics, U. Ill., 1961, PhD in Nuclear Engring, 1966. Asst. prof. nuclear engring. U. Ill., Urbana, 1966-70, assoc. prof., 1970-77, prof., 1977-84, asst. dean engring., 1981-82; prof. nuclear engring. N.C. State U., Raleigh, 1984-89, dir. nuclear reactor program, 1984-89; prof. mech. engring. U. Tex., Austin, 1989-2000, dir. Nuclear Engring. Teaching Lab., 1989-2000; adj. prof. nuclear engring. N.C. State U., Raleigh, 2000—. Cons. Argonne and Los Alamos nat. labs.; mem. crosssect. evaluation working group Brookhaven Nat. Lab. Contbr. sects. to books, articles to profl. publs. AEC fellow, 1963-65; NSF grantee, 1968— Fellow Am. Nuclear Soc.; mem. Am. Nuclear Soc. (standards com.), Am. Phys. Soc. Achievements include contributing in the generation of basic nuclear data and development of new instruments and experimental techniques. Home: 516 Westbrook Dr Raleigh NC 27615-7321

WEHRLE, LEROY SNYDER, economist, educator; b. St. Louis, Feb. 5, 1932; s. Fred Joseph and Eleanor (Snyder) W.; m. JoAnn Griffith, Aug. 29, 1959; children— Chandra Lee, Lon Joseph. BS, Washington U., St. Louis, 1953; MA in Econs, Yale, 1956, PhD with honors, 1959. Asst. instr. Yale, 1958-59; with econ. sect. AID mission to Laos, 1960-61; sr. staff economist President's Council Econ. Advisers, 1961-62; spl. econ. adviser to U.S. Ambassador Unger, Vientiane, 1962; dep. dir. AID mission to Laos, 1963-64; asst. dir. AID mission, also econ. counsellor to U.S. ambassador, Saigon, 1964-67; asso. dir. AID Mission, Saigon, 1964-67; dept. asst. adminstr. Vietnam, AID, Dept. State, 1967-68; univ. fellow Harvard, 1968-69; sr. fellow Brookings Instn., 1969-70; dir. Ill. Inst. for Social Policy, Springfield, 1970-72; aide to Lt. Gov. Paul Simon, 1972; prof. economics Sangamon State U., 1972-88; founding ptnr., chief exec. officer Health Econs. and Mkt. Analysis Inc., Springfield, 1987-94; pres. Healthcare Cost Analysis, Inc., 1994—. Chmn. bd. Tie Collar, Ltd. Mem. spl. study group Alliance Progress, 1962; mem. Rockefeller Latin Am. Mission, 1969; chmn. study team world food and nutrition study Nat. Acad. Sci., 1976-77. Served with AUS, 1953-55. Recipient William A. Jump meml. award, 1966 Home and Office: 2001 S Bates Ave Springfield IL 62704-3304 E-mail: wehrle@springnet1.com.

WEHRWEIN, AUSTIN CARL, newspaper reporter, editor, writer; b. Austin, Tex., Jan. 12, 1916; s. George S. and Anna (Ruby) W.; m. Judith Oakes, 1950; children: Sven Austin, Paul, Peter, Joanna Judith. AB, U. Wis., 1937; LL.B., Columbia U., 1940; student, London Sch. Econs., 1948. Reporter Washington Bur., UP, 1941-43, 46-48; information specialist E.C.A., London, Copenhagen, Oslo, Stockholm, 1948-51; financial writer Milw. Jour., 1951-53; staff corr. Time, Inc., Chgo., 1953-55; reporter Chgo. Sun-Times, 1955-56, fin. editor, 1956-57; chief Chgo. bur. N.Y. Times, 1957-66; editorial writer Mpls. Star, 1966-82. Editor The Observer, 1984-87. Served with USAAF, 1943-45; mem. staff Stars and Stripes 1945-46, Shanghai, China. Recipient Pulitizer prize for internat. reporting, 1953; Disting. Journalism award U. Wis., 1963; cert. of merit ABA Gavel competition, 1968, 80; Gavel award, 1969, 71 Home and Office: 2309 Carter Ave Saint Paul MN 55108-1640

WEHRWEIN-HUNT, JERI LYNN, elementary education educator; b. New Richmond, Wis., Aug. 13, 1952; d. Harlan Fredric and Olive Angeline (Steies) Wehrwein; 1 child Katie Lynn. BS in Elem. Edn., BS in Spl. Edn., St. Cloud State U., 1973; MEd, U. Minn., 1990. cert. elem. and spl. edn. tchr., Minn. Coord. social studies curriculum Minneapolis Pub. Schs., 1977-78, tchr., 1973—2001, asst. spl. edn. camp program coord., 1982, coord. and tchr. gifted program, 1984-86; title I and family involvement coord., 2001—. Recipient recognition for outstanding environmental activities in the classroom, Minn. Atty. Gen., 1994. Mem. Am. Fedn. Tchrs., Minn. Fedn. Tchrs. Roman Catholic. Avocations: interior decorating, singing, theater. Office: Jenny Lind Elem Sch 5025 Bryant Ave N Minneapolis MN 55430-3500 E-mail: hjh55126@aol.com.

WEI, BENJAMIN MIN, engineering educator, educator; b. Hebei, China, Aug. 11, 1930; s. Fu Shun and Yuan Qing (Zhang) W.; m. Diana Yun Dee; 1 child: Victor Mark. BSME, Chung Cheng Inst. Tech., 1953; MSME, Concordia U., 1970; PhD, Pa. State U., 1981. Mech. engr. Ordnance Corps Arsenal, Taipei, Taiwan, 1953-59; tchr. Wenshan High Sch., 1960-61; teaching asst. New Brunswick (Can.) U., 1962-64; supr. Domtar Constrn. Materials Co., Can., 1964-66; computer programmer McGill U., Can., 1966-67, Montreal (Can.) U., 1967-68; tchr. Pierrefond Comprehensive High sch., Que., 1970-73; prof. Norfolk (Va.) State U., 1974—. Hon. prof., cons. Taiyuan U. Polytech. Contbr. articles to profl. jours. Mem. Statistical Quality Control of China. Home: 1152 Janaf Pl Norfolk VA 23502-2631

WEI, FONG, nephrologist; b. Shanghai, May 2, 1941; came to U.S., 1941; s. Tseh Heen and Waling (Chung) W.; m. Theodora Mary Zopko, July 16, 1966; children: Christopher, Alexander. BA, Yale U., 1963; MD, Tufts U., 1967. Diplomate Am. Bd. Internal Medicine, Am. Bd. Nephrology; specialist in clin. hypertension. Intern Boston City Hosp., 1967-68, resident, 1968-69, Bronx (N.Y.) Mcpl., 1969-70; fellow in nephrology U. N.C., Chapel Hill, 1970-72; pvt. practice Princeton, N.J., 1974—. Clin. assoc. prof. Robert Wood Johnson Med. Sch., New Brunswick, N.J., 1975—; pres. med. staff Med. Ctr. Princeton, 1981-82; prin. investigator Bristol Myers Squibb, Princeton, 1984—, Merck and Co., Princeton, 1988—; cons. Princeton U., 1990—; pres. Princeton Med. Group, 1982—. Med. advisor Princeton Regional Homemakers Assn., 1975—. Fellow ACP; mem. Am. Soc. Nephrology, Internat. Soc. Nephrology, Am. Soc. Hypertension. Office: Princeton Med Group 419 N Harrison St Princeton NJ 08540-3521

WEI, GUO-QING, computer scientist; b. Jing-Tan, Jiangsu, China, Oct. 1, 1962; came to U.S., 1998; s. Lian-Gen and Xiao-Min (Dong) W.; m. Xiao-Wen Yin, Sept. 16, 1963; children: Catherine, Lucia. BSc, Nanjing (China) Inst. Tech., 1983, MSc, 1986; PhD, Southeastern U., Nanjing, 1989. Asst. prof. Chinese Acad. Scis., Beijing, 1989-91; sr. rsch. scientist German Aerospace Rsch. Establishment, Munich, 1991-98; sr. mem. tech. staff Siemens Corp. Rsch., Inc., Princeton, NJ, 1998—. Contbr. numerous articles to profl. jours. Recipient Best Paper award Chinese Acad. Scis., 1991, Best Paper award German Assn. pattern Recognion and Austrian Assn. pattern Recognition, 1994, Olympus European Found. prize, 1997. Mem. IEEE (sr.). Avocations: walking, swimming, table-tennis. Office: Siemens Corp Rsch Inc 755 College Rd E Princeton NJ 08540-6632 E-mail: wei@scr.siemens.com.

WEI, JAMES, chemical engineering educator, academic dean; b. Macao, China, Aug. 14, 1930; came to U.S., 1949, naturalized, 1960; s. Hsiang-chen and Nuen (Kwok) W.; m. Virginia Hong, Nov. 4, 1956; children: Alexander, Christina, Natasha, Randolph (dec.). BS in Chem. Engring, Ga. Inst. Tech., 1952; MS, MIT, 1954, ScD, 1955; grad., Advanced Mgmt. Program Harvard, 1969. Research engr. to research assoc. Mobil Oil, Paulsboro, N.J., 1956-62; sr. scientist Princeton, 1963-68; mgr. corp. planning N.Y.C., 1969-70; Allan P. Colburn prof. U. Del., Newark, 1971-77; Sherman Fairchild distinguished scholar Calif. Inst. Tech., 1977; Warren K. Lewis prof. MIT, Cambridge, 1977-91, head dept. chem. engring., 1977-88; Pomeroy and Betty Smith prof. chem. engring., dean Sch. Engring. and Applied Sci. Princeton (N.J.) U., 1991—. Vis. prof. Princeton, 1962-63, Calif. Inst. Tech., 1965; cons. Mobil Oil Corp.; cons. com. on motor vehicle emissions Nat. Acad. Sci., 1972-74, 79-80; mem. sci. adv. bd. EPA, 1976-79; mem. Presdl. Pvt. Sector Survey Task Force on Dept. Energy, 1982-83 Bd. editors Chem. Tech, 1971-80, Chem. Engring. Communications, 1972—; cons. editor chem. engring. series, McGraw-Hill, 1964—; editor-in-chief: Advances in Chemical Engineering, 1980; Contbr. papers, monographs to profl. lit., The Structure of Chemical Processing Industries, 1979. Trustee Am. U. Beirut, 1998—, Smith Coll., 1999—. Recipient Am. Acad. Achievement Golden Plate award, 1966 [e]m. AIChE (dir. 1970-72, Inst. lectr. 1968, Profl. Progress award 1970, Walker award 1980, Lewis award 1985, v.p. 1987, pres. 1988, Founders award 1990), Am. Chem. Soc. (award in petroleum chemistry 1966), Nat. Acad. Engring. (nominating com. 1981, 96, peer com. 1980-82, membership com. 1983-85, Draper award com. 1995-97, chair chem. engring. sect. 1998-99), AAAS, Am. Acad. Arts and Scis., Academica Sinica of Taiwan, Sigma Xi. Home: 571 Lake Dr Princeton NJ 08540-5632 Office: Princeton U Engring Quadrangle Princeton NJ 08544-0001 E-mail: jameswei@princeton.edu.

WEI, JOHN HUA-FANG, engineering executive; b. Shanghai, China, Oct. 11, 1963; s. Keming and Quanbao Tang W.; 1 child, John Tiger. BS, Shanghai Jiao Tong U., 1985; MS, Stanford U., 1989; PhD, Dartmouth Coll., 1992. CAD/CAM engr. Shanghai Rsch. Inst. Tool and Die Tech., 1985-87; assoc. MIT, Cambridge, 1992-93; tech. staff Sharp Microelectronics Tech. Inc., Camas, Wash., 1994; design engr. LSI Logic Corp., Milpitas, Calif., 1994-97; tech. staff Equator Techs. Inc., Campbell, 1997-98; prin. engr. NeoMagic Corp., Santa Clara, 1998-99; mgr. IC design and silicon architect PMC-Sierra, Inc., 1999—. Contbr. articles to profl. jours. Mem. IEEE, Sigma Xi. Achievements include 4 patents in field. Avocations: snow skiing, golf, ice skating, rollerblading, oil painting. E-mail: hfwei@alumni.stanford.org.

WEI, QINGYI, cancer research educator; b. Nanjing, Jiangsu, China, Apr. 30, 1956; parents Yongxing Wei and Huifeng; m. Jingrong Yan, Oct. 1, 1983; children: Michael Yang, Herbie Hao. MD, Nanjing Med. Coll., 1983; MS, Chinese Acad. Preventive Med., Beijing, 1986; PhD, Johns Hopkins U., 1993. Rsch. assoc. Chinese Acad. Preventive Medicine, Beijing, 1986-87, Johns Hopkins U. Sch. Hygiene and Pub. Health, Balt., 1992-93; asst. prof. U. Tex. M.D. Anderson Cancer Ctr., Houston, 1993-98, assoc. prof., 1998—. Contbr. rsch. articles to profl. jours. Grantee, NIH, 1996, 1997, 2000. Avocations: reading, music, ping pong.

WEI, SU-HUAI, physicist, researcher; b. Shanghai, People's Republic of China, Oct. 14, 1957; came to U.S., 1981; s. Liangqing Wei and Fulan Gao; m. Fanyu Pei, Aug. 12, 1985; children: Peng-Peng Faustine, Di Sonia. BS, Fudan U., Shanghai; MS, Coll. William and Mary, 1983, PhD, 1985. Postdoctoral fellow Nat. Renewable Energy Lab. (formerly Solar Energy Rsch. Inst.), Golden, Colo., 1985-88, rsch. assoc., 1989, staff scientist, 1990-91, sr. scientist, 1992—. Contbr. over 160 articles to profl. jours. Fellow: Am. Phys. Soc.; mem.: Material Rsch. Soc. Achievements include development of the general potential linearized augmented plane wave method for electronic structure calculations; of the first principles theory on the electronic structure and stability of semiconductor and metal alloys, interfaces, superlattices and defects. Office: Nat Renewable Energy Lab 1617 Cole Blvd Golden CO 80401-3305 E-mail: swei@nrel.gov.

WEI, TIE-QUAN, biochemist; b. Feshan, Canton, China, Sept. 3, 1956; came to U.S., 1988; s. Yuan-Pu Wei and Shu-Gui Wang; m. Yun Yue, Nov. 20, 1986; children: Le, Jason. BS, Nankai U., Tianjing, China, 1982; MS, Chinese Acad. Scis., Beijing, 1986; PhD in Biochemistry, U. Ill., Chgo., 1993. Rsch. assoc. China-Japan Friendship Hosp., Beijing, 1986-88; postdoctoral fellow Loyola Med. Ctr., Chgo., 1993-95; devel. biochemist DuPont Med. Products, Newark, 1995-96; sr. biochemist Dade Behring Inc., 1996—. Contbr. articles to profl. jours. Recipient Sci. Advancement award Chinese Acad. Scis., 1987, Travel award GenBio, Inc., 1995. Fellow Nat. Acad. Clin. Biochemistry, mem. Am. Assn. Clin. Chemistry (diplomate). Achievements include discovery and purification of Casein Kinase II from human erythrocyte membrane. Home: 115 George Ct Bear DE 19701-1882 Office: Dade Behring Inc Glasgow Site 707 PO Box 6101 Newark DE 19714-6101 E-mail: weitq@dadebehring.com.

WEI, WANLI, biomedical scientist, physician; b. Xi'an, Shaanxi Province, China, Jan. 11, 1969; d. Yangxue Wei and Yiqing He. MD, Xi'an Med. U., China, 1995; PhD, Beijing Inst. Pharmacology and Toxicology, China, 1998. Asst. prof. Beijing Inst. Pharmacology and Toxicology, 1998—99; rsch. scientist NIH, Balt., 1999—. Mem.: Am. Soc. Biochemistry and Molecular Biology, Soc. Neurosci. Office: LCMB/NIA/Nat Inst Health 5600 Nathan Shock Dr Baltimore MD 21224 Business E-Mail: weiwa@grc.nia.nih.gov.

WEI, YEHUA DENNIS, geography educator; b. Zhejiang, China, Oct. 24, 1963; BS in Urban Planning, Hangzhou (China) U., 1984; MA in Urban Studies, U. Akron, 1991; PhD in Geogrphy, UCLA, 1998. Assoc. prof. U. Wis., Milw., 1997—. Mem. Assn. Am. Geographers, Assn. Asian Studies, Chinese Profls. Geog. Info. Sys. Office: U Wis Milw Dept Geography Milwaukee WI 53201 Fax: 414-229-3981.

WEI, YING, chemist; b. Harbin, China, Aug. 29, 1952; d. Wen-Jia Wei and Su-Zhen Xu; m. Jian-Ming Jiang, Jan. 28, 1981 (div. Feb. 1997); 1 child Mike Jiang. BS in Chemistry, Hei Long Jiang U., China, 1982; MS, Rennes (France) I U., 1984, PhD, 1986. Postdoc. fellow A&M U., College Station, Tex., 1989—90, Lamar U., Beaumont, 1990—91; IT corp. lab. supr. IT Corp., Cosby, 1991—95; city lab. mgr. City of Houston/Water Prodn., 1996—. Contbr. articles to profl. jour. Mem.: Am. Water Works Assn. Home: 3414 Almond Creek Dr Houston TX 77059 Office: City of Houston 2300 Federal Rd Houston TX 77015 E-mail: ying.wei@cityofhouston.net.

WEIANT, ELIZABETH ABBOTT, retired biology educator; b. New Britain, Conn., July 4, 1913; d. William Armstrong and Flora (Abbott) W. BS, MS, Tufts U., 1943; MA, Radcliffe Coll., 1952; EdD, Boston U., 1970. Instr. biology Tufts Coll., Medford, Mass., 1943-56, asst. prof., 1957-61; asst. prof. biology Simmons Coll., Boston, 1961-71, assoc. prof., 1972-79, chmn. dept., 1977-79, ret., 1979; corr. Evening Citizen, Laconia, N.H., 1987-98, Franklin-Tilton Telegram, Franklin, 1990-2000. Rschr. OSRD, USPHS, NSF, 1943-61; sr. rsch. fellow Max-Planck Inst., Seewiesen, Fed. Republic Germany, 1958; physiologist for product validation Cordis Corp., Miami, Fla., 1970 Contbr. articles to profl. jours. Mem. Hist. Dist. Commn., Sanbornton, N.H., 1979-83; sec., mem. Sanbornton Conservation Commn., 1979-83, Trustees of Trust Fund, Sanbornton, 1985-96; bd. dirs., sec. N.H. affiliate Am. Heart Assn., Manchester, 1981-85; bd. dirs., mem. coms. Franklin (N.H.) Regional Hosp., 1984-91; pres. Sanbornton Hist. Soc., 1980-82; publicity chmn. Friends N.H. Music Festival. Recipient Disting. Svc. award Tufts U., 1970, Tower award Westbrook Coll., Portland, Maine, 1974, Woman of Yr. award Tilton-Northfield Bus. and Profl. Women, 1980, Heart of Gold award Am. Heart Assn., 1986, award for Pub. Svc. Belknap County Pomona Grange, 1990, Gov.'s Outstanding Vol. award, 1992. Mem. Am. Inst. Biol. Scis., Sigma Xi (sec. Tufts U. chpt. 1947-59), Grange. Republican. Home: PO Box 11 Sanbornton NH 03269-0011

WEIBLEY, GRAYCE L. retired writer; b. Bath, Pa., Dec. 3, 1921; d. Harvey Samuel and Clara Magdalene Miller; m. Marvin H. Weibley, Dec. 4, 1943; children: Marvin Weibley, Jr. (Deceased), Gayle I. Diploma, Famous Writers Sch., Westport, CT, 1971, Inst. of Children's Lit., 1975. Sec. Consumers Gas Co., Reading, Pa., 1939—43; office clk. QM-USMC, Camp Lejeune, 1944; x-ray therapist Dr. A.M. Sharpe, Chester, 1955; office mgr. Penncrest H.S., Media, 1956—60; staff sec. Bartol Rsch. Found., Springfield, 1962—66; libr. Elkton Christian Schools, Elkton, 1998—2001. Chaplain Nat. League of Am. Pen Women, Washington, 1995; dramatic monologues Nursing Homes & Schools, NC, PA, and MD, 1950—2002. Recipient Most Meaningful Short, St. David's Christian Writers, PA, Best Entry, Black Mountain Christian Writers, NC, 1994. R-Liberal. Baptist. Achievements include development of Set up and organized the Elkton Christian School's 6,500-book library. Avocations: reading, writing, needlecrafts, puzzles. Home: 36 Trent Road Elkton MD 21921-7584 Personal E-mail: gramar5@juno.com.

WEICHER, JOHN CHARLES, federal agency administrator; b. Chgo., Mar. 8, 1938; s. John Jr. and Ruth Agnes (Waits) W.; m. Alice Jean Landt, Sept. 30, 1972; children: John Victor, Stephany Jean Ruth. AB, U. Mich., 1959; PhD, U. Chgo., 1968. Acting asst. prof. U. Calif., Irvine, 1965-67; assoc. and asst. prof. econs. Ohio State U., Columbus, 1967-77; with div. policy rsch. OEO, Washington, 1972-73; dir. div. econ. policy HUD, 1973-74, dep. asst. sec. econ. affairs, 1975-77; dir. econs. and fin. markets program Urban Inst., 1977-81; F.K. Weyerhaeuser scholar in pub. policy Am. Enterprise Inst, 1981-87; assoc. dir. econ. policy Office of Mgmt. and Budget, 1987-89; asst. sec. policy devel. and rsch. HUD, 1989—; asst. secy. housing and comnr., fed. housing admin. U.S. Dept H.U.D., 2001—. Author: Urban Renewal: Federal Program for Local Problems, 1972, Housing: Federal Policies and Programs, 1980, Maintaining the Safety Net, 1984; contbr. articles to profl. jours. Presbyterian. Avocation: sports. Office: US Dept HUD Office of Housing & Fed Housing Admin 451 7th St SW Washington DC 20410-9000*

WEICHERT, JAMEY PAUL, scientist; b. Austin, Minn., Oct. 6, 1956; m. Judy R. Landberg; children: Andrew, Emily, Cassie. BS, U. Minn., 1980; PhD, U. Mich., 1985. Sr. assoc. rsch. scientist U. Mich., Ann Arbor, 1985-98; asst. prof. U. Wis., Madison, 1998—. Cons. in field. Mem. Radiologic Soc. N.Am., Am. Chem. Soc., Molecular Imaging Soc., Soc. Nuclear Medicine Avocations: racquetball, woodworking. Office: U Wis Radiology E3/311 CSC 600 Highland Ave Madison WI 53792 E-mail: jpweichert@facstaff.wisc.edu.

WEICHMAN, DOUGLAS JOHN, fleet manager county government; b. Lakeview, Mich., May 23, 1956; s. George Ludwig and Phyllis Bertha (Baker) W.; m. Teresa Marie Bevier, May 3, 1980; children: Kyle Douglas, Rebecca Marie. BSc, Ferris State U., 1978; postgrad. instr.'s course Alternate Fuel, U.S. Dept. Transportation, Tampa, Fla., 1995. Supr. equipment maintenance Purolator Security, Detroit, 1978-79; shop supr. McLouth Steel, Trenton, Mich., 1979-81; fleet svc. mgr. Met. Dade County, Miami, Fla., 1982-90; dir. fleet mgmt. Palm Beach County, W. Palm Beach, 1990—. Mem. accident rev. bd., W. Palm Beach, Fla., 1995—. Presenter TV Program, Govt. Svc. TV Network; contbr. articles to profl. jours. Cub scout leader, Boy Scouts Am., Jupiter, Fla., 1995—; bd. dirs. Clean Cities Coalition, Hollywood, Fla., 1996 (govt. appointee); chmn. Palm Beach County United Way, W. Palm Beach, 1996. Recipient Alternative Fuels Grant, State of Fla. Comty. Affairs, 1994, 95. Mem. Nat. Assn. Fleet Adminstrs. (chair), Fla. Assn. Govtl. Fleet Adminstrs. Avocations: boating, golf, racquetball. Home: 17885 Bridle Ln Jupiter FL 33478-4717 Office: Palm Beach County 3700 Belvedere Rd Ste D West Palm Beach FL 33406-1577

WEICHSEL, JOHN, town manager; b. Germany, Dec. 26, 1932; children: Barry, Amy Weichsel Rosen. BA, U. Pa., 1954, M Govtl. Adminstrn., 1956. Adminstrv. asst. City of Kalamazoo, 1955-59; village mgr. Village of Ellenville, N.Y., 1959-66; town mgr. Town of Southington, Conn., 1966—. Bd. dirs. Bradley Meml. Hosp., Southington, 1990—. Recipient 45-Yr. plaque ICMA, Washington, 2000. Mem. N.Y. City and Town Mgmt. Assn. (pres.), Internat. City and County Mgrs. Assn. Home: 124 Beechwood Dr Southington CT 06489 Office: Town of Southington 75 Main St Southington CT 06489

WEIDA, LEWIS DIXON, marketing analyst, consultant; b. Moran, Ind., Apr. 23, 1924; s. Charles Ray and Luella Mildred (Dixon) W.; student Kenyon Coll., 1943, Purdue U., 1946; B.S., Ind. U., 1948; M.S., Columbia U., 1950. Mgr. statis. analysis unit Gen. Motors Acceptance Corp., N.Y.C., 1949-55; asst. to exec. v.p. Am. Express Co., 1955-82. Served with USAAF, 1943-46; PTO. Mem. Internat. Platform Assn. Democrat. Club: Masons. Home: 25 Tudor City Pl New York NY 10017-6819

WEIDAW, KENNETH ROE, musician, educator, consultant; b. Toledo, Apr. 7, 1920; s. Fred Andrew and Ola Mae (Harris) W.; m. Margaret Ruth Lazear, Dec. 14, 1940;children: Patricia Ruth, Pamela Mae, Kenneth Roe Jr., Karen Louise. B in Music Edn., Vandercook Coll., 1942; MusB, Roosevelt U., 1942; MusM, U. So. Calif., 1953. Freelance musician, 1940—; several adminstrv. positions various music schs., colls. and vets. adminstrns., Chgo. and Los Angeles, 1940-54; tchr., coord. music Arcadia (Calif.) Unified Schs., 1952-81; musician Glendale (Calif.) Symphony, 1961-83, L.A. Rams Band, 1965-69, 74-80; regional coord. Am. Scandinavian Student Exch., Laguna Beach, Calif., 1980-84, student group escort, 1987—; area coord. Fgn. Study League and E.F. Inst. for Cultural Exch., L.A., 1975-79. Musician L.A. City Concert Band, 1958—81; condr. San Gabriel (Calif.) Valley Jr. Symphony, 1962—66; adjudicator, clinician, 1940—; adj. prof. Calif. State U., L.A., 1984—2000; investment exec., Temple City, Calif., 1971—. Musician for (films) Paint Your Wagon and Heaven Can Wait; contbr. articles to profl. jours. Mem. Sun City (Ariz.) Concert Band, 1998—, Sun City Renaissance Brass, 1999-2000. With USN, 1942-45. Recipient Am. Bicentennial medal, 1976; named Tchr. of Year, Santa Anita Industry-Edn. Council, 1972, Outstanding Music Educator, Los Angeles County Bd. Edn., 1983; Ann. Ken Weidaw Outstanding Music Student award named in his honor Arcadia Music Club, 1982. Mem.: L.A. County Music Educators Assn., Assn. Calif. Sch. Adminstrs., Am. Sch. Band Dirs. Assn., Calif. Music Educators Assn. (pres. 1980—83), Music Educators Nat. Conf., Plan Cons. Specializing in Investment/Retirement Planning (CEO 1985—, registered rep., plan mem. securities corp. 1998—, titan value equities corp. 1991—98), Fin. Planning Assn., Am. Fedn. Musicians (life), So. Calif. Sch. Band and Orch. Assn. (life; pres. 1975—77), Phi Mu Sigma, Pi Kappa Lambda. Avocations: golf, travel. Office: Plan Cons PO Box 493 Temple City CA 91780-0493

WEIDEMAN, WARREN MILO, producer; b. Houston, Mar. 4, 1944; s. George and Marion (Rand) W. BA, U. Ark., 1970. Creative dir. Weidman & Whitney Advt., Hartford, Conn., 1972-77; mktg. dir. CMR-Playboy Enterprise Coll. Divsn., 1977-79; mktg. cons. 20th Century Fox, Universal, 1979-84; co-founder Krown, Inc., Beverly Hills, Calif., 1984-88; mng. dir. Krown/Y&R, Culver City, 1988-91; pres. 1st Look Prodns., L.A., 1991-95; pres., CEO Harmony Entertainment, 1995—. Spkr. in field. V.p. Free Arts Clinic for Abused Children, Malibu, Calif., 1985-95. with USAF, 1962-66. Office: Harmony Entertainment 420 S Beverly Dr Ste 100 Beverly Hills CA 90212-4410

WEIDEMANN, CELIA JEAN, social scientist, international business and financial development consultant; b. Denver, Dec. 6, 1942; d. John Clement and Hazel (Van Tuyl) Kirlin; m. Wesley Clark Weidemann, July 1, 1972; 1 child, Stephanie Jean. BS, Iowa State U., 1964; MS, U. Wis., Madison, 1970, PhD, 1973; postgrad., U. So. Calif., 1983. Advisor UN Food & Agr. Orgn., Ibadan, Nigeria, 1973-77; ind. rschr. Asia and Near East, 1977-78; program coord., asst. prof., rsch. assoc. U. Wis., Madison, 1979-81; chief institutional and human resources U.S. Agy. for Internat. Devel., Washington, 1982-85; team leader, cons. Sumatra, Indonesia, 1984; dir. fed. econs. program Midwest Rsch. Inst., Washington, 1985-86; pres., founder, pres. emeritus Weidemann Assocs., Arlington, Va., 1986-2000; pres. Weidemann Found., 2000—. Cons. U.S. Congress, Aspen Inst., Ford Found., World Bank, Egypt, Nigeria, Gambia, Pakistan, Indonesia, AID, Thailand, Jamaica, Panama, Philippines, Sierra Leone, Kenya, Jordon, Poland, India, Egypt, Russia, Finnish Internat. Devel. Agy., Namibia, pvt. client Estonia, Lativa, Russia, Japan, Internat. Ctr. Rsch. on Women, Zaire, UN Food and Agriculture Orgn., Ghana, Internat. Statis. Inst., The Netherlands, Global Exch., 1986-87, Asian Devel. Bank, Mongolia, Nepal, Vietnam, Bangladesh, Indonesia, Philippines. Author: Planning Home Economics Curriculum for Social and Economic Development, Agricultural Extension for Women Farmers in Africa, 1990, Financial Services for Women, 1992, Egyptian Women and Microenterprise: The Invisible Entrepreneurs, 1992, Small Enterprise Development in Poland: Does Gender Matter?, 1994, Microenterprise and Gender in India, 1995, Supporting Women's Livelihoods: Microfinance That Works for the Majority , 2002; contbr. Fellow Am. Home Econs. Assn., 1969-73; grantee Ford Found., 1987-89. Mem. Nat. Rsch. Coun., Nat. Acad. Sci. (peer reviewer), Soc. Internat. Devel., Am. Sociol. Assn., Assn. for Women in Devel. (pres. 1989, founder, bd. dirs.), Coalition for Women's Econ. Devel. and Global Equality (co-chair), Internat. Devel. Conf. (bd. dirs., exec. com.), Am. Home Econs. Assn. (Wis. internat., chmn. 1980-81), Internat. Platform Assn., Pi Lambda Theta, Omicron Nu. Avocations: mountain trekking, piano/pipe organ, canoeing, photography, poetry. Office: Weidemann Assocs Inc 933 N Kenmore St Ste 401A Arlington VA 22201-2236 E-mail: jweidemann@aol.com.

WEIDEMANN, JULIA CLARK, retired principal, educator; b. Batavia, N.Y., May 21, 1937; d. Edward Thomas and Grace Eloise (Kenna) Clark; m. Rudolph John Weidemann, July 9, 1960 (dec.); 1 child, Michael John (dec.). BA in English, Daemen Coll., 1958; MS in Edn., SUNY, Buffalo, 1961, MEd in Reading Edn., 1973, postgrad, 1985-86. Cert. sch. adminstr., supr. Tchr Buffalo Pub. Schs., 1958-61, 66-67; remedial reading tchr. West Seneca (N.Y.) Cen. Sch. Dist., 1972-79, coord. chpt. I reading program, 1974-79, reading coord., 1980-87; prin. Parkdale Elem. Sch. East Aurora (N.Y.) Union Free Sch., 1987—. Adj. prof. edn. Canisius Coll., Medaille Coll., Daemen Coll.; tchr. cons. Scott Foresman Lang. Arts Textbooks; sch. support team mem. N.Y. State Edn. Dept.; chmn. elem. com. staff devel. West Seneca Ctrl. Sch., 1985-87; mem. adv. coun. Medaille Coll.; chmn. various confs.; lectr. in field. Author numerous poems; invited poet Women's Impact Gallery, Buffalo, N.Y., 1996, 97. Mem. West Seneca Dist. Computer Adv. Com., 1980-87, East Aurora Hist. Soc., 1990—; mem. cmty. adv. coun. SUNY, Buffalo, 1994—, Women's Health Initiative, 1994-96; mem. Women's Action Coalition of Buffalo, 1994; pres. Roycroft Wordsmiths; mem. steering com. Kids Voting N.Y., 1996-99. Scholar Rosary Hill Coll., 1954, N.Y. State Regents, 1954; recipient Reading award Niagara Frontier Reading Coun., 1986. Mem. AAUW (life, pres. Buffalo br. 1994-95, exec. bd. dirs., named gift ednl. found., state bd. dirs. equity in edn. com. 1995—), Assn. Compensatory Edn. (pres. 1984-85, exec. bd. Region VI 1983-87, conf. chmn. Region VI 1985-87), Internat. Reading Assn. (acting chmn. 3d ea. regional reading conf. 1980), Niagara Frontier Reading Assn. (pres. 1979-80, fin. com. chmn., bd. dirs. 1973—), Daemen Coll. Alumni Assn. (bd. govs. 1987, chmn. alumni reunion weekend, chmn. sr. reception, Disting. Alumna 1989), Assn. Supervision and Devel., Assn. Tchr. Educators, Delta Kappa Gamma (pres., Ruth Fraser scholar 1986), Beta Zeta (pres.), Phi Delta Kappa (Buffalo-South chpt. 1989). Democrat. Roman Catholic. Home: 21 Nye Hill Rd East Aurora NY 14052-2651

WEIDEMEYER, CARLETON LLOYD, lawyer; b. Hebbville, Md., June 12, 1933; BA in Polit. Sci., U. Md., 1958; JD, Stetson U., 1961. Bar: Fla. 1961, D.C. 1971, U.S. Dist. Ct. (mid. dist.) Fla. 1963, U.S. Ct. Appeals (5th cir.) 1967, U.S. Ct. Appeals (D.C. cir.) 1976, U.S. Supreme Ct. 1966, U.S. Ct. Appeals (11th cir.) 1982. Rsch. asst. Fla. 2d Dist. Ct. Appeals, 1961-65; ptnr. Kalle and Weidemeyer, St. Petersburg, Fla., 1965-68; asst. pub. defender 6th Jud. Cir., 1966-69, 81-83; ptnr. Wightman, Weidemeyer, Jones, Turnbull and Cobb, Clearwater, 1968-82; pres. Carleton L. Weidemeyer, P.A. Law Office, 1982—; pres. So. Mcpl. Corp., 1997—. Guest lectr. Stetson U., 1978—80; lectr. estate planning seminars; bd. dirs. Watson Ctr. for the Blind, 1998—; trustee Tampa Bay Rsch. Inst., 2000—, Francis Prasse Scholarship Trust, 1984—; mem. bd. advisors to Fla. Sheriff's Youth Ranches, 1997—2001. Author: (handbook) Arbitration of Entertainment Claims, Baltimore County's Second District, The Emerging Thirties, 1990, Area History, Baltimore County, 1990, History of Musicians' Association of Clearwater, Local 729, AFM, 1999; editor Ad Lib mag., 1978-81; contbr. numerous articles to profl. jours. and geneal. pubs.; performer This Is Your Navy Radio Show, Memphis, 1951-52; leader Polka Dots, The Jazz Notes, 1976—; mem. St. Paul Ch. Orch., Fla. Hist. Soc., 1973—, Md. Hist. Soc., 1990—, Pinellas County Estate Planning Assn., 1997—; performer Clearwater Jazz Holiday, 1980, 81, co-chmn., 1981. Bd. advisors Musician Ins. Trust; trustee Francis G. Prasse Meml. Scholarship Trust, 1984—; mem. planned giving com. Upper Pinellas Assn. Retarded Citizens, 1996-2001; bd. trustees Tampa Bay Rsch. Inst., 2001—; adv. com. Fla. Sheriff Youth Ranches, 1997—; bd. dirs. Pinellas Ctr. for Visually Impaired, 1999-2000; bd. dirs. Watson Ctr. for the Blind, 2000—. Served with USN, 1951-54. Mem. SAR, Musicians Assn. Clearwater (pres. 1976-81), Fla.-Ga. Conf. Musicians (sec., treas. 1974-76), NRA, ABA (sr. bar sect.), Fed. Bar Assn., Fla. State Hist. Soc., Md. Hist. Soc., Greater St. Petersburg Musicians Assn., Clearwater Bar Assn. (probate divsn.), Am. Fedn. Musicians (internat. law com. pres. so. conf. musicians 1979-80), Nat. Geneal. Soc., Clearwater Genealogy Soc., Md. Geneal. Soc., Augustan Soc., Lancaster (Pa.) Geneal. Soc., Pinellas (Fla.) Geneal. Soc. (lectr. 1995—), Carroll County (Md.) Geneal. Soc., Balt. County Geneal. Soc., Lancaster Mennonite Hist. Soc., Navy Hurricane Hunters, Sons Union Vets. Civil War, Md. Hist. Soc., Catonsville (Md.) Hist. Soc., Am. Legion, German Am. Geneal. Assn., DAV Fleet Res., Masons, Scottish Rite (Tampa), Egypt Temple Shrine, Moose, Sertoma (bd. dirs. Clearwater chpt. 1984-96, v.p. 1989-92), Phi Delta Phi, Sigma Pi, Kappa Kappa Psi. Home: 2261 Belleair Rd Clearwater FL 33764-2761 Office: Legal Arts Bldg Ste 1 501 S Fort Harrison Ave Clearwater FL 33756-5317

WEIDEN, PAUL LINCOLN, cancer researcher, oncologist, educator; b. Portland, Oreg., Aug. 21, 1941; BA, Harvard U., 1963, MD, 1967. Intern U. Hosps., Cleve., 1967-68, resident medicine, 1968-69; fellow hematology and oncology U. Wash., Seattle, 1971-73; med. dir. Nat. Marrow Donor Program Collection Ctr., 1988-2001, Dendreon Corp., Seattle, 2001—; cons. Bartlett Regional Hosp., Juneau, Alaska, 2001—. Chmn. stem cell transplantation com. Virginia Mason Hosp., Seattle, 1991—2001, prin. investigator cmty. clin. oncology program, 1993—2001, med. dir. cancer clin. rsch. unit, 1995—2001, chmn. rsch. adv. com., 2000—01, emeritus physician, 2001—; clin. prof. U. Wash. Med. Sch., 1991—. Fellow ACP; mem. AMA, Am. Soc. Clin. Oncology, Am. Soc. Hematology. Office: 3005 First Ave Seattle WA 98121 E-mail: plweiden@dendreon.com.

WEIDENAAR, DENNIS JAY, economics educator; b. Grand Rapids, Mich., Oct. 4, 1936; s. John and Jennie (Beukema) W.; m. Kristin Andrews, July 14, 1943; children: Kaarin Jaye, John Andrews. AB, Calvin Coll., Grand Rapids, 1958; MA, U. Chgo., 1961; PhD, Purdue U., 1969. Asst. prof. econs. Purdue U., West Lafayette, Ind., 1966-72, assoc. prof., 1972-77, prof., 1977-83; interim dean Krannert Sch. of Mgmt., 1983-84, assoc. dean, 1984-99; dean Krannert Grad. Sch. Mgmt., 1990-99, prof. econs., 1999—. Cons. TRW, B.F. Goodrich, Ea. Panhandle; bd. dirs. Lafayette Ins. Co. Author: Economics. Contbr. articles to profl. jours. Bd. dirs. Ind. Coun. on Econ. Edn., Lafayette, 1974-83, Lafayette Ins. Co. Recipient The Leavey Awd for Excellence in Pvt. Enterprise Edn., Freedom's Found., Valley Forge, 1983, Distinguished Service Awd., Joint Council on Econ. Edn., N.Y., 1986, Golden Key Nat. Honor Soc., 1985. Mem. Rotary, Delta Sigma Pi, Beta Gamma Sigma (bd. dirs., pres. 2002--), Phi Delta Kappa. Presbyterian. Home: 217 Rosebank Ln West Lafayette IN 47906-8614 Office: Purdue U Krannert Sch Mgmt West Lafayette IN 47907

WEIDENBAUM, MURRAY LEW, economist, educator; b. Bronx, N.Y., Feb. 10, 1927; s. David and Rose (Warshaw) Weidenbaum; m. Phyllis Green, June 13, 1954; children: Susan, James, Laurie. BBA, CCNY, 1948; MA, Columbia U., 1949; MPA, Princeton U., 1954, PhD, 1958; LLD, Baruch Coll., 1981, U. Evansville, 1983, McKendree Coll., 1993. Fiscal economist Bur. Budget, Washington, 1949—57; corp. economist Boeing Co., Seattle, 1958—62; sr. economist Stanford Rsch. Inst., Palo Alto, Calif., 1962—63; mem. faculty Washington U., St. Louis, 1964—, prof., chmn. dept. econs., 1966—69, Mallinckrodt prof., 1971—, dir. Ctr. for Study Am. Bus., 1974—81, Washington U., St. Louis, 1982—95; chmn. Ctr. for Study Am. Bus. Washington U., 1995—2000; asst. sec. econ. policy Treasury Dept., 1969—71; chmn. Coun. of Econ. Advs., 1981—82; hon. chmn. Weidenbaum Ctr. on the Economy, Govt. and Pub. Policy, St. Louis, 2001—. Chmn. rsch. adv. com. St. Louis Regional Indsl. Devel. Corp., 1965—69; exec. sec. Pres.'s Com. on Econ. Impact of Def. and Disarmament, 1964; mem. U.S. Fin. Investment Adv. Panel, 1970—72; cons. various firms and instns.; chmn. U.S. Commn. to Rev. the Trade Deficit, 1999—2000. Author: Federal Budgeting, 1964, Modern Public Sector, 1969, Economics of Peacetime Defense, 1974, Economic Impact of the Vietnam War, 1967, Government-Mandated Price Increases, 1975, The Future of Business Regulation, 1980, Rendezvous With Reality: The American Economy After Reagan, 1988, Rendezvous With Reality: The American Economy After Reagan, paperback edit., 1990, Business, Government, and the Public, 1990, Small Wars, Big Defense, 1992, The Bamboo Network, 1996, Business and Government in the Global Marketplace, 1999; mem. editl. bd.: Publius, 1971—, mem. editl. bd.: Jour. Econ. Issues, 1972—75, mem. editl. bd.: Challenge, 1974—81, mem. editl. bd.: , 1983—, mem. editl. bd.: Business and the Contemporary World, 1997—2000. With U.S. Army, 1945. Named Banbury fellow, Princeton U., 1952—54; named to Free Market Hall of Fame, 1983; recipient Alexander Hamilton medal, U.S. Dept. Treasury, 1971, Disting. Writer award, Georgetown U., award for disting. tchg., Freedoms Found., 1980, award for best book in econs., Assn. Am. Pubs., 1992. Fellow: Assn. for Pvt. Enterprise Edn. (Adam Smith award 1986), City Coll. Alumni Assn. (Townsend Harris medal 1969), Soc. Tech. Comm., Nat. Assn. Bus. Economists, Cosmos. Office: Washington Univ Weidenbaum Ctr 1 Brookings Dr Saint Louis MO 63130-4899

WEIDENBRUCH, ANNA MAE, nurse; b. Owosso, Mich., July 26, 1926; d. Robert Harry and Della Jane (Gander) Thompson; m. Manley Lavern Nixon, Aug. 3, 1946 (div. 1961); children: Terry Lee, Douglas Kent, LaVerna Ann, Norma Jean; m. Donald F. Clewley, Aug. 27, 1961 (dec. 1973); m. Heinz

Weidenbruch, 1984 (dec. 1999). ADN, Lansing (Mich.) C.C., 1983; BS in Health Studies, Western Mich. U., Kalamazoo, 1993. RN, Mich. Staff nurse Sparrow Hosp., Lansing, 1958-62, Ingham Med. Hosp., Lansing, 1962-64, Lansing Gen. Hosp., 1964-66, 77-88, Hazel I. Findlay Country Manor, St. Johns, Mich., 1987-89, Staff Builders, Okemos, 1990-96; ret., 1996. Democrat. Avocations: knitting, crocheting, embroidery, traveling, dancing. Home: 9855 E Irvington Rd Unit 189 Tucson AZ 85730-5234 E-mail: aweidenbruch@qwest.net., annaw@voyager.net.

WEIDENFELD, EDWARD LEE, lawyer; b. Akron, Ohio, July 15, 1943; s. Sam and Beatrice (Cooper) W.; m. Sheila Rabb, Aug. 11, 1968; children: Nicholas, Daniel. BS, U. Wis., 1965; JD, Columbia U., 1968. Bar: N.Y. 1968, U.S. Supreme Ct. 1972, D.C. 1973. Pvt. practice, N.Y.C., 1969-71, 73-82, Washington, 1982—. Spl. cons. N.Y.C. Dept. Bldgs., 1967; counsel, dir. energy staff Com. on Interior and Insular Affairs, U.S. Ho. of Reps., 1971—73; mem. faculty Am. Law Inst.-ABA CLE Programs; mem. Internat. Del. to Observe Philippine Election, 1986, Internat. Del. to Observe Republic Korea Election, 1987, Pakistan Election, 1988, Chilean Election, 1989, Albanian Election, 1997; mem. D.C. Bar Task Force on the Omnibus Trusts and Estates Amendment Act of 2000, 1999—2001; lectr. to profl. groups. Editor in chief Atomic Energy Law Jour., 1975-76; editor Conspectus Current Estate Planning Jour., 1998-2001; contbg. author: Generations: Planning Your Legacy, 1999. Mem. Pres.'s Commn. on White House Fellowships, 1977; nat. chmn. Lawyers for Reagan/Bush, 1980; chief dep. counsel Reagan/Bush Campaign, 1980; chmn. Reagan/Bush '84 Legal Adv. Bd., 1984; mem. D.C. Rep. Com., 1984-92, vice chmn., 1984-88; mem. Coun. Adminstrv. Conf. of U.S., 1981-92, sr. fellow, 1992-95; overseer dept. def. regional ctrs., sec.-treas. Salvation Army Adv. Bd.; trustee Danny Kaye and Sylvia Fine Kaye Found.; chmn. bd. overseers The Nat. Def. U. Recipient medal of Peter the Great, Russian Fedn., 2000. Mem. ABA, D.C. Bar Assn., Am. Law Inst. (life), Assn. Bar City N.Y., D.C. Estate Planning Coun. Clubs: Met. (Washington). Office: 1828 L St NW Ste 500 Washington DC 20036-3806 E-mail: eweidenf@aol.com.

WEIDENFELD, SHEILA RABB, television producer, author; b. Cambridge, Mass., Sept. 7, 1943; d. Maxwell M. and Ruth (Cryden) Rabb; m. Edward L. Weidenfeld, Aug. 11, 1968; children: Nicholas Rabb, Daniel Rabb. BA, Brandeis U., 1965. Assoc. prodr. Metromedia, Inc., Sta. WNEW-TV, N.Y.C., 1965-68; talent coord. That Show with Joan Rivers, NBC, 1968-71; coord. NBC network game programs, 1968-71; prodr. Metromedia, Inc., Sta. WTTG-TV, Washington, 1971-73; creator/prodr. Take It From Here, NBC (WBC-TV), 1973-74; press sec. to first lady Betty Ford, spl. asst. to Pres. Gerald R. Ford, 1974-77; mem. Pres.'s Adv. Commn. on Hist. Preservation, 1977-81; TV prodr., moderator On the Record, NBC-TV, Sta. WRC-TV, Washington, 1978-79; pres. D.C. Prodns., Ltd., 1978; prodr., host Your Personal Decorator, 1987; mem. Sec. State's Adv. Commn. on Fgn. Svc. Inst., 1972-74; founding mem. Project Censured Panel of Judges, 1976—. Bd. dirs. First Star. Author: First Lady's Lady, 1979. Mem. U.S. Holocaust Meml. Coun., 1987-97; corporator Dana Hall Sch., Wellesley, Mass.; bd. dirs. Wolf Trap Found., Women's Campaign Fund, 1978-79; bd. dirs. D.C. Contemporary Dance Theatre, 1986-88, D.C. Rep. Ctrl. Com., 1984—, D.C. Preservation League, 1987-90; chmn. C&O Canal Nat. Hist. Park Commn., 1988—; bd. dirs. Am. Univ. Rome, 1988—. Recipient awards for outstanding achievement in the media AAUW, 1973, 74, Silver Screen award A Campaign to Remember for the U.S. Holocaust Meml. Coun., 1989, Bronze medal Internat. Film and Video Festival N.Y., 1990; named hon. consul gen. of Republic of San Marino to Washington; knighted by Order of St. Agatha, Republic of San Marino, 1986. Mem. NATAS (Emmy award 1972), Washington Press Club, Am. Newspaper Women's Club, Am. Women in Radio and TV, Cosmos Club, Consular Corps, Sigma Delta Chi. Home and Office: 3059 Q St NW Washington DC 20007-3081

WEIDENTHAL, MAURICE DAVID (BUD WEIDENTHAL), educational administrator, journalist; b. Cleve., Nov. 26, 1925; s. William and Evelyn (Kolinsky) W.; m. Grace Schwartz, Apr. 14, 1957; 1 child, Susan Elizabeth Weidenthal Saltzman. BA, U. Mich., 1950. Mem. staff Cleve. Press, 1950-81, editorial writer, 1950-51, asst. city editor, 1956-58, edn. editor, 1958-81; v.p. public affairs Cuyahoga Community Coll. Dist., Cleve., 1981-88; dir. Urban Colls. Project RC-2000, Tempe, Ariz., 1989—. Editor The Urban Report, Cleve., 1989—. Mem. pub. affairs com. Greater Cleve. Growth Assn., 1981-88; mem. bd. advisors Coun. for Advancement and Support of Edn., 1981-88, Nat. Coun. Mktg. and Pub. Rels., 1981—; alt. bd. dirs. St. Vincent Quadrangle, 1983-88; trustee Hebrew Free Loan Assn., 1975-86. With AUS, 1944-45. Decorated Air medal. Mem. Edn. Writers Assn., Soc. Profl. Journalists, (bd. dirs.), Cleve. City Club (bd. dirs. 1969-76), Cleve. Press Club. Home: 25858 Fairmount Blvd Cleveland OH 44122-2214 Office: 4250 Richmond Rd Cleveland OH 44122-6104 E-mail: u2w@aol.com., bud.weidenthal@tri-c.cc.oh.us.

WEIDMAN, JOHN CARL, II, education educator, consultant; b. Ephrata, Pa., Oct. 3, 1945; s. John Carl and Mary Elizabeth (Grube) W.; m. Carla Sue Fassnacht, Aug. 20, 1967; children: Jonathan Scott, Rebecca Mary. AB in Sociology cum laude, Princeton U., 1967; AM, U. Chgo., 1968, PhD, 1974. Acting asst. prof. edn. U. Minn., Mpls., 1970-74, asst. prof. edn., sociology and Am. studies, 1974-77; sr. rsch. assoc. Bur. Social Sci. Rsch., Inc., Washington, 1977-78; assoc. prof. edn. and sociology U. Pitts., 1979-86, prof. edn. and sociology, 1986—, chmn. dept. adminstrv. and policy studies, 1986-93. Cons. Nat. Ctr. Adminstrv. Justice, Youthwork, Inc., Upper Midwest Tri-Racial Gen. Assistance Ctr., Acad. for Ednl. Devel., Mongolia, Asian Devel. Bank, Indonesia, Laos and Mongolia, German Acad. Exch. Svc., Sema-Belgium; UNESCO chair higher edn. rsch. Maseno U. Coll., Kenya, 1993. Author: rsch. monographs; mem. editl. bd. Rev. of Higher Edn., 1984-88, Am. Ednl. Rsch. Jour., 1991-92, 96-98; co-author: Research on Higher Education in Developing Countries: Suggested Agendas and Research Strategies, 1991, Implementing a Faculty Assessment System: A Case Study of the University of Pittsburgh-UsA, 1994, Higher Education Costs and Tuition, 1996, Higher Education in Korea: Tradition and Adaptation, 2000, Socialization of Graduate and Professional Students: A Perilous Passage?, 2001, Finance and Higher Education, 2001; cons. editor Jour. Higher Edn., 1989—; contbr. chpts. to books, articles to profl. jours. Bd. dirs. Sch. Vol. Assn. Pitts., 1982-90, pres., 1984-87. Grantee U.S. Office Edn., 1971-73, Spencer Found., 1973-76, Nat. Inst. Edn., 1976-79, NEH, 1985-86, Asian Devel. Bank, Laos, 1995-96, Mongolia, 1997-2000; Fulbright scholar U. Augsburg, Germany, 1986-87. Mem. Am. Ednl. Rsch. Assn. (sec. postsecondary divsn. 1987-89), Am. Sociol. Assn., Assn. Study of Higher Edn., Comparative and Internat. Edn. Soc., Phi Delta Kappa. Office: U Pitts 5S38 Posvar Hall 230 S Bouquet St Pittsburgh PA 15260

WEIDMANN, K. TIMOTHY, not-for-profit fundraiser, writer; b. Bronxville, NY, May 28, 1950; s. Carl Frederick and Kathryn Henrietta Weidmann; m. Deborah Ann Emanuel, Sept. 18, 1976; 1 child Sarah 1 child Seth 1 child Jesse Florea. AB, Harvard Coll., Cambridge, MA, 1972; MDiv, Yale Div. Sch., New Haven, CT, 1980—80. Mktg. rep. IBM, White Plains, NY, 1981—83; assoc. dir. Yale U., New Haven, 1983—87; assoc. v.p. Northwestern U., Evanston, Ill., 1987—2001; sr. cons. Marts & Lundy, Inc., Lyndhurst, NJ, 2001—. V.p. devel. ALS Les Turner Found., Chicago, Ill., 1990—95; chair of devel. com. Vt. Studio Ctr., Johnson, Vt., 2001—. Author: (book) Lives and Legacies: An Encyclopedia of People Who Changed the World, 1999, (magazine) Breakaway, 1997, Clubhouse, 1998. Sr. warden St. John's Ch., New Haven, 1986—87; vestry mem. St. Mark's Ch., Evanston, Ill., 1990—92. Recipient Scholarship, Harvard Club of Westchester, 1968; fellow fellowship, Roothbert Fund, 1977-80, Leopold Schepp Found., 1977-80, Vt. Studio Ctr., 2000. Fellow: Timothy Dwight Coll., Yale (residential fellow 1985—87); mem.: Am. Healthcare Profls., Am. Fundraising Profls., Coun. on Aid and Support of Edn. Episcopalian. Achievements include Built infrastructure for corporate philantrophy at Yale; built infrastructure for grateful patient philanthropy as basis of fund=raising at Northwestern University Medical School. Avocations: reading, squash, travel. Home: 9018 Sleeping Bear Rd Skokie IL 60076 Personal E-mail: weidmann@martsandlundy.com.

WEIDNER, C. KEN, II, finance educator, consultant; b. Dallas, Nov. 16, 1959; s. Charles Leyman Weidner and Olga Despina Hogan; m. Barbara Ann Harris, June 30, 2000; 1 child Erica Leslie. BA in Mgmt., U. Ill., Springfield, 1987; MBA, U. Ill., Chgo., 1989, PhD, 1997. V.p. Mgmt. Ho., Inc., Inverness, Ill., 1989—93; mgmt. and orgn. devel. specialist U. Chgo. Hosps., 1993—96; asst. prof. orgn. devel. Loyola U. Chgo., 1996—2000; asst. prof. mgmt. St. Joseph's U., Phila., 2000—. Pres., dir. of practice ValueWorks, Inc., Phoenixville, Pa., 1996—. Contbr. articles to profl. jours. Recipient Best Practices award, Am. Hosp. Assn., Chgo., 1994, Dissertation award, ASTD, 1996, Outstanding Reviewer award, Acad. Mgmt. Edn. and Devel., 2001. Mem.: Phila. Regional Orgn. Devel. Network, Orgn. Devel. Network (bd. dirs. Chgo. chpt. 1998—2000). Avocations: sailing, music, reading. Office: St Joseph's U 5600 City Ave Philadelphia PA 19131 Fax: 610-935-4890. E-mail: weidner@sju.edu.

WEIDNER, EDWARD WILLIAM, university chancellor, political scientist; b. Mpls., July 7, 1921; s. Peter Clifford and Lillian (Halbe) W.; m. Jean Elizabeth Blomquist, Mar. 23, 1944 (dec. Apr., 1997); children: Nancy Louise, Gary Richard, Karen, William; m. Marjorie M. Fermanich, June 6, 1998. BA magna cum laude, U. Minn., 1942, MA, 1943, PhD, 1946; postgrad., U. Wis., 1943-45; LHD (hon.), No. Mich. U., 1969; PhD (hon.), Linköping U., Sweden, 1975. Staff mem. Nat. Mcpl. League, 1944, research assoc., 1944-45; cons. govts. div. U.S. Bur. Census, 1945, statistician, 1946; lectr. U. Wis., Madison, 1945; instr. U. Minn., Mpls., 1945-47, asst. prof., 1947-49, asst. dir. research in inter-govtl. relations, 1946-53; asst. prof. UCLA, 1949-50; faculty Mich. State U., East Lansing, 1950-62, from assoc. prof., dir. govtl. research bur., to prof. polit. sci., 1952-62, chmn. polit. sci. dept., 1952-57; coordinator, chief adviser Vietnam Project, 1955-57; dir. Inst. Research on Overseas Programs, 1957-61; vice chancellor E.W. Ctr., 1962-65; prof. polit. sci., dir. ctr. for devel. change U. Ky., Lexington, 1965-67; chancellor U. Wis., Green Bay, 1966-86, prof. polit. sci., 1966-89, chancellor emeritus, prof. emeritus, 1989—, dir. Cofrin Arboretum, 1986-89. Planning dir. Weidner Ctr. for the Performing Arts, 1987-93; bd. dirs. Univ. Bank, Green Bay; cons. Fgn. Ops. Adminstrn., Vietnam, 1954-55, Baltimore County (Md.) Reorgn. Commn., 1953-54, Ford Found., Pakistan, 1956, Nat. Assn. Fgn. Student Advisers, 1959-60, Pres.'s Task Force Fgn. Econ. Assistance, 1961, Dept. State, 1962-63, AID, 1964-65, Lees Coll., 1971-72, Green Bay Bot. Garden, 1997-98; mem. Gov. Mich. Commn. Inter-Govtl. Rels., 1954-55. Author: (with William Anderson) American Government, 1951, State and Local Government, 1951, (with others) The International Programs of American Universities, 1958, Intergovernmental Relations as Seen by Public Officials, 1960, (with William Anderson, Clara Penniman) Government for the Fifty States, 1960, The World Role of Universities, 1962, Technical Assistance in Public Administration Overseas, 1964; editor: Development Administration in Asia, 1970. Mem. Wis. Gov.'s Commn. on UN, 1975-81; trustee Prairie Sch., 1969-91, mem. adv. bd., 1991—; bd. dirs. Inst. for Shipboard Edn., 1976-89; mem. Lab. Ornithology, Cornell U., bd. dirs. 1989-98; chmn. adv. bd. Lakeland chpt. ARC, 1981-84; mem. N.Am. adv. group UN Environ. Programme, 1983-90; bd. advisers Nature Conservancy Wis., 1984-91; bd. dirs. Heritage Hill Found., 1987-92, 95-97, pres. 1991-92; bd. dirs. Assn. Am. Colls., 1978-80, Brown County, Family Svc. Assn., 1988-93; chmn. Brown County Cultural Coun., 1991-94; mem. nat. coun. ASPA, 1947-50; mem. internat. coun. UN U., 1974-80; bd. dirs. Am. Coun. on Edn., 1971-74, sec. bd., 1971-72; mem. nat. coun. Am. Polit. Assn., 1950-52. Recipient Outstanding Achievement award U. Minn., 1975. Mem. Wis. Soc. Ornithology, Wilderness Soc., World Wildlife Fund, Interfaith Alliance, Common Cause, Nature Conservancy, Audubon Soc., Am. Birding Assn., Green Bay Area C. of C. (bd. dirs. 1970-74), Mcpl. Clks. Edn. Found. (bd. dirs. 1980-97), Phi Beta Kappa, Pi Sigma Alpha. Home: 1656 Twin Lakes Cir Green Bay WI 54311-4207 E-mail: osggg@netnet.net.

WEIDNER, JAMES RICHARD, pediatrician; b. Camden, N.J., Feb. 15, 1966; BA in Biology, Franklin & Marshall Coll., 1988; MD, Temple U., 1992. Diplomate Am. Bd. Pediatrics. Resident in pediatrics Childrens Hosp., Phila., 1992-95; staff mem. West Jersey Hosp., Vorhees, N.J., 1995—. Mem. N.J. Med. Soc., Am. Acad. of Pediatrics. Home: 22 Eclipse Ave Sewell NJ 08080-1913 Office: 619 S White Horse Pike Audubon NJ 08106-1314

WEIDNER, ROBERT WRIGHT, musician, music educator, musicologist; b. Brookfield, Wis., Oct. 21, 1923; s. Oswald Frederick and Minnie Marie (Giencke) W.; m. Jean Dionne Rockwell; children: Robert Rockwell Weidner, Diane Jean Weidner. BS, Milw. State Tchrs. Coll., 1949; MA, Eastman Sch. of Music U. R.I., 1951, PhD, 1960. Band dir., tchr. history North Divsn. H.S., Milw., 1949-50; music dir. Oostburg (Wis.) Pub. Schs., 1951-52; band dir., music prof. Ohio No. U., Ada, 1952-55; band dir., prof. music Tex. Luth. Coll., Seguin, 1955-56; dir. music Abbotsford (Wis.) Pub. Schs./Dorchester (Wis.) Pub. Schs., 1956-58; prof. music, dir. orchestra Nebr. Wesleyan U., Lincoln, 1959-62; prof. music, dept. head U. Dubuque (Iowa), 1962-65; coord. grad. studies in music Ea. Ill. U., Charleston, 1987-89, prof. music, 1965-93, retired, 1994. Composer Tex. Luth. Coll. alma mater, 1956; editor (book) Christopher Tye: The Instrumental Music, 1965, Tye's Actes of the Apostles, 1970. Bd. dirs. Charleston Civic Assn., Charleston, 1991-97. With U.S. Army, 1943-46, ETO. Mem. Am. Musicol. Soc. Mem. Dem. Socialists of Am. Avocation: reading. Home: 1002 Scovill St Urbana IL 61801-6874 E-mail: rwweidner@aol.com.

WEIERS, JIM, state representative; b. SD; m. Gina Weiers; 4 children. Pres., CEO BHF, Inc.; mem. Ariz. Ho. of Reps., 1995—, speaker, 2001—. Republican. Office: Speaker of the House 1700 W Washington St Phoenix AZ 85007 Business E-Mail: jweiers@azleg.state.az.us.*

WEIERSTALL, RICHARD PAUL, retired pharmaceutical chemist; b. Jersey City, Nov. 5, 1942; s. William August and Emily (Haughey) W.; m. Gail Janet Thomsen, Aug. 17, 1968; children: Eric, Kurt, Karen. BS, Rutgers U., 1966, MS, 1969; PhD, U. Calif., San Francisco, 1973. Unit head drug metabolism Sandoz Pharm., East Hanover, N.J., 1973-74; dir. tech. svc. Banner Gelatin Products, Chatsworth, Calif., 1974-76; v.p. tech. svc. Banner Gelatin Prod., 1976-81; dir. pharm. sci. Ayerst Labs Inc., Rouses Point, N.Y., 1981-87; asst. v.p. Wyeth Ayerst Rsch., 1987-95, asst. v.p. quality assurance, 1995-99; ret., 1999. Mem. Am. Assn. Pharm. Sci., Am. Pharm. Assn. Home: 7 Stewart St Rouses Point NY 12979-1511 E-mail: rweiers@northnet.org.

WEIGAND, JAN CHRISTINE, elementary education educator, computer specialist; b. Kirksville, Mo., July 22, 1952; d. Charles Leo and Helen Frances (Myers) Jeffries; m. Douglas Walter Weigand, July 29, 1978; 1 child, Jeffrey Douglas. BS in Edn., Valparaiso (Ind.) U., 1974; MEd in Tech. in Edn., Nat.-Louis U., Wheaton, Ill., 1999; MA in Edn. Tchg. and Leadership, St. Xavier U., Chgo., 2001. Tchr. 2d grade Harrison St. Sch., Geneva, 1974-77, tchr. 1st grade, 1977—, computer coord., 1987—. Mem. NEA, Ill. Edn. Assn., Internat. Reading Assn., No. Ill. Reading Coun., Geneva Edn. Assn. Methodist. Avocations: genealogy, crafts. Office: Harrison St Sch 201 Harrison St Geneva IL 60134 E-mail: jweigand@geneva.k12.il.us.

WEIGEL, HENRY DONALD, civil engineer; b. Somers Point, N.J., Dec. 14, 1964; s. Henry Frank and Joan Alma (Sampson) W. BSCE, Villanova U., 1987. Lic. ocean operator USCG, 1987. Capt., mate various sportfishing vessels, Ocean City, N.J., 1977-88; asst. engr. Adams, Rehmann & Heggan Assoc., Hammonton, 1987-88, project engr., 1990—. With USN, 1988-90. Mem. Nat. Assn. Profl. Engrs., Villanova U. Engring. Alumni Soc., Cape May County Party and Charter Boat Assn. Episcopalian. Office: Adams Rehmann & Heggan Assocs 850 White Horse Pike S Hammonton NJ 08037-2018 Home: 17 Linsay Ln Woodbine NJ 08270-3126

WEIGEL, PAUL HENRY, biochemistry educator, researcher, consultant; b. N.Y.C., Aug. 11, 1946; s. Helmut and Jeanne Weigel; m. Nancy Shulman, June 15, 1968 (div. Dec. 1987); 1 child, Dana J.; m. Janet Oka, May 17, 1992. BA in Chemistry, Cornell U., 1968; MS in Biochemistry, Johns Hopkins U., Balt., 1969, PhD in Biochemistry, 1975. NIH postdoctoral fellow Johns Hopkins U., Balt., 1975-78; asst. prof. U. Tex. Med. Br., Galveston, Tex., 1978-82, assoc. prof., 1982—94, prof. biochemistry and cell biology, 1987-94, vice chmn. dept. human biol. chemistry and genetics, 1990-93, acting chmn. dept. human biology, chemistry and genetics, 1992-93; prof., chmn. dept. biochemistry and molecular biology U. Okla. Health Scis. Ctr., Okalahoma City, 1994—; co-founder Hyalose LLC, 2000—. Mem. NIH Pathobiochemistry Study Sect., Washington, 1985-87; cons. Teltech, Mpls., 1985—, Hyalose LLC 2000—. Contbr. articles to profl. jours.; patentee in field. Treas. Bayou Chateau Neighborhood Assn., Dickinson, Tex., 1981-83, v.p., 1983-84, pres., 1984-86. With U.S. Army, 1969-71. Grantee NIH, 1979—, Office Naval Rsch., 1983-87, Tex. Biotech., 1989-94, Ctr. Advanced Sci. Tech., 2000-, Okla. Ctr. Advancement Sci. and Tech.; recipient Disting. Tchr. award U. Tex. Med. Br., 1989, Disting. Rsch. award, 1989. Mem. Am. Chem. Soc., Am. Soc. Cell Biology, Am. Soc. Biochemistry and Molecular Biology (mem. pub. affairs adv. com.). Democrat. Lutheran. Avocations: raquetball, basketball card collecting, poetry, camping. Home: 817 Hollowdale Edmond OK 73003-3022 Office: U Okla Health Scis Ctr Dept Biochem & Mol Biology Bmsb Rm 860 Oklahoma City OK 73190-0001 E-mail: paul-weigel@ouhsc.edu.

WEIGEL, RICHARD GEORGE, psychologist, educator; b. St. Louis, Feb. 23, 1937; s. George D. and Irene K. (Bretz) W.; children: Paul K., Laura K. BA, DePauw U., 1959; MA, U. Mo., Columbia, 1962, PhD in Psychology, 1968. Diplomate in clin. psychology Am. bd. Profl. Psychology; lic. psychologist Utah. Counselor/asst. prof. psychology Oreg. State U., Corvallis, 1964-67, acting dir. Counseling Ctr., 1967; asst. prof. to prof. and chmn. counseling psychology program Colo. State U., Ft. Collins, 1967-78; sr. cons. psychologist Rohrer, Hibler & Replogle, Inc., Denver, 1978-90, mgr., 1981-86; dir. and adj. prof. psychology Student Counseling Ctr., Ill. State U., Normal, 1990-92; dir. Counseling Ctr. U. Utah, Salt Lake City, 1992—, clin. prof. psychology, ednl. psychology and psychiatry, 1992—, asst. v.p. student devel., 1996-97, interim v.p. for student affairs, 1997-99. Pvt. practice psychology, Ft. Collins, 1970-78; adj. prof. Denver U. Sch. Profl. Psychology, 1977-78, Counseling Psychology Program, Ctr. for Spl. and Advanced Programs of U. No. Colo., Greeley, 1975-78, vis. assoc. prof. counseling psychology program, summer 1975; lectr. continuing edn. for nurses Poudre Valley Meml. Hosp., Ft. Collins, 1975; selection psychologist Peace Corps, 1973-74; asst. prof. psychology divsn. continuing edn. Oreg. State Sys. Higher Edn., Salem, 1965; ind. practice marriage counseling, Corvallis, Oreg., 1965-67; clin. psychologist Mo. Tng. Sch. for Boys, summer 1964; instr. psychology U. Mo., Columbia, 1963-64; counselor Counseling Svc., Stephens Coll., Columbia, 1963-64, Univ. Testing and Counseling Svc., U. Mo., Columbia, 1961-62; instr. psychology, resident advisor George Williams Coll., Lake Geneva, Wis., summer 1961; tchg./rsch. asst. psychology U. Mo., 1960-61; rsch. asst. Purdue U., West Lafayette, Ind., 1960; VA clin. psychology trainee Indpls., 1959-60; vis. scientist/lectr. APA, Drury Coll., 1974; lectr. in field; condr. workshops in field; v.p. Bd. Psychologist Examiners State of Colo., 1973-76. Assoc. editor Cons. Psychology Jour.: Practice and rsch., 1991-93, editl. bd., 1990-97; editl. bd. Jour. Coll. Student Devel., 1970-73, 92—, Profl. Psychology: Rsch. and Practice, 1990-92, Group Dynamics: Theory, Research & Practice, 1999—; reviewer Jour. Counseling Psychology, 1976, 94-96, Counseling Psychologist, 1994-98, Jour. Cons. and Clin. Psychology, 1977; editl. cons. Wadsworth-Brooks/Cole Pub. Co., 1974-78, Univ. Park Press, 1976; contbr. numerous articles to profl. jours.; co-author: Innovative Psychological Therapies, 1975, Innovative Medical-Psychiatric Therapies, 1976. Bd. dirs. Mental Health Assn., Benton County, Oreg., 1966-67; mem. Soc. Indiana Pioneers, 19905; mem. profl. adv. bd. Denver U. Sch. Profl. Psychology, 1976-78. NIMH grantee, 1977-82, Colo. State U. grantee, 1976-77, Oreg. State U. grantee, 1965-66, 66-67; Paul Harris fellow Rotary, 1981-86. Fellow APA (task force on revision of accreditation criteria 1977-78, vis. scientist 1974, divsn. cons. psychology pres.-elect 1995-96, pres. 1996-97, past pres. 1997-98, sec. 1993-95, exec. com. 1990-98, com. fellows 1989-93, chair 1991-93, program com. 1990, counseling psychology divsn. awards com. 1993-95, 98, edn. and tng. com. 1975-78, 91-93, coll. counseling interest group 19915, clin. psychology divsn., group psychology and group psychotherapy divsn. com. on fellows 1991-93, 95—, chair 1992-93, pres. 2000—), Am. Psychol. Soc.; mem. AAUP, Assn. Univ. and Coll. Counseling Ctr. Dirs. (governing bd. 1993-95), Rocky Mountain Psychol. Assn. (pres. 1973-74, treas. 1971-72, Disting. Svc. award 1987), Rsch. Consortium of Counseling and Psychol. Svcs. in Higher Edn. (bd. dirs. 1993-95), Internat. Assn. Counseling Svcs. (site visitor 1991-95), Am. Coll. Pers. Assn., Utah Psychol. Assn., Colo. State Bd. Psychologist Examiners (vice chmn. 1974-76, del. to Am. Assn. State Psychology Bds. 1976), Coun. of Counseling Psychology Tng. Programs (bd. dirs. 1974-79, liaison to Am. Assn. State Psychology Bds. 1979), Newcomen Soc. U.S., Sigma Xi, Psi Chi, Phi Gamma Delta, Phi Mu Alpha, Phi Kappa Phi (hon., Golden Key). Avocation: history. Office: University of Utah 201 S 1460 East Rm 42-b Salt Lake City UT 84112-9061 E-mail: rweigel@saff.utah.edu.

WEIGEL, TRACEY LEE, thoracic surgeon; b. Englewood, N.J., Jan. 30, 1961; d. Robert Edwin and Margaret Marie Weigel. BA, U. Va., 1982; MD, U. Rochester, 1986. Resident in surgery Brown U., Providence, 1986-93; surg. oncology fellow Meml. Sloan-Kettering Cancer Ctr., N.Y.C., 1993-95; cardiothoracic surgery resident U. Wis., Madison, 1995-97; asst. prof. surgery U. Pitts., 1997-99, Meml. Sloan Kettering/Cornell U., N.Y.C., 1999-2001; assoc. prof. surgery & head, thoracic surgery Univ. Wis., 2001—. Contbr. articles to profl. jours. Fellow ACS, Am. Coll. Chest Physicians, Soc. Surg. Oncology, Soc. Am. Gastrointestinal Endoscopic Surgeons, Soc. Surgery Alimentary Tract. Office: UWHC 600 Highland Ave CSC H4/346 Madison WI 53792 E-mail: weigel@surgery.wisc.edu.

WEIGELE, RICHARD SAYRE, police officer; b. Passaic, N.J., Oct. 5, 1949; s. Louis Charles and Marjorie (Sayre) W. BA, Hope Coll., Holland, Mich., 1972; MPA, Kean Coll. N.J., Union, 1989. Police officer Summit (N.J.) Police Dept., 1973-80; mobile intensive care paramedic Overlook Hosp., Summit, 1977—; first response tng. coord. Union County Police acad., Scotch Plains, N.J., 1980—; police sgt., 911 mcpl. coord. Mountainside (N.J.) Police Dept., 1980—, commdr. Emergency Svcs. Unit, 1998—. Paramedic preceptor Overlook Hosp., 1980—, pre-hosp. trauma life support instr., 1993—, pediatric prehosp. emergency care instr., 1995—; CPR instr. Am. Heart Assn., Summit, 1978; police instr. Union County Police Acad., 1980—; EMS text reviewer Brady Publishing, 1996. Officer Summit First Aid Squad, 1975-80; vol. Overlook Hosp., 1974-81; mem. Liberty Corner First Aid Squad, 1993-98; instr. ARC, Somerville, N.J., 1992-98. With N.J. Army NG, 1972-78. Recipient Award of Merit N.J. State Police Benevolent Assn., 1974, Award of recognition, Union County Police Acad., 1990. Mem. Nat. Assn. EMT/Paramedics (charter), N.J. Police Honor Legion, Internat. Police Assn. (reception officer 1989—), Mountainside Police Benevolent Assn. (Police Officer of the Yr. 1986), Pi Alpha Alpha. Ref. Ch. of Am. Avocations: skiing, biking, computers, community service. Home: 268 Crabtree Ct Basking Ridge NJ 07920-3154 Office: Mountainside Police Dept 1385 Route 22 Mountainside NJ 07092-2699

WEIGEND, GUIDO GUSTAV, geographer, educator; b. Zeltweg, Austria, Jan. 2, 1920; came to U.S., 1939, naturalized, 1943; s. Gustav F. and Paula (Sorgo) W.; m. Areta Kelble, June 26, 1947 (dec. 1993); children: Nina, Cynthia, Kenneth. BS, U. Chgo., 1942, MS, 1946, PhD, 1949. With OSS, 1943-45; with mil. intelligence U.S. War Dept., 1946; instr. geography U. Ill., Chgo., 1946-47; instr. then asst. prof. geography Beloit Coll., 1947-49; asst. prof. geography Rutgers U., 1949-51, assoc. prof., 1951-57, prof., 1957-76, acting dept. chmn., 1951-52, chmn. dept., 1953-67, assoc. dean, 1972-76; dean Coll. Liberal Arts, Prof. geography Ariz. State U., Tempe, 1976-84, prof. geography, 1976-89; ret., 1989. Fulbright lectr. U. Barcelona, 1960-61; vis. prof. geography Columbia U., 1963-67, NYU, 1967, U. Colo., summer 1968, U. Hawaii, summer 1969; liaison rep. Rutgers U. to UN, 1950-52; invited by Chinese Acad. Scis. to visit minority areas in Chinese Cent. Asia, 1988; mem. U.S. nat. com. Internat. Geog. Union, 1951-58, 61-65; chmn. Conf. on Polit. and Social Geography, 1968-69 Author articles, monographs, bulls. for profl. jours.; contbr.: (4th edit.) A Geography of Europe, 1977; geog. editor-in-chief: Odyssey World Atlas, 1966. Bd. adjustment Franklin Twp., N.J., 1959; mem. Highland Park (N.J.) Bd. Edn., 1973-75, v.p., 1975; mem. Ariz. Coun. on Humanities and Pub. Policy, 1976-80; vice chmn. Phoenix Com. on Fgn. Rels., 1976-79, chmn., 1979-81; mem. exec. com. Fedn. Pub. Programs in Humanities, 1977-82; bd. dirs. Coun. Colls. Arts and Scis., 1980-83; bd. dirs. Phoenix Chamber Music Soc., 1995—, pres., 2000—); commr. N. Cen. Assn. Colls. and Schs., 1976-80, bd. dirs. commn. on instns. of higher edn., 1980-83. Research fellow Office Naval Research, 1952-55, Rutgers Research Council, 1970-71; grantee Social Sci. Research Council, 1956, Ford Found., 1966, Am. Philos. Soc., 1970-71, German Acad. Exchange Service, 1984; Fulbright travel grantee Netherlands, 1970-71. Mem. Assn. Am. Geographers (chmn. N.Y. Met. divsn. 1955-56, editl. bd. 1955-59, mem. coun. 1965-66, chmn. N.Y.-N.J. divsn. 1965-66), Am. Geog. Soc., Phoenix Chamber Mus. Soc. (bd. dirs. 1995—, pres. 2000—), Sigma Xi (pres. Ariz. State U. chpt. 1989-91). Home: 2094 E Golf Ave Tempe AZ 85282-4046 Office: Ariz State U Dept Geography Tempe AZ 85287

WEIGENSBERG, IRVING JOSEPH, radiation oncologist; b. Newark, Aug. 14, 1931; s. Abraham and Frieda (Mintz) W.; m. Marilyn Bierman, June 14, 1953; children: Marc, Irene Fahrenwald, Paula Feynman, David. AB, Washington U., 1953, MD, 1956. Diplomate Am. Bd. Radiology. Intern Jewish Hosp., St. Louis, 1956-57; resident in radiology Hosp. U. Pa., Phila., 1960-64; instr. div. radiation therapy Wash. U. Sch. Medicine Dept. Radiology, St. Louis, 1964—66; med. dir. dept. radiation oncology Meth. Med. Ctr., Peoria, Ill., 1971—93; clin. asst. prof. radiology U. Ill. Coll. Medicine, 1972—93; ret. Mem. adv. com. dept. radiology U. Ill., Peoria, 1985-93; vis. prof. dept. radiation oncology Albert Einstein Med. Ctr., Phila., 1988, Loyola U. Med. Ctr., Chgo., 1988; vis. prof., spl. cons. divsn. radiation therapy U. Hosp. Eppendorf, U. Hamburg, Germany, 1996, 2000. Contbr. articles to med. jours.; contbr. chpt. to book Tumor Bd. Case Mgmt., 1997. Bd. dirs. Am. Cancer Soc., St. Louis and Peoria, 1968-86, Ill. divsn., 1975-81, pres. Peoria County unit, 1973-76; pres. Friends of the Gateway Festival Orch., 1965-70; mem. Gov.'s Adv. Coun. on Cancer, Ill., 1980-93. Mem. AMA, Am. Coll. Radiology, Am. Radium Soc., Am. Soc. Therapeutic Radiology and Oncology, Am. Brachytherapy Soc.

WEIGER, JOHN GEORGE, foreign language educator; b. Dresden, Germany, Feb. 6, 1933; came to U.S., 1938, naturalized, 1945; s. Willy and Elisabeth (Prinz) W.; m. Leslie Lawrence Carpenter, Dec. 28, 1955; children: Robert Boyden, Mark Owen, Heidi Elaine. BA, Middlebury Coll., 1955; MA, U. Colo., 1957; PhD (NDEA fellow), Ind. U., 1966. Instr. U. Colo., Boulder, 1955-57, Lawrence Coll., Appleton, Wis., 1957-58; instr. Romance langs. U. Vt., Burlington, 1958-62, asst. prof., 1964-67, assoc. prof., 1967-73, prof., 1973-98, prof. emeritus, 1998—, vice chmn. Romance lang. dept., 1964-68, chmn., 1994-98, asst. dean Coll. Arts and Scis., 1968-69, assoc. dean, 1969-71, dean, 1971-76; instnl. rep. for Rhodes scholarships, Danforth fellowships, Turrell Fund scholarships, 1971-76; program chmn. George Aiken lecture series, 1975; vis. lectr. U. Bologna, 1978, 87, U. Venice, Italy, 1987, U. Valencia, Spain, 1987; Cervantes lectr. Fordham U., 1990. Cons. Eirik Borve, Inc., 1979-80. Author: Introduction to the Youthful Deeds of the Cid, 1969, The Valencian Dramatists of Spain's Golden Age, 1976, Cristobal de Virues, 1978, Hacia la Comedia, 1978, The Individuated Self: Cervantes and the Emergence of the Individual, 1979, The Substance of Cervantes, 1985, In the Margins of Cervantes, 1988; editor: Las Hazañas del Cid, 1981, La Infelice Marcela, 1985; mem. editl. bd.: Bull. of Comediantes, 1978-2000; editl. bd.: Hispania, 1993-01; contbr. articles to profl. jours., also chpts. to books. U. Vt. Faculty Research fellow, 1967, 83, 86; Am. Council Learned Socs. grantee, 1978; U. Vt. Univ. scholar for the humanities, 1985-86. Mem. MLA (chmn. comedia sect. 1970-71), Renaissance Soc. Am., Am. Assn. Tchrs. Spanish and Portuguese (chmn. com. hon. mems. and fellows 1984), The Comediantes, Internat. Assn. Hispanists, Cervantes Soc. Am., Phi Beta Kappa, Phi Sigma Iota, Phi Eta Sigma (hon.). Home: 63 Woodbine Rd Shelburne VT 05482-6702 E-mail: jweiger@adelphia.net.

WEIGERT, ANDREW JOSEPH, sociology educator; b. N.Y.C., Apr. 8, 1934; s. Andrew Joseph and Marie Teresa (Kollmer) W.; m. Kathleen Rose Maas, Aug. 31, 1967; children: Karen Rose, Sheila Marie. BA, St. Louis U., 1958, PhL, 1959, MA, 1960; BTh, Woodstock (Md.) Coll., 1964; PhD, U. Minn., 1968. NIMH trainee U. Minn., Mpls., 1965-67; asst. prof. sociology U. Notre Dame, Ind., 1968-72, assoc. prof., 1972-76, prof., 1976—, chmn. dept., 1980-84, 88-89. Vis. assoc. prof. Yale U., New Haven, 1973-74; participant nat. and regional profl. meetings. Co-author: Family Socialization, 1974, Interpretive Sociology, 1978, Society and Identity, 1986; author: Everyday Life, 1981, Social Psychology, 1983, Life and Society, 1983, Mixed Emotions, 1991, Self, Interaction, and Natural Environment, 1997; adv. editor various sociology jours.; contbr. numerous articles to profl. jours., chpts. to books. Recipient tchg. awards, 1999, 2002; NSF grantee, 1969. Avocation: woodlot and prairie management. Office: U Notre Dame Dept Sociology Notre Dame IN 46556

WEIGHT, ALEC CHARLES, retired management consultant; b. Plymouth, Eng., July 20, 1939; s. Charles William and Jean Stirling (Thomson) W.; m. Barbara Anne Carpenter, Mar. 10, 1962 (div. Oct. 1979); children: Glenn, Paul, Andrew; m. Mary-Linn Wright, July 19, 1980; children: Christopher, Matthew, Ryan. B of Chem. Engring., McMaster U., Hamilton, Can., 1961; MS, Waterloo (Can.) U., 1973. Registered profl. engr., Ont. Plant engr. Procter and Gamble, Hamilton, 1961-69, plant mgr., 1969-73; assoc. McKinsey and Co., Toronto, Can., 1973-78; ptnr. Booz Allen and Hamilton, N.Y.C., 1978-90, mng. ptnr. Wassenaar, The Netherlands, 1990-93, ptnr. Sydney, Australia, 1993-98; ret., 1998. Republican. Avocations: skiing, sailing, watercolors. Home: 2710 Broke Spoke Way Park City UT 84060

WEIGHT, DOUG, professional hockey player; b. Warren, Mich., Jan. 21, 1971; Student, Lake Superior State Coll., Mich. Center N.Y. Rangers, 1990-93; traded Edmonton Oilers, 1993, center, 1993—2001, St. Louis Blues, 2001—. Named to CCHA All-Rookie team, 1989-90, NCAA All-Am. West 2d team, 1990-91, CHA All-Star 1st team, 1990-91; selected for NHL All-Star Game, 1996. Address: St. Louis Blues Savvis Center Saint Louis MO 63101-2709*

WEIGHTMAN, ESTHER LYNN, emergency trauma nurse; b. Tawas City, Mich., June 13, 1966; d. Garrie Lee and Naomi Ruth (Atwood) Schneller; m. Robert Thomas Weightman, Dec. 31, 1996; children: Erin Elizabeth, Kaili Marie. BS in Christian Secondary Edn., Ozark Bible Inst. & Coll., Neosho, Mo., 1988; BSN, Ind. Wesleyan U., Marion, 1991; MS in Cmty. Health Nursing, U. Colo. Health Scis. Ctr., Denver, 1995. RN, Colo.; cert. ACLS, pediatric advanced life support, trauma nurse core course; Profl. Spl. Svcs. licensee Colo. Dept. Edn. Staff nurse emergency dept. Marion Gen. Hosp., 1991-92, Penrose-St. Francis Healthcare Sys., Colorado Springs, Colo., 1992-95; staff nurse registry QS Nurses Corp., 1992-2001; staff devel. nurse 302d ASTS-USAFR, Peterson AFB, Colo., 1994-2001; staff nurse emergency dept. Med. Ctr. of Aurora, 1997-2001; staff nurse St. Peter's Hosp., Helena, Mont., 2001—02, VA Mont. Healthcare Sys., Ft. Harrison, 2002—. Mentor various healthcare instnl. facilities, 1991—; vol. tchr. health classes Knowledge is Power, Red Cross Shelter, Colorado Springs, 1995-96. Mem.: Emergency Nurses Assn., Res. Officers Assn., Sigma Theta Tau. Avocations: French, cooking, orchestra (trumpet).

WEIGLE, ROBERT EDWARD, civil engineer, research director; b. Shiloh, Pa., Apr. 27, 1927; s. William Edgar and Hilda Geraldine (Fans) W.; m. Mona Jean Long, Aug. 13, 1949; 1 child, Geoffrey Robert. BCE in Structures, Rensselear Poly. Inst., 1951, MS in Mechanics, 1957, PhD in Mechanics, 1959. Registered profl. engr., N.Y., Pa. Assoc. rsch. scientist Rensselear Poly. Inst., Troy, N.Y., 1955-59; chief scientist Watervliet Arsenal, 1959—62; tech. dir., then dir. Benet Weapons Lab., 1962—77; tech. dir. U.S. Army and Armament R & D Command, 1977-82; dir. U.S. Army Rsch. Office, 1982-88; dir. phys. sci. lab. N.Mex. State U., Las Cruces, 1988-96; dir. emeritus phys. sci. lab. N. Mex. State U., 1996—. Chmn. numerous DoD and Army coms.; dir. emeritus Phys. Sci. Lab. N.Mex. State U., 1996. Contbr. articles to profl. jours. Recipient Meritorious Civilian Service award for cannon breech design U.S. Army, 1964, U.S. Army Materiel Command citation for engineering achievement in Vietnam, 1966, Presidential citation for development of cannon firing simulator, 1965, Exceptional Civilian Svc. medal U.S. Army, 1988, Rank of Meritorious Exec. Pres. Reagan, 1982; elected to Am. Acad. of Mechanics, 1972. Mem. NSPE, ASME, AAAS, ASTM, Soc. Exptl. Mechanics, Am. Def. Preparedness Assn. (Crozier prize 1985), Nat. Conf. Advancement Rsch. (program com. 1987, exec. conf. com., host rep. NCAR-46 ann. conf. 1992), Army Sci. Bd. (chmn. rsch. and new initiatives group 1992), Tau Beta Pi, Chi Epsilon, Sigma Xi.

WEIGLEY, RUSSELL FRANK, history educator; b. Reading, Pa., July 2, 1930; s. Frank Francis and Meta Beulah (Rohrbach) W.; m. Emma Eleanor Seifrit, July 27, 1963; children: Jared Francis Guldin, Catherine Emma Rohrbach. BA, Albright Coll., 1952; MA, U. Pa., 1953, PhD, 1956; HLD (hon.), Albright Coll., 1978. Instr. history U. Pa., Phila., 1956-58; asst. prof. Drexel Inst. Tech., 1958-60, assoc. prof., 1960-62, Temple U., Phila., 1962-64, prof. history, 1964-85, Disting. Univ. prof., 1985-98, prof. emeritus, 1998—. Vis. prof. Dartmouth Coll., Hanover, N.H., 1967-68; U.S. Army vis. prof. mil. history rsch. U.S. Army War Coll., U.S. Army Mil. History Rsch. Collection, Carlisle Barrakcs, Pa., 1973-74; pres. Am. Mil. Inst., Washington, 1975-76. Author: Quartermaster General of the Union Army: A Biography of M.C. Meigs, 1959, Towards an American Army: Military Thought from Washington to Marshall, 1962, History of the United States Army, 1967, 84, The Partisan War: The South Carolina Campaign of 1780-82, 1970, The American Way of War, 1973, Eisenhower's Lieutenants, 1981 (Atheneum of Phila. Spl. award for Nonfiction by a Phila. Author, 1983), The Age of Battles: The Quest for Decisive Warfare from Breitenfeld to Waterloo, 1991, A Great Civil War: A Military and Political History, 1862-1865, 2000 (Lincoln prize 2001); editor: The American Military: Readings in the History of the Military in American Society, 1969, New Dimensions in Military History, 1976, Philadelphia: A 300-Year History, 1982. Mem. hist. adv. commn. Dept. of Army, Washington, 1976-79, 88—, Pa. Hist. Records Adv. Com., Harrisburg, 1977-79; bd. dirs. Masonic Libr., Mus. of Pa., The Grand Lodge of Masons of Pa., Phila., 1990-95, 97—; Supreme Coun., Scottish Rite, No. Masonic Jurisdiction, 1999. Penrose Fund grantee Am. Philos. Soc., 1958; fellow John Simon Guggenheim Meml. Found., 1969-70; recipient Samuel Eliot Morison prize Am. Mil. Inst., 1989, Lincoln prize, 2001. Mem. Hist. Soc. Pa. (vice chmn. 1989-93, councilor 1983-89, 92-98, emeritus 1998—), Pa. Hist. Assn. (pres. 1975-78, v.p. 1967-75, coun. 1967—, editor jour. 1962-67), Am. Hist. Assn., Orgn. Am. Historians, Soc. Mil. Hist. (Disting. Book award 1992), So. Hist. Assn., Soc. Am. Historians Inc., Interuniv. Seminar on Armed Forces and Soc., Am. Philos. Soc., Masons (33d degree, Scottish rite supreme coun. northern Masonic jurisdiction 1999). Democrat. Unitarian Universalist. Home: 327 S Smedley St Philadelphia PA 19103-6717 Office: Temple U Dept History Philadelphia PA 19122 E-mail: rweigley@unix.temple.edu.

WEIGNER, BRENT JAMES, secondary education educator; b. Pratt, Kans., Aug. 19, 1949; s. Doyle Dean and Elizabeth (Hanger) W.; m. Sue Ellen Weber Hume, Mar. 30, 1985; children: Russell John Hume, Scott William Hume. BA, U. No. Colo., 1972; MEd, U. Wyo., 1977, PhD, 1984. Cert. Nat. Bd. for Profl. Tchg. Stds. Cert. Counselor, coach Olympia Sport Village, Upson, Wyo., summer 1968; dir. youth sports F.E. Warren AFB, Cheyenne, summers 1973, 74; instr. geography Laramie County Community Coll., 1974-75; tchr. social sci. McCormick Jr. High Sch., 1975—, Laramie County Sch. Dist. 1, Cheyenne, 1975—; head social studies dept. McCormick Jr. High Sch., 1987-99, 2001—02; curriculum adv. coun. chmn. Laramie County Sch. Dist. No. 1, 1988-89. Lectr. ednl. methods U. Wyo., 1989, mem. clin. faculty, 1992-94; nat. chmn. Jr. Olympic cross-country com. AAU, Indpls., 1980-81; pres. Wyo. Athletic Congress, 1981-87; tchr. cons. Nat. Geog. Soc. Geography Inst., summer 1991, North Pole Marathon cons. Global Expdns., 2002-; bd. dirs. Shadow Mountain Lodge, Aspen, Colo., 1992-93, United Med. Ctr. of Wyo. Found., 1995—. Fgn. exch. student U. Munich, 1971-72; head coach Cheyenne Track Club, 1976—, pres., 1980; race dir. Wyo. Marathon, 1978—; deacon 1st Christian Ch., Cheyenne, 1987-90, elder, 1991-93; rep. candidate gen. election Wyo. Legis., 1991; bd. dirs. Cheyenne Boys and Girls Club, 1999—. Named Wyoming State bd. edn. Disting. Educator, Wyo. U.S. West Outstanding Tchr., 1989, Wyo. Coun. for the Social Studies K-8 Tchr. of Yr., 1994-95, Jr. High Coach of Yr., Wyo. Coaches Assn., 1996, Vol. of Yr., office Youth Alternatives, 2000; fellow Taft Found., 1976, Earthwatch-Hearst fellow, Punta Allen, Mex., summer 1987, Christa McAuliffe fellow, 1991-92, Wyo. Christa Mcauliffe Fellowship Selection Com., 1994, 95, 01; Fulbright grantee, Israel, summer 1984; Fulbright scholar Ghana and Senegal, 1990; People-to-People Internat. Ambassador to Vietnam, 1993; recipient Masons of Wyo. Disting. Tchr. award 1994. Mem. NEA, Nat. Network for Ednl. Renewal, Nat. Coun. Social Studies, Nat. Coun. Geog. Edn., Dominican Rep. Nat. Coun. for Geog. Edn. (Cram scholarship 1992), Wyo. Geog. Alliance (steering com., Amazon Workshop Fellowship 1998), Cheyenne Tchrs. Edn. Assn. (govtl. rels. com., instrn. and profl. devel. com.), U. No. Colo. Alumni Assn., Cheyenne C. of C., Wyo. Heritage Soc., Wyo. Edn. Assn. (World Book Ency. classroom rsch. project cons. 1976—, accountability task force 1989-90), Fulbright Alumni Assn. (life), U. Wyo. Alumni Assn. (life), Cheyenne Sunrise, Lions (bd. dirs. Cheyenne 1987, pres. 1995-96, 1st v.p. 1993-94, Melvin Jones Fellowship, 1995), Phi Delta Kappa (life, bd. dirs. Cheyenne 1989—, v.p., edn. award for rsch. 1990, pres. 1992-93, editl. found. rep. 1993-94, area 4-D coord. 1994-95, Gerald Read Internat. Seminar scholar 1994; mem. outstanding doctoral dissertation com. 1994, 96), Phi Delta Kappa (Ed. award for Svc. 2000). Achievements include world record holder as first person in the world to run ultramarathon races on all seven continents; Adventure Network Internat. South Pole Ultramarathon champion, 1999-2002. Home: 402 W 31st St Cheyenne WY 82001-2527 Office: McCormick Jr HS 6000 Education Dr Cheyenne WY 82009-3991 E-mail: RunWyo@msn.com.

WEIGOLD, MICHAEL F. advertising executive, educator, advertising executive, consultant; b. New York, Oct. 7, 1958; s. Frederick W. and Lorraine Weigold; children: Sean. PhD, U. Fla., Gainesville, 1989. Assoc. prof. dept. advt. U. Fla., Gainesville, 1994—. Home: 4830 NW 43rd St Gainesville FL 32606 Office: Univ Fla Weimer Hall PO Box 118400 Gainesville FL 32611-8400 Personal E-mail: mweigold@jou.ufl.edu.

WEIHAUPT, JOHN GEORGE, geosciences educator, scientist, university administrator; b. La Crosse, Wis., Mar. 5, 1930; s. John George and Gladys Mae (Ash) W.; m. Audrey Mae Reis, Jan. 28, 1961. Student, St. Norbert Coll., De Pere, Wis., 1948-49; BS, U. Wis., 1952, MS, 1953, U. Wis.-Milw., 1971; PhD, U. Wis., 1973. Exploration geologist Am. Smelting & Refining Co., Nfld., 1953, Anaconda Co., Chile, S.Am., 1956-57; seismologist United Geophys. Corp., 1958; geophysicist Arctic Inst. N.Am., Antarctica, 1958-60, Geophys. and Polar Research Center, U. Wis., Antarctica, 1960-63; dir. participating Coll. and Univ. program, chmn. dept. phys. and biol. sci. U.S. Armed Forces Inst., Dept. Def., 1963-73; assoc. dean for acad. affairs Sch. Sci., Ind. U.-Purdue U., Indpls., 1973-78, prof. geology, 1973-78; asst. dean (Grad. Sch., prof. geoscis. Purdue U.), 1975-78; prof. geology, assoc. acad. v.p., dean grad. studies and research, v.p. Univ. Research Found., San Jose (Calif.) State U., 1978-82; vice chancellor for acad. affairs U. Colo., Denver, 1982-86, prof. geoscis., 1987—. Sci. cons., mem. sci. adv. bd. Holt Reinhart and Winston, Inc., 1967— ; sci. editor, cons. McGraw-Hill Co., 1966— ; hon. lectr. U. Wis., 1963-73; geol. cons., 1968— ; editorial cons. John Wiley & Sons, 1968; editorial adv. bd. Dushkin Pub. Group, 1971— Author: Exploration of the Oceans: An Introduction to Oceanography; mem. editorial bd. Internat. Jour. Interdisciplinary Cycle Research, Leiden; co-discoverer USARP Mountain Range (Arctic Inst. Mountain Range), in Victoria Land, Antarctica, 1960; discoverer Wilkes Land Meteorite Crater, Antarctic. Mem. Capital Community Citizens Assn.; mem. Madison Transp. Study Com., Found. for Internat. Energy Research and Tng.; U.S. com. for UN Univ.; mem. sci. council Internat. Center for Interdisciplinary Cycle Research; mem. Internat. Awareness and Leadership Council; mem. governing bd. Moss Landing Marine Labs.; bd. dirs. San Jose State U. Found. Served as 1st lt. AUS, 1953-55, Korea. Mt. Weihaupt in Antarctica named for him, 1966; recipient Madisonian medal for outstanding community service, 1973; Outstanding Cote Meml. award, 1974; Antarctic medal, 1968 Fellow Geol. Soc. Am., Explorers Club; mem. Antarctican Soc., Nat. Sci. Tchrs. Assn., Am. Geophys. Union, Internat. Council Corr. Edu., Soc. Am. Mil. Engrs., Wis. Alumni Assn., Soc. Study Biol. Rhythms, Internat. Soc. for Chronobiology, Marine Tech. Soc., AAAS, Univ. Indsl. Adv. Council, Am. Council on Edn., Expdn. Polaire France (hon.), Found. for Study Cycles, Assn. Am. Geographers, Nat. Council Univ. Research Adminstrs., Soc. Research Adminstrs., Man-Environ. Communication Center, Internat. Union Geol. Scis., Internat. Geog. Union, Internat. Soc. Study Time, Community Council Pub. TV, Internat. Platform Assn., Ind., Midwest assns. grad. schs., Western Assn. Grad. Schs., Council Grad. Schs. in U.S., Wis. Alumni Assn. of San Francisco, Kiwanis, Carmel Racquet Club (Rinconada), The Ridge at Hiwan (Evergreen, Colo., pres. 1991-93). Achievements include discovery of the Wilkes Land Anomaly and of the USARP Mt. Range in Victoria Land, both in Antarctica; also credited with revision of the discovery date of Antarctic continent by 3 centuries. Home: 23906 Currant Dr Golden CO 80401-9243 Office: U Colo Campus Box 172 PO Box 173364 Denver CO 80217-3364

WEIHING, JOHN LAWSON, plant pathologist, state senator; b. Rocky Ford, Colo., Feb. 26, 1921; s. Henry John and Clara Adele (Krull) W.; m. Shirley Ruth Wilkerson, Aug. 18, 1948; children: Lawson James, Martin Roy, Adell Ann, Warren John. BS in Agronomy, Colo. State U., 1942; MSc in Agronomy, U. Nebr., 1949, PhD in Botany and Plant Pathology, 1954. Instr. plant pathology U. Nebr., Lincoln, 1950-54, asst. prof., 1954-56, assoc. prof., 1956-60, prof., 1960-61, 62-64, 66-71, prof., interim chmn. plant pathology dept., 1961-62, prof., dir. Panhandle Rsch. and Extension Ctr. Scottsbluff, 1971-84, with Alumni Office, Panhandle Found. Scottsbluf, 1984-86; prof., chmn. plant sci. dept. Ataturk U., Erzurum, Turkey, 1964-66; mem. dist. 48 Nebr. Legislature, Lincoln, 1987-91. Cons. Am. Hydrponics Systems, Inc., Grapevine, Tex., 1969-72. Creator U. Nebr. TV series Backyard Farmer, The Equation of Nature, 1959-60. Campaign chmn. United Way, Scottsbluff and Gering, Nebr., 1978. Lt. U.S. Army, 1942-46. Recipient Honor award Soil Conservation Soc. Am., 1982, Merit award Gamma Sigma Delta, 1977, Disting. Svc. award Nebr. Turfgrass Found., 1982, Nebr. Coop. Extension, 1970; named to Nebr. Hall Agrl. Achievement, 1987. Mem. Am. Phytopathol. Soc. (chmn. nat. extension com. 1963, pres. north cen. dir. 1971-72), AAAS, Am. Inst. Biol. Scis., Nebr. State Hist. Soc. (trustee 1992—), Scottsbluff/Gering United C. of C. (pres. 1980-81), Rotary (bd. dirs. 1977-80), Elks. Republican. Presbyterian. Avocation: archeology. Home: 1605 Holly Dr Gering NE 69341-1954

WEIHRICH, HEINZ, management educator; b. Germany; came to U.S., 1959; s. Paul and Anna Weihrich; m. Ursula Weihrich, Aug. 3, 1963. BS, UCLA, 1966, MBA, 1967, PhD, 1973; Dr. (hon.), San Martin de Porres U., Peru, 2000. Assoc. Grad. Sch. Mgmt. UCLA, 1968-73; from asst. to assoc. prof. Ariz. State U., Tempe, 1973-80; prof. global mgmt. and behavioral sci. U. San Francisco, 1980—. Mem. faculty China Europe Internat. Bus. Sch., Shanghai, Grad. Sch. Bus. Adminstrsn., Switzerland; global mgmt. cons. in field. Author: (with Harold Koontz and Cyril O'Donnell) Management, 7th edit., 1980, Japanese, Chinese and Indonesian edits., 8th edit., 1984, Singapore edit., 1985, Indonesian edit., 1986, Philippines edit., Bengali edit., 1989, Taiwan edit., 1985 (with Harold Koontz) 9th edit., 1988, Singapore edit., 1988, Chinese edit., 1989, Spanish edit., 1990, best-seller Spanish speaking world, Korean edit., 1988, 90, Pengurusan (Malaysian) edit., 1991, Czech edit., 1993. Hungarian edit., 1992, Management: A Global Perspective, 10th edit. (with Harold Koontz), 1993, Spanish edit., 1993, best-seller Spanish speaking world, Chinese, 1998, Singapore edit., 1993, Korean edit., 1996, Croatian edit., 1995, 11th edit., 1998, Administracão Fundamentos da Teoriae da Cienca, Primeiro Volume 1986, Administracão Organizacão Planejamento e Controle, Segundo Volume, 1987, Administracão Recursos Humanos: Desenvolvimento de Administradores, Terceiro Volume, 1987, (with Harold Koontz and Cyril O'Donnell) Management: A Book of Readings, 5th edit., 1980, (with George Odiorne and Jack Mendleson) Executive Skills: A Management by Objectives Approach, 1980, (with Harold Koontz) Measuring Managers--A Double-Barreled Approach, 1981, (with Harold Koontz and Cyril O'Donnell) Essentials of Management, 3d edit. 1982, Taiwan, Philippines, Chinese and India edits., 4th edit., 1986, Singapore edit., 1986, 5th edit., 1990, (with Harold Koontz) Manajamen, Jilid 1, Indonesian edit., 1987, Manajamen, Jilid 2, 1986, Elementos de Administración, 3d edit., 1983, 4th edit. 1988, 6th edit., Management Excellence--Productivity through MBO, 1985, Singapore edit. 1986, Japanese edit., 1990, Greek edit., Produttivita con L' Italian edit. 1987, Administracion, 1985, Management Basiswissen, German edit., 1986, Excelencia Administrativa (Mex.), Spanish edit., 1987, Chinese edit., 1997, (with Harold Koontz and Cyril O'Donnell) Adminstracion Moderna, Tomo 1, 1986, (with Harold Koontz) Management: A Global Perspective, internat. edit., 1993, Administración: Una Perspectiva Global, 1994, Korean edit., 1993, 96, Croatian edit., 1996, Czech edit., 1993, 96, Elementos de Administracion - Enfoque Internactional, Exta Edicion, 2002; editor: (with Jack Mendleson) Management: An MBO Approach, 1978; contbr. numerous articles and papers to profl. jours. Grantee Am. Mgmt. Assn., 1970. Fellow Internat. Acad. Mgmt., mem. Acad. Mgmt., Assn. Mgmt. Excellence (trustee 1985-87), Assn. Bus. Simulation Exptl. Learning, Acad. Internat. Bus., Beta Gamma Sigma, Sigma Iota Epsilon. Roman Catholic. Office: U San Francisco 2130 Fulton St San Francisco CA 94117-1080

WEIKART, DAVID POWELL, educational research foundation administrator; b. Youngstown, Ohio, Aug. 26, 1931; s. Hubert James and Catherine (Powell) W.; m. Phyllis Saxton, Aug. 24, 1957; children: Cynthia, Catherine, Jennifer, Gretchen. AB, Oberlin Coll., 1953, DSc (hon.), 1992; PhD, U. Mich., 1966. Cert. sch. psychologist, Mich. Dir. spl. svcs. Ypsilanti (Mich.) Pub. Schs., 1957-70; pres. High Scope Ednl. Rsch. Found., Ypsilanti, 1970-2000, pres. emeritus, 2001—. Dir. High Scope Inst., 1991, Netherlands, 1995, Ireland, 1999, U.K. Author: Young Children in Action, 1979, Changed Lives, 1984, Challenging the Potential, 1992, Significant Benefits, 1993, Educating Young Children, 1995, 2d edit., 2002, Lasting Difference, 1997; editor: How Nations Serve Young Children, 1991, Families Speak, 1994, What Should Young Children Learn, 1999. Mem., Nat. Commn. on Children, 1990-93. 1st lt. USMC, 1953-55. Recipient Lela Rowland award Nat. Mental Health Assn., Washington, 1987. Mem. Nat. Assn. for Edn. of Young Children (Lifetime Achievement award 1999). Avocation: camping. E-mail: davew@highscope.org.

WEIKERT, JERARD LEE, real estate broker; b. Zanesfield, Ohio, Dec. 25, 1929; s. Paul Hoover and Thelma May (McKeever) W.; m. Beth Ann Houston, Aug. 24, 1983. Grad., Officer Candidate Sch., 1952; BA, Wittenberg U., 1961; MS, George Washington U., 1966. Enlisted U.S. Army, 1951, advanced through grades to col., 1967, ret., 1972; self-employed profl. horse trainer and judge Fairfax County, Va., 1972—; v.p. sales and plans Keyes Gateway, Inc., Dayton, Ohio, 1983—; pres. Darrowby Inc. Real Estate Brokerage Consultancy, 1994—. Judge Am. Horse Show Assn., 1972—. Contbr. articles to U.S. Army and horse jours. Chmn. Human Rels. Bd., Springfield, Ohio, 1991-92; mem. Planning Commn., Clark County, Ohio, 1991-93; v.p., exec. bd. Community Leadership Acad., Springfield, 1991-93; fin. dir. Tackett for State Senate, Ohio, 1992. Decorated Legion of Merit (2), Combat Infantry Badge Mem. U.S. Dressage Fedn. (exec. bd.), Dayton Dressage Assn. (chmn. bd. dirs. 1995—), Dayton Area Bd. Realtors (chmn. equal opportunity com. 1988-90, profl. stds. com. 1991-93, grievance com. 1993-94, chmn. grievance com. 1995-97, chmn. profl. standards com. 1999), Dayton Racquet Club, Troy Country Club. Democrat. Avocations: antique bronzes and icons, geneaology.

WEIKSNER, SANDRA S. lawyer; b. D.C., Nov. 9, 1945; d. Donald B. and Dick (Cutter) Smiley; m. George B. Weiksner, Aug. 19, 1969; children: Michael, Nicholas. BA in Psychology, Stanford U., 1966, JD, 1969. Teaching fellow Stanford U., Calif., 1969-70; assoc. Cleary, Gottlieb, Steen & Hamilton, N.Y.C., 1970-77, ptnr., 1978—. Vis. lectr. Yale Law Sch., 1991-92. Bd. dirs. N.Y. Law Sch.; mem. Union Theol. Sem. Fellow Am. Bar Found., Am. Coll. Trusts and Estates Counsel, Internat. Acad. Estate and Trust Law; mem. ABA, N.Y. State Bar Assn., Assn. Bar of City of N.Y., Conn. Bar Assn. Democrat. Unitarian Universalist. Home: 164 E 81st St New York NY 10028-1804 Office: Cleary Gottlieb Steen & Hamilton 1 Liberty Plz Fl 43 New York NY 10006-1404

WEIL, ANDREW THOMAS, physician, educator; b. Phila., June 8, 1942; s. Daniel Pythias and Jenny (Silverstein) Weil. BA, Harvard U., 1964, MD, 1968. Intern Mt. Zion Hosp. Med. Ctr., San Francisco, 1968-69; assoc. Harvard Bot. Mus., Cambridge, Mass., 1971-84; fellow Inst. Current World Affairs, N.Y.C., 1971-75; lectr. U. Ariz., Tucson, 1983—, dir. program in integrative medicine, clin. prof. medicine, 1996—. Author: Natural Mind, 1972, Marriage of the Sun and Moon, 1980, Chocolate to Morphine, 1983, Health and Healing, 1984, Natural Health, Natural Medicine, 1990, Spontaneous Healing, 1995, 8 Weeks to Optimum Health, 1997, Eating Well for Optimum Health, 2000, The Healthy Kitchen, 2002, (newsletter) Self-Healing, (website) drweil.com. Served to lt. USPHS, 1969-70. Fellow Linnean Soc. London; mem. Am. Acad. Achievement, Sigma Xi. Democrat. Buddhist. Avocations: gardening, backpacking. Home: 6700 S X9 Ranch Rd Vail AZ 85641-6202 Office: Ariz Health Scis Ctr PO Box 245153 Tucson AZ 85724-5153 E-mail: mnhardin@ix.netcom.com.

WEIL, CASS SARGENT, lawyer; b. N.Y.C., Nov. 6, 1946; s. Theodore and Ruth Frances (Sargent) W. BA, SUNY, Stonybrook, 1968; JD cum laude, William Mitchell Coll. of Law, 1980. Bar: Minn. 1980, U.S. Dist. Ct. Minn. 1980, U.S. Ct. Appeals (8th cir.) 1980, Wis. 1984, U.S. Ct. Appeals (7th cir.) 1984; cert. bankruptcy law specialist, consumer and bus. Am. Bd. Certification. Assoc. J.R. Kotts & Assoc., Mpls., 1980-81, Wagner, Rutchick & Trojack, St. Paul, 1981-83; ptnr. Zohlmann & Weil, Wilmar, Minn., 1983, Peterson, Franke & Riach, P.A., St. Paul, 1983-91, O'Connor & Hannan, Mpls., 1991-94, Moss & Barnett, P.A., Mpls., 1994—. Editor: Minn. Legal Forms, Bankruptcy, 1983, 87, 91, 92, 93. Recipient Leading Am. Atty. award Am. Rsch. Corp., 1994, 96, 98, 2000, Minn. Top Lawyers Mpls. St. Paul Mag., 1998. Mem. Minn. Bar Assn. (vice chmn. bankruptcy sect. 1984-88, chairperson 1988-89), Wis. Bar Assn., Am. Bankruptcy Inst., Turnaround Mgmt. Assn., Comml. Law League Am., Order of Barristers. Democrat. Jewish. Office: Moss & Barnett PA 4800 Wells Fargo Ctr Minneapolis MN 55402 also: 90 S 7th St Ste 4800 Minneapolis MN 55402 Business E-Mail: weilc@moss-barnett.com.

WEIL, DENIE SANDISON, foundation administrator; b. St. Louis, Mar. 16, 1931; d. James Calvin and Eliza (Tillman) Sandison; m. Frank A. Weil, Feb. ll, 1951; children: Deborah, Amanda, Sandison, William. AB, Radcliffe Coll., 1954. Dep. dir. rsch. Vera Inst., N.Y.C., 1974-77; program officer German Marshall Fund U.S., Washington, 1977-82; writer, cons., 1983-85; pres. Citizens' Participation Project, Washington, 1986-88. Bd. dirs. Fiduciary Trust Co. Internat., N.Y.C. Contbr. articles on career mgmt. to Working Women. Trustee, v.p. Irvington (N.Y.) Inst. Med. Rsch., 1958-77, Abbott House, Irvington, 1965-75, Jewish Assn. for Svcs. for Aged, N.Y.C., 1969-77; trustee Arena Stage, Washington, 1984—, pres., 1991—; trustee Radcliffe Coll., Cambridge, Mass., 1972-83; bd. overseers Harvard U., Cambridge, 1981-87. Mem. Harvard Club (N.Y.C., bd. mgrs. 1987—), Cosmopolitan Club (N.Y.C.). Democrat. Home: 1516 28th St NW Washington DC 20007-3058

WEIL, D(ONALD) WALLACE, business administration educator; b. Cleve., July 20, 1923; s. Laurence J. and Carol S. (Wallace) W.; m. Jane A. Bittel, Dec. 29, 1947; children— John Wallace, Charles Andrew, Margaret Jane, Carol Wyn. BA, Oberlin Coll., 1947; JD, Willamette U., 1950. Pres. James Foundry Corp., Fort Atkinson, Wis., 1960-70; faculty bus. adminstrn. U. Wis., Eau Claire, 1971-74, chmn. dept. bus. adminstrn., 1974-77, prof., 1985—; pres. Diversified Industries, Inc., St. Louis, 1977-81, UHI Corp., Los Angeles, 1981-85. Dir. U.H.I. Corp. Diversified Industries, Inc., St. Louis, Sales Investments, Mgmt. Inc., Elmwood, Wis., Jane B. Inc., Eau Claire Served with AUS, 1942-45. Mem. Am. Security Council, Nat. Council Small Bus. Mgmt. Devel., Phi Kappa Phi, Beta Gamma Sigma. Republican. Congregationalist. Home: 1530 Canfield St Eau Claire WI 54701-4018 Office: U Wis-Eau Claire Dept Bus Adminstrn Eau Claire WI 54701

WEIL, FRANK A. investment banker, lawyer; b. Bedford, N.Y., Feb. 14, 1931; s. Sylvan and Ruth Alice (Norman) W.; m. Denie Sandison, Feb. 10, 1951; children: Deborah Weil Harrington, Amanda, Sandison, William. AB cum laude, Harvard U., 1953, LL.B., 1956. Bar: N.Y. 1956. Practiced in, N.Y.C., 1957-60; gen. partner Loeb, Rhoades & Co., 1960-71; pres. Abacus Fund, Inc., 1968-72; chief fin. officer, dir. Paine, Webber, Jackson & Curtis, N.Y.C., 1972-77; asst. sec. industry and trade Dept. Commerce, Washington, 1977-79; partner firm, bd. chmn., Ginsburg, Feldman, Weil & Bress, 1979-83, Wald, Harkrader & Ross, Washington, 1983-85; chmn., chief exec. officer, dir., Abacus and Assocs., Inc., 1985—; chmn. bd. SyVox Corp., Exxel/Atmos, Inc. Dir. Geico, Dorr-Oliver, Inc., Stamford, Conn., 1968-77, Hamburg Savs. Bank, N.Y.C., 1975-77, J.B. Lippincott Co., Phila., 1975-77, Govt. Research Corp., 1975-77, 79-85; dir., pres. Norman Found., 1953-77, 79, 92, chmn. bd. trustee, Ednl. Alliance. Trustee Tchrs. Coll., Columbia U., 1976-79, Montefiore Hosp., 1960-77; trustee, vice chmn. No. Westchester Hosp., 1971-77; past vice chmn. bd. govs. Atlantic Inst. Internat. Affairs; past pres. Ednl. Alliance, trustee, 1957-77; trustee, sec. Fedn. Jewish Philanthropies, N.Y.C., 1965-77; trustee, chmn. Harvey Sch., 1969-76; trustee Hurricane Island Outward Bound Sch., 1974—, Washington Opera, 1984-85, Asia Soc., 1993—; bd. dirs., pres., vice chmn., Hickrill Found., Inc., 1953-77, 79—; chmn. bd. dirs. Coun. Excellence in Govt., 1984—, chmn., 1988-93, Am. Assembly, 1992—, Smithsonian Inst., 1994—, chmn., 1997—; mem. vis. com. Kennedy Sch. Govt., Harvard U., chmn., 1998—; chmn. tax com., mem. N.Y. State Econ. Devel. Bd., 1975-77, mem. Appleseed Found. bd., 1995—; chmn., mem. N.Y. State Bd. Equalization and Assessment, 1976-77; adv. bd. Sch. Advanced Internat. Studies, Johns Hopkins U., 1979-88; mem. N.Y. State Council on Fiscal and Econ. Priorities, 1985-89, N.Y. Coun. Fgn. Rels.; mem. N.Y. State Adv. Commn. on Liability Ins., 1986. Mem. Century Assn., Harvard Club, River Club, Met. Club. Home: 1516 28th St NW Washington DC 20007-3058 Office: Abacus & Assocs Inc 147 E 48th St # 3fl New York NY 10017-1223

WEIL, GORDON LEE, energy executive; b. Mineola, N.Y., Mar. 12, 1937; s. Irving and Sadye (Gordon) Weil; m. Roberta Meserve, Apr. 6, 1962; children: Anne Inger, Richard Clement. BA cum laude, Bowduin Coll., 1958; Diploma of Advanced European Studies, Coll. Europe, Belgium, 1959; PhD, Columbia U., 1961. Dir. UN Semester Drew U., N.Y.C. and Madison, N.J., 1962—63; dep. ofcl. spokesman EEC, Washington, N.Y.C., Brussels, 1963—66; contbr. Washington Post, Newsweek, Bus. Abroad, Brussels, 1966—68; rsch. assoc. Twentieth Century Fund, N.Y.C., 1968—70; press sec. Sen. George McGovern, Washington, 1970—72; vis. prof. govt. Bowdoin Coll., Brunswick, Maine, 1973—74; corr., prodr. WNET/13, N.Y.C., 1973—75; pres. Polit. Intelligence, Inc., Harpswell, Maine, 1974—79; commr. bus. regulation State of Maine, Augusta, 1979—80, pub. adv., 1981—82; dir. Main Office Energy Resources, 1980—82; pres. Weil and Howe, Inc., 1982—, Weil Pub. Co., Inc., 1989—2000; chmn. Weil Cos., 2000—. Chmn. New Eng. Energy Dirs., 1982; staff chmn. Nat. Govs. Assn. Subcom. Energy Conservation and Renewable Resources, 1981—82; vice chmn. New Eng. Power Planning Com., 1982; chmn., bd. dirs. Energy Testing Lab. Maine, 1979—82; gen. mgr. Dirigo Elec. Coop., 1983—89; lectr. Am. govt. Colby Coll., Waterville, Maine, 1977; lectr. internat. trade Baruch Coll., CUNY, N.Y.C., 1969—70; prof. European instns. Coll. Europe, Bruges, Belgium, 1966—67; lectr. internat. law Am. U., Washington, 1963—64; lectr. Am. govt. Rutgers U., New Brunswick, NJ, 1962. Author: The European Convention on Human Rights, 1963, A Handbook on the European Economic Community, 1965, Trade Policy in the '70s, 1969, A Foreign Policy for Europe, 1970, The Benelux Nations, 1970; author: (with Ian D. Davidson) The Gold War: The Story of the World's Monetary Crisis, 1970; author: The Long Shot: George McGovern Runs for President, 1973, The Consumer's Guide to Banks, 1975, American Trade Policy: A New Round, 1975, Election '76: A Complete Guide to the New Campaign, 1976, Sears, Roebuck, U.S.A., 1977, The Welfare Debate of 1978, 1978. Selectman, chmn. Town of Harpswell, Maine, 1997—2000; bd. dirs. Am. Lung Assn. of Maine, 1987—93. With U.S. Army, 1961—62. Fellow Rockefeller found., 1966—68. Mem.: Phi Beta Kappa (senator 1985—). Democrat. Office: PO Box 1990 150 Capitol St Augusta ME 04332-1990 E-mail: Gordon.Weil@weilnet.com.

WEIL, JACK BAUM, clothing manufacturing company executive; b. Denver, Nov. 13, 1928; s. Jack Arnold and Beatrice (Baum) W.; m. Elizabeth Fried, 1956 (div. 1969); children: Steven Eugene, Judith B. Weil Oksner; m. Candace Helene Taylor, 1973 (div. 1983). BA, Tulane U., 1952. V.p. Rockmount Ranch Wear Mfg. Co., Denver, 1954—, designer, sales mgr., 1957—. Designer western apparel. Head planning group Humboldt Island Hist. Dist., Denver; planning com. City of Denver Chessman Park, 1996—; chmn. Commty. Coll. Denver Found. bd. dirs.; committeeman Denver Rep. Party, 1974—; del. Rep. county, dist. and state convs., 1974—; sec. Rep. Party Com., 1st Congl. Dist. Colo., 1993-94, chmn. 1995-99; sec. Colo. Rep. State Ctrl. Com., 1999—; mem. Colo. State Rep. Exec. Com., 1996—; bd. dirs. 1st Universalist Ch., Denver; mem. admissions com. Tulane U., 1994—; del. Rep. Nat. Conv., 1992, 96, nat. credentials com. 1st lt. U.S. Army, 1952-54. Mem. West Coast Western Mktg. Assn., Midwest Western Wear and Equipment Assn. (bd. dirs.), N.W. Western Wear & Equipment Travelers Assn. (pres. Mpls.), S.E. Western, English and Equine Assn. (bd. dirs. Altanta), Denver Western Wear and Equipment Assn., Hat Inst. Am. (del. 1974—), Denver Athletic Club, Town Club, Lincoln Club (bd. dirs. 1997—), Rump Club, Kappa Delta Phi. Avocations: painting, politics, physical fitness, travel. Home: 1025 Humboldt St Denver CO 80218-3121 Office: Rockmount Ranch Wear Mfg Co 1626 Wazee St Denver CO 80202-1314

WEIL, JEFFREY GEORGE, lawyer; b. Allentown, Pa., Apr. 28, 1951; s. Russel G.E. and Irene Marie (Kozlowski) W.; children: Michael, Stephen, Brooke; m. Rachel Eisner, 1994. AB, Princeton U., 1973; JD, Harvard U., 1976. Bar: Pa. 1976, U.S. Dist. Ct. (ea. dist.) Pa. 1976, U.S. Ct. Appeals (3d cir.) 1976, U.S. Supreme Ct., 1988. Assoc. Dechert, Price & Rhoads, Phila., 1976-84, ptnr., 1984—, chmn. firm hiring com., 1987-89, mem. firm exec. com., 1990-94. Chmn. com. United Way Southeastern Pa., Phila., 1982-85, trustee, 1983-89, mem. funding policy com., 1987-90; participant Community Leadership Seminar Program, Phila., 1986; bd. dirs. Hawk Mountain Sanctuary, 1993-99, chmn. bd. dirs., 2000—; bd. dirs. Pa. Wildlife Fedn., 1996-99. Mem. ABA (vice chmn. adminstrn. law com. on pub. advs. and pub. representation 1985-88, mem. antitrust sect. pvt. litigation subcom. 1991—), Pa. Bar Assn., Phila. Bar Assn. (fed. cts. com. 1985—), Princeton U. Alumni Schs. Com., Princeton Club Phila. Avocations: fly-fishing, reading. Home: 2 Esprit Ter Wayne PA 19087-5713 Office: Dechert Price & Rhoads 1717 Arch St Lbby 3 Philadelphia PA 19103-2713

WEIL, JOHN WILLIAM, technology management consultant; b. N.Y.C., Feb. 3, 1928; s. Frank Leopold and Henrietta Amelia (Simons) W.; m. Joan Leatrice Landis, June 15, 1950; children— Nancy Ellen, Linda Jill. BS, MIT, 1948; PhD, Cornell U., 1953. Various positions in nuclear reactors and computers Gen. Electric Co. (various locations), 1953-70; v.p. advanced systems and tech. Honeywell Info. Systems, Inc., Waltham, Mass., 1970-74; v.p., chief tech. officer Bendix Corp., Southfield, Mich., 1974-77, sr. v.p., chief tech. officer, 1977-83; v.p. advanced tech. and engrng. Allied Corp., 1983; pres. Modular Bio Systems, Inc., 1983-85, Weil Assocs., Inc., Bloomfield Hills, Mich., 1985-97. Founder Met. Detroit Sci. and Engrng. Coalition, 1977, sec., 1977-80, pres., 1980-82; chmn. Mich. Biotech. Inst., 1981-85, trustee, 1985-92; mem. Army Sci. Bd., 1982-84. Contbr. articles to prof. jours. AEC fellow, 1950-51 Home and Office: 218 Guilford Rd Bloomfield Hills MI 48304-2737 E-mail: johnww@weilhome.com.

WEIL, JOHN DAVID, financial executive; b. Chgo., Sept. 28, 1947; s. Leslie Joseph and Carlyne (Strauss) W.; m. Marcie Bornfriend, July 4, 1981; children: Jessica Lauren, Michael Brandon, Samantha Leigh. BS in Econs., U. Ill., 1969; MBA in Fin., Northwestern U., 1971. Asst. to chmn. bd. Stanwood Industries, Lake Forest, Ill., 1971-74; pres. Kent Paper Co., Ridgewood, N.Y., 1974-81; pres., CEO Am. Envelope Co., Chgo., 1982-94; operating affiliate McCown De Leeuw & Co., 1995—; dir. Dimac Holdings, 1998—. Pres., CEO U.S.A. Internat. Data Response Corp., Scottsdale, Ariz., 1998—99; CFO DIMAC Holdings, 1999—2001; dir., corp. sec. On Stage Entertainment, 2001—. Mem. Envelope Mfrs. Am. (bd. dirs. 1986-94), Northmoor Country Club, Ancala Country Club. Office: 8777 E Via de Ventura Ste 100 Scottsdale AZ 85258

WEIL, LEONARD, banker; b. 1922; married With U.S. Dept. State, Vienna, Austria, 1946; with Union Bank, Los Angeles, 1946-62; pres., CEO Mfrs. Bank, 1962-86, pres. emeritus, 1986—. Adj. asst. prof. fin. Anderson Grad. Sch. Mgmt., UCLA (ret.) Trustee UCLA Found.; bd. visitors UCLA Grad. Sch. Mgmt.; past pres. Town Hall; bd. dirs. Braille Inst. Served with U.S. Army, 1943-45 Mem. Calif. Bankers Assn. (bd. dirs., past pres.), Am. Mgmt. Assn., Am. Econs. Assn., Am. Bankers Assn. (past dir.). Office: PO Box 571150 Tarzana CA 91357-1150 Address: 4501 La Barca Pl Tarzana CA 91356-5029

WEIL, LOUIS ARTHUR, III, retired newspaper publishing executive; b. Grand Rapids, Mich., Mar. 14, 1941; s. Louis Arthur, Jr. and Kathryn (Halligan) W.; m. Mary Elizabeth Buckingham, Sept. 7, 1963 (div. June 1977); children: Scott Arthur, Christopher Davison, Timothy Buckingham; m. Daryl Hopkins Goss, Jan. 26, 1980. BA in English, Ind. U., 1963; DHL (hon.), Mercy Coll., Grand Valley State U. Various positions Times Herald, Port Huron, Mich., 1966-68; personnel dir., pub. Journal and Courier, Lafayette, Ind., 1968-73; gen. mgr., pub. Gannett Westchester Rockland Newspapers, White Plains, N.Y., 1973-74, pres., gen. mgr., 1974-77, pres., pub., 1977-79; v.p. devel. Gannett Co., Inc., N.Y.C., 1979-83, sr. v.p. planning and devel., 1982-86; chmn., pub. Gannett Westchester Rockland Newspapers, White Plains, 1984-86; pres. The Detroit News, 1986-89, pub., 1987-89; U.S. pub. Time Mag., 1989-91; pub., chief exec. officer, exec. v.p. Ariz. Republic, Phoenix Gazette, Ariz. Bus. Gazette, 1991-96; chmn., pres., CEO Central Newspapers, Inc., Phoenix, 1996-2000. Bd. dirs. Ctrl. Newspapers, Inc., Prudential. Trustee, mem. adv. bd. Ariz. Cancer Ctr. at U. Ariz., Am. Grad. Sch. Internat. Mgmt.; bd. dirs. Ariz. Cmty. Found., Heard Mus.; campaign chmn. Valley of the Sun United Way, 1992; past chmn. Greater Phoenix Leadership; past pres. bd. trustees Phoenix Art Mus. With USN. Office: 5112 N 40th St Ste 101 Phoenix AZ 85018

WEIL, PETER HENRY, lawyer; b. N.Y.C., Nov. 20, 1933; s. Frank L. and Henrietta Amelia (Simons) W.; m. Helen Fay Kolodkin, Dec. 18, 1960; children: Karen W. Markus, Frank L. BA cum laude, Princeton U., 1954; LLB cum laude, Harvard U., 1957. Bar: N.Y. 1957, U.S. Dist. Cts. (so. and ea. dists.) N.Y. 1972. Assoc. Weil, Gotshal & Manges, N.Y.C., 1958-62; from assoc. to ptnr. Kaye Scholer, 1962-95, ret., 1995. Lectr. SMU Inst. on Comml. Financing, 1985-94, Banking Law Inst., 1987-89. Author: Asset Based Lending: An Introductory Guide to Secured Financing, P.L.I., 1989, 3d edit., 1996. Fellow Am. Coll. of Commercial Fin. Lawyers; former chmn. N.Y. bd. overseers, former bd. govs. Hebrew Union Coll., Jewish Inst. Religion, Cin., N.Y.C., Los Angeles, Jerusalem. With U.S. Army 1957-58. Mem. Ringwood Golden Master Volleyball Team, U.S. Nat. Champions, 1983 Mem. ABA, Assn. of Bar of City of N.Y. (banking law com. 1975-78).

WEIL, RANDOLPH ALLEN, executive; b. Champaign, Ill., Nov. 23, 1951; s. Nicholas Andrew and Audrey Florence W.; m. Susan Kay Rostad, Feb. 26, 1977; 1 child, Alexander Rostad. BS in Econs., U. Ill., Chgo., 1973; MBA, U. Calif., Berkeley, 1974. Gen. sales mgr. Cummins Engrng. Co., Downers Grove, Ill., 1975-83; gen. mgr. ops. Sub of Cummins Engrng. Co., Chgo., 1983-85; v.p., gen. mgr. global parts The Budd Co., Dallas, 1985-87; dir. coastal ops. Allied Tube & Conduit, Harvey, Ill., 1987-88; dir. distbn. ops. Square D. Co., Florence, Ky., 1988-92; v.p. logistics AT&T NEtwork Systems, Morristown, N.J., 1992-94; v.p. svc. logistics NCR Corp., Dayton, Ohio, 1994-99. Dir. Jr. Achievement, Dayton, 1996-99, Boy Scouts Am., Columbus, 1978-80. Mem. Am. Prodn. & Inventory Control Soc., Coun. Logistics Mgrs. Avocations: bicycling, swimming, opera, remodelling, gardening.

WEIL, RAYMOND RICHARD, soil scientist; b. Detroit, May 27, 1948; s. Ulrich L. and Hilde C. (Levy) W.; m. Susan R. Boscov, Feb. 22, 1968 (div. Feb. 1982); children: Benjamin S., Joshua J.; m. Patricia Lynn Driggers, Feb. 5, 1983. BS, Mich. State U., 1970; MS, Purdue U., 1972; PhD, Va. Poly. Inst. and State U., 1977. Cert. profl. soil scientist. Vol. Peace Corps, Ethiopia, 1970; farm mgr. Nat. Sharecropper's Fund, Wadesboro, N.C., 1972-73; instr. Va. Poly. Inst. and State U., Blacksburg, 1975-77; lectr. U. Malawi, Lilongwe, 1977-79; from asst. prof. to assoc. prof. U. Md., College Park, 1979-91, prof., 1991—. Cosn. Forest Dept., Sri Lanka Govt., 1981; adv. bd. Com. on Agr. Sustainability for Developing Countries, Washington, 1988—; mem. task force Ecosystem Farm, Accokeek (Med.) Found., 1990—, chair medium size farm bd. Future Harvest Project, 1995—, advisor Govt. Ethiopia Agrl. Rsch. Orgn., 2001. Author: Lab Manual for Intro Soil Science, 1998; co-author: Nature and Properties of Soil: A Study Guide, 1984; co-author: Nature and Properties of Soils, 13th edit., 2002; contbr. articles to profl. jours. Named Fulbright-Hayes Scholarship Exch. fellow, Zimbabwe, 1985, Fulbright-Hayes Africa Regional Rsch. scholar, Tanzania, 1994, Nat. Def. Edn. Act fellow, Ind., Md., 1991, Md. Agr. Exptl. Sta., 1991-94, U.S. AID, Malawi, 1988-92, USDA Agrl. Rsch. Edn., 1996—. Mem. Am. Soc. Agronomy (internat. div. chair 1993-94, bd. dirs. 1998—), Soil Sci. Soc. Am., Internat. Soil Sci. Soc. Achievements include development of new methods of matching fertilizer use to soil requirements in peasant farming sectors by mapping soil and plant nutrient status, of improved cropping system for sustainable production of cereals and legumes; development of new soil management system to reduce groundwater contamination by nitrates; contributions to understanding how best to manage organic wastes such as animal manure and sewage sludge in farming systems; development of new method for indigenous nutrient sources to enhance soil fertility, practical measures of soil quality. Office: U Md Dept Natural Resource Scis College Park MD 20742-0001 E-mail: rw17@umail.umd.edu.

WEIL, RICHARD, III, surgeon, medical educator; b. N.Y.C., Feb. 22, 1936; s. Richard Jr. and Allene (Hall) W.; m. Polly Edgar, Aug. 22, 1959; children: Wendy, Richard. AB, Princeton U., 1957; MD, Columbia U. Coll. Physicians and Surgeons, 1961. Diplomate Am. Bd. Surgery, Nat. Bd. Med. Examiners. Intern in surgery Presbyn. Hosp., 1961-62, asst. resident in surgery, 1962-63, 65-67, chief resident in gen. surgery, 1968; chief resident in pediat. surgery Babies Hosp., 1969, chief resident in vasc. surgery, 1969, asst. attending surgeon, chmn. surg. house staff com., 1970-74, dir. kidney transplantation, 1973-74; asst. in surgery Columbia U. Coll. Physicians and Surgeons, 1967-68, instr. surgery, 1969, asst. prof. surgery, 1970-74; fellow in transplantation surgery U. Minn., 1970; assoc. prof. surgery U. Colo., 1974-79, prof. surgery, 1979-87, dir. transplantation, 1980-87; prof. surgery, dir. transplantation NYU, 1987-93; assoc. dean medicine, prof. surgery Brown U., Providence, 1993-98. Cons. surgeon Manhattan VA Hosp., 1989-92, Denver VA Hosp., 1980-87, Denver Gen. Hosp., 1980-87, St. Anthony-Ctrl. Hosp. Denver, 1980-87; attending surgeon Bellevue Hosp. Ctr., 1989-93 Contbr. more than 130 articles to profl. jours. including Surg. Forum, Am. Jour. Surgery, Transplantation, Surgery, Jour. Pediat. Surgery, Surgery, Gynecology & Obstets., among others. Capt. U.S. Army Med. Corps, 1963-65, Germany. Mem. Am. Assn. Tissue Banks, ACS, Am. Fedn. Clin. Rsch., Am. Soc. Transplant Surgeons, Am. Soc. for Artificial Internal Organs, Am. Surg. Assn., Assn. for Acad. Surgery, Allen O. Whipple Surg. Soc. (recorder 1976-78), Ctrl. Surg. Assn., Clin. Immunology Soc., Denver Acad. Surgery, Harvey Soc., Intermountain End-Stage Renal Disease Network (exec. com. 1975-79), Internat. Cardiovasc. Soc., N.Y. Ctr. for Liver Transplantation, N.Y. Clin. Soc., N.Y. Regional Transplant Program (pres. 1991-92), N.Y. Surg. Soc., Rocky Mountain Vasc. Surg. Soc., Soc. Internat. de Chirurgie, soc. Univ. Surgeons, Transplantation Soc., Western Assn. Transplant Surgeons, United Network for Organ Sharing (councilor for Colo., Wyo., Nebr., Kans., Iowa, Mo. 1986-87).

WEIL, ROBERT IRVING, lawyer, arbitrator, mediator, retired judge; b. N.Y.C., Apr. 6, 1922; s. Irving Julius and Esther (Aisenstein) W.; m. Carol Ethel Tannenbaum, Nov. 6, 1946 (div. 1953); children: David Irving, Timothy Robert; m. Dorothy Granet Kornhandler, Sept. 12, 1958. AB, UCLA, 1943; MS in Journalism, Columbia U., 1944; JD, U. So. Calif., L.A., 1951. Bar: Calif. 1951, U.S. Dist. Ct. (cen. dist.) Calif. 1951, U.S. Supreme Ct. 1961. Assoc. Pacht, Tannenbaum & Ross, L.A., 1951-54; ptnr. Tannenbaum, Steinberg & Shearer, Beverly Hills, Calif., 1954-58, Aaronson, Weil & Friedman, L.A., 1958-75; judge Calif. County Superior Ct., 1975-90; pvt. practice, 1990—. V.p. L.A. Police Commn., 1973-75; chmn. Calif. Ctr. for Jud. Edn. and Rsch., Emoryville, 1989-90; lectr., seminar leader Calif. Jud. Coll., Berkeley, 1981—, The Rutter Group, L.A., 1981—. Co-author: California Practice Guide: Civil Procedure Before Trial, 1983; contbr. articles to profl. jours. Mem. ABA, Am. Judges Assn., Calif. Judges Assn. (pres. 1985-86, v.p. 1993-94), Pres.'s award 1987, v.p. 1993, Edn. award 1997), L.A. County Bar Assn., L.A. Copyright Soc., Beverly Hills Bar Assn. Avocations: writing, reading, travel, theatre. Home and Office: 2686 Claray Dr Los Angeles CA 90077-2017 E-mail: robertweil@worldnet.att.net.

WEIL, ROLF ALFRED, economist, university president emeritus; b. Pforzheim, Germany, Oct. 29, 1921; came to U.S., 1936, naturalized, 1944; s. Henry and Lina (Landauer) W.; m. Leni Metzger, Nov. 3, 1945; children: Susan Linda, Ronald Alan. BA, U. Chgo., 1942, PhD, 1950; D. Hebrew Letters, Coll. Jewish Studies, 1967; L.H.D., Loyola U., 1970; D.H.L., Bowling Green State U., Ohio, 1986; LHD, Roosevelt U., 1988. Rsch. asst. Cowles Commn. for Rsch. in Econs., 1942-44; rsch. analyst Ill. Dept. Revenue, 1944-46; mem. faculty Roosevelt U., Chgo., 1946—, prof. fin. and econs., also chmn. dept. fin., 1954-65, dean Coll. Bus. Adminstrn., 1957-64, acting pres., 1965-66, pres., 1966-88, pres. emeritus, 1988—. Past pres. Selfhelp Home for the Aged, Chgo.; cons. to non-profit orgns., 1988—. Author: Through these Portals-from Immigrant to College President, 1991; contbr. articles on fin. Bd. dirs. trustees Roosevelt U., Selfhelp of Chgo., Inc. Mem. Am. Econ. Assn., Cliff Dwellers Club. E-mail: rweil@roosevelt.edu.

WEIL, ROMAN LEE, accounting educator; b. Montgomery, Ala., May 22, 1940; s. Roman L. and Charlotte (Alexander) W.; children: Alexis Cherie, Charles Alexander Roman, Lacey Lorraine. BA, Yale U., 1962; MS in Indsl. Adminstrn, Carnegie-Mellon U., 1965, PhD in Econs., 1966. CPA, CMA, Ill. From instr. to prof. U. Chgo., 1965-93, Sigmund E. Edelstone prof. acctg., 1993-97, V. Duane Rath prof. acctg., 1997—, dir. Dir.'s Coll., 1998—; Mills B. Lane prof. indsl. mgmt. Ga. Inst. Tech., 1974-76; mem. adv. com. replacement cost implementation SEC, 1976-77. Prof. acctg. Stanford (Calif.) U., 1984, prof. econs., 1985, prof. law, 1990-96; prof. acctg. and law NYU Sch. Law, 1985; mem. adv. coun. Fin. Acctg. Stds., 1989-94; mem. task force on consolidations Fin. Acctg. Stds. Bd., 1984-89, mem. task force on discounting, 1989-99, mem. task force on fin. instruments, 1994-98, mem. adv. coun., 1989-94; dir. Dir.'s Coll., 1999-; co-founder Chgo./Stanford/Wharton Dir.'s Consortium, 2002-. Author: Fundamentals of Accounting, 1975, Financial Accounting, 10th edit., 2002, Accounting: The Language of Business, 10th edit., 1998, Inflation Accounting, 1976, Replacement Cost Accounting, 1976, Managerial Accounting, 1979, 7th edit., 2000, Litigation Svcs. Handbook, 3d edit., 2001; editor: Handbook of Modern Accounting, 1977, 3rd edit., 1983, Handbook of Cost Accounting, 1980, Acctg. Rev., 1974-79, Fin. Analysts Jour., 1980-88. NSF grantee, 1967-81 Mem. AICPA, Ill. Soc. CPAs, Am. Econ. Assn., Inst. Mgmt. Scis., Nat. Assn. Accts. (cert. mgmt. acct.), Am. Acctg. Assn., Inst. Managerial Acctg., Assembly Am. Collegiate Schs. Bus. (acctg. accreditation com. 1987-88), Oenonomy Soc. (co-chmn.). Home: #306 600 N Kingsbury St Chicago IL 60611 Office: U Chgo Grad Sch Bus 1101 E 58th St Chicago IL 60637-1511 E-mail: roman.weil@gsb.uchicago.edu.

WEIL, STEPHEN EDWARD, retired museum official; b. N.Y.C., June 24, 1928; s. Sidney and Beatrice (Sachs) W.; m. Rose Reicherson, Oct. 15, 1950 (div.); children: Rachel J., David N., Michael D.; m. Elizabeth Carbone, Sept. 7, 1974 (div.); m. Wendy Luke, Apr. 8, 1990. AB, Brown U., 1949; LL.B., Columbia U., 1956. Bar: N.Y. 1956. Assoc. firm Rosenman, Colin, Kaye, Petschek & Freund, N.Y.C., 1956-63; v.p., gen. mgr. Marlborough-Gerson Gallery, 1963-67; adminstr., sec., trustee Whitney Mus. Am. Art, 1967-74; dep. dir., sec. Hirshhorn Mus. and Sculpture Garden, Smithsonian Instn., Washington, 1974-95; emeritus sr. scholar, 1995—. Mem. cultural property adv. com. USIA, 1995-2000; chair adv. com. Museum Loan Network, 1995—. Co-author: Art Works - Law, Policy, Practice, 1974, Art Law - Rights and Liabilities of Creators and Collectors, 1986; author: Beauty and the Beasts, 1983, Rethinking the Museum, 1990, A Cabinet of Curiosities, 1995, Making Museums Matter, 2002; editor: A Deaccession Reader, 1997; co-editor: Art Galleries and Museums, 1973. Mem. mus. adv. panel N.Y. State Coun. on Arts, 1974-78; mem. adv. panel Inst. for Mus. Scis.; trustee Brown U., 1989-95. Mem. Am. Assn. Mus. (treas., v.p., councilor), Am. Fedn. Arts (trustee 1988-95). Jewish. Home: 800 25th St NW Washington DC 20037-2207 Office: Ctr for Edn and Mus Studies Smithsonian Instn Washington DC 20560-0427 E-mail: sweil@scems.si.edu.

WEIL, THOMAS ALEXANDER, electronics engineer, retired; b. N.Y.C., Jan. 22, 1930; s. Frank Leopold and Henrietta Amelia (Simons) W.; m. Dianne Isaacs; children: Deborah, Elizabeth, Alexander. BSEE, MIT, 1951. Engr. modulator sect. Raytheon Co., Watertown, Mass., 1951-55, sect. mgr. transmitters, 1955-69, dept. mgr. transmitters, 1969-77, staff scientist equipment devel. labs., 1972-95, lab. mgr. radar systems, 1977-79, lab. mgr. advanced devel., 1979-80, program mgr. oil shale program, 1980-84; cons. in field, 1995—. Contbr. 3 chpts. to books, 37 articles to profl. jours.; holder 10 patents in field. Recipient Excellence in Tech. award Raytheon co., 1990; Raytheon Co. fellow, 1989. Fellow IEEE (tech. papers com. Modulator Symposia, Microwave Tube Symposia, Germeshausen award 1994). Universalist-Unitarian. Avocations: classical music, photography, mountain climbing, cosmology. Home: 14 Lanark Rd Wellesley MA 02481-3029 *Evolution and survival of the fittest have left mankind aggressive and prone to make war. Peace depends on finding how to overcome this heritage. Shouldn't we be working on how to resteer mankind's instincts?.*

WEIL, THOMAS P. health services consultant; b. Mount Vernon, N.Y., Oct. 2, 1932; s. H.M. and Alice (Franc) W.; m. Janet Whalen, Feb. 13, 1965. BA, Union Coll., 1954; MPH, Yale U., 1958; PhD, U. Mich., 1964. S.S. Goldwater fellow Mount Sinai Med. Ctr., N.Y.C., 1957-58; assoc. cons. J.G. Steinle Assocs., Garden City, N.Y., 1958-61; asst. prof. UCLA, 1962-65; assoc. dir. Touro Infirmary, New Orleans, 1964-66; prof., dir. U. Mo., 1966—71; v.p. E.D. Rosenfeld Assocs., N.Y.C., 1971-75; pres. Bedford Health Assocs. Inc., N.Y., N.C., 1975-2000. Chmn. Health Edn. & Applied Rsch. Found., Washington, 1981-83; bd. dirs. Albany (N.Y.) Med. Ctr., Inc., 1974-77; cons. to numerous hosps., med. schs., health related orgs., 1958-2000. Contbr. articles profl. jours. Named vis. prof. W.K. Kellogg Found., Sydney, Australia, 1969; recipient svc. award Am. Assn. Healthcare Cons., 1982; Weil Disting. Prof. in Health Svcs. Mgmt., U. Mo. established in 1991. Fellow APHA (emeritus), Am. Assn. Healthcare Cons. (emeritus), Am. Coll. Healthcare Execs. (emeritus). Jewish. Avocations: English Cocker Spaniels, Appaloosa Quarter Horses.

WEILAND, CHARLES HANKES, lawyer; b. Billings, Mont., Feb. 19, 1921; s. George Michael and Elizabeth (Hankes) W. AB cum laude, Johns Hopkins U., 1942; JD, Harvard U., 1948. Bar: Ill. 1949, U.S. Dist. Ct. (no.

dist.) Ill. 1949, U.S. Ct. Appeals (7th cir.) 1949, U.S. Supreme Ct. 1968. Assoc. Lord, Bissell & Brook, Chgo., 1948-55, ptnr., 1956-83. Chmn. Cook County Inquiry Bd., Supreme Ct. Ill. Atty. Regis. and Disciplinary Commn., 1974-75 Served with AUS, 1942-46. Mem. Ill. Bar Assn., Chgo. Bar Assn. Clubs: The Lawyers Club of Chgo. Republican.

WEILAND, JONATHON A. nursing and rehabilitation facility administrator; b. Allentown, Pa., Feb. 5, 1970; s. Edward J. Weiland and Nancy J.G. Chemello. BS, Pa. State U., 1992. Lic. nursing home adminstr. Pa., N.J. Asst. mgr. Avco Fin. Svcs., State College, Pa., 1992-95; admissions dir. Leader Nursing & Rehab., Bethlehem, 1996, ManorCare Health Svcs., Easton, 1996-98; asst. adminstr. HCR Manor Care, 1998—2001, adminstr. Pottstown, Pa., 2001—. Mem.: Pa. State U. Alumni Assn., Am. Mgmt. Assn., Nittany Lions. Avocations: weightlifting, reading, skiing. Office: HCR-Manor Care 724 N Charlotte St Pottstown PA 19464

WEILAND, JULIETTE MARIE, public relations executive, freelance writer and photographer; b. St. Cloud, Minn., Oct. 5, 1944; d. Raymond Henry and Marie Julie (Fradette) Peterson; m. James Edward Weiland, Sept. 18, 1965; children: James Edward Jr., Timothy Paul, Kristin Juliette, Stephanie Marie. BS, U. Minn., 1967; student, U. Calif., Berkeley, 1978-83, Silvermine Sch. Art, New Canaan, Conn., 1987, Am. Mgmt. Assn., 1993. Cert. English tchr. Tchr. English Anoka Hennepin Sch. Dist., Coon Rapids, Minn., 1968-71, tutor ESL Anoka, 1971-73, Cherry Creek Sch. Dist., Englewood, Colo., 1975-76; pvt. tutor ESL Bethel, Conn., 1976-78; ptnr., owner, author Pamphleteers & Co., Wilton, 1986-96; pub. rels. dir. Nursing & Home Care, 1988-95; owner Breathe Easy Environ. Assocs., 1991-96. Freelance writer, Acton, Mass., 1982-84. Author: (short story) Somewhere There's A Child Waiting For Me, 1984; newspaper columnist on polit. govt. issues, 1987-89, The Hour - Public Relations for Small Business Owners, 2000-02; co-editor The Wilton Voter, Wilton LWV, 1994-95; photographer various newspapers, mags., reports; contbr. numerous articles to profl. jours. Co-chair Open Door Soc. for Adoptive Parents, Acton, 1980-83; pub. rels. dir. LWV Conn., Hamden, 1986-88, comm. cons., 1988-89; publicity dir. Crop Walk for Hungry, Wilton, 1987-88; mem. Graffiti Task Force, Norwalk, 1998-99. Mem. NAFE, Pub. Rels. Soc. Am. (treas. 1998, v.p. 1999, chmn. job bank 1997-2000, pres. 2000, nominating chmn. 2001-02), Internat. Freelance Photographers Orgn., Nat. Fedn. Press Women, Fairfield County Pub. Rels. Assn., Conn. Press Club (pres. 2000-02, 3rd prize external ann. report for non-profits 1990, 2d prize 1991, 3d prize news photo 1991), Healthcare Pub. Rels. and Mktg. Soc. Greater N.Y., Wilton C. of C. Democrat. Roman Catholic. Avocation: photography. Home: 67 Signal Hill Rd Wilton CT 06897-1930 Office: Juliette Weiland & Co 67 Signal Hill Rd Wilton CT 06897-1930 E-mail: jmwpr@wilton-ct.com., jweiland@optonline.net.

WEILAND, MARK BRADLEY, corporate lawyer; b. Hinsdale, Ill., June 15, 1956; s. William Sheplar and Dorothy (Costello) W.; m. Susan Jean Hill, Nov. 14, 1987; children: William, Abigail. BA, U. Ill. Champaign, 1978; JD, U. Chgo.-Kent Coll. Law, 1981. Asst. state's atty. Dupage Co., Ill., 1982-86; atty. William D. Lyman and Assocs., Oakbrook Terr., 1986-87; gen. counsel/v.p. and corporate sec. Profl. Svc. Industries, Inc., Lombard, 1987—. Chmn. Advocate's Assembly, Silver Spring, Md., 1993—, Lawyer's Roundtable. Mem. ABA, Ill. Bar Assn., Am. Soc. Testing and Materials (mem. com. D-18 1998—), Chgo. Bar Assn., Columbia Yacht Club. Republican. Roman Catholic. Avocations: fly fishing, boating, woodworking. Office: Ste 400 1901 S Meyers Rd Oakbrook Ter IL 60181-5208 Fax: 630-691-1498. E-mail: mark.weiland@psiusa.com.

WEILAND, PAUL S. lawyer; b. Mt. Kisco, N.Y., Dec. 18, 1968; s. Peter G. and Mary Rose Weiland; m. Marcy N. Weiland, July 31, 1993; 1 child Katherine M. BA, U. So. Calif., 1992; PhD, Ind. U., 1996; JD, Harvard U., 1999. Assoc. Goodwin Procter, Boston, 1999-2001; atty. Dept. Justice, Washington, 2001—. Chair Harvard Law Sch. Environ. Law Soc. Alumni Adv. Bd., Cambridge, Mass., 2000—. Co-author: (book) Managing for the Environment, 1999 (Best Book award 2000, 2001). Mem. ABA, Am. Polit. Sci. Assn., Am. Soc. for Pub. Adminstrn., Environ. Law Inst. (assoc.). Office: Dept Justice PO Box 4390 Washington DC 20044-4390

WEILBACHER, WILLIAM MANNING, advertising and marketing consultant; b. Albany, N.Y., June 23, 1928; s. William Carl and Gladys (Manning) W.; m. Martha Ethel Meyer, May 19, 1962; children: Barbara Taylor, Elizabeth Manning. BS, Yale U., 1949; MS, Columbia, 1951. Supr. product analysis Nat. Biscuit Co., 1951-53; v.p., dir. rsch. Dancer-Fitzgerald-Sample, Inc., 1953-62, sr. v.p., 1971-73, exec. v.p., 1973-74, vice chmn., 1974-79; bd. dir., sr. v.p. McCaffrey & McCall, 1962-66; exec. dir. Ctr. for Advanced Practice, 1966; ptnr. Jack Tinker and Ptnrs., Interpub. Inc., 1966-69; v.p., dir. rsch. J. Walter Thompson Co., 1969-70; pres. Master Jazz Recs., Inc., 1967—. D-F-S Realty Inc., 1975-79, D-F-S Holdings Inc., 1974-79, Bismark Corp., 1979—, Second Mktg. Opinion, Inc., 1981—. Lectr. advt. Grad. Sch. Bus., Columbia U., 1956-64, adj. prof. mktg., 1976-77, 81-82, 83; lectr. mktg. CCNY, 1955-57; adj. prof. mktg. Grad. Sch. Bus., NYU, 1965-70, 80-81, 88; Spencer vis. prof. S.I. Newhouse Sch. Pub. Comms., Syracuse U., 1982-86; mem. Radio-TV Ratings Rev. Com., 1958-65; bd. dirs. Audit Bur. Circulation, 1964-71, Broacast Rating Coun., 1963-67; mem. tech. adv. com. Robert Wood Johnson Found., 1994—; adv. bd. The Ency. of Advt., 1998—. Author: (with L.O. Brown, R. S. Lessler) Advertising Media, 1957, (with H.C. Barksdale) Marketing Research; Selected Readings and Analytic Commentaries, 1966, (with R.A. Bauer, S.A. Greyser) Advertising in America: The Consumer View, 1968, Marketing Management Cases, 1970, 4th edit. 1986, Advertising, 1979, 2d edit. 1984, Cases in Advertising, 1981, Auditing Productivity, 1981, Choosing an Advertising Agency, 1983, Current Advertiser Practices in Compensating Their Advertising Agencies, 1983, 86, 89, 92, 95, Choosing and Working with Your Advertising Agency, 1991, Managing Agency Relations, 1991, Brand Marketing, 1993, contbg. editor: Marketing Handbook, 1965. Vice chmn. tech. com. Advt. Rsch. Found., 1960-63, chmn., 1963-65, bd. dirs., 1965-67. Mem. Am. Assn. Advt. Agys. (past vice chmn. rsch. com.), Market Rsch. Coun. (pres. 1970-71), Yale Club of N.Y.C., Alpha Kappa Psi, Beta Gamma Sigma. Home: Box 2002 30 Bismark Way Dennis MA 02638-2207

WEILER, ANGELA M. librarian, writer; b. Cortland, N.Y., Feb. 23, 1952; d. Nicola S. and Gloria Maria Stefano; children: Briana. BA, Syracuse U., 1974, MLS, 1997. Reference libr. Cazenovia (N.Y.) Coll., 1996—97; circulation coord., instrn. coord. SUNY-Morrisville Coll. Libr., 1997—. State libr. contract adv. team SUNY, Albany, 2000—. Author short stories; contbr. articles to jours. Grantee Applied Rsch. grant, SUNY Morrisville Alumni Assn., 1998; scholar Regents scholar, N.Y. State Bd. Regents, 1970. Mem.: Ea. N.Y. Assn. Coll. and Rsch. Librs., SUNY Librs. Assn. (chair instrn. com. 2002—), Beta Phi Mu. Avocations: literature, music, art, theater , cinema. Office: SUNY Morrisville College Eaton St Morrisville NY 13408 Office Fax: 315-684-6115. Business E-Mail: weileram@morrisville.edu. E-mail: cynarios@yahoo.com.

WEILER, DOROTHY ESSER, librarian; b. Hartford, Wis., Feb. 21, 1914; d. Henry Hugo and Agatha Christina (Dopp) Esser; A.B. in Fgn. Langs., Wash. State U., 1935; B.A.L., Grad. Library Sch., U. Wash., 1936; postgrad. U. Ariz., 1956-57, Ariz. State U., 1957-58, Grad. Sch. Librarianship, U. Denver, 1971; m. Henry C. Weiler, Aug. 30, 1937; children— Robert William, Kurt Walter. Tchr.-librarian Roosevelt Elem. Schs., Dist. #66, Phoenix, 1956-59; extension librarian Ariz. Dept. Library and Archives, Phoenix, 1959-67; library dir. City of Tempe (Ariz.), 1967-79; assoc. prof., dept. library sci. Ariz. State U., 1968; vis. faculty Mesa Community Coll., 1980-84. Mem. public relations com. United Fund; treas. Desert Samaritan Med. Ctr. Aux., 1981, v.p. community relations Hosp., 1982, vol. asst. chaplain, 1988—, pastoral care vol. Named Ariz. Librarian of Yr., 1971; recipient Silver Book award Library Binding Inst., 1963. Mem. Tempe Hist. Soc., Ariz. Pioneers Hist. Soc., Am. Radio Relay League, Am. Bus. Women's Assn., ALA, Southwestern Library Assn., Ariz. State Libr. Assn. (pres. 1973-74), Ariz. Libr. Pioneer. Roman Catholic. Clubs: Our Lady of Mt. Carmel Ladies' Sodality, Soroptimist Internat. Founder, editor Roadrunner, Tumbling Tumbleweed; contbr. articles to mags. Home: 1605 E Southern Ave Tempe AZ 85282-5610

WEILER, EDWARD J. federal agency administrator; b. Chgo., 1949; PhD, Northwestern U., 1976. Staff scientist, chief ultraviolet/visible and gravitational astrophysics NASA, 1979, chief scientist Hobble Space Telescope, 1979—96, dir. origins program, 1996—98, assoc. adminstr. space sci., 1998—. Office: NASA Hdqrs Mail Code S 300 E St SW Washington DC 20546

WEILER, JEFFRY LOUIS, lawyer; b. N.Y.C., Dec. 31, 1942; s. Kurt and Elaine (Kabb) W.; m. Susan Karen Goodman, June 8, 1964; children: Philip K., June M. BS, Miami U., Oxford, Ohio, 1964; JD, Cleve. State U., 1970. Bar: Ohio 1970, Fla. 1981; CPA, Ohio 1968. Acct. Meaden & Moore, CPAs, Cleve., 1964-65; IRS agt. U.S. Dept. Treasury, 1965-70; assoc. Ulmer & Berne, 1970-71; ptnr. Benesch, Friedlander, Coplan & Aronoff, LLP, 1971—. Adj. assoc. prof. Cleve.-Marshall Coll. Law, Cleve. State U., 1980-87. Contbr. to profl. pubs. Fellow Am. Coll. Trust and Estate Counsel; mem. ABA (sect. taxation, estate and gift tax subcom.), Ohio State Bar Assn. (bd. govs. estate planning trust and probate law sect. 1999—), Cleve. Estate Planning Inst. (chmn. 1980), Cleve. Tax Inst. (chmn. 1983), Cleve. Bar Assn. (treas. 1993-96, trustee 1988-91), Tax Club of Cleve. (sec. 1996-97, v.p. 1997-99, pres. 1999-2000). Avocations: photography, sailboat racing, ice skating. Home: 24714 Maidstone Ln Beachwood OH 44122-1614 Office: Benesch Friedlander Coplan & Aronoff LLP 2300 BP Tower 200 Public Sq Cleveland OH 44114-2301 E-mail: jweiler@bfca.com.

WEILER, JENNIFER DAWN, family therapist; b. Alamosa, Colo., Sept. 5, 1973; d. William Lewis and Karan Rae Johnson; m. Gregory David Weiler, May 31, 1997. BA, Mesa State Coll., Grand Junction, Colo., 1995; MA, U. Colo., Denver, 2001. Child adv. Horizon House, Grand Junction, 1994-95; mental health worker Cleo Wallace Ctr., Westminster, Colo., 1995-98; multisystemic family therapist Savio House, Denver, 1998—. Mem. ACA, Multisystemic Therapy Group (cert.). Avocations: skiing, crafts, woodworking, cooking, reading. Office: Savio House 325 King St Denver CO 80219 E-mail: jennweiler@aol.com.

WEILER, KURT WALTER, radio astronomer; b. Phoenix, Mar. 16, 1943; s. Henry Carl and Dorothy (Esser) W.; m. Geertje Stoelwinder, June 8, 1979; children: Corinn Nynke Yoon, Anil Erick Jivan, Sanna Femke Lee. BS, U. Ariz., 1964; PhD, Calif. Inst. Tech., 1970. Guest investigator Netherlands Found. for Radioastronomy, Groningen, 1970-74; sci. collaborator Inst. for Radioastronomy, Bologna, Italy, 1975-76; sr. scientist Max Planck Inst. for Radioastronomy, Bonn, West Germany, 1976-79; program dir. NSF, Washington, 1979-85; radio astronomer Naval Rsch. Lab., 1985—. Mem. Halley steering com. NASA, Washington, 1981-85. Author: WSRT Users Guide, 1973, 75; editor: Low Frequency Astrophysics from Space, 1990; editor Radio Astronomy from Space, 1987, Radio Astronomy at Long Wavelengths, 2000; contbr. more than 150 articles to profl. jours. and mags. Mem. Am. Aston. Soc., Royal Astron. Soc., Internat. Astron. Union, Internat. Sci. Radio Union, Nederlandse Astronomen Club, Jaguar Club, Nat. Capital Club. Office: Naval Rsch Lab Code 7213 4555 Overlook Ave SW Washington DC 20375-0001

WEILER, SCOTT MICHAEL, machine tool manufacturing company executive; b. Fargo, N.D., Jan. 9, 1952; s. F.S. and Lorraine M. (Kopach) W.; m. Sandra L. Meyer, Aug. 28, 1971 (div. July 1986); 1 child, Kimberly. Application engr. Devlieg Machine Co., Royal Oak, Mich., 1973-84, project mgr., 1984-89, Giddings & Lewis, Fraser, Mich., 1989-94, Ingersoll CM Systems, Midland, 1994—, dir. engring. ops. & projects, 1997-99; mgr. svc. Johann A. Krause, Auburn Hills, 2000—. Mem. Soc. Mfg. Engrs., Am. Mgmt. Assn., Project Mgmt. Inst. Office: 901 Doris Rd Auburn Hills MI 48326-2716

WEILER, STEPHAN, economist, educator; b. Stanford, Calif., Dec. 2, 1965; s. Hans and Frauke Weiler. BA with honors, MA, Stanford U., 1988; PhD, U. Calif., Berkeley, 1994. Project analyst Cath. Relief Svcs., Rabat, Morocco, 1988-90; rsch. asst. prof. Regional Rsch. Inst., Morgantown, W.Va., 1994-96; regional economist, asst. prof. Colo. State U., Ft. Collins, 1996-2000, regional economist, assoc. prof., 2001—. Co-dir. Ctr. Rsch. Colo. Econ., 2001—. Contbr. articles to profl. jours. Mem. Am. Econ. Assn., Regional Sci. Assn. Office: Colo State U Econs Dept Fort Collins CO 80523 E-mail: stephan.weiler@colostate.edu.

WEILER, TODD DAVID, lawyer; b. Augusta, Ga., May 4, 1967; s. Wayne D. and Yvonne Elizabeth (Black) W.; m. Elizbeth A. Gordon, Aug. 2, 1991; children: Tyman T., London G., Nicholas Styles. BS, Brigham Young U., 1990, JD, 1996. Bar: Utah 1996, U.S. Dist. Ct. Utah 1996, U.S. Ct. Appeals (10th cir.) 1996. Assoc. Scalley & Reading, Salt Lake City, 1996-99, Parry, Anderson & Mansfield, Salt Lake City, 1999—. Republican. Mem. Lds Ch. Office: Parry Anderson & Mansfield 60 E South Temple Ste 1270 Salt Lake City UT 84111 E-mail: toddweiler@parrylaw.com.

WEILERT, RONALD LEE, data processing executive; b. Alhambra, Calif., July 12, 1948; s. Edwin H. and Leona M. (Pierson) W.; m. Geri A. Ode, July 31, 1971; children: Jeff, Kathy, Joanna, Kristin, Jenny. BS in Engring. Mgmt., USAF Acad., 1971; MA in Indsl. Engring., Cen. Mich. U., 1974. Commd. 2d lt. USAF, 1971, advanced through grades to capt., 1974, resigned, 1978; salesman Scott Paper Co., L.A., 1978-79; salesman, dir. sales Consumer Systems Corp., Oakbrook, Ill., 1979-84; from salesman to v.p. Oracle Corp., Lisle, 1984-93; pres., CEO Baan Internat., 1993-95; pres. bd. Oswego Found. for Ednl. Excellence, 1995—. Owner, pres. Four Seasons Car Washes, Inc., 1987—; pres WRI, LLC, 1997—. Mem., v.p. sch. bd. Dist. 308, Oswego, Ill., 1987-91; dist. chmn. Meramech Hill dist. Three Fires coun. Boy Scouts Am., 1996-98. Mem. Lds Ch. Home: 3838 E Plainfield Rd Oswego IL 60543-9642 E-mail: rweilert@aol.com.

WEIL-GARRIS BRANDT, KATHLEEN (KATHLEEN BRANDT), art historian; b. Surrey, Eng. d. Kurt Hermann and Charlotte (Garris) Weil; m. Werner Brandt (dec. 1983). BA with honors, Vassar Coll., 1956; postgrad., U. Bonn, Germany, 1956-57; MA, Radcliffe U., 1958; PhD, Harvard, 1966; MA, Oxford U., 1998. Asst. prof. NYU, N.Y.C., 1963-67, assoc. prof., 1967-72, prof., 1973—; asst. prof. NYU Inst. Fine Arts, 1966-67, assoc. prof., 1967-72, prof., 1973—; vis. prof. Harvard U., Cambridge, Mass., 1980; editor in chief The Art Bulletin, N.Y.C., 1977-81; Slade prof. Oxford U., 1998. Cons. on Renaissance art Vatican Mus., 1987—; vis. fellow Bibliotheca Hertziana (Max-Planck Inst.) Rome. Author: Leonardo and Central Italian Art, 1974, Problems In Cinquecento Sculpture, 1977; author: (with J. d'Amico) The Renaissance Cardinal's Ideal Palace, 1981, (with C. Acicini, J. Draper, N. Penny) Giovinezza di Michelangelo, 1999-2000; contbr. numerous articles to profl. jours.; editor: Michelangelo: la cappella Sistina: documentazione e interpretazione, vol. III, 1996. Mem. Am. com. Medici Archive Project, 1996—; bd. dirs. Raccolta Vinciana, 1997—. Decorated officer Order of Merit (Italy); recipient rsch. award Humboldt Found., 1985, Disting. Tchg. award Lindback Found., 1967, Golden Dozen Tchr. award NYU, 1993, Alumni Great Tchr. award, 1996; Guggenheim fellow, 1976; grantee Henkel Found., 1987, Samuel H. Kress Found., 1999. Mem. Coll. Art Assn. (bd. dirs. 1973-74, 77-81), Renaissance Soc. Am. (editl. bd. 1992—), Soc. Archtl. Historians, N.Y. Acad. Scis., Phi Beta Kappa (v.p. NYU chpt. 1979-81). Avocations: art films, conservation, music, dance. Office: NYU Inst Fine Arts 1 E 78th St New York NY 10021-0119

WEILL, GEORGES GUSTAVE, mathematics educator; b. Strasbourg, France, Apr. 9, 1926; came to U.S., 1956; s. Edmond and Germaine (Falck) W. Ed., Ecole Polytechnique, Paris, 1950; E.N.S., Telecom., Paris, 1952; Licence de Mathematiques, U. Paris, France, 1954, D.Sc. in Physics, 1955; PhD in Math, U. Calif. at Los Angeles, 1960. Research scientist Compagnie Generale de Telegraphie Sans Fil, France, 1952-56; research fellow dept. elec. engring. Calif. Inst. Tech., Pasadena, 1956-59; teaching asso. math. U. Calif. at Los Angeles, 1959-60; research fellow math. Harvard, 1960-62; lectr., research asso. Yale, 1962-64; vis. asst. prof. Belfer Grad. Sch. Sci., Yeshiva U., 1964-65; assoc. prof. math. Poly. U., Bklyn., 1964-65, prof., 1966-95, prof. math. emeritus, 1995—. Adj. prof. math. Cooper Union, N.Y.C. Mem. Am. Math. Soc., Societe Mathematique de France, IEEE (sr. mem.), Sigma Xi, Pi Mu Epsilon. Office: Polytechnic Univ 333 Jay St Brooklyn NY 11201-2990

WEILL, SANFORD I. bank executive; b. N.Y.C., Mar. 16, 1933; s. Max and Etta (Kalika) W.; m. Joan Mosher, June 20, 1955; children: Marc P., Jessica M. BA, Cornell U., 1955, student Grad. Sch. Bus. and Pub. Adminstrn., 1954-55. Chmn. bd., chief exec. officer Carter, Berlind & Weill (name changed to CBWL-Hayden, Stone, Inc. 1970, to Hayden Stone, Inc. 1972, to Shearson Hayden Stone 1974, to Shearson Loeb Rhoades), N.Y.C., 1960-84, dir., chmn. exec. com., 1981-83, pres., 1983-85, Am. Express Co., 1983—85, chmn., CEO Fireman's Fund Ins. Co. subs., 1984-85; chmn., CEO Am. Express Insurance Svcs., Inc. , 1984—85; chmn., pres., chief exec. officer Comml. Credit Co., Balt., 1986—88; chmn., CEO Primerica Corp., N.Y.C., 1988—93, pres., 1988—92; chmn. Primerica Holdings Inc.; chmn., CEO Travelers Group, 1993—98, Citigroup, New York, 1998—. Bd. dirs. Fed. Res. Bank N.Y., AT&T Corp., United Technologies Corp; vice chmn. adv. council The Johnson Grad. Sch. of Mgmt.; founder Acad. of Fin. Mem. bd. overseers Joan and Sanford I. Weill Med. Coll. and Grad. Sch. Med. Scis. of Cornell U. (formerly Cornell Med. Coll.), 1982-, chmn., 1986-; chmn. bd. trustees Carnegie Hall, N.Y.C.; trustee N.Y. Presbyn. Hosp.; bd. overseers Meml. Sloan-Kettering Cancer Ctr.; bd. dirs. Balt. Symphony Orch. Mem. N.Y. Soc. Security Analysts Clubs: Cornell (N.Y.C.), Century Country (Purchase, N.Y.), Harmonie (N.Y.C.). Office: 399 Park Ave New York NY 10022-4614 also: Citigroup 153 E 53rd St New York NY 10043-0001*

WEIMANN, ROBERT BRUCE, retired surgeon; b. Camden, N.J., May 18, 1931; s. Max Ludwig and Ruth Elizabeth (Karl) W.; m. Carol Lee Cain, June 1, 1957; children: Robert Steven, Theodore Harrison, Lauren Lee. AB, Duke U., 1952; MD, Thomas Jefferson U., Phila., 1956. Diplomate Am. Bd. Gen. and Thoracic Surgeons. Intern Thomas Jefferson U. Hosp., Phila., 1956-57; resident surgery Temple U. Med. Ctr., 1957-61; resident thoracic surgery Baylor U. Affiliated Hosps., Houston, 1961-62; mem. staff Cooper Med. ctr., Camden; chief sect. surgery West Jersey Health Systems; prof. surgery emeritus U. Medicine and Dentistry N.J.-Rutgers; ret., 1994. Bd. mem. Am. Cancer Soc., Camden County, N.J., 1963-80. Mem. ACS, Am. Coll. Chest Surgeons, Pan-Pacific Surg. Assn., Del. Valley Vascular Surg. Soc., S. Jersey Vascular Soc. Republican. Methodist. E-mail: weimannmd@aol.com.

WEIMAR, ROBERT HENRY, clinical hypnotherapist; b. Chgo., July 4, 1946; BA in Psychology, U. Ill., 1968; MS in Community Mental Health, No. Ill. U., 1971. Cert. med. hypnotherapist. Cons., edn. coord. No. Community Mental Health Ctr., Ashland, Wis., 1978-79; pvt. practice counselor and cons., 1981-88; alcohol prevention coord. Bad River Chippewa Tribe, Odanah, Wis., 1982-88; prodr. freelance radio programs Ashland, 1984-90, Lynchburg, Va., 1984-90; pvt. practice in hypnotherapy , 1990—. Coord. Va. Divsn. Drug Abuse Control, Richmond, 1972—74; planner N.Y. State Drug Abuse Control Commn., N.Y.C., 1974—75; mental health counselor Ctrl. Health (Bridges), Lynchburg, 1988—90, mental health cons., 1990—; prodr. (self hypnosis audio tapes) What's On It; adj. instr. psychology Nat. Coll., 2000—. Prodr.: Weimar Hypnosis Audio Tape Series on Inductive Therapy; contbr. articles to profl. jours. Recipient Outstanding Svc. award Nat. Indian Bd. on Alcohol and Drug Abuse, 1987. Office: Hypnosis For Health PO Box 10321 Lynchburg VA 24506 E-mail: hypnosu@hypnosumric@zzn.com.

WEIMER, DAVID LEE, educator; b. Buffalo, May 23, 1950; s. Leo Nickolas and Dorthy May (Tates) W.; m. Melanie Frances Manion, June 7, 1990. BS in Engring and BA in Urban Studies, U. Rochester, 1973; M of Pub. Policy, U. Calif., 1975, MA in stats., 1976, PhD, 1978. Grad, intern office rsch. and stats. Social Security Adminstrn., 1974; teaching asst. grad. sch. pub. policy U. Calif., Berkeley, 1975-76; instr. dept. polit. sci. U. Rochester (N.Y.), 1977-78, asst. prof., 1978-82; economist office of policy, planning and analysis U.S. Dept. Energy, 1980-81; assoc. prof. U. Rochester, 1982-86, deputy dir. pub. policy analysis program, 1982-89, prof. polit. sci., pub. policy analysis, 1986-2000; prof. dept. polit. sci. Robert M. La Follette Sch. Pub. Affairs U. Wis., Madison, 2000—. Chevron disting. vis. prof. faculty bus. adminstrn. Simon Fraser U., 1986; disting. vis., prof. Robert M. La Follette Inst. Pub. Affairs U. Wis., Madison, 1989-90; disting. pub. policy lectr. pub. policy program U. N.C., Chapel Hill, 1992; vis. prof. dept. polit. sci. and pub. adminstrn. Peking U., 1993; found. dir. Ctr. For Pub. Policy Studies LIngnan Coll., Hong Kong, 1994-95. Author: Improving Prosecution? The Inducement and Implementation of Innovations for Prosecution Management, 1980, The Strategic Petroleum Reserve: Planning, Implementation and Analysis, 1982, Policy Analysis and Economics: Developments, Tensions, Prospects, 1991; co-editor: Oil Price Stocks, Market Response and Contingency Planning, 1984, Responding to International Oil Crises, 1988, Policy Analysis: Concepts and Practice, 3d edit., 1999, Instl. Design, 1995, Cost Benefit Analysis, 1996, Political Economy of Property Rights, 1997, Organizational Report Cards, 1999; editor Jour. Policy Analysis and Mgmt., 1985-89; author articles. Dir. U.S. Go Congress, Rochester, 1991. Bridging fellow Dept. Pharmacology and Toxicology U. Rochester, 1983. Mem. Assn. Pub. Policy Analysis and Mgmt., Am. Soc. Pub. Adminstrn., Am. Polit. Sci. Assn., Am. Econ. Assn., Am. Risk and Ins. Assn., Am. Go Assn., Phi Beta Kappa. Avocation: Go (Asian game). Office: Robert M La Follette Sch Pub Affairs U Wis Dept Polit Sci Madison WI 53706

WEIMER, DAWN, sculptor; b. Denver, June 11, 1943; d. Morton Weil and Elsie Ione (Gudgel) Griswold; m. Thomas Eugene Weimer, June 14, 1964; 1 child, Heath. Executed bronzes for City of Westminister, Colo., 1996, City of Fort Collins, Colo., 1996-97, City of Loveland, Colo., 1996-97, City of Greeley, Colo., 1996-97, The Shaner Group, State College, Pa., 2000, The Hotel Savery, Des Moines, 2000, Loveland Good Samaritan Village, 2000; represented in permanent collections Lockheed-Martin Corp., Bethesda, Md., Express Pers. Internat. Hdqs., Oklahoma City, Okla., Bliss Industries Inc. Internat. Hdqs., Ponca City, Okla., Am. Quarter Horse Mus., Amarillo, Tex., Colo. State U., Ft. Collins, Smithsonian Nat. Mus. Am. History, Washington; one-woman shows include Bank One, Loveland, 1997, Ft. Morgan County Mus. Recipient Best of Show, First Place award Draft Horse Classic, 1996, Philip Isenberg award Pen and Brush Sculpture Exhibit, 1994, Anna Hyatt Huntington award Am. Artists Pro League, 1993, Best of Show Western Heritage Show, 1998. Mem. Nat. Sculpture Soc., Catharine Lorillard Wolfe Art Club (Leila Gardin Sawyer award 1992), We. Art Assn., We. Heritage Artists. Office: 2727 Eldorado Springs Dr Loveland CO 80538-5321 E-mail: info@dawnweimer.com.

WEIMER, DOUGLAS REID, lawyer; b. Somerset, Pa., Apr. 10, 1953; s. Reid A. and Thelma L. (Lint) W. Student, U. Pa., 1975; BA summa cum laude, U. Pitts., 1975; JD, U. Notre Dame, 1978; postgrad., Oxford U., 1993, Cambridge U., 1996. Bar: Pa. 1978, D.C. 1986, U.S. Supreme Ct. 1986. Law clk. to atty. gen. Pa. Dept. of Justice, Harrisburg, 1974; fed. intern USDA, Washington, 1975, instr., 1991; law clk. to chief judge U.S. Army JAG Corps, 1976; law clk. U.S. Dept. Edn., 1977; atty. U.S. SEC, 1978-79; legis. atty. Congl. Rsch. Svc. Libr. of Congress, 1979—; atty., special detail Office of Gen. Counsel, U.S. Copyright Office, 1994-95. Teaching asst. law sch. U. Notre Dame, Ind., 1976-78; atty. Office of Tech. Assessment, U.S. Congress, Washington, 1988-90; mem. U.S. Del. to Berne Conv., Geneva, 1992; cons. in field. Contbr. articles to profl. jours. Mem. Fed. Bar Assn. (bd. dirs. Younger Lawyers div. 1983-86, Svc. award 1986), D.C. Bar Assn., Pa. Bar Assn., Soc. of Cincinnati (Pa.), Order of Founders and Patriots of Am. (states atty. 1988-2000), SAR (libr. 1986-91), Sons of the Revolution (asst. sec. 1985-92, historian 1992-97, 99-2000), Soc. of Colonial Wars (asst. sec. 1985-92, dep. registrar 1993-94), Soc. of the War of 1812 (historian 1987-96), U. Pitts. at Johnstown Alumni Assn. (coun. 1996—), Racquet Club Phila., Cosmos Club (legal affairs com. 1993-97, history com. 1997—), Phi Eta Sigma (sec. 1973-74), Lambda Iota Tau, Alpha Mu Gamma, Pi Gamma Mu, Phi Alpha Delta (v.p. 1977-78). Avocations: travel, literature, antiques, genealogy, swimming. Home: # 811 2801 New Mexico Ave NW Apt 811 Washington DC 20007-3910 Office: Libr Congress Congrl Rsch Svc Lmm 230 Ald Libr Washington DC 20540-0001

WEIMER, GARY W. academic medical center development executive; b. Louisville, Mar. 28, 1944; s. G. Wilfred and Wanda Ruth (Green) Weimer; married. AB, Princeton U., 1966; M.T.S., Harvard U., 1971. Reporter, copy editor The Vindicator, Youngstown, Ohio, 1970; dir. devel. programs Oberlin (Ohio) Coll., 1971-78; dir. devel. U. Calif., Santa Barbara, 1978-82; v.p. Hiram (Ohio) Coll., 1982-87; sr. devel. officer Case Western Res. U., Cleve., 1987-90; dir. devel. U. Hosps. of Cleve., 1991—2001, sr. v.p. devel., 2002—. Trustee U. Calif. Santa Barbara Found., 1979-82, Robert Maynard Hutchins Ctr. for the Study of Dem. Insts., Santa Barbara, 1979-81. With U.S. Army,

1968-69, Vietnam. James A. Garfield fellow Hiram Coll., 1982, Rockefeller Bros. Theol. fellow Rockefeller and Booth-Ferris Founds., Harvard Divinity Sch., 1966-67; decorated Bronze Star, Air medal, U.S. Army Am. Spirit Honor medal.

WEIMER, JOHN L. state official; b. Thibodaux, Oct. 2, 1954; m. Penny Hymel Weimer; 3 children. BS (with honors), Nicholls State U., 1980; JD, La. State U., 1980. Pvt. practice law, 1980—95; judge 17th Judicial Dist. Ct., 1995—98, 1st Cir. Ct. of Appeal, Dist. 1, Divsn. B, 1998—; justice Supreme Ct. State of La., 2001—. Adj. prof. law Nicholls State U. , 1982—97, prof. law, 1982—97. Mem. Thibodaux Vol. Fire Dept. Recipient Crimefighter's Outstanding Jurist award . Mem.: Lafourche Parish Student Govt. Day Program (creator, coord.), Citizens' Summit Justice Reform (regional co-chmn. 1997), Assumption C. of C., Houma-Terrebonne C. of C., Thibodaux C. of C., Nicholls State U. (mem. alumni bd., former vol. legal counsel), Lafourche Parish Bar Assn., La. State Bar Assn. (del.), Rotary Club. Achievements include development of Lafourche Parish Drug Treatment Court. Mailing: 301 Loyola Ave New Orleans LA 70112*

WEIMER, PETER DWIGHT, mediator, lawyer, corporate executive; b. Grand Rapids, Mich., Oct. 14, 1938; s. Glen E. and Clarabel (Kauffman) W.; children: Melanie, Kim; m. Judith Anne Minor. BA, Bridgewater Coll., 1962; JD, Howard U., 1969. Cert. mediator Supreme Ct. Va. Assoc. counsel Loporto & Weimer Ltd., Manassas, Va., 1970-75; chief counsel Weimer & Cheatle Ltd., 1975-79, Peter D. Weimer, P.C., Manassas, 1979-83; pres., mediator Mediation Ltd., 1981—2002. Pres. Citation Properties, Inc., Manassas, 1971-93; pres. Preferred Rsch. of No. Va., Inc., 1985-89, Pro Rsch. Inc., 1989-93, Pro Mgmt., Inc., 1990—; cons. Continental Title & Escrow, Inc., 1992-96. Address: PO Box 1616 Manassas VA 20108-1616 E-mail: pjweimer@gte.net.

WEIMER, ROBERT JAY, geology educator, energy consultant, civic leader; b. Glendo, Wyo., Sept. 4, 1926; s. John L. and Helen (Mowrey) W.; m. Ruth Carol Adams, Sept. 12, 1948; children: Robert Thomas, Loren Edward (dec.), Paul Christner, Carl Scott. BA, U Wyo., 1948, MA, 1949; PhD, Stanford U., 1953. Registered profl. engr., Colo. Geologist Union Oil Co. Calif., 1949-54; cons. geologist U.S. and fgn. petroleum exploration, 1954—; prof. geology Colo. Sch. Mines, 1957-83, prof. emeritus, 1983—, Getty prof. geology, 1978-83; vis. prof. U. Colo., 1961, U. Calgary, Can., 1970, Inst. Tech., Bandung, Indonesia, 1975. Fulbright lectr. U. Adelaide, South Australia, 1967; disting. lectr. and continuing edn. lectr. Am. Assn. Petroleum Geologists, Soc. Expl. Geophysicists; ednl. cons. to petroleum cos., 1964—; mem. energy rsch. adv. bd. Dept. Energy, 1985-90, Bd. on Mineral and Energy Resources, Nat. Rsch. Coun., 1988. Editor: Guide to Geology of Colorado, 1960, Symposium on Cretaceous Rocks of Colorado and Adjacent Area, 1959, Denver Earthquakes, 1968, Fossil Fuel Exploration, 1974, Studies in Colorado Field Geology, 1976, Petroleum System, Denver Basin, 1996. Trustee Colo. Sch. Mines Research Found., 1967-70; pres. Rockland Found., 1982-83; bd. dirs. Foothills Art Ctr., 1997—. With USNR, 1944-46. Recipient Disting. Alumnus award U. Wyo., 1982, Mines medal Colo. Sch. Mines, 1984, Brown medal, 1990, Parker medal Am. Inst. Profl. Geologists, 1986, Exemplary Alumni award U. Wyo., 1994. Fellow Geol. Soc. Am. (chmn. Rocky Mountain sect. 1966-67), AAAS; mem. Am. Assn. Petroleum Geologists (hon. pres. 1992, Sidney Powers medal 1983, Dist. Educator award 1996), Soc. for Sedimentary Geology (hon., sec.-treas. 1966-67, v.p. 1971, pres. 1972, Twenhofel medal 1995), Colo. Sci. Soc. (hon., pres. 1981), Rocky Mountain Assn. Geologists (hon., pres. 1969, found. bd. 1976-86, Scientist of Yr. 1982), Nigerian Mining and Geoscis. Soc. (hon.), Can. Soc. Petroleum Geologists (hon.), Wyo. Geol. Assn. (hon.), Colo. Sch. Mines Alumni Assn. (hon., Coolbaugh award 1996), Am. Geol. Inst. Found. (sec., treas. 1984-88), Geol. Soc. Am. Found. (bd. dirs.), Nat. Acad. Engring. (ch. sec. 11 1999, ISEM Hedberg award 2001), Northwoodside Inc. Land Conservancy Found. (v.p. 1995-96, pres. 1997—), Mt. Vernon Country Club (Golden, bd. dirs. 1956-59, 81-84, pres. 1983-84). Home: RR 3 25853 Mt Vernon Rd Golden CO 80401-9699 E-mail: rweimer@mines.edu.

WEIMER, WILLIAM ARTHUR, computer company executive, consultant; b. Freeport, Ill., May 9, 1934; s. Lee Henry Weimer and Bonnie Butterfield; m. Julie Ellen Richards, Sept. 10, 1995; children: Lee J., Mark W., Jay A., Kent J. BS in Physics, Purdue U., 1956. Various sales, system engring, human resources IBM, 1956-89, mgr. Europe's external edn. dept. Belgium; spkr., cons. U.S., Europe, 1990-91, 93—; with European Inst. of Tech., Verona, Italy, 1991; pres. EuroPace, Paris, 1992-93. Contbr. articles to profl. jours. Avocations: hiking, cooking, reading, genealogy. Home: 34 Windward Dr Asheville NC 28803

WEIN, ALAN JEROME, urologist, educator, researcher; b. Newark, Dec. 15, 1941; s. Isadore R. and Jeanette Frances (Abrams) W. AB cum laude, Princeton U., 1962; MD, U. Pa., 1966. Diplomate, trustee emeritus Am. Bd. Urology. Intern mixed surgery Hosp. U. Pa., Phila., 1966-67, resident surgery, 1967-68; resident urology U. Pa., 1969-72, fellow Harrison Dept. Surg. Rsch. Urology Sch. Medicine, 1968-69, asst. instr. surgery Sch. Medicine, 1967-68, asst. instr. urology, 1969-71, instr., 1971-72, asst. prof., 1974-76, assoc. prof., 1976-83, prof., 1983—, asst. chief urology, 1974-79, dir. Urodynamic Evaluation Ctr., 1974—, chmn. div. urology, 1981—, chief urology, 1981—. Dir. resident edn. com. div. urology Sch. Medicine U. Pa., 1976—, coord. program urologics oncology, 1976—; chief urology VA Hosp., Phila., 1974-82, attending urologist, 1982-96; asst. surgeon Children's Hosp. Phila., 1974—; cons. CDC Coun. Incontinence, 1990—; assoc. surgeon Pa. Hosp., Phila., 1977—; attending urologist Grad. Hosp., Phila., 1980-97. Author: (with D.M. Barrett) Controversies in Neuro-Urology, 1984, Voiding Function and Dysfunction: A Logical and Practical Approach, 1988, 2d edit., 1995, (with A.R. Mundy and T.P. Stephenson) Urodynamics: Principles, Practice and Application, 1984, 2d edit., 1994, (with P.M. Hanno) A Clinical Manual of Urology, 1987, 2d edit., 1994, (with Hanno, Staskin and Krane) Interstitial Cystitis, 1990; editl. bd. asst. Urol. Survey, 1978-81; editl. bd. cons. Investigative Urology, 1978-81; mem. editl. bd. World Jour. Urology, 1982—, Am. Urol. Assn. Update series, 1983—, Urol. Survey, 1987—, Internat. Jour. Impotence Rsch.: Basic and Clin. Studies, 1989-99, Urology, 1991—; ad hoc reviewer Cancer, 1985—; cons. editor Sexuality and Disability, 1985—; asst. editor Jour. Urology, 1980-89, ad hoc reviewer clin. sect., 1989—, editl. bd. investigative sect., 1989—; assoc. editor Neurourlogy and Urodynamics, 1982—; contbr. over 600 articles and abstracts to profl. jours. Mem. coun. urology Nat. Kidney Found., Inc.; mem lectrs. bur. Am. Cancer Soc., 1984—; mem. adv. panel Nat. Assn. for Incontinence, 1987—; mem. adv. bd. Simon Found., 1987—; mem. med. adv. bd. Institial Cystitis Assn., 1987—; chmn. bladder health coun. Am. Found. Urologic Disease, 1990-95; trustee Am. Bd. Urology, 1990-96. Maj. MC, U.S. Army, 1972-74. Grantee VA, 1974-79, 79, 81, 81-84, 82-85, 85-88, 88-92, Eaton Labs., 1975-76, 78-80, McCabe Rsch. Fund, 1975-82, 87-88, Merrell Nat. Labs., 1979-82, 1980-82, Nat. Kidney Found., 1980-81, NIH, 1980-83, 83-88, 84-87, 87—, Roche Labs., 1981, Smith Kline and French Labs., 1982, 86-88, Eli Lilly Labs., 1986-88, 91, Found. Interstitial Cystitis, 1986-87, 87-88, Sterling Drug Co., 1991; recipient F. Brantley Scott award Am. Found. for Urologic Disease, 1996, Hugh Hampton Young award, 1997, AUA Disting. Svc. award, 2000, AUA Disting. Contbn. award, 2001. Fellow ACS; mem. AAAS, AMA (cons. com. drug evaluation 1977-90), Am. Acad. Clin. Neurophysiology, Am. Assn. Surgery of Trauma, Am. Assn. Clin. Urologists, Am. Assn. Genito-Urinary Surgeons, Am. Surg. Assn., Am. Soc. Pharmacology and Exptl. Therapeutics, Am. Soc. Andrology, Am. Soc. Clin. Oncology, Am. Urol. Assn. (chmn. practical cases urology 1982—, rsch. com. 1985—, editl. com. mid-Atlantic sect. 1988—, pub. rels. adv. bd. 1998—, Disting. Svc. award 2000), Assn. Acad. Surgery, Can. Urol. Assn., Clin. Soc. Genito-Urinary Surgeons, Ea. Coop. Oncologic Group, Endourol. Soc., Internat. Continence Soc., Nat. Assn. VA Physicians, N.Y. Acad. Scis., Coll. Physicians Phila., John Morgan Soc., Pa. Med. Assn., Pa. Oncologic Soc., Phila. Acad. Surgery, Phila. County Med. Soc., Phila. Profl. Standards Rev. Orgn., Phila. Urologic Soc. (pres. 1990-91), Ravdin-Rhoads Surg. Soc., Urol. Assn. Pa., Radiation Therapy Oncology Group (genitourinary working com. 1980—), Royal Soc. Medicine, Soc. Internat. d'Urologie, Soc. Basic Urologic Rsch., Soc. Sex Therapy and Rsch., Soc. Govt. Svc. Urologists, Soc. Pelvic Surgeons, Soc. Univ. Surgeons, Soc. Univ. Urologists (counselor 1996—, pres. 1999-2000), Soc. Urologic Oncology, Univ. Urologic Forum, Urodynamics Soc. (exec. com. 1980—, Lifetime Achievement award 1996), Urologic Rsch. Soc., Urologist's Corr. Club, Sigma Xi. Home: 1224 Mirabeau Ln Gladwyne PA 19035-1048 Office: Hosp U Pa 1 Rhoads Pavilion 3400 Spruce St Philadelphia PA 19104-4206

WEINBACH, ARTHUR FREDERIC, computing services company executive; b. Waterbury, Conn., May 3, 1943; s. Max and Winifred (Eckstein) W.; m. Joanne Kaplan, Nov. 20, 1970; children: Michael Scott, Jonathan David. BS in Econs., U. Pa., 1965, MS in Acctg., 1966. CPA. With Touche Ross & Co., N.Y.C., 1966-75, ptnr. Stamford, Conn., 1976-79; v.p. Automatic Data Processing, Inc., Roseland, N.J., 1980-81, sr. v.p. adminstrn. and fin., 1982-91, exec. v.p., 1992-94, pres., 1994-98, CEO, 1996—, also bd. dirs., 1989—, chmn., 1998. Bd. dirs. Schering-Plough Corp., First Data Corp. Bd. dirs. Boys Hope, 1991—, Overlook Hosp. Found., 1991-98, Metro N.J. U. Pa. Club, 1993-99, N.J. Inst. Tech., 1998—, N.J. Seeds, 1997—, United Way of Tri-State, 1998—. Jewish. Home: One Twin Oak Rd Short Hills NJ 07078-1208 Office: ADP Inc 1 A D P Blvd Roseland NJ 07068-1786

WEINBACH, LAWRENCE ALLEN, computer company executive; b. N.Y.C., Jan. 8, 1940; s. Max N. and Winifred E. Weinbach; m. Patricia Leiter, Dec. 1961; children: Wendy, Peter, Daniel. BS in Econs., U. Pa., 1961. CPA. With Andersen Worldwide, N.Y.C., 1961-97, mng. ptnr. Stamford, Conn., 1974-80, N.Y.C., 1980-83, mng. ptnr. N.Y. Met. area, 1983-87, COO, 1987-89, mng. ptnr., CEO, 1989-97; chmn., pres., CEO Unisys Corp, Blue Bell, Pa., 1997—. Bd. dirs. Avon Products, Inc., Unisys Corp., UBS, AG. Trustee Carnegie Hall, U. Pa., Catalyst; mem bd. overseers Wharton Sch., U. Pa.; mem. Greater Phila. First, Phila.; life trustee emeritus Northwestern U.; trustee cancer ctr. bd. U. Pa.; mem. adv. com. NYSE Listed Co., Nat. Security Telecomm. Mem. Harmonie Club, Beta Gamma Sigma, Beta Alpha Psi. Office: Unisys Corp Unisys Way Blue Bell PA 19424-0001

WEINBAUM, SHELDON, biomedical engineer; b. Bklyn., July 26, 1937; s. Alexander Weinbaum and Frances Clare (Stark) Colby; m. Alexandra Tamara Weinbaum, June 10, 1962; children: Alys Eve, Daniel Eden. BAE, Rensselaer Polytech. Inst., Troy, 1959; MS, Harvard U., 1960, PhD, 1963. Mem. rsch. staff Sperry Rand Rsch. Lab., Sudbury, Mass., 1963-64; prin. rsch. scientist Avco Everett Rsch. Lab., Everett, 1964, G.E. Space Sci. Lab., Valley Forge, Pa., 1964-67; assoc. prof. CCNY, 1967-72, H. Kayser Prof., 1980-85; CUNY Disting. Prof., 1986—; dir. N.Y. Ctr. Biomed. Engring. CUNY, 1994-99. Vis. prof. Imperial Coll. Sci. and Tech., London, 1973—74, MIT, 1980—81; Russell S. Springer vis. prof. U. Calif., Berkeley, 1979—80; sr. fellow Sci. Rsch. Coun. Gt. Britain, 1973—74. Chair legal action com. CCNY, 1992—96. Recipient Pub. Svc. award, Fund for City of N.Y., 1988, Rsch. award, European Soc. Biomechanics, 1994, Spl. Creativity award, NSF, 1985—87; fellow Gordon McKay prize, Harvard U., 1959—60, NSF, 1961—63, John Simon Guggenheim, 2002. Fellow: NAE (acad. adv. coun. 1998—2000), ASME (H.R. Lissner award 1994, Melville medal 1996, Classic Paper award Heat Transfer divsn. 2000), Nat. Acad. Sci., Am. Inst. Med. Bio. Engring., Am. Phys. Soc.; mem.: Biomed. Engring. Soc. (bd. dirs. 1989—92, Whitaker Disting. lectr. 1997). Achievements include contributions in the broad application of engineering principles to the understanding of biological and medical processes; including Weinbaum-Caro model for transport in artery wall, water and solute transport in capillary interendothelial clefts; new interpretation of Starling hypothesis, Weinbaum-Jiji bioheat equation, plasma skimmings and red cell screening in blood flow; leaky junction-cell turnover hypothesis, for LDL transport, model for intraocular fluid mechanics, transport models for the arterial intima and artherogenesis; fluid shear hypothesis for activation of osteocytes, mechano-sensory mechanisms for bone growth and brush border microvilli in kidney, fundamental fluid mechanics; contributions include particle and boundary interactions at low Reynolds number, non-linear lubrication theory in highly compresible porous media, high altitude near wake, mechanics of skiing. Office: City Coll City of New York Convent Ave & 137th St New York NY 10031 E-mail: weinbaum@ccny.cuny.edu.

WEINBERG, ALVIN MARTIN, physicist; b. Chgo., Apr. 20, 1915; s. J.L. and Emma (Levinson) W.; m. Margaret Despres, June 14, 1940 (dec. 1969); children: David, Richard; m. Gene K. DePersio, Sept. 20, 1974. AB, U. Chgo., 1935, A.M., 1936, PhD, 1939; LL.D., U. Chattanooga, Alfred U.; D.Sc., U. Pacific, Denison U., Wake Forest U., Kenyon Coll., Worcester Poly. Inst., U. Rochester, Stevens Inst. Tech., Butler U., U. Louisville, U. Bridgeport. Research assoc. math. biophysics U. Chgo., 1939-41, Metall. Lab., 1941-45; joined Oak Ridge Nat. Lab., 1945, dir. physics div., 1947-48, research dir. lab., 1948-55, dir. lab., 1955-74; dir. Office Energy R&D, Fed. Energy Adminstrn., 1974, Inst. Energy Analysis, Oak Ridge, 1975-85; disting. fellow Oak Ridge Associated Univs., 1985—. Mem. Pres.'s Sci. Adv. Com., 1960-62, Pres.'s Medal of Sci. Com. Author: Reflections on Big Science, (with E.P. Wigner) Physical Theory of Neutron Chain Reactors, 1958, Continuing the Nuclear Dialogue, 1985, Nuclear Reactions: Science and Trans-Science, 1992, The First Nuclear Era: The Life and Times of a Technological Fixer, 1994; co-author: The Second Nuclear Era, 1985; co-editor: The Nuclear Connection, 1985, Strategic Defenses and Arms Control, 1987; editor: Eugene Wigner's Collected Works on Nuclear Energy. Recipient Atoms for Peace award, 1960, E.O. Lawrence award, 1960, U. Chgo. Alumni medal, 1966, Heinrich Hertz award, 1975, N.Y. Acad. Scis. award, 1976, Enrico Fermi award, 1980, Harvey prize, 1982, Eugene Wigner award in reactor physics, 1992. Mem. Nat. Acad. Scis. (applied sci. sect.), Am. Nuclear Soc. (pres. 1959-60, Alvin M. Weinberg award 1996), Nat. Acad. Engring., Am. Acad. Arts and Scis., Am. Philos. Soc., Royal Netherlands Acad. Sci. (fgn. asso.) Home: 111 Moylan Ln Oak Ridge TN 37830-5351 Office: Oak Ridge Associated Univs PO Box 117 Oak Ridge TN 37831-0117

WEINBERG, DALE GLASER, technical writer, consultant, trainer; b. N.Y.C., Oct. 21, 1948; d. Milton and Joyce I. (Litsky) Glaser; m. Howard Weinberg, June 20, 1971 (separated); 1 child, Tracy J. BS in English Edn., NYU, 1971; MS in English Edn., Iona Coll., New Rochelle, N.Y., 1975. Lic. secondary tchr. English, N.Y. Programmer, documentation adminstr. ITT Continental Baking, Rye, N.Y., 1971-78; owner, pres. Techically Write, Eastchester, 1978—. Cons., course leader, tchr. writing seminars throughout U.S., Am. Mgmt. Assn., N.Y.C., 1980; designer, tchr. bus. writing Am. Mgmt. Assn.-Operation Enterprise, Hamilton, N.Y., 1998; ind. tech. writing and tng. cons., 1978—. Editor: Money Smarts, 1982, A Funny Thing Happened on the Way to the Interview, 1995; designer, editor, prodr. 3 major publs. Eastchester (N.Y.) Mid. Sch., 1993—; assoc. editor Calif. Ride Reporter, 1993—. Recipient Spl. Svc. award/citation for publs. Eastchester Mid. Sch., 1994. Mem. IEEE Profl. Comm. Soc. (assoc.), Soc. Tech. Comm. (sr.), Assn. Computing Machinery. Avocations: scuba diving, yoga, skiing, theater, reading, travel. Office: Technically Write 19 Soundview Dr Eastchester NY 10709-1526

WEINBERG, DAVID B. investor; b. Chgo., Feb. 19, 1952; s. Judd A. and Marjorie (Gottlieb) W.; m. Lynne Ellen Mesirow, July 6, 1980. AB cum laude, Harvard U., 1974; JD, Georgetown U., 1977. Bar: Ill. 1977, U.S. Dist. Ct. (no. dist.) Ill. 1977, U.S. Ct. Appeals (7th cir.) 1978. Law clerk to Hon. William G. Clark Supreme Ct. Ill., 1977-79; assoc. Lord, Bissell & Brook, Chgo., 1979-84, ptnr., 1985-89, Mayer, Brown & Platt, Chgo., 1989-96; chmn., CEO Judd Enterprises, Inc., 1996—; pres. Digital BandWidth LLC, 1996—; dir. NFR Security, Inc., Rockville, Md., 2001—. Ill. Supreme Ct. com. Profl. Responsibility, Chgo., 1984-94, chmn. subcom. lawyers certification. Chmn. bd. trustees Ravinia Festival Assn., Highland Park, Ill., 1998—2001; vice chmn. bd. trustees Northwestern U., 1999—. Mem. Chgo. Club, Standard Club Chgo. (d ir. 1988-90), Econ. Club Chgo., Lake Shore Country Club, Arts Club Chgo., Comml. Club Chgo., Civic Com. Office: Judd Enterprises Bank One Plz 21 S Clark St Ste 3140 Chicago IL 60603-2090

WEINBERG, EUGENE DAVID, microbiologist, educator; b. Chgo., Mar. 4, 1922; s. Philip and Lenore (Bergman) W.; m. Frances Murl Izen, Sept. 5, 1949; children— Barbara Ann, Marjorie Jean, Geoffrey Alan, Michael Benjamin. BS, U. Chgo., 1942, MA, 1948, PhD, 1950. Instr. dept. microbiology Ind. U., Bloomington, 1950-53, asst. prof., 1953-57, asso. prof., 1957-61, prof., 1961—, head microbiology sect., med. sci. program, 1978—. Served with AUS, 1942-45. Mem. AAAS, Am. Soc. Microbiology. Office: Ind U Biology Dept Jordan Hall Bloomington IN 47405 Fax: 812-855-6705. E-mail: eweinber@indiana.edu.

WEINBERG, GERHARD LUDWIG, history educator; b. Hannover, Germany, Jan. 1, 1928; came to U.S., 1940, naturalized, 1949; s. Max Bendix and Kate Sarah (Gruenebaum) W.; m. Janet Kabler White, Apr. 29, 1989. BA, N.Y. State Coll. Tchrs., Albany, 1948; MA, U. Chgo., 1949, PhD, 1951; LHD honoris causa, SUNY, Albany, 1989; PhD (hon.), U. Hannover, 2001. Research analyst War Documentation project Columbia U., 1951-54; vis. lectr. history U. Chgo., 1954-55, U. Ky., Lexington, 1955-56; dir. project microfilming captured German documents Am. Hist. Assn., 1956-57; asst. prof. U. Ky., 1957-59; mem. faculty U. Mich., Ann Arbor, 1959-74, prof. history, 1963-74, chmn. dept., 1972-73; William Rand Kenan, Jr. prof. history U. N.C., Chapel Hill, 1974-99, prof. emeritus, 1999—, acting chmn. dept., 1989-90. Vis. prof. Bonn U., 1983, USAF Acad., 1990-91; Shapiro sr. scholar-in-residence U.S. Holocaust Meml. Mus., 2001--; bd. dirs. World War II Studies Assn., 1968—; cons. in field. Author: Guide to Captured German Documents, 1952, Germany and the Soviet Union, 1939-41, 1954, The Foreign Policy of Hitler's Germany, 1933-36, 1970, The Foreign Policy of Hitler's Germany, 1937-39, 1980, World in the Balance: Behind the Scenes of World II, 1981, A World at Arms: A Global History of World War II, 1994, Germany, Hitler and World War II, 1995; co-author: Soviet Partisans in World War II, 1964; editor: Hitlers zweites Buch, 1961, 95, Transformation of a Continent, 1975; bd. editors Jour. Modern History, 1970-72, Central European History, 1970-72, Kansas Humanities Series, 1987—, Internat. History Rev., 1990-2000, Jour. Intelligence History, 2001—. Chmn. Ann Arbor Democratic Com., 1961-63; mem. Mich. Dem. Central Com., 1963-67; mem. adv. com. on the air force history program Sec. of Air Force, 1987-90; mem. adv. com. army history program Sec. Army, 1996—, chmn., 1998—; mem. dept. defence Hist. Records Declassification Adv. Panel, 1996—. Wwith AUS, 1946-47. Fellow Social Sci. Research Council, 1962-63; fellow Am. Council Learned Socs., 1965-66; fellow Guggenheim Found., 1971-72; fellow Nat. Endowment Humanities, 1978-79 Mem. Am. Hist. Assn. (George Louis Beer prize 1971, 95, v.p. rsch. 1982-84), So. Hist. Assn. (chmn. European sect. 1989), Conf. Group for Ctrl. European History (chmn. 1982), Coordinating Com. Women in Hist. Profession, German Studies Assn. (exec. com. 1989-92, Halverson prize 1981, v.p. 1994-96, pres. 1996-98), World War II Studies Assn., Am. Acad. Arts and Scis., Phi Beta Kappa. Jewish. Home: 1416 Mount Willing Rd Efland NC 27243-9646 E-mail: gweinber@email.unc.edu.

WEINBERG, H. BARBARA, art historian, educator, curator paintings and sculpture; b. N.Y.C., Jan. 23, 1942; d. Max and Evelyn Kallman; m. Michael B. Weinberg, Aug. 30, 1964. AB, Barnard Coll., 1962; MA, Columbia U., N.Y.C., 1964, PhD, 1972. From asst. prof. to prof. art history Queens Coll. and Grad. Sch., CUNY, 1972-94; curator Am. paintings and sculpture Met. Mus. Art., 1990-98; Alice Pratt Brown curator Am. paintings and sculpture Met. Mus. Art, 1998—. Author: The Decorative Work of John La Farge, 1977, The American Pupils of Jean-Léon Gérome, 1984, The Lure of Paris: Nineteenth-Century American Painters and Their French Teachers, 1991, Thomas Eakins and the Metropolitan Museum of Art, 1994; co-author: American Impressionism and Realism: The Painting of Modern Life, 1885-1915, 1994, Am. Drawings and Watercolors in The Metropolitan Mus. of Art: John Singer Sargent, 2000; John Singer Sargent in The Metropolitan Mus. Art, 2000; mem. editorial bd. Am. Art Jour., 1984—. Mem.: Phi Beta Kappa. Office: Met Mus Art 1000 5th Ave New York NY 10028-0113

WEINBERG, HEDY LEAH, journalist; b. Utica, N.Y., Oct. 15, 1939; d. S. Joshua and Priva (Konowitz) Kohn; m. Michael Davis Weinberg, Aug. 7, 1960; children: Benjamin Thomas, Shira Beth, Adam Jerome. BA, NYU, 1961; student, Brandeis U., 1957-60; M in Spl. Studies, U. Denver, 1985. Substitute tchr. N.Y. Bd. Edn., Bklyn., 1961-64; staff writer, contbg. editor Sr. Edition USA, Denver, 1987-91; instr. writing divsn. extended studies U. Colo., 1992-94; v.p. Weinberg Group, Inc., 1996—. Co-author: Living with Hepatitis C: A Survivor's Guide, 1997, 3d edit., 2002 (1st Place Non-Fiction, Colo. Press Women 1998), My Mom Has Hepatitis C, 2000, Living with Hepatitis B: A Survivor's Guide, 2002. Recipient Journalism award Leukemia Soc. Am., 1987, Third Place Personality Profile, Nat. Fedn. Press Women, 1989, First Place Articles/Essays, Nat. Writers Assn., 1995. Mem. Am. Soc. Journalists and Authors, Authors Guild, Soc. Profl. Journalists, Colo. Authors League, Denver Woman's Press Club. Office: 4025 S Oneida St Denver CO 80237-2045 E-mail: hedy_twgi@msn.com.

WEINBERG, HERSCHEL MAYER, lawyer; b. Bklyn., Oct. 13, 1927; s. Jacob and Gertrude (Wernick) W. BA, Bklyn. Coll., 1948; LL.B., Harvard U., 1952. Bar: N.Y. 1952. Atty. firm Payne & Steingarten, N.Y.C., 1952-57, Jacobs, Persinger & Parker, N.Y.C., 1957-61; partner firm Rubin, Rubin, Weinberg, & Di Paola, 1961-78, Weinberg Tauber & Pressman, 1979-90; pvt. practice N.Y.C., 1990—. Served with AUS, 1946-47. Mem. Assn. of Bar of City of N.Y., N.Y. State Bar Assn. Clubs: Harvard (N.Y.C.). Home: 50 Sutton Pl S New York NY 10022-4167 Office: 110 E 59th St New York NY 10022-1304

WEINBERG, HUBERT, plastic surgeon; b. Clermont-Ferrant, France, Feb. 2, 1950; came to U.S., 1955; s. Paul and Esther Weinberg; m. Rita Weinberg, June 24, 1974; children: Deborah, Nevin, Michael, Jennifer, Lauren, Aimee. BA, Yeshiva U., 1971; MD, Cornell U., 1975. Diplomate Am. Bd. Plastic Surgery. Intern, resident Mt. Sinai Hosp.; instr. Mt. Sinai Med. Ctr., N.Y.C., 1982-84, assoc. prof., 1984-97, prof., 1998-2000; clin. prof., 2000—; assoc. attending physician Mt. Sinai Med. Ctr., N.Y.C., 1984-97, dir. microsurgery rsch. dept., 1982-2000, attending physician, 1998—, Westchester Med. Ctr., Valhalla, N.Y., 2000—. Adj. prof. N.Y. Med. Coll., 2000—. Author: (with others) Musculoskeletal Oncology, 1992; contbr. articles to profl. jours. including Current Surgery, Plastic Reconstrn. Surgery, and Jour. Reconstructive Microsurgery. Recipient 2d pl. award Plastic Surgery Ednl. Found., 1983. Fellow ACS, N.Y. Acad. Scis. (1st prize awards 1987, 93); mem. Am. Soc. Plastic and Reconstructive Surgeons, Am. Assn. Plastic Surgeons. Avocations: computer graphics, gardening, landscaping. Office: Westchester Med Ctr Burn Ctr Macy Pavilion Valhalla NY 10595 E-mail: weinbh01@doc.mssm.edu.

WEINBERG, JOHN LEE, federal judge; b. Chgo., Apr. 24, 1941; s. Louis Jr. and Jane Kitz (Goldstein) W.; m. Sarah Kibbee, July 6, 1963; children: Ruth, Leo. BA, Swarthmore Coll., 1962; JD, U. Chgo., 1965. Bar: Ill. 1966, Wash. 1967, U.S. Dist. Ct. (we. dist.) Wash. 1967, U.S. Ct. Appeals (9th cir.) 1967. Law clk. to Hon. Henry L. Burman Ill. Appellate Ct., Chgo., 1965-66; law clk. to Hon. Walter V. Schaefer Ill. Supreme Ct., 1966; law clk. to Hon. William T. Beeks U.S. Dist. Ct. Wash., Seattle, 1967-68; atty. Perkins Coie Law Firm, 1968-73; magistrate judge U.S. Dist. Ct.; U.S. Magistrate judge Seattle, 1973—. Author: Federal Bail and Detention Handbook, 1988. Mem. ABA, Am. Judicature Soc., Wash. State Bar Assn., Seattle-King County Bar Assn., Fed. Magistrate Judges Assn. (nat. pres. 1982-83). Avocations: sports and physical fitness activities, bridge. Office: US Magistrate Judge 304 US Courthouse 1010 5th Ave Seattle WA 98104-1195

WEINBERG, JOHN LIVINGSTON, investment banker; b. N.Y.C., Jan. 5, 1925; s. Sidney James and Helen (Livingston) W.; m. Sue Ann Gotshal, Dec. 6, 1952; children: Ann K. (dec.), John, Jean. AB cum laude, Princeton U., 1948; MBA, Harvard U., 1950. With Goldman, Sachs & Co., N.Y.C., 1950—, ptnr., 1956-76, sr. ptnr., 1976-90, co-chmn. mgmt. com., 1976-84, sr. ptnr., chmn. mgmt. com., 1984-90, sr. chmn., 1990-2001, ret., 2001. Sr. chmn. The Goldman Sachs Group, Inc., 2002; bd. dirs. Knight-Rider, Inc., Tricon Global Restaurants, Inc.; mem. Conf. Bd. Dir. emeritus N.Y. and Presbyn. Hosps. 2d lt. USMCR, 1942-46, capt., 1951-52. Fellow AAAS; mem. Va. Neurol. Inst., Coun. on Fgn. Rels., Bus. Coun. (grad.), DeWitt Wallace Fund for Meml. Sloan Kettering Cancer Ctr. Office: Goldman Sachs Group Inc Ste 1002 375 Park Ave New York NY 10152 E-mail: john.l.weinberg@gs.com.

WEINBERG, LEONARD BURTON, political scientist; b. N.Y.C., Nov. 10, 1939; s. Max R. and Rose (Levin) W.; m. Ellen Bach, Aug. 23, 1966 (div.); 1 son, David; m. Sinikka Palomaki, June 4, 1986. BA, Syracuse U., 1961, PhD, 1967; MA, U. Chgo., 1963. Instr. polit. sci. U. Wis., Milw., 1966-67; asst. prof. polit. sci. U. Nev., Reno, 1967-71, assoc. prof., 1971-78, prof., 1978—, chmn. dept., 1979-82. Vis. prof. U. Florence, Italy, 1992. Author: Comparing Public Policies, 1977, After Mussolini, 1979, The Rise and Fall of Italian Terrorism, 1987, Introduction to Political Terrorism, 1989; editor: Political Parties and Terrorist Groups, 1992, Revival of Right-Wing Extremism in the 1990s, 1996, Political Violence and the Democratic Experience. 2000; co-editor: Encounters with the Radical Right, 1992, The Transformation of Italian Communism,

1994, Revival of Right-Wing Extremism in the 1990s, 1997, The Emergence of a Euro-American Radical, 1998. Recipient Fulbright Rsch. award, 1984; Italian Govt. Borsa di Studio, 1965-66; Fulbright grantee, 1965-66, Harry F. Guggenheim grantee, 1995-96. Mem. Am. Polit. Sci. Assn., Internat. Polit. Sci. Assn. (political sociology com.), Conf. Group on Italian Politics of Am. Polit. Sci. Assn., Phi Kappa Phi. Jewish. Office: U Nev Dept Polit Sci Reno NV 89557-0001 E-mail: WeirBrl@unr.nevada.edu.

WEINBERG, LILA SHAFFER, writer, editor; d. Sam and Blanche (Hyman) Shaffer; m. Arthur Weinberg, Jan. 25, 1953; children: Hedy Merrill Cornfield, Anita Michelle Miller, Wendy Clare Rothman. Editor Ziff-Davis Pub. Co., 1944—53; assoc. chief manuscript editor jours. U. Chgo. Press, 1966—80, sr. manuscript editor books, 1980—98; mem. faculty Sch. for New Learning DePaul U., Chgo., 1979—89. Vis. faculty continuing edn. programs U. Chgo., 1984-92. Author: (with A. Weinberg) The Muckrakers, 1961 (selected for White House Library 1963), Verdicts Out of Court, 1963, Instead of Violence, 1963, Passport to Utopia, 1968, Some Dissenting Voices, 1970, Clarence Darrow: A Sentimental Rebel, 1980; contbr. articles and revs. to various publs. Bd. dirs. Hillel Found. U. Chgo., 1988-96. Recipient Friends of Lit. award Chgo. Found. Lit., 1980, Social Justice award Darrow Community Ctr., 1980, Disting. Body of Work award Friends of Midwest Authors, 1987. Mem. Soc. Midland Authors (dir. 1977-83, pres. 1983-85, Best Biography award 1980), ACLU, Clarence Darrow Commemorative Com., YIVO, Authors' League. Home: 5421 S Cornell Ave Chicago IL 60615-5646 E-mail: lilawein@aol.com.

WEINBERG, LORETTA, state legislator; b. N.Y.C., Feb. 6, 1935; d. Murray Isaacs and Raya Hamilton; m. Irwin S. Weinberg, July 25, 1960 (dec. Feb. 1999); children: Daniel J., Francine S. BA, UCLA, 1956. Former aide N.J. Assemblyman D. Bennett Mazur, Trenton; mem. N.J. Assembly, 1992—. Mem. Teaneck Coun., 1990-94. Recipient Legis. Leadership award No. N.J. Chiropractic Assn., 1992, Woman of Achievement award Bus. and Profl. Women's Club of East Bergen, 1993, Carrie Chapman Catt award No. N.J. NOW, 1997, Ethical Recognition award Ethical Culture Soc. of Bergen County, 1998; named Citizen of Yr. N.J. Jewish War Vets., Legislator of Yr., 2000. Mem. Nat. Coun. Jewish Women (life mem., Hannah G. Solomon award 1995, Disting. Achievement award Women's Commn.). Democrat. Jewish. Office: State of NJ 545 Cedar Ln Teaneck NJ 07666-1740

WEINBERG, LOUISE, law educator, author; b. N.Y.C. m. Steven Weinberg; 1 child, Elizabeth. AB summa cum laude, Cornell U.; JD, Harvard U., 1969, LLM, 1974. Bar: Mass. Sr. law clk. Hon. Chas. E. Wyzanski, Jr., Boston, 1971-72; assoc. in law Bingham, Dana & Gould, 1969-72; teaching fellow Harvard Law Sch., 1972-74; lectr. law Brandeis U., Waltham, Mass., 1974; assoc. prof. law Suffolk U., Boston, 1974-76, prof., 1977-80; vis. assoc. prof. law Stanford U., Palo Alto, Calif., 1976-77; vis. prof. law U. Tex., Austin, 1979; prof. law Sch. Law, U. Tex., 1980-84, Thompson prof. law, 1984-90, Andrews and Kurth prof. law, 1990-92; Fulbright and Jaworski regents rsch. prof. U. Tex., 1991-92, Angus G. Wynne, Sr. prof. civil jurisprudence, 1992-97, Fondren chair faculty excellence, 1995—, Eugene R. Smith Centennial rsch. prof. law, 1993-97, holder William B. Bates chair adminstrn. justice, 1997—. Vis. scholar Hebrew U., Jerusalem, 1989; Forum fellow World Econ. Forum, Davos, Switzerland, 1995—; pub. spkr., lectr. in field. Author: Federal Courts: Judicial Federalism and Judicial Power, 1994, and ann. supplements; co-author: Conflict of Laws, 1990, 2d edit., 2002; contbr. chpts. to books, articles to profl. jours. Bd. dirs. Ballet Austin, 1986-88, Austin Coun. on Fgn. Affairs, 1985—. Recipient Disting. Educator award Tex. Exes Assn., 1996. Mem.: Am. Constn. Soc. for Law and Pub. Policy, Maritime Law Assn., Tex. Asian C. of C., Assn. Am. Law Schs. (chmn. com. on conflict laws 1991—93, exec. com. sect. on fed. cts. 2001—02, program chair 2002—, chair-elect 2002—03), The Philos. Soc. Tex., Am. Law Inst. (consultative com. complex litigation 1989—93, consultative com. enterprise liability 1990—95, adv. group fed. judicial code revision project 1996—2001), Scribes, Phi Kappa Phi, Phi Beta Kappa. Office: U Tex Sch Law 727 Dean Keeton St Austin TX 78705-3224 E-mail: lweinberg@mail.law.utexas.edu. *Personal philosophy: The right thing is usually also the humane and liberal thing.*

WEINBERG, LOUISE, artist, curator; b. Chgo., Nov. 5, 1954; d. Samuel Charles and Nancy (Stein) W. Student, U. Wis.-Parkside, Kenosha, 1975; BFA, U. Wis., Madison, 1983, MFA, 1986. Gallery asst. U. Wis.-U. Galleries, Madison, 1979-83; curatorial asst. Madison Art Ctr., 1983-85, registrar, 1985-86; asst. curator, registrar Queens Mus. Art, Flushing, N.Y., 1986-89; mng. dir. Feuerman Studios, N.Y.C., 1989-99; arts adminstr., curator Louise Weinberg & Assocs., Long Island City, N.Y., 1994—; exhbn. coord. Queens Mus. Art, Flushing, 2000-01, Hudson River Mus., Yonkers, NY, 2001—02. Cons. for art collection Rayovac Corp., Madison, 1985; juror art exhbn. Hicksville (N.Y.) Art Assn., 1990, Nat. Art League, Douglaston, N.Y., 1999; artist cons., guest curator Flushing Coun. on Culture and the Arts, 1996—; cons. Artists' Videos, 1998-2001; juror Nat. Art League, Douglaston, N.Y., 1999; curatorial panelist MTA Arts for Transit, 2002; art tour guide The New We. Frontier, Flushing Town Hall, 2002; facilitator IMAGINE N.Y., Mcpl. Arts Soc., 2002. One-woman shows include Ctr. Gallery, Madison, Wis., 1982, Vashti de Verteuil, N.Y.C., 1989, Women's Studio Workshop, Rosendale, N.Y., 1990, U.S. Fed. Bldg., Jamaica, N.Y., 1995, McHenry County Coll., Crystal Lake, Ill., 1996, Matrix Gallery, Sacramento, Calif., 1998, So. Oreg. U., Ashland, 1999; exhibited in group shows at Ceres Gallery, N.Y.C., 1997, City Without Walls, Newark, Smithtown Arts Ctr., Art Gallery San Francisco State U., 1997, Columbia (Mo.) Coll., 1997, New Arts Program, Kutztown, Pa., 1997, 98, 99, 2000, Art Gallery Seton Hall U. Sch. Law, Newark, 1997, Hera Gallery, Wakefield, R.I., 1997, Firehouse Art Gallery, Nassau C.C., Garden City, N.Y., 1997, 99, Slocumb Galleries, East Tenn. State U., Johnson City, 1997, Heckscher Mus. Art, Huntington, N.Y., 1997, Chautauqua (N.Y.) Ctr. for Visual Arts, 1997, Cooperstown (N.Y.) Art Assn., 1997, Smithtown Arts Coun., 1999, Mills Pond House, St. James, N.Y., 1997, 99, 2000, Allentown, Pa., 1998, The Mariboe Gallery at the Peddie Sch., Hightstown, N.J., 1998, The Chrysler Mus. Art, Norfolk, Va., 1998, Sawtooth Galleries, Winston-Salem, N.C., 1998, Soho 20 Gallery, N.Y.C., 1999, The Target Gallery, Torpedo Factory Art Ctr., Alexandria, Va., 1999, U. Gallery St. John's U., Jamaica, 1999, Arts Ctr. Gallery CMS U., Warrensburg, Mo., 1999, Monarch Contemporary Art Ctr., Tenino, Wash., 1999, Montclair State U., Upper Montclair, N.J., 1999, Meml. Hall for Arts, Wilmington, Vt., 1999, City Without Walls, Newark, 1999, 2000, Sharjah (Va.) Arts Mus., 2000, Garland Artists Group, Dallas, 2000, Herndon Gallery Antioch (Ohio) Coll., 2000, Appleton Art Ctr., Wis., 2000, Islip Art Mus., N.Y., 2000, The Art Club, N.Y.C., 2000, Printmaking Coun. NJ, Somerville, 2000-2001, Bronx Mus. Arts, N.Y., 2000, San Jacinto Coll. South, Houston, 2000, Dublin Arts Council, Dublin, OH, 2001, numerous others; contbr. artwork to profl. jours.; author catalog essays. Grad. fellow U. Wis., 1984, artist's fellow Palenville (N.Y.) Interarts Colony, 1989-90, artists fellow Va. Ctr. for Creative Arts, 1992-93; Manhattan Graphics Ctr. scholar, 1989; Artists' grantee Artist's Space, 1990. Mem. Coll. Art Assn., New Mus. Art, Pyramic Atlantic Book Arts Ctr., City Without Walls, Orgn. Ind. Artists. Avocations: reading, travel, writing, walking. Home and Office: 10-09 46th Rd Long Island City NY 11101 Fax: (718) 706-9061. E-mail: minniew@mindspring.com.

WEINBERG, MARC ALAN, cardiologist; b. N.Y.C., Apr. 30, 1948; s. Milton and Sarah Weinberg; m. Rochelle Fay Weinberg, June 20, 1971; children: Laura, Deborah, Glenn. BA, Hofstra U., 1969; MD, Yale U., 1973. Bd. cert. in cardiovasc. disease and critical care Am. Bd. Internal Medicine. Chief cardiology Huntington (N.Y.) Hosp., 1991-95, chief cardiac rehab., 1997—. Fellow ACP, Am. Coll. Cardiology. Office: West Carver Med Assocs 200 W Carver St Huntington NY 11743-3303

WEINBERG, MARTIN HERBERT, retired psychiatrist; b. Bklyn., Sept. 3, 1923; s. Abe and Ida (Levine) W.; m. Elizabeth Carwardine, Sept. 20, 1951; children: Mark David, Sheila Ann, Keith Warren. BS, CCNY, 1947; licentiate, Royal Coll. Surgeons, Edinburgh, Royal Coll. Physicians, Royal Faculty Physicians and Surgeons, Glasgow. Diplomate: Am. Bd. Psychiatry and Neurology, certified mental hosp. adminstr. Intern Kings County Med. Center, Bklyn., 1952; resident psychiatry Essex County Overbrook Hosp., Cedar Grove, N.J., 1954-56; staff psychiatrist Ancora State Hosp., Hammonton, 1956, chief service, 1957, clin. dir., 1958-60, asst. med. dir., 1960-62, dep. med. dir., 1962-67; med. dir. Trenton Psychiat. Hosp., 1967-73; dir. div. mental health and hosps. N.J. Dept. Instns. and Agys., 1973-74; med. dir. Trenton Psychiat. Hosp., 1974-79; surveyor psychiat. programs Joint Commn. Accreditation of Hosps., 1979-80; asst. supt. clin. services Phila. State Hosp., 1980-81; individual practice medicine specializing in psychiatry, 1981-86; ret., 1986. Staff psychiatrist Woods Sch., Langhorne, Pa., to 1986; cons. N.J. Neuropsychiat. Inst., 1981-83, New Lisbon State Sch., to 1985. Fellow Am. Psychiat. Assn., AAAS; mem. N.J. Psychiat. Assn. (past pres.) Home: 26 Diane Dr Trenton NJ 08628-2621

WEINBERG, MILTON, JR. cardiovascular and thoracic surgeon; b. Sumter, S.C., Aug. 8, 1924; s. Milton and Ethel (Harper) W.; m. Joan Ehrenstrom, Nov. 24, 1956; children: Caryl, Susan, Amy. Student, Duke U., 1941-43, MD, 1947. Diplomate Am. Bd. Surgery, Am. Bd. Thoracic Surgery. Attending surgeon Rush Presbyn.-St. Luke's Med. Ctr., Chgo., 1957-90, emeritus attending, 1990—; attending surgeon Cook County Hosp., 1956-80, Luth. Gen. Hosp., Park Ridge, 1986—; mem. governing coun., 1996—2001; assoc. prof. Rush Med. Coll., Chgo., 1969-78, prof. surgery, 1978-90, emeritus prof., 1990—; clin. prof. U. Chgo., 1990-99. Chmn. dept. surgery Luth. Gen. Hosp., Park Ridge, 1988-94, vice-chmn. dept. surgery, 1994—; pres. med. staff Rush Med. Ctr., Chgo., 1977-79; presenter movies at mtgs. ACS. Mem. editorial bd. Annals of Thoracic Surgery, 1968-79; contbr. articles to profl. jours., chpts. to surg. textbooks. Trustee The Presbyn. Home, Evanston, Ill., 1984—; bd. dirs. Chgo. Symphony Orch., 1985-95; advisor Charitable Found. Bd., 1996-2002. Maj. U.S. Army, 1951-53. Decorated Bronze Star. Fellow ACS, Am. Coll. Chest Physicians, Am. Coll. Cardiology; mem. Am. Assn. Thoracic Surgery, Soc. Thoracic Surgeons, Soc. Vascular Surgery, Internat. Cardiovascular Soc., Ctrl. Surg. Soc. Avocations: fly fishing, fly rod building. Home: 983 Kirkhill Ln Lake Forest IL 60045-4209 Office: Luth Gen Hosp 1775 Dempster St Park Ridge IL 60068-1173 Fax: (847) 482-1774. E-mail: weinbergm@prodigy.net.

WEINBERG, PAUL JAY, real estate company officer; b. N.Y.C., May 22, 1944; s. Robert and Mildred Weinberg; m. M. Ellen Weinberg (div. Jan. 1985); 1 child Mark. BS, Cornell U., 1966; MA, McGill U., 1970; PhD, NYU, 1977. V.p. human resources Am. Express, N.Y.C., 1972—87; assoc. prof. Baruch Coll., 1993—95; v.p. human resources Kimco Realty Corp., New Hyde Park, NY, 1997—. Cons., N.Y.C., 1987—97. Author: European Labor and Multinationals, 1977. U.S. rep. Internat. Labor Orgn., Geneva, 1981—82. E-mail: kimcopw@aol.com.

WEINBERG, ROBERT ALLAN, biochemist, educator; b. Pitts., Nov. 11, 1942; s. Fritz E. and Lore (Reichhardt) Weinberg; m. Amy Schulman Weinberg, Nov. 19, 1976; children: Aron, Leah Rosa. S.B., MIT, 1964, Ph.D, 1969; PhD (hon.), Northwestern U., 1984. Instr. Stillman Coll., Tuscaloosa, Ala., 1965—66; research fellow Weizmann Inst., Rehovoth, Israel, 1969—70, Salk Inst., LaJolla, Calif., 1970—72; from asst. prof. to assoc. prof. dept. biology & ctr. cancer rsch. MIT, Cambridge, 1973—82, prof. biology, 1982—, Daniel K. Ludwig prof. for cancer rsch. Mem. Whitehead Inst., Cambridge, 1984—; elected mem. Inst. of Medicine, 2000. Contbr. Recipient Bristol Myers award, 1984, Brown-Hazen award N.Y. State Dept. Health, 1984, Sloan prize, Gen. Motors Cancer Rsch. Found., 1987, Rsch. Recognition award, Samuel Roberts Noble Found., 1990, Gairdner Found. Internat. award, 1992, Harvey Prize, Technion, 1994, G.H.A. Clowes Meml. award, 1996, Nat. Medal of Sci., 1997. Mem.: NAS (sci. award 1984). Avocations: genealogy, house building. Office: Whitehead Inst 9 Cambridge Ctr Cambridge MA 02142-1479*

WEINBERG, ROGER DAVID, communications executive; b. Balt., Feb. 10, 1954; s. James Henry Weinberg and Anne (Horowitz) Meyers; m. Jacquelyn Scully, Apr. 5, 1986. BA cum laude gen. honors program, U. Pa., 1976; grad., Broadcast Acad. Richmond, 1979. Copywriter Heilig-Meyers Co., Richmond, Va., 1976-82, dir. video tng., 1982-88, asst. v.p. corp. communications, 1988-97, v.p. corp. comm., 1997—. Prodr. numerous videotapes. Vol. reader Va. Voice for Print Handicapped, Richmond, 1980—, bd. dirs., 1998—. Mem. charter mem. (inductee) Va. Voice Vol. Hall of Fame. Jewish. Avocations: music, photography, television trivia. Home: 7616 Cornwall Rd Richmond VA 23229-6718 Office: Heilig-Meyers Co 12560 W Creek Pkwy Richmond VA 23238-1115

WEINBERG, SAMUEL, pediatric dermatologist; b. N.Y.C., Jan. 12, 1926; s. Harry and Rose (Stecher) W.; m. Pearl Oksner, Dec. 12, 1948; children: Ronald Andrew, Robin Ann. MB, Chgo. Med. Sch., 1947, MD, 1948. Clin. asst. prof. dermatology Med. Ctr. NYU, N.Y.C., 1961-84, prof. dermatology, 1984—. Author: Color Atlas of Pediatric Dermatology, 1975, 2nd rev. edit., 1990, 3rd rev. edit., 1998. Capt. USAF, 1951-53. Recipient Clark W. Finnerud award Dermatology Found., 1999. Fellow ACP, Am. Acad. Pediat. (Alvin Jacobs award 1998), Am. Acad. Dermatology (chmn. pediat. dermatology sect. 1978-81, mem. com. dermatol. subsplty. 1984-86, mem. task force on pediat. dermatology 1981-84), Nassau Acad. Medicine; mem. Soc. Pediat. Dermatology (charter, pres. 1980-81). Office: NYU Med Ctr 530 1st Ave New York NY 10016-6497

WEINBERG, SIDNEY R. physician; b. N.Y.C., Sept. 2, 1912; s. Hyman and Minnie (Slotnick) W.; m. Goldie Winkler, June 12, 1938 (wid. Oct. 1984); children: Jane, Emily, Winkler G.; m. Hilda B. Lasdon, Feb. 28, 1986. MD, NYU, 1937; MD (hon.), U. Madrid, 1960. Asst. to assoc. prof. urology N.Y. Downstate Coll. of Medicine, 1954-63, clin. prof. urology, 1963-73; dir. urology Jewish Hosp. of Bklyn.; dir. renal dialysis and urologist V.I., 1973-83; med. staff Hospice of Palm Beach County and Hospice by the Sea, Palm Beach County, Fla. Co-author: Urology in General Practice, 1962; author: Simultaneous Prostatectomy and Herniorrapy, 1968, Jewish Combatants in the Wars of Early America, 1998. Mem. West End Temple of Neponsit, Reform Judaism. 1st lt. U.S. Army Res., 1938-39, 41-42. Mem. AMA, Am. Coll. Surgeons, Am. Assn. Urology, Internat. Soc. of Urology. Republican. Avocations: tennis, bicycle trips, Bonzai and regular horticulture.

WEINBERG, STEVEN, physics educator; b. N.Y.C., NY, May 3, 1933; s. Fred and Eva (Israel) Weinberg; m. Louise Goldwasser, July 6, 1954; 1 child Elizabeth. BA, Cornell U., 1954; postgrad., Copenhagen Inst. Theoretical Physics, 1954—55; PhD, Princeton U., 1957; AM (hon.) , Harvard U., 1973; ScD (hon.) , Knox Coll., 1978, U. Chgo., 1978, U. Rochester, 1979, Yale U., 1979, CUNY, 1980, Clark U., 1982, Dartmouth Coll., 1984, Columbia U., 1990, U. Salamanca, 1992, U. Padua, 1992, Bates Coll., 2002; D (hon.) , U. Barcelona, 1966, D (hon.) , 1996; PhD (hon.) , Weizmann Inst., 1985; DLitt (hon.) , Washington Coll., 1985. Rsch. assoc., instr. Columbia U., 1957-59; rsch. physicist Lawrence Radiation Lab., Berkeley, Calif., 1959-60; mem. faculty U. Calif., 1960-69, prof. physics, 1964-69; vis. prof. MIT, 1967-69, prof. physics, 1969-73; Higgins prof. physics Harvard U., 1973-83; sr. scientist Smithsonian Astrophys. Lab., 1973-83; Josey prof. sci. U. Tex., Austin, 1982—; sr. cons. Smithsonian Astrophys. Obs., 1983—. Cons. Inst. Def. Analyses, Washington, 1960—73, ACDA, 1973; Sloan fellow, 1961—65; chair in physics Coll. de France, 1971; mem. Pres.'s Com. on Nat. Medal of Sci., 1979—82, Coun. of Scholars, Libr. of Congress, 1983—85; sr. adv. La Jolla Inst.; mem. Com. on Internat. Security and Arms Control, NRC, 1981, Bd. on Physics & Astronomy, 1989—90; dir. Jerusalem Winter Sch. Theoretical Physics, 1983—84; mem. adv. coun. Tex. Superconducting Supercollider High Energy Rsch. Facility, 1987; Loeb lectr. in physics Harvard U., 1966—67, Morris Loeb vis. prof. physics, 1983—; Richtmeyer lectr., 1974; Scott lectr. Cavendish Lab., 1975; Silliman lectr. Yale U., 1977; Lauritsen Meml. lectr. Calif. Inst. Tech., 1979; Bethe lectr. Cornell U., 1979; de Shalit lectr. Weizmann Inst., 1979; Cherwell-Simon lectr. Oxford U., 1983; Bampton lectr. Columbia U., 1983; Einstein lectr. Israel Acad. Arts and Scis., 1984; Hilldale lectr. U. Wis., 1985; Clark lectr. U. Tex., Dallas, 1986; Dirac lectr. U. Cambridge, 1986; Klein lectr. U. Stockholm, 1989; Brittin lectr. U. Colo., 1994; Sackler lectr. U. Copenhagen, 1994; Gibbs lectr. Am. Math. Soc., 1996; Bochner lectr. Rice U., 1997; Sanchez lectr. Tex. A&M Internat. U., 1998; Witherspoon lectr. Washington U., 2001; mem. Supercollider Sci. Policy Com., 1989—93. Author: Principles and Applications of the General Theory of Relativity, 1972, The First Three Minutes: A Modern View of the Origin of the Universe, 1977, The Discovery of Subatomic Particles, 1982; author: (with R. Feynman) Elementary Particles and the Laws of Physics; author: Dreams of a Final Theory, 1992, The Quantum Theory of Fields - Vol. I: Foundations, 1995, Modern Applications, Vol. II, 1996, Supersymmetry, Vol. III, 2000, Facing Up: Science and Its Cultural Adversaries, 2001; rsch. and publs. on elementary particles, quantum field theory, cosmology, coeditor monographs on math. physics Cambridge U. Press , mem. adv. bd. Issues in Sci. and Tech., 1984—87, mem. sci. book bom. Sloan Found., 1985—91, editl. bd. Jour. Math. Physics, 1986—88, mem. bd. editors Daedalus, 1990—, Jour. Math. Physics, 1998—, mem. bd. assoc. editors Nuc. Physics B, —. Bd. advisors Santa Barbara Inst. Theoretical Physics, 1983—86; bd. overseers SSC Accelerator, 1984—86; bd. dirs. Headliners Found., 1993—. Recipient J. Robert Oppenheimer Meml. prize, 1973, Dannie Heineman prize in math. physics, 1977, Am. Inst. Physics U.S. Steel Found. sci. writing award, 1977, Nobel prize in Physics, 1979, Elliott Cresson medal, Franklin Inst., 1979, Madison medal, Princeton U., 1991, Nat. medal of Sci., NSF, 1991, Andrew Gemant prize, Am. Inst. Physics, 1997, Piazzi prize, Govts. Sicily and Palermo, 1998, Lewis Thomas prize, Rockefeller U., 1999. Mem.: NAS, Tex. Inst. Letters, Philos. Soc. Tex., History of Sci. Soc., Royal Soc. London, Am. Philos. Soc., Coun. Fgn. Rels., Internat. Astron. Union, Am. Phys. Soc., Am. Acad. Arts and Scis., Cambridge Sci. Soc., Headliners Club, Saturday Club (Boston), Tuesday Club (Austin), Phi Beta Kappa.

WEINBERG, STEVEN LEWIS, lawyer; b. N.Y.C., Aug. 22, 1961; s. Harry and Florence Weinberg. BA in Polit. Sci., SUNY, Binghamton, 1982; JD, Union U., Binghamton, 1985. Bar: N.Y. 1987, U.S. Ct. Appeals (2d cir.) 1987, U.S. Dist. Ct. (no., so., and ea. dists.) N.Y. 1987. Asst. dist. atty. Queens Dist. Atty., Kew Gardens, N.Y., 1985-87; trustee Gotesman Wolgel Secuda Malomy & Flynn P.C., N.Y.C., 1987—. Dep. mayor Village of Thomaston, Great Neck, NY, 1997—. Office: Gottesman Wolgel Secunda Malamy & Flynn PC 11 Hanover Sq New York NY 10005

WEINBERG, SYLVAN LEE, cardiologist, educator, author, editor; b. Nashville, June 14, 1923; s. Abraham J. and Beatrice (Kottler) W.; m. Joan Hutzler, Jan. 29, 1956; children: Andrew Lee, Leslie. BS, Northwestern U., 1945, MD, 1948. From intern to resident, fellow Michael Reese Hosp., Chgo., 1947-51; attending physician Good Samaritan Hosp., Dayton, Ohio, 1953-99, chief of cardiology, 1966-99, founding dir. coronary care unit, 1967-99; clin. prof. medicine Wright State U., 1975—; dir. med. edn. Dayton Heart Hosp., 2000—. Former panelist Med. Affairs, nat. TV; pres. Weinberg Marcus Cardiomed. Group, Inc., 1970-99; pres. Arts & Comms. Internat., Inc., 1995—. Author: An Epitaph for Merlin and Perhaps for Medicine, 1983, The Golden Age of Medical Science and the Dark Age of Health Care Delivery, 2000; founding editor Dayton Medicine, 1980—, Heart & Lung, 1972-87, The American Heart Hosp. Jour., 2002—; editor-in-chief Am. Heart Hosp. Jour., 2002-; contbr. articles to profl jours. Capt. U.S. Army, 1951-53, Korea. Recipient Army Commendation medal, Richard A. DeWall MD award for excellence in cardiology, Am. Heart Assn., 2001, Outstanding Pub. Svc. award, Ohio State Senate, 1980. Fellow ACP (Ohio Laureate award 1997), Am. Coll. Cardiology (editor in chief jour. ACCEL 1985-2000, pres. 1993-94), Am. Coll. Chest Physicians (pres. 1984); mem. Montgomery County Med. Soc. (pres. 1980). Avocations: writing, travel, golf. Home: 4555 Southern Blvd Dayton OH 45429-1118 Office: Dayton Heart Hosp 707 S Edwin Moses Blvd Dayton OH 45408 E-mail: slwjal@aol.com.

WEINBERG, WILLIAM HENRY, chemical engineer, chemical physicist, educator; b. Columbia, S.C., Dec. 5, 1944; s. Ulrich Vivian and Ruth Ann (Duncan) W. BS, U. S.C., 1966; PhD in Chem. Engring, U. Calif., Berkeley, 1970; NATO postdoctoral fellow in phys. chemistry, Cambridge U., Eng., 1971. Asst. prof. chem. engring. Calif. Inst. Tech., 1972-74, assoc. prof., 1974-77, prof. chem. engring. and chem. physics, 1977-89, Chevron disting. prof. chem. engring. and chem. physics, 1981-86; prof. chem. engring. and chemistry U. Calif., Santa Barbara, 1989—, assoc. dean Coll. Engring., 1992-96; chief tech. officer Symyx Techs., Santa Clara, Calif., 1996—. Vis. prof. chemistry Harvard U., 1980, U. Pitts., 1987-88, Oxford U., 1991; Alexander von Humboldt Found. fellow U. Munich, 1982; cons. E.I. DuPont Co. Author: (with Van Hove and Chan) Low-Energy Electron Diffraction, 1986; editor 4 books in field; mem. editl. bd. Jour. Applications Surface Sci., 1977-85, Handbook Surfaces and Interfaces, 1978-80, Surface Sci. Reports, 1980—, gen. editor, 1992—, Applied Surface Sci., 1985—, Langmuir, 1990-96, Surface Sci., 1992—, Jour. Combinatorial Chemistry, 1998—; contbr. articles to profl. jours., chpts. to books. Recipient Giuseppe Parravano award Mich. Catalysis Soc., 1989, Disting. Teaching award Coll. of Engring., U. Calif. Santa Barbara, 1995; fellow NSF, 1966-69, Alfred P. Sloan Found., 1976-78, Camille and Henry Dreyfus Found., 1976-81. Fellow AAAS, Am. Phys. Soc. (Nottingham prize 1972), Am. Vacuum Soc.; mem. AIChE (Colburn award 1981), Am. Chem. Soc. (LaMer award 1973, Kendall award 1991, Arthur W. Adamson award 1995), N.Am. Catalysis Soc., Nat. Acad. Engring., Phi Beta Kappa. Office: Symyx Technologies 3100 Central Expy Santa Clara CA 95051-0801 E-mail: hweinberg@symyx.com.

WEINBERGER, ADRIENNE, artist, appraiser; b. Washington, Apr. 28, 1948; d. Samuel Aaron and Marta (Barta) W.; m. Edward Herschel Egelman, Mar. 21, 1980; children: Serge Maurice, Liana Dora. BA, Goucher Coll., 1970; MEd, Johns Hopkins U., 1973; MA, Northwestern U., 1974; postgrad., Sch. of Mus. of Fine Arts, 1979-82. Lectr. Art Inst. Chgo., 1973-75; lectr., docent trainer Mus. of Fine Arts, Boston, 1978-82; mus. educator Yale Ctr. Brit. Art, Yale Art Gallery, New Haven, 1984-86; instr., coord. alumni coll. Albertus Magnus Coll., 1987-89; instr. Mpls. C.C., 1989-94; propr. Studio 95, Edina, Minn., 1995-99, Charlottesville, Va., 1999—. Panelist New England Regional Confs., Am. Assn. Muss., Mass., Conn., 1976-77; mem., workshop leader New Haven Green Found., New Haven 350 Com., 1987-88; pres. Cmty. Art Fund., 2000—. Author, illustrator, pub.: New Haven Coloring Book, 1987, Culcha-Man Visits New York City, 1988, CulchaMan Visits Washinton, D.C., 1988. Participant Edina Futures Forum, 1990; dir. Edina-Woodhill Assn., 1997—98; mem. State Affirmative Action Commn., 1996—98; del. chair, mem. nominating com. Dem. State Conv., St. Paul, 1994, del., chair Rochester, 1996, St. Cloud, 1998, del. Norfolk, 2000; mem. Dem. State Exec. Com., 1997—99; sec. Dem.-Farmer Labor Party, Edina, Eden Prairie, 1990—94, chair, 1994—96; mem. Dem. State Cen. com., 1994—99; treas. 3d Congl. Dist. Dem.-Farmer Labor Party, 1996—99; mem. adv. bd. gifted edn. svcs. Edina Pub. Schs., 1993—96; bd. dirs. Consortium for Advancement of Arts, 2001—, Leadership Charlottesville, 2002—. Recipient Juror's award Berkshire Mus., Pittsfield, Mass., 1981, New Haven Brush & Palette Club, 1985, Edina Art Ctr., 1991. Mem. Am. Soc. Appraisers (accredited sr. appraiser; sec. Twin Cities chpt. 1997-99, pres. Richmond chpt. 2000—), Charlottesville C. of C. (Amb. Corps. 2000, legis. action com., initiator cmty. art fund 2000—). Avocations: travel, reading, politics, advising on education. Office: Studio 95 3100 Waverly Dr Charlottesville VA 22901-9576 E-mail: studio95@guanotronic.com.

WEINBERGER, ALAN DAVID, lawyer, corporate executive; b. Washington, July 31, 1945; s. Theodore George and Shirley Sunshine (Gross) W.; m. Lauren Myra Kaminski, Dec. 2, 1979; children: Mark Henry, Benjamin Charles. BA, NYU, 1967, JD, 1970; LLM, Harvard U., 1973. Bar: N.Y. 1971, D.C. 1978, U.S. Supreme Ct. 1980. Assoc. White & Case, N.Y.C., 1970-72; founding law prof. Vt. Law Sch., South Royalton, 1973-75; atty. SEC and Fed. Home Loan Bank Bd., Washington, 1977-81; founder, chmn. bd. dirs., CEO The ASCII Group Inc., 1984—; founder, chmn. bd. dirs. Tech. Net, Inc., Bethesda, Md., 1995. Mem. adv. bd. Ashton Tate Inc., Torrance, Calif., 1986-87; sponsor, agt. All Union Fgn. Trade Acad., Acad. Nat. Economy of USSR in U.S.A., 1988-90; chmn. U.S. adv. bd. Moscow State U. of Commerce, 1992—; chmn. govt. affairs com. Computer Tech. Industry Assn., 1993-95; mem. U.S. adv. bd. U.S.-UK Fulbright Commn., 1999—. Author: White Paper to Reform Business Education in Russia, 1996; law rev. editor NYU Sch. Law, 1970. Named one of Top 25 Most Influential Execs. in Computer Industry, Computer Reseller News, 1988; recipient CEO of Yr. award Cyber Chanels, 1999; named eInnovator of Yr. Cyber Channels Assn., 2000. Mem. Nat. Orgn. on Disability (CEO coun.), D.C. Bar Assn., Order of Coif, Kenwood Country Club. Avocation: tennis. Office: ASCII Group Inc 7101 Wisconsin Ave Bethesda MD 20814-4871

WEINBERGER, ARNOLD, retired electrical engineer; b. Bardejov, Czechoslovakia, Oct. 23, 1924; came to U.S., 1939; s. Henry C. and Bina (Shapira) W.; widowed; children: Paul I., Ronda B., Keith A. BSEE, CCNY, 1950. Engr. Nat. Bur. Standards, Washington, 1950-60; rsch. staff mem. IBM, Yorktown Heights, N.Y., 1960-66, engr., Poughkeepsie, N.Y., 1966-91, ret., 1991. Contbr. articles on computer arithmetic, logic, large-scale integration, system organization, memories, design automation. Patentee in field. With U.S. Army, 1944-46, ETO. Fellow IEEE (Outstanding sect. award 1981). Avocation: table tennis.

WEINBERGER, CASPAR WILLARD, publishing executive, former secretary of defense; b. San Francisco, Aug. 18, 1917; s. Herman and Cerise Carpenter (Hampson) W.; m. Jane Dalton, Aug. 16, 1942; children: Arlin Cerise, Caspar Willard. AB magna cum laude, Harvard U., 1938, LLB, 1941; LLD (hon.), U. Leeds, Eng., 1989; LittD (hon.), U. Buckingham, 1995, Rennselear Poly., U. San Francisco. Bar: Calif., 1941, U.S. Ct. Appeals (D.C. cir.) 1990. Law clk. U.S. Judge William E. Orr, 1945-47; with firm Heller, Ehrman, White & McAuliffe, 1947-69, ptnr., 1959-69; mem. Calif. Legislature from 21st Dist., 1952-58; vice chmn. Calif. Rep. Ctrl. Com., 1960-62, chmn., 1962-64, Com. Calif. Govt. Orgn. and Econs., 1967-68; dir. fin. Calif., 1968-69; chmn. FTC, 1970; dep. dir. Office Mgmt. and Budget, 1970-72, dir., 1972-73; counsellor to the Pres., 1973; sec. HEW, 1973-75; gen. counsel, v.p., dir. Bechtel Power Corp., San Francisco, 1975-80, Bechtel, Inc., 1975-80, Bechtel Corp., 1975-80; sec. U.S. Dept. Def., Washington, 1981-87; counsel Law Firm of Rogers & Wells, Washington and N.Y.C., 1988-94; chmn. Forbes Magazine, New York, 1989—. Formerly staff book reviewer San Francisco Chronicle; moderator weekly TV program Profile, Bay Area, sta. KQED, San Francisco, 1959-68; Frank Nelson Doubleday lectr., 1974; co-host World Bus. Review, 1996-99. Author: Fighting for Peace: Seven Critical Years in the Pentagon, 1990, The Next War, 1996; author: (with Gretchen Roberts) In the Arena: A Memoir of the 20th Century, 2001; co-author (with Peter Schweizer): In the Arena, A Memoir of the 20th Century, 2001. Chmn. Pres.'s Com. on Mental Retardation, 1973-75; former mem. Trilaterial Commn.; former mem. adv. coun. Am. Ditchley Found.; former bd. dirs. Yosemite Inst.; former trustee St. Luke's Hosp., San Francisco, Mechanics Inst.; former chmn. nat. bd. trustees Nat. Symphony, Washington; former bd. govs. San Francisco Symphony; chmn. bd. USA-ROC Econ. Coun., 1991-94; co-chmn. Winston Churchill Travelling Fellowships Found., 1989-99; trustee Winston Churchill Meml. Trust, 1994—; bd. dirs. Chatham House Found., Inc., 1996—; mem. coun. on fgn. rels. Capt., inf. AUS, 1941-45; PTO. Decorated Bronze Star, Grand Cordon of Order of the Rising Sun (Japan), Hon. Knight Grand Cross Civil Div. Order of Brit. Empire, Order of Brillians Star with Grand Cordon, Taiwan; recipient Presdl. medal Freedom with distinction, 1987, Merite First Class, Mex., 1987, George Catlet Marshall medal, 1988, Civil award Hilal-i-Pakistan, 1989. Mem. ABA, State Bar Calif., D.C. Ct. Appeals, Century Club (N.Y.), Bohemian Club (San Francisco), Pacific Union Club (San Francisco), Harvard Club (Washington). Episcopalian (former treas. Diocese of Calif.). Office: Forbes Mag Office of Chmn 1101 17th St NW Ste 406 Washington DC 20036-4720

WEINBERGER, DANIEL R. psychiatrist, neurologist; b. N.Y.C., May 24, 1947; married; 1 child. BA, Johns Hopkins U., 1969; MD, U. Pa., 1973. Diplomate Am. Bd. Psychiatry and Neurology. Intern L.A. County-Harbor Gen. Hosp., Torrance, Calif., 1973-74; grad. fellow in medicine UCLA Sch. Medicine, 1973-74; clin. fellow in psychiatry Harvard U., 1974-77; resident in psychiatry Mass. Mental Health Ctr., Boston, 1974-76, chief resident, 1976-77; assoc. in medicine, divsn. psychiatry Peter Bent Brigham Hosp., 1974-76; asst. clin. prof. psychiatry George Washington U., Washington, 1978-81, assoc. clin. prof., 1982, assoc. clin. prof. neurology and psychiatry, 1984; resident in neurology George Washington U. Med. Ctr., 1980-83; dir. rsch. ward adult psychiatry br., intermural rsch. program NIHM, 1977-78, staff psychiatrist, 1977-81; head clin. neuropsychiatry and neurobehavior unit NIMH/St. Elizabeth's Hosp., 1981-82, chief sect., 1983-86, chief clin. brain disorders br., 1986—; dir. movement disorder, dementia clinic, experimental therapeutics br. Nat. Inst. Neurol. Diseases and Stroke, 1983-86; dir. behavioral neurology svc. St. Elizabeth's Hosp., 1983-88. Part-time gen. practice Bridgewater Med. Ctr., East Bridgewater, Mass., 1974-76; emergency rm. physician Cardinal Cushing Gen. Hosp., Brockton, Mass., 1974-77; examiner Am. Bd. Psychiatry and Neurology; part-time gen. practice psychiatry and neurology, Washington, 1978—; scientists promotion review com. NIMH, 1984-87; elected to coun. Assembly of Scientists NIMH/Nat. Inst. Neurological Diseases and Stroke, 1985-88; Roerig vis. prof. U. N.Mex., 1990, U. Mich., 1992; adv. bd. Alzheimer Disease Found., 1990—, Adams Super Ctr. Brain Studies, Tel Aviv, 1993—; Neal Mysell lectr. Harvard Med. Sch., 1993; steering com. in vivo NMR Ctr., NIH, 1993—. Mem. editorial bd. Biol. Psychiatry, 1986—, Internat. Jour. Schizophrenia Rsch., 1987—, Jour. Neuropsychiatry and Clin. Neurosci., 1987—, Psychiatry, 1987—, Progress in Neuropsychiatry and Psychopharmacology, 1989—, Jour. Clin. Brain Imaging, 1989—, Psychiatry Research: Neuroimaging, 1990—, Jour. Psychiatry and Neurosci., 1990—, Neuropsychopharmacology, 1991—, Development and Psychopathology, 1991—, Harvard Review of Psychiatry, 1992—; contbr. articles to profl. jours.; patentee in field. Capt. USPHS, 1977-86. Recipient Morton Prince award Am. Psychopathol. Assn., 1984, Judith B. Silver award Nat. Alliance for Mentally Ill, 1985, Arthur S. Flemming award Washington Jaycees, 1986, Established Investigator award NARSAD, 1990, Lieber award, 1993, Dean award Am. Coll. Psychiatrists, 1994. Fellow Am. Coll. Neuropsychopharmacology (Joel Elkes internat. award 1989); mem. AMA, AAAS, Am. Psychiat. Assn. (Found. Fund prize for rsch. 1991), Am. Acad. Neurology (sci. program com. 1993—), Am. Neuropsychiatric Assn., Soc. Biol. Psychiatry (A.E. Benett Found. award clin. science 1981), Behavioral Neurology Soc., Soc. Neurosci. (pub. lectr. 20th ann. meeting 1990), Washington Neurology Soc., Washington Psychiat. Soc., Phi Beta Kappa, Alpha Omega Alpha, Inst. Medicine. Office: NIMH Clinical Brain Disorders Branch 10 Center Dr Rm 4S235 Bldg 10 Bethesda MD 20892-1379 Office Fax: 301-480-7795.*

WEINBERGER, FRANK, information management consultant; b. Chgo., Sept. 18, 1926; s. Rudolph and Elaine (Kellner) W.; m. Beatrice Natalie Fixler, June 27, 1953; children: Alan J., Bruce I. BSEE, Ill. Inst. Tech., Chgo., 1951; MBA, Northwestern U., 1959; DBA, U.S. Internat. U., San Diego, 1996. Registered profl. engr., Ill, Calif. Engr. Admiral Corp., Chgo., 1951-53; sr. engr. Cook Rsch., 1953-59; mem. tech. staff Rockwell Internat., Downey, Calif., 1959-80, info. systems advisor, 1980-95; info. mgmt. cons., 1995—. Pres. Temple Israel, Long Beach, Calif., 1985-87, bd. dirs. 1973-85. With USN, 1944-46. Mem. Assn. for Computer Machinery. Democrat. Jewish. Avocation: microcomputers. Home and Office: 3231 Yellowtail Dr Los Alamitos CA 90720-5253 E-mail: weinberger@covad.net. *Don't ask "what can I do?" Instead, survey the needs, prepare the information, and give your best recommendation.*

WEINBERGER, GEORGE IAN, dermatologist; b. Bronx, N.Y., Mar. 1, 1949; s. Frederick and Ruth (Gendler) W.; m. Joyce Fishman, July 19, 1970; children: Michelle, Shari, Seth. BS, Muhlenburg Coll., 1969; MD, N.J. Med. Sch., 1973. Intern Henry Ford Hosp., Detroit, 1973-74, resident in dermatology, 1974-77; pvt. practice North Plainfield, N.J., 1979—. Maj. USAF, 1977-79. Fellow Am. Acad. Dermatology; mem. AMA, Dermatol. Soc. N.J. (v.p. 1987-88, pres. 1989), N.J. Med. Soc. Office: 190 Greenbrook Rd North Plainfield NJ 07060-3903

WEINBERGER, HAROLD PAUL, lawyer; b. N.Y.C., Mar. 12, 1947; s. Fred and Elaine (Schonfeld) W.; m. Toby Ann Strassman, Dec. 15, 1968; children: James David, Karen Ellen. BA, CCNY, 1967; JD, Columbia U., 1970. Bar: N.Y. 1971, U.S. Dist. Cts. (so., ea., and no. dists.) N.Y. 1972, U.s. Ct. Appeals (2d cir.) 1972. Law clk. to presiding justice U.S. Ct. Appeals (2d cir.), N.Y.C., 1970-71; assoc. Kramer Levin Naftalis Frankel LLP, 1971-77, ptnr., 1978—. Recipient John Ordronaux prize Columbia U. Law Sch., 1970. Mem. ABA (intellectual property law sect. 1999—), Assn. Bar City N.Y. (com. fed. legislation 1975-78, com. on products liability 1983-86, mem. com. on trademarks and unfair competition 1995-97). Democrat. Jewish. Home: 336 Central Park W New York NY 10025-7111 Office: Kramer Levin Naftalis & Frankel LLP 919 3rd Ave New York NY 10022-3902 E-mail: hweinberger@kramerlevin.com.

WEINBERGER, JANE DALTON, retired nurse, volunteer; b. Maine, Mar. 29, 1919; m. Caspar Willard Weinberger, Aug. 16, 1942; children: Caspar Willard and Arlin Weinberger. Student, U. Maine, 1936-38, student, 1938-41; BSN, Somerville Hosp. Sch. Nursing, 1940; postgrad., Boston U., 1941. Reg. nurse Calif. Vol. St. Luke's Hosp., San Francisco, 1947-77; owner, editor, author Windswept House Pubs., Mt. Desert, Maine, 1984—; ret., 1999—. Author: (Children's Books) The Little Ones, Lemon Drop, Tabitha Jones, Wee Peter Puffin, Fanny and Sarah, Cory the Cormorant, That's What Counts, VIM: A Very Important Mouse, Mrs. Witherspoon's Eagles; (adult biography): As Ever, Canned Plums and Other Vissitudes of Life. Bd. Trustees Nat. Symphony Assn., 1970—, Capitol Children's Mus., 1970-85; bd. dirs. Folger Shakespeare Libr., 1970—, chmn. 1981-86; founding mem. New Globe Theatre, London, 1999; bd. vols. D.C. Gen. Hosp., 1970-75, hon. bd. mem. 1975—; bd. dirs. Jackson Lab. (Cancer Rsch. Inst.), 1984—, mem. Internat. Coun. Jackson Lab., 1990—; mem. women's com. Washington Performing Arts Soc., 1970—; sponsor The Internat. Hospitality Soc., Washington, 1970-85, other vol. orgns.; Rep. coms. campaign mgr., San Francisco, 1964-68. 2nd lt. U.S. Army Nurse Corps, 1942-43, PTO. Recipient Svc. to Humanity award, Alpha chpt. Chi Eta Phi, 1974, Deborah Morton award, Westbrook (Maine) Coll., 1992. Mem. Maine Media Women, Nat. News Women, Maine Writers and Pubs. Alliance, Jr. Army Navy Guild (hon.), Soc of Sponsors USN, The Century Club of Calif., Congressional Club (Washington), Pal's Club, (Sacramento,Calif.). Episcopalian. Avocations: cooking, gardening, swimming, boating, collecting glass paperweights, minature porcelain boxes. Office: Windswept House PO Box 159 Mount Desert ME 04660-0159

WEINBERGER, LILLA GILBRECH, bookseller; b. Pasadena, Calif., Oct. 8, 1941; d. George Herbert and Lilla Dorothy Gilbrech; m. Christopher Pearce (div. 1969); m. Andrew Harvey Weinberger, Nov. 10, 1974; children: Gideon, Tobias. Student, Occidental Coll., 1959-61; BA in Comparative Lit., U. Calif., Berkeley, 1963. Child care officer London County Coun., 1964-65; libr. asst. Huntington Libr., San Marino, Calif., 1965-66; rschr., edn. pub. welfare rsch. svc. Libr. Congress, Washington, 1966-72; freelance photographer, writer L.A., 1973-84; dir., cmty. coord. Women's Svc. Ctr., Pittsfield, Mass., 1984-91; co-owner Reader's Books, Sonoma, Calif., 1991—. Pres., bd. dirs. Women's Statewide Legis. Network, Mass., 1988-90; mem. Gov.'s Commn. on the Status of Women, Mass., 1987-91. Recipient poetry award Bantam Doubleday Dell Pub., 1994; named Woman of Yr. Berkshire County Women's Groups, 1990, Indy award Sonoma County Ind., 1998. Mem. No. Calif. Ind. Booksellers Assn. (former sec., exec. bd. dirs.), Am. Booksellers Assn. (bd. dirs.). Democrat. Office: Readers Books 127 E Napa St Sonoma CA 95476-6709

WEINBERGER, MARK, federal agency administrator; m. Nancy Weinberger; children: Rachel, Noah, Sean, Benjamin. Grad., Emory U.; MBA, Case We. Res.; LLM in Taxation, Georgetown U. Co-founder Washington Counsel, P.C. (merged with Ernst & Young); dir. U.S. nat. tax practice Ernst & Young LLP; asst. sec. treasury for tax policy U.S. Dept. Treasury, Washington, 2001—. Chief of staff, counsel Pres. Bipartisan Commn. on Entitlement and Tax Reform; sr. advisor Kemp Commn.; commr. Nat. Commn. on Retirement Policy; apptd. mem. Social Security Adv. Bd. Office: US Dept Treasury Tax Policy 1500 Pennsylvania Ave NW Washington DC 20220*

WEINBERGER, MARTIN ANDREW, computer company executive; b. Santa Monica, Calif., Sept. 9, 1962; s. Tibor Weinberger and Katalin Klara Avedissian. BSEE, UCLA, 1984; postgrad. in computer engring., U. So. Calif. Microsoft cert. sys. engr.; Microsoft cert. product specialist; sun expert level 1000 engr.; Digital Equipment Corp. Network Product Bus. Unit Level II Engr. Sr. engr. Northrop Electronics, Hawthorne, Calif., 1985-87; sr. engr. data systems divsn. Litton Industries, Van Nuys, 1987-90; prin., owner, pres. Genesis Software Applications, Santa Monica, 1990—; device driver engr. Peerless Systems Corp., El Segundo, Calif., 1997-2000; 3d level engr. Unisource AT&T Internat., The Hague, Netherlands, 1997; chief software engr. I.N. Inc., Los Alamitos, Calif., 2000—. Developer: (software) MediSec. Democrat. Avocations: violin, snow skiing, ice skating, swimming. Office: Genesis Software Applications PMB 753 2118 Wilshire Blvd Santa Monica CA 90403-5784

WEINBERGER, MILES M. physician, pediatric educator; b. McKeesport, Pa., June 28, 1938; divorced; 4 children; m. Leslie Kramer, Aug. 22, 1992. AB, U. Pitts., 1960, MD, 1965. Diplomate Am. Bd. Pediatrics, Am. Bd. Allergy and Immunology, Am. Bd. Pediatric Pulmonology. Intern U. Calif. Med. Ctr., San Francisco, 1965-66, pediatric resident, 1965-67; research assoc NIH, Bethesda, Md., 1967-69; allergy and pulmonary fellow U. Colo., Denver, 1969-71; staff Ross Valley Med. Clinic, Greenbrae, Calif., 1971-73; clin. pharmacology fellow U. Colo., Denver, 1973-75; divsn. dir. U. Iowa, Iowa City, 1975—. Cons. D.C.Hosp. for Sick Children, 1967-69, allergy and immunology Family Practice Program, Sonoma County Community Hosp., U. Calif. Sch. Medicine, 1972-73; clin. instr. pediatrics Georgetown U. Sch. Medicine, Washington, 1967-69; staff pediatrician part-time West Side Neighborhood Health Ctr., Denver, 1970-71; pediatric sr. staff mem. Nat.Jewish Hosp. and Research Ctr., 1973-75; clin. asst. U. Colo. Med.Ctr., 1974-75; assoc. prof. pediatrics, chmn. pediatric allergy and pulmonary div. U. Iowa Coll. Medicine, 1975-80, assoc. prof. pharmacology, 1975-79, dir. Cystic Fibrosis Ctr., 1977— , prof. pediatrics, 1980—, dir. pediatric allergy and pulmonary div., 1975—. Author: Managing Asthma, 1990; contbr. numerous articles to profl. jours., chpts. to books, also audio-visual materials, commentaries, pub. letters and presentations in field Recipient Clemens von Pirquet award Am. Coll. Allergy, 1974; grantee NIH, 1980-85, Cystic Fibrosis Ctr., Pharm. Mfrs. Assn. Fellow Am. Acad. Pediatrics (allergy sect. 1972, sect. on clin. pharmacology and therapeutics 1978, diseases of chest 1978); mem. Am. Acad. Allergy, Am. Soc. Clin. Pharmacology and Therapeutics, Soc. for Pediatric Rsch., Am. Thoracic Soc. (pres. Iowa Thoracic Soc. 1992-93), Camp Superkids of Iowa (adv. bd. 1981—), Am. Lung Assn. (pediatric pulmonbary ctr. task force com. 1984-86). Home: 7 Cottage Grove Dr NE Iowa City IA 52240-9171 Office: U Iowa Dept Pediatrics Iowa City IA 52242 E-mail: miles-weinberger@uiowa.edu.

WEINBERGER, MYRON HILMAR, medical educator; b. Cin., Sept. 21, 1937; s. Samuel and Helen Eleanor (Price) W.; m. Myrna M. Rosenberg, June 12, 1960; children: Howard David, Steven Neal, Debra Ellen. BS, Ind. U., Bloomington, 1959, MD, 1963. Intern Ind. U. Med. Ctr., Indpls., 1963-64, resident in internal medicine, 1964-66, asst. prof. medicine, 1969-73, assoc. prof., 1973-76, prof., 1976—, dir. Hypertension Research Ctr., 1981—; USPHS trainee in endocrinology and metabolism Stanford U. Med. Ctr., Calif., 1966-68, USPHS spl. fellow in hypertension, 1968-69. Contbr. articles to profl. jours. Recipient Tigerstedt award Am. Soc. Hypertension, 1996, Page-Bradley Lifetime Achievement award Am. Heart Assn. Coun. for High Blood Pressure Rsch., 1999. Fellow ACP, Am. Coll. Cardiology, Am. Coll. Nutrition, Am. Soc. for Clin. Pharmacology and Therapeutics; mem. AAAS, Am. Fedn. Clin. Research, AMA, Am. Heart Assn. (lifetime achievement award coun. for high blood pressure rsch. 1999), Am. Soc. Nephrology, Internat. Soc. Nephrology, Central Soc. Clin. Research, Endocrine Soc., Internat. Soc. Hypertension, Soc. for Exptl. Biology and Medicine Home: 135 Bow Ln Indianapolis IN 46220-1023 Office: Ind U Hypertension Research Ctr 541 Clinical Dr Indianapolis IN 46202-5233 E-mail: mweinbe@iupui.edu.

WEINBERGER, ROBERT, analytical chemist; b. N.Y.C., June 26, 1951; s. Albert and Florence (Krell) W.; m. Elizabeth Reinitz, Feb. 29, 1984; children: Julie, Jeremy. BS, CCNY, 1973, MA, 1976; PhD, Seton Hall, 1983. Group leader Reed & Carnrick, Kenilworth, N.J., 1973-78; sr. scientist Technicon Instruments, Tarrytown, 1978-81; rsch. fellow Seton Hall, South Orange, 1982-83; dir. rsch. Applied Biosys., Ramsey, 1983-90; pres. CE Techs., Chappaqua, N.Y., 1990—. Instr. Am. Chem. Soc. courses, 1990—; contract rschr. Author: Practical Capillary Electrophoresis, 1993, 2d edit., 2000, Separation Solutions (monthly column); contbr. articles to profl. jours. Office: CE Technologies PO Box 140 Chappaqua NY 10514-0140 E-mail: robertweinberger@aol.com.

WEINBLATT, CHARLES SAMUEL, university administrator, employment consultant; b. Toledo, Dec. 23, 1952; s. Morris and Clara (Volk) W.; m. Frances Barbara Auslander, Aug. 12, 1973; children: Brian J., Lauren M. BA, U. Toledo, 1974. Cert. edn. and tng. counselor, Ohio. Psychiat. counselor St. Vincent Hosp., Toledo, 1974-77; vocat., rehab. counselor Goodwill Industries, 1977-85; employment cons., pvt. practice, 1985—; tng. counselor UAW Chrysler, Perrysburg, Ohio, 1987; dir. divsn. orgn. devel. and leadership U. Toledo, 1988—. Employment svcs. cons. Employers' Assn. Toledo, 1985-90; outplacement cons. Toledo Pub. Schs., 1986; spkr. in field of labor and mgmt. rels., employee involvement. Author: Job Seeking Skills for Students, 1987. Mem. Toledo Vision Com., 1989-90. Recipient Quality Improvement award Chrysler, 1987, cert. Am. Inst. Banking, 1989. Mem. ASTD, Ohio Continuing Higher Edn. Assn., Toledo Area Human Resource Assoc., World Future Soc. Jewish. Avocations: music, sports, gardening. Home: 5118 Brenden Way Sylvania OH 43560-2223 Office: U Toledo Seagate Campus 401 Jefferson Ave Toledo OH 43604-1063 E-mail: cweinbl@utnet.utoledo.edu.

WEINBRENNER, GEORGE RYAN, aeronautical engineer; b. June 10, 1917; s. George Penbrook and Helen Mercedes (Ryan) W.; m. Billie Marjorie Elwood, May 2, 1955. BS, MIT, 1940, MS, 1941; AMP, Harvard U., 1966; ScD (hon.), Mapua Inst. Tech., Manila, 1994. Commd. 2d lt. USAAF, 1939, advanced through grades to col., 1949; def. attaché Am. Embassy, Prague, Czechoslovakia, 1958-61; dep. chief staff intelligence Air Force Sys. Command, Washington, 1962-68; comdr. fgn. tech. divsn. USAF, Wright-Patterson AFB, Ohio, 1968-74; comdr. Brooks AFB, Tex., 1974-75; ret., 1975; exec. v.p. B.C. Wills & Co., Inc., Reno, 1975-84; chmn. bd. Hispaño-Technica S.A. Inc., San Antonio, 1977—. Lectr. Sch. Aerospace Medicine Brooks AFB, Tex., 1975-84; adv. dir. Plaza Nat. Bank, San Antonio; cons. Def. Dept., 1981, Dept. Air Force, 1975-84. Decorated D.S.M., Legion of Merit, Bronze Star, Air medal, Purple Heart, Ordre Nat. du Merite, Medaille de la Resistance, Croix de Guerre (France). Fellow AIAA (assoc.); mem. World Affairs Coun., Air Force Assn. (exec. sec. Tex. 1976-94), Assn. Former Intelligence Officers (nat. dir.), Air Force Hist. Found. (dir.), U.S. Strategic Inst., Nat. Mil. Intelligence Assn., Tex. Aerospace & Nat. Def. Tech. Devel. Coun., Am. Astron. Soc., Aerospace Ednl. Foun. (trustee), Disabled Am. Vets. (life), Mil. Order World Wars, Am. Legion, Assn. Old Crows, Army-Navy Club (Washington), Kappa Sigma. Roman Catholic. Home: 7400 Crestway Dr Apt 903 San Antonio TX 78239-3094 Office: AFA Texas 118 Broadway Ste 234 San Antonio TX 78205-1945 E-mail: afatexas@member.afa.org.

WEINBROT, HOWARD DAVID, English educator; b. Bklyn., May 14, 1936; s. William and Rose (Shapiro) W. BA, Antioch Coll., Yellow Springs, Ohio, 1958; MA with honors (Woodrow Wilson fellow 1959, grad. fellow 1959-63), U. Chgo., 1959, PhD, 1963. Teaching fellow U. Chgo., 1962-63; instr. English Yale U., 1963-66; asst. prof., then assoc. prof. U. Calif., Riverside, 1966-69; mem. faculty U. Wis., Madison, 1969—, prof. English, 1972-84, Ricardo Quintana prof., 1984-87, Vilas prof., 1987—. Andrew Mellon vis. prof. Inst. Advanced Studies, Princeton, N.J., 1993-94. Author: The Formal Strain, 1969, Augustus Caesar in Augustan England, 1978, Alexander Pope and the Traditions of Formal Verse Satire, 1982, Essays on 18th-Century Satire, 1988, Britannia's Issue, 1993; also numerous articles, revs.; editor: New Aspects of Lexicography, 1972, Northrop Frye and 18th Century Studies; co-editor: The 18th Century: A Current Bibliography for 1973, 1975, Poetry in English, An Anthology, 1987, Eighteenth-Century Contexts, 2001. Fellow Inst. for Advanced Studies, Princeton, N.J, 1993-94, 2001; Guggenheim fellow, 1988-89. Mem. Am. Soc. 18th Century Studies (mem. editl. bd. 1977-80, exec. com. 96-99), Johnsonians, Johnson Soc. (sec.-treas. 1970-75, v.p. 2000—), Midwest Am. Soc. Eighteenth Century Studies, Eighteenth Century Scottish Studies. Home: 1505 Wood Ln Madison WI 53705-1456 Office: U Wis Dept English 600 N Park St Madison WI 53706-1403 E-mail: weinbrot@facstaff.wisc.edu.

WEINEL, PAMELA JEAN, nurse administrator; b. Olney, Md., Dec. 14, 1956; d. Clarence Dawson and Jean Elizabeth (Woodward) Weinel; m. Nathan Richards, May 6, 1995. AA in Edn., Montgomery Coll., Rockville, Md., 1976; BSN, U. Balt., Balt., 1986, M in Science Adminstrn., 1998; MBA, U. Balt., 2001. Oncology staff nurse George Washington U. Med. Ctr., Washington, 1986-88, Bone Marrow Transplant coord., 1988-90; adminstrv. coord. Walter Reed Army Med Ctr., 1990-98; advice nurse Kaiser Permanente, Kensington, Md., 1991-98; rsch. program mgr. Clin. Rsch. and Protocol Mgmt. Office U. Md. Greenebaum Cancer Ctr., Balt., 1999—. Cons., mem. People to People Internat., Russia, 1992, Vietnam, 93; roundtable facilitator Internat. BMT Symposium, Omaha, 1992; lectr. Contemporary Forums, San Francisco, 1994. Contbr. Sponsor for adults Resurrection Roman Cath. Ch., Burtonsville, Md., 1997—2002, CCD instr. 7th grade, 1997—2002. Named Nat. Dean's List, 1995—96, One of Outstanding Young Women in Am., 1997. Mem.: NAFE, Oncology Nursing Soc. (cert., Bone Marrow Transplant spl. interest group), Am. Coll. Oncology Adminstrs., Am. Acad. Med. Adminstrs., World Affairs Coun. of Washington, Sigma Iota Epsilon, Phi Kappa Phi, Phi Theta Kappa, Sigma Theta Tau (scholar 1996). Avocations: travel, photography, writing. Office: Greenbaum Cancer Ctr U Md 22 S Greene St # N9e17 Baltimore MD 21201-1544 Fax: 410-328-1180.

WEINER, ALAN E. accountant, lawyer; b. Bklyn., Nov. 17, 1942; BBA, CCNY, 1963; JD, Bklyn. Law Sch., 1968; LLM, NYU, 1972. Bar: N.Y. 1969, U.S. Tax Ct. 1969, U.S. Supreme Ct. 1995; CPA N.Y. 1967. Staff acct. Kamerman & Kamerman, N.Y.C., 1963-68; assoc. law firm Wien & Malkin, 1968-69; tax mgr. Touche Ross & Co. (now Deloitte & Touche LLP), L.I., N.Y., 1969-75; tax dir. Wolf & Co., N.Y.C., 1975; sr. tax ptnr. Holtz Rubenstein & Co., LLP, L.I., 1975—. Instr. Hofstra U., 1973-76; lectr. Found. for Acctg. Edn., N.Y.C., 1974—, pres., 2000-2001. Columnist Suffolk County Life Underwriters Assn., 1976-79; author: All About Limited Liability Companies and Partnerships, 1994, DFK International Worldwide Tax Overview, 2000; editl. adviser The Tax Adviser, 1997-2001; editor fed. tax column The CPA Jour., 1983-85; mem. adv. bd. Financial Manager mag., 1988-90; contbr. articles to profl. jours. Pres. Estate Planning Coun. of Suffolk County (N.Y.), 1978-79; founder, chmn. L.I. Accts. Blood Drive, 1982-84; trustee L.I. chpt. Leukemia Soc. Am., 1987-98. Mem. AICPA (coun. 1997-2000), N.Y. State Soc. CPAs (pres. 1999-2000, pres.-elect 1998-99, treas. 1995-97, bd. dirs. 1992-95, chmn. tax divsn. exec. com. 1993-95, chmn. Clinton tax proposals task force 1993, ltd. liability co. task force 1992, chmn. tax plenary session 1991, chmn. partnership tax com. 1989-91, chmn. fed. tax com. Nassau chpt. 1986-87, chmn. estate planning coun. Nassau chpt. 1973-74), Nassau County Bar Assn. (mem. tax law com. 1973—), Am. Assn. Atty.-CPA's, Suffolk County Bar Assn. (mem. tax law com. 1980—, chmn. bi-county com. atty./accts. 1990-91), DFK Internat. (exec. com. mem. 2000—, v.p. of the Ams. 1997-2000, chmn. internat. tax com. 1990-95). Office: Holtz Rubenstein & Co LLP 125 Baylis Rd Melville NY 11747-3823 Fax: 631-752-1742. E-mail: aeweiner@hrcpa.com.

WEINER, ANDREW JAY, lawyer; b. Hartford, Conn., Dec. 19, 1950; m. Debra Lewin, May 29, 1977; children: Joshua Isaac, Hannah Leah. BA, Yale Coll., 1972; JD, Harvard U., 1976. Bar: N.Y. 1977. Planner N.Y.C. Dept. City Planning, 1972-73; assoc. Shearman & Sterling, N.Y.C., 1976-84; ptnr. Gordon Hurwitz Butowsky Weitzen Shalov & Wein, 1984-89, Morrison & Foerster LLP, N.Y.C., 1990—. Office: Morrison & Foerster Ste 306 1290 Avenue Of The Americas Fl 41 New York NY 10104-0050 E-mail: aweiner@mafo.com.

WEINER, ANNE LEE, social worker; b. Chelsea-Malden, Mass., Nov. 2, 1932; d. Nathan and Edith E. (Sigel) Varnick; m. Paul J. Weiner, Jan. 25, 1959; children: Berdine R., Ronald M. Diploma in med. sec., Chandler Sch. for Women, 1952; AA in Social Work, Middelsex C.C., 1974; BSW, Salem Coll., 1987. Med. sec. New Eng. Med. - Boston U. Hosp., Boston, 1952-1960; social worker Lynn-Union Hosp., Lynn, Mass., 1968-1982; home care social worker Mass. Elder Care, Peabody, 1982-1987; nursing home social worker Logan Homes, Wingate Homes, Hill Haven Homes, Mass., 1987-99. Mem. region bd. Hadassah steering com. social work, Hadassah, Boston and Fla. Atlantic region; active Hist. Soc. Peabody; organizer social work support groups, North Shore, Mass. Mem. No. New Eng. Hadassah (pres. Peabody chpt.). Office: Lakes of Delray # 114 Watersedge J Delray Beach FL 33484 E-mail: lighthousealw@aol.com.

WEINER, ANTHONY DAVID, congressman; b. Bklyn. BA, SUNY, Plattsburgh, 1985. Washington DC and N.Y. aide to U.S. Congressman Charles Schumer; city councilman Dist. 48, N.Y.C., 1991-98, mem. pub. safety, consumet affairs, transp. coms., chmn. subcom. crime in pub. housing; mem. 106th Congress from 9th N.Y. dist., 1999—; mem. judiciary com.; mem. sci. com., 1998—. Bd. dirs. Boys Town, Jerusalem, Shaare Zedek Hosp., Israel. Office: 1901 Emmons Ave Ste 212 Brooklyn NY 11235-2700 also: US Ho of Reps 222 Cannon Ho Office Bldg Washington DC 20515*

WEINER, CHARLES R. federal judge; b. Phila., June 27, 1922; s. Max and Bessie (Chairney) W.; m. Edna Gerber, Aug. 24, 1947; children: William, Carole, Harvey. Grad., U. Pa., 1947, MA, 1967, PhD, 1972; LL.B., Temple U., 1950. Bar: Pa. bar 1951. Asst. dist. atty. Philadelphia County, 1952-53; mem. Pa. Senate from Phila. County, 1952-67, minority floor leader, 1959-60, 63-64, majority floor leader, 1961-62; U.S. dist. judge Eastern Dist. Pa., 1967—; now sr. judge. Mem. Phila. County Bd. Law Examiners, 1959— Mem. Pres.'s Adv. Commn. Inter-Govtl. Rels., Phila., Pub. Policy Com., Phila. Crime Prevention Assn., Big Bros. Assn.; mem. Pa. Bd. Arts and Scis.; trustee, exec. com. Fedn.

Jewish Philanthropies of Phila., Allied Jewish Appeal of Phila.; bd. dirs. Mental Health Assn. of Pa., Phila. Psychiat. Ctr., Phila. Tribune Charities, Phila. Wharton Ctr. Parkside YMCA, Jewish Publ. Soc. Am., The Athenaeum, and others. With USN, 1942—46. Recipient Phila. Fellowship award; Founder's Day award Temple U.; Alumni award U. Pa.; Founder's award Berean Inst.; others. Mem. ABA, Pa. Bar Assn., Phila. Bar Assn., Am. Law Inst. Office: US District Ct 6613 US Courthouse Ind Mall W 601 Market St Philadelphia PA 19106-1713

WEINER, CHERRY, literary agent; b. Melbourne, Australia, July 16, 1947; d. Michael and Giza (Fedder) Epstein; m. Jacob Norman Weiner, June 18, 1972; children: Tracy, Teri. Self employed literary agent, Manalapan, N.J., 1976—. Named Literary Agent of Yr. Wordcraft Cir., 1997, 99. Fax: 732-792-0506. E-mail: cherry8486@aol.com.

WEINER, CLAIRE MURIEL, freelance writer; b. Bronx, N.Y., Dec. 18, 1951; d. David and Norma (Berry) W. BA, U. Miami, Coral Gables, Fla., 1973; MA, U. Md., 1980. Pub. rels. specialist Hialeah Recreation Div., Hialeah, Fla., 1974-77; freelance writer North Miami Beach, 1977-78, Germantown, Md., 1989—, Montgomery County, 1981—. Govt. affairs liaison for new ednl. data base co. being formed, Montgomery County, 1982—; acting comm. dir. Ednl. Info. Svcs., 1996—. Contbr. articles to local newspapers; contbr. travel articles to profl. jours, mags. Active membership com. newsletter Greater Miami Jewish Fedn., 1974-77; charter mem. Women for Today chpt. B'nai B'rith Women, Washington, 1985-89. Named Hon. Citizen of Historic Williamburg. Life fellow Am. Biog. Inst. Rsch. Assn., World Lit. Acad.; mem. NAFE, Internat. Platform Assn., Nat. Trust for Hist. Preservation. Jewish. Home: 18828 Sky Blue Cir Germantown MD 20874-5398

WEINER, CLAIRE ZUNDELL, theatrical director; b. Worcester, Mass., June 19, 1933; d. Edward A. and Mary (Abramson) Shapiro; children: Aaryn Anne, Elliot Michael. Student, Clark U., SUNY, Miami-Dade Coll. Instr. fundamentals of theatre Dade County (Fla.) Cmty. Sch. Sys., 1965-68; tchr. theatre arts Roberson Centre of the Arts, Binghamton, N.Y., 1969-70; artist-in-theatre Colgate U., Hamilton, 1968-70; freelance feature writer Norwich (N.Y.) Eve. Sun, 1969-72; dir. Norwich Sr. High Theatre, 1968-72; dir. cultural activities for youth Norwich Youth Commn., 1969-72; resident dir., actress Gold Crown Dinner Theatre & Touring Co., Downey, Calif., 1972-76; dir. Theatre for Youth City of Santa Clara, 1979-80; dir. The Center Players, Long Beach, 1977-78; resident dir./playwright Arrowhead Theatre, San Jose, 1990—, resident dir./actor, Reader's Theatre for Original Plays, 1992-94. Mem. Miami Actor sCo., Miami, Fla., 1965-68, Gainesville (Fla.) Little Theatre, 1956-58, Jacksonville (Fla.) Little Theatre, 1958-62, Gallery Theatre, Coral Gables, Fla., 1961-62, Miami Beach Players, 1962-64, Arlington Players, Jacksonville, 1958-61; dir. Norwich Adult Weekly Summer Repertory Theatre, 1969-72, Norwich Weekly Children's Theatre in Mime, 1969-72; originator 1st area multi-sch. project Tino WorkShop Theatre, Fremont H.S. Dist., 1980—; guest dir. West Valley Civic Light Opera, 1982; advisor N.Y. State Coun. on Arts, 1968-70; tchr. theatre arts Norwich Bd. Edn. summer 1970, Met. Edn. Dist., San Jose, 1998. Author: The Rabbi's Daughter, 1987, Between the Night Shadows, 1989, Thresholds, 1990, Billington's, 1992, What Do I Wear Now? The Breast Cancer Legacy, 1995, Gettin On With It, 2001, The WaterStreet Diaries: a work in progress, 2001, (in pen name Claire Z. Cameron) The Home, 2002; guest spkr., 1992—; animation voice-overs E.J. Sound/Hosca Prodn., Inc., San Jose; featured poet Norwich Sun, N.Y., 2000—. Youth leader B'nai B'rith; reader for the blind San Jose Pub. Libr. Mem. Am. Ednl. Theatre Assn., Internat. Platform Assn. Home: 5363 Joseph Ln San Jose CA 95118

WEINER, CLARE FRANCES, social worker, psychotherapist; b. Phila., Dec. 3, 1929; d. Jack and Jessie (Rosengarten) Weinbaum; m. George C. Wheeler, Jan. 21, 1978; children by previous marriage: Justin M., Kate J., Lucian J. BS, Temple U., 1951; MSW, U. Wis., 1967. Diplomate Am. Bd. Examiners in Clin. Social Work. Social worker Ohio Valley Mental Retardation Evaluation Unit, Athens, Ohio, 1968-69; social worker inpatient psychiat. svc. VA Hosp., Albany, N.Y., 1969-70; chief social worker Schenectady County Outpatient Mental Health Clinic, 1970-76; adult treatment team leader, supervising social worker Saratoga County Mental Health Ctr., N.Y., 1976-81; pvt. practice psychotherapy individuals, couples, families Schenectady, 1975—. Fellow N.Y. State Soc. for Clin. Social Workers, Nat. Assn. Social Workers (diplomate); mem. Gestalt Inst. Cleve., Burnt Hills Oratorio Soc. Avocations: music, hiking, quilting. Office: 29 Front St Schenectady NY 12305-1301

WEINER, DEBORAH DORIS, non-profit executive; b. Bronx, N.Y., Feb. 13, 1930; d. Daniel Noah and Rose Mendelson; children: Gail T. Allan, Bruce B. Weiner. MSW, SUNY, Stony Brook, 1989. Cert. social worker, N.Y. Case mgr. Family Svc. Assn., Hempstead, N.Y., 1988; dir. Ret. and Sr. Vol. Program, Smithtown, 1989—. Mem. adv. bd. N.Y. State Assembly Com., Albany, 1989—; mem. N.Y. State Office of Aging Adv. Com., 2000-. Mem. NASW, Nat. Assn. Ret. and Sr. Vol. Program Dirs. (del. 1993-96, v.p. 1996-2001), Am. Soc. Aging, Nat. Coun. Aging, Zonta Suffolk County (bd. dirs. 1990—). Jewish. Avocations: reading, travel, golf, theater. Office: Ret Sr Vol Program 1 W Main St Smithtown NY 11787-2629

WEINER, EARL DAVID, lawyer; b. Balt., Aug. 21, 1939; s. Jacob Joseph and Sophia Gertrude (Rachanow) W.; m. Gina Helen Priestley Ingoglia, Mar. 30, 1962; children: Melissa Danis Balmain, John Barlow. AB, Dickinson Coll., 1960; LL.B., Yale U., 1968. Bar: N.Y. 1969. Assoc. Sullivan & Cromwell, N.Y.C., 1968-76, ptnr., 1976—. Adj. prof. Rutgers U. Sch. Law, 1987-88; bd. dirs. Solvay Techs. Inc., Hedwin Corp., The Acting Co., vice chair, 1992—, v.p., 1991-92. Gov. Bklyn. Heights Assn., 1980-87, pres., 1985-87, adv. com., 1987—; gov. The Heights Casino, 1979-84, pres., 1981-84; trustee Bklyn. Bot. Garden, 1985—, chmn. 1998—; trustee Green-Wood Cemetery, 1986—, Bklyn. Hosp. Ctr., 1998—; bd. advisors Dickinson Coll., Carlisle, Pa., 1986-90, chmn., 1988-90, trustee, 1988-2002, vice chmn., 1998-2002; mem. adv. com. East Rock Inst., 1988—; bd. visitors U. Md. Ctr. for Environ. Svcs., 2002—. Lt. USN, 1961-65. Fellow Fgn. Policy Assn. (sr.); mem. ABA, N.Y. State Bar Assn., Assn. Bar City N.Y. Office: Sullivan & Cromwell 125 Broad St Fl 28 New York NY 10004-2489

WEINER, EDWARD, civil engineer, federal agency administrator; b. Bklyn., Mar. 31, 1941; s. Abe C. and Elsie (Botwinick) W.; m. Joanne Jessen, Sept. 9, 1967 Idiv. Mar. 1988); children: Jennifer Lynn, Michael Andrew; m. Janis Lynn Wolford, Oct. 7, 1995. BA, BCE, NYU, 1963; MS in Civil Engring., Purdue U., 1964; M. in Pub. Adminstrn., U. So. Calif., 1978. Registered profl. engr. Hwy. research engr. Bur. of Pub. Rds., then Fed. Hwy. Adminstrn., Washington, 1964-70; mgr. urban analysis program Office Sec. of Transp., 1970-77, sr. policy analyst, 1978—, mobility and infrastructure team leader, 2001—. Sec. Task Force on Pub. Transp., Transp. Research Bd., 1971-72, mem. Com. on Travel Behavior and Values, Oct. 1973—; group 1 council, transp. systems planning and adminstrn., 1984-90; mem. com. Intergovernmental Relations and Policy Process, Telecomm. and Travel Behavior; guest lectr. George Washington U., U. Va., Portland State U., U. Wis.; U.S. rep. internat. working groups on urban travel. Co-editor: Emerging Transportation Planning Methods, 1978; author, co-author: Urban Transportation Planning in the U.S., 1987, revised edit., 1999, National Transportation System Initiative, 1999; (monographs) Role of Taxicabs in Urban Transportation, 1974, Glossary of Urban Public Transportation Terms, 1978, Modal Split, 1966; co-editor Internat. Assn. for Travel Behavior newsletter, 1985-88; contbr. over 70 articles to profl. jours.; mem. editorial adv. bd. Transp., 1978-80, 92-2000. Asst. troop leader Girl Scouts Am., Silver Spring, Md., 1981-82; v.p. Unitarian Universalist Ch. of Silver Spring, 1984, pres., 1985-86, v.p., 1998-99. Edn. for Public Mgmt. fellow U.S. Dept. Transp., 1978; recipient Bronze medal Dept. Transp., 1981, Spl. Achievement award, 1990, 95, 98, 99, 2000. Mem. ASCE, Transp. Research Bd. Home: 16615 Harbour Town Dr Silver Spring MD 20905-4082 Office: US Dept Transp P-30 400 7th St SW Washington DC 20590-0001 E-mail: ed.weiner@ost.dot.gov.

WEINER, FERNE, psychologist; b. N.Y.C., June 14, 1928; d. Irving Kapp and Peggy (Finkelstein) Hessberg; m. Howard Weiner, July 20, 1948; children: Irving Kenneth, Laurie. BA, Skidmore Coll., 1965; MA, Sarah Lawrence Coll., 1971; PhD, U. Hawaii, 1975. Lic. psychologist, Conn., Hawaii. Asst. prof. West Oahu Coll. U. Hawaii, Honolulu, 1975-77; staff psychologist Cmty. Guidance Clinic, Manchester, Conn., 1978-83; chief cons. psychologist Consultation and Evaluation Ctr., Meriden, 1984-85; psychologist cons. Disability Determination Svcs., Hartford, 1986-87, Honolulu, 1988—; police psychologist Honolulu Police Dept., 1988. Pvt. practice, Greenwich, Conn., 1983-87, Honolulu, 1988—; cons. Adopt-A-Sch. Project, Honolulu, 1991-94; interviewer, therapist Sexual Abuse Treatment Team, Manchester, 1979-83; cons., trainer Conn. schs., day care, ch. groups, 1979-87. Contbr. articles to profl. jours. Active Disaster Assistance Mgmt. Team, Hawaii, 1994-95; v.p., sec. Queens Court at Kapiolani Bd., Honolulu, 1992-95; admissions rep. Hawaii Sarah Lawrence Coll., Honolulu, 1970-80; cons. to adoptees search Orphan Voyage, Conn., 1980-87; mentor Girl Scout Coun. Am., Oahu, 1993-94. Mem. Am. Psychol. Assn. (clin. psychotherapy and neuropsychology divsn.), Hawaii Psychol. Assn., Nat. Registry Health Svcs. Providers, Outrigger Canoe Club, Honolulu Club. Democrat. Jewish. Avocations: aerobics, interior design, property renovation, gourmet cooking, travel. Address: 9776 Claiborne Sq La Jolla CA 92037-1158 E-mail: wfeine1@san.rr.com.

WEINER, GEORGE DAVID, medical association executive, researcher; b. N.Y.C., Aug. 10, 1942; s. Harry and Edith May (Whitworth) W., m. Janet Elaine Buring, Jan. 20, 1979; children: Amy Lynn Lochner, Joshua Louis Lochner. AB, Cornell U., 1966, MS in Regional Planning, 1968, PhD, 1976. Asst. prof. Syracuse U., N.Y., 1976-78; assoc. social scientist Rand Corp., Santa Monica, Calif., 1978-81; asst. prof. Cleve. State U., 1981-85; v.p., dir. The MetroHealth Sys., Cleve., 1985-97; v.p. policy analysis & rsch. Ctr. for Health Affairs, 1997-2001; sr. rsch. fellow Fedn. for Cmty. Planning, 2001—. Adj. assoc. prof. Case Western Reserve U., Cleve., 1994—; mem. data com., Ohio Hosp. Assn., Columbus, Ctr. for Health Affairs, Cleve.; project dir. Am. Internat. Health Alliance, Washington, 1995—. Coun. mem. Shaker Heights, Ohio; chmn., mem. Landmarks Commn., Shaker Heights; trustee Clark Metro Devel. Corp., Cleve., 1995-97, Larchmere Devel. Corp., Cleve., 1995-97, The Art Studio, 1999. Fellow R.K. Mellon Found., 1967, USPHS, 1968, 69-72, Williamson fellow in applied rsch., 2000. Mem. APHA, AHSR, Cornell Club (Northeastern Ohio chpt., treas.), Print Club of Cleve. Avocations: print making, sculpting, hist. preservation, architecture, skiing. Home: 2883 Warrington Rd Shaker Heights OH 44120-2420 Office: Fedn for Cmty Planning 1226 Huron Rd E Cleveland OH 44115-1702

WEINER, GEORGE JAY, internist; b. Plainview, N.Y., Mar. 1, 1956; m. Teresa Emily Wilhelm, July 30, 1983; children: Aaron, Miriam, Nathan. BA, Johns Hopkins U., 1978; MD, Ohio State U., 1981. Resident in internal medicine Med. Coll. Ohio, Toledo, 1981-85; hematology/oncology fellow U. Mich., Ann Arbor, 1985-89; asst. prof. medicine U. Iowa, Iowa City, 1989-94, assoc. prof., 1994-99, prof., 1999—, dir. Cancer Ctr., 1998—. Dir. Holden Comprehensive Cancer Ctr., U. Iowa. Achievements include devel. of new approaches to cancer immunotherapy. Office: Univ of Iowa 5970 JPP Iowa City IA 52242

WEINER, GERALD ARNE, stockbroker; b. Chgo., Dec. 20, 1941; s. Irwin S. and Lilyan (Stock) W.; m. Barbara I. Allen, June 18, 1967; children: Rachel Anne, Sara Naomi. BSS, Loyola U., Chgo., 1964; student, U. Vienna, 1962-63; MS, Georgetown U., 1966; postgrad., Ind. U., 1966-72, S.E. Asian Areas Cert., 1967. Pacification specialist AID, Laos, 1965; instr. polit. sci. Loyola U., Chgo., 1970-72; asst. v.p. A.G. Becker & Co., 1973-78; sr. v.p. Oppenheimer & Co., 1978-83, J. David Securities, Inc., Chgo., 1983-84, Morgan Stanley , Chgo., 1984—. Exec. edn. for securities industry Wharton Sch. Bus. U. Pa., 1988-90. Trustee Highland Park Police Pension Fund. Mucia fellow, 1969. Mem. Midwest Bonsai Soc., Multiplex Club. Republican. Jewish. Office: Morgan Stanely 70 W Madison St Ste 300 Chicago IL 60602-4278

WEINER, GERSHON RALPH, physician; b. Detroit, Apr. 12, 1935; s. Morris and Phyllis Weiner; m. Myra H. Levenson, July 1956 (div. May 1972); children: Bruce J., Sandra C. Mishory, Stuart J.(dec.) ; m. M. Jean (Jeannie) Mann, Dec. 31, 1975; 1 child Joel Edward Jackson. BS, Wayne State U., 1955; DO, Des Moines U., 1963. Diplomate Nat. Bd. Examiners, Am. Osteo Bd. Phys. Medicine and Rehab. (bd. examiner 1982-91). Intern Mt. Clemens (Mich.) Gen. Hosp., 1963-64; family practice Detroit and Warren, Mich., 1964-71; practice in emergency medicine Macomb (Mich.) County hosps., 1964-73; dep. med. examiner Macomb County, 1965-74; resident, fellow in physical medicine and rehab. Wayne State U. Sch. Medicine, Detroit, 1971-74; chief resident, 1973-74; practice medicine specializing in physical medicine and rehab. Wayne and Macomb Counties, 1974—. Team physician wheelchair basketball team Detroit Sparks, 1971-72; rehab. med. cons. Detroit League Handicapped Goodwill Industries, 1972-76; lectr. phys. therapy Wayne State U., 1972-74; lectr., cons., med. dir. rehab. svcs., BiCounty Cmty. Hosp., Warren, Riverside Osteo. Hosp., Trenton, Mich., 1974—; clin. asst. prof. Mich. State U.; cons. Henry Ford Wyandotte Hosp., Wyandotte, Mich., 2002-; spkr. in field. Contbr. articles to profl. jours. Served to capt. USAF, 1955-58. Fellow Am. Osteo. Coll. Phys. Medicine and Rehab. (trustee 1982-89, pres. 1984-85); mem. Am. Osteo. Assn., Am. Congress Rehab. Medicine, Mich. Osteo. Assn., Macomb County Osteo. Assn. Jewish. Avocations: photography, reading, community service.

WEINER, HAROLD M. retired radiologist; b. Phila., Apr. 30, 1937; s. Louis A. and Anna (Becker) W.; divorced; children: Lori, Julie. BA summa cum laude, Temple U., 1958, MD with hons., 1962. Diplomate Am. Bd. Radiology, Nat. Bd. Med. Examiners. Intern Polyclinic Hosp., Harrisburg, Pa., 1962-63; resident in pathology VA Hosp., Phila., 1965, resident in radiology, 1966-68; staff radiologist Sacred Heart Hosp., Norristown, Pa., 1969-73, chief radiologist, 1973-94; chmn. infectious disease com., 1976-77, patient care com., 1977-80, med. audit com., 1981-87; sec.-treas. med. staff, 1982-85; radiologist Suburban Gen. Hosp., Norristown, Pa., 1994-95; ret., 1997. Presenter numerous papers med. meetings. Served to capt. M.C. USAF, 1963-65. Decorated Legion of Honor Chapel of Four Chaplains. Mem. Am. Heart Assn. (coun. on cardiovascular radiology), Pa. Radiologic Soc., Pa. Med. Soc., Montgomery County Med. Soc. (chmn. continuing edn. com. 1980-84, bd. dirs. 1983-89, v.p. 1983-84, pres. 1985-86, del. to Pa. Med. Soc. 1979-92, chair nominating com. 1988-89), Phila. Coll. Physicians and Surgeons, Phila. Roentgen Ray Soc., Am. Coll. Radiology (alt. councilor 1983-85), N.Y. Acad. Scis., Radiolog. Soc. N.Am., World Affairs Coun., Alpha Omega Alpha. Avocations: photography, art, bridge, music, travel.

WEINER, HENRY, biochemistry educator; b. Cleve., May 18, 1937; s. Philip and Hilda (Dapeer) Weiner; m. Esther Riza Blankfeld, June 12, 1960; children: Suzanna Lynn, Alexander James. BS in Chem. Engring., Case Inst. Tech., 1959; PhD, Purdue U., 1963. Postdoctoral Brookhaven Nat. Lab., Upton, N.Y., 1963-65, Karolinska Inst., Stockholm, 1965-66; prof. biochemistry Purdue U., West Lafayette, Ind., 1966—. Editor: Enzymology and Molecular Biology of Carbonyl Metabolism, others; contbr. articles to books and profl. jours. Officer civic and religious orgns., West Lafayette. Recipient Merit award NIH, 1989. Avocations: baking, wood turning, travel. Office: Purdue U Dept Biochemistry West Lafayette IN 47907-1153 Office Fax: 765-494-7897. E-mail: hweiner@purdue.edu.

WEINER, HOWARD MARC, physician; b. Feb. 25, 1946; BSc, Marietta Coll., 1967; MD, U. Cin., 1971; MPH, Med. Coll. Wis., 1994. Diplomate Am. Bd. Forensic Examiners, Diplomate Am. Bd. Internal Medicine, Am. Bd. Allergy, Asthma & Immunology, Am. Bd. Preventive Medicine/Occupl. Medicine, Am. Bd. Ind. Med. Examiners. Intern in medicine Temple U. Hosp., Phila., 1971-72, resident in internal medicine, 1972-74; fellow in allergy and clin. immunology Hosp. of U. Pa., 1974-76; pres., physician Allergy & Asthma Assocs. West Boca, Boca Raton, Fla., 1988—; pres., med. dir. Med. Assessment Inst. Inc., 1997—. Chmn. ethics com. Palm Beach County Med. Soc., West Palm Beach, Fla., 1994-97; bd. dirs. Primus Physicians Svcs., Inc., So. Fla. Mem. Omicron Delta Kappa Soc., Pi Kappa Epsilon. Office: 9980 Central Park Blvd N Boca Raton FL 33428-1762

WEINER, IRVING BERNARD, psychologist; b. Grand Rapids, Mich., Aug. 16, 1933; s. Jacob H. and Mollie Jean (Laevin) W.; m. Frances Shair, June 9, 1963; children: Jeremy Harris, Seth Howard. BA, U. Mich., Ann Arbor, 1955, MA, 1957, PhD, 1959. Diplomate Am. Bd. Profl. Psychology. From instr. to prof. psychiatry and pediat. U. Rochester, N.Y., 1959-72; head divsn. psychology U. Rochester Med. Center, 1968-72; prof. psychology, chmn. dept. Case Western Res. U., 1972-77, dean grad. studies, 1976-79; vice chancellor for acad. affairs U. Denver, 1979-83, prof. psychology, 1979-85; v.p. for acad. affairs Fairleigh Dickinson U., Teaneck, N.J., 1985-89, prof. psychology, 1985-89; prof. psychiatry U. South Fla., Tampa, 1989—. Adv. editor John Wiley & Sons, 1967-93, 99—, Lawrence Erlbaum Assocs., 1993-99; psychology edn. rev. com. NIMH, 1977-81. Author: Psychodiagnosis in Schizophrenia, 1966, Psychological Disturbance in Adolescence, 1970, rev. edit., 1992, Rorschach Handbook, 1971, Child Development, 1972, Principles of Psychotherapy, 1975, rev. edit., 1998, Development of the Child, 1978, Child and Adolescent Psychopathology, 1982, Rorschach Assessment of Children and Adolescents, 1982, rev. edit., 1995, Adolescence, 1985, rev. edit., 1995, Handbook of Forensic Psychology, 1987, rev. edit., 1999, Principles of Rorschach Interpretation, 1998; editor: Readings in Child Development, 1972, Clinical Methods in Psychology, 1976, 83, Jour. Personality Assessment, 1985-93, Rorschachiana, 1989-96; mem. editl. bd. Profl. Psychology, 1971-76, Jour. Adolescent Health Care, 1979-87, Children and Youth Svcs. Rev., 1979-91, Jour. Pediat. Psychology, 1981-87, Devel. and Behavioral Pediat., 1985-96, Studi Rorschachiani, 1985—, European Jour. Psychol. Assessment, 1985—, Jour. Adolescent Rsch., 1986-91, Jour. Personality Disorders, 1986-92, Psychol. Assessment, 1994—. Recipient Disting. Profl. Achievement award Genesee Psychol. Assn., 1974 Fellow APA, Am. Psychol. Soc., Acad. Clin. Psychology, Acad. Forensic Psychology; mem. Assn. Advancement Psychology, Soc. Personality Assessment (pres. 1976-78, Disting. Contbn. award 1983), Assn. Internship Ctrs. (exec. com. 1971-76), Soc. Rsch. in Adolescence, Soc. for Rsch. in Child and Adolescent Psychopathology, Soc. for Exploration Psychotherapy Integration, Soc. Pediat. Psychology, Am. Psychol. Law Soc., Internat. Rorschach Soc. (pres. 1999—), Phi Beta Kappa, Sigma Xi, Phi Kappa Phi. Home and Office: 13716 Halliford Dr Tampa FL 33624-6903 E-mail: iweiner@hsc.usf.edu.

WEINER, JEROME HARRIS, mechanical engineering educator; b. N.Y.C., Apr. 5, 1923; s. Barnet and Dora (Muchar) W.; m. Florence Mensch, June 24, 1950; children: Jonathan David, Eric Daniel. B. Mech. Engring., Cooper Union U., 1943; A.M., Columbia U., 1946, PhD, 1952. Mem. faculty Columbia U., N.Y.C., 1952-68, prof. mech. engring., 1960-68, acting chmn. dept., 1961-62; L. Herbert Ballou Univ. prof. Brown U., Providence, 1968-93; L. Herbert Ballou Univ. prof. emeritus, 1993—. Author: (with B.A. Boley) Theory of Thermal Stresses, 1960, Statistical Mechanics of Elasticity, 1983. Fulbright research scholar Rome, Italy, 1958-59, Haifa, Israel, 1965- 66; Guggenheim fellow, 1965-66 Mem. Am. Phys. Soc., Am. Math. Soc., ASME Home: 24 Taber Ave Providence RI 02906-4113 Office: Brown U 79 Waterman St Providence RI 02912-9079

WEINER, JODY CARL, lawyer, author, producer; b. Chgo., Oct. 19, 1948; s. Leo and Sarah J. Weiner; m. Nancy S. Calef, Mar. 4, 1993. BA, U. Wis., 1970; JD, DePaul U., 1974. Bar: Ill. 1974, U.S. Dist. Ct. (no. dist.) Ill. 1974, U.S. Ct. Appeals (6th and 7th cirs.) 1975, Calif. 1989, U.S. Dist. Ct. (no. dist.) Calif. 1989. Assoc. Law Offices Frazin & Frazin, Chgo., 1974-77; ptnr. Muslin & Weiner, 1977-80; pvt. practice, 1980-85; sr. assoc. Law Offices James Duryea Jr., San Francisco, 1989-91; pvt. practice, 1991—. Gen. mgr. The Island Hotel, Koh Samui, Thailand, 1994-96; corp. counsel Skyy Spirits, LLC, San Francisco, 1995—. Author: Raise Your Other Right Hand, 1991, Prisoners of Truth, 2001; assoc. prodr.: (feature film) Mama's Boy, 2000; (documentary) A Conversation with Koko, 1999. Cons., advisor Artist Guild San Francisco, 1996-99, Gorilla Found., Woodside, Calif., 1998-99, Eureka Theatre, San Francisco, 1998-2000; dir. Golda Found., Calif., 2001-. Office: 846 Filbert St San Francisco CA 94133-2627 E-mail: jodycarlweiner@aol.com.

WEINER, KAREN COLBY (KAREN LYNN COLBY), psychologist, lawyer; b. Oak Park, Ill., Oct. 28, 1943; d. Leonard L. and Mildred Irene (Berman) Colby; m. J. Laevin Weiner, July 26, 1964; children: Joel Laevin, Doren Robin, Anthony Justin. BA, Mich. State U., East Lansing, 1964; JD, U. Detroit, 1977, MA, 1986, PhD, 1988. Bar: Mich. 1977, D.C. 1978. Speech therapist Oak Park Sch. Dist., 1965-68; law clk. justice G. Mennen Williams Mich. Supreme Ct., Lansing, 1977-79; assoc. Dickinson, Wright, Moon, Van Dusen & Freeman, Detroit, 1979-83; intern in psychology Detroit Psychiat. Inst., 1986-88; psychologist Northland Clinic, Southfield, Mich., 1987-88, Counseling Assocs., Southfield, 1988—; postdoctoral intern Wyandotte (Mich.) Hosp. and Health Ctr., 1988-90; dir. psychol. svcs., quality assurance coord. Counseling Assocs., Southfield, 1991-99. Hearing panelist Atty. Discipline Bd., Detroit, 1982-95; hearing referee Mich. Civil Rights Commn., Detroit, 1983-91; mem. Mich. Bd. Psychology, 1999—; adj. prof. U. Detroit Mercy, 2001—. Contbr. articles to profl. jours. Mem. adv. bd. Mich. chpt. Anti-Defamation League, 1981-90. Fellow Mich. Psychol. Assn. (mem. ethics com. 1992—, chmn. legis. com. 1993, chmn. ethics com. 1997-99); mem. APA, Mich. Soc. for Psychoanalytic Psychology (pres. 1995-97, sec. 1991-92, treas. 1992-94), Women Lawyers Assn. Mich. (pres. 1981-82, pres. Found. 1982-83), Mich. Bar Assn. (chmn. spl. com. for expansion under represented groups in law 1980-83). Jewish. Home: 2501 Long Lake Rd West Bloomfield MI 48323 Office: 29260 Franklin Rd Ste 115 Southfield MI 48034-1144 E-mail: drkcw@aol.com.

WEINER, KENNETH BRIAN, lawyer; b. N.Y.C., Oct. 13, 1954; s. Irwin I. and Elayne B. (Biffer) W.; m. Sandra Hong, Apr. 30, 2000. BSCE, Case Western Res. U., 1976; JD summa cum laude, N.Y. Law Sch., 1986. Bar: N.Y. 1986, Washington 1997; registered profl. engr., N.J. Quality control engr. Cosmic Constrn. Co., Newport News, Va., 1976-77; project engr., geotech. engr. Mueser Rutledge Cons. Engrs., N.Y.C., 1977-86; assoc. Olwine, Connelly, Chase, O'Donnel & Weyner, 1986-91, Ballard Spahr Andrews & Ingersoll LLP, Washington, 1992, Reid & Priest LLP, Washington, 1992-95, ptnr., 1996-98, Thelen Reid & Priest LLP, Washington, 1998—. Contbr. articles to profl. jours. Mem. Aircraft Owners and Pilots Assn., Mooney Aircraft Pilots Assn. Avocation: flying. Office: Thelen Reid & Priest LLP 701 Pennsylvania Ave NW Washington DC 20004-2608 E-mail: kweiner@thelenreid.com.

WEINER, LAWRENCE, lawyer; b. Phila., Aug. 20, 1942; s. Robert A. and Goldie Weiner; m. Jane M. Coulthard, Feb. 28, 1976; 1 child, Kimberly. BS in Econs., U. Pa., 1964, JD, 1967. Bar: Pa. 1967, U.S. Dist. Ct. (ea. dist.) Pa. 1967, Fla. 1970, U.S. Dist. Ct. (so. dist.) Fla. 1976, U.S. Ct. Appeals (5th cir.) 1976, U.S. Tax Ct. 1984. Assoc., ptnr. Blank, Rome, Klaus & Comisky, Phila., 1967-71, 1975-77; ptnr. Weiner & Weisenfeld, P.A., Miami Beach, Fla., 1971-73, Pettigrew & Bailey, Miami, 1973-75; pres. Lawrence Weiner, P.A., 1977-83; ptnr. Spieler, Weiner & Spieler, P.A., 1983-89, Weiner & Cummings, P.A., Miami, 1989-94, Weiner, Cummings & Vittoria, Miami, 1994—. Lectr. Wharton Sch. U. Pa., Phila., 1968-70; instr. bus. law and acctg. Community Coll. Phila., 1967-70; lectr. estate planning various non-lawyer groups, Miami, 1972—. Mem. Fla. Bar (liaison non-lawyers groups 1980-87), Pa. Bar Assn., Phila. Bar Assn., Dade County Bar Assn. (chmn. ins. com. 1977-78, probate law com. 1992—). Democrat. Jewish. Office: Weiner Cummings & Vittoria 1428 Brickell Ave Ste 400 Miami FL 33131-3436

WEINER, LAWRENCE CHARLES, artist; b. Bronx, N.Y., Feb. 10, 1942; One-man shows include Hirshhorn Mus. and Sculpture Garden, Washington, 1990, San Francisco Mus. Modern Art, 1992, Walker Art Ctr., Mpls., 1994, Städtische Galerie Chemnitz, Germany, 1994, Phila. Mus. Art, 1994, Radio Düsseldorf, Germany, 1994, Leo Castelli Gallery, N.Y., 1994, N.Y. Pub. libr., 1995, Mus. Ludwig Köln, 1995, Mus. Boijmans Van Beuningen, Rotterdam, 1996, The Lawrence Weiner Poster Archive, Kunsthalle Nüurnberg, 1998; exhibited in group shows Mus. Modern Art, N.Y., 1970, Art Inst. Chgo., 1974, Tate Gallery, London, 1982, Mus. Contemporary Art, L.A., 1983, Deutsche Guggenheim, Berlin, 2000, Kunstmuseum Rolfsburg, 2000; represented in permanent collections Mus. Modern Art, N.Y., Guggenheim Mus., N.Y., Van Abbe Mus., Eindhoven, The Netherlands, Staatliches Mus. Mönchengladbach, Germany, Ctr. Georges Pompidou, Paris, Nat. Gallery Australia, Canberra, others. Recipient Arthur Köpcke prize, Copenhagen, 1991, Wolfgang Hahn prize, 1995, Skowhegan medal for painting, 1999; fellow Nat. Endowment Arts, 1976, 83; John Simon Guggenheim fellow, 1994. Home: 297 W 4th St New York NY 10014-2207

WEINER, LEONARD JAY, surgery educator; b. Nov. 25, 1935; AB, UCLA, 1957; MD, Albert Einstein Coll. Medicine, 1961. Intern Yale U., New Haven, 1961-62; resident in gen. surgery U. Pa. Hosp., Phila., 1962-67; asst. prof. surgery Valley Forge Army Hosp., 1967-68; resident in plastic surgery, asst. prof. surgery U. Ariz., Tucson, 1969-72; asst. prof. surgery U.S. Army, Vietnam, 1968-69; prof. surgery U. Louisville, 1994—2002, dir. emeritus divsn. plastic and reconstructive surgery, 1994—. Officer M.C., U.S. Army, 1968-69, Vietnam. Mem. Am. Soc. Plastic and Reconstructive Surgeons (bd. dirs. 1980-87), Am. Soc. Aesthetic Plastic Surgeons (bd. dirs. 1982-88), Ky. Soc. for Plastic and Reconstructive Surgeons (pres. 1975-76).

WEINER, LESLIE PHILIP, neurology educator, researcher; b. Bklyn., Mar. 17, 1936; s. Paul Larry and Sarah (Paris) W.; m. Judith Marilyn Hoffman, Dec. 26, 1959; children: Patrice, Allison, Matthew, Jonathan. BA, Wilkes Coll., 1957; MD, U. Cin., 1961. Diplomate Am. Bd. Psychiatry and Neurology. Intern in medicine SUNY, Syracuse, 1961-62; resident in neurology Johns Hopkins Hosp., Balt., 1962-65, fellow, 1967-69; resident Balt. City Hosp., 1962-63; fellow in virology Slow Virus Lab., Nat. Inst. Neurol and Communicative Disorders-Stroke, NIH, Balt., 1969; asst. prof. neurology Johns Hopkins U., 1969-72, assoc. prof., 1972-75; prof. neurology and microbiology U. So. Calif. Sch. Medicine, L.A., 1975—, chmn. dept. neurology, 1979—, Richard Angus Grant Sr. chair in neurology, 1987—. Chief neurologist U. So. Calif. Univ. Hosp., 1991-96, mem. bd. govs.; chief neurologist L.A. county-U. So. Calif. Med. Ctr., 1979-94,; chmn. U. So. Calif. Gen. Clin. Res. Ctr., 1994-95; bd. dirs. John Douglas French Found., L.A., 1987-2000; mem. neurosci. tng. study sect. NIH, 1990-93; chmn., mem. sci. adv. bd. Hereditary Disease Found., 1992—, chmn., 1994-96; mem. programs rsch. adv. com. Nat. Multiple Sclerosis Soc., 2000—. Contbr. over 120 articles on neurology, immunology and virology to med. jours., chpts. to books; assoc. editor: Neurobase, 1994-95, Neuronet; mem. editl. bd. Infectious and Geographic Neurol., 1994—; assoc. editor: Neurobase. Bd. dirs. Starbright Found., L.A., 1991—99. Capt. M.C. U.S. Army, 1965—67. Grantee, Conrad Hilton Found., 1995—97, Kenneth Norris Found., 1995—, NIH, 1999—, Race to Erase MS Nancy Davis Ctrs. Without Walls, 2000—, McDonald Found., Oxnard Found., Gogan Found., Heron Found. Fellow: Am. Acad. Neurology; mem.: AAAS, Nat. MS Soc. (mem. adv. com. rsch. program 2000—, grant 2000—), Coalition Advancement Med. Rsch., Assn. Univ. Profs. Neurology, L.A. Acad. Medicine, Johns Hopkins U. Soc. Scholars, Soc. Neurosci., Am. Neurology Assn., Am. Health Assistance Found., Alpha Omega Alpha. Democrat. Jewish. Avocations: collecting books, concerts, plays. Home: 625 S Rimpau Blvd Los Angeles CA 90005-3842 Office: 1975 Zonal Ave # Kam410 Los Angeles CA 90089-0105 Fax: 323-442-3015. E-mail: lweiner@hsc.usc.edu.

WEINER, LOWELL B. corporate communications executive; m. Leslie Weiner; 1 child. BM, Ind. U., 1972, MM, 1974; PhD, NYU, 1980. Formerly with Hill and Knowlton, Ketchum Pub. Rels.; formerly dir. pub. rels. and internat. comm. Schering-Plough Corp.; asst. v.p. pub. rels. Wyeth, Madison, NJ, 1995—. Trustee Colonial Symphony. Office: Wyeth 5 Giralda Farms Madison NJ 07940-1027 E-mail: weinerl@wyeth.com.

WEINER, MARC V. health services facility executive; b. Boston, Aug. 15, 1952; s. George and Edith (Kaitz) W.; m. Deborah G., Jan. 21, 1983; children: Kelly, Matthew. BA, Guilford Coll., 1974; MHA, Tulane U., 1976. CFO Naval Submarine Med. Ctr., Groton, Conn., 1976-80; chief operating officer Irvington (N.J.) Gen. Hosp., 1980-85; CFO Cottage Hosp., Grosse Pointe, Mich., 1985-88; sr. v.p. St. Francis Hosp., Poughkeepsie, N.Y., 1988-94; COO Barnert Hosp., Paterson, N.J., 1994-96; regional v.p. PhyAmerica Physician Group, Inc., 1996-99; mng. dir. The Cons. Gateway, Oakland, N.J., 1996—. Exec. v.p., COO PhyAm. Physician Group, Inc., 1999—. Fellow Am. Coll. Healthcare Execs., No. Metro. Healthcare Assn.; mem. Assn. Healthcare Execs. N.J., Am. Hosp. Assn. Home: 25 Oneida Ave Oakland NJ 07436-3006 E-mail: marc.weiner@phyamerica.net.

WEINER, MAX, educational psychology educator; b. Hartford, Conn., May 7, 1926; s. Harry Sam and Gertrude (Cohen) W.; m. Gloria Sall, Feb. 24, 1960; children: William Ronald, Jennifer Sharon. BA, U. Conn., 1950; MA, Trinity Coll., 1953; PhD, Yale U., 1957. Sci. tchr. Meriden (Conn.) Pub. Schs., 1952-55; guidance dir. White Plains (N.Y.) Pub. Schs., 1956-59; assoc. prof. Bklyn. Coll., CUNY, 1959-68; prof. Grad. Sch. CUNY, 1968-81, acting univ. dean, tchr. edn., 1973-74, exec. officer PhD program edn. psychology, 1970-76, dir. Ctr. for Advanced Study Edn., 1970-78, acting dean rsch. Grad. Sch., 1978-79; dean edn. Fordham U., N.Y.C., 1981-93, prof. ednl. psychology, 1981-97, prof. and dean emeritus, 1997—. Cons. psychologist SUNY Health Sci. Ctr., Bklyn., 1967-89; mem. nat. commn. on excellence in edn. adminstrn. Univ. Coun. for Edn. Adminstrn., 1985-87; mem. nat. adv. commn. Coll. Bd. Equity 2000, 1993-2000. Contbr. articles to profl. jours. Treas. N.Y. Alliance for Pub. Schs., N.Y.C., 1987-93; mem. Mayor's Commn. on Spl. Edn., N.Y.C., 1984-85; bd. dirs. Arthritis Found., Atlanta, 1974-76; trustee Beth El Synagogue, New Rochelle, N.Y., 1985-2001, La Scuola, N.Y., 1986—; bd. visitors Scranton U. Sch. Edn., 1992-2002. Fellow Japan Soc. Promotion Scis., 1978. Fellow APA, Am. Psychol. Soc., N.Y. Acad. Scis.; mem. ACA (life), AAAS, Arthritis Health Professions Assn. (pres. 1974-75), Am. Ednl. Rsch. Assn., Assn. Colls. and Schs. Edn. in State Univs. and Land Grant Colls. and Affiliated Pvt. Univs. (mem. exec. com. 1986-89, 92-93), Assn. for Measurement and Evaluation in Guidance (senator 1966-72, sec. 1973-75), Nat. Coun. Measurement in Edn., Westchester Assn. Hebrew Schs. (pres. 1982-84), Sigma Xi, Phi Delta Kappa, Kappa Delta Pi. Office: Fordham U Grad Sch Edn Neparan Rd Tarrytown NY 10591

WEINER, MERVYN, retired mergers and acquisitions executive; b. Boston, Aug. 21, 1935; s. Samuel and Celia Sophia (Weiner) W.; m. Marjorie J. Kapelsohn, June 1962 (div. May 1978): children: Joshua, Michael; m. Deborah B. Cleveland, Feb. 14, 1999. BS, U. Mass., 1957; MS, Tufts U., 1962; MBA with honors, Boston U., 1967. Group leader New England Nuclear, Boston, 1962-68; mgr. mktg. Hoffmann-LaRoche, Nutley, N.J., 1968-75; mgr. corp. strategic planning Pfizer, Inc., N.Y.C., 1975-77; v.p. mktg. Nichols Inst., San Pedro, Calif., 1977-78; cons. Marina del Rey, 1978-80; dir. corp. devel. Bristol-Myers Squibb Co., N.Y.C., 1980-92, v.p. corp. devel. health care group, 1992-95, ret., 1995. Adj. prof. Calif. State U., Long Beach, 1978-80. Contbr. articles to profl. jours. Tufts U. rsch. fellow, 1962. Mem. AAAS, Am. Chem. Soc., Am. Assn. Advancement Med. Instrumentation, N.Y. Acad. Scis., Biomedical Mktg. Assn. Avocations: sailing, fishing, tennis, music, art, literature. Home: 18 Rock Spring Rd West Orange NJ 07052-3007

WEINER, MORTON DAVID, banker, insurance agent; b. Balt., Aug. 19, 1922; s. Max and Rose (Wolfe) W.; children: Bruce, Lori, Julie, Jeff. BS, Towson State Coll., 1942; grad. exec. program, UCLA, 1959. Pres., dir. AVNET, Inc., N.Y.C., 1963-69; pres., owner Morton D. Weiner & Co., Inc., 1969-70; dir. USLIFE Corp., 1968-70; chmn. bd. Nat. Investors Life Ins. Cos., 1970-77; exec. v.p. Norris Grain Co., 1971-78; pres., chief exec. officer Norin Corp., 1971-78; chmn. bd. Maple Leaf Mills, Ltd., Toronto, Ont., Can., 1974-78; chmn., dir. South Atlantic Fin. Corp., 1978-80, Atico Fin. Corp., 1980-81; chmn. Morton D. Weiner & Co., 1981—. Bd. dirs. City Nat. Bank Fla. Served to capt. Signal Corps, U.S. Army, 1942-46, CBI. Office: 1065 95th St Bay Harbor Islands FL 33154

WEINER, NORMAN, pharmacology educator; b. Rochester, N.Y., July 13, 1928; m. Diana Elaine Weiner, 1955; children: Steven, David, Jeffrey, Gareth, Eric. BS, U. Mich., 1949; MD, Harvard U., 1953. Diplomate Am. Bd. Med. Examiners. Intern 2d and 4th Harvard Med. Svc., Boston City Hosp., 1953-54; rsch. med. officer USAF, 1954-56; instr. dept. pharmacology-biochemistry Sch. of Aviation Medicine, San Antonio, 1954-56; from instr. to asst. prof. Harvard Med. Sch., Boston, 1956-67; prof. pharmacology U. Colo. Health Sci. Ctr., Denver, 1967—, disting. prof., 1989, chmn. dept. pharmacology, 1967-87. Vis. prof. U. Calif., Berkeley, 1973-76; interim dean U. Colo. Sch. Medicine, 1983-84; Allan D. Bass lectr. sch. medicine Vanderbilt U., Nashville, 1983, divsn. v.p. Abbott Labs., Abbott Park, Ill., 1985-87; Pfizer lectr. Tex. Coll. Osteo. Medicine, Ft. Worth, 1985; disting. prof. UCHSC, 1989. Editor: Drugs and the Developing Brain, 1974, Structure and Function of Monoamine Enzymes, 1977, Regulation and Function of Monoamine Enzymes, 1981, Neuronal and Extraneuronal Events in Autonomic Pharmacology, 1984. Recipient Rsch. Career Devel. award USPHS, 1963, Kaiser Permanente award, 1974, 81, Otto Krayer award Am. Soc. Pharmacology and Exptl. Therapeutics, 1985; Spl. fellow USPHS, London, 1961-62; Disting. Volwiler Rsch. fellow Abbott Labs., 1988; Norman Weiner Festschrift, 1993; Julius Axelrod medal for outstanding scholarship in catecholamine rsch., 1993. Mem. N.Y. Acad. Scis., Assn. Med. Sch. Pharmacology, Am. Soc. Neurochemistry, Western Pharmacology Soc., Am. Coll. Neuropsychopharmacology, Soc. Neurosci., Biochem. Soc., Internat. Brain Rsch. Orgn., Internat. Soc. Neurochemistry, Rsch. Soc. on Alcoholism, Phi Beta Kappa, Sigma Xi, Alpha Omega Alpha, Phi Eta Sigma, Phi Lambda Upsilon, Phi Kappa Phi. Office: U Colo Health Sci Ctr Pharmacology Dept 4200 E 9th Ave Denver CO 80220-3706

WEINER, PATRICIA HERMANN, performing arts administrator, concert manager, artist manager; b. Cape Town, Republic of South Africa, July 7, 1941; came to U.S., 1962; d. Gunther and Beatrice (Frankel) Hermann; m. Jay Joseph Weiner, Mar. 31, 1969; children: Jason Lee, Wendy Lynn. BA in Music and Communications, Western Conn. State U., 1986. Outreach coord. Aston Magna, Danbury, Conn., 1986-88; assoc. dir. Berkshire Friends of Baroque Music, 1986-88; dir. concerts and press info. Sch. of Music Yale U., New Haven, 1988-91; mgr. New Music Consort, N.Y.C., 1991; prin. Weiner Mgmt. Co. Artist Mgmt., 1991-96; dir. major gifts Datahr Rehab. Ctr., Brookfield, Conn., 1996-98, mem. devel. bd., 1997-99; devel. dir. Music and Art Ctr. for the Handicapped, Bridgeport, Conn., 1997-99. Bd. dirs. Music Mountain, Falls Village, Conn. Assoc. prodr. (opera) Burning Bright Yale U., 1993. Founder Ives Festival Artists, Danbury, 1979; bd. dirs. Charles Ives Ctr., Danbury, 1979-80; publicity dir. Norwalk Youth Symphony, 1984-88; mgr., v.p. Western Conn. Symphony Orch., 1984-87; adminstr. Beth Israel Med. Ctr., N.Y.C., 1967 active pub. rels. devel. civic orgns. Avocations: music, playing flute, cooking. Address: 150 Brushy Hill Rd Danbury CT 06810-8431

WEINER, RICHARD, public relations executive; b. Bklyn., May 10, 1927; s. George M. and Sally (Kosover) W.; m. Florence Chaiken, Dec. 9, 1956; children: Jessica Weiner Lampert, Stephanie Weiner Iosbaker BS, U. Wis., 1949, MS, 1950. Pres. Creative Radio Assocs., Madison, Wis., 1951-52, Weiner-Morton Assocs., Madison, 1952-53; sr. v.p. Ruder & Finn, Inc., N.Y.C., 1953-68; pres. Richard Weiner, Inc., 1968-86; pres. N.Y. div. Porter/Novelli, 1987-88, sr. counselor, 1988—. Author: Professional's Guide to Public Relations Services, 1968, News Bureaus in the U.S., 1970, Syndicated Columnists, 1972, Professional's Guide to Publicity, 1979, Military Publications, 1979, College Alumni Publications, 1980, Investment Newsletters, 1981, Webster's New World Dictionary of Media and Communications, 1996. Bd. dirs. Medicare Rights Ctr. Fellow Pub. Rels. Soc. Am. (accredited counselor, Silver Anvil award 1965, 84, 86, 87, John Hill award 1984, Gold Anvil award 1990), Am. Arbitration Assn. Jewish. Office: Porter/Novelli 350 Lexington Ave New York NY 10017-5806 E-mail: dweiner@porternovelli.com. *The essence of life is growth, adaptation, change. I hope to continue to succeed in living vigorously.*

WEINER, RICHARD DAVID, psychiatrist, researcher; b. N.Y.C., Nov. 25, 1945; BS, MIT, 1967; M of Systems Engring., U. Pa., 1969; MD, PhD, Duke U., 1973. Diplomate Am. Bd. Psychiatry and Neurology. Prof. psychiatry Duke U. Med. Ctr., Durham, N.C., 1997—, dir. electroconvulsive therapy program, 1991—; chief, mental health svc. line VA Med. Ctr., 1993—. Office: Duke U Med Ctr PO Box 3309 Durham NC 27702-3309

WEINER, RICHARD LENARD, hospital administrator, educator, pediatrician; b. N.Y.C., May 23, 1951; s. Irving and Martha E. (Pell) W. BA in Biology cum laude, NYU, 1972; MD, Albert Einstein Coll. Medicine, 1975. Diplomate Am. Bd. Pediat. Resident in pediats. Bronx Mcpl. Hosp. Ctr./Albert Einstein Coll. Medicine, 1975-78; instr. in pediat. Albert Einstein Coll. of Medicine, Bronx, N.Y., 1978-80, asst. prof. pediat., 1980-95, assoc. prof. pediat., 1995—; pediatrician New Rochelle (N.Y.) Hosp. Med. Ctr., 1978-80; asst. dir. pediat. Hosp. of Albert Einstein Coll. of Medicine, Bronx, 1980-86; assoc. dir. pediat. Einstein-Weiler Hosp. MMC, 1986-97; dir. pediat. evaluation unit Einstein-Weiler Hosp., 1990-94; dir. divsn. faculty practice Albert Einstein Coll. Medicine/Montefiore Med. Ctr., 1993-99; dir. pediatrics Montefiore Med. Group, 1999—. Coord. pediatric med. edn. New Rochelle Hosp., 1978-80; chmn. pvt. practice governance coun. dept. pediatrics Albert Einstein Coll. of Medicine, 1988-91, 97-99; pres. Temple Beth Abraham Tarrytown, N.Y., 1995-96. Mem. editl. bd. Primary Care/Emergency Decisions, 1984-88; contbr. articles to Jour. Pediat., Pediat., Pediat. Infectious Diseases, Emergency Decisions. Recipient Physician's Recognition award AMA, 1982, 86; named one of Best Doctors in N.Y., N.Y. Mag., 1998-2002. Mem. Am. Acad. Pediats., Am. Physicians Fellowship for Medicine in Israel, Ambulatory Pediat. Assn., N.Y. Acad. Scis., N.Y. Pediat. Soc., Pediat. Alumni Assn. (coord. 1980-2000), Phi Beta Kappa, Beta Lambda Sigma. Jewish. Office: 1500 Astor Ave Bronx NY 10469-5900 Fax: 718-881-7752.

WEINER, ROBERT STEPHEN, federal agency administrator; b. Paterson, N.J., Apr. 3, 1947; s. Jess Joseph Weiner and Dorothea Violet (Slavin) Tabor. BA, Oberlin Coll., 1969; MA, U. Mass., 1974. Student coord. Hampshire County, dir. telephone bank Kennedy for U.S. Senate, Amherst, Mass., 1970; dir. nat. voter registration Young Dems. Am., Washington, 1971-72; dir. voter registration, media dir. get out the vote Dem. Nat. Com., 1972; legis. asst. Congressman Edward Koch, 1974-75; staff dir. subcom. health and long-term care U.S. Ho. of Reps., 1975-76, staff dir. com. aging, 1976-80; sr. assoc. Mgmt. Recruiters Internat., Springfield, Mass., 1981-83; dir. Robert Weiner Assocs., Amherst, 1983-86; media dir., press sec. com. narcotics U.S. Ho. of Reps., Washington, 1987-90, press sec./comms. dir. com. on govt. ops., 1990-95; dir. comm. Ho. Judiciary com. Minority and Cong. John Conyers Jr., 1995; dir. pub. affairs White House Drug Policy Office, Washington, 1995—2002; pres. Robert Weiner Assocs., Pub. Affairs and Issues, 2002—. Dir. gen. press rm. Dem. Nat. Convention, Atlanta, 1988, N.Y.C, 1992, Chgo., 1996, L.A., 2000; cons. Carter-Mondale Transition, Washington, 1976-77, Congressman Claude Pepper, Washington, 1975-89. Represented in permanent exhbns. Nat. Mus. Am. History, Smithsonian Instn., Washington; contbr. numerous articles to profl. jours. Dem. nominee for U.S. Congress, Mass., 1986; chmn. Road Runners Am. Nat. 10 Mile Championship, Amherst, 1984; vice chmn. Dem. Town Com., Amherst, 1984-87; legis. chmn. Pioneer Valley Gray Panthers, Amherst, 1981-87; nat campaign aide Kennedy for Pres., Washington, 1980. Named Communicator of Yr., Washington Crime News Svcs., 1988, 89, 90; 2d place U.S. Nat. Masters Track Championship, 1994, 97. Mem. Nat. Dem. Club (bd. govs. 2002—), Sugarloaf Mountain Athletic Club (pres. 1984-86), White House Athletic Ctr. (exec. bd. 1995-2001), Potomac Valley Track Club, Capitol Hill Runners (pres. 1991—). Avocations: running, attending performing arts, hiking. Home: 1104 Sanford Ln Accokeek MD 20607-2324 Office: PO Box 28271 1750 Pennsylvania Ave NW Washington DC 20038-8271

WEINER, RONALD GARY, accounting firm executive; b. Newark, Nov. 24, 1945; s. Seymour and Beatrice (Goldberg) W.; m. Vicki Miles, Sept. 8, 1973; children: Jennie, Maureen. BSBA, Babson Coll., 1966; postgrad., NYU, 1968-69, Harvard U., 1982. CPA, N.Y., N.J., Pa. Mgmt. cons., acct., pres. Perelson Weiner LLP, N.Y.C., 1971—. Bd. dirs. Nautica Enterprises, Inc., Babson Interactive. Officer, bd. dirs. Jewish Cmty. Rels. Coun. N.Y.; trustee Babson Coll., Citizens Budget Com., N.Y.C.; officer, bd. govs., Am. Jewish Com.; v.p., bd. dirs. Irvington Inst. Immunol. Rsch.; mem. adv. com. Nat. Polish Am. Jewish Am. Coun. Fellow Wexner Heritage Found., Adenauer Exch. Program. Mem.: AICPA, Chief Execs. Orgn., N.Y. State Soc. CPAs, N.J. Soc. CPAs, Pa. Soc. CPAs, Mt. Ridge Country Club, Harvard Club, Harmonie Club, Econ. Club, Accts. Club Am. Office: Perelson Weiner LLP One Dag Hammarskjold Plz New York NY 10017-2286 Fax: (212) 605-3128. E-mail: ron@pwcpa.com.

WEINER, RONALD MARTIN, microbiology and cell biology educator, research scientist; BS, Bklyn. Coll., 1964; MS, L.I. U., 1967; PhD, Iowa State U., 1970. Instr. dept. bacteriology Iowa State U., Ames, 1969-70; asst. prof. dept. microbiology U. Md., College Park, 1970-75, assoc. prof. dept. microbiology, 1975-86, acting chmn. dept. microbiology, 1980-81, prof. dept. cell biology and molecular genetics, 1986—2001; joint appointment Ctr. Marine Biotech., 1987-93, prof. cell and molecular biology program, 1990—93; program dir. cell biology and microbial observatories NSF, 2001—. Vis. scientist NIH, 1985—89; program dir. cell biology NSF, 2000—; mem. panel granting agys.; svc. on numerous univ. and govt. coms. and commns.; spkr. over 125 seminars; rschr. in field; mentor to more than 50 grad. students, postdoctoral fellows and vis. profs.; Gordon conf. invitee. Author 25 book chpts.; reviewer, mem. editl. bd. 10 jours.; contbr. over 85 articles to profl. jours.; multiple patents in field. Recipient Panhellenic Outstanding Tchr. award, 1997, Outstanding Faculty recognition, Kappa Delta, 1998, PACON Ocean award, 1998, numerous grants in field; scholar, Fulbright, 1990. Fellow Am. Acad. Microbiology (colloquium chair) Life Sci. Coun. (mem. strategic planning com.); mem. AAAS, Am. Soc. Microbiology (Svc. award 2000), Indsl. Microbiology Soc., Sigma Xi, Phi Kappa Phi. Office: Univ Md Microbiology Bldg Dept Cell Biology & Molecular Genetics College Park MD 20742-0001 E-mail: RW19@umail.umd.edu.

WEINER, ROY SAMUEL, medical educator, health facility administrator; b. Suffern, N.Y., July 28, 1941; s. Harry and Sylvia (Friefeld) Weiner; m. Marjorie Nancy Gordon, July 5, 1964; children: Adam Seth, Craig Jacog, Sara Beth. BA, Williams Coll., 1963; MD, SUNY, Bklyn., 1967. Chief divsn. med. oncology U. Fla., Gainesville, 1976-93, prof. medicine, 1981-93, prof. immunology and med. microbiology, 1981-83; planning dir. U. Fla. Cancer Ctr., 1992-93; dir. Tulane Cancer Ctr., New Orleans, 1993—; prof. medicine and pediat. Tulane U. Med. Ctr., 1993—. Mem. steering com. HCA Healthcare, Nashville, 1997—. Contbr. Mem. La. Cancer and Lung Trust Fund, 1997—; med. advisor Am. Cancer Soc., 1988—93, pres., 1987—88. Mem.: So. Assn. Oncology (program chair 1999), Am. Assn. Cancer Rsch. (fin. com., chair pub. rels. and comm. com.), Am. Soc. Hematologists, Am. Soc. Clin. Oncologists, Assn. Oncology. Jewish. Avocations: skiing, wine connoisseur. Office: Tulane Cancer Ctr 1430 Tulane Ave # Sl68 New Orleans LA 70112-2699

WEINER, STEPHEN MARK, lawyer; b. Boston, Mar. 20, 1943; s. Meyer and Esther (Lowenstein) W.; m. Roslyn G. Weiner, Dec. 19, 1967 (div. 1992); children: Jeremiah, Ben, Miriam, Isaac. AB magna cum laude, Harvard U., 1964; LLB, Yale U., 1968. Bar: Mass. 1968. Teaching fellow Boston Coll. Law Sch., Chestnut Hill, Mass., 1968-69; assoc. Goodwin, Proctor & Hoar, Boston, 1969-71; spl. asst. to Gov. Francis W. Sargent Commonwealth of Mass., 1971-74; chmn. Mass. Rate Setting Commn., 1972-78; assoc. prof. Boston U. Sch. Law, 1978-81, dir. Ctr. for Law and Health Scis.; mem. Goulston & Storrs, Boston, 1981-90, Mintz, Levin, Cohn, Ferris, Glovsky and Popeo, P.C., Boston, 1990—. Chair health law sect. Mintz, Levin, Cohn, Ferris, Glovsky and Popeo, P.C.; adj. prof. law Boston U. Sch. Law, 1993-94, Suffolk U. Sch. Law, 1997—; vis. lectr. Yale Law Sch., 1994-95. Mem. editl. bd. New Eng. Jour. Human Svcs., 1979-81; adv. bd. Hosp. Risk Mgmt., 1979-83; contbr. articles to profl. jours. Legal adv. com. AIDS Action Coun., Washington; dir., treas. AIDS Action Com., Mass., 1989—97; bd. dirs. GLAD, Inc., 1999—2000, Boston Film Video Found.; del. Mass. Easter Seal Soc.; trustee Beth Israel Hosp. , Boston, 1979—95, Spaulding Rehab. Hosp., Boston, 1979—95, Corp. Ptnrs. Healthcare Sys., Inc., Boston, 1994—2001, Boston Ballet, treas., 2001—; overseer Boston Lyric Opera; dir. New Eng. Conservatory Lab. Charter Sch.; trustee Huntington Theater Co., Boston; mem. govt. task force to evaluate Mass. Determination of Need Program, 1979—80; profl. adv. coun. Mass. Dept. Elder Affairs, 1979—81; Mass. atty. gen. Mass. Adv. Com. on Health Care and Tobacco Control. Mem. ABA, Nat. Health Lawyers Assn., Mass. Bar Assn., Boston Bar Assn. Home: 7 Beethoven Ave Walpole MA 02081 Office: Mintz Levin Cohn Ferris Glovsky and Popeo PC 1 Financial Ctr Boston MA 02111-2657 E-mail: sweiner@mintz.com.

WEINER, STEPHEN ARTHUR, lawyer; b. Bklyn., Nov. 20, 1933; s. Joseph Lee W. and Ruth Lessall (Weiner); m. Mina Rieur, Sept. 1, 1958; children: Karen, James. BA summa cum laude, Harvard U., 1954; JD cum laude, Yale U., 1957. Bar: N.Y. 1958, U.S. Supreme Ct. 1963. Assoc. Winthrop, Stimson, Putnam & Roberts, N.Y.C., 1958-65, ptnr., 1968—2000, vice chmn. mgmt. com., 1984-97; acting prof. law U. Calif., Berkeley, 1965-68; ptnr. Pillsbury Winthrop, LLP, N.Y.C., 2001—, sr. counsel, 2002—. Mem. com. on character and fitness 1st dept. appellate divsn. N.Y. Supreme Ct., 1998—, spl. master, 1999—; mem. N.Y. State Jud. Inst. on Professionalism in the Law, 1999—. Contbr. articles to legal pubs. Comment editor Yale Law Jour., 1956-57. Fellow Am. Coll. Trial Lawyers, Am. Bar Found.; mem. Assn. of Bar of City of N.Y. (chmn. recruitment of lawyers com., chmn. com. on Stimson medal), Fed. Bar Coun. (chmn. com. on 2d cir. cts., trustee), Order of Coif, Phi Beta Kappa. Home: 190 Harbor Rd Sands Point NY 11050-2636 Office: Pillsbury Winthrop, LLP One Battery Park Pla New York NY 10004-1490 E-mail: sweiner@pillsburywinthrop.com.

WEINER-HEUSCHKEL, SYDELL, theater educator; b. N.Y.C., Feb. 18, 1947; d. Milton A. and Janet (Kay) Horowitz; children: Jason, Emily; m. Rex Heuschkel, Sept. 3, 1992. BA, SUNY, Binghamton, 1968; MA, Calif. State U., L.A., 1974; postgrad., Yale U., 1968-70; PhD, NYU, 1986; MS, Calif. State U., Dominguez Hills, 1996. Lic. marriage and family therapist. Prof. theater arts, chmn. dept., dir. honors program Calif. State U. Dominguez Hills, Carson, 1984—. Guest lectr. Calif. Inst. Arts, 1988. Appeared in play Vikings, Grove Shakespeare Festival, 1988; dir. Plaza Suite, Brea (Calif.) Civic Theatre, 1982, Gypsy, Carson Civic Light Opera, 1990, Same Time Next Year, Muckehthaler, 1987, Slow Dance on the Killing Ground, Alternative Repertory Theatre, 1989; co-author: School and Community Theater Problems: A Handbook for Survival, 1978, (software) Public Speaking, 1991; contbr. Am. Jour. Psychotherapy, 1997, Jour. Clin. Psychology, 1998. Yale U. fellow, 1969; recipient Lyle Gibson Disting. Tchr. award, 1989. Mem. Screen Actors Guild, Am. Fedn. TV and Radio Artists, Calif. State U. Women's Coun. (treas. 1989-91), Phi Kappa Phi. E-mail: sweiner@csudh.edu.

WEINERT, HENRY M. biomedical company executive; b. Nordhausen, Kassel, Fed. Republic Germany, May 31, 1940; s. Heinrich V. Nennenstiehl and Martha H. Weinert; m. Helen Koopmans, Feb. 14, 1966 (div. June 1982); children: Jason C., Brian T.; m. Kerri V. Keaton, Sept. 25, 1989. BA in Sci., Columbia Coll., 1962; MBA, Harvard Grad. Sch. Bus., 1970. Med. rsch. assoc. Columbia Univ., N.Y.C., 1964-65; exec. v.p., founder Clin. Diagnostic Lab., New Haven, 1966-68; dir. planning, bus. devel. Lederle Labs./Am. Cyan., Pearl River, N.Y., 1970-73, mktg. dir., 1973-74; bus. devel. mgr. Corning (N.Y.) Glass Works, 1974-77; pres., founder Boston Biomed. Cons., Waltham, Mass., 1977—. Spl. ltd. ptnr. MedVenture Assocs., San Francisco, 1965—, Interwest Ptnrs., San Francisco, 1989; presenter, lectr. in field. Patentee laser fabrication of microsuture needles; contbr. articles to profl. jours. Pres. Svc. Soc., Columbia Coll., 1959; chmn. Student Union Com., Columbia Coll., 1961; treas. Class 1962, Columbia Coll., 1962-64; others. Recipient Alumni Achievement award Columbia Coll., 1962; grantee NIH, 1964-66. Mem. Biomed. Mktg. Assn. (bd. dirs. 1978-86, Recognition award 1986), Am. Assn. Clin. Chemistry, Van Slyke Soc. (bd. mem. 1991—). Lutheran. Avocations: reading science fiction and mystery novels, sailing, cars, landscaping. Home: 86 Myles Standish Rd Weston MA 02493-2124 Office: Boston Biomed Cons 1000 Winter St Ste 1600 Waltham MA 02451-1469 E-mail: hweinert@bostonbiomed.com.

WEINFELD, ALBERT, retired radiologist and educator; b. N.Y.C., Jan. 6, 1934; MD, SUNY, Downstate, 1957. Diplomate Am. Bd. Radiology. Intern Bellevue Hosp., Cornell U., N.Y.C., 1957-58; resident in radiology Cornell Affiliate Hosps., 1958-61; attending in radiology Jackson Meml. Med. Ctr., U. Miami, Fla., 1962-98; prof. radiology U. Miami, 1992-98, emeritus prof., 1998—. Fellow Am. Coll. Radiology.

WEINGAND, DARLENE ERNA, librarian educator, consultant; b. Oak Park, Ill., Aug. 13, 1937; d. Edward Emil and Erna (Heidenway) W.,; m. Wayne Anthony Weston, Sept. 7, 1957 (div. June 1976); children: Kathleen Mary, Lynda Anne, Judith Diane, Barbara Jeanne; m. James Elberling, May 1977 (div. 1980); m. Roger Paul Couture, Apr. 7, 1984. BA in History and English, Elmhurst Coll., 1972; MALS, Rosary Coll., 1973; PhD in Adult Edn./Libr. Sci., U. Minn., 1980. Asst. prof. U. Wis., Madison, 1981-86, assoc. prof., 1986-92, prof., 1992-99, prof. emerita, 1999—, SLIS acting dir., 1991, summer 86, SLIS asst. dir., 1990-94, adminstr. SLIS Continuing Edn. Svcs., 1981-99. Cons. in mktg., continuing edn., libr. futures, info. issues, and mgmt., 1980—; invited mentor Snowbird Leadership Inst., 1990, 92; vis. fellow Curtin U. Tech. Perth, Australia, 1990; Fulbright lectr. U. Iceland, 1988; lectr. 2d World Conf. on Continuing Edn. for Libr. and Info. Sci., Barcelona, 1993, Internat. Fedn. Libr. Assn.; adj. prof. U. Hawaii Manoa, 1999—. Author: Future Driven Library Marketing, 1998, Marketing/Planning Library and Information Services, 1999, Administration of the Small Public Library, 4th edit., 2001, Budgeting and the political Process in Libraries: Customer Svc. Excellence, 1997, Simulation Games, 1992 (with others), Connections: Literacy and Cultural Heritage: Lessons from Iceland, 1992, Managing Today's Public Library: Blueprint for Change, 1994, author (with others) Continuing Professional Education and Internat. Fed. of Libr. Assoc.: Past, Present, and a Vision for the Future, 1993, Keeping the Book$: Public Library Financial Management, 1992; contbr. articles to profl. jours. Recipient excellence award Nat. Univ. Continuing Edn. Assn., 1989, Econ. and Cmty. Devel. award, 1989, outanding achievement in audio applications award Internat. Teleconferencing Assn., 1991, LITA/Libr. Hi-Tech award, 1996, disting. alumna award Dominican U., 1998. Mem. ALA, Internat. Fedn. Libr. Assns. (ALA rep.), Assn. for Libr. and Info. Sci. Edn. (bd. dirs. 1990-93, rsch. grantee 1992, Russia project fellow 1994), Hawaii Libr. Assn., Wis. Assn. for Adult and Continuing Edn., Phi Delta Kappa, Beta Phi Mu. Office: U Hawaii-Manoa 26 Hamilton Libr Honolulu HI 96815

WEINGARDT, JOHN W. accountant; b. Indpls., Oct. 22, 1961; s. Jake E. and Betty J. (Crouch) W.; m. Kristina L. Gullion, Aug. 31, 1985; children: Ashley, Abigail, John Robert. BS in Acctg. and Econs., U. Indpls., 1984. CPA, Ind. Tax sr. Ernst & Young, Indpls., 1984-87; tax mgr. Laventhol & Horwath, 1987-89; pres. John W. Weingardt CPA, PC, 1989-92; mng. ptnr. Peachin, Schwartz & Weingardt, PC, 1992—. Instr. Ind. U.-Purdue U., Indpls., 1986-93. Treas. Geist Christian Ch., Indpls., 1994, 95. Mem. AICPA, Ind. CPA Soc. (fed. tax com.). Avocation: antique autos. Home: 10235 Woods Edge Dr Fishers IN 46038-9351 Office: Ste 150 9449 Priority Way West Dr Indianapolis IN 46240-6421

WEINGART, ROBERT PAUL, financial consultant; b. East Orange, N.J., Oct. 3, 1937; s. Paul Edward and Loretta Madeline (Heagney) W.; m. Susan Beresford Lyman, July 22, 1967 (div.); children: Nicole, Melinda, Deborah, Lindsey. BA in Sci., U. Notre Dame, 1959, BSME, 1960; MBA, U. Mich., 1970. Lic. securities rep.; cert. investment specialist; registered fin. planner, fin. cons. Sales engr. New Departure Hyatt (Divsn. GMC), Sandusky, Ohio, 1960-70; dist. mgr. Xerox Corp., Pasadena, Calif., 1970-73; fin. cons. Grosse Point Farms, Mich., 1973—. Chmn. U.S. Navy Recruiting Dist. Assistance Coun. for State of Mich. Contbr. articles to profl. jours. Chmn. St. Alan's Parish Coun., Troy, Mich., 1997-98; precinct del., candidate Mich. Rep. Party, Troy. Comdr. USNR, 1962-94. Mem. USN Inst., Assn. Naval Aviation, Internat. Assn. Fin. Planning, Internat. Assn. Registered Fin. Cons., Knight Sovereign Mil. Order of Temple of Jerusalem. Republican. Roman Catholic. Avocation: golf, reading. Home: 2020 Somerset Blvd Apt 106 Troy MI 48084-3902 Office: 21 Kercheval Ave Ste 270 Grosse Pointe Farms MI 48236-3633

WEINGARTEN, JOSEPH LEONARD, aerospace engineer; b. N.Y.C., June 5, 1944; s. Herman H. and Irene Jane (Binzer) (dec.) W.; m. Cindy L. Carter; 1 child, Toby. B Mech. Engring., NYU, 1966; postgrad., Air War Coll., 1976. Chief engr. Air Transportability Test Loading Agy. Wright-Patterson AFB, Wright-Patterson AFB, Ohio, 1972-74; project engr. dept. engring. USAF, 1966-72, sr. project engr. dept. engring., 1974-76, planning and project engr. dept. engring., 1976-81, chief mgmt. ops. dept. engring., 1981-83, sr. tech. planner dept. engring., 1983-92; tech. asst. DCS Engring. and Tech. Mgmt. Air Force Material Command, 1992-93; founder, CEO Huffman Wright Inst., 1993-98; cons. Main Net Inc., Urbana, Ohio, 1997—. CEO Weingarten Gallery, Dayton, Ohio, 1967—; pres., v.p., sec., treas., bd. dirs. Ohio Designer Craftsmen, Columbus; sec. Ohio Designer Craftsmen Enterprise, Columbus, 1982-90; chmn. continuing edn. design dept. Affiliate Socs. Coun., Dayton, 1971-74, chmn. edn. coord. com. Kettering Inst., Wright State U., 1974-76, chmn. scientist and engr. awards panel, 1990-91, mem., 1992-94. Contbr. articles on systems engring. to Aeronautical Sys. divsn. Mech. Engring. Jour. (1st place award nat. contest 1970), Procs. 4th Intersoc. Conf. on Transp., Air Force Sys. Command, USAF Spl. Purpose Report, Gems and Minerals, Friends Jour. USAF Mus., Ceramics Monthly, The Crafts Report, Macintosh Software. Scoutmaster Troop 81, Boy Scouts Am., Kettering, Ohio, 1985—91, com. mem., 1991—93, dist. chmn. Wright Bros. Dist., 2000—, dist. chmn. Sequoia Dist. Miami Valley Coun., 1991—93, asst. coun. commr., 1993—2000; pres. Friends of Montessori Sch., South Dayton, 1978—94. Capt. USAF, 1967—71. Recipient Disting. Eagle award Boy Scouts Am., 1992, Silver Beaver award Boy Scouts Am., 1995, Pinnacle award Eastern Region Microage, Inc., 1999; named as one of 5 bus. execs. of yr. Miami Valley Bus. Advisor/Cox Pub., 1998. Mem. AIAA (sr. mem., air transport systems tech. com. 1976-78, 80-82, Lawrence Sperry award 1977), ASME (sr. mem.), Am. Nat. Standards Inst. (materials handling 5 com. 1966-70), Soc. Automotive Engrs. (aircraft ground support equipment com. 1969-75). Achievements include 11 patents for expendable air cargo pallet, mail container, collapsible air cargo container, process for reinforcing extruded articles, process for large scale extrusions, air flotation cargo handling system, integral aircraft barrier net, load distributive cargo platform, laminated plastic packaging material, computer printer paper support, and investment casting mold base; developments include 3g cargo restraint criteria used worldwide on aircraft/spacecraft/shuttles, rope extraction system for C-5A, system for large scale structural plastics extruxions, advanced planning documents for Air Force, report in new type of DOD procurement system; other achievements include the design and creation of jewelry sold in museums and retail stores.

WEINGARTEN, SAUL MYER, lawyer; b. Los Angeles, Dec. 19, 1921; s. Louis and Lillian Dorothy (Alter) W.; m. Miriam Ellen Moore, Jan. 21, 1949; children: David, Steven, Lawrence, Bruce. AA, Antelope Valley Coll., 1940; AB, UCLA, 1942; cert., Cornell U., 1943; JD, U. Southern Calif., 1949. Bar: Calif. 1950, U.S. Supreme Ct., 1960, Calif. Supreme Ct., 1950, Fed. Dist. Ct., 1950, U.S. Ct. of Mil. Appeals, 1951, U.S. Supreme Ct., 1961. Prin. Saul M. Weingarten Assocs., Seaside, Calif., 1954—. Atty. City of Gonzales, Calif., 1954-74, City of Seaside, 1955-70; gen. counsel Redevel. Agy., Seaside, 1955-76, Security Nat. Bank, Monterey, Calif., 1968-74; bd. dirs., exec. com. Frontier Bank, Cheyenne, Wyo., 1984-99; pres. Quaestor, Inc., 1991-98. Author: Practice Compendium, 1950; contbr. articles to profl. jours. Del. Internat. Union of Local Authorities, Brussels, Belgium, 1963, 73; candidate state legislature Dem. Com., Monterey County, 1958; counsel Monterey Peninsula Mus. of Art, Inc., 1972-80; gen. counsel Monterey County Symphony Assn., Carmel, Calif., 1974-98, Mountain Plains Edn. Project, Glasgow, Mont., 1975-81; chmn. fund raising ARC, Monterey, 1964; chmn., bd. dirs. fund raising United Way, Monterey, 1962-63; pres., bd. dirs. Alliance on Aging, Monterey, 1968-82; bd. dirs. Family Svc. Agy., Monterey, 1958-66, Monterey County Cultural Coun., 1986-94, Clark Found., 1982—; dir., mem. exec. com. Monterey Bay Performing Arts Ctr., 1990. Served to commdr. USN, 1942-46, 50-54, Korea. Grad. fellow Coro Found., 1949-50. Mem. Calif. Bar Assn., Monterey County Bar Assn., Monterey County Trial Lawyers Assn., Rotary (pres. 1970-71, 82-83), Commonwealth Club, Meadowbrook Club. Jewish. Avocations: travel. Home: 4135 Crest Rd Pebble Beach CA 93953-3008 Office: Ste D 1123 Fremont Blvd Seaside CA 93955-5759 E-mail: lsm147@juno.com.

WEINGARTNER, H(ANS) MARTIN, finance educator, educator; b. Heidelberg, Germany, Apr. 4, 1929; came to U.S., 1939, naturalized, 1944; s. Jacob and Grete Weingartner; m. Joyce Trellis, June 12, 1955; children—Steven M., Susan C. De La Paz, Eric H., Kenneth L. AB, SB, U. Chgo., 1950, AM, 1951; MS, Carnegie Mellon U., 1956, PhD, 1962. Economist Dept. Commerce, 1951-53; instr. Grad. Sch. Indsl. Adminstrn., Carnegie Mellon U., 1956-57; instr., then asst. prof. Grad. Sch. Bus., U. Chgo., 1957-63; assoc. prof. fin. Alfred P. Sloan Sch. Mgmt., Mass. Inst. Tech., 1963-66; prof. Grad. Sch. Mgmt., U. Rochester, N.Y., 1966-77; Brownlee O. Currey prof. fin. Owen Grad. Sch. Mgmt., Vanderbilt U., Nashville, 1977-98, Brownlee O. Carrey Prof. of Fin., emeritus, 1998—; dir. Computer Consoles, Inc., 1974-89. Cons. to industry. Author: Mathematical Programming and the Analysis of Capital Budgeting Problems, 3d edit, 1974, (with George Benston and Dan Horsky) An Empirical Study of Mortgage Redlining, 1978; also articles.; Deptl. editor: Mgmt. Sci, 1967-73. Served with AUS, 1951-53. Mellon fellow, 1954-55; Ford Found. fellow, 1955-56, recipient first prize Dissertation Competition, 1963. Mem.: Coun. Sci. Soc. Pres. (alumni mem.), Inst. for Ops. Rsch. and the Mgmt. Scis., Inst. Mgmt. Scis. (v.p. fin. 1978—84, pres. 1985—86), Beta Gamma Sigma. Home: 1616 Ash Valley Dr Nashville TN 37215-4202 Office: Vanderbilt U Owen Grad Sch Mgmt 401 21st Ave N Nashville TN 37203 E-mail: H.M.Weingartner@Vanderbilt.edu..

WEINGARTNER, RUDOLPH HERBERT, philosophy educator; b. Heidelberg, Germany, Feb. 12, 1927; came to U.S., 1939, naturalized, 1944; s. Jacob and Grete (Kahn) W.; m. Fannia Goldberg-Rudkowski, Dec. 28, 1952 (dec. Nov. 1994); children: Mark H., Eleanor C.; m. Regitze E.G. Winkelhorn Hamburger, June 13, 1997. AB, Columbia U., 1950, MA, 1953, PhD, 1959. Fellow Inst. Philos. Research, San Francisco, 1953-55; instr. philosophy Columbia, 1955-59; from asst. prof. to prof., chmn. dept. philosophy San Francisco State Coll., 1959-68; prof. philosophy Vassar Coll., Poughkeepsie, 1968-74, chmn. dept., 1969-74, Taylor prof. philosophy, 1973-74, dean Coll. Arts and Scis.; prof. philosophy Northwestern U., Evanston, Ill., 1974-87; provost U. Pitts., 1987-89, prof. philosophy, 1987-94, chmn. dept. philosophy, 1991-93. Author: Experience and Culture: The Philosophy of Georg Simmel, 1962, The Unity of the Platonic Dialogue: The Cratylus, The Protagoras, The Parmenides, 1973, Undergraduate Education: Goals and Means, 1992 (Frederick W. Ness book award 1993), Fitting Form to Function: A Primer on the Organization of Academic Institutions, 1996, The Moral Dimensions of Academic Administration, 1999; editor: (with Joseph Katz) Philosophy in the West, 1965; exhibited sculptures in Mendelson Gallery, 1992, 94, UP Gallery, 1992, Assoc. Artists Pitts. Gallery, 2000; contbr. articles to profl. jours. Bd. dirs. Chamber Music Chgo., 1982-87, pres., 1986-87; mem. bd. advisors Pitts. Symphony, 1991-2000, mem. bd. dirs., chmn. artistic com.; mem. adv. bd. Sch. Music Carnegie Mellon U., Pitts., 1992—. Social Sci. Rsch. Coun. fellow, 1958-59; Guggenheim fellow, 1965-66; Am. Coun. Learned Socs. fellow, 1971-72; residency Rockefeller Found. Study and Conf. Ctr. in Bellagio, 1994. Mem. Am. Philos. Assn., Assn. Am. Colls. (bd. dirs. 1985-89, task force on gen. edn. 1985-88, editorial bd. liberal edn. jours. 1986-94), Assoc. Artists Pitts. (artist mem.), Phi Beta Kappa. Home: 5448 Northumberland St Pittsburgh PA 15217-1129 E-mail: rudywein@pitt.edu.

WEINGAST, MARVIN, laboratory executive; b. Bklyn., Jan. 1, 1943; s. Abe and Rose (Altein) W. BS, L.I. U., 1967, MS, 1971; postgrad., Poly. Inst., 1967-68. Analytic and pollution chemist Amerada Hess Corp., Pt. Reading, N.J., 1969-73; asst. lab. dir. Chem. Constrn., North Brunswick, 1973-74; dir. Indsl. Hygiene Lab. Nat. Starch and Chemical, Bridgewater, 1974—. Grant com. mem. Ctr. for Hazardous and Toxic Substance Mgmt., Newark, 1988—; mem. Sourland Regional Citizens Planning Coun., Neshanic, N.J., 1989—. Contbr. to book: Small Business Programs, 1980; contbr. articles to profl. jours. Recipient Chemistry Dept. award L.I. U., 1967, Teaching fellowship Poly. Inst., 1967, L.I. U., 1968. Mem. MENSA, Am. Chem. Soc., Am. Conf. Chem. Labeling, Soc. Toxicology. Achievements include development of improved system for identification of hazardous chemicals; organization of first global monitoring of indsl. workers to hazardous workplace chemicals. Office: Nat Starch & Chem Co 10 Finderne Ave Bridgewater NJ 08807-3355 Home: 299 Gemini Dr Hillsborough NJ 08844-4978 E-mail: weingast@weingast.com.

WEINGEIST, THOMAS ALAN, ophthalmology educator; b. N.Y.C., Jan. 28, 1940; s. Samson and Fausta (Haim) W.; m. Carol Perera, Mar. 19, 1963 (div. Aug. 1977); children: Aaron P., Rachel; m. Catherine McGregor, Aug. 18, 1977; children: Robert M., David M. BA, Earlham Coll., 1963; PhD, Columbia U., 1969; MD, U. Iowa, 1972. Resident in ophthalmology U. Iowa, 1972-75, fellow in retina, 1976, asst. prof. ophthalmology, 1976-80, assoc. prof., 1980-83, prof., 1983—, prof., head dept. ophthalmology, 1986—. DeVoe lectr. Columbia U., 2001; Doheny lectr. U. S.C., 2002. Mem. editl. bd. Documenta Ophthalmologica, The Netherlands, 1989-94, Ophthalmology World News, 1994-96; med. editor Argus/Ophthalmology's World News, 1996-98; med. editor EyeNet mag., 1999-2001. Fellow: Am. Acad. Ophthalmology (editl. bd. jour. 1982—, assoc. sec. for self-assessment 1988—93, sec. continuing edn. 1993—, trustee 1993—, sr. sec. clin. edn. 1994—, pres. 2002—, Honor award 1979, Sr. Honor award 1989); mem.: Assn. Univ. Profs. Ophthalmology (pres. 1995, bd. dirs.), Am. Medico-Legal Found., Vitreous Soc., Retina Soc., Macula Soc. Avocations: photography, tennis. Home: 3 Heather Ct Iowa City IA 52245-3226 Office: U Iowa Dept Ophthalmology Iowa City IA 52242

WEINGER, STEVEN MURRAY, lawyer; b. Chgo., Feb. 7, 1954; s. Paul and Joan (Taxay) W.; children: Blake, Paige, Haley. BA, Hampshire Coll., 1975; JD, U. Chgo., 1978. Bar: Fla. 1979, Ill. 1979, U.S. Dist. Ct. (so. dist.) Fla. 1979, U.S. Ct. Appeals (5th cir.) 1980, U.S. Ct. Appeals (11th cir.) 1981, U.S. Supreme Ct. 1982, U.S. Dist. Ct. (mid. dist.) Fla. 1989. Mem. faculty U. Miami Sch. Law, Coral Gables, Fla., 1978-79; ptnr. Kurzban, Kurzban & Weinger, P.A., Miami, 1979—. Bd. dirs. Sunrise Cmty. for Mentally Retarded, Miami, United Cerebral Palsy Tallahassee, Inc., Palmer-Trinity Sch., Miami, GobleStage, Inc., 1999—. Recipient Chmn.'s award Sunrise Cmty. for Mentally Retarded, 1987; honoree United Cerebral Palsy in South Fla., 1995, Fla. Assn. Rehab. Facilities, 1996, United Cerebral Palsy Assn., 1997. Mem. ABA, Assn. Trial Lawyers Am., Fla. Assn. Trial Lawyers. Office: Kurzban Kurzban & Weinger 2650 SW 27th Ave Fl 2D Miami FL 33133-3003 E-mail: swmiami@aol.com.

WEINGROW, HOWARD L. financial executive, investor; b. N.Y.C., Dec. 6, 1922; s. Nathan and Anna (Mintzes) W.; m. Muriel Corrine Franzblau, Nov. 24, 1946; children: Terry Vaccaro, Caron Abby Haim. Owner Legion Fluorescent Corp., N.Y.C., 1946-56; ptnr. Hechler & Weingrow, Inc., 1956-58, Hechler, Lifton & Weingrow, Inc., N.Y.C., 1958-78; exec. v.p. Tanscontinental Investing Corp., 1960-67, pres., 1967-70; prin. Lifton & Weingrow, N.Y.C., 1970—; co-chmn. Marcade Group, Inc., 1986-91, bd. dirs., 1986-93; pres. Medis Techs., Ltd. (MDTL) , 1992—, Stanoff Corp., 1980—, Wesak Internat., 1992-94; chmn. Wesak Chrysler, 1992-94; pres. Medis Techs. Ltd. Bd. dirs. Preferred Health Care, N.Y.C., Four Winds Inc., N.Y.C., Medis-El, Medis Techs. Ltd.; founder Ctr. for Chilhood Asthma, 2002, Weingrow Family Pediatric Urology Lab., L.I. Jewish Hosp., 1989, The Howard L. and Muriel Weingrow Collection of Avant-Garde Art and Lit., Hofstra U., 1972; chmn. Vision Telemedia, Inc., 1995-98. Treas. Dem. Nat. Com., Washington, 1970-72; mem. bd. govs. Hofstra U. Law Sch., 1977-79; dep. fin. chmn. Pres. Carter, Washington, 1976, 80; trustee Hofstra U., Hempstead, N.Y., 1973-76, James S. Brady Presdl. Found., 1982, Children's Med. Fund, L.I. Jewish Children's Hosp., Lake Success, N.Y., 1986—, Am. Jewish Congress, 1988-96; treas. Nassau County Mus. Fine Arts, 1988—, North Shore, L.I. Jewish Hosp. Sys., 1999—; advisor to Pres. Lyndon Johnson, OEO, Washington; fin. advisor to the Govt. of Grenada and Office of Prime Minister Garry, 1977-79. Decorated Air medal with 13 silver oak leaf clusters, DFC; recipient Presdl. medal Hofstra U. Office: Stanoff Corp 805 3rd Ave Fl 15 New York NY 10022-7513 Fax: 212-935-9216.

WEINHAUER, WILLIAM GILLETTE, retired bishop; b. N.Y.C., Dec. 3, 1924; s. Nicholas Alfred and Florence Anastacia (Davis) W.; m. Jean Roberta Shanks, Mar. 20, 1948; children: Roberta Lynn, Cynthia Anne, Doris Jean. BS, Trinity Coll., Hartford, Conn., 1948; MDiv, Gen. Theol. Sem., 1951, STM, 1956, ThD, 1970. Ordained to ministry Episcopal Ch., 1951. Pastor Episcopal parishes Diocese N.Y., 1951-56; prof. N.T. St. Andrews Theol. Sem., Manila, Philippines, 1956-60; asst. prof. N.T. Gen. Theol. Sem., 1961-71; rector Christ Ch., Poughkeepsie, N.Y., 1971-73; bishop Episcopal Diocese of Western N.C., Black Mountain, 1973-90, ret., 1990. Vis. prof. religion Western Carolina U., Cullowhee, N.C., 1991-98; adj. faculty Seabury-Western Theol. Sem., Evanston, Ill., 19991-94. Served with USN, 1943-46. Mem. Soc. Bibl. Lit.

WEINHOEFT, JOHN JOSEPH, data processing executive; b. Springfield, Ill., Nov. 23, 1952; s. Henry and Mary F. Weinhoeft; m. Kerry D. McKean, May 19, 1984; children: Bryan, Bill (dec.). Assoc., Springfield Coll., 1972. Lead operator fin. dept. State of Ill., Springfield, 1970-72, shift supr. fin. dept., 1973-77, tech. asst. to ops. mgr., 1977-78, system coordinator adminstrv. services, 1978-84, sr. systems architect resource mgmt. cen. mgmt. services, 1984-93; sr. pub. svc. adminstr., 1993—. Author: SNA: An IBM Standard, 1986, rev. edit., 1987, Capacity Management for IBM Mainframes, 1987, SAA: IBM's Master Plan, 1988, ESA/370: IBM's Architecture for the 1990s, 1989, IBM 3390 Disk Technology, 1990, The System/390 Report, 1991, Downsizing for Cost-Effective Enterprise Computing, 1993; editor: IBM 4381 Processors, 1987, Inside Sierra, 1988, The 3990/3390 Disk Report, 1990. Webelos den leader Boy Scouts Am., 1995-99. Mem. Cen. Ill. Personal Computer Users Group (v.p. 1987-88, pres. 1988-89), ComputerFest Inc. (founding mem., bd. dirs., sec. 1987-90), Checker Car Club Am. (bd. dirs. 2002—, sec. 2002—). Home: 2525 S Glenwood Ave Springfield IL 62704-4535 Office: Cen Mgmt Svcs 201 W Adams St Springfield IL 62704-1874 E-mail: john_weinhoeft@cms.state.il.us.

WEINHOLD, VIRGINIA BEAMER, interior designer; b. Elizabeth, N.J., June 21, 1932; d. Clayton Mitchell and Rosemary (Behrend) Beamer; divorced; children: Thomas Craig, Robert Scott, Amy Linette. BA, Cornell U., 1955; BFA summa cum laude, Ohio State U., 1969; MA in Design Mgmt., Ohio State U., 1982. Freelance interior designer, 1969-72; interior designer, dir. interior design Karlsberger and Assocs. Inc., Columbus, Ohio, 1972-82; assoc. prof. dept. design Ohio State U., 1982—, grad. studies chairperson, 1986-89, 1995-96; lectr. indsl. design Ohio State U., 1972, 79-80. Trustee Found. for Interior Design Edn. and Rsch., 1991-97. Mem. Inst. Bus. Designers (chpt. treas. 1977-79, nat. trustee 1979-81, nat. chmn. contract documents com. 1979-84, chpt. pres. 1981-83), Constrn. Specifications Inst., Interior Design Educator's Coun. (nat. treas. 1989-93), Interior Design Educator's Coun. Found. (nat. treas. 1992-94), Illuminating Engring. Soc. (chpt. v.p. 1997-98), AIA (assoc.), Internat. Interior Design Assn. (nat. dir. 1994-97). Prin. works include Grands Rapids (Mich.) Osteo. Hosp., Melrose (Mass.) Wakefield Hosp., Christopher Inn, Columbus, John W. Galbreath Hdqrs., Columbus, Guernsey Meml. Hosp., Cambridge, Ohio, Trinity Epis. Ch. and Parish House, Columbus, Hale Hosp., Haverhill, Mass., Ohio State U. Dept. Indsl. Design Lighting Lab., others. Author: IBD Forms and Documents Manual, Interior Finish Materials for Health Care Facilities, Subjective Impressions: Lighting Hotels and Resturants, 1989, Effects of Lighting on The Perception of Interior Spaces, 1993. Home: 112 Glen Dr Columbus OH 43085-4010 Office: Ohio State U Dept Design 128 N Oval Mall Columbus OH 43210-1318

WEINHOUSE, SIDNEY, biochemist, educator; b. Chgo., May 21, 1909; s. Harry and Dora (Cutler) Weinhouse; m. Sylvia Krawitz, Sept. 13, 1935 (dec. Aug. 1957); children: Doris Joan, James Lester, Barbara May; m. Adele Klein, Dec. 27, 1969. BS, U. Chgo., 1933, PhD, 1936; D.MS (hon.) (hon.) , Med. Coll. Pa., 1973; D.Sc. (hon.) (hon.) , Temple U., 1976, U. Chieti, Italy, 1979, Jefferson Med. Coll., 1983. Eli Lilly fellow U. Chgo., 1936—38, Coman fellow, 1939—41; staff OSRD, 1941—44; with Houdry Process Corp., 1944—47; biochem. research dir. Temple U. Research Inst., 1947—50, prof. chemistry, 1952—77; emeritus prof. biochemistry Temple U. Med. Sch., 1977—; emeritus prof. Jefferson Med. Coll., 1991; sr. scientist Lankenau Med. Research Ctr., 1987—. Head dept. metabolic chemistry Lankenau Hosp. Research Inst. and Inst. Cancer Research, 1950—57; chmn. div. biochemistry Inst. Cancer Research, 1957—61; assoc. dir. Fels Research Inst., Temple U. Med. Sch., Phila., 1961—64, dir., 1964—67; mem. bd. sci. advisers Inst. Environ. Health, NIH. Contbr. ; editor: Jour. Cancer Research, 1969—79. Bd. dirs. Am. Cancer Soc. Mem.: NAS, Am. Assn. Cancer Research, Am. Soc. Biol. Chemists, Am. Chem. Soc. Home: 1919 Chestnut St Philadelphia PA 19103

WEINIG, RICHARD ARTHUR, lawyer; b. Durango, Colo., Mar. 23, 1940; s. Arthur John and Edna (Novella) W.; m. Barbara A. Westerlund, June 16, 1964. BA in Polit. Sci., Stanford U., 1962, postgrad. in Soviet Studies, 1962-65; JD, U. Calif., San Francisco, 1971. Bar: Alaska 1971, U.S. Dist. Ct. Alaska 1971, U.S. Ct. Appeals (9th cir.) 1978, U.S. Supreme Ct. 1979. Assoc. Burr, Pease & Kurtz, Anchorage, 1971-73, Greater Anchorage Area Borough, 1973-75, Municipality of Anchorage, 1975-82; ptnr. Pletcher & Slaybaugh, Anchorage, 1982-88, Pletcher, Weinig & Merriner, Anchorage, 1988-99. Mem. editl. bd. Hastings Law Jour. Active Stanford U. Young Republicans, 1961-65, Sierra Club, Mountaineering Club, Knik Canoyers and Kayakers of Alaska, Alaska Ctr. for Environ. Mem. ABA, Alaska Bar Assn., Anchorage Bar Assn., NRA. Republican. Presbyterian. Office: Pletcher Weinig & Fisher 800 E Dimond Blvd Ste 3-620 Anchorage AK 99515-2045 Office Fax: 907-349-7758. E-mail: richard@akinsurancedefense.com.

WEINKAUF, WILLIAM CARL, instructional media company executive; b. Fond du Lac, Wis., Apr. 7, 1934; s. Carl Alfred and Erma Gertrude (Lueck) W.; m. Carole Jean Hill, May 3, 1958 (div.); children: Carl William, Mary Gretchen, Donald Hill; m. Jean Boyne Hawks, Sept. 10, 1988. BA, Ripon Coll., 1955; postgrad., U. Wis., 1954, 57-58. Dir. Wis. Cen. Lumber Co., 1959-63; with Carlton Films, Beloit, Wis., 1965-68; founder, pres. IMCO, Inc., Green Lake, 1968—. Founder, pres. initiator of distribution of ednl. instructional materials catalogs, IMCO Pub. Co., 1978—; bd. dirs. The Peterson System, Inc.; co-founder, chmn. Affluence Unltd., Inc., Dallas, 1986; founder, pres. Weinkauf Technologies, LLC, Dallas, 1996. Chmn. coun. Cub Scouts Am., 1968-69; mem. exec. com. county Reps., 1970-71; trustee United Ch. Christ, Green Lake, 1965-66; deacon United Ch. Christ, Dallas, 1989-93, chmn. bd. deacons, 1992-93. Mem. Nat. Audio Visual Assn. (chmn. legis. com. Wis. 1975—), Nat. Sch. Supply and Equipment Assn. (bd. dirs. 1986-87), U.S. Res. Officers Assn. (chpt. pres. 1966-70), Green Lake C. of C., Sigma Nu, Masons (32d degree), KT. Office: 2215 Commerce St Dallas TX 75201-4345

WEINKE, CHRIS, football player; b. St. Paul, July 31, 1972; Attended, Fla. State Univ. Quarterback Carolina Panthers, 2001—; winner Heisman Trophy. Achievements include ranking second in NFL history for passing yards as a rookie. Office: Carolina Panthers 800 S Mint St Charlotte NC 28202*

WEINKOPF, FRIEDRICH J. lawyer; b. Bautsch, Germany, Feb. 17, 1930; Referendar, U. Marburg, Germany, 1954; LLM, U. Pa., 1958; JD, Chgo.-Kent Coll. Law, 1967. Bar: Ill. 1967. Ptnr. Baker & McKenzie, Chgo. Office: Baker & McKenzie 1 Prudential Plz 130 E Randolph St Fl 3600 Chicago IL 60601-6315

WEINMAN, GLENN ALAN, lawyer; b. N.Y.C., Dec. 9, 1955; s. Seymour and Iris Rhoda (Bergman) W. BA in Polit. Sci., UCLA, 1978; JD, U. So. Calif., 1981. Bar: Calif. 1981. Assoc. counsel Mitsui Mfrs. Bank, L.A., 1981-83; assoc. McKenna, Conner & Cuneo, 1983-85, Stroock, Stroock & Lavan, L.A., 1985-87; sr. counsel Buchalter, Nemer, Fields & Younger, 1987-91; ptnr. Keck, Mahin & Cate, 1991-93; sr. v.p., gen. counsel Western Internat. Media Corp., 1993-96; v.p. gen. counsel and human resources, sec. Guess?, Inc., 1996-2000; also bd. dirs.; chief adminstrv. officer Competitive Knowledge, Inc., 2000; v.p., gen. counsel, sec. Luminent, Inc., Chatsworth, Calif., 2000-01; exec. v.p., COO InsoVery Svcs. Group, Woodland Hills, 2001—. Bd. dirs. Guess? Retail Inc., Guess? Licensing, Inc., Guess.com., Inc. Mem. ABA (corp. banking and bus. law sect., com. on savs. instns., com. on banking law corp. counsel sect.), Calif. Bar Assn. (bus. law sect., com. fin. instns. 1989-91, com. consumer svcs. 1991-94), L.A. County Bar Assn. (corp. legal depts. sect., bus. and corps. law sect., subcom. on fin. instns.), Calif. Fashion Assn. (exec. bd. 1997-2000), , Am. Apparel Mfrs. Assn. (govt. rels. com. 1997-2000), Legion Lex, U. So. Calif. Law Alumni Assn., Phi Alpha Delta. Avocation: tennis. Office: 21031 Ventura Blvd Ste 601 Woodland Hills CA 91364-2203 E-mail: gaweinman@aol.com.

WEINMAN, HOWARD MARK, lawyer; b. N.Y.C., May 6, 1947; s. Joseph and Kate (Dorn) W.; m. Pamela Eve Brodie, Jan. 6, 1980; children: David Lewis, Nathaniel Saul. B.A. magna cum laude, Columbia U., 1969; M.P.P., Harvard U, 1973, J.D. cum laude, 1973; LL.M. with highest honors in Taxation, George Washington U., 1981. Assoc., Fried, Frank, Harris, Shriver & Kampelman, Washington and N.Y.C., 1973-78; legis. atty. Joint Com. on Taxation, U.S. Congress, Washington, 1978-80; assoc. Sachs, Greenebaum, & Tayler, Washington, 1980-82; assoc. Crowell & Moring, Washington, 1982-84, ptnr., 1984—; adj. prof. internat. tax Georgetown U. Law Ctr., 1988-89. Contbr. articles to profl. jours. Mem. ABA (sect. on taxation), Kenwood Club, Phi Beta Kappa. Jewish. Home: 5404 Center St Bethesda MD 20815-7101 Office: Crowell & Moring 1001 Pennsylvania Ave NW Fl 10 Washington DC 20004-2595

WEINMAN, STEVEN ALAN, emergency nurse, researcher, writer, educator, consultant; b. St. Louis, July 17, 1962; s. Stanley I. Weinman and Diana Raye (Kessler) Schrader; m. Carol Angela Daiber, July 27, 1986; children: Erin Elizabeth, Sarah Katherine. Diploma in Nursing, Jewish Hosp. of St. Louis, 1986; BSN, Webster U., Kansas City, 1996; postgrad., Webster U., 2001—. RN, Mo., N.Y., N.J.; cert. emergency nurse. Emergency nurse Jewish Hosp. of St. Louis, 1986-87, Truman Med. Ctr.-West, Kansas City, Mo., 1987-93, clin. nurse mgr., 1987-93; clin. educator, 1993-95; emergency nurse St. Luke's Northland Hosp., Kansas City, Mo., 1996-97; prin. ptnr. Emergency Care Cons. Greater N.Y., Somerville, NJ, 1996—; instr. dept. emergency medicine N.Y. Hosp.-Cornell Med. Ctr., N.Y.C., 1997-2001; dir. Office Continuing Med. Edn. Excerpta Medica, Inc. divsn. Elsevier Sci., Hillsborough, 2001—. Clin. rsch. assoc. Clin. Multiphase Rsch., Wilton, Conn., 1991—93, nurse rschr., 1991—2000; rsch. coord. dept. emergency medicine Truman Med. Ctr., Kansas City, 1991—96; mem. editl. adv. bd. Roadrunner Press/ENA, 1999—2001; per diem instr. in emergency and trauma care N.Y. Presbyn. Hosp.-Cornell Med. Ctr., N.Y.C., 2001—. Editor textbooks and monographs; mem. editl. bd. Clin. CORNERSTONE, Excerpta Medica, Inc.;

contbg. author books and book chpts; contbr. articles to profl. jours. Mem. adv. bd. Kansas City chpt. ARC, 1991-94; chief nurse first aid Kansas City Spiritfest, 1989-95. Recipient Spl. Recognition award Emergency Nursing Found. Mem.: AONE, NJSNA, Nat. Assn. EMS Educators, Global Alliance for Med. Edn., Alliance for Continuing Med. Edn., Soc. Trauma Nurses, Am. Trauma Soc., Emergency Nurses Assn. (treas. Greater Kansas City chpt. 1989—91, pres. 1994, state coun. exec. com. 1993—95, sec. 1991, state del. 1991—95, Recognition award 1991, 1993, 1994, 2000, 2001, Edn. award 1993, Educator of Yr. 1994, 1996, Disting. Svc. award 2000). Avocations: photography, writing, computers/electronics, traveling. Home: 29 W Spring St Somerville NJ 08876-1627 Office: 105 Raider Blvd Ste 101 Hillsborough NJ 08844

WEINMANN, ERIC, retired lawyer; b. Teplice, Czech Republic, July 29, 1913; came to U.S., 1942; s. Ing Edmund and Josefine (Taussig) W.; m. Camilla Behn, May 4, 1946 (div. 1953); children: Edward Marvin, Gail Greenwood; m. Mary Ethel Carothers, Dec. 21, 1974. Diploma, Handelshochschule, Berlin, 1935; MA, Columbia U., 1943, JD, 1957; LLM, Georgetown U., 1963. Bar: N.Y. 1957, D.C. 1958, U.S. Supreme Ct. 1963. Assoc. counsel Legal & Monetary Subcom., Ho. of Reps., Washington, 1957-60; atty. SEC, 1960-63; counsel SBA, 1963-89. Contbr. articles to profl. jours. Trustee emeritus Folger Shakespeare Libr., Washington, 1985. Mem. Met. Club City of Washington, City Tavern Assn., N.Y. Athletic Club. Avocations: skin diving, mountain climbing, dressage riding. Home: 3244 Nebraska Ave NW Washington DC 20016-2704

WEINMANN, JOHN GIFFEN, lawyer, diplomat; b. New Orleans, Aug. 29, 1928; s. Rudolph John and Mary Victoria (Mills) W.; m. Virginia Lee Eason, June 11, 1955; children: Winston Eason, Robert St. George Tucker, John Giffen Jr., Mary Virginia Lewis, George Gustaf. BA, Tulane U., 1950, JD, 1952. Bar: La. 1952. Pvt. practice law Phelps Dunbar and predecessor firm, New Orleans, ptnr., 1955-80, of counsel, 1981-83, 85-89, 1993—; gen. counsel Times-Picayune Pub. Corp., Rathborne Land Co., 1968-80; pres., dir. Waverly Oil Corp., 1981-89; amb. to Finland Am. Embassy, Helsinki, 1989-91; amb., chief of protocol of White House Dept. of State, Washington, 1991-93. Lectr. bills and notes New Orleans chpt. Am. Inst. Banking, 1958-59; bd. dir. Eason Oil Co., 1961-81, chmn., 1977; bd. dir. 1st Nat. Bank of Oklahoma City, 1978-84, Am. Life Ins. Co. of N.Y., 1981-88, Allied Investment Corp., 1985-88; asst. sec. Am. Bar Endowment, 1971-74, bd. dirs., sec., 1975-80 Mem. adv. bd. Tulane Law Rev., 1965-92. Bd. govs. Tulane Med. Ctr., 1968-81; bd. adminstrs. Tulane Ednl. Fund, 1981-98, emeritus, 99—, chmn. devel. com., 1985-89, co-chmn. Tulane Parents Fund, 1980-81, bd. chmn., 1993-98; nat. chmn. ann. giving Campaign for Tulane, 1983-85; bd. dirs. Coun. for Better La., 1987-89, Tulane Children's Ctr., 1981-84, WYES Ednl. TV Sta., 1981-82; trustee S.W. Legal Found., 1978-80, Metairie Park Country Day Sch., vice chmn., 1976-77, chmn., 1978-80, U.S. commr. gen. for 1984 La. World Expn., 1983-85; U.S. del. Bur. Internat. Expositions, Paris, 1984-85, chmn. del., 1985; state fin. co-chmn. George Bush for Pres., and Victory La. '88, 1987-89. Named Outstanding Law Alumnus Tulane U., 1985, Outstanding Alumnus Class of 1950, Tulane Coll., 2000, Disting. Tulane U. Alumnus, 2002; selected Rex, King of Carnival, New Orleans, 1996. Mem. ABA (chmn. jr. bar conf. 1963-64, mem. ho. dels. 1964-66, 70, 72-76, sec. com. ethics evaluation 1965, rep. to conv. Union des Jeunes Avocats de France, 1964, chmn. sect. bar activities 1969-70), La. Bar Assn. (sec. treas. 1965-67, Outstanding Young Lawyer award), La. Soc. Colonial Wars (gov. 1976), Swiss-Am. Cultural Exch. Found. (hon. com. 1994—), Phi Beta Kappa, Order of Coif, Delta Kappa Epsilon, Omicron Delta Kappa. Episcopalian. Home: 611 Hector Ave Metairie LA 70005-4415 Office: Waverly Enterprises 601 Poydras St Ste 2690 New Orleans LA 70130-6026

WEINMANN, JUDY MUNGER, nurse; b. Georgetown, Tenn., June 1, 1943; d. Paul and Martha Edith (Smith) Powell; m. David Finley Munger, Dec. 6, 1963 (div. June 1985); children: David Finley Jr., Robert Powell. Grad., Erlanger Hosp., Chattanooga, 1964; AS, Cleveland (Tenn.) State Coll., 1982; BS, U. Tenn., 1984. RN Tenn., cert. occupl. health nurse specialist (COHN-S), Tenn. Med. staff nurse Bradley Meml. Hosp., Cleveland, 1964; office nurse William I. Proffitt, M.D., 1964-65; occupational health nurse Singer-Cobble Co., Chattanooga, 1966-67, Burlington Woolens Co., Cleveland, 1967-68, Am. Uniform Co., Cleveland, 1972-73; sch. nurse Cleveland State Coll., 1968-72, Bradley High Sch., Cleveland, 1973-79; occupational health nurse M&M/Mars, 1979-91; dir. nursing Open Arms Care Corp., Ooltewah, Tenn., 1992-93, Tenn. Home Health, Hixson, 1993; dir. cmty. edn./case mgmt. Med. Shares Home Care, Chattanooga, 1994—2000; adminstr. occupational health svcs. Parkridge Med. Ctr., 2000—02; account exec. Med Shares Home Care, 2002—. Presenter in field. Nurse ARC, Cleveland, 1979—; chmn. Bradley County Substance Abuse Com., Cleveland, 1980-87; com. mem. Am. Cancer Soc., Chattanooga, 1984—. Recipient Schering award as Tenn. outstanding occupational health nurse Schering-Plough Co., 1989. Mem.: Case Mgrs. Soc. Am., Cleve. Area Safety Coun. (Safety award 1988), Chattanooga Occupational Health Nurses Assn. (v.p., bd. dirs., Pres.'s award 1989), Chattanooga Nurses Assn., Tenn. Occupational Health Nurses Assn. (bd. dirs. 1986—), Tenn. Nurses Assn., Sigma Theta Tau. Democrat. Baptist. Avocations: dancing, reading, music, gardening, crafts. Home: 1200 King Arthur Rd Chattanooga TN 37421-4020

WEINMANN, RICHARD ADRIAN, lawyer; b. N.Y.C., Oct. 15, 1917; s. Randolph and Mae (Korber) W.; m. Bert Millicent Landes, Dec. 26, 1946; children: Harriet Joan, Elaine, Anita; m. Ginger Grace Rich, 1999. LLB, Bklyn. Law Sch., 1948; LLM, NYU, 1953. Bar: N.Y. 1958, U.S. Dist. Ct. (so. dist.) N.Y. 1960; U.S. Dist. Ct. (ea. dist.) N.Y. 1960, U.S. Ct. Appeals (2d cir.) 1965, U.S. Supreme Ct. 1964. Ptnr. Sipser, Weinstock & Weinmann, N.Y.C., 1953-71; sole practice, 1972—. Guest lectr. seminars; mem. staff Cornell U. Sch. Indsl. and Labor Relations; panel arbitrator Fed. Mediation and Conciliation Svc. Am. Arbitration Assn. Suffolk and Nassau Counties Pub. Employment Relations Bds. N.Y. State; N.Y. State Employment Rels. Bd. Committeeman Nassau County (N.Y.), 1965—; former mem. legal adv. bd. Union Lawyers Ednl. Conf. Served with AUS, 1943-46. Mem. ABA, ACLU, VFW, N.Y. State Bar Assn., Indsl. Rels. Rsch. Assn., B'nai B'rith.

WEINREB, MICHAEL PHILIP, physicist; b. Lakewood, N.J., Feb. 2, 1939; s. Sol and Lillian (Bolotsky) W.; m. Alice Kogan, Aug. 28, 1966; children: Jenya, Elizabeth. BA, U. Pa., 1960; MA, Brandeis U., 1963, PhD, 1966. Physicist NASA, Cambridge, Mass., 1965-70, U.S. Dept. Transp., Cambridge, 1970, Nat. Oceanic and Atmospheric Adminstrn., Washington, 1970—. Adj. prof. math. Am. U., Washington, 1984-85. Contbr. articles to profl. jours. Recipient Gold medal U.S. Dept. of Commerce, 1998, Bronze medal, 1994. Mem. Optical Soc. Am., Am. Meteorol. Soc., Am. Geophys. Union, Phi Beta Kappa. Avocation: music. Office: NOAA NESDIS 5200 Auth Rd Camp Springs MD 20746-4304

WEINREICH, GABRIEL, physicist, minister, educator; b. Vilnius, Lithuania, Feb. 12, 1928; came to U.S., 1941, naturalized, 1949; s. Max and Regina (Szabad) W.; m. Alisa Lourié, Apr. 19, 1951 (dec. 1970); m. Gerane Siemering Benamou, Oct. 23, 1971; children: Catherine, Marc, Daniel, Rebecca, Natalie. AB, Columbia U., 1948, MA, 1949, PhD, 1954. Ordained priest Episcopal Ch., 1986. Mem. staff Bell Telephone Labs., Murray Hill, N.J., 1953-60; mem. faculty U. Mich., Ann Arbor, 1960—, prof. physics, 1964-95; prof. emeritus, 1995—; Collegiate prof. U. Mich., 1974-76. Adj. min. St. Clare's Episcopal ch., Ann Arbor, 1985-90; rector St. Stephen's Episcopal Ch., Hamburg, Mich., 1993-96. Author: Solids: Elementary Theory for Advanced Students, 1965, Fundamental Thermodynamics, 1968, Notes for General Physics, 1972, Geometrical Vectors, 1998; editor: Mechanics of Musical Instruments, 1995. Recipient Disting. Teaching award U. Mich., 1968, Klopsteg award Am. Assn. Physics Tchrs., 1992, Internat. medal French Acoustical Soc., 1992. Fellow Acoustical Soc. Am. (assoc. editor Jour. 1987-89). Home: 754 Greenhills Dr Ann Arbor MI 48105-2718 Office: Randall Lab U Mich Ann Arbor MI 48109-1120 E-mail: weinreic@umich.edu.

WEINRICH, BRIAN ERWIN, mathematician, computer scientist; b. Passaic, N.J., Jan. 8, 1952; s. Erwin H. and Ann E. (Gall) Weinrich. BS, Pa. State U., 1974, MA, 1978; MS, Shippensburg (Pa.) U., 1983; postgrad. in computer engring., U. Fla., 2002—. Mathematician U.S. Dept. Agr., Agrl. Rsch. Svc., University Park, Pa., 1974-80; instr. math and computer sci. Shippensburg U., 1980-84; assoc. prof. maths. and computer sci. California U. of Pa., 1984-97, assoc. prof. emeritus of mathematics and computer scis., 1997—. Cons. in field; mem. Wall St. Jour. Panel, 1990—; devel. articulation agreements in Malaysia California U. of Pa., 1992—; vis. sr. lectr. in computer sci. Inti Coll., Subang Jaya, Malaysia, 1993—2001; cons. in math., sys. and database programming, 2001—02. Author (with A. S. Rogowski): (book) Water Movement and Quality on Strip-Mined Lands: A Compilation of Computer Programs, 1984; author: (with others) Surface Mining, 1990; contbr. articles to profl. jours. Mem. mission bd. Calvary Bapt. Ch., State College, Pa., 1975—80; visitation team Prince St. United Brethren Ch., Shippensburg, 1982—84; Bible study leader, asst. Sunday sch. tchr. Libr. Bapt. Ch., 1986—92. Fellow, U. Fla., 2002—; grantee, U.S. Dept. Age, 1982—89. Mem.: Assn. Computing Machinery, Math. Assn. Am., Am. Biog. Inst. (bd. advisors 1989—), Computer Soc. of IEEE. Republican. Home: 1001 SW 16th Ave Apt 67 Gainesville FL 32601 Office: U Fla Dept computer and Info Sci and Engring PO Box 116120 Gainesville FL 32611

WEINRICH, JAMES DONALD, psychobiologist, internet consultant; b. Cleve., July 2, 1950; s. Albert James and Helen Weinrich. AB, Princeton U., 1972; PhD, Harvard U., 1976. Postdoctoral fellow, then instr. Johns Hopkins U., Balt., 1980-82; rsch. assoc., then asst. rsch. prof. psychiatry Boston U., 1983-87; asst. rsch. psychobiologist, project mgr. U. Calif., San Diego, 1987-89, asst. rsch. psychobiologist, ctr. mgr., 1989-91, sr. investigator sexology, 1991-93, prin. investigator sexology project, 1994-99; prin. PhD Home Pages Cons. Firm, 2000—. Author: Sexual Landscapes, 1987; co-editor: Homosexuality: Social, Psychological and Biological Issues, 1982, Homosexuality: Research Implications for Public Policy, 1991; cons. editor Jour. of Sex Rsch., 1997-2000; mem. editl. bd. Jour. of Bisexuality, 2000—. Recipient Hugo Beigel award Soc. for Sci. Study of Sex, 1987. Mem. Am. Coll. Sexologists (cert.), Phi Beta Kappa. Avocations: naturism, photography. Office: Univ Calif San Diego PO Box 151365 San Diego CA 92175-1365 E-mail: jweinrich@ucsd.edu.

WEINRICH, JOHNATHAN EDWARD, lawyer; b. N.Y.C., Sept. 17, 1949; s. John Edward and Anne (Murray) W.; children: Joy Teresa, Johnathan Joseph; m. Evelyn; 1 child, Kristina Lynn. BA, SUNY, Binghamton, 1974; JD magna cum laude, Vt. Law Sch., 1977. Bar: N.Y. 1978, U.S. Dist. Ct. (ea. and so. dist.) N.Y. 1978, U.S. Tax Ct. 1981, U.S. Ct. Appeals (2d cir.) 1980. Sr. staff atty. Legal Aid Soc., N.Y.C., 1979-81; ptnr. Rutberg & Weinrich, 1981-83; prin., owner Johnathan E. Weinrich Law Firm, 1983—. Legis. counsel N.Y.C. Councilman Ralph Colon, 1987-92, N.Y.C. Councilman David Rosado, 1992-96, N.Y.C. Councilman Federico Perez, 1997-98, N.Y. State Senator David Rosado, 1997-2000; mem. Gov.'s Metro Task Force on Correctional Services, N.Y.C., 1984; trustee Vt. Law Sch., 1975-76. Editor Vt. Law Rev., 1976-77. Counsel Excise Bonds, 1990—, Kings County Soc. Prevention Cruelty to Children, 1992—, Local One Security Officers Union, 1998—. Recipient State of N.Y. Legis. Resolution #759, 1989, N.Y. Coun. Proclaimation, 1992, N.Y. State Senate Resolution, 2000. Mem. ABA, N.Y. State Trial Lawyers Assn., Assn. Trial Lawyers Am., Bklyn. Bar Assn., Kings County Criminal Bar Assn., Legal Aid Alumni Assn., N.Y. State Defenders Assn., N.Y. State Assn. Criminal Def. Attys. (charter 1987—), Royal Order of Scotland. Lodge: Masons. Democrat. Roman Catholic. Address: 15 Maiden Lane Ste 800 New York NY 10038

WEINSCHEL, ALAN JAY, lawyer; b. Bklyn., Feb. 9, 1946; m. Barbara Ellen Schure, Aug. 20, 1967; children: Lawrence, Adam, Naomi. BA, Bklyn. Coll., 1967; JD, NYU, 1969. Bar: N.Y. 1970, U.S. Dist. Ct. (so. and ea. dists.) N.Y. 1973, U.S. Ct. Appeals (2d cir.) 1979, U.S. Ct. Appeals (9th cir.) 1986, U.S. Ct. Appeals (3d cir.) 1993, U.S. Ct. Appeals (7th cir.) 1996. Assoc. Breed, Abbott & Morgan, N.Y.C., 1969-74, Weil, Gotshal & Manges, N.Y.C., 1974-78, ptnr., 1978—. Lectr. Practising Law Inst., Ohio Legal Ctr., Am. Mgmt. Assn., Law Jour. Seminars, Law and Bus. Seminars, Glasser Legalworks, Insight Seminars, Mfrs.' Alliance. Author: Antitrust Intellectual Property Handbook, 2000. Trustee N.Y. Inst. Tech., Old Westbury, N.Y., 1969-76, Temple Sinai, Roslyn, N.Y., 1981-87, 89-95. Capt. U.S. Army res., 1969-74. Mem. ABA (editl. bd. Antitrust Devels. 1981-87), N.Y. State Bar Assn. (chmn. antitrust sect. 1993-95), Assn. Bar of City of N.Y. Office: Weil Gotshal & Manges 767 5th Ave New York NY 10153-0119 E-mail: alan.weinschel@weil.com.

WEINSHENKER, NAOMI JOYCE, clinical psychiatrist, educator, researcher; b. Ridgewood, N.J., Mar. 28, 1961; d. Theodore and Anne Betty (Jaffe) W. BA summa cum laude, Yale U., 1983; MD, U. Pa., 1989. Diplomate Am. Bd. Psychiatry and Neurology. Rotating intern Overlook Hosp., Summit, N.J., 1989-90; resident in adult psychiatry Mass. Mental Health Ctr., Harvard U. Med. Sch., Boston, 1990-92, fellow in child and adolescent psychiatry, 1992-93, Boston Children's Hosp., Harvard U. Med. Sch., 1993-94; staff psychiatrist Choate Health Systems, Woburn, Mass., 1994-96; asst. prof. clin. psychiatry U. Medicine and Dentistry of N.J., Newark, 1996-2000; asst. prof. clin. psychiatry Sch. Medicine NYU, 2000—. Staff psychiatrist Univ. Behavioral HealthCare, Newark, 1996—97; asst.dir. Univ.Hosp. Psychiat. Outpatient Ctr., 1998—2000; mem. faculty NYU Child Study Ctr., 2000—; cons. child outpatient svcs. Tri-City Mental Health and Retardation Ctr., Inc., Medford, Mass., 1996. Contbr. articles to profl. jours.; editl. asst. Emergency Medicine mag., 1983-84. Vol. psychiatry unit, coord. psychiatry vols., Yale-New Haven Hosp., 1979-83; vol. recruitment coord. Phila. Adult Spl. Olympics, 1985. Mem. Am. Psychiat. Assn., Am. Acad. Child/Adolescent Psychiatry, N.J. Psychiat. Assn. (Essex County rep. Tri-County chpt. 1997-98, treas. 1998-99, sec. 1999-00, v.p. 2000-2001, pres.-elect 2001—), N.J. Coun. Child/Adolescent Psychiatry, Phi Beta Kappa, Sigma Xi. Democrat. Jewish. Avocations: singing, viola, musical theatre, nutrition and vegetarianism, weight training and aerobics. Office: NYU Child Study Ctr 550 First Ave New York NY 10016

WEINSHILBOUM, RICHARD M. pharmacologist, educator, biomedical researcher; b. Eldorado, Kans., Mar. 31, 1943; s. Robert Saul and Rose Lazer Weinshilboum; m. Lily Shuling, June 4, 1965; children: Rebecca Y., David H. BA, U. Kans., 1962; MD, U. Kans., Kansas City, 1967; LLD (hon.) , New Eng. U., 1995. Cert. bd. cert. in internal medicine, bd. cert. in clin. pharmacology. Resident in internal medicine Mass. Gen. Hosp., Boston, 1967—69, 1971—72; rsch. assoc. NIMH, Bethesda, Md., 1969—71; prof. molecular pharmacology and exptl. therapeutics and medicine Mayo Med. Sch., Mayo Clinic, Rochester, Minn., 1979—. Contbr. articles to profl. jours. Scholar Burroughs-Wellcome in Clin. Pharmacology, 1981—86. Mem.: Am. Soc. Clin. Pharmacology and Therapeutics (Rawls-Palmer award 1979, Oscar B. Hunter award 1998). Jewish. Achievements include major contributions to the fields of pharmacogenetics and pharmacogenomics of drug metabolism. Avocation: tennis. Office: Mayo Clinic 200 Fist St SW Rochester MN 55905

WEINSTEIN, ALAN EDWARD, lawyer; b. Bklyn., Apr. 20, 1945; s. John and Matilda W.; m. Patti Kantor, Dec. 18, 1965; children: Steven R., David A. AA, U. Fla., 1964; BBA, U. Miami, Fla., 1965, JD cum laude, 1968. Bar: Fla. 1968, U.S. Dist. Ct. (so. dist.) Fla. 1968, U.S. Ct. Appeals (5th cir.) 1969, U.S. Supreme Ct. 1973, U.S. Ct. Appeals (4th & 11th cirs.) 1981. Assoc. Cohen & Hogan, Miami Beach, Fla., 1968-71; pvt. practice, 1972-81; sr. ptnr. Weinstein & Preira, 1981-92; prin. Law Offices of Alan E. Weinstein, Miami, 1992—. Lectr. in field. Mem. ABA (criminal and family law sect. 1968—, white collar crime commn. 1986—), Nat. Assn. Criminal Def. Lawyers, 1st Family Law Am. Inn of Court, Fla. Bar Assn. (criminal and family law sect. 1968—, ethics com. 1987-88, bench/bar com. 1988-89, grievance com. 1999-2002, chmn. 2002), Fla. Criminal Def. Attys. Assn. (pres. 1978-79), Fla. Assn. Criminal Def. Lawyers (treas. 1989-90), Miami Beach Bar Assn., Soc. Wig and Robe, Phi Kappa Phi. Avocations: marlin fishing, reading, travel. Office: 1801 West Ave Miami FL 33139-1431 E-mail: defense1@bellsouth.net.

WEINSTEIN, ALLEN, educator, historian, non-profit administrator; b. N.Y.C., Sept. 1, 1937; s. Samuel and Sarah (Popkoff) W.; m. Adrienne Dominguez, June 14, 1995; children: Andrew Samuel, David Meier. BA, CCNY; MA, Yale U., PhD, 1967. Prof. Smith Coll., Northampton, Mass., 1966-81, Georgetown U., Washington, 1981-83; pres. R.M. Hutchins CSDI, Santa Barbara, Calif., 1984; prof. Boston U., 1985-89; founder, pres. The Ctr. for Democracy, Washington, 1985—. Author: Prelude to Populism, 1970, Freedom and Crisis, 1974, 3d edit., 1981, Perjury, 1978 (NISC award 1978), new edit., 1998, Between the Wars, 1978; co-author: The Haunted Wood: Soviet Espionage in America, 1999, The Story of America, 2002; editor: Am. Negro Slavery, 1968, 3d edit., 1981, HST and Israel, 1981; mem. editl. bd. The Washington Post, 1981; exec. editor The Washington Quar., 1982-83. Exec. dir. The Democracy Program, Washington, 1982-83; acting pres. Nat. Endowment for Democracy, Washington, 1983-84; chmn. edn. com. U.S. Inst. Peace, Washington, 1986—; mem. U.S. Observer del., Feb., 1986 Philippines election, co-author report; vice chmn. U.S. del. UNESCO World Conf. on Culture, 1982, UNESCO/IPDC meeting, 1983; chmn. Internat. IMPAC/Dublin Lit. award, 1996—. Recipient Meade prize in history CCNY, 1960, Egleston prize Yale U., 1967, Binkley-Stephenson prize Orgn. Am. Historians, 1968, UN Peace medal, 1986, Coun. of Europe silver medal, 1990, 96; Fulbright lectr., Australia, 1968, 71; Commonwealth Fund lectr. U.S. History, U. London, 1981; Fourth of July Orator Faneuil Hall, Boston, 1987. Fellow Woodrow Wilson Ctr., NEH; mem. Soc. Am. Historians, Cosmos Club. Democrat. Jewish. Office: The Ctr for Democracy 1101 15th St NW Ste 505 Washington DC 20005-5002

WEINSTEIN, ANDREW H. lawyer; b. Pitts., Oct. 5, 1943; s. Adolph J. and Meta I. (Schwarz) W.; m. Susan Balber, Aug. 11, 1968; children: Jodi L., Toby M., Jamie M. BSBA, Duquesne U., 1965; JD, U. Pitts., 1968; LLM in Tax Law, NYU, 1969. Bar: Pa. 1969, U.S. Tax Ct. 1969, Fla. 1970, U.S. Dist. Ct. (so. dist.) Fla., U.S. Ct. Fed. Claims. Trial atty. IRS, L.A., 1969-70, Miami, Fla., 1970-73; ptnr. Glass, Schultz, Weinstein & Moss, Coral Gables, 1973-80, Holland & Knight, Miami, 1980—. Contbr. articles to profl. jours. Bd. dirs. New World Symphony, Miami, Performing Arts Found., Zool. Soc. Fla. Fellow Am. Coll. Tax Counsel; mem. ABA (tax sect. com., chmn. subcom. 1981-87, chmn. CLE subcom., adminstrv. practice com., chmn. chief coun. liaison subcom.), The Fla. Bar Assn. Republican. Avocations: golf, swimming, travel. Office: Holland & Knight 701 Brickell Ave Ste 3000 Miami FL 33131-2898

WEINSTEIN, BARRY ALAN, architect; b. Chgo., Oct. 31, 1943; s. Reuben and Dorothy (Weiss) W.; m. Margery Gail Spector, June 12, 1966; children: Scott Howard, Allison Beth. BArch, U. Ill., 1967. Architect-in-tng. C.F. Murphy Assocs., Chgo., 1967-69, Norman A. Koglin Assocs., Chgo., 1969-71; project mgr., tech. dir. R.M.M. Inc., 1971-74; ptnr. Berger-Weinstein Assocs., 1974-81; owner B. Weinstein Assocs., 1981—. Instr. Harrington Inst. of Interior Design, Chgo., 1972-74; adj. prof. Triton Coll., 1988. Recipient Hon. award Am. Architecture State of the Art in the '80s, 1985. Mem.: ALA, Nat. Coun. Archtl. Registration Bds. Home and Office: 1166 Wade St Highland Park IL 60035-3451 E-mail: bwa1166@attbi.com.

WEINSTEIN, CHARLES DAVID, psychologist; b. Los Angeles, Oct. 1, 1953; s. Roy Cyril and Helen Bernice (Tellefsen) W.; m. Ann-Marie Pianta, Mar. 19, 1988; children: Patrick O'Keefe Miller, Nicholas Alexander Weinstein, Natalie Helena Weinstein, Michael Roy Peter Weinstein. AB with honors, Brown U., 1975; MA in Psychology, U. So. Calif., 1981, PhD in Psychology, 1983. Diplomate in Clin. Psychology, Am. bd. Profl. Psychology, 1996. From asst. dir. to dir. Pomona (Calif.) Open Door Community Mental Health Clin., 1976-78; assessor Mid-Valley Diagnostic Ctr, Covina, Calif., 1979; psychology trainee Jerry L. Pettis VA Hosp., Loma Linda, 1979; program coordinator for human relations ctr. U. So. Calif., Los Angeles, 1979-80, teaching asst., 1980-81; project assoc. Univ. Family Studies Project, 1980-82; neuropsychol. assessor of children Children's Hosp. of Los Angeles, 1982-83; predoctoral intern U. So. Calif. Med. Ctr., Los Angeles, 1982-83, clin. asst. prof. psychiatry, 1984—, clin. assoc. dept. psychology, 1985—; clin. onsite supr. Loyola Marmount U., 1983-84; psychologist, postdoctoral fellow San Fernando Valley (Calif.) Child Guidance Clinic, 1983-84; psychologist Woodland Hills (Calif.) Med. Group, 1984—; clin. dir. Santa Clarita Valley Spl. Children's Ctr., Newhall, Calif., 1985-88. Contbr. articles to profl. jours. Active Calif. Scholastic Fedn. NIMH fellow, 1979-80. Mem. Am. Psychol. Assn. (mem. com. clin. child psychology 1985), Calif. State Psychol. Assn., Los Angeles County Psychol. Assn., Sigma Xi (assoc.). E-mamil. Office: 4849 Van Nuys Blvd Ste 210 Sherman Oaks CA 91403-2126 E-mail: Charles805@aol.com.

WEINSTEIN, DAVID AKERS, lawyer; b. Denver, Apr. 9, 1942; s. Sam and Rowena May (Akers) W.; m. Gayle Ann Sunshine. BA, U. Colo., 1963; JD, U. Denver, 1967. Bar: Colo. 1967, N.Y. 1970, Ohio 1972, Wis. 1993, U.S. Dist. Ct. Colo., U.S. Ct. Appeals (10th and fed. cirs.). Atty. U.S. Patent and Trademark Office, Washington, 1967-70, Gen. Foods Corp., White Plains, N.Y., 1970-71, Borden Inc., Columbus, Ohio, 1971-77; pvt. practice Denver, 1977-91; atty.-spl. counsel Reinhart, Boerner Van Deuren Norris & Rieselbach, 1991-94, Holme, Roberts & Owen, Denver, 1994-96; ptnr. Dorsey & Whitney, 1996-97. Legal cons. Republic of Bulgaria Patent Office, Sofia, 1996, Govt. of Egypt Trademark Office, Cairo, 1997-99, Govt. of Jordan Ministry of Industry & Trade, 1999; mediator, mem. CPR/INTA Panel of Mediators. Author: How to Protect Your Creative Work, 1987, How to Protect Your Business, Professional & Brand Names, 1990. Past pres., bd. dirs. Colo. Lawyers for the Arts, Denver. Mem. Am. Intellectual Property Law Assn., Copyright Soc. U.S.A., Internat. Trademark Assn. Office: Ste 2600 1600 Broadway Denver CO 80202-4989

WEINSTEIN, EDWARD MICHAEL, architect, consultant; b. Bklyn., May 5, 1947; s. Hyman and Freda (Rochkes) W.; m. Melanie Jane Ross, June 22, 1969; children: Valerie, David. BS, CCNY, 1969. Registered architect; lic. N.Y., N.J. Jr. architect N.Y.C. Dept. Ports and Terminals, 1970-72, architect, 1972-75, sr. urban designer, 1975-80, dir. waterfront devel., 1980-84, asst. commr., 1984-87; pres. EMW Assocs., Hastings-On-Hudson, N.Y., 1984—; ptnr. The Hastings Design Group, 1987—2001; prin. Edward M. Weinstein, Planning and Architecture, 2001—. Adv. bd. Metro Marine Express Ltd., N.Y.C., 1989-91. Active Planning Bd., Hastings-on-Hudson, 1990-2000, Waterfront Ctr.; trustee Greenburgh Hebrew Ctr., Dobbs Ferry, N.Y., 1986-89, 92—; v.p. N.Y. Port Promotion Assn., N.Y.C., 1984-87; adv. com. on waterfront devel. N.Y. State Assembly; chair Village of Hastings-on-Hudson Waterfront Revitalization Com., 1999—. Recipient Gold Key award House Plan Assn., 1969. Mem. AIA, Am. Assn. Port Authority, N.Y. Soc. Architects, The Waterfront Ctr., CCNY Alumni Assn., Bklyn. Tech. H.S. Alumni Assn. (life), Am. Inst. of Certified Planners. Democrat. Jewish. Avocations: tennis, art. Office: EMW Planning and Architecture 14 Spring St Hastings On Hudson NY 10706 E-mail: ewarkitect@aol.com.

WEINSTEIN, ELLEN, performing company executive; BFA in Dance, SUNY. Dancer Garden State Ballet, Savannah Ballet; tchr., choreographer Nat. Dance Inst., N.Y.C., 1985—89, assoc. artistic dir., 1989—94, artistic dir., 1995—. Cons. Nat. Dance Inst. Nat. Outreach Program. Choreographer (films) Disney, Polaroid's 50th Anniversary Celebration, Radio City Music Hall. Office: National Dance Institute 594 Broadway Rm 805 New York NY 10012*

WEINSTEIN, GERALD D. dermatology educator; b. N.Y.C., Oct. 13, 1936; m. Marcia Z. Weinstein; children: Jeff, Jon, Debbie. BA, U. Pa., 1957, MD, 1961. Diplomate Am. Bd. Dermatology. Intern Los Angeles County Gen. Hosp., 1961-62; clin. assoc. dermatology br. Nat. Cancer Instn. NIH, Bethesda, Md., 1962-64; resident dept. dermatology U. Miami, Fla., 1964-65; asst. prof. Dept. Dermatology U. Miami, 1966-71, assoc. prof., 1971-74, prof., 1975-79; prof., chmn. dept. dermatology U. Calif., Irvine, 1979—, acting dean Coll. Medicine, 1985-87. Attending staff VA Med. Ctr., Long Beach, Calif., 1979—, UCI Med. Ctr., Orange, Calif., 1979—, St. Joseph Hosp., Orange, 1980—. Contbr. articles to profl. jours., chpts. to books. Recipient Lifetime Achievement award Nat. Psoriasis Found., 1994; co-recipient award for psoriasis rsch. Taub Internat. Meml., 1971; NIH spl. postdoctoral fellow, 1965-67. Mem. Am. Acad. Dermatology (chmn. task force on psoriasis 1986—, bd. dirs. 1984-88). Office: U Calif Irvine Coll Medicine Dept Dermatology C340 Med Scis Bldg 1 Irvine CA 92697-0001

WEINSTEIN, HERBERT, chemical engineer, educator; b. Bklyn., Mar. 10, 1933; s. Abraham and Pauline (Feldman) W.; m. Judith Cooper, Apr. 6, 1957; children: Michael Howard, Edward Marc, Ellen Rachel. B.Engring. in Chem. Engring, Coll. City N.Y., 1955; MS in Chem. Engring, Purdue U., 1957; PhD, Case Inst. Tech., 1963. Staff mem. Los Alamos Sci. Lab., 1956-58; research engr. NASA Lewis Research Center, Cleve., 1959-63; asst. prof. chem. engring. Ill. Inst. Tech., 1963-66, assoc. prof., 1966-72, prof., 1972-77; dir. Center for Biomed. Engring., 1973-77; prof. CUNY, 1977—; Herbert G. Kayser prof. of chem. engring., 1987—. Vis. rsch. assoc., mem. Med. Rsch. Inst. Michael Reese Hosp. and Med. Ctr., Chgo., 1965-77; vis. prof. mech. engring. Technion-Israel Inst. Tech., 1972-73; vis. prof. biomed. engring. Rush

Med. Coll., Chgo., 1973-76; summer prof. Exxon Rsch. and Engring. Co., annually, 1981-92; Lady Davis vis. prof. Technion-Israel Inst. Tech., 1985; cons. to industry, rsch. labs. Mem.: Am. Inst. Chem. Engrs., Sigma Xi. Jewish. Achievements include research publs. and patents on fluidization, chem. reactor engring., fluid mechanics, biomed. engring. Office: CUNY Dept Chem Engring New York NY 10031 E-mail: hweinst@che-mail.engr.ccny.cuny.edu.

WEINSTEIN, I. BERNARD, oncologist, geneticist, research administrator; b. Madison, Wis., Sept. 9, 1930; married, 1952; 3 children. BS, U. Wis., 1952, MD, 1955, DSc (hon.), 1992. Nat. Cancer Inst. spl. rsch. fellow bacteriology/immunology Harvard Med. Sch./MIT, Boston, 1959-61; career scientist Health Rsch. Coun., City of N.Y., 1961-72; assoc. vis. physician Francis Delafield Hosp., 1961-66; from asst. attending physician to assoc. attending physician Presbyn. Hosp., 1967-81, attending physician, 1981—; from asst. to assoc. prof. medicine Columbia U. Coll. Phys. and Surg., N.Y.C., 1978-90; prof. medicine Columbia U., 1973—, prof. pub. health, 1978—, prof. genetics and devel., 1990—, Frode Jensen prof. medicine, 1990—, dir. comprehensive cancer ctr., 1985-96. Advisor Lung Cancer Segment, Carcinogenesis Program, Nat. Cancer Inst., 1971-74, Chem. and Molecular Biol. Segment, 1973-76; mem. interdisciplinary comm. program Smithsonian Inst., 1971-74, Pharmacology B Study sect., NIH, 1971-75, numerous sci. and adv. coms. Nat. Cancer Inst., Am. Cancer Soc., 1976-88; advisor Roswell Park Meml. Inst., Buffalo, Brookhaven Nat. Lab., Divsn. Cancer Cause and Prevention, Nat. Cancer Inst., Coun. on Analysis and Projects, Am. Cancer Soc., Internat. Agy. for Rsch. on Cancer, WHO, Lyon, France; Nakasone vis. prof., Tokyo, 1987; GM Cancer Rsch. Found. vis. prof. Internat. Agy. Rsch. Cancer, Lyon, 1988; mem. adv. coun. Nat. Inst. Environ. Health Scis., 1995—; chmn. Bristol-Myers Squibb Cancer Awards, 1993-96. Assoc. editor Cancer Rsch., 1973-76, 86-95, Jour. Environ. Pathology and Toxicology, 1977-84, Jour. Cellular Physiology, 1982-89, Oncogene, 1989-99, Clin. Cancer Rsch., 1998—. Named Louise Weissberger lectr., U. Rochester, 1981, Mary Ann Swetland lectr., Case Western Res. U., 1983, Daniel Laszlo Meml. lectr., Montefiore Med. Ctr., 1983, Samuel Kuna Disting. lectr., Rutgers U., 1985, Ester Langer lectr., U. Chgo., 1989, Harris Meml. lectr., MIT, 1989, Rufus Cole lectr., 1997, travel fellow, European Molecular Biology Orgn., 1970—71; recipient Meltzer medal, 1964, Clowes award, Am. Assn. Cancer Rsch., 1987, Silvio O. Conte award, Environ. Health Inst., 1990, Nakahara award, 1996, Anthony Dipple Carcinogenesis award, 2000, Disting. Achievement award, Am. Soc. Preventive Oncology, 2001, Am. Assn. Cancer Rsch./Am. Cancer Soc. award, 2001. Mem.: AAAS (coun. del. 1985—88), N.Y. Acad. Sci., Am. Soc. Clin. Investigation, Internat. Soc. Quantum Biology, Am. Soc. Microbiology, Am. Assn. Physicians, Am. Acad. Arts and Scis., Inst. Medicine/Nat. Acad. Sci., Am. Assn. Cancer Rsch. (pres. 1990—91). Achievements include research in cellular and molecular aspects of carcinogenesis, environmental carcinogenesis, molecular epidemiology, cancer prevention. Office: Cancer Ctr Columbia Univ 701 W 168th St New York NY 10032-2704 E-mail: weinstein@cuccfa.cc.columbia.edu.

WEINSTEIN, IRWIN MARSHALL, internist, hematologist; b. Denver, Mar. 5, 1926; m. Judith Braun, 1951. Student, Dartmouth Coll., 1943—44, Williams Coll., 1944—45; MD, U. Colo., Denver, 1949. Diplomate Am. Bd. Internal Medicine. Intern Montefiore Hosp., N.Y.C., 1949—50, jr. asst. resident in medicine, 1950—51; sr. asst. resident in medicine U. Chgo., 1951—52, resident in medicine, 1952—53, instr. in medicine, 1953—54, asst. prof. medicine, 1954—55; vis. assoc. prof. medicine U. Calif. Center for Health Scis., L.A., 1955—56, assoc. clin. prof., 1957—60, clin. prof., 1970—; hon. prof., 1996—; sect. chief in medicine, hematology sect. Wadsworth Gen. Hosp., VA Center, L.A., 1956—59; pvt. practice medicine specializing in hematology and internal medicine Los Angeles, 1959—; mem. staff Cedars-Sinai Med. Center, L.A., 1959—; chief of med. staff Cedars-Sinai Med. Ctr., 1972—74, bd. govs., 1974—. Assoc. bd. govs. hematology subcom. Am. Bd. Internal Medicine; mem. staff U. Calif. Ctr. Health Scis., Wadsworth Gen. Hosp., VA Ctr.; vis. prof. Hadassah Med. Ctr., Jerusalem, 1967; adv. for health affairs to Hon. Alan Cranston, 1971—92; mem. com. on space biology and medicine Space Sci. Bd.; active UCLA Comprehensive Cancer Ctr. Contbr. articles to profl. publs.; editor (with Ernest Beutler): Mechanisms of Anemia, 1962. Recipient Pioneer in Medicine award, Cedars-Sinai Med. Ctr., 1997. Master: ACP (gov. So. Calif. region I 1989—93); fellow: Israel Med. Assn. (hon.); mem.: AAAS, Western Soc. Clin. Rsch., Royal Soc. Medicine, Reticulo-Endothelial Soc., N.Y. Acad. Sci., Inst. of Medicine NAS, L.A. Soc. Nuc. Medicine, L.A. Acad. Medicine, Internat. Soc. Internal Medicine, Internat. Soc. Hematology, Assn. Am. Med. Colls., Am. Soc. Internal Medicine, Am. Soc. Hematology (exec. com. 1974—78, chmn. com. on practice 1978—87, mem. coun. 1974—78), Am. Fedn. Clin. Rsch., Alpha Omega Alpha. Office: 9509 Heather Rd Beverly Hills CA 90210-1739

WEINSTEIN, JACK BERTRAND, federal judge; b. Wichita, Kans., Aug. 10, 1921; s. Harry Louis and Bessie Helen (Brodach) W.; m. Evelyn Horowitz, Oct. 10, 1946; children: Seth George, Michael David, Howard Lewis. BA, Bklyn. Coll., 1943; LLB, Columbia, 1948; LLD (hon.), Bklyn. Law Sch., Yeshiva U., Albany Law Sch., Hofstra Law Sch., L.I. U., Yale U. Bar: N.Y. 1949. Assoc. Columbia Law Sch., 1948-49; law clk. N.Y. Ct. Appeals Judge Stanly H. Fuld, 1949-50; ptnr. William Rosenfeld, N.Y.C., 1950-52; mem. faculty Columbia Law Sch., 1952-67, prof. law, 1956-67, adj. prof., 1967-97; U.S. judge (Eastern Dist. N.Y.), 1967-93, chief judge, 1980-88; sr. judge Ea. Dist. N.Y., 1993—. Vis. prof. U. Tex., 1957, U. Colo., 1961, Harvard U., 1982, Georgetown U., 1991, Bklyn. Law Sch., 1988-97, others; counsel N.Y. Joint Legis. Com. Motor Vehicle Problems, 1952-54, State Sen. Seymour Halpern, 1952-54; reporter adv. com. practice and procedure N.Y. State Temp. Commn. Cts., 1955-58; adv. com. practice N.Y. Judicial Conf., 1963-66; adv. com. rules of evidence U.S. Jud. Conf., 1965-75, mem. com. jurisdiction, 1969-75, mem., 1983-86; mem. 2d Cir. Jud. Coun., 1982-88, U.S. Jud. Conf., 1983-86, others in past. Author: (with Morgan and Maquire) Cases and Materials on Evidence, 4th edit, 1965, (with Maguire, Chadbourne and Mansfield, 5th edit.), 1971, 6th edit., 1975, (with Mansfield, Abrams and Berger), 9th edit., 1997, (with Rosenberg) Cases and Materials on Civil Procedure, 1961, rev. edit, (with Smit), 1971, (with Smit, Rosenberg and Korn), 1976, (with Korn and Miller) New York Civil Procedure, 9 vols., rev. edit, 1966, Manual of New York Civil Procedure, 1967, Basic Problems of State and Federal Evidence, 1976, (with Berger) Weinstein's Evidence, 7 vols., 1967, rev. edit., 1993, Revising Rule Making Procedures, 1977, A New York Constitution Meeting Today's Needs and Tomorrow's Challenges, 1967, Disaster, A Legal Allegory, 1988, (with Greenawalt) Readings for Seminar on Equality and Law, 1979, (with Murphy) Readings for Seminar in Individual Rights in a Mass Society, 1990-91, (with Berger) Readings for Seminar in Science and Law, (with Feinberg) Mass Torts, 1992, 94, Individual Justice in Mass Litigation, 1995. Chmn. N.Y. Dem. adv. com. on Constl. Conv., 1955; bd. dirs. N.Y. Civil Liberties Union, 1956-62, Cardozo Sch. Law, Conf. on Jewish Social Studies, 1980-88; nat. adv. bd. Am. Jewish Congress, 1960-67, CARE, 1985-90, Fedn. Jewish Philanthropies, 1985-94; chmn. lay bd. Riverside Hosp. Adolescent Drug Users, 1954-55. Lt. USNR, 1943-46. Mem. ABA, N.Y. State Bar Assn., Assn. of Bar of City of N.Y., Nassau County Bar Assn., Am. Law Inst., Soc. Pub. Tchrs. Law (Eng.), Am. Acad. Arts and Scis. Jewish. Office: US Dist Ct US Courthouse 225 Cadman Plz E Brooklyn NY 11201-1818

WEINSTEIN, JAY A. social science educator, researcher; b. Chgo., Feb. 23, 1942; s. Lawrence E. and Jacqueline L. (Caplan) W.; m. Diana S. Staffin, Sept. 16, 1961; m. Marilyn L. Schwartz, Nov. 25, 1972; children— Liza, Bennett. AB, U. Ill., 1963, PhD, 1973; MA, Washington U., St. Louis, 1965. Teaching fellow U. Ill., Urbana, 1963-64; teaching asst. McGill U., Montreal, Que., Can., 1966-68; instr. Sir George Williams U., Can., 1967-68; lectr. Simon Fraser U., Vancouver, B.C., Can., 1968; asst. prof. North Central Coll., Naperville, Ill., 1970-71, U. Iowa, 1973-77; prof. social sci. Ga. Inst. Tech., Atlanta, 1977-86; head dept. sociology Eastern Mich U., 1986-90, faculty rsch. fellow, 1990-91; grantee ednl. devel. project USIA-Soros Found., Albania, 1992—; dir. Applied Rsch. Unit, 1996—. Cons. World Bank Study Social and Econ. Vulnerability in Albania, 1997, World Bank Study on Closing the Vulnerability Gap, Albania, 1997—98; project dir. Ea. Mich.-U-Ypsilanti Cmty. Outreach Partnership Ctr.; cons. pvt. and pub. agencies; rschr. in field. Author: Madras: An Analysis of Urban Ecological Structure in India, 1974, Demographic Transition and Social Change, 1976, Sociology-Technology: Foundations of Postacademic Social Science, 1982, The Grammar of Social Relations: The Major Essays of Louis Schneider, 1984; editor: Paradox and Society, 1986; (with Vinod Tewari and V.L.S. Prakash Rao) Indian Cities: Ecological Perspectives, Social and Cultural Change: Social Science for a Dynamic World, 1997, 1987, The Holocaust: A Sociological Analysis, 1997, Demography: The Science of Population, 2000; Studies in Comparative International Development, 1978-88; mem. editorial bd. Social Development Issues, 1977-85; specialized contbr. Calcutta Mcpl. Gazette, 1979—; editor: Social and Cultural Change, 1974-75; ed. Michigan Soc. Review, 1997—, editorial reviewer Jour. Asian Studies, Social Devel. Issues, Tech. and Culture, Am. Sociologist, Technol. Forecasting and Social Change; contbr. chpts. to book, articles to profl. jours. Recipient Charles Horton Cooley award for outstanding contbns. to sociology in Mich., 1998; Fulbright prof. Ahmedabad, India, 1975-76, Hyderabad, India, 1981-82; grantee Ga. Tech. Found., 1981-82, World Order Studies Course, 1994-97, State of Mich. Rsch. Excellence Fund; Steinberg fellow, 1967. Mem. Am. Sociol. Assn., Soc. for Applied Sociology (v.p. 1998—, mem. exec. bd. 2000—), Mich. Sociol. Assn. (pres. 1988-89, v.p. 1994-95), Sigma Xi. Jewish. Office: Eastern Mich U Sociology Dept Ypsilanti MI 48197 E-mail: weinst@aol.com.

WEINSTEIN, JOEL DAVID, orthopedic surgeon; b. Memphis, Aug. 9, 1936; s. Jake and Rose (Wahl) W.; m. Judith Lefkovits, June 10, 1959; children: David, Jeffrey, Peter. BA, Princeton U., 1958; MD, Columbia U., 1962. Diplomate Am. Bd. Orthop. Surgery. Intern Presbyn. Hosp., N.Y.C., 1962-63; resident in gen. surgery Bellevue Med. Ctr., 1965-66; resident in otrhop. surgery N.Y. Orthop. Hosp., 1966-69, chief resident, 1969-70; orthop. surgeon Katzman, Tarsney, Weinstein, Tenafly, N.J., 1970-75; pvt. practice Englewood, 1975-78; surgeon Englewood Orthop. Assocs., 1978—. Pres. med. staff Englewood Hosp., 1989-90, assoc. chief dept. orthop. surgery, 1997—; from instr. to assoc. clin. prof. Columbia U., N.Y.C., 1970-96. Capt. USAF, 1963-65. Fellow Am. Acad. Orthop. Surgery; mem. Stinchfield Orthop. Club. Avocations: golf, tennis, sailing. Office: Englewood Orthop Assocs 401 S Van Brunt St Ste 3 Englewood NJ 07631-4600

WEINSTEIN, JOYCE, artist; b. June 7, 1931; d. Sidney and Rose (Bier) W.; m. Stanley Boxer, Nov. 28, 1952. Student, CCNY, 1948-50, Art Students League, 1948-52. Exec. coord. Women in Arts Found., Inc., 1975-79, 81-82, coord. bd., 1983-87. One-person shows include Perdalma Gallery, N.Y.C., 1953-56, L.I. U., Bklyn., 1969, U. Calif.-Santa Cruz, 1969, T. Bortolazzo Gallery, Santa Barbara, Calif., 1972, Dorsky Gallery, N.Y.C., 1972, 74, Galerie Ariadne, N.Y.C., 1975, Gloria Cortella Gallery, N.Y.C., 1976, Meredith Long Contemporary Gallery, N.Y.C., 1978, 79, 88-90, Martin Gerard Gallery, Edmonton, Alta., Can., 1981, 82, 84, Galerie Wentzel, Cologne, Fed. Republic of Germany, 1982, 87, Haber Theodore Gallery, N.Y.C., 1983, 95, Gallery One, Toronto, Ont., Can., 1983, 2002, Paul Kuhn Gallery, Calgary, 1985, Eva Cohn Gallery, Highland Park, Ill., 1985, Meredith Long & Co., Houston, 1988, 90, Alena Adlung Gallery, N.Y.C., 1989, Flanders Art Gallery, Mpls., 1999 Harmon-Meek Gallery, Naples, Fla., 2000, Gallery One, Toronto, 2002; exhibited in group shows at Marlborough Gallery, N.Y.C., 1968, Bula Mus. Art, Calcutta, India, 1970, Phoenix Gallery, N.Y.C., 1988, Provident Nat. Bank, 1988, Alena Adlung Gallery, 1989, 90, Edmonton Art Mus., 1975, 77, 83, 85, 89, Rose Fried Gallery, N.Y.C., 1970, Hudson River Mus., 1971, Dorsky Gallery, 1972, 94, Suffolk Mus., Stony Brook, N.Y., 1972, N.Y. Cultural Ctr., 1973, Stamford (Conn.) Mus., 1973, Landmark Gallery, N.Y.C., 1974, Women's Interart Ctr., N.Y.C., 1974, 75, 78, New Sch. Social Rsch., N.Y.C., 1975, Bklyn. Mus., 1975, Galerie Ariadne, 1975, Mus. of Modern Art, N.Y.C., 1981, The Queens Mus. N.Y., 1984, The Centre de Creacio Contemporania, Barcelona, Spain, 1987, Fairleigh Dickinson U., Hackensack, N.J., 1976, Gloria Cortella, Inc., 1976, Northeastern U., Boston, 1977, Lehigh (Pa.) U., 1977, Meredith Long Contemporary Gallery, 1977, 78, 79, 80, Galerie Wentzel, 1981-85, Martin Gerard Gallery, 1981-84, Gallery One, 1983, 84, Haber Theodore Gallery, 1982-85, Jerald Melberg Gallery, Charlotte, N.C., 1984, Richard Green Gallery, N.Y.C., 1986, Rosel Art Fair, Basel Switzerland, 1986, Meredith Long & Co., 1988-90, Broome St. Gallery, N.Y.C., 1991, 97, Andre Zarre Gallery, N.Y.C., 1990, Cork Gallery, N.Y.C., 1990, Chgo. Internat. Art Exbn., 1990, Queens Coll., N.Y.C., 1991, Miami Art Fair, 1993, Bklyn. Botanic Gardens, 1994, Dorothy Blau Gallery, Bay Harbor Islands, Fla., 1997-98, Harmon-Meek Gallery, Naples, Fla., 1998-99, Flanders Contemporary Art, Mpls., 1999; represented in permanent collections: Pa. Acad. Fine Arts, N.J. State Mus., Ciba-Geigy Corp., New Sch. Social Rsch., Bula Mus. Art, U. Calif., Mus. Modern Art, N.Y.C., McMullen Gallery, Edmonton, Ga., De Spisset Mus., U. Santa Clara, Edmonton Art Gallery Mus., The Hines Collection, Boston, others; represented by Smith Anderson Gallery, Palo Alto, Calif., Flanders Art Gallery, Harmon-Meek Gallery, Naples, Fla., Flanders Contemporary Art, Mpls., Dorothy Blau Gallery, Bay Harbor Island, Fla., Gallery One, Toronto. Recipient Lambert Fund award Pa. Acad. Fine Arts, 1955, Susan B. Anthony award NOW, 1983. Home: 46 Fox Hill Rd Ancramdale NY 12503-5311

WEINSTEIN, KENNETH R. think-tank executive; b. N.Y.C., Nov. 4, 1961; s. Victor and Hannelore S. Weinstein; m. Amy B. Kauffman, Nov. 10, 1996; children: Raina, Harrison. BA, U. Chgo.; DEA in Soviet Studies, Institut d'Etudes Politiques de Paris; PhD in Polit. Sci., Harvard U. Rsch. fellow Hudson Inst., Indpls., 1991—94; dir. rsch. The New Citizenship Project, Washington, 1994—96; dir. govt. reform project The Heritage Found., 1996—98; dir. Washington office Shalem Ctr., 1998—99; v.p. and dir. Washington office Hudson Inst., 1999—. Adj. prof. govt. Goergetown U., Washington, 1999—2000. Fellow Carrere Travelling fellow, Harvard U., 1986, Chateaubriand Fellowship for Social Sci. Rsch., French Fgn. Ministry, 1989; scholar, Govt. France, 1986. Jewish. Home: 1426 35th St NW Washington DC 20007 Office: Hudson Inst Ste 300 1015 18th St NW Washington DC 20036 Office Fax: 202-223-8537. E-mail: ken@hudsondc.org.

WEINSTEIN, LEONARD HARLAN, institute program director, educator; b. Springfield, Mass., Apr. 11, 1926; s. Barney Willard Weinstein and Ida Pauline (Feinberg) Weinstein Clark; m. Sylvia Jane Sherman, Oct. 15, 1950; children: Beth Rachel, David Harold (dec.). BS, Pa. State U., 1949; MS, U. Mass., 1950; PhD, Rutgers U., 1953. Postdoctorial fellow Rutgers U., New Brunswick, N.J., 1953-55; plant physiologist Boyce Thompson Inst., Yonkers, N.Y., 1955-63, program dir. Ithaca, 1963-91, bd. dirs., 1976-96; dir. ecosystem rsch. ctr. Cornell U., 1988-90, William Boyce Thompson scientist emeritus, 1993—, adj. prof. dept. natural resources, 1979—. Mem. rsch. adv. com. Oak Ridge Nat. Lab, 1985-87. Contbr. over 175 articles to profl. jours., chpts. to books. Mem. sci. adv. bd. EPA, Washington, 1988-91; mem. com. natural resources NASULGS, 1986-89. Grantee NIH, NSF, HEW, Am. Cancer Soc., NASA, EPA, DOE, USDA. Mem. Am. Soc. Plant Physiologists, Sigma Xi, Pi Alpha Xi, Gamma Sigma Delta. Home: 608 Cayuga Heights Rd Ithaca NY 14850-1424 Office: Cornell U 125 Boyce Thompson Inst Tower Rd Ithaca NY 14853

WEINSTEIN, MARIE PASTORE, psychologist; b. N.Y.C., Oct. 3, 1940; d. Edward and Sarah (Mancuso) Pastore; children: Arielle Rebecca Dorros, Damon Alexander. BA in Polit. Sci. and Lit., Ind. U.; MS in Psychology, L.I. U.; PhD in Ednl. Psychology, CCNY, 1986. Cert. sch. psychologist; lic. psychologist, N.Y. Pvt. practice, 1978—; dir., adminstr. learning ctr. Guidance Ctr. Flatbush, Bklyn., 1978—82; clin. team coord./psychologist Lorge Upper and Lower Sch., N.Y.C., 1982—85; psychologist devel. disabilities ctr. Roosevelt Hosp., 1985—87; chief psychologist Blueberry Treatment Ctrs., Bklyn., 1987—89; cons. psychologist Safe Space, N.Y.C., 1989—; law guardian Panel of Forensic Psychologists, 1994—. Cons. psychologist United Cerebral Palsy Hearst Presch., Bklyn., 1988-89, Charles Drew Day Ctr., Queens Village, N.Y., 1982-85, Warbasse Nursery Sch., Bklyn., 1981-85, YWCA Montessori Sch., 1993-94; adj. asst. prof. Baruch Coll. CUNY, 1989; pvt. practice, Bklyn.; rsch. cons. Children's TV Workshop, N.Y.C., 1979; clin. cons. Bedford Stuyvesant Mental Health Ctr., Bklyn., 1990, Youth Counseling League, N.Y.C., 1993; cons. dist. 2 N.Y.C. Bd. Edn., 1988; guest lectr. Met. Hosp. Dept. Psychiatry, N.Y.C., 1988, Dist. 3 Bd. Edn., 1993; edn. cons. Lit. Vols. N.Y., 1974-76. Contbg. author to children's ency., 1970. Bd. dirs. Artists in Search of. . . . Fellow Am. Orthopsychiat. Assn. (program com. 1990—); mem. APA, Internat. Congress on Child Abuse and Neglect, Manhattan Fedn. Child and Adolescent Svcs. Office: 26 Court St Ste 2112 Brooklyn NY 11242-1121

WEINSTEIN, MARK JAY, opera general director; b. N.Y.C., Oct. 7, 1955; s. Lawrence and Rhoda Joy (Stucker) W.; m. Susanne Irene Marsee, May 15, 1987; 1 child, Zachary. BA, Carleton Coll.; MBA, Harvard U. Asst. product mgr. Gen. Mills, Inc., Mpls., 1979-81; assoc. Strategic Planning Assocs., Washington, 1981-83; pres. Pierre Deux, Pleasantville, N.Y., 1993; exec. dir. N.Y.C. Opera, 1983-96; v.p. ops. Nat. Artists Mgmt. Co., N.Y.C., 1996-97; exec. dir. Pitts. Opera, 1997-99, gen. dir., 1999—. Co-chair Nat. Endowment Arts Challenge Grants Panel, Washington, 1994; chmn. AGMA Pension and Health Funds; on site evaluator Nat. Endowment Arts, Washington, 1995, 97, 99, 2001-02; chair Arts Leadership, 2000, 2001; bd. dirs. Greater Pitts. Arts Alliance; bd. dirs., treas. Opera Am., 1999--. Home: 5600 Northumberland St Pittsburgh PA 15217-1238 Office: Pitts Opera 801 Penn Ave Pittsburgh PA 15222-3609

WEINSTEIN, MARTIN, aerospace manufacturing executive, materials scientist; b. Mar. 3, 1936; s. Benjamin and Dora (Lemo) W.; m. Sandra Rebecca Yaffie, June 5, 1961; children: Hilary Ann, Sarah Elizabeth, Joshua Aaron. BS in Metals Engring., Rensselaer Poly. Inst., 1957; MS, MIT, 1960, PhD, 1961. Mgr. materials sci. Tycolabs., Waltham, Mass., 1961-69; tech. dir. turbine support divsn. Chromalloy Am. Corp., San Antonio, 1968-71, v.p., asst. gen. mgr., 1971-74, pres., 1975-79, Chromalloy Compressor Techs., San Antonio, 1979-82; group pres. Chromalloy Gas Turbine, 1982-86, chmn., CEO N.Y.C., 1986—. Supervisory mng. dir. Turbine Support Europe, Tilburg, Netherlands, 1975—; bd. dirs. Turbine Support Thailand, Bankok, Chromalloy U.K., Nottingham, Eng., Internat. Coating Co., Tokyo, Japan, Chromalloy, France, Malichaud Orleans, France. Patentee diffusion coating of jet engine materials; contbr. articles to profl. jours. Bd. dirs. Jewish Fedn., 1981-85, Chamber Players of San Antonio, 1979-83, NCCJ, 1982-85, Sequa Corp., N.Y.C., 1999—; mem. vis. com. dept. metallurgy and materials sci. MIT, 1992-2001. Recipient Turner Meml. award Electrochem. Soc., 1963, Achievement award NASA, 1963; Am. Iron and Steel Inst. fellow, 1960. Mem. Am. Soc. Metals, Am. Inst. Metall. Engrs., N.Y. Acad. Sci., Sigma Xi. Home: 111 Sheffield San Antonio TX 78213-2626 Office: Chromalloy Gas Turbine Corp 200 Park Ave New York NY 10166-0005 E-mail: mw@chronalloy.com.

WEINSTEIN, MARTIN JAMES, lawyer; b. Washington, Jan. 31, 1959; m. Amy Cooper, Apr. 14, 1991. BA, Dartmouth Coll., 1981; JD, Univ. Va., 1984. Bar: D.C. 1985, Md. 1985, Ga. 1990. Assoc. Howrey & Simon, Washington, 1984-88; trial atty. U.S. Dept. Justice, 1988-89; asst. U.S. atty. U.S. Dept. Justice, U.S. Atty's Office, Atlanta, 1989-96; ptnr. Foley & Lardner, Washington, 1996—; chmn. compliance, counselling Govt. Enforcement Practice Group. Contbr. articles to profl. jours. Recipient Federal Law Enforcement Officers Prosecutorial award Fed. Law Enforcement, 1995, The John Marshall award U.S. Dept. Justice, 1995. Office: Foley & Lardner 3000 K St NW Ste 500 Washington DC 20007-5143 E-mail: mweinstein@foleylaw.com.

WEINSTEIN, MELVIN PHILLIP, physician educator; b. Long Branch, N.J., Apr. 27, 1944; s. Joseph and Selma Joyce (Nathanson) W.; m. Dustra Lee Anderson, July 13, 1969; children: Joanna Lee, Michael Jacob. BA in Zoology with distinction, Rutgers U., 1966; MD, George Washington U., 1970. Diplomate Nat. Bd. Med. Examiners, Am. Bd. Internal Medicine, Am. Bd. Infectious Diseases, Am. Bd. Pathology (Med. Microbiology). Intern Hartford (Conn.) Hosp., 1970-71, resident, 1973-75; fellow in infectious diseases U. Colo. Health Sci. Ctr., Denver, 1975-77, fellow in clin. microbiology, 1983; asst. prof. medicine U. Medicine and Dentistry N.J., New Brunswick, 1977-83, assoc. prof. medicine and pathology, 1983-91, prof. medicine and pathology, 1991—; staff Robert Wood Johnson U. Hosp. Cons. staff St. Peter's U. Hosp., 1998—; cons. Roosevelt Hosp., Edison, N.J., 1986-89; vis. assoc. prof. Rutgers U., New Brunswick, 1986—; vis. prof. Rutgers U. Coll. Pharmacy, 1998—; trustee Am. Bd. Med. Microbiology, Washington, 1991-97; mem. area com. on microbiology and subcom. antimicrobial susceptibility testing Nat. Com. Clin. Lab. Standards, Wayne, Pa., 1993—, vice chair area com. on microbiology, 1998—; dir. Microbiology Lab., Robert Wood Johnson U. Hosp., New Brunswick, 1983—, HIV-Antibody Counselling and Testing Svc., 1985-87, 91—; chief divsn. of allergy, immunology and infectious diseases Robert Wood Johnson Med. Sch., 2001—; lectr. in field. Mem. editl. bd. Jour. Clin. Microbiology, 1984-99, Am. Jour. Infection Control, 1987-2000, Diagnostic Microbiology and Infectious Disease, 1989—; sect. editor Clin. Infectious Diseases, Manual Clin. Microbiology, 8th edit.; contbr. chpts. to books, articles to profl. jours. Comdr. USPHS, 1971-73. Henry Rutgers Rsch. fellow, 1965-66. Fellow ACP, Infectious Diseases Soc. Am., Am. Acad. Microbiology; mem. Am. Fedn. Clin. Rsch., Am. Soc. Microbiology, Soc. Hosp. Epidemiologists Am., N.J. Infectious Disease Soc. (founding mem.), Alpha Omega Alpha. Avocations: tennis, golf. Office: Robert Wood Johnson Med Sch 1 Robert Wood Johnson Pl New Brunswick NJ 08901-1928

WEINSTEIN, MICHAEL ALAN, political science educator; b. Bklyn., Aug. 24, 1942; s. Aaron and Grace (Sosin) W.; m. Deena Schneiweiss, May 31, 1964. BA summa cum laude, NYU, 1964; MA in Polit. Sci., Case Western Res. U., 1965, PhD, 1967. Asst. prof. polit. sci. Case Western Res. U., summer 1967, Va. Poly. Inst., 1967-68; asst. prof. Purdue U., 1968-70, assoc. prof., 1970-72, prof., 1972—; Milward Simpson disting. prof. polit. sci. U. Wyo., 1979. Author: (with Deena Weinstein) Living Sociology, 1974, The Polarity of Mexican Thought, 1976, The Tragic Sense of Political Life, 1977, Meaning and Appreciation, 1978, The Structure of Human Life, 1979, The Wilderness and the City, 1982, Unity and Variety in the Philosophy of Samuel Alexander, 1984, Finite Perfection, 1985, Culture Critique: Fernand Dumont and New Quebec Sociology, 1985, (with Helmut Loiskandl and Deena Weinstein) Georg Simmel's Scopenhauer and Nietzsche, 1986; (with Deena Weinstein) Deconstruction as Cultural History/The Cultural History of Deconstruction, 1990, La Déconstruction un Jeu Symbolique, 1990, (with Deena Weinstein) Georg Simmel: Sociological Flâmeur/Bricoleur, 1991, Photographic Realism as a Moral Practice, 1992, (with Deena Weinstein) Postmodern(ized) Simmel, 1993, (with Arthur Kroker) Data Trash: The Theory of the Virtual Class, 1994, Culture/Flesh: Explorations of Postcivilized Modernity, 1995, Peter Vierecki Reconciliation and Beyond, 1997, East/West: Globalizing Civilization, 2000; artist in residence Columbia Coll., 2002; mem. editl. bd. Humanitas, Social Philosophy Rsch. Book Series. Recipient Best Paper prize Midwest Polit. Sci. Assn., 1969; Guggenheim fellow, 1974-75; Rockefeller Found. humanities fellow, 1976; fellow Center Humanistic Studies, Purdue U., 1981, Lily Endowment Tchg. grant, 2001. Mem. Phi Beta Kappa. Home: 800 Princess Dr West Lafayette IN 47906-2038 Office: Dept Polit Sci Purdue U West Lafayette IN 47907 *And which is worse, to be arbitrary or to be contradictory? I have attempted to be the most consistent rationalist of all by refusing to harmonize what is irreconcilable in the name of reason.*

WEINSTEIN, MICHAEL MAGEN, economics journalist, educator; b. Phila., Sept. 7, 1948; s. Matthew B. and Rosalie (Magen) W.; m. Frances Schwartz, Nov. 22, 1974; children: Zachary, Lev. BA with great distinction, Stanford U., 1970; student, U. Chgo., 1970-71; PhD, MIT, 1979. Mem. faculty Haverford (Pa.) Coll., 1975-89, chmn. dept., 1981-89; pres. M.B.W. Mgmt. Corp., Narberth, Pa., 1986—; pres., founder W.A.D. Fin. Counseling Inc., 1989—; mem. editorial bd. New York Times, 1989—. Cons. in field. Author: Recovery and Redistribution Under the NIRA, 1980; also articles. NSF fellow U. Chgo., 1970-71, MIT, 1971-74. Mem. Am. Econs. Assn., Econ. History Assn., Phi Beta Kappa. Office: NY Times 229 W 43rd St New York NY 10036-3959

WEINSTEIN, MILTON CHARLES, health policy educator; b. Brookline, Mass., July 14, 1949; s. William and Ethel (Rosenbloom) W.; m. Rhonda Kruger, June 14, 1970; children: Jeffrey William, Daniel Jay. AB, AM, Harvard U., 1970, MMP, 1972, PhD, 1973. Asst. prof. John F. Kennedy Sch. Govt., Harvard U., Cambridge, Mass., 1973-76, assoc. prof., 1976-80; prof. policy and decision scis. Harvard Sch. Pub. Health, Boston, 1980-86, Henry J. Kaiser prof. health policy and mgmt., 1986—; prof. medicine Harvard Med. Sch., 1992—; v.p. Innovus Rsch. Inc., Medford, Mass., 1998—. Adj. prof. cmty. and family medicine Dartmouth Med. Sch., Hanover, N.H., 1981-87; cons. U.S. Office Tech. Assessment, 1979-87, HHS, 1979—, VA, 1984-86, EPA, 1983—, Smith Kline and French, 1984-87, Ciba-Geigy, 1987-98, New Eng. Med. Ctr., 1986-87, Intermountain Health Care, 1987—, Bristol Myers-Squibb, 1989-92, E.I. Dupont de Nemours Co., 1989-91, Schering-Plough Corp., 1991-98, Hoechst Marion Roussel, 1992-98, Pharmacia and Upjohn, Inc., 1992-98, Berlex Corp., 1992-98, Fournier Rsch., 1998; mem. adult treatment panel Nat. Cholesterol Edn. Program, NIH; co-chair Panel on

Cost-Effectiveness in Health and Medicine, USPHS, 1993-96. Author: Clinical Decision Analysis, 1980, Hypertension: A Policy Perspective, 1976, Cost-Effectiveness in Health and Medicine, 1996; mem. editl. bd. Med. Decision Making, 1981—, Jour. Environ. Econs. and Mgmt., 1986-88, Jour. Clin. Oncology, 1996-99; assoc. editor Med. Decision Making, 1994-2001. NSF fellow, 1972. Mem. Inst. Ops. Rsch. Mgmt. Scis., Inst. Medicine of NAS (com. on priorities for new vaccine devel., com. to evaluate the NIH artificial heart program), Soc. Med. Decision Making (trustee 1980-82, pres. 1984-85), Internat. Health Econs. Assn., Soc. Risk Analysis, Internat. Soc. Tech. Assessment in Health Care, Internat. Soc. Pharmacoens. and Outcomes Rsch., Am. Med. Joggers Assn., U.S. Speedskating (bd. dirs. 1996-2000), Phi Beta Kappa. Office: Harvard U Sch Pub Health Ctr for Risk Analysis 718 Huntington Ave Fl 2 Boston MA 02115-5924

WEINSTEIN, NANCY LOU, interior designer; b. Covington, Ky., Apr. 8, 1946; m. Mel Weinstein, Sept. 19, 1964; 1 child, Jennifer Nicole. Pvt. practice interior design, Long Beach, Calif., 1966. Dir. Easter Seals Internat. Design House, 1985. Contbr. articles to mags., newspapers. Named Hon. Order of Ky. Cols., 1959. Mem. Interior Design Soc., Design Internat., Orange County (Calif.) Charter 100, Women in Business, Nat. Assn. of Women Bus. Owners, Long Beach C. of C. Avocation: travel.

WEINSTEIN, RANDY, engineering educator; BS, U. Va., 1993; PhD, MIT, 1998. Asst. prof. chem. engring. Villanova (Pa.) U., 1998—. Office: Villanova U 800 Lancaster Ave Villanova PA 19085

WEINSTEIN, RANDY FRANKLIN, school system administrator; b. Norwalk, Conn., Dec. 22, 1953; s. Sydney Lewis Weinstein and Jeane Elizabeth Kolburne; m. Rebecca Louise Weinstein, Aug. 12, 1988; 1 child Tyler Franklin. BA, Westfield State U., 1976. CEO Kolburne Sch., Inc., New Marlboro, Mass., 1972—; pres. N. Star Rare Books, Gt. Barrington, 1997—. Author: (book) Against the Tide: Commentaries on a Collection of African American, 1997 (award Am. Inst. Graphic Arts, 1997), The Unassuming Grant: Ulysees S. Grant, 2002. Mem.: Kiwanis. Jewish. Home and Office: 684 S Main St Great Barrington MA 01230 Office Fax: 413-644-9596. E-mail: nsrb@vgernet.net.

WEINSTEIN, ROBERT, hematologist, researcher; b. Brooklyn, NY, Aug. 10, 1949; s. Rachel Weinstein, George Weinstein; m. Brenda Leigh Laufs; children: Rebecca, Jessica. MD, New York University School of Medicine, New York, NY, 1971—75. Chief, Hematology and Transfusion Medicine St. Elizabeth's Medical Center of Boston, Boston, 1994—, Director, Non-Invasive Vascular Laboratory, 1987—96. President American Society for Apheresis, Tucson, 1999—2000; Chairman, Hemapheresis Committee American Association of Blood Banks, Bethesda, MD, 2001—; Member, Committee on Practice American Society for Hematology, Washington, 2000—; Member, Medical Advisory Committee American Red Cross Blood Services New England Region, Dedham, MA, 2000—; Member, Committee on Transfusion Medicine Massachusetts Medical Society, Waltham, MA, 1998. Contbr. Textbook (Morton-Grove Rasmussen Award, 2000). President Temple Beth Avodah, Newton Centre, MA, 200—02. Mem.: American Society of Hematology (Member, Committee on Practice 2000—04), American Association of Blood Banks (Chair, Hemapheresis Committee 2001—03), American Society for Apheresis (President 1999—2000). Jewish. Office: St. Elizabeth's Medical Center of Boston 736 Cambridge Street MMR 3 HEM Boston MA 02135 Office Fax: 617-789-3349. Business E-Mail: Robert_Weinstein_MD@cchcs.org.

WEINSTEIN, RONALD S. pathologist, educator; b. Schenectady, N.Y., Nov. 20, 1938; s. H. Edward and Shirley (Diamond) W.; m. Mary Dominica Corabi, July 12, 1964; children: Katherine Eiliesh, John Benjamin. BS, Union Coll., Schenectady, 1960; MD, Tufts U., 1965. Diplomate: Am. Bd. Pathology; 1972. Chemist Marine Biol. Lab., Woods Hole, Mass., 1960-62; intern Mass. Gen. Hosp., Boston, 1965-66, clin. and research fellow, 1965-70, resident in pathology, 1966-70; dir. Mixter Lab., 1966-70; vice chmn. pathology Aerospace Med. Research Labs., Dayton, Ohio, 1970-72; asso. prof. pathology Tufts U., 1972-75; Harriet Blair Borland prof., chmn. dept. pathology Rush Med. Coll. and Rush-Presbyn.-St. Luke's Med. Center, Chgo., 1975-90; prof., head dept. pathology U. Ariz. and U. Med. Ctr., Tucson, 1990—; dir. Ariz. Telemedicine Program, 1996—. Teaching fellow Harvard Med. Sch., 1966-70; dir. Central Pathology Lab., Nat. Bladder Cancer Group, 1983-89, mem. editorial bd. Pathology, 1991—, J. Urologic Pathology, 1992—. Mem. editorial bd. Ultrastructural Pathology, 1979—, Human Pathology, 1980—, assoc. editor, 1983-92, mem. editorial bd. Lab. Investigation, 1983—; assoc. editor Advances in Pathology, 1985-91, editor, 1991—; contbr.: articles profl. jours. Served as maj. USAF, 1970-72. Ford Found. fellow, 1959; Congressional intern, 1959; USPHS fellow, 1965-68 Mem.: AMA, Am. Telemed. Assn. (v.p. 2001—), Internat. Coun. Soc. Pathology (v.p. 1992—98, pres. 1998—), Internat. Soc. Urologic Pathology (pres.-elect 1992—94, pres. 1995—96), Chgo. Pathol. Soc. (pres. 1979—80), Assn. Pathology (chmn., sec. treas. 1989—90, v.p. 1998—), U.S. and Can. Acad. Pathology (pres. 1988—89), Internat. Acad. Pathology (councilor 1980—82, internat.councilor 1982—84), Am. Soc. Cell Biology. Office: U Ariz Dept Pathology 1501 N Campbell Ave Tucson AZ 85724-0001

WEINSTEIN, ROY, physics educator, researcher; b. N.Y.C., Apr. 21, 1927; s. Harry and Lillian (Ehrenberg) W.; m. Janet E. Spiller, Mar. 26, 1954 (dec. 1995); children: Lee Davis, Sara Lynn; m. Gail A. Birdsell, July 26, 1996. BS, MIT, 1951, PhD, 1954; ScD (hon.), Lycoming Coll., 1981. Rsch. asst. Mass. Inst. Tech., 1951-54, asst. prof., 1956-59, Brandeis U., Waltham, Mass., 1954-56; assoc. prof. Northeastern U., Boston, 1960-63, prof. physics, 1963-82, exec. officer, chmn. grad. div. of physics dept., 1967-69, chmn. physics dept., 1974-81; spokesman MAC Detector Stanford U., 1981-82; dean Coll. Natural Scis. and Math. U. Houston, 1982-88; prof. physics, 1982—; dir. Inst. Beam Particle Dynamics U. Houston, 1985-95; assoc. dir., spokesman Tex. Ctr. for Superconductivity, 1987-89. Vis. scholar and physicist Stanford (Calif.) U., 1966-67, 81-82; bd. dirs. Perception Tech., Inc., Winchester, Mass., Omniwave Inc., Gloucester, Mass., Wincom Inc., Woburn, Mass.; cons. Visidyne Inc., Burlington, Mass., Houston Area Rsch. Ctr., Stanford U., Hodotector Inc., Houston, Park Square Engring., Marietta, Ga., Harvard U., Cambridge, Mass., Cambridge Electron Accelerator, mem. adv. com., 1967-69; adv. com. and portfolio evaluation com. Houston Venture Ptnrs., 1990-99; chmn. bd. dirs. Xytron Corp., 1986-91; dir., mem. exec. com. Houston Area Rsch. Ctr., 1984-87; chmn. organizing com. Internat. Conf. on Meson Spectroscopy, 1974, chmn. program com., 1977, mem. organizing com., 1980; chmn. mgmt. group Tex. Accelerator Ctr., Woodlands, 1985-90; chmn. Tex. High Energy Physicists, 1989-91; keynote spkr. MIT Alumni series, 1988; permanent mem. exec. com. Large Vol. Detector (Underground Neutrino Telescope, Italy), 1988—; organizer session High Temperature Superconducting Magnets 3d and 4th World Congress on Superconductivity, Munich, 1993, Orlando, 1994. Author: Atomic Physics, 1964, Nuclear Physics, 1964, Interactions of Radiation and Matter, 1964; editor: Nuclear Reactor Theory, 1964, Nuclear Materials, 1964; editor procs.: 5th Internat. Conf. on Mesons, 1977; contbr. articles to profl. jours. Active Lexington (Mass.) Town Meeting, 1973-84; vice chmn. Lexington Coun. on Aging, 1977-83. With USNR, 1945-46. Recipient Founders award World Congress Superconductivity, 1988, Materials/Devices award Internat. Superconductivity Technology Ctr., Japan, and Materials Rsch. Soc., U.S., 1995, High Current award, 1997, Excellence award for great achievements in the field of bulk superconducting materials Internat. Program Com. Processing and Applications of Large Superconducting Rare Earth Grains Worshop, 1999, NSF Rsch. awards, 1961-96, Tex. Rsch. award, 1986-87, 90-2000, U.S. Dept. Energy award 1974, 77, 87-97, NASA award, 1990-98, ARO award, 1994—, Elec. Power Rsch. Inst. award, 1990-95, Welch Found. award, 1997—, Nat. Cancer Inst. award, 2000—; NSF fellow Bohr Inst., Copenhagen, 1959-60, Stanford U. 1969-70, Guggenheim fellow Harvard U., 1970-71. Fellow Am. Phys. Soc. (organizer session SSC and High Energy Physics 1984); mem. Am. Assn. Physics Tchrs., Masons, Sigma Xi, Phi Kappa Phi (chpt. pres. 1977-79, Nat. Triennial Disting. Scholar prize 1980-83), Pi Lambda Phi. Unitarian Universalist. Achievements include measurement of fine structure of positronium; first measurement of rho meson coupling to gamma rays, of phi meson decay to two muons; early observation of break down in SU3 symmetry; demonstration of electron-muon universality, discovery of non-applicability of Lorentz contraction to length measured by a single observer; disproof of splitting of A2 meson; independent discovery of upsilon meson (bottom quark); achievement of highest magnetic field for any permanent magnet, in YBa2Cu307, 10.1 Tesla; achievement of highest current density in textured superconductor, 0.3 megA/cm2. Home: 4368 Fiesta Ln Houston TX 77004-6603 Office: U Houston IBPD 632 SR1 Houston TX 77204-5005

WEINSTEIN, RUTH JOSEPH, lawyer; b. N.Y.C., Mar. 26, 1933; d. David Arthur and Toby (Landau) J.; m. Marvin Walter Weinstein, June 3, 1962; children: Rosalyn S., Steven M., Barbara E. AB magna cum laude, Radcliffe Coll., 1954; LLB, Harvard U., 1957. Bar: N.Y. 1957, D.C. 1966. Assoc. Hale Russell & Gray and predecessor firms, N.Y.C., 1957-66, ptnr., 1966-85, Winthrop Stimson Putnam & Roberts, N.Y.C., 1985-98, sr. counsel, 1999-2000, Pillsbury Winthrop, N.Y.C., 2000—. Chairperson Practising Law Inst. Forum, N.Y.C., 1978. Mem. sch. bd. Union Free Sch. Dist. 5, Rye Town, N.Y., 1976-79, pres., 1978-79; mem. The Friends of Crawford Park. Mem. ABA, Assn. of Bar of City of N.Y. (com. on Aeronautics Assn. 1987-90), Harvard-Radcliffe Club of Westchester. Avocations: boating, skiing. Home: 21 Meadowlark Rd Rye Brook NY 10573-1209 Office: Pillsbury Winthrop 1 Battery Park Plz New York NY 10004-1490

WEINSTEIN, SHARON SCHLEIN, corporate communications executive, educator; b. Newark, Apr. 15, 1942; d. Louis Charles and Ruth Margaret (Franzblau) Schlein; m. Elliott Henry Weinstein, May 7, 1978. BA, U. Pa., 1964; MA, New Sch. for Social Rsch., N.Y.C., 1985. Sr. editor Merrill Lynch, N.Y.C., 1972-74; pub. rels. officer Chase Manhattan Bank, 1974-79; mgr. corp. communication Sanford C. Berstein & Co., 1980-83; v.p. corp. affairs Nat. Westminster Bancorp, 1983-95; dir. corp. comms. Nat. Securities Cleaning Corp., 1995-98; asst. v.p. corp. comm. Guardian Life Ins. Co., 1998—. Adj. asst. prof. NYU, 1988—. Home: 161 W 15th St New York NY 10011-6720

WEINSTEIN, SIDNEY, retired university program director; b. N.Y.C., July 1, 1920; s. Jacob and Yetta W.; m. Celia Kahn, Mar. 6, 1943 (dec.); children: Risa, Jeri; m. Florence Landau, June 21, 1988. BA, Bklyn. Coll., 1951; MA, Columbia U., 1955; DPA, Indsl. Coll. Armed Forces, 1964. Contract adminstr. U.S. Corps Engrs., 1941-43; mgmt. analyst Dept. Army, N.Y.C., 1946-55; dir. data processing procurement GSA, 1956-68, dep. asst. commr. automated data mgmt. services, 1968-72, asst. commr. automated data and telecommunications, 1972-75; exec. dir. Assn. Computing Machinery, N.Y.C., 1975-85; assoc. prof., dir. affiliates program Ctr. Research Info. Systems, Leonard N. Stern. Sch. Bus. NYU, 1985-99, ret., 1999. Cons. to chmn. U.S. CSC Served with USAF, 1943-46. Recipient Exceptional service award U.S. Govt., 1975 Mem. ABA (arbitrator 1989—), Coun. Engring. and Sci. Soc. Execs. (dir.), N.Y. Soc. Assn. Execs., Assn. Indsl. Coll. Armed Forces, Assn. Fed. Execs. Inst., Assn. Computing Machinery, Soc. Info. Mgmt. Home: 360 E 72nd St New York NY 10021-4753 E-mail: s_weinstein@msn.com., s_weinstein@msn.com.

WEINSTEIN, SIDNEY TOM, information technology executive; BS in Mil. Engring., U.S. Mil. Acad., 1956; MS in Bus. Adminstrn., U. Rochester, 1970; PhD (hon.) , Def. Intelligence Coll. Commd. lt. U.S. Army, 1956, advanced through grades to comdr., 1981, dep. comdr. intelligence & security commd., 1980—81, comdr. intelligence ctr. & sch., 1981—84, dep. chief of staff intelligence, 1984—89, ret., 1989; sr. v.p. Electronic Warfare Assoc., Inc., Herndon, Va., 1989—. Office: Electronic Warfare Assoc Inc 13873 Park Center Road Herndon VA 20171*

WEINSTEIN, STANLEY, Buddhist studies educator; b. Bklyn., Nov. 13, 1929; s. Louis Arthur and Ruth (Appleson) W.; m. Lucie Ruth Krebs, Sept. 23, 1951; 1 son, David Eli. BA, Komazawa U., Tokyo, 1954-58; MA, U. Tokyo, 1960; PhD, Harvard U., 1966; MAH (hon.), Yale U., 1974. Lectr. Sch. Oriental and African Studies, London, 1962-68; assoc. prof. Buddhist studies Yale U., New Haven, 1968-74, prof., 1974—, chmn. council East Asian studies, 1982-85. Author: Buddhism under T'ang, 1987. Served with U.S. Army, 1952-54. Ford Found. fgn. area fellow, 1958-62; NEH sr. fellow, 1974-75 Mem. Am. Oriental Soc., Assn. Asian Studies Home: 270 Ridgewood Ave Hamden CT 06517-1426 Office: Yale U Dept Relig Studies PO Box 208287 New Haven CT 06520-8287

WEINSTEIN, STEPHEN BRANT, communications executive, researcher, writer; b. N.Y.C., Nov. 25, 1938; s. Max S. and Evelyn A. (Brandt) W.; m. Judith Louise Benham, June 10, 1961; children: Brant M., Anna M. SB, MIT, 1960; MS, U. Mich., 1962; PhD, U. Calif. at Berkeley, 1966. Mem. tech. staff Philips Rsch. Labs., Eindhoven, The Netherlands, 1967-68, Bell Labs., Holmdel, N.J., 1968-79; v.p. tech. strategy Am. Express Co., N.Y.C., 1979-84; exec. dir. subscriber systems rsch. Bellcore, Morristown, N.J., 1984-93; fellow, mgr. comm. tech. rsch. C&C Rsch. Lab., NEC USA, Inc., 1994—2001; ptnr. Comm. Theory & Tech. Cons., 2002—. Editor-in-chief Jour. Comms. and Networks, 1999—. Author: Getting the Picture: A Guide to CATV and the New Electronic Media, 1986; co-author: Data Communication Principles, 1992; contbr. articles to profl. jours.; patentee in field. Fellow IEEE (bd. dirs. 2002—, editor-in-chief Comms. mag. 1984-89, chmn. press 1979-82, Centennial medal 1984), IEEE Comms. Soc. (pres. 1996-97, v.p. tech. affairs 1994-95, dir. publs. 1990-93, editor-in-chief KICS Jour. Comm. and Networks 1999-00). Avocations: skiing, digital photography. Home and Office: 150 Woodland Ave Summit NJ 07901-2029 E-mail: weinstein5@home.com.

WEINSTEIN, STEVEN, lawyer; b. Phila., May 3, 1946; s. Leon and Elizabeth (Evantash) W.; m. Karin Elkis, Feb. 16, 1986. BA, Rutgers U., 1968, JD, 1975. Bar: N.J. 1975, Pa. 1975, U.S. Dist. Ct. 1979, U.S. Dist. Ct. (ea. dist.) Pa. 1975, U.S. Supreme Ct. 1979, U.S. Ct. Appeals (3d cir.) 1981, U.S. Ct. Claims 1986, U.S.D.C. (N.J.) (mediator). Assoc. Lewis Katz P.C., Cherry Hill, N.J., 1975-78; pvt. practice law Collingswood, 1978-84; ptnr. Blank, Rome, Comisky & McCauley, Cherry Hill, 1984—. Lawyer Camden (N.J.) County Counsel, 1982—84; v.p. N.J. County Counsels Assn., 1983. Trustee Camden County Coll., Blackwood, N.J., 1983, West Jersey Hosps. Found., Camden, 1984-96, chmn. 1989-91; trustee Rowan Coll., N.J., 1990-96, chmn. 1992-94, trustee devel. fund. bd., 1989-90; mem. N.J. Bus.-Higher Edn. Forum. Mem.: ABA, Haddonfield Bd. Edn., Camden County Bar Assn., Israel-Am. Affiliates (South Jersey chpt.), Ben Gurion U. of the Negev (chair), N.J. Higher Edn. Alliance (chair), N.J. Governing Bds. Assn. (sec. 1993—94, vice-chair 1996), Soc. Fellows, Am. Coun. Trustees & Alumni. Democrat. Jewish. Office: Blank Rome Comisky & McCauley Woodland Falls Corporate Park 210 Lake Dr E Ste 200 Cherry Hill NJ 08002-1163 E-mail: weinstein@blankrome.com.

WEINSTEIN, STUART LESLIE, orthopaedic surgeon; b. Chgo., Aug. 18, 1946; s. Sheldon and Carolyn June Weinstein; m. Lynn K. Weinstein, Aug. 16, 1970; 1 child, William Stuart. AB in Polit. Sci., U. Ill., 1968; MD, U. Iowa, 1972. Diplomate Am. Bd. Orthopedic Surgery. Intern in medicine U. Calif., San Francisco, 1972-73; resident in orthopedic surgery U. Iowa, Iowa City, 1973-76, asst. prof. orthopedic surgery, 1976-80, assoc. prof. orthopedic surgery, 1980-84, prof. orthopedic surgery, 1984-87, Ignacio V. Ponseti prof. orthopedic surgery, 1987—, Ignacio V. Ponseti chair orthopedic surgery, 2000—. Dir. Am. Bd. Orthopaedic Surgery, 1994—, pres., 2000-01. Editor (textbook): Turek's Orthopaedics, 1994, Lovell and Winter's Pediatric Orthopaedics, 2 vols., 2001, Pediatric Spine, 2 vols., 2001; assoc. editor: Jour. Bone and Joint Surgery, 1988—92, sec. bd. trustees: , 1999—2001, treas. bd. trustees: , 2001—02; editor: Bull. Pediatric Orthopedic Soc. Chgo., 1986—89; mem. editl. bd.: Jour. Pediatric Orthopaedics. Recipient Kappa Delta award Orthopaedic Rsch. Soc., 1998, Bristol-Myers Squibb/Zimmer award for disting. achievement in orthopaedic rsch., 1999. Fellow Am. Acad. Orthopaedic Surgeons (coun. on edn. 1997—, bone and joint decade chair 1998—); mem. Am. Orthopaedic Assn. (pres. 1997-98), Scoliosis Rsch. Soc. (bd. dirs. 1986-88, Hibbs award 1998), Pediatric Orthopaedic Soc. N.Am. (pres. 1992-93, Wood Lovell award 1991, Arthur Huene award 1994, Mercer Rang award 2000), Internat. Ctr. Orthopaedic Edn. (chmn. 1992—). Office: U Iowa Dept Orthopedic Surgery 01026 JPP Univ Hosp Iowa City IA 52242

WEINSTEIN, WILLIAM JOSEPH, lawyer; b. Detroit, Dec. 9, 1917; s. Joseph and Bessie (Abromovitch) W.; m. Evelyn Ross, Apr. 5, 1942 (dec.); children: Patricia, Michael; m. Rose Sokolsky, Oct. 25, 1972. LLB, Wayne State U., 1940. Bar: Mich. 1940, U.S. Dist. Ct. (ea. and so. dists.) Mich. 1940, U.S. Ct. Appeals (6th cir.) 1951, U.S. Ct. Appeals (9th cir.) 1972. Ptnr. Charfoos, Gussin & Weinstein, Southfield, Mich., 1951-54, Charfoos, Gussin, Weinstein & Kroll, Detroit, 1955-59, Gussin, Weinstein & Kroll, P.C., Detroit, 1965-73, Weinstein, Kroll & Gordon, P.C., Detroit, 1973-85; pvt. practice Southfield, 1985-87, Bloomfield Hills, Mich., 1987—. Mem. std. jury instrn. com. Mich. Supreme Ct. 1965-72. Contbr. articles to legal jours. Maj. gen. USMCR, 1941-75. Decorated Bronze Star with Combat V, Legion of Merit (2), Purple Heart (2). Recipient Disting. Alumnus award Wayne State U. Law Sch., 1968. Mem. Mich. Bar Assn. (chmn. negligence sect. 1962-63), Am. Coll. Trial Lawyers, Internat. Acad. Trial Lawyers, USN League (nat. v.p. 1971-72), Tam-o-Shanter Club (Orchard Lake, Mich.), St. Andrews Country Club (Boca Raton, Fla.). Home (Summer): 3922 Wabeek Lake Dr E Bloomfield Hills MI 48302-1261 Home: 7205 Gateside Dr Boca Raton FL 33496 E-mail: marinewein@aol.com.

WEINSTEIN, WILLIAM STEVEN, technical engineer; b. Newark, Aug. 28, 1947; s. Abraham Weinstein and Hilda (Bushman) Blonde; m. Ellen Faith Weinberger, Dec. 24, 1972; children: Lenard Scott, John Ryan. Engr. Precision Indsl. Design, Newark, 1967-68; enlisted USAF, 1968, tech. sgt., technician, 1968-82, resigned, 1982; engr. MPCS Video Industries, N.Y.C., 1982-83; equipment maintenance supr. CBS, 1983—. Mem. N.Y. Acad. Scis. Home: 255 Greenbriar Cir Tobyhanna PA 18466-3008

WEINSTEIN-BACAL, STUART ALLEN, lawyer, educator; b. Stuttgart, Germany, May 23, 1948; s. Marvin Stuart and Mae (Beal) W.; m. Holly Laurette Thompson, Aug. 7, 1982; children: Rachel Lee, Maximillian II, Sarah Nicole. BA, U. Va., 1970, MEd, 1973; JD cum laude, U. Miami, 1979. Bar: D.C. 1979, Va. 1981, V.I. 1985, P.R. 1988. Tchr., pvt. tutor various schs., Conn., Fla., Costa Rica, 1973-76; mem. prof. staff Merchant Marine and Fisheries Com. U.S. Ho. of Reps., Washington, 1978; assoc. Cameron, Hornbostel & Adelman, 1979-80, Burch, Kerns & Klimek, PC, Washington, 1980-81; staff atty. C.A.C.I., 1982-83; sr. assoc. Dudley, Dudley & Topper, St. Thomas, U.S. Virgin Islands, 1984-85; v.p. , gen. counsel Redondo Construction Corp., San Juan, PR, 1985-89; founder Indiano, Williams & Weinstein-Bacal, 1989-2000; owner Weinstein-Bacal & Assocs., P.S.C., Old San Juan, 2000—. Early neutral evaluator U.S. Dist. Ct. P.R. Contbr. articles to profl. jours. Capt. USAR, 1970-85. Mem. ABA, Am. Arbitration Assn. (pres., Caribbean region adv. coun. 1988—, arbitrator 1989—), Res. Officers Assn., Colegio de Abogados de P.R., U. Va. Alumni Assn., Nature Conservancy, Sovereign Order of the Oak (knight comdr.), Rotary Club of San Juan (bd. dirs. 1991-95), Middleburg Tennis Club, Bankers Club P.R., Phi Alpha Delta. Avocations: sailing, golf, tennis, riding, gourmet cooking, travel. Home: Villas Del Mar E # 7D Carolina PR 00979 also: Mallory Chase Farm 35919 Turkey Roost Rd Middleburg VA 20117-3401 Office: Gonzalez Padin Bldg-Penthouse 154 Rafael Cordero St Plz Armas Old San Juan PR 00901 E-mail: sawbacal@aol.com.

WEINSTOCK, ALAN ROBERT, internist; b. Stamford, Conn., Nov. 11, 1940; s. David and Lena Florence (Robinson) W.; m. Madeline Jane Oidick, June 10, 1967; children: Jeffrey, Debra, Jonathan. AB in Biology, Franklin and Marshall Coll., 1962; MD, Georgetown U., 1967. Diplomate Am. Bd. Internal Medicine, Am. Bd. Family Practice. Clin. practice Holzman, Wechler, Hurwitz, Washington, 1973-74, Altschuler & Weinstock, Silver Spring, Md., 1974-84; pvt. practice Alan R. Weinstock, MD, 1984—. Chmn. dept. family practice Holy Cross Hosp., Silver Spring, 1988-89. Maj. M.C., U.S. Army, 1969-71. Fellow ACP, Am. Acad. Family Physicians; mem. AMA, Am. Soc. Internal Medicine, Montgomery County Med. Soc., Jacobi Soc. Washington (pres. 1983-84), Med Chi Md. Avocations: golf, travel. Office: 10313 Georgia Ave Silver Spring MD 20902-5006 E-mail: aweinstock@msn.com.

WEINSTOCK, GARY ALAN, internist, allergist; b. Bronx, N.Y., Aug. 13, 1954; m. Bonnie Siber, Aug. 27, 1978; 2 children. BA, Hofstra U., 1975; MD, Union U., 1979. Diplomate Am. Bd. Internal Medicine, Am. Bd. Allergy and Immunology; lic. MD, N.Y. Resident in internal medicine Cornell Cooperating Hosps., North Shore U. Hosp., 1979-82; fellow in pulmonary diseases Health Scis. Ctr. SUNY at Stony Brook, 1982-83, fellow in allergy and clin. immunology, 1983-86; clin. assoc. Cornell (N.Y.) U. Med. Coll., 1980-82; asst. clin. instr. Dept. of Medicine Health Scis. Ctr., SUNY at Stony Brook, 1982-86; clin. instr. medicine Cornell (N.Y.) U. Med. Coll., 1992-96; clin. asst. prof. medicine NYU Med. Coll., 1996—; provisional attending Dept. of Medicine North Shore U. Hosp., 1986-88, asst. attending Dept. of Medicine, 1988-91, sr. asst. attending Dept. of Medicine, 1991—. Teaching ward attending, Med. Svc. at North Shore U. Hosp., 1986—, ann. lectr. to med. housestaff on allergic diseases, 1986—; med. advisor Support for Asthmatic Youth Founding Chpt. of Nat. Network, North Shore U. Hosp., 1989—; med. advisor for adolescent svcs.Asthma and Allergy Found. of Am., 1993—, nat. bd. dirs., 1994-01, bd. dirs. N.Y. State, 1994-99; lectr. in field. Contbr. articles to profl. jours. and newsletters. Recipient USPHS Individual Nat. Rsch. Svc. award, 1983-86; grantee for Support for Asthmatic Youth, Allen and Hansburys Respiratory Inst., 1991, 92, 93, 94, Fisons, For Preparation of Asthma Ednl. Materials, 1994, 95, Fisons, For Asthma Camp Edn. Programs, 1994. Fellow Am. Acad. Allergy and Immunology; mem. ACP, AMA, Med. Soc. of State of N.Y., Am. Thoracic Soc., Am. Acad. Allergy and Immunology (allied health sect. com. 1993-00, travel grant recipient 1985), Nassau County Med. Soc., L.I. Allergy Soc., N.Y. State Allergy Soc. Office: 310 E Shore Rd Ste 308 Great Neck NY 11023-2432

WEINSTOCK, GEORGE DAVID, financial services company executive; b. Vienna, Austria, Jan. 31, 1937; came to U.S., 1940; s. Paul and Ernestine Esther (Stark) W.; m. Lorna Smith, July 17, 1965; children: Pamela Ellen, Andrea Joan. AB, Columbia U., 1958, BSEE, 1959, MS, 1962; cert., Coll. for Fin. Planning, Denver, 1985. cert. fin. planner. Sr. engr. ITT, Nutley, N.J., 1959-61; sr. mem. tech. staff RCA, N.Y.C., 1961-65; project dir. Computer Scis. Co., Paramus, N.J., 1965-69; v.p., dir., sec. Ultimacc Systems, Inc., Maywood, 1969-78; v.p. Satnick Devel. Group, Hoboken, 1978-84; sr. v.p. Knitwaves, Inc., Moonachie, 1984-85; chmn. bd. Bancroft Group, Inc., Paramus, 1985-88; pres. Atrium Adv. Group, Inc., 1990—. Mem. faculty Fairleigh Dickinson U., Baruch Coll., Coll. Fin. Planning. Author: System 360/DOS Operation, 1971, Multi-Taxation of Retirement Plans, 1991, Retirement Planning and Employee Benefits, 1992, Solving the Pre-59 1/2 Distribution Ten Percent Penalty Tax, 1992. Com. mem. United Jewish Cmty. Bergen County, 1988; pres. N.J. Estate Planning Coun., 1993-95, trustee, 1995—. Mem. IEEE, Inst. for CFPs, Nat. Assn. Accts. Jewish. Home: 216 Barnstable Dr Wyckoff NJ 07481-2146 Office: Atrium Adv Group Inc PO Box 15 East 80 Rte 4 Paramus NJ 07653-0015

WEINSTOCK, HAROLD, lawyer; b. Stamford, Conn., Nov. 30, 1925; s. Elias and Sarah (Singer) W.; m. Barbara Lans, Aug. 27, 1950; children—Nathaniel, Michael, Philip. BS magna cum laude, N.Y. U., 1947; JD, Harvard, 1950. Bar: Conn. bar 1950, Ill. bar 1950, Calif. bar 1958. Atty. SEC, Washington, 1950-52, IRS, 1952-56; tax atty. Hunt Foods & Industries, Inc., Los Angeles, 1956-58; pvt. practice Beverly Hills, Calif., 1958-71, Los Angeles, 1971—; mem. Weinstock, Manion, Reisman, Shore & Neumann (and predecessor firms), 1958—. Lectr. extension div., estate planning courses U. Calif. at Los Angeles, 1959— ; estate planning and taxation courses Calif. Continuing Edn. of the Bar, 1960— Author: Planning An Estate, 4th edit., 1995; contbr. articles to profl. publs. Nat. trustee Union Am. Hebrew Congregations, 1976-79; trustee Jewish Cmty. Found., L.A., 1993-99; adv. bd. Estate Planning Inst. UCLA Law Sch., 1979-92, NYU Inst. on Fed. Taxation, 1986-95. Mem. ABA, Calif. Bar Assn., Beverly Hills Bar Assn. (chmn. probate and trusts com. 1967-68), Los Angeles Bar Assn., Beverly Hills Estate Planning Council (pres. 1968-69), Estate Counselors Forum of Los Angeles (pres. 1963-64) Jewish (pres. temple 1974-76). Office: Weinstock Manion 1875 Century Park E Fl 15 Los Angeles CA 90067-2501

WEINSTOCK, JUDITH, obstetrician/gynecologist; b. Mt. Vernon, N.Y., Mar. 30, 1952; MD, Baylor U., 1982. Diplomate Am. Bd. Ob-Gyn. Intern L.I. Coll. Hosp., Bklyn., 1982-83, resident in ob-gyn., 1983-86, attending physician, 1986—. Mem. Assn. Womens Surgeons, Bklyn. Gynecol. Soc., N.Y. Soc. Ob-gyn., N.Y. Med. Soc. Office: Bklyn Womens Health Care 9 Pierrepont St Brooklyn NY 11201-3302 also: 421 78th St Brooklyn NY 11209-3403

WEINSTOCK, LEONARD, lawyer; b. Bklyn., Aug. 18, 1935; s. Samuel Morris and Evelyn (Reiser) W.; m. Rita Lee Itkowitz, May 25, 1963; children: Gregg Douglas, Valerie Lisa, Tara Diane. BS, Bklyn. Coll., 1956; JD, St. John's U., Bklyn., 1959. Bar: N.Y. 1961, U.S. Supreme Ct. 1964, U.S. Ct. Appeals (2d cir.) 1963, U.S. Dist. Ct. (ea. and so. dists.) N.Y. 1963, U.S. Tax Ct. 1963. Assoc. Bernard Helfenstein law practice, Bklyn., 1962-63; supr. All

State Ins. Co., 1963-64; atty. Hertz Corp., N.Y.C., 1964-65; ptnr. Nicholas & Weinstock, Flushing, N.Y., 1965-68; v.p., ptnr. Garbarini & Scher, P.C., N.Y.C., 1968—. Lectr. Practicing Law Inst., N.Y.C., 1975—; arbitrator Nassau County Dist. Ct., Mineola, N.Y., 1979—. U.S. Dist. Ct. (ea. dist.) N.Y. 1986—; mem. Med. Malpractice Mediation Panel, Mineola, 1978—. Legal counsel Massapequa Soccer Club, N.Y., 1981—; county committeeman Dem. Party, Massapequa Park, N.Y., 1979—. With U.S. Army, 1959-62. Mem. ABA, N.Y. State Bar Assn., Nassau County Bar Assn. (mem. med. jurisprudence ins. com. 1978), N.Y. Trial Lawyers Assn. Avocations: stamp collecting, softball, racquetball. Home: 38 Barstow Rd Great Neck NY 11021-2218 Office: Garbarini and Scher PC 432 Park Ave S New York NY 10016-8013

WEINSTOCK, MARTIN ARTHUR, dermatologist, epidemiologist, educator; b. N.Y.C., Oct. 31, 1956; s. Irvin and Mae Weinstock; m. Gail Gilkey, June, 1981; children: Hannah, Clara. BA in Math. summa cum laude, Williams Coll., 1977; MPhil, Columbia U., 1981, PhD, 1982, MD, 1983. Diplomate Am. Bd. Dermatology; lic. Mass., R.I. Resident in internal medicine U. Pitts. Hosps., 1983-84; resident in dermatology Harvard U. Hosps., Boston, 1984-87; rsch. fellow in clin. epidemiology Harvard Med. Sch., 1987-88; chief of dermatology, staff physician Dept. Vets. Affairs Med. Ctr., Providence, 1988—. Staff physician Mass. Gen. Hosp. Chelsea Health Ctr., Boston, 1985-86, South Boston Community Health Ctr., 1986-88, Children's Hosp., Boston, 1987-88; dir. R.I. pigmented lesion unit, photomedicine, staff physician Roger Williams Med. Ctr., Providence, 1988-97, R.I. Hosp., 1997—; asst. prof. Brown U., Providence, 1988-94, assoc. prof., 1994-98, prof., 1998—. Mem. editl. bd. Jour. Am. Acad. Dermatology, 1993—, Jour. Cutaneous Medicine and Surgery, others; contbr. articles to profl. jours.; reviewer for grants; reviewer for sci. jours. Chair skin cancer adv. group Am. Cancer Soc. Grantee NIH, VA. Mem. APHA, Internat. DermatoEpidemiology Assn. (founder, pres. 1996-98), Nat. Assn. VA Dermatologists (v.p. 1991-92, pres. 1992-93, nominating com. 1993-97), Am. Acad. Dermatology, Soc. Epidemiologic Rsch., Soc. Investigative Dermatology (com. on sci. programs, abstract reviewer, 1993—), New Eng. Dermatol. Soc., R.I. Dermatol. Soc., R.I. Med. Soc., Phi Beta Kappa, Sigma Xi. Home: 22 Hilltop Ave Barrington RI 02806-3516 Office: VA Med Ctr 111D 830 Chalkstone Ave Providence RI 02908-4734

WEINSTOCK, ROBERT, physics educator; b. Phila., Feb. 2, 1919; s. Morris and Lillian (Hirsch) W.; m. Elizabeth Winch Brownell, Apr. 22, 1950; children: Frank Morse, Robert B. Weinstock-Collins. AB, U. Pa., 1940; PhD, Stanford U., 1943. Instr. physics Stanford U., Calif., 1943-44, instr. math., 1946-50, acting asst. prof. math., 1950-54; research assoc. in radar countermeasures Radio Rsch. Lab. Harvard U., Cambridge, Mass., 1944-45; asst. prof. U. Notre Dame, Ind., 1954-58, assoc. prof. math., 1958-59; vis. assoc. prof. math. Oberlin Coll., Ohio, 1959-60, assoc. prof., 1960-66, prof. physics, 1966-83, emeritus prof., 1983—. Author: Calculus of Variations, 1952; contbr. numerous tech. articles to profl. jours. Fellow AAAS, Ohio Acad. Sci.; mem. ACLU, Am. Assn. Physics Tchrs., Am. Phys. Soc., History of Sci. Soc., British Soc. for the History of Sci., Sigma Xi. Avocations: concert going, reading, walking, travel, letter writing. Home: 37 Kendal Dr Oberlin OH 44074-1902 E-mail: zweinsto@oberlin.net.

WEINSTOCK, WALTER WOLFE, systems engineer; b. Phila., Aug. 18, 1925; s. Abraham and Jeanne (Feldman) W.; m. Doris Alpert, Sept. 21, 1946; children— Steven Eric, Bruce Alan. BSE.E., U.Pa., 1946, MSE.E., 1954, PhD, 1964. Design engr. Philco, 1946-49; with RCA Corp., 1949-87; prin. scientist RCA Corp. (Missile and Surface Radar div.), Moorestown, N.J., 1979-87; cons., 1987—. Mem. planning and steering adv. group Surface Ship Security Panel, Dept. Navy, 1979-82 Contbg. author: Modern Radar, 1965, Practical Phased Array Antenna Systems, 1991; contbr. articles to profl. jours. Recipient David Sarnoff award for Outstanding Achievement in Enrging. RCA, 1972 Fellow IEEE; mem. Tau Beta Pi, Eta Kappa Nu, Sigma Tau, Pi Mu Epsilon. Patentee in field. Home: 6 Beryl Rd Cheltenham PA 19012-1206 E-mail: walter.w.weinstock@lmco.com., walt1925@earthlink.net.

WEINTRAUB, ABNER EDWARD, information services executive; b. Miami, Fla., Aug. 30, 1954; s. William Albert Weintraub and Miriam (Mayers) Lemberg; m. Kimbal Reisig, Aug. 31, 1979; 1 child, Sarah Lee. BS, U. N.C., 1983. Prin. rschr. DynaSearch Group, Orlando, Fla., 1983-86, dir. rsch., 1986-94; mgr. consumer markets rsch. Sprint/United Telephone of Fla., Altamonte Springs, 1995—. Originator databases, 1985-86; patentee in field. Mem. Soc. for Investigation of Unexplained (assoc. investigator 1982—). Democrat. Avocations: amateur physics, cryptozoology, composing, music. Office: 1Rate Services LLC 6220 S Orange Blossom Trl Ste 194 Orlando FL 32809

WEINTRAUB, ARTHUR E. health service association executive; b. N.Y.C., July 18, 1935; s. Jacob and Sarah (Jaffe) W.; m. Carole, Apr. 14, 1962; children: Jill, David. BA, Hunter Coll., 1956; M in Planning, NYU, 1965. Project planner U.S. Army Corps Engrs., N.Y.C., 1956-64; chief long range planning Tri-State Regional Planning Commn., 1964-67; sr. v.p. Mid Hudson Pattern, Poughkeepsie, N.Y., 1967-78; exec. dir. Hudson Valley Health Sys. Agy., Tuxedo, 1978-82; pres. No. Met. Hosp. Assn., Newburgh, 1982—. Adj. faculty SUNY, New Paltz, 1982-91, New Sch. U., N.Y.C., 1992—; sr. lectr. N.Y. Med. Coll., Valhalla, 1992—. Contbr. articles to profl. jours. Trustee St. Luke's Hosp., Newburgh, 1972-78; pres. Bd. Edn., Newburgh, 1974-82; mem. health law adv. bd. Pace U. Law Sch., White Plains, N.Y., 1995—, Ch. Conf. Metro Hosp. Assns., 1997. NEH fellow Princeton U., 1977; recipient Disting. Cmty. Svc. award Orange County C. of C., 1970, Am. Red. Cross, 1996, Family Health Ctr., 1997, Arthritis Found., 2001. Office: No Met Hosp Assn 400 Stony Brook Ct Newburgh NY 12550-6522 E-mail: awein@normet.org.

WEINTRAUB, BERNARD STEPHEN, chest physician; b. L.A., Oct. 15, 1951; s. Harry and Rita Selma Weintraub; m. Marcia Kuehn, Nov. 6, 1988. BS, UCLA, 1972; MD, U. Calif., San Francisco, 1976. Diplomate Am. Bd. Chest Physicians. Intern Long Beach VA Hosp., 1976-77; resident U. Oreg., Portland, 1977-79; pulmonary fellow Cedars-Sinai Med. Ctr., L.A., 1980-82; emergency medicine physician, 1982-84; pvt. practice in pulmonary medicine and critical care Santa Monica, Calif., 1985—. Founding mem. Cogent Healthcare, Laguna Hills, Calif. Mem. Am. Coll. Chest Physicians, Am. Thoracic Soc., Calif. Med. Assn., L.A. County Med. Assn. Avocations: skiing, percussion music. Office: #335 2021 Santa Monica Blvd Ste 335 Santa Monica CA 90404-2201

WEINTRAUB, E(LIOT) ROY, economics educator; b. Bklyn., Mar. 22, 1943; s. Sidney and Sheila E. (Tarlow) Weintraub; m. Nell Maxine Soloway, Nov. 25, 1989; children from previous marriage: Matthew, Garth. AB, Swarthmore Coll., 1964; MS, U. Pa., 1967, PhD, 1969. Asst. profl. Rutgers U., New Brunswick, NJ, 1968—70; assoc. prof. Duke U., Durham, NC, 1970—75, prof. econs., 1975—, chmn. econs. dept., 1982—86, dean arts and scis., 1993—95. Author: Conflict and Cooperation, 1974, Microfoundations, 1979, Mathematics for Economists, 1983, General Equilibrium Analysis, 1985, Stabilizing Dynamics, 1991, Home Economics Became a Mathematical Science, 2002, The Future and the History of Economics, 2002; cons. editor Cambridge U. Press, 1980—90, Duke U. Press, 1996—. Advisor Kudzu Alliance, Durham, 1979—82; trustee Carolina Friends Sch., 1975—78. Mem.: History of Sci. Soc., History of Econs. Soc., Am. Econ. Assn. Home: 6905 Falconbridge Rd Chapel Hill NC 27517-7881 Office: Duke U Dept Econs Durham NC 27708

WEINTRAUB, JACOB MICHAEL, pediatrician; b. Detroit, Sept. 22, 1948; s. Morris and Betty (Hornick) W.; m. Johnell Cuddeback, Sept. 19, 1976; 1 child, Elizabeth J. AB, U. Chgo., 1970; MD, U. Mich., 1974. Diplomate Am. Bd. Pediats. Resident in pediat. Emory U. Affiliated Hosp., Atlanta, 1974-77; asst. pediat. program dir. Mich. State U./Kalamazoo Ctr. for Med. Studies, Kalamazoo, 1982-87; dir. pediat. Pheasant Ridge Ctr. Children's Psychiat. Hosp., 1987-97; clin. asst. prof. Mich. State U., Ctr. for Med. Studies, 1998—. Interim hosp. dir. Pheasant Ridge Ctr., Kalamazoo, 1990-91; med. cons. Kalamazoo Guidance Clinic, 1995—; pediat. cons. Disability Determination Svcs., 1994—. Bd. dirs. Temple B'nai Israel, Kalamazoo, 1984-87. Fellow Am. Acad. Pediats. Office: 2615 Stadium Dr Kalamazoo MI 49008-1654

WEINTRAUB, JOSEPH BARTON, publishing executive; b. Phila., Dec. 2, 1945; s. George and Edith (Lubner) W.; m. Denise Waters, June 14, 1974. BA, U. Pitts., 1966; MA, U. Chgo., 1967, PhD, 1973. Assoc. faculty U. Ind., Gary, Ind., 1970-74; mktg. specialist journalism div. U. Chgo. Press, 1974-75, sr. copywriter journalism div., 1975-78; periodical specialist ABA, Chgo., 1978-80, mktg. mgr., 1980-92, dir. publ. planning, 1992-97, dir. book publ., 1997-99; mgr. dir. mktg. U. Chgo. Press, 1999—. Mktg. cons. Teachers Coll. Record, N.Y.C., 1977-79, Repertoire Internat. de la Litterature de l'Art, N.Y.C., 1977-79, Am. Lung Assn., 1980-82. Writer You, 2000; contbr. essays, translations, plays, poems, short fiction to lit. revs. and small press anthologies. Recipient award Ill. Art Coun., Barrington Art Coun. Mem. Phi Beta Kappa. Avocations: writing, language study. Office: U Chgo Press 1427 E 60th Street Chicago IL 60637-5418

WEINTRAUB, RUSSELL JAY, lawyer, educator; b. N.Y.C., Dec. 20, 1929; s. Harry and Alice (Lieberman) W.; m. Zelda Kresshover, Sept. 6, 1953; children— Sharon Hope, Harry David, Steven Ross. BA, NYU, 1950; JD, Harvard U., 1953. Bar: N.Y. 1955, Iowa 1961, Tex. 1980. Tchg. fellow Harvard U. Law Sch., 1955-57; asst. prof. law U. Iowa, 1957-61, prof., 1961-65, U. Tex., 1965—, Marrs McLean prof. law, 1970-80, Bryant Smith chmn., 1980-82, John B. Connally chmn., 1982-98, Powell chmn., 1998—. Vis. prof. law U. Mich., 1965, UCLA, 1967, U. Calif., Berkeley, 1973-74, Bklyn. Law Sch., 1990, 95, Inst. Internat. Comparative Law, Paris, 1975, Florence, Italy, 1997, Barcelona, 1999, 2002, London, 2000, U. Houston, 1979-80, Inst. Internat. and Comparative Law, Oxford, Eng., 1982-83, 86-87, 92, Dublin, Ireland, 1991, La. State U., Aix-en-Provence, France, 1993, Tulane U., Spetses, Greece, 1998, Australian Nat. U., 2001; Ronald Graveson Meml. lectr. King's Coll., London, 2000; lectr. Hague Acad. Internat. Law, 1984; cons. U.S. Dept. State, 1995—; cons. in field. Author: International Litigation and Arbitration, 1994, 3d revised edit., 2001, ann. supplement; (with Eugene Scoles) Cases and Materials on the Conflict of Laws, 1967, 2d rev. edit., 1972, supplement, 1978, Commentary on the Conflict of Laws, 1971, 4th rev. edit., 2000; (with Hamilton and Rau) Cases and Materials on Contracts, 1984, 2d rev. edit., 1992; (with Hay and Borchers) Cases and Materials on the Conflict of Laws, 11th rev. edit., 2000, annual supplement; contbr. articles to profl. jours. Trustee U. Iowa Sch. Religion, 1960-65. With U.S. Army, 1953-55. Recipient Disting. Prof. award U. Tex. Sch. Law, 1977, Teaching Excellence award, 1979, cert. of meritorious service Am. Bar Assn., 1977, cert. of meritorious service Tex. Bar Assn., 1978, Best Tchr. award U. Houston, 1980, Carl Fulda award scholarship in internat. law, 1993. Mem. Am. Law Inst., Am. Bar Found. (life), Tex. Bar Found., Scribes. Jewish. Home: 7204 Sungate Dr Austin TX 78731-2141 Office: U Tex Sch Law 727 E Dean Keeton Austin TX 78705-3224 E-mail: rweintraub@mail.law.utexas.edu. *The only true happiness lies in useful work done to the best of your ability.*

WEINTRAUB, SAM, reading educator; b. St. Louis, Apr. 24, 1927; s. Julius and Jeannette (Schwartz) W.; 1 child, Robert. BA, Ohio State U., 1948, BS, 1950, MEd, 1954; EdD, U. Ill., 1960. Tchr. Wyandotte Pub. Schs., Mich., 1950-53, Campus Sch. Wis. STate Coll., La Crosse, 1953-54; asst. prof. Case Western Res. U., Cleve., 1960-61, U. Chgo., 1964-68; assoc. prof. Ind. U., Bloomington, 1968-74; prof. SUNY-Buffalo, Amherst, 1974-95, prof. emeritus, 1995—. Vs. prof. Tex. Woman's U., Denton, 1980-81; cons. in field. Author, editor: Ann. Summary of Investigations Relating to Reading, 1968-97; co-editor: Improving Reading Research, 1976; co-editor jour. Reading Rsch. Quar., 1969-79. Named to Reading Hall of Fame. Fellow Nat. Conf. Rsch. in English (pres. 1978-79); mem. Internat. Reading Assn. (Spl. Svc. award 1987, Wm. S. Gray citation of merit 1997), Nat. Coun. Tchrs. English, Am. Ednl. Rsch. Assn., Niagara Frontier Reading Coun. (v.p. 1990-91, Spl. Svc. award 1990). Avocations: reading, traveling.

WEINTRAUB, SIDNEY, economist, educator; b. N.Y.C., May 18, 1922; s. Reuben and Anna Weintraub; m. Gladys Katz, Aug. 11, 1946; children: Jeffrey, Marcia Weintraub Plunkett, Deborah Weintraub Chilewich. BBA, CCNY, 1943; B.J., MA in Journalism, U. Mo., 1948; MA in Econs., Yale U., 1958; PhD in Econs, Am. U., 1966. Commd. fgn. service officer Dept. State, 1949, dep. asst. sec. of state for internat. fin. and devel., 1969-74; asst. adminstr. for interagy. devel. coordination AID, 1974-75, exec. dir. interagy devel. coordination com., 1974-75; ret., 1975; sr. fellow Brookings Instn., Washington, 1978-79; Dean Rusk prof. Lyndon B. Johnson Sch. Public Affairs, U. Tex., Austin, 1976-96; prof. emeritus, 1996; also co-dir. Program for U.S.-Mex. Policy Studies Lyndon B. Johnson Sch. Public Affairs, U. Tex.; William E. Simon chair in polit. economy Ctr. Strategic and Internat. Studies, 1993—. Disting. vis. scholar Ctr. for Strategic and Internat. Studies, Washington, 1990. Author: Free Trade with Mexico, 1984, A Marriage of Convenience: Relations Between Mexico and The United States, 1990, NAFTA: What Comes Next, 1994, NAFTA at Three: A Progress Report, 1997, Financial Decision-Making in Mexico: To Bet a Nation, 2000; contbr. articles to profl. jours. Served with U.S. Army, 1943-46. Recipient Disting. Career Service award AID, 1975 Mem.: Am. Econ. Assn., Am. Fgn. Service Assn., Coun. on Fgn. Rels., Cosmos (Washington). Office: Ctr Strategic and Internat Studies 1800 K St NW Washington DC 20006-2202 *Once having been thrust into the Second World War, my main intellectual interest has been in foreign affairs. I had concluded, as President Kennedy did later, that domestic issues can hurt but misplaced foreign policy can kill. My drive has been to understand what motivates nations, what stimulates people within different nations, what is the U.S. national interest, and to become as expert as my talents would allow about such crucial issues as domestic security, international economic interaction, social mobility, and human development generally. This remains my ambition.*

WEINTRAUB, STANLEY, arts and humanities educator, writer; b. Phila., Apr. 17, 1929; s. Ben and Ray (Segal) W.; m. Rodelle Horwitz, June 6, 1954; children: Mark, David, Erica. BS, West Chester (Pa.) State Coll., 1949; MA, Temple U., 1951; PhD, Pa. State U., 1956. Instr. Pa. State U., University Park, 1953-59, asst. prof., 1959-62, asso. prof., 1962-65, prof. English, 1965-70, research prof., 1970-86, Evan Pugh prof. Arts and Humanities, 1986-99, Evan Pugh prof. Emeritus, 2000—; dir. Inst. for Arts and Humanistic Studies, 1970-90. Vis. prof. U. Calif. at Los Angeles, 1963, U. Hawaii, 1973, U. Malaya, 1977, Nat. U. Singapore, 1982 Author: Private Shaw and Public Shaw, 1963, The War in the Wards, 1964, Reggie, 1965, The Art of William Golding, 1965, Beardsley, 1967, The Last Great Cause, The Intellectuals and the Spanish Civil War, 1968, Evolution of a Revolt: Early Postwar Writings of T.E. Lawrence, 1968, The Literary Criticism of Oscar Wilde, 1968, Journey to Heartbreak, 1971, Whistler: A Biography, 1974, Lawrence of Arabia: the Literary Impulse, 1975, Four Rossettis, A Victorian Biography, 1977, Aubrey Beardsley: Imp of the Perverse, 1976, The London Yankees: Portraits of American Writers and Artists in England, 1894-1914, 1979, The Unexpected Shaw. Biographical Approaches to G.B. Shaw and His Work, 1982, A Stillness Heard Round the World: The End of the Great War, 1985, Victoria. An Intimate Biography, 1987, Long Day's Journey into War: December 7, 1941, 1991, Bernard Shaw: A Guide to Research, 1992, Disraeli: A Biography, 1993, The Last Great Victory-The End of World War II, July/August 1945, 1995, Shaw's People. Victoria to Churchill, 1996, Uncrowned King: The Life of Prince Albert, 1997, MacArthur's War: Korea and the Undoing of an American Hero, 2000, The Importance of Being Edward, King in Waiting, 1841-1901, 2000, Silent Night. The Remarkable 1914 Christmas Truce of 1914, 2001; editor: An Unfinished Novel by Bernard Shaw, 1958, C.P. Snow: A Spectrum, 1963, The Yellow Book: Quintessence of the Nineties, 1964, The Savoy: Nineties Experiment, 1966, The Court Theatre, 1966, Biography and Truth, 1967, Evolution of a Revolt: Early Postwar Writings of T.E. Lawrence, 1968, The Literary Criticism of Oscar Wilde, 1968, Shaw: An Autobiography 1856-1898, 1969, Shaw: An Autobiography, The Playwright Years, 1898-1950, 1970, Bernard Shaw's Nondramatic Literary Criticism, 1972, Directions in Literary Criticism, 1973, Saint Joan Fifty Years After: 1923/24-1973/74, 1973, The Portable Bernard Shaw, 1977, (with Anne Wright) Heartbreak House. A Facsimile of the Revised Typescript, 1979, (with Richard Aldington) The Portable Oscar Wilde, 1981, Modern British Dramatists, 1900-1945, 1982, The Playwright and the Pirate. Bernard Shaw and Frank Harris: A Correspondence, 1982, British Dramatists Since World War II, 1983, Bernard Shaw, the Diaries, 1885-1897, 1986, Bernard Shaw on the London Art Scene, 1885-1950, 1989, (with Rodelle Weintraub) Dear Young Friend. The Letters of American Presidents to Children, 2000, also editor Comparative Literature Studies, 1987-92, Shaw, The Ann. of Bernard Shaw Studies, 1956-89. Pres. Jewish Community Council of Bellefonte (Pa.) State Coll., 1966-67. Served to 1st lt. AUS, 1951-53, Korea. Decorated Bronze Star medal.; Guggenheim fellow, 1968-69; recipient Disting. Humanist award Pa. Humanities Council, 1985 Mem. The Authors' Guild, PEN. Home: 840 Outer Dr State College PA 16801-8233 Office: Pa State U 202 Ihlseng Bldg University Park PA 16802-1705 E-mail: sqw4@psu.edu. *I subscribe to Bernard Shaw's declaration in the Preface to Man and Superman that "This is the true joy in life, the being used for a purpose recognized by yourself as mighty one; the being thoroughly worn out before you are thrown on the scrap heap; the being a force of Nature instead of a feverish selfish little clod of ailments and grievances complaining that the world will not devote itself to making you happy.".*

WEINTRAUB, WILLIAM SETH, epidemiologist; b. N.Y.C., Dec. 30, 1948; s. Herbert and Claire (Stahl) W.; m. Veronica Halward, Mar. 30, 1975; children: Stephanie, Adam, Ellis. BS, Tufts U., 1971; MD, Johns Hopkins U., 1975. Intern Boston U., 1975-76, resident, 1976-77; fellow in cardiology Mt. Sinai Hosp., N.Y.C., 1977-79; rsch. fellow U. Pa., Phila., 1979-80, asst. prof., 1980-86; assoc. prof. Emory U., Atlanta, 1986-94, prof., 1994—. Home: 105 Breakwater Cir NE Atlanta GA 30328-1804 Office: Emory U Divsn Cardiology Wmb 319 1639 Pierce Dr Atlanta GA 30322-0001

WEINTZ, JACOB FREDERICK, JR. retired investment banker; b. N.Y.C., June 27, 1926; s. Jacob Frederick and Grace (Cortelyou) W.; m. Elisabeth Hamlin Brewer, Nov. 26, 1955; children: Elizabeth Hunt Cerf, Polly Warren, Eric Cortelyou, Karl Frederick. Student, Norwich U., 1943-44; BA, Stanford U., 1948; MBA, Harvard U., 1951. Salesman Vick Chem. Co., N.Y.C., 1948-49; assoc. buying dept. Goldman, Sachs & Co., 1951-54, assoc. new bus. dept., 1954-65, ptnr., 1965-84; ltd. ptnr. Goldman, Sachs Group L.P., 1984—. Pres., chmn. bd. dirs. Stonebridge Condominium Assn., Snowmass Village, Colo., 1978-85; trustee Pace U., 1981-97, Norwich U., Stanford U., 1985-95, Sierra Club Found., 1984-90, 92—, treas.; trustee Harbor Lights Found., N.Y.C.; mem. corp. Greenwich Hosp.; vice chmn. bd. dirs. Guiding Eyes for Blind, 1984-93; bd. dir. The Forum for World Affairs, Stanford, Conn., 1988-94; mem. Ctr. Internat. Security and Arms Control Stanford U.; pres. Harvard U. Bus. Sch. Alumni Assn., 1988-90; del. Coun. Governing Bds., Albany, N.Y.; chmn. bd. dirs. N.Y. Young Rep. Club, 1957-58; mem. exec. com. Greenwich Rep. Town Com., Conn., 1962-69, The Task Force on Def. Spending, The Economy and the Nation's Security, BENS-ED Commn. on Fundamental Def. Mgmt. Issues; mem. Stanford in Washington Coun.; mem. pres.'s coun. AmeriCares Found., New Canaan, Conn.; mem. vis. com. Inst. Internat. Studies Stanford U. With USAAF, 1944-45. Recipient La Medaille de la Ville de Paris, 1990, Stanford Gold Spike award, 1992. Mem. Ambs. Round Table (Stamford), Bond Club (N.Y.), Newcomen Soc. N.Am., Down Town Assn., Harvard Club, Riverside Yacht Club, Manhattan Yacht Club, Stanford (Calif.) Golf Club, Flying Scot Sailing Assn. (pres. 1968-69), Theta Chi. Republican. Episcopalian. Home: Harbor Lights 43 Jones Park Dr Riverside CT 06878-2205 Office: Goldman Sachs & Co 85 Broad St New York NY 10004-2456

WEIR, ALEXANDER, JR. utility consultant, inventor; b. Crossett, Ark., Dec. 19, 1922; s. Alexander and Mary Eloise (Field) W.; m. Florence Forschner, Dec. 28, 1946; children: Alexander III, Carol Jean, Bruce Richard BSChemE, U. Ark., 1943; MChemE, Poly Inst. Bklyn., 1946; PhD, U. Mich., 1954; cert., U. So. Calif. Grad. Sch. Bus. Adminstrn., 1968. Chem. engr. Am. Cyanamid Co., Stamford Rsch. Labs., 1943-47; with U. Mich., 1948-58; rsch. assoc., project supr. Engrng. Rsch. Inst., U. Mich., 1948-57; lectr. chem. and metall. engrng. dept. U. Mich., 1954-56, asst. prof., 1956-58; cons. Ramo-Woolridge Corp., L.A., 1956-57; mem. tech. staff, sect. head, asst. mgr. Ramo-Wooldridge Corp., 1957-60, incharge Atlas Missile Captive test program, 1956-60; tech. adv. to pres. Northrop Corp., Beverly Hills, Calif., 1960-70; prin. scientist for air quality So. Calif. Edison Co., L.A., 1970-76, mgr. chem. sys. R & D, 1976-86, chief rsch. scientist, 1986-88; utility cons. Playa Del Rey, Calif., 1988—. Rep. Am. Rocket Soc. to Detroit Nuc. Coun., 1954-57; chmn. session on chem. reactions Nuc. Sci. and Engrng. Congress, Cleve., 1955; U.S. del. AGARD (NATO) Combustion Colloquium, Liege, Belgium, 1955; Western U.S. rep. task force on environ. R & D goals Electric Rsch. Coun., 1971; electric utility advisor Electric Power Rsch. Inst., 1974-78, 84-87; industry advisor dept. chemistry and biochemistry Calif. State U., L.A., 1981-88. Author: Two and Three Dimensional Flow of Air through Square-Edged Sonic Orifices, 1954; (with R.B. Morrison and T.C. Anderson) Notes on Combustion, 1955, also tech. papers; inventor acid rain prevention device used in 5 states. Sea scout leader, Greenwich, Conn., 1944-48, Marina del Rey, Calif., 1965-70; bd. govs., past pres. Civic Union Playa del Rey, chmn. sch., police and fire, nominating, civil def., army liaison coms.; mem. Senate, Westchester YMCA, chmn. Dads sponsoring com., active fundraising; chmn. nominating com. Paseo del Rey Sch. PTA, 1961; mem. L.A. Mayors Cmty. Adv. Com.; asst. chmn. advancement com., merit badge dean Cantinella dist. L.A. Area coun. Boy Scouts Am. Recipient Nat. Rsch. Coun. Flue Gas Desulfurization Industrials Scale Reliability award NAS, 1975, Power Environ. Achievement award EPA, 1980, Excellence in Sulfur Dioxide Control award EPA, 1985. Mem. AIChE, Am. Geophys. Union, Navy League U.S. (v.p. Palos Verdes Peninsula coun. 1961-62), N.Y. Acad. Scis., Sci. Rsch. Soc. Am., Am. Chem. Soc., U.S. Power Squadron (hon. capt. of fleet 1997), St. Andrew Soc. So. Calif., Clan Macnachtan Assn., Clan Buchanan Soc. Am., Clan Farquharson Assn., Betty Washington Lewis Soc. of Children of Am. Revolution (past pres.), Ark. Soc. of Children of Am. Revolution (past pres.), Santa Monica Yacht Club (lifetime hon. cannoneer), Sigma Xi, Phi Kappa Phi, Phi Lambda Upsilon, Alpha Chi Sigma, Lambda Chi Alpha. Office: 8229 Billowvista Dr Playa Del Rey CA 90293-7807

WEIR, ANNE, writer; b. Boston, Feb. 9, 1942; d. John Weir and Martha (Kingman) Perry; children: Emily Weir, Sarah Noel, Katherine Joy. BA, Swarthmore Coll., 1964; MEd, U. Maine, 1984. Cert. elem. and secondary edn. tchr. Editor: MARLOWE: Being In the Life of the Mind, 1996, A BOOK OF CERTAINTIES, 1998, THE COLOR BOOK, 1998, Marlowe, corrected and augmented, 1999, Christopher's Journey, Acts & Scenes, News, The Bird's Eye, 1996-2000, A Native Woman poems, 1999, American City, 2000, A Codebook for the Plays, 2000, WAKING, An Academic Celebration, 2001, A Teacher's Holiday, "Streamlines" A Study in Bibliography, New Songs, 2001, The Reincarnation of Love, 2002. Office: Marlowe Books PO Box 10364 Portland ME 04104-0364

WEIR, BRYCE KEITH ALEXANDER, neurosurgeon, neurology educator; b. Edinburgh, Scotland, Apr. 29, 1936; came to U.S., 1992; s. Ernest John and Marion (Stewart) W.; m. Mary Lou Lauber, Feb. 25, 1976; children: Leanora, Glyncora, Brocke. BSc, McGill U., Montreal, Que., Can., 1958, MD, CM, 1960, MSc, 1963. Diplomate Am. Bd. Neurol. Surgery, Nat. Bd. Med. Examiners. Intern Montreal Gen. Hosp., 1960-61; resident in neurosurgery Neurological Inst., Montreal, 1962-64, 65-66, N.Y. Neurol. Inst., N.Y.C., 1964-65; neurosurgeon U. Alta., Edmonton, Can., 1967-92, dir. div. neurosurgery Can., 1982-86, Walter Anderson prof., chmn. dept. surgery Can., 1986-92; surgeon-in-chief U. Alta. Hosps., 1986-92; Maurice Goldblatt prof. surgery and neurology U. Chgo., 1992—2002, dir. Brain Rsch. Inst., 1993—2001, interim dean biol. scis. divsn. and Pritzker Sch. Medicine, v.p. med. affairs, 2001—02. Past pres. V Internat. Symposium on Cerebral Vasospasm; mem. neurology A study sect. NIH, 1991—93; invited speaker at over 135 profl. meetings; vis. prof. over 68 univs., including Yale U., Cornell U., Columbia U., Duke U., U. Toronto, U. Calif., San Francisco; 18 named lectureships, including White lectr. , Harvard U., Gainey lectr., Mayo Clinic. Author: Aneurysms Affecting the Nervous System, 1987, Subarachnoid Hemorrhage-Causes and Cures, 1998, Cerebral Vasospasm, 2001; co-editor: Primer on Cerebrovascular Diseases, 1997; mem. editl. bd. Jour. Neurosurgery, chmn. bd, 1993—94, mem. editl. bd. Neurosurgery Quar., Jour. Cerebrovascular Disease, Neurosurgery; contbr. over 265 articles to med. jours. Named Officer of the Order of Can., 1995. Fellow: ACS, Royal Coll. Surgeons Can., Royal Coll. Surgeons Edinburgh (hon.); mem.: Interurban Neurosurg. Soc. (chmn.), Nat. Acad. Scis., Inst. Medicine, Soc. Neurol. Surgsons (Grass gold medal 1992), Japan Neurosurg. Soc. (hon.), Am. Acad. Neurol. Surgeons, James. IV Assn. Surgeons, Am. Surg. Assn. Achievements include contributions to the understanding of cerebral vasospasm and the surgical management of intracranial aneurysms.

WEIR, EDWARD KENNETH, cardiologist, educator; b. Belfast, No. Ireland, Jan. 7, 1943; came to U.S. 1973; s. Thomas Kenneth and Violet Hilda (ffrench) W.; m. Elizabeth Vincent Pearman, May 29, 1971; children: Fergus G., Conor K. BA, U. Oxford, U.K., 1964; MA, BM, BCh, U. Oxford, Eng.,

1967, DM, 1976. Diplomate Am. Bd. Internal Medicine. Intern Churchill Hosp., Oxford, Eng., 1968, Radcliffe Infirmary, Oxford, 1968, resident, 1970-71, Hammersmith Hosp., London, 1969, Groot Schuur Hosp., Cape Town, South Africa, 1969-70, registrar in cardiology, 1971-73; postdoctoral rsch. fellow U. Colo., Denver, 1973-75; cons. pediatric cardiologist U. Cape Town Med. Sch., 1975-76; cons. cardiologist U. Natal Med. Sch., Durban, South Africa, 1976-77; assoc. prof. medicine U. Minn., Mpls., 1978-85, prof. medicine, 1985—, prof. physiology, 1999—. Staff physician VAMC, Mpls., 1978—, chief of cardiology, 2000—; dir. Grover Confs. on Pulmonary Circulation, 1984-2000. Co-editor: Pulmonary Hypertension, 1984, The Pulmonary Circulation in Health and Disease, 1987, Pulmonary Vascular Physiology and Pathophysiology, 1989, The Diagnosis and Treatment of Pulmonary Hypertension, 1992, Ion Flux in Pulmonary Vascular Control, 1993, The Pulmonary Circulation and Gas Exchange, 1994, Nitric Oxide and Radicals in the Pulmonary Vasculature, 1996, Pulmonary Edema, 1998, Oxygen Regulation of Ion Channels and Gene Expression, 1998, The Fetal and Neonatal Pulmonary Circulations, 2000, Interactions of Blood and the Pulmonary Circulation, 2002. Fulbright scholar, 1973-75; Sr. Internat. Fogarty fellow, 1993. Fellow Am. Coll. Cardiology, Royal Coll. Physicians London; mem. Am. Heart Assn. (Minn. affiliate bd. dirs. 1989-93, Nat. Cardiopulmonary Coun. (exec. com. 1992—), Pulmonary Circulation Found. (treas. 1985-2001). Office: VA Med Ctr 1 Veterans Dr # 111C Minneapolis MN 55417-2300 *What you "achieve" in life is much less important than what you do for those around you. One hundred years after their death, very few people are remembered for what they achieved.*

WEIR, DAME GILLIAN CONSTANCE, concert organist, harpsichordist; b. Martinborough, New Zealand, Jan. 17, 1941; d. Cecil Alexander and Clarice M. Foy (Bignell) W. Grad., Royal Coll. Music, London, 1965; DMus (hon.), U. Victoria of Wellington, New Zealand, 1983; DLitt (hon.), Huddersfield U., 1997; DMus (hon.), Hull U., 1999, Exeter U., 2001; Doctorate (hon.), U. Ctrl. Eng., 2001. Artist in residence numerous univs. including Washington U., St. Louis, U. Western Australia, others; vis. lectr. Royal No. Coll. Music, Manchester, Eng., 1974-89; vis. prof. organ Royal Acad. Music, London, 1997-98; Prince Consort prof. Royal Coll. of Music, London, 1999—; spkr. BBC programs on music and performance; subject of Melvyn Bragg's TV documentary South Bank Show, 2000. Concert appearances with leading Brit. Orchs. and Boston Orch., Seattle Orch., Australian ABC Orch., Wurttemberg Chamber and other fgn. orchs.; appeared in major internat. festivals including Edinburgh, Flanders, Aldeburgh, Bath, Proms, Europalia; appeared at concert halls including Royal Festival Hall, Royal Albert Hall, Lincoln Ctr., N.Y., Sydney Opera House; numerous radio and TV appearances in Brit. and world-wide including Royal Festival Hall Jubilee; organ cons.; adjudicator internat. competitions; contbr. The Messiaen Companion, 1995; contbr. articles to profl. jours.; recs. include complete organ works of Olivier Messiaen, others; TV documentary film on career, 1982, BBC TV programs The King of Instruments, 1989. Decorated comdr., dame comdr. Order Brit. Empire; recipient Turnovsky award 1985, Evening Std. award for outstanding solo performance, 1998-99. Fellow Royal Coll. Organists (hon., mem. coun. 1977—, mem. exec. 1981-85, pres. 1994-96, 1st Woman pres.), Royal Can. Coll. Organists (hon.), Royal Coll. Music (hon.); mem. Royal Acad. Music (hon.), Inc. Soc. Musicians (pres. 1992-93), Albert Schweitzer Assn. (Silver medal 1998), Soloists' Ensemble (pres. 1997). Office: care Karen McFarlane Artists 2385 Fenwood Rd Cleveland OH 44118-3803

WEIR, JOHN R. science educator, retired; b. Tenefly, N.J., July 8, 1919; s. Joseph Ralph and Bertha (Louis) W.; m. Frances Shilling, Aug. 1, 1945; 1 child, Leslie Ralph. BS in Phys. Sci., Thiel Coll., 1942; postgrad., Fresno State Coll., Calif. State U., San Jose State U., Stanford U., UCLA. Cert. gen. secondary tchg., Calif. Tchr. San Benito County (Calif.) H.S., 1947—52, Merced (Calif.) Union H.S., 1952-79; ret., 1979. With USAF, 1942—46. Mem. Am. Assn. Ret. Persons (legis. com. chair), Calif. Ret. tchrs. Assn. (state legislation com.). Democrat. Methodist. Avocations: woodworking, gardening, political advocacy. E-mail: jrfsweir@cyberlink.com.

WEIR, MORTON WEBSTER, retired academic administrator, educator; b. Canton, Ill., July 18, 1934; s. James and Frances Mary (Johnson) W.; m. Cecelia Ann Rumler, June 23, 1956; children: Deborah, Kevin, Mark. AB, Knox Coll., 1955; MA, U. Tex., 1958, PhD, 1959. Rsch. assoc., asst. prof. child devel. U. Minn., Mpls., 1959; asst. prof. child devel. U. Ill., Urbana, 1960-64, assoc. prof., 1964-68, prof., 1968-93, prof. emeritus, 1993—, head dept. psychology, 1969-71, vice chancellor acad. affairs, 1971-79, v.p. acad. affairs, 1982-88, chancellor, 1988-93, chancellor emeritus, 1993—, sr. found. rep., 1993-99; dir. Boys Town Center Study Youth Development, 1979-80. Contbr. numerous articles to profl. jours. Trustee Knox Coll., 1984—, chmn., 1995-99; trustee Menninger Found., 1993—; dir. RHR Internat. Co., 1986—. With AUS, 1960. NSF Predoctoral fellow, 1957-59 Fellow AAAS; mem. Soc. Rsch. in Child Devel. (chmn. bd. publs. 1971, chmn. fin. com. 1993-95), Sigma Xi, Phi Beta Kappa Phi.

WEIR, PETER DOUGLAS, accountant; b. Glendale, Calif., Oct. 11, 1959; s. Douglas Brenton and Diane Isabel (Leppert) W.; m. Allison Margaret Bowen, June 7, 1986; children: Heather Elizabeth, Michelle Christine. BA, U. Calif., Santa Barbara, 1981. CPA. Acct. Stonefield Josephson, An Accountancy Corp., L.A., 1981-87; ptnr. Brown & Weir, An Accountancy Corp., Glendale, 1987-94; pvt. practice Calif., 1995—. Office: Peter D Weir An Accountacy Corp 505 N Brand Blvd Ste 750 Glendale CA 91203-3330

WEIR, PETER FRANK, lawyer; b. Mar. 26, 1933; s. Robert Henry and Ruth Sophie W.; m. Jean M., Sept. 27, 1958; children: Bradford F., Elizabeth A. BA, Williams Coll., 1955; LLB, Harvard U., 1958; MBA, N.Y.U., 1967. Bar: N.Y. 1959, Ga. 1957. Assoc. Winston & Strawn (formerly Cole and Deitz), N.Y.C., 1959-66; ptnr., 1966-92; ret. ptnr., 1992; pvt. practice, 1993—; chmn., CEO Northeast Internat. Soya, Inc., 1980—. Bd. dirs. Episc. Ch. Found., 1981-93, sec., 1989-93, also treas., chn. fin. com ., 1982-89, chmn. audit com., 1982-88; mem. exec. com. N.Y. Regional Coun., 1975-81, chmn. 1979-81, mem. steering com., 1981-93; mem. adv. bd. First Am. Title Ins. Co. of N.Y., Inc., 1984-95. Bd. dirs., counsel Point O'Woods Assn., N.Y., 1976-91, v.p., 1982-91; alt. bd. dirs. Fire Island Assn., 1976-86, 92—; sec. and dir. Elderworks Found., 1982-92; dir. Episc. Preaching Found., 1995—; sec. and dir. The Point O'Woods Cmty. Trust, Inc., 1998—. Served with Air N.G., 1958-63. Mem. ABA, Internat. Bar Assn., N.Y. State Bar Assn., Assn. of Bar of City of N.Y., Church Club (trustee 1988-91), Downtown Assn. Club, Williams Club, Club at Point O'Woods (v.p., gov. 1970-79), Hillsboro Club. Republican. Home: 49 E 86th St Apt 12C New York NY 10028-1060 Office: 555 5th Ave 9th Fl New York NY 10017

WEIR, PETER LINDSAY, film director; b. Sydney, Australia, Aug. 21, 1944; s. Lindsay Weir and Peggy Barnsley; m. Wendy Stites, 1966; 2 children. Educated, Scots Coll., Sydney, Vaucluse Boys H.S., Sydney U. Worked in real estate until 1965; worked as stagehand in TV, Sydney, 1967; dir. film sequences in variety show, 1968; dir. amateur univ. revs., 1967-69; dir. for Film Australia, 1969-73; made own short films, 1969-73, ind. feature film producer, dir. and writer, 1973—. Films include: Cars That Ate Paris, 1973, Picnic at Hanging Rock, 1975, The Last Wave, 1977, The Plumber (TV), 1978, Gallipoli, 1980, The Year of Living Dangerously, 1982, Witness, 1985, The Mosquito Coast, 1986, Dead Poets Society, 1989, Green Card, 1990, Fearless, 1993, The Truman Show, 1997, The Far Side of the World, 2003. Recipient various film awards. Mem. Australia A.M. Office: CAA care John Ptak 9830 Wilshire Blvd Beverly Hills CA 90212-1804

WEIR, SONJA ANN, artist; b. Hazleton, Pa., Oct. 12, 1934; d. Stephen and Anna (Prehatny) Tatusko; m. Richard Clayton Weir, Jan. 14, 1956; children: Robert, Carl, Donna, Lisa, Nancy. Studied with Mary Ellen Silkotch, 1963-83; student, Art Students League, N.Y.C., 1985-87. Artist Knickerbocker Toy Co., Middlesex, N.J., 1980; represented by Agora Gallery, Soho, N.Y., 1999. Guest speaker career day Bridgewater H.S., 1993-94. One-woman shows include Johnson & Johnson, Piscataway, N.J., 1992, Somerset County Libr., Bridgewater, N.J., 1992-94, Manville (N.J.) Pub. Libr., 1994-99; exhibited in group shows at Raritan Valley Art Assn., 1982-83, 95, 98 (Best in Show award 1983, 2d prize 1995, 1st place for oil 1998), Ariel Gallery, N.Y.C., 1991, Am. Artists Profl. League, 1991, 94, Barren Art Ctr., Woodbridge, N.J., 1993, Agora Gallery, Soho, N.Y., 1995-99, Somerset County Libr., 1998-99, Am. Artists Profl. League, 1999, Atrium Gallery, Morristown, N.J., 2001, Agora Gallery, N.Y.C., 2001; featured in Artis Apectrum mag., vol. 11/6, 1999, Star Ledger, 2000, Agora Gallery, N.Y.C., 2001; represented in permanent collections N.W.B. Bank of South Bound Brook, N.J., Summit Bank. Featured in Artis Spectrum mag., 1999. Fellow: Nat. Am. Artists Profl. League (v.p. N.J. chpt. 1988—91, publicity com. 1988—91, show chmn. 1989—91, pres. N.J. chpt. 1992—95, editor newsletter 1992—99, nat. exec. bd. 1998—2000, pres. N.Y. chpt. 2002); mem.: Miniature Art Soc. Fla., Raritan Valley Arts Assn. (pres. 1982—84), Nat. Miniature Assn. (assoc.), Nat. Mus. Women in the Arts. Home: 25 Madison St South Bound Brook NJ 08880-1244

WEIR, STEPHEN JAMES, financial executive; b. Calgary, Alta., Can., Mar. 22, 1940; s. Jack W. and Elizabeth T. (Speirs) W.; m. Janet R Suggitt, July 1961; children: James, Jennifer. C.A., U. Man., 1962; MBA, U. Western Ont., Can., 1967. Accountant, Winnipeg, Man., 1957-63; mgr. credit and control 3M Co. of Can., London, Ont., 1963-65; asst. credit mgr. corporate credit Bank of Montreal, 1967-72; treas. Dominion Textile Inc., Montreal, 1972-77; compt., 1977-81; v.p. internat. divsn. Dominion Textile Inc., 1981-83, v.p. consumer div., 1983-84, v.p. ops. service, 1984-85, v.p. APP/IND div., 1985-87, v.p. fin. ops., 1987-88; v.p. fin. Telemedia Inc., Montreal, 1988-90, exec. v.p., chief fin. officer, 1990—. Mem. Can. Inst. Chartered Accountants, Financial Execs. Inst.. Office: Telemedia Inc 1411 Peel St Montreal QC Canada H3A 1S5 E-mail: sweir@telemedia-inc.com.

WEIR, THOMAS CHARLES, banker; b. Sandwich, Ill., Oct. 18, 1933; s. Glendon V. and Eleanor (Hoge) W.; m. Angela Di Giovanni. Grad., Pacific Coast Banking Sch., U. Wash., 1966. Mgr. consumer loans Barnett Nat. Bank, Cocoa, Fla., 1955-58; with 1st Interstate Bank Ariz., 1958-79; head retail banking div. 1st Nat. Bank Ariz., various locations, 1974-79, exec. v.p., 1975-79; chmn., chief exec. officer Home Fed. Savs., Tucson, 1979-87; chmn. Ariz. Commerce Bank, 1987-88; pres. Tucson Resources, Inc., 1988-89; pres., chief exec. officer Tucson Electric Power Co., 1989-90; fin. cons. Tucson, 1990—; pres. WD Enterprises, Inc., 1994—, Dependable Personnel, Inc., 1994—. Bd. dirs. Apollo Group, Inc.; pres. Dependable Nurses, Inc., Phoenix, 1994-96. With AUS, 1953-55. Mem.: Tucson Country, White Mountain Country. Republican. Episcopalian.

WEIRICH, ROBERT WAYNE, musician, educator; b. Massillon, Ohio, Feb. 6, 1950; s. Richard Wayne and Mary Margaret Weirich; m. Karen Lynn Kushner, May 20, 2000. Bachelor Music, Oberlin Conservatory Music, Oberlin, OH, 1968—72; Master Music, Yale U., New Haven, CT, 1974—76, Dr. Musical Arts, 1977—81. Asst. prof. piano Tulane U., New Orleans, 1977—79; asst. / assoc. prof. piano Northwestern U., Evanston, Ill., 1979—85; artist / faculty Peabody Conservatory Music, Baltimore, Md., 1985—95; prof. piano Conservatory Music Mo., U. Mo., Kansas City, Mo., 1998—. Artistic dir. Skaneateles Festival, Skaneateles, NY, 1990—99; pres. Coll. Music Soc., 2002—, bd. mem. performance, 1995—97. Composer: Going Home (song cycle) (Barnhart Prize), Steamboat Stomp (horn & piano) (Britter on the Bay); author: (magazine column) Clavier Magazine (EPA Prizes, 1989). Recipient Artistic Excellence Award, Pope Found., New York, NY; fellow Trustees Faculty Fellowship, U. Mo. Curators, Kans. City, MO, 2002; grantee Solo Recitalist Grant, Nat. Endowment for the Arts, Wash., DC, 1990. Mem.: Am. Music Ctr., Music Teachers Nat. Assn. (Dist. Svc. 1995), Pi Kappa Lambda. Home: 6609 State Line Road Kansas City MO 64113 Office: UMKC Conservatory of Music 4949 Cherry Street Kansas City MO 64110 E-mail: weirichr@umkc.edu.

WEIS, ANDREW JEROME (ANDY WEIS), musician, educator; b. St. Marys, Pa., July 28, 1954; s. Leo Benten and Audrey Mary (Wendel) W.; m. Virginia Lee Wortman, June 15, 1984 (div.); 1 child, Audrey Anna. Profl. diploma, Berklee Coll. Music, 1975; student, Navy Sch. Music, 1980. Drum tchr. jazz camps Monterey Jazz Festival and Youth Music Monterey. With U.S. Army, 1980-83. Mem. Am. Fedn. Musicians. Roman Catholic. Avocations: drum restoration, drum consulting. Home and Office: 625 Major Sherman Ln Monterey CA 93940-4620

WEIS, JOSEPH FRANCIS, JR. federal judge; b. Pitts., Mar. 12, 1923; s. Joseph Francis and Mary (Flaherty) Weis; m. Margaret Horne Weis, Dec. 27, 1958; children: Maureen, Joseph Francis, Christine. BA, Duquesne U., 1941—47; JD, U. Pitts., 1950; LLD (hon.) , Dickinson Coll., 1989. Bar: Pa. 1950. Pvt. practice, Pitts., 1950—68; judge Ct. Common Pleas, Allegheny County, 1968-70, U.S. Dist. Ct. (we. dist.) , 1970—73, U.S. Ct. Appeals (3d cir.), Pitts., 1973—99, sr. judge, 1999—. Lectr. trial procedures, 1965—; adj. prof. law U. Pitts., 1986—; chmn. Fed. Cts. Study Com., Jud. Conf. Com. on Experiment to Videotape Trial Proceedings within the 3rd Cir., Internat. Jud. Conf. the Joint Am.-Can. Appellate Judges Conf., Toronto, 1986, London, 85; futurist subcom. bicentennial com. Ct. Common Pleas, Allegheny County, Pa., 1988; participant programs legal medicine, Rome, London; mem. Am.-Can. Legal Exch., 1987; apptd. by Chief Justice Rehnquist U.S. Jud. Conf., Com. on Internat. Jud. Rels., 1998—2001; com. on adminstrn. bankruptcy sys., subcom. on jud. improvements Jud. Conf. U.S. , 1983—87, chmn. civil rules com. , 1986—87, chmn. standing com. rules of practice and procedure , 1988. Contbr. articles to profl. jours. Active Mental Health and Mental Retardation Bd., Allegheny County, 1970—73, Leukemia Soc., 1970—73, Disabled Am. Vets., Cath. War Vets, Mil. Order of the World Wars; trustee Forbes Hosp. Sys., Pitts., 1969—74; bd. adminstrn. Cath. Diocese Pitts., 1971—83. Capt. U.S. Army, 1943—48. Decorated Bronze Star, Purple Heart with oak leaf cluster; recipient St. Thomas More award, 1971, Phillip Amram award, 1991, Edward J. Devitt Disting. Svc. to Justice award, 1993, History Makers award, 1997. Fellow: Am. Bar Found., Internat. Acad. Trial Lawyers (hon.); mem.: ABA (chmn. appellate judges' conf. 1981—83), Inst. Jud. Adminstrn., Am. Judicature Soc., Acad. Trial Lawyers Allegheny County (past pres.), Allegheny Bar Assn. (past v.p.), Pa. Bar Assn., 4th Armored Divsn. Assn., Am. Legion, Knights of Malta, KC. Home: 225 Hillcrest Rd Pittsburgh PA 15238-2307 Office: US Ct Appeals US PO & Courthouse 7th & Grant St Rm 513 Pittsburgh PA 15219

WEIS, MARGARET EDITH, writer, editor; b. Independence, Mo., Mar. 16, 1948; d. George Edward and Francis Irene (Reed) W.; m. Robert William Baldwin, Aug. 22, 1970 (div. 1981); children: David William, Elizabeth Lynn; m. Donald Bayne Stewart Perrin, 1996. BA in Creative Writing, U. Mo., 1966-70. Proofreader Herald Pub. House, Independence, Mo., 1970-73, advt. dir., 1973-82; dir. div. Independence (Mo.) Press, 1977-82; editor TSR Inc, Lake Geneva, Wis., 1982-86. Freelance writer; co-owner Sovereign Press, Williams Bay, Wis., www.sovstone.com. Author: (short story) The Test of the Twins, 1984, (books) The Endless Catacombs, 1984, Tower of Midnight Dreams, 1984, (with Tracy Hickman) The Dragonlance Chronicles, Vols. 1-3, 1984, 85, Dragonlance Legends, Vols. 1-3, 1985, 86, The Darksword Trilogy, Vols. 1-3, 1987, (with Roger Moore) Riddle of The Griffon, 1985, (under Margaret Baldwin) The Boys Who Saved The Children, 1982, Kisses of Death, 1983, (with Pat O'Brien) Wanted: Frank and Jesse James, The Real Story, 1981, (with Janet Pack) Children of The Holocaust, 1986, My First Thanksgiving, 1983, (with Gary Pack) Computer Graphics, 1984, Robots and Robotics, 1984, (short story) The Thirty Nine Buttons, 1987, (novella) (with Tracy Hickman) The Legacy, 1987, Wanna Bet?, 1987; editor: The Art of Dungeons and Dragons, 1985, Leaves of the Inn of the Last Home, 1987, The Art of Dragonlance, 1987, Dragonlance Tales, vol. 1, 2, 3, 1987, (with Tracy Hickman) The Rose of the Prophet, 1989, (with Tracy Hickman) Death's Gate, vol. 1, 1990, vols. 2, 3, 4, 5, 6, 7, Star of the Guardian, vol. 1, The Lost King, 1990, King's Test vol. 2, 1991, King's Sacrifice Vol. 3, 1991, Ghost Legion Vol. 4, 1991, Dragons of Summer Flame, 1996, (with Don Perrin), Doom Brigade, 1997, Mag Force 7 novels, 3 vols., The Soulforge, 1998, Brothers in Arms, 1999, (with Tracy Hickman) Starshield, Vols. 1-3, 1997, Legacy of the Darksword, 1997, War of Souls, 3 vols., 2000; editor: Kender, Gully Dwarves and Gnomes, 1989, Love and War, 1991, Reign of Istar, 1993, Dragons of War, 1996, Dragons of Chaos, 1997, Relics and Omens, 1998, Sovereign Stone Role-Playing Games, 1999, Sovereign Stone novels, (with Tracy Hickman) vol. 1, Well of Darkness, 2000, vol. 2, Guardians of the Lost, 2001, (with Don Perrin) Draconian Measures, 2000. Named to Writer's Hall of Fame, 2002; recipient Origins award, 2001. Avocations: role-playing games, flyball, racing.

WEIS, MONICA ROSEMARY, English educator; b. Rochester, N.Y., Nov. 9, 1942; d. Raymond Peter and Josephine Marie (McGrath) W. BA, Nazareth Coll. Rochester, 1965; MA, Bread Loaf Sch. English, 1973; postgrad., Oxford (Eng.) U., 1976; PhD, U. Va., 1985. Joined Sisters of St. Joseph, Roman Cath. Ch., 1960; cert. English tchr. grades 7-12, N.Y. Tchr. Our Lady of Lourdes Sch., Brighton, N.Y., 1964-72, vice prin., 1970-71; tchr. St. Lawrence Sch., Greece, 1972-74; prof. English Nazareth Coll. Rochester, 1974—, Rosemary A. White prof. English and Am. lit., 2000—, coord. English and edn., 1982-92. Writing cons. U. Cen. Fla., Orlando, 1988-91; vis. scholar Boston Coll., 1989; vis. fellow Yale U., 1996. Contbr. articles to profl. jours. Recipient Excellence in Tchg. award sr. faculty Nazareth Coll., 1997-98; rsch. grantee Nazareth Coll., Grasmere, Eng., 1986, Rochester, 1991, 92, 95. Mem. MLA, Coll. English Assn. (bd.dirs. 1990-93, 98-2001), Nat. Coun. Tchrs. English, Internat. Thomas Merton Soc. (adv. bd. 1993-95, 99-2001, v.p. 1995-97 Office: Nazareth Coll Rochester 4245 East Ave Rochester NY 14618-3790 E-mail: mrweis@naz.edu.

WEIS, ROBERT FREEMAN, supermarket company executive; b. Sunbury, Pa. m. Patricia Ross; children: Jennifer, Colleen, Jonathan. Grad., Mercersburg Acad., 1937; BA, Yale U., 1941. With Weis Markets, Sunbury, Pa., 1946—, v.p., treas., bd. dirs., treas., 1995—, chmn. bd. dirs., 2002—. Chair steering com. capital campaign Susquehanna U., Selinsgrove, Pa., past vice chmn. bd. trustees; past pres. bd. trustees Sunbury Cmty. Hosp., trustee; bd. dirs. Lown Cardiovascular Rsch. Found., Brookline, Mass. Past pres. Sunbury C. of C.; past chmn. bd. dirs. First Nat. Trust Bank Sunbury, ereritus dir.; past dir. Susquehanna Bancshares; treas. Sunbury chpt. United Jewish Appeal. Office: Weis Markets Inc 1000 S 2d St PO Box 471 Sunbury PA 17801-0471

WEISBACH, LOU, advertising executive; Pres., CEO, founder Ha-Lo Industries, Inc., Niles, Ill., 1972-99, chmn., 1999—. Office: HALO Industries Inc 5800 W Touhy Ave Niles IL 60714*

WEISBERG, ADAM JON, lawyer; b. Cocoa Beach, Fla., June 5, 1963; s. Melvin H. Weisberg and Joan Julie (Carney) Vargo; m. Cheryl Lynn Scupp, June 25, 1994. BS in Bus. Econs., Rider Coll., 1985; JD, N.Y. Law Sch., 1988. Bar: N.Y. 1989, N.J. 1989, U.S. Dist. Ct. 1989, Fla. 1991. Law clk., asst. prosecutor Middlesex County Prosecutors Office, New Brunswick, N.J., 1988-90; workers' compensation atty. Levinson Axelrod Wheaton, Edison, 1990-91; trial atty. workers compensation Richard J. Simon, Esq., New Brunswick, 1991-92; pvt. practice lawyer, 1992—; pres. Asbury Music Co., Belmar, N.J. Mem. ABA, N.J. Bar Assn., Middlesex County Bar Assn., Monmouth County Bar Assn., Assn. Criminal Def. Lawyers. Avocations: fishing, surfing. Office: Monmouth Exec Plz II 1300 Highway 35 Ste 201 Ocean NJ 07712-3531 also: 200 Livingston Ave New Brunswick NJ 08901-2152

WEISBERG, BRUCE STEVEN, bank executive; b. Haverhill, Mass., July 17, 1958; s. Charles Raymond and Miriam Weisberg. BS in Hotel Adminstrn., U. N.H., 1980; cert. of graduation, Williams Coll., 1988, U. Wis., 1999, Metrowest Acad., 2001. Fin. control clk. USTrust/UST Corp., Boston, 1984, treas., 1984-85, treas., compliance officer, 1986-88, v.p., treas., compliance officer, 1988-90, v.p., dir. gen. acctg., 1991-96, v.p. adminstrn./fin. retail banking, 1996-98, v.p. adminstrn. and fin. Office of the Pres., 1998-2000; v.p. adminstrn. Middlesex Savs. Bank, Natick, 2000—. Campaign co. leader United Way of Mass. Bay, Boston, 1993-99; bd. dirs., treas. Natick Organic Cmty. Farm, 1999—; co-chmn. Natick Friends of the Fourth, 2002—. Mem. Bank Adminstrn. Inst. (v.p. Boston chpt. 1990-92, pres. 1992-94), Greater Boston Bus. Coun. (treas., bd. dirs. 1999-2000). Democrat. Jewish. Avocations: travel, cooking, walking, gardening, music. Home: 37 Hopewell Farm Rd Natick MA 01760-5570 Office: Middlesex Savs Bank 6 Main St Natick MA 01760-4534

WEISBERG, DAVID CHARLES, lawyer; b. N.Y.C., June 25, 1938; s. Leonard Joseph and Rae M. (Kimberg) W.; m. Linda Gail Kerman, Aug. 27, 1975; children: Leonard Jay, Risa Beth. AB, U. Mich., 1958; LLB, Harvard U., 1961. Bar: N.Y. 1962, U.S. Dist. Ct. (so. and ea. dists.) N.Y. 1965, U.S. Supreme Ct. 1970. Assoc. Dreyer & Traub, Bklyn., 1962, Lee Franklin, Mineola, N.Y., 1962-65; pvt. practice, Patchogue, 1965-67, 77-80; ptnr. Bass & Weisberg, 1967-77, Davidow, Davidow, Russo & Weisberg, Patchogue, 1981-82, Davidow, Davidow, Weisberg & Wismann, Patchogue, 1982-87, Davidow, Davidow & Wismann, Patchogue, 1988-92, Weisberg & Wismann, Patchogue, 1992-98; propr. The Lawyer's Equalizer, 2000—. Assoc. justice and justice Village of Patchogue, 1968-70, village atty., 1970-85; spl. asst. dist. atty. Suffolk County, Patchogue, 1970-85; assoc. estate tax atty., appraiser N.Y. State Dept. Taxation and Fin., Hauppauge, N.Y., 1975-85; lectr. estate tax Suffolk County Acad. Law, 1976-84, negligence law, 1994; cons. in field. Law chmn. Suffolk County Dem. Com., N.Y., 1975-85; bd. dirs. Temple Beth El of Patchogue. With USAR, 1961-62. Mem. ATLA, N.Y. State Bar Assn., Suffolk County Bar Assn., Nassau-Suffolk Trial Lawyers Sect., Lions (pres. Medford 1978-79, 2d v.p. 1984-85). Avocations: bicycling, skiing. E-mail: dcw@lawyersequalizer.com., dcw608@yahoo.com.

WEISBERG, HERBERT FRANK, political science educator; b. Mpls., Dec. 8, 1941; s. Nathan R. and Jean (Schlessinger) W.; m. Judith Ann Robinson, Dec. 16, 1979; 1 child, Bryan Bowen. BA, U. Minn., 1963; PhD, U. Mich., 1968. Asst. prof. polit. sci. U. Mich., Ann Arbor, 1967-73, assoc. prof. polit. sci., 1973-74, Ohio State U., Columbus, 1974-77, prof. polit. sci., 1977—. Author: Central Tendency and Variation, 1992; co-author: Theory Building and Data Analysis, 1984, Controversies in Voting Behavior, 2001, Survey Research Polling and Data Analysis, 1996, Classics in Congressional Politics, 1999; editor: Political Science: Science of Politics, 1985, Democracy's Feast: Elections in America, 1995; co-editor Am. Jour. Polit. Sci., 1979-82, Great Theatre: The American Congress in the 1990's, 1998, Reelection 1996: How Americans Voted, 1999. Mem.: Am. Polit. Sci. Assn. (program chmn. 1983), Midwest Polit. Sci. Assn. (pres. 2001—02), Phi Kappa Phi, Pi Sigma Alpha, Phi Beta Kappa. Home: 742 Gatehouse Ln Columbus OH 43235-1732 Office: Ohio State U Dept Polic Sci 2140 Derby Hall 154 N Oval Mall Columbus OH 43210-1330

WEISBERG, LEONARD R. engineering executive, researcher, retired; b. N.Y.C., Oct. 17, 1929; s. Emanuel E. and Esther (Raynes) W.; m. Frances Simon, Mar. 23, 1980; children: Glenna Weisberg Andersen, Orren Weisberg Falk, Frances Weisberg Brookner. BA magna cum laude, Clark U., 1950; MA, Columbia U., 1952. Rsch. asst. Watson Labs. IBM, N.Y.C., 1953-55; with RCA Labs., Princeton, N.J., 1955-71, mem. tech. staff, 1955-66, head rsch. group, 1966-69, dir. semicondr. device rsch. lab., 1969-71; dir. materials rsch. lab. Itek Corp., Lexington, Mass., 1972-74, v.p., dir. ctrl. rsch. lab., 1974-75; dir. electronics tech U.S. Dept. Def., Washington, 1975-79; v.p. rsch. and engring. Honeywell Inc., Mpls., 1980-94, ret., 1994. Mem. adv. group on electron devices U.S. Dept. Def., 1981-99. Contbr. articles to profl. jours. Recipient award for initiating VHSIC program U.S. Dept. Def., 1979. Fellow IEEE; mem. Am. Phys. Soc., Sigma Xi Home: 1250 S Washington St # 202 Alexandria VA 22314-4455 E-mail: LenW5678@aol.com.

WEISBERG, LYNNE WILLING, psychiatrist, consultant; b. N.Y.C., Apr. 11, 1948; d. Stanley S. and Pearl R. Willing. BA, Barnard Coll., 1969; PhD, U. Mich., 1972; MD, SUNY, Downstate, 1978. Diplomate Am. Bd. Psychiatry and Neurology, Am. Bd. Adolescent Psychiatry. Intern NYU Med. Ctr., 1978-79; resident in adult psychiatry Mt. Sinai Hosp., N.Y.C., 1979-81; fellow in child psychiatry Columbia Med. Ctr., 1981-83; staff psychiatrist Fair Oaks Hosp., Summit, N.J., 1983-85, asst. dir. child and adolescent psychiatry, 1985-88, assoc. dir. child and adolescent psychiatry, 1988-92; dir. child and adolescent outpatient psychiat. svcs. Psychiat. Assocs. N.J. at Fair Oaks Hosp., 1992—; pvt. practice Morris County, N.J., 1993—. Cons. Bonnie Brae Sch., Millington, N.J., 1984-92. Author: When Acting Out Isn't Acting, 1991. Horace Rackham Prize fellow, 1972. Mem. AMA, Med. Soc. N.J., Am. Soc. Clin. Psychopharmacology. Office: 135 Columbia Tpke Ste 201 Florham Park NJ 07932-2104

WEISBERGER, BARBARA, artistic director, educator, choreographer; b. Bklyn., Feb. 28, 1926; d. Herman and Sally (Goldstein) Linshes; m. Sol Spiller, Sept. 3, 1945 (div. 1948); m. Ernest Weisberger, Nov. 15, 1949; children: Wendy, Steven. BS in Edn., Psychology, Pa. State U., 1945; L.H.D. (hon.), Swarthmore Coll., 1970; D.F.A. (hon.), Temple U., 1973, Kings Coll., 1978, Villanova U., 1978, U. New England, 1996. Founder, dir., tchr. Wilkes-Barre (Pa.) Ballet Theater, 1953-63; founder, dir. Pa. Ballet, Phila., 1962-82, Carlisle (Pa.) Project, 1984—; artistic advisor Peabody Dance, Balt., 2001—. Vice chmn. dance panel Nat. Endowment for the Arts, Washington, 1975-79. Performed with Met. Opera Ballet, N.Y.C., 1937, 38, Mary Binney

Montgomery Co., Phila., 1940-42, ballet mistress, choreographer, Ballet Co. of Phila. Lyric Opera, 1961-62, ; choreographic works include Italian Concerto, Bach, Symphonic Variations, Franck; also operas for, Phila. Lyric Opera Co. Named Disting. Dau. of Pa., 1972, Disting. Alumna, Pa. State U., 1972; recipient 46th ann. Gimbel Phila. award, 1978. Mem. Psi Chi. Home and Office: 571 Charles Ave Kingston PA 18704-4711 Fax: 570-287-7778.

WEISBERGER, JOSEPH ROBERT, retired judge; b. Providence, Aug. 3, 1920; s. Samuel Joseph and Ann Elizabeth (Meighan) W.; m. Sylvia Blanche Pigeon, June 9, 1951; children: Joseph Robert, Paula Ann, Judith Marie. AB, Brown U., 1942; JD, Harvard U., 1949; LLD (hon.) , R.I. Coll., Suffolk U., Mt. St. Joseph Coll.; DCL (hon.) , Providence Coll.; DHL (hon.) , Bryant Coll.; LLD (hon.) , Roger Williams Coll., 1992; LLD (hon.) , Brown U., 1992, Constantine U., 1997; LLD, So. New England Sch. Law, 1998; DHL (hon.) , Salve Regina U., 2001. Bar: Mass. 1949, R.I. 1950. With Quinn & Quinn, Providence, 1951-56; solicitor Glocester, R.I., 1953-56; judge Superior Ct. R.I., Providence, 1956-72; presiding justice R.I. Superior Ct., 1972-78; justice R.I. Supreme Ct., 1978—, chief justice, 1993—2001; ret., 2001. Adj. prof. U. Nev., 1986—; mem. faculty Nat. Jud. Coll.; vis. lectr. Providence Coll., Suffolk Law Sch., Roger Williams Coll.; Chmn. New Eng. Regional Conf. Trial Judges, 1962, 63, 65; chmn. New Eng. Regional Commn. Disordered Offender, 1968-71, R.I. Com. Adoption on Rules Criminal Procedure, 1968-72, chmn. of R.I. Adv. Com. Corrections, 1973, Nat. Conf. State Trial Judges ABA, 1977-78; exec. com. Appelate Judges Conf. ABA, 1979—, vice chmn., 1983-85, chmn., 1985-86; bd. dirs. Nat. Ctr. for State Cts., 1975-81. Chmn. editorial bd. Judges Jour., 1973-75. Pres. R.I. Health Facilities Planning Coun., 1967-70; chmn. Gov. R.I. Coun. Mental Health, 1968-73; moderator Town of East Providence, 1954-56; mem. R.I. Senate, 1953-56, minority leader, 1955-56; vice chmn. bd. trustee R.I. Hosp., 1968-92, St. Joseph's Hosp., trustee, 1962—. Lt. comdr. USNR, 1941-46. Recipient Erwin Griswold award Nat. Jud. Coll., 1989; named to R.I. Hall of Fame; Paul Harris fellow Rotary Internat. Fellow Am. Bar Found.; mem. ABA (ho. of dels., task force on criminal justice stds. 1977-79, exec. com. appellate judges' conf. 1979-95), KC, R.I. Bar Assn., Am. Judges Assn. (gov.), Inst. Jud. Adminstrn., Am. Judicature Soc. (Herbert Harley award 1990), Am. Law Inst., Order of St. Gregory (knight comdr. with star 1989, Goodrich award for Svc. 1995), Phi Beta Kappa (past pres. Alpha chpt. Brown U.). Home: 60 Winthrop St Riverside RI 02915-2624 Office: RI Supreme Ct 250 Benefit St Ste 7 Providence RI 02903-2724 E-mail: jweisberger@courts.state.ri.us. *My professional life for the last 45 years has been occupied with judicial duties. I have been blessed with the opportunity to meet ever changing challenges and to attempt to solve a myriad of problems. These opportunities have been rewarding and absorbing. I consider judicial work to be a great privilege.*

WEISBIN, CHARLES RICHARD, nuclear engineer; b. Bklyn., Jan. 4, 1944; s. Alma (Schwartz) Lovitt; m. Alison Norma Weisbin, June 20, 1964; children: Daniel Mark, Amy Gayle. MS in Nuclear Engring., Columbia U., 1965, DSc in Nuclear Engring., 1969. Group leader Oak Ridge (Tenn.) Nat. Lab., 1977-80, section head, 1980-89, dir. robotics and intelligence systems, 1986-89; mgr. telerobotics tech. Jet Propulsion Lab., Pasadena, Calif., 1991-92, mgr. robotic systems and advanced computer tech. sect., 1989-93, mgr. rover and telerobotic tech., 1993-95, Mars program technologist, 1994-96, mgr. robotics and Mars exploration tech., 1995-98; dep. mgr. Cross Enterprise Tech. Devel. Program, NASA, 1999-2000; dir. Ctr. for Engring. Systems Advanced Rsch. Oak Ridge (Tenn.) Nat. Lab., 1982-89; dep. Strategic Sys. Tech. Program Office NASA, 2001—, thrust mgr. surface sys., 1999-2000. Mem. joint tech. panel on robotics DOD Joint Dirs. Labs., 1986—89; assoc. prof. computer sci. U. Tenn., Knoxville, 1984—89; program chmn. 2d Internat. Conf. on Artificial Intelligence IEEE Computer Soc., 1985; co-chmn. U.S. NASA Telerobotics Working Group, 1990—98; robotics and telepresence com. Space Tech. Interagy. Group, 1992—96. Author: Sensitivity and Uncertainty Analysis of Reactor Performance Parameters, 1982; contbr. Recipient Execptional Svc. medal, NASA, 1993, 1999, Nova award, 1998, Thomas O. Paine award for advancement of human exploration to Mars, 1998, Outstanding Leadership in surface robotics award, 2000, Decadal Planning Team Achievement award, 2001. Mem.: IEEE (Cert. Appreciation 1987), Robotics and Automation Soc., Am. Nuclear Soc. (program chmn. 1977—79), Tau Beta Pi, Sigma Chi. Republican. Jewish. Achievements include development of initiation of robotics and intelligent systems at Oak Ridge; research in sensitivity analysis, non-destructive assay of spent nuclear fuel, supervised inspection, and emergency response robotics. Home: 775 Starlight Heights Dr La Canada Flintridge CA 91011-1854 Office: Jet Propulsion Lab 4800 Oak Grove Dr Pasadena CA 91109-8001

WEISBROD, CARL, lawyer, public official; b. N.Y.C., Oct. 5, 1944; s. Walter and Hilda (Pelzer) W.; m. Jody Adams, Jan. 21, 1979; 1 child, William. BS, Cornell U., 1965; JD, NYU, 1968. Bar: N.Y., 1968; U.S. Dist. Ct. (so. dist.) N.Y., 1969. Asst. commr. N.Y.C. Housing Dept., 1970-72; counsel, chief exec. officer Wildcat Svc. Corp., N.Y.C., 1972-77; gen. counsel Manpower Demonstration Rsch. Corp., 1977-78; dir. Mayor's Office of Midtown Enforcement, 1978-84; exec. dir. City Vol. Corps, 1984-86, N.Y.C. Planning Commn., 1986-87; pres. 42d St. Devel. Project, N.Y.C., 1987-90; pres., chief exec. officer N.Y.C. Econ. Devel. Corp., 1990-94; pres. Alliance for Downtown N.Y., 1995—; dir. Sept. 11 Fund, 2001—. Chmn. N.Y.C. Loft Bd., 1982-84. Contbr. articles to profl. jours. Trustee The Ford Found., 1996, NYU Downtown Hosp., 1999—; dir. Tarragon Realty Advisors, Inc., 1995—; dir. Lower Manhattan Devel. Corp. Office: Alliance for Downtown NY 120 Broadway New York NY 10271-0002 E-mail: cwiesbrod@downtownny.com.

WEISBROD, KEN (JOSEPH LOUIS WEISBROD), marketing professional; b. Los Angeles, July 31, 1957; s. Louis Isadore and Dolores Joan (Adamczyk) W.; m. Kary Lin Shirley, Jan. 25, 1992 (separated May 10, 2002); children: Katherine Irene, Benjamin Joseph. Cert., Gemological Inst. Am, 1988. Jewelry designer House of Time Jewelers, Granada Hills, Calif., 1968-79; pres. Ken Weisbrod Prodns., Inc., Chatsworth, 1979-85; v.p. The Ramolap Co., 1985—. Dir. prodn. Katherine's of Broadway Market, Chatsworth, 1987—. Designer jewelry for numerous art exhibits, 1969-75. Mem. Advt. Prodn. Assn. L.A., Greater L.A. Zoo Assn., Advertising Prodn. Assn. L.A. Democrat. Roman Catholic. Office: Ramolap Co PO Box 5359 Chatsworth CA 91313-5359

WEISBROT, MARVIN MYRON, retired healthcare administrator, consultant; b. Phila., Oct. 20, 1928; s. Lewis Harold Weisbrot and Rose (Horn) Weisbrot/Abel; m. Jan Levin, Feb. 14, 1954; 1 child, Michele Ann. BA, U. Pa., 1950; BS, Phila. Coll. Pharmacy, 1959; MBA, Temple U., 1973. Registered pharmacist, N.J. Pres. Drug Ctrs., Inc., Burlington, N.J., 1956-71; adminstrv. officer VA Med. Ctr., Tampa, Fla., 1973-74, adminstrv. officer, clin. studies coord. Drug Dependence Treatment Ctr. Phila., 1974-80; lectr. psychiatry Sch. Medicine U. Pa., 1974-93; adminstrv. officer, co-investigator, rsch. coord. Psychiatry Svc. VA Med. Ctr., 1980-90, clin. rsch. Med. Rsch. Svc., 1990-93; cons. on addictive disease Roxane Labs., Columbus, Ohio, 1995-97. Bd. dirs. Drenk Mental Health Ctr., Mt. Holly, N.J., chair program com., v.p., bd. dirs., 2001—; trustee Meml. Health Alliance, Mt. Holly, 1988-98; cons. addictive disease Bio Devel. Corp., McLean, Va., 1993-95; cons. health edn. Evesham (N.J.) sch. dists., 1995; cons. to Ministry of Health, Portugal, 1993-96, France, 1993; mem. profl. adv. coun. Cmty. Nursing Svcs. Burlington County. Author: Comparison of Modalities of Treatment for Narcotic Addiction, 1973;; contbr. papers and monographs to profl. jours. Mem., cons. Mcpl. Alliance for Drug and Alcohol Awareness and Edn. (DARE), Mt. Laurel, N.J., 1993-2001; mem. Legion of Honor, Chapel of Four Chaplains, Phila., 1977. 1st lt. U.S. Army, 1951-54. Named Outstanding Young Man of Yr., Jaycees, 1962, 64. Fellow Am. Coll. Apothecaries. Jewish. Avocations: photography, travel, golf. Home: 327 Carleton Ln Mount Laurel NJ 08054-3113 E-mail: poppermw@aol.com.

WEISBUCH, ROBERT ALAN, English educator; b. Rochester, N.Y., Nov. 22, 1946; s. Irving Arthur and Ferne (Paull) W.; m. Susan Ann Remington, July 23, 1972 (div. 1979); 1 child, Max; m. Louise Wicks Freymann, Aug. 6, 1983 (div. 1994); children: Sarah, Michael; m. Candy Jaye Cooper, Aug. 27, 1994; 1 child, Gabriel. BA magna cum laude, Wesleyan U., Middletown, Conn., 1968; MPhil in English, Yale U., 1970, PhD in English, 1972. Asst. prof. English U. Mich., Ann Arbor, 1972-76, assoc. prof., 1976-85, prof., 1985—, assoc. chmn. dept. English, 1981-84, chmn., 1987-94, assoc. prof. rsch., assoc. dean faculty programs Rackham Sch. Grad. Studies, 1994-95, assoc. v.p. rsch., 1994-95, interim dean Grad. Sch., 1995-96; pres. The Woodrow Wilson Nat. Fellowship Found., 1997—; dir. Mellon Fellowships Humanistic Studies, 1998—. Author: Emily Dickinson's Poetry, 1975, Atlantic Double-Cross, 1986; co-editor Dickinson and Audience, 1995. Am. Coun. Learned Socs. fellow, 1976-77, Rackham fellow, U. Mich., 1983; recipient Amoco teaching award U. Mich., 1986 Mem. Phi Beta Kappa. Avocations: radio, wine, baseball. E-mail: bobweis@woodrow.org.

WEISBURGER, ELIZABETH KREISER, retired chemist, editor; b. Greenlane, Pa., Apr. 9, 1924; d. Raymond Samuel and Amy Elizabeth (Snavely) Kreiser; m. John H. Weisburger, Apr. 7, 1947 (div. May 1974); children: William Raymond, Diane Susan, Andrew John. BS, Lebanon Valley Coll., 1944, DSc (hon.), 1989; PhD, U. Cin., 1947, DSc (hon.), 1981. Rsch. assoc. U. Cin., 1947-49; col. USPHS, 1951-89; postdoctoral fellow Nat. Cancer Inst., Bethesda, Md., 1949-51, chemist, 1951-73, chief carcinogen metabolism and toxicology br., 1972-75, chief Lab. Carcinogen Metabolism, 1975-81, asst. dir. chem. carcinogenesis, 1981-89, ret. Cons. in field; lectr. Found. for Advanced Edn. in Scis., Bethesda, 1980-95; adj. prof. Am. U., Washington, 1982-83. Asst. editor-in-chief Jour. Nat. Cancer Inst., 1971-87; mem. editl. adv. bd. Chem. Health and Safety, 1994-99, Jour. Applied Toxicology, 1996—; contbr. articles to profl. jours. Trustee Lebanon Valley Coll., 1970—, pres. bd. trustees, 1985-89. Recipient Meritorious Svc. medal USPHS, 1973, Disting. Svc. medal, 1985; Hillebrand prize Chem. Soc. Washington, 1981, Charles Gordon award, 1999. Fellow AAAS (nominating com. 1978-81); mem. Am. Chem. Soc. (Garvan medal 1981, Tillmanns-Skolnick award divsn. chem. health and safety 2001), Am. Assn. Cancer Rsch., Soc. Toxicology, Am. Soc. Biochem. and Molecular Biology, Royal Soc. Chemistry, Am. Conf. Govtl. Indsl. Hygienists (Herbert Stokinger award 1996), Grad. Women in Sci. (hon.), Iota Sigma Pi (hon.). Lutheran.

WEISBURGER, JOHN HANS, medical researcher; b. Stuttgart, Germany, Sept. 15, 1921; came to U.S., 1943, naturalized, 1944; s. William and Selma (Barth) W.; children: William, Diane, Andrew. AB, U. Cin., 1947, MS, 1948, PhD, 1949; MD (hon.), U. Umeå, Sweden, 1980. Officer USPHS, 1950-72; mem. staff Nat. Cancer Inst., NIH, Bethesda, Md., 1950-61, head carcinogen screening sect., 1961-72; dir. bioassay segment, Carcinogenesis Programs Nat. Cancer Inst., 1971-72; v.p. rsch. Am. Health Found., Valhalla, N.Y., 1972-87; dir. Naylor Dana Inst. for Disease Prevention, 1972-87, dir. emeritus, sr. mem., 1987—; rsch. prof. pathology N.Y. Med. Coll., 1974—; pres. Weisburger Assocs., North White Plains, N.Y., 1987—. Mem. biochemistry and nutrition study sect. NIH, 1957—58; mem. interdepartmental panel on carcinogens FDA, USDA, USPHS, 1962—71; chmn. carcinogenesis subcom. Nat. Large Bowel Cancer Project, 1972—75; mem. expert panel on nitrites and nitrosamines USDA, 1973—77; mem. Nat. Cancer Inst. Clearinghouse on Environ. Carcinogens, 1976—78; co-chmn. organizing com. US-Japan Coop. Workshop on GI Tract Cancer, 1979; chmn. sci. rev. panel NJ State Commn. Cancer Rsch., 1988—90; co-chmn. internat. symposium on health effects of tea, NY, 1991; chmn. nutrition and cancer sect. 3d Anticarcinogenesis & antimutagenesis conf., Italy, 1991; chmn. study sect. NIH-Nat. Cancer Inst., Bethesda, Md., 1991; rsch. fellow Japanese Found. for Promotion of Cancer Rsch. Nat. Cancer Ctr. Rsch. Inst., Tokyo, 1992; adv. com. rev. RDA Food & Nutrition Bd. NAS, 1993; lectr. numerous lectures in field; chmn. numerous confs. national & internat. Assoc. editor Jour. Nat. Cancer Inst., 1960-62, Xenobiotica, 1971—, Archives of Toxicology, 1977-87, Internat. Jour. Toxicology, 1982—, Preventive Medicine, 1988—; mem. internat. editl. adv. bd. Food and Chem. Toxicology, 1967—; assoc. editor Cancer Rsch., 1969-80, mem. cover editl. bd., 1987-99; mem. editl. bd. Chemico-Biol. Interactions, 1969-88, Carcinogenesis, 1979-87, Inst. Sci. Info. Atlas of Sci., 1987-89, Cancer Epidemiology Biomarkers Prevention, 1991-98, Cancer Detection Prevention, 1994—; mem. guest editl. bd. Japanese Jour. Cancer Rsch., 1987—. With AUS, 1944-46; col. USPHS, 1950-72. Decorated D.S.M., 1964; recipient Meritorious Svc. medal USPHS HEW, 1970, Outstanding Service award Westchester div. Am. Cancer Soc., 1984, Meyer and Anna Prentis award Mich. Cancer Ctr., 1987; named one of 1000 most cited scientists, ISI List, 1981. Leadership plaque N.J. State Commn. Cancer Rsch., 1990. Fellow N.Y. Acad. Scis., Am. Coll. Nutrition; mem. Am. Assn. Cancer Rsch. (hon. mem., rep. to European Assn. Cancer Rsch. 1985-89), Am. Chem. Soc. (hon., com. environ. improvement 1992-94, chmn. lectr. chemistry and health 31st Middle Atlantic regional meeting 1997), Am. Gastroent. Assn., Am. Conf. Govt. Indsl. Hygienists, Am. Soc. Biochem. Molecular Biologists, Am. Soc. Preventive Oncology (founding mem., bd. dirs. 1983-90, Disting. Svc. award 1990), Biochem. Soc. (London, emeritus), Environ. Mutagen Soc., European Assn. Cancer Rsch. (coun. 1985-90), Japan Cancer Assn. (hon. life), Soc. Exptl. Biol. Medicine, Soc. Toxicology (chmn. bd. publs. 1968-71, councilor 1972-74, amb. toxicology Mid-Atlantic divsn. 1990, hon. mem. 1995, Award of Merit 1981), Westchester Chem. Soc. (Disting. Scientist 1996), Sigma Xi, Alpha Chi Sigma (pres. Washington profl. chpt. 1967-68), Phi Lambda Upsilon. Achievements include research and over 550 publs. on lifestyle and chronic disease prevention, relevant mechanisms, and medical care cost reduction. Home: 4 Whitewood Rd White Plains NY 10603-1137 Office: Am Health Found Naylor Dana Inst Valhalla NY 10595-1599 *In my lifetime a revolutionary change occurred in our knowledge of the causes and the mechanisms involved in the major premature killing diseases—heart disease, hypertension, stroke, many forms of cancer. These key advances stemmed from the partnership between the federal government, public-supported societies and academic institutions that encourage health research. The impact of these diseases can be reduced in virtually all countries of the world provided their political bodies can agree that peaceful endeavors and cooperation in fostering better health for their people can be made a high priority goal. Medical science now can implement successful prevention efforts. I am glad I have lived through this period and have played a role in this development.*

WEISCHADLE, DAVID EMMANUEL, education educator; b. Sayreville, N.J., Oct. 4, 1941; s. Richard G. and Christina (Dailey) W.; m. Mary Ann Piscopo, June 22, 1968; children: David E. II, Douglas E. BS, Rutgers U., 1963, EdM, 1964, EdD, 1970. Cert. tchr., supr., prin., supt., N.J. Tchr. Edison (N.J.) Pub. Schs., 1964-65, 67-69; program specialist N.J. Urban Sch. Devel. Coun., Trenton, 1969-70; dir. planning Trenton Pub. Schs., 1970-73; prof. Montclair State U., Upper Montclair, N.J., 1973—, chair dept. counseling, human devel. and ednl. leadership, 2000—. Pres. DW Global Strategies, Inc., Princeton, N.J. Author: (novel) 228, 1997; contbr. 100 articles to profl. jours. Capt. U.S. Army, 1965-67, Republic of Vietnam. Recipient Outstanding Achievement for Vietnam Vet award, Pres. of U.S., 1979, Achievement award Assessment and Devel. Ctr., N.J., 1989-90, Individual Achievement award, ASTD, 1988, N.J. Disting. Svc. medal Gov. N.J., 2000. Mem. ASTD (award 1988), ASCD, Ednl. Adminstrn. Profs. N.J. (pres. 1987-89, 1995-97), N.J. Staff Devel. Coun., N.J. Vietnam Vets. Meml. Commn., others. Avocations: reading, travel, politics. Home: 6 Ribsam St Trenton NJ 08619-3605 Office: Montclair State U Normal Ave Montclair NJ 07043 E-mail: weischadled@mail.montclair.edu.

WEISENBURGER, THEODORE MAURICE, retired judge, poet, educator, writer; b. Tuttle, N.D., May 12, 1930; s. John and Emily (Rosenau) W.; children: Sam, Jennifer, Emily, Todd, Daniel, Dwight, Holly, Michael, Paul, Peter; m. Maylyne Chu, Sept. 19, 1985; 1 child, Irene. BA, U. N.D., 1952, LLB, 1956, JD, 1969; BFT, Am. Grad Sch. Internat. Mgmt., Phoenix, 1957. Bar: N.D. 1963, U.S. Dist. Ct. N.D. 1963. County judge, tchr. Bensen County, Minnewaukan, N.D., 1968-75, Walsh County, Grafton, 1975-87; trial judge Devils Lake Sioux, Ft. Totten, 1968-84, Turtle Mountain Chippewa, Belcourt, 1974-87; U.S. magistrate U.S. Dist. Ct., Minnewaukan, 1972-75; Justice of the Peace pro tem Maricopa County, Ariz., 1988-92; instr. Rio Salado C.C., 1992—. Tchr. in Ethiopia, 1958-59. Author: Poetry and Other Poems, 1991. 1st lt. U.S. Army, 1952-54. Recipient Humanitarian award U.S. Cath. Conf., 1978, 82, Right to Know award Sigma Delta Chi, 1980, Spirit of Am. award U.S. Conf. Bishops, 1982. Home: 4353 E Libby St Phoenix AZ 85032-1732 E-mail: tweisenburger@msn.com.

WEISENFELD, ROBERT BELLER, chemist, researcher; b. Newark, July 15, 1953; s. Roland and Ruth Beller Weisenfeld; m. Tahmineh Entessar, Aug. 18, 1984; 1 child, Aryan Entessar. BS in Chemistry, Rensselaer Poly. Inst., 1975; PhD in Chemistry, U. Pitts., 1979. Postdoctoral rschr. in chemistry Yale U., New Haven, 1979-81; chemist Monsanto Co., St. Louis, 1981—. Patentee in field; contbr. articles to profl. jours. Mem.: Am. Chem. Soc. Avocations: swimming, reading. Home: 412 Greenstone Dr Chesterfield MO 63017 Office: Monsanto Co 800 N Lindbergh Blvd Saint Louis MO 63167

WEISER, DAVID JOSEPH, psychiatrist; b. Montreal, Que., Can., June 28, 1945; came to U.S., 1970; s. Louis and Sarah (Richler) W.; m. Estare Kurz, Apr. 22, 1967; children: Philip, Steven. BS, McGill U., 1966, MD, 1970. Diplomate Am. Bd. Psychiatry and Neurology; cert. group therapist. Intern in social pediats. Montefiore Hosp. & Med. Ctr., Bronx, N.Y., 1970-71; resident in psychiatry Albert Einstein Coll. Medicine, Bronx Psychiat. Ctr., 1971-74; psychiatrist Briarcliff Manor, N.Y., 1976—; attending psychiatrist Phelps Meml. Hosp., 1976-92; psychiat. cons. St. Basil Acad., Garrison, NY, 2001—. Cons. psychiatry No. Westchester BOCES, 1980-83, BriarCrest Nursing Home, Briarcliff Manor, 1987-92, Marymount Coll., Tarrytown, N.Y., 1987-92, Bedford (N.Y.) Ctrl. Sch. Dist., 1982-91, Phelps Day Treatment Ctr., Tarrytown, 1978-81; clin. asst. prof. Cornell U. Med. Coll., N.Y.C., 1982-92; dir. Yonkers (N.Y.) Cmty. Svc. Ctr., 1992-96; lectr. N.Y. Hosp., No. Westchester Hosp., Phelps Meml. Hosp., St. Joseph's Hosp., Harlem Valley Psychiat. Ctr., Lawrence Hosp. Fellow: Am. Psychiat. Assn. (sec. Westchester chpt. 1983—86, program coord. 1981—83); mem.: Hudson Ind. Practitioners Assn. (treas. 1988—91), Westchester Group Psychotherapy Soc. (membership chairperson 1994—), Am. Group Psychotherapy Assn., Am. Assn. Psychiat. Adminstrs., Am. Neuropsychiat. Assn. Democrat. Jewish. Avocations: tennis, bicycling, singing, reading, movies. Office: 144 N State Rd Briarcliff Manor NY 10510-1443 Fax: (914) 762-6415. E-mail: deweiser@aol.com.

WEISER, ERIK SAUL, materials research engineer, project manager; b. Quantico, Va., Feb. 8, 1972; s. Sidney Leon and Debbie B. Weiser; m. Andrea Sue Karlsberg, Jan. 31, 1973. BS in Materials Sci. and Engring., Ga. Inst. Tech., 1995, MS in Materials Engring., 1997; postgrad., Coll. of William and Mary. Sr. materials rsch. engr. NASA Langley Rsch. Ctr., Hampton, Va., 1992—. Program mgr. NASA Langley Rsch. Ctr., 1999—. Contbr. articles to profl. jours.; patentee in field. Republican. Avocations: sailing, jogging, weightlifting, traveling. Office: 6A W Taylor St Rm 120B Hampton VA 23681-2102

WEISER, MARTIN JAY, lawyer; b. N.Y.C., Mar. 20, 1943; s. Jack J. and Esther (Attias) w.; m. Pamela D. Morgan, Sept. 4, 1966; children: Nicole, Jennifer. BA, Temple U., 1964; JD, Bklyn. Law Sch., 1967; LLM, NYU, 1975. Cert. tchr., N.Y.; Bar: N.Y. 1967; U.S. Dist. Ct. (ea. dist.) N.Y. 1975, U.S. Dist. Ct. (so. dist.) N.Y., 1990. Assoc. Newman & O'Malley, N.Y.C., 1967-69; ptnr., pres. Raiskin, Weiser & Donofrio, P.C., 1970—. Counsel Metro N.Y. Oldsmobile Dealers Assn., 1988. Bd. dirs. East Hills, N.Y. Assn., 1986-87; v.p. Rio Assn., 1988, bd. dirs., pres., 1988—. Mem. N.Y. County Lawyers Assn., Nassau Bar Assn., N.Y. State Trial Lawyers Assn., Assn. Trial Lawyers of Am., Car and Truck Leasing Assn. Am., Inst. for Safety Analysis, Nob Hill Club (v.p. 1985-86). Office: Weiser & Assocs PC 215 Lexington Ave New York NY 10016-6023

WEISER, PAUL DAVID, manufacturing company executive; b. N.Y.C., May 30, 1936; s. Irving Julius and Rose (Peckerman) W.; m. Paula Lee Block, June 19, 1960; children: Amy Helen, Deborah Susan. BS in Metallurgy, M.I.T., 1959; LL.B. (editor law rev.), U. Calif., Berkeley, 1963. Bar: Calif. 1963. Assoc. firm Mitchell, Silberberg & Knupp, Los Angeles, 1963-68; sec., gen. counsel Hitachi Koki Imaging Solutions, Inc. (formerly Dataproducts Corp.), 1968—, sr. v.p., sec. Calif.; chmn. adv. com. shareholder communications SEC, 1981. Contbr. articles legal publns. Served with USAR, 1959-60. Mem. Am. Bar Assn., Am. Soc. Corp. Secs. Jewish. Office: 1757 Tapo Canyon Rd Simi Valley CA 93063-3391

WEISER, RALPH RAPHAEL, business executive; b. N.Y.C., May 25, 1925; children: Jane, Jeffrey. BA, NYU, 1947; JSD, Harvard U., 1950. Bar: N.Y. 1950. Ptnr. Lotterman & Weiser, Esq., N.Y.C., 1955-64; pres. Dragor Shipping Inc., 1964-65; chmn. Nat. Equipment Rental, 1965-67; exec. v.p. Am. Export Industries, 1967-69; pvt. practice investment, 1970-84; chmn. World Fuel Svc. Corp. (NYSE-INT), Miami, Fla., 1984—. Sgt. USAAF, 1943-45, PTO. Office: World Fuel Svcs Corp 700 S Royal Poinciana Blvd Miami FL 33166-6600

WEISER, SHERWOOD MANUEL, hotel and corporation executive, lawyer; b. Cleve., Mar. 9, 1931; s. Aaron A. and Helen (Scheiner) W.; m. Judith A. Zirkin, July 31, 1955; children: Douglas J., Warren P., Bradley A. BS, Ohio State U., 1952; LLB, Case Western Res. U., 1955. Bar: Ohio 1955. Ptnr. Weiser & Weiser, Attys., Cleve., 1955-65, Weiser & Lefton, Attys., Cleve., 1965-69; chmn., chief exec. officer TCC, Miami, Fla., 1970—. Bd. dirs. United Nat. Bank, Miami, Carnival Cruise Lines, Miami, Wyndham Hotels, Interstate Hotels. Trustee Fla. Internat. U. Found., Miami, 1984-94, U. Miami, 1988—, New World Symphony, Miami, 1987—; trustee, chmn. bd. Ransom-Everglades Sch., Miami, 1974-84; co-chmn. bd. advisors Coconut Grove Playhouse, 1986-90; chmn. Performing Arts Ctr. Found., 1994—. Mem. Am. Hotel and Motel Assn., Cleve. Bar Assn., Soc. of Benchers, Order of Coif. Jewish. Avocations: tennis, sailing, art. Office: Continental Hospitality Holdings 3250 Mary St Miami FL 33133-5232

WEISER, STANLEY, screenwriter; b. N.Y.C., Mar. 15, 1949; BFA in Film, NYU, 1973. Ind. film writer various studios, Calif., 1980—. Screenwriter (films) Coast to Coast, 1980, Project X, 1987, (with Oliver Stone) Wall Street, 1987, (TV movie) Murder in Mississippi, 1990 (Emmy nomination, DGA award), Fatherland, 1994, Witness to the Mob, 1998, (with Phil Alden Robinson) Freedom Song, 2000; script cons. Any Given Sunday, 1999. Co-recipient Outstanding Original TV Movie or Mini-Series, Writers Guild Am. Mem. TV Acad. of Sci. and Arts, Writers Guild Am. West (co-winner award for Freedom Song, 2001), Acad. Motion Picture Arts and Scis. Office: care Writers Guild Am West 7000 W 3d St Los Angeles CA 90048-2420 also: care ICM 8899 Beverly Blvd Los Angeles CA 90048-2412 also: William Morris Agy 151 S El Camino Dr Beverly Hills CA 90212-2704

WEISERT, KENT ALBERT FREDERICK, lawyer; b. Passaic, N.J., Sept. 9, 1949; s. Frederick William and Waleska Anna Sophia (Bischoff) W.; m. Deborah Jean Searing, Mar. 12, 1983; 1 child, Christianna Lillian. BA magna cum laude, Rutgers U., 1971, JD, 1974. Bar: N.J. 1974, U.S. Dist. Ct. N.J. 1974, U.S. Tax Ct. 1975, U.S. Ct. Appeals (3d cir.) 1978, U.S. Supreme Ct. 1987. Adminstrv. asst. trust dept. Howard Savs. Bank, Newark, 1973-74; ptnr. Schwartz, Tobia & Stanziale, Montclair, 1975—2001; pvt. practice law Bloomfield, 2001—. Arbitrator U.S. Dist. Ct., Newark, 1985—. Contbr. chpt. to book New Jersey Transaction Guide, 1987. Pres. ch. coun. Holy Trinity Luth. Ch., Nutley, N.J., 1982-83; mem. Greater N.J. Estate Planning Coun.; trustee, v.p. Oakside Bloomfield Cultural Ctr. Mem. N.J. State Bar Assn., Essex County Bar Assn., Rutgers Law Sch. Alumni Assn., Nat. Trust Hist. Preservation, N.J. Hist. Soc., Phi Beta Kappa, Phi Alpha Theta, Pi Delta Epsilon. Republican. Lutheran. Avocations: classical music, antiques, mil. and gen. history, hist. presevation, tennis. Home: 51 Fairway Bloomfield NJ 07003-5515 Office: Kent A.F. Weisert, Esq. 51 Fairway Bloomfield NJ 07003

WEISFELD, JAY STANLEY, public health physician; b. Milw., Feb. 10, 1947; s. Albert Henry Weisfeld and Evelyn A. Gottlieb. BA in Med. Scis., U. Wis., 1969; MD, Med. Coll. Wis., 1972; MPH, Harvard U., 1977. Intern USPHS, Boston, 1972-73; epidemiologist Ctrs. for Disease Control, Atlanta, 1973-94; cons. Rochester, Vt., 1995—. Instr. Harvard U., Boston, 1996—. Fellow Am. Bd. Preventive Medicine (diplomate), Am. Coll. Preventive Medicine; mem. Phi Eta Sigma. Avocations: forestry, hiking. Home: PO Box 158 Rochester VT 05767-0158 E-mail: Jwvt@aol.com.

WEISFELD, SHELDON, lawyer; b. McAllen, Tex., Feb. 20, 1946; s. Morris and Pauline (Horwitz) W.; m. Eve F. Weisfeld, Jan. 23, 1994; 1 child, Raquel Paolina. BBA, U. Tex., 1967; postgrad., Nat. U. Mex., Mexico City, 1969; JD, U. Houston, 1970. Bar: Tex. 1971, U.S. Dist. Ct. (so. dist.) Tex. 1978, U.S. Dist. Ct. (we. dist.) Tex. 1995, U.S. Ct. Appeals (5th cir.) 1978, U.S. Ct. Appeals (11th cir.) 1981, U.S. Supreme Ct. 1982. Pvt. practice, Austin, Tex., 1973-77; pvt. practice law Brownsville, 1980—. Asst. fed. pub. defender U.S. Dist. Ct. (so. dist.) Tex., Brownsville, 1977-80. Mem. Nat. Assn. Criminal Def. Lawyers, Tex. Criminal Def. Lawyers (dir.), ABA, ACLU Tex. (bd. dirs.), Fed. Bar Assn., State Bar Tex., Cameron County (Tex.) Bar Assn., Hidalgo County (Tex.) Bar Assn., Rotary Club, B'nai B'rith. Democrat. Office: 855 E Harrison St Brownsville TX 78520-7173 Fax: 956-544-7446. E-mail: isweisfeld@aol.com.

WEISFELDT, MYRON LEE, physician, educator; b. Milw., Apr. 25, 1940; s. Simon Charles and Sophia (Price) W.; m. Linda Nan Zaremski, Dec. 29, 1963; children— Ellyn Joy, Lisa Janel, Sara Michelle Student, Northwester U., 1958-60; BA, Johns Hopkins U., 1962, MD, 1965. Intern and resident Columbia-Presbyn. Med. Ctr., N.Y.C., 1965-67; fellow in cardiology Mass. Gen. Hosp., Boston, 1970-72; asst. prof. medicine Johns Hopkins U., Balt., 1972-78, prof. medicine, 1978-91, Robert L. Levy prof. cardiology, 1979-91; Samuel Bard prof. medicine, chair dept. Columbia-Presbyn. Med. Ctr., N.Y.C., 1991—2001; William Osler prof. medicine, dir. dept. medicine Johns Hopkins Med. Sch., 2001—; physician in chief Johns Hopkins Hosp., 2001. Dir. cardiology Johns Hopkins Med. Inst., Balt., 1975-91, Peter Belfer Lab. for Johns Hopkins, Ischemic Heart Disease Spl. Ctr. Rsch., 1977-91; nat. pres. Am. Heart Assn., 1989-90; cardiology adv. com. Nat. Heart, Lung and Blood Inst., 1986-90, chmn., 1988-90; mem. adv. coun. Nat. Inst. on Aging, 1999—. Editor: The Aging Heart, 1980; editorial bd. Jour. Clin. Investigation, 1984-88, Circulation, 1980-86, 88—, Jour. Am. Coll. Cardiology, 1987-93, Jour. Molecular and Cellular Cardiology, 1975-80, 86-89, Circulation Rsch., 1988-94. Served with USPHS, 1967-69 NIH grantee, 1977-91; recipient Golden Heart award Am. Heart Assn., 1998. Fellow AAAS, ACP, Am. Coll. Cardiology; mem. Assn. Univ. Cardiologists, Am. Soc. Clin. Investigation, Assn. Am. Physicians, Assn. Prof. Medicine, Inst. of Medicine, Phi Beta Kappa, Alpha Omega Alpha, Interurban Clin. Club. Jewish. Office: Johns Hopkins Medicine 1830 E Monument St Ste 9026 Baltimore MD 21287 Home: 1002 Rolandvue Ave Baltimore MD 21204 E-mail: mlw5@jhmi.edu.

WEISGALL, JONATHAN MICHAEL, lawyer; b. Balt., Mar. 17, 1949; s. Hugo David and Nathalie (Shulman) W.; m. Ruth Macdonald, June 3, 1979; children: Alison, Andrew, Benjamin. BA, Columbia Coll., 1970; JD, Stanford U., 1973. Bar: D.C. 1974, N.Y. 1974, U.S. Supreme Ct. 1982, Marshall Islands 1983. Law clk. to judge U.S. Ct. Appeals (9th cir.), San Francisco, 1973-74; assoc. Covington & Burling, Washington, 1974-79; from assoc. to ptnr. Ginsburg, Feldman, Weil & Bress, 1980-83; pvt. practice, 1983-99; v.p. Legis. and Regulatory Affairs MidAmerican Energy Holdings Co., 1995—. Adj. prof. Georgetown U. Law Ctr. Author: Operation Crossroads: The Atomic Tests at Bikini Atoll, 1994; exec. prodr. documentary film Radio Bikini. Chmn. bd. dirs. Ctr. for Energy Efficiency and Renewable Techs.; trustee Arena Stage, Washington; bd. dirs. Meet the Composer. Mem. Geothermal Energy Assn. (past v.p., bd. dirs., pres.), Geothermal Resources Coun. (bd. dirs.), Phi Beta Kappa. Jewish. Home: 5309 Edgemoor Ln Bethesda MD 20814-1323 Office: Ste 300 1200 New Hampshire Ave NW Washington DC 20036-6812 E-mail: jweisgall@aol.com.

WEISGARBER, ROBERT LEE, corporate financial executive; b. Rockwood, Tenn., Mar. 21, 1952; s. Robert Lee and Claudia Virginia (McCormick) W.; m. Ann Denise Wall, June 10, 1976. BS in Acctg., Wright State U., Dayton, Ohio, 1976; MBA, Harvard U., 1981. CPA, Tex. Fin. analyst Exxon Co., USA, Houston, 1977-79; cons. Price Waterhouse, 1981-82; asst. treas. Milchem Inc., 1982-86; controller Internat. Paint Co., 1986-93; v.p. adminstrn. Texberry Container Corp., 1993-95; CFO SteelWorks, Inc., 1995-98, DSI Toys, Inc., Houston, 1999—. Served with U.S. Army, 1970-73. Mem. Am. Inst. CPA's, Tex. Soc. CPA's. Avocation: genealogy. Home: 206 Venice St Sugar Land TX 77478-3255 Office: DSI TOYS, INC 1100 W Sam Houston Pky Houston TX 77043 E-mail: rweisgarber@dsitoys.com.

WEISHAUS, JOEL, writer; b. Bklyn., July 11, 1939; s. Leo and Sophie W. Asst. traffic mgr. Monroe Greenthal Advt., N.Y.C., 1958-60; traffic mgr. Richard Meltzer Advt., San Francisco, 1964-65; ednl. materials Cons. Counseling & Resource Ctr., Santa Fe, 1992-2000; advisor web-specific writing Portland (Oreg.) State U., 2001—. Writer-in-residence Helene Wurlitzer Found., 1977-78, 86. Author: Threading the Petrified Glyph, 1997; editor: On the Mesa: An Anthology of Bolinas Writing, 1971, Bits & Snatches: The Selected of Sam Thomas, 1973; translator: Oxherding-A Reworking of the Zen Text, 1971. With U.S. Army, 1962-63. PEN Am. Ctr. grantee, 1971, Mary Roberts Reinhart Found. grantee, 1977, Witter Bynner Found. Poetry grantee, 1990. Buddhist.

WEISKITTEL, RALPH JOSEPH, real estate broker; b. Covington, Ky., Jan. 1, 1924; s. Nelson I. and Hilda (Nieman) W.; m. Audrey Bushelman, June 19, 1948; children— Thomas, Carol Anne, Barbara Jane. Eve. student, Xavier U., Cin., 1946-47. Mem. staff Cin. Enquirer, 1942-43, 45—, home sect. editor, 1958-63, bus. editor, 1963-77; v.p. corp. markets Koetzle Corp. (Realtors), 1977-79; v.p. Devitt and Assocs. (Realtors), 1979-90; v.p. sales and mktg. Toebben Cos., 1990-91; sr. v.p. The Chelsea-Moore Co., 1991-94; v.p. sales Cline Realtors, Cin., 1994-2001; comml. broker Huff Realty, Ft. Mitchell, Ky., 2001—. Dir. New Comty. Developers, Inc. Mem. city council, Ft. Wright, Ky., 1960-68; mem. St. Agnes Parish Council, 1974-77; mem. bishop's adv. council Diocese of Covington. Served with AUS, 1943-46. Mem. Nat. Assn. Real Estate Editors, Soc. Am. Bus. Writers. Clubs: Cin. Athletic. Home: 1571 St Anthony Dr Covington KY 41011-3752 Office: Huff Realty 250 Grandview Dr Fort Mitchell KY 41017

WEISL, EDWIN LOUIS, JR. foundation executive, lawyer; b. N.Y.C., Oct. 17, 1929; s. Edwin L. and Alice (Todriff) W.; m. Barbara Butler, June 12, 1974; 1 child, by previous marriage, Angela Jane. AB, Yale, 1951; LL.B., Columbia, 1956. Bar: N.Y. 1956, D.C. 1968. Assoc. Simpson Thacher & Bartlett, N.Y.C., 1956-64, mem. firm, 1964-65, 69-73; adminstr. parks, recreation and cultural affairs, commr. parks City of N.Y., 1973-75; asst. atty. gen. of U.S. in charge of land and natural resources division, 1965-67; asst. atty. gen. in charge civil div., 1967-69; asst. spl. counsel, preparedness investigating com. U.S. Senate, 1957-58; former pres. Internat. Found. for Art Research. Dir. N.Y. State Dem. campaign, 1964; mem. The 1001, World Wildlife Fund; mem. vis. com. dept. European paintings Met. Mus. Art; bd. dirs. Robert Lehman Found.; mem. corp. Presbyn. Hosp., N.Y.C.; bd. dirs. Old Master Exhbn. Soc. N.Y.; mem. Villa I Tatti Coun, Harvard Ctr. for Renaissance Studies. Lt. (j.g.) U.S. Navy, 1951-53. Mem. Explorers Club, Warrenton Hunt Club, Century Assn., Fauquier Club. Office: 50 E 77th St New York NY 10021-1842

WEISMAN, AVERY, psychiatrist; b. Detroit, Dec. 13, 1913; s. Alec and Sadie Belle (Danto) W.; m. Erma Carman, Dec. 30, 1950 (dec. 1982); m. Lois London, July 8, 1988. AB, U. Mich., 1935, BS, 1936, MD, 1940. Diplomate Am. Bd. Psychiatry and Neurology. Intern Montefiore Hosp., Pitts., 1940-41; resident in Neurology Wayne County Gen., Eloise, Mich., 1941-42; resident in Neuropath and Neurology Boston City Hosp., 1942-44; resident in psychiatry to sr. psychiatrist Mass. Gen. Hosp., Boston, 1944—; instr. to prof. of psychiatry emeritus Med. Sch. Harvard U., 1944—. Disting. vis. prof. Northwestern U. Med. Sch., 1986-90; numerous vis. professorships; cons. Mass. Gen. Hosp., 1995. Author: Existential Core of Psychoanalysis, 1965, On Dying and Denying, 1972, Psychological Autopsy, 1968, Realization of Death, 1975, Coping Capacity, 1984, Coping with Cancer, 1989, Vulnerable Self, 1993, (novel) The Next Taboo, 2002; contbr. articles to profl. jours. Recipient Deutsch award Boston Psychoanalytic soc., 1950, Sutherland award Sloan Kettering Cancer Ctr., 1982, Disting. Svc. award Yeshiva U., 1983, Avery Weisman Lectureship Found. of Thanatology, 1988, Pollin Found. award 1989, Hackett award Acad. Psychosomatic Medicine, 1992. Fellow Am. Psychiat. Assn.; mem. Am. Psychoanalytic Assn., Am. Acad. Neurology, Psychosomatic Acad., Am. Assn. Suicidology (pres. 1977, Dublin award). Jewish. Home: 7476 E Beryl Ave Scottsdale AZ 85258-1019 E-mail: averydw@aol.com.

WEISMAN, GARY ANDREW, biochemist; b. Bklyn., June 18, 1951; s. Joseph Herman and Elaine (Melman) W.; m. Sandra Kay Hille, Aug. 4, 1979; children: Laura Joanne, Pamela Michelle, Veronica Evelyn. BS, Polytechnic U., 1972; postgrad., U. Bordeaux, France, 1972-74; PhD, U. Nebr., 1980. Postdoctoral rsch. assoc. Cornell U., N.Y.C., 1980-85; asst. prof. U. Mo., Columbia, 1985-92, assoc. prof., 1992-98, prof., 1998—. Spl. reviewer NIH; reviewer NSF, Jour. Membrane Biology and Eur. Jour. Cancer, Am. Jour. Physiology. Contbr. articles to profl. jours. Grantee USDA, 1987—, NIH, 1988—, CF Found., 1994—, Am. Diabetes, 1995—. Mem. AAAS, Am. Chem. Soc., Am. Soc. Biochem. and Molecular Biology, Am. Diabetes Assn., Am. Heart Assn., N.Y. Acad. Scis. Home: 1804 University Ave Columbia MO 65201-6004 Office: U Mo Dept Biochemistry M121 Med Scis Bldg Columbia MO 65212-0001 E-mail: weismang@missouri.edu.

WEISMAN, IRVING, social worker, educator; b. N.Y.C., May 6, 1918; s. Max and Sadie (Berkowitz) W.; m. Cyrille Gold, May 1, 1941; children: Seth, Adam. BS, CCNY, 1939; MS, U. Buffalo, 1942; Ed.D., Columbia U., 1962. Cert. social worker N.Y. State. Caseworker Nat. Refugee Service, N.Y.C., 1941; warden's asst. Fed. Detention Hdqrs., Bur. Prisons, U.S. Dept. Justice, 1942-43; psychiat. social worker to chief social worker VA, Camden and Union City, N.J., 1946-49; case supr. Altro Health and Rehab. Service, N.Y., 1949-50; field instr., lectr. Columbia U. Sch. Social Work, 1950-57, assoc. prof., 1957-62, prof., 1962-84, prof. emeritus, 1984, adj. prof., 1984, acting dean, 1964-65; assoc. dean Hunter Coll. Sch. Social Work, 1967-69; exec. officer doctoral program social work Grad. Ctr. CUNY, 1975-78; clin. practice William Alanson White Inst., 1976-79. Vis. prof. Sch. Social Work Barry U., 1984—85; adj. prof. Sch. Social Work San Diego State U., 1988—90; curriculum chmn. Inst. Continuing Learning U. S.D., 1990—2000; UN adv. on social welfare to Ceylon, Sri Lanka, 1963—64; sr. Simon rsch. fellow U. Manchester, England, 1970—71; cons. U.S. Office Juvenile Delinquency and Youth Devel., U.S. Children's Bur., NIMH, NIDA, HEW, N.Y.C. Dept. Pers., Westchester County (N.Y.) Dept. Mental Health, Cmty. Svc. Soc., Coun. Social Work Edn., Mobilization for Youth, N.Y.C., Universidad Católica Madre y Maestra, Santo Domingo, Dominican Republic, 1983—84, United Jewish Appeal-Fedn. Jewish Philanthropies of N.Y.C., 1986—87; condr. continuing edn. workshops, various univs. Contbr. articles to profl. jours., also monographs. With U.S. Army Air Corps., 1943-46. HEW and HHS grantee, 1961-62, 64-76, 77-81 Mem. Inst. Continued Learning, U.C. San Diego. Home: 4612 Monongahela St San Diego CA 92117-2415

WEISMAN, JOEL, nuclear engineering educator, engineering consultant; b. N.Y.C., July 15, 1928; s. Abraham and Ethel (Marcus) W.; m. Bernice Newman, Feb. 6, 1955; 1 child, Jay (dec.) B.Ch.E., CCNY, 1948; MS, Columbia U., 1949; PhD, U. Pitts, 1968. Registered profl. engr., N.Y. Plant engr. Etched Products, N.Y.C., 1950-51; from jr. engr. to assoc. engr. Brookhaven Nat. Lab., Upton, N.Y., 1951-54; from engr. to fellow engr. Westinghouse Nuclear Energy Systems, Pitts., 1954-59, from fellow engr. to mgr. thermal and hydraulic analysis, 1960-68; sr. engr. Nuclear Devel. Assocs., White Plains, N.Y., 1959-60; assoc. prof. nuclear engring. U. Cin., 1968-72, prof. nuclear engring., 1972-96, dir. nuclear engring. program, 1977-86, dir. lab. basic and applied nuclear research, 1984-94, prof. emeritus nuclear engring., 1996—. Co-author: Thermal Analysis of Pressurized Water Reactors, 1970, 2d edit., 1979, 3rd edit., 1996, Introduction to Optimization Theory, 1973, Modern Power Plant Engineering, 1985; editor: Elements of Nuclear Reactor Design, 1977, 2d edit., 1983; contbr. tech. articles to profl. jours.; patentee in field. Mem. Cin. Environ. Adv. Council, 1976-78; mem. Cin. Asian Art Soc., 1977—, v.p., 1980-82, pres., 1982-84; mem. exec. bd. Air Pollution League Greater Cin., 1980-90. Sr. NATO fellow, Winfrith Lab., U.K. Atomic Energy Authority, 1972; sr. fellow Argonne Nat. Lab., Ill., 1982; NSF research grantee, 1974-78, 82-85, 86-89; recipient Dean's award U. Cin. Coll. Engring., 1987. Fellow Am. Nuclear Soc. (v.p. Pitts. sect. 1957-58, mem. exec. com. thermal-hydraulics div. 1989-92); mem. Am. Inst. Chem. Engrs., Sigma Xi Democrat. Jewish. Avocation: Japanese art. Home: 3419 Manor Hill Dr Cincinnati OH 45220-1522 Office: U Cin Dept Mech Ind & Nuclear Engr Cincinnati OH 45221-0001

WEISMAN, JOHN, author; b. N.Y.C., Aug. 1, 1942; s. Abner I Weisman and Syde (Lubowe) Kremer; m. Susan Lee Povenmire, Feb. 12, 1983. AB, Bard Coll., 1964. Mng. editor Coast mag., Los Angeles, 1969-70; staff writer Rolling Stone, San Francisco, 1971, Detroit Free Press, 1971-73; assoc. editor TV Guide, Radnor, Pa., 1973-77, bur. chief Washington, 1977-89; sr. fellow Annenberg Washington program Northwestern U., 1989-91. Author: (nonfiction) Guerrilla Theatre, 1973, Shadow Warrior, 1989, Rogue Warrior, 1992 (No 1 bestseller NY Times Book Rev), (novels) Evidence, 1980, Watchdogs, 1983, Blood Cries, 1987, Rogue Warrior II, Red Cell, 1994 (bestseller NY Times), Green Team, 1995 (bestseller NY Times), Task Force Blue, 1996 (bestseller NY Times), (anthology) Unusual Suspects, 1996, Designation Gold, 1997 (bestseller NY Times), The Best American Mystery Stories of 1995, 1995, SEAL Force Alpha, 1998 (bestseller NY Times), Option Delta, 1999, Echo Platoon, 2000, Detachment Bravo, 2001. Active Clarke County Rep Comt, Va. Mem.: AFIO, Internat. Defensive Pistol Assn., Bard Coll. Alumni Assn., Naval and Mil. Club (London), Cosmos Club, Army and Navy Club. E-mail: jweisman@ix.netcom.com.

WEISMAN, LORENZO DAVID, investment banker; b. Guatemala, Apr. 22, 1945; came to U.S., 1957; s. Eduardo and Suzanne (Loeb) Weisman; m. Danielle Maysonnave, June 22, 1971; children: Melissa Anne, Alexia Maria, Thomas Alexander. BA in History and Lit. cum laude, Harvard U., 1966; postgrad., Conservatoire Nat. D'Art Dramatique, Paris, 1966-71; MBA in Fin., Columbia U., 1973. V.p. Dillon, Read & Co., Inc., N.Y.C., 1977-80, sr. v.p., 1980-82, mng. dir. London, 1982-84; pres., chief exec. officer Dillon Read Ltd., 1984-93; head Internat. Dillon Read & Co., N.Y.C., 1993—97; head L.Am. corp. fin. UBS Warburg, 1997—2001; co-founder & mng. mem. Hill St. Capital LLC, 2002—. Com. univ. resources Harvard U., 1991, mem. adv. com. David Rockefeller Ctr. for L.Am. Studies, 1995—; mem. internat. bd. overseers Columbia Bus. Sch., 1992; mem. bd. overseers Institut Français/Alliance Française, N.Y., 1995—. Trustee Institut Français/Alliance Française, N.Y.C., 1995. Mem. Harvard Club (N.Y.C.), Travelers Club (Paris), Knickerbocker Club (N.Y.C.).

WEISMAN, MARTIN JEROME, manufacturing company executive; b. N.Y.C., Aug. 22, 1930; s. Lewis E. and Estelle (Scherer) W.; m. Sherrie Cohen, Jan. 27, 1952; children: Jane Dory, Andrea Sue, Amy Ellen. B in Chem. Engring., N.Y.U., 1951. Sr. chem. engr. Ideal Toy Corp., Hollis, N.Y., 1951-57; research chemist Chesebrough-Ponds, Stamford, Conn., 1957-62; mgr. nail products lab. Max Factor and Co., Hollywood, Calif., 1962-81; v.p., tech. dir. Sher-Mar Cosmetics div. Weisman Industries, Inc., Canoga Park, 1981-97; owner Weisman Industries, Inc., Westlake Vlg., CA, 1997-2000; ret., 2000. Patentee in field. Mem. Soc. Cosmetic Chemists, Los Angeles Soc. Coatings Tech., Am. Chem. Soc. Home: Weisman Industries 32132 Canyon Crest Ct Westlake Village CA 91361-4800 E-mail: shermar@worldnet.att.net.

WEISMAN, MELODY, guidance counselor; b. N.Y.C., Apr. 1, 1945; d. Harold and Arlene (Plumb) Keller; m. Richard Nathan Weisman, Jan. 23, 1971; children: David, Peter. BA, SUNY, Cortland, 1967; MEd, Lehigh U., 1981. Cert. secondary English tchr., NY.; cert. guidance counselor, secondary English tchr., Pa. Tchr. Vitalistic Therapeutic, Allentown, Pa., 1986-90; guidance counselor Saucon Valley Sch. Dist., Hellertown, 1990—2000, spl. edn. counselor, 2000—. Contbg. author: Make It, 1981. Sec. bd. dirs. Bethlehem (Pa.) Area Pub. Libr., 1991-94. Mem. NEA, Pa. Sch. Counselors Assn., Pa. Edn. Assn., Am. Counseling Assn., Saucon Valley Edn. Assn. Home: 2320 Black River Rd Bethlehem PA 18015-5402

WEISMAN, PAUL HOWARD, lawyer; b. Los Angeles, Oct. 14, 1957; s. Albert L. and Rose J. (Zimman) W.; m. Allison L. Minas, Oct. 19, 1985. BA cum laude, U. Calif., Davis, 1979; JD, Loyola U., Los Angeles, 1982. Bar: Calif. 1982. Tax atty. legis. and regulations div. office of chief counsel Dept. of Treasury IRS, Washington, 1982-83, tax atty. dist. counsel/office of chief counsel L.A., 1983-87; tax atty. Law Offices of Paul H. Weisman, 1987—. Registered players contract rep. Nat. Football League Players Assn. Co-author BNA Tax Mgmt. Portfolio 638 Federal Tax Collection Procedure, publs. in field. Participant vol. Income Tax Assistance, L.A., 1981-83; alt. mem. Los Angeles County Assessment Appeals Bd. Mem. San Fernando Valley Bar Assn., Beverly Hills Bar Assn. (co-chmn. tax ct. prose program). Republican. Avocations: sports, running, art, music, politics.

WEISMAN, R(OBERT) BRUCE, physical chemist, educator; b. Balt., Nov. 23, 1950; s. Samuel and Eva (Abramson) W.; m. Kathleen Mary Beckingham, July 25, 1986; 1 child, Caroline Mary. BA, Johns Hopkins U., 1971; PhD, U. Chgo., 1977. Postdoctoral fellow U. Pa., Phila., 1977-79; asst. prof. Rice U., Houston, 1979-84, assoc. prof., 1984-93, prof., 1993—. Mem. editl. bd. Rev. Sci. Instruments, 1991-93; contbr. more than 75 articles to profl. and sci. jours. Grad. fellow Fannie and John Hertz Found., 1973-76, NSF, 1971-73; postdoctoral fellow NSF, 1977-78; rsch. fellow Alfred P. Sloan Found., 1985-89. Mem. AAAS, Am. Chem. Soc., Am. Phys. Soc., Electrochem. Soc. (mem.-at-large Fullerenes Divsn. 2000—), Sigma Xi. Office: Rice U Dept Chemistry Houston TX 77005 E-mail: weisman@rice.edu.

WEISMANN, DONALD LEROY, art educator, artist, filmmaker, writer; b. Milw., Oct. 12, 1914; s. Friedrich Othello and Stela Priscilla (Custer) W.; m. M. Virginia Stant; children: Anne Wilder, Christopher Thomas. BS, U. Wis., Milw., 1935; PhM, U. Wis., Madison, 1940; PhD, Ohio State U., 1950. Asst. prof. art Ill. State U., Normal, 1940-42, 47-48, Wayne U., Detroit, 1949-51; prof., head dept. art U. Ky., Lexington, 1951-54; prof., chmn. dept. art U. Tex., Austin, 1954-58, Univ. prof. arts, 1959-81, prof. emeritus, 1981—. Cons. Ford Found., N.Y.C., 1958, 66, U.S. Nat. Com. UNESCO, 1953, Rockefeller Found., 1956, Nat. Council Arts., 1966-72; spl. cons. USIS, Forence, Italy, 1961-62 Author: Language and Visual Form, 1968, Visual Arts as Human Experience, 1970, Duncan Phyfe & Drum, 1984, Follow the Bus with the Greek License Plates, 1981, Frank Reaugh, Painter to the Longhorns, 1985, The Stuff of Stories, 1999, Artifacts, Fictions and Memory, 2001; contbr. articles, poems, stories and revs. to profl. jours.; painter, collagist one-man shows, Cushman Gallery, Houston, Nye Gallery, Dallas, Petite Gallery, N.Y.C., Art Mus. U. N. Mex., group shows, Bocur Gallery, N.Y.C., Chgo. Art Inst., Dallas Mus. Fine Arts, Rockefeller Ctr., N.Y.C., Vanucci Gallery, Pistoia, Italy, Villa Monte Carlo Chapala, Jalisco, Mexico; film-maker numerous productions. Served to lt. (j.g.) USN, 1942-45, PTO. Recipient Letter of Commendation Pres. U.S., 1972; honoree for book Some Folks Went West, 12th Ann. Writers Conf., Austin, 1960; grantee U. Tex. Rsch. Inst., Italy, Eng., 1961-62, 71, Pub. Broadcast Corp., 1970, 72; named fine arts scholar Harvard U., 1941 Mem. Nat. Humanities Faculty Home: 4513 Edgemont Dr Austin TX 78731-5223 Office: Am Studies U Tex Austin TX 78712

WEISMANTEL, GREGORY NELSON, management consultant and software executive; b. Houston, Sept. 8, 1940; s. Leo Joseph and Ellen Elizabeth (Zudis) W.; m. Marilyn Ann Fanger, June 18, 1966; children: Guy Gregory, Christopher Gregory, Andrea Rose. BA in English, U. Notre Dame, 1962; MBA in Internat. Bus., Loyola U., Chgo., 1979. With mgmt. staff Gen. Foods Corp., White Plains, N.Y., 1966-80; pres., chief exec. officer Manor House Foods, Inc., Addison, Ill., 1980-82, Weismantel & Assocs., Downers Grove, 1982-84; v.p. perishable div. Profl. Marketers, Inc., Lombard, 1984-86, group v.p. sales and mktg. services, dir. corp. strategy, 1986-87; v.p. mng. prin. CPG Industry, Louis A. Allen Assoc. Inc., Palo Alto, Calif., 1987-88; pres., chief exec. officer The Vista Tech. Group, Ltd., St. Charles, Ill., 1989-2000, chmn. bd., 2001—. Bd. dirs. Epicurean Foods, Ltd., Chgo.; pres., CEO The Vista Tech. Group, Ltd., The Vista Mgmt. Group. Chmn. fin. St. Edward's High Sch. Jubilee, Elgin, Ill., 1982-85; bd. dirs. Dist. 301 Sch. Bd., Burlington, Ill., 1980-84, St. Edward's Found., Elgin, 1982—. Capt. U.S. Army, 1962-66. Recipient ICP/Chgo. Software Assoc. Re-Engring. award, 1994-96; State of Ill. grantee, 1989, Build Ill. Investment Fund. Mem. Grocery Mfg. Sales Execs., Chgo. Software Assn., Chg. C. of C. (small bus. com.). Clubs: Merchandising Execs., Food Products, Am. Mktg. (Chgo.). Roman Catholic. *Success can only occur when a person realizes that life is not a rehearsal.*

WEISNER, DAVID, illustrator; b. Bridgewater, N.J. m. Kim Khang; 2 children. BFA in Illustration, R.I. Sch. Design. Illustrator Houghton Mifflin, N.Y.C. Author (illustrator): Freefall, 1988 (Caldecott Honor, 1989), Hurricane, 1990, Tuesday, 1991 (Caldecott medal, 1992), The Loathsome Dragon, 1987, Moo, 1996, Sector 7, 1997. Home: 730 E Hadley St Milwaukee WI 53212*

WEISPFENNIG, KLAUS, chemical engineer, educator; b. Gelsenkirchen, Germany, Jan. 25, 1962; came to U.S., 1990; s. Alfred Sigfried August and Gertrud Elsbeth (Nispel) W.; m. Maria-Victoria Tejada-Simon, May 15, 1996. BS, RWTH, Aachen, Germany, 1990, MS, 1991; PhD, Mich. State U., 1997. Rsch. asst. RWTH, Aachen, 1985-89, Mich. State U., East Lansing, 1990-96, vis. rsch. assoc., 1997-98; devel. engr. Baker Petrolite-Baker Hughes, Sugarland, Tex., 1998—. Cons. Ital Traco N.Am., Inc., East Lansing, 1996. Editor, translator: Fruit Distillation Today: A Guideline for Small Distilleries, 1997; contbr. articles to profl. jours. Mem. AIChemE. Avocations: ice hockey, squash, tennis, outdoor activities. Office: Baker Petrolite-Baker Hughes 12645 W Airport Blvd Sugar Land TX 77478-6120 E-mail: Klaus.Weispfennig@bakerpetrolite.com.

WEISPFENNING, JOHN THOMAS, communications educator, consultant; b. Cooperstown, N.D., July 30, 1960; s. Walter William and Edna Margaret (Gums) W.; m. Christine M. Kelly, June 15, 1991. BS, Moorhead State U., 1982; MS, N.D. State U., 1985; PhD, Purdue U., 1992. Asst. program dir. Sta. KVOX, Moorhead, Minn., 1981-82; announcer Sta. KQWB, Fargo, N.D., 1982-84; sta. mgr. Sta. KCSD, Sioux Falls, S.D., 1985-88; instr. mass comm. Sioux Falls Coll., 1985-88; instr. interviewing Purdue U., West Lafayette, Ind., 1988-91; vis. lectr. Ind. U., Indpls., 1991-92; asst. prof. U. Maine, Orono, 1992-95; assoc. prof., dept. chair Otterbein Coll., Westerville, Ohio, 1995—, chair comm. dept., 1999—. Prodr., host (radio program) South Dakota Focus, 1985-88. Mem. Assn. Edn. in Journalism and Mass Comm., Broadcast Edn. Assn., Ctrl. States Comm. Assn., Speech Comm. Assn. Ohio (exec. dir. 1996-99). Democrat. Presbyterian. Avocations: reading, fitness, music. E-mail: jweispfenning@otterbein.edu.

WEISS, ALAN, musician, educator, clinician; b. Boston, July 9, 1954; s. Daniel and Riva (Adlerstein) W.; m. Ann Marie Rosandich, Oct. 11, 1986. MusB, Boston U., 1977, MusM, 1986. Prin. flutist Va. Symphony, Norfolk, 1977-78; sub-prin. flutist Iceland Nat. Symphony, Rekjavik, 1978-79; co-prin. flutist State Orch. of Mex., Toluca, 1981-82, Mexico City Philharm., 1982-84, Boston Classical Orch., 1988—; prof. flute, chamber music Boston U., 1987-96; from flute faculty to dir. Tanglewood Inst. Boston U., Lenox, Mass., 1987-94, artistic dir., 1996-94; artist-in-residence XIV Schubert Internat. Music Festival and Competition, Ovada, Italy. Solo flutist (world premier performances and on Nat. Pub. Radio) Fall of the House of Usher, 1988, Orphee by Phillip Glass, 1993; recitalist Sta. WGBH-FM, 1988—; soloist Romanian Radio Orch., 1995; soundtrack (PBS movie) Edgar Allan Poe, 1995; solo performance for compact disc, Orchard #494, 1998, Albany Records #457, 2001; rec. on Carlton Classics. Trustee Boston Classical Orch., 1989-93, founder youth competition, 1990-98. 1st Am. flutist to solo with George Enesco Philharmonic, Bucharest, Romania. Mem. Boston Musician's Assn., Pi Kappa Lambda. Republican. Jewish. Avocations: reading, travel. Fax: 617-361-9270. E-mail: alanflute@yahoo.com.

WEISS, ALAN ARTHUR, mathematician, researcher; b. Cleve., Dec. 5, 1955; s. Leonard Benjamin and Annabelle Weiss; m. Judy Brenda Goldhirsch, July 1, 1978; children: Benjamin Leonard, David Charles. BS in Math., BS in Physics, Case Western Res. U., 1976; MS in Math., NYU, 1979, PhD in Math., 1981. Mem. tech. staff Bell Labs., Murray Hill, NJ, 1981—2001, disting. mem. tech. staff, 2001—. Lectr. in field. Co-author: Large Deviations for Performance Analysis, 1995. Recipient Best Paper award, ACM Sigmetrics, 1995. Jewish. Achievements include patents pending for voice/data multiplexer; parallel event-driven simulation; optical cross-connect optimization. Avocations: cycling, reading, magic, singing. Office: Bell Labs Room 2 C-318 600 Mountain Ave Murray Hill NJ 07974

WEISS, ALLAN JOSEPH, transport company executive, lawyer; b. Boston, Nov. 1, 1932; s. Mark and Eve S. (Kane) W.; m. Sherrill Roecker, Feb. 18, 1973; children: Stephanie Eve, Mark Allan. BS, U.S. Mcht. Marine Acad., 1955; JD, Cornell U., 1961. Bar: N.Y. 1961, D.C. 1962, Calif. 1965, U.S. Supreme Ct. 1965. Trial atty. admiralty and shipping U.S. Dept. Justice, 1961-67, chief trial atty. admiralty office, 1967-74; Pacific counsel Sea-Land Service, Inc., Oakland, Calif., 1974-76, dep. gen. counsel, 1977-78, gen. counsel, 1978-82, sec., 1979-82; assoc. gen. counsel Sea-Land Industries, 1979-82; pres. Freights Unltd., Inc., 1982—; gen. counsel Toledo, Peoria & Western Rwy., 1991-96. Adj. prof. law McGeorge Sch. Law, 1974-76 Served with U.S. Navy, 1956-57. Mem. Fed. Bar Assn., Calif. Bar Assn., D.C. Bar Assn., San Francisco Bar Assn., Maritime Law Assn. U.S., Cornell U. Law Assn., Kings Point Alumni Assn. Home: 89 Loft Dr Martinsville NJ 08836-2246 Office: Freights Unlimited Inc 89 Loft Dr Martinsville NJ 08836-2246 E-mail: allanw@bellatlantic.net.

WEISS, ALVIN HARVEY, chemical engineering educator, catalysis researcher and consultant; b. Phila., Apr. 28, 1928; s. Louis and Helen F. (Wilinsky) W.; children: Linda S., Louis B.; m. Devorah Schwartz, June 10, 1979 BSChemE, U. Pa., 1949, PhD in Phys. Chemistry, 1965; MSChemE, Newark Coll. Engring., 1955. Registered profl. engr., Mass., Del. Chem. engr. Fiber Chem. Corp., Cliffwood, N.J., 1949-51, Colgate-Palmolive Co., Jersey City, 1953-55, Houdry Process and Chems. Co., Linwood, Pa., 1956-63; rsch. assoc., lectr. U. Pa., Phila., 1963-66; prof. chem. engring. Worcester (Mass.)

Poly. Inst., Mass., 1966-94, prof. emeritus, 1994—. Vis. prof. Northeastern U., Boston, Mass., 2000-; NASA-ASEE summer faculty fellow Stanford U., Ames Research Ctr., 1967, 68; affiliate scientist Worcester Found. Exptl. Biology, 1972-74; Fulbright-Hays sr. faculty fellow to dept. chem. engring. Ben-Gurion U. of Negev, Beersheva, Israel, 1973-74, vis. prof. chem. engring., 1974; U.S. coord. U.S.-USSR Coop. Sci. Program in Chem. Catalysis, Topic IV, 1973-76, prin. investigator (with M.M. Sakharov), 1976-78; prin. investigator (with K.I. Ione) U.S.-USSR Coop. Sci. Program in Chem. Catalysis, Topic III, 1978-80; Fulbright-Hays vis. lectr. dept. chem. engring. Mid. East Tech. U., Ankara, Turkey, 1974, vis. prof., 1991; vis. rsch. scientist dept. organic chemistry Weizmann Inst., Rehovoth, Israel, 1974; vis. lectr. Inst. Isotopes and Ctrl. Inst. Chemistry, Hungarian Acad. Scis., Budapest, 1976; vis. prof. Inst. Cultural Rels. and Inst. Isotopes, Hungarian Acad. Scis., 1978, 80; UNIDO chief tech. advisor to Petrochem. Complex of Bahia Blanca, Argentina, 1980; sr. rsch. fellow chem. sys. lab. Army Chem. Ctr., Md., 1981; UNIDO expert in chem. process devel. Rsch. Inst. for Chem. Industry, Beijing, Peoples Republic of China, 1982; UNIDO expert in catalysis to YARPET Petrochem. Complex, Yarimca, Turkey, 1986-87; bd. dirs. U.S. com. for sci. coop. with Vietnam; vis. lectr. Nat. Ctr. for Sci. Rsch., Hanoi, Inst. of Indsl. Chemistry, Ho Chi Minh City, 1986; vis. prof., vis. scientist Ctr. for Advanced Microgravity Materials Processing, Northeastern U., Boston, 2000—. Translator: (with M. Delleo, G. Dembinski and J. Happel) Catalysis by Non-Metals (O.V. Krylov), 1970; contbr. articles to profl. jours.; patentee in field. With U.S. Army, 1951-53. Named Outstanding Rschr. and Creative Scholar, Worcester Poly. Inst., 1984; recipient Sci. Achievement award Worcester Engring. Soc., 1984; rsch. grantee NSF, PRF, NASA, DOD, DOE. Fellow AIChE (rsch. com. 1968-80, symposia chmn. 1973-84); mem. AAUP, Catalysis Soc. (bd. dirs., sec. 1968-88), Catalysis Soc. New England (founding pres. 1967-68, bd. dirs. 1968—), Am. Chem. Soc. (New England petroleum divsn. rep. 1970-88, session chmn. 1973—), Deutsche Gesellschaft für Chemische Apparatewesen.

WEISS, ANDRE, psychiatrist; s. Melchior and Magda (Sziklas) W.; m. Renee Veit, 1952; children: Madeleine Eve Fagan, Stephen Philip. BS, U. Geneva, 1950, MD, 1954. Intern Sewickley Valley (Pa.) Hosp., 1955-56; resident Ctrl. Islip (N.Y.) State Hosp., 1956; pvt. practice in gen. medicine Aberdeen, Md., 1957-64; resident in psychiatry Sheppard Pratt Hosp., Balt., 1964-67; psychiatrist out patient dept., instr. psychiatry John Hopkins Med. Sch., 1966-67; med. officer WHO, Geneva, 1968-76; staff psychiatrist Sheppard Pratt Hosp., Balt., 1977-78, Taylor Manor Hosp., Ellicott City, 1984-93, Cmty. Mental Health Ctr., Catonsville, 1991-2000; pvt. practice Geneva, 1978-84, Columbia, Md., 1991—, Silver Spring, 1995—2001. Author: Typhus in Concentration Camps (Brit. Imperial War Mus. recognition); exhibitor stamp collection (Grand award), 1964. Mem. Am. Psychiat. Assn.

WEISS, ANTONIO FRANCESCO, investment banker; b. N.Y.C., Sept. 28, 1966; s. Piero Ernesto and Carole Severson W.; m. Susannah Gordon Hunnewell, June 5, 1993; 1 child, NiccolÒ Francesco Hunnewell. BA, Yale U., 1988; MBA, Harvard U., 1994. Sr. editor The Paris Rev., N.Y.C., 1988-90; fin. analyst Donaldson, Lufkin & Jenrette, 1991-92; assoc. Lazard, Frères & Co., LLC, 1994-96; v.p. Lazard, Freres & Co., LLC, 1997-98, mng. dir., 1999—. Bd. dirs. Lazard Vitale Borghesi SpA, Milan; adv. ed. The Paris Rev., N.Y.C. Loeb fellow Harvard U., Cambridge, Mass., 1994, Baker scholar, 1994. Mem. Racquet and Tennis Club (N.Y.C.), Links Club (N.Y.C.). Home: 1165 5th Ave New York NY 10029-6931 Office: Lazard Freres & Co LLC 30 Rockefeller Plz New York NY 10112-0002

WEISS, ARMAND BERL, economist, association management executive; b. Richmond, Va., Apr. 2, 1931; s. Maurice Herbert and Henrietta (Shapiro) W.; m. Judith Bernstein, May 18, 1957; children: Jo Ann Michele, Rhett Louis. BS in Econs., Wharton Sch. Fin., U. Pa., 1953, MBA, 1954; DBA, George Washington U., 1971. Cert. assn. exec. Officer USN, 1954-65; spl. asst. to auditor gen. Dept. Navy, 1964-65; sr. economist Ctr. for Naval Analyses, Arlington, Va., 1965-68; project dir. Logistics Mgmt. Inst., Washington, 1968-74; dir. systems integration Fed. Energy Adminstrn., 1974-76; sr. economist Nat. Commn. Supplies and Shortages, 1976-77; tech. asst. to v.p. Sys. Planning Corp., 1977-78; chmn. bd., pres., CEO Assns. Internat. Inc., 1978—; chmn. bd. dirs., CFO Rail Digital Corp., 1988-91; v.p., treas. Tech. Frontiers, Inc., 1978-80; sr. v.p. Weiss Pub. Co., Inc., Richmond, Va., 1960—. V.p. Condo News Internat., Inc., 1981; v.p., bd. dirs. Leaders Digest Inc., 1987-88; sec., bd. dirs. Mgmt. Svcs. Internat. Inc., 1987-88; adj. prof. Am. U., 1979-80, 89-90; vis. lectr. George Washington U., 1971; assoc. prof. George Mason U., 1984; treas. Fairfax County (Va.) Dem. Com., 1992-94, assisted Pres. Clinton, v.p. Gore transition at White House, 1993; pres. Washington Mgmt. and Bus. Assn., 1993—; chmn. U.S. del., session chmn. NATO Symposium on Cost-Benefit Analysis, The Hague, Netherlands, 1969, NATO Conf. on Operational Rsch. in Indsl. Systems, St. Louis, France, 1970; pres. Nat. Coun. Assns. Policy Scis., 1971-77; chmn. adv. group Def. Econ. Adv. Coun. Dept. Def., 1970-74; resident assoc. Smithsonian Instn., 1973—; expert cons. Dept. State, GAO; undercover agt. FBI, 3 yrs. Co-editor: Systems Analysis for Social Problems, 1970, The Relevance of Economic Analysis to Decision Making in the Department of Defense, 1972, Toward More Effective Public Programs: The Role of Analysis and Evaluation, 1975; editor: Cost-Effectiveness Newsletter, 1966-70, Operations Rsch./Systems Analysis Today, 1971-73, Operation Rsch./Mgmt. Sci. Today, 1974-87, Feedback, 1969-93, Condo World, 1981, The Democrat, 1997-2000; assoc. editor Ops. Rsch., 1971-75; pub. IEEE Scanner, 1983-89, Spl. and Individual Needs Tech. (SAINT) Newsletter, 1987-88, Jour. Parametrics, 1984-88. Del. Pres.'s Mid-Century White House Conf. on Children and Youth, 1950; scoutmaster Japan, U.S.; leader World Jamborees, France, Can., U.S., 1945-61; Eagle scout, 1947; U.S. del. Internat. Conf. on Ops. Rsch., Dublin, Ireland, 1972; organizing com. Internat. Cost-Effectiveness Symposium, Washington, 1970; spkr. Internat. Conf. Inst. Mgmt. Scis., Tel Aviv, 1973, del., Mexico City, 1967; mem. bus. com. Nat. Symphony Orch., 1968-70, Washington Performing Arts Soc., 1974-88; bus. mgr. Nat. Lyric Opera Co., 1983—, Internat. Assn. Med. Sci. Educators, 1997-98, Data Adminstrv. Mgmt. Assn. Nat. Capital, 1992—, Potomac Pedalers Touring Club, 1990—, Am. Friends of London Sch. Econs., 1988-97; mem. mktg. com. Fairfax Symphony Orch., 1984-91; bd. dirs. McLean (Va.) Orch., 1992-94; exec. com. Mid Atlantic coun. Union Am. Hebrew Congregations, 1970-79, treas., 1974-79, mem. nat. MUM com., 1974-79; mem. dist. com. Boy Scouts Am., 1972-75; bd. dirs. Nat. Coun. Career Women, 1975-79, Va. Acad. Scis., 1991—; pres. Jewish temple, 1970-72; adminstr. Daniel Heumann Fund for Spinal Cord Rsch., 2000—; treas. Quest for the Cure, 2000--. Recipient Silver medal 50-yard free style and half mile swimming meet. No. Va. Sr. Olympics, 1990, Gold, Silver, Bronze medals, 2001. Fellow AAAS, Washington Acad. Scis. (gov. 1981-92, v.p. 1987-88, pres.-elect 1989-90, pres. 1990-91, past pres. 1991-92), Ops. Rsch. Soc. Am. (chmn. meetings com. 1969-70, chmn. cost-effectiveness sect. 1969-70), Washington Ops. Rsch./Mgmt.. Sci. Coun. (editor newsletter 1969-93, sec. 1971-72, pres. 1973-74, trustee 1975-77, bus. mgr. 1976-93, Moving Spirit award 1994), Internat. Inst. Strategic Studies (London), Am. Soc. Assn. Execs. (membership com. 1981-82, assn. mgmt. co. sect. coun. 1995-98, cert.), Inst. Ops. Rsch. and the Mgmt. Scis., Am. Econ. Assn., Wharton Grad. Sch. Alumni Assn. (exec. com. 1970-73), Nat. Eagle Scout Assn., VFW, Am. Legion, Navy League of U.S., Greater Wash. Soc. Assn. Execs. (new ventures com. 1995-97), Alumni Assn. George Washington U. (governing bd. 1974-82, chmn. univ. publs. com. 1976-78, Alumni Svc. award 1980), Alumni Assn. George Washington U. Sch. Govt. and Bus. Adminstrn. (exec. v.p. 1977-78, pres. 1978-79), George Washington U. Doctoral Assn. (sr. v.p. 1968-69), Nat. Assn. Acad. Sci. (del. 1991-93), Wharton Sch. Washington (sec. 1967-69, pres. 1969-70, exec. dir. 1987-2001, Joseph Wharton award 1991, Lifetime Svc. award 2000). Home: 6516 Truman Ln Falls Church VA 22043-1821 E-mail: aiboss@aol.com.

WEISS, ARNOLD HANS, b. Nurnberg, Germany, July 25, 1924; m. Artemis Lychos, May 5, 1956; children: Daniel L., Andrew A. BA, U. Wis., 1951, JD, 1952. Bar: Wis. 1953, D.C. 1958. Atty. advisor Office Gen. Counsel U.S. Treasury, 1953-60; atty. Inter Am. Devel. Bank, 1960-61, dep. gen. counsel, 1961-70, gen. counsel, 1970-77; ptnr. Arent, Fox, Kintner, Plotkin & Kahn, Washington, 1977-90; cons. Chevy Chase, Md., 1991; sec., gen. counsel Emerging Markets Corp., Washington, 1992—. With U.S. Army, 1942-47; served to lt. col. JAGC USAR, 1948-62. Decorated Bronze Star Mem.: ABA, Inter-Am. Bar Assn., Am. Soc. Internat. Law, Columbia Country Club (Chevy Chase, Md.), Army and Navy Club (Washington), Univ. Club D.C. Office: Emerging Markets Corp 2001 Pennsylvania Ave NW # 1100 Washington DC 20006-1850

WEISS, CHARLES, JR. educator; b. San Francisco, Dec. 20, 1937; s. Charles and Dorothy (Wilkes) W.; m. Edith Gayle Brown, July 24, 1969; children: Jed Ariel, Tamara Ginger. BA summa cum laude, Harvard U., 1959, PhD, 1965. Post-doctoral fellow U. Calif., Berkeley, 1967-69; chemist Lawrence Berkeley Lab., U. Calif., 1969; staff scientist IBM Watson Lab., Columbia U., N.Y.C., 1969-71; sci. and tech. advisor World Bank, Washington, 1971-86; prin. Internat. Tech. Mgmt. and Fin., 1987-91, Innovation Ptnrs., 1987-91; pres. Global Tech. Mgmt., 1991—. Lectr. U. Pa., Phila., 1986-90; vis. lectr. Woodrow Wilson Sch., Princeton U., 1989-94; professorial lectr. Sch. Advanced Internat. Studies, Johns Hopkins U., 1994-97; disting. prof., chair sci., tech. and internat. affairs Sch. Fgn. Svc., Georgetown U., 1997—; corp. bd. mem. Vols. in Tech. Assistance, Arlington, Va., 1974-85; mem. U.S. Nat. Climate Adv. Com., Washington, 1978-81, Coun. of Fgn. Rels., 1985—. Editor: Mobilizing Technology for World Development, 1979, Technology, Finance and Development, 1984, Choice and Management of Technology, 1987; contbr. articles to profl. jours. Pres. Bethesda Jewish Congregation, 1988-90; land use chair Bannockburn Cmty. Assn., 1990-94. Capt. U.S. Army, 1965-67. Fellow NSF, 1959-62, NIH, 1962-65, Woodrow Wilson Found. (hon.). Mem. AAAS, Internat. Orgn. Chem. Scis. for Devel. (exec. officer biotic exploration fund), Am. Chem. Soc., Soc. Internat. Devel., Phi Beta Kappa. Avocations: ethnographic art and music. Office: Sch Fgn Svc Georgetown Univ 37th & O Sts NW Washington DC 20057-0001 E-mail: weissc@georgetown.edu.

WEISS, CHARLES ANDREW, lawyer; b. Perryville, Mo., Jan. 24, 1942; s. Wallace Francis and Iola Francis Weiss; m. Marie Suzanne Desloge, June 10, 1972; children: Christopher, Robert, Julie, Anne. BJ with highest honors, U. Mo., 1964, AB in History, 1965; JD cum laude, Notre Dame U., 1968. Bar: Mo. 1968, U.S. Dist. Ct. (ea. dist.) Mo. 1968, U.S. Ct. Appeals (8th cir.) 1968, U.S. Supreme Ct. 1972, U.S. Ct. Appeals (9th cir.) 1974, U.S. Ct. Appeals (2d cir.) 1977, U.S. Ct. Appeals (5th cir.) 1992. Law clk. to chief judge U.S. Ct. Appeals (8th cir.), 1968; ptnr. Bryan Cave, St. Louis, 1969—. Lectr. St. Louis U. Law Sch., 1970-73. Supr. Red Cross Water Safety Program, Perry County, Mo., 1962-64; dir. Neighborhood Youth Corps., Perry County, 1965-66; pres. Perry County Young Democrats Club, 1965-67; committeeman Boy Scouts Am., 1982-86. Fellow Am. Coll. Trial Lawyers; mem. ABA (ho. of dels. 1986—), Met. Bar Assn. St. Louis (pres. 1984-85), Mo. Bar Assn. (bd. govs. 1985, v.p. 1994-95, pres.-elect 1995-96, pres. 1996-97), Mo. Athletic Club (St. Louis), The Riverlands Assn., Inc. (pres. 1991-93), Jefferson Nat. Parks Assn. (chmn. 1993-2000), Notre Dame Club St. Louis (dir. 1983—), Notre Dame Law Assn. (dir., pres. 1997—). Roman Catholic. Office: Bryan Cave 211 N Broadway Saint Louis MO 63102-2733

WEISS, CHARLES MANUEL, environmental biologist; b. Scranton, Pa., Dec. 7, 1918; s. Morris and Fannie (Levy) W.; m. Shirley Friedlander, June 7, 1942. BS, Rutgers U., 1939, postgrad., 1939-40, Harvard U., 1940; PhD, Johns Hopkins U., 1950. Fellow in marine microbiology, research assoc. in marine biology Woods Hole Oceanographic Instn., Mass., 1939-47; chemist, biologist Balt. Harbor Project, Johns Hopkins U. Dept. San Engring., 1947-50; basin biologist div. water pollution control USPHS, N.Y.C., 1950-52; biologist med. labs. Army Chem. Ctr., Edgewood, Md., 1952-56; prof. environ. biology U. N.C., Chapel Hill, 1956-89, prof. emeritus, 1989—, creator/sponsor C. & S. Weiss Urban Livability program, 1992—. Cons. limnology Duke Power Co., 1980-94; mem. ad hoc panel waste treatment Space Sci. Bd., Nat. Acad. Sci., 1966-68, chmn. panel mgmt. of spacecraft solid and liquid wastes, 1968-69, subcom. atmosphere and water contaminants of manned spacecraft, 1971; mem. triennial water quality standards rev. com. N.C. Dept. Natural Resources and Community Devel., 1982-83; cons. Nat. Health Service, Santiago, Chile, 1971 Author: Water Quality Investigations, Guatemala: Lake Atitlan 1968-70, 1971, Water Quality Investigations, Guatemala: Lake Amatitlan 1969-70, 1971, The Trophic State of North Carolina Lakes, 1976, The Water Quality of the Upper Yadkin Drainage Basin, 1981, Water Quality Study, B. Everett Jordan Lake, N.C., 1981-85, 87; editor N.C. Conf. AAUP Newsletter, 1985-91. Mem. Chapel Hill Planning Bd., 1969-76, chmn., 1970-72, 75-76; trustee Chapel Hill Preservation Soc., 1972; bd. dirs. Triangle Opera, 1986, 89, 91-2002; mem. adv. coun. Santa Fe Chamber Music Festival, 1990-91, 97-98, trustee, 1991-97, 98—; bd. dirs. The Chamber Orch. of the Triangle, 1997—. Co-recipient Gifford Phillips award Santa Fe Chamber Music Festival, 2000; Bigelow fellow Woods Hole Oceanographic Instn., 1970—. Fellow AAAS, APHA, N.Y. Acad. Scis.; mem. AAUP (chpt. pres. 1980-81, pres. N.C. conf. 1982-83, William S. Tacey award Assembly of State Confs. 1992), Am. Chem. Soc., Am. Geophys. Union, Am. Fisheries Soc., Am. Soc. Limnology and Oceanography, Ecol. Soc. Am., Soc. Internat. Limnologie, Water Pollution Control Fedn. (chmn. rsch. com. 1966-71), Am. Water Works Assn. (chmn. subcom. water quality sampling for quality control in reservoirs 1978-80), Am. Soc. Microbiology, Sigma Xi, Delta Omega. Home: 155 N Hamilton Rd Chapel Hill NC 27517-5628 Office: U NC Sch Pub Health CB7431 Chapel Hill NC 27599-7400

WEISS, DAVID ALAN, international trade consultant; b. Washington, June 22, 1953; s. Leonard and Mary Louise (Barker) W.; m. Mamie Kresses, June 2, 1991. BA, Hamilton Coll., 1975; MS in Fgn. Svc., Georgetown U., 1978. Staff asst. Office of Senator Thomas F. Eagleton, Washington, 1970-71; rsch. fellow Carnegie Endowment for Internat. Peace, 1975-76; spl. asst. to dir. Peace Corps, 1978-80; fgn. svc. officer U.S. Dept of State, 1980-90; with econ. office Am. Embassy, Port-au-Prince, Haiti, 1981-83; with secretariat staff Office of Sec. of State, 1983-84; sr. spl. asst. to dep. sec. of state U.S. Dept. of State, 1985-87; dir. European Community high tech and east-west trade policy Office of European Affairs, U.S. Trade Rep., Washington, 1987-89; exec. dir. for policy coordination Exec. Office of The Pres., U.S. Trade Rep., 1989-92; dep. asst. U.S. Trade Rep. for North Am. Affairs, 1992-95, asst., 1995-97; prin., dir. trade policy Verner, Liipfert, Bernhard, McPherson & Hand, Washington, 1997—. Mem. Am. Fgn. Svc. Assn., Diplomatic and Consular Officers Ret. Office: Verner Liipfert Bernhard McPherson & Hand 901 15th St NW Washington DC 20005-2306

WEISS, DAVID STEVEN, chemist; b. Newark, Mar. 3, 1944; BS in Chemistry, Lehigh U., 1965; PhD in Chemistry, Columbia U., 1969. Asst. prof. U. Mich., Ann Arbor, 1972-78; rsch. assoc. Eastman Kodak Co., Rochester, N.Y., 1978—. Co-author: (book) Organic Photoreceptors for Imaging Systems, 1994, Organic Photoreceptors for Xerography, 1998; assoc. editor Jour. Imaging Science and Technology, 1988—; contbr. over 60 articles to profl. jours.; patentee in field. Mem. AAAS, Am. Chem. Soc. (Rochester sect. chmn. 1997), Inter Am. Photochem. Soc., Sigma Xi, Tau Beta Pi, Phi Beta Kappa. Avocations: Genesee region orchid soc. past pres., Rochester area triathletes, track club. Office: Eastman Kodak Co Research Labs Rochester NY 14650-0001

WEISS, DIETER WALDEMAR, economics educator, consultant; b. Berlin, Dec. 2, 1935; s. Waldemar Weiss and Elsa Radke. Diploma in engring., Tech. U., Berlin, 1960, PhD, 1962. With policy planning sect. Fed. Ministry Econ. Cooperation, Bonn, Germany, 1962-65; chief Mid. East dept. German Devel. Inst., Berlin, 1965-80; prof. Freie U., 1980—. John Foster Dulles vis. prof. Princeton U., 1994; mem. German econ. adv. mission to Pres. Anwar Sadat, Egypt, 1977. Author, co-author 10 books; contbr. over 120 articles to profl. jours. Named to Order of the Arab Republic of Egypt, Govt. Egypt, Cairo, 1977. Office: Freie U Berlin Goethestr 80 10623 Berlin Germany E-mail: dweiss@wiwiss.fu-berlin.de.

WEISS, DONALD A. naval officer; b. Jamestown, N.D. Graduate, U.S. Naval Acad., 1968. Advanced through grades to rear adm. USN; naval aviator Kingsville, Tex., 1970; various assignments USS Independence, USS America; detailer Jr. Officer Aviation Assignment Branch, 1980-82; comdg. officer Gunslingers, 1982-85; attack/strike fighter readiness officer U.S. Atlantic Fleet, 1985-; comdg. officer USS Concord, 1989-91, USS Saratoga, 1992-94; dir. ops. Defense Spl. Weapons Agy., 1994-96; comdr. USS Carl Vinson Battle Group, 1996-98, U.S. Naval Forces, Japan, 1998-00; dir. Asian Pacific affairs officer U.S. Sec. Def., Washington, 2000-01. Govt. fellow Harvard U., 1995.

WEISS, DONALD L(OGAN), retired sports association executive; b. Aurora, Ill., Aug. 22, 1926; s. Harry H. and Esther (Cook) W.; m. Charlene Thomas, Aug. 23, 1947; children: Deborah Lynn Weiss Geline, Barbara Jane Weiss Juckett, Pamela Sue Weiss Van der Lee. Student, Cornell Coll., Mt. Vernon, Iowa, 1943, 46; B.J., U. Mo., 1949. Newsman AP, Huntington, W.Va., 1949-51, sports writer-editor N.Y.C., 1951-63; publs. editor, info. dir. U.S. Golf Assn., 1963-65; dir. info. Nat. Football League, 1965-68, dir. public relations, 1968-77, exec. dir., 1977-94. Contbr. articles on golf and football to profl. publs., 1963— . With submarine svc., USN, 1944-46. Recipient Journalistic Achievement awards Sigma Delta Chi, Kappa Tau Alpha, 1948-49, Trustees' award Ohio U., 1978, Nat. citation Nat. H.S. Athletic Coaches Assn., 1990, Pete Rozelle award New Orleans Touchdown Club, 2000. Methodist. Office: 280 Park Ave New York NY 10017-1216

WEISS, EARLE BURTON, physician; b. Waltham, Mass., Nov. 23, 1932; s. Murray E. and Ruth R. (Pill) W.; m. Ruth Lithwick, Dec. 1, 1963; children—Ilana, Joshua. BS with honors, Northeastern U., 1955; MS, MIT, 1957; MD, Albert Einstein Coll. Medicine, 1961. Intern King's County Hosp., Bklyn., 1961-62; resident Boston City Hosp., 1962-64, Nat. Heart Inst. fellow, 1964-66; assoc. chief of medicine Tufts Med. Svc., 1969-71; founder/first dir. respiratory ICU, physician pulmonary svc. Boston City Hosp., 1964-71; dir. div. respiratory diseases St. Vincent Hosp., Worcester, Mass., 1971-89, also acting med. dir., 1985-87; prof. medicine U. Mass. Med. Sch., 1977—; sr. pulmonary rsch. scientist, dept. anesthesia Rsch. Labs. Brigham and Womens Hosp., Boston, 1989—. Cons. FDA, 1975-77; lectr. in medicine Tufts Med. Sch.; assoc. prof. life scis. Worcester (Mass.) Poly. Inst.; vis. prof. Faculty of Medicine, dept. of anesthesia Harvard Med. Sch., 1990—, vis. prof. U. Guadalajara, Mexico, 1973, 77; med. dir. Found. Rsch. in Bronchial Asthma and Related Diseases; Tb cons. Commonwealth of Mass., 1972-89; dir. regional inpatient Tv, Worcester County; vis. prof. U. Guadalajara, Mex., 1973, 77; prof. extraordinario faculty of medicine U. Guadalajara Med. Sch., 1977, 82. Author: Bronchial Asthma, 2d edit., 1976, 3d edit., 1993, Status Asthmaticus, 1978; contbr. (with artist Frank H. Netter) Ciba Collection: The Respiratory System and Clinical Symposia; contbr. articles to profl. jours., abstracts, audio tapes and book chpts. Capt. USAF, 1965-70. Recipient 1st Dr. J. McKeever Meml. award for outstanding med. educator, 1970, The Acad. Honor Soc. Fellow ACP, Am. Coll. Chest Physicians, Royal Coll. Physicians (assoc.); mem. AAAS, AMA, Mass. Thoracic Soc. (pres. 1976-78, Chadwick medal for meritorious contbn. 1990), Mass. Med. Soc., Am. Thoracic Soc. (co-founder clin. assembly, rep. councilor 1979-82, chmn. med. devices com. 1972-79), Am. Assn. Clin. Scientists, Am. Soc. Internal Medicine, Soc. Free Radical Rsch., N.Y. Acad. Scis., Interasthma, Sigma Xi. Achievements include first to use mech. ventilation in respiratory failure of chronic lung disease, arterial blood gas profiles in status asthma, the theory of the role of calcium and oxygen toxic products in causing asthma and airways reactivity. Avocations: oil painting, cello, family. Home: 57 South St Natick MA 01760-5526 Office: Brigham and Womens Hosp Dept Anesthesia Rsch L Boston MA 02115 E-mail: eweiss@bics.bwh.harvard.edu., drwe@attbi.com.

WEISS, EDITH BROWN, law educator; b. Salem, Oreg., Feb. 19, 1942; d. Leon M. and Edith E. Brown; m. Charles Weiss, Jr., July 24, 1969; children: Jed, Tamara. AB, Stanford U., 1963; JD, Harvard U., 1966; PhD, U. Calif., Berkeley, 1973; DDL (hon.), Chgo.-Kent Coll. Law, 1993. Bar: D.C. 1967, U.S. Ct. Claims 1967, U.S. Ct. Customs and Patent Appeals 1967, U.S. Ct. Mil. Appeals. Atty. advisor ACDA, Washington, 1966-68; rsch. assoc. Columbia U., N.Y.C., 1970-72, Brookings Instn., Washington, 1972-74; asst. prof. civil engring. and politics Princeton U., 1974-78; prof. law Georgetown U., Washington, 1978—, Francis Cabell Brown prof. internat. law, 1996—. Cons. UN Environ. Program, 1974—78, 1994—97, 2000—01, UNU, 1983—98; assoc. gen. counsel internat. law EPA, 1990—92; chmn. com. on rsch. on global environ. change Social Sci. Rsch. Coun., 1989—94; spl. legal advisor N. Am. , 1965; mem. Commn. on Environmental Cooperation, 1995—2000; bd. trustees Ctr. for Internat. Environ. Law, 2001—02; mem. inspection panel World Bank, 2002—07. Author: (with Jacobson) Engaging Countries: Strengthening Compliance with International Environment Accords, 1998, (with Jackson) Reconciling Environment and Trade, 2001, In Fairness to Future Generations: International Law, Common Patrimony and Intergenerational Equity, 1989, Environmental Change and International Law, 1992; mem. bd. editors Am. Jour. Internat. Law, Jour. Internat. Econ. Law, Global Governance, Environment, Transnat. Press, Global Environ. Politics, Internat. Environ. Agreements, Politics, Law and Econs., Berkeley Jour. Internat. Law, Internat. Review Environmental Strategy; contbr. articles to profl. jours. Recipient Dinkelspiel award Stanford U., 1963, Leland T. Chapin award, 1962, Mellinkoff award, 1963; Harold and Margaret Sprout award, 1979, Elizabeth Haub prize, 1994, Prominent Woman in Internat. Law award Am. Soc. Internat. Law, 1996; Woodrow Wilson fellow, 1968. Mem. ABA (v. chmn. internat. environ. law com.), Am. Soc. Internat. Law (chmn. ann meeting 1979, exec. coun. 1981-85, v.p. 1983-85, pres. 1994-96, Cert. Merit 1990), NAS (environ. studies bd. 1981-84, vice chair U.S. nat. com. for SCOPE 1984-85, water sci. and tech. bd. 1985-88, commn. on geoscis., environment and resources 1992-95), Internat. Inst. Applied Sys. Analysis (vice chair U.S. nat. com. 1993-98), Coun. Fgn. Rels., Am. Law Inst., Internat. Coun. Environ. Law, Cousteau Soc. (coun. advs.), Japanese Inst. Global Environ Strategies (bd. dirs. 1996—), Nat. Ctr. for Atmospheric Rsch. (adv. coun.2001—) Bannockburn Civic Assn., Phi Beta Kappa, Sigma Xi. Office: Georgetown U Law Ctr 600 New Jersey Ave NW Washington DC 20001-2075 E-mail: weiss@law.georgetown.edu.

WEISS, EGON ARTHUR, retired library administrator; b. Vienna, Austria, June 7, 1919; Came to U.S., 1938; s. Arthur and Martha (Schrecker) W.; m. Renee Hansi Weiss, July 11, 1942; children— Helen Louise, Steven Arthur Student, Berea Coll., Ky., 1938-40; AB, Harvard U., 1947; MA, Boston U., 1949; MSL.S., Simmons Coll., Boston, 1951. Prof. asst. Brookline (Mass.) Pub. Library, 1949-51, br. dir., 1951-58; asst. dir. library U.S. Mil. Acad., West Point, N.Y., 1958-62, libr., dir. libr., 1962-87, libr. emeritus, 1987—. Libr. cons., 1987—; trustee Southeast N.Y. Libr. Rsch. Coun., Poughkeepsie, 1966—; mem. John Cotton Dana Com., N.Y.C., 1975-79; cons. Pergamon Press, McLean, Va., 1983—. Co-author: Catalog Military Science Coll., 4 vols., 1969; contbr. to Funk & Wagnalls Ency., 1965—; appraiser rare books and spl. collections. Chmn. Black Rock Forest Preservation Council, Cornwall, N.Y., 1981— ; trustee Mus. Hudson Highlands, Cornwall-on-Hudson, N.Y., 1968; vice chmn. Citizens Adv. Com., Cornwall, 1963-64; pres. Friends of Cornwall (N.Y.) Pub. Libr., 1989—, chmn. gifts and bequests, 1984—; counsellor Friends of West Point Libr., 1987—; trustee David Libr. of Am. Revolution, Pa., 1986—; alt. del. The White House Conf. on Libr. and Info. Svcs., 1991. Served to lt. col. U.S. Army, 1942-46, ETO Mem. ALA (pres. armed forces sect. 1966), Spl. Libraries Assn. (chmn. mil. library div. 1970), Archons of Colophon, Res. Officers Assn. (pres. Orange County 1965—), Assn. U.S. Army (bd. govs. 1984—) Clubs: Harvard (v.p. schs. and scholarship) (Poughkeepsie, N.Y.). Lodges: Toastmasters (edn. v.p. Newburgh, N.Y. 1968), Masons. Avocations: reading; swimming; tennis; playing violin. Home: Apt B6 7450 Olivetas Ave La Jolla CA 92037-4955 E-mail: egonandrene@aol.com.

WEISS, ELAINE LANDSBERG, community development management official; b. N.Y.C. d. Louis and Sadie Blossum (Schoenfeld); divorced. BA in Philosophy and Polit. Sci., Bklyn. Coll., 1960; postgrad., NYU Law Sch., 1960-62; MA in Sociology, Hunter Coll., N.Y.C., 1969. Social investigator N.Y.C. Dept. Social Services, 1963-64; intern, fellow Eleanor Roosevelt Meml. Found., Nat. Assn. Intergroup Relations Ofcls., 1964-65; asst. dir. housing and asst. project dir. Operation Equality, Nat. Urban League, 1965-67; program assoc. housing div. ch. missions Am. Bapt. Home Mission Socs., 1967-70; pres. E.L. Weiss Assocs., 1970-76; exec. dir. Suffolk Community Devel. Corp., Coram, N.Y., 1976-89, E.L. Weiss Assocs., N.Y.C., 1990—, Grenadier Realty Corp., 1990-92; COO Morningside Heights Housing Corp., 1992-95; exec. dir. Fairmont Housing Corp. (N.J.) subsidiary YWCA Hudson County, 1995-97, Westchester Residential Opportunities, Inc., White Plains, N.Y., 1997-98, Saparn Realty, Inc., 1998-2001, N.Y. Soc. Deaf, 2001—. Mem. citizens adv. com. N.Y.C. Dept. Housing Preservation and Devel.; exec. com. L.I. Community Devel. Orgn.; past 2d v.p. Suffolk Housing Task Force; chmn. Suffolk County Citizens Adv. Com., 1981-82. Recipient cert. of commendation L.I. Council Chs., 1981. Mem. Nat. Assn. Housing Ofcls., N.Y. State Assn. Housing and Redevel. Ofcls., Am. Contract Bridge League (life master). Home: PO Box 1532 East Quogue NY 11942-1339

WEISS, ERIC GLENN, physician; b. White Sands, N.Mex., Mar. 19, 1962; s. Richard Fred and Harriet (Stuart) W.; m. Debra R. Weiss, June 12, 1988; children: Morgan Rachel, Adam Howard, Brett Phillip. BS in Biochemistry, Pa. State U., 1984; MD, Temple U., 1988. Diplomate Am. Bd. Surgery, Am. Bd. Colon and Rectal Surgery. Resident in surgery Albert Einstein Med. Ctr., Phila., 1988-93; fellow in colorectal surgery Cleveland Clinic Fla., Ft. Lauderdale, 1993-94, staff colorectal surgeon, 1994—, assoc. residency program dir., 1998—, chmn. surg. endoscopy, 1996—, chmn. grad. med. edn., 1999—. Co-editor: Diagnosis and Treatment of Fecal Incontinence, 2000. Fellow ACS, Am. Soc. Colon and Rectal Surgeons; mem. Am. Coll. Gastroenterology. Office: Cleveland Clinic Fla 2950 Cleveland Clinic Blvd Weston FL 33331 E-mail: weisse@ccf.crg.

WEISS, ERNEST, federal agency administrator; b. Detroit, Oct. 28, 1918; s. Louis and Eugenie (Glick) W.; m. Gloria Caroline Hacker, Feb. 21, 1943; children: Lynn Carol, Gail Corynn. BBA, CUNY, 1942; postgrad., Am. U., 1948-54. With Gen. Svc. Adminstrn. VA, 1946-52, ICC, Washington, 1952-67, asst. to mng. dir., 1955-63, asst. mng. dir., 1963-67; exec. dir. Nat. Transp. Safety Bd., 1967-72; sr. staff scientist George Washington U., 1973-78; commr. Montgomery County (Md.) Commn. on Health, 1990-96. Recipient Meritorious Achievement award Transp. Dept., 1968. Mem. Phi Sigma Alpha. Home: 3312 Brooklawn Ter Chevy Chase MD 20815-3901

WEISS, GEORGE HERBERT, mathematician, consultant; b. N.Y.C., Feb. 19, 1930; s. Morris and Violet (Mayer) W.; m. Delia Esther Orgel, Dec. 20, 1961; children: Miriam Judith, Alan Keith, Daniel Jonathan. BA, Columbia U., 1951; MA, U. Md., 1953, PhD, 1958. Physicist USN, White Oak, Md., 1951-61; asst. prof. U. Md., College Park, 1959-63; fellow Rockefeller U., N.Y.C., 1963-64, Weizmann Inst., Rehovot, Israel, 1958-59; mathematician NIH, Bethesda, Md., 1964—. Cons. GM, IBM, GE. Author: Lattice Dynamics in the Harmonic Approximation, 1963, 2d edit., 1971, The Master Equation in Chemical Physics, 1977, Contemporary Problems in Statistical Physics, 1994, Aspects and Applications of the Random Walk, 1994, Introduction to Crystallographic Statistics, 1995. With U.S. Army, 1954-56. Recipient Disting. Svc. in Math. award Washington Acad. Sci., 1967, Disting. Svc. award NIH, 1970. Avocations: photography, music, chess, philately. Office: NIH Bethesda MD 20816 E-mail: ghw@helix.nih.gov.

WEISS, GERHARD HANS, German language educator; b. Berlin, Aug. 6, 1926; came to U.S., 1946; s. Curt Erich and Gertrud (Grothus) W.; m. Janet Marilyn Smith, Dec. 27, 1953; children: John Martin, Susan Elizabeth Weiss Spencer, James David. BA, Washington U., St. Louis, 1950, MA, 1952; PhD, U. Wis., 1956. Prof. German U. Minn., Mpls., 1956—, assoc. dean, 1967-71, 79, chmn. dept. German, 1987-95, interim dir. Ctr. Austrian Studies, 1999-2001. Mem. German-Am. Textbook Commn., Braunschweig, Fed. Republic Germany, 1985-88. Author: Begegnung mit Deutschland, 1970; editor: Unterrichtspraxis, 1975-80, Minn. Monographs in the Humanities, 1964-70; contbr. articles to profl. jours. Served to lt. col. USAR, 1946-75. Recipient Cross Merit, Fed. Republic Germany, 1982. Mem. MLA, Am. Assn. Tchrs. German (pres. 1982-83, cert. of merit 1981, Disting. German Educator award 1991, elected hon. mem. 1995), German Studies Assn. (v.p. 1997-98, pres. 1999-00), Am. Coun. Tchg. Fgn. Langs. (Nelson Brooks award 1987). Methodist. Home: 4101 Abbott Ave S Minneapolis MN 55410-1004

WEISS, GERSON, physician, educator; b. N.Y.C., Aug. 1, 1939; s. Samuel and Lillian (Wolpe) W.; m. Linda Gordon, Dec. 24, 1959; children: Jonathan, David, Michele, Andrew. BA, NYU, 1960, MD, 1964. Diplomate Am. Bd. Ob-Gyn. (mem. divsn. reproductive endocrinology 1985-90, pres. bd. 1999-2002). Intern, fellow dept. medicine Johns Hopkins Sch. Medicine, 1964-65; resident ob-gyn NYU Med. Ctr., 1964-69; rsch. fellow physiology U. Pitts. Sch. Medicine, 1971-73; asst. prof. ob-gyn NYU Med. Ctr., 1971-76, asso. prof., 1976-80, prof., 1980-85; dir. div. reproductive endocrinology NYU Med. Center, 1975-85; prof. ob-gyn U. Med. and Dentistry N.J.-N.J. Med. Sch., 1986—, chmn. dept., 1986—; dir. divsn. reproductive endocrinology Hackensack (N.J.) U. Med. Ctr., 1996—. Rep. Am. Bd. Med. Specialists. Mem. editl. bd. Fertility and Sterility Jour., 1986-93, Gyn.-Ob. Investigation; contbr. rsch. articles reproductive endocrinology and gynecology to med. jours. Served to maj. MC U.S. Army, 1969-71. Rsch. grantee NIH, 1975—, United Cerebral Palsy Found., 1977-83, Mellon Found., 1982-85; John Polachek Found. Med. Rsch. fellow. Mem. ACOG, Am. Ob-Gyn. Soc., Am. Bd. Ob-Gyn. (bd. dirs., treas. 1997-98, pres. 1998-2002, chmn. 2002-, ob-gyn. residency rev. com. 1995-2000, coun. univ. chairs ob-gyn, pres.-elect, 1998-99, pres. 2000-02), Am. Bd. Med. Spltys. (coun. 2002--), Endocrine Soc. Gynecol. Investigation, N.Y. Obstet. Soc. (pres. 1990-91), N.Y. Gynecol. Soc. (pres. 1989-90), Soc. Study of Reprodn., Phi Beta Kappa, Sigma Xi, Alpha Omega Alpha. Home: 390 1st Ave Apt 11D New York NY 10010-4935 Office: UMDNJ NJ Med Sch Dept Ob-Gyn 185 S Orange Ave Newark NJ 07103-2757

WEISS, GREGORY LEE, sociology educator; b. Canton, Ohio, Aug. 19, 1949; m. Janet S. Jonas. BA, Wittenberg U., 1971; MS, Purdue U., 1972, PhD, 1975. Fellow USPHS Purdue U., West Lafayette, Ind., 1971-75, instr. Sch. of Continuing Edn., 1974-75; asst. prof. sociology Roanoke Coll., Salem, Va., 1975-81, assoc. prof. sociology, 1981-87, prof., 1987—, chair dept. sociology, 1996-99, dir. assessment, 1999—2001. Dir. Ctr. for Cmty. Rsch., 1983-91. Author: The Sociology of Health Hearing and Illness, 1994, The Sociology of Health Hearing and Illness, 4th edit., 2002; co-author: Annual Research in the Spociology of Health Care; contbr. articles to profl. jours. Bd. dirs. Bradley Free Clinic, Roanoke, Planned Parenthood, Roanoke, League for Animal Protection, SPCA Pet Therapy. Recipient Outstanding Svc. award Bradley Free Clinic, 1981; Institutional Lab. Improvement grant NSF, Washington, 1994. Mem.: APHA, Va. Social Sci. Assn. (pres. 1985—86, scholar award 1982), So. Sociol. Soc., Am. Assn. Higher Edn., Am. Sociol. Assn. (cons. 1991—, Tchg. Endowment Fund grants 1997). Home: 182 Forest Dr Salem VA 24153-6860 Office: Roanoke Coll Dept Sociology Salem VA 24153 E-mail: weiss@roanoke.edu.

WEISS, HARLAN LEE, lawyer; b. Washington, Dec. 6, 1941; s. Richard Stanley and Ethel (Shulman) W.; m. Elaine Sharon Schooler, Feb. 14, 1971; children: Rachel Shayna, Brian Adam. BA, U. Md.-College Park, 1963; JD with honors, U. Md.-Balt., 1966. Bar: Md. 1967, D.C. 1967, U.S. Dist. Ct. Md. 1967, U.S. Dist. Ct. D.C. 1967, U.S. Ct. Appeals (D.C. cir.) 1968, U.S. Ct. Appeals (4th cir.) 1977, U.S. Supreme Ct. 1970. Law clk. Ct. Appeals of Md., 1966-67; assoc. Surrey & Morse and predecessors, Washington, 1967-72, Sachs, Greenebaum, Taylor, Washington, 1972-76, ptnr., 1976-90; mem. Kivitz & Liptz, LLC, Chevy Chase, Md., 1990. Mem. Jud. Conf. D.C., 1978-79. Home: 12017 Cheyenne Rd Gaithersburg MD 20878-2011 Office: 650 Barlow Bldg 5454 Wisconsin Ave Chevy Chase MD 20815-6901

WEISS, HERBERT KLEMM, retired aeronautical engineer; b. Lawrence, Mass., June 22, 1917; s. Herbert Julius and Louise (Klemm) W.; m. Ethel Celesta Giltner, May 14, 1945 (dec.); children: Janet Elaine, Jack Klemm (dec.). BS, MIT, 1937, MS, 1938. Engr. U.S. Army Arty. Bds., Ft. Monroe, Va, 1938-42, Camp Davis, N.C., 1942-44, Ft. Bliss, Tex., 1944-46; chief WPN Systems Lab., Ballistic Research Labs., Aberdeen Proving Grounds, Md, 1946-53; chief WPN systems analysis dept. Northrop Aircraft Corp., 1953-58; mgr. advanced systems devel. mil. systems planning aeronutronic div. Ford Motor Co., Newport Beach, Calif., 1958-61; group dir., plans devel. and analysis Aerospace Corp., El Segundo, 1961-65; sr. scientist Litton Industries, Van Nuys, 1965-82; cons. mil. systems analysis, 1982-90. Mem. Sci. Adv. Bd. USAF, 1959-63, sci. adv. panel U.S. Army, 1965-74, sci. adv. commn. Army Ball Research Labs., 1973-77; advisor Pres.'s Commn. Law Enforcement and Adminstrn. Justice, 1966; cons. Office Dir. Def., Research and Engring., 1954-64. Contbr. articles to profl. jours. Patentee in field Recipient Commendation for meritorious civilian service USAF, 1964, cert. appreciation U.S. Army, 1976. Fellow AAAS, AIAA (assoc.); mem. IEEE, Ops. Rsch. Soc. Am., Cosmos Club. Republican. Home: PO Box 2668 Palos Verdes Peninsula CA 90274-8668 *The difference between having something to do and having to do something is a pain in the neck. Anything worth doing takes more doing than it is worth except for the fun of it.*

WEISS, HOWARD A. violinist, concertmaster, conductor, music educator; b. Chgo. s. Morris X. and Rose Weiss. B.Music, Chgo. Musical Coll. of Roosevelt U., 1960; M.Music with honors, Roosevelt U., 1966. Founder, music dir., condr. Rochester Philharm. Youth Orch., N.Y., 1970-89; music dir., condr. Siena (Italy) Festival String Orch., 1998—; prof. violin Eastman Sch. Music, Rochester, 1981—, Nazareth Coll., Rochester, 1983-85. Adv. bd. Young Audiences of Rochester, 1975—, Rochester Chamber Orch., 1981—. Concertmaster Rochester Philharm. Orch., 1967-87, concertmaster emeritus, 1987— , concertmaster Rochester Oratorio Soc., 1987—, Chgo. Chamber Orch., 1962-70, Va. Symphony, 1964, San Francisco Ballet Orch., 1962, Eastern Music Festival, Greensboro, N.C., 1976-80, Grand Teton Music Festival Seminar, Jackson Hole, Wyo., 1983-86, Bear Lake Mus. Festival, Utah, 1992-93, Siena Festival, Italy, 1998—; 1st violinist Cleve. Orch., 1965-67; violin soloist more than 45 concertos with Cleve. Orch., Rochester Philharm., New Orleans Philharm., Chgo. Grant Park Symphony, Siena Festival, Italy, Cin. Chamber Orch., Chgo. Chamber Orch., Rochester Chamber Orch.; soloist U.S. premiere Carl Nielsen violin concerto, 1967; soloist Rochester, N.Y. premieres of violin concertos of Berg, Nielsen and Vaughan Williams; violin soloist with conductors James Levine, David Zinman, Alexander Schneider, Walter Hendl, Gerard Schwarz; soloist in complete concerti, (5) of J.S. Bach for Violin and Orch. with Rochester Bach Festival; soloist in complete concerti, (3) of Haydn for Violin and orch. with Rochester Chamber Orch.; soloist rec. Amram Elegy for Violin and Orchestra, David Zinman, Rochester Philharm. Orch., on RCA Red Seal; performed chamber music with: Misha Dichter, Leonard Rose, Lynn Harrell, Yo-Yo Ma, Elly Ameling, Jaime Laredo, Walter Trampler, Lillian Fuchs, James Buswell, Gary Karr, Alan Civil, Lukas Foss; violinist of Brockport Piano Trio, 1971-74; leader of Hartwell String Quartet, 1975-78; asst. concertmaster, participant Casals Festival, P.R., 1975-80; as music dir. and condr. Rochester Philharm. Youth Orch. recorded 21 LPs including symphonies by Franck, Sibelius, Shostakovich, Dvorak, Borodin and Rachmaninoff, made 12 tours, including 4 abroad, Eng. and Scotland, 1984, Germany, Austria and Switzerland, 1986, Dominican Republic, 1987, Jamaica, 1989, and appears on Voice of Am. Named Outstanding Grad. of 1966, Roosevelt U., 1973; recipient Monroe County (N.Y.) Medallion, 1986. Home: 228 Castlebar Rd Rochester NY 14610-2914

WEISS, JAMES LLOYD, cardiology educator; b. Chgo., Jan. 15, 1941; s. Edward Huhner and Ruth (Wingerhoff) W.; m. Susan Forscher Weiss, July 23, 1967; children: Ethan James, Lisa Fleur. BA, Harvard Coll., 1963; MD, Yale U., 1968. Intern, resident U. Mich. Hosp., Ann Arbor, 1968-70; staff fellow NIH, Bethesda, Md., 1970-72; resident medicine Johns Hopkins Hosp., Balt., 1972-73, fellow cardiology, 1973-75, dir. Heart Station, 1976—, asst. prof. Medicine, 1975-81, assoc. prof. Medicine, 1981-90, prof. Medicine, Cardiology, 1990—, Michael J. Cudahy prof. of cardiology, 1992—, assoc. dean admissions and acad. affairs, 1999—, dir. cardiology fellowship and tng. program, 1999—. Mem. editl. bd.: Johns Hopkins Med. Letter, 1991—, mem. editl. bd.: Jour. Am. Coll. Cardiology, 1995—; contbr. Recipient Harvard Book prize, 1959. Fellow Am. Coll. Cardiology, AHA Coun. on Circulation; mem. Harvard Club N.Y.C., Ctr. Club. Office: Cardiology Divsn Johns Hopkins Hosp 600 N Wolfe St Baltimore MD 21287-0005

WEISS, JAMES MICHAEL, financial analyst, portfolio manager; b. Chgo., July 20, 1946; s. Harold Cornelius and Elizabeth Josephine (Jesse) W.; m. Kathleen Jane Postorino, July 18, 1970; children: Elizabeth, Ann, Jane, William. BA, Marquette U., 1968; MBA, U. Pa., 1972. CFA; chartered investment counselor. Credit analyst Provident Nat. Bank, Phila., 1972; ptnr., sr. portfolio mgr. Stein Roe & Farnham Investment Counsel, Chgo., 1972-87, 1st v.p., prin., sr. portfolio mgr., 1987-90, sr. v.p., prin., sr. portfolio mgr., 1991-92; exec. v.p., sr. portfolio mgr. IDS Adv. Group, Inc., Mpls., 1993-95; pres., chief investment officer IDS Equity Advisors, 1995; sr. v.p., dep. chief investment officer Equities, State St. Rsch. & Mgmt. Co., Boston, 1995-97, exec. v.p., mem. mgmt. com., dep. head of equities, 1998-99, exec. v.p. mem. mgmt. com., chief invest. officer, bd. dirs., 1999—. Bd. dirs. Tropp & Co., Chgo.; v.p. Stein Roe Cash Reserves Fund, Chgo., 1982-87. Author: (with others) Handbook of Cash Flow and Treasury Management, 1987; contbr. articles to profl. jours. Commr. Glenview (Ill.) Zoning Bd., 1978-80; trustee Glenview Village Bd. Trustees, 1980-86; chmn. Marquette U. Exec. Senate, Chgo., 1984-87; mem. Glenview Bus. Area Redevel. Com., 1990-93; mem. bus. adv. coun. Elmhurst (Ill.) Coll., 1986-93; founding bd. dirs. Glenview Edn. Found., 1990-93; bd. trustees The Fenn Sch., Concord, Mass., 1996-2002; co-chmn. Fenn Sch. Capital Campaign, 1997-2000. With U.S. Army, 1968-70. Recipient Cert. Merit Village of Glenview, 1987. Mem.: Investment Counsel Assn., Fin. Analysts Fedn., Investment Analysts Soc., Marquette U. Alumni Assn. (nat. bd. dirs. 1989—91, liberal arts bd. 2000—, Nat. Svc. award 1995), Indian River Country Club (Vero Beach, Fla.), Boston Coll. Club, Wedgewood Pines Club (Stow, Mass.), North Shore Country Club (Glenview). Avocations: golf, travel, writing. Home: 251 Caterina Hts Concord MA 01742-4774 Office: 1 Financial Ctr Boston MA 02111-2621 E-mail: jweiss6@aol.com.

WEISS, JAMES MOSES AARON, psychiatrist, educator; b. St. Paul, Oct. 22, 1921; s. Louis Robert and Gertrude (Simon) W.; m. Bette Shapera, Apr. 7, 1946; children: Jenny Anne Weiss Ford, Jonathan James. AB summa cum laude, U. Minn., 1941, ScB, 1947, MB, 1949, MD, 1950; MPH with high honors, Yale U., 1951. Diplomate: Am. Bd. Psychiatry and Neurology (examiner 1963-83). Teaching asst. psychology St. Thomas Coll., St. Paul, 1941-42; intern USPHS Hosp., Seattle, 1949-50; resident, fellow psychiatry Yale Med. Sch., 1950-53; from instr. to asst. prof. psychiatry Washington U., St. Louis, 1954-60; mem. faculty U. Mo., 1959—, First Prof. psychiatry, 1961—, founding chmn. dept., 1960-91, prof. community medicine, 1971—, univ. prof. emeritus, 1991—. Vis. prof. Inst. Criminology, Cambridge (Eng.) U., 1968-69, All-India Inst. Med. Scis. and U. Malaya, 1984; internat. cons., 1958— ; founding co-chmn. Asian-Am. Consortium on Psychiat. Disorders, 1986—; Kohler disting. lectr. St. Louis U., 1988. Author numerous articles in field; editor, co-author: Nurses, Patients, and Social Systems, 1968; corr. editor: Jour. Geriatric Psychiatry, 1967-93; founding editor, chmn. bd. Jour. Operational Psychiatry, 1970-90; editorial advisor Community Mental Health Jour., 1979-87; trustee Mo. Rev., 1982-83. Mem. adv. bd. Mo. Probation and Parole, 1st pres., 1995-97. Served with M.C., AUS, 1942-46, PTO; to capt. M.C., AUS, 1953-54. Decorated Philippine Liberation medal, 1945; recipient Sir Henry Wellcome award, 1955, Israeli bronze medal, 1963, Basic Books award, 1974, Disting. Service commendation Nat. Council Community Mental Health Ctrs., 1982, 83, 86, Guhleman award for Clin. Excellence U. Mo., 1987, Hon. Achievement award U.Mo., 1991, Disting. Svc. award VA, 1991; named Chancellor's Emissary U. Mo., 1979, Alumnus Magnus award, St. Thomas U., 1992; faculty fellow Inter-Univ. Council, 1958, sr. research fellow Am. Council Edn. and NSF, 1984 Found. fellow Royal Coll. Psychiatrists; fellow Royal Soc. Medicine, Am. Psychiat. Assn. (life), Am. Pub. Health Assn. (life), Am. Coll. Preventive Medicine (emeritus), AAAS, Am. Coll. Psychiatrists (life), Am. Assn. Psychoanalytic Physicians (hon.); mem. Assn. Mil. Surgeons U.S. (hon. life), Assn. Western Profs. Psychiatry (chmn. 1970-71), Mo. Acad. Psychiatry (1st pres. 1966-67), Mo. Psychiat. Assn. (life, pres. 1987-88), Assn. de Methodologie et Documentation en Psychiatrie, Mil. Order World Wars, Phi Beta Kappa, Sigma Xi, Psi Chi, Alpha Omega Alpha, Alpha Epsilon Sigma, Gamma Alpha. Clubs: Scholars (Cantab.); Wine Label (London); Univ. (Columbia). Achievements include research on suicide, homicide, antisocial behavior, aging, social psychiatry. Home: Crow Wing Farm RR 2 Box 2 Columbia MO 65201-9802 Office: U Mo Dept Psychiatry Columbia MO 65212-0001 E-mail: doxbj@aol.com. *Only this endures: creativity, the pursuit of excellence, and continuing concern for human civilization.*

WEISS, JAY M(ICHAEL), psychologist, educator; b. Passaic, N.J., Mar. 20, 1941; s. Benjamin and Anne (Pearl) W.; m. Meryl Etta Levenson, June 9, 1963; children: Jennifer, Jason. BA, Lafayette Coll., 1962; PhD, Yale U., 1967. Asst. prof. Rockefeller U., N.Y.C., 1969-73, assoc. prof., 1973-84; prof. dept. psychiatry Med. Ctr., Duke U., Durham, N.C., 1984-92; prof. dept psychiatry behavioral scis. Emory U. Sch. Medicine, Atlanta, 1992-95, Jenny Culbreth Adams prof. psychiatry and behavioral scis., 1995—. Adj. assoc. prof. NYU, 1973-84, CCNY, 1979-84. MacArthur Found. fellow, 1984-89. Fellow AAAS, Soc. for Behavioral Medicine, Am. Coll. Neuropsychopharmacology. Office: Emory West Campus Emory Univ 1256 Briarcliff Rd NE Atlanta GA 30306-2656

WEISS, JOAN OPPENHEIMER, social worker, educator; b. Balt., Apr. 10, 1930; d. Reuben and Selma (Levy) Oppenheimer; m. Milton Gottesman, Oct. 19, 1952 (div. 1958); m. Stanley Weiss, Nov. 6, 1960; children: Betsy, Michael, Jonathan. BA, Barnard Coll., 1952; MSW, Cath. U., 1956. Caseworker Jewish Social Svc. Agy., Washington, 1956-62, Family and Child Svcs., Washington, 1962-64; social worker divsn. med. genetics Johns Hopkins U., Balt., 1968-88; founding exec. dir. Alliance of Genetic Support Groups, Chevy Chase, 1988-96; co-dir. Human Genome Edn. Model Project, 1993—. Instr. Child Devel. Ctr., Georgetown U., Washington, 1981—95; cons. Genetics Ctr., Johns Hopkins U., 1988—90; co-dir. Human Genome Edn. Model Project, 1993—2001; chmn. GenEthics Consortium, 1997—98; chmn. genetic standards for clin. practice com. NASW. Co-author Starting and Sustaining Genetic Support Groups, 1996; co-editor: Genetic Disorders and Birth Defects in Families and Society, 1983, Genetic Support Groups: A Partnership of Volunteers and Professionals, 1986; contbr. articles to profl. jours. Mem. profl. adv. bds. several vol. genetic orgns., 1973—. Maternal and Child Health grantee, 1989-96, March of Dimes Birth Defects Found. grantee, 1991. Mem. NASW, Am. Soc. Human Genetics (social issues com.), Am. Coll. Med. Genetics, Nat. Soc. Human Genetics, Nat. Soc. Genetic Counselors, Genetic Alliance. Avocations: travel, theatre, reading, music.

WEISS, JOEL ALEXANDER, environmental and manufacturing executive; b. Washington; s. Jack Lawrence and Margaret (Siegal) W.; m. Sandra Jean Spaulding, July 6, 1969; children: Martin, Robert, Eric, Amy. B of Engring. Sci., Johns Hopkins U., 1969; AM, Harvard U., 1970, PhD, 1975. Rsch. physicist U.S. Naval Rsch. Lab., Washington, 1966-75; program mgr. U.S. Dept. Energy, 1975-78, exec. asst., 1978-80; mgr. Washington ops. Acurex Corp., Mtn. View, Calif., 1980-84; dir. tactical warfare Gould Inc., Glen Burnie, Md., 1984-87; mgr. rsch. & technology Martin Marietta Aero & Naval Systems, Balt., 1987-90; v.p. bus. devel. Marietta Tech. Svcs. Inc., Bethesda, Md., 1990-93; dir. strategic planning Sandia Nat. Labs., Albuquerque, 1993-95; v.p. bus. devel. Lockheed Martin Energy Programs, Bethesda, Md., 1995-2000; pres. Lockheed Martin Energy Techs., Inc., 1999-2000; exec. v.p., prin. QuadraTech Group, LLC, Arlington, Va., 2001—; pres. EnergoTech, LLC, a QuadraTech Co., 2001—. Patentee in field. Mem. Sigma Xi, Tau Beta Pi. Avocation: computers. Office: EnergoTech LLC 2231 Crystal Dr Ste 815 Arlington VA 22202 E-mail: joel.a.weiss@energotechllc.com.

WEISS, JONATHAN ARTHUR, lawyer; b. May 1, 1939; s. Paul and Victoria Brodkin Weiss. BA, Yale U., 1960, LLB, 1963; student, U. Chgo. Law Sch., 1960—61. Bar: NY 1967, DC 1994, Vet.'s Ct. (2d and 3d cirs.), U.S. Supreme Ct. 1967. Mng. atty. Neighborhood Legal Svcs., Washington, 1964-66, Mobilization for Youth Legal Svcs., N.Y.C., 1969-71; with Ctr. on Welfare Law, Columbia U. Law Sch., 1967-69; dir. Legal Svcs. for Elderly, 1971—. Lectr. Hebrew U., Jerusalem, 1966; vis. prof. Tex. So. U. Law Sch., Houston, 1971; adj. prof. Yeshiva U. Cardozo Law Sch., N.Y.C., falls 1983-85. Co-author, editor: The Law and the Elderly, 1976; co-author: Right and Wrong a Philosophical Dialogue and Between Father and Son, 1968; contbr. numerous articles and revs. to law and philos. jours. and newspapers, French and Russian transls. of novels, screenplay and play. Bd. dirs. N.Y. Civil Liberties Union, Disability Legal Def. Fund, World Trust Fund Inc. Recipient Disting. Scholar medal Hofstra U., 1972; Fulbright scholar, 1966. Mem. ABA (mem. Adv. Coun. ethics 2000 com.), Native Am. Bar Assn., N.Y. State Bar (internat. sect. human rights). Democrat. Office: Legal Svcs for Elderly 130 W 42d St New York NY 10036

WEISS, JOSEPH, physician; b. Kosice, Czechoslovakia, June 23, 1913; came to U.S., 1949; s. Abraham Adolf and Johanna (Nagy) W.; m. Eva Farkas, Apr. 24, 1944; 1 child, Julia. MD, Charles U., Prague, Czechoslovakia, 1947. Diplomate Am. Bd. Family Practice. Clin. asst. Charles U., 1947-48; resident in medicine Lebanon Hosp., Bronx, N.Y., 1949-51; clinician N.Y.C. Dept. Health, 1954-85; clin. instr. medicine N.Y. Med. Coll., N.Y.C. and Valhalla, N.Y., 1973-90. Bd. dirs. La Guardia-Health Ins. Plan Greater N.Y., 1979-85, chmn. peer rev. com., 1985-96, pres., 1996, Semmelweis Sci. Soc., N.Y.C., 1973-74; pres. Am.-Hungarian Med. Assn., N.Y.C., 1973-74. Recipient Presdl. Scroll Semmelweis Sci. Soc., 1974, medal Internat. Conv. Pathophysiology, Prague, 1975, Internat. Symposium Cardiomyopathies, Bratislava, Czechoslovakia, 1985. Fellow InterAm. Coll. Physicians and Surgeons, Am. Geriat. Soc., Am. Acad. Family Practice; mem. AMA, N.Y. State Med. Soc. (diploma for 50 yrs. in medicine), Queens County Med. Soc., N.Y. Acad. Scis. Home: 69-33 170th St Flushing NY 11365-3309

WEISS, KENNETH ANDREW, lawyer, law educator; b. New Orleans, Jan. 16, 1951; s. Irving and Julia (Mayer) W. BA, Tulane U., 1972, JD with honors, 1975; LLM in Taxation with highest honors, George Washington U., 1981. Bar: La. 1975, D.C. 1976. Edit. writer, Washington corr. The Times-Picayune, New Orleans and Washington, 1973-79; news editor Congl. Quarterly, Washington, 1979-81; mng. editor Reporters Com. for Freedom of the Press, 1981-82; assoc. McGlinchey Stafford, New Orleans, 1982-84, dir., 1984—. Prof. Tulane U. Law Sch., New Orleans, 1987—, La. State U. Law Sch., 2000—; mem. trust code com. La. Law Inst., Baton Rouge, 1993—, mem. successions and donations com., 1996—; mem. planning com. Tulane Tax Inst., 1996—; chair Tulane U. Law Sch. Ann. Estate Planning Seminar, 1995—2001, Tulane U. Estate Planning Inst., 2002—. Co-author: Bankers' Guide to Establishing, Managing and Operating Common Trust Funds, 1986, Business Uses of Life Insurance, 1986, Executive Compensation, 1990; assoc. editor Tulane Law Rev., 1974-75, mem. bd. adv. editors, 1992—; contbr. articles to profl. jours. Bd. dirs. Longue Vue House and Gardens Adv. Corp., 1993-95, bd. dirs. Longue Vue Found., 1995—; trustee Greater New Orleans Ednl. TV Found., Sta. WYES-TV, 1994-98; bd. dirs. So. Repertory Theatre, 1996-2001, pres., 1998-99; bd. advisors Project Lazarus, 1996-2000, pres. 1997-99; mem. profl. adv. com., Jewish Endowment Found., 1982—; mem. planned gifts adv. com. Tulane U., 1989—; active Met. Area Com. Leadership Forum, New Orleans, 1983; fellow Inst. Politics Loyola U., New Orleans, 1989-90; mem. devel. com. Greater New Orleans Found., 1995—. bd. dirs., Innocence Project New Orleans, 2002-,. Recipient Addy award for polit. advt., 1989, awards for investigative reporting; Phi Delta Phi scholar, 1972-73. Fellow Am. Coll. Trust and Estate Counsel; mem. La. State Bar Assn. (taxation sect., bd. cert. tax atty., bd. cert. estate planning and adminstrn. specialist), New Orleans Bar Assn., Nat. Coun. Planned Giving (greater New Orleans chpt.), New Orleans Estate Planning Coun., Order of the Coif. Republican. Jewish. Office: McGlinchey Stafford 643 Magazine St New Orleans LA 70130-3477

WEISS, KENNETH JAY, education educator, reading specialist, administrator; b. N.Y.C., Mar. 26, 1950; s. Daniel and Ida (Berson) W.; m. Roberta Carol Ungar, June 10, 1973; children: Seth, Richard. BA, C.W. Post Coll., 1972; MBA, Long Island U., 1982; EdM, Rutgers U., 1989, EdD, 1993. Cert. tchr. reading specialist, adminstr., N.J. Assoc. prof. edn., dir. grad. literacy edn. program Nazareth Coll., Rochester, N.Y., 1993—. Mem. Nat. Coun. Tchrs. English, Internat. Reading Assn., Nat. Reading Conf., Nat. Conf. Rsch. in Lit. and Lang. Arts, Kappa Delta Pi.

WEISS, KIMBERLY SUE, physician assistant, academic administrator; b. Balt., Oct. 3, 1967; BS, St. Francis Coll., Loretto, Pa., 1989, MMS, 1994. Cert. physician asst. Physician asst. Johns Hopkins Hosp., Balt., 1989-92, Kennedy Krueger Inst., Balt., 1992-97, Owensville (Md.) Primary Care, 1997—2000; acad. coord. Anne Arundel C.C., Arnold, Md., 1997—2000; pharm. sales rep. Gate Pharms., North Wales, Pa., 2000—. Avocation: piano. Office: Anne Arundel CC 101 College Pkwy Arnold MD 21012-1857

WEISS, KLAUDIUSZ R. neuroscientist; b. Le Mans, France, June 7, 1944; s. Edward Weiss and Irene-Hadassa Edelman; m. Julia Przybos, Jan. 15, 1947. PhD, SUNY, Stony Brook, 1973. Asst. prof. dept. psychiatry Columbia U., N.Y.C., 1986-87, assoc. prof. dept. psychiatry, 1986-90; prof. dept. physiology Mt. Sinai Sch. Medicine, 1990—. Contbr. articles to profl. jours. Office: Mt Sinai Sch Medicine 1 Gustave Levy Pl New York NY 10029 Fax: 212-289-0637. E-mail: klaudiusz.weiss@mssm.edu.

WEISS, LAWRENCE N. lawyer; b. N.Y.C., Aug. 9, 1942; s. Joseph and Martha (Guggenheimer) W.; m. Osnat Gad. BA, CCNY, 1963; LLB summa cum laude, Columbia U., 1966. Bar: N.Y. 1966, U.S. Ct. Appeals (2d cir.) 1967, U.S. Dist. Ct. (so. and ea. dists) N.Y. 1968, U.S. Supreme Ct. 1971, U.S. Ct. Appeals (3d cir.) 1968, U.S. Ct. Appeals (6th cir.) 1980, U.S. Tax Ct. 1977. Assoc. Kaye, Scholer, Fierman, Hays & Handler, N.Y.C., 1966-67, 67-73; law clk. to judge N.Y. Ct. Appeals, Albany and N.Y.C., 1967; assoc. Botein, Hays, Sklar & Herzberg, N.Y.C., 1973-76, Weisman, Celler, Spett, Modlin & Wertheimer, N.Y.C., 1976, ptnr., 1977-79, counsel, 1979-81; prin. Lawrence N. Weiss, P.C., 1981—; Pantaleoni & Weiss, 1993—. Arbitrator Civil Ct., N.Y.C., 1985—; mediator U.S. Dist. Ct. (ea. dist.) N.Y. and N.Y. Supreme Ct. Mem. Assn. Bar of City of N.Y. (com. on legal edn. and admission to bar), N.Y. State Bar Assn. (chair com. CLE, com. on fed. judiciary, spl. com. on copyright, vice chair com on UN, subcom. internat. cts., litig. sect., judiciary com.). Avocations: Shakespearean studies, equestrian activities, scuba. Home: 107 E 37th St New York NY 10016-3065 E-mail: pandw@akula.com.

WEISS, LEON ALAN, lawyer; b. Cleve., Mar. 6, 1942; s. Benjamin J. and Anne N. (Rose) W.; m. Marilou Rippner, Feb. 6, 1965 (div. 1972); m. Ellen A. Wolf, May 7, 1997. BS, Bucknell U., 1963; JD, Case Western Res. U., 1966. Bar: Ohio 1966, U.S. Dist. Ct. (no. dist.) Ohio 1966, U.S. Ct. Appeals (6th cir.) 1966. Assoc. Rippner Schwartz & Carlin, Cleve., 1966-70; pvt. practice, 1970-79; ptnr. Reminger & Reminger, 1979—. Fellow: Am. Coll. Trust and Estate Counsel; mem.: Cleve. Bar Assn., Ohio Bar Assn. Office: Reminger & Reminger Co LPA 1400 Midland Bldg 101 Prospect Ave W Cleveland OH 44115

WEISS, LEONARD, senate official, mathematician, engineer; b. N.Y.C., Mar. 14, 1934; s. Max and Sadie (Albert) W.; m. Sandra Joyce Raynes, June 15, 1958; children: Madelyn, Eugene. B.E.E., CCNY, 1956; MS, Columbia U., 1959; PhD, Johns Hopkins U., 1962. Lectr. CCNY, 1956-59; staff scientist Research Inst. for Advanced Studies, Balt., 1962-64; asst. prof. Brown U., Providence, 1964-66, assoc. prof., 1966-68; prof. U. Md., College Park, 1968-78; legis. asst. to Senator John Glenn of Ohio, 1976-77; cons. Naval Research Lab., Washington, 1970-77; staff dir. Senate Subcom. on Energy, Nuclear Proliferation and Govt. Processes, 1977-86, Senate Com. Govtl. Affairs., 1987-99; cons. Lawrence Livermore Nat. Lab., 1999—. Editor: Ordinary Differential Equations, 1972; contbr. articles to profl. jours.; author legislation on nuclear proliferation, energy, health and safety, govt. orgn., and govt. mgmt. Alfred P. Sloan research fellow, 1966-68, IEEE Congl. fellow, 1976, Stennis Congl. fellow, 1997. Mem. AAAS, IEEE, Sigma Xi. Home and Office: 11701 Auth Ln Silver Spring MD 20902-1644 E-mail: lensan@worldnet.att.net.

WEISS, LOREN ELLIOT, lawyer, law educator; b. Cleve., Sept. 28, 1947; s. Harry and Gertrude (Rapport) W.; m. Gina Dalton. BA with honors, UCLA, 1969; JD cum laude, U. San Diego, 1972. Bar: Calif. 1972, U.S. Dist. Ct. (so. dist.) Calif. 1972, Utah 1983, U.S. Dist. Ct. (cen. dist.) Calif. 1983, U.S. Dist. Ct. Utah 1983, U.S. Ct. Appeals (9th cir.) 1972, U.S. Ct. Appeals (10th cir.) 1986. With various law firms, San Diego, 1972-80; owner, gen. mgr. Mid-Mountain Lodge, Park City, Utah, 1980-83; pvt. practice, Salt Lake City, 1983—89; of counsel Purser, Okazaki & Berrett, 1989-93; pvt. practice, 1993—96; prin. Weiss Berrett Petty, 1996—2001; of counsel VanCott, Bagley, Cornwall & McCarthy, 2001—. Mem. Utah Com. Bar Examiners, 1989-93; mem. ann. meeting com. Utah State Bar, 1985-91, chmn., 1994-95; liaison, panel atty. rep. U.S. Jud. Conf. Com. on Defender Svc., 1992-95; mem. mandatory cont. legal edn. bd. Utah Judicial Conf., 1995—; adj. prof. J. Reuben Clark Law Sch., Brigham Young U., 1990-98. Contbr. articles to legal jours. Trustee Utah Trout Found., Salt Lake City, 1988-96. Mem. FBA, Calif. Bar Assn., Utah Bar Assn., Nat. Assn. Criminal Def. Lawyers (co-chmn. continuing legal edn. com. 1992-93, co-chair indigent svcs. com. 1994-95), Am. Bd. Trial Advocates. Avocations: fly fishing, reading. Office: Ste 1600 50 S Main St Salt Lake City UT 84144-2044 Fax: 801-534-0058. E-mail: lweiss@vancott.com.

WEISS, LOUISE ANNETTE, music educator; b. Litchfield, Ill. m. Dennis R. Weiss. BME, So. Ill. U., 1979, MME, 1996. Cert. tchr. K-12, Ill. Tchr. music Greenfield (Ill.) Cmty. Unit, 1979-81, Mulberry Grove (Ill.) Schs., 1981-87; instr. music Greenville (Ill.) Coll., 1988—. Adjudicator various mus. contests, 1979—; conducted band clinic, Ramsey (Ill.) H.S., 1992. Ch. musician Mulberry Grove Meth. Ch., 1981—, tchr. Sunday sch., 1996—. Mem. Nat. Assn. Coll. Wind and Percussion Instrs., Music Tchrs. Nat. Assn., Music Educators Nat. Conf., Kappa Delta Pi. Office: Greenville Coll Dept Music 315 E College Ave Greenville IL 62246-1145 E-mail: lweiss@greenville.edu.

WEISS, MARK ANSCHEL, lawyer; b. N.Y.C., NY, June 20, 1937; s. George and Ida (Galin) W.; m. Joan Roth, June 8, 1958; children: Rebecca, Sarabeth, Jonathan, Deborah. AB, Columbia U., 1958; LLB magna cum laude, Harvard U., 1961. Bar: N.Y. 1961, D.C. 1962, U.S. Supreme Ct. 1965. Assoc. Covington & Burling, Washington, 1961-66, 69-70, ptnr., 1970—; spl. asst. to Under Sec. Treasury Dept., 1966-68; spl. asst. to sec., 1968-69. Mem. editl. adv. bd. Electronic Banking Law and Commerce Report. Mem. ABA, D.C. Bar, Fed. Bar Assn. (chmn. banking law com.). Office: Covington & Burling 1201 Pennsylvania Ave NW Washington DC 20004-2401

WEISS, MARTIN, consulting environmental engineer; b. Stoneham, Mass., Apr. 30, 1934; s. Manuel and Ethel Edna (Pekowsky) W.; m. Marsha H. Sobell, May 8, 1958; children: Barbara Gene, Robert Charles. BSCE, Northeastern U., 1957, MSCE, 1966. Registered profl. engr., Mass.; diplomate Am. Acad. Environ. Engrs.; cert. waste water treatment plant operator, Mass. Engr. Metcalf & Eddy, Wakefield, Mass., 1958-63, v.p, gen. mgr., 1981-86; project mgr. Camp, Dresser & McKee, Cambridge, 1963-67; plant mgr., chief engr. Met. Dist. Commn., Boston, 1967-81; project dir. Roy F. Weston, West Chester, Pa., 1986-87; pres. Capitol Environ. Engring., North Reading, Mass., 1988—; dir. Nat. Coun. of Northeastern U. Presenter in field to profl. orgns., 1970—; editl. advisor Pollution Engring., 1977. Contbr. articles to profl. jours. Chmn. pack com. Cub Scouts Am., Newton, Mass., 1971-72; treas. Meml. Sch. PTA, Newton, 1972-73; mem. Newton Adv. Planning Commn., 1972; chmn. North Reading (Mass.) Conservation Commn., 1992—. Mem. Water Environ. Fedn. (bd. dirs. 1981-84, exec. com. 1983, Quarter Century Club, Hatfield award 1974), Assn. Met. Sewer Agys. (bd. dirs. 1976-80, treas. 1980), Am. Water Works Assn., Boston Soc. Civil Engrs., New Eng. Water Environ. Assn. (pres. 1980), Thomson Country Club (bd. dirs. 1993—). Avocation: golf. Home: 26 Cleek Ct North Reading MA 01864-3420 Office: Capitol Environ Engring Park Place E 348 Park St Ste 207E North Reading MA 01864-2154 E-mail: martinweiss@aol.com.

WEISS, MARTIN HARVEY, neurosurgeon, educator; b. Newark , Feb. 2, 1939; s. Max and Rae W.; m. R. Debora Rosenthal, Aug. 20, 1961; children: Brad, Jessica, Elisabeth. AB magna cum laude, Dartmouth Coll., 1960, BMS, 1961; MD, Cornell U., 1963. Diplomate Am. Bd. Neurol. Surgery (bd. dirs. 1983-89, vice chmn. 1987-88, chmn. 1988-89). Intern Univ. Hosps., Cleve., 1963-64, resident in neurosurgery, 1966-70; sr. instr. to asst. prof. neurosurgery Case Western Res. U., 1970-73; asso. prof. neurosurgery U. So. Calif., 1973-76, prof., 1976-78, prof., chmn. dept., 1978—, Martin H. Weiss chair in neurol. surgery, 1997—. Chmn. neurology B study sect. NIH; mem. residency rev. com. for neurosurg. Accreditation Commn. for Grad. Med. Edn., 1989—, vice chmn., 1991—93, chmn., 1993—95, mem. appeals coun. in neurosurg., 1995—; Courville lectr. Loma Linda U. Sch. Medicine, 1989; vis. prof. Harvard Med. Sch., 1988; Edgar Kahn vis. prof. U. Mich, 1987; W. James Gardner lectr. Cleve. Clinic, 1993; Edwin Boldrey vis. prof. U. Calif., San Francisco, 1994; hon. guest San Francisco Neurol. Soc., 1994, Australian Neurosurg. Soc., 1996; Arthur Ward vis. prof. U. Wash., 1988; John Raff vis. prof. U. Oreg., 1995; vis. prof. Tufts U., 1996; Afrox traveling prof. South African Congress Neurol. Surgeons, 1989; Loyal Davis lectr. Northwestern U., 1990; vis. prof. U. Melbourne, 1996, U. Sydney, 1996; Wagner lectr. U. Medicine and Dentistry N.J., 1997; Altman lectr. U. Pa., 2001; hon. guest Royal Coll. Physicians Endocrine Sect., London, 2001; vis. prof. U. Erlangen/Nurnberg, 1999, U. Geneva, 1999. Author: Pituitary Diseases, 1980; editor-in-chief Clin. Neurosurgery, 1980-83; assoc. editor Bull. L.A. Neurol. Socs., 1976-81, Jour. Clin. Neurosci., 1981—; mem. editl. bd. Neurosurgery, 1979-84, Neurol. Rsch., 1980—, Jour. Neurosurgery, 1987—, chmn., 1995—, assoc. editor, 1996—. Served to capt. USAR, 1964-66. Spl. fellow in neurosurgery NIH, 1969-70; recipient Jamieson medal Australasian Neurosurg. Soc., 1996. Mem. ACS (adv. coun. neurosurgery 1985-88), Soc. Neurol. Surgeons (v.p. 1999, pres.-elect 2000—, pres. 2001-02), Neurosurg. Soc. Am., Am. Acad. Neurol. Surgery (exec. com. 1988-89, v.p. 1992-93), Rsch. Soc. Neurol. Surgeons, Am. Assn. Neurol. Surgeons (bd. dirs. 1988-91, sec. 1994-97, pres.-elect 1998-99, pres. 1999-2000, past pres. 2000-2001), Congress Neurol. Surgeons (v.p. 1982-83), Western Neurosurg. Soc., Neurosurg. Forum, So. Calif. Neurosurg. Soc. (pres. 1983-84), Phi Beta Kappa, Alpha Omega Alpha. Home: 357 Georgian Rd La Canada Flintridge CA 91011-3520 Office: 1200 N State St Los Angeles CA 90033-1029 E-mail: weiss@hsc.usc.edu.

WEISS, MARY ALICE, insurance economics educator; b. Cleve., June 12, 1957; d. Richard Alfred And Julianna (Scerbik) W.; m. J. David Cummins. BSBA, Quincy Coll., 1979; MS in Ins. Econs., U. Pa., 1982, PhD in Ins. Econs., 1984. Lectr. La Salle Coll., Phila., 1983; asst. prof. U. S.C., Columbia, 1984, Rider Coll., Lawrenceville, N.J., 1984-86, Temple U., Phila., 1986—. Cons. IBM, N.Y., 1985-87; speaker nat. and internat. ins. confs. Reviewer Jour. Risk and Ins., 1985—, book rev. editor, 1986—; contbr. articles to profl. jours. Active Clean Water Action, Phila., 1986—; faculty advisor Gamma Iota Sigma, Phila., 1987—. Huebner fellow Huebner Found., U. Pa., 1979-82; presdl. scholar Quincy Coll., 1975-79. Mem. Am. Risk & Ins. Assn. (coms., nat. & internat. conf. speaker), Western Econ. Assn., Penjerdel Employee Benefit Assn. Democrat. Avocation: antiques. Home: 625 New Gulph Rd Bryn Mawr PA 19010-3650 Office: Temple U Ritter Hall Annex Rm 479 Philadelphia PA 19122

WEISS, MAX TIBOR, retired aerospace company executive; b. Hajduananas, Hungary, Dec. 29, 1922; came to U.S., 1929, naturalized, 1936; s. Samuel and Anna (Hornstein) W.; m. Melitta Newman, June 28, 1953; children: Samuel Harvey, Herschel William, David Nathaniel, Deborah Beth. BEE, CCNY, 1943; MS, MIT, 1947, PhD, 1950. Rsch. assoc. MIT, 1946-50; mem. tech. staff Bell Tel. Labs., Holmdel, N.J., 1950-59; assoc. head applied physics lab. Hughes Aircraft Co., Culver City, Calif., 1959-60; dir. electronics rsch. lab. The Aerospace Corp., L.A., 1961-63, gen. mgr. labs. div., 1963-67, gen. mgr. electronics and optics div., 1968-78, v.p., gen. mgr. lab. ops., 1978-81, v.p. engring. group, 1981-86; v.p. tech. and electronics system group Northrop Corp., 1986-91, v.p., gen. mgr. electronics systems div. Hawthorne, Calif., 1991-94; corp. v.p., dep. gen. mgr. electronics/systems integration Northrop Grumman Corp., Bethpage, N.Y., 1994-96, corp. v.p., 1996. Asst. mgr. engring. ops. TRW Systems, Redondo Beach, Calif., 1967-68; mem. sci. adv. bd. USAF; bd. dirs. Concorde Solutions, Inc., Concord, Calif. Contbr. articles to physics and electronics jours.; patentee in electronics and communications. With USNR, 1944-45. Fellow Am. Phys. Soc., IEEE (Centennial medal, 1983, Fredrik Philips award, 1993), AIAA, AAAS; mem. NAE, Sigma Xi. E-mail: maxweiss@mediaone.net.

WEISS, MICHAEL DAVID, mathematician, mathematical economist; b. Chgo., Nov. 12, 1942; s. Harry Edward and Gertrude (Plotkin) W. BA, Brandeis U., 1964; PhD, Brown U., 1970; MA, U. Md., 1984. Asst. prof. math. Wayne State U., Detroit, 1969-74; ops. research analyst Ketron, Inc., Arlington, Va., 1974-76; math. statistician USDA, Washington, 1976-85, agrl. economist, 1985-97; cons., 1998—. Adj. assoc. prof. U. Md., 1998-99. Author: (U.S. Govt. rsch. monographs) Conceptual Foundations of Risk Theory, 1987, The Automated Weather/Yield System, 1983; contbr. rsch. publs. to jours., books, others. Mem. Am. Math. Soc., Soc. for Indsl. and Applied Math. (pres. Washington-Balt. sect. 1993-98, vis. lectr. 1992—), Sigma Xi. Achievements include research in entropy theory, fuzzy set theory, risk theory, food-safety economics, weather/yield modeling, and the economics of precision farming. Home and Office: 7797 Heatherton Ln Potomac MD 20854-3264 E-mail: michaelweiss@erols.com.

WEISS, MYRNA GRACE, business executive; b. N.Y.C., June 22, 1939; d. Herman and Blanche (Stiftel) Ziegler; m. Arthur H. Weiss; children: Debra Anne Huddleston, Louise Esther Pennington. BA, Barnard Coll., 1958; MA, Hunter Coll., 1968; MPA, NYU, 1978; cert. in Mktg., U. Pa. Tchr., N.Y.C. and Vallejo, Calif., 1959-68; dir. admissions Columbia Prep. Sch., N.Y.C., 1969-72; dir. PREP counselling NYU, 1973-74; dept. head Hewitt Sch., 1974-79; mgr. Met. Ins. Co., 1979-84; mktg. exec. Rothschild, Inc., 1984-85; pres. First Mktg. Capital Group Ltd., 1985—; mng. dir. Wrap Co. Internat. N.V., 1992-97; advisor Lared Group, N.Y.C., 1987-97; CEO, pres., bd. dirs. Ibnet, 1998—2002. Advisor Gov.'s Hwy. Safety Com., N.Y.C., 1985-88; pres. Fin. Women's Assn. N.Y., 1984-85. Bd. dirs. 92nd Y, N.Y.C., 1972-90, ARC, N.Y.C., 1989-96, 97—, asst. treas., 1993-96, 97—. Mem. Internat. Women's Forum (bd. dirs. 1990-92), Econ. Club N.Y., Women's Econ. Roundtable (bd. dirs. 1988-90). Office: 1st Mktg Capital Group Ltd 1056 5th Ave New York NY 10028-0112 E-mail: mzweiss@ibnet.com.

WEISS, NANCY P. artist; b. Chgo., June 12, 1938; d. Manny and Helen (Spero) Passman; m. Lenard Garsen Weiss, Aug. 30, 1958; children: Pamela Lee, Elizabeth Susan. Student, U. Colo., 1956-57, U. Calif., Berkeley, from 1958, CCAC, Oakland, Calif., 1980-81, San Francisco Art Inst., 1984-85. Artist, 1950—. Exhibited in shows at Bolinas (Calif.) Mus., 1992-2002, Galleria Le Logge, Assisi, Italy, 1997, 98, 99; contbr. to The Calif. Art Rev., 1990. Chair Berkeley Civic Arts Commn. City of Berkeley, 1980-85; mem. adv. bd. No. Calif. chpt. Nat. Mus. Women in the Arts; bd. dirs. Eureka Theatre Co., San Francisco. Democrat. Jewish. Avocations: walking, yoga, tennis. Fax: (415) 362-3110.

WEISS, RANDALL A. television and radio producer, supermarket executive; b. Gary, Ind., Sept. 3, 1952; s. Arthur and Sylvia (Mednick) W.; m. Adrienne J. Weiss, Feb. 5, 1973; children: Benjamin, Caleb, Joshua, James, Abigail, Emma. AA, Coll. DuPage, 1977; BA, Dallas Bapt. U., 1993; MA in Religious Studies, Greenwich U., 1994; diploma of practical theology, Christ for the Nations Inst., 1993; PhD, Greenwich U., 1995; MS in Jewish Studies, Spertus Inst. Jewish Studies, 1996; DMin, Faraston Theol. Sem., 1996. Ordained to Ministry, Christ for Nations Alumni Ministers Fellowship. Gen. mgr. We Care Food Stores, Inc., Knox, Ind., 1975-84; pres., CEO We Care Food Stores, Inc. subs. Five Star Foods, 1984—; prodn. mgr. Excellence in Christian Broadcasting; comml. real estate developer Magnum Value Properties, LLC; TV sta. owner KKCC, Oklahoma City, Sta. KTAV-LP, Lancaster, Calif. Songwriter, pub. Lordship Music Pub., BMI; asst. prof. on adj. faculty ICI U.; dean Jewish studies dept. Columbia Evang. Sem.; bd. regents Columbia Evangelical Sem. (formerly Faraston Theol. Sem.); Am. rep. Australian Christian Channel. Author: Jewish Sects of the New Testament Era, Does Jacob's Trouble Wear a Cross?: Christianity: A Jewish Religion, In Search of the Lost Jewish Atonement; writer, artist: (TV show) Crosstalk, 1994--, (prime time TV spl.) Passover: The Jewish Connection to the Last Supper, Hanukkah: It's Not A Jewish Christmas, Days of Awe: The Jewish High Holidays, (TV) Father's Day; author (CD rom) Crosstalk Bible study software: Does Jacob's Trouble Wear a Cross?, Jewish Sects of the New Testament Era; writer, prodr. albums Munchy Manna, Never Seen a U-Haul on a Hearse, Lead Me to the Rock. Worship in the Holy Land, Good News Jew's Blues; writer, prodr. single projects I Don't Need no Designer Jeans, Never Seen a U-Haul on a Hearse, Jesus is Lord; contbg. editor World Evangelism mag. Bd. dirs. World Missionary Evangelism. Nominated NRB Christian T.V. Program of Yr., 2000. Mem. Full Gospel Bus. Men's Fellowship Internat. (life, banquet spkr.), Soc. for Pentecostal Studies, Evang. Theol. Soc., Nat. Religious Broadcasters, Alliance for Cmty. Media, Fellowship of European Broadcasters. Avocations: fishing, travel, reading, music. Office: Five Star Foods 1209 S Heaton St Knox IN 46534-2398

WEISS, RANDALL DUNN, economist; b. Washington, May 28, 1946; s. Emanuel G. and Mili (Dunn) W.; m. Laura Burstein, July 3, 1968; 1 child, Stephanie. AB magna cum laude wth highest hons. in econs., Harvard U., 1968, AM, 1971, PhD, 1973. Asst. prof. econs. U. Md., College Park, 1973-77; staff economist Joint Com. on Taxation, U.S. Congress, Washington, 1977-83, chief economist, 1983-84, dep. chief staff, 1985-89; prin., dir. tax econs. Deloitte & Touche LLP, 1989—. Cons. World Bank, Washington, 1974, U.S. Dept. Labor, Washington, 1975; mem. adv. bd. Office Tax Analysis, U.S. Dept. Treasury, Washington, 1986-87, Joint Com. Taxation, 1995—. Contbr. articles to profl. jours. Woodrow Wilson Found. fellow, 1968; NSF grad. fellowship, 1968-72. Mem. Am. Econ. Assn., Phi Beta Kappa. Office: Deloitte & Touche 1001 Pennsylvania Ave NW Washington DC 20004-2505

WEISS, RENÉE KAROL, editor, writer, musician; b. Allentown, Pa., Sept. 11, 1923; d. Abraham S. and Elizabeth (Levitt) Karol; m. Theodore Weiss. BA, Bard Coll., 1951; student, Conn. Sch. Dance; studied violin with, Sascha Jacobinoff, Boris Koutzen, Emile Hauser, Ivan Galamian. Mem. Miami U. Symphony Orch., 1941, N.C. State Sympnony, 1942-45, Oxford U. Symphony, Opera Orchs., Eng., 1953-54, Woodstock String Quartet, 1956-60, Bard Coll. Chamber Ensemble, 1950-66, Hudson Valley Philharmonic, 1960-66, Hudson Valley String Quartet, 1965, Princeton Chamber Orch., 1980-93; orchestral, chamber work, 1966—. Participant Theodore and Renée Weiss poetry writing workshops Princeton U., 1985, Hofstra Coll., 1985, modern poetry workshop Cooper Union, 1988, Princeton Adult Edn.; tchr. modern dance to children Bard Coll., Kindergarten Tivoli, N.Y. Pub. Sch., 1955-58. Author: (children's books) To Win A Race, 1966, A Paper Zoo, 1968 (best books for children N.Y. Times, Book World 1968, N.J. Author's award 1968, 70, 88), The Bird From the Sea, 1970, Biography: David Schubert: Works and Days, 1984; co-editor, mgr. Quar. Rev. Lit., 1945—; author of poetry with Theodore Weiss; poetry readings (with Theodore Weiss) at various colls. in U.S. and abroad, including China. Mem. PEN (Nora Magid Lifetime Achievement award with Theodore Weiss 1997). Home and Office: Q R L Poetry Series 26 Haslet Ave Princeton NJ 08540-4914

WEISS, RHETT LOUIS, business executive, lawyer; b. Kyushu, Japan, May 22, 1961; came to U.S., 1961; s. Armand Berl and Judith (Bernstein) W.; m. Kristen Sue Krieger, Oct. 11, 1987; children: Aaron Bradford, Alexander Donald, Andrew Franklin, Alison Judith. BS in Mgmt. cum laude, Tulane U., 1983; JD, Coll. William and Mary, 1986; exec. internat. bus. cert., Georgetown U., 1996; postgrad., U. N.C., 2000. Bar: Va. 1986, D.C. 1993, N.Y. 1995, U.S. Ct. Appeals (4th cir.) 1986, U.S. Tax Ct. 1987, U.S. Dist. Ct. (we. dist.) Va. 1989, U.S. Bankruptcy Ct. (we. dist.) Va. 1989, U.S. Dist. Ct. (ea. dist.) Va. 1989, U.S. Bankruptcy Ct. (ea. dist.) Va. 1996. Chief ops. officer First Fed. Savs. Bank Shenandoah Valley, Front Royal, Va., 1990-92; sr. atty. Weil, Gotshal & Manges LLP, Washington, 1992-97; dir. strategic relocation/expansion svcs., mem. mgmt. com. Bus. Incentives Group, KPMG Peat Marwick LLP, McLean, Va., 1997-99; founder, CEO, chmn. DEALTEK, Ltd., Syracuse, NY, 1999—; former prin., dir. Adamson, Crump, Sharp & Weiss, P.C., Front Royal. Bd. dirs. Pentathlon Corp., Winchester, Va., Assns. Internat. Inc., McLean, Va., Weiss Pub. Co., Inc., Richmond, Va.; asst. town atty., counsel to Front Royal Planning Commn., 1987-90. Author: Portfolio Transactions: The Anatomy of a Deal, 1994, The Basics of Successful Negotiating, 1994, The Negotiating Process: Optimizing Give and Take, 1995, 96, 97, Doing Global Business in a United States Foreign-Trade Zone, 1996, 97, Sales and Use Tax-Exempt Construction: An Innovative Economic Development Tool to Help Land the Deal, 1997, Facility Development, Expansion and Operations: The Major Tax and Related Cost Aspects, 1998, Doing a Deal in the U.S.: Incentives and the Project Negotiation Process, 1998, Business Expansion and Facility Development: Incentives and the Project Development Process, 1999, 2000, Working With Economic Developers, 2000; Web-Enabled Site Selection: Getting the Information You Need at Internet Speed, 2000, Economic Development in the Electronic Age, 2001, 02, Use Incentives to Make the Best Location Choice, 2001, Using the Internet to Move Technology Around the Globe Without Ever Leaving Home, 2002. Bd. dirs. Blue Ridge Arts Coun., Inc., 1987-92, v.p., 1989-90, pres., 1990-91; bd. dirs. Front Royal Little Theatre, Inc., 1988-89, Front Royal Warren County Unit Am. Heart Assn., 1991-92, Lord Fairfax C.C. Edn. Found., 1991-94, Build-A-Future Found., 1994-98, v.p., 1997-98; Shenrapawa dist. chmn. Shenandoah area coun. Boy Scouts Am., 1988-89, coun. treas., 1991-92, coun. bd. dirs., 1987-94; adv. com. Small Bus. Assistance Ctr., Lord Fairfax C.C.; mem. Seaton Elem. Sch. devel. team D.C. Pub. Schs. Ptnrs. In Edn. Program, 1994-96; soccer coach Southwestern Youth Assn., 1998-2001. Recipient Nat. Quality Dist. award Boy Scouts Am., 1988, 89, Statuette award, 1992. Fellow John Marshall Soc. of Va. Bar Assn.; mem. ABA, Internat. Econ. Devel. Coun., Internat. Econ. Devel. Coun., D.C. Bar (vice chmn. comml. trans. com. 1994-96, vice chmn. real property trans. com. 1996-97, chmn. 1997-98, real estate, housing and land use sect.), Va. State Bar, N.Y. Bar, Va., N.C. and S.C. Econ. Developers Assn., So. Econ. Devel. Coun., Greater Syracuse C. of C. (entrepreneurial coun., chair visibility com. 2002--), Ctrl. N.Y. Internat. Bus. Alliance (founding dir. 2002--), Rotary (bd. dirs. 2002--), Valley Estate Planning Coun. (bd. govs. 1989-92, pres. 1992), Front Royal-Warren County C. of C. (bd. dirs. 1989-92, pres. 1990-91), Country Club Fairfax (Va.), Delta Tau Delta (sec. 1980-81), Beta Gamma Sigma, Beta Alpha Psi. Avocations: cars, outdoors, travel, music, sports. Office: 100 Madison St Ste 1200 Syracuse NY 13202 Home: 3767 Highland Ave Skaneateles NY 13152-9356 E-mail: rweiss@dealtek.com.

WEISS, ROBERT ALAN, surgeon; b. Chgo., Mar. 8, 1956; s. Harold Richard and Nancy (Rogoff) W.; m. Tina Haberer. MD, Chgo. Med. Sch., North Chicago, Ill., 1982. Diplomate Nat. Bd. Med. Examiners, Am. Bd. Ophthalmology, Am. Soc. Oculoplastic and Reconstructive Surgery. Flexible intern Cook County Hosp., Chgo., 1982-83; resident ophthalmology house staff Cornell U., N.Y. Hosp. & Meml. Sloan Kettering Cancer Ctr., N.Y.C., 1983-86, fellow ophthalmic oncology and orbital disease, 1986-87; fellow oculoplastic and reconstructive surgery Emory U. Med. Ctr., Atlanta, 1987-88; asst. clin. prof. ophthalmology Cornell U. Med. Ctr., N.Y.C., 1988-90; clin. assoc. prof. ophthalmology and neurosurgery U. Ill., Chgo. Med. Ctr., 1991—; attending oculoplastic surgeon Chgo. Eye Inst., 1991—. Asst. dir. Cornell Med. Ctr. Robert Ellsworth-Ophthalmic Oncology Ctr., N.Y.C., 1988-90; credentialled specialist U. Ill. Divsn. Svcs. Cripped Children, Chgo., 1991—; co-dir. U. Ill. Retinoblastoma Bd., Chgo., 1992—; vis. prof. Lions Club, Bolivian Am. Med. Soc., S.Am. Med. Soc., Israel, Bolivia, Columbia, Equador, Philippines, Egypt, 1991, 93, 94, 98, 99, 2000. Editor: Principles and Practice of Ophthalmic Plastic and Reconstructive Surgery, 1996. Recipient Golden Apple Tchg. award U. Ill., Chgo., 1994; named tchr. of yr. Chgo. Curriculum in Ophthalmology, 2000. Fellow Am. Soc. Oculoplastic and Reconstructive Surgery, Am. Acad. Ophthalmology, Alpha Omega Alpha. Avocations: gardening, photography, painting. Office: Chgo Eye Inst 3982 N Milwaukee Ave Chicago IL 60641-2703

WEISS, ROBERT FRANCIS, former academic administrator, religious organization administrator, consultant; b. St. Louis, Aug. 27, 1924; s. Frank L. G. and Helen M. (Beck) W. BA, St. Louis U., 1951, Ph.L., MA, St. Louis U., 1953, S.T.L., 1961; PhD, U. Minn., 1964. Joined Soc. of Jesus, 1946; ordained priest Roman Catholic Ch., 1959; tchr. Rockhurst High Sch., Kansas City, Mo., 1953-56; adminstrv. asst. to pres. St. Louis U., 1961-62; asst. dean Rockhurst Coll., Kansas City, Mo., 1964-66, dean, v.p., asst. prof. edn., 1966-72, pres., 1977-88, St. Louis U. High Sch., 1973-77, interim pres., 1992; asst. for higher edn. and continuing formation Mo. Province S.J., St. Louis, 1989-92, 97—, treas., 1992—. Mem. Commn. on Govtl. Rels., Am. Coun. Edn., 1985-87; bd. dirs. Kansas City Regional Coun. for Higher Edn., 1978-88, Boys Hope Girls Hope, 1977—. Contbr. chpts. to books, articles to profl. jours. Trustee St. Louis U., 1973-87, 91—, Loyola U., New Orleans, 1973-82, 85-88, United Student Aid Funds, Inc., 1977-94, U. San Francisco, 1987-99, Marymount Coll., Salina, Kans., 1986-88, St. Louis U. H.S., 1989-99, Fontbonne Coll., St. Louis, 1973-77, Sacred Heart Program, Radio and TV Apostolate, St. Louis, 1990-96, pres., 1992-96, bd. dirs, 2000—; bd. dirs. Creighton U., Omaha, 1981-97, Our Little Haven, 1992—, St. Elizabeth Acad., St. Louis, 1997—, Loyola Acad. St. Louis, 2000—. 1st sgt. U.S. Army, 1943-46. Decorated Bronze Star. Mem. Am. Assn. for Higher Edn., Rainbow Divsn. Vets. Assn. (nat. chaplain 1976-84, 88-90, pres.-elect 1990-91, pres. 1991-92, assoc. nat. chaplain 1992—), Alpha Sigma Nu, Alpha Phi Omega. Home and Office: 4511 W Pine Blvd Saint Louis MO 63108-2109 E-mail: treasurer@jesuits-mis.org. *The only way for me to look at life is in the light of faith, which I consider one of God's greatest gifts. Life for me is an opportunity to serve God and as many of my neighbors as I can. I am basically an optimist. There is so much beauty around us, so many good people, so many marvels to behold— that I thank the Lord for giving me the ability to know and experience this life and to look forward to eternal life with God, the Source of all life. Any success I have had I attribute to taking advantage of the opportunities that God has put in my path.*

WEISS, ROBERT JEROME, psychiatrist, educator; b. West New York, N.J., Dec. 9, 1917; s. Harry and Dora (Samuels) W.; m. Minnie Thompson Moore, Apr. 21, 1945; children— Scott Tillman, James Woodrow, Elizabeth Thompson. Student, Johns Hopkins, 1937; AB, George Washington U., 1947; MD,

Columbia, 1951; MA (hon.), Dartmouth, 1964. Intern Columbia div. Bellevue Hosp., 1951, asst. resident medicine, 1953; resident psychiatry N.Y. Psychiat. Inst., 1954-56; asst. attending Vanderbilt Clinic, 1957-58, Presbyn. Hosp., N.Y.C., 1958-59; chief psychiatry Mary Hitchcock Meml. Hosp., 1959-70; career tchr. trainee Nat. Inst. Mental Health, 1956-58; tchr., research Columbia Coll. Phys. and Surg., 1956-59; prof. psychiatry, founder, chmn. dept. Dartmouth Med. Sch., 1959-70; psychiatrist Beth Israel Hosp., 1988-90; attending physician Presbyn. Hosp., 1975-85, cons., 1985—. Vis. prof. cmty. medicine Harvard Med. Sch., 1970-75, assoc. dir. cmty. health, 1970-95, assoc. dean health care planning; prof. psychiatry and social medicine Columbia Coll. Physicians and Surgeons, 1975-86, also dir. Ctrs. for Cmty. Health, 1975-86; De Lamar prof. pub. health practice, dean Columbia U. Sch. Pub. Health, 1980-86, dean and De Lamar prof. of pub. health practice, prof. psychiatry, prof. social medicine, prof. emeritus, 1986—; vis. prof. cmty. medicine U. N.Mex. Med. Sch., 1986-89; adj. prof. arts and sci. U. Maine, Orono, 1997—; cons. Nat. Ctr. for Health Svcs. Rsch., 1975-86, NIMH, 1977-86; chmn. psychiatry tng. com. NIMH, 1967-68, mem. coord. panel, 1965-67, ad hoc com. interdisciplinary tng. program, 1966, mem. agenda com., 1966; cons. AT&T, 1990-92; chmn. bd. Academica, 1992, Employee Managed Care Corp., 1994-96; prin. Weiss, Baldacci & Fletcher. Co-editor: Columbia U. Coll. Physicians and Surgeons Complete Home Medical Guide, 1986, editor emeritus 2d and 3d edits., 1989; contbr. articles to profl. jours., chpts. to books. Founder dept. psychiatry Dartmouth Med. Sch., 1959. Served to maj. AUS, 1941-46. Recipient Bi-Centennial medal Columbia Coll. Phys. and Surg., 1967 Fellow Am. Psychiat. Assn. (life); mem. Am. Assn. Chmn. Depts. Psychiatry (pres. 1979-80). Achievements include first telemedicine 2-way transmission between medical centers; demonstrated social supports reduce disability due to mental illness; research in special health care delivery, health care preventive psychiatry. Home: 10 Cromwell Dr Orono ME 04473-3639 E-mail: rweiss7765@aol.com.

WEISS, ROBERT M. urologist, educator; b. N.Y.C., Jan. 13, 1936; s. David and Laura W.; m. Ilana Shemer, May 20, 1973; children: Erik Daniel, Dana Alexandra. BS magna cum laude, Franklin and Marshall Coll., Lancaster, Pa., 1957; MD, SUNY, Bklyn., 1960; MA (hon.), Yale U., 1976. Diplomate: Am. Bd. Urology, Nat. Bd. Med. Examiners. Intern Cornell Med. Div., Bellevue Hosp., N.Y.C., 1960-61; resident in gen. surgery Beth Israel Hosp., 1961-62; resident in urology Squier Urol. Clinic, Presbyn. Hosp., 1963-64, 65-67; vs. fellow Columbia U. Coll. Physicians and Surgeons, 1964-65, adj. assoc. prof. pharmacology, 1975-77, adj. prof. pharmacology, 1977—; mem. faculty Yale U. Med. Sch., New Haven, 1967—, prof. urology, 1976-88, prof., chief sect. of urology, 1988—, interim chmn. dept. surgery, 1999-2001; attending urology Yale-New Haven Hosp., 1967-88, head sect. of urology, 1988—, interim chief dept. surgery, 1999—2001. Cons. West Haven VA Hosp., Waterbury (Conn.) Hosp. Contbr. articles to med. publs. Trustee Am. Bd. Urology, 1998—. With USAR, 1962-63. Fellow ACS, Am. Acad. Pediatrics; mem. AAAS, Am. Assn. Genito-Urinary Surgeons, Am. Surg. Assn, Am. Physiol. Soc., Soc. Gen. Physiologists, Assn. Univ. Urologists, Soc. Pediatric Urology, Am. Urol. Assn., Clin. Soc. Genito-Urinary Surgeons, Phi Beta Kappa, Sigma Xi. Office: Yale U Sch of Medicine Dept Urology PO Box 208041 New Haven CT 06520-8041

WEISS, ROBERT MICHAEL, dentist; b. Bklyn., June 5, 1940; s. Henry and Rena (Bluth) W.; m. Irene Marilyn Sternick, June 30, 1962; children: Lori Ann, Julie Lynn, Karen Michelle. Trustees scholar, L.I. U., 1958-61; DDS, NYU, 1965; postdoctoral cert., LD Pankey Inst. for Advanced Dental Edn., 1979. Pvt. practice dentistry, Avon, Conn., 1967—; pres. Avon Dental Group, P.C., 1972—; clin. prof. Coll. Dentistry U. Conn., 2000—. Nat. cons. Conn. Gen. Ins. Co. for ins. coverage for Gen. Electric Co., 1980—; advisor dental assisting program Briarwood Coll.; cons. CNA Ins. Co., 1988—; mem. mentorship program U. Conn. Coll. Dentistry; bd. dirs. Sentinel Bank; mentor program U. Conn. Coll. Dentistry. Chmn. Children's Dental Health Week, Hartford County, Conn., 1971; chmn. Jewish Adult Edn., West Hartford, Conn., 1986-87; trustee Temple Beth Israel, 1983—. Served to capt. USAF, 1965-67. Fellow Acad. Gen. Dentistry, Am. Acad. Gen. Dentistry, Pierre Fauchand Acad. (hon.); mem. ADA, Am. Soc. Preventive Dentistry (pres. Conn. chpt.), Acad. Osseointegration, Internat. Congress Oral Implantologists, Hartford Dental Soc. (exec. com. 1993—, chmn. centennial yr., chmn. 100th anniversary 1996-97), Conn. State Dental Assn. (ho. of dels. 1992—), Chronic Fatigue Immune Dysfunction Syndrome (Conn. bd. dirs. 1992—), So. New Eng. Assn. Practice Adminstrn., Starnard Beach Assn. (pres. 1984-86), Avon Jr. C. of C. (pres. 1971-72), Masons, Alpha Omega, Sigma Alpha Mu. Home: 13 Alpine Meadow Ln Avon CT 06001-3935 Office: Avon Dental Group 20 W Avon Rd Ste 2 Avon CT 06001-3540

WEISS, ROBERT ORR, speech educator; b. Kalamazoo, Apr. 8, 1926; s. Nicholas John and Ruth (Orr) W.; m. Ann Lenore Lawson, Sept. 16, 1951; children: Elizabeth Ann, John Lawson, James Robert, Virginia Lenore. BA, Albion Coll., 1948; MA, Northwestern U., 1949, PhD, 1954. Instr. speech Wayne State U., Detroit, 1949-51; instr. pub. speaking Northwestern U., Evanston, Ill., 1954-55; mem. faculty DePauw U., Greencastle, Ind., 1955—, H.B. Gough prof. speech, 1965-97, head comm. arts and scis., 1963-78, 85-86, 93. Author: Public Argument, 1995; editor: Speaker and Gavel, 1968-75, Speaking Across the Curriculum, 1990—; co-editor: Current Criticism, 1971; contbr. articles to profl. jours. Served with AUS, 1945-46. Recipient Fred C. Tucker Disting. Career award, 1995, Lifetime award, Nat. Ednl. Debate Assn., 1997, Presdl. citation Nat. Communication Assn., 1999. Mem. AAUP (pres. DePauw U. chpt. 1961-62), Nat. Communication Assn. (legis. assembly 1966-68), Am. Forensic Assn. (sec.-treas. 1958-59), Ctrl. States Communication Assn., Internat. Communication Assn., Phi Beta Kappa, Delta Sigma Rho-Tau Kappa Alpha (nat. v.p. 1981-83, pres. 1983-85), Sigma Nu. Home: 722 Highridge Ave Greencastle IN 46135-1402 E-mail: robertweiss@depauw.edu.

WEISS, ROBERT STEPHEN, medical manufacturing company financial executive; b. Oct. 25, 1946; s. Stephen John and Anna Blanche (Lescinski) W.; m. Marilyn Annette Chesick, Oct. 29, 1970; children: Christopher Robert, Kim Marie, Douglas Paul. BS in Acctg. cum laude, U. Scranton, 1968. CPA, N.Y. Supr. KPMG (formerly Peat, Marwick, Mitchell & Co.), N.Y.C., 1971-76; asst. corp. contr. Cooper Labs., Inc., Parsippany, N.J., 1977-78; group contr. Coopen Vision, Inc., 1980; v.p., corp. contr. Cooper Labs., Palo Alto, Calif., 1981-83, The Cooper Cos., Inc. (formerly CooperVision, Inc.), Palo Alto, 1984-89; v.p., treas., CFO The Cooper Cos., Inc., Pleasanton, 1989—, sr. v.p., 1992-95, exec. v.p. fin., 1995—. Bd. dirs. The Cooper Cos., Inc., Pleasanton, Calif. With U.S. Army, 1969-70. Decorated Bronze Star with oak leaf cluster, Army Commendation medal. Mem. AICPA, N.Y. State Soc. CPAs. Home: 1775 Spumante Pl Pleasanton CA 94566-6478 Office: The Cooper Companies Inc Ste 590 6140 Stoneridge Mall Rd Pleasanton CA 94588 E-mail: rweiss@cooperco.com.

WEISS, RONALD PHILLIP, lawyer; b. Springfield, Mass., Apr. 28, 1947; s. Kermit Paul and Fay Roslyn (Robinovitz) W.; m. Janet Faye Landon, June 15, 1969; children: Emily, Katherine. BA, Dartmouth Coll., 1968; JD, U. Pa., 1972. Bar: Mass. 1972, U.S. Dist. Ct. Mass. 1975, U.S. Tax Ct. 1979, U.S. Ct. Appeals (1st cir.) 2000. Assoc. Bulkley, Richardson and Gelinas, Springfield, Mass., 1972-78; ptnr. Bulkley, Richardson and Gelinas, LLP, 1978—. Pres. Estate Planning Coun. Hampden County, 1979-81; trustee Mass. Continuing Legal Edn. Inc., 1978-81. Author: (with others) Drafting Wills and Trusts in Massachusetts, 1990, 92, 94; editor: (with others) Massachusetts Corporate Tax Manual, 1986. Trustee Springfield Symphony Orch., 1986—, v.p., 1988—89, pres., 1989—91, chmn., 1991—94; mem. bd. advisors U. Mass. Family Bus. Ctr., 1992—; mem. adv. panel Hanson Initiative for Lang. and Literacy, MGH Inst. Health Professions, 2001—; counsel Cmty. Found. of Western Mass.; mem. appropriations com. Town of Longmeadow, Mass., 1990—96, chmn., 1991—92, 1995—96; trustee Jewish Fedn. Greater Springfield, 1986—90. Mem. ABA, Mass. Bar Assn. (chmn. taxation sect. 1978-81, bd. dels. 1979-81), Mass. Bar Found., Hampden County Bar Assn., Rotary. Office: Bulkley Richardson and Gelinas LLP 1500 Main St Ste 2700 Springfield MA 01115-0001

WEISS, SAMUEL ABRAHAM, psychologist, psychoanalyst; b. N.Y.C. s. Kasiel and Sophie Sima (Schechter) W.; m. Alice Langer, May 20, 1958; children: Benjamin Z., Naomi E., Susan J. BA, Yeshiva U., 1944; MA, NYU, 1948, PhD, 1957. Diplomate in clin. psychology, Am. Bd. Profl. Psychology. Intern Bellevue Psychiat. Hosp., N.Y.C., 1955-56; assoc. rsch. scientist NYU Med. Ctr., 1956-59, rsch. scientist, 1959-68, assoc. dir. amputee psychology rsch., 1958-66; assoc. prof. psychology Yeshiva U., 1961-71; psychol. cons. Stern Coll. for Women, Yeshiva U., 1960-71; psychologist, psychotherapist, psychoanalyst in pvt. practice. Cons. N.Y. State Div. Vocat. Rehab., 1958-73. Contbr. articles to profl. jours. Fellow AAAS (Rosette award 1991), APA (editl. cons. rehab. psychology 1972-80), Am. Psychol. Soc. Jewish. Achievements include new research on medical factors in phantom limb pain and rehabilitation. Home: 80-40 Lefferts Blvd Kew Gardens NY 11415-1723 Office: 7 Park Ave Apt 66 New York NY 10016-4356

WEISS, SCOTT ALAN, real estate agent; s. Stuart Rollin Weiss and Sandy Carol Courson, Dan Christopher Courson (Stepfather); m. Corey Elizabeth Weilbacher, June 17, 2000. BA in Journalism, La. State U., 1997; postgrad. in law, South Tex. U., 2001—. Cert. CCIM. Comml. real estate broker Metronational, Houston, 1997—2000. Fellow fed. intern fellow, Houston FBA, 2002. Mem.: Currents Internat. Trade Law (mng. editor 2002), South Tex. Law Rev. (asst. editor 2001—02). Jewish. Avocations: running, reading. Office: South Texas Coll Law Ste 400 1303 San Jacinto Houston TX 77002-7000 E-mail: scottweiss@ev1.net.

WEISS, SCOTT TILLMAN, internist, research epidemiologist, educator; b. N.Y.C., Apr. 16, 1946; s. Robert Jerome and Minnie Thompson (Moore) W.; m. Deborah Jackson, June 2, 1968; children: Benjamin, Matthew. BA, Haverford Coll., 1968; MS in Pub. Health, Harvard U., 1977; MD, Case Western Res. U., 1972. Diplomate internal medicine, pulmonary disease Am. Bd. Internal Medicine. Intern medicine Harvard Med. Svc., Boston City Hosp., 1972-73; resident medicine Beth Israel Hosp., 1973-75; rsch. fellow Channing Lab., Brigham and Worans Hosp., 1975-77; chief resident medicine Beth Israel Hosp., 1977-78; instr. internal medicine Harvard U., Boston, 1977-80, asst. prof., 1980-85, assoc. prof., 1985-96; prof. environ. health Harvard Sch. Pub. Health, 1996—; prof. medicine Harvard Med. Sch., 1996—; dir. genetic epidemiology Brigham and Women's Hosp., 1996—; dir. respirator and environ. epidemiology Channing Lab. Brigham and Women's Hosp., Boston, 1996—. Editor Atopy and Airways Responsiveness in the Obstructive Airways Diseases, 1989. Fellow ACP, Am. Coll. Chest Physicians; mem. Am. Thoracic Soc. Office: Brigham and Women's Hosp 181 Longwood Ave Boston MA 02115-5804 E-mail: scott.weiss@channing.harvard.edu.

WEISS, SHERMAN DAVID, lawyer, consultant; b. Detroit, Dec. 26, 1929; s. Abraham and Eva (Lieberman) W.; m. Lorraine Gloria Moss, Apr. 5, 1952; children: Roger Kevin, Diane Leslie, Linda Beth. Student, U. Ill., 1947-48; BSC., Roosevelt U., 1951; JD, Chgo.-Kent Coll. Law, 1957. Bar: Ill. 1958, U.S. Dist. Ct. (no. dist.) Ill. 1958, U.S. Ct. Appeals (7th cir.) 1965. Mem. Deutsch & Kurlan, Chgo., 1959-60, Brody and Gore, Chgo., 1960-62, Arnstein, Gluck, Weitzenfeld and Minow, Chgo., 1963-65; asst. sec., asst. v.p. Walter E. Heller Internat. Corp., 1965-75, Imperial Leather & Sportswear Ltd., L.A., 1975-76; exec. v.p. Roth Carpet Mills, Santa Monica, Calif., 1977-78; sr. research rep. Greenwich Assocs., 1985-87. Cons. fin. and bus. mgmt., L.A., 1979—; adj. prof. law John Marshall Sch. Law, Chgo., 1966-67. Case editor Chgo.-Kent Law Rev., 1956-57. Bd. dirs. Met. YMCA Chgo., 1961-64; gen. counsel Leukemia League Ill., 1960-70. Served with U.S. Army, 1952-54. Mem. Ill. Bar Assn., ABA. Jewish. Home: 30 Parterre Foothill Ranch CA 92610-2341 E-mail: shrmwrm@hotmail.com.

WEISS, SHIRLEY F. urban and regional planner, economist, educator; b. N.Y.C., Feb. 26, 1921; d. Max and Vera (Hendel) Friedlander; m. Charles M. Weiss, June 7, 1942. BA, Douglass Coll., Rutgers U., 1942; postgrad., Johns Hopkins U., 1949-50; M in Regional Planning, U. N.C., 1958; PhD, Duke U., 1973. Assoc. research dir. Ctr. for Urban and Regional Studies U. N.C., Chapel Hill, 1957-91, lectr. in planning, 1958-62, assoc. prof., 1962-73, prof., 1973-91, prof. emerita, 1991—; joint creator-sponsor Charles and Shirley Weiss Urban Livability Program, U. N.C., 1992—; research assoc. Inst. for Research in Social Sci., U. N.C., 1957-73; research prof. U. N.C., Chapel Hill, 1973-91, acting dir. women's studies program Coll. Arts and Scis., 1985, faculty marshal, 1988-91. Mem. tech. com. Water Resources Rsch. Inst., 1976-79; mem. adv. com. on housing for 1980 census Dept. Commerce, 1976-81; cons. Urban Inst., Washington, 1977-80; mem. rev. panel Exptl. Housing Allowance Program, HUD, 1977-80; mem. adv. bd. on built environ. Nat. Acad. Scis.-NRC, 1981-83, mem. program coordinating com. fed. constrn. coun. of adv. bd. on built environ., 1982-83; mem. Planning Accreditation Bd., Site Visitation Pool, Am. Inst. Cert. Planners and Assn. Collegiate Schs. Planning, 1985—; mem. discipline screening com. Fulbright Scholar awards in Architecture and City Planning, Coun. for Internat. Exchange of Scholars, 1985-88; mem. N.Mex. adv. bd. The Enterprise Found., Santa Fe, 1997—; mem. governing bd. Acad. Freedom Fund, AAUP, 1997-2000. Author: The Central Business District in Transition: Methodological Approaches to CBD Analysis and Forecasting Future Space Requirements, 1957, New Town Development in the United States: Experiment in Private Entrepreneurship, 1973; co-author: A Probabilistic Model for Residential Growth, 1964, Residential Developer Decisions: A Focused View of the Urban Growth Process, 1966, New Communities U.S.A., 1976; co-author, co-editor: New Community Development: Planning Process, Implementation and Emerging Social Concerns, vols. 1, 2, 1971, City Centers in Transition, 1976, New Communities Research Series, 1976-77; mem. editl. bd.: Jour. Am. Inst. Planners, 1963-68, Rev. of Regional Studies, 1969-74, 82-92, Internat. Regional Sci. Rev., 1975-81. Trustee Friends of Libr., U. N.C., Chapel Hill, 1988-94, Santa Fe Chamber Music Festival, adv. coun., 1990-91, 97-98, trustee, 1991-97, 98—; bd. dirs. Triangle Opera, 1986-89, 91-2002, Chamber Orch. of the Triangle, 1997—. Recipient Cornelia Phillips Spencer Bell award in recognition of contbns. to life and success of U. N.C. at Chapel Hill, 1996, Disting. Alumni award in recognition of outstanding contbns. in field of city and regional planning Alumni Assn. Dept. City and Regional Planning, U. N.C. at Chapel Hill, 1996, Mary Turner Lane award Assn. Women Faculty, 1994, (with Charles M. Weiss) Gifford Phillips award Santa Fe Chamber Music Festival, 2000; Adelaide M. Zagoren fellow Douglass Coll., Rutgers U., 1994. Emeritus fellow Urban Land Inst. (sr. fellow, exec. group, cmty. devel. coun. 1978—); mem. Am. Inst. Planners (sec., treas. southeast chpt. 1957-59, v.p. 1960-61), Am. Inst. Cert. Planners, Am. Planning Assn., Am. Econ. Assn., So. Regional Sci. Assn. (pres. 1977-78), Regional Sci. Assn. (councillor 1971-74, v.p. 1976-77), Nat. Assn. Housing and Redevelopment Ofcls., Interamerican Planning Soc., Internat. Fedn. Housing and Planning, Town and Country Planning Assn., Internat. Urban Devel. Assn., Econ. History Assn., Am. Real Estate and Urban Econs. Assn. (regional membership chmn. 1976-82, 84-85, dir. 1977-80), AAUP (chpt. pres. 1976-77, pres. N.C. Conf. 1978-79, mem. nat. coun. 1983-86, William S. Tacey award Assembly of State Confs.), Douglass Soc., Order of Valkyries, Phi Beta Kappa. Home: 155 N Hamilton Rd Chapel Hill NC 27517-5628

WEISS, STANLEY H. physician, epidemiologist, educator, epidemiologist, researcher, epidemiologist, consultant, oncologist; b. Bklyn., Jan. 28, 1954; s. Simon and Claire Weiss; m. Robin Joanna Kase, July 12, 1981; children: Madeline Joy, Jeremy Michael. BA (summa cum laude), Yale Coll., 1974; MD, Harvard Med. Sch., 1978. Diplomate Am. Bd. Internal Medicine, Am. Bd. Med. Oncology; lic. physician, N.Y., N.J. Dir. Pathology Diagnosis Registry Peter Bent Brigham Hosp., Boston, 1976-78; mem. house staff Montefiore Hosp. & Med. Ctr., Bronx, N.Y., 1978-81, assoc. attending, 1981-82; med. staff fellow Nat. Cancer Inst., Bethesda, Md., 1982-87; epidemiology fellow, 1983-87; chief AIDS & retroviral epidemiology U. Medicine and Dentistry of N.J.-N.J. Med. Sch., Newark, 1987—, dir. div. infectious diseases epidemiology, 1988—, asst. prof., 1987-93, assoc. prof., 1993—. Adj. asst. prof. F. Edward Hebert Sch. Medicine, Bethesda, 1986—88; spl. cons. WHO, Geneva, 1987, Geneva, 88; exec. sci. com. N.J. Cmty. Rsch. Initiative, Newark, 1988—98; sci. adv. com. Clin. Dirs. Network, Cmty. Program Clin. Rsch. on AIDS, 1990—96; chmn. 6th Internat. Conf. on Human Retrovirology: HTLV, Absecon, NJ, 1993—94; sr. rsch. fellow Windwards Island Rsch. and Edn. Found., St. Georges Med. Sch., Grenada, 1996—. Mem. editl. bd.: AIDS Rsch. and Human Retroviruses, 1990—98, mem. editl. bd.: AIDS, 1990—93; contbr. over 250 articles and abstracts to profl. jours. Recipient Travel award Am. Soc. Clin. Oncology, 1985, Barge Prize for Excellence in Math. Yale U., 1971; named Humanities Fellow UMDNJ-N.J. Med. Sch., 1988, Fellow Infectious Diseases Soc. Am., 1989—. Fellow ACP; mem. AAAS, AMA, AAUP, APHA (co-chair epidemiology sect. program com. 1994-97, mem. governing coun. 1997—, whip governing coun. epidemiology 1998—), Am. Coll. Epidemiology, Internat. Retrovirology Assn. (exec. bd. 1994-98), Acad. Medicine N.J., Am. Fedn. Clin. Rsch., Am. Soc. Clin. Oncology, Am. Assn. Cancer Rsch., Am. Soc. Microbiology, Am. Soc. Internal Medicine, Internat. AIDS Soc., Internat. Immunocompromised Host Soc., Internat. Soc. Infectious Diseases, N.J. Infectious Diseases Soc. (founding), Oncology Soc. N.J., Soc. Gen. Internal Medicine, Soc. Epidemiologic Rsch., Sydenham Soc., N.J. Pub. Health Assn. (chair AIDS com. 1994-97, exec. bd. 1994—, N.J. Med. Sch. rep. 1997—, chair epidemiology 1998—, at-large rep. 1999—), N.J. SAS Users Group, Oncology Soc. N.J., Peer Rev. Orgn. N.J., Phi Beta Kappa, Sigma Xi. Avocations: bridge, reading, swimming, gardening, traveling. Home: 42 Ridge Dr Livingston NJ 07039-3716 Office: UMDNJ NJ Med Sch Bldg ADMC 16 30 Bergen St Ste 1614 Newark NJ 07107-3000 E-mail: weiss@umdnj.edu.

WEISS, STEPHEN J. lawyer; b. N.Y.C., Sept. 12, 1938; s. Morris and Frances (Dinkin) W.; m. Madeline Adler, Aug. 12, 1962; children: Lowell Andrew, Valerie Elizabeth, Bradley Lawrence. BS, Queens Coll., 1959; LL.B., Cornell U., 1962; LL.M., Georgetown U., 1966. Bar: N.Y. 1963, D.C. 1966, U.S. Supreme Ct. 1975. Atty. SEC, Washington, 1962-65; assoc. firm Arent Fox Kintner Plotkin & Kahn, 1965-70, ptnr., 1971-94, Holland & Knight LLP, Washington, 1994—. Lectr. securities, corp. law, dirs. and officers liability and ins. Am. Law Inst., ABA, Fed. Bar Assn., Practicing Law Inst., Bur. Nat. Affairs, Exec. Enterprises, Aspen Law & Bus. Orgn. Mgmt., Inc., Inst. for Internat. Rsch., Profl. Liability Underwriting Soc.; mem. adv. bd. Securities Regulation and Law Report, Bur. Nat. Affairs, 1980—. Author: Regulation D-A Practical Guide, 1994, Navigating the D&O Maze: A Handbook for Purchasers of Directors and Officers Liability Insurance, 1997, Navigating the EPLI Maze: A Handbook for Purchasers of Employment Practices Liability Insurance, 1998; insurance columnist Directors & Boards Mag., 1998--; contbr. articles to profl. jours. Mem. nat. com. Cornell Law Sch. Fund, 1987-88. Mem. ABA (fed. regulation securities com. 1970—, chmn. Rule 10b-5 subcom. 1976-78, chmn. civil liabilities subcom. 1978-81, chmn. com. fgn. corrupt practices legislation 1976-77, Guiding Principles Task Force bus. ins. com. 1994-95, devels. in bus. financing com. 1982—), Fed. Bar Assn. (chmn. securities law comm. 1968-70, mem. exec. coun. of securities law com. 1971—, chmn. coun. on financing and taxation 1971-72, chmn. publs. bd. 1977-78, nat. coun. 1972-80, Leadership commendation 1973, Disting. Svc. award), Profl. Liability Underwriting Soc. (adv. bd., Cornell Law Club Washington (pres. 1971-79). Office: Holland & Knight LLP 2099 Pennsylvania Ave NW Washington DC 20006 E-mail: sweiss@hklaw.com.

WEISS, STEPHEN MAX, healthcare administrator, surgeon, educator; b. Phila., Nov. 20, 1947; s. Walter and Rita (Griffin) W. BS, Ursinus Coll., 1969; MD, Temple U., 1973; MBA, Allentown Coll., 1998. Diplomate Am. Bd. Surgery, recert.; lic., Pa. Surgery resident Pa. Hosp., Phila., 1973-78; fellow in surg. oncology Thomas Jefferson U., 1978-79; from asst. prof. surgery to assoc. prof. surgery Jefferson Med. Coll., 1979-93; attending surgeon Thomas Jefferson Univ. Hosp., 1979-87; asst. surgeon Pa. Hosp., 1984-87; attending surgeon, chmn. dept. surgery, dir. surg. res. prg. Mercy Cath. Med. Ctr., Darby, Pa., 1987-93, chmn. dept. surgery, dir. surg. residence program, 1987-93; attending surgeon Mercy Haverford Hosp., Havertown, Pa., 1991-93; clin. assoc. prof. surgery Coll. Medicine Pa. State U., 1993-95; chmn. dept. surgery, dir. surg. residency program Pinnacle Health Sys. (merger Polyclinic Med. Ctr. and Harrisburg Hosp.), Harrisburg, Pa., 1993—. Gen. and oncologic surgeon Capital Area Surg. Assocs., P.C., Harrisburg, 1994—; cons. Wilmington (Del.) VA Hosp., 1979-86, Wills Eye Hosp., Phila., 1981-87; adj. asst. prof. surgery Sch. Medicine, U. Pa., 1984-88; mem. com. on sci. bus. Phila. Acad. Surgery, 1987-88, sec., 1989-92, 2d v.p., 1993, 1st v.p., 1994, pres., 1995; assoc. examiner Am. Bd. Surgery, 1992, 95. Contbr. numerous articles and abstracts to profl. jours. Bd. dirs. Phila. divsn. Am. Cancer Soc., 1983-92, chmn. profl. edn. com., 1986-88, pres., 1990-91, bd. dirs., 1994-95. Recipient Vol. Achievement award Phila. divsn. Am. Cancer Soc., 1987; jr. faculty clin. fellow Am. Cancer Soc., 1979-82, clin. fellow, 1976-77; grantee Am. Cancer Soc., 1988, Nat. Cancer Inst., 1993. Fellow ACS (mem. Phila. chpt. 1986-93, mem. cen. Pa. chpt. 1993-95, pres. cen. Pa. chpt. 1995, 97, field liaison commn. on cancer Thomas Jefferson Univ. Hosp. 1982-87); mem. AMA, Am. Coll. Radiology (mem. instnl. rev. bd. Radiation Oncology Study Ctr. 1982-85, 92, chmn. surg. com. Radiation Therapy Oncology Group 1982-88), Am. Soc. Parenteral and Enteral Nutrition, Assn. for Acad. Surgery, Am. Radium Soc., Soc. Surg. Oncology, Am. Coll. Physician Execs., Phila. County Med. Soc., Sigma Xi. Office: 226 Academy St N Ahoskie NC 27910-3239

WEISS, STEVEN WILMAR, internet security company executive; b. Saginaw, Mich., July 26, 1952; s. Edward Richard and Lucille Edna Weiss; m. Charlene Diana Weiss, June 11, 1977 (div. Aug. 1999); children: Robin Leah, Jillian Rose. BS in Math., USAF Acad., 1974; MS in Ops. Rsch., Air Force Inst. Tech., 1983. Cert. flight instr., airline transport pilot, FAA. Commd. 2d lt. USAF, 1974, advanced through grades to lt. col., 1990, computer sys. analyst, 1983-87, instr. pilot RAF Woodbridge, U.K., 1987-90, squadron ops. officer Albuquerque, 1990-93, wing total quality mgmt. advisor, 1993-95, wing resource advisor, 1995-96, ret., 1996; project mgr., sr. analyst Correa Enterprises Inc., 1996-99; v.p. ops. Cryptodynamics Inc., 1999-2000; ops. analyst Scientific Rsch. Corp., 2000—. Decorated Air medal. Mem. Air Force Assn., Mil. Ops. Rsch. Soc., Ret. Officers Assn., Mensa. Avocations: fishing, flying, gardening. Home: 4416 Red Tail Ct NW Albuquerque NM 87114-4129

WEISS, STUART LLOYD, television and radio producer, tax attorney; b. Bklyn., June 29, 1945; m. Donna Cusick, July 23, 1995; children: Tara Brooke, Joseph John. BA in Econs., Queens Coll., Flushing, N.Y., 1966; JD, Bklyn. Law Sch., 1969. Bar: N.Y. 1970, U.S. Tax Ct. Art tchr. N.Y.C. Pub. Sch. System, 1970-71; atty. M. Friedman and Co., N.Y.C., 1971-74; pres. The S.L. Weiss Co., Inc., Pelham, N.Y., 1975—, Zbig Vision, Ltd., Pelham, 1985-91. Assoc. producer music video Imagine, 1986 (Silver Lion award 1987, Rio Festival award 1987); exec. producer various TV shows including Steps, 1987 (Monitor award 1987), The Fourth Dimension, 1988; producer TV show The Orchestra, 1990 (Emmy award, Prix Italia, Festival award Internat. Electronic Cinema Festival). Pres. Westchester Spl. Olympics, Westchester, N.Y., 1985. Mem. Queens Coll. Alumni Assn. (bd. dirs. 1975-83, Disting. Alumni award 1976). Avocations: golf, travel, music. Office: 438 5th Ave Pelham NY 10803-1257

WEISS, SUSAN F. accountant; b. Providence, Mar. 9, 1965; d. Frank and Maria (Felsner) Weiss. BS in Acctg., R.I. Coll., 1988; postgrad., Bryant Coll., 2000—. Cert. mgmt. acct. Acctg. intern Ann & Hope Svc. Corp., Cumberland, R.I., 1986-88; sr. cost acct. Quebecor Printing, Inc., Providence, 1988-98; cost acct., material requirements project mgr. Union Industries, Inc., 1998; cost acctg. mgr. AAI.Fostergrant, Smithfield, R.I., 1999—. Mem. Am. Soc. Women Accts. (pres. R.I. chpt. 2001-02), Inst. Mgmt. Accts. Avocation: ballet. Home: 86 Meadowcrest Dr Cumberland RI 02864-6434 Office: 500 George Washington Hwy Smithfield RI 02917-1926 E-mail: sweiss@aaifgg.com.

WEISS, SUSETTE MARÉ, technical and photographic consultant, mass communications and media relations specialist, investor; b. New Orleans, June 14, 1959; d. Stanley and Dorothy Lee (Cambre) Weiss. AA in Photojournalism, La. State U., Monroe, 1977; PhD in Comparative Religion, Universal Life Coll., Modesto, Calif., 1990. Cert. retinal angiographer; cert. ophthalmic asst. Prodn. supr., lab. mgr. Colorpix Custom Photogs., Inc., New Orleans, 1978-84; ophthalmic photographer Ochsner Clinic, 1984-85; dir. ophthalmic photography Omni/Medivision, Metairie, 1986-87; audiovisual meeting planner, technician and cons. New Orleans, 1988-89; tech. and photographic supr. Retina and Vitreous Assocs. of Ala., Mobile, 1989; dir. photography Dauphin West Eye, Ear, Nose and Throat Specialists, 1989-91; tech. sales rep., tech. specialist Nikon, Inc., Melville, N.Y., 1992-95; contractual cons. Simply Susette, Inc., New Orleans, 1995—, pvt. investor, 2001—. Mass comm. specialist with emphasis in photographic imaging and media rels. Inventor stereo-imaging calibrator and quantitative stereopsis technique; author: Redefining the Wheel: Stereo-Photomicroscopy and Ophthalmology, 150 Years of Advancement; contbr. photography to Inc. Mag., Mademoiselle, Good Housekeeping, Income Opportunities, Mari Times, 1998-99; videographer Chrysler Corp. comml.; Rep. Conv. speech coverage aired by ABC, CBS, NBC, C-SPAN, 1998; exclusive media coverage and photos for New Orleans Mus. of Art's Famous Native-Am. Painting Acquistion, Times Picayune Newspaper, 1998; nat. test trial photos selected to demonstrate the tech. advancements in Neopan 400 film, Fuji Film, Photokina 1990 World News Conf. Recipient Best of Show photography award Biol. Photographers' Assn., 1991, 1st pl. gen. photography award Biol. Photographers' Assn., 1991. Mem. Ophthalmic Photographers' Soc. (audio-visual chair 1991, audio-vusial co-chair 1992 nat. edn. meeting), Am. Soc. Mag. Photographers, Profl. Photographers Am., Biol. Photographers Assn., Lakeview Civic Assn. Achievements include ongoing rsch. and devel. in new techniques and applications of teletronic comms. and imaging for the med. and comml. field. Home and Office: 5905 Colbert St New Orleans LA 70124-2910 E-mail: ssusette@bellsouth.net.

WEISS, THEODORE RUSSELL, poet, editor; b. Reading, Pa., Dec. 16, 1916; s. Nathan and Mollie T. (Weinberg) W.; m. Renée Karol, July 6, 1941. BA, Muhlenberg Coll., 1938, Litt.D. (hon.), 1968; MA, Columbia U., 1940, postgrad., 1940-41; Litt.D. (hon.), Bard Coll., 1973. Instr. English U. Md., 1941, U. N.C., 1942-44, Yale U., 1944-46; prof. English, Bard Coll., 1946-68; vis. prof. poetry MIT, 1961-62; resident fellow creative writing Princeton U., 1966-67, prof. English and creative writing, 1968-87, emeritus, William and Annie S. Paton prof. ancient and modern lit., 1977-87, emeritus. Fannie Hurst vis. prof. lit. Washington U., St. Louis, 1978; prof. English poetry Cooper Union, 1988; poet-in-residence Monash U., Melbourne, Australia, 1982; lectr. New Sch. Social Research, 1955-56, N.Y.C. YMHA, 1965-67; lectr. for USIS in various countries; guest Inst. for Advanced Study, Princeton, N.J., 1986-87, 87-88, Villa Serbelloni, Bellagio, Italy, 1989; guest lectr. Peking U., Shanghai U., People's Republic China, 1991. Editor, pub. Quar. Rev. Lit., 1943— ; editor poetry series Princeton U. Press, 1974-78; mem. poetry bd. poetry series Wesleyan U. Press, 1964-70; juror in poetry for poetry series, Bollingen Com., 1965, Nat. Book Awards, 1967, 77; author: Selections from the Note-Books of G.M. Hopkins, 1945; author: The Breath of Clowns and Kings: Shakespeare's Early Comedies and Histories, 1971, The Man from Porlock, Selected Essays, 1982; (poems) The Catch, 1951; Outlanders, 1960, Gunsight, 1962, The Medium, 1965, The Last Day and the First, 1968, The World Before Us: Poems, 1950-70, 1970, Fireweeds, 1976, Views and Spectacles, Selected Poems, 1978, Views and Spectacles, New and Selected Shorter Poems, 1979, Recoveries, 1982, A Slow Fuse, 1984, Collected Poems, 1987, paper back edit., 1988, A Sum of Destructions, 1994, Selected Poems, 1995; also articles and recs. Recipient Wallace Stevens award, 1956, Creative Arts award Brandeis U., 1977, Shelley Meml. award Poetry Soc. Am., 1989, Lifetime Achievement award Pen/Nora Magid, 1997, Oscar Williams and Gene Derwood award, 1997; fellow Ford Found., 1953-54, Ingram Merrill Found., 1974-75, Guggenheim Found., 1986-87 hon. fellow Ezra Stiles Coll., Yale U.; grantee Nat. Found. Arts and Humanities, 1967-68; subject of films Living Poetry, 1988, Yes, With Lemon, 1996. Home: 26 Haslet Ave Princeton NJ 08540-4914

WEISS, VOLKER, university administrator, educator; b. Rottenmann, Austria, Sept. 2, 1930; came to U.S., 1953, naturalized, 1960; s. Othmar and Pauline (Morianz) W.; m. Peg Hake, Sept. 14, 1957; children: Erick V., Christopher J. Dipl.Ing. Physics, Tech. U. Vienna; Dipl.Ing. Physics (Fulbright scholar), 1955; PhD in Solid State Sci. and Tech, Syracuse U., 1957. Rsch. metallurgist DEMKA Steel, Utrecht, The Netherlands, 1952; asst. prof. metallurgy Syracuse U., 1957-60, prof. materials sci., 1965—, prof. engring. and physics, 1986—, chmn. solid state sci. and tech. program, 1960-77, assoc. dean sponsored programs, 1972-78; dir. Inst. Energy Rsch., 1976-80, v.p. rsch. and grad. affairs, 1978-86, dir. engring physics program, 1988-99, chmn. dept. mechanical, aerospace, mfg. engring., 1992-94. U.S.-Can Prof., 1993-99; cons. indsl. firms Dept. Transp.; bd. dirs., past pres. Syracuse Friends of Chamber Music, Tech. Club Syracuse; v.p., bd. dirs. Discovery Ctr. of Sci. and Tech., 1979—; NATO sr. scientist fellow, Germany and Gt. Britain, 1967-68. Editor: Sagamore Conf. Procs, 1962-86; contbr. articles on mech. behavior of materials and phys. metallurgy to profl. jours. Fellow Am. Soc. Metals; mem. ASME, ASTM, Am. Physical Soc., Sigma Xi. Home: 238 Scottholm Ter Syracuse NY 13224-1738 Office: Syracuse U 251 Link Hl Syracuse NY 13244-0001 E-mail: vweiss1@twcny.rr.com.

WEISS, WALTER STANLEY, lawyer; b. Newark, Mar. 12, 1929; s. Jack and Mollie (Orkin) W.; m. Misty M. Moore; children from previous marriage: Jack Stephen, Andrew Scott. AB, Rutgers U., 1949, JD, 1952. Bar: D.C. 1952, N.J. 1956, Calif. 1961. Trial atty. IRS, Phila., Los Angeles, 1957-62; asst. U.S. atty., chief tax div. Los Angeles, 1962-63; ptnr. firm Goodson & Hannam, 1963-67; mng. ptnr. firm Long & Levit, 1967-79; ptnr. firm Greenberg & Glusker, 1979-81, Rosenfeld, Meyer and Susman, Beverly Hills, Calif., 1981-93; prin. Law Office of Walter S. Weiss, L.A., 1993—. Judge pro tem L.A. and Santa Monica (Calif.) Mcpl. Cts., 1994—. Contbr. articles to legal jours. Served to capt. JAGC USAF, 1953-56. Named Arbitrator Nat. Assn. Securities Dealers, 1974 Fellow Am. Coll. Trial Lawyers; mem. ABA, Los Angeles County Bar Assn., Beverly Hills Bar Assn. Home: 12349 Ridge Cir Los Angeles CA 90049-1183 Office: 12400 Wilshire Blvd Ste 1300 Los Angeles CA 90025-1055 E-mail: wsweiss@aol.com.

WEISS, WENDY RUTH, artist, educator; b. Newark, Sept. 22, 1957; d. Jay Kenneth and Joan Burke (Tutin) W. BA, Colo. Coll., 1979; MFA, U. Kans., 1983. Asst. prof. textiles, clothing and design U. Nebr., Lincoln, 1986-93, assoc. prof., 1993—, dir. Hillestad Textiles Gallery, 1995—, dir. project Different Voices: New Art from Poland, 1995-2000. One-woman shows include Art and Design Bldg. Gallery, U. Kans., 1983, Lawrence (Kans.) Arts Ctr., 1986, Rogers Gallery, U. Mo., Columbia, 1990, Miller Gallery, Indiana U. Pa., 1992, Elder Gallery, Nebr. Wesleyan U., 1992, Rall Gallery, Doane Coll., Crete, Nebr., 1996, Surface Design Assn. internat. conf. U. Kans., 1997; installer handwoven textiles for performance space for dancer Joan Stone, Auroville, Ind., 1997, Sioux City Art Ctr., 1998, Norfolk Art Ctr., Nebr., 2001, Norstrand Gallery, Wayne, Nebr., 2000, Asian Centre Gallery, U. BC, 2002; participant nat. and internat. juried exhbns., including Mid. Tenn. State U. Art Gallery, Murfreesboro, 1989, Octagon Ctr. for Arts, Ames, Iowa, 1990, Adams Art Gallery, Dunkirk, N.Y., 1991, Creative Arts Guild, Dalton, Ga., 1991, Sheraton-Washington Hotel, 1992, others; group shows at Gallery of Dept. Art and Art History, U. Nebr., Lincoln, 1990, U. Nebr. Omaha Art Gallery, 1991, Ctrl. Time Zone Sculpture Orgn., Batavia, Ill., 1991, Ctrl. Mus. Textiles, Lodz, Poland, 1993, Topeka Pub. Libr., 1993, Raiffeisenhof, Graz, Austria, 1993, 94, Mus. Nebr. Art, Kearney, 1994, Mulvane Art Mus., Washburn U., Topeka, 1995, Univ. Art Gallery, U. S.D., Vermillion, 1995; contbr. articles to profl. publs., procs. Recipient Women's Artist award Lincoln/Lancaster Women's Comm., 1997, Women's Artist award Lincoln/Lancaster Women's Commn., McDonald's Spirit of Svc. award, 2001; Nebr. Arts Coun. Master Artist fellow, 1995, Nebr. Arts Coun. fellow, 2001, Winterthur residential fellow, 2002; grantee various projects, orgns. Mem. Am. Craft Coun., Surface Design Assn. (state rep.), Handweavers Guild Am., Nebr. Women's Caucus for Art (pres. 1996, mem. program com. 1997). Office: Univ Nebr Dept Text Clothing Design Lincoln NE 68583-0802

WEISSBACH, HERBERT, biochemist, researcher; b. N.Y.C., Mar. 16, 1932; s. Louis and Vivian (Ruhalter) W.; m. Renee Kohl, Dec. 27, 1953; children—Lawrence, Nancy, Marjorie, Robert BS, CUNY, 1953; MS, George Washington U., 1955, PhD, 1957. Chemist Nat. Heart Inst., Bethesda, Md., 1953-68; acting chief NIH, 1968-69; assoc. dir. Roche Inst. Molecular Biology, Nutley, N.J., 1969-83, dir., 1983-96; v.p. Hoffmann-La Roche, 1983-96; disting. rsch. prof., dir. ctr. for molecular biology and biotechnology Fla. Atlantic U., Boca Raton, Fla., 1997—. Adj. prof. George Washington U., 1964-69, Columbia U., 1969-85, U. Medicine and Dentistry N.J., Newark, 1981-93, Princeton U., 1984-85. Editor: Molecular Mechanisms of Protein Biosynthesis, 1977, Archives of Biochemistry and Biophysics; contbr. articles to profl. jours. Recipient Superior Svc. award HEW, 1968, Enzyme award Am. Chem. Soc., 1970, Disting. Alumni award George Washington U., 1994. Mem. Am. Chem. Soc., Am. Soc. Biol. Chemists, Am. Soc. Pharmacology and Exptl. Therapeutics, Am. Soc. Microbiology, Nat. Acad. Scis., AAAS Home: 8008 Desmond Dr Boynton Beach FL 33437-5011 Office: Fla Atlantic U 777 Glades Rd Boca Raton FL 33431-6424 E-mail: hweissba@fau.edu.

WEISSBARD, DAVID RAYMOND, minister; b. Albany, N.Y., July 10, 1940; s. Alfred Henry and E. Ramona (Van Wie) W.; m. Mary Linda Roberts, Mar. 31, 1963 (dec. May 1987); children: Melissa Anne, Michele Lee Weissbard Burns, Andrew Van Wie (dec.), Meredith Lynn Weissbard Andrews; m. Karen Wells, Sept. 1, 1990; 1 child, Hilary Rebecca. BA, St. Lawrence U., 1962, MDiv., 1965; diploma in applied social studies, U. Southampton, Eng., 1973. Ordained to ministry Unitarian Universalist Assn., 1965; cert. social worker, Eng. Student min. 1st Universalist Ch., Dexter, N.Y., 1963-65, Henderson, 1963-65; min. 1st Parish in Bedford (Mass.) Unitarian Universalist Ch., 1965-74; sr. min. Fairfax Unitarian Ch., Oakton, Va., 1974-79, The Unitarian Universalist Ch., Rockford, Ill., 1979—. V.p. Cen. Midwest Dist. Unitarian Universalist Assn., 1989-92. Producer, host weekly TV program Fusion, WIFR-TV, 1980—. Mem. religious policy com. Rockford Sch. Dist., 1991; founder I Support Pub. Schs., 1998. Recipient Skinner award Unitarian Universalist Assn., 1979; named One of Rockford's 15 Most Interesting People, 1990, Rockford's Best Preacher by Readers of Rockford Register-Star, 1997. Mem. ACLU (co-pres. No. Ill. chpt.), Greater Rockford Clergy Assn., Unitarian Universalist Mins. Assn. (treas. 1976-78). Democrat. Home: 1805 Clinton St Rockford IL 61103-4805 Office: The Unitarian Ch 4848 Turner St Rockford IL 61107-5099

WEISSBARD, SAMUEL HELD, lawyer; b. N.Y.C., Mar. 3, 1947; children: Andrew Joshua, David S. BA, Case Western Res. U., 1967; JD with highest honors, George Washington U., 1970. Bar: D.C. 1970, U.S. Supreme Ct. 1974, Calif. 1998. Assoc. Fried, Frank, Harris, Shriver & Kampelman, 1970-73, Arent, Fox, Kintner, Plotkin & Kahn, 1973-78; prin. Weissbard & Fields, P.C., 1978-83; shareholder, v.p. Wilkes, Artis, Hedrick & Lane, Washington, 1983-86; ptnr. Foley & Lardner, 1986-97, L.A., 1997-98, co-chair creditors' rights workout and bankruptcy group Washington, 1992-95; sr. counsel Cox, Castle & Nicholson, L.L.P., Newport Beach, Calif., 1998—2001; exec. v.p., gen. counsel Makar Properties, LLC, 2001—. Editor in chief George Washington U. Law Rev., 1969-70. Bd. dirs. Luther Rice Soc., George Washington U., 1985-87, Atlanta Coll. Art, 1993, Nat. Learning Ctr., 1993-96, Georgetown Arts Commn. and gen. counsel 1995-96; Chmn. steering com. of Lawyer's Alliance for Nat. Learning Ctr. and Capital Children's Mus., 1989-90; mem. steering com. DC/NLC Don't Drop Out Campaign, 1992,93, bd. dirs., 1994-96; devel. com. Shelter for the Homeless, 1998-99. Recipient John Bell Larner medal, 1970. Mem. ABA, D.C. Bar, Calif. Bar Assn., Orange County Bar Assn., Georgetown Bus. and Profl. Assn. (bd. dirs. 1993-96, sec., gen. counsel 1993-97), Orange County Bus. Assn. (legis. com. 1998-99), Order of Coif. Office: Makar Properties LLC 4100 MacArthur Blvd Ste 4100 Newport Beach CA 92660 E-mail: sweissbard@makarproperties.com.

WEISS-CORNWELL, AMY, interior designer; b. Mpls., Dec. 8, 1950; d. August Carl and Margaret Amelia (Wittman) Weiss; m. Dan Cornwell, July 31, 1995; 1 child, Emma Elizabeth. AA in Home Econs., Cerritos Coll.; student, Long Beach State U., Santa Ana Jr. Coll. Asst. to interior designer Bobbi Hart at Pati Pfahler Designs, Canoga Park, Calif., 1974-75; interior designer B.A. Interiors, Fullerton, 1976-78, Birns Cos., Rancho Mirage, 1978-79; staff interior designer Assoc. Design Studios, Costa Mesa, 1979-81; interior designer Carole Eichen Interiors, Fullerton, 1981, Sears, Roebuck and Co., Alhambra, Calif., 1982-84; sr. corp. designer, mgr. design studio Barratt Am., Irvine, 1984-88; owner, retail designer Amy Weiss Designs, Coronado, 1988—. Designer in residence San Diego Design Ctr., 1990—92; participant Pacific Design Ctr.; Designer on Call program, 1994—95. Prin. works include interior designs for residences, yachts; comml. interiors including lobbies and offices. Mem. Am. Soc. Interior Designers (Globe-Guilders steering com. 1989-92, chmn. Christmas party, co-chmn. Christmas on Prado 1989, 89, designer for ASID showcase house 1992, 93), Bldg. Industry Assn. (sales and mktg. coun. awards com. 1993, mem. sales and mktg. coun. 1986-88, mem. home builders coun. 1994, 2d place M.A.M.E. award 1987, 1st place M.A.M.E. award 1986, 2d place S.A.M. award 1987), Building Industry Assn. Remodeler's Coun., Nat. Kitchen and Bath Assn., Coronado C. of C., Coronado Cays Yacht Club (in charge entertainment and spl. events 1997, in charge Regalia Shop 1998, in charge Commodore's Ball and Opening Day 1999), Rotary. Office: Amy Weiss Designs 1123 Marysville Ave Chula Vista CA 91913 Fax: 619-482-0438. E-mail: AmyWeissDesigns@cox.net.

WEISSE, ALLEN BARRY, educator, cardiologist, author, historian; b. N.Y.C., Dec. 6, 1929; s. Charles and Frieda (Lewitt) W.; m. Laura Van Raalte, Aug. 5, 1967; children: Danielle, Charles. BA, NYU, 1950; MD, SUNY, Bklyn., 1958. Diplomate Am. Bd. Internal Medicine, Am. Bd. Cardiovascular Disease. Intern Mt. Zion. Hosp. and Med. Ctr., San Francisco, 1958-59; jr. resident in medicine VA Hosp., 1959-60; resident in medicine U. Calif. svc. San Francisco Gen. Hosp., 1960-61; trainee in cardiovascular rsch. U. Utah Med. Sch., Salt Lake City, 1961-63; instr. medicine Seton Hall Coll. Medicine (now N.J. Med. Sch., Jersey City, 1963-65, U. Medicine and Dentistry N.J.-N.J. Med. Sch., Newark, 1965-67, asst. prof., 1967-69; assoc. prof. U. Medicine and Density N.J.-N.J. Med. Sch., 1969-74, prof., 1974—. Attending physician Jersey City Med. Ctr., 1964-67, East Orange (N.J.) Va. Hosp., 1967-85, U. Hosp. Newark, N.J., 1980-2001, Martland Hosp. Unit and Coll. Hosp. U. Medicine and Dentistry N.J., 1967-80—, dir. cardiac care unit, 1972-79, pres. med.-dental staff, 1979-81, dir. Echocardiography Lab., 1980-97; asst. attending physician B.S. Pollak Hosp. for Chest Diseases, 1965-71. Author: (with C. Mangel) Medicine: The State of the Art, 1984, Conversations in Medicine: The Story of 20th Century Medicine in the Words of Those Who Created It, 1984, Medical Odysseys: The Different and Sometimes Unexpected Patterns to 20th Century Medical Discoveries, 1991, The Man's Guide to Good Health, 1991, The Staff and the Serpent: Pertinent and Impertinent Observations on the World of Medicine, 1998; contbr. over 150 articles and abstracts to med. jours., chpts. to books. Bd. dirs. Union County Heart Assn., 1972-83. 1st lt. USAF, 1952-54. Recipient Charles L. Brown award U. Md., 1977. Fellow Am. Coll. Cardiology, ACP.; mem. AAAS, Am. Heart Assn. (coun. on basic sci., coronary care com. N.J. affiliate), Am. Fedn. for Clin. Rsch., Am. Physiol. Soc., N.J. Med. Soc. (sec. cardiovascular sect. 1968-69, chmn. 1969-70), Am. Soc. Echocardiography, Med. Hist. Soc. N.J. (pres. 2000-02), Am. Assn. Hist. Medicine, Am. Osler Soc. Democrat. Jewish. Avocations: music, tennis, swimming. Home: 164 Hillside Ave Springfield NJ 07081 Fax: 973-379-1372. E-mail: weisseab@umdnj.edu.

WEISSENBERGER, HARRY GEORGE, lawyer; b. Berlin, Fed. Republic of Germany, Aug. 20, 1928; s. Georg Wilhelm and Gabriele Anna (Hochberg) W.; m. Margaret Looper, Dec. 23, 1950 (dec.); children: Carol Weissenberger Schlicht, Harry George Jr., Bruce Lee. Student, Swiss Inst. Tech., 1946-47; BEE, Ga. Tech. Inst., 1950; JD, Emory U., 1952; LLM, George Washington U., 1956. Bar: Ga. 1952, U.S. Dist. Ct. (no. dist.) Ga. 1952, U.S. Ct. Appeals (4th cir.) 1952, U.S. Supreme Ct. 1956, U.S. Ct. Customs and Patent Appeals 1956, Mo. 1957, U.S. Dist. Ct. (ea. dist.) Mo. 1957, U.S. Ct. Appeals (8th cir.) 1957, Mich. 1961, U.S. Dist. Ct. (we. dist.) Mich. 1961, U.S. Ct. Appeals (7th cir.) 1961, Calif. 1964, U.S. Dist. Ct. (no. and cen. dists.) Calif. 1964, U.S. Ct. Appeals (9th cir.) 1964, U.S. Dist. Ct. (ea. dist.) Calif. 1974, U.S. Dist. Ct. (we. dist.) Tex. 1976, U.S. Dist. ct. (so. dist.) Calif. 1982, U.S. Ct. Appeals (Fed. cir.) 1982. Examiner U.S. Patent Office, Washington, 1955-56; assoc. Bruninga & Sutherland, St. Louis, 1956-58, Sutherland, Polster & Taylor, St. Louis, 1958-59, Price & Heneveld, Grand Rapids, Mich., 1959-61, ptnr., 1961-63, Mellin, Hanscom & Hursh, San Francisco, 1963-67, Mellin, Hursh, Moore & Weissenberger, 1967-74, Phillips, Moore, Weissenberger, Lempio & Strabala, San Francisco, 1974-76, Phillips, Moore, Weissenberger, Lempio & Majestic, San Francisco, 1976-78, Newport Beach, 1978-81, Weissenberger & Peterson, Newport Beach, 1982-86, Laguna Hills, Calif., 1986-90, Weissenberger, Peterson, Uxa & Myers, Laguna Hills, 1990-93; pvt. practice atty., 1993-99; of counsel Stout, Uxa, Buyan & Mullins, Irvine, Calif., 1999—2001. Dir., gen. counsel Ctr. for Sutton Movement Writing, Inc., Newport Beach, Calif., 1983-93. Mem. Indsl. League Orange County, 1982-93. Served to 1st lt. USAF, 1953-55. Recipient Honored Citizen award Orange County Bd. Suprs., 1992. Mem. Calif. Bar Assn., Am. Intellectual Property Law Assn., Orange County Patent Law Assn. (pres. 1985), Am. Arbitration Assn., Rotary (chpt. bd. dirs. 1988-94, 98, pres. 1991-92, Rotarian of the Yr. award 1989). Republican. Presbyterian. Office: 2408-B S Grand Ave Ste 200 Carthage MO 64836 E-mail: weisspat@aol.com.

WEISSENBORN, ANNE ADKINS, lawyer; b. Circleville, Ohio, Feb. 15, 1939; d. Joseph W. Jr. and Eleanor Y. (Yeagley) Adkins; m. Ernest W. Weissenborn, Apr. 11, 1970; 1 child, Elizabeth Anne. BA, Western Coll. Women, Oxford, Ohio, 1961; MA, Johns Hopkins Sch. Advanced Internat. Studies, Washington, 1964; MEd, Harvard U., 1968; JD, Cath. U., Washington, 1977. Bar: Md. 1977, D.C. 1980. Program specialist U.S. Office Edn., Washington, 1963-65; tchr. African Am. Inst., Dar es Salaam, Tanzania, 1965-66; program asst. African-Am. Inst., Washington, 1968, 69; instr. The Western Coll., Oxford, 1969-71; cons. Trans-Century Corp., Washington, 1972-75; atty. Fed. Election Commn., 1977-87, sr. atty., 1987—. Bd. dirs. Allied Silver Spring (Md.) Interfaith Svcs. for Srs., 1996—; founding pres., bd. dirs. Shaw Cmty. Ministry, Washington, 1991—. Mem. Bar Assn. D.C., Western Coll. Alumnae Assn. (trustee 1996-2000, pres. 2000-02). Mem. Christ Cong. Ch. (moderator 1988). Home: 10021 Raynor Rd Silver Spring MD 20901-2124 Office: Fed Election Commn 999 E St NW Washington DC 20239-0004 E-mail: weissenborn@starpower.net.

WEISSKOPF, BERNARD, pediatrician, child behavior, development and genetics specialist, educator; b. Berlin, Dec. 11, 1929; came to U.S., 1939, naturalized, 1944; s. Benjamin and Bertha (Loew) W.; m. Penelope Allderdice, Dec. 26, 1965; children: Matthew David, Stephen Daniel. BA, Syracuse U., 1951; MD, U. Leiden, Netherlands, 1958. Diplomate Am. Bd. Med. Mgmt. Intern Meadowbrook Hosp., East Meadow, N.Y., 1958-59, resident, 1959-60, Johns Hopkins Hosp., Balt., 1962-64; fellow child psychiatry Johns Hopkins U. Sch. Medicine, 1962-64; asst. prof. pediatrics U. Ill. Coll. Medicine, Chgo., 1964-66; faculty U. Louisville, 1966—, prof. pediatrics, 1970-2000, emeritus prof. pediat., 2000—, assoc. in psychiatry, pathology and ob-gyn., 1966-2000, dir. Child Evaluation Ctr., 1966-2000. Chmn. Gov.'s Adv. Com. Early Childhood, Gov.'s Council on Early Childhood, Ky., 1986-88. Contbr. articles to profl. jours. Trustee Jewish Hosp., Louisville, 1974-77. Served to capt. USAF, 1960-62. Fellow Am. Acad. Pediatrics, Am. Assn. Mental Deficiency; mem. Am. Soc. Human Genetics, So. Soc. Pediatric Rsch., Am. Soc. Law and Medicine, Am. Coll. Physician Execs. Home: 6409 Deep Creek Dr Prospect KY 40059-9422 Office: Weisskopf Ctr for Evaluation of Children 571 S Floyd St Ste 100 Louisville KY 40202-3828 E-mail: bernweisul@aol.com.

WEISSMAN, JACK (GEORGE ANDERSON), retired editor; b. Chgo., June 6, 1921; s. Ben and Ida (Meyerson) W.; m. Bernice Platt, Nov. 13, 1949; children: Bruce, David, Ellen Montgomery. BA in Edn., Northwestern U., 1943, MS in Journalism, 1944. Asst. editor Bankers Monthly, Chgo., 1944-45; mng. editor Practical Knowledge, 1945-50; with pub. relations dept. Roosevelt U., 1947-50; editor Opportunity Mag., 1950-89, ret. Author: Make Money at Home, 1963, How to Make Correct Decisions, 1964, Money Making Businesses You Can Start for $500 Or Less, 1965, Making It Big in Selling, 1987. Served to cpl. USAAF, 1945-46 Mem. Sigma Delta Chi, Phi Delta Kappa Jewish.

WEISSMAN, MICHAEL LEWIS, lawyer; b. Chgo., Sept. 11, 1934; s. Maurice and Sue (Goldberg) Weissman; m. Joanne Sherwin, Dec. 19, 1961; children: Mark Douglas, Greg Steven, Scott Adam, Brett Anthony. Student White scholar, U. Chgo., 1951-52; BS in Econs, Northwestern U., 1954; MBA in Acctg., U. Pa., 1956; JD, Harvard U., 1958; postgrad. Fulbright scholar, U. Sydney, Australia, 1958-59; postgrad., Hague Acad. Internat. Law, 1959. Bar: D.C. 1958, Ill. 1959. Asst. prof. bus. law Roosevelt U., Chgo., 1959-61; pvt. practice, 1959—; mem. firm Aaron, Aaron, Schimberg & Hess, 1969-78; sr. ptnr. Boorstein & Weissman, 1978-82, Weissman, Smolev & Solow, 1982-88, Foley & Lardner, 1988-92, McBride Baker & Coles, Chgo., 1992—2001; exec. v.p., gen. counsel Bridgeview Bank Group; of counsel Holland & Knight LLP, 2002—. Asst. prof. Roosevelt U., 1960—62; adj. prof. law John Marshall Law Sch., 2001—02; lectr. Lake Forest (Ill.) Coll., 1979—80; chmn. Banking Group, Union League Club Chgo.; panelist Robert Morris Assocs., Banking Law Inst., Midwest Fin. Conf., Greater O'Hare Assn., Miss. Law Inst., Bank Lending Inst., Chgo. Assn. Commerce and Industry, State of Art Seminars, Infocast Inc., SBA, Fed. Res. Bank Chgo., Lenders Ednl. Inst., Bank Adminstrn. Inst. Found., Lender's Forum. Author: (book) Lender Liability, 1988, Commercial Loan Documentation and Secured Lending, 1990, How to Avoid Career-Ending Mistakes in Commercial Lending, 1996, The Lender's Edge, 1997; mem. editl. bd.: Commercial Damages, 1985—; contbr. articles to profl. jours. Mem. adv. bd. Affective Disorders Clinic, U. Ill. Med. Sch., 1979—81. Scholar White, U. Chgo., 1951—52, Fulbright, U. Sydney, 1958—59. Mem.: ABA, Robert Morris Assn., Comml. Fin. Assn. Ednl. Found. (adv. bd.), Turnaround Mgmt. Assn. (steering com. Chgo. chpt.), Harvard Law Soc. Ill., Assn. Comml. Fin. Attys. (bd. dirs.), Ill. Inst. CLE (bd. dirs. 1989—2000, chmn. 2001—02), Ill. Bankers Assn. (mem. com. bank counsel 1987—88, vice chmn. 1988—89), Chgo. Bar Assn., Ill. Bar Assn., Beta Alpha Psi. Home: 2067 Old Briar Rd Highland Park IL 60035-4245 Office: Holland & Knight LLP 500 W Madison St Ste 4000 Chicago IL 60661-2511 also: Bridgeview Bank Group 1740 N Halsted St Chicago IL 60614 Business E-Mail: weissman@bridgeviewbank.com. E-mail: weissman@mbc.com.

WEISSMAN, SUSAN, social services professional; b. N.Y.C., Feb. 11, 1938; d. Samuel and Anne (Kunis) Miller; m. Irwin Weissman, June 2, 1957; children: Debra, Emily. BS, Queens Coll., 1976; MSW, Columbia U., 1978; postgrad., CUNY, 1996. Lic. social worker, N.Y.; cert. elem. tchr. Pvt. practice clin. social worker, N.Y.C., 1978-81; social worker L.I. (N.Y.) Jewish Hosp., 1978-80, psychoednl. therapist, 1979-80; founder, exec. dir. Park Ctr. Preschs., N.Y.C., 1981-91; with Child Care Cons. Corp., 1991-94; prin. Susan Weissman Cons. Corp., 1985—. Lectr. Learning Annex , N.Y.C., 1986—90, Borough of Manhattan C.C., CUNY, 1987; pres. Child Care Cons. Corp., 1990—94; co-pres. Eldercare Svc. Providers, 1995; mem. adv. bd. Mothers Network, 1992—96; mem. parents adv. bd. Showtime TV Network, 1993—96; spl. events chmn. Pearl Theatre, 1992—97; trustee Pearl Theatre Co., 1992—97; pres. Smart Parent Prodns., 1996—; prodr. Smart Parent Expo, 1996—; exec. dir., founder, co-dir. Next Step Assn., 2000—. Author: Parents Guide to DayCare, 1986; contbr. articles to Parent's Mag., Working Woman, Parent Guide, others. Bd. dirs. Child Care, Inc., N.Y.C., 1986-88. Mem. NAFE, Nat. Assn. Edn. Young Children, Early Childhood Edn. Soc., Nat. Assn. Child Care Mgmt., Nat. Assn. Social Workers. Avocations: cooking, entertaining, travel. Home: 50 Murray St Apt 408 New York NY 10007 Office: Susan Weissman Cons Corp and Smart Parent Prodns Inc 570 7th Ave Rm 403 New York NY 10018-1604

WEISSMAN, SUZANNE HEISLER, analytical chemist; b. The Dalles, Oreg., June 20, 1949; d. Donald Eugene and Roberta Myrth (Van Valkenburgh) Heisler; m. Steven Jay Weissman, May 29, 1976. BS, Oreg. State U., 1971; MS, U. Ill., 1973, PhD, 1975. Rsch. and teaching asst., then vis. asst. prof. U. Ill., Urbana, 1971-76; sr. scientist Lovelace ITRI, Albuquerque, 1976-80; mem. tech. staff Sandia Nat. Labs., 1980-86, supr., 1986-92, mgr., 1992—. Mem.: Am. Chem. Soc., N. Mex. Assn. for Women in Sci. and Engring. (v.p. 1981—82). Office: Sandia Nat Labs PO Box 5800 Albuquerque NM 87185-0100

WEISSMAN, WILLIAM R. lawyer; b. N.Y.C., Aug. 16, 1940; s. Emanuel and Gertrude (Halpern) W.; m. Barbra Phylis Gershman; 1 child, Adam; stepchildren: Eric, Jace, Julie Greenman. BA, Columbia U., 1962, JD cum laude, 1965. Bar: N.Y. 1965, D.C. 1969, U.S. Dist Ct. (no. dist.) Tex. 1965, U.S. Dist. Ct. (so. and ea. dists.) N.Y. 1977, U.S. Ct. Appeals (5th cir.) 1966, U.S. Ct. Appeals (D.C. dir.) 1969, U.S. Ct. Appeals (9th cir.) 1973, U.S. Ct. Apeals (2d and 3d cirs.) 1974, U.S. Ct. Appeals (10th cir.) 1979, U.S. Ct. Appeals (11th cir.) 1981, U.S. Supreme Ct. 1968. News dir., progrm dir. WKCR-FM, N.Y.C., 1960-62; law clk. U.S. dist. judge, Dallas, 1965-66; trial atty. antitrust divsn. Dept. Justice, Washington, 1966-69; spl. asst. U.S. atty., 1967; assoc. Wald, Harkrader & Ross, 1969-72, ptnr., 1973-85, Piper & Marbury LLP, Washington, 1986-99, Piper Marbury Rudnick & Wolfe LLP, Washington, 2000—02, Piper, Rudnick, LLP, Washington, 2002—. Instr. D.C. Bar continuing legal edn. program Georgetown U. Law Sch., Washington, 1980-89; environ. regulation course Exec. Enterprises, Inc., 1985-95. Mem. editl. bd. Jour. Environ. Regulation, 1991-95, Environ. Regulation & Permitting, 1995-2000. Parliamentarian Arlington County Dem. Com., 1971-75; mem. Arlington (Va.) County Tenant-Landlord Commn., 1973-77, chmn. 1975-77. Mem. ABA, ASTM (E-50 com. environ. assessment 1996—, rec. sect., 1998-99, vice chmn. 2000—), Columbia U. Washington Club (bd. dirs. 1987-93). Jewish. Home: 3802 Lakeview Ter Falls Church VA 22041-1313 Office: Piper Rudnick LLP 1200 19th St NW Fl 7 Washington DC 20036-2430 E-mail: william.weissman@piperrudnick.com.

WEISSMANN, GERALD, medical educator, researcher, writer, editor; b. Vienna, Austria, Aug. 7, 1930; came to U.S., 1938; s. Adolf and Greta (Lustbader) W.; m. Ann Raphael, Apr. 1, 1953; children: Lisa, Andrew. BA with honors, Columbia U., N.Y.C., 1950; MD, NYU, 1954. Diplomate Am. Bd. Internal Medicine. Intern Mt Sinai Hosp., N.Y.C., 1954-55, asst. resident medicine, 1957-58; chief resident medicine Bellevue Hosp., 1959-60; fellow depts. biochemistry and medicine Arthritis and Rheumatism Fedn., NYU, 1958-59; rsch. asst. dept. medicine NYU Sch. Medicine, 1959-60, instr. medicine, 1959-62, asst. prof., 1962-65, assoc. prof., 1966-70, prof., 1970—, dir. div. cell biology, 1969-73, dir. div. rheumatology of dept. medicine, 1973-2000; dir. Ctr. Biotech. Studies, 2000—. USPHS spl. rsch. fellow dept. biophysics Strangeways Lab., Cambridge, Eng., 1960-61; sr. investigator Arthritis and Rheumatism Found., N.Y.C., 1961-65; career rsch. scientist Health Rsch. Coun. N.Y.C., 1966-71; instr. physiology Marine Biol. Lab., Woods Hole, Mass., 1973-77, investigator, 1970—, trustee, 1993—; vis. investigator ARC Inst. Animal Physiology, Babraham, Eng., 1964-69, Centre de Physiologie et d'Immunologie Cellulaires, Hosp. St. Antoine, Paris, 1973-74, William Harvey Rsch. Inst., London, 1987; mem. postdoctoral fellowships rev. com. Pfizer Internat., N.Y.C., 1983-89; mem. scholarship selection com. Pew Scholars in Biomed. Scis., New Haven, 1984-94; lectr. Johns Hopkins U., 1976, 89, Med. Coll. Ga., Augusta, 1980, Med. Coll. Pa., 1988, William Harvey Rsch. Inst., London, 1987, others; nat. adv. bd. Ellison Med. Found, 1997—. Author: The Woods Hole Cantata, 1995, They All Laughed at Christopher Columbus, 1987, The Doctor With Two Heads, 1990, The Doctor Dilemma, 1992, Democracy and DNA, 1996, Darwin's Audubon, 1998, The Year of the Genome, 2001; editor-in-chief Inflammation, 1975-2001, Advances in Inflammation Rsch., 1979—, MD Mag., 1989-94; mem. editl. bd. Clin. Immunology and Immunopathology, 1972-88, Advances in Prostaglandin, Thromboxane and Leukotriene Rsch., 1975—, Am. Jour. Medicine, 1976-88, Tissue Reactions, 1979, Immunopharmacology, 1982; contbr. over 300 articles to profl. jours. Capt. M.C., U.S. Army, 1955-57. Recipient Allesandro Robecchi prize Internat. League Against Rheumatism, 1972, Marine Biol. Lab. award, 1974, 1979, U. Bologna medal, Italy, 1978, Lila Gruber Cancer Rsch. award Am. Acad. Dermatology, 1979, Solomon A. Berson Med. Alumni Achievement award NYU, 1980, Merit award NIH, 1987, Centennial award Marine Biol. Lab., 1988, C.M. Plotz award N.Y. Arthritis Found., 1993, Paul Klemperer award N.Y. Acad. Medicine, 1997, others; Guggenheim Found. fellow, N.Y.C., 1973-74. Fellow AAAS; mem. Am. Coll. Rheumatology (pres. 1982-83, Disting. Investigator award 1992, master 1996), Am. Fedn. Clin. Rsch., Soc. Exptl. Biology and Medicine, Am. Soc. Pharmacology and Exptl. Therapeutics, Am. Soc. Exptl. Pathology, Assn. Am. Immunologists, Am. Soc. Cell Biology, Am. Soc. Clin. Investigation, Am. Soc. Biol. Chemistry and Molecular Biology, Assn. Am. Physicians, Harvey Soc. of N.Y. (pres. 1981-82), Interurban Clin. Club, PEN Am. Ctr., Phi Beta Kappa, Alpha Omega Alpha. Avocation: tennis. Office: NYU Med Ctr Dept Medicine 550 1st Ave New York NY 10016-6402

WEISSTEIN, NAOMI, neuroscientist, psychology educator, writer; b. N.Y.C., Oct. 16, 1939; d. Samuel and Mary (Menk) W.; m. Jesse Lemisch, June 14, 1965. BA with honors, Wellesley Coll., 1961; PhD with distinction, Harvard U., 1964; postgrad., U. Chgo., 1964-65. Rsch. assoc. Yale U., summer 1964; USPHS postdoctoral trainee in math. biology U. Chgo., fall 1964, lectr., rsch. assoc. dept. psychiatry, 1965-66; from asst. prof. to prof. psychology Loyola U., Chgo., 1966-73; tech. staff Bell Labs., Murray Hill, N.J., 1973; prof. psychology SUNY, Buffalo, 1973—. Cons. Xerox Corp., Rochester, N.Y., 1973-74; vis. rsch. fellow dept. psychology Princeton U., 1979-80; mem. faculty exch. dept. psychology Moscow State U., 1978; presenter sci. meetings; spkr. Brown U., Stanford U., U. Pa., Princeton U., Rockefeller U., MIT, Moscow State U., others. Author: (with V. Blaisdell & J. Lemisch) The Godfathers: Freudians, Marxists, and the Scientific and Political Protection Societies, 1976; cons. editor: Jour. Exptl. Psychology, 1973-75, Cognitive Psychology, Spatial Vision; mem. editl. bd.: Signs: A Jour. of Women in Culture and Soc.; contbr. articles to profl. jours. including Sci., Jour. Exptl. Psychology, Psychol. Rev., Vision Rsch., Perception & Psychophysics; rec. album: Mountain Moving Day, 1972, retitled, Papa Don't Lay That S--- on Me, remastered, 2002; patentee in vision field. Recipient NIKE award for contbn. to women in soc., Europe, 1998, Vet. Feminists of Am. award for founders of women's liberation in U.S., 1997, Vet. Feminists of Am. award for Feminist Educators, 2001; Durant scholar; Hon. Woodrow Wilson fellow, 1961-64, NSF predoctoral fellow, 1961-64, NIMH postdoctoral fellow, 1979-80, Guggenheim fellow, 1980-81; Rsch. grantee NIH, NEI, NSF, others. Fellow AAAS (emeritus), APS, NAS (nat. rsch. coun., com. on vision), Optical Soc. Am., Assn. for Rsch. in Vision and Ophthalmology (program com. 1977-80, program chair 1980), Am. Psychol. Soc., Am. Psychol. Assn., Ea. Psychol. Assn., Psychonomic Soc., Lake Ont. Visionary Establishment (program com. 1976-78), Phi Beta Kappa, Sigma Xi. Home: 890 W End Ave Apt 8B New York NY 10025-3521 Office: SUNY Dept Psychology Park Hall Buffalo NY 14260 E-mail: utopia1@attglobal.net.

WEISSTEIN, ULRICH WERNER, English literature educator; b. Breslau, Germany, Nov. 14, 1925; came to U.S., 1950, naturalized, 1959; s. Rudolf and Berta (Wende) W.; m. Elisabeth Rieckh; children: Cristina, Cecily, Eric Wolfgang, Anton Edward. Student, Goethe-Universität, Frankfurt, 1947-50, 51-52, U. Iowa, 1950-51; MA, Ind. U., 1953, PhD, 1954; Doctorate (hon.), U. Lund, Sweden, 1993. Instr. Lehigh U., Bethlehem, Pa., 1954-58, asst. prof., 1958; asst. prof. English and comparative lit. Ind. U., Bloomington, 1959-62, assoc. prof., 1962-66, prof. German and comparative lit., 1966-90, chmn. comparative lit. program, 1985-89; dir. Ind. U.-Purdue U. Studienprogramm U. Hamburg, 1981-82. Vis. prof. U. Wis., summer 1966, Middlebury Sch. German, summer 1970, U. Hamburg (Germany), spring 1971, spring 1982, U. Vienna, 1976, Stanford U., 1979 , Graz U., Austria, 1985, 95, 96, U. Bologna, Italy, 1991, U. Antwerp, Belgium, 1992, U. Salzburg, 1997; external examiner comparative lit. U. Hong Kong, 1974-76. Author: Heinrich Mann, 1962, The Essence of Opera, 1964, Max Frisch, 1967, Einführung in die Vergleichende Literaturwissenschaft, 1968, English version: Comparative Literature and Literary Theory, 1973; Spanish version: Introduccion a la Literatura Comparada, 1975, Chinese version, 1987, Japanese version, 1976, Korean version, 1979; Forschungsbericht zur Vergleichenden Literaturwissenschaft, 1968-1977, 1981, Links und links gesellt sich nicht: Gesammelte Aufsätze zum Werk Heinrich Manns und Bertolt Brechts, 1985; editor: Literatur und Bildende Kunst: Ein Handbuch zur Theorie und Praxis eines komparatistischen Grenzgebiets, 1992; editor German sect. Twayne World Authors series, 1964-86, Yearbook of Comparative and General Literature, 1960-90, Oper Im Brennpunkt, 2001, Expressionism as an International Literary Phenomenon, 1973; co-editor: Literature and the Other Arts, 1981, Texte und Kontexte: Festschrift für Norbert Fuerst, 1973, Intertextuality: German Literature and Visual Art from the Renaissance to the Twentieth Century, 1993, Musico-Poetics Today Calvin S. Brown in Memoriam, 2000; translator: The Grotesque in Art and Literature (W. Kayser), 1963. Recipient Grosses goldenes Ehrenzeichen des Landes Steiermark, 1996; Guggenheim fellow, 1974-75; MLA grantee, 1958-59. Mem.: MLA (exec. coun. 1979—85, sec. 1985—89), Gesellschaft der Freunde der Oper in Graz (pres. 1991—97), Coun. Internat. Exchange Scholars (area com. for West Germany and Austria 1983—85), Am. Comparative Lit. Assn., Internat. Comparative Lit. Assn. Home: Baiernstrasse 54/IV 8020 Graz Austria

WEIST, WILLIAM BERNARD, lawyer; b. Lafayette, Ind., Dec. 23, 1938; s. Bernard Francis and Frances Loretta (Doyle) W.; m. Rosemary Elaine Anderson, Apr. 30, 1963; children: Sean M., Cynthia A. BBA, U. Notre Dame, 1961; JD, U. Louisville, 1970. Bar: Ky. 1971, Ind. 1971, U.S. Dist. Ct. (no. and so. dists.) Ind. 1971. Bank examiner Fed. Res. Bank, St. Louis, 1966-67; Trust officer Citizens Fidelity Bank, Louisville, 1967-71; pvt. practice Fowler, Ind., 1971—. Bd. dirs. Benton Fin. Corp., Fowler, Fowler State Bank; pros. atty. 76th Jud. Cir., Benton County, Ind., 1975-98. Capt. USAF, 1961-65. Fellow Ind. Bar Found. (charter mem.),; mem. Ind. State Bar Assn., Ind. Prosecuting Attys. Assn. (pres. 1979), Ind. Prosecuting Attys. Coun. (chmn. 1989), Nat. Dist. Attys. Assn. (bd. dirs.), Columbia Club (Indpls.), Elks, KC. Avocations: golf, reading. Home: 1000 E 5th St Fowler IN 47944-1520 Office: Weist Bldg Grant Ave Fowler IN 47944-0101

WEISWASSER, STEPHEN, electronics manufacturing executive; b. Detroit, Nov. 21, 1940; BA, Wayne State U.; postgrad., Johns Hopkins U.; JD magna cum laude, Harvard U. Ptnr. Wilmer, Cutler & Pickering; sr. v.p. Capital Cities/ABC, Inc.; pres., CEO Americast, 1995-98; ptnr. Covington & Burling, Washington, 1998-99; exec. v.p., gen. counsel Gemstar Internat. Group Ltd., Pasadena, Calif., 1999—, also bd. dirs. Woodrow Wilson Nat. fellow Johns Hopkins U. Office: Gemstar Internat Group Ltd Ste 800 135 N Los Roldes Ave Pasadena CA 91101 Office Fax: 626-792-0257.

WEISZ, PAUL B(URG), physicist; b. Pilsen, Czechoslovakia, July 2, 1919; , naturalized, 1946; s. Alexander and Amalia (Sulc) Weisz; m. Rhoda A.M. Burg, Sept. 4, 1943; children: Ingrid R., P. Randall. Student, Tech. U. Berlin, 0193—1939; BS, Auburn U., 1940; ScD, Swiss Fed. Inst. Tech., Zurich, 1965, ScD (hon.) , 1980. Research physicist Bartol Research Found., Swarthmore, Pa., 1940—46, Mobil Oil Corp. (formerly Socony Mobil Oil Corp.), 1958—61, sr. scientist, 1961—69, mgr. process research sect., 1967—69; mgr. Central Research Lab. Mobil Research & Devel. Corp., Princeton, NJ, 1969—82, sr. scientist and sci. adv., 1982—84; Disting. prof. chem. and bio-engring. sci. U. Pa., 1984—90, prof. emeritus, 1990—. Adj. prof. Pa. State U., 1992—; cons. rsch. and tech. strategy, 1984—; mng. dir. BioCell Tech. LLC, 1996—; vis. prof. Princeton U., 1974—76, mem. adv. coun. dept. chem. engring., 1973—78; mem. adv. and resource coun. Princeton U. Sch. Engring., 1974—78; chmn. ctr. policy bd. Ctr. for Catalytic Sci. and Tech., U. Del., 1977—81; mem. energy rsch. adv. bd. U.S. Dept. Energy, 1985—90. Editor: Advances in Catalysis, 1956—93; editl. bd. Jour. Catalysis, 1962—83, Chem. Engring. Comms., 1972—78, Heterogeneous Chem. Revs., 1993—96, monthly columnist Sci. of the Possible, Chemtech, 1980—83, contbr. numerous articles to sci. jours., holder 80 patents. Recipient ann. award, Catalysis Club Phila., 1973, Lavoisier medal, Chem. Soc. France, 1983, Perkin medal, Soc. Chem. Industries, U.S. Nat. medal of Tech., 1992. Fellow: Am. Inst. Chemists (Chem. Pioneer award 1974), Am. Phys. Soc.; mem.: NAE, AIChE (R.H. Wilhelm award 1978), N.Y. Acad. Scis., Am. Chem. Soc. (sci. award South Jersey sect. 1963, E.V. Murphree award 1972, 1977, Chemistry of Contemporary Tech. Problems award 1986, Carothers award 1987), Nassau Club (Princeton). Mem. Soc. Of Friends. Fax: 814-237-3202. E-mail: pweisz@aol.com.

WEISZ, RACHEL, actress; b. London, Mar. 7, 1971; BA, U. Cambridge, England. Motion picture and T.V. actress. Films include Chain Reaction, 1996, Going All the Way, 1997, Amy Foster, 1997, Land Girls, 1997, I Want You, 1998, The Mummy, 1999, The Taste of Sunshine, 1999, , Enemy at the Gate, 2000, Beautiful Creatures, 2000, The Mummy Returns, 2001; About a Boy, 2002, others, (TV film) My Summer with Des, 1998. Office: c/o CAA 9830 Wilshire Blvd Beverly Hills CA 90212*

WEISZ, RITA LANYCE, social worker; b. Harvey, N.D., June 2, 1951; d. Robert LeRoy and Bernice Lucille (Meier) W. BS, Union Coll., Lincoln, Nebr., 1973. Lic. social worker, N.D. With Union Coll., Lincoln, Nebr., 1973-74; dietary supr., social worker Wahpeton (N.D.) Rehab. Ctr., 1974-77; asst. cook Nibble Nook, Ellendale, N.D., 1978; social worker Stutsman County Social Svcs., Jamestown, 1978-80, Burleigh County Social Svc., Bismarck, 1980-85; asst. regional supr. West Cen. Human Social Ctr., 1985-89, regional supr., 1989—. Mem. mental health adv. bd. Med Ctr. One, 1991—. Bd. dirs. Little Bros./Little Sister, Bismarck, 1984-86; prog. leader Pathfinders, Hurdsfield, 1983-85. Home: 2881 Warwick Loop Apt C Bismarck ND 58504-7640 Office: West Central Human Svc Ctr 500 S 2nd St Bismarck ND 58504-5536

WEITHORN, STANLEY STEPHEN, lawyer; b. N.Y.C., Aug. 28, 1924; s. Louis W. and Florence O. (Mandel) W.; m. Corinne J. Breslow, Dec. 26, 1949 (dec. 1987); children: Lois Ann, Michael J.; m. Muriel Casper, Sept. 9, 1990; 1 stepchild, Corey Casper. BSBA, Hofstra U., Hempstead, N.Y., 1947; JD, NYU, 1954, LLM in Taxation, 1956. Bar: N.Y. 1955. Assoc. firm Olwine, Connelly, Chase O'Donnell & Weyher, N.Y.C., 1956-61; ptnr. firm Lewis, McDonald & Varian, 1961-62; pvt. practice, 1962-63, 67-68; ptnr. firm Wormser, Koch, Keily & Alessandroni, 1963-66; sr. ptnr. firm Baer, Marks & Upham (successor to Upham, Meeker & Weithorn), 1968-88, Epstein, Becker & Green, N.Y.C., 1988-89; sr. counsel Reid & Priest, 1989-94, Morrison & Foerster, Palo Alto, Calif., 1994—. Spl. prof. law Hofstra U., 1974-78; adj. prof. law U. Miami, Fla., 1975-79; mem. adv. com. U. Miami Law Ctr. Ann. Inst. Estate Planning, 1974-80; coordinator fed. budget and tax policy course nat. policy studies program New Sch. Social Rsch., N.Y.C., 1975; mem. fund raising mgmt. adv. com. Grad. Sch. Mgmt. and Urban professions, New Sch. for Social Rsch., N.Y.C., 1977-84; mem. adv. com. N.Y. U. Inst. on Fed. Taxation, 1980-90; program chmn. Practicing Law Inst. confs., N.Y.C., 1962-78, N.Y. Law Jour. confs., 1980, NYU Inst. on Fed. Taxation confs., 1955-88; tax cons. Pres's. Coun. on Environ. Quality, 1970; lectr. fed. taxation to univ. insts., non-profit org. confs., profl. bus. meetings. Author: Penalty Taxes on Accumulated Earnings and Personal Holding Companies, 1963, Tax Techniques for Foundations and Other Exempt Organizations, 7 vols, 1964, The Accumulated Earnings Tax, 1966; Contbg. editor, mem. adv. bd.: Tax Mgmt, 1959-68; feature columnist: Nat. Law Jour, 1978-79; Contbr. articles to profl. jours. Co-chmn. Port Washington-Manhasset (N.Y.) unit New Dem. Coalition, 1968-69; tax adviser nat. finance com. McGovern for Pres., 1971-72, mem. N.Y. fin. com., 1971-72; bd. dirs., exec. com. Equal Employment Coun. Inc., N.Y.C., 1968-71; bd. dirs., exec. sec. New Priorities Edn. Fund, 1969-70; bd. dirs., exec. com., sec., co-chmn. Fund for New Priorities in Am., 1969—; bd. dirs., treas. Cow Bay Manpower Devel. Corp., Port Washington, 1969-71; bd. dirs., chmn. exec. com., pres. L.I. (N.Y.) Pub. Affairs Coun., 1973-78; bd. dirs., pres. Mental Health Assn. Nassau County, N.Y., 1980-85, Herman and Amelia Ehrmann Found., 1977—; bd. dirs. Jewish Family and Children's Svcs., San Francisco, 1994—; mem. legacy com. United Cerebral Palsy, N.Y.C., 1975-90; bd. dirs. Community Action for Legal Svcs., 1976-78, Frederick and Amelia Schimper Found., 1977—, Florence Weithorn Warner Found., N.Y.C., 1967-72, N.Y. Fedn. Reform Synagogues, 1973-78, Nat. Coalition for Children's Justice, 1980-90, N.Y. Fedn. Reform Synagogues, 1973-78, Am. Inst. for Philanthropic Studies, L.A. and N.Y.C., 1981-92, Nat. Health Council, 1984-92, Laurent and Alberta Gerschel Found., 1986—, Interns for Peace, 1985—, Am.-Israeli Civil Liberties Coalition, 1987—, Inst. Am. Values, 1987-91, Fund for Human Dignity, 1989-90, Found. Fund, 1986—, L.I. Community Found., 1989-93, Cancer Prevention Rsch. Inst., 1989—, Green Seal, 1989-92; mem. Emergency Task Force on Juvenile Delinquency Prevention, 1976-79; mem. adv. panel N.Y. chpt. Am. Jewish Com., 1978-80; mem. com. on deferred giving Fedn. Jewish Philanthropies N.Y., 1978-86; mem. legal and tax panel United Jewish Appeal/Fedn. Jewish Philanthropies, N.Y., 1986—; nat. chair Planned Giving Program, Am. Assocs. Ben-Gurion U. Negev, 1992—, mem. exec. com. N.W. region; mem. com. tax policy Nat. Assembly Vol. Health, Social Welfare Orgns. Inc., N.Y.C., 1961-73; mem. com. bequests and legacies Nat. Jewish Hosp., Denver, 1965-78; mem. estate planning com. ARC of Greater N.Y., 1970—; mem. leadership coun. United Jewish Appeal, N.Y.C., 1966-70; mem. adv. com., project on ch., state and taxation NCCJ, 1980-85; mem. legacy adv. coun. Am. Jewish Congress, N.Y.C., 1968-72; mem. Internat. Coun. on Environ. Law, 1982—; mem. Pres.'s adv. com. ACLU Found., 1983—; chmn. Uptown Tax Discussion Group, 1957-69, Exempt Orgns. Discussion Group, 1973-79, Fresh Meadows Civic Assn., 1961-63; mem. legal activities policy bd. Tax Analysts, 1974—. Served with AUS, 1943-46, ETO. Recipient Allard K. Lowenstein Meml. award Am. Jewish Congress, 1988; honoree Mental Health Assn. Nassau County, N.Y., 1991. Fellow Am. Coll. Tax Counsel; mem. ABA (chmn. subcom. exempt orgns. 1965-69, subcom. charitable contbns. 1971-75), Am. Soc. Technion-Israel Inst. Tech. (bd. dirs. N.W. region 1992—), N.Y. State Bar Assn. (exec. com. 1967-69), Assn. of Bar of City of N.Y., Internat. Acad. Estate and Trust Law (exec. coun. 1974-78, 90—), Univ. Club, Knickerbocker Yacht Club (bd. dirs. 1986-88). Jewish (trustee synagogue 1970-74). Home: 150 Central Park S # 1610 New York NY 10019-1566 Office: Morrison & Foerster 755 Page Mill Rd Palo Alto CA 94304-1018 *No one truly is an altruist. We all attempt to do what most fulfills us. For some this motivates apparently selfish behavior; for others it is quite the opposite. However, why we act as we do affects only the actor whereas what we do affects society. Look to the deed, not to the doer; good deeds make for a better world.*

WEITKAMP, WILLIAM GEORGE, retired nuclear physicist; b. Fremont, Nebr., June 22, 1934; s. Alvin Herman and Georgia Ann (Fuhrmeister) W.; m. Audrey Ann Jensen, June 2, 1956; children— Erick, Jay, Gretchen, Laurie. BA, St. Olaf Coll., 1956; MS, U. Wis., 1961, PhD, 1965. Rsch. asst. prof. U. Wash., Seattle, 1965-67; asst. prof. U. Pitts., 1967-68; tech. dir., rsch. prof. Nuclear Physics Lab., U. Wash., Seattle, 1968-95; ret., 1995; rsch. prof. emeritus, 1995—. With USAF, 1956-59. Acad. guest Eidgenossische Technische Hochschule Zurich, Switzerland, 1974-75. Home: 2019 E Louisa St Seattle WA 98112-2207 Office: Univ Wash CENPA Box 354290 Seattle WA 98195-0001 E-mail: weitkamp@u.washington.edu.

WEITZ, BRUCE (PETER WEITZ), actor; b. Norwalk, Conn., May 27, 1943; s. Alvin Weitz and Sybil Weitz Rubel; m. Cecilia Hart, 1973 (div. 1980) BA, MFA, Carnegie Inst. Tech. Performer Long Wharf Repertory Theater, Norwalk, 1967, Guthrie Theater, Mpls., 1967-69, Arena Stage, Washington, 1970-76, Shakespeare-in-the Park prodns., N.Y.C., 1976-80, others; star: (TV series) Hill Street Blues, 1981-87 (Emmy nominations 1981-83, Emmy award for best supporting actor 1984); actor: (TV films) including Every Stray Dog and Kid, 1981, Death of a Centerfold: The Dorothy Stratton Story, 1981, A Reason to Live, 1985; If It's Tuesday, This Must Be Belgium, 1988, The Baby "M" Story, 1988, A Deadly Silence, 1989, Rainbow Drive, 1990, Leona Helmsley: The Queen of Mean, 1990, Babe Ruth, 1991, The O.J. Simpson Story, 1995, Mixed Blessings, 1995, Her Hidden Truth, 1995, Sudden Terror: The Hijacking of School Bus #17, 1996, The Legend of the Ruby Silver, 1996, Justice for Annie: A Moment of Truth Movie, 1996, Breaking the Surface: The Greg Louganis Story, 1996, Joe and Max, 2002, (films) No Place to Hide, 1992, Molly & Gina, 1993, The Liars' Club, 1993, Windrunner, 1995, Prehysteria 3, 1995, Cops n Roberts, 1995, Coyote Summer, 1996, Velocity Trap, 1997, Deep Impact, 1998, The Landlady, 1998, Shattered Illusions, 1998, Memorial Day, 1998, Fool's Gold, 1998, Gut Feeling, 1999, Quality Time, 2000, Mach 2, 2000, The Entrepreneurs, 2000, Focus, 2001, Facing the Enemy, 2001, No Place Like Home, 2001, Half Past Dead, 2002, (Broadway plays) including Death of a Salesman, Norman, Is That You?, The Basic Training of Pavlo Hummel, 1978-80; TV series appearances include The White Shadow, Paris, Midnight Caller, Anything But Love, 1989, Byrds of Paradise, 1994. Office: care William Morris Agy 151 S El Camino Dr Beverly Hills CA 90212-2704*

WEITZ, HARVEY, lawyer, educator; b. Bklyn., Aug. 16, 1933; AB, Bklyn. Coll.; JD, Bklyn. Law Sch. Bar: N.Y. 1954, U.S. Dist. Ct. (ea. and so. dists.) N.Y. 1956. Diplomate Am. Bd. Profl. Liability Attys. Ptnr. Schneider, Kleinick, Weitz, Damashek & Shoot, N.Y.C., 1966—; dean N.Y. State Trial Lawyers Inst.; adj. prof. Bklyn. Law Sch.; spl. master Supreme Ct., 1980-84. Author: A Compendium of the Art of Summation, Weitz on Automobile Litigation: The No-Fault Handbook; editor in chief Trial Lawyers Quar., 1972-80. Served with U.S. Army. Fellow Internat. Acad. Trial Lawyers, Internat. Soc. Barristers, Roscoe Pound Found.; mem. N.Y. State Trial Lawyers Assn. (bd. dirs.), Trial Lawyers for Pub. Justice (bd. dirs.), Am. Bd. Trial Advocates (nat. bd. mem.), ATLA (bd. govs. 1981-93, nat. sec. 1986-87), N.Y. State Trial Lawyers Assn. (pres. 1980-82), Bklyn. Law Sch. Alumni Assn. (bd. dirs.), Inner Circle of Advocates, Nat. Forensic Ctr. (mem. adv. panel), N.Y. State Bar (lectr.), Nat. Practice Inst. (lectr.), Assn. of the Bar, N.Y. County Lawyers Assn. (lectr.), N.Y.C. Trial Lawyers Assn. Office: Schneider Kleinick Weitz Damashek & Shoot 233 Broadway Fl 5 New York NY 10279-0050 E-mail: hweitz@lawyer1.com.

WEITZ, JEANNE STEWART, artist, educator; b. Warren, Ohio, Apr. 30, 1920; d. William McKinley and Ruth (Stewart) Kohlmorgan; m. Loyal Wilbur Weitz, Aug. 1, 1940 (dec. 1986); children: Gail, Judith, John, Marc. BS in Art and English, Youngstown U., 1944; MEd in Art, U. Tex., El Paso, 1964; postgrad., Tex. Tech U., 1976. Indsl. engr. Republic Iron & Steel, Youngstown, Ohio, 1942-43; art tchr. pub. schs., Bessemer, Pa., 1943-44, El Paso (Tex.) Independent Sch. Dist., 1944-50, 54-78, art. cons., 1978-87; art tchr. Hermosa Beach (Calif.) Independent Sch. Dist., 1950-53, El Paso Mus. Art, 1960-65; lectr. in art U. Tex., El Paso, 1963-66; instr. El Paso Community Coll., 1970-78; free-lance artist, lectr. El Paso, 1987-91; supr. student tchr. U. Tex., 1989-91; mgr. Sunland Art Gallery, 1994-95. Represented in group exhibitions at Sun CarnivalExhbn., 1961, El Paso Mus. Art, 1962; author highsch. curriculum guide; exhibited at LVAA Shows, 1990 (5 First Places), Westside Art Guild, 1992, LVAA, 1992 (1st in Watercolor). Coordinator art edn. El Paso Civic Planning Coun., 1985-86; chmn. art edn., art resources dept. City of El Paso, 1982-83. Recipient Purchase award El Paso Art Assn. Spring Show, 1995, 1st pl. award KCOS (PBS), 1996, 1st pl. award Westside Art Guild, 1996, 2d pl. El Paso Art Assoc., 1998, 1st pl. award West Side Art Guild, 1998, 99, H.M. El Paso Pastel Soc. Show, 1998. Mem.: Pastel Soc. N.Mex. (v.p. 2002), Rio Grande Art Assn., N.Mex. Watercolor Soc., Pastel Soc. El Paso (v.p. 1999—2000), Rio Bravo Watercolorists (sec. 1998), Nat. Soc. Am. Pen Women, Westfield Art Guild (pres. 1993—95), Nat. Art Edn. Assn. (sec. 1988—93, two 1st place award LVAA shows 1989). Lower Valley Art Assn. (Hon. Mention award 1988), El Paso Mus. Art Guild, Nat. Soc. Arts and Letters (sec. El Paso chpt. 1988—), Tex. Art Edn. Assn. (conf. planner, local orgn. 1981, Hon. Mention award 1972). Republican. Presbyterian. Avocations: printmaking, travel. Home: 1800 Paige Pl NE Albuquerque NM 87112-4747 E-mail: jweitz@prodigy.net.

WEITZ, JOHN, designer, writer; b. Berlin, May 25, 1923; came to U.S., 1940, naturalized, 1943; s. Robert and Hedy (Jacob) W.; m. Susan Kohner, Aug. 30, 1964; children: Paul John, Christopher John; children by previous marriage: Karen Weitz Curtis, Robert. Student, Hall Sch., London, 1936, St. Paul's Sch., 1936-39; certificate, Oxford-Cambridge Sch., 1938. Founder John Weitz Designs, Inc., N.Y.C., 1954—. Designer various cos., until 1954; author: Value of Nothing, Man in Charge (Best Seller list 1974), Friends in High Places, 1982, Hitler's Diplomat, 1992, Hitler's Banker, 1997. Bd. dirs. emeritus The Allen-Stevenson Sch., N.Y.C.; bd. dirs. William J. Donovan Found., Vets. of OSS, Am. Coun. n Germany; mem. pres.'s coun. Mus. City of N.Y. Capt. M.I. AUS, 1942-46, ETO. Decorated First Class Cross Order of Merit (Fed. Republic Germany), 1988, Comdr.'s Cross (Fed. Republic Germany), 1995; recipient Sports Illustrated award, 1959, NBC Today award, 1960, Phila. Mus. award, 1960, Caswell Massey awards 1963-66, Harpers Bazaar medallion, 1966, Moscow diploma, 1967, Coty award, 1974, Cartier Design award, 1981, Mayor's Liberty medal, N.Y.C., 1986, Cutty Sark Career Achievement award, 1986, Dallas Menswear Mart award, 1990, Pres.'s award of Fashion Inst. of Tech., 1990, Ellis Island medal of Honor, 1992; named to Internat. Best Dressed List Hall of Fame, 1971. Mem. Union Club, Spl. Forces Club, Old Pauline Club (v.p., London), The Naval Club (London), Vintage Sports Car Club Am., Sports Car Club Am., Road Racing Drivers Club, USN Acad. Sailing Squadron, Sag Harbor Yacht Club, N.Y. Yacht Club. Office: JOHN WEITZ INC 3 E 66th St New York NY 10021-5812

WEITZ, JOHN JEROME, JR. city planner; b. Mobile, Ala., Aug. 19, 1961; s. John J. and Marcheta (Knight) W.; m. Patricia L. Weitz, Oct. 20, 1990; 1 child, John Jerome III. BA, Emory U., Atlanta, 1983; M City Planning, Ga. Inst. Tech., Atlanta, 1985; D Philosophy Urban Studies, Portland (Oreg.) State U., 1998. Cert. planner. Planner technician City of Roswell, Ga., 1985-87; planner II Fulton County Dept. Planning and Econ. Devel., Atlanta, 1987-88; zoning adminstr. Albany-Dougherty Planning Commn., Albany, 1988-89; sr. planner Ga. Mountains Regional Devel. Ctr., Gainesville, 1989-94; urban growth mgmt. specialist State of Oreg., Salem, 1994-97; cons. Benkendorf Assocs., Portland, 1994-96; planning divsn. mgr. Cowlitz Coun, Kelso, Wash., 1997-99; planning dir. City of Roswell, 1999-2000; pres. Jerry Weitz & Assocs., Inc., Alpharetta, 2001—; part-time asst. prof. pub. adminstrn. Kennesaw (Ga.) State U., 2001; asst. prof. pub. adminstrn. Troy State U., Atlanta, 2001—. Citizens adv. group Atlanta Regional Commn., 1987; exec. com. Ga. Planning Assn., Atlanta, 1993—94, v.p. legislative affairs, 2000—. Author: Sprawl Busting: State Programs to Guide Growth, 1999. Coun. mem. City of Gillsville, Ga., 1994; mem. design rev. bd. City of Beaverton, Oreg., 1997-99. Recipient Outstanding Achievement award Alpharetta Jaycees, 1986. Mem. Am. Planning Assn., Urban Affairs Assn., Internat. City/County Mgmt. Assn., Assn. Collegiate Schs. Planning, Ga. Planning Assn. (disting. profl. achievement in planning award 2000). Avocations: fishing, camping, golf. Home: 1045 Mid Broadwell Rd Alpharetta GA 30004-1027 E-mail: jerryweitz@aol.com.

WEITZEL, JOHN PATTERSON, lawyer; b. Pitts., Aug. 24, 1923; s. Albert Philip and Elizabeth (Patterson) W.; m. Elisabeth Swan, Mar. 20, 1965; children: Mary Middleton, Paul Patterson. Student, Deerfield (Mass.) Acad., 1937-40; AB, Yale U., 1946; LL.B., Harvard U., 1949. Bar: Mass. 1949, U.S. Supreme Ct. 1960. Assoc. Herrick, Smith, Donald, Farley & Ketchum (now Herrick & Smith), Boston, 1949-53, ptnr., 1961-86, Palmer & Dodge, Boston, 1986-93; of counsel, 1993—; spl. asst. to asst. sec. treasury, 1953-55; asst. to under sec. treas, 1955-56; asst. gen. counsel Treasury Dept., 1956-59, dep. to sec. treasury, 1959-60, asst. sec. treasury, 1960-61; U.S. exec. dir. World Bank, 1960-61. Mem. planning bd. NSC, 1959-61; cons. to sec. def., 1973. Mem. Mass. Council Arts and Humanities, 1966-71; overseer, dir. sec. Boys and Girls Clubs, Boston; mem. corp. Mass. Gen. Hosp., Boston Mus. Sci.; trustee Roxbury Latin Sch. Served with USAAF, 1943-45. Mem. Am., Boston bar assns., Am. Law Inst. Clubs: Harvard (Boston), Union Boat (Boston). Home: 45 Devon Rd Chestnut Hill MA 02467-1851 Office: Palmer & Dodge LLP 111 Huntington Ave Boston MA 02199-7613

WEITZEL, JOHN QUINN, bishop; b. Chgo., May 10, 1928; s. Carl Joseph and Patricia (Quinn) W. BA, Maryknoll (N.Y.) Sem., 1951, M of Religious Edn., 1953; PMD, Harvard U. Ordained priest Roman Cath. Ch., 1955. With ednl. devel. Cath. Fgn. Mission Soc. of Am., Maryknoll, 1955-63, nat. dir. vocations for Maryknoll, dir. devel. dept. and info. services, 1963-72, mem. gen. council, 1972-78; asst. parish priest Cath. Ch., Western Samoa, 1979-81, pastor, vicar gen. Western Samoa, 1981-86; consecrated bishop, 1986; bishop Cath. Ch., Am. Samoa, 1986—. Office: Diocese Samoa-Pago Pago PO Box 3594 Pago Pago AS 96799-3594

WEITZEN, JEFFREY, computer manufacturing company executive; b. Perth Amboy, N.J., Apr. 15, 1956; BA in Econs., Wesleyan U.; MBA, U. Chgo. Various positions AT&T, 1980-98, exec. v.p. bus. markets divsn., until 1998; pres. Gateway, Inc., San Diego, 1998—, CEO, 2000—01, also bd. dirs. Bd. dirs. San Diego Zool. Soc. Mem. U.S. C. of C. (bd. dirs.). Office: Gateway Inc 14303 Gateway Pl Poway CA 92064-7140*

WEITZER, RONALD, sociology educator; b. Apr. 25, 1952; BA, U. Calif., Santa Cruz, 1975; PhD, U. Calif., Berkeley, 1985. Prof. George Washington U., Washington, 1988—. Author: Transforming Settler States: Communal Conflict and Internal Security in Northern Ireland and Zimbabwe, 1990, Policing Under Fire: Ethnic Conflict and Police-Community Relations in Northern Ireland, 1995; editor: Sex for Sale: Prostitution, Pornography, and the Sex Industry, 1999. Recipient grant NSF, 1992-94, 95-98. Office: George Washington Univ Dept Sociology Washington DC 20052-0001 Fax: 202-994-3239. E-mail: weitzer@gwu.edu.

WEITZMAN, ARTHUR JOSHUA, English educator; b. Newark, Sept. 13, 1933; s. Louis I. and Cecele W.; m. Catherine Ezell, Aug. 8, 1982; children: Peter A., Anne E. BA, U. Chgo., 1956, MA, 1957; PhD, NYU, 1964. Instr. English, Bklyn. Coll., 1960-63; asst. prof. Temple U., Phila., 1963-69; assoc. prof. Northeastern U., Boston, 1969-72, prof., 1972-98. Editor: Letters Writ by a Turkish Spy (G.P. Marana), 1970; founder, co-editor: The Scriblerian, 1968— ; co-editor: Milton and the Romantics, 1980-81; contbr.: revs. and articles to profl. jours. and newspapers including Los Angeles Times, Boston Globe, Miami Herald NEH fellow, 1972-73; Mellon fellow, 1976; research grantee Temple U.; research grantee Northeastern U. Mem. MLA, Am. Soc. 18th Century Studies, Nat. Assn. Scholars, Assn. Lit. Scholars and Critics. Jewish. Home: 4 Bellis Cir Cambridge MA 02140-3240 Office: Northeastern U Dept English 406 Holmes Boston MA 02115 E-mail: weitzman@neu.edu.

WEITZMAN, BERNARD, film company executive, consultant; b. Springfield, Mass., Sept. 29, 1923; m. Barbara Rogers, July 22, 1951; children: Douglas, Casey, James. BSCE, U. Ala., 1947; JD, Southwestern U., 1962; MA in Cinema-TV, U. So. Calif., 1967. V.p. legal and bus. affairs Desilu Prodns. Inc., Hollywood, Calif., 1954-67; v.p., gen. mgr. Universal Studios, Universal CIty, 1967-74; sr. v.p. MGM Inc., Culver City, 1974-77; exec. v.p. Lorimar Inc., Burbank/Culver CIty, 1977-87; sr. v.p. AME Inc., Burbank, 1987-90; pres., CEO Sussex Ltd. Inc., Encino, Calif., 1990—. Mem. Acad. Motion Picture Arts & Scis., Acad. TV Arts & Scis., Radio-TV Mus., Motion Picture Pioneers, Am. Arbitration Assn., USC Trojan Club. Office: Sussex Ltd Inc 16633 Ventura Blvd Ste 540 Encino CA 91436-1814 E-mail: berniebar@aol.com.

WEITZMAN, LINDA SUE, lawyer; b. Phila., July 27, 1959; d. Gerald and Elaine Weitzman. BA, Emory U., 1981; JD, U. Miami, 1984. Bar: Fla. 1984, Ga. 1989, U.S. Dist. Ct. (so. dist.) Fla. 1990. Assoc. Weiner, Shapiro & Rose, Miami; clk. Judge Mary Ann MacKenzie; in house counsel KRC Enterprises Inc., Ft. Lauderdale, Fla.; pvt. practice Coral Gables, 1989-99, Delray Beach, 1999-2001, West Palm Beach, 2001—. Mem. Am. Cancer Soc. Mem. ABA, ATLA, Dade County Bar Assn., Palm Beach County Bar Assn., Atty.'s Title Ins. Fund. Office: 4102 Washington Rd West Palm Beach FL 33405 Fax: 561-659-2996.

WEITZMAN, MARC HERSCHEL, lawyer; b. Milw., Feb. 1, 1950; s. J. Leonard and Esther (Charne) W.; m. Natalyn Ann Gipstein, Oct. 5, 1980; children: Benjamin, Marissa, Laura, Emily. BA, U. Calif., Santa Barbara, 1972; JD, Western State U., 1976. Bar: Calif. 1978, U.S. Dist. Ct. (cen. dist.) Calif. 1979, U.S. Ct. Appeals (9th cir.) 1981, U.S. Supreme Ct. 1987. Atty. State Compensation Ins. Fund, Long Beach, Calif., 1979-82, State Farm Ins. Co., Costa Mesa, 1982-85; assoc. Grancell, Grancell & Marshall, Santa Ana, 1985-88; ptnr. Hertz & Weitzman, Huntington Beach, 1988-89; pvt. practice Seal Beach, 1989—. Judge pro tem State of Calif. Divsn. Indsl. Rels.-Divsn. Indsl. Accidents, Norwalk, 1986—, Long Beach, 1984—, Santa Ana, 1995—; cert. workers' compensation specialist Calif. Bd. Legal Specialization-State Bar Calif., 1988—; arbitrator State of Calif. Divsns. Indsl. Rels. and Indsl. Accident, 1991. Mem. L.A. County Bar Assn., Orange County Bar Assn., Orange County Workers' Compensation Def. Assn., So. Calif. Rehab. Exch., Long Beach Bar Assn. Office: 3010 Old Ranch Pkwy Ste 200 Seal Beach CA 90740-2750

WEITZMAN, ROBERT HAROLD, investment company executive; b. Chgo., July 15, 1937; s. Nathan and Selma Weitzman; m. Marilynn Beth Felzer, Sept. 5, 1965; children— Joshua C., Eliza S. BA in Bus., Econs., Grinnell Coll., 1959; JD, DePaul U., 1963. Bar: Ill 1963. Vice pres. Weitzman Enterprises, Chgo., 1955-63; assoc. Lissner, Rothenberg, Reif & Barth, 1963-68; real estate counsel Continental Ill. Nat. Bank and Trust Co., 1968-74; v.p., group head Continental Ill. Investment Trust, 1974-76; founding ptnr. Group One Investments, 1977—. Lectr. in field. Editor: Real Estate Finance Handbook, 1979. Contbr. articles to profl. jours. Trustee, advisor Weitzman Found., 1963-77, mng. trustee, 1978— ; cons., advisor Ill. chpt. Big Bros. Am. Orgn., 1969-72; trustee The Wis. Real Estate Investment Trust, 1980, 81. Recipient Outstanding Young Man Am. award U.S. Jaycees, 1973 Mem. Ill. Bar Assn., Chgo. Bar Assn., Nat. Assn. Rev. Appraisers and Mortgage Underwriters (charter mem. cert. rev. appraiser designation), Real Estate Securities and Syndication Inst. (bd. dirs. Ill. chpt. 1982-90, pres. 1984, regional v. p. 1988, specialist in real estate securities designation 1988, chmn. nat. com. on continuing edn. 1989, 90). Real Estate Investment Assn. (founding mem., Nat. bd. dirs. 1990—, exec. com. nat assn. and Ill. chpt. 1990—, chmn. nat. com. for advanced edn., 1990-95, nat. pres. 1996-98, nat. chmn. 1999—, specialist in real estate investment designation 1990), Am. Inst. Banking, Internat. Coll. Real Estate Cons. Profls., Internat. Real Estate Bd. Home: 535 Carriage Way Deerfield IL 60015-4534 Office: Group One Investments 77 W Washington St Ste 1005 Chicago IL 60602-2805 E-mail: r.weitzman@g1invest.com.

WEITZMAN, SARAH BROWN, retired staff developer; b. Port Washington, N.Y., Feb. 6, 1935; d. Philip E. Jr. and Mildred Marion (Toole) Brown; m. Arthur H. Weitzman, Nov. 21, 1965. BS in English Lit., NYU, 1956, MA in English Lit., 1957. Tchr. English N.Y.C. Bd. Edn., 1957-63, 67-85; instr. writing NYU, N.Y.C., 1963-67; staff developer U.F.T., 1985-91. Author poetry. Nat. Endowment for the Arts fellow, 1984. Mem. Poetry Soc. Am. Home: 1470 1st Ave New York NY 10021-2277

WEITZMAN, STEPHEN MICHAEL, educator; b. Jamaica, N.Y., Sept. 29, 1945; s. Joseph and Ida (Rutchick) W.; m. Diane Kaminsky, Aug. 22, 1976; children: Joshua, Greg. BA, Queens Coll., 1967; MS in Edn., Hofstra U., 1969; postgrad., Rutgers U., 1971-72; MBA, N.Y. Inst. Tech., 1980; MS in Jewish Studies, Spertus Coll., 2000. Instr. Jersey City (N.J.) State Coll., 1969-71; tchr. Yeshiva Ch'San Sofer, Bklyn., 1969-72, Temple Isaiah, Stony Brook, N.Y., 1980—, Smithtown (N.Y.) Sch. Dist., 1972—. Adj. prof. Hofstra U., Hempstead, N.Y., 1970-72, Newark State Coll., Union, N.J., 1971-72, C.W. Post Coll., Greenvale, N.Y., 1974-92. Contbr. articles to profl. jours. Bldg. rep. Smithtown Tchrs. Assn., 1972-86, newsletter editor, 1972-76; pres. Temple Isaiah, 1989, 91, 97, v.p., ritual com. chair, adult edn. chair, social action chair, chair youth group com., pub. chair, capital campaign co-chair; program v.p., regional v.p., rel. edn. chair, youth devel. chair, nominating com. chair Greater N.Y. Coun. Reform Synagogues, N.Y.C., 1987-; mem. commns. and task forces Union Am. Hebrew Congregations, N.Y.C., 1994-, trustee, 2000—; bd. dirs. Am. Jewish Congress, Suffolk, N.Y., 1985-95. Recipient Cmty. Svc. award Student Activities award, CMC Coun. award Queens Coll., 1967, Irving J. Fain Social Action award, 1985, Grinspoon-Steinhardt award for excellence in Jewish edn., 2002. Avocations: philately, model railroading. E-mail: smweitzman@aol.com.

WEITZMANN, WILLIAM HENRY, education educator, photographer; b. Phila., Apr. 8, 1943; s. Henry P. and Anna H. Weitzmann; m. Susan L. Bower, June 25, 1966; children: Todd W., Amy L. BA in Indsl. Arts Edn., Pa. State U., 1966; MA in Indsl. Tech., Trenton State Coll., 1972. Cert. tchr. tech. edn. and indsl. arts. Tchr. indsl. arts East Stroudsburg (Pa.) Sch. Dist., 1966-68; curriculum coord., tchr. Stroudsburg (Pa.) Area Sch. Dist., 1968—; owner W.H. Weitzmann Photographer, Stroudsburg, 1976—. Adj. prof. East Stroudsburg (Pa.) U., 1982, 98—; bd. dirs. North Eastern Pa. Sch. Employees Fed. Credit Union, Stroudsburg. Photographs appeared in one-man show East Stroudsburg (Pa.) U., 1982. Scoutmaster Boy Scouts Am., Stroudsburg, 1973-93. Recipient award of merit Boy Scouts Am.-Pocono Dist., 1985, Silver Beaver award Boy Scouts Am.-Minsi Trails Coun., 1988, citation Pa. Ho. of Reps., 1990, 93, commendation The Gov.'s Office, 1993, commendation The Senate Pa., 1993, commendation Monroe County Commrs., 1993, Founders award North Ea. Pa. Fed. Credit Union, 1998; ITEC Microcomputer Competitive grantee Pa. Higher Edn. Assistance Agy., Stroudsburg, 1987. Mem. NEA, Pa. State Edn. Assn., Tech. Edn. Assn. Pa. (v.p. 1993-98, pres.-elect 1999, dep. pres. 2000, pres. 2001, conf. workshop chmn. 1996-98, Outstanding V.p. Svc. award 1996). Avocation: classical automobile restoration. Home: 523 Queen St Stroudsburg PA 18360-2215 Office: Stroudsburg Area Sch Dist 1100 W Main St Stroudsburg PA 18360-1332 E-mail: bill.weitzmann@teaponline.org.

WEIXLMANN, JOSEPH NORMAN, JR. English educator, dean; b. Buffalo, Dec. 16, 1946; s. Joseph Norman and Mary C. (Degenhart) W.; m. Sharron Pollack, Mar. 14, 1982; children: Seth Jacob, Adira Jenna, Benjamin Ari. AB, Canisius Coll., 1968; MA, Kans. State U., 1970, PhD, 1973. Instr. U. Okla., Norman, 1973-74; asst. prof. Tex. Tech U., Lubbock, 1974-76; from asst. prof. to prof. Ind. State U., Terre Haute, 1976—, assoc. dean, 1987-92, acting dean, 1992-94, dean, 1994—. Author: John Barth, 1976, American Short-Fiction Criticism, 1982; co-editor: Black American Prose Theory, 1984, Belief vs. Theory in Black American Literary Criticism, 1986, Black Feminist Criticism, 1988, Studies in Black Am. Lit. Ann., 1984-88; editor African Am. Rev. jour., 1976—; contbg. editor High Plains Lit. Rev., 1987—; adv. editor Langston Hughes Rev., 1982—. Fellow NDEA, 1970-72, NEH, 1980; Nat. Endowment for Arts grantee, 1988-95. Mem. MLA (exec. com. divsn. Black Am. Lit. and Culture 1985—), Coll. Lang. Assn., Langston Hughes Soc., Zora Neale Hurston Soc., Coun. Colls. Arts and Scis., Coun. Lit. Mags. and Presses (grantee 1977-96, Editor's grantee 1986), Coun. Editors Learned Jours. Office: Ind State Univ Stalker Hl # 213 Terre Haute IN 47809-0001 Home: 6344 Wydown Blvd Saint Louis MO 63105-2213

WEIZMANN-JARAMILLO, MARIA PIA, ESL educator; b. Oslo, Norway, June 3, 1968; d. Liv Vigdis and Antonio Manchinu; m. Luigi Jaramillo. AA, No. Virgina C.C., 1992; BS Criminal Justice, Fla. Met. U., 2000; BA French, U. of South Fla., 2002; MBA, Fla. Met. U., 2002. Real estate sales agt. Shannon & Luchs, Springfield, Va., 1987—89; exec. asst. to the pres. Consensus Builders, Inc., Tampa, Fla., 1999—2000; receptionist & translator Marine Tech. Corp., Hampton, Va., 1989—94; receptionist/administrative asst. Khalsa Chirporactic/Boston Orthopedics, Cambridge, Mass., 1994—95; dir. of ops. and human resources Khalsa Chiropractic/Boston Orthopedics, 1995—97; billing & collections analyst Neurology Associates, Tampa, 1997—99; instr. ESL Fla. Met. U., 2000—02. Author: (textbook) The Grammar Reference: American English, 2002; editor: (history & recipe book) 101 Recipes: Escargots!, 2002. Vol., petitioner The Humane Soc., Tampa and Washington, D.C., 1996—2002; asst. to case mgrs. Hillsborough County Comprehensive Sanctions Ctr., Tampa, 2000—00; vol. academic tutor Northside Mental Health Ctr. (for female juveniles), 1999—99. Mem.: Phi Sigma Iota - Internat. Fgn. Lang. Honor Soc. Avocation: dancing, swimming, researching and writing. Office: Florida Metropolitan University 3319 West Hillsborough Avenue Tampa FL 33614 Personal E-mail: mariapiaj@yahoo.com.

WEKEZER, JERZY WLADYSLAW, civil engineering educator; b. Czestochowa, Poland, June 27, 1946; came to U.S., 1982; s. Kazimierz and Janina (Rosikon) W.; m. Mariola Nowak, July 15, 1969 (div. July 1980); 1 child, Michal; m. Henryka Debska, Dec. 27, 1983; 1 child, Joanna Amy. BSCE, Gdansk Tech. U., Poland, 1969, PhD in Applied Mechanics, 1974. Registered profl. engr., Alaska, Fla. Lectr., asst. prof. Gdansk Tech. U., Poland, 1969-81; rsch. assoc. Inst. Fluid-Flow Machinery, Gdansk, 1973-74; lectr. U. Basrah, Iraq; vis. asst. prof. U. So. Calif., L.A., 1983-85; assoc. prof. U. Alaska, Anchorage, 1985-87, prof., 1987—94, head, civil engring. dept., 1990-94; dept. chmn. civil and environ. engring. Fla. Agrl. and Mech. U./Fla. State U. Coll. Engring., Tallahassee, 1994—. Cons. Autogenesis, Anchorage, 1990, Fed. Hwy. Adminstrn., 1991-96, ARCO Alaska, Inc., 1992-93. Co-author two books, monographs; reviewed jour. articles. Fellow: ASCE (Disting. Prof.). Avocations: jogging, travel. Office: FAMU-FSU Coll Engring Dept Civil & Environ Engring 2525 Pottsdamer St Tallahassee FL 32310-6046

WEKKIN, GARY DON, political science educator, researcher; b. Durand, Wis., June 6, 1949; s. Donald and Nellie Almeda (Newell) W.; m. Julia Maurene Pierson, June 26, 1971; children— Clifford Donald, Erik Lloyd. B.A., U. Wis.-Madison, 1971; M.A., U. B.C., Vancouver, 1972, Ph.D., 1980. Grad. asst. Inst. Internat. Relations, Vancouver, 1973-74; del. selection coordinator Wis. Democratic Party, Madison, 1975-76; lectr. U. Wis. Ctr., Janesville, Wis., 1978-81; vis. asst. prof. U. Mo., Kansas City, 1981-82; asst. prof. polit. sci. U. Central Ark., Conway, 1982-86, assoc. prof., 1986—; referee Ark. Polit. Sci. Jour., Conway, 1983— . Author: Democrat vs Democrat, 1984. Contbr. articles to profl. jours. U.S., Gt. Britain, Australia. Campaign mgr. Ada Deer for Sec. State, Madison, 1978; mem. exec. com. Dane County Democrats (Wis.), 1976-77; del. Ark. State Conv., Hot Springs, 1984; advisor U. Central Ark. Young Dems., Conway, 1982— . Recipient Dr. MacKenzie Am. Alumni award U. B.C., 1971-72; grantee U. Central Ark. Research Council, 1985, U. Wis. Ctr. System, 1980. Mem. Am. Polit. Sci. Assn. (grantee 1987), Midwestern Polit. Sci. Assn., Acad. Polit. Sci., So. Polit. Sci. Assn., Com. for Party Renewal. Presbyterian. Avocation: mil. strategy games. Home: 11 Tucker Creek Rd Conway AR 72034-2913 Office: U Central Ark Dept Polit Sci Conway AR 72032

WELBER, DAVID ALAN, accountant; b. York, Pa., Oct. 14, 1949; s. Harry and Julia Welber. BS in Acctg., York Coll., 1975. CPA, Pa.; cert. fin. planner, Coll. for Fin. Planners. Acct. Einhorn, Butler, Gingerich & Co., York, 1974-82; ptnr. Bergdoll & Martin, 1984-86; prin. David A. Welber, CPA, 1982-84, 86—. V.p. Bell Socialization Svcs., 1994-96. Bd. dirs. Jewish Family Svcs.,Exch. Club Ctr. for Prevention of Child Abuse, Harrisburg, Pa.,1979-96, Rehab. and Indsl. Tng. Ctr., York, 1987-90, Bell Socialization Svcs., 1991—, pres.1996-98; mem. coun. Colony Park Homeowners Assn., York, 1982-84; co-chmn. Ohev Sholom Bd. Edn., York, 1987-90. Mem. Pa. Inst. CPAs (mem. personal fin. planning com. 1987—, Edn. award 1973), Exch. Club York (treas. 1984-90, pres. 1991-92), Greater York Rep. Club (treas. 1995—). Republican. Jewish. Avocations: reading, dancing, history, tropical birds, Browsing the web, Caribbean and classical music, collecting and smoking pipes. Office: 212 E Market St York PA 17403-2013

WELBORN, W. MILLER, transportation service executive; Co-founder, chmn. Welborn Transport, Tuscaloosa, Ala.; v.p. to acting CEO Boyd Bros. Transp., Claton, 1997-99, pres., CEO, 1999-2000, vice-chmn. bd. dirs., 2000—. Office: Boyd Bros Transp 3275 Highway 30 Clayton AL 36016-3003

WELBORNE, JOHN HOWARD, railway company executive, lawyer; b. July 24, 1947; s. William Elmo and Pauline Cornwell (Schoder) W.; m. Mary Martha Lampkin, Oct. 8, 1994. AB, U. Calif.-Berkeley, 1969; MPA, UCLA, 1974; JD, U. Calif.-Davis, 1977. Bar: Calif. 1977, D.C. 1980. Congl. intern Congressman John V. Tunney, Washington, 1969; assoc. firm Adams, Duque & Hazeltine, L.A., 1979-84, of counsel, 1984-96; gen. counsel Magnum Software Corp., Chatsworth, Calif., 1989-98. Mgmt. cons., 1971—; dir. Pueblo Viejo Devel. Corp., 1979-88, Union Hardware & Metal Co., 1981—; pres. Angels Flight Railway Co., L.A., 1995—; COO Calif. Sesquicentennial Found., 1996-97; dir. Childrens Hosp. L.A. Centennial Celebration, 1998-2001. Contbr. articles to profl. jours. Mem. cen. bus. dist. project adv. com., downtown strategic plan adv. com., chmn. open space task force, mem. South Park task force City of L.A. Cmty. Redevel. Agy.; mem. L.A. Philharm. Men's Com., 1978-89; pres. L.A. County Host Com. for Olympic Games, 1984; mem. exec. com. Citizens's Task Force for Cen. Libr. Devel., L.A., 1981-83; bd. dirs. Children's Bur., L.A., 1982-88, El Pueblo Park Assn., 1983-89, L.A. Chpt. ARC, 1986-89, Angels Flight Rlwy. Found., 1995—, Friends of the USC Librs., 1999—, Inner City Law Ctr., 1992-95, Los Amigos del Pueblo, L.A. Libr. Assn., 1983-89, 92—, Windsor Sq. Assn., 1980-87, 1999—, L.A. Beautiful, 1982-85, Pershing Sq. Restoration Campaign, 1986-87, Children's Bur. Found., 1997—; bd. dirs. In the Wings divsn. Music Ctr., Los Angeles County, 1982-86, pres. 1984-85; bd. dirs., officer L.A. 200 Com., 1978-91; bd. councilors U. So. Calif. Sch. Pub. Adminstrn., 1983-89; mem. adv. bd. The L.A. Conservancy, 1986—; trustee Windsor Sq-Hancock Park Hist. Soc., 1983-86, Nat. Trust Hist. Preservation, 1997—; fellow Amundsen Inst. U.S.-Mex. Studies, 1987. Capt. Adj. Gen.'s Corps., U.S. Army, 1970-71, USAR, 1972-79. Decorated Army Commendation medal with oak leaf cluster; Cross of Merit 1st class (Fed. Republic Germany). Mem. ABA, D.C. Bar Assn., State Bar Calif., Ordre des Coteaux de Champagne, Confrerie Saint-Etienne d'Alsace, Calif. Vintage Wine Soc. Episcopalian. Office: Angels Flight Railway PO Box 712345 Los Angeles CA 90071-7345

WELCH, ALEXIS B. nursing administrator; b. Kinston, N.C., Jan. 28, 1953; d. Alex and Clara Barwick; m. Larry Welch, Oct. 24, 1976; children: Sarah, Jason. AS, Mt. Olive Coll., 1973; BSN, Atlantic Christian Coll., 1975; M in Art Adult Edn., East Carolina U., 1982. RN, N.C. Staff nurse, nurse educator Lenoir Meml. Hosp., Kinston, 1975-80; nurse educator James Sprunt C.C., Kenansville, N.C., 1981-89; nurse educator, DON, dean Lenoir C.C., Kinston, 1989—. Pvt. duty Home Health, N.C., 1989-99. Mem. adv. com. troop 746 Boy Scouts Am., Albertson, 1999—; tchr. devel. coord. local ch., Albertson, 1999—; youth group pres. local ch., Albertson, 1994-99. Mem.: ANA, N.C. Nurses Assn., N.C. Assn. Degree Nursing Coun. (past sec.-treas. 1992—94), Phi Kappa Phi. Mem. Lds Ch. Office: Lenoir C C Kinston NC 28502 E-mail: abw801@email.lenoir.cc.nc.us.

WELCH, ARNOLD DEMERRITT, pharmacologist, biochemist; b. Nottingham, N.H., Nov. 7, 1908; s. Lewis H. and Stella M. (Batchelder) W.; m. Mary Grace Scott, June 15, 1933 (dec.); children: Michael Scott, Stephen Anthony, Gwyneth Jeanne Sinizer; m. Erika Petrová, Mar. 15, 1966. BS, U. Fla., 1930, MS, 1931, D.Sc. (hon.), 1973; PhD, U. Toronto, 1934; MD, Washington U., St. Louis, 1939. Research asst. U. Fla., 1929-31; fellow pharmacology U. Toronto, 1931-35; asst. pharmacology Washington U., 1935-36, instr., 1936-40; dir. pharmacol. research Sharp and Dohme, Inc., Phila., 1940-44, dir. research, 1943-44; prof. pharmacology, dir. dept. Sch. Medicine, Western Res. U., 1944-53; Fulbright sr. research scholar Oxford U., 1952; prof. pharmacology, chmn. dept. Sch. Medicine, Yale U., 1953-67, Eugene Higgins prof. pharmacology, 1957-67; dir. Squibb Inst. Med. Research, 1967-72; v.p. R&D E.R. Squibb & Sons, Inc.; pres. Squibb Inst. Med. Research, Princeton, N.J., 1972-74; chmn. dept. biochem. and clin. pharmacology St. Jude Children's Research Hosp., Memphis, 1974-81, rschr., mem. emeritus, 1981-83. Cancer expert Nat. Cancer Inst., NIH, 1983-86, acting dep. dir. divsn. of cancer treatment, 1984; scientist emeritus and rschr. NIH, 1986-88; mem. com. on growth NRC, chmn. panel mech. action, 1946-48, chmn. sect. chemotherapy, 1948-52, chmn. com. on growth, 1952-54; mem. sci. adv. bds. Leonard Wood Meml., 1947-53, Nat. Vitamin Found., 1953-56, St. Jude Children's Rsch. Hosp., Memphis, 1968-71; mem. divsn. biology and medicine NSF, 1953-55; mem. study sect. pharmacology and exptl. therapeutics USPHS, 1952-56, 1959-63, chmn., 1960-63, chmn. study sect. chemotherapy, 1963-65; mem. coordinating com. cancer chemotherapy Nat. Cancer Svc. Ctr., USPHS, 1955-57; mem. rsch. adv. coun. Am. Cancer Soc., 1956-59; mem. adv. coun. biol. sci. Princeton U., 1969-75; mem. working cadre Nat. Large Bowel Cancer program Nat. Cancer Inst., 1975-80; sci. adv. bd. La Jolla Cancer Rsch. Found., 1978-81; mem. Memphis Med. Seminar, 1977-83, pres., 1981-82. Assoc. editor: Cancer Research, 1950-58, Pharmacological Revs., 1962-66, Ann. Rev. Pharmacol., 1965-69; Am. editor: Biochem. Pharmacology, 1958-62, vice chmn. internat. bd. editors, 1962-83, chmn., 1983-93; mem. adv. bd. Advances in Pharmacology and Chemotherapy, 1962-85; mem. bd. editors Handbuch der experimentellen Pharmakologie, 1966-85; contbr. articles to profl. jours., chpts. in books. Recipient alumni award U. Fla., 1953, Washington U., 1957, Torald Sollmann award Am. Soc. Pharmacology and Exptl. Therapeutics, 1966, Chester Stock award Meml. Sloan-Kettering Cancer Ctr., 1987, J. Heyrovsky gold medal Czechoslovak Acad. Scis., 1990; Commonwealth fellow Inst. für Therapeutische Biochemie, U. Frankfurt, Germany, and Acad. Scis., Prague, Czechoslovakia, 1964-65. Fellow AAAS; mem. Am. Soc. Pharmacol. and Exptl. Therapeutics, Assn. Am. Physicians, Am. Assn. Cancer Rsch., Am. Soc. Biol. Chemistry and Molecular Biology, Am. Soc. Clin. Pharmacology and Therapeutics, Am. Soc. Hematology, Am. Chem. Soc., Soc. Exptl. Biology and Medicine, Biochem. Soc. (Gt. Britain), Cosmos Club (Washington), Phi Beta Kappa, Sigma Xi, Alpha Omega Alpha, Phi Kappa Phi, Delta Tau Delta. Home: 5212 Renaissance Ave San Diego CA 92122-5602

WELCH, ASHLEY JAMES, engineering educator; b. Ft. Worth, May 3, 1933; married, 1952; 3 children. BS, Tex. Tech U., 1955; MS, So. Meth. U., 1959; PhD in Elec. Engring., Rice U., 1964. Aerophys. engr. Gen. Dynamics, Ft. Worth, 1957-60; instr. elec. engring. Rice U., 1960-64, from asst. to assoc. prof., 1964-68, dir. engring. computing facility, 1970-75, dir. biomed. engring. program, 1971-75, 95-96; prof. elec. and biomed. engring. U. Tex., Austin, 1975—, Marion E. Forsman Centennial prof. engring., 1985—, faculty advisor undergraduate biomedical engring. students, 2002—. Fellow: IEEE, Am. Inst. for Med. and Biol. Engring., Am. Soc. Lasers Surg. Medicine (bd. dirs. 1989—92, 1999—2002, W.B. Mark award 2002). Achievements include research in laser-tissue interaction, application of lasers in medicine. Office: U Tex at Austin Dept Elec & Computer Engring Austin TX 78712

WELCH, CHARLES EDGAR, JR. retired English language educator, writer; b. Phila., July 20, 1918; s. Charles Edgar and Eva Dudley (Morris) W.; widower. BS in Edn., West Chester U., 1947; MA in Early Am. History, U. Pa., 1948, PhD in Folklore, 1970; cert. in 20th Century poetry, Oxford (Eng.) U., 1948. Cert. tchr., Pa. Lectr. English, Phila. Coll. Pharmacy and Sci., 1947-50, asst. prof., 1951-60, assoc. prof., 1960-69, prof., 1969-77, emeritus prof., 1977—, chmn. dept. langs. and social scis., 1950-77. Adj. prof. ESL, Temple U., Phila., 1977-96; part-owner Trevose Summer Theater, 1950-52; contbr., cons. Ledger Syndicate, 1950-70; actor, asst. stage mgr. New Angola (Pa.) Summer Theater, 1955; program dir. Folk Fair, Nationalities Svc. Ctr., Phila., 1955-75; contbr. to humanities program Thomas Jefferson U.; writer Milestones, Phila.; a host You and Your Health, Sta. WFIL-TV, 1958-70; folklorist for documentary on Phila. Mummers Parade Look Who's Having Fun, 1986. Author: Oh! Dem Golden Slippers: A History of the Philadelphia Mummers Parade, 1970, revised, 1993, (with A. Osol): A Sesquicentennial of Service 1821-1971 of the Philadelphia College of Pharmacy and Science; contbr. articles and book revs. to profl. jours., newspapers and mags. Stage mgr. fund raising program, fund raiser Erlanger Theater, Phila., Internat. House, Phila. Mem. Acad. Natural Scis., Pa. Hist. Soc., Pa. Acad. Arts, Nat. Mus. Women in Arts (charter). Republican. Avocation: writing. Home: 2423 Pine St Philadelphia PA 19103-6416

WELCH, CLAUDE (CLAUDE RAYMOND WELCH), theology educator; b. Genoa City, Wis., Mar. 10, 1922; s. Virgil Cleon and Deone West (Grenelle) W.; m. Eloise Janette Turner, May 31, 1942 (div. 1970); children— Eric, Thomas, Claudia; m. Theodosia Montignel Blewett, Oct. 5, 1970 (dec. 1978); m. Joy Neuman, Oct. 30, 1982. BA summa cum laude, Upper Iowa U., 1942; postgrad., Garrett Theol. Sem., 1942-43; BD cum laude, Yale U., 1945, PhD, 1950; DD (hon.), Ch. Div. Sch. of Pacific, 1972, Jesuit Sch. Theology, 1982; LHD (hon.), U. Judaism, 1976. Ordained to ministry Meth. Ch., 1947. Instr. religion Princeton (N.J.) U., 1947-50, asst. prof., 1950-51, vis. prof., 1962; asst. prof. theology Yale U. Div. Sch., New Haven, 1951-54, assoc. prof., 1954-60; Berg prof. religious thought, chmn. dept. U. Pa., Phila., 1960-71, assoc. dean Coll. Arts and Scis., 1964-68, acting chmn. dept. philosophy, 1965-66; prof. hist. theology Grad. Theol. Union, Berkeley, Calif., 1971—, dean, 1971-87, pres., 1972-82. Vis. prof. Garrett Theol. Sem., 1951, Pacific Sch. Religion, 1958, Hartford Sem. Found., 1958-59, Princeton Theol. Sem., 1962-63, U. Va., 1987; Fulbright sr. lectr. U. Mainz, Germany, 1968; Sprunt lectr. Union Theol. Sem., Richmond, Va., 1958; Willson lectr. Southwestern U., Georgetown, Tex., 1994; dir. study of grad. edn. in religion Am. Coun. Learned Socs., 1969-71; del. World Conf. on Faith and Order, 1963. Author: In This Name: the Doctrine of the Trinity in Contemporary Theology, 1952, (with John Dillenberger) Protestant Christianity, interpreted through its Development, 1954, 2d rev. edit., 1988, The Reality of the Church, 1958,

Graduate Education in Religion: A Critical Appraisal, 1971, Religion in the Undergraduate Curriculum, 1972, Protestant Thought in the 19th Century, vol. 1, 1799-1870, 1972, vol. 2, 1870-1914, 1985; Editor, translator: God and Incarnation in Mid-19th Century German Theology (Thomasius, Dorner and Biedermann), 1965; Contbr. to publs. in field. Recipient decennial prize Bross Found., 1970; Guggenheim fellow, 1976; NEH research fellow, 1984, Fulbright research fellow, 1956-57. Mem. Am. Acad. Religion (pres. 1969-70), Coun. of Socs. for Study of Religion (chmn. 1969-74, 85-90), Soc. for Values in Higher Edn. (pres. 1967-71), Am. Soc. Ch. History, Am. Theol. Soc., Phi Beta Kappa. Home: 123 Fairlawn Dr Berkeley CA 94708-2107 E-mail: claudew2@juno.com.

WELCH, DAVID WILLIAM, lawyer; b. St. Louis, Feb. 26, 1941; s. Claude LeRoy Welch and Mary Eleanor (Peggs) Penney; m. Candace Lee Capages, June 5, 1971; children: Joseph Peggs, Heather Elizabeth, Katherine Laura. BSBA, Washington U., St. Louis, 1963; JD, U. Tulsa, 1971. Bar: Okla. 1972, Mo. 1973, U.S. Dist. Ct. (we. dist.) Mo. 1973, U.S. Dist. Ct. (ea. dist.) Mo. 1974, U.S. Ct. Appeals (8th cir.) 1977, U.S. Ct. Appeals (7th cir.) 1991. Contract adminstr. McDonnell Aircraft Corp., St. Louis, 1965-66; bus. analyst Dun & Bradstreet Inc., Los Angeles, 1967-68; atty. U.S. Dept. Labor, Washington, 1972-73; ptnr. Moller Talent, Kuelthau & Welch, St. Louis, 1973-88, Lashly & Baer, St. Louis, 1988-96, Armstrong Teasdale LLP, St. Louis, 1996—. Author: (handbook) Missouri Employment Law, 1988; contbr. book chpts. Missouri Bar Employee-Employer Law, 1985, 87, 89, 92, 94, Missouri Discrimination Law, 1999; co-editor: Occupational Safety and Health Law, 1996. Mem. City of Creve Coeur Ethics Commn., 1987-88, Planning and Zoning Commn., 1988-96; bd. dirs. Camp Wyman, Eureka, Mo., 1982—, sec., 1987-88, 2nd v.p. 1988-89, 1st v.p. 1990-92, pres., 1992-94. Mem. ABA, Fed. Bar Assn., Mo. Bar Assn., Okla. Bar Assn., St. Louis Bar Assn., Kiwanis (bd. dirs. St. Louis 1979—, sec. 1982-83, 93-94, v.p. 1983-84, 88-90, 92-93, Man of Yr. award 1985). Democrat. Mem. Christian Ch. (Disciples Of Christ). Avocations: travel, landscaping, music. Home: 536 N Mosley Rd Saint Louis MO 63141-7633 Office: Armstrong Teasdale 1 Metropolitan Sq Ste 2600 Saint Louis MO 63102-2740

WELCH, DOMINIC, publishing consultant; Former pres., pub. The Salt Lake Tribune, Salt Lake City. Office: 143 S. Main St. 400 Tribune Bldg Salt Lake City UT 84111*

WELCH, EDWIN HUGH, academic administrator; b. Balt., Apr. 11, 1944; s. Lester Kenneth and Catherine (Dodrer); m. Janet Gail Boggess, Nov. 22, 1977. BA, Western Md. Coll., 1965; STB, Boston U. Sch. Theology, 1968; postgrad., London Sch. Econs. and Polit. Sci., 1968-69; PhD, Boston U., 1971. Assoc. prof., chmn. W.Va. Wesleyan Coll., Buckhannon, 1971-75, Lebanon Valley Coll., Annville, Pa., 1975-79, dir. weekend coll., 1979-80; dean Lakeland Coll., Sheboygan, Wis., 1980-81; provost Wartburg Coll., Waverly, Iowa, 1981-89; pres. U. Charleston, W.Va., 1989—. Chmn. Iowa Deans Confs., Des Moines, 1984-89; title III evaluator Iowa Wesleyan Coll., Mt. Pleasant, 1983-85; pres. W.Va. Intercollegiate Athletic Conf., 1994-96. Contbr. articles to edn. jours. Bd. dirs. Bus. and Indsl. Devel. Corp., BB&T, Charleston Area Med. Ctr.; Health Sys.; creator, dir. Cmty. Leadership Devel. Program, Waverly, 1986-88; bd. dirs., pres. Lebanon (Pa.) Family Planning Assn., 1976-81. Named Tchr. of Yr., W.Va. Wesleyan Coll., 1974. Mem. Nat. Assn. Ind. Colls. and Univs., W.Va. Ind. Coll. & Univ. (exec. com.) Balt. Conf. United Meth. Ch. (ordained), Appalachian Coll. Assn. (chmn.), Coun. Ind. Colls., Rotary Internat. (past pres. Charleston chpt.). Democrat. Methodist. Office: U Charleston Office of Pres 2300 Maccorkle Ave SE Charleston WV 25304-1045

WELCH, GREG RONALD, publishing executive; b. Huntington Beach, Calif., Nov. 19, 1973; s. Myrna Lacy. Art gallery mgr. Koenig, Newtown, Conn., 1998—2001; pub. ARTistic FX Mag., New Britain, 2001—. Office: FX Pub LLC Ste 303 99 West Main St New Britain CT 06051 Office Fax: 860-826-7755. Personal E-mail: G.R.Welch@att.net. Business E-Mail: ARTisticFX@att.net.

WELCH, JACK HAMILL, retired internist; b. Columbus, Ohio, July 14, 1915; s. John Orr and Evelyn (Bigger) W.; m. Mary Elaine Childs, Apr. 25, 1943 (div. 1976); children: David, Pamela, Michael; m. Alice Elizabeth Welch, May 6, 1978. BA, Ohio State U., 1936; MD, Duke U., 1940. Diplomate Am. Bd. Internal Medicine, Nat. Bd. Med. Examiners. Intern, then resident Henry Ford Hosp., Detroit, 1940-42, 46-48; pvt. practice internal medicine Columbus, 1948-50, Hollywood, Calif., 1950-52, San Fernando Valley, L.A., 1952-83; ret., 1983. Author: Battalion surgeon WWII, 1996. Mem. Visions of Cmty. , 1984—94, chair, 1990—92; initiator Peace and Justice com. United Ch. of Christ, Fresno, 1990—97; co-founder, bd. dirs. Fresno Ctr. for Non Violence, 1992—, Black.White Dialogue Group, Fresno, 1997—. With M.C. U.S. Army, 1942—45, ETO. Decorated bronze star. Mem. AMA, ACP, Physicians for Social Responsibility (ho. dels. 1987-88), Fgn. Policy Assn. Democrat. Mem. United Ch. Christ. Avocations: singing, writing, family, walking, TV, golf. Home: 6432 N Dolores Ave Fresno CA 93711

WELCH, JAMES E. artist; b. Nora, Va., July 14, 1943; Student, Art Sch. Soc. Arts and Crafts, 1963-64, Ctr. Creative Studies, 1973. Illustrator Best of Pastel, 1995, Portrait Inspirations, 1996, Love, 1998, Angel of Love, 1999; exhbns. include Left Bank Gallery, 1982, 83, 87, 88, 95, Lansing Art Gallery, 1982, 85, 86, 88, 95, 98, Midland Ctr. for the Arts, 1982, 85, 86, Our Town Birmingham, 1986-88, 97-2000 (2d place award 1986, 87), Krasl Art Ctr., St. Joseph, Mich., 1986, Kendall Sch. Design, 1986, Detroit Inst. Art, 1987, Flint Inst. Arts, 1987, Ea. Mich. U., 1987, Macomb Ctr. for the Arts, 1988, Mt. Clemens Art Ctr., 1988, 93, Saginaw Art Mus., 1988, 89, 92, 99, Pontiac Creative Art Ctr., 1989, New Visions Gallery, 1989-90, U. Mich. Hosp., 1989, South Bend Art Ctr., 1990, Elle Sharp Mus., 1990. Mem. Survivors Art Found. Recipient purchase award Bank Commerce, 1985; Viewer's Choice award Midland Ctr. Arts, 1982, 85, Outstanding award, 1985; 2d place award Midwest States Kendall Sch. Design, 1986, purchase and People's Choice awards State of Arts, 1988, 1st place award Grand Valley Artists, 1988, purchase award, Viewers' Choice award Krasl Art Ctr., 1990, Klienschmidt award Saginaw Art Mus., 1992, 2d place award Lansing Art Gallery, 1995, Phil & Marion Agree award, 1995, Sponsors award Chrysler Corp., 1998, Award of Merit Manhattan Arts Internat., 1999. Mem. Saginaw (Mich.) Arts Guild (hon.), Greater Flint Arts Coun. (hon. mention 1993, 96, 2d place award 1995). Avocations: travel, hiking. Home: 585 S US 23 Harrisville MI 48740-9583

WELCH, JANET MARTIN, librarian; b. Chgo., Jan. 12, 1945; d. Lowell Arthur and Bella S. Martin; m. H. William Welch, Dec. 30, 1967; children: Scott Martin, Dana Michelle. BA magna cum laude, Bucknell U., 1967; MLS, Rutgers U., 1968. Project intern State Librs., Pa., N.J., Ill., 1966-67; dir. Rsch. Lab./NL Industries, Highstown, N.J., 1967-69; sci. libr. SUNY, Albany, 1969-71; dir. Resource Ctr. Ft. Ann (N.Y.) Ctrl. Sch., 1971-72; jount author, sr. rsch. assoc. Tucson Pub. Libr., 1973-74; editl./network cons. Pahlavi Nat. Libr., East Norwich, N.Y., 1974-76; learning resource cons. North Country C.C., Elizabethtown, 1976-77; exec. dir. Rochester (N.Y.) Regional Libr. Coun., 1977-97; state libr., asst. commr. N.Y. State Edn. Dept., Albany, 1997—. Adj. prof. SUNY. Buffalo, 1986—; cons. N.Y. State Regions, 1986—. Editor NYLA semi-ann. publ. PR Alert, 1992; mem. editl. bd. The Bottom Line: Mng. Libr. Fins., 1986, others. Mem. governing bd. Greater Rochester Project, 1995—; del. White House Conf. on Librs. and Info. Svcs., 1991, N.Y. State Gov.'s Conf. on Librs., Albany, 1990-91; bd. dirs. N.Y. State Coun. on Humanities, N.Y.c., 1988-93. Recipient Ann. award for Legis. Success, ALA, 1996; Pres.'s award for pub. awareness of Librs., N.Y. Libr. Assn., 1995, also Spirit of Librarianship award, 1993, Outstanding Svc. to Librs. award, 1986. Office: NY State Libr 10 C 34 Cultural Ctr Albany NY 12234-0001

WELCH, JASPER ARTHUR, JR. security company executive, consultant; b. Baton Rouge, Jan. 5, 1931; s. Jasper Arthur and Oramay Ballinger (Young) W.; m. Frances Carroll Wright, Mar. 28, 1953 (div. Nov. 1984); children: Jasper Arthur III, Carroll Welch Pawlikowski, Brent Ballinger; m. Jane Ann Alford Tudor, Dec. 31, 1985. BS in Physics, La. State U., 1952; MA in Physics, U. Calif., Berkeley, 1954, PhD in Physics, 1958. Commd. officer 2d lt. USAF, 1952, advanced through grades to maj. gen., 1975; chief analyst Hdqs. USAF, Washington, 1969-71; chief strategic analysis Office Sec. Def., 1971-74; chief strategic concepts Hdqs. USAF, 1974-75, asst. chief staff for analysis, 1975-79; coord. def. policy NSC, 1979-81; asst. dept. chief staff Hdqs. USAF, 1981-83; retired, 1983; tech. cons. Jasper Welch Assocs., Arlington, Va., 1983—. Bd. dirs. Sci. Applications Intrnat. Corp., San Diego; mem. tech. adv. coun. Sikorsky Aircraft, Stratford, Conn., 1984—; mem. adv. coun. NASA, Washington, 1985-89; chmn. mil. adv. panel to dir. CIA, Washington, 1986-98; mem. nat. security panel U. Calif., 2000— Author: Atomic Theory of Gas Dynamics, 1965; contbr. articles to sci. jours., including Phys. Rev., Strategic Rev. Youth dir. St. Matthews Epis. Ch., Pacific Palisades, Calif., 1969-74, St. Andrews Epis. Ch., Arlington, 1969-74; mem. found. bd. Santa Fe Chamber Music Festival, 1998—. Decorated D.S.M. with oak leaf cluster, Legion of merit with two oak leaf clusters. Mem. NAE (found. bd. 1999—), Am. Geophys. Union, Am. Phys. Soc., Coun. on Fgn. Rels. Avocations: music, theater, gardening, hiking, racing sailboats. Office: Sci Applications Internat Corp 1710 SAIC Dr Mc Lean VA 22102

WELCH, JEANIE MAXINE, librarian; b. L.A., Jan. 22, 1946; d. Howard Carlton and Roberta Jean (Dunsmuir) W. BA, U. Denver, 1967, MA, 1968; M of Internat. Mgmt., Am. Grad. Sch. Internat. Mgmt., 1981. Asst. libr. Am. Grad. Sch. Internat. Mgmt., Glendale, Ariz., 1968-83; reference libr. Lamar U., Beaumont, Tex., 1983-85, head reference, 1985-87; reference unit head U. N.C., Charlotte, 1988-98, asst. coord. reference svcs., 1998-2000, bus. ref. libr., 2000—. Author: The Spice Trade, 1994, The Tokyo Trial, 2002; contbr. articles to profl. jours. Chpt. pres. NOW, Beaumont, 1985-87, state sec., Tex., 1986; exec. bd. Ariz. State Libr. Assn., 1976-80. Rsch. grantee Tex. Libr. Assn., 1986; named Dun & Bradstreet Info. Svcs. Online Champion of Yr., 1996. Mem.: ALA, Acad. Internat. Bus., Acad. Internat. Bus., Soc. Mil. Historians, N.C. Libr. Assn., Phi Beta Delta. Democrat. Methodist. Office: U NC Atkins Libr Charlotte NC 28223 E-mail: jmwelch@email.uncc.edu.

WELCH, JERRY, oil company executive; b. Marion, Ohio, Mar. 13, 1963; s. Arthur Leroy and Donna R. (Ellwood) W.; m. Sharon Carol Lee, 1995; children: Joseph Peterson, Shellie Peterson, James Peterson. BA, U. Colo., 1984. Exec. Amoco Oil, Houston, 1984—; CEO Brit. Inc., Paris. Mem. Internat. Platform Assn. Republican. Avocations: auto racing, tennis, sailing, swimming. Home: 31650 Hwy 44 E Eustis FL 31650 also: PO Box 470512 Lake Monroe FL 32747-0512

WELCH, J(OAN) KATHLEEN, entrepreneur; b. Pensacola, Fla., Jan. 28, 1950; d. Leslie Peter and Frances Louise (Hughes) Morales. AOS in Massage Therapy, 2000, degree Tuina, 2001. Cert. advanced clin. hypnotist 1997, massage therapist 1998, canine massage therapist 2000, equine massage therapist 2000. Salesperson Arthur Murray Dance Studio, Colo., Fla., Pa. and N.J., 1970-81; sales rep. Warner-Lambert Co., Morris Plains, N.J., 1981-83; supr., mgr. Dance Club Internat., Chatham, 1983-90; dist. rep. Nat. Fedn. Ind. Bus., 1990-95; pres. I Am Consulting, 1993—; radio sales rep. Fress Media, 1995-96; acct. exec. Atlantic Lucent Techs., 1997; computer programmer Mailcraft, Inc., 1997-98. Developer sales program Dance Club Internat.; judge Nat. Dance Coun. Am., 1977—90, dance coach, 1975—90; coach winners U.S. Ballroom Championships Hustle divsn., 1978, choreographer, 1971—90, competitor, 1972—81; condr. New Age lectrs., seminars and workshops, 1994—; practitioner Kofutu Touch Healing, 1994—; Reiki practitioner, 1995—; Kinesiology practitioner, 1995—; Regenesis practitioner, 1996—; tchr. meditation, yoga, Tai Chi, Chee Gung (Qigong), 1995—. Co-prodr., promoter, talent scout for TV program: Astrology Today (formerly It's in the Stars), 1989-94; performed on nat. TV with leading personalities including George Raft, Donald O'Connor, and Mike Douglas. Recipient awards Arthur Murray Studio, 1971-81, 1st place counselor award Arthur Murray All Star Tournament, 1977, 1st place Supr. award Dance Club Internat., 1st place Registrar award Dance Club Internat. in the Tournament of Champions, 1984; ranked No. 1 rep. in Profls. Corner, N.Y. div. Nat. Fedn. Ind. Bus., 1991, ranked No. 2 rep., 1992; named Internat. Woman of Yr., 1993. Mem. Imperial Soc. Tchrs. of Dancing (assoc. Ballroom br., Latin-Am. br.), Am. Dance Tchrs. Assn. Mem. Unity Ch. Avocations: travel, yoga, astrology, theater, metaphysics and new age studies. Home and Office: PO Box 181277 Denver CO 80218 E-mail: jkathleenwelch@hotmail.com.

WELCH, JOHN DANA, urologist, arts association executive; b. Canton, Ill., Mar. 14, 1938; m. Myrna Lee Loring, Dec. 23, 1962; children: Timothy Lance, Christina Dawn. BS, U. Ill., 1960, MD, 1963. Diplomate Am. Bd. Urology, Nat. Bd. Med. Examiners, Fla. Bd. Med. Examiners. Rotating intern Tampa (Fla.) Gen. Hosp., 1963-64, resident in urology, 1964-68; pvt. practice, Sarasota, Fla., 1970-98. Bd. dirs. Bay Area Renal Stone Ctr., 1986-98; chief surgery HCA Doctors Hosp., 1981, chief of staff, 1983, trustee, 1988-91. Bd. dirs. Asolo Ctr. for Performing Arts, 1982-95, sec., 1989-90, v.p., 1990-93, pres., 1993-94; pres., founder Sarasota Film Festival, 1998—. Maj. USAF, 1968-70. Mem. Fla. Med. Assn., Sarasota County Med. Soc., Am. Urological Assn. (SE sect.), Fla. Urological Soc. (pres. 1986), Am. Lithotripsy Soc. Home and Office: 650 Mourning Dove Dr Sarasota FL 34236-1926 E-mail: SRQDOC@aol.com.

WELCH, JOHN F., JR. retired utilities executive; BS chem. engring., U. Mass., 1957; MS chem. engring., U. Illinois, 1958, PhD chem. engring., 1960. Joined General Electric Co., 1960, v.p., 1979—81, chmn. bd., CEO Conn., 1981—2001, retired, 2001. Mailing: PO Box 861 Shelton CT 06484*

WELCH, JOSEPH DANIEL, lawyer; b. University City, Mo., Feb. 1, 1952; s. Robert Joseph and Mary Virginia (Church) W.; m. Sharon Susan Filipek, Mar. 16, 1973; children: Eric Ryan, Christopher Joseph, Colin Andrew, Maria Nicole, Theresa Katherine. BA cum laude, St. Louis U., 1974, JD, 1977. Bar: Mo. 1977, U.S. Dist. Ct. (ea. and we. dists.) Mo. 1977, U.S. Ct. Appeals (8th cir.) 1984, U.S. Supreme Ct. 1994. Assoc. Ely & Cary, Hannibal, Mo., 1977-79; ptnr. Ely, Cary & Welch, 1979-82, Ely, Cary, Welch & Hickman, Hannibal, 1982-99, Cary, Welch & Hickman, L.L.P., Hannibal, 1999—2001, Cary, Welch, Hickman, Walden & Porter, L.L.P., 2002—. Mem. Nat. Network of Estate Planning Attys, 2000-, Mississippi River Pky. Commn., St. Paul, 1988-95, head Mo. del., 1988; prof. bus. law Hannibal-LaGrange Coll., 1993-98; mem. Nat. Heritage Corridor Commn., Washington, 1990-96; speaker various orgns. Editor: Year in Review-Bankruptcy, 1991-94, co-author, 1988-90; speaker various profl. orgns.; contbr. articles to profl. jours. Bd. dirs. Hannibal Pks. and Recreation Dept., 2000-, Mark Twain Area Physician's Recruitment Assn., Hannibal, 1984-85, Hannibal Free Pub. Libr., 1980-82, Hannibal C. of C., 1978-80, pres. Hannibal Ctrl. Bus. Devel., Inc., 1982-85; mem. Mo. Right-to-Life, 1977—; community adv. bd. St. Elizabeth Hosp., 1985-86; Birthright of Hannibal, Inc., 1980—, Holy Family Sch. Bd., 1990-95. Acad. scholar St. Louis U., 1970-74; recognition for Significant Contribution to Bush Administrn., Dept. Interior, 1993. Mem. ATLA, Mo. Assn. Trial Lawyers., Mark Twain Astron. Soc. (co-founder), Nat. Network of Estate Planning Attys. Roman Catholic. Avocations: parenting, basketball, tennis, boating, creative writing. Home: 601 Country Club Dr Hannibal MO 63401-3033 Office: Cary Welch and Hickman LLP 1000 Center St Hannibal MO 63401-3449

WELCH, LAWRENCE ANDREW, JR. lawyer; b. Memphis, Apr. 5, 1961; s. Lawrence A. and Dorothy (Foust) W.; m. Lisa Carol Garland Sept. 19, 1987; children: Jennifer Leigh, Lawrence Andrew III. BS in Bus. Administrn., Christian Bros. Coll., 1983; JD, Memphis State U., 1990. Bar: Tenn. 1990, U.S. Dist. Ct. (ea. dist.) Tenn. 1991, U.S. Ct. Appeals (6th cir.) 1992. Mem. Milligan & Coleman, Greeneville, Tenn., 1990-94; sole practitioner, 1994—. Mem. ABA (litigation sect., legal malpractice com.), Tenn. Defense Lawyer Assn., Tenn. Bar Assn., Greene County Bar Assn. Republican. Presbyterian. Home: 58 Woodcrest Cir Greeneville TN 37745-0521 Office: 313 E Bernard Ave Greeneville TN 37745-5013

WELCH, LLOYD RICHARD, electrical engineering educator, communications consultant; b. Detroit, Sept. 28, 1927; s. Richard C. and Helen (Felt) W.; m. Irene Althea Main, Sept. 12, 1953; children: Pamela Irene Towery, Melinda Ann Bryant, Diana Lia Worthington. BS in Math., U. Ill., 1951; PhD in Math., Calif. Inst. Tech., 1958. Mathematician NASA-Jet Propulsion Lab., Pasadena, Calif., 1956-59; staff mathematician Inst. Def. Analyses, Princeton, N.J., 1959-65; prof. elec. engring. U. So. Calif., L.A., 1965-99, prof. emeritus, 1999—. Cons. in field of elec. comms. Contbr. articles to profl. jours. Served with USN, 1945-49, 51-52. Fellow IEEE; mem. Nat. Acad. Engring., Am. Math. Soc., Math. Assn. Am., Phi Beta Kappa, Sigma Xi, Phi Kappa Phi, Pi Mu Epsilon, Eta Kappa Nu Office: U So Calif Elec Engring Bldg 500A Los Angeles CA 90089-0001 E-mail: lloydwelch@earthlink.net.

WELCH, MARTHA GRACE, physician, researcher; b. Buffalo, June 21, 1944; d. Thomas Harris and Jane Elizabeth (Todd) W.; m. Anthony H. Horan, July 7, 1970 (div. May 1985); 1 child, Thomas Bramwell Welch Horan. BA, N.Y.U., 1966; MD, Columbia U., 1971. Diplomate Am. Bd. Psychiatry and Neurology. Intern Greenwich (Conn.) Hosp. Assn., 1971-72; resident Albert Einstein Coll. Med., Bronx, N.Y., 1972-74, fellow, 1974-77, instr., 1977-79; dir., founder The Mothering Ctr., Greenwich, 1978—; asst. clin. prof. psychiatry Columbia U., N.Y.C., 1997—. Author: Holding Time, 1989, (with others) Autistic Children, 1983; contbr. articles to profl. jours. Pres. alumni coun. Columbia U. Coll. Physicians and Surgeons, 2001-2002 Recipient Alumni Achievement award Middlebury (Vt.) Coll., 1995. Mem. Am. Psychiat. Assn. Avocations: reading, skiing, tennis, sewing, biking, music. Office: 15 E 91st St New York NY 10128-0648

WELCH, MICHAEL FRANCIS, educator, author; b. Kansas City, Mo., Jan. 8, 1960; s. Edmund Francis and Diane Janet Welch. BA, Benedictine Coll., 1982; MA, U. Mo., Kansas City, 1983; MS, Ill. State U., 1984; PhD, U. North Tex., 1987. Social sci. rsch. analyst Fed. Bur. of Prisons, Fort Worth, 1985-87; assoc. prof. St. John's U., Queens, N.Y., 1987-93; assoc. prof. criminology Rutgers U., New Brunswick, 1993—. Adv. bd. Justice Profl., 1993—. Author: Corrections: A Critial Approach, 1996, Punishment in America, 1999, Flag Burning, Moral Panic and the Criminalization of Protest, 2000; co-editor Social Pathology, 1996—; editl. bd. Jour. of Crime and Justice, 1998—. Mem. Coalition to Support Cuban Detainees. Mem. ACLU, Amnesty Internat., Am. Soc. of Criminology, Acad. of Criminal Justice Scis. Avocations: guitarist, subway surfing.

WELCH, MICHAEL JOHN, chemistry educator, researcher; b. Stoke-on-Trent, Staffordshire, Eng., June 28, 1939; came to U.S., 1965; s. Arthur John W. and Mary (Welch); m. Teresa Jean Conocchiolli, Apr. 22, 1967 (div. 1979); children: Colin, Lesley. BA, Cambridge U., Eng., 1961; MA, Cambridge U., 1964; PhD, London U., 1965. Asst. prof. radiation chemistry in radiology Washington U. Sch. Medicine, St. Louis, 1967-70, assoc. prof., 1970-74; assoc. prof. dept. chemistry Washington U., 1971-75, prof. dept. chemistry, 1978—; prof. radiology Washington U. Sch. Medicine, 1991—, prof. molecular biology and pharmacology, 1993—; prof. biomed. engring. program Washington U., 1996; co-dir. Mallinckrodt Inst. Dir. radiol. scis. dept. Washignton U., 1990—; mem. diagnostic radiology study sect. NIH, 1986-89, chmn., 1989-91; mem. sci. adv. com. Whitaker Found., 1995—. Author: Introduction to the Tracer Methods, 1972; editor: Radiopharmaceuticals and Other Compounds Labeled with Shortlived Radionuclides, 1977; assoc. editor Jour. Nuclear Medicine, 1989—; contbr. chpts. to books, more than 400 articles to profl. jours. Recipient Georg Charles de Hevesy Nuclear Medicine Pioneer award, 1992; scholar St. Catharine Coll. Cambridge U., 1958-61. Mem. Soc. Nuclear Medicine (trustee, pres. 1984, Paul C. Aebersold award 1980, de Hevesy Nuclear Pioneer award 1992), Radiopharm. Sci. Coun. (pres. 1980-81), Am. Chem. Soc. (St. Louis award 1988, award for nuclear chemistry 1990, Mid-West award 1991), Chem. Soc. London, Radiation Rsch. Soc., Inst. Medicine, Sigma Xi Office: Washington U Sch Medicine Edward Mallinckrodt Inst Radiology 510 S Kingshighway Blvd Box 8225 Saint Louis MO 63110-1016 E-mail: welchm@mir.wustl.edu.*

WELCH, OLIVER WENDELL, retired pharmaceutical executive; b. Jacksonville, Tex., Jan. 9, 1930; s. Jackson Andrew and Annie Laura (Trapp) W.; m. Wanda Virginia Urrey, Nov. 14, 1948. BA, Tex. Tech U., 1952; MA, Columbia U., 1958. Pharm. rep., supr. mktg. rsch., manpower devel. Warner Lambert Co., Morris Plains, N.J., 1962-72; mgr. corp. devel. Boehringer Mannheim Corp., N.Y.C., 1972-75; v.p. Biomed. Data Co., 1975-77; assoc. dir., dep. dir. regulatory affairs Sterling Winthrop Inc., 1977-94; ret., 1994. Cons. Sanofi Winthrop, Inc., N.Y.C., 1995. Mem. Regulatory Affairs Profls. Soc., Drug Info. Assn., Order St. John of Jerusalem. Republican. Episcopalian. Avocations: music, travel, theatre. *Pursue excellence. Pay attention to detail. Expect a positive result.*

WELCH, PATRICK, health insurance company executive; BS, Seattle U.; MS, MBA, U. Wash. Chmn., pres. and CEO GNA Corp., Gen. Electric Capital Corp.; chmn. bd. Sentinel Group Funds, Inc.; chmn., CEO and pres. Nat. Life Group; pres. CIGNA HealthCare, 2002—. Office: 1 Liberty Pl Philadelphia PA 19192*

WELCH, PATRICK JAMES, economics educator, author, consultant; b. Chgo., Feb. 8, 1944; s. Lourde John and Regina Frances W.; m. Geraldine Frances Nasiatka, Apr. 15, 1968. BSBA, Marquette U., 1966, MA in Econs., 1968; PhD in Econs., U. Pitts., 1974. Instr. econs. St. Ambrose Coll., Davenport, Iowa, 1968-70; asst. prof. St. Louis U., 1974-78, assoc. prof., 1978-83, prof., 1983—, prof. sch. pub. health, 1985—, prof. pub. policy studies, 1987—. Vis. economist Fed. Res. Bank St. Louis, 1982; spl. asst. dir. strategic planning Ralston Purina Agri-Prod Group, St. Louis, 1983; cons. competitive analysis Monsanto Co., St. Louis, 1984-86; cons. antitrust and competitive analysis various clients, 1988—. Co-author: Economics: Theory and Practice, 1982, rev. 6th edit., 1998; editor: Forum for Social Economics, 1995—; contbr. articles to profl. jours. chpts. in books. Mem. Human Rights Commn. Archdiocese of St. Louis, 1992—99; bd. dirs. Epworth Children & Family Svcs., 2000—. Grantee NSF, 1973. Mem.: Assn. Social Econs. (bd. dirs. 1989—91), Nat. Assn. Bus. Economists (pres. St. Louis chpt. 1992—93), Webster Grove Hist. Soc. (bd.dirs., pres. 2001—). Avocation: jazz musician. Home: 320 S Gray Ave Saint Louis MO 63119-3608 Office: St Louis U Dept Econs 3674 Lindell Blvd Saint Louis MO 63108-3302

WELCH, PHILIP BURLAND, electronics and office products company executive; b. Portland, Maine, Nov. 15, 1931; s. Philip Gerald Welch and Clara Jenny (Berry) Hawxwell; m. Sheila Mae Preston, May 19, 1960; children: Jahna Holly Welch Roth, Victoria Preston Welch Johnsen. Student, Berklee Coll., 1955-58. Profl. trumpeter, arranger, composer, N.Y.C., 1958—65; dist. sales mgr. Rheem Mfg. Co., Phila., 1965—66, regional sales mgr., 1966—70; nat. sales mgr. Akai Am. Ltd., Anaheim, Calif., 1970-73, BSR, USA, Blaupunkt, N.Y., 1973-76; nat. sales and mktg. mgr. Philips High Fidelity Labs, Ft. Wayne, Ind., 1976-79; dir. mktg. Pioneer Electronics, Moonachie, N.J., 1979-82; pres. Schneider N.Am. Ltd., Dayton, 1982-83; v.p. Lyons & Assocs., Indpls., 1986-88; pres. Nat. Electric Mktg. Co., Jacksonville, Fla., 1975-88, Hemisphere Enterprises Corp., Jacksonville, 1988-91, Phil Welch Enterprises, Jacksonville, 1989-99, ret., 1999. Cons. ContraTech Corp., Portland, Oreg., 1986-87, Kukje Internat., N.Y.C., 1986, FCI Inc., N.J., 1985, Multiform Products, Inc., Jacksonville, 1989-90, gen. mgr., v.p., 1990-96; pres. Atlantic Office Sources, Inc., Jacksonville, 1996-99. Contbr. articles to profl. jours. With USAF, 1950-54. Named Man of Decade Audio/Video Cons. USA, 1982, Man of Yr. Soc. of Audio Cons., 1974. Republican. Avocations: flying, golf. Home and Office: 12821 Julington Forest Dr W Jacksonville FL 32258-3454 E-mail: philwelchind@aol.com.

WELCH, REED LYNN, political scientist, educator; b. Wichita Falls, Tex., Dec. 19, 1966; s. Robert Godfrey and Arlene Lynn Welch; m. Jennifer Laura Foess, June 27, 1989; children: Regan, Emily, William, Lindsey. BA, Brigham Young U., 1990; PhD, Tex. A&M U., 1997. Instr. Tex. A&M U., Coll. Sta., Tex., 1994—2000; prof. polit. sci. We.Tex. A&M U., Canyon, 2000—. Mem. Lds Ch. Office: West Texas A&M University WTAMU Box 60807 Canyon TX 79016-0001

WELCH, RHEA JO, special education educator; b. Jacksonville, Ill., Jan. 26, 1957; d. James Daniel and Bobbye Jo (Weatherford) W.; m. Bert Hamm, Nov. 1996; 1 child, James Alexander. BA, William Woods U., Fulton, Mo., 1980; cert., U. Ill., Springfield, 1981; postgrad., MacMurray Coll., 1985, 86, 88, So. Ill. U., 1990, 91. Cert. 6-12 tchr., spl. edn., Ill. Tchr. recreational skills Ill. Sch. for Visually Impaired, Jacksonville, 1984; cross categorical tchr. Sangamon Area Spl. Edn. Dist., Springfield, 1988-89; tchr.'s aid Four Rivers Spl. Edn. Dist., Jacksonville, 1981, substitute tchr. spl. edn., 1982-86, tchr. learning disabilities, 1987, tchr. students with severe behavioral disorders, 1989—. Mem. human rights com. Jacksonville Devel. Ctr., 1992—; pub. speaker; project dir. for community svc. programs Garrison Sch., Ill. Adv. Coun. on Voluntary Action-Serve Ill.; originator Class Time Community Svc. Volunteerism Four Rivers Spl. Edn. Dist.; coord. Spl. Olympics Ivan K. Garrison Sch., 1992-93; speaker Ill. Coun. Children With Behavior Disorders, 1997. Vol. ARC, instr. HIV-AIDS, CPR, First Aid. Named Staff Mem. of Month, Ivan K. Garrison Alternative Sch., 1992, 2001; recipient 2 Disting. Svc.

citations, 1992; grantee, Kraft Food Co., 1991—92. Mem. Coun. for Exceptional Children, Nat. Soc. for Experiential Edn. Episcopalian. Office: Four Rivers Spl Edn Dist 936 W Michigan Ave Jacksonville IL 62650-3113

WELCH, RICHARD L. priest, lawyer; b. Naples, Italy, Dec. 22, 1953; s. Richard and Alice (Nevin) W. BA, St. Alphonsus Sem., Suffield, Conn., 1977; MRE, Mt. St. Alphonsus, Esopus, N.Y., 1979, MDiv, 1981; JCL, U. St. Thomas Aquinas, Rome, 1995. Parish priest, P.R., 1981-87; rector Catholic cathedral Caguas, 1987-93; rector Notre Dame Sch., 1987-93; rep. Rome Human Life Internat., Rome, 1994—, pres., 1997—. Author: (books) Blood of the Martyrs, 1994, Culture of Death Vs. Culture of Life, 1995. Bd. dirs. For Human Life Internat, U.S., Can., Ireland, Australia, New Zealand, 1997, pres., 1997— Named Eagle Scout Boy Scouts of Am., 1968. Roman Catholic. Office: HLI 4 Family Life Front Royal VA 22630 also: Via Merulana 31 I-00185 Rome Italy

WELCH, RICHARD LEROY, personal improvement company executive; b. Lincoln, Nebr., Oct. 15, 1939; s. Raymond Nathanial and Helen Lila (Ludwig) W.; m. Donna Lee Gysegem, Nov. 3, 1991; children: Terri L. Flowerday, Julie A. Kuhl; 1 stepchild, Shannon Panzo. Student, U. Nebr.; PhD (hon.), Devonshire U., Eng., 2000. Agt. Gurantee Mut. Life, Lincoln, Nebr., 1960-61; agt., mgr. Mut. of Omaha, 1962-68; gen. agt. Loyal Protective Life, Omaha, 1969-70; mgr. Mut. Benefit Life, Dallas, 1971-73; br. mgr. Great West Life, San Jose, Calif., 1973-74; pres. Internat. Speedreading Inst., Phoenix, 1975-80; CEO, founder Educom, Inc./Subliminal Dynamics, Dynamic Brain Mgmt., Aurora, Colo., 1980—. Mem. adv. bd. Great West Life, San Jose, 1973; pres. bd. dirs. Internat. Speedreading Inst., Phoenix, 1975-80, Subliminal Dynamics, Inc., San Jose, 1980-93, Educom, Inc., Aurora, 1993—; scientist, spkr., author, educator in field. Author: Brain Management, 1996. Inductee Lincoln H.S. Athletic Hall of Fame, 2000. Mem. Shriners, Masons (32d degree). Democrat. Avocations: sports, music, travel. Office: Educom Inc DBA Subliminal Dynamics 19744 E Union Dr Aurora CO 80015-3486 Fax: (303) 627-2870. E-mail: subdyn@subdyn.com.

WELCH, RICHARD LON See ABELL, RICHARD BENDER

WELCH, ROBERT ALAN, obstetrician-gynecologist, perinatologist maternal-fetal medicine; b. Perrysburg, Ohio, Aug. 1, 1951; s. Robert Chester and Dorothy Jean (Hamilton) W.; m. Sally Elizabeth Straits, June 24, 1972; children: Olivia, Robert Jr., Kathryn. BS, U. Toledo, 1973; MD, La. State U., 1980; MSA, Ctrl. Mich. U., 2000. Diplomate Am. Bd. Maternal Fetal Medicine. Resident in ob-gyn. Wayne State U., Detroit, 1980-84, fellow in perinatal dept., clin. instr., 1984-86; exec. chief resident Detroit Med Ctr., 1983-84; assoc. prof. ob-gyn. Wayne State U., Detroit, 1986-91; dir. maternal and fetal medicine Providence Hosp., Southfield, 1991-95, chmn., program dir. dept. ob-gyn., 1995—, med. dir. women's svcs., 1998—. Dir. high risk pregnancy unit Hutzel Hosp., Detroit, 1986; lectr. in field. Patentee modified surgical gloves, self-capping needle, digital device for dispensing medicine, cervical ring; contbr. articles to profl. jours., chpts. to books. Recipient Morris Bachman award, Stephenson Prize award Detroit Med. Ctr., 1983-84. Fellow: Am. Coll. Ob-Gyn. (Mich. sect. adv. com., Searle Donald F. Richardson Meml. prize 1986, Ephraigm McDowell award 1985); mem.: AAAS, AMA, Soc. Maternal Fetal Medicine, Oakland County Med. Soc., Am. Coll. Physician Execs., Am. Fedn. Clin. Rsch., Am. Assn. Med. Edn. and Rsch. in Substance Abuse, Assn. Profs. in Gynecology and Obs., N.Y. Acad. Sci., Am. Fertility Soc., Am. Inst. Ultrasound in Medicine, Am. Soc. Gynecologic Laparoscopists, Wayne County Med. Soc., Mich. State Med. Soc. Avocation: microcomputing. Office: Providence Hosp Dept Ob-Gyn Southfield MI 48075 also: PO Box 2043 16001 W 9 Mile Rd Southfield MI 48075-4818

WELCH, ROBERT BALLINGER, investment planner; b. Baton Rouge, Nov. 16, 1936; s. Jasper Arthur and Oramay (Ballinger) W.; m. Janice I. Perrine; children: Robert B. Jr., Mary Inger, Carlton Arthur; m. Judith Dorene Brace, Apr. 17, 1971. BA in Comm. and Mktg., U. Ill., 1961. Lic. investment broker and planner. Advt. account mgr., TV writer, dir. sales Nat. Advt. Agy. & TV Broadcasting, Baton Rouge, Dallas, Houston, until 1972; gen. ptnr. real estate devel. Nat. Firms, New Orleans, 1972-80, investment broker, 1980—. Mem. adv. bd. Computer Mentors. Co-prodr.: (TV documentary) No Bells at Carville, 1959 (Emmy award). Mem. student life adv. bd. Tulane U. Mem. Carl G. Jung Soc. (treas., bd. dirs.), Sigma Chi (regional officer). email). Home and Office: 106 Westchester Pl New Orleans LA 70131-2044 E-mail: judyandbob@hotmail.com(temp.

WELCH, ROBERT BOND, ophthalmologist, educator; b. Balt., May 24, 1927; s. Robert S.G. and Sally (Bond) W.; m. Elizabeth Truslow, May 30, 1953. AB, Princeton U., 1949; MD, Johns Hopkins U., 1953. Diplomate: Am. Bd. Ophthalmology. Intern in internal medicine Duke U. Hosp., 1953-54; resident in ophthalmology Wilmer Inst., Johns Hopkins U., 1954-57, chief resident in ophthalmology, 1959, co-dir. retina service, 1959-84, dir. retina service, 1984-85; retinal cons. in ophthalmology Walter Reed Army Hosp., 1961—, Bethesda Naval Hosp, 1976-99; assoc. prof. ophthalmology Johns Hopkins U.; chmn. dept. ophthalmology Greater Balt. Med. Ctr., 1985-91. Author: (with others) The Wilmer Institute 1925-1975, 1976; author: The Wilmer Opthalmological Institute 1925-2000, 2000; editor Transactions Am. Ophthal. Soc., 1984-91; mem. editorial staff Retina mag., 1980-86. Served with USNR, 1945-47. Recipient Disting. Alumnus award, Johns Hopkins U., 2001. Mem. Am. Ophthal. Soc. (v.p. 1992-93, pres. 1993-94, editor 1984-90), Retina Soc. (pres. 1981-83), Pan. Pacific Surg. Assn. (v.p. 1972-80), Md. Soc. Eye Physicians and Surgeons (pres. 1963-64), Md. Club., Elkridge Club, South River Club. Democrat. Episcopalian. Home: 4409 Atwick Rd Baltimore MD 21210-2811 Office: 86 State Cir Annapolis MD 21401-1906

WELCH, RONALD J. actuary; b. Luling, Tex., June 26, 1945; s. Billie C. and Irene (Anton) W.; m. Leslie Ann Herman, Oct. 9, 1971; children: Kelley, Stephen. BBA, U. Tex., 1966; MS, Northeastern U., 1968. V.p., actuary Am. Nat. Ins. Co., Galveston, Tex., 1975-80, sr. v.p., actuary, 1980-86, sr. v.p., chief actuary, 1986-95, exec. v.p., chief actuary, 1995—. Bd. dirs. Standard Life & Accident Ins. Co., Oklahoma City, Am. Nat. Property & Casualty Ins., Springfield, Mo., Am. Nat. Life Ins. Co. of Tex., Galveston, Farm Family Life Ins. Co., Farm Family Casualty Ins. Co.; chmn. bd. Garden State Life Ins. Co., League City, Tex. Fellow Soc. of Actuaries; mem. Am. Acad. Actuaries. Office: Am Nat Ins Co 1 Moody Plz Galveston TX 77550-7947

WELCH, ROSS MAYNARD, plant physiologist, researcher, educator; b. Lancaster, Calif., May 8, 1943; s. Lloyd C. and Theda W. (Slane) W.; m. Jill Susanne Varley, Aug. 22, 1965; children: Renell Cherie, Brent Ross BS, Calif. Poly. U., 1966; MS, U. Calif., Davis, 1969, PhD, 1971. Plant physiologist USDA Agrl. Rsch. Svc., Ithaca, N.Y., 1971—; rsch. assoc. Cornell U., 1971-75, asst. prof. plant nutrition, 1975-81, assoc. prof. plant nutrition, 1981-87, prof., 1987—; co-organizer food sys. for improved health program Coll. Agr. and Life Scis., Cornell U., 1994—. Disting. vis. scientist Murdoch U., Perth, Australia, 1980-81; vis. disting. scholar and lectr. U. Adelaide, Australia, 1991—. Editor: Crops as Sources of Nutrients for Humans, 1984; co-editor: Micronutrients in Agriculture, 2d edit., 1989; contbr. over 160 rsch. articles and 55 rev. articles to profl. jours. Fellow Am. Soc. Agronomy (Rsch. award N.E. br. 1992), Soil Sci. Soc. Am.; mem. Am. Soc. Plant Physiologists, AAAS, Am. Soc. Assn., Corp. Sci. Soc. Am., Am. Soc. Agronomy, Masons (master 1984-85), Sigma Xi. Republican. Mem. United Ch. of Christ. Achievements include discovery that nickel is an essential element for all higher plants; discovery that zinc plays a role in maintaining the integrity of root-cell plasma membranes. E-mial. Home: 24 Hickory Cir Ithaca NY 14850-9673 Office: US Plant Soil & Nutrition Lab Tower Rd Ithaca NY 14853 E-mail: rmw1@cornell.edu.

WELCH, S(TEPHEN) ANTHONY, university administrator, Islamic studies and arts educator; b. Phila., Apr. 29, 1942; s. Arnold DeMerritt and Mary Scott Welch; m. Hyesoon Kim; children: Nicholas, Bronwen, Emily. Student, U. Munich, Free U. of Berlin; BA in German Lit. with honors, Swarthmore Coll., 1965; MA, Harvard U., 1967, PhD History of Art and Architecture, 1972. Lectr. dept. history in art U. Victoria, B.C., 1971-72, asst. prof., 1972-75, assoc. prof., 1975-80, prof., 1980—, assoc. dean, 1982-85, Dean of Faculty of Fine Arts, 1985-98, exec. dir. office of internat. affairs. Vis. prof. U. Minn., U. Wash., U. Chgo.; specialist in Iranian painting, Mughal painting in India, Islamic calligraphy and Sultanate architecture in medieval India. Author: Shah 'Abbas and the Arts of Isfahan, 1973, Artists for the Shah, 1976, Collection of Islamic Art, Prince Sadruddin Aga Khan, 4 Vols., 1972-78, Calligraphy in the Arts of the Muslim World, 1979, Arts of the Islamic Book, 1982, Treasures of Islam, 1985; contbr. articles to scholarly and profl. jours. Office: Office Internat Affairs Univ Victoria Victoria BC Canada V8W 2Y2 E-mail: world@oia.uvic.ca.

WELCH, TILLMIN GENE, small business owner; b. Edinburg, Tex., Oct. 23, 1951; s. Henry Othell and Mary Mildred (Sodders) W.; m. Carrie Beth Brown, Jan. 7, 1978. BS in Radio, TV and Film, U. Tex., 1975. Salesman, asst. mgr. McMorris Ford Inc., Austin, Tex., 1975-78; owner, mgr. A-Fast Bail Bonds, Edinburg, 1978—. Named One of Outstanding Young Men of Am., 1985. Mem. Soc. Profl. Sales Execs. (Sales Mktg. Exec. award 1977), Profl. Bondsmen of U.S., Profl. Bondsmen of Tex. (trustee 1986-87, 89—, v.p. 1987-89), Edinburg C. of C. (social com.), Tex. BAILPAC (chmn. 1989—), Phi Sigma Kappa (social chmn., v.p. 1971-72, bd. trustees 1983-85). Home: 4608 N 5th St Mcallen TX 78504-2946 Office: A Fast Bail Bonds 3107 S Us Highway 281 Edinburg TX 78539-9696

WELCH, VERN A. retired corn breeder; b. Phillipsburg, Kans., Jan. 19, 1928; s. Virgil H. and Neva E. (Bruner) W.; m. Barbara A. Schultz, Nov. 19, 1960; children: Timothy A., Kimberly A. BA, U. Nebr., 1952. Asst. corn breeder Cornhusker Hybrid Co., Fremont, Nebr., 1950-56, Dekalb Agr. Rsch., Inc., Fremont, 1956-64, corn breeder, 1965-86, J.C. Robinson/Golden Harvest, Fremont, 1987-92, rsch. ops. coord. Waterloo, 1993-97. Patentee semi-dwarf maize, 1981. Mem. Am. Soc. Agronomy, Crop Sci. Soc. of Am. Avocations: photography, computers, travel. Home: 21506 Pinehurst Ave Elkhorn NE 68022-2209 E-mail: vbwelch@msn.com.

WELCH, WILLIAM CHARLES, neurosurgeon; b. N.Y.C., Mar. 24, 1961; s. William Barker and Carolyn (Ferrandino) W.; m. Bonnie Katz, Apr. 18, 1998. BS, CCNY, 1983; MD, SUNY Downstate Med. Ctr., Bklyn., 1985. Intern in gen. surgery and resident in neurosurgery Stong Meml. Hosp., Rochester, N.Y., 1985-91; fellow in neurosurgical oncology and spinal surgery Montefiore Med. Ctr., Bronx, 1991-93; asst. prof. neurologic surgery U. Pitts. Presbyn. U. Hosp., 1993-98, co-dir. spine splty. ctr., 1995-2000, dir. spine splty. ctr., 2001—, dir. neurosurg. spine svcs., 1997—, assoc. prof. neurologic, orthop. surgery, sch. rehab. scis., 1998—. Chief editor Operative Spine Surgery, 1999. Lt. comdr. USNR, 1988-98. Office: Dept Neurol Surgery U Pitts Presbyn Univ Hosp 200 Lothrop St Pittsburgh PA 15213-2546 E-mail: wwelch@neuronet.pitt.edu.

WELCH, WILLIAM F. lawyer; b. Logansport, Ind., June 17, 1918; s. George W. and Alyce W.; m. Jean Louise Knauss, Mar. 5, 1949; children: Brian W., Sarah L. McNaught. BA, DePauw U., 1940; JD, U. Mich., 1948. Bar: Ind. 1948, U.S. Dist. Ct. (so. dist.) Ind. 1948, U.S. Ct. Claims 1948, U.S. Ct. Appeals (7th cir.) 1952, U.S. Tax Ct. 1955, U.S. Supreme Ct. 1974. From assoc. to ptnr. McHale, Cook & Welch P.C., Indpls., 1948—2002, also past chmn. bd.; of counsel Bingham McHale LLP, 2002—. Trustee Citizens Gas and Coke, Indpls. Trustee DePauw U., Greencastle, Ind. Lt. comdr. USNR, 1941-46, PTO. Fellow Am. Bar Found., Ind. Bar Found., Indpls. Bar Found.; mem. 7th Cir. Bar Assn. (bd. govs., pres. 1991-92). Office: Bingham McHale LLP 1100 Chamber of Comm Bldg 310 N Meridian St Indianapolis IN 46204-1709

WELCOME, LINDA PAAR, interior designer; b. South Bend, Ind., June 12, 1949; d. Robert Steven and Dolores Paar; 1 child, James William Adams. BS in Fine Arts/Art Edn., Ind. Univ., 1975; MS in Interior Design, Ind. State Univ., 1979. Cert. interior design/art educator, K-h.s. and coll. Instr., interior design Purdue-Ind. Univ., Indpls., 1976; instr., in-residence artist Indpls. Art League, 1978-79; graphic art designer State of Ind., Indpls., 1977-78; owner/pres. Welcome Interiors, 1980—; former radio personality The Welcome Interior Design Show, Silver Spring, Md., 1987-88. Interior designer Embassy of Kuwait, Washington; interior design cons. Embassy Iraq, Washington; designer Nat. Symphony Decorator Show Houses, Design for Living Show, Washington, 1989—. Designer projects pub. in Family Circle Mag., Luxury Home, Real Estate Mag., local newspapers. Avocations: painting, silversmithing. Office: Welcome Interiors 2205 Seminary Rd Silver Spring MD 20910-1370

WELD, ALISON GORDON, artist; b. Ft. Knox, Ky., June 10, 1953; d. Paul Woodbury and Mary Jean (Cameron) W.; m. Charles Robert Russell, July 1, 1990. Student, Wolverhampton (Eng.) Poly., 1974-75; BFA, Alfred U., 1975; MFA, Art Inst. Chgo., 1979. Curatorial asst. Am. Mus. Natural History, N.Y.C., 1980-83; curator Robeson Gallery, Rutgers U., Newark, 1983-88; asst. curator fine art N.J. State Mus., Trenton, 1988-99. Solo exhbns. E.L. Stark Gallery, N.Y.C., Morris Mus., Morristown, N.J., Susan Schreiber Gallery, N.Y.C., U. Bridgeport, Conn., 1996, Hunterdon Mus. Art, 1998, Ednl. Alliance, N.Y.C., Pacifico Fine Art, N.Y.C., Mulloy Coll. Art Gallery, 2002, Robert Steele Gallery, N.Y.C.; curator: Dream Singers, Story Tellers: An African American Presence, Fukui Fine Arts Mus., Japan, N.J. State Mus., 1992-94, (show of self-taught and mainstream artists) A Density of Passions, N.J. State Mus., 1989, Art by African Americans in the Collection of the New Jersey State Museum, 1998. Artist grantee N.J. State Coun. Arts, 1983-84, artist Rutgers Ctr. for Innovative Printmaking, 1994.

WELD, JONATHAN MINOT, lawyer; b. Greenwich, Conn., Feb. 25, 1941; s. Alfred White and Sally (Duggan) W.; m. Jane Paige, June 19, 1965; children: Elizabeth, Eric. AB in History cum laude, Harvard U., 1963; JD, Cornell U., 1967. Bar: N.Y. 1967, U.S. Ct. Appeals (2d cir.) 1969, U.S. Dist. Ct. (ea. and so. dist.) N.Y. 1970. Assoc. Shearman & Sterling, N.Y.C., 1967-75, ptnr., 1976—. London, 1982-85. Bd. dirs. Bank of N.S. Internat.; chmn., bd. dirs., The Evergreens. Bd. dirs. Bklyn. Hosp., St. Ann's Sch., Bklyn. Botanic Garden; former bd. dirs. Bklyn. Home for Children, Harvard Coll. Fund, Winant and Clayton Vols. Mem. ABA, N.Y. State Bar Assn. Office: 599 Lexington Ave Fl C2 New York NY 10022-6030

WELD, ROGER BOWEN, religious organization administrator; b. Greenfield, Mass., Dec. 1, 1953; s. Wayland Mauney and Luvycie (Bowen) W.; m. Patricia Ann Kaminski, June 7, 1978 (div. 1979); m. Cynthia Lou Lang, Apr. 15, 1995 (div. 2001). Grad., Sacred Acad. Jamilian U. of the Ordained, Reno, 1976-77, Seminary, 1978-82; student, U. Nev., 1983-85; postgrad., Sacred Coll. Jamilian Theology, 1988-90. Ordained to ministry, Internat. Comty. of Christ Ch. of Second Advent, 1977; appointed Rabban priest Internat. Comty. of Christ, 1993. Adminstrv. staff Internat. Cmty. of Christ Ch. of Second Advent, Reno, 1977—, exec. officer dept. canon law, 1985—2001, exec. officer advocates for religious rights and freedoms, 1985—, exec. officer spkrs. bur., 1985—2001, exec. officer office pub. info., 1986—2001, mgr. Jamilian Univ. Press, 1987—, dir. advt. prodns., 1988—; founder, pres. Crown Rsch. Found., 1992—. Mem. Chamber of Concerned Christians for Separation of Ch. and State. Author: Twelve Generations of the Family of Weld: Edmund to Wayland Mauney, 1986, A Steamboat in the Desert--A History of Steamboat Springs, Nevada, 1998; dir. photography, supervising editor: (video documentary) Gene Savoy's Royal Roads to Discovery, 1993, The Gran Vilaya Expeditions, Reclaiming a Legendary Lost City From the High Jungles of Peru, 1996. Staff sgt. USAF, 1971-75. Named Life Mem., Sacred Oversee, 1991. Mem.: Nev. Clergyman's Assn., Andean Explorers Found. (Explorer's medal 1990), Ocean Sailing Club (exec. sec. 1988—94, v.p. 1994—2001, vice-commodore 2001—, Participant's Silver Medallion 1989, Survivors medal Feathered Serpent III Grand Ophir Sea Expedition 1998, Dolphin award 1999). Avocations: photography, cinematography, videography, print media. Office: Andean Explorers Found & Ocean Sailing Club 16026 S Virginia St Reno NV 89511 E-mail: rweld@aefosc.org. *In the volatile arena of international politics, mankind's hope rests upon the acceptance of its spiritual destiny, not dwelling on its material past.*

WELDEN, ARTHUR LUNA, biology educator; b. Birmingham, Ala., Jan. 27, 1927; s. Arthur Luna and Mary Woodson (Smith) W.; m. Frances Merkl Colvin, Aug. 19, 1950; children: Charles Woodson, Arthur Frederick. AB, Birmingham-So. Coll., 1950; MS, U. Tenn., 1951; PhD, U. Iowa, 1954. Asst. prof. Millikin U., Decatur, Ill., 1954-55; instr. in botany Tulane U., New Orleans, 1955-59, asst. prof., 1959-63, assoc. prof., 1963-68, prof. biology, 1968-79, Ida Richardson prof. botany, 1979-93, chmn. dept. biology, 1979-83, prof. emeritus, 1994—. Panel chmn. So. Assembly, Biloxi, Miss., 1970-71; program dir. Mesoam. Ecology Inst., New Orleans, 1982-87. Assoc. editor Tulane Studies in Zoology and Botany, 1966-78; contbr. articles to profl. jours. Served with U.S. Army, 1945-47. Grantee Am. Philos. Soc., 1957, NSF, 1960-75, NSF and Consejo Nacional de Mex., 1976-79, fellow AAAS, 1992; named to Socio Honorario, Sociedad Mexicana de Mex., 1982. Mem. Mycol. Soc. Am. (councilor 1967-69), Orgn. for Tropical Studies (life), Sigma Xi. Democrat. Home: 7826 Willow St New Orleans LA 70118-4056 Office: Tulane U Dept Biology 6823 Saint Charles Ave New Orleans LA 70118-5698

WELDON, DAVID BLACK, company director; b. London, Can., June 27, 1925; s. Douglas Black and Margaret (Black) W.; m. Ina G. Perry, July 7, 1951; children: Susan, Douglas, Anthony, Mardie, Kate BA with honors, U. Western Ont., London, 1947, LLD (hon.). With Midland Walwyn Inc. and predecessor cos., Toronto, Ont., 1950—; ret. Midland Doherty Fin. Corp. and predecessor cos., 1989; chancellor U. Western Ont., 1984-88, chancellor emeritus, 1994—. Dir. Dover Industries Ltd., Toronto. Trustee Ont. Jockey Club; bd. dirs. Royal Agrl. Winter Fair, Toronto, 1970— , pres., 1980-82. Served with inf. Can. Army, 1944-45 Mem. Order of Can. Progressive Conservative. Anglican. Clubs: Toronto (bd. mgrs. 1983-85), York, Toronto Golf; London Hunt, London; Ristigouche Salmon (Quebec, Que., Can.); Griffith Island Avocations: breeding and racing standardbred horses; fishing; hunting. Home: Prospect Farms Arva ON Canada N0M 1C0 also: 18A Hazelton Ave Apt 408 Toronto ON Canada M5R 2E2

WELDON, DAVID JOSEPH, JR. congressman, physician; b. Amityville, N.Y., Aug. 31, 1953; s. David Joseph and Anna (Mallardi) W.; m. Nancy Sourbeck, Aug. 18, 1979; children: Kathryn, David. BS, SUNY, Stony Brook, 1978; MD, SUNY, Buffalo, 1981. Intern Letterman Army Med. Ctr., 1981-82, resident in internal medicine, 1982-84; pvt. practice, Melbourne, Fla., 1987—; mem. 104th Congress from 15th Fla. dist., Washington, 1995—. Pres. Space Coast Family Forum, Melbourne, 1988-91. Elder Zion Christian Fellowship, Palm Bay, Fla., 1991—. Maj. USAR, 1981—. Mem. AMA, ACP, Fla. Med. Assn. Office: US House of Reps 332 Cannon Bldg Washington DC 20515-2001

WELDON, JEFFREY ALAN, lawyer; b. Billings, Mont., May 6, 1963; s. Richard Allen and Monica (Michaud) Weldon; m. Leslie Helen Boileau, July 7, 1990; 2 children. BA, U. Mont., 1986, MPA, 1994, JD, 1996. State senator, Mont., 1993-97; assoc. atty. Moulton Bellingham, Longo & Mather, P.C., Billings, 1997-2000; chief legal counsel Office of Pub. Instrn., State of Mont., Helena, 2000—. E-mail: jweldon@state.mt.us.

WELDON, THEODORE TEFFT, JR. manufacturing executive; b. Evanston, Ill., July 19, 1932; s. Theodore Tefft and Dorothe Galbraith (Stover) W.; m. Barbara Ann Eskilson, Aug. 17, 1957; children: Lisa Courtney Weldon LeFevre, Theodore Tefft III, Margaret Helen. BA, Dartmouth Coll., 1954. Retail store salesman Sears Roebuck & Co., Gary, Ind., 1954-58, retail store mgr. Kankakee, Ill., 1958-62, sales mgr. Craftsman Chgo., 1962-69, advt. mgr. Craftsman, 1969-70, mktg. mgr. tires, 1970-81, sr. buyer sporting goods, 1981-82, nat. gen. catalog mgr., 1982-86; dir. home TV shopping Sears/QVC, 1986-92. Cons. Drake, Beam, Morin, Inc., Chgo., 1992-94, Focus Media, Inc., L.A., 1993-96, Std. Mktg. Corp., Naperville, Ill., 1993-98, King World Direct, L.A., 1993-97, Guthy-Renker, Las Vegas, 1997-98, Sears Roebuck and Co., 1997-2000, Ovation Group, 1997—, Home Depot, 1997-98, Kmart, 1997-98, Walmart, 1997-98, Pearle Vision, 1998, 3M, 1998, Tyee, 1998-2000, Target Stores, 1998, Panasonic 1997-2000; v.p. mktg. Link Tools Internat., USA, 1998—, Content = Commerce Inc., 2001--. Mem. Jr. Achievemnt, Chgo., 1966-68; rep. Winnetka (Ill.) Village Caucus, 1972-74; advisor Children's Theatre of Winnetka, 1972—; pres. Sunset Improvement Assn., Winnetka, 1975—. Avocations: internat. travel, theatre, swimming, biking, golf. Home and Office: 426 Sunset Rd Winnetka IL 60093-4232

WELDON, THOMAS DAVID, medical products manufacturer; b. West Lafayette, Ind., Aug. 17, 1955; s. Norman Ross and Carol Janet (Warne) W.; divorced; children: Marijke Lee, David Joesph, Michael John. BS in Indsl. Engring., Purdue U., 1977; MBA, Ind. U., 1981. Indsl. engr. Sq. D Co., Cedar Rapids, Iowa, 1977-79; instr. Ind. U., Bloomington, 1981-82; corp. strategic planner Key Pharms., Miami, Fla., 1982-84; sr. cons. Arthur Young and Co., 1984-85, mgr., 1985-87; chmn. Novoste Corp., Atlanta, 1987—, also bd. dirs.; CEO, chmn. The Innovation Factory, 1999—. Pres. contest coordinator Nat. Jr. Achievement Inc., Bloomington, Ind., 1979-87, instr. applied econs. , Miami chpt., 1984-87. Presbyterian. Avocations: collecting artwork and books, volleyball, sailing, scuba. Office: Innovation Factory Ste 200 2750 Premiere Pkwy Duluth GA 30097

WELDON, VIRGINIA V. retired corporate executive, physician; b. Toronto, Sept. 8, 1935; came to U.S., 1937; d. John Edward and Carolyn Edith (Swift) Verral; children: Ann Weldon Doyle, Susan Weldon Mohart. AB cum laude, Smith Coll., 1957; MD, SUNY-Buffalo, 1962; LHD (hon.), Rush U., 1985. Diplomate Am. Bd. Pediat., Am. Bd. Pediatric Endocrinology and Metabolism, Nat. Bd. Med. Examiners (bd. dirs. 1987-89). Intern Johns Hopkins Hosp., Balt., 1962-63, resident in pediatrics, 1963-64; fellow pediatric endocrinology Johns Hopkins U., 1964-67, instr. pediatrics, 1967-68, Washington U., St. Louis, 1968-69, asst. prof., 1969-73, assoc. prof., 1973-79, prof., 1979-89, v.p. Med. Ctr., 1980-89, dep. vice chancellor med. affairs, 1983-89; v.p. sci. affairs Monsanto Co., 1989, v.p. pub. policy, 1989-93, sr. v.p. pub. policy, 1993-98; dir. Ctr. for Study Am. Bus., Washington U., 1998-99. Mem. gen. clin. rsch. ctrs. adv. com. NIH, Bethesda, Md., 1976-80, mem. rsch. resources adv. coun., 1980-84; bd. dirs. GenAm. Fin. Corp., Quintiles Transnat., CPI Corp.; bd. dirs., advisor Monsanto Co., 1989-98. Contbr. articles to sci. jours. Trustee Calif. Inst. Tech., 1996—, Whitaker Found., 1997-99, Whitfield Sch., 1997—, Grand Ctr., St. Louis Sci. Ctr.; commr. St. Louis Zool. Park, 1983-92; bd. d irs., vice chmn., chmn. St. Louis Symphony Orch.; bd. dirs. United Way Greater St. Louis, 1978-90, St. Louis Regional Health Care Corp., 1985-91; mem. risk assessment mgmt. commn. EPA, 1992-97; mem. Pres.'s Com. of Advisors on Sci. and Tech., 1994-2000; mem. adv. com. on agrl. biotech. USDA, 2000-01. Fellow: AAAS, Am. Acad. Pediat.; mem.: St. Louis Med. Soc., Soc. Pediat. Rsch., Endocrine Soc., Am. Pediat. Soc., Assn. Am. Med. Colls. (disting. svc. mem., del., chmn. coun. acad. socs. 1984—85, chmn. assembly 1985—86), Nat. Acads. (nat. assoc.), Inst. Medicine, Knights of Malta, Equestrian Order of Holy Sepulchre, Alpha Omega Alpha, Sigma Xi. Roman Catholic. Home: 242 Carlyle Lake Dr Saint Louis MO 63141-7544

WELDON, W(AYNE) CURTIS (CURT WELDON), congressman; b. Marcus Hook, Pa., July 22, 1947; m. Mary Gallagher; children: Karen, Kristin, Kimberly, Curt, Andrew. BA in Humanities, West Chester State Coll., 1969; AAS in Fire Sci., Del. County C.C., Media, Pa., 1972; state instrn. cert., Cheyney State Coll.; postgrad., Cabrini Coll., Temple U., St. Joseph's U. Lic. tchr. Pa. From tchr. to head tchr. Walnut St. Sch., Darby-Colwyn-William Penn Sch. Dist., Pa., 1972-76; dir. tng. and manpower CIGNA (INA Corp.), Del. County, 1976-87; mayor City of Marcus Hook, 1977-81; councilman Del. County Council, 1981-87, from vice-chmn. to chmn., 1984-87; mem. U.S. Congress from 7th Pa. dist., Washington, 1987—; mem. armed svcs. com. and sci. com. Past chmn. Del. Valley Regional Planning Commn.; asst. dir. Elem. Secondary Edn. Act Title I Program, 1972-76; environ. specialist Project KARE, 1972-76; chmn. R&D House Nat. Security Com. Readiness; mem. Com. on Sci. Energy and Environ. Tech.; co-chmn. Congl. Fire Svcs. Caucus, Globe Ocean Protection Task Force, Congl. Missil Def. Caucus, US-FSU Energy Caucus. Named Man of Yr. Chester Bus. and Profl. Assn., Most Effective Freshman Legislator Am. Security Coun., Citizen of the Yr. Del. County C. of C., Clean Air Champion Sierra Club, Man of Yr. Internat. Soc. Fire Protection Engrs., 1988, taxpayers hero Citizen's Against Government Waste; recipient Outstanding Govt. Leadership award Nat. Recycling Coalition, Fed. Legis. award Pa. Dirs. Assn. Community Action Agys., Spirit of Enterprise award U.S. C. of C., Golden Bulldog Watchdogs of Treasury award. Office: US Ho of Reps 2466 Rayburn Ho Office Bldg Washington DC 20515-0001*

WELDON, WILLIAM C. pharmaceutical executive; Grad. Quinnipiac U. With Johnson & Johnson and subs., 1971—; CEO Johnson & Johnson, New Brunswick, NJ, 2002—. Office: Johnson & Johnson 1 Johnson & Johnson Plaza New Brunswick NJ 08933*

WELDON, WILLIAM FORREST, electrical and mechanical engineer, educator; b. San Marcos, Tex., Jan. 12, 1945; s. Forrest Jackson and Rubie Mae (Wilson) W.; m. Morey Sheppard McGonigle, July 28, 1968; children:

William, Embree, Seth Forrest. BS in Engring. Sci., Trinity U., San Antonio, 1967; MSME, U. Tex., 1970. Registered profl. engr., Tex. Engr. Cameron Iron Works, Houston, 1967-68; project engr. Glastron Boat Co., Austin, Tex., 1970-72; chief engr. Nalle Plastics Co., 1972-73; rsch. engr. U. Tex., 1973-77, tech. dir. Ctr. Electromechanics, 1977-85, dir. Ctr. Electromechanics, 1985-93, prof., 1985-2000, Josey Centennial prof. in energy resources, 1992-2000, Josey Centennial prof. emeritus, 2000—. Mem. permanent com. Symposium on Electromagnetic Launch Tech., 1978-97, vice chmn., 1995-98, naval rsch. adv. com., 1992-97, 2001-; cons. numerous cos. and govts., 1973—; chief scientist Office Naval Rsch.-Europe, 1998-99; tech. dir. Office Naval Rsch. Internat. Field Office, 1998-99. Contbr. over 285 articles to profl. publs. Bd. dirs. Water Control & Improvement Dist. No. 10, Travis County, Tex., 1984-97. Recipient Peter Mark medal Electromagnetic Launch Symposium, 1986, IR 100 award Indsl. Rsch. mag., 1983, Navy Superior Pub. Svc. award, 1998, 99. Fellow ASME; mem. IEEE (sr.), NSPE. Achievements include 35 patents for rotating electrical machines, pulsed power, and electromagnetic propulsion.

WELDON-LINNE, C. MICHAEL, pathologist, microbiologist; b. Danville, Ill., Dec. 25, 1953; s. Curtis Lane and A. Charline Linne; m. Madeleine Marie Weldon, Dec. 27, 1976; children: Aleksandra Patrice, Mariel Charline, Alyssa Faith. BS, Northwestern U., 1977, MD, 1978. Diplomate Am. Bd. Pathology, Am. Bd. Med. Examiners. Resident in pathology Evanston (Ill.) Hosp.-Northwestern McGaw Med. Ctr., 1978-81, chief resident in pathology, 1981-82; staff pathologist, dir. microbiology and virology Adv. Ill. Masonic Med. Ctr., Chgo., 1982—; assoc. chmn., chief divsn. clin. pathology Ill. Masonic Med. Ctr., 1994—. Clin. asst. prof. U. Ill., Chgo., 1984—; mem. faculty Nat. Ctr. Advanced Med. Edn., Chgo., 1983—; bd. dirs. Metromed Health Sys., Inc., 1999- 2002; v.p., 2001— 2002. Contbr. chpts. to books, articles to profl. jours. Fellow Am. Soc. Clin. Pathologists, Coll. Am. Pathologists, Am. Soc. Microbiology, Inst. Medicine Chgo.; mem. AMA, Ill. Soc. Pathologists (sec., treas., bd. dirs. 1986-92), Alpha Omega Alpha. Roman Catholic. Avocations: painting, toy soldier collecting, gardening. Office: Adv. Ill Masonic Med Ctr 836 W Wellington Ave Chicago IL 60657-9224 E-mail: michael.weldon-linne-md@advocatehealth.com.

WELDON-LINNE, MADELEINE MARIE, lawyer; b. Oak Park, Ill., July 3, 1954; d. William Glynn and Patricia Butler Weldon; m. C. Michael Weldon-Linne, Dec. 27, 1976; children: Aleksandra, Mariel, Alyssa. BS, Northwestern U., 1975; JD, DePaul U., 1981. Bar: Ill., Wis. Atty. Pretzel & Stouffer, Chgo., 1981-84; atty., ptnr. Bullaro & Carton, 1984-96; founding ptnr., atty. Weldon-Linne & Vogt, 1996—. Author (book rev.) Perspectives in Biology, 2000; contbr. articles to profl. jours. Mem. ABA, Wis. Bar Assn., Profl. Liability Underwriter Soc., Am. Soc. Hosp. Risk Mgmt., Trial Net. Roman Catholic. Office: Weldon-Linne & Vogt Ste 1400 105 W Madison St Chicago IL 60602

WELGE, DONALD EDWARD, food manufacturing executive; b. St. Louis, July 11, 1935; s. William H. and Rudelle (Fritze) W.; m. Mary Alice Childers, Aug. 4, 1962; children: Robert, Tom. BS, La. State U., 1957. With Gilster-Mary Lee Corp., Chester, Ill., 1957—, pres., gen. mgr., 1965—. Dir. Buena Vista Bank of Chester; pres. Buena Vista Bankcorp. Former chmn. St. John's Luth. Bd. Edn. 1st lt. Transp. Corp, U.S. Army, 1958-63. Named So. Ill. Bus. Leader of Yr. So. Ill. U., 1988. Mem. Perryville C. of C. (pres. 1989), Chester, Ill. C. of C. (past pres.), Alpha Zeta, Phi Kappa Phi. Republican. Lutheran. Home: 5 Knollwood Dr Chester IL 62233-1416 Office: Gilster Mary Lee Co PO Box 227 Chester IL 62233-0227

WELGE, JACK HERMAN , JR. lawyer; b. Austin, Tex., Sept. 12, 1951; s. Jack Herman and Regina Victoria (Hunger) W.; m. Frances Ava Roddy Avent, Dec. 23, 1977; children: Kirsten Frances Page Welge, Kathleen Ava Regina Welge. BA, U. Tex., 1974; JD, St. Mary's U., 1977. Bar: Tex. 1977, U.S. Dist. Ct. (ea. dist.) Tex. 1979, U.S. Dist. Ct. (no. dist.) Tex. 1982, U.S. Ct. Appeals (5th cir.) 1983, U.S. Supreme Ct., 1984; cert. family law Tex. Bd. Legal Specialization 1984. Asst. dist. atty. Gregg County Criminal Dist. Atty., Longview, Tex., 1978-79; assoc. Law Office of G. Brockett Irwin, 1979-81; judge Mcpl. Ct. of Record, 1979-81; ptnr. Adams & Sheppard, 1981-83; pvt. practice, 1983—. Of counsel East Tex. Assn. for Abused Families, Longview, 1985-90. Hair profl. divsn. Gregg County United Way, 1996—97; mem. vestry Trinity Episcopal Ch., Longview, 1993—96, 2001—; bd. dirs. Longview Mus. and Arts Ctr., 1991—94, East Tex. Coun. on Alcoholism and Drug Abuse, Longview, 1981—83, Longview Cmty. Theater, 1979—82, East Tex. Assn. for Abused Families, Longview, 1983—85, Salvation Army, 1994—, chmn., 1997. Mem. State Bar of Tex. (pro bono coll., contested custody case panel, protective case panel, Gregg County lawyers pro bono project, Outstanding Contbn. award 1990, Disting. Svc. award 1993, 95, Outstanding Pro Bono Atty. 1994, 97), N.E. Tex. Bar Assn., Rotary (pres. Longview club 1987-88, Paul Harris fellow 1982, 23 Yrs. Perfect Attendance 2001), Gregg County Bar Assn. (pres. 1983), Gregg County Family Law Coun., Tex. Acad. Family Law Specialists, East Tex. Knife and Fork Club (pres. 1983-84), Mason, Delta Theta Phi (dean 1977, Bickett Senate), Delta Upsilon (Tex. chpt. found. bd. 1974-78). Office: 413-415 S Green St PO Box 3624 Longview TX 75606-3624 E-mail: welgjhjr@hotmail.com.

WELHOUSE, LUCILLE MARIE, musician, educator; b. Superior, Wis., Sept. 15, 1919; d. Joseph Aloysius and Genevieve Rose (Moran) Weber; m. Joseph John Welhouse, Sept. 3, 1949; children: Gereon, Mark, James, Randal, Paul, Daniel, Stephen. BA in Music Edn., Coll. St. Scholastica, Duluth, Minn., 1942. Stenographer Kimberly-Clark Army Air Corp., 1942-43; tchr. music Pub. Sch., Calif., Wis., 1944-47; prof. viola player Symphony and Quartet, Green Bay, Wis., 1959—; pvt. piano/violin/viola tchr., 1962—. Bd. dirs. Green Bay Civic Symphony Orch., Suzuki, Green Bay Symphony, Piano Tchrs. Forum; co-organizer N.E. Wis. Talent Edn., Green Bay, 1978—; Suzuki co-organizer Piano Tchrs. Forum, Green Bay, 1973—, pres., 1973; mem. Green Bay Symphony Orch., Heritage String Quartet, 1980—2000. Co-organizer Montessori Sch., Green Bay, 1963. Mem. Am. String Tchrs. Assn., Nat. Guild Piano Tchrs. (audition chmn. 1970-92), Wis. Music Tchrs. Assn. (cert., Cert. of Experience-Piano 1984, Cert. of Experience-Strings 1984, Emeritus Cert. 1989)), SAA, Am. Suzuki Assn., Internat. Suzuki Assn., Wis. Suzuki Assn., Musicians' Union, Green Bay Civic Symphony. Republican. Roman Catholic. Avocations: travel, gardening. Home: 1153 Loch Dr Green Bay WI 54304-2248

WELIKSON, JEFFREY ALAN, lawyer; b. Bklyn., Jan. 8, 1957; s. Bennet Joseph and Cynthia Ann Welikson; m. Laura Sanders, Aug. 19, 1979; children: Gregory Andrew, Joshua Stuart. BS, U. Pa., 1976, MBA, 1977; JD, Harvard U., 1980. Bar: N.Y. 1981; CPA, N.Y. Assoc. Shearman & Sterling, N.Y.C., 1980-83; staff counsel Reliance Group Holdings Inc., 1983-84, dir. legal dept., 1984-85, asst. v.p., corp. counsel, 1985-88, v.p., asst. gen. counsel, asst. sec., 1988-94; exec. v.p., gen. counsel, sec. Reliance Nat. Ins. Co., 1994-2000; sr. v.p., corp. sec., head corp. law Lehman Bros., 2000—. Contbg. editor Harvard U. Internat. Law Jour., 1979-80. Mem. ABA, Assn. Bar of City of N.Y., Am. Corp. Counsel Assn. Office: Lehman Brothers Holdings Inc 399 Park Ave New York NY 10022

WELISH, MARJORIE, poet; b. N.Y.C., June 2, 1944; d. Aaron Welish and Hester Hellman. BS, Columbia U., 1968. Freelance art critic, 1968—. Adj. assoc. prof. Pratt Inst., 1990; adj. assoc. prof. Brown U., Providence, 1990, vis. assoc. prof., 1993-94; vis. prof. New Sch. U., N.Y.C., 2000—. Author: (poems) The Windows Flew Open, 1991, Casting Sequences, 1993, Else, in Substance, 1999, The Annotated "Here" and Selected Poems, 2000, Begetting Textile, 2000; (art criticism) Signifying Art and Essays on Art After 1960, 1999. Fellow Howard Found., 1998-99, Fund for Poetry, 1987, 89, 99, fellow N.Y. Found. Arts, 1990-91; residency grantee Internat. Studio Program, 1995, Artists' Mus., 1998-99; grantee Pollock-Krasner, 1997. Mem. PEN, MLA, Acad. Am. Poets, Poetry Soc. Am., Internat. Writers Assn., Coll. Art Assn., Internat. Assn. Art Critics. Home and Office: 225 W 10th St New York NY 10014-2974

WELKE, ELTON GRINNELL, JR. publisher, writer; b. Berkeley, Calif., June 15, 1941; s. Elton Grinnell and Elsie Maud (Shattuck) W.; m. Anna Lange, July 28, 1963 (div. 1980); children: Allison Espy, Erik Grinnell; m. Bonnie Jean Lum, Jan. 24, 1981; 1 child, Erin Irene. BA in Zoology, U. Calif., Berkeley, 1962. Staff writer Sunset mag., Menlo Pk., Calif., 1962-65, assoc. editor, 1965-69, sr. editor, 1978-80; travel editor Better Homes & Gardens, Des Moines, 1969-71; mng. editor Apt. Life mag., 1971-72; exec. editor Sunset Spl. Interest mags., Menlo Pk., 1972-78; freelance editorial cons. San Francisco and Seattle, 1981-84; v.p., dir. Livingston & Co., Seattle, 1984-89; publisher Microsoft Press, 1989-98; chmn. North Wave Comms., Inc., Alaska, 1996—, Elton-Wolf Pub. Co., Seattle, 1999—. Bd. dirs. Smart Starters Corp.; cons. Holland Am. Line, Seattle, 1983-84, Livingston & Co. Advt., Seattle, 1983-84, Pacifica Bank, Bellevue, Wash., 1998—. Author: How to Survive Being Alive, 1977, Place's to go With Children Around Puget Sound, 1987. Bd. dirs. Olympic Nat. Pk. Assocs., Washington, 1965-69, March of Dimes, Western Washington, 1987-92, chmn. campaign com., 1989-92. Recipient 1st Pl. award Washington Press Assn., 1985, 86, 88, WPA award, 1987. Mem. Soc. Am. Travel Writers, PRSA, Internat. Assn. Bus. Communicators (Golden Quill award 1985), Safari Club, Bellevue Club, Alpha Delta Phi. Republican. Avocations: gardening, plant collecting, fly fishing, cattle ranching, Asian art. Home and Office: 11329 NE 103d St Kirkland WA 98033-5178

WELKER, JAMES ANTHONY, physician; b. Pitts., Oct. 27, 1969; s. James Edward and Janet Rachael Welker. BS, Ohio No. U., 1991; DO, Phila. Coll. Osteo. Medicine, 1995. Intern U. Medicine and Dental of N.J., Stafford, 1995-96; resident in internal medicine Washington Hosp., 1996-99; dir. hospitalist sect., hospitalist, mem. tchg. faculty Harbor Hosp. Ctr., Balt., 1999—, mem. office of e-health initiative workgroup , Pain Mgmt. Task Force, grad. med. edn. Med. cons. Nutrition Superstores.com, West Palm Beach, Fla., 1999-2002; cons. and software developer for med. info. sys.; founding ptnr. real estate investment co.; prin. investigator multi-instnl. clin. trials.; presenter at sci. and ednl. confs. Contbr. articles to profl. jours. Vol. physician Mobile Med. Care, Rockville, 1997-99. Med. scholarship Frederick A. Presscott, M.D., 1992-95, Pa. Osteo. Med. Assn., 1994; recipient Preceptor award Am. Coll. of Gen. Practitioners, 1994. Roman Catholic. Avocations: exercising, outdoors. Office: Harbor Hosp Ctr Baltimore MD 21225 E-mail: jimwelker@hotmail.com.

WELKER, WALLACE IRVING, neurophysiologist, educator; b. Batavia, N.Y., Dec. 17, 1926; PhD in Psychology, U. Chgo., 1954. Mem. faculty U. Wis. Med. Sch., 1957—, prof. neurophysiology, 1965-90, emeritus prof., 1990—. Served with AUS, 1945-47. Sister Kenny Found. scholar, 1957-62; recipient NIH Career Devel. award, 1962-67 Mem. Am. Anat. Soc., Neurosci. Soc. Office: 1802 Fordem Ave Apt 14 Madison WI 53704-7116

WELKER, WILLIAM ANDREW, reading specialist; b. Shamokin, Pa., Apr. 26, 1947; s. William Howard and Dorothy Irene (Bertolette) W.; m. Margaret Jean Bainbridge, Mar. 1, 1969; children: William, Richard, Tiffany, Daniel. BS, U. Pitts., 1969, MEd, 1970; EdD, W.Va. U., 1989. Cert. tchr. health, phys. edn. K-12, Pa., W.Va., reading specialist K-12, Pa., W.Va., secondary prin. 5-12, W.Va., elem. prin. K-5, Pa., lang. arts 7-9, W.Va. Tchr. health phys. edn. Philip Murray Elem. Sch., Pitts., 1969-70, Swissvale (Pa.) Elem. Sch., 1970; tchr. 6th grade Edgington Lane Elem. Sch., Wheeling, W.Va., 1970-72; tchr. reading and English Ctrl. Cath. H.S., 1972-76; tchr. reading Warwood Mid. Sch., 1976—; adj. asst. prof. W.Va. U., Morgantown, 1991—. Mem. steering com. Rschrs. In-Sch. Environ, Ohio County Schs., Wheeling, 1990-94. Contbr. articles to profl. jours. Commr. Wheeling Human Rights Commn., 1990-93. Named WV Wrestling Sportswriter of Yr., 1981, 85, 89, 96, 2000, Nat. Wrestling Sportswriter of Yr., Wrestling USA Mag., 1987, WV Wrestling Man of Yr., Wrestling USA Mag., 2001, NFHS Sect. 2 Disting. Active Ofcl. of Yr., 2001, Nat. Wrestling Ofcl. of Yr., Wrestling USA Mag., 2002; mini-grantee W.Va. Edn. Fund, Charleston, 1987, 89, 90. Mem. Internat. Reading Assn. (Columnist Svc. award 1991), Wheeling Island Lions Club. Avocations: writing, sports officiating, wrestling clinician, interpreter. Home: 110 N Huron St Wheeling WV 26003-2226 Office: Warwood Mid Sch 150 Viking Dr Wheeling WV 26003-7028 E-mail: mattalkwv@hotmail.com.

WELKOWITZ, WALTER, biomedical engineer, educator; b. Bklyn., Aug. 3, 1926; s. Samuel and Shirley (Rosenblum) W.; m. Joan Horowitz, June 17, 1951; children: David, Lawrence, Julie. BS, The Cooper Union, N.Y.C., 1948; MS, U. Ill., 1949, PhD, 1954. Profl. engr., N.J. Rsch. assoc. U. Ill., Urbana, 1948-54, Columbia U., N.Y.C., 1954-55; asst. to pres., gen. mgr. Gulton Industries, Inc., Metuchen, N.J., 1955-64; prof., chmn. elec. engring. Rutgers U., Piscataway, 1964-86, prof. biomed. engring., 1986—, chmn. biomedical engring., 1986-90. Cons. Gulton Industries, Metuchen, N.J., 1964-74. Author: Engineering Hemodynamics: Application to Cardiac Assist Devices, 1977, 2d edit., 1987; co-author: Biomedical Instruments: Theory and Design, 1976, 2d edit., 1992; author numerous chpts. in books; contbr. more than 100 articles to profl. jours. With U.S. Navy, 1944-46. Rutgers U. Rsch. Coun. fellow, 1974-75; recipient Centennial medal IEEE, 1984, Excellence in Rsch. award Rutgers Bd. Trustees, 1985, IEEE Career Achievement award Soc. Engring. Med. Biology, 1991; Llewellyn Thomas vis. prof. U. Toronto, Can., 1989. Fellow IEEE (engring. in medicine and biol. soc. career achievement award 1991), N.Y. Acad. Medicine, Am. Inst. of Medicine and Biol. Engring. Achievements include 26 patents for Electron Tube, Ultrasonic Flowmeter, Ultrasonic Transducer, Piezoelectric Heart Assist Apparatus, Method and Apparatus for Non-Invasive Monitoring Dynamic Cardiac Performance, and others. Home: PO Box 2289 Lenox MA 01240-5289 Office: Rutgers U Biomed Engring PO Box 909 Piscataway NJ 08855-0909 E-mail: wwelkowitz@aol.com.

WELL, IRWIN, language educator; b. Cin., Apr. 16, 1928; s. Sidney and Florence (Levy) W.; m. Vivian Max, Dec. 27, 1950; children: Martin, Alice, Daniel. BA, U. Chgo., 1948, MA, 1951; PhD, Harvard U., 1960; D (hon.), Nevsky Inst., Petersburg, Russia, 1999. Teaching fellow Harvard U., Cambridge, Mass., 1955-58; asst. prof. Brandeis U., Waltham, 1958-65; assoc. prof. Northwestern U., Evanston, Ill., 1966-70, prof. Russian, Russian Lit., 1970—. Pres., mem. bd. dirs. Am. Coun. Tchrs. of Russian., Washington, 1967—. Author numerous books in field; contbr. articles to scholarly jours. Recipient Pushkin medal Internat. Assn. of Russian Profs. Jewish. Avocations: music, singing. Office: Northwestern U Slavic Dept Evanston IL 60208-0001

WELLBERG, EDWARD LOUIS, JR. insurance company executive; b. Eagle Pass, Tex., June 5, 1945; s. Edward L. Wellberg and Nell L. (Kownslar) Walker; children: Elizabeth, Ashley, Jennifer; m. Yvonne Hill, Feb. 4, 1989. Student, St. Mary's U., San Antonio, 1978. CLU, Life Underwriters Tng. Coun. Fellow. Sales agt. Washington Nat. Ins. Co., San Antonio, 1969-82; ptnr. Mazur Bennett Wellberg Assocs., 1982-91; mktg. exec. Wellberg Assocs., 1991—. Bd. dirs. Tex. State Ins. Bd. Adv. Coun., Austin, 1988-94. Contbr. articles to trade publs. Mem. Am. Soc. CLU's, Tex. Assn. Ins. and Fin. Advisors (bd. dirs. 1983-86, 92-93, pres. 1996, state nat. com. 1997-2000), Tex. Life Underwriters Polit. Action Com. (vice chmn. 1981-83, 88-90, chmn. 1990-92, state nat. committeeman 1997-2000), San Antonio Assn. Ins. and Fin. Advisors (pres. 1982). Home: 1707 Ashley Cir San Antonio TX 78232-4710 Office: 14400 Northbrook Dr Ste 200 San Antonio TX 78232-5038 E-mail: wellberg@aol.com.

WELLBORN, CHARLES IVEY, science and technology business consultant; b. Houston, Dec. 9, 1941; s. Fred W. and Emily R. (Gladu) W.; m. JD McCausland, Aug. 14, 1965; children: Westly O., Kerry S. BA in Econs., U. N.Mex., 1963, JD, 1966; LLM, NYU, 1972. Bar: N.Mex. 1963, U.S. Dist. Ct. N.Mex. 1966. Assoc. Neal & Matkins, Carlsbad, N.Mex., 1966-68, Robinson & Stevens, Albuquerque, 1969-71; ptnr. Schlenker, Parker, Payne & Wellborn, 1971-76, Parker & Wellborn, Albuquerque, 1976-82, Modrall, Sperling, Roehl, Harris & Sisk, Albuquerque, 1982-95; pres., CEO Sci. & Tech. Corp. at U. N.Mex., 1995-2000; pres. Wellborn Strategies LLC, 2000—. Contbr. articles to law revs. Bd. dirs. N.Mex. Symphony Orch., 1988-91, U. N.Mex. Anderson Schs. Mgmt. Found., 1989-94, N.Mex. First, 1989-93, 2000—, Accion N.Mex., 1995-97; vice chair U. N.Mex. Found., Inc., 1990-95; mem. Gov.'s Bus. Adv. Coun., 1989—, SBA Fin. Svcs. Adv., N.Mex., 1989; mem. venture capital mgmt. adv. com. N.Mex. State Investment Coun., 1991-98; mem. Econ. Forum, 1986-2002, chmn., 1995-96; chmn. Roots and Wings Found., 1989-93; v.p. N.Mex. Dem. Bus. Coun., 1992-96; mem. Gov.'s Prayer Breakfast Com., 1991-2002, chair, 2000-2002; mem. City-County Classification Exploration Group, 2002—. Sgt. USAF, 1968-69, Korea. Fellow Am. Bar Found.; mem. ABA (ho. of dels. 1984-91), Albuquerque Bar Assn. (pres. 1977-78), N.Mex. Bar Found. (pres. 1980-82), State Bar N.Mex. (pres. 1982-83). Democrat. Roman Catholic. Office: Wellborn Strategies LLC 3819 La Hacienda Dr NE Albuquerque NM 87110-6115 E-mail: chuckwellborn@hotmail.com.

WELLBORN, OLIN GUY, III, law educator, educator; b. Galveston, Tex., Oct. 21, 1947; s. Olin Guy Jr. and Betty Jean (Merriman) W.; m. Jodi Boston, July 1, 1983; children: Olivia Boston, Olin Guy IV. AB in English magna cum laude, Harvard U., 1970, JD magna cum laude, 1973. Law clk. U.S. Ct. Appeals, San Francisco, 1973-74; asst. prof. U. Tex. Sch Law, Austin, 1974-77, prof., 1977—, William C. Liedtke sr. prof., 1985—, assoc. dean acad. affairs, 1987-91. Vis. prof. Harvard Law Sch., 1978, U. Mich. Law Sch., 1987; co-reporter Tex. Rules of Evidence, 1981—84; advisor standing com. adminstrn. rules of evidence State Bar Tex., 1983—88, 1994—2001; faculty Tex. Ctr. for Judiciary, 1992—. Author (with John F. Sutton Jr.): Cases and Materials on Evidence, 6th edit., 1987; author: 7th edit., 1992, 8th edit., 1996, Teacher's Manual to Accompany Cases and Materials on Evidence, 1992, 1996; author: (with Steven Goode and M. Michael Sharlot) Guide to the Texas Rules of Evidence: Civil and Criminal, 1988; author: 2d edit., 1993, Courtroom Handbook on Texas Evidence, 1994, 9th rev. edit., 2002; author: (with Steven Goode) Courtroom Evidence Handbook, 1995; author: 4th edit., 2001, Courtroom Handbook on Federal Evidence, 1995, 8th rev. edit., 2002; author: (with David W.Robertson, William Powers Jr., David A.Anderson) Cases and Materials on Torts, 2d edit., 1998; author: Teacher's Manual to Accompany Cases and Materials on Torts, 1998, Cases and Materials on the Rules of Evidence, 2000, Teacher's Manual to Accompany Cases and Materials on the Rules of Evidence, 2000; contbr. articles to profl. jours. Mem. Phi Beta Kappa. Office: U Tex Sch Law 727 E Dean Keeton Austin TX 78705-3224

WELLE, TALMAN JAMISON, music educator; b. Tacoma, July 14, 1963; s. Arthur Thomas and Martha Ann (Thatcher) Welle; m. Laurie Lynn St. George, Dec. 28, 1985 (div. Aug. 5, 1995); 1 child Shannon Christine. MusB, Ctrl. Wash. U., 1985, MusM, 1987. Prof. piano Olympic Coll. , Bremerton, Wash., 1988—. Musician: (CD) Portrait of Marti, 1995, Work of Martha Thatcher, 1999, Concert Villa Lobos and Gershwin, 2001. Mem.: Wash. State Music Assn., Music Tchrs. Nat. Assn. (cert. tchr. piano 1999), Nat.Guild of Piano Tchrs. (chmn. 1988). Avocation: competitive bodybuilding. Home: 3045 NE Chippewa Ct Poulsbo WA 98370 Office: Olympic Coll 1600 Chester Ave Bremerton WA 98310 E-mail: talmanmusicman@aol.com.

WELLEN, DANA THOMAS, system administrator; b. Warwick, R.I., Dec. 20, 1957; s. Robert G. and Thomasina (Morris) W.; m. Debra Ann Ciccarelli, July 18, 1987. AS, R.I. Jr. Coll., 1979. Electronic engring. technologist Semiconductor Corp., East Greenwich, R.I., 1979-88, adminstr. computer sys., computer programmer, 1987—, assoc. elec. engr., 1988—. Mem. Sun Users Group. Avocations: fishing, golf, bowling, photography. Home: 87 Helen Ave Coventry RI 02816-6347

WELLEN, ROBERT HOWARD, lawyer; b. Jersey City, Aug. 19, 1946; s. Abraham Louis and Helen Rose (Krieger) W.; m. Anita Fass, June 16, 1968; children: Elizabeth, Judith Maria. BA, Yale Coll., 1968; JD, Yale U., 1971; LLM in Taxation, Georgetown U., 1975. Bar: Conn. 1971, D.C. 1972, Colo. 1982. Assoc. Fulbright & Jaworski, Washington, 1975-76, participating assoc., 1976-79, ptnr., 1979-93, Ivins, Phillips & Barker, Washington, 1993—. Adj. prof. law Georgetown U. Law Ctr., 1982-85. Contbr. articles to legal publs. Served to lt. JAGC, USNR, 1971-75. Mem. ABA (past asst. sec., past chmn. com. on corp. tax, sect. taxation, past supr. editor sect. taxation newsletter), Fed. Bar Assn. (coun. taxation), Phi Beta Kappa. Jewish. Office: Ivins Phillips & Barker 1700 Pennsylvania Ave NW Washington DC 20006-4704 E-mail: rwellen@ipbtax.com.

WELLER, ANTHONY, writer, musician; b. Macon, Ga., Sept. 18, 1957; s. George Anthony and Gladys (Lasky) W.; m. Valérie Diane Moniez, Aug. 4, 1989 (div. Dec. 1993); m. Kylée Lizbeth Smith, Aug. 23, 1997. BA in Music, Yale U., 1980; pvt. study poetry with, Peyton Houston, 1976-95; pvt. study composition, Julián Orbón, 1978-85; pvt. study guitar, Rey de la Torre, 1975-79. Self employed writer and musician, N.Y.C., 1980-85, Amsterdam and Paris, 1985-86, Girne, Cyprus, 1987-90, Gloucester, Mass., 1991—. Author: (novels) The Polish Lover, 1998, The Garden of the Peacocks, 1996, (travel memoir) Days and Nights on the Grand Trunk Road, 1997; guitarist, co-leader Chamber Jazz, 1992—; guitarist Jon Jarvis Trio, 1994—, Herb Pomeroy Trio, 1997—; numerous recs. of CDs. Recipient Yale prize Acad. Am. Poets, 1980, Lowell Thomas medal for fgn. reporting U. Mich. and Soc. Am. Travel Writers, 1993; CAPS grantee, 1983-84. Mem. Kingsley Trust Assn., Kyrenia Soc., Musicians Union. Avocation: travel. Home: 3 Adams Hill Rd Gloucester MA 01930-1303

WELLER, CHERYL K. Internet service provider executive, educator; b. Rochester, Pa., Apr. 2, 1959; d. Glenn Stanley and Annabelle Lee (English) W. BA in English, Coll. Wooster, 1981; MA in English, Slippery Rock U., 1987; postgrad., Duquesne U. Instr. English Slippery Rock (Pa.) U., 1988-90; author centennial history Greek Cath. Union, 1990-92; instr. comms. Robert Morris Coll., 1992-96; owner, web-site developer Get-A-Site Internet Archs, Tucson, 1996—; instr. tech. writing C.C. Beaver County, 1997-98; tchr. St. Gregory Coll. Prep., 1998—. Editor: 20th Century History of Beaver County, 1989 (Best New Titles Pa. Mus. Commn. 1990); author: A Steadfast Commitment, 1993. Recipient Honorable Mention Sparrowgrass Poetry Forum, 1994; named Poet of Merit Am. Poetry Assn., 1989. Mem. NCTE, AAUW, Am. Conf. on Romanticism, Coll. English Assn. Avocations: antiques, cycling, tennis, racketball. Office: St Gregory Coll Prep English Dep 3231 N Craycroft Rd Tucson AZ 85712-5207 E-mail: ckprof@getasite.com.

WELLER, DEBRA ANNE, elementary educator; b. New Orleans, Feb. 4, 1954; d. James Garretson and Elizabeth Gene (Blakely) Hyatt; m. Bruce Weller, June 15, 1974; children: Jenny, Todd. AA in Art, St. Petersburg Jr. Coll., 1974; BA in Art Edn., Glassboro State Coll., 1983; MS in Curriculum and Instrn., Nat. U., 1991. Cert. tchr. Profl. storyteller, Mission Viejo, Calif., 1980—; tchr. Capistrano Unified Sch. Dist., San Juan Capistrano, 1989—; elem. tchg. asst. prin. Bathgate Elem., 1998—, stds. curriculum specialist. Edn. dir. South Coast Storytellers Guild, Costa Mesa, Calif., 1990—; workshop presenter Orange County Dept. Edn., Costa Mesa, 1991—, Imagination Celebration, Irvine, Calif., 1993—; bd. mem. Calif. Kindergarten Assn. Author: (pamphlets) Image-U-Telling Clubs, 1995, Storytelling, the Cornerstone of Literacy, also articles. Sec. Mission Viejo Cultural Com., 1995—. Cultural Arts grantee Dana Point (Calif.) Cultural Commn., 1993. Mem. NEA, Nat. Storytelling Network (Pacific region liaison), Calif. Tchrs. Assn., Calif. Kindergarten Assn. (bd. dirs.). Mem. Lds Ch. Avocations: calligraphy, composing, playing banjo, dulcimer and guitar.

WELLER, DOUGLAS LAFONTAINE, patent lawyer; b. Balt., Dec. 20, 1956; s. Weston Douglas and Jeanne Marie Weller; m. Frances Elizabeth Farrow, Sept. 7, 1991; 1 child, Weston John. BSEE, U. Calif., Davis, 1979; JD, U. Calif., Berkeley, 1983; MDiv, Western Sem., Portland, Oreg., 1990. Bar: Calif. 1983. Atty. Hewlett-Packard Co., Palo Alto, Calif., 1983-87; pvt. practice Santa Clara, 1987—. Prodr. TV show Search for Truth, San Jose, Calif., 2000. Chmn., elder Valley Ch., 1999—. Office: 431 Magnolia Ln Santa Clara CA 95051-5637 E-mail: patentcnsl@aol.com.

WELLER, ELIZABETH BOGHOSSIAN, child and adolescent psychiatrist; b. Aug. 7, 1949; m. Ronald A. Weller, Feb. 18, 1978; children: Andrew, Christine. BS, Am. U., Beirut, Lebanon, 1971, MD, 1975. Lic. psychiatrist, Lebanon, Mo., Ohio, Pa. Intern Am. U. of Beirut, 1974-75; resident Renard Hosp./Washington U., St. Louis, 1975-78; fellow U. Kans. Med. Ctr., Kansas City, 1978-79; asst. prof. psychiatry U. Kans. Med. Sch., 1979-85; chief child/adolescent psychiatry Ohio State U., Columbus, 1985-94, assoc. chair dept. psychiatry, 1994-96; prof. psychiatry and pediat. U. Pa., 1996—, chair dept. psychiatry child and adolescent psychiatry, 1996-99, vice chair dept. psychiatry, prof. psychiatry/pediatrics, 1996—. Fred Allen chair dept. psychiatry Children's Hosp. of Phila., med. dir. Child Guidance Ctr., 1996-99. Co-author: Psychiatric Disorders in Child/Adolescent, 1990, Current Perspectives on Major Depressive Disorders in Children, 1984, Children's Interview for Psychiatric Syndromes, 1999. Fellow APA, Am. Acad. Child/Adolescent Psychiatry; mem. AMA, ACP, World Fedn. for Mental Health, Soc. of Biol. Psychiatry, Pa. Psychiat. Assn. Office: 34th St and Civic Ctr Blvd Philadelphia PA 19104-4399 E-mail: weller@email.chop.edu.

WELLER, GERALD C. congressman; b. Streator, Ill., July 7, 1957; Degree in Agriculture, U. Ill., 1979. Aide to U.S. Congressman Tom Corcoran, 1977-78; aide to U.S. Sec. of Agriculture John R. Block, 1981-85; active family farm, 1985-88; rep. State of Ill., 1988-94; mem. 104th-106th Congresses from 11th Ill. dist., 1994—; asst. majority whip; mem. ways and means com. Rep. House Republican steering com.; mem. Newt Gingrich's policy com.; exec. com. NRCC, House Banking Com., House Veterans Affairs Com., House Transp. and Infrastructure Com. Mem. 1st Christian Ch. of Morris, Ill. Mem. Nat. Republican Legis. Assn. (nominated Legislator of Yr.). Office: US House Reps 1210 Longworth HOB Washington DC 20515-1311*

WELLER, GUNTER ERNST, geophysics educator; b. Haifa, June 14, 1934; came to U.S., 1968; s. Erich and Nella (Lange) W.; m. Sigrid Beilharz, Apr. 11, 1963; children: Yvette, Kara, Britta. BS, U. Melbourne, Australia, 1962, MS, 1964, PhD, 1968. Meteorologist Bur. Meteorology, Melbourne, 1959-61; glaciologist Australian Antarctic Exps., 1964-67; from asst. prof. to assoc. prof. geophysics Geophys. Inst., U. Alaska, Fairbanks, 1968-72, prof., 1973-98, dep. dir., 1984-86, 90-98; prof. emeritus Geophys. Inst., U. Ala., 1998—; project dir. NASA-UAF Alaska SAR Facility, 1983-93. Program mgr. NSF, Washington, 1972-74; pres. Internat. Commn. Polar Meteorology, 1980-83; chmn. polar rsch. bd. NAS, 1985-90, Global Change Steering Com. Sci. com. on Antarctic Rsch., 1988-92; chmn. Global Change Working Group Internat. Arctic Sci. Com., 1990-97; dir. Ctr. for Global Change and Arctic Sys. Rsch., U. Alaska, 1990—; dir. Coop. Inst. Arctic Rsch., 1994—; exec. dir. Arctic Climate Impact Assessment, Arctic Coun., 2000—. Contbr. numerous articles to profl. jours. Recipient Polar medal Govt. Australia, 1969; Mt. Weller named in his honor by Govt. Australia, Antarctica; Weller Bank named in his honor by U.S. Govt., Arctic. Fellow AAAS (exec. sec. arctic divsn. 1982-93), Arctic Inst. N.Am.; mem. Internat. Glaciological Soc., Am. Meteorol. Soc. (chmn. polar meteorology com. 1980-83), Am. Geophys. Union. Home: PO Box 81024 Fairbanks AK 99708-1024 Office: U Alaska Coop Inst Arctic Rsch Fairbanks AK 99775-7740 E-mail: gunter@gi.alaska.edu.

WELLER, JANE KATHLEEN, emergency nurse; b. Balt., May 26, 1948; d. Donald Boyd and Jane Lee (Collins) Sealing; m. Richard Earl Weller, Oct. 20, 1973 (div. Dec. 1978); 1 child, Jennifer Lee. AA in Nursing, Essex Community Coll., Balt., 1971; BS in Health, U. Md., 1983, MS in Health, PhD, U. Md., 1998. RN, Md. Nurse, clin. dir. Bon Secour Hosp., Balt., 1971—. Mem. Nat. Emergency Nurses Assn., Md. Emergency Nurses Assn., Md. Accident Injury Prevention Network. Lutheran. Avocations: symphony, cooking, reading. Home: 8737 Sicklebar Way Ellicott City MD 21043-6569 Office: Mont Gen Hosp Olney MD 20861

WELLER, KEITH A. lawyer, corporate officer; b. Camden, N.J. AB, St. Joseph's U., 1984; JD, NYU, 1987. Bar: Pa. 1987, D.C. 1989, N.Y. 1991. Atty. Drinker Biddle & Reath, Phila., 1987-91, Brown & Wood LLP, N.Y.C., 1991-95; dir., sr. assoc. gen. counsel Brinson Advisors, Inc., 1995—. Officer numerous investment cos. Articles editor NYU Jour. of Internat. Law and Politics, 1985-87. Mem. Union League of Phila.

WELLER, ROBERT PAUL, anthropologist, consultant; b. Phila., Dec. 8, 1953; s. Sol. W. and Miriam D. W.; m. Alice E. Ingerson, Nov. 5, 1979; children: Ezra, Hannah. BA, Yale U., 1974; PhD, the Johns Hopkins U., 1980. Asst. prof. Duke U., Durham, N.C., 1980-86, asst. dean, 1986-90; rsch. assoc., assoc. prof. Boston U., 1990-96, prof., 1999—. Cons. World Bank, Washington, 1994—, U.S. Dept. State, Washington, 1999, 00; adv. bd. Chinese Sociology and Anthropology, Canberra, Australia, 1992-95. Author: Unities and Diversities in Chinese Religion, 1987, Resistance, Chaos and Control in China, 1994, Alternate Civilities: Chinese Culture and the Prospects for Democracy, 1999; co-editor: Unruly Gods: Divinity and Society in China, 1996. Grantee NSF, Washington, 1977, Himalaya Found., Taiwan, 1998. Mem. Am. Anthropological Assn., Assn. Asian Studies (coun. mem. 1999-01). Office: ISEC Boston Univ 10 Lenox St Brookline MA 02446-4042 E-mail: rpweller@bu.edu.

WELLER, ROBIN LEA, elementary school educator, secondary school educator; b. Jacksonville, Ill., Aug. 9, 1955; d. James Robert and Lois Lea Ford; m. Michael Lewis Weller, June 22, 1975; children: Christopher Lewis, Robert Michael, Morgan Lea. B in Elem. Edn., U. Ill., Springfield, 1985. Owner Robin's Nest Flower Shop, Greenfield, Ill., 1976—81; lang. arts instr., counselor Greenfield Elem. Sch., 1985—; GED instr. Greene County IIP, Roodhouse, 1993—. Methodist. Avocations: painting, gardening, music. Home: 302 Walnut St Greenfield IL 62044 Office: Greenfield Elem Sch 115 Prairie St Greenfield IL 62044 E-mail: rweller1955@yahoo.com.

WELLER, ROY OLIVER, neuropathologist; b. London, May 27, 1938; s. Leonard Arthur and Myrtle Weller; m. Francine Michelle Cranley, Dec. 22, 1960; children: Adrienne, Timothy. BSc in Anatomy with honors, Guy's Hosp., 1959, MB BS, 1962, PhD in Pathology, 1967, MD, 1971. House officer, intern Guy's Hosp., London, 1961-62, lectr. in pathology, 1963-67, sr. lectr., cons., 1968-72; postdoctoral fellow NIH, N.Y.C., 1967-68; sr. lectr. U. Southampton, 1973-78, prof. neuropathology U.K., 1978—. Dep. dean of medicine U. Southampton, 1980-84, curator U. Libr., 1984-88, dir. pathology, 1989-93; editor Neuropathology and Applied Neurobiology, 1989-98. Author: Pathology of Peripheral Nerves, 1977, Atlas of Neuropathology, 1984; editor: Clinical Neuropathology, 1983, Systemicpathology-Neuropathology, 1991; contbr. over 170 articles to profl. jours. Rsch. grant Multiple Sclerosis Soc., 1990—. Fellow Royal Coll. Pathology; mem. Royal Coll. Pathology, British Neuropathol. Soc. (pres. 2001—), Internat. Soc. Neuropathology (v.p. 2000—). Achievements include research on neuropathology including Multiple Sclerosis and Alzheimer's disease. Home: 22 Abbey Hill Rd Winchester S023 7AT England Office: Dept Path Mail Point 813 Southampton Gen Hosp Southampton S016 6YD England E-mail: row@soton.ac.uk.

WELLER, SOL WILLIAM, chemical engineering educator; b. Detroit, July 27, 1918; s. Ira and Bessie (Wieselthier) W.; m. Miriam Damick, June 11, 1943; children: Judith, Susan, Robert, Ira BS, Wayne State U., 1938; PhD, U. Chgo., 1941. Asst. chief coal hydrogenation U.S. Bur. Mines, Pitts., 1945-50; head fundamental rsch. Houdry Process Corp., Linwood, Pa., 1950-58; mgr. propulsion rsch. Ford Aeronutronic Co., Newport Beach, Calif., 1958-61; dir. chem. lab. and materials rsch. lab. Philco-Ford Co., 1961-65; prof. chem. engring. SUNY-Buffalo, 1965—; emeritus, 1989; C.C. Furnas prof. SUNY-Buffalo, 1983—. Vis. fellow Oxford U., 1989. Author numerous sci. papers, book chpts., ency. entries Fulbright lectr. Madrid, 1975, Istanbul, 1980 Mem. Am. Chem. Soc. (chmn. Orange County sect. 1964, H.H. Storch award 1981, E.V. Murphree award 1982, Schoellkopf medal 1984, Dean's award 1991), ASTM (founder com. D32 on catalysts). Achievements include patents in field. Office: SUNY Buffalo 305 Furnas Hall Buffalo NY 14260-4200 Fax: 716-645-3822.

WELLER, THOMAS HUCKLE, physician, former educator; b. Ann Arbor, Mich., June 15, 1915; s. Carl V. and Elsie A. (Huckle) Weller; m. Kathleen R. Fahey, Aug. 18, 1945; children: Peter Fahey, Nancy Kathleen, Robert Andrew, Janet Louise. AB, U. Mich., 1936; MS, 1937, LL.D. (hon.), 1956; MD, Harvard, 1940; Sc.D., Gustavus Adolphus U., 1975, U. Mass., 1985; L.H.D., Lowell U., 1977. Diplomate Am. Bd. Pediatrics. Teaching fellow bacteriology Harvard Med. Sch., 1940—41, research fellow tropical medicine, pediatrics, 1947—48, instr. comparative pathology, tropical medicine, 1948—49, asst. prof. tropical pub. health Sch. Pub. Health, 1949—50, assoc. prof., 1950—54, Richard Pearson Strong prof. tropical pub. health, 1954—85, prof. emeritus, 1985—, head dept., 1954—81; intern bacteriology and pathology Children's Hosp., Boston, 1941, intern medicine, 1942, asst. resident medicine, 1946, asst. dir. research div. infectious diseases, 1949—55; mem. commn. parasitic diseases Armed Forces Epidemiol. Bd., 1953—72, dir., 1953—59. Contbr. articles. Maj. M.C. U.S. Army, 1942—46. Named Stern Symposium honoree, 1972; recipient Mead Johnson award for devel. tissue culture procedures in study virus diseases, Am. Acad. Pediats., 1953, Kimble Methodology award, 1954, Nobel Prize in physiology and medicine, 1954, George Ledlie prize, 1963, Weinstein Cerebral Palsy award, 1973, Bristol award, Infectious Diseases Soc. Am., 1980, Gold medal and diploma of honor, U. Costa Rica, 1984, First Sci. Achievement award, VZV Rsch. Found., 1993, Walter Reed medal, Am. Soc. Tropical Medicine, 1996. Fellow: Am. Acad. Arts and Scis., Royal Soc. Tropical Medicine and Hygiene (hon.); mem.: Am. Soc. Tropical Medicine and Hygiene, Soc. Pediat. Rsch., Am. Assn. Immunologists, Soc. Exptl. Biology and Medicine, Assn. Am. Physicians, Am. Pediat. Soc., Am. Epidemiol. Soc., Harvey Soc., NAS, AMA, Alpha Omega Alpha, Sigma Xi, Phi Beta Kappa. Home and Office: 56 Winding River Rd Needham MA 02492-1025

WELLES, JOHN GALT, retired museum director; b. Orange, N.J., Aug. 24, 1925; s. Paul and Elizabeth Ash (Galt) W.; m. Barbara Lee Chrisman, Sept. 15, 1951; children: Virginia Chrisman, Deborah Galt, Barton Jeffery, Holly Page. BE, Yale U., 1946; MBA, U. Pa., 1949; LHD (hon.), U. Denver, 1994. Test engr. Gen. Electric Co., Lynn, Mass., 1947; labor rels. staff New Departure divsn. Gen. Motors Corp., Bristol, Conn., 1949-51; mem. staff Mountain States Employers Coun., Denver, 1952-55; head indsl. econs. divsn. U. Denver Rsch. Inst., 1956-74; v.p. planning and devel. Colo. Sch. Mines, Golden, 1974-83; regional adminstr. EPA, Denver, 1983-87; exec. dir. Denver Mus. Natural History, 1987-94, exec. dir. emeritus, 1994—. Contbr. articles to profl. jours., newspapers. Sr. cons. Secretariat, UN Conf. Human Environment, Geneva, 1971-72; cons. Bus. Internat., S.A., Geneva, 1972; trustee Tax Free Fund of Colo., N.Y., 1987-2000, Denver Pub. Libr. Friends Found., 1996—; mem. Rocky Mountain regional adv. bd. Inst. Internat. Edn., 1996—; exec. com. Denver Com. on Fgn. Rels., 1987—; bd. dirs. Gulf of Maine Found., 1995—; chmn. Colo. Front Range Project, Denver, 1979-80. Recipient Disting. Svc. award Denver Regional Coun. Govts., 1980, Barnes award EPA, 1987. Mem.: AAAS, Am. Assn. Mus. (ethics com. 1991—94, v.p. 1992—95), World Future Soc., Cactus Club (Denver), Univ. Club (Denver), Denver Exec. Club (pres. 1967—68), Blue Key, Tau Beta Pi. Republican. Episcopalian. E-mail: jgwbcw@aol.com.

WELLES, VIRGINIA CHRISMAN, land use planner; b. Denver, June 17, 1954; d. John Galt and Barbara Lee (Chrisman) W.; m. Dwight Lyman Gertz, Oct. 9, 1982. Student, Hampshire Coll., 1972-74; BA in Polit. and Econ. Sys., Yale Coll., 1976; M in City Planning, MIT, 1981. Planning cons. Sugarloaf Mountain Corp., Carrabassett Valley, Maine, 1982-84; regional dir. EIP/N.E., Boston, 1984-85; project mgr. MetroWest Growth Mgmt. Com., Natick, Mass., 1985-88; planner, environ. enalyst Exec. Office Transp. and Constrn., State of Mass., 1988-89, Ctrl. Transp. Planning Staff, Boston, 1989-91; gen. ptnr. Welles Farms Partnership, 1991—. Chair Loon Preservation Com., 1991-93; trustee Squam Lakes Assn., 1988-91, Squam Lakes Conservation Trust, 1988-92, Audubon Soc., N.H., 1988-95, sec., 1993-95, chair edn. com., 1994-95; sec. Lincoln Nursery Sch. Bd., 1994-96; dir. Walden Conservancy, 1994-97; assoc. dir. Mass. Audubon Soc., 1995-98, dir., 1998—, chair adv. com., 2001—; mem. distbn. com., Crossroads Cmty. Found., 1999—. Pub. Policy fellow MIT, 1979-81. Democrat.

WELLFORD, HARRY WALKER, federal judge; b. Memphis, Aug. 6, 1924; s. Harry Alexander and Roberta Thompson (Prothro) Wellford; m. Katherine E. Potts, Dec. 8, 1951; children: Harry Walker, James B., Buckner P., Katherine T., Allison R. Student, U. N.C., 1943—44; BA, Washington and Lee U., 1947; postgrad. , U. Mich., 1947—48; LLD, Vanderbilt U., 1950. Bar: Tenn. 1950. Atty. McCloy, Myar & Wellford, Memphis, 1950—60, McCloy, Wellford & Clark, Memphis, 1960—70; judge U.S. Dist. Ct., 1970—82, U.S. Ct. Appeals (6th cir.), Cin. and Memphis, 1982—92, sr. judge, 1992—2002, ret., 2002. Chmn. Tenn. Hist. Commn., Tenn. Constnl. Bicentennial Commn., 1987—88; charter drafting com. City of Memphis, 1967, Tenn. Am. Revolution Bicentennial Commn., 1976; com. on adminstrn. fed. magistrates sys. Jud. Conf. Subcom. Adminstrn. Criminal Law Probation; clk. session, commr. Gen. Assembly; campaign chmn. Senator Howard Baker , 1964—66; elder Presbyn. Ch.; moderator Memphis Presbytery, 1994. Recipient Sam A. Myar award, Memphis State Law U., 1963. Mem.: Omega Delta Kappa, Phi Beta Kappa. Office: US Ct Appeals Clifford Davis Federal Bldg 167 N Main St Ste 1116 Memphis TN 38103-1887 Fax: 901-495-1356.

WELLIN, KEITH SEARS, investment banker; b. Grand Rapids, Mich., Aug. 13, 1926; s. Elmer G. and Ruth (Chamberlin) W.; m. Carol D. Woodhouse, Sept. 5, 1951 (dec. 1970); children: Cynthia Wellin Plum, Peter, Marjorie Wellin King. BA, Hamilton Coll., 1950; MBA, Harvard U., 1952. With E.F. Hutton & Co., Inc., Chgo., 1952-71, regional v.p., dir., 1962-66, pres., 1967-71, vice chmn., 1970-71; sr. v.p., treas., dir. Reynolds Securities Inc., 1971-74, pres., dir., 1974-78; exec. v.p., dir. Dean Witter Reynolds Orgn., from 1978; chmn. Dean Witter Reynolds Inter-Capital, from 1978; former vice chmn. Dean Witter Reynolds Inc. Chmn. bd. Moorco Internat., Houston; former gov., mem. exec. com. Assn. Stock Exchange Firms; mem. governing council Securities Industry Assn. Mem. investment com., trustee Hamilton Coll. Served to 2d lt., inf. AUS, 1945-47. Mem.: Knickerbocker (N.Y.C.); Clove Valley Rod and Gun (La Grangeville, N.Y.); Round Hill (Greenwich, Conn.); River Club. Home: Seaside Farm PO Box 335 Friendship ME 04547-0335 Office: c/o Dean Witter Reynolds 1345 Avenue Of The Americas New York NY 10105-0302

WELLIN, THOMAS, music director; m. Annette Wellin; children: Claire, Christopher, Patrick. BMus summa cum laude, Ind. U.; MMus, U. Maine; postgrad., Acad. Mus. Chigiana, Siena, Italy; studied with Julius Herford, Ruggiero Ricci, Franco Rerrara, Gustav Meier. Music dir., condr. Bismarck (N.D.)-Mandan Symphony Orch., 1990—. Guest condr. Fargo-Moorhead Symphony; lectr. in field. Condr. summer concerts Pops on the Prairie, New Year's Eve Viennese Gala, Dickinson State U., I-94 Music Festival, Beulah, N.D., 4th of July Spectacular on State Capitol Mall, (CD) Vivaldi's The Four Seasons. Performing Artists fellow N.D. Coun. Arts. Office: Bismarck-Mandan Symphony Orch PO Box 2031 Bismarck ND 58502-2031*

WELLINGTON, CAROL STRONG, law librarian; b. Altadena, Calif., Jan. 30, 1948; d. Edward Walters and Elizabeth (Leonards) Strong; m. David Heath Wellington, May 27, 1978; 1 child, Edward Heath. BA, Lake Forest (Ill.) Coll., 1969; MLS, Simmons Coll., 1973. Libr. Hill & Barlow, Boston, 1973-88, Peabody & Arnold LLP, Boston, 1988—. Mem. Am. Assn. Law Librs., Assn. Boston Law Librs. (v.p. 1979-80, pres. 1980-81), Spl. Librs. Assn., Law Librs. New England, Maugus Club (dir. 1991—). Office: Peabody & Arnold LLP 50 Rowes Wharf Fl 7 Boston MA 02110-3339 E-mail: cwellington@peabodyarnold.com.

WELLINGTON, HARRY HILLEL, lawyer, educator; b. New Haven, Aug. 13, 1926; s. Alex M. and Jean (Ripps) W.; m. Sheila Wacks, June 22, 1952; children: John, Thomas. AB, U. Pa., 1947; LLB, Harvard U., 1952; MA (hon.), Yale U., 1960. Bar: D.C. 1952. Law clk. to U.S. Judge Magruder, 1953-54, Supreme Ct. Justice Frankfurter, 1955-56; asst. prof. law Stanford U., 1954-56; mem. faculty Yale U., 1956—, prof. law, 1960—, Edward J. Phelps prof. law, 1967-83, dean Law Sch., 1975-85, Sterling prof. law, 1983-92, Sterling prof. emeritus law, 1992—, Harry H. Wellington prof. lectr., 1995—; pres., dean, prof. law N.Y. Law Sch., N.Y.C., 1992-2000, dean emeritus, prof., 2000—. Ford fellow London Sch. Econs., 1965; Guggenheim fellow; sr. fellow Brookings Instn., 1968-71; Rockefeller Found. fellow Bellagio Study and Conf. Ctr., 1984; faculty mem. Salzburg Seminar in Am. Studies, 1985; John M. Harlan disting. vis. prof. N.Y. Law Sch., 1985-86; review person ITT-SEC; moderator Asbestos-Wellington Group; cons. domestic and fgn. govtl. agys.; trustee N.Y. Law Sch.; bd. govs. Yale U. Press; mem. jud. panel, exec. com. Ctr. Public Resources Legal Program; Harry H. Wellington lectr., 1995—. Author: with Harold Shepherd) Contracts and Contract Remedies, 1957, Labor and the Legal Process, 1968, (with Clyde Summers) Labor Law, 1968, 2d edit., 1983, (with Ralph Winter) The Unions and the Cities, 1971, Interpreting the Constitution, 1990; contbr. articles to profl. jours. Mem. ABA, Bar Assn. Conn., Am. Law Inst., Am. Arbitration Assn., Am. Acad. Arts and Scis., Common Cause (nat governing bd.). Office: NY Law Sch 57 Worth St New York NY 10013-2959 also: Yale U Sch Law New Haven CT 06520

WELLINGTON, JEAN SUSORNEY, librarian; b. East Chicago, Ind., Oct. 23, 1945; d. Carl Matthew and Theresa Ann Susorney; m. Donald Clifford Wellington, June 12, 1976; 1 child, Evelin Patricia. BA, Purdue U., 1967; MA in LS, Dominican U., River Forest, Ill., 1969; MA, U. Cin., 1976. Head Burnam Classical Libr. U. Cin., 1970—. Compiler: Dictionary of Bibliographic Abbreviations Found in the Scholarship of Classical Studies and Related Disciplines, 1983. Mem. Art. Librs. Soc. N.Am. (chair Ohio br. 1984-85). Office: U Cin Classics Libr PO Box 210191 Cincinnati OH 45221-0191

WELLINGTON, LINDA See **HATTON, BRENDA**

WELLINGTON, ROBERT HALL, manufacturing company executive; b. Atlanta, July 4, 1922; s. Robert H. and Ernestine V. (Vossbrinck) W.; m. Marjorie Jarchow, Nov. 15, 1947; children: Charles R., Robert H., Christian J., Jeanne L. BS, McCormack Sch. of Engring. and Applied Scis. (formerly Northwestern Tech. Inst.), 1944; MSBA, MBA, U. Chgo., 1958. With Griffin Wheel Co., 1946-61; v.p. parent co. Amsted Industries, Inc., Chgo., 1961-74, exec. v.p., 1974-80, pres., chief exec. officer, 1981-88, chmn. bd., chief exec. officer, 1988-90. Served to lt. USN, 1943-46. Office: Amsted Industries Inc 205 N Michigan Ave Fl 44 Chicago IL 60601-5927

WELLINGTON, ROSEMARY, economic development coordinator; b. Petoskey, Mich., Aug. 1, 1953; d. James Doud and Mary Margaret (Thompson) Wellington; m. Dan L., June 16, 1974 (div. 1997); children: Jennifer Mary, Joshua Daniel. BS in Sociology, No. Mich. U., Marquette, 1977; postgrad., No. Mich. U., 1987—; student, U. Ariz., 1998, Econ. Devel Inst. I, U. Okla., 1998, Econ. Devel. Inst. II, U. Okla., 1998. Activities coordinator E.U.P. Mental Health Bd., Sault, Mich., 1978-80; client services asst. E.U.P. Mental Health Bd, 1980; assoc. dir. U.P. Health Systems Agy., 1980-82; U.P. field coordinator Riegle for Mich., 1982, Marquette, 1988; community educator Chippewa County Health Dept., 1983-84; legal asst. U.P. Legal Services, Sault, 1983-85; camp lic. cons. Mich. Dept. of Social Services, Mich., 1985-86; career cons. Six County Consortium for Employment, Marquette, 1985-92; regional rep. U.S. Senator Carl Levin, Escanaba, Mich., 1992-97; devel. coord. K.I. Sawyer Devel. Dept. (now Sawyer Internat. Airport and Bus. Ctr.), County of Marquette, 1997—. Del. Mich. Dem. State Ctrl. Com., 1986-91; chair Marquette County Health Care Access project adv. com., 1987-90; publicity chair United Way Marquette County, 1987-89; mem. Marquette Women's Ctr. Life Skills adv. com., 1987-88; appointee Alger-Marquette Community Mental Health Bd., 1989-93; vice chmn., mem. fin. com. Marquette County Irwin for Congress, 1988, coord., 1988; mem. adv. bd. spl. projects No. Mich. U.; mem. exec. com. Marquette County Dem. Party, 2000—. Mem. Mich. Assn. Community Mental Health Bds. (del., legis. com.), U.P. Pers. Assn., Women in Aviation Internat., UP Econ. Devel. Alliance, Mich. Econ. Devel. Assn., Air Force Assn., Ctr. for Urban Econ. Devel. Methodist. Avocations: sewing, needlepoint, tennis, dancing, downhill skiing. Home: 774 Lakewood Ln Marquette MI 49855-9518

WELLINGTON, WILLIAM GEORGE, entomologist, ecologist, educator; b. Vancouver, B.C., Can., Aug. 16, 1920; s. George and Lilly (Rae) W.; m. Margret Ellen Reiss, Sept. 22, 1959; children: Katherine Jean, Stephen Ross. BA, U. B.C., 1941; MA, U. Toronto, 1945, PhD, 1947. Meteorol. officer Can. Meteorol. Service, Toronto, 1942-45; research entomologist Can. Dept. Agr., Sault Ste. Marie, Ont., 1946-51; head bioclimatology sect. Can. Dept. Forestry, Sault Ste. Marie, Ont., Victoria, B.C., 1951-67, prin. scientist Victoria, 1964-68; prof. ecology U. Toronto, 1968-70; dir. Inst. Animal Resource Ecology, U. B.C., Vancouver, 1973-79, prof. plant sci. and resource ecology, 1970-86, hon. prof. dept. plant sci., 1986—, prof. emeritus, 1986—; Killam sr. research fellow U. B.C., 1980-81. Inaugural lectr. C.E. Atwood Meml. Seminar Series, Dept. Zoology, U. Toronto, 1993; vis. prof. N.C. State U., 1972, 75, 81, San Diego State U., 1975, Laval U., 1981, U. Calgary, 1983, Simon Fraser U., 1987. Contbr. articles to profl. jours. Named Prof. of Yr., Faculty Agrl. Sci., U. B.C., 1986 Fellow Entomol. Soc. Can. (pres. 1976-78, Gold medal 1968), Royal Soc. Can., Explorers Club; mem. Am. Meteorol. Soc. (award 1969), Entomol. Soc. Am. (C. J. Woodworth award 1979), Japanese Soc. Population Ecology, Entomol. Soc. Ont. Clubs: Am. Philatelic Soc. Anglican. Home: 2350 130A St Surrey BC Canada V4A 8Y5 Office: U BC ARE and Dept Plant Sci Vancouver BC Canada V6T 1W5

WELLISCH, WILLIAM JEREMIAH, social psychology educator; b. Vienna, Austria, July 3, 1938; came to U.S., 1940; s. Max and Zelda (Schanser) W.; m. Geraldine Eve Miller (dec. Feb. 1970); children: Garth Kevin, Miriam Rhoda; m. Claudine Abbey Truman, Sept. 5, 1971; children: Rebecca Colleen, Marcus Joshua, Gabriel Jason. MA in Sociology, U. Mo., 1965, PhD in Sociology, 1968. Researcher urbanization Hemispheric Consultants, Columbia, Mo., 1968-69; cons. to local govt. ofcl. on L.Am. Bi-cultural Consultants, Inc., Denver, 1969-70; prof. Red Rocks Coll., Lakewood, Colo., 1970-76, 77—. Author: Bi-Cultural Development, 1971, Honduras: A Study in Sub-Development, 1978. Mem. citizen's adv. bd. Sta. KCFR Pub. Radio, Denver, 1989—. Republican. Mem. Unification Ch. Avocations: still-life photography, landscape gardening. Home: 2201 Lamar St Edgewater CO 80214-1051 Office: Red Rocks CC 13300 W 6th Ave Golden CO 80401-5357

WELLISZ, STANISLAW, economics educator; b. Warsaw, Poland, Mar. 28, 1925; came to U.S., 1941; s. Leopold and Jadwiga (Landau) W.; m. Anna Blaszkicwicz; children: Tadeusz, Krzyszrof. BA magna cum laude, Harvard Coll., 1946, MA, 1949; postgrad., U. Cambridge, England, 1949-52; PhD, Harvard U., 1953; D (hon.), Warsaw U., 1998. Asst. prof. U. Chgo., 1957-60, assoc. prof., 1960-63; prof. Columbia U., N.Y.C., 1964-94, Kathryn and Shelby Cullom Davis prof. econs. & internat. affairs, 1994—. Vis. prof. Warsaw U., 1989-97. Author: The Economics of the Soviet Bloc, 1964; co-author: The Political Economy of Growth, 1993; co-editor: Stabilization in Poland, 1993. NSF fellow, 1975, 82; named officer Polish Order Merit, Govt. Poland, 1997. Office: Columbia U Dept Econs New York NY 10027 E-mail: SW11@columbia.edu.

WELLIVER, WARREN DEE, lawyer, retired state supreme court justice; b. Butler, Mo., Feb. 24, 1920; s. Carl Winfield and Burdee Marie (Wolfe) W.; m. Ruth Rose Galey, Dec. 25, 1942; children: Gale Dee (Mrs. William B. Stone), Carla Camile (Mrs. Dayton Stone), Christy Marie. BA, U. Mo., 1945; JD, U. Mo., 1948. Bar: Mo. 1948. Asst. pros. atty. Boone County, Columbia, 1948-54; sr. ptnr. Welliver, Atkinson and Eng, 1960-79; tchr. law Law Sch. U. Mo., 1948-49; mem. Mo. Senate, 1977-79; justice Supreme Ct. Mo., Jefferson City, 1979-89. Mem. Gov. Mo. Adv. Coun. Alcoholism and Drug Abuse, chmn. drug coun., 1970-72; chmn. Task Force Revision Mo. Drug Laws, 1970-71; liaison mem. coun. Nat. Inst. Alcoholism and Alcohol Abuse, 1973-76; mem. Cen. Regional Adv. Coun. Comprehensive Psychiat. Svcs., 1990-92. Bd. dirs. Nat. Assn. Mental Health, 1970-76, regional v.p., 1973-76; pres. Mo. Assn. Mental Health, 1968-69, Stephens Coll. Assocs., 1965-79; pres. Friends of Libr., U. Mo., 1976, bd. dirs., 1979-92; chmn. Dem. Com., 1954-64; hon. fellow Harry S. Truman Libr. Inst., 1979—; bd. dirs. Supreme Ct. Hist. Soc., 1982—; vice chair adv. bd. U. Mo. Multiple Sclerosis Inst., 1992—; bd. curators Stephen's Coll., 1980-92. With USNR, 1941-45. Recipient Disting. Alumni medal and award U. Mo., 1994. Fellow Am. Coll. Trial Lawyers, Am. Bar Found., Mo. Bar Found.; mem. ABA, Mo. Bar Assn. (pres. 1967-68), Boone County Bar Assn. (pres. 1970), Am. Judicature Soc., Am. Legion (past post comdr.), Multiple Sclerosis Soc. (Gateway chpt. bd. dirs. 1986-92), Order of Coif, Country Club of Mo., Columbia Country Club (past pres.). Home: 3430 Woodrail Ter Columbia MO 65203-0926

WELLMAN, BARCLAY ORMES, furniture company executive; b. Jamestown, N.Y., May 13, 1936; s. Albert Austin and Leona (Greenlund) W.; m. Diane Taylor, July 2, 1960; children: Barclay Ormes Jr., Taylor A., Alexandra C. BA, Dartmouth Coll., 1959; grad., U.S. Army War Coll., 1982. Interior designer Wellman Bros., Inc., Jamestown, 1963-64, treas., 1964—, pres., 1978—. Trustee Lakeview Cemetery Assn., Jamestown, 1978—, Sheldon Found., Jamestown, 1981—. Maj. gen. U.S. Army, ret. Mem. Am. Soc. Interior Designers (v.p. 1972-74), Am. Appraisers Assn., Am. Legion, Res. Officers Assn., Sr. Army Res. Comdrs. Assn., Sportsmens Club, Moon Brook Country Club, Delta Kappa Epsilon. Republican. Presbyterian. Avocation: fishing. Home: 1235 Prendergast Ave Jamestown NY 14701-3146 Office: Wellman Bros Inc 130 S Main St Jamestown NY 14701-6623

WELLMAN, CARL PIERCE, philosophy educator; b. Lynn, Mass., Sept. 3, 1926; s. Frank and Carolyn (Heath) W.; m. Farnell Parsons, June 20, 1953; children: Timothy, Philip, Lesley, Christopher. BA, U. Ariz., 1949; MA, Harvard U., 1951, PhD, 1954; postgrad., U. Cambridge, Eng., 1951-52. Instr. Lawrence U., Appleton, Wis., 1953-57, asst. prof., 1957-62, assoc. prof., 1962-66, prof., chmn. dept. philosophy, 1966-68; prof. philosophy Washington U., St. Louis, 1968-88, Hortense and Tobias Lewin Disting. prof. humanities, 1988-99, Hortense and Tobias Lewin Disting. prof. emeritus, 1999—. Mem. rev. panel rsch. grants NEH, 1968—71. Author: The Language of Ethics, 1961, Challenge and Response: Justification in Ethics, 1971, Morals and Ethics, 1975, Welfare Rights, 1982, A Theory of Rights, 1985, Real Rights, 1995, An Approach to Rights, 1997, The Proliferation of Rights, 1999. Recipient Uhrig Distinguished Teaching award Lawrence U., 1968; Am. Council Learned Socs. fellow, 1965-66; NEH sr. fellow, 1972-73; Nat.

Humanities Center fellow, 1982-83 Mem. Am. Philos. Assn., Internat. Assn. for Philosophy Law and Social Philosophy (hon. pres.). Home: 625 S Skinker Blvd # 902 Saint Louis MO 63105-2301 E-mail: wellman@twinearth.wustl.edu.

WELLMAN, GERALD EDWIN, JR. safety and fire inspector; b. Steubenville, Ohio, Feb. 27, 1948; s. Gerald Edwin Sr. and Rose Marie (Bonacci) W.; 1 child, Jerad Anthony. AS Data Processing, BSBA, West Liberty State Coll., 1974; MS in Safety Mgmt., W.Va. U., 1991, cert. of advanced study, 1995. With production, mechanical Wheeling and Pitts. Steel Corp., Beech Bottom, W.Va., 1966-76, with production, mechanical, safety Steubenville, Ohio, 1976—, also safety and fire insp., safety coord.;, 1993, 95. Mem. wellness com. Wheeling and Pitts. Steel Plant; safety coord. Wheeling and Pitts. Steel Corp. Hazardous Material Team; safety chmn., trustee local 1190 United Steel Workers Am.; mem. Am. Iron and Steel Inst. R.R. Com. Contbr. articles to profl. jours. With U.S. Army, 1967-69, Vietnam. Mem. Am. Iron and Steel Inst. (railroad com.), West Liberty State Coll. Alumni Club, West Liberty State Coll Hilltops Club, W.Va. U. Alumni Club, Mountaineer Athletic Club, Dapper Dan Club Upper Ohio Valley, Brooke High Sch. Boosters Club, W.Va. Sheriffs Assn., Follansbee Blue Waves Boosters Club, Nat. Fire Protection Assn., Nat. Safety Coun., W.Va. Safety Coun., Western Pa. Safety Coun., U.S. Steel Workers Am., Eagles Club, Am. Soc. Safety Engrs. (nominating com. 1989—), Alpha Kappa Psi. Avocations: golf, swimming, basketball, baseball, coaching youth football. Home: 311 Hillcrest Dr Wellsburg WV 26070-1943

WELLMAN, HENRY M. psychology educator; b. Hickory, N.C., Mar. 9, 1948; s. Henry M. and Martha M. Wellman; m. Karen K. Lind; children: Edward M., Daniel L. BA, Pomona Coll., 1970; PhD, U. Minn., 1975. Asst. prof. Ariz. State U., Tempe, 1975-77; prof. U. Mich., Ann Arbor, 1977—. Mem. exec. bd. U. Mich. Children's Ctrs., Ann Arbor, 1980—; mem. sci. adv. bd. Max Planck Inst. for Human Devel., Berlin, 1995—. Author: The Child's Theory of Mind, 1990, Children Talk about the Mind, 1995; editor: Essays in Developmental Psychology, 1997—, Brit. Jour. Developmental Psychology, 1990-98; contbr. more than 100 articles to profl. jours. Recipient Career Devel. award Nat. Inst. Child Health and Human Devel., 1983-88. Fellow APA, Am. Psychol. Soc. (founding fellow), Ctr. for Advanced Study in the Behavioral Scis. Office: Dept Psychology U Mich 525 E University Ann Arbor MI 48109-1109

WELLNER, MARCEL NAHUM, physics educator, researcher; b. Antwerp, Belgium, Feb. 8, 1930; came to U.S., 1949; s. Jules and Lucie (Rapoport) W.; m. Magdeleine Misselyn, Apr. 7, 1961; children: Pierre, Lucie. BS, MIT, 1952; PhD, Princeton U., 1958. Instr. Brandeis U., Waltham, Mass., 1957-59; mem. Inst. Advanced Study, Princeton, N.J., 1959-60; rsch. assoc. Ind. U., Bloomington, 1960-63; vis. scientist Atomic Energy Rsch. Establishment, Harwell, Eng., 1963-64; from asst. prof. to prof. Syracuse (N.Y.) U., 1964-95, prof. emeritus, 1995—; rsch. prof. SUNY Upstate, Syracuse, 1995—. Author gen. physics textbook; contbr. numerous articles on quantum field theory , fractals and excitable media to profl. jours. Mem. Am. Phys. Soc.

WELLNITZ, CRAIG OTTO, lawyer, English language educator; b. Elwood, Ind., Dec. 5, 1946; s. Frank Otto and Jeanne (Albright) W.; m. Karen Sue Thomas, Apr. 13, 1974 (div. Sept. 1987); children: Jennifer Suzanne, Anne Katherine; m. Carol L. Hinesley, Jan. 23, 1988. BA, Purdue U., 1969; MA, Ind. U., 1972; JD, Ind. U.-Indpls., 1978. Bar: Ind. 1978, U.S. Dist. Ct. (so. dist.) Ind. 1978, U.S. Supreme Ct. 1983, U.S. Ct. Appeals (7th and Fed. cirs.) 1984, U.S. Dist. Ct. (no. dist.) 1990; registered mediator, Ind. Instr. Danville Jr. Coll., Ill., 1972-74, S.W. Mo. State U., Springfield, Mo., 1974-75; ptnr. Coates, Hatfield, Calkins & Wellnitz, Indpls., 1978-98; pub. defender criminal divsn. Marion Superior Ct., Marion County, 1979-88, master commr. criminal divsn., 1988-96, registered mediator, 1998—; ptnr. Coates, Hatfield & Wellnitz, Indpls., 1999—. Instr. U. Indpls., 1981-82; mem. adj. faculty dept. English Butler U., Indpls., 1982—; instr. English Ind. U.-Purdue U., Indpls., 1987-90; pres. Ind. Account Mgmt., Inspls., 1985-94; v.p. Carol Craig Assocs., Indpls., 1987—; lectr. in field. Co-author: Successful Judgment Collection in Indiana, 1996, Emerging Trends in Indiana Commercial Collections, 2001; columnist A Jury of Your Peers, 1984-86. Vice committeeman Indpls. Rep. precinct, 1978; chmn. fin. com. St. Luke's United Meth. Ch., 1985-87; sponsor Christian Children's Fund, 1990—; active Am. Mus. Natural History, Indpls. Zoo, Children's Mus. Indpls., The Royal Oak Found. Postgrad. study grantee S.W. Mo. State U., Springfield, 1975. Mem.: MLA, AAUP, Broad Ripple Village Assn., Internat. Spkrs. Network., Spkrs. U.S.A., Libr. Congress Assocs., Smithsonian Assocs., Ind. Trial Lawyers Assn., Ind. Bar Assn., Internat. Assn. Comml. Collectors, Creditors Internat., Am. Collectors Assn. Internat., Def. Rsch. Inst., Rivera Club Indpls., Columbia Club, Elks. Office: One Indiana Sq Ste 2335 Indianapolis IN 46204-2012 E-mail: Indplslaw@aol.com.

WELLON, ROBERT G. lawyer; b. Port Jervis, N.Y., Apr. 18, 1948; s. Frank Lewis and Alice (Stevens) W.; m. Jan Montgomery, Aug. 12, 1972; children: Robert F., Alice Wynn. AB, Emory U., 1970; JD, Stetson Coll. Law, 1974. Assoc. Turner, Turner & Turner, Atlanta, 1974-78; ptnr. Ridley, Wellon, Schwieger & Brazier, 1978-86; of counsel Wilson, Strickland & Benson, 1987—2000; pvt. practice, 2000—. Adj. prof. Atlanta Law Sch., 1981-94; adj. prof. law Emory U. Sch. of Law, 1995—. Gov.'s task force chmn. Atlanta 2000, 1978; exec. com., treas., 2nd v.p. Atlanta Easter Seals Soc., 1983-88; rep. Neighborhood Planning Unit, 1981-83; adminstrv. bd. Northside United Meth. Ch. Served with USAR, 1970-76. Recipient Judge Joe Morris award Stetson Coll. Law, St. Petersburg, 1974, Charles E. Watkins svc. award 1995). Mem. ABA (ho. of dels. 1999—), Fla. Bar, State Bar of Ga. (professionalism com. 1994—), Atlanta Bar Assn. (bd. dirs. 1978-88, pres. 1986-87, bd. trustees CLE), Lawyers Club Atlanta, Old War Horse Lawyers Club, Charles Longstreet Weltner Family Law Inn of Ct. (pres. 1997-2001), Atlanta Found. for Psychoanalysis, Inc. (bd. dirs. 1994-, exec. com. 1997—). Methodist. Office: Ste 1800 Promenade II 1230 Peachtree St NE Atlanta GA 30309 E-mail: rgwlaw@earthlink.net.

WELLS, ARTHUR STANTON, retired manufacturing company executive; b. Kingsport, Tenn., Jan. 8, 1931; s. Arthur Stanton and Blanche Welch (Duncan) W.; m. Ellen N. Blackburn, June 15, 1957; children: Arthur S., Thomas B., Emily B., Richard R. BS, Yale U., 1953; MBA, Harvard U., 1957. Fin. analyst Eastman Kodak Co., Kingsport, Tenn., 1957-65; mgr. profit analysis Xerox Corp., Rochester, N.Y., 1966-68, asst. treas. Stamford, Conn., 1969-76, treas., 1976-79; v.p. fin. Barnes Group Inc., Bristol, 1979-86, exec. v.p. fin., 1987-93, pres., CEO, 1994-96, also dir., 1994-96. Bd. dirs. Nash Engrng. Co., Trumbull, Conn., 1995—98. Trustee, treas. Wilton (Conn.) Libr. Assn., 1972-78; trustee Lincoln Acad., New Castle, Maine, 2002—; bd. dirs. New Eng. Opera Assn., 1972-78; assoc. bd. dirs. Conn. Bank and Trust Co., Hartford, 1984-90; chmn. bd. trustees, exec. com. Conn. Pub. Expenditure Coun., Inc., 1990-93. With AUS, 1953-55. Mem. Fin. Execs. Inst. Democrat. Home: 4 CCIA Rd South Bristol ME 04568-4710

WELLS, CARL, III, professional sports team executive; Founder Precision Preparation, Inc., 1979; team owner PPI Motorsports, Hickory, NC, 1982—. Office: PPI Motorsports 3051 1st Ave Ct SE Hickory NC 28602-4044

WELLS, CAROL MCCONNELL, genealogist, retired archivist; b. Phila., Feb. 21, 1918; d. William Hugh McConnell and Edith Mary Lower; m. Tom Henderson Wells, Dec. 31, 1943 (dec.); children: Lucy, Sarah, Tom, Christopher, Julia, Peter. BA, Pa. State Coll., 1939; MA, Northwestern State U., 1973. Archivist Northwestern State U., Natchitoches, La., 1974-88; editor So. Studies, 1982-88. Spkr. in field. Author: Williamson County, Tennessee: A Genealogical Abstract of the County Court Minutes, 1800-1804, 1987, 88, Davidson County, Tennessee, County Court Mnutes 1783-1792, 1990, Davidson County, Tennessee, County Court Minutes, 1792-1799, 1991, Davidson County, Tennessee, County Court Minutes 1799-1803, 1991, many others. Mem. Natchitoches Hist. Found., 1994—. Lt. (j.g.) USNR, 1942-44. Named Woman of Yr. C. of C., 1975; recipient Clio award Phi Alpha Theta, 1988. Mem. DAR, PEO Sisterhood, Phi Mu, Phi Beta Kappa, Phi Kappa Phi. Republican. Anglican Catholic. Avocation: gardening. Home: 607 Williams Ave Natchitoches LA 71457 E-mail: granny@cp-tel.net.

WELLS, CAROLYN CRESSY, social work educator; b. Boston, July 26, 1943; d. Harris Shipman Wells and Marianne Elizabeth (Monroe) Glazier; m. Dale Reed Konle, Oct. 11, 1970 (div. Sept. 3, 1982); m. Dennis Alan Loeffler, Sept. 29, 1990. BA, U. Calif., Berkeley, 1965; MSW, U. Wis., 1968, PhD, 1973. Cert. ind. clin. social worker, marriage and family therapist. Vol. VISTA, Espanola, N.Mex., 1965-66; social worker Project Six Cen. Wis. Colony, Madison, 1968, Milw. Dept. Pub. Welfare, 1969, Shorewood (Wis.) Manor Nursing Home, 1972; sch. social worker Jefferson (Wis.) County Spl. Edn., 1977-78; lectr. sociology and social work Marquette U., Milw., 1972-73, dir. social work program, 1973-90, 93—, assoc. prof. social work, 1981-94, prof. social work, 1994—; social work therapist Lighthouse Counseling Assocs., Racine, Wis., 1989-91, The Cambridge Group, 1991-92; Achievement Assocs., 1992-95. Vis. lectr. social work U. Canterbury, Christchurch, N.Z., 1983. Author: Social Work Day to Day, 1982, rev. edit., 1988, Social Work Ethics Day to Day, 1986; co-author: The Social Work Experience, 1991, rev. edit., 1996. Mem. Wis. Coun. on Social Work Edn., pres., 1980-82, sec., 1985-87, mem. exec. com., 1993-96. Mem. NASW, Am. Assn. Profl. Hypnotherapists, Coun. on Social Work Edn. (mem. publs. and media com. 1989-91, site visitor for accreditation 1987—), Acad. Cert. Social Workers, Assn. Baccalaureate Program Dirs. Democrat. Avocations: writing, silent sports. Home: 4173 Sleeping Dragon Rd West Bend WI 53095-9296 Office: Marquette U Social Work Program 526 N 14th St Milwaukee WI 53233-2211

WELLS, CHARLES TALLEY, state supreme court justice; b. Orlando, Fla., Mar. 4, 1939; Bar: Fla. 1965, U.S. Dist. Ct. (mid. dist.) Fla., U.S. Ct. Appeals (5th and 11th cirs.) 1966, U.S. Supreme Ct. 1969, U.S. Dist. Ct., U.S. Dist. Ct. (so. dist.) Fla. 1976, U.S. Ct. of Claims 1990. Trial atty. U.S. dept justice, Washington, 1969; pvt. practice Maguire, Voohris and Wells, PA, Orlando, Fla., 1965—68, 1970—75, Wells, Gattis, Hollowes & Carpenter, PA, Orlando, 1976—94; justice Fla. Supreme Ct., Tallahassee, 1994—. Methodist. Office: Fla Supreme Ct Supreme Ct Bldg 500 S Duval St Tallahassee FL 32399-1925*

WELLS, CHRISTINE, foundation executive; b. Grayling, Mich., Aug. 6, 1948; d. Chester John and Mary W. BA, Mich. State U., 1970, MLIR, 1982; MLS, U. Mich., 1976. Head libr. Lansing State Jour., E. Lansing, Mich., 1973-82; mng. editor libr. svcs. USA TODAY, Washington, 1982-87; libr. dir. Gannett Co., Inc., 1985-87, chief staff, chmn. and CEO office, 1988-89; v.p. adminstrn. Gannett Found., 1989-90; v.p. internat. The Freedom Forum, 1991—; exec. dir. The Newseum, 1993-94; sr. v.p. internat. The Freedom Forum, 1994—. Mem. bd. overseers Internat. Press Ctr. and Club, Moscow; mem. bd. visitors Coll. Sci., Mich. State U. Recipient Dising. Alumni award U. Mich., 1991. Mem. ALA, Spl. Librs. Assn. (Profl. award 1994). Office: The Freedom Forum 1101 Wilson Blvd Ste 2300 Arlington VA 22209-2265

WELLS, CHRISTINE VALERIE, music educator; b. Flushing, N.Y., Sept. 25, 1948; d. Roland Clifford and Frances Marie (Da Ros) Stoehr; m. Jonathan Freda Wells, June 20, 1970 (dec. Nov. 1989); children: Jennifer Lee Magee, Kevin Michael, Frederick Joseph. BMus cum laude, Bucknell U., 1970; MA, U. Md., 1974. Elem. vocal music tchr. Prince George's County Pub. Schs., Upper Marlboro, Md., 1970—; cantor, substitute organist Holy Trinity Cath. Ch., Glen Burnie, 1980-81, St. Stanislaus Kostka Ch., Balt., 1983-2000; organist Holy Rosary Ch., 2000—. Choir dir. Gregorian Singers, Glen Burnie, 1981—90; music dir. numerous plays Pasadena Theatre Co., Millersville, Md., 1981—; music dir. for plays Act II Dinner Theatre, Rosedale, Md., 1994—95, Timonium (Md.) Dinner Theatre, 1994—95, Music and Drama and Goddard Space Flight Ctr., 1997—; soprano Friday Morning Music Club Chorale, Washington, 2001—. Active fundraising Leukemia Soc., Am. Heart Assn., Glen Burnie; cantor, organist, lector Good Shepherd Cath. Ch., Glen Burnie, 1982—. Mem. Nat. Mus. Women in the Arts (charter). Republican. Roman Catholic. Avocations: traveling, music and theater, baseball, swimming, reading. Home: 303 Glenwood Ave Glen Burnie MD 21061-2233 Office: Columbia Park Elem Sch 1901 Kent Village Dr Hyattsville MD 20785-3999 E-mail: cvwells@netzero.net.

WELLS, CHRISTOPHER BRIAN, lawyer; b. Belleville, Ill., Jan. 23, 1948; s. Frederick Meyers and Ethel Pauline (Morris) W.; m. Gaynelle Vansandt, June 6, 1970; 1 child, Deva Marie. BA in Econs., U. Kans., BS in Bus., 1970, JD, 1973. Enforcement atty. SEC, Seattle, 1977-82; ptnr. Lane, Powell, Spears , Lubersky, LLP, 1982—. Capt. U.S. Army, 1973-77. Mem. ABA, Wash. State Bar Assn., King County Trial Lawyers Assn., Wash. Soc. CPA's., Kans. Bar Assn., Securities Industry Assn. (legal and compliance divsn.). Democrat. Office: Lane Powell Spears Lubersky LLP 1420 5th Ave Ste 4100 Seattle WA 98101-2338 E-mail: wellsc@lanepowell.com.

WELLS, CLAUDIA MAE ELLIS, nutritionist, educator; b. Reform, Ala., Apr. 25, 1911; d. Leven Handy and Mary (Sibley) Ellis; m. John Walter Wells, Sept. 10, 1935; 1 child, John Walter. BS in Home Econs., U. Ala., 1931, MS, 1933. Registered dietitian. Dietitian U. Ala., 1931-33; tchr. home econs., sci. Ala. high schs., 1942-50; sci. tchr. Marietta (Ga.) High Sch., 1950-53, head sci. dept., 1953-56; instr. biology U. Ga. Ctr., Marietta, 1953-56; asst. prof. nutrition and food sci. U. Ky., 1956-76. Organizer Ga. Sci. Fairs, 1954-56, Lafayette (Ky.) High Sch. Band Club, Ctrl. Ky. Youth Orch. Assn., 1956-58; presenter papers in field. Author: History of Aiken Garden Club, 1990, Laborers Together, 1995, History of Pickens County Alabama and Families, 5 biographies, 1998; contbr. articles to profl. jours. Active ARC, YWCA, PTA, Ala., Ga., Ky.; sponsor Bapt. Student Union U. Ky., 1964; assoc. Young People's Dir., mem. Bapt. Tng. Union, Cmty. Missions divsn. Woman's Missionary Union, chmn., 1963-64, Elkhorn (Ky.) Assn.; tchr. ladies' Sunday Sch. class Aiken (S.C.) 1st Bapt. Ch., 1976-98, pres. ch. tng. group, 1978, 80, chm. nominating com., 1978-79; pres. Aiken Garden Club, 1978-80; active Aiken Garden Coun., 1978-80, parliamentarian, 1979-84; vol. Multiple Sclerosis Soc., 1980; pres. Sunshine Club, 1988-90, mem. sr. adult choir, 1990—; active Nat. Arbor Day Found., 1995—. Named Honorable Order of Ky. Col., 1976; honoree 50th Anniversary of Coll. Home Econs., U. Ala., 1981; named to Faculty Hall of Fame, U. Ky. Mem. NEA, Am. Ednl. Assn., Ga. Edn. Assn., Biology Tchrs. Am., Inst. Technologists, Inst. Food Technologists (historian Bluegrass sect. 1965-71), Am. Home Econs. Assn., Ky. Home Econs. Assn., Am. Dietetic Assn., Ky. Dietetic Assn. (pub. rels. chmn. 1968-71, co-editor bull. 1971-75), Bluegrass Dietetic Assn. (v.p. 1963-64, pres. 1964-65), Sigma Xi. Avocations: flower and vegetable gardening. Home: Apt 102 190 Wexford Dr Anderson SC 29621-1755

WELLS, DAMON, investment company executive; b. Houston, May 20, 1937; s. Damon and Margaret Corinne (Howze) W. BA magna cum laude, Yale U., 1958; BA, Oxford U., 1964, MA, 1968; PhD, Rice U., 1968. Owner, CEO Damon Wells Interests, Houston, 1958—; pres. Damon Wells Found., 1993—. Author: Stephen Douglas: The Last Years, 1857-61, 1971 (Tex. Writer's Roundup prize 1971), paperback edit., 1990. Bd. dirs. Child Guidance Ctr. of Houston, 1970-73; trustee Christ Ch. Cathedral Endowment Fund, 1970-73, 84-88, chmn., 1987-88, Kinkaid Sch., 1972-86, Kinkaid Sch. Endowment Fund, 1981-86; hon. friend of Somerville Coll., Oxford U., 1988—; mem. Sr. Common Room, Pembroke Coll., Oxford U., 1972—; trustee Camp Allen retreat of Episc. Diocese of Tex., 1976-78; founding bd. dirs. Brit. Inst. U.S., 1979-80; mem. pres.'s coun. Tex. A&M U., 1983-89. Named Hon. Comdr. Most Excellent Order of Brit. Empire by Her Majesty Queen Elizabeth II, 1991, Outstanding Alumnus Yr. by Kinkaid Sch., 1994; fellow Jonathan Edwards Coll. (assoc.), Yale U., 1982—, Sterling fellow Yale U., 2000—, hon. fellow Pembroke Coll., Oxford U., 1984—. Mem. English-Speaking Union (nat. dir. 1970-72, v.p. Houston br. 1966-73), Coun. Fgn. Rels., Houston Country Club, Houston Club, Yale Club (N.Y.C.), United Oxford and Cambridge U. Club (London), Cosmos Club (Washington), Buck's Club (London), Coronado Club (Houston), Little Ship Club (London). Episcopalian. Home: 5555 Del Monte Dr Houston TX 77056-4100 Office: 2001 Kirby Dr Ste 806 Houston TX 77019-6088 Fax: 713-528-4832.

WELLS, DEWEY WALLACE, lawyer; b. Raleigh, N.C., Oct. 14, 1929; s. B.C. and Alma (Blanchard) W.; m. Ann D. Wells, Aug 25, 1951; children: Robert, Betty W., Daniel, Brady, Jeff. AA, Mars Hill Coll., 1950; BS, Wake Forest U., 1952, JD, 1954. Bar: N.C. 1954, U.S. Dist. Ct. (ea. dist.) N.C. 1960, U.S. Ct. Appeals (4th cir.) 1961, U.S. Dist. Ct. (mid. and we. dist.) N.C. 1985. Exec. sec. N.C. Jud. Council, Raleigh, 1954-55; ptnr. LeRoy, Wells, Shaw, Hornthal & Riley, Elizabeth City, N.C., 1958-85, Womble, Carlyle, Sandridge & Rice, PLLC, Winston Salem, 1985—. Judge Superior Ct., 1st Jud. Dist. N.C., 1974. Trustee N.C. Natural Heritage Trust, 1990-96, chmn. 1996—. 1st lt. USAR, 1954-58. Fellow Am. Coll. Trial Lawyers; mem. N.C. Bar Assn. (pres. 1980-81). Republican. Baptist. Home: 1890 Pilot Ridge Rd Blowing Rock NC 28605-8917 Office: Womble Carlyle Sandridge & Rice 1 W 4th St Winston Salem NC 27102-0084

WELLS, FAY GILLIS, writer, lecturer, broadcaster, aviation historian; b. Mpls., Oct. 15, 1908; d. Julius Howells and Minnie Irene (Shafer) Gillis; m. Linton Wells, Apr. 1, 1935 (dec. 1976); 1 child, Linton Wells II. Student, Mich. State Coll., 1925-28. Freelance corr. in USSR N.Y. Herald Tribune and AP, 1930-34, aviation mags., 1930-36; fgn. corr. Italy-Ethiopian War N.Y. Herald Tribune, 1935-36, spl. Hollywood corr., 1937-38; contbr. book revs. Saturday Rev., 1939-42; dep. chief of mission U.S. Comml. Co., Portuguese West Africa, 1942-46; syndicated boating columnist, 1960-62; White Ho. corr. Storer Broadcasting Co., 1964-77. Aircraft pilot, 1929; designer yacht interiors Alta Grant Samuels, 1958-62; now co-chmn. Internat. Forest of Friendship; hon. co-chmn. Nat. Air Heritage Coun.; mem. com. to select 1st journalist in space, 1985—; judge of trophy winners Nat. Air Space Mus., 1988—. Recipient Sherman Fairchild Internat. Air Safety Writing award, 1965, Amelia Earhart medal, 1967, Golden Age of Flight award Nat. Air and Space Mus.-Dept. Transp., 1984, Elder Statesman of Aviation, 1984, award Internat. Conf. Women Engrs. and Scientists, 1984, Lifetime Achievement award Women in Aerospace Scis., 1996, Achievements award San Diego Aerospace Mus., 1997, Disting. Alumni award Elizabeth N.J. Edn. Coun., 1997, Pres.'s Personal award of excellence, 1997, Inspiration award Internat. Orgn. Women Pilots, 1997, Honors award Women in Aviation, 1990; named to Hall of Fame, Women in Aviation Pioneers, 1992; asteroid # 4820 named in her honor, 1995. Mem. NAFE, DAR, Aviation/Space Writers Assn., Am. Women in Radio and TV (pres. Washington chpt. 1968-69, CBS Charlotte Friel award 1972, Ester Tufty Meml. award 1998, Woman of Yr. award 2001), White Ho. Corrs. Assn. (hon. life), Aircraft Owners and Pilots Assn., The Ninety-Nines (founding mem., Most Valuable Pilot, Washington chpt. 1975, Spirit of Inspiration award 1996), OX5 Aviation Pioneers (Outstanding Woman of Yr. award 1972), Internat. Soc. Woman Geographers, Broadcast Pioneers, Zonta Internat. (life hon.), Nat. Aero. Assn. (named elder statesman 1984, Katherine Wright award 2001, Amelia Earhart Festival award 2002), Overseas Press Club (founding mem. 1939), Nat. Press Club, Internat. Forest Friendship (founding mem., co-gen. chmn. 1976—, Fay Gillis Wells Gazebo dedicated 1991). Home: 4211 Duvawn St Alexandria VA 22310-2024 E-mail: faywells@erols.com.

WELLS, GLADYSANN, library director; MLS, SUNY, Albany. Legis. session rsch. aide N.Y. State Legislature, 1972—73; legis. reference libr. N.Y. State Libr., Albany, 1973—78; with Sen. Rsch. Svc., 1978—80; Sen. Libr., 1980; dir. Ariz. State Libr., 1997—. Editor several books on the economy of the northeast; contbr. articles to profl. jours. Avocations: cross country skiing, hiking, snow shoeing. Office: Ariz State Libr 1700 W Washington Ste 200 Phoenix AZ 85007-2896*

WELLS, GORDON LEE, science educator; b. Dallas, Dec. 2, 1948; s. Phillip C. and Marilyn L. Wells; m. Carolyn S. Kerns; children: Elizabeth Stubbe, Phillip. BA, Marshall U., Huntington, 1971; MS, Fla. State U., Tallahassee, 1972—75; postgrad., U. Mich., Ann Arbor, 1984—86. Cert. profl. tchg. cert. W. Va., 1971. Instr. Fla. Keys Cmty. Coll., Key West, Fla., 1975—76; assoc. prof. Ohio Valley Coll., Vienna, 1976—. Computer cons., Vienna, 1986—; presenter in field. Author: The Effects of Oil and its Water Soluble Extracts on Marine Phytoplankton, 1975; contbr. chapters to books. Pres. Vienna Civitan Club, Vienna, 1983—84, pres.-elect, 1982—83; cubmaster BSA Cub Scout Pack 104, 1990—92; asst. coach Vienna Recreation League, 1988—93. Recipient OVC President's All Out award, Ohio Valley Coll., 1999, Faculty Christian Svc. award, Ohio Valley Coll. Student Body, President's award, Vienna Civitan Club, 1984; fellow Sch. of Edn. Merit fellowship, U. of Mich., 1985, Thomas A & Elizabeth Mann Diamond fellowship, 1984, 1985; grantee Spectroscopy Grant, Spectroscopy Soc. of Pitts., 1998, Tchg. and Tech. Collaborative Grant, Appalachian Coll. Assn., 1997—99. Mem.: NSTA (grantee 2000—), Sci. Tech. Engring. and Math. Consortium (co-chair for Share Fair 2002 2001—02), Human Anatomy and Physiology Soc., Omicron Delta Kappa, Phi Delta Kappa. Office: Ohio Valley Coll 1 Campus View Dr Vienna WV 26105 Office Fax: 304-865-6001. Business E-Mail: glwells@ovc.edu.

WELLS, JAMES ROBERT, pharmaceutical company executive; b. Moundsville, W.Va., Apr. 5, 1940; s. Robert H. and Maxine (Mason) W.; m. Lynne Holt, Mar. 28, 1981. BS, Wheeling Jesuit U., 1962; PhD, U. Pitts., 1967. Profl. and managerial positions in R&D DuPont Co., Wilmington, Del., 1967-76, prodn. supt. Orange, Tex., 1976-77, rsch. mgr. Wilmington, Del., 1977-79, mgr. strategic planning, 1979-87, mgr. external alliances, 1987-91; dir. external alliances DuPont Merck Pharm. Co., 1991-92, v.p. bus. devel., 1992-95, v.p. internat., 1995—. Bd. dirs. Dupont-Sankyo Pharm. Co., Ltd., Tokyo. Patentee in field. Pres. West Orange-Cove Sch. Bd., Orange, Tex., 1976-77. Mem. Am. Chem. Soc., Licensing Execs. Soc., Drug Info. Assn. Achievements include granting 2 U.S. patents, 1974, 1975. Avocations: sailing, gardening, reading fiction. Home: 24 Drake Rd Chesapeake City MD 21915-1709 Office: DuPont Pharm Co 974 Centre Rd Wilmington DE 19805-1269 E-mail: jrwells@crosslink.net.

WELLS, JAMES T. development and brokerage executive, consultant; b. Salt Lake City, Mar. 24, 1939; s. Calvin Young and Arvilla (Thomas) W.; m. Luana P., July 7, 1967; children: Rebecca Ann, Elizabeth Marie, Rachel Diane, Jamie Danielle, Eden Michelle, Don Carlos, Natalie Rose. BA in Econs. and Bus. Law, U. Utah, 1964, MBA in Fin. and Acctg., 1966. Cert. real estate broker, Calif. Corp. staff fin. analyst Radio Corp. Am., N.Y.C., 1966-67, divsn. overhead budget adminstrn. Van Nuys, Calif., 1967-68; cons. KMPG Peat Marvick LLP (CPA), L.A., 1968-69; mgr. 3d party leasing and fin. Xerox Data Sys., Inc., El Segundo, Calif., 1970-72; v.p. fin. Holstein Industries, Inc., Costa Mesa, 1972-76; CEO, pres. Svc. Sta. and Mini Mart Sales, Inc., Wildomar, 1976—2001. Pres. Mesa Verde Cmty., Inc., Calif., 1991-94. Author: Recent Real Estate Trends, 1966. Mem. Nat. Assn. Realtors, Calif. Assn. Realtors. Republican. Mem. Lds Ch. Avocation: church ministry. Office: Svc Sta and Mini Mart Sales Inc 23905 Clinton Keith Rd #114 Wildomar CA 92595

WELLS, JERRY WAYNE, police official; b. Hodgenville, Ky., Dec. 17, 1950; s. Lawrence and Margaret Evelyn W. BA in History, Western Ky. U., 1973; postgrad., So. Police Inst., Louisville, 1987; MS in Criminal Justice Adminstrn., Ea. Ky. U., 1990; grad., Ky. Dept. Criminal Justice Tng., 1993, FBI Nat. Acad., Quantico, Va., 1998. Cert. police officer, police mgmt. instr., Ky. Audio visual technician, police dispatcher Western Ky. U., Bowling Green, 1972-74, police officer, detective and sgt., 1975-76; police officer City of Bowling Green, 1976-83, police sgt., 1983-87, police capt., 1987-94, sector comdr., capt., 1994-99, capt. profl. stds. unit, 2000—. Part-time tchr. police related topics; also legal mgmt. rschr. Mem., grad. Leadership Bowling Green, 1989. Mem. Fraternal Order Police (treas. 1981-84, svc. award 1979, 81), Internat. Assn. Chiefs of Police, Western Ky. U. Alumni Assn., So. Police Inst. Alumni Assn., Ea. Ky. U. Alumni Assn., Leadership Bowling Green Alumni Assn., Coll. Law Enforcement Alumni Assn., FBI Nat. Acad. Assocs. Republican. Baptist. Avocations: racquetball, bowling, golf, traveling, historical research. Home: PO Box 684 Bowling Green KY 42102-0684 Office: Bowling Green Police Dept 911 Kentucky St Bowling Green KY 42101-2105 E-mail: wellj21@bgky.org.

WELLS, JOHN STEWART, physician, psychiatrist; b. San Francisco, June 15, 1934; BA, Stanford U., 1956; MD, U. Iowa, 1965. Diplomate Am. Bd. Psychiatry and Neurology, Am. Bd. Forensic Examiners. Pvt. practice medicine specializing in psychiatry, Arcadia, Calif., 1969—; dep. dir. Los Angeles County Dept. Mental Health, L.A., 1970-93; asst. clin. prof. psychiatry U. So. Calif., 1978—, now emeritus; ret. Served to lt. USN, 1957-61. Fellow (life) Am. Psychiat. Assn.; mem. So. Calif. Psychiat. Soc. Democrat. Presbyterian. Avocation: skiing, backpacking, bridge, swimming, travel. E-mail: jwellsmd@earthlink.net.

WELLS, JON BARRETT, engineer; b. Sewickley, Pa., Oct. 21, 1937; s. Calvin and Martha Barrett (Byrnes) W.; m. Nancy Lou LaFrance, Nov. 18, 1967; children: James Jonathan, Tiffany Lynn. BSEE, Calif. Poly U., 1961. Various positions Bell & Howell Co. Datatape Div., Pasadena, Calif., 1961-73, chief engr., 1973-75, engring. mgr. Calif., 1975-87; remittance projects mgr. Lundy Fin. Systems, Rancho Cucamonga, 1987-92; engring. mgr. Recognition Internat. (formerly Lundy Fin. Systems), Irving, Tex., 1992-96; project mgr.

BancTec (formerly Recognition Internat.), 1996—. Pres. Datatape Fed. Credit Union, Pasadena, 1978-93; v.p. Recognition Tech. Users Assn., Boston, 1987—; sec. Am. Nat. Standard Inst. X9B6, Washington, 1989-92. Patentee in field; contbr. articles to publs. Sec., founder Pasadena Neighborhood Housing Svcs., Pasadena, 1976-80. Mem. IEEE, Pasadena IBM Personal Computer Users Group, U.S. Power Squadrons, Aircraft Owners and Pilots Assn., Internat. Underwater Explorers Soc. Republican. Avocations: flying, boating, scuba diving, computers. Home: 32921 Arrowhead Dr Trabuco Canyon CA 92679-4322 Office: BancTec Inc 2701 E Grauwyler Rd Irving TX 75061-3414 E-mail: jon.wells@banctec.com.

WELLS, KATHLEEN ANNE, social services administrator; b. Santa Monica, Calif., Apr. 6, 1951; d. Gordon Thomas and Mary Clare (Sharer) Gibbs; m. Dennis Franklin Wells, June 29, 1978; 1 child Jennifer Stacey Wells Carroll. BA in Comm. Arts, U Ala., Huntsville, 1988. Materials mgmt. coord. Saginaw divsn. GM, Athens, Ala., 1976-82; purchasing coord. ConAgra, Inc., Decatur, 1982-85; customer end. cons. McCormack & Dodge, Huntsville, 1986-89; aide to mayor City of Madison, 1989-90; sr. info. designer D & B Software, Huntsville, 1990-91; asst. dir. Nat. Resource Ctr. on Child Sexual Abuse Nat. Children's Advocacy Ctr., 1991-94, project dir. nat. tng. program on effective treatment, 1992-94; exec. dir. HOPE Pl., Inc., 1995-98, cons., 1994-95; exec. dir. Crisis Svcs. of North Ala., 1999—. Bd. dirs. Ala. Coalition Against Domestic Violence, Montgomery, 1995—, pres., 1996—98; mem. N.Am. Coalition for the Homeless, Huntsville, 1995—, Gov.s' Domestic Violence Adv. Coun., 1997—98, Ala. State Batterer's Program Cert. Com., 1999—, Nat. Coun. Juvenile and Family Ct. Judges/Ala. Model Code Com., 1998—; leadership Huntsville/Madison County, 2001—02; exec. bd. Madison County Coordinating Coun. Families & Children, 2002—; bd. dirs. HOPE Pl., 1984—93. Recipient award for outstanding svcs. to families, Gov. State of Ala., 1987, award for outstanding svcs. and dedication to families, U.S. Dept. of Justice, 1990, Disting. Grad. award, Nat. Cath. Edn. Assn., 2001. Mem.: United Way Exec. Dir.'s Assn., Nat. Coalition Against Domestic Violence. Roman Catholic. Home: 95 Oakland Trce Madison AL 35758-7501 Office: CSNA Inc PO Box 368 Huntsville AL 35804-0368

WELLS, KITTY (MURIEL DEASON WRIGHT), country western singer; b. Nashville, Aug. 30, 1919; d. Charles Carey and Murtle Bell (Street) Deason; m. Johnnie Robert Wright, Oct. 30, 1937; children: Ruby Jean Wright Taylor, Bobby Wright, Carol Sue Wright-Sturdivant. Grad. high sch. Country music singer; sang gospel in chs. as a child; performed on radio, early 1930s; with John and Jack and the Tenn. Mountain Boys, late 1930's-early 1940's, regular on Grand Ole Opry, from 1952, now with Johnny Wright, Bobby Wright and the Tennessee Mountain Boys; songs include: Release Me, It Wasn't God Who Made Honky Tonk Angels, Making Believe; albums include Kitty Wells & Roy Drusky, Vol. 1 & 2, Back to Back Patsy Kline, 1995, (with Red Foley, Webb Pierce, others) Duets, 1995; author: Kitty Wells Cookbook. Bd. dirs. Nashville Meml. Hosp. Recipient award as number 1 female singer Cashbox Mag., 1953-62, Billboard 1954-65, award of yr. for top female country vocalist Record World mag. 1965, award for highest artistic achievement in rec. arts 1964, various awards Downbeat mag., award as all-time queen of country music Music Bus. mag. 1964, Woman of Yr. award 1974, named Top Female Artist of Decade, Record World mag. 1974, named to Country Music Hall of Fame 1976. Mem. Country Music Assn., Nat. Assn. Rec. Arts and Scis. Mem. Ch. of Christ. Achievements include being the first woman to hit No. 1 on the country charts with "It Wasn't God Who Made Honky Tonk Angels.".

WELLS, LESLEY, judge; b. Muskegon, Mich., Oct. 6, 1937; d. James Franklin and Inez Simpson Wells; m. Charles F. Clarke, Nov. 13, 1998; children: Lauren Elizabeth, Caryn Alison, Anne Kristin, Thomas Eliot. BA, Chatham Coll., 1959; JD cum laude, Cleve. State U., 1974; cert., Nat. Jud. Coll., 1983, 85, 87, cert., 89. Bar: Ohio 1975, U.S. Dist. Ct. (no. dist.) Ohio 1975, U.S. Supreme Ct. 1989. Pvt. practice, Cleve., 1975; ptnr. Brooks & Moffet, 1975-79; dir., atty. ABAR Litigation Ctr., 1979-80; assoc. Schneider, Smeltz, Huston & Ranney, 1980-83; judge Ct. of Common Pleas, 1983-94, U.S. Dist. Ct. (no. dist.) Ohio 6th Cir., Cleve., 1994—. Adj. prof. law and urban policy Cleve. State U., 1979-82. Editor, author: Litigation Manual, 1980. Past pres. Cleve. Legal Aid Soc.; legal chmn. Nat. Women's Polit. Caucus, 1981-82; chmn. Gov.'s Task Force on Family Violence, Ohio, 1983-87; mem. biomed. ethics com. Case Western Res. U. Med. Sch., 1985-94; mem. N.W. Ordinance U.S. Constn. Commn., Ohio, 1986-88; master Burton Inn of Ct., 1989—, counselor, 1993, pres., 1998-99; trustee Rosemary Ctr., 1986-92, Miami U., 1988-92, Urban League Cleve., 1989-90, Chatham Coll., 1989-94. Recipient Superior Jud. award Supreme Ct. Ohio, 1983, J. Irwin award Womenspace, Ohio, 1984, award Womens City Club, 1985, Disting. Alumna award Chatham Coll., 1988, Alumni Civic Achievement award Cleve. State U., 1992, Golden Gavel award Ohio Judges Assn., 1994, Outstanding Alumni award Cleve. Marshall Law Alumni Assn., 1994, Greater Cleve. Achievement award YWCA, 1995. Mem. ABA (coun. litigation sect. 1996-99), Am. Law Inst., Ohio Bar Assn., Ohio Womens Bar Assn., Cleve. Bar Assn. (Merit Svc. award 1983), Cuyahoga County Bar Assn., Nat. Assn. Women Judges, Philos. Club Cleve. Office: 18-A US Court House 201 Superior Ave Cleveland OH 44113-1836

WELLS, LINDA ANN, editor-in-chief; b. N.Y.C., Aug. 9, 1958; d. H. Wayne and Jean (Burchell) W.; m. Charles King Thompson, Nov., 1993. BA in English, Trinity Coll., 1980. Edit. asst. Vogue Mag., N.Y.C., 1980-83, assoc. editor beauty, 1983-85; style reporter New York Times, 1985, beauty editor, food editor, 1985-90; founding editor, editor-in-chief Allure Mag., 1990—. Spkr. Am. Womens' Econ. Devel., N.Y., 1988-89, Brand Futures Group, N.Y., 1999. Contbr. numerous articles to N.Y. Times Mag., Allure Mag., 1985—. Chmn. N.Y. Shakespeare Festival, 1993, 94; bd. fellows Trinity Coll., 1998—; bd. visitors Mary Inst. Country Day Sch., St. Louis. Recipient Fragrance Found. award 1991, 99, 2000, 2001, Nat. Mag. Design award, 1994, Legal Def. and Edn. Fund Equal Opportunity award NOW, 1994, Trinith Coll. Alumni Achievement award, 2000, Cosmetic Exec. Women Achiever award, 2001. Mem. Am. Soc. Mag. Editors (bd. dirs. 1993-97). Office: Allure Mag Conde Nast Publs 4 Times Sq Fl 10 New York NY 10036-6522

WELLS, LIONELLE DUDLEY, psychiatrist, educator; b. Winnsboro, S.C., Nov. 22, 1921; s. Lionelle Dudley and Mary Wells; m. Mildred Wohltman, June 28, 1945 (dec. 1986); children: Lucia, Lionelle, John, Diane; m. Eilene Bromfield, Sept. 23, 1989. BS, U. S.C., 1943; MD, Med. U. S.C., 1945; grad., Boston Psychoanalytic Inst., 1960. Diplomate Am. Bd. Psychiatry and Neurology; lic. physician, S.C., Mass.; cert. in psychoanalysis. Intern Met. Hosp., N.Y.C., 1945-46; psychiatry resident VA Hosp., North Little Rock, Ark., 1948-50; asst. resident in Psychiatry Graylyn, Bowman-Gray Sch. Medicine, Winston-Salem, 1950-51; instr. psychiatry U. Ark., 1949-51, Mass. Gen. Hosp./Harvard Med. Sch., Boston, 1955-69; clin. instr. psychiatry Harvard Med. Sch., 1969-78; lectr. psychiatry Boston U. Sch. Medicine, 1977-98; asst. clin. prof. psychiatry Harvard Med. Sch., 1978-93; lectr. psychiatry Tufts U. Med. Sch., Boston, 1981—. Cons. staff Newton-Wellesley Hosp., Newton, Mass., 1983-95, hon. staff, 1995—; assoc psychiatrist Mass. Gen. Hosp., Boston, 1975-82, psychiatrist, 1982-96, sr. psychiatrist, 1996—; courtesy staff Waltham Deaconess Hosp. and Med. Ctr., 1977-99; cons. Edith Nourse Rogers Meml. VA Med. Ctr., Bedford, Mass., 1966—; cons. in psychiatry VA Outpatient Clinic, Boston, 1959-2002, others in past; chmn. bd., chief exec. officer Bay State Health Care, 1984-91; nominating com. Am. Managed Care and Rev. Assn., 1988-89, others. Contbr. articles to profl. jours. Recipient Robert Wilson award, Med. U. S.C., 1943, 44. Fellow Am. Coll. Physician Execs., Am. Psychiat. Assn. (life); mem. AMA, Am. Psychoanalytic Assn., Am. Assn. Geriatric Psychiatry, Internat. Gero-Psychiatry Assn., Mass. Psychiat. Soc., Mass. Med. Soc., Boston Psychoanalytic Soc. and Inst., Boston Soc. for Gerontologic Psychiatry (mem. chmn. and dir. 1974-76). Home and Office: 73 Rolling Ln Weston MA 02493-2474 E-mail: ldwellsmd@attbi.com

WELLS, LLOYD ALLAN, psychiatrist, educator; b. Providence, Mar. 4, 1948; s. Lloyd Alvin and Elizabeth Hunter Wells; m. Denise Marie Coutu, Dec. 15, 1973; children: Aynslee, Llyd, Ethan. BA, Harvard Coll., 8, 1968; PhD, U. Rochester, 1973, MD with distinction, 1974. Diplomate Am. Bd. Psychiatry and Neurology. Cons. Mayo Clinic, Rochester, Minn., 1974—2001, assoc. prof., 1983—, sect. head, 1980—91, vice-chmn. edn., 1999—. Contbr. articles to profl. jours. Active Olmsted County Task Force on Family Violence, Rochester, Minn., 1982—83, Olmsted County Task Force on Guidelines for Hospitalization, Rochester, 1989. Named Tchr. of Yr., Assn. for Acad. Psychiatry, 1998; named to Tchg. Hall of Fame, Mayo Graduate Sch. Medicine, 1987; recipient Fisher award, Internat. Hibernation Soc., 1969, Writing award, Perspectives in Biology and Medicine, 1976; fellow Falk fellow, Am. Psychiatric Assn., 1976—77, Laughlin fellow, Am. Coll. Psychiatrists, 1977. Fellow: Am. Psychiat. Assn. (psychiat. nursing com. 1977—80); mem.: Am. Acad. Child and Adolescent Psychiatry (com. on substance abuse 1988—93), Am. Assn. for the History of Medicine (Harvey Osler award 1972), Am. Assn. Dirs. of Psychiatry Residency Training Pprograms (child and adolescent caucus), Soc. Profs. of Child and Adolescent Psychiatry (assoc. edn. chmn. 2001—02), Assn. for the Advancement of Philosophy and Psychiatry, Am. Acad. Psychoanalysis (managed care com., edn. com. 1998—2002), Am. Soc. Adolescent Psychiatry (coun. on fellowships, treas., dir. ednl. resources 1990—94), Am. Bd. Psychiatry and Neurology, Inc. (assoc. examiner), Acad. Psychosomatic Medicine (ednl. dir. 1983), Minn. Psychiat. Soc. (nominating com. 1979, ethics com. 1989), Sigma Xi. Home: 623 8th Ave SW Rochester MN 55902 Office: Mayo Clinic Rochester MN 55905 Business E-Mail: wells.lloyd@mayo.edu.

WELLS, MABEL GILBERT, social work educator; b. Hurt, Va., Dec. 15, 1932; d. Enoch and Victoria Queen (Cook) Gilbert; m. James Earl Wells, May 30, 1961 (div. Aug. 1968); children: Lisa Kay, Margo Cecile. BA, Howard U., 1955, MSW, 1957; PHD, Bryn Mawr Coll., 1978. Child welfare worker Dept. Pub. Welfare D.C., 1957-58; psychiat. social worker Dept. Mental Hygiene State Calif., Fresno, 1958-64; child welfare supr. Dept. Pub. Welfare Madera (Calif.) County, 1964-66; asst. prof. social work Fresno State Coll., 1966-69, Smith Coll., Northampton, Mass., 1969-71; admissions assoc. Bryn Mawr (Pa.) Coll., 1971-73; asst. prof. Va. Commonwealth U., Richmond, 1973-77, assoc. prof., 1977—. Bd. dirs. Dept. Social Svcs. State Va., Richmond, 1986-90, chair, 90-91; mem. commn. ednl. planning Coun. Social Work Edn., Alexandria, Va., 1988-91. Contbr. articles to profl. jours. Bd. dirs. Richmond Urban League, 1988-91. Mem. NASW, Nat. Assn. Black Social Workers, Acad. Cert. Social Workers, Coun. on Social Work Educators, Va. Assn. for Preservation of Family (bd. dirs. 1990-91), Child Welfare League Am., Delta Sigma Theta. Baptist. Avocations: choir, bell choir. Office: Va Commonwealth U 1001 W Franklin St # 2027 Richmond VA 23284-9041

WELLS, MARGARET ANN, piano educator; b. Corsicana, Tex., May 20, 1952; d. Chester Owen and Ollie Bernice (Pickens) Sprinkle; m. Byron Stephen Wells, Dec. 28, 1974; 1 child, Jennifer Ann. B of Music, U. Tex., 1975. Cert. tchr. music. Piano tchr. Mansfield Studio, Corsicana, Tex., 1968-70; music tchr. Shawnee Mission (Kans.) Ind. Sch. Dist., 1977-78; pvt. piano tchr. Wells Piano Studio, Kansas City, Mo., 1977-78; choir dir. St. John United Ch., Pflugerville, Tex., 1979-84; pvt. piano tchr. Wells Piano Studio, Pflugerville, 1980-84, Lewisville, Tex., 1984-94; choir dir. Round Grove United Ch., 1984—; pvt. piano tchr. Wells Piano Studio, Flower Mound, Tex., 1994—. Adjudicator for piano festivals and competitions, 1987—; music coord., choir dir. Gen. Synod United Ch. of Christ, Ft. Worth, 1989; choir dir., pianist South Ctrl. Conf. United Ch. of Christ, 1994—99. Named Tchr. of Yr. Denton Music Tchrs. Assn., 1989. Mem. Carrollton Music Tchrs. Assn. (student affiliate chair 1991-93, pres. yearbook adv. chair 1993-95, v.p. 1992-93, Gillock contest chmn. 1996—, cert. chair 1995-2000, music tchrs. forum chair, publicity chair, pres. 2000—, Tchr. of Yr. 1992, 95, 98, Pre-Collegiate Tchr. of Yr. 1992, 2001), Dallas Music Tchrs. Assn., Am. Coll. of Musicians, Jr. Pianists Guild, Alpha Xi Delta, Sigma Alpha Iota. Avocation: needlework. Home and Office: 309 Salisbury Ln Flower Mound TX 75028-7150

WELLS, MARK KENDALL, military officer, educator; b. Lubbock, Tex., May 4, 1953; s. Maurice Lee and Dorothy Jean Wells; m. Donna Carol Wells, June 29, 1975; children: Nathaniel K., Emily C. BS, USAF Acad., 1975; MA, Tex. Tech. U., 1983; PhD, Kings Coll., London, Eng., 1992. Comd. 2d lt. USAF, 1975, advanced through grades to col., 1975—96, pilot 29th FTW, Craig AFB Ala., 1975—76, aircraft comdr. KC-135 92 BMW, Fairchild AFB Spokane, Wash., 1977—80, instr. pilot T-37, 64th FTW, Reese AFB Lubbock, Tex., 1980—83, asst. prof. history USAF Acad. Colorado Springs, Colo., 1983—86, flight comdr. PIT, Randolph AFB San Antonio, 1987—88, dep. dept. head history USAF Acad. Colorado Springs, Colo., 1993—99, permanent prof. and head, 2000—. Author: Courage and Air Warfare, 1995 (Soc. for Mil. History Outstanding Book award, 1997); editor: Airpower: Promise and Reality, 2000. Fellow NEH, 1985. Fellow La Societe Napoleonienne Internat.; mem. Soc. Mil. History, Air Force Assn., Air Force Hist. Found., Assn. Grad. USAF Acad., Dadalians, Nat. Order Mil. Pilots, Phi Alpha Theta. Avocations: flying, reading. Home: 1670 Ridgeview Cir Monument CO 80132 Office: HQ USAFA/DFH 2354 Fairchild Dr Ste 6F37 U S A F Academy CO 80840 E-mail: mark.wells@usafa.af.mil.

WELLS, MARTHA JOHANNA, elementary education educator; b. Rock Springs, Wyo., Feb. 25, 1941; d. Harold Richard and Mae Amber Rose (Langmack) Frey; children: Timothy Duane, Amber Jo Sutter. BA, Wayne State, 1964. Cert. tchr. grades K-9. Kindergarten tchr. Cherokee (Iowa) Cmty. Schs., 1960-63, Harris-Lake Park (Iowa) Cmty. Schs., 1964-66, Norfolk (Nebr.) Cmty. Schs., 1966-68; sr. primary tchr. Emmetsburg (Iowa) Cmty. Schs., 1969-75, first grade tchr., 1975-82, kindergarten tchr., 1982-92, second grade tchr., 1992-2000. Critical reader adv. bd. Perfection Form Co., Des Moines, 1985-86; team mem. for evaluation on Paulina (Iowa) Schs.-Dept. Edn., 1985; presenter in field. Vol. helper Party for John Glenn, Marcie Frevert's Home, Emmetsburg, 1983; bd. dirs. Emmetsburg Pub. Libr. Recipient Iowa Reading Tchr. of Yr. award, 2000, cert. of recognition Iowa Ho. of Reps., 2000, Ron Ferry award, 2000, Honor award Uniserve Unit 10, 1999-2000, cert. of recognition NEA-Iowa State Edn. Assn., 2000. Mem. Internat. Reading Assn., Iowa Reading Assn. (zone coord. 1983-93, dir. at large 1993-95, dir. membership 1995-98, hospitality chairperson regional conf. 1995—, Appreciation cert. 1983), Iowa State Edn. Assn. (team interviewer 1994), Emmetsburg Edn. Assn. (profl. rights and responsibilities com. 1992-2000), Palo Alto Clay Kossuth Reading Coun. (newspaper in edn. com. 1990-92), Meth. Women, Kiwanis. Democrat. Avocations: golf, bridge, dance, walking, reading. Home: 1603 8th St Emmetsburg IA 50536-1442 E-mail: mwells@ncn.net

WELLS, MARY ELIZABETH THOMPSON, minister; b. Dallas, Oct. 9, 1936; d. Owen Perry and Ruth Marie (Baker) Thompson; children: Tadd Whitney, Britony Ruth. BA in Sociology, Syracuse (N.Y.) U., 1958; MA in Child Devel., Tufts U., 1964, MEd in Counseling Psychology, 1974; grad. studies in Theology, St. Vincent de Paul Sem., 1996—. Asst. dir. pub. relations Inst. for Crippled and Disabled, N.Y.C., 1958-59; head tchr. Eliot-Pearson Children's Sch., Tufts U., Medford, Mass., 1964-66; psychotherapist Mental Health Ctr. of Greater Cape Ann, Gloucester, 1974-89; min.-chaplain St. Paul's Episcopal Ch., Delray Beach, Fla., 1998—. Mem. Am. Psychol. Assn., Am. Orthopsychiat. Assn., Gulfstream Bath & Tennis Club, Assn. Clinical Pastoral Educators, Assn. Profl. Chaplains. Home: 1009 Langer Way Delray Beach FL 33483-6713 Office: St Paul's Episcopal Ch 188 S Swinton Ave Delray Beach FL 33444-3698

WELLS, MELISSA FOELSCH, foreign service officer; b. Tallinn, Estonia, Nov. 18, 1932; emigrated to U.S., 1936, naturalized, 1941; d. Kuno Georg and Miliza (Korjus) Foelsch; m. Alfred Washburn Wells, 1960; children: Christopher, Gregory. BS in Fgn. Service, Georgetown U., 1956. Fgn. svc. officer Dept. State, Washington, 1958-61, consular officer Trinidad, 1961-64; econ. officer mission OECD, Paris, 1964-66; econ. officer London, 1966-71; internat. economist, 1971-73; dep. dir. maj. export projects Dept. Commerce, 1973-75; comml. counselor Brazil, 1975-76; amb. to Guinea-Bissau and Cape Verde Dept. of State, 1976-77; U.S. rep. ECOSOC, UN, N.Y.C., 1977-79; resident rep. UNDP, Kampala, Uganda, 1979-81, dir. IMPACT program Geneva, 1982-86; amb. to Mozambique, 1987-90; amb. to Zaire (Kinshasa), Kinshasa, 1991-93; under-sec. gen. for adminstrn. and mgmt. UN, N.Y., 1993-94; cons. Sao Paulo, Brazil, 1995-97; amb. to Republic of Estonia Dept. of State, 1998—. Mem. Am. Fgn. Service Assn. Office: Casa Wells Plz Leoncio Bento 7 38830 Agulo Gomera Canary Islands Spain

WELLS, NATALIE CLARKE, anesthesiologist; b. Phila., Jan. 21, 1961; d. Nathanael Greene and Barbara Ann (O'Neill) W. BA, Smith Coll., Northampton, Mass., 1982; MD, U. Fla., 1986. Diplomate Am. Bd. Anesthesiology. Resident in gen. surgery U. Fla., Gainesville, 1986-89, resident in anesthesiology, 1989-92; attending anesthesiologist JLR Anesthesia, Fla. Hosp., Orlando, 1991—2001; med. dir. Physician's Surg. Care Ctr., Winter Park, Fla., 1995—99; attending anesthesiologist Anesthesiologists of Greater Orlando, 2001—. Mem. Am. Soc. Anesthesiologists, Fla. Soc. Anesthesiologists, Soc. Ambulatory Anesthesia, Soc. Cardiovasc. Anesthesiologists. Office: Anesthesiologists of Greater Orlando 2000 N Orange Ave Ste 202 Orlando FL 32804

WELLS, PALMER DONALD, performing arts executive; b. Keokee, Va., Jan. 31, 1937; s. Lon S. Wells and Ada Mae (Russell) Craft. BA in Journalism, U. Ky., 1960. Co-founder, producing dir. Theatre in the Square, Marietta, Ga., 1982—. V.p. IBM Drama Club, White Plains, N.Y., 1976. Appeared in The Three Penny Opera, 1963; director plays The Glass Menagerie, 1965, Dark of the Moon, 1966, The Little Foxes, 1983, Tobacco Road, 1985, Mary Shelly's Frankenstein, 1988; director musicals The 1940's Radio Hour, 1987. Founder Lonesome Pine Players, Cumberland, Ky., 1960; mem. Cobb Landmarks Soc., Marietta, 1990. With U.S. Army, 1961-63. Democrat. Avocations: pottery, Spanish. Home: 43 Mcdonald St Marietta GA 30064-3217 Office: Theatre in the Square 11 Whitlock Ave Marietta GA 30064-2321

WELLS, PATRICIA TRENT, retail marketing executive; b. N.Y.C., June 29, 1943; d. Ralph Harold and Lorraine Mary (Parker) Trent; m. Peter Scoville Wells, Dec. 8, 1973. BA in History, Marymount Manhattan Coll., N.Y.C., 1992; MA in Folk Art Studies, NYU, 1999. Ops. mgr. customer svc. Bell Atlantic, N.Y.C., 1970-84, mktg. mgr., 1984-90, assoc. dir. internal auditing, 1990—, supervising sr. auditor, 1990—2000; sr. specialist retail markets Verizon Corp., 2001—. Pres. Marymount Manhattan Coll. Adv., Bd. Mem. Sovereign Mil. Order of Temple of Jerusalem, N.Y. Jr. League, Inst. of Internal Auditors. Home: 449 E 78th St New York NY 10021-1649 Office: Verizon Corp 1095 Ave Americas New York NY 10036

WELLS, PAULINE M. accountant; b. Newfane, N.Y., June 8, 1974; d. William Hayes and Dorothy May Wells. BS in Computer Info Sys. magna cum laude, BBA in Acctg. magna cum laude, Niagara U., 1996; MBA, Rochester Inst. Tech., 2001. Acct. Xerox Corp., Webster, N.Y., 1996—. USAA All Am. scholar, 1996. Mem. Inst. Mgmt. Accts., Delta Epsilon Sigma. Avocation: bowling. E-mail: Pauline.Wells@usa.xerox.com.

WELLS, PETER NATHANIEL, judge, lawyer; b. Ogdensburg, N.Y., May 13, 1938; s. John Harris and Mary Theresa (Houlihan) W.; m. Diana Barry Wells, Apr. 8, 1967; childen: Mary, Sarah, Matthew. BS in Polit. Sci., Manhattan Coll., 1960; LLB, Boston Coll., 1963. Bar: N.Y. 1963, U.S. Dist. Ct. (no. dist.) N.Y. 1967, U.S. Dist. Ct. (we. dist.) N.Y. 1971, U.S. Ct. Appeals (d cir.) 1974, U.S. Ct. Appeals (3d cir.) 1978, U.S. Supreme Ct. 1974. Asst. atty. gen. State of N.Y., 1964-68; assoc. Costello, Cooney & Fearon, Syracuse, N.Y., 1968-70, ptnr. 5, 1970-76, Williams, Micale & Wells, Syracuse, 1976-88, Mackenzie Smith Lewis, Michell & Hughes, Syracuse, 1988; surrogate ct. judge Onondaga County, 1989—. Mem. EPTL-SCPA Legis. adv. com. of N.Y. State. Editl. bd. Warren's Heaton on Surrogate Ct. Chmn. Dewitt Republican Com., 1976-87; town justice Dewitt, N.Y., 1987-88. Served with USAR, 1963-69. Mem. ABA, N.Y. State Bar Assn., Onondaga County Bar Assn., Def. Rsch. Inst., Upstate Trial Lawyers Assn., N.Y. State Surrogates Assn. (pres. 1999-2001), Cavalry Club, Manlius Club (N.Y.). Roman Catholic. Home: 100 Downing Rd De Witt NY 13214-1503 Office: Surrogate Ct Chambers Onondaga County Courth Syracuse NY 13202

WELLS, PETER SCOVILLE, marketing executive; b. N.Y.C., Apr. 25, 1938; s. Jonathan Godfrey and Eleanore Shannon (Scoville) W.; m. Patricia Ann Trent, Dec. 8, 1973; 1 child by previous marriage, Peter Scoville. Asst. to contr. Laird & Co., N.Y.C., 1961-63; asst. to ptnr. charge ops. Goldman Sachs, 1963-64; mgr. new bus. dept. B.J. Herkimer Co., 1964-67; divisional policy and procedures adminstr. Paine, Webber, Jackson & Curtis, Inc., 1967-70, asst. to exec. cashier, 1970-73, asst. v.p., mgr. employment svcs., adminstr. equal employment opportunity, 1973-80; pers. officer, exec. recruiter N.Y. Stock Exch., 1980-86, mgr. employment; sr. v.p. Wesley Brown & Bartle, 1986-87; sr. v.p., dir. Alliance Mktg., Inc., 1987; ptnr. Richards & Wells, 1988-90, Brookman Assocs., Inc., 1990—. With AUS, 1958-66. Mem. SAR, Vet. Corps Artillery, Mil. Order Loyal Legion, Knights of Malta, Order of Lafayette, Knights Templar, L'Ordre Mondial des Gourmets Degustateurs, Phi Kappa Psi. Home: 449 E 78th St New York NY 10021-1649 also: 80 Bullock Rd PO Box 244 Chadds Ford PA 19317

WELLS, RAYMOND O'NEIL, JR. mathematics educator, researcher; b. Dallas, June 12, 1940; s. Raymond O. and Hazel (Rand) W.; m. Rena Schwarze, Aug. 1, 1963; children: Richard Andrew, René Michael. BA, Rice U., 1962; MS, NYU, 1964, PhD, 1965. Asst. prof. math. Rice U., Houston, 1965-69, assoc. prof., 1969-74, prof. math., 1974-2000, prof. edn., 1993-2000; chmn. dept. math., 1976-79; chmn. dept. edn. Rice U., Houston, 1994-98, dir. sch. math. project, 1987-2000, dir. computational math. lab., 1990-2000, prof. math emeritus, 2000—, asst. to pres., 2000-01; v.p. external affairs, prof. math. Internat. U., Bremen, 2001—. Vis. asst. prof. Brandeis U., Waltham, Mass., 1967-68; vis. prof. U. Göttingen, Germany, 1974-75, U. Colo., Boulder, 1983-84, U. Bremen, Germany, 1995-96, Internat. Univ. Bremen, 1998-2001; adj. prof. cmty. medicine Baylor Coll. Medicine, 1994—; active Inst. for Advanced Study, Princeton, N.J., 1970-71, 79-80; exch. visitor NAS, Sofia, Bulgaria, 1984; planning com. Internat. U., Bremen, 1997-99. Author: Differential Analysis on Complex Manifolds, 1973, Mathematics in Civilization, 1973, Twister Geometry and Field Theory, 1990, Wavelet Analysis: The Scaleable Structure of Information, 1998; editor: Mathematical Heritage of Herman Weyl, 1989, (book series) Expositions in Mathematics, 1988—; contbr. numerous articles to sci. jours. Pres. Stages Repertory Theater, Houston, 1989-90. Recipient Alexander von Humboldt Sr. U.S. Scientist award U. Göttingen, 1974-75; Fulbright fellow, 1968, Guggenheim fellow, 1974. Fellow AAAS (coun. 1989—); mem. Am. Math. Soc. (coun., editor 1978-88), Cosmos Club Washington. Home: Lüder-von-Bentheim Str 12 28209 Bremen Germany Office: Internat Univ Bremen PO Box 750561 28725 Bremen Germany E-mail: wells@iu-bremen.de.

WELLS, ROBERT DIAL, soil scientist; b. Newcastle, Tex., Jan. 1, 1920; s. Hawes Coleman and Mabel Crain Wells; m. Myrtle Weaver; children: Nancy(dec.) , Margie, Sally, Evelyn, Robert Ken, William Ben(dec.). BS, Tex. A&M U., 1940; postgrad., Iowa State U., 1966. Soil scientist USDA Soil Conservation, Ga., 1941—65, state soil scientist SC, 1965—76; fighter pilot mem. ready res. U.S. Marine Corps , 1947—50, 1952—74, active duty, capt., 1951—52, ret. col., 1974; fin. planner, 1976—78; soil cons., 1978—90; ret., 1990. Author: Soil Survey Douglas County Georgia, 1959, Soil Survey Meriwether County Georgia, 1963. Lt. USMC, 1942—46, with USMC Reserve, 1947—74. Republican. Avocations: reading, jogging, flower growing. Home: 4550 Storkland Ave Columbia SC 29206-1245

WELLS, ROBERT HARTLEY, chemistry professional; b. Springfield, Mass., Mar. 23, 1926; s. Cecil and Anna (Coates) W.; m. Mary G. Frinzi, May 30 1952 (wid. May 1969); children: Michael J., Brian H., Donald L.; m. Alice G. Asplund, June 20, 1970. BS in Chemistry, U. Maine, 1948, MS in Chemistry, 1950. Instr. in chemistry Lafayette Coll., Easton, Pa., 1950-51; rsch. chemist Celanese Corp., Summit, N.J., 1952-56, S.D. Warren, Westbrook, Maine, 1956-58; epoxy rsch. engr. CIBA Corp., Toms River, N.J., 1958-66; sect. head Foundry Products Borden Cem., Bainbridge, N.Y., 1966-70; sr. rsch. engr. Amoco Chem., Naperville, Ill., 1970-73; product mgr. epoxies Wilmington (Del.) Chem., 1973-76; product mgr. epoxy resins AZS Corp., Lakeland, Fla., 1976-83; cons. chemist, 1983—. Patentee in field; contbr. articles to profl. jours.; photographer exhibits in field. Mem. Toms River Sch. Bd., 1962-66, Garden State Symphony, Toms River, 1963-66; pres. Toms River Jaycees, 1962; photographer SPCA, Lakeland, 1993-2001; vol. photographer Fla. Presbyn. Homes, 1997—; photographer Lakeland Vols. in Medicine, 2001—. Sgt. U.S. Army, 1944-46. Mem. AAAS, Am. Chem. Soc., Photog. Soc. (mem. chmn. 1993-95, Merit Svc. award 1994), Photog. Soc. Am., Am. Contract Bridge League, Polk County Camera Club (pres. 1988-91), Sigma Xi, Kappa Phi Kappa. Republican. Methodist. E-mail: aspwells@msn.com.

WELLS, ROBERT LOUIS, priest; b. Alexandria, La., Mar. 18, 1939; s. Charles Alexander Jr. and Elouise (Hinton) W.; m. Michal Ann McCubbin, Mar. 12, 1966 (div. Oct. 1982); children: Steve, David (dec.), Melissa; m. Carol Hunter, Apr. 3, 1983; 1 child, Matthew. BA, La. State U., 1961; MDiv, Golden Gate Bapt. Theol. Sem., 1965. Pastor Second Bapt. Ch., Lubbock, Tex., 1966-78; exec. dir. Contact Lubbock, Inc., 1979-91; religion tchr. All Saints Episcopal Sch., Lubbock, 1988-91, dir. counseling, 1988-91; pvt.

practice, 1982-91; asst. rector St. Paul's Episcopal Ch., Waco, Tex., 1991-95; chaplain Canterbury Assn. at Baylor U., 1991-95; exec. dir. The William Temple Episcopal Ctr., Galveston, 1995—2002; dir. cmty. hope St. Luke's Episcopal Hosp., Houston, 2002—. Chmn. bd. dirs. Contact USA, Inc., Harrisburg, Pa., 1971-82; treas. secretariat Life Line Internat., Harrisburg, 1979-87. Editor (NASCOD jour.) Chiasma, 1984. Chmn. Community Planning Coun., Lubbock, 1976-79; bd. dirs. United Way of Lubbock, Inc., 1977-78; mem. City-County Child Welfare Bd., Lubbock, 1968-71, South Plains Info. and Referral Bd., Lubbock, 1981, Nat. Assn. Eagle Scouts, Boy Scouts Am., 1979—; chaplain U. Tex. Med. Br., chmn. coun. on religious ministry, 1995-99; Sunday assisting priest Trinity Episcopal Ch., Galveston, 1996-2002; adv. bd. Galveston Hist. Found., 1996-99; bd. trustees Bishop Quin Found., 2001-. Parish Minister's fellow The Fund for Theol. Edn., Inc., 1975-76; named Citizen of Yr. Lubbock unit Tex. chpt. NASW, 1980. Mem. Assn. for Psychol. Type, Masons, Rotary, Lambda Chi Alpha. Democrat. Episcopalian. Avocations: scuba diving, swimming, photography, travel. Home: 9221 Sunbonnet Dr Galveston TX 77584 Office: St Lukes Episcopal Hosp Cmty Hope PO Box 20269 Galveston TX 77225-0269 E-mail: frwells@airmail.net.

WELLS, ROGER STANLEY, software engineer; b. Seattle, Apr. 13, 1949; s. Stanley A. and Margaret W. BA, Whitman Coll., 1971; postgrad., U. Tex., Austin, 1973-74; BS, Oreg. State U., 1977. Software evaluation engr. Tektronix, Beaverton, Oreg., 1979-83; computer engr. Aramco, Dhahran, Saudi Arabia, 1983-84; software engr. Conrac Corp., Clackamas, Oreg., 1984-85, Duarte, Calif., 1985; software analyst Lundy Fin. Systems, San Dimas, 1986-89; pvt. practice Seattle, 1989-92; sr. project engr. Illuminet, Olympia, 1993-2000, mem. Exec. Yr. 2000 com., 1998-99; configuration mgr. New Edge Networks, Vancouver, 2000; sr. product engr. Wind River Systems, Beaverton, Oreg., 2000-01; tech. advisor E-corps Wash. Svc. Corps, 2002—. Bd. dirs. The Lydia Whitney Found., Collinsville, Conn. Bd. dirs. The Sci. Fiction Mus., Salem, Oreg., 1993—; co-founder, bd. dirs., pres. Oreg. Sci. Fiction Conv., 1979-81. Mem. IEEE, Am. Philatelic Soc., Nat. Assn. Parliamentarians, Am. Inst. Parliamentarians (chpt. v.p. 1996-97, pres. 1997-98), Fantasy Amateur Press Assn., Portland Sci. Fiction Soc., N.W. Sci. Fiction Soc., Mensa, Assn. Computing Machinery, L.A. Sci. Fantasy Soc., Melbourne (Australia) Sci. Fiction Club, Toastmasters Internat. (pres. 1980, v.p. edn. 1994-95, area gov. 1994-95, dist. 32 parliamentarian 1996-99). Achievements include designing software program to transfer billing records for regional telephone companies. Avocations: traveling, public speaking, science fiction, stamp collecting. Home: PO Box 92 Yakima WA 98907-0092

WELLS, SAMUEL ALONZO, JR. surgeon, educator; b. Cuthbert, Ga., Mar. 16, 1936; s. Samuel Alonzo and Martha Steele W.; m. Barbara Anne Atwood, Feb. 13, 1964; children: Sarah, Susan. Student, Emory U., 1954—57, MD, 1961. Intern Johns Hopkins Hosp., Balt., 1961—62, resident in internal medicine, 1962—63; asst. resident in surgery Barnes Hosp., St. Louis, 1963—64; resident in surgery Duke U., Durham, NC, 1966—70; guest investigator dept. tumor biology Karolinska Inst., Stockholm, 1967—68; asst. prof. surgery Duke U., Durham, NC, 1970—72, assoc. prof., 1972—76, prof., 1976—81; clin. assoc. surgery br. Nat. Cancer Inst., NIH, Bethesda, Md., 1964—66, sr. investigator surgery br., 1970—72, cons. surgery br., 1975—; prof., chmn. dept. surgery Washington U., St. Louis, 1981—98; dir. ACS, Chgo., 1998—99, dir. Ctr. Clin. Trials and Evidence-Based Medicine, 1999—. Dir. Duke U. Clin. Rsch. Ctr., 1978—81; prof. surgery Duke U. Sch. Medicine, 2000—. Mem. editl. bd.: Annals of Surgery, 1975—93, Mem. editl. bd.: Surgery, 1975—93, Mem. editl. bd.: Jour. Surg. Rsch., 1981—93, editor in chief : World Jour. Surgery, 1983—92, editor in chief : Current Problems in Surgery, 1989—. Pres. GM Cancer Rsch. Found., 1996—. Lt. comdr. USPHS, 1964—66. Mem.: ACS (residency rev. com. for surgery 1987—93, bd. regents 1989—98, chmn. 1991—93, vice chmn. 1995—, exec. dir. 1998—, group chmn. oncology group 1998—), Soc. Internationale de Chirurgie (pres. 2001), Soc. Surg. Oncology (pres. 1993—94), Halsted Soc. (pres. 1987), Nat. Cancer Adv. Bd., Inst. of Medicine of NAS, Am. Soc. Clin. Investigation, Soc. Clin. Surgery (treas. 1980—86, v.p. 1986—88, pres. 1988—90), Soc. Univ. Surgeons (exec. coun. 1976—78), Am. Surg. Assn. (mem. coun. 1986—91, pres. 1995—96, recorder), Am. Bd. Surgery (exec. com. 1986—89, vice chmn. 1987—88, chmn. 1988—89, diplomate, bd. dirs.), Alpha Omega Alpha. Office: Dept Surgery Box 17969 Duke U Sch Medicine Durham NC 27715

WELLS, SAMUEL FOGLE, JR. research center administrator; b. Mullins, S.C., Sept. 13, 1935; s. Samuel Fogle and Mildred Inez (Meeks) W.; m. Novella R. Cloninger, June 15, 1957 (div. 1969); children: Lauren, Anthony (dec.), Jeffrey (dec.); m. Sherrill Perkins Brown, June 7, 1969; 1 child, Christopher Wentworth. AB, U. N.C., 1957; MA, Harvard U., 1961, PhD, 1967. Instr. Wellesley (Mass.) Coll., 1963-65; asst. prof. U. N.C., Chapel Hill, 1965-70, assoc. prof., 1970-78; dir. internat. security studies program Woodrow Wilson Ctr., Washington, 1977-87, assoc. dir., 1985-88, 99—, dep. dir., 1988-98. Cons. Office of Sec. of Def., Washington, 1974-77; trustee Z. Smith Reynolds Found., Winston-Salem, 1977-83. Author: The Challenges of Power: American Diplomacy, 1900-1921, 1990; editor and contbr. to books: Economics and World Power: An Assessment of American Diplomacy Since 1789, 1984, Limiting Nuclear Proliferation, 1985, Strategic Defenses and Soviet-American Relations, 1987, Security in the Middle East: Regional Change and Great Power Strategies, 1987, Superpower Competition and Security in the Third World, 1988, The Helsinki Process and the Future of Europe, 1990, New European Orders, 1919 and 1991, 1996, The Quest for Sustained Growth: Southeast Asian and Southeast European Cases, 1999; contbr. articles to profl. jours. Capt. USMC, 1957-60. Woodrow Wilson fellow, 1957, Danforth Found. fellow, 1957, Peace fellow Hoover Instn., 1972-73, Woodrow Wilson Internat. Ctr. for Scholars fellow, 1976-77. Mem. Am. Hist. Assn., Internat. Inst. for Strategic Studies, Orgn. Am. Historians, Soc. for Historians of Am. Fgn. Rels., Internat. Studies Assn., Coun. on Fgn. Rels. Avocations: hiking, soccer. Home: 1509 Woodacre Dr Mc Lean VA 22101-2538 Office: Woodrow Wilson Internat Ctr 1300 Pennsylvania Ave NW Washington DC 20004-3027 E-mail: wellssam@wwic.si.edu.

WELLS, STEVEN WAYNE, lawyer; b. Ft. Walton Beach, Fla., Sept. 8, 1960; s. H. Wayne and Shirley A. W.; m. Lisa Stieler, May 20, 1983; Robert, James, Jessica. BA in Comm., Mich. State U., 1982; JD with distinction, Detroit Coll. of Law, 1985. Bar: Mich. Asst. prosecutor Oakland County, Pontiac, Mich., 1985-88; mng. ptnr. Schnelz, Bondy & Wells, PC, Troy, 1988-93; shareholder, mng. ptnr. Cross Wrock, PC, Detroit, 1993-99; prin. shareholder Schnelz, Wells, Monaghan & Wells PC, Birmingham, Mich., 1999—. Lectr., presenter in field. Contbr. articles to State Bar Jour. Pres. Bloomfield Village Bd. Fellow Mich. Bar Assn.; ABA, ATLA, Detroit Bar Assn., Mich. Trial Lawyers Assn., Nat. Dist. Attys. Assn. Avocations: golf, tennis, coaching youth baseball, soccer. Address: 255 S Old Woodward Ave Ste 200 Birmingham MI 48009-6184

WELLS, THOMAS B. federal judge; b. 1945; BS, Miami U., 1967; JD, Emory U., 1973; LLM, NYU, 1978. Atty. Graham & Wells, Vidalia, Ga., Hurt, Richardson, Garner, Todd & Cadenhead, Atlanta, Shearer & Wells, Atlanta; city atty. City of Vidalia; county atty. Toombs County, Ga.; judge U.S. Tax Ct., Washington, 1986—, chief judge, 2000—. With USNR, 1967—70. Mem. ABA. Office: US Tax Ct 400 2nd St NW Washington DC 20217-0002

WELLS, VICTOR HUGH, JR. retired advertising agency executive; b. Bloomington, Ill., Apr. 19, 1924; s. Victor Hugh and Wilma Julia (Codlin) W.; m. Jacqueline L. Wade, Nov. 25, 1949; children— Victor Hugh, III, Polly Jo, Ken Douglas. BS, Bradley U., 1948. Copywriter Chgo. Tribune, 1949-54, Earle Ludgin & Co., Chgo., 1954-58, creative dir., 1959-64; group creative dir. Tatham-Laird, 1958-59; founder, creative dir., pres. Rink Wells & Assos. (advt. agy.), 1964-72; exec. v.p., dir. creative services N.W. Ayer Inc., 1972-84, N.Y.C., 1984-86, also bd. dirs.; cons. N. W. Ayer Inc., 1986-91; ret., 1991. Served to 2d lt. AC U.S. Army, 1943-45. Recipient various advt. creative awards, including Clio, Andy awards.

WELLS, ZELLA FAYE, school system administrator; b. Prestonsburg, Ky., Oct. 15, 1948; d. Robert Jackson and Nancy Jane (Stephens) Wallace; m. Frank Allen Wells Jr., Aug. 11, 1972 (div. Dec. 1992). AS, Prestonsburg C.C., 1968; BA, U. Ky., 1970, MA, 1973, Ed.D, 1999. Tchr. Floyd County Schs., Prestonsburg, 1970-72; tchr., instrnl. supr., asst. prin., asst. supt. Johnson County Schs., Paintsville, Ky., 1972—95, 1996—2001; disting. educator Ky. Dept. Edn., Frankfort, 1995-96; state mgr. Floyd County (Ky.) Sch. Sys. Adj. instr. Prestonsburg C.C., 1983-91. Mem. Ky. Edn. Profl. Stds. Bd., Frankfort, 1996-2000, Morehead State U. Big Sandy Adv. Bd., Prestonsburg, 1996—, Ky. Testing and Internship Adv. Bd., Frankfort, 1993-98, Ky. Edn. Assn. Pub. Edn. Task Force, Frankfort, 1996-98. Named Disting. Educator, Ky. Dept. Edn., Frankfort, 1993; recipient Disting. Svc. award Ky. Coun. Tchrs. of Math., 1993, Outstanding Math. Edn. Achievement award Ea. Ky. Coun. Tchrs. of Math., 1993. Mem.: ASCD, Ky. Assn. Sch. Supts., Ky. Assn. Sch. Adminstrs., Univ. Coun. for Edn. Adminstrn., Ky. Assn. Tchr. Educators, Nat. Coun. Tchrs. Math., Am. Ednl. Rsch. Assn., U. Ky. Alumni Assn., Sierra Club, Phi Delta Kappa. Avocations: canoeing, running, birding. Home: PO Box 1024 Paintsville KY 41240-5024 Office: Floyd County Bd Edn 106 N Front St Prestonsburg KY 41653

WELLS BRADLEY, CHARLENA RENEE, editor, writer; b. Cleve., Oct. 2, 1964; BA in Comm., Cleve. State U., 1988. Libr. asst., typist John Carroll U., University Heights, Ohio, summer 1982; asst. sociology dept., registration asst. Cleve. State U., 1985-88; project asst. Jones, Day, Reavis & Pogue, Cleve., 1988-94; asst. writer Righteousness Newsletter, 1990-93; editor-in-chief, writer Holiness Inc., 1993—; project asst. Jones, Day, Reavis & Pogue, 1988-94; adminstrv. exec. USA Mobile Comms., 1994; file adminstrv. clk. Pioneer Stds. Electronics Inc., 1994; mktg. rep. APT Publs., 1996—; adminstrv./registration asst. MBA degree program Case Western Res. U., Cleve., 1996—; telephone operator Roetzel & Andress, 1996—; property asst. Trammell Crow Co., Cleve., 1997-98; counter mgr. lingerie dept. Dillard's, 1998-99, assoc., 1999—; telemarketer Allied Capital Corp., 1999—; sr. sec., outsourcing rep. Kaiser Permanente, Cleve., 2000—; account specialist MBNA Am. Bank, 2001—; pres. Wells Bradley Advice Mail, 2001—. Outsourcing rep. CCS, Kaiser Permanente, Cleve., 2000—; radio asst. Sta. WABQ, Cleve., spring 1987; beauty advisor Fashion Fair Dilliards, 1998; selling specialist J.C. Penney, 1998; bus. builder Shaklee Products, 1998; sr. sec. Kaiser Permanente, 2000—; ind. beauty cons. Mary Kay Cosmetics, 2002—; sr. v.p., sec. Wells Creations. Nursing asst. St. Vincent Charity Hosp., Cleve., 1987; facilitator/exhibit guide Cleve. Children's Mus., 1986; guest spkr. AME Zion Ch., Cleve., 1993, Assembly Missionary Bapt. Ch., Cleve., 1994; lay min. St. Anthony Messenger, 2001; vol. child care ministry Mega Ch., 2001—; Christian actress, psalmist Parma Heights Bapt. Ch., 1998—; co-hostess Sta.-WCIN, Cin., 1991. Acad. scholar John Carroll U., 1982. Avocations: tennis, chess, singing, reading, writing. Home: 11308 Clarebird Ave Cleveland OH 44105 also: 3203 Brunswick Ave Lawrenceville NJ 08648-2409 Office: MBNA 25875 Science Park Dr Beachwood OH 44122 also: Wells Creations 21936 Lakeshore Blvd Euclid OH 44132

WELLS-HENDERSON, RONALD JOHN, investment counselor; b. Shanghai, Jan. 28, 1934; s. William Noel and Sylvia Mary (Gowen) Wells-H.; m. Kathleen Louise McDonnell, Sept. 14, 1957; children— Anne, John. B.A., U. Wash., 1955; M.B.A., Northwestern U., 1957. Chartered fin. analyst. Security analyst Continental Bank, Chgo., 1957-59; fin. analyst Boeing Co., Seattle; trust investment mgr. Seattle Trust, 1970-80; prin. KAS Investment Cons., Seattle, 1980—. Treas., Civil Affairs Assn., 1975-79; curator-treas. Seattle King County Mil. History Soc., 1978-80. Contbr. articles to profl. jours. Mem. Seattle Art Mus., Bellevue Art Mus., 1957—. Served to lt. col. USAR, 1955-83. Gazzam Found. scholar, 1952-55. Mem. Seattle Soc. Fin. Analysts, Inst. Chartered Fin. Analysts, Assn. for Investment Mgmt. and Rsch., Washington Water Trails Assn. Episcopalian. E-mail: RonW-H@prodigy.net. Home: 13005 SE 46th St Bellevue WA 98006-2042 Office: KAS Investment Cons PO Box 5617 Bellevue WA 98006-0117

WELLS-MAXWELL, VIOLET, writer, artist; b. Redkey, Ind., Aug. 3, 1927; d. James William Philebaum and Etta Catherine Hunt; m. Paul Eugene Wells, Sept. 5, 1947 (dec. May 1975); children: Carol Parrott, Randy Wells, Joy Wells; m. Rudolph Neff Maxwell, Sept. 22, 1990. BBA, Olivet Nazarene U., 1949. Sec. Olivet Nazarene U., Kankakee, Ill., 1947-49; receptionist Speech Clinic Ohio State U., 1950-54; art and music instr. Ea. Nazarene Coll., Boston, 1955-69; art tchr., 1960-99; receptionist Office for Fin. Aid to Students Mt. Vernon (Ohio) Nazarene Coll., 1970-73; realtor assoc. Gtr. Ohio Realty, Mt. Vernon, 1974-76; real estate assoc. Century 21 Dalbec, Willsboro, N.Y., 1976-82; nutrition supr. Shaklee Products, Mt. Vernon, Ohio, 1990—2002. Exhbns. include Dixie Days Street Fair, Mt. Vernon, 1997, Dan Emmett Festival, 1994-96, Mt. Vernon (Ohio) News, 1988, Lake Holm Ch. Gallery, Mt. Vernon, 1988, Heritage Hall Gallery, Mt. Vernon, 1996-98. Mem. ch. choir, Mt. Vernon, 1970-75; active Celebration of the Arts high sch., middle sch., Mt. Vernon, 1992-99. Mem. Poetry Appreciation, Mt. Vernon Pub. Libr. Avocations: Mark Twain, reading poetry, singing, restoring art work. Studio: 500 N Gay St Mount Vernon OH 43050-1708 E-mail: vjw@ecr.net.

WELLSTONE, PAUL, senator; b. Arlington, Va., July 21, 1944; s. Leon and Minnie W.; m. Sheila Wellstone, 1963; children: David, Marcia, Mark. BA, U. N.C., 1965, PhD Polit. Sci., 1969. Tchr. Carleton Coll., Minn.; U.S. senator from Minn., 1991—. Mem. U.S. Senate coms. small bus., energy and natural resources, Indian affairs, labor and human resources, Senate Dem. policy com., chmn. subcom. rural economy and family farming; mem. com. fgn. rels., 1997—; mem. com. health, edn., labor & pensions, 1991—; ranking mem. fgn. rels. subcom. on Near Eastern and South Asian affairs, health, education, labor and pensions subcom. on employment safety and tng. Author: How the Rural Poor Got Power, Powerline. Dir. Minn. Community Energy Program. Office: US Senate 136 Hart Senate Office Bldg Washington DC 20510-0001*

WELLY, MICHAEL ANTHONY, elementary school educator; b. Tiffin, Ohio, Jan. 31, 1958; s. Martin Ralph and Clara Alice (Kimmet) W. BS, Bowling Green State U., 1980. Elem. tchr. St. Bernards Sch., New Washington, Ohio, 1980—2001, St. Helen Sch., 2001—; co-dir. Power of the Pen, 2001—. Dir. sci. fair St. Bernards Sch., 1980—, sch. mus. dir., 1984-89, sci. tournament dir., 1989-99, student coun. advisor, 1993—; mem. local profl. devel. com. 1998—; tchg. cons. Ohio Geographic Alliance, 1998—. Bd. dirs. Bucyrus (Ohio) Little Theatre, 1986-97; EMT New Washington Ambulance, 1983-2000, asst. adminstr., 1990-2000; EMT New Riegel (Ohio) Emergency Med. Svcs., 1983-88; mem. Diocesan Curriculum com., Toledo Diocese, 1994-96. Named DARE Tchr. of Yr. Crawford County Sheriff Dept., 1992-93, 95. Mem. Nat. Coun. Tchrs. English, Nat. Cath. Edn. Assn., Crawford County Reading Assn. Avocations: theater work, record collecting, old time radio programs. Office: St Helen Sch 5086 Burkhardt Rd Dayton OH 45431

WELMAKER, FORREST NOLAN, lawyer; b. McKinney, Tex., Aug. 13, 1925; s. Felix E. and Forrest Love (Baker) W.; div.; children: Forrest Nolan Jr., Mary Elizabeth Welmaker Young, Byron Skillin. BBA, U. Tex., 1950, LLD, 1953. Bar: Tex. 1953, U.S. Dist. Ct. (so. and we. dists.) Tex. 1956, U.S. Ct. Appeals (5th cir.) 1956, U.S. Tax Ct. 1959, U.S. Supreme Ct. 1956. Pvt. practice, San Antonio, 1953—. Past bd. dirs., officer United Fund San Antonio, San Antonio chpt. ARC, Children Welfare Bur. San Antonio, San Antonio YMCA. Capt. USNR, 1943-46, PTO, 1950-52, Korea. Fellow Tex. Bar Found., San Antonio Bar Found.; mem. San Antonio Bar Assn. (past bd. dirs., v.p., pres.), Tex. Assn. Def. Counsel, San Antonio Res. Officer Assn., Tex. Bar Assn. (past bd. dirs.), San Antonio Pla. Club, San Antonio German Club. Episcopalian. Avocations: handball, boating. Home: 114 W Brandon Dr San Antonio TX 78209-6404 E-mail: nwelmaker@ev1.net.

WELNA, CECILIA, mathematics educator; b. Kensington, Conn., July 15; d. Joseph and Sophie (Roman) W. BS, St. Joseph Coll., 1949; MA, U. Conn., 1952, PhD, 1960. Instr. Mt. St. Joseph Acad., 1949-50; asst. instr. U. Conn., 1950-55; instr. U. Mass., Amherst, 1955-56; prof., chmn. dept. math. and physics U. Hartford, 1957-82, dean Coll. Edn., Nursing and Health Professions, 1982-91, prof. math., 1991—. Mem. Math. Assn. Am., Nat. Council Tchrs. Math., Assn. Tchrs. Math. Conn., Sigma Xi. Office: U Hartford Dana 295A Bloomfield Ave West Hartford CT 06117 E-mail: seawell31@aol.com.

WELNA, JEROME SHELDON, agriculturist, consultant; b. Lynch, Nebr., Sept. 3, 1923; s. Lorayne M. Welna, May 15, 1945 (div. May 1961); children: Linda, Jeannette, Gregory, Debra; m. Jeannette Gertrude Welna, Feb. 18, 1972. BSc in Agr., Calif. State Polytechnic Co., San Luis Obispo, 1951; cert. computer programming, Minn. Sch. Bus., Mpls., 1967. Dir. edn., assoc. scientist Salsbury Labs., Charles City, Iowa, 1951-58; poultry cons. Doughboy Industries, Inc., New Richmond, Wis., 1958-61, San Diego, 1961-71; various mgmt. positions Schering-Plough Corp., Kenilworth, N.J., 1971-94; poultry health cons. Prescott, Ariz., 1994-95; poultry health specialist, cons., 1996—. Cons., 1952—; spkr. in field. Author: Poultry House Sanitation, Flock Health, and Hatching Egg Care, 1962, Escherichia Coli in Turkeys, 1962, also numerous poultry disease manuals. With USN, 1943-45, ETO, PTO. Republican. Episcopalian. Avocations: scuba diving, photography, woodworking, writing, WWII history. Office: PO Box 4159 Prescott AZ 86302

WELPOTT, JACK WARREN, photographer, educator; b. Kansas City, Kans., Apr. 27, 1923; s. Ray Calvert and Dolores (Davenroy) W.; m. Doris Jean Franklin, June 12, 1949; children— Jan Marie, Matthew David; m. Judy Dater, May 22, 1969; m. Wendy Brooke Gray, May 11, 1986. BS, Ind. U., 1949, MS, 1954, M.F.A., 1959. Mem. acad. staff Ind. U., 1949-59; mem. faculty San Francisco State U., 1959-93, ret., 1993. Artist in residence RISD, 1984; workshop leader Columbia Coll., 1985, Friends of Photo, 1985, Humboldt State U., 1985, Parsons Sch. Design, Paris, 1985, Volcano Hawaii, 1986, numerous others in France, England, Switzerland, Japan and Mexico. One man shows include, U. Calif., Davis, Art Inst. Chgo., 1972, Wall Street Gallery, Spokane, 1973, Gallery 113, Santa Cruz, Calif., 1974, San Francisco Mus. Art, 25 year retrospective, 1976, U. So. Calif., 25 year retrospective, 1977, Ind. U., 25 year retrospective, 1977, Silver Image Gallery, Seattle, 1977, Ohio State U., 1978, Center for Creative Photography, U. Ariz., 1979, Colo. Mountain Coll., 1980, Bard Coll., 1981, Jehu Gallery, San Francisco, 1981, Galerif Voor Fotografie, Antwerp, Belgium, 1983, R.I. Sch. Design, 1984, La Photographie Creative, Pavillon des Arts, Paris, 1984, New Sch. Social Research, N.Y.C., 1984, Foto Biennale Enschede, Netherlands, 1984, Vision Gallery, San Francisco, 1984, Min Gallery, Tokyo, 1987, Osaka (Japan) Cultrual Ctr., 1989, Retrospective Vision Gallery, San Francisco, 1992; two man shows include Musee Reattu, Arles, France, 1976, Photographers Gallery, Palo Alto, Calif., 1986, group exhbns. include Santa Barbara Mus., Mus. Modern Art, Mexico City, Photography in Am, Whitney Mus., N.Y.C., Photography in the 20th Century, George Eastman House, California Photography, Oakland Mus., San Francisco Mus. Art, U. Oreg. Commitment to Vision, 1986, U. Colo. Photographics, 1986, numerous others, Met. Mus. Art, N.Y.C., De Cordova Mus., Lincoln, Mass.; represented in permanent collections Graham Nash Collection, Mus. Modern Art, N.Y.C., Whitney Mus. Art, N.Y.C., Art Inst. Chgo., Biblioteque Nat, Paris, Tokyo Coll. Photography, Open U., London, Internat. Mus. Photography, Rochester, N.Y., San Francisco Mus. Art, Musee Reattu, Arles, Frances, Oakland (Calif.) Mus., U. Colo., Center Creative Photography, Tucson, U. N.Mex., Pasadena Art Mus., Australian Nat. Gallery, Houston Mus. Fine Arts, Fogg Art Mus., Cambridge, Mass., Gallery Van Haarlem, Netherlands; author: The Halide Conversion, 1989; contbr. photos to books. Served with USAAF, 1943-46. NEA fellow, 1979; grantee Polaroid, 1983, Marin Arts Coun., 1991. Home: PO Box 496 Inverness CA 94937-0496 E-mail: jax@svn.net.

WELSCH, KENNETH ROBERT, estate planner, mortgage consultant; b. Chgo., Feb. 28, 1938; s. Philip and Violet (Rose) W.; m. Renee R. Chardell, Oct. 15, 1979; children: Kenneth M., Kimberly J. Welsch Bentel; stepchildren: Lisa A. Templeton, Joel E. Gappa, John E. Gappa. BS in Chemistry, U. Ill., Chgo., 1961; cert. in mgmt., Dartnell Inst. of Mgmt., Chgo., 1973. Cert. estate planner, advanced underwriter. Assoc. gen. agt. A. Eppel & Assocs., North Brook, Ill., 1975-80; estate planner Welsch, Bertolino & Assocs., River Grove, 1980-83, Welsch, Kasper & Assocs., Hoffman Estates, 1983-87, Barrington (Ill.) Fin. Group, 1987—. Pres. Barrington Sq. Homeowners Assn., Hoffman Estates, Ill. 1983-87; v.p. No. Ill. Bus. & Profl. Assn., Inc., Northbrook, 1975-80; resource authority Nat. Assn. Ret. Persons, Chgo., 1984-85. Named Life Ins. Agt. of Yr. Life Ins. Industry, 1975. Mem. Internat. Assn. Fin. Planning (practitioner divsn.). Avocations: boating, photography. Office: Barrington Fin Group PO Box 3008 Barrington IL 60011-3008 E-mail: kennethwelsch@msn.com.

WELSER-MÖST, FRANZ, conductor; b. Linz, Austria, Aug. 16, 1960; s. Andreas von Bennigsen and Marilies (Wetzelsberger) Möst. Chief condr. Sinfonieorkester Norrköping, Sweden, 1986-91, Stadtorchester Winterthur, Switzerland, 1987-90; music dir. London Philharm., 1990—. Conducting debut Salzburg Festival, Austria, 1985; Am. debut St. Louis, 1989; condr. Vienna Opera, 1987, Berlin Opera, 1991. Office: care Artists Mgmt Co Pf 1131 FL-9490 Vaduz Liechtenstein also: Severance Hall 11001 Euclid Ave Cleveland OH 44106*

WELSH, SIR ALFRED JOHN, lawyer, consultant; b. Louisville, May 10, 1947; s. Elvin Alfred and Carol (Kleymeyer) W.; m. Lee Mitchell, Aug. 1, 1970; children: Charles Kleymeyer, Kathryn Thomas. BA, Centre Coll., 1969; JD, U. Ky., 1972; LLM in Internat. Law cum laude, U. Brussels, 1973. Bar: Ky. 1972, U.S. Dist. Ct. (we. and ea. dists.) Ky. 1972, U.S. Ct. Appeals (6th cir.) 1972. Asst. atty. Ky. Atty. Gen. Office, Frankfort, 1973-74; legis. counsel to congressman Ho. of Reps., Washington, 1974-77; mng. ptnr. Adams, Hayward and Welsh, Louisville, 1977—, Boone Welsh and Hayward Internat. Law. Hon. counsel of Belgium, 1983—; econ. devel. advisor Kingdom of Belgium; mem. Ky. Econ. Adv. Coun., 1991-94; pres. Transcontinental Trading Cons., Ltd.; del. North African Mideast Econ. Summit Conf., Morocco, 1994; bd. dirs. Intervention Resources Ctr., Inc. Bd. dirs. Greater Louisville Swim Found., 1983-94, exec. com., 1994—; bd. dirs. Louisville com. Coun. Fgn. Rels., 1993—, also pres.; bd. dirs. Jefferson County Alcohol and Drug Abuse Found., Louisville, 1986-98, Internet. Resolve, Louisville Internat. Cultural Ctr.; mem. econ. task force of Ky. Legis. Agts. Decorated knight Order of the Crown (Belgium). Mem. ABA (internat. law sect., commn. on impairment), ATLA, Ky. Bar Assn. (bd. dirs. 1981-82, pres. young lawyers divsn. 1981-82), Ky. Acad. Trial Lawyers, Am. Judicature Soc., Louisville C. of C. Democrat. Presbyterian. Avocations: swimming, water polo, soccer. Office: Barristers Hall 1009 S 4th St Louisville KY 40203-3207

WELSH, DONALD EMORY, publisher; b. Youngstown, Ohio, Oct. 6, 1943; s. Edward Francis and Clevelle Rose W.; m. Elizabeth Bourne Floyd, June 25, 1966; children: Leah Bourne, Emory Philip. AB, Columbia U., 1965; JD, Cleveland Marshall Sch. Law, 1969. Bar: Ohio 1969. Trust devel. officer Cleve. Trust Co., 1968-70; advt. sales rep. Fortune mag., Time, Inc., N.Y.C., 1970-75; advt. dir. Rolling Stone mag., 1975-77, v.p., assoc. pub., 1977-78; pub. Outside mag., N.Y.C., 1978-82; pub. Muppet mag. and pres. Lorimar Pub. Group (formerly Telepictures Publs., Inc.), 1982-87; pres. Welsh Pub. Group, Inc., 1987-94; exec. v.p. Marvel Comics Group, N.Y.C., 1994-96; chmn. Group XXVII Comms., 1997-2000; pres. pub. group Digital Convergence Inc., 2000-2001; chmn. Budget Living Commn., 2001—. Trustee Outward Bound, U.S.A.; former bd. dirs. Big Apple Circus. Mem. ABA. Mag. Pubs. Assn. (past bd. dirs.), Century Assn., Racquet and Tennis Club, Sharon Country Club (Conn.), Ocean Reef Club (Fla.). Home: 501 E 79th St New York NY 10021-0735 Office: Budget Living Commn 317 Madison Ave Ste 2300 New York NY 10017 E-mail: DonaldEWelsh@aol.com.

WELSH, DORIS MCNEIL, early childhood education specialist; b. Kansas City, Mo. d. Zelbert Melbourne and Anna May (Main) McNeil; children: J. Randall, Valerie M. BA, U. Calif., Berkeley, 1950, MA, 1952; postgrad., U. San Francisco, 1980-82. Cert. tchr., counselor, supr., Calif. Asst. dir. Bing Sch., Stanford, Calif., 1966-76; family devel. specialist Children's Hosp., 1976-78; rsch. cons. Stanford U. Med. Ctr., 1970-87; dir. One Fifty Parker Sch., San Francisco, 1978-99; assoc. Lawrence Hall of Sci., U. Calif., Berkeley, 1996—. Citizen amb. del. edn. and childcare People to People Internat., St. Petersburg, Russia, Vilnius, Lithuania, Budapest, Hungary, 1993; pres. bd. dirs. Support for Parents of Spl. Children, San Francisco, 1986-87; bd. dirs. Family Svc. Assn. Mid-Peninsula, Palo Alto, Calif., 1970-80; leader Summer Camp for Pre-Schoolers, East Palo Alto, 1970-73; leader parenthood discussion groups U. Chgo., 1963-64; lectr. in field; cons., 1999—. Vol. Irving Mental Hosp., Chgo., 1963. Mem. Nat. Assn. Edn. Young Children, Assn. Childhood Edn. Internat., World Affairs Coun., Audubon Soc., Sierra Club. Avocations: natural sciences, hiking, horseback riding, gardening. Office: 26630 Ascension Dr Los Altos CA 94022-2001

WELSH, GEORGE FRANKLIN, plastic surgeon, educator, healthcare consultant; b. Charles City, Iowa, Oct. 13, 1940; s. George S. Welsh and Aldeen (Paris) Welsh Taylor; m. Rosemary Dahlen, June 23, 1973; children: Christopher Franklin, Penelope Cosette, Bradford Alexander. BA, Carleton Coll., 1962; BS, U. N.D., 1964; MD, Harvard U., Boston, 1966; M Health and Hosp. Adminstrn., Xavier U., Cin., 1994. Diplomate Am. Bd. Surgery, Am. Bd. Plastic Surgery; cert. Commn. Med. Mgmt. Commd. officer USAF, 1966, advanced through grades to lt. col., 1974; intern USAF Hosp., San Antonio,

1966-67; flight surgeon USAF, Thailand, 1967-69; resident in surgery Mayo Clinic, Rochester, Minn., 1969-73; resident in plastic surgery U. Okla. Health Sci. Ctr., Oklahoma City, 1973-75; plastic surgeon USAF, Dayton, Ohio, 1975-78, dir. base med. svcs. United Arab Emirates, 1991; ret. USAFR, 1996; pvt. practice, Cin., 1978—. Cons. on healthcare adminstrn., Cin., 1994—; asst. clin. prof. surgery Wright State U. Sch. Medicine, Dayton, 1975-78; vol. asst. prof. surgery U. Cin. Sch. Medicine, 1978-2002. Contbr. articles to med. jours., including Surg. Clinics N.Am., Jour. Thoracic and Cardiovasc. Surgery, So. Med. Jour., Plastic and Reconstructive Surgery, Aesthetic Plastic Surgery, Brit. Jour. Plastic Surgery, Mil. Medicine, Health Care Fin. Mgmt., Jour. Health Care Fin., Quality Progress, Physician Exec. Mem. Leadership Cin., 1981; citizen amb. People to People Internat., Albania, Russia, 1994, Cuba, 2000; vice-chmn. Hamilton County Alcohol and Drug Addiction Svc. Bd., Cin., 1999—. Fellow ACS; mem. Am. Coll. Healthcare Execs., Am. Coll. Physician Execs. (cert.), Am. Soc. Plastic Surgeons, Am. Soc. for Aesthetic Plastic Surgery, Millard Plastic Surg. Soc. (past pres.), English Spkg. Union (past pres. Cin. br.), Soc. Colonial Wars Ohio (dep. gov. gen.), Harvard Club Ohio Valley (regional dir.). Avocations: public health and medical-surgical missions. Office: Aesthetic Plastic Surgery Ctr 6200 Pfeiffer Rd Ste 320 Cincinnati OH 45242-5861

WELSH, JAMES JOHN, computer consultant; b. Huntington, N.Y., Nov. 4, 1966; s. Brian James and Alice Theresa (Weiler) W.; m. Diane Romano, July 9, 1988; children: Matthew James, Daniel Joseph, Jake Alexander. AS, Champlain Coll., 1990. Programmer Whalstrom & Co., Inc., Stamford, Conn., 1990-91; cons. software WELCON, Port Chester, N.Y., 1991-92; dir. mktg. Dancik-On-Disk Internat., Ltd., Raleigh, NC, 1993—98; pres. Weller Enterprioses, Inc., Wilson, 1995—2000; owner The Welsh Tile Co., Charlottesville, Va., 2000—. Republican. Lutheran. Avocations: cycling, oil painting, weight lifting, music. Office: Welsh Tile Co 105 S Panhops Dr Ste B-5 Charlottesville VA 22963

WELSH, JOHN BERESFORD, JR. lawyer; b. Seattle, Feb. 16, 1940; s. John B. and Rowena Morgan (Custer) W. Student, U. Hawaii, 1960, Georgetown U., 1960; BA, U. Wash., 1962; LLB, 1965. Bar: Wash. 1965. Staff counsel Joint Com. on Govtl. Cooperation, 1965-66; asst. atty gen. Dept. Labor and Industries, 1966-67; atty. Legis Counsel; acting as counsel Pub. Health Com., Labor Com., Pub. Employees Collective Bargaining Com., Com. on State Instns. and Youth Devel., State of Wash., 1967-73; sr. counsel Wash. Ho. of Reps., Ho. Com. on Social and Health Svcs., Olympia, WA, 1973-86; atty., spkr. Ho. of Reps., 1973; counsel Ho. Com. Human Svcs., 1987-91, 93-95, Ho. Com. on Health Care, 1987—. Counsel Ho. Com. on Trade and Econ. Devel., 1995-98, Joint Select Com. on Nurse Delegation, 1995-98, Joint Select Com. on Oral Health, 1996. legal cons. Gov's. Planning Commn. Vocat. Rehab., 1968, Gov.'s Commn. on Youth Involvement, 1969; envoy from Gov. Wash. to investiture of Prince of Wales, London, 1969, fac. Nat. Conf. State Legislatures, Denver, 1977, New Orleans, 1977; fac. Coun. Licensure, Enforcement and Regulation, San Francisco, 1984, Orlando, Fla., 1985, Denver, 1986, Kansas City, Mo., 1987, Washington, 1988, Indpls., 1989, Seattle, 1990, Ft. Lauderdale, Fla., 1991, Albuquerque, 1992, Boston, 1994, San Antonio, 1995, Norfolk, 1997; steering com., 1986-90, legis. issues com., 1986-88, Coun. of State Govts. com. on suggested state legis., 1988-95, subcom. scope and agenda, 1988-95. Vol. Hampton Rds. U.S. Naval Mus., mem. gov's. state medal merit com., 1986—. Recipient Gov.'s award for Excellence in State Health Care Policy, 2002. Mem. Wash. Bar Assn., Govtl. Lawyers Assn., Nat. Health Lawyers Assn., Soc. des Amis du Musee de l'Armee, Paris, English Speaking Union, La Societe Napoleoienne (pres.), Medals Soc. Am., Sons of Union Veterans of the Civil War, Custer Battlefield Hist. & Mus. Assn., 8th Army Air Force Hist. Assn., Northwest Hist. Assn. (bd. dirs.), The Colonial Williamsburg Found., Napoleonic Alliance (bd. dirs.), Alliance Francaise (Seattle), Friends of Willie & Joe, Phi Delta Phi. Home: 1700 Evergreen Park Lane SW Olympia WA 98502

WELSH, JOHN FRANCIS, retired advertising executive; b. New Haven, May 19, 1916; s. Pierce Jerome and Irene (Kennedy) W.; m. Margaret Burke, Sept. 18, 1947; children: Peter Burke, Diana Margaret. BA, Yale U., 1937. With Warwick & Legler, Inc., N.Y.C, 1946-81; exec. v.p., mgmt. supr., mem. mgmt. com.; vice chmn. Warwick, Welsh & Miller, Inc., 1973-81. Served with AUS, 1941-45. Decorated Bronze Star, Croix de Guerre France). Mem.: Tokeneke (Darien). Home: 98 Ridge Acres Rd Darien CT 06820-2616

WELSH, JUDITH SCHENCK, communications educator; b. Patchogue, L.I., N.Y., Feb. 5, 1939; d. Frank W. and Muriel (Whitman) Schenck; m. Robert C. Welsh, Sept. 16, 1961; children: Derek Francis, Christopher Lord (dec.). BEd, U. Miami (Fla.), 1961, MA in English, 1968. Co-organizer Cataract Surg. Congress med. meetings, 1963-76; grad. asst. instr. Dale Carnegie Courses Internat., 1967; adminstr. Office Admissions, Bauder Fashio Coll., Miami, 1976-77, instr. comms., 1977—, also pub. coll. monthly paper. Freelance writer regional and nat. publs.; guest spkr. Optifair Internat., N.Y.C., 1980, Fla. Freelance Writers Assn. ann. conf., Ft. Lauderdale, 1991, Suncoast Writers' Conf., Tampa, Fla., 2000, Book Island Festival, Fernandina, Fla., 2000; guest spkr., mem. seminar faculty Optifair West, Anaheim, Calif., 1980, Optifair Midwest, St. Louis, 1980, Face to Face, Kansas City, Mo., 1981; conf. dir. So. Fla. Writers Conf., Nat. Writers Assn./U. Miami, 1997—98, 1999—2000. Co-editor: The New Report on Cataract Surgery, 1969, Second Report on Cataract Surgery, 1974; editor: Surgidev's Cataract Surgery N.O.W., 1982—; contbr. Miami Today, Ft. Lauderdale Sun/Sentinel, Prime Times, Club Life, Gainesville Sun, The Oklahoman, South Fla. mag., Miami Herald; staff writer (internet cos.): AOS, staff writer (internet cos.): Press-Release-Writing.Com. Mem. NAFE, Fla. Freelance Writers Assn., Nat. Writers Club (award), Nat. Writers Assn. (conf. dir. 1997-2000), Coral Reef Yacht Club, Riviera Country Club, Rotary Internat. (Paul Harris award), Delta Gamma. Congregationalist. Home and Office: 1600 Onaway Dr Miami FL 33133-2516

WELSH, MARY MCANAW, family mediator, educator; b. Cameron, Mo., Dec. 7, 1920; d. Francis Louis and Mary Matilda (Moore) McAnaw; m. Alvin F. Welsh, Feb. 10, 1944 (dec.); children: Mary Celia, Clinton F., M. Ann. AB, U. Kans., 1942; MA, Seton Hall U., 1960; EdD, Columbia U., 1971. Reporter Hutchinson (Kans.) News Herald, 1942-43; house editor Worthington Pump & Machine Corp., Harrison, N.J., 1943-44; tchr., housemaster, coord. Summit (N.J.) Pub. Schs., 1960-68; prof. family studies N.Mex. State U., Las Cruces, 1972-85; adj. faculty dept. family practice Tex. Tech Regional Acad. Health Ctr., El Paso, 1978-82, Family Mediation Practicce, Las Cruces, 1986—. Author: A Good Family is Hard to Found, 1972, Parent, Child and Sex, 1970; contbr. articles to profl. jours.; writer, presenter home econs. and family study series KRWG-TV, 1974; moderator TV series The Changing Family in N.Mex./LWV, 1976. Mem. AAUW (pres. N.Mex. 1981-83), N.Mex. Coun. Women's Orgn. (founder, chmn. 1982-83), Delta Kappa Gamma, Kappa Alpha Theta. Democrat. Roman Catholic. Home and Office: 1975 Avenida Antigua Las Cruces NM 88005

WELSH, MICHAEL LOUIS, business executive; b. Clayton, Ga., June 14, 1959; s. John F. and Mary Ann (Casimes) W.; m. Susie Googe, June 5, 1982; children: Sarah Alex, Daniel, Grace, Samuel BBA magna cum laude, U. Ga., 1981, MACC, 1986. Consolidation acct. Tex. Instruments, Dallas, 1981-82, fin. analyst, 1982-84; v.p. cons. MISA, Atlanta, 1986-87; consolidation analyst Coca-Cola Enterprise, 1987-88; mid-Atlantic supr., mgr. Coca-Cola Bottling Co., Columbia, Md., 1988-90; div. mgr. Coca-Cola Enterprises-North, 1990-91; ops. controller Cott Beverages USA, Columbus, Ga., 1993-95; v.p. adminstrn. Thompson Hardwoods, Inc., Hazlehurst, 1995-98; owner Michael Welsh Media, Evans, 1998—. Acctg. and system implementation cons., Dallas and Athens, Ga., 1982-86. Youth leader Ascension Ch., Dallas, 1982-83, St. Michael's Ch., Stone Mountain, Ga., 1986-88, St. John's Episc. Ch., Ellicott City, Md., 1988-91; leader Approved Workers Are Not Ashamed-AWANA, 1995-98, 2000-02, Altamaha Youth Soccer Assn., pres. 1996-98, co-founder; bd. trustees Westside Bapt. Ch., 2000-02; treas. Riverchase Homeowners Assn., 2002. Mem. U. Ga. Alumni Soc. (pres. Dallas chpt. 1983-84), Blue Key, Golden Key, Phi Kappa Phi, Beta Gamma Sigma, Phi Eta Sigma, Beta Alpha Psi, Phi Kappa Psi. Baptist. Avocations: sports, reading. Office: Michael Welsh Media PO Box 1983 Evans GA 30809-1983

WELSH, PETER CORBETT, museum consultant, historian; b. Washington, Aug. 28, 1926; s. Arthur Brinkley and Susan Jane (Putney) W.; m. Catherine Beatrice Allen, Nov. 27, 1951 (div. 1969); children— Susan Jane, Peter Corbett; m. Caroline Levert Mastin, Sept. 8, 1970; 1 child, James Munson Corbett. BA, Mt. Union Coll., Alliance, Ohio, 1950; postgrad., U. Va., 1950-51; MA (Hagley fellow), U. Del., 1956. Research asst., fellowship coordinator Eleutherian Mills-Hagley Found., Wilmington, Del., 1956-59; assoc. curator dept. civil history Mus. History and Tech., Smithsonian Instn., 1959-61; curator Growth U.S., 1962-64, curator dept. civil history, 1964-69, asst. dir. gen. mus. of instn., 1969-70, dir. Office Mus. Programs, 1970-71; dir. N.Y. State Hist. Assn., Cooperstown, 1971-74; vis. prof. Cooperstown Grad. Program, N.Y. State Hist. Assn.; dir. Cooperstown Grad. Programs, 1971-74; dir. spl. projects N.Y. State Mus., Albany, 1975-76; dir. Bur. Mus., Pa. Hist. and Mus. Commn., 1976-84; pres. The Welsh Group, 1984-86; curator The Adirondack Mus., Blue Mountain Lake, N.Y., 1986-88, sr. historian, 1988-89; mus. cons., lectr., 1989—. Adj. prof. SUNY; cons. FDR Mus. and Little White House, Warm Springs, Ga., 1968-72; trustee Landon Sch., Bethesda, Md., 1964-70; bd. dirs., mem. exec. com. Ctr. for Conservation of Hist. Art and Artifacts, 1979-83; bd. dirs. Lake Placid Ctr. for the Arts, 1992-96; mem. publs. adv. com. The Adirondack Mus., 2002--. Author: Tanning in the United States: A Brief History, 1964, American Folk Art: The Art and Spirit of the People, 1967, Track and Road: The American Trotting Horse, 1820-1990, 1968, The Art of Enterprise: A Pennsylvania Tradition, 1983, Jacks, Jobbers and Kings: Logging the Adirondacks, 1850-1950, 1996; contbr. articles to profl. publs.; editor Smithsonian Jour. History, 1967-70. Served to 1st lt. AUS, 1951-54. Mem. Am. Hist. Assn., Am. Studies Assn., Am. Assn. Mus., N.Y. State Assn. Mus. (council 1971-75), Am. Assn. State and Local History (publ. com.), Soc. History of Tech., Sigma Nu. Clubs: Country of Harrisburg. Democrat. Roman Catholic. Office: 34 Second St Tupper Lake NY 12986-2011

WELSH, RONALD ARTHUR, physician, educator; b. Houston, Oct. 13, 1926; s. Leo Arthur and Octavia Virginia (Franssen) W.; m. Mary Jeanne Duncan, June 24, 1950; children: Mary Jeanne, William, James. AB, U. Tex., 1947, MD, 1950. Intern USPHS, Hosp., New Orleans, 1950-51; resident in pathology USPHS, Balt., 1951-55; chief pathology USPHS Hosp., Galveston, Tex., 1955-57; asst. prof. pathology L. Tex. Med. Br., 1955-57, La. State U., New Orleans, 1957-59, asso. prof., 1959-61, prof., 1961-98; chief surg. pathology Charity Hosp., New Orleans, 1975-93. Cons. forensic pathology Orleans Parish Coroner, 1961-79; cons. path. Va. Hosp., New Orleans, 1971—; Mem. La. Commn. on Narcotics and Rehab., 1970-72; Bd. dirs. La. div. Am. Cancer Soc., 1960-89, La. div. Am. Cancer Soc. (nat. div.), 1966-68, nat. del. dir., 1980-86. Served with USNR, 1944-46; Served with USPHS, 1950-57. Recipient Distinguished Prof. award La. State U. Alumni Assn., 1973-74, Asclepian award Am. Cancer Soc., New Orleans unit, 1992; honored with establishment of Ronald A. Welsh professorship pathology La. State U., 1998. Mem. AMA, Internat. Acad. Pathology, Am. Soc. Clin. Pathologists, Coll. Am. Pathologists, Assn. Pathologists, La., Orleans Parish med. socs., Phi Beta Kappa, Alpha Omega Alpha, Nu Sigma Nu. Republican. Episcopalian. Home: 2429 Octavia St New Orleans LA 70115-6533 Office: 1901 Perdido St New Orleans LA 70112-1328

WELSH, WILLIAM DANIEL, geriatric medicine family practice physician; b. Balt., May 18, 1950; s. Joseph Leo and Bessie Mary (Tangires) W.; m. Loraine Lynn Barkhaus, July 11, 1985; children: Sean William, Ryan Daniel. Student, Johns Hopkins U., 1971; BS in Biology cum laude, Fairleigh Dickinson U., 1972; DO, Coll. Osteo. Medicine-Surgery, Des Moines, 1975. Diplomate Nat. Bd. Osteo. Physicians; cert. ATLS; approved supr. physician assts. Osteophatic Med. Bd. Calif.; radiography and fluoroscopy x-ray supr., operator Calif. Intern Martin Place Hosp., Madison Heights, Mich., 1975-76, resident in internal medicine, 1976-77; pvt. practice Detroit, 1977-79; pvt. practice, Whittier, Calif., 1979—. Instr. ACLS, L.A., 1980-92; bd. dirs. Whittier Hosp. Med. Ctr., 1981, vice chief staff, 1982-84, med. dir. family asthma forum, 1979-88, med. dir. Summit Place alcohol treatment program, 1983-88; med. dir. Mirada Hills Rehab. Hosp., La Mirada, Calif., 1980-88; former clin. preceptor Coll. Osteo. Med. Pacific, Pomona, Calif., clin. assoc. prof. internal medicine; mem. dept. family practice, physician rev. com. Friendly Hills Regional Med. Ctr., La Habra, Calif., 1994-97; mem. staff Presbyn. Intercmty. Hosp., Whittier, Whittier Hosp. Med. Ctr., chmn. by laws com. 1999-2001, mem. exec. com. 1999-2001; med. dir. Berryman Health Convalescent Hosp. Participant Calif. Beach Clean Up Day, 1996. Recipient Physician Recognition award AMA, 1991, 95, 96, Commn. of Merit Rep. Nat. Com., 1995. Mem. Am. Osteo. Assn., Am. Coll. Osteo. Family Physicians, Osteo. Physicians and Surgeons Calif., Am. Coll. Osteopathic Family Practitioners (bd. cert. family practice 1991, geriatrics 2000), L.A. Osteopathic County Med. Assn. Avocations: boating, skiing, reading, tennis. Home: 16871 Marina Bay Dr Huntington Beach CA 92649-2913 Fax: 562-592-4225. E-mail: wdwelsh@juno.com., wdwelshdo@ipninet.com.

WELSHONS, WADE VINCENT, biomedical sciences educator; b. Berkeley, Calif., Oct. 6, 1951; s. William John and Harriett Jean Welshons; m. Susan Carol Nagel, Jan. 1, 1998; children: John William, Samantha Marie. BA, Yale U., 1973; PhD, Harvard U., 1981. Asst. prof. U. Mo., Columbia, 1987-94, assoc. prof., 1994—. Mem. AAAS, Endocrine Soc., Harvard Club of St. Louis, Yale Club of St. Louis. Office: U Mo Dept Biomed Sci E102 Vet Medicine Columbia MO 65211-5120 E-mail: WelshonsW@missouri.edu.

WELSOME, EILEEN, journalist; b. N.Y.C., Mar. 12, 1951; d. Richard H. and Jane M. (Garity) W.; m. James R. Martin, Aug. 3, 1983. BJ with honors, U. Tex., 1980. Reporter Beaumont (Tex.) Enterprise, 1980-82, San Antonio Light, 1982-83, San Antonio Express-News, 1983-86, Albuquerque Tribune, 1987-94, Westword Newspaper, Denver, 2000-01. Author: The Plutonium Files, 1999. Recipient Clarion award, 1989, News Reporting award Nat. Headliners, 1989, John Hancock award, 1991, Mng. Editors Pub. Svc. award AP, 1991, 94, Roy Howard award 1994, James Aronson award, 1994, Gold Medal award Investigative Reporters and Editors, 1994, Sigma Delta Chi award, 1994, Investigative Reporting award Nat. Headliners, 1994, Selden Ring award, 1994, Heywood Broun award, 1994, George Polk award, 1994, Sidney Hillman Found. award, 1994, Pulitzer Prize for nat. reporting, 1994, PEN/Martha Albrand award for first nonfiction, 2000; PEN/West Literary award for rsch. nonfiction PEN, 2000; John S. Knight fellow Stanford U., 1991-92. E-mail: ewelsome@aol.com.

WELT, PHILIP STANLEY, lawyer, consultant; b. Freeport, N.Y., July 5, 1959; s. Morris and Rose (Offenberg) W.; m. Karen Teresa Gault, May 22, 1994. BBA summa cum laude, Hofstra U., 1983; MBA, Columbia U., 1988; JD cum laude, NYU, 1995. Bar: N.J. 1995, N.Y. 1995; U.S. Dist. Ct. N.J. 1995, U.S. Dist. Ct. (so. and ea. dists.) N.Y. 1996, U.S. Ct. Appeals (2d cir.), 1997, U.S. Ct. Appeals Armed Forces, 2000, U.S. Supreme Ct. 1999; CPA, N.Y. Sr. mgr. Deloitte & Touche, N.Y.C., 1983-92; assoc. Reboul MacMurray Hewitt Maynard & Kristol, 1993, Davis Polk & Wardwell, N.Y.C., 1994, 1996-2001; jud. clk. U.S. Dist. Ct. N.J., Newark, 1995-96; special asst. dist. atty. Kings Co., N.Y., 1999—; asst. gen. counsel Am. Internat. Group, Inc., 2001—. Bd. dirs., treas. Pub. Interest Law Found., N.Y.C., 1993-94; guest spkr. Boy Scouts Am., Nassau County, 1984-91, Nat. Assn. Accts., N.Y./N.J., 1988-92, others. Sr. editor Columbia Jour. World Bus., 1986-88; sr. exec. editor Ann. Survey Am. Law, 1993-95; contbr. articles to profl. jours. Vol. income tax asst. Dept. Treasury, IRS, N.Y.C., 1981-87; vol. Variety-The Children's Charity, N.Y.C., 1985-87; advisor Friends of Jon Kaiman, Nassau County, 1995. Provost's scholar Hofstra U., 1981-83, Deloitt & Touche fellow Columbia U., 1986-88; recipient Appreciation cert. Dept. Treasury, IRS, 1981-87, Variety, 1985-87, Bovenaan Outstanding Cmty. Svc. award Hofstra U., 1983, Orison S. Marden Moot Ct. Advocacy award NYU Sch. Law, 1993, Seymore A. Levy meml. award, 1995. Mem. ABA, AICPA, N.Y. State Bar Assn., N.Y. State Soc. CPAs, Beta Alpha Psi, Beta Gamma Sigma. Avocations: golf, rock climbing, photography, philately, amateur radio. Home: 157 Mountain Wood Rd Stamford CT 06903-2107 Office: Am Internat Group Inc 70 Pine St New York NY 10270 E-mail: psw12Wcolumbia.edu.

WELTE, A. THEODORE, chamber of commerce executive; b. Mankato, Minn., Feb. 11, 1944; s. Arthur William and Bernice (Town) M.; m. Kathleen P. Browne, May 3, 1969; 1 child, Jason N. BA in Sociology, Psychology, Mankato State U., 1966, MA in Econs., 1972; cert., U. Notre Dame, 1987; cert. mgmt., Stonehill Coll., 1990. Cert. chamber exec. Program officer, br. officer Peace Corp, Washington, 1968-69; rsch. dir. Tech. Found., W.Va. Tech., Montgomery, 1969-70; project dir. Self-Help, Inc., Brockton, Mass., 1972-73; regional planner, planning supr. Old Colony Planning Coun., 1974-81; pres., CEO Metro West C of C., 1981-90, MetroWest C. of C., Framingham, Mass., 1990—. Trustee Brockton Regional Econ. Devel. Corp., 1982-90; treas. Brockton Area Pvt. Industry Coun., 1987-89. Cubmaster pack 68 Boy Scouts Am., Easton, Mass., 1989-90, com. chair troop 86, 1991-94, bd. dirs. Algonquin/Knox Trail coun., 1991—, v.p. exploring, 1996-99. Mem. New Eng. Assn. C. of C. Execs. (sec. 1990-91, 2d v.p. 1991-92, 1st v.p. 1992-93, pres. 1993-94), Mass. Assn. C. of C. Execs. (pres. 1988-89), Rotary (sec. Brockton 1988-90, v.p. Framingham 1990-92, pres. 1993-94). Presbyterian. Office: MetroWest C of C 1671 Worcester Rd Ste 201 Framingham MA 01701-5400 E-mail: ted@metrowest.org.

WELTER, LINDA ALLAIRE, development executive; b. Bayonne, N.J., Aug. 11, 1949; d. Godfrey Adolf and Grace Elizabeth (Buss) W. BA in Philosophy and Polit. Sci., Drew U., 1971, postgrad., 1972-73, Harvard U., 1985; MBA, Boston Coll., 1987. Development asst. Harvard U., Cambridge, Mass., 1980-83, development assoc., 1983-85, dir. class and area programs, 1985-86, sr. development officer, 1986-87; from capital campaign dir. to asst. v.p. for resources Wellesley (Mass.) Coll., 1987-93; v.p., gen. mgr. for development ops. ARC, Washington, 1993-94; dir. major gifts U. Calif., Berkeley, 1994—. Instr. Stonehill Coll., Easton, Mass.; lectr. Northeastern U., Boston; cons. Vassar Coll.; fundraising cons. Dimock Comty. Health Ctr., Boston, 1992. Vol. co-chair fundraising Ruah; mem. capital campaign com. Fenway Cmty. Health Ctr.; vol. Nat. Network on Women as Philanthropists. Mem. Women in Development (bd. dirs., chair city svc. project), Coun. for Advancement and Support of Edn. (teaching faculty 1985—), Women in Philanthropy. Avocations: Alpine and Nordic skiing, sailing, mountain climbing, writing, photography. Address: 7 Alveston St Jamaica Plain MA 02130-2804 Office: U Calif Univ Rels 2440 Bancroft Way Berkeley CA 94704-1603

WELTER, WILLIAM MICHAEL, marketing and advertising executive; b. Evanston, Ill., Nov. 18, 1946; s. Roy Michael and Frances (DeShields) W.; m. Pamela Bassett, June 11, 1971; children: Barclay, Robert Michael. BS, Mo. Valley Coll., 1966. Account exec. Leo Burnett Co., Inc., Chgo., 1966-74; v.p., account supr. Needham Harper Worldwide, 1974-80; v.p. mktg. Wendy's Internat., Inc., Dublin, 1981, sr. v.p. mktg., 1981-84, exec. v.p., 1984-87; owner, chief exec. officer Haunty & Welter Advt. Agy., Worthington, 1987-91; sr. exec. v.p. mktg. Rax Restaurants Inc., Dublin, 1992; exec. v.p. mktg. Metromedia Steakhouses, Inc., Dayton, 1992-93; sr. v.p. mktg. Metromedia Co., 1993-95; exec. v.p., chief mktg. officer Heartland Foods Inc., Dublin, 1995-96; exec. v.p. brand mgmt. Late Nite Magic, Inc., Las Vegas, Nev., 1996—99; pres., CEO W.M. Welter & Assocs., 1996—; pres. Wings West LLC, 1999—, Buffalo Wild Wings, Inc., Las Vegas, 2001—. Founder Santa's Silent Helpers, Columbus, Ohio, 1985 Mem. Advt. Fedn. Las Vegas, Spanish Trail Country Club. Avocations: golf, fishing. Home: 1517 Angelberry St Las Vegas NV 89117-1372 Office: 8084 W Sahara Las Vegas NV 89117 Fax: 702 360-8379. E-mail: billwingman@cs.com.

WELTERS, ANTHONY, health services executive; BA in economics, Manhattanville Coll.; JD, NYU. Atty. SEC; exec. asst. to Sen. Jacob Javits; sr.-level positions Amtrak and U.S. Dept. Transp.; chmn. bd. and CEO Americhoice, 1989—. Vice chmn. bd. Morehouse Sch. Medicine; mem. bd. Healthcare Leadership Coun., NYU Law Sch., Wolf Trap Found. Recipient Horatio Alger award, 1998. Office: Americhoice 8045 Leesburg Pike Ste 650 Vienna VA 22182*

WELTMAN, DAVID LEE, lawyer; b. Springfield, Mass., Jan. 12, 1933; s. Sol Walter and Esther (Ziskind) W.; m. Lois Handmaker, Sept. 2, 1956; children: John, Elizabeth, Herman, Sally. AB, Yale U., 1954; LLB, Harvard U., 1957. Bar: Mass. 1957. Assoc. Mintz, Levin & Cohn, Boston, 1957-60; v.p. Ansonia Mills, Inc., Taunton, Mass., 1960-63; assoc. Foley, Hoag & Eliot, Boston, 1963-67, ptnr., 1967—. Sec., clk. Charles River Assocs., Boston, 1965-97, Brigham Med. Group Found., 1972—, Siemens-Nixdorf Info. Systems, Burlington, Mass., 1979-94, Am. Brush Co., Clairmont, N.H., 1982-92. Chmn. leadership devel. coun. Jewish Fedn. and Welfare Funds, 1966-68; trustee New Eng. Med. Ctr., Boston, 1970-82, Combined Jewish Philanthropies, Boston, 1970—, Hebrew Coll., Boston, 1995—; chmn. Newbury Coll., Boston, 1972—, Lown Cardiovasc. Rsch. Found., 1993—; incorporator Mus. Sci., Boston, 1972-92, Boston U. Med. Ctr., 1965-96; pres. Beaver Country Day Sch., Chestnut Hill, Mass., 1975-80, Jewish Cmty. Ctr., Brookline and Newton, 1968-71; bd. overseers South Shore Hosp. Found., Weymouth, Mass., 1990—. Recipient Young Leadership award Combined Jewish Philanthropies, 1968, Class of 1954 award Yale U., 1989, Founders Day award Beaver Country Day Sch., 1991. Mem. ABA, Boston Bar Assn., Nat. Health Lawyers Assn., Cohasset Golf Club, Cohasset Yacht Club, Downtown Club. Avocations: tennis, sailing. Home: 90 Gammons Rd Cohasset MA 02025-1406 Office: Foley Hoag & Eliot 1 Post Office Sq Ste 1700 Boston MA 02109-2175

WELTON, ALICE GORDON (ALICE GUILFOY), artist; b. Balt., May 26, 1948; d. John Berryman and Helen (Gaddy) Guilfoy; m. James Frank Welton, Nov. 23, 1968; children: Jaime Alan, Eric Grahame. Student, No. Ill. U., 1966-67, Elgin C.C., 1976-79, 87-89; studied sculpture and pottery with, Dale Raddatz and Michael Brown, 1972-74; studied watercolor with, Alan Yau, 1981-83. Lic. commodities broker, series 3, 1997. Draftsperson Western Electric, Rolling Meadows, Ill., 1968-69; tech. illustrator Hallicrafters, Palatine, 1969-70; advt. mgr. ABC Records & Tapes, Elk Grove, 1970-71; performer, studio singer Chgo., 1972-76; fine artist Welton Fine Arts, Elgin, Ill., 1977—. Instr. gifted art program U46 Sch. Dist. Coleman Sch., Elgin, 1982; presenter watercolor workshop U. Wis., Whitewater, 1982, Des Plaines (Ill.) Art Guild, 1987, handmade paper workshop Mary Bell Galleries, Chgo., 1989, Lincoln Coll., 1990; guest artist Artist to Artist, 1990. One-woman shows include Ill. Inst. Tech., Chgo., 1987, Mary Bell Galleries, Chgo., 1983, 84, 85, 86-87, 88, 89, 90, 92, 95, Judith Posner Gallery, Milw., 1989, 93, Mary Bell Galleries, 1995; exhibited in group shows at Mazur-Mazur Gallery, Deerfield, Ill., 1982, Mary Bell Galleries, 1983, 84, 86, 88, 93, 94, 95, 96, No. Ill. U. Swen Parson Gallery, DeKalb, 1986, Art Expo, N.Y.c., 1988, Katy Gingrass Galleries, Milw., 1993, Corp. Artworks, Schaumburg, Ill., 1993, 94; juried and nat. competitions House Gallery Mus., Oklahoma City, 1981, Westmoreland County Mus. Art, Greensburg, Pa., 1982, others; corp. collections include United Airlines, Arthur Young, Amoco, Prudential Ins. of Chgo., OCE USA, Chgo. Title and Trust, La Salle Internat. Group, Inc., Marshall Field and Co., Nat. Assn. Ind. Insurers; represented by Mary Bell Galleries, Chgo., Boritzer, Gray, Hamano Gallery, L.A., Corp. Art Works, Schaumburg, Katie Gingrass Gallery, Windsor Gallery, Dania, Fla. 2d degree Black Belt instr. Kwon's Taekwondo, Bloomingdale, Ill., 1992-93. Recipient Sparring Gold medal Wis. State Champion World Taekwondo Fedn., exec. sr. div. 1991, Forms Gold medal, Sparring Bronze medal Ill. State Champion, 1992, Forms Gold medal, Sparring Silver medal Nat. Champion World Taekwondo Fedn. Hampton (Va.) Coliseum, 1992. Mem. Am. Watercolor Soc. (assoc.), Midwest Watercolor Soc., Ill. Watercolor Soc., Ga. Watercolor Soc., Chgo. Artist Coalition. Avocations: martial arts, reading, commodities trading, writing, designing Japanese gardens and landscaping.

WELTON, CHARLES EPHRAIM, lawyer; b. Cloquet, Minn., June 23, 1947; s. Eugene Frances and Evelyn Esther Welton; children: Spencer, Marshall. BA, Macalester Coll., 1969; postgrad., U. Minn., 1969-70; JD, U. Denver, 1974. Bar: Colo. 1974, U.S. Dist. Ct. Colo. 1974, U.S. Supreme Ct. 1979, U.S. Ct. Appeals (10th cir.) 1980; cert. civil trial advocate Nat. Bd. Trial Advocacy, 2001. Assoc. Davidovich & Wanifuchi, Denver, 1974-77, Charles Welton and Assocs. and successor firms, Denver, 1978-86; ptnr. OSM Properties, 1982-97; prin. Brock House, LLC, 1997—. Prin. Charles Welton, P.C., 1986—; adj. prof. Inst. Advanced Legal Studies U. Denver, 1991-98; polit. and social commentator; lectr. in field; instr. Nat. Inst. Trial Advocacy, 1998-2001, Lorman Ednl. Svcs., 1999-2001. Author instrnl. materials; editor profl. publications; contbr. articles to profl. jours. Sch. pres. PTSA, Denver, 1983-84; coach Colo. Jr. Soccer League, 1980-85; coach Odessey of Mind (formerly Olympics of Mind), 1986-88; bd. dirs. Virginia Vale Swim Club, officer, 1989-91; bd. dirs. Pioneer Jr. Hockey Assn., 1990-92. Served alt. mil. duty Denver Gen. Hosp., 1970-72. Mem. ATLA, Denver Bar Assn. (facilitator bench/bar retreat 1995, 96, chmn. legal fee arbitration com. 2002—), Colo. Bar Assn. (interprofl. com.), Colo. Trial Lawyers Assn. (bd. dirs. 1985-90, chmn. seminar com. 1986-88, exec. com. 1987-88, legis. com. 1988-94, case assistance com. 1995—, keyperson 1997—), Am. Bldg. a Lasting Earth (founder), Exec. Ventures Group of Am. Leadership Forum (founding adv. bd. 1987-90). Democrat. Home: 680 Vista Ln Lakewood CO 80215-6037 Office: The Brock House 1800 Gaylord St Denver CO 80206-1211 E-mail: welton@charleswelton.com.

WELTON, MICHAEL PETER, dentist; b. Milw., Apr. 19, 1957; s. Lloyd Peter and Allegra (Nimmer) W.; m. Lucia Aldon, Jan. 29, 1994. BS in Biology cum laude, Carroll Coll., 1979; DDS, U. Minn., 1983. Commd. lt. USN, 1983; resident Naval Hosp. Camp Pendleton, Oceanside, Calif., 1983-84; with periodontics dept. Naval Dental Clinic, Yokosuka, Japan, 1984-85; clinic dir. Negishi Dental Annex, Yokohama, Japan, 1985-87; gen. dentist Br. Dental Clinic, Mare Island Naval Sta., Vallejo, Calif., 1987-90; pvt. practice gen. dentistry. Vacaville, 1990—. Legis. extern Am. Student Dental Assn., Washington, 1982; student rep. Minn. Dental Assn., Mpls., 1980. Fellow Acad. Dentistry Internat.; mem. ADA, Calif. Dental Assn. (ho. of dels. 1996-98, com. rules and order 1998), Napa-Solano Dental Soc. (exec. com. 1995-98, bd. dirs. 1990-95, pres. 1997), Art Deco Soc. Calif., No. Calif. Golf Assn., Vacaville C. of C., Tilden Park Golf Club, Delta Sigma Delta (treas. Mpls. chpt. 1982-83, Outstanding Mem. award 1982-83), Ducks Unltd. (dinner com. 1997—), Rotary (bd. dirs. Vacaville 1997-99, sec. 1999—, Paul Harris fellow 1997). Avocations: golf, skiing, tennis, reading, gardening, hunting. Office: 3000 Alamo Dr Ste 103 Vacaville CA 95687-6345 Home: 59 Emerald Cir Vallejo CA 94589-2737

WELTY, CHARLES DOUGLAS, lawyer; b. Houston, Mar. 16, 1952; s. Charles I. and Jane Douglas (Mullane) W.; m. Anita Katherine Blair, Feb. 24, 1986. BA, Rice U., 1974; JD, U. Va., 1982. Bar: N.Y. 1983, D.C. 1984, Va., 1988, U.S. Supreme Ct. 1996. Assoc. Lord, Day & Lord, N.Y.C., 1982-84; pvt. practice Washington, 1984-86; assoc. Eckert, Seamans et. al., 1986-88; pvt. practice Arlington, Va., 1988-91; ptnr. Welty & Blair, P.C., 1991—. Sr. editor Va. Jour. Internat. Law, 1980-82. Lt. USN, 1974-79, Indian Ocean. Mem. Federalist Soc., Fed. Am. Inn of Court, The Army & Navy Club (Washington), Va. Bar Assn., Christian Legal Soc. Office: Welty & Blair PC 2111 Wilson Blvd Ste 550 Arlington VA 22201-3051

WELTY, JOHN DONALD, academic administrator; b. Amboy, Ill., Aug. 24, 1944; s. John Donald and Doris (Donnelly) W.; m. Sharon Welty; children: Anne, Elisabeth, Bryan, Darren, Heather. BS, Western Ill. U., 1965; MA, Mich. State U., 1967; Ed.D., Ind. U., 1974. Asst. v.p. for student affairs SW State U., Marshall, Minn., 1973-74; dir. residences SUNY-Albany, 1974-77, assoc. dean for student affairs, 1977-80; v.p. for student and univ. affairs Indiana U. of Pa., 1980-84, pres., 1984-91, Calif. State U., Fresno, 1991—. Lectr. in field; chair Am. Humanics. Contbr. articles to profl. jours. Recipient Chancellor's award SUNY, 1977, Chief Exec. Leadership award Coun. for Advancement and Support of Edn., 1999, John Templeton Found. award for leadership in student character devel., 1999. Mem. Fresno Bus. Coun., Fresno Econ. Devel. Commn., Sunnyside Country Club. Lodges: Rotary. Roman Catholic. Office: Calif State U 5241 S Maple Ave Fresno CA 93725-9739 E-mail: johnw@csufresno.edu.

WELTY, JOHN RIDER, lawyer; b. Waynesboro, Pa., Nov. 5, 1948; s. Richard Samuel and Mary Catherine (Rider) W.; m. Susan Eileen Mescall, Aug. 7, 1970; children: John R. II, David Richard, Brian James. BA in Econs., Shippensburg State U., 1970; JD, Am. U., 1975. Bar: Pa. Economist bur. econ. analysis U.S. Dept. of Commerce, Washington, 1970-76; staff atty. to sr. atty. Carpenter Tech. Corp., Reading, Pa., 1976-82, assoc. gen. counsel, 1982-89, dir. law, 1989-90, dir. law, asst. sec., 1990-91, gen. counsel, asst. sec., 1991-92, gen. counsel, sec., 1992-93, v.p., gen. counsel, sec., 1993—. Founder Drexelwood Cmty. Assn., Wyomissing, Pa., 1981-82; bd. dirs. Cornwall Terr. Cmty. Assn., Sinking Spring, Pa., 1977-79; mem. Sch. Bd., Conrad Weiser Area Sch. Dist., 1992-97; asst. commr. Hawk Mountain coun. Boy Scouts Am., 1991-96. Mem. ABA, Pa. Bar Assn., Am. Corp. Counsel Assn., Pa. Self Insurers Assn. (bd. dirs. 1978-81), Phi Alpha Delta, Alpha Phi Omega. Republican. Avocations: tennis, golf, reading. Office: Carpenter Tech Corp PO Box 14662 1047 N Park Rd Wyomissing PA 19610-1339

WELTY, KENNETH HARRY, civil engineer; b. Spirit Lake, Iowa, July 16, 1933; s. Kenneth Bertram and Josephine Louise (Tott) W.; m. Patricia Julienne Fremming, June 22, 1958; chidlren: David Keith, Michael Kent, Lisa Ann Welty Pagliocchini. BS in Civil Engring., U. Ariz., 1961. Highway engr. trainee U.S. Bur. Pub. Rds., Washington, 1961-64; highway rsch. engr. U.S. Dept. Trans. Fed. Highway Adminstrn., 1964-67, highway engr. Office Planning, 1967-98; ret., 1998. Leader Boy Scouts Am., Springfield, Va., 1970-82; watch coord. Fairfax County Neighborhood Watch, Springfield, 1990--. With U.S. Army, 1955-57. Mem. Tau Beta Pi. Methodist. Home: 6423 Cabell Ct Springfield VA 22150-1326

WELTZ, MARTIN DAVID, oncologist, hematologist; b. Phila., Jan. 18, 1948; m. Sharon Frankfort; children: Michael, Adam. BS in Biology, Bklyn. Coll., 1969; DO, U. for Health Scis., 1973; postgrad., Johns Hopkins U. Diplomate Nat. Bd. Med. Examiners for Osteo. Physicians and Surgeons, Am. Bd. Internal Medicine, (subspecialty of med. oncology, subspecialty of hematology, subspecialty hospice and palliative medicine). Commd. 2d lt. USMC, 1973, advanced through grades to lt. col., 1981; intern Walter Reed Army Med. Ctr., Washington, 1973-74, resident, 1974-76, fellow hematology and med. oncology sect., 1976-79, attending physician dept. internal medicine, 1979-81, staff hematologist, med. oncologist, dir. med. edn., 1979-80, chief divsn. head Clin. Cancer Chemo-Pharmacology Rsch. Lab., 1979-80, asst. chief, dir. clin. pharmacy hematology-med. oncology, 1980-81; resigned USMC, 1981; pvt. practice, v.p. Hematology-Oncology Cons., Greenbelt, Md., 1983—, v.p., sec., 1986—; pres. med.-dental staff Laurel Regional Hosp., 1993-99; chmn. dept. internal medicine Washington Adventist Hosp., 1997-2001. V.p., sec., 1986—; attending med. staff AMI Drs. Hosp., Prince George's County, Lanham, Md., 1983, Washington Adventist Hosp., Takoma Park, Md., 1983—, sec.-treas. dept. internal medicine, 1991-94, asst. chmn., 1994-97; asst. chief hematology/med. oncology Prince Georges Hosp. Ctr., 1986—; staff Laurel Regional Hosp., 1983—, chmn. hematology-med. oncology, 1989—, med. dir. Hospice in Prince George's County, 1989—, chmn. dept. internal medicine, 1989-92, chmn. tumor bd., 1989—, chmn. employees ann. benefit med.-dental staff, 1990—, chmn. med. exec. com., 1993—, pres. med. and dental staff, 1993—, trustee, 1993—; ; bd. dirs. Dimensions Corp., Landover, Md., sec.-treas. bd. dirs., 1990—; pres. Med. Dental Staff laurel Regional Hosp., 1993—; vice chmn. Dept. Internal Medicine, Washington Adventist Hosp., 1994—; chmn. Dimensions Health Care Network PHO, 1994—; med. dir. Hospice in Prince Georges County, 1990—, Hospice of the Chesapeake, 2000—; bd. dirs. Universal Health Care Network, Medi-Cen of Md.; bd. dirs., found. chmn. med. exec. com., pres. med.-dental staff Laurel Region Hosp., 1993—; bd. dirs. Dimensions Healthcare Network, Dimensions Health Care Corp. Medi-Cen of Md. and Universal Healthcare Corp., Cancer Care, Inc.; med. dir. hospice, P.G. County, 1992-99; chmn., founder tumor bd. Laurel Regional Hosp. and Washington Adventist Hosp., 1988—; chmn. transfusion com. Washington Adventist Hosp., 1990—; sec. Laurel Hosp. Found., 2000—. Contbr. articles to profl. jours. Bd. dirs. Am. Cancer Soc., Prince George's County, 1981—; med. advisor cansurmount program Am. Cancer Soc., Montgomery County, Md., 1982-90; ring dir. Ea. Regional Karate Tournament, Montgomery Coll., Rockville, Md., 1987—; mem. advisor Md. Blood Ctr., 1987-88; mem. med. adv. bd. Hospice Prince George's County, Largo, Md., 1991—, active archtl. and design com., capital campaign com., bldg. com., 1992—; mem. com. Parent Fund and Centurion Campaign; bd. dirs. Found. Laurel Regional Hosp., 1993—, others. Fellow ACP, Acad. Medicine N.J.; mem. AMA, Am. Soc. Internal Medicine, Am. Soc. Clin. Oncology, Am. Soc. Hematology, Acad. Hospice and Polliative Medicine, Am. Coll. Clin. Pharmacology, Am. Coll. Osteo. Internists, Am. Soc. Clin. Oncologists, Am. Coll. Physician Execs., Am. Soc. Clin. Pharmacology and Therapeutics, Am. Soc. Contemporary Medicine and Surgery, Am. Fedn. for Clin. Rsch., Royal Soc. Medicine (London), Md. Osteo. Assn., Oncology Soc. N.J., N.J. Soc. Internal Medicine, N.Y. Acad. Scis., N.Y. Oncology Soc., Md. Soc. Clin. Oncology, George Washington U. Parent Assn., Luther Rice Soc., Johns Hopkins Alumni Assn. Office: Greenway Center Dr Greenbelt MD 20770 E-mail: martinweitz@aol.com.

WELU, JAMES A. art museum director; b. Dubuque, Iowa, Dec. 15, 1943; s. Andrew L. and Anna E. (Riley) W. BA, Loras Coll., 1966; MA, U. Notre Dame, 1967, MFA, 1968; PhD, Boston U., 1977. Instr. St. Mary-of-the-Woods (Ind.) Coll., 1968-70; asst. curator Worcester (Mass.) Art Mus., 1974-76, assoc. curator, 1976-80, instr., 1977-78, 80-81, chief curator, 1980-86, dir., 1986—. Instr. Clark U., Worcester, 1980. Panelist Mass. Coun. on Arts and Humanities, Boston, 1981-82, 90, Utilization of Mus. Resources Nat. Endowment for the Arts, 1988; trustee Williamstown Regional Art Conservation Lab., Inc., Mass., 1981-86; mem. panel Utilization Mus. Resources, NEA, 1988. Boston U. grantee, 1973, NEA Mus.' Profl. grantee, 1976-81; Samuel H. Kress Found. fellow, 1973; recipient Netherland-Am. Found. award Netherland Found., 1973, Disting. Alumni award Boston U. Grad. Sch., 1986. Mem.: Historians Netherlandish Art, New Eng. Mus. Assn., Am. Assn. Mus. (accreditation commr. 2000—), Coll. Art Assn. Am., Am. Fedn. Arts (trustee), Assn. Art Mus. Dirs. (pres. 1999—2000, trustee). Home: 10 Massachusetts Ave Worcester MA 01609-1649 Office: Worcester Art Mus 55 Salisbury St Worcester MA 01609-3196

WEMPNER, GERALD ARTHUR, engineering educator; b. Waupun, Wis. s. Paul Christian and Thekla Nelda (Jung) W.; m. Lorraine Bischel, Sept. 6, 1952 (div. Apr. 1983); children: Susan K., Paul J. BS, U. Wis., 1952, MS, 1953; PhD, U. Ill., 1957. Instr. U. Ill., Urbana, 1953-57, asst. prof., 1957-59; assoc. prof. U. Ariz., Tucson, 1959-62; prof. U. Ala., Huntsville, 1964-73, Ga. Inst. Tech., Atlanta, 1973-91, prof. emeritus, 1991—. Vis. prof. U. Calif., Berkeley, 1962-63. Author: Mechanics of Solids, 1973; co-author: Mechanics of Deformable Bodies, 1961, Mechanics of Solids, 1995; contbr. articles to profl. jours. With U.S. Army, 1946-48. NSF fellow, Stanford (Calif.) U., 1963-64, Sr. fellow Alexander von Humboldt Found., Germany, 1973, Killam fellow U. Calgary, Can., 1983. Fellow ASME (asssoc. editor 1976-83), Am. Acad. Mechanics. Avocations: art, sculpture, photography, woodwork. Home and Office: 3397 Hidden Acres Dr Doraville GA 30340-4445

WEN, GEYI, applied physics educator; b. Pingjiang, Hunan, China, Dec. 28, 1962; s. Zhiwu and Meiran Li Wen; m. Jun Yuan Wen, Jan. 22, 1988; 1 child Lan. BS, Xidian U., Xian, China, 1982, MS, 1984, PhD, 1987. Lectr. S.E. U., Nanjing, China, 1988-90; assoc. prof. U. Electronic Sci. and Tech. China, Chengdu, 1990-92, prof., 1993—. Vis. rschr. U. Calif., Berkeley, 1992-93j; vice chmn. Inst. Applied Physics, U. Electronic Sci. and Tech. China, 1996-97, chmn., 1997—; vis. prof. U. Waterloo, Can., 1998; EM rschr. Rsch. in Motion, Can., 1998—. Author: Modern Methods for Electromagnetic Computation, 1996, Advances in Electormagnetic Theory, 1999; contbr. articles to profl. jours. Recipient Talent through Century award Sichuan Province, Chengdu, China, 1994, Sci. and Tech. Progress award China Soc. Sci. and Tech., 1996, Talent through Century award Nat. Edn. Com., Beijing, 1996. Mem. IEEE (editl. bd. IEEE Transactions on Microwave Theory & Techniques 1992—), China Soc. Computational Physics (mem. couns. 1992—), China Inst. Electronics (editl. bd. Jour. Electromagnetic Waves 1997—). Avocations: table tennis, Chinese chess. Office: Rsch in Motion 295 Phillip St Waterloo ON Canada N2L 3W8 E-mail: gwen@rim.net.

WEN, HUNGTAO JOSEPH, management educator; b. July 20, 1958; PhD, Va. Commonwealth U., 1993. Asst. prof. N.J. Inst. Tech., Newark, 1994-98, assoc. prof., 1999—. Office: N J Inst Tech Sch Mgmt 211 Stewart Ave Newark NJ 07102-1982

WEN, SHEREE, computer company executive; BS in Physics, Natural Tsiug Hua U, Taiwan; PhD, U. Calif., Berkeley, 1979. Rsch. divsn. staff IBM, 1979-81, dept. mgr. Materials, Characterization and Analysis, 1981-84, program mgr. Tech., 1984-86, sr. mgr of Optics 1986, prog. mgr., tech. asst. to sr. v.p.; pres. WenLab USA Inc., N.Y.C. Patentee in field; Contbr. articles to profl. jours. Recipient John E. Dom Achievement award Am. Soc. for Metal, 1978, Outstanding tech. Achievement award, IBM, 1986, invention Achievement award, IBM, 1987; The Robert Lansing Hardy gold Metal The Metals, Materials & Minerals Soc. (TMS-AIME); the AIME as the most promising young Materials Scientist in Am., 1979 Mem. TMS-AIME's Process Monitor & Control Com. (chmn.), Materials Design & Mfg. Divsn. Award Com.; Indsl. Liaison for U. Calif. at Berkeley's ctr. for Materials. Office: WEN Tech Corp 999 Central Park Ave Yonkers NY 10704-1088 Fax: 914-376-7092.

WEN, SHIH-LIANG, mathematics educator; b. Peoples Republic of China; came to U.S., 1959; s. S.W. and C.F. (Hsiao) W.; m. Liang Tao; children: Dennis, Andy, Jue, Nannan. BS, Nat. Taiwan U., Taipei, 1956; MS, U. Utah, 1961; PhD, Purdue U., 1968. Assoc. research engr. The Boeing Co., Seattle, 1961-63; with dept. math. Ohio U., Athens, 1968—, successively asst. prof., assoc. prof. and prof., chmn. dept. math., 1985-93. Rsch. analyst Applied Math Rsch. Lab. USAF, Wright-Patterson AFB, Ohio, summer, 1972; vis. rsch. scientist Courant Inst. Math. Scis. NYU, 1978-79; hon. prof. Jiangxi U., People's Republic of China, 1985; disting. vis. prof. Lanzhou U., People's Republic of China, 1989. Mem. Am. Math. Soc., Soc. for Indsl. and Applied Math., Math. Assn. Am. Avocations: fishing, bridge, music. Office: Ohio Univ Dept Of Math Athens OH 45701

WEN, SIHAI, research engineer, materials scientist; b. Wuhu, Anhui, China, Oct. 26, 1970; s. Shizhong and Meizhu (Hu) W.; m. Xianping Li, Oct. 25, 1995. BS, Nanchang Inst. Aero-Tech., Jiangxi, China, 1992; MS, South China U. Tech., Guangzhou, Guangdong, China, 1995. Rsch. asst. South China U. Tech., Guangzhou, 1992-95; rsch. engr. Guangzhou U., 1995-98; scholar, rsch. asst. SUNY, Buffalo, 1998—. Excellent Student scholar Nanchang Inst. Aero-Tech., 1988-92; grad. scholar South China U. Tech., 1992-95; recipient Mark Diamond Rsch. Fund award, SUNY, 2001. Mem. N.Y. Acad. Scis., Soc. for Advancement of Material and Process Engring., Am. Soc. Metals Internat., Minerals, Metals and Materials Soc. Home: 211-5775 Vine St Niagara Falls L2J 1K8 Canada Office: SUNY 321 Jarvis Hall Buffalo NY 14260-4400 E-mail: sihaiwen@acsu.buffalo.edu.

WEN, XIAOQING, engineer, researcher, educator; b. Beijing, China, Apr. 23, 1964; came to U.S., 1998; s. Tingzhe Wen and Yanxiu Qu; m. Kanako Hayashido; 1 child, Bryant Wen. B in Engring., Tsinghua U., Beijing, 1986; M in Engring., Hiroshima (Japan) U., 1990; PhD, Osaka (Japan) U., 1993. Sys. engr. IC Instruments Co., Osaka, 1993; asst. prof. engring. Akita (Japan) U., 1993-97; rsch. fellow U. Wis., Madison, 1995-96; R&D dir. SynTest Technologies, Inc., Sunnyvale, Calif., 1998—. Cons. Internat. Langs. Engring. Co. Ltd., Boulder, Colo., 1995-97, Excel Co. Ltd., Osaka, 1995-97, Sharp Co. Ltd., Nara, Japan, 1996-97. Contbr. articles to profl. jours. Recipient Rsch. Encouragement award Inst. Elec., Info. and Comm. Engrs., Japan, 1994. Mem. IEEE, Info. Processing Soc. Japan (Rsch. Encouragement award 1994). Avocations: movies, swimming, jogging, reading, walking. Office: 505 S Pastoria Ave Ste 101 Sunnyvale CA 94086-7583 E-mail: wenew@earthlink.net.

WEN, YUMING, research scientist; b. Wuhu, Anhui Province, China, Jan. 9, 1969; arrived in U.S., 2000; s. Shizhong Wen and Meizhu Hu; m. Yiqun Chen; 1 child Victor. Bachelor's degree, Shandaong U. Sci. and Tech., Tai'an, Shandong, China, 1993; Master's degree, S.W. Jiaotong U., Chengdu, Sichuan, China, 1996; postgrad., U. R.I., 2000—. GIS asst. tutor S.W. Jiaotong U., Chengdu, 1994—95; GIS rsch. asst. Inst. Geography, Chinese Academy of Scis., Beijing, 1996—98; tchg. asst. tutor U. Auckland, New Zealand, 2000; rsch. asst. U. R.I., Kingston, 2000—. GIS software developer Inst. Geography, Chinese Acad. Scis., Beijing, 1996—97. Contbr. articles to profl. jours. and procs. Scholar postgrad. scholar, S.W. Jiaotong U., 1995—96. Mem.: IEEE, Computer Soc., Am. Soc. for Photogrammetry and Remote Sensing. Office: U RI CIK 106 1 Greenhouse Rd Kingston RI 02881 Office Fax: 401-874-4561. Personal E-mail: ywen@geoinfofocus.com. Business E-Mail: wenym@yahoo.com.

WENDEBORN, RICHARD DONALD, retired manufacturing company executive; b. Winnipeg, Man., Can. came to U.S., 1976; naturalized, 1988; s. Curtis and Rose (Lysecki) W.; m. Dorothy Ann Munn, Aug. 24, 1957; children: Margaret Gayle, Beverley Jane, Stephen Richard, Peter Donald, Ann Elizabeth. Diploma, Colo. Sch. Mines, 1952; grad. advanced mgmt. program, Harvard U., 1974. With Can. Ingersoll-Rand Co., Montreal, 1952—, gen. mgr., v.p., dir., 1968, pres., 1969-74, chmn. bd., 1976—; exec. v.p. Ingersoll-Rand Co., Woodcliff Lake, N.J., 1976-89; ret., 1989. Mem. Can Govt. Oil and Gas Tech. Exch. Program with former USSR, 1972—, Minerals and Metals Mission to China, 1972—. Mem. Resource Fund Colo. Sch. Mines; past pres., dir. Town and River Civic Assn. Mem. Machinery and Equipment Mfrs. Assn. Can. (bd. dirs. 1974—, past chmn.), Royal Palm Yacht Club (commodore 1994), Internat. Order of Blue Gavel (past Commodore's Club, past pres. Royal Palm br. dist. 8), Useppa Island Club, Tau Beta Pi. Home: 9990 Cypress Lake Dr Fort Myers FL 33919-6020 E-mail: Dickandda@aol.com.

WENDEL, CHARLES ALLEN, lawyer; b. Lockport, N.Y., Aug. 13, 1942; s. Harold Henry and Doris Lillian (Gardner) W.; m. Helen W. Roberts, June 23, 1973; children: William Charles, Jonathan David. BChem Engring., Rensselaer Poly Inst., 1964; JD, Am. U., 1968. Bar: N.Y. 1969, Va. 1971, D.C. 1980, U.S. Ct. Appeals (fed. and 4th cirs.), U.S. Dsit. Ct. (ea. and we. dists.) Va., U.S. Supreme Ct. Patent examiner U.S. Patent and Trademark Office, Washington, 1964-66; patent trainee Union Carbide Corp., 1966-68, patent atty. N.Y.C., 1968-70; assoc., then ptnr. Stevens, Davis, Miller & Mosher, Arlington, Va., 1970-83; ptnr. firm Wegner & Bretschneider, Washington, 1983-85; assoc. solicitor U.S. Patent and Trademark Office, 1985-88; assoc. Lyon & Lyon, Washington, 1988-90; founding ptnr. Parkhurst, Wendel & Rossi, Alexandria, Va., 1990-95. Contbr. articles to profl. jours. Mem. Va. State Bar (patent trademark copyright sect., chmn. 1977-78), Am. Intellectual Patent Law Assn., Patent Lawyers Club Washington (prs. 1982-83), Delta Theta Phi. Republican. Office: Parkhurst & Wendel LLP 1421 Prince St Ste 210 Alexandria VA 22314-2805

WENDEL, CHRISTOPHER MARK, environmental experience designer; b. Mpls., Mar. 29, 1954; s. Adolph Henry and Cordelia Marie (Ruthenbeck) W.; m. Catherine Mary Boe, Sept. 13, 1975; children: Amy, Adam. BS in Design, U. Minn., 1979; postgrad., Robert Morris Coll., 1988-90; MBA in Mktg., Seton Hall U., 1994. Designer Polivka-Logan Designers, Wayzata, Minn., 1975-79, Lakeside Ltd., Mpls., 1979-80, Omnicon Ltd., Chgo., 1981-82; design dir. CEI, 1982-86; sr. designer Giltspur, Pitts., 1986-90; v.p., creative dir. Exhibitgroup N.Y., Edison, 1990-93; corp. v.p. design and new product devel. Exhibitgroup/Giltspur, 1993—2001; prin. ChrisWendel, 2001—. Patentee in field. Recipient Bronze Idea award, 1995, iF award for Good Indsl. Design, 1996, Best New Product award Exhibitor mag., 1996. Mem. Indsl. Designers Soc. Am., Harley Owners Group. Republican. Lutheran. Avocations: skiing, tennis, golf, motorcycling. Office Fax: 908-789-3317. E-mail: cw@chriswendel.com.

WENDEL, JOAN AUDREY, music educator; b. N.Y.C., Dec. 1, 1931; d. Adam and Edna Sophia Wohlfart; m. Ralph Aurel Wendel, July 21, 1962 (dec. May 1998); 1 child, Tracy Lynn. BA summa cum laude, Dowling Coll., 1969; MA, Adelphi U., 1971. Cert. elem. tchr., N.Y. Sec. A.C. Edwards Inc., Sayville, N.Y., 1950-53; office mgr. John V. Potter Ins., East Islip, 1953-59, Pilger Agy., Patchogue, 1959-66; tchr. Connetquot CSD of Islip, Bohemia, 1969-91; pvt. music tchr., 1979-93; music dir. Christ Luth. Ch., Cape Coral, Fla., 1996—, Sounds of Fla., Cape Coral, 1999—. Mem. Music Tchrs. Nat. Assn., Music Educators Nat. Conf., Assn. Luth. Ch. Musicians, Ft. Myers Music Tchrs. Assn. (v.p. 1999), Order Eastern Star (worthy matron 1964, assoc. grand marshal 1973, grand musician 1987). Republican. Lutheran. Avocations: walking, golf, music, reading. Home: 2218 SE 10th Ter Cape Coral FL 33990-6217 Office: Christ Luth Ch 2911 Del Prado Blvd S Cape Coral FL 33904-7297

WENDEL, JOSEPH ARTHUR, retired secondary education educator; b. Somerville, N.J., Mar. 19, 1926; s. Peter Fred and Lillian Stewart Wendel. BA, Kenyon Coll., 1950; MA in English, U. Iowa, 1967. Tchr. Malcolm Gordon Sch., Garrison, N.Y., 1952-54, St. Bernard's Sch., Gladstone, N.J., 1954-56, Princess Elizabeth Sch., St. John, N.B., Can., 1957-60, Fay Sch., Southborough, Mass., 1960-63; tchr., adminstr. Kingsbrook Acad., Mendham, N.J., 1972-74; asst. headmaster, tchr. St. Paul's Sch., Garden City, N.Y., 1974-83; tchr. Arlington Christian Sch., Fairburn, Ga., 1985-95. Tchr., area rep. U.S. Peace Corps, Asella, Ethiopia, 1963-65; tchr., asst. prof. Haile Selassie I. U., Addis Ababa, Ethiopia, 1967-71; tchr. Tex. Mil. Inst., San Antonio, 1983-84; instr. English Davis & Elkins Coll., Elkins, W.Va., 1984-85. Tutor Literacy Vols. Ea. Panhandle, Martinsburg, W.Va., 1995—; vol. Berkeley County Schs., Martinsburg, 1995—. Quartermaster 3/C USN, 1944-46, PTO. Home: 814 W Burke St Martinsburg WV 25401-2302

WENDEL, RICHARD FREDERICK, economist, educator, consultant; b. Chgo., Apr. 29, 1930; s. Elmer Carl and Victoria Matilda (Jeffrey) W.; m. Leslie Jane Travis, June 15, 1957; children: John Travis, Andrew Stewart. AB, Augustana Coll., 1951; MBA, U. Pa., 1957, PhD (fellow 1962-64), 1966. Asst. to pres. Flexonics Corp., Maywood, Ill., 1957-59; sales rep., product mgr. Kordite div. Nat. Distillers Corp., Macedon, N.Y., 1959-62; instr. Wharton Sch., U. Pa., 1964-65; asst. prof. mktg. Grad. Sch. Bus. Adminstrn., Washington U., St. Louis, 1965-69; asso. prof. U. Conn., 1969-74, prof., 1974-90, prof. emeritus, 1990. Mem. U.S. Census Field Adv. Commn., 1967-69; mem. acad. adv. commn. Bur. Labor Stats., U.S. Bur. Census Survey of Consumer Expenditures, 1971-76; mem. Conn. Export Devel. Council, Dept. Commerce, 1972-76; dir. Neon Software Inc. Author: (with M.L. Bell) Economic Importance of Highway Advertising, 1966; (with W. Gorman) Selling: Preparation. Persuasion. Strategy., 1983, 88; editor: Readings in Marketing, 1973-74, 75-76, 77-78, 78-79, 79-80, 80-81, (with C.L. Lapp) Add to Your Selling Know-How, 1968; editorial staff: jour. Mktg., 1965-74. Bd. dirs. Roper Center. Served with USAF, 1951-55. Center for Real Estate and Urban Econs. grantee, 1969-70 Mem. Am. Mktg. Assn., N.Y. Acad. Scis. Republican. Episcopalian. Home: 106 S Queen St Chestertown MD 21620-1522

WENDELBURG, NORMA RUTH, composer, pianist, educator; b. Stafford, Kans. d. Henry and Anna Louise (Moeckel) W. MusB, Bethany Coll., 1943; MusM, U. Mich., 1947, Eastman Sch. Music, 1951, postgrad., 1964-65, 66-67, PhD in Composition, 1969; postgrd., Mozarteum, 1953-54, Vienna Acad. Music, 1955. Tchr. music edn., piano Wayne (Nebr.) State Coll., 1947-50; asst. prof. Bethany Coll., Lindsborg, Kans., 1952-53, U. Iowa, 1956-58; asst. prof. composition, theory, piano Hardin-Simmons U., Abilene, Tex., 1958-66, chmn. grad. com. Sch. Music, 1960-66, founder, chmn. ann. univ. festival contemporary music, 1959—; assoc. prof. music Dallas Bapt. Coll., 1973-75; rsch. asst. to dir. grad. studies Eastman Sch. Music, 1966-67; assoc. prof., chmn. dept. theory and composition S.W. Tex. State U., 1969-72; mem. faculty Friends Bible Coll., Haviland, Kans., 1977-83. Guest composer colls. including U. Ottawa, 1984; performed in Eng. and Prague; performed Am. Conservatory Mus., Charles Ives Ctr. for Am. Music, 1990—; various solo recitals and festivals. Composer: Symphony, 1967, Suite for Violin and Piano, 1965, Song Cycle for Soprano, flutes, Piano, 1974, Music for Two Pianos, 1985, Affirmation, 1982, Interlacings (organ), 1983, (recorded) Suite No. 2 for Violin and Piano, 1989, Fantasy for Trumpet and Piano, 1990, Sonata for Clarinet and Piano, Sinfonietta, 1994, Concerto for Clarinet and Orch.; performances Mosaic, Smetana Hall, Prague, 1999, Symphony Orch. of Prague, 1999, Symphony Hall, Boston, 1998, Concertino for Oboe and String Orch., Alice Tully Hall Lincoln Ctr., N.Y.C., 1999, Warsaw Rhapsody, Warsaw Philharm. Orch., Lutoslawski Hall, 1999, performed and recorded Warsaw Rhapsody, Warsaw, 1999, CD Mosaic, 2001. Recipient Meet the Composer award N.Y. State Coun. Arts, 1979; named Kans. Composer of Yr., Kans. Fed. Music Clubs, 2000; Composition scholar Composers' Conf. Middlebury (Vt.), 1950, Berkshire Ctr., 1953; Fulbright awardee, 1953-55; Resident fellow Huntington Hartford Found., 1955-56, 58, 61; MacDowell Colony fellow, 1958, 60, 70; Nat. Festival Performing Arts fellow, 1989. Mem. ASCAP (Composition awards 1988-2001), Music Tchrs. Nat. Conf., Am. Soc. Univ. Composers, Minn. Composers Forum, Am. Women Composers, Music Club (Hutchinson), Sigma Alpha Iota. Republican. Avocations: travel, photography, gardening. Address: 2206 N Van Buren St Hutchinson KS 67502-3738

WENDELN, DARLENE DORIS, English language educator; b. Indpls., July 18, 1956; d. Robert Edward and Doris Mae (Brabender) W. BS, U. Indpls., 1978; MS, Ind. U., 1986. Lic. tchr., Ind. Secondary English tchr., coach Centerville (Ind.)-Abington Sch. Corp., 1978—. Coach girls' tennis regional and sectional championships. Mem. NEA, Nat. Coun. Tchrs. English, Ind. H.S. Tennis Coaches Assn., U.S. Tennis Assn. Lutheran. Avocations: bicycling, tennis, golf, reading. Office: Centerville High Sch Willow Grove Rd Centerville IN 47330

WENDELSTEDT, HARRY HUNTER, JR. umpire; b. Balt., July 27, 1938; m. Cheryl Maher, Nov. 2, 1970; children: Harry III, Amy. Student, Essex Community Coll.; BS in Edn., U. Md. Profl. baseball umpire, 1962—; with minor leagues, Ga.-Fla., 1962, (Northwest), 1963, Tex., 1964, (Internat.),

1965, maj. leagues (Nat.), 1966-98; umpire All-Star Game, 1968, 76, 83, 92, Nat. League championship series, 1970, 72, 77, 80, 82, 84, 88, 90, 96, World Series, 1973, 80, 86, 91, 95; umpire supr. Nat. Baseball League, 1999—. Owner, operator Harry Wendelstedt Umpire Sch. Named Top Umpire in Maj. League Baseball Md. Profl. Baseball Players Assn., 1975, Best Umpire in Nat. League Chgo. Tribune, 1982, Best Ball and Strike Umpire Sports Illustrated, 1982, Major League Umpire of Yr., 1992, Fla. Diamond Club, 1993. Mem. Major League Umpires Assn. (4 term past pres.) Address: care Wendelstedt Sch for Umpires 88 S Saint Andrews Dr Ormond Beach FL 32174-3857

WENDER, IRA TENSARD, lawyer; b. Pitts., Jan. 5, 1927; s. Louis and Luba (Kibrick) W.; m. Phyllis M.Bellows, June 24, 1966; children: Justin B., Sarah T; children by previous marriage: Theodore M., Abigail A., John B. Swarthmore Coll., 1942-45; JD, U. Chgo., 1948; LLM, NYU, 1951. Atty. Lord, Day and Lord, N.Y.C., 1950-52, 54-59; asst. dir. internat. program in tax. Harvard U. Law Sch., 1952-54; lectr. N.Y. U. Sch. Law, N.Y.C., 1954-59; ptnr. Baker and McKenzie, Chgo., 1959-61; founding ptnr. N.Y.C. office, 1961-71; sr. ptnr. Wender, Murase & White, 1971-82; of counsel, 1982-86; chmn. C. Brewer and Co., Ltd., Honolulu, 1969-75; pres., CEO A. G. Becker Paribas Inc., 1978-82; chmn., CEO Sussex Securities Inc., 1983-85; of counsel Patterson, Belknap, Webb & Tyler, N.Y.C., 1986-87, ptnr., 1988-93; of counsel, 1994—. Chmn. Perry Ellis Internat., Inc., N.Y.C., 1994; bd. dirs. REFAC Corp., N.Y.C., Dime Bancorp, N.Y.C.; bd. mgrs. Swarthmore Coll, 1978-89; pres., bd. mgrs. PARC Vendome Condominium, 1990-94; trustee Putnet (Vt.) Sch., 1985-92, 93—, vice chmn., 1998—; trustee Brearley Sch., N.Y.C., 1980-85. Author: (with E.R. Barlow) Foreign Investment and Taxation, 1995. Dir., treas. Fountain House, Inc., N.Y., 1998—; dir. Am. Near East Refuge Aid, Washington; mem. Coun. on Fgn. Rels. Mem. ABA, N.Y. State Bar Assn., Assn. of Bar of City of N.Y. Home: 115 E 67th St New York NY 10021-5951 Office: Patterson Belknap Webb & Tyler LLP Ste 2200 1133 Avenue Of The Americas New York NY 10036-6731

WENDER, PHYLLIS BELLOWS, literary agent; b. N.Y.C., Jan. 6, 1934; d. Lee and Lillian (Frank) Bellows; m. Ira Tensard Wender, June 24, 1966; children: Justin Bellows, Sarah Tensard. BA, Wells Coll., 1956. Asst. advt dir. Book Find Club, N.Y.C., 1957-58; publicity dir. Grove Press, 1958-61, Dell Pub. Co., N.Y.C., 1961-63; theatrical agt. Artists Agy. Inc., 1963-68; agt. Wender & Assocs., 1968-81; writers' agt. Rosenstone/Wender, 1981—. Bd. dirs. Just Women Inc., Bklyn., 1982, mem. adv. com., 1983-87; bd. dirs. Fortune Soc., N.Y.C., 1977-80; trustee Wells Coll., Aurora, N.Y., 1981-90. Mem. Women's Media Group (dir. 1988-90), Cosmopolitan Club. Office: Rosenstone Wender 38 East 29th St 10th Flr New York NY 10016 Office Fax: 212-725-9447.

WENDLAND, CLAIRE, nursing administrator, geriatrics nurse; b. Havre, Mont., July 5, 1952; d. Sam W. and W. Inez (Dent) Berge; m. John Wendland, Sept. 20, 1975; children: Erin Mariah, Jared Keefe. ADN, No. Mont. Coll., 1973, BSN, 1993. RN, Mont. Staff nurse II pediatric unit Mont. Deaconess Med. Ctr., Great Falls, 1973-75; supr. staff nurse Lutheran Home of the Good Shepherd, Havre, 1985-87, dir. insvc. edn., 1987-88, DON, 1989-93, adminstr., 1993-99; cmty. programs coord. No. Mont. Health Care Inc., 1999—, dir. vol. and sr. svcs. Mem. Evang. Luth. Ch. Am. Mem. Mont. Dirs. Long Term Care, Mont. Health Care Assn., Mont. Gerentol. Soc., Nat. League Nursing.

WENDLINGER, ROBERT MATTHEW, communications and memory consultant; b. N.Y.C., 1922; s. Harry and Rose (Pollock) W.; m. Dalis Peralta, 1955 (div. 1973); children: David, Marcella, Marta; m. Joan Hays Cole, June 23, 1984. Student, U. Calif., Berkeley, 1942-43, Columbia U., 1947-52. Script editor Radio Free Europe, N.Y.C., 1950-52; assoc. editor Ind. Film Jour., 1953-57; gen. mgr. Kermit Rolland and Assocs., Princeton, N.J., 1957-59; exec. asst. in charge editl. svcs. United Hosp. Fund of N.Y., N.Y.C., 1959-60; editl. assoc. in pub. rels. N.Y. Life Ins. Co., 1960-65; mgr. info. sect. Com. for Air and Water Conservation, Am. Petroleum Inst., 1965-66; with Bank of Am. NT & SA, San Francisco, 1967-78, adminstrv. officer, 1967-70, asst. v.p. comm., 1970-78; pres. Comm. Cons. and Svcs., Berkeley, Calif., 1978-82; pub. rels. Nestle Corp., White Plains, N.Y., 1983-84; pres. Proust Press, Oakland, Calif., 1994—. Mem. grad. faculty St. Mary's Coll., Moraga, Calif., 1975-78; mem. Astron Corp. Author: (with James M. Reid, Jr.) Effective Letters: A Program in Self-Instruction, 1964, 3d edit., 1978, Japanese edit., 1996, The Memory Triggering Book: Using Your Memories to Enhance Your Life and Your Relationships, 1995; contbr.: Everybody Wins: TA Applied to Organizations, 1973, Affirmative Action for Women, 1973, McGraw-Hill Ency. Professional Management, 1978. Fellow Am. Bus. Comm. Assn.; mem. Indsl. Comm. Coun. (past pres.). Office: 6239 College Ave Oakland CA 94618-2331

WENDORF, DENVER FRED, JR. anthropology educator; b. Terrell, Tex., July 31, 1924; s. Denver Fred and Margaret (Hall) W.; m. Anna Christy Bednar, Apr. 27, 1996; children: Frederick Carl, Michael Andrew, Gail Susan, Cynthia Ann, Kelly Peta, Scott Frederick. BA, U. Ariz., 1948; MA, Harvard U., 1950, PhD, 1953. Rsch. assoc. Mus. N.Mex., Santa Fe, 1950-56, assoc. dir., 1958-64; assoc. prof. Tex. Tech U., Lubbock, 1956-58; prof. anthropology So. Meth. U., Dallas, 1964—, chmn. dept. anthropology, 1968-74, Henderson-Morrison prof. prehistory, 1974—2002, prof. emeritus, 2002—. Dir. Ft. Burgwin Rsch. Ctr., Taos, N.Mex., 1957-76. Author: The Prehistory of Nubia, 1968, The Midland Discovery, 1955, Paleoecology of the Llano Estacado, 1961, A Guide to Salvage Archaeology, Prehistory of the Eastern Sahara, 1980; contbr. articles to profl. jours. Chmn. Tex. State Antiquities Com., 1969-82; mem. Nat. Park System Adv. Bd., 1983-87, chmn., 1985-87; mem. Cultural Properties Adv. Bd., 1984-90. With AUS, 1943-47. Decorated Purple Heart; decorated Bronze Star. Mem. Soc. for Am. Archaeology (treas. 1974-77, pres. 1979-81), Nat. Acad. Scis., Soc. of Profl. Archaeologists (pres. 1995-97). Home: 12242 Montego Plz Dallas TX 75230-1720

WENDORF, HULEN DEE, retired law educator, writer; b. West, Tex., Oct. 29, 1916; s. Reinhardt and Laura (Blume) W.; m. Mary Jane Pfeffer, June 13, 1939; children: Robert Joseph, Donald Joseph, Florence Ann. BS, U.S. Mil. Acad., 1939; JD, Yale U., 1951. Bar: Conn. 1951, Tex. 1961, U.S. Ct. Mil. Appeals 1952, U.S. Supreme Ct. 1958, U.S. Dist. Ct. 1960. Commd. 2d lt. U.S. Army, 1939, advanced through grades to col., ret. as chief of adminstrv. law div. Office Judge Adv. Gen., 1959; practice El Paso, Tex., 1959-61; prof. law Baylor U. Law Sch., 1961-86, prof. emeritus, 1986—. Former chmn. and long-time mem. Citizens Adv. Com. to Juvenile Judge; former dir. Heart of Tex. Legal Aid Assn. Author: Texas Law of Evidence Manual, 1983, 5th rev. edit., 1998, also 3 law sch. casebooks; columnist United Retirement Bull.; contbr. various articles to law revs. Rsch. dir. Texans War on Drugs, 1980-81; chmn. Food Bank, 1981—. Decorated Legion of Merit, Bronze Star, Army Commendation medal Mem. Waco-McLennan County Bar Assn. (former dir., former v.p.), Phi Delta Phi. Home: 2808 Cumberland Ave Waco TX 76707-1324 *Enjoying the work you do, the support of a good family, and a strong religious faith are the cornerstones of a good life. Do your best work when the boss is not looking.*

WENDORF, RICHARD HAROLD, library director, scholar; b. Cedar Rapids, Iowa, Mar. 17, 1948; s. Harold Albert and Jeanne Ellen (Hamblin) W.; m. Barbara Hilderman, 1970 (div. 1983); m. Diana Thanet French, 1984 (div. 1995); children: Reed Thanet Wendorf-French, Carolyn Thanet Wendorf-French; m. Elizabeth Morse, 1997. BA, Williams Coll., 1970; PhB, U. Oxford, Eng., 1972; MA, Princeton U., 1974, PhD, 1976. From asst. prof. English to assoc. prof. English Northwestern U., Evanston, Ill., 1976-86, assoc. dean, 1984-88, prof. English and art history, 1986-89; libr. dir. Houghton Libr., Harvard U., Cambridge, Mass., 1989-97; Stanford Calderwood dir. and libr. Boston Athenaeum, 1997—. Sr. lectr. fine arts Harvard U., 1990-97, acting libr. Fine Arts Libr., 1991-92; lectr. Phi Beta Kappa Assocs., 1992-96; dir. NEH summer seminars for coll. tchrs. Northwestern U., 1987, Harvard U., 1990, 92, 96; Robert Sterling Clark vis. prof. art history Williams Coll., 1993; trustee Mus. Fine Arts, Boston. Author: William Collins and Eighteenth-Century English Poetry 1981, The Elements of Life: Biography and Portrait Painting in Stuart and Georgian England, 1990, paperback edit., 1991, Sir Joshua Reynolds: The Painter in Society, 1996; editor: Articulate Images: The Sister Arts from Hogarth to Tennyson, 1983, Rare Book and Manuscript Libraries in the Twenty-First Century, 1993, (with Charles Ryskamp) The Works of William Collins, 1979; contbr. essays in field; mem. editl. bd. Studies in 18th Century Culture, 1985-89, Word and Image, 1992-95, 96-2000, Yale edit. Writings of Samuel Johnson, Old-Time New Eng., 1996-99. Rsch. grantee Folger Shakespeare Libr., Washington, 1976, Am. Philos. Soc., Phila., 1977, 82, Henry E. Huntington Libr., 1979, Yale Ctr. for Brit. Art, 1983; jr. rsch. fellow Am. Coun. Learned Socs., 1978-79; summer stipend NEH, 1979; sr. rsch. fellow Am. Coun. Learned Socs., 1981-82; NEH rsch. fellow Newberry Libr., Chgo., 1988-89; fellow John Simon Guggenheim Meml. Found., 1989-90. Mem.: The Johnsonians (chmn. 1994—95, 1997—98), Nat. Com. on Stds. in Arts, Colonial Soc. Mass., Soc. Brit. Art Historians, Coll. Art Assn., Am. Soc. 18th Century Studies (pres. Midwest regional soc. 1986, Annibel Jenkins Biography prize 1998), Am. Antiquarian Soc., Keats-Shelley Assn. Am. (bd. dirs. 1993—98), Signet Soc. (assoc.), Union Club Boston, Cambridge Sci. Club, Saturday Club, Grolier Club, Phi Beta Kappa (exec. bd. Chgo. 1984—87, nominating com. 1998—2002). Office: Boston Athenaeum 10 1/2 Beacon St Boston MA 02108-3777

WENDORF, VIRGINIA LOU, retired accountant; b. Oak Park, Ill., Dec. 11, 1930; d. David Cyrus and Mildred Bernice (Tolley) Stineback; m. Jere Granville Marcum, June 17, 1955 (div. Nov. 1957); 1 child, Cody; m. Howard Henry Wendorf, June 7, 1958 (div. 1973); children: Thomas, Patricia. BSBA, Roosevelt U., 1975. CPA. Sr. acct., audit staff Fox & Co. CPAs, Chgo., 1975-79; from sr. auditor to mgr. fin. reporting & analysis Chgo. Transit Auth., 1980-92. Recipient fin. reporting achievement award Govt. Fin. Officers Assn., 1989, 90, 91, leadership award YWCA, Chgo., 1984, award for outstanding contbn. to transit auth. Am. Pub. Transit Assn., 1990. Mem. City Plan Commn., Burlington, Iowa, 1993—, chair, 1993-94.

WENDT, CHARLES WILLIAM, soil physicist, educator; b. Plainview, Tex., July 12, 1931; s. Charles Gottlieb and Winnie Mae (Bean) W.; m. Clara Anne Diller, Oct. 15, 1955; children: Charles Diller, John William, Elaine Anne, Cynthia Lynne. BS in Agronomy, Tex. A&M U., 1951, PhD in Soil Physics, 1966; MS in Agronomy, Tex. Tech U., 1957. Research asst. Tex. Tech Coll., 1953-55, instr. agronomy, 1957-61, asst. prof., 1961-63; research asst. soil physics Tex. A&M U., 1963-65, research assoc., 1965-66; asst. prof. Tex. A&M U. (Agrl. Research and Extension Center), Lubbock, 1966-69, assoc. prof., 1969-74, prof., 1974-91, prof. emeritus, 1991—. Cons. cotton prodn. Ministry of Agr. Sudan, summer 1960; cons. Irrigation Assn., 1977-81, Office of Tech. and Assessment, 1982, S.E. Consortium for Internat. Devel., 1989, Rhone Poulenc Agrl. Co., 1992-93; prin. backstop scientist U.S. AID West African Rsch. Program on Soil-Plant0Water Mgmt., 1982-91; chmn. agrl. sect. Southwestern and Rocky Mountain divsn. AAAS, 1982-83. Contbr. articles to profl. jours., chpt. to book. Del. Lubbock County Rep. Conv., 1978; elder Westminster Presbyn. Ch.; Tex. rep. to Great Plains Coun. 1 com. on evapotranspiration; bd. dirs. Presbyn. Ctr., Inc., Growing Recruits for Urban Bus., Growing Recruits for Urban Bus., The South Plains Food Bank, 1999—, Presbyn. Women's Clinic, 1999—; bd. dirs. divsn. land use and devel. 1st lt. U.S. Army, 1951-53. Named Outstanding Researcher High Plains Research Found., 1982; recipient Superior Achievement award for rsch., soil and crop scis. dept. Tex. A&M Univ., 1987, Vice Chancellors award in excellence as mem. TROPSOILS Rsch. team Tex. A&M U., 1996; grantee industry and water dists. Dept. Interior, U.S. AID, EPA. Mem. Soil Sci. Soc. Am., Am. Soc. Agronomy, Optimist Club (1st v.p., bd. dirs.). Home: 4518 22nd St Lubbock TX 79407-2515 Office: Texas Agrl Expt Station RR 3 Lubbock TX 79403-9803 E-mail: absendt@aol.com., absendt@home.com.

WENDT, DAVID J. cardiologist; b. N.Y.C., Oct. 30, 1954; s. Vernon E. and Hildegard M. Wendt. MD, Wayne State U., 1982. Diplomate in internal medicine, cardiology and cardiac electrophysiology Am. Bd. Internal Medicine. Cardiology fellow U. Iowa, Iowa City, 1986-89; electrophysiology fellow Duke U., Durham, N.C., 1989-92; pvt. practice Chattanooga Heart Inst., 1992—. Med. dir. cardiac E.P. lab. Erlanger Hosp., Chattanooga, 1995—. Contbr. articles to profl. jours. Bd. dirs. Tenn. Inst. of Healing Arts, Chattanooga. Fellow Am. Coll. Cardiology; mem. AMA, Am. Heart Assn. (mem. clin. coun.), Wilderness Med. Soc. Avocations: backpacking, bicycling, photography, music. Office: Chattanooga Heart Inst 2501 Citico Ave Chattanooga TN 37404-1127

WENDT, E. ALLAN, international affairs consultant; b. Chgo., Nov. 8, 1935; s. John Arthur Frederic and Dorothy Hannah (Stephenson) W. BA magna cum laude, Yale U., 1957; Certificat d'Etudes Politques, Institut d'Etudes Politques, Paris, 1959; MPA, Harvard U., 1967. Econ. comml. officer Am. Embassy, Saigon, Vietnam, 1967-71; fin. officer U.S. Mission to European Cmtys., Brussels, 1971-74; State Dept. fellow Coun. on Fgn. Rels., N.Y.C., 1974-75; dir. Office Internat. Commodities Dept. State, Washington, 1975-79; counselor for econ. and comml. affairs Am. Embassy, Cairo, 1979-81; dep. asst. sec. of state for internat. energy and resources policy Dept. State, 1981-86, sr. rep. for strategic tech. policy, 1987-92, with rank of amb., 1988-92, U.S. amb. to Republic of Slovenia Ljubljana, 1993-95, spl. rep. Internat. Donor Activities in Kosovo, 1998-2000; internat. affairs cons., 2000—. Councillor Atlantic Coun. of U.S. Contbr. articles to profl. jours. and newspapers. Mem. adv. bd. Nat. Youth Leadership Forum. Recipient award for heroism Dept. State, 1968, Presdl. Meritorious Svc. award, 1986, Superior Honor award Dept. State, 1992. Mem. Coun. Fgn. Rels., Washington Inst. Fgn. Affairs. Episcopalian.

WENDT, ELIZABETH WARCZAK, retired insurance company executive; b. Chgo., Aug. 27, 1931; d. John George and Elizabeth Marion (Jankowski) Warczak; m. John Edward Wendt, Oct. 31, 1953 (div.); children: John Alan, Brian Arthur, James Michael. Student Loyola U., Chgo., 1951-52; BSBA, St. Mary-of-the-Woods Coll., 1980; postgrad. Chgo. Kent Coll. Law, 1981-82. Asst. to actuary Globe Life Ins. Co., Chgo., 1970-74; asst. compliance officer Globe Life/Ryan Ins. Group, Chgo., 1974-86; mgr. credit product devel., 1986-96; ret. 1996; mem. FLMI Soc. Chgo., 1983—; co. rep. Consumer Credit Ins. Assn., Chgo., 1983-89; co. rep., mem. Handout Com. Life & Health Compliance Assn., 1979-96. Election judge, 1984—. Mem. United Farm Workers Support Com., Chgo. Fellow Life Mgmt. Inst. Democrat. Roman Catholic.

WENDT, GARY CARL, finance company executive; b. Portage, Wis., Mar. 13, 1942; s. Walter Carl and Dorothy Mae (Neesam) W.; children: Sarah, Rachel. BS in Civil Engring., U. Wis., 1965; MBA, Harvard U., 1967. V.p. La. Co. Inc., Houston, 1967-71, Diversified Advisor, Miami, 1971-75, GE Credit Corp., Stamford, Conn., 1975-84, COO, 1984-86; pres., CEO GE Capital Svcs. (formerly Gen. Electric Credit Corp.), 1986—; CEO, chmn., Conseco, Inc., Carmel, IN, 2000—. Trustee Boy's and Girl's Club of Stamford, past campaign chmn. capital fund campaign; past chmn. Stamford United Way; chmn. Conn. Bus. Edn. Coun.; trustee Outward Bound USA; chmn. corp. adv. com. Fairfield County Community Found. Recipient of His Royal Highness Prince Philips award, 1996, Corporate award for Outstanding Svs., to Outward Bound, Stamford Vol. Ctr Heart of Gold Soc. award, Herbert Hoover Humaniarian award, The Boys and Girl Club of Am., 1994, Recipirnt of The Nat. Ethnic Coalition Org. Ellis Island Medal, 1993, Recipient of the SACIA Walter H. Wheeler Jr. Business Leadership award, 1993, Disting Svs. Citation from The Coll. Engring. at U. Wis., Recipient of The Nat. Conf. of Christian and Jews Nat. Human Rels. award, 1990, Recipient of The Outward Bound Corp. Leadership award, 1990, The SACIA Excalibur Leadership award, 1990, Regional Plan Assn. Leadership award, 1990. Mem. Southwestern Area Commerce and Industry Assn. of Conn. (bd. dirs., past chmn.), The Regional Plan Assn. (mem. bd., past chmn.), mem nat. bd of governors, Boys and Girls Club of Am., mem. bd., of govs. for United Way of Tri State. Office: Conseco Inc 11825 N Pennsylvania St Carmel IN 46032*

WENDT, HANS W. life scientist; b. Berlin, July 25, 1923; s. Hans O. and Alice (Creutzburg) W.; m. Martha A. Linger, Dec. 23, 1956 (div.); children: Alexander, Christopher, Sandra; m. Judith A. Hammer, June 25, 1988. MSc, U. Hamburg, Germany, 1949; PhD in Psychopharmacology, U. Marburg, Germany, 1953. Diplomate in psychology. Rsch. asst. U. Marburg, 1949-53; rsch. assoc. Wesleyan U. and Office Naval Rsch., Middletown, Conn., 1952-53; asst. prof., field dir. internat. project U. Mainz, Germany, 1955-59; engring. psychologist to prin. human factors scientist Link Aviation, Apollo Simulator Systems, Binghamton, N.Y., 1959-61; assoc. to prof. psychology Valparaiso (Ind.) U., 1961-68; prof. psychology Macalester Coll., St. Paul, 1968-93; sr. rsch. fellow Chronobiology Labs. U. Minn., 1980—; prin. investigator A.v. Humboldt Geomedicine Collaboration (astrobiology), 1994—. Cons. and reviewer, 1961—; hon. prof. sci. U. Marburg, Germany, 1971—; vis. prof. U. Victoria, B.C., Can., U. Marburg, U. Bochum, U. Bielefeld, U. Goettingen, all Germany, 1966-89. Contbr. articles to profl. jours., chpts. to books. Recipient Disting. Sr. Scientist award, Alexander von Humboldt Found., 1976. Home: 2180 Lower Saint Dennis Rd Saint Paul MN 55116-2831

WENDT, JOHN ARTHUR FREDERIC, JR. lawyer; b. Cleve. s. John Arthur Frederic and Martha Ann (Hunter) W.; m. Marjorie Rickard Richardson, Oct. 2, 1962; children: Eric A., John A. F. III, Hilary H.; m. Dorothy Fay Nuttall, Dec. 29, 1976. AB with honors, U. Mich., 1942; JD, U. Colo., 1951. Bar: Colo. 1951, U.S. Dist. Ct. Colo. 1951, U.S. Ct. Appeals (10th cir.) 1957, U.S. Supreme Ct. 1971. Assoc. Tippit, Haskell & Welborn, Denver, 1953-58; ptnr. Wendt & Kistler, 1958-62, Wendt Law Offices, Aspen, 1971-81, Delta, 1985—; dist. atty. 9th Jud. Dist. Colo., 1965-69; judge Pitkin County, Colo., 1971-78; dist. atty. 7th Jud. Dist. Colo., 1981-85; judge Cedaredge, Colo., 1986—2002. Contract mediator, Colo. Judiciary, 1995—. Chmn. Delta County Planning Commn., 1991-94. Maj. U.S. Army, 1942-46, 51-53. Decorated Purple Heart (2), Silver Star, Bronze Star (2). Mem. Am. Arbitration Assn., Acad. Family Mediators, Colo. Bar Assn. (gov. 1965-71, 82, 85, 87-96), Pitkin County Bar Assn. (pres. 1971-72), Delta County Bar Assn. (pres. 1986-89), 7th Jud. Dist. Bench-Bar Com., 187th Infantry (disting.), U.S. Equestrian Team (chmn. Colo. chpt. 1976-86), Masters of Fox Hounds Assn., M.F.H. Roaring Fork Hounds, U.S. Pony Clubs, Inc. (gov. 1996-2000), Phi Kappa Psi, Phi Delta Phi, Phi Beta Kappa. Republican. Episcopalian. Home: Lenado Farm 882 2175 Dr Austin CO 81410 Office: PO Box 94 540 Main St Delta CO 81416-1834

WENDT, LINDA M. educational association administrator; b. Garmisch Partenkirchen, Germany; m. Martin J. Wendt; 1 child, Angelica. BS, Western Mich. U., 1967. Cert. fund raising exec., Va. Tchr. Mich. (Tex.) Pub. Schs., 1968-80; small bus. owner Battle Creek, Mich., 1980-85; supr. Allied Stores, 1985-86; pres. Jr. Achievement, 1986—. Steering com. Ctr. for Workforce Excellence, Battle Creek, 1991—; edn. subcom. Econ. Devel. Forum, Battle Creek, 1991—; v.p. Volunteerism in Action, Battle Creek, 1988-91; chair Oper. GRAD Oversight, Battle Creek, 1995—. Com chair Cereal Fest, Battle Creek, 1986-91; campaign divsn. chair United Arts Coun., Battle Creek, 1990; campaign vol. United Way, Battle Creek, 1986—; bd. dirs. Thornapple Arts Coun., Downtown Battle Creek Assn.; campaign vol. March of Dimes, Muscular Dystrophy; vol. Battle Creek Symphony; mem. nat. leadership coun. Jr. Achievement; bd. dirs. Rotary Dist. Found., 2000—, Battle Creek Rotary Club Found., 1998—. U.S.-China Ednl. Inst. fellow, 1995. Mem. AAUW, Rotary (com chair 1993—, bd. dirs.), Battle Creek C. of C. Avocations: tennis, boating. Office: Jr Achievement Inc 4941 Walnut Ridge Battle Creek MI 49017

WENDT, MARILYNN SUZANN, elementary school educator, principal; b. Bay City, Mich., Oct. 6, 1939; d. Clarence Henry and Margaret Viola (Rugenstein) W. AA, Bay City Jr. Coll., 1959; BA, Ctrl. Mich. U., 1962, MA, 1964; EdD, Wayne State U., 1971. Cert. elem. adminstr., Mich. Tchr., teaching prin. Baxman Sch., Bay City, 1959-62; tchr., guidance counselor, dir. elem. edn. Essexville (Mich.)-Hampton Schs., 1962-66; tchr., dir. elem. edn., dir. curriculum rsch. Bloomfield Hills (Mich.) Schs., 1966-78; elem. prin., staff development trainer, learning improvement ctr. supr. Waterford (Mich.) Schs., 1978—. Consortium facilitator Mich. Dept. Edn. Exptl. & Demonstration Ctr., Lansing, 1975-76; part time faculty mem. Wayne State U., Detroit, 1972-78. Co-author: Rational Basis for Planning School Accountability, 1976; contbr. articles to profl. jours. Trustee, v.p. Waterford Twp. Libr., 1990-95; trustee St. Mark's Bd. Edn., West Bloomfield, Mich., 1991-95. Recipient Outstanding Educator award U.S. Office of Edn.-Harold Howe II, 1968, Disting. Svc. award Bloomfield Hills Schs., 1980. Mem. ASCD, Nat. Coun. Tchrs. English, Internat. Reading Assn., Mich. Reading Assn. (Celebrate Literacy award 1989, Adminstr. of Yr. 1991), Mich. ASCD (editor newsletter, conf. planner), Oakland County Reading Assn., Oakland County State & Fed. Program Specialists, Delta Kappa Gamma (v.p. 1990-93, Woman of Distinction 1982). Avocations: reading, swimming.

WENDT, STEVEN WILLIAM, business educator; b. Rockford, Ill., Sept. 18, 1948; s. Roy W. Wendt and Betty Lou (Phillips) Wendt Oser. AAS, Clark County Community Coll., North Las Vegas, Nev., 1982; BS, U. Nev., 1985, MBA, 1987. Cert. vocat. adult educator, Nev. Electronics tech. engr. Rockford Automation, Inc., 1972-74; owner, operator S.W. Ltd., Rockford, 1972-76, S.W. Enterprises, Henderson, Nev., 1977—; instr. electronics Nev. Gaming Sch., Las Vegas, 1977-83; gen. mgr., corp. sec. treas. Customs by Peter Schell, 1977-83; field engr. Bell & Howell Mailmobile Ops. div., Zeeland, Mich., 1982-90; instr. bus. U. Nev., Las Vegas, 1985-2000; dir. Wing Fong & Family Microcomputer Labs. Coll. Bus. and Econs. U. Nev., 1990-97. Sr. arbitrator Better Bus. Bur., Las Vegas, 1982—; bus. cons. Small Bus. Devel. Ctr., Las Vegas, 1985—; incorporator, v.p. Info. Sys., Warren, Mich., 1990-91; fin. officer, gen. ptnr. Obsidian Pub. Press, Henderson, Nev., 1991-96; mem. faculty senate U. Nev., 1993-96; bd. dirs. Gem Crafters Inc., Warren; CAD/CAM dir. Casino Displays, Las Vegas, 2000—. Author: Intro to Microcomputers, For Future PC Experts, 1992. Treas. U. Nev. Grad. Student Assn, 1986-87. Served with USN, 1967-71. Recipient Cert. Appreciation UNICEF, 1984. Mem. IEEE, Computer Soc., Assn. Info. Systems, Fin. Mgmt. Assn. (Nat. Honor Soc. 1985), Strategic Gaming Soc., U. Nev. Computer User Group (exec. com., chair stds. com.), U. Nev. Alumni Assn., Am. Legion, VFW (life), Phi Lambda Alpha. Avocations: geology, numismatics, philatelics. Home: 1325 Chestnut St Henderson NV 89015-4208 Office: U Nev 4505 S Maryland Pkwy Las Vegas NV 89154-4208 E-mail: swwendt@usa.com.

WENDT, THOMAS GENE, finance executive; b. Watertown, Wis., May 14, 1951; s. Walter Harry and Gladys Florence (Munzel) W. BBA, U. Wis., Whitewater, 1973. CPA, Wis. Auditor Coopers & Lybrand, Milw., 1973-75; supr. Conley, McDonald, Sprague & Co., 1975-80; CFO E. Cen./Select Sires, Waupun, Wis., 1981—, also rec. sec., bd. dirs. Bd. dirs. Moravian Homes Inc., Mueller Apts., Inc., Marquardt Meml. Manor, Inc., Watertown, Wis., 1985—, sec. and treas. bd. dirs., 1986—. Mem. Marquardt Found., 1988—; bd. dirs. Zinsendorf Hall, 1989—, sec., treas., 1989—, forward campaign chmn., 1988; pres. bd. trustees Watertown Moravian Ch., 1981-84, bd. elders, 1990-93, ch. sec., 2000—; adv. del. Western Dist. Synod, Wis., 1982, 86, 90, 96; bd. dirs. Moravian Homes of Sturgeon Bay, 1991—; bd. dirs. Hus Apts., Inc., 1993—, sec., treas., 1993—; sec. Watertown Moravian Ch., 2000—. Mem. AICPA, Wis. Inst. CPAs, Milw. Art Mus. Avocations: athletics, music, art. Office: E Central/Select Sires PO Box 191 Waupun WI 53963-0191

WENDT, VERNON EARL, internist, cardiologist; b. Cleve., Mar. 26, 1931; s. Raymond C. and Esther L. (Naujoks) W.; m. Hildegarde Caroline Moeller, Aug. 14, 1953; children: David, Frederick, Kathryn, Elizabeth, Doralyn, James, Vernon Earl, Jr. BS in Zoology and Chemistry cum laude, Baldwin-Wallace Coll., 1952; MD, Columbia U., 1956. Diplomate Am. Bd. Internal Medicine. Intern Detroit Receiving Hosp., 1956-57, resident, 1959-62; US-PHS postdoctoral fellow in cardiology Wayne State U. Sch. of Medicine, Detroit, 1962-65, from instr. to asst. prof. medicine, 1961-65; dir. rsch. Blodgett Meml. Med. Ctr., Grand Rapids, 1965-67; pvt. practice internal medicine and cardiology, 1967—2000. Capt. med. corps. USAF, 1957-59. Fellow: ACP, Am. Coll. Angiology, Am. Coll. Cardiology; mem.: Mich. Health Coun. (trustee 1998—), Am. Acad. Anti-Aging Medicine, Coun. on Geriatric Cardiology, Kent County Med. Soc., Mich. Soc. Internal Medicine (pres. 1991—92), Am. Lung Assn. of Mich. (pres. 1978—80), Am. Heart Assn. of Mich. (trustee 1973—93, pres. 1987—88). Lutheran. Avocations: golf, gardening, walking. Home and Office: 1620 Andover Rd SE Grand Rapids MI 49506 E-mail: vhwendt@worldnet.att.net.

WENDZEL, ROBERT LEROY, political science educator; b. May 28, 1938; married; 3 children. BA in Polit. Sci. magna cum laude, Kalamazoo Coll., 1960; PhD in Polit. Sci., U. Fla., 1965. Assoc. prof. polit. sci. U. Maine, Orono, 1977-81, 82-83; prof. internat. affairs U.S. Air War Coll., Maxwell AFB, Ala., 1981-82; asst. dean arts & scis., prof. polit. sci., coord. internat. affairs program U. Maine, 1984-86; prof. internat. politics U.S. Air War Coll., Maxwell AFB, 1986-87, ednl. advisor to the Commandant, 1987-2000; Paschal P. Vacca prof. liberal arts U. Montevallo, Ala., 2000—01; Merrill prof. polit. sci. Utah State U., Logan, 2001. Internat. affairs com., U. Maine, 1970-86, budget adv. com., 1983-86, coord. internat. affairs program, 1984-86. Author: International Relations: A Policymaker Focus, Thai edit., 1989, Relacoes Internacionais, 1985, International Politics: Policymakers and Policymaking, 1981, International Relations: A Policymaker Focus, 1977, 2d edit., 1980; co-author: America's Foreign Policy in a Changing World, 1994, Defending America's Security, 1988, 2d edit., 1990, To Preserve the Republic: The Foreign Policy of the United States, 1985, Games Nations Play, 9th edit., 1996; contbr. articles to profl. jours. Mem. Phi Beta Kappa. Home: 160 Old Field Dr Montgomery AL 36117-3938 E-mail: blw052838@aol.com.

WENEGRAT, SAUL S. arts administrator, art educator, consultant; b. Jersey City, Mar. 28, 1933; s. John and Tillie (Freeman) W. BA, Rutgers U., 1960; MPA, Harvard U., 1962; cert., London U., 1975. Dir. art program Port Authority of N.Y. & N.J., N.Y.C., 1962-95; prof. grad. divsn. Fashion Inst. Tech., 1987-95; v.p. Forums Internat., 1995—; cons. arts advisor Wooasavage and Assocs., Archs., 2001—. Pub. art panelist N.J. State Com. Arts, Trenton, 1985-95, Conn. State Com. Arts, Hartford, 1988, N.Y.C. Cultural Affairs, 1980-88, Met. Transit Authority, N.Y.C., 1994-95. Editor: Art for the Public, 1985. Capt. USAF, 1953-57. Recipient Doris Freedman award Mayor of N.Y.C., 1984, Merit cert. Mcpl. Art Soc., 1980, 85; Carnegie fellow, 1960, Fels fellow, 1960. Mem. Nat. Assn. Corp. Art Adminstrn. (chmn. bd. 1985-95), Harvard Club. Avocations: bridge, walking, museums. Home: 2 Beekman Pl New York NY 10022-8058

WENER, MAUREEN G. association executive; b. Chgo., June 25, 1973; d. Clifford R. Wener and Marsha T. Cowles. B, U. Kans., 1995; postgrad., Northea. Ill. U., 1998—99. Chief of staff State Sen. John Cullerton, Chgo., 1999—; external rels. specialist Rotary Internat., Evanston, 1999—. Vol. leader 200 for 2000, Chgo., 1999—; precinct committeewoman 44th Ward, Chgo., 1997-2000; province collegiate chairwoman Delta Gamma, Evanston, 1999-2000; treas. Friends of Kathy Ryg, 2002—. Avocations: exercise, reading, travel. Office: Rotary Internat 1560 Sherman Ave Evanston IL 60201 Fax: (847) 680-7497. E-mail: wenerm@yahoo.com.

WENG, GEORGE JUENG-CIOUS, engineering educator; b. Oct. 8, 1944; s. Wan-Chung and Kuang-chieh (Hsieh) Weng; m. Jacki Li; children: Shawn, Cidney;children from previous marriage: Bruce, Joyce. BS, Taiwan U., 1967; MPhil, Yale U., 1971, PhD, 1974. Rsch. fellow Delft (The Netherlands) U. Tech., 1973-74; postdoctoral fellow Yale U., UCLA, 1974-76; sr. rsch. engr. GM Rsch. Lab., Warren, Mich., 1976-77; asst. prof. mech. and aerospace engring. Rutgers U., New Brunswick, N.J., 1977-80, assoc. prof., 1980-84, prof., 1984-92, disting. prof., 1992—, grad. dir., 1995-98. Contbr. more than 135 articles to profl. jours.; editor Acta Mechanica, 1985—; tech. editor Jour. Engring. Materials and Tech., trans. ASME, 1992-97; editl. bd. Internat. Jour. Plasticity, 1985—, Acta Mechanica Solida Sinica, 1997—, JSME Internat. Jour., 1997—. NSF grantee, 1978-. Fellow ASME, Am. Acad. Mechanics. Achievements include work in mechanics of materials, micromechanics of composite materials, shape-memory alloys, ferroelectric ceramics, nanograined materials. Home: 65 Sycamore Way Warren NJ 07059 Office: Sch Engring Rutgers U New Brunswick NJ 08903 E-mail: weng@jove.rutgers.edu.

WENG, HAN-RONG, neuroscientist, researcher; b. Shantou, Guangdong, China, Mar. 22, 1958; arrived in Sweden, 1989; came to U.S., 1997; s. Kaixiu Weng and Ruixiang Xu; m. Xiaoling Luo, July 13, 1985; 1 child, Hongsheng. MD, Sun Yat-Sen U. Med. Scis., Guangzhou, China, 1983, postgrad., 1983-86; PhD, Faculty Medicine U. Lund, Sweden, 1996. Medical diplomate. Rschr. Rsch. Inst. Neurosci. Guangzhou (China) Med. Coll., 1986-89; rsch. fellow dept. physiology and neurosci. U. Lund, 1996-97; rsch. fellow dept. neurosurgery Sch. Medicine Johns Hopkins U. and U. Md. Dental Sch., Balt., 1997-2000; rsch. scientist dept. anesthesiology MD Anderson Cancer Ctr. U. Tex., 2001—. Inventor in neurosci. rsch. field. Mem. Internat. Assn. Study of Pain, Soc. Neurosci., N.Y. Acad. Scis. Avocations: reading, swimming, tennis, travel, music. Office: U Texas Dept Anesthesiology 1515 Holcombe Blvd Box 42 Houston TX 77030

WENG, JOHN JUYANG, computer science educator, researcher; b. Shanghai, Apr. 15, 1957; came to U.S., 1983; m. Min Guo, 1985; children: Colin S., Rodney D. BS in Computer Sci., Fudan U., Shanghai, 1982; MS in Computer Sci., U. Ill., 1985, PhD in Computer Sci., 1989. Rsch. asst. U. Ill., Urbana, 1984-88; rschr. Computer Rsch. Inst. Montreal, Can., 1989-90; vis. asst. prof. U. Ill., 1990-92; asst. prof. Mich. State U., East Lansing, 1992-98, assoc. prof., 1998—. Author: (chpt.) Early Visual Learning, 1996; co-author: (chpt.) Handbook of Pattern Recognition and Computer Vision, 1993, Motion and Structures from Image Sequences, 1993, Visual Navigation, 1997. Mem. IEEE (Computer Soc., assoc. editor IEEE Transactions on Image Processing 1994-97; assoc. editor Transactions on Pattern Analysis and Machine Intelligence 2000—), Am. Soc. Engring. Edn., Sigma Xi, Phi Beta Delta. Achievements include contributions to understanding and computation of estimation of motion and structure from image sequences; co-inventor of Cresceptron, an experimental system for recognizing and segmenting objects from natural images; director of SHOSLIF project for a general framework for visual learning by computers; an originator of the developmental approach to artificial intelligence; dir. SAIL developmental robot project. Office: Mich State Univ 3115 Engring Bldg East Lansing MI 48824

WENG, WEN-KAI, physician, medical researcher; b. Taipei, China, Dec. 11, 1962; arrived in U.S., 1990; s. Hua-Min and Lee (Chu) W. MD, Chung-Shan Med. & Dental Coll., Taichung, China, 1988; PhD, U. Minn., 1996. Rsch. asst. U. Minn., Mpls., 1990-96; resident in internal medicine U. Tex./Houston Med. Sch., 1996-99; fellow in oncology Stanford U., Calif., 1999—. Ad hoc reviewer Blood-Jour. Am. Soc. Hematology, 1996. Dir. acad. com. Minn. Chinese Soc. Biomed. Sci., Mpls., 1993-96; cons. Minn. Chinese Student Assn., Mpls., 1993-96. With Rep. of China Army, 1988-90. Recipient fellowship U. Minn. Grad. Sch., 1995-96, rsch. fellowship Lymphoma Rsch. Found., 2002-04, Nat. Rsch. Svc. award NIH, 1994-95. Mem. Chinese Med. Assn., Sigma Xi (Charles and Dorothy Andrew Bird award 1996). Avocations: wildlife photography, birding, rock climbing, computers. Office: Stanford U Divsn Oncology Medicine 1000 Welch Rd Ste 202 Palo Alto CA 94304-1808

WENGER, BRUCE EDWARD, art educator, educator; b. Grand Rapids, Mich., Mar. 10, 1948; s. Gerald and Beatrice June (Bremer) W.; m. Grace Ann Glick, Dec. 30, 1982 (div. Jan. 1995); 1 child, Jesse. BS in Art, Western Mich. U., 1970; MFA, Ohio U., 1973. Prints specialist Ohio U., Athens, 1971-72; lectr. drawing Ea. Mich. U., Ypsilanti, 1974; asst. prof. art Houghton (N.Y.) Coll., 1978-86, head dept., 1982-86; asst. prof. Rochester (N.Y.) Inst. Tech. Coll. Imaging Arts and Sci., 1986—. Exhibited in group shows Melville C. Brown Gallery, Laramie, Wyo., Stamford (Conn.) Art Assn., NYU, Art West Gallery, Jackson, Wyo., Memphis State U., Chattahoochee Valley Art Assn., La Grange, Ga., Viridian Gallery, N.Y.C., Schoharie County Arts Coun., Cobleskill, N.Y., Minot (N.Dak.) State Coll., 100% Real Art Gallery, Spokane, Wash., U. Ill., Chgo., U. Maine, Presque Isle, Pyramid Arts Ctr., Rochester, Day Spring Art Fair, Toronto, Ont., Can., Huntington (W.Va.) Galleries, also others. Recipient hon. mention Melville C. Brown Gallery, Schoharie County Arts Coun., Three Rivers Arts Festival, Pitts., purchase award Drawing and Print Exhbn., Ft. Hays, Kans., Ann. Maine Maritime Flatwork Exhbn., Mich. Biennial Painters and Printmakers, Grand Rapids. Office: Rochester Inst Tech Coll Imaging Arts and Sci One Lomb Memorial Dr Rochester NY 14623 E-mail: bewfaa@rit.edu.

WENGER, DERRICK ELIOT, securities analyst; b. Tulsa, May 20, 1961; s. Virgil Eugene and Jo Anne (Putney) W.; m. Ana Maria Salazar, Aug. 25, 1989. BSBA, Georgetown U., 1983; MBA, Harvard U., 1988. FMP trainee GE, Rockville, Md., 1983-84; assoc. Credit Suisse, N.Y.C., 1984-86; intern Fidelity Mgmt. & Rsch., Boston, 1987; assoc. Paine Webber, N.Y.C., 1988-89; exec. v.p. Evergreen Asset Mgmt., Purchase, N.Y., 1989-96; ptnr., dir. rsch. Forest Investment Mgmt., Old Greenwich, Conn., 1996-2000; dir. convertible rsch. Jefferies & Co. Inc., N.Y.C., 2000—. Mem. Am. Assn. Individual Investors, N.Y. Soc. Security Analysts, Fin. Analysts Fedn., Assn. Investment Mgmt. and Rsch. Republican. Home: 96 Meadow Rd Riverside CT 06878-2520 Office: Jefferies & Co Inc 520 Madison Ave New York NY 10022

WENGER, JAY LAMAR, psychologist; b. Hershey, Pa., Jan. 16, 1954; s. Melvin Sensenig and Janette Louise Wenger; m. Suzanne Marie Shenk; 1 child Kira. BS in Math., Millersville U. of Pa., 1976, BA in Psychology, 1989; MS in Psychology, Pa. State U., 1991, PhD in Psychology, 1994. Tchr. math. Locust Grove Mennonite Sch., Smoketown, Pa., 1977—87; prof. psychology U. West Ala., Livingston, 1994—. Contbr. rsch. articles to profl. jours. Vice-chmn. Wesley Found. of U. West Ala. Scholar Fulbright scholar, Tallinn (Estonia) Pedagog. U., 2001—02. Mem.: APA, Christian Assn. for Psychol. Studies, Southeastern Psychol. Assn. Avocations: travel, photography. Office: U West Ala Washington St Livingston AL 35470 Home Fax: 205-652-3717; Office Fax: 205-652-3717. Personal E-mail: jwenger@uwa.edu. Business E-Mail: jwenger@uwa.edu.

WENGER, LARRY BRUCE, law librarian, law educator; b. Everett, Wash., Dec. 21, 1941; s. Lester Edwin Wenger and Selma Marie (Norberg) W. Saterstrom; m. Marilyn Diane Watt, June 26, 1965; children: Bruce Daniel, Kathleen Marie. BA, U. Wash., 1964, JD, 1967; MLS, Simmons Coll., 1969. Reference libr. Sch. Law Harvard U., Cambridge, Mass., 1967-69; asst. law libr. SUNY, Buffalo, 1969-71, law libr., assoc. prof. law, 1971-76; law libr., prof. law U. Va., Charlottesville, 1976—. Cons. to law librs.; bd. dirs. Nat. Ctr. for Preservation Law. Editor: Marine Affairs Bibliography. Mem. Am. Assn. Law Librs., Internat. Assn. Law Librs. (pres. 1995-2001), Bibliog. Soc., Bibliog. Soc. Am. Home: 2630 Meriwether Dr Charlottesville VA 22901-9513 Office: U Va Law Libr 580 Massie Rd Charlottesville VA 22903-1739

WENGER, LOWELL EDWARD, physics educator; b. Middlebury, Ind., Nov. 17, 1948; s. Theodore E. and Lavina A. W.; m. Andrea J. Goral, Dec. 26, 1976; children: Joel, Erin. BS, Purdue U., 1971, MS, 1973, PhD, 1975. From asst. prof. to prof. dept. physics Wayne State U., Detroit, 1976-98, prof., chair dept. physics, 1998—. Alfred Sloan fellow Sloan Found., 1978-79, Fulbright Rsch. fellow The Netherlands, 1982-83. Mem. Am. Phys. Soc., Materials Rsch. Soc., Sigma Xi (pres. local chpt. 1996—). Office: Wayne State Univ Dept Physics Detroit MI 48201 E-mail: wenger@physics.wayne.edu.

WENGER, NANETTE KASS, cardiology educator; b. N.Y.C., Sept. 3, 1930; d. Aaron Zelig and Edith (Malkin) Kass; m. Julius Wenger; children: Deborah, Judith, Beth. BA summa cum laude, Hunter Coll., 1951; MD, Harvard Coll., 1954. Intern Mt. Sinai Hosp., N.Y.C., 1954-55, chief resident in cardiology, 1956-57; sr. resident in medicine Grady Meml. Hosp., Atlanta, 1958, mem. med. staff internal medicine/cardiology, 1959—; fellow in cardiology Sch. Medicine, Emory U. at Grady Meml. Hosp., 1958-59; instr. medicine Schs. Medicine and Dentistry, Emory U., Atlanta, 1959-62, assoc. in medicine, 1962-64, asst. prof. cardiology, 1964-68, assoc. prof., 1968-71, prof., 1971—; mem. med. staff Crawford W. Long Hosp., 1977—. Dir. cardiac clinics, Grady Meml. Hosp., 1960—, dir. project for cardiac evaluation and med. and vocat. rehab., 1966—; cons. cardiology VA Med. Ctr., Atlanta, 1988—, Pan Am. Health Orgn., Santiago, Chile, 1985; participant numerous profl. symposiums and confs.; mem. cardiovascular and renal drugs adv. com. U.S. FDA, 1978-82, cons. to com., 1982—; cons. nat. cardiovascular health program YMCA, 1974-79; co-chairperson nat. plan for cardiac rehab. com. Div. Vocat. Rehab., Social and Rehab. Svcs.,HEW, 1973—; mem. Internat. Task Force for Prevention of Coronary Heart Disease, 1989—; founding fellow Coun. on Geriatric Cardiology, 1986, bd. dirs., 1987—, chairperson long-range planning com., 1988—. Mem. editorial bd. various profl. publs. including Cardiac Rehab. Quarterly, 1974-79, Primary Care, 1975-79, Internat. Jour. Sports Cardiology, 1983—, Med. Month, 1983-84, Jour. Cardiovascular and Pulmonary Medicine, 1983—, Geriatric Cardiology, 1986—, Nutrition, Metabolism and Cardiovascular Disease, 1989—; reviewer publs. including Am. Jour. Medicine, 1972—, Am. Jour. Cardiology, 1979—, Am. Heart Jour., 1975—, European Heart Jour., 1983—. Active Ga. affiliate Am. Heart Assn., 1960—, chairperson Heart Sunday program, 1968-69, program chairperson Fulton County Heart Unit, 1969-71, bd. dirs., 1969-79, 80-82, pres., 1977-78; fellow coun. clin. cardiology, Am. Heart Assn., 1970, chairperson rehab. com., 1972-75, chairperson artherosclerosis task force, 1973-74, program v.p., 1975-76, bd. dirs., 1975-79, mem./past mem. numerous other coms.; mem. med. adv. and cardiovascular health coms. Butler St. YMCA, 1980-82. Recipient Myrtle Wreath award Atlanta Hadassah, 1967, Aaward of Achievement, Nat. Ctr. for Vol. Action, 1978; recipient Bronze Disting. Svc. medallion Ga. affiliate Am. Heart Assn., 1970-71, Silver Disting. Svc. medallion, 1978, Gold Disting. Svc. medallion, 1979; honoree Women of Yr. issue Time Mag., 1976. Fellow ACP, Am. Coll. Cardiology (gov. Ga. chpt. 1983-86, mem. bd. trustees 1987-89, mem. various coms.); mem. AMA, WHO (mem. expert adv. panel on cardiovascular disease 1989—), Am. Assn. Cardiovascular and Pulmonary Rehab. (mem. bd. trustees 1985-88, chairperson ethics com. 1985—, 2nd Ann. Lecture award 1987), Nat. Heart, Lung and Blood Inst., Internat. Soc. and Fedn. Cardiology (pres. sci. coun. on rehab. of cardiac patients 1984-88), Med. Assn. Ga., Med. Assn. Atlanta, Atlanta Clin. Soc.(emeritis), Soc. for Prevention of Heart Disease and Rehab. (hon.), Philippine Heart Assn. (hon.), Philippine Coll. Cardiology (hon.), Omicron Delta Kappa. Office: Emory Univ Sch Medicine 69 Butler St SE Atlanta GA 30303-3033

WENGER, RONALD DAVID, surgeon; b. Phila., May 1, 1944; s. Christian Showalter and Helen Grace (Heisey) W.; m. Judith Kay Anderson, Jan. 24, 1970; children: Clayton, Lera. BA, Ohio Wesleyan U., 1966; MD, Case Western Res. U., 1970. Diplomate Am. Bd. Surgery. Intern U. Oreg. Med. Sch., Portland, 1970-71; fellow Mayo Clinic Surgery Dept., Rochester, Minn., 1973-77; clin. prof. surgery U. Wis. Med. Sch., Madison, 1977—; pvt. practice, 1977—; asst. chief surgery St. Mary's Hosp., 1980-00; chief surgery Dean Med. Ctr., 1988-93. Mem. ACS (also Wis. chpt.), AMA, SAGES, Wis. State Med. Soc., Madison Surg. Soc., Wis. Surg. Soc., Soc. for Surgery of Alimentary Tract. Avocations: skiing, bicycling, sailing, travel, reading. Home: 726 Farwell Dr Madison WI 53704-6032 Office: 1912 Atwood Ave Madison WI 53704-5221

WENGERT, TIMOTHY, church history educator, clergyman; b. Teaneck, N.J., Oct. 1, 1950; s. Norman Irving and Janet (Mueller) W.; m. Barbara Ann Farlow, Nov. 17, 1973 (dec. May 2001); children: Emily, David. AB, U. Mich., 1972, MA, 1973; MDiv, Luther Sem., St. Paul, 1977; PhD, Duke U., 1984. Ordained to ministry Evangel. Luth. Ch. in Am., 1977. Asst. pastor Luth. Ch. of the Master, Edina, Minn., 1977-78; pastor Cross Luth. Ch., Roberts, Wis., 1983-89; prof. Luth. Theol. Sem. Phila., 1989—. Author: Philip Melanchthon's Annotationes in Johannem, 1987, Human Freedom, Christian Righteousness, 1998, Law and Gospel, 1997; editor: (with Charles Brockwell) Telling the Churches' Stories, 1995, (with Robert Kolb) The Book of Concord; assoc. editor The Luth. Quar, 1997—. Grantee Deutscher Akademischer Austauschdienst, 1980-81, 95, Herzog August Bibliothek, 1991, 94, Lilly Theol. Rsch. grantee, faculty fellow, 1999—; recipient Melanchthon prize City of Bretten, Germany, 2000. Mem. Sixteenth Century Studies Conf., Soc. for Reformation Rsch., Am. Soc. for Ch. History. Office: Luth Theol Sem 7301 Germantown Ave Philadelphia PA 19119-1726 E-mail: twengert@ltsp.edu.

WENGLER, MARGUERITE MARIE, educational therapist; b. Kokomo, Ind., Nov. 18, 1943; d. Eugene Ferdinand and Flavia Marie (Marullo) Scalzo; m. James Burton Wengler, Oct. 4,1969; children: James Eugene, Dale Douglas, Lauren Christine. BS in Edn., Hofstra U., 1964; MA in Moderate Spl. Needs Edn., Assumption Coll., 1991. Cert. elem. edn. tchr., N.Y., Mass, spl. needs tchr., Mass. Spl. needs dir. Montessori Primary and Upper Schs., Lexington, Mass.; spl. edn. tchr. Lincoln-Sudbury Pub. Schs., Sudbury, 1987-88; from assoc. lectr. to sr. lectr. Program Advanced Lng. Curry Coll., Milton, 1993—, outreach dir., 1997-98. Dir. Learning Success Helpline, Acton, Mass., 1984—; profl. devel. provider towards tchr. cert. Dept. of Edn. state of Mass. Author: 60 Minutes to Much Higher Grades, coll. edit., 1995, 60 Minutes to Much Higher Grades, H.S. edit., 1997; contbg. author A Closer Look, 1995; mng. editor Shared Visions of Teaching and Learning, 1997-2001. Del. People to People/Citizen Amb., China, 1994; dir., founder A Friend in Need, Acton, Mass., 1990-96, bd. dirs. Recipient Grant to Friend in Need United Way, 1991-94, Cmty. Chest, 1993; grantee State of Mass., 1989-91. Mem. AAUP, Learning Disabilities Network. Home: 14 Francine Rd Acton MA 01720-3611 Office: Program Advancement Lng Curry Coll Blue Hill Ave Milton MA 02186-2302

WENGLOWSKI, GARY MARTIN, economist; b. Rochester, N.Y., Sept. 2, 1942; s. Henry Bernard and Isabelle (Franc) W.; m. Joyce Richards, Oct. 3, 1964; children: Gary Martin, Catherine Jean. BS in Econs., U. Pa., 1964, MA, 1965, PhD in Econs., 1967. With Goldman Sachs & Co., N.Y.C., 1967—, v.p., dir. econ. rsch., 1972-78, ptnr., 1978-86, ltd. ptnr., 1986-99; ret. ptnr., 1999—. Adj. prof. Baruch Coll., 1998—; chmn. vis. com. econ. dept. U. Pa., 1985-98. Author: Industry Profit Forecasting, 1972, Industry Profit Forecasting—Progress Report, 1975. Trustee CARE Found., 1991—, Haystack Mountain Sch., 1993—. Named Best Economist on Wall St., Ann. Instnl. Investor Mag. Polls, 1976-86; NDEA fellow, 1965, 67. Fellow Nat. Assn. Bus. Economists; mem. Am. Econ. Assn., Deer Isle Yacht Club (vice commodore 1993-94, commodore 1994-2000). Home: 32 Partridge Ridge Rd Katonah NY 10536-3500

WENIGER-PHELPS, NANCY ANN, media specialist, photographer; b. Kingman, Kans., Sept. 4, 1948; d. Watson and Reva Jo (Schlup) W. BA in Phys. Edn., Ottawa (Kans.) U., 1970; MA in LS, U. Denver, 1980. Cert. K-12 media specialist, secondary phys. edn. tchr., Ariz. Phys. edn. tchr. Grand Junction (Colo.) Sch. Dist., 1970-73; dist. mgr. World Book Ency., 1973-74; personal sec. Younger Bail Bond Svc., Grand Junction, 1974-76; media specialist K-12, phys. edn. tchr. Kingman (Kans.) Unified Sch. Dist., 1976-78, Ovid (Colo.) Sch. Dist., 1980-82, Sargeant Sch. Dist., Monte Vista, Colo., 1982-84, Antonito Sch. Dist., Ovid, 1984-85; photographer's asst. Bill Westenberg Photography, Alamosa, 1985-86; sch. media specialist Window Rick (Ariz.) Unified Sch. Dist., 1986-96. Profl. photographer; trainer adult and student storytellers; head dist. lib. computer program. Author: Photographic Uses in the Library; exhibited in group shows Gallup (N.Mex.) Gallery, 1989, Window Rock Elem. Sch., 1989, Sunflower Shop, Wichita, Kans. 1989-90, 96-98, also Alamosa, Colo., 1985-87, 1st Nat. Bank, Kingman (Kans.), Fernley (Nev.) Phys. Therapy, 1993. Mem. Washoe County Friends of Libr., Reno, Nev., vol. book sorter, vol. book sale. Mem. AAHPERD, ALA, Am. Fedn. Tchrs., Internat. Platform Assn., Ariz. Fedn. Tchrs., Window Rock Fedn. Tchrs., Ariz. Edn. Media Assn., Assoc. Photographers Internat. Ariz. Edn. Assn., Alpha Delta Kappa. Home: 3305 Farm District Rd Fernley NV 89408-8608

WENK, EDWARD, JR. civil engineer, policy analyst, educator, writer; b. Balt., Jan. 24, 1920; s. Edward and Lillie (Heller) Went; m. Carolyn Frances Lyford, Dec. 27, 1941; children: Lawrence Shelley Went, Robin Edward Alexander Went, Terry Allan Went(dec.). BE, Johns Hopkins U., 1940, DEng, 1950; MSc, Harvard U., 1947; DSc (hon.), U. R.I., 1968; LHD (hon.), Johns Hopkins U., 1989. Registered profl. engr. Head structures div. USN David Taylor Model Basin, Washington, 1942-56; chmn. dept. engring. mechanics S.W. Research Inst., San Antonio, 1956-59; sr. specialist sci. and tech. Legis. Reference Service, Library of Congress, Washington, 1959-61, chief sci. policy research div., 1964-66; tech. asst. to U.S. President's sci. adviser and exec. sec. Fed. Council for Sci. and Tech., White House, Washington, 1961-64; exec. sec. Nat. Council on Marine Resources and Engring. Devel., Exec. Office of Pres., 1966-70; prof. engring. and pub. affairs U. Wash., Seattle, 1970-83, prof. emeritus, 1983—, dir. program in social mgmt. tech., 1973-79; tech. advisor to gov. State of Wash., 1993-96. Lectr. numerous univs.; cons. in pub. policy for environ. and tech. affairs, risk assessments, human and orgnl. error, futures, ocean engring., info. tech., decision theory; Nat. Adv. Com. on Oceans and Atmosphere, 1972-73; vice chmn. U.S. Congress Tech. Assessment Adv. Coun., 1973-79; adviser Congress, GAO, NSF, EPA, NOAA, White House, UN Secretariat, Wash. State, Alaska, U.K., Australia, Sweden, The Philippines, Alaska Oil Spill Commn., 1989, Wash. State Marine Oversight Bd., 1992, pub. interest groups, 1997, U.S. Dept. Transportation; vis. scholar Woodrow Wilson Internat. Ctr. for Scholars, 1970-72, Harvard U., 1976, Woods Hole Oceanographic Instn., 1976, U. Sussex, 1977, Bellagio Ctr., Rockefeller Found., 1977, 90. Author: The Politics of the Ocean, 1972, Margins for Survival, 1979, Tradeoffs-Imperatives of Choice in a High-Tech World, 1986, Making Waves—Engineering, Politics and the Social Management of Technology, 1995, The Double Helix: Technology and Democracy in the American Future, 1999; editor: Engring. Mechs. Jour., 1958-60, Exptl. Mechs. Jour., 1954-56; mem. editl. bd. Tech. Forecasting, Tech. in Soc.; contbr. articles to profl. jours.; designer Aluminaut submarine, 1959; author of concept of tech. assessment, 1964. Bd. dirs. Human Interaction Rsch. Inst., 1980-90, Smithsonian Sci. Info. Exch., 1977-82, URS Corp., 1973-88; mem. Interfaith Alliance. Ensign USNR, 1944-45. Recipient Navy Meritorious Civilian Svc. award, 1946, authors prize Gov. Wash., 1974, ann. prize Edn. Press Assn., 1997; named Disting. Alumnus Johns Hopkins U., 1979, Tchr. of Yr., Wash. State Engrs., 1980, Tchr. of Yr., Students in Pub. Adminstrn., 1986, Disting. Alumnus, Balt. Poly. Inst., 1991; Ford Found. grantee, 1970; Rockefeller Found. Belagio fellow, 1976, 90; 1st Stuckenburg lectr. Wash. U., 1988; Regents lectr. U. Calif., Berkeley, 1989. Fellow ASME (exec., Ralph Coats Roe medal 1999), AAAS; mem. ASCE, NSPE, Soc. Exptl. Stress Analysis (past pres. and William M. Murray lectr.), Internat. Assn. Impact Assessment (pres. 1981-82), NAE (chmn. com. on pub. policy 1970-75), Nat. Acad. Pub. Adminstrn., Am. Soc. for Pub. Adminstrn. (chmn. com. on sci. and tech. in govt. 1974-78), Assembly Engring. and Marine Bd. NRC, Nat. Oceanography Assn. (v.p. pub. affairs 1970-72), Cousteau Soc. (chmn. adv. bd. 1975-97), USA Club of Rome (bd. dirs. 1997-98), Cosmos Club (Washington), Explorers Club, Sigma Xi (nat. lectr.), Tau Beta Pi, Chi Epsilon. Home: 900 University St # 13L Seattle WA 98101 *Each of us has the opportunity, indeed responsibility, to contribute to the human experience and to enrich the lives of future generations. In a world of change, cultural diversity and uncertainty, we must be ourselves and not merely slaves of conventional thought. We must act on the basis of what we believe to be right rather than only from the desire to be loved.*

WENKER, MARILYN J. artist, educator; b. Glendale, Calif., June 1, 1946; BA in Fine Arts, Burlington Coll., 1990; MFA in Writing and Painting, Bard Coll., 1992; MFA in Creative Writing, Syracuse U., 1996. Home: 85 Eastern Pky Brooklyn NY 11238 E-mail: wenker@aaahawk.com.

WENKERT, DEBORAH, pediatric rheumatologist, researcher; b. Ames, Iowa, July 2, 1958; d. Ernest and Ann (Davis) W.; m. Roger Alan Young, Aug. 1988; children: Benjamin Sidney Young, Jonathan Davis Young, Nathaniel Theodore Young. BA, Rice U., 1979; MD, U. Tex., 1987. Diplomate Am. Bd. Pediatrics and Pediat. Rheumatology. Technician, rschr. Baylor Coll. Medicine, Houston, 1979-81; intern Children's Hosp., St. Louis, 1987-88, resident, 1988-90; fellow New Eng. Med. Ctr., Boston, 1990-93; postdoctoral Harvard U., Cambridge, Mass., 1991-94; instr. Washington U. Med. Sch., St. Louis, 1994-98; v.p. Bench Master Inc., 1998—; asst. prof. St. Louis U. Med. Sch., 1999—. Mem.courtesy staff Shriners Hosp. for Crippled Children, St. Louis, 2001—. Cancer Rsch. Inst. fellow, 1991; Physician Scientist awardee NIH, 1993.. Fellow Am. Acad. Pediat., Am. Coll. Rheumatology.

WENNER, CHARLES RODERICK, lawyer; b. New Haven, Jan. 10, 1947; s. Charles Bellew and Joan Rhoda (Morrison) W.; m. Jovita C. Vergara, June 11, 1999; children: Abigail Jessica, Charles Roderick Jr. BS, Coll. Charleston, 1969; JD, U. Conn., 1973. Bar: Conn. 1974, D.C. 1977. Law clk. Conn. Superior Ct., Hartford, 1973-74; staff atty. SEC, Washington, 1974-76, spl. counsel to chmn., 1976-77; assoc. Fulbright & Jaworski, 1977-81, ptnr., 1981—. Lectr. law Sch. Law U. Conn., 1973-74. Trustee Calvary United Meth. Ch., Arlington, Va., 1993-95, 97-98; counselor Gospel Mission of Washington, 1991—; bd. dirs. Operation Friendship Internat., Inc., Washington, 1993—. Recipient Am. Hist. award DAR, Charleston, 1969. Mem. ABA, D.C. Bar Assn. Methodist. Avocations: running. Home: Apt 105 1101 S Arlington Ridge Rd Arlington VA 22202-1922 Office: Fulbright & Jaworski 801 Pennsylvania Ave NW Fl 3-5 Washington DC 20004-2623

WENNER, GENE CHARLES, arts management executive; b. Catasauqua, Pa., Dec. 21, 1931; s. Clinton G. and Bertha (Taggert) W.; m. Carole Brunner, Aug. 15, 1953; children: Robert Larren, Laurel E. Wenner Carsell BS in Music, West Chester (Pa.) State Coll., 1953; M.Ed. in Music, Pa. State U., 1954. Tchr. music Phila. pub. schs., 1945-55, 56-60; assoc. prof. Kutztown (Pa.) State Coll., 1960-66, dir. coll. choir, 1960-66; fine arts adv. Pa. Dept. Edn., 1966-69, U.S. Office Edn., 1969-71; asst. dir. arts in edn. program John D. Rockefeller 3d Fund, 1971-78; arts edn. coordinator Office Commr., U.S. Office Edn., 1978-79; pres. Am. Music Conf., Wilmette, Ill., 1979-81; v.p. for programs Nat. Found. Advancement in Arts, Miami, Fla., 1983-87; pres. Arts and Edn. Cons., Inc., Reston, Va., 1987-91; sr. cons. Bus. & Industry for Arts Edn., 1990-91; exec. dir. Charlotte (N.C.) Community Sch. for the Arts, 1991-96; pres. Arts & Edn. Cons., Inc., Pittsfield, Mass., 1996—. Fund raising cons. Nat. Pub. Radio, Nat. Music Found., Mohawk Theater Capital Campaign, Goldman Meml. Band, Jacob's Pillow, Berkshire C.C. Non-Profit mgmt. Counsel, Mass. Coll. Liberal Arts; mus. dir. Allentown (Pa.) Mcpl. Oper. 1962-63, Allentown Civic Little Theatre, 1964, Little Theatre Alexandria, Va., 1971; dir. Hershey (Pa.) Little Theatre, 1967-68, Hershey Community Chorus, 1967-69 Composer: I'll Never Forget You, 1968, Chorale of Dedication, 1974, Great Things God Hath Done, 1986, In My ather's House,

1986; original music and script Adventures in the Arts, Hershey, 1968; also original TV music, I Am the Way, 1985, When You Remember, 1985; author papers, reports in field. Served with AUS, 1955-56. Named Best Mus. Dir. Little Theatre Alexandria Mem. Music Educators Nat. Conf., Network Performing and Visual Arts Schs. Clubs: Masons. Home and Office: 3 Walden Ln Pittsfield MA 01201-1554 E-mail: aecwenn@concentric.net.

WENRICH, JOHN WILLIAM, college president; b. York, Pa., June 8, 1937; s. Ralph Chester and Helen Louise (McCollam) W.; m. Linda Larsen, June 23, 1961 (dec. Sept. 1966); 1 child, Thomas Allen; m. Martha Gail Lofberg, Sept. 1, 1967; 1 child, Margaret Ann AB, Princeton U., 1959; MA, U. Mich., 1961, PhD, 1968. Fgn. service officer Dept. State, Washington, 1962-65; rep. Internat. Devel. Found., N.Y.C., 1965-66; project dir. U. Mich., Ann Arbor, 1966-69; asst. to pres. Coll. San Mateo, Calif., 1969-71; v.p. Ferris State U., Big Rapids, Mich., 1971-75, pres., 1984-88, Canada Coll., Redwood City, Calif., 1975-79, Santa Ana Coll., 1979-84; chancellor San Diego Community Coll. Dist., 1988-90, Dallas County Community Coll., 1990—. Co-author: Leadership in Administration of Technical and Vocational Education, 1974, Administration of Vocational Education. Recipient Meritorious Service medal Dept. State, 1966; Hinsdale scholar Sch. Edn. U. Mich., 1968 Avocations: bridge; tennis; travel. Home: 3504 Springbrook St Dallas TX 75205-4337 Office: 701 Elm St Dallas TX 75202-3200

WENSINGER, ARTHUR STEVENS, language and literature educator, writer; b. Grosse Pointe, Mich., Mar. 9, 1926; s. Carl Franklin and Suzanne (Stevens) W. Grad., Phillips Acad. Andover, 1944; BA, Dartmouth Coll., 1948; MA, U. Mich., 1951; postgrad., U. Munich, 1948, 50-51, U. Innsbruck, 1953-54; PhD, U. Mich., 1958. Instr., asst. prof., assoc. prof. Wesleyan U., Middletown, Conn., 1955-68, prof. German and humanities, 1968-93, Marcus Taft prof. German and humanities, 1977-93, prof. emeritus, 1994—, chmn. dept. German lang. and lit., 1971-93, also sr. tutor Coll. Letters; pres. Friends of Davison Art Ctr. Mem. selection com. German Acad. Exch. Svc., 1980-92. Author: Hogarth on High Life, 1970, Plays by Arthur Schnitzler, 1982-1983, 1995; translator, editor (with W. Gropius): The Theater of the Bauhaus, 1961, translator, editor (with W. Gropius): rev. edit., 1996, translator, editor: The Letters and Journals of Paula Modersohn-Becker, 1983, translator, editor (with W. Gropius): 2d edit., 1990, translator, editor: Querelle: The Film Book, 1983, translator, editor: Franz Kafka: Pictures of a Life, 1984; translator: The Sons, 1989, Marlene Dietrich: Portraits, 1984, Shabbat (Peter Stefan Jungk), 1985, Hanna Schygulla and R.W. Fassbinder, 1986, Kaethe Kollwitz: The Work in Color, 1988, Niklas Frank, In the Shadow of the Reich, 1991, (plays) Arthur Schnitzler; co-translator: Günter Grass, Two States-One Nation?, 1990; contbr. ; editor: Stone Island (Peter S. Boynton), 1973; co-editor: Hesse's Siddhartha, 1962; continuing editor: Correspondence of Norman Douglas, 1868-1952, : exbhn. and symposium catalog articles on Norman Douglas, continuing translator: plays of Schnitzler; contbr. , articles to profl. jours.; , translator in field. Wesleyan Ctr. for Humanities fellow, 1974, Reynolds fellow, 1950-51, Fulbright fellow, 1954-55, Danforth fellow, 1959, Ford Found. fellow, 1970-71; Inter Nations grantee, 1978, 82, NEH rsch. grantee, 1993. Mem. MLA, Am. Assn. Tchrs. German, Heinrich von Kleist Gesellschaft, Internat. Brecht Soc., Kafka Soc. Am., Auden Soc., Soc. Preservation New Eng. Antiquities, Conn. Acad. Arts and Scis., Yale Libr. Assocs., Haddam, Conn. Land Trust, Phi Beta Kappa, Phi Kappa Phi, Delta Tau Delta. Home: Candlewood Farm 95 Jacoby Rd Higganum CT 06441-4225 Office: Wesleyan U Fisk Hall Middletown CT 06459-6082 E-mail: awensinger@wesleyan.edu.

WENSITS, JAMES EMRICH, newspaper editor; b. South Bend, Ind., Oct. 8, 1944; s. John Andrew and Melva Mae (Betz) W.; m. Wendy Anne Reygaert, June 12, 1965; children: Cheryl Wensits Lightfoot, John, Kristin Wensits Hough, Amy; m. Catherine Marie Palmer Pope, Nov. 27, 1987 (dec. Sept. 1996); 1 stepchild, Christina Pope; m. Carol Schaal, Oct. 19, 1998. BA in Journalism, Purdue U., 1966. Reporter South Bend Tribune, 1966-92, assoc. editor, 1992—. Office: South Bend Tribune 225 W Colfax Ave South Bend IN 46626-1001

WENTE, VAN ARTHUR, consultant, retired government official; b. Johnston City, Ill., Jan. 11, 1925; s. Edward H. and Pauline Lucille (Barham) W.; m. Jane Van Derveer Updike, Sept. 22, 1962; children: Gretchen Jane, Robert Edward. BSChemE, Washington U., St. Louis, 1945; grad., Nat. Def. U., 1977. Chem. engr. Firestone Tire & Rubber Co., Pottstown, Pa., 1945-50, USN Research Lab., Washington, 1950-56; info. officer U.S. Atomic Energy Agy., Germantown, Md., 1956-59, sci. advisor, 1959-61; documentation head NASA, Washington, 1961-64, systems head, 1965-80, sci. and tech. info. dir., 1981-89, sr. exec. svc., 1983-89. Mem. adv. group on aerospace R & D info. NATO, 1983-89. Contbr. articles to profl. jours., chpts. to books. Chairperson ch. coun. Concord-St. Andrews United Meth. Ch., 2000—; treas. Montgomery Interclub Sr. Tennis League, 1997—. Recipient Presdl. award Mgmt. Improvement, 1970. Fellow Nat. Fedn. Abstracting and Info. Svcs. (hon., bd. dirs. 1986-88); mem. AIChE, Am. Soc. for Info. Scis., Chem. Engrs. Washington (treas. 1957-58, sec. 1958-59), Kenwood Golf and Country Club (bd. govs. 1995-2000, chair tennis com. 1998-00), Mil. Officers Club, Omicron Delta Kappa, Sigma Xi. Avocations: tennis, music, photography. Home and Office: 5919 Gloster Rd Bethesda MD 20816-1144 E-mail: van.wente@att.net.

WENTS, DORIS ROBERTA, psychologist; b. L.A., Aug. 26, 1944; d. John Henry and Julia (Cole) W. BA, UCLA, 1966; MA, San Francisco State U., 1968; postgrad., Calif. State U., L.A., 1989-90, Claremont (Calif.) Grad. U, 1990—. Lic. ednl. psychologist, credentialed sch. psychologist, Calif. Sch. psychologist Diagnostic Sch. for Neurologically Handicapped Children, L.A., 1969-86; pvt. practice Monterey Park, Calif., 1986—. Instr. Calif. State U., L.A., 1977. Co-author: Southern California Ordinal Scales of Development, 1977. Mem. Western Psychol. Assn., L.A. World Affairs Coun., L.A. Conservancy, Zeta Tau Alpha (officer Santa Monica alumnae chpt. 1970—, Cert. of Merit 1979), Sigma Xi. Avocations: travel, watersports, theatre, bridge, photography. Office: Claremont Grad U Dept Psychology Claremont CA 91711 E-mail: Dori.Wents@cgu.edu.

WENTWORTH, ALAN F. neurosurgeon; b. St. Ansgar, Iowa, July 2, 1931; s. Laydon S. and Charlotte K. Wentworth; m. Ruth C. Wentworth, Oct. 13, 1956; children: Michael, Kathryn, Margaret, Richard. BA, U. Iowa, 1954, MD, 1956. Diplomate Am. Bd. Neurol. Surgery. Commd. ensign USN, 1956, advanced through grades to comdr., resigned, 1970, flight surgeon, 1958-59, resident in neurosurgery, 1960-64, staff neurosurgeon, 1964-70; pvt. practice neurosurgery Neurol. Surgeons Ltd., Green Bay, Wis., 1970-97, ret., 1997. Chief neurosurg. divsn. USN Hosp., Phila., 1964-70. Bd. dirs. St. Vincent Hosp., Green Bay, 1990-99, Weidner Ctr. for Performing Arts, Green Bay, 1999—. Fellow ACS; mem. U.S. Power Squadrons (officer, past dist. comdr., tchr. 1975-99). Avocations: sailing, boating, photography, computer communications. E-mail: AWentworth@aol.com.

WENTWORTH, BETTE WILSON, artist, educator; b. Paducah, Tex., Aug. 14, 1938; d. Herbert Woodrow and Mertice (Foster) Wilson; m. Nicholas Noyes Wentworth, Apr. 25, 1964; children: Mark Benning, Alan Hunter. BA, U. Tex., 1961; postgrad., Sch. Social Work Smith Coll., 1961-62, Glassell Sch. of Art, Houston, 1976-80. Social caseworker De Pelchin Faith Home, Houston, 1962-66; artist, 1968-97, Austin, 1997-99; art tchr. continuing edn. Spring Br. Independent Sch. Dist., Houston, 1980-91. Juror Tenneco Internat. Children's Exhibit, 1983, Scholastic Art awards Houston Independent Sch. Dist., 1984. Exhibited in solo show at North Fourth Cafe, Albuquerque, 1997, group shows at The Art League of Houston, 1982 (2d place), 83, Watercolor Art Soc., Houston, 1983, 84, 85, 87 (1st place), 88, Jewish Cmty. Ctr. 1983, Galveston Art League, 1983, Town and Country Gallery, 1987, Aries Gallery, 1989, Aquamedia, Wash., 1988, Waterloo Watercolor Group Spring Show, 1997. Pres. Bunkerhill West Civic Club, 1988; vol. Trinity Hosp. Aux., 1999; pres. Brenham Fine Arts League, 2001—02; bd. dirs. Altharetta Yeargin Art Mus., Seton Hosp. Vol. Aux., vol. Mem. Watercolor Art Soc. Houston (chmn. 13th nat. exhibition), The Art League Houston, Waterloo Watercolor Group. Episcopalian. Avocations: walking, reading, mysteries. Home and Office: PO Box 339 491 Oak Forest Rd Bellville TX 77418-9617

WENTWORTH, DIANA VON WELANETZ, author; b. L.A., Mar. 4, 1941; d. Eugene and Marguerite (Rufi) Webb; m. Frederic Paul von Welanetz, Nov. 2, 1963 (dec. Mar. 19, 1989); 1 child, Lexi Welanetz Bursin; m. Theodore S. Wentworth, Dec. 9, 1989; stepchildren: ChristinaWentworth Coyne, Kathryn Allison Wentworth Purdy. Student, UCLA, 1958-60. Ptnr. von Welanetz Cooking Workshop, L.A., 1968-85; host TV series New Way Gourmet, 1983-86; founder Inside Edge Found. Edn., Calif., 1985-93. Spkr. in field. Author: The Pleasure of Your Company, 1976 (Cookbook of Yr.), With Love from Your Kitchen, 1976, The Art of Buffet Entertaining, 1978, The Von Welanetz Guide to Ethnic Ingredients, 1983, L.A. Cuisine, 1985, Celebrations, 1985, Chicken Soup for the Soul Cookbook, 1995, Send Me Someone, 2001. Treas. Louise L. Hay Found., Carson, Calif., 1988—; advisor Women of Vision, Calif., 1995—. Mem. Internat. Food, Wine & Travel Writers Assn., Internat. Assn. Cooking Profls., Angels of Arts/Orange County Performing Arts Ctr., Ctr. Club. Avocations: painting, fine art, travel writing, design. Office: 4631 Teller Ave Ste 100 Newport Beach CA 92660-8105 E-mail: diana@sendmesomeone.com.

WENTWORTH, JACK ROBERTS, business educator, consultant; b. Elgin, Ill., June 11, 1928; s. William Franklin and Elizabeth (Roberts) W.; m. Rosemary Ann Pawlak, May 30, 1956; children: William, Barbara Student, Carleton Coll., 1946-48; BS, Ind. U., 1950, MBA, 1954, DBA, 1959. Coord. displays Cadillac divsn., Gen. Motors Corp., Detroit, 1954-56; asst. prof. bus., assoc. dir. research Sch. of Bus. Ind. U., Bloomington, 1957-60, assoc. prof., dir. rsch., 1960-70, prof., 1970-93, chmn. MBA program, 1970-76, chmn. dept., faculty rep. NCAA, 1978-85, dean Sch. of Bus., 1984-93, Arthur M. Weimer prof., 1993-97, Arthur M. Weimer prof. emeritus, 1997—. Mktg. cons., Bloomington, 1960—; bd. dirs. Kimball Internat., Jasper, Ind. Editor: (monograph) Marketing Horizons, 1965; exec. editor Bus. Horizons, 1960-70 Served to 1st lt. USAF, 1950-53 Recipient Teaching award MBA Assn., 1973, 78, 81, 84, 85, Svc. award Assn. for Bus. and Econ. Rsch., 1983. Mem. Am. Mktg. Assn. (v.p. 1971-73), Grad. Mgmt. Admissions Coun. (chmn. bd. trustees 1977-78), Univ. Club, Masons, Beta Gamma Sigma (pres. Alpha of Ind. chpt. 1971-72, bd. govs. 1986-98, nat. pres. 1994-96). Republican. Methodist. Avocations: athletic events; travel; bicycling; model railroading; magic. Office: Indiana Univ Sch Bus Bloomington IN 47405

WENTWORTH, MICHAEL JUSTIN, curator; b. Detroit, June 15, 1938; s. Harold Arnold and Marian (Jones) W. MFA, U. Mich., 1962; PHD, Harvard U., 1976. Curator, acting dir. Smith Coll. Mus. Art, Northhampton, Mass., 1968—69; dir. Rose Art Mus., Brandies U., Waltham, 1970—74; assoc. prof. Wellesley Coll., 1976; curator Boston Athenaeum, 1985—. Author: Tissot: Catalogue Raisonné of Prints, 1976, James Tissot, 1984, Tissot, 1988, 50 Books in the Collection of the Boston Athenaeum, 1994, The Boston Library Society, 1995. Office: Boston Athenaeum 10 1/2 Beacon St Boston MA 02108-3777 E-mail: wentworth@bostonathenaeum.org.

WENTWORTH, MURRAY JACKSON, artist, educator; b. Boston, Jan. 18, 1927; s. Harold Squires and Mary Louise (Murray) W.; m. Elaine Magnuson, June 16, 1953; 1 child, Janet Louise. Diploma, Art Inst. Boston, 1950. Advt. artist Agy. Art Svcs., Boston, 1950-58; instr. Art Inst. Boston, 1958-78; artist, instr. Norwell, Mass., 1968—. Group shows, Allied Artists Am., 1980, 82 (Silver medal 1980), Allied Art Am., 1982 (Obrig prize 1982), Am. Watercolor Soc., 1980 (Dolphin fellow 1980), Rocky Mount Nat. Exhibition, 1982 (Grumbacher award 1982). Cpl. U.S. Army, 1945-47. Recipient Hudson Valley Art Assn. award, 1991, Whitney Meml. award, 1996, Guild Boston Artists award, 1992, Watercolor award Acad. Artists' Assn., 1997, Daler Rowney award, 1998, Hudson Valley Art Assn. Watercolor award, 1998. Mem. NAD (Pike Meml. award 1986, award of merit 1997), Allied Artists Am. (Mina Mora Meml. award for watercolor 1997), Am. Watercolor Soc., New Eng. Watercolor Soc. (Grumbacher gold medal 1989). Home: 132 Central St Norwell MA 02061-1306

WENTWORTH, THEODORE SUMNER, lawyer; b. Bklyn., July 18, 1938; s. Theodore Sumner and Alice Ruth (Wortmann) W.; m. Sharon Linelle Arkush, 1965 (dec. 1987); children: Christina Linn, Kathrun Allison; m. Diana Webb von Welanetz, 1989; 1 stepchild, Lexi von Welanetz. AA, Am. River Coll., 1958; JD, U. Calif., Hastings, 1962. Bar: Calif. 1963, U.S. Dist. Ct. (no. and ctrl. dists.) Calif., U.S. Ct. Appeals (9th cir.), U.S. Supreme Ct.; cert. trial specialist; diplomate Nat. Bd. Trial Advocacy; assoc. Am. Bd. Trial Advocates. Assoc. Adams, Hunt & Martin, Santa Ana, Calif., 1963-66; ptnr. Hunt, Liljestrom & Wentworth, 1967-77; pres. Solabs Corp.; chmn. bd., exec. v.p. Plant Warehouse, Inc., Hawaii, 1974-82; prin. Law Offices of Wentworth, Paoli & Purdy, Newport Beach & Temecula, Calif.; judge pro tem Superior Ct. Attys. Panel Harbor Mcpl. Ct. Owner Eagles Ridge Ranch, Temecula, 1977—. Author (M. Evans): Build a Better Spouse Trap, 2002. Pres., bd. dirs. Santa Ana-Tustin Cmty. Chest, 1972; v.p., trustee South Orange County United Way, 1973-75; pres. Orange County Fedn. Funds, 1972-73; bd. dirs. Orange County Mental Health Assn. Mem. ABA, Am. Bd. Trial Advocates (assoc.), State Bar Calif., Orange County Bar Assn. (dir. 1972-76), Am. Trial Lawyers Assn., Calif. Trial Lawyers Assn. (bd. govs. 1968-70), Orange County Trial Lawyers Assn. (pres. 1967-68), Lawyer-Pilots Bar Assn., Aircraft Owners and Pilots Assn., Bahia Corinthian Yacht Club, Pacific Club, Newport. Achievements include research in vedic prins., natural law, quantum physics and mechanics. Office: 4631 Teller Ave Ste 100 Newport Beach CA 92660-8105 also: 41530 Enterprise Cir S Temecula CA 92590-4816 E-mail: ocrawfirm@aol.com.

WENTWORTH, WILLIAM EDGAR, journalist; b. Newton, N.H., Nov. 4, 1931; s. Charles Bertrand and Mildred Frances (Ingalls) W. BA in Journalism, U. Tenn., Knoxville, 1958. Reporter Rochester (N.H.) Courier, 1959; reporter, copy editor Foster's Daily Democrat, Dover, N.H., 1959-68; copy editor Florida Today, Melbourne, Fla., 1968-93, ret., 1993. Author: (book) Vital Records, 1790-1829, 1995, Journals of Enoch Hayes Place, 1998; editor: (periodical) Genealogical Record, 1995—. Data entry-online Dover Pub. Libr., N.H., 1993—; libr. Woodman Inst. Mus., Dover. Sgt. USAF, 1950-54. Mem. Strafford County Genealogical Soc., Citizens Against Government Waste, Srs. Coalition, N.H. Hist. Soc., N.H. Soc. Genealogists, Maine Soc. Genealogists, New Eng. Hist. Genealogical Soc. Republican. Baptist. Avocation: genealogy research. Home: 13 Olde Madbury Ln Dover NH 03820-5439 E-mail: edwent@ttlc.net.

WENTZ, CATHERINE JANE, elementary education educator; b. Boise, Idaho, Aug. 11, 1948; d. Frank Paul and Litha Zella (Langer) W. BA, Boise State U., 1970, MA, 1975. Tchr. 2d grade Longfellow Sch., Boise, 1970-72, Taft Elem. Sch., Boise, 1972-84; tchr. 1st grade Cole Elem. Sch., 1984-87, Garfield Elem. Sch., Boise, 1987-92, Horizon Elem. Sch., Boise, 1992—. Instr. Spalding Edn. Found., Boise, 1980—. Active Horizon PTO. Mem. NEA, Idaho Coun. Internat. Reading Assn., Boise Edn. Assn., Idaho Edn. Assn., Orton Dyslexia Soc., Alpha Delta Kappa. Avocations: singing, dancing, acting, piano, tennis. Home: 2063 E Lochmeadow Ct Meridian ID 83642-5789 Office: Horizon Elem Sch 730 N Mitchell St Boise ID 83704-9783

WENTZ, CHARLES ALVIN, JR. environmentalist, chemical engineer; b. Edwardsville, Ill., Oct. 12, 1935; s. Charles Alvin and Frances Margaret (Bohm) W.; m. Sandra Niederecker, Dec. 11, 1961 (div. Jan. 1982); children: Sharon, Christopher, Suzanne, Sheila; m. Joan Domigan, Aug., 1983. BSChemE, U. Mo., Rolla, 1957, MSChemE, 1959; PhDChemE, Northwestern U., 1961; MBA, So. Ill. U., 1985. Registered profl. engr. Various exec. positions Phillips Petroleum Co., Bartlesville, Okla., 1961-82; pres. New Park Waste Treatment, Inc., New Orleans, 1982-83, ENSCO, Inc., El Dorado, Ark., 1983-84; pres., CEO Wentz Healthcare, Inc., Lebanon, Ill., 1984—; CEO Internat. Sci. Mgmt., Inc., Edwardsville, 1985—; mgr., waste and safety Argonne (Ill.) Nat. Lab., 1988-91; assoc. dean Chulalongkorn U., Bangkok, 1994; ptnr. Bohm Heirs Partnership, 2000—. Vis. prof. So. Ill. U., Edwardsville, 1984-86 Author: Hazardous Waste Management, 1989, 2d edit., 1995, (with others) Occupational and Environmental Safety, 1990, Encyclopedia of Environmental Control Technology, vol. 5, 1992, Safety, Health and Environmental Protection, 1998; editor spl. issues Environ. Progress, 1988, 89; patentee in field; contbr. articles to profl. jours. Mem. adv. bd. Ill. Hazardous Waste Rsch. and Info. Ctr., 1989-91. Mem.: ACS, AIChE, Nat. Safety Coun., Acad. Chem. Engrs. U. Mo. Rolla Alumni Assn., Greater Edwardsville Area Cmty. Found., Lincoln Sch. Alumni Found., Sigma Xi. Avocations: hunting, fishing, gardening, cooking. Office: Internat Sci Mgmt Inc 5953 Old Poag Rd Edwardsville IL 62025-7341 E-mail: jdomigan@aol.com.

WENTZ, CHRISTOPHER JAMES, state agency administrator; b. St. Louis, Apr. 28, 1955; s. Walter William and Mary Elenor (Wamser) W.; m. Christine Marie Schulte, Oct. 13, 1978; children: Ashley Kristen, Ryan Christine. BS in Biology, S.W. Mo. State U., Springfield, 1977. Technician Century Geophys. Corp., Tulsa, Okla., 1978-80; energy policy analyst State of N.Mex. Energy Dept., Santa Fe, 1980—. N.Mex. rep. Western Interstate Energy Bd., Denver, 1983—, Western Govs. Assn., Denver, 1989—, Interstate Oil and Gas Compact Commn., Oklahoma City, 1984-90; pres. Friends of the Corrales (N.Mex.) Libr., 1994-96. Mem. Nat. Assn. State Energy Ofcls. Avocations: hiking, hunting, fishing, golf, gardening. Home: PO Box 2174 Corrales NM 87048-2174 Office: NMex Energy Dept Conserv & Mgmt Div PO Box 6429 1220 St Francis Dr Santa Fe NM 87505

WENTZ, DEBRA LINOWITZ, professional association executive; b. Cape May, N.J., May 25, 1952; d. Sol. Myron and Ruth (Levy) Linowitz. BA, Goucher Coll., 1973; MA, U. Conn., 1975, PhD, 1980, U. Paris, 1978; Exec. MBA, U. Pa., 1982. Sr. copywriter, dir. pub. rels. Berry & Whittey Assocs., Hartford, Conn., 1973-77; pres., mktg. coord. Cabinet Wentz, Créteil, France, 1977-79; dir. publs. and pub. rels. Giuffre Med. Ctr., Phila., 1979-83; v.p. mktg. and bus. devel. Johnston Assocs. Inc., Princeton, N.J., 1983-84; mgr. planning and pub. affairs N.J. Housing and Mortgage Fin. Agy., Trenton, 1987-89, dir. planning and intergovernmental rels., 1989-93; v.p. mktg., pub. rels., planning devel. Cornerstone Treatment Facilities Network, N.Y.C., 1993-95; CEO N.J. Assn. Mental Health Agys. Inc., Mercerville, NJ, 1995—. Mem. Children's Sys. of Care, NJ Statewide Implementation Adv. Task Force, Redirection II Statewide Task Force; cons. in field, spkr. Recipient adminstr. recognition award, NAMI NJ, 1999, award for tireless and invaluable work to advance and support position of mentally ill, Cmty. Mental Health Found., 1999, 1st Place Advocacy Schizophrenia Reintegration award, Eli Lilly & Co., 2001, Ann Klein award, Cmty. Health Law Project, 2002. Mem.: NJ Bus. and Industry Assn., Employers Assn. NJ, Assn. Ambulatory Behavioral Health Care, Nat. Coun. Cmty. Behavioral Healthcare (pub. policy com. and divsn. state assns.), Nat. Psychiat. Health Sys., Am. Soc. Assn. Execs. Avocations: antiques, study of Victorian era, French landuage and culture, chocolate, cuisine. Office: NJ Assn Mental Health Agys 3575 Quakerbridge Rd Ste 102 Mercerville NJ 08619

WENTZ, EDWARD, music educator; b. Milw., Jan. 22, 1941; m. Dorena Canfield, July 24, 1971; 1 child Jennifer. BA, Northland Coll., 1966. Cert. Tchg. credential 1990. Dir. elem. band Murrieta Valley Unified Sch. Dist., Murrieta, Calif., 1998—; dir. mid. sch. band Perris Unifiec Sch. Dist., Perris, 1996—98; dir. mid./h.s. band Woodcrest Christian Schools, Riverside, 1991—96. Musician: arranger and composer of many band selections, 2002 (BRAVO Award, 2002). Nominee BRAVO Nominee, LA Ctr. For The Performing Arts, 2002. R-Consevative. Home: 29596 Kanan Rd Sun City CA 92586

WENTZ, JEFFREY LEE, information systems executive; b. Philippi, W.Va., Nov. 29, 1956; s. William Henry and Edith Marie (McBee) W.; m. Phuong Thi Thanh, Nov. 17, 2001. AS in Data Processing, BS in Acctg., Fairmont (W.Va.) State Coll., 1978. Programmer/analyst U.S. Dept. Energy, Morgantown, W.Va., 1978-79; analyst Middle South Svcs., New Orleans, 1979-81; sr. analyst Bank of Am., San Francisco, 1981-83; pres., info. sys. cons. Wentz Cons. Inc., 1983-2000; dir. tech. solutions Charles Schwab & Co., 2000—.

WENTZ, RICHARD EUGENE, religious studies educator; b. Palmerton, Pa., Jan. 10, 1928; s. Walter E. and Mary Susanna (Snyder) W.; m. Yvonne Louise Delauder, June 25, 1955; children: Selena Louise, Susanna Marie, Melissa Roulette; m. Cynthia G. Carsten, Dec. 21, 1991; 1 child, Shawn Marie. AB, Ursinus Coll., Collegeville, Pa., 1948; BD, Lancaster (Pa.) Theol. Sem., 1951; PhD, George Washington U., 1971. Master English and Bible, Mercersburg (Pa.) Acad., 1955-62; asst. prof. religious studies Pa. State U., University Park, 1962-72; prof. religious studies Ariz. State U., Tempe, 1972—, prof. emeritus, 1999—. Disting. vis. prof. U. Tulsa, 1991. Author: Religion in the New World, 1990, John Williamson Nevin, American Theologian, 1997, The Culture of Religious Pluralism, 1998, Pennsylvania Dutch Folk Spirituality, 1993, Why People Do Bad Things in the Name of Religion, 1993; editor-in-chief Anglican Theol. Rev., 1989-91; contbr. articles to religious jours., including Christian Century, Ch. History, Parabola, Founds., Jour. Am. Acad. Religion, Religion in Life, Japanese Jour. Religious Studies, Encounter, Anglican Theol. Rev.; editl. bd. Pennsylvania German Studies; contbg. editor New Mercersburg Rev. Lilly Endowment grantee, 1975; rsch. scholar Nanzan Inst. for Religion and Culture, Nagoya, Japan, fall 1987. Mem. Am. Acad. Religion (pres. western region 1989). Avocations: wood carving, furniture refinishing, storytelling. Home: HC 1 Box 1426 Strawberry AZ 85544-9737 Office: Ariz State U Dept Religious Studies Tempe AZ 85287-3104 E-mail: richardwentz@asu.edu.

WENTZ, SIDNEY FREDERICK, insurance company executive, foundation executive; b. Dallas, Mar. 27, 1932; s. Howard Beck and Emmy Lou (Cawthon) W.; m. Barbara Strait, Sept. 9, 1961; children: Eric, Jennifer, Robin. AB, Princeton U., 1954; LLB, Harvard U., 1960. Bar: N.Y. 1961. Atty. White & Case, N.Y.C., 1960-65, Western Electric Co., 1965-66, AT&T Corp., 1966-67; with Crum & Forster Inc., Morristown, N.J., 1967—, v.p., gen. counsel, 1967-71, sr. v.p., gen. counsel, 1971-72, exec. v.p., 1972, pres., 1972-87, chmn. bd., 1987-88, chmn. exec. com., 1988-90, also bd. dirs.; chmn. bd. Robert Wood Johnson Found., Princeton, 1989-99. Trustee Morristown Meml. Hosp., 1974-96, Drew U., 1991—. Served to lt. (j.g.) USNR, 1954-57. Mem. Morris County Golf Club, Sakonnet (R.I.) Golf Club, Baltusrol Golf Club, Jupiter Hills (Fla.) Golf Club, Loblolly Pines (Fla.) Golf Club.

WENTZ, WENDELL FRANKLIN, columnist, writer; b. Eufaula, Ala., Mar. 24, 1939; s. Hermann Wendell and Johnnie Mae (Jones) W.; children: Hermann Wendell II, Anna C. Vaughan, Sarah C. Morris, Larry Eugene Cruce II; m. Joanna B. Wentz, Jan. 21, 2000. AB, Mercer U., Macon, Ga., 1961. Pastor Liberty Bapt. Ch., Georgetown, Ga., 1956-57, Mitchell (Ga.) Bapt. Ch., 1957-70, Benton (Ala.) Bapt. Ch., 1970-77, First Bapt. Ch., Lowry City, Mo., 1977-79, Lakeland Bapt. Ch., Clinton, 1979-80; with material svcs. Kansas City Power & Light Co., 1979—; columnist Clinton Daily Dem., 1989—. Freelance writer. Avocations: photography, gardening, reading. Home: Frog Rock 930 NE 231 Rd Clinton MO 64735-9717 Office: Kansas City Power & Light 400 SW Highway P Clinton MO 64735-9093

WENTZ, WILLIAM HENRY, JR. aerospace engineer, educator; b. Wichita, Kans., Dec. 18, 1933; BS in Mech. Engring. cum laude, Wichita State U., 1955, MS in Aeronautical Engring., 1961; PhD in Engring. Mechanics, U. Kans., 1969. Lic. profl. engr., Kans. Liaison engr. Beech Aircraft, 1952-53; propulsion engr. Boeing Co., Wichita, Kans., 1955; instr. mech. engring. Wichita State U., 1957-58; aerodynamicist Boeing Co., Wichita, 1958-63; from asst. prof. to assoc. prof. aeronautical engring. Wichita State U., 1963-75, prof. aeronautical engring., 1975-83, Gates-Learjet prof. aeronautical engring., 1983-86, disting. prof. aerospace engring., 1986-98, dir. Ctr. Basic and Applied Rsch. Inst. Aviation Rsch., 1986-89, exec. dir. Nat. Inst. Aviation Rsch., 1988-97; sr. fellow Nat. Inst. Aviation Rsch., 1997-98; disting. prof. emeritus aerospace engring., exec. dir. emer. Nat. Inst. Aviation Rsch., 1999; ret. Dir. rsch. projects Boeing Co., 1960, 61, NASA, 1964-66, 66-68, 70-71, 71-83, 86-87, 86-88, 82-87, Dept. of Def., 1986-88, Kans. Tech. Enterprise Corp., 1988-96, FAA, 1986-96. Contbr. articles to profl. jours. With USAF, 1955-57. Recipient Disting. Engr. Svc. award Wichita State U., 1999, Kans. Aviation Honors award Gov. Bill Graves, 1999; Sci. Faculty fellow NSF, 1967-68. Fellow AIAA (assoc., past chmn. Wichita sect., Outstanding advisor student chpt. 1964, 65, 70, Gen. Aviation award 1981, Engr. of Yr. award Wichita sect. 1992, Engr. of Yr. award Region V 1991-92; mem. Soc. Automotive Engrs. (Ralph R. Teeter award 1973), Sigma Gamma Tau, Tau Beta Pi.

WENTZEL, KAREN LYNN, secondary education educator; b. Granite City, Ill., May 22, 1949; d. Mike J. and Virginia L. (Prewett) Firtos; m. Joseph A. Wentzel Jr., June 2, 1967 (div. 1989); 1 child, David J. AA, St. Louis Community Coll., 1988; BA summa cum laude, Fontbonne Coll., 1990; MEd, U. Mo., St. Louis, 1994. Cert. secondary tchr., Mo. Instr. writing Meramec Coll., St. Louis, 1990-91; tchr. Div. of Youth Svcs., 1991; tchr. lang. arts North Kirkwood Mid. Sch., 1991—98; tchr. Kirkwood H.S., 1998—. Features editor newspaper Fontbanner, 1990; mng. editor newsletter Hogan Highlights, 1991. Recipient Meramec's Exemplary Svc. award, 1991. Mem. Mo. Mid. Sch. Assn., Nat. Coun. Tchrs. English, Phi Theta Kappa, Sigma Tau Delta, Phi Delta Kappa, Chi Sigma Iota, Phi Kappa Phi. Avocations: classical ballet, tap and jazz dancing. Home: 4908 Fite Dr Imperial MO 63052-1412 Office: Kirkwood HS 801 W Essex Kirkwood MO 63122

WENTZLER, NANCY ANNE, economist; b. Montoursville, Pa., July 6, 1951; d. John McConnell and Betty (Hynan) W. BS, Pa. State U., 1973; MA, U. Wis., 1976, PhD, 1978. Asst. prof. Pa. State U., University Park, 1977-83; econs. advisor Dept. Labor, Washington, 1980-83; dep. br. chief Office Mgmt. and Budget, 1983-86, dep. adminstr., 1986-89; inspector gen., economist Commodity Futures Trading Commn., 1989-90; dep. dir. Office Thrift Supervision, 1990-94, office comptr. currency, 1994—. Equal opportunity counselor Office Mgmt. and Budget, Washington, 1986-87; cons., economist Dept. of Labor, Washington, 1980-83; instr. Va. Tech., Washington, 1989—. Contbr. articles to profl. jours. NIMH fellow U. Wis., Madison, 1977-78. Mem. Am. Econs. Assn., So. Econs. Assn., Western Econs. Assn. Home: 6511 Sunburst Way Alexandria VA 22315-3460 Office: Comptr of Currency 250 E St NE # Srsw Washington DC 20002-4923

WENZEL, JOAN ELLEN, artist; b. N.Y.C., July 23, 1944; d. Irwin S. and Pearl (Silverman) Rever; m. Allen Jay Wenzel, June 12, 1966 (div. June 1987); 1 child, Kimberly Anne; m. Robert Harold Messing, July 23, 1987 (dec.). Student, Syracuse U., 1962-64; BS in Painting, NYU, 1966, MA in Painting, 1976; postgrad., Harvard U., 1967. One-woman shows include Coplan Gallery, Boca Raton, Fla., 1997, Esperante Sculpture Ctr., 1996, Lighthouse Sch. and Gallery, Tequesta, Fla., 1996, Helander Gallery, Palm Beach, Fla., 1985, 89, 95, Adamar Fine Art, Miami, 1993, Gallery Contemporena, Jacksonville, Fla., 1993, Alexander Brest Mus., Jacksonville, 1993, Albertson Peterson Gallery, Winter Park, Fla., 1992, Amerifest, Miami, 1991, Gallery Yves Arman, N.Y.C., 1982, Palm Beach County Court House, West Palm Beach, Fla., 1991, One Brickell Square, Miami, 1992; exhbns. include Aldrich Mus., Ridgefield, Conn., 1977, Queens Mus., N.Y.C., 1981. Democrat. Jewish. Home: 2275 Ibis Isle Rd W Palm Beach FL 33480-5307

WENZEL, LEONARD ANDREW, engineering educator; b. Palo Alto, Calif., Jan. 21, 1923; s. Robert N. and Frances A. (Browne) W.; m. Mary E. Leathers, Oct. 21, 1944; children: Frances B., Alma L., Jesse R., Sara V.; m. Constance L. Houser, Jan. 1, 2000. BSChemE, Pa. State U., 1943; MSChemE, U. Mich., 1948, PhD in Chem. Engring., 1950. Registered profl. engr., Pa. Jr. rsch. engr. Phillips Petroleum Co., Bartlesville, Okla., 1943-44; jr. rsch. scientist Mellon Inst., Pitts., 1944; rsch. engr. Colgate-Palmolive, Jersey City, 1949-51; asst. prof. engring. Lehigh U., Bethlehem, Pa., 1951-56—, assoc. prof., 1956-60, prof., 1960-88, chmn. dep. chem. engring., 1962-83, prof. emeritus, 1988—. Project dir. UNESCO, Bucaramanga, Colombia, 1969-70, cons. in chem. engring., Maracaibo, Venezuela,, 1970-73; cons. Air Products and Chems., Allentown, Pa., 1951-80, Exxon, Baytown, Tex., 1983-86; chief scientist Arencibia Techs., Inc., Allentown, 1987-93; pres. L.A. Wenzel, Inc., Bethlehem, 1988—; dir. of tech. Eco-Gen Techs., Inc., Bethlehem, 1993-96. Co-author: Principles of Unit Operations, 1960, Introduction to Chemical Engineering, 1961, Chemical Process Analysis: Mass and Energy Balances, 1987. Bd. dirs. South Bethlehem Neighborhood Ctr., 1986—, Bethlehem Housing Authority, 1988-2002. Lt. (j.g.) USN, 1944-46, PTO. Fellow Am. Inst. Chem. Engrs.; mem. Am. Chem. Soc., Am. Soc. for Engring. Edn. Avocations: stamps, gardening, travel. Home: 2110 Henderson St Bethlehem PA 18017-4925 Office: Lehigh Univ Bldg #111 Bethlehem PA 18015 E-mail: law2@lehigh.edu.

WENZEL, LOREN ALVIN, accounting educator; b. Dec. 12, 1945; s. Alvin Karl Gustav and Lois LaVonne (Kuechenmeister) W.; children: Lisa Anne (Wenzel) Szumilas, Karl Louis, Sara Kirsten Wenzel; m. Nylah Onalee. DBA, U. Memphis, 1990. Asst. prof. acctg. Wichita (Kans.) State U., 1987-88; prof. acctg. Mankato (Minn.) State U., 1988-98, U. Md. European Divsn., Heidelberg, Germany, 1996-97, Buena Vista U., Storm Lake, Iowa, 1998-99, Austin Peay State U., Clarksville, Tenn., 1999-2000, Marshall U., Huntington, W.Va., 2000—, prof., head divsn. accountancy and legal environment, 2000—, Elizabeth McDowell Lewis endowed chair Lewis Coll. Bus., 2000—. Contbr. articles to profl. publs. Office: Marshall U Lewis Coll Bus Div Acctancy/Legal Environ One John Marshall Dr Huntington WV 25545 E-mail: wenzel@marshall.edu.

WENZEL, LYNN, writer, editor; b. San Francisco, Mar. 22, 1944; d. Ralph Everett and Roberta (Hansen) Shallenberger; m. Jeffrey Bruce Wenzel, June 28, 1964; children: Jennifer Ann, Michael Charles. BA magna cum laude, William Paterson U., 1976. Editor Womanspace, Hackensack, N.J., 1980-85; asst. editor New Directions for Women, Englewood, 1988-89, mng. editor, 1989-94; writer feature stories for nat. antique mag. Handed Down, Nevada City, Calif., 1996—. Writers features, mags., newspapers, Newsweek, N.Y. Times, Newsday, On the Issues, among others, N.J., 1979—; editor lit. and visual arts Bergen County N.J. Sch., Hackensack, 1992, Maywood, N.J., 1974-93; graphic artist New Directions for Women, Englewood, 1974-93, Marine Field Trip Manual, N.Y.C., 1989-93. Author: I Hear America Singing, 1989, Past & Promise, 1992; poetry and photography for photo-greeting cards Foto-Feelings, 1993. Apptd. constnl. bicentennial com. on women and the constn. Teaneck Mayor's Office, Teaneck, N.J., 1987. Recipient The World is Moving award Bd. Freeholders, 1993. Mem. NOW, No. N.J. Nat. Orgn. for Women (co-pres. 1985-87, chairwoman media task force 1987-89, 12th Annual Feminist Achievement award 1992), Bergen County Alliance for Women (chairwoman publicity/media 1986-88), Nat. Writers Union, Internat. Women's Writing Guild. Unitarian-Universalist. Avocations: antiques, reading, genealogy, photography, interior design.

WENZEL, RICHARD PUTNAM, internist; b. Phila., Jan. 8, 1940; m. Jo Gail Wenzel; children: Amy, Richard. BS, Haverford (Pa.) Coll., 1961; MD, Jefferson Med. Coll., 1965; MSc, London U., 1986. Diplomate Am. Bd. Internal Medicine, Am. Bd. Infectious Diseases. Intern Phila. Gen. Hosp., 1965-66; resident in internal medicine U. Md. Hosp., Balt., 1966-68, fellowship infectious diseases, 1968-69, chief resident in internal medicine, 1969-70; asst. in medicine U. Md. Med. Sch., 1969-70; hosp. epidemiologist U. Va. Med. Ctr., Charlottesville, 1972-86; asst. prof. internal medicine U. Va. Sch. of Medicine, 1972-76, assoc. prof., 1976-81, prof. internal medcine, 1981-86; dir. divsn. clin. epidemiology U. Iowa Coll. Medicine, Iowa City, 1986-89, prof. medicine, preventive medicine, 1986-95, dir. hosp. epidemiology and statewide epidemiology svcs., 1986-95, dir. divsn. gen. medicine, clin. epidemiology and health svcs. rsch., 1989-95; prof., chair dept. internal medicine Med. Coll. Va./Va. Commonwealth U., Richmond, 1995. Founding chair dept. epidemiology MS degree granting program Grad. Sch. Arts and Scis., U. Va., Charlottesville, 1981-86; pres. ho. staff assn. of interns, residents and fellows U. Md. Hosp., 1968-69; cons. U.S. HO. Reps. Ethics Adv. Bd. Ethics Regarding Freedom of Info. and Infection Surveillance Data, Washington, 1979-80, NIH small bus. innovation rsch, 1988; infection control cons. U. Calif. Systemwide Task Force on AIDS, 1987; spl. cons. NIH Study Sect. Epidemiology and Disease Control (#2), 1987-92. Author: Assessing Quality Care: Perspective for Clinicians, 1992, Prevention and Control of Nosocomial Infections, 1987, Handbook on Hospital Acquired Infections, 1981; founding editor Infection Control and Hospital Epidemiology, 1979—, Clinical Performance and Quality Health Care, 1993—; editorial bd. Jour. of Hosp. Infection, London, 1984—, Enfermedades Infecciosas y Microbiologia Clinica, 1990—, New England Jour. of Medicine, 1992—, others; contbr. numerous articles to profl. jours. Recipient Sir Henry S. Wellcome medal prize, 1971, Major Louis Livingston Seaman prize, 1974, Burlington No. Found. Faculty Achievement award, 1990; Sr. Internat. fellowship, NIH, 1985-86. Fellow ACP, Infectious Diesease Soc. of Am. (coun. mem. 1988-91), Am. Coll. Epidemiology, Am. Acad. of Microbiology; sr. internat. fellow NIH, 1985-86; mem. Am. Assn. of Physicians, Am. Clin. and Climatological Assn., Am. Epidemiological Soc., So. Soc. for Clin. Investigation, Am. Fedn. for Clin. Rsch., Am. Soc. for Microbiology, Assn. for Practitioners in Infection Control, Surg. Infection Soc., Soc. for Epidemiologic Rsch., Hosp. Infections Soc. (Europe), Assn. Am. Physicians, Am. Soc. Clin. Investigation. Address: U Va Commonwealth Dept Internal Med PO Box 980663 Richmond VA 23298-0663 E-mail: rwenzel@hsc.vcu.edu.

WENZLAFF, RICHARD M. psychologist; b. Chgo., June 26, 1953; s. Adolph Herman and Catherine Elizabeth Wenzlaff; m. Ann R. Eisenberg, Jan. 1, 1989; children: Rachel, Adam. BA, Tex., San Antonio, 1978; MA, Trinity U., San Antonio, 1980; PhD, U. Tex., Austin, 1984. Intern U. Tex. Health Sci. Ctr., San Antonio, 1983-84; postdoctoral fellow UCLA, 1984-85; asst. prof. U. Tex., San Antonio, 1985-91, assoc. prof., 1991-2000, prof., 2000—. Contbr. articles to profl. jours. Mem. Am. Psychol. Soc., Am. Psychol. Assn., Soc. Exptl. Social Psychology. Office: U Tex Dept Psychology San Antonio TX 78249

WENZLER, EDWARD WILLIAM, architect; b. Milw., Feb. 17, 1954; s. William Paul and Dolores Ann (Rahn) W.; m. Georgine Marie Eggert, Apr. 3, 1976; children: Christopher E., Michael E. BArch, U. Milw., 1978. Registered architect Wis., 1981, Minn., 1996, Ill., 2001. Architect Gordon Sibeck, Dallas, 1978-79; assoc. Wenzler and Assocs., Milw., 1979-84, ptnr., 1984-91, pres., 1991—. Prin. works include Oak Hill Terr, Waukesha, Wis., The Student Ctr. Addition at U. Wis.-Whitewater, Laurel Oaks Retirement Cmty, Glendale, Wis., Ctr. for the Arts at U. Wis.-Whitewater, Seven Oaks Skilled Care Facility, Glendale, Weidner Ctr. Addition at U. Wis.-Greenbay, Indsl. Electric Wire and Cable, New Berlin, Wis., Miron Constrn. Corp. Hdqrs., Appleton, Wis. Mem. AIA, Nat. Coun. Archtl. Registration Bds., Constrn. Specification Inst. Home: 19600 Gebhardt Rd Brookfield WI 53045-4823 E-mail: ewenzler@wenzlerarchitects.com.

WEPNER, SHELLEY BETH, education educator, software developer; b. Phila., Oct. 23, 1951; d. Bernard and Carole Frances (Abramson) Markovitz; m. Roy Henry Wepner, Aug. 3, 1974; children: Leslie Marcia and Meredith Susan (twins). BS magna cum laude, U. Pitts., 1972; MS, U. Pa., 1973, EdD, 1980. Cert. reading specialist, prin., supr., elem. tchr., N.J. Reading tchr. West Deptford (N.J.) Sch. Dist., 1973-74; reading resource tchr. Middletown (N.J.) Sch. Dist., 1974-75, Title I tchr., 1975-76; reading specialist Marlboro (N.J.) Sch. Dist., 1976-78, curriculum cons., 1978-80, supr. curriculum and instrn., 1980-82; prof. edn. William Paterson U., Wayne, N.J., 1989, chair dept. curriculum and instrn., 1991-94, asst. to dean, 1994-97; dir. ctr. edn., assoc. dean, prof. edn. Widener U., 1997—. Cons. Tchr. Support Software, Gainesville, Fla., 1988-99, East Brunswick (N.J.) Sch., 1989. Co-author: Using Computers in the Teaching of Reading, 1987, Moving Forward with Literature: Basals, Books, and Beyond, 1993; co-editor: Linking Literacy and Technology, 2000, The Administration and Supervision of Reading Programs, 1989, 2d edit., 1995, 3rd edit., 2002, Process Reading and Writing: A Literature Based Approach, 1992; author software Read-A-Logo, 1987 (Methods and Media award 1989), Reading Realities, 1989 (Top Five award, Methods and Media award), updated, 2001, Reading Realities Elem. Series, 1990 (Top 36 award, Methods and Media award), updated, 2001; contbr. over 95 articles to profl. jours. Chmn. gifted and talented Coles Sch. PTA, Scotch Plains, N.J., 1989-90. Mem. Am. Assn. Tchr. Educators (chair tech. and tchr. edn. com. 2001-2003), Pa. Assn. Colls. Tchr. Edn., Coll. Reading Assn. Internat. Soc. for Tech. in Edn., Internat. Reading Assn., N.J. Reading Assn. (bd. dirs. 1982-85), Phi Delta Kappa, Phi Kappa Phi. Avocations: traveling, walking, aerobics, reading. Home: 29 Todd Ridge Rd Titusville NJ 08560-1421 Office: Widener Univ One University Pl Chester PA 19013 E-mail: shelley.b.wepner@widener.edu.

WEPPELMAN, ROGER MICHAEL, retired regulatory compliance officer; b. Pitts., Nov. 4, 1944; s. Roger John and Margaretta Bertha Weppelman; m. Marsha Lee Beers, July 17, 1971. BS, U. Pitts., 1965, PhD, 1970. Instr. U. Pitts., 1970-71; rschr., adminstr. Merck & Co., Rahway, N.J., 1973-89; regulatory affairs officer Monsanto Co., St. Louis, 1989-99. Adj. prof. Rutgers U., New Brunswick, N.J., 1982-89. Inventor in field. Am. Cancer Soc. fellow U. Calif., Berkeley, 1971-73. Mem. Phi Beta Kappa, Sigma Xi.

WEPPLER, JAY ROBERT, merchant banking executive; b. Montclair, N.J., May 16, 1943; s. George Robert and Cornelia (Menard) W.; m. Cynthia Anne Stone, June 21, 1969 (div. Jan. 1982); children: Ashley Menard, George Reid Willcutt; m. Pauline Ann Kelly, Sept. 27, 1983. Student, U. Conn., 1961-64; BS, Johnson Coll., 1966. Asst. sec. Chem. Bank, N.Y.C., 1972-74, asst. v.p. San Francisco, 1974-77, v.p., gen. mgr. Sydney, NSW, Australia, 1978-80, Hong Kong, 1980-82, v.p., regional mgr. London, 1982-85, v.p. Wilmington, Del., 1985-86, v.p., group head N.Y.C., 1987-88; sr. v.p., mgr. corp. fin. GE Capital, Stamford, Conn., 1988-92; mng. ptnr. Buckingham Ptnrs., Darien, 1992-95; exec. v.p., dir. investment banking Auerbach, Pollack & Richardson, Stamford, 1995—; exec. v.p. Auerbach Fin. Group, 1995-99; chmn., pres., CEO Unico, Inc., 1999—2001; vice chmn. TCN Networks, Inc., Greenwich, Conn., 2002—. Lt. USNR, 1968-71. Mem. Hurlingham Club, Univ. Club, Royal Hong Kong Jockey Club, RAC-Pall Mall. Republican. Home: 15 Lafayette Ct Greenwich CT 06830-5325

WERBA, GABRIEL, public relations consultant; b. Paris, Feb. 28, 1930; came to U.S., 1941; s. Aron and Dina (Lewin) W.; m. Barrie Celia Sakolsky, June 1, 1952; children: Dean Steffen, Annmarie Alexandra Bragdon. BA in Journalism, U. Tex., 1948; postgrad., NYU Grad. Sch. Bus., 1948-49, NYU Sch. Law, 1961-62. Account exec. Harold C. Meyers & Co., N.Y.C., 1959-61; dir. pub. rels. and advt. Yardney Electric Corp., 1961-63, 57-59; sr. assoc. Shiefman & Assocs., Detroit, 1963-66; account exec. Merrill Lynch, 1966-70; exec. v.p. Shiefman Werba & Assocs., 1970-73; sr. v.p., exec. v.p., pres., chief oper. officer Anthony M. Franco, Inc., 1973-88; pres., chief exec. officer The Werba Group, Inc. and Gabriel Werba and Assocs., Inc., 1988-94; prin. Durocher, Dixson, Werba, L.L.C., 1994—. Bd. dirs. Erudite Corp., Detroit. Contbr. articles to profl. jours. Bd. dirs. Oakland Citizens League, Detroit, 1970-93, Detroit Symphony Orch. Hall, Detroit Chamber Winds, 1985-91, The Common Ground Sanctuary, Royal Oak, Mich., The Attic Theatre, Detroit, 1989-93, The Children's Ctr., Detroit; mem. strategic planning com., chmn. comm. com., bd. dirs., 1989-95, 1996-2002, adv. bd., 1995-96, 2002—; bd. dirs. NATAS, Detroit, 1993-98, The Jewish Cmty. Coun. Met. Detroit, 1989-95, Margaret W. Montgomery Hosp., 1993-95, adv. bd. 1988-93; bd. dirs. Lawrence P. Doss Found., 2002—, first vice-chmn., 2002—; mem. comm. com. Detroit Inst. Arts, 1986-92, exhibits com., 1990-2001. Named to, PRSA-Detroit Hall of Fame, 2002. Mem. Nat. Investor Rels. Inst. (past dir., pres. Detroit chpt., spkr., panelist), Pub. Rels. Soc. Am. (bd. dirs. Detroit chpt. 1988-94, pres. 1992-93, past treas. Detroit Counselors' sect., co-chair, sect. coun., past nat. chmn. fin. sect., spkr., panelist), Fin. Analysts Soc. Detroit (past chmn. pub. info. com.), Am. Mensa (bd. dirs. 1975-91, nat. chmn. 1979-83), Internat. Mensa (bd. dirs. 1979-83, 85-93), Adcraft Club. Avocations: art collecting, concerts, theater. Office: Durocher Dixson Werba LLC 16th Floor Buhl Bldg 535 Griswold St Detroit MI 48226-3604 Home: 21920 River Ridge Tr Farmington Hills MI 48335 E-mail: werba@ddwpr.com.

WERBACH, MELVYN ROY, psychiatrist, writer; b. N.Y.C., Nov. 11, 1940; s. Samuel and Martha (Robbins) W.; m. Gail Beth Leibsohn, June 20, 1967; children: Kevin, Adam. BA, Columbia Coll., N.Y.C., 1962; MD, Tufts U., Boston, 1966. Diplomate Am. Bd. Psychiatry and Neurology. Intern VA Hosp., Bklyn., 1966-67; resident in psychiatry Cedars-Sinai Med. Ctr., L.A., 1969-71; dir. psychol. svcs., clin. biofeedback UCLA Hosp. and Clinics, 1976-80; pres. Third Line Press, 1986—; prof. integrative medicine Capital U. Integrative Medicine, Washington, 2001—. Asst. clin. prof. Sch. Medicine, UCLA, 1978-00; mem. nutritional adv. bd. Cancer Treatment Ctrs. Am., 1989-93; mem. adv. com. The Dead Sea Confs., Israel, 1990—; mem. adv. com. Found. for Micronutrients in Medicine, Switzerland, 1999—; mem. internat. adv. bd. Internat. Joseph H. Navach Project, Human Energy Sys. Lab., U. Ariz., Tucson, 2000—. Author: Third Line Medicine, 1986, Nutritional Influences on Illness, 1987, Nutritional Influences on Illness, 2d edit., 1993, Nutritional Influences on Mental Illness, 1991, Nutritional Influences on Mental Illness, 2d edit., Healing Through Nutrition, 1993, Foundations of Nutritional Medicine, 1997, Textbook of Nutritional Medicine, 1999, Case Studies in Natural Medicine, 2002; co-author: Botanical Influences on Illness, 1994, Botanical Influences on Illness, 2d edit., 2000; mem. editl. bd.: Jour. of Nutritional Medicine, 1993—, mem. editl. bd.: Alt. Medicine, 1994—, columnist: various jours., mem. adv. bd.: numerous jours.; contbr. articles to profl. jours., to books. Mem. Am. Coll. Nutrition, Biofeedback Soc. Calif. (hon. life mem., pres. 1977, Cert. Honor 1985), Australian Coll. Nutritional and Environ. Medicine (hon.).

WERBER, FRED ALAN, dermatologist; b. L.A., Mar. 12, 1951; s. Ben Harvey and Anne (Rapoport) W.; m. Terri Lee Werber, June 12, 1980. BS, Whittier Coll., 1973; MD, U. Calif., Irvine, 1980. Diplomate Am. Bd. Dermatology. Intern, resident U. Calif., Irvine; dermatologist Ventura, Calif., 1980—. Diplomate Am. Bd. Dermatology. Avocation: marathon running. Office: 2967 Loma Vista Rd Ventura CA 93003-2915

WERBITT, WARREN, gastroenterologist, educator; b. Phila., Jan. 29, 1939; s. Saull Boris and Pearl (Weiner) W.; m. Drue Natalie Engman Werbitt, Aug. 30, 1964; children: Julie Michele, Jeffrey Brian. BS in Pharmacy, Temple U., 1960; D in Osteopathy, U. Osteo. Med. and Health Sci., Des Moines, 1966; MD, Allegheny U. Hosps. Med. Coll., Pa., 1973. Diplomate Am. Osteo. Bd. Internal Medicine, also sub-splty. bd. Gastroenterology; diplomate Am. Bd. Internal Medicine, also sub-splty. bd. Gastroenterology. Intern Doctor's Hosp., Columbus, Ohio, 1966-67, resident in internal medicine, 1967-68, Kennedy Meml. Hosps., Cherry Hill, N.J., 1968-69, Mercy Cath. Med. Ctr., Phila., 1969-70, Allegheny U. Hosps.- Med. Coll. Pa. divsn., Phila., 1971-72, fellow in gastroenterology, 1970-71, 72-74, instr., 1973—, attending physician and cons. in gastroenterology, 1977-94; instr. Phila. Coll. Osteo. Medicine, 1973-75, chmn. divsn. gastroenterology, 1975-77; clin. assoc. prof. medicine U. Medicine and Dentistry, N.J., 1977—; attending physician and cons. in gastroenterology Vet. Adminstrn. Hosp., Phila., 1972-75; chmn. Div. Gastroenterology, Dept. Medicine Phila. Coll. Osteopathic Medicine, 1975-77; chmn. Dept. Medicine Kennedy Meml. Hosp. U. Med. Ctr., Cherry Hill, 1979-81, chmn. subsect. Gastroenterology, 1979-87. Contbg. editor The N.J. Jour. for Ostepathic Physicians and Surgeons, 1980—; mem. scientific adv. com. Phila. chpt. Nat. Found. Ileitis & Colitis, Inc., 1982—; contbr. articles to profl. jours. Recipient Profl. Svc. award Med. Soc. N.J., 1991. Fellow Am. Coll. Physicians, Am. Coll. Gastroenterology, Acad. Med. N.J.; mem. AMA, Am. Soc. Gastrointestinal Endoscopy, Am. Gastroenterology Assn., Am. Soc. Parenteral and Enteric Nutrition, Am. Inst. Ultrasound in Medicine, Am. Assn. Gynecologic Laparoscopists, Phila. Gastrointestinal Rsch. Forum, State Med. Soc. N.J., Camden County Med. Soc., N.J. Endoscopic Soc., Del. Valley Soc. for Gastrointestinal Endoscopy, South Jersey Gastroenterological Soc., Am. Osteopathic Assn., N.J. Soc. Osteopathic Physicians and Surgeons, Am. Coll. Osteopathic Internists, Camden County Osteopathic Assn., Am. Cancer Soc. (bd. dirs. N.J. chpt.), Crohn's and Colitis Found. Am. Inc. (Phila. and Del.), Pres.'s Circle Am. U., N.Y. Acad. Scis., John Sherman Myers Soc., Med. Club Phila., Lambda Omicron Gamma. Avocations: golf, running, music, reading, American History. Office: Profl Gastroenterology Assn 1939 Route 70 E Ste 250 Cherry Hill NJ 08003-4507

WERBOW, STANLEY NEWMAN, language educator; b. Phila., Apr. 19, 1922; s. Morris and Sadie (Newman) W.; m. Naomi Esther Ecker, June 1, 1952; children: Susan Linda, Emily Frances, Carol Martha. BA, George Washington U., 1946; postgrad., Middlebury Coll., 1946, 47, U. Mich., 1948; PhD, Johns Hopkins, 1953. Tchr. Ea. High Sch., Washington, 1946-47; research analyst specialist U.S. Dept. Def., 1952-53; mem. faculty U. Tex., Austin, 1953—, prof., 1965-69, 78-97, chmn. dept. Germanic langs., 1969-71, dean Coll. Humanities, 1971-78, acting dean Coll. Fine Arts, 1980-81, prof. emeritus, 1997—. Vis. prof. U. Marburg, 1963, U. N.Mex. German Summer Sch., 1984, 87, 89. Author: Martin von Amberg, 1957, (with Lehmann, Rehder, Shaw) Review and Progress in German, 1959; Editor: Formal Aspects of Medieval German Poetry, 1970. Served with Signal Corps AUS, 1943-45. Decorated Bronze Star medal; Bundesverdienstkreuz erster klasse W. Ger.; recipient Fulbright award to Netherlands, 1950-51; Guggenheim fellow, 1960; Fulbright research scholar Germany, 1960-61 Mem. Modern Lang. Assn. (pres. South Central assn. 1976—), Medieval Acad., Internat. Assn. Germanists, Phi Beta Kappa, Phi Kappa Phi, Delta Phi Alpha. Home: 4205 Prickly Pear Dr Austin TX 78731-2017 Office: Univ Texas Dept Germanic Studies Austin TX 78712 E-mail: s.werbow@mail.utexas.edu.

WERDEGAR, KATHRYN MICKLE, state supreme court justice; b. San Francisco; d. Benjamin Christie and Kathryn Marie (Clark) Mickle; m. David Werdegar; children: Maurice Clark, Matthew Mickle. Student, Wellesley Coll., 1954—55; AB with honors, U. Calif., Berkeley, 1957; JD with highest distinction, George Washington U., 1962; JD, U. Calif., Berkeley, 1990. Bar: Calif. 1964, U.S. Dist. Ct. (no. dist.) Calif. 1964, U.S. Ct. Appeals (9th cir.) 1964, Calif. Supreme Ct. 1964. Legal asst. civil rights divsn. U.S. Dept. Justice, Washington, 1962—63; rsch. atty. Calif. State Study Commn. on Mental Retardation, 1963—64; assoc. U. Calif. Ctr. for Study of Law and Soc., Berkeley, 1965—67; spl. cons. State Dept. Mental Health, 1967—68; cons. Calif. Coll. Trial Judges, 1968—71; dir. criminal law divsn. Calif. Continuing Edn. of Bar, 1971—78; assoc. dean acad. and student affairs, assoc. prof. Sch. Law, U. San Francisco, 1978—81; sr. staff atty. Calif. 1st Dist. Ct. Appeal, 1981—85, Calif. Supreme Ct., 1985—91; assoc. justice Calif. 1st Dist. Ct. Appeal, 1991—94, Calif. Supreme Ct., San Francisco, 1994—. Regents' lectr. U. Calif., Berkeley, 2000. Author: Benchbook: Misdemeanor Procedure, 1971, Misdemeanor Procedure Benchbook, 1975, 1983; contbr. California Continuing Education of the Bar books; editor: California Criminal Law Practice series Discovery, 1975, California Uninsured Motorist Practice, 1973, I California Civil Procedure Before Trial, 1977. Bd. dirs. Calif. Supreme Ct. Hist. Soc. Recipient Charles Glover award, George Washington U., 1962, J. William Fulbright award for disting. pub. svc., George Washington U. Law Sch. Alumni Assn., 1996, excellence in achievement award, Calif. Alumni Assn., 1996, Roger J. Traynor Appellate Justice of Yr. award, 1996, Justice of Yr. award, Consumer Attys. of Calif., 1998, also 5 Am. Jurisprudence awards, 1960—62, Citation award, Book Hall Sch. Law U. Calif., Berkeley, 2002. Mem.: Am. Law Inst., Nev./Calif. Women Judges Assn., Calif. Judges Assn., Nat. Assn. Women Judges, Calif. Supreme Ct. Hist. Soc. (bd. dir.), Order of the Coif. Office: Calif Supreme Court 350 McAllister St San Francisco CA 94102-4797

WERDEN, DAVID RAY, music educator; b. Davenport, Iowa, Apr. 21, 1947; s. Lawrence Otis and Dorothy Lucille W.; m. Joyce Carol Schuessler, Aug. 31, 1968 (div. Sept. 1979); 1 child, Carolyn Joyce; m. Denise Marie Werner, Feb. 2, 1980; children: Jennifer Judith, Alan David. MusB, U. Iowa, 1970; MusM, U. Conn., 1993. Clinician music edn. Boosey & Hawkes, Libertyville, Ill., 1979-89; pvt. music instr. Gales Ferry, Conn., 1980—; instr. U. Conn., Storrs, 1989-96; clinician music edn. Custom Music Co., Ferndale, Mich., 1989—, Sterling Mus. Instruments, Eng., 1989—; staff, musician USCG Acad. Band, New London, Conn., 1970-96, computer sys. coord., 1986-96; soloist, clinician Euphonium, Minnetonka, Minn., 1996—; tuba player Sheldon Theater Brass Band, Red Wing, 1996—; web devel. coord. Integrated Network Techs., Burnsville, 1996—. Author: The Blaikley Compensating System, 1980, Euphonium Music Guide, 1990, Scoring for Euphonium; editor: The Brass Musician, 1986, Euphonium Excerpts, 1992; contbr. articles to profl. jours.; composer arrangements for solo brass and chamber ensembles. Sr. chief USCG, 1970-96. Named Euphonium Player of Yr. Sounding Brass Mag., Eng., 1980. Mem. Internat. Trombone Assn., Tubists Universal Brotherhood Assn. (euphonium coord. 1982-84, bd. dirs. 1987-89, hon. bd. advisors 1989-97), Pi Kappa Lambda. Avocations: computer programming, music arranging, web page design. Home: 15800 Lake Street Ext Minnetonka MN 55345-1921 Office: INTxx 101 W Burnsville Pkwy Ste 102 Burnsville MN 55337-2571

WERDER, HORST HEINRICH, lawyer; b. Stettin, Germany, Aug. 13, 1924; BS, Columbia U., 1949, JD, 1951. Bar: N.Y. 1952, Ill. 1962. Ptnr. Haseltine & Lake, N.Y.C., 1952-61, Baker & McKenzie, Chgo., 1961-89. Mem. Columbia U. Club of S.W. Fla., Mich. Shores Club (Wilmette, Ill.). Office: 1001 Arbor Lake Dr Naples FL 34110-7080 Fax: 239-594-8498.

WERESH, THELMA FAYE, sculptor, artist; b. Baca County, Colo., Mar. 15, 1919; d. William Lee Cotton and Myrtle Mae (Quiet) Cotton-Winston; m. Andrew Anthony Weresh, Jan. 28, 1939; children: Charlotte Maria, Catherine Ann. BA, Coll. St. Mary, 1967. Art tchr. Ralston (Nebr.) Pub. Schs., 1967-73, Father Flanagan's Boys Home, Boys Town, Nebr., 1973-75. Bd. dirs. Alliance of Arts Coun., Lincoln, Nebr., 1975; chmn. Visual Arts Commn., Loveland, Colo., 1990-91. One person exhibn. includes Ariel Gallery, N.Y., 1991; featured in Artist's Profile KRMA TV, 1995. Recipient SOHO Internat. 1st Place, 1990, 1st Place United Coun., 1990, 2nd Place, 1991, 1st Place George Lewis, 1991, 1st Place Southwest Art, 1992, 1st Place Women Artists, 1992, Spl. award Mus. N.W., 1992, First Annual Hall of Fame award Revue mag., 1996. Mem. Allied Artists Am., Loveland (Colo.) Sculpture Group. Home: 2009 Lakewood Dr Loveland CO 80538-3423

WERFEL, SANDRA DIANE, clinical social worker; b. Kew Gardens, N.Y., Feb. 23, 1947; d. Israel Harry and Charlotte (Lustryn) Leibowitz; m. Mark Werfel, Oct. 25, 1970; children: Justin Keith, Erica Elizabeth. BA, Queens Coll., 1968; MSW, Simmons Coll., 1970. Diplomate in Clin. Social Work; lic. social worker, Va., Md., Washington, D.C. Staff social worker Child Guidance

Ctr., Greater Lynn, Mass., 1970-73; supervising social worker Union Hosp. Cmty. Mental Health Ctr., Lynn, 1973-77; instr., supr. Boston U. Sch. Social Work, 1974-77; cons. Paragon Assocs., McLean, Va., 1980-82, Enterprise Sch., Vienna, 1982-83, Marriage and Family Clinic, Annandale, Va., 1982-85, Silver Hill Svcs. to Families and Children, Temple Hills, Md., 1984-87; founder, pres. Met. Stress Cons., Burke, Va., 1985-87, Burke Family Counseling and Consultation Ctr., 1987—. Mem. adv. com. Family Day Care Program, No. Va. Jewish Cmty. Ctr., Fairfax, 1984-87, Elem. Age Programs, 1987-88; mem. sch. com. Congregation Beth-El, Alexandria, Va., 1983-85. Recipient Maida H. Solomon honorable mention citation Simmons Coll. Sch. Social Work, 1979; scholar NIMH, 1968, 69. Mem.: NASW, Obsessive-Compulsive Found., Anxiety Disorders Assn. Am., Greater Washington Soc. Clin. Social Work, Acad. Cert. Social Workers. Avocations: reading, music, needlework, bike riding. Office: Burke Profl Ctr 5206 Rolling Rd Ste B Burke VA 22015-1605

WERFEL, SCOTT, computer programmer; b. Newark, June 19, 1960; s. Sanford and Rita Rosalind (Hermelin) W.; m. Janet Werfel, June 3, 1990. BS in Math. and Physics, Northwestern U., 1982; MS in Applied Math., Rutgers U., 1987. Actuary Parkway Ins. Co., Bridgewater, NJ, 1995—. Home: 4 Holly Dr Hightstown NJ 08520-2212

WERFELMAN, WILLIAM HERMAN, JR. public relations executive; b. Bridgeport, Conn., July 11, 1953; s. William H. and Helen D. (Rainier) W.; m. Patricia Aileen Maytrott, Aug. 28, 1977; children: Lauren Aileen, Juliana Aileen. BA in English, St. Bonaventure U., 1975; postgrad., Georgetown U., 1975-76. Staff writer Post-Telegram newspapers, Bridgeport, 1976-79; product publicity specialist Dictaphone Corp., Rye, N.Y., 1979-81; supr. press rels. GE, Fairfield, Conn., 1981-84; mgr. corp. pub. rels. Olin Corp., Stamford, 1984-90; dir. pub. rels./comm., 1990-94; v.p. external comms. Home Ins. Co., 1994-95; v.p. media rels. N.Y. Life Ins. Co., N.Y.C., 1995—. Mem., chmn. Zoning Bd. Appeals, Redding, Conn., 1977-89, 92-99; party recruitment chmn. Rep. Town Com., Redding, 1976-90. Recipient Fin. World Bronze award for ann. report, 1992. Mem. Internat. Assn. Bus. Communicators (Best Pub. Rels. results 1982), Pub. Rels. Soc. Am., Nat. Assn. Investors (Best Ann Report 1988, 90). Republican. Roman Catholic. Avocations: fiction writing, investments. Home: 195 Gallows Hill Rd Redding CT 06896-1423 Office: NY Life Ins Co 51 Madison Ave New York NY 10010-1603

WERHANE, PATRICIA HOGUE, finance educator; b. Ontario, Oreg., Sept. 20, 1935; m. Charles William Werhane (dec.); children: Hillary, Kelly Althoff, Marijke, Stephanie. MA, PhD, Northwestern U., 1969. Prof. Am. Coll. Switzerland, Leysin, 1972—75, Loyola U., Chgo., 1975—93; Ruffin prof. bus. ethics Darden Sch. U. Va., Charlottesville, 1993—. Co-dir. Olsson Ctr. for Applied Ethics. Author: (books) Moral Imagination and Management Decision-Making, 1999, Adam Smith and his Legacy for Modern Capitalism, 1991, Organization Ethics in Health Care, 2000, Employment and Employee Rights, 2002, Ethical Issues in Business, 7th edit., 2002. Office: U Va Darden Sch 100 Darden Blvd Charlottesville VA 22903

WERHUN, ANTHONY T. emergency medicine physician, educator; b. Apr. 30, 1957; BS, King's Coll., 1979; MD, Jefferson Med. Coll., 1983. Emergency medicine physician Lehigh Valley Hosp., Allentown, Pa., 1986—; clin. asst. prof. medicine Pa. State Coll. Medicine, 1996—. Home: 1172 Kressler Rd Allentown PA 18103-6039 E-mail: l302n@aol.com.

WERKHEISER, STEVEN LAWRENCE, financial specialist; b. Oct. 6, 1945; s. Laverne Eugene and Dorothy M. W.; m. Michelle Sue Phelan; children: Steven Lawrence, Kirsten Elizabeth. Student, L.A. Pierce Coll., 1964-66; BA, UCLA, 1970, MS, 1971. Mcpl. bond trader/underwriter Blyth & Co., L.A., 1971-72, 1972-73, mgr. mcpl. bond dept., 1974; fin. analyst Northrop Corp., Hawthorne, Calif., 1974-75, fin. planning analyst, 1976-80; v.p. trading R.H. Moulton & Co., L.A., from 1980; divsn. fin. specialist, mgr. planning and adminstrn. Northrop Corp., Hawthorne; corp. fin. cons. L.A., 1975-92; bus. devel., treas., CFO Ticom Corp., Warren, Mich., 1992-95; also bd. dirs.; bus. devel. Northrop Gruman, 1995-98; CFO Italbiz, 2000—. Bd. dirs. Monadnock Corp. With AUS, 1966-68. Mem. Fin. Mgmt. Assn., L.A. Bond Club, In the Wings, Assn. MBAs, UCLA Alumni Assn. Republican. Methodist. Home: 25102 Avenida Ignacio Valencia CA 91355-3033

WERKING, RICHARD HUME, librarian, historian, academic administrator; b. Charleston, S.C., Sept. 29, 1943; s. F. Woody and Mary S. (Prissinger) W. BA, U. Evansville, 1966; MA in Am. History, U. Wis., 1967, PhD in Am. History, 1973; MA in Librarianship, U. Chgo., 1975. Instr. history Northland Coll., Ashland, Wis., 1967-68; pers. staffing specialist U.S. Civil Svc. Commn., Indpls., 1968-69; reference libr. Lawrence U., Appleton, Wis., 1975-77; head reference dept., asst./acting libr. dir. U. Miss., Oxford, 1977-81, asst. prof. history, 1977-81; assoc. libr. dir., asst. prof. history Trinity U., San Antonio, 1981-83, libr. dir., assoc. prof. history, 1983-91; libr. dir., assoc. dean, prof. history U.S. Naval Acad., Annapolis, Md., 1991—. Author: The Master Architects: Building the U.S. Foreign Service, 1977; contbr. articles to profl. jours., chpts. to books, also papers, monographs and revs. With U.S. Army, 1962. Sparks fellow Phi Kappa Phi, 1966, postdoctoral fellow Coun. on Libr. Resources, 1974. Mem. ALA (chmn. coll. librs. sect. 1987-88), Orgn. Am. Historians. Office: US Naval Acad Nimitz Libr 589 Mcnair Rd Annapolis MD 21402-1323 E-mail: rwerking@usna.edu.

WERKMAN, ROSEMARIE ANNE, former public relations professional, civic worker; b. Washingtonville, N.Y., Apr. 21, 1926; d. Alexander and Michelina (Russo) Di Benedetto; m. Henry J. Werkman, June 29, 1947; children: Elizabeth, Kristine, Hendrik. Student, U. Miami, Fla. Billing clk. Stern's Dept. Store, N.Y.C., 1945; clk., typist Doubleday-Doran Book Pub., 1945-46; receptionist Moser & Cotins Advt. Agy., Utica, N.Y., 1947-48, Washingtonville Sch., 1960-75. Author: (biography/autobiography) Love, War and Remembrance, 1992; author short stories; poetry pub. in several anthologies. Mem. Dem. Com., Blooming Grove; bd. dirs. Blooming Grove Hist. Assn.; mem. com. Update: Blooming Grove Master Plan; mem. Orange County Coun. Disabled; bd. dirs. Rehab. Support Svcs; charter mem. Orange County Citizens Found.; mem. steering com. Blooming Grove (N.Y.) BiCentennial Celebration, 1999; participant restorations Habitat for Humanity, 2001—. Named Poet of Merit, Am. Poetry Assn., 1989, Poet Laureate Orange County, N.Y., 2002; recipient Notable Civic Contbns. award Blooming Grove/Washingtonville C. of C., 1996, Rose award, 1996. Mem. Blooming Grove C. of C. (v.p.), Orange County Classic Choral Soc., Clearwater (Fla.) Chorus. Democrat. Roman Catholic. Avocations: reading, gardening, furniture refinishing, singing.

WERKMAN, SIDNEY LEE, psychiatry educator; b. Washington, May 3, 1927; AB, Williams Coll., 1948; MD, Cornell U., 1952. Diplomate Am. Bd. Psychiatry and Neurology, Am. Bd. Child Psychiatry. Intern U. Va. Hosp., Charlottesville; resident in psychiatry Yale U., 1953-55, St. Elizabeth's Hosp., Washington, 1955-56; assoc. prof. psychiatry George Washington U., 1960-69; prof. U. Colo. Sch. Medicine, Denver, 1969-87; dir. div. adolescent psychiatry Children's Hosp. of Washington, 1965-69; clin. prof. Georgetown U. Sch. Medicine, Washington, 1989—; psychiatrist Capital Area Permanente Med. Group, 1990—. Cons. grants NIMH, Washington, 1982— , guest researcher, 1984-85 Author: The Role of Psychiatry in Medical Education, 1966, Only a Little Time: A Chronicle of Dying, 1972, Bringing Up Children Overseas, 1977 Bd. dirs. Med. U. So. Africa, Performing Arts Soc., Washington Concert Operas. Master sgt. U.S. Army. Fellow Commonwealth Fund, Florence, Italy, 1963-64, NEH, 1979 Mem. Am. Psychiat. Assn., Am. Acad. Child Psychiatry, Group for Advancement Psychiatry, Am. Orthopsychiat. Assn. (bd. dirs. 1970-73), Colo. Psychiat. Soc. Office: Ste AG 29 3636 16th St NW Ste Ag29 Washington DC 20010-8138

WERLE, ROBERT GEARY, academic administrator; b. Washington, Mar. 28, 1944; s. Francis Bernard and Evelyn Mae (Case) W. BA, Christian Bros. Coll., 1970; MEd, U. Toronto, Ont., Can., 1976. Cert. Ednl. Adminstr. Tchr. La Salle H.S., Cin., 1970-73; tchr., adminstr. Roncalli H.S., Omaha, 1973-77; asst. prin. O'Hara H.S., Kansas City, Mo., 1977-79; dir. Stritch Retreat Ctr., Memphis, 1979-82; vocation dir. La Salle Inst., St. Louis, 1982-84; admissions counselor Christian Bros. U., Memphis, 1984-85, dir. campus ministry, 1985-86, dir. campus activities, 1986-91, assoc. dir. Stritch Conf. Ctr., 1991-94. Archivist Christian Bros. U., C.B. Midwest Dist.; curator of art Christian Bros. U. Mem. Soc. Am. Archivists, Religious Archives Assn., De La Salle Regional Archivist Assn. (founder, chair USA-Toronto region 1989—), Art Today (sec. 1997-98, treas. 1998-2000, membership chair 2000-01), Memphis/Shelby Urban Art Commn., Pi Kappa Phi (adv. 1986-89, 94-96, Founder's Svc. award 1989, Alumni award 1995), Memphis in May Archives Com. (Founders award 1994), Records Mgr. Assn. (ARMA). Democrat. Roman Catholic. Avocations: reading, graphic design, drafting. Office: Christian Bros Univ O Donnell Archives 2455 Avery Ave Memphis TN 38112-4824 E-mail: rwerle@cbu.edu.

WERLIN, LAWRENCE B. obstetrician, gynecologist, reproductive endocrinologist; b. Albany, N.Y., 1948; s. Esther (Caplan) W.; m. Sally Rosso, Dec. 24, 1970; children: Rachel, Evan, Emma. BA, Boston U., 1970; MD, Mt. Sinai Sch. Medicine, N.Y.C., 1976. Diplomate Am. Bd. Ob-Gyn. Intern Harbor Gen. Hosp., Torrance, Calif., 1976-77, resident in ob-gyn., 1977-80; fellow in reproductive endocrinology NIH, Bethesda, Md., 1980-82; mem. staff Hoag Meml. Hosp., Newport Beach, Calif. Nat. Reproductive Medicine fellow, 1980-82. Mem. AAAS, Am. Soc. Reproductive Medicine, Soc. for Assisted Reproductive Tech., Pacific Coast Fertility Soc. Office: Coastal Fertility Med Ctr 4900 Barranca Pkwy Ste 103 Irvine CA 92604-8603 E-mail: werlmd@coastalfertility.com.

WERLING, DONN PAUL, environmental educator; b. Ft. Wayne, Ind., Oct. 14, 1945; s. Paul Henry and Lydia Sophia (Rebber) W.; m. Diane Mueller, July 11, 1970; 1 child, Benjamin Paul. BS, Valparaiso U., 1967; MS, Mich. State U., 1968; MEd, Loyola U., 1970; PhD, U. Mich., 1979. Dir. nature project Raymond Sch., Chgo. Bd. Edn., 1969-72; dir. Evanston (Ill.) Environ. Assn., 1973-81; dir. Henry Ford Estate U. Mich., Dearborn, 1983—2002, adj. asst. prof. edn., 1984-95, adj. assoc. prof., 1996—; exec. dir. History Ctr., Ft. Wayne, Ind., 2002—. Founder N.Am. Voyageur Conf., 1977. Author: Environmental Education and Your School Site, 1973, A School-Community Stewardship Model, 1979, Lake Michigan and Its Lighthouses, 1982, Lakes and Lighthouses, 1989, Lighthouse Library of the Great Lakes, 1993, Lore and Legacy, 1994, Keepers of Tomorrow, 1998, Henry Ford: Hearthside Perspective, 1999, Henry Ford and His Uncommon Friends, 1999. Mem. state master plan com. on environ. edn., State of Ill, Springfield, 1970; mem. adv. com. Ill. Coastal Zone, Chgo., 1978; bd. dirs. Ill. Shore Coun. Girl Scouts U.S., 1978-82, Chgo. Maritime Soc., 1982; co-chmn. ad hoc com. estab. Nat. Auto Heritage Area, signed into law, 1998. Recipient Mayor's award City of Evanston, 1976, Russell E. Wilson award U. Mich. Sch. Edn., 1979, Svc. award Ill. Shore Coun. Girl Scouts U.S., 1978, J. Lee Barrett award Met. Detroit Tourist and Conv. Bur., 1986, award for interpretative excellence Nat. Assn. for Interpretation, 1989, 2000; named to Outstanding Young Men of Am., Jaycees, 1975. Mem. Nat. Assn. Interpretation (founder), Am. Assn. Mus., Great Lakes Lighthouse Keepers Assn. (founder, pres. 1982-86), Tourist and Travel Assn. S.E. Mich. (chmn. 1984-86), Kiwanis. Avocations: historic restoration, gardening, writing, composing, singing, Chris ian and bluewater music. Office: History Ctr 302 E Berry Fort Wayne IN 46802 E-mail: dpwerling@comcast.com.

WERLY, JOHN MCINTYRE, historian, educator, retired; b. Rochester, N.Y., Nov. 6, 1939; s. Berlyn McIntryre and Grace (Steinhauser) W.; m. Bonnie Windolf, July 8, 1961; children: Aric, Robyn, Scott. BA, Trinity Coll., Hartford, Conn., 1961, MA, 1966; PhD in U.S. History, Syracuse U., 1972. Instr. history Robinson Sch., West Hartford, Conn., 1963-68; teaching asst. U. S. history Syracuse (N.Y.) U., 1969-70; instr. U.S. history SUNY, Cortland, 1970-72; asst. prof. history Southeastern Mass. U., North Dartmouth, 1972-78, assoc. prof., 1978-84; prof. U. Mass., Dartmouth, 1984—2002, prof. emeritus, 2002—. Community lectr. in field. Contbr. articles to profl. jours. Recipient Mass. Commonwealth Citation for Outstanding Performance, 1987. Mem. Orgn. Am. Historians. Home: 20 Stillman St South Dartmouth MA 02748-3540 Office: U Mass Dartmouth North Dartmouth MA 02747 E-mail: jwerly@umassd.edu.

WERMAN, DAVID SANFORD, psychiatrist, psychoanalyst, educator; b. N.Y.C., Jan. 1, 1922; s. Morris and Blanche (Heftel) W.; m. Marjolijn R. de Jager, Oct. 25, 1958 (div. 1975); children: Marco W., Claudia J. BA, Queens Coll., 1942; postgrad., Columbia U., 1946-47; MD, Cert. d'Etudes Medicales, U. Lausanne, Switzerland, 1952. Diplomate Am. Bd. Obstetrics and Gynecology, Am. Bd. Psychiatry and Neurology. Intern Beth Israel Hosp., N.Y.C., 1953-54, resident, 1954-57, Montefiore Hosp., Bronx, N.Y., 1964-67; pvt. practice specializing in ob-gyn. N.Y.C., 1957-64; faculty acad. psychiatry U. N.C., Chapel Hill, 1967-76, assoc. prof., instr. psychoanalytic tng. program, 1974—; prof. psychiatry Duke U. Med. Ctr., Durham, N.C., 1976—, supervising and tng. analyst psychoanalytic tng. program, 1981-97, Honored prof. psychiatry, 1990—, prof. emeritus, 1992—, supervising and tng. analyst emeritus, 1997—. Cons. Durham VA Hosp. Author: The Practice of Supportive Psychotherapy, 1984. Contbr. chpts. to books, articles to profl. jours. With AUS, 1943-45 Named Outstanding Tchr. psychiatry U. N.C., 1975, honored tchr. psychiatry Duke U., 1978, hon. prof., 1990. Fellow ACS, Am. Psychiat. Assn., Am. Coll. Psychoanalysts, others Home and Office: 12 Foster Ct Croton On Hudson NY 10520-3303 Fax: 914-271-1358.

WERMAN, THOMAS EHRLICH, record producer; b. Newton, Mass., Mar. 2, 1945; s. Lester and Ruth (Ehrlich) W.; m. Susan Lynne Gould, Aug. 25, 1968; children— Julia Gould, Nina Eve, Daniel Lester BA, Columbia U., 1967, MBA, 1969. Asst. account exec. Grey Advt., N.Y.C., 1969-70; asst. to dir. Epic Records Artistes and Repertoire, 1970-73; dir. talent acquisition Epic Records, 1973-76, staff producer, 1976-80; v.p., exec. producer CBS Records, Inc., L.A., 1980-81; sr. v.p. Elektra Records, 1981-82; pres. Julia's Music Inc., L.A., 1981—; v.p. artists and repertoire EMI-Capitol Entertainment Properties, 1997-98; owner/operator Stonover Farm Bed and Breakfast, Lenox, Mass., 2001—. Recipient N.Y.C. Civilian Commendation award for heroism, 1968, 14 platinum records awards Rec. Industry Assn. Am., 1977—, 10 Gold Record awards, 1977—. Mem. Nat. Assn. Recording Arts and Scis. Democrat. Jewish.

WERMUTH, MARY LOUELLA, secondary education educator; b. Oakland County, Mich., May 2, 1943; d. Burt and Ila A. (Cole) W.; m. David J. Kohne, Dec. 28, 1975; 1 child, John B. BA, Oakland U., 1965, MA, 1969, 81. Tchr. Rochester Cmty. Schs., Rochester Hills, Mich., 1965-96; instr., counselor Internat. Acad., Bloomfield Hills, 1996—. Farmer, 1964—; presenter in field; bd. dirs. Mich. Future Problem Solving; exchange tchr. New South Wales, Australia, 1996; ptnr. Old Indian Enterprises, 1982—; faculty Internat. Acad., dean humanities, 1996-2000; ednl. travel cons. Author: Images of Michigan, 1981, Michigan Centennial Farm History, 1986. Pres. Horizons Residential Ctrs., Inc., New Baltimore, Mich., 1984—; artistic dir. Phoenix Theater Co., 1997—2001, prodr.; ptnr. Rediscovery Ctr., Holly, Mich., 2000—; bd. dirs. Amerris Ind. Schs., 2000—. Recipient Disting. Alumni award Oakland U., 1976. Mem. NEA, Rochestern Edn. Assn., Mich. Edn. Assn., Mich. Coun. Tchrs. English (coms. 1985, 87), Oakland U. Alumni Assn. (pres. 1971-73), Mich. Centennial Farm Assn. (bd. dirs. 1979—), Mich. Assn. Gifted Edn. (v.p. 1991-93), Oakland County Tchrs. English (coms. 1985-93). Office: Internat Acad 1020 E Square Lake Rd Bloomfield Hills MI 48304-1957

WERMUTH, PAUL CHARLES, retired English educator; b. Phila., Oct. 28, 1925; s. Paul C. and Susan (Manga) W.; m. Barbara Ethel Braun, Aug. 26, 1951; children— Geoffrey Paul, Paul Charles, Alan John, Stephen Mark. AB, MA, Boston U., 1951; PhD, Pa. State U., 1955. Instr. Clarkson Coll., Potsdam, N.Y., 1951-52; part-time instr., grad. asst. Pa. State U., 1952-55; asst. prof. Coll. William and Mary, 1955-57; mem. faculty Central Conn. State Coll., New Britain, 1957-68, asso. prof. English, 1966-68; prof. English Northeastern U., 1968-90, prof. emeritus, 1990—, chmn. dept., 1968-75. Vis. prof. Middlebury Coll., 1963-64 Author: Modern Essays on Writing and Style, 2d edit, 1969, Essays in English, 1967, Bayard Taylor, 1974, Selected Letters of Bayard Taylor, 1997, also articles. Served with USAAF, 1943-46. Danforth summer study grantee, 1961 Mem. Modern Lang. Assn., AAUP, Mensa. Home: 73 Mostyn St Swampscott MA 01907-1616 Office: English Dept Northeastern Univ Boston MA 02115 E-mail: pwermuth@quik.com.

WERNER, ANDREW JOSEPH, physician, endocrinologist, musicologist; b. Budapest, Hungary, June 5, 1936; came to U.S., 1956; s. Steven and Clara (Gutfreund) W.; m. Elaine Audrey Friedenn; 1 child, Andrea Lisa. MD, Med. Coll. of Va., 1962. Intern Kings County Hosp. Downstate Med. Ctr., Bklyn., 1962-63; resident in internal medicine N.Y. Med. Coll. Flower and 5th Ave. Hosps., N.Y.C., 1963-65; NIH fellow in endocrinology Mt. Sinai Hosp., 1965-66; attending physician Mt. Sinai Med. Ctr., 1966—; mem. professorial faculty Mt. Sinai Sch. of Medicine, 1966—; cons. in endocrinology Hosp. for Joint Diseases-Orthopedic Inst., 1979—. Cons. in endocrinology North Gen. Hosp., N.Y.C., 1992—. Author: Wolfgang Amadeus Mozart, Summa Summarum, 1990; co-author: Malignant Tumors of the Thyroid: Clinical Concepts and Controversies, 1992. Patron Met. Opera Assn. Recipient Festungs medallion State of Salzburg, Austria, 1989, Pro Patria Hungarica award Republic of Hungary, 1997. Fellow Am. Coll. Endocrinology, N.Y. Acad. Medicine; mem. Am. Diabetes Assn., Endocrine Soc., N.Y. Acad. Scis., Am. Assn. Clin. Endocrinologists, The Philharmonic-Symphony Soc. of N.Y., Am. Inst. for Verdi Studies, Internat. Stiftung Mozarteum-Salzburg (Austria), Internat. Salzburg Assn. (pres. N.Y.C. and Salzburg 1989—). Office: 1112 Park Ave New York NY 10128-1235

WERNER, BETTY JEAN, music educator; b. Galveston, Tex., Aug. 13, 1924; d. Robert Arnold and Mae Ernestine (Locke) Sneyd; m. Eugene H. Werner, June 25, 1945; children: Betty Ann, Donald Eugene. B Music Edn. with honors, So. Meth. U., 1943. Elem. sch. music tchr. Galveston Pub. Schs., 1944-45, Austin (Tex.) Pub. Schs., 1945-47, Dallas Pub. Schs., 1947-48; pvt. piano tchr. Dallas, 1949-66, Overland Park, Kans., 1967—2000, Kansas City, Mo., 2000—. Mem. Music Tchrs. Nat. Assn. (cert. piano tchr., nat. chair H.S. auditions 1983-86, nat. conv. com. 1987-91, nat. exec. bd. 1983-96), Nat. Guild Piano Tchrs., Kans. Music Tchrs. Assn. (v.p. for assns. 1990-94, Outstanding Tchr. award 1988), Mu Phi Epsilon. Republican. Presbyterian. Home: 9805 Jefferson Ct Kansas City MO 64114

WERNER, BURTON KREADY, insurance company executive; b. St. Louis, Apr. 24, 1933; s. Elmer L. and Helen (Kready) W.; m. Joanna Catherine Hill, Oct. 17, 1959; children: Lisa Anne, Cynthia Catherine, Bradford Kready. AB cum laude, Amherst Coll., 1954; MBA, U. Pa., 1958. CPCU. Sec. Insurers Svc. Corp., St. Louis, 1958-65, exec. v.p., 1965-75, pres., also bd. dirs., 1975-88; v.p., bd. dirs. Safety Mut. Casualty Corp., 1958-76, pres., 1976-87, chmn., 1987-91; also bd. dirs.; chmn. Safety Nat. Casualty Corp., St. Louis, 1991-99, chmn. emeritus, 1999—. Chmn. SIG Holdings, Inc., St. Louis, 1991-96, Delphi Fin. Group, Inc., bd. dirs.; originator unemployment compensation reinsurance for non-profit orgns. under pub. law 91-373. Guarantor St. Louis Mcpl. Opera; trustee Churchill Sch., St. Louis Country Day Sch.; mem. Humane Soc. Mo., Arts and Edn. Coun. St. Louis, Associated Industries Mo., Mo. Bot. Garden, Mo. Hist. Soc., St. Louis Symphony Soc., City Art Mus., St. Louis Landmark Assn, Maui Meml. Med. Ctr. Found., Inc., Hui No'Eau Visual Arts Ctr., Maui Arts and Cultural Ctr. Capt. USAF, 1954—56. Named to Hon. Order Ky. Cols. Fellow: Truman Libr.; mem.: Better Bus. Bur. St. Louis, Am. Soc. CPCU, Nat. Assn. Safety and Claims Orgns., Maui Arts & Cultural Ctr, St. Louis McDonnell Planetarium, St. Louis Zoo Assn., Wailea Golf Club, Casa y Pesca Las Cruces Club, Windfall Club, Univ. Club, Racquet Club, Napili Kai Beach Club, Boone Valley Golf Club, Jupiter Hills Club, Delta Kappa Epsilon. Episcopalian. Office: Safety Nat Casualty Corp 2043 Woodland Pkwy Ste 200 Saint Louis MO 63146-4235 E-mail: bk.werner@sncc.com.

WERNER, ELIZABETH HELEN, librarian, Spanish language educator; b. Palo Alto, Calif., June 21, 1944; d. Fielding and Lucy Elizabeth (Hart) McDearmon; m. Michael Andrew Werner, Aug. 21, 1976. BA, Mills Coll., 1966; MA, Ind. U., 1968; MLS, U. Md., 1973. Instr. Spanish, McDaniel Coll., Westminster, Md., 1968—72; libr., assoc. prof. Clearwater (Fla.) Christian Coll., 1975—. Sec. Sunline Libr. users group Tampa Bay Libr. Consortium, Tampa, Fla., 1993—94, 1998—2000, 2002—. Contbr. book revs. to profl. jours. Com. mem. Upper Pinellas County Post Office Customers' Adv. Coun., Clearwater, 1992—. Mem. Fla. Libr. Assn., Assn. Christian Librs. (Christian libr. consortium team coord. 1998—), Fla. Assn. Christian Librs. (pres. 1991-94, sec. 1987-90, 95-98, 2000), Friends of the Clearwater Libr., Am. Assn. Tchrs. Spanish and Portuguese. Avocations: reading, choir, travel, language study. Office: Clearwater Christian Coll 3400 Gulf To Bay Blvd Clearwater FL 33759-4514

WERNER, GLORIA S. librarian; b. Seattle, Dec. 12, 1940; d. Irving L. and Eva H. Stolzoff; m. Newton Davis Werner, June 30, 1963; 1 son, Adam Davis. BA, Oberlin Coll., 1961; ML, U. Wash., 1962; postgrad. UCLA, 1962-63. Reference librarian UCLA Biomed Library, 1963-64, asst. head pub. services dept., 1964-66, head pub. services dept., head reference div., 1966-72, asst. biomed. librarian public services, 1972-77, asso. biomed. librarian, 1977-78, biomed. librarian, assoc. univ. librarian, dir. Pacific S.W. regional Med. Library Service, 1979-83; asst. dean library services UCLA Sch. Medicine, 1980-83; assoc. univ. librarian for tech. services, 1983-89, dir. libraries, acting univ. librarian, 1989-90, univ. librarian, 1990-2002; adj. lectr. UCLA Grad. Sch. Library and Info. Sci., 1977-83. Editor, Bull. Med. Library Assn., 1979-82, asso. editor, 1974-79; mem. editorial bd. Ann. Stats. Med. Sch. Libraries U.S. and Can., 1980-83; mem. accrediting commn. Western Assn. Schs. and Colls., N.W. Assn. Schs. and Colls. Mem. ALA, Assn. Rsch. Librs. (bd. dirs. 1993-98, v.p./pres.-elect 1995-96, pres. 1996-97, past pres. 1997-98). Office: UCLA Rsch Libr Adminstrv Office 405 Hilgard Ave Los Angeles CA 90095-9000

WERNER, JOANNE LOUCILLE, financial executive; b. Midland, Mich., Jan. 20, 1940; d. Ewald George and Martha (Yuchlal) W. AAS, Ea. Nazarene Coll., Quincy, Mass., 1972; BAS, Boston U., 1977; MBA, Suffolk U., Boston, 1979. Prog. asst. Dept. Def., Washington, 1966-68, budget analyst, 1968-70, Dept. of Navy, Washington, 1970-72, GSA, Boston, 1972-77, sr. budget analyst, 1977-79; sr. fin. mgmt. specialist HUD, 1979-90; founder, dir., coord. Network Industry Leaders Internat., Quincy, 1990; ind. contractor courier svcs., 1994-95; data quality analyst South Shore Hosp., 2001. Part-time exec. Gillette Co., Boston, 1995-97. Editor newsletter Baystatement, 1980-81. Vol. med. supplies mgr. Mass. Emergency Mgmt. Agy., Quincy, 1995. With USNR. Sioux Falls Coll. grantee, 1959; named Sailor of Yr. USNR, 1985. Mem. Am. Soc. Women Accts. (bd. dirs. 1986-88, 90-91), Habitat for Humanity Internat. (vol., family selection com., family partnership liaison 1997-98). Avocations: music, reading, nutrition, travel. Home and Office: 994 Summit Lake Drive West Palm Beach FL 33406 E-mail: joanne1449@hotmail.com.

WERNER, JOSEPH ANTHONY, occupational therapist; b. S.I., N.Y., Dec. 7, 1957; s. Joseph Anthony and Edna Marie (Lichenstein) W.; m. Meiba Werner, June 20, 1982; children: Joseph Anthony, Michael Stephen. BS in Occupl. Therapy, SUNY, Bklyn., 1981. Cert. sensory integration specialist Sensory Integration Internat. Occupl. therapist Occupl. Therapy Cons., Ridgefield, N.J., 1986-89, Sea Pines Rehab. Hosp., Melbourne, Fla., 1989-91; pvt. practice in occupl. therapy Joseph Werner Therapies, Palm Bay, 1991-93; co-owner, occupl. therapist, v.p. Child and Family Cons., Melbourne, 1993—. Bd. dirs. Early Intervention Team, Melbourne, 1997. Mem. Am. Occupl. Therapy Assn. (cert. in pediat.), Fla. Occupl. Assn. Avocations: jogging, reading, enjoying my family. Home: 970 Peachland Ave NE Palm Bay FL 32907-1225 Office: Child and Family Cons 1800 Penn St Ste 12 Melbourne FL 32901-2625

WERNER, LORA SIEGMANN, environment health scientist; b. June 22, 1970; BS, Rensselaer Polytechnic Inst., 1992; MPH, Johns Hopkins U., 1999. Regional rep. Agy. for Toxic Substances and Disease Registry, Phila., 1999—; hazardous materials program mgr. Fed. Emergency Mgmt. Agy., 1998-99. Environ. cons., sr. assoc. ICF Kaiser, Fairfax, Va., 1992-98. Contbr. articles to profl. jours. including Am. Soc. Profl. Emergency Planners. Office: 1650 Arch St 3HS00 Philadelphia PA 19103 E-mail: lora_s_werner@hotmail.com.

WERNER, MICHAEL J. biotechnologist; Sr. health advisor US Senate Majority Leader George Mitchell; counsel for legis. and policy Am. Coll. Physicians-Am. Soc. Internal Medicine; v.p. bioethics Biotechnology Industry Orgn. Staff Task Force on Health Reform, 1993; sr. advisor Md. Gov. William Donald Schaefer; spkr. in field. Treas. Americans for Better Care of the Dying. Mem.: Am. Soc. Law, Medicine & Ethics, Am. Health Lawyers Assn. Office: Biotechnology Industry Orgn 1225 Eye St NW Ste 400 Washington DC 20005*

WERNER, PATRICE (PATRICIA ANN WERNER), college president; b. Jersey City, May 31, 1937; d. Louis and Ella Blanche (Smith) W. BA in French, Caldwell Coll., 1966; MA in French, McGill U., 1970; PhD in French, NYU, 1976; postgrad. Inst. Ednl. Mgmt., Harvard U., 1991. Joined Dominican Sisters of Caldwell, 1954. Sch. tchr. Archdiocesan Sch. Systems, N.J., Ala.,

1954-62; tchr. French, Latin Jersey City, Caldwell, N.J., 1962-72; instr. French Caldwell Coll., 1973-76, dir. continuing edn., 1976-79, chair dept. fgn. langs., assoc. prof. French, 1979-85, acad. dean, prof. French, 1985-94, pres., 1994—. Trustee Caldwell Coll.; mem. corp., trustee Providence Coll.; coll. bd. Dominican Higher Edn. Coun. Vice chair exec. com. Ind. Coll. Fund N.J., bd. trustees; bd. dirs. Neylan Commn. Mem. NAICU, Am. Assn. Higher Edn. , Assn. Ind. Colls. and Univs. N.J. (bd. dirs., sec.), N.J. Presidents Coun. (exec. bd., treas.), Coun. of Ind. Colls., N.J. Assn. Colls. and Univs., Am. Coun. on Edn., Assn. Am. Colls. and Univs., Assn. Cath. Colls. and Univs., Assn. Governing Bds. of Colls. and Univs., N.J.'s Long Range Plan for Higher Edn. Steering Com. Avocations: tennis, reading, avid sports fan, travel. Office: Caldwell Coll 9 Ryerson Ave Caldwell NJ 07006-6195

WERNER, R(ICHARD) BUDD, retired business executive; b. Lorain, Ohio, Aug. 27, 1931; s. Paul Henry and Bessie Marie (Budd) W.; m. Janet Sue Kelsey, Aug. 28, 1932; children: Richard Budd Jr., David Kelsey, Mary Paula. BS in Commerce, Ohio U., 1953. CPA, Ohio. Sr. auditor Arthur Andersen & Co., Cleve., 1955-59; various fin. positions Glidden Co., 1959-65; v.p., asst. treas. Harshaw divsn. Kewanee Oil Co., 1965-72; v.p. fin., treas. Weatherhead Co., 1973-77; v.p. finance, treas. Hauserman, Inc., 1977-81; v.p. fin., CFO SPX Corp., Muskegon, Mich., 1981-94, sr. v.p. planning and devel., 1994-95; exec. in residence coll. of bus. Ohio U., Athens, 1995—. Mem. Lakewood (Ohio) City Coun., 1972-73; mem. North Muskegon (Mich.) Sch. Bd., 1981-85; bd. mem. Appalachian Cmty. Vis. Nurse Assn., Hospice, Health Svc. Inc., 1999—, ACENET Ventures, Inc., 2000—. Lt. Q.M.C., U.S. Army, 1953-55. Mem. Fin. Execs. Inst. Office: Ohio U Copeland Hall Athens OH 45701

WERNER, ROBERT JOSEPH, college dean, music educator; b. Lackawanna, N.Y., Feb. 13, 1932; s. Edward Joseph and Marian L. (Gerringer) W.; m. Sharon Lynne Mohrfeld, June 22, 1957; children: Mark J., Kurt M., Erik J. BME, Northwestern U., 1953, MusM, 1954, PhD, 1967. Dir. instrumental music Evanston (Ill.) Twp. H.S., 1956-66; assoc. prof. mus. Harpur Coll. SUNY, Binghamton, 1966-68, dir. Contemporary Music Project, 1968-73; dir. Sch. Mus. U. Ariz., Tucson, 1973-85, dean fine arts, 1981-82; dean Coll.-Conservatory of Music U. Cin., 1985-2000, dean emeritus, 2000—. Editor: Comprehensive Musicianship: An Anthology of Evolving Thought, 1971; contbtr. articles to profl. jours. Mem. exec. bd. Tucson Symphony Orch., 1974-85; bd. dirs. Cultural Commn. Tucson, 1974-75, Cin. Symphony Orch., 1985-2000, Cin. Opera, 1985-2000, Cin. Ballet, 1985-2000; mem. artistic directorate Am. Classical Music Hall of Fame. With U.S. Army, 1954-56. Mem. Nat. Assn. Schs. Music (pres. 1989-91), Coll. Music Soc. (pres. 1977-78), Internat. Soc. for Music Edn. (pres. 1984-86, treas. 1986-97), Music Educators Nat.Conf., McDowell Soc., Coll. Music Soc., Psi Upsilon, Phi Mu Alpha Sinfonia.

WERNER, ROBERT L. lawyer, consultant; b. N.Y.C., Feb. 28, 1913; s. Abraham L. and Elsa (Ludwig) W.; m. Raye Davies, Oct. 13, 1945; children: William, John. AB, Yale U., 1933; LLB, Harvard U., 1936. Bar: N.Y. 1936, U.S. Supreme Ct. 1936, also various fed. cts. and adminstrv. agys. 1936. Spl. asst. to U.S. atty. So. Dist. N.Y., 1936, asst. U.S. atty. 1937-40, confidential asst., 1940-42; 1st asst. civil div. U.S. Dept. Justice, Washington, 1946-47; spl. asst. to atty. gen. U.S., 1946-47; mem. law dept. RCA, N.Y.C., 1947, v.p., gen. atty., 1951-62, exec. v.p., gen. atty., 1962-66, exec. v.p., gen. counsel, 1966-78, dir., 1963-79, cons., 1978-83. Mem. adv. bd. Internat. and Comparative Law Ctr. Southwestern Legal Found., Dallas, 1966—, treas., 1970-72, vice chmn., 1972-73, chmn. advisory bd., 1974-76, found. trustee 1976-88, hon. trustee 1988—; lectr. Conf. Bd., Practicing Law Inst., others; mem. nat. adv. council corp. law depts. Practising Law Inst., 1974-78; com. on restrictive bus. practices U.S. council Internat. C. of C., 1973-78; N.Y. Lawyers' Com. for Civil Rights under Law, 1972-78. Trustee Ithaca Coll., N.Y., 1968-88, hon. trustee, 1988—, chmn. bd., 1976-78; trustee Salisbury (Conn.) Sch., 1975-77, N.Y. Chiropractic Coll., 1986-89; bd. dirs. Midtown Arts Common at St. Peter's Ch., 1983-89. Capt. U.S. Army, 1942-44; to lt. col. USAAF, 1944-46, ETO. Recipient Disting. Service award Ithaca Coll., 1988. Fellow Am. Bar Found.; mem. Internat., Fed., Am., N.Y. State, City N.Y., FCC bar assns., IEEE (sr.), Am. Legion, Harvard Law Sch. Assn., Assn. Gen. Counsel (emeritus), U.S. Naval Inst., Internat. Law Assn. (Am. br.), Nat. Legal Aid and Defender Assn. (dir. 1974-79), Am. Judicature Soc., Newcomen Soc., N.Y. County Lawyers' Assn., Am. Soc. Internat. Law, Yale Club, Harvard Club N.Y., Nat. Lawyers Club, Army and Navy Club (Washington), Coral Beach Club (Bermuda). Home: 116 E 68th St New York NY 10021-5955

WERNER, ROGER HARRY, archaeologist; b. N.Y.C., Nov. 11, 1950; s. Harry Emile and Rena (Roode) W.; m. Kathleen Diane Engdahl, Feb. 20, 1982; children: Meryl Lauren, Sarah Melise, Jeremy Marshall; 1 stepchild, Amber Fawn. BA, Belknap Coll., 1973; MA, Sonoma State U., Rohnert Park, Calif., 1982. Curatorial aide Anthro. Lab. Sonoma State Coll., 1975-76, curatorial asst., 1976-77, staff archaeologist, 1977-80, Planning Dept., Lake County, Calif., 1977; cir. riding archaeologist western region Nat. Park Service, Tucson, 1978; prin. investigator ASI Cartography and Geog. Info. Sys., Stockton, Calif., 1979—; v.p. bus. ptnr. devel. Internet Ventures Inc., 1995-97. Cons. Calif. Indian Legal Svcs., Ukiah, 1977, Geothermal Rsch. Impact Projection Study, Lakeport, Calif., 1977—, Delta Net Comms., Stockton, Calif., 1995—; instr. Ya-Ka-Ana Indian Ednl. Ctr., Santa Rosa, Calif., 1978-79; lead archaeologist No. Calif., WESTEC Svcs., Inc., San Diego, 1979-81; adj. prof. U. Puget Sound, summer 1995. Sec. Colonial Hts. PTA, 1983-84, 2d v.p., 1985-86, historian, 1986-87, v.p., 1987-88; cons., instr. Clovis Adult Sch., 1984-85; instr. U. Pacific Lifelong Learning Ctr., 1987—, San Joaquin Delta Coll., 1990—, Calif. State U., Fresno, 1992—; bd. dirs. Valley Mountain Regional Ctr., 1987-88, treas., 1988-89, v.p., 1989-90, pres.-elect, 1990-91, pres., 1991-92; bd. trustees Stockton Chorale, treas., 1992-93, youth chorale rep., 1993-94; active Spl. Olympics, Stockton, Calif.; adminstr. Minor A divsn. Sundown Little League of Stockton, Inc., 1998, Cultural Heritage Bd., City of Stockton, 2000—. Anthropology dept. research grantee, Sonoma State U., 1980. Mem. Geol. Soc. Am., Soc. for Am. Archaeologists, Great Basin Anthropol. Conf., Soc. for Calif. Archaeology, Assn. for Retarded Citizens. Democrat. Avocations: reading, community activities, computers, antiques, collectibles. Home: 1117 Aberdeen Ave Stockton CA 95209-2625 Office: ASI Archaeology and Cultural Resources Mgmt 1117 Aberdeen Ave Stockton CA 95209

WERNER, THOMAS LEE, hospital administrator; b. Hazen, N.D., Dec. 8, 1945; married. BA, Union Coll., 1967; MA, U. Nebr., 1969. Asst. dir. pers. Portland (Oreg.) Adventist Med. Ctr., 1971-72; v.p. Verticare Ambulatory Care Program, Portland, 1972-73; adminstr. Tillamook (Oreg.) CountyGen. Hosp., 1973-77, Walla Walla (Wash.)Gen. Hosp., 1977-81; exec. v.p. Fla. Hosp. Med. Ctr., Orlando, 1981-85, pres., 1985-2000, Adventist Health Systems, Winter Park, Fla., 2000—. Office: Adventist Health Systems 111 N Orlando Ave Winter Park FL 32789-3675*

WERNER-JACOBSEN, EMMY ELISABETH, developmental psychologist; b. Eltville, Germany, May 26, 1929; came to U.S., 1952, naturalized, 1962; d. Peter Josef and Liesel (Kunz) W. BS, Johannes Gutenberg U., Germany, 1950; MA, U. Nebr., 1952, PhD, 1955; postgrad., U. Calif., Berkeley, 1953-54. Research asso. Inst. Child Welfare, U. Minn., 1956-59; vis. scientist NIH, 1959-62; asst. prof. to prof. human devel., rsch. child psychologist U. Calif., Davis, 1962-94, rsch. prof., 1995—. Sr. author: The Children of Kauai, 1971, Kauai's Children Come of Age, 1977; author: Cross-Cultural Child Development: A View from the Planet Earth, 1979, Vulnerable, but Invincible, 1982, 3d edit., 1998, Child Care: Kith, Kin and Hired Hands, 1984, Overcoming the Odds, 1992, Pioneer Children on the Journey West, 1995, Reluctant Witnesses: Children's Voices From the Civil War, 1998, Through the Eyes of Innocents: Children Witness World War II, 2000, Unschuldige Zeugen, 2001, Journeys From Childhood to Mid Life: Risk, Resilience and Recovery, 2001, A Conspiracy of Decency: The Rescue of the Danish Jews in World War II, 2002; contbr. articles to profl. jours. Fellow Am. Psychol. Soc., German Acad. Social Pediats. (hon.), Soc. for Rsch. in Child Devel.

WERNICK, EDITH ELAINE, pianist, educator; b. Columbus, Ohio, July 30, 1944; d. Maurice and Evelyn (Stone) Wernick. Pupil Loy Kohler, Jerry Lowder, George Haddad, Dave Wheeler, Lee Knoll. Cert. piano musicianship-pedagogy Nat. Piano Found. Pvt. tchr. piano, guitar, organ, accordian, keyboard, Columbus, 1963—. Instr. Van's Music Studio, Columbus, 1965-77; formerly tchr. Coyle's Music, Columbus; judge Columbus Music Coop. Recital, 2000. Rec. sec. Franklin County Young Dems., 1976-77; fin. sec. women singles unit B'nai B'rith, 1977—; tchr. Hauer Music Store, Columbus; mem. exec. com. Sabra Hadassah Edn. Com., 1977. Mem. Music Tchrs. Nat. Assn., Nat. Piano Guild, Ohio Music Tchrs. Assn., Columbus Music Tchrs. Assn., Internat. Libr. Music Svc. for Profl. Music Tchrs., Nat. Honor Roll of Guild Tchrs. Jewish. Home: 9116 Harper St SW Stoutsville OH 43104

WERNICK, EDWARD RAYMOND, company executive, computer consultant; b. Irvington, N.J., Mar. 11, 1955; s. Edward Joseph and Ann (Czech) W.; m. Ione Sharon Greenbaum, Nov. 2, 1984; 1 child, Elissa Ann. BS in Computer Sci., Kean Coll., 1977. Computer analyst N.Y. Life Ins., N.Y.C., 1978-81; computer cons. Horizons, 1981-84; data base adminstr. oracle Standard & Poors, 1984-88; tchr. sybase Sybase, 1988-89; data base adminstr. sybase Merrill Lynch, 1989-91, Paramount Comms., Old Tappan, N.J., 1991-95; v.p. Crossmar, Parsippany, 1995-98; pres., CEO Femasque Inc., 1998—. Computer, fin. cons., pvt. practice, Oradell, N.J., 1981—; pres. FEMASQUE, Inc., 1998—. Designer stage lighting for more than 80 plays, 1974-88; writer relational scripts for Australian govt., 1994; exhibited sculpture in India, 1991, Brazil, 1992, Oslo, Norway, 1994. Mem. Rep. Nat. Com.; sec. Stockton (N.J.) Rifle Club, 1974; pres. Irvington (N.J.) Masquers, 1978. Named Outstanding Young Rep. Union, N.J., Rep. Com., 1976; Best of Show sculpture Art Assoc., Irvington, N.J., 1979; 100 yd. standing rifle champion Stockton (N.J.) Rifle Club, 1974. Mem. Assn. for Computing Machinery, Sybase Internat. Users Group, Relational Database Users Group, Oradell Arts Com., Internet Users Group. Roman Catholic. Avocations: lighting design, theater, logic. Home: 920 Oradell Ave Oradell NJ 07649-1925 Office: Crossmar 111 Sylvan Ave Englewood Cliffs NJ 07632 E-mail: ednnj42@aol.com.

WERNICK, RICHARD FRANK, composer, conductor; b. Boston, Jan. 16, 1934; s. Louis and Irene (Prince) W.; m. Beatrice Messina, July 15, 1956; children: Lewis, Adam, Peter (dec.). BA, Brandeis U., 1955; MA, Mills Coll., 1957. Instr. music U. Buffalo, 1964-65; asst. prof. music, dir. univ. symphony U. Chgo., 1965-68; conductor Pa. Contemporary Players, 1968-93; prof. music U. Pa., 1968-96, prof. emeritus, 1996—. Co-founder Community Youth Orch. of Delaware County; cons. Contemporary Music, The Phil. Orch., 1983-89, spl. cons. to the music dir., 1989-93; bd. dirs. Theodore Presser Co. Music dir. Royal Winnipeg Ballet Can., 1957-58; composer: Haiku of Basho, 1967, A Prayer for Jerusalem, 1971 (Naumburg award 1975), Moonsongs from the Japanese, 1972, Kaddish Requiem, 1973, String Quartet 2, 1973, Songs of Remembrance, 1974, Visions of Terror and Wonder, 1976 (Pulitzer prize 1977), Contemplations of the Tenth Muse, Book I, 1976, Book II, 1978, Introits and Canons, 1977, A Poison Tree, 1979, Concerto for Cello and Ten Players, 1980, In Praise of Zephyrus, 1981, Piano Sonata: Reflections of a Dark Light, 1982, Sonata for cello and piano: Portraits of Antiquity, 1982, The Oracle of Shimon bar Yochai, 1983, Concerto for Violin and Orch., 1983-84 (Friedheim 1st prize 1986); Oracle II for soprano, oboe and piano, 1985, Concerto for Viola and Orch., 1985-86, Musica Ptolemeica brass quintet, 1987, Symphony #1, 1988, String Quartet #3, 1988, Concerto for Piano and Orch. (Friedheim award 1992), 1989-90, Fragments of Prophecy, 1990, String Quartet #4, 1991 (Friedheim 1st prize 1991), Concerto for Saxophone Quartet and Orch., 1991, Cello Concerto #2, 1992, Symphony #2, 1993, ...and a time for peace, 1994, String Quartet #5, 1995, Cassation Music Tom Jefferson Knew, 1995, trio for violin, cello, piano, 1996, Da'ase for solo guitar, 1996, Fagotto Memories for solo bassoon, 1997, Sonata for violin and piano, 1997, Duettino for violin and oboe, 1997, String Quartet 6, 1998, Musica da Camerata, 1999, Telino's Acrobats, 1999, Piano Sonata # 2, 2000, The Name of the Game, 2000, Sonata # 2 for Cello and Piano, 2001, Cello Sonata #2, 2001, Quintet for Horn & String Quartet, 2002. Recipient music award Nat. Inst. Arts and Letters, 1976, Nat. Endowment Arts grantee, 1975, 79, 82; Fellow Ford Found., 1962-64, Guggenheim Found., 1976. Mem. ASCAP. Democrat. E-mail: rfwernick@aol.com.

WERNICK, SANDRA MARGOT, advertising and public relations executive; b. Tampa, Sept. 13, 1944; d. Nathan and Sylvia (Bienstock) Rothstein. BA in English, U. Fla., 1966. Tchr. English Miami Beach (Fla.) Sr. High Sch., 1967; adminstrv. asst. pub. rels. Bozell & Jacobs, Inc., N.Y.C., 1968-69; asst. to dir. pub. rels. Waldorf-Astoria, 1969-70; dir. advt. and pub. rels. Hyatt on Union Square, San Francisco, 1974-82; pres. Wernick Mktg. Group, 1982—; exec. dir. Sales and Mktg. Execs. of the Bay Area, 1995-2000; mng. ptnr. The Stanford Group, 1998-99. Bd. dirs. Nat. Kidney Assn., San Francisco, 1985-87; advisor Swords to Plowshares, San Francisco, 1988-89; mem. mktg. com. to bd. bd. Boy Scouts of Greater East Bay, 1995-2000. Recipient Award of Merit, San Francisco Advt. and Cable Car Awards, 1979, Award of Excellence, San Francisco Art Dirs. 1978, Disting. Mktg. award Sales and Mktg. Internat., 1997, awards Am. Hotel and Motel Assn., 1981, 1982, awards of excellence San Francisco Publicity Club, 1990, 1994, 1995-98, 1990. Mem. NAFE, Women in Comms. (bd. dirs. 1987-89), Am. Women in Radio and TV (bd. dirs. 1989-90), Pub. Rels. Soc. Am., San Francisco Publicity Club (pres. 1989), Variety Club, Profl. Bus. Women's Assn., Calif. Pacific Med. Ctr. (aux. 1988-95). Democrat. Jewish. Office: 1690 Broadway Ste 705 San Francisco CA 94109-2107 E-mail: sandie@wernickmarketinggroup.com.

WERPY, STEVE, music educator; b. Ada, Minn., July 30, 1953; s. Quentin and Ada (Merkins) Werpy. MA, U. of Minn., Minneapolis, MN, 1978—83; BS, Minn. State University-Moorhead, Moorhead, MN, 1971—76; PhD, Northwestern U., Evanston, IL, 1995—95; grad. studies in music, U. N.D., Grand forks, 2002—. Cert. K-12 Music tchr. Mont., 2000. Dir. 5-12 band and 7-12 music Killdeer (N.D.) Pub. Schools, 1976—77; dir. 10-12 band and choir Estevan (Sask) Comprehensive Sch., Canada, 1977—79. Dir. k-12 choir and classroom music Ada Pub. Schools, Ada, Minn., 1979—81; 5-12 band and 7-12 choir Littlefork-Big Falls Pub. Schools, Littlefork, Minn., 1983—86; 1-6 classroom music long-term substitute Forest Lake Pub. Schools, Forest Lake, Minn., 1988—89; k-6 classroom music long-term substitute Osseo Pub. Schools, Osseo, Minn., 1989—89; k-12 music Savage Pub. Schools, Savage, Mont., 1989—92; 9-12 band and beginner band Sidney Pub. Schools, Sidney, Mont., 1992—94; asst. prof. of music edn. U. of Houston, Houston, 1995—2000; k-12 music Savage Pub. Schools, Savage, Mont., 2000—02; tchg. asst., band U. of ND, Grand Forks, ND, 2002—. Contbr. book; musician: (rock cd) Shadow on My Soul: The Story of Kevin Carter, 2001; dir.: (band performance) Houston I.S.D. Middle Sch. Honor Band, 1999, (orch.performance) Texas Region 17 High Sch Honor Orch., 1999. Ch. musician Christ the King Luth. Ch., Houston, 1995—2000; summer camp staff No. Lights Coun., B.S.A., Fargo, ND, 1972—2001. Recipient Grad. Sch. Fellowship, Northwestern U., 1986-1988, Enron Tchg. Excellence Award, U. of Houston, 1998. Mem.: Music Educators Nat. Conf., Nat. Band Assn. Dfl. Lutheran. Avocations: camping, travel. Office: Univ ND Music Dept Grand Forks ND

WERRIES, E. DEAN, food distribution company executive; b. Tescott, Kans., May 8, 1929; s. John William and Sophie E. Werries; m. Marjean Sparling, May 18, 1962. BS, U. Kans., 1952. With Fleming Foods Co., Topeka, 1955-89, exec. v.p., 1973-76, exec. v.p. Eastern ops. Phila., 1976-78, pres. Oklahoma City, 1978-81; pres., chief operating officer Fleming Cos., Inc., 1981-88, also dir., pres., chief exec. officer, 1988-89, chmn., CEO, 1989-93. Chmn. bd. Sonic Corp., 1995-99. Sec. of Commerce State of Okla., 1995. With U.S. Army, 1952-54, Korea. Mem. Nat. Am. Wholesale Grocers Assn. (bd. dirs. 1979-93), Food Mktg. Inst. (bd. dirs. 1984—, chmn. 1989-91), Ind. Grocers Alliance (bd. dirs. 1984-94). Republican. Presbyterian.

WERRONEN, BETSY WARREN, political organization administrator; BA in Polit. Sci., Newton Coll. Sacred Heart, 1965. Legis. asst. to Sen. Thruston B. Morton, 1966-68; exec. asst. to Sen. Edward W. Brooke, 1968-75; dir. legis. nuclear energy and taxes Edison Electric Inst., 1979-81, chief lobbyist on nuclear power issues, 1979-81; acting asst. sec. of state for legis. affairs Dept. of State, Washington, 1981-85, prin. dep. asst. sec. of state for legis. affairs, 1987-89; prin. dep. asst. sec. for congl., intergovtl., pub. affairs Dept. of Energy, 1985-86; founder, pres. Warren and Co., 1989—; fin. chmn. Rep. Com. DC Rep. Party, Washington, 1998-2000, chmn. Rep. Com., 2000—. Mem. nat. steering com., congl. steering com. Women for Bush/Quayle, 1992; co-chair Ward 2, 1996-98; alternate del. Rep. Nat. Conv., 1996, 2000. Apptd. U.S. election observer, El Salvador, 1988; bd. dirs. Fgn. Student Coun., 1993-97. Mem. League of Rep. Women (1st v.p. 1997-99, pres. 1999—). Office: DC Rep Party 310 1st St SE Washington DC 20003*

WERSCHULZ, ARTHUR GUSTAV, computer and information sciences educator; b. Louisville, Dec. 22, 1950; s. Harry W. and Lee Fay (Levin) W.; m. Patricia Ann Patterson, Dec. 23, 1972; children: Aaron, Nathaniel. BS in Math., Carnegie-Mellon U., 1972, MS in Math., 1973, PhD in Math., 1977. Asst. prof. math. U. Md. Baltimore County, Catonsville, 1976-82; assoc. prof. math. and computer sci. Fordham U., N.Y.C., 1982-91, prof. math. and computer sci., 1991-95, prof. computer sci., 1995—. Vis. scholar Columbia U., N.Y.C., 1982-99; adj. sr. rsch. scientist, 1999—. Author: Computational Complexity of Differential and Integral Equations: An Information-Based Approach, 1991; co-author: (with J.F. Traub) Complexity and Information, 1998. Jewish. Office: Fordham Univ Dept Computer and Info Scis 113 W 60th St New York NY 10023-7484 E-mail: agw@dsm.fordham.edu.

WERSHALS, PAUL LEONARD, lawyer; b. Bklyn., July 10, 1942; AA in Bus. Adminstrn., Midwest Inst. Bus. Adminstrn., 1963; BS in Bus. Adminstrn., Babson Coll., 1965; JD, Suffolk U., 1969; LLM, NYU, 1975. Bar: N.Y. 1974, U.S. Supreme Ct. 1974. Mem. Nassau County Assigned Counsel Defender Plan; mem. legal com., citizens adv. com. for cablevision Town of North Heampstead, N.Y., 1976-97. Mem. Sen. Michael J. Tully's legis. adv. com., 1982-97; dir. Great Neck (N.Y.) Sr. Citizens Ctr., Inc., Town of North Hempstead, 1985-89. Mem. Am. Judges Assn., N.Y. State Trial Lawyers Assn., Nassau County Bar Assn. (arbitrator 1981—, mem. arbitration tribunal panel 1984—), Great Neck (N.Y.) Lawyers Assn. (bd. dirs. 1973—, sec. 1981-84,pres. 1985, chmn. bd. dirs. 1986-87), Phi Alpha Delta (mem. moot ct.). Office: 10 Cuttermill Rd Great Neck NY 11021-3201 Fax: 516 829-6219.

WERT, BARBARA J. YINGLING, special education consultant; b. Hanover, Pa., May 18, 1953; d. Richard Bruce and Jacqueline Louise (Myers) Yingling; m. Barry Thomas Wert, Aug. 23, 1975; children: Jennifer Allison, Jason Frederick. BS in Elem. Edn., Kutztown (Pa.) U., 1975; MS in Spl. Edn., Bloomsburg (Pa.) U., 1990; PhD, Pa. State U., 2002. Cert. in elem. edn., spl. edn., Pa.; cert. early childhood, Pa. Dir. children's program Coun. for United Ch. Ministries of Reading, Reading, Pa., 1975-76; instr. Berks County Vo-Tech., Oley Valley, 1976-77; asst. tchr. Ostrander Elem. Sch., Wallkill, N.Y., 1982-85; spl. needs surp., instrnl. support tchr., cons. Danville (Pa.) Child Devel. Ctr., 1986—; dir. Little Learners Pre-Sch., Northumberland, Pa., 1991-94, ednl. cons., 1991—. Pvt. cons. Families with Spl. Needs, Northumberland, 1991—; adj. prof. spl. edn., Bloomsburg U., 1995, 97, 98, 99, 00. Recipient Parent Profl. Partnership award 1993. Mem. ASCD, Coun. for Exceptional Children (exec. bd. dirs. divsn. early childhood 1991—, sec. 1991-93, newsletter editor, v.p. 1993-94, pres. 1995-96), Nat. Assn. for Edn. Young Children (v.p. Pa. divsn. for early childhood 1993—, tchr. edn. divsn., coun. for behavior disorders divsn., learning disabilities divsn.), Local Autism Support and Advocacy Group. Avocations: photography, needlework, hiking, reading. Home: RR 1 Box 372-n Northumberland PA 17857-9717

WERT, JAMES JUNIOR, materials scientist, educator; b. Barron, Wis., Jan. 9, 1933; s. James Lewis and Bernice Janet (Walker) W.; m. Jane Alice Thornton, Aug. 16, 1958; children: Thaddeus Thornton, Melissa Jane. BS, U. Wis., 1957, MS, 1958, PhD, 1961; postgrad., Carnegie Tech. Inst., 1958-59. Assoc. engr. Westinghouse Electric Corp., Pitts., 1958-60; rsch. scientist A.O. Smith Corp., Milw., 1961-62; mem. faculty Vanderbilt U., Nashville, 1962—, prof. material sci. and engring., 1967—, chmn. dept., 1969, chmn. materials, mechanics and structures div., 1969-72, chmn. materials sci. dept., 1975-82, chmn. dept. mech. and materials engring., 1976-82, George A. Sloan prof. metallurgy, 1976-96, Sloan prof. metallurgy and prof. mech. engring. emeritus, 1997—; mayor City of Forest Hills, Tenn., 1990-95. Dir. Ctr. for Coatings Sci. and Tech., Vanderbilt U., 1969-74; co.-dir. Ctr. for Materials Tribology, 1987—; vis. prof. Cambridge U., 1974; sr. Fulbright lectr. Mid. East; cons. Avco, 1964-71, Temco, 1964-71, Arnold Engring. Ctr., Tullahome, Tenn., 1966-71, Nat. Acad. Scis., 1969-70; pres. Technology Assocs., Inc., Nashville, 1975-85; pres. James Wert & Assocs., 1985—. Contbr. articles to profl. jours.; patentee nuclear fuels and cladding materials. Served with AUS, 1953-55. Ampco fellow, 1957-58; Westinghouse-Bettis fellow, 1958-59; Foundry Edn. fellow, 1952-57; recipient Adams award Am. Welding Soc., 1969, Teaching award Tau Beta Pi, 1970, 78. Fellow ASME, ASM Internat.; mem. ASTM, AIME, Am. Welding Soc., Am. Soc. Metals, Hillwood Country Club, Vines Golf and Country Club, Sigma Xi, Tau Beta Pi, Phi Eta Sigma, Alpha Sigma Mu, Pi Kappa Alpha, Pi Tau Sigma, Omicron Kappa Delta Methodist. Home: 2510 Ridgewood Dr Nashville TN 37215-4518 E-mail: jimwert@worldnet.att.net.

WERT, JONATHAN MAXWELL, II, management consultant; b. Port Royal, Pa., Nov. 8, 1939; s. Jonathan Maxwell I and Helen Leona (Leonard) W.; m. Wendy J. Mast; children: Jonathan Maxwell III, Kimberly Dee, Jon Adam, Justin Tyler, Amanda Elizabeth, Gabriel Chadwick. BS in Biology, Austin Peay State U., 1966, MS in Biology, 1968; PhD in Adminstrn., U. Ala., 1974. Park supt., chief interpretive services Bur. State Parks Pa. Dept. Environ. Resources, Harrisburg, 1968-69; chief naturalist Bays Mountain Park Environ. Edn. Ctr., Kingsport, Tenn., 1969-71; environ. and energy edn. specialist TVA, Knoxville, 1971-75; cons. energy, environment, conservation U. Tenn., 1975; sr. assoc.-energy Extension Svc., Coop. Extension Svc., Pa. State U., 1977-80; pres. Energy-Environ. Consultants, Port Royal, Pa., 1981-85, Mgmt. Diagnostics, Inc., Port Royal, 1985—. Author: Writing Environmental Education Grant Proposals, 1974, Environmental Education Study Projects for High School Students, 1974, Environmental Education Study Projects for College Students, 1974, Developing Environmental Study Areas, 1974, Developing Environmental Education Curriculum Material, 1974, Finding Solutions to Environmental Problems . . . A Process Guide, 1975, Assessing an Issue in Relation to Environmental, Economic, and Social Impact . . . A Process Guide, 1976, Energy Conservation Measures for Mobile Home Dwellers, 1978, Selected Energy Conservation Options for the Home, 1978, Selected Energy Management Options for Small Business and Local Government, 1978, Life Lines: A Book of Poetry, Prose, and Axioms, 1983, Survivorship and Growth in Employment: A Question and Answer Guide, 1983; mem. adv. bd.: Environ. Edn. Report, 1974— ; cons. editor: Jour. Environ. Edn, 1975; contbr. articles to profl. jours. Counselor Boy Scouts Am., 1975. Served with USMC, 1958-61. Recipient Conservation award Am. Motors Co., 1976 Mem. U.S. Energy Assn., Inst. Mgmt. Cons., Orgn. Devel. Inst., Inst. of Mgmt. Cons. (cert. mgmt. cons. 1987), Soc. for (profl. mgmt. cons.). Lutheran. Home: RR 5 Box 250 Mifflintown PA 17059-9576 Office: Mgmt Diagnostics Inc PO Box 240 Port Royal PA 17082-0240 E-mail: jwert@mdi-wert.com.

WERT, ROBERT CLIFTON, lawyer; b. Pleasantville, N.J., Jan. 8, 1944; s. Clifton Robert and Anna Louise (McLarren) W.; m. Grace Elizabeth Dunbar, Dec. 16, 1967; children: Andrew, Amy, Bethany, Laura. BS in Acctg., Temple U., 1965, JD, 1968; grad., JAG Sch., 1982, Command & Gen. Staff Coll., 1984, U.S. Army JFK Spl. Warfare Ctr, 1987. Bar: Pa. 1968, U.S. Dist. Ct. (ea. dist.) Pa. 1968, U.S. Ct. Mil. Appeals 1969, U.S. Supreme Ct. 1981. Commd. 2d lt. mil. police USAR, 1965, advanced through ranks to lt. col., 1984, ret., 1990; mil. judge U.S. Army, Okinawa, Japan, 1970-73, chief trial counsel, 1973, staff judge adv. Valley Forge Army Hosp., 1973-74, chief trial counsel N.J., 1974-76, chief legal asst. and claims, 1976-77, ret., 1990; chief staff counsel Southeastern Penn Transp. Authority, Phila., 1977-78, acting chief counsel, 1978-80, gen. counsel, 1980-84, dept. gen. mgr., 1984-86; exec. dir. Blank Rome Comisky & McCauley, 1986—. Owner Insulco, King of Prussia, Pa., 1972-79; co-owner Master Page Inc., Malvern, Pa., 1985-93. Bd. dirs. Evang. Assn. for Promotion of Edn., St. David's, Pa., Ea. Coll., 1988—, Crime Prevention Assn. Charitable Giving, Phila., 1991—; bd. dirs. Crime Prevention Assn., Phila., 1988-2001, chair exec. com., 1992-94, 1998-2001, treas., 1994-96, v.p., 1997-98; pres. Charlestown Townwatch, 1980-2000; coord. Twp. Emergency, 1984-99; vice-chair bd. supr. Charlestown Twp., 1998-2000;mem. bd. trustees Great Valley Presbyn. Ch., 2001—; deacon, Sunday Sch. supt., mem. bldg. com., chmn. property com. Ch. of the Savior, Wayne, Pa.; bd. dirs., asst. treas. Adv. Meth. Ch., Phila. Decorated Meritorious Svc. medal, Army Achievement medal, Overseas Svc. medal, Nat. Def. Svc. medal, various Res. decorations; recipient Pa. Gov.'s award, 1989. Mem. Assn. of Legal Adminstrs., Phila. Bar Assn., Temple U. Law Alumni Assn. (exec. com. 1995-96), Masons. Avocation: woodworking. Office: Blank Rome Comisky & McCauley LLP One Logan Sq Philadelphia PA 19103-6998 E-mail: wert@blankrome.com.

WERTH, VICTORIA PATRICIA, dermatologist, educator; b. Chgo., Sept. 1, 1954; d. Michael Wolf and Gloria Ruth (Goldsmith) W.; m. Kevin Jon Williams, Jan. 1, 1983; children: Nathan, Erik, Adrienne. BA in Chemistry, MS in Phys. Chemistry, Cath. U., 1976; MD, Johns Hopkins U., 1980. Diplomate Am. Bd. Internal Medicine, Am. Bd. Dermatology, Am. Bd. Immunodermatology and Immunopathology. Intern in medicine Northwestern Meml. Hosp., Chgo., 1980-81, resident in internal medicine, 1981-83; resident in dermatology NYU, N.Y.C., 1983-86, chief resident in dermatology, 1985-86, rsch. fellow in dermatology, 1986-88, clin. instr. in dermatology, 1986-89, asst. prof. dermatology, 1986-88; rsch. collaborator med. dept. Brookhaven Nat. Lab./Assoc. Univs., Inc., 1986-87; asst. prof. dermatology U. Pa. Sch. Medicine, 1989-98, assoc. prof. dermatology, 1998—; chief divsn. dermatology Phila. VA Hosp., 1989—. Lectr. in field. Author: University of Pennsylvania Manual of Dermatologic Diagnosis and Treatment, 1990, In-Conn's Current Therapy, 1991; contbr. articles to profl. publs. Mem. AMA, Am. Coll. Physicians, Am. Acad. Dermatology (task force on govt. medicine), Dermatology Found., Soc. Investigative Dermatology, Am. Coll. Rheumatology, Phi Beta Kappa. Home: 425 Wister Rd Wynnewood PA 19096-1808 Office: VA Hosp Divsn Dermatology University and Woodland Ave Philadelphia PA 19104 E-mail: werth@mail.med.upenn.edu.

WERTHAMER, NATHAN RICHARD, physicist; b. Milw., Feb. 9, 1935; BA, Harvard Coll., 1956; PhD in physics, U. Calif., 1961. Rsch. assoc. U. Calif., San Diego, 1961-62; mem. tech. staff Bell Labs, 1962-75; mem. corp. planning dept. AT&T, 1975-76; chmn. N.Y. State Energy Rsch. and Devel. Authority, 1976-78; sr. advisor sci. and tech. dept. Exxon Corp., 1978-83; exec. dir. Becton Dickinson Devel. Corp., 1983-89; exec. officer Am. Phys. Soc., 1990-93; mgmt. cons. Chelsea Technols, N.Y.C., 1993—. Fellow AAAS, Am. Phys. Soc. Office: Chelsea Technols 43 W 16th St Apt 7D New York NY 10011-6321

WERTHEIM, MARY DANIELLE, elementary education coordinator; b. N.Y.C. d. Daniel Leo and Helen Loretta (Sudimick) Conroy; m. Stanley Claude Wertheim, Mar. 9, 1963. BA in English with honors, CCNY, 1960, MA, 1979. Coord. English and lang. arts Horace Mann Lower Sch., Riverdale, N.Y., 1969—. Pvt. investor Wertheim Trust, N.Y.C., 1985—; pres. winner's cir. Horace Mann Investment Club, Riverdale, 1989—. Founder, advisor Horace Mann Lower Sch. Cmty. Svc. Group, Riverdale, 1980—; active Rep. nat. Com., 1980—. Mem.: ASCD, Nat. Assn. Investors Corp., The Internat. Netsuke Soc. (sec. N.Y. chapter), Priory Scholars, Am. Firm, Mensa, The Grolier Club. Avocations: desk top publishing, manuscript collecting, frogs, Sherlock Holmes. Home: 180 Cabrini Blvd New York NY 10033-1138 Office: Horace Mann Lower Sch 4440 Tibbett Ave Bronx NY 10471-3416 E-mail: herbieboo@aol.com.

WERTHEIM, MITZI MALLINA, technology company executive; b. N.Y.C. d. Rudolf and Myrtle B. (McGraw) Mallina; m. Ronald P. Wertheim, Feb. 25, 1965 (div. July 1988); children: Carter, Tiana. BA, U. Mich., 1960. Asst. dir. div. research Peace Corps, Washington, 1961-66; sr. program officer Cafritz Found., 1970-76; dep. undersec. navy, 1977-81; with Fed. Sector Div. IBM, 1981-94; v.p. enterprise solutions SRA Corp., 1994-98, CNA Corp., 1998—. Woodrow Wilson vis. fellow, 1979, 80 Bd. dirs. Nat. Coalition Sci. and Tech., 1983—86; mem. vis. com. MIT, 1983—89; bd. dirs. Youth Policy Inst., 1986—91, VITA, 1990—2000; founder MIT Seminar XXI, 1985—. Recipient Federally Employed Women award Def. Dept., 1980; Disting. Pub. Svc. medal Navy Dept., 1981; fellow Maxwell Sch. Syracuse U., 1996-97. Mem.: Naval Studies Bd., Coun. on Fgn. Rels. Episcopalian. Home: 3113 38th St NW Washington DC 20016-3726

WERTHEIM, ROBERT HALLEY, national security consultant; b. Carlsbad, N.Mex., Nov. 9, 1922; s. Joseph and Emma (Vorenberg) W.; m. Barbara Louise Selig, Dec. 26, 1946; children: Joseph Howard, David Andrew. Student, N.Mex. Mil. Inst., 1940-42; BS, U.S. Naval Acad., 1945; MS in Physics, M.I.T., 1954; postgrad., Harvard U., 1969. Commd. ensign U.S. Navy, 1945, advanced through grades to rear adm., 1972; assigned Spl. Projects Office, Washington, 1956-61, Naval Ordnance Test Sta., China Lake, 1961-62, Office Sec. Def., Washington, 1962-65; head Missile br. Strategic Systems Project Office, 1965-67, dep. tech. dir., 1967-68, tech. dir., 1968-77, dir., 1977-80; sr. v.p. Lockheed Corp., 1981-88; cons. nat. def., 1988—. Emeritus mem. Draper Lab., Inc.; mem. U. Calif. Pres. Adv. Coun.; mem. sci. adv. group Dept. Def., Dept. Energy, U.S. Strategic Command; mem. nat. security adv. Lawrence Livermore Nat. Lab. Decorated D.S.M. with cluster, Legion of Merit, Navy Commendation medal, Joint Svc. Commendation medal; recipient Rear Adm. William S. Parsons award Navy League U.S., 1971, Chmn. Joint Chiefs of Staff Disting. Pub. Svc. award, 1996, Sec. of Def. medal for outstanding pub. svc., 1996. Fellow AIAA, Calif. Coun. Sci. Tech.; mem. Am. Soc. Naval Engrs. (hon. mem., Gold medal 1972), Nat. Acad. Engring., U.S. Naval Inst., Bernardo Heights Country Club, Masons, Sigma Xi, Tau Beta Pi. Home: 17705 Devereux Rd San Diego CA 92128-2084 Office: Sci Applications Internat Corp 1200 Prospect St La Jolla CA 92037-3608

WERTHEIMER, ESTHER, sculptor; b. Poland; Student, Montreal Mus. Fine Arts, 1958-63, Internat. Acad., Austria, 1966, Acad. Belle Arte, Florence, Italy, 1967-68; BA, Loyola of Montreal, 1973; MA, Goddard Coll., 1975. Sculptures installed at Maimonides Hosp., Montreal, Can., Recreation Ctr., Pt. St. Lucie, Fla., Itami City Cultural Hall, Hyogo Prefecture, Japan, Okaloosa-Walton C.C., Niceville, Fla., Upper Iowa U., Fayette, Okayama Mcpl. Ctr., Japan, Health Care Ctr., Kyoto, Japan, Royal Palm Plaza, Boca Raton, Fla., Hikifune Cultural Ctr., Sumida-ku, Tokyo, 21st Century forest Park, Fukushima, Japan, Yumeji Mus. Okayama, Katsushika Performing Art Ctr., Tokyo, City of Hamura, Tokyo, Fukuoka City Hall, Japan, Hakone Open-Air Mus., Kanagawa-ken, Sun Bank, Palm Springs, Calif., North Miami Beach, Fla., Atrium of Alcan Aluminum Ltd., Montreal, Glouster City Hall for Carling Park of Commerce, East Ottawa, Joliette Mus., Que., Carling Exec. Pk., Ottawa, Cote St-Luc City Hall and Libr., Montreal, Conf. Bd. of Can., Ottawa, Douglas Hosp., Montreal, others. Recipient awards Montreal Mus. Fine Arts, 1956-63, Borsa di Studio, Italian Govt., 1967-68, Govt. Que. Bource de l'Enseignement Superieur, 1974, Gold medal INT Tourismo, Rome, EUR Europa Premio, Rome, B'nai B'rith Internat. Arts award, 1997, others; grantee Can. Coun. Travel, 1967, Elizabeth T. Greenshields Meml., 1969, Govt. Can., 1989, 94. Home: 6507 Brava Way Boca Raton FL 33433-8239 also: 6695 Somerled Ave Montreal QC H4V 1T5 Canada Fax: 561-392-0065. E-mail: ewertheimer@ewertheimer.com.

WERTHEIMER, FREDRIC MICHAEL, public policy advocate; b. Bklyn., Jan. 9, 1939; s. Irving Wertheimer and Mildred (Klein) Van Brink; m. Linda Cozby, June 15, 1969. BA, U. Mich., 1959; LL.B., Harvard U., 1962. Bar: N.Y. bar 1963, D.C. bar 1971. Atty. SEC, 1963-66; legis. counsel Congressman Silvio Conte, 1967-68; counsel House Small Bus. Com., 1969-70; lobbyist, legis. dir., v.p. Common Cause, Washington, 1971-81, pres., 1981-95; news polit. analyst CBS News, Washington, 1996; pres. Democracy 21, 1997—. Fellow Press Politics and Policy Ctr. Harvard U., 1996; J. Skelly Wright fellow, vis. lectr. Yale Law Sch., 1997; polit. analyst ABC News, 1999-2000. Author: Common Cause Manual on Money and Politics. With U.S. Army, 1962-63. Fellow Inst. Politics Harvard U., 1972. Jewish. Home: 3502 Macomb St NW Washington DC 20016-3162

WERTS, MERRILL HARMON, retired management consultant; b. Nov. 17, 1922; s. Mack Allen and Ruth Martha (Badger) W.; m. Dorothy Wilson, Mar. 22, 1946; children: Stephen M., Riley J., Todd J., Kelly M. BS, Kans. State U., 1947; MS, Cornell U., 1948. Beef sales mgr. John Morrell & Co., Topeka and Memphis, 1948-53; dir. mktg. Kans. Dept. Agr., Topeka, 1953-55; sec.-treas. Falley's Markets, Inc., 1955-58; v.p. S.W. State Bank, 1958-65; pres. First Nat. Bank, Junction City, Kans., 1965-78; pvt. practice mgmt. cons., 1978-98; ret., 1998. Mem. Kans. Sen., 1978-88; mem. Kans. Pub. Employee Rels. Bd., 1989-94, Kans. Comns. on Future of Health Care, 1991-94; chmn. Kans. WWII Commemoration Com., 1995-96, Kans. Commn. on Vets. Affairs, 1995-98, Geary County Pub. Bldg. Commn., 1996-99; bd. dirs. Stockgrowers State Bank, Maple Hill, Kans. Mem. Kans. Bank Mgmt. Commn., 1967-71; mem. adv. com. U.S. Comptroller of Currency, 1971-72; mem. Topeka Bd. Edn., 1957-61; pres. Junction City-Geary County United Fund, 1967-68, Junction City Indsl. Devel., Inc., 1966-72; trustee Kans. State U. Endowment Assn., 1958-2001, Kans. Pub. Policy Inst., 1995-99, Kans. Synod Presbyn. Westminster Found., 1965-72; bd. dirs. Kans. Hist. Soc., 1989-97. 1st lt., inf., AUS, 1943-46. Decorated Bronze Star medal, Purple Heart, Combat Inf. badge; named to Inf. Officer Candidate Hall Fame, 1981, Civilian Aide to Sec. of Army for Kans., 1991-95; named Outstanding State Legis. Am. Legis. Exch. Coun., 1988. Mem. Kans. State U. Alumni Assn. (pres. 1957), Am. Legion, VFW, DAV, Kans. Bankers Assn., Assn. U.S. Army (Gen. Creighton W. Abrams medal 1997), U.S., Kans. (bd. dirs., v.p. 1979-84), Junction City C.C. (pres. 1975-76), Kans. Farm Bur., Kans. Livestock Assn., Junction City Country Club (past pres.), Masons, Shriners, Jesters, Rotary (dist. gov. 1973-74), Sigma Phi Epsilon. Republican. Presbyterian. Address: 1228 Miller Dr Junction City KS 66441-3312

WERTSCH, PAUL ANTHONY, family physician, medical administrator; b. Oshkosh, Wis., Dec. 3, 1943; s. Paul G. and Lila E. Wertsch; m. Kay A. Heggestad, Sept. 7, 1968; children: Johanna, Gregory. BS, U. Wis., 1966, MD, 1970. Diplomate Am. Bd. Family Practice. Intern St. Paul-Ramsey Med. Ctr., 1971; resident in family practice Gallup (N.Mex.) Indian Hosp., 1973; ptnr. Monona Grove Clinic, Madison, Wis., 1973-78; founder, pres., dir. Wildwood Family Clinic, 1978—; clin. assoc. prof. Med. Sch. U. Wis. Chief med. staff St. Mary's Hosp. Med. Ctr., Madison, 1988—90; v.p. Madison Maennerchor, 1998—. Bd. dirs. WisMedPac, 2000—; v.p. Madison Maenerchor, 1999—. Lt. comdr. USPHS, 1971-73. Fellow Am. Acad. Family Practice: mem. AMA (rep. St. Mary's Hosp. Med. Ctr. staff to organized med. staff sect. 1992—), State Med. Soc. Wis. (bd. dirs. 1993-2002), Wis. Med. Soc. (pres.-elect 2002), Dane County Med. Soc. (pres. 1990-91), Alpha Chi Rho (Ziegler award 1990), Nu Sigma Nu (pres. 1969-70). Republican. Roman Catholic. Avocations: bioethics, politics, farming. Home: 4221 Venetian Ln Madison WI 53718-6655 Office: Wildwood Family Clinic 4901 Cottage Grove Rd Madison WI 53716-1392 E-mail: pwertsch@facstaff.wisc.edu.

WERTSMAN, VLADIMIR FILIP, librarian, information specialist, author, translator; b. Secureni, Romania, Apr. 6, 1929; came to U.S., 1967; s. Filip and Anna Wertsman. LLM summa cum laude, U. A.I. Cuza, Romania, 1953; MLS, Columbia U., 1969. Judge lower and appellate cts., Romania, 1953-67; examiner stock certs. 1st Nat. City Bank, N.Y.C., 1967-68; reference libr. sci. div. Bklyn. Pub. Libr., 1969-74, sr. libr. Canarsie br., 1974-77, sr. libr. Greenpoint br., 1977-80, sr. libr. Leonard br., 1980-82; sr. libr., Slavic and Romanian specialist Donnell Libr. Ctr. N.Y. Pub. Libr., 1982-86; sr. libr. Learner's Adv. and Job Info. Ctr., 1987-93. Author, editor: The Romanians in America, 1748-1974, 1974, The Ukrainians in America, 1608-1975, 1976, The Russians in America, 1727-1970, 1977, The Armenians in America, 1618-1976, 1978, The Romanians in America and Canada, 1980, Librarian's Companion: A Handbook of Thousands of Facts and Figures on Libraries/Librarians, 1987, 2d edit., 1996, Career Opportunities for Bilinguals and Multilinguals: A Directory of Resources in Education, Employment and Business, 1991, 2d edit., 1994, What's Cooking in Multicultural America, 1996, New York: The City in Over 500 Memorable Quotations From American & Foriegn Sources, 1996, paperback edit., 1999, Directory of Ethnic and Multicultural Publishers, Distributors and Resource Organizations, 3d edit., 1995, 4th edit., 1999; co-author: Ukrainians in Canada and United States, 1981, Free Voices in Russian Literature, 1950s-1980s, 1986; editl. cons. Harvard Ency. Am. Ethnic Groups, 1980; contbr. Books, Libraries and Information in Slavic and East European Studies, 1986, Immigrant Labor Press in North America, 1840s-1970s, 1987, Through American Eyes, 1989, Ency. of N.Y.C., 1995; mem. adv. bd., contbr.: Gale Ency. Multicultural Am., 1995, 99; contbr. articles, book revs. to profl. jours. Recipient Disting. Lit. Achievement award Am. Soc. Writers, 1977. Mem. ALA (chair multilingual libr. materials and svcs. com. 1976-88, spl. merit award 1988, chair pub. and multicultural material com. of Emie Round Table Ala. 1989—), Am. Assn. Advancement of Slavic Studies, Am. Romanian Acad. Arts & Scis., Delta Tau Kappa. Avocations: chess playing, travel, stamp collecting, dancing. Home: 60 Babcock St Apt 96 Brookline MA 02446-5920 E-mail: vlavik@aol.com. *America is by its very nature of historical formation and development a multiethnic, multicultural and multilingual society. And if variety is the spice of life then American ethno-linguistic and cultural mosaique is the spice of our society. America's pluralism is also a microcosm of the entire world its citizens representing virtually all continents.*

WERTZ, DOROTHY CORBETT, sociologist; b. Buffalo, May 18, 1937; d. William Joseph and Helen (Leggett) Corbett; m. Richard Wayne Wertz, Jan. 29, 1967. AB, Radcliffe Coll., 1958; postgrad., London Sch. Econ., 1959; MA, Harvard U., 1961, PhD, 1966. Instr. Bryn Mawr Coll., 1963-65; asst. prof. Boston Coll., 1966-68, Bridgewater (Mass.) State Coll., 1969-71; instr. Lowell (Mass.) Technol. Inst., 1971-72; asst. prof. U. Bridgeport, Conn., 1972-73; assoc. prof. U. New Haven, 1973-74, Suffolk U., Boston, 1975-81; NSF fellow Sch. of Pub. Health Boston U., 1981-84, assoc. rsch. prof. Sch. of Pub. Health, 1984-86, rsch. prof. Sch. of Pub. Health, 1986—; sr. scientist Shriver Ctr., Waltham, 1991—2000; rsch. prof. U. Mass., 2000—. Cons., advisor Sci. Coun. Can., Ottawa, 1987-90, World Health Orgn., Geneva, 1993—; researcher, reviewer Royal Commn. on New Reproductive Techs., Ottawa, 1988-92; cons. NIH, Bethesda, 1990-91. Author: Lying-In: A History of Childbirth in America, 1989, Ethics and Human Genetics, 1989, Guidelines on Ethical Issues in Medical Genetics and the Provision of Genetics Services, 1995; contbr. articles to profl. jours. Recipient Silver Gavel award ABA, 1991. Mem. APHA, Am. Soc. of Human Genetics (social issues com. 1991-94), European Soc. Human Genetics, Human Genome Orgn. Achievements include organization of worldwide surveys regarding ethical views. Office: U Mass Med Sch, Shriver Divsn 200 Trapelo Rd Waltham MA 02452-6319

WERTZ, JOHN ALAN, secondary school educator; b. Mpls., May 28, 1945; s. John Edward and Florence (Carlson) W.; m. Margaret M. Schlangen, 1993. BS, Hamline U., 1967; MS, St. Cloud State Coll., 1973; postgrad., George Washington U., 1985. Tchr. social sci. St. Cloud Cmty. Schs., St. Cloud, Minn., 1967—2002. Trainer and field rep. New Games Found., San Francisco, 1980-83; tchr.-coach Apollo H.S. Mock Trial team, 1987-2000. Mem. com. social action Minn. Synod, Luth. Ch. Am., 1971-74; chair social action com. Salem Luth. Ch. Coun., St. Cloud, 1974-76; mem. affirmative action com. St. Cloud Cmty. Schs., 1975-78, co-chair student assistance com., 1982-83, mem. site coun. Apollo H.S., 1994-96, co-chair site coun. Apollo H.S., 1995-96; chair St. Cloud Human Rights Commn., 1979-83; adv. Ctrl. Minn. Sexual Assault Ctr., 1981-83; bd. dirs. St. Cloud Area Tenants' Assn., 1975-77, St. Cloud Area Spl. Olympics, 1982-83, United Way St. Cloud Area, 1996-2001, Minn. Edn. Assn., 1996-99, Great River Roundtable, 1997—, sec., 1997-98; mem. Edn. Minn. Transition Bd., 1998-99, Edn. Minn. Governing Bd., 1999—2002; bd. dirs. St. Cloud Area Family YMCA, 2001—; candidate for Minn. State Legislature, 2000, 2002. Recipient Merit award St. Cloud Area Coun. for Handicapped, 1976; grad. St. Cloud Area Leadership Program, 1995. Mem. ASCD, NEA, Am. Fedn. Tchrs., Edn. Minn., St. Cloud Edn. Assn. (chair govtl. rels. coun. 1978-83, 88-96), Am. Hist. Soc. Germans from Russia, St. Cloud Area C. of C. (edn. divsn. 1992-97, vice-chmn. PreK-12 com. 1993-94, chair edn. recognition com. 1994-96, Thayer Youth Leadership steering com. 1995-97). Avocations: theatre arts, travel. Home: 816 Rilla Rd Saint Cloud MN 56303-1037 Office: Apollo High Sch 1000 44th Ave N Saint Cloud MN 56303-2036 E-mail: jawertz@aol.com.

WERTZ, KENNETH DEAN, real estate executive; b. Oklahoma City, July 14, 1946; s. Walter K. and Kathryn L. (Moore) W.; children: Adam Troy, Kirsten Paige. BS in Acctg., Okla. State U., 1968, MS in Acctg. and Econs., 1969; JD, U. San Francisco, 1978. CPA, Okla., Calif; lic. real estate broker, Okla. Sr. acct. Deloitte, Haskins & Sells, San Francisco, 1969-70, 71-75; v.p. acquisitions, mng. dir. Landsing Corp., Menlo Park, Calif., 1975-86; pres. Detrick Salsberry Mgmt. Inc., Tulsa, 1987-88; v.p. asset mgmt. Corporex Co., Cin., 1989-90; exec. v.p. real estate Brunner Cos., Dayton, Ohio, 1990-92; pres. Pillar Real Estate Advisors, 1992—. Lt. col. Med. Svc. corps U.S. Army, 1968-98. Decorated Army Commendation medal with three oak leaf clusters, Meritorious Svc. medal. Mem. Am. Inst. CPA's, Okla. Soc. CPA's, Calif. Soc. CPA's, Nat. Assn. Securities Dealers (fin. prin., registered sales rep.). Republican. Methodist. Avocations: cycling, snow and water skiing, racquetball, camping, fishing. Home: 835 Huntersknoll Ln Cincinnati OH 45230-4343 Office: Pillar Real Estate Advisors 5335 Far Hills Ave Ste 318 Dayton OH 45429-2317

WESBERRY, JAMES PICKETT, JR. financial management consultant, auditor, international organization executive; b. Columbia, S.C., Sept. 22, 1934; s. James P. and Ruby L. (Perry) W.; m. Lea Esdras Casteneda, June 13, 1975; children: Jonathan Jesse, Perry Latimer, Ruby Lee Nilda; children by previous marriage: James Pickett III, Elisa Marie, Lillian Sue, Paul Armand. BBA, Ga. State U., 1955; LLD (hon.), Atlanta Law Sch., 1967; MPA, Am. U., 1983. CPA, Ga.; cert. internal auditor, fraud examiner, govt. fin. mgr., fin. svcs. auditor. Page U.S. Ho. Reps., 1949-51; acct., mgmt. cons. Atlanta, 1956-67; v.p. fin. and adminstrn. Computer Tech. South, 1969-70; sr. cons. Inst. Pub. Adminstrn., N.Y.C., 1967-69, 70-76; cons. to comptr. gen. Peru, 1970-74, Ecuador, 1974-78; adv., prof. Latin Am. Inst. Auditing Scis. Peruvian and Ecuadorean Sch. Govtl. Auditing, 1971-78; dir. sys., stds. and procedures Days of Inns Am., Inc., 1979-80; chief auditor OAS, Washington, 1980-82; cons. World Bank, 1982-83; prin. advisor acctg. and auditing pub. sector Latin Am. and Caribean Region, 1994-97; dir. America's accountability/anti-corruption project Casals & Assocs., Alexandria, Va., 1997—2001, dir. Mex. accountability audit, anti-corruption project, 2001—. Founder, pres. Accountability 21, 1998—; advisor to pres. of Latin Am. Orgn. of Supreme Audit Instn., 1993—2000; sr. adv. to comptr. gen. U.S., 1983—85; dir. internat. ops. Price Waterhouse, 1985—88; sr. fin. advisor AID, 1988—93; pres., CEO Inst. Pub. Adminstrn., 1993—94, trustee; dir. N.Y. Bur. Mcpl. Rsch., 1993—94; mem. panel of experts in acctg. and auditing UN, 1972—82; adj. prof. Am. U., Washington, 1981—85; founding dir. Internat. Consortium Govtl. Fin. Mgmt., 1977—88, 1994—97, pres., 1984—87; cons., tchr. all Spanish-speaking We. Hemisphere nations Brazil, Haiti, Jamaica, The Netherlands Antilles, Guyana, Peoples Republic China, The Philippines, Can., U.S. Co-author: UN Handbook on Government Auditing for Developing Countries; editor: Latin American Manual of Professional Auditing in the Public Sector, Spanish Lang. newsletter Pistas de Auditoria, 1985-92; mem. editl. bd. Pub. Budgeting and Fin. Mgmt., 1982-92, The Govt. Accts. Jour.; contbr. articles to profl. jours. Mem. Ga. Senate, 1962-67, Fulton County Dem. Exec. Com., 1962-66. Decorated Order of Merit (Peru), 1972, Comptr. Gen. Venezuela, 1998; recipient Outstanding Career Achievement award USAID, 1993. Mem. AICPA (hon. life, chmn. interam. com. 1988-95), Interam. Acctg. Assn. (cert. assoc., bd. dirs. 1989-95, chmn. pub. sector com. 1989-91, 2000-2001, exec. com. 1994-95, Vet. Acct. Am. award 1987, lifetime acct. of Am. 1995), Am. Acctg. Assn., Assn. Govt. Accts. (Authors award 1981-82, 89-90, chmn. internat. affairs com. 1981-82, 89-91), Inst. Internal Auditors (v.p. Latin Am. 1978-79, internat. rels. com. 1977-82, 84-88, regional dir. Latin Am. 1986-88, chpt. bd. govs. 1981-87, v.p. 1982-84, pres. 1984-85, vice chmn. internat. membership com. 1989-90, chpt. Disting. Svc. award 1987, Bradford Cadmus Meml. award internat. orgn. 1989, Outstanding Author's award 1990), Honduras CPA Soc. (Hon. award 1990), Jr. Chamber Internat. (life senator), Quito (Ecuador) Inst. Internal Auditors (life bd. dirs.), Lina Coll. Pub. Accts. (hon.), Lima Jr. C. of C. (hon.), Pinchicha Coll. Pub. Accts. (hon.), Ecuador Fedn. Pub. Accts. (hon.). Baptist. Office: Casals & Assocs 1199 N Fairfax St Alexandria VA 22314-1437 also: Arbol #34 Colonie San Angel 01000 Mexico City Mexico Home: PO Box 2087 Laredo TX 78044-3087 E-mail: jimwes@casals.com.

WESBROOK, FREDERIC P. health facility administrator, physician; MD, Ind. U. Sch. Medicine, Indpls., 1970. Bd. cert. in Internal Medicine 1975, lic. State of Wisc. Intern Ind. U. Hosp., Indpls., 1971; resident Fitzsimmons Army Med. Ctr., Denver, 1975; pres. Marshfield (Wis.) Clinic, 2000—. Mem.: State Med. Soc. Wis. Office: Marshfield Clinic 1000 N Oak Ave Marshfield WI 54449*

WESBURY, STUART ARNOLD, JR. health administration and policy educator; b. Phila., Dec. 13, 1933; s. Stuart Arnold and Jennie (Glazewska) W.; m. June Carol Davis, Feb. 23, 1957; children: Brian, Brent, Bruce, Bradford. BS, Temple U., 1955; MHA, U. Mich., 1960; PhD, U. Fla., 1972. Sr. health svcs. officer USPHS, 1955, served as adminstrv. officer, hosp. and clinic pharmacist, resigned, 1958; adminstrv. asst. Del. Hosp., 1960-61; asst. adminstr. Bronson Meth. Hosp., 1961-66; assoc. dir., asst. prof. U. Fla. Tchg. Hosp., 1966-67, dir., assoc. prof., 1967-69; v.p. Computer Mgmt. Corp., Gainesville, Fla., 1969-72; dir., prof. grad. studies in health svcs. mgmt. U. Mo., Columbia, 1972-78; pres. Am. Coll. Healthcare Execs., Chgo., 1979-91; sr. v.p. TriBrook Group, Inc., Westmont, 1992-94; prof. Sch. of Health Adminstrn. and Policy Ariz. State U., Tempe, 1994-2000, dir., exec. edn. programs Coll. Bus., 1996-2000, prof. emeritus, 2000—. Chmn. bd. trustees Blood Sys., Inc., Scottsdale, Ariz. Co-author: Why We Spend Too Much on Health Care; contbr. articles to profl. jours. Bd. dirs. Health Task, Inc., Atlanta, Boys Clubs, Gainesville, Heartland Inst.; chmn. bd. dirs. Mid-Am. chpt. ARC, 1988-91, DuPage County Dist., 1984-87; active Boy Scouts Am.; chmn. adminstrv. bd. Meth. Ch.; trustee Nat. Blood Found.; Rep. Congl. candidate Dist. 13, Ill. Fellow Am. Coll. Health Care Adminstrs. (hon.), Am. Coll. Healthcare Execs. (Silver Medal award 1991); mem. APHA, Am. Hosp. Assn., Hosp. Mgmt. Sys. Soc., Assn. Univ. Programs in Health Adminstrn. (chmn. 1977-78), Am. Assn. Healthcare Cons. (hon.), Rotary (past pres.). Home and Office: 6711 E Camelback Rd Unit 25 Scottsdale AZ 85251-2064 Fax: 480-990-7334. E-mail: stu.wesbury@asu.edu.

WESCOTT, WILLIAM BURNHAM, oral maxillofacial pathologist, educator; b. Pendleton, Oreg., Nov. 10, 1922; s. Merton Girard and Josephine (Creasey) W.; m. Barbara L., Dec. 31, 1944 (dec. June 12, 1969); children: William Douglas, Diane Elizabeth; m. Gloria Greer-Collins, Aug. 28, 1989. DMD, U. Oreg., Portland, 1951, MS, 1962. Asst. prof. to assoc. dean admin. U. Oreg. Dental Sch., Portland, 1953-72; co-dir. oral disease rsch. VA, Houston, 1972-75, dir. dental edn. ctr. L.A., 1980-85; acting dir. Reg. Med. Edn. Ctr., Birmingham, Ala., 1978-80; chief dental svc. Dept. of Veteran's Affairs, San Francisco, 1985-94; clin. prof. U. Calif., 1994—; cons. Northern System of Clinics Dept. Vets. Affairs, 1994—. Dental surgeon, Oreg. Air N.G., Portland, 1954-68; cons. Madigan Army Med. Ctr., Ft. Lewis, W. Va., 1971-74, VA Med. Ctrs., No. Calif., 1985—, prof. pathology Duke U. Med. Sch., 1977-79. Contbr. 80 articles to profl. jours. and several chpts. to profl. books; 4 chpts. to books. Dist. chmn. Boys Scouts Am., Portland, 1965-67; bd. dirs. Am. Cancer Soc., Portland, 1964-67; comdr. Veterans Foreign Wars Post 5731, Gridley, Calif., 1994-95, comdr., 1996-98; chmn. Mil. Vets Ct. of Honor Meml., No. Calif., 1997—. With Oreg. N.G., 1938-40; with U.S. Army, 1940-42; lt. col. USAF, 1942-68. Decorated DFC with oak leaf cluster, USAF, Oreg. N.G. Merit Svc. Medal, Portland, Fedn. des Anciens Combattants Français medal, 1944. Fellow Am. Acad. Oral and Maxillofacial Pathology, Omicron Kappa Upsilon, Sigma Xi. Avocations: woodworking, fishing. Home: 437 Justeson Ave Gridley CA 95948-9434 Office: U Calif Sch of Dentistry S 512 San Francisco 3rd & Parnassus San Francisco CA 94143-0424 E-mail: globil@manznet.com.

WESELY, EDWIN JOSEPH, lawyer; b. N.Y.C., May 16, 1929; s. Joseph and Elizabeth (Peles) W.; children: Marissa Celeste, Adrienne Lee; m. Marcy Brownson, Sept. 23, 1992. Ed., Deep Springs Coll., 1945-47; AB, Cornell U., 1949; JD, Columbia U., 1954. Bar: N.Y. 1954, D.C. 1985, U.S. Supreme Ct. 1960, others. Law clk. to judge U.S. Dist. Ct. (so. dist.) N.Y., 1954-55; asst. U.S. atty. So. Dist. N.Y., 1955-57; assoc. Winthrop, Stimson, Putnam & Roberts, N.Y.C., 1957-63, ptnr., 1964-2000; sr. counsel Pillsbury Winthrop LLP, 2001—. Spl. master numerous cases; chmn. spl. com. on effective discovery in civil cases U.S. Dist. Ct. (ea. dist.) N.Y., 1982-84, com. on civil caseflow, 1985-88, com. on civil litigation, 1988—, civil justice reform adv. group, 1990-95; mem. com. on pretrial phase civil cases Jud. Coun. 2d Cir., 1984-86, standing com. on improvement civil litigation, 1986-89; ex-officio Civil Justice Reform Act adv. group U.S. Dist. Ct. (so. dist.) N.Y.; pres. CARE, 1986-89, chmn., 1978-86, 89-90, internat. bd. dirs., 1981-90, pres., 1987-90; bd. dirs. Internat. Rescue Com.; bd. dirs., exec. com. Internat. Ctr. in N.Y., 1990—, chmn., 1998—. Trustee Deep Springs Coll., 1991-2000; vice-chair, 1998-2000. Decorated Order of Civil Merit (Republic of Korea); recipient World Humanitarian award Fgn. Press Assn., 1988, Commendation Bd. Judges U.S. Dist. Ct. (ea. dist.) N.Y., 1993. Fellow Am. Coll. Trial Lawyers; mem. ABA (spl. adv. com. on internat. activities 1990-93, litigation sect. chmn. com. on discovery 1977-78, spl. com. study discovery abuse 1977-82, chmn. task force on liaison with internat. profl. assns. on matters of mutual concern 1989-93, Civil Justice Reform Act task force 1991-93, task force on the state of the justice sys. 1993-95, fed. initiatives task force 1995-98, co-chmn. task force on fed. and local rules 1997-98), UN Assn. U.S.A. (bd. dirs. 1991—),

Assn. of Bar of City of N.Y. (com. chmn., organized demostration observation panel), Coun. on Fgn. Rels., River Club. Office: Pillsbury Winthrop LLP One Battery Park Pla New York NY 10004-1490 E-mail: eweselye@pillsburywinthrop.com.

WESELY, MARISSA CELESTE, lawyer; b. N.Y.C., Apr. 25, 1955; d. Edwin Joseph and Yolanda Teresa (Pyles) W.; m. Frederick Hamerman; 1 child, Emma Elizabeth Wesely Allen. BA magna cum laude, Williams Coll., 1976; JD cum laude, Harvard U., 1980. Bar: N.Y. 1981. Assoc. Simpson Thacher & Bartlett, N.Y.C., 1980-82, 84-88, ptnr., 1989—, assoc. London, 1982-84. Lectr., cons. Harvard Inst. Internat. Devel., Beijing, 1981, Jakarta, Indonesia, 1982; guest lectr. Yale Law Sch., New Haven, 1991; spkr. Am. Conf. Inst., Practicing Law Inst., Bankers Assn. for Fgn. Trade, N.Y. State Bar Assn. confs., 1993—. Bd. dirs. City Lore, N.Y.C. Mem. N.Y.C. Bar Assn., N.Y. State Bar Assn. (mem. exec. com. sect. internat. law and practice), Internat. Bar Assn., Phi Beta Kappa.

WESELY, YOLANDA THEREZA, retired sociologist, marketing professional, researcher; b. São Paulo, Brazil, Nov. 9, 1927; came to U.S., 1946; d. Richard Milton and Etelvina (Pacheco E Silva) Pyles; m. Edwin Joseph Wesely, July 1, 1950 (div. 1990); children: Marissa C., Adrienne Lee. BA in Math., Barnard Coll., 1950; MA in Sociology, Columbia U., 1968, PhD in Sociology with honors, 1975. CLU, 1984. With The Equitable, N.Y.C., 1974-76, dir. spl. studies, 1976-78, exec. asst. to chmn. and vice chmn. of the bd., 1978-79, dir. market research, 1979-84, asst. v.p. market rsch., 1984-88; ret. Co-founder Sociologists in Bus. Bd. dirs. Westchester Older Women's League, 1989-92; vice chairperson bd. dirs. Union Theol. Sem., N.Y.C., 1980-88, chair nominating com., 1984, com. on divestiture of investments in South Africa; trustee Scarsdale Congl. Ch., 1989-91, moderator, 1992-94, vice moderator, chair clergy rels. com., 2001—; dir. Westchester Civil Liberties Union, 1991-94; treas. WESPAC Found., 1995—. Mem. Older Women's League, Phi Beta Kappa. Democrat. Congregationalist. Home: 6 Chateaux Cir Scarsdale NY 10583-4144 E-mail: ytwesely@aol.com.

WESENER, BARBARA A. association executive; d. Melvin Rudolph and Delores Angela (Wagner) W.; m. Clinton Lee Toms, June 27, 1981. BA Alverno Coll., Milw., 1970. Cert. assn. exec. Tchr. Piux XI H.S., Milw., 1970-72, Divine Savior-Holy Angels H.S., Milw., 1972-76; asst. dir. continuing edn. Marquette U., 1976-79; asst. dir. pub. rels. Internat. Found. Employee Benefit Plans, 1979-86; exec. dir. Wis. Ready Mixed Concrete Assn., 1986—. Mem. Pub. Rels. Soc. Am. (accredited), Nat. Ready Mixed Concrete Assn. (bd. dirs. 1999-2002), Wis. Soc. Assn. Execs. (pres. 2000). Avocations: travel, gardening, reading. Office: Wis Ready Mixed Concrete Assn 9415 W Forest Home Ave 203 Hales Corners WI 53130-1680 E-mail: wrmca@execpc.com.

WESKAMP, KELLEY S. loan account manager, real estate company executive; b. Boulder City, Nev., Jan. 9, 1964; d. Dale P. and Phyllis J. (Cooper) W. BA in English Lang. Lit. with distinction, Loretto Heights Coll., 1985. Cons. Ely Leadership Mgmt., Lakewood, Colo., 1985-88; budget asst. Bureau Reclamation, Denver, 1988-90; real estate owned technician FDIC, 1990-93; real estate specialist Westfall and Co., Westminster, 1993-95, account mgr., 1995-97, Castle Advisors subs. Chgo. Title, 1998-99; sr. account mgr. Litton Loan Servicing, Houston, 1999—. Participant Bench Mark Study, Pete Marwick Assocs., 1997. Contbr. article to mag. Democrat. Roman Catholic. Avocations: weaving, reading, travel, cooking. Home: 12080 W Mexico Ave Lakewood CO 80228-3909

WESLER, KEN, performing arts company executive; b. Phila., Apr. 3, 1964; s. Irwin Harvey and Marcia Elaine (Trilling) W.; m. Deborah Lee Rader, Nov. 2, 1986; children: Alexander, Samantha. BA, Temple U., 1994. Prodn. mgr. The Wilma Theatre, Phila., 1983-89; gen. mgr. Gretna Prodns., Inc., Mt. Gretna, Pa., 1989, 90, Walnut St. Theatre, Phila., 1989-95; exec. dir. The Grand Opera House, Wilmington, 1995—. Guest lectr. Cabrini Coll., Phila., 1988, Temple U., Phila., 1988—. Bd. dirs. MBNA Excellence in Edn. Found., Downtown Visions. Mem. The Wilma Theater. Office: The Grand Opera House 818 N Market St Wilmington DE 19801-3011 E-mail: kwesler@comcast.net.

WESLEY, ARTHUR BERNELL, II, music educator, musician; b. Brookhaven, Miss., Sept. 18, 1945; s. Arthur and Norma Lee Wesley; children: Toni Wesley-Ellis, Arthur Bernell III, Vinetta Amber. Student, Fla. A&M U., 1963—64; Ed.Specialist in Adminstrn. in Higher Edn. (ED S), Ala. A&M U., Huntsville, Alabama, 1993—95; MusM Edn. (M.M.ED.), Vander Cook Coll. of Music, Chicago, Illinois, 1968—71; BS in Music Edn., Miss. Valley State U., Itta Bena, Mississippi, 1964—67. Asst. dir. of bands/asst. prof. of music Miss. Valley State U., Itta Bena, 1967—74; dir. of bands/asst. prof. of music Ala. A&M U., Huntsvile, 1974—. Musician (composer, arranger). Recipient Coll. Band Dir. of the Yr., Birmingham Grid Forecasters, 1983, 1986, 1989, 1991, 1993, 1995—99. Mem.: NEA, Music Educators Nat. Conf., Kappa Kappa Psi, Phi Mu Alpha Sinfonia. Baptist. Office: Ala A&M U PO Box 246 Normal AL 35762 Home Fax: 256-851-5974; Office Fax: 256-851-5974. Personal E-mail: aweslwy2@aamu.edu.

WESLEY, JOHN MERCER, artist; b. Los Angeles, Nov. 25, 1928; s. Ner Wesley and Elsa Marie (Patzwaldt) W.; m. Hannah Allen Green, Dec. 18, 1971; children: Christine Alice, Ner. Student, Los Angeles City Coll., UCLA, 1947-50. One-man shows include, Robert Elkon Gallery, N.Y.C., 1963-80, 84, Premio Internat., Instituto Torcuato di Tella, Buenos Aires, 1967, Documenta 5, Kassel, 1972, Carl Solway Gallery, Cin., 1972, 85, 89, Galerie Rudolf Zwirner, Cologne, 1973, Rush Rhees Gallery, U. Rochester, 1974, PS 1, N.Y.C., 1978, Reinhard Onnasch Ausstellungen, Berlin, 1982-83, 101 Spring St. Gallery, N.Y.C., 1987, fiction/non fiction, N.Y.C., 1990, 91, Chinati Found., Marfa, Tex., 1990, 98, Daniel Weinberg Gallery, Santa Monica, Calif., 1992, 98, Portikus, Frankfurt, 1993, Stedelijk Mus., Amsterdam, 1993, Kunstverein, Ludwigsburg, Germany, 1993, daad-Galerie, Berlin, 1993, Galerie Rolf Ricke, Cologne, 1994, José Freire Gallery, N.Y.C., 1994, Jessica Fredericks Gallery, N.Y.C., 1996, 98, 99, 2000, 01, 02, Galerie Haus Schneider, Karlsruhe, Germany, 1996, Danese Gallery, N.Y.C., 1998, P.S.1 Contemporary Art Ctr., N.Y.C., 2000-01, Sert Gallery, Harvard U., 2001, Gagosian Gallery, London, 2001, Daniel Weinberg Gallery, L.A., 2002; group exhbns. include, Whitney Mus., 1968, 69, 76, Indpls. Mus., 1976, Royal Academy, London, 1991, Mus. Contemporary Art, L.A., 1992-93, Mus. Beaux Arts, Montreal, 1992-93, Deichtorhallen, Hamburg, 1997, Kunsthaus, Zürich, 1997; represented in permanent collections Albright-Knox Mus., Buffalo, Mus. Modern Art, N.Y.C., U. Tex., Austin, Mpls. Soc. Fine Arts., Chinati Found., Marfa, Tex., Rose Art Gallery, Brandeis U., Waltham, Mass., U. Kentucky, Lexington, Kunstmuseum, Basel, Switzerland, Dayton (Ohio) Mus. Art, Portland (Oreg.) Art Mus., Whitney Mus., Stedelijk Mus., Speed Mus., Louisville, Ky. Guggenheim fellow, 1976; grantee Nat. Endowment Arts, 1989. Address: 52 Barrow St New York NY 10014-3723

WESLEY, LATONYA RASHAWN, legislative assistant; b. Detroit, Oct. 22, 1974; Student, Spelman Coll., 1992-94; BA in Polit. Sci., Mich. State U., 1997; postgrad., U. Balt., 2002—. Legis. corrd. U.S. Senate, Washington, 1998-99; adminstrv. asst. APA, 1999-2000, legis. asst., 2000—. Contbr. to Psychol. Sci. Agenda. Legis. intern Mich. State Senate, Lansing, 1997; vol. Atlanta Project, 1993, Econ. Crisis Ctr., East Lansing, Mich., 1996, Debbie Stabenow Campaign for U.S. Ho. of Reps., East Lansing, 1996, Make a Difference Day, Ft. Meade, Md., 1998-99, AIDS Walk, Washington, Walk for Wellness-Am. Heart Assn., Balt., 1999, ARC, East Lansing, 1997; mentor, tutor Cornerstone Charter Sch., Washington, 1998; telefundraiser Am. Cancer Soc., East Lansing, 1997; mentor Brent Elem. Sch., Washington, 1998. Mem. Mich. State U. Alumni Assn., Zeta Phi Beta (grammateus 2000-01, Md. del. Rho Eta Zeta chpt. 2001). Office: APA 750 1st St NE Washington DC 20002 Fax: 202-336-6063. E-mail: lwesley@apa.org., meow1920@excite.com.

WESLEY, MARILYN CLARKE, English language educator; b. Middletown, N.Y., Dec. 14; d. Richard Edgar and Flora (Sorg) Clarke; m. Thomas James Hayes, 1967 (div. 1980); children: Jeremy Thomas, Jordan Clarke; m. Norman Wesley, July 25, 1980. BA, SUNY, Oneonta, 1967; MA, Syracuse U., 1970, PhD, 1988. Women's studies instr. SUNY, Oneonta, 1987; adj. prof. English Hartwick Coll., 1988-91, asst. prof. English, 1991-2001, Cora M. Babcock prof. English, 1998—. Cons. NEH grants Four County Libr., Oneonta, 1993-94; poetry editor Phoebe, 1994—. Author: Refusal and Transgression in Joyce Carol Oates, 1993, Secret Journeys: The Trope of Women's Travel in American Literature, 1998; contbr. articles to profl. jours. Avocations: practicing poet, Victorian architecture. Office: Hartwick Coll Dept English Oneonta NY 13820 E-mail: wesleym@hartwick.edu.

WESLEY, STEPHEN BURTON, training professional; b. Louisville, July 13, 1949; s. Leon and Montie C. (Burton) W.; m. Kun Wanna Jarusin, May 22, 1972; 1 child, Thomas Jayson. AA, Somerset (Ky.) Coll., 1969; student, Community Coll. of Air Force, Maxwell, AFB, 1970-77; AA, Watterson Coll., 1977; student, U. Louisville, 1978-80. Cert. energy mgr., lighting efficiency profl. Electronics tech. Kegco, Somerset, 1973-74; instrument tech. Ky. Air Nat. Guard, Louisville, 1974-78; application engr. Johnson Controls, Inc., 1978-81, sales engr., 1981-88, energy svcs. mgr., 1988-96; regional tng. dir. Excel Telecom., 1995—. Adv. bd. Ivy Tech Vocat. Sch., Jeffersonville, Ind., 1988-90. Inventor pitot tube removal tool. Lay dir. Walk to Emmaus, Elizabethtown, Ky., 1989. Sgt. USAF, 1969-73. Mem. Assn. Energy Engrs. Methodist. Avocations: fishing, reading, church work, investments, genealogy. Home and Office: 9129 Gayle Dr Louisville KY 40272

WESLEY, STEPHEN HARRISON, pharmaceutical company executive; b. Knoxville, Tenn., Aug. 13, 1961; s. Robert Louis and Doris Ruth (Rogers) W.; m. Kittie Conner, May 28, 1988; children: Robert Allen, Kellie Elizabeth. BA in Econs., U. Tenn., 1984. Sales rep. Newark Electronics, Knoxville, Tenn., 1984-85; sales engr. Carolina Controls Co., 1986-88; profl. rep. Winthrop Pharmaceuticals, 1988-90, med. ctr. specialist Nashville, 1990—; wound care market specialist Convatec divsn. Bristol-Myers Squibb, Knoxville, 1995—; editor-in-chief, Healthlook Mag. Silhouette Publs. Co., Inc., 1998-99; regional sales mg. Cardinal Distbn., 2000—. Healthcare cons. Convatec divsn. Bristol-Myers Squibb; editor emeritus Healthlook Mag. Active Boy Scouts Am. Recipient Mayor's Merit award City of Knoxville, 1974, Silver Pen Editl. award The Nashville Banner, 1993. Mem. Maverick Med. Corp. Investment Club (sec., treas.). Avocations: reading, weight training, home remodeling. Home and Office: 2804 Pebblestone Ln Knoxville TN 37938-3934

WESLEY, VIRGINIA ANNE, real estate property manager; b. Seattle, Apr. 29, 1951; d. Albert William and Mary Louise (Heusser) W. BA in Speech, U. Hawaii, Hilo, 1978. Cert. property mgr. Mgr. office, traffic Radio Sta. KIPA, Hilo, 1972-74; reporter West Hawaii Today, Kailua-Kona, Hawaii, 1974; mgr. office U. Hawaii, Hilo, 1975-78; dir. property mgmt. First City Equities, Seattle, 1978-88, Winvest Devel. Corp., Seattle, 1988-89; with Quadrant Corp, Bellevue, Wash., 1992-98; dir. property mgmt. Fisher Properties, Inc., Seattle, 1998—. Instr. Bellevue (Wash.) C.C., 1982-85. Bd. dirs. Mayor's Small Bus. Task Force, Seattle, 1981-83, 1st Hill Improvement Assn., Seattle, 1982—; active Goodwill Games, Seattle, 1990, Kauri Investments, Ltd., Seattle, 1991-92. Mem. Inst. Real Estate Mgmt., Internat. Coun. Shopping Ctrs., Comml. Real Estate Women, Women's Bus. Exch., Seattle-King County Bd. Realtors, Big Island Press Club, Phi Kappa Phi. Home: 5143 S Wildwood Ln Seattle WA 98118-4252 E-mail: gingerw@fishprop.com.

WESLING, DONALD TRUMAN, English literature educator; b. Buffalo, May 6, 1939; s. Truman Albert and Helene Marie (Bullinger) W.; m. Judith Elaine Dulinawka, July 28, 1961; children: Benjamin, Molly, Natasha. BA, Harvard U., 1960, PhD, 1965; BA, Cambridge U., Eng., 1962. Asst. prof. U. Calif. at San Diego, La Jolla, 1965-67, assoc. prof., 1970-80, prof., 1981—. Lectr. U. Essex, Colchester, Eng., 1967-70. Author: Wordsworth and Landscape, 1970, Chances of Rhyme, 1981, The New Poetries, 1985, The Scissors of Meter, 1996, (with T. Slawek) Literary Voice, 1995. Mem. Amnesty Internat. Office: U Calif Lit # 0410 La Jolla CA 92093 Home: 3609 Ingraham St San Diego CA 92109-6717

WESNER, JOHN WILLIAM, engineering manager; b. Newark, July 14, 1936; s. John William and Gaselle Alice (Pollak) W.; m. Monica Anneliese Fischer, May 1, 1965; children: Katrin, Francis William. BSME, Carnegie Inst. Tech., 1958; MSME, Calif. Inst. Tech., 1959; PhD in Mech. Engring., Carnegie Mellon U., 1968. Registered profl engr., N.J. Sr. engr. Westinghouse Atomic Power Divs., Madison, Pa., 1964-68; mem. tech. staff Bell Telephone Labs., Holmdel, N.J., 1968-76; supr. AT&T Bell Labs., Middletown, 1976-96, Lucent Techs., Holmdel, 1996—. Chmn. ad hoc adv. com. NSF Program in Engring. Design, Washington, 1987-92; adv. bd. to mech. engring. dept. Carnegie Mellon U. Co-author: Winning with Quality; mem. editl. bd. Bell Labs Tech. Jour.; contbr. articles to profl. jours.; patentee in field. Mem. dist. com. Boy Scouts Am., Freehold, N.J., Pitts., Lexington, Ky., Germany. 1st lt. U.S. Army, 1963-64. George Westinghouse scholar Carnegie Inst. Tech., 1954-58; grad. fellow NSF, 1958-60; recipient Silver Beaver award Boy Scouts Am. Fellow ASME (v.p. sys. and design 1996—, design engring. div. chair 1991-92, chair edn. com. 1983-87, chair design for manufacturability com. 1987-89, Dedicated Svc. award 1990), Mensa, Hon. Order of Ky. Cols., Sigma Xi, Beta Theta Pi, Phi Kappa Phi, Pi Tau Sigma, Tau Beta Pi. Roman Catholic. Avocations: model railroading, war gaming. Office: Lucent Techs 101 Crawfords Corner Rd Holmdel NJ 07733-1900

WESOKY, SHARON RUTH, political scientist, educator; b. Cleve., Apr. 10, 1969; d. Howard Louis Wesoky, Carolyn (Scheibel) Wesoky; m. Jim Fitch. PhD, Cornell U., 1999. Asst. prof. Polit. Sci. Allegheny Coll., Meadville, Pa., 1998—. Author: Chinese Feminism Faces Globalization, 2001; cinematographer:. Office: Dept Polit Sci Allegheny College Meadville PA 16335 Office Fax: 814-332-2310. Business E-Mail: swesoky@allegheny.edu.

WESP, WENDY LOUISE, vocalist, songwriter; b. Hackensack, N.J., Dec. 25, 1954; d. Robert Edward and Beverly M. (De Koning) W. Diploma tchr. early childhood edn., Bergen C.C., Paramus, 1979; diploma in adminstrn. office tech., Plaza Tech. Sch., Paramus, N.J., 1996. Tchr. Rutherford (N.J.) Child Care Ctr., 1975-80, 93-95, Sandy Lane Nursery, Belleville, N.J., 1981-83; auditor, clk. indsl. engring. dept. United Parcel Svc., Secaucus, 1990-92; music contractee/contractor Barry Jason Orchs., Ft. Lee, 1986-2000; vocalist Dom Perry Orchs., Brunswick, 1988—. Hank Joel Orchs., LenBornstein Orch. Rec. contract artist In House Rec. Co., South Ozone Park, N.Y., 1986-87; with Temp. Excellence, Paramus and Fairfield, N.J., 1997—; performed with Nick Massey Four Seasons Band, 1981, Calumet (of Mitch Ryder Band), Peter Tork (of the Monkies) Band, 1983, Glass House Music, 2B Reel Music, 1989, others; contractor various orch. agys., Don Dee Agy. Enterprises, Hillsdale, N.J., D.C. Entertainment, 1984—; freelance musician, All Prodns., Teleco Toy Music-Vocals 1988, numerous others; pvt. vocal tchr., Paterson, 1995; mem. band Broadway, also others, 1984—; founder band Affinity, Cause, Total Strangers, Fortress; gal friday CSA Audio, 1997-98, with Am. Pers. and Quincy Mutual Ins. Co; co-owner 2 cos.; vocalist Joe Franklin radio show, other radio performances. Writer numerous songs, songwriter with Len Rothbart and G. Baros; performed at World Trade Ctr., Town Hall, St. Anthony's Feast, Fashion Arts Ctr., N.Y.C., various other venues; mem. band Destiny, 1980s. Entertainer polit. event Gracie Mansion, N.Y.C., 1964, Jersey City Housing Bur., 1988, 98, Rutherford Sr. Ctr. '99, 1990-2000, Ridgewood (N.J.) Arts Ctr., 1995, others. Recipient Billboard Mag. Cert. of Achievement for original song. Mem. BMI. Avocations: poetry, skating, dancing, antiques. Office: PO Box 61 Totowa NJ 07511-0061

WESSE, DAVID, higher education administrator, consultant; b. Chgo., May 5, 1951; s. Herman Theodore and Lorraine Joan (Holland) W.; m. Deborah Lynn Smith, Oct. 11, 1975; children: Jason David, Eric Joseph. AA, South Suburban Coll., 1971; postgrad., Purdue U., 1971-72; BEd, Ill. State U., 1973; MS, Loyola U., Chgo., 1983. Adminstr. Reuben H. Donnelley Corp., Chgo., 1974-76; adminstrv. mgr. Loyola U., 1976-79, Joint Commn. on Accreditation of Healthcare Orgns., Oakbrook Terrace, 1979-81; adminstrv. dir., asst. sec. Northwestern U., Evanston, 1981-97; higher edn. cons. KPMG Peat Marwick, LLP, Chgo., 1997-2000; exec. dir. U. Houston, 2000; prin. Joslyn Assocs., Oregon, Ill., 2000—; asst. v.p. U. North Fla., 2000—. Seminar leader Nat. Assn. Coll. Aux. Svcs., 1998. Contbr. numerous articles to profl. publs. Pres., bd. dirs. Riverdale (Ill.) Libr. Dist., 1975, Riverdale Youth Commn., 1975; bd. dirs. Better Bus. Bur. Chgo. and No. Ill., 1991-97, Adminstrv. Mgmt. Soc. Found., 1998—. Recipient Svc. Recognition award Riverdale Libr. Dist., 1975, Excellence in Journalism award Nat. Assn. Coll. Aux. Svcs., 1989. Mem. Adminstrv. Mgmt. Soc. (bd. dirs. Chgo. chpt. 1983-88, pres. 1986-87, bd. regents 1986-88), Acad. Adminstrv. Mgmt. (bd. regents 1992-94), Profl. Office Mgmt. Assn. Chgo. (bd. dirs. 1992-93, sec. 1993-95, pres. 1995), Nat. Mgmt. Assn. (chpt. pres. 1995), Nat. Assn. Coll. and Univ. Bus. Officers (com. mem. 1986-87, 89-90, cost reduction awards 1986-88, 90, 92), Midwest Higher Edn. Commn. (com. mem. 1996-97), Assn. Coll. Adminstrn. Profls. (seminar leader 1995, 98, 99), Chgo. Area Bus. and Support Svc. Adminstrs. (founder 1988), Big Ten Bus. and Support Svc. Adminstrs. (founder 1992), Pvt. Univ. Bus. and Support Svc. Adminstrs. (founder 1996), U. North Fla. Adminstrv. and Profl. ASsn. (pres. 2002--), Phi Theta Kappa, Lambda Epsilon. Lutheran. Office: Joslyn Assocs Ste 1805 3500 University Blvd Jacksonville FL 32277 E-mail: d.wesse@worldnet.att.net.

WESSEL, HENRY, photographer; b. Teaneck, N.J., July 28, 1942; s. Henry and Jennie (Cincotta) W.; children by previous marriage: Nicholas, Rider. BA, Pa. State U., 1966; M.F.A., SUNY, Buffalo, 1972. Propr., mgr. comml. photog. studio, State Coll., Pa., 1966-68; cinematographer for documentary film Dept. HEW, 1967; instr. dept. art Pa. State U., Phila., 1967-69; prof. dept. photography San Francisco Art Inst., 1973-98, chmn. grad. program photography, 1977-78, chmn. dept. photography, 1987-93; asst. prof. San Francisco State U., 1974-75; vis. lectr. photography various colls. and art schs., 1967-81; propr., dir. Photographic Resources, Point Richmond, Calif., 1977—. Vis. artist Mills Coll., 1987-88 One-man show at Mus. Modern Art, N.Y.C., 1973, Mus. Contemporary Art, L.A., 1998; represented in permanent collections, Mus. Modern Art, N.Y.C., Phila. Mus. Art, Boston Mus. Fine Arts, Library of Congress, Am. Arts Documentation Center, Exeter, Eng., Nat. Gallery of Can., Ottawa; author: Henry Wessel, 1987, House Pictures, 1992, Night Walk, 2000, Odd Photos, 2002. Guggenheim fellow, 1971, 78; Nat. Endowment Arts fellow, 1975, 77, 78 Home: PO Box 475 Richmond CA 94807-0475

WESSEL, MORRIS ARTHUR, retired pediatrics educator; b. Providence, Nov. 1, 1917; s. Morris Jacob and Bessie (Bloom) W.; m. Irmgard Rosenzweig, June 1, 1952; children: David, Bruce, Paul, Lois. BA, Johns Hopkins U., 1939; MD, Yale U., 1943. Diplomate Am. Bd. Pediatrics. Intern Babies Hosp., N.Y.C., 1943-44; fellow in pediat. Mayo Found., Rochester, Minn., 1947-48; rooming-in fellow in pediat. Yale U. Sch. Medicine, 1948-51; asst. dir. pediatric outpatient clinic Yale-New Haven Hosp., 1951-52, dir. pediatric outpatient clinic, 1952-57; staff pediatrician, collaboration project Yale U. Sch. Medicine, 1957-62, instr. pediatrics, 1950-53, clin. asst. prof., 1963-61, clin. assoc. prof., 1961-75, clin. prof., 1975-97; ret. Cons. pediatrician Clifford Beers Child Guidance Clinic, 1967—; bd. dirs. Clifford Beers Guidance Clinic, New Haven, 1950-55, Women's Health Svc., New Haven, 1992-97, Child Welfare League, N.Y.C., 1979-91. Author: Parents Book on Raising a Healthy Child, 1987. Maj. AUS, 1944-47, ETO. Mem. Am. Acad. Pediat. (Practitioner Rsch. award 1994, C. Anderson Aldrich award 1997), Soc. Adolescent Medicine, Conn. Med. Soc., New Haven County Med. Soc. Office: Clifford Beers Clinic 93 Edwards St New Haven CT 06511 Fax: (203) 387-1927. E-mail: mwessel@snet.net.

WESSEL, PETER, lawyer; b. N.Y.C., N.Y., Feb. 2, 1952; s. Harry Nathan Jr. and Charlene (Freimuth) W.; married Vicki Brodsky Scheck; children: Daniel, Elizabeth, Justin Scheck, Matthew Scheck. BS, Syracuse U., 1974, MPA, JD, 1980. Bar: N.Y. 1981, U.S. Dist. Ct. (no., so., ea. and we. dists.) N.Y. 1981, Fla. 1984, U.S. Ct. Mil. Appeals, 1988, U.S. Ct. Appeals (2d cir.) 1988, U.S. Supreme Ct. 1988. Confidential law clk. to Hon. David F. Lee Jr. N.Y. Supreme Ct., 1980-82; sr. atty. criminal def. div. The Legal Aid Soc., N.Y.C., 1982-87; pvt. practice, 1987—. Notes and comments editor Syracuse Law Rev., 1979-80; contbr. articles to profl. jours. Robert M. Anderson award for Writing and Legal Scholarship, 1980, Neal Brewster scholar, 1977-78, Syracuse U. Coll. Law scholar 1978-79, Louis Waters Meml. scholar, 1979-80, Hiscock, Cowie, Bruce & Lee scholar, 1979-80; Martindale-Hubbell a-v rated. Mem. ABA, N.Y. State Bar Assn., Assn. of Bar of City of N.Y., Fla. Bar Assn., Nat. Assn. Criminal Def. Lawyers, N.Y. State Assn. Criminal Def. Lawyers, N.Y. State Defender Assn., N.Y. State Trial Lawyers Assn., N.Y. County Lawyers Assn., N.Y. Criminal Bar Assn.

WESSELINK, DAVID DUWAYNE, finance company executive; b. Webster City, Iowa, Sept. 5, 1942; s. William David and Lavina C. (Haahr) W.; m. Linda R. DeWitt, Dec. 27, 1971; children: Catherine, Bill. BA in Bus., Ctrl. Coll., 1964; MBA, Mich. State U., 1970. Tchr. Peace Corps, Turkey, 1964-66, Karabuk Koleji, Turkey, 1967-68, Robert Koleji, Turkey, 1969-70; rsch. analyst Household Fin. Corp., Chgo., 1971-73, asst. dir. rsch., 1973-77, asst. treas. Prospect Heights, Ill., 1977, v.p., dir. rsch., 1977-82, group v.p., CFO, 1982-86, sr. v.p., CFO, 1986—; v.p., treas. Household Internat., 1988-93; sr. v.p., CFO Advanta Corp., 1993-98; exec. v.p., CFO Metris Cos., Saint Louis Park, Minn., 1998-2000, vice chmn., 2000—. Bd. dirs. CFC Internat., Chicago Heights, Ill., Am. Fin. Svcs. Assn., Saxon Capital Corp., Glen Allen. Bd. dirs. Ctrl. Coll., Pella, Iowa, 1990—. Mem. Fin. Execs. Inst., Chgo. Coun. on Fgn. Rels., Econ. Club Chgo. Office: Metris Cos 10900 Wayzata Blvd Minnetonka MN 55305 E-mail: david.wesselink@metriscompanies.com.

WESSELKAMPER, SUE, academic administrator; m. Tom Wesselkamper; 2 children. BA History, Govt., Edgecliff Coll.; M Social Work, U. Mich.; PhD Social Welfare, CUNY. Head cmty., social svs. program New River Cmty. Coll.; dir. social work field instrn. program Radford U., Va.; dean sch. arts and scis., assoc. prof. social work Coll. New Rochelle, NY; pres. Chaminade U. Honolulu, 1995—. Author: Enhancing Identity Through Cross-Cultural Interaction , An Intercultural Approach to Contemporary Ethnicity , Issues in Implementing Cultural Diversity Content, Role of the Social Worker in Health Planning. Chmn. bd. dirs. Family Svcs. Westchester County, NY; mem. adv. com. Pew Charitable Trust 3d Black Colls. Project on Student Retention; mem. Hawaii Cath. Conf., Hawaii State Network of Am. Coun. on Edn.'s Women Leaders in Higher Edn. Avocations: reading, movies, hiking, travel. Office: Chaminade U of Honolulu 3140 Waialae Ave Honolulu HI 96816*

WESSELMANN, GLENN ALLEN, retired hospital executive; b. Cleve., Mar. 21, 1932; s. Roy Arthur and Dorothy (Oakes) W.; m. Genevieve De Witt, Sept. 6, 1958; children: Debbie, Scott, Janet. AB, Dartmouth, 1954; MBA with distinction, Cornell U., 1959. Research aide Cornell U., Ithaca, N.Y., 1958-59; adminstrv. resident Meml. Hosp., N.Y.C., 1957-58, adminstrv. asst., 1959-61, asst. adminstr., 1961-65, asst. v.p., 1965-68; v.p. for adminstrn. Meml. Hosp. for Cancer and Allied Diseases, N.Y.C., 1968-79; exec. v.p., chief operating officer St. John Hosp., Detroit, 1979-84; pres., CEO St. John Health System, 1984-95, vice chmn., 1995-97; chmn., pres., CEO St. John Hosp. & Med. Ctr., 1984-94, ret., 1995. Mem. bus. adv. bd. City of Detroit, 1991-95, chmn., 1993-94; mem. exec. com. Greater Detroit Area Health Coun.; bd. dirs. Caymich Ins. Co. Ltd., Mich. Health Care Alliance, SelectCare, Detroit Econ. Growth Corp. Trustee Sisters of St. Joseph Health System 1981-94, Sisters of St. Joseph Health Svc., 1983-95, St. John Hosp. and Med. Ctr., 1979-95, St. John Health System, 1984-95, The Oxford Inst., 1984-95, Eastwood Clinics, 1992-95; pres. Providence Ch. Corp., Hilton Head Island, S.C., chmn. ch. fin. ocm., corp. pres. session; mem. bus. adv. bd.! City of Detroit, 1991-95, chmn. 1993-94. Served with MC AUS, 1955-57. Fellow ACHE; mem. Am. Hosp. Assn., Internat. Hosp. Fedn., Mich. Hosp. Assn. (trustee, chmn. 1994-95, mem. exec. com.), Assn. Am. Med. Colls. (Coth rep.), Am. Cancer Soc. (regional adv. bd. 1994-95), Med. Group Mgmt. Assn., Soc. Health Service Adminstrs., Sigma Phi Epsilon. Home: 63 Big Woods Dr Hilton Head Island SC 29926-2604

WESSELS, BRUCE W. materials scientist, educator; b. N.Y.C., Oct. 18, 1946; m. Beverly T. Wessels; children: David, Kirsten. BS in Metallurgy and Materials Sci., U. Pa., 1968; PhD in Materials Sci., MIT, 1973. Tech. staff GE R&D Ctr., 1972-77, acting branch mgr., 1976; from asst. prof. to assoc. prof. Northwestern U., Evanston, Ill., 1977-83, prof. materials sci. and engring., 1984—, Walter P. Murphy prof., 1998—, prof. elec. and computer engring., 1987—. Vis. sci. Argonne Nat. Lab., 1978; mem. program com. Internat. Conf. Superlattices, Microdevices and Microstructures, 1987. Editor 5 books including (with G.Y. Chin) Advances in Electronic Materials, 1986; mem. editl. bd. Jour. Electronic Materials, 1982-88, 98—; contbr. articles to profl. jours.; patentee in field. Fellow ASM; mem. TMS, The Minerals, Metals and Materials Soc. (chmn. electronic materials com. 1987-89, conf. program chmn. 1986-87, key reader Trans. of AIME 1985-92, bd. dirs. 1993-98, vice-chmn. exec. coun. electronic, magnetic and photonic materials divsn. 1991-92, chmn. 1993-95, v.p. 1995, pres. 1996, bd. trustees AIME 1996-97), Electrochem. Soc. Materials Rsch. Soc. (symposium organizer 1993, 95), Am. Phys. Soc., Sigma Xi, Tau Beta Pi. Office: Materials Science-Engring Northwestern U 2225 N Campus Dr Evanston IL 60208-3108 E-mail: b-wessels@northwestern.edu.

WESSER, YVONNE, artist; b. London, 1935; came to U.S., 1957; m. David R. Wesser (div.); children: Marius, Pavelle. BA in Religion, CUNY, 1991. One-woman shows include Main St. Gallery, Brewster, N.Y., 1975, Little Carnegie Art Gallery, N.Y.C., 1980, 34th St. Theatre Gallery, N.Y.C., 1980, Lida Gallery, N.Y.C., 1982, Gallery 84, N.Y.C., 1984, 85, Discovery Art Gallery, Glen Cove, N.Y., 1987, Plaza Gallery, City Hall Bldg., Binghampton, N.Y., 1987, Stehle-Rd. Gallery, Midland, Tex., 1987, Pleiades Gallery, N.Y.C., 1991; exhibited in group shows at Galeria Mesa, Ariz., 1988, Scoharie County Arts Coun., Cobbleskill, N.Y., Cen. Mo. State Univ. Art Ctr. Gallery, Warrensburg, 1989, Viridian Gallery, N.Y.C., 1990, Columbus (Ohio) Art Gallery, 1991, Jacob Javits Fed. Bldg., N.Y.C., 1991, Multi Media Gallery, N.Y.C., 1991, The Corner Gallery, N.Y.C., 1991, Broadway Mall Gallery, N.Y.C., 1991; represented in permanent collections including Barky Hosp., Saigon, Vietnam, Art Students League, N.Y.C., Nat. Art Mus. of Sport U. New Haven, West Haven, Conn.; commns. include for Barsky Hosp., John Disiere, Larry Freed. Mem. Whitney Mus., Mus. Modern Art, Burr Artists. Recipient Elmer Perkin award Mus. Modern Art, N.Y.C., 1986, Juror's Merit award Alexandria Mus., N.Y.C., 1986, 2d prize Mus. of Contemporary Art, L.A., 1989, 1st prize Whitney Mus., N.Y.C., 1987. Mem. Nat. Assn. Women's Pen League, Visual Individualists United, N.Y. Acad. Sci. Roman Catholic. Avocations: poetry, religious studies, swimming, reading, hiking. Home: 12 E 86th St Apt 1631 New York NY 10028-0517

WESSLER, MARY HRAHA, real estate company executive; b. Des Moines, Nov. 4, 1961; d. Francis M. and Shirley A. (Malone) Hraha; 1 child, Nick. BA in Mass Comm., Iowa State U., 1984; postgrad., U. Denver, 1990. Dir. mktg. Real Estate Mgmt. Corp., Scottsdale, Ariz., 1984-87; v.p. Great West Mgmt. and Realty, Ltd., Denver, 1987-97; reg. v.p. AIMCO, 1997-98; v.p. JPI, 1999—2001, Omni Properties, Inc., Denver, 2001—. Instr., spkr. in field, Multi-Housing World NAA and IREM. Bd. dirs., past pres. Apt. Assn. Metro. Denver, 1990—. Mem. Nat. Apt. Assn. (bd. dirs. and v.p. Region 8, 2000—), Colo. Apt. Assn. (bd. dirs. 1990—). Home: 4185 S Granby Cir Aurora CO 80014 E-mail: mwessler@omniprop.com.

WESSLER, MELVIN DEAN, farmer, rancher; b. Dodge City, Kans., Feb. 11, 1932; s. Oscar Lewis and Clara (Reiss) W.; m. Laura Ethel Arbuthnot, Aug. 23, 1951; children: Monty Dean, Charla Cay, Virgil Lewis. Grad. high sch. Farmer, rancher, Springfield, Colo., 1950—. Dir., sec. bd. Springfield Co-op. Sales Co., 1964-80, pres. bd., 1980— . Pres., Arkansas Valley Co-op. Council, SE Colo. Area, 1965-87, Colo. Co-op. Council, 1969-72, v.p. 1974, sec. 1980-86; community com. chmn. Baca County, Agr. Stablzn. and Conservation Svc., Springfield, 1961-73, 79—, vice chmn. Baca County Com., 1980-90; mem. spl. com. on grain mktg. Far-Mar-Co. Mem. adv. bd. Denver Bapt. Bible Coll., 1984-89; chmn. bd. dirs. Springfield Cemetery Bd., 1985—; apptd. spl. com. Farmland Industries spl. project Tomorrow, 1987—. Recipient The Colo. Cooperator award Colo. Coop. Coun., 1990. Mem. Colo. Cattlemen's Assn., Colo. Wheat Growers Assn., Southeast Farm Bus. Assn. (bd. dirs. 1991-95), Big Rock Grange (treas. 1964-76, master 1976-82), Southwest Kans. Farm Bus. Assn. (dir. 1996—, pres. 1999-2001). Address: 18363 County Road Pp Springfield CO 81073

WESSLER, PETER, music educator; b. Peoria, Ill., Aug. 15, 1957; s. Max Alden and Ardith Wessler; m. Carol Denise Warren, Oct. 9, 1982; children: Jonathan, Daniel. B in Music Edn., Bradley U., 1980; M in Music Edn., Ill. State U., 1986. Cert. tchr. Ill. Tchr./orch. dir. Peoria Pub. Schools, Dist. 150, 1980—; affiliate instr. music Bradley U., 1997—. Violinist Peoria Symphony Orch., 1977—; condr. concert orch. Ctrl. Ill. Youth Symphony, Peoria, 1981—96. Youth counselor, mem., dir. youth bd. Trinity Luth. Ch., Peoria, Ill., 1980—87, bd. of word and sacrament, 1987—89, watch ministry steering com., 1996, adult choir dir., 1992—. Recipient Russell F. Peters Outstanding Tchr. award, Kiwanis Club of Peoria, 1999; grantee Jordan Fundamentals grantee, Nat. Assn. for Improvement of Edn., 2000. Mem.: Am. Fedn. Teachers, Am. String Tchrs.' Assn. with Nat. Sch. Orch. Assn., Ill. Music Educators' Assn., Nat. Assn. Music Edn., Assn. Luth. Ch. Musicians, Phi Mu Alpha Sinfonia. Lutheran. Avocations: travel, exercise/fitness. Home: 2525 W Barker Ave Peoria IL 61604 Office: Woodruff HS 1800 NE Perry Ave Peoria IL 61603 Personal E-mail: pwes75@aol.com. E-mail: peter.wessler@psd150.org.

WESSLER, STANFORD, physician, educator; b. N.Y.C., Apr. 20, 1917; S. Hugo and Minerva (Miller) W.; m. Margaret Barnet Muhlfelder, Dec. 17, 1942; children— John Stanford, Stephen Lawrence, James Hugh. Grad., Fieldston Sch., N.Y.C., 1934; BA, Harvard, 1938; MD, N.Y.U., 1942. From fellow to asst. prof. medicine Harvard U. Med. Sch., 1946-64; from resident to assoc. chief med. svc. Beth Israel Hosp., Boston, 1946-64; prof. medicine Washington U. Sch. Medicine, St. Louis, 1964-74, John L. and Adalaine Simon prof., 1966-74; prof. medicine, assoc. dean postgrad. programs NYU Sch. Medicine, 1974-90; physician in chief Jewish Hosp., St. Louis, 1964-74; assoc. physician Barnes Hosp., 1964-74; attending physician NYU Med. Center, Univ. Hosp., N.Y.C., 1974-90, Bellevue Hosp. Center, N.Y.C., 1974-90, Manhattan VA Hosp. Med. Ctr., 1974-90. Mem. coms. NRC, Inst. of Medicine, Nat. Heart, Lung and Blood Inst.; bd. dirs. N.Y. Heart Assn., 1980-86; pres. Council Continuing Med. Edn., N.Y., 1979-85. Contbr. articles on vascular disease.; mem. editorial bds. jours. in field. Served with M.C. AUS, 1943-46. Recipient James A. Mitchell award, 1972. Mem. Am. Physiol. Soc., Am. Soc. Clin. Investigation, Assn. Am. Physicians, Am. Heart Assn. (investigator 1955-59, bd. dirs. 1971-76, chmn. publs. com. 1972-76, chmn. coun. on thrombosis 1974-76, v.p. 1974-76, mem. sci. adv. com. 1986-90, Merit award 1978, Disting. Achievement award 1989), Alpha Omega Alpha. Home: 575 Osgood St #1202 North Andover MA 01845-1975

WESSLING, ROBERT BRUCE, lawyer; b. Chgo., Oct. 8, 1937; s. Robert Euans and Marguerite (Rickert) W.; m. Judith Ann Hanson, Aug. 26, 1961; children: Katherine, Jennifer, Carolyn. BA, DePauw U., 1959; JD, U. Mich., 1962. Bar: U.S. Dist. Ct. (cen. dist.) Calif. 1963, U.S. Ct. Appeals (9th cir.) 1965. Assoc. Latham & Watkins, L.A., 1962-70, ptnr., 1970-94, of counsel, 1995—. Bd. govs. Fin. Lawyers Conf., Los Angeles, 1974-2000. Mem. World Affairs Coun., L.A., Town Hall, L.A.; trustee DePauw U. Mem. ABA, Los Angeles Bar Assn., Phi Beta Kappa, Phi Delta Phi, Phi Eta Sigma, Order of Coif. Democrat. Methodist. Avocations: tennis, travel. Office: 633 W 5th St Ste 4000 Los Angeles CA 90071-2005 E-mail: bbwessling@aol.com.

WESSNER, DEBORAH MARIE, telecommunications executive, computer consultant; b. St. Louis, Aug. 15, 1950; d. John George and Mary Jane (Beetz) Eyerman; m. Brian Paul Wessner, Sept. 15, 1972; children: Krystin, David. BA in Math. and Chemistry, St. Louis U., 1972; M Computer Info. Sci., U. New Haven, 1980. Statistitian Armstrong Rubber Co., New Haven, 1972-74; programmer analyst Sikorsky div. United Techs., Stratford, Conn., 1974-77; project engr. GE, Bridgeport, 1977-79, software mgr. Arlington, Va., 1979-81; mgr. software ops. Satellite Bus. Systems, McLean, 1981-83; v.p. ops. DAMA Telecommunications, Rockville, Md., 1983-87; dir. network ops. and adminstrn. Data Gen. Network Svcs., 1987-91; dir. bus. ops. Sprint Internat., Reston, Va., 1991-92; v.p. network adminstrn. Citicorp, Washington, 1992-93, v.p. telecomm. product mgmt. Reston, Va., 1994-95, v.p. product mgmt., 1996-97, v.p., dir. Yr. 2000 program, 1997-99; v.p. global procurement C&W, 2000—. Assoc., cons. KDB Assocs., Columbia, Md., 1986—. Mem. exec. bd. Howard County PTA. Mem. Am. Bus. Women's Assn., NAFE. Avocations: sailing, windsurfing, tennis.

WESSON, HERB J. state representative; b. Cleve. m. Fabian Wesson; children: Douglas, P.J., Herb III, Justin. BA in History, Lincoln U., Pa., 1999. Served as chief of staff LA County Supr. Yvonne Brathwaite Burke; served as chief dep. LA City Councilman Nate Holden; mem. Calif. State Assembly, 1998—, served on appropriations, health, utilities, and commerce com., served on bus. and professions com., chair govtl. orgn. com., speaker, 2002—. Mem. Mid-City C. of C., Culver City C. of C.; former mem. adv. bd. African Cmty. Resource Ctr.; bd. dirs. Martin Luther King, Jr. Gen. Hosp. Found., Second Dist. Edn. Found. Recipient Pub. Svc. award, Greater LA C. of C., Crusader State Leadership award, Calif. Alliance for Pride and Equality, Legis. of Yr. award, Youth Employment Sys., 1999—2000, Pub. Official award, Stonewall Dem. Club, 2000, Legis. of Yr. award, Planned Parenthood LA, 2001, Calif. Assessors' Assn., 2001. Office: Speaker of the House PO Box 942849 Sacramento CA 94249-0001*

WEST, ALEXANDRA (ANNIE WEST), artist, creative director; b. Chgo., Dec. 10, 1963; Degree, U. Provence, Aix-Marseilles, France, 1984; BA in French Studies, U. Mich., 1986; MFA, Sch. Art Inst. Chgo., 1992. Studio artist Whitney Mus. Am. Art, N.Y.C., 1993; creative dir. The Hub/New Line Cinema, 1996—. Artist resident Banff (Can.) Ctr. for Arts, 1994, Sculpture Space, Utica, N.Y., 1995, Ucross Found., Wyo., 1996; vis. artist Temistocles 44, Mexico City, 1994; panelist San Francisco Camera Work, San Francisco, 1995, Conn. Tchrs. Conf., 1996; guest curator Digital Film Festival, N.Y.C., 1998. Exhibited in shows at Beacon St. Gallery, Chgo., 1989, Chgo. Gallery, 1990, Gallery II, Chgo., 1991, Ceres Gallery, N.Y., 1993, Whitney Mus. Am. Art, N.Y., 1993, Hyde Park Art Ctr., Chgo., 1994, Miranushi/Lederman Prodns., Amsterdam, 1994, Temistocles 44, 1994, Cheap Art, Hamburg, 1994, Randolph St. Gallery, Chgo., 1991, 94, San Francisco Camera Work, 1995, Gallery 450, N.Y., 1995, Washington Project for Arts, Washington, 1995, Aldrich Mus. of Contemporary Art, Conn., 1995, Colgate U. Art Gallery, N.Y., 1995, P.P.O.W. Gallery, N.Y., 1995, ATA Gallery, San Francisco, 1996, Exit Art, N.Y.C., 1997; included in Joan Flasch Artists' Book Collection, Art Inst. Chgo., MOMA/Franklin Furnace Archive. Fellow Ernst Haas Photography, 1995, Nat. Endowment for Arts, 1995-96; Art Matters grantee, 1994.

WEST, ALICE CLARE, artist; b. Oct. 5, 1951; BA, San Francisco State U., 1975; MFA, U. Calif., Berkeley, 1986. One-woman shows include Rolando Castellon Contemporary Art Gallery, San Francisco, 1988, Mace-Space for Art, San Francisco, 1993, San Francisco Mus. Modern Art Rental Gallery, 1993; group exhibits include Mission Cultural Ctr.-Galeria Museo, San Francisco, 1981, Moscone Ctr., San Francisco, 1982, Sun Gallery, Hayward, Calif., 1983, Richmond (Calif.) Art Ctr., 1983, (Juror's prize 1983), Worth Ryder Art Gallery-U. Calif., Berkeley, 1984, 85, Meml. Union Gallery-U. Calif., Davis, 1985, Colorbox, San Francisco, 1986, Pro Arts, Oakland, Calif., 1987, U. Art Mus., Berkeley, 1987, Rolando Castellon Contemporary Art Gallery, San Francisco, 1987, Santa Rosa (Calif.) Jr. Coll., 1989, SOMAR Gallery, San Francisco, 1990, 98, Clary-Miner Gallery, Buffalo, N.Y., 1991, Gallery Rte. One, Point Reyes, Calif., 1991, Calif. Mus. Art, Santa Rosa, 1992, Columbia (Mo.) Coll., 1994, Crocker Art Mus., Sacramento, 1994, San Francisco Art Commn. Gallery, 1994, Palace of Fine Arts, San Francisco, 1994, Triton Mus. Art, Santa Clara, 1995, San Francisco Mus. Modern Art Rental Gallery, 1995, Calif. Mus. Art, Santa Rosa, 1996, (Juror's prize 1996), 97, Ctr. for Visual Art, Oakland, Calif., 1996, 97, San Francisco Mus. Modern Art Rental Gallery, 1999, 2000, Weber State U., Ogden, Utah, 2000, Sanchez Art Gallery, 2001, Somar Gallery, San Francisco, 2001; represented in permanent collections Levinson Bros., Inc., S.A.P. Am., Del Mondo, LLC, Sanchez Art Ctr., Pacifica, Calif., SOMAR Gallery, San Francisco, 2001, and pvt. collections. Recipient Juror's prize Hayward 22nd Annual Exhbn., 1984, John Michael Welcome prize U. Calif. Berkeley Art Dept., 1985. Home and Office: 4047 Cesar Chavez St San Francisco CA 94131-1918

WEST, A(RNOLD) SUMNER, chemical engineer; b. Phila., Jan. 12, 1922; s. Arnold and Mary (Sumner) W.; m. Beverly Helen Lehman, Oct. 5, 1946; children: Barbara Ann, Richard Sumner. BSChemE, U. Pa., 1943; MS, Pa. State U., 1946. With Rohm and Haas Co., Phila., 1946-87, rsch. engr., 1946-62, rsch. supr., 1962-72, mgr. research dept., 1972-77, sr. tech. specialist govt. and regulatory affairs, 1978-87; owner, prin. A.S. West Assocs., Huntingdon Valley, 1987—. Cons. dept. chem. engring. U. Pa., 1952-72; mem. indsl. and profl. adv. com. Coll. Engring., Pa. State U., 1978-84, chmn. chem. engring. div., 1980-81, chmn. com., 1982-83 Editor: AIChE Safety and Health News, 1996—. Mem. Lower Moreland Twp. (Montgomery County) Authority, 1970, sec., 1971—; vice-chmn. bd. dirs. Chemical Heritage Found., 1984-92; pres. United Engring. Trustees, 1986-87. Fellow Am. Inst. Chem. Engrs. (dir. 1964-66, treas. 1973-75, v.p. 1976, pres. 1977); mem. Engrs. Joint Council (dir. 1976-79), Am. Assn. Engring. Socs. (vice chmn. public affairs council 1981, chmn. council 1982-83), Am. Chem. Soc., Nat. Soc. Profl. Engrs., Soc. Automotive Engrs., Water Environ. Fedn. Clubs: The Valley (Huntingdon Valley). Home and Office: 3896 Sidney Rd Huntingdon Valley PA 19006-2347 E-mail: aswest@worldnet.att.net.

WEST, ARTHUR JAMES, II, retired biologist, educator; b. Boston, Dec. 14, 1927; s. Arthur James and Lillian (Laming) W.; m. Carolyn Barbara Ross, June 4, 1948 (div. May 1972); children: Arthur James, Gregory Thomas, Donald Robert; m. Linda Jean Cummings, July 21, 1985 (div. Sept. 1993); children: Melissa Ida, Benjamin Cummings; m. Pamela Kay Yenco, Oct. 2, 1999. BS, Suffolk U., 1951, MA in Edn., 1956; MS, U. N.H., 1962, PhD in Zoology, 1964. Faculty Suffolk U., Boston, 1952-68, assoc. prof. biology, 1964-65, prof., 1965-68, co-chmn. biology, 1964-68; dean, prof. div. natural sci. New Eng. Coll., Henniker, N.H., 1968-70; prof., chmn. dept. biology Suffolk U., 1970-72, 78-88; assoc. program dir. Pre-coll. Edn. in Scis./NSF, 1972-73; prof. dept. biology Suffolk U., 1973-89, prof. emeritus, 1989—. Acad. v.p. for curriculum devel. U. San Juan Capistrano, 1992-93; owner, operator Subway of Farmington and Skowhegan, Maine, 1990-98, chmn. adv. coun. 1993-94, Art W. Enterprises Nev. Corp., 1997-2001; treas. Dahl Assocs., Inc., 1991-98, Lamb Assocs., Inc., 1990—; CEO, Mountain View Chocolate Shoppe, 2001—; dir. R.S. Friedman Cobscook Bay Lab., 1975-88; mem. exec. com. MIT/SEA Grant Consortium Program, 1979-85; asst. prof., chmn. biology Mass. Coll. Optometry, 1957-60; instr., chmn. sci. Emerson Coll., 1956-59; staff Norwich U., 1960; cons. Ginn & Co. Sci. Publs., 1967-70; hon. cons., parasitologist Akvapatologisk Lab., 1987; civil svc. examiner Mass. Dept. Natural Resources, 1965-72; bd. dirs. Life Enrichment Advancing People (LEAP), 1997—. Founding pres. Keltown Civic Assn., 1954; chmn. Woburn United Fund, 1958; mem. Woburn Sch. Com., 1955-60, chmn. 1957; chmn. Woburn YMCA, 1958, Woburn Rep. City Com., 1959, New Vineyard Town Com., 1990; vice-chmn. Franklin County Rep. Com.; mem. commn. on ocean mgmt. Mass. Served with USN, 1946-47, with Res., 1947-52. NSF grantee, 1968-71, 70-71, 75-82. Mem. Mass. Bay Marine Studies Consortium (pres. 1982-85), Mass. Marine Educators, Inc. (com. 1978-86), AAAS, Am. Inst. Biol. Scis., Nat. Marine Edn. Assn. (dir. 1976-78, pres. 1985-86), Ea. Star, Rotary, Masons, Sigma Xi (Suffolk U. club pres. 1972), Sigma Zeta, Phi Beta Chi (pres. 1951), Beta Beta Beta, Phi Sigma. Home: PO Box 104 New Vineyard ME 04956-0104 E-mail: awesty@ime.net., awestyusa@netscape.net.

WEST, BARBARA A. educator; b. Buffalo, Aug. 5, 1967; d. Kathleen M West, Peter C West; life ptnr. Fran Murphy. BA, Colgate U., 1989; MA, PhD, U. Rochester, 1995. Asst. prof. U. Pacific, Stockton, Calif., 1995—2000, assoc. prof., 2000—. Vis. instr. Eotvos Lorand Tudomanyegyetem, Budapest, Hungary, 1993—94; adj. instr. SUNY, Brockport, NY, 1994—95. Author: The Danger is Everywhere!, 2002 (Teacher of the Year, School of International Studies, University of the Pacific, 2001); editor: Anthropology of East Europe Rev., 2001—. Mem.: Assn. Feminist Anthropology (treas. 2001—). Atheist. Avocation: travel. Office: U of the Pacific 3601 Pacific Ave Stockton CA 95211

WEST, BENJAMIN B. advertising executive; b. 1951; BA, Washington and Lee U. With West Advt. & Mktg., Tampa, Fla., 1973-80; pres., CEO & founder WestGroup Inc, 1980-96; pres. WestWayne Inc. (merger of WestGroup with Tucker Wayne/Luckie & Co.), FL, 1996-99; CEO WestWayne Inc., 1999—. Office: WestWayne Inc 4018 Jackson St Ste 3600 Tampa FL 33602*

WEST, BILL, writer, artist, photographer, composer; b. Chgo. s. Joseph James and Catherine Theresa W. AB in English, Loyola U., Chgo.; MA in English, PhD in English and Am. Literatures, Northwestern U., Evanston, Ill. Tchg. asst. Northwestern U., Evanston, Ill.; instr. in English Ill. Inst. Tech., Georgetown U.; asst. prof. in English Ill. Inst. Tech., Loyola U., Chgo., prof. emeritus. Author: Sacred Numbers, American Summer Suite, Kaimami, The Heians, The Sparrow with the Slit Tongue and Beautiful Oiwa: Ghost Tales of Old Japan; contbr. poetry to anthologies and mags.; illustrator Canopy Mag., Iota Poetry Quar. Mag., Aabye's Baby Mag., The Inquirer Mag., NIH's Haiku 2000 Anthology, Presence Mag., Writer's Own Mag., Azami Mag., Prijatelj Mag., The Brobdingnagian Times Mag., Raw NerVZ Mag., Yumtzilob: Tijdschrift over den Ams. Mag., Calligraphy for Azami Mag., Iota Poetry Quar. Mag., Krax Mag., Presence Mag., Handshake Mag., Lotus Mag.; guest artist Hidden Oak mag, Inclement mag. Mem. SAG, Poets and Writers, Internat. Artists and Writers Assn., Tanka Soc. Am. Avocations: tennis, bicycle riding, gardening.

WEST, BLAIR, investment banker, consultant; b. Toronto, Ont., Can., Dec. 10, 1965; s. Robert Scott and M. Ray (Marshal) W.; m. Ann Michele Byrne; children: Hunter Alexander, Madison Ann, Parker Alexander. BA, Wheaton Coll., 1987; MBA, U. Chgo., 1995. Lic. real estate broker, N.Y., NASD series 7 and 63. V.p. Barnett Bank, Tampa, Fla., 1988-93, Credit Suisse First Boston, N.Y.C., 1995-2000; mng. dir., owner Crusader Investments, 2000—. Mem. Met. Club, Penn Club. Avocations: golf, sailing, reading. Office: Crusader Investments 230 Park Ave Ste 1000 New York NY 10169

WEST, BOB, pharmaceutical company executive; b. Ellenville, N.Y., Mar. 7, 1931; s. Harry and Elsie May Wicentowsky; m. Betty Parker, May 9, 1957 (div.); children: Debra Ellen, Elizabeth Ann, Sharon Lynn; m. Jacqueline Cutler, Jan. 3, 1982. BS, Union U., 1952; MS, Purdue U., 1954, PhD, 1956; postgrad. mgmt. seminar, U. Chgo., 1972. Pres., dir. research Food, Drug, Chem. Svcs., Stamford, Conn., 1975—; pres., dir. research Bob West Assocs., Inc., 1975—. Pres. Drug Info. Assn., Phila., 1974-75; sci. adv. bd. Fountain Pharms., Inc., Largo, Fla., 1993—, Dovetail Techs., Inc., College Park, Md., 1996—, Phytopede, Inc., Sarasota, Fla., 1999—. Editorial bd. Drug Info. Assn. Jour., Phila., 1977-85; contbr. articles to profl. jours. Mem. ASPET, Am. Soc. Toxicology, Acad. Pharm. Scis., Assn. Rsch. Dirs., Drug Info. Assn., Assn. Univ. Tech. Mgrs. Home and Office: Food Drug Chem Svcs 7925 Meadow Rush Loop Sarasota FL 34238-4319 E-mail: bjwest1@prodigy.net.

WEST, CAROL CATHERINE, law educator; b. Phila., May 23, 1944; d. Scott G. and Helen (Young) West. BA, Miss. U. for Women, 1966; MLS, U. So. Miss., 1984; JD, U. Miss., 1970. Pub. svcs. law libr. U. Va., Charlottesville, 1966-67; catalog law libr. U. Miss., Oxford, 1967-70; legis. reference libr. Miss. Legislature, Jackson, 1970-75; law libr. Miss. Coll., 1975-94, prof. law, 1975—. Del. White House Conf. Libr. and Info. Svcs., 1991; cons. to Parliament of Armenia, 1995, Parliament of Tanzania, 1997; mem. bd. commrs. Miss. Libr. Commn., 1993—98; mem., sec. Miss. Task Force on Gender Fairness in the Cts. Mem.: ABA, Miss. Women's Polit. Network (bd. dirs. 1998—2000), Miss. Libr. Assn., Miss. Women Lawyers Assn. (bd. dirs. 1991—93), Hinds County Bar, Miss. Bar Assn. (Susie Blue Buchanan award 2001). Methodist. Office: Miss Coll Law Sch 151 E Griffith St Jackson MS 39201-1302

WEST, CHARLES CONVERSE, theologian, educator; b. Plainfield, N.J., Feb. 3, 1921; s. George Parsons and Florence (Farish) W.; m. Ruth Floy Carson, Sept. 6, 1944; children: Russell Arthur, Walter Lawrence, Glenn Andrew. BA, Columbia U., 1942; B.D., Union Theol. Sem., N.Y.C., 1945; PhD, Yale U., 1955. Ordained to ministry Presbyterian Ch. U.S.A., 1946; missionary, fraternal worker Bd. Fgn. Missions Presbyn. Ch. U.S.A., 1946-56; instr., chaplain Cheeloo U., Hangchow, China, 1948-49; instr. Nanking Theol. Sem., 1949-50; indsl. mission work Gossner Mission, Mainz-Kastel, Germany, 1950-51; lectr. Kirchliche Hochschule, Berlin, 1951-53; Lectr. Hartford Sem. Found., 1955-56; asso. dir. Ecumenical Inst., Bossey, Switzerland under World Council Chs., 1956-61; chargé de cours U. Geneva, 1956-61; instr. Peking Nat. U., 1948; assoc. prof. Christian ethics Princeton Theol. Sem., 1961-63, Stephen Colwell prof. Christian ethics, 1963-91, prof. emeritus, 1991—, acad. dean, 1979-84. Mem. Commn. to Form Statement Faith U.P. Ch. U.S.A., 1961-67, chmn. internat. affairs adv. com., 1963-66; Chmn. U.S. Com. for Christian Peace Conf., 1965-72; chmn. working com. Dept. Studies in Mission, Evangelism World Council Chs., 1967-68; member Commn. on Internat. Affairs, Nat. Council Chs., 1968-73 Author: Communism and the Theologians, 1958, Outside the Camp, 1959, Ethics, Violence and Revolution, 1969, The Power to be Human, 1971, Perspective on South Africa, 1985, Power, Truth and Community in Modern Culture, 1999; editor: The Sufficiency of God, Essays in Honor of Dr. W.A. Visser't Hooft, 1963; assoc. editor: Religion in Eastern Europe, 1985—; translator: J. Hamel-A Christian in East Germany, 1960. Mem. Am. Soc. Christian Ethics (v.p. 1972-73, pres. 1973-74), Am. Theol. Soc. (v.p. 1982-83, pres. 1983-84), Presbytery N.Y.C., Ams. for Dem. Action., Christians Associated for Rels. with Eastern Europe (pres. 1988-92). Home: 9 Hedge Row Rd Princeton NJ 08540-5047 Office: Princeton Theological Seminary CN821 Princeton NJ 08542 E-mail: c.c.west@att.net.

WEST, CHRISTOPHER EUGENE, military officer; b. Memphis, Jan. 16, 1963; s. John Walter West, Sr. and Clara Lucille Block; 1 child, Christopher Gabriel. AS, S.W. Tenn. C.C., 1987; BA, U. Memphis, 1989. Patient care specialist Gorgas Army Hosp., Rep. of Panama, 1981-84; acad. tutor U. Memphis, 1986-89; co. exec. officer 1st/26th Inf. Regiment, Fort Jackson, S.C., 1989-93; dir. mktg. and pub. rels. Personnel Plus, Memphis, 1993-97; comdr. Hdqtrs. Co./467th Engr. Btn., 1997—. Intern Office of U.S. Sen. Bill Frist, Memphis, 1996; cons. Office of Pub. Affairs, U.S. Army Corps of Engrs., Memphis, 2000. Editor: U.S. Army Engr. Mag./Helena, Vicinity Project. Pub. affairs dir. Memphis Police Ambs., 1996; civil mil. coord. Convoy of Hope, memphis, 2000. 1st lt. U.S. Army, 1989-93. Recipient Gen. Douglas MacArthur Leadership award, Washington, 2001, Outstanding Jr. Officer of Yr. award Res. Officers assn. of the U.S. Major Gen. Strom Thurmond, 1999; decorated Bronze Order of the De Fluery medal Army Engr. Assn., Hon. Order of St. Barbara. Mem. Pi Sigma Alpha. Republican. Baptist. Avocations: reading, writing, Internet, polit. sci. Office: HHC 467th Engr Btn 25262 Avery Ave Memphis TN 38112-4898

WEST, CHRISTOPHER JOHN (KIT WEST), visual and special effects supervisor; b. London, Feb. 6, 1936; s. Lionel Clifford and Dorothy (Collins) W.; m. Diane Lorraine Jefferson; 1 child, Rebecca. Student, Kings Coll., London. With camera dept. Realist Films, London; cameraman Bowie Films; owner, supr. Kit West Prodns. Supr. spl. effects on numerous films including Pink Panther Strikes Again, Raiders of the Lost Ark (Oscar award 1982), Return of the Jedi (British Film Academy award 1984), Young Sherlock Holmes, 1986 (Oscar award nomination 1986), Empire of the Sun, 1987, Casualties of War, 1989, Conquest of Paradise, Stargate, 1992, Dragon Heart, 1994 (Oscar nomination 1997, Saturn award nomination 1998 Acad. Sci. Fiction, Fantasy and Horror Films), Daylight, 1995, 96, Kull the Conquerer, 1996-97, Black Dog, 1997-98, Enemy at the Gates, 1999-2000, Ali, 2001. Mem. Acad. Motion Picture Arts and Scis., Brit. Acad. Film and TV Arts, U.S. Visual Effects Soc. (founding), Alliance of Spl. Effects & Pyrotechnic Operators, Inc. Mem. Tory Party. Anglican. Home and Office: Kit West Prodns 2 Albany Close London SW14 7DX England Address: 954 N Croft Ave Apt 205 Los Angeles CA 90069-4243 Fax: 323 654-3722. E-mail: kit.west@amserve.net.

WEST, CLARK DARWIN, pediatric nephrologist, educator; b. Jamestown, N.Y., July 4, 1918; s. Clark Darwin and Frances Isabel (Blanchard) W.; m. Ruthann Asbury, Apr. 12, 1944 (div.); children: Charles Michael, John Clark, Lucy Frances; m. Dolores Lachenman, Mar. 1, 1986. AB, Coll. of Wooster, 1940; MD, U. Mich., 1943. Intern Univ. Hosp., Ann Arbor, Mich., 1943-44, resident in pediatrics, 1944-46; fellow in pediatrics Children's Hosp. Research Found., Cin., 1948-49, research asso., 1951-89, asso. dir., 1963-89, dir. div. immunology and nephrology, 1958-89; with cardiopulmonary lab. chest service Bellevue Hosp., N.Y.C., 1949-51; attending pediatrician Children's Hosp., 1951-89; asst. prof. pediatrics U. Cin., 1951-55, asso. prof., 1955-62, prof., 1962-89. Mem. coms. NIH, 1965-69, 1972-73 Mem. editorial bd.: Jour. Pediatrics, 1960-79, Kidney Internat., 1977-89, Clin. Nephrology, 1989-96; contbr. articles to profl. jours. Served to capt. M.C., AUS, 1946-47. Decorated Army commendation medal; recipient recognition award Cin. Pediat. Soc., 1980, Mitchell Rubin award, 1986, Henry L. Barnett award, 1995, Daniel Drake medal, 1996, John P. Peters award, 1996. Mem. Soc. Pediatric Research (sec.-treas. 1958-62, pres. 1963-64), Am. Pediatric Soc., Am. Soc. Pediatric Nephrologists (pres. 1973-74), Am. Physiol. Soc., Am. Assn. Immunologists, Am. Soc. Nephrology, Internat. Pediatric Nephrology Assn., Sigma Xi, Alpha Omega Alpha. Achievements include research on immunopathogenesis and treatment of glomerulonephritides and in the complement system. Home: 11688 Aristocrat Dr Harrison OH 45030-9753 Office: Children's Hosp Med Ctr Cincinnati OH 45229

WEST, CORNEL, humanities educator, writer; b. Tulsa, June 2, 1953; s. Clifton L. W.; 1 child from previous marriage, Clifton; m. Elleni Gebre Amlak. BA, Harvard U., 1973; PhD, Princeton U., 1977. Prof. religion Union Theol. Sem., N.Y., 1977-84, 87-88, Yale U. Divinity Sch., New Haven, 1984-87; prof. religion, dir. dept. Afro-Am. Studies Princeton (N.J.) U., 1988-94; prof. Afro-Am. studies, philosophy of religion Harvard U., Cambridge, Mass.,

1994—99, Alphonse Fletcher jr. prof., 1999—2002; Class of 1943 Univ. prof. of religion Princeton U., 2002—. Am. corr. Le Monde Diplomatique; vis. prof. U. Paris; DuBois fellow Harvard U., 1994-99. Author: Prophesy Deliverance! An Afro-American Revolutionary Christianity, 1982, Prophetic Fragments, 1988, The American Evasion of Philosophy: A Genealogy of Pragmatism, 1990, Breaking Bread: Insurgent Black Intellectual Life, 1991, The Ethical Dimensions of Marxist Thought, 1991, Race Matters, 1993, Beyond Eurocentrism and Multiculturalism, Vol. I: Prophetic Thought in Postmodern Times, 1993, Vol. II: Notes on Race, Class and Power, 1993, Keeping Faith: Philosophy and Race in America, 1993, (with Paula Giddings) Regarding Malcolm X, 1994, (with Michael Lerner) Jews and Blacks: Let the Healing Begin, 1995, Future of the Race, 1996, Restoring Hope, 1997, The Cornel West Reader, 2000; co-prodr. (with Derek "D.O.A." Allen, Clifton West & Mike Daily) album, Sketches of my Culture, 2001. Recipient Literary Lion award N.Y. Pub. Libr., 1993. Office: Princeton U. Dept of Religion, 1879 Hall Princeton NJ 08544-1066*.

WEST, DOE, bioethicist, social justice activist, psychology researcher; b. Tucson, July 14, 1951; d. George Oliver and Dorothy Marie (Watson) W. AA, Dutchess C.C., 1975; BS, SUNY, New Paltz, 1977; BA, Logos Bible Coll., 1986, MDiv, 1993; MS, Boston U., 1980; PhD, Northeastern U., 2001. Dir. 504/compliance officer dept. health and hosps. City of Boston, 1979-81, commr. handicap affairs, 1981-84; pres. Myth Breakers, Inc., 1984—. Sr. rsch., Assoc. N.E. Family Studies, 2002-; project coord. task force on human subject rsch. Fernald State Sch., 1994. Postdoctoral fellow Ctr. for Psychol. Rehab. Boston U., 1999-2002. Home: PO Box 600585 Newton MA 02460- E-mail: doewest@aol.com.

WEST, DONNA C. licensing executive; b. Lancaster, Pa., Oct. 10, 1956; d. Donald A. and Catherine M. (Sammet) Ziegler; m. Robert C. West, May 16, 1987; 1 child, Cathy. Student, U. Nev., 1974, Nat. Judicial Coll., 1985. DUI adjudicator DMV & PS, Carson City, Nev., so. dist. mgr. Las Vegas, asst. chief licensing divsn. Gov. award for team bldg., 1995. Mem. So. Nev. DUI Task Force, Organ Donor Coalition, Leadership Las Vegas. Office: Dept Motor Vehicles 8250 W Flamingo Rd Las Vegas NV 89147-4111

WEST, EARLE HUDDLESTON, communications company professional; b. Nashville, Sept. 13, 1955; s. Earle H. and Tommie West; m. Diane M. Matthews, Oct. 7, 1978; children: Benjamin, Lauren, Sarah, Nathan. BS in Math., Harding U., 1976; MSEE, Ga. Tech. U., 1978; MBA, St. Edwards U., 1981. Engr. Semiconductor div. Motorola, Austin, 1978-82; mgr. AT&T Bell Labs., Holmdel, N.J., 1982—. Deacon Freehold (N.J.) Ch. of Christ, 1989. Mem. Ch. of Christ. Home: 32 Georgian Bay Dr Morganville NJ 07751-1322 Office: AT&T 101 Crawfords Corner Rd Holmdel NJ 07733-1985

WEST, EDWARD ALAN, graphics communications executive; b. L.A., Dec. 25, 1928; s. Albert Reginald and Gladys Delia (White) W.; m. Sonya Lea Smith, Jan. 2, 1983; children: Troy A., Tamara L.; stepchildren: Debra, Chris, Donna. AA, Fullerton Coll., 1966; student, Cerrotos Coll., 1957, UCLA, 1966-67. Circulation mgr. Huntington Park (Calif.) Signal Newspaper, 1946-52; newspaper web pressman Long Beach (Calif.) Press Telegram, 1955-62; gravure web pressman Gravure West, Los Angeles, 1966-67; sales engr. Halm Jet Press, Glen Head, N.Y., 1968-70; salesman Polychrome Corp., 1970-74; supr. reprographics Fluor Engring & Construction, Irvine, Calif., 1974-81; dir. reprographics Fluor Arabia, Dhahran, Saudi Arabia, 1981-85, Press Telegram, Long Beach, 1986-97; with Suburban LA Newspaper Group, 1998—. Printing advisor Saddleback C.C., Mission Viejo, Calif., 1979, 80. Author: How to Paste up For Graphic Reproduction, 1967. Sgt. USMC, 1952-55, Korea. Decorated Korean War Svc. medal with 3 battle stars, Combat Action ribbon, Good Conduct medal, UN Svc. medal, Navy commendation medal, Nat. Def. Svc. medal. Mem.: Internat. Assn. Legions of Honor (emeritus), In-Plant Printing Assn. (cert. graphics comm. mgr. 1977, editor newsletter 1977, pres.Orange County chpt. 1979—80, Internat. Man of Yr. award 1980), 1st Marine Divsn. Assn. (life), Royal Order of Jesters Ct. 161, Order of Quetzalcoatl, Internat. High Twelve 500 (Capistrano pres. 1995, 1996), KT, Masons (50-yr. mem.), Shriners (pres. South Coast club 1991, editor blue and gold unit Legion of Honor El Bekal Temple 1989—92, comdr. Legion of Honor (life) 1992, Shriner of Yr. award 1994), Western Shrine Assn. (emeritus) (comdr. 1996—97), Am. Legion, VFW (life). Presbyterian. Home: 198 Monarch Bay Dr Dana Point CA 92629-3437 Office: Suburban LA Newspaper Group 1210 N Azusa Canyon Rd West Covina CA 91790-1003 *Personal philosophy: With God's help anything is possible.*

WEST, FELTON, retired newspaper writer; b. Houston, May 9, 1926; s. Felton Eber and Clara Viola (Ross) W.; m. Jean Frances Osborn, Oct. 27, 1945; children— Felton Dale, Bruce Eugene, Wade Osborn, Barbara Jean. Student, U. N.Mex., 1944-46; BJ, U. Houston, 1952, M.Litt., 1957. Mem. staff Houston Post, 1943-95, Washington corr., 1961-65, chief Austin (Tex.) capitol bur., 1966-85, columnist, 1985-93, editorial writer, 1993-95, ret., 1995. Served with USNR, World War II. Mem. Soc. Profl. Journalists, Phi Kappa Phi. Home and Office: 209 Barrington Dr Liberty Hill TX 78642-4297 E-mail: few2@evi.net.

WEST, GAIL BERRY, lawyer; b. Cin. d. Theodore Moody and Johnnie Mae (Newton) B.; m. Togo D. West, Jr., June 18, 1966; children: Tiffany Berry, Hilary Carter. BA magna cum laude, Fisk U., 1964; MA, U. Cin., 1965; JD, Howard U., 1968. Bar: D.C. 1969, U.S. Supreme Ct. 1978. Staff atty. IBM, 1969-76; spl. asst. to sec. HUD, 1977-78; staff asst. to spl. asst. to Pres., Washington, 1978-80; dep. asst. sec. for manpower res. affairs installations Dept. Air Force, 1980-81; atty. AT&T, Washington, 1983-84; exec. dir. govt. affairs Bell Comms. Rsch. Inc., 1984-95; dir. govt. rels. Armstrong World Industries, Inc., 1995—. Mem. exec. com. ARC, Washington, 1974-85; bd. dirs. Family and Child Svcs., Washington, 1974-87; bd. trustees Corcoran Gallery Art, 1983-2000, Arena Stage, 1992-99, Decatur House, WETA, 1995-2001, Fisher House Found., Inc.; bd. dirs. Meridian House, 1994-2000; mem. cathedral chpt. Nat. Cathedral. Ford Found. fellow, 1965-68 Mem. ABA, D.C. Bar Assn., Unified Bar D.C. Democrat. Episcopalian. Home: 4934 Rockwood Pkwy NW Washington DC 20016-3211 Office: 1150 Connecticut Ave NW Washington DC 20036-5405

WEST, GLENN EDWARD, investment banking executive; b. Kansas City, Mo., Nov. 19, 1944; s. Ernest and Helen Cecil (Johnson) W.; m. Vicki Lynn Knox, May 22, 1970; children: Keele Kay, Kollen Chandler, Ashley Knox. BS in Acctg. and Mktg. cum laude, Northwest Mo. State U., 1966; student, U. Colo. Inst. Orgn. Mgmt., 1974, Notre Dame U. Acad. Orgn. Mgmt., 1977. Auditor Arthur Young & Co., Kansas City, 1966-68; sales mgr. Procter & Gamble, 1968-69; mgr. pub. rels. St. Joseph (Mo.) Area C. of C., Mo., 1969-71, mgr. econ. devel., 1971-74; exec. v.p. Lawrence (Kans.) C. of C., 1974-81, Greater Macon (Ga.) C. of C., 1981—; pres. Greater Austin Co. of C., 1987-99; mng. dir. Hoak Breadlove Wesneski & Co, Austin, 1999—. Contbr. articles to profl. jours. Chpt. chmn. ARC, Macon, 1984; pres. Quality of Life Found. Austin, Greater Austin Sports Found.; ctrl. campaign chair Capital Area United Way, 1995. Served with USNG, 1967-73. Recipient Leadership award Kiwanis, St. Joseph, 1974. Mem. Kans. Assn. Commerce and Industry (bd. dirs. 1977-79, leadership award 1981), Kans. C. of C. Execs. (bd. dirs. 1977-80, pres. 1979), Ga. C. of C. Execs. (bd. dirs. 1982—), Am. C. of C. Execs. (bd. dirs. 1979-81, 83-84, vice chmn. 1989—, chmn. 1991, cert. chamber exec. 1980), C. of C. of U.S. (adv. com. 1981-89, bd. dirs. 1995, U. Tex. IC2 fellow), Rotary, Barton Creek Country Club. Republican. Methodist. Office: Breedlove Hoak Wesneski & Co 701 Brazos Ste 500 Austin TX 78701 E-mail: gwest@hbwco.com.

WEST, GREGORY ALAN, physician; b. Houston, Aug. 1, 1950; s. Wayne Garland and Frankie Onalita (Russell) W.; m. Catherine Ann Sharp, June 18, 1976 (div. Oct. 1980); 1 child, Benjamin M.; m. Linda French Lucas, Apr. 13, 1985 (div. 1994); children: Robert, Scott; m. Cynthia Lee Swainston, Apr. 30, 1997. BA, Austin Coll., 1972; PhD, U. Louisville, 1980, MD, 1982; MDiv, Louisville Presbyn. Theol. Sem, 1981. Diplomate Am. Bd. Pediat., 1987, Am. Bd. Emergency Medicine, 1990, 99, with additional cert. in pediat. emergency medicine, 1997. EMT Louisville Emergency Med. Svc., 1977-79; intern in pediatrics U. Louisville Affiliated Hosps., 1982-83, resident in pediatrics, 1983-85; staff physician emergency dept. St. Anthony Hosp., Louisville, 1985-86, King's Daus. Hosp., Madison, Ind., 1985-95, med. dir. emergency med. svcs., 1989-91; staff physician emergency dept. Tri-County Cmty. Hosp., La Grange, Ky., 1991-92, Hardin County Meml. Hosp., Elizabethtown, 1995-99, Harrison County Hosp., Corydon, Ind., 2000—. Contbr. articles to profl. jours. Recipient pediatric radiology award and chmn.'s achievement award U. Louisville Affiliated Hosps. Fellow Am. Acad. Emergency Medicine, Am. Acad. Pediatrics; mem. Omicron Delta Kappa. Episcopalian. Avocations: tae kwon do karate, scuba diving, travel.

WEST, HUGH STERLING, aircraft leasing company executive; b. Kansas City, Kans., Apr. 5, 1930; s. Gilbert Eugene and Dorothy (Johnson) W.; m. Willa Alden Reed, Jan. 16, 1954; children: Karen, Phillip, Susan. BS, U. Va., 1952; BS in Aero., U. Md., 1959; grad., U.S. Naval Test Pilot Sch., 1959. Commd. 2d lt. USMC, 1948, advanced through grades to maj., 1961; exptl. flight test pilot U.S. Naval Air Test Ctr., Patuxent River, Md.; resigned, 1961; program mgr. Boeing Aircraft Co., Seattle, Phila., 1961-66, dir. airworthiness, comml. airplane divsn., 1969-71; dir. aircraft sales Am. Airlines, Tulsa, 1971-76; v.p. equipment mgmt. GATX Leasing Corp., San Francisco, 1976-80; v.p. tech., ptnr. Polaris Aircraft Leasing Corp., 1980-85; v.p., co-founder U.S. Airlease, Inc. divsn. Ford Motor Co., 1986-96; ret., 1996. Pres. Hugh S. West & Assocs., Comml. Aircraft Cons. Mem. Soc. Exptl. Test Pilots, Army Navy Country Club. Republican. Episcopalian. Home and Office: 387 Darrell Rd Hillsborough CA 94010-6763

WEST, IRMA MARIE, retired occupational health physician; b. Hespeler, Ont., Can., Dec. 31, 1917; arrived in U.S., 1929; d. Frances Albert Calvert and Vera Mary (Alderson) Calvert-Price; m. Ernest James West, Oct. 17, 1948 (div. Mar. 1953); 1 child, Michael David. AB, Willamette U., 1940; MD, Med. Coll. Pa., 1947; MPH, U. Calif., Berkeley, 1953. Bd. cert. Preventive Medicine and Public Health. Computer NACA (now NASA), Moffett Field, Calif., 1941-43; med. officer, cons., chief occupl. health State of Calif. Dept. Pub. Health, Berkeley, 1951-73, assoc. dep. dir., chief occupl. health br., rsch. sect., 1974-80. Chair traffic safety com. Alameda County Med. Assn., Oakland, Calif., 1964-73; chair com. on pesticides APHA, N.Y., 1963-68. Contbr. sci. papers to profl. jours. and books. Mem. Sacramento County Hist. Soc., 1988—, Old City Cemetery Com., Sacramento, 1988—. Recipient award for traffic safety rsch. Calif. Hwy. Patrol, 1966, Cmty. Svc. awards County and City of Sacramento, 1989-94. Mem. AAUW, AMA, Calif. Med. Assn. (editl. bd. Western Jour. Medicine 1973-80), Sierra Sacramento Valley Med. Soc. (vice-chair hist. com. 1982—), Torch Club (past pres.). Democrat. Unitarian Universalist. Avocations: writing, medical history. Home: 8428 Citadel Way Sacramento CA 95826-3006 E-mail: Imariewest@aol.com.

WEST, JAMES JOSEPH, lawyer; b. Tarentum, Pa., Nov. 26, 1945; s. Samuel Elwood and Rose (McIntyre) W.; m. Kathleen Geslak, Aug. 19, 1967; children: Joseph Allen, Yvonne Michelle, KaiLynn Ann. BS in Econs., St. Vincent Coll., 1967; JD, Duquesne U., 1970. Bar: Pa. 1971, U.S. Dist. Ct. (we. dist.) Pa. 1971, U.S. Ct. Appeals (3d cir.) 1971, U.S. Dist. Ct. (mid. dist.) Pa., 1980. Law clk. to presiding justice U.S. Dist. Ct., Pa., 1970-74; asst. U.S. atty. chief appellate sect. U.S. Atty.'s Office, Pitts., 1974-79; dep. dir. criminal law Pa. Atty. Gen.'s Office, Harrisburg, 1979-82; 1st asst. U.S. atty. U.S. Dist. Ct. (mid. dist.) Pa., 1982-84, U.S. atty., 1984-93; assoc. Sprague & Sprague, Phila., 1993-95; pvt. practice Harrisburg, Pa., 1995—. Mem. Nat. Environ. Enforcement Council. Recipient Outstanding Performance award U.S. Dept. Justice, 1974-78, Commendation Gov. of Pa., 1981. Mem. Pa. Bar Assn., Allegheny County Bar Assn., Dauphin County Bar Assn. Republican. Roman Catholic. Home: 1222 Cardinal Way Rd Hummelstown PA 17036-8548 Office: James West 105 N Front St Harrisburg PA 17101-1483 E-mail: jwestlaw@aol.com.

WEST, JAMES LEMUEL WILLS, III, English educator, historian; b. Roanoke, Va., Nov. 15, 1946; s. James L.W. West Jr. and Lucy Kate Bradley; 4 children. BA, U. S.C., 1968, PhD, 1971. From instr. to prof. English Va. Tech., Blacksburg, 1971-85; prof. English Pa. State U., University Park, 1986-92, Disting. prof., 1992-2000, Sparks prof., 2000—. Dir. Pa. State Ctr. for History of the Book, 1992—. Author: American Authors and the Literary Marketplace, 1988, William Styron, A Life, 1998; editor: Fitzgerald's Trimalchio, 2000. Fellow Nat. Humanities Ctr., N.C., 1981-82, J.S. Guggenheim Found., N.Y.C., 1985-86, NEH, Washington, 1994-95, 98-99; vis. fellow Am. Acad. in Rome, 1994. Mem. Soc. History of Authorship, Reading and Pub. (v.p. 1996-2000, pres. 2000—), Internat. Dreiser Soc. (pres. 1998-2000), F. Scott Fitzgerald Soc. Avocations: cooking, travel, cigars. Office: Dept English Pa State U University Park PA 16802 E-mail: jlw14@psu.edu.

WEST, JAMES ODELL, JR. finance executive; b. Newport News, Va., Mar. 1, 1960; s. James Odell and Margaret Alice (Schweida) W.; m. Elizabeth Ann Healy, May 21, 1983; children: James Odell III, William Charles. BA in History, Coll. of William and Mary, 1983, MBA, 1990. Analyst govt. contract adminstrn. Newport News Shipbuilding, 1984-90, supr., govt. audit liaison, 1990-93; dir. capital budgeting Tenneco, Inc., Houston, 1993—. Capt. USAR, 1984-93. Mem. Am. Mgmt. Assn., Beta Sigma. Republican. Avocations: cycling, weight training. Home: 74 Rumplecreek Pl The Woodlands TX 77381 Office: Tenneco Inc PO Box 4100 The Woodlands TX 77387-4100

WEST, JAN GLASCOCK, researcher; b. Dallas, Sept. 12, 1956; d. B.J. and Rose Ann Glascock; m. J. Ken West, May 5, 2001; children: Jaclyn, Stephanie. BS, So. Methodist U., 1976, MS, 1982, PhD, 1996. CEO, Nat. Bus. Rsch. Inst., Inc., Dallas, 1982—. Founder database of universal survey questions and normative data, 1982—. Mem. APA. Office: Nat Bus Rsch Inst Inc 15305 Dallas Pkwy 3d Fl Addison TX 75001-4637 E-mail: janwest@nbrii.com.

WEST, JOHN BURNARD, physiologist, physician, educator; b. Adelaide, Australia, Dec. 27, 1928; came to U.S., 1969; s. Esmond Frank and Meta Pauline (Spehr) W.; m. Penelope Hall Banks, Oct. 28, 1967; children: Robert Burnard, Joanna Ruth. MB, BChir, Adelaide U., 1951, MD, 1958, DSc, 1980; PhD, London U., 1960; PhD (hon.), U. Barcelona, Spain, 1987. Resident Royal Adelaide Hosp., 1952, Hammersmith Hosp., London, 1953-55; physiologist Sir Edmund Hillary's Himalayan Expdn., 1960-61; dir. respiratory research group Postgrad. Med. Sch., London, 1962-67, reader medicine, 1968; prof. medicine and physiology U. Calif., San Diego, 1969—. Wiltshire lectr., London, 1971, Schwidetzky lectr., 1975, Fleischner lectr., 1977, Robertson lectr. Adelaide U., 1978, McClement lectr. NYU, 1996; leader Am. Med. Rsch. Expdn. to Mt. Everest, 1981; U.S. organizer China-U.S. Conf. on respiratory failure, Nanjing, 1986; mem. life scis. adv. com. NASA, 1985-88, task force sci. uses of space sta., 1984-87, aerospace med. adv. com., 1988-89, chmn. sci. verification com. Spacelab SLS-1, 1983-92; prin. investigator Spacelabs SLS 1, 2, LMS, Neurolab, 1983—; co-investigator European Spacelabs, D2, Euromir, 1987—; mem. commn. on respiratory physiol. Internat. Union Physiol. Scis., 1985—; mem. commn. on clin. physiol., 1991—, mem. commn. gravitation physiol., 1986—; mem. study sect. NIH, chmn., 1973-75. Author: Ventilation/Blood Flow and Gas Exchange, 1965, Respiratory Physiology-The Essentials, 1974, Translations in Respiratory Physiology, 1975, Pulmonary Pathophysiology-The Essentials, 1977, Translations in Respiratory Physiology, 1977, Bioengineering Aspects of the Lung, 1977, Regional Differences in the Lung, 1977, Pulmonary Gas Exchange (2 vols.), 1980, High Altitude Physiology, 1981, High Altitude and Man, 1984, Everest-The Testing Place, 1985, Best and Taylor's Physiological Basis of Medical Practice, 1985, 91, Study Guide for Best and Taylor, 1985, High Altitude Medicine and Physiology, 1989, The Lung: Scientific Foundations, 1991, 2d edit., 1997, Lung Injury, 1992, Respiratory Physiology: People and Ideas, 1996, High Life: A History of High Altitude Physiology and Medicine, 1998. Recipient Ernest Jung prize for medicine, Hamburg, 1977; Presdl. citation Am. Coll. Chest Physicians, 1977; Reynolds prize for history Am. Physiol. Soc., 1987; I.J. Flance lectr. Washington U., 1978; G.C. Griffith lectr. Am. Heart Assn., 1978; scholar Macy Found., 1974; Kaiser teaching award 1980; W.A. Smith lectr. Med. Coll. S.C., 1982, S. Kronheim lectr. Undersea Med. Soc., 1984, D.W. Richards lectr. Am. Heart Assn., 1980, E.M. Papper lectr. Columbia U., 1981, I.S. Ravdin lectr. ACS, 1982, Burns Amberson lectr. Am. Thoracic Soc., 1984, Harry G. Armstrong lectr. Aerospace Med. Assn., 1984. Annual Space Life Scis. lectr. Federation Associated Socs. of Exptl. Biology, 1991, Hermann Rahn lectr. SUNY Buffalo, 1992, Menkes lectr. Johns Hopkins, 1992; Jeffries Med. Rsch. award AIAA, 1992; Macalllum lectr. U. Toronto, Can., 1989, Macleod lectr. Southampton U., U.K., 1990, Bulatto lectr. U. Philippines, Manila, 1990, Mohaideen lectr. L.I. Coll., Bklyn., 1992, Bullard lectr. Uniformed Svcs. U., Bethesda, Md., 1993, Raven lectr. Am. Coll. Sports Medicine, Dallas, 1995, Waksman lectr. N.J. Thoracic Soc., 1998, James Hardy lectr. Yale U., 1998, Gillian Hanson lectr. Intensive Care Soc., London, 1998, George Dock lectr. Huntington Hist. Soc., Pasadena, 1999; Simon Rodbard lectr. Am. Coll. Chest Physicians, Chgo., 1999; James V. Warren Med. Humanities lectr., Ohio State U., 2000; Doris J.W. Escher lectr. Montefiore Med. Ctr., N.Y.C., 2001; D.A. Stewart lectr. in History of Medicine U. Man., Winnipeg, 2002; external examiner Nat. U. Singapore, 1995; founder, editor-in-chief High Altitude Medicine and Biology, 2000—. Fellow Royal Coll. Physicians (London), Royal Australasian Coll. Physicians, Royal Geog. Soc. (London), AAAS (med. sci. nominating com. 1987-93, coun. del. sect. med. scis.), Am. Inst. for Med. and Biol. Engring. (founder fellow 1992), Internat. Soc. for Mountain Medicine (pres. 1991-94); mem. NAS (com. space biology and medicine 1986-90, subcom. on space biology 1984-85, com. advanced space tech. 1992-94, panel on small spacecraft tech. 1994), Nat. Bd. Med. Examiners (physiology test com. 1973-76), Am. Physiol. Soc. (pres. 1984-85, coun. 1981-86, chmn. sct. on history of physiology 1984-92, hist. pubs. adv. com., Ray Daggs award 1998, Guyton Tchg. award 2002), Am. Acad. Arts and Scis., Am. Soc. Clin. Investigation, Physiol. Soc. Gt. Britain, Am. Thoracic Soc. (Edward Livingston Trudeau medal 2002), Assn. Am. Physicians, Am. Acad. Arts and Scis., Western Assn. Physicians, Russian Acad. Sci. (elected fgn. mem.), Explorers Club, Fleischner Soc. (pres. 1985), Harveian Soc. (London), Royal Instn. Gt. Britain, Royal Soc. Medicine (London), Hurlingham Club (London), La Jolla Beach & Tennis Club. Home: 9626 Blackgold Rd La Jolla CA 92037-1110 Office: U Calif San Diego Sch Medicine 0623 Dept Medicine La Jolla CA 92093

WEST, JOHN H(ENRY), III, clergyman, educator; b. Moorestown, N.J., 1954; s. John Henry Jr. and Gwendolyn (Clark) W.; m. Patricia Lynn Murray. BA in History, Lincoln (Pa.) U., 1976; MDiv, Pitts. Theol. Sem., 1979. Assoc. pastor Martin Luther King Jr. Meml. Bapt. Ch., Pitts., 1977-78, Cornerstone Bapt. Ch., Pitts., 1978-79; chaplain, intern John J. Kane Hosp., 1978-79; chaplain Lincoln U., 1979-94, instr. religion, 1981-84, asst. prof., 1984—, chair dept. religion, 1984—; pastor Siloam Bapt. Ch., Norristown, Pa., 1984—. Pres. West Inspirational Network, Lincoln Univ., 1988—. Bd. dirs. Downtown (Pa.) Indsl. and Agrl. Sch., 1989; bd. dirs., v.p. Lincoln Community Assn. Mem. Am. Bapt. Chs., U.S.A., Nat. Bapt. Chs., U.S.A., Inc., Oxford Area Ministerium, Ministeries to Blacks in Higher Edn., Soc. Bibl. Lit., So. Chester County NAACP. Democrat. Avocations: computers, sports, music, travel, reading. Home: 1223 Willow St Norristown PA 19401-3305

WEST, JOHN MERLE, retired physicist, nuclear consultant; b. Stilwell, Okla., Jan. 18, 1920; s. James M. and Maude B. (Bacon) W.; m. Navlion Farmer, Oct. 5, 1945; children: J. Cornel, L. Clark. BS in Phys. Sci. and Math. with highest honors, Northeastern State U., 1939; MS in Physics, U. Iowa, 1941. Physicist, supr. Du Pont Co., Carney's Point, N.J., 1941-42, Pryor, Okla., 1942-43, U. Chgo. Manhattan Project, 1943-44, Hanford Works Manhattan Project, 1944-46, GE, Hanford Works, Richland, Wash., 1946-49; asst. dir. reactor engring., project mgr. Argonne Nat. Lab., Lemont, Ill., 1949-57; exec. v.p. Gen. Nuclear Engring. Corp., Dunedin, Fla., 1957-65; v.p. nuclear activities Combustion Engring. Inc., Windsor, Conn., 1965-84; sr. v.p. Nuclear Combustion Engring. Inc., 1984-85. Nuclear cons., Cape Coral, Fla., 1985—. Contbr. numerous articles to profl. jours., papers at profl. meetings; holder numerous patents. Recipient Charles Coffin award GE, 1949. Fellow Am. Nuclear Soc. (charter mem., Walter Zinn award 1983); mem. NAE, Engrs. Club. Republican. Presbyterian. Home and Office: 1608 SE 40th Ter Cape Coral FL 33904-7467

WEST, JOHN THOMAS, retired surgeon; b. Live Oak, Fla., June 23, 1924; s. James Whitaker and Lelah Eulalia (Moore) W.; m. Ruth Marit Blakely, June 18, 1948; children: Phyllis Ann, Rebecca Ruth, James Carl, Jeffrey Moore, Paul Blakely. BS, U. Mich., 1946; MD, Vanderbilt U., 1951. Diplomate Am. Bd. Surgery. Commd. officer USPHS, 1951, advanced through grades to capt., 1963; rotating intern USPHS Hosp., Seattle, 1951-52; chief surgery USPHS Alaska Native Hosp., Anchorage, 1957-60, resident gen. surgery, 1954-57; chief surgery USPHS Hosp., Seattle, 1963-69, USPHS Indian Hosp., Phoenix, 1969-71; sr. investigator surg. br. Nat. Cancer Inst., USPHS, Bethesda, Md., 1960-63; ret., 1971; clin. assoc. prof. Tex. Tech U., Lubbock, 1974-77; pvt. practice La Grange, Ga., 1971-74, 77-94; ret., 1994. Mem. active staff West Ga. Med. Ctr., La Grange, 1971-74, 77-94. Bd. dirs. Ga. divsn. Am. Cancer Soc., 1972-77, 77-92. Recipient Meritorious Svc. medal USPHS, 1968. Fellow ACS, Soc. Surg. Oncology. Presbyterian. Achievements include report of facilitation of major hepatic resection by an innovation in the surgical exposure of the liver. Home: 134 Hickory Ln Lagrange GA 30240-8622 E-mail: jtwrbw@mindspring.com.

WEST, JOSEPH KING, judge; b. Yonkers, N.Y., Sept. 11, 1929; s. Ralph and Nellie (Brown) W.; m. Shirley Arvene Gray, July 3, 1954; children: Rebecca, Joseph K. BS, Howard U., Washington, 1952; JD, Bklyn. Law Sch., 1961. Bar: U.S. Supreme Ct. 1962, N.Y. 1962, U.S. Dist. Ct. (so. dist.) N.Y. 1974. Asst. corp. counsel City of Yonkers, N.Y., 1964-65; asst. dist. atty. Pros. Office, White Plains, 1965-82; city ct. judge Yonkers City Ct., 1983-84; county ct. judge Westchester Jud. Ct., White Plains, 1985-99; supervising judge Criminal Cts. 9th Jud. Dist. Dutchess, Orange, Putnam, Rockland and Westchester Counties, 1991-98; state supreme ct. justice State of New York, 1999—. Bd. dirs. St. Joseph's Med. Ctr.; adv. bd. Yonkers Big. Bros./Big Sisters. 1st lt. U.S. Army, 1952-56. Mem. Westchester County Bar Assn., Yonkers Lawyers Assn., Alpha Phi Alpha. Avocations: sports, walking, tennis, piano. Office: Westchester County Ct 111 Dr Martin Luther King Jr B White Plains NY 10601-2509

WEST, KENNETH EDWARD, lawyer; b. Phila., June 30, 1963; s. Edward Brown and Delores Ann (Brooks) W.; m. Cheryl Y. Tolerico; children: Jessie Marie, Brooks T., Jennifer Zevra. BS, Pa. State U., 1985; JD, Villanova U., 1988. Bar: Pa. 1988, U.S. Dist. Ct. (ea. dist.) Pa. 1990, U.S. Dist. Ct. N.J. 1988; lic. real estate agent, Pa. Assoc. Pachtman, Douglass & Assocs., Folsom, Pa., 1988-90; ptnr. Douglass, West & Riley, Drexel Hill, 1990-93, Douglass, West & Assocs., Drexel Hill, 1993—. Mem. bancruptcy conf. U.S. Dist. Ct. (ea. dist.) Pa. Mem. Pa. Trial Lawyers Assn., Del. County Bar Assn. Avocations: squash, raquetball. Office: Douglass West & Assocs 830 N Landsdowne Ave Drexel Hill PA 19026-1526 E-mail: kendwa@aol.com.

WEST, KENNETH D. economist, educator; b. Urbana, Ill., May 31, 1953; m. Lisa Vogel Vogel; children: Benjamin T., Hannah E. PhD in Econ., MIT, 1979. Sys. engr. Data Gen. Corp., Westboro, Mass., 1974—79; asst. prof. Princeton U., NJ, 1983—88; Ragnar Frisch prof. U. Wis., Madison, 1988—. Rsch. assoc. Nat. Bus. Econ. Rsch., Cambridge, 1993—. Co-editor: Am. Econ. Review, 1994—96, Jour. Money, Credit and Banking, 2001—. Fellow Alfred P. Sloan Rsch. fellow, Sloan Found., 1989. Fellow: Econometric Soc.; mem.: Am. Econ. Assn. Office: Univ Wis Dept Econ 1180 Observatory Dr Madison WI 53706 Office Fax: 608-262-2033. Business E-mail: kdwest@facstaff.wisc.edu.

WEST, KENNETH IRWIN, automotive executive; b. Aza Kuwae, Okinawa, Japan, July 1, 1966; (parents Am. citizens); s. Jackie Eugene and Ritsuko Maki West. Diploma in small engine repair, Foley-Belsaw Inst., Kansas City, Mo., 1983; A in Bus. and Auto/Diesel Tech., U. Northwestern Ohio, 1985; diploma in computer repair, Internat. Corr. Sch., 1991. Gen. mgr. Great Bear Auto Ctr., Huntington Beach , Calif., 1987—. Avocations: building models, computer programming, computer graphics, multiplayer online gaming, building high performance street cars.

WEST, LEE ROY, federal judge; b. Clayton, Okla., Nov. 26, 1929; s. Calvin and Nicie (Hill) W.; m. MaryAnn Ellis, Aug. 29, 1952; children: Kimberly Ellis, Jennifer Lee. BA, U. Okla., 1952, JD, 1956; LL.M. (Ford Found. fellow), Harvard U., 1963. Bar: Okla. 1956. Individual practice law, Ada, Okla., 1956-61, 63-65; faculty U. Okla. Coll. Law, 1961-62; Ford Found. fellow in law teaching Harvard U., Cambridge, Mass., 1962-63; judge 22d Jud. Dist. Okla., Ada, 1965-73; mem. CAB, Washington, 1973-78, acting chmn., 1977; practice law Tulsa, 1978-79; spl. justice Okla. Supreme Ct., 1965; judge U.S. Dist Ct. (we. dist.) Okla., 1979-94; sr. judge U.S. Dist. Ct. (we. dist.), Okla., 1994—. Editor: Okla. Law Rev. Served to capt. USMC, 1952-54. Recipient Humanitarian award Nat. Conf. Cmty. and Justice, 2000, Jud. Excellence award Okla. Bar Assn., 2000. Mem. U. Okla. Alumni Assn. (dir.), Phi Delta Phi (pres. 1956), Phi Eta Sigma, Order of Coif. Home: 6500 E Danforth Rd Edmond OK 73034-7601 Office: US Dist Ct 3001 US Courthouse 200 NW 4th St Oklahoma City OK 73102-3027

WEST, MACDONALD, real estate executive; b. Bournemouth, England, July 15, 1943; came to U.S., 1968; s. Joseph Stanley and Maisie Siswick (Hollom) W.; m. Charlotte Denise Duvall, Nov. 1, 1980. Diploma, London U. Coll. Estate Mgmt., 1968; MBA, Columbia U., 1970. Trainee surveyor Navy Works Dept., Admiralty, London, 1960-64; sr. assoc. Robinson & Roods, 1965-68; dir. cost control Nat. Liberty Corp., Valley Forge, Pa., 1970-71; v.p., dir. Philipsborn Cos., Coral Gables, Fla., 1972-76, Allen Morris Co., Miami, 1976-89; sr. v.p., chief oper. officer Allen Morris Constrn. Co., 1978-89, also sr. v.p. asset mgmt. divsn.; pres. Miami Lakes (Fla.) Devel., Inc., 1989-91; exec. v.p. The Graham Cos., Miami Lakes, 1989-91; pres., CEO The Macdonald West Co., Coral Gables, 1991—; mng. dir. The Allen Morris Co., 2000—. Deacon U. Bapt. Ch., Coral Gables, 1977—. Fellow Royal Instn. Chartered Surveyors; mem. Counselors Real Estate (pres. 1995), Nat. Assn. Realtors (chmn. 2001), Am. Arbitration Assn., Nat. Assn. Indsl. and Office Parks, Indsl. Assn. Dade County, Realtor Assn. Greater Miami (pres. 2000), Builders Assn. South Fla. (pres. 1996), Nat. Assn. Home Builders, Miami City Club, Ocean Reef Club, Rotary (Miami club). Republican. Home: 5325 Orduna Dr Coral Gables FL 33146-2640 Office: 1390 S Dixie Hwy Ste 2225 Miami FL 33146-2945 E-mail: macwest@bellsouth.net.

WEST, MARSHA, elementary school educator; b. DeQueen, Ark., Sept. 1, 1950; d. Marshall T. and Mildred L. (Davis) Gore; m. Larry T. West, May 19, 1972; 1 child, Zachary. BS in Edn., So. State Coll., Magnolia, Ark., 1971; MEd, U. Ark., 1975; postgrad., Henderson State Coll., Arkadelphia, Ark., Purdue U.; specialist's degree, U. Ga., 1991. Cert. elem. and spl. edn. tchr., Tex., elem. tchr., early childhood, mid. sch. tchr., media specialist, Ga. Spl. edn. resource tchr. Gatesville (Tex.) Ind. Sch. Dist.; tchr. early childhood spl. edn. Bryan (Tex.) Ind. Sch. Dist.; elem. tchr. Tippecanoe Sch. Corp., Lafayette, Ind., Clarke County Sch. Dist., Athens, Ga., media specialist. Mem. ALA, NEA, Am. Assn. Sch. Librs., Ga. Assn. Educators, Ga. Assn. Instrnl. Tech., Ga. Libr. Media Assn. (dist. V chair, pres.), Clarke County Assn. Educators, Kappa Delta Pi. Office: David C Barrow Elem Sch 100 Pinecrest Dr Athens GA 30605-1459

WEST, MICHAEL ALAN, retired hospital administrator; b. Waseca, Minn., Aug. 4, 1938; s. Ralph Lel and Elizabeth Mary (Brann) W.; m. Mary Thissen, Jan. 21, 1961; children— Anne, Nancy, Douglas. BA, U. Minn., 1961, MHA, 1963. Sales corr. Physicians and Hosps. Supply Co., Mpls., 1959-60; adminstrv. resident R.I. Hosp., Providence, 1962-63, adminstrv. asst., 1963-65, asst. dir., 1965-68; exec. asst. dir. Med. Center U. Mo., Columbia, 1968-70, assoc. dir., 1970-74, asst. prof. community health and med. practice, 1968-74; v.p. for adminstrn. Luth. Gen. Hosp., Park Ridge, Ill., 1974-80, exec. v.p., 1980-84; pres., CEO Akron Gen. Med. Ctr., Ohio, 1984-97, Akron Gen. Health Sys., 1997—2002. Bd. dirs. Vol. Hosps. Am. Inc.; chair VHA-Ctrl., Inc. Bd. dirs. Great Trails Coun. Boy Scouts Am. Mem. Am. Coll. Healthcare Execs., Akron Regional Hosp. Assn. (chmn.), Portage Country Club, Akron City Club, Catawba Island Club. Home: 495 Woodbury Dr Akron OH 44333-2780

WEST, MICHAEL DAVIDSON, English educator; b. Morristown, N.J., Apr. 13, 1937; s. David Haller and Isabel Emily (Smith) W.; m. Deborah Hall Green, June 17, 1961; 1 child, Alexandra. AB, Harvard U., 1959, AM, 1961, PhD, 1965. Teaching fellow Harvard U., Cambridge, Mass., 1961-64; instr. Wesleyan U., Middletown, Conn., 1964-65, asst. prof., 1965-72; instr. Middlesex Community Coll., 1967-68; assoc. prof. English U. Pitts., 1972-76, prof. English, 1976—. Fulbright lectr. U. Copenhagen. Author: Transcendental Wordplay: America's Romantic Punsters and the Search for the Language of Nature, 2000; contbr. articles to profl. jours. Sr. fellow Wesleyan Ctr. for Humanities, Middletown, 1970, Am. Coun. Learned Socs. fellow, N.Y., 1978-79, Peterson fellow Am. Antiquarian Soc., 1985, Huntington-NEH fellow Huntington Libr., 1985-86, Newberry Libr. fellow, 1985-86, hon. fellow Inst. Advanced Studies in the Humanities, U. Edinburgh, Scotland, 1987; recipient DeGolyer prize SW Rev. So. Meth. U., 1987, First prize Fraute O'Connor Essay Contes, 2002. Mem. MLA (tchg. award 1972), N.E. MLA (Ohio U. Press Book award 1999, Thirtieth Anniversary award 2000), Renaissance Soc. Am., Phi Beta Kappa (Christian Gauss award). Home: 416 Morewood Ave Pittsburgh PA 15213-1814 Office: U Pitts English Dept CL 526 Pittsburgh PA 15260 E-mail: mikewest@pitt.edu.

WEST, MICHAEL J. real estate developer, business owner; b. Asheville, N.C., Oct. 4, 1957; s. John H. West and Gail M. (Williams) Helton; m. Janice J. Hollifield, June 2, 1993. Student, Asheville-Buncombe Coll., Asheville, N.C., 1983, 93, Blue Ridge Coll., Hendersonville, N.C., 1988. Mgr. Mill End Carpets, Asheville, 1976-80; machining technologist Perfection Gear, 1983-97; real estate broker Fairview (N.C.) Realty, 1993-95; real estate developer Fletcher, N.C., 1996—; owner bus. software and pub. co. Westworld Unltd. Tax advisor Vol. Income Tax Assistance, A.B. Tech. Coll., 1994. Mem. Inst. Mgmt. Accts. Avocations: intellectual enlightenment, physical fitness, fly fishing. Home: PO Box 5753 Asheville NC 28813-5753 E-mail: westworld_unlimited@yahoo.com.

WEST, NANCY LEE, music educator, performance artist, entertainer; b. Evansville, Ind., Dec. 5, 1929; d. Harold Addison and Helen Beatrice (Roland) Hill; m. Owen L. West, Aug. 2, 1952; children: Gail Ann, Janet Lee, Robert Owen. BFA, Wesleyan U., Ill., 1952. Pvt. practice, Gibson City, Ill., 1952-57, Urbana, 1957-59, Buckhannon, W.Va., 1959-68, Eureka, Ill., 1968—; music tchr. Elliott (Ill.) Elem. Sch., 1953-54; piano soloist various events. hotels, restaurants in W.Va. and Ill., 1953—; dance orch. leader various parties, clubs, benefits, Ill., 1985—; piano accompanist various musical prodns., performances in W.Va. and Ill., 1953—. Cello player Symphony Orch., Bloomington, Ill., 1950-52. Mem. adv. bd. Ctrl. Ill. Youth Symphony, Peoria, 1969-78; mem. women's bd. Eureka Coll. Recipient Purchase award Walnut Grove Fine Arts Assn., Eureka, 1978, Best of Show award, Clarksburg, W.Va., 1966, One Person Show award Volkwein Music, Pitts., 1967; winner Grand prize Salem Coll., W.Va., 1965. Mem. Am. Coll. Musicians, Music Tchrs. Nat. Assn., Am. Fedn. Musicians, AAUW, Peoria Area Music Tchrs. Assn. Mem. Christian Ch. Avocations: sewing, crafts, reading, dancing. Home and Office: 810 N Main St Eureka IL 61530-9412

WEST, NETTIE J.R. music educator; b. Schoharie, N.Y., Oct. 12, 1925; d. Everett C. and Christina M. Maria (Youngs) Ruland; m. J. Russell Langwig, Sept. 11, 1948 (div. 1976); children: J. Russell, John Everett, Christina; m. Robert L. West, Oct. 8, 1983; stepchildren: Betsy, Katie, Laurel. BS, BM cum laude, Skidmore Coll., 1947; MA, U. Buffalo, 1968; cert. Suzuki tchg., Sch. for Strings, N.Y.C., 1983, Ithaca Coll., 1978-79. Music instr. Suzuki Sounds Violin Sch., Lagrangeville, N.Y., 1984—; orch. tchr. Hyde Park (N.Y.) H.S., 1983-84; Suzuki violin tchr. The Music Box, Poughkeepsie, 1997-99, Hudson Valley Philharm. Music Sch., Poughkeepsie, 1979-80; sub. tchr. Arlington Sch., Wappingers Dist., 1976-80; violinist Woodstock (N.Y.) Chamber Orch., 1983—. Attendee internat. confs. Suzuki Method, Matsumoto, Japan, 1983, 89, 99, Alberta Canada, 1985, Berlin, Germany, 1987, Adelaide, Australia, 1991, Dublin, Ireland, 1995. Mem. Religious Soc. Friends, Bulls-Head Oswego Meeting, 1980—, mem. worship group Green Haven Corr. Fac., 1980—; facilitator Alternatives to Violence Project, 1980—, coord. 1986-89; mem. Martha's Vineyard Hist. Assn. Mem. Suzuki Assn. Am., Inc., Music Educators Nat. Conf., N.Y. State Sch. Music Assn., Lagoon Pond Assn. Inc. of Martha's Vineyard. Avocations: swimming, skiing, bird watching, reading, attending concerts.

WEST, NORMAN ELLSWORTH, artist; b. Exeter, N.H., May 16, 1952; s. Norman Ellsworth and Alice Marie West. BS, Plymouth State Coll., 1976; BFA, Maine Coll. of Art, 1980. Leader color workshops regional schs., York County, 1981—; artist in residence Holderness Acad., Plymouth, N.H., 1989-91; set designer Shenanigans Prodns., Portland, Boston, 1993-96; tchr. Heartwood Coll. of Art, Kennebunk, Maine, 1994—. Dir. Heartwood Coll. Art Gallery, 2002. One person shows include West Kuhn Gallery, Cape Neddick, Maine, 1988, Van Ward Gallery, Ogunquit, Maine, 1994, 98; group shows include Currier Gallery, Manchester, N.H., 1988, 89, Barn Gallery, Ogunquit, 1988, Mast Core Galleries, Kennebunkport, Maine, 1988, 89, Ogunquit Art Assn., 1988—, Maine Coast Artists, Rockport, Maine, 1989, 90. Bd. dirs. Shellfish Commn., Ogunquit, Maine, 1996—; clam warden Town of Ogunquit, 1997-99. Mem. Ogunquit Art Assn. (curator invited sculptor's exhibit 1996—), Ogunquit Arts Collaborative (v.p. 2000—), Ogunquit Rotary Club. Home: PO Box 1560 Ogunquit ME 03907

WEST, PAUL NODEN, author; b. Eckington, Derbyshire, Eng., Feb. 23, 1930; came to U.S., 1961, naturalized, 1971; s. Alfred Massick and Mildred (Noden) W. Student, Oxford U., 1950-53; MA, Columbia U., 1953. Asst. prof. English Meml. U. Nfld., Can., 1957-58, assoc. prof., 1958-60; faculty Pa. State U., 1962-95, prof. English and comparative lit., 1968-95; prof. emeritus, 1995—. Crawshaw prof. Colgate U., 1972; Melvin Hill disting. vis. prof. Hobart and William Smith Colls., 1973; vis. English prof. Cornell U., 1986; disting. writer in residence Wichita State U., 1982; vis. prof. English Brown U., 1992; fiction judge Creative Artists Pub. Svc. Program, N.Y.C., 1974, 81; writer-in-residence U. Ariz., 1984; judge Katherine Ann Porter Prize for Fiction, 1984, Artists Found. Author: Byron and the Spoiler's Art, 1960, rev. edit., 1990, I Said the Sparrow, 1963, The Snow Leopard, 1965, Tenement of Clay, 1965, The Wine of Absurdity, 1966, Alley Jaggers, 1967, I'm Expecting to Live Quite Soon, 1970, Words for a Deaf Daughter, 1970, Caliban's Filibuster, 1972, Colonel Mint, 1973, Gala, 1976, The Very Rich Hours of Count von Stauffenberg, 1980, Out of My Depths: A Swimmer in the Universe, 1983, Rat Man of Paris, 1986, Sheer Fiction, 1987, The Universe and Other Fiction, 1988, The Place in Flowers Where Pollen Rests, 1988, Lord Byron's Doctor, 1989, Portable People, The Women of Whitechapel and Jack the Ripper, 1991, Sheer Fiction: II, 1991, James Ensor, 1991, Love's Mansion, 1992, Tenement of Clay, 2d edit., 1993, Sheer Fiction, III, 1994, A Stroke of Genius, 1995, The Tent of Orange Mist, 1995 (memoir) My Mother's Music, 1996 (novel) Sporting with Amaryllis, 1996, Terrestrials, 1997, Life With Swan, 1999, O.K.: The Corral, The Earps, and Doc Holliday, 2000, The Dry Danube: A Hitler Forgery, 2000, The Secret Lives of Words, 2000, A Fifth of November, 2001, Master Class, 2001, Oxford Days, 2002, Cheops: A Cupboard for the Sun, 2002; contbr. Washington Post and N.Y. Times, 1962—, Harper's Mag., Paris Rev., Yale Rev., Parnassus, Agni, Conjunctions, War, Literature and the Arts, First Intensity, Tin Roof; fiction judge N.Y. Found. for the Arts, Nat. Book award, 1990. Served with RAF, 1954-57. Decorated Chevalier de l'Ordre des Arts et des Lettres (France); recipient Aga Khan Fiction prize, 1973, Hazlett Meml. award for Excellence in Arts (lit.), 1981, Lit. award Am. Acad. and Inst. Arts and Letters, 1985, Pushcart prize 1987, 91, The Best Am. Essays award, 1990, Outstanding Achievement medal Pa. State U., 1991, Grand Prix Halpérine Kaminsky award, 1992, Lannan Fiction award, 1993, Tchg. award Northeastern Assn. Grad. Schs., 1994, Art of Fact prize SUNY, 2000; named Lit. Lion N.Y. Pub. Libr., 1987; Guggenheim fellow, 1963; NEA Creative Writing fellow, 1979, 84; nominated for Médicis, Femina and Meilleur Livre Étranger prizes, France, 1991, Lannan Lit. Videos 35, Nat. Book Critics award for fiction, 1996; named to Honor Roll The Yr. in Fiction, DLB Yearbook, 1996. Office: Elaine Markson Agy 44 Greenwich Ave Fl 3 New York NY 10011-8389 *The unexamined life may not be worth having, but the examined life is endurable only to an open mind, through which life historically flows, keeping that mind as incomplete as our knowledge of the universe itself.*

WEST, RALPH LELAND, veterinarian; b. Grand Rapids, Minn., Apr. 23, 1915; s. Ralph Leland and Elsie (Wardall) W.; m. Mary Elizabeth Brann, June 14, 1937; children: Michael Alan, Janet Lee West Friedrich, Thomas James. DVM, Iowa State U., 1936; MS, Purdue U., 1972. Pvt. practice, Waseca, Minn., 1936-42, 46-70; grad. asst. Sch. Vet. Medicine Purdue U., West Lafayette, Ind., 1970-72; asst. dir. sci. activities Am. Vet. Med. Assn., Schaumburg, Ill., 1972-77, dir. sci. activities, 1977-87. Contbr. articles to jours. in field. Mem. Pk. Bd., Waseca, 1948-50, Youth Commn., 1948-52; mem., chmn. Waseca Hosp. Bd., 1954-64; trustee Sunny Acres Village Inc., Denver, 1988-95. Maj. U.S. Army, 1942-46, ETO. Recipient Stange award Iowa State U., 1983. Mem. AMVA (award 1990), Am. Assn. Ret. Vets. (dir. 1987-90), Am. Vet. History Soc., Colo. Vet. Med. Assn., Minn. Vet. Med. Assn., Iowa State U. Vet. Alumni Assn., Phi Zeta. Republican. Avocations: reading, TV sports, stock market. Home: 1719 E Bijou St Apt 611 Colorado Springs CO 80909-5751 E-mail: WDrwest1@aol.com.

WEST, REXFORD LEON, retired banker; b. Syracuse, N.Y., Feb. 18, 1938; s. Rexford A. and Nina (Crysler) W.; m. Grace Carlile, Apr. 24, 1999; children from previous marriage: Lisa, Julie, Gregory, Kristen. AAS, Auburn C.C., N.Y., 1957; BS magna cum laude, Syracuse U., N.Y., 1972; Advanced Mgmt. Program, Harvard Bus. Sch., Boston, 1984. Accountant Marine Midland Bank, Syracuse, N.Y., 1959-67, v.p., asst. treas., 1967-72; v.p., contr. Marine Midland Services Corp., Buffalo, 1972-76; v.p. ops. divsn. Marine Midland Bank, N.A., 1976-77, sr. v.p., sr. ops. officer, 1977-79, exec. v.p., sr. ops. officer, 1979-85, divsn. exec. ops., 1985-87, sector exec. ops. and fin. mgmt., 1987-90, sr. exec. v.p. corp. engring., 1990-92; exec. v.p. adminstrv. svc. Fleet Bank, Melville, 1992-94; exec. v.p. loan servicing Fleet Mortgage Group, Columbia, S.C., 1994-96; ret., 1996. Served with U.S. Army, 1957-61

WEST, RICHARD VINCENT, art museum director; b. Prague, Czechoslovakia, Nov. 26, 1934; came to U.S., 1938, naturalized, 1947; s. Jan Josef and Katherine Frieda (Mayer) Vyslouzil; 1 child, Jessica Katherine Student, UCLA, 1952-55, Music Acad. of the West, 1958-60; BA with highest honors, U. Calif., Santa Barbara, 1961; postgrad., Akademie der Bildenden Kuenste, Vienna, 1961-62, Hochschule fur Musik und darstellende Kuenste, 1961-62; MA, U. Calif., Berkeley, 1965. Curatorial intern Cleve. Art Mus., 1965-66, Albright-Knox Art Gallery, Buffalo, 1966-67; curator Mus. Art Bowdoin Coll., Brunswick, Maine, 1967—72; dir. Crocker Art Mus., Sacramento, 1973-82, Santa Barbara Mus. Art, 1983-91; pres. Artmuse Assocs., Benicia, 1991-92; dir. Newport (R.I.) Art Mus., 1992-94, Frye Art Mus., Seattle, 1995—. Mem. Joint Yugoslav-Am. Excavations at Sirmium, 1971; bd. dirs. Sacramento Regional Art Coun., 1973-77; bd. overseers Strawbery Banke, 1993-99. Author: Painters of the Section d'Or, 1967, Language of the Print, 1968; The Walker Art Building Murals, 1972, Munich and American Realism in the 19th Cen., 1978, An Enkindled Eye: The Paintings of Rockwell Kent, 1985, Standing in the Tempest: Painters of the Hungarian Avant-Garde, 1991, America in Art, 1991, A Significant Story: American Painting and Decorative Arts from the Karolik Collection, 1993; editor: Contemporary American Marine Art, 1997, Circle of Lyon: 7 French Painters of Reality, 1998, Children of the Yellow Kid: The Evolution of the American Comic Strip, 1998, Carlo Maria Mariani: The Mysterious Enchantment of Beauty, 1999, This Tranquil Land: Hudson River Paintings from the Herson Collection, 2000, Winold Reiss: Native American Portraits, 2000, Graham Nickson: Dual Natures, 2000, Representing LA: Pictorial Currents in Southern California Art, 2001, The Perception of Appearance, 2002; exhbn. catalogues, also various revs. and articles. Founding mem. New England Community Mus. Consortium; active USCG Aux., 1989—. Served with USN, 1956-57. Ford Found. fellow, 1965-67; Smithsonian fellow, 1971 Mem. Assn. Art Mus. Dirs., Am. Assn. Mus., Coll. Art Assn., Internat. Coun. Mus., Western Assn. Art Mus. (pres. 1975-78), Calif. Assn. Mus. (bd. dirs. 1980-82, v.p. 1986-91), Newport Reading Rm., Rotary, Rainier Club. Office: Frye Art Mus 704 Terry Ave Seattle WA 98104-2019

WEST, ROBERT GRADY, lawyer; b. Dallas, Aug. 13, 1947; s. Robert Sorrells and Thelma Grady W.; m. Marsha Lee Riegert, June 5, 1971; children: Kathryn Lee, Laura Elaine. BA, Midwestern State U., 1969; JD, U. Tex., 1972. Bar: Tex. 1972, U.S. Dist. Ct. (no. dist.) Tex. 1975, U.S. Dist. Ct. (ea. dist.) Tex. 1992, U.S. Ct. Appeals (5th cir.) 1976. Assoc. McGown, Godfrey, Decker, McMackin, Shipman & McClane, Ft. Worth, 1972-77, ptnr., 1977-88, Decker, McMackin & McClane, Ft. Worth, 1988-90, Decker, Jones, McMackin, McClane, Hall & Bates, Ft. Worth, 1990-93; assoc. Michener, Larimore, Swindle, Whitaker, et al, 1993-98, ptnr., 1999-2000, Whitaker, Chalk, Swindle & Sawyer, 2000—. Bd. regents Midwestern State U., Wichita Falls, Tex., 1992-98; dir. Grace Found., Dallas, 1990-92; mem. Tex. Ctr. Legal Ethics & Professionalism, 1994—, Leadership Ft. Worth, 1984. Mem. Am. Assn. Profl. Landmen, State Bar Tex., Tarrant County Bar Assn. Presbyterian. Avocations: travel, musical theatre, walking, volunteering. Office: Whitaker Chalk Swindle & Sawyer 3500 City Ctr Tower II 301 Commerce St Fort Worth TX 76102-4186 E-mail: rwest@whitakerchalk.com.

WEST, ROBERT LEE , JR. marketing professional; b. Wilmington, N.C., Oct. 5, 1958; s. Robert L. Sr. and Elsie S. (Skipper) W.; m. Shari H., Aug. 1, 1998. BSBA, U. N.C., Pembroke, 1981; postgrad., U. Pa., 1988—90. Divsn. controller Royster Co., Norfolk, Va., 1982-84; regional fin. mgr. Rohm & Haas Co., Phila., 1984-86; head Asian ops. Franklin Mint, Hone Kong, 1986-88, head corp. cost improvement Phila., 1988-89, head European ops. London, 1989-90; v.p. fin. & ops. Paradise Galleries, Inc., San Diego, 1990-91; v.p., chief fin. officer Georgetown Collection, Inc., Portland, Maine, 1992-95; v.p. worldwide ops. Nat. Media Corp., Phoenix, 1995-97; pres., founder DCA Internat., 1990—; CEO, pres. Georgetown Collection, Inc., Portland, Maine, 1997-98; chief oper. officer, pres. LL Knickerbocker, Lake Forest, Calif., 1998-99; v.p., gen. mgr. Chevrolet Catalog, San Diego, 1999—. Cons. to CEO J Crew, N.Y.C., 1990-91. V.p. Maxton (N.C.) Conservative Response, 1980-82; lay leader Good Shepherd Luth. Ch., Irvine, Calif. Named one of Top Exec. Leading Direct Mktg., Phila. Inquirer Mag. Mem. Am. Mgmt. Assn., Am. Fin. Assn., Inst. Mgmt. Accts., World Affairs Coun. Republican. Avocations: biking, church activities, model railroading, tennis, long distance running. Office: DCA Dynamic Cons Assocs Ste 300 4 Venture Irvine CA 92618 Address: 26741 Portola Pkwy Ste 1E Box 130 Foothill Ranch CA 92610

WEST, ROBERT MACLELLAN, science education consultant; b. Appleton, Wis., Sept. 1, 1942; s. Clarence John and Elizabeth Ophelia (Moore) W.; m. Jean Sydow, June 19, 1965; 1 child, Christopher. BA, Lawrence Coll., 1963; SM, U. Chgo., 1964, PhD, 1968. Rsch. assoc. Princeton (N.J.) U., 1968-69; asst. prof. Adelphi U., Garden City, N.Y., 1969-74; curator of geology Milw. Pub. Mus., 1974-83; dir. Carnegie Mus. Natural History, Pitts., 1983-87, Cranbrook Inst. Sci., Bloomfield Hills, Mich., 1987-91; prin. RMW Sci. Action, Washington, 1992-95; pres. Informal Sci., Inc., 1993-98, Informal Learning Experiences, Inc., Washington, 1999—. Adj. prof. U. Wis., Milw., 1974-83; com. mem. Indo-U.S. Subcom., 1990-96. Contbr. articles to profl. jours. Bd. dirs. Friends of the New Zoo, Pitts., 1984-87; treas. East Mich. Environ. Action Coun., Birmingham, Mich., 1987-92. Recipient Arnold Guyot prize Nat. Geographic Soc., 1982; named Man of Yr. in Sci. by Vectors Pitts., 1988; NSF fellow, 1965-68, NSF rsch. grantee, 1970-82, Nat. Geographic Soc. rsch. grantee, 1973, 76, 77, 79, 80, 82. Mem. Nat. Ctr. Sci. Edn. (bd. dirs. 1984-88, 92—), Nepal Natural History Soc. (advisor 1992—), Soc. Vertebrate Paleontology, Geol. Soc. Am., Paleontology Soc., The Mus. Group, Am. Assn. Mus., Rotary. Avocations: nature, history, sports. Office: Informal Learning Experiences Inc PO Box 42328 Washington DC 20015-0928 E-mail: ile@informallearning.com.

WEST, ROBERT VAN OSDELL, JR. retired petroleum executive; b. Kansas City, Mo., Apr. 29, 1921; s. Robert Van Osdell and Josephine (Quistgaard) W.; divorced; children: Robert Van Osdell III, Kathryn Anne, Suzanne Small, Patricia Lynn; m. Helen L. Boecking, 1978. BS, U. Tex., 1942, MS, 1943, PhD, 1949. Registered profl engr., Tex. Petroleum engr. Slick Urschel Oil Co., 1949-56; pres. Slick Secondary Recovery Corp., 1956-59; v.p. Texstar Corp., 1959; pres. Texstar Petroleum Co. subs. Texstar Corp., 1959-64; founder Tesoro Petroleum Corp., San Antonio, 1964, chmn. bd. dirs., chief exec. officer, 1971-88, chmn. bd., 1989-92, chief exec. officer, 1964-92; retired. Bd. dirs. Frost Nat. Bank. Mem. engring. found. adv. coun. U. Tex., mem. at large and life Centennial Commn.; former bd. visitors McDonald Obs. and Astronomy; mem. devel. bd. U. Tex. San Antonio Health Sci. Ctr.; assoc. mem. bd. visitors U. Tex. M.D. Anderson Cancer Ctr., Houston; Trinity U. Assoc., San Antonio; mem. adv. coun., trustee St. Mary's U. Sch. Bus.; past trustee San Antonio City Public Service Bd.; trustee S.W. Research Inst.; past chmn. San Antonio Econ. Devel. Found.; bd. dirs. World Affairs Council, San Antonio; chmn. St. Luke's Luth. Hosp. Found., San Antonio; emeritus chmn. bd. trustees San Antonio Symphony; founder, former chmn. bd. dirs. Tiwanaku Archaeol. Found., Bolivia.; founder, former chmn. exec. com. Caribbean/L.Am. Action, Washington; trustee Ams. Soc. N.Y.; chmn. gen. campaign United Way of San Antonio and Bexar County, 1986, vice chmn. bd. trustees, 1988—; chmn. pub. sector campaign subcom. United Way of Am., 1988—. Named Disting. Grad., U. Tex. Coll. Engring., 1973; recipient People of Vision award Nat. Soc. Prevention of Blindness, 1982, Internat. Citizens award World Affairs Coun., 1986, Good Scout award Boy Scouts Am., 1987, Alexis de Tocqueville award United Way of San Antonio and Bexar County, 1990. Mem. Ind. Petroleum Assn. Am., Soc. Petroleum Engrs. (past chmn. San Antonio-Austin chpt.), 25 Yr. Club Petroleum Industry, Pvt. Enterprise Edn. (Herman W. Lay Meml. award 1986), Am.'s Soc., All-Am. Wildcatters Club, Sigma Chi (Significant Sig award 1979). Episcopalian. Office: 1250 NE Loop 410 Ste 805 San Antonio TX 78209-1533

WEST, ROBERTA BERTHA, writer; b. Saline County, Mo., Sept. 7, 1904; d. Robert and Amanda Melvina (Driver) Baur; m. Harold Clinton West, Aug. 27, 1932; children: Arle Faith W. Lohof, Lydia Ann (Lydia) F H. Hyde, Danna Rose F H. Burns. AB, William Jewell Coll., 1928; AM, U. Mo., 1930. Cert. tchr., Mo., Mont. Elem. and secondary sch. tchr. Mo. and Mont. Schs., 1922-47; supt. schs. Hogeland (Mont.) Schs., 1947-48, 55; prof. fgn. langs. Will Mayfield Coll., Marble Hill, Mo., 1930; columnist Quad County Star, Viburnum, 1982—; writer and researcher ch. history, 1964-91. Cons. hist. com. Yellowstone Conf. Meth. Ch., 1971-84; compiler Mont. list of Meth. Mins. 1784-1984. Author: Northern Montana Methodist History, 3 vols., 1974, Faith, Hope and Love in the West, 1971; editor: Brother Van by Those Who Knew Him, 1975, reprinted, 1989,; also contbr. articles. Recipient 1st John M. Templeton prize, 1959, Wedgwood Jasper Plate 70th Anniversary of Class of 1927 Wm. Jewell Coll., 1997. Mem. Alpha Zeta Pi. Democrat. Avocation: crocheting. Home: PO Box 583 Viburnum MO 65566-0583 Office: Quad County Star Viburnum MO 65566

WEST, STEPHEN ALLAN, lawyer; b. Salt Lake City, Mar. 23, 1935; s. Allan Morrell and Ferne (Page) W.; m. Martha Sears, Mar. 21, 1960; children: Stephen Allan, Jr., Page, Adam. JD, U. Utah, 1961, BS in Philosophy, 1962. Law clk. to judge U.S. Dist. Ct., Utah, 1961-62; assoc. Marr, Wilkins & Cannon, Salt Lake City, 1962-65, ptnr., 1965-67; atty. Jennings, Strouss, Salmon & Trask, Washington, 1967-68, Marriott Corp., Washington, 1968-71, asst. gen. counsel, 1971-74, v.p. and assoc. gen. counsel, 1974-87, v.p. and dep. gen. counsel, 1987-93; sr. v.p., gen. counsel Marriott Internat., Inc., 1993-94; pres. Tex. San Antonio mission Ch. of Jesus Christ of Latter-day Saints, 1995-98, Gen. Authority, 1998—. Mem. exec. bd. Interfaith Conf. Met. Washington, 1989-93, vice chmn., 1992-93; mem. exec. bd. Christa McAuliffe Inst. Task Force of Nat. Found. for Improvement Edn. Mem. ABA (exec. coun. young lawyers sect. 1964-65), Utah Bar Assn. (exec. com. young lawyers sect. 1962-67), D.C. Bar Assn., Utah Profl. Rels. Com., U. Utah Alumni Assn. (Disting. Alumni award 1971), Skull and Bones, Owl and Key, Phi Delta Phi, Sigma Chi. Office: Ch Jesus Christ Latter-day Saints 47 E South Temple Salt Lake City UT 84150-1700 Home: 1117 Fox Farm Rd Logan UT 84321-4807

WEST, SYNTHA JANE TRAUGHBAR, mental health services professional; b. Gladewater, Tex., Oct. 22, 1938; d. Jimmy J. and Virginia Lavon (Wood) Traughber; m. Royce Glen West; children: Rock David, Royal Jim. BA, Baylor U., 1961; MEd, Tex. A&M U., 1965, PhD, 1971. Lic. profl. counselor, marriage and family therapist, cert. counselor, expert in traumatic stress and bereavement trauma. Adj. asst. prof. East Tex. State U., Commerce, 1975—76; lead H.S. counselor Longview (Tex.) Ind. Sch. Dist., 1975—77; head H.S. counselor Marshall (Tex.) Ind. Sch. Dist., 1977—80; counselor Tyler Jr. Coll., 1992; mid. and H.S. counselor Winona (Tex.) Ind. Sch. Dist., 1980—97; mental health therapist Walker & Assocs., Tyler, 1997—98, Andrews Ctr., Tyler, 1998—99. Dir. guidance Brewer H.S., White Settlement, Tex., 1971—75, Kerens (Tex.) Ind. Sch. Dist., Kerens, 1966—69, Rains Ind. Schs. Dist., Emory, Tex., 1966; spkr. in field. Author: Today's Dreams, Tomorrow's Realities, 2001, (poetry) Poetry Gems 2000, 2001, America at the Millennium, 2000. Pianist, asst. First Bapt. Ch., Owentown, Tex., 2000—; bd. dirs. Gladewater (Tex.) Former Students, 1997—. Nominee Tex. Women's Hall of Fame, 1999, 2000; named Ms. Congeniality, Ms. Tex. Sr. Pageant, 2000, Ms. Tex. Sr., 2001. Mem.: Tex. Ret. Sch. Pers., Piney Woods Counseling Assn., Tex. Counseling Assn., Sheriff's Assn. Tex. Avocations: dancing, twirling batons, patriotic flag routing, piano. Home: 12446 Chapman Rd Tyler TX 75708-3210

WEST, TERENCE DOUGLAS, furniture company design executive; b. Twin Falls, Idaho, Sept. 12, 1948; s. Clark Ernest and Elsie Erma (Kulm) W. BS, San Jose State U., 1971. Indsl. designer Clement Labs., Palo Alto, Calif., 1970-74, U.S. Govt., Washington, 1974-78; dist. mgr., arch., designer programs Steelcase, 1978-82, nat. mgr., arch., designer program, 1982-84, dir. indsl. design, 1984-96; dir. product devel. Steelcase Japan Ltd., 1992-94, Steelcase Asia Pacific Ltd., 1994-95; dir. market planning Steelcase Inc., 1995-97, dir. corp. strategy and devel., 1997-2000, dir. advanced concepts, R&D Europe, 2000—. Guest lectr. San Jose State U., 1988, Lehigh U., 1988, Art Ctr. Coll. Design, Pasadena, Calif., 1989, Kendall Coll. of Design, 1990, Waseda U. Tokyo, 1994; Devos lectr., Grand Rapids, Mich., 1990; guest spkr.

Mfg. Sys. Engring. for 21st Century Conf., 1989, Internat. Facilities Mgmt. Assn. Conf., 1989, Internat. Facilities Exec. Conf., 1991; mem. bd. advisors Art Ctr. Coll. Design, Pasadena, 1990—; design jurist Women's Archtl. League Portland, Oreg. Sch. Design, Portland chpt. AIA, 1979, Internat. Design Ann. Rev., 1991, Internat. Design mag., 1991. Contbr.: Behaviour and Information Technology, 1987; also articles and designs to profl. jours.; patentee sensor seating. Mem. com. San Jose Urban Coalition, 1971-72; mem. Mayor's Com. for Commemorative Sculpture, Grand Rapids, 1990-95; mem. bldg. com. Grand Rapids Art Mus. Fulbright fellow on design and design edn.; recipient numerous group design awards. Mem. Am. Ctr. For Design, Indsl. Designers Soc. Am. (guest spkr. Denver 1991), Design Mgmt. Inst. Democrat. Lutheran. Home: 9655 Ravine Rdg SE Caledonia MI 49316-8243 Office: PO Box 1967 Grand Rapids MI 49501-1967

WEST, THOMAS LOWELL, JR. insurance company executive; b. Cedar Bluff, Va., June 7, 1937; s. Thomas Lowell and Kathleen West; m. Katharine Thompson, Feb. 13, 1960; children: Thomas Lowell III, John Gardner, Katharine Covington. BS in Indsl. Engring., U. Tenn., 1959. CLU, 1967; chartered fin. cons., 1987. Asst. supr. Aetna Life Ins. Co., Memphis, 1960-62, supr., 1962-67, asst. gen. agt., 1967-69, gen. agt. Jackson, Miss., 1969-80; regional v.p. Aetna Life & Casualty, Hartford, Conn., 1980-85; v.p. Aetna Life Ins. and Annuity Co., 1985-88, sr. v.p. exec. com. and investment com., 1988-94, also bd. dirs. V.p. Aetna Fin. Services, Hartford, 1986-87; pres., bd. dirs. Structured Benefits, Inc., Hartford, 1985-94, Systemized Benefits Adminstrn., Inc., SBFI, 1988; pres., dir. exec. com., mgmt. com., investment com. The Variable Annuity Life Ins. Co., 1994-98; chmn., CEO, dir. Am. Gen. Retirement Svcs., vice chmn. Am. Gen. Corp., 1998; VALIC and Am. Gen. Annunity Ins. Co.; exec. v.p., dir. Am. Gen. Series Portfolio Co.; mem. bd. dirs. Houston Symphony; pres., CEO Variable Annuity Mktg. Co.; chmn., pres., CEO Am. Gen. Fund Group; bd. dirs. Info-One, Walker West Worldwide, Intermark Lang. Svcs.; mem. adv. bd. Salvage.sale.com, annuityscout-.com; pres., CEO Pocket Techs.; chmn., CEO Walker West Worldwide, Inc., 2000-. Named to Hall of Fame, Jackson Assn. Life Underwriters, 1977. Mem. Soc. Fin. Svc. Profls., Am. Soc. Pension Actuaries (assoc.), Assn. for Advanced Life Underwriters (assoc.), Nat. Assn. Ins. and Fin. Advisors, Nat. Assn. for Variable Annuities (bd. dirs., chmn.), Investment Co. Inst. (bd. govs.), Fin. Planning Assn. Republican. Presbyterian. Avocations: tennis, running, E-type Jaguars, Mercedes Benz. Home: 2120 Brentwood Dr Houston TX 77019-3512 E-mail: twestjr@aol.com.

WEST, TOGO DENNIS, JR. lawyer, former cabinet member, former aerospace executive; b. Winston-Salem, N.C., June 21, 1942; s. Togo Dennis and Evelyn (Carter) W.; m. Gail Estelle Berry, June 18, 1966; children: Tiffany Berry, Hilary Carter. BSEE, Howard U., 1965, JD cum laude, 1968; LLD (hon.), Winston-Salem U., 1996, Gannon U., 1998. Bar: D.C. 1968, N.Y. 1969, U.S. Ct. Mil. Appeals 1969, U.S. Supreme Ct. 1978, U.S. Ct. Claims 1981. Elec. engr. Duquesne Light and Power Co., 1965; patent researcher Sughrue, Rothwell, Mion, Zinn and McPeak, 1966-67; legal intern U.S. EEOC, 1967; law clk. firm Covington & Burling, Washington, 1967-68, summer assoc., 1968, assoc., 1973-75, 76-77; law clk. to Judge Tyler U.S. Dist. Ct. for So. Dist. N.Y., 1968-69; assoc. dep. atty. gen. U.S. Dept. Justice, Washington, 1975-76; gen. counsel Dept. Navy, 1977-79; spl. asst. to sec. and dep. sec. Dept. Def., 1979-80, gen. counsel, 1980-81; ptnr. Patterson, Belknap, Webb & Tyler, 1981-90; sr. v.p. govt. rels. Northrop Corp., 1990-93; sec. of Army, 1993-98; chair Panama Canal Commn., 1997; sec. U.S. Dept. of Veterans Affairs, Washington, 1998—. Adj. prof. Duke U. Sch. Law, 1980-81; bd. cons. Riggs Nat. Bank, Washington, 1990-93; bd. dirs. Krispy Kreme Doughnuts, Inc., Bowater, Inc., Washington Hosp. Ctr.; bd. trustees Mitretek Sys., Inc., 2001—. Mng. editor: Howard Law Jour, 1968. Commr. D.C. Law Rev. Comm., 1982-89, chmn., 1985-89; mem. Nat. Council of Friends of John F. Kennedy Ctr. for Performing Arts, 1984-91, treas., 1987-91; bd. govs. Antioch U. Sch. Law, 1983-87, vice chmn., 1986-87; bd. visitors Wake Forest U. Sch. Law, 1991-94; chmn. Greater Washington Bd. Trade, legis. bur., 1987-89, bd. dirs., 1987-93, mem. exec. com. 1987-92; mem. fed. legis. com., 1990-93; chmn. Kennedy Ctr. Community and Friends Bd., 1991-2001; mem. Washington Lawyers' Com. Civil Rights Under Law, 1987-93, D.C. Com. on Pub. Edn., 1988-93, chmn., 1990-91; trustee The Aerospace Corp., 1983-90, Ctr. for Strategic and Internat. Studies, 1987-90, Nat. Lawyers Com. for Civil Rights Under Law, 1987-93, Inst. for Def. Analyses, 1989-91, Protestant Episcopal Cathedral Found., 1989-95, Shakespeare Theatre at The Folger, 1990-93, N.C. Sch. Arts, 1990—, Aerospace Edn. Found. of Air Force Assn., 1991-93; bd. dirs. D.C. Law Students in Ct. Program, 1986-92, World Affairs Coun., 1991-93, 2000—, Atlantic Coun., 1991-93, 2000—; mem. fin. com. Episcopal Diocese of Washington, 1989—, mem. standing com., 1990-92; sr. warden St. John's Ch., Lafayette Sq.; mem. Coun. Fgn. Rels., 1996—; chmn. trustee coun. YMCA Metro. Wash., 1990-92; mem. nat. adv. com. UN Assn. USA, 1991-93; D.C. Ct. Appeals Admissions Com., 1990-93; bd. trustees Assn. of U.S. Army, 2001—. Served to capt. Judge Adv. Gen. Corps U.S. Army, 1969-73. Decorated Legion of Merit; recipient Disting. Pub. Svc. medal Dept. Def., 1981, Eagle Scout award with Bronze Palm Boy Scouts Am., 1957, Disting. Eagle Scout award 1995, Svc. to Howard U. award, 1965., Meritorious Svc. medal, Medal of Merit, Brazil, Disting. Civil Svc. medal, 1998, Dept. Vet. Affairs, 2000. Mem. ABA, Nat. Bar Assn., Washington Coun. Lawyers (dir. 1973-75), Sigma Pi Phi, Phi Alpha Delta, Omega Psi Psi, Alpha Phi Omega. Clubs: Metropolitan, University (Washington). Office: Covington & Burling 1201 Pennsylvania Ave NW Washington DC 20004

WEST, W. RICHARD, museum director; b. San Bernardino, Calif., Jan. 6, 1943; s. W. Richard Sr. and Maribelle (McCrea) W.; m. Mary Beth Braden, June 29, 1968; children: Amy Elizabeth, Benjamin Braden. BA magna cum laude in Am. History, U. Redlands, 1965; AM in Am. History, Harvard U., 1968; JD, Stanford U., 1971; LHD (hon.), Bacone Coll., 1992, Ottawa U., 1994, U. Okla., 1995. Bar: Calif., D.C., U.S. Ct. Appeals (8th cir.), U.S. Supreme Ct. Clk. to Hon. Benjamin C. Duniway U.S. Ct. Appeals (9th cir.), 1971-72; assoc. Fried, Frank, Harris, Shriver & Jacobson, Washington, 1973-79, ptnr., 1979-88; dir. direct support component Am. Indian Lawyer Tng. Program, Inc., 1976-77; ptnr. Gover, Stetson Williams & West P.C., Albuquerque, 1988-90; founding dir. Smithsonian Instn's Nat. Mus. Am. Indian, Washington, 1990—. Treas. Am. Indian Lawyer Tng. Program, Inc., 1973—; adj. prof. Indian law Stanford U., 1977. Mem. edit. bd. Am. Indian Historian, 1969-71; note editor Stanford Law Review, 1970-71; contbr. articles to profl. jours. Coord., treas. Native Am. Coun. Regents Inst. Am. Indian Arts, 1975-80; bd. visitors Stanford Law Sch., 1978-81; trustee Phelps Stokes Fund, 1981-87, Bush Found., 1991—, Bacone Coll., 1986-89, chmn., 1988-89, Morning Star Found., 1987-93, U. Redlands, 1991—, alumni bd., 1987-89, Ednl. Found. Am., 1993-96; bd. dirs. Amerindian Circle, Inc., 1981-88, Nat. Indian Justice Ctr., 1982-89; cultural edn. com. Smithsonian Inst., 1987-90; nat. support com. Native Am. Rights Fund, 1990—; adv. com. Winslow Found., 1991—; hon. coun. Wings Am., 1993—; mem. Environ. Def. Fund, bd. trustees, 1986—. Recipient Career Achievement award U. Redlands, 1987, Disting. Svc. award, 1992, award Appreciation and Recognition, Cheyenne and Arapaho Tribes Okla., 1990, Spirit of the People award Okla. Inst. Indian Heritage, 1990; named (with another) Amb. of Yr. Red Earth Indian Ctr. Okla., 1993. Mem. Am. Indian Bar Assn. (charter pres. 1976-77). Mem. Cheyenne and Arapaho Tribes Okla. Office: Nat Mus of Am Indian 470 Lenfant Plz SW Ste 7102 Washington DC 20024-2124*

WEST, WALLACE MARION, cultural organization administrator; b. N.Y.C., Aug. 30, 1921; s. Florian and Mary (Wziatek) Wesolowski. BSBA, L.I. U., 1966; cert. mus. mgmt., Columbia U. Estimating engr. Sperry Rand Corp., Lake Success, N.Y., 1957-65; sys. analyst Grumman Aerospace, Bethpage, 1965-71; exec. dir. Queens Coun. on Arts, Jamaica, 1971-76, Hall of Sci. of City of N.Y., Flushing, 1976-79; pres. Am. Inst. Polish Culture, Pinellas Park, Fla., 1982—. Cons. arts mgmt. N.Y. State Coun. on Arts, 1968-71. Author: Handbook for Directors of Non-Profit Corporations, 1974; editor: Sharing Our Heritage, 1996; editor Polish Heritage Quarterly, 1985-99; contbr. articles to profl. jours. Recipient Order of Merit Republic of Poland, 1992; named Notable Am. of Bicentennial Era Am. Biog. Inst., 1976. Mem. Am. Inst. Polish Culture (pres., Polonian of Yr. 1985), Am. Coun. Polish Culture (bd. dirs., Founders award 1992, Spl. Achievement award 2000, editor 1985-99), Polish Am. Soc., Polish Inst. Arts/Scis. in Am., Polish Am. Pulaski Assn., Polish Am. Congress (Heritage award 2001), Kosciuszko Found., Pilsudski Inst. Am. Republican. Roman Catholic. Avocations: photography, crafts, electronics, swimming. Home: 6507 107th Ter Pinellas Park FL 33782-2432 Office: Am Inst Polish Culture 9190 49th St Pinellas Park FL 33782-5228 E-mail: wallyw830@cs.com.

WEST, WILLIAM FLOYD, political scientist, educator; b. Seattle, July 6, 1949; s. William Floyd and Constance West; m. Patricia J. McDaniel, Aug. 16, 1990; children: Elizabeth. Nicole McDaniel-Carder, Jackson, Michelle McDaniel-Carder, Grant. BS, US Mil. Acad., West Point, NY, 1971; PhD, Rice Univ., Houston, TX, 1981. Prof./dir. of masters program Tex. A&M Univ., College Station, Tex., 2001—, prof., pol. sci., 1981—2001. Officer US Army, Fort Bragg, NC, 1971—75. Author: (book) Administrative Rulemaking, Controlling the Bureaucracy. Leutenant US Army, 1971—75, Fort Bragg, NC. Recipient Gardner Award for Best Dissertation, Rice Univ., Houston, TX, 1981. Achievements include Author Of Numerous Articles. Home: 915 Dartmoor Drive Austin TX 78746-511 Office: Texas A&M Univ Bush School 4220 Texas A&M Univ College Station TX 77843-0001

WEST, WILLIAM ROBERT, history educator; b. Woodbury, N.J., Feb. 4, 1947; s. William Robert Sr. and Genevieve Jane (Cooper) West; m. Rhonda Gaye Foster, Apr. 4, 1981; children: Shaun Cooper Foster West, Ryan William Foster West. BA, Ky. Wesleyan Coll., 1970; MA, Western Ky. U., 1973; postgrad., U. Louisville, U. Shanghai, U. Denver, U. Wash., others. Ky. secondary cert. life. Tchr. Daviess County Pub. Schs., Owensboro, 1971-86; prof. history U. Ky., Owensboro (Ky.) C.C., 1984—. Ky. C.C. faculty senate coun. rep. univ. studies; U. Ky. C.C.S. coun. mem., 1994-97; parent rep. local sch. based coun. Mem. Leadership Owensboro Class of 1988, Leadership Ky. Class of 1997; exec. dir. Owensboro Sister Cities Program, 1990—; mem. state mgmt. team Ky. Sister Cities, 1991—; internat. rep. Shawnee Trails Coun. Boy Scouts Am. Recipient cert. of merit Ky. Ednl. TV-Ashland Oil Found., 1982; rsch. scholar Lyndhurst Found., 1984, scholar Japan Endowment at U. Wash., 1983, N.E. Asia Coun. of Assn. for Asian Studies, 1983; travel grantee U.S.-Japan Found., 1983. Mem. Am. Assn. Individual Investors, Nat. Geographic Soc., Nat. Trust Historic Preservation, Hon. Order Ky. Cols., U.S.-China Peoples Friendships Assn. (nat. bd. dirs. 1997-2001), UN Assn. U.S.A., Ky. C.C. Humanities Assn., The So. Hist. Assn. (European history sect.), others. Democrat. Unitarian Universalist. Avocations: reading, traveling, fostering internat. perspective through edn. Home: 5829 Jack Hinton Rd Philpot KY 42366-9641 Office: Univ Ky Owensboro C C 4800 New Hartford Rd Owensboro KY 42303-1800

WESTACOTT, EMRYS, philosophy educator; b. Nottingham, U.K., Oct. 22, 1956; came to U.S., 1986; s. Frederick Charles and Kathleen Mary (Powell) W.; m. Victoria Valentine Cobb, July 19, 1985; 2 children, Sophie, Emily. BA, U. Sheffield, U.K., 1979; MA, McGill U., Montreal, Que., Can., 1984; postgrad., U. Tex., Austin, 1986—. Bus conductor East Midland Motors, Chesterfield, U.K., 1975-76; teaching asst. McGill U., 1981-82; exec. officer Dept. Health and Social Security, Sheffield, 1984-86; teaching asst., instr. dept. philosophy U. Tex., Austin, 1986—94; visiting asst. prof., dept. philosophy Southwestern U., 1995—96; asst. prof. Alfred U., Alfred, NY, 1996—2001, assoc. prof., 2001—. Author (with E. Horner): (publications) Thinking Through Philosophy, 2000. Dow Hickson fellow McGill U., 1980, recipient Guy DeSaultes prize, 1982. Office: Univ Tex Austin Dept Philosophy Waggener Hall Austin TX 78712

WESTALL, ANDREW JON, legislative staff member, urban planner; b. San Diego, Jan. 14, 1973; s. Frederick Charls and Janet (Robertson) W. BA in Polit. Sci.-Pub. Svc., U. Calif., Davis, 1996; MA in Urban Planning, UCLA, 1999. Acad. rsch. intern Office of City Councilmem. Deborah Ortiz, Sacramento, 1995-96; DC office intern Office of Andrew Cuomo, HUD, Washington, 1995; capitol office intern Office Assembly Mem. Carole Migden, Sacramento, 1996; viewpoint columnist The Daily Bruin, L.A., 1997; dist. cons. Office of Assembly Mem. Deborah Ortiz, Sacramento, 1997; pres. Grad. Students Assn., UCLA, 1997-98; adminstrv. asst. The Durfee Found., Santa Monica, Calif., 1996-98; campaign worker Working Families for Deborah Ortiz, State Senate, Sacramento, 1998; cons. Nat. Assn. Latino Elected and Apptd. Ofcls., L.A., 1998—; field rep., rschr. Office of Asssembly Mem. Robert M. Hertzberg, Van Nuys, Calif., 1999—. Advisor Sacramento County Adult and Aging Commn., 1996. Author: Reapportionment, Redistricting and the Latin Community Toward 2000, 2000. Recipient award U. Calif. Pres. Washington Ctr., 1995. Mem. ACLU, Am. Planning Assn., U. Calif. Davis Alumni Assn., Chi Pi (pres. Sigma Delta chpt. 1995). Democrat. Episcopalian. Avocations: hiking, basketball. Office: Office Assembly Mem Robert M. Hertzberg 6150 Van Nuys Blvd Ste 305 Van Nuys CA 91401-3345 E-mail: Andrew.Westall@asm.ca.gov.

WESTBERRY, DAVID M. executive search consultant; b. Savannah, Ga., Aug. 26, 1951; s. John R. and Marianne (Stopfer) W.; m. Carolyn Diane Manton, Apr. 27, 1987. AA, Pensacola Jr. Coll., 1976; BA in Acctg., U. West Fla., Pensacola, 1978. CPA, Fla. Sr. acct. KPMG Peat Marwick, Jacksonville, Fla., 1979-81; v.p. Robert Half Internat., 1981-82, Pierce Catterton, Houston, 1983; sr. mgr. exec. search KPMG Peat Marwick, Dallas, 1983-89; mng. dir. Ward Howell Internat., 1989-95, exec. com., 1992-95; ptnr. LAI, 1995-98; mng. dir. Korn Ferry Internat., 1998—. Mem. adv. coun. U. West Fla. Coll. Bus., Pensacola, 1992—. Trustee U. West Fla. Found., Pensacola, 1994—. Sgt. USAF, 1971-74, South Korea. Home: 6429 Pemberton Dr Dallas TX 75230-4126

WESTBERRY, JOHN ELLIOTT, mathematics educator; b. Knoxville, Tenn., Aug. 8, 1922; s. John Elliott and Annie (Richardson) W.; m. Gaynelle Hines, July 8, 1942 (dec. May 1992); 1 child, Larry; m. Maxine Willis, Mar. 18, 1993. BS, Livingstone Coll., 1941; MS, Atlanta U., 1949; MA, U. Mich., 1954. Asst. prof. Tex. Coll., Tyler, 1949-50, Tex. State U., Houston, 1950-54; registrar, dir. admissions Tex. So. U., 1954-94, assoc. prof., 1975—. Tech. sgt. U.S. Army, 1942-45, ETO. Named one of 100 Most Influential Blacks, Ebony mag., 1974, 75, 76, Am.'s Best Tchrs. Ednl. Comms., Inc., 1998. Mem. Am. Assn. Coll. Registrars and Admissions Officers (sec.-treas. 1980-83), Math. Assn. Am., Tex. Assn. Coll. Registrars and Admissions Officers (pres. 1982), Phi Beta Sigma (pres. 1974-76). Democrat. Avocations: reading, speaking. Home: 5306 Stuyvesant Ln Houston TX 77021-3145 Office: Tex So U 3100 Cleburne St Houston TX 77004-4501

WESTBIE, BARBARA JANE, retired graphics designer; b. Little Rock, Nov. 3, 1946; d. Freeman Bryant Davis and Virginia Lee Thompson; children: Suzanne Michelle, Derrek Christopher. Grad. in graphic design, U. Calif., Davis, 1992; student, Miramar Coll., San Diego, 1976, Chabot Coll., Hayward, Calif., 1974. Exec. dir. Ambiance, Danville, Calif., 1980—84; dir. Lake Gallery, Tahoe City, 1985—87; art cons. Reed Gallery, 1988—90; ret. Art dir., creative cons. Associated Students Re-Entry Ctr. Chico State U., Calif., 2001—. Inventor Fat Fuzzy/Iknonotrisc Family, 1981, artist (poster/logo) Project Mana Fundraising Event, 1988, (brochure/media kit) Chocolate Festival, 1989. Vol. crisis intervention counselor CIS/Tahoe Women's Svcs., Kings Beach, 1989—91; lead counselor Emotions Anonymous 12-Step Program, North Lake Tahoe Area, 1990—93; vol. pk. svc. Washoe Lake State Pk., Carson City, Nev., 1993—94; coord. new vols. ARC, Chico, 2000—01, vol. Butte County, 2000—. Named Vol. of Yr., Tahoe Women's Svcs., 1989; recipient Disting. Svc. award, CIS/Tahoe Women's Svcs., 1989—90. Mem.: Smithsonian Instn. (assoc.). Protestant. Avocations: skiing, reading, gardening, writing, painting.

WESTBROOK, GARY WAYNE, music educator, consultant; b. Burlington, N.C., June 29, 1966; s. Betty Briggs Smith. MusB, East Carolina U., 1989; MusM, U. N.C., 1996, DPhil Music Edn., 2002. Dir. bands So. Nash High Sch., Spring Hope, NC, 1989—90, Blenheim Mid. Sch., Blenheim, SC, 1990—92, South Florence High Sch., Florence, 1992—95; dir. athletic bands and percussion studies Concord Coll., Athens, W.Va., 2001—. Percussionist Florence Symphony Orch., Florence, 1990—94; instructor/arranger percussion Liberty High Sch., Bedford, 1995—; drummer Necessary Jazz Combo, Tazewell, 2000—; instructor, pit arranger Carolina Gold Sr. Drum and Bugle Corps, Raleigh, NC, 2001—; Member, Pit Section Leader Bridgemen Drum and Bugle Corps, Bayonne, NJ, 1986—87; adj. instr. percussion Pfeidder U., Meisenheimer, 1999—2001, Concord Coll., 1999—2001. Contbr. articles to profl. jours. Mem.: Music Educators Nat. Conf., Music Tchrs. Nat. Assn., Percussive Arts Soc., Internat. Assn. Jazz Edn. Pentecostal. Avocations: hiking, bicycling, swimming, basketball. Home: 103 J Montvale Ave Bluefield VA 24605 Office: Concord Coll Department of Music Athens WV 24712 Personal E-mail: Blwinkl@stargate.net.

WESTBROOK, JACK HALL, metallurgist, consultant; b. Troy, N.Y., Aug. 19, 1924; s. Russell Tippett and Grace Hall (Wager) W.; m. Elizabeth Kirkland, Sept. 20, 1947 (dec.); children: Nicholas, Kathryn, Melissa, Kirkland, Daniel. B in Metall. Engring., Rensselaer Poly. Inst., 1944, M in Metall. Engring., 1947; ScD, MIT, 1949. Registered profl. engr., N.Y. With Gen. Electric Corp., Schenectady, N.Y., 1949-85, mgr. materials info. svcs., 1971-82, cons. engring. and mfg., 1982-85; pres., prin., cons. Sci-Tech Knowledge Sys., Scotia, 1985-91, Brookline Techs., Ballston Spa, 1991—. Trustee Engring. Info. Inc., N.Y.C., 1977-80, chmn. indsl. data comm., mem. exec. com. Codata, 1988-94; cons. in field. Editor: Intermetallic Compounds, 1967, 21 other books; co-editor: Intermetallic Compounds: Principles and Practice, Vols. 1 and 2, 1994, Vol. 3, 2002. Mem. zoning bd. Town of Ballston, N.Y.; bd. edn. Ballston Spa Sch. Dist., 1966-72. With USN, 1944-46. Recipient Turner award Electrochem. Soc., 1957, Hofmann prize Lead Devel. Assn., 1971; NAS traveling fellow to USSR, 1971. Fellow AAAS, Am. Ceramic Soc., Am. Soc. Metals (Campbell lectr. 1976, Jeffries lectr. 1979, Sauveur award 2001), Am. Inst. Chemists; mem. ASTM (Templin award 1959), AIME, Inst. Materials (U.K.), Nat. Acad. Engring. Avocations: old house restoration, history of sci. and tech. Home and Office: 5 Brookline Rd Ballston Spa NY 12020-3523 E-mail: jackwestbrook@earthlink.net.

WESTBROOK, JAMES EDWIN, lawyer, educator; b. Camden, Ark., Sept. 7, 1934; s. Loy Edwin and Helen Lucille (Bethea) W.; m. Elizabeth Kay Farris, Dec. 23, 1956; children: William Michael, Robert Bruce, Matthew David. BA with high honors, Hendrix Coll., 1956; JD with distinction, Duke U., 1959; LLM, Georgetown U., 1965. Bar: Ark. 1959, Okla. 1977, Mo. 1982. Assoc. Mehaffy, Smith & Williams, Little Rock, 1959-62; asst. counsel, subcom. of U.S. Senate Jud. Com., Washington, 1963; legis. asst. U.S. Senate, 1963-65; asst. prof. law U. Mo., Columbia, 1965-68, asst. dean, 1966-68, assoc. prof., 1968-70, prof., 1970-76, 80—, James S. Rollins prof. law, 1974-76, 80—, Earl F. Nelson prof. law, 1982-99, emeritus prof., 1999—, interim dean, 1981-82; dean U. Okla. Coll. Law, Norman, 1976-80. George Allen vis. prof. law, U. Richmond, 1987; vis. prof. law Duke U., 1988, Washington U., St. Louis, 1996, 2001; reporter Mid-Am. Assembly on Role of State in Urban Crisis, 1970; dir. Summer Internship Program in Local Govt., 1968; cons. various Mo. cities on drafting home-rule charters; mem. Gov.'s Adv. Coun. on Local Govt. Law, 1967-68, Fed. Practice Com. U.S. Dist. Ct. (we. dist.) Mo., 1986-90; chmn. Columbia Charter Revision Commn., 1973-74; mem. spl. com. labor relations Mo. Dept. Labor and Indsl. Rels., 1975; mem., chmn. subcom. on domestic violence Task Force on Gender and Justice, Mo. Jud. Conf., 1990-93; mem. com. to rev. govtl. structure of Boone County, Mo., 1991. Author: (with L. Riskin) Dispute Resolution and Lawyers, 1987, supplement, 1993, 2d edit., 1997, abridged edit. of 2d edit., 1998; contbr. articles to profl. jours. Chair search com. for chancellor U. Mo., Columbia, 1992, chair search com. for provost, 1998. Mem. ABA, Nat. Acad. Arbitrators, Assn. Am. Law Schs. (chmn. local govt. law round table coun. 1972), Ctrl. States Law Sch. Assn. (pres. 1982-83), Mo. Bar Assn. (vice chmn. labor law com. 1986-87, chmn. 1987-88, Spurgeon Smithton award 1995), Order of Coif, Blue Key, Alpha Chi. Roman Catholic. Home: 3609 S Woods Edge Rd Columbia MO 65203-6606 Office: U Mo Sch Law Columbia MO 65211-0001

WESTBROOK, JAY LAWRENCE, law educator; b. Morristown, N.J., Dec. 11, 1943; s. Joel W. and Elaine Frances (Summers) W.; m. Pauline June Travis, Feb. 15, 1969; 1 child, Joel Mastin. BA in Polit. Sci./Philosophy, U. Tex., 1965, JD, 1968. Bar: Tex. 1968, D.C. 1969, U.S. Ct. Appeals (D.C. cir.) 1969, U.S. Supreme Ct. 1976, U.S. Ct. Appeals (4th cir.) 1978, U.S. Ct. Appeals (2d cir.) 1979. Assoc. Surrey & Morse (name now Jones, Day, Reavis, Pogue), Washington, 1969-74; ptnr. Surrey & Morse (name now Jones, Day, Reavis, Pogue, Surrey & Morse), 1974-80; mem. law faculty U. Tex., Austin, 1980—, Benno C. Schmidt Chair Bus. Law, 1991—. Vis. prof. U. London, 1990, Harvard Law Sch., 1991-92; advisor Tex. Internat. Law Jour., 1985-91; reporter Am. Law Inst. Transnat. Insolvency Project, 1994-2000; co-leader U.S. delegation to UN Commn. on Internat. Trade Law Working Group on Model Law Internation Insolvency, 1995-97, 99; sr. advisor Nat. Bankruptcy Rev. Com., 1997; mem. State Dept. Adv. Com. on Pvt. Internat. Law, 1997-2000. Co-author: As We Forgive Our Debtors: Bankruptcy and Consumer Credit in America, 1989 (Silver Gavel award ABA 1989), The Law of Debtors and Creditors: Text, Cases and Problems, 4th edit., 2001, Teacher's Manual, The Law of Debtors and Creditors, 4th edit., 2001, The Fragile Middle Class, 2000; contbr. articles to profl. jours. Grantee U. Tex. Law Sch. Found., 1982, U. Rsch. Inst., 1982-83, NSF, 1983-86, Policy Rsch. Inst., Lyndon Johnson Sch. Pub. Affairs, 1984, Tex. Bar Found., 1985, Nat. Inst. Child Health and Human Devel., 1986, Nat. Conf. Bankruptcy Judges, 1991, 93. Mem. ABA (bus. bankruptcy com., vice chair internat. bankruptcy subcom. 1999—, Meyer rsch. grant 1986), Am. Law Inst., Am. Coll. Bankruptcy, Nat. Bankruptcy Conf., State Bar Tex. (governing coun. internat. sect. 1987-89), Internat. Bar Assn., Internat. Bankruptcy Com. (com. J), Internat. Acad. Comml. and Consumer Law, Order of Coif. Office: U Tex Sch Law 727 E Dean Keeton St Austin TX 78705-3224

WESTBROOK, KENT COLEMAN, surgeon, educator; b. Hot Springs, Ark., Feb. 13, 1940; MD, U. Ark., 1965. Diplomate Am. Bd. Surgery. Intern U. Ark. Hosp., Little Rock, 1965-66, surg. resident, 1966-70; fellow in surg. oncology M.D. Anderson Tumor Inst., Houston, 1970-72; staff U. Ark. Hosp. Prof., U. Ark. Sch. Medicine. Mem. AMA, Southwestern Surg. Congress. Office: Univ Ark Med Ctr Slot 520 4301 W Markham St Little Rock AR 72205-7101

WESTBROOK, MICHAEL GEORGE, secondary school educator; b. Miami, Fla., June 8, 1946; s. Paul Otis Westbrook and Georgia (Chrisman) Kinner; m. Linda Michele Eidson, July 6, 1968. BA, Fla. State U., 1968; MEd, Rollins Coll., 1984. Cert. tchr. and prin. Tchr. Ft. Meade (Fla.) H.S., 1968—74, Kathleen H.S., Lakeland, 1974—79, Lake Gibson H.S., Lakeland, 1979—84, dean, 1984—87; asst. prin. Lakeland H.S., 1987—95, tchr., 2001—02; prin. Harrison Arts, 1995—2001. Mem. Greater Lakeland Area Presenters, 1997—2001, City Lakeland Planning Task Force, 1999—2001; bd. dirs. Cultural Arts Bd. Polk County, 1996—2001, Assn. Sch. Based Adminstrs., Polk County, 1997—2001. Mem.: Kiwanis (bd. dirs. 2001—). Methodist. Avocations: travel, art, photography.

WESTBY, TIMOTHY SCOTT, lawyer, researcher; b. Fargo, N.D., Apr. 16, 1957; s. Joseph Arlo and Dorothy Mae (Nye) W.; m. Ann Amoroso Westby, June 16, 2001. SBChemE, MIT, 1979; PhDChemE, U. Tex., 1984; JD, U. Houston, 1994. Bar: Tex., U.S. Dist. Ct. (so. dist.) Tex., U.S. Ct. Appeals (fed. cir.). Researcher Energy Lab., MIT, Cambridge, 1976-79; rsch. asst. U. Tex., Austin, 1979-84, teaching asst., 1981-83; assoc. rsch. engr. Shell Devel. Co., Houston, 1984-87, rsch. engr., 1987-91, sr. rsch. engr., 1991-94; assoc. Conley, Rose & Tayon, P.C., 1994—. Mem. adv. com. Ohio Combustion Rsch., Columbus, 1985-90, Pa. Coal Rsch. Coop., University Station, 1986-89; adj. prof. chemistry Rice U., 1998—. Contbr. articles to profl. jours.; patentee method for in situ coal drilling, patentee coal blends having improved ash viscosity. Campaigner United Way, Houston, 1989-91. Scholar MIT, 1975-79; fellow U.S. dept. Energy, 1979-82, Getty Oil Co., 1983-84. Mem. ABA, AIChE, ASTM (com. D-5 1989-94), ASME (advisor rsch. com. on corrosion and deposits from flue gases 1988—), N.Am. Catalysis Soc., Southwestern Catalysis Soc., Am. Intellectual Property Law Assn., Fed. Cir. Bar Assn., State Bar of Tex., Houston Bar Assn., Houston Intellectual Property Law Assn., Porsche Club Am. (bd. dirs., treas. 2001—). Avocations: golf, sailing, skiing, racing sports cars. Office: Conley Rose & Tayon PC 600 Travis Ste 1800 Houston TX 77002-2912 E-mail: twestby@crtlaw.com.

WESTCOTT, BRIAN JOHN, manufacturing executive; b. Rexford, N.Y., June 19, 1957; s. John Campbell and Norma (Cornell) W.; m. Andrea Belrose, Apr. 23, 1988; children: Sarah Katharine, Paul Brian. BS, Lehigh U., 1979; MS, Stanford U., 1980, PhD, 1987. Engr. Combustion Engring., Windsor, Conn., 1980-81; rsch. engr. Gen. Electric Corp. Rsch., Niskayuna, N.Y., 1981-83; rsch. fellow Stanford (Calif.) Grad. Sch. Bus., 1987-88; mgr. Gen. Electric Corp. Mgmt., Bridgeport, Conn., 1988-89; prin. A.T. Kearney Tech. Inc., Redwood City, Calif., 1989—; chief exec. officer Westt, Inc., Menlo Park, 1990—; CEO e Innovate, 1999—. Author: (with others) Paradox and

Transformation, 1988; contbr. articles to profl. jours.; inventor, patentee in field. Mem. Menlo Park Vitality Task Force, 1993-94. Recipient Tech 500 award Westt, Inc., 1996, 97, 98, Inc. 500 award, 1997, Silicon Valley Tech fast 50 award, 1997, 98, San Francisco and San Jose award for top 100 fastest growing pvt. cos.; co. named among Top 50 Fastest Growing Pvt. Cos. in San Francisco and San Jose, 2001; postdoctoral rsch. fellow Stanford U. Grad. Sch. Bus., 1987, 88; rsch. fellow Electric Power Rsch., Stanford, 1983-87. Mem. ASME. Avocations: sports, politics. Office: Westt Inc 1090 Obrien Dr Menlo Park CA 94025-1409 E-mail: brian.westcott@westt.com.

WESTCOTT, JOAN CLARK, poet; b. Union City, Pa., Feb. 8, 1919; d. William Clyde and Marjorie (Clark) W. BA, Vassar Coll., 1941; grad., Katherine Gibbs Sec. Sch., Boston, 1942. Clk. Boston Port Embarkation, 1942—43; sec. Harvard U., Cambridge, 1943-45, Players Theater, Sarasota, Fla., 1947-49, AEC, UCLA, 1950-52; sec. to John Loveton L.A., 1953-54; sec. to J. West Arch., Sarasota, 1955-60. Author: (poetry) Fragments of Stained Glass, 1967, More Fragments of Stained Glass, 1968, Bits of Chaff, 1970, Taffeta and Lace, 1976, Ribbon of Light, 1980, Fragments of Stained Glass III, 1988, Homeward Bound, 1997. Poetry books plus papers in Rare Books and Spl. Collections Libr., U. Fla., Gainesville. Mem. Planetary Soc., Habitat Nat. Wildlife Fedn., Women in the Arts, Union of Concerned Scientists. Avocations: gardening, reading, playing piano, needlepoint, raising Siamese cats. Home: John Knox Village 4100 E Fletcher Ave Tampa FL 33613

WESTCOTT, ROBERT FREDERICK, consultant; b. Detroit; s. Edgar Cecil and Lois Gertrude (Strongman) W.; m. Nora P., Jan. 28, 1950 (div. June 1975); children: Mark A., Robert F. Jr., Douglas K., Craig M.; m. Jeanne Marienthal Weislow, Dec. 23, 1998; children: David G., James E., Philip J. BS, Mich. State U., 1948; MBA, U. Detroit, 1953. Owner, mgr. Keystone Market, Detroit, 1948-50; advance sales Swift & Co., 1950-51; prodn. quality control Snow Corp., N.Y.C., 1951-53; sales & promotion Rath Packing Co., Waterloo, Iowa, 1953-55; cons. Booz, Allen & Hamilton, Chgo., 1955-60; v.p. corp. dir. Spencer Stuart & Assoc., 1960-66; pres. Westcott Assocs., Inc., 1966-93. With U.S. Army, 1942-45. Mem. Carlton Club, Long Boat Key Club. Democrat. Avocation: travel. Home: 180 E Pearson St Apt 4707 Chicago IL 60611 also: 501 Bayport Way Longboat Key FL 34228-2621

WESTEBBE, BARBARA LIEBST, writer, sculptor; b. Newton, Kans., Dec. 8, 1925; d. Harold Charles and Marie Josiphine (Whitcomb) Liebst; m. Richard Manning Westebbe, Dec. 18, 1947; children: Mark, Shelly, Bruce, Susy. Student, Kans. State Tchrs. Coll., 1945; grad., Utrecht (Holland) U., 1954; postgrad., George Washington U., 1955, 56, 57. Tchr. 8th grade Deerhead Sch., Medicine Lodge, Kans., 1945; illustrator, engr. Culver Aircraft Corp., Wichita, 1946; mem. Sen. Arthur Capper staff U.S. Senate, Washington, 1946-47; asst. to chmn. Nat. Assn. Motor Bus Operators, 1947-48; office mgr. to Dr. R. McFarland Human Engring. Dept. Sch. Pub. Health, Harvard U., Cambridge, Mass., 1949-51; prin. Am. H.S., Den Haag, Holland, 1953-54; editor of Den Haag transls. of Den Ramp series Am. Acad. Scis., Holland, 1954-56; writer weekly column Athens (Greece) Post Newspaper, 1961-65; founder, dir. Life Conservation, Inc., Fredricksburg, Va., 1973—. Exhibited in group exhbns. at Pierce Coll., Athens, 1966; editor (poems under pseudonym Colleen Cody) Fed. Poet, 1967-70; author poems; writer quar. column Downs Syndrome Mag., 1990-94. Bd. dirs. Nat. Womens Party, 1946-66; mem. archtl. review bd. Stafford County Svcs., Falmouth, Va., 1989—; mem. Fredricksburg Ctr. Creative Arts, 1990—. Recipient Citizen of Yr. award Am. Legion. Mem. Nat. Edn. Soc., Alpha Zigma Tau. Avocations: gardening, teaching special artists, pets, sculpting. Home and Office: 807 Holly Corner Rd Fredericksburg VA 22406-5360

WESTEBBE, EVELYN ROSENTHAL, social worker; b. Orange, N.J., June 6, 1926; d. Leon J. and Bertha (Lewit) Rosenthal; m. Donald M. Westebbe, June 21, 1953 (div. July 1981); children: Jonathan, David, Sharon. BS, U. Mich., 1948; MSW, U. Pa., 1950. Acad. cert. social worker; diplomate in clin. social work. Psychiatric social worker Jewish Community Svc., Jamaica, N.Y., 1949-53, Albany (N.Y.) Med. Ctr. Cerebral Palsy Ctr., 1953-54, Vt. Children's Aid Soc., Burlington, 1954-57; sr. psychiat. social worker Rutland Mental health Svc., 1962-72; psychiatric social worker So. Vt. Women's Health Ctr., Rutland, 1972-89; pvt. practice, 1980—. Rutland County coord. Forum on Family Violence; founding chair Frieda Vargish Meml. Inst.; student supr. Antioch New Eng. Grad. Program; group leader Crash Program State of Vt.; incest survivors group therapist Herstory House for Battered Women's Shelter. Mem. Gov.'s Com. on Children and Youth; bd. dirs. Rutland Mental Health Svc.; county chair Nat. Found. for Infantile Paralysis. Mem. NASW (charter, register clin. social workers), Vt. Assn. Mental Health (bd. dirs.). Jewish. Avocations: creative arts, skiing, tennis. Home and Office: 8 Notch Rd Rutland VT 05701-9642

WESTENDORF, ELAINE SUSAN, social worker; b. Beruit, Lebanon, Jan. 7, 1956; came to U.S., 1957; d. Glen Albert and Barbara (Redlick) L. AA, Fresno City Coll., 1979; BA in Psychology, U. Calif., Santa Cruz, 1981; MSW, San Francisco State U., 1985. Cert. coll. instr., coll. counselor. Intern Star Lodge Drug and Alcohol Treatment Ctr., Scotts Valley, Calif., 1983; with employees assistance program NASA, Moffett Field, 1983-84; psychiat. social worker intern Cath. Social Services Children's Counseling Ctr., Santa Clara, 1984, Kaiser Permanente-Psychiatry, Redwood City, 1984-85; psychiat. social worker San Benito County Mental Health, Hollister, 1985-88, San Benito County Schs., Hollister, 1985-88, Personal Performance Cons., Mountain View, Calif., 1988-90; pvt. practice, 1990—. Cons. San Benito County Schs., 1985-88. Mem. Nat. Assn. Social Workers, Assn. Clin. Social Workers. Democrat. Avocations: scuba diving, hiking, crafts. Office: 800 Pollard Rd Ste B20 Los Gatos CA 95030

WESTER, ELIZABETH ANNE, counselor; b. Jacksonville, Fla., Feb. 23, 1968; d. Wallace Eugene and Mary Elizabeth Wester. BA, Western State Coll., Gunnison, Colo., 1990; MA, Lenoir-Rhyne Coll., 1999. Lic. profl. counselor, N.C. Outpatient therapist Counseling Svcs. of Catawba County, Hickory, N.C., 1997-2000; lic. profl. counselor Statesville, 2000—. Mem.: ACA, Internat. ASsn. Play Therapy, NC Alliance for the Mentally Ill (bd. dirs. 1996—98), Altrusa Internat., Jr. Svc. League., Chi Sigma Iota. Avocations: cooking, gardening. Home: 216 Rose St Mooresville NC 28117 Office: 119 N Tradd St Ste B Statesville NC 28677 Fax: (704) 871-0098. E-mail: leisa@vnet.net.

WESTER, KEITH ALBERT, film and television recording engineer, real estate developer; b. Seattle, Feb. 21, 1940; s. Albert John and Evelyn Grayce (Nettell) W., m. Judith Elizabeth Jones, 1968 (div. Mar. 1974); 1 child, Wendy Elizabeth; m. Joan Marie Bursler, Feb. 2001. AA, Am. River Coll., Sacramento, 1959; BA, Calif. State U., L.A., 1962; MA, UCLA, 1965. Lic. multi-engine rated pilot. Prodn. asst. Sta. KCRA-TV, Sacramento, 1956; announcer Sta. KSFM, 1960; film editor, sound rec. technician Urie & Assocs., Hollywood, Calif., 1963-66; co-owner Steckler-Wester Film Prodns., 1966-70; owner Profl. Sound Recorders, Studio City, Calif., 1970—. Aero-charter, Studio City, 1974—, Wester Devel., Sun Valley, Coeur d'Alene, Idaho, 1989—, also Studio City, 1989—; majority stockholder Channel 58 TV, Coeur d'Alene/Spokane, 1993-99. Prodn. sound mixer: (films) Cradle to Grave, 2002, Carolina, 2001, Orange County, 2001, Princess Diaries, 2000, The Perfect Storm, 1999 (acad. award co-nominee for best sound 2001), Never Been Kissed, 1999, Runaway Bride, 1999, Armageddon, 1998 (Acad. award co-nominee 1999), Mouse Hunt, 1997, Air Force One, 1997 (Acad. award co-nominee for best sound 1998), Shadow Conspiracy, 1996, G.I. Jane, 1997, The Rock, 1996 (Acad. award co-nominee for best sound, 1997), Waterworld, 1995 (Acad. award co-nominee for best sound 1996), The Shadow, 1994, Wayne's World II, 1993, Coneheads, 1993, Body of Evidence, 1992, Indecent Proposal, 1992, School Ties, 1991, Frankie and Johnny, 1991, Another You, 1991, Thelma and Louise, 1990, Shattered, 1990, Desperate Hours, 1989, Joe vs. the Volcano, 1989, Black Rain, 1989 (Acad. award co-nominee 1990), Sea of Love, 1988, Real Men, 1985, Mask, 1984, Thief of Hearts, 1983, Young Doctors in Love, 1982, First Monday in October, 1981. Mem. NATAS (Emmy award An Early Frost 1986, Emmy nominations in 1982, 84, 85, 87), SAG, Acad. Motion Picture Arts and Scis., Brit. Acad. Film and TV Arts (award nomination for The Rock 1997, The Perfect Storm 2001), Cinema Audio Soc. (sec. 1985-91, Sound award 1987), Soc. Motion Picture and TV Engrs., Internat. Sound Technicians, Local 695, Assn. Film Craftsmen (sec. 1967-73, treas. 1973-76), Aircraft Owners and Pilots Assn. (Commemorative Air Force col.), Am. Radio Relay League (K6DGN). Home: 4146 Bellingham Ave Studio City CA 91604-1601 Office: Profl Sound Recorders Ste 308 6324 Variel Ave Woodland Hills CA 91367-7770

WESTER, M(ARY) SUE HIEBERT, occupational medicine physician; b. St. Paul, Jan. 26, 1938; d. Homer Leonard Hiebert and Grace Elizabeth Blake; m. Donald Robert Wester, Oct. 12, 1962; children: Stephen, Adrienne, Ian, Kimberly. BA magna cum laude, Kans. State U., 1960; postgrad., U. Kans., Kansas City, 1960-62; MD, U. Minn., 1964. Diplomate Am. Bd. Preventive Medicine in Occupl. Medicine. Intern Bethesda Luth. Hosp., St. Paul, 1964-65; resident U. Cin. Coll. Medicine, 1979-80; cons. physician Gen. Mills, Inc., Mpls., 1966-74, staff physician, 1974-80, dir. plant med. svcs., 1980-83, dir. med. svcs., 1983-86, dir. employee health svcs., 1986—2001. Mem. editl. staff Jour. Occupl. and Environ. Medicine, 1989-99. Mem. pub. edn. com. Am. Cancer Soc., Mpls., 1975-79; pres. bd. dirs. Hammer Residences, Minnetonka, Minn., 1987-89; mem. bd. Meml. Blood Ctr., Mpls., 1989-99 Grantee Am. Heart Found., 1958. Fellow Am. Coll. Occupl. and Environ. Medicine (bd. dirs. 1992-99, mem. ethics, pers. and bldg. com. 1989-99, chmn. edn. and conf. coun. 1993-96); mem. AMA, APHA, Am. Acad. Family Practice, North Ctrl. Occupl. Medicine Assn. (pres. 1982), Minn. Med. Assn. (del. 1982-85), Hennepin County Med. Soc. (RESPONSE child abuse coordinating com. 1982-88), Mpls. Acad. Medicine, Phi Kappa Phi.

WESTERBAND, ALEX, surgeon, educator; b. Cap-Haitien, Haiti, Sept. 8, 1957; s. Adrien and Ursule Westerband; m. Catherine Madeleine Trometer, May 19, 1988; children: Alexandra, Eric Albert. BS, Inst. St. Louis De Gonzague, Port-Au-Prince, 1975; MD, Sch. Med. State U. Haiti, 1982; postgrad., U. Louis Pasteur Strasbourg, France, 1984-88. Diplomate Am. Bd. Surgery - Vascular Surgery, Am. Bd. Surgery - Gen. Surgery. Clin. asst. Ctr. Hospitalier Gen., Wissenbourg, France, 1984-88; intern, resident L.I. Jewish Med. Ctr., New Hyde Park, N.Y., 1988-91; resident Case Western Res. U. Hosp., Cleve., 1991-94, fellow vascular surgery, 1995-97; asst. prof. clin. surgery U. Ariz. Coll. Medicine, Tucson, 1997—2002, assoc. prof. clin. surgery, 2002—; clin. instr. surgery Case Western Res. U., 1995-97; attending vascular surgeon So. Ariz. VA Health Care Sys., Tucson, 1997—; assoc. staff vascular surgery U. Med. Ctr., 1999—. Contbr. articles to profl. jours and chpts. to books. Co-dir. Red Cross Youth, Port-Au-Prince, 1978-82. Fellow ACS; mem. Internat. Soc. for Endovascular Specialists, Internat. Coll. Surgeons, Assn. VA Surgeons, Assn. Academic Surgery, Am. Assn. Vascular Surgery, Peripheral Vascular Surgery Soc., We. Vascular Surgery Soc. Office: So Ariz VA Health Care Sys Surg Care Line (2-112) 3601 S 6th Ave Tucson AZ 85723-0001 E-mail: halex94@aol.com.

WESTERBERG, ARTHUR WILLIAM, chemical engineering educator; b. St. Paul, Oct. 9, 1938; s. Kenneth Waldorf and Marjorie Claire (Darling) W.; m. Barbara Ann Dyson, July 14, 1963; children: Kenneth (dec.), Karl. BS, U. Minn., 1960; MS, Princeton U., 1961; PhD, Imperial Coll., London, 1964. Pres. Farm Engring. Sales Inc., Savage, Minn., 1964-65; sr. analyst Control Data Corp., San Diego, 1965-67; asst. prof., assoc. prof., prof. U. Fla., Gainesville, 1967-76; prof. chem. engring. Carnegie-Mellon U., Pitts., 1976—, chmn. dept., 1980-83, Swearingen prof., 1982—, dir. Design Research Ctr., 1978-80, Univ. prof., 1992—; dir. Engring. Design Research Ctr., 1986-89. Co-author: Process Flowsheeting, 1979, Systematic Methods of Chemical Process Design, 1997. Recipient Murphree award Am. Chem. Soc., 1997, Coll. of Engring., Carnegie Mellon (Steven J. Fenves Sys. Engring. award, 1998), Disting. Prof. award, 2002. Fellow AIChE (lectr. 1989, Computers and Systems Tech. divsn. award 1983, Walker award 1987, McAfee award 1990, Founders Outstanding Contbns. Chem. Engring. award 1995); mem. NAE, Am. Soc. Engring. Edn. (chem. engring. divsn. lectr. 1981, GE Sr. Rsch. award 1999). Home: 5564 Beacon St Pittsburgh PA 15217-1972 Office: Chem Engring Dept Carnegie Mellon U Pittsburgh PA 15213 E-mail: a.westerberg@cmu.edu.

WESTERDAHL, JOHN BRIAN, nutritionist, health educator; b. Tucson, Dec. 3, 1954; s. Jay E. and Margaret (Meyer) W.; m. Doris Mui Lian Tan, Nov. 18, 1989; 1 child, Jasmine Leilani. AA, Orange Coast Coll., 1977; BS, Pacific Union Coll., 1979; MPH, Loma Linda U., 1981; PhD, Pacific Western U., 2001. Registered dietitian, master herbalist; cert. nutrition specialist; bd. cert. anti-aging health practitioner. From nutritionist, health educator to dir. Castle Med. Ctr., Kailua, Hawaii, 1981—98, dir. wellness and lifestyle medicine and nutritional svc., 1998—; dir. nutrition and health rsch. Health Sci., Santa Barbara, Calif., 1989-90; sr. nutritionist, project mgr. Shaklee Corp., San Francisco, 1990-96; dir. nutrition Dr. McDougall's Right Foods, Inc., South San Francisco, 1996—; mem. faculty staff, dir. continuing edn. Am. Acad. Nutrition, 1996—98, dir. wellness and lifestyle medicine and nutritional svcs., 1998—; staff nutritionist Millennium Restaurant, San Francisco, 1995—. Radio talk show host Nutrition and You KGU Radio, Honolulu, 1983—89, KWAI Radio, Honolulu, 1999—; nutrition com. mem. Hawaii div. Am. Heart Assn., Honolulu, 1984—87; mem. nutrition study group Gov.s Conf. Health Promotion and Disease Prevention, Hawaii, 1985. Author: Medicinal Herbs: A Vital Reference Guide, 1998, The Millennium Cookbook: Extraordinary Vegetarian Cuisine, 1998; editor: Nourish Mag., 1995-96; nutrition editor: Veggie Life Mag., 1995—. Mem.: several other profl. assns., Seventh-day Adventist Dietetic Assn., Hawaii Dietetic Assn., Hawaii Nutrition Coun. (v.p. 1983-86, pres.-elect 1988-89, pres. 1989), Inst. Food Technologists, Am. Soc. Pharmacognosy, Am. Coll. Nutrition, Am. Dietetic Assn. (Hawaii coord. vegetarian nutrition dietetic practice group), Am. Acad. Anti-Aging Medicine, Am. Coll. Sports Medicine, AAAS. Republican. Seventh-Day Adventist. Avocations: swimming, scuba diving. Office: Castle Med Ctr Wellness & Lifestyle Med Ctr 640 Ulukahiki St Kailua HI 96734 *Personal philosophy: "Beloved, I wish above all things that thou mayest prosper and be in health, even as thy soul prospereth." 3 John 2.*

WESTERFIELD, CAROLYN ELIZABETH HESS, city planner; b. New Haven, May 3, 1933; d. Orvan Walter and Carol Woodruff (Maurer) Hess; m. Holt Bradford Westerfield, Dec. 17, 1960; children: Pamela Bradford Bingham, Leland Avery. BA, Wellesley Coll., 1954; postgrad., Yale U., 1954-55, M of City Planning, 1959. Planner, office mgr. Tech. Planning Assocs., New Haven, 1955-57, 61-62; assoc. planner City Plan Dept., 1956-59; planner, editor State of Conn. Devel. Commn., 1959-61; cons., 1962—; prin. planner South Cen. Conn. Planning Region, 1979-87; asst. plan dir. Town of Fairfield (Conn.), 1987; planning and zoning adminstr. Town of North Branford (Conn.), 1987-89. Devel. pvt. programs New Haven Hosp.-Boston City Hosp., 1952-54; lectr. city planning U. New Haven, 1988—. Mem. alumni bd. Yale U. Sch. Architecture, 1964-76, 85-96, pres., 1993-95; bd. dirs. alumni orgns. Prospect Hill Sch., New Haven, St. Thomas Day Sch.; class officer Wellesley Coll.; mem. Econ. Devel. Commn. Consortium, Hamden, Conn., mem. design rev. com.; clk. Ethics Commn. Mem. Am. Planning Assn., Am. Inst. Cert. Planners, Conn. Women in Planning and Devel., Alliance for Architecture (steering com. 1995—), New Haven Colony Hist. Soc., Jr. League New Haven (various exec. position), Watch Hill Improvement Soc. (pres. 1971-73), Conn. Child Welfare Assn., Yale U. Women's Orgn. (pres. 1979-81). Avocations: music, arts, sports, cultural exchange. Home and Office: 115 Rogers Rd Hamden CT 06517-3541

WESTERFIELD, HOLT BRADFORD, political scientist, educator; b. Rome, Italy, Mar. 7, 1928; s. Ray Bert and Mary Beatrice (Putney) W.; m. Carolyn Elizabeth Hess, Dec. 17, 1960; children: Pamela Bradford, Leland Avery. Grad., Choate Sch., 1944; BA, Yale U., 1947; MA, Harvard U., 1951, PhD, 1952. Instr. govt. Harvard U., 1952-56; asst. prof. polit. sci. U. Chgo., 1956-57; mem. faculty Yale U., 1957—, prof. polit. sci., 1965-2000, chmn. dept., 1970-72, Damon Wells prof. internat. studies, 1985-2000; prof. emeritus, 2000—; rsch. assoc. Washington Center Fgn. Policy Research, Johns Hopkins Sch. Advanced Internat. Studies, 1965-66. Vis. prof. Wesleyan U., Middletown, Conn., 1967, 71; bd. visitors U.S. Joint Mil. Intelligence Coll., Washington, 1998—. Author: Foreign Policy and Party Politics: Pearl Harbor to Korea, 1955, The Instruments of America's Foreign Policy, 1963; editor: Inside CIA's Private World: Declassified Articles from the Agency's Internal Journal, 1955-92, 1995. Sheldon traveling fellow Harvard, 1951-52; Henry L. Stimson fellow Yale, 1962, 73; sr. Fulbright-Hays scholar, 1973; hon. vis. fellow Australian Nat. U., 1973. Mem. Am. Polit. Sci. Assn. (Congl. fellow 1953-54), Internat. Polit. Sci. Assn., Internat. Studies Assn. Home: 115 Rogers Rd Hamden CT 06517-3541 Office: Yale Univ Dept Polit Sci PO Box 208301 New Haven CT 06520-8301

WESTERFIELD, PUTNEY, management consulting executive; b. New Haven, Feb. 9, 1930; s. Ray Bert and Mary Beatrice (Putney) W.; m. Anne Montgomery, Apr. 17, 1954; children: Bradford, Geoffrey, Clare. Grad., Choate Sch., 1942-47; BA, Yale, 1951. Co-founder, v.p. Careers, Inc., N.Y.C., 1950-52; mgr. S.E. Asia Swen Publs., Inc., Manila, Philippines, 1952; mem. joint adv. commn. Korea, 1953-54; polit. officer Am. embassy, Saigon, Vietnam, 1955-57; asst. to pub. Time mag., N.Y.C., 1957-59, asst. circulation dir., 1959-61, circulation dir., 1961-66, asst. pub., 1966-68, Life mag., N.Y.C., 1968; pub. Fortune mag., 1969-73; pres. Chase World Info. Corp., 1973-75; v.p. Boyden Assocs. Internat., San Francisco, 1976-80, sr. v.p., western mgr., 1980-84, pres., chief exec. officer N.Y.C. and San Francisco, 1984-90, mng. dir., 1990—. Chmn. bd. dirs. Upside Media Inc. Bd. dirs. Urban League, N.Y.C., 1969-71, Children's Village, 1968-71, Mediterranean Sch. Found., 1969-71, Nat. Boys Club, 1970-73, U.S. -S. Africa Leaders Exch. Program, 1971—, Bus. Coun. for Internat. Understanding, 1974-76, Yale-China Assn., 1975-78, East Meets West Found., 1991—; trustee Choate Sch., Wallingford, Conn., 1967-76, Westover Sch., Middlebury, Conn., 1975-79, Watch Hill Chapel Soc., 1963-77, Assn. Yale Alumni, 1972-75, 80-83. Mem. Burlingame Country Club, Pacific Union Club, Bohemian Club. Home and Office: 10 Greenview Ln Hillsborough CA 94010-6424 E-mail: putneyw@pacbell.net.

WESTERFIELD, RICHARD, music director; BA in Music, Yale Coll., 1979; MMus, Yale Sch. Music, 1986; MBA, Dartmouth U., 1990. Condr. N.Y. Philharmic, 1993; assoc. condr. Boston Symphony Orch.; music dir. Ala. Symphony Orch., Birmingham, Harrisburg Symphony; asst. prof. Brown U. Guest condr. NY Philharm., Pitts. Symphony, Buffalo Philharm., Montreal Symphony, Netherlands Radio Symphony, Melbourne Symphony, Sydney Symphony, Adelaide Symphony, NY Chamber Symphony, San Diego Symphony, L'Orchestre de Bretagne, Augsburg Philharm. Orchester, Heidelberg Symphony, BBC Symphony, Wales, Edmonton Symphony, Tapiola Sinfonietta, Oreg. Bach Festival, Balt. Symphony, Phoenix Symphony, Kansas City Symphony, Tucson Symphony, Colo. Symphony, Indpls. Symphony, Grand Rapids Symphony, Pacific Symphony, Chgo.'s Grant Park Festival Orch., Can. Nat. Arts Ctr. Orch., Kitchener-Waterloo Symphony, Minn. and Fla. Orchs., Orch. of St. Luke's, New World, Jacksonville, Fla., West Coast and Colo. Springs Symphonies, R.I. and Tulsa Philharm. Orchs., Aukland Philharmonia, Singapore Symphony, Japan's Osaka Century and Hiroshima Symphonies, Bucharest, Cluj and Moldova Philharm. Orchs., Finland's Koupio and Oulu Symphonies, Mexico City Camerata Nacional. Office: Ala Symphony Orch 3621 6th Ave S Birmingham AL 35222-2407

WESTERGAARD, GEORGE HENRY, secondary education educator; b. Sumas, Wash., Aug. 4, 1942; s. Henry C. and Mary T. Westergaard; m. Donna M. Westergaard, June 20, 1964; 1 child, Kristen. BA in Edn., Ctrl. Wash. State Coll., 1964; MS in Interdisciplinary Studies, U. Oreg., 1969; DA in History, Carnegie Mellon U., 1976. Cert. secondary edn. tchr., Wash. Tchr. social studies and English Woodrow Wilson Jr. H.S., Yakima, Wash., 1964-67, Cal Young Jr. H.S., Eugene, Oreg., 1967-73; mem. staff, asst. rsch. historian Carnegie Mellon U., Pitts., 1971-73; tchr. social studies, counselor Thomas Jefferson Jr. H.S., Eugene, 1973-83; tchr. govt., econs., global studies, and psychology South Eugene H.S., 1983-88, tchr. social scis., chair social studies dept., 1988-94, tchr. advanced placement govt. and politics, 1994-99; tchr. advanced placement psychology, comp. govt., politics Sammamish H.S., Bellevue, Wash., 1999—. Cons. AP Govt. ad Politics workshops, 1990—; adj. prof. edn. U. Oreg., summer 1991; mem. social studies task force State of Oreg., 1997-99; nat. reader, question leader AP Gov. and Politics; adj. prof. Pacific Luth. U., 2001, 2002. Fellow Ind. Study in the Humanities, 1986. Avocations: photography, fishing, hiking. Home: 2323 167th Ave NE Bellevue WA 98008

WESTERHAUS, CATHERINE K. social worker; b. Corydon, Ind., Oct. 13, 1910; d. Anthony Joseph and Permelia Ann (Mathes) Kannapel; m. George Henry Westerhaus, Apr. 15, 1950. BEd in Music, Kans. U., 1934; MSW, Loyola U., Chgo., 1949. Cert. Acad. Cert. Social Workers. Clin. social worker Friendly Acres Home of Aged, Newton, Kans.; county welfare dir., state adult svcs. supr. Newton-Harvey County, State of Kans.; vol. cert. social worker Newton. Project dir.: Memories of War Years, 1995, The War Years Including Veterans of Harvey County, Kansas, 1995; contbr. articles to profl. jours. Vol. to veterans, home-bound and disabled people, residents in nursing homes, patients in hospitals. With USNR, 1945-46. Named Kans. Social Worker of Yr., 1975, Kans. 5th Dist. Legionnaire of Yr., 1998. Mem. NASW (cert.), Kans. Soc. Cert. Social Work, Am. Legion (comdr. Wayne G. Austin post 1981-82, del Nat. Conv. 1997, Legionnaire of Yr. Dept. Kans. 1998). Home: 20215 SE 30th Ave Pratt KS 67124-8371

WESTERHAUS, DOUGLAS BERNARD, lawyer; b. Marion, Kans., Jan. 11, 1951; s. Edwin Gerard and Bernadine (Ullman) W.; m. Susan Elizabeth Scott, Aug. 20, 1973 (div. Jan. 1979); m. Karen Sue Giersch, Sept. 20, 1980 (div. Aug. 1997); children: John Joseph, Jamie Lynn, Jeffrey Michael; m. Victoria Lee Ruhga, March, 1998. BSBA, Kans. U., 1973, JD, 1976. Bar: Kans. 1976, U.S. Dist. Kans. 1976, U.S. Supreme Ct. 1980. Assoc. Harper & Hornbaker, Junction City, Kans., 1976-78, ptnr., 1978-80; prin. Westerhaus Law Office, Marion, Kans., 1980-86; pres. Hydrogen Energy Corp., 1986-91, also bd. dirs.; staff atty. THORN Ams., Inc., dba Rent-A-Ctr., Wichita, Kans., 1991-95, chief counsel human resources, 1995-96, assoc. gen. counsel, 1996-97; dir. Field Human Resources, 1997-98; exec. v.p. Mr. Goodcents Franchise Sys., Inc., 1999—2001, sr. v.p. and gen. counsel, 2002—. Atty. City of Grandview Plaza, Kans. 1977-80, City of Lehigh, Kans. 1980-86, Marion County, 1981-85; gen. counsel The Hydrogen Energy Corp., Kansas City, Mo. 1984-86, Marion Die & Fixture, 1980-86. Bd. dirs. St. Luke's Hosp., Marion, 1985-86. Mem. ABA, Kans. Bar Assn. (chmn. Lawyer Referral Commn. 1979-84, Outstanding Service award 1984), Marion County Bar Assn. (pres. 1985), Sedgwick County Bar Assn. Republican. Roman Catholic. Home: 12813 King St Overland Park KS 66213-4416

WESTERHOFF, GARRET PETER, environmental engineer, executive; b. Fairlawn, N.J., Oct. 12, 1935; s. Garret Peter and Elizabeth (Ullmer) W.; m. Helga Ann Kasch, May 31, 1958; children: Garret Peter, Eric John, Paul Keith. BS in Civil Engring., N.J. Inst. Tech., 1957, MS in Sanitary Engring., 1967. Registered profl. engr., N.J., N.Y., Ohio, Va., Ariz., Calif., Md., Fla., Ala., La., Maine, Mass., Nebr., N.Mex., Nev., N.C., Pa., Wash.; cert. profl. planner; diplomate Am. Acad. Environ. Engrs. Loss prevention engr. Factory Mutual Engring. Co., 1960-64; project engr. Jersey Engring. Assocs., 1964-65; from v.p. to chmn., CEO Malcolm Pirnie, Inc., White Plains, N.Y., 1967—. Mem. rsch. adv. coun. Nat. Water Rsch. Inst.; internat. rapporteur on water quality and treatment in U.S. Internat. Water Supply Assn., World Congress, Budapest, 1993, Durban, S. Africa, 1995; tech. cons. Office Drinking Water U.S. EPA; presenter in field. Contbr. articles to profl. jours. 1st lt. USAF, 1957-60. Mem. ASCE, NAE, NSPE, Am. Water Works Assn. (former stds. coun., chmn. Internat. Water Supply Assn. N.Am. com., former chmn. water supply planning and coord. com., former trustee engring. and constrn. divsn., former chmn. water reuse coom., former chmn. water treatment plant wastes disposal com., former chmn. alum recovery rsch. adv. com., rsch. adv. coun. Rsch. Found.), Water Environment Fedn. Avocations: fishing, photography, writing. Office: Malcolm Pirnie Inc 104 Corporate Park Dr Ste 1 White Plains NY 10604-3335 E-mail: gwesterhoff@pirnie.com.

WESTERHOFF, JOHN HENRY, III, clergyman, theologian, educator; b. Paterson, N.J., June 28, 1933; s. John Henry and Nona Celia (Walsh) W.; m. Alberta Louise Barnhart, Dec. 27, 1955 (div. 1991); childen: Jill Louise, John Jeffrey, Beth Anne; m. Caroline Askew Hughes, Oct. 27, 1991. BS, Ursinus Coll., 1955; STB, Harvard U., 1958; EdD, Columbia U., 1974; DD, Ursinus Coll., 1990. Ordained to ministry United Ch. of Christ, 1958, Episcopal Ch., 1978; pastor Congl. Ch., Presque Isle, Maine, 1958-60, assoc. pastor Needham, Mass., 1960-64; pastor 1st Congl. Ch., Williamstown, 1964-66; edn. sec., editor Colloquy (United Ch. Bd. for Homeland Ministries), N.Y.C., 1966-73; Lentz lectr. Harvard U. Div. Sch., 1973-74; prof. Duke U. Div. Sch., Durham, N.C., 1974-94; dir. Inst. Pastoral Studies, Atlanta, 1992—; interim rector St. Bartholomew Episcopal Ch., 1993-94; assoc. rector St. Lukes

Episcopal Ch., 1994—. Author: Values for Tomorrows Children, 1970, A Colloquy on Christian Education, 1972, Generation to Generation, 1974, Tomorrow's Church, 1976, Will Our Children Have Faith?, 1976, McGuffey and His Readers, 1978, Who Are We?, 1978, Learning Through Liturgy, 1978, Inner Growth-Outer Change, 1979, The Church's Ministry in Higher Education, 1979, Liturgy and Learning Through the Life Cycle, 1980, Christian Believing, 1980, Bringing Up Children in The Christian Church, 1980, A Faithful Church, 1981, The Spiritual Life: Learning East and West, 1981, Building God's People, 1983, A Pilgrim People, 1984, Living the Faith Community, 1985, On the Threshold of God's Future, 1986, Living Into Our Baptism, 1990, Schooling Christians, 1992, The Spiritual Life: Foundation for Preaching and Teaching, 1994; A People Called Episcopalians, 1995, Holy Baptism: A Guide for Parents and Godparents, 1996, Grateful and Generous Hearts, 1997, To Love and to Cherich Till Death Do Us Part, 1998, Sensing Beauty, 1998, A People on a Pilgrimage, 1999, Will Our Children Have Faith?, 2000; editor: Religious Edn, 1979-89. Mem. Assn. Profs. and Researchers in Religious Edn., Religious Edn. Assn. Democrat. Episcopalian. Office: Saint Luke's Episcopal Ch 435 Peachtree St NE Atlanta GA 30308-3228

WESTERHOUT, GART, b. The Hague, The Netherlands, June 15, 1927; arrived in U.S., 1962, naturalized, 1969; s. Gerrit and Magdalena (Foppe) W.; m. Judith Mary Monaghan, Nov. 14, 1956; children: Magda C., Gart T., Brigit M., Julian C. Drs., Leiden U., Netherlands, 1954, PhD, 1958. Asst. Leiden U. Observatory, 1952-56, sci. officer, 1956-59, chief sci. officer, 1959-62; prof., dir. astronomy U. Md., 1962-73, chmn. div. math. and phys. scis. and engring., 1972-73, prof. astronomy, 1973-77; sci. dir. U.S. Naval Observatory, Washington, 1977-93; vis. astronomer Max Planck Inst. Radio Astronomy, Bonn, Germany, 1973-74, mem. adv. bd. Germany, 1976-79. Mem. astronomy adv. bd. NSF, 1963-67; vice chmn. divsn. phys. sci. NRC, 1969-73; mem. com. on radio frequencies, 1971-92; trustee Assoc. Univs. Inc., 1971-74; mem. Inter Union Commn. on Allocation of Frequencies, 1974-82; mem. sci. coun. Stellar Data Ctr., Strasbourg, France, 1978-84, chmn., 1981; chmn. working group on astrometry, astronomy survey com. NAS, 1979-81; mem. adv. bd. Haystack-N.E. Radio Obs. Consortium, 1974-77; mem. Arecibo adv. bd. Nat. Astronomy and Ionosphere Ctr., 1977-80, chmn., 1979-80; mem. U.S. nat. com. CODATA, 1985-91. Contbr. on radio astronomy, spiral structure of our Galaxy and astrometry to profl. jours. Recipient citation for teaching excellence Washington Acad. Scis., 1972; U.S. Sr. Scientist award Alexander von Humboldt Stiftung, Ger., 1973; NATO fellow, 1959. Mem. Internat. Astron. Union (chmn. working group on astron. data 1985-91), Internat. Sci. Radio Union (pres. commn. on radio astronomy 1975-78), Am. Astron. Soc. (councillor 1975-78, v.p. 1985-87), Royal Astron. Soc. Roman Catholic. Home: 811 W 38th St Baltimore MD 21211-2203

WESTERLAND, MAUREEN A. fundraiser; b. Teaneck, N.J., Aug. 29, 1944; d. Michael Joseph and Lorraine (McAvoy) McDermott; m. Barry C. Westerland, Jan. 13, 1973; children: Craig, Kirsten. BS in Phys. Therapy, U. N.C., 1966; MA, MEd in Counseling Psychology, Columbia U., 1974. Dir. devel. Seniors Inc., Denver, 1984-87; exec. dir. Aurora (Colo.) Edn. Found., 1987-88; dir. devel. Morris Area Girl Scout Coun., Randolph, N.J., 1988-90, Morristown (N.J.) Neighborhood House, 1990-91; asst. v.p. univ. advancement N.J. Inst. Tech., Newark, 1991-95; dir. devel. Summit Speech Sch., New Providence, N.J., 1995—. Trustee Chatham (NJ) Edn. Found., 1992—99. Mem. adv. bd. Jr. League, Summit, N.J. Mem. Nat. Soc. Fund Raisers (trustee 1996—, Outstanding Fund Raising Profl. award in N.J. 2000). Avocations: skiing, reading, cooking. Office: Summit Speech Sch 705 Central Ave New Providence NJ 07974-1140

WESTERLUND, ELAINE M. psychologist, educator; b. Boston, Nov. 19, 1945; d. Alden F. and Virginia A. (Peterson) W.; m. Joseph F. Doherty; 1 child, Neil A. Doherty. BS, Northeastern U., 1980; EdM, Boston U., 1982, EdD, 1987. Lic. psychologist, Mass.; diplomate Am. Bd. Psychol. Specialties, Am. Psycho-therapy Assn. Psychology trainee Solomon Carter Fuller Mental Health Ctr, Roxbury, Mass., 1981-82, Laboure Ctr. Mental Health Clinic, South Boston, 1982-83; psychology intern South Shore Mental Health Ctr., Quincy, 1983-84; co-founder, peer counselor, group facilitator Incest Resources, Inc., Cambridge, 1980-82, psychotherapist, 1982-88, dir., 1988—; pvt. practice, 1988—. Cons., guest lectr. in field; tchg. fellow Boston U., 1982-84; founding mem. Deaf Women's Counseling Project, Cambridge, Mass.; pioneer survivor self-help movement in U.S.; developer program and treatment models for survivors. Author: Responding to Incest: In Memory of Nancy, 1987, Women's Sexuality After Childhood Incest, 1992; contbr. articles to profl. jours. Recipient Outstanding Alumni award Health Scis., Northeastern U., 1999. Mem. Am. Psychotherapy Assn., Mass. Psychol. Assn., Am. Coll. Forensic Examiners, Mass. Assn. of Deaf, Psi Chi, Pi Lambda Theta, Sigma Epsilon Rho. Office: One Arnold Cir Cambridge MA 02139-2250

WESTERMAN, ALBERT BARRY, marine surveyor and consultant; b. Phila., July 8, 1941; s. William Edward and Alice Beverly (Martin) W.; m. Madeline Rose Laugginger, July 23, 1943 (div. July 1974); children: Debra Lee Westerman Bordelon, Allan Keith; m. Lynn Marie Nesser, May 31, 1947; children: David William, Dawn Marie. Student, U. Md., Augsburg, Germany, 1961, Bucks County Tech., 1966, Tulane U., 1970-71, La. State U., 1987. Journeyman machinist Honeywell Corp., Tampa, Fla., 1967-68; resident surveyor Owensby & Kritikos, Inc., Gretna, La., 1968-70; field constrn. supr. Ocean Drilling & Exploration Co., New Orleans, 1970-73; gen. mgr. Weldit Engring. Ltd., Scunthorpe, Eng., 1973; v.p. Ocean-Oil Internat. Engring. Corp., New Orleans, 1973-74; pres. Internat. Cons. & Brokers, Inc., Metairie, La., 1974-76; v.p. Am. Gulf Shipping, Inc., 1982-88; pres., dir. Nat. Radiometric Agy., Inc., 1987—; pres. Albert B. Westerman & Co., Inc., 1973—. Author, editor: Procedure and Operations Manual, 1987. With U.S. Army, 1960-61. Mem. NRA, Nat. Assn. Marine Surveyors, Soc. Naval Archs. and Marine Engrs., Am. Boat and Yacht Coun., Propeller Club. Lutheran. Avocations: diving, hunting, fishing. Home: 2800 Sells St Metairie LA 70003-3543 Office: Nat Radiometric Agy PO Box 7784 Metairie LA 70010-7784 E-mail: al@alwesterman.com.

WESTERMAN, LIANE MARIE, research scientist executive; b. Long Branch, N.J., June 20, 1949; d. Charles Wilson and Edith Doris (Johnson) Case; m. S. Thomas Westerman; children: David Aaron, Charles Paul. BA in Psychology, Monmouth U., West Long Branch, N.J., 1972; MA in Teaching, Coll. of N.J., 1979. Cert. tchr. of handicapped, N.J. Tchr. spl. edn., dir. afternoon program S.E.A.R.C.H., Ocean, N.J., 1972-74; tchr. spl. edn. Jackson (N.J.) Twp. Sch. System, 1974-79; exec. dir. Otologic Edn., Inc., Shrewsbury, N.J., 1980-88; dir. clin. rsch. Nat. Patent Analytical Systems, Inc., Roslyn Heights, N.Y., 1983-86, v.p. rsch., 1986-88; pres. Westerman Rsch. Assocs., Inc., Shrewsbury, N.J., 1988—. Participant numerous convs., profl. organs. and spl. interest groups, U.S.A., Israel and The Netherlands, 1974—; software devel. expert to knowledge engr. for Visual Perceptual System, 1984—; v.p. Otologic Edn., Inc., Shrewsbury, 1988—. Co-contbr. articles and chpts. to profl. publs.; U.S. and Can. patentee computer-aided drug-abuse detection. Fundraiser Am. Heart Assn., 1991; active MADD; activist Nat. Audubon Soc. Mem. Am. Acad. Otolaryngology, Head and Neck Surgery (assoc.), Internat. Regulatory Affairs Profls. Soc., Nat. Graphic Soc., Assn. Clin. Pharmacologists, Regulatory Affairs Profls. Soc., Monmouth County Assn. Children with Learning Disabilities, Psi Chi, Sigma Xi. Avocations: travel, classical music, creative writing. Office: Westerman Rsch Assocs Inc 499 Broad St Shrewsbury NJ 07702-4003

WESTERMAN, ROSEMARY MATZZIE, nurse, administrator; b. Sewickley, Pa., May 20, 1949; d. Joseph Edward and Martha (Aquino) Matzzie; m. Philip M. Westerman, Aug. 7, 1971. BSN, Duquesne U., 1971, MSEd, 1975. RN, Pa. Head nurse Dept. Vet. Affairs VA Med. Ctr., Pitts., 1982-83; assoc. chief, nursing svc., edn. W. S. Middleton Meml. VA Hosp., Madison, Wis., 1983-85, Dept. VA Affairs VA Med. Ctr., Chilicothe, 1985-91, assoc. chief nursing svc., long term. care, 1991-93; assoc. chief nurse VA Med. Ctr., Augusta, Ga., 1993-97, chief nurse Muskogee, Okla., 1997—; clin. nurse specialist Office of the Med. Inspector Vet. Health Adminstrn., Washington. Active Literacy Vol. of Am. Mem. ANA (cert. nursing adminstrn. advanced), Assoc. Am. Coll. Health Care Execs. Nursing Orgn. of VA, VA Nurse Execs., Sigma Theta Tau. Home: 4001 Olney Laytonsville Rd Olney MD 20832-1801

WESTERMANN-CICIO, MARY LOUISE, academic administrator, library studies educator; b. N.Y.C., Mar. 11, 1953; d. A. Louis and Anne U. (Skelly) Morse; m. Edward L. Cicio, June 20, 1998. BS in Biology, L.I. U., 1975, MS in Libr. Sci., 1976, MPA in Health Care Adminstrn., 1986; MA in History, SUNY, Stony Brook, 1992, PhD, 2001. Con. med. libr. Nassau-Suffolk Health Systems Agy., Melville, N.Y., 1976-77; dir. John N. Shell Libr. Nassau Acad. Medicine, Gardent City, 1977-78; instr. L.I. U., Greenvale, 1977-88, adj. prof., 1983-88; asst. prof. Palmer Grad. Libr. Sch., 1988-95, asst. dean, 1995—. Trustee L.I. Libr. Resources Coun., 1986-91; mem. adv. bd. Sr. Connections Program, Adelphi U., 1987-92; bd. dirs. Nassau County coun. Girl Scouts, 2002—. Recipient E. Hugh Behymer award L.I. U., 1976, Disting. Alumni award Palmer Sch. L.I. U., 1993, Jackson Turner Maid award SUNY at Stony Brook, 1993. Mem. ALA, Med. Libr. Assn. (sec. med. socs. sect. 1981-82, instr. continuing edn. 1982, chmn. med. soc. sect. 1986-87; cert. health scis. librianship, Murry E. Gottlieb award 1998), Acad. Health Info. Professions, Spl. Librs. Assn. (sec. L.I. chpt. 1978-80, bd. dirs. 1982-84, pres. elect 1988, pres. 1989-90), Cath. Libr. Assn. (instr. workshop, Libr. of Yr. award 1992), Suffolk-Nassau on-Line Retrievers (chmn. 1981), Med. and Sci. Librs. of L.I. (pres. 1980-81), Nassau County Libr. Assn. (chmn. health svcs. com. 1978-81, 83-93, bd. dirs. 1990-92), Beta Beta Beta, Beta Phi Mu (bd. dirs. Beta Mu chpt. 1987-89, Golden Anniversary award 1999), Pi Alpha Alpha. Office: LI Univ CW Post Campus Palmer Sch Libr and Info Scis Greenvale NY 11548 E-mail: westerma@liu.edu.

WESTERMEYER, JOSEPH JOHN, psychiatrist; b. Chgo., Apr. 8, 1937; m. Rachel Moga; children: Michelle, Joseph; 5 foster children. Student, U. Notre Dame and St. Thomas Coll., 1955-57; BS in Biology and Chemistry, U. Minn., 1959, MD, 1961, MA in Anthropology, 1969, MPH, PhD, 1970. Diplomate Am. Bd. Psychiatry and Neurology, Am. Bd. Family Practice. Rotating intern St. Paul-Ramsey Hosp., 1961-62; gen. practice medicine Payne Ave. Med. Clinic, St. Paul, 1962-65; dep. chief div. pub. health AID, Laos, 1965-67; resident in psychiatry U. Minn., Mpls., 1967-70, instr., 1970-71, asst. prof., 1971-74, assoc. prof., 1974-78, prof. psychiatry, 1978—, prof., chair, 1989, adj. prof. anthropology, adj. prof. psychology, 1979—, dir. med. student edn. dept. psychiatry, 1976-82; mem. psychiatry staff, outpatient psychiat. practice U. Minn. Hosps. and Clinics, 1970-89; prof., chmn. dept. psychiatry and behavioral sci. Okla. U. Med. Ctr., Oklahoma City, 1989—; founder, dir. acute in-patient service U. Minn. Hosps. and Clinics, Mpls., 1970-72, founder, dir. day hosp., 1971-73, cons. primary care clinic, 1970-83, founder, dir. outpatient clinic for refugees from S.E. Asia, 1977-82, founder, dir. program for alcohol and drug dependence, 1982—, founder, dir. internat. clinic dept. psychiatry, 1984—. Mem. ad hoc com. on Indochinese refugees Minn. Dept. Pub. Welfare, 1980-82; cons. methadone program Minn. VA Hosp., 1977-84, dept. psychiatry Mpls. VA Hosp., 1978-85; mem. case devel. com. for computer-based exam. Nat. Bd. Med. Examiners, 1983-88; mem. com. on mental and behavioral assessment and disorder in pilots FAA and AMA, 1984-85; chmn., co-editor devel. of a teaching manual on drug/alcohol dependence WHO, 1982-85, chmn., co-editor task force and report on methadone treatment in opiate dependence, 1982-85, research cons. internat. collaborative study of drug dependence intervention and treatment in primary health care, 1982-85; cons. in field; vis. prof. various colls.; lectr. in field. Author: A Primer on Chemical Dependency: A Clinical Guide to Alcohol and Drug Problems, 1976, Poppies, Pipes and People: A Study of Opium and Its Use in Laos, 1983, (with C. Williams) Refugees Mental Health Issues in Resettlement Countries, 1986, A Clinical Guide to Drug and Alcohol Problems, 1986; (with A. Arif) A Manual for Substance Abuse Education, 1988, An Update on Methadone, 1988; The Psychiatric Care of Migrants, 1989; editor: Anthropology and Mental Health, 1976; co-editor: (with E. Foulks, R. Wintrob and A. Favazza) Transcultural Psychiatry, 1977; contbr. revs. and articles to profl. jours., chpts. to books; mem. editorial bd. Am. Jour. Drug and Alcohol Abuse, 1973— , Jour. Operational Psychiatry, 1977-86, Am. Jour. Pub. Health, 1980-83, 83-87, Advances in Alcohol and Substance Abuse, 1980— , Alcoholism: Clin. and Exptl. Research, 1980-86, Alcohol and Research World, 1981— ; social sci. editor Substance Abuse Newsletter, 1979-83; rev. reader Am. Jour. Psychiatry, 1978—, Transcultural Psychiat. Revs., 1980-84, Archives Gen. Psychiatry, 1981—, White Cloud Jour., 1981—, Jour. Nervous and Mental Disease, 1977—, Current Anthropology, 1979, 83, 85, Culture, Medicine and Psychiatry, 1979-80, various others. Recipient Meritorious Service award U.S. AID, 1967; Ginzburg fellow Group for Advancement of Psychiatry, 1969-70, NIH summer fellow Grad. Session in Epidemiology, U. Minn. Continuation Ctr., 1970, 72, 78; research grantee Office Internat. Programs, U. Minn., 1974-75, 78, 81, NIMH, 1973-74, 80-81, 82-84, Nat. Inst. Alcohol Abuse and Alcoholism, 1974-77, 78-79, Grad. Sch. U. Minn., 1977-78, Office Drug Abuse Prevention, U. Minn., 1977-78, Minn. Med. Found., 1974-75, 81, 82-83, Nat. Inst. Drug Abuse, 1977-78, 83-85, State Minn., 1979-80, Ctr. Urban and Regional Affairs, U. Minn., 1982-83, career tchr. grantee Alcohol, Drug Abuse and Mental Health Adminstrn., HEW, 1973-75, Biomed. research support grantee U. Minn. Med. Sch., 1977-78, Minn. Med. Found., 1977, tng. grantee Office Alcohol and Other Drug Abuse Programming, U. Minn., 1979-83, Indochinese Health Professionals, 1979-81, Archie; recipient numerous other research grants. Fellow Am. Anthropol. Assn., Am. Assn. Family Practice, Am. Psychiat. Assn. (com. on drug abuse 1985—); mem. World Psychiat. Assn. (transcultural sect.), Am. Soc. Social Psychiatry, Soc. Med. Anthropology, Assn. Med. Educators and Researchers in Substance Abuse (award for disting. contributions to the field 1987), AAAS, Assn. Behavioral Sci. and Med. Edn., Assn. Acad. Psychiatrists, Am. Pub. Health Assn., Research Soc. on Alcoholism, World Psychiat. Assn. (sect. on transcultural psychiatry), Soc. for Study of Psychiatry and Culture (steering com. 1979— , secretariat 1984-85), Am. Med. Soc. on Alcoholism (state chmn. 1979—), Am. Acad. Psychiatrists in Alcoholism and Addictions, Soc. Traumatic Stress Studies, Minn. Psychiat. Assn. (mem. chem. dependency subcom. 1979— , mem. Minn. mental health interdisciplinary interest group rep. 1980-85, pres. 1984-86), Minn. State Med. Assn. (resource group on alcoholism and other chem. dependencies 1976-81), Okla. Med. Assn., Alpha Omega Alpha. Home: 1935 Summit Ave Saint Paul MN 55105-1430

WESTERN, KARL AUGUST, physician, epidemiologist; b. Trenton, N.J., July 6, 1940; s. August Earl and Lillian Theresa (Murphy) W.; m. Aileen Martin Worthington, May 2, 1964; children: Ann Worthington, Mark August. AB, Georgetown U., 1961, MD, 1965; diploma of tropical pub. health, London Sch. Tropical Medicine & Hygiene, 1972. Intern Bellevue Hosp.-Cornell Meml.-Sloan Kettering Joint Program, N.Y.C., 1965-66, resident, 1966-67; medical epidemiologist Ctr. Disease Control, Atlanta, 1967-70; resident supr. infectious diseases L.A. County-USC Med. Ctr., 1971-72; medical epidemiologist Va. State Health Dept., Richmond, 1972-74; dept. head Pan Am. Health Orgn., Washington, 1975-79; asst. dir. Nat. Inst. Allergy & Infectious Diseases, Bethesda, Md., 1979—. Adj. assoc. prof. Uniformed Services U. Health Scis., Bethesda, 1981—, Tulane U., New Orleans, 1986—. Served as med. dir. USPHS, 1967-97. Recipient Okeke award U. London, 1972, Meritorious Service award, 1970, Commendation award, 1983, Outstand. Service award, 1987, USPHS. Mem. AMA, Am. Soc. Tropical Medicine & Hygiene (editor Tropical Med. news, 1987-99), Am. Pub. Health Assn. (sec. epidemiology sect. 1973-78), Nat. Council Internat. Health (chair annual meeting 1986). Republican. Roman Catholic. Home: 6436 31st St NW Washington DC 20015-2342 Office: Nat Inst Allergy Infectious Diseases/NIH 9000 Rockville Pike Bethesda MD 20892-7630

WESTERVELT, CHARLES EPHRAIM, JR. lawyer; b. Columbus, Ohio, Mar. 10, 1922; s. Charles Ephraim and Winifred Reed (Wells) W.; m. Melba Louise Kuhlman, Mar. 3, 1946; children: John Charles, Kirk Thomas, Todd William, Reed Matthew. BA, Ohio State U., 1943, LLB and JD, 1948. Ptnr. Graves & Westervelt, Columbus, 1948-53; chief right of way atty. Ohio Turnpike Commn., 1953-55, asst. to exec. dir., 1956; pvt. practice C.E. Westervelt Jr., Westerville, Ohio, 1956—. Trustee Westerville Pub. Libr., 1958-75; twp. clk. Geona Twp., Ohio, 1960-72, mem. vol. fire dept., 1970-95; various offices Westerville Hist. Soc., 1948—. With USAAF, ETO, 1943-46. Decorated Air medal with 4 oak leaf clusters. Mem. Phi Beta Kappa. Republican. United Methodist. Avocations: reading, gardening, camping, fishing, genealogy. Home: 7974 Africa Rd Westerville OH 43082-8818 Office: 18 W College Ave Westerville OH 43081-2104

WESTERVELT, JAMES JOSEPH, retired insurance company executive; b. Bklyn., July 8, 1946; s. Cornealius V. and Regina Elizabeth (May) W.; m. Sue Jane Brubaker, Aug. 5, 1972; children: Kevin K., Natalie M. MBA, Manhattan Coll., 1967. Mgr. auditing Peat, Marwick & Mitchell, N.Y.C., 1967-78; dir. auditing City Investing, 1978-81; asst. v.p., asst. contr. The Hartford Financial Svcs. Group, Inc., Conn., 1981-89, v.p., group contr., 1989-94, sr. v.p., group contr., 1994—2001; CFO HIMCO, 1998—2001; group contr. Hartford Fin. Svc. Group, 1998—99; sr. v.p., CFO Himco, 1999—2001; sr. v.p. Hartford Fin. Svc., Inc.; ret., 2002—. With U.S. Army, 1968-69. Mem. AICPA, Hawaii Soc. CPAs, Conn. Soc. CPAs, Am. Ins. Assn. Roman Catholic. Avocations: skiing, wine tasting, tennis, chess, electronics.

WESTFALL, CAROL ANN, artist, educator; b. Everett, Pa., Sept. 7, 1938; d. Carroll Francis and Doris Lucille (Hawkins) Dooley; m. Jon David Westfall, Jan. 27, 1962 (div. Aug. 1976); children: Camille, Maigann; m. Andrew J. Del Preore, Aug. 14, 1992. BFA, RISD, 1960; MFA, Md. Inst., 1972. Instr. Md. Inst., Balt., 1968-72; asst. prof. fine arts Montclair State Coll., Upper Montclair, NJ, 1972-79, assoc. prof., 1979-87, prof., 1987—2002, v.p. senate Sch. Fine and Performing Arts, 1987-89. Vis. prof. Columbia U. Tchrs. Coll., N.Y.C., 1976-86; artist-in-residence Memphis Coll. Art, 1985, Am. Craft Mus., N.Y.C., 1987; mem. artists in schs. panel N.J. Coun. on Arts, Trenton, 1978-88; study leader India tour Textile Mus., Washington, 1987; resident Artpark, Lewiston, N.Y., 1989; guest prof. Seian Coll., Kyoto, Japan, 1992. Co-author: Plaiting: Step by Step, 1976; exhibited at Lausanne Biennale, 1975, Am. Craft Mus., 1987, Kyoto (Japan) Internat. Textile Exhbn., 1989, 97, 99. Recipient purchase award N.J. State Mus., 1975; Indo-Am. fellow, 1980-81, fellow N.J. Coun. on Arts, 1987; rsch. grantee Montclair State Coll., 1987, 89, 90, 91, 94, 98, 99, 2000, 01. Mem. N.Y. Rug Soc. Office: Montclair State U Dept Art and Design Upper Montclair NJ 07043

WESTFALL, DAVID, lawyer, educator; b. Columbia, Mo., Apr. 16, 1927; s. Wilhelmus David A. and Ruth (Rollins) W.; children: Elizabeth Stewart, William Beatty, Thomas Curwen, Katharine Putnam. AB, U. Mo., 1947; LLB magna cum laude, Harvard U., 1950. Bar: Ill. 1950, Mass. 1956. Assoc. Bell, Boyd, Marshall & Lloyd, Chgo., 1950-55; asst. prof. law Harvard Law Sch., 1955-58, prof., 1958—, John L. Gray prof., 1983—, Carl F. Schipper Jr. prof., 1996—. Author: Estate Planning Cases and Text, 1985, Every Woman's Guide to Financial Planning, 1984, Family Law, 1993; co-author: Estate Planning Law and Taxation, 4th edit., 2000; co-editor: Readings in Federal Taxation, 1983. Served as 1st lt. JAGC, AUS, 1951-53. Fellow Am. Coll. Trust and Estate Counsel (acad.); mem. ABA, Mass. Bar Assn., Am. Law Inst., Phi Beta Kappa, Phi Delta Theta. Office: 1525 Massachusetts Ave Cambridge MA 02138-2903 Home: 1525 Massachusetts Ave Cambridge MA 02138-2903

WESTFALL, MORRIS, state legislator; b. Apr. 5, 1939; s. Raymond Earl and Ethel Faye (Neill) W.; m. Sharon Kay Douglas, Dec. 19, 1964; children: Craig Lin, Christi Dawn. BS, U. Mo., 1962. Mem. Mo. Ho. of Reps., Jefferson City, 1971-81, Mo. Senate from 28th dist., Jefferson City, 1994—; asst. minority floor leader, minority whip, 1995—. State exec. dir. agrl. stabilization conservation svc. USDA, Mo., 1981-93. Mem. U. Mo. Alumni Assn., Saddle Club. Office: State Capitol Building Jefferson City MO 65101-1556 E-mail: morris_westfall@senate.state.mo.us.

WESTFIELD, FRED M. economics educator; b. Essen, Germany, Nov. 7, 1926; came to U.S., 1940; s. Dietrich and Grete (Stern) W.; m. Joyce A. Horwitz Nochlin, Nov. 15, 1968; stepchildren: Steven Nochlin, Keith Nochlin. BA magna cum laude, Vanderbilt U., 1950; PhD in Indsl. Econs., MIT, 1957. Teaching asst., instr. MIT, Cambridge, 1952-53; lectr. Northwestern U., Evanston, Ill., 1953-57, asst. prof., 1957-60, assoc. prof., 1960-65; prof. econs. Vanderbilt U., Nashville, 1965-98, mem. faculty coun. Coll. Arts and Sci., 1974-76, mem. faculty senate, 1979-82, 94-95, dir. undergrad. studies dept. econs. and bus. adminstrn., 1984-87, mem. grad. faculty coun., 1991, prof. econs. emeritus, 1998—. Vis. prof. U. Colo., summers 1973-74; condr. seminars, lectr., participant univs. and rsch. orgns.; Fulbright sr. lectr. U. Nac. del Sur, Argentina, 1986; cons. Coun. Econ. Advisers, Exec. Office Pres., 1968, World Bank and Water and Power Devel. Authority, Pakistan, 1970-72, World Bank and East African Power and Light Co., Kenya, 1975, NSF, 1975, FTC, 1976-78, World Bank, UN Devel. Program and Econ. Planning Bd. South Korea, 1975-76; expert witness Tenn. Pub. Svc. Commn., 1980-89, Consumer Advocate Tenn. Atty. Gen., 1994; also others. Mem. editorial bd. Utilities Policy, 1990—; mem. bd. editors So. Econ. Jour., 1973-75; editorial referee Am. Econ. Rev., Jour. Polit. Economy, Econometrica, So. Econ. Jour., Econ. Inquiry; contbr. articles and book revs. to profl. jours. With U.S. Army, 1945-46. Fellow Gen. Edn. Bd., MIT, Ford Found., 1958-59. Mem. Am. Econ. Assn., Econometric Soc. (program com. 1967, chmn. conf. sessions), So. Econ. Assn. (v.p. 1976-77, chmn. conf. sessions), Phi Beta Kappa. Home: 1097 Lynnwood Blvd Nashville TN 37215-4540

WESTHAVER, LAWRENCE ALBERT, electronics engineer, consultant; b. Washington, Oct. 24, 1936; s. James Waldo and Hattie Virginia (Bush) W.; m. Jo Ann Turner, Jan. 5, 1957; children: Lawrence Albert Jr., Wendy Jo Westhaver Burke, Bonnie Jo Westhaver Green. Cert. engring., U. Va., 1966. Electronic design, cons. Westhaver Assocs., Inc., Laurel, Md., 1971—; engring. draftsman Office Rsch. and Devel. Nat. Security Agy., Arlington Hall, Va., 1955-57, engring. technician Office Rsch. and Engring. Ft. G.G. Meade, Md., 1958-66, electronic engr. Office Rsch. and Engring., 1967-82, sr. engr. Office of Rsch. and Engring., 1982-84; sr. engr. Communications Systems Support Group, Laurel, 1984-93. Patentee method for photographic aperture control, photographic light integrator, switching current regulator, photographic test equipment, electronic tuner for stringed musical instruments, microcomputer-based Ni-Cd battery charger, and color-correcting filter for underwater photography. Avocations: scuba diving, snorkeling, biking, hiking, bird watching. Home: 8609 Portsmouth Dr Laurel MD 20708-1819 E-mail: larry@westhaver.com.

WESTHEIMER, DAVID KAPLAN, novelist; b. Houston, Apr. 11, 1917; s. Adolf and Esther (Kaplan) W.; m. Doris Gertrude Rothstein, Oct. 9, 1945; children: Fred, Eric. BA, Rice Inst., Houston, 1937. Successively asst. amusement editor, radio editor, mag. editor, TV editor Houston Post, 1939-41, 45-46, 50, 53-60, columnist, 1984-88. Author: Summer on the Water, 1948, The Magic Fallacy, 1950, Watching Out for Dulie, 1960, Von Ryan's Express, 1964, My Sweet Charlie, 1965, Song of the Young Sentry, 1968, Lighter Than a Feather, 1971, Over the Edge, 1972, Going Public, 1973, The Avila Gold, 1974, The Olmec Head, 1974, Rider on the Wind, 1979, Von Ryan's Return, 1980, The Great Wounded Bird, and other poems, 2000, (with John Sherlock) The Amindra Gamble, 1982, Sitting It Out, 1992, Death Is Lighter Than a Feather, 1995, Delay En Route, 2002, (with Karen Westheimer) LoneStar Zodiac, 1995, (play) My Sweet Charlie, 1966, (TV films) Trouble Comes to Town, 1972, A Killer Among Us, 1990. Served to capt. USAAF, 1941-45, ETO; served to capt. USAF, 1950-53; lt. col. USAF; ret. Decorated Air medal, D.F.C. Mem. ACLU, NAACP, Writer's Guild Am. West. Author's Guild, Ret. Officers Assn., Calif. Writers Club. Democrat. Avocation: reading. Home and Office: 11722 Darlington Ave Apt 2 Los Angeles CA 90049-5525 E-mail: dwestheime@aol.com.

WESTHEIMER, FRANK HENRY, chemist, educator; b. Balt., Jan. 15, 1912; s. Henry Ferdinand and Carrie (Burgunder) Westheimer; m. Jeanne Friedmann, Aug. 31, 1937; children: Ruth Susan, Ellen. AB, Dartmouth Coll., 1932, SCD (hon.) , 1961; MA, Harvard U., 1933, PhD, 1935; ScD (hon.) , U. Chgo., 1973, U. Cin., 1976; ScD (hon.) , Tufts U., 1978, U. N.C., 1983, Bard Coll., 1983, Weizmann Inst., 1987; ScD (hon.) , U. Ill., Chgo., 1988. Rsch. assoc. U. Chgo., 1936—37, instr., 1937—41, asst. prof., 1941—44, assoc. prof., 1946—48, prof. chemistry, 1948—53; vis. prof. Harvard U., 1953—54, prof. chemistry, 1954—82, sr. prof., 1982—83, prof. emeritus, 1983—, chmn. dept., 1959—62; Overseas fellow Churchill Coll., U. Cambridge, England, 1962—63. Mem. Pres.'s Sci. Adv. Com., 1967—70; rsch. supr. Explosives Rsch. Lab., Nat. Def. Rsch. Com, 1944—45; presenter in field. Mem. editl. bd.: Jour. Chem. Physics, 1942—44, mem. editl. bd.: , 1952—54, mem. editl. bd.: , 1960—69; contbr. articles to profl. jours. Recipient Naval Ordnance Development award, 1946, Army-Navy cert. of appreciation, 1946, James Flack Norris award in phys.-organic chemistry, 1970, Willard Gibbs medal, 1970, Theodore W. Richards medal, 1976, Richard Kokes award, 1980, Charles Frederick Chandler medal, 1980, Rosenstiel award, 1981, Nichols medal, 1982, Robert A. Welch award, 1982, Cope award, 1982, Ingold medal,

1983, Nat. Medal of Sci., 1986, Paracelsus medal, 1988, Priestley medal, 1988, Repligen award, 1992, Nakanishi award, 1997; fellow, Columbia U. NRC, 1935—36, Guggenheim Found., 1962—63, Fulbright-Hays Found., 1974, Exchange fellow, NAS, China, 1982, Japan Soc. Promotion of Sci., 1982. Mem.: Royal Soc., Am. Acad. Arts and Scis. (sec. 1985—90), Am. Philos. Soc. (council 1981—84), Nat. Acad. Sci. (council 1971—75, 1976—79, chmn. com. survey chemistry 1964—65, award in chem. scis. 1980). Home: 3 Berkeley St Cambridge MA 02138-3409 E-mail: westheimer@chmistry.harvard.edu.

WESTHEIMER, GERALD, optometrist, educator; b. Berlin, Germany, May 13, 1924; naturalized, 1944, came to U.S., 1951; s. Isaak and Ilse (Cohn) W. Optometry diploma, Sydney (Australia) Tech. Coll., 1943, fellowship diploma, 1950; BSc, U. Sydney, 1947; PhD, Ohio State U., 1953; DSc (hon.), U. NSW, Australia, 1988; ScD (hon.), SUNY, 1990. Practice optometry, Sydney, 1945-51; research fellow Ohio State U., 1951-53; prof. physiol. optics U. Houston, 1953-54; asst. prof., then assoc. prof. physiol. optics Ohio State U., 1954-60; postdoctoral fellow neurophysiology Marine Biol. Lab., Woods Hole, Mass., 1957; vis. researcher Physiol. Lab., U. Cambridge, Eng., 1958-59; mem. faculty U. Calif. at Berkeley, 1960—, prof. physiol. optics, 1963-68, chmn. group physiol. optics, 1964-67, prof. physiology, 1968-89, prof. neurobiology, 1989—, head div. neurobiology, 1987-92; adj. prof. Rockefeller U., N.Y., 1992—. Sackler lectr. Tel Aviv U. Med. Sch., 1988, D.O. Hebb lectr. McGill U., 1991, Grass Found. lectr. U. Ill., 1991, Wertheimer lectr. U. Frankfort on the Main, 1998; mem. com. vision NRC, 1957-72; mem. visual scis. study sect. NIH, 1966-70, chmn. visual scis. B study sect., 1977-79; mem. vision, research and tng. com. Nat. Eye Inst., NIH, 1970-74, chmn. bd. sci. counselors, 1981-83; mem. exec. council com. vision NAS-NRC, 1969-72; mem. communicative scis. cluster Pres.'s Biomed. Rsch. Panel, 1975. Author rsch. papers; editor: Vision Rsch., 1972-79; editl. bd. Investigative Ophthalmology, 1973-77, Exptl. Brain Rsch., 1973-89, Optics Letters, 1977-78, Spatial Vision, 1985—, Ophthalmic and Physiological Optics, 1985—, Vision Rsch., 1985-92, Jour. of Physiology, 1987-94. Recipient Von Sallman prize Columbia U., 1986; Prentice medal Am. Acad. Optometry, 1986, Bicentennial medal Australian Optometric Assn., 1988. Fellow AAAS, Royal Soc. London (Ferrier lectr. 1992, editl. bd. procs. 1990-96, 2000—), Am. Acad. Arts and Scis., Optical Soc. Am. (Tillyer medal 1978, assoc. editor jour. 1980-83), Am. Acad. Optometry; mem. Royal Soc. New So. Wales, Soc. Neurosci., Assn. Rsch. in Vision and Ophthalmology (Proctor medal 1979), Internat. Brain Rsch. Orgn., Physiol. Soc. Gt. Britain, Sigma Xi. Home: 582 Santa Barbara Rd Berkeley CA 94707-1746 E-mail: gwest@socrates.berkeley.edu.

WEST-HILL, GWENDOLYN, poet, educator, artist, evangelist; b. Indpls., July 30, 1951; d. Wendell Waldon West and Joyce Moody Young; m. David Lee Spencer, March 12, 1972 (div. Mar. 1982); children: Hasan Abdul Spencer, Laila Marscia Spencer; m. David Lee Hill, July 25, 1985 (dec. July 1995). BA in Elem. Edn., Ind. U., 1973; Degree in Bus. Adminstrn., Butler U., 1983; degree in Comml. Art, Chas Wharton Sch. Art, 1984; student, Ga. Med. Inst., 1992. Prin., CEO T-Shirt Haven, Atlanta, 1990—. Author: Poems for the Family, 1990, Prism of Thoughts, 1998, Giving It Back To You, 2000, My Brother Phillip West, 2002; contbr. poems to newspapers, mags., and anthologies. Missionary House of Refuge Prayer, Coll. Park, Ga., 1993—, Metro World Outreach Ctr., Stonemountain, Ga., 1998.; evangelist Metro World Outreach Ctr., The Potter's House, T.D. Jakes Ministries, Dallas, 1999. Recipient Eubie Blake award Ind. Black Expo, Indpls., 1985. Fellow Delta Sigma Theta (Gamma Nu chpt.). Pentecostal. Avocations: singing, drawing, writing, travel, teaching. Home: 4251 Parkview Ct Stone Mountain GA 30083-1294 Office: House of Refuge Prayer Mission College Park GA 30337-6243 E-mail: gospelqueen20022002@yahoo.com.

WESTIE, FRANK ROBERT, social sciences educator; b. Houghton, Mich., Mar. 9, 1921; s. Elmer Westie and Anna Josephine Sandell; m. Margaret Louise Blum, July 1, 1944; children: Katharine, Kurt, Anne. PhD, Ohio State U., 1951. Pres. Glen Arbor Enterprises, Mich., 1989—2002; adj. prof. Ariz. State U., Tempe, Ariz., 1982—2000; pres. Inverness Woods, Inc., Bloomington, Ind., 1964—82; prof. Ind. U., 1949—82. Mem. bd. Fulbright Com., Wash., DC, 1970; faculty grants chmn. Soc. Sci. Rsch. Coun., N.Y.C., 1970; pres. North Ctrl. Sociol. Assn., 1970; mem. coun. Am. Sociol. Soc., Wash., DC, 1950. Author: (novels) Ash Wednesday '45, 1996; contbr. articles to profl. jours. 1st lt. USAF. Decorated 9 combats. Mem.: Author's Guild, Soc. Sci. Rsch. Coun. Avocation: musical composition.

WESTIN, ALAN FURMAN, political science educator; b. N.Y.C., Nov. 11, 1929; s. Irving and Etta (Furman) W.; m. Beatrice Patricia Shapoff, June 20, 1954; children: David, Debra, Jeremy. BA, U. Fla., 1948; LLB, Harvard U., 1951, PhD, 1965. Bar: D.C. 1951. Sr. fellow Yale U. Law Sch., New Haven, 1956-57, vis. prof. polit. sci., 1960-61; asst. prof. govt. Cornell U., Ithaca, N.Y., 1957-59; assoc. prof. pub. law and govt. Columbia U., N.Y.C., 1959-66, prof., 1966-96, prof. emeritus, 1997—; dir. Ctr. Rsch. and Edn. in Am. Liberties, 1965-71; founder, pres. Ednl. Fund Individual Rights, N.Y.C., 1978-86; pres. Changing Workplaces, Englewood, N.J., 1982-87; program assoc. Harvard U., 1968-72; cons. IBM, 1973-75, U.S. Office Tech. Assessment, 1973—; pres. Ctr. Social and Legal Rsch., 1987—, Ref. Point Found., 1987-98; ptnr. Privacy Cons. Group, Washington, 1993—; chmn., CEO Toolkit Software, 1996—; CEO, Privacy Knowledge, 2001—; dir. Privacy Exchange.org, 1998—, Japan-U.S. Privacy and Data Protection Program, 1999—. Cons. on privacy to Equifax, Citicorp, IBM, Am. Express, U.S. Social Security Adminstrn., Chrysler, Health Data Exch., N.Y. State Identification and Intelligence Sys., Bell Atlantic, Glaxo Wellcome, Eli Lilly; cons. on employee rights Fed. Express, Aetna Life and Casualty, Citicorp, IBM, 1980-86; acad. advisor nat. pub. surveys on privacy Louis Harris and Assocs., 1979, 90, 91, 92, 93, 94, 95, 96, 97, 98, 99, 2000; nat. pub. surveys on cons. privacy, Can., 1992, 94, U.K., Germany, 1999; dir. privacy and human genome project U.S. Dept. Energy, 1992-95; chmn. emm. adv. panels U.S. Office Tech. Assessment, 1975-92; chmn. Res. Coun. Healthy Cos., 1991-95; spkr. nat. bus., profl., govt. confs., 1960—; pres. Privacy & Am. Bus. Inst., 1993—. Author: The Anatomy of a Constitutional Law Case, 1958, reprinted, 1990 (put in Notable Trials Libr. 1995), Privacy and Freedom, 1967 (George Polk award, Sidney Hillman award, Melcher award, Van Am. Soc. award 1967), (with Barry Mahoney) The Trial of Martin Luther King, 1975, (with Michael A. Baker) Databanks in a Free Society, 1972; editor: Whistle Blowing! Loyalty and Dissent in the Corporation, 1980, Information Technology in a Democracy, 1971 (with Alfred Feliu) Resolving Employment Disputes Without Litigation, 1988, (with John D. Aram) Managerial Delemmas: Cases in Social, Legal, and Technological Change, 1988; editor-in-chief: The Civil Liberties Rev., 1973-79; polit. sci. editor: Casebook Series, 1960-66; contbr. numerous chpts. to books, articles to legal and popular publs.; mem. editl. bd. Employee Rights and Responsibilities Jour., Information Age, Jour. Computing and Society, Transnational Data Report: writer-narrator: CBS-TV Series, The Road to the White House, 1964; cons. spl. programs: ABC-TV; advisor Off Limits: Your Health, Your Job, Your Privacy, PBS Network, 1994; pub. editor-in-chief Privacy and American Business, 1993—. Mem. Nat. Wiretapping Commn., 1973-76; vice-chmn. N.J. Commn. Individual Liberty, 1977-81; sr. cons. U.S. Privacy Protection Study Commn., 1975-77. Recipient Mark Van Doren award Columbia U., 1972; recipient Disting. Alumnus award Delta Sigma Rho-Tau-Kappa Alpha, 1965; grantee Rockefeller Found., 1983, Russell Saga Found., 1969-71, 81-82 Mem. Nat. Acad. Scis. (computer sci. and engring. bd. 1969-72), Am. Polit. Sci. Assn., Assn. Computing Machinery (chmn. task force privacy 1972-73) Home: 1100 Trafalgar St Teaneck NJ 07666-1928 also: Ctr Social Legal Rsch 2 University Plaza Dr Ste 414 Hackensack NJ 07601-6209 *As fast as technological and social changes are in our age, the enduring matters are how we try to live our personal lives, how we relate to the people we work with, and how strongly we support civility and democratic values in our communities and nation.*

WESTIN, HELEN TILDA, writer, songwriter; b. Laporte, Minn., Oct. 14, 1918; d. Theodore Olsen and Hannah Christina (Pedersen) Granvold; m. Kermit Wallace Westin, Oct. 25, 1936; 1 child, Gail Westin Ochiai. Sec. LaSalle Mgmt. Co., Detroit, 1946-50; acct. State of Oreg., Salem, 1953-54. Author: Introducing the Song Sheet, 1976; creator game Song Twisters, 1988; composer various songs; publ. Keiko's Song, 1997; contbr. numerous articles to Nat. Sheet Music Soc. Mem. City Roses Sheet Music Club (charter). Home: 912 NE 113th Ave Portland OR 97220-2208

WESTIN, RICHARD AXEL, law educator, lawyer, consultant; b. London, July 8, 1945; came to U.S., 1952; s. Gosta Victor and Muriel Yalden (Thomson) W.; m. Judith A. Parke,r Sept. 3, 1978; m. 2d, Elizabeth J. Cook, June 13, 1981. BA, Columbia U., 1967, MBA, 1968; JD, U. Pa., 1972. Bar: Calif. 1973, Vt. 1975, U.S. Dist. Ct. (no. dist.) Calif. 1972, U.S. Dist. Ct. Vt. 1975. Cons. World Bank, 1969-72; assoc. Dewey, Ballantine, Bushby, Palmer & Wood, N.Y.C., 1972-75; tax counsel Vt. Life Ins. Co., Montpelier, 1975-79; prof. law U. Houston Law Ctr. Cons., dir. Millenium Leasing Corp., Paradise Land and Cattle, Inc. Author: Tax Lexicon, 1984, Natural Resource Taxation, 1987, Federal Tax Planning, 1990; author: (with others) Tax Fraud and Money Laundering, Accounting Periods and Methods, 1993; contbr. articles to profl. jours. Mem. ABA (leader task force on liquidation/reins). Home: 3141 Warrenwood Wynd Lexington KY 40502-3578

WESTLAND, CYNTHIA LANE, management consultant, engineer; b. Weymouth, Mass., Sept. 10, 1953; d. Robert Edson and Mary Eleanor (Calvi) Lane. BS Indsl. Engring., Northeastern U., 1976. Quality coord. Stone & Webster Engring., Boston, 1971-76; quality engr. Kaiser Engrs., 1976-80; quality mgr. Microcom, Norwood, Mass., 1980-82; sr. engr. Aritech, Framingham, 1982-84; supr. cons. Coopers & Lybrand, Boston, 1984-86; pres. 21st Century Engring., Newton, Mass., 1986-89; prin. Mercer Mgmt. Cons., Lexington, 1989-92, Rath & Strong, Lexington, 1992—. Author: Quality, The Myth and The Magic, 1990. Mem. Am. Soc. Women Engrs. (sr.), Am. Soc. Quality Control (Golden Quill 1991), NAFE, Goal/Quality, Productivity and Competitiveness. Republican. Avocations: skiing, sailing, Chung Moo Doe. Office: Rath and Strong 92 Hayden Ave Ste 1 Lexington MA 02421-7963 Home: 148 Russell St Woburn MA 01801-4709

WESTLEY, JOHN RICHARD, economist; b. Fairmont, Minn., Feb. 25, 1939; s. Richard and Margaret (Kindschi) W.; m. Sidney Kathryn Bohanna, Mar. 26, 1966(div. Sept. 1977); children: Elizabeth Laura, Karen Margaret, Marian Bohanna; m. Joan Nancy Ehrlich, Apr. 12, 1980; 1 child, Katherine Matthea. BA in Philosophy, Yale U., 1961; MA in Econs., Columbia U., 1966; PhD in Econs., Am. Univ., 1983. Internat. economist U.S. Dept. Treasury, Washington, 1966-69; loan officer U.S. AID, Addis Ababa, Ethiopia, 1970-72, economist Nairobi, Kenya, 1973-75, Washington, 1976-78, program officer New Delhi, India, 1979-84, dir. mission to Bangladesh Dhaka, 1985-87, assoc. asst. adminstr. bur. Africa Washington, 1987-90, dir. mission to Kenya Nairobi, 1990-94; dir. Mission to Egypt US AID, Cairo, 1994-98; v.p. Internat. Fund Agrl. Devel., Rome, 1998—. Author: Agriculture and Equitable Growth, 1986. With U.S. Army, 1961-64. Mem. Am. Econ. Assn., Phi Beta Kappa. Presbyterian. Home and Office: IFAD Via del Serafico 107 00142 Rome Italy

WESTLING, JON, university administrator; b. Yakima, Wash., June 7, 1942; s. Norman L. and Jean R. (Bergamini) W.; m. Elizabeth A. Wüthrich, Oct. 14, 1977; children: Emma E., Matthew R., Andrew N. BA, Reed Coll., 1964; postgrad., St. John's Coll. Oxford (Eng.) U., 1964-67, UCLA, 1971-74. Instr. history Centre Coll., Danville, Ky., 1967-68; asst. prof. history and humanities Reed Coll., Portland, Oreg., 1968-71; assoc. dir. Boston Univ. Prodns., 1974-76; asst. to pres. Boston U., 1976-79, assoc. provost, 1979-83, provost ad interim, 1983-84, provost, 1984-88, exec. v.p., 1988-90, interim pres., 1990, exec. v.p., provost, 1991-95, provost, pres.-elect, 1995-96, pres., 1996—2002, pres. emeritus, 2002—. Bd. dirs. Century Bank. Bd. dirs. Jobs for Mass., Inc., 1998—, Boston 2000, 1987—2000; trustee Boston Mus. Sci., 1990—; mem. corp. Nat. Braille Press, Inc., 1998—; trustee Am. Coll. Greece, 1998—; bd. dirs. Boston History Collaboration, 2000—, treas., 2001—. Gen. Motors Nat. scholar, 1960-64, Rhodes scholar, 1964-67. Home: 135 Ivy St Brookline MA 02446-3904 Office: Boston U Office Pres 147 Bay State Rd Boston MA 02215-1708 also: Boston University 121 Bay State Road Boston MA 02215

WESTLUND, MARIBETH, secondary school educator; b. Chgo., Apr. 29, 1961; d. Francis Joseph and Catherine Marie Balda. BS, Ill. State U., 1983; MEd, DePaul U., 1993. Cert. ednl. adminstr., tchr. Ill. Tchr. Our Lady of Knock Cath. Sch., Calumet City, Ill., 1985—86; dept. chair of social studies, tchr. Schaumburg H.S., Schaumburg High School, 1986—. Nominee Golden Apple Educator Nominee, Golden Apple Found., 2002. Mem.: AAUW, NOW, Nat. Coun. Social Studies. Avocations: travel, hiking, bicycling, tennis. Office: Schaumburg HS 1100 W Schaumburg Rd Schaumburg IL 60194 Personal E-mail: mbwestlund@yahoo.com. E-mail: mwestlund@d211.org.*

WESTMAN, JACK CONRAD, child psychiatrist, educator; b. Cadillac, Mich., Oct. 28, 1927; s. Conrad A. and Alice (Pedersen) W.; m. Nancy K. Baehre, July 17, 1953; children— Daniel P., John C., Eric C. MD, U. Mich., 1952. Diplomate Am. Bd. Psychiatry and Neurology. Intern Duke Hosp., Durham, N.C., 1952-53; resident U. Mich. Med. Ctr., 1955-59; dir. outpatient svcs. Children's Psychiat. Hosp., Ann Arbor, Mich., 1961-65; assoc. prof. U. Mich. Med. Sch., 1964-65; coord. diagnostic and treatment unit Waisman Ctr., U. Wis., Madison, 1966-74, prof. psychiatry, 1965-96, prof. emeritus, 1997—. Cons. Joint Commn. on Mental Health of Children, 1967-69, Madison Pub. Schs., 1965-74, Children's Treatment Ctr., Mendota Mental Health Inst., 1965-69 Author: Individual Differences in Children, 1973, Child Advocacy, 1979, Handbook of Learning Disabilities, 1990, Who Speaks for the Children?, 1991, Licensing Parents, 1994, Born to Belong, 1997, Parenthood in America, 2001; editor Child Psychiatry and Human Devel., 1984-99; contbr. articles to profl. jours. Vice-pres. Big Bros. of Dane County, 1970-73; v.p. Wis. Assn. Mental Health, 1968-72; co-chmn. Project Understanding, 1968-75; pres. Wis. Cares, 1998—. With USNR, 1953-55. Fellow Am. Psychiat. Assn., Am. Coll. Psychiatrists, Am. Acad. Child and Adolescent Psychiatry, Am. Orthopsychiat. Assn. (bd. dirs. 1973-76); mem. Am. Assn. Psychiat. Svcs. for Children (pres. 1978-80), Multidisciplinary Acad. Clin. Edn. (pres. 1992-98). Home: 1234 Dartmouth Rd Madison WI 53705-2214 E-mail: jwestman@facstaff.wisc.edu.

WESTMAN, ROBERT ALLAN, management consultant; b. Marbleton, Que., Can., Feb. 22, 1926; s. James Amon and Flora Gladys (Gilbert) W.; m. Esther Florence Renshaw, July 2, 1949; children: Michael, Joel, Robin, Andrew. Student Chemistry, Physics, U. Bishop's Coll., Que., Can., 1942-43; BASc, U. Toronto, 1949; postgrad. Bus. Adminstrn., U. Pa., 1955-56. V.p. spl. projects Ogden Metals, Inc., Cleve., 1970-74; chmn. Warren (Ohio) Fabricating Corp., 1974-78; v.p., gen. mgr. C-L Metals, Niles (Ohio), Inc., 1978-79; pres. Inred Iron, Inc., Roseland, N.J., 1981-85, R.A. Westman & Assoc., Warren, 1979—. Bd. dirs., cons. Felber Studios, Inc., Ardmore, Pa., 1984—. Patentee cast clad steel plate. Rep. ward leader, Sunnyvale, Ca., 1961-62. Served with RCAF, 1943-45. Mem. Assn. Iron and Steel Engrs. (assoc.), Am. Iron and Steel Inst. (assoc.). Clubs: Duquesne (Pitts.). Presbyterian. Home and Office: 8984 Inverrary Dr SE Warren OH 44484-2551

WESTMAN, STEVEN RONALD, rabbi; b. Chgo., Sept. 16, 1945; s. Kurt S. and Hilda (Schmoller) W.; m. Sherri, Nov. 30, 1980; children: Rachel Dara, Emily Nicole, Molly Sarah Levin. BA, U. Ill., 1967; B of Hebrew Letters, Hebrew Union Coll., 1969, MA in Hebrew Letters, 1972, DDiv., 1997. Ordained rabbi, 1972. Asst. rabbi Congregation Rodeph Shalom, Phila., 1972-75; rabbi Temple Israel, Stroudsburg, Pa., 1975-83, Temple Beth Torah, Wellington, Fla., 1983-95, Temple Beth El Israel, Ft. Pierce, 1995-00, Temple Beth El, West Palm Beach, 2000—. Mem. Commn. for Jewish Edn., West Palm Beach, Fla., 1990-94; bd. dirs. Jewish Cmty. Day Sch., West Palm Beach, 1988-91, Jewish Cmty. Ctr., 1987-89; pres. Palm BEach County Bd. Rabbis, 1989-92. Bd. dirs. Palms West Hosp., Loxahatchee, Fla., 1986-91, Pocono Hosp., East Stroudsburg, Pa., 1979-83; found. bd. dirs. Hospice of Monroe County, East Stroudsburg, 1978-83; bd. dirs. Palm Beach Liturgical Culture Soc., West Palm Beach, 1986-95. Recipient Tower of David award State of Israel Bonds, 1988, Leadership award Jewish Fedn. of Palm Beach County, 1985. Mem. Cen. Conf. of Am. Rabbis, Rotary. Home: 13587 Jonquil Pl West Palm Beach FL 33414-8557 Office: Temple Beth El 2815 N Flagler Dr West Palm Beach FL 33407 E-mail: rabbiwestman@aol.com. *The theme and spirit of my rabbinate are found in the words of Pirkey Avot, the ethics of the Fathers: "Be of the disciples of Aaron, loving peace and pursuing peace, loving your fellow creatures and bringing them close to the Torah." (Avot 1:12).*

WESTMORE, MICHAEL GEORGE, make-up artist, writer; b. Hollywood, Calif., Mar. 22, 1938; s. Montague George and Edith Adeline W.; m. Marion Christine Bergeson, Dec. 4, 1966; children: Michael George, Michele, McKenzie. BA, U. Calif., Santa Barbara, 1961. Apprentice make-up artist Universal City Studios, Universal City, Calif., 1961-63, staff make-up artist, 1964, asst. head dept. make-up lab., 1965-71; freelance make-up artist various studios, Hollywood, 1971-87; make-up supr. and designer Paramount Studios, 1987—. Instr. theatre arts dept. Los Angeles Valley Coll., 1966-71; pres. Cosmetic Control Ctrs., Inc., 1971-76; pres. Hollywood Magic Cosmetics, 1985-87; rsch. cons., lectr. therapeutic cosmetics for med. assns. Author: The Art of Theatrical Make-Up for Stage and Screen, 1971, also chpts. in books; co-author: Star Trek Makeup FX Journal, Star Trek-Alines & Artifacts; make-up artist for TV spls. Eleanor and Franklin (emmy award NATAS 1976), Why Me? (Emmy award 1984), Three Wishes of Billy Grier (Emmy award 1985), Star Trek (Emmy award 1988, 92, 93, 95, 96), Amazing Stories (Emmy award 1987), (films) 2010 (Acad. award nomination Acad. Motion Picture Arts and Scis. 1985), Mask (Acad. award 1986), Clan of the Cave Bear (Acad. award nomination 1987), Star Trek First Contact (Acad. award nomination 1996). Served with AUS, 1956. Recipient Best Spl. Effects Make-up on TV for Geppetto award, Hollywood Make-up Artists Guild, 2001, Order of Achievement award, Lambda Chi Alpha. Mem. Internat. Alliance Theatrical Stage Employees, Soc. Make-up Artists, Vikings of Scandia, Lambda Chi Alpha (life) Address: 4616 Balboa Blvd Encino CA 91316-4105

WESTMORELAND, BARBARA FENN, neurologist, electroencephalographer, educator; b. 1940; BS in Chemistry, Mary Washington Coll., 1961; MD, U. Va., 1965. Diplomate Am. Bd. Psychiatry and Neurology and certification of added qualification in clin. neurophysiology (vice chair). Intern Vanderbilt Hosp., Nashville, 1965-66; resident in neurology U. Va. Hosp., Charlottesville, 1966-70; fellow in electroencephalography Mayo Clinic, Rochester, Minn., 1970-71, assoc. cons. neurology, 1971-73; asst. prof. neurology Mayo Med. Sch., 1973-78, assoc. prof., 1978-85, prof., 1985—. Co-author: Medical Neurosciences, 1978, rev. edit., 1986, first author 3d edit., 1994. Mem. Am. Epilepsy Soc. (treas. 1978-80, pres. 1987-88), Am. EEG Soc. (sec. 1985-87, pres. 1991-92), Cen. Assn. Electroencephalographers (sec.-treas. 1976-78, pres. 1979-80, chair neurology resident in-svc. tng. exam 1994-99), Am. Acad. Neurology (chair elect of sect. clin. neurophysiology 1998-2000, chair sect. clin. neurophysiology 2000-2002, vice chair exam com. for cert. in clin. neurophysiology of Am. bd. Psychiatry and Neurology 1998—), Mayo History of Medicine Soc. (pres. 1990-91), Sigma Xi (pres. chpt. 1987-88).

WESTMORELAND, T. ANDREW, university president; b. Batesville, Ark., Feb. 22, 1957; s. Fred E. and Elda L. W.; m. Jeanna S., May 17, 1980; 1 child, Riley Elizabeth. BA, Ouachita Bapt. U., 1979; MA, U. Ark., 1996, EdD, 1997. From devel. officer to pres. Ouachita Bapt. U., Arkadelphia, Ark., 1985—. Bd. dirs. Arkansans for Drug-Free Youth, Little Rock, 1998—, Bapt. Health Corp., Little Rock, 1998—, Clark County Indsl. Commn., Arkadelphia, 1990-93. Mem. Nat. Assn. Ind. Colls. & Univs. (bd. dirs. 2000—), Rotary. Avocations: travel, reading. Office: Ouachita Bapt U PO Box 3753 Arkadelphia AR 71998-3753

WESTMORELAND, THOMAS DELBERT, JR. chemist; b. near Vivian, La., June 2, 1940; s. Thomas Delbert and Marguerite Beatrice (Moore) W.; m. Martha Verne Beard, Jan. 1, 1966; children: Anne Laura, Kyle Thomas. BS, U. North Tex., 1963, MS, 1965; PhD, La. State U., 1971, postdoctoral fellow, 1971-72. Tchr., rsch. dir. Lewisville (Tex.) H.S., 1964; summer devel. program student Tex. Instruments, Inc., Dallas, 1966; sr. exptl./analytical engr. Power Systems divsn. United Technologies, South Windsor, Conn., 1972-76; sr. rsch. chemist Pennzoil Co., Shreveport, La., 1976-82, rsch. assoc., 1983-93; sr. environ. engr. Pennzoil Products Co. Tech. Ctr., The Woodlands, Tex., 1993-96; lectr. U. Houston, 1996-98; adj. prof. Tomball (Tex.) Coll., 1997, Montgomery Coll., Conroe, Tex., 1997-2000; health and safety officer Lexicon Genetics Inc., The Woodlands, 1998—2000, mgr. corp. safety, 2001—. Contbr. sci. articles to profl. jours.; patentee in field. Recipient E.I. duPont Tchg. award La. State U., 1968-69. Mem. Nat. Fire Protection Assn., Am. Chem. Soc. (treas. 1978-79, chmn. 1979-80), Assn. Rsch. and Enlightenment, Soc. Automotive Engrs., Jaycees (state dir. Conn. 1976, gov.'s civic leadership award Conn. 1975-76, C. William Brownfield Meml. award 1976), Masons (Scottish Rite, 32nd degree), Sigma Xi (sec.), Phi Eta Sigma (pres. 1959-60), Alpha Chi Sigma, Kappa Mu Epsilon. Home: 588 Melmont St Conroe TX 77302-3116 Office: 4000 Research Forest Dr The Woodlands TX 77381-4229 E-mail: twestmoreland@lexgen.com.

WESTOFF, CHARLES FRANCIS, demographer, educator; b. N.Y.C., July 23, 1927; s. Frank Barnett and Evelyn (Bales) Westoff; m. Joan P. Uszynski, Sept. 11, 1948 (div. Jan. 1969); children: David, Carol; m. Leslie Aldridge, Aug. 1969 (div. Feb. 1993); m. Jane De Lung, May 1997. AB, Syracuse U., 1949, MA, 1950; PhD, U. Pa., 1953. Instr. sociology U. Pa., 1950—52; research assoc. Milbank Meml. Fund, N.Y.C., 1952—55; research assoc. Office Population Research Princeton U., 1955—62, Maurice P. During '22 prof. demographic studies and sociology, 1962—99, sr. rsch. demographer, 1999—, chmn. dept. sociology, 1965—70, assoc. dir. Office Population Research, 1962—75, dir., 1975—92; assoc. prof. sociology N.Y.U., also chmn. dept. sociology Washington Sq. Coll., 1959—62; vis. sr. fellow East-West Population Inst., Honolulu, 1979—81; Disting. vis. prof. Am. U., Cairo, 1979; mem. vis. com. Harvard-M.I.T. Joint Center for Urban Studies, 1980—83. Exec. dir. Commn. Population Growth and Am. Future, 1970—72; mem. adv. com. on population stats. U.S. Bur. Census, 1973—79; chmn. Nat. Com. for Rsch. on 1980 Census, 1981—88; bd. dirs. Alan Guttmacher Inst., 1977—88, 1989—97; sr. tech. advisor Demographic Health Surveys, 1984—; bd. dirs. Population Resource Ctr., 1985—, Population Ref. Bur., 1988—94, Population Commns. Internat., 1992—98; com. on population NAS, 1983—88. Co-author: Family Growth in Metropolitan America, 1961, The Third Child, 1963, College Women and Fertility Values, 1967, The Later Years of Childbearing, 1970, From Now to Zero, 1971, Reproduction in the United States, 1965, 1971, Toward the End of Growth: Population in America, 1973, The Contraceptive Revolution, 1976, Demographic Dynamics in America, 1977, Age at Marriage, Age at First Birth and Fertility in Africa, 1992, Unmet Need: 1990-1994, 1995, Childbearing Attitudes and Intentions, 1995, Mass Media and Reproductive Behavior in Africa, 1997, Replacement of Abortion by Contraception in Three Central Asian Republics, 1998; contbr. articles on demography and sociology to profl. jours.; co-author: Unmet Need at the End of the Century, 2002. Recipient Irene Taeuber award for Outstanding Rsch. Contbns., 1995, 1995. Fellow: Am. Acad. Arts and Scis., Am. Sociol. Assn.; mem.: Internat. Union Sci. Study Population, Population Assn. Am. (bd. dirs. 1960—62, 1968—70, 1st v.p. 1972—73, pres. 1974—75), Planned Parenthood Fedn. Am. (dir. 1978—81), Inst. Medicine-NAS. Home: 1 Highland Rd Princeton NJ 08540 Office: Princeton U Wallace Hall Princeton NJ 08544

WESTON, ARTHUR WALTER, chemist, scientific and business executive; b. Smith Falls, Ont. Can., Feb. 13, 1914; came to U.S., 1935, naturalized, 1952; s. Herbert W. and Alice M. (Houghton) W.; m. V. Dawn Thompson, Sept. 10, 1940; children: Roger L., Randall K., Cynthia B. BA, Queen's U., Kingston, Ont., 1934, MA, 1935; PhD, Northwestern U., 1938. Postdoctoral fellow Northwestern U., Evanston, Ill., 1938-40; with Abbott Labs., North Chgo., 1940-79, dir. rsch. and devel., 1959-61, v.p. rsch. and devel., 1961-68, dir. company, 1959-68, v.p. sci. affairs, 1968-77, v.p. corp. licensing, 1977-79; v.p., dir. San-Abbott, Japan, 1976-79; cons. Abbott Labs., North Chgo., Ill., 1979-85; pres. Arthur W. Weston & Assocs., Lake Forest, 1979—. Contbr. profl jours. and books. Patentee in field. Mem. Office Sci. Rsch. and Devel., War Manpower Commn., 1942-45; mem. exec. com. indsl. chemistry, div. chemistry and chem. tech. NRC, 1961-65; mem. indsl. panel on sci. and tech. NSF, 1974-80; mem. ad hoc com. chem. agts. Dept. Def., 1961-65. Mem. Rsch. Dirs. Assn. Chgo. (pres. 1965-66), Am. Chem. Soc. (trustee Chgo. 1965—, dir. Chgo. sect. 1952-59, nat. com. corp. assocs. 1967-72), Dirs. Indsl. Rsch., Indsl. Rsch. Inst. (bd. dirs. 1970-73), Phi Beta Kappa, Sigma Xi, Phi Lambda Upsilon. Home and Office: 349 Hilldale Pl Lake Forest IL 60045-3031

WESTON, DAWN THOMPSON, artist, researcher; b. Joliet, Ill., Apr. 15, 1919; d. Cyril C. and Vivian Grace Thompson; student (scholar) Penn Hall Jr. Coll., Chambersburg, Pa., 1937-38; BS, Northwestern U., 1942, postgrad. in reading and speech pathology, 1960-61, MA in Ednl. Adminstrn., 1970; postgrad. U. Ill., 1964; student Art Inst. Chgo., 1954, Pestalozzi-Froebel, Chgo., 1955, Phila. Inst. for Achievement Human Potential, 1963; m. Arthur Walter Weston, Sept. 10, 1940; children: Roger Lance, Randall Kent, Cynthia Brooke. Therapist, USN Hosp., Gt. Lakes, Ill., 1940-45; tchr. Holy Child and Waukegan (Ill.) High Schs., 1946-54, Lake Forest High Sch., 1966-69; elem. and jr. high art dir. Lake Bluff (Ill.) Schs., 1954-58; pioneer ednl. dir. Grove

Sch. for Brain-Injured, Lake Forest, Ill., 1958-66, now life mem., treas. corp., chmn. bd., 1982-87. One woman shows include Evanston Woman's Club, Northwestern U., Deerpath Gallery, Lake Forest; The Hein Co., Waukegan; numerous group shows, 1939-76; represented in permanent collections: ARC, Victory Meml. Hosp., Waukegan, Sierra Assos., Chgo., numerous pvt. collections U.S., Can., Japan, Africa; works include: Poisonous Plants of Midwest set of etchings for Country Gentleman mag., 1956, Clouds mural, 1981; ind. researcher, lectr. on shifting visual imagery due to trauma, 1982-99; mem. 1st found. bd. for srs. in Lake Forest, Ill., 1999; chair Grove Sch. Inc., 1996-97; chmn. July 4th parade 100th Anniversary Child-Serve Greater Chgo., 1994. Mem. Presdl. Gold Chain, Trinity Coll., 1979; del. ann. conf. Meth. Ch., 1982-90; lay leader Grace United Methodist Ch., Lake Bluff, Ill., 1990-93. Named Citizen of Yr., Grove Sch., 1978, room at sch. named in her honor, 1982; cert. tchr./adminstr., Ill. Mem. Art Inst. Chgo., Penn Hall Alumni Assn. (Chgo. pres. 1938-40), Deerpath Art League (mem. bd. dirs.), Pi Lambda Theta. Research on uneven growth, 1969—. Home and Office: 349 Hilldale Pl Lake Forest IL 60045-3031

WESTON, FRANCINE EVANS, secondary education educator; b. Mt. Vernon, N.Y., Oct. 8, 1946; d. John Joseph and Frances (Fantino) Pisaniello. *Dr. Weston voiced her gratitude to her maternal grandfather by dedicating "Beautifully Old" to him in 1984. She fondly acknowledges here: The paternal grandparents who allowed her to spend what seemed like hours happily, though cacophonously, "playing" their piano, the various aunts who took her to Radio City, Horn-N-Hardart and for wheelbarrow rides, the godparents who took her to the rodeo, and especially the maternal grandmother for whom she picked raspberries, who typed her first essay contest entry (three times), and who was the only person who could make "You're just like your father," sound like a compliment.* BA, Hunter Coll., 1968; MA, Lehman Coll., 1973; cert., Am. Acad. Dramatic Arts, N.Y.C., 1976; PhD, NYU, 1991. Cert. elem., secondary tchr., N.Y. Tchr. Yonkers (N.Y.) Bd. Edn., 1968—; aquatic dir. Woodlane Day Camp, Irvington-on-Hudson, N.Y., 1967-70, Yonkers Jewish Community Ctr., 1971-75. Creative drama tchr. John Burroughs Jr. H.S., Yonkers, 1971-77; stage lighting designer Iona Summer Theatre Festival, New Rochelle, N.Y., 1980-81, Yonkers Male Glee Club, 1981-89, Roosevelt H.S., 1980-97; freelance, 1998—; rsch. specialist Scholarship Locating Svc., 1992-94, Yonkers Civil Def. Police Aux., 1994—; master electrician NYU Summer Mus. Theatre, 1979-80; appointed program developer for Cadet Acad. of Police & Fire Scis., Pub. Safety Magnet, Roosevelt H.S., 2001. *Although an explosion at school on 3/10/97 changed Dr. Weston's life forever by substantially impairing her hearing, she resumed her professional life as an outstanding educator and active member of Yonkers' volunteer citizenry. Fortified with hearing aids and 300 hours of speechreading exercises, she stalwartly returned to the classroom and to the auxiliary police. Her volunteer responsibilities are restructured to administrative duties, but her contribution and value to the Yonkers Public School System remains unchanged. Never a clockwatcher, she continues to provide expert instruction, emotional support, tutorial help, guidance and inspiration as a Teacher/ Program Developer and activities sponsor.* Actress in numerous comty. theater plays including A Touch of the Poet, 1979; dir. stage prodns. including I Remember Mama, 1973, The Man Who Came to Dinner, 1975; author: A Descriptive Comparison of Computerized Stage Lighting Memory Systems With Non-Computerized Systems, 1991, (short stories) A Hat for Louise, 1984, Old Memories: Beautiful and Otherwise, 1984; lit. editor: (story and poetry collection) Beautifully Old, 1984; editor: Command Post Dispatch quar., 1997—. Mem. Yonkers Civil Def. Police Aux., 1994—, adminstrv. asst. to commanding officer, 1996—, lt., capt. adminstrn., 2002—; steering com. chairperson Roosevelt H.S.-Middle States Assn. of Schs. and Colls. Self-Evaluation, 1985—88. Named Tchr. of Excellence, N.Y. State English Coun., 1990; recipient Monetary award for Teaching Excellence, Carter-Wallace Products, 1992; named to Arrid Tchrs. Honor Roll, 1992. Republican. Roman Catholic. Avocations: swimming, animal related activities, anything theatrical. Office: Roosevelt High Sch Tuckahoe Rd Yonkers NY 10710

WESTON, I. DONALD, architect; b. Bklyn., Feb. 16, 1928; s. Martyn N. and Betty (Lash) W.; m. Sylvia Stone, Oct. 23, 1952; children: Suzanne, Pamela. BArch, MIT, 1950; MArch, Pratt Inst., 1959, M in City and Regional Planning, 1981. Cert. Nat. Coun. Archtl. Regis. Bd.; lic. architect N.Y., Mass. Ptnr., prin. Martyn & Don Weston Architects, Bklyn., 1956—. Dir. Bklyn. Arts Coun., 1998—. Co-authored 2 studies for determining methods of reducing the cost of pub. housing, 1960. Mem. Mayor's Blue Ribbon Panel to Investigate the Bldg. Process in N.Y.C., 1987-88; pro bono pub. mem., sec. Cadman Plz. Co-op., Bklyn., 1972-78. Fellow AIA (mem. Bklyn. chpt. 1954—, chmn. urban design com. Bklyn. chpt. 1994—, pres. 1964-65); mem. Architects Coun. of N.Y.C. (pres. 1970-72), N.Y.C. Art Commn.; mem. Nat. Sculpture Soc. (v.p. 1990-94), Fine Arts Fedn. N.Y. (v.p. 1981—, pres. 1984-87, 90-91, hon. v.p. 1992—), Art Commn. Assocs. (pres. 1991-92). Avocations: tennis, golf, community activism. Office: Martyn & Don Weston Arch 100 Remsen St Brooklyn NY 11201-4256

WESTON, JOAN SPENCER, production director, communications executive, editor; b. Barton, Vt., Aug. 11, 1943; d. Rolfe Weston and Dorothy Lena (Spencer) Schoppe. BA magna cum laude, U. Mass., 1965. Tchr. high sch. Gorham (Maine) Schs., 1965-66; tchr. Sherwood Hall Sch., Mansfield, Eng., 1966-67; tchr. middle sch. Meden Sch., Warsop, Eng., 1967-68; dept. head high sch. Goffstown (N.H.) Schs., 1968-82; dir. circulation T.H.E. Jour., Acton, Mass., 1982-83; prodn. mgr. The Robb Report, 1983-87, prodn. dir., 1988; prodn. cons. Spencer Weston Assocs., Portland, Maine, 1988-93; prodn. dir. New Age Pub. Inc., Watertown, Mass., 1993-96, Pvt. Colls. and Univs., Inc., Westford, 1996—. Mem. Boston Prodn. Mgrs. Group (charter), Phi Beta Kappa. Avocations: travel, music, psychology, antiques. Office: Pvt Colls and Univs 2 LAN Dr Ste 100 Westford MA 01886-3547 E-mail: jsweston@privatecolleges.com.

WESTON, SIR JOHN (SIR PHILIP JOHN WESTON), company non-executive director, retired diplomat; b. Apr. 13, 1938; s. Philip George and Edith Alice Bray (Ansell) W.; m. Margaret Sally Ehlers, 1967; 3 children. Grad. with 1st class honors, Worcester Coll., Oxford (Eng.) U.; student Chinese lang., Hong Kong, 1964-66, Peking, China, 1967-68. Joined diplomatic svc. Govt. of Gt. Britain, 1962, served Fgn. Office, 1962-63, 69-71, with Treasure Ctr. for Adminstrv. Studies, 1964, permanent rep. to EEC, 1972-74, asst. pvt. sec. to sec. state fgn. affairs and commonwealth affairs, 1974-76, counsellor, head EEC presidency secretariat Fgn. and Commonwealth Office, 1976-77, counsellor Brit. Embassy, 1978-81, head def. dept. Fgn. and Commonwealth Office, 1981-84, asst. under-sec. state Fgn. and Commonwealth Office, 1984-85, min. Brit. Embassy, 1985-88, dep. sec. to cabinet Cabinet Office, 1988-89, dep. under-sec. state def. Fgn. and Commonwealth Office, 1989-90, polit. dir. Fgn. and Commonwealth Office, 1990-92, amb., permanent rep. to NATO, also accredited to Western European Union, 1992-95; U.K. amb. to UN, U.K. permanent rep. UN Security Coun., N.Y.C., 1995-98. Non-exec. dir. Brit. Telecom, Rolls Royce plc, 1998—, Hakluyt & Co. Ltd., 2001—; vis. fellow Old Souls Coll., Oxford (Eng.) U., 1977-78; hon. pres. U.K. Cmty. Found. Network, 1998—. Chmn. governing body Sherborne Sch., 2001-; trustee Nat. Portrait Gallery; Am. assoc. Royal Acad., 1999-; bd. govs. Ditchley Found., 2000-; mem. coun. Internat. Inst. Strategic Studies, 2001--. Served Royal Marines, 1956-58. Decorated knight comdr. St. Michael and St. George (Eng.); Order of Merit with star (Fed. Republic Germany). Address: 13 Denbigh Gardens Richmond Surrey TW10 6EN England

WESTON, JOHN FREDERICK, business educator, consultant; b. Ft. Wayne, Ind., Feb. 6, 1916; s. David Thomas and Bertha (Schwartz) W.; children: Kenneth F., Byron L., Ellen J. BA, U. Chgo., 1937, MBA, 1943, PhD, 1948. Instr. U. Chgo. Sch. Bus., 1940-42, asst. prof., 1947-48; prof. The Anderson Sch. UCLA, 1949—, Cordner prof. The Anderson Sch., 1981-94, prof. emeritus recalled The Anderson Sch., 1986—, dir. rsch. program in competition and bus. policy, 1969—, dir. Ctr. for Managerial Econs. and Pub. Policy, 1983-86. Econ. cons. to pres. Am. Bankers Assn., 1945-46; disting. lecture series U. Okla., 1967, U. Utah, 1972, Miss. State U., 1972, Miami State U., 1975. Author: Scope and Methodology of Finance, 1966, International Managerial Finance, 1972, Impact of Large Firms on U.S. Economy, 1973, Financial Theory and Corporate Policy, 1979, 2d edit., 1983, 3d edit., 1988, Mergers, Restructuring and Corporate Control, 1990, Takeovers, Restructuring and Corporate Governance, 3d edit., 2000, Managerial Finance, 9th edit, 1992; assoc. editor: Jour. of Finance, 1948-55; mem. editorial bd., 1957-59; editorial bd. Bus. Econs., Jour. Fin. Rsch., Managerial and Decision Econs.; manuscript referee Am. Econ. Rev., Rev. of Econs. and Statistics, Engring. Economist, Bus. Econs., Fin. Mgmt. Bd. dirs. Bunker Hill Fund. Served with Ordnance Dept. AUS, 1943-45. Recipient Abramson Scroll award Bus. Econs., 1989-94; McKinsey Found. grantee, 1965-68; GE grantee, 1967; Ford Found. Faculty Rsch. fellow, 1961-62. Fellow Nat. Assn. Bus. Economists; mem. Am. Finance Assn. (pres. 1966, adv. bd. 1967-71), Am. Econ. Assn., Western Econ. Assn. (pres. 1962), Econometric Soc., Am. Statis. Assn., Royal Econ. Soc., Fin. Analysts Soc., Fin. Mgmt. Assn. (pres. 1979-80) Home: 258 Tavistock Ave Los Angeles CA 90049-3229 Office: UCLA 258 Tavistock Ave Los Angeles CA 90049-3229

WESTON, LAURIE BETH, psychiatrist; b. Washington, Oct. 4, 1951; d. Burt H. Weston and Doreen Elizabeth Berger; m. Craydon Dean McDonald, Dec. 4, 1982; children: Ian Cameron McDonald, Brendan Roarke McDonald, Tavis Hunter McDonald, Morgynne Elizabeth McDonald. BA, Kalamazoo Coll., 1974; MD, Med. Coll. Va., 1982. Diplomate Nat. Bd. Med. Examiners, Am. Bd. Psychiatry and Neurology, added qualification in geriatric psychiatry, Am. Bd. Adolescent Psychiatry. Med. dir. Unified Counseling Svcs., Lancaster, Wis., 1987-88; psychiatrist Lakeland Counseling Ctr., Elkhorn, 1988-93; psychiatrist, med. dir. Drs. McDonald, Weston and Assocs., Lake Geneva, 1991-93, Dr. McDonald, Weston Assoc., Flagstaff, Ariz., 1993—; univ. psychiatrist No. Ariz. U., 1993-95; med. dir., psychiatrist Mt. Vista Family Health Ctr., 1994-96. Counseling psychiatrist Ariz. Divsn. Devel. Disabilities, Flagstaff, 1995—, Geriatric Svcs. of Cen. Mass., Worcester, 1986-87. Asst. scoutmaster Boy Scouts Am., Flagstaff, 1998—, asst. Cub Scout leader, 1993-97; pres. Med. Sch. class Med. Coll. Va., 1979-80. Mem. Am. Psychiat. Assn., Phi Sigma, Phi Kappa Phi. Democrat. Avocations: camping, hiking, swimming, genealogy, traveling. Office: Drs McDonald Weston and Assocs 1100 N San Francisco St Ste C Flagstaff AZ 86001-3260

WESTON, PHYLLIS JEAN, art gallery director; b. Cleve., Mar. 17, 1921; d. Armin and Wilma H. (Wasserman) Hornstein; m. Leo F. Weston, Oct. 18, 1963; children: H. Todd Cobey, John Cobey. Student, Yale U. V.p., dir. AB Closson Jr. Art Gallery, Cin., 1964—; instr. I.L.R., U. Cin., 1995—2001. Art cons. Proctor & Gamble Co., Cin., 1983—; cons., lectr. in art. Curator Ohio Gov. Residential Found. Bd. dirs. Cin. Opera Guild, Internation Visitors Ctr., Inc., Cin. Chamber Orch., C.A.S.A., others; founder Enjoy the Arts, Cin. Commn. on the Arts, The Post Corbett awards; adv. judge Congl. Art Competition Sch. Creative and Performing Arts; mem. Citizens Against Substance Abuse. Recipient Post Corbett award, 1989, Prima award, 1999; named Woman of the Yr. Cin. Enquirer, 1987. Home: 4 Taft Road Ln Cincinnati OH 45206-1805 Office: 401 Race St Cincinnati OH 45202-2804

WESTON, PRISCILLA ATWOOD, library director; b. May 6, 1925; BA, U. N.H., 1947, cert. in libr. techniques, 1974. Libr. dir. Mansfield Libr., Temple, N.H., 1964—. Curator Temple Hist. Soc., 1964—; mem., sec. Temple Conservation Commn., 1978-88; mem. Temple Sch. Bd., 1952-55, ch. historian; dir. Hillsboro County Farm Bur., 1964-65. Mem. Greenville Woman's Club, Miller Grange (master 1964-65). Avocations: reading, gardening, genealogy, choir. Office: Mansfield Libr PO Box 210 Temple NH 03084-0210

WESTON, ROGER LANCE, banker; b. Waukegan, Ill., Mar. 2, 1943; s. Arthur Walter and Vivian Dawn (Thompson) W.; children: Cynthia Page, Kent Andrew, Arthur Eladio, Rebecca Dawn, Alice Sinclair, Elliot Churchill, Evan Walter, Spencer Lance. BS, MacMurray Coll., 1965; MBA, Washington U., St. Louis, 1967. Investment adviser Harris Trust & Savs. Bank, Chgo., 1967-69; sr. investment counselor Security Suprs., 1969-70; gen. ptnr. Sierra Capital Group, 1970-85; exec. v.p., treas., chief fin. officer Telemed Corp., Hoffman Estates, Ill., 1971-79; vice chmn. Bank Lincolnwood, 1979-85; pres., CEO, GSC Enterprises, Lincolnwood, 1979-85; chmn. bd. dirs., pres., CEO, GreatBanc, Inc., Aurora, Ill., 1986—. Mem. Barrington Hills (Ill.) Zoning Bd. Appeals, 1987, com. Asian art Art Inst. Chgo., 1987; mem. nat. coun., mem. Hatchery devel. com. John M. Olin Sch. Bus., Washington U. Mem. Washington U. Eliot Soc. (Chgo. nat. com., chmn. membership com. 1996-92), Univ. Club. Republican. Presbyterian. Office: Great Banc Inc 2300 Barrington Rd Hoffman Estates IL 60195

WESTON, SAUNDRA OLIVIA (SAUNDRA LAIDLAW), computer technician, minister; b. Loiret, France, Sept. 23, 1954; d. Cleophus Hamiter, Olivia Hamiter; m. Michael LeRoy Laidlaw. AAS, Milw. Tech. Coll., 1996; B in Elective Studies, St. Cloud State U., 2002. Ordained to ministry 1999. Data entry operator Blue Cross & Blue Shield United Wis., Milw., 1987, acctg. technician, 1987—89, microcomputer technician, 1989—93, microcomputer project analyst II, 1993—96, sys. adminstr., 1996—99; software programmer EMR Innovations, St. Cloud, Minn., 1999—2001, quality assurance technician, 2001—. Cons., Milw., 1992—99. Author: (book) One That God Away, 2002. V.p. Overcomers Internat., St. Cloud, 2002; pastor Temple Faith Ch., 2000—. Finalist State Amb., Milw. Area Tech. Coll., 1996; recipient Lamp of Knowledge, 1996. Pentecostal. Avocation: travel. Home Fax: 320-202-0334. Personal E-mail: soweston@earthlink.net.

WESTPHAL, DOUGLAS HERBERT, retired engineering company executive; b. Houston, Feb. 21, 1940; s. Herbert Hugo and Olga Clara (Brune) W.; m. Blanche Elizabeth Berkley; children: Barbara Ann, Christi Ann. BS in Mech. Engring., U. Houston, 1964. Ops. technician Sinclair Refining Co., Houston, 1964-67; asst. buyer Sinclair Oil Corp., N.Y.C., 1967-69; buyer BP Oil Corp., Atlanta, 1969-70; procurement engr. Standard Oil Co., Cleve., 1970-73; sr. buyer Alyeska Pipeline Svc. Co., Anchorage, 1973-76, Fluor Engrs. and Constructors, Inc., Houston, 1976-80; mgr. purchasing and stores Coastal Refining and Mktg., Inc., Corpus Christi, Tex., 1980-89; mgr. project procurement Fluor Daniel, Inc., Houston, 1989-93; mgr. procurement MES Engring., 1993-94; mgr. project procurement Fluor Daniel, Inc., Sugar Land, Tex., 1994-99; retired, 1999; purchasing agt. Kobelco Am., 1999—. Mem. Corpus Christi Kennel Club, 1982-90, show chmn., 1989; life mem. Houston Livestock Show and Rodeo, club chmn. 1999—; mem. ch. coun. Trinity Luth. Ch., Frelsburg, Tex., fin. sec., 1992, pres., 1993-94. Mem. ASME, NSPE, Gulf Coast Purchasing Mgmt. Assn. (pres. 1986-87, bd. dirs. 1987-90), Houston Farm and Ranch Club (life), Hold 'Em & Hit 'Em Club (pres.), Kappa Kappa Psi (hon. band fraternity). Democrat. Lutheran. Home and Office: 9822 Penton Dr Sugar Land TX 77478-1025

WESTPHAL, JOSEPH W. academic administrator; m. Linda Westphal; 4 children. PhD in political, Univ. Mo.; BA, Adelphi Univ. Chancellor Univ. Maine Sys., 2002—; sr. policy adv. U.S. Environment Protection Agency; exec. dir. Congressional Sunbelt Caucus, 1988—95; spl. asst. Dept. Interior; prof. Okla. State Univ., head political sci. dept. Served House Com.; adj. prof. Georgetown Univ. Contbr. articles. Acting sec. U.S. Army, asst. sec. U.S. Army, 1998. Mem.: Patton Boggs, LLP (sr.), Wash. Law Firm (sr.). Office: U Maine Sys 107 Maine Ave Bangor ME 04401*

WESTPHAL, ROGER ALLEN, electrical engineer; b. Waterloo, Iowa, Feb. 17, 1946; s. Clifford Henry and Pauline Vere (Kleinow) W.; foster children: Rajathi, Ponnammal. BSEE, U. Fla., 1981, MS, 1990. Registered profl. engr., Fla. Instrumentation technician Gen. Dynamics, Ft. Worth, 1966-68, Gen. Dynamics/Convair, Edwards AFB, Calif., 1968-72; electronics technician Lockheed Calif. Co., Burbank, 1973-74, field svc. rep., 1974-78; engring. technician engring. scis. dept. U. Fla., Gainesville, 1980-84, instr. elec. engring. dept., 1984-86, 90; engr. elec. utility Gainesville Regional Utilities, 1987—. Mem. Friends of Classic 89, Gainesville, Friends of Five, Gainesville; supporting mem. Smithsonian, Washington. With USN, 1968-71. Mem. IEEE, Am. Solar Energy Soc., Internat. Solar Energy Soc., Phi Kappa Phi, Eta Kappa Nu, Tau Beta Phi. Republican. Methodist. Avocations: farmer, carpenter, wine making. Home: PO Box 846 Gainesville FL 32602-0846 Office: Gainesville Regl Utilities # A 136 PO Box 147117 Gainesville FL 32614-7117 E-mail: westphalra@gru.com.

WESTPHAL, RUTH LILLY, educational media company; b. Glendale, Calif., July 27, 1931; d. Glen R. Lilly and Margaret Elizabeth John; m. H. Frederick Westphal, June 25, 1953. BA in Edn., UCLA, 1953; MA in Edn. Sys. Tech., Chapman Coll., 1968. Life tchg. credential, Calif. Pub. sch. tchr., L.A., Glendale, Calif., East Whittier, 1953-65; edn. sys. analyst Litton Industries, Anaheim, 1965-67; dir. of devel. Trainex Corp., Garden Grove, 1967-69; CEO Concept Media Corp., Irvine, 1969-2000; pub. Westphal Pub., 1980—. Author: (book) Plein Air Painters of California: The Southland, 1982 (Western Books award 1982), P.A.P.C.: The North, 1986; author, prodr. numerous ednl. films. Co-founder Friends of LaHabra (Calif.) Libr., 1960-65; mem. exec. com. Hist. Collections Coun., Orange County Mus. Art, 1996-99. Named one of Top 100 Prodrs., AV Video Multimedia Prodr. Mag., 1999. Republican/Libertarian. Avocations: art history, economics, boating. Office: Concept Media Corp 2493 DuBridge Ave Irvine CA 92606

WESTPHAL, WILLIAM HENRY, staff nurse; b. Pt. Washington, Wis., Oct. 29, 1946; s. Henry Vernon and Milda Emma (Sudbrink) W.; m. R. Elaine Stumreiter, Dec. 14, 1974. Cert. oper. rm. technician, Brook Army Med. Ctr., 1967; LPN with honors, Lakeshore Tech. Coll., 1971, ADN with honors, 1979; BBA, Lakeland Coll., 1993. LPN, RN, Wis.; ACLS. Staff nurse, surg. nurse orthopedics, gen. surgery, urology St. Nicholas Hosp., Sheboygan, Wis., 1969-79; surg. asst. orthopedics Sheboygan Clinics, 1979-89; staff nurse Sheboygan County Instns., 1989-95; surg. nurse Flambeau Med. Ctr., Park Falls, 1996—. Treas. LPN state chpt. Wis. Fedn. LPN, Sheboygan, 1971-79. Mem. Park Falls planning comm., 1995—. Sgt. 1st class U.S. Army, 1967-77, Vietnam, 1968-69. Sgt. 1st class U.S. Army, 1967—77, Vietnam, 1968-69. Mem. Am. Fedn. Nurses and Health Profls. (Wis. nurses union 1989-95), KC (3d degree knight). Roman Catholic. Avocations: world travel, photography, woodcraft, golf.

WESTRA, SJIRK JAN, radiologist; b. Heiloo, The Netherlands, Mar. 22, 1957; s. Johannes George and Elisabeth Anna (Overhoff) W.; m. Joan Sabitha Kalideen, Oct. 8, 1982 (div. Jan. 2000). Diploma, Het Rhedens Lyceum, Velp, The Netherlands, 1975; MD, Rijksuniversiteit, Groningen, The Netherlands, 1984. Diplomate in radiology and in pediatric radiology Am. Bd. Radiology. Resident pediatrics U. Hosp., Leiden, The Netherlands, 1984-86; resident radiology Acad. Med. Ctr. U. Amsterdam, The Netherlands, 1986-90; clin. instr. UCLA Med. Ctr., 1990-91, asst. prof., 1991-99; assoc. prof. Childrens Meml. Hosp., Chgo., 1999—2001; with dept. radiology Mass. Gen. Hosp., Boston. Vis. prof. Red Cross Children's Hosp., Cape Town, South Africa, 1997; mem. protective svcs. team, Children's Meml. Hosp., Chgo., 1999—, mem. instnl. rev. bd., UCLA, 1997-99. Contbr. articles to profl. jours. Recipient Joseph H. Holmes award, Jour. Clin. Ultrasound, 1991; Editor's Recognition award, Radiology Jour., 1998, 99. Mem. Radiol. Soc. N.Am., Am. Roentgen Ray Soc., Soc. Pediatric Radiology (rsch. com.), Am. Inst. Ultrasound in Medicine (sr. mem.), Assn. Univ. Radiologists, Am. Soc. Pediatric Neuroradiology. Avocations: reading, skiing, travel, clarinet. Office: Mass Gen Hosp Dept Radiology 34 Fruit St White 250 Boston MA 02114 E-mail: swestra@partners.org.

WESTRICK, HEIDI LYNN, medical/surgical nurse; b. Johnstown, Pa., Dec. 15, 1966; d. Thomas and Karol Anne (Kirchner) Zwiener; m. Daniel D. Westrick, Sept. 4, 1999. Diploma, Conemaugh Valley Meml. Hosp., Johnstown, 1987; RN, BSN, U. Pitts., Johnstown, 1993. Cert. in trauma nursing, peritoneal dialysis, CPR, med./surg. nurse, cardiac monitoring. Nurse Conemaugh Valley Meml. Hosp., Johnston, Pa., 1987—; admissions coord. Conemaugh Rehab. Unit, Crichton Ctr. Advanced Rehab., 1996—. Mem. Conemaugh Valley Meml. Alumni (sec. peer rev. com.), Alumni of U. Pitts. at Johnstown. Office: 1086 Franklin St Johnstown PA 15905 E-mail: daniel@forspeed.com.

WESTROPE, MARTHA RANDOLPH, psychologist, consultant; b. Gaffney, S.C., May 19, 1922; d. Gordon Robert and Hannah (Brown) W.; 1 adopted child, Ashley Randolph. BS, Winthrop Coll., 1942; MA, U. N.C., 1944; PhD, State U. of Iowa, Iowa City, 1952. Lic. psychologist, S.C. Pvt. practice, Greenville, S.C., 1960—; part-time pvt. practice, 1987-96; part-time staff mem. Spartanburg (S.C.) Mental Health Clinic, 1971-73, Greenville Mental Health Ctr., 1974-85, Patrick B. Harris Psychiat. Hosp., Anderson, S.C., 1985-87; med. cons. S.C. Vocat. Rehab. Dept., Greenville, 1987-91, part-time med. cons., 1993-99. Cons. S.C. Parole Bd. for Psychol. Evaluation, S.C. Dept. Corrections, 1983-87. Mem. Am. Psychol. Assn., Southeastern Psychol. Assn., S.C. Psychol. Assn., Am. Assn. for Advancement of Psychology, Greenville County Mental Health Assn., Am. Group Psychotherapy Assn., Coun. for the Nat. Register of Health Svc. Providers in Psychology. Democrat. Presbyterian. Avocations: wildlife preservation, fine arts, collecting dolls, stamps. Home: 11 Darien Way Greenville SC 29615-3236

WESTRUM, HELEN JOSEPHINE, writer, retired educator; b. Mahnomen, Minn., Nov. 6, 1928; d. Roy Arthur and Bertha Florence (Smith) Dirl; m. Wesley Theodore Westrum. BS, Mont. State U., 1951, MS, 1966; EdD, Oreg. State U., 1974. Tchr. home econ. Libby (Mont.) H.S., 1950-52, Whitefish (Mont.) H.S., 1952-54; home economist Grant County Pub. Utility Dist., Wash., 1954-62, Pacific Power and Light Co., Roseberg, Oreg., 1964-65; mem. faculty Ea. Wash. U., Cheney, 1966-88, program dir. home econ., 1985-88, prof. emeritus, 1988—. Vis. lectr. U. Mont., Missoula, 1963-64; adj. faculty Coll. Fin. Planning, Denver, 1983. Co-author: Competencies for Home Economics, 1978. Recipient Outstanding Tchr. award Wash. Vocat. Assn., 1986. Mem. PEO (chaplain 1993-94), Diaconia (v.p. 1991—), Eastern Star. Avocations: water color and oil painting, historical research. E-mail: piper@omnicast.

WESTWOOD, JAMES NICHOLSON, lawyer; b. Portland, Oreg., Dec. 3, 1944; s. Frederick Alton and Catherine (Nicholson) W.; m. Janet Sue Butler, Feb. 23, 1980; children: Laura, David. BA, Portland State U., 1967; JD, Columbia U., 1974. Bar: Oreg. 1974, U.S. Dist. Ct. Oreg. 1974, U.S. Ct. Appeals (9th cir.) 1978, U.S. Supreme Ct. 1981, U.S. Ct. Appeals (fed. cir.) 1984, U.S. Ct. Appeals (D.C. cir.) 1997. Assoc. Miller, Anderson, Nash, Yerke & Wiener, Portland, 1974-76, 78-81; asst. to pres. Portland State U., 1976-78; ptnr. Miller, Nash, Wiener, Hager & Carlsen, Portland, 1981-99, Stoel Rives LLP, Portland, 1999—. Recipient Disting. Svc. award Portland State U. Found., 1984, Outstanding Alumni award Portland State U., 1992. Mem. ABA (chmn. forest resources com. 1987-89), Oreg. Bar Assn. (chmn. appellate practice sect. 1996-97), Am. Acad. Appellate Lawyers, Univ. Club (bd. govs. 1994), City Club (pres. 1991-92), Park Blocks Found. (pres. 1999—). Republican. Unitarian Universalist. Home: 3121 NE Thompson St Portland OR 97212-4908 Office: Stoel Rivers LLP 900 SW 5th Ave Ste 2600 Portland OR 97204-1268 E-mail: jnwestwood@stoel.com.

WESTWOOD, MELVIN NEIL, horticulturist, pomologist; b. Hiawatha, Utah, Mar. 25, 1923; s. Neil and Ida (Blake) W.; m. Wanda Mae Shields, Oct. 12, 1946; children: Rose Dawn, Nancy Gwen, Robert Melvin, Kathryn Mae. Student, U. Utah, 1948-50; BS in Pomology, Utah State U., 1952; PhD in Pomology, Wash. State U., 1956. Field botanist Utah State U., Logan, 1951-52, supt. Howell Field Sta., 1952-53; rsch. asst. State Coll. Wash., 1953-55; rsch. horticulturist Agrl. Rsch. Svc. USDA, Wenatchee, Wash., 1955-60; assoc. prof. Oreg. State U., Corvallis, 1960-67, prof., 1967-80, prof. emeritus, 1986—; rsch. dir. Nat. Clonal Germplasm Repository, 1980-83, nat. tech. advisor, 1984-86. Author: Deciduous Fruit and Nut Production, 1976, Temperate-Zone Pomology: Physiology and Culture, 1978, 3d edit., 1993, Contract Military Air Transport: From the Ground Up, 1995, Pear Varieties and Species, 1996; author: (with others) Cherry Nutrition, 1966, Pear Rootstocks, 1987, Management and Utilization of Plant Germplasm, 1988, Maintenance and Storage: Clonal Germplasm, 1989, Genetic Resources of Malus, 1991; contbr. articles to profl. jours. With U.S. Air Transport Command, 1943-45, USAAF, 1946-47. Grantee NSF, 1966; recipient Hartman Cup award Oreg. Hort. Soc., 1989, Earl Price Excellence in Rsch. award Oreg. State U., 1983. Fellow Am. Soc. Hort. Sci. (bd. dirs. 1974-75, chmn. com. environ. quality 1971, adv. coun. 1974-79, mem. pomology sect. 1967-74, publs. com. 1971-74, pres. Western region 1974, Joseph Harvey Gourley award for Pomology 1958, 77, Stark award for Pomology 1969, 77, Outstanding Rschr. award 1986); mem. AAAS, Am. Soc. Plant Physiologists, Am. Pomological Soc. (mem. adv. bd. 1970-75, mem. exec. bd. 1980-84, Paul Howe Shepard award 1968, 82, Wilder medal 1980), UN Assn. USA, Ams. United for Separation of Ch. and State, Amnesty Internat., Phi Kappa Phi, Gamma Sigma Delta. Baptist. Achievements include patent for Autumn Blaze ornamental pear; research on Pyrus (pear), Malus (apple) and Prunus (plum, cherry, peach) and on the physiology of rootstock genera. Office: Oreg State U Dept Horticulture Corvallis OR 97331

WETEKAM, DONALD J. career officer; BS, USAF Academy, Colorado Springs, 1973; M in Engring. Adminstrn., U. Utah, 1978. Commd. 2d lt. USAF, 1973, advanced through grades to brigadier gen., 1999; officer in charge 4th Munitions Maintenance Squadron, Seymour Johnson AFB, N.C., 1974-75, 635th Munitions Maintenance Squadron, U-Tapao Royal Thai Naval, Airfield, Thailand, 1975-76; munitions svc. officer, officer in charge 388th Tactical Fighter Wing, Hill AFB, Utah, 1976-79; officer in charge 313th Aircraft Maintenance Unit, Hahn Air Base, Germany, 1981-84; maintenance staff officer HQ Tactical Air Command, Langley AFB, Va., 1984-86; comdr. 56th Equipment Maintenance Squadron, MacDill AFB, Fla., 1986-89; F-15 and standard avionics logistics program mgr. HQ USAF, Pentagon, 1989-93; comdr. 49th Logistics Group, Holloman AFB, N.M., 1994-95; dir. aircraft mgmt. directorate Oklahoma City Air Logistics Ctr., Tinker AFB, 1995-97, vice comdr., 1997-98; dir. logistics Hdqrs. Pacific Air Forces, Hickam AFB, Hawaii, 1998—2000; dep. dir. combat weapons systems Hdqrs. Air Combat Command, Langley AFB, Va., 2000, dir. maintenance and logistics, 2000—02; comdr. Warner Robins AFB, Ga., 2002—.

WETENHALL, JOHN, museum director; b. June 1, 1957; s. Jack Wetenhall and Jane (Rinaud) Keating. AB cum laude, Dartmouth Coll., 1979; MA, Williams Coll., Williamstown, Mass., 1982, Stanford U., 1985, PhD, 1988; MBA, Vanderbilt U., 1999. Fellow Smithsonian Instn., Washington, 1986-87, 88-89; lectr. Santa Clara (Calif.) U., 1985, U. Minn., Mpls., 1988; curator painting and sculpture Birmingham (Ala.) Mus. Art, 1989-95; dir. Checkwood Mus. Art, Nashville, 1995-2001; exec. dir. John and Mable Ringling Mus. Art, Sarasota, Fla., 2001—. Founder Thomas Art Projects, Birmingham, 1992-95, Carell Woodland Sculpture Trail, Nashville, 1996-99; cons. Vietnam Women's Meml. Project, Washington, 1988-89, U. So. Calif. Pub. Art Program, 1991. Author: (with Karal Ann Marling) Iwo Jima: Monuments, Memories and the American Hero, 1991, (with David Cass) (catalogue) Italian Paintings, 1850-1910, 1982; editor: (catalogue) Splendors of the American West, 1990; contbr. articles to profl. jours.; appearance in Am. Masters: Alexander Calder, PBS, 1998. Chair Livelier City Ctr. com. Ops. New Birmingham, 1994—95, chair cultural dist. forum, 1992—94; chair nat register peers, design excellence program Gen. Svcs. Adminstrn., 1998—; chair Nashville Rotary Adopt-A House Program; mem. Leadership Manatee, 2002. Recipient Award of Excellence Tenn. Assn. Mus., 1996, 2001, Gold and Silver medals for ednl. programming Southeastern Mus. Conf., 1999; B. Gerald Cantor fellow, 1986, Nat. Endowment for the Arts grantee, 1991, Lyndon Baines Johnson Found. Moody Travel grantee, 1986, John F. Kennedy Libr. Found. grantee, 1986. Mem. Am. Tchrs. Assn. of the Martial Arts (sensei), Rotary (Paul Harris fellow), Beta Gamma Sigma. Avocations: white water kayaking, flying, Aiki Ju Jitsu (blackbelt). Office: Ringling Mus of Art 5401 Bayshore Rd Sarasota FL 34243 E-mail: jwetenhall@ringling.org.

WETHERALL, ROBERT SHAW, librarian; b. Jesup, Ga., Aug. 18, 1944; s. Robert and Elizabeth (Shaw) W; m. Cynthia Jane Campbell, July 31, 1976; children— Robert G., Gerritt C. B.A. in History, U. Del., 1966, M.A. in History, 1968; M.L.S., Drexel U., 1973. Cert. profl. libr., N.J. Libr. Cumberland County Libr., Bridgeton, N.J., 1973-76; asst. dir., 1976-80, dir., 1981-89; dir. Dover (Del.) Pub. Libr., 1989—; mem. Cumberland County Audio-Visual Aids Commn., Bridgeton, 1981-89; pres. South Jersey Regional Libr. Coop., Inc., 1986-88, treas., 1988-89. Served with USAF, 1968-72. Mem. ALA, Del. Libr. Assn. (pres. 1992-93, action implementation com.). Office: Dover Pub Libr 45 S State St Dover DE 19901-7311

WETHERBEE, JAMES D. astronaut; b. Flushing, N.Y., Nov. 27, 1952; s. Dana A. and Wetherbee; m. Robin DeVore Platt; 2 children. BS in Aerospace Engrng., U. Notre Dame, 1974. Commd. ensign USN, 1975, advanced through grades to capt.; naval aviator Attack Squadron 72, USS John F. Kennedy, 1977—80; with Systems Engrng. Test Directorate; project officer, test pilot; with Strike Fighter Squadron 132; astronaut NASA, Houston, 1984—, dir. Flight Crew Ops. Directorate. Mem.: Soc. Exptl. Test Pilot. Achievements include logged over 5,000 hours flying time; 345 carrier landings in over 20 different types of aircraft; logged over 1,262 hours in space; pilot STS-32 Columbia (1990); mission comdr. STS-52 Columbia (1992), STS-63 Discovery (1995), STS-86 Atlantis (1997) and STS-102 Discovery (2001). Office: Astronaut Office/CB NASA Johnson Space Ctr Houston TX 77058*

WETHERILL, EIKINS, lawyer, stock exchange executive; b. Phila., Oct. 3, 1919; s. A. Hecksher and Edwina (Brunner) W. LL.B., U. Pa., 1948. Practiced in Phila., 1948-55, Norristown, 1955-98; assoc. firm Evans, Bayard & Frick, 1948-50; ptnr. Reilly, Hepburn, Earle & Wetherill, 1950-55; firm Henderson, Wetherill, O'Hey & Horsey, 1955-98; pres. Phila. Stock Exchange, Inc., 1965-81. Bd. dirs. Germantown Savs. Bank; fin. commentator CBS-TV News, 1966-68; chmn. bd. Sta. WHYY-TV, 1970-76, dir., 1976-90; dir. 1st Pa. Corp., 1st Pa. Bank, solicitor to lt. gov. Pa., 1951-55, asst. U.S. atty. gen., 1953-55, treas., Montgomery County, 1956-59; pres. Montgomery County Bd. Commrs., 1960-63; chmn. Pa. Securities Commn., 1963-65; commr. Delaware Valley Regional Planning Commn., 1965—, chmn., 1968-69, 70-71, 78-79. Former bd. dirs. Greater Phila. Partnership; chmn. Phila. Drama Guild, 1975-80, dir., 1980-87; trustee Davis and Elkins Coll., 1973-91. Served to capt., cav. Signal Corps, OSS, AUS, 1941-45. Mem. Am., Phila. bar assns., Delta Psi. Clubs: Phila. (Phila.), Racquet (Phila.). Episcopalian.

WETHERILL, GEORGE WEST, geophysicist; b. Phila., Aug. 12, 1925; s. George West and Leah Victoria (Hardwick) Wetherill; m. Phylllis May Steiss, June 17, 1950 (dec. 1995); children: Rachel, George, Sarah; m. Mary Bailey, 1998. PhB, U. Chgo., 1948, SB in Physics, 1949, SM, 1951, PhD in Physics, 1953. Mem. staff dept. terrestrial magnetism Carnegie Inst., Washington, 1953—60; prof. geophysics and geology UCLA, 1960—75, chmn. dept. planetary and space sci., 1968—72; dir. dept. terrestrial magnetism Carnegie Inst., Washington, 1975—91, mem. sci. staff, 1991—2001, dir. emeritus, 2001—. V.p. Snickersville Gen. Store, Inc., Bluemont, Va., 1976—80; cons. NASA, NSF, NAS. Editor Ann. Rev. of Earth and Planetary Sci., 1981—96, assoc. editor, 1972—80, Meteoritics and Planetary Sci., Icarus; contbr. articles to profl. jours. With USN, 1943—46. Recipient G.K. Gilbert award, Geol. Soc. Am., 1984, Profl. Achievement citation, U. Chgo. Alumni Assn., 1985, Nat. medal of Sci., 1997. Fellow: Meteoritical Soc. (v.p. 1971—74, 1981—83, pres. 1983—85, Leonard medal 1981), Am. Geophys. Union (pres. planetology sect. 1970—72, H.H. Hess medal 1991), Am. Acad. Arts and Scis.; mem.: NAS (J. Lawrence Smith award 2000), Am. Astron. Soc. Divsn. Planetary Scis. and Dynamic Astronomy (G.P. Kuiper prize 1986), Internat. Astron. Union, Internat. Assn. Geochemistry and Cosmochemistry (pres. 1977—80), Geochem. Soc. (v.p. 1973—74, pres. 1974—75), Am. Philos. Soc., Internat. Soc. Study of Origin of Life, Religious Soc. Free Quakers. Episcopalian. Office: Carnegie Inst 5241 Broad Branch Rd NW Washington DC 20015-1305 E-mail: wetherill@dtm.ciw.edu. *Seek him that maketh the Pleiades and Orion, and turneth the shadow of death into morning. Amos 5:8.*

WETHERINGTON, ROGER VINCENT, journalism educator, newspaper copy editor; b. Jacksonville, Fla., Mar. 12, 1942; s. Roger Vincent and Ruby Estelle (Jones) W.; m. Andra Marie Miller, Aug. 31, 1972; 1 child, Brady Miller. BA in English Lit., Columbia U., 1965; MA in Journalism (with hons.), U. So. Calif., 1979, PhD in Comm., 1986. Copyboy, reporter, asst. city editor Daily News, N.Y.C., 1963-76; lectr. journalism Calif. State U., Long Beach, 1976-78, 87-90, asst. prof. Northridge, 1979-84; asst. prof. comm. St. John's U., Jamaica, N.Y., 1990-93, assoc. prof., 1993—, dir. journalism, 2001—. Copy editor N.Y. Times, N.Y.C., 1992-; assoc. editor St. John's Today, 1990-98, editor, 1998-2000. Recipient media award for incisive reporting Cancer Care, Inc., 1974, faculty devel. award Calif. State U.-Northridge, 1983; teaching fellow Gannett Found., 1977. Mem. Assn. for Edn. in Journalism and Mass Comm., Am. Copy Editors Soc., Soc. Profl. Journalists, Investigative Reporters and Editors, Deadline Club. Avocation: opera. Office: St John's U 8000 Utopia Pky Jamaica NY 11439-0002 E-mail: wetherir@stjohns.edu.

WETHINGTON, CHARLES T., JR. academic administrator; AB, Ea. Ky. U., 1956; postgrad., Syracuse U., 1958-59; MA, U. Ky., 1962, PhD, 1965. Instr. ednl. psychology U. Ky., Lexington, 1965-66; dir. Maysville (Ky.) C.C., 1967-71; asst. v.p. c.c. system U. Ky., Lexington, 1971-81, v.p. c.c. system, 1981-82, chancellor c.c. system, 1982-88, chancellor c.c. system and univ. rels., 1988-89, interim pres., 1989-90, pres., 1990—2001, pres. emeritus, 2001—. Chmn. legis. com. State Dirs. Community and Jr. Colls., 1983-85, chmn. nat. coun., 1985-86; commn. on colls. So. Assn. Schs. and Colls., 1978-84, vice chmn. exec. commn., 1984, trustee, 1986-89; mem. So. Regional Edn. Bd., 1988-2000, mem. exec. com., 1989-93, vice-chmn., 1991-93; pres. Southeastern Conf., 1993-95, chair exec. com. NCAA, 1999-2001. Bd. dirs. Bluegrass State Skills Corp., 1984-91, vice-chmn. bd. dirs., 1986-87; bd. visitors C.C. Air Force, 1986-90; jud. nominating commn. 22nd Jud. Dist., Fayette County, Ky., 1988-91, So. Growth Policies Bd., 1990-2000; bd. dirs. NCAA Found., 1999—; active Bus.-Higher Edn. Forum, 1999-2001. With security svc. USAF, 1957-61. Home: 2926 Four Pines Dr Lexington KY 40502 Office: U Ky 5-52 Wm T Young Libr Lexington KY 40506-0456 E-mail: cwething@email.uky.edu.

WETHINGTON, NORBERT ANTHONY, medieval scholar; b. Dayton, Ohio, Sept. 14, 1943; s. Norbert and Sophie Lillian W.; m. Martha M. Vannice, Aug. 13, 1966. BA, U. Dayton, 1965; MA, John Carroll U., 1967; postgrad., Baldwin Wallace Coll., 1968—70; PhD, U. Toledo (Ohio), 1997. Grad. asst., tchg. assoc. John Carroll U., Cleve., 1965—67; English tchr. Padua Franciscan High Sch., Parma, 1967—70; instr., chmn. dept. tech. writing and speech N. Ctrl. Tech. Coll., Mansfield, 1978—80, dir. pub. and cmty. svc. technologies, 1980—94; dir. humanities Terra State C.C., 1994—96, assoc. dean of instr., 1996—97; affiliate scholar Oberlin Coll., 1998—. Cons. in field. Contbr. articles. V.p. Sandusky County Bd. Health, 1979—80. Mem.: Nat. Coun. Tchrs. English, Ohio Vocat. Assn. (pres. tech. edn. divsn. 1985—86, Disting. Svc. award 1987), Am. Vocat. Assn., Nat. Coalition Ind. Scholars, MLA. Democrat. Roman Catholic. Mailing: PO Box 842 Fremont OH 43420-0842

WETLI, PEGGY MARIE, performing company executive; b. Green Bay, Wis., Oct. 10, 1949; d. Alois Bernard and Viola Marie Wetli; m. Timothy Hugh McCloskey, Mar. 17, 1990. BA, U. Minn., Mpls. Founder, CEO CLIMB Theater, Inver Grove Heights, Minn., 1975—. Author 15 plays for children. Recipient Outstanding Cmty. Svc. award Minn. chpt. NASW, Outstanding Achievement award for Leadership in Arts YWCA of St. Paul, Minn., 1991; named Woman of Distinction Sta KARE II-TV, 1996. Avocations: weightlifting, wateraerobics. Office: CLIMB Theater Inver Grove Heights MN 55076 E-mail: peg@climb.org.

WETMORE, KEVIN JESS, JR. theatre educator; b. New Haven, Feb. 1, 1969; s. Kevin Jess and Eleanor Maher Wetmore; m. Maura Rebecca Chwastyk, Oct. 20, 2001. BA, Bates Coll., 1991; MA, U. Leeds, Eng., 1992; PhD, U. Pitts., 1999. Tchg. fellow U. Pitts., 1993-99; prof. theatre Denison U., Granville, Ohio, 1999—. Artistic dir., founder Unseam'd Shakespeare Co., Pitts., 1994-96. Author: African Adaptation of Greek Tragedy, 2001; contbr. articles to profl. jours. Grantee Toshiba Found., Pitts., 1996. Mem. Am. Soc. Theatre Rsch., Soc. Am. Fight Dirs., Internat. Ho. of Japan. Avocations: herpetoculture, reading, film, skiing, martial arts. Office: Denison U Dept Theatre Granville OH 43023 E-mail: wetmore@denison.edu.

WETMORE, WILLIAM THOMSON, writer, small business owner; b. Boston, Nov. 29, 1930; s. William Thomson Wetmore and Joan Deery Dixon; m. Margaret Finley, Dec. 21, 1957; children: Charles, Michael, Joan. BA, Harvard U., 1954. Owner Cascade Mountain Vineyards, Amenia, N.Y., 1972—. Author: All the Right People, 1965, A Matter of Blue Chips, 1967, House of Flesh, 1969, Here Comes Jamie, 1972. With USMC, 1948-49. Mem. N.Y. Farmers (pres.). Home: 249 Flint Hill Rd Amenia NY 12501

WETSCH, JOHN ROBERT, information systems specialist; b. Dickinson, N.D., Aug. 27, 1959; s. Joseph John (dec.) and Florence Mae (Edwards) W.; m. Laura Jean Johnson, Aug. 29, 1981; children: Julie Elizabeth, Katherine Anne, John Michael, Joseph Harold. BS, Excelsior Coll., Albany, 1984; MA, Antioch U., 1989; PhD, Nova S.E. U., 1994; BS, U. N.D., 2001; M in Astronomy, U. Western Sydney, 2002. Radiation physics instr. Grand Forks (N.D.) Clinic, 1983-85; sr. programmer PRC, Inc., Cavalier Air Force Sta., N.D., 1987-91, PARCS project-SAFEGUARD sys.; pres. Dakota Sci. Inc., Langdon, N.D., 1988-95; instr. U. N.D.-Lake Region, Devils Lake, 1988-91; systems adminstr. U.S. Courts Nat. Fine Ctr., Raleigh, N.C., 1991-94; project leader U.S. Postal Svc., Raleigh (N.C.) Integrated Bus. Sys. Solution Ctr., 1994—2001; v.p. R & D HYTEC Consulting, Inc., 1997—; tech. fellow engr. Northrop-Grumman Info. Tech., 2001—. Cons. on Wave Obs./N.D. Proposal, Gov.'s Office, Bismarck, 1991; founder, developer Dakota Sci., Inc., Langdon, 1988-95; instr. divsn. continuing edn. Wake Tech. C.C., 1993-99; mem. adj. faculty computer info. systems N.C. Wesleyan Coll., 1997-2001; adj. faculty N.C. State U., 1999-2000, Capella U., Mpls., 2000—. Author: Distributed UNIX System Administration, 1998; (with others) COMPUTE!'s 2nd Book of Amiga, 1988; contbr. articles to COMPUTE! Jour. of Progressive Computing, 1987, other profl. jours. Program coord. Lake Region Outreach, U. N.D., Cavalier Air Force Sta., 1988—91; mem. bd. alumni trustees USNY-Regents Coll., Albany, 1995—2000, v.p., 1996—97, pres., 1997—2000, ex-officio mem. bd. overseers, 1997; pres. Zeta Rho chpt. Pi Kappa Alpha, Grand Forks, 1981; pres. Alumni Assn. Excelsior Coll., 1999—2001; ex-officio voting Excelsior Coll. Bd. Trustees, 1999—2001, bd. trustees, 2001—. Named Larimore-Mathews scholar, U. N.D., Grand Forks, 1978, N.D. Acad. Sci. scholar, 1978, SMITS scholar, N.D. Acad. Sci., 1990; recipient Westinghouse Sci. Talent Search award, 1978, Nova Southeastern U. Leadership award, Internat. Alumni Assn., 1998. Mem.: IEEE Computer Soc., IEEE, AAAS, N.Y. Acad. Sci., Dakota Astron. Soc. (pres. 1987—91, co-founder), Assn. for Computing Machinery. Republican. Roman Catholic. Achievements include missile simulation; microcomputer short range weather forecasting algorithm, study in astronomy and culture, system administration assessment of U.S. Courts and establishment and assessment of information control systems for the U.S. Courts National Fine Center. E-mail: dr_wetsch@prodigy.net.

WETSCH, LAURA JOHNSON, lawyer; b. Fargo, N.D., Nov. 18, 1959; d. Ronald Lee Johnson and Jacqualene Lee (Goudie) Johnson Trefz; m. John Robert Wetsch, Aug. 29, 1981; children: Julie Elizabeth, Katherine Anne, John Michael. AA, Bismarck (N.D.) State Coll., 1980; BA, U. N.D., 1982, JD, 1985. Bar: N.D. 1985, N.C. 1992. Law clk. to Hon. Patrick A. Conmy, U.S. Dist. Ct. for N.D., Bismarck, 1985-88; pvt. practice, Langdon, N.D., 1988-91; assoc. Jordan Price Wall Gray Jones & Carlton, PLLC, Raleigh, N.C., 1992-99; dir., v.p. legal affairs Hytec Cons., Inc., Cary, 1999—; of counsel Joyce L. Davis & Assocs., Raleigh, 1999—. Instr. bus. and criminal law U. N.D.-Lake Region, Cavalier, 1990-91; instr. paralegal studies Ctrl. Carolina C.C., Sanford, N.C., 1991-92; instr. bus. law Wake Tech. C.C., Raleigh, 1992-93. Author, editor (pamphlet) Crime Survivors Handbook, 1996; editor N.D. Women Lawyers Assn. Newsletter, 1990-91; contbr. articles to profl. jours. Vol. mediator and arbitrator Burleigh County Housing Authority, Bismarck, 1986-88; concessions co-chmn. Sanderson H.S. Band Boosters, 1996-2000; curbside cons. in employment law, N.C. Ctr. for Nonprofits, 1998. Mem. Nat. Employment Lawyers Assn., N.C. Bar Assn. (citizen edn. com. young lawyers divsn. 1994-96, chmn. membership svcs. com. young lawyers divsn. 1996-97), N.C. Acad. Trial Lawyers, Wake County Bar Assn. (fee arbitration com. 2001—). Democrat. Roman Catholic. Office: 2 Hannover Sq Ste 1730 Raleigh NC 27601-1767 E-mail: lwetsch@jldavis.com.

WETSCHLER, ED, editor; b. N.Y.C., Nov. 3, 1946; s. Herman and Elsie (Singer) W.; m. Carol M. Loftus, Jan. 24, 1988. AB, U. Rochester, 1968; MA, CUNY, 1973. Tchr. Erasmus Hall High Sch., Bklyn., 1968—84; freelance writer, theatre critic Entertainment, N.Y., 1980—84; assoc. editor Diversion Mag. (Hearst), N.Y.C., 1984—89, sr. editor, 1989—95, exec. editor, 1995—2001, editor-in-chief, 2002—. Contbg. author: Berlitz Guide to New York. Mem.: N.Y. Travel Writers Assn., Am. Soc. Mag. Editors. Avocations: gardening, cooking, music. Office: Diversion 1790 Broadway Fl 6 New York NY 10019-1412 E-mail: ewetschler@hearst.com.

WETSTONE, JANET MEYERSON, designer, journalist; b. Spartanburg, S.C., 1928; d. Louis Alexander and Ella (Levinson) Meyerson; m. Richard J. Wetstone, Sept. 21, 1947 (div. Dec. 1973); children: John B., Gregory S., Linda Wetstone Sherman. Student, U. Mo., 1945-47, Ga. State U., 1970, 80. Interior designer Jan's Interiors, Atlanta, 1965-68; pres. Wetstone Crafts Co., 1968—, Jan Westone Crafts Co., 1998—. Instr. women in bus. Emory U., 1972; cons. Plaid Enterprises Inc. Author: Rags to Riches with Mod-Podge, 1969; Specially Yours Decorating With Sheets, 1977; Needle-Podge Book, 1976; Creative Frame Maker, 1972; prin. works include Fast-Cast Designs Arts Kits for QVC Network., Home Shopping Networks, 1999; patentee craft paint Mod-Podge, frame-maker. Pres., founder Experts at Sea, Inc.; pres. edn. guild Ringling Mus., Sarasota, Fla., 1963-64, chair 1st creative art carnival, 1963-64; decorating chair Jimmy Carter Election Night, Atlanta, 1976. Nominee Fla. State Legis., 1988; dir. comms. Carter-Mondale 1980 campaign, Atlanta, 1980; chmn. visual arts Sarasota Centennial, 1985-86. Mem. United INventors and Scientists Am., Women in Film (v.p. 1982-83), Fla. Assn. Realtors, Million Dollar Club, Phi Sigma Sigma. Democrat. Avocations: riding, painting, golf. Home: 3969 Glen Oaks Manor Dr Sarasota FL 34232-1045 Fax: (941) 365-9009. E-mail: janwetstone@msn.com.

WETTACH, THOMAS C. lawyer; b. Pitts., Oct. 8, 1941; s. William and Alice (Sauer) W.; m. Bette J. Creveling; children: Christine L., Heidi L. BA in Physics, Washington & Jefferson Coll., 1963; JD with honors, U. N.C., 1966. Bar: Pa., U.S. Ct. Appeals (2d, 3d, 4th and Fed. cirs.), U.S. Patent & Trademark Office, U.S. Supreme Ct. Assoc. Webb Burden Robinson & Webb, Pitts., 1966-69, Blenko Leonard & Buell, Pitts., 1969-70; ptnr. Yeager Stein & Wettach, 1970-74, Reed Smith Shaw & McClay, Pitts., 1974-93; Cindrich & Titus, 1993—. Past pres. Techlaw Group, Multi-City, 1987—; chmn. Techlex Group/RSSM, Pitts.,1 986—. Pres. Thornburg Borough Coun., 1978—; mem. Health Systems Agy., Southwestern Pa., 1976-86. Mem. ABA, Pa. Bar Assn., Pitts. Intellectual Property Assn., Allegheny County Bar Assn. Office: Cindrich & Titus 4 Gateway Ctr Fl 20 Pittsburgh PA 15222-1220

WETTER-KUBECK, DAISY FISHER, dietitian, consultant; b. Lubbock, Tex., Jan. 27, 1936; d. Arthur Frederick and Margaret Elizabeth Fisher; m. John Francis Wetter, Aug. 24, 1958 (div. June 1975); children: James Robert, Jeffrey Mark; m. Edmund Kubeck, Nov. 29, 1997. BS cum laude, Linfield Coll., McMinnville, Oreg., 1956; MS, Purdue U., 1959. Cert. surveyor healthcare fin.; registered dietitian; lic. dietitian, Tex. Coop. rsch. agt. USDA, West Lafayette, Ind., 1957-59; grad. tchg. asst. Purdue U., 1957-59, dietitian Women's Resident Halls, 1958-59; instr. food, nutrition, advanced nutrition North Ctrl. Coll., Naperville, Ill., 1960-61; mgr. sch. lunch program/jr. h.s. tchr. Geneva (Ill.) Pub. Schs., 1961-64; long-term care unit nutritionist, surveyor Tex. dept. Human Svcs., San Antonio, 1986-96; dietary cons. San Marcos, 1996—. Contbr. articles to profl. jours. Mem. com. for halfway houses Tex. Youth Commn., Austin, 1984; vol. dietitian Sr. Citizens Ctr./Meals on wheels, San Marcos, Tex., 1982; mem. parent adv. com. San Marcos H.S., 1981-85; mem. citizens adv. coun., exec. bd. Parkway Sch. dist., Chesterfield, Mo., 1973-74, PTA exec. bd., v.p., 1972-74; exec. bd., treas., cmty. projects chmn., yearbook chmn. Oak Tree Farms, Mo. Garden Club, 1969-75; mem. ch. bd. Manchester United Meth. Ch., 1972-73. Mem. Am. Dietetic Assn. (bd. dirs. gerontol. nutrition dietetic practice group 1998—), Am. Heart Assn. (nutrition com. 1997-98), Tex. Nutrition Coun. (co-chmn. statewide workshops, v.p., parliamentarian, nominating chmn.), San Antonio Dietetic Assn. (presenter in field), Tex. Dietetic Assn. (gerontol. practice group 1984—, cons. dietitians in health care facilities practice group 1981—), Omicron Nu, Pi Gamma Mu, Mu Phi Epsilon. Democrat. Avocations: gardening, travel. Home and Office: 126 Algarita St San Marcos TX 78666-2504

WETTERWALD, AUDREY LYNN, dance educator; b. Chelmsford, Mass., Dec. 22, 1968; d. Edmund E. Jr. and Audrey Jane (Cooper) W. BFA, Lake Erie Coll., 1990. Cert. tchr. Ohio; registered dance educator. Dance educator Ashtabula (Ohio) Arts Ctr., 1990-92, Ashtabula City Schs., 1991-92, Phillips-Osborne Sch., Painesville, Ohio, 1990-96, Kirtland/Mentor (Ohio) Dances, 1991-96; dir. Dance Expressions Unltd., Mass., 1996—. Choreographer numerous dance concerts and musicals; appeared in Chorus Line, 1990, Tapestry, 1999, Nutcracker, 1999-2000, Impulse Dance Co., 1999, Sleeping Beauty, 2000. Active World Wildlife Fund, Sponsor the Whales, United Cerebral Palsy Found., Am. Cancer Soc., Epilepsy Found, Sponsor the Wolves. Dance Tchrs.' Club of Boston scholar, 1983-85. Mem. AAHPERD, Nat. Dance Edn. Assn., Nat. Dance Assn., Nat. Registry of Dance Educators, Internat. Tap Assn., Pythian Sisters, Arts Coun. Coop, Dance Tchr.'s Club Boston, Greater Lowell C. of C. Avocations: reading, sports, crafts, sewing. Office: 73 Progress Ave #1 Tyngsboro MA 01879-2725 E-mail: danceexpressionsunlimited@attbi.com.

WETZEL, EDWARD THOMAS, business executive; b. Indpls., Apr. 16, 1937; s. Edward George and Sarah Catherine Wetzel; m. Christine E. Healy; children from previous marriage: Raymond, Cynthia. BA, Bethany (W.Va.) Coll., 1959; MBA, U. Mass., 1963. Market rsch. analyst Gen. Electric Co., Pittsfield, Mass., 1960-63; asst. v.p. DMS, Inc., Greenwich, Conn., 1964-70; pres. Industry News Svc., Inc., Wilton, 1970-92; v.p. Wright Investors Svc., Bridgeport, 1992-97; pres. Retirement Living Info. Ctr., Inc., 1997—. Pres. Wilton Vol. Ambulance Corps, 1976-81, 83-87. Recipient Disting. Citizen award Town of Wilton, 1986. Mem. Strategic Leadership Forum, Info. Industry Assn., Kiwanis (prs. bd. dirs. Wilton chpt. 1991-92). Office: 19 Ledgewood Rd Redding CT 06896-2916

WETZEL, FRANKLIN TODD, spinal surgeon, educator, researcher; b. Wilmington, Del., Mar. 7, 1955; s. Franklin Huff and Jean Hartman (Clouser) W.; m. Patricia Ann Cassanos, May 23, 1981 (div. June 1993); m. Cathleen Ann Myers, Nov. 21, 1993 (div. May, 2002); 1 child, Colin Todd. AB, Harvard Coll., 1977; MD, U. Pa., 1981. Diplomate Am. Bd. Orthop. Surgery. Resident Yale U., New Haven, 1981-86, instr. Med. Sch., 1986-87; fellow S. Henry LaRocca, MD, New Orleans, 1987-88; asst. prof. Pa. State U., Hershey, 1988-91, assoc. prof., 1991-93, U. Chgo., 1993—, dir. Spine Ctr., 1993—, vice chair dept. surgery; chief sect. orthopedic surgery L.A. Weiss Hosp., Chgo., 1998—, chair divsn. of surgery, 2000—. Reviewer Clin. Orthops., Phila., 1993—. Assoc. editor Spine, 1990—; contbr. articles to profl. jours. Physician Armenian Gen. Benevolent, Hershey, 1988; mem. alumni coun. Wilmington Friends Sch., 1991—. Fellow Am. Acad. Orthop. Surgery; mem. Cervical Spine Rsch. Soc., N.Am. Spine Soc., Am. Neuromodulation Soc. (bd. dirs. 1994—), Acad. Orthop. Soc., Am. Pain Soc., Harvard Club (interviewer 1995—), Sigma Xi. Presbyterian. Avocations: vertebrate palentology, vintage cars, military history, baseball, tennis, squash. Office: U Chgo Spine Ctr 4646 N Marine Dr Chicago IL 60640-5759 E-mail: twetzel@mcis.bsd.uchicago.edu.

WETZEL, HEINZ, foreign language educator; b. Ziesar, Germany, May 11, 1935; immigrated to Can., 1965; s. Ernst and Katharina (Jentzsch) W.; m. Marianne Dummin, Mar. 19, 1957; children: Andreas, Suzanne, Claudia. Staatsexamen, Free Univ., Berlin, 1960; Dr. phil., U. Göttingen, Fed. Republic Germany, 1967. Asst. prof. German dept. Queen's U., Kingston, Can., 1965-69; assoc. prof., grad. sec. German dept. U. Toronto, Can., 1969-72, prof. German dept. Can., 1972—, chmn. German dept., 1984-89. Vis. prof. U. Calif., San Diego, 1973, Technische U. Braunschweig, Germany, 1973, Humboldt U. Berlin, 1995, 97, 99. Author: (book) Konkordanz zu den Dichtungen Georg Trakls, 1971, Klang und Bild in den Dichtungen Georg Trakls, 2d edit., 1972, Banale Vitalitaet und laehmendes Erkennen, Drei vergleichende Studien zu T.S. Eliots, The Waste Land, 1974; editor: Seminar: A Journal of Germanic Studies, 1980-85; contbr. 50 articles to German and comparative lit. to profl. jours. Fellowships and grants from Social Scis. and Humanities Rsch. Coun. of Can. Mem. MLA of Am., Can. Assn. Univ. Tchrs. German. E-mail: h.wetzel@rogers.com.

WETZEL, JODI (JOY LYNN WETZEL), history and women's studies educator; b. Salt Lake City, Apr. 5, 1943; d. Richard Coulam and Margaret Elaine (Openshaw) Wood; m. David Nevin Wetzel, June 12, 1967; children: Meredith (dec.), Richard Rawlins. BA in English, U. Utah, 1965, MA in English, 1967; PhD in Am. Studies, U. Minn., 1977. Instr. Am. studies and family social sci. U. Minn., 1973-77, asst. prof. Am. studies and women's studies, 1977-79, asst. to dir. Minn. Women's Ctr., 1973-75, asst. dir., 1975-79; dir. Women's Resource Ctrs. U. Denver, 1980-84, mem. adj. faculty history, 1981-84, dir. Am. studies program, dir. Women's Inst., 1983-84; dir. Women in Curriculum U. Maine, 1985-86, mem. coop. faculty sociology, social work and human devel., 1986; dir. Inst. Women's Studies and Svcs. Met. State Coll. Denver, 1986—, assoc. prof. history, 1986-89, prof. history, 1990—. Speaker, presenter, cons. in field; vis. prof. Am. studies U. Colo., 1985. Co-author: Women's Studies: Thinking Women, 1993; co-editor: Readings Toward Composition, 2d edit., 1969; contbr. articles to profl. publs. Del. at-large Nat. Women's Meeting, Houston, 1977; bd. dirs. Rocky Mountain Women's Inst., 1981-84; treas. Colo. Women's Agenda, 1987-91. U. Utah Dept. English fellow, 1967; U. Minn. fellow, 1978-79; grantee NEH, 1973, NSF, 1981-83, Carnegie Corp., 1988; named to Outstanding Young Women of Am., 1979. Mem. Am. Hist. Assn., Nat. Assn. Women in Edn. (Hilda A. Davis Ednl. Leadership award 1996, Sr. Scholar 1996), Am. Assn. for Higher Edn., Am. Studies Assn., Nat. Women's Studies Assn., Golden Key Nat. Honor Soc. (hon.), Alpha Lambda Delta, Phi Kappa Phi. Office: Met State Coll Den Campus Box 36 PO Box 173362 Denver CO 80217-3362

WETZEL, KARL JOSEPH, physics educator; b. Waynesboro, Va., May 29, 1937; s. Mark Ernest and Margaret K. (Jungbluth) W.; m. Barbara Carol Damutz, Aug. 3, 1968; children: Sebastian P., Christopher M. BS in Physics, Georgetown U., 1959; MS in Physics, Yale U., 1960, PhD in Physics, 1965. Physicist Nat. Bur. Standards, Washington, 1959; postdoctoral fellow Inst. Nuclear Physics, Darmstadt, Germany, 1965-67, Argonne (Ill.) Nat. Lab., 1967-69; asst. prof. physics U. Portland, Oreg., 1969-72, assoc. prof., 1972-80, prof., 1980-2000, prof. emeritus, 2001—, chmn. sci. dept., 1980-86, dean Grad. Sch., 1987-98. Cons. in field; adj. prof. State of Oreg. Dept. Continuing Edn., Portland, 1976-96. Contbr. articles to profl. publs. Bd. dirs. Friendly House Ctr., Portland, 1979-82, Choral Arts Ensemble, Portland, 1988-95, 98—. NSF fellow, 1965, 76-77; recipient Pres.' award Oreg. Mus. Sci. and Industry, 1972, Outstanding Advisor award Am. Coll. Test/Nat. Academic Advising Assn., 1984. Mem. Am. Phys. Soc., AAUP. Achievements include first to describe experiments using germanium detectors with neutron-capture gamma-ray spectroscopy; first measurement of Delbrück effect in photon scattering. Office: U Portland 5000 N Willamette Blvd Portland OR 97203-5743

WETZEL, ROBERT GEORGE, botany educator; b. Ann Arbor, Mich., Aug. 16, 1936; s. Wilhelm and Eugenia (Wagner) W.; m. Carol Ann Andree, Aug. 9, 1959; children: Paul Robert, Pamela Jeanette, Timothy Mark, Kristina Marie. BS, U. Mich., 1958, MS, 1959; PhD, U. Calif. at Davis, 1962; PhD (hon.), U. Uppsala, Sweden, 1984. Rsch. assoc. Ind. U., Bloomington, 1962-65; asst. prof. botany Mich. State U., East Lansing, 1965-68, assoc. prof., 1968-71, prof., 1971-86, U. Mich., Ann Arbor, 1986-90; Bishop prof. biology U. Ala., Tuscaloosa, 1990—2001; prof. environ. scis. U. N.C., 2001—. Cons. Internat. Biol. Program, London, 1967-75; chmn. Internat. Seagrass Commn., 1974-75; founding mem. Internat. Lake Environment Com., 1986—. Author: Limnology, 1975, 3d rev. edit., 2001, Limnological Analyses, 1979, 3d rev. edit., 2000, To Quench Our Thirst: Present and Future Freshwater Resources of the United States, 1983, Freshwater Ecosystems: Revitalizing Educational Programs in Limnology, 1996; editor: Periphyton of Freshwater Ecosystems, 1983, Wetlands and Ecotones, 1993, Recent Studies on Ecology and Management of Wetlands, 1994, Wetland Ecology, 1995, Lake Okeechobee: A Synthesis, 1995, Limnology of Developing Countries, vol. 1 1995, Limnology of Developing Countries, Vol. 2, 1999, Vol. 3, 2001, Watershed Management for Potable Water Supply, 2000, Confronting Climate Change in the Gulf Coast Region, 2001; contbr. numerous articles on ecology and freshwater biology sys. to profl. jours.; mem. editl. bd. Aquatic Botany, 1975—, Jour. Tropical Freshwater Ecology, 1987—, Internat. Jour. Salt Lake Resources, 1991—, Biogeochemistry, 1993—, Lakes and Reservoirs, 1995—, Aquatic Ecology, 1996—, Boreal Environment Rsch., 1996—, Jour. Limnology, 1999—; N.Am. editor Archiv für Hydrobiologie, 1989—. Served with USNR, 1954-62. Recipient First T. Erlander Nat. professorship Swedish Nat. Research Council and U. Uppsala, 1982-83, award of Distinction U. Calif. at Davis, 1989; AEC grantee, 1965-75; NSF grantee, 1962— ; ERDA grantee, 1975-77; Dept. Energy grantee, 1978— Fellow AAAS; mem. Royal Danish Acaad. Scis. (elected fgn. mem. 1986), Am. Acad. Arts and Scis. (elected 1993), Am. Inst. Biol. Scis., Am. Soc. Limnology and Oceanography (edtl. bd. 1971-74, v.p. 1979-80, pres. 1980-81, G.E. Hutchinson medal 1992), Aquatic Plant Mgmt. Soc., Ecol. Soc. Am., Internat. Assn. Ecology, Freshwater Biol. Assn. U.K., Internat. Assn. Theoretical and Applied Limnology (gen. sec. treas. 1968—, Baldi Meml. award 1989, Naumann-Thienemann medal 1992), Internat. Phycological Soc., Mich. Acad. Scis., N.Am. Benthological Soc., Phycological Soc. Am., Internat. Assn. Great Lakes Rsch., Internat. Consortium Salt Lake Rsch. (edtl. bd. 1991—), Japanese Soc. Limnology, Mich. Bot. Soc., Internat. Assn. Aquatic Vascular Plant Biologists (founder, pres. 1979—), Water Assn. Finland (edtl bd. 1990—), Asociacion Argentina de Limnologia (hon.), Brazilian Soc. Limnology, Finnish Limnological Soc. (edtl. bd. 1989—), Internat. Lake Environ. Comm. Found. (exec. bd. 1986—), Netherlands Soc. Aquatic Ecology (editl. bd. 1996—), Soc. Wetland Scientists (Lifetime Achievement award 2000), Sigma Xi, Phi Sigma. Home: 102 Songbird Ln Chapel Hill NC 27514-2650 Office: U North Carolina Dept Environ Scis-Engring Chapel Hill NC 27599-7431

WETZEL, WENDY SUE, women's health nurse practitioner, holistic health nurse; b. Milw., Jan. 10, 1949; d. L. James and Hazel J. (Frodermann) Metzler; 1 child, Christopher John. Diploma in nursing, Madison (Wis.) Gen. Hosp., 1971; BSN, Pub. Health Nurse cert., Statewide Nursing Program, Sacramento, 1985; MSN, Sonoma State U., Rohnert Park, Calif., 1989. RN, Calif.; ASPO-cert. childbirth educator; cert. holistic nurse Am. Holistic Nurses Cert. Corp., 1997, cert. healing touch practitioner Healing Touch Inst., 1995. Staff nurse in obstetrics USAF Hosp., Clark AFB, The Philippines, 1971-72; staff nurse in neonatal ICU U. Calif., Sacramento, 1972-74; charge nurse Shriner's Hosp. for Crippled Children, Spokane, Wash., 1974-76; office nurse George Kibler, M.D., Fairfield, Calif., 1978-79; head nurse James C. Heinrich, M.D., 1979-88; ultrasonographer, nurse practitioner North Bay Ob-Gyn., 1988-95; nurse practitioner A Woman's Place, Flagstaff, Ariz., 1995—. Pvt. practice childbirth educator, 1976-90; owner, mgr. Health Resources Cons., Fairfield, 1983-95; instr. Calif. State U., 1989-94; rschr. in field. Contbr. articles to profl. jours. Fellow Am. Coll. Childbirth Educators (chmn. co-founder, pres. 1979), Am. Holistic Nurses Assn. (dir. at large 1989-93, treas. 1991-97, state coord. 1989-93, S.W. regional dir. 1993-97, Holistic Nurse of Yr. 1989, Charlotte McGuire scholar 1988), Sigma Theta Tau (charter Lambda Gamma chpt.). Office: 3100 N West St Flagstaff AZ 86004-1650

WETZELL, RICHARD F. historian, researcher; b. Hannover, Germany, Aug. 5, 1961; s. Otto Wolfgang and Helen Wetzell. BA, Swarthmore Coll., 1984; MA, Columbia U., 1985; PhD, Stanford U., 1991. Asst. prof. history U. Md., College Park, 1991—93; post-doctoral fellow Ctr. European Studies Harvard U., Cambridge, Mass., 1993—95; asst. prof. history U. Md., College Park, 1995—2000; rsch. fellow German Hist. Inst., Washington, 2000—. Author: Inventing the Criminal: A History of German Criminology, 1880-1945, 2000. Fellow Dissertation Rsch. fellow, German Acad. Exch. Svc., 1988—89, Hon. Charlotte W. Newcombe fellow, Woodrow Wilson Nat. Fellowship Found., 1989—90, Dissertation fellow, Mabelle McLeod Lewis Meml. Fund, 1990—91, James Bryant Conant Post-Doctoral fellow, Ctr. European Studies, Harvard U., 1993—94, rsch. fellow, German Hist. Inst., 2000—; grantee, NEH, 1993, rsch. grantee, Harry Frank Guggenheim Found., 1994—95. Mem.: Social Sci. History Assn., History of Sci. Soc., German Studies Assn., Am. Soc. Legal History, Am. Hist. Assn., Phi Beta Kappa. Office: German Hist Inst 1607 New Hampshire Ave NW Washington DC 20009 Office Fax: 202-483-3430. Business E-Mail: r.wetzell@ghi-dc.org.

WEVERS, JOHN WILLIAM, retired Semitic languages educator; b. Baldwin, Wis., June 4, 1919; emigrated to Can., 1951; s. Bernard and Wilemina (Te Grootenhuis) W.; m. Grace Della Brondsema, May 22, 1942; children: Robert Dick, John William, Harold George, James Merritt. AB, Calvin Coll., Grand Rapids, Mich., 1940; ThB, Calvin Sem., 1943; ThD, Princeton Theol. Sem., 1945; DD (hon.), Knox Coll., Toronto, 1973; DHC (hon.), Leiden U., 1985. Lectr., then asst. prof. O.T. and Semitic langs. Princeton Theol. Sem., 1946-51; mem. faculty U. Toronto, Ont., Can., 1951—, prof. Near Eastern studies Can., 1963—, prof. emeritus Can., 1984—, grad. chmn. Can., 1972-75, chmn. dept. Can., 1975-80. Chmn. adminstrv. council Presbyn. Ch. Can., 1960-65 Author: Commentary on the Book of Ezekiel, 1969, Septuaginta Vetus Testamentum Graecum: Genesis, 1974, Deuteronomium, 1977, Numeri, 1981, Leviticus, 1986, Exodus, 1991; also text histories, 1974, 78, 83, 86, 92, Notes on the Greek Text of Exodus, 1990, Genesis, 1993, Deuteronomy, 1995, Leviticus, 1997, Numbers, 1998. Bd. govs. Ctrl. Hosp., Toronto, 1963-96, chmn., 1967-80; chmn. Hosp. Coun. Met. Toronto, 1974-75; bd. govs. Ont. Hosp. Assn., 1974-84, pres., 1978-79. Recipient Queen's Jubilee medal, 1978 Fellow Royal Soc. Can.; mem. Oriental Club Toronto, Internat. Orgn. Septuagint and Cognate Studies (pres. 1972-80, hon. pres. 1989—), Can. Bibl. Studies (hon. life), Akademie Wissenschaften Goettingen (corr.), Arts and Letters Club (Toronto). Home: 116 Briar Hill Ave Toronto ON Canada M4R 1H9 Office: U Toronto Near and Middle East Civs Toronto ON Canada M5S 1A1 E-mail: jwevers@utoronto.ca.

WEXELBAUM, MICHAEL, lawyer; b. Bklyn., Aug. 12, 1946; s. Joseph and Beatrice (Skurnick) W.; m. Cynthia Debra Schorr, Apr. 15, 1973 (dec. 1984); children: Joshua David, Stephanie Faye; m. Joan Brenda Math, Aug. 21, 1994; stepchildren: Jonathan David Kaye, Matthew Lawrence Kaye, Julie Dana Kaye. BA in Econs., Bucknell U., 1968; JD, NYU, 1971. Bar: N.Y. 1972, U.S. Dist. Ct. (so. and ea. dists.) N.Y. 1973, U.S. Dist. Ct. (ea. dist.) Wis. 1998. Assoc. Sherman, Citron & Karasik, P.C., N.Y.C., 1972-80, ptnr., head litigation dept., 1980-2001; ptnr. litigation dept. Snow Becker Krauss P.C., 2001—. Arbitrator Nat. Arbitration Forum, 1999—. Arbitrator Am. Arbitration Assn. and Gen. Arbitration Coun. of Textile and Apparel Industries, N.Y.C., 1982—. Mem. Bankruptcy Lawyers Bar Assn., Lawyers Assn. Textile and Apparel Industries (bd. govs.), Am. Arbitration Assn. (arbitrator), Nat. Arbitration Forum (arbitrator). Democratic. Jewish. Avocations: tennis, skiing, biking, theatre. Home: 85 Norrans Ridge Dr Ridgefield CT 06877-4237 Office: Snow Becker Krauss PC 605 Third Ave New York NY 10158-0125 Office Fax: 212-455-0455. E-mail: mwexelbaum@sbklaw.com.

WEXLER, ANNETTE FRANCES, writer; b. Bronx, N.Y., Mar. 28, 1930; d. Samuel and Celia (Gotkin) Levine; m. Solomon Wexler, June 19, 1948 (div. Aug. 1981); children: Steven, Ronald, Bruce, Alan. AA, Middlesex C.C., 1981; BA, Kean U., 1983. Corr. The Daily Jour., Elizabeth, N.J., 1978-81; reporter The News Tribune, Woodbridge, 1982-88; contbg. editor Bus. Jour. N.J., Morganville, 1986-91, Garden State Home & Garden, Morganville, 1986-91, Dun & Bradstreet Reports, N.Y.C., 1992-94; contbg. writer The N.Y. Times, 1990-96, The Star-Ledger, Newark, 1990—; pub. rels. writer and editor Middlesex County Coll., Edison, 2000—; contbg. editor N.Y. Real Estate, N.Y.C., 1997—. Author: (poetry) Illusions, 1980. Advisor to sr. citizens Jewish Cmty. Ctr., Edison, 1982-85; supr. children's activities Cong. Beth Shalom,. Iselin, N.J., 1964-69. Recipient award Comms. Contest, Nat. Fedn. Press Women, 1990. Mem. N.J. Press Women. Avocations: Scrabble, bridge, jogging, golf, skiing. Home and Office: 57 Judson St Apt 2A Edison NJ 08837-2438 E-mail: awexler@bellatlantic.net.

WEXLER, DONALD, psychiatrist, educator; b. Bklyn., Apr. 27, 1923; s. Harry and Gussie (Cooperstein) W.; m. Suzanne Fay Siris, July 22, 1952 (div. June 6, 1981); children: Elisabeth Ann, Marea Jean, William Siris. BA, Wesleyan, Middletown, Conn., 1945; MD, NYU Sch. Medicine, 1948. Diplomate Am. Bd. Psychiatry and Neurology, 1958. Intern Lincoln Hosp., Bronx, N.Y., 1948-49; fellow child psychiatry Univ. Hosp., Ann Arbor, 1949-51, Child Guidance Clinic of Met. Detroit, Detroit, 1951-52; chief resident Boston Hosp., 1955-56; asst. clin. prof. psychiatry Harvard Med. Sch., Boston, 1968-73; assoc. prof. Boston U., 1973—; med. dir. physician asst. program Northeastern U., Boston, 1977—; pvt. practice, Cambridge, Mass., 1957—; cons. group therapy EDRVA Med. Ctr., Bedford, 1979—. Fellow Am. Psychiat. Assn., Am. Group Psychotherapy Assn. Avocations: photography, tennis. Home: 24 Arlington St Cambridge MA 02140-2713 Office: 3 Concord Ave Cambridge MA 02138-3616

WEXLER, GEORGE, retired art educator, artist; b. Bklyn., Jan. 18, 1925; s. Morris and Sarah W.; m. Claire Seidner Wexler, Jan. 4, 1947; children: Andrew, James, Daniel. Diploma, The Cooper Union, N.Y.C., 1948; BA, NYU, 1950; MA, Mich. State U., 1954. Art instr. Mich. State U., E. Lansing, 1950-57; prof. art SUNY, New Paltz, 1957-87, prof. emeritus, 1987—. Landscape painter. Exhbns. include over 20 one-man shows. Cpl. U.S. Army, 1943-46.

WEXLER, HASKELL, film producer, cameraman; b. Chgo., 1922; s. Simon Wexler; m. Nancy Ashenhurst (div.); two children; m. Marian Witt (div.); 1 son, Mark; m. Rita Taggart. Ednl. documentaries, Chgo., for eleven years; cinematographer films: The Hoodlum Priest, The Best Man, America America, The Loved One, In the Heat of the Night, Who's Afraid of Virginia Woolf? (Acad. award), The Thomas Crown Affair, American Graffiti, One Flew Over the Cuckoo's Nest, Introduction to the Enemy, Bound for Glory (Acad. award), Coming Home, Colors, Three Fugitives, 1988, Blaze, 1989, Lookin' to Get Out, Matewan, Other People's Money, The Babe, Mulholland Falls, 1995, Rich Man's Wife, 1995, (with others) Days of Heaven, (with others) Rolling Stones-IMAX, The Secret of Roan Inish, Canadian Bacon, Limbo, 1999, HBO 61—, 2001; writer, dir., photographer: Medium Cool, 1969; wrote and directed Latino, 1985, feature documentary Bus Riders Union, documentary Five Days in March. Received star on Hollywood's Walk of Fame, 1996. Mem. Acad. Motion Picture Arts and Scis. (bd. govs. cinematographers br.). Office: Skouras Agy 631 Wilshire Blvd Ste 2C Santa Monica CA 90401-1513 Address: 1247 Lincoln Blvd # 585 Santa Monica CA 90401-1700

WEXLER, HERBERT IRA, retail company executive; b. Newark, Sept. 6, 1916; s. Irving and Jeanette (Lesser) W.; m. Elaine L. Ellis, Oct. 10, 1948; children: Susan, Peter, Toni. Student, Rutgers U., 1939-41; student Advanced Mgmt. Program, Harvard U., 1956. From stock boy to asst. buyer L. Bamberger & Co., 1935-47; from buyer appliances to sr. v.p., exec. com., dir. R.H. Macy & Co., N.Y.C., 1947-73; pres., CEO, chmn. bd. dirs. Marcade Group Inc., 1973-86, cons., bd. dirs., 1987-97. Vice chmn. Greater N.Y. coun. Boy Scouts Am.; organizer, fundraiser Yale Grace New Haven Hosp.; mem. Gov. Harriman's Com. to Investigate Fraud and Misrepresentation in Consumer Products; mem. adv. coun. to bd. trustees Greens Farms Acad., Westport, Conn.; gen. chmn. State of Israel Bond Drive, 1980, testimonial, 1978; gen. chmn. N.Y. Cmty. Svc. Soc.; chmn. N.Y. sect. for fundraising Denver Jewish Hosp; dir. Children's Blood Found. N.Y. Hosp. Served to capt. U.S. Army, 1941—46. Named Key Man of Yr. Am. Jewish Com. and B'nai B'rith, 1957; named B'nai B'rith Man of Yr., 1976; recipient Disting. Service award Am. Jewish Com. and Anti-Defamation League, 1960, Award of Honor Fedn. Jewish Philanthropies of N.Y., 1961, Scroll of Honor United Jewish Appeal of Greater N.Y., 1964, Man of Yr. award Conn. Digestive Disease Soc., 1973 Mem. Harvard Club, Birchwood Country Club. Home: Greenfield Hunt 49 Palmer Brg Fairfield CT 06430-7830

WEXLER, JOAN G. dean, law educator; b. N.Y.C., Nov. 25, 1946; m. Marvin Wexler, June 16, 1968 (div.); children: Matthew Eric, Laura Page. BS with honors and distinction, Cornell U., 1968; MA in Teaching, Harvard U., 1970; JD, Yale, 1974. Judicial law clerk for Judge Jack B. Weinstein U.S. Dist. Ct. (ea. dist.), N.Y., 1974-75; assoc. Debevoise & Plimpton, N.Y.C., 1975-77; asst. prof. law NYU Sch. Law, 1978-81, assoc. prof. law, 1981-85; prof. law Bklyn. Law Sch., 1985—, assoc. dean acad. affairs, prof. law, 1987-94, acting dean, prof. law, 1994, dean, pres. and prof. law, 1994—. Spkr. in field; evaluator trust adminstrn. and estate adminstrn. courses N.Y. State Banking Assn., 1993; mem. planning com. Bench and Bar Conf. Fed. Bar Coun., 1995, 2003, chair Winter Bench and Bar Conf., Feb. 2002, bd. dirs. Fed. Bar Coun. Found.; mem. planning com. Workshop on Family and Juvenile Law Am. Assn. Law Schs., Washington, 1993; atty. mem. Jud. Conf. of State of N.Y., 2000—. Contbr. articles to profl. jours. Bd. dirs. Downtown Bklyn. Devel. Assn., 1992-96, Fund for Modern Cts., 1994—, Assn. of the Bar of the City of N.Y. Fund, 1994-96; active Commn. on Alcohol and Substance abuse in the Profession, 1999—; mem. Commn. on Univ. Relations, Cornell U., 2001—. Fellow Am. Bar Found., Practising Law Inst. (mem. com. on programs and publs., alternate mem. exec. com., bd. of trustees); mem. ABA (vice chairperson sect. legal edn. and admissions new deans' seminar planning com. 1995-96, ind. law sch. com. 1996-97, 2000-2002, continuing legal edn. com. 1997-2001), Am. Law Inst., Fed. Bar Coun. Found. (pres. 1998-99, chair nominating com. 1998, pres. award 2002), N.Y. State Bar Assn. (com. on children and the law 1993-97, com. on legal edn. and admission to the bar 1994—), N.Y. Women's Bar Assn. (bd. dirs. 1988-91, v.p. 1987-88, 92-93, spl. recognition award 1996, pres. award, 2002), Assn. of the Bar of the City of N.Y. (ad hoc com. on AIDS 1987-88, ad hoc com. on surrogate parenting 1986-88, com. on family ct. and family law 1989-92, nominating com. 1992-93, 99, long range planning com. 1992-95, com. on matrimonial law 1985-89, 92-95, com. on honors 1994-97, v.p. 1996-97, chair com. on honors 1997-2000), Pres.'s Coun. of Cornell Women, Downtown Bklyn. Coun. Exec. Com; mem., Com. on univ. rels., 2001-, com. to restore the Thurgood Marshall landmark courthouse 2001-. Home: 1045 Nine Acres Ln Mamaroneck NY 10543-4706 Office: Bklyn Law Sch 250 Joralemon St Brooklyn NY 11201-3700

WEXLER, RICHARD LEWIS, lawyer; b. Chgo., June 19, 1941; s. Stanley and Lottie (Pinkert) W.; m. Roberta Seigel, June 13, 1962; children: Deborah (Mrs. Jonathan Sokobin), Joshua, Jonathan. Student, U. Mich., 1959-1962; JD cum laude, John Marshall Law Sch., 1965. Bar: Ill. 1965, U.S. Dist. Ct. (no. dist.) Ill. 1967. Gen. counsel Metro. Planning Council, Chgo., 1965-67; ptnr. Wexler, Kane, Rosenzweig & Shaw, 1967-71, Taussig, Wexler & Shaw, Chgo., 1971-78, Wexler, Siegel & Shaw, Ltd., Chgo., 1978-83, Sachnoff & Weaver, Ltd., Chgo., 1983-91, chair real estate dept., 1985-91, mng. ptnr., 1985-90; ptnr., chmn. real estate dept. Lord Bissell & Brook, 1991-97, mem. compensation com., 1995. Legal cons. Zoning Laws Study Commn., Ill. Gen. Assembly, Springfield, 1969-71, Urban Counties Study Commn., Springfield, 1971-72; legal counsel Ill. Coastal Zone Mgmt. Program, Springfield, 1979-81, Northeastern Ill. Planning Commn., Chgo., 1969—. Contbr. numerous articles to profl. jours. Pres. Jewish Fedn. Met. Chgo., 1986-88, mem. numerous coms., also bd. dirs., 1978-90; pres. Jewish United Fund, 1986-88; bd. dirs. Coun. Jewish Fedns., 1980, mem. exec. com., 1985—, v.p., 1988—, chmn. planning steering com., 1990-95, chmn. fedn./agy. rels. com., 1988-90; co-chmn. Task Force on Poverty and Low Income, 1985-87; nat. vice-chmn. United Jewish Appeal, 1988, nat. chmn., 1996-98, regional allocations chmn., 1987-88, chmn. region II, 1988-90, budget com., 1989-92, allocations com., 1990-91, campaign exec., 1991-2000; chmn. Operation Exodus II, 1993-94, chmn. nat. mktg. com., 1994-95, chmn. 1997 campaign planning and budget com., nat. chmn., 1997-98, pres. bd. trustees, 1998-2000; co-chair United Jewish Appeal Fedns. N.Am., 1998-2000; bd. dirs. Jewish Edn. Soc. N.Am., 1982-85, Hebrew Immigrant Aid Soc., 1988—, Nat. Conf. on Soviet Jewry, 1989-95, vice chmn., 1989-92, nat. chmn., 1992-94; bd. dirs. Nat. Jewish Cmty. Rels. Adv. Coun., 1988-90, vice chmn., 1988-92; chmn. Jewish Com. Rels. Coun. Chgo., 1988-89. Fellow Eta Lambda; mem. ABA, Ill. State Bar Assn. (Lincoln award, Legal Writing, 1966). Avocations: tennis, reading, travel. Office: Lord Bissell & Brook 115 S La Salle St Ste 3400 Chicago IL 60603-3801 E-mail: rwexler@lordbissell.com.

WEXLER, ROBERT, congressman; b. Queens, Jan. 2, 1961; m. Laurie Wexler; children: Rachel, Zachary, Hannah. BA in Polit. Scis., U. Fla., 1982; JD, George Washington U. Law Sch., 1985. Mem. Fla. State Senate, 1990-96, U.S. Congress from 19th Fla. dist., 1997—; mem. internat. rels. com., judiciary com. Recipient Senatorial Leadership award Fla. Prosecutor's Assn.; named Legis. of the Year Palm Beach Police Benevolent Assn., Top Environ. Senator Fla. Leagues Conservation Voters, 1996. Democrat. Office: Ho Rep 213 Cannon Ho Office Bldg Washington DC 20515-0919*

WEXLER ROBOCK, STEPHANIE ELLEN, human services and career development specialist, researcher; b. Bronx, N.Y., July 28, 1952; d. Benjamin and Pauline (Zalewitz) Wexler; m. Jerry Robock, May 4, 1980; children: Zachary, Maxwell. BA in Cultural Anthropology cum laude with honors, Lehman Coll., CUNY, 1973; MA in Counselor Edn., NYU, 1979; postgrad., Columbia U., 1982, Mercy Coll., 1985, Fordham U., 1994—. With social work, dir. recreational therapy area nursing homes and health-related facilities, Bronx, Mt. Vernon, N.Y., 1972-77; ind. rschr. Hellenic Gerontol. Inst., Athens, Greece, 1979; dir. R & D N.Y. State Divsn. Youth, 1980-83; sr. pers. cons., assessment, outplacement Pers. Systems, Inc., N.Y.C., Peekskill, Pomona, N.Y., 1986—; dir. JCC on the Hudson, Tarrytown, 1998—. Advisor, mem. grant com. Gerontol. Ctr., NYU, N.Y.C., 1980; career devel. specialist, trainer Fedn. Employment and Guidance Svc., 1982-86; cons., trainer, evaluator in field, Westchester, N.Y.C. and Conn., 1983—; coord./trainer Profl. Devel. Inst., N.Y.C., 1984-90; co-ordinator career devel. Croton Sch. Dist., 1984; dir. Career Devel., Transition and Assessment Svcs. JCC on the Hudson, Tarrytown, N.Y, 1995—; presenter in field. Designer Computer Based Career Devel. software, 1986. Mem. Environ. Def. Fund, N.Y.C., 1992—, Yorktown PTA, 1991—, Nat. PTA, 1991—. Rsch. grantee Hellenic Gerontol. Inst., 1980. Mem. ACA, AHEAD, NCDA, NECA, Nat. Career Devel. Assn., Nat. Cert. Career Counselors, Nat. Cert. Counselors. Avocations: ice skating, rock climbing, reading, computer programming. Office: Wexler-Robock PO Box 421 Baron de Hirsch Rd Crompond NY 10517

WEXNER, LESLIE HERBERT, retail executive; b. Dayton, Ohio, 1937; BSBA, Ohio State U., 1959, HHD (hon.), 1986; LLD (hon.), Hofstra U., 1987; LHD (hon.), Brandeis U., 1990; PhD (hon.), Jewish Theol. Sem. Founder, pres., chmn. bd. The Limited, Inc., fashion chain, Columbus, 1963—. Dir., mem. exec. com. Banc One Corp., Sotheby's Holdings Inc., vis. com. Grad. Sch. Design Harvard U.; mem. bus. adminstrn. adv. coun. Ohio State U.; chmn. Retail Industry Trade Action Coalition. Bd. dirs. Columbus Urban League, 1982-84, Hebrew Immigrant Aid Soc., N.Y.C., 1982—; co-chmn. Internat. United Jewish Appeal Com.; nat. vice chmn., treas. United Jewish Appeal; bd. dirs., mem. exec. com. Am. Jewish Joint Distbn. Com., Inc.; trustee Columbus Jewish Fedn., 1972, Columbus Jewish Found., Aspen Inst., Ohio State U., Columbus Capital Corp. for Civic Improvement; former trustee Columbus Mus. Art, Columbus Symphony Orch., Whitney Mus. Am. Art, Capitol South Community Urban Redevel. Corp.; former mem. Governing Com. Columbus Found.; founding mem., first chair The Ohio State U. Found; exec. com. Am. Israel Pub. Affairs Com. Decorated cavaliere Republic of Italy. Named Man of Yr. Am. Mktg. Assn., 1974. Mem. Young Presidents Orgn., Sigma Alpha Mu. Clubs: B'nai B'rith. Office: Limited Inc PO Box 16000 3 Limited Pkwy Columbus OH 43230-1450*

WEYANDT, DANIEL SCOTT, naval officer, engineer, physicist; b. Altoona, Pa., Dec. 26, 1962; s. Blair Sherwood and Madolyn Rae (Dunmire) W.; m. Laura Anne Weatherington, Oct. 27, 2001; 2 children from previous marriage: Alexander James Collins, Jeremy Auden Collins. BS, Juniata Coll., Huntingdon, Pa., 1984; MS in Physics, Pa. State U., 1992; MBA, U. R.I., 1995. Commd. USN, 1984, advanced through grades to lt. comdr., 1996; divsn. officer USS John C. Calhoun, Charleston, S.C., 1987, USS Simon Bolivar, Charleston, 1986-89; rsch. officer Naval Undersea Warfare Ctr. Divsn., Newport, R.I., 1992-95; sr. engr., countermeasures mgr. Electronic Sensors and Sys. divsn. Northrop Grumman corp., Balt., 1995-99; fellow engr., leading engr. torpedo def. oceanic and naval sys. divsn. Northrop Grumman Electronic Sys., Annapolis, 1999—; res. duty, tng. officer, adminstrv. officer COMSUBRON 8 Det 1106, 1995-98; asst. dep. comdr. COMSUBRON 8, 1995-98; ops. specialist, tng. officer COMSUBEASTLANT DET 1005, 1998—. Decorated Navy achievement medal, Navy commendation medal. Mem. Am. Soc. Naval Engrs., Am. Phys. Soc., Altoona Horseshoe Chorus (assoc. dir. 1978—), Chorus of the Chesapeake, Sigma Pi Sigma. Republican. Methodist. Avocations: music, water sports, fitness. Home: PO Box 89 Hesston PA 16647-0089 Office: Northrop Grumman Corp PO Box 1693 Baltimore MD 21203-1693 E-mail: daniel_s_weyandt@md.northgrum.com.

WEYGAND, BOB A. former congressman; b. Attleboro, Mass., May 10, 1948; BA in Fine Arts, U. R.I., 1971, BS in Civil and Environ. Engring., 1976. Project mgr. R.I. Dept. Nat. Resources, 1973-82; owner Weygand, Orciuch & Christie, Inc., 1982-92; mem. R.I. Ho. of Reps. from 84th dist., 1985-93; lt. gov. State of R.I., 1993-97; mem. 105th-106th Congress from 2d R.I. dist., 1997—2001; pres., CEO New England Board Higher Edu. , Boston, 2001—. Mem. budget com., banking and fin. svcs. com.; chmn. R.I. house com. on corps., 1990; chmn. E. Providence Planning Bd., 1979-84, R.I. Small Bus. Advocacy Coun., 1993-97, R.I. Long Term Care Coord. Coun., 1993-97, R.I. Delegation/White House Conf. on Aging, 1995; presdl. appointee White House Conf. on Small Bus., 1995. Bd. dirs. Save the Bay, 1984-87, United Way, 1993—, Meeting St. Ctr., 1993—, Big Bros. of R.I.; pres., bd. dirs. R.I. Parks Assn., 1983-92; chmn. R.I. Land Use Commn., 1987-92. Recipient Legislator of Yr. award R.I. League Cities and Towns, 1988, Exceptional Pub. Svc. award FBI, 1992, Disting. Svc. Star State of R.I., 1992. Mem. Am. Soc. Landscape Architects; Am. Planning Assn. (Outstanding Pub. Svc. award New Eng. chpt. 1992, Leadership award 1992). Office: New Englan Board Higher Edu 45 Temple Pl Boston MA 02111 Office Fax: 617-338-1577. E-mail: rweygand@nebhe.org.*

WEYHER, HARRY FREDERICK, III, merchant banker; b. N.Y.C., Mar. 9, 1956; s. Harry F. and Barbara (McCusker) W.; m. Anda Gailitis, July 7, 1984; children: Harry F. IV, Jesse D. BA, Middlebury Coll., 1977. Treas. Bunge Corp., N.Y.C., 1977-90; v.p. fin. Gerald Metals Inc., Stamford, Conn., 1990-96; ptnr. Littlejohn & Co., LLC, Greenwich, 1996-01; pres. Vy Capital LLC, Westport, 2001—. Mem. Racquet & Tennis Club, L.I. Wyandanch Club. Home: 215 Ridgefield Rd Wilton CT 06897-2432 Office: Vy Capital LLC 181 Post Rd W Westport CT 06880

WEYHER, MARY JANE, civic worker; b. Salt Lake City, Dec. 26, 1947; d. John Walter and Helen (Brown) Jarman; m. William Carl Weyher, Nov. 27, 1970; children: Sam, Zach, Anna, Willy. Student Foothill Coll., 1966-67; BA, U. Utah, 1971. Tchr. Neighborhood House, Salt Lake City, 1970-71, Head Start, 1972-74. Vice chmn. 2136 Rep. Dist., 1984—; bd. dirs. Girls Village, 1984—, Sarah Daft Home, 1984—; mem. edn. com. Planned Parenthood,

1985—; mem. hospitality com. Rowland Hall St. Mark's Sch. Home and Sch. Assn. Episcopalian. Avocations: skiing, swimming, reading, tennis. Home: 1442 Circle Way Salt Lake City UT 84103-4434

WEYMAN, STEVEN ALOYSIUS, military officer, retired; b. Fort Thomas, Ky., May 31, 1957; s. Edward Joseph Weyman and Carol Jean (Steffen) Jackson; m. Kathleen Anne Bradford, June 2, 1990; 1 child, Jennifer Elizabeth. BS in Math., No. Ky. U., 1978; MS in Comm. Sys. Tech., Naval Postgrad. Sch., 1988. Commd. 2d lt. U.S. Army, 1978, advanced through grades to lt. col., 1995; bn. signal officer 8th Engr. Bn., 1st Cav. Divsn., Ft. Hood, Tex., 1979-81, 2nd M.I. Bn., Pirmasens, Germany, 1982-85; co. comdr. B Co., 307th M.I. Bn., Ludwigsburg, Germany, 1985-86; signal combat devel. project officer Combined Arms Command, Ft. Leavenworth, Kans., 1988-91; student U.S. Army Command Gen. Staff Coll., 1991-92; bn. exec. officer 123rd Signal Bn., 3rd Inf. Divsn., Kitzingen, Germany, 1992-94; asst. divsn. signal officer 3rd Inf. Divsn., Wuerzburg, Germany, 1994-95; operational readiness evaluation team chief 5th U.S. Army (West), Ft. Lewis, Wash., 1995-97; def. info. sys. network deployed program mgmt. chief Def. Info. Sys. Agy., Arlington, Va., 1997-2000; student Armed Forces Staff Coll., Norfolk, 1998; ret. Def. Info. Sys. Agy., Arlington, 2000; student Armed Forces Staff Coll., Norfolk, 1998; tech. acct. mgr. Intel Online Svcs., 2000—01; dep. program mgr., prin. engr. Arrowhead Space and Telecomm. Inc., 2001—. Decorated Legion of Merit. Mem. U.S. Signal Corps Assn. (Bronze Order of Mercury 1995), Armed Forces Comm. Electronics Assn. Avocations: computers, travel, reading, sports. Home: 43921 Felicity Pl Ashburn VA 20147-4860 E-mail: steve@weyman.net., weymans@arrowheadsat.com.

WEYRAUCH, PAUL TURNEY, retired army officer, educator; b. Alpine, Tex., July 22, 1941; s. Paul Russell and Margaret Fischer (Fletcher) W.; m. Nancy Virginia Haight, Dec. 18, 1965; children: Julie Lynn, Paul C. BS, U.S. Mil. Acad., West Point, N.Y., 1963; MBA, Tulane U., 1976; Tchg. Cert., S.W. Tex. State U., 1995, MEd, 1997, prin.'s cert., 1998. Commd. 2d lt. U.S. Army, 1963, advanced through grades to brig. gen.; bn. comdr. 1st Bn., 5th F.A., Ft. Riley, Kans., 1978-80; asst. chief of staff 1st Inf. Div., 1980-81; comdr. 1st Cav. Div. Arty., Ft. Hood, 1982-85; chief of staff U.S. Army F.A. Ctr., Ft. Sill, Okla., 1985-86; asst. chief of staff for plans and policy Allied Forces So. Europe, Naples, Italy, 1986-89; chief of staff III Corps and Ft. Hood, 1989-91; ret., 1991; tchr. math. Richarte H.S., Georgetown, Tex., 1995-97, prin., 1997—; planning and zoning commr. City of Georgetown, 1994-96, chmn. planning and zoning commn., 1995-96. Tchr. Sunday sch. local Protestant chs., pres. chapel couns., leader, coord. Bible studies. Decorated D.S.M., Def. Superior Svc. Medal, Legion of Merit, Bronze Star medal with V. device, Bronze Star medal with 1 oak leaf cluster, Meritorious Svc. medal with 3 oak leaf clusters. Mem. 1st Cav. Div. Assn. Avocations: running, collecting military insignia. Home: 320 S Ridge Cir Georgetown TX 78628-8213

WEYRAUCH, WALTER OTTO, law educator; b. Lindau, Germany, Aug. 27, 1919; came to U.S., 1952; s. Hans Ernst Winand and Meta Margarete (Lönholdt) W.; m. Jill Carolyn White, Mar. 17, 1973; children from previous marriages: Kurt Roman (dec.), Corinne Harriet Irene, Bettina Elaine (dec.). Student, U. Freiburg, 1937, U. Frankfurt Main, Germany, 1940-43, Dr. iur, 1951; LL.B., Georgetown U., 1955; LL.M., Harvard, 1956; J.S.D., Yale, 1962; Golden Dr. diploma (hon.) , U. Frankfurt Main, 2001. Referendar, Frankfurt, Germany, 1943-48; atty. German cts. U.S. Ct. Appeals, Allied High Commn., 1949-52; expert on trade regulations, visit in U.S. under auspices Dept. State, 1950; Harvard U. Dumbarton Oaks Library and Collection, Washington, 1953-55; asst. in instrn. Law Sch., Yale, 1956-57; assoc. prof. law U. Fla., Gainesville, 1957-60, prof., 1960-89, Clarence J. TeSelle prof. law, 1989-94, Stephen C. O'Connell chair, 1994—, disting. prof. law, 1998—; hon. prof. law Johann Wolfgang Goethe U., Franfurt Main, 1980—. Vis. cons. U. Calif. at Berkeley, Space Scis. Lab., 1965-66; vis. prof. law Rutgers U., 1968; vis. prof. polit. sci. U. Calif. at Berkeley, 1968-69; vis. prof. law U. Frankfurt, 1975; cons. Commn. of Experts on Problems of Succession of the Hague Conf. on Pvt. Internat. Law, U.S. Dept. State, 1968-71; Rockefeller Found. fellow, Europe, 1958-59; Richard G. Huber disting. lectr. Law Sch. Boston Coll., 1999. Author: The Personality of Lawyers, 1964, Zum Gesellschaftsbild des Juristen, 1970, Hierarchie der Ausbildungsstätten, Rechtsstudium und Recht in den Vereinigten Staaten, 1976, Gestapo V-Leute: Tatsachen und Theorie des Geheimdienstes, 1989, 2nd edit., 1992; author: (with Sanford N. Katz) American Family Law in Transition, 1983; author: (with Katz and Frances E. Olsen) Cases and Materials on Family Law: Legal Concepts and Changing Human Relationships, 1994; author, editor: Gypsy Law: Romani Legal Traditions and Culture, 2001; contbr. , . Mem. Law and Soc. Assn., Internat. Soc. on Family Law, Assn. Am. Law Schs. (chmn. com. studies beyond 1st degree in law 1965-67), Order of Coif. Home: 2713 SW 5th Pl Gainesville FL 32607-3113 Office: U Fla Coll Law Gainesville FL 32611

WEYRICH, PAUL MICHAEL, political organizations executive; b. Racine, Wis., Oct. 7, 1942; s. Ignatius A. and Virginia M. (Wickstrom) W.; m. Joyce Anne Smigun, July 6, 1963; children: Dawn, Peter, Diana, Stephen, Andrew. AA, U. Wis., 1962. Ordained deacon Melkite Greek Eparchy, 1990. News dir., announcer, program dir. SLIP, WAXD-FM, Kenosha, Wis., 1960-63; reporter Milw. Sentinel, 1963-64; polit. reporter, newscaster CBS, Milw., 1964-65; news dir. Sta. KQXI, Denver, 1966; press sec. U.S. Sen. Gordon Allott of Colo., 1967-73; spl. asst. to Sen. Carl T. Curtis, Nebr., 1973-77; founder, pres. Heritage Found., 1973-74; nat. chmn. Free Congress PAC, Coalitions for Am., 1987—, BOD, Amtrak, 1987-93. Founder, pres. Free Congress Found.; pres. Krieble Inst. of Free Congress Found., 1989-96, America's Voice, 1991-97; nat. editor Transport Central, 1968-71; treas. Coun. Nat. Policy, 1981-92; bd. dirs. All News Radio WEEI, Boston, 1984-90, Krieble Inst. Russia; nat. chmn. Com. for Effective State Govt.; chmn. bd. Yorktownuniversity.com, 1999—. Author: The Role of Rails series, 1964; pub. Polit. Report, 1975-89, The New Electric Rwy. Jour., 1988-96, Spotlight on Congress, 1989-93; host (daily talk show) Direct Line, 1993-98; co-host The New Electric Rwy. Jour., 1994-96, Ways & Means, 1994—. Recipient Youth of Yr. award Racine Optimist Club, 1960, Excellence in Reporting citation Milw. Common Council, 1964, Documentary of Yr. award for Wis. TV, 1965, Crystal Ball award for predicting outcome 1996 presdl. election Washington Post, 1996, Thomas Jefferson award for servant leadership Coun. Nat. Policy, 1997. Mem. Ctrl. Electric Railroaders Assn., Internat. Policy Forum (chmn. 1983-84); former mem. HUD Adv. Commn. on Regulatory Barriers to Affordable Housing. Greek Catholic. Home: 12615 Lake Normandy Ln Fairfax VA 22030-7262 Office: Free Congress Found 717 2nd St NE Washington DC 20002-4368 E-mail: paulwey@free.congress.org.

WHALE, ARTHUR RICHARD, lawyer; b. Detroit, Oct. 28, 1923; s. Arthur B. and Orpha Louella (Doak) W.; m. Roberta Lou Donaldson, Oct. 29, 1949; children: Richard Donaldson, Linda Jean. BSChemE, Northwestern U., 1945; LLB, George Washington U., 1956. Bar: D.C. 1957, Mich. 1957, Ind. 1977, U.S. Patent and Trademark Office 1957. Chem. engr. Ansul Chem. Co., Marinette, Wis., 1946-47, Parke, Davis & Co., Detroit, 1947-50, writer med. lit., 1950-52; chem. engr. Bur. Ships, U.S. Dept. Navy, Washington, 1952-55, dep. sect. head, indsl. gas sect., 1954-55; patent engr. Swift & Co., Washington, 1955-56; patent atty. Upjohn Co., Kalamazoo, 1956-65; asst. mgr. organic chems. sect. patent dept. Dow Chem. Co., Midland, Mich., 1965-66, mgr., 1967-73, mng. counsel, 1973-75; asst. sec., gen. patent counsel Eli Lilly & Co., Indpls., 1975-86; of counsel Miller, Morriss, & Pappas, Lansing, Mich., 1986-89, Baker & Daniels, Indpls., 1987—. Lectr. Practicing Law Inst., John Marshall Law Sch. Contbr. articles to profl. jours. Pres. Nat. Inventors Hall of Fame Found., 1978-79; bd. dirs. Holcomb Rsch. Inst., INdpls, 1982-86. Served to lt. (j.g.) USNR, 1943-46. Mem. State Bar Mich. (chmn. patent trademark copyright sect. 1967-69), D.C. Bar Assn. (mem. patent trademark copyright div.), Midland County Bar Assn. (pres. 1974-75), Am. Bar Assn. (mem. patent trademark copyright sect.), Assn. Corp. Patent Counsel, Nat. Coun. Patent Law Assns. (chmn. 1979-80), Am. Intellectual Property Law Assn. (pres. 1974-75), Ashlar Lodge, Masons, Shriners. Republican. Presbyterian. Avocation: golf. also: 2363 Gulf Shore Blvd N Naples FL 46103 Office: Baker & Daniels 300 N Meridian St Ste 2700 Indianapolis IN 46204-1782 Home: 2363 Gulf Shore Blvd N Naples FL 34103-4356 E-mail: arwhale@bakerd.com.

WHALEN, ALBERTA DEAN, retired community health nurse; b. Oakland, Calif., Apr. 27, 1929; d. Govie and Lula (Rutledge) Smith; m. Joseph T. Whalen, May 29, 1954; children: Michael, Joseph, William. Grad., Providence Coll. Nursing, 1951; postgrad., Chabot Coll., Las Positas Coll. RN, Calif. Surgical/recovery room nurse Peralta Hosp., Oakland, Calif., 1951-55; surg., recovery rm. nurse Providence Hosp., 1956; recovery room nurse Eden Hosp., Castro Valley, Calif., 1957; pvt. duty nurse Valley Meml. Hosp., Livermore, 1966-68; nurse Daphne M. Chisolm, MD, 1984-86; home nursing, 1987-95. Pvt. duty nurse Hacienda Care Ctr., Livermore, Calif., 1993-95. Vol. ARC, 1974—, CPR and std. 1st aid instr., rep. in fair booths and 1st aid stas., disaster teams, coord. Tri Valley Area, 1995; vol. cmty. health nurse for Livermore Libr. sr. blood pressure clinics, 1984-99; rec. sec. Cath. Nurses Assn., South Alameda County, 1958-60; mem. Newly Merged Summit Med. Group, Oakland, Calif.; active St. Rose Hosp. Found., Hayward, Calif.; mem. St. Charles Borromeo Cath. Ch., mem. welcoming com., 1968-86; founding mem. welcoming com. St. Michaels Cath. Ch., Livermore, 1988—, Golden Friends, 1988—, Eucharistic min., 1991—; pub. affairs chmn. Tri Valley Livermore Pleasanton Dublin ARC, 1996-97; nurse coord. Tri Valley ARC, 1996-98; pub. affairs chmn. Acalanes H.S. Class of '47 50 Yr. Reunion, 1997; pub. affairs chmn. H.S. Class of '47 55th Yr. Reunion, 2002, Grief Support St. Michaels/St. Charles, Livermore, Calif.; chair Providence Class 1951; mem. Tri Valley Ballroom Dance Group, 1996—. Recipient nursing pin ARC, 1980, 20 yr. pin 1995, 25 yr. pin 1999, Exceptional Svc. award 1996, Honor award spl. citation for exceptional vol. svc., 1996, 99; named Instr. of Yr. Tri Valley ARC Ctr., 1995. Mem. ARC, Providence Hosp. Valley Meml. Hosp. Founds., Livermore Art Assn. (pub. chmn. 1978-81, art show hostess). Avocations: travel, arts, family functions.

WHALEN, CHARLES WILLIAM, JR. author, business executive, educator; b. Dayton, Ohio, July 31, 1920; s. Charles William and Colette (Kelleher) W.; m. Mary Barbara Gleason, Dec. 27, 1958; children— Charles E., Daniel D., Edward J., Joseph M., Anne E., Mary B. BS, U. Dayton, 1942, HHD (hon.), 1980; MBA, Harvard U., 1946; postgrad., Ohio State U., 1959-60; LLD, Central State U., Ohio, 1966. Vice pres. Dayton Dress Co., 1946-52; faculty U. Dayton, 1952-66; mem. 90th-95th Congresses 3d Dist. Ohio; pres. New Directions, Washington, 1978-79; fellow Woodrow Wilson Internat. Center for Scholars, 1980; adj. prof. Sch. Internat. Service, Am. U., 1981. Mem. Ohio Ho. of Reps., 1954-60, Ohio Senate, 1960-66; mem. Internat. Vol. Svcs., Inc., 1985-95; v.p. Washington Inst. Fgn. Affairs, 1982-98; mem. U. Dayton adv. bd. Ctr. for Internat. Studies, 1990-96; bd. dirs. Harvard Bus. Sch., Washington, 1982-84, 91-94. 1st lt. AUS, 1943-46. Recipient Disting. Alumnus award U. Dayton Alumni Assn., 1975, Alumni Lifetime Achievement award U. Dayton Sch. Bus. Adminstrn., 2001. Mem.: Capitol Hill, Kenwood Country, Dayton Bicycle. Roman Catholic.

WHALEN, JOHN PHILIP, retired educational administrator, clergyman, lawyer; b. Troy, N.Y., Jan. 4, 1928; s. Philip Joseph and Mary Catherine (Doyle) W. BA summa cum laude, St. Mary's Sem. and Univ., Balt., 1949; STL, Cath. U., 1953, MA, 1954, STD summa cum laude, 1965; JD, George Washington U., 1976; postgrad., Johns Hopkins U., 1959-60, U. Md., College Park, 1958-59, Fordham U., 1953-54; LHD (hon.), Marymount U., 1987. Ordained priest Roman Cath. Ch., 1953. Instr. Mater Christi Sem., Albany, 1953-58; asst. prof. Mt. St. Mary's Coll., Emmitsburg, Md., 1959-61; assoc. prof. Cath. U. Am., Washington, 1961-67, acting pres., 1968-69; pastor St. Mary's Ch., Oneonta, N.Y., 1970-72; pres. Consortium of Univs. of Washington area, 1972-88; mng. editor New Cath. Ency., 1963-67; pres., editor-in-chief Corpus Publs., 1967-94, ret., 1994. Cons. 12 colls. and univs.; founder, chmn. Univ. Support Svcs., Inc., 1986-94, pres., CEO, founder; cons. student loans, capital access trust, capital loans to colls., 1999-2000; founder, prin. Power Systems, Inc.; founder Whalen Holdings, LLC; founder prin. Full Measure, LLC, Whalen Holdings, LLC, JMJ Whalen Found., Inc.; bd. dirs. U.S. Fund for Improvement Postsecondary Edn., 1988-91. Mem. editl. bd. Law and Edn.; weekly columnist Evangelist, Albany; contbr. to Nat. Geog. mag.; contbr. articles to edni. and theol. jours. Pres. Univ. Extension Ednl. Corp., 1974—94; mem. Fed. City Coun., 1982—, Coun. for Ct. Excellence, 1984—90; chmn. Ctr. Advanced Studies of the Ams., 1984—90; bd. dirs. Sta. WETA-TV, 1968—69, Washington Ctr. for Met. Studies, 1968—69, Cath. U. Am., 1968—69, Nat. Shrine of Immaculate Conception, 1968—69, Dumbarton Coll., 1970—72, Trinity Coll., 1969—72, St. Mary's Coll., South Bend, Ind., 1970—74, St. Anselm's, 1979—85, Mt. Vernon Coll., 1982—84, CBR Found., 2001—, Met. Bd. Trade, Washington, 1975—90, sec bd. dirs., 1983—85. Named Man of the Yr., 1984; recipient Disting. Alumnus award George Washington U., 1988. Mem. Nat. Cath. Edn. Assn., Cath. Theol. Soc. Am. (dir. 1966-68), Higher Edn. Group Washington (pres. 1974-75), Tired Hands Club (pres. 1982-84), Cosmos Club (Washington), City Club, Rotary. Office: 1614 Parham Rd Silver Spring MD 20903-2256

WHALEN, JOHN SYDNEY, management consultant; b. Moncton, N.B., Can., Sept. 26, 1934; s. Harry Edward and Sarah Maude (Bourgeois) W.; m. Margaret Joan Carruthers, May 3, 1958; children: Bradley Graham, Elizabeth Ann. Grad., Can. Inst. Chartered Accts., 1959. Chartered acct. Coopers & Lybrand (formerly McDonald, Currie & Co.), St. John, N.B., 1954-63; with Kaiser Services, Oakland, Calif., 1963-75, telecommunications mgr., 1966-69, asst. controller, 1969-70, controller, 1970-74; mgr. corp. acctg. Kaiser Industries Corp., Oakland, 1975; controller Kaiser Engrs., Inc., 1975-76, v.p. fin. and adminstrn., 1976-82; mgmt. cons., owner Whalen & Assocs., Inc., Alamo, Calif., 1983—. Pres. Round Hill Holdings, Inc., 1993-99. Mem. Commonwealth Club. Home: 2216 Nelda Way Alamo CA 94507-2004 Office: 3195 Danville Blvd Ste 4 Alamo CA 94507-1920 E-mail: sydwhalen@aol.com.

WHALEN, LORETTA THERESA, religious educational administrator; b. Bklyn., May 21, 1940; d. William Michael and Loretta Margaret (Malone) Whalen; children: Ann Lindsay, Margaret Force. RN, St. Vincent's Hosp., N.Y.C., 1960; BSN, U. Pa., 1965; MA in Edn., Fordham U., 1971; cert. in sociology religion, Louvain U., Belgium, 1974; PhD in Global Edn., The Union Grad. Sch., 1994. Staff nurse Holy Family Hosp., Atlanta, 1967-69; Latin Am. communication dir. Med. Mission Sisters, Maracaibo, Venezuela, 1969-71; intensive care nurse St. Vincent's Hosp., N.Y.C., 1971-72; mem. ministry team Med. Mission Sisters, various locations, 1972-74, dir. communications Phila., 1974-77; asst. to exec. Interreligious Peace Colloquium, Washington, 1977; freelance writing, photography Ch. World Svc., N.Y.C., 1978-79; dir. Office Global Edn. Nat. Council Chs., 1980-99. Co-author: Make a World of Difference: Creative Activities for Global Learning, 1990, Tales of the Heart: Affective Approaches to Global Education, 1991; mem. editorial bd., rev. editor Connections Mag., 1984-87; contbr. articles to profl. jours. Mem. Peace and Justice Commn., Archdiocese of Balt., 1985-89. Mem. Amnesty Internat., Bread for the World, NOW, World Wildlife Fund, Greenpeace, Sigma Theta Tau. Democrat. Roman Catholic. Avocations: photography, writing, racquetball, interior design, travel.

WHALEN, LUCILLE, retired academic administrator; b. Los Angeles, July 26, 1925; d. Edward Cleveland and Mary Lucille (Perrault) W. BA in English, Immaculate Heart Coll., Los Angeles, 1949; MSL.S., Catholic U. Am., 1955; D.L.S., Columbia U., 1965. Tchr. elem. and secondary parochial schs., L.A., Calif., 1945—52; tchr., libr. Conaty Meml. H.S., 1950—52; reference/serials librarian, instr. in library sci. Immaculate Heart Coll., 1955-58; dean Immaculate Heart Coll. (Sch. Library Sci.), 1958-60, 65-70; assoc. dean, prof. SUNY, Albany, 1971-78, 84-87, prof. Sch. Info. Sci. and Policy, 1979-87; dean grad. programs, libr. Immaculate Heart Coll. Ctr., Los Angeles, 1987-90; ref. libr. (part-time) Glendale Community Coll., 1990—. Dir. U.S. Office Edn. Instn. Author, editor: (with others) Reference Services in Archives, 1986. author: Human Rights: A Reference Handbook, 1989. Mem. ACLU, Common Cause, Amnesty Internat. Democrat. Roman Catholic. Home: 320 S Gramercy Pl Apt 101 Los Angeles CA 90020-4542 Office: Glendale CC 1500 N Verdugo Rd Glendale CA 91208-2809

WHALEN, MICHAEL, company executive; b. Hartford, Nov. 3, 1963; s. Robert and Penelope Whalen; m. Susan Smith, Aug. 15, 1995; children: Emily, Conor. BS, Princeton U., 1985; MBA, U. Chgo., 1993. Product mgr. Xerox Corp., Rochester, NY, 1993—2000; CEO Elucida Rsch. LLC, Beverly, Mass., 2000—. Capt. U.S. Army, 1985—89. Office: Elucida Rsch LLC PO Box 7100 Beverly MA 01915 Office Fax: 978-921-4195. Business E-Mail: mwhalen@elucidaresearch.com.

WHALEN, PATRICIA THERESE, marketing and public relations educator, consultant; b. Columbus, Ohio, June 26, 1955; d. Daniel Edward and Rose Eileen Whalen. BA in English, Ohio State U., 1977; MS in Bus. Adminstrn., Ind. U., 1981; PhD, Mich. State U., 1999. Sales promotion specialist Clark Components Div., Buchanan, Mich., 1978-81, supr., advt. and pub. rels., 1981-82; mgr. corp. comm. Clark Equipment Co., 1982-84, dir. govt. affairs South Bend, Ind., 1984-86; dir. pub. rels. COMSAT World Systems Div., Clarksburg, Md., 1986-87, dir. mktg. communications Washington, 1987-90; dir. mktg. COMSAT Mobile Comm., 1990-94; instr. dept. advt. Mich. State U., 1995—; asst. prof. integrated mktg. comms. Northwestern U., Madill Sch. Journalism, 1999—2001; dir. prof. devel. Internat. Advt. Assocs., 2001—. Seminar speaker in field. Contbr. articles to profl. jours. Bd. dirs. Jr. Achievement, Niles, Mich., South Bend, Ind., 1982-86, Tri-county Pvt. Industry Coun., St. Joseph County, Mich., 1983-85. Mem. Pub. Rels. Soc. Am. (tech. com. 1982—, Silver Anvil award 1982), Soc. Satellite Profls. (bd. dirs. 1990-93). Roman Catholic. Avocations: golf, snow skiing, tennis, internat. travel, pub. speaking. Home: 5307 Davis St Skokie IL 60077-1536 E-mail: p_whalen@nwu.edu.

WHALEN, PAUL LEWELLIN, lawyer, educator, mediator; b. Lexington, Ky. s. Elza Boz and Barbara Jean (Lewellin) W.; m. Teena Gail Tanner, Jan. 26, 1985; children: Ashley, Lars, Lucy. BA, U. Ky.; JD, Northern Ky. U.; cert., Bonn U., Fed. Republic Germany, 1981; student, U.S. Army J.A.G. Sch., 1988; diploma, USAF Squadron Officers Sch., 1998. Bar: W.Va. 1984, U.S. Ct. Appeals (6th cir.) 1984, Ky. 1985, U.S. Ct. Appeals (4th cir.) 1985, Ohio 1993. Assoc. Geary Walker, Parkersburg, W.Va., 1984-85; prin. Paul L. Whalen, Ft. Thomas, Ky., 1985—; advisor Families with Children from China, 1998—; prof. Def. Acquisition U., WP AFB; prof. pub. contract law Air Force Inst. Tech., 1999-2000; atty. Dept. of Air Force, Office of Chief Trial Atty. Contract Law Ctr., Wright Patterson AFB, 1988—89; hearing officer, prosecutor Ky. Dept. Ednl. Profl. Stds. Bd., 1995—97; mem. arbitration panel No. Ky., 1997—, Montgomery County, Ohio, 1998—; hearing officer Ky. Dept. Edn. IDEA, 1999—2000. Mem. Leadership No. Ky., Ft. Thomas Bd. Edn., 1987—99, chmn., 1990—94; mem. Ky. Bd. Edn., 2000—, Ky. Commn. on Human Svcs.; pres. ch. coun. Highland United Meth. Ch., 2000; mem. Campbell County Foster Care Rev. Bd., Newport, Ky., 1986; bd. dirs. Ky. Coun. Child Abuse, Inc. Com. for Kids; dir. Ky. Sch. Bd. Assn., 1993—98; mem. Air Force Bicycle Team Ride Across Iowa, 1997—2000. Recipient Commendation No. Ky. Legal Aid, 1986-2001. Fellow Commonwealth Inst. Leadership; mem. Fed. Bar Assn., No. Ky. Bar Assn., Optimist Club, Kiwanis Club, Phi Alpha Delta. Democrat. Methodist. Avocations: freelance writing, stamp collecting, politics, amateur radio, bicycling. Home: 113 Ridgeway Ave Fort Thomas KY 41075-1333 Office: PO Box 22 Fort Thomas KY 41075 E-mail: plewellinwhalen@aol.com. *Notable cases include: Givan vs. Ask Realty, Ky. App., 788 S.W. 2d 503, 1990, establishing that a real estate broker has a fiduciary relationship with seller even though he may be sub-agent; Oconto Electric, Inc., ASBCA No. 36789, 88-3 BCA, 21,188, regarding timeliness of appeals to bds. of contract appeals; 256F.3d 409 (6th Cir. 2001), succesful writ of habeas corpus.*

WHALEN, THOMAS BRIAN, anesthesiologist; b. Bristol, Pa., July 24, 1959; s. Richard George and Alice (Connolly) W. BS in Biology, St. Joseph's U., 1981; MD, Pa. State U., 1985. Diplomate Am. Bd. Anesthesiology, Am. Acad. Pain Mgmt. Intern St. Francis Med. Ctr., Pitts., 1985-86; resident in anesthesiology Duke U. Med. Ctr., Durham, N.C., 1986-88; fellow in pain mgmt., obstetric and pediat. anesthesia Med. U. S.C., Charleston, 1988-89; pvt. practice S.C., 1989-91, Atlanta, 1992-93; asst. prof. U. Tex. S.W. Med. Sch., Dallas, 1994, clin. asst. prof., 1995; pvt. practice, 1995-2001, Atlanta, 2001—; dept. vice chair Presbyn. Hosp., Plano, 1998, 99, chair, 2000—01. Mem. Am. Soc. Anesthesiologists, Soc. for Ambulatory Anesthesia, Ga. Soc. Anesthesiologists. Republican. Presbyterian. Avocation: equestrian activities, running, hiking. Office: 108 Paces Run Atlanta GA 30339-3788 E-mail: twhalenmd@yahoo.com.

WHALEN, WAYNE W. lawyer; b. Savanna, Ill., Aug. 22, 1939; s. Leo R. and Esther M. (Yackley) W.; m. Paula Wolff, Apr. 22, 1970; children: Amanda, Clementine, Antonia, Nathaniel, Daniel. BS, U.S. Air Force Acad., 1961; JD, Northwestern U., 1967. Bar: Ill. 1967, U.S. Ct. Appeals (7th cir.) 1968, U.S. Supreme Ct. 1972. Commd. 1st lt. USAF, 1961, ret., 1964; assoc. Mayer, Brown & Platt, Chgo., 1967-74, ptnr., 1974, Skadden, Arps, Slate, Meagher & Flom (Ill.), Chgo., 1984—. Bd. dirs. Van Kampen Funds, Oak Brook, Ill. Author: Annotated Illinois Constitution, 1972. Del. 6th Ill. Constitutional Conv., 1969-70, chmn. style drafting and submission com. Named Outstanding Young Lawyer, Chgo. Bar Found., 1970. Mem. Chgo. Club. Office: Skadden Arps Slate Meagher & Flom (Ill.) 333 W Wacker Dr Ste 2100 Chicago IL 60606-1220

WHALEY, CHARLES E. writer, consultant; b. Bloomington, Ind., Aug. 12, 1948; s. Lawrence Ellsworth and Mary Beth (Bennett) W. BS, Ind. U., 1973, MS, 1975, EdS, 1977; postgrad. U. Houston; postgrad., U. South Fla. Tchr. Ctr. for World Studies, Grand Rapids, Mich.; tchr. social studies Leon County Schs., Tallahassee; instr. social studies Devel. Rsch. Sch. Fla. State U.; dir. Fla. Gov.'s Summer Coll.; program coord. instrnl. strategies br. Ky. Dept. Edn., Frankfort. Author: Future Images: Futures Studies for Grades 4-12, 1986, The Futures Primer for Classroom Teachers, 1987, Enhancing Thinking & Creativity with Futures Studies, 1991, also other books, chpts. and articles. Named Ky. Col., 1985; recipient Disting. Svc. award, Ky., 1987, 94, Disting. Svc. award for Gifted Edn. State of Ind.; grantee NDEA, ESEA, also others. E-mail: edub47@earthlink.net.

WHALEY, CHARLES HENRY, IV, communications company executive; b. Elmhurst, N.Y., Jan. 15, 1958; s. Charles Henry III and Edna Mae (Squires) W.; m. Jeanette Marie Smith, Sept. 26, 1987. AAS in Electrical Tech., Queensborough Community Coll., Bayside, N.Y., 1979. Testing engr. GTE/Telenet, Mount Laurel, N.J., 1979-81; field service engr. Gen. Dynamics Communications Co., St. Louis, 1981-82; ops. engr. United Techs. Communications Co., Pine Brook, N.J., 1982-84, sr. ops. engr. N.Y.C., 1984-85, ops. supr., 1985-86; project mgr. Telex Computer Products, 1986; pres. Pertel Comms. of N.E., 1990—, Metrocom Tech. Svcs., 1997—. Democrat. Presbyterian. Avocations: computers, classic automobiles, contemporary music, U.S. history, study of industrial/mechanical evolution. Office: Pertel Comm of NE Inc 750 Main St Hartford CT 06103 E-mail: chw4@aol.com., cwhaley@pertelne.com.

WHALEY, CHRISTOPHER DAVID, manufacturing engineer, consultant; b. Fulton, N.Y., Feb. 21, 1965; s. Lawrence Arthor and Shirley May (Beebe) W.; m. Nina Terresa Barucco (div.); children: Stefan, Aric. BS in Physics, SUNY, Oswego, 1986; BS in Polit. Sci., SUNY, Cortland, 1991; AAS in Mech. Engrng. Tech., Ononadoga C.C., Syracuse, N.Y., 1988. Rsch. and devel. toolmaker The Eraser Co., Syracuse, 1983-85; design engr. Greno Industries, Scota, N.Y., 1985-87; mfg. and design engr. Majestic Mold, Phoenix, N.Y., 1987-89; mfg. engr. GE Co., Syracuse, 1989-92; v.p. mfg. engr. Display Prodrs., Bronx, N.Y., 1992-95; v.p. engring. and ops. Viz Mold & Die Ltd., Northvale, N.J., 1995; pres. Merlin Mold & Mfg., Port Chester, N.Y., 1995—, CW Assocs., Port Chester, 1995—. Cons. Viz Plastics & Mold, Northvale, N.J., 1992—, Shar-Jo Industries, Fulton, N.Y., 1989—; tooling designer GTS Industries, Clifton, N.J., 1992—. Author: U.S. Naval Repair Manual, 1986. Asst. wrestling coach Mexico (N.Y.) Acad. Schs., 1983-85. Mem. Soc. Plastic Engrs. Republican. Avocations: formula style road racing, motorcross racing, remote control gas car racing. Office: 247 Cape Horn Rd Fulton NY 13069-3666

WHALEY, JOSEPH S. physician; b. Yuma, Ariz., Nov. 29, 1933; s. Joseph S. and Elizabeth (Johnson) W.; m. Doris N. Pettie, June 7, 1957; children: Craig T., Dawna T. BA, U. Ariz., 1954; MD, Hahnemann Med. Coll., 1958. Bd. cert. Am. Bd. Family Practice. Intern Letterman Army Hosp., 1958-59; physician pvt. practice, Tucson, 1963—. Capt. USAF, 1959-63. Fellow Am. Acad. Family Physicians (pres. Ariz. chpt. 1972-73); mem. AMA, Phi Beta Kappa, Sigma Pi Phi. Democrat. Baptist. Avocations: golf, tennis, fishing. Office: 368 E Grant Rd Tucson AZ 85705-5783

WHALEY, ROBERT HAMILTON, judge; m. Lucinda Schilling Whaley; 3 children. BA, Princeton U., 1965; JD, Emory U., 1968. Litigator land and natural resources divsn. Dept. Justice, 1969-71; asst. U.S. atty. U.S. Dist. Wash. (ea. dist.), 1971-72; assoc. Winston & Cashatt, Spokane, Wash., 1972-76, ptnr., 1976—; judge Spokane County Superior Ct., 1992-95, U.S. Dist. Ct. (ea. dist.) Wash., Spokane, 1995—. Office: US Dist Ct Ea Dist Wash PO Box 283 920 Riverside Ave W Spokane WA 99210

WHALEY, ROSS SAMUEL, environmentalist, educator; b. Detroit, Nov. 7, 1937; s. Lyle John and Margaret Nielson (Semple) W.; m. Beverly Mae Heemstra, June 14, 1958; children— Heather Jean, Susan Lesli, Lindsay John BS, U. Mich., 1959, PhD, 1969; MS, Colo. State U., 1961. Asst. prof., assoc. prof., prof. Utah State U., Logan, 1965—70, dept. head, 1967—70; assoc. dean Colo. State U., Ft. Collins, 1970—73; dept. head U. Mass., Amherst, 1973—76, dean, 1976—78; dir. econ. research USDA Forest Service, Washington, 1978—84; pres. SUNY Coll. Environ. Scis. and Forestry, Syracuse, 1984—2000, prof., 2000—. Cons. UN FAO, Rome, 1983-84, UN, Budapest, Hungary, 1974, U.S. Peace Corps., South Am., 1972, Geddes, Brecher, Qualls & Cunningham, Denver, 1971-72 Contbr. articles to profl. jours. Bd. dirs. Glynwood Ctr., Au Sable Inst. Environ. Studies, Natural History Mus. of the Adirondacks, Adirondack Nature Conservancy. Fellow Soc. Am. Foresters (pres. 1991). Mem. Christian Ref. Ch. Avocations: reading, swimming, hiking, fly fishing, cross country skiing. Office: SUNY/ESF 326 Marshall Hall 1 Forestry Dr Syracuse NY 13210

WHALEY, STORM HAMMOND, retired government official, consultant; b. Sulphur Springs, Ark., Mar. 15, 1916; s. Storm Onus and Mabel Etta (Prater) W.; m. Jane Florence Bucy, Oct. 6, 1935; children: Carroll Jean Whaley Anderson, Ann Marie Whaley Adams, Rebecca Glenn Whaley Dyess. BA, John Brown U., 1935; LL.D. (hon.), 1959; postgrad., Am. U. Law Sch., 1954; D.Sc. hon., U. Ark. for Med. Scis., 1983. Mgr. Sta. KUOA, Siloam Springs, Ark., 1935-53, Sta. KGER, Long Beach, 1948-53, KOME, Tulsa, 1951-53; asst. to Congressman J.W. Trimble, 1953-54; asst. to pres. U. Ark., 1954-59, acting pres., 1959-60, v.p. health scis., 1960-70; assoc. dir. communications NIH, Bethesda, Md., 1970-92; retired, 1992. Mem. U.S. del. World Health Assembly, 1962, 63, 64; mem. nat. adv. health council USPHS, 1963-66; chmn. ad hoc com. Report to Pres. and Congress Regional Med. Programs, 1967; mem. U.S. Sr. Exec. Service, 1979 Author: They Call It, 1951. Del. Democratic Nat. Conv., 1940, 44, 48, 52. Recipient Superior Service award HEW, 1974, SES Performance award, 1982, Superior Service award USPHS, 1987; named Outstanding Alumnus, John Brown U., 2001. Fellow AAAS; mem. Broadcast Pioneers, Ark. Broadcasters Assn. (life), Internat. Sci. Writers Assn., NIH Alumni Assn. (bd. dirs. 1992—, sec.-treas.. 1997-2001), Nat. Press Club, KT, Masons (33d deg.), Omicron Delta Kappa, Lambda Chi Alpha. Home and Office: 4400 E West Hwy Bethesda MD 20814-4524 E-mail: hail@erols.com.

WHALEY, WALLACE W. military officer; b. NC; BSCE, The Citadel, 1968; postgrad., Air Command and Staff Coll., 1980. Commd. USAF, 1968, advanced through grades to maj. gen., 1995; provider pilot 311th Tactical Airlift Squadron, Da Nang Air Base, Vietnam, 1969—70; starlifter pilot, instr. 14th Mil. Airlift Squadron, Norton AFB, Calif., 1970—72; galaxy simulator instr., flight examiner 3d Mil. Airlift Squadron, Charleston AFB, SC, 1972—73; command post duty officer, C-5 flight examiner, pilot 436th Mil. Airlift Wing, Dover AFB, Del., 1973—74; res. C-5 and C-141 pilot, asst. squadron ops. officer 349th Mil. Airlift Wing, Travis AFB, Calif., 1974—83; WC-130 pilot, dep. comdr. ops. 920th Weather Reconnaissance Group, Keesler AFB, Miss., 1983; pilot, dep. comdr. ops. 446th Mil. Airlift Wing, McChord AFB, Wash., 1983—84; comdr. 928th Tactical Airlift Group, O'Hare Air Res. Forces Facility, Chgo., 1984—86; vice comdr. 446th Mil. Airlift Wing, McChord AFB, Wash., 1986—88; comdr. 349th Mil. Airlift Wing, Travis AFB, Calif., 1988—90; dep. to chief of AF Res. Hdqrs. USAF, Washington, 1990—93; comdr. 14th AF, AF Res. Command, McClellan AFB, Calif., 1993—98, March AFB, 1998—2000; dir. ops. Hdqrs. AF Res. Command, Robins AFB, Ga., 2000—. Decorated SDM, Legion of Merit with oak leaf cluster, DFC, Air medal with four oak leaf clusters. Mem.: Assn. of The Citadel, Res. Officers Assn., Air Force Assn. Office: Robbins AFB Robins AFB GA 31098-5009

WHALEY-BUCKEL, MARNIE, social service administrator; b. Madison County, Ohio, July 16, 1946; d. H. John and Frances (Kramer) Hostetler; m. John Benjamin Whaley, Sept. 14, 1974 (wid. Mar. 1977); 1 child, Monica Anne; m. Raymond J. Buckel, May 17, 1991; 1 adopted child, Dimitri R.A. Buckel. BA in Social Work, Bluffton Coll., 1969; MSW, Ohio State U., 1983. Lic. ind. social worker, Ohio. Counselor Family Counseling, Lima, Ohio, 1969-70; social worker psychiat. unit St. Rita's Hosp., 1970-74; emergency counselor Northwest Ctr. for Human Resources, 1975-78, outpatient therapist, 1977-80, coord. emergency svcs., 1979-82; intern coord. pub. rels. Northwest Couseling, Columbus, Ohio, 1982-83; coord. community rels. Madison County Hosp., London, 1983-85; assoc. dir. Madison County Health Ctr Inc., 1985-89; exec. dir. Bd. Alcohol, Drug Addiction and Mental Health Svcs., 1989-94; pvt. practice Cath. Social Svcs., Dayton, Ohio, 1997—. Chmn. Allen County Welfare Adv. Bd., Lima, 1979-82; vice chmn. Act. Inc., Columbus, 1989-91, chmn., 1991-93; Ohio Hospice Adv. Bd., London, 1990-91, pvt. cons., agy. adminstrn., mediation, 1995—. Chmn. bd. ch. edn. Big Darby Bapt. Ch., Plain City, Ohio, 1987, clk., 1989—, sec.-treas., 1988, 89,, chmn. constitution com., 1990. Mem. NASW, Mental Health Adminstrs., Phi Kappa Phi, Delta Sigma Mu. Avocations: sewing, crafts, gardening, flowers. Office: Cath Social Svcs MV 922 W Riverview Ave Dayton OH 45407-2424 also: Positive Perspectives 2355 Derr Rd Springfield OH 45503-2455 E-mail: buckelmu@cssmu.org.

WHALIN, ROBERT W. physicist; B in Physics, U. Ky.; M in Physics, U. Ill.; PhD of Phys. Oceanography, Tex. A&M U. Registered Profl. Engr. Dir. Army Rsch. Lab. Army Rsch. Lab., Adelphi, Md., 1998—; dir. U.S. Army Engr. Waterways Experiment Sta., Vicksburg, Miss., 1992—98; tech. dir. U.S. Army Engrs. Waterways Experiment Sta., 1985—92, U.S. Army Corps Engrs. Coastal Engring. Rsch. Ctr., Fort Belvoir, Va., 1982—85. Adj. prof. Miss. State U., Tex. A&M U., U. Miss.; mem. external rsch. adv. com. Miss. State U.; engring. adv. coun. mem. U. Fla.; rsch. adv. com. for Army High Performance Computing Rsch. Ctr. U. Minn.; adv. bd. mem. Dept. Civil Engring. U. New Orleans. Contbr. Mem.: ASCE, Sr. Exec. Assn., Army Engr. Assn., Soc. Am. Mil. Engrs., Tsunami Soc., Permanent Internat. Assn. Navigation Congresses, Am. Soc. Engring. Edn., Sigma Xi, Phi Kappa Phi, Phi Eta Sigma. Office: US Army Rsch Lab AMSRL-VS-EA-PA 2800 Powder Mill Rd Adelphi MD 20783-1197*

WHALLON, WILLIAM, literature educator; b. Richmond, Ind., Sept. 24, 1928; s. Arthur J. and Adelaide (Wheeler) W.; m. Joanne Holland, Aug. 22, 1957; children: Andrew, Nicholas. BA, McGill U., 1950; PhD, Yale U., 1957. From asst. prof. to prof. Mich. State U., East Lansing, 1963—. Author: Formula, Character, and Context, 1969, Problem and Spectacle, 1980, Inconsistencies, 1983, (poetry) A Book of Time, 1990, (scenarios) The Oresteia / Apollo & Bacchus, 1997, The Jesus Rule, 2002. Fellow Center for Hellenic Studies, 1962-63; Fulbright prof. comparative lit., U. Bayreuth, 1984-85. Home: 1655 Walnut Heights Dr East Lansing MI 48823-2943

WHAM, DAVID BUFFINGTON, secondary school educator; b. Evanston, Ill., May 25, 1937; s. Benjamin and Virginia (Buffington) W.; m. Joan Field Wilber, Mar. 9, 1968 (div. May 1972); children: Benjamin, Rachel. AB cum laude, Harvard U., 1959; MA, So. Ill. U., Carbondale, 1967. Instr. U. Wyo., Powell, 1963-65, So. Ill. U., Carbondale, 1965-67; legis. asst. U.S. Congress, Washington, 1969-78; freelance writer Chgo., 1980-89; tchr. Chgo. Pub. Schs., 1994—. Speechwriter Adlai Stevenson for Gov. campaign, 1986, Dawn Netsch for Gov. campaign, 1994. Author: My Farewell to Bohemia, 1968, The Comic Genuflection, 1984, A Wave of Bright Boys, 1994. With U.S. Army, 1959-62. Recipient fiction award Columbia Pacific U., 1994. Mem. Harvard Club Chgo. (interviewer 1984—), Spee Club Harvard, Hasty Pudding Club Harvard. Democrat. Episcopalian. Home: 860 Hinman Ave # 724 Evanston IL 60202 Office: 125 S Clark St Chicago IL 60603-5200

WHAM, DOROTHY STONECIPHER, state legislator; b. Centralia, Ill., Jan. 5, 1925; d. Ernest Joseph and Vera Thelma (Shafer) Stonecipher; m. Robert S. Wham, Jan. 26, 1947; children: Nancy S. Wham Mitchell, Jeanne Wham Ryan, Robert S. II. BA, MacMurray Coll., 1946; MA, U. Ill., 1949; D of Pub. Adminstrn. (hon.), MacMurray Coll., 1992. Counsellor Student Counselling Bur. U. Ill., Urbana, 1946-49; state dir. ACTION program, Colo./Wyo. U.S. Govt., Denver, 1972-82; mem. Colo. Ho. of Reps., 1986-87, Colo. Senate, 1987-2000, chair jud. com., 1988-2000. With capital devel. com., health, environ., welfare, instns., legal svcs. Mem. Civil Rights Commn. Denver, 1972-80; bd. dirs. Denver Com. on Mental Health, 1985-88, Denver Symphony, 1985-88. Mem. APA, AAUW, LWV, Colo. Mental Health Assn. (bd. dirs. 1986-88), Civitan. Republican. Avocations: travel, furniture refinishing. Home: 3430 S Race St Englewood CO 80110

WHAM, GEORGE SIMS, retired publishing executive; b. Laurens, S.C., Jan. 27, 1920; s. George Sims and Nellie (Melette) W.; m. Beth Keeler, Sept. 13, 1947; children— Norman Brent, Bonnie Beth, Barry Keeler. BS, Clemson U., 1941; MS, U. Tenn., 1947; PhD, Pa. State U., 1951. Textile technologist USDA, 1947-49; research assoc. Sch. Chemistry and Physics, Pa. State U., 1949-51; prof., asst. dean Tex. Women's U., 1951-54; sr. editor Good Housekeeping mag., N.Y.C., 1954-60, v.p., tech. dir., 1961-87; tech. cons., 1987-98. Disting. vis. prof. U. N.C., 1987-88; dir. R&D, Phillips Van Heusen, Inc., 1960-61; guest lectr. Purdue U., U. Md., Ariz. State U., U. Conn., U. Del., Clemson U., U. R.I., Mich. State U.; leader U.S. del. Internat. Standards Confs., 1968, 71, 86, 87. Contbr. articles to profl. jours. Pres. Governing Council, Hightstown, N.J., 1960-62; mem. Bd. Edn., Hightstown, 1959-61. Served to maj. AUS, 1941-46. Decorated Silver Star, Purple Heart. Mem. Am. Assn. Textile Chemists and Colorists (past pres., Harold C. Chapin award), Am. Nat. Standards Inst. (chmn. bd. dirs. 1986-88, chmn. textile standards bd. 1966-68, Howard Coonley medal 1985, George S. Wham Leadership medal 1990), Consumer Coun. (chmn. 1985), Sigma Xi, Phi Psi, Omicron Nu. Home: 201 Ward St Hightstown NJ 08520-3313

WHAM, WILLIAM NEIL, publisher; b. N.Y.C., Dec. 28, 1934; s. William and Jessie (Neill) W.; m. Lynn McCorvie, Mar. 6, 1966; children: McCorvie, Avery. BS, Syracuse U., 1956. Salesman Mut. N.Y., N.Y.C., 1959-61; regional sales mgr. Doubleday Pub. Co., 1961-64, Reinhold Pub. Co., N.Y.C., 1964-68; sales mgr. United Bus. Publs., 1968; pres., pub. jours. Internat. Scientific Communications, Inc., Shelton, Conn., 1968—. Founder: sci. jours. Am. Lab., Internat. Lab., Am. Biotech. Lab., Am. Clin. Lab., Internat. Biotech. Lab., Am. Lab. News, European Clin. Lab., Internat. Lab. News, Am. Environ. Lab., Mng. The Modern Lab., UK Lab., Jour. of Capillary Electrophorisis and Microchip Tech. Served with AUS, 1956-58. Home: 157 Pinewood Trl Trumbull CT 06611-3312 Office: Internat Sci Communications Inc 30 Control Dr Shelton CT 06484-6111

WHANG, SUKOO JACK, pathologist, microbiologist; b. Seoul, South Korea, Feb. 3, 1934; arrived in U.S., 63, naturalized; m. Chung A. Park, Nov. 30, 1963; children: Selena, Stephanie, John. BS, Oreg. State U., 1957; MS, UCLA, 1960, PhD, 1963; MD, Korea U., Seoul, 1972. Diplomate Am. Bd. Tropical Medicine, Am. Bd. Forensic Medicine, Am. Bd. Pathology, Am. Bd. Med. Microbiology. Intern Good Samaritan Hosp., Dayton, Ohio, 1973—74; resident White Meml. Med. Ctr., L.A., 1974—77, clin. pathologist, 1977—90, chmn. infection control com., 1977—87, dir. Sch. Med. Tech., 1977—87; dep. med. examiner L.A. County Coroner's Dept., 1991—2000; med. dir. Dimensions Med. Lab., Northridge, 1990—. Recipient Physician's Recognition award, AMA, 1980—. Fellow: ACP, Coll. Am. Pathologists (Pathology Continuing Med. Edn. award 1984—), Am. Coll. Forensic Medicine, Am. Coll. Tropical Medicine, Am. Soc. Clin. Pathologists. Republican. Seventh Day Adventist. Avocations: swimming, reading. Home: 1325 Via Del Rey South Pasadena CA 91030 Fax: 323-258-2156.

WHANGBO, MYUNG HWAN, chemist; s. Een and Kie Yul Whangbo, Kie Yul Whangbo; m. Jin Ok Lee; children: Jennifer, Albert. BS in Chemistry, Seoul Nat. U., Korea, 1964—68, MS in Chemistry, 1968—70; PhD in Chemistry, Queen's U., Kingston, Ont., Can., 1971—74. Postdoctoral fellow Queen's U., Kingston, Canada, 1975—76; postdoctoral assoc. Cornell U., Ithaca, NY, 1976—77; asst. prof. N.C. State U., Raleigh, NC, 1978—81, assoc. prof., 1981—87, prof., 1987—. Contbr. articles. Recipient Alumni Assn.'s Outstanding Rsch. award, N.C. State U., 1988, 2001, Ho-Am prize for Basic Sci., The Ho-Am Found., 1999, Alexander von Humboldt Rsch. award for Sr. US Scientists, Alexander von Humboldt Found., 1994, Sigma Xi Rsch. award, Sigma Xi, 1981, Camille and Henry Dreyfus Tchr. Scholar award, Dreyfus Found., 1980. Mem.: Materials Rsch. Soc., Am. Chem. Soc. (dist. lectr. N.C. section 2002). Home: 5208 Pine Dr Raleigh NC 27606 Office: NC State University Box 8204 Raleigh NC 27695-8204 Office Fax: 919-515-7832. Business E-Mail: mike_whangbo@ncsu.edu.

WHAPLES, ROBERT MACDONALD, economic history educator; b. Augsburg, Fed. Republic Germany, Mar. 23, 1961; came to U.S., 1963; s. Gene C. and Marlene (Dreher) W.; m. Regina T. Tatarewicz, June 16, 1984; children: Thomas, Antonina, Rebecca, Rose, Charles. BA in Econs. and History, U. Md., 1983; PhD in Econs., U. Pa., Phila., 1990. Asst. editor Jour. Econ. History, Phila., 1985-88; asst. prof. history U. Wis., Milw., 1988-91; asst. prof. econs. Wake Forest U., Winston-Salem, 1991-96, assoc. prof., 1996—. Assoc. dir. EH.Net. Author: (with Dianne Betts) Historical Perspectives on American Economy, 1994; contbr. articles to profl. publs. Recipient Allen Nevins prize for outstanding dissertation in Am. econ. history, 1990. Mem. Am. Econ. Assn. (assoc. dir. 1996—), Econ. History Assn., Social Sci. History Assn., Cliometric Soc. Office: Wake Forest U Dept Econs Winston Salem NC 27109

WHARAM, MOODY DEWITT, JR. physician, medical educator; b. Washington, July 22, 1941; s. Moody DeWitt Sr. and Ethyl May (Morris) W.; m. Sheila Mairead Reese, June 22, 1968; children: Julia M., J. Franklin, Anne M. BA, Harvard U., 1963; MD, U. Va., 1969. Diplomate Am. Bd. Radiology. Intern in medicine and pediatrics Georgetown U. Med. Ctr., Washington, 1969-70; NIH fellow in radiation oncology U. Calif. Med. Ctr., San Francisco, 1970-73, resident, clin. instr., 1973-74; asst. prof. radiology Sch. Medicine Duke U., Durham, N.C., 1974-75; asst. prof. oncology and radiol. sci. Sch. Medicine Johns Hopkins U., Balt., 1975-80, assoc. prof. oncology, radiol. sci., pediatrics and neurosurgery, 1980-93, prof., 1993—. Acting dir. divsn. radiol. oncology Johns Hopkins Oncology Ctr., Balt., 1991-93, dir. divsn. radiol. oncology, 1994-2000. Lt. (j.g.) USNR, 1963-65. Mem. Am. Coll. Radiology, Am. Soc. Therapeutic Radiology and Oncology, Am. Soc. Clin. Oncology, Internat. Soc. Pediatric Oncology. Roman Catholic. Office: Johns Hopkins Hosp 401 N Broadway Rm 1460 Baltimore MD 21231-2410

WHARE, WANDA SNYDER, lawyer; b. Columbia, Pa., Nov. 5, 1959; d. William Sylvester and Dorothy Jacqueline (Luttman) W.; m. James Robert Snyder, Nov. 14, 1987; 1 child, Eric James. BA, Franklin & Marshall Coll., 1981; JD, Dickinson Sch. Law, 1984. Bar: Pa. 1984. Asst. counsel Pa. Dept. Labor and Industry, Harrisburg, 1984-87; assoc. Gibbel, Kraybill & Hess, Lancaster, Pa., 1987-89; corp. counsel Irex Corp., 1990-98, chmn. awareness subcom., 1995-97, mem. continuous improvement coun., 1995-97; corp. counsel Specialty Products & Insulation Co., 1998—2001; v.p., sec. Specialty Products Investments, Inc., Wilmington, Del., 1998—2001; asst. sec. Specialty Products Insulation Co., 2000—01; assoc. Nikolaus & Hohenadel LLP, 2001—. Parish-staff rels. com. First Meth. Ch., Lancaster, 1987—92, com. on status and role of women, 1989—95, chmn., 1992—95, adminstrv. team, 2001—; chmn. com. on status and role of women Ea. Pa. Conf. of United Meth. Ch., 1996—98. Office: Nikolaus & Hohenadel LLP 212 N Queen St Lancaster PA 17603 E-mail: wandaswhare@aol.com., wwhare@nikolaushohenadel.com.

WHAREN, ROBERT ELLSWORTH, JR. neurosurgeon, educator; b. Harrisburg, Pa., June 2, 1953; s. Robert E. and Jean L. (Sheats) W.; m. Mary Beth Blascovich, June 12, 1982; children: Laura, Amy, Stephanie. BA in Chemistry, U. Chgo., 1975; MD, Pa. State U., Hershey, 1979. Diplomate Am. Bd. Neurol. Surgery, Nat. Bd. Med. Examiners. Intern Mayo Grad. Sch. Medicine, Mayo Clinic, Rochester, Minn., 1979-80, resident in neurologic surgery, 1980-85; extern Grady Meml. Hosp.-Emory U., Atlanta, 1984; asst. prof. neurol. surgery U. Pitts. Sch. Medicine, 1985-86; full-time active staff dept. neurol. surgery Montefiore Hosp., Pitts., 1985-86; instr. neurologic surgery Mayo Med. Sch., Jacksonville, Fla., 1986-90, asst. prof., 1990—2000, chmn. dept., 1986—, assoc. prof., 2000—; staff cons. Mayo Clinic, 1986—; chmn. dept. neurosurgery Mayo Clinic Jacksonville, 1986—, bd. govs., 1994—2002. Chmn. dept. neurosurgery St. Luke's Hosp., Jacksonville, 1993—, bd. dirs., 1992-95, mem. exec. med. staff, 1993—, chmn. neurology and neurosurgery practice team, 1996—; presenter at nat. and internat. meetings; vis. prof. Med. Coll. Ga., Augusta, 1992; guest spkr. in field. Contbr. articles to med. jours., chpts. to books. Mayo Clinic neurosurg. travel grantee, 1985. Mem. AMA, Am. Assn. Neurol. Surgeons (liaison to ASTM 1988—), Congress Neurol. Surg. (liaison to ASTM 1988-98), Neurosurg. Soc. Am. (membership com. 1996—), Soc. for Neuro-Oncology, Internat. Soc. Photodynamic Therapy, Fla. Neurosurg. Soc., Neurosurg. Rsch. Soc. Western Ont., North Ctrl. Fla. Cancer Treatment Group, Duval County Med. Soc., Sigma Xi. Office: Mayo Clinic Jacksonville 4500 San Pablo Rd S Jacksonville FL 32224-1865

WHARTON, DANNY CARROLL, zoo biologist; b. Ontario, Oreg., Mar. 13, 1947; s. Carroll Curtis and Norma (Grigg) W.; m. Marilyn Christine Hoyt, Sept. 22, 1973; children: Amanda, Catherine, Margaret, Arcadio. BA in Psychology, Coll. Idaho, 1969; MA in Internat. Adminstrn., Sch. for Internat. Tng., 1975; PhD in Biology, Fordham U., 1990. Rsch. assoc. Foresta Inst., Carson City, Nev., 1973-74; curatorial asst. Woodland Park Zool. Garden, Seattle, 1974-79; asst. curator N.Y. Zool. Soc./The Wildlife Conservation Soc., Bronx, 1979-85; assoc. curator N.Y. Zool. Soc., 1985-89, curator, 1989—; dir. Ctrl. Pk. Wildlife Ctr., N.Y.C., 1994—; adjunct sci. faculty Columbia U. Chmn. Internat. Advisors Internat. Snow Leopard Trust, Seattle, 1986; mem. US-USSR Environ. Agreement of U.S. Fish and Wildlife Svc., 1983. Contbr. articles to profl. jours.; editor Jour. Zoo Biology, 1996-98, exec. editor, 1998—. Vol. U.S. Peace Corps., Ecuador, 1969-71. Fulbright scholar, U. Münster, Fed. Republic Germany, 1976-77. Fellow Am. Assn. Zool. Parks and Aquariums (chmn. gorilla species survival plan 1992—, chmn. snow leopard species survival plan 1986—, co-chmn. marsupial and monotre,e taxon adv. group 1990-94; mem. Soc. for Conservation Biology, Internat. Union for Conservation of Nature/Species Survival Commn. (mem. captive breeding specialist group). Office: Wildlife Conservation Soc Ctrl Park Wildlife Ctr 830 5th Ave New York NY 10021-7001 E-mail: dwharton@wcs.org.

WHARTON, HUGH DAVIS, III, lawyer, judge; b. Buffalo, June 1, 1940; s. Hugh Davis and Helen Bricka (McAuliffe) W.; m. Patricia Granville Ditton, June 20, 1964 (div. Apr. 1982); children: Jennifer Wharton, Gregory Paul, Michael David. BA, Princeton U., 1961; JD, Yale U., 1964. Bar: Alaska 1965, Colo. 1965, Calif. 1969. Asst. atty. gen. State of Alaska, Juneau, 1964-65; chief law clk. to Judge Doyle, U.S. Dist. Ct., Denver, 1965-66; field rep. U.S. OEO, Office of Pres., Kansas City, Mo., 1966-67, San Francisco, 1967-69, dep. regional atty. Western region, 1969-71, regional atty., 1971-73; city atty. City of Livermore, Calif., 1973-74; regional atty. Western region U.S. Dept. Energy, San Francisco, 1974-80; pvt. practice San Francisco, Santa Rosa, 1980—; adminstrv. law judge City and County of San Francisco, 1984-01; judge pro tem Superior Ct., 1990—. Pres. Golden Gate Bus. Assn., San Francisco, 1989-92; mem. bd. dirs. United Way of the Bay Area, 1989-2001; candidate for supr. City and County of San Francisco, 1982, 84, candidate for muni judge, 1988; mem. vol. bd. dirs. San Francisco Gen. Hosp., 1983-88; pres. Diamond Hts. Cmty. Assn., San Francisco, 1987-90. Recipient John W. Gardner Disting. Leadership award United Way, 1992. Mem. State Bar of Calif., Bay Area Lawyers for Individual Freedom. Democrat. Episcopalian. Avocations; politics, travel, fitness, classic cars, Thai culture.

WHARTON, JOHN JAMES, JR. research physicist; b. Warrensburg, Mo., May 28, 1949; s. John James and Carol Jean (West) W.; m. Anne Elizabeth Connolly, Sept. 21, 1985; children: Elizabeth, Angela, J.J., Eric. BSEE, U. Mo., 1971; MS, Air Force Inst. Tech., 1977; PhD, U. Ariz., 1984. Asst. prof. physics U.S. Air Force Acad., Colorado Springs, Colo., 1978-80; assoc. prof. physics, dep. dept. head Air Force Inst. Tech., Dayton, Ohio, 1983-87; program mgr. Def. Advanced Rsch. Projects Agy., Rosslyn, Va., 1987-91; dir. Info. Mgmt. Ctr. Veridian Systems, Ann Arbor, Mich., 1991—. Adj. assoc. prof. Coll. Engring., U. Mich., 1996—. Mem. IEEE, Optical Soc. Am. (bd. dirs. 1990-92), Am. Phys. Soc., Mensa, Tau Beta Pi. Home: 7409 Steeple Chase Ct Saline MI 48176-9031 Office: Veridian Systems PO Box 134008 Ann Arbor MI 48113-4008

WHARTON, LENNARD, engineering company executive; b. Boston, Dec. 10, 1933; s. Nathaniel Philip and Deeda (Levine) W.; m. Judith R. Gordon, Dec. 26, 1957; children: Ruth, Rebecca, Nathaniel. BS in Chem. Engring, MIT, 1955; BA, MA, Cambridge U., 1957; A.M., Harvard U.; A.M. (NSF fellow 1957-60), 1960, PhD (Jr. fellow Soc. of Fellows 1960-63), 1963. Registered profl. engr., N.J., Ill. Prof. dept. chemistry U. Chgo., 1963-80; v.p. engring. ITE Imperial Corp., 1972-73; v.p. tech. Studebaker-Worthington, Barrington, Ill., 1978-79, McGraw Edison Co., Rolling Meadows, 1979-80, v.p. engring. and tech. Worthington group Mountainside, N.J., 1980-85; corp. v.p. tech. Material Research Corp., Pearl River, N.Y., 1985-87; v.p. Packer Engring. Inc., Naperville, Ill., 1987-95, chmn. bd., 1994-95; pres. Evidentia Engring. Inc., Short Hills, N.J., 1995—. Sloan fellow, 1964-66; named Outstanding Young Man of Chgo. Chgo. Jr. Assn. Commerce and Industry, 1968 Mem. IEEE (sr.), Nat. Fire Protection Assn., Am. Inst. Chem. Engrs. Office: 10 Park Pl Short Hills NJ 07078-2826

WHARTON, RALPH NATHANIEL, psychiatrist, educator; b. Boston, June 15, 1932; s. Nathaniel Philip and Deeda (Levine) W.; children: Naida, Philip, Laura. AB cum laude, Harvard U., 1953; MD, Columbia U., 1957, degree in psychoanalysis, 1970. Intern Cornell divsn. Bellevue Hosp., N.Y.C., 1957-58; resident Columbia-Presbyn. Med. Ctr., 1961-64; practice medicine specializing in psychiatry/pharm., 1964—; assoc. psychiatry Coll. Physicians and Surgeons, 1964-69, asst. prof. clin. psychiatry, 1969-72, assoc. prof., 1972-83, prof., 1984—; sr. rsch. psychiatrist N.Y. State Psychiat. Inst., 1964-70; assoc. attending psychiatry Columbia-Presbyn. Hosp., 1970—. Ex-officio mem. bd. trustees, pres. Soc. Practitioners Columbia-Presbyn. Med. Center, 1980-82, attending psychiatrist, 1984—; exec. dir. Wharton Fund for Brain Rsch.; med. dir. Black Sea project Macalester Coll., 1994-98. Author: Landmark Papers, Lithium Carbonate for Affective Disorders, 1966; contbr. numerous papers and publs. in profl. jours. Mem. alumni coun. Coll. Physicians and Surgeons, Columbia U., 2002—. Served to capt. M.C., U.S. Army, 1958-61. Named one of Best Drs. N.Y. mag. Fellow N.Y. Acad. Medicine, Am. Psychiat. Assn., Am. Coll. Psychoanalysts (pres. 1996, bd. dirs. 1996-2001), Internat. Assn. Study of Pain (founder); mem. AMA (mem. legis. action com.), Soc. Biol. Psychiatry, Royal Soc. Medicine, Lotos Club, Salon de Virtuosi (founding bd. mem. 1991—), Harvard Club, Harmonie Club. Office: Columbia-Presbyn Med Ctr Atchley Pavilion Ste 322 161 Ft Washington Ave New York NY 10032-3713 also: 1070 Park Ave Ste 1D New York NY 10128-1000 E-mail: rnw1@columbia.edu.

WHARTON, THOMAS WILLIAM, mining executive; b. St. Louis, Nov. 20, 1943; s. Thomas William and Elaine Margaret (Bassett) Wharton; children from previous marriage: Thomas William, Christopher John. BSc in Econs., U. Mo., 1967; M in Health Adminstrn., U. Ottawa, Ont., Can., 1978. Asst. to exec. dir. Ottawa Civic Hosp., 1978-80; exec. dir. Cariboo Meml. Hosp., Williams Lake, B.C., Can., 1980-83; dir. clinic and rehab. services Workers' Compensation Bd., Vancouver, 1983-89; dir. Conquistador Gold Mines, 1989-98; pres. Diagnostic and Health Cons., 1989—; dir. Citrine Holdings, Ltd., Can., 1994-98; v.p. corp. devel. and med. affairs MTI Corp., Can., 2000—. Bd. dirs. Ecom Netrix Corp., Emeryville, Calif., Can. Med. Placement Svc., Vancouver, Canada, 1997—99, Lusilvemures, Vancover, B.C., Canada, 2000—. Named Lord of the Manors of Wharton and Kirkby Stephen, Eng., 1991; recipient Founder award, Cariboo Musical Soc., 1983. Avocations: music, art.

WHATCOTT, MARSHA RASMUSSEN, elementary education educator; b. Fillmore, Utah, Mar. 29, 1941; d. William Hans and Evangelyn (Robison) Rasmussen; m. Robert LaGrand Whatcott, Sept. 14, 1961; children: Sherry, Cindy, Jay Robert, Justin William. Assoc., So. Utah State U., 1962; BS, Brigham Young U., 1968. Cert. tchr. early childhood, Utah. Tchr. 1st grade Provost Elem. Sch., Provo, Utah, 1968-84, kindergarten tchr., 1984-91, tchr. 3d grade, 19912001. Music specialist Provost Elem., 1984-87, 91-92, 93-94, art specialist, 1984-85, math. specialist, 1988-89, sci. specialist, 1994-95, 96, 97, 98-99, 99-2000; phys. edn. specialist, 1998-99, 99-2000, phys. edn. health-Olympic specialist, 2000-01; del. Utah Edn. Assn., 1989-90; bldg. rep. Provo Edn. Assn., 1993-94, 94-95; choir dir., music arranger 3d grade choir Provo City Winter Festival, Lights on Ceremony, 1995-2000; assessment and placement specialist, 2000-01. Mem. polit. action com. Provo Sch. Dist., 1982, 90, mem. profl. devel. com. Bonniville Uniserve (Provo, Alpine and Nebo Sch. Dist.), 1994-95; choir dir., music arranger 3d grade choir City Winter Festival, 1995-2000; vol. Opening and Closing Ceremonies, 2002 Olympic Games, Salt Lake City, 2001-2002. Recipient Millard County Utah PTA scholarship, 1959-62, Golden Apple award Provo City PTA, 1984, Recognition Disting. Svc. in Edn. award Utah State Legis., 1992; named Outstanding Educator in Utah Legis. Dist. # 64, 1992, Utah State Senate Edn. Spl. award, 2001. Mem.

Utah Edn. Asn. (del. 1989-90), Provo Edn. Assn. (bldg. rep. 1993-94, 94-95), Bonneville Uniserve (profl. devel. com.). Mem. Lds Ch. Avocations: music, gardening, art, drama, crafts. Office: Provost Elem Sch 629 S 1000 E Provo UT 84606-5204

WHATLEY, JACQUELINE BELTRAM, lawyer; b. West Orange, N.J., Sept. 26, 1944; d. Quirino and Eliane (Gruet) Beltram; m. John W. Whatley, June 25, 1966 (dec. July 1998). BA, U. Tampa, 1966; JD, Stetson U., 1969. Bar: Fla. 1969, Alaska 1971; cert. real estate law splst. Assoc. Tucker, McEwen, Smith & Cofer, Tampa, Fla., 1969-71; pvt. practice Anchorage, 1971-73; ptnr. Gibbons, Tucker, Miller, Whatley & Stein, P.A., Tampa, 1973—; pres., 1981—. Bd. dirs. Travelers Aid Soc., 1982-94; trustee Humana Women's Hosp., Tampa, 1987-93, Keystone United Meth. Ch., 1986-89, 99—. Mem. ABA, Fla. Bar Assn. (real estaet cert. com. 1993-95), Alaska Bar Assn., Tenn. Walking Horse Breeders and Exhibitors Assn. (v.p. 1984-87, dir. Fla. 1981-87, 90-93, 97-99, adv. com. Tenn. Walking Horse Celebrateion 1994-97), Fla. Walking and Racking Horse Assn. (bd. dirs. 1988-89, pres. 1980-82), Athena Club (Tampa). Republican. Methodist. Home: PO Box 17595 Tampa FL 33682-7595 Office: 101 E Kennedy Blvd Ste 1000 Tampa FL 33602-5146 E-mail: whatley@gte.net.

WHATLEY, WILLIAM WAYNE, JR. lawyer; b. Dothan, Ala., Dec. 12, 1958; s. William Wayne Whatley Sr. and Emily Carol (Hudgens) Vandemark; m. Joy Thompson Campbell, Oct. 4, 1997. BA, U. Ala., 1981, JD, 1984. Bar: Ala. 1984, U.S. Dist. Ct. (mid. and no. dists.) Ala. 1985, U.S. Ct. Appeals (11th cir.) 1985, U.S. Dist. Ct. (so. dist.) Ala. 1986, U.S. Supreme Ct. 1997. Staff atty. Ala. Ct. Criminal Appeals, Montgomery, 1984-85; asst. atty. gen. State of Ala., 1985-87, asst. atty. gen. criminal litigation divsn., 1987-88; asst. atty. gen., dir. Ala. Medicaid Fraud Control Unit, 1988-92, dep. atty. gen., 1992-96; pvt. practice, 1996—. Office: 8101 Seaton Pl Ste B Montgomery AL 36116

WHEALEY, LOIS DEIMEL, humanities scholar; b. N.Y.C., June 20, 1932; d. Edgar Bertram Deimel and Lois Elizabeth (Hatch) Washburn; m. Robert Howard Whealey, July 2, 1954; children: Richard William, David John, Alice Ann. BA in History, Stanford U., 1951; MA in Edn., U. Mich., 1955; MA in Polit. Sci., Ohio U., 1975. Tchr. 5th grade Swayne Sch., Owyhee, Nev., 1952-53; tchr. 7th grade Ft. Knox (Ky.) Dependent's Sch., 1955-56; tchr. adult basic edn. USAF, Oxford, 1956-57; tchr. 6th grade Amerman Sch., Northville, Mich., 1957-58; tchr. 8th grade English, social studies Slauson Jr. High Sch., Ann Arbor, 1958-59; adminstrv. asst. humanities conf. Ohio U., Athens, 1974-76, 83. Part-time instr. Ohio U., Athens, 1966-68, 75, VISTA with Rural Action, 1996-98. Contbr. articles to profl. jours. Mem. Athens County Regional Planning Commn., 1974—78, treas., 1976—78; mem. Ohio coord. com. Internat. Women's Yr., 1977; v.p. Black Diamond Girl Scout Coun., 1980—86; chair New Day for Equal Rights Amendment, 1982; mem. Athens City Bd. Edn., 1984—90, v.p., 1984, pres., 1985; mem. Tri-County Vocat. Sch. Bd., Nelsonville, Ohio, 1984—90, v.p., 1988—89; mem. adv. com. Ohio River Valley Water Sanitation Commn., 1986—95; Ohio outreach liaison Nat. Town Meeting for Sustainable Am., 1999; bd. dirs. Ohio Environ. Coun., 1984—90, sec., 1986—90; bd. dirs. Ohio Alliance for Environ., 1994—98, v.p., 1998; bd. dirs. Organize Ohio, 1999—, bd. pres., 2001—; bd. dirs. Ohio Women, Inc., 1995—, sec., 1997—; bd. dirs. Ohio Meadville Dist. Unitarian-Universalist Assn., 1975—81, Unitarian Universalist Svc. Com., 2001—. Recipient Unsung Unitarian Universalist award Ohio-Meadville Dist. Unitarian Universalist Assn., 1984, Thanks badge Black Diamond Girl Scout Coun., 1986, How-to award Ednl. Press Assn. Am., 1990, Donna Chen Women's Equity award Ohio U., 1994, Cmty. Svc. award Athens County Cmty. Svcs. Coun., 1998; named Woman of Achievement, Black Diamond Girl Scout Coun., 1987, Peacemaker Appalachian Peace and Justice Network, 1998. Mem. AAUW (pres. Athens br. 1969-70, 89-90, 93-2001, AAUW/Ohio bd. 1995—), LWV (pres. 1975-77), Phi Lambda Theta (life). Democrat. Avocations: classical music, genealogy. Home: 14 Oak St Athens OH 45701-2605

WHEALEY, ROBERT HOWARD, historian; b. Freeport, N.Y., May 16, 1930; s. Howard Edgar and Ethel Ann (Rooney) W.; m. Lois Deimel, July 2, 1954; children: Richard, David, Alice. BA, U. Del., 1952; MA, U. Mich., 1954, PhD, 1963. Instr. U. Maine, Orono, 1961-64; asst. prof. Ohio U., Athens, 1964-67, assoc. prof., 1967-2001, emeritus, 2001. Author: Hitler and Spain, 1989. Dem. U.S. congl. candidate, Athens, 1972. With U.S. Army, 1955-56. Fulbright Found. award, 1977-78. Mem. ACLU (bd. dirs. Athens chpt. 1994—), Am. Hist. Assn. Mem. Unitarian Ch. Avocations: stamp collecting, swimming. Home: 14 Oak St Athens OH 45701-2605 Office: Ohio U History/Bentley Athens OH 45701

WHEAT, J. MARC, U.S. State Department official; b. Ft. Wayne, Ind., Oct. 22, 1964; s. Thomas E. Wheat and Suzanne L. Morris; m. Marie G. Gilliland, May 22, 1993. JD, George Mason U., 1995. Legis. asst. Rep. Dennis Hastert, 1987—90; dir. tax and budget policy Citizens for a Sound Economy, Washington, 1990-92; counsel com. on energy and commerce U.S. Ho. of Reps., 1995—2001; sr. Congl. advisor for Senate affairs U.S. Dept. State, 2001—. Lead com. counsel legis. Ryan White CARE Act Amendments of 2000, 2000, Breast and Cervical Cancer Prevention and Treatment Act, Children's Health Act of 2000, Nat. Inst. Biomed. Imaging and Engring. Est. Act; lectr. parliamentary law The Leadership Inst., 1994—. Trustee, 1st v.p. Meml. Found. Germanna Colonies, Culpepr, Va., 1996; bd. mem. Oakseed Ministries, 2000—; mem. Va. Bd. Med. Assistance Svcs., 2001—; deacon McLean Presbyn. Ch. Mem. Va. Bar Assn., D.C. Soc. SAR (life mem., treas. 1995-2000, Meritorious Svc. medal 1998), Avocations: history, genealogy. Home: 4966 N 34th Rd Arlington VA 22207-2872 Office: US Dept State Ste 7325 Washington DC 20520 Office Fax: 202-647-2762. E-mail: marc.wheat@patron.com.

WHEAT, JOHN NIXON, lawyer; b. Liberty, Tex., Dec. 15, 1952; s. Thomas Allen and Dora (Arrendell) W. BA, Tulane U., 1975; JD, St. Mary's U., San Antonio, 1977. Bar: Tex. 1978, U.S. Dist. Ct. (ea. dist.) Tex. 1978, U.S. Ct. Appeals (5th cir.) 1979. Law clk. U.S. Dist. Ct. Ea. Dist. Tex., Beaumont, 1978-79; pvt. practice The Wheat Firm, Liberty, Tex., 1979—. Vice chmn. Chambers-Liberty County Navigation Dist., 1994-99, chmn., 1999—; pres. chpt. 10 Sons of Republic of Tex.; bd. dirs. Express Theater, Houston, Sam Houston Libr. and Rsch. Ctr.-Tex. State Archive. Mem. ABA, Tex. Bar Assn., Liberty-Chambers County Bar Assn., Houston Bar Assn., Tower Club of Beaumont, Magnolia Ridge County Club, Knights of Neches, Delta Theta Phi. Republican. Episcopalian. Avocations: ranching, hunting, riding, philosophy. Office: 1704 Cos Ave PO Box 10050 Liberty TX 77575-7550

WHEAT, MYRON WILLIAM, JR. cardiothoracic surgeon; b. Sapulpa, Okla., Mar. 24, 1924; s. Myron William and Mary Lee (Hudiburg) W.; m. Erlene Adele Plank, June 12, 1949 (div. June 1970); children: Penelope Louise, Myron William III, Pamela Lynn, Douglas Plank; m. Carol Ann Karmgard, June 18, 1970 (div. Apr. 1996); 1 child, Christopher West. AB, Washington U., St. Louis, 1949; MD cum laude, Washington U., 1951. Diplomate Am. Bd. Surgery, Am. Bd. Thoracic Surgery. Instr., clin. fellow Washington U., St. Louis, 1956-58; asst. prof. surgery U. Fla., Gainesville, 1958-65, prof. surgery, 1965-72; dir. profl. svcs., chief clin. physician U. Fla. Shands Teaching Hosp., 1968-72; prof. surgery, dir. thoracic and cardiothoracic surgery U. Louisville Sch. Medicine, 1972-75; clin. prof. surgery U. Louisville Sch. of Medicine, 1975—; cardiothoracic surgeon Cardiac Surg. Assocs., P.A., St. Petersburg, Fla., 1975-91; cons., thoracic surgery Bay Pine VA Hosp., 1994—; clin. prof. surgery U. So. Fla. Sch. Medicine, Tampa, 1995—; cardiothoracic surgeon Cardiac Surg. Assocs., P.A., Clearwater, Fla., 1991—. Clin. prof. surger U. South Fla., 1995—; cons. Bay Pines VA Hosp., St. Petersburg, Fla., 1991—. Author (with others) 14 books; contbr. over 100 articles to profl. jours.; developed drug therapy for acute dissecting aneurysms of the aorta. 1st lt. USAF, 1943-46, ETO. Named First Howard W. Lillenthal Meml. lectr. Mt. Sinai Hosp., 1963; recipient DFC Air medal, Presdl. Citation. Fellow Am. Coll. Cardiology (chmn. bd. govs. 1968-69), Am. Coll. Surgeons (gov.); mem. Am. Surg. Assn., Am. Assn. for Thoracic Surgery, So. Surg. Assn., So. Thoracic Surg. Assn., Soc. Thoracic Surgeons, Soc. Thoracic Surgeons Great Britain and Ireland, Alpha Omega Alpha. Republican. Avocation: field trials-bird dogs. Home and Office: PO Box 136 Largo FL 33779-0136

WHEAT, WILLIS JAMES, retired university dean, management educator; b. Oklahoma City, Feb. 28, 1926; s. Willis R. and Aubyn (Roach) W.; m. Julia Francis Maguire, July 4, 1946; children: Willis J., Chatham James. BS, Okla. State U., Stillwater, 1949, MS, 1950; DPA in Pub. Adminstrn., U. Pacific, 1968; LLD, Tex. Wesleyan Coll., 1962; DrCommlSci, Oklahoma City U., 1980. Prof. mgmt., dean Sch. Bus. Oklahoma City U., 1954-64; exec. v.p., dir. mktg. Liberty Nat. Bank & Trust Co., Oklahoma City, 1964-87; mem. faculty Stonier Grad. Sch. Banking, Rutgers U., New Brunswick, N.J., 1975-87; pres. Oklahoma City U., 1979-80, dean Meinders Sch. Bus., 1987-89; mem. faculty Essentials of Banking Sch., Norman, Okla., 1980-82, Grad. Sch. Banking of the South, Baton Rouge, 1981-83. Bd. dirs., chmn. United Bank Okla., 1987-95; bd. dirs. Pace Co., Baldor Electric Co. Contbr. articles to profl. jours. Chmn. Oklahoma City Plan Adv. Com., 1974-81, Okla. Employment Security Commn., Oklahoma City, 1981-89; trustee, mem. exec. com. Oklahoma City U., 1975-87. Served with U.S. Army, World War II. Recipient Disting. Svc. citation U.S. SBA, 1978, Disting. Svc. award Oklahoma City U., 1980, Okla. Coun. Econ. Edn., 1982. Mem. Am. Bankers Assn., Soc. Advancement of Mgmt. (past pres.), Nat. Coun. for Small Bus. Mgmt. Devel., Okla. Polit. Sci. Assn., Okla. Coun. on Econ. Edn., Masons, Shriners, Jesters, Delta Sigma Pi, Beta Gamma Sigma. Methodist. Office: PO Box 60804 Oklahoma City OK 73146-0804

WHEATLAND, RICHARD, II, fiduciary services executive, museum executive; b. Boston, Nov. 25, 1923; s. Stephen and Dorothy (Parker) W.; m. Cynthia McAdoo, Feb. 13, 1954; 1 child, Sarah Wheatland Fisher. AB, Harvard U., 1944, postgrad., 1946-47; JD, Columbia U., 1949. Various positions with Marshall Plan adminstrn. Office Spl. Rep. in Europe, Dept. State, Paris, 1950-53; v.p. N.Y. Airways, N.Y.C., 1953-68; pres. Acadia Mgmt. Co., Inc., Boston, 1968-93, chmn., 1993—. Bd. dirs., v.p. Pingree Assocs., Bangor, Maine. Mem. Mayor's Com. Insl. Leaders for Youth, N.Y.C., 1963-66; mem. corp. New Eng. Forestry Found.; mem., former chmn. Fund for Preservation of Wild Life and Natural Areas, Boston, 1980-92, bd. dirs. 1980-91; trustee Penobscot Marine Mus., Searsport, Maine, 1968-90, hon. trustee, 1990—, ; bd. dirs. Friends of Pub. Garden, Boston, 1972-89, 90-96, 97—, Beacon Hill Civic Assn., Boston, 1985-89, Boston Natural Areas Fund, 1987—, asst. treas., 1993-94, treas. 1994-96, bd. dirs. 1997, acting chair, 1997—; treas. Frank Hatch for Gov. com., Boston, 1977-78; chmn., bd. trustees & overseers Peabody Essex Mus. (formerly Peabody Mus. of Salem), Salem, Mass., 1992—, trustee, 1972-92, pres., 1983-92. Lt. (j.g.) USN, 1943-46, PTO. Mem. Am. Assn. Mus. (bd. dirs. trustee com. 1976-86, govt. affairs com. 1985-89), Mus. Trustee Assn. (founder, bd. dirs. 1986—, sec. 1986-92), City Club Corp. (former bd. mgrs., former treas.). Avocations: jogging, sailing, travel. Office: Acadia Mgmt Co Inc 31 Milk St Ste 1104 Boston MA 02109-5129

WHEATLEY, CHARLES HENRY, III, biomedical technology company executive, lawyer; b. Balt., Aug. 11, 1932; s. Charles Henry Jr. and Rebecca W. (Cloud) Wheatley; m. Charlotte Beryl Davis, June 11, 1955; children: Charles H. IV, Craig A., Cheryl L.W. Wilhelm. *Descendant of Robert Burns, Scottish poet; grandchildren: Tyler C., Travis A., Caitlin K., Emma E. Wheatley, Regan L., Kristen N. Wilhelm. Sisters and brothers in law: Elaine W., Raymond L. Jacobs, Lois W., Andrew J. Schultz, Katherine W., Herman S. Roemer, Dorothy W., Calvin E. Plitt. Daughters and son in law: Kimberly R., Elaine L. Wheatley Jeffery J.Wilhelm Nieces: Elaine J. Bousman, Carole R. Hickey, Jean K., Mollie W. Roemer, Catherine S. Santee. Nephews: Andrew J. Jr., Frank C. Schultz, Calvin E. Plitt, Jr. Grandparents: Mary B., Charles H. Wheatley Sr., Caroline H., Walter G. Cloud. Father and Mother in law: Esther B., Delbert M. Davis.* BA in Polit. Sci. with hons., Western Md. Coll., 1954; JD with hons., U. Md., 1959. Bar: Md. 1960, D.C. 1981, U.S. Supreme Ct. 1964. Tchr. Carroll County Pub. Schs., Westminster, Md., 1955-56; officer, judge advocate U.S. Army, 1957-62; law clk. assoc. judge William R. Horney Md. Ct. Appeals, Annapolis, 1959-60; pvt. practice Md. and Washington, 1960—; mem. Md. Ho. of Dels., Annapolis, 1962-66; pres., COO, advisor corp. rels., dir. Cell Works, Inc., Balt., 1997—. Real estate, ins. exec. AID Realty & Ins. Co., Balt., 1960—; adj. coll. instr. Western Md. Coll., Westminster, 1963-65, Villa Julie Coll., 1980-86, Balt. Cmty. Coll., 1966-72; mem. adv. bd. Balt. C.C., 1986—; chmn. bd., CEO Regional Mfg. Inst., Balt., 1993-96; nat. del. White House Conf. on Small Bus., Washington, 1985; pres. Fish Am., Inc., 1990—, Replex, Inc., 1986—, Life, Inc., 1994—; spkr. in field. *Founded World Wide Health Info.com. Sponsored "Planned Unit Development" and "Adequate Facilities" Zoning Ordinances, Baltimore City Council, Maryland to ensure well planned community development. Originated first statewide Maryland prepaid legal services. Incorporated one of the first commercial space launch companies in the world. Consultant in law office automation Maryland and American Bar Sponsored first mandatory seatbelt and teenage driver education in Maryland legislature. Chaired Baltimore City Council Capital Budget Committee for inner harbor development. Established "language signs for the deaf" as foreign language credit in Maryland schools. Designed first statewide educational support staff personnel organization in Maryland State Teachers Association.* Contbr., editor: (weekly newspaper) Maryland Teacher, 1974-77; guest News Makers program WJZ-TV, 1985; contbr. articles to profl. jours. Md. del. Md. State Constitutional Convention, Annapolis, 1967-68; councilman Balt. City Coun., 1971-74. 1st lt. JAG U.S. Army, 1957-62. Received Cell Works Co. Computerworld-Smithsonian Science Innovation laureate award, 1999. Mem.: Md. State Tchrs. Assn. (exec. sec. 1974—77), Supreme Ct. Bar, Dist. Columbia Bar Assn., Md. State Bar Assn., Md. Commn. Mfg. Competitiveness, Order of Coif, Pi Gamma Mu. Methodist. Avocations: education, music, writing, photography, health. Office: 707 Wheatley Dr Westminster MD 21157

WHEATLEY, GEORGE MILHOLLAND, medical administrator; b. Balt., Mar. 21, 1909; s. William Francis and Teresa Genevieve (Milholland) W.; m. Eleanor Dodge, June 28, 1933 (dec. June 1969); children: George Milholland, Jr., Mary Ellen Rausch, Sarah Grinnell Nichols, William Bradford; m. Virginia Connelly Garling, Feb. 21, 1970 (dec. 1997); m. Lady Lorna Doone Snow, Sept. 6, 1997 (dec. Nov. 1998). BS, Cath. U., 1929; MD, Harvard U., 1933; MPH, Columbia U., 1942. Diplomate Am. Bd. Pediatrics, Am. Bd. Preventive Medicine. Intern Hartford Hosp., Conn., 1933-35; house officer pediatrics Johns Hopkins Hosp., Balt., 1935-36; rsch. fellow N.Y. Post. Grad. Hosp., N.Y.C., 1936-37; prin. pediatrician Health Dept., 1937-40; asst. med. dir. Met. Life Ins. Co., 1940-45, asst. v.p., 1945-69, v.p., chief med. dir., 1969-74; med. dir. Dept. Social Svcs., Hauppauge, N.Y., 1974-95; ret., 1995. Founder, 1st chmn. com. for joint action with Am. Coll. Surgeons, Assn. Surgery of Trauma, and Nat. Safety Coun.; 1st chmn. accident prevention com. Am. Acad. Pediatrics. Author: Health Observation of School Children, 3d edit., 1965; contbr. articles to profl. jours. Bd. dirs. Med. Alert Found. Internat., Calif., 1974-84. Recipient Disting. Svc. award Am. Heart Assn., 1968. Fellow Am. Acad. Pediatrics (pres. 1960-61, trustee Partnership for Child Health 1987—, Clifford Grulee award 1964, Injury and Poison Prevention award 1993); mem. Union League Club, Piping Rock Club. Avocations: civil war history, water-color painting. E-mail: georgewheatley@aol.com.

WHEATLEY, JOSEPH KEVIN, physician, urologist; b. N.Y.C., Jan. 5, 1946; s. Patrick Owen and Catherine (Malloy) W.; m. Anne Johanna Foody, Aug. 22, 1970; children: Joseph, Thomas. BSChemE, Manhattan Coll., 1967; MSChemE, U. Del., 1969; MD, N.J. U. of Medicine, 1974. Diplomate Am. Bd. Urology. Rsch. engr. NASA, Houston, 1965, 66, Exxon, Florham Park, N.J., 1968-69; urology resident Emory Univ., Atlanta, 1975-79, assoc. prof. urology, 1979—; clin. urology practice Urology Assocs., 1986—; chief of urology Kennestone Hosp., Marietta, Ga., 1990-93. Medicare care cons. Ga. Found. med. Care, Atlanta, 1982—; tchr. Atlanta VA Med. Ctr., Atlanta, 1979—; mem. hosp. exec. com. Kennestone Hosp., Marietta, 1990-93. Contbr. chpts. to books and articles to profl. jours. Active various Rep. actitives, 1992—. Named Top Drs. in Atlanta Atlanta Mag., 1995-96. Fellow ACS; mem. AMA, Urol. Assn., Urodynamics Soc., Am. Fertility Soc., Soc. of Reproductive Surgeons, Lithotripsy Soc. Roman Catholic. Avocations: skiing, hiking, biking trips, tennis, computers. Home: 692 N Saint Marys Ln NW Marietta GA 30064-1454 Office: Urology Assocs 55 Whitcher St NE Ste 250 Marietta GA 30060-1169

WHEATLEY, LUCILE MARIS, civic worker; b. Corvallis, Oreg., Mar. 24, 1917; d. Paul Vestal and Mary Elizabeth (Davis) Maris; m. Melvin Ernest Wheatley, Jr., June 15, 1939; children: Paul Melvin, James Maris, John Sherwood (dec.). BA cum laude, Am. U., 1938. Cert. tchr., Va. Chmn. L.A. Portraits Am. Women, 1968-70. A founder Parents and Friends Lesbians and Gays, Denver, 1981, speaker, workshop leader, Colo. and Calif., 1981—; active LWV, Denver, 1973-84; active citizen protests at Rocky Flats Nuclear Plant, Denver, 1981, 82. Recipient Human Rights award, Universal Fellowship Met. Cmty. Congregations, 1985, Peace and Justice award, Ill. Sch. Theology, Denver, 1987, Affirmation award, Calif.-Pacific Conf., United Meth. Ch., 1994, Nat. Affirmation award, 1994, citation, City Coun. of L.A., 2000, Lifetime Achievement award, Denver Parents, Family, Friends of Lesbians and Gays, 2000. Democrat. Avocations: grandparenting, travel, music, reading, Public Broadcasting System programs. Home: 859A Ronda Mendoza Laguna Hills CA 92653-5940 E-mail: lmwheatley@webtv.net.

WHEATLEY, MELVIN ERNEST, JR. retired bishop; b. Lewisville, Pa., May 7, 1915; s. Melvin Ernest and Gertrude Elizabeth (Mitchell) W.; m. Lucile Elizabeth Maris, June 15, 1939; children: Paul Melvin, James Maris, John Sherwood (dec.). AB magna cum laude, Am. U., 1936, DD, 1958; BD summa cum laude, Drew U., 1939; DD, U. of Pacific, 1948. Ordained to ministry Meth. Ch., 1939. Pastor area Meth. ch., Lincoln, Del., 1939-41; assoc. pastor First Meth. Ch., Fresno, Calif., 1941-43; pastor Centenary Meth. Ch., Modesto, 1943-46, Cen. Meth. Ch., Stockton, 1946-54, Westwood Meth. Ch., L.A., 1954-72; bishop Denver Area, 1972-84; ret., 1984. Instr. philosophy Modesto Jr. Coll., 1944; summer session instr. Hebrew-Christian heritage U. of Pacific; instr. Homiletics U. So. Calif., So. Calif. Sch. Theology, Claremont; lectr. St. Luke's Lectures, Houston, 1966; mem. Bd. of Ch. and Soc., Commn. on Status and Role of Women, United Meth. Ch., 1976-84; condr. European Christian Heritage tour, 1961, Alaska and Hawaii Missions, 1952, 54. Author: Going His Way, 1957, Our Man and the Church, 1968, The Power of Worship, 1970, Family Ministries Manual, 1970, Christmas Is for Celebrating, 1977; contbr. articles to profl. jours. Chmn. Community Rels. Conf. So. Calif., 1966-69; pres. So. Calif.-Ariz. Conf. Bd. Edn., 1960-68; hon. trustee Iliff Sch. Theology; hon. dir., active mem. Parents and Friends of Lesbians and Gays, 1980—. Recipient Disting. Alumnus award Am. U., 1979, Ball award Meth. Fedn. Social Action, 1984, Prophetic Leadership award The Consultation on Homosexuality, Tolerance and Roman Cath. Theology, 1985, Human Rights award Universal Fellowship of Met. Community Congregations, 1985, award for social justice Calif.-Pacific Meth. Fedn. for Social Action, 2000, Lifetime Achievement award Denver Parents, Families and Friends of Lesbians and Gays, 2000. Home: 859 Ronda Mendoza Unit A Laguna Hills CA 92653-5940 E-mail: lmwheatley@webtv.net.

WHEATLEY, SHARMAN B. art educator, artist; b. N.Y.C., Nov. 21, 1951; d. Norman Alexander and Marjorie Grace (Biggs) Johnson; m. Simon J. Wheatley, June 21, 1975; children: Gregory Drew, Justin West. BA in Art Edn., Wagner Coll., 1973; MA in Art Edn., Coll. of New Rochelle, 1979. Cert. art educator, N.Y.; provisional cert. art educator, Conn. Art educator for multi-handicapped students Bd. Coop. Edn. Svcs., New City, N.Y., 1973-75; art educator Ardsley Pub. Schs., 1975-76; art and humanities educator The Ursuline Sch., New Rochelle, 1976-83; owner, dir. of tour co. Big Apple Enrichment Tours, Larchmont, 1981-83; libr. publicist Monroe Pub. Libr., Conn., 1987-88; newspaper editor Trumbull Times, 1988; art educator Trumbull Pub. Schs., 1989-91; theatrical prodr. Little Theatre Prodns., Wilton, 1993-96; art educator Wilton Pub. Schs., 1991—. Summer crafts supr. Ardsley Pub. Schs., N.Y., 1971-79. Artist, illustrator cover design for Street Bagel mag., 1982; exhibited in group shows at Larchmont Libr., 1982, Union Trust Bank, Darien, Conn., 1983; cover illustrator Litton Pubs., N.Y.C., 1980. 1st v.p., treas., corr. sec. mem. parents coun. Monroe PTO, Conn., 1985—. Recipient 2d prize Darien Arts Coun., 1983, Adams Interior Design Ctr. award Darien Arts Coun., 1983. Mem. NEA, Conn. Edn. Assn., Met. Mus. Art, N.Y. Mus. Modern Art. Avocations: writing, dancing, sculpting, drawing, reading. Home: 44 Oakwood Dr Monroe CT 06468-2134

WHEATLEY, THOMAS EDWARD, English language educator; b. Augusta, Ga., Nov. 13, 1957; s. William Carl Jr. and Mary (Brasfield) W.; m. Margaret Mary Mackay, Aug. 4, 1984. BA, Rhodes Coll., 1979; MA Ctr. Medieval Studies, U. York, Eng., 1983; MA, PhD, U. Va., 1991. Instr. ESL Luth. Social Svcs., Jacksonville, Fla., 1982; asst. prof. Hamilton Coll., Clinton, N.Y., 1990-97, Elderhostel instr., 1994—, chair Medieval and Renaissance studies, 1996—, assoc. prof., 1997—, faculty advisor disability action group, 2000—. Author: Mastering Aesop, 2000, (chpt. in book) Blackwell's Companion to Chaucer, 2001; editor: Sources and Analogues of Chaucer's Canterbury Tales, 2001. Vol. Peace Corps, Ivory Coast, 1979-81; bd. dirs. Sculpture Space, Utica, N.Y., 2000—. Grantee Am. Philos. Soc., 1993, NEH, 1993, Emerson grants Hamilton Coll., 1997, 99; Mellon Faculty fellow in humanities Harvard U., 1993-94. Mem. MLA, New Chaucer Soc., Early Book Soc. Avocations: violin, gardening, cooking. Office: Hamilton Coll 198 College Hill Rd Clinton NY 13323 E-mail: ewheatle@hamilton.edu.

WHEATLEY, WILLIAM ARTHUR, architect, musician; b. Knoxville, Tenn., Sept. 23, 1944; s. Arthur Cornwallis and Inda Mary (Benway) W.; m. Celeste Ann George, Mar. 25, 1970 (div.); children: Charles Arthur, James Harris Giddings; m. Rosaria Giovanna Cilia, June 10, 1995. Student, Rice U., 1962-66; BA, U. St. Thomas, 1972. Registered architect, Pa., Md., N.J. Design draftsman W.W. Alexander, Houston, 1966-70; chief prodn. W.W. Scarborough, 1970—72; project arch. Ronald H. Waldie & Assocs., 1972-74; pres. Wheatley & Assocs., Inc., 1974-81; project arch. Brooks Assn., 1977—79; mgr. design Stone Bldg. Systems, Inc., 1979-81; project arch. Bechtel, 1981—84; prin. Wheatley & Assocs., 1984-87; project mgr. STV/Sanders & Thomas, Pottstown, Pa., 1987-88, MDC Sys. Divsn. Day & Zimmermann Internat., Inc., Phila., 1988-97; prin., exec. v.p. MDC Sys., Inc., 1997-2000; chmn. MDC Sys. UK Ltd., Aberdeen, Scotland, 1999—2001; pres. Wheatley US Ltd. , Bala Cynwyd, Pa., 2000—; chmn. Wheatley UK Ltd. , London, 2002—; ptnr. ICS, LLC, 2002—. Composer piano solos, chorales, oratorio and cantata, 1961—; contbr. articles to profl. jours. Del. Tex. Rep. Convs., 1980, 82, 84; bd. dirs. Found. for Anglican Cath. Tradition. Mem. AIA, ABA (assoc.), Am. Coll. Forensic Examiners, Royal Archtl. Inst. of Can., Am. Arbitration Assn., Pa. Soc. Architects, Bldg. Ofcls. and Code Adminstrs. Internat., The Mastersingers (bd. dirs. 1989-92, treas. 1990-91), Archeol. Inst. Am., Choral Soc. Montgomery County (bd. dirs. 1990-96, pres. 1992-95). Anglican. Avocations: writing music, poetry and fiction, drawing, painting, sculpture. Office: Wheatley US Ltd Two Bala Plz Ste 300 Bala Cynwyd PA 19004-1501 also: Wheatley UK Ltd Thistle Pl Aberdeen AB10 1UZ Scotland Fax: 610-658-6318.

WHEATON, ALICE ALSHULER, administrative assistant; b. Burbank, Calif., Mar. 20, 1920; d. Elmore and Anzy Jeanette (Richards) Wheaton; m. Robert Edward Alshuler, Sept. 19, 1942 (div. 1972); children: John Robert, Katherine Alshuler Voss. BA in Edn., UCLA, 1942. Cert. prof. sec. Internat. Assn. Adminstrv. Profls.; cert. tchr. Owner, dir. The Fitness Studio, Washington, 1974-85; staff asst. Pres. Coun. Phys. Fitness and Sports, 1980-89; coord. Fed. Inter Agy. Health Fitness Coun., 1980-89; expert cons. U.S. Office Pers. Mgmt., 1986-89; adminstrv. asst. North County Bank, Escondido, Calif., 1990-95; sec. Pala Mesa Village Homes Assn., 1994-96, office mgr., 1997—. Cons. Pres. Coun. Phys. Fitness and Sports. Editor: The Federal FitKit-Guidelines for Federal Agencies, 1988. Recipient Gold Key award L.A. Area United Way, 1966. Mem. Internat. Assn. Admin. Profls. (pres. Palomar chpt. 1993-95), UCLA Gold Shield Hon. (pres.), UCLA Alumni Assn. (assoc. v.p., Disting. Com. Svc. award 1968), PEO (officer 2001-02), San Diego Hist. Soc., North County Kappa Kappa Gamma Alumnae Assn. (pres. 1995-97, 99-2000, province dir. alumnae 2000—). Republican. Episcopalian. Avocations: historical research, gardening.

WHEATON, MARILYN, music educator, pianist, organist; b. Warren, Ohio, Feb. 1, 1933; d. Russell and Donabelle Irene Donehue; m. Warren Randall Wheaton, June 20, 1953; 1 child, Janean Renee Vaupel-Wilson. BS in Music Edn. cum laude, Kent State U., 1955. Cert. Yamaha music instr. Pvt. piano and organ tchr., Ohio and Ariz., 1950—; profl. pianist, organist, accompanist, 1946—; elem. music supr. Austintown Pub. Schs., Youngstown, Ohio, 1955-61. Founder, dir. Potter's Clay Christian singing group, Phoenix, 1981-85; choir dir., organist, pianist at various chs., Ohio and Ariz., 1942—; rep. for elem. music texts and programs Mahoning County Schs., Youngstown, 1959-60; tchr., organizer student trips to numerous concerts; tchr., dir. choirs and soloists for dist. and state competitions, 1955—. Composer (poems to music) Seven Last Words of Christ; also anthems, introits, reponses; arranges music for beginning and handicapped students. Dir., accompanist Terry's

Variety Show, Austintown, 1951, Potter's Clay, 1980-85. Kent State U. and Youngstown U. scholar, 1951-55. Mem. Music Tchrs. Nat. Assn., Delta Omicron (life, charter mem., pres. Delta Upsilon chpt.). Avocations: travel, camping, reading, walking. Home and Office: 3245 W Yucca St Phoenix AZ 85029-4133

WHEATON, ROBIN LEE, lawyer; b. Flint, Mich., July 29, 1948; s. Richard George and Roberta Jean (Schmiedeknecht) W.; m. Barbara Jean Bright, Oct. 18, 1968; children: Shane Matthew, Ashley Sarah, Joshua David. Student, C.S. Mott C.C., Flint, 1971-72; BA, U. Mich., Flint, 1974; JD, U. Detroit, 1977. Bar: Mich. 1978. Pvt. practice, Flint, 1980—. Bd. dirs. Am. Heart Assn., Flint, 1988-92. With U.S. Army, 1968-70, Vietnam. Decorated Bronze medal with V device, Purple Heart with oak leaf cluster, Army commendation medal with oak leaf clusters. Office: 1003 Church St Flint MI 48502-1011

WHEDON, GEORGE DONALD, medical administrator, researcher; b. Geneva, July 4, 1915; s. George Dunton and Elizabeth (Crockett) W.; m. Margaret Brunssen, May 12, 1942 (div. Sept. 1982); children: Karen Anne, David Marshall. AB, Hobart Coll., 1936, ScD (hon.), 1967; MD, U. Rochester, 1941, ScD (hon.), 1978. Diplomate Am. Bd. Internal Medicine, Am. Bd. Nutrition. Intern in medicine Mary Imogene Bassett Hosp., Cooperstown, N.Y., 1941-42; asst. in medicine U. Rochester Sch. Medicine; also asst. resident physician medicine Strong Meml. Hosp., Rochester, 1942-44; instr. medicine Cornell U. Med. Coll., 1944-50, asst. prof. medicine, 1950-52; chief metabolic diseases br. Nat. Inst. Arthritis, Diabetes, Digestive and Kidney Diseases, NIH, Bethesda, Md., 1952-65, asst. dir., 1956-62, dir., 1962-81, sr. sci. adv., 1981-82; sr. assoc., dir. conf. program Kroc Found., Santa Ynez, Calif., 1982-84; adj. prof. medicine (endocrinology) UCLA Sch. Medicine, 1982-84; dir. med. rsch. programs Shriners Hosps. for Crippled Children, Tampa, 1984-91. Mem. subcom. on calcium, com. dietary allowances Food and Nutrition Bd., NRC, 1959-64; cons. to office manned space flight NASA, 1963-78, chmn. Am. Inst. Biol. Scis. med. program adv. panel to, 1971-75, chmn. NASA life scis. com., 1974-78, mem. space program adv. coun., NASA, 1974-78; cons. on endocrinology and metabolism adv. com. Bur. Drugs, FDA, 1977-82; mem. subcommn. on gravitational biology Com. on Space Rsch., Internat. Union Physiol. Scis., 1979-85; mem. rsch. adv. bd. Shriners Hosps., 1981-84; mem. subcom. spacecraft maximum allowable concentrations, com. toxicology, bd. on environ. studies and toxicology Commn. on Life Scis. NRC, 1989-99; cons. in medicine Wadsworth Gen. Hosp. VA Ctr., L.A., 1982-84; mem. U.S. Del. of U.S.-Japan Coop. Med. Sci. Program, 1984-93; mem. Internat. Soc. Gravitational and Space Physiol., 1991—. Mem. editorial bd. Jour. Clin. Endocrinology and Metabolism, 1960-67; adv. editor Calcified Tissue Rsch., 1967-76; contbr. articles to profl. publs. Mem. med. alumni coun. Sch. Medicine, mem. trustees' coun. U. Rochester, 1971-76, vice chmn. trustees' coun., 1973-74, chmn., 1974-75; trustee Dermatology Found., 1978-82; bd. dirs. Osteogenesis Imperfecta Found., 1991-97, med. adv. coun., 1993-96. Recipient Superior Svc. award USPHS, 1967, Alumni citation U. Rochester, 1971, Alumni citation Hobart Coll., 1986, Medal Excellence, 1998, Exceptional Sci. Achievement medal NASA, 1974, NASA award of Merit, 1996. Fellow Royal Soc. Medicine; mem. AAAS, Am. Fedn. Med. Rsch., Assn. Am. Physicians, Aerospace Med. Assn. (Arnold D. Tuttle Meml. award 1978), Internat. Bone and Mineral Soc., Md. Acad. Scis. (sci. coun. 1964-70, 81-82), Endocrine Soc. (Robert H. Williams Disting. Leadership award in endocrinology 1982, Ayerst award 1974), Am. Physiol. Soc., Am. Inst. Nutrition, Am. Acad. Orthopaedic Surgeons (hon.), Am. Soc. Bone and Mineral Rsch., Orthopaedic Rsch. Soc., Am. Soc. Gravitational/Space Biology (Founders award 1994), Theta Delta Chi. Episcopalian. Home: 880 Mandalay Ave Apt N1014 Clearwater FL 33767-1257

WHEDON, RALPH GIBBS, manufacturing executive; b. Elizabeth, N.J., Aug. 10, 1949; s. Ralph Gibbs and Jane (MacMaster) W.; m. Lorna Jean Neebe, June 3, 1972; children: Deborah, David. Student, Clarkson Coll., 1968-70; BS, St. Lawrence U., 1972; student, Rensselaer Polytech. Inst., 1978; MBA, De Paul U., 1985. CPA, Ohio. Credit rep. Internat. Harvester Credit Corp., Albany, N.Y., 1972-75, ops. supr., 1975-79; mgr. export ops. Internat. Harvester Co., Chgo., 1979-86; treas. Pettibone Corp., Des Plaines, Ill., 1986-91; mgr. cash resources Bailey Controls Co., Wickliffe, Ohio, 1991-95, acting dir. treas., 1992-95, mgr. adminstrn., 1993-95; dir. MIS HMI Industries, Cleve., 1995-97; project mgr. Unum Am., Portland, Maine, 1997-98; mgr. Unum Provident, 1998—. Sec. Tube Form, 1995-97; sec. Bliss Mgg., 1995-97; sec. Newton Falls Holding Co., 1995-97. Bd. dirs. Naperville (Ill.) Cmty. Chorus, 1985-87; trop leader Boy scouts Am., Naperville, 1985-91; mem. adv. coun. United Way, 1993-95; mem. adv. coun. Cleve. Treas. Club, 1992-97, bd. dirs., 1994-96; pres. Brightwood Lakes Assn., 1996-97; treas. S.J.E.C. Found., 1996-97. Episcopalian. Avocations: sailing, flying. Home: 82 Curtis Rd Portland ME 04103-2924 also: 7 Fairwind Way Ellsworth ME 04605-2935

WHEELAHAN, TIMOTHY MICHAEL, physical therapist; b. New Orleans, Mar. 24, 1957; s. Keith John and Helen Rose Wheelahan; m. Diane McKellar, Dec. 6, 1986; children: Megan, Mary Lauren, Madeline Rose. BS in Phys. Therapy, La. State U., New Orleans, 1981; MEd, La. State U., Shreveport, 1985. Lic. phys. therapist, La. Phys. therapist Meml. Hosp., Danville, Va., 1981-82, La. State U. Med. Ctr., Shreveport, 1982-86, asst. prof. phys. therapy, 1986; phys. therapist Crescent Cit Phys. Therapy, New Orleans, 1986-87, Red River Phys. Therapy, Shreveport, 1987-92; phys. therapy ptnr. Sheveport Phys. Therapy, 1992—. Contbr. articles to profl. jours. Bd. dirs. La. Dance Found., N.W. La. Eye Bank, Vol. for Youth Justice, Think First. Mem. Am. Phys. Therapy Assn. (membership chmn. 1992-96, orthopedic sect., geriat. sect.; past edn. chmn. Shreveport chpt.; student liaison La. chpt.). Republican. Methodist. Home: 5010 Belle Chasse Bossier City LA 71112

WHELAN, R(ICHELIEU) E(DWARD), lawyer; b. N.Y.C., July 10, 1945; s. Richard Fairfax and Margaret (Murray) W. BS, Springfield (Mass.) Coll., 1967; MS, Iona Coll., 1977; JD, Pace U., 1981. Bar: N.Y. 1982, Minn. 1983, Colo. 1989, Tex. 1990, U.S. Dist. Ct. (no dist.) Calif. 1982, (so. dist.) Tex. 1991, U.S. Internat. Trade 1982, U.S. Ct. Appeals (2d cir.) 1982, (9th cir.) 1983, (5th cir.) 1993, U.S. Supreme Ct. 1994, U.S. Tax Ct. 1998; bd. cert. criminal law, trial advocacy. Lt. of detectives White Plains (N.Y.) Police Dept., 1969-81; area counsel IBM, Armonk, N.Y., 1981-89; gen. counsel Kroll Assocs. (Asia), Hong Kong, 1989-91; pvt. practice, Houston, 1991—. Mem.: ABA (mem. sentencing guidelines com.), Tex. Assn. Criminal Def. Lawyers, Pro Bono Coll. State Bar Tex., New York County Lawyers Assn., N.Y. State Bar Assn., Coll. of State Bar Tex., Nat. Assn. Criminal Def. Lawyers (life; mem. death penalty com., champion adv. bd.). Office: 440 Louisiana St Houston TX 77002-1639

WHEELER, ALBIN GRAY, army officer, educator, retail executive; b. Huntington, W.Va., Mar. 16, 1935; s. Harvey Gray and Hattie Benson (Weddle) W.; m. Beatrice Thomas, May 17, 1958; children: Dianne, Michelle, Patrice. BA, Marshall U., 1958; MBA, Pepperdine U., 1975; postgrad., Army War Coll., 1976, Harvard U., 1990. Enlisted U.S. Army, 1952, commd. 2d lt., 1959, advanced through grades to maj. gen., 1982; comdr. divsn. spt. command, chief of staff 1st Inf. Divsn., Ft. Riley, Kans., 1978-80; dep. comdr. U.S. Army Logistics Ctr., Ft. Lee, Va., 1980-81; chief exec. officer Army AF Exch. Svc.-Europe, Munich, 1981-83; comdr. 2d Spt. Command, VII U.S. Corps, Germany, 1983-85; pres. Indsl. Coll. Armed Forces, Washington, 1985-89; dir. human resources Army Materiel Command, 1989-91; CEO Army and Air Force Exch. Svc., Dallas, 1991-93; ret. U.S. Army, 1993; exec. dir. Arent Fox Kitner Plotkin & Kahn, Washington, 1993-96. Bd. dirs. Yeager Scholars, Marshall U., 1986—; pres. bd. advisors Army Quartermaster Found.; bd. dirs. Army Distaff Found. Decorated Def. and Army D.S.M., Bronze Star with two oak leaf clusters, Legion of Merit with two oak leaf clusters; inducted into Army Quartermaster Hall of Fame, 1999. Mem. Marshall U. Alumni Assn. (disting. alumnus 1983).

WHEELER, ANTHONY CLYDE, human resources executive; b. Johannesburg, South Africa, Feb. 23, 1953; came to U.S., 1975; s. Anthony Clyde and Marie Claude (DuPont) W.; m. Susan Weaver, 1976 (div. Sept. 1983); m. Allison O'Meara, Apr. 26, 1986; children, Anthony Mark, Bradley Alan. BS, Tex. A&M U., 1979. Sr. pers. rep. Brown & Root, Inc., Houston, 1979-85; human resources mgr. N.L. Industries, 1985-86; dir. human resources WNS, Inc., 1986-89; benefits cons. Donovan Benefits System, 1989-90; dir. adminstrn. The York Group, Inc., 1991—. Mem. Leadership Houston, 1989—. Capt. USAR, 1983—. Tex. A&M athletic scholar, 1979—. Mem. Soc. for Human Resource Mgmt., Houston Human Resource Mgmt. Assn., Res. Officers Assn., Tex. A&M Assn. Former Students, Tex. A&M Lettermen's Assn. Roman Catholic. Avocations: golf, running, tennis, raquetball, scuba. Office: The York Group Inc 8554 Katy Fwy Ste 200 Houston TX 77024-1851

WHEELER, BARBARA J. management consultant; b. Coral Gables, Fla., June 1, 1960; d. Robert Henry and Mary Jean (Seiler) W. BA, Miami U., 1982. Commd. 2nd lt. USAF, 1984, advanced through grades to capt., 1988, chief command control comm., def. sect., XIDB project mgr., intelligence agency; resigned, 1992; prin. cons. Litton-PRC, McLean, Va., 1994-97; dir. TRW Mgmt. Cons., Reston, 1998-2000; strategic and program mgmt. counsulting, writer Montgomery Village, Md., 2000—. Mem. NAFE, Am. Prodn. and Inventory Control Soc., Project Mgmt. Inst. (cert.), Am. Legion. Avocations: reading, lecturing, travel, ice skating. E-mail: bjwheeler@comcast.net.

WHEELER, BETTY ELLER, association executive; b. Elkin, N.C., Feb. 21, 1938; d. Wade Edward and Dempsie (Smith) Eller; m. Stanley B. Wheeler, May 29, 1959 (div. June 1981); children: Mark Edward, Jonathan Burke. BA in Sociology, Tex. Tech U., 1958, postgrad., 1958-59. Elem. sch. tchr., Slaton, Tex., 1959-60; dist. dir. Camp Fire Girls, Lubbock, 1960-63; child welfare worker Lubbock (Tex.) City-County Child Welfare, 1964-67; officer Lubbock County (Tex.) Juvenile Probation, 1967-68; vol. staff Nat. Camp Fire Girls, Tex. and N.Mex., 1975-76; cons. social services Milam's Children's Tng. Cen., Lubbock, 1975-76; asst. exec. dir. Lubbock Day Care Assn., 1972-77; cons. fund raising Easter Seal Soc., Lubbock, 1978; dir. Christian Edn. St. Paul's Epis. Ch., 1971-83; interim dir. All Saints Epis. Sch., 1980-81; exec. dir. YWCA Lubbock, 1981—. Bd. dirs. Tex. Coalition Juvenile Justice 1986-90; adv. council Cultural Affairs Council 1985-90, Teen Connection 1987-88. Bd. dirs. Lubbock Heritage Soc. 1985-88; delegate St. Dem. Conv., Austin 1986, 2002; chmn. Elec. Utility Bd. 1982, City-County Health Bd., Citizens Com. for Lubbock County Juvenile Detention Ctr., South Plains Youth Council, Dupre and Parsons Elem. Schs. PTA Bds., Tex. Tech Arts and Scis. Adv. Council, United Way, Lubbock Symphony Guild; del. 1970 Gov.'s Conference on Children and Youth; vol. Salvation Army Soup Kitchen; chmn. child care adv. coun. Nat. YWCA, 1998—; polit. campaign worker Dem. Party; participant in numerous other civic activities. Named one of Outstanding Young Women Am., Lubbock Bus. and Profl. Women's Club, 1968, Lubbock's Woman of the Yr., Altrusa Club, 1968, Disting. Alumna Coll. Arts and Scis. Tex. Tech. U.; recipient Human Rels. award City of Lubbock. Mem. Nat. Assn. YWCA Execs., United Way Exec. Dirs. Assn. (past chmn.), South Plains Chpt. Nat. Soc. Prevention Child Abuse (bd. dirs.), Head Start Del. Assn. (chmn. 1995-2000), Interagency Action Council, Exec. Forum., Jr. League (community v.p. 1978-79, exec. com. 2 yrs., bd. dirs. 4 yrs., sustaining advisor 2 yrs.), Delta Delta Delta (mem. adv. council). Avocation: youth work. Home: 3310 55th St Lubbock TX 79413-4806 Office: YWCA 3101 35th St Lubbock TX 79413-2312

WHEELER, BEVERLY (BARNES), cardiology and cardiothoracic nurse specialist; b. St. Stephens, N.B., Can., Nov. 9, 1946; parents Am. citizens; d. Robert George and Elizabeth B. (Rideout) Barnes; divorced; children: Jeffrey, Tami. AA, Mohegan C.C., Norwich, Conn., 1981; BSN and cert. in gerontology, George Mason U., 1989, MSN, 1991; post-grad. study, Mich. State U., 1999. RN, Va.; cert. and registered clin. nurse specialist, Va.; cert. ACLS. Various civilian adminstrv. positions U.S. Navy, Groton, Conn., Arlington, Va., 1974-87; vis. nurse Comprehensive Health Agy., Springfield, 1984-86; nursing agy. pers. SRT Med.-Staff Internat., 1982-88; legal asst. Office of Asst. Sec. of Navy for Rsch., Engring. and Sys., Washington, 1987-89; staff nurse Arlington Hosp., 1986-90, Fairfax Hosp., Falls Church, Va., 1991—; cardiology/cardiothoracic surgery clin. nurse specialist Nat. Naval Med. Ctr., Bethesda, Md., 1989—. Adj. clin. nursing instr. Marymount U., Arlington, Va., 2000—; mem. test devel. com. Am. Nurses Credetialing Ctr., 1996-99; textbook cons., 1994—; legal cons. and expert witness; rschr. in field. Contbr. articles to profl. nursing jours. Vol. Am. Heart Assn., 1994—2002. Mem. ANA, NAFE, ANCC, Va. Nurses Assn. Episcopalian. Avocations: aerobics, reading, gardening, crocheting. Home: 10302 Annaberg Ct Burke VA 22015-2833 Office: Nat Naval Med Ctr 8901 Wisconsin Ave Bethesda MD 20889 E-mail: beverly.wylie@erols.com.

WHEELER, BURTON M. literature educator, higher education consultant, college dean; b. Mullins, S.C., Mar. 12, 1927; s. Paul and Elizabeth (Cleveland) W.; m. Jacquelyn Mulkey, Aug. 20, 1950; children— Paul, Geoffrey, Kristin AB, U. S.C., 1948, MA, 1951; PhD, Harvard U., 1961. Teaching fellow Harvard U., Cambridge, Mass., 1953-56; mem. faculty Washington U., St. Louis, 1956-96, prof., 1974-96; prof. emeritus, 1996—; dean Coll. Arts and Scis. Washington U., St. Louis, 1966-78, interim dean univ. librs., 1988-89. Cons., panelist Danforth Found., St. Louis, 1958-82; mem. GPEP panel Assn. Am. Med. Colls., Washington, 1981-84; cons.-evaluator North Cen. Assn., Chgo. Author: Close to Me, But Far Away, 2001; contbr. articles to profl. jours. Eli Lilly Found. fellow, 1965-66 Mem. Soc. Values in Higher Edn., Kent Fellow, Phi Beta Kappa (senator, chmn. qualifications com., chmn. com. on chpts.). E-mail: bwheeler@artsci.wustl.edu.

WHEELER, C. HERBERT, architect, consultant, educator; b. Merchantville, N.J., June 6, 1915; s. Clarence Herbert and Louise Emma (Pennell) W.; m. Cicely Pointer, Aug. 29, 1940; children: Pamela, Janet, Betsy. BArch, U. Pa., 1937; MArch, MIT, 1940, postgrad., 1953, 56, Alexander Hamilton Inst., 1947. Registered architect N.Y., N.J., Pa., Mich.; cert. Nat. Council Archtl. Registration Bds. Archtl. designer Austin Co., N.Y.C., 1938-41; from architect to chief architect J.G. White Engring. Co., 1941-55; mgr. engring. Stran Steel Corp., Detroit, 1955-58; mgr. environ. sys. Curtiss-Wright Corp., Quehanna, Pa., 1958-64; prof. archtl. engring. Pa. State U., University Park, 1964-80, prof. emeritus, 1980—. Author: Public Organizations and Public Architecture, 1987; co-author: Emerging Techniques of Architectural Practice, 1966, Emerging Techniques of Architectural Programming, 1969. Served to maj. C.E., U.S. Army, 1942-46. Decorated Commendation Ribbon U.S. Army CE, 1945. Fellow AIA (emeritus, internat. relations com. 1981-84, v.p. Central Pa. chtp. 1984), Union Internat. des Architects Paris (permanent sec. profl. devel. work group 1980-85, coll. dels. 1981-85), mem. Am. Soc. Engring. Edn. (emeritus, chmn. archtl. engring. div. 1970), constrn. Specifications Inst., Ret. Officers Assn., Theta Xi (v.p. St. Louis 1953-54). Republican. Episcopalian/Methodist. Avocations: travel; precanceled stamp collecting; geography; literature. Home: 638 Franklin St State College PA 16803-3459 Office: PA State U 104 Engring A Unit University Park PA 16802

WHEELER, CATHY JO, government official; b. Birmingham, Ala., Feb. 14, 1954; d. Charles Edwin and Hazel Josephine (Hollis) Wheeler; m. David Arthur Tate, 1994. BA, U. Montevallo, 1975; postgrad., U. Ala., 1982-84. With Social Security Adminstrn., Birmingham, 1975—, sr. employment devel. specialist, 1983-85, mgr. tech. tng. dept., 1985-91, staff advisor to asst. regional commr. Process Ctr. Ops., 2000-01, fin mgmt specialist, 2001—. V.p. Fed. Women's Program, Birmingham, Ala., 1984—85; treas., charter mem. Federally Employed Women, Birmingham, 1984—88. Mem. Art Alumni Adv. Bd., 1997—2001, v.p., 1998—2000. Mem.: ASTD (treas. 1987—88, pres. elect 1989, pres. 1990, asst. regional dir. 1991—92), Univ Montevallo Nat Alumni Asn (bd. dirs. 1991—94, v.p. fin. 1994—98, pres.-elect 1998—2000, pres. 2000—02, parliamentarian 2002—), Ala Designer-Craftsmen, Soc Govt Meeting Planners (v.p. 1989—90, sec. 1990—91), Riverchase Women's Club, Jaycees (v.p. mgmt. devel. Hoover Ala. chpt. 1988—89), Chi Omega Alumni Asn (treas. 1991, advisor 1991—). Avocations: photography, reading, travel. Home: 4001 Fairchase Ln Birmingham AL 35244-1300 Office: Social Security Adminstrn 2001 12th Ave N Birmingham AL 35285 E-mail: cathyjowheeler@bellsouth.net.

WHEELER, CLARENCE JOSEPH, JR. physician; b. Dallas, Sept. 25, 1917; s. Clarence Joseph Sr. and Sadie Alice (McKinney) W.; m. Alice Mary Freels, Dec. 6, 1942; deceased; m. Patsy Lester Butler, Sept. 2, 1995; children: Stephen Freels, C.J. III, Robert McKinney, Thomas Michael, David Ritchey. BS in Math., So. Meth. U., 1941, BA in Psychology, 1946; MD, John Hopkins U., 1950. Diplomate Am. Bd. Surgery; cert. provider ACLS and advanced trauma life support, Am. Heart Assn. Intern John Hopkins Hosp., Balti., 1950-51; resident in surgery Barnes Hosp., St. Louis, 1951-54; fellow thoracic surgery U. Wis. Hosp., Madison, 1954-56, instr. surgery, 1955-56; attending surgeon Welborne Clinic Baptist Hosp., Evansville, Ind., 1956-57; mem. consulting staff Tex. Children's Hosp., 1957-70; courtesy and consulting staffs Pasadena Hosp., Spring Br. Hosp., others, Houston, 1957-70; mem. active staff Hermann Hosp., 1957-70, St. Luke's Hosp., Houston, 1957-70, Meth. Hosp., Houston, 1957-70, St. Joseph's Hosp., Houston, 1957-70, Meml. Hosp., Houston, 1957-70, Ben Taub Gen. City/County Hosp., Houston, 1957-70, Diagnostic Hosp., &, 1957-70; attending surgeon Lindley Hosp., Duncan, Okla., 1970-71; sr. attending, chief surgery Gordon Hosp., Lewisburg, Tenn., 1971-73; chief thoracic surgery Lewisburg Community Hosp., 1973-75; mem. active med. staff, med. dir. Carver Family Health Clinic, 1975-82; dir. emergency dept. Meth. Med. Ctr. Ill., Peoria, 1975-82; mem. staff Contract Emergency Med. Care, Houston and Dallas, 1982-88; med. dir. substance abuse unit Terrell (Tex.) State Hosp., 1988-90; med. dir. Schick-Shadel Hosp., Dallas-Ft. Worth, 1991—, med. dir., chief of staff Ft. Worth, 1991-93; med. dir. Skillman Med. Ctr., Dallas, 1993-95, Centers for Preventative Medicine, Dallas, 1996—. Instr. surgery U. Wis. Med. Sch., 1955-56; clin. instr. Baylor Coll. Medicine, Houston, 1959-70; lectr. U. Tex. Postgrad. Sch., Houston, 1957-70; clin. asst. prof. U. Ill. Sch. Medicine, Peoria, 1977-82; sr. med. advisor Thua Tien Province, So. Vietnam, 1968-69; chief of surgery Bien Vien Hué So. Vietnam, 1968-69. Treas. Samuel Clark Red Sch. PTA, Houston, 1959-61; bd. dirs. Salvation Army Boys Club, Houston; mem. Am. Mus. of Nat. History, Met. Mus. Art, Smithsonian Inst., Dallas Symphony Assn., Dallas Opera Soc., Dallas Theatre Ctr., Theatre Three Assn. Capt. USMCR, 1942-45, PTO. Decorated DFC with three stars, Air medal with four stars, Pacific Combat Theatre Ribbon with three stars, Purple Heart, Vietnamese Medal of Health (1st class), Vietnamese Medal Social Welfare, Navy Commendation medal, Presdl. Unit citation medal, Meritorious Bronze Star. Fellow ACS, Am. Coll. Angiology, Am. Coll. Chest Physicians, Royal Soc. Medicine, Internat. Coll. Surgeons, Am. Coll. Gastroenterology, Southern Surg. Congress, Southwestern Surg. Congress, Internat. Assn. Proctologists; mem. AAAS, AMA, Am. Thoracic Soc., Nat. Tb Assn., Am. Assn. History of Medicine, Am. Soc. Contemporary Medicine and Surgery, Am. Soc. Addiction Medicine (cert.), Am. Heart Assn., Am. Cancer Soc., Am. Soc. Abdominal Surgeons, Marine Corps Officer's Assn., Naval Res. Officer's Assn., Nat. Geog. Soc., Mil. Order of the World Wars, Navy League, Indsl. Med. Assn., So. Med. Assn., Tex. Med. Assn., Tex. Thoracic Soc., Tex. Heart Assn., Tex. Anti-Tb Assn., Postgrad. Med. Assembly So. Tex., St. Louis Med. Soc., Dallas County Med. Soc., Marshall County Med. Soc. (pres.), Harris County Med. Soc., Houston Heart Assn., Houston Gastroent. Soc., Houston Surg. Soc., Greater Dallas Res. Officers Assn., Sierra Club, Rotary, Kappa Sigma, Phi Eta Sigma, Kappa Mu Epsilon, Psi Chi. Episcopalian. Address: 601 Palomar Ln Richardson TX 75081-4416 E-mail: cjwjrmd@aol.com.

WHEELER, CLAYTON EUGENE, JR. dermatologist, educator; b. Viroqua, Wis., June 30, 1917; s. Clayton Eugene and Vista Beulah (Heal) W.; m. Susie Brooks Overton, Oct. 11, 1952; children: Susan Brooks, Margaret Ann, Elizabeth Clayton. BA, U. Wis., 1938, MD, 1941. Diplomate Am. Bd. Internal Medicine, Am. Bd. Dermatology (dir. 1970-79, vice pres. 1977-78, pres. 1978-79). Intern Cin. Gen. Hosp., 1941-42; resident in internal medicine U. Mich. Hosps., 1942-44, research fellow endocrinology and metabolism, 1947-48, resident in dermatology, 1948-51; from asst. prof. to prof. dermatology U. Va. Med. Sch., 1951-62; prof. dermatology U. N.C. Med. Sch., Chapel Hill, 1962—, chmn. div., 1962-72, chmn. dept., 1972-87, chmn., exec. com. Med. Faculty Practice Plan, 1986-90. Cutaneous commn. Armed Forces Epidemiol. Bd., 1961-72; dermatology tng. grants com. NIAMD, 1963-67, residency rev. com. dermatology, 1973-79, chair, 1975-79; chair task force ednl. programs faculty Nat. Program Dermatology, 1969-74; trustee Dermatology Found., 1975-79. Author: Practical Dermatology, 3d edit, 1967, also articles. Served to maj. M.C. AUS, 1944-47. Recipient U. N.C. Med. Alumni Disting. faculty award, 1986, Disting. Svc. award U. N.C. Med. Alumni, 1997; honored with establishment of Clayton E. Wheeler Jr. Professorship of Dermatology position, 1991, recipient David Martin Carter Mentorship Award, 2002. Mem. Soc. Investigative Dermatology (bd. dirs. 1970-73, pres. 1974-75, Rothman award 1979, hon. mem. 1993), Assn. Profs. Dermatology (bd. dirs. 1969-71, 76-79, sec.-treas. 1971-74, pres. 1975-76), Am. Dermatol. Assn. (pres. 1982-83, hon. mem. 1997), Am. Acad. Dermatology (past dir., pres.-elect 1983-84, pres. 1984-85, past pres. 1985-86, hon. mem. 1988, masters in dermatology 1993, Gold medal 1993), Am. Skin Assn. (David Martin Carter award 2002), Phi Beta Kappa, Alpha Omega Alpha. Methodist. Home: 2120 N Lakeshore Dr Chapel Hill NC 27514-2027 Office: U NC Cb # 7287 Chapel Hill NC 27599-0001 E-mail: spryor@med.unc.edu.

WHEELER, DAVID LAURIE, university dean; b. Saginaw, Mich., July 30, 1934; s. Clayton Final and Blanche Beatrice (Hunt) W.; m. Jane Louise Manchester, Sept. 6, 1958; children: Elizabeth, Anne. AB, U. Mich., 1956, AM, 1958, PhD, 1962. Asst. dean student service Ill. State U., Normal, 1967-68, assoc. dean, 1968-69, assoc. dean grad. sch., 1969-72; dean grad. sch. West Tex. State U., Canyon, 1972-79, Ball State U., Muncie, Ind., 1979-96, dean emeritus, 1996—. Cons. McGraw-Hill Pub. Co., N.Y.C., Van Nostrand Reinhold Pub. Co., N.Y.C. Editor: The Human Habitat: Contemporary Readings, 1971. Woodrow Wilson fellow, 1961; recipient Commdrs. Pub. Svc. award Dept. of Army, 1996. Mem. Assn. Am. Geographers, Nat. Coun. Univ. Rsch. Adminstrs., Western History Assn., Tex. State Hist. Assn., U.S. Army War Coll. Found., Rotary, Sigma Xi, Phi Kappa Phi, Kappa Sigma. Republican. Presbyterian. E-mail: wheeler2@gj.net.

WHEELER, DAVID WAYNE, freelance/self-employed accountant; b. Charlottesville, Va., June 1, 1952; s. Daniel Gordon and Marion Elaine (Booth) W. BS in Acctg., Va. Poly. Inst. and State U., 1975. CPA, Va. Staff acct. Robert M. Musselman, Charlottesville, Va., 1971-76; pvt. practice acctg., 1976-77; sec., treas. Wheeler & Hancher Ltd., 1977-79; pres. David W. Wheeler Ltd., 1980—. Contbr. articles to profl. jours. Treas., bd. dirs. East Rivanna Vol. Fire Dept., Albemarle County, Va., 1983-91; bd. dirs. Literacy Vols. of Am., Charlottesville, Albemarle, 1988-90; treas./adv. bd. Va. Piedmont divsn. March of Dimes, 1999—. Mem. AICPA (taxation div.), Va. Soc. CPAs (bd. dirs. 1992-93, chpt. sec. 1990-91, v.p. 1991-92, pres. 1992-93), Oak Ridge Fox Hunt Club (treas. 1985—). Baptist. Avocations: golf, hunting, fishing. Home: 1112 Beaverdam Rd Keswick VA 22947-2148 Office: The Massie-Smith House 211 4th St NE Charlottesville VA 22902-5205

WHEELER, DONALD KEITH, community and economic development specialist; b. Miami, Fla., Oct. 30, 1960; s. Clifford Keith and Elizabeth Grace (Bonilla) W. AA in Broadcasting, Miami-Dade Community Coll., 1981; BA in Polit. Sci., U. Fla., 1983; M of Pub. and Internat. Affairs, U. Pitts., 1985. Planning intern Am. Cancer Soc., Miami, 1985; assoc. planning and systems devel. Area Agy. on Aging, 1985-86; rsch. assoc. Fla. Internat. U., North Miami, 1986-87, adminstrv. coord., vis. instr., 1987-88; planner, grantwriter SER Jobs for Progress, Miami, 1988-90; tribal planner Miccosukee Tribe of Indians, Dade County, Fla., 1990—; assoc. logistics officer UN Devel Programme, 1993-94; health planner Health Coun. South Fla., 1994-96; pres., dir. grant programs Barry U., Miami Shores, Fla., 2001—. Mem. Miccosukee Tribal Community Rev. Bd., Dade County, 1990. Advisor Am. Cancer Soc., Miami, 1980-83. Recipient Outstanding Svc. award Am. Cancer Soc., 1981, Outstanding Community Svc. award The Miami Herald, 1979. Mem. Acad. Polit. Sci., Am. Soc. Pub. Adminstrn., Ptnrs. of the Ams., Toastmasters Internat. (pres. 1989, 96), Sigma Phi Epsilon. Baptist. Avocations: writing, reading, tennis, swimming. Home: B-309 9351 Fontainebleau Blvd Miami FL 33172-4610 Office: Barry U 11300 NE 2nd Ave Miami FL 33161-6695

WHEELER, DOUGLAS LANPHIER, history educator, writer; b. St. Louis, July 19, 1937; s. Russell Charles and Lucille (Wengler) W.; m. Katherine Wells; children: Katherine Gladney, Lucille Lanphier. AB in History, Dartmouth Coll., 1959; MA in History, Boston U., 1960, PhD in History, 1963; postgrad., Lisbon U. (Portugal), 1961-62. Vis. asst. prof. Morgan State Coll., Balt., 1965; from asst. prof. to prof. U. N.H., Durham, 1965—2002, chair dept. history, 1971-74, Prince Henry the Navigator prof. of Portuguese History and the Discoveries, 1995—2002. Vis. asst. prof. U. Coll. Rhodesia, Salisbury, Richard Welch Meml. fellow in Advanced Rsch. Intelligence, Harvard U., Cambridge, 1984-85. Author: Republican Portugal, 1978, Ditadura Militar Portuguesa, 1988, Historical Dictionary of Portugal, 1993, 2d edit., 2001; co-author: Angola, 1971; co-editor: In Search of Modern Portugal, 1983; editor Portuguese Studies Newsletter, 1976-91, Portuguese Studies Rev., 1991—; bd. editors European Studies Quarterly, 1983—; mem. editorial bd.

Mediterranean Studies. Moderator Community Ch. of Durham, 1983-84, com. mem. 1969—; bd. mem. Mill Pond Ctr., Arts Ctr. Durham, 1982-98, Theatre by the Sea, Portsmouth, N.H., 1981-85; dir. N.H. Coun. World Affairs, Durham, 1974—. 1st Lt. USAR, 1963-65. Decorated grand officer Order of Prince Henry The Navigator (Portugal), 1993; Fulbright grantee, Fulbright Commn., U. Lisbon, 1961-62, Fulbright Hays Faculty Rsch., U.S. Govt., 1969-70, Gulbenkian Found., Lisbon, 1972—; recipient Cert. Achievement, U.S. Army Intelligence Sch., Md., 1965. Mem. Internat. Conf. Group on Portugal (coord. 1978—), Soc. for Spanish and Portuguese Hist. Studies (gen. sec. 1981-84), Nat. Mil. Intelligence Assn., Assn. Former Intelligence Officers, Nat. Intelligence Studies Ctr. Democrat. Avocations: reading, travel abroad, tennis, amateur theatricals, playwriting. Home: 27 Mill Rd Durham NH 03824-3006 E-mail: dwheeler@hypatia.unh.edu.

WHEELER, DOUGLAS PAUL, conservationist, government official, lawyer; b. Bklyn., Jan. 10, 1942; s. Robert S. and Lottie (Neubauer) W.; m. Heather A. Campbell, Aug. 28, 1965; children— Clay Campbell, Christopher Campbell AB in Govt. with honors, Hamilton Coll., Clinton, N.Y., 1963; LLB, Duke U., 1966. Bar: N.C. 1966, D.C. 1999. Assoc. Levine, Goodman & Murchison, Charlotte, N.C., 1966-69; legis. atty. to asst. legis. counsel U.S. Dept. Interior, Washington, 1969-72, dep. asst. sec. Fish and Wildlife and Pks., 1972-77; exec. v.p. Nat. Trust for Hist. Preservation, 1977-80; pres. Am. Farmland Trust, 1980-85, now life mem.; exec. dir. Sierra Club, San Francisco, 1985-86; v.p. Conservation Found., Washington, 1986-88, exec. v.p., 1989-91; sec. for resources State of Calif., 1991-99; ptnr. Hogan & Hartson LLP, Washington, 1999—. Vis. lectr. Duke U. Sch. Law. Hon. life mem. bd. visitors Duke U. Sch. of Law; mem. bd. visitors Bren Sch. Environ. Mgmt., U. Calif., Santa Barbara, Tahoe-Baikal Inst.; candidate N.C. Ho. of Reps., 1968; mem. D.C. Rep. Ctrl. Com., 1984-85; active nat. coun. World Wildlife Fund, Am. Farmland Trust/The Conservation Fund; chmn. biodiversity conservation working group N.Am. Commn. for Environ. Cooperation. Lt. JAGC, USNR, 1969-75. Recipient commendation U.S. Dept. Interior, 1976, Achievement award, 1980, Conservation award Gulf Oil Corp., 1985, Charles S. Murphy award for pub. svc, 1995, Presdl. award for sustainable devel., 1996, Nat. Conservation Leadership award The Conservation Fund, 1997. Mem. ABA, N.C. Bar Assn., Sierra Club (life), Am. Farmland Trust (life). Episcopalian. Home: 4541 45th St NW Washington DC 20016-4473 E-mail: dpwheeler@hhlaw.com.

WHEELER, EDD DUDLEY, lawyer; b. Macon, Ga., July 19, 1940; m. Frances Schnelker Rouhslange, Feb. 12, 1974; children: Diana Kaye, Catherine Anne, Emily Clare. BS, USAF Acad., 1962; MPA, U. Okla., 1968; PhD, Emory U., 1971; JD, Am. U., 1979. Bar: Ga. 1979, U.S. Dist. Ct. (no. dist.) Ga., U.S. Supreme Ct. 1991. Commd. 2d lt. USAF, Macon, 1962, advanced through grades to lt. col. Atlanta, 1976, ret. Tucker, Ga., 1978; pvt. practice Macon, 1979-83, Tucker, Ga., 1984-91; assoc. dir. Law & Econs. Ctr. Emory U., Atlanta, 1983-84. Spl. asst. atty. gen. Ga. Atty. Gen. Office, Atlanta, 1987-88; pres. Cronus, Inc., Atlanta, 1989-91; fed. adminstrv. law judge, 1991—. Author: From Games of God to Bubba's Field: A Century of the Modern Olympic Games, 1995, The Knot which Is Great within Us: Poems on Life, Law, and Other Imperfections, 1997. County commr. Bibb County Bd. of Commrs., Macon, 1980-82. Fellow Ga. Bar Found.; mem. Ga. Bar Assn., Com. on Lawyer Professionalism (reporter 1986-87). Episcopalian. Office: 3598 Midvale Cv Tucker GA 30084-3208

WHEELER, EDWARD NORWOOD, chemical consultant; b. Yancey, Tex., Oct. 11, 1927; s. Wilber Basel and Clara Clementine (Stafford) W.; m. Luella Jean Brossette, Nov. 21, 1950; children: Gordon A., Sterling R., Darrell S., Charlotte, Murray H. BS, Tex. A&I U., 1947, BSChemE, 1949; MA, U. Tex., 1951, PhD, 1953. Rsch. chemist Celanese Chem. Co., Corpus Christi, 1953-55, group leader, 1955-62, section mgr., 1962-67, dir. rsch., 1967-72, dir. devel., 1972-74, planning dir. N.Y.C., 1974-75, dir. rsch. devel. planning, 1975-76, v.p. rsch. devel. planning, 1976-79, v.p. rsch. & devel. Dallas, 1979-83; cons. and expert witness White and Case, Hong Kong and N.Y.C., 1986-91. Mem. adv. coun. U. Tex. Natural Sci. Found. Contbr. articles to profl. jours., patentee 14 inventions. Treas. Dallas Bethlehem Ctr., 1985-89; hon. life mem., mem. adv. coun. U. Tex. Coll. Natural Sci. Found.; bd. trustees Tex. A&M U.-Kingsville Found., 1994-98; pres. North Tex. Conf. Coun. on Fin. and Adminstrn., United Meth. Ch., 1992-96. Recipient Disting. Alumnus award Tex. A&I U., Kingsville, 1981. Mem. Am. Chem. Soc., Indsl. Rsch. Inst., Synthetic Organic Chem. Mfrs. Assn. (bd. govs. 1977-81), Littlefield Soc. U. Tex. Methodist. Avocations: gardening, genealogy, cooking. Home and Office: 9238 Moss Haven Dr Dallas TX 75231-1412

WHEELER, ELTON SAMUEL, financial executive; b. Salinas, Calif., Oct. 25, 1943; s. Luther Elton and Naomi E. (Beatty) W.; m. Moretha Jean Miller, June 17, 1995; children: Pamela Kathleen, Leslie Elizabeth-Anne, Deborah Suzanne, Jonathan Samuel. BS, Calif. State U., 1966. CPA, Calif. Acct. Pricewaterhouse Coopers, Oakland, Calif., 1967-70, Adams Properties, Inc., San Francisco, 1970-71, treas., 1972-75, v.p., CFO, 1976-77, Adams Capital Mgmt. Co., San Francisco, 1977-79, pres., CEO, 1979-87; pres., CEO, bd. dirs. Calif. Real Estate Investment Trust, 1980-88, Franklin Select Real Estate Income Trust, 1989-2000, Franklin Advantage Real Estate Income Trust, 1990-96. With USMCR, 1966-72. Mem. Nat. Assn. Real Estate Investment Trusts, Inc (sec., treas., bd. govs. 1984-89), Am. Inst. CPAs, Calif. Soc. CPAs, United Way of Tuolumne-Calaveras Counties (pres., dir., treas. 1989-98), Rotary (Sonora, Calif., pres. 1994-95), Rotary Internat. (dist. 5220 dir. 1998-99, asst. gov. 2000-01, dist. conf. chair 2001-02). Home: 16399 Crestridge Ave Sonora CA 95370-8752 Office: PO Box 3718 Sonora CA 95370-3718 E-mail: swheeler@samwheelercpa.com.

WHEELER, FRANK KNOWLES BLASDELL, retired military officer, business consultant; b. Mpls., Oct. 29, 1912; s. Walter Hall and Eva Maude (Blasdell) W.; widowed, Oct. 1991; children: Mary Ann Wheeler Masher, Frances Blasdell Wheeler Kindle, Charles Knowles. BSME, U.S. Naval Acad., 1935, PhD (Equivalent) Electronics, 1944. Registered profl. engr., Calif. Commd. ensign USN, 1935, advanced through grades to capt., 1954; commdg. officer U.S.S. Kearney, 1944-46; mem. various fleets/electronics staffs USN, 1946-60, ret., 1960; mfg. mgr. Hewlett Packard Co., Palo Alto, Calif., 1960-70; co. mfg. mgr. Fairchild, Mountain View, 1970-72; pres., bus. cons. Wheeler & Assocs., Los Altos Hills, 1972—. Mem. IEEE. Republican. Presbyterian. Avocations: electronics, preparing historical video productions. Home and Office: 27174 Elena Rd Los Altos CA 94022

WHEELER, GEORGE CHARLES, materials and processes engineer; b. Balt., Oct. 9, 1923; s. George Charles and Julia Elizabeth (Watrous) W.; m. Dorothy W. Whittemore, Sept. 13, 1947; children: Scott, Craig, Mark, Matthew, Tracy, Bruce; m. Clare Frances Weiner, Jan. 21, 1978. BS in Metall. Engring., Lehigh U., 1944. Various engring. and supervisory positions GE, Mass. and N.Y., 1944-62; mgr. materials, welding and nondestructive test engring. Knolls Atomic Power Lab., G.E., Schenectady, N.Y., 1962-68; mgr. nondestructive testing G.E. Power Sys., 1968-85; pres., CEO Wheeler Nondestructive Testing, Inc., 1985-95, Materials and Processes Cons., Schenectady, 1995—; mgr. tech. svcs. Am. Soc. for Nondestructive Testing, Columbus, Ohio, 1993-94. Cons. UN, N.Y.C., 1985-98, IAEA, Vienna, Austria, 1985-98, ASNT, 1997—, others; guest lectr. Rensselaer Poly. Inst., Troy, N.Y., Union Coll., Schenectady, 1978-87; mem. math. sci. and tech. com. Schenectady County C.C., 1978-85, adj. prof., 1987-97; U.S. del. Internat. Stds. Orgn., com. TC 135/SC7 NDT Pers. Qualification, 1987-97, convenor working group #2, ISO-9712; mem. ASNT Cert. Mgmt. Bd., 1994-98, chmn. 1976-80, 86-89. Author: Guide to Personnel Cert., 1990, Guide to Developing Certification Exams, 1992; Level II Study Guide: Radiographic Testing, 1998, Level II Study Guide: Ultrasonic Testing, 1999; contbg. editor JMaterials Evaluation, Jour. of ASNT; tech. editor Nondestructive Testing Handbook, 3d edit., vol. 3. Fellow Am. Soc. Nondestructive Testing (hon. life mem., bd. dirs. 1976-85, pres. 1983-84, chmn. cert. com. 1976-80, 86-89); mem. ASTM (com. internat. stds., com. nondestructive testing), NRA (life), Am. Soc. Metals (life), Nature Conservancy (life), Adirondack Mountain Club, Adirondack Forty-Sixers. Avocations: mountaineering, flying, firearms, photography, cross country skiing, golf. E-mail: geocharles@aol.com.

WHEELER, GERALDINE HARTSHORN, historian, essayist; b. Pomona, Calif., Feb. 5, 1919; d. Albion True and Beatrice Osa (Barnes) Hartshorn; m. Lloyd Franklyn Wheeler, Dec. 2, 1938 (dec. Mar. 1996); children: Russell Lloyd, Robert Gerald. AA, Santa Barbara (Calif.) C.C., 1950's. Co-owner Atheling's, Santa Barbara, Calif., 1971-76, Pomona, 1976-90; chmn. bd. trustees Atheling Heritage Trust, Claremont, Calif., 1994—. Pub., editor: mag. Athling's, 1974—75, pub., editor: newsletter Grand Priory of America Order of St. Lazarus, 1974—86; editor: St. Margaret's Jour., 1975—; author: (essays) A World Full in 1891, 1975—, President John Adams - A Profile, 1975—, Ralph Waldo Emerson--A Profile, 1975, The Many Masks of Communism, 1975, A Tale of St. Nicholas, 1995, Post Cards and Postal Cards, 1996, Pocahontas Kinships, 1996. Vol. PTA, Fontana and Santa Barbara, 1945-60; active Hist. Soc. Pomona Valley, 1950—; mem. various coms. and choir First Congl. Ch., Santa Barbara, 1952-72; leader Cub Scouts Am., Santa Barbara, 1953-56; grey lady unit chmn. Santa Barbara chpt.-ARC, 1958-62; women's project bd. v.p., activities chmn., active various coms. Santa Barbara Hist. Soc., 1960-74; exec. sec. 1960 Nixon for Pres. Campaign, Santa Barbara, 1960; mem. spkrs. bur. Nixon for Gov. Campaign, Santa Barbara, 1962; mem. Rep. state ctrl. com. State of Calif., 1962-64; blitz chmn. Rockefeller for Pres. Campaign, Santa Barbara, 1964; coord. vol. svcs. Office of Civil Def., City of Santa Barbara, 1965-76; coord. tv series on earthquakes Sta. KEYT, Office of Civil Def., Santa Barbara, 1968; bd. dirs. Calif. Ctrl. Coast Area, U.S.O., 1968-76, treas. bd., 1970-76; supporter Vis. Nurses and Hospice Assn., 1994—; others. Decorated Dame of Grace, Mil. and Hospitaller Order of St. Lazarus of Jerusalem, Cert. of Merit, 1973, The Alan Weaver Hazelton award; recipient Cert. of Merit, Santa Barbara Jr. Coll., 1954-55, Medal of Appreciation SAR, 1972, Cert. of Award Nat. Soc. Daus. of Founders and Patriots of Am., 1977. Mem. Calif. Hist. Soc., New Eng. Hist. and Geneal. Soc., The Pomona Ebell (pres. 1998-2000), Wilson Ctr. Assocs., Smithsonian Assocs., Nat. Trust for Hist. Preservation, Am. Farmland Trust, Nat. Woman's History Mus. Republican. Avocations: book collecting, reading, genealogy, classical music, needlework. Home: 1047 E Baseline Rd Claremont CA 91711-1577

WHEELER, GRACE R. retired market researcher; b. Phila., May 17, 1927; d. Norman F.S. Russell and Ella Dewees Eisenbrey; m. Philip Price Sharples, Oct. 9, 1954 (div.); children: Martha Sharples Daniels, Grace Sharples Cooke, Russell Price Sharples; m. Alexander Bowman Wheeler, Aug. 16, 1980 (dec.). BA, Bennington Coll., 1948; MBA, Temple U., 1968. Rsch. analyst ARCO, Phila., 1948-51, Alderson & Sessions, Phila., 1951-54; owner Gen. Rsch. Assn., Bryn Mawr, Pa., 1974-88; ret., 1988. Contbr. (sch. history): ...better than riches..., 1989; author, editor exhibit catalog, 1976. Adv. bd., Montessori Genesis II, Phila., 1980—; founder Gladwyne (Pa.) Montessori Sch., 1960; mem. William Penn Charter Sch. Bd., 1973—, head of bd., 1975-85; mem. bd., Darby Creek Valley Assn., Drexel Hill, Pa., 1998—. Republican. Mem. Soc. Of Friends. Avocations: land stewardship, gardening. Home: 3824 Darby Rd Bryn Mawr PA 19010

WHEELER, GWEN, medical, surgical, and critical care nurse; b. Bogalusa, La., Oct. 5, 1949; d. John David and Marie (Taylor) Easterling; m. Thomas D. Wheeler, July 20, 1968; children: Thomas D. Jr., Daniel Blair. AD, S.W. Miss. Jr. Coll., Summit, 1986; student, St. Josephs Coll., 1990-95, U. So. Miss., 1995—98; M in Nursing Sci., Southeastern La. U., 2000. Cert. critical care nurse, ACLS, advance trauma life support system, RN, cert. adult nurse practitioner. Emergency rm. staff nurse Riverside Med. Ctr., Franklinton, La., 1992, nursing supr., 1992-94, staff nurse emergency room, 1998—2001; ICU staff nurse Bogalusa (La.) Cmty. Med. Ctr., Franklinton, La., 1994—98; adult nurse practitioner Franklinton Rural Health Clinic, 2001—. Mem. AACN, La. Nursing Assn., Emergency Nurses Assn.

WHEELER, HAROLD AUSTIN, SR. lawyer, former educational administrator; b. Montverde, Fla., Oct. 5, 1925; s. Bureon Kylus and Susan Ella (Bible) W.; m. Myrtle Edna Suggs, Sept. 30, 1949; children: Brenda Lynn, Harold Austin, Stephen Wayne, Donna Kay. BSBA, U. Fla., 1950; MEd, Fla. Atlantic U., 1970; JD, U. Miami (Fla.), 1973, LLM, 1977. CPA, Fla., 1962; bar: Fla. 1973. Auditor to supr. auditor Fla. State Auditing Dept., 1950-62; asst. supt. fin. and acctg. Fla. Pub. Schs., Palm Beach County, 1962-65, dir. fin., treas. Dade County, 1966-81. Mem. AICPA, Fla. Inst. CPA, Fla. Bar Assn., Assn. Sch. Bus. Ofcls. of U.S. and Can., Kiwanis (life mem.). Democrat. Baptist. Home: 6695 SW 112th St Miami FL 33156-4856

WHEELER, HEWITT BROWNELL, surgeon, educator; b. Louisville, July 21, 1929; s. Arville and Lois (Vance) W.; m. Elizabeth Jane Maxwell, July 21, 1956; children: Stephen, Elizabeth, Jane, Mary. Student, Vanderbilt U., 1945-48; MD, Harvard U., 1952. Diplomate Am. Bd. Surgery (bd. dirs. 1984-90). Cushing fellow Harvard Med. Sch., Boston, 1953, Peters fellow, 1956, research fellow, 1959-60, instr. surgery, 1961-64, clin. assoc. surgery, 1964-67, asst. clin. prof. surgery, 1967-70, assoc. prof. surgery, 1970-71; asst. in surgery Peter Bent Brigham Hosp., 1959-60, jr. assoc. surgery, 1961-64, assoc. surgery, 1964-69, sr. assoc. surgery, 1969-71; asst. chief surgery Roxbury VA Hosp., 1961-62, chief surgery, 1962-71, chief of staff, 1968-71; cons. surgery U. Mass. Med. Sch., Worcester, 1966-71; prof., chmn. dept. surgery U. Mass. Med. Sch. at Worcester, 1971-96, Harry M. Haidak disting. prof. surgery, 1985-98, prof. emeritus, 1998—; chief staff U. Mass. Hosp., 1974-76, surgeon-in-chief, 1976-96; exec. dir. Ctr. for Advanced Clin. Tech., 1995—; affiliate prof. biomed. engring. Worcester Poly. Inst., 1974—; lectr. surgery Harvard Med. Sch., 1974-96; chief surgery St. Vincent Hosp., Worcester, 1971-75. Cons. Meml. Hosp., Worcester City Hosp., 1970-96, Worcester Hahnemann Hosp., 1974-94, Peter Bent Brigham Hosp., 1973-96; chmn. surg. research program com. VA, Washington, 1965-67, nat. participant surg. cons., 1965-69, chmn. ad hoc adv. com. surgery, 1969-71. Pres. Mass. Compassionate Care Coalition, 2000—; trustee Ctrl. Mass. Health Care Found., 1975—77, Worcester Found. for Biomed. Rsch., 1996—, Hospice Ctrl. Mass. Inc., 1997—, U. Mass. Meml. Found., 1998—, Boston Med. Libr., 1996—. 1st lt. M.C. AUS, 1953—55. Mem. ACS (bd. govs. 1984-90, coun. Mass. chpt. 1973-76, pres. 1980), AAAS, AMA, Am. Surg. Assn., Soc. Univ. Surgeons, Internat. Cardiovascular Soc., New Eng. Surg. Soc. (treas. 1977-84, v.p. 1986-87, pres. 1989-91), Boston Surg. Soc. (pres. 1995-96), Worcester Surg. Soc. (pres. 1973-75), Transplantation Soc., Mass. Med. Soc. (100th Shattuck lectr. 1990), Worcester Dist. Med. Soc. (sec. 1996-99, v.p. 1999-00, pres. 2000-01), New Eng. Vascular Soc. (v.p. 1985-86, pres. 1988-89). Achievements include rsch. in exptl. transplantation, blood vessel surgery, method to detect blood clots, improving end-of-life care. Home: 10 Old English Rd Worcester MA 01609-1306 E-mail: h.brownell.wheeler@umassmed.edu.

WHEELER, JAMES JULIAN, lawyer; b. Independence, Mo., Mar. 20, 1921; s. Luther I. and Edith (Hesler) W.; m. Janet L. Esau, Apr. 28, 1951; children: Linnell Gretzinger, Robert W. LLB, U. Mo., 1948. Bar: Mo. 1948, U.S. Dist. Ct. (ea. dist.) Mo. 1956. Prosecuting atty. County of Chariton, Mo., 1950-54, probate judge, 1974-75; circuit judge 9th Judicial Circuit Court, 1976-82; sole practice Keytesville, 1948-74, 82—. Served as cpl. USMC, 1941-46, PTO. Mem. ABA, Mo. Bar Assn., Am. Judicature Soc., Assn. Trial Lawyers Am. Democrat. Home: 112 Kennedy Ave Keytesville MO 65261 Office: 304 Walnut St Keytesville MO 65261-1064

WHEELER, JOHN ARCHIBALD, physicist; b. Jacksonville, Fla., July 9, 1911; s. Joseph Lewis and Mabel (Archibald) Wheeler; m. Janette Hegner, June 10, 1935; children: Isabel Letitia Wheeler Ufford, James English, Alison Christie Wheeler Lahnston. PhD, Johns Hopkins U., 1933; ScD (hon.), Western Res. U., 1958, U. N.C., 1959, U. Pa., 1968, Middlebury Coll., 1969, Rutgers U., 1969, Yeshiva U., 1973, Yale U., 1974; PhD (hon.), U. Uppsala, 1975; ScD (hon.), U. Md., 1977, Gustavus Adolphus U., 1981, Cath. U. Am., 1982, U. Newcastle-upon-Tyne, 1983, Princeton U., 1986, U. Conn., 1989, U. Maine, 1992, Tufts U., 1992; LLD (hon.), Johns Hopkins U., 1977; LittD (hon.), Drexel U., 1987. NRC fellow, N.Y., Copenhagen, 1933—35; from asst. prof. to assoc. prof. physics U. N.C., 1935—38; asst. prof. physics Princeton U., 1938—42, assoc. prof., 1945—47, prof., 1947—76, Joseph Henry prof. physics, 1966—76, Joseph Henry prof. physics emeritus, 1976—; prof. physics and dir. Ctr. for Theoretical Physics, U. Tex., Austin, 1976—86; Ashbel Smith prof. U. Tex., 1979—86, Blumberg prof., 1981—86, Smith and Blumberg prof. emeritus, 1986—. Cons. and physicist on atomic energy projects Princeton U., 1939—42, U. Chgo., 1942, E.I. duPont de Nemours & C, Wilmington, Del., Richland, Wash., 1943—45, Los Alamos, 1950—53; dir. Project Matterhorn (H-bomb) Princeton U., 1951—53; Guggenheim fellow, Paris and Copenhagen, 1949—50; summer lectr. U. Mich., U. Chgo., Columbia U; Lorentz prof. U. Leiden, 1956; Fulbright prof. Kyoto U., 1962; vis. fellow Clare Coll., Cambridge U., 1964; Ritchie lectr. Edinburgh, 1958; vis. prof. U. Calif.-Berkeley, 1960; Battelle prof. U. Wash., 1975; I.I. Rabi vis. prof. Columbia U., 1983; sci. advisor U.S. Senate del. to 3d ann. conf. NATO Parliamentarians, Paris, 1957; mem. adv. com. Oak Ridge Nat. Lab., 1957—65, U. Calif., Los Alamos and Livermore, 1972—77; v.p. Internat. Union Physics, 1951—54; chmn. join com. on history of theoretical physics in 20th century Am. Phys. Soc. and Am. Philos. Soc., 1960—72; sci. adv. bd. USAF, 1961—62; chmn. Dept. Def. Advanced Rsch. Projects Agy. Project 137 (now Project Jason), 1958; mem. U.S. Gen. Adv. Com. Arms Control and Disarmament, 1969—72, 1974—77. Author: Geometrodynamics, 1962; author: (with others) Gravitation Theory and Gravitational Collapse, 1965; author: Spacetime Physics, 1966; author: (with E. Taylor) Spacetime Physics, 2d edit., 1992; author: (in German) Einstein's Vision, 1968; author: (with C.W. Misner and K.S. Thorne) Gravitation, 1973; author: (with M. Rees and R. Ruffini) Black Holes, Gravitation Waves and Cosmology, 1974; author: Frontiers of Time, 1979, A Journey into Gravity and Spacetime, 1990, At Home in the Universe, 1994; author: (with I. Ciufolini) Gravitation and Inertia, 1995; author: also translations, 1991—92; author: (with Kenneth Ford) Geons, Black Holes and Quantum Foam: A Life in Physics, 1998; editor (with W. Zurek): Quantum Theory and Measurement, 1983; contbr. 375 articles to profl. jours. Trustee Battelle Meml. Inst. , 1959—89, S.W. Rsch. Inst., San Antonio, 1977—92, Unitarian Ch., 1965. Recipient A. Cressy Morrison prize for work on nuc. physics, N.Y. Acad. Scis., 1947, Albert Einstein prize, Strauss Found., 1965, Enrico Fermi award, AEC, 1968, Franklin medal, Franklin Inst., 1969, Nat. medal of Sci., 1971, Herzfeld award, 1975, Outstanding Grad. Tchg. award, U. Tex., 1981, Niels Bohr Internat. Gold medal, 1982, Oersted medal, Am. Assn. Physics Tchrs., 1983, J. Robert Oppenheimer Meml. prize, 1984, Matteucci medal, Nat. Acad. Sci. Rome, Soc. of the Forty, 1994, Wolf Found. prize in Physics, Jerusalem, 1997. Fellow: AAAS (dir. 1965—68), Am. Phys. Soc. (pres. 1966); mem.: NAS, Royal Danish Acad. Scis., Royal Soc. (London), Accademia Nazionale dei Lincei, Internat. Union Physics (v.p. 1951—54), L'Academie Internationale de Philosophie des Sciences (v.p. 1987—90), Tex. Philos. Soc., Royal Acad. Sci. (Uppsala, Sweden), Philos. Soc. of Tex., Am. Philos. Soc. (councillor 1963—66, v.p. 1971—73, councillor 1976—79, Franklin medal 1989), Am. Acad. Arts and Scis., Internat. Astron. Union, Am. Math. Soc., Princeton Club (N.Y.C.), Century Assn. (N.Y.C.), Sigma Xi, Phi Beta Kappa. Unitarian Universalist. Office: Princeton U Dept Physics Princeton NJ 08544-0001 E-mail: jawheeler@pupgg.princeton.edu. *We will first understand how simple the universe is when we recognize how strange it is.*

WHEELER, JOHN CHARLES, telecommunications professional; b. Charleston, W.Va., June 28, 1947; s. Charles Andrew Wheeler and Edith Christine (Cooper) Shumate; m. Karen Eilleen Ward, Jan. 9, 1976 (dec. Sept. 1994); children: Richard Wayne, William Shawn. Grad. H.S., Hinton, W.Va. Supr. cmty. dial offices Bell Atlantic Switching, Beckley, W.Va., 1972-81, traffic svc. position sys. project coord. Charleston, 1981-83, traffic operator position sys. project coord. Beckley, 1983-90, supr. electromech. switching control ctr., 1983-90, supr. digital conversions Beckley, Logan, Lewisburg, W.Va., 1985-89, team leader electronic switching sys./interoffice facilities Beckley, 1990—. Quality instr. Bell Atlantic, Charleston, 1993-94. Author: Angel's Past Present Future, 1995. Treas. Shady Spring (W.Va.) H.S., Band Boosters, 1993-96; mem. Raleigh County Bd. Edn. Planning and Devel., Beckley, 1993-2001, Better Schs. Coun., State of W.Va., Beckley, 1995. With U.S. Army, 1965-72. Mem. Kiwanis Club Beckley (bd. dirs. 1993-94, 2001-02, pres. 1994-95, immediate past pres. 1995-96, Disting. Svc. award 1994). Democrat. Baptist. Avocations: water skiing, fishing, restoring vintage muscle cars such as Corvetts. E-mail: mustgo@inetone.net.

WHEELER, JOHN CRAIG, astrophysicist, writer; b. Glendale, Calif., Apr. 5, 1943; s. G.L. and Peggy Wheeler; m. Hsueh Lie, Oct. 29, 1967; children: Diek Winters, J. Robinson. BS in Physics, MIT, 1965; PhD in Physics, U. Colo., 1969. Asst. prof. astronomy Harvard U., Cambridge, Mass., 1971-74; assoc. prof. U. Tex., Austin, 1974-80, prof., 1980—, Samuel T. and Fern Yanagisawa Regents prof. astronomy, 1985—, chmn. astronomy dept., 1986-90. Vis. fellow Joint Inst. Lab. Astrophysics, Boulder, Colo., 1978-79, Japan Soc. for Promotion of Sci., 1983; 1st vis. prof. Assn. Univs. for Rsch. in Astronomy, 1990; vis. sr. scientist Inst. for Theoretical Physics, U. Calif., Santa Barbara, 1997; gen. mem. Aspen (Colo.) Ctr. for Physics; mem. exec. com. Tex. Symposium on Relativistic Astrophysics. Author: The Krone Experiment, 1986, Cosmic Catastrophes, 2000; editor: Accretion Disks in Compact Stellar Systems, 1993, Supernovae, 1990, Disk Instabilities in Close Binary Systems, 1999, Proceedings of the 20th Texas Symposium on Relativistic Astrophysics. Recipient awards U. Tex., 1984, 86, 99, Pres.'s Assocs. Tchg. Excellence award, 1999; Fulbright fellow, Italy, 1991; Dads Assn. Centennial Tchg. fellow U. Tex., 1999. Mem. Internat. Astron. Union, Am. Astron. Soc. (v.p. 1995—), Sigma Xi. Avocations: running, writing, reading. Office: U Tex Dept Astronomy Austin TX 78712

WHEELER, JOHN HARVEY, political scientist, writer; b. Waco, Tex., Oct. 17, 1918; m. Norene Burleigh; children: David Carroll, John Harvey III, Mark Jefferson. BA, Ind. U., 1946, MA, 1947; PhD, Harvard U., 1950. Instr. dept. govt., asst. dir. Summer Sch., Harvard U., 1950; asst. prof. Johns Hopkins U., 1950-54; assoc. prof. Washington and Lee U., 1954-56, prof. polit. sci., 1956-60; fellow in residence Ctr. for Study Dem. Instns., 1960-69; program dir., 1970-75; chmn., pres. Inst. Higher Studies, Carpinteria, Calif., 1975—. Martha Boaz rsch. prof. in acad. info. systems U. So. Calif. Libr. Systems, 1986—, Martha Boaz disting. rsch. prof., 1987—; cons. Fund for Republic, 1958-61; adj. prof. New Sch., 1986—, ISIM, 1989—; founder, bd. dirs. The Virtual Acad., 1987; mem. faculty Western Behavioral Scis. Inst., 1990—; mem. BESTnet, Nat. Rsch. and Edn. Network; pres. C-Mode Inst., 1992—; bd. dirs. Silicon Beach Comm. Author: The Conservative Crisis, 1958, (with Eugene Burdick) Fail-Safe, 1962, repub., 1999 (film 1962) asst. exec. prodr., (TV re-make 2000), Democracy in a Revolutionary Era, 1968, The Politics of Revolution, 1971, The Virtual Library, 1987, The Virtual Society, 1988, 2d edit., 1992, Atlantoz 2005, 2002; editor, contbg. author: Beyond Punitive Society, 1973, Structure of Ancient Wisdom, 1983, Bioalgebra of Judgment, 1986, Fundamental Structures Human Reflexion, 1990; editor: (with George Boas) Lattimore, The Scholar, 1953; co-founder, joint chief editor: (with James Danielli) Jour. Social and Biol. Structures, 1973-95; joint editor Goethe's Science, 1986; developed computer-mediated "Freshman Academy", 1993; contbr. articles on constitutionalism and Francis Bacon to profl. jours. Keynote spkr. Subiaco Writing Festival, 2002. Served with AUS, 1941-46. Recipient Mouton Tor award, 2001. Office: Inst Higher Studies PO Box 704 Carpinteria CA 93014-0704 E-mail: verulan@mindspring.com.

WHEELER, JOHN OLIVER, geologist; b. Mussoorie, India, Dec. 19, 1924; s. Edward Oliver and Dorothea Sophie (Danielsen) W.; m. Nora Jean Hughes, May 17, 1952; children: Kathleen Anna Wheeler Hunter, Jennifer Margaret Wheeler Crompton. BASc. in Geol. Engring, U. B.C., 1947; PhD in Geology, Columbia U., 1956; D.Sc. (hon.), U. B.C., 2000. Geologist Geol. Survey Can., Ottawa, Ont., 1951-61, Vancouver, B.C., 1961-65, rsch. scientist, 1965-70, rsch. mgr., 1970—, chief regional and econ. geology div., 1970-73, dep. dir. gen., 1973-79; rsch. scientist Geol. Survey Can. (Cordilleran div.), 1979-90, rsch. scientist emeritus, 1990—. Gen. editor: Geology of Canada, 8 vols., 1989-98; compiler of regional geol. maps of we. Can., Can. and no. N.Am. and Greenland; contbr. articles to profl. jours. Recipient Queen's Silver Jubilee medal, 1977, Can. 125 medal, 1994, Earth Sci. Sector and Dept. awards Nat. Resources Can., 1996, Spl. award of B.C.-Yukon Chamber of Mines for outstanding contbn. to Can. Cordilleran geology, 2000. Fellow Royal Soc. Can., Geol. Assn. Can. (pres. 1970-71, Logan medal 1983, Disting. fellow 1996), Geol. Soc. Am. (councillor 1971-74), Can. Geosci. Council (pres. 1981); mem. Can. Inst. Mining and Metallurgy., Can. Geol. Found. (pres. 1974-79) Clubs: Can. Alpine, Am. Alpine. Anglican. Office: Geol Survey Can 101-605 Robson St Vancouver BC Canada V6B 5J3

WHEELER, JOHN WATSON, lawyer; b. Murfreesboro, Tenn., Sept. 11, 1938; s. James William and Grace (Fann) W.; m. Dorothy Anita Pressgrove, Aug. 5, 1959; children: Jeffrey William, John Harold. BS in Journalism, U. Tenn., 1960, JD, 1968. Bar: Tenn. 1968, U.S. Dist. Ct. (ea. dist.) Tenn. 1968, U.S. Supreme Ct. 1974, U.S. Ct. Appeals (6th cir.) 1975. Editor The Covington (Tenn.) Leader, 1963-65; adminstrv. asst. to lab. dir. UT-AEC Rsch. Lab., Oak

Ridge, Tenn., 1965-68; assoc. Hodges, Doughty & Carson, Knoxville, 1968-72, ptnr., 1972—. Mem. commn. to study Applellate Cts. in Tenn.; chair U.S. Magistrate Merit Selection Panel, Ea. Dist., Tenn., 1991; mem. Bankruptcy Judge Merit Selection Panel, Ea. Dist. Tenn., 1992-94; chmn. Hist. Soc., U.S. Dist. Ct. (ea. dist.) Tenn. Mem. organizing com. Tenn. Supreme Ct. Hist. Soc. Lt. U.S. Army, 1961-63, capt. Res. Fellow Am. Bar Found. (life, Tenn. chair 1999—), Tenn. Bar Found. (life); mem. ABA (ho. of dels. 1986-2000), Tenn. Bar Assn. (pres. 1989-90, bd. govs. 1981-91), Nat. Conf. Bar Pres., Am. Inns. of Ct. (master of bench, emeritus), Internat. Assn. Def. Counsel, So. Conf. Bar Pres., 6th Cir. Jud. Conf. (life), Fox Den Country Club. Republican. Lutheran. Avocations: golf, travel. Home: 12009 N Fox Den Dr Knoxville TN 37922-2540 Office: Hodges Doughty & Carson PO Box 869 Knoxville TN 37901-0869

WHEELER, KATHERINE WELLS, state legislator; b. St. Louis, Feb. 8, 1940; d. Benjamin Harris and Katherine (Gladney) Wells; m. Douglas Lanphier Wheeler, June 13, 1964; children: Katherine Gladney, Lucille Lanphier BA, Smith Coll., 1961; MA, Washington U., St. Louis, 1966. Founder auction N.H. Pub. TV, Durham, 1973-76; pub. mem. N.H. Pub. Broadcasting Coun., 1975-80; founding mem. bd. govs. N.H. Pub. TV, 1980-88; elected N.H. Ho. of Reps., Concord, 1988, 90, 92,94; mem. N.H. Senate, 1996-98, 98—, v.p. ops., chmn. ins., vice-chmn. health & human svcs. coms. Coord. internat. visitors program N.J. Coun. World Affairs, 1981-95; bd. dirs. The Clinic. Bd. dirs. Planned Parenthood No. New England, 1989-95, Gt. Bay Sch. and Tng. Ctr., Newington, N.H., 1989-97, Devel. Svcs. Strafford County, Inc., 1991—; vice chairperson Strafford County Legis. Del., 1993-94; active Commn. on Health, Human Svcs. and Elderly Affairs N.H. Ho. of Reps., Concord, 1988-96; bd. dirs. N.H. Pub. Health Assn., 1996—, Northeast Action, 1996; pres. elect N.H. Order of Women Legislators, 1997—. Named Woman of Yr., Union Leader Newspaper, 1984, Citizen of Yr., Homemakers of Strafford County, 1990, N.H. sect. NASW, 1993, Legislator of Yr., N.H. Nurses Assn., 1996, N.H. Acad. Pediat., 1996; recipient Elizabeth Campbell Outstanding Pub. TV Vol. award Nat. Friends Pub. Broadcasting, 1984, Meritorious Svc. award N.H. Women's Lobby, 1992, Dist. Contbn. award N.H. Psychol. Orgn., Inc., 1994, Cert. of Achievement for Outstanding Legis. Leadership N.H. Citizen Action, 1994; Fleming fellow Leadership Inst., Ctr. for Policy Alternatives, Washington, 1997-98. Mem. AAUW, LWV, Am. Assn. Ret. Persons, Order of Women Legislators, N.H. Smith Coll. Club (v.p. 1974-76, pres. 1976-78, v.p. class of 1961, 1991-96), N.H. Assn. Social Workers (Legislator of Yr. 1993), N.H. Psychol. Orgn. Inc. (Disting. Contbn. award 1994). Democrat. Mem. United Ch. of Christ. Home and Office: 27 Mill Rd Durham NH 03824-3006

WHEELER, KATHRYN S. editor; b. Grosse Ile, Mich. d. Emich Duane and Anna K. Solms; m. William Donald Wheeler, Sept. 23, 1989. BA, Hope Coll., 1976; student, U. Mont., 1981. Editor Herman Miller Inc., Zeeland, Mich., 1977-80; copywriter Exclamation Point Advertising, Billings, Mont., 1981-84; sr. copywriter Aves Advertising, Grand Rapids, Mich., 1985-89; staff writer David Perkins & Assocs., 1990-94; editor School Zone Publishing, 1994-95; sr. editor Instructional Fair Group (now McGraw-Hill Children's Pub.), 1998—. Cons. in ednl. writing, 1994—, adj. prof. Grand Valley State U., 1986-90. Editor: ednl. CD and book series; author: Tunnel 2000, 1999, The Suspicious Stranger, 1999, No Room for Neighbors, 1999, Finders Keepers, 2000, Patty Saves the Day, 2001, Patriotic Traditions, 2002. Advertising cons. Sara Smolenski Campaign, 1996, bd. mem. Carol Irons Com., 1989. Grantee Mich. Coun. for the Arts, 1988. Mem. Soc. Children's Book Writers and Illustrators. Democrat. Episcopalian. Office: McGraw Hill Childrens Pub 3195 Wilson Ave Grand Rapids MI 49544

WHEELER, LARRY RICHARD, accountant; b. Greybull, Wyo., Nov. 30, 1940; s. Richard F. and Olive B. (Fredrickson) W.; m. Patricia C. Marturano, Dec. 3, 1977; children: Anthony, Richard, Teresa, Kara. BS, U. Wyo., 1965. CPA, Colo. Staff acct. H. Greger CPA, Ft. Collins, Colo., 1965-66; sr. acct. Lester, Wickham & Draney, Colorado Springs, 1966-67; acct., contr., treas. J.D. Adams Co., 1967-74; ptnr. Wheeler Pierce & Hurd, Inc., 1974-80; gen. mgr., v.p. Schneebeck's, Inc., 1980-81; prin. L.R. Wheeler & Co., PC, 1981-94; pres. Wheeler & Gilmartin Assocs., PC, 1994-95, L.R. Wheeler & Co., PC, Colorado Springs, 1995—. Dir. Schneebeck's Industries, Williams Printing, Inc., Colorado Springs Small Bus. Devel. Ctr. Active U.S. Taekwondo Union; bd. dirs. Domestic Violence Prevention Ctr. Paul Stock Found. grant, 1962. Mem. AICPA, Colo. Soc. CPA's, Nat. Assn. Cert. Valuation Analysts. Office: 317 E San Rafael St Colorado Springs CO 80903-2405

WHEELER, LAWRENCE JEFFERSON, art museum director; BA cum laude in History and French, Pfeiffer Coll., 1965; MA in European History, U. Ga., 1969, PhD in European History, 1972; cert., Fed. Execs. Inst., Charlottesville, Va., 1977, U. N.C., 1982. Asst. prof. European history Pfeiffer Coll., Misenheimer, N.C., 1970-74; dep. sec. N.C. Dept. Cultural Resources, Raleigh, 1977-85; asst. dir. mus. and dir. devel. Cleve. Mus. Art, 1985-94; staff liaison for bldg. and staffing N.C. Mus. Art, Raleigh, 1977-83, dir., 1994—. Cons. on fundraising and pub. rels. N.C. Mus. History, Raleigh; coord. 400th anniversary celebration Sir Walter Raleigh's voyages festival, 1984. Bd. dirs. Am. Arts Alliance, 1991-92. Named N.C. Man of Yr., News and Observer newspaper, Raleigh, N.C. . Mem. Am. Assn. Mus. (chmn. dvel. and membership profl. com. 1990-92, sr. reviewer mus. assessment program 1992—), Inst. Mus. Svcs. (reviewer 1988—), Art Mus. Devel. Assn. (pres. 1987-88). Home: 44 Cedar St Chapel Hill NC 27514-2712 Office: NC Mus Art 4630 Mail Service Ctr Raleigh NC 27699-4630 Fax: 919-733-8034.

WHEELER, M. CASS, health science association administrator; Stockbroker NY Stock Exch. firm , Dallas, 1969—73; with AHA, Austin , 1973—, COO Dallas, 1982, sr. v.p., field ops., 1996, CEO, 1997—. Chmn. bd. Nat. Health Coun. Office: Am Heart Assn 7272 Greenville Ave Dallas TX 75231-5129*

WHEELER, MALCOLM EDWARD, lawyer, law educator; b. Berkeley, Calif., Nov. 29, 1944; s. Malcolm Ross and Frances Dolores (Kane) W.; m. Donna Marie Stambaugh, July 25, 1981; children: Jessica Ross, M. Connor. SB, MIT, 1966; JD, Stanford U., 1969. Bar: Calif. 1970, Colo. 1992, U.S. Dist. Ct (cen. dist.) Calif. 1970, U.S. Ct. Appeals (9th cir.) 1970, U.S. Ct. Appeals (10th cir.) 1973, U.S. Dist. Ct. (no., so., ea. and cen. dists.) Calif. 1975, U.S. Ct. Appeals (11th cir.) 1987, U.S. Ct. Appeals (D.C. cir.) 1987, U.S. Supreme Ct. 1976, U.S. Ct. Appeals (3d cir.) 1989, (4th cir.) 1992, (8th cir.) 1993, (5th cir.) 1995, (Fed. cir.) 1998. Assoc. Howard, Prim, Smith, Rice & Downs, San Francisco, 1969-71; assoc. prof. law U. Kans., Lawrence, 1971-74; assoc. Hughes Hubbard & Reed, Los Angeles, 1974-77, ptnr., 1977-81, 83-85, cons., 1981-83; ptnr. Skadden, Arps, Slate, Meagher & Flom, 1985-91; dir. Parcel, Mauro, Hultin & Spaanstra P.C., Denver, 1991-98, Wheeler Trigg & Kennedy, P.C., Denver, 1998—. Vis. prof. U. Iowa, 1978, prof., 1979; prof. U. Kans., Lawrence, 1981-83; chief counsel U.S. Senate Select Com. to Study Law Enforcement Undercover Activities, Washington, 1982-83. Mem. editorial bd. Jour. Products Liability, 1984—; bd. editors Fed. Litigation Guide Reporter, 1986—; contbr. articles to profl. jours. Mem. ABA, Calif. Bar Assn., Colo. Bar Assn., Am. Law Inst. Home: 100 Humboldt St Denver CO 80218-3932

WHEELER, MARK ANDREW, SR. lawyer; b. Pitts., Feb. 14, 1963; s. Andrew Mate Wheeler and Anna Ruth (Whitfield) W.; m. Irina P. Wheeler, May 10, 1993; children: Mark Andrew Jr., Lauren Anna, Layne Allison, Livia Arden. BA in Philosophy, Hampden-Sydney Coll., 1985; JD, W.Va. U., 1991. Bar: Pa. 1992, U.S. Dist. Ct. (we. dist.) Pa. 1993; ordained to ministry Lighthouse Ch., 1997. Staff litigator W.Va. U. Coll. Law Legal Clinic, Morgantown, 1991-92; jud. clk. Mahoning County, Youngstown, Ohio, 1991-92; pvt. practice Reynoldsville, Pa., 1993—, Clarion, 1994—. Legal cons. S.T. & E., Inc., Punxsutawney, Pa., 1993—, Jefferson County Gun Owners Assn., Brookville, Pa., 1994—, Crimestoppers of Jefferson County, Brookville, 1993-94, Five Star Homes, Inc., 1995-97, Bembeng Cons., Inc., 1994—. Bd. dirs. Reynoldsville Area Indsl. Bd., 1993-96; mem. exec. dist. com. Boy Scouts Am., Dubois, Pa., 1993—; bd. dirs. Reynoldsville Pub. Libr. Assn., 1993-96; mem. Dubois Christian and Missionary Alliance Ch., mem. choir, 1995—. Mem. ABA, ATLA, Internat. Platform Assn., Pa. Bar Assn. (young lawyers divsn., chair zone 7), Am. Ctr. for Law and Justice, Pa. Trial Lawyers Assn., Pa. Assn. Notaries, Jefferson County Bar Assn., Western Pa. Trial Lawyers Assn., Clarion County Bar Assn., Nat. Eagle Scout Assn. Republican. Avocations: songwriting, public speaking, home renovation, car restoration. Office: PO Box 176 512 Main St Reynoldsville PA 15851-1335 also: PO Box 770 Clarion PA 16214-0770

WHEELER, MICHELE LYNN, financial analyst; b. Santa Maria, Calif., Jan. 5, 1964; d. Thomas Almon and Patricia (O'Bid) W. BSBA, U. Nev., 1986, MBA, 1990. Acct. exec. Citicorp, Las Vegas, 1986; mgmt. analyst I Clark County, 1986-88, mgmt. analyst, 1988-91, sr. fin. analyst, 1991—. Participant, mem. Clark County Leadership Forum, 1993. Named Outstanding Mgmt. Student U. Nev., 1986. Mem. ASPA, Am. Pub. Works Assn., Govt. Fin. Officers Assn., Jr. League Las Vegas (chmn. 1993-94, 94-95), U. Nev. Alumni Soc., Phi Kappa Phi. Republican. Roman Catholic. Avocations: skiing, mountain biking, scuba diving, golf, tennis. Home: PO Box 97195 Las Vegas NV 89193-7195 Office: Clark County 225 Bridger Ave Las Vegas NV 89101-6101

WHEELER, ORVILLE EUGENE, university dean, civil and mechanical engineering educator; b. Memphis, Dec. 31, 1932; s. Eugene Lloyd and Sarah Josephine (Craig) W.; m. Mary Bea Rychlik, June 6, 1956; 1 dau., Lynnette Layne. B.Engring. cum laude, Vanderbilt U., 1954; MS in Civil Enging, U. Mo., 1956; PhD, Tex. A&M U., 1966. Registered profl. engr., Ala., Tenn., Wis. With Chance Vought Co., Dallas, 1959-60, Hayes Aircraft Co., Birmingham, Ala., 1960-61, Brown Engring. Co., Huntsville, 1961-62, NASA, Huntsville, 1962-66; design specialist Gen. Dynamics Co., Ft. Worth, 1966-72; chief structures engr. Bucyrus Erie Co., Milw., 1972-78; prof. civil and mech. engring., dean Herff Coll. Engring. Memphis State U., 1978-87, Herff prof. structural mechanics, 1987—. Served with USN, 1956-59. Mem. ASCE, ASTM, Assn. for Computing Machinery, Memphis Engrs. Club. Methodist. Home: 3307 E Monticello Cir Memphis TN 38115-0640 Office: Dept of Engring U Memphis Memphis TN 38152-0001

WHEELER, OTIS BULLARD, retired English educator and university official; b. Mansfield, Ark., Feb. 1, 1921; s. Clarence Charles and Georgia Elizabeth (Bullard) W.; m. Doris Louise Alexander, Jan. 17, 1943; children: Ann Carolyn, Ross Charles; m. Anne Carol Loveland, Mar. 23, 1991. BA, U. Okla., 1942; MA, U. Tex., 1947; PhD, U. Minn., 1951. Mem. faculty La. State U., Baton Rouge, 1952—, prof. English, 1965-81, prof. emeritus, 1981—, chmn. dept., 1974, asst. dean grad. sch., 1962-67, vice chancellor for acad. affairs, 1974-80, acting chancellor, 1981. Fulbright-Hayes lectr. U. Innsbruck, Austria, 1968-69 Author: The Literary Career of Maurice Thompson, 1965; photographer: (with R.W. Heck) Religious Architecture in Louisiana, 1995. Served with U.S. Army, 1942-46, 51-52. Decorated Bronze Star medal. Mem. Phi Kappa Phi, Omicron Delta Kappa. Democrat. Methodist. Home: 657 Highland Oaks Dr Baton Rouge LA 70810-5348

WHEELER, PETER MARTIN, federal agency administrator, educator; b. Bronx, N.Y., Nov. 10, 1939; s. James and Mary A. (Doyle) W.; m. Mary Gaffey, Aug. 7, 1982; children: Bernadette, Peter, Mary Beth, James, Sam, Andrea. BA, Iona Coll., New Rochelle, N.Y., 1961; MPA, U. So. Calif., 1985, DPA (Dr. Pub. Administrn.), 1992. Claims rep., field rep. Social Security Adminstrn., Bronx, 1961-64, claims authorizer Balt., 1964-65, comms. specialist, 1965-70, dep. assoc. commr., 1973-91, assoc. commr., 1992-99, sr. policy officer, 1999—2002; asst. exec. sec. Office of Sec. Dept. of Health, Edn. and Welfare, Washington, 1970-73; ret., 2002. Rep. Internat. Conf. on Social Welfare, Holland, 1972, Kenya, 1974; cons. Can. health and Welfare Agy. Ottawa, 1989; adj. prof. George Washington U., Washington, 1994—. Mem. U.S. study team Benefits & Svcs. for Poor Children Eng., 1973. Recipient Nat. Inst. Pub. Affairs award U. So. Calif., 1969-70. Mem. Internat. Social Security Assn. (social security adminstrn. rep., mem. study com. rsch. Geneva, Vienna). Roman Catholic. Achievements include research on revitalizing SSAs rsch. capacity, rebuilding Social Security Administration's quality assurance and research/evaluation systems. Home: 3238 Birchmede Dr Ellicott City MD 21042-2302

WHEELER, RAYMOND LOUIS, lawyer; b. Ft. Sill, Okla., Feb. 10, 1945; s. Raymond Louis and Dorothy Marie (Hutcherson) W.; m. Priscilla Wheeler, July 1, 1966 (div. 1982); children: Jennifer, Hilary; m. Cynthia Lee Jackson, July 14, 1984 (div. 1994); children: Matthew Raymond, Madeline Elizabeth; m. Freddie Kay Park, June 10, 1995. BA, U. Tex., 1967; JD, Harvard U., 1970. Bar: Calif. 1972, U.S. Dist. Ct. (no., cen., ea., so. dists.) Calif., U.S. Ct. Appeals (9th cir., 7th cir.), U.S. Ct. Appeals (7th cir.), U.S. Supreme Ct. Law clk. to hon. Irving L. Goldberg U.S. Ct. Appeals 5th cir., 1970-71; assoc. Morrison & Foerster, San Francisco, 1971-76, ptnr., 1976-90, Palo Alto, Calif., 1990—. Chmn. labor and employment law dept. Morrison & Foerster, San Francisco, 1984-88, 92—; lectr. labor and EEO law. Exec. editor Harvard Law Rev., 1969-70; editor in chief The Developing Labor Law; mem. nat. adv. bd. Berkeley Jour. Employment and Labor Law, 1980—; contbr. articles to law jours. Fellow Coll. Labor and Employment Lawyers; mem. ABA (chmn. com. on law devel. under labor rels. act 1990-93, coun. mem. sect. labor and employment 1994-02). Republican. Office: Morrison & Foerster 755 Page Mill Rd Palo Alto CA 94304-1018 E-mail: rwheeler@mofo.com.

WHEELER, R(ICHARD) KENNETH, lawyer, educator; b. Washington, July 25, 1934; s. Nathaniel Dudley and Ruth Lee (Matthews) W.; m. Christine Kandris, Jan. 11, 1990; children by previous marriage: Jennifer L., Ruth E. BA, Emory and Henry Coll., U. Richmond, 1957; LLB, U. Richmond, 1964. Bar: Va. 1963, D.C. 1977, U.S. Tax Ct. 1978. Assoc., then ptnr. Hunton, Williams, Gay, Powell & Gibson and successor firms, Richmond, 1963-88; sr. ptnr. Kane, Wheeler, Fenderson & Jeffries, 1988-90; counsel Durrette, Irvin, Lemons & Fenderson, P.C., 1990-94; sr. ptnr. Wallace, Harris & Wheeler, 1994-95. Adj. prof. law T.C. Williams Sch. Law, U. Richmond, 1966, 83, bd. dirs., 1977-79; adj. prof. law Va. Commonwealth U., 1970; lectr. trial practice U. Va., 1981-82, 85, 87; arbitrator Am. Arbitration Assn. Served to capt. USMCR, 1957-61. Williams scholar U. Richmond, 1961-63. Mem. Am. Law Inst., Va. State Bar (chmn. com. liaison with law schs. 1977-78, chmn. com. legal edn. and admission to bar 1978-80, spcl. com. on professionalism 1987-88), Web Soc., McNeill Law Soc., Marine Corps League (life), Rector's Club (U. Richmond, life), Pi Sigma Alpha, Phi Delta Phi, Omicron Delta Kappa (hon.).

WHEELER, RICHARD PAUL, English educator, dean; b. Newton, Iowa, Sept. 9, 1943; s. Clifford Don and Irene Maxine Wheeler; m. Pat Gill, Mar. 28, 1997. BA, Cornell Coll., 1965; MA, SUNY, Buffalo, 1967, PhD, 1970. From asst. prof. to assoc. prof. U. Ill., Urbana, 1969-87, prof., 1987—, head English dept., 1987-89, dean grad. coll., 1989—, head anthropology. Evaluator English dept. U. Oreg., Eugene, 1996, U. Minn., Mpls., 1997, U. Tenn., Memphis, 1998. Author: Shakespeare's Development and the Problem Comedies, 1981; co-author: The Whole Journey: Shakespeare's Power of Development, 1986; editor: Creating Elizabethan Tragedy, 1988, Critical Essays on Shakespeare's Measure for Measure, 1999. Mem. MLA, Shakespeare Assn. Am., Coun. Grad. Schs., Assn. Grad. Schs., Coun. Rsch. Policy and Grad. Edn. Democrat. Home: 512 W Springfield Champaign IL 61820 Office: U Ill 801 S Wright St Champaign IL 61820-6210 Fax: 217-333-8019. E-mail: rpw@uiuc.edu.

WHEELER, RURIC E. educator; b. Clarkson, Ky., Nov. 30, 1923; s. Mark H. and Mary (Sullivan) W.; A.B., Western Ky. U., 1947; M.S., U. Ky., 1948, Ph.D., 1952; m. Joyce Ray, May 31, 1946; children: Eddy Ray, Paul Warren. Instr. math. U. Ky., 1948-52; asst. prof. statistics Fla. State U., 1952-53; asso. prof. math. Samford U., 1953-55, prof., head dept., 1955-65, chmn. div. natural scis., 1965-67, asst. to acad. dean, 1967-68; dean Howard Coll. Arts and Scis., 1968-70, v.p. acad. affairs, 1970-87, univ. professor, 1987—; cons. in field; dir. NSF Inst., 1961, Ala. Vis. Scientist Program, 1962-67. Mem. Birmingham Manpower Area Planning Council, 1972-75. Trustee Gorgas Found., 1968—, chmn., 1988-92; mem. Jefferson County Ednl. Consortium, 1981-93, pres. 1986-90; mem. Commn. to Upgrade Jefferson County Schs., 1982-86. Served to lt. USAAF, 1943-46. Mem. Am. Edn. Assn., Am. Math. Soc., Am. Math. Assn. (chmn. S.E. sect. 1966-67, vis. lecture program 1989—), Nat. Council Tchrs. Math., Assn. Math. Tchrs. Ala. (pres. 1963), Assn. So. Bapt. Colls. and Schs. (sec. 1973, v.p. 1974, pres. 1975, deans sect.), Ala. Acad. Sci. (pres. 1967-69), Am. Assn. Higher Edn., Assn. Ala. Coll. Adminstrs. (exec. com. 1976— , pres. 1978-79), Am. Assn. U. Adminstrs. (exec. com Ala. sect. 1972-74, v.p. 1974-76, pres. 1976-77), Am. Conf. Acad. Deans, So. Conf. Deans Faculties and Acad. Vice Presidents (pres. 1982), Conf. Acad. Deans of So. States (pres. 1985-86). Baptist (deacon). Rotarian (pres. 1982). Author: Modern Math, 1966, 8th edit., 1994, alt. edit., 1981, Fundamental Concepts of Math, 1968, 2d edit., 1976, Modern Math for Business, 1969, 4th edit., 1986, A Programmed Study of Number Systems, 1972, Finite Mathematics, 1974, 3d edit., 1985, Intuitive Geometry, 1975, Mathematics, an Everyday Language, 1979, Student Activities Manual, Elementary Mathematics, 1984, Finite Mathematics (A Problem Solving Approach), 1991, Mathematicas un Lenguaje Cotidiano, 1982, Activities Manual for Elementary School Teachers, 1988, Introduccion a los Conjuntos Numericos, 1976, Modern Mathematics for Elementary School Teachers, 1994. Home: 1347 Badham Dr Birmingham AL 35216-2939

WHEELER, STEPHEN FREDERICK, legal administration; BA in Polit. Sci., Mt. Union Coll., Alliance, Ohio, 1968; MS in Adminstrn. of Justice, Am. U., 1974. Probation officer 19th Dist. Juvenile and Domestic Rels. Ct. Prince William County, Manassas, Va., 1972-75; ct. systems planner Office of Jud. Planning Ky. Jud. Coun., Frankfort, 1975-76; co-dir. Ky. pretrial svcs. Adminstrv. Office of Cts. Ky. Ct. of Justice, 1976-81; ct. adminstr. Jud. Dist. 27A, Gastonia, N.C., 1982-87, Colorado Springs (Colo.) Mcpl. Ct., 1987—. Ct. systems cons. Nat. Criminal Justice Collaborative, Sea Island, Ga., 1981-85. Office: City of Colorado Springs Mcpl Ct PO Box 2169 Colorado Springs CO 80901-2169 E-mail: swheeler@ci.colospgs.co.us.

WHEELER, STEVE DEREAL, neurologist; b. Chgo., Sept. 15, 1951; s. Clarence and Tommie L. (Andrews) W.; m. Debra B. Buckingham; children: Winter N., Ryan S., Gabrielle S. Student, Mich. State U., 1970-73; MD, Dartmouth Coll., 1976. Diplomate Am. Bd. Psychiatry and Neurology, Nat. Bd. Med. Examiners; lic. Mich., Ohio, Fla. Intern Thomas Jefferson U., Phila., 1976-77; emergency physician River Dist. Hosp. Emergency Cons., Inc., St. Clair, Mich., 1977-78; fellow Dartmouth Med. Sch., 1978; resident U. Miami, Fla., 1978-81; fellow Washington U., St. Louis, 1981-82; instr. in neurology Med. Coll. Pa., Phila., 1982-83; electroencephalograph reader, attending neurologist VA Med. Ctr., 1982-83; asst. neurologist, attending neurologist Muscle Clinic U. Hosps. Cleve., 1983-86; electromyographer Rainbow Babies and Children's Hosp., U. Hosps. Cleve., 1983-86; chief neuromuscular diseases divsn., asst. prof. neurology Case Western Res. U., Cleve., 1983-86, co-dir. muscle disease ctr. and lab., 1985-86; clin. assoc. prof. of neurology U. Miami, 1987-89; pvt. practice Miami, 1987—; dir., co-founder Ryan Wheeler Headache Treatment Ctr., 2001—. Lectr. Myasthenia Gravis Found., Vermilion, Ohio, 1984, Cleve., 1983—86; vol. assoc. prof. U. Miami Sch., 1992—97, vis. lectr., 1983—2001; chief headache divsn. Neurologic Ctr. for South Fla.; neurology cons. Low Back Pain Team U. Hosps. Cleve., 1984—86; mem. quality assurance com. Coral Reef Hosp., Miami, 1987—88; cons. dir. planning Bapt. Headache Clinic Bapt. Hosp., Miami, 1993—95; mem. adminstrv. com. Deering Hosp. Pain Mgmt. Ctr., Miami, 1993—94; mem. sleep diagnostic ctr. com. Bapt. Hosp., 1990—92, 1994—98, advisor to headache support group, 1995—; lectr. in field. Author: (chpt.) Intensive Care For Neurological Trauma and Disease, 1982, (chpt.) Migraine and the Primary Headaches, 2002; mem. editl. bd.: Headache jour., 2001—, ad hoc reviewer: Headache, 2000, ad hoc reviewer: Cephalalgia, 1999—, ad hoc reviewer: Jour. Nat. Med. Assn., 2001—. Named Internat. Man Yr., 1991-92; recipient Celebration Excellence Black Achiever award Family Christian Assn. Am., 1992. Fellow Royal Soc. Medicine, Am. Acad. Neurology; mem. ACP, Am. Headache Soc., So. Med. Assn. (chmn. psychiatry and neurology sect. 2000-02), Nat. Headache Found., Internat. Headache Soc., Fla. Med. Assn., Fla. Soc. Neurology, Fla. Soc. Internal Medicine, N.Y. Acad. Scis., Muscular Disease Soc. Northeastern Ohio (trustee 1984-86), Dade County Med. Assn., So. Pain Soc., Internat. Assn. Study of Pain, Dartmouth Club Greater Miami, Am. Coun. for Headache Edn. Achievements include research in plasmapheresis in treatment of acute Guillain-Barre Syndrome; repeat neuroimaging in headache when first study normal, migraine with cluster features, hemicrania continua. Office: Ryan Wheeler Headache Treatment Ctr 20601 Old Cutler Rd Miami FL 33189

WHEELER, STEVEN M. lawyer; b. Evanston, Ill., Jan. 5, 1949; AB, Pricneton U., 1971; JD with distinction, Cornell U., 1974. Bar: Ariz. 1974. Mem. Snell & Wilmer, Phoenix, ptnr., 1980—. Mng. editor Cornell Law Review, 1973-74; contbr. articles to profl. jours. Mem. ABA, Order Coif, Phi Kappa Phi. Office: Snell & Wilmer 1 Arizona Ctr Phoenix AZ 85004-0001

WHEELER, SUSAN, poet, educator; b. Pitts., July 16, 1955; d. Ray Barton and Grace Louise (Skeen) W.; m. Philip Furmanski, Aug. 23, 1991; stepchildren: Lisa, Jonathan. BA in Lit., Bennington Coll., 1977; postgrad., U. Chgo., 1979-81. Dir. pub. programs and info. Art Inst. Chgo., 1981-85; freelance cons., editor and writer, 1983-91; dir. pub. affairs art and sci. NYU, 1989-95. CETA writer and instr. Vt. Coun. on the Arts, 1977-78; instr. liberal arts Sch. of Art Inst. Chgo., 1984-85; instr. Poets in Pub. Svc., N.Y.C., 1989-91; instr. New Sch. for Social Rsch., N.Y.C., 1994—; Thornton writer-in-residence Lynchburg Coll., 1995; lectr. Rutgers U., 1995-96, NYU, 1997-98, U. Iowa Writers Workshop, 2000, Princeton U., 1999—. Author: (poetry collections) Bag o' Diamonds, 1993 (winner Poetry Soc. Am. Norma Farber 1st Book award 1994), Smokes, 1998 (Four Way Books award 1998), Source Codes, 2001; poems anthologized in The Best Am. Poetry, 1988, 91, 93, 96, 98 (Pushcart prize 1994), Roth's Poetry Ann., 1990; contbr. poems to jours. including New Yorker, Witness, Slate, New Am. Writing, Paris Rev.; contbr. articles and essays to books and jours. Recipient Grolier award for poetry, 1987, Prize for Poetry, Roberts Found., 1988; Vt. Coun. Arts grantee, 1978-79, Fund for Poetry grantee, 1990; N.Y. Found. for Arts fellow, 1993-95, 97-99, John Simon Guggenheim Found. fellow, 1999-2000. Mem. PEN (membership com.), Acad. Am. Poets, Poetry Soc. Am., Poetry Project at St. Mark's Ch., Poets and Writers, Writers Guild, Nat. Writers Union. Home: 37 Washington Sq W Apt 10A New York NY 10011-9100 E-mail: susanwheeler@earthlink.net.

WHEELER, SUSIE WEEMS, retired educator; b. Cassville, Ga., Feb. 24, 1917; d. Percy Weems and Cora (Smith) Weems-Canty; m. Dan W. Wheeler Sr., June 7, 1941; 1 child, Dan Jr. BS, Fort Valley (Ga.) State U., 1945; MEd, Atlanta U., 1947, EdD, 1978; postgrad., U. Ky., 1959-60; EdS, U. Ga., 1977. Tchr. Bartow County Schs., Cartersville (Ga.) City Schs., 1938-44, Jeanes supr., 1946-58; supr., curriculum dir. Paulding Sch. Sys.-Stephens Sch., Calhoun City, 1958-64; summer sch. tchr. Atlanta U., 1961-63; curriculum dir. Bartow County Schs., 1963-79; ret., 1979. Pres., co-owner Wheeler-Morris Svc. Ctr., 1990—; mem. Ga. Commn. on Student Fin., 1985-95. Coord. Noble Hill-Wheeler Meml. Ctr. Project, 1983—. Recipient Oscar W. Canty Cmty. Svc. award, 1991, Woman in History award Fedn. Bus. and Profl. Women, 1995, New Frontiers Cmty. Svc. award, 1997, Outstanding Achievement for Preserving Georgia Hist., 2000; recognition 50 plus years, Delta Sigma Theta Sorority, Inc., 2002. Mem. AAUW (v.p. membership 1989-91, Ga. Achievement award 1993, Edn. Found. award Cartersville-Bartow br.), Ga. Assn. Curriculum and Supervision (pres.-elect 1973-74, pres. 1974-75, Johnnye V. Cox award 1975), Delta Sigma Theta (pres. Rome alumnae chpt. 1978-80, mem. nat. bd. 1984, planning com. 1988—, Dynamic Delta award 1967, 78), Ga. Jeanes Assn. (pres. 1968-70). Home: 105 Fite St Cartersville GA 30120-3410

WHEELER, THOMAS EDGAR, communications technology executive; b. Redlands, Calif., Apr. 5, 1946; s. Charles Taylor and Martha (Edgar) W.; married; children: Nicole Pierce, David Maxwell. BS, Ohio State U., 1968. Asst. dir. Ohio State U. Alumni Assn., Columbus, 1968-69; v.p. Grocery Mfrs. Am., Inc., Washington, 1969-76; exec. v.p. Nat. Cable TV Assn., 1976-79, pres., chief exec. officer, 1979-85, NABU: The Home Computer Network, 1985-86; chmn., chief exec. officer NuCable Resources Corp., Washington, 1986-94; pres., chief exec. officer Cellular Telecommunications Industry Assn., 1992—. Author: Leadership Lessons from the Civil War, 1999. Bd. trustees John F. Kennedy Ctr. for Performing Arts; bd. dirs. Cibernet Corp., Found. for Nat. Archives, Omni Sky Corp., Pub. Broadcasting Svc. Democrat. Office: Cellular Telecom Ind Assn 1250 Connecticut Ave NW Ste 200 Washington DC 20036-2655

WHEELER, VIRGINIA ANN, secondary school educator; b. Atlanta, May 16, 1954; d. Vincent D. and Carrie L. (Huiet) W. B Music Edn., Shorter Coll., Rome, Ga., 1976; MusM, Ga. State U., Atlanta. Music tchr. Floyd Middle Sch., Mableton, Ga., 1976-85; choral dir. South Cobb H.S., Austell, 1985-99, Dobbins Mid. Sch., Powder Springs, 1999—. Pianist Powder Springs (Ga.) 1st United Meth. Ch. Recipient Heritage Music Festival award, 1989, Fla. Music Fantasy award, Orlando, 1990, Manhattan Skyline Choral Festival, 1991.

Mem. Nat. Music Educators Assn., Am. Choral Dirs. Assn., Ga. Music Educators Assn. Avocations: spending time at the beach, walking, shopping. Office: Dobbins Mid Sch 637 Williams Lake Rd Powder Springs GA 30127-5719

WHEELER, WARREN G(AGE), JR. retired publishing executive; b. Boston, Dec. 6, 1921; s. Warren Gage and Helen (Hoagl) W.; m. Jean Frances Moseley, Feb. 22, 1945; children: Richard, Michael, Ann, Duncan. BS, Bowdoin Coll., 1943; B.J., U. Mo., 1947, MA, 1948. With South Bend (Ind.) Tribune (name changed to Schurz Communications, Inc. 1976), 1948-82, gen. mgr., 1964-71, exec. v.p., 1971-75, pres., 1975-82. Campaign chmn. United Cmty. Svcs., South Bend, 1960, pres., 1964; treas. South Bend Urban League, 1962-63; trustee St. Joseph's Hosp., South Bend, 1969-77; gen. chmn. St. Joseph County (Ind.) Hosp. Devel., 1969-71; deacon, elder, pres. session 1st Presbyn. Ch., South Bend; chmn. bd. trustees United Ch. Marco Island, 1992-93, ch. pres., 1996-99; trustee Marco Healthcare Ctr., 2000-02. With USN, 1943-46. Protestant recipient Brotherhood award South Bend-Mishawaka chpt. NCCJ, 1970 Mem. Am. Newspaper Pubs. Assn., Am. Mgmt. Assn., Newspaper Personnel Relations Assn. (pres. 1955-56), Hoosier State Press Assn. (dir. 1967-70), Inland Daily Press Assn. (pres. 1972, pres. found. 1974-78), South Bend Press Club, Hideaway Beach Club (dir. 1995-2000), Sigma Delta Chi, Kappa Tau Alpha, Kappa Mu. Home: 6000 Royal Marco Way Apt 657 Marco Island FL 34145-1886

WHEELER, WILLIAM EARL, general surgeon; b. Fort Benning, Ga., Feb. 23, 1952; s. Thomas Harvey and Martha (Donaldson) W.; m. Rebecca Sue Shafer, May 6, 1984; children: Thomas Andrew, William Matthew. AA, East Ctrl. C.C., 1972; BS, Millsaps Coll., 1974; MD, U. Miss., 1977. Diplomate Am. Bd. Surgery. From asst. prof. to assoc. prof. Marshall Univ., Huntington, W.Va., 1983-91; staff surgeon VA Med. Ctr., 1983—91; chief surg. svc. VA med. Ctr., 1985—91; staff & burn surgeon Cabell Huntington Hosp., 1983—91; staff surgeon St. Mary's Hosp., 1983—91, Upstate Carolina Med. Ctr., Gaffney, 1991—, chief surg. sect., 1994—95, chief of staff, 1999—2000; staff surgeon Mary Black Meml. Hosp., Spartanburg, 1992—. Asst. clin. prof. surgery Med. Coll. SC, Charleston, SC, 1994—; mem. courtesy staff Spartanburg Regional Med. Ctr., 2001—. Camp physician, committeeman Boy Scouts Am., Huntington, 1986-91; water safety instr. ARC, Decatur, Miss., 1971-80; elder Limestone Presbyn. Ch., Gaffney, 1994-96, fin. com., 1993-2002. Recipient Eagle Scout award, Boy Scouts Am., 1967. Fellow Am. Coll. Surgeons; mem. AMA, Am. Burn Assn., S.C. Med. Assn., So. Med. Assn., Kiwanis (pres. Gaffney chpt. 1997-98). Avocations: golf, swimming, skiing. Home: 118 Greenbriar Dr Gaffney SC 29341-1016 Office: 117 E Montgomery St Gaffney SC 29340-3058

WHEELER, W(ILLIAM) SCOTT, composer, conductor, music educator; b. Washington, Feb. 24, 1952; s. Malcolm Frederick and Aurora Dorothy (Anas) W.; m. Christen Struthers Frothingham, Jan. 5, 1985; children: Margaret Lee, Catherine Elizabeth. BA, Amherst Coll., 1973; MFA, Brandeis U., 1978, PhD, 1984. Artistic dir. Dinosaur Annex Music Ensemble, Boston, 1975—; dir. Cambridge (Mass.) Chorale, 1976-78; tchr. music, condr. Emerson Coll., Boston, 1978—. Composer (choral) A Babe is Born, ,1979, (chamber) Winter Hills, 1987 (Somerville Arts Coun. Commn.), (symphony) Northern Lights, 1987 (Koussevitzky commn.), (opera) The Construction of Boston (libretto by Kenneth Koch), 1989, (choral) The Angle of the Sun, 1994 (Nat. Endowment for the Arts). Guggenheim fellow, 1988-89. Mem. Am. Music Ctr., ASCAP. Episcopalian. Home: 6 Sunset Ave North Reading MA 01864-1427 Office: Emerson Coll Div Performing Arts 120 Boylston St Boston MA 02116-4624 E-mail: scott_wheeler@emerson.edu.

WHEELER, WILMOT FITCH, JR. diversified manufacturing company executive; b. Southport, Conn., June 5, 1923; s. Wilmot Fitch and Hulda Day (Chapman) W.; m. Barbara Rutherfurd, Sept. 30, 1944 (dec. Sept. 1971); children: Wilmot Fitch III, James Alexander, John R. (dec.), Susan; m. Nonnye Landers, Dec. 20, 1973; children: Tracy Lynne, Alexa Margaret. BA, Yale U., 1945; postgrad., NYU, 1947-48; LLD honoris causa, Sacred Heart U., 1999. Staff engr. Stevenson, Jordan & Harrison, Inc. (mgmt. cons.), 1946-51; with Am. Chain & Cable Co., Inc., N.Y.C., 1951-76, pres., chmn., CEO, 1966-76; chmn., dir. Jelliff Corp., Southport, Conn., 1976—; prin. Case & Co. Inc. (mgmt. cons.), 1977-82; trustee Dollar Savs. Bank, 1974-83, chmn., CEO, 1982-83; chmn., trustee, CEO Dollar Dry Dock Savs. Bank, 1983-84. Vice chmn., chmn., bd. dirs., CEO Manhattan Nat. Corp., 1986-90; v.p. William T. Morris Found., 1976—; bd. dirs. Am. Mut. Liability Ins. Co., 1969-89, Am. Policyholders Ins. Co., 1969-89, Am. Dist. Telegraph Co., 1968-88, Bristol Co. of Can. Ltd., 1955-76, Brit. Wire Products Ltd. (Eng.), 1955-76, Cables Automotrices, S.A. (Mexico), 1955-76, Dominion Chain Co. Ltd., 1955-76, FATA, SpA (Italy), 1975-76, Hersey Products Corp., 1976-86, Instrumentos Bristol, S.A. (Mexico), 1955-76, Manhattan Life Ins. Co., 1972-93, Arthur G. McKee & Co., 1972-79, Parsons Controls Ltd., 1955-76, People's Bank, 1988-98, People's Mut. Holdings, 1975-98, Pratt-Read Corp., 1978-85, Pujol y Tarrago S.A. (Spain), 1969-85, Sormir Petroleum, Inc., 1994-98, Union Ctrl. Life Ins. Co., 1990-93, Wilmot F. Wheeler Found., 1944—. Trustee Am. Farm Sch., 1981-93, Bridgeport Hosp., 1977-94, U. Bridgeport, 1978-88. With AUS, 1943-46. Decorated Bronze Star. Mem. Yale Club (N.Y.C.), Country Club Fairfield. Episcopalian. Home: PO Box 429 Southport CT 06490-0429 Office: Jelliff Corp PO Box 758 354 Pequot Ave Southport CT 06490-1369

WHEELESS, LEON LUM, pathology educator; b. Jackson, Miss., Nov. 6, 1935; s. Leon Lum and Frances (King) W.; m. Waldine Marie Jones, Aug. 27, 1957; children: Susan, Diane, Linda. SB, MIT, 1958; MS, U. Rochester, 1962, PhD, 1965. Scientist Bausch & Lomb Corp., Rochester, N.Y., 1958-69, dir. biomed. rsch., 1969-71; assoc. prof. pathology and elec. engring. U. Rochester, 1971-84, prof. elec. engring., 1984-91; dir. analytical cytology divsn. U. Rochester Med. Ctr., 1975-97, prof. pathology and lab. medicine, 1984-97, prof. urology, 1989-97, prof. oncology, 1996-2001, emeritus prof. pathology and lab. medicine and urology, 1997—. Cons. NIH, 1976—. Patentee in field. Frequent NIH grantee, 1972-2000; recipient Gest Lectureship award Am. Soc. Cytology, 1975. Mem. IEEE (sr., Centennial award 1984), Internat. Soc. Analytical Cytology (charter, pres. 1982-84, Disting. Svc. award 1996), Engring. in Medicine and Biology Soc. (pres. 1974-75), Sigma Xi. Avocations: sailing, skiing, camping. Home: 47 Woodcliff Ter Fairport NY 14450-4208 Office: Univ Rochester Med Ctr Dept Pathology Rochester NY 14642-0001 E-mail: leon_wheeless@urmc.rochester.edu.

WHEELEY, NANCY JANINE, librarian; b. Steubenville, Ohio, July 22, 1944; d. B. Otto and Kathleen Marie (Wilson) W. BA, Muskingom Coll., 1966; MLS, U. Pitts., 1967. Spl. projects libr. Miss. U. for Women, Columbus, 1967—. Mem. Lowndes County (Miss.) Rep. Exec. Com., Columbus Arts Coun. Guild, 1996—. Mem. AAUW, Am. Bus. Women's Assn. (pres. 2002-), Miss. Libr. Assn., Pilot Internat. Baptist. Avocations: Lifeline, Columbus Pilgrimage, Antiquities Soc., choral groups, politics. Office: Fant Meml Libr W-1625 Columbus MS 39701

WHEELING, ROBERT FRANKLIN, computer consultant; b. Springboro, Pa., Sept. 10, 1923; s. Alfred Abraham and Louwaive Letty (Hollabaugh) W.; m. Luella Mae Race, June 2, 1951; 1 child, Eric Wayne. BSEE, Pa. State Coll., 1944; MS in Math., U. Rochester, 1949; postgrad., Brown U., 1947-51. Project engr. Eastman Kodak Co., Rochester, N.Y., 1944-47; mathematician Mobil Research and Devel. Corp., Paulsboro, N.J., 1952-70; mgr. computer technology Mobil Oil Corp., N.Y.C., 1971-72; engring. cons. Mobil Research and Devel. Corp., Princeton, N.J., 1973-84; pvt. practice computer cons. Naples, Fla., 1985—. Contbr. chpt. to book Optimizers, 1964; contbr. articles to profl. jours.; patentee in field. Mem. Mathematical Assn. of Am., Assn. for Computing Machinery (lectr. 1963). Avocations: robotics, carpentry. Home and Office: 2718 Shoreview Dr Naples FL 34112-5840

WHEELOCK, DONALD F. music educator, composer; b. Stamford, Conn., June 17, 1940; s. Ralph Douglas and Cynthia (Doliber) W.; children: Ingrid, Sarah, Benjamin; m. Anne Hunter, Feb. 8, 1997. AB, Union Coll., Schenectady, N.Y., 1962; MMus, Yale U., 1966. Instr. music Colgate U., Hamilton, NY, 1966—69; asst. prof. music Amherst (Mass.) Coll., 1969—74; faculty Smith Coll., Northampton, Mass., 1974—, prof. music, 1985—95, Alper Glass prof. music, 1995—. Composer 2 symphonies, 4 string quartets, many solo instrumental, ensemble and orchestral works. Office: Smith Coll Music Dept Northampton MA 01063

WHEELOCK, DOUGLAS H. astronaut, military officer; b. Binghamton, N.Y., May 5, 1960; s. Olin and Margaret Wheelock; m. Cathleen Hollen; 1 child. BS in Applied Scis. and Engring., U.S. Mil. Acad., West Point, N.Y., 1983; MS in Aerospace Engring, Ga. Inst. Tech., 1992. Commd 2d lt. U.S. Army, West Point, NY, 1983; student Army Aviation Sch., Ft. Rucker , Ala., 1983—84; from sect. leader to troop cmmdr. Pacific Theater U.S. Army Aviation; rsch. and devel. engr. Aviation Directorate of Combat Devels., Fort Rucker , Ala.; mem. class 104 U.S. Naval Test Pilot Sch.; from exptl. test pilot to divsn. chief for fixed wing testing of airborne signal and imagery intelligence systems. U.S. Army Aviation Tech. Test Ctr., 1997—98; astronaut NASA Johnson Space Ctr., Houston, 1998—; support engr. for 5 space missions, lead engr, for 2 NASA, 2000—. Named Outstanding Spokesman for Freedom, VFW, 1990, Disting. Grad., U.S. Army Initial Entry Flight Tng. Course, 1984; recipient Gamble award, U.S. Naval Test Pilot Sch., 1995, Group Acheivement award, NASA, 1997. Avocations: baseball, flying, coaching youth sports, hiking, sports. Office: Astronaut Office/CB Johnson Space Ctr Houston TX 77058

WHEELOCK, KEITH WARD, retired consulting company executive, educator; b. Phila., Oct. 17, 1933; s. Ward and Margot Trevor (Williams) W.; m. Susan Bowen Kimball, June 15, 1956 (div. Nov. 1975); children: Helen Fraser, James Voorhees; m. Bente Lorentzen Ott, July 1978 (div. June 1988); m. Georgia Whiddén, May 17, 1997. BA, Yale U., 1955; MA, U. Pa., 1957; MS, MIT, 1972. Fgn. svc. officer Dept. State, Washington, 1960-69; dir. programs and policy divsn. N.Y.C. Housing and Devel. Adminstrn., 1970-71; devel. officer Moody's Investors Svc., Inc., N.Y.C., 1972-74, v.p. internat. ops., 1974-75, exec. v.p., 1975-76; pres. The Fantus Co., Millburn, N.J., 1976-83; mem. Sr. Dun & Bradstreet Mgmt. Group, 1979-83; prin. Wheelock Cons., 1983-88; project dir. Mng. Growth in N.J., 1986-90; assoc. prof. Raritan Valley C.C., 1992—. Rsch. asst. Fgn. Policy Rsch. Inst., U. Pa. Author: Nasser's New Egypt, A Critical Analysis, 1960, New Jersey Growth Management, 1989. Mem. Montgomery (N.J.) Twp. Com., 1986-88; pres. adv. coun. Eisenhower Exch. Fellowship. Sloan fellow MIT, 1972. Home: 325 Mountain View Rd Skillman NJ 08558-2412 E-mail: kwheelock@rcn.com.

WHEELOCK, KENNETH STEVEN, chemist; b. Kansas City, Mo., Sept. 18, 1943; s. Kenneth Lewis and Clara Mae (Hanenkratt) W.; m. Mary Corinne Percy, June 30, 1972; children: Michael Steven, Celeste Marie. BSc, U. Mo., Kansas City, 1965; PhD, Tulane U., New Orleans, 1970; JD magna cum laude, Western New Eng. Coll., 1998. Bar: Mass.; registered patent atty. Chemist Exxon Rsch. & Devel. Labs., Baton Rouge, 1969-72, rsch. chemist, 1972-77, staff chemist, 1977-83, sr. staff chemist, 1983-86; assoc. prof. physics La. State U., 1987; sr. rsch. chemist Phillips Petroleum Co., Bartlesville, Okla., 1987-91; chmn. Prakti Katalysts, 1992-93; patent agt. GE Plastics, Pittsfield, Mass., 1993-98, counsel intellectual property, 1998—. Cons. dept. chemistry Tulane U., New Orleans, 1970-75. Advisor Jr. Achievement, Baton Rouge, 1971; sec. Baton Rouge Orchid Soc., 1983, Bartlesville Gifted and Talented, 1989; vestry St. Stephen's, Pittsfield, 1999-2002. NDEA trainee, Tulane U., New Orleans, 1965-67, NASA fellow, 1967-69. Fellow Am. Inst. Chemists (profl. rels. com. 1991, 92, patents com. 1992); mem. Am. Chem. Soc. (program chmn. petroleum div. 1976-77, Snyder award Legal Ethics 1998), Licensing Execs. Soc., Assn. Univ. Tech. Mgrs., N.Y. Acad. Sci., Sigma Xi. Episcopalian. Achievements include 20 patents; preparation and determination of crystal structure of (211) phase of 123 superconductors; invention of randomly cross-linked smectites, of high surface area supported perovskite catalysts and method for preparation; selective auto exhaust catalysts; theory of finely divided metals; bonding model for zerovalent acetylene and olefin complexes; fluidized catalytic cracking catalysts, sulfur tolerant catalytic reforming. Office: GE Plastics One Plastics Ave Pittsfield MA 01201

WHEELOCK, LARRY ARTHUR, retired engineer, consultant; b. Chgo., Nov. 20, 1938; s. Preston J. and Rozella (Schonert) W.; m. Ruth E. Pruess (div. Sept. 1975); children: John P., J. Robert, William D., Thomas K.; m. Norma Jane Fair, Oct. 22, 1984. BSEE, U. Evansville, 1962. Registered profl. engr., Ind.; cert. instrument rated comml. pilot, airframe and powerplant mechanic with inspection authorization, FAA. Co-op student engr. Naval Avionics Facility, Indpls., 1958-59, Naval Weapons Support Ctr., Crane, Ind., 1959-62, elec. engr., 1963-78, Delco Electronics, Kokomo, 1962-63; sr. mfg. eng. Ford Aerospace & Comm., Bedford, 1979-80; plant engr. Ethyl Corp., Terre Haute, 1980-81; plant mgr. Tredegar Industries/Ethyl Corp., 1981-91. Cons. in field. Patentee in field. Bd. dirs. Hulman Regional Airport Authority, 1991-95, pres., 1992; pres. Greene County Airport Bd. Commrs., Bloomfield, Ind., 1972-81. Mem. IEEE, Aircraft Owners & Pilots Assn., Exptl. Aircraft Assn., AntiquAircraft Assn., Internat. Flying Farmers, Flying Engrs. Internat. (pres. 1994, 95), Mensa, Internat. Assn. Flying Rotarians, Rotary Internat. Avocations: aviation, agriculture, mechanics, amateur radio, computers. Home: 7480 State Road 42 Terre Haute IN 47803-9778 also: PO Box 309 Raymondville TX 78580-0309 E-mail: lawheelock@earthlink.net.

WHEELOCK, THOMAS DAVID, professor chemical engineering; b. Cusi, Chih, Mexico, May 15, 1925; came to U.S., 1938; s. Harry Ellis and Lottie Lucretia (Quist) W.; m. Edra Violet Smith, Aug. 9, 1952; children: David C., Ann K. BS, Iowa State Coll., 1949, PhD, 1958. Sales engr. Chem. Equipment Co. of Calif., Chgo., 1949-51; chem. engr. FMC Corp., Charleston, W.Va., 1951-54; instr. Iowa State U., Ames, Iowa, 1957-58, asst. prof., 1958-61, assoc. prof., 1961-64, prof. chem. engring., 1964-94, univ. prof., 1994—2001, prof. emeritus, 2001—. Editor: Coal Desulfurization/Chemical and Physical Methods, 1977, Processing and Utilization of High-Sulfur Coals III, 1990; patentee in field; contbr. articles to profl. jours. With USN, 1943-46. Recipient The 1990 Gov.'s Sci. Medal for sci. achievement, Iowa, 1991. Fellow Am. Inst. Chem. Engrs., Iowa Acad. Sci.; mem. Am. Chem. Soc., Am. Soc. for Engring. Edn., Soc. Mining, Metallurgy & Exploration, Sigma Xi, Osborn Research Club. Presbyterian. Avocations: photography, travel, genealogy. Home: 437 N Franklin Ave Ames IA 50014-3513 Office: Iowa State U 2114 Sweeney Hl Ames IA 50011-2230

WHEELON, ALBERT DEWELL, physicist; b. Moline, Ill., Jan. 18, 1929; s. Orville Albert and Alice Geltz (Dewell) W.; m. Nancy Helen Hermanson, Feb. 28, 1953 (dec. May 1980); children: Elizabeth Anne, Cynthia Helen; m. Cicely J. Evans, Feb. 4, 1984. B.Sc., Stanford U., 1949; PhD, Mass. Inst. Tech., 1952. Teaching fellow, then rsch. assoc. physics MIT, Boston, 1949-52; with Douglas Aircraft Co., 1952-53, Ramo-Wooldridge Corp., 1953-62; dep. dir. sci. and tech. CIA, Washington, 1962-66; with Hughes Aircraft Co., L.A., 1966-88, chmn., chief exec. officer, 1987-88. Vis. prof. MIT, 1989; mem. Def. Sci. Bd., 1968-76; mem. Pres.'s Fgn. Intelligence, 1983-88; mem. Presdl. Commn. on Space Shuttle Challenger Accident, 1986; trustee Aerospace Corp., 1990-93, Calif. Inst. Tech., Rand Corp., 1993-2001. Author Electromagnetic Scintillation: Vol. 1 and 2, 2001; contbr. 30 papers on radiowave propagation and guidance systems. Recipient R.V. Jones Intelligence award, 1994. Fellow IEEE, AIAA (Von Karman medal 1986, Goddard Astronautics award 1997), Am. Phys. Soc.; mem. NAE, Sigma Chi. Episcopalian. Independent. Address: 181 Sheffield Dr Montecito CA 93108-2242

WHELAN, ELIZABETH ANN MURPHY, epidemiologist; b. N.Y.C., Dec. 4, 1943; d. Joseph and Marion (Barrett) Murphy; m. Stephen T. Whelan, Apr. 3, 1971; 1 child, Christine B. BA, Conn. Coll., 1965; MPH, Yale U., 1967; MS, Harvard U., 1968, ScD, 1971. Coordinator County study Planned Parenthood, 1971-72; research assoc. Harvard Sch. Pub. Health, Boston, 1975-80; exec. dir. Am. Council Sci. and Health, N.Y.C., 1980-92, pres., 1992—. Mem. com. on pesticides and toxics EPA; mem. U.S. Com. of Vital Stats., HHS; mem. Nat. Adv. Com. on Meat and Poultry Inspection USDA; guest lectr. Queen Elizabeth 2 (Cunard Line). Author: Sex and Sensibility, 1973, Making Sense Out of Sex, 1974, Panic in the Pantry, 1975, 92, A Baby?...Maybe, 1975, Boy or Girl?, 1976, The Pregnancy Experience, 1977, Preventing Cancer, 1978, The Nutrition Hoax, 1983, A Smoking Gun, 1984, Toxic Terror, 1984, 86, 93, Balanced Nutrition, 1988; contbr. articles to profl. jours. and consumer publs. Bd. dirs. Food and Drug Law Inst., Nat. Agrl. Legal Fund, Media Inst., N.Y. divsn. Am. Cancer Soc. Recipient Disting. Achievement medal Conn. Coll., 1979, award Am. Pub. Health Assn. Environ., 1992, Disting. Alumnus award Yale U., 1994-95, Ethics award Am. Inst. Chemists, 1996. Mem. APHA (Early Career award 1982, Homer Calver award 1992), Am. Inst. Nutrition, Am. Med. Writers Assn. (Walter Alvarez award 1986), U.S. Com. Vital Stats. Office: Am Council Sci and Health 1995 Broadway Fl 2 New York NY 10023-5882 E-mail: whelan@acsh.org.

WHELAN, JAMES ROBERT, communications executive, international trade and investment consultant, author, educator, mining executive; b. Buffalo, July 27, 1933; s. Robert and Margaret (Southard) W.; children from previous marriage: Robert J., Heather Elizabeth; m. Guadalupe Aguirre, 1990. Student, U. Buffalo, 1951-53, U. R.I., 1955-57; BA, Fla. Internat. U., 1974. Staff corr., fgn. corr., country mgr., divsn. mgr. UPI, Buffalo, 1952-53, staff corr., fgn. corr., country mgr., div. mgr. Providence, 1955-57, Boston, 1957-58, Buenos Aires, Argentina, 1958-61, Caracas, Venezuela, 1961-66, San Juan, P.R., 1966, 68; regional dir. corp. rels., then v.p. ops. ITT World Directories, ITT, 1968-70; Latin Am. corr. Scripps-Howard Newspaper Alliance, Washington, 1970-71; mng. editor Miami (Fla.) News, 1971-73; free-lance writer, 1973-74; pres., editor, pub. Hialeah (Fla.) Pub. Co., 1975-77; v.p., editl. dir. Panax Corp., Washington, 1977-80; v.p., editor Sacramento Union, 1980-82; editor, pub. Washington Times, 1982-84; mng. dir. CBN News, 1985-86; pres. Capital Comm. Internat., 1986—; editor-in-chief Conservative Digest, 1988-89; vice chmn. Inter-Am. Found., Arlington, Va., 1991-94; external affairs advisor Inter-Am. Investment Corp., 1992-93; dir. strategic planning Cocetel Holding, Santiago, Chile, 1993-94; pres. Minera Silver Standard S.A., 1994—, Silver Std., Mex., 1995—. Free-lance writer; scholar World Assn. Internat. Studies, Stanford U., 1999—; vis. prof. Polit. Sci. Inst., U. Chile, 1993-95; assoc. prof. Finis Terrae U., 1993—; adj. prof. U. Md., 1992-93; guest lectr. ednl. instns., including Boston U., U. Miami, Ctrl. U. Venezuela, Cath. U., Andrès Bello U., Chile, U. Chile, U. Tex., Austin, U. Concepcion, U. Santiago; guest prof. U. Fla., 1973. Author: Through the American Looking Glass; Central America's Crisis, 1980, Allende: Death of a Marxist Dream, 1981, Catastrophe in the Caribbean: The Failure of America's Human Rights Policy in Central America, 1984, The Soviet Assault on America's Southern Flank, 1988, Out of the Ashes: Life, Death and Transfiguration of Democracy in Chile, 1833-1988, 1989, Hunters in the Sky, 1991, Desde las Cenizas: Vida, Muerte y Transfiguracion de la Democracia en Chile, 1833-1988, 1993, 2nd edit., 1995. Bd. dirs. Christian Community Service Agy., Miami, 1973, Hialeah-Miami Springs (Fla.) C. of C., 1976-77, Wolf Trap Found., 1984-87; bd. dirs. Nat. Council for Better Edn.; chmn. print media div. United Way campaign, Sacramento, 1981; bd. govs. Council on Nat. Policy, Washington, 1981-87; del. Commn. of Californias, 1981; chmn. Council for Inter-Am. Security Ednl. Inst., 1986-90; mem. spl. task force on pub. safety Greater Washington Bd. Trade; mem. Nat. Commn. on Free and Responsible Media, 1983-84; bd. dirs. Nat. Bus. Consortium for Gifted and Talented Children, 1985-87; bd. govs. Internat. Policy Forum, 1985—; mem. Presdl. Bd. Fgn. Scholarships (Fulbright Commn.), 1986-92, exec. planning com., 1987-92. With Signal Corps U.S. Army, 1953-55. Nieman fellow Harvard U., 1966-67; recipient citation of excellence Overseas Press Club, 1971, Unity award Lincoln U., 1976, Golden Press award Am. Legion Aux., 1977, Freedom award Valley Forge Found., 1981, Bernardo O'Higgins award Chilean Govt., 1990, presented at Chilean Embassy by Amb. Octavio Errazuriz. Mem. Nat. Press Club, Overseas Press Club, Univ. Club (Washington), Georgetown Club, Cosmos Club, Harvard Club (N.Y.C.), Club de Ofcls. de Fuerza Aerea (Santiago), Club Militar Lo Curro (Santiago), Instituto O'Higginiano de Chile.

WHELAN, JOHN WILLIAM, lawyer, law educator, consultant; b. Cleve., Apr. 23, 1922; s. Walter Edmund and Stacia Miriam W.; m. Maryrose Shields, May 29, 1947; children: Moira Ann Whelan Dykstra, Thomas M. AB, John Carroll U., 1943; JD, Georgetown U., 1948. Assoc. prof. law Columbus U., Washington, 1948-50; asst. prof. law U. Va., Charlottesville, 1955-56; asso. prof. law U. Wis., Madison, 1956-59; prof. law Georgetown U., Washington, 1959-67, U. Calif., Davis, 1967-75, Hastings Coll. Law U. Calif., San Francisco, 1975-91; prof. emeritus Hasting Coll. Law U. Calif., 1991—. Vis. prof. Nihon U. Coll. Law, Tokyo, summer 1989; cons. to atty. gen. Trust Ty. Pacific Islands, 1976-78; mem. atomic energy com. Bd. Contract Appeals, 1965-73; hearing examiner Medi-Cal Fiscal Intermediary Contract, 1979-82; adminstrn. law judge constrn. contracts Trust Ter. Pacific Island, 1984-86; cons. on govt. contracts to Polish govt., 1992. Author: (with R.S. Pasley) Federal Government Contracts, 1975; (with K.H. York) Insurance, 1983, 2d edit., 1988, Federal Government Contracts, 1985, 2d edit. 2002, Supplement, 1989, Understanding Government Contracts, 1994; (with K.H. York, Leo Martinez) Insurance, 4th edit., 2001; editor: Yearbook of Procurement Articles, 1965-90; mem. editl. bd. Pub. Procurement Law Rev. (U.K. pub.), 1991—; contbr. articles to profl. jours. Served with inf. AUS, 1943-45; served with J.A.G., 1950-55, Decorated Bronze Star; Ford Found. grantee, 1958-59, 63-64, summer 1970 Mem.: ABA, Fed. Cir. Bar Assn., Bds. of Contract Appeals Bar Assn., Nat. Contract Mgmt. Assn., D.C. Bar Assn., Fed. Bar Assn. Home: 306 Bristol Pl Mill Valley CA 94941-4005 Office: U Calif Hastings Coll Law 200 Mcallister St San Francisco CA 94102-4707

WHELAN, JOSEPH L. neurologist; b. Chisholm, Minn., Aug. 13, 1917; s. James Gorman and Johanna (Quilty) W.; m. Gloria Ann Rewoldt, June 12, 1948; children: Joe, Jennifer. Student, Hibbing Jr. Coll., 1935-38; BS, U. Minn., 1940, MB, 1942, MD, 1943. Diplomate Am. Bd. Psychiatry and Neurology. Intern Detroit Receiving Hosp., 1942-43; fellow neurology U. Pa. Hosp., Phila., 1946-47; resident neurology U. Minn. Hosps., Mpls., 1947-49; chief neurology svc. VA Hosp., 1949; spl. fellow electroencephalography Mayo Clinic, Rochester, Minn., 1951; practice medicine specializing in neurology Detroit, 1949-73, Petoskey and Gaylord, Mich., 1973-87; asst. prof. Wayne State U., 1957-63. Chief neurology svcs. Grace Hosp., St. John's Hosp., Bon Secour Hosp., Detroit; cons. neurologist No. Mich. Hosps., Charlevoix Area Hosp.; instr. Med. Sch. U. Minn., 1949; cons. USPHS, Detroit Bd. Edn. Contbr. articles to profl. jours. Founder, mem. ad hoc Com. to Force Lawyers Out of Govt. Fellow Am. Acad. Neurology (treas. 1955-57), Am. Electroencephalography Soc.; mem. AMA, AAAS, Assn. Rsch. Nervous and Mental Diseases, Soc. Clin. Neurologists, Mich. Neurol. Assn. (sec.-treas. 1967-76, Disting. Physician award 1988), Mich. Med. Soc., No. Mich. Med. Soc., Grosse Pointe (Mich.) Club. Address: 9797 N Twin Lake Rd NE Mancelona MI 49659-9203

WHELAN, RICHARD J. retired academic administrator; b. Emmett, Kans, June 23, 1931; s. Richard Joseph and Margaret Alma (Cox) W.; m. Carol Ann King, Nov. 21, 1959; children— Mark Richard, Cheryl Lynne BA, Washburn U., 1955; Ed.D., U. Kans., 1966. Dir. edn. Menninger Clinic, Topeka, 1959-62; dir. edn. children's rehab. unit U. Kans. Med. Ctr., Kansas City, 1966-99; prof. spl. edn. and pediatrics, chmn. dept. spl. edn. U. Kans., Lawrence, 1966-72, 78-80, 83-88, assoc. dean grad. studies and outreach, 1988-94, Ralph L. Smith disting. prof. child devel., 1968-99, dean sch. edn., 1992-94, prof. emeritus, 1999—; div. dir. U.S. Office Edn., Washington, 1972-74; cons. Blue Valley Sch. Dist., Overland Park, Kans., 1999—; complaint investigator Kans. Bd. of Edn., 2000—. Cons. colls. and univs., state and fed. agys.; chmn. policy bd. Evaluation Tng., Kalamazoo, 1975-81 Author, editor: Promising Practices..., 1983, Emotional and Behavioral Disorders, 1998; cons. editor Ednl. Research Ency., 1982; contbr. articles to profl. jours., chpts. to books Chmn. adv. bd. Kans. Bd. Edn., Topeka, 1982-92; mem. adv. bd. Shawnee Mission Sch. Dist., Kans., 1984-92; mem. Gov.'s Task Force on Early Childhood, 1984-92; hearing officer various sch. dists. Kans. Bd. Edn., Bur. Indian Affiars; mediator and trainer. Mem. Soc. for Learning Disabilities (pres. 1980-81), Council for Exceptional Children, Assn. for Persons with Severe Handicaps (bd. dirs. 1975-79), Kans. Council for Exceptional Children (pres. 1963-64, Service award 1978, award for excellence 2000), Phi Kappa Phi Avocations: reading, music, golf, running, flying. Home: 7400 West 148th St Overland Park KS 66223 E-mail: rwhelan@kumc.edu.

WHELAN, ROGER MICHAEL, lawyer, educator; b. Montclair, N.J., Nov. 12, 1936; s. John Leslie and Helen Louise (Callahan) W.; m. Rosemary Bogdan, Aug. 26, 1961; children: Helen, Theresa, John, James, Kathleen (dec.), Julie, Jennifer. AB cum laude, Georgetown U., 1959, JD, 1962. Bar: D.C. 1962, U.S. Dist. Ct. D.C. 1962, U.S. Ct. Appeals (D.C. cir.) 1962, U.S. Supreme Ct. 1968, U.S. Dist. Ct. Md. 1985. Assoc. Fried, Rogers & Ritz, Washington, 1961-66; ptnr. Doctor & Whelan, 1967-72; judge U.S. Bankruptcy Ct., 1972-83; sr. mem. Verner, Liipfert, Bernhard, McPherson & Hand, Chartered, 1984-89; outside counsel Shaw, Pittman, Potts & Trowbridge, 1989-00, Washington & Md. law firms, 00—. Dir. Lincoln Ctr. for Legal Studies, Arlington, Va., 1974-84; disting. lectr. Columbus Sch. Law, Cath. U. Am., Washington, 1975—; bd. govs. Conf. on Consumer Fin. Law, 1995—. Sec. local campaign com., Alexandria, Va., 1964; trustee YMCAA, Silver Spring, Md., 1972-74. Recipient award D.C. Cir. Jud. Conf., 1984. Fellow:

Am. Coll. Bankruptcy (bd. regents 1989—95, bd. dirs. 1995—2002); mem.: FBA (chmn. bankruptcy subcom. 1988, exec. com. 1993—, pres. 1999—2000), Assn. Former Bankruptcy Judges (sec.-treas. 1996—), Am. Bankruptcy Inst. (bd. dirs. 1991—97, exec. com. 1993—95, chmn. legis. com. 1991—99), Walter Chandler Inn of Ct. (master emeritus 1990—). Republican. Roman Catholic. Avocations: fishing, hunting, boating. Home: 17908 Ednor View Ter Ashton MD 20861-9757

WHELAN, STEPHEN THOMAS, lawyer; b. Phila., July 28, 1947; s. Stephen Thomas and Virginia King (Ball) W.; m. Elizabeth Ann Murphy, Apr. 3, 1971; children: Christine B. Whelan. BA magna cum laude, Princeton U., 1968; JD, Harvard U., 1971. Bar: N.Y. 1972, U.S. Dist. Ct. (so. dist.) N.Y. 1975. Assoc. Mudge Rose Guthrie & Alexander, N.Y.C., 1971-75, Thacher Proffitt & Wood, N.Y.C., 1975-77, ptnr., 1978—, chmn. corp. dept., 1992-97; lectr. politics dept. Princeton U., 1999—. Author: The ABCs of the UCC: Article 2A (Leases), 1997, New York's Uniform Commercial Code Article 2A, 1994; contbr. articles to profl. jours. Bd. dirs. Atlantic Legal Found., 1997—; active N.Y. County Rep. Com., 1985—; active Princeton U. Alumni Coun., 1993—; trustee The Cloister Inn of Princeton U., 1996—. Fellow Am. Coll. Investment Counsel; mem. ABA (chmn. subcom. on leasing 1994—), N.Y. State Bar Assn., Equipment Leasing Assn. Am. (fed. govt. rels. com. 1992-97, legal com. 1995-97), S.R. (bd. dirs. N.Y. 1979—). Roman Catholic. Avocations: road racing, secondary school students mentor, golf. E-mail: SWhelan@tpwlaw.com.

WHELAN, SUSAN, member of parliament; d. Elizabeth and Eugene Whelan. Degree in commerce, U. Windsor, B in Laws, 1988; JD, U. Detroit. Bar: Ont. 1990. Assoc. Yuffy, Roberts, Goldstein, Manzocco, Windsor, 1988-93; M.P. for Essex-Windsor House of Commons, 1993—, parliamentary sec. to Min. Nat. Revenue, 1993-96, mem. standing com. pub. accouts, 1994-96, assoc. mem. standing com. on fin., 1994-96, vice chair fin. com., 1996-97, mem. justice subcom. on draft regulations on firearms, 1996-97, mem. subcom. on rev. of spl. import measures act, 1996, chair industry com., 1997—2002. Former dir. Essex Region Conservation Found., Alzheimer Soc. Windsor and Essex County. Named "Hon. Susan E. Whelan", Minister for Internat. Coop., 2002. Mem. Law Soc. Upper Can., Can. Bar Assn., Essex County Law Assn. Office: 109 Justice Bldg Ottawa ON Canada K1A 0A6*

WHELAN, VERONICA, family practice physician, geriatrician; b. San Diego, Apr. 27, 1950; d. Charles Peter and Elora Alice (Biggs) W.; m. A. Baldwin Keenan, June 26, 1971; children: Lee Richard, Nora Briana, Claire Simone, Keenan Whelan. BA in Math., U. Calif., Irvine, 1972, MD, 1981. Diplomate Am. Bd. Family Practice, Am. Bd. Geriatric Medicine. Staff physician Talbert Med. Group (formerly FHP Health Care, Santa Ana, Calif., 1984—. Assoc. prof. U. Calif. Irvine Med. Sch., 1985— Mem. Am. Acad. Family Physicians, Assn. Clin. Faculty. Office: Talbert Med Group 1002 N Fairview St Santa Ana CA 92703-1811

WHELAN, WILLIAM PAUL, retired research scientist; b. Brooklyn, Ny, Sept. 22, 1923; s. William Paul and Clara Florence Whelan; m. Margaret Helena Flynn (dec. Oct. 18, 1983); children: Christine, William, Mark. AB, Coll. of the Holy Cross, Worcester, MA, 1943, MS, 1947; PhD, Columbia Univ., New York, NY, 1952. Rsch. chemist Uniroyal, Inc., Wayne, NJ, 1952—66, sr. rsch. scientist Middlebury, 1966—85. Author: (paper) Journal of Fire Retardent Chemistry. 1st leutenant USAF, 1943—46, Africa. Mem.: Am. Chem. Soc. Achievements include patents for Inventor, 12 Patents, 1961-1994. Avocations: singing, gardening, studying languages, playing table tennis. Home: 27 Orchard Lane Woodbury CT 06798-3918

WHELAN, WINIFRED OLWYN, theology studies educator; b. Chgo. d. Francis Whelan and Mary Agnes Quinn. BA, Alverno Coll., 1953; MA, Marquette U., 1968; PhD, Northwestern U., 1985. Tchr. religion St. Benedict Sch., Chgo., 1966—70; dir. religious edn. St. Dismas Ch., Waukegan, 1970—72, St. Linus Ch., Oak Lawn, 1972—74, St. Dismas Ch., Winnetka, 1974—79; prof. theology St. Bonaventure (N.Y.) U., 1985—2002. Contbr. articles to profl. jours. Mem.: Coll. Theology Soc. Home and Office: 2572 W Argyle Chicago IL 60625-2604 E-mail: whelan@sbu.edu.

WHELCHEL, BETTY ANNE, lawyer; b. Augusta, Ga., Dec. 22, 1956; d. John Davis and Charnell (Ramsey) W.; m. Douglas Charles Kruse, June 20, 1987. AB, U. Ga., 1978; JD, Harvard U., 1981. Bar: D.C. 1981, N.Y. 1984, gaikokuho-jimu-bengoshi (fgn. lawyer) Japan, 1988-89. Atty.-advisor U.S. Dept. Treasury, Washington, 1981-84; assoc. Shearman & Sterling, N.Y.C., 1984-87, 89-90, Tokyo, 1987-89; dep. gen. counsel Deutsche Bank N.Am., N.Y., 1990—; lead counsel Deutsche Bank Asset Mgmt., 1999—. Staff atty. Depository Instns. Deregulation Com., Washington, 1983-84. Mem. Assn. of the Bar of the City of N.Y. (com. on diversity, com. on fgn. and comparative law 1992-97, chmn. 1996-99, coun. on internat. affairs 1996-99). Office: Deutsche Bank AG 345 Park Ave New York NY 10154 E-mail: betty.a.whelchel@db.com.

WHELCHEL, SANDRA JANE, writer; b. Denver, May 31, 1944; d. Ralph Earl and Janette Isabelle (March) Everitt; m. Andrew Jackson Whelchel, June 27, 1965; children: Andrew Jackson, Anita Earlyn. BA in Elem. Edn., U. No. Colo., 1966; postgrad., Pepperdine Coll., 1971, UCLA, 1971. Elem. tchr. Douglas County Schs., Castle Rock, Colo., 1966-68, El Monte (Calif.) schs., 1968-72; br. libr. Douglas County Librs., Parker, Colo., 1973-78; zone writer Denver Post, 1979-81; reporter The Express newspapers, Castle Rock, 1979-81; history columnist Parker Trail newspapers, 1985-93; columnist Gothic Jour., 1994; writing tchr. Aurora Parks and Recreation, 1985-91; writing instr. Arapahoe C.C., 1991-2000; exec. dir. Nat. Writers Assn., 1991—. Lectr. on writing and history Durango Writer's Workshop, 1996-97, Estes Park Writer's Retreat, 1996-97, Pikes Peak Writer's Workshop, 1997, Sinipee Writer's Workshop, 1998, Oasis for Seniors, 2000, Denver Women's Press Club, 1999, Rocky Mountain Gold Conf., 1999, Colo. Writers Fellowship, 2000, Colo. Ind. Publishers, 2000; spkr. Internat. Olympiad of Mind, Paris, 2000. Editor Authorship mag., 1992-98; lit. agent NWLA, 1996-99; contbr. short stories and articles to various publs. including: Genre Sampler, Writer's World, Writer's Open Forum, Writer's Jour., Reunions, Fresno Bee, Ancestry Newsletter, Empire mag., Calif. Horse Rev., Host mag., Jack and Jill, Child Life, Children's Digest, Peak to Peak mag.; author (non-fiction books): Your Air Force Academy, 1982, A Guide to the U.S. Air Force Acad., 1990, Parker, Colorado: A Folk History, 1990, The Beginning Writer's Writing Book, 1996, A Folk History of Parker and Hilltop, 1996; co-author: The Writer's Office, 1998, The Register, 1989, (coloring books) A Day at the Cave, 1985, A Day in Blue, 1984, Pro Rodeo Hall of Champions and Museum of the American Cowboy, 1985, Pikes Peak Country, 1986, Mile High Denver, 1987. Mem.: Colo. Author's League (awards com. 1999—2000, who's who com. 2001), Parker Area Hist. Soc. (pres. 1987—89), Nat. Writer's Club (treas. Denver Metro chpt. 1985—86, v.p. membership 1987, sec, 1990, bd. dirs., pres. 1990—91, v.p. programs 1992, v.p. membership 2002). *Personal philosophy: Tenacity and perseverance are keys to success. Optimism and self-belief open the door. The goals achieved through these elements are the most thrilling and savory.*

WHELESS, JAMES WARREN, neurologist; b. Glens Falls, N.Y., Apr. 18, 1956; s. True and Adelphine Ada (Bump) W.; m. Annette Carolyn Hyland, Apr. 7, 1984; children: Catherine Elizabeth, Margaret Caroline. BS, U. Okla., Oklahoma City, 1978, MD, 1982. Diplomate Am. Bd. Pediatrics, Am. Bd. Psychiatry and Neurology with spl. qualification in child neurology, with spl. qualification in clin. neurophysiology. Intern, then pediatric resident U. Okla.-Tulsa Med. Coll., 1982-85; fellow in child neurology Northwestern U., Chgo., 1985-88; fellow in clin. neurophysiology/epilepsy Med. Coll. Ga., Augusta, 1988-89; asst. prof. neurology and pediatrics U. Tex., Houston, 1989-95, dir. epilepsy monitoring unit, 1989—, assoc. prof. neurology and pediatrics, 1995-2000, prof. neurology and pediats., 2000—; dir., dir. pedia. epilepsy sect., head clin. EEG Tex. Comprehensive Epilepsy Program, 1998—. Exec. bd. internat. epilepsy consortium Nat. Tuberous Sclerosis Assn. Contbr. articles to profl. jours., chpt. to book; mem. editl. bd.: Jour. of Child Neurology, The Stroke Interventionalist, Formulary. Camp physician Kamp Kleidoscope, Livingston, Tex., 1995—; mem. profl. bd. Nat. Tuberous Sclerosis Assn., Citizens United for Rsch. in Epilepsy; mem. exec. bd. Internat. Epilepsy Consortium. Pres.'s Fund grantee U. Tex.-Houston, 1990, Children's Miracle Network Telethon grantee Hermann Children's Hosp.; rsch. grantee NIH. Fellow Am. Acad. Neurology, Child Neurology Soc.; mem. AMA, Am. Epilepsy Soc., Am. Acad. Pediatrics, Epilepsy Assn. of Houston/Gulf Coast (chmn. profl. adv. bd. 1992-94). Avocations: running, camping, hiking, travel, reading. Office: U Tex-Houston Dept Neurology 6431 Fannin St Ste 7044 Houston TX 77030-1501

WHELIHAN, ALAN STUART, real estate developer, automotive executive; b. Phila., Sept. 17, 1932; s. John Franklin and Dorothy Dodge W.; m. Joan Murrell, June 20, 1959; children: Pamela, Deborah, Linda, Jacqueline. BS in Engring., Princeton U., 1954; MBA, U. Pa., 1960. Elect. engr. Philco Corp., Phila., 1954-55; product line mgr. govt. and indsl. divsn. RCA, Camden, N.J., 1959-65; gen. mgr. Chem. Micromilling Co., Pensauken, 1965-66; mgmt. cons. Peat Marwick Mitchell & Co., Washington, 1966-72; asst. commr. Fed. Supply Svc., Arlington, Va., 1973-79; dir. planning and coordination U.S. Metric Bd., 1979-82; dir. metric program U.S. Dept. Commerce, Washington, 1983-94; pres. VAW, LLC, Frederick, Md., 1994—. Dir. Am. Nat. Stds. Inst., 1973-75, Am. Nat. Metric Coun., Washington, 1990-92. Lt. Comdr. USNR, 1955-57. Mem. IEEE (sr. mem.), Soc. Automotive Engrs. (metric adv. bd. 1990—), Congl. Country Club. Republican. Avocation: collecting antique automobiles. Office: W Properties LLC Stanford Indsl. Park 4975 Winchester Blvd Frederick MD 21703-7400 Home: 3009 Anna's Terrace Frederick MD 21703

WHELPLEY, DAVID B., JR. lawyer; b. Akron, Ohio, Apr. 21, 1964; s. David B. and JoAnn D. Whelpley; m. Teresa E. Dugger, Oct. 21, 1989; children: David III, Austin, Hannah. BS cum laude, Clemson U., 1986; JD, Emory U., 1989. Bar: N.C. 1989, Ga. 1989. Ptnr. Kilpatrick Stockton LLP, Charlotte, NC, 1989—. Advisor Legal Svcs. N.C., Raleigh, 1997—98. Mem. exec. bd. Theatre Charlotte, 1995—2002; bd. dirs. Mecklenburg County Register Deeds Adv. Bd., 1995—2002. Mem.: ABA (mem. com.), N.C. Bar Assn. (mem. com.). Avocations: travel, skiing, hiking. Office: Kilpatrick Stockton LLP 3500 One Wachovia Ctr 301 S College St Charlotte NC 28202-6000

WHELPLEY, DENNIS PORTER, lawyer; b. Mpls., Feb. 16, 1951; s. John Olsen and Harriet Marie (Porter) W.; m. Patricia Jan Adamy, Nov. 27, 1976; children: Heather Nicolle, Christopher Eric. BA, U. Minn., 1973, JD magna cum laude, 1976. Bar: Minn. 1976. Assoc. Oppenheimer Wolff & Donnelly, St. Paul, 1976-83, ptnr., 1983—. Mem. Order of Coif (Minn. chpt.), Phi Beta Kappa (Alpha of Minn. chpt.), Psi Upsilon (Mu chpt.), Dellwood Hills Golf & Country Club. Avocations: golf, tennis, squash, bridge. Home: 49 Locust St Mahtomedi MN 55115-1542 Office: Oppenheimer Wolff & Donnelly 45 S 7th St Ste 3300 Minneapolis MN 55402-1614 E-mail: dwhelpley@oppenheimer.com.

WHELPLEY, WILLIAM ALBERT, management consultant, educator; b. Iowa City, Oct. 7, 1963; s. William Albert Sr. and Sara Gayle Whelpley. BS in Econs. and History, Carnegie Mellon U., 1985, MS in Finance, 1989. Asst. economist Fed. Reserve Bank of Richmond, Va., 1985-87; prin. Whlpley Assoc., Inc., Princeton, N.J., 1987-92; v.p. Cowen & Co., N.Y.C., 1992-95; ind. cons. Donaldson, Lufkin & Jenrette, 1995-96; adj. prof. mgmt. N.Y. Poly. Inst., Bklyn., 1996-98; mng. cons. Renaissance Worldwide, Inc., N.Y.C., 1996-99; ptnr. Batman-Burke & Co., Iselin, N.J., 1999—; prin. NetsUP, Inc., 1999—. Featured spkr., UNIX Expo+, N.Y.C., 1996. Contbr. articles to profl. jours. Alumni advisor Carnegie Mellon U., Pitts., 1985—. Office: NetsUP Inc 14 Commerce Dr Cranford NJ 07016 E-mail: ww2j@msn.com., whelpley@netsup-usa.com.

WHETTEN, JOHN D. food products executive; b. Chgo., June 8, 1940; s. Lester and Kate (Allred) W.; m. Becky Pearse; children: Carma, Rebecca, Mary Coza. BS, Brigham Young U., 1965; MBA, U. Calif., Berkeley, 1967. Advt. and mktg. mgr. The Clorox Corp., Oakland, Calif., 1967-79; pres., CEO Challenge Dairy Products, Inc., Dublin, 1982—; CEO DairyAmerica, Inc., 1995-98. U.S. rep. Internat. Dairy Mktg. and Promotion Ann. Meeting, 1996. Co-chair U.S. Butter Task Force, 1990—97; mem. nat. steering com. Brigham Young U. Sch. Mgmt., 1992—95; mem. nat. adv. coun. Utah Valley State Coll., 1999—2001; bd. dirs. U.S. Diry Export Coun., 1995—98, Epidermolysis Bullosa Med. Rsch. Found., 1991—. Mem.: Western Assn. Milk Mktg. Coop. (bd. dirs. 1992—2002, sec. 1994—2002), Barbecue Industry Assn. (dir. 1974—79, pres. 1977—78), Dairy Mktg. Coop. Fedn. (pres. 1992—), Dairy Export Incentive Program Coalition (pres. 1994—), Am. Dairy Products Inst. (bd. dirs. 1982—98, hon. life dir. 1999—), Am. Butter Inst. (bd. dirs. 1982—, v.p. 1995—99, pres. 1999—2001, Pres.'s Disting. Svc. award 1991). Office: Challenge Dairy Products Inc 11875 Dublin Blvd Ste B230 Dublin CA 94568-2818 E-mail: john@challengedairy.com.

WHETTEN, JOHN THEODORE, geologist, researcher; b. Willimantic, Conn., Mar. 16, 1935; s. Nathan Laselle and Theora Lucille (Johnson) W.; m. Carol Annette Jacobsen, July 14, 1960; children— Andrea, Krista, Michelle. AB with high honors, Princeton U., 1957, PhD, 1962; MS, U. Calif., Berkeley, 1959. Mem. faculty U. Wash., Seattle, 1963-81, research instr. oceanography, 1963-64, asst. prof., 1964-68, assoc. prof., 1968-72, prof. geol. scis. and oceanography, 1972-81, chmn. dept. geol. scis., 1969-74; assoc. dean Grad. Sch., 1968-69; geologist U.S. Geol. Survey, Seattle, 1975-80; asst. div. leader geoscis. div. Los Alamos Nat. Lab., 1980-81, dep. div. leader earth and space scis. div., 1981-84, div. leader earth and space scis. div., 1984-86, assoc. dir. energy and tech., 1986-92, assoc. dir. quality, policy and performance, 1992-93; lab. affiliate, 1994—; cons. in nat. lab. partnerships and tech. transfer Motorola Corp., 1994-97; sr. cons. Motorola U., 1998-2001, Motorola Labs, 2001—. Mem. adv. com. Pacific N.W. Nat.. Lab., 1999—. Contbr. articles to profl. jours. Fulbright fellow, 1962-63 Home and Office: 381 Kings Point Rd Lopez Island WA 98261-8223 E-mail: johnandcarol@rockisland.com.

WHETTEN, LAWRENCE L. international relations educator; b. Provo, Utah, June 12, 1932; s. Lester B. and Kate (Allred) W.; m. Gabriele Indra, Oct. 28, 1974 (dec. May 1985). BA, Brigham U., 1954, MA, 1955; PhD with honors, NYU, 1963. Sr. polit. analyst Hdqrs. USAFE, Wiesbaden, Fed. Republic Germany, 1963-70; resident dir. grad. program in internat. relations U. So. Calif., Munich, Fed. Republic Germany, 1971-78, dir. studies USC/SIR grad. program in Germany Fed. Republic Germany, 1978-86; Erich Voegelin Gast prof. Munich U., 1987-88; lectr. Boston U., 1988—; lectr. Profl. Assoc. Ctr. Def. and Strategic Studies S.W. Mo. State U., Springfield, 1991—. Cons. Fgn. Policy Inst., Phila., 1969-71, 76-79, R & D Assocs., Munich, 1977; prof. Hochschule für Politik, Munich U.; adj. prof., profl. assoc. Ctr. for Def. and Strategic Studies, S.W. Mo. State U., 1991—. Author: Germany's Ostpolitik, 1971, Contemporary American Foreign Policy, 1974, The Canal War: Four Power Conflict, 1974, Germany East and West, 1981. Author, editor: Present State Communist Internationalism, 1983, The Interaction of Political Reforms Within the East Block, 1989. Served to capt. USAF, 1960-63 Penfield fellow NYU, 1957-59; grantee Ford Found., 1970, Royal Inst. Internat. Affairs, London, 1970, Thyssen Found., Cologne, Germany, 1974-82, 89, Volkswagen Found., 1982-85 Mem. Am. Acad. Polit. and Social Scis., Internat. Inst. Strategic Studies, Am. Assn. Advancement of Soviet Studies, Gesellschaft für Auslandskunde, German Am. Assn. Home: Widenmayerstrasse 41 80538 Munich Germany

WHICHARD, WILLIS PADGETT, law educator, former state supreme court justice; b. Durham, N.C., May 24, 1940; s. Willis Guilford and Beulah (Padgett) W.; m. Leona Irene Paschal, June 4, 1961; children: Jennifer Diane, Ida Gilbert. AB, U. N.C., 1962, JD, 1965; LLM, U. Va., 1984, SJD, 1994. Bar: N.C. 1965. Law clk. N.C. Supreme Ct., Raleigh, 1965-66; ptnr. Powe, Porter, Alphin & Whichard, Durham, 1966-80; assoc. judge N.C. Ct. Appeals, Raleigh, 1980-86; assoc. justice N.C. Supreme Ct., 1986-98; dean and prof. law Campbell U. Instr. grad. sch. bus. adminstrn. Duke U., 1978; vis. lectr. U. N.C. Sch. Law, 1986-98. Contbr. articles to profl. jours. Rep. N.C. Ho. of Reps., Raleigh, 1970-74; senator N.C. Senate, 1974-80, chair numerous coms. and commns.; N.C. legis. rsch. commn., 1971-73, 75-77, land policy coun., 1975-79; bd. dirs. Sr. Citizens Coordinating Coun., 1972-74; chair local crusade Am. Cancer Soc., 1977, state crusade chair, 1980, chair pub. issues com., 1980-84; pres., bd. chmn. Downtown Durham Devel. Corp., 1980-84; bd. dirs. Durham County chpt. ARC, 1971-79; Durham county campaign dir. March of Dimes, 1968, 69, chmn., 1969-74, bd. dirs. Triangle chpt., 1974-79; bd. advisors Duke Hosp., 1982-85, U. N.C. Sch. Pub. Health, 1985-96, U. N.C. Sch. Social Work, 1989—; bd. visitors N.C. Ctrl. U. Sch. Law, 1987—; mem. law sch. dean search com. U. N.C., 1978-79, 88-89, self-study com., 1985-86; pres. N.C. Inst. Justice, 1984-94; bd. dirs. N.C. Ctr. Crime and Punishment, 1984-94. Staff sgt. N.C. Army NG, 1966-72. Recipient Disting. Service award Durham Jaycees, 1971, Outstanding Legis. award N.C. Acad. Trial Lawyers, 1975, Outstanding Youth Service award N.C. Juvenile Correctional Assn., 1975, Citizen of Yr., Eno Valley Civitan Club, Durham, 1982, Faith Active in Pub. Life award N.C. Council of Churches, 1983, Outstanding Appellate Judge award N.C. Acad. Trial Lawyers, 1983, inducted Durham High Sch. Hall of Fame, 1987. Mem. ABA, N.C. Bar Assn. (v.p. 1983-84, 2001-02), Durham County Bar Assn., U. N.C. Law Alumni Assn. (pres. 1978-79, bd. dirs. 1979-82), Nat. Guard Assn. (judge advocate 1972-73, legis. com. 1974-76), Order of Golden Fleece, Order of Grail, Order of Old Well, Amphoterothen Soc., Order of Coif, Phi Alpha Theta, Phi Kappa Alpha. Clubs: Durham-Chapel Hill Torch (pres. 1984-85), Watauga (Raleigh, pres. 1994-95). Democrat. Baptist. Home: 5608 Woodberry Rd Durham NC 27707-5335 Office: Wiggins Sch Law Campbell Univ PO Box 158 Buies Creek NC 27506-0158 E-mail: Whichard@webster.campbell.edu., whichoo1@earthlink.net.

WHIDDEN, ROBERT LEE, JR. healthcare consultant; b. Beverly, Mass., Oct. 10, 1943; s. Robert Lee and Phyllis Alma (Patch) W.; m. Lois Ann Lapeza, Mar. 4, 1972. AB in English, Harvard U., 1965. Div. dir. Lowell (Mass.) Gen. Hosp., 1970-75; asst. adminstr. Union Hosp., Lynn, Mass., 1975-85; pres. Surgi/1 div., 1984-86, R.L. Whidden and Co., Andover, Mass., 1986—. Query, Andover, 1986—. Prin. cons. Charlton Meml. Hosp., Fall River, Mass., 1987—, Boston Regional Med. Ctr., Stoneham, Mass., 1988—; hosp. rep. delegated rev. com. Eastern Mass. Profl. Standards Rev. Orgn., bd. dirs., 1984—; ex-officio mem. Integrated Data Demonstration Grant Com. Blue Cross Mass., 1982—; health care advisor Govt. of Anguilla, Brit. West Indies, 1989-91; cons. health affairs Brit. Dept. Territories, 1990—. Bd. dirs. Lowell Area Continuing Edn. Ctr., Nat. Found. Environ. Control, 1971, Hospice of North Shore, Inc.; bd. dirs., chmn. Northshore Manpower Coalition; mem. corp. edn. adv. bd. North Shore Community Coll., 1981—; mem. North Shore Econ. Coun., 1981—; mem. Mass. Health Data Adv. Council. Nat. Merit scholar, 1960-61; named to Hon. Order Ky. Cols. Mem. Am. Coll. Health Care Execs. (diplomate), Mass. Hosp. Assn. (mem. program rev. com. 1982—, chmn. mgmt. com. 1984—, mem. facilities and svc. com. class of 1987), New Eng. Hosp. Assembly, Am. Soc. Law and Medicine, Health Care Mgmt. Assn., Am. Mgmt. Assn., Order Paul Revere Patriots, Phi Beta Kappa, Myopia Polo Club (patron), Hasty Pudding Club, Andover Tennis Club. Episcopalian. Home and Office: 3 Spruce Cir Andover MA 01810-4020 E-mail: rwhidden@aol.com.

WHIFFEN, JAMES DOUGLASS, surgeon, educator; b. N.Y.C., Jan. 16, 1931; s. John Phillips and Lorna Elizabeth (Douglass) W.; child from a previous marriage, Gregory James; m. Sally Vilas Runge, Aug. 21, 1993. BS, U. Wis., 1952, MD, 1955. Diplomate: Am. Bd. Surgery. Intern Ohio State U. Hosp., 1955-56; resident U. Wis. Hosp., 1956-57, 59-61; instr. dept. surgery U. Wis. Med. Sch., 1962-64, asst. prof., 1964-67, asso. prof., 1967-71, prof., 1971-96, vice chmn. dept., 1970-72, acting chmn., 1972-74; asst. dean Med. Sch., 1975-96; prof. emeritus U. Wis. Med. Sch., 1996—; mem. exam. council State of Wis. Emergency Med. Services, 1974-77. Bd. dirs. Wis. Heart Assn. Served to lt. comdr. USNR, 1957-59. John and Mary R. Markle scholar in acad. medicine, also; Research Career Devel. award NIH, 1965-75 Fellow A.C.S., Am. Soc. Artificial Internal Organs. Clubs: Maple Bluff Country. Achievements include research publs. on biomaterials, thrombo-resistant surfaces and the physiology of heart-lung bypass procedures. Home: 17 Cambridge Ct Madison WI 53704-5906 Office: 600 Highland Ave Madison WI 53792-0001 E-mail: JWhiffen@facstaff.wisc.edu.

WHIGHAM, MARK ANTHONY, computer scientist; b. Mobile, Ala., Jan. 14, 1959; s. Tommie Lee Sr. and Callie Mae (Molette) W. BS in Computer Sci., Ala. A&M U., 1983, MS in Computer Sci., 1990; postgrad., Ala. A&M Univ., 1995—. Computer programmer U.S. Army Corps of Engrs., Huntsville, Ala., 1985-88; programmer analyst, coord. acad. computing Ala. A&M U., Normal, 1988-89, programmer analyst II, DEC systems coord., instr. part-time computer sci. dept., 1989-91; systems engr. Advanced Bus. Cons. Inc.-La. div. Dow Chem. Co., 1991-93; owner Whigham's Computer Cons., 1990—; sys. engr. DOW Chem. Co.-USA La. Divsn., Plaquemine, La., 1991-93; instr. computer info. system Calhoun C.C., Decatur, Ala., 1993-97; network specialist/cons. Ala. A&M U., Normal, 1994—; computer info. sys. instr. Calhoun C.C., Decatur, Ala., 1994—; mgmt. info. sys. dir., CIO J.F. Drake Tech. Coll., Huntsville, 1997-98; software engr. Colsa Corp., 1998—99; dir. info. tech. Lane Coll., 1999—2000; instr. computer sci. Lawson State CC, 2000—. Instr. computer sci. dept. Ala. A&M U., 1989-91; network specialist, cons. Ala. A&M U., Normal, 1994—. Active Huntsville Interdenominational Ministerial Fellowship, Huntsville, 1984. Mem. Nat. Assn. Sys. Programmers, Ala. Coun. for Computer Edn., Assn. for Computing Machinery, Huntsville Jaycees, Nat. Soc. Black Engrs., Assn. Info. Tech. Profls., So. Poetry Assn., Nat. Arts Soc., Internat. Black Writers and Artists Assn., Optimists, U.S. Chess Fedn. (cert. chess coach), Future Bus. Leaders of Am.-Phi Beta Lambda, Sigma Tau Epsilon, Alpha Phi Omega. Baptist. Avocations: chess, skating, reading, playing piano. Office: Lawson State CC 3060 Wilson Rd Birmingham AL 35209-1542 Home: Apt 202 917 Valley Ridge Dr Birmingham AL 35209-1542 Office Fax: 205-929-6362. Business E-Mail: mwhigham@cougar.ls.cc.al.

WHILDIN, DONNA, retired medical/surgical nurse; b. Altoona, Pa., May 28, 1939; d. Arthur M. and Laura (Temple) Kyper; children: Michael, Lori, Ann Marie. AS, Cumberland County Coll., Vineland, N.J., 1969. Staff nurse, relief night supr. Newcomb Med. Ctr.; staff nurse Millville (N.J.)-South Jersey Hosp. System, Bridgeton-South Jersey Hosp. System, ret., 2001. Mem. AACCN.

WHILDIN, LEONORA PORRECA, nurse midwife, nursing; b. Boston, Dec. 7, 1926; d. John and Anna (Annunziata) Porreca; m. William Miller Whildin; children: Susan Lee, Robert Miller, Walter Thomas. BS, Boston U., 1954; MS, Columbia U., 1971. RN, Mass., N.Y., N.J.; cert. nurse midwife, N.Y. Cadet nurse corps. Boston City Hosp., 1943-46, staff, asst. head nurse neurology, neurosurgery, 1946-48, scrub nurse neurosurgery, 1948-50; civilian nurse Dept. of Army, Bremerhaven, Germany, 1948; pub. health nurse Bklyn. Vis. Nurse Assn., 1954-56; instr. Helene Fulde Sch. of Practical Nursing, N.Y., 1956-57; pub. health nurse V.N.A. Morris Co., Morristown, N.J., 1967; instr. All Souls Hosp. Sch. of Nursing, 1968-69; guest lectr. Seton Hall U., South Orange, 1978. Del. Am. Nurses Assn, Mass., 1954; By-Laws Com. Am. Coll. Nurse Midwives, N.Y., 1972, By-Laws Com. Am. Coll. Nurse Midwives (N.J. chpt.), 1980; bd. mem. V.N.A. Morris Co., Morristown, N.J., 1977-78; v.p. bd. health, Randolph Twp., Randolph, N.J., 1972-74. Coun. woman Randolph Twp., 1972-78; mayor (1st woman mayor) Randolph Twp., 1977; Dem. party county com., Morris Co., Morristown, N.J., 1972-96; Dem. party state com., N.J., 1992-98; vol. United Way of Morris County. Mem. APHA, ANA, LWV, Mass., N.Y., N.J. (bd. mem. 1964-66), Sigma Theta Tau. Democrat. Avocations: ice skating, knitting, crafts, baking. Home: 82 Radtke Rd Randolph NJ 07869-3815

WHILLOCK, DAVID EVERETT, communication educator, dean, consultant; b. Fayetteville, Ark., Oct. 9, 1952; s. Everett Andrew and Bernelle Louise (Wilson) W.; m. Rita Gayle Kirk, June 30, 1978; 1 child, Robert Kirk. BA, Hendrix Coll., 1976; MA, U. Ark., 1979; PhD, U. Mo., 1986. Prof. film, TV Kearney (Nebr.) State Coll., 1979-80; prof. film, TV, video Stepehn F. Austin State U., Nacogdoches, Tex., 1980-84, U. Ala., Huntsville, 1986-91, Tex. Christian U., Ft. Worth, 1991—, interim dean Coll. Comm., 1999—2002, assoc. dean Coll. Comm., 2002—; mgr. Sta. KTCU, 1994-99. Prodr. Speakinc Corp., Huntsville, 1980-90, Bransby Prodns., Huntsville, 1987-90; cons. Ronnie Flippo for Gov. campaign, Huntsville, 1989-90, Bill Smith for Senate campaign, Huntsville, 1989-90, Jennings Outdoors, Huntsville, 1990. Producer TV commls., videos; dir. plays, TV series Women in Focus, 1980-84. Mem. Huntsville Arts Coun., 1990, Van Cliburn Found., 1999—. Grantee Tex. Endowment for Humanities, 1985. Mem. Am. Film Inst., Soc. Cinema Studies, Univ. Film and Video Assn., Collegiate Players, Popular Culture Assn., Nat. Comm. Assn., Profl. Assn. Dive Instrs., Nat. Assn. Underwater Instrs. Avocations: photography, white-water rafting, camping, hiking, scuba diving. Home: 4150 Woodside Knls Grapevine TX 76051-6518 Office: Tex Christian U Coll Comm Fort Worth TX 76129

WHINERY, MICHAEL ALBERT, physician; b. Watsford, Eng., June 30, 1951; s. Leo Howard and Doris Eileene W. and Alma Piper; m. Tatijana Dunnebier, 1976 (dec. Jan. 1981); m. Judy Renee Wright, Apr. 30, 1982; children: Rhiannon Daire Eileene, Terron Rae Lee. BS, Okla. U., 1976; D of Osteopathy, Okla. State U., 1980. Diplomate Am. Bd. Family Practice. Intern Hillcrest Health Ctr., Oklahoma City, 1980-81; with McLoud Clinic, McLoud, 1981-98; staff physician Okla. Vets. Ctr., Claremore, 2000—. House physician McLoud Nursing Ctr., 1988—; med. examiner Pottawatomie County Health, McLoud, 1983--. Author: Poetic Voices of America, 1991; composer lyrics and music at Stella Gospel Rec. Studio, 1993, A Soldier Last Prayer.. Mem. Presdl. Order Merit Nat. Repub. Senatorial Com., Washington, 1991, Presdl. Task Force, 1983—, Senatorial Commn. Repub. Senatorial Inner Circle, Washington, 1991; mem. U.S. Congrl. Adv. Bd., 1993. With USMC, Vietnam era. Recipient Acknowledgement of Outstanding Contbn. in Clin. Rsch. award SANDOZ Labs., 1992, Rep. Presdl. Legion of Merit, 1994, Rep. Majority medal, U.S. Senate, 1997, Rep. Task Force medal of merit, 1997. Mem. Am. Legion, C. of C., Jr. C. of C., U.S. Senatorial Club (preferred mem.), U.S. Congressional Act Bd. (state advisor 1990-91). Baptist. Avocations: fishing, music, composing and writing lyrics. Office: PO Box 988 3001 W Bluestarr Claremore OK 74018 E-mail: MWhinery@ODVA.State.OK.US.

WHINNERY, JOHN ROY, b. Read, Colo., July 26, 1916; s. Ralph V. and Edith Mable (Bent) Whinnery; m. Patricia Barry, Sept. 17, 1944; children: Carol Joanne, Catherine, Barbara. BS Elec. Engring., U. Calif., Berkeley, 1937, PhD, 1948. With GE, 1937—46; part-time lectr. Union Coll., Schenectady, 1945—46; assoc. prof. elec. engring. U. Calif., Berkeley, 1946—52, prof., vice chmn. div. elec. engring., 1952—56, chmn., 1956—59, dean Coll. Engring., 1959—63, prof. elec. engring., 1963—80, Univ. prof. Coll. Engring., 1980—. Rsch. sci. electron tubes Hughes Aircraft Co., Culver City, 1951—52; vis. mem. tech. staff Bell Tel. Labs., 1963—64; mem. sci. and tech. com. Manned Space Flight, NASA, 1963—69; chmn. Commn. Engring. Edn., 1966—68; standing com. controlled thermonuclear rsch. AEC, 1970—73; mem. Pres.'s Com. on Nat. Sci. Medal, 1970—73, 1979—80. Author (with Simon Ramo): Fields and Waves in Communication Electronics, 1944; author: (with Ramo and Van Duzar) Fields and Waves in Communication Electronics, 3rd edit., 1994; author: (with D.O. Pederson and J.J. Studer) Introduction to Electronic Systems, Circuits and Devices; contbr. tech. articles. Named to Hall of Fame, Modesto (Calif.) H.S., 1983, ASEE Hall of Fame, 1993; recipient Lamme medal, Am. Soc. Engring. Edn., 1975, Centennial medal, 1993, Engring. Alumni award, U. Calif.-Berkeley, 1980, Nat. Medal of Sci., NSF, 1992; fellow, Guggenheim, 1959. Fellow: IRE (bd. dirs. 1956—59), IEEE (life; bd. dirs. 1969—71, sec. 1971, Edn. medal 1967, Centennial medal 1984, Medal of Honor 1985), Am. Acad. Arts and Scis., Optical Soc. Am.; mem.: IEEE Microwave Theory and Techniques Soc. (disting. lectr. 1989—92, Microwave Career award 1977, Okawa prize in info. and telecom. 1997), NAS, NAE (Founders award 1986), Eta Kappa Nu (eminent mem.), Tau Beta Pi, Sigma Xi, Phi Beta Kappa. Congregationalist. Home: 1804 Wales Dr Walnut Creek CA 94595-2472 Office: U Calif Dept Elect Engring Berkeley CA 94720-1770

WHINSTON, ARTHUR LEWIS, lawyer; b. N.Y.C., Feb. 5, 1925; s. Charles Nathaniel and Charlotte (Nalen) W.; m. Melicent Ames Kingsbury, Mar. 19, 1949; children: Ann Kingsbury, James Pierce, Melicent Ames, Louise Ellen, Patricia Kingsbury. B.C.E., Cornell U., 1945; MSE., Princeton U., 1947; JD, N.Y. U., 1957. Bar: N.Y. 1957, Oreg. 1964, U.S. Supreme Ct 1966, U.S. Patent Office 1958, U.S. Ct. Appeals (fed. cir.) 1959; registered profl. engr., N.Y., Oreg. Engr. Chas. N. & Selig Whinston, N.Y.C., 1947-50; lectr. Coll. City N.Y., 1950-51; structures engr. Republic Aviation Corp., Farmingdale, N.Y., 1951-57; practice in N.Y.C., 1957-64, Portland, Oreg., 1964—; patent lawyer Arthur, Dry & Kalish, 1957-64; partner Klarquist Sparkman, LLP, 1964—; chmn. Oreg. Bar com. on patent, trademark and copyright law, 1968-69, 77-78, mem. com. unauthorized practice law, 1970-73, chmn., 1972-73, com. on profl. responsibility, 1973-75. Served as ensign, C.E. USNR, 1945-46. Recipient Fuertes medal Cornell U. Sch. Civil Engring., 1945 Mem. ABA, Oreg. Bar Assn., N.Y. Bar Assn., Multnomah County Bar Assn., Am. Intellectual Property Law Assn., N.Y. Intellectual Property Law Assn., Oreg. Patent Law Assn. (pres. 1977-78), Profl. Engrs. Oreg. (past state legis. chmn.), Sigma Xi, Chi Epsilon, Phi Kappa Phi. Clubs: Multnomah Athletic. Republican. Unitarian Universalist. Home: 3824 SW 50th Ave Portland OR 97221-2112 Office: One World Trade Ctr Ste 1600 Portland OR 97204

WHINSTON, STEPHEN ALAN, lawyer; b. Stamford, Conn., Mar. 27, 1948; s. Alfred Leonard and Rose (Eisgrau) W.; m. Joan Lenett, June 4, 1978; children: Stephanie Portnoy, Brian Arasim, Joshua. BA, Colgate U., 1970; JD, Case Western Res. U., 1973. Bar: Pa. 1973, U.S. Dist. Ct. (ea. dist.) Pa. 1973, U.S. Ct. Appeals (3d cir.) 1973, U.S. Ct. Appeals (8th cir.) 1995, U.S. Ct. Appeals (2d cir.) 2000, U.S. Supreme Ct. 2001. Trial atty. U.S. Dept. Justice, Washington, 1974-79, sr. trial atty., 1979-83; atty. Berger & Montague, P.C., Phila., 1983-85, shareholder, 1986—. Bd. dirs. Disabilities Law Project, Phila., 1989—, Jewish Fedn. Housing, Inc., Cherry Hill, N.J., 1994-96. Mem. Pa. Prison Soc. (bd. dirs.). Avocation: music. Office: Berger & Montague PC 1622 Locust St Philadelphia PA 19103-6305 E-mail: saw@bm.net.

WHIPPLE, FRED LAWRENCE, astronomer; b. Red Oak, Iowa, Nov. 5, 1906; s. Harry Lawrence and Celestia (MacFarl) W.; m. Dorothy Woods, 1928 (div. 1935); 1 son, Earle Raymond; m. Babette F. Samelson, Aug. 20, 1946; children: Dorothy Sandra, Laura. Student, Occidental Coll., 1923-24; AB, UCLA, 1927; PhD, U. Calif., 1931; AM (hon.), Harvard, 1945; ScD, Am. Internat. Coll., 1958; DLitt (hon.), Northeastern U., 1961; DSc (hon.), Temple U., 1961, U. Ariz., 1979; LLD (hon.), C.W. Post Coll., L.I. U., 1962. Teaching fellow U. Calif. at Berkeley, 1927-29, Lick Obs. fellow, 1930-31; instr. Stanford U., summer 1929, U. Calif., summer 1931; staff mem. Harvard Obs., 1931-77; instr. Harvard U., 1932-38, lectr., 1938-45; research asso. Radio Research Lab., 1942-45, asso. prof. astronomy, 1945-50, prof. astronomy, 1950-77, chmn. dept., 1949-56, Phillips prof. astronomy, 1968-77. Dir. Smithsonian Astrophys. Obs., 1955-73, sr. scientist, 1973—; mem. Rocket Rsch. Panel U.S., 1946-57; U.S. subcom. NASA, 1946-52, U.S. Rsch. and Devel. Bd. Panel, 1947-52; chmn. Tech. Panel on Rocketry; mem. Tech. Panel on Earth Satellite Program, 1955-59; other coms. Internat. Geophys. Year, 1955-59; mem., past officer Internat. Astron. Union; cons. missions to U.K. and MTO, 1944; del. Inter-Am. Astrophys. Congress, Mexico, 1942; active leader project on Upper-Atmospheric Rsch. via Meteor Photog. sponsored by Bur. Ordnance, U.S. Navy, 1946-51; b. Bur. Ordnance, U.S. Navy (Office Naval Rsch.), 1951-57, USAF, 1948-62; mem. com. meteorology, space sci. bd., com. on atmospheric scis. Nat. Acad. Scis.-NRC, 1958-65; advisor Sci. Adv. Bd., USAF, 1963-67; spl. cons. com. Sci. and Astronautics U.S. Ho. Reps., 1960-73; chmn. Gordon Rsch. Confs., 1963; dir. Optical Satellite Tracking Project, NASA, 1958-73; project dir. Orbiting Astron. Obs., 1958-72; dir. Meteorite Photography and Recovery Program, 1962-73, cons. planetary atmospheres, 1962-69; mem. space scis. working group on Orbiting Astron. Observatories, 1959-70; chmn. sci. coun. geodetic uses artificial satellites Com. Space Rsch., 1965-70. Author: Earth, Moon and Planets, rev. edit, 1968, Orbiting The Sun: Planets and Satellites of The Solar System, The Mystery of Comets, 1985; co-author: Survey of the Universe; Contbr.: sci. papers on astron. and upper atmosphere to Ency. Brit; mags., other publs.; Asso. editor: Astronomical Jour, 1954-56, 64-71; editor: Smithsonian Contributions to Astrophysics, 1956-73, Planetary and Space Science, 1958-83, hon. editor, 1983—, Science Revs, 1961-70; editorial bd.: Earth and Planetary Sci. Letters, 1966-73; inventor tanometer, meteor bumper; a developer window as radar countermeasure, 1944. Decorated comdr. Order of Merit for rsch. and invention, Esnault-Pelerie award France; recipient Donohue medals for ind. discovery of 6 new comets, Presdl. Cert. of Merit for sci. work during World War II, J. Lawrence Smith medal Nat. Acad. Scis. for rsch. on meteors, 1949, medal for astron. rsch. U. Liege, 1960, Space Flight award Am. Astronautical Soc., 1961, Disting. Fed. Civilian Svc. award, 1963; Space Pioneers medallion for contbns. to fed. space program, 1968, Pub. Svc. award for contbns. to OAO2 devel. NASA, 1969, Leonard medal Meteoritical Soc., 1970, Kepler medal AAAS, 1971, Career Svc. award Nat. Civil Svc. League, 1972, Henry medal Smithsonian Instn., 1973, Alumnus of Yr. Achievement award UCLA, 1976, UCLA medal, 1997, Golden Plate award Am. Acad. Achievement, 1981, Gold medal Royal Aston. Soc., 1983, Bruce medal Astron. Soc. Pacific, 1986, Benjamin Franklin fellow Royal Soc. Arts, London, 1968—; depicted on postal stamp of Mauritania, 1986, St. Vincent, 1994, Living Legend Medallion, U.S. Congrl. Libr., 2000. Fellow Am. Astron. Soc. (v.p. 1962-64, 1987 Russell lecturer), Am. Rocket Soc., Am. Geophys. Union (Fred L. Whipple yearly lectr. estab. in honor planetary div. 1990), Royal Astron. Soc. (assoc.); mem. AAAS, Nat. Acad. Scis., AIAA Astronautics (aerospace tech. panel space physics 1960-63), Astronautical Soc. Pacific, Solar Assos., Internat. Sci. Radio Union (U.S.A. nat. com. 1949-61), Am. Meteoritical Soc., Am. Standards Assn., Am. Acad. Arts and Scis., Am. Philos. Soc. (councillor sect. astronomy and earth scis. 1966-70), Royal Soc. Scis. Belgium (corr.), Internat. Acad. Astronautics (sci. advisory com. 1962-65), Internat. Astronautical Fedn., Am. Meteorol. Soc., Royal Astron. Soc. (assoc.), Phi Beta Kappa, Sigma Xi, Pi Mu Epsilon. Clubs: Examiner (Boston); Cosmos (Washington). Office: 60 Garden St Cambridge MA 02138-1516

WHIPPLE, HARRY M. newspaper publishing executive; b. Tulsa, June 30, 1947; children: Garth, Erin. Student, Ind. U., 1965-68, U. Evansville, 1965-68, Ark Poly. Coll., 1965-68. Gen. mgr. Mt. Vernon (Ind.) Pub Co., 1972-75; asst. pub. Pioneer Newspapers (formerly Scripps League Newspapers), Monongahela, Pa., 1975-77; advt. dir. Rockford (Ill.) Morning Star and Register Republic, 1977-81; pres., pub. Valley News Dispatch, The Herald, North Hills News Record, Tarentum, Pa., 1981-84; v.p., regional mgr. Midwest Gannett Media Sales/Gannett Nat. Sales, Chgo., 1984-87; pres. TNI Ptnrs., Tucson, 1987-92; pres., pub. The Cincinnati Enquirer, 1992—. Bd. trustees Zool. Soc. Cin.; co-chair adv. bd. Nat. Underground R.R. Freedom Ctr.; chmn. bd. dirs. Greater Cin. Ctr. for Econ. Edn. Mem. Greater Cin. C. of C. (chmn. bd. trustees). Office: Cincinnati Enquirer 312 Elm St Fl 20 Cincinnati OH 45202-2754

WHIPPLE, JENNIFER JEAN, botanist; b. San Jose, Calif., Mar. 15, 1951; d. Edward Keith and Harriet Jean W.; s. Roderick Alan Hutchinson, May 26, 1979 (dec. Mar. 1997). Student, U. Calif., San Diego, 1970; BS in Botany, U. Calif., Davis, 1973; MA in Biology, Humboldt State U., 1981. Biol. technician Nat. Park Svc., Yellowstone Nat. Park, Wyo., 1985-92; botanist, data mgr. Greater Yellowstone Conservation Data Ctr. The Nature Conservancy, 1993; botanist Nat. Park Svc., 1993—. Instr. Yellowstone Inst., 1999—. Co-author: Wyoming Rare Plant Field Guide, 1994. Mem. AAAS, Am. Soc. Plant Taxonomists, Wyo. Native Plant Soc., Calif. Bot. Soc., Mont. Native Plant Soc., Idaho Native Plant Soc. Avocation: photography. Home: PO Box 118 Yellowstone National Park WY 82190 Office: Nat Park Svc PO Box 168 Yellowstone National Park WY 82190 E-mail: jennifer_whipple@nps.gov.

WHIPPLE, JUDITH ROY, book editor; b. N.Y.C., May 14, 1935; d. Edwin Paul and Elizabeth (Levis) Roy; m. William Whipple, Oct. 26, 1963. AB, Mount Holyoke Coll., 1957. Head libr. Am. Sch. Lima (Peru), S.A., 1957-59; asst. editor children's books G.P. Putnam's Sons, N.Y.C., 1959-62; assoc. editor W.W. Norton & Co., Inc., 1962-68; editor Four Winds Press, 1968-75; editor-in-chief Scholastic Gen. Book Divsn., 1975-77; pub. Four Winds Press subs. Scholastic Inc., N.Y.C., 1977-82; pub., v.p. Macmillan Pub. Co., 1982-89, exec. editor, 1989-94; editl. dir. Cavendish Children's Books, Tarrytown, NY, 1994—2002. Mem. PEN, Children's Book Coun. (pres. 1977, bd. dirs. 1970-79), Women's Nat. Book Assn., Soc. Children's Book Writers and Illustrators. Avocations: gardening, swimming, piano, travel. E-mail: jrwhipple@stny.rr.com.

WHIPPLE, KENNETH, utilities executive; b. 1934; BS, MIT, 1958. With Ford Motor Co., Dearborn, Mich., 1958—, systems mgr. Ford Credit, 1966-69, mgr. mgmt. svcs. dept. fin. staff, 1969-71, systems analysis mgr. fin. staff, 1971-74, asst. contr. internat. fin. staff, 1974-75, v.p. fin. Ford Credit, 1975-77, exec. v.p. Ford Credit, 1977-80, pres. Ford Credit, 1980-84, v.p. corp. strategy, 1984-86; v.p. chmn. Ford of Europe, 1986-88; exec. v.p., pres. Ford Fin. Svcs. Group, Dearborn, 1988—99; chmn. bd., CEO CMS Energy, Mich., 2002—. Office: CMS Energy Fairlane Plz S Ste 1100 330 Town Center Dr Dearborn MI 48126*

WHIPPLE, ROBERT CLIFTON, music educator, conductor; b. Lewiston, Idaho, Aug. 21, 1937; s. Clifton Claude and Lita Isabel (McIntosh) Whipple. MusB, U. of Idaho, 1959. Music tchr. Gem County Pub. Schools, Emmett, Idaho, 1959—61, Moscow (Idaho) Pub. Schools, 1961—66; music dir. and condr. Ill. Valley Symphony Orch., Ottawa, Ill., 1966—71; music dir. Timber Lake Playhouse, Mount Carroll, 1971—73; music dir. and condr. Illowa Chamber Orch., Sterling, 1973—76; pvt. studio tchr., 1973—; music dir., condr. Sterling Festival Orch., 1981—94. Editor: (profl. jour.) The Scroll. Named Outstanding Young Educator, Moscow Idaho Jaycees, 1966; recipient Cmty. Svc. Award, Sterling (Ill.) Chamber of Commerce and Industry, 1978. Mem.: Am. String Teachers Assn. with Nat. Sch. Orch. Assn. (pres. 2000—02), Music Educators Nat. Conf., Phi Mu Alpha Sinfonia.

WHIPPLE, WILLIAM, JR. engineering consultant, writer; b. Cinclare, La., Feb. 4, 1909; s. William and Genevieve (Randolph) W.; m. Dixie Ancrum, Mar. 30, 1935 (dec. Oct. 1955); children: Anne Calhoun, William III, Claire Randolph; m. Renée Pauline Exiga, July 21, 1956 (div. May 1974); 1 child, Philip; m. Frances Edith Cheek, June 1, 1974 (dec. July 1983); m. Alice Terry Goodloe, Dec. 1, 1984. BS, U.S. Mil. Acad., 1930; BA, Oxford (Eng.) U., 1933, MA, 1937; Civil Engr., Princeton U., 1936. Registered profl. engr., N.J. Commd. 2d lt. Corps Engrs., U.S. Army, 1930, advanced through grades to brig. gen., ret., 1960; chief engr. N.Y. World's Fair Corp., Flushing Meadow, N.Y., 1960-64; pvt. practice cons. engr. N.Y.C., 1964-65; dir. Water Resources Rsch. Inst. Rutgers U., New Brunswick, N.J., 1965-79, rsch. prof. Coastal and Environ. Inst., 1979-81; asst. dir. divsn. water resources Dept. Environ. Protection, Trenton, 1981-89, coord. nonpoint cource control program divsn. water resource, 1989-90; prin. Greeley Polhemus Group, Chester, Pa., 1990-2000; pvt. practice cons. Princeton, N.J., 1999—. Author: New Perspectives on Water Supply, 1994, Comprehensive Water Planning and Regulation, 1996, Water Resource: A New Era for Coordination, 1998; contbr. articles to publs. on water resources. Chmn. Flood Control Com., Princeton, N.J., 1975-81. Recipient Trustees award N.J. inst. Tech., 1985, govt. award Water Resource Assn. of Delaware River Basin, 1987, Toulmin award for best articles Mil. Engr., 1975, Formal Commendation from Pres. of U.S., 1971. Fellow AAAS, ASCE (life, chmn. urban water resources rsch. coun. 1973-75, Lifetime Achievement award Inst. Environment and Water Resources 2001), Soc. Am. Mil. Engrs. (life), Am. Water Resources Assn. (pres. 1993, Icko Iben award 1978, William Ackerman medal 1989, Boggess award; mem. Am. Acad. Environ. Engrs. (diplomate), Univs. Coun. on Water Resources (chmn. 1976-78), Sigma Xi. Avocations: tennis, walking with dog, history and biography. Home and Office: 2 Hedge Row Rd Princeton NJ 08540-5055

WHIPPLE, WILLIAM PERRY, foundation administrator; b. Cedar Rapids, Iowa, Nov. 1, 1913; s. Robert Milo and Jeanette (Fry) W.; m. Gayle Schroeder, Sept. 18, 1937; children: John William, Robert Milo. BA, Coe Coll., 1935, hon. doctorate, 1996. Prin. Whipple Ins. Agy., Cedar Rapids, 1935-57; pres. Whipple and Winterberg, 1957-71; chmn. Frank B. Hall of Iowa, Inc., 1971-74; pres. Hall Found., Inc., 1974-95, also bd. dirs.; chair Hall-Perrine Found., 1995—. Exec. in residence Colo. State U., Fort Collins, 1973; bd. dirs. Fire Mark Cir. of Ams., Chamblee, Ga., Interocean Reins. Corp., Cedar Rapids, 1st Fed. Savs. and Loan, Cedar Rapids, Nissen Corp., Cedar Rapids, 1966-72, Banks of Iowa, Inc., Des Moines, 1982-85. Trustee Cedar Rapids Pub. Library, Coe Coll., chmn.; hon. bd. dirs. Methwick Manor, Cedar Rapids, Linn County ARC, Greater Cedar Rapids Found. Recipient Outstanding Layman award YMCA, Cedar Rapids, 1986, Alumni Achievement award, Coe Coll., 1990, Founders Day award Coe Coll., 2001, First Community Svc. award, Cedar Rapids Rotary, 1993. Mem. Rotary (Paul Harris fellow 1987), Elks. Republican. Presbyterian. Avocations: signevierist, stamp collecting. Home: 1224 13th St NW Cedar Rapids IA 52405-2404 Office: Hall-Perrine Found 115 3d St SE Cedar Rapids IA 52401-1222

WHIPPS, EDWARD FRANKLIN, lawyer; b. Columbus, Ohio, Dec. 17, 1936; s. Rusk Henry and Agnes Lucille (Green) W.; children: Edward Scott, Rusk Huot, Sylvia Louise, Rudyard Christian. BA, Ohio Wesleyan U., 1958; JD, Ohio State U., 1961. Bar: Ohio 1961, U.S. Dist. Ct. (so. dist.) Ohio 1962, U.S. Dist. Ct. (no. dist.) Ohio 1964, U.S. Ct. Claims 1963, U.S. Supreme Ct. 1963, Miss. 1965, U.S. Ct. Appeals (6th cir.) 1980. Assoc. George, Greek, King & McMahon, Columbus, 1961-66; ptnr. George, Greek, King, McMahon & McConnaughey, 1966-79, McConnaughey, Stradley, Mone & Moul, Columbus, 1979-81, Thompson, Hine & Flory, Columbus, 1981-93; prin. Edward F. Whipps & Assocs., 1993-94, 2000—; ptnr. Whipps & Wistner, 1995-99. Founder, trustee Creative Living, Inc., 1969—; trustee, v.p. Unverferth House, Inc., 1989; trustee Eagle Scholarship Trust. Host: (TV) Upper Arlington Plain Talk, 1979-82, Bridging Disability, 1981-82, Lawyers on Call, 1982—; U.A. Today, 1982-86, The Ohio Wesleyan Experience, 1984— . Mem. Ohio Bd. Psychology, 1992—, pres. 2001-02; active Upper Arlington (Ohio) Bd. Edn., 1971-80, pres., 1978-79; bd. alumni dirs. Ohio Wesleyan U., 1975-79; trustee Walden Ravines Assn., 1992-96, pres. 1993-96. Mem. ABA, Columbus Bar Assn., Ohio State Bar Assn., Assn. Trial Lawyers Am., Ohio Acad. Trial Lawyers, Franklin County Trial Lawyers Assn., Am. Judicature Soc., Columbus Bar Found., Ohio Bd. Psychology, Columbus C. of C., Upper Arlington Area C. of C. (trustee 1978—), Lawyers Club, Barrister Club, Columbus Athletic Club, Nat. Football Found. & Hall of Fame, Columbus Touchdown Club, Downtown Quarterback Club, Ohio State U. Faculty (Columbus) Club, Ohio State U. Golf Club, Highlands Golf Club (dir. 2001—), Delta Tau Delta (nat. v.p. 1976-78). Republican. Home: 51 Highland Ct Pataskala OH 43062-8910 Office: Edward F Whipps & Assocs 500 S Front St Columbus OH 43215-7619 *Personal philosophy: Commitment to personal growth, the development of interpersonal relationships, the rule of law and a firm belief in the unique value of every individual in a holographic universe are the primary factors seen in my approach to life.*

WHISENANT, B(ERT) R(OY), JR. insurance company executive; b. Brownsville, Tex., Oct. 10, 1950; s. Bert R. and Jimmie Lee (Tallon) W.; m. Margaret Elizabeth Bugge, Aug. 21, 1970; children: Michelle, Bert III, Bryan, Monette. BBA in Ins., S.W. Tex. State U., 1972. Ptnr. Bert Whisenant Ins., McAllen, Tex., 1972—. Pres. JJ & BW, Inc. Investment Co., McAllen, 1987—; bd. dirs. Ind. Agy., Inc., Harlingen, Tex., 1977—. Contbr. articles to Tex. Insuror, 1984. Recipient Blue Ribbon Honors award Aetna Life and Casualty, Co., 1974, Charter Pacesetter award West Coast Life Ins. Co., 1982. Mem. Ind. Ins. Agts. Am. (bd. dirs. 1984—), Ind. Ins. Agts. Tex. (com. person 1986—), Ind. Ins. Agts. McAllen (pres. 1985-86), Associated Risk Mgrs. of Tex., Upper Valley Life Underwriters (sec.-treas. 1978), Jaycees (bd. dirs., chaplain 1974). Lodges: Optimists (pres. McAllen club 1986), Rotary. Republican. Avocations: snow and water skiing, surfing, piloting. Office: 816 E Hackberry Ave Mcallen TX 78501-5739

WHISENHUNT, DONALD WAYNE, history educator; b. Meadow, Tex., May 16, 1938; s. William Alexander Whisenhunt and Beulah (Johnson) King; m. Betsy Ann Baker, Aug. 27, 1960; children: Donald Wayne Jr., William Benton. BA, McMurry Coll., 1960; MA, Tex. Tech U., 1962, PhD, 1966. Tchr. Elida (N.Mex.) High Sch., 1961-63; from asst. to assoc. prof. history Murray (Ky.) State U., 1966-69; assoc. prof., chmn. dept. Thiel Coll., Greenville, Pa., 1969-73; Dean Sch. Liberal Arts and Scis., Ea. N.Mex. U., Portales, 1973-77; v.p. acad. affairs U. Tex., Tyler, 1977-83; v.p., provost Wayne (Nebr.) State Coll., 1983-91, interim pres., 1985; prof. history, chmn. dept. Western Wash. U., Bellingham, 1991—. Fulbright lectr. Peoples Republic of China, 1995. Author: Environment and American Experience, 1974, Depression in the Southwest, 1979, Chronological History of Texas, Vol. 1, 1982, Vol.2, 1987, Texas: Sesquicentennial Celebration, 1984; editor: Encyclopedia USA, 1988—, Poetry of the People: Poems to the President, 1929-1945, 1996, Tent Show: Arthur Names and His Famous Players, 2000, It Seems to Me: Selected Letters of Eleanor Roosevelt, 2001. Democrat. Methodist. Office: Western Wash U Dept History Bellingham WA 98225

WHISHER, BRADLEY EDWARD, insurance company executive, financial consultant; b. Plattsburg, N.Y., Nov. 4, 1954; s. Floyd Edward and Angeline (Molinero) W.; children: Lindsay L., Kimberly A., Bradley E. Jr. BSBA, Ithaca Coll., 1976; student, Am. Coll., Bryn Mawr, Pa., 1991—. CLU, chartered fin. cons. Asst. mgr., sales rep. Prudential Ins. Co., Albany, N.Y., 1976-80; asst. mgr., cons. Home Life Ins. Co., 1980-86; mgr. life and fin. svcs. Jardine Ins. Brokers Inc., Schenectady, 1986; pres. Bradley E. Whisher Co., Albany, 1992—; pres. the View Restaurant at Indian Kettles Bramaan Enterprises LLC, DBA, 2001—. Mem. pension adv. com., St. Clare's Hosp. Found., Schnectady; registered rep. Nathan & Lewis Securities, 1986—. Past pres. Schenectady chpt. Am. Cancer Soc., sec., 1996—. Mem. Nat. Assn. Life Unerwriters, Am. Soc. CLU, Internat. Assn. Fin. Planners, Million Dollar Round Table (honor roll), Rotary (chmn. Niskayuna Hank Whisher track meet 1991—). Avocations: skiing, hunting, fishing, boating. Home: 209 Shaker Ridge Dr Niskayuna NY 12309 Office: 3 Wembley Sq Ste 104 Albany NY 12205-3836 E-mail: bewco@captial.net.

WHISLER, JAMES STEVEN, lawyer, mining and manufacturing executive; b. Centerville, Iowa, Nov. 23, 1954; s. James Thomas and Betty Lou (Clark) W.; m. Ardyce Dawn Christensen, Jan. 20, 1979; children: James Kyle, Kristen Elyse. BS, U. Colo., Boulder, 1975; JD, U. Denver, 1978; MS, Colo. Sch. Mines, Golden, 1984; AMP, Harvard Bus. Sch., 1998. Bar: Colo. 1978; CPA, Ariz. Assoc. gen. counsel, sec. Western Nuclear, Inc., Denver, 1979-81; exploration counsel Phelps Dodge Corp., N.Y.C., 1981-85, legal and adminstrv. mgr. Phoenix, 1985-87, v.p., gen. counsel, 1987-88, sr. v.p., gen. counsel, 1988-91; pres. Phelps Dodge Mining Co., 1991-98; pres., COO Phelps Dodge Corp., Phoenix, 1997-99, chmn., pres., CEO, 2000—. Bd. dirs. Phelps Dodge Corp., Burlington No. Santa Fe Corp., So. Peru Copper Corp., Am. West Holdings Corp., Copper Devel. Assn., Internat. Copper Assn., Nat. Mining Assn.; mem. Bus. Coun. Mem.: AIME, AICPA, Mining and Metallurgical Soc. Am., Colo. Bar Assn., Soc. Mining Engrs., Links Club. Office: Phelps Dodge Corp One N Central Ave Phoenix AZ 85004-2306

WHISNAND, REX JAMES, association housing executive; b. Van Nuys, Calif., Jan. 2, 1948; s. Harold Theodore Whisnand and Laura Fay Brigham Whisnand Brown; m. Cathy Ladeane Bennett, Apr. 1, 1978; 1 child, Bryce James. BS in Agrl. Bus. Mgmt., Calif. Poly State U., San Luis Obispo, 1970; BSBA, Calif. State U., Sacramento, 1976; MPA in Housing Adminstrn., U. San Francisco, 1985; grad., U.S. Naval Submarine Sch., New London, Conn., 1972; postgraduate, Inst. for Organization Mgmt.; EdD in Orgn. and Leadership, U. San Francisco, 2000. Generalist W & W Hardware Store, Orcutt, Calif., 1964-70; state park ranger Calif. Dept. Parks and Recreation, Lompoc and Sacramento, 1969-75; exec. asst. Constrn. Industry Legis. Coun., Sacramento, 1974-75; dir. assn. svcs. Bldg. Industry Assn. Superior Calif., 1976-79; exec. v.p. West Bay divsn. Bldg. Industry Assn. No. Calif., Redwood City, 1980-84; exec. v.p. Bldg. Industry Assn., Tacoma/Pierce County, 1984-86; supr. Lumberjack Store, Lodi, Calif., 1988-90; exec. v.p. Rental Housing Owners Assn. of So. Alameda County, Hayward, 1990-96; field rep., crew leader census 2000 Am. Housing Survey, 1997-98; exec. peninsula dist. Boy Scouts Am., 1999; field ops. supr. Am. Housing Survey, 2000; field rep. westat survey U.S. Pub. Health Svc., 2000—; exec. dir. Housing Conservation and Devel. Corp., San Francisco, 2002—. Com. mem. Calif. Bldg. Industry Assn., Sacramento, 1976-84; mem. exec. officers coun., local govt. com. Calif. Apt. Assn., 1991-96; mem. Alameda County Housing Rsch. Adv. Bd., Hayward, Calif., 1990-93; bd. dirs. Credit Union Execs. Soc., Internat. Credit Assn., Pronet; adj. faculty U. San Francisco; guest svc. rep. Oakland Athletics, 1997-2002. Editor Pierce County Builder, 1984-86 (Assn. Achievement award Nat. Assn. Home Builders 1984-85), Superior California Builder Mag., 1978-80. Active 20-30 Club Internat. #1, Sacramento, 1976-80, officer, 1981-82; mem. South Sacramento Area Cmty. Planning Adv. Bd., 1978-79; grad. Pleasanton Leadership, 1995; chmn. Coastside Coalition for Safe Hwys., Half Moon Bay, 1983-84; bd. congregations Family Emergency Shelter Coalition Alameda County, 1995-96; active Pleasanton Gen. Plan Econ./Fiscal Growth Com., 1994-96, Bay Area Indsl. Edn. Coun., 1995-96, Hayward Coalition for Youth, 1995-96; officer Half Moon Bay C. of C., 1982-84; cert. basketball coach Nat. Youth Sports Assn., 1994-97. With USNR, 1970-76, U.S. Army, N.G., 1990-92. Named Outstanding Young Man. in Am., Jr. C. of C., Foster City, Calif., 1983. Mem. Internat. Assn. Bus. Communicators (pres. Sacramento chpt. 1979, pres. Peninsula chpt. 1981), Am. Soc. Assn. Execs. (cert.), No. Calif. Soc. Assn. Execs. (bd. dirs. 1994-97, com. chmn. 1993-95), Pleasanton C. of C. (econ. devel. com. 1990-96), Wash. State Home Builders Assn. (pres. exec. officers coun. 1985), Western Conf. Assn. Execs. (com. mem. 1995-96), San Francisco Planning and Urban Rsch. Assn. (mem. housing com. and homeless com. 2002), Hayward C. of C. (govt. rels. coun. 1990-95), Calif. Vocat. Indsl. Clubs Am. (bd. dirs. 1977-80), Calif. Polytech. Alumni Assn., World Future Soc., Alpha Gamma Rho (charter, com. chair 1969-99). Episcopalian. Avocation: dog training, genealogy. Home: 5435 Black Ave Ste 3 Pleasanton CA 94566-5966

WHISNANT, JACK PAGE, neurologist; b. Little Rock, Oct. 26, 1924; s. John Clifton and Zula I. (Page) W.; m. Patricia Anne Rimmey, May 12, 1944; children: Elizabeth Anne, John David, James Michael. BS, U. Ark., 1948, MD, 1951; MS, U. Minn., 1955. Intern Balt. City Hosp., 1951-52; resident in medicine and neurology Mayo Grad. Sch. Medicine, Rochester, Minn., 1952-55, instr. neurology, 1956-60, asst. prof., 1960-64, asso. prof., 1964-69, prof., 1969—; Meyer prof. neurosci. Mayo Med. Sch.; chmn. dept. neurology Mayo Clinic, Mayo Med. Sch., Mayo Grad. Sch. Medicine, 1971-81; chmn. dept. health scis. research Mayo Clinic and Mayo Med. Sch., 1987-93. Cons. neurology Mayo Clinic, 1955-96 , head sect. neurology, 1963-71; dir. Mayo Cerebrovascular Clin. Research Center, 1975-96. Contbr. articles on neurology and cerebrovascular disease to med. jours. Trustee YMCA, Rochester, pres., 1977. With USAAF, 1942-45. Decorated Air medal. NIH grantee, 1959-96. Fellow Am. Heart Assn., Am. Acad. Neurology (pres. 1993-95); mem. AMA, Am. Neurol. Assn. (pres. 1981-82), Am. Bd. Psychiatry and Neurology (bd. dirs. 1983-90, pres. 1989), Zumbro Valley Med. Soc., Minn. Med. Assn., Minn. Soc. Neurol. Scis., Ctrl. Soc. Neurol. Rsch. (pres. 1964), Alumni Assn. Mayo Found. Presbyterian. Home: 1005 7th Ave NE Rochester MN 55906-7074 Office: Mayo Found Dept Health Scis Rsch 201 1st St SW Rochester MN 55905-0001 E-mail: whisnant1924@att.net., whisnant@mayo.edu.

WHISTLER, BRADLEY JAMES, state government official; b. Juneau, Alaska, Mar. 22, 1958; s. Robert Leo and Beverly Jean Whistler; children: Kelly Anne, Brian Robert. BA, Western Wash. U., Bellingham, 1980; DMD, Oreg. Health Scis. U., Portland, 1984; postgrad., U. Alaska-S.E., 1994—. Tax examiner Alaska Dept. Revenue, Juneau, 1984-86, tax specialist, 1986-88; rsch. analyst Alaska Dept. Health & Social Svcs., 1988-90, health planner, 1990-93, health planner, state dental dir., 1993—. Author: Alaska Department of Health and Social Services Database Directory, 1989, 1990 Alaska Hospital Survey, 1991; author, editor: Health Alaskans 2000, 1994; editor: Meeting the Challenge, 1994. Bd. dirs. Alaska Rural Health Ctr., Fairbanks, 1995—. Mem. Am. Pub. Health Assn., Am. Health Planners Assn., Assn. State and Territorial Dental Dirs., Am. Assn. Pub. Health Dentistry, Alaska Pub. Health Assn. (pres. 1994-96, exec. bd., Short Term Svc. award 1995), Alaska Health Educators Consortium, Am. Soc. Pub. Adminstrn. Avocations: softball, weight training, fishing. Home: PO Box 32936 Juneau AK 99803-2936 Office: Alaska Dept Health & Social Svcs PO Box 110612 Juneau AK 99811-0612

WHISTLER, ROY LESTER, chemist, educator, industrialist; b. Morgantown, W.Va., Mar. 31, 1912; s. Park H. and Cloe (Martin) W.; m. Leila Anna Barbara Kaufman, Sept. 6, 1935 (dec. 1994); 1 child, William Harris. BS, Heidelberg Coll., 1934, D.Sc. (hon.), 1957; MS, Ohio State U., 1935; PhD, Iowa State U., 1938; D.Litt. (hon.), St. Thomas Inst., 1982; D.Agr., Purdue U., 1985. Instr. chemistry Iowa State U., 1935-38; research fellow Bur. Standards, 1938-40; sect. leader dept. agr. No. Regional Rsch. Lab., 1940-46; prof. biochemistry Purdue U., 1946-76, Hillenbrand distinguished prof., asst. dept. head, 1974-82, Hillenbrand disting. prof. emeritus Ind., 1982—; chmn. Inst. Agrl. Utilization Research, 1961-75; pres. Lafayette Applied Chemistry Inc., 1980-96. Vis. lectr. U. Witwatersrand, South Africa, 1961, South Africa, 65, South Africa, 77, South Africa, 85, Acad. Sci., France, 1975, Vladivostock Acad. Sci., Russia, 1976, numerous other countries; lectr. Bradley Polytech. Inst., 1941—42; adj. prof. Whistler Ctr. Carbohydrate Chemistry (named by Purdue U. 1984) , advisor, bd. dirs.; indsl cons. dir. Pfanstiehl Lab., Inc., 1940—2000, Greenwich Pharm., Inc., 1946—52, Larex, 1999—. Author: Polysaccharide Chemistry, 1953, Industrial Gums, 1959, 2d rev. edit., 1976, 3d rev. edit., 1992; rev. edit.: Methods of Carbohydrate Chemistry, series, 1962—; co-author: Guar, 1979, Carbohydrates for Food Scientists, 1997; editor: Starch-Chemistry and Technology, 2 vols., 1965, 67, rev. edit., 1984, 3d edit. 1999; editl bd. Jour. Carbohydrate Research, 1960-91, Starchs Chemistry and Technology, 1985; bd. advisors: Advances in Carbohydrate Chemistry, 1950-96, Organic Preparations and Procedures Internat., 1970—, Jour. Carbo-Nucleosides-Nucleotides, 1973-77, Stärke, Starch, 1979-99; contbr. numerous articles to profl. jours. Recipient Sigma Xi rsch. award Purdue U., 1953, Medal of Merit, Japanese Starch Tech. Soc., 1967, German Saare medal, 1974, Thomas Burr Osborne award Am. Assn. Cereal Chemists, 1974, Sterling Henricks award USDA, 1991, 93, Nicholas Appert award Inst. Food Technologists, 1994; Roy L. Whistler internat. award in carbohydrates established in his hon., Rsch. bldg. named in his honor Purdue U., 1997; Fred W. Tanner lectr., Chgo., 1994; Named Hillenbrand Disting. prof. Fellow AAAS, Am. Chem. Soc. (chmn. Purdue sect. 1949-50, carbohydrate divsn. 1951, cellular divsn. 1962, nat. councilor 1953-87, bd. dirs. 5th dist. 1955-58, chmn. com. edn. and students, chmn. sub-com. polysaccharide nomenclature, symposium dedicated in his honor 1979, hon. fellow award cellulose divsn. 1983, Hudson award 1960, Anselme Payen award 1967, Carl Lucas Alsburg award 1970, Spencer award 1970, 75, Disting. Svc. award 1983, named one of 10 outstanding chemists Chgo. sect. 1948), Am. Inst. Chemists (pres. 1982-83, Gold medal 1992), Am. Assn. Cereal Chemists (pres. 1978), Internat. Carbohydrate Union (pres. 1972-74); mem. Lafayette Applied Chemistry (pres. 1970-94), Argentine Chem. Soc. (life), Rotary (pres. 1966), Sigma Xi (pres. Purdue sect. 1957-59, nat. exec. com. 1958-62, hon. life mem. 1983—), Phi Lambda Upsilon, Rotary (pres. 1966). Office: Whistler Ctr for Carbohydrate Rsch 1160 Food Sci Bldg Lafayette IN 47907

WHITACRE, EDWARD E., JR. telecommunications executive; b. Ennis, Tex., Nov. 4, 1941; BS in Indsl. Engring., Tex. Tech U., 1964. With Southwestern Bell Telephone Co., 1963-85; various positions in ops. depts. Tex., Ark., Kans.; pres. Kans. divsn. Topeka, 1982-85; group pres. Southwestern Bell Corp., 1985-86, v.p. revenues and pub. affairs, vice-chmn., chief fin. officer, 1986-88, pres., COO, 1988-89, chmn., CEO, 1990—, also bd. dirs. Bd. dirs. Anheuser-Busch Cos., Inc., May Dept. Stores Co., Emerson Electric Co., Burlington No. Santa Fe, Inc.; with Learning Nat. Adv. Bd. Bd. regents Tex. Tech. U. and Health Scis., Lubbock; nat. pres. Boy Scouts Am.; trustee com. econ. devel. State N.Y., S.W. Rsch. Inst.; bd. govs. S.W. Found. Biomed. Rsch.; mem. govs. bus. coun. State of Tex.; chmn. campaign United Way, San Antonio, 1998. Recipient Internat. Citizen of Yr. award World Affairs Coun. San Antonio, 1997, Spirit of Achievement award Nat. Jewish Med. and Rsch. Ctr., 1998, Freeman award San Antonio C. of C., 1998; named to Tex. Bus. Hall of Fame, 1997. Presbyterian. Office: SBC Communications Inc 175 E Houston St San Antonio TX 78205-2255*

WHITACRE, TERESA A. quality engineer; b. Jeannette, Pa., Feb. 4, 1966; d. Connie P. Fidei; m. Dennis M. Whitacre, Aug. 20, 1988; children: Bradley J., Owen J. AA in Liberal Arts, Westmoreland C.C., 1988; BS in Quality Engring., Pacific Western U., 1994; postgrad., Kennedy Western U., 2001—. Quality technician NuKote, Derry, Pa., 1992—94; quality engr. BICO Inc., Indiana, 1994—95, Classic Industries, Latrobe, 1997; quality analyst, pres. Marketech Systems, 1995—; quality systems mgr. Carlo Tech. Plastics, 1998—. Author: Quality Technology: A Guide, 1996. Sunday sch. tchr. First Ch. of God, Latrobe, 1998—2001. Mem.: Am. Soc. for Quality (sr.; chair 1995—96, newsletter editor 1998—2002, cert. quality technician, quality engr., quality analyst, quality mgr.). Avocations: camping, fishing, devotional reading, computers. Office: Marketech Systems PO Box 308 Latrobe PA 15650

WHITACRE, VICKI ANN, emergency physician; b. Columbus, Ohio, Nov. 29, 1945; d. Victor Calvin and Ruth Helene (Dougan) Whitacre; m. Richard C. Treat, Aug. 2, 1970 (div. June 1975); m. Arthur Neal Moose, July 7, 1977; children: Natina Nicole, David Arthur L., Natasia Helene; stepchildren: Bryan Friday, Neala Moose, Anita Moose. BS in Zoology, Ohio U., 1967; MD, Ohio State U., 1971. Lic. physician, Ohio, Ky. Intern in pediats. Children's Hosp., Columbus, 1971-72; staff physician emergency dept. U. Ky., Lexington, 1972-73, resident in emergency medicine, 1973-75, resident in pediats., 1975-76; dir. emergency physicians Bethesda Hosp., Zanesville, Ohio, 1979-84, emergency physician, 1976-2001; med. dir. Muskingum County Pub. Health Dept., 2000—. Pre-natal clinic physician Muskingum County PHD, Zanesville, 1986-99; med. dir. Muskingum Behavior Health, Zanesville, 1986-99; established pre-hosp. care/control for Muskingum County Area Emergency Med. Adv. Coun., 1977-84; mem. Am. Bd. Emergency Medicine. Bd. dirs. Family Health Svcs. E. Ctrl. Ohio, Inc., Newark, 1996—, Joe Berg Sci. and Math. Found., 1977—; mem. ADN adv. com. Ohio U., Zanesville. Recipient Muskingum Couunty Family Y Woman of Achievement award in med. professions, 2002; charter mem. Southeastern Ohio Women's Hall of Fame, 1985. Mem. AMA, Ohio State Med. Assn., Am. Coll. Emergency Physicians, Muskingum County Acad. Medicine (sec.-treas. 1977—), Phi Beta Kappa, Alpha Lambda Delta. Republican. Presbyterian. Avocations: doll collecting, art, jewelry, reading. Home: 2435 Dunzweiler Dr Zanesville OH 43701-8670 Office: Muskingum County Public Health Dept Bethesda Hosp 205 N 7th St Zanesville OH 43701

WHITAKER, A(LBERT) DUNCAN, lawyer; b. Ft. Wayne, Ind., Jan. 3, 1932; s. Robert Lynn and Rhoda Irene (Duncan) W.; m. Adelaide B. Saccone, Aug. 13, 1955; children: Brent Robert, Alene G., Karen E. BA, Yale U., 1954; JD, U. Mich., 1957. Bar: Mich. 1957, U.S. Ct. Appeals D.C. 1959, U.S. Supreme Ct. 1961. Atty. antitrust div. U.S. Dept. Justice, 1957-59; assoc. Howrey & Simon, Washington, 1959-65, ptnr., 1965-97; pro bono atty., 1997—. Lectr. George Washington U., George Mason U. Law Sch. Contbr. articles to profl. jours. Mem. ABA, Fed. Bar Assn., D.C. Bar Assn., Order of Coif, Phi Beta Kappa Clubs: Metropolitan. Office: Howrey Simon Arnold and White 1299 Pennsylvania Ave NW Ste 1 Washington DC 20004-2420 E-mail: whitakerd@howrey.com., whitd1332@aol.com.

WHITAKER, ARTHUR LUTHER, retired minister, psychologist; b. Malden, Mass., July 23, 1921; s. Robert William and Elizabeth Arveen (Hinton) W.; m. Virginia Aileene Carter, June 6, 1948; children: Ronald, Paul, Mark, Keith. BA, Gordon Coll., 1949; BD, Harvard U., 1952; MST, Andover Newton Theol. Sem., 1954, D in Ministry, 1973. Ordained to ministry Baptist Ch., 1951; lic. counseling psychologist and health provider, Mass.; diplomate Internat. Acad. Behavioral Medicine, Am. Bd. Forensic Examiners and Medicine, Am. Coll. Forensic Examiners, Am. Bd. Psychol. Svcs. Pastor Calvary Bapt. Ch., Haverhill, Mass., 1950-55; field rep. Am. Bapt. Home Mission, N.Y.C., 1955-56; pastor Mt. Olivet Bapt. Ch., Rochester, N.Y., 1956-66, Pilgrim Bapt. Ch., St. Paul, 1966-70; assoc. exec. min. Am. Bapt. Chs. Mass., Boston, 1970-78; exec. min. Am. Bapt. Chs. N.Y., Syracuse, 1978-83; Protestant chaplain VA Med. Ctr., 1984-86; ret. exec. min. Am. Bapt. Chs. USA-N.Y. State Region, 1986—; counselor, vis. lectr. Harvard U. Divinity Sch., Cambridge, Mass., 1990-2000, Interfaith Counseling Svc. Inc., Newton, 1990-92. Lectr. social psychology U. Rochester, 1958-66; cons. U.S. Commn. Civil Rights, U.S. Govt., Rochester, 1964, Nat. Office NAACP, Rochester, 1964-65; vis. prof. Afro-Am. studies Gordon Coll., Wenham, Mass., 1972; trustee Colgate Rochester Divinity Sch., Gordon Coll., Keuka Coll. Contbr. articles and revs. to profl. jours. Active Mass. Dem. Party, Boston; hon. mem. nat. steering com. Gore 2000; contbg. mem. Dem. Nat. Com., 1995—; keynote spkr. 7th ann. Martin Luther King, Jr. Meml. Luncheon, North Shore Black Women's Assn., 2000. Tech. sgt. U.S. Army, 1943-46, ETO. Named Alumnus of Yr., Gordon Coll. Alumni Assn., Wenham, 1972; Whitaker Hall named in honor Mt. Olivet Bapt. Ch., Rochester, N.Y., 1991; Arthur L. Whitaker award Am. Bapt. Chs. Mass., annually 1992—. Mem. APA, Mass. Psychol. Assn., Harvard Divinity Sch. Alumni Assn. (sec. 1990-92, Outstanding Svc. award 1998, commemorative luncheon spkr. Dr. Martin Luther King Jr. celebration, miniature 1775 Minuteman statue recipient, African-Am. heritage com.), Andover Newton Theol. Sch. Alumni Assn. (pres. 1996-97). Avocations: music, spectator sports, drama, swimming, reading. Home: 292 Chestnut W # 27-E Randolph MA 02368-2331

WHITAKER, AUDIE DALE, hospital laboratory medical technologist; b. Cin., Jan. 19, 1949; s. Audie and Wanda Edith (Weaver) W.; m. Sandra Sue McPhail, Aug. 22, 1970; children: Audie David Nathaniel, Andrea Grace, Alexandra Christine. BA, Olivet Nazarene U., 1971; Degree in Med. Tech., Silver Cross Hosp., Joliet, Ill., 1972; MS in Biology, Ball State U., 1999. Med. tech. Riverside Hosp., Kankakee, 1971-72, Silver Cross Hosp., Joliet, 1972-77; lab. mgr. Lakeshore Community Hosp., 1977-90; evening lab. supr. Community Hosp., Anderson, Ind., 1990-93; med. technologist Community Hosp. of Anderson, 1990—. Lectr. in field. Health care rep. Local Emergency Preparedness Com., Hart, Mich., 1988-90; sec., deacon, bd. dirs. West Shore Christian Fellowship, Muskegon, 1987-90, vice chmn. edn. com., 1988-90; mem. Rep. Nat. Com. S.W. Nazarene Ch. Dist. grantee, 1967, Directed Study grantee, 1970-71, rsch. grantee Sigma Xi, 1993; grad. rsch. grantee Ball State U., 1994. Mem. Am. Soc. Clin. Pathologists. Republican. Avocations: acting, poetry, astronomy. Home: 1705 N Tillotson Ave Muncie IN 47304-2601 Office: Community Hosp 1515 N Madison Ave Anderson IN 46011-3457

WHITAKER, BRUCE EZELL, college president; b. Cleveland County, N.C., June 27, 1921; m. Esther Adams, Aug. 22, 1947; children: Barry Eugene, Garry Bruce. BA, Wake Forest U., 1944; BD, So. Bapt. Theol. Sem., 1947, ThM, 1948, PhD, 1950; postgrad., George Peabody Coll., 1952; DL, Wake Forest U., 1987. Ordained to ministry Bapt. Ch., 1945; pastor Smithfield, Ky., 1945-49; instr. sociology and philosophy Ind. U., 1947-50; prof. religion Cumberland U., Lebanon, Tenn., 1950-51, Belmont Coll., Nashville, 1951-52; prof. sociology, asst. to pres. Shorter Coll., Rome, 1952-53; asso. pastor, minister edn. Atlanta, 1953-54; state sec., student dept. Bapt. State Conv., N.C., 1954-57; pres. Chowan Coll., Murfreesboro, 1957-89, pres. emeritus, 1989—. Mem. adv. com. to Nd. Higher Edn., 1962-66; to N.C. Commn. Higher Edn. Facilities, 1964—; pres. N.C. Conf. Social Svc., 1965-67, Assn. Governing Bds., 1973-82, Assn. So. Baptist Colls. and Schs., 1967-68, Assn. Eastern N.C. Colls., 1968-69; bd. dirs. Regional Edn. Lab. for Carolinas and Va. Pres. bd. trustees N.C. Found. Church-Related Colls., 1970-74; bd. dirs., v.p. Nat. Coun. Ind. Jr. Colls., 1974-75, pres., 1975-76; mem. adv. coun. presidents Assn. Governing Bds., from 1973; mem. N.C. Bd. Mental Health, from 1966; bd. dirs. Am. Assn. Cmty. and Jr. Colls., 1976-82; pres. N.C. Assn. Colls. and Univs., 1977-78; chmn. N.C. Commn. Mental Health/Mental Retardation Sers., 1978-81; mem. N.C. Commn. on Mental Health, Developmental Disabilities, and Alcohol and Drug Svcs., 1995—. V.p. Bapt. State Conv. N.C., 1989-91. Named Tarheel of Week Raleigh News and Observer, 1962, Boss of Year N.C. Jaycees, 1972; tribute paid in Congl. Record, 1962, 89; Whitaker Libr. at Chowan Coll. named for him; Whitaker Sch. at Butner, N.C. named for him; selected one of nation's 18 most effective coll. pres. in 1985, funded study Exxon Found.; featured in We the People of North Carolina, 1989. Mem. N.C. Lit. and Hist. Assn. (pres. 1970-71), Am. Acad. Polit. and Social Scis., NEA, Am. Assn. Community and Jr. Colls. (dir. 1976-82, Leadership Recognition award 1989), Nat. Assn. Ind. Colls. and Univs. (dir. 1977-78, 81-85), Am. Assn. Higher Edn., Am. Coun. Edn. (bd. dirs. 1985-89), Internat. Platform Assn., Omicron Delta Kappa. Clubs: Capital City (Raleigh, N.C.), Capitol Club (Raleigh); Rotary (chmn. dist. student exchange com. 1969-72, Paul Harris fellow); Optimist; Beechwood Country (Ahoskie, N.C.); Harbor (Norfolk, Va.). Office: PO Box 40 Murfreesboro NC 27855-0040

WHITAKER, CLEM, JR. advertising and public relations executive; b. Sacramento, Aug. 30, 1922; s. Clem and Harriett (Reynolds) W.; 1 child, Isabella Alexandra. Student, Sacramento Jr. Coll., 1942, U. Calif.-Berkeley, 1943. Reporter, Sacramento Union, 1938-40; staff mem. Campaigns, Inc.-Whitaker & Baxter, San Francisco, 1946-50, partner, 1950-58, pres., 1958—; partner Whitaker & Baxter Advt. Agy., San Francisco, 1950-58, pres., 1958—. Co-pub. Calif. Feature Svc., San Francisco, 1950—; chmn. Wye Energy Group. Bd. dirs. San Francisco Opera Assn. With USAAF, 1942-46, ETO. Mem. Cercle de L'Union, Villa Tavernea. Home: 2040 Broadway St San Francisco CA 94115-1500 Office: Box 334 2443 Fillmore St San Francisco CA 94115-1814

WHITAKER, EILEEN MONAGHAN (EILEEN MONAGHAN), artist; b. Holyoke, Mass., Nov. 22, 1911; d. Thomas F. and Mary (Doona) Monaghan; m. Frederic Whitaker. Ed., Mass. Coll. Art, Boston. Annual exhibits in nat. and regional juried shows; represented in permanent collections, Frye Mus., Seattle, NA, Hispanic Soc., N.Y.C., High Mus. Art, Atlanta, U. Mass., Norfolk (Va.) Mus., Springfield (Mass.) Mus. Art, Reading (Pa.) Art Mus., Nat. Acad., U. Mass., Okla. Mus. Art, St. Lawrence U., Wichita State U., Retrospective show, Founders Gallery U. San Diego, 1988, invitational one-person show Frye Art Mus., 1990; included in pvt. collections; featured in cover article of American Artist mag., Mar. 1987, in article Art of Calif. mag., July 1991; invitational Am. Realism Exhbn. Cir. Gallery, San Diego, 1992; author: Eileen Monaghan Whitaker Paints San Diego, 1986. Recipient numerous major awards, including Allied Artists Am., Am. Watercolor Soc., 1st prize Providence Water Color Club, Wong award Calif. Watercolor Soc., De Young award Soc. Western Artists, 1st award Springville (Utah) Mus., Ranger Fund purchase prize, Orbrig prize NA, Walter Biggs Meml. award, 1987; silver medal Am. Watercolor Soc., Watercolor West; fellow Huntington Hartford Found., 1964. Mem. Nat. Acad. Design (Academician NA William P. and Gertrude Schweitzer prize for excellence in watercolor 171st Annual Exbhn. 1996); mem. Am. Watercolor Soc. (Dolphin fellow), Watercolor West (hon.), San Diego Watercolor Soc. (hon.), Providence Watercolor Club (award), Phila. Watercolor Club.. Home: 1579 Alta La Jolla Dr La Jolla CA 92037-7101 E-mail: fandemwhitaker@aol.com.

WHITAKER, EVANS PARKER, academic administrator; b. Shelby, N.C., Nov. 4, 1960; s. Howard Vernon and Helen Louise (Parker) W. BSBA, Gardner-Webb U., 1983; MEd in Instn. Advancement, Vanderbilt U., 1986, PhD in Edn. and Human Devel., 1999. Dir. found. and corp. rels. Gardner-Webb U., Boiling Springs, N.C., 1983-86; exec. asst. to pres. Gardner-Webb Coll., 1986-88, assoc. v.p., 1990-92; v.p. devel. Wingate (N.C.) U., 1992-96; dir. endowment and trust devel. N.C. Bapt. Found., Cary, 1988-90; dir. development Belmont U., Nashville, 1996-97, v.p. univ. advancement, 1998—. Bd. trustees Leukemia/Lymphoma Soc. Tenn.; bd. dirs. Bapt. Employee Credit Union, Cary. President Boiling Springs Rotary, 1988; mem. Shelby (N.C.) Rotary, 1991. Vanderbilt U. scholar, 1985; recipient Resolution of Appreciation, Gardner-Webb U., 1987, 88, Grenzebach Dissertation of the Yr. award, 2000, Warwick Dissertation of the Yr. award, 2000. Mem. Am. Assn. Higher Edn., Assn. for Study Higher Edn., Coun. for Advancement and Support of Edn., Am. Edn. Rsch. Assn. Home: 509 Brennan Lane Franklin TN 37067 Office: Belmont Univ 1900 Belmont Blvd Nashville TN 37212-3757

WHITAKER, GILBERT RILEY, JR. academic administrator, business economist; b. Oklahoma City, Oct. 8, 1931; s. Gilbert Riley and Melodese (Kilpatrick) W.; m. Ruth Pauline Tonn, Dec. 18, 1953; children: Kathleen, David Edward, Thomas Gilbert. BA, Rice U., 1953; postgrad., So. Methodist U., 1956-57; MS in Econs., U. Wis., Madison, 1958, PhD in Econs. (Ford Found. dissertation fellow), 1961. Instr., Sch. of Bus. Northwestern U., 1960-61, asst. prof. bus. econs., Sch. of Bus., 1961-64, asso. prof., Sch. of Bus., 1964-66, research assoc. Transp. Center, Sch. of Bus., 1962-66; asso. prof. Washington U., St. Louis, 1966-67, prof., 1967-76, adj. prof. econs., 1968-76, asso. dean Sch. Bus. Adminstrn., 1969-76; dean, prof. bus. econs. M.J. Neeley Sch. Bus., Tex. Christian U., 1976-79; dean U. Mich., 1979-90; prof. Sch. Bus. Adminstrn. U. Mich., 1979-97; provost, v.p. acad. affairs U. Mich., Ann Arbor, 1990-93, provost, exec. v.p. acad. affairs, 1993-95; sr. advisor Andrew W. Mellon Found., 1996—; dean Jesse Jones Graduate Sch. of Mgmt./Rice U., Houston, 1997—. Dir. Am. Assembly of Collegiate Schs. of Bus., 1984-91, v.p., pres.-elect, 1988-89, pres., 1989-90, dir. Washington campus, 1980-89, chmn., 1985-88; bd. dirs. Lincoln Nat. Corp., 1986-2002; Johnson Controls, Inc., 1985-2001; Structural Dynamics Rsch. Corp., 1986-2001; sr. economist banking and currency com. U.S. Ho. of Reps., 1964; mem. Grad. Mgmt. Admissions Coun., 1972-75, chmn., 1974-75; bd. dirs. Washtenaw County United Way, 1990-96. Author: (with Marshall Colberg and Dascomb Forbush) books including Business Economics, 6th edit., 1981, (with Roger Chisholm) Forecasting Methods, 1971. Bd. trustees, sec.-treas. JSTOR, 1995-2002. With USN, 1953-56. Mem. Am. Econ. Assn., Ft. Worth Boat Club. Home: 6425 Mercer St Houston TX 77005-3733 Office: Rice University Jesse Jones Grad Sch of Mgmt 6100 Main St # Ms531 Houston TX 77005-1892 E-mail: grwhit@rice.edu.

WHITAKER, GLENN VIRGIL, lawyer; b. Cin., July 23, 1947; s. Glenn M. and Doris (Handlon) W.; m. Jennifer Lynn Angus, Oct. 22, 1990. BA, Denison U., 1969; JD, George Washington U., 1972. Bar: Md. 1972, D.C. 1973, Ohio 1980. Law clk. to judge U.S. Dist. Ct., Balt., 1972-73; assoc. O'Donoghue and O'Donoghue, Washington, 1973-76; trial atty. civil div. U.S. Dept. Justice, 1976-78, spl. litigation counsel, 1978-80; ptnr. Graydon, Head & Ritchey, Cin., 1980-92, Voyrs, Sater, Seymour & Pease, Cin., 1992—. Emeritus master of bench Potter Stewart Inn of Ct., Cin., 1985—; adj. prof. law Coll. Law U. Cin.; mem. Am. Bd. Trial Advocates. Fellow Am. Coll. Trial Lawyers; mem. ABA, Ohio Bar Assn., D.C. Bar Assn., Md. Bar Assn., Cin. Bar Assn. Avocations: hiking, exploring. Office: Vorys Sater Seymour & Pease 221 E 4th St Ste 2100 Cincinnati OH 45202-5133

WHITAKER, HEIDI SUE, accountant, auditor, information systems specialist; b. Framingham, Mass., Sept. 21, 1964; d. Charles Harvey and Judith R. (Reich) Whitaker; m. Raymond Serverian, Oct. 8, 1988 (div. Dec. 1997); 1 child, William Michael. BS in Acctg., BS in Mgmt. Info. Sys., U. Ariz., 1987; Master Cert. in Info. Tech. Project Mgmt, George Washington U., 1999; postgrad. in Law, Tex. Wesleyan Sch. Law, 2002—. Acctg. clk. Inventory Auditors, Inc., Denver, 1984; leasing and adminstrv. asst. James Presley Co., Tucson, 1985-86; office mgr. Sid's Appliance and TV, 1986; assoc. acct., acct. GTE Calif., Thousand Oaks, Calif., 1987-89; auditor I and II GTE Svc. Corp., Westlake Village, 1989-91, sr. auditor, 1991-94; staff acct., staff adminstr. regulatory acctg. GTE Telephone Ops., Irving, Tex., 1994-96; bus. process specialist sys. GTE Long Distance, 1996-97; program mgr. info. tech. GTE Bus. Devel. and Integration, 1997-99; IT audit mgr. EXCEL Comms., Inc., 1999-2000, sr. IT audit mgr., 2000—02; audit mgr. Citigroup, 2002—. Mem. Project Mgmt. Inst., 1996—. Sec, bd. dirs. Congregation Kol Ami, 1997-98, sisterhood pres., 1997-99, chmn. reengring. com., 1997-99, treas. bd. dirs., 1999-2002, exec. v.p. bd. dirs., 2002-; chair Highland Village Balloon Fest Stage Entertainment, 1998-99. Mem. Inst. Mgmt. Accts. (CMA), Inst. Internal Auditors, Lions (Lionette 1990-95, tail twister Flower Mound 1996-98, pres. Highland Village 1999-2000). Avocations: arts and crafts, word puzzles, roller-blading. Office: Citigroup 250 Carpenter Fwy Irving TX 75062

WHITAKER, JAMES DENNIS, retired retailer, mayor; b. Lexington, Nebr., Oct. 20, 1936; s. James Ebbert and Kathleen Whitaker; m. Nancy Jolene Whitaker, June 14, 1959; children: Kimberly Anne Nichols, David James Whitaker. BS, U. Nebr., 1959; JD, U. Denver, 1961. Bar: Colo. 1961, Nebr. 1963. Lawyer Kilroy, Meiklejohn Law Firm, Denver, 1961-63; with Whitaker Furniture Co., North Platte, Nebr., 1963-87, pres., 1975-87; mayor City of North Platte, 1996—. Legis. com. Nebr. League of Municipalities, Lincoln, 1997—; bd. dirs. Great Plains Regional Med. Ctr., North Platte, North Platte Devel. Corp. Gen. chmn., v.p. Nebrakaland Days, North Platte, 1967-76; vice chmn. Urban Renewal Authority, North Platte, 1969-78; mem., chmn. Civil Svc. Commn., North Platte, 1989-96, Airport Authority, North Platte, 1989-96. Named Young Man of Yr. North Platte Jaycees, 1972, Retailer of Yr. Nebr. Retail Merchants Assn., 1980; apptd. Admiral in the Nebr. Navy, Gov. State of Nebr., 1972, 80; recipient Disting. Svc. award Nebr. U. Alumni Assn., 1982. Mem. North Platte Rotary Club (Paul Harris fellow 1997), Elks, Moose, C. of C. (bd. dirs. 1996—). Republican. Methodist. Avocations: running, photography. Home: 2311 Birchwood Rd North Platte NE 69101-5914 Office: City of North Platte 211 W 3rd St North Platte NE 69101-3911

WHITAKER, JOEL, publisher, editor, elected public official; b. Indpls., May 27, 1942; s. Quincy Myers and Sigur Elizabeth (Moore) W.; m. Donna Kay, Apr. 27, 1986. BS in Bus. Journalism, Ind. U., 1964, MA in Journalism, 1971; JD, Temple U., 1979. Reporter St. Petersburg (Fla.) Times, 1964, copy editor, 1966-68, Wall St. Journal, N.Y.C., 1968-73; bus. news editor Phila. Evening and Sunday Bull., 1973-78; law clk. Fellheimer, Krakower & Eicen, Phila., 1978-79; mng. editor Bank Letter, N.Y.C., 1979-80; editor, pres. Whitaker Newsletters Inc., Fanwood, N.J., 1980—. Chmn. Fanwood Planning Bd., 1981-85; trustee Fanwood cmty. Found. 1998—; mem. Downtown Redevel. Commn., Fanwood, 1983-85; mem. Union County (N.J.) local adv. commn. on alcoholism and drug abuse, 1993-97, chmn., 1994-95, vice chmn. 1997; councilman Borough of Fanwood, 1998—, coun. pres., 2000—. Mem. Newsletter Publishers Assn. (bd. dirs. 1983-92, found. trustee 1986—, treas. 1989-93), Soc. Profl. Journalists (treas. N.J. profl. chpt. 1997—), Nat. Press Club (Washington), Rotary (bd. dirs. Fanwood-Scotch Plains club 1996-98), Army and Navy Club (Washington). Republican. Roman Catholic. Office: Whitaker Newsletters Inc 313 South Ave Fanwood NJ 07023-1364

WHITAKER, JOHN KING, economics educator; b. Burnley, Lancashire, Eng., Jan. 30, 1933; came to U.S., 1967; s. Ben and Mary (King) W.; m. Sally Bell Cross, Aug. 24, 1957; children: Ann Elizabeth, Jane Claire, David John. BA in Econs, U. Manchester, 1956; A.M., Johns Hopkins U., 1957; PhD, Cambridge U., 1962. Lectr. U. Bristol, Eng., 1960-66; prof., 1966-69; vis. prof. U. Va., Charlottesville, 1967-68, prof. econs., 1969-86, chmn. dept. econs., 1979-82, Paul Goodloe McIntire prof. of econs., 1986-92, Georgia Bankard prof. of econs., 1992—. Author: The Early Economic Writings of Alfred Marshall, 1867-1890, 2 vols., 1975, The Correspondence of Alfred

Marshall, Economist, 3 vols., 1996. Mem. Am. Econ. Assn., Royal Econ. Soc., History of Econs. Soc. Home: 1615 Yorktown Dr Charlottesville VA 22901-3046 Office: U Va Dept Econs Rouss Hall Charlottesville VA 22901 E-mail: jw9s@virginia.edu.

WHITAKER, LINTON ANDIN, plastic surgeon; b. Navasota, Tex., Nov. 16, 1936; s. Ira Andin and Lena Rivers (Stedman) W.; m. Renata Grasmanis, Dec. 20, 1963; children: Derek Andin (dec.), Ingrid Marlena, Brandon Andrew. BA, U. Tex., 1958; MD, Tulane U., 1962. Diplomate Am. Bd. Surgery, Am. Bd. Plastic Surgery. Founder, dir. ctr. human appearance U. Pa. Med. Ctr., Phila., 1988—; resident in gen. surgery Dartmouth Affiliated Hosps., Hanover, N.H., 1965-69; resident in plastic surgery U. Pa. Hosp., Phila., 1969-71; chief plastic surgery Grad. Hosp., 1971-77, U. Pa. Hosp., Phila., 1987—, attending surgeon, 1971—; chief plastic surgery Children's Hosp. Phila., 1981—2001, attending surgeon, 1971—; v.p. med. staff Children's Hosp., Phila., 1992-94, pres. med. staff, 1994-96; attending physician VA Hosp., 1971—, Phila. Gen. Hosp., 1971-77; assoc. in plastic surgery Sch. Medicine, U. Pa., Phila., 1971-73, asst. prof. in plastic surgery, 1973-76, assoc. prof., 1976-81, prof., 1981—; founder, dir. ctr. human appearance U. Pa. Med. Ctr., 1988—. Vis. prof. South Australia Craniofacial Unit, Adelaide, Australia and New Zealand, 1981, U. Hawaii, 1983, Brown U., Providence, 1983, Mass. Gen. Hosp., Boston, 1984, U. Utah, Salt Lake City, 1984, U. B.C., Vancouver, 1986, U. Pitts., 1988, U. Calif., San Diego, 1992, Ohio Valley Soc. for Plastic and Reconstructive Surgery, 1992, N.Y. U., 1994; Curts vis. prof. Dartmouth U. Med. Ctr., Hanover, N.H., 1990, Kazanjian vis. prof. Mass. Gen. Hosp., Boston, 1990; First Seiichi Ohmori Meml. lectr. All Asiatic Congress on Aesthetic Surgery, Tokyo, 1988; vis. speaker Inst. Cosmotology and Inst. Stomatology, Moskow, Russia, 1985, vis. prof. Seoul Nat. U. and vis. speaker Korean Soc. for Plastic Surgeons, 1994; hon. vis. spkr. Chinese Plastic Surgery Soc., Beijing, 1996; lectr., speaker at univs., assns. in field. Co-author: Atlas of Cranio-maxillofacial Surgery, 1982, Aesthetic Surgery of the Facial Skelton, 1992; editor (with P. Randall): Symposium on the Reconstruction of Jaw Deformity, Clinics in Plastic Surgery, 1987, 1991; co-editor: Yearbook of Plastic and Reconstructive Surgery, 1980—97; assoc. editor: Seminars in Complementary Medicine, 2001—, mem. editl. bd.: Jour. Cutaneous Aging and Cosmetic Dermatology, 1988—; contbr. Capt. U.S. Army Med. Corps, 1963-65. Foederer fellow Foederer Fund for Excellence, 1985-88; NIH grantee, 1976-79, 81-87, 82-85, 89, Plastic Surgery Edn. Found. Rsch. grantee, 1980-82; recipient James IV Surg. Traveller award, 1979. Fellow Am. Coll. Surgeons, Am. Soc. Ophthalmic Plastic and Reconstructive Surgery (hon.); mem. AMA (mem. coun. sci. affairs, diagnostic and therapeutic tech. assessment reference panel 1982), Am. Assn. Plastic Surgeons (mem. program com. 1988, chmn. 1989, Rsch. grantee 1984-85), Am. Surg. Assn., Am. Alpine Workshop in Plastic Surgery (founding mem.), Am. Cleft Palate Assn. (chmn. com. classification craniofacial anomalies 1976-80, mem. program com. for 1978 mtg. 1977, mem. long-range planning com. 1980, mem. coun. 1981-84, chmn. internat. rels. com. 1981-83), Am. Cleft Palate Ednl. Found. (bd. dirs. 1975-84, chmn. rsch. com. 1975-78, chmn. instrl. courses 1980-81), Am. Soc. Aesthetic Plastic Surgery, Am. Soc. Craniofacial Surgery (mem. coun. 1992—), Am. Soc. Maxillofacial Surgeons, Am. Soc. Plastic and Reconstructive Surgeons (mem. pub. rels com. 1974-76, mem. plastic surgery speakers bur. 1977—), Am. Soc. Plastic and Reconstructive Surgeons Ednl. Found. (chmn. ednl. assessment com., maxillofacial truama and craniofacial anomalies 1975-78, mem. clin. symposia com. 1978-82, chmn. clin. symposia com. 1981-82), Internat. Cleft Palate & Related Craniofacial Anomalies Soc. (mem. program com. 1981, 89), Internat. Soc. Aesthetic Surgery, Internat. Soc. Craniofacial Surgeons (founding mem., organizer, mem. exec. com. 1987—, sec and treas. 1993-95, pres. 1995-97), Phila. Med. Soc., Phila. Acad. Surgery, Coll. Physicians Phila., Assn. Acad. Surgery, Northeastern Soc. Plastic Surgeons N.Y. (chmn. program com. 1987, mem. programcom. 1988), Plastic Surgery Rsch. Coun., John Morgan Soc., Robert H. Ivy Soc., The Columbian Soc. Plastic, Maxillofacial and Hand Surgery (hon.), Academia Medica Lombarda (Italy, hon.). Sociedad Jamie Planas de Cirugia Plastica (Spain, hon.), Mt. Kenya Safari Club (hon.), Soc. Former Residents and Assocs. Plastic Surgery (hon.), Japan Soc. Craniomaxillofacial Surgeons (hon.), asian Pacific Cranofacial Assn., Phila. Club, Merion Cricket Club. Avocations: mountaineering, skiing, wines. Office: U Pa Med Ctr 10 Penn Tower 3400 Spruce St Philadelphia PA 19104-4206 E-mail: lwhitake@mail.med.upenn.edu.

WHITAKER, MARK THEIS, magazine editor; b. Lower Merion, Pa., Sept. 7, 1957; s. Cleophus Sylvester and Jeanne (Theis) W.; m. Alexis Lynn Gelber, May 5, 1985; children: Rachel Eva, Matthew Edward. BA summa cum laude, Harvard U., 1979; postgrad., Oxford (Eng.) U., 1979-81; LLD (hon.), Wheaton Coll. Assoc. editor Newsweek mag., N.Y.C., 1981-83, gen. editor, 1983, sr. writer, 1984-86, sr. editor, bus. editor, 1987-91, asst. mng. editor, 1991-95, mng. editor, 1996-98, editor, 1998—. Marshall scholar Brit. Marshall Fund, Oxford U., 1979-81. Mem. Nat. Assn. Black Journalists, Am. Soc. Mag. Editors (bd. dirs.), Coun. on Fgn. Rels., Century Assn., Phi Beta Kappa. Office: Newsweek 251 W 57th St New York NY 10019-1802

WHITAKER, MARSHA JONES, author, educator; b. Balt., Nov. 12, 1959; d. Arthur John Jones Jr. and Joyce Irene Jones Smith; m. Marvin J. Whitaker Sr., May 31, 1991; 1 child, Marvin J. Jr. AA, U. Md., 1985, BS, 1996. Coord., legal writer State of Md., Office of State's Atty., Balt., 1986—; owner, prin. Learning By Reading Inc., 1998—. Author, editor: Marvin's Adventure in the Owl, 1997, Marvin's Adventures in the Talking, 1997, Marvin's Adventures in the Universe, 1998, Marvin's Adventures in Learning About Cells, 2000, Marvin's Adventures in Learning About Mammals, 2001. Recipient Editor's Choice award Nat. Libr. of Poetry, 1995, 96, 97, 98, Golden Apple award Balt. Pub. Schs., 1998. Democrat. Avocations: writing poetry, books, lyrics, music. E-mail: marshawhitaker3@att.net.

WHITAKER, MICAL ROZIER, theater director, educator; b. Metter, Ga., Feb. 10, 1941; s. Ellis and Alma Mical Whitaker; m. Georgenia Lyons Whitaker, Sept. 1, 1978 (div. June 0, 1991); children: Georgenia Lyons. BFA, NC A&T State U., Greensboro, NY, 1989. Founder and dir. East River Players, New York, NY, 1964—76; prodr. Ossie Davis and Ruby Dee Story Hour, 1975—77; asst. prof. Ga. So. U., Statesboro, Ga., 1981—. Cons. Children's TV Productions Sesame St., 1969; artistic dir. Richard Allen Ctr. Culture and Art, 1978—82; writer and dir. Teleprompter Cable TV, New York, NY, 1971; founder and coord. Lincoln Ctr. St. Theatre Festivals, New York, NY, 1979—81. Dir.: (festival) Words from the Renaissance, (birthday pageant) A Place of Sunshine, (tragedy) Othello, (ceremony) The Audelco Awards, (historical drama) The Drinking Gourd, (tragi-comedy) The Real Queen of Hearts Ain't Even Pretty, (fables for children) Story Theatre, The Last Night at Ballyhoo, The Foreigner, Purile Victorious, (musical) Tambourines to Glory, Before the Flood; dir., dir.: Everyman and Roach, The fantasticks, (play) A Glance From God, To Be Young, Gifted and Black, Shades of Harlem, Eyes, One More Sunday, Black Nativity, Home, On the Brink of the Mountaintop, Ceremonies in Dark Old Men, High on People, The Importance of Being Earnest, St. Louis Woman, (drama) Agamemnon, A Christmas Carol, The Miracle Worker, In Splendid Error, Who's Afraid of Virginia Woolf, The Biko Inquest, Johnny Moonbeam and the Silver Arrow, The Amen Corner, (play) Boochie, From the Mississippi Delta, Spunk, Maricella de la Luz, Long Day's Journey into Night, Stairs to the Roof; actor: As You Like It; dir., actor: Everyman and Roach, Merlin, The Bloodknot, Ma Rainey's Black Bottom; actor, actor: I'm Not Rappaport, Twelfth Night, The Cherry Orchard. Recipient Dir. Musical, Audelco Awards, 1975, Emmy, Seattle Chpt., 1979-1980, G.S.C. Masquers award, G.S.C., 1982, Jefferson citation Directing, Kuumba Theatre, 1979, Spl. award St. Theatre, NYC, 1973, Renaissance and Cultural Devel. award, Black Image Awards, 2000, YMCA Little Theatre Award Set Design, YMCA, 1963, AUDELCO award St. Theatre, AUDELCO, 1977, AUDELCO award Directing, 1979; fellow Nat. Endowment Humanities fellowship, Duke U., 1991, Fulbright-Hays and U.S. Dept. Edn. fellowship, Ga. Consortium, 1992. Mem.: NAACP. Achievements include Founded Candler Company Cultural Center Communication. Avocations: travel, reading, home decorating, theatre. Home: 515 Washington Street Metter GA 30439 Office: Georgia Southern University Po 8091 Statesboro GA 30460 Office Fax: 912-681-0822. E-mail: mrwhit@gasou.edu.

WHITAKER, RONALD STEPHEN, lawyer; b. Cleve., Oct. 26, 1957; s. Wilbert S. and Dolores J. Whitaker; m. Carolyn M. Conyers, Sept. 29, 1984; children: Christopher, Chelsea. BA, UCLA, 1980, JD, 1983. Bar: Calif. 1983, U.S. Dist. Ct. (cen. dist.) Calif., 1983, U.S. Dist. Ct. (so. dist.) Calif., 1984, U.S. Dist. Ct. (ea. dist.) Calif., 1993, U.S. Ct. Appeals (9th cir.) 1983. Assoc. Ritter, Winne & Rodriguez, L.A., 1983-86, Spray, Gould & Bowers, L.A., 1986-88, prin., 1988-91; shareholder, founding mem. Robinson, Dilando & Whitaker, 1991—. Mem. ABA, Am. Bd. Trial Advocates, Def. Rsch. Inst., L.A. County Bar Assn., Nat. Bar Assn., John M. Langston Bar Assn. Republican. Avocations: basketball, softball. Office: Robinson Dilando & Whitaker 800 Wilshire Blvd Ste 1100 Los Angeles CA 90017-2615 E-mail: rwhitaker@rdwlaw.com.

WHITAKER, RUTH REED, state legislator, retired newspaper editor; b. Blytheville, Ark., Dec. 13, 1936; d. Lawrence Neill and Ruth Shipton (Weidemeyer) Reed; m. Thomas Jefferson Whitaker, dec. 29, 1961; children: Steven Bryan, Alicia Morrow. BA, Hendrix Coll., 1958. Copywriter, weather person KTVE TV, El Dorado, Ark., 1958-59; nat. bridal cons. Treasure House, 1959; bridal cons. Pfeifers of Ark., Little Rock, 1959-60; dir. of continuity S. M. Brooks Advt. Agy., 1960-61; layout artist C. V. Mosby Co., St. Louis, 1961-62; editor, owner Razorback Am. Newspaper, Ft. Smith, Ark., 1979-81; ret., 1981; mem. from dist. 3 Ark. State Senate, 2000—. Host Crawford Conversations TV show; contbr. author indsl. catalog, 1979 (Addy award). State sec. Rep. Party of Ark., 1992-94, mem. Ark. Electoral Coll., 1996, del. Rep. Nat. Conv., 1996; ; mem. Ben Geren Regional Park Commn., Sebastian County, Ark., 1984-89, pres., 1990; past pres. Jr. Civic League; mem. Ft. Smith Orchid Com.; mem. com. of 21 United Way; publicity chmn. Sebastian County Rep. Com., 1983-84; state press officer Reagan-Bush Campaign, 1984; exec. dir. Ark. Dole for Pres., 1995-96; pres. Women's Aux. Sebastian County Med. Soc., 1974; mem. Razorback Scholarship Fund; class agt. alumni fund Hendrix Coll., 1990, 91, 92; mem. Sparks Woman's Bd.; 1st vice chmn. 3d Dist. Rep. Party; state committeewoman Rep. Party Ark.; chmn. Crawford County Rep. Com.; apptd. by Gov. of Ark. to Commr. Ark. Ednl. TV Network Commn., sec. 1998-99; mem. city coun., City of Cedarville, Ark., 1998. Recipient Disting. Vol. Leadership award Nat. Found. March of Dimes, 1973, Appreciation award Ft. Smith Advt. Fedn., 1977, 78, Hon. Parents of Yr. award U. Ark., 1984, Recognition award United Cerebral Palsy, 1980. Mem. AAUW, Alden Soc. Am. (life), Ft. Smith C. of C., Ark. Nature Conservancy, Am. Legion Aux., Frontier Rschrs. Soc. (pres. 1995-96), Daus. Union Vets. Presbyterian. Avocations: philanthropy, genealogy, writing, photography, ornithology. Home: PO Box 349 Cedarville AR 72932-0349

WHITAKER, SANDRA SUE, soprano, educator; b. South Bend, Ind., June 20, 1949; d. William George and Bertha May (Culp) McPhail; m. Audie Dale Whitaker, Aug. 22, 1970; children: Audie David, Andrea, Alexandra. BA in Music Edn., Olivet Nazarene U., Bourbonnais, Ill., 1974; MM in Music, Am. Conservatory of Music, Chgo., 1994; MM in Voice, Ball State U., 1993, DA in Voice, 1998. Music tchr. Joliet (Ill.) Pub. Schs., 1974-77; singer, presenter S.W. for the Arts, 1977—; grad. asst. Ball State U., Muncie, Ind., 1991-96; voice tchr. Ind. Wesleyan U., Marion, 1996-97; music tchr. Muncie Cmty. Pub. Schs., 1998—. Mem. ch. choir Parker Christ Fellowship, Parker City, Ind., 1996—. Ball State U. grantee, 1991-93, 93-96. Mem. Nat. Assn. Tchrs. of Singing, Sigma Alpha Iota, Pi Kappa Lambda. Avocation: visual art. Home: 1705 N Tillotson Ave Muncie IN 47304-2601 Office: SW for the Arts 1705 N Tillotson Ave Muncie IN 47304-2601

WHITAKER, SCOTT, federal agency administrator; B in Polit. Sci., Palm Beach Atlantic Coll.; M in Govt., Johns Hopkins U. Staff mem. Senate Asst. Majority Leader Don Nickles, policy adviser, 1997—; asst. sec. for legislation Dept. HHS, Washington, 2001—. Office: Dept HHS Legislation 200 Independence Ave SW Washington DC 20201*

WHITAKER, SHIRLEY ANN, telecommunications company marketing executive; b. Asmara, Eritea, Ethiopia, Oct. 13, 1955; (parents Am. citizens); d. Calvin Randall and Ruth (Ganeles) Peck; m. John Marshall Whitaker, June 16, 1973; 1 child, Kathryn Ann. AA, Tacoma Community Coll., 1974; BA, Wash. State U., 1977, MBA, 1978. Planning adminstr. for econ. rsch. GTE NW, Everett, Wash., 1978-80; specialist in demand analysis western region GTE Svc. Corp., Los Gatos, Calif., 1980-81, fin. analyst Stamford, Conn., 1981-83, staff specialist demand analysis and forecasting, 1983-84; group mgr. for rate devel. Nat. Exch. Carrier Assn., Whippany, N.J., 1984-87; mgr. pricing strategy and migration GTE Calif., Thousand Oaks, 1987-88; mgr. market forecasting GTE Telephone Ops. Hdqrs., Irving, Tex., 1989-90, dir. revenue analysis, 1990-92, dir. market rsch., 1992-93, dir. process re-engring., 1993-94, dir. network and resource mgmt., 1994-97; gen. sales mgr. customer contact GTE Network Svcs., Victorville, Calif., 1997-2000; dir. employee devel. Verizon Comm., N.Y.C., 2000—01, dir. support and response ctrs. Trenton, NJ, 2001—. Mem. Am. Mktg. Assn. (mem. chair 1984), Beta Gamma Sigma, Phi Kappa Phi, Rotary (sec. 2000). Avocation: sailing.

WHITAKER, SUSANNE KANIS, veterinary medical librarian; b. Clinton, Mass., Sept. 10, 1947; AB in Biology, Clark U., 1969; MS in Library Sci., Case Western Res. U., 1970. Regional reference librarian Yale Med. Library, New Haven, 1970-72; med. librarian Hartford Hosp., Conn., 1972-77; asst. librarian Cornell U., Ithaca, N.Y., 1977-78; vet. med. librarian Coll. Vet. Medicine, Cornell U., 1978-98, vet. pub. svcs. libr., 1998—. Mem. Med. Libr. Assn. (sec.-treas. vet. med. librs. sect. 1983-84, chmn. 1984-85, chmn. pub. rels. com. 2000—), Med. Libr. Assn. (upstate N.Y. and Ont. chpt.), Acad. Health Info. Profls. Home: 23 Wedgewood Dr Ithaca NY 14850-1064 Office: Cornell U Coll Vet Medicine Flower-Sprecher Libr Ithaca NY 14853-6401 E-mail: skw2@cornell.edu.

WHITAKER, THOMAS PATRICK, lawyer; b. Washington, Sept. 22, 1944; s. Thomas J. and Mary K. (Finn) W.; m. Donna Mae Brenish, Feb. 16, 1974; children: Laura, Kevin. BA, George Washington U., 1966, MPA, 1973, JD, 1979; postgrad., Naval War Coll., 1984. Bar: Va. 1979. Staff asst. Adminstrn. Office of U.S. Cts., Washington, 1972-73, analyst, 1975-77; cons. Planning Research Corp., McLean, Va., 1973-75; mgmt. analyst CAB, Washington, 1977-82; program analyst Social Security Adminstrn., Falls Church, Va., 1982—. Served to lt. (j.g.) USNR, 1966-71, Vietnam, capt. with Res. 1983-97. Acting U.S. Naval Attache, Malaysia, 1992. Mem. U.S. Naval Inst., Naval Res. Assn., Res. Officers Assn. Home: 9817 Days Farm Dr Vienna VA 22182-7306 E-mail: twhitake@hotmail.com.

WHITBECK, JILL KARLA, lawyer; b. Bangkok, Jan. 17, 1968; d. Joseph Kern Walter and Ruth Ann Tucker; m. Christopher Lee Whitbeck, July 20, 1991; children: Jasmine Claire, Donald Joseph, Jade Karin, Jennifer Morgan. BA, Calif. Luth. U., 1990; JD, Pepperdine U. Sch. Law, 1993. Bar: Nev. 1993, U.S. Dist. Ct. Nev. 1994. Atty. Laxalt & Nomura, Reno, 1993-94, Edward M. Bernstein & Assocs., Reno, 1994-97, Law Offices of White & Meany, Reno, 1997-2000; sole practitioner, 2000—. Deaconess, sch. bd. New Beginnings Child Devel. Ctr., Washoe Valley, Nev., 1998—. Mem. ABA, ATLA, Nev. Trial Lawyers Assn., No. Nev. Women Lawyers Assn., Nev. State Bar Assn., Washoe County Bar Assn. Republican. Mem. Christian Ch. Office: 955 S Virginia St Ste 220 Reno NV 89502 Fax: (775) 337-8873. E-mail: jkwhitbeck@aol.com.

WHITBOURNE, SUSAN KRAUSS, psychology educator; b. Buffalo, Dec. 16, 1948; d. Theodore Calman Krauss and Lisbeth Kaethe Hauser Rock; m. Richard Desmond O'Brien, Sept. 19, 1981; children: Stacey Beth, Jennifer Louise O'Brien. BA, SUNY, Buffalo, 1970; PhD, Columbia U., 1974. Lic. psychologist, Mass. Asst. prof. SUNY, Geneseo, 1973-75; from. asst. prof. to assoc. prof. U. Rochester, N.Y., 1975-84; prof. U. Mass., Amherst, 1984—. Cons. VA, Bath, N.Y., 1974-84, Max Planck Inst., Berlin, 1988, Sandoz Pharms., Rochester, 1976. Author: The Aging Body, 1985, Adult Development, 1986, The Me I Know: A Study of Adult Identity, 1986, The Aging Individual, 1996, (with R. Halgin) Abnormal Psychology, 1994; consulting editor Psychology & Aging, 1986-90. Faculty coord. United Way U. Mass., 1994-95. Fellow APA (pres. divsn. 20 1995-96), Am. Psychol. Soc. (exec. bd.), Gerontol. Soc. Am. (exec. bd.). Democrat. Jewish. Avocations: piano, knitting, trumpet, sports, aerobics. Office: U Mass Dept Psychology Amherst MA 01003-7710

WHITBREAD, THOMAS BACON, English educator, author; b. Bronxville, N.Y., Aug. 22, 1931; s. Thomas Francis and Caroline Nancy (Bacon) W. BA, Amherst Coll., 1952; A.M., Harvard U., 1953, PhD, 1959. Instr. English, U. Tex. at Austin, 1959-62, asst. prof., 1962-65, asso. prof., 1965-71, prof., 1971—. Vis. asso. prof. Rice U., 1969-70; mem. lit. adv. panel Tex. Commn. on Arts and Humanities, 1972-76 Author (poetry): Four Infinitives, 1964, Whomp and Moonshiver, 1982; contbg. author: Prize Stories, 1962, The O. Henry Awards, 1962; editor: Seven Contemporary Authors, 1966. Recipient third Aga Khan prize for fiction Paris Rev., 1960, Lit. Anthology Program award Nat. Endowment for Arts, 1968, Outstanding Freshman Tchr. award Phi Eta Sigma, 1972-73 Mem. AAUP, Tex. Inst. Letters (Poetry award 1965, 83), Nat., Am. amateur press assns., Phi Beta Kappa. Democrat. Home: 1014 E 38th St Austin TX 78705-1835 Office: U Tex Dept English Austin TX 78712 E-mail: whitbread@mail.utexas.edu.

WHITBURN, GERALD, insurance company executive; b. Wakefield, Mich., July 12, 1944; s. Donald and Ruby E. (Nichols) W.; m. Charmaine M. Heise, May 3, 1969; children: Bree, Luke. BS, U. Wis., Oshkosh, 1966; MA, U. Wis., Madison, 1968; postgrad., Harvard U., 1988, 00, U. Pa., 1997. Aide Gov. Warren P. Knowles, Wis., 1966-69; personal asst. USN sec. John H. Chafee, Washington, 1969-72; automobile dealer, real estate developer Merrill, Wis., 1973-80; exec. asst. to Senator Robert W. Kasten U.S. Senate, Washington, 1981-87; dep. sec. Wis. Dept. Adminstrn., Madison, 1987-89; sec. Wis. Dept. Industry, Labor and Human Rels., 1989-91, Wis. Dept. Health and Social Svcs., Madison, 1991-95; sec. exec. office of health and human svcs. Commonwealth of Mass., Boston, 1995-96; pres., CEO, dir. Ch. Mut. Ins. Co., Merrill, Wis., 1996—; dir. Alliance of Am. Insurers. Mem. U.S. Labor Sec.'s Commn. on Achieving Necessary Skills, Washington, 1990-92. Contbr. articles to newspapers. Del. Rep. Nat. Conv., 1988, 92. Recipient Disting. Alumni award U. Wis., Oshkosh, 1991. Home: 2079 Sunset Dr Tomahawk WI 54487-9301 Office: Ch Mut Ins Co 300 Schuster Ln Merrill WI 54452

WHITBURN, MERRILL DUANE, English literature educator; b. Mpls., Apr. 29, 1938; s. George and Marie Ellen (Carlstedt) W.; m. Diane Robertson, June 15, 1960; children: Stephen, Mark, Elizabeth. AB, U. Mich., 1960, AM, 1968; PhD, U. Iowa, 1973. With Western Electric Co., N.Y.C. and Indpls., 1965-67; asst. prof. Tex. A&M U., College Station, 1973-77, assoc. prof., 1977-79; assoc. prof. English Rensselaer Poly. Inst., Troy, N.Y., 1979-83, prof., 1983-89, Louis Ellsworth Laflin prof., 1989—, chmn. dept., 1979-85, 88-95. Co-owner Pride and Prejudice Books, Ballston Lake, N.Y., 1985—. Author: Rhetorical Scope and Performance: The Example of Technical Communication, 2000; co-author: (booklet) Guide for Departments of English, 1985; contbr. articles to profl. publs. Recipient Disting. Svc. award Tex. A&M U., 1976, Disting. Teaching award, 1979, Jay R. Gould award for excellence in tchg. tech. comm. Soc. Tech. Comm., 1995; grantee Fund for the Improvement of Postsecondary Edn., 1983. Mem. Nat. Coun. Tchrs. English (best article in tech. writing award 1981), Coun. for Programs in Tech. and Sci. Communication.

WHITBY, RICHARD WILLIAM, newspaper editor, journalism educator; b. S.I., N.Y., Aug. 12, 1952; BA in Contemporary Arts, Ramapo Coll. N.J., 1980. Asst. nat. editor N.Y. Daily News, N.Y.C., 1997—. Adj. prof. comms. Ramapo Coll. N.J., Mahwah, 2000—. Office: N Y Daily News 450 W 33d St New York NY 10001 E-mail: rwhitby@edit.nydailynews.com., whitby.richard@verizon.net.

WHITCHURCH, CHARLES AUGUSTUS, art gallery owner, humanities educator; b. Long Beach, Calif., Sept. 29, 1940; s. Charles August and Frances Elizabeth (White) Whitchurch; m. Michéle Elizabeth Cartier, Aug. 17, 1968 (div. 1977); children: Gialisa Elizabeth, Marisa Tatiana; m. Mary Susan Ornelas, Jan. 28, 1984. BA in History, Santa Clara U., Irvine, 1962; MA in Comparative Lit., U. Calif., Irvine, 1970. Cert. grad. secondary teaching credential. Asst. ops. officer United Calif. Bank, Inglewood, 1965-66; tchr. English Laguna Beach (Calif.) High Sch., 1966-68; teaching assoc., fellow U. Calif., Irvine, 1968-70; prof. lit. and humanities Golden West Coll., Huntington Beach, Calif., 1971—, dir. honors program, chair. hon. coun., 2000—; owner, dir. Charles Whitchurch Fine Arts, 1978—. Cons. Pyo Gallery, Seoul, Dem. Peoples Rep. Korea, 1989-90, Gordon Gallery, Santa Monica, Calif., 1989-96, Pinnacle Creations, 1999—; judge, spkr. in field. Author mus. catalogues; contbr. articles to profl. jours. Founding mem., mem. adv. coun. Modern Mus. Art, Santa Ana, Calif., 1987-92. NEA grantee; named One of Outstanding Young Men Am., 1977. Mem.: Found. Creative Arts (bd. dirs. 1996—), Robert Gumbiner Found. for the Arts (bd. dirs. 1994—95), Assn. Literary Scholars and Critics, Art Dealers Assn. Calif. (bd. dirs. 1988—2001, sec. 1988—90, pres. 1990—92), Nat. Coun. Tchrs. English, Santa Clara Alumni Assn., The Libra Group (pres. 1994—2001), Huntington Beach Art Assn. (founding mem. 1990), Phi Sigma Tau, Alpha Sigma Nu. Avocations: swimming, weight tng., writing, reading. E-mail: cwhitchurch@gwc.cccd.edu.

WHITCOMB, CAMILLE GRIMES, psychologist; b. Annapolis, Md., Aug. 2, 1930; d. Clifton Garvin and Frances (Sellers) G.; m. Bruce Frederick Henderson, Nov. 23, 1952 (div. 1984); children: Leslie Henderson Weddell, Barbara Henderson Green, Elizabeth Henderson Garrett, Thomas C.G.; m. James Howard Whitcomb, Mar. 22, 1991. BS, Coll. William and Mary, 1952; MA, Fairfield U., 1980; PhD, Southeastern U., 1983. Psychologist Am. Sch. Sao Paulo, Brazil, 1965-74, Silver Hill Found., New Canaan, Conn., 1975-83; pvt. practice, 1983—91, , Hobe Sound, Fla., 1991—. Cons. on testing to internat. schs., S.Am., 1966-74; founder, pres. Cons. in Internat. Living, New Canaan, 1980-91; coord. Sci. in Edn. Women in Sch. Conn. and N.Y. 1984-91. Contbr. numerous articles, newspaper columns on testing and diagnostics. Bd. dirs. Hobe Sound Child Care Ctr., 1993—, New Horizons of Treasure Coast, Ft. Pierce, Fla., 1994-2000; bd. govs. Lablolly, Hobe Sound, 1998—; trustee Bishop's Sch., La Jolla, Calif., 2000—. Scholar Daus. of Cincinnati. Mem. Am. Psychol. Soc., Soc. Personality Assessment, AAUW (v.p., sec., pres. Ct. and Fla. 1974-99).

WHITCOMB, JAMES HALL, geophysicist, foundation administrator; b. Sterling, Colo., Dec. 10, 1940; s. Clay Thane and Julia Melvina Whitcomb; m. Sandra Lynn McMurdo, July 13, 1965 (div. 1978); m. Teresa R. Idoni, Feb. 3, 1989; children: Lisa Michelle, Marisa Giulia, Sabina Maria. Geophysics engring. degree, Colo. Sch. of Mines, 1962; MS in Oceanography, Geophysics, Oreg. State U., 1964; PhD in Geophysics, Calif. Inst. Tech., 1973. Grad. rsch. asst. dept. oceanography Oreg. State U., Corvallis, 1962-64; geophysicist ctr. astrogeology U.S. Geol. Survey, Flagstaff, Ariz., 1964-66; Fullbright-Hayes program rsch. fellow seismol. inst. U. Uppsala, Sweden, 1966-67; grad. rsch. asst. seismol. lab. Calif. Inst. Tech., Pasadena, 1967-73, sr. rsch. fellow seismol. lab., 1973-79; assoc. prof. attendant rank dept. geol. scis. U. Colo., Boulder, 1979-82, fellow Coop. Inst. Rsch. in Environ. Scis., 1979-84; v.p. technical applications and mktg. ISTAC, Inc., Pasadena, 1984-88; program dir. seismology NSF, Washington, 1989-99, acting dep. divsn. dir., 1999—. Expert witness U.S. Ho. Reps. Com. on Sci. and Tech., 1977; mem. geodynamics rev. bd. Jet Propulsion Lab., 1980-82, com. on geodesy Nat. Acad. Scis., 1982-85; pres. Boulder Systems, Inc., Pasadena, 1987-88. Recipient Outstanding Achievement award U.S. Geol. Survey, 1964, Dir.'s award for mgmt. excellence NSF, 1995; scholar State of Colo., 1958-62, Mobil Oil Co., 1960; fellow Sweden-Am. Found., 1966. Mem. AAAS, Am. Geophysical Union, Seismol. Soc. Am., Soc. Exploration Geophysicists (scholar 1963), Tau Beta Pi, Phi Kappa Phi, Sigma Xi. Office: Nat Sci Found Geosciences 4201 Wilson Blvd Arlington VA 22230-0002

WHITCOMB, JAMES HOWARD, communications company executive; b. Lewiston, Maine, June 12, 1927; s. Edwin H. and Alice (McLaughlin) W.; m. Eleanor Keady, June 7, 1952; children: Susan W. Ahern, James H., Michael K. BA, Bowdoin Coll., 1948; MBA, Harvard U., 1951. Field rep. Aetna Casualty and Surety Co., Boston, 1948-49; retail zone mgr. Time, Inc., N.Y.C., 1951-53; account exec. N.W. Ayer Co., Phila., 1953-57, account supr. N.Y.C., 1957-59; product mgr. Gen. Foods Corp., White Plains, N.Y., 1959-62, mktg. dir. Japan, 1962-64, gen. mgr. Australia, 1964-66, mng. dir. Eng., 1967-69; pres. Gen. Foods Europe, 1969-76, v.p. parent co., 1969—; pres. Gen. Foods, Latin Am., 1976-80, Gen. Foods internat. market devel., mktg. and adminstrn., 1980-83, Gen. Foods World Trade, 1983-86; pres. western hemisphere Bus. Internat. Corp., N.Y.C., 1986—. Mem.: Harvard Bus. Sch. (N.Y.C); Bay Head Yacht (N.J.); New Canaan (Conn.) Country; Harbour Ridge Country (Stuart, Fla.). Home: 6 Breen Rd Westerly RI 02891-5006 Office: Bus Internat Corp 1 Dag Hammarskjold Plz New York NY 10017-2201

WHITCOMB, JAMES HOWARD, JR. investment banker; b. Bryn Mawr, Pa., Nov. 15, 1954; s. James Howard Sr. and Eleanor Keady W.; m. Havilande Bayard Brown, Oct. 11, 1986; children: James Howard III, Ashton Bayard, Christiana Prescott. BA with honors, Williams Coll., 1976; MBA, U. Va.,

1981. Sr. v.p. Lehman Bros., N.Y.C., London, 1981-93; mng. dir. Chem. Securities, N.Y.C., 1995-97; sr. v.p. NatWest Markets, 1997-98; dir. Shattuck Hammond Ptnrs. LLC, 1998—2001, prin., 2001—. Bd.trustees Southport Conglist. Ch., 1998—2000, Southport Conservancy, 2000—02. Fellow Fgn. Policy Assn.; mem. Pequot Yacht Club, Fairfield County Hunt Club, Williams Club (N.Y.C.), U. Va. Club. Avocations: foreign relations, sailing, skiing, travel. Home: 249 Old South Rd Southport CT 06490 Office: 630 5th Ave New York NY 10111-0100

WHITCOMB, JAMES STUART, videographer, photographer, production company executive; b. Buffalo, May 7, 1957; s. C. Stuart and Helen Nancy (O'Reilly) W. BA in Journalism/Broadcasting, SUNY, Buffalo, 1983. Cert. master herbalist, iridologist. Pres., owner Ad Astra Prodns., Williamsville, N.Y., 1987—; co-owner, videographer, photographer STB Prodns., 1989—; owner legal books and computer software co. JSW Pub., 1997—. Videographer, editor nature/stress reduction Videos A Celebration of the Four Seasons, 1991, Autumn on Cape Code and Martha's Vineyard, 1993, Gardens, Blossoms & Blooms, 1994, A Walk Through St. Francis Woods, 1994, Nantucket Noel: Christmas on Nantucket, 1994, Reflections: Nature's Watercolors, 1995, Autumn in Vermont, 1995, A Day On the Farm, 1995, Window Shopping, 1995, Singalong with your Old Favorites, 1997, A Celebration of the Four Seasons II: Seasons of the Seashore, 1997, Kids and Animals, 1998; videographer, writer promotion video Internat. Modeling and Talent Assn., 1990; videographer numerous prodns. for modelling, fashion, and spl. interest. Supporter St. Joseph's Indian Sch., Chamberlain, S.D. Mem. People for Ethical Treatment of Animals, Wilderness Soc., Am. Hiking Soc., Nat. Audubon Soc., Farm Sanctuary, Best Friends Animal Sanctuary, Assn. for Rsch. and Enlightenment, Adirondack Mountain Club. Avocations: skiing (former instr.), hiking (former mountain guide). Home: 71 Rinewalt St Williamsville NY 14221-5736 Office: Ad Astra and STB Prodns PO Box 1725 Williamsville NY 14231-1725

WHITCOMB, RICHARD TRAVIS, aeronautical consultant; b. Evanston, Ill., Feb. 21, 1921; s. Kenneth Frederick and Gladys (Travis) Whitcomb. BS in Aero. Engring., Worcester Poly. Inst., 1943, DEng (hon.) , 1956; DSc (hon.) , Old Dominion U., 1985. Aero. research scientist Langley Research Ctr. NASA, Hampton, Va., 1943—58, head transonic aerodynamics br., 1958—80, disting. research assoc., 1980—85; pvt. practice aero. cons., 1980—90. Patentee aero. equipment. Recipient Collier Trophy, Nat. Aero. Assn., 1955, Nat. Medal for Sci., Office of the Pres. U.S., 1973, Wright Bros. trophy, Nat. Aero. Assn., 1974, award in Aeronautical Engring., NAS, 2000. Fellow: AIAA (hon. Reed award 1969, Daniel Guggenheim medal 2002); mem.: Nat. Acad. Engring. Avocations: music, reading, exercise.

WHITCRAFT, JAMES RICHARD, JR. accountant; b. Muncie, Ind., Jan. 27, 1947; s. James R. and Hazel V. (Garner) W.; m. Pamela D. Imel, July 29, 1977; children: Christopher K., Kelle D. BS, Ball State U., 1969, MBA, 1972. CPA, Ind., Mich. Sr. staff acct. Arthur Andersen & Co., Indpls., 1969-77; audit mgr. Holdeman, Fulmer, Elkhart, Ind., 1977-81; owner Dick Whitcraft, CPA, Elkhart, 1981-84; mng. ptnr. Whitcraft & Pletcher, LLP, CPA's, Elkhart and Goshen, 1984—. Tres. Life Recovery Ctr., Inc., 1985-92, Presbyn. Ch., 1985-87; bd. dirs., treas. Elkhart County YMCA, 1989—; pres. Big Bros./Big Sisters of Elhart County, 1977-78. With U.S. Army, 1969-71. Mem. AICPA, Ind. Assn. CPA's, Elkhart C. of C. (com. chmn. 1979-89), Blue Key, Sigma Chi (life), Elcona County Club. Republican. Lodge: Optimists (pres. Elkhart chpt. 1981-82, 84). Office: Whitcraft & Pletcher LLP CPAs 524 S 2nd St Elkhart IN 46516-3220 Home: 19148 Calvin Hill St Cassopolis MI 49031-9542

WHITE, ALAN EDWARD, computer company executive; b. Logan, W.Va., July 24, 1949; s. William Edward and Annabel White; m. Susan Rader, May 20, 1972; children: Megan, Elissa, Andrew. BS in Physics, W.Va. Tech., Montgomery, 1971. With tech. sales Preiser Sci., St. Albans, W.Va., 1972-75, Process Instruments Inc., Charleston, 1975-76; v.p. Std. Instrumentation, 1976-80; sys. engr. Warren Tech. Assocs., Circleville, Ohio, 1984-87; mgr. engring. BH-F Sys. Ltd., Toledo, 1987-91; v.p. engring. Advanced Control Solutions, Inc., Sylvania, 1991—. Asst. scoutmaster Boy Scouts Am., 1994—. With W.Va. N.G., 1971-77. Recipient Alumnus of Yr. award W.Va. Tech., 1999. Mem. Toledo Astronomical Assn., Instrument Soc. Am., Nat. Eagle Scout Assn. Republican. Mem. Christian Ch. (Disciples Of Christ). Avocations: backpacking, trap shooting, restoring vintage BMWs, building telescopes, watersports. Office: Advanced Control Solutions Inc 8750 Resource Park Dr Sylvania OH 43560

WHITE, ALAN FREDERICK, academic administrator; b. Evansville, Ind., Dec. 17, 1937; s. Hubert Ruben and Nota Lizzee (Culver) W.; m. Patricia Lynn Townsend, Nov. 7, 1959; children: Gregory Townsend, Samuel Townsend. AB, Miami U., Oxford, Ohio, 1963; MS, MIT, 1971. Dir. U. Hawaii Ctr. Crosscultural Tng. and Rsch., Hilo, 1967-70, exec. asst. to pres. Honolulu, 1971-73; Alfred P. Sloan fellow MIT, Cambridge, 1970-71, assoc. dir. exec. edn., 1973-78, dir. exec. edn., 1978-85, assoc. dean for exec. edn., 1985-95, sr. assoc. dean, COO, lectr., 1991. Cons. AT&T, Brit. Petroleum, Young Pres. Orgn.; bd. dir. SBS Tech., JonesUniversity.com, Internat. Consortium for Exec. Edn. Rsch.; bd. advisors The StartupAvenue.com, Toffler Assoc.; mem. Internat. Mgmt. Devel., 1985—. Contbr. articles to profl. jours. Mem. Consortium of Univ. Dirs. of Exec. Edn., Japan Mgmt. Inst. (adv. bd.), Mgmt. Scis. for Health (bd. dirs.). Avocations: oil painting, tennis, swimming, golf, gardening. Home: 13 Pickman Dr Bedford MA 01730-1009 Office: MIT Mit 50 Memorial Dr Cambridge MA 02139

WHITE, ALEXANDER B. retired internist; b. Krosno, Poland, June 4, 1923; came to U.S., 1950; s. Mendel and Leah (Platner) Bialywlos; m. Inez Kay Libby, Feb. 28, 1953; children: Denise, Les, Julie. MD, U. Munich, 1950. Diplomate Am. Bd. Internal Medicine and Nephrology. Pres. Med. Group, Olympia Fields, Ill., 1958-90; dir. Dialysis Ctr., 1978-94; ret., 1997. Capt. U.S. Army, 1953-55. Fellow ACP, Am. Coll. Cardiology. Avocations: swimming, travel. Home: 12160 N 123d Way Scottsdale AZ 85259-3353 Fax: 480-661-7211. E-mail: albiwhite@pol.net.

WHITE, ALFRED KENNETH, JR. lawyer; b. Pitts., Jan. 6, 1929; s. Alfred Kenneth Sr. and Mira Carlotta (Frey) W.; m. Virginia Ann Schwering, Sept. 1, 1956; children: Christopher F., Derek S. BA cum laude, Gettysburg (Pa.) Coll., 1951; JD, Yale U., 1957. Bar: N.Y. 1959, U.S. Dist. Ct. (so. and ea. dists.) N.Y. 1967. Atty. Vick Chem. Co., N.Y.C., 1957-59; gen. atty., sec. L. E. Waterman Pen Co. Ltd./Barker Automation, Inc., 1959-62; spl. atty. Procter & Gamble Co., Cin., 1962-66, counsel internat. div., 1966-90, gen. counsel-internat., 1990-91, v.p., gen counsel-internat., 1991-94; of counsel Douglas M. Case Law Firm, 1995—. Vice chmn. Internat. & Comparative Law Ctr., Southwestern Legal Found., Dallas, 1985-90, symposium chmn., 1991-94; adv. bd. U.S./Can. Law Inst., Cleve. Maj. USAR, 1946-48, 51-54. Mem. ABA, Internat. Bar Assn., Cin. Bar Assn., Camargo Hunt Club (sec. 1997—), Bankers Club, The Camargo Club. Republican. Episcopalian. Avocations: equestrian, antique silver and furniture, travel. Home and Office: 8885 Spooky Ridge Ln Cincinnati OH 45242-7350

WHITE, ALICE ELIZABETH, physicist, researcher; b. Glen Ridge, N.J., Apr. 5, 1954; d. Alan David and Elizabeth Joyce (Jones) W.; m. Donald Paul Monroe, Oct. 13, 1990; children: Ellen Elizabeth White Monroe, Janet Clare White Monroe. BA in Physics, Middlebury (Vt.) Coll., 1976; MA in Physics, Harvard U., 1978, PhD in Physics, 1982. Postdoctoral mem. tech. staff AT&T Bell Labs., Murray Hill, N.J., 1982-84, mem. tech. staff, 1984-88; dir. Bell Labs Lucent Technologies, 1988—. Contbr. over 100 articles to profl. pubs.; patentee in field. Recipient Alumni Achievement award Middlebury Coll., 1994. Fellow Am. Phys. Soc. (Maria Goeppert-Mayer award 1991); mem. IEEE, Optical Soc. of Am., Phi Beta Kappa. Office: Bell Labs Lucent Technol Rm 1D-339 PO Box 636 New Providence NJ 07974-0636

WHITE, ALICE VIRGINIA, volunteer health corps administrator; b. Wichita, Kans., June 30, 1946; d. Harry Houston White and Margaret V. (Milligan) Gabbert. BA in Russian (hons.) and Spanish, U. Kans., 1967; MS in Counseling, Kans. State U., Ft. Hays, 1973; PhD in Journalism, U. Tex., 1991. Tchr. Russian and Spanish Ingalls Sch. Dist., Kansas City, Mo., 1967-72; instr. Dodge City (Kans.) C.C., 1972-73, 84; tchr. Arrowhead West, Inc., 1984-85; asst. dir. Ctr. for Bus. & Industry Dodge City (Kans.) Community Coll., 1984-85, dir. community rels. and resource devel., 1985-87; co-founder, treas. Breitenbach Farms, Inc., Dodge City, 1970-79, pres., 1979-85; asst. to dean for devel. Coll. Comm., U. Tex., Austin, 1990-93, asst. instr. journalism, 1988-90, lectr. pub. rels., 1992; asst. immunization strategic coord. Tex. Dept. Health, 1993-95, coord. spl. health initiatives, 1995-96; mgr. Tex. Vol. Health Corps, 1996—; liaison Tex. Alliance for Healthy Communities, 1999—. Media judge Headliners Found., Austin, 1989, Tex. Hosp. Assn., 1990, 91; dir. job placement Kans. Elks Tng. Ctr. for Handicapped, 1984-85; mgr. dental office, 1973-83; bd. dirs. Dispute Resolution Ctr., 1992-93; adv. bd. N.E. Caregivers of Austin, 2002-. Treas. Ford County Hist. Soc., 1972-77, Ofcl. Bicentennial Com. Ford County, 1975-77; active Leadership Kans., 1986, Leadership Austin, 1990-91; co-founder Leadership Dodge, 1987; founder Walk-a-Dog project Williamson County SPCA, Austin State Sch., 1991; media judge Tex. PTA, 1992, Tex. Med. Assn., 1993; mem. chancellors coun. U. Tex. Sys.; mem. endowment com. United Way Capital Area, 1994—; mem. Animal Trustees Austin Inc., Ctrl. Tex. Soc. Prevention of Cruelty to Animals, Ready Teddy, the Emergency Med. Svcs. Bear-A-Medic Mascot; mem. Gov.'s Blue Ribbon Selection Com. for Tex. Vol. awards, 1998, 99; mem. Gov.'s Unified State Planning/Cmty. Svc. Com., 1997, 98; mem. Leadership Tex., 1999; 2d v.p. Pub. Health Mus. of Tex., 1999—; treas. Pet Helpers, Inc., 2000—; active Animal Trustees of Austin's Vol. Spotlight, 2000, Tex. Youth Commn., 2001, 02; mem. selection com. for Tex. vol. awards Tex. Dept. Human Svcs., 2001; hon. laboratorian Tex. Dept. Health. Recipient Most Creative Vol. Project award Tex. Mental Health and Mental Retardation, 1992, Athena winner Women's C. of C., 1987, Kans. PRIDE honoree, 1988; U. Tex. fellow, 1987-89; named of one of 100 Best-Managed Farms in U.S., Farm Futures Mgr., 1983; named endowments at Austin Cmty. Found., Wichita (Kans.) Cmty. Found., Arthur E. and Cornelia Scroggins Found., Dodge City, Kans. Mem. AAUW (treas. 1977-78, pres. Kans. 1979-81, gift honoree 1973, 81, 91), Nat. Assn. Individual Investors (life), Pub. Rels. Soc. Am. (mentor, profl. advisor U. Tex. 1985-96), Tex. Pub. Rels. Soc. (bd. dirs. 1993), Women in Comm. (liaison to student chpt. 1989-91), Tex. Exes Alumni Assn. (life), U. Kans. Alumni Assn. (nat. bd. dirs. 1977-82), Austin C. of C., U. Tex. Pres.' Assocs., U. Tex. Littlefield Soc., U. Kans. Chancellor's Club, Austin-Travis County Humane Soc. (life), Waterloo Benevolent Soc. of United Way Capital Area, Leave a Legacy Tex. Style, KLRU Pub.-TV Prodrs. Circle, Phi Beta Kappa (treas. Austin Alumni Assn.), Phi Kappa Phi, Chi Omega. Home: 1861 Coronado Hills Dr Austin TX 78752-2116 Office: Texas Alliance for Healthier Communities 1100 W 49th St Austin TX 78756-3101 E-mail: alice.white@tdh.state.tx.us.

WHITE, ANN WELLS, community activist; b. Kansas City, Mo., Mar. 16, 1927; d. William Gates and Annie Loretta (Morton) Wells; m. Norman E. White, Oct. 2, 1949 (div. Dec. 1977); children: Thomas Wells, Norman Lee. BJ, U. Mo., 1948. Asst. to pres. Cities in Schs., 1978-79. Lobbyist Common Cause, Atlanta, 1972-73; vol. Jimmy Carter's Peanut Brigade, 1976, Carter/Mondale campaign, 1980; bd. dirs., vice chair Atlanta Area Svcs. for the Blind, 1973-81; Gov.'s Commn. on the Status of Women, Atlanta, 1974-76; office mgr. Carter/Mondale Transition Office, Atlanta, 1976; chair evaluation com. United Way Met. Atlanta, 1980-90; bd. dirs. Mems. Guild, The High Mus. of Art, Atlanta, 1982-83, Hillside Hosp., Atlanta, 1989-94, Ga. Forum, Atlanta, 1988-91; bd. dirs. Planned Parenthood of Atlanta area, 1975-89, pres., 1978-81; bd. dirs. Planned Parenthood Fedn. Am., N.Y.C., 1980-86, chair ann. meeting, New Orleans, 1986; legis. chair, lobbyist Ga. Women's Polit. Caucus, 1984-90; convenor, founding chair Georgians for Choice, 1989. Democrat. Presbyterian. Home: 3750 Peachtree Rd #519 Atlanta GA 30319-1322

WHITE, ANNETTE JONES, retired early childhood educator, administrator; b. Albany, Ga., Aug. 29, 1939; d. Paul Lawrence and Delores Christine (Berry) Jones; m. Frank Irvin White, Nov. 13, 1964; children: Melanie Francine, Sharmian Lynell. BA, Spelman Coll., 1964; MEd, Va. State U., 1980. Tchr. Flint Ave Child Devel. Ctr., Albany, 1966-67; tchr., supr. Flintside Child Devel. Ctr., 1967-68; tchr., dir. Albany Ga. Community Sch., 1968-69; tchr. Martin Luther King Community Ctr., Atlanta, 1975-77, The Appleton Sch., Atlanta, 1977-78; sec., proofreader The Atlanta Daily World, 1978-80; tchr. kindergarten Spelman Coll., Atlanta, 1981-88, dir. nursery and kindergarten, lectr. in edn., 1988-97, asst. dir. Marian Wright Edelman Ctr., 1997-98. Cons., presenter child devel. assoc. program Morris Brown Coll., Atlanta, 1991; presenter Ga. Assn. of Young Children, 1992, ann. child care conf. Waycross (Ga.) Coll., 1993. Contbr. articles to profl. jours. including Am. Visions, Sage, So. Exposure, S.W. Georgian, Atlanta Tribune, Atlanta Daily World, Double Stitch, Choosing to Learn/An Alternative GED Curriculum Guide, 1996. Mem. Peace Action, Washington, 1990—. Children's Def. Action Coun., Washington, 1990—. Native Am. Rights Fund, Nat. Mus. Native Ams., Albany Civil Rights Mus. Mem. Nat. Coun. Negro Women, Sierra Club. Avocations: cane weaving, crocheting, cooking, drawing, reading.

WHITE, ANTHONY ROY, JR. composer, educator; b. Lakeport, Calif., Jan. 14, 1949; s. Anthony Roy White, Sr. and Merrie (Haynes) Wilkinson; m. Karen Jean Lamb, Dec. 21, 1980; 1 child, Jesse Solomon Sheibley. BA in Anthropology, Calif. State U., Sacramento, 1972, MA in Edn., 1982; MA in English, Portland State U., 2000. Instr. in devel. English Clark College, Vancouver, Wash., 1990-97; grad. asst. Portland State U., 1998-2000; instr. English Coll. Sequoias, 2000—01, Merced (Calif.) Coll., 2001—. Composer in residence Third Angle New Music Ensemble, 2000. Composer: variety of commissioned chamber and concert works, 1989—; composer, author, producer, dir. (movement drama) In the Wound, 1996; poem included in Portland Rev. Faculty senator Assn. Higher Edn. NEA, Washington Edn. Assn., Clark Coll., Vancouver, !993-95. Recipient 1st prize Acad. Am. Poets; Artist Trust Music fellowship Wash. State Arts Commn., NEA fellow Wash. State Arts Commn., 1995. Mem. ASCAP, NEA, MLA, Nat. Coun. Tchrs. of English, Artist Trust of Wash., Phi Kappa Phi. Avocations: backpacking, trout fishing, gardening, wine making, sailing. E-mail: whitet@merced.ca.cc.us.

WHITE, AUGUSTUS AARON, III, orthopedic surgeon; b. Memphis, June 4, 1936; s. Augustus Aaron and Vivian (Dandridge) W.; m. Anita Ottemo; children: Alissa Alexandra, Atina Andrea, Annica Akila. AB in Psychology cum laude, Brown U., 1957; MD, Stanford U., 1961; PhD, Karolinska Inst., Sweden, 1969; Advanced Mgmt. Program, Harvard U., 1984; DHL (hon.), U. New Haven, 1987; DMS (hon.), Brown U., 1997; DS (hon.), So. Conn. State U., 2000. Diplomate Nat. Bd. Examiners, Am. Bd. Orthopaedic Surgery. Intern U. Mich. Hosp., Ann Arbor, 1961-62; asst. resident in gen. surgery Presbyn. Med. Center, San Francisco, 1962-63; asst. resident in orthopaedic surgery Yale Med. Center, New Haven, 1963-65, sr. instr., resident orthopaedic surgery, 1965-66; asst. prof. orthopaedic surgery Yale Med. Sch., 1969-72, assoc. prof., 1972-76, prof., 1977-78, dir. biomech. research dept. orthopedics, 1970-78; prof. orthopedic surgery Harvard Med. Sch., 1978—; orthopedic surgeon-in-chief Beth Israel Deaconess Med. Ctr., Boston, 1978-92, orthopedic surgeon-in-chief emeritus, 1996—2001; sr. assoc. orthopedic surgery Children's Hosp. Med. Ctr., 1979-89; assoc. in orthopedic surgery Brigham & Women's Hosp., 1980-89; cons. div. surgery Sidney Farber Cancer Inst., 1980—; Ellen and Melvin Gordon prof. of med. edn. Harvard Med. Sch., 2002. Rschr. biomechanics lab. Beth Israel Deaconess Med. Ctr.; chair sci. adv. bd., dir. OrthoLogic, Inc., Phoenix; sci. adv. bd. Am. Shared Hosp. Svcs., San Francisco; cons. orthopaedic surgery West Haven (Conn.) VA Hosp., 1970-78, Hill Health Ctr., New Haven, 1970-78; chief orthopedic surgery Conn. Health Care Plan, 1976-78; mem. adv. coun. Nat. Inst. Arthritis, Metabolism and Digestive Disease, NIH, 1979-82; mem. admission scom. Yale Med. Sch., 1970-72; presenter, moderator Symposium on Cervical Myelopathy, San Francisco, 1987; chmn. grant rev. com. NIH, 1985; founding mem., bd. overseers Brown U. Sch. of Medicine, 1996—; bd. overseers WGBH Radio/TV, Boston, 1996-98, trustee 1998—; bd. dirs. Zimmer, Inc.; Alfred R. Shands Jr. lectr., Am. Orthopaedic Assn., 2001, Pres. guest lectr., Scoliosis Rsch. Soc., 2001. Author: (monographs) Analysis of the Mechanics of the Thoracic Spine in Man, Leprosy, The Foot and The Orthopaedic Surgeon at Am. Acad. Orthopaedic Surgeons, 1970; (books) Clinical Biomechanics of the Spine, 1978, 2d edit., 1990, (with M. Panjabi) Biomechanics in the Musculoskeletal System, 2001 ; Symposium on Idiopathic Low Back Pain, 1982, Your Aching Back-A Doctor's Guide to Relief, 1983, rev. and updated edit., 1990, translated in German, 1992; guest editor Clin. Orthop. and Related Rsch., 1999; contbr. articles to profl. jours., chpts. to sci. books. Trustee Brown U., Providence, 1971-76, bd. fellows, 1981-92, fellow emeritus, 1992—, chmn. corp. com. on minority affairs, 1981-86, chmn. corp. com. on med. edn., 1989-96, chmn. vis. com. on diversity; trustee Northfield Mt. Hermon Sch., Northfield, Mass., 1976-81; bd. dirs. The Partnership, Boston, 1984—. Capt. AUS, 1966-68. Decorated Bronze Star medal; named 1 of 10 Outstanding Young Men U.S. Jr. C. of C., 1969, Selected for Exceptional Black Scientist poster series CIBA-GEIGY Corp., 1982; recipient Martin Luther King, Jr. Med. Achievement award, 1972, Kappa Delta award, nat. prize for outstanding research in orthopaedics field, 1975; nat. award for spinal research Eastern Orthopaedic Assn., 1980; Disting. Service award Northfield Mt. Hermon Sch. Alumni Assn., 1983; William Rogers award Associated Alumni Brown U., 1984; Outstanding Achievement award Delta Upsilon, 1986; Am.-Brit.-Canadian Travelling fellow Am. Orthopedic Assn., 1975 Fellow Am. Acad. Orthopaedic Surgeons (chmn. diversity com. 1997—), Scoliosis Rsch. Soc.; mem. Orthopaedic Rsch. Soc., Cervical Spine Rsch. Soc., Internat. Soc. for Study Lumbar Spine, Internat. Soc. Orthopaedic Surgery and Traumatology, Nat. Med. Assn. (Orthopaedic Scholar award 1994), Cervical Spine Rsch. Soc. (pres. 1988), N.Am. Spine Soc., Acad. Orthopaedic Soc. (co-chmn. com. on diversity), J. Robert Gladden Orthopaedic Soc. (pres. 2000), Fedn. of Spine Assns. (pres. 1998), Sigma Xi, Sigma Pi Phi, Delta Upsilon (pres. Brown U. chpt. 1956).

WHITE, B. JOSEPH, academic administrator; Dean bus. administrn. U. Mich., Ann Arbor, 2002—, interim pres., 2002—. Office: U Mich Ann Arbor Office of the Pres 2074 Fleming Admin Bldg Ann Arbor MI 48109-1340 Business E-Mail: bjwhite@umich.edu..

WHITE, BARBARA EHRLICH, art history educator; b. N.Y.C., Oct. 20, 1936; d. Stanley Ehrlich and Ruth (Krimsky) Ehrlich; m. Leon S. White, Aug. 6, 1961; children: Joel, David. BA, Smith Coll., 1958; MA, Columbia U., 1960, PhD, 1965. Lectr. Queens (N.Y.) Coll., 1959-61, Boston U., summer 1965, Tufts U., Medford, Mass., 1965-66, asst. prof., 1966-87, adj. prof. art history, 1987—. Author: Renoir: His Life, Art and Letters, 1984, French edit., 1985; editor: Impressionism in Perspective, 1978; contbr. articles to profl. jours. NEH younger scholar fellow, 1969-70; Samuel Kress grantee, 1969-70. Mem. Coll. Art Assn., 19th Century Scholar's Collaborative, Women's Caucus for Art. Office: Tufts U Dept Art History 11 Talbot Ave Medford MA 02155-5812

WHITE, BARRY BENNETT, lawyer; b. Boston, Feb. 13, 1943; s. Harold and Rosalyn (Schneider) W.; m. Eleanor Greenberg; children: Joshua S., Adam J., Benjamin D. AB magna cum laude, Harvard U., 1964, JD magna cum laude, 1967. Bar: Mass. 1967, U.S. Dist. Ct. Mass. 1967, U.S. Ct. Appeals (1st cir.) 1967. Assoc. Foley Hoag & Eliot, Boston, 1969-74, ptnr., 1975—, mem. exec. com., 1981-92, 93—, chmn. exec. com., 1987-91, mng. ptnr., 1991-92, 93—, mem. exec. com., 1991-96, sec., 1992-93. Chmn. Lex Mundi, 1994. Editor Harvard Law Rev., 1965-67. Sec., gen. counsel, exec. com. Greater Boston C. of C., Initiative for Competitive Inner City; bd. dirs., exec. com. Mass. Assn. Mental Health, 1985—, pres., 1993-95; bd. dirs. Boston Mcpl. Rsch. Bur., Vol. Lawyers Project, 1987-93, Support Ctr. of Mass., 1988-95; mem. Jewish Family and Children's Svcs., Boston, 1979-87; bd. visitors Boston U. Grad. Sch. Dentistry, 1981—; bd. trustees Jewish Cmty. Rels. Coun., 1988-92; chmn. com. for Clinton/Gore New Eng. Lawyers, 1992-96; chmn. Tsongas for Pres. Com., 1991-98. With USPHS, 1967-69. Mem. ABA, Mass. Bar Assn., Boston Bar Assn., Internat. Bar Assn., Am. Acad. Hosp. Attys., Am. Hosp. Assn. (adj. task force on health planning 1982-84, contbg. editor hosp. law manual 1981-84), Harvard Club Boston, Badminton and Tennis Club. Democrat. Office: Foley Hoag & Eliot 1 Post Office Sq Ste 1700 Boston MA 02109-2175 E-mail: bbwhite@fhe.com.

WHITE, BENJAMIN STEVEN, mathematician, researcher; b. Boston, Sept. 29, 1945; s. Norman Kenneth White and Mildred Ruth (Silverman) Stahl; m. Helen Katherine Frazer, June 12, 1966; children: Adam Frazer, Ethan Abraham. SB, MIT, 1967; MA, U. Ariz., 1968; PhD Courant Inst., NYU, 1974. Sr. mathematician Raytheon Co., Newport, R.I., 1969-70; sys. analyst Time-Sharing Resources, N.Y.C., 1970-71; vis. mem. Courant Inst., NYU, 1974-75; instr. applied math. Calif. Inst. Tech., Pasadena, 1975-78; mem. tech. staff Jet Propulsion Lab., 1978-81; corp. rschr. Exxon Rsch. and Engring. Co., Annandale, N.J., 1981-91, head applied math. group, 1986-89; sr. rsch. assoc. Exxon Mobil Corp. Strat. Rsch., 1999—. Instr. NYU, Bronx, 1971-72; v.p. Perceptive Systems, Inc., Pasadena, 1981. Contbr. articles to profl. jours. Mem. AAAS, Soc. Indsl. and Applied Math., Am. Math. Soc. Democrat. Home: 345 Shunpike Rd Chatham NJ 07928-1633 E-mail: benjamin.s.white@exxonmobil.com.

WHITE, BERTRAM MILTON, chemicals executive; b. Boston, Nov. 17, 1923; s. Samuel Louis and Jennie Anne (Cohen) W.; m. Bernice Hannah Ginns; children: Mark Alan, Leland Jeffrey. BS, Lowell Inst. Tech., Cambridge, Mass., 1943. Product mgr. Philipps Bros. Chems. Inc., Holbrook, Mass., 1952-65, Sobin Chems. Inc., South Boston, 1965-69; pres. Solvent Chems. Co., Inc., Malden, Mass., 1969-73; v.p. I.C.C. Chems. Inc., N.Y.C., 1973-80; sr. v.p. Asoma Chems. Inc., Boston, 1980-83, Laporte Chems. USA, Hackensack, N.J., 1983-84; pres. Gen. Plastics and Chems. Co., Natick, Mass., 1984-91, GFI Chems. Inc., Sudbury, 1991-93; vice chmn. E & F King & Co. Inc., Norwood, 1994-96; cons. Holtrachem Inc., 1997-2000. Bd. dirs. Sudexco N.V., Brussels, Recochem Inc., Montreal, Que., Can.; cons. Holtrachem Group, Natick, 1996-2000, Lithium Co., LLC, White Plains, N.Y., 1997-2000, BMW Chems. Inc., 1998—, Salvage.com, Houston, 2000-01; pres. BMW Chems., Inc., Natick, Mass., cons. for SalvageSale.com., Houston. Served with Corps of Engring. U.S Army, 1943-46, ETO. Decorated Purple Heart. Mem. Drug Chem. and Allied Trades Assn., New Eng. Chemists Club, N.Y.C. Chemists Club, Salesmen's Assn. of Am. Chem. Industry. Jewish. Avocations: tennis, golf, boating. Fax: 508-651-0294. E-mail: bmwchem@msc.com., bmwchem@aol.com.

WHITE, BETTY MAYNARD, retired social worker; b. N.Y.C., May 22, 1922; d. William and Madge (Hooks) Maynard; m. Charles E. White, Sept. 8, 1941; 1 child, Charles B. BA, Hunter Coll., 1964; MSW, Columbia U., 1969. Case worker Bur. Child Welfare, Jamaica, N.Y., 1964-69; supr. foster care Spl. Svcs. Children, 1969-73, case supr. application sec., famiily svcs., group svcs., 1973-83; supr. II. borough coord., divsn. med. rev. Office Home Care Svcs., 1983-84, dir. divsn. med. rev., 1984; pvt. practice, 1986-90. Mem. NASW, Acad. Cert. Social Workers, Hunter Coll. Alumni Assn. Democrat. Roman Catholic. Home: 3548 Tryon Ave Apt 3D Bronx NY 10467-1567

WHITE, BEVERLY JANE, cytogeneticist; b. Seattle, Oct. 9, 1938; Grad., U. Wash., 1959, MD, 1963. Diplomate Nat. Bd. Med. Examiners, Am. Bd. Pediatrics, Am. Bd. Med. Genetics; lic physician and surgeon, Wash., N.J., Calif. Rsch. trainee dept. anatomy Sch. Medicine U. Wash., Seattle, 1960-62, pediatric resident dept. pediatrics, 1967-69; rotating intern Phila. Gen. Hosp., 1963-64; rsch. fellow med. ob-gyn. unit Cardiovascular Rsch. Inst. U. Calif. Med. Ctr., San Francisco, 1964-65; staff fellow lab. biomed. scis. Nat. Inst. Child Health and Human Devel. NIH, Bethesda, Md., 1965-67, sr. staff fellow, attending physician lab. exptl. pathology Nat. Inst. Arthritis, Metabolism and Digestive Diseases, 1969-74, acting chief sect. cytogenetics, 1975-76, rsch. med. officer, attending physician sect. cytogenetics lab. cellular biology and genetics, 1974-86, dir. cytogenetics unit, interinstitute med. genetics program clin. ctr., 1987-95; dir. cytogenetics Corning Clin. Labs., Teterboro, N.J., 1995-96; assoc. med. dir. cytogenetics Nichols Inst.-Quest Diagnostics, San Juan Capistrano, Calif., 1996-97, med. dir. cytogenetics, 1998—2000, Nichols Inst. - Quest Diagnostic, San Juan, 2002—; med. dir. genetics Nichols Inst.-Quest Diagnostics, San Juan Capistrano, Calif., 2000—02. Vis. scientist dept. pediat. divsn. genetics U. Wash. Sch. Medicine, 1983-84; intramural cons. NIH, 1975-95; cons. to assoc. editor Jour. Nat. Cancer Inst., 1976; cons. dept. ob-gyn. Naval Hosp., Bethesda, 1988-89; lectr., presenter in field. Recipient Mosby Book award, 1963, Women of Excellence award U. Wash. and Seattle Profl. chpt. Women in Comm., 1959, Reuben award Am. Soc. for Study Sterility, 1963. Fellow Am. Coll. Med. Genetics (founding), Am. Acad. Pediatrics; mem. AMA. Am. Soc. Human Genetics, Assn. Genetic Technologists (program com. 1989). Home: 14 Toulon Laguna Niguel CA 92677 Office: Nichols Inst Quest Diagnostics Inc Dept Cytogenetics San Juan Capistrano CA 92690-6130 E-mail: bjwsur@aol.com.

WHITE, BONNIE YVONNE, management consultant, retired educator; b. Long Beach, Calif., Sept. 4, 1940; d. William Albert and Helen Iris (Harbaugh) W. BS, Brigham Young U., 1962, MS, 1965, EdD in Ednl. Adminstrn., 1976; postgrad., Harvard U., 1987. Tchr. Wilson High Sch., Long Beach, Calif.,

1962-63; grad. asst. Brigham Young U., Provo, Utah, 1963-65; instr., dir. West Valley Coll., Saratoga, Calif., 1965-76; instr., evening adminstr. Mission Coll., Santa Clara, 1976-80; dean gen. edn. Mendocino Coll., Ukiah, 1980-85; dean instrn. Porterville (Calif.) Coll., 1985-89, dean adminstrv. svc., 1989-93. Rsch. assoc. SAGE Rsch. Internat., Orem, Utah, 1975-99. Mem. AAUW, Faculty Assn. Calif., Cmty. Colls., Calif., Coun. Fine Arts Deans, Assn. Calif. C.C. Adminstrs., Assn. Calif. C.C. Adminstrs. Liberal Arts, Zonta (intern), Soroptimists (intern). Republican. Mem. Lds Ch.

WHITE, BRITTAN ROMEO, manufacturing company executive; b. N.Y.C., Feb. 13, 1936; s. Brittan R. and Matilda H. (Baumann) W.; m. Esther D. Friederich, Aug. 25, 1958 (dec. May 1981); children: Cynthia E., Brittan R. VII; m. Peggy A. Lee, Aug. 30, 1990. BSChemE, Drexel U., 1958; MBA, Lehigh U., 1967; JD, Loyola U., Los Angeles, 1974; MA, Pepperdine U., 1985. Bar: Calif., U.S. Dist. Ct. Calif.; registered profl. engr., Calif. Process engr. Air Reduction Co., Bound Brook, N.J., 1958-64; area supr. J.T. Baker Chem. Co., Phillipsburg, 1964-66; asst. plant mgr. Gamma Chem. Co., Great Meadows, 1966-69; plant mgr. Maquite Corp., Elizabeth, 1969-70; purchasing mgr. Atlantic Richfield Co., Los Angeles, 1970-79; dir. mfg. Imperial Oil, 1979-82; mgr. chem. mgmt. program Hughes Aircraft Co., 1982-94; pres. The Crawford Group, 1994—. Bd. dirs. Diversified Resource Devel. Inc., Los Angeles, 1979—; seminar moderator and speaker Energy Conservation Seminars, 1979-83. Editor Rottweiler Rev., 1979-81; chief award judge Chem. Processing mag., 1976, 78, 80; contbr. articles to profl. jours. Vice chmn. Bd. Zoning and Adjustment, Flemington, N.J., 1970-72; pres. bd. dirs. Homeowners' Assn., Palm Springs, Calif., 1983-90, Prescott, Ariz., 1997—; vice chmn. State Legis. Com., 1998—; mem. indsl. adv. com. sci., tech. and globalization program Embry-Riddle Aeronaut. U., 1998—. Capt. C.E., U.S. Army, 1958-60, res., 1960-68. Mem. ABA, Am. Inst. Chem. Engrs., Am. Chem. Soc., Mensa, Psi Chi. Lodges: Elks. Republican. Avocations: antiques, show dogs, psychology. Home: 1091 Pine Country Ct Prescott AZ 86303-6403 Office: The Crawford Group PO Box 3020 Prescott AZ 86302-3020 E-mail: bpwhite@msn.com.

WHITE, BRUCE DAVID, law and ethics educator, consultant; b. Elizabethton, Tenn., Jan. 10, 1951; s. Darold S. and Anna Ruth (Lewis) W.; m. Sarah Jo Pugh, Dec. 28, 1974; children: Sarah Elizabeth, Meredith Ruth, Rebecca Mae. BS in Pharmacy, U. Tenn., 1974, JD, 1976; DO, North Tex. State U., Tex. Coll. Osteo. Medicine, 1985. Bar: Tenn. 1977, U.S. Dist. Ct. (we. dist.) Tenn. 1979; diplomate Am. Bd. Pediats. Asst. prof. U. Tenn. Health Scis. Ctr., Memphis, 1977-81, assoc. prof., 1981; lectr. U. Miss., Oxford, 1980-81; asst. prof. North Tex. State U., Tex. Coll. Osteo. Medicine, Ft. Worth, 1981-85; ptnr. Swafford & White, Memphis, 1979-81; resident in pediats. U. Louisville, 1985-88; asst. prof. pediatrics. Meharry Med. Coll., 1988-93; asst. prof., asst. dir. Ctr. Clin. Rsch. Ethics, Vanderbilt U. Med. Ctr., 1988-94; fellow clin. med. ethics U. Chgo., 1989-91; dir. Clin. Ethics Ctr. St. Thomas Hosp., Nashville, 1993-98; prof. McWhorter Sch. Pharmacy, Samford U., Birmingham, Ala., 1994—; of counsel Moody Whitfield & Castellarin, 1999—. V.p. Integrity Svcs., L.L.C., Nashville, 1998-99; of counsel Moody Whitfield & Castellarin, 1999—; dir. Healthcare Ethics and Law Inst. Samford U., Birmingham, 1998—. Author: (with H. Wetherbee) Cases and Mateials on Pharmacy Law, 1980; (with W.B. Swafford) Tennessee Pharmacy Law Handbook, 1980, Mississipi Pharmacy Law Handbook, 1981. Fellow Am. Soc. Pharmacy Law, Am. Coll. Legal Medicine, Masons. Office: 95 White Bridge Rd Ste 509 Nashville TN 37205-1490

WHITE, BRUCE EMERSON, JR. graphic design executive; b. Winston-Salem, N.C., Feb. 26, 1961; s. Bruce Emerson and Earline Syble (Nelson) W.; m. Wendy Melynn Potter; children: Monica Joy, Nicole Melynn, Bryson Elliott. With Arby's, Inc., Ft. Lauderdale, Fla., 1977-92, field rep., 1984-87, ops. devel. mgr. Miami, 1987-91, franchise dist. mgr., 1992; dist. mgr. Trefz & Trefz, Inc., Augusta, Ga., 1992-98; owner White Market Enterprises, Uniforms & Sportswear, 1993-98, Wild Mountain Designs, Mocksville, 1999—, Bruwen & Assocs., Mocksville, 1999—. Bd. dirs. resource com. Big Bros./Big Sisters Charlotte, N.C., 1994-99, bd. dirs., Mocksville, N.C., 2000—; grad. Leadership York County, 1999. Recipient Outstanding Leadership award. Mem. Rock Hill (S.C.) C. of C., York (S.C.) C. of C., Mocksville C. of C. Republican. Mem. Ch. of Christ. Fax: 336-940-3179. E-mail: wildmtdesigns@mocksville.com., wildmtdesign@hotmail.com.

WHITE, BURTON LEONARD, retired psychologist, writer, consultant; b. Boston, June 27, 1929; s. Jack J. and Evelyn S. W.; m. Janet Hodgson-White; children— Laura, Emily, David, Daniel. BSM.E., Tufts Coll., 1949; BA, Boston U., 1956, MA, 1957; PhD, Brandeis U., 1960. Research assoc. Brandeis U., 1960-62, M.I.T., 1962-65; sr. research assoc. Harvard Grad. Sch. Edn., 1965-78; head Center Parent Edn., Newton, Mass., 1978-99, ret., 1999. Author: books including Human Infants, 1971, Experience and Environment, Vol. I, 1973, Vol. II, 1978, The First Three Years of Life, 1975, latest edit. 1995, The Origins of Competence, 1979, Educating the Infant and Toddler, 1988, Raising A Happy, Unspoiled Child, 1994, The New First Three Years of Life, 1995; contbr. articles to profl. jours. Served with AUS, 1951-53. Home: 115 Pine Ridge Rd Newton MA 02468-1616

WHITE, C. MICHAEL, pharmacy educator, researcher; b. Schenectady, N.Y., Mar. 27, 1972; s. Harry Lawrence and Nancy Marie White. BS in Pharmacy, Albany Coll. Pharmacy, 1994, PharmD cum laude, 1996. Registered pharmacist, Conn. Fellow in cardiology Hartford (Conn.) Hosp., 1996-98, co-dir. arrhythmia rsch., 1998—, dir. cardiovasc. pharmacology fellowship, 1998—, clin. pharmacist cardiac ICU, 1999—; adj. asst. prof. clin. pharmacy U. Conn. Sch. Pharmacy, Storrs, 1996-98, asst. prof. pharmacy practice, 1998—. Clin. pharmacy specialist in critical care and cardiology Conn. VA Health Sys., West Haven, 1989-99; frequent spkr. to physicians, pharmacists and nurses on drug-related topics; mem. instnl. rev. bd. U. Conn., 1999—; jour. reviewer in field, 1997—. Contbr. over 60 articles to sci. jours., including Lancet, Formulary, Conn. Medicine, Am. Jour. Health-Sys. Pharmacists (Best Rsch. Publ. award 2000), Pharmacotherapy, Jour. Clin. Pharmacology, Annals Pharmacotherapy, Hosp. Pharmacy, Internat. Jour. Pharm. Compounding, Anesthesia and Analgesia, Jour. Cardiovasc. Pharmacology, Am. Jour. Cardiology. Mem. Am. Soc. Health Sys. Pharmacists (expert panelist 1999), Am. Coll. Clin. Pharmacology (membership com. 1998—), Am. Assn. Colls. Pharmacy, Am. Coll. Clin. Pharmacists, Conn. Soc. Health Sys. Pharmacists, Conn. Soc. Hospital Pharmacists (silver medal rsch. awards 1998, 99, gold medal rsch. award 1999, bronze medal rsch. award 1999, Meritorious Achievement awrd 2000), Rho Chi. Avocations: chess, walking. Home: 267 Marlborough St Newington CT 06111-4339 Office: Hartford Hosp Drug Info Ctr 80 Seymour St Hartford CT 06102-8000

WHITE, CALVIN JOHN, zoo executive, financial manager, zoological association executive; b. Twillingate, Nfld., Can., Feb. 28, 1948; s. Harold and Meta Blanche (Abbott) W.; m. Lorna Joan Maclachlan; children: Chelsea Elizabeth, Evan Alexander. B in Commerce, U. Toronto, Ont., Can., 1971. Fin. analyst Can. GE Co. Ltd., Toronto, 1971-72, Ford Motor Co. Can., Oakville, Ont., 1972-74; sr. fin. analyst Municipality of Met. Toronto, 1974-77, asst. dir. budget and ops. analysis, 1977-81, dir. budget analysis and internal control, 1981-86; CEO Toronto Zoo, 1986—. Bd. dirs. Toronto Conv. and Visitors Assn., Can. Mus. Assn., Can. Assn. Zoos and Aquariums, Ctr. for Endangered Reptiles, 1989-91, Rouge Park Alliance, Toronto Chongqing Assn. Fellow Am. Zoo and Aquarium Assn.; mem. Am. Assn. Zoo Keepers, Inst. Pub. Adminstrn. Can. (bd. dirs. 1989-91), Toronto Zoo Found. (bd. dirs. 1991—, CEO 1994—), World Conservation Union, World Zoo Orgn., Toronto Sportmen's Assn., Mensa. Office: Toronto Zoo 361A Old Finch Ave Scarborough ON Canada M1B 5K7 E-mail: cwhite@torontozoo.ca.

WHITE, CALVIN LAMONT, engineer; b. Chico, Calif., Nov. 14, 1947; s. Calvin Hardy White and Jean Elizabeth (Detree) Hardy; m. Elsie Jean, June 28, 1968; 1 child: Calvin Frederick. BS in Mech. Engr., U. Calif., Davis, 1969; MS in Mater. Sci., U. Minn., 1971; PhD, Mich. Tech. U., Houghton, 1974. Mem. rsch. staff Oak Ridge (Tenn.) Nat. Lab., 1974-86; prof. Mich. Tech. U., Houghton, 1986—, chair dept. materials sci. and engring., 1996—. Recipient Material Sci. Rsch. award U.S. Dept. of Energy, 1984. Fellow ASM Internat.; mem. AAAS, Am. Welding Soc., Materials Rsch. Soc., The Metall. Soc. Inc. (bd. dirs. 1988-91), Am. Soc. Engring. Edn., Sigma Xi. Avocations: hunting, fishing. Office: Mich Tech U Materials Sci and Engring Houghton MI 49931

WHITE, CARL EDWARD, JR. pharmaceutical administrator; b. Huntington, W.Va., Apr. 4, 1955; s. Carl Edward Sr. and Peggy Joan (Church) W.; m. Denise Karen McDaniel, May 26, 1979; children: Daniel Aaron, David Kenton, Caitlin Ruth. BS, Purdue U., 1977; MBA, Ga. State U., 1996. Profl. sales rep. Ciba-Geigy Pharms., Huntington, 1977-85, dist. sales mgr., 1985-93, area bus. dir Atlanta, 1993-94; dist. bus. mgr., 1994-98; sr. dist. mgr. Novartis Pharms., Roswell, Ga., 1998—. Bd. dirs. Coventry Homeowners' Assn., Peachtree City, Ga., 1991, Park Brooke Homeowners' Assn., Alpharetta, Ga., 1996; chmn. deacons First Bapt. Ch., Peachtree City, 1992. Republican. So. Bapt. Avocations: computers, singing, gardening. Home: 3905 Brookline Dr Alpharetta GA 30022-6436

WHITE, CAROLYN, author, storyteller; b. Bklyn., Mar. 27, 1948; d. Aaron and Sylvia White; m. Winston A. Wilkinson, Aug. 17, 1969. Diploma in French lit., U. Dijon, France, 1968; BA in English, Harper Coll. SUNY, 1969; MA, Mich. State U., 1972, PhD in Comparative Lit., 1974. Profl. storyteller, Mich. Spkr. in field; co-prodr., featured storyteller radio series Michigan Storyhouse, 2000—; mem. Mich. Arts and Humanities Touring Program, 2000—. Author: A History of Irish Fairies, 1976, The Tree House Children, 1994 (Am. Booksellers Mag. Pick of the List), Whuppity Stoorie, 1997, The Adventure of Louey and Frank, 2001, (poetry) The Voyage of Penelope; contbr. stories to lit. publs. Creative Writers grantee Mich. Coun. for Arts. Mem. Soc. Children's Book Writers and Illustrators. Avocations: tai chi, contra dancing, canoeing, travel. Home and Office: 1661 Mt Vernon Ave East Lansing MI 48823

WHITE, CECIL RAY, librarian, consultant; b. Hammond, Ind., Oct. 15, 1937; s. Cecil Valentine and Vesta Ivern (Bradley) W.; m. Frances Ann Gee, Dec. 23, 1960 (div. 1987); children: Timothy Wayne, Stephen Patrick. BS in Edn., So. Ill. U., 1959; postgrad., Syracuse U., 1961; MDiv, Southwestern Bapt. Sem., 1969; MLS, No. Tex. State U., 1970, PhD, 1984. Libr. Herrin (Ill.) H.S., 1964-66; acting reference libr. Southwestern Sem., Ft. Worth, 1968-70, asst. libr., 1970-80; head libr. Golden Gate Bapt. Sem., Mill Valley, Calif., 1980-88, West Oahu Coll., Pearl City, Hawaii, 1988-89; dir. spl. projects North State Coop. Libr. System, Yreka, Calif., 1989-90; dir. libr. St. Patrick's Sem., Menlo Park, 1990—. Library cons. Hist. Commn., So. Bapt. Conv., Nashville, 1983-84, Internat. Bapt. Sem., Prague, Czech Republic, 1996; mem. Thesaurus Com., 1974-84; adv. bd. Cath. Periodical and Lit. Index, 1995—. Bd. dirs. Hope and Help Ctr., 1986-88, vice chmn., 1987-88. With USAF, 1960-64. Lilly Found. grantee Am. theol. Assn., 1969. Mem. ALA, Am. Theol. Libr. Assn. (coord. cons. svc. 1973-78, program planning com. 1985-88, chmn. 1986-88), Nat. Assn. Profs. Hebrew (archivist 1985—), Assn. Coll. and Rsch. Librs., Cath. Libr. Assn. (mem. exec. bd. 1999—), Phi Kappa Phi, Beta Phi Mu. Democrat. Baptist. Home: 229 Rome Place Hayward CA 94544 Office: St Patricks Sem 320 Middlefield Rd Menlo Park CA 94025-3563 E-mail: cecilrwhite@hotmail.com., stpats@ix.netcom.com. *Personal philosophy: Except for the gift of life and faith, the best gift that has been given to me, and which I can give, is the unique gift of oneself in friendship. No one else can give it, and it cannot be bought at any price.*

WHITE, CHARLES B. academic administrator; b. Oct. 21, 1943; BA, MS, San Diego State U., 1969; PhD, U. Ga., 1974. Prof. psychology Trinity U., San Antonio, 1980—, assoc. v.p., 1989-98, v.p. info. resources adminstrv. affairs, 1999—. Office: 715 Stadium Dr San Antonio TX 78212-3104 E-mail: cwhite@trinity.edu.

WHITE, CHARLES OLDS, aeronautical engineer; b. Beirut, Apr. 2, 1931; s. Frank Laurence and Dorothy Alice (Olds) W.; m. Mary Carolyn Liechty, Sept. 3, 1955; children— Charles Cameron, Bruce Blair. B.S. in Aero. Engring., MIT, 1953, M.S., 1954. Aero. engr. Douglas Aircraft Long Beach, 1954-60, aero. engr. Ford Aerospace & Communication Corp., Calif., 1960-79, sr. engr. specialist, 1979-80, staff office of gen. mgr. DIVAD div., 1980-81, tech. mgr. DIVAD Fuzes, 1981-82, supr. design and analysis DIVAD div., 1982-85; tech. mgr. Advanced Ordnance Programs, 1985-87, PREDATOR Missile, 1987-90, cons. 1990-93; engring. tech. prin. Aerojet Corp., 1993-94; tech. prin. OCSW Ammunition Olin Ordinance, 1994-97, cons., 1997—. Mem. AIAA, AAAS, Nat. Mgmt. Assn., Am. Aviation Hist. Soc., Sigma Gamma Tau. Republican. Presbyterian. Clubs: Masters Swimming, Newport Beach Tennis. Contbr. articles to profl. jours.

WHITE, CHARLES R. mayor; b. Boston; m. Maria White; 4 children. Grad., Riverside CC. Mayor City of Moreno Valley, 1997. Mem. Moreno Valley City Coun., 1996—; mem. So. Calif. Assn. Govt., Regional Coun., Transp. & Comm. Policy Com., Magnetic Levitation Task Force, Growth Visioning Com.; bd. Riverside Transit Agency; mem., chmn. March Joint Powers Commn., 1999, vice chmn., 2001, chmn., 02. Served Planning Commr., Redevelopment Project Area Com., Traffic Safety Adv. Com., Disaster Preparedness Com., Mayor's Drug Task Force; treasurer Friends Moreno Valley Sr. Ctr.; pres. Moreno Valley Elks Lodge; vice comdr. Moreno Valley VFW Post; jr. deacon Moreno Valley Masonic Lodge; pres. Sunnymead Little League; v.p. Sunnymead PTA; co-founder Moreno Valley Youth Fedn. Served USAR. Mem.: Idylwild Am. Legion Post (life). Office: 14177 Frederick St PO Box 88005 Moreno Valley CA 92552*

WHITE, CHRISTOPHER DAVID, manufacturing executive, consultant; b. Boston, Sept. 18, 1964; s. Edwin Clarance and Evelyn Marie White; m. Meg Miller, May 9, 1998; children: Drew, Alexander. BS, U. Ala., Tuscaloosa, 1988. Cert. engr., IOPP, 2000. Gen. mgr. Tweeter ETC., Canton, Mass., 1993—98; pres. The Filling Sta., Walpole, 1998—. Exec. cons. Tube Coun. of N.Am., Wayne, NJ, 2000—. Contbr. articles. Exec. com. THSP Condo Trust. Mem.: PGA, Tube Coun. of N.Am. (exec. com. 2000—), A-Club, Masons (Master Mason 1993—). Republican. Episcipalian. Avocations: music, travel, sports. Office: The Filling Station 87 West St Walpole MA 02081 Office Fax: 508-850-5178. Business E-Mail: CDW@thefillingstation.net.

WHITE, CHRISTOPHER TODD, language educator; b. Columbia, Mo., Dec. 7, 1965; s. Eric B. and Barbara K. White. BA, U. Nebr., Lincoln, 1990; MA, U. Mo., Kansas City, 1994, U. Nev., Las Vegas, 1998; PhD, U. So. Calif., L.A., 1998—. Adj. lectr. Rockhurst Coll., Kansas City, Mo., 1994—95; editl. asst. BkMk Press, 1993—95; adj. lectr. English U. Mo., 1993—95; acad. advisor Ednl. Talent Search, Las Vegas, Nev., 1995—96; asst. prof./lectr. U. Nev., 1996—98; instr. Glendale C.C., Calif., 1998—; tchr., rsch. asst. dept. anthropology U. So. Calif., L.A., 1998—. Dir. Homosexual Info. Ctr., L.A., 2001—, ONE Inst. and Archives, L.A., 2001—02. Editor: San Dieguito and La Jolla: Collected Papers of Claude N. Warren and Colleagues, 2002; asst. editor Risk Takers and Trend Setters: Biographies of the Pre-Stonewall Gay Activists and Supporters, 2002; editor: U. Nev.-Las Vegas Jour. Anthropology, 1995—; contbr. ; editl. adv. bd. Collegiate Press, 2002, referee Popular Culture Rev. Recipient Patricia Roccio Award in Anthropology, U. Nev.-Las Vegas, 1997; scholar Hal Call Mattachine scholar, Inst. for Study of Human Resources, 2000—01. Mem.: Homosexual Info. Ctr. (sec.-treas. 2001—), Southwestern Anthropol. Assn., Soc. of Lesbian and Gay Anthropologists (sec.-treas. 1998—), Soc. of Linguistic Anthropology, Am. Anthropol. Assn., Am. Fedn. Tchrs. Democrat. Buddhist. Avocations: camping, book collecting, piano, running, bicycling. Home: 3216 Community Ave La Crescenta CA 91214 Office: Univ of Southern Calif Dept Anthropology Los Angeles CA 90089-0661

WHITE, CLARA JO, small business owner, consultant; b. County Cherokee, Tex., June 1926; d. William and Elmira (Johnson) Walker; m. Jeff Davis White, May 5, 1950; children: Anita, Jackie, Mona Lisa, Jeris, Gina. Cert., Ft. Worth Bus. Coll., 1947; AA, Riverside City Coll., 1986; cert. mgmt. and supervisory devel., U. Calif., Riverside, 1986, cert. counseling skills, 1990. Cert. Graphoanalyst 1977; cert. master graphoanalyst 1979; cert. mus. docent tng., 1977. Owner, pres. White Handwriting Analysis Svc., Riverside, Calif., 1982—. Cons. Graphoanalysisy, Riverside, 1977—; instr. Internat. Congress and Resident Inst., Internat. Graphoanalysis Soc., 1989, discussion group leader, 88; seminar presenter U. Calif., Riverside, 1993—99; presenter in field; analyzed handwriting Lady Margaret Beaufort, 1992, Mary Queen of Scots, 1994, Hillary Rodham Clinton, 1994, Pres. Bill Clinton, 1997, Georgia O'Keeffe, 1999, presidents George Washington, Abraham Lincoln, John F. Kennedy, 2000, others. Asst. editor: (commemorative book) Reflections, 1986; contbr. poems to anthologies. Mem. YWCA, Riverside, Nat. Geographic Soc., 1995—, The Nat. Mus. Women in Arts, 1998—; mem. children's conf. planning com. Riverside Mental Health Assn., 1981—; mem. U.S. Olympic Com., 1984; v.p. Heritage House Mus., Riverside, 1981—, co-pres., 1985-86, pres. 1986-87; historian Riverside Juvenile Hall Aux., 1984—, pres., 1987—; vol. teacher's aide County of Riverside Juvenile Ct. Schs., 1979—; mem. Riverside Mus. Assocs., bd. dirs., 1985-87, vol. 1985-88, aux. historian 1984—, pres., 1987-88; mem. Met. Mus. Assocs., 1960—; participant 24th Internat. Congress on Arts and Comms., Oxford (Eng.) U., 1997. Recipient Cert. of Appreciation vol. svcs. program Riverside County Probation Dept., 1986, County Riverside Suprs., 1988; award F.H. Butterfield Sch., 1980, Golden Poet award The Homer Honor Soc., 1987, 90, cert. appreciation Nat. Law Enforcement Officers Meml. Fund, 1998, cert. Libr. of Congress, 1998; named Vol. of Yr., recipient community svc. cert. Riverside City Coll., 1982; named to Hall of Fame, Riverside Juvenile Hall Aux., 1984; recipient Cert. of Appreciation, Riverside Mental Health, 1990, First Pl. award writing-poetry Am. Biog. Rsch. Assn., 1991, Trophy award for Outstanding Svc. to Community Sta. KQLH-FM, Trophy Pl. Vol. Ctr. of Riverside, 1991, Trophy award and Individual Svc. award, Riverside County Juvenile Hall of Fame, 1990-91, Cert. Recognition Riverside County Probation Dept., 1991, Cert. Recognition Calif. Legis.-State Assembly, 1991, Cert. Appreciation So. Calif. Chpt. IGAS, 1990-91, Cert. Appreciation Riverside County Bd. Suprs. and Riverside County Probation Dept., 1993, Participation award 21st Internat. Congress Arts and Comm., Scotland, 1994, Lisbon, Portugal, 1999, Cert. of Appreciation, 26th Children's Conf. Com., 1999, Internat. Gold Medal of Honor for disting. participation ABI/IBC 26th Congress On Arts and Comm., Lisbon, Portugal, 1999, Graphoanalyst of Yr. award So. Calif. chpt. Graphoanalysts, 2000; her poem Peace included in Scottish Library Archives, 1994. Mem. AAUW, NAFE, Internat. Graphoanalysis Soc. (life, cert. master graphoanalyst, 2d and 1st v.p., pres. So. Calif. chpt., pres. excellence award 1982, 83, 84, Merit cert. 1981, Pres. Merit citation 1988, Achievement cert. 1995), U.S. Olympic Soc., Smithsonian Inst. (assoc.), Calif. Probation, Parole, and Corrections Assn. (cert. of tng. 1995), Riverside C. of C., The Rsch. Coun. of Scripps Clinic and Rsch. Found., Women's Networking Club (Riverside), Confederation of Chivalry (life, grand coun., dame officer), DAV Aux. (life), Top Cops Nat. Assn. Police Orgns., World War II Meml. Soc. (charter). Clubs: Women's Networking (Riverside). Avocations: sewing, music and art, collecting antiques, dancing, walking and exercise. Home and Office: 7965 Helena Ave Riverside CA 92504-3513

WHITE, CORALIE HEARD, music educator; b. Monroe, La., Nov. 8, 1941; d. Winifred Pearl Johnson; m. Jack Weldon White, Nov. 10, 1957; children: Jack Jr., Allison Anne, Ashley Susan, Elizabeth Coralie. BMus, N.E. La. State Coll., 1962; MMus, N.E. La. U., 1975. Nat. cert. tchr. of piano. Tchr. N.E. La. U., Monroe, 1975-98; keyboardist Monroe Symphony, 1975-98; pvt. piano tchr. West Monroe, La., 1962-98. Church organist, Monroe and West Monroe, 1953-96; adjudicator piano festivals; calliopist area cities, 1994-98; accompanist Symphony Auditions, 1973-98. Soloist Monroe Symphony, South Ark. Symphony, N.E. La. U. Symphony, N.E. La. U. Band. Named to Outstanding Young Women of Am., 1975, L.A.'s Outstanding Young Women, 1975. Mem. DAR, PEO, Musical Coterie, Trenton Soc. Book Club, Jr. League, Delta Kappa Gamma (v.p. 1975-98). Home: 412 Maridale Dr West Monroe LA 71291-2356

WHITE, DALE ANDREW, journalist; b. Jacksonville, Fla., Feb. 17, 1958; s. John Andrew and Jeannelle Corinne White. B in Journalism, U. Fla., 1983. Reporter UPI, Miami, Fla., 1980, Orlando (Fla.) Sentinel Star, 1981; corr. Fla. Times-Union, Gainesville, 1982; reporter, columnist, editl. writer, editor Sarasota Herald-Tribune, Bradenton, Fla., 1983—. Contbr. short stories to profl. publs. Recipient Chmn.'s award N.Y. Times, 1987, 3d place Editorial Writing award Fla. Soc. Newspaper Editors, 1993, 1st place Ind. Reporter Media award Fla. Sch. Bds. Assn., 1996. Office: PO Box 1695 Bradenton FL 34206-1695

WHITE, DANA EILEEN, public health service officer; b. New Orleans, Nov. 30, 1969; d. Charlie Jr. and Carolyn J. White. BS, Xavier U. of La., New Orleans, 1993; MPA, Troy State U., New Orleans, 1997. Clk. La. Office of Pub. Health, New Orleans, 1993—94, disease intervention specialist, 1994—98; interviewer, asst. site coord. Wash. State U., Pullman, 1998—2001; rsch. and evaluation asst. King County Pub. Health, Seattle, 1998—2001; rsch. analyst Northwest Crime & Social Rsch., Inc., 2000—01; pub. health prevention specialist Ctrs. for Disease Control and Prevention, 2001—. Democrat. Baptist. Home: 5252 Constance St New Orleans LA 70115-1850

WHITE, DAVID ALAN, JR. manufacturing company executive; b. Chgo., Feb. 18, 1942; s. David Alan and Janet (Fate) W.; m. Catherine Elizabeth Harman, June 12, 1971; children: Christopher Alan, John Michael. BS, U.S. Mil. Acad., 1964; MBA, U. Pa., 1971. Planning analyst Cooper Industries, Houston, 1971-74; exec. asst. The Cooper Group, Raleigh, 1974-76; v.p. fin. and planning Cooper Energy Svcs. Group, Mt. Vernon, Ohio, 1976-80; v.p., gen. mgr. Cooper Power Tools, Columbia, S.C., 1980-88; v.p. corp. planning and devel. Cooper Industries, 1988-96, sr. v.p. strategic planning, 1996—99. Capt. U.S. Army, 1964-69. Decorated Army Commendation medal. Republican. Episcopalian. Avocations: golf, reading. Office: Cooper Industries Inc PO Box 4446 Houston TX 77210-4446 E-mail: white@cooperindustries.com.

WHITE, DAVID CALVIN, electrical engineer, energy educator, consultant; b. Sunnyside, Wash., Feb. 18, 1922; s. David Calvin Sr. and Leafie Eloise (Scott) W.; m. Glorianna Guilii, July 30, 1949 (dec. Dec. 1965); 1 child, Julie Anne White Coman (dec.); m. Margot Ann Fuller, June 4, 1966; 1 child, Constance Anne. BS, Stanford U., 1946, MS, 1947, PhD, 1949. Registered profl. engr. Elec. engr. Kaiser Industries, Vancouver, Wash., 1941-42, 43-45; assoc. prof. elec. engring. U. Fla., Gainesville, 1949-52; asst. prof. elec. engring. MIT, Cambridge, 1952-54, assoc. prof., 1954-58, prof., 1958-62, Ford prof. engring., 1962-92, dir. energy lab., 1972-89, Ford prof. engring. emeritus, 1992—. Pres., dir. Energy Conversion, Inc., 1961-64; cons. Gulf Oil, 1976-84, Johnson Controls, 1980-98; sr. advisor and vis. prof. Birla Inst., India, 1968-70; mem. council U. Benin, Nigeria, 1972; trustee Lowell Tech. Inst., Mass., 1972-74; mem. corp. Woods Hole Oceanographic Inst., Mass., 1977-84; mem. research coordinating panel Gas Research Inst., Chgo., 1977-85; chmn. adv. council Electric Power Research Inst., Palo Alto, Calif., 1984-86, mem., 1980-87. Author: (with others) Electromechanical Energy Conversion, 1959 Commr. Electric Light Plant, Concord, Mass., 1959-64, Kalmia Woods Water Dist., Concord, 1960-63 Named hon. prof. Instituto Politecnico Nacional, Mex., 1961 Fellow IEEE; mem. Nat. Acad. Engring., Am. Acad. Arts and Scis., Am. Soc. Engring. Edn. (George Westinghouse award 1961), New Seabury Country Club, Boca Delray Mar Country Club, Phi Beta Kappa, Sigma Xi, Tau Beta Pi, Eta Kappa Nu. Republican. Avocations: golf, boating. Home: 8 Chart Way Popponesset Island Mashpee MA 02649 also: PO Box 809 Mashpee MA 02649-0809 Office: MIT 77 Massachusetts Ave Rm E40-473 Cambridge MA 02139-4307 also: 23401 Water Circle Boca Raton FL 33486 E-mail: dcmfwhite@aol.com.

WHITE, DAVID HYWEL, physics educator; b. Cardiff, Wales, June 4, 1931; came to U.S., 1959, naturalized, 1966; s. William Richard and Bessie (Morgan) W.; m. Frances Mary Shearman, July 23, 1954; children: Richard Gerwyn, Christopher David. BS, U. Wales, 1953; PhD, Birmingham U., 1956. Asst. lectr. Birmingham U., 1958-59; asst. prof. U. Pa., 1961-64; asso. prof. Cornell U., Ithaca, N.Y., 1964-69, prof., 1969-78; sr. physicist, head exptl. facilities div. Isabelle Project, Brookhaven Nat. Lab., Upton, L.I., N.Y., 1978-86; group leader nuclear and particle physics rsch. P divsn. Los Alamos (N.Mex.) Nat. Lab., 1986-88, lab. fellow, 1998—. Cons., 1967-69, 76-78, 99—. Author: Elementary Electronics, 1967; Editor: Scintillation Counters, 1966. NSF sr. postdoctoral fellow, 1970; JSPS fellow, 1981 Fellow Am. Phys. Soc., AAAS. Home: 913 Calle Vistoso Santa Fe NM 87501-1031

WHITE, DAVID LAWRENCE, mechanical engineer, retail manager; b. Cheverly, Md., June 16, 1965; s. Kenneth William and Betty Mary (Brunacci) W.; m. Reena Shah, May 21, 1994; children: Savanah, Brianna. BS in mech. engring., Va. Polytech. Inst., 1987; MBA, Case Western Reserve U., 1993. Cert. EIT, 1987. Dist. sales engr. Torrington Ingersoll-Rand, Cleveland, 1987-92; devel. adv. USAID, Washington, 1992-93; internat. bus. devel. RELTEC Corp., Cleveland, 1993—95, internat. sales Delhi and Charna, India, 1995—97; area mgr. Torrington Ingersoll-Rand, Mumbai, India, 1997—2001; product mktg. mgr. Ingersoll-Rand, Shippensburg, Pa., 2002—. Roman Catholic. Home and Office: 59 Field St Torrington CT 06790-1008 Office: Ingersoll-Rand 312 Ingersoll Dr Shippensburg PA 15217

WHITE, DAVID OLDS, researcher, former educator; b. Fenton, Mich., Dec. 18, 1921; s. Harold Bancroft and Doris Caroline (Olds) W.; m. Janice Ethel Russell, Sept. 17, 1923; children: John Russell, David Olds Jr., Benjamin Hill BA, Amherst Coll., 1943; MS, U. Mass., 1950; PhD, U. Oreg., 1970. Tchr. human physiology Defiance (Ohio) Coll., summer 1950; sci. tchr. Roosevelt Jr. High Sch., Eugene, Oreg., 1951-52; prin. Glide (Oreg.) High Sch., 1952-56; tchr. Munich Am. Elem. Sch., 1957-69; prin. Wurzburg (Fed. Republic Germany) Am. High Sch., 1959-60, Wertheim (Fed. Republic Germany) Am. Elem. Sch., 1960-61; tchr. Dash Point Elem. Sch., Tacoma, 1961-63, Eugene (Oreg.) Pub. Schs., 1963-81. Internat. rschr. in field. Contbr. articles to profl. publs.; patentee electronic model airplane. Staff sgt. U.S. Army, 1942-45, PTO. Fulbright grantee, 1956-57, 72-73. Mem. NEA, Fulbright Alumni Assn., Phi Delta Kappa. Avocations: skiing, camping, tennis, hunting, piano. Home: 4544 Fox Hollow Rd Eugene OR 97405-3904

WHITE, DEBRA SAUNDERS, technology executive; b. Mason City, Iowa, Jan. 8, 1957; d. Roger Allen and Irene Boone Saunders; m. Cecil White Jr., Aug. 27, 1988; children: Elizabeth Paige, Cecil III. BA, U. Va., 1979; MBA, Coll. William and Mary, 1993; postgrad., George Washington U., 2000—. Account mgr. IBM, Norfolk, Va., 1979-93; chief info. officer St. George's Sch., Newport, R.I., 1993-98, Hampton (Va.) U., 1999—. Mem. Va. Rsch. Tech. Adv. Commn., Hampton; chairperson Internet com. Advanced Network Minority Serving Inst., Washington. Team mother Midget Foxhill Football, Hampton. Recipient Indpls. Minority Bus. Leader award City of Indpls., 1989; recognized Cyberstar, Black Issues in Higher Edn., 2002. Mem. Alpha Kappa Alpha. Avocation: skiing. Home: 21 Sarfan Dr Hampton VA 23664 Office: 130 E Tyler St Hampton VA 23669-5403 E-mail: debra.white@hamptonu.edu.

WHITE, DIRK BRADFORD, printing company executive; b. St. Joseph, Mo., Aug. 18, 1955; s. John Paul and Sandra Sue (Dedmon) W.; m. Julie Maureen Eisenreich, June 30, 1979; children: Kristen Elizabeth, Paul Aaron. BS in Mktg., Southwest Mo. State U., 1977. Estimator I.J. Eagle Printing Co., Inc., Kansas City, Mo., 1978-83; customer svc. mgr. Eagle Lithographing Co., 1983-88, v.p. prodn., 1988-90, sr. v.p., gen. mgr., 1990-92; mgr. prodn. control Spangler Inc., Kans., 1992-96; mgr. Banta Publs.-Kansas City, Liberty, Mo., 1996—. Mem. Printing Industries Am., Graphic Arts Tech. Found., Kappa Alpha. Avocations: fly fishing, bicycling, wilderness camping and hiking, mountaineering, photography. Home: 8309 Mullen Rd Lenexa KS 66215-4133

WHITE, DON WILLIAM, rancher, minister; b. Santa Rita, N.Mex., June 27, 1942; s. Thomas Melvin and Barbara (Smith) W.; m. Jacqueline Diane Bufkin, June 12, 1965; children: Don William Jr., David Wayne. BBA, Western N.Mex. U., 1974, MBA, 1977. Field acct. Stearns Roger Corp., Denver, 1967-70; controller, adminstrv. mgr. USNR Mining and Minerals Inc., Silver City, N.Mex., 1970-72; devel. specialist County of Grant, 1973-77; divisional controller Molycorp. Inc., Taos, N.Mex., 1977-78; mgr. project adminstrn. Kennecott Minerals Co., Hurley, 1978-83; sr. v.p. Sunwest Bank Grant County, Silver City, 1983-84, exec. v.p., 1984-85, pres., chief exec. officer, 1985-97; rancher Deming, 1997—; Owner-walking w ranch pastor Berean New Bapt. Ch. Bd. dirs. Bank of Grant County. Bd. dirs. Sunwest Bank of Grant County, Silver City/Grant County Econ. Devel., 1983—; councilman Town of Silver City, 1977; chmn. Dems. for Senator Pete Domenici, 1986; pres. Gila Regional Med. Found., 1989-92; pres. SWNM Econ. Devel. Corp., 1984-2000; trustee Indian Hills Bapt. Ch., 1988-89; chmn. State of N.Mex. Small Bus. Adv. Coun.; vice chmn. vocat. edn. adv. com. Western N.Mex. U., 1989; mem. Silver Schs.-Sch./Bus. Partnership Coun. Named Outstanding Vol., Silver City/Grant County Econ. Devel., 1987, 94, FFA, 1985, Western N.Mex. U. Outstanding Alumni, 1998. Mem. Am. Bankers Assn., N.Mex. Bankers Assn., Bank Adminstrn. Inst., Assn. Commerce and Industry (bd. dirs. 1988-91), N.Mex. Mining Assn. (assoc.), Rotary (past pres., dist. gov. rep.). Avocations: snow skiing, water skiing, hunting, fishing, golf. Office: 12025 Dwyer Rd NW Deming NM 88030-2305

WHITE, DONALD HARVEY, physics educator emeritus; b. Berkeley, Calif., Apr. 30, 1931; s. Harvey Elliott and Adeline White; m. Beverly Evalina Jones, Aug. 8, 1953; children: Jeri, Brett, Holly, Scott, Erin. AB, U. Calif., Berkeley, 1953; PhD, Cornell U., 1960. Rsch. physicist Lawrence Livermore (Calif.) Nat. Lab., 1960-71, cons., 1971-90; prof. physics Western Oreg. U., Monmouth, 1971-95; ret. Vis. rsch. scientist Inst. Laue-Langevin, Grenoble, France, 1977-78, 84-85, 91-92. Author: (with others) Physics, an Experimental Science, 1968, Physics and Music, 1980. Pres. Monmouth-Independence Cmty. Arts, 1983. DuPont scholar, 1958; Minna-Heineman Found. fellow, Hannover, Germany, 1977. Mem. Am. Phys. Soc., Oreg. Acad. Sci. (pres. 1979-80), Phi Kappa Phi (pres. West Oreg. chpt. 1989-90) Democrat. Presbyterian. Home: 322 Stadium Dr S Monmouth OR 97361

WHITE, DONNA RAE, English educator, writer; b. Ft. Walton Beach, Fla., Oct. 6, 1955; d. Earl Ray White and Mildred Ann Wilson. BA in English, Ark. Tech. U., 1976; MA in English, U. Tex., Austin, 1983; PhD in English, U. Minn., 1991. Mgr. Barney's Used Books, Russellville, Ark., 1983-86; editor The Edwin Mellen Press, Lampeter, Wales, 1989-90; asst. prof. English Clemson (S.C.) U., 1992-98, Ark. Tech. U., Russellville, 2001—. Vis. lectr., Ark. Tech. U., Russellville, 1999-2001. Author: A Century of Welsh Myth in Children's Literature, 1998 (Mythopoeic Scholarship award 1999), Dancing with Dragons: Ursula K. Le Guin and the Critics, 1999; editor Books for Children, Clemson, S.C., 1992-98. Bd. dirs., Pope County Libr., Russellville, 1985-86; judge, Book Pubs. of Tex. Award, Tex. Inst. Letters, Ft. Worth, 1998, Spur Award, We. Writers of Am., 1997. Rsch. grantee, Oreg. Humanities Ctr., 1996; grantee NEH, 1993, 94, rsch. scholar Nat. Welsh-Am. Found., 1989. Mem. MLA, Children's Lit. Assn. (chair scholarship com. 1996-99, bd. dirs. 1999-2000). Avocations: travel, reading. Office: Ark Tech U Dept English Russellville AR 72801

WHITE, DOUGLAS ALLAN, legislative aide, data archivist; b. Madison, Wis., May 14, 1970; s. Mathew James and Anna Mae (Schuette) W. BA in Polit. Sci. with honors, U. Hawaii at Manoa, Honolulu, 1997, MA in Polit. Sci., 1999. Data archivist Hawaii Mapping Rsch. Group, Honolulu, 1996—; legis. aide Hawaii Ho. of Reps., 1997—2002. Cpl. USMC, 1988-93. Mem. Am. Polit. Sci. Assn., Am. Radio Relay League, Phi Beta Kappa. Avocations: offshore yacht racing, inshore yacht racing, amateur radio.

WHITE, DOUGLAS JAMES, JR. lawyer; b. N.Y.C., Mar. 20, 1934; s. Douglas James and Margaret (Stillman) W.; m. Denise Beale, May 28, 1960; children: Brian Douglas, James Roderick. BA, U. Oreg., 1955; LLB, Willamette U., 1958. Bar: Oreg. 1958. Law clk. to assoc. justice Oreg. Supreme Ct., Salem, 1958-59; assoc. Schwabe, Williamson & Wyatt (formerly known as Mautz, Souther, Spaulding, Kinsey & Williamson), Portland, Oreg., 1959-69; shareholder, gen. ptnr. Schwabe, Williamson & Wyatt, P.C. (formerly known as Schwabe, Williamson, Wyatt, Moore & Roberts), 1969-79, sr. ptnr., 1979-93; shareholder, 1994-98; of counsel, 1999—. Trustee Jesuit H.S., Beaverton, 1991-94; bd. dirs. St. Vincent de Paul Child Devel. Ctr., Portland, 1979-90, Portland Coun., Soc. St. Vincent de Paul, 1989-92, Portland House of Umoja, 1995—; bd. dirs., officer Maryville Nursing Home, Beaverton, 1993-99, St. Vincent de Paul Conf. of St. Thomas More, Portland, 1966—; active Saturday Acad. Beaverton, 1982—. Mem.: Oreg. State Bar Assn. (real estate and land use sect. exec. com. 1984—85), Flyfisher Club Oreg., Multnomah Athletic Club (Portland chpt.). Republican. Roman Catholic. Avocations: fly-fishing, cross-country skiing, bridge, hiking. Home: 6725 SW Preslynn Dr Portland OR 97225-2668 Office: Schwabe Williamson & Wyatt 1211 SW 5th Ave Ste 1600 Portland OR 97204-3713

WHITE, DOUGLAS RICHIE, anthropology educator; b. Mpls., Mar. 13, 1942; s. Asher Abbott and Margaret McQuestin (Richie) W.; m. Jayne Chamberlain (div. Feb. 1971); m. Lilyan Amdur Brudner, Mar. 21, 1971; 1 child, Scott Douglas. BA, U. Minn., 1964, MA, 1967, PhD, 1969. Asst. prof. U. Pitts., 1967-72, assoc. prof., 1972-76, U. Calif., Irvine, 1976-79, prof., 1979—. Dep. dir. Lang. Attitudes Rsch. Project, Dublin, 1971—73; vis. prof. U. Tex., Austin, 1974—75, Ecole des Hautes Etudes en Sci. Sociales, Paris, 1999—2002, Inst. Nat. d'Etudes Démographique, 2000; chmn. Linkages: World Devel. Res. Coun., Md., 1986—, pres., Md., 1986—90. Co-editor: Research Methods in Social Networks, 1989, Anthropology of Urban Environments, 1972, Kinship, Networks and Exchange, 1998; founder, gen. editor World Cultures Jour., 1985-90; contbr. sci. software packages; contbr. articles to profl. jours. Recipient Sr. Disting. U.S. Scientist award, Alexander von Humboldt Stiftung, Bonn, Germany, 1989—91, Bourse de Haute Niveau award, Ministry Rsch. and Tech., Paris, 1992; fellow, Ctr. for Advanced Studies, Western Behavioral Sci. Inst., La Jolla, Calif., 1981—84. Mem. Social Sci. Computing Assn. (pres. elect 1991, pres. 1992.), Santa Fe Inst. (mem. working groups 1999, 2000, 2001). Democrat. Home: 8633 Via Mallorca Unit C La Jolla CA 92037 Office: U Calif School Social Sci Irvine CA 92697-0001

WHITE, EDITH ROBERTA SHOEMAKE, elementary school educator; b. Hattiesburg, Miss., Feb. 24, 1948; d. Robert Ellis and Helen C.M. (Hinton) Shoemake; m. Robert Q. White, May 31, 1992 (dec. Sept. 2000). Student, Perkinston (Miss.) Jr. Coll., 1968; BS, U. So. Miss., 1970, MA, 1985. Cert. elem. tchr., Miss. Tchr. Ouachita Parish Schs., Monroe, La., Meridian (Miss.) City Schs., Lauderdale County Schs., Meridian, Perry County Schs., New Augusta, Miss.; mid. sch. tchr. Hancock County Schs., Bay St. Louis, Pass Christian (Miss.) Pub. Schs. Dist. Mem. NEA, Miss. Assn. Educators. Methodist. Home: 124 Clower Ave Long Beach MS 39560-3302

WHITE, EDMUND WILLIAM, chemical engineer; b. Phila., July 8, 1920; s. Edmund Britten and Grace Salome (Faunce) W.; m. Kathrine Nathalie Cadwallader, Apr. 24, 1948; children: Christine Louise, William Cadwallader, Thomas Edmund, James Christopher. BA, Columbia Coll., 1940; BS, Columbia Sch. Engring., 1941, MChemE, 1942; PhD, Lehigh U., 1952. Registered profl. engr., Ohio. Jr. chemist Westvaco Chlorine Products Corp., South Charleston, W.Va., 1942-44; chem. engr. C.L. Mantel, N.Y.C., 1946-47, Diamond Alkali Co., Painesville, Ohio, 1947-49; grad. asst. Lehigh U., Bethlehem, Pa., 1949-51; sr. chemist Cities Svc. R & D Co., various cities, NJ, 1951-59, 1964—65, Athabasca Inc., Edmonton, Alberta, Canada, 1960-64; project mgr. U.S. Dept. Navy, Washington, 1965-66; rsch. chem. engr. Naval Surface Warfare Ctr., Annapolis, Md., 1966-95; ret., 1995. Cons. in field; mem. U.S. del. to ISO TC 28 mtgs. in Budapest, 1990, Phila., 1992, Paris, 1994; mem. U.S. tech. adv. group in ISO TC 28; mem. Quadripartite Navies group on Fuels, Lubricants and Allied Products, mem. U.S. del. and co-chair mtg., 1993; presenter in field. Contbr. articles to profl. jours. Treas., v.p., pres. sch. PTAs, Silver Spring, Md., 1968-79; den father, mem. troop com. Boy Scouts Am., Silver Spring, 1966-75. Ensign USN, 1944-46. Fellow ASTM (chairperson task force, sect. subcom., com. 1967—, mem. award of merit com. 1996-98, mem. coord. com. on Flash Point 1989-99, Award of Merit 1990, Scroll of Honor 1993, Award of Excellence 1999); mem. AIChE (50 Yr. award), Am. Chem. Soc. (50 Yr. award), Potomac Curling Club (bd. dirs., pres. 1982-84), Internat. Assn. for Stability and Handling of Liquid Fuels (hon. mem., mem. steering com. 1985-95, Hon. Membership award 1999), Sigma Xi. Republican. Achievements include 4 patents and 2 Canadian patents; research in consensus standardization, fuel stability testing, fuel stability, synthetic fuels, separation processes, wax oxidation, mixing and chlorine-caustic electrolytic cell. Home: 908 Crest Park Dr Silver Spring MD 20903-1307 E-mail: ednwhite@erols.com.

WHITE, EDWARD GIBSON, II, lawyer; b. Lexington, Ky., Nov. 7, 1954; s. Russell Edwin White and Betty Lee White-Estabrook; m. Cynthia Ann Reisz, Mar. 10, 1979; children: Edward Gibson III, William Elliot, John Alexander, Albert Grahm. BA, U. Tenn., Chattanooga, 1980; JD, U. Tenn., Knoxville, 1983. Bar: Tenn. 1983, U.S. Dist. Ct. (ea. dist.) Tenn. 1984, U.S. Ct. Appeals (6th cir.) 1985. Assoc. Hodges, Doughty & Carson, Knoxville, 1983-87, ptnr., 1988—. Bd. dirs. Knoxville affiliate The Susan G. Komen Breast Cancer Found., Inc., Elizabeth R. Griffin Rsch. Found. Mem. ABA (litigation sect. 1985—), Tenn. Bar Assn. (interprofl. code com. 1989—, med./legal com. 1991—), Knoxville Bar Assn. (treas. 1995-96, continuing legal edn. com. 1985-86, 88-91, chmn. 1992-94, mem. naturalization com. 1985-87, bd. govs. 1993-94, pres. elect 1996, pres. 1997, Pres.'s award 1992), Tenn. Def. Lawyers Assn., Def. Rsch. Inst. (med./legal com. 1985—), Am. Bd. Trial Advocates, Knoxville Bar Found. (bd. dirs.), U. Tenn. Pres.'s Club, Univ. Club, Cherokee Country Club, Knoxville Racquet Club. Republican. Avocations: tennis, golf, boating, water sports, fishing. Office: Hodges Doughty & Carson 617 Main St # 869 Knoxville TN 37902-2602

WHITE, EDWARD ALFRED, lawyer; b. Elizabeth, N.J., Nov. 23, 1934; BS in Indsl. Engring., U. Mich., 1957, JD, 1963. Bar: Fla. 1963, U.S. Ct. Appeals (5th cir.) 1971, U.S. Ct. Appeals (11th cir.) 1981, U.S. Supreme Ct. 1976. Assoc. Jennings, Watts, Clarke & Hamilton, Jacksonville, Fla., 1963-66, ptnr., 1966-69, Wayman & White, Jacksonville, 1969-72; pvt. practice, 1972—. Mem. aviation law com. Fla. Bar, 1972-94, chmn., 1979-81, bd. govs., 1984-88, admiralty com., 1984—, chmn., 1990-91, chmn. pub. relations com., 1986-88, exec. coun. trial lawyers sect., 1986-91, chmn. admiralty cert. com., 1995-97. Fellow Am. Bar Found.; mem. ABA (vice chmn. admiralty law com. 1995—), Fla. Bar Assn. (bd. cert. civil trial lawyer, bd. cert. admiralty lawyer), Jacksonville Bar Assn. (chmn. legal ethics com. 1975-76, bd. govs. 1976-78, pres. 1979-80), Assn. Trial Lawyers Am. (sustaining mem. 1984—), Acad. Fla. Trial Lawyers (diplomate), Fla. Coun. Bar Assn. Pres.'s, Lawyer-Pilots Bar Assn., Am. Judicature Soc., Maritime Law Assn. (proctor in admirality), Southeastern Admiralty Law Inst. (bd. dirs. 1982-084, chmn., pres. 1994). Home: 1959 Largo Rd Jacksonville FL 32207-3926 Office: 901 Blackstone Bldg 233 E Bay St Jacksonville FL 32202-3452 Fax: 904-356-6508.

WHITE, EDWARD ALLEN, electronics company executive; b. Jan. 1, 1928; s. Joseph and Bessie (Allen) W.; m. Joan Dixon, Dec. 22, 1949 (div. Aug. 1978); children: Dixon Richard, Leslie Ann; m. Nancy Rhoads, Oct. 6, 1979. BS, Tufts U., 1947. Vice chmn. White Electronic Designs Corp., Phoenix, 1951—. Pres. Ariz. Digital Corp., Phoenix, 1975—91, Interactive Digital Corp., Phoenix, 1992—. Patentee in field. Bd. dirs. Gov.'s Coun. Children, Youth and Families, Phoenix, 1982-84, Planned Parenthood Fedn. Am., 1984-88; pres., bd. dirs. Planned Parenthood Ctrl. and No. Ariz., 1984-88; trustee Internat. House, N.Y.C., 1973-75, Tufts U., 1973-83. Recipient Horatio Alger award, 1962. Mem.: World Pres.'s Orgn., Paradise Valley Country Club, Tau Beta Pi. Home: 5786 N Echo Canyon Cir Phoenix AZ 85018-1242 Office: White Electronic Designs Corp 3601 E University Dr Phoenix AZ 85034-7254 E-mail: ewhite@whiteedc.com.

WHITE, ELIZABETH LOCZI, academic researcher, civil engineer; b. McKees Rocks, Pa., Mar. 9, 1936; d. Victor and Elizabeth (Vezendy) Loczi; m. William Blaine White, Mar. 27, 1959; children: Nikki Elizabeth White Vezendi, W. Brion (dec.). BSCE, U. Pitts., 1958; MSCE, Pa. State U., 1969, PhD in Civil Engring., 1975. Registered profl. engr., Pa. Civil engr. IV Pa. Dept. Hwys., Harrisburg, 1958-59; part-time rsch. asst. Pa. State U., University Park, 1964-74; Anna L. Rhodes Hawkes fellow AAUW, State College, Pa., 1974-75; rsch. assoc. Pa. State U., University Park, 1975-83, sr. rsch. assoc., 1983—. Hydrologic cons., State College, Pa., 1975—. Fellow Nat. Speleological Soc. (editor caving pubs. 1961—); mem. Grad. Women in Sci. (life, treas.), Nat. Soc. Profl. Engrs., AAUW, Sigma Sigma Sigma. Republican. Hungarian Reformed. Avocations: cave exploration, hiking. Home: RR 1 Box 527 Petersburg PA 16669-9211 Office: Pa State U Dept Civil Engring 212 Sackett Bldg University Park PA 16802-1408

WHITE, ELMER, physicist, researcher; b. Atlanta, June 22, 1926; s. William Tallahassee and Gladys W.; m. Louise Turner, June 18, 1960; children: Allisa Michele, Derek Elmer. BS, Ohio State U., 1952; student, Air Force Inst. Tech., 1961-63; PhD in Mgmt., LaJolla U., 1982. Engring. designer GE, Evendale, Ohio, 1954-56; physicist Wright-Patterson AFB, Dayton, 1960-67, Lawrence Livermore Lab., Livermore, Calif., 1967-71, Naval Ocean Syss., San Diego, 1972-86; physicist Naval Rsch. Lab. Stennis Space Ctr., Miss., 1986-94; ret., 1994. Contbr. articles to profl. jours. Served in USN, 1943-45. Mem. Acoustic Soc. Am. Home: 130 Moonraker Dr Slidell LA 70458-5521

WHITE, EMMET, JR. retirement community administrator; b. Newark, Oct. 18, 1946; s. Emmet Sr. and June (Howlett) White; m. Betty Orr, June 7, 1970; children: Benjamin, Suzanne, George. BA, Lafayette Coll., 1968; JD, Coll. of William and Mary, 1971. Bar: Hawaii 1972; cert. nursing home adminstr., Hawaii. Law ptnr. Mau & White AAL, Honolulu, 1975-83, White & Tom AAL, Honolulu, 1983-95; CEO, adminstr. Arcadia Retirement Residence, 1996—. Bd. trustees Ctrl. Union Ch., Honolulu, 1980-84, chmn. 1983-84, moderator, 1987. Col. USAR, 1968-94. Mem.: Hawaii Long Term Care Assn. (chmn. 2001—02), Hawaii Bar Assn. Avocations: family activities, physical activities. Office: Arcadia Retirement Residence 1434 Punahou St Honolulu HI 96822-4754 E-mail: ewhite@arcadia-hi.org.

WHITE, ERSKINE NORMAN, JR. management company executive; b. N.Y.C., July 21, 1924; s. Erskine Norman and Catharine (Putnam) W.; m. Eileen E. Lutz, Nov. 5, 1949; children: Erskine Norman III, Carol White Wolfe, Catharine White Brush. BE, Yale U., 1947; MS, MIT, 1949. Staff mem. rsch. devel. bd. Dept. Def., 1949; plant mgr. Gorham Mfg. Co. (became Gorham Corp. 1961, Gorham div. Textron Inc. 1968), Asheville, N.C., 1956-57, 1956-57, exec. v.p., 1964-68, pres., 1968-69, dir., 1960-69; group v.p. Textron Inc., Providence, 1969-71, exec. v.p. ops., 1971-75, exec. v.p., 1975-79, exec. v.p. corp. affairs, 1979-81; pres. E.N. White Mgmt. Corp., Providence, 1981-95. V.p., treas. Cadwagan Assoc. Trustee Women and Infants Hosp., R.I., 1974-93, RISD, 1966-72, 82-95, chmn. fin. com., 1988-95, treas., 1990-95, Low Country Cmty. Devel. Corp., Hilton Head Island, S.C., 1999-; bd. dirs., exec. com. New England Coun., 1979-81; chmn. NCCJ, 1987-89. With USN, 1944-46, PTO. Mem. NAM (bd. dir. 1974-80, regional v.p. 1975, div. vice chmn. 1978-80, exec. com.), Urban League (bd. dir. R.I. chpt. 1989-97), Greater Providence C. of C. (bd. dir., pres. 1978), R.I. C. of C. Fedn. (pres. 1979), Sigma Xi, Tau Beta Pi.

WHITE, EUGENE VADEN, retired pharmacist; b. Cape Charles, Va., Aug. 13, 1924; s. Paul Randolph and Louise (Townsend) W.; m. Laura Juanita LaFontaine, Aug. 28, 1948; children: Lynda Sue, Patricia Louise. BS in Pharmacy, Med. Coll. Va., 1950; PharM (hon.), Phila. Coll. Pharmacy and Sci., 1966; DSc (hon.), Shenandoah U., 2001. Pharmacist McKim & Huffman Drug Store, Luray, Va., 1950, Miller's Drug Store, Winchester, 1950-53; pharmacist, ptnr. Shiner's Drug Store, Front Royal, 1953-56; pharmacist, owner Eugene V. White, Pharmacist, P.C., Berryville, 1956-98, ret., 1998. Sturmer lectr. Phila. Coll. Pharmacy and Sci., 1979; Lubin vis. prof. U. Tenn. Sch. Pharmacy, Memphis, 1974; mem. bd. visitors Sch. Pharmacy, U. Pitts., 1969. Author: The Office-Based Family Pharmacist, 1978; created first office practice in community pharmacy, 1960, developed patient medication profile record, 1960. 2d lt. USAAC, 1943-45. Recipient Nat. Leadership award Phi Lambda Sigma, 1979, Outstanding Pharmacy Alumnus award Med. Coll. Va. Sch. Pharmacy Alumni Assn., 1989; Eugene V. White scholarship named in his honor Shenandoah U. Sch. Pharmacy, 1996, Eugene V. White Disting. Lecture Series established by Delta Xi chpt. Kappa Psi Pharm. Fraternity, Shenandoah U. Sch. Pharmacy, 1998. Fellow Am. Coll. Apothecaries (J. Leon Lascoff award 1973); mem. Am. Pharm Assn. (Daniel B. Smith award 1965, Remington Honor medal 1978), Va. Pharm. Assn. (Pharmacist of Yr. award 1966, Outstanding Pharmacist award 1992). Methodist. Avocations: reading, woodworking, computer. E-mail: evwhite@visuallink.com.

WHITE, EUGENE A. retired physician, neuroradiologist; b. Birmingham, Ala., Oct. 29, 1935; s. Roger O. and Gregory C. (Durr) W.; m. June Ardis Johnson, Feb. 6, 1965; children: Theodore O., Forrest E., Darlene E. BA summa cum laude, Fisk U., 1956; MD, Case Western Res. U., 1964. Diplomate Am. Bd. Radiology. Postdoctoral fellow dept. neuroradiology Karolinska Hosp., Stockholm, 1969-70; radiologist Forest City Hosp., Cleve., 1970-72, Luth. Hosp., Cleve., 1972-73; from instr. to asst. prof. radiology Case Western Res. Med. Sch., 1973-77, asst. clin. prof. radiology, 1977-99; neuroradiologist in pvt. practice Drs. Hill & Thomas Inc., Beachwood, Ohio, 1977-99, ptnr., v.p. neuroradiology svcs., 1988-99, also bd. dirs. Mng. dir. Assoc. Med. Enterprises, Beachwood, 1980-87; clin. cons. Technicare Corp., Solon, Ohio, 1984-86. Contbr. articles to profl. jours. Bd. dirs. League Park Ctr., Cleve., 1976-82, Murtis Taylor Cmty. Ctr., 1986-92, Fisk U., Nashville, 1988—, Adrienne Kennedy Soc., 1989—, Great Lakes Theatre Festival, Cleve., 1992—, Cleve. Internat. Program, 1994—, Geric Found., 1996—; chmn. bd. dirs. Creative Writing Workshop, 1995—, Coun. of Internat. Programs, 1999--, chmn. bd., 2002, mem. com. on fgn. rels., 2002 Mem.: NAACP (life), Internat. Symposium Neuroradiology, Am. Roentgen Ray Soc., Am. Coll. Neuroradiology, Am. Coll. Radiology, Hermit Club, Cleveland Skating Club, Pasteur Club, Phi Beta Kappa, Alpha Phi Alpha (life). Avocations: music, tennis, theater, international relations, philosophy. Home: 3199 Van Aken Blvd Shaker Heights OH 44120 E-mail: eaw5@stratos.net.

WHITE, FLORENCE MAY, learning disabilities specialist; b. Ottawa, Kans., Sept. 1, 1936; d. O.C. Robert and Effie Lynne (Walker) Arnold; m. Donald L. White, June 1, 1958 (dec. Jan. 1996); children: Tab Vincent, Jacque Sue, Michelle May. BA, Ottawa U., 1958; MS, Kans. U., 1974; postgrad., Kans. U. Med. Ctr., 1975-76. Cert. reading specialist, learning disabilities specialist; cert. elem. and mid. sch. edn.: lang. arts, social studies, elem. curriculum. Classroom tchr. 2d grade Wellsville (Kans.) Elem., 1958-59; learning disabilities tchr. Olatha (Kans.) Spl. Edn. Coop., 1971-74; learning disabilities specialist, tchr. 7-9 Ottawa Mid. Sch., 1974-77; learning disabilities specialist, tchr. Paola Spl. Edn. Coop., Richmond, Kans., 1980-95; tchr. learning disabilities classes elem. level Ctrl. Heights Elem. Sch., 2001—. Pub. rep., speaker on learning disabilities to civic groups and local orgns., 1972-75. Den mother Boy Scouts Am. and Brownies, Ottawa, 1968-70; chair state GOP women's polit. activities Rep. State Party, Topeka, 1964-67; chair scholarship contest DAR, Ottawa dist., 1984-96; Sunday sch. tchr. Meth. Ch., Ottawa; crafts tchr. local 4-H, Ottawa; mem. Central Heights PTA (projects com. 1980-95); mem. Ottawa Arts Coun. State of Kans. scholar State Spl. Edn. Dept., 1976. Mem. Internat. Reading Assn., Kans. Reading Assn., Franklin County Reading Coun. (exec. bd. 1993-94, v.p., pres.-elect 1989-91, pres. 1991-92), PEO, Alpha Delta Kappa (projects com. 1988—, environment com., hospitality com.). Roman Catholic. Avocations: oil painting, reading, travel, music, flower arranging.

WHITE, FREDERICK ANDREW, physics educator, physicist; b. Detroit, Mar. 11, 1918; s. Andrew Bracken and Mildred (Witzel) W.; m. Dorothy Janet Sibley, Nov. 7, 1942 (dec.); children: Wendell William, Lawrence Sibley, Eric Sibley, Roger Randolph (dec.). BS, Wayne State U., 1940; MS, U. Mich., 1941; postgrad., U. Rochester, 1943-46; PhD, U. Wis., 1959. Insp. U.S. Army Ordnance, Rochester, N.Y., 1941-43; rsch. asst. Manhattan project U. Rochester, 1943-45; grad. instr. rsch. Manhattan project U. Rochester, 1946; rsch. asst., rsch. assoc., cons. physicist Gen. Electric Co. Knolls Atomic Power Lab., Schenectady, 1947-62; adj. prof. nuclear sci. Rensselaer Poly. Inst., Troy, N.Y., 1961-62, prof. nuclear engring. and environmental engring., indsl. liaison scientist, 1962-81, prof. emeritus, 1981—; staff Bell Telephone Labs., 1969; rsch. and liaison scientist Rochester Gas & Electric Co., N.Y., 1978-96; adj. prof. physics SUNY, Albany, 1981-88. Cons. NASA, 1965-80; organist and acoustic cons., 1952—. Author: American Industrial Research Laboratories, 1961, Mass Spectrometry in Science and Technology, 1968, Our Acoustic Environment, 1975; Mass Spectrometry: Applications in Science and Engineering, 1986. Mem. AIAA, IEEE, Optical Soc. Am., Am. Guild Organists. Achievements include developing mass spectrometric instrumentation and its uses in measurements relating to nuclear and atomic physics; co-discoverer last naturally-occurring stable isotope. Home: 2456 Hilltop Rd Niskayuna NY 12309-2405 Office: Rensselaer Poly Inst Linac Lab Troy NY 12181 E-mail: whitef@taconic.net.

WHITE, GARY FRANCIS, investigation professional; b. Boston, Oct. 12, 1945; s. Edward Francis and Ruth Audrey (Buchan) White; m. Janice Gertrude Weldon, June 23, 1968 (div. Jan. 1991); children: G. Christopher, Joel D., Kerri L., Kevin D., Ryan M.; m. Susan Ellen Harrison, June 6, 1992; stepchildren: James Harrison, Constance Mitchell. BS in Acctg., Bentley Coll., 1969; MBA, Fairleigh Dickinson U., 1976. Spl. agt. FBI, 1969-96; corp. mgr. investigations Raytheon Co., Lexington, Mass., 1996—. Mem. New Eng. Insps. Gen. Coun., Boston, 1988-94; lectr. in field. Participant Project Bread-Walk for Hunger, Boston, 1988—; res. dep. sheriff Middlesex County, Mass. Recipient numerous FBI Commendations. Mem. Cert. Fraud Examiners, Am. Soc. Indsl. Security, Soc. Former Spl. Agts. FBI, Assn. Insps. Gen. Roman Catholic. Avocations: singing, horticulture. Home: 40 Hawkins Glen Dr Salem NH 03079 Office: Raytheon Co 141 Spring St Lexington MA 02421-7899

WHITE, GARY RICHARD, electrical engineer, plant operator; b. Detroit, Nov. 15, 1962; s. Thomas Richard and Davene (Reynolds) W. BSEE, Wayne State U., 1986. Electronics engr. U.S. Army Info. Sys. Engring. Command, Ft. Belvoir, Va., 1987-88, Ft. Shafter, Hawaii, 1988-92; elec. worker U.S. Navy Pub. Works Ctr., Pearl Harbor, 1992-96, plant operator helper, 1996—. Mem. IEEE, NRA, NSPE, Assn. Computing Machinery, Am. Assn. Individual Investors, Am. Mgmt. Assn. Avocations: weightlifting, biking, hardware and software, rock concerts, movies. Office: PO Box 19055 Honolulu HI 96817-8055

WHITE, GAYLE CLAY, aerospace company executive; b. Wyandotte, Mich., Sept. 28, 1944; s. John Leonard and Irene Frances (Clay) W.; m. Sharon Wong, June 8, 1968; children: Lai Jean, Quinn Yee. BBA, Ea. Mich. U., 1967; MBA, Utah State U., 1971; MPA, Auburn U., 1976; postgrad., Nova U., 1985-99. Computer system analyst USAF Logistics Command, Odgen, Utah, 1967-71, U.S.-Can. Mil. Officer Exec., Ottawa, Ont., 1971-73; mgr. software devel. USAF Data System Design Ctr., Montgomery, Ala., 1973-77; data base adminstr. Supreme Hdqrs. Allied Powers Europe, Casteau, Belgium, 1977-81; mgr. software configuration System Integration Office, Colorado Springs, Colo., 1981-83; mgr. computer ops. N.Am. Aerospace Def. Command, 1983-84; dir. ops. 6 Missile Warning Squadron, Space Command, Cape Cod, Mass., 1984-86, comdr., 1986-87; mgr. program devel. Rockwell Internat., Colorado Springs, 1987-96; mgr. bus. devel. The Boeing Co., 1996-99; ret. Mem. faculty computer sci. and bus. Regis U., Colorado Springs, 1981-97; sr. mem. exec. staff Computer Scis. Corp., 1999—. Treas. Christian Ctr. Ch., Colorado Springs, 1989-95; v.p. European Parents, Tchrs. and Students Assn., 1979-81. Recipient Mil.-Civilian Rels. award, Otis Civilian Adv. Coun., 1987, cert., Data Processing Mgmt. Assn., 1973, Service award, NDIA, 1998, Air Force Assn. Legion of Merit, 2001, medal of merit, Colo. Air Force Assn., 2001, Significant Serv. award, Nat. Def. Indsl. Assn., 1998. Mem.: C. of C. Mil. Affairs Com., Christian Businessmen's Assn., Nat. Security Indsl. Assn. (bd. dirs. Rocky Mountain chpt. 1990—97, vice chmn. space com. 1999—2000, vice chmn. ctrl. region 1996—97, space com. bd. dirs. 1993—, pres. 1997—99, chmn. nat. space com. 2000—, Exceptional Svc. award 2001), SHAPE Officers Assn., Air Force Assn. (v.p. membership Lance Sijan chpt. 2000—), Global Positioning Sys. Internat. Assn., Inst. Nav. (treas. Rocky Mountain sect. 1996—97), Armed Forces Comm. Electronics Assn., Lynmar Racquet Club, Alpha Kappa Psi. Republican. Avocations: racquetball, camping, coin collecting. Office: Computer Scis Corp 1250 Academy Park Loop Ste 240 Colorado Springs CO 80910-3707 E-mail: gwhite22@csc.com.

WHITE, GEORGE, government official, physical scientist; b. Bklyn., Dec. 19, 1937; s. Samuel Louis and Mollie (Telson) W.; m. Susan Jane Doppelhammer, Apr. 13, 1969; 1 child, Jeffrey Steven. BS, CUNY, 1960; MS, NYU, 1964; postgrad., Am. U., 1966-68. Rsch. asst. Rockefeller Inst., N.Y.C., 1960, NYU, N.Y.C., 1961-64; rsch. scientist Atlantic Rsch. Corp., Alexandria, Va., 1965-72; sr. staff officer Nat. Acad. Scis., Washington, 1973-80; divsn. chief, asst. to dir. U.S. Bur. Mines, Dept. Interior, 1981-96; lectr. chemistry No. Va. C.C., Alexandria, Va., 1972-78, Bronx C.C., 1961-64; spl. asst. to Congressman Ed Pastor, 1995-98. Staff editor: Chemistry of Coal Utilization, 1980, Minerals and Materials, 1983-87, Minerals Position of the U.S., 1985-90. Named Presdl. Sci. Intern, Nat. Sci. Found., Dept. Transp., 1972; Legis. fellow U.S. Congress, 1992. Mem. AAAS, Am. Chem. Soc., Am. Inst. Mining Engrs., Washington Chem. Soc. Democrat. Jewish. Home: Annandale, Va. Died 2002.

WHITE, GEORGE COOKE, theater director, foundation executive; b. New London, Conn., Aug. 16, 1935; s. Nelson Cooke and Aida (Rovetti) W.; m. Elizabeth Conant Darling, July 5, 1958; children: George Conant, Caleb Ensign, Juliette Darling. Student, U. Paris, 1956; BA, Yale U., 1957, MFA, 1961; student, Shakespeare Inst., 1959; ArtsD (hon.), Conn. Coll., 1994. Stage mgr. Imperial Japanese Azumakabuki Co., 1955; asst. mgr. Internat. Ballet Festival, Nervi, Italy, 1955; prodn. coordinator Talent Assos., 1961-63; adminstrv. v.p. score prodns. Paramount Pictures, 1963-65; founder, pres. Eugene O'Neill Meml. Theatre Found., 1965—2000; adviser, dir. Theatre One, Conn. Coll. Women, 1967-70; exec. dir. The Johnny Mercer Found., 1999; regional theater cons. Nat. Ednl. TV Network; guest lectr. Wagner Coll., 1970; acting dir. Hunter Coll. Hunter Arts, 1972-73. Adj. prof. U. N.C.; prof. theater adminstrn. program Yale U., 1978-91; co-chmn. Yale Drama Sch.; mem. exec. com. Theatre Libr. Assn., 1967; bd. govs. Am. Playwrights Theatre; mem. bd. ANTA, 1967-68; mem. Mayor N.Y.C.'s. Theatre Adv. Com.; advisory bd. Internat. Theatre Inst.; panel mem. Exptl. Theatre; U.S. State Dept. cultural exchange grantee to Australia; guest adminstr. Australian Nat. Playwrights Conf., 1973; U.S. del. Internat. Theatre Inst. Congress, Moscow, 1973; mem. Conn. Commn. on Arts, 1978-93, mem. exec. com., 1979-83, vice chair, 1992-93; co-founder Caribbean-U.S. Theatre Exchange; dir. Actors Theatre St. Paul, 1979, 80, 82, 83, 86, Hartman Repertory Theatre, 1980; guest dir. Chinese Theater Assn., Beijing, 1984, 87, Hedgerow Theatre, 1986; mem. nominating com. Antoinette Perry Awards, 1984-86, 88, 94-96, 98-2002, adminstrv. com. Am. Theater Wing, 1997; dir. Anna Christie Beijing Cen. Dramatic Theater, 1984, 87; bd. dirs. New London Day. Appeared in TV series Citizen Soldier, 1959-61; appeared in off-Broadway prodn. John Brown's Body. Trustee Goodspeed Opera House, 1966-68, Nat. Theatre Conf., 1973—, Eastern Conn. Symphony, Dance Arts Coun., Conn. Opera Assn., Conn. Pub. TV, 1973-83, Mitchell Coll., 1994—, Arts & Bus. Coun., 1994—, Arts Internat., 2001--, Boston Conservatory, 2000--; trustee Conn. Edn. Telecommunications Corp., 1973-83, chmn., 1982; mem. planning bd. Op. Rescue; bd. dirs. Rehearsal Club, Centre for Inter-Am. Rels., Theater of Latin Am., Manhattan Theatre Club, 1970-80, Met. Opera Guild; Performance mag.; exec. com. Yale Drama Alumni, 1963-73; mem. Yale Alumni Bd.; bd. overseers drama dept. Brandeis U.; adv. bd. Am. Musical Theatre Program, Hartford Conservatory, Bd. Arts & Bus. Coun., Brandeis Creative Arts Award Jury, Theater and New Music Theatre Works Panel, NEA; mem. Waterford (Conn.) Rep. Town Meeting, 1975-77; presdl. appointment to Nat. Coun. NEA, 1992; mem. Nat. Coun. Arts, 1992-97; bd. dirs. Day Pub. Co., RKO Pictures; mem. Coast Guard Auxillary, Crew mem. U.S. Coast Guard Barque Eagle. Served with AUS, 1957-59; Flotilla Cmdr, U.S. Coast Auxillary, 1998-99. Named Officer first class, Royal Swedish Order of Polar Star; recipient spl. citation, New England Theatre Conf., 1968, 1998, Margo Jones award, 1968, Pub. Svc. award, New London County Bar Assn., 1975, Disting. Citizen's award, Town of Waterford, 1976, Distin. Svc. award, Conn. mag., 1981, Contbns. to State award, 1981, Lifetime Contbn. to Theatre award, Am. Theater Assn., 1989, Contbn. to Conn. Arts award, Quinnipiac Coll., 1989, Medal of Arts, Russian Federation, Chevalier des artes et des lettres (France), 1983, gold medal, Cairo Internat. Experimental Theater Festival; grantee Internat. Communications Agy. cultural exch. grantee to People's Republic of China, 1980. Fellow Royal Soc. Arts, Coll. of Am. Theatre; mem. Chinese Theatre Assn. (hon.). Clubs: Century; Cosmos (Washington); Thames (New London); White's Point Yacht. Office: O'Neill Theater Ctr 305 Great Neck Rd Waterford CT 06385-3825 Home: 30 Sutton Pl New York NY 10022

WHITE, GEORGE EDWARD, law educator, lawyer; b. Northampton, Mass., Mar. 19, 1941; s. George LeRoy and Frances Dorothy (McCafferty) W.; m. Susan Valre Davis, Dec. 31, 1966; children: Alexandra V., Elisabeth McC. BA, Amherst Coll., 1963; MA, Yale U., 1964, PhD, 1967; JD, Harvard U., 1970. Bar: D.C. 1970, Va. 1975, U.S. Supreme Ct. 1973. Vis. scholar Am. Bar Found., 1970-71; law clk. to Chief Justice Warren U.S. Supreme Ct., 1971-72; asst. prof. law U. Va., 1972-74, assoc. prof., 1974-77, prof., 1977-86, John B. Minor prof. law and history, 1987-92, disting. univ. prof., John B. Minor prof. law and history, 1992—. Vis. prof. Marshall-Wythe Law Sch. spring 1988, N.Y. Law Sch., fall 1988. Author books, including: The American Judicial Tradition, 1976, 2d edit., 1988, Tort Law in America: An Intellectual History (gavel award ABA 1981), 1980, Earl Warren: A Public Life (gavel award ABA 1983), 1982, The Marshall Court and Cultural Change, 1988, 2d edit., 1991 (James Willard Hurst prize 1990), Justice Oliver Wendell Holmes: Law and the Inner Self, 1993 (gavel award ABA 1994, Scribes award, 1994, Littleton-Griswold prize 1994, Triennial Order of the Coif award 1996), Intervention and Detachment: Essays in Legal History and Jurisprudence, 1994; Creating the National Pastime: Baseball Transforms Itself, 1903-1953, 1996, The Constitution and The New Deal, 2000; editor Studies in Legal History, 1980-86, Delegate in Law, 1986-97. Mem. AAAS, Am. Law Inst., Am. Soc. Legal History (bd. dirs. 1978-81), Soc. Am. Historians. Office: Law Sch U Va Charlottesville VA 22903-1789 E-mail: gew@virginia.edu.

WHITE, GEORGE MALCOLM, architect; b. Cleve., Nov. 1, 1920; m. Susanne Neiley Daniels, Apr. 21, 1973; children: Stephanie, Jocelyn, Geoffrey, Pamela. BS, MS, MIT, 1942; MBA, Harvard, 1948; LL.B., Case Western Res. U., 1959. Design engr. Gen. Electric Co., Schenectady, 1942-47; practice architecture and law Cleve., 1948-71; Architect of Capitol, Washington, 1971-95; vice chmn. Leo A. Daly, 1996—. Bd. dirs. 3D Internat. Works include First Unitarian Ch., Cleve., 1959, Preformed Line Products Co. Office Bldg., Cleve., 1960, Mentor Harbor Yacht Club, 1968, restoration, Old Senate and Supreme Ct. Chambers, U.S. Capitol, 1975, Libr. of Congress James Madison Meml. Bldg., 1979, U.S. Capitol Power Plant Extension, 1979, master plan for U.S. Capitol, 1981, Hart Senate Office Bldg., 1982, restoration of the west cen. front U.S. Capitol Bldg., 1987, Thurgood Marshall Fed. Judiciary Bldg., 1992, U.S. Capitol west terr. restoration and courtyard addt., 1993. Former mem. D.C. Zoning Commn., U.S. Capitol Police Bd., U.S. Capitol Guide Bd., U.S. Ho. of Reps. Page Bd., Adv. Coun. on Hist. Preservation, Internat. Ctr. Com., Nat. Conservation Adv. Coun., Nat. Capital Meml. Commn., art adv. com. Washington Met. Area Transit Auth.; former acting dir. U.S. Bot. Garden; former mem. bd. dirs., chmn. design com. Pennsylvania Ave. Devel. Corp.; former bd. dirs. Nat. Bldg. Mus.; former trustee Fed. City Coun.; mem. bd. regents Am. Archtl. Found; former chmn. archtl. adv. com. Restoration of Statue of Liberty; chmn. com. for Statue of Liberty Mus.; mem. nat. panel arbitrators Am. Arbitration Assn.; former mem. vis. com. dept. architecture and planning MIT; mem. bd. cons. Nubian monuments at Philae, Egypt; mem. internat. com. cons. for Egyptian Mus., Cairo; chmn. rev. com. Nat. Capital Devel. Commn. for Canberra, Australia. Recipient Gold medal Archtl. Soc. Ohio, 1971, Burton award for Disting. Pub. Svc. Cleve. Club, 1991. Fellow AIA (Thomas Jefferson award 1992), ASCE (hon.), Nat. Soc. Profl. Engrs., Nat. Acad. Forensic Engrs.; mem. Sigma Xi, Eta Kappa Nu, Lambda Alpha, Tau Beta Pi. Office: Leo A Daly 1201 Connecticut Ave NW Washington DC 20036-2683 Address: 3 Chalfont Ct Bethesda MD 20816-1805

WHITE, GERALD ANDREW, retired chemical company executive; b. L.I., N.Y., Aug. 2, 1934; s. Charles Eugene and Grace Mary (Trojan) W.; m. Mary Alice Turvey, June 8, 1957; children— Kevin, Patricia, Timothy, Megan B in Chem. Engring., Villanova U., 1957; cert. advanced mgmt. program, Harvard Bus. Sch., 1975. Staff engr. Air Products and Chems., Inc., Allentown, Pa., 1962-65, mgr. systems devel., 1965-66, group controller, 1969-72, corp. controller, 1974-76, v.p. planning, 1977-82, v.p. fin., chief fin. officer, 1982-92, sr. v.p. fin., chief fin. officer, 1992-95. Pres. United Way in Lehigh County, 1981; bd. dirs. Pa. Coun. on Econ. Edn., 1981-95; trustee, treas. Allentown Art Mus., 1984; trustee, chmn. bd. trustees De Sales U, Center Valley, 1983. Lt. USN, 1957-62. Recipient J. Stanley Morehouse Meml. award Villanova U. Coll. Engring., 1983 Mem. AIChE, Fin. Execs. Inst. (pres. northeastern Pa. chpt. 1974-75), Fin. Execs. Rsch. Found. (trustee 1992-96), Tau Beta Pi. Avocation: squash.

WHITE, GILBERT, federal agency administrator; BS Elec. Engring., So. Carolina State U.; postgrad. in Engring. Mgmt., George Washington U. Payload safety mgr. Space Station Freedom Program Office NASA, 1992—99; mgr. Internat. Space Station Ops. NASA Enterprise Safety and Mission Assurance Div. Office of Safety and Mission Assurance, 1999—. Office: NASA Hdqrs Mail Code Q 300 E St SW Washington DC 20546*

WHITE, GILBERT F(OWLER), geographer, educator; b. Chgo., Nov. 26, 1911; s. Arthur E. and Mary (Guthrie) W.; m. Anne Elizabeth Underwood, Apr. 28, 1944; children: William D., Mary, Frances. BS, U. Chgo., 1932, SM, 1934, PhD, 1942; LLD (hon.), Hamilton Coll., 1951, Swarthmore Coll.; LL.D. (hon.), Earlham Coll., Richmond, Ind., Mich. State U., Augustana Coll.; ScD (hon.), Haverford Coll.; hon. degree, Northland Coll. Geographer Miss. Valley Com. of P.W.A., 1934, Nat. Resources Bd., 1934-35; sec. land and water com. Nat. Resources Com. and Nat. Resources Planning Bd., 1935-40; with Exec. Office Pres., Bur. Budget, 1941-42; asst. exec. sec. Am. Friends Service Com., 1945-46; relief adminstr. in France, 1942-43; interned Baden-Baden, 1943-44; sec. Am. Relief for India, 1945-46; pres. Haverford Coll., 1946-55; prof. geography U. Chgo., 1956-69; prof. geography, dir. Inst. Behavioral Sci., U. Colo., Boulder, 1970-78, Gustavson disting. prof. emeritus, 1979—; dir. Natural Hazards Info. Ctr., 1978-84, 92-94; exec. editor Environment mag., 1983-93. Vis. prof. Oxford U., 1962-63; cons. Investigations Lower Mekong Basin, 1961-62, 70; U.S. mem. UNESCO adv. com. on arid zone research, 1954-55; mem. mission Am. Vol. Agys. Relief Germany, 1946; vice chmn. Pres.'s Water Resources Policy Commn., 1950; mem. com. natural resources Hoover Commn., 1948; chmn. UN Panel Integrated River Basin Devel., 1956-57; chmn. Task Force Fed. Flood Control Policy, 1965-66; sci. adv. to adminstr. UN Devel. Program, 1966-71; chmn. adv. bd. Energy Policy Project, 1972-74; chmn. Am. Friends Service Com., 1963-69; chmn. com. on man and environment IGU, 1969-76; chmn. steering com. High Sch. Geography com., 1964-70; mem. Tech. Assessment Adv. Council, 1974-76; chmn. environ. studies bd. NRC, 1975-77; pres. Sci. Com. on Problems of Environment, 1976-82; chmn. bd. Resources for Future, 1973-79; co-chmn. U.S.-Egypt Joint Consultative Com. on Sci. and Tech., 1981-86; mem. adv. group on greenhouse gases World Meteorol. Orgn., Internat. Council of Scientific Unions, UN Environ. Program., 1986-90; chmn. tech. rev. com. Nev. Nuclear Waste Project, 1987-93; mem. adv. group on water UN Environ. Program, 1989-93, working group for Action Plan for Aral Sea Basin, USSR, 1990-93; chmn. nat. rev. com. Status U.S. Floodplain Mgmt., 1989; bd. dirs. Am. Soc. Flood Plain Mgrs. Found., 1996—. Author: Human Adjustment to Floods, 1942, Science and Future of Arid Lands, 1960, Social and Economic Aspects of Natural Resources, 1962, Choice of Adjustment to Floods, 1964, Strategies of American Water Management, 1969; co-author: Drawers of Water, 1972, Assessment of Research on Natural Hazards, 1975, Flood Hazard in the United States, 1975, The Environment as Hazard, 1978, also various govt. reports, 1937-45; editor: Natural Hazards: Local, National and Global, 1974, Environmental Aspects of Complex River Development, 1977; co-editor: Environmental Issues, 1977, The World Environment, 1972-1982, 1982, Environmental Effects of Nuclear War, 1983. Reicpient Daly medal Am. Geog. Soc., 1971, Eben award Am. Water Resources Assn., 1972, Caulfield medal, 1989, Alumni medal U. Chgo., 1979, Outstanding Achievement award Nat. Coun. for Geog. Edn., 1981, Sasakawa UN Evniron. prize, 1985, Tyler prize, 1987, Laureat d'Honneur award Internat. Geog. Union, 1988, Vautrin Lud Internat. Geog. prize, 1992, Hubbard medal Nat. Geog. Soc., 1994, Volvo Environment prize, 1995. Mem. AAAS, NAS (mem. commn. on natural resources 1973-80, chmn. 1977-80, chmn. com. on water 1964-68, chmn. com. on sustainable water supplies of Middle East 1996-99, Environ. award 1980, Pub. Welfare medal 2000), Assn. Am. Geographers (pres. 1962, Outstanding Achievement award 1955, 74, Anderson medal 1986, U.S. Nat. Medal Sci 2000), Internat. Coun. Sci. Unions (mem. steering com. on study of environ. consequences of nuclear war 1983-87, mem. adv. com. on environ. 1990-96), Internat. Water Resources Assn. (Millenium award 2000), Russian Geog. Soc. (hon.), Royal Geog. Soc. (hon.), Russian Acad. Scis. (fgn.), Am. Philos. Soc., Cosmos Club (Washington, award 1993), Sigma Xi, Mem. Soc. Friends. Home: 624 Pearl St Apt 302 Boulder CO 80302-5072 E-mail: gilbert.white@colorado.edu.

WHITE, GORDON ELIOT, historian; b. Glen Ridge, N.J., Oct. 25, 1933; s. Maurice Brewster and Sarah Fullilove (Gordon) W.; m. Nancy Johnson, 1955 (div. 1957); m. Mary Joan Briggs, Aug. 6, 1960 (dec. Nov. 1987); children: Sarah Elizabeth and Gordon O'Neal Brewster (twins), David McIntyre; m. Francis C. Barrineau, 1989 (div. 1996); m. Angela Tyler, Mar. 27, 1999. BA, Cornell U., 1955; MS in Journalism, Columbia U., 1957. Lic. master mariner USCG; lic. pilot FAA. Stringer Nassau Daily Rev.-Star, Rockville Centre, L.I., N.Y., 1948-50; stringer Freeport (N.Y.) Leader, 1949-50; sports writer Morris County (N.J.) Citizen, 1950-51; stringer Ithaca (N.Y.) Evening News, 1951-55; photo editor, editorial writer Cornell Daily Sun, 1951-55; copy editor Am. Banker, N.Y.C., 1958; Washington corr. Chgo. Am., 1958-61; chief Washington bur. Deseret News, Salt Lake City, 1961-88. Also corr. in Europe, U.S. and Antarctic for WJR, Detroit; KSL-KSL-TV, Salt Lake City, also KGMB, Honolulu; free lance writer with U.S. Navy, Army and Air Force, 1959; cons. Nat. Air and Space Mus.; auto racing, mil. aviation electronics historian. Author: Offenhauser, the Legendary American Racing Engine and the Men Who Built It, 1996, The Indianapolis Racing Cars of Frank Kurtis, 1940-1963, 2000, Kurtis-Kraft: Masterworks of Speed & Style, 2001, Lost Race Tracks, 2002. Advisor auto racing Nat. Mus. Am. History, Smithsonian Instn., 1989—; curator Miller-Offenhauser Archive of historic race engine blueprints. Recipient 1st prize for newsphoto Sigma Delta Chi, 1954; Raymond Clapper Meml. award White House Corrs. Assn., 1978; award for excellence in reporting Exec. Dept. and White House; award for excellence in reporting Nat. Press Club, 1979; Nat. Sigma Delta Chi award for disting. work as Washington Corr., 1979; Roy W. Howard award for outstanding public service by a newspaper corr., 1979; award for disting. investigative reporting Investigative Reporters and Editors, 1980; Reser-Tuthill award for writing on history of automobile racing, Indpls., 1985 Mem. Sigma Delta Chi, Pi Kappa Phi, Pi Delta Epsilon. Clubs: Nat. Press (Washington). Episcopalian. Home and Office: PO Box 129 Hardyville VA 23070 E-mail: gewhite@crosslink.net.

WHITE, GWENDOLYN A. recreational facility executive; b. Detroit, Sept. 14, 1955; d. Charles E. Hunter and Margaret J. Hannold; children: Stevan H., Cathleen G. Cert. pvt. pilot, alcohol misuse prevention program. Horse breeder, trainer Pers. Bus./Paso Fino Horse Assn., Edinburg, Va., 1979—92; unit sec. Shenandoah Co. Meml. Hosp., Woodstock, 1980—91; sec., mgr. Pioneer Lodge, Inc., Willow, Alaska, 1992—2001; CEO BAL, Inc. dba Willow Air Svc., 1997—. Mem.: Women in Aviation Internat., Aircraft Owners & Pilots Assn., Willow C. of C. Methodist. Avocations: photography, writing, snow machining, cross country skiing, horseback riding. Office: BAL Inc dba Willow Air Svc PO Box 42 Willow AK 99688

WHITE, HALBERT LYNN , JR. economist, educator, consultant; b. Kansas City, Mo., Nov. 19, 1950; s. H. Lynn and Emily (Roach) W.; m. Kim A. Titensor, Oct. 25, 1986 (div. Dec. 2001); children: Richard H. Weeks, Rachel A. Weeks. AB, Princeton U., 1972; PhD, MIT, 1976. Asst. prof. U. Rochester, N.Y., 1976-80; assoc. prof. U. Calif., San Diego, 1980-84, prof., 1984-95, prof. above scale, 1995—. Vis. assoc. prof. MIT, Cambridge, 1984; mem. adv. bd. Merrill Lynch Acad., 1994-95; mem. adv. bd. Stone Analytics, Inc.; chmn. LaJolla (Calif.) Data Sys., 1988-91, NeuralNet R&D Assocs., 1992—; commodity trading advisor, 1993-2000; pres. QuantMetrics Corp., 1998—; chmn. Bates White & Ballentine, LLC, 1999—; cons. in field. Author: Asymptotic Theory for Econometricians, 1984, rev. edit., 2000, Estimation, Inference and Specification Analysis, 1994; co-author: Artificial Neural Networks - Approximation and Learning Theory, 1992, A Unified Theory of Estimation and Inference for Nonlinear Dynamic Models, 1988, Advances in Econometric Theory, 1998, Cointegration, Causality and Forecasting, 1999; editor: Abstracts of Working Papers in Economics, 1985—; contbr. articles to profl. jours.; patentee in field. Recipient Best Article award Internat. Jour. Forecasting, 1996-97, Multa Scripsit award Econometric Theory jour., 1997, Chancellor's Assocs. award for excellence in rsch. in arts, humanities and social scis., 2002; Guggenheim fellow Guggenheim Found., 1988-89; NSF grantee, 1980—; Jour. Econometrics fellow, 1995. Fellow Econometric Soc., Am. Acad. Arts and Scis.; mem. IEEE (sr.), Internat. Assn. Fin. Engrs., Am. Fin. Assn., Internat. Inst. of Forecasters, Am. Math. Soc., Am. Statis. Assn., Internat. Neural Network Soc. (governing bd. 2001—), Big Band and Jazz Hall of Fame (bd. dirs. 1997—, v.p. 1999-2000, sec. 2000—), Friends of Tiger Band (bd. dirs. 1998—), Jazz Soc. L.A., Jazz Soc. Lower So. Calif. (treas. 1988). Avocations: music performance and composition, antiques. Office: U Calif San Diego Dept Econs # 0508 La Jolla CA 92093 E-mail: hwhite@weber.ucsd.edu.

WHITE, HAROLD F. bankruptcy judge, retired federal judge; b. Hartford, Conn., Apr. 29, 1920; s. Harry T, and Maude Evelyn (McCarthy) W.; m. Edna Jeanette Murie, 1943; children; Frances, Susan, Harold. BSc, Ohio U., 1946; JD, U. Akron, 1952. Bar: Ohio 1952. Chief police prosecutor City of Akron, Ohio, 1953; asst. prosecutor Summit County, Akron, 1957-58; bankruptcy referee, bankruptcy judge U.S. Cts., 1958-94, on recall as sr. bankruptcy judge, 1994—, on recall as bankruptcy judge, 1995-2001. Trustee Summit County Kidney Found; elder Westminster Presbyn. Ch., Akron. Named Disting. Alumni Ohio U., 1979, Outstanding Alumni U. Akron Sch. Law, 1983; recipient John Quine adj. lectr. of law award U. Akron Sch. Law, 1991. Fellow Ohio State Bar Assn. (hon. life); mem. Akron Bar Assn., Nat. Conf. Bankruptcy Judges (twice gov. 6th cir.), Commercial Law League, Am. Bankruptcy Inst. Office: Rm 455 2 S Main St Akron OH 44308-1880

WHITE, HAROLD JACK, pathologist; b. Bklyn., Jan. 4, 1920; s. Abraham and Jennie (Warshawsky) W.; m. Lucette Darby, July 19, 1962; children: Elizabeth, Darby, Matthew, Esther. BS, Harvard U., 1941; MD, U. Geneva, 1952. Diplomate Am. Bd. Pathology. Intern, resident in pathology Yale U. Sch. Medicine, New Haven, 1953-58, fellow, 1957-58; assoc. pathologist Brigham and Women's Hosp., Boston, 1962-66; chief lab. svc. VA Hosp., West Roxbury, Mass., 1962-66, Little Rock, 1966-80; sr. scientist, acting head biomed. sci. dept. GM Rsch. Labs., Warren, Mich., 1980-85, cons., 1985—. Prof. pathology, microbiology U. Ark. Med. Sch., Little Rock, 1966—; vis. scientist dept. comparative medicine, MIT, Cambridge, 1988—. Contbr. over 100 articles, abstracts in pathology, microbiology, immunology, toxicology, biomedicine to profl. jours. 1st lt. USAAF, 1942-46. Fellow Coll. Am. Pathologists, Internat. Coll. Pathology. Home: 24 Bass Rocks Rd Gloucester MA 01930-3276 Office: 35 Main St Gloucester MA 01930-5730

WHITE, HAROLD R. insurance and health care information company executive; b. Bklyn., Jan. 16, 1936; s. Harold George and Margurite (Huot) W.; m. Dolores Angelina Iannuzzi, Jan. 23, 1965; children: Michael A., Denise M. AAS, Staten Island (N.Y.) Community Coll., 1961; BBA, The Coll. of Ins., N.Y.C., 1969. Sales agent Am. Mut. Ins., N.Y.C., 1961-62; mktg. adminstrv. asst. The Hartford Group, 1962-70, asst. sec. Hartford, Conn., 1971-88; sales engr. Insco System Corp., Neptune, N.J., 1970-71; sr. account exec. Health Info. Systems, Inc., W. Hartford, Conn., 1988-91; dealer Foxwoods Resort Casino, Ledyard, 1992—. Treas. Andover, Hebron and Marlborough Youth Svcs., Hebron, Conn., 1984-86; pres. Malborough (Conn.) Assn. for Sr. Housing, 1985-96, bd. edn. 1980-84; mem. bd. fin. Town of Marlborough, 1984-85, mem. bd. selectmen, 1985-86. Airman 1st class USAF, 1954-58. Republican. Avocations: politics, govt. Home: 56 Kellogg Rd Marlborough CT 06447-1238 Office: Foxwoods Resort Casino RR 2 Ledyard CT 06339-9802

WHITE, HARRY EDWARD, JR. lawyer; b. Menominee, Mich., Apr. 26, 1939; s. Harry Edward and Verena Charlotte (Leisen) W.; m. Mary P.A. Sheaffer, June 7, 1980. BS in Fgn. Svc., Georgetown U., Washington, 1961; LLB, Columbia U., 1964. Bar: N.Y. 1965, U.S. Supreme Ct. 1970, U.S. Dist. Ct. (so. dist.) N.Y. 1979, U.S. Tax Ct. 1980. Assoc. Milbank, Tweed, Hadley & McCloy, N.Y.C., 1964-65, 67-73, ptnr., 1974—. Contbr. chpts. to books, articles to legal jours. Served with M.I., U.S. Army, 1965-66, Vietnam. Decorated Bronze Star. Mem. ABA, Internat. Bar Assn., N.Y. State Bar Assn. (chmn. taxation com. internat. law practice sect. 1987-90, co-chmn. exempt orgns. com. tax sect. 1987-88), Internat. Law Assn., ssn. Bar City N.Y., Internat. Fiscal Assn. Republican. Roman Catholic. Home: 333 E 55th St New York NY 10022-8316 Office: Milbank Tweed Hadley & McCloy 1 Chase Manhattan Plz Fl 47 New York NY 10005-1413 E-mail: hwhite@milbank.com.

WHITE, HARRY HOUSTON, neurologist; b. Batesville, Ark., Jan. 21, 1934; s. Harry H. and Margaret V. White; m. Serena Rankin, Dec. 21, 1957; children: Rebecca, David, Maria. AB, U. Kans., 1955, MD, 1958. Diplomate Am. Bd. Psychiatry and Neurology (examiner 1970—). Asst. prof. neurology U. Kans., Kansas City, 1965-69, assoc. prof. neurology, 1969-72; prof. neurology U. Mo., Columbia, 1972-75, 88—; attending neurologist Menninger Found., Topeka, 1975-80; pvt. practice Durango, Colo., 1980-84, Columbia, 1984-88. Capt. U.S. Army, 1962-64. Markle Found. scholar, 1969. Fellow Am. Acad. Neurology; mem. Am. Neurol. Assn., Alpha Omega Alpha. Office: Truman VA Hosp 800 Stadium Dr Columbia MO 65201

WHITE, HELENE R. sociologist, educator; b. Paterson, N.J., July 11, 1949; d. Sidney and Madeleine Beck Raskin; m. Larry H. White, June 18, 1972. BA, Douglass Coll., 1971; MPhil, Rutgers U., New Brunswick, N.J., 1975, PhD, 1976. Asst. to full prof. Rutgers U., New Brunswick, 1975—. Co-principal investigator Nat. Inst. Drug Abuse, Washington, 1978—; grant reviewer Nat. Inst. Health, DC, 1992—96; principal investigator Alcoholic Beverage Med. Rsch. Found., Md., 1992—; behavioral and social adv. coun. Alcoholic Beverage Med. Rsch. Found., Baltimore, Md., 1997—; principal investigator Robert Wood Johnson Found., Princeton, NJ, 1997—. Editor: (book) Alcohol, Science and Society, 1982, Society, Culture and Drinking Patterns Re-examinned, 1991; guest editor (journ.) Journal of Drug Issues, 1996; contbr. articles sci. journ., chapters to books. Recipient Pub. Svc. Award, Criminal Justice Alcoholism Coalition. Mem.: Am. Soc. Criminology, Discovery Inst. (bd. dirs., v.p.), Alcohol and Drugs Section, Am. Soc. Assn. (chair in formation 1991—92, chair-elect 2001—02, chair 2002—). Avocations: golf, cooking, working out. Office: Rutgers U Ctr Alcohol Studies 607 Alison Rd Piscataway NJ 08854-8001 Fax: 732-445-3500. Business E-Mail: hewhite@rci.rutgers.edu.

WHITE, HERBERT SPENCER, research library educator, university dean; b. Vienna, Austria, Sept. 5, 1927; came to U.S., 1938, naturalized, 1944; s. Leon and Ernestine (Lichteneger) Hochweis; m. Mary Virginia Dyer, Feb. 19, 1953; 1 son, Jerome. BS in Chemistry, CCNY, 1949; MSLS, Syracuse U., 1950. Intern Libr. of Congress, Washington, 1950, mem. tech. info. divsn., 1950-53; tech. libr. AEC, Oak Ridge, Tenn., 1953-54; organizer, mgr. corp. libr. Chance Vought Aircraft, Dallas, 1954-59; mgr. engring. libr. IBM Corp., Kingston, N.Y., 1959-62, mgr. tech. info. ctr. Poughkeepsie, 1962-64; exec. dir. NASA Sci. and Tech. Info. Facility, College Park, Md., 1964-68; v.p. info. mgmt. Leasco Systems & Rsch. Corp., Bethesda, 1968-70; sr. v.p. Inst. Sci. Info., Phila., 1970-74, corp. dir., 1971-74; pres. Stechert-Macmillan, Inc., Pennsauken, N.J., 1974-75; prof., dir. Rsch. Ctr. Grad. Libr. Sch. Ind. U., Bloomington, 1975-80, dean Sch. Libr. and Info. Scis., 1980-90, disting. prof., 1991-95; prof. emeritus, 1995—. Adj. prof. U. Ariz. Sch. Libr. Scis., 1995—; vis. prof. Alberta, San Jose State, Hawaii; cons., lectr. Author: Librarianship Quo Vadis?, 2000, others; contbr. articles to profl. publs.; columnist Libr. Jour. Mem. Pres.'s Adv. Com. for Adminstrn. Title II-B Higher Edn. Act, 1965-68, Libr. Rsch. Planning Com. for 1980s, U.S. Dept. Edn., v.p. Green Valley Cmty. Coordinating Coun., 1997—; grant reviewer Inst. Mus. and Librs., 1998—. Spl. honoree, U. of Essen (Germany) Conf., 1992. Fellow Spl. Libraries Assn. (pres. 1969-70, J.C. Dana award 1985, Hall of Fame 1994); mem. ALA (councillor 1988-92, planning com. 1989-91, Dewey medal 1987), Am. Soc. Info. Sci. (pres. 1973-74, W. Davis award 1977, award of merit 1981, named Pioneer, 1987), Assn. Libr. and Info. Sci. Edn. (chmn. govtl. rels. com. 1980-88), Am. Fedn. Info. Processing Socs. (dir. 1972-78), Federation Internationale de Documentation (Netherlands, bd. dir. 1976-78, treas. 1978-82), Soc. for Scholarly Pub. (bd. dirs. 1981-82), Assn. Rsch. Libraries (com. on libr. edn, 1983-85), Coun. Libr. Resources (rsch. priorities task force 1984-88, Ind. Libr. Lifetime Achievement award 1990), Beta Phi Mu (Svc. award 1995). Address: 5950 N Fountains Ave #7102 Tucson AZ 85704-7863

WHITE, HUGH VERNON, JR. lawyer; b. Suffolk, Va., July 24, 1933; s. Hugh Vernon and Mary Lois (Claud) W.; m. Mary Margaret Flowers, Nov. 25, 1961; children: Hunter, William, John. BS in Civil Engring., Va. Mil. Inst., 1954; LLB, Washington & Lee U., 1961. Bar: Va. 1961. Engr. E.I. DuPont de Nemours & Co., Parlin, N.J., 1954-55; exec. dir. Va. Legis. Study Commn., Richmond, Va., 1961-63; assoc. Hunton & Williams, 1963-69, ptnr., 1969-99, sr. counsel, 1999—. Bd. dirs. Chesapeake Corp., Richmond, Va. Mem. Richmond First, 1966—, pres., 1971; bd. trustees Va. Hist. Soc., 1997—, Randolph-Macon Woman's Coll., 1997—. YMCA of Greater Richmond, 1996—, chmn. 2000-01. Lt. USAF, 1955-58. Mem. ABA, Va. Bar Assn., Richmond Bar Assn., Phi Beta Kappa, Omicron Delta Kappa. Clubs: Commonwealth, Country (Richmond). Presbyterian. Home: 512 S Gaskins Rd Richmond VA 23233-5710 Office: Hunton & Williams Riverfront Plaza East Tower PO Box 1535 Richmond VA 23218-1535

WHITE, IRENE, insurance professional; b. Taumuning, Guam, Jan. 3, 1961; d. Antonio Gill and Irma Magdalena (Idrogo) Gill; m. William Paul Franck, Aug. 4, 1979 (div. July 1984); m. Richard Nelson White, May 12, 1989 (div. Dec. 1993); 1 child, Karen Elizabeth. Cert. ins. adjuster, Tex., assoc. in claims; chartered property casualty underwriter, 1997. Ins. adjuster Gen. Accident Group, San Antonio, 1983-85, Crum & Forster Ins., San Antonio, 1985-89, Aetna Life & Casualty, San Antonio, 1979-83, adjuster, analyst, cons., complex case mgr. Dallas, 1989-96; sr. account exec., regional mgr. Travelers, 1996—. Big sister Big Bros. and Sisters, San Antonio, 1987-89; vol. counselor March of Dimes, San Antonio, 1988-89; catechist St. Mark the Evangelist Cath. Ch., Plano, Tex., 1999—. Republican. Avocations: gardening. Office: Travelers 10440 N Central Expy Dallas TX 75231-2221 E-mail: irene.white@travelers.com.

WHITE, JAMES, JR. psychiatric, mental health nurse, consultant; b. Muskogee, Okla., Nov. 24, 1944; s. James Sr. and Mary Bd. (Brassfield) W.; children: Stacie R., Stephen W. BA, Northeastern State U., 1969; MS, Pittsburg State U., 1972, BSN, 1982; PhD, Columbia Pacific U., 1984. Diplomate Am. Bd. Forensic Examiners, Soc. for Study of Neuronal Regulation; CSW, advance register nurse practitioner, cert. rehab. counselor, cert./lic. psychologist, nationally bd. cert. counselor. Exec. dir. Sanilac County Mental Health, Sandusky, Mich., 1975-78, Crawford County Mental Health, Pittsburg, 1978-80; psychologist Psychol. and Ednl. Svcs., 1982—84; psychiatric practitioner Family Counseling and Resource Ctr., Joplin, 1983-86; pvt. practice, 1986-88; med. sociologist Mich. Health Ctr., Detroit, 1988-91; psychiatric practitioner Wayne County Sheriff and Sinai Hosp. Psychiatry, 1990—; clin. coord. Detroit Health Care for Homeless, 1991—. Chmn. recipient right com. Lafayette Clinic, Detroit, 1991—, coun. mem., 1990—. Lt. U.S. Army, 1969-82. Mem. ANA for Nurses in Advanced Practice, Am. Psychatric Nurses Assn., Am. Acad. Nurse Practitioners (Mich. State Rep. 1991—), Am. Bd. Med. Psychotherapists (cert., clin. assoc.), Coun. Psychiatric and Mental Health Nursing, Am. Acad. Pain Mgmt. Avocations: biking, swimming, boating. Home: 42029 Utah Dr Sterling Heights MI 48313-2965 Office: Inst for Inner Resource 75 W Square Lake Rd Troy MI 48098-2929 E-mail: info@expertsinmind.com.

WHITE, JAMES BARR, lawyer, real estate investor, consultant; b. Haverhill, Mass., June 13, 1941; s. Ned and Shirlee (Euster) W.; m. Carol Klein, June 23, 1963; children: Michael Andrew, Laurie Alison, Elizabeth Ellen. BS, Tufts U., 1962; LLB, Columbia U., 1965; MPA, Harvard U., 1988. Bar: Mass. 1965. Assoc. Goulston & Storrs, Boston, 1965-71, ptnr., 1971-74, Palmer & Dodge, Boston, 1974-89; pres. ELAW Corp., Concord, Mass., 1992—. Mem. adv. com. MIT Ctr. for Real Estate Devel., Cambridge, 1987-89; dir. Nat. Realty Com., Washington, 1987-89. Chmn., mem. Town of Wayland (Mass.) Planning Bd., 1974-78; mem. Route 128 Area Com., Lincoln, Mass., 1985-87; mem. Town of Lincoln Planning Bd., 1991-2001, Town of Lincoln Hist. Dist. Commn., 1992-2001; bd. overseers New Eng. Conservatory, 1995-98; chmn., bd. govs. Quansoo Beach Assn., Martha's Vineyard, Mass., 1998—; dir. Boston History Ctr. and Mus., Inc., 1999—, pres., 2000—. Mem. Handel and Haydn Soc. (gov. 1985-90, overseer 1990-94), Bostonian Soc. (bd. dirs. 1990—). Home: 38 Bedford Rd Lincoln MA 01773-2037 Office: ELAW Corp Office of Pres 175 Sudbury Rd Concord MA 01742-3419

WHITE, JAMES BOYD, law educator; b. Boston, July 28, 1938; s. Benjamin Vroom and Charlotte Green (Conover) W.; m. Mary Louise Fitch, Jan. 1, 1978; children: Emma Lillian, Henry Alfred; children by previous marriage: Catherine Conover, John Southworth. AB, Amherst Coll., 1960; AM, Harvard U., 1961, LLB, 1964. Assoc. Foley, Hoag & Eliot, Boston, 1964-67; asst. prof. law U. Colo., 1967-69, assoc. prof., 1969-73, prof., 1973-75; prof. law U. Chgo., 1975-83; Hart Wright prof. law and English U. Mich., Ann Arbor, 1983—. Vis. assoc. prof. Stanford U., 1972 Author: The Legal Imagination, 1973, (with Scarboro) Constitutional Criminal Procedure, 1976, When Words Lose Their Meaning, 1981, Heracles' Bow, 1985, Justice as Translation, 1990, "This Book of Starres", 1994, Acts of Hope, 1994, From Expectation to Experience, 1999, The Edge of Meaning, 2001. Sinclair Kennedy Traveling fellow, 1964-65; Nat. Endowment for Humanities fellow, 1979-80, 92; Guggenheim fellow, 1993; vis. scholar Phi Beta Kappa, 1997-98. Mem. AAAS, Am. Law Inst. Office: U Mich Law Sch 625 S State St Ann Arbor MI 48109-1215

WHITE, JAMES C. manufacturing quality management executive; b. Des Moines, Nov. 13, 1958; s. James D. White and Doris J. Brown; m. Carla J. Maples; children: Abbie, David, Travis; children: Jason Lathrop, Jonathon Lathrop, Jacob Maples. BS in Human Resources/Bus. Mgmt., Park U., Independence, Mo., 1994. Cert. ISO/QS 9000 lead auditor. Author: (book) David Goes Fishing, 2001. Cpl. U.S. Army, 1985—86. Personal E-mail: unicorn08@hotmail.com.

WHITE, JAMES CHARLES, production company executive; b. Binghamton, N.Y., Mar. 3, 1948; s. Charles Edward and Beverly Jean (Palmer) W.; m. Kathie A. Whalen, Apr. 17, 1971; children: Bryan, Bridget, David. BS in Comm., Emerson Coll., 1975. Prodr. Marshall's Inc., Woburn, Mass., 1981-84; exec. prodr. HBM, Inc., Boston, 1985-87, Della Femina-McNamee, Boston, 1987-89; sr. exec. prodr. Whitewater Prodn. Co., North Hampton, N.H., 1989-98, BTDT Pictures, North Hampton, 1999—. With U.S. Army, 1968-71, Germany. Democrat. Roman Catholic. Office: BTDT Pictures PO Box 543 North Hampton NH 03862-0543

WHITE, JAMES EDWARD, geophysicist, educator; b. Cherokee, Tex., May 10, 1918; s. William Cleburne and Willie (Carter) W.; m. Courtenay Brumby, Feb. 1, 1941; children: Rebecca White Vanderslice, Peter McDuffie, Margaret Marie White Jamleson, Courtenay White Forte. BA, U. Tex., 1940, MA, 1946; PhD, MIT, 1949. Dir. Underwater Sound Lab., MIT, Cambridge, 1941-45; scientist Def. Research Lab., Austin, Tex., 1945-46; research assoc. MIT, 1946-49; group leader, field research lab. Mobil Oil Co., Dallas, 1949-55; mgr. physics dept. Denver Research Center, Marathon Oil Co., 1955-69; v.p. Globe Universal Scis., Midland, Tex., 1969-71; adj. prof. dept. geophysics Colo. Sch. Mines, Golden, 1972-73, C.H. Green prof., 1976-87, prof. emeritus, 1986—; L.A. Nelson prof. U. Tex., El Paso, 1973-76. Esso vis. prof. U. Sydney, Australia, 1975; vis. prof. MIT, 1982, U. Tex.-Austin, 1985, Macquarie U., Sydney, 1988; del. U.S.-USSR geophysics exch. Dept. State, 1965; mem. bd. Am. Geol. Inst., 1972; mem. space applications bd. NAE, 1972-77; NAS exch. scientist US-USSR, Zagreb, Yugoslavia, 1973-74; del. conf. on oil exploration China Geophys. Soc.-Soc. Exploration Geophysicists, 1981; cons. world bank Chinese U. Devel. Project II, 1987. Author: Seismic Waves: Radiation, Transmission, Attenuation, 1965, Underground Sound: Application of Seismic Waves, 1983, (with R.L. Sengbush) Production Seismology, 1987, Seismic Wave Propagation: Collected Works of J.E. White, 2000; editor: Vertical Seismic Profiling (E.I. Galperin), 1974; contbr. articles to profl. jours.; patentee in field. Recipient Halliburton award, 1987, Kapitsa Gold medal Russian Acad. Natural Scis., 1996. Fellow Acoustical Soc. Am.; mem. NAE, Soc. Exploration Geophysicists (hon., Maurice Ewing medal 1986), Cosmos Club, Sigma Xi. Unitarian Universalist. Office: Colo Sch Mines Dept Geophysics Golden CO 80401

WHITE, JAMES FLOYD, theology educator; b. Boston, Jan. 23, 1932; s. Edwin Turner and Madeline (Rinker) W.; m. Marilyn Atkinson, Aug. 23, 1959 (div. 1982); children: Louise, Robert, Ellen, Laura, Martin; m. Susan Jan Waller, Oct. 28, 1982 (div. 1993); m. Claire Duggan, Mar. 2, 1997. Grad., Phillips Acad., Andover, Mass., 1949; AB, Harvard U., 1953; BD, Union Theol. Sem., 1956; PhD, Duke U., 1960. Ordained to ministry United Meth. Ch., 1955. Instr. Ohio Wesleyan U., Delaware, 1959-61, Meth. Theol. Sch. in Ohio, Delaware, 1960-61; prof. Perkins Sch. Theology, So. Meth. U., Dallas, 1961-83, U. Notre Dame, Ind., 1983-99; Bard Thompson prof. Drew U., 2000—02; vis. prof. Yale U., 2002—. Author: Cambridge Movement, 1962, New Forms of Worship, 1971, Introduction to Christian Worship, 1980, Protestant Worship, 1989, Roman Catholic Worship (1st place award Cath. Press Assn. 1996), Christian Worship in North America, 1997, also others; mem. editl. bd. Religious Book Club, 1980-93. Named one of 100 Most Influential People in Am. Religion, Christian Century mag., 1982; honored by book published in his honor: The Sunday Service of the Methodists: Studies in Honor of James F. White, 1996. Mem. N.Am. Acad. Liturgy (pres. 1979, Berakah award 1983), Am. Soc. Ch. History, Liturgical Conf., Societas Liturgica. Avocations: hiking, travel, book and antiques collecting.

WHITE, JAMES PATRICK, law educator; b. Iowa City, Sept. 29, 1931; s. Raymond Patrick and Besse (Kanak) W.; m. Anna R. Seim, July 2, 1964. BA, U. Iowa, 1953, JD, 1956; LLM, George Washington U., 1959; LLD (hon.), U. Pacific, 1964, John Marshall Law Sch., 1989, Weidner U., 1989, Campbell U., 1993; Jur D (hon.), Whittier Coll., 1992; LLD (hon.), Campbell U., 1993, Southwestern U., 1995, Quinnipiac U., 1995, Calif. Western Law Sch., 1997; LLD, Roger Williams U., 1999, New England Sch. of Law, 2001, Seattle U., 2001, We. New Coll., 2002. Bar: Iowa 1956, D.C. 1959, U.S. Supreme Ct. 1959. Teaching fellow George Washington U. Law Sch., 1958-59; asst. prof. U. N.D. Law Sch., Grand Forks, 1959-62, asso. prof., acting dean, 1962-63, prof., asst. dean, 1963-67; dir. agrl. law rsch. program, prof. law Ind. U. Law Sch., Indpls., 1967—, also dir. urban legal studies program, 1971-74; dean acad. devel. and planning, spl. asst. to chancellor Ind. Univ., 1974-83. Mem. for N.D., Commn. on Uniform State Laws, 1961-66; cons. legal edn. ABA, Indpls., 1974-2001. Contbr. papers to tech. lit. 1st lt. JAGC, USAF, 1956-58. Recipient Thomas More award, St. Mary's U., 1965; fellow Carnegie postdoctoral fellow, U. Mich. Ctr. for Study Higher Edn., 1964—65. Fellow: Soc. for Advanced Legal Studies (Eng.) (chair Fulbright com. awards in law 1989—92), Indpls. Bar Found., Am. Bar Found. (life); mem.: ABA (cons. legal edn. 1974—2001, cons. emeritus 2001—, Kutak award medal 2001), Indpls. Bar Assn., Am. Law Inst. (life), Iowa Bar Assn., Ind. Bar Assn., Woodstock Club (Indpls.), Order of Coif (life). Roman Catholic. Home: 7707 N Meridian St Indianapolis IN 46260-3651 Office: Ind U 550 W North St Indianapolis IN 46202-3162 E-mail: jwhite@uipui.edu.

WHITE, JAMES RICHARD, lawyer; b. McKinney, Tex., Jan. 22, 1948; s. James Ray and Maxine (Brown) W.; children: Nicole Olivia, Mandi Leigh, James Derek. BBA, So. Meth. U., 1969, MBA, 1970, JD, 1973, LLM, 1977. Bar: Tex. 1973, U.S. Tax Ct. 1975, U.S. Supreme Ct. 1989, U.S. Ct. Appeals (5th cir.) 1989); cert. Comml. Real Estate Law Tex. Bd. Legal Specialization. Assoc. Elliot, Meer, Vetter, Denton & Bates, Dallas, 1973-74, Atwell, Cain & Davenport, Dallas, 1974-75; atty. Sabine Corp., 1975-77; assoc. Brice & Barron, 1977-79; ptnr. Millard & Olson, 1979-82, Johnson & Swanson, Dallas, 1982-83, Winstead, Sechrest & Minick P.C., Dallas, 1983—, hiring ptnr., 1987-2001, exec. com., 2000-01. Mem. staff Southwestern Law Jour., Dallas, 1971-73; mem. So. Meth. U. Moot Ct. Bd., Order Barristers, Dallas, 1972-73; prof. North Lake Coll., Dallas, 1985; bd. dirs. Tex. Assn. Young Lawyers, Austin, 1980-82; sec. bd. dirs. Dallas Assn. Young Lawyers, 1976-80. Contbr. articles to profl. jours. Chmn. bd. dirs. Tex. Lawyers Credit Union, Austin, 1980-82; pres. North Tex. Premier Soccer Assn., Dallas, 1979-81; v.p. Lake Highlands Soccer Assn., 1995-96, pres., 1996—; mem. regional mobility task force Real Estate Coun., City of Dallas, 1991-92, mem. downtown revitalization com., 1995-97; mem. Dallas Indsl. Devel. Bd., 1992-93, Dallas Higher Edn. Authority Bd., 1994-96; spkr.'s bur. and accreditation divsn. World Cup USA '94; mem. exec. coun. Recreational Interleague Assn. Dallas, 2002—. Mem. ABA (mem. title ins. and survey, mortgage loan origination and structure com., mortgage financing and opinion, non-traditional comml. real estate fin. coms.), Tex. Bar Assn. (cert. 1973, mem. mortgage loan opinion com.), Tex. Coll. Real Estate Attys., Coll. State Bar Tex. Methodist. Avocations: soccer, golf, skiing, racquetball. Home: 8003 Hundley Ct Dallas TX 75231-4728 Office: Winstead Sechrest & Minick 5400 Renaissance Tower 1201 Elm St Ste 5400 Dallas TX 75270-2199 E-mail: jrwhite@winstead.com.

WHITE, JAN TUTTLE (MRS. BENJAMIN WINTHROP WHITE), information technology executive; b. Bridgeport, Conn., Nov. 5, 1943; d. Michael and Jennie Agnes (Leko) Soltis; m. David Dustin Tuttle, Oct. 7, 1972 (div. Apr. 1988); m. Benjamin Winthrop White, May 6, 1989. BS in Math., Bates Coll., 1965; MBA in Mktg. and Ops. Rsch., Columbia U., 1967. Cert. comml. real estate broker, Mass. With corp. staff IBM Corp., Armonk, N.Y., 1966, systems engr. N.Y.C., 1967-69, mktg. rep. to Harvard U., corp. staff, sys. engr., Harvard U. account mgr. Cambridge, Mass., 1969-72; asst. to dir. info. processing svcs. MIT, 1972-75; mng. dir. Tuttle Family Trust, 1975-81; VAX product mktg. mgr., then sr. product mgr. Digital Equipment Corp., Marlborough, 1981-86, artificial intelligence market devel. mgr., 1986-87, fin. systems group market devel. mgr., 1987-90, market devel. mgr. banking/investments group, 1990; program mgr. MIT Internat. Fin. Svc. Rsch. Ctr., Hudson; med. systems mgr. Beth Israel Deaconess Med. Ctr., Boston, 1990—. Spkr. in field; sponsor Harvard Host Family Program. Appeared in Disney channel documentary film Silver Men, 1987, Boston Mus. Sci. introductory film for opening of Mugar Omni Theatre, 1987; contbr. (books) An Olde Concord Christmas, 1980, Boston Symphony Orch. Cookbook, 1983, Boston Cooks, 1991. Chmn. Concord Coun. Boston Symphony Orch., assoc. assn. vols., supporter Tanglewood scholarship programs, capt. Centennial Major Gifts campaign; active guild bd. Opera Co. Boston, patron Fledermaus Ball; life mem., chmn. Emerson Hosp. Aux.; trustee, mem. mgmt. rev. com. Women's Ednl. and Indsl. Union; edn. com. chmn. Ladies Assn.; life mem., bd. Concord Antiquarian Mus., nom. com. edn. long-range planning com., chmn. edn. com., costumes and textiles com., exhbt. designer An Old Concorde Christmas, established family meml. fund; bd. adv. Sci. Mus. Exhibit Collaborative, Garden Club Concord, Boston Mus. Sci.; life mem. Mus. of Fine Arts, Boston, Nat. Trust for Scotland, Friends of Loch Lomond, Friends of the Beth Israel Med. Ctr, Harvard Neighbors; mem. fin. com. Trinitarian Congl. Ch.; trustee, life mem. Women's Ednl. and Indsl. Union; bd. dirs., life mem. Hannah Duston Garrison House Assn., Mus. Fine Arts, Boston; life mem. Friends of the New Eng. Deaconess Hosp., Boston, Friends of the Beth Israel Deaconess Med. Ctr., Boston; patron mem. Friends of Music at the Mus. of Fine Arts, Boston; mem. Isabella Stewart Gardner Mus.; invitational alumni Hurricane Island (Maine) Outward Bound Sch., underwriter Silver Anniversary video 1987; water safety instr., sr. life saving instr., First Aid instr. Red Cross Nat. Aquatic Sch., 1964. Recipient numerous industry achievement awards; nominated White House fellow, 1971. Mem. Am. Assn. Artificial Intelligence, Inst. for Mgmt. Scis., Ops. Rsch. Soc. Am., Hannah Duston Garrison house Assn. (life, bd.), Harwich Hist. Assn. (life), Stratford Hist. Soc. (life), Cambridge Hist. Soc., Bates Coll. Class 1965 (sec., treas., reunion chmn., com. chmn. 25th reunion major gifts), Columbia U. Grad. Sch. Bus. Alumni Assn. (nat. chmn. membership, bd. dirs.), Mass. Hort. Soc., Conn. Soc. Genealogists, Nat. Assn. Underwater Instrs. (cert. scuba diver), So. Mass. Yacht Racing Assn., Columbia Bus. Club Boston (founding dir., bd. dirs.), Columbia U. Club New Eng. (founding dir.), Columbia Club N.Y., Concord Country Club, Harvard Club (Boston, N.Y.C.), Harvard Neighbors, Harvard U. art Mus., Harvard Faculty Club, Stone Horse Yacht Club, Women's City Club (com. membership), Royal Scottish Automobile Club, So. Mass. Yacht Racing Assn., Friends of Loch Lomond (life), Mass. Hort. Soc., Arnold Arboretum Harvard U., Housatonic Boat Club. Republican. Avocations: the arts, sports, horticulture, environ. preservation, geneology. Home: 20 Chapel St Ste C101 Brookline MA 02446-5445 Office: Beth Israel Deaconess Med Ctr 110 Francis St Ste 9-A Boston MA 02215-5501 Fax: (617) 566-8165. E-mail: janwhite20@aol.com.

WHITE, JEFFERY HOWELL, lawyer; b. Tyler, Tex., Aug. 4, 1959; s. Bluford D. and Tempie R. (Tunnell) W.; m. Michael Anne Mackley, May 21, 1989; children: Kristin, Alex, Landry. BS in History, So. Ark. U., 1983; JD, Oklahoma City U., 1986. Bar: Tex. 1987. Assoc. Dean White, Canton, Tex., 1986-90; asst. dist. atty. Van Zandt Co., 1991-94; ptnr. Elliott Elliott & White, 1994-97; pvt. practice Tex., 1997—. Mem. Van Zandt County Bar Assn. (v.p. 1999-2000, pres. 2000-01), Tex. Criminal Def. Lawyers Assn. (sustaining), Tex. State Bar (dist. 1-A grievance com. 1996—). Democrat. United Methodist. Avocations: golf, tennis, spectator sports. Home: Box 1200 Van TX 75790-1200 Office: 157 N Buffalo St Canton TX 75103-1353

WHITE, JEFFREY GEORGE, healthcare consultant, educator; b. Lawrence, Mass., Apr. 16, 1944; s. Alfred James and Ruth Virginia (Maylum) W.; children: Jennifer L., Tracy E. AB in Econs., Bowdoin Coll., 1966; MBA, U. N.H., 1985. Asst. pers. dir., then asst. adminstr. Maine Med. Ctr., Portland, 1967-71; asst. adminstr. Regional Meml. Hosp., Brunswick, Maine, 1971, adminstr., 1971-74; assoc. dir. Elizabeth Ann Seton Hosp. (now Mid-Maine Med. Ctr.), Waterville, 1974-75; assoc. adminstr. Mid-Maine Med. Ctr., 1975-79, v.p. ops., 1979-83; asst. dir. Wentworth-Douglass Hosp., Dover, N.H., 1983-85; exec. v.p. Frisbie Meml. Hosp., Rochester, 1985-89, pres., 1989-92; sr. cons., prin. Helms & Co., Inc., Concord, 1992—. Preceptor dept. health mgmt. and policy U. N.H., Durham, 1985-92, adj. asst. prof., 1991-93, asst. prof., 1993-97, dean's leadership coun. sch. health human svcs., 1998—; bd. dirs. River Woods at Exeter. Vol. pub. TV sta.; bd. dirs. Greater Seacoast United Way, 1991-94, chmn. comty. campaign, 1993; pres. Greater Rochester C. of C., 1990. Fellow Am. Coll. Healthcare Execs. (past regent for N.H.); mem. N.H. Hosp. Assn. (trustee emeritus). Republican. Avocations: tennis, skiing, reading, travel. Home: 37 Mill Pond Rd Durham NH 03824-2722 Office: Helms & Co Inc 1 Pillsbury St Concord NH 03301-3556

WHITE, JEFFREY MUNROE, lawyer; b. Lewiston, Maine, Jan. 16, 1948; BS in Applied Physics magna cum laude, Tufts U., 1970; JD, Boston Coll., 1975. Bar: Maine 1975, U.S. Ct. Appeals (1st cir.) 1979. Semiconductor engr. Fairchild Semiconductor, 1970-72; ptnr., head antitrust and trade regulation group Pierce, Atwood, Portland, Maine. Lectr., contbr. to profl. publs. on antitrust, litig., and intellectual property topics. Chmn. Cape Elizabeth Sch. Study Com., 1990-91. Mem. ABA (mem. antitrust, intellectual property and litigation sects.), N.E. Bar Assn. (dir. 1982-85), Maine State Bar Assn. (co-chmn. com. continuing legal edn. 1981-83), Maine Trial Lawyers Assn., Cumberland County Bar Assn. Office: Pierce Atwood Monument Sq Portland ME 04101 E-mail: jwhite@pierceatwood.com.

WHITE, JENNIFER PHELPS, counselor; b. Palo Alto, Calif., Aug. 31, 1943; d. Delmer Frank and Luella Elizabeth (McHugh) Phelps; m. Charles Evan White, Oct. 29, 1965; children: George Kevin, Colleen Elizabeth. AA in Liberal Arts, Foothill Jr. Coll., 1964; BA in Sociology & Anthropology, U. N.Mex., 1967, MPA, 1987. Lic. profl. mental health counselor N.Mex. Counseling and Therapy Bd. Sales clk. Barron Park Pharmacy, Palo Alto, 1960-64; caseworker State of N.Mex., Albuquerque, 1968-70; info. sys. coord. City of Albuquerque, 1971-75; rsch. specialist Pub. Interest Rsch. Group, 1976-77; interviewer Sandia Market Rsch., 1980-81; acad. adviser, counselor U. N.Mex., 1981-88; rehab. specialist Intracorps, 1988-89; dir. career svcs. ctr. YWCA, 1989-96; athletic advisor U. N.Mex., Albuquerque, 1996—. Mem. women in transition Planning Commn. State of N.Mex., Albuquerque, 1990—; mem. career guidance project adv. com. Commn. on Status of Women, Albuquerque, 1993-95; employment cons. Genesis Project, Albuquerque, 1989-91; mem. steering com. United Staff U. N.Mex., 1996—, staff coun., 2000—. Chair women's affirmative action coun. City of Albuquerque, 1976-82; mem. steering com. Choice Pac, Albuquerque, 1984—; mem. Human Rights Coalition, 1995—. Named Outstanding N.Mex. Women, Office of Gov., State of N.Mex., 1994; recipient Grassroots Accomplishment award Nat. Coun. Negro Women, Las Mujeres de Lulac, 1994, Human Rights award City of Albuquerque, 1995. Mem. NOW (mem. Albuquerque and N.Mex. chpts., bd. dirs., pres., coord. 1975—, lobbyist N.Mex. State Legislature 1978-87), Nat. Abortion Rights Action League/Right to Choose (bd. dirs. 1980-93), Career Devel. Assn., Women Work! Nat. Network (Svc. awards 1994-95), Women's Housing Coalition (bd. dirs., pres., v.p. 1989—, project change bd. dirs. 1996—). Democrat. Avocations: political activist, Pre-Columbian anthropology, sewing. Home: 416 Montclaire Dr SE Albuquerque NM 87108-2630 Office: Univ NMex Athletic Dept Main Campus Albuquerque NM 87131-0001

WHITE, JERRY T. academic administrator; b. Caribou, Maine, Nov. 24, 1943; s. Perley P. and Hazel White; m. Jean B. White, Nov. 24, 1973; children: Jerry, Nathan, Katherine, Nicholas, Sebastian. BS in Edn., U. Maine, Machias, 1967; MS in Edn., U. Maine, Orono, 1980, Cert. of Advanced Study, 1983. Bus. edn. tchr. Maine Sch. Dist. #24, Van Buren, 1967-69, dept. chair bus. edn., 1973-80, asst. h.s. prin., 1980-83; supt., prin. Maine Sch. Dist. #7, North Haven, 1983-90; supt. schs. Maine Sch. Dist. #33, Frenchville, 1990—2001, Maine Sch. Dist. #65, 2001—. Chair No. Maine Tech. Prep. Commn., Presque Isle, 1992—2001; v.p. No. Aroostook Regional Airport, Frenchville, 1993—2001; sec.-treas. Carleton Project, Presque Isle, 1999—. Sgt. USAF, 1969—73. Named Maine Supt. of the Yr., Am. Assn. Sch. Adminstrs., 1989; recipient Cyber Sch. award, Jessie B. Cox Charitable Found., 1998; grantee U.S. Dept. Edn., 1992. Mem. Optimist Club (pres. 1996-98). Avocations: canoe building, skiing, sailing, golf. Office: Maine Sch Dist #65 69 Main St North Haven ME 04853 E-mail: super9021@aol.com.

WHITE, JERUSHA LYNN, lawyer; b. Kansas City, Mo., Nov. 30, 1950; d. Riley Vaughn and Edith Blynn (Ringen) W.; m. Larry D. Hancock, Jan. 5, 1969 (div. 1973); m. Stephen Perry Wasson, Nov. 30, 1978 (div. 1985); m. Charles Beam Westley, Feb. 14, 1994 (div.). AS, State Fair C.C., 1974; BS, Cen. Mo. State U., 1978; JD, U. Mo., Kansas City, 1981. Bar: Mo. 1981. With Montgomery Ward & Co., Sedalia, Mo., 1968-69, 73-74, Parkhurst Mfg. Co., Sedalia, 1969-71, United Farm Agy., Sedalia, 1972-73, Howard Truck & Equipment Co., Sedalia, 1974-75, McGraw-Edison Co., Sedalia, 1975-76, Rival Mfg. Co., Sedalia, 1977-78; buyer Hotel Equipment Co., Century City, Calif., 1978; law clk. Legal Aid Western Mo., Kansas City, 1979-80, Horowitz & Shurin PC, Kansas City, 1980-81; assoc. Steve Borel/Steve Streen, 1982-83; pvt. practice Sedalia, 1983-85; ptnr. Cope, Schuber & White, 1985-86; staff atty. Hyatt Legal Svcs., 1986-88; asst. dist. counsel U.S. Army Corps Engrs., Kansas City, 1988-2000, 2002—; staff judge advocate conract atty. advisor Ft. Leavenworth, Kans., 2000—02. Mem. ABA, Mo. Bar Assn. Democrat. Presbyterian. Home: 6717 NW Chinquapin Ct Kansas City MO 64151-2326 Office: US Army Corps Engrs 601 E 12th St Rm 715 Kansas City MO 64106 E-mail: jerushawhite@aol.com., jerusha.l.white@usace.army.mil.

WHITE, JESSE, state official; b. Alton, Ill., 1934; BS, Ala. State U., 1957. With Chgo. Cubs; tchr., adminstr. Chgo. Pub. Sch. Sys.; mem. Ill. Gen. Assembly, Springfield, chmn. com. on human svcs., mem. edn. com., mem. select com. on children and aging; recorder of deeds State of Ill., Springfield,

1992-98, sec. of state, 1999—. Founder Jesse White Tumbling Team, 1959; Dem. committeeman 27th Ward, Chgo., 1996—; libr. State of Ill. State Libr.; archivist State of Ill.; mem. Ill. N.G. With USAF. Recipient Archbishop Richard Chenevix Trench award, 1999; Inductee Southwestern Athletic Conf. Hall of Fam, 1995, Chgo. Pub. League Basketball Coaches Assn. Hall of Fame, 1995. Office: 213 State Capitol Springfield IL 62706*

WHITE, JILL CAROLYN, lawyer; b. Santa Barbara, Calif., Mar. 20, 1934; d. Douglas Cameron and Gladys Louise (Ashley) W.; m. Walter Otto Weyrauch, Mar. 17, 1973. BA, Occidental Coll., L.A., 1955; JD, U. Calif., Berkeley, 1972. Bar: Fla. 1974, Calif. 1975, U.S. Dist. Ct. (no. and mid. dists.) Fla., U.S. Ct. Appeals (5th and 11th cirs.), U.S. Supreme Ct. Staff mem. U.S. Dept. State, Am. Embassy, Rio de Janeiro, 1956-58; with psychol. rsch. units Inst. Human Devel., Inst. Personality Assessment and Rsch., U. Calif., Berkeley, 1961-68; adj. prof. criminal justice program U. Fla., Gainesville, Fla., 1976-78; pvt. practice immigration and nationality law, 1976—. Contbr. articles to profl. jours. Mem.: Gainesville Area Innovation Network, Fla. Bar (immigration and nationality law cert. com. 1994—99, chmn. cert. com. 1997—98, cert. in immigration and nationality law 1995—), Bar Assn. 8th Jud. Cir. Fla., Am. Immigration Lawyers Assn. (bd. dirs. Ctrl. Fla. chpt. 1985—94, 1995—96, 1997—2000, chmn. Ctrl. Fla. chpt. 1988—89, co-chmn. so. regional liaison com. 1990—92, nat. bd. dirs. 1988—89), Altrusa. Democrat. Office: 2830 NW 41st St Ste C Gainesville FL 32606-6667 E-mail: jwhite49@earthlink.net.

WHITE, JOAN MICHELSON, artist; b. Hartford, Conn., Jan. 4, 1936; d. William Allen and Mitzi (Lurie) Michelson; m. Harvey Marshall White, June 28, 1958; children: Randi Lynn, Andrew Steven. BA, Ctrl. Conn. State U., 1958; postgrad., Wesleyan U., 1980. Cert. tchr., Conn. One woman shows include Canton (Conn.) Gallery on the Green, 1977, Saltbox Gallery, West Hartford, Conn., 1986, Key Gallery, N.Y.C., 1982, Hartford Jewish Cmty. Ctr., 1980; mem. Hartford Art Sch. Aux.; mem. adv. bd. U. Hartford Joseloff Gallery; docent Wadsworth Atheneum, Hartford, 1998—. Group shows include Silvermine Guild New Eng. Exhbn., 1977, 79, Springfield (Mass.) Art League Nat. Exhbn., 1980, 83, 86, The Galleries, Wellesley, Mass., 1983, Stephen Haller Fine Arts, N.Y.C., 1987, 88, Penrose Gallery, Nantucket, Mass., 1984, Conn. Artists Showcase, Conn. Commn. on the Arts, Hartford, 1986, Provincetown (Mass.) Art Assn. and Mus., 1986, Old Lyme (Conn.) Art Works, 1985, Greene Gallery, Guilford, Conn., 1986, Signature Gallery, West Hartford, Conn., 1986-94, Allan Stone Gallery, N.Y.C., 1984, Shippee Gallery, N.Y.C., 1984, Heritage State Park Mus., Holyoke, Mass., 1988, Southern Conn. State U., New Haven, 1989, Farmington Valley Arts Ctr., Avon, Conn., 1992, John Slade Ely House, New Haven, 1993, Ute Stebich Gallery, Lenox, Mass., 1994, North Coast Collage Soc., Seattle, 1994, Small Walls Gallery, Hartford, Conn., 1999-99. Docent Wadsworth Atheneum, Hartford, Conn. Mem. Conn. Watercolor Soc. (bd. dirs. 1980-82), West Hartford Ctr. for Visual Arts, Conn. Women Artists, Conn. Acad. Fine Arts. Home: 73 Avondale Rd West Hartford CT 06117-1108

WHITE, JOE LLOYD, soil scientist, educator; b. Pierce, Okla., Nov. 8, 1921; s. Claud Amos and Alta Maurice (Denney) W.; m. Wanita Irene Robertson, May 29, 1945; children— Lerrill, Darla, Ronna, Bren, Janeil Student, Connors State Agrl. Coll., 1940-42; BS, Okla. State U., 1944, MS, 1945; PhD, U. Wis., 1947. Asst. prof. agronomy Purdue U., West Lafayette, Ind., 1947-51, assoc. prof., 1951-57, prof., 1957-88. Cons. Bancroft Co., William H. Rorer Co., Chattem Chem. Co., Merck Sharp & Dohme Rsch. Lab. Patentee in field Fellow NSF, 1965-66, Guggenheim Found., 1972-73; Fulbright scholar, 1973; recipient Sr. U.S. Scientist award Alexander von Humboldt Found., 1980-81 Fellow AAAS, Am. Soc. Agronomy, Am. Inst. Chemists, Soil Sci. Soc. Am., Mineral Soc. Am., Royal Soc. Chemistry; mem. Am. Chem. Soc., Clay Minerals Soc. (disting.), Am. Pharm. Assn., Coblentz Soc., Geochem. Soc., Internat. Soil Sci. Soc., Internat. Assn. Colloid and Interface Scientists, N.Y. Acad. Sci., Royal Soc. Chemists (chartered chemist), Soc. Petroleum Engrs. of AIME, Internat. Zeolite Assn., Soc. Applied Spectroscopy, Sigma Xi, Phi Kappa Phi, Phi Lambda Upsilon Mem. Ch. of Christ Achievements include patents for use of zeolites in ruminant nutrition, for stable dried aluminum hydroxide gel, for method and composition for treatment of hyperphosphatemia; establishment of the role of carbonate in inhibiting crystallization of aluminum hydroxide; definitive characterization of aluminum-containing adjuvants used in vaccines. Home: 2505 Roselawn Ave Lafayette IN 47904-2319 Office: Purdue U Dept Agronomy West Lafayette IN 47907

WHITE, JOHN ARNOLD, physics educator, research scientist; b. Chgo., Jan. 30, 1933; s. Maxwell Richard and Dorothy Edith (Arnold) W.; m. Rebecca Anne Cotten, June 20, 1964; children: Lauren, Thomas, Julia. BA, Oberlin Coll., 1954; MS, Yale U., 1955, PhD, 1959. Instr. physics Yale U., 1958-59, Harvard U., 1959-62; research assoc. Yale U., 1962-63; research physicist Nat. Bur. Standards, Washington, 1963-64; research assoc. U. Md., College Park, 1965-66; assoc. prof. Am. U., Washington, 1966-68, prof., 1968-97, prof. emeritus, 1997—. Cons. Nat. Bur. Standards, 1965-72; mem. tech. staff Bell Telephone Labs., summers 1954, 60-62; vis. scientist MIT, fall 1972, Nat. Bur. Standards, Washington, summer 1981; vis. prof. Inst. for Phys. Sci. and Tech., U. Md., College Park, fall 1993. Author sci. papers on atomic structure and fluorescence, magnetism, lasers, speed of light, thermodynamic fluctuations, critical point phenomena, extended renormalization group theory of fluids. Recipient (with Zoltan Bay) Boyden Premium Franklin Inst., Phila., 1980; honor scholar, 1950-54; Noyes Clark fellow, 1954-57; NSF fellow, 1957-58; grantee NSF, 1966, 67, 69, 71; grantee Office Naval Research, 1973, 74; Am. Soc. Engring. Edn. faculty fellow Naval Research Lab., Washington, summer 1985; Dept. Energy Office Basic Energy Scis. grantee, 1986, 88, 90. Fellow Am. Phys. Soc.; mem. AAUP, Washington Philos. Soc., Phi Beta Kappa, Sigma Xi. Home: 7107 Fairfax Rd Bethesda MD 20814-1234 Office: Am U Dept Physics Washington DC 20016-8058 E-mail: jwhite@american.edu.

WHITE, JOHN DAVID, composer, theorist, cellist; b. Rochester, Minn., Nov. 28, 1931; s. Leslie David and Millie (Solum) W.; m. Marjorie Manuel, Dec. 27, 1952; children: Jeffrey Alan, Michele Kay, David Eliot. BA magna cum laude, U. Minn., 1953; MA, U. Rochester, 1954, PhD, performance cert., U. Rochester, 1960. Mem. faculty Kent (Ohio) State U., 1956-58, 60-63, 65-73, prof. music, assoc. dean Grad. Sch., 1967-73; asst. prof. U. Mich., 1963-65; dean Sch. Music, Ithaca (N.Y.) Coll., 1973-74; vis. prof. U. Wis., 1975-78; chmn. music dept. Whitman Coll., 1978-80; prof. U. Fla., 1980-97, prof. emeritus, 1997—. Prin. cellist, Eastman Philharmonia, 1959, Akron Symphony Orch., 1969-73; cellist Fla. Baroque Ensemble, 1980-97, Fla. Arts Trio, 1986-93; dir. Fla. Musica Nova, 1991-97; author: (with A. Cohen) Anthology of Music for Analysis, 1965, Understanding and Enjoying Music, 1968 (pub. in Japanese 1978), Music in Western Culture, 1972, The Analysis of Music, 1976, 2d edit., 1984, Guidelines for College Teaching of Music Theory, 1981, 2d edit., 2002, Comprehensive Musical Analysis, 1994, Theories of Musical Texture in Western History, 1995; editor: Music and Man; editl. bd. Jour. for Musicological Research, Jour. Music Theory Pedagogy; contbr. articles to profl. jours.; Composer: Symphony No. 2, 1960, Blake Songs, 1961; (for flute, violin and viola) Divertimento, 1961; opera The Legend of Sleepy Hollow, 1962; Three Choruses From Goethe's Faust, 1965, Three Joyce Songs, 1966, Ode to Darkness, 1967, Cantos of the Year, 1969; (for clarinet and piano) Variations, 1971, Whitman Music, 1970; (for chorus and orchestra) Three Madrigals, 1971, Russian Songs for Voices and Winds, 1972, Prayer (Solzhenytsin), 1973, String Quartet 1, 1975; (for piano) Variations, 1976, Suite, 2001; Ode on the Morning of Christ's Nativity (Donne), 1977; (for violin, cello and piano) Music for Oriana, 1978, Pied Beauty, 1980; (for cello and piano) Sonata, 1981, Zodiac, 1981, Music for violin and piano, 1982, The Soft Voice, 1983, Concerto for Flute and Wind Ensemble, 1983; (for trombone and piano) Dialogues, 1984, Sonata, 2001, Symphony for Wind Band (3rd Symphony), 1985; (for cello and orch.) Concerto da Camera, 1985, Symphony for a Saint (4th Symphony), 1986, Music for Cello and Percussion, 1988, Songs of the Shulamite, 1989; (for piano and orch.) Mirrors, 1990, But God's Own Descent (5th Symphony), 1991, Music of the Open Road, 1993, Daylight and Moonlight, 1993, O Sing to the Lord a New Song, 1993, Illusions for Three, 1994; (for trumpet and cello) Tryptich, 1994, Ars Poetica, 1995, Colors of Earth and Sky (6th Symphony), 1995, Summer Storm Madrigals, 1996; (for horn and piano) Time and the Water, 1996, O Sing to the Lord a New Song, 1997; Maria Laudata, 1998, God's Own Descent, 1998, The Song of Ruth, 1999, Symbolic Interaction for Orchestra, 1999; (for harpsichord) Suite, 1999, The Heavens are Telling, 1999, Flower Songs, 2000; (for piano and wind ensemble) Concerto, 2000; recs. on Advent, Mark, Capstone and Opus One Labels. With AUS, 1954-56. Recipient Benjamin award, 1960, award Nat. Fedn. Music Clubs, 1962, internat. composition award U. Wis.-Oriana Trio, 1979, composition award Am. Choral Dirs. Assn., 1984; grantee NEA; Fulbright rsch. fellow, 1995-96. Fellow Am. Scandinavian Found., 1997; mem. ASCAP (awards 1965—), Soc. Composers, Inc. (nat. coun. 1987-89, 93-96), Soc. Music Theory, Pi Kappa Lambda, Delta Omicron, Phi Mu Alpha, Phi Beta Delta. Home: 29862 Troutdale Park Pl Evergreen CO 80439-7730 E-mail: jdwhite48@earthlink.net.

WHITE, JOHN JOSEPH, III, lawyer; b. Darby, Pa., Nov. 23, 1948; s. John J. Jr. and Catherine (Lafferty) W.; m. Catherine M Staley, Dec. 9, 1983. BS, U. Scranton, 1970; MPA, Marywood U., 1977; JD, Loyola U., New Orleans, 1983. Bar: Pa. 1983, U.S. Dist. Ct. (ea. dist.) Pa. 1983, N.J. 1984, U.S. Ct. Appeals (3d cir.) 1983, U.S. Dist. Ct. N.J. 1984, U.S. Tax Ct. 1984, D.C. 1985, U.S. Supreme Ct. 1987. Exec. dir. Scranton (Pa.) Theatre Libre, Inc., 1973-77; pub. Libre Press Inc., Scranton, 1977-83; pvt. practice Phila., 1983—. Pres. eMercury, Inc., Lansdowne, Pa., 1987—; N.Am. agt. Palacky U. Med. Sch., Olomouc, Czech Republic, 1995—2001. Founder, pub. Metro Mag., 1977-83. Founder, Scranton Pub. Theatre, 1976; exec. dir. Scranton Theatre Libre, Inc., 1973. Capt. USAF, 1970-73; lt. col. Res., 1973-89, col. ANG, 1999-2000, ret. 2000. Mem.: ABA, Phila. Bar Assn., Nat. Acad. Elder Law Attys., Mil. Order of Fgn. Wars, Air Force Assn. (chpt. pres. 1975—), Phi Delta Phi Internat. Legal Frat. Democrat. Roman Catholic. Avocations: jogging, art collecting. E-mail: lawfirmusa@aol.com.

WHITE, JOHN KENNETH, politics educator; b. Providence, Oct. 10, 1952; s. Harold Allison and Margaret Mary (Morrissey) W.; m. Yvonne J. Prevost, July 1, 1995; 1 child, Jeannette Brigitte. BA, U. R.I., 1975; MA, U. Conn., 1976, PhD, 1980. Assoc. prof. SUNY, Potsdam, 1980-88; prof. Cath. U., Washington, 1988—. V.p. Ctr. for Party Devel., 1992-99; co-chair Com. for Party Renewal, 1994-99. Author: The Fractured Electorate, 1983, The New Politics of Old Values, 1990, Still Seeing Red, 1998, (with Daniel M. Shea) New Party Politics: From Hamilton and Jefferson to the Information Age, 2000, The Values Divide: American Politics and Culture in Transition, 2002. Roman Catholic. Office: Dept Politics Dept Politics Cath Univ Am Washington DC 20064-0001 E-mail: white@cua.edu.

WHITE, JOHN LEE, theology studies educator; b. Washington; s. Frank William and Clarice May (Mistler) White; m. Myrna Ruth Wacker, Sept. 3, 1961; children: John Barak, Karis Anne, Kristen Burga. BA, William Jewell Coll., Liberty, Mo., 1962; BD, Colgate Rochester Div. Sch., 1966; MA, Vanderbilt U., 1968, PhD, 1970. Asst. prof. religion Mo. Sch. Religion, Columbia, 1969—75, assoc. prof. religion, 1976—81; assoc. prof. theology Loyola U., Chgo., 1981—87, prof. theology, 1987—. Cons. NEH, Washington, 1980; editl. cons. Fortress Press, Phila., 1985—87; bd. dirs. Polebridge Press, Santa Clara, Calif., 1988—2000. Author: Light from Ancient Letters, 1986, The Apostle of God: Paul and the Promise of Abraham, 1999; editor: Studies in Ancient Letter Writing, 1982. Recipient Faculty Devel. award, Loyola Endowment for Humanities, 1992; fellow, Am. Assn. Learned Socs., 1972. Mem.: Westar Inst., Soc. Bibl. Lit. (assoc. in coun. 1979—81), Chgo. Soc. Bibl. Rsch. (pres. 1988—89). Home: 2138 E Briar Springfield MO 65804

WHITE, JOHN MICHAEL, chemistry educator; b. Danville, Ill., Nov. 26, 1938; married, 1960; 3 children. BS, Harding Coll., 1960; MS, U. Ill., 1962, PhD in Chemistry, 1966. From asst. to assoc. prof. U. Tex., Austin, 1966—76, prof. chemistry, Hackerman prof. chemistry, 1985—2000, Robert A. Welch chair chemistry, dir. Materials Chem. Ctr., 2001—. Mem. Am. Chem. Soc., Am. Phys. Soc. Achievements include research in surface and materials chemistry. Office: U Tex Dept Chemistry Welch Hall #3.310 Austin TX 78712

WHITE, JOHN P, federal agency administrator; BS in Indsl. and Labor Rels., Cornell U.; MA in Econs., PhD in Econs., Syracuse U. Sr. v.p. nat. security rsch. programs Rand Corp., 1968-77; asst. sec. Def. Manpower, Res. Affairs, and Logistics, 1977-78; dep. dir. Office Mgmt. and Budget, 1978-81; CEO, chmn. bd. dirs. Interactive Sys. Corp., 1981-88; gen. mgr. integration and sys. products divsn., v.p. Eastman Kodak Co., 1988-92; faculty dir. Ctr. for Bus. and Govt. Harvard U. Kennedy Sch. Govt., 1992-95; dep. sec. Dept. of Def., Washington, 1995-97; faculty Harvard U. Kennedy Sch. Govt., 1998—; sr. ptnr. Global Tech. Ptnrs., Washington, 1998—. Officer USMC. Office: Kennedy Sch Gov Harvard U 79 SFK St Cambridge MA 02138 Also: Global Tech Partners 99 Summer St Ste 1820 Boston MA 02110

WHITE, JOHN PATRICK, lawyer; b. Boston, Oct. 14, 1946; s. John Marion and Margaret Patricia (Gannon) W.; m. Gemma Mary Flattly, Feb. 9, 1980; 1 son, John Myles. BS in Chem. Engring., Columbia U., 1968, MA in Biochemistry, 1971, MPh in Molecular Biology, 1975; JD, Fordham U., 1977. Bar: N.Y. 1978, U.S. dist. ct. (ea. and so. dists.) N.Y. 1978, U.S. Ct. Customs and Patent Appeals 1979, U.S. Ct. Appeals (Fed. cir.) 1982. Legis. dir. Cmty. Coun. Greater N.Y., 1971-77; assoc. Cooper, Dunham, Clark, Griffin & Moran, N.Y.C., 1977-81, ptnr., 1981-88, Cooper & Dunham, LLP, N.Y.C., 1988—. Owner Shallow Brook Farm, Stillwater, N.J.; breeder Reg Angus Cattle, Ringneck Pheasants and Carriage Horses; dir. Oncogene Sci., Inc., BioTech. Gen. Corp.; instr. Practicing Law Inst. Contbr. articles to sci. and legal jours. Democratic dist. leader, 1975-81; vice chmn. Dem. Com. N.Y. County, 1977-81; jud. del. 1st jud. dept., 1975, 76, 77, 79; adminstr. screening panel 2d Mcpl. Ct. Dist.; pub. mem. Columbia U. Recombinant DNA Biosafety Com. Columbia U. faculty fellow, 1969-71; NIH grantee, 1969-71. Mem. ABA, Am. Chem. Soc., Am. Intellectual Property Law Assn., N.Y. Intellectual Property Law Assn., Assn. Bar City N.Y., Fed. Bar Coun. (com. patents), Club: Columbia of N.Y.C, Four In Hand Club, Upperville, Va. Office: Cooper & Dunham Ste 2200 1185 Avenue Of The Americas New York NY 10036-2615

WHITE, JOHN VINCENT, surgeon, consultant; b. Chgo., May 7, 1952; BS, Northwestern U., 1974; MD, Columbia U., 1978. Diplomate Am. Bd. Surgery. Instr. surgery Columbia U., N.Y.C., 1982-83; asst. prof. surgery Temple U., Phila., 1984-88, assoc. prof. surgery, 1988-94, prof. surgery, 1994-99; chmn. dept. surgery Luth. Gen. Hosp., Park Ridge, Ill., 1999—. Adj. sr. fellow Sch. Health Econs. U. Pa., Phila., 1994—; tech. cons. Boston Scientific Corp., Natick, Mass., 1995—; surg. cons. Dept. of Health N.Y. State, 1993; surg. tech. cons. Congl. Office of Tech. Assessment, Washington, 1995; laser tech. cons. Office of Naval Rsch., Washington, 1993-97. Editor: Hemodilution in Patient Care, 1989, Alternatives to Open Vascular Surgery, 1995, Surgical Clinics of North America, 1998; founding editor: Jour. Laparoendoscopic Surgery, 1990. Recipient Samuel D. Gross award Phila. Acad. Surgery, 1992. Mem. Am. Soc. Laser Medicine and Surgery, Soc. Univ. Surgeons (mem. found. bd. dirs. 1994-98), Del. Valley Vascular Soc. (pres. 1995—), Soc. Vascular Surgery (mem. com. outcomes analysis 1994—), Alpha Omega Alpha. Office: Lutheran Gen Hosp 1775 Dempster St Park Ridge IL 60068-1173 Fax: (847) 696-3394. E-mail: john.white-md@advocatehealth.com.

WHITE, JOHN WESLEY, JR. retired university president; b. Nashville, Oct. 20, 1933; s. John W. and Ernestine (Engle) W.; m. Martha Ellen Bragg, June 24, 1956; children: Marcus Wesley, Michelle Suzanne. Student, Martin Jr. Coll., 1952-54; BA, Vanderbilt U., 1956, BD, 1959; MA, George Peabody Coll., 1966, PhD, 1968; LHD, U. Nebr., 1983; LLD, Kwansai Gakuin U., Japan, 1991. Dean admissions, dir. student affairs Martin Coll., 1960-65; asst. to acad. v.p. George Peabody Coll., 1965-67; assoc. dean for humanities Oklahoma City U., 1968-70, dean Coll. Arts and Scis., 1970-77, assoc. prof. English, 1968-73, prof., 1973-77; pres. Nebr. Wesleyan U., 1977-97, chancellor, 1997-98, pres. emeritus, 1998—. Cons., spkr. in field; bd. dirs. Woodmen Accident and Life Co.; chmn. Nebr. Ednl. Temecom. Commn., 1996-97. Past pres. U. Senate, United Meth. Ch.; bd. dirs. Cooper Found., Lincoln Symphony Orch., Madonna Rehab. Hosp. Eli Lilly Sr. scholar Vanderbilt U., 1959. Mem. Nat. Assn. Ind. Colls. and Univs. (bd. dirs. 1989-93, 95-97), Lincoln C. of C. (bd. dirs. 1990-93), Rotary (pres. West Oklahoma City 1976), Kappa Delta Pi, Phi Kappa Phi, Alpha Mu Gamma, Blue Key. *Two principles have been paramount in my life: One, related to the attitude toward myself, is that we can help to shape life, not simply endure it. We are "creative" creatures, not just "surviving" creatures. The second principle, related to the attitude toward others, is that communication is essential to coexistence; and only as we make a real effort to hear what is meant, rather than simply what is said or written, are we able to communicate effectively.*

WHITE, JON MANCHIP, retired English educator; b. Cardiff, Wales, June 22, 1924; came to U.S., 1967; s. Gwilym Manchip White and Eva Elizabeth Ewbank; m. Valerie Leighton, 1946 (dec. 1995); children: Bronwen, Rhiannon. BA, Cambridge (Eng.) U., 1947, diploma in archaeology and anthropology, 1948, MA, 1950. Sr. exec. officer BBC TV, London, 1950-52, Her Majesty's Fgn. Svc., London, 1952-56; story editor, screenwriter London, Paris, Rome, Madrid, 1957-66; prof. English U. Tex., El Paso, 1967-77; Lindsay Young Chair of English U. Tenn., Knoxville, 1977-94. Author 14 novels, 1 book short stories, 2 books poetry, 3 books travel, 3 historical biographies, 4 books archaeology and anthropology; author, prodr. numerous radio and TV programs, screenplays; editor numerous books. Served with Royal Navy and Welsh Guards, WWII. Mem.: Welsh Acad., Phi Beta Kappa. Avocations: fly fishing, Formula One motor racing, fiesta brava. Home: 5620 Pinellas Dr Knoxville TN 37919

WHITE, JOSEPH CHARLES, manufacturing and retailing company executive; b. Toronto, Ont., Can., Aug. 14, 1922; s. Joseph Cleveland and Edith Parker (Johnson) W.; m. G. Evelyn Vipond, July 15, 1944; children— Ronald, Richard, JoAnne Chartered acct., Queens U., Kingston, Ont.; B.Commerce, U. Toronto. Vice-pres., dir. Agnew-Surpass, Inc., Brantford, Ont., Can., 1964-78; v.p., dir. Genesco Can., Inc., Cambridge, Can., 1978-82, exec. v.p., dir. Can., 1982-87, pres., gen. mgr. retail op., 1986-87. Dir., v.p. Genesco Group Inc.; dir. Genesco Fin. Ltd.; pres. Brantford Art Gallery, 1994-95, Brantford Probus Club, 1995-96. Chmn. Ross MacDonald Found., Brantford, Ont., 1983-86; pres. YMCA, Brantford, 1968-69; chmn. Brant County Post-Secondary Edn. Corp., Brantford, 1973-76. Served with Royal Can. Air Force, 1943-45 Mem. Ont. Inst. Chartered Accts., Can. Council Distbn. (pres. 1972-73), Brant County C. of C. (treas. 1966-68) Mem. United Ch. of Can. Avocations: downhill skiing; tennis. Office: Genesco Can Inc 401 Fountain St Cambridge ON Canada N3H 4V5 Home: 40 Museum Drive Unit 420 Orillia ON L3V 7T9 Canada

WHITE, JOY MIEKO, communications executive; b. Yokohama, Japan, May 1, 1951; came to U.S., 1951; d. Frank Deforest and Wanda Mieko Mellen; m. George William White, June 5, 1948; 1 child, Karen. BA in Comms., Calif. State U., Fullerton, 1974, student, 1977, Orange Coast C.C., 1981, Golden West C.C., 1990. Cert. secondary tchr., Calif.; cert. tchr. Coast C.C.s Dist. Secondary tchr. Anaheim (Calif.) Union H.S. Dist., 1977-80; tech. writer Pertec Computer Corp., Irvine, Calif., 1980-81; supr. large sys. divsn. Burroughs, Mission Viejo, 1981-83; mgr. Lockheed divsn. CalComp, Anaheim, 1983-86; owner, pres. Communicator's Connection, Irvine, Calif., 1986-90; pres. Info Team, Inc., 1989—. Mem. adj. faculty, coord. tech. comm. program Golden West Coll., Huntington Beach, Calif., 1987-90; instr. U. Calif., Irvine, 1987-89, Calif. State U., Fullerton, 1988-91; condr. numerous workshops, profl. presentations, 1982—; sec. Santa Ana Dist. chpt. U.S. SBA Assn. for Minority-Owned Bus., 1991-96. Active Performing Arts, Costa Mesa, 1986—; troop leader Girl Scouts U.S., 1995—, life mem., 1994—. Fellow Soc. Tech. Comm. (assoc., internat. assoc., sr., Orange County chpt. 1987, Mem. of Yr.); mem. NAFE, Soc. Profl. Journalists, Women in Comms. (pres. Orange County Profl. chpt. 1989-90), Nat. Assn. Women Bus. Owners, Rembrandts Wine Club (Yorba Linda), Girl Scouts U.S. (life). Democrat. Avocations: writing short stories, needlework, camping, fishing. Home: 3531 Brentridge Dr Corona CA 92881-8445 Office: 23328 Forest Canyon Diamond Bar CA 91765 also: 1877 S Highgate Ct Dayton OH 45432-1880

WHITE, JOYCE LOUISE, librarian; b. Phila., June 7, 1927; d. George William and Louisa (Adams) W. BA, U. Pa., 1949; MLS, Drexel U., 1963; MA in Religion, Episc. Sem. S.W., 1978. Head libr. Penniman Libr. Edn. U. Pa., Phila., 1960-76; archivist St. Francis Boys' Home, Salina, Kans., 1982-84; libr. Brown Mackie Coll., 1983-86; libr., dir. St. Thomas Theol. Sem., Denver, 1986-95; libr., dir. Archbishop Vehr Theol. Libr. Archdiocese of Denver, 1995-96. Author: Biographical and Historial Yarnall Library, 1979; asst. editor: Women Religious History Sources, 1983; contbr. articles to profl. jours. and chpts. to books. Vol. libr. St. John's Cath., Denver, 1993—. Mem. Ch. and Synagogue Libr. Assn. (life, founding, pres. 1969-70, exec. sec. 1970-72, exec. bd. 1967-76, ann. conf. chair 1996). Avocations: gardening, cats, church libraries. Office: St John's Cathedral Libr 1350 Washington St Denver CO 80203-2008

WHITE, JUDITH LOUISE, social worker, counselor; b. Lodi, Ohio, Feb. 27, 1939; d. Henry and Charlotte Virginia (Spahr) Schmelzer; m. Downer Dale White, Sept. 4, 1959; children: Mark, Kelly, Kristy, David. AA, Northland Pioneer Coll., 1980; postgrad., No. Ariz. U., 1984—, Ariz. State U., 1985—; BS in Human Svcs., Prescott Coll., 1992. Tchr. White Mountain Apache Heart Start Program, Whiteriver, Ariz., 1976-80, child svcs. coord., 1976-80; cons. Nat. Indian Head Start, 1980—; family svcs. coord. Whiteriver Elem. Sch., 1987—. Trainer Indian Child & Family Conf., Phoenix and Albuquerque, 1982-86, Fetal Alcohol Syndrome-Indian Health Services, Whiteriver, 1984—; cons. White Mountain Apache Head Start Resource Access Project, 1984—; assoc. tchr. Northland Pioneer Jr. Coll., Holbrook, Ariz., 1985—; trainer pilot parent program; coord. Whiteriver Pilot Parents. Mem. Coalition for Chronically Ill Chilkdren, Phoenix, 1985—, White Mt. Apache Child Protective Team, Kinishba Coun. Prevent Child Abuse. Mem. NASW (presenter conf. 1990), Coun. Exceptional Children, Nat. Assn. Edn. Young Children, White Mt. Assn. Edn. Young Children. Avocations: music, reading, theater, art. Home and Office: 660 N Spring Creek Trail Cornville AZ 86325

WHITE, JUNE MILLER, mathematics educator, education consultant; b. E. Bernstadt, Ky., June 13, 1938; d. James Fulton and Ida Mae (Hansel) Miller; m. Richard Allen White, Aug. 27, 1960; children: Jennifer Lynn, Richard Allen Jr. BS with high honors, Denison U., 1960; MA, U. Rochester, 1969; PhD, Bryn Mawr Coll., 1980. Engring. asst. AT&T, Kansas City, Mo., 1960-61; math. tchr. William Chrisman H.S., Independence Pub. Schs., Independence, 1961-62, Brighton (N.Y.) H.S., 1962-69, Conestoga H.S., Tredyffrin-Easttown Pub. Schs., Berwyn, Pa., 1970-72; chair math. dept. Hill Top Prep. Sch., Rosemont, 1972-76, curriculum coord., 1976-81; instr. math. St. Petersburg Jr. Coll., Clearwater, Fla., 1982-84, dir. math. program, 1984—2002, prof. math. edn., 2002—. Presenter at various confs. Author: A Collection of Mathematics Applications for College Students, 1989; editor SPECTRUM, 1983-95; contbr. articles to profl. jours. Elder Northwood Presbyn. Ch., Clearwater, 1986-90; chmn. blood drive ARC, King of Prussia, Pa., 1973-74; chmn. citizens adv. com. Upper Merion Pub. Schs., King of Prussia, 1975-76. Mem. Am. Math. Assn. of Two Yr. Colls., Math. Assn. Am. (v.p. Fla. and Caribbean sect. 1988-91, sec. 1994-99, pres.-elect 1999, pres. 2000), Nat. Coun. Tchrs. Math., Fla. Assn. Cmty. Colls., Rsch. Coun. for Diagnostic and Prescriptive Math., Pinellas County Assn. for Children and Adults with Learning Disabilities (bd. dirs. 1987-88), Phi Beta Kappa. Avocations: camping, sailing, travel. Home: 4951 Bacopa Ln S Unit 103 Saint Petersburg FL 33715-2617 E-mail: whitejune@spjc.edu.

WHITE, KAREN RUTH JONES, information systems executive; b. Ft. Meade, Md., Oct. 8, 1953; d. Frank L. Jones and Inge H. Lesser; m. M. Timothy Heath, Apr. 23, 1973 (div. Aug. 1976); m. Carl W. White, May 30, 1993. AS in Electronic Data Processing, N.H. Tech. Inst., Concord, 1977; BS in MIS with high honors, Northeastern U., Boston, 1984, MS in Info. Sys., 1997. Programmer Chubb Life Ins. Co., Concord, N.H., 1977-79, Retailers Electronics Account Processing, Woburn, Mass., 1979-82; sr. programmer, analyst N.H. Ins. Group, Manchester, 1982-84; prin. systems analyst Wang Labs., Inc., Lowell, Mass., 1984-89; project mgr. TASC, Inc., Reading, 1989-2000; mng. cons. PM Solutions, Franklin, Ohio, 2000—. Bd. dirs. Brandywyne Common Assn., Derry, N.H., 1991-94; mem. St. Paul's Sch. Advanced Studies Pgm Alumni Assn., Concord, N.H. With U.S. Army Res., 1974-84. Decorated Army Commendation medal, 1980. Mem.: AAUW, NAFE, IEEE (computer soc., tech. com. in software engring., program chair 5th reengring. forum 1996, dep. conf. chair 6th reengring. forum 1998, mem. exec. adv. bd. 1996—99), Project Mgmt. Inst. (Mass. Bay chpt. program dir. 1992—93, project chair PMI '96 1994—96, dir. seminars/symposium 1996—98, PMI 2000 adv. group 1999—2000, ethics rev. com. 2000—, awards rev. com. 2001—), Engring. Mgmt. Soc., Nat. Soc. Fund Raising Execs., Sigma Epsilon Rho. Home: 50 Merrill Rd Weare NH 03281-4708 Office: PM Solutions 50 Merrill Rd Weare NH 03281-4708

WHITE, KATHERINE ELIZABETH, retired pediatrician; b. Syracuse, N.Y., Mar. 23, 1920; d. Rufus Macandie and Marguerite Mary (Eselin) W.; m. Nicholas V. Oddo, Feb. 12, 1947 (dec. 1966); 1 child, Sandra S. Qualls. BA, Syracuse U., 1941, MD, 1943. Intern Syracuse U. Med. Ctr., 1944-45; asst. resident Buffalo Children's Hosp., 1945-46, chief resident, 1946-47; instr. pediatrics L.A. Children's Hosp., 1947; pvt. practice, Long Beach, Calif., 1947-90; mem. med. staff Miller Children's Hosp., 1966—, trustee, 1968—. Adv. bd. and life mem. Children's Clinic (bd. dirs. 1968-87, Recognition award, 1991), Long Beach; bd. trustees Long Beach Meml. Med. Ctr. (Achievement award, 1997). Recipient Meml. Med. Ctr. Found., 1984, 90, Found. for Children's Health Care, 1987, Humanitarian award Kiwanis, 1990. Fellow Am. Acad. Pediatrics; mem. AMA, Am. Med. Women's Assn., Calif. Med. Assn., L.A. County Med. Assn., Long Beach Med. Assn., Soroptimist (Woman of Distinction 1989, Hall of Fame award 1990), Women and Philanthropy Calif. State U., Phi Beta Kappa. Republican. Roman Catholic. Home: 6354 Riviera Cir Long Beach CA 90815-4767 E-mail: bknlb@aol.com.

WHITE, KATHRYN CAMILLE, management consultant; b. Denville, N.J., Oct. 19, 1966; d. Leo Anthony and Rosanna (del Piero) W. BA in Econs., Johns Hopkins U., 1988. Market rsch. analyst Stouffer Harborplace Hotel, Balt., 1989-91, adminstr. transient sales, 1991-92; analyst HCIA Inc., 1992-95, mgmt. cons. Boston, 1995—. Mem., sec., bd. dirs. Hands on Balt., Inc., 1993-95. Mem. NOW.

WHITE, KEITH BRANDON, music company executive, writer, musician; b. Detroit, Sept. 27, 1975; s. John Delbert and Emma Jean White. Student, U. Mich., 1993—97, Wayne State U., 1997, Marygrove Coll., 2002—. Cert. sub. tchr. Mich. Info. svcs. asst. Wayne State U., Detroit, 1997—98; info. specialist Alpha Data Svcs., Inc., 1999; sales exec. FM98 WJLB, 2000; tchr. asst. Innovative Ednl. Programs, 1999—. CEO Phonosynthesis, Inc., Detroit, 2001—. Mem.: NAACP. Democrat. Avocations: reading, dancing, theater, travel, billiards. Office: Phonosynthesis Inc 581 Fiske Dr Detroit MI 48214

WHITE, KEITH GORDON, bank executive, artist; b. Cleve., Nov. 18, 1959; s. Luther John and Anna Gai (Redmond) W.; m. Gabriela Elisabeth Weising, July 9, 1997. AB in English, Dartmouth Coll., 1982; Cert. Fine Arts, N.Y. Studio Sch., 1995; MCP, Microsoft Corp., 1996. Microsoft cert. trainer. Credit analyst Mfrs. Hanover Trust, N.Y.C., 1985-86; analyst Royal Bank Can., 1986-87; tchr. N.Y.C. Bd. Edn., 1987-95, Rhodes Prep. Sch., N.Y.C., 1992-94; lead artist New Fellowship Bapt. Ch., Nashua, N.H., 1996-2000; MIS dir. The Dwight Sch., N.Y.C., 1995-96, dir. media svcs. project mgr., chmn. computer sci. dept., 1995-96; systems engr. Valinor, 1996-97; project mgr. Alpine Computer Systems, 1997-98; v.p. Credit Suisse First Boston, 1999—. Bd. dir. Artist Cmty. Fed. Credit Union, N.Y.C., 1990-92; dir. tech. PTW Harlem Cmty. Computer Ctr., N.Y.C., 1995-96. One-man painting exhbns. include East Germany, 1991, Hanover CEBIT, 1992, Amherst, N.H., 2000-01; exhibited in group shows at N.Y. Studio Sch., 1996, 2000, Art Machine, 2000, Gracie Park, 2000; represented by Arts Forum Gallery, N.Y.C., 14th Street Painters, 2000, Transparent, Arts Forum Gallery, 2001; reviewed in various publs. including Boston Globe, The Amherst Citizen, others. Grantee Artist Space, 1991, scholarship Philip Morris Co. Inc., 1993, 94, 95. Mem. N.Y. City Dartmouth Alumni Assn. (bd. dirs.), Dartmouth Club (chmn. tech. com., recipient Resnikoff Vol. Svc. award 2000). Avocation: marathons (finisher N.Y.C. 1995). Home: PO Box 6201 New York NY 10128-0012

WHITE, KENDRED ALAN, lawyer; b. Madisonville, Tenn., Oct. 2, 1938; s. Leonard A. and Nora (Clyde) W.; m. Peggy Ann Cowling, Aug. 24, 1963; children: Jonathan C., Erik K., Lauren A. BS, U. Tenn., 1961, JD, 1964. Bar: Tenn. 1964, U.S. Dist. Ct. (ea. dist.) Tenn. 1966, U.S. Supreme Ct. 1971. Pvt. practice law, Madisonville, 1964—. Mem. hearing com. Bd. of Profl. Responsibility, Tenn. Supreme Ct., 1982-85; bd. dirs. Vol. Fed. S&L, Madisonville. With USAF, 1958-64. Fellow Tenn. Bar Found.; mem. ABA, Tenn. Bar Assn., Phi Delta Phi (province pres. 1996—). Republican. Baptist. Avocation: travel.

WHITE, KENNETH RAY, health administration educator, consultant; b. Okmulgee, Okla., June 28, 1956; s. Miles Delano and Ollie Jane (Roberts) W. BS, Oral Roberts U., 1979; MPH, U. Okla., Oklahoma City, 1980; BSN, MSN, Va. Commonwealth U., 1995, PhD in Health Svcs. Orgn. and Rsch., 1996. Dir. planning Mercy Health Ctr., Oklahoma City, 1980-81, adminstrv. asst., 1981-86, v.p. mktg., 1987-89; v.p. ops. Harris Hosp.-HEB, Bedford, Tex., 1986-87; sr. cons. Mercy Internat., Farmington Hills, Mich., 1989-93; instr. health adminstrn. Va. Commonwealth U., Richmond, 1993-95, asst. prof., assoc. dir. profl. grad. programs dept. health, 1995-2001; assoc. prof., dir. MHA program, 2001—. Contbr. articles to profl. jours. Bd. dirs., officer March of Dimes, Oklahoma City, 1980-89, Am. Heart Assn., Oklahoma City, 1984-89, Cross-over Clinic vol. , 1999. Named Outstanding Alumni, U. Okla., 1983, ACHE Regent's award, 1999, Va. Outstanding Nurse, 1999. Fellow Am. Coll. Healthcare Execs., Sigma Theta Tau, Phi Kappa Phi. Avocations: travel, home renovation, foreign films. Office: Va Commonwealth U Med Coll Va PO Box 980203 Richmond VA 23298-0203

WHITE, KERR LACHLAN, retired physician, foundation administrator; b. Winnipeg, Man., Can., Jan. 23, 1917; s. John Alexander and Ruth Cecelia (Preston) Stevenson; m. Isabel Anne Pennefather, Nov. 26, 1943; children: Susan Isabel, Margot Edith. BA with honors (Oliver Gold medal), McGill U., 1940, MD, CM, 1949; DM (hon.) , U. Leuven, 1978; postgrad., London Sch. Hygiene and Tropical Medicine, 1960; DSc (hon.) , McMaster U., 1983. Intern, resident in medicine Mary Hitchcock Meml. Hosp., Hanover, NH, 1949—52; Hosmer fellow McGill U. and Royal Victoria Hosp., Montreal, Canada, 1952—53; asst. prof. medicine U. N.C. Sch. Medicine, Chapel Hill, 1953—57, assoc. prof. medicine and preventive medicine, 1957—62; Commonwealth advanced fellow Med. Rsch. Coun., Social Medicine Rsch. unit London Hosp., 1959—60; chmn., prof. epidemiology and community medicine U. Vt., Burlington, 1962—64; prof. Sch. Hygiene and Pub. Health Johns Hopkins U., Balt., 1965—76, chmn. dept. health care orgn., 1965—72; dir. Inst. Health Care Studies United Hosp. Fund N.Y., 1977—78; dep. dir. health scis. Rockefeller Found., N.Y.C., 1978—97, ret., 1997. Chmn. U.S. Nat. Com. Vital and Health Stats., 1975—79; mem. health adv. panel Office of Tech. Assessment, U.S. Congress, 1975—82; cons. Nat. Ctr. Health Stats., 1967—83, WHO, 1967—. Editor: Manual for Examination of Patients, 1960, Medical Care Research, 1965, Health Care: An International Study, 1976, Epidemiology as a Fundamental Science, 1976, Task of Medicine, 1988, Healing the Schism, 1991; mem. editl. bd.: Med. Care, 1962—73, mem. editl. bd.: Inquiry, 1967—79, mem. editl. bd.: Internat. Jour. Epidemiology, 1971—81, mem. editl. bd.: Internat. Jour. Health Svcs., 1971—; contbr. chapters to books, articles to profl. jours. Trustee Case-Western Res. U., 1974—79; bd. dirs. Found. for Child Devel., 1969—80. With Can. Army, 1942—45. Recipient Pew Primary Care Achievement award, 1995, Baxter Found. award, 1996, Wood award for lifetime contbns. to primary care rsch., 1999. Fellow: APHA (gov. coun. 1964—68, 1971—73, coun. med. care sect. 1962—65), NAS (Inst. Medicine coun. 1974—76, chmn. membership com. 1975—77), ACP, AAAS, Am. Heart Assn., Am. Acad. Preventive Medicine, Royal Soc. Medicine (hon.); mem.: AMA, Kerr L. White Inst. Health Svcs. Rsch. (hon. dir. 1995—), Internat. Epidemiol. Assn. (hon.; life, pres. 1974—77, treas., exec. com. 1964—71, 1974—77, coun. 1971—81), Am. Hosp. Assn. (adv. coun. ednl. and rsch. trust 1965—68), Assn. Tchrs. Preventive Medicine (coun. 1963—68), Century Club (N.Y.C.), Cosmos Club (Washington), Alpha Omega Alpha, Sigma Xi. E-mail: klw2j@virginia.edu.

WHITE, K(ING) PRESTON, JR. systems engineering educator, researcher, consultant; b. Dec. 31, 1948; s. K. Preston and Rosamond (Conley) White; m. Charlotte Rebekah O'Cain, Apr. 9, 1977 (dec.); 1 child William Preston. BSE, Duke U., 1970, MS, 1972, PhD, 1976. Grad. tchg. and rsch. asst. Duke U., Durham, NC, 1970—75; asst. prof. dept. ops. rsch. and sys. analysis Poly. Inst. NY, Bklyn., 1975—77; asst. prof. dept. mech. engring., dept. engring. and pub. policy Carnegie-Mellon U., Pitts., 1977—79; asst. prof. sys. engring. U. Va., Charlottesville, 1979—85, assoc. prof., 1985—2000, prof., 2000—, interim dept. chmn., 1996, Capstone program dir., 1996—. V.p. ERICA, Inc., Charlottesville, 1993; disting. vis. prof. SEMATECH, Austin, 1993—94; rschr., cons. in field; jour. referee; bd. dirs. Va. Modeling, Analysis and Simulation Ctr. Contbr. articles to profl. jours., chpts. to books; U.S. editor: Internat. Abstracts in Ops. Rsch., assoc. editor: IEEE Transactions on Electronics Packaging Mfg.; contbr. . Recipient Outstanding Educator award, Boeing, 2001. Mem.: IEEE (sr.; winter simulation conf.), Soc. Automotive Engrs., Sys., Man and Cybernetics Soc., Am. Soc. Engring. Edn., Ops. Rsch. Soc. Am., Inst. Indsl. Engrs. (sr.), Pi Tau Sigma (ABET award for ednl. innovation 1990), Sigma Xi, Omega Rho (charter), Tau Beta Pi. Home: 1033 Findlay Mountain Rd Shipman VA 22971-9801 Office: U Va Dept Systems Engring PO Box 400747 151 Engineers Way Charlottesville VA 22904-4747 E-mail: kpwhite@virginia.edu.

WHITE, LARRY D. retired political science educator; b. Paola, Kans., Nov. 22, 1937; s. Carl B. and Elsie I. White; m. Marilee A. Foster, Jan. 22, 1966. AA, Independence (Kans.) C.C., 1957; BS in Edn., Pittsburg (Kans.) State U., 1959, MS in Polit. Sci., 1960; ArtsD in Govt., Econs., Sociology, Idaho State U., 1974. Instr., coach Highland (Kans.) C. Coll., 1960-65, Prestonsburg (Ky.) C.C., 1965-68; from instr. to asst. prof. polit. sci. U. Wis. Colls., Rice Lake, 1969-82, assoc. prof. polit. sci. Menasha, 1982-98, prof. polit. sci., 1998—, dept. chmn., 1988-92, 95-98; ret., 2000. E-mail: ldwhite@c212.com.

WHITE, LAWRENCE J. economics educator; b. N.Y.C., June 1, 1943; s. Martin H. and Florence M. (Meiman) W. AB, Harvard U., 1964, PhD, 1969; MS in Econs., London Sch. Econs., 1965. Econ. adviser Harvard Devel. Adv. Svc., Pakistan and Indonesia, 1969-70; asst. prof. econs. Princeton U., N.J., 1970-76; mem. faculty Stern Sch. Bus., NYU., 1976—; prof. econs. Stern Sch. Bus., NYU, 1979—, chmn. dept., 1990-95; sr. staff economist U.S. Council Econ. Advisers, 1978-79; dir. econ. policy office, antitrust div. Dept. Justice, Washington, 1982-83. Mem. Fed. Home Loan Bank Bd., 1986-89; cons. in field. Author: The Automobile Industry Since 1945, 1971, Industrial Concentration and Economic Power in Pakistan, 1974, Reforming Regulation: Processes and Problems, 1981, The Regulation: Processes and Problems, 1981, The Regulation of Air Pollutant Emissions from Motor Vehicles, 1982, The Public Library in the 1980s: The Problems of Choice, 1983, International Trade in Ocean Shipping Services: The U.S. and the World, 1988, The S&L Debacle: Public Policy Lessons for Bank and Thrift Regulation, 1991; editor or co-editor: The Deregulation of the Banking and Securities Industries, 1979, Mergers and Acquisitions: Current Problems in Perspective, 1982, Technology and the Regulation of Financial Markets: Securities, Futures and Banking, 1986, Private Antitrust Litigation: New Evidence, New Learning, 1988, The Antitrust Revolution, 1989, Bank Management and Regulation, 1992, Structural Change in Banking, 1993, The Antitrust Revolution: The Role of Economics, 2d edit., 1994, The Antitrust Revolution: Economics, Competition, and Policy, 3d edit., 1999; N.Am. editor Jour. Indsl. Econs., 1984-87, 90-95. NSF fellow, 1965-69 Mem. Am. Econ. Assn., Phi Beta Kappa Office: NYU Stern Sch Bus 44 W 4th St New York NY 10012-1126

WHITE, LEE CALVIN, lawyer; b. Omaha, Sept. 1, 1923; s. Herman Henry and Ann Ruth (Ackerman) W.; m. Cecile R. Zorinsky, Nov. 19, 1989 (dec. Apr. 1996); children: Bruce D., Rosalyn A., Murray L., Sheldon R., Laura H., Lori J. BS in Elec. Engring., U. Nebr., 1948, LL.B., 1950. Bar: Nebr. 1950, D.C. 1958. Atty. legal div. TVA, 1950-54; legis. asst. to Senator John F. Kennedy, 1954-57; asst. to Joseph P. Kennedy; mem. Hoover Commn., 1954-55; counsel U.S. Senate Small Bus. Com., 1957-58; adminstrv. asst. to Senator John S. Cooper, 1958-61; asst. spl. counsel to Pres. Kennedy, 1961-63; assoc. counsel to Pres. Johnson, 1963-65, spl. counsel, 1965-66; chmn. Fed. Power Commn., 1966-69. Campaign mgr. R. Sargent Shriver (Democratic candidate v.p. U.S.), 1972; dir. Central Hudson Gas and Electric Corp., 1984-88. Bd. govs. N.Y. Merc. Exchange, 1984—88, 1987—91. With USAR, 1943—46. Mem. D.C. Bar (gov. 1977-80) Home: 435 N St SW Washington DC 20024-3701 Office: 1350 New York Ave NW Ste 1100 Washington DC 20005-4710 E-mail: lee.white@spiegelmcd.com.

WHITE, LEON SAMUEL, college administrator; b. West Palm Beach, Fla., Mar. 31, 1946; s. Edward Julius and Carmeta Francis (Ferguson) W.; m. Anne Fryer, Sept. 29, 1969; children: Nigel, Kanika Pele. BS, Tuskegee Inst., 1969, MEd, 1973; PhD, Ohio State U., 1976; cert. in journalism, Columbia U., 1970. Rsch. assoc. Ohio State U., Columbus, 1974-76; coord. counseling St. Augustine's Coll., Raleigh, N.C., 1976-77, dean of students, 1977-81, Savannah (Ga.) State Coll., 1981-84; vice chancellor student affairs Elizabeth City (N.C.) State U., 1984-96; ednl. cons. Thomas White, PA Consultants, West Palm Beach, 1996-97, Hertford, N.C., 1996-97; v.p. student affairs Cheyney U. of Pa., 1997-2000; counselor Elizabeth City (N.C.) Middle Sch., 2000—01, RCCDC YouthBuild Program, Elizabeth City, 2001—. Contbr. articles to profl. jours. Psychol. cons. Franklin County Drug Treatment Program, Columbus, Ohio, 1975-76; mentor Boys Club of Raleigh, 1978-81; vol. counselor Tidelands Cmty. Mental Health, Savannah, 1982-84. Tuskegee Inst. scholar, 1963, grad. internship, 1971. Mem. So. Assn. Coll. Student Pers., Nat. Assn. Pers. Workers, Am. Assn. Counseling and Devel., Phi Delta Kappa. Democrat. Methodist. Avocations: writing, gardening, swimming, tennis, running. Home: PO Box 2502 Elizabeth City NC 27906-2502 Office: RCCDC YouthBuild 303 W Ehringhaus St Elizabeth City NC 27909 E-mail: dr_leonwhitee@hotmail.com.

WHITE, LERRILL JAMES, clinical pastoral educator; b. Lafayette, Ind., Mar. 13, 1948; s. Joe Lloyd and Wanita Irene (Robertson) W.; m. Deborah June Brown, Dec. 27, 1969; children: Krister Colin Brant, Kourtney Cassidy Benay. BA, Abilene Christian U., 1970, MS, 1973; MDiv, Princeton Theol. Sem., 1975; postgrad., Pa. State U., 1980-89. Ordained to ministry Ch. of Christ, 1975. Clin. chaplain Ft. Logan Mental Health Ctr., Denver, 1975-76, Meml. Med. Ctr., Corpus Christi, Tex., 1976-78; sr. pastor Centre Community Ch. of Christ, State Coll., Pa., 1978-87; assoc. dir. pastoral care Geisinger Med. Ctr., Danville, 1983-87; dir. pastoral care Yuma (Ariz.) Regional Med. Ctr., 1987-95; pastor Mohawk Valley Cmty. Ch., Roll, Ariz., 1995-99; asst. dir. clin. pastoral edn. St. Luke's Episcopal Hosp., Houston, 2000—. Pres. well i b enterprises inc., 1995—; author, presenter tng. courses, 1987—. Contbr. articles to profl. jours.; creator interview instrument P.C. Ranking Instrument, 1981. Bd. dirs. Behavioral Health Svcs., Yuma, 1991-96; mem., coach Yuma Youth Soccer Assn., 1987-93; mem., treas. Internat. Pastoral Care Network for Social Responsibility, Inc., 1987—. Mem. Assn. Clin. Pastoral Edn. (supr. 1983—), Assn. Profl Chaplains (bd. cert.), Ariz. Chaplain's Assn. (exec. com. 1988-93, pres. 1989-90), Cola-Gila Kiwanis (pres. 1995-2000). *Making choices about how we live our lives in a responsible and meaningful way is ultimately what life is about and becomes our legacy for generations to come.*

WHITE, LINDA SUE, cardiology technician; b. Gary, Ind., Apr. 14, 1964; d. Ralph Warren and Anna Elizabeth (Chadourne) W. Cert., Ill. Med. Tng. Ctr., 1986, Commonwealth Coll., Merrillville, Ind., 1988; student, Internat. Corr. Schs., 1991-93, N.Y. Inst. Photography, 1997-99. With Video King, Merrillville, 1983-85, Olan Mills, Portage, Ind., 1984-85; EKG tech. Porter Meml. Hosp., Valparaiso, 1986-87; med. asst. Dr. Brown, Crown Point, 1988-89; office mgr., med. asst., office nurse Dr. Pargaonker, Merrillville, 1989-92; med. asst. Dr. J. Timothy Ames, Valparaiso, 1992-98, Dr. F. J. Halloran, Arlington Heights, Ill., 1998-99, Clin. Cardiology Cons., S.C., Melrose Park, 1999-00, Chhabra Med. Corp., Portage, Ind., 2000—01; office mgr. Dr. Ram C. Gupta MD, Merrillville, 2001—02, Hilltop Cmty. Health Ctr., Valparaiso, 2002—. Mem. Am. Assn. Med. Assts. (cert. 1996, recert. 2000). Democrat. Baptist. Avocations: photography, needlework. Home: 399 Keystone Dr Valparaiso IN 46385-8829 Office: Hilltop Cmty Health Ctr 460 S College Ave Valparaiso IN 46383 E-mail: survivorsrose_2000@yahoo.com.

WHITE, LINDA DIANE, lawyer; b. N.Y.C., Apr. 1, 1952; d. Bernard and Elaine (Simons) Schwartz; m. Thomas M. White, Aug. 16, 1975; 1 child, Alexandra Nicole. AB, U. Pa., 1973; JD, Northwestern U., 1976. Bar: Ill. 1976. Assoc. Walsh, Case, Coale & Brown, Chgo., 1976-77, Greenberger & Kaufmann (merged into Katten, Muchin), Chgo., 1977-82, ptnr., 1982-85, Sonnenschein Nath & Rosenthal, Chgo., 1985—. Co-pres. Midwest Regional adv. bd. U. Pa. Co-pres. Midwest regional adv. bd. U. Pa.; mem. trustees coun. Penn Women; mem. Samuel Zell and Robert Lurie Real Estate Ctr., The Wharton Sch., U. Pa. Mem. ABA (real property fin. com., comml. leasing com., real property, probate and trust law sect. 1987—), Ill. Bar Assn., Chgo. Bar Assn., Practicing Law Inst. (chmn. program on negotiating comml. leases 1995-99, real estate law adv. com.). Office: Sonnenschein Nath & Rosenthal 8000 Sears Tower 233 S Wacker Dr Ste 8000 Chicago IL 60606-6491 E-mail: lwhite@sonnenschein.com.

WHITE, LINDA LEE LOCY, secondary educator; b. Detroit, Sept. 12, 1943; d. John Lorenzo and Vivian Bethia (Greenlee) Locy. BA, Western Mich. U., 1965; MA in Speech Comm., San Francisco State U., 1982. Cert. secondary tchr., Calif. English tchr. Hillside Jr. H.S., Kalamazoo, 1965-67, Sinaloa Jr. H.S., Novato, Calif., 1975-83; mentor tchr. Novato Unified Sch. Dist., 1993-96, program overseer-at-risk student tutorial, 1997—99, English tchr., Journalism tchr., 1968—73, 1983—93. Bd. dirs. Hear Me & Co., San Francisco, 1997-98, Bay Area Women's Resource Ctr., San Francisco, 1977-78; grief counselor Marin Cmty. Counseling, San Rafael, 1991—; active Internat. Women's Conf., Nairobi, Kenya, 1985. Tech. grant Calif. State Dept. of Edn., 1987; learning fellowship Buck Inst. for Edn., 1997. Avocations: hiking, reading, golfing. Home: 634 Plum St Novato CA 94945-2561

WHITE, LORAY BETTY, TV talk show host, writer, television producer, vocalist, actress, television director; b. Houston , Nov. 27, 1934; d. Harold White and Joyce Mae (Jenkins) Mills; m. Sammy Davis Jr., 1957 (div. 1958); 1 child, Deborah R. DeHart. Student, UCLA, 1948-50, 90-91, Nichiren Shoshu Acad., 1988-92; AA in Bus., Sayer Bus. Sch., 1970; study div. mem. dept. L.A., Calif. Study Group of Japan, 1970-86. Editor, entertainment writer L.A. Community New, 1970-81; exec. sec. guest rels. KNBC Prodns., Burbank, Calif., 1969-75; security specialist Xerox X10 Think Tank, L.A., 1975-80; exec. asst. Ralph Powell & Assocs., 1980-82; pres., owner, producer LBW & Assocs. Pub. Rels., 1980—; owner, producer, writer, host TV prodn. co. Pub. Pub. Rels., 1987—. Dir., producer L.B.W. Prodn. "Yesterday, Today, Tomorrow, L.A., 1981—; with CBS news dept./Bogey's Corner, The Vol. Brigade Corps, KCBS News, 1999. Actor: (films) Ten Commandments, 1956; singer: (films) The Jazz Review, 1960—65; headline singer Radio City Music Hall, N.Y.C., 1961, Can Can Cafe Concert in Mex., 1967—75, feature singer Hilton Hotel Mex., featured singer Hotel Maria Isabel, Acapulco, Disneyland, Calif.; singer: TV, 1981—, (Broadway plays) Joy Ride; appearances in the following (endorsements) Budweiser Beer, Old Gold Cigarettes, Salem Cigarettes, TV commls. including Cheer, Puffs Tissue, Coca Cola, Buffern, others, entertainment editor (newspaper) L.A. Community News, 1970—73, writer (column) Balance News, 1980—82. Vol. ARC, 1995, L.B.W. & Assocs., Ltd. Ann. Prodn. of Mother and Daughter of the Yr. Tribute, 1999, L.B.W. & Assocs., United Peace and Cultural Exch. Dinner and Awards Show, 1999; mem. Habitat for Humanity Internat, Nat. Com. Preserve Soc. Sec. and Medicare, 1998-99, Nat. Black Network Assn., AARP, So. Calif. Com. Sr. Citizens, re-elect Scott Wildmen Rep. campaign; mem. resident adv. bd. Burbank Housing Authority, HUD, 2002—; mem. Com. to Reelect Ted McConkey to Burbank City Coun., 1999; bd. dirs. Chabmlee Found. of Calif., 1998-99; exec. prodr. The Fifth L.B.W. and Assocs. Internat. Ann. Achievement Awards Show, 1999. The Sixth L.B.W. and Assocs. Internat. Ann. Achievement Awards Show, 2000. Recipient Cert. of Honor, ARC, 1984, Internat. Orgn. Soka Gakkai Internat. of Japan, Cmty. Vols. of Am. award, 1994, Mother and Daughter of Yr. Tribune, 2000-01, 6th Internat. Achievement award L.B.W. and Assoc.; named Performer of Yr. Cardella Demillo, 1976-77. Mem. ARC (planning, mktg., prodn. event com. 1995), UCLA Alumni Assn., Lupus Found. Am. (So. Calif. chpt.), Nat. Fedn. Blind, Myohoji-Hokkeko Internat., Libr. of Congress Assocs. (charter). Buddhist. Avocations: singing, acting, TV writing and producing. E-mail: lbwbootsie@aol.com. *Accepting challenges in life is a choice. The choice is always yours. I've chosen never to give up-to always give my best. To constantly keep a growing and open mind. To remember to strengthen and reinforce the quality of my integrity no matter what. Be a winner to yourself.*

WHITE, MARCIA LYNNE, accountant; b. Jacksonville, Fla., Aug. 12, 1956; d. George William and Harriet Catherine (Tabb) Asinc; m. Joseph Anthony White (div. 1986). BSBA, Kennesaw State Coll., Marietta, Ga., 1981. Construction acct. Georgia-Pacific Corp., Atlanta, 1981-83, supr. payroll controls, 1983-84, gen. acctg. supr. HQ divsn., 1984-86, acctg. mgr. control bd. mktg., 1986-87, asst. contr. Doraville container, 1987-88, adminstrv. mgr. containerboard mktg., 1988-89, mktg. controller pulp & bleached bd. divsn., 1989-92, asst. to controller ops., 1992-93, sr. bus. analyst corp. plan & devel., 1993-95, sr. mgr. BPI, 1995-96, bus. mgr. bleached bd., 1996-97, bus. mgr. market pulp, 1997—.

WHITE, MARILEA, school social worker; b. Kewanee, Ill., Oct. 24, 1941; d. Glenn William and Genevieve (Risedorf) W. BA, Ill. Wesleyan U., 1963; MSW, U. Ill., 1965. Lic. social worker, Ill. Social worker Baby Fold, Normal, Ill., 1965-70; adult probation officer McLean County, Bloomington, 1970-79; social worker MARC Ctr., 1979-89; sch. social worker Tri-County Spl. Edn., 1989—. Bd. dirs., com. mem. Habitat for Humanity, McLean County, 1984—. Mem. Acad. Cert. Social Workers, Amnesty Internat. Presbyterian. Avocations: camping, gardening, reading, handiwork. Office: Tri-County Spl Edn 105 E Hamilton Rd Bloomington IL 61704-7574

WHITE, MARILYN DOMAS, information science educator; b. Franklin, La., Aug. 16, 1940; d. George Julian and Norma Edwina (Melancon) Domas; m. Roger Stuart White, Aug. 31, 1968; 1 child, Joshua Stuart. BA, Our Lady of the Lake Coll., San Antonio, 1962; MS, U. Wis., 1963; PhD, U. Ill., 1971. Dir. Commerce Libr. U. Wis., Madison, 1963-65; head Social Sci./Bus. Libr. So. Ill. U., Edwardsville, 1965-67; cons. So. Ill. U./U.S. AID Adv. Team, South Vietnam, 1967; asst. prof. SUNY, Buffalo, 1972-74; lectr., vis. asst. prof. U. Md., College Park, 1976-77, asst. prof. info sci., 1977-82, assoc. prof. info. sci., 1982—. Cons. USIA, Washington and abroad, 1977-83, Inst. for Def. Analyses, Bowie, Md.,Supercomputing Rsch. Ctr., 1990-91, Am. Health Care Assn., Washington, 1990-92, Am. Coun. on Edn., 1995. Contbr. articles to Libr. Quar., Libr. & Info. Sci. Rsch., to Jour. Documentation, Jour. Am. Soc. for Info. Sci., others; editor (rev. editor): (Jours.) Libr.& Info. Sci. Rsch. James Lyman Whitney grantee ALA, 1983, Spl. Libr. Assn. rsch. grantee, 1993-94, Coun. Libr. Resources grantee, 1995-96, Info. Sci. Abstracts grantee, 1997-98. Mem. Am. Soc. for Info. Sci., Spl. Libr. Assn. Office: U Md Coll Info Studies Hornbake 4117F South Wing College Park MD 20742-0001

WHITE, MARTHA VETTER, allergy and immunology physician, researcher; b. Richmond, Va., Oct. 23, 1951; d. Robert Joseph and Miriam Ernestine (Thomas) Vetter; m. Frederick Joseph Kozub, Oct. 11, 1975 (div. June 1982); m. John Irving White, Feb. 18, 1984; children: Josh, Christie. Student, Vanderbilt U., Nashville, 1969-71; BA, U. Richmond, 1973; MD, Va. Commonwealth U., Richmond, 1978. Cert. m. Bd. Pediatrics, Am. Bd. Allergy and Immunology. Pediatric intern and resident Va. Commonwealth U., Richmond, 1978-81; locum tenens Pub. Health, Va., 1981-82; fellow Allergy and Immunology U. Southern Calif., L.A., 1983-84, Georgetown U., 1983-84; sr. staff fellow Food and Drug Adminstrn., Bethesda, Md., 1984-85; NSRA fellow Nat. Inst. Allergy and Infectious Diseases, 1985-88; sr. staff fellow, 1988-93; rsch. dir. Inst. for Asthma and Allergy, Wheaton, Md., 1993—. Cons. Sandoz Pharms., Marion Merrell Dow, Glaxo, Boehringer Ingleheim, Ciba-Geigy, Miles Genentech; rschr. Glaxo, Abbott, Pfizer, Marion Merrell Dow, Miles, Rhône Poulenc Rhoen, Sanofi, Adams, Astra, Merck, Neurbiol. Techs., 3M, Zeneca, Wyeth, Smith-Kline Beecham; bd. dirs. Allery & Asthma Network/Mothers of Asthmatics, 1987—; med. editor MA Report, 1986—; assoc. editor Allergy, Asthma and Immunology Guide, 1989-90. Contbr. numerous scientific papers, abstracts, chpts. and reviews in field. Recipient Norwich Eaton Rsch. award, 1987; Merrell Dow scholar in allergy, 1989; Geigy fellow, 1984. Mem.: Soc. Prin. Investigators (pres.), Am. Thoracic Soc., Am. Coll. Allergy and Immunology, Adm. Acad. Allergy and Immunology, Am. Acad. Pediat., Am. Assn. Immunologists, Gamma Sigma Epsilon, Psi Chi, Beta Beta Beta. Office: Inst Asthma and Allergy 11160 Viers Mill Rd # 414 Wheaton MD 20902

WHITE, MARTIN CHRISTOPHER, academic administrator; b. Anderson, S.C., Oct. 16, 1943; s. Jesse Martin and Christine Freida (Powell) W.; m. Linda Ann Fleming, July 31, 1965; children: Martin Lynn, Andrew Christopher. AB, Mercer U., 1965; MDiv, So. Bapt. Theol. Sem., 1968; PhD, Emory U., 1972. Prof. Elon Coll. (N.C.), 1972-76, dean acad. affairs, 1976-82, v.p. for acad. and student affairs, 1982-86; pres. Gardner-Webb U., Boiling Springs, N.C., 1986—. Cons. So. Assn. Colls. and Schs., Atlanta, 1982—. Contbr. articles in field. Bd. dirs. United Way, Shelby, N.C., 1987. Woodrow Wilson fellow,

1971. Mem. Soc. Bibl. Lit., Nat. Assn. Bapt. Profs. of Religion, N.C. Ind. Coll. Assn., Alpha Chi, Omicron Delta Kappa. Lodges: Rotary (bd. dirs. Burlington, N.C. chpt. 1986). Democrat. Baptist. Avocations: golfing, tennis, music, traveling. Home: 101 River Chase Dr Shelby NC 28152-7723 Office: Gardner-Webb U Campus Mail Dept Boiling Springs NC 28017

WHITE, MARY JO, lawyer; b. Kans. City , Mo., Dec. 27, 1947; d. Carl and Ruth King Monk; m. John W. White, Jan. 24, 1970. BS, Coll. William & Mary, 1970; MA in Psychology, New Sch. for Soc. Rsch., 1971; JD, Columbia U., , 1974. Bar: New York 1975. Law Clerk to Hon. Marvin E. Frankel, So. Dist. N.Y. , NY, 1975—76; assoc. Debevoise & Plimpton, 1976—78, litig. ptnr., 1983—90, ptnr., chair of litig., 2002—; asst. U.S. atty. So. Dist. N.Y., chief appellate atty. of criminal div. , 1978—81; instr. in Profl. Responsibility and Ethics Columbia Law Sch., 1982—; chief asst. U.S. atty. Ea. Dist. N.Y. , Bklyn., 1990—93; U.S. atty. So. Dist. N.Y., Manhattan, 1993—2002. Chairperson Atty. Gen. Janet Reno's advisory com. of U.S. Attys., 1993—94. Recipient Women of Power and Influence award, NOW, "Magnificent 7" award, Bus. & Profl. Women USA, Law Enforcement Person of the Year award, Soc. of Profl. Investigators, Human Relations Award, Anti-Defamation League Lawyer's Div., 1996, Edward Weinfeld award for disting. contbn. to Admin. of Justice, N.Y. County Lawyers' Assn., 1998, Nat. Law Jour. 2002 list of Top Women Litigators, John P. O'Neill Pillar of Justice award, Respect for Law Alliance, 2002, Sandra Day O'Connor award for Distinction in Public Svc., 2002, dir. of FBI's Jefferson Cup award for contbn. to Rule of Law in the fight against terrorism and crime, 2002, George H. W. Bush award for excellence in counter-terrorism and the Agency Seal Medallion, CIA, 2002; fellow Am. Coll. of Trial Lawyers. Mem.: ABA, N.Y. State Bar Assn., Assn. of the Bar of City of N.Y. (established tutorial prog. for minority canidates for admin. to bar). Achievements include First women to serve as U.S Atty. for So. Dist. of N.Y; first chairperson of Atty. Gen. Janet Reno's Advisory Com.of U.S. Attys. Office: Debevoise & Plimpton 919 Third Ave New York NY 10022

WHITE, MARY ANN, bank executive; b. Blackey, Ky., June 21, 1932; d. William Bradley and Audrey Ison; divorced; 1 child, William R. Student, Cannon Trust Sch., Charlotte, N.C., 1974; grad. Nat. Grad Trust Sch., Northwestern U., Evanston, Ill., 1978. With 1st Nat. Bank and Trust Co., Georgetown, Ky., 1953—, asst. trust officer, 1962-64, asst. cashier, 1964-74, asst. trust officer, asst. v.p., 1974-76, v.p., trust officer, 1976—. Treas. Sr. Citizens Exec. Bd., Georgetown; bd. dirs. Urban Renewal and Cmty. Devel. Agy. Bd., Georgetown, C. of C., Georgetown; pres. Scott County Bus. Women's Club, Georgetown. Mem. Fin. Women Internat. (sec., treas., v.p.). Avocations: flower gardening, cooking, travel. Office: 1st Nat Bank and Trust Co 101 W Main St Georgetown KY 40324-1320

WHITE, MATTHEW C. advertising executive; m. Maria White; children: Lauren, Ashley. Pres. E. James White Comms., Herndon, Va. Mem. Am. Assn. of Advt. Agencies (bd. govs.), Am. Soc. of Travel Agts. (allied mktg. com.), Am. Passenger Rail Coalition (bd. dirs.), Travel Industry of Am., Assn. of Travel Mktg. Execs. Office: E James White Comms Ste 150 13665 Dulles Technology Dr Herndon VA 20171*

WHITE, MICHAEL JAMES, healthcare facilities administrator; b. Malone, N.Y., May 19, 1950; s. Lyle J. and Patricia M. (Finnegan) W. AAS in Nursing, SUNY, Canton, 1973; BSN, Case Western Res. U., 1978; MS in Healthcare Mgmt., LaSalle U., 1988; PhD, Kennedy-Western U., 1996. Cert. case mgr. Adminstrv. supr. The Inst. for Rehab. & Rsch., Houston, 1978-81; regional dir. NSI Svcs., Inc., 1981-85; dir. home care Tulane U. Med. Ctr., New Orleans, 1985-88; supr. case mgmt. Sanus/N.Y. Life Health Plan, Houston, 1988-91; lectr. 3d party reimbursement and medicare Sch. of Nursing U. Tex. Health Sci. Ctr., 1988-96; dir. splty. svcs. Vis. Nurse Assn., Houston, 1992; mng. ptnr. Sills, White and Assocs., managed care cons., 1988-96; dir. quality and resource mgmt. Bayshore Med. Ctr., Pasadena, Tex., 1994-96; group dir. clin. operations Columbia/HCA Healthcare Corp., Nashville, 1996-98; corp. dir. clin. ops. LifePoint Hosps., Inc., 1998—. Chmn. nurses campaign United Way, Houston; adv. bd. ARC, Houston. Mem. ANA (rep. nat. ho. of dels.), Tex. Nurses Assn. (numerous local offices including pres., bd. dirs., state level rep. ho. of dels., coms.), Assn. Rehab. Nurses (local and state bd. dirs., state sec.-treas.), Case Mgmt. Soc. Am. (pres. local chpt., sec.-treas. state chpt.), Sigma Theta Tau. Home: 209 Rising Sun Ln Old Hickory TN 37138 Office: LifePoint Hosps Inc 103 Powell Ct Ste 200 Brentwood TN 37027

WHITE, MICHAEL SHAY, security officer, mariner; b. Portsmouth, Va., Oct. 12, 1968; s. Leonard Ray White and Hilda Elaine Hollier; m. Renee Eva Fisher; children: Nicholas Fisher, Katherine Fisher, Alexandra Fisher, Jessica. A in Law Enforcement Tech., Asheville (N.C.) Buncombe Tech. C.C., 1996. Professional first responder, cert. open water diver, first aid/CPR, lic. firearms tng., cert. jujitsu. Relief engr./deckhand Bay Towing, Norfolk, Va., 1999—2000; deckhand C&P Towing, Portsmouth, 2000; lead deckhand Vane Bros. Bunkering (Doris Hamlin), Philadelphia, 2000—. Sec. AB Tech Criminal Justice Assn., Asheville, NC, 1994—96. Recipient Safety award, Glacier Park, Inc., 1991—92. Republican. Methodist. Avocations: reading, writing, travel. Office: Vane Bros Bunkering Line Inc 4925 Ft Mifflin Rd. W Philadelphia PA 19153 Personal E-mail: michaelwhite3268@yahoo.com. Business E-Mail: dorishamlin2000@yahoo.com.

WHITE, MICHELLE JO, economics educator; b. Washington, Dec. 3, 1945; d. Harry L. and Irene (Silverman) Rich; m. Roger Hall Gordon, July 25, 1982. AB, Harvard U., 1967; MSc in Econs., London Sch. Econs., 1968; PhD, Princeton U., 1973. Asst. prof. U. Pa., Phila., 1973-78; from assoc. prof. to prof. NYU, N.Y.C., 1978-83; prof. econs. U. Mich., Ann Arbor, 1984—, dir. PhD program in econs., 1992-94, 98—; prof. econs. U. Calif., San Diego, 2000—. Vis. asst. prof. Yale U., New Haven, 1978; vis. prof. People's U., Beijing, 1986, U. Warsaw, 1990, U. Wis., Madison, 1991, U. Munich, Germany, 1992, 2002, Tilburg U., The Netherlands, 1993, 95, U. Chgo., 1993, Copenhagen Bus. Sch., 1995, Uppsala U., Sweden, 1997, Hebrew U., Israel, 1997, U. Calif. Law Sch. Berkeley, 1999; rsch. assoc. Nat. Bur. Econ. Rsch., 2002--; cons. Pension Benefit Guaranty Corp., Washington, 1987, World Bank, 1999; chmn. adv. com. dept. econs. Princeton U., 1988-90. Editor: The Non-profit Sector in a Three Sector Economy, 1981, Financial Distress and Bankruptcy: Economic Issues, 1997; contbr. numerous articles to profl. jours. Bd. dirs. Com. on Status of Women in Econs. Profession, 1984-86. Resources for Future fellow, 1972-73; grantee NSF, 1979, 82, 88, 91, 93, 96, 2002, Sloan Found., 1984, Fund for Rsch. in Dispute Resolution, 1989; Fulbright scholar, Poland, 1990. Mem. Am. Econ. Assn., Am. Law and Econ. Assn. (bd. dirs. 1991-92, 2001-, chair nominating com. 2002), Am. Real Estate and Urban Econs. Assn. (bd. dirs. 1992-95), Social Scis. Rsch. Coun. (bd. dirs. 1994—, treas. 1996—), Midwest Econs. Assn. (1st v.p. 1996-97). Office: U California-San Diego Dept Economics 9500 Gilman Dr La Jolla CA 92093-0508

WHITE, MICHELLE LANATTA, journalist; b. Pittsburgh, Pa., Nov. 19, 1963; d. Willie Jay and Betty Ruth White. BA, Point Pk. Coll., Pittsburgh, Pennsylvania, 1986. Feature writer Gateway Publ., Pittsburgh, Pa., 1982—84; tech. writer Nason Corp., New York, NY, 1986—92; cons. govt., Pittsburgh, Pa., 1993—. Prodr. pub. affair programming KQV-1410 News Radio, Pittsburgh, Pa., 1996; news radio announcer Wpit Am, Pittsburgh, Pa., 1993. Contbr. articles to profl. jours. Spokesperson Alliance of Ret. Persons, Pittsburgh, Pa., 2001—02; coord. Pitts. Black Media Fedn., 1982—86. Methodist.

WHITE, MILES D. pharmaceutical company executive; B in Mech. Engring., MBA, Stanford U. With Abbott Labs., 1984—, v.p. diagnostic sys. and ops., 1993-94, sr. v.p. diagnostic ops., 1994-98, exec. v.p., dir., 1998-99, CEO, dir. and chmn., 1999—. Office: Abbott Labs 100 Abbott Park Rd Abbott Park IL 60064-6400*

WHITE, MORRIS FRED, JR. physicist; b. Richmond, Va., June 26, 1957; s. Morris Fred Sr. and Alma (Liggins) W.; m. Gloria Hicks; 1 child, Samantha Sevynne. BS, Hampton U., 1980; MS, Va. State U., Petersburg, 2001. Physicist E.I. duPont, Aiken, S.C., 1981-85, Philip Morris U.S.A., Richmond, 1985—. Contbr. articles to profl. jours. Mem. Soc. Physics Students. Republican. Presbyterian. Achievements include 3 patents for novel cigarette filters. Avocations: model rocketry, tennis. Office: Philip Morris USA PO Box 26583 Richmond VA 23261-6583 E-mail: morris.f.white@pmusa.com.

WHITE, MORTON GABRIEL, philosopher, writer; b. N.Y.C., Apr. 29, 1917; s. Robert and Esther (Levine) Weisberger; m. Lucia Perry, Aug. 29, 1940 (dec.); children: Nicholas Perry, Stephen Daniel; m. Helen Starobin, June 30, 1997. BS, CCNY, 1936; L.H.D., CUNY, 1975; A.M., Columbia U., 1938, PhD, 1942. Instr. philosophy Columbia U., 1942-46; instr. physics CCNY, 1942-43; asst. prof. philosophy U. Pa., 1946-48, Harvard U., 1948-50, asso. prof., 1950-53, prof., 1953-70, chmn. dept., 1954-57, acting chmn. dept., 1967-69; prof. Inst. Advanced Study, 1970-87; prof. emeritus, 1987—. Guggenheim research fellow, 1950-51; vis. prof. Tokyo U., 1952, 60, 66, U. Oslo, 1977-78; Neesima lectr. Doshisha U., Kyoto, 1985, CUNY, 1968-69, Rutgers U., 1987-88, 88-89; mem. Inst. Advanced Study, 1953-54, 62-63, 67-68, 68-69. Author: The Origin of Dewey's Instrumentalism, 1943, Social Thought in America, 1949, The Age of Analysis, 1955, Toward Reunion in Philosophy, 1956, Religion, Politics, and the Higher Learning, 1959, (with Lucia White) The Intellectual Versus the City, 1962; Editor: (with Arthur M. Schlesinger, Jr.) Paths of American Thought, 1963, Foundations of Historical Knowledge, 1965, Science and Sentiment in America, 1972, Documents in the History of American Philosophy, 1972, Pragmatism and the American Mind, 1973, The Philosophy of the American Revolution, 1978, What Is and What Ought to Be Done, 1981, (with Lucia White) Journeys to the Japanese, 1952-79, 1986, Philosophy, The Federalist and the Constitution, 1987, The Question of Free Will, 1993, A Philosopher's Story, 1999. Fellow Center Advanced Study Behavioral Scis., 1959-60; fellow Am. Council Learned Socs., 1962-63 Mem. Am. Acad. Arts and Scis., Am. Antiquarian Soc., Am. Philos. Soc. Office: Inst for Advanced Study Princeton NJ 08540

WHITE, NANCY ELIZABETH, psychologist, artist; b. San Angelo, Tex., Feb. 8, 1935; d. John William and Vivian Olive (Harrison) Whitten; m. Kirkwood Coulter Myers, Nov. 25, 1954 (dec.); children: Kirkwood Coulter, Nancy Elizabeth; m. Robert Arthur White, Apr. 25, 1959 (dec. Oct. 1977); children: Mark Hadley, John Bradford. BFA, U. Houston, 1976, MA, 1978; PhD in Clin. Psychology, Union Inst., Cin., 1985. Diplomate Am. Bd. Sexology (clin. supr.), Nat. Registry Neurofeedback Providers; lic. marriage and family therapist, chem. dependency therapist; cert. neurotherapist, quantitative EEG. Profl. artist, Houston, 1970-77; art therapist Galveston County Hosp., Texas City, 1976-77; psychotherapist Houston, 1978—. Nat. seminar leader Practical Application Intimate Relationship Skills, Houston, 1989—; owner, dir. The Meta Ctr., Houston, 1989-99; pres. The Tex. Meta Corp., 1980-99; owner, dir. The Enhancement Inst., 2000—; mem. field faculty Norwich U.; bd. adv. Practical Application Intimate Relationship Sklls Found. Fay Sch., The Lumatron Corp., The Pairs Found., The Quantitative EEG Cert. Bd. One-woman shows include Erdon Gallery, Houston, 1971-72, Houston Bar Ctr., 1971; group shows include: Alfred Lee Gallery, Houston, 1975, Sol Del Rio Gallery, San Antonio, 1976. Recipient merit award S.W. Watercolor Soc., 1976; 1st prize Jewish Cmty. Ctr., 1976; citation Tex. Fine Arts, 1977; merit award Watercolor Art Soc. Houston, 1977. Fellow Am. Acad. Clin. Sexologists; mem. Am. Assn. Marriage & Family Therapy (clin.), Am. Assn. Sex Educators, Counselors & Therapists (cert.), Internat. Acad. Profl. Counseling and Psychotherapy, APA (clin.), Acad. Cert. Neurotherapists (cert.), Am. Art Therapy Assn. (registered art therapist, cert. chem. dependency specialist), Soc. Neuronal Regulation (sec. 1994-96), Watercolor Art Soc. Houston, Profit Seekers Investment Club (treas. 1965-70). Home: 9023 Briar Forest Dr Houston TX 77024-7220 E-mail: nancywhite@enhancementinstitute.com.

WHITE, NEIL H. pediatrician, educator; b. N.Y.C., June 25, 1949; s. Alan Maurice White and Edith Berman White Lebett; m. Ann T., Sept. 21, 1949; children: Michael Steven, Justin Alan. BS, SUNY, Albany, 1971; MD, Albert Einstein Coll. Medicine, 1975. Diplomate Am. Bd. Pediatrics, Am. Bd. Pediatric Endocrinology; cert. diabetes educator. Resident in pediatrics St. Louis Children's Hosp., 1975-77; fellow in endocrinology Washington U., St. Louis, 1977-80, asst. prof. pediatrics, 1980-87, assoc. prof. pediat., 1991—2000, prof. pediat., 2000—, prof. medicine, 2001—; assoc. prof. pediatrics U. Mich., Ann Arbor, 1987-91. Dir. pediat. endocrine and metabolism Washington U. Sch. Medicine, 1997—, co-unit leader pediatric patient-oriented rsch. unit, assoc. dir. GCRC, 1997—. Mem.: Endocrine Soc., Lawson Wilkins Pediat. Endocrine Soc., Am. Pediatric Soc., Soc. Pediat. Rsch., Coun. on Diabetes in Youth, Am. Diabetes Assn. (pres. St. Louis chpt. 2000—, award 1998). Office: Washington U 1 Childrens Pl Saint Louis MO 63110-1002

WHITE, NELSON HENRY, writer, publisher, realtor; b. Balt., Oct. 29, 1938; s. Thomas Robert and Edith Eyre W.; m. Sergei Saint-Germain, Aug. 29, 1972 (div. Dec. 30, 1992); m. Sheila Ann Emery White, Apr. 1, 1994. BA in History, U. Redlands, Calif., 1968; D in Divinity, Light of Truth Ch., Pasadena, Calif., 1971; D in Theology, Pasadena Inst., Pasadena, Calif., 1973. Teaching cert., Calif. 1969. Opr. Religious Supply and Book Store, Pasadena, Calif.; sr. calibration lab. technician NASA Ames Rsch. Ctr., Moffet Field, 1991-96; ret., 1996. Estate conservator Superior Ct., Martinez, Calif., 1997. Author over 130 books; contbr. articles to profl. jours. Deputy sheriff San Bernardino County, 1959-61; import specialist U.S. Customs Svc., Terminal Island, Calif., 1970; mem. Contra Costa County Sheriff's Posse, 2001--. Named Knight and officer Gross Priorat Österreck Templer Orden, Klagenfürt, Austria, 1989. Mem. Mensa, The Richmond Chor, Pro-Constitution Polit. Action Group. Avocations: private pilot, amateur radio, 4-wheel drive enthusiast, photography, camping, hiking. E-mail address. Home: PO Box 21172 El Sobrante CA 94820-1172 Office: Assist 2 Sell Emery Realty 5069 Appian Way El Sobrante CA 94803-1901 E-mail: whtmagick@aol.com.

WHITE, NEVA LOIS, librarian, consultant; b. Newton, Kans., Dec. 14, 1915; d. Elmer Jay and Sadie Melissa (Byler) W. BA, Goshen Coll., 1944; ABLS, U. Mich., 1946, postgrad., summer 1946. Libr. Goshen (Ind.) Coll., 1944-49; relief worker Mennonite Ctrl. Com., Hong Kong, 1949-52; med. libr. Joseph Smith Med. Library, Wausau, Wis., 1952-53; libr. Marquette U., Milw., 1953-59; libr. cons. Wyo. Contract Team USAID, Kabul, Afghanistan, 1959-66; libr. Kans. State U. Library, Manhattan, 1966-83. Reviewer Library Jour., 1958-71; libr. prof. emerita Kans. State U., Manhattan, 1983—. Author: Now We Are Many, 1975, A White Family History, 1991. Democrat. Roman Catholic. Home: 2465 Vaughn Dr Manhattan KS 66502-2627

WHITE, NORVAL CRAWFORD, architect; b. N.Y.C., June 12, 1926; s. William Crawford and Caroline Ruth (Taylor) W.; m. Joyce Leslie Lee, May 24, 1958 (div.); children: William Crawford, Thomas Taylor, Gordon Crawford, Alistair David; m. Camilla Cecilia Crowe, June 7, 1992. BS, Mass. Inst. Tech., 1949; student, Sch. Fine Arts, Fontainbleau, 1954; M.F.A., Princeton, 1955. Designer, assoc. Lathrop Douglass (Architect), 1955-59; prin. Norval C. White (Architect), N.Y.C., 1959-62, 66-67; partner Rowan & White (Architects), 1962-66, Gruzen & Partners, N.Y.C., 1967-70; prin. Norval C. White & Assos., 1970-74; ptnr. Levien, Deliso & White, 1974-80, Levien Deliso White Songer, 1980-86. Asst. prof. architecture Cooper Union, 1961-67; prof. architecture City Coll., CUNY, 1970-95, prof. emeritus, 1995—, chmn. dept. 1970-77. Author (with E. Willensky): AIA Guide to New York City, 1968, AIA Guide to New York City, 4th edit., 2000; author: The Architecture Book, 1976, New York: A Physical HIstory, 1987, The Guide to the Architecture of Paris, 1991;prin. works include Seiden House, Tenafly, N.J., 1960, Essex Terrace (housing), Bklyn., 1970, N.Y.C. Police Hdqrs., 1973, Brookhaven Parks (L.I.) Sanitary Landfill, 1971, Forsgate Indsl. Park, South Brunswick, N.J., 1978—86, Del Vista Condominiums, Miami, 1981, 61 Christopher Street, Greenwich Village, 1987, White House, Salisbury, Conn., 1998. Trustee Bklyn. Inst. Arts and Scis., 1973-82, Bklyn. Pub. Libr., 1993-96; gov. Bklyn. Mus., 1973-82, adv. com., 1982—; mem. N.Y.C. Art Commn., 1975-86, sec., 1975-77, v.p., 1978-80. Served with USNR, 1944-46. Fellow AIA; mem. Soc. Archtl. Historians, N.Y. State Assn. Architects. Clubs: Century Assn. (N.Y.C.). Democrat. Home and Office: PO Box 241 Salisbury CT 06068-0241 E-mail: norval@discovernet.net.

WHITE, ORTRUDE B. architect; b. St. Louis, Feb. 7, 1943; d. Ewald W. and Ortrude (Schnaedelbach) Busse; m. W.P. Dinsmoor White, July 31, 1965; 1 child, Erika D.; m. Myles Greene Smith, Feb. 19, 1984; 1 child, Toby A. BArch, Cornell U., 1965; MRP, U. N.C., 1968; Cert. in Orgnl. Devel., Calif. Inst. Integral Studies, San Francisco, 1993. Lic. architect, Va. Architect/planner Boston Redevel. Authority, 1967-69; rsch. officer Ctr. for Environ. Studies, London, 1969-71; architect Environ. Design Group, Reston, Va., 1973-75; chief architect Va. Housing Redevel. Authority, Richmond, 1975-81; dir. resdl. planning and design Kiawah Island Co., Charleston, S.C., 1981-83; prin. Niles Bolton Assocs., Atlanta, 1983-88; pres. Ortrude White & Assocs., 1988—. Loeb fellow Harvard U., 1979, AIA Found. fellow, 1992. Mem. AIA (chair housing com. 1983, chair women in arch. com. 1988, chair practice mgmt. com. 1994-95, Atlanta chpt. pres. 1997). Unitarian Universalist. Avocations: watercolor painting, whitewater canoeing, tennis. Office: Ortrude White & Assocs 881 Ponce De Leon Ave NE Atlanta GA 30306-4252 E-mail: ortrude@mindspring.com.

WHITE, PERRIN CHARLES, endocrinologist; b. Bklyn., Jan. 12, 1951; AB, Harvard Coll., 1972; MD, Harvard Med. Sch., Boston, 1976. Intern dept. pediatrics Johns Hopkins Hosp., Balt., 1976-77, asst. resident pediatrics, 1977-78; postdoctoral fellow Rockefeller U., N.Y.C., 1978-80; asst. pediatrician N.Y. Hosp., 1980-81; rsch. assoc. Sloan-Kettering Inst., 1981-85; asst. prof. pediatrics Cornell U. Med. Coll., 1981-87, dir. lab. of molecular endocrinology, 1985-94, assoc. prof. pediatrics, 1987-91, prof. pediatrics, 1991-94, U. Tex. Southwestern Med. Ctr., Dallas, 1994—; chief of endocrinology Children's Med. Ctr., 1994—. Recipient Young Investigator award Am. Soc. Histocompatibility and Immunogenetics, 1984, Merit award NIH, 1994-2001. Mem. Soc. for Pediatric Rsch. (Mead Johnson award 1996), Endocrine Soc. (Ernst Oppenheimer award 1991), Am. Soc. for Clin. Investigation. Office: U Tex SW Med Ctr 5323 Harry Hines Blvd Dallas TX 75390-9063

WHITE, PERRY D. music educator; b. Manchester, Iowa, Oct. 24, 1961; s. Jon William White (dec.) and Sandra M. Heefner; m. Dalene S. Zimmerman, July 23, 1994. BA, Luther Coll., 1983; MMus, U. Mo., Kansas City, 1988; D in Musical Arts, U. Okla., 1998. Dir. vocal activities Winnetonka H.S., Kansas City, Mo., 1986-90; dir. choral activities Iowa Ctrl. C.C., Ft. Dodge, 1991-95, Kilgore (Tex.) Coll., 1997-98, Monmouth (Ill.) Coll., 1998—. Concert chair Maple Leaf Cmty. Concerts, Monmouth, 1998—. Mem. Am. Choral Dirs. Assn., Music Educators Nat. Conf. Home: 1220 N Park Cir Monmouth IL 61462-9695 Office: Monmouth Coll Music Dept 700 E Broadway Monmouth IL 61462-1998 E-mail: pwhite@monm.edu.

WHITE, RALPH EDWARD, chemical engineer, educator; b. Clovis, N.Mex., Nov. 6, 1942; s. Wilford Weldon and Fannie (Edens) W.; m. Carolyn Jean McDaniel, Feb. 24, 1969 (div. Oct. 1981); 1 child, David Stewart; m. Marjorie Nicholson, Oct. 13, 1981; children: Robert Edward, Priscilla Anne, Lillian Leigh, Samuel Joseph. BS in Engring., U. S.C., 1971; MS in Chem. Engring., U. Calif., Berkeley, 1973, PhD in Chem. Engring., 1977. Registered profl. engr., Tex. Asst. prof. Tex. A&M U., College Station, 1977-81, assoc. prof., 1981-85, prof., 1985-92, assoc. head dept. chem. engring., 1990-92; prof. chem. engring. U. S.C., Columbia, 1993—, chmn. dept. chem. engring., 1993—, disting. scientist, 1993—, dir. Ctr. Electrochem. Engring., 1995—. Cons. Dow Chem. Co., Freeport, Tex., 1979-93, Exxon Corp., 1981-82, GM Corp., Dearborn, Mich., 1984-87, Allied Corp., 1985-86. Editor: Comprehensive Treatise on Electrochemistry, 1981-84, Modern Aspects of Electrochemistry, 1982-95; ECS Proc. of Symposiums (9), 1986-94. Recipient Silver Medal award for best paper Jour. of Am. Electroplaters and Surface Finishers Soc., 1993. Mem. The Electrochem. Soc. (nat. treas. 1990-94, Electrodeposition Divsn. Rsch. award 1992, Battery Divsn. Rsch. award 1991). Achievements include patent on electrochemical method for producing hydrogen and sulfur. Home: 5 Brandywine Ln Columbia SC 29206-1366 Office: Univ of South Carolina Dept Chem Engring Swearingen 2c13 Columbia SC 29208-0001

WHITE, RALPH PAUL, automotive executive, consultant; b. Watertown, Mass., Aug. 1, 1926; s. Irving William and Margaret Sarah (McGowan) W.; m. Shirley Irene Christie, Nov. 22, 1947; children: Karin Ann, Eric John. BS in Indsl. Engring., Columbia U., 1951; postgrad., Yale U., 1958-59. Instr. engring. mechanics U. Conn., Torrington, 1956-57; mgr. data processing. B.F. Goodrich Co., Shelton, Conn., 1958-61; ptnr., mgmt. cons. Bavier, Bulger & Goodyear, New Haven, 1961-66; v.p. Davidson Rubber Co., Dover, N.H., 1966-69, pres., 1969-80; group v.p. parent co. Ex-Cell-O, Troy, Mich., 1980-83; pres. Troy (N.H.) Mills Inc., 1983-86, chief exec. officer, 1983-89, chmn., 1987-89, also bd. dirs.; cons., 1989—. Bd. dirs. J.A. Wright Co., Keene, N.H., J.D. Cahill Co., Hampton, N.H., Exeter Trust Co. Mem. N.H. Indsl. Devel. Authority, 1972-80, 85-88, Pease Devel. Authority, State of N.H., 1990-93, N.H. Bus. Fin. Authority, 1992—; exec. bd. Whittemore Sch. Bus., U. N.H., Durham, 1984—. Mem. Am. Inst. Indsl. Engrs., Soc. Automotive Engrs., N.H. Bus. and Industry Assn. (bd. dirs. 1970-80, pres. 1972-73, vice chmn. 1984-86), Abenaqui Country Club, Rye Beach Club, Coral Beach Club. Republican. Roman Catholic. Avocations: skiing, golf. Home: 70 Woodland Rd # 667 North Hampton NH 03862-2234 E-mail: rpw99@aol.com.

WHITE, RAYE MITCHELL, educational administrator; b. Gilmer, Tex., Jan. 21, 1944; d. R.E. and Addie Belle (Collum) Mullican; children: Victoria, William Brett. BS, East Tex. State U., 1966, MS, 1973; EdD, U. Ga., 1984. Cert. tchr., supr., Tex. Tchr. Arabian Oil Co., Ras Tanura, Saudi Arabia, 1978-84; cons. Region VII Edn. Svc. Ctr., Kilgore, Tex., 1985; curriculum dir. Gilmer Ind. Sch. Dist., 1985-87, 92-96; tchr., coord. at-risk mentoring program L.V. Stockard Middle Sch., Dallas, 1987-89; curriculum dir. Chapel Hill Ind. Sch. Dist., Tyler, Tex., 1989-92; part-time prof. U. Tex., 1991-93; owner Internat. Golf, Longview and Tyler, Tex., 1996—. Mem. editorial bd. The Reading Tchr., 1987-90. Mem. ASCD, Internat. Reading Assn., Nat. Coun. Tchrs. English, Phi Delta Kappa, Kappa Delta Pi, Delta Kappa Gamma. Home: 1796 Fm 852 Gilmer TX 75644-5094 Office: Internat Golf 2608 Gilmer Rd # 3 Longview TX 75604-1820

WHITE, RAYMOND PETRIE, JR. dentist, educator; b. N.Y.C., Feb. 13, 1937; s. Raymond Petrie and Mabel Sarah (Shutze) White; m. Betty Pritchett, Dec. 27, 1961; children: Karen Elizabeth, Michael Wood. Student, Washington and Lee U., 1955—58; D.D.S., Med. Coll. Va., 1962, PhD, 1967. Diplomate Am. Bd. Oral and Maxillofacian Surgery. Postdoctoral fellow anatomy Med. Coll. Va., Richmond, 1962—67, resident in oral surgery, 1964—67; asst. prof. U. Ky., Lexington, 1967—70, asso. prof., 1970—71, chmn. dept. oral surgery, 1969—71; prof., asst. dean adminstrn. Va. Commonwealth U., Richmond, 1971—74; prof. Sch. Dentistry U. N.C., Chapel Hill, 1974—, Dalton L. McMichael disting. prof., 1993—; dean Sch. Dentistry, U. N.C., 1974—81, assoc. dean Sch. Medicine, 1981—92. Mem. staff U. N.C. Hosps., mem. exec. com., 1974—98, sec., 1977—78, assoc. chief staff, 1981—92; mem. adv. panel on dentistry U.S. Pharmacopeial Conv., 1985—; sr. program cons. The Robert Wood Johnson Found., 1982—90. Author (with E.R. Costich): Fundamentals of Oral Surgery, 1971; author: (with Bell and Proffit) Surgical Correction of Dentofacial Deformities, 1980; author: (with W.R. Proffit) Surgical Orthodontic Treatment, 1990; author: (with M.R. Tucker, B.C. Terry, J.E. Van Sickels) Rigid Fixations for Maxillofacial Surgery, 1991; co-editor: Internat. Jour. Adult Orthodontics and Orthodontic Surgery, 1985—; asst. editor: Jour. Oral and Maxillofacial Surgery, 1993—; contbr. Bd. dirs. Am. Fund for Dental Health, 1978—86, v.p., 1982—85. Recipient Disting. Svc. award, Am. Fund Dental Health, 1987, Dentist Found. N.C., 1981, John C. Brauer award for acad. distinction, U. N.C. Alumni Assn., 2000. Mem.: AAAS, ADA, N.C. Assn. Oral and Maxillofacial Surgeons, Am. Assn. Oral and Maxillofacial Surgeons (gen. chmn. sci. sessions com. 1974—76, chmn. strategic planning com. 1990—96, Outstanding Svc. award as committeeman 1976, William Gies award 2000), Chalmers J. Lyons Acad. Oral Surgery, Inst. Medicine of NAS, Internat. Assn. Dental Rsch. (pres. Ky. sect. 1970), N.C. Dental Soc., Sigma Xi, Omicron Kappa Upsilon, Sigma Zeta, Alpha Sigma Chi, Delta Tau Delta, Psi Omega. Roman Catholic. Home: 1506 Velma Rd Chapel Hill NC 27514-7601 Office: U NC Sch Dentistry Dept Oral/Maxillofacial Surgery Chapel Hill NC 27599-7450 E-mail: ray_white@dentistry.unc.edu.

WHITE, RAYMOND LESLIE, geneticist; b. Orlando, Fla., Oct. 23, 1943; s. Lawrence and Marjorie White; m. Joan Palmer Distin, June 1, 1968; children: Juliette, Jeremy. BS in Microbiology, U. Oreg., 1965; PhD in Microbiology, MIT, 1971; postdoctoral studies, Stanford. Rsch. assoc., instr. MIT, Cambridge, 1971-72; postdoctoral fellow Sch. Medicine Stanford (Calif.) U., 1972-75; asst. prof. Dept. Microbiology U. Mass. Sch. Medicine, Worcester, 1975-78, assoc. prof. Dept. Microbiology, 1978-80; investigator Howard Hughes Med. Inst. U. Utah Med. Ctr., 1980-94; assoc. prof. Dept. Cellular, Viral and Molecular Biology U. Utah Sch. Medicine, 1980-84, co-chmn. Dept. Human Genetics, 1984-94, prof. Dept. Oncological Scis., 1985—; prof. Dept. of Human Genetics U. Utah Sch. of Medicine, 1985—; chmn. Dept. Oncological Scis. U. Utah Sch. Medicine, 1994—, dir. Huntsman Cancer Inst.,

1994—2000; chief sci. officer DNA Scis., Inc., 2000—. Ad hoc mem. NIH Gen. Med. Sci. Inst. Coun., 1984, mem. NIH study sect., 1979-83. Consulting editor Jour. Clin. Investigation; subject area editor Genomics, 1987-90; contbr. articles to profl. jours. Woodrow Wilson fellow, 1965-66, NIH grad. fellow, 1966-71, Jane Coffins Childs Found. fellow, 1971-75; Nat. Cancer Inst. Cancer Ctr. Support grantee, 1995—; recipient Sword Hope award Am. Cancer Soc., 1995, Lewis S. Rosenstiel award Disting. Work Basic Med. Scis., Brandeis U., 1992, Rosenblatt award for excellence, 1993, Nat. Med. Rsch. award Nat. Health Coun., 1991, Friedrich von Recklinghausen award Nat. Neurofibromatosis Found., 1990, Charles S. Mott prize Gen. Motors Cancer Rsch. Found., 1990, Raymond Bourfine award, Paris, 2002. Mem. NAS, Am. Soc. Human Genetics (Allen Cancer Rsch. award 1989, assoc. editor Cancer Rsch.), Utah Acad. Scis. Achievements include the development of a new technology for mapping and ultimately identifying human genes causing disease and the discovery of fundamental genes and genetic mechanisms important in the inherited and cellular pathways to cancer. Avocations: sailing, biking, rafting, fishing, hiking. Office: DNA Scis Inc 6540 Kaiser Dr Fremont CA 94555-3613

WHITE, REBECCA E. advocate; b. Washington, Nov. 17, 1945; d. Edward and Anna Pendleton White. BS, D.C. Tchrs. Coll., 1971; postgrad., Pepperdine U., 1993. Cert. tchr., D.C., Calif. Tchr. English D.C. Pub. Schs., Washington, 1971-73; paralegal specialist U.S. Dept. Justice, 1973-81; adminstr. U.S. Dept. Vet. Affairs VA Med. Ctr., L.A., 1982-89, 94-96, Sepulveda, Calif., 1992-94; patient/employee advocate U.S. Dept. Vet. Affairs, L.A., 1982-89, 92-96; tchr. English L.A. Unified Sch. Dist., 1989-91, children's advocate, 1989—; tchr. English Inglewood (Calif.) Unified Sch. Dist., 1996-97, children's advocate, 1996-98. Cmty. advocate Baldwin Hills Cmty., L.A., 1983—; children's advocate L.A. County Schs., 1999—; mem. L.A. World Affairs Coun., 1999—. Mem. NEA, Calif. Tchrs. Assn. Avocations: writing, hiking, entertaining, reading. Office: LA County Office of Edn Foster Youth Svcs 639 S New Hampshire Ave Los Angeles CA 90005

WHITE, RENEE ALLYN, judge; b. Bronx, N.Y., Sept. 22, 1945; d. Lawrence and Ann (Kaufman) W.; m. Michael W. Moore, Oct. 23, 1993. BA, Hofstra U., 1966; JD, Bklyn. Law Sch., 1969. Bar: N.Y. 1969, U.S. Dist. Ct. (ea. and so. dists.) N.Y. 1977, U.S. Supreme Ct. 1978. Trial atty. Criminal Def. divsn. The Legal Aid Soc., N.Y.C., 1969-74; atty. in charge Criminal Justice sect. Office of Projects Devel. Appealate divsn. First Dept., 1974-78; adminstrv. law judge City N.Y. Office Adminstrv. Trials and Hearings, 1978-84; judge N.Y.C. Civil Ct., 1984, Criminal Ct. City of N.Y., 1985-88; acting supreme ct. justice, supervising judge of N.Y. County Criminal Ct., 1988-90; acting supreme ct. justice, criminal term, 1990—. Lectr. in field, mem. criminal procedure law com. of the office of ct. adminstrn. Editor: Criminal Trial Advocacy, 1977; contbr. in field. Mem. ABA, N.Y. State Bar Assn. (chmn. criminal justice sect. 1985-87, mem. house of dels. 1985-88, 91-95, elected nominating com. 1989-90, co-chair, spl. com. on AIDS and the law 1992-95, chair CLE com. on jud. sect., 1994-99, task force on ct. reorgn. 1997-2002), Assn. of Bar of City of N.Y. (coun. on jud. adminstrn. 1990-94), N.Y. Women's Bar Assn.

WHITE, RHEA AMELIA, information scientist, consciousness researcher; b. Utica, N.Y., May 6, 1931; d. John Raymond and Rhea Jane (Parry) W. BA, Pa. State U., 1953; MLS, Pratt Inst., Bklyn., 1965; postgrad., SUNY, Stony Brook, 1990-92. Rsch. fellow Parapsychology Lab. Duke U., Durham, N.C., 1954-58; editor Jour. Am. Soc. Psychical Rsch., N.Y.C., 1959-62, 84-00, editor-in-chief, 2001—; libr. dept. psychiatry Maimonides Med. Ctr., Bklyn., 1965-67; dir. info. Am. Soc. Psychical Rsch., N.Y.C., 1965-80; reference libr. East Meadow (N.Y.) Pub. Libr., 1965-95; founder, dir. Parapsychology Sources of Info. Ctr., Dix Hills, N.Y., 1981-90; editor Rsch. in Parapsychology, Metuchen, N.J., 1981-85, Theta, Durham, N.C., 1981-86; founder, editor Parapsychology Abstracts Internat., Dix Hills, 1983-89, Exceptional Human Experience, Dix Hills, 1990; founder, producer PsiLine Database, 1983—; mng. editor Advances in Parapsychol. Rsch., N.Y.C., 1977; founder, dir. Exceptional Human Experience Network, New Bern, 1990-94, 95—. Rsch. fellow Menninger Found., Topeka, 1963-65; abstractor Psychol. Abstracts, Washington, 1967-91; cons. Scarecrow Press, Metuchen, N.J., 1980-85; referee Jour. Parapsychology, Durham, 1981-85; sr. rsch. cons. Ctr. Sci. Anomalies Rsch., 1981—; chmn., keynote spkr. conf. on women and parapsychology Parapsychology Found., Dublin, Ireland, 1991; keynote speaker Acad. Religion and Psychical Rsch. Conf., 1992; founder, editor EHE News, Dix Hills, 1994, New Bern, 1995—; instr. exceptional human experience course Portland (Oreg.) State U., 1999. *White has developed a new approach to autobiographical writing called the "exceptional human experience (EHE) autobiography technique," which is aimed at enhancing one's awareness and realization of the meaning of one's life. The method has been taught informally and in classes, and it has been used in doctoral research. White is currently writing her own EHE autobiography and will follow it with a book on how to write an EHE autobiography.* Author: Parapsychology: Sources of Information, 1973, Surveys in Parapsychology, 1975, Parapsychology: New Sources of Information, 1990; (with M. Murphy) The Psychic Side of Sports, 1978; parapsychology book reviewer Libr. Jour., N.Y.C., 1974-86, Reprint Bull., 1974-79, (with Michael Murphy) In the Zone, 1995; regional editor European Jour. Parapsychology, 1975-90; mem. editl. bd. Advances in Parapsychol. Rsch., 1980-85, Archaeus, 1985-93; contbr. over 100 articles to profl. jours. Recipient Hans Peter Luhn award Am. Soc. Info. Sci., N.Y.C. chpt., 1965; Coll. Human Scis. hon. fellow Internat. Inst. Integral Human Scis. Mem. Parapsychol. Assn. (mem. coun. 1958, 62-63, 82-85, pres. 1984, dir. 1986, Lifetime Outstanding Rsch. award 1992, spkr. conf. 1993), Soc. Psychical. Rsch., Acad. Religion and Psychical Rsch. (mem. bd. 1982-84, publs. com. 1982-97), Spiritual Frontiers Fellowship, Internat. Assn. Near-Death Studies, Soc. Sci. Study of Religion, Soc. Sci. Exploration, AAUW, Nassau County Libr. Assn., Internat. Assn. Religion and Parapsychology, Internat. Inst. Integral Human Scis., Inst. Noetic Scis., Am. Anthrop. Assn., Soc. for Anthropology of Consciousness, Internat. Soc. for Study Subtle Energies and Energy Medicine, Found for Shamanic Studies. Avocations: hiking, gardening, animals, reading, listening to music. Home and Office: 414 Rockledge Rd New Bern NC 28562-9553 E-mail: ehenwhite@coxnc.rr.

WHITE, RICHARD BOOTH, management consultant; b. N.Y.C., Aug. 26, 1930; s. Frank K. and Doris (Booth) W.; m. Mary Kane Russell, Dec. 9, 1961; children: Katherine Learned, Richard Booth (dec.), Anne Tristram, Leslie Russell. BA, Yale U., 1952. Asst. account exec. Batten, Barton, Durstine & Osborn, N.Y.C., 1955, account exec., 1956-58, account supr., 1958-63, v.p., 1959-70, mgmt. supr., 1963-76, sr. v.p., 1970-76, exec. v.p., 1976-83, also dir., chmn. exec. com.; dir. BBDO Internat. Inc.; sr. dir., ptnr. Spencer Stuart & Assocs., N.Y.C., 1984-98; ind. cons., 1998—. Mem. town coun., New Canaan, Conn. 1st lt. USMCR, 1952-54. Mem. Yale Club (N.Y.C.), Country Club of New Canaan, Beta Theta Pi. Presbyterian. Home: 27 Bank St New Canaan CT 06840-6202

WHITE, RICHARD EDMUND, marketing executive; b. Reading, Pa., June 8, 1944; s. Carl Marshall and Miriam Elizabeth (Curry) W.; m. Kristen Margaret Lloyd, June 17, 1967; children: Ross, Peter, Andrew. BS in Econs., U. Pa., 1967; MBA with distinction, U. Mich., 1968. Gen. mgr. mktg. H. J. Heinz Co., Pitts., 1970-81; dir. mktg. Seven Up Co., St. Louis, 1981-83; v.p. mktg. & sales Herr Foods, Inc., Nottingham, Pa., 1984—. Bd. dirs. Conard-Pyle Co. Chmn. fin. com. Sewickley Borough Coun., Pa., 1977—81; pres. So. Chester County Devel. Found., Jennersville, 1988—94, So. Chester County YMCA, West Grove, 1988—93, bd. mgrs., 1988—93, Avon Grove United Way, 1988—93, pres., 1988—93; chmn. So. Chester County Med. Ctr., 1988—2001, bd. dirs., 1988—2001, Brandywine YMCA Assn.; chmn. bd. dirs. Jenners Pond, 2001—, Health and Welfare Found. So. Chester County, pres. Mem. Am. Mgmt. Assn. (mktg. coun.). Republican. Avocations: physical fitness, reading. Home: 7 Sullivan Chase Dr Avondale PA 19311-9347 Office: Herr Foods Inc PO Box 300 Nottingham PA 19362-0300 E-mail: richard.white@herrs.com.

WHITE, RICHARD MANNING, electrical engineering educator; b. Denver, Apr. 25, 1930; s. Rolland Manning and Freeda Blanche (Behny) W.; m. Chissie Lee Chamberlain, Feb. 1, 1964 (div. 1975); children: Rolland Kenneth, William Brendan. AB, Harvard U., 1951, AM, 1952, PhD in Applied Physics, 1956. Rsch. assoc. Harvard U., Cambridge, Mass., 1956; mem. tech. staff GE Microwave Lab., Palo Alto, Calif., 1956-63; prof. elec. engring. U. Calif., Berkeley, 1963—, Chancellor's prof., 1996-99. Chmn. Grad. Group on Sci. and Math. Edn., U. Calif. at Berkeley, 1981-85; co-dir. Berkeley Sensor and Actuator Ctr., 1986—, Co-author: Solar Cells: From Basics to Advanced Systems, Microsensors, 1991, Electrical Engineering Uncovered, 1997, Acoustic Wave Sensors, 1997; editor ElectroTechnology Rev.; patentee in field. Guggenheim fellow, 1968. Fellow AAAS, IEEE (Cledo Brunetto award 1986, Achievement award 1988, Disting. lectr. 1989, Cady award 2000); mem. Nat. Acad. Engring., Acoustical Soc. Am., Am. Phys. Soc., Phi Beta Kappa, Sigma Xi. Avocations: photography, hiking, skiing, running, music. Office: U Calif Sensor & Actuator Ctr EECS Dept Ctr Berkeley CA 94720-0001

WHITE, RICHARD THOMAS, radiologist; b. Binghamton, N.Y., May 10, 1941; s. William Joseph and Winifred (Murphy) W.; 1 child by previous marriage, Kevin Michael; m. Rory Lynn Leyman. BS, SUNY, Binghamton, 1967; DO, Chgo. Coll. Osteo. Medicine, 1972. Intern Bi County Hosp., Warren, Mich.; staff radiologist Bi-County Hosp., 1977-79; resident Detroit Hosp., Children's Hosp., Detroit, 1973-76; fellow Johns Hopkins Hosp., Balt., 1976; asst. prof. radiology Mich. State U., East Lansing, 1980-84, cons. ultra-sound rsch., 1980-83, cons. nuclear magnetic rsch., 1982-83; asst. prof. radiology U. Tex., Houston, 1984-85, U. Ill., Chgo., 1985-88; chief radiology VA Med. Ctr., Bath, N.Y., 1988—; clin. prof. radiology U. Rochester (N.Y.) Sch. Medicine and Dentistry, 1989—. Cons. varsity sports, 1980-84, handicapped athletes Spl. Olympics, Washington, 1978-84, Detroit Red Wings hockey team, 1977-84; cons. in radiology St. James Hosp., Hornell, N.Y., 1989—. Med. dir. Mich. Spl. Olympics Ctrl. Mich. U., Mt. Pleasant, 1977-84; bd. dirs. Spl. Olympics, Mich., 1980-84, N.Y. Spl. Olympics, 1996-2000; med. advisor Amateur Hockey Assn. USA, Colorado Springs, Colo., 1980-84. With U.S. Army, 1960-66; lt. col. USAR, 1990-96, ret. Recipient Outstanding Contbn. award Spl. Olympics, 1980; named Team Physician U.S. Nat. Hockey Team, Mich. Amateur Hockey Assn., 1979, 81, 83. Mem. AMA, Am. Osteo. Assn., Am. Osteo. Coll. Radiology, Assn. Mil. Physicians and Surgeons, Am. Osteopath Assn., Radiol. Soc. N.Am., Am. Coll. Radiology, Am. Inst. Ultrasound in Medicine, Am. Acad. Sci., Soc. Med. Cons. to U.S. Armed Forces, Kiwanis, Am. Legion.

WHITE, ROBERT JAMES, newspaper columnist; b. Mpls., Nov. 6, 1927; s. Robert Howard and Claire Lillian (Horner) W.; m. Adrienne Hoffman, Sept. 24, 1955; children: Claire, Pamela, Sarah. BS, U.S. Naval Acad., 1950. V.p. White Investment Co., Mpls., 1957-67; editl. writer Mpls. Tribune, 1967-73, assoc. editor, 1973-82; editor editl. pages Mpls. Star Tribune, 1982-93, columnist, 1993-95, contbg. columnist, 1996—. Recipient cert. of excellence Overseas Press Club, 1981. Mem. Coun. Fgn. Rels., Mpls. Club. Congregationalist. Home: Summit House 400 Groveland Ave #2212 Minneapolis MN 55403 E-mail: rjw823@aol.com.

WHITE, ROBERT BROWN, medical educator; b. Ennis, Tex., Jan. 5, 1921; s. Robert Brown and Willia Elizabeth (Latimer) W.; m. Jimmie Estelle Sims, Oct. 18, 1942; children: Robert B., Canelia White Layton, Margaret White Gilbert. BS, Tex. A & M Coll., 1941; MD, U. Tex., 1944; cert., Western New Eng. Psychoanalytic Inst., 1959. Intern Phila. (Pa.) Gen. Hosp., 1944-45; psychiat. residency John Sealy Hosp., Galveston, Tex., 1945-46, 48-49; psychiatry fellow Austen Riggs Ctr., Stockbridge, Mass., 1949-51, staff psychiatrist, 1951-62; assoc. prof. U. Tex. Med. Br., Galveston, 1962-67, prof., 1967—, Marie Gale prof. of psychiatry, 1981-93; prof. emeritus, 1993—; tng. analyst New Orleans (La.) Psychoanalytic Inst., 1966-76. Tng. analyst Houston-Galveston Psychoanalytic Inst., 1974-94; analyst emeritus, 1994—. Author: Elements of Psychopathology, 1975; contbr. chpts. to books and articles to profl. jours. Capt. U.S. Army, 1946-48. Recipient David Rapaport prize Western New Eng. Psychoanalytic Inst., New Haven, 1959; Ohio State award Ohio State Univ., 1976. Fellow Am. Psychiat. Assn., Am. Coll. Psychiatrists, Am. Coll. Psychoanalysts (bd. regents 1988-91); mem. Am. Psychoanalytic Assn., Alpha Omega Alpha. Democrat. Avocations: photography, carpentry. Home: 1013 Harbor View Dr Galveston TX 77550-3109 Office: Univ Tex Med Br Galveston TX 77550

WHITE, ROBERT DENNIS, pediatrician; b. South Bend, Ind., Dec. 29, 1949; s. Alfred Butler and Mary Ruth (Gibbens) W.; m. Kathy Lynn Samuels, Aug. 15, 1970; children: Luke Alfred, James Samuels, Kieran Claire, Benjamin Robert. Student, U. Notre Dame, 1967-69; BA, John Hopkins U., 1969-70, MD, 1970-74. Diplomate Am. Bd. Pediatrics. Resident in pediatrics Johns Hopkins Hosp., Balt., 1974-76, fellow in neonatology; sr. rsch. scientist Wellcome Rsch. Labs., London, 1980; dir. regional newborn program Mem. Hosp., South Bend, Ind., 1981—. Adj. prof. psychology U. Notre Dame, 1989—, clin. asst. prof. pediatrics Ind. U. Sch. Med., 1983—. Co-author: Recommended Standards for Newborn ICU Design, 1999; co-editor: Lifespan Perspectives on Health and Illness, 1999. Co-chair Child Abuse Task Force, So. Bend, Ind., 1991—. Fellow Am. Acad. Pediatrics Office: Meml Hosp 615 N Michigan St South Bend IN 46601-1087

WHITE, ROBERT JOEL, lawyer; b. Chgo., Nov. 1, 1946; s. Melvin and Margaret (Hoffman) W.; m. Gail Janet Edenson, June 29, 1969 (div. Dec. 1982); m. Penelope K. Bloch, Dec. 22, 1985. BS in Accountancy, U. Ill., 1968; JD, U. Mich., 1972. Bar: Calif. 1972, N.Y. 1985, U.S. Dist. Ct. (cen., ea., so. dists.) Calif. 1972, U.S. Ct. Appeals (9th cir.) 1978, U.S. Ct. Appeals (5th cir.) 1983, U.S. Ct. Appeals (6th cir.) 1984, U.S. Supreme Ct. 1977. Staff auditor Haskin & Sells, Chgo., 1968-69; assoc. O'Melveny & Myers, L.A., 1972-79, ptnr., 1980-2001, chair reorgn. and restructuring dept., 1986—; CEO O'Melvey Cons. LLC, 2001—. Vis. lectr. U. Mich. Law Sch., Ann Arbor, 1986; lectr. Profl. Edn. Sys., Inc., Dallas, 1987, L.A., 1987, 89, Phoenix, 1990, Practicing Law Inst., San Francisco and N.Y.C., 1989-93, 2001—, Southwestern Legal Found., Dalalas, 1991, UCLA Bankruptcy Inst., 1993, UCLA, 1993; mem. L.A. Productivity Commn., 1993-96. Contbr. articles to profl. jours. Active Constl. Rights Found., 1980—; active Am. Cancer Soc., 1989—, mem. L.A. bd. dirs., 1995—; mem. Nat. Bankruptcy Conf., exec. com., 1999—. Fellow Am. Coll. Brankruptcy; mem. ABA (litigation sect., mem. comml. law and bankruptcy com. 1972—), L.A. County Bar Assn. (comml. law and bankruptcy sect., chmn. fed. cts. com. 1981-82, exec. com. 1982—), Assn. Bus. Trial Lawyers (bd. govs. 1983-85), Fin. Lawyers Conf. (bd. govs. 1986—, pres. 1990-91), Am. Bankruptcy Inst. Avocations: skiing, running, U.S. history. Office: O'Melveny & Myers 1999 Ave of Stars Los Angeles CA 90067-6035

WHITE, ROBERT L. G., JR. aerospace company executive; b. Orange, N.J., Dec. 20, 1941; s. Robert L.G. and Gertrude Marie (Wilson) W.; m. Joan Adam, May 9, 1970; children: Robert L.G. III, Sonya Lynn. BS in Metallurgical Engring., Lafayette Coll., 1964. Sr. engr. Crucible Steel Co., 1964-68; various positions Curtiss-Wright Corp., Woodridge, N.J., 1968-76, plant mgr. nuclear facility, 1976-80, dir. gas turbine overhaul, 1980-83; v.p., gen. mgr. Curtiss-Wright/Marquette, Inc., Fountain Inn, S.C., 1983-87; pres. GEC-Marconi Aerospace Inc., Whippany, N.J., 1987-94, Breeze-Eastern, Union, 1994-98; pres. aerospace products group Transtechnology Corp., Liberty Corner, 1998—. Office: Breeze-Eastern 700 Liberty Ave Union NJ 07083-8198

WHITE, ROBERT LEE, electrical engineer, educator; b. Plainfield, N.J., Feb. 14, 1927; s. Claude and Ruby Hemsworth Emerson (Levick) W.; m. Phyllis Lillian Arlt, June 14, 1952; children: Lauren A., Kimberly A., Christopher L., Matthew P. BA in Physics, Columbia U., 1949, MA, 1951, PhD, 1954. Assoc. head atomic physics dept. Hughes Rsch. Labs., Malibu, Calif., 1954-61; head magnetics dept. Gen. Tel. and Electronics Rsch. Lab., Palo Alto, 1961-63; prof. elec. engring., materials sci. and engring. Stanford U., 1963, chmn. elec. engring. dept., 1981-86, William E. Ayer prof. elec. engring., 1985-88; exec. dir. The Exploratorium, San Francisco, 1987-89; dir. Inst. for Electronics in Medicine, 1973-87, Stanford Ctr. for Rsch. on Info. Storage Materials, 1991—. Initial ltd. ptnr. Mayfield Fund, Mayfield II and Alpha II Fund, Rainbow Co-Investment Ptnrs., Halo Ptnrs.; vis. prof. Tokyo U., 1975; cons. in field. Author: (with K.A. Wickersheim) Magnetism and Magnetic Materials, 1965, Basic Quantum Mechanics, 1967; Contbr. numerous articles to profl. jours. With USN, 1945-46. Fellow Guggenheim Oxford U., 1969-70, Canton Hosp., Swiss Fed. Inst. Tech., Zürich, 1977-78, Christensen fellow Oxford U., 1986, IEEE Magnetics Soc. Disting. lectr., 1998; Sony sabbatical chair, 1994. Fellow Am. Phys. Soc., IEEE; mem. Sigma Xi, Phi Beta Kappa. Home: 450 El Escarpado Stanford CA 94305-8431 Office: Stanford U Dept Material Sci Engr Stanford CA 94305 E-mail: white@ee.stanford.edu.

WHITE, ROBERT M., II, newspaper executive, editor, publisher; b. Mexico, Mo., Apr. 6, 1915; s. L. Mitchell and Maude (See) W.; m. Barbara Whitney Spurgeon, Aug. 19, 1948 (dec. Feb., 1983); children: Barbara Whitney, Jane See, Laura L., Robert M. III. Grad., Mo. Mil. Acad., 1933; AB, Washington and Lee U., 1938, LL.B. (hon.), 1972. Writer of newspaper articles, Australia, Africa, S.Am., Europe, USSR, 1966, 86, People's Republic China, 1972, 77; reporter Mexico (Mo.) Eve. Ledger, 1938-39, editor, pub., 1945; vis. prof. Sch. Journalism, Mo. U., 1968-69; reporter UP Bur., Kansas City, 1939-40; pres. Ledger Newspapers, Inc., Mexico, Mo., 1945-86. Spl. cons. to pub. Chgo. Sun-Times, 1956-58; pres. See TV Co., Mexico, 1966-81; editor, pres., bd. dirs. N.Y. Herald Tribune, 1959-61; juror Pulitzer prize journalism, 1964-65; bd. dirs. World Press Freedom Com. Co-author: A Study of the Printing and Publishing Business in the Soviet Union. President Gen. Douglas MacArthur Found., 1981-91. Lt. col. AUS, 1940-45. Decorated Bronze Star; recipient nat. disting. service award for editorials Sigma Delta Chi, 1952, 68; editorial award N.Y. Silurians, 1959; Disting. Service to Journalism award U. Mo., 1967; Pres. award of merit Nat. Newspapers Assn., 1967; Ralph D. Casey Minn. award disting. service in journalism, 1983; finalist Journalist in Space 1986—. Mem. Am. Soc. Newspaper Editors (dir. 1968-69, chmn. freedom of info. com. 1970-72), Am. Newspaper Pubs. Assn. (nat. treas. 1963, dir. 1955-63, chmn. internat. group 1982-86), Washington Inst. Fgn. Affairs, Inland Daily Press Assn. (chmn. bd. 1958-59, pres., past sec., v.p.), Mo. Press Assn. (dir., v.p. 1981-83, pres. 1983-84, Hall of Fame 1998), Mo. Press-Bar Commn. (chmn. 1972-74), Internat. Press Inst. (chmn. Am. com. 1982-85), Nat. Press Club, Bohemian Club, Burning Tree Club, Cosmos Club, Sigma Delta Chi (nat. pres. 1967, pres. found. 1968), Beta Theta Pi. Office: Apt 1037 4000 Massachusetts Ave NW Washington DC 20016-5113

WHITE, ROBERT MARSHALL, physicist, government official, educator; b. Reading, Pa., Oct. 2, 1938; s. Carl M. and Miriam E. White; m. Sara Tolles; children: Victoria, Jonathan. BS in Physics, MIT, 1960; PhD, Stanford U., 1964. Vis. scientist Osaka (Japan) U., 1963; NSF postdoctoral fellow U. Calif., Berkeley, 1965-66; asst. prof. physics Stanford U., Palo Alto, Calif., 1966-70; NSF postdoctoral fellow Cambridge U., England, 1970-71; mgr. solid state rsch. area XEROX Parc, 1971-78, mgr. storage tech., 1978-83, prin. scientist, 1983-84; v.p. rsch. and tech. Control Data Corp. Data Storage Products Group, Mpls., 1984-86; chief tech. officer, v.p. rsch. and engring. Control Data Corp., 1986-89; v.p., dir. advanced computer techs. Microelectronics & Computer Tech. Corp., Austin, Tex., 1989-90; undersec. of commerce for tech. Dept. Commerce, Washington, 1990-93; prof., head dept. electrical and computer engring. Carnegie Mellon U., Pitts., 1993-99, dir. Data Storage Sys. Ctr., 1999—. Vis. scientist Ecole Polytechnique, Paris, 1976-78, U. Pernambuco, Brazil, 1978, Max Planck Inst., Stuttgart, 1981; cons. prof. applied physics, Stanford U., 1992-93; adj. prof. dept. physics U. Minn., 1987-89; guest Chinese Acad. Scis., 1982; bd. dirs. Found. Nat. Medals Sci. and Tech., Silicon Graphics, STMicroelectronics, ENSCO, Read-Rite. Author: Quantum Theory of Magnetism, 1970 (Russian transl., 1972, Polish transl., 1979); Long Range Order in Solids, 1979 (Russian transl., 1982); Quantum Theory of Magnetism, 1983; Introduction to Magnetic Recording, 1985. Contbr. articles to profl. jours. Bd. advisors Inst. Tech. U. Minn., 1987; mem. State Minn. Com. on Sci. and Tech. Rsch. and Devel., 1987-90; mem. adv. bd. U. Ill. Coll. Engring. Recipient Alexander von Humboldt Prize, Fed. Republic of Germany, 1981. Fellow AAAS, IEEE (disting. lectr. Magnetics Soc., mem. editorial bd. SPECTRUM, IEEE Disting. Pub. Svc. award 1993), Am. Phys. Soc.; mem. NAE, NRC (mem. nat. materials adv. bd., chmn. com. magnetic materials 1984, material sci. and engring., nat. steering com. advanced steady state neutron source, vice chmn. IUPAP commn. on magnetism), Conf. Magnetism and Magnetic Materials (adv. com. 1976-78, 80-95, program com. 1973-75, chmn. 1981, chmn. Intermag. Conf. 1991), Internat. Conf. Magnetism (program chmn. 1985), Found. Nat. Medals Sci. and Tech. (bd. dirs. 1993—); mem. Panel and Advanced Computing of the Japanese Tech. Evaluation Ctr.; mem. Nat. Adv. Com. on Semiconductors, 1990-92, Mfg. Forum, 1991, Nat. Critical Techs. Panel, 1990-91. Office: Carnegie Mellon U Elec & Computer Engring Dep Pittsburgh PA 15213-3890

WHITE, ROBERT MAYER, meteorologist; b. Boston, Feb. 13, 1923; s. David and Mary (Winkeller) W.; m. Mavis Seagle, Apr. 18, 1948; children: Richard Harry, Edwina Janet. BA, Harvard, 1944; MS, Mass. Inst. Tech., 1949, Sc.D., 1950; D.Sc. (hon.), L.I. U., 1976, Rensselaer Poly. Inst., 1977, U. Wis., Milw., 1978; ScD (hon.), U. Bridgeport, 1984, U. R.I., 1986, Clarkson U.; PhD (hon.), Johns Hopkins U., 1982, Drexel U., 1985, Ill. Inst. Tech., 1994. Project scientist Air Force Cambridge Research Center, 1950-58, chief meteorol. devel. lab., 1958-59; asso. dir. research dept. Travelers Ins. Co., 1959-60; pres. Travelers Research Center, Inc., 1960-63; chief U.S. Weather Bur., 1963-65; adminstr. Environ. Sci. Services Adminstrn., 1965-70, NOAA, 1970-77; pres. Joint Oceanographic Inst., Inc., 1977-79; chmn. Climate Research Bd., exec. officer Nat. Acad. Scis., 1977-79; Washington; adminstr. Nat. Research Council, 1979-80; pres. Univ. Corp. Atmospheric Research, 1980-83, Nat. Acad. Eng., 1983-95; Karl T. Compton lectr. MIT, Cambridge, 1995-96; sr. fellow Univ. Corp. Atmospheric Rsch., 1995—. Sr. fellow H. John Heinz III Ctr. for Sci., Econs. and Environment, 1996—2000; pres. Wash. Adv. Group, 1996—2001. Author: articles in field; mem. editl. bd.: Am. Soc. Engring. Edn. Jour. Bd. overseers Harvard U., 1977—79; mem. vis. com. Kennedy Sch. Govt., Harvard U.; bd. dirs. Resources for the Future, 1980—. Capt. USAAF, World War II. Decorated Legion of Hon. France; recipient Godfrey L. Cabot award, Aero Club Boston, 1966, Cleveland Abbe award, Am. Meteorol. Soc., 1969, Jesse L. Rosenberger medal, U. Chgo., 1971, Rockefeller Pub. Svc. award, 1974, David B. Stone award, New Eng. Aquarium, 1975, Neptune award, Am. Oceanic Orgn., 1977, Matthew Fontaine Maury award, Smithsonian Instn., 1976, Internat. Conservation award, Nat. Wildlife Fedn., 1976, Internat. Meteorol. Orgn. prize, 1980, Tyler prize for Environ. Achievement, U. Calif., 1992, Vannevar Bush award, Nat. Sci. Bd., 1998. Fellow: Am. Acad. Arts and Scis., Australian Acad. Tech. Scis. and Engring., Am. Geophys. Union, World Acad. Art and Scis., AAAS, UCAR (sr.), Am. Meteorol. Soc. (coun. 1965—67, 1977—, pres. 1980, Charles Franklin Brooks award1978); mem.: Royal Acad. Engring. (U.K.), Russian Acad. Engring., Royal Acad. Engring. (hon.), Engring. Acad. Japan (fgn. assoc.), Am. Philos. Soc., Finnish Acad. Tech. (fgn.), Nat. Action Coun. Minorities in Engring. Inc., Coun. Fgn. Rels., Marine Tech. Soc., NAE (coun. 1977, pres. 1983—95), Cosmos Club (Washington). Home: Somerset House II 5610 Wisconsin Ave Apt 1506 Bethesda MD 20815-4439 Office: 1275 K St NW Ste 1025 Washington DC 20005-4089 E-mail: rwhite@theadvisorygroup.com.

WHITE, ROBERT MCKINLEY, JR. oncologist, federal agency administrator; b. Hackensack, N.J., Jan. 1, 1950; s. Robert M. and Janet (Carter) W. BA in Chemistry with honors, Wesleyan U., 1972; MD, N.J. Med. Sch., 1976. Diplomate Nat. Bd. Med. Examiners, Am. Bd. Internal Medicine, Am. Bd. Med. Oncology. Resident dept. medicine N.J. Med. Sch., Newark, 1976-77; clin. assoc., investigator endocrine sect. metabolism br. NCI, Bethesda, Md., 1977-80; resident dept. medicine Georgetown U. Hosp., Washington, 1980-81, fellow in med. oncology V.T. Lombardi Cancer Ctr., 1981-83; asst. prof. medicine and oncology Howard U. Cancer Ctr., 1983-88, assoc. prof. medicine and oncology, 1988-93; med. officer divsn. oncology drugs and pulmonary products FDA, Rockville, Md., 1987-93, med. officer divsn. oncology drugs, 1993—. Contbr. articles to med. jours. Capt. USAF Res., 1983-91. Recipient Man of Yr. award North Jersey unit Nat. Assn. Negro Business and Profl. Women's Clubs, 1997, Commednable Svc. award FDA, 1996. Fellow ACP (direct); mem. Am. Soc. Clin. Oncology, ACS, Endocrine Soc., NIH Judo Club. Avocations: scuba diving, judo, research for a re-analysis of the Tuskegee Syphillis Study. Home: 12054 Eaglewood Ct Silver Spring MD 20902-1876

WHITE, ROBERT MILES FORD, life insurance company executive; b. Lufkin, Tex., June 9, 1928; s. Sullivan Miles and Faye Clark (Scurlock) F.; m. Mary Ruth Wathen, Nov. 10, 1946; children: Martha, Robert, Benedict, Mary, Jesse, Margaret, Maureen, Thomas. BA, Stephen F. Austin State U., 1948; BBA, St. Mary's U., San Antonio, 1955; MS in Fin. Services, Am. Coll., Bryn Mawr, Pa., 1981, MS in Mgmt., 1986. CLU. Tchr. Douglas (Tex.) Pub. Schs., 1946-47, Houston Pub. Schs., 1948-51; office mgr. Heat Control Insulation Co., San Antonio, 1951-53; acct. S.W. Acceptance Co., San Antonio, 1953-55; sec.-treas. Howell Corp., San Antonio, 1955-64; agt. New Eng. Mut. Life Ins.

Co., San Antonio, 1964-71; br. mgr. Occidental Life Ins. Co. of Calif., San Antonio, 1971-84; gen. agt. Transam. Occidental Life Ins. Co., 1984—. Regional planner Estate Planning for the Disabled; mem. citizens liaison com. San Antonio Ind. Sch. Dist., 1972-78, EEO Coun., 1974-80; Mem. San Antonio Estate Planners Coun., S.W. Pension Conf., Nat., Tex., San Antonio assns. life underwriters, Am. Soc. CLU's., Internat. Assn. Fin. Planners, Gen. Agts. and Mgrs. Assn., Am. Risk and Ins. Assn., Internat. Platform Assn., Tex. Hist. Soc., East Tex. Hist. Soc., San Antonio, S.E. Tex. Geneal. Soc., S.E. Tex. Hist. Soc., Sons of Republic of Tex., SAR, Kappa Pi Sigma. Republican. Roman Catholic. Home: 701 E Sunshine Dr San Antonio TX 78228-2516 Office: 5372 Fredericksburg Rd Ste 114 San Antonio TX 78229-3559

WHITE, ROBERT RANKIN, writer, historian, hydrologist; b. Houston, Feb. 8, 1942; s. Rankin Jones and Eleanor Margaret (White) W. BA in Geology, U. Tex., 1964; MS in Hydrology, U. Ariz., 1971; PhD in Am. studies, U. N.Mex., 1993. Hydrologist Tex. Water Devel. Bd., Austin, 1972-74, U.S. Geol. Survey, Las Cruces, N.Mex., 1974-78, Santa Fe, 1978-80, Albuquerque, 1980-89; writer, historian, 1989—. Mem. planning bd. N.Mex. Art History Conf., Taos, N.Mex., 1987-99. Author: The Lithographs and Etchings of E. Martin Hennings, 1978, The Taos Soc. of Artists, 1983 (rev. edit. 1998); co-author: Pioneer Artists of Taos, 1983, Bert Geer Phillips and The Taos Art Colony, 1994, The New Mexico Painters, 1999; contbr. articles to profl. jours. Bd. dirs. Friends of U. N.Mex. Librs., Albuquerque, 1984-90. With U.S. Army, 1965-68. Mem. NRA (life), Hist. Soc. N.Mex. (pres. 1991-93), N.Mex. Book League (pres. 1994, exec. dir. 1996-2001), Taos County Hist. Soc. Episcopalian. Home and Office: 1409 Las Lomas Rd NE Albuquerque NM 87106-4529

WHITE, ROBERT ROY, retired chemical engineer; b. Bklyn., Mar. 1, 1916; s. Laurance S. and Grace A. (Diffin) W.; m. Elizabeth R. Clark, July 2, 1940; children: Robert Roy, William Wesley, Elizabeth Ann, Margaret. BS, Cooper Union Inst. Tech., 1936; postgrad., Bklyn. Poly. Inst., 1936-37; MS (Horace H. Rackham predoctoral fellow 1938), U. Mich., 1938; PhD, 1941; postgrad., DePaul U. Law Sch., 1940-41, MIT, 1962. Jr. chem. engr. Calco Chem. Co., Bound Brook, N.J., 1936-37; rsch. chem. engr. Dow Chem. Co., 1937-38; chem. engr. Stnd. Oil Co. Calif., 1940, Universal Oil Products Co., 1940-42; faculty U. Mich., 1942-60, prof. chem. engring., 1945-60, assoc. dean Horace H. Rackham Sch. Grad. Studies, 1958-60; assoc. dean U. Mich. Coll. Engring., 1958-60; dir. U. Mich. Inst. Sci. and Tech., 1959-60; v.p., gen. mgr. R & D Atlantic Refining Co., Phila., 1960-62; sr. staff mgmt. svc. divsn. Arthur D. Little, Inc., 1962; v.p. devel. Champion Papers, Inc., Hamilton, Ohio, 1962-66; pres. rsch. divsn. W.R. Grace & Co., 1966-67; dean Sch. Mgmt., Case Western Res. U., Cleve., 1967-71; mng. dir. Karl Kroyer S.A., Denmark, 1970; spl. asst. to pres., dir. forum Nat. Acad. Sci., Washington, 1971-1981. Adj. prof. chem. engring. U. Md., 1982-85, Cath. U. Am., Am. U.; v.p. JC Tech., 1986—; cons. in field. Author: (with others) Unit Operations, 1950; Contbr. articles to profl. jours. Recipient Henry Russell award U. Mich., 1945; teaching award Phi Lambda Upsilon chpt. U. Mich., 1949; sesquicentennial award U. Mich., 1967; prof. award Cooper Union Inst., 1975; McCormack-Freud hon. lectr. Ill. Inst. Tech. Mem.: SAR, AIChE (Jr. award 1945, Presentation award 1951, Profl. Progress award 1956), AAAS, Am. Soc. Engring. Edn. (George Westinghouse award 1955), Am. Chem. Soc., Founders and Patriots Soc., Order Crown of Charlemagne, St. Andrews Soc., Baron Magna Charta, Nat. Yacht Club, Cosmos Club, Iota Alpha, Tau Beta Pi, Phi Kappa Phi, Phi Lambda Upsilon, Alpha Chi Sigma, Sigma Xi. Office: 2440 Virginia Ave NW Washington DC 20037-2601 Fax: 202-467-4002. E-mail: robroy82@erols.com.

WHITE, ROBERT STEPHEN, physics educator; b. Ellsworth, Kans., Dec. 28, 1920; s. Byron F. and Sebina (Leighty) W.; m. Freda Marie Bridgewater, Aug. 30, 1942; children: Nancy Lynn, Margaret Diane, John Stephen, David Bruce. AB, Southwestern Coll., 1942, DSc hon., 1971; MS, U. Ill., 1943; PhD, U. Calif., Berkeley, 1951. Physicist Lawrence Radiation Lab., Berkeley, Livermore, Calif., 1948-61; head dept. particles and fields Space Physics Lab. Aerospace Corp., El Segundo, 1962-67; physics prof. U. Calif., Riverside, 1967-92, dir. Inst. Geophysics and Planetary Physics, 1967-92, chmn. dept. physics, 1970-73, prof. emeritus physics dept., rsch. physicist, 1992—. Lectr. U. Calif., Berkeley, 1953-54, 57-59. Author: Space Physics, 1970, Why Science?, 1998; contbr. articles to profl. jours. Officer USNR, 1944-46. Sr. Postdoctoral fellow NSF, 1961-62; grantee NASA, NSF, USAF, numerous others. Fellow AAAS, Am. Phys. Soc. (exec. com. 1972-74); mem. AAUP, Am. Geophys. Union, Am. Astron. Soc. Home: 5225 Austin Rd Santa Barbara CA 93111-2905 E-mail: stevewhite2@cox.net.

WHITE, ROBERT, JR MCKAY, musician, consultant; s. Robert McKay White; m. Joy Esterson, Dec. 17, 1952; children: James, Tyler. BS in Music Edn., Lebanon Valley Coll., Annville, PA, 1973—77; M. Ed. in Adminstrn. and Supervision, Loyola Coll. in Md., Baltimore, MD, 2000—02. Certificate in Administration and Supervision Md. State Dept of Edn., 2002, Advanced Professional Certificate Md. State Dept of Edn., 1998. Music resource tchr. Howard County Pub. Schools, Ellicott City, Md., 2000—, instrumental music tchr., 1996—2002, fine arts resource tchr., 1993—96, instrumental music tchr., 1978—93. Cons. / item writer Westat, Rockville, Md., 2002—02. Recipient Finalist for the Music Educator of the Yr., Howard County Parents for Sch. Music, 1997. Mem.: Howard County Edn. Assn., ASCD. Home: 3310 Oakwood Drive New Windsor MD 21776 Office: Howard County Public Schools 10910 Route 108 Ellicott City MD 21042 Personal E-mail: rwhite@mail.howard.k12.md.us. E-mail: rwhite@mail.howard.k12.md.us.

WHITE, ROBERTA LEE, financial analyst; b. Denver, Sept. 18, 1946; d. Harold Tindall and Araminta (Campbell) Bangs; m. Lewis Paul White, Jr., Jan. 23, 1973 (div. Sept. 1974). BA cum laude, Linfield Coll., 1976; postgrad., Lewis and Clark Coll. Lic. tax preparer, Oreg. Office mgr. Multnomah County Auditor, Portland, Oreg., 1977-81; rsch. asst. Dan Goldy and Assocs., 1981-83; regional asst. Vocat. Rehab., Eugene, Oreg., 1983-85; internal auditor Multnomah County, Portland, 1985-89; cons., 1989-91; fin. analyst City of Portland, 1991-93; comptroller Wordsmith Svcs., Portland, 1993-97; fin. analyst City of Portland, 1997—. Mem. Com. for Implementation of the ADA, Portland, 1991-93. Treas. Mary Wendy Roberts for Sec. of State, Portland, 1992, Re-Elect Mary Wendy Roberts, Portland, 1990, Elect Hank Miggins Com., 1994; mem. Oreg. Women's Polit. Caucus, Portland, 1982-85, City Club, Portland, 1978-81. Democrat. Mem. Christian Ch. (Disciples Of Christ). Avocations: reading, hiking, opera, symphony, ballet. Home: 1620 NE Irving St Apt 80 Portland OR 97232-2244 Office: City of Portland Office of Mgmt/Fin Facil Svcs Divsn Rm 1204 1204 1120 SW 5th Ave Portland OR 97204-1912

WHITE, ROGER BRADLEY, priest; b. Chgo., Feb. 13, 1952; s. Alfred Harry and Mildred Alfrida (Bergstrom) W. AB, U. Ill., 1974; MA, Yale U., 1976, MPhil, 1977, MA in Religion, 1979. Ordained Deacon Episcopal Ch., 1982, ordained priest, 1983. Lectr. in history Yale U., New Haven, 1978-82, asst. dean Berkeley Divinity Sch., 1981-82; curate Ch. of the Holy Spirit, Lake Forest, Ill., 1982-85; rector St. Andrew's Parish, Kent, Conn., 1985—. Sec. bd. trustees Berkeley Divinity Sch. at Yale, 1991-99; sec. bd. mgrs. Ch. Missions Pub. Co., Hartford, Conn., 1991—; mem. scholarship rev. com. Soc. for Increase of the Ministry, Hartford, 1997—; chair com. of examining chaplains Diocese of Conn., Hartford, 1990-97. Author: (meditations) Day By Day, 1997; editor: Ultra jour., 1988-90; book rev. editor Conn. Diocesan Newspaper, Hartford, 1990-95. Pres. bd. trustees Greenwoods Counseling Svcs., Litchfield, Conn., 1992-96; bd. dirs. Kent Affordable Housing, 1990—; chaplain coord. Litchfield County Jail, 1988-93; trustee Oratory of the Little Way, Gaylordsville, Conn., 1987-92. Mem. Elizabethan Club Yale U., Hist. Soc. of Episcopal Ch., Phi Beta Kappa. Avocations: reading, walking, music, cooking. Office: St Andrew's Parish PO Box 309 Kent CT 06757-0309

WHITE, ROGER L., JR. graphic designer, art director; b. Ft. Lauderdale, Fla., Feb. 16, 1961; s. Roger Lee and Bonnie Sue (Brooks) White. Cert. in Art History, Am. Coll. Paris, 1982; BFA, Parsons Sch. of Design, 1983. Designer, art dir. Late Show with David Letterman, N.Y.C., 1985—; art dir. Late Night with David Letterman, 1993—; illustrator Saturday Night Live, 1987-94, N.Y. Times, 1993; designer Between the Lions PBS, N.Y.C., 1999—, Court TV, N.Y.C., 1999; illustrator Newsweek Mag., 1999—; web designer Uproar.com, 1997-98. Instr. The Mac Learning Ctr., N.Y.C., 2001-2002, Tony Randal's Nat. Actors Theatre, N.Y.C., 1997-99. Prin. works include theater marquee Ed Sullivan Theater, 1993, logo design Late Show with David Letterman, 1993, 5 Questions, Title Animation, Late Late Show with Craig Koilborn, CBS, 2001. Recipient Emmy Contribution award Acad. TV Arts & Scis., 1986, 87; nominee Emmy award, 1994. Mem. Assn. for Computing Machinery, Art Students League, Broadcast Designers Assn. Avocations: painting, skiing. Office: White Lie Design 160 W End Ave Apt 3K New York NY 10023-5603 E-mail: whiteLied_2000@yahoo.com.

WHITE, RONALD JOSEPH, life and biomedical scientist, physiology educator; b. Opelousas, La., Dec. 4, 1940; s. John Wesley and Alma Louise (La Salle) W.; m. Margaret Helen Launey, June 8, 1963; children: Joseph La Salle, Angela Alma, Margaret Leslie. BS in Chemistry, U. S.W. La., 1963; PhD in Phys. Chemistry, U. Wis., 1968. NSF postdoctoral fellow in theoretical chemistry U. Oxford, Eng., 1967-68; rsch. assoc. Bell Tel. Labs., Murray Hill, N.J., 1968-70; from asst. prof. to assoc. prof. math. U. S.W. La., Lafayette, 1970—76, prof. math., dir. Univ. Honors Program, 1976—80; rsch. assoc. dept. physiology and biophysics U. Miss. Med. Ctr., Jackson, 1973-75; sr. scientist GE Co./Mgmt. and Tech. Svcs. Co., Washington and Houston, 1980-85; chief scientist Life/Biomed. Scis. and Applications Divsn. NASA Life/Biomed. Scis. and Applications Divsn. NASA Hdqs., Washington, 1985—96; rsch. prof. physiology Uniformed Svcs. U. Health Scis., Bethesda, Md., 1985—96; prof. dept. otorhinolaryngology Baylor Coll. Medicine, Houston, 1996—; assoc. dir. Nat. Space Biomed. Rsch. Inst., 1997—. Editor (assoc. life scis.): Simulation, 1974—75; editor: (spl.) Medicine and Sci. in Sports and Exercise, 1996; contbr. numerous chpts. to books, papers to profl. jours. Vice pres. Assn. Gifted and Talented Students, La, 1977-80; pres. La. Collegiate Honors Coun., 1978-79. Recipient NASA traineeship, 1963-66, Woodrow Wilson fellowship (hon.), 1963, Am. Inst. Chemists award, 1963, Med. Info. Processing Best Paper award 15th ann. Hawaii Internat. Conf. on Systems Scis., 1982, Hon. Mem. award Soc. NASA Flight Surgeons, 1992, Exceptional Achievement medal NASA, 1992. Mem.: Internat. Acad. Astronautics (bd. trustees 1997—, chair life scis. 2001—, commr. space life scis. 2001—), Am. Soc. for Gravitational and Space Biology (charter mem.), Am. Phys. Soc., Aerospace Med. Assn., Sigma Xi (rsch. award 1976), Phi Kappa Phi. Home: 1303 Primrose Ln Seabrook TX 77586-4718 Office: NSBRI One Baylor Plz NA 425 Houston TX 77030

WHITE, RONALD LEON, financial management consultant; b. West York, Pa., July 14, 1930; s. Clarence William and Grace Elizabeth (Gingerich) W.; m. Estheranne Wieder, June 16, 1951; children: Bradford William, Clifford Allen, Erick David. BS in Econs, U. Pa., 1952, MBA, 1957. Cost analysis supr. Air Products & Chem. Corp., Allentown, Pa., 1957-60; cost control mgr. Mack Trucks, Inc., 1960-64; mgmt. cons. Peat, Marwick, Mitchell & Co., Phila., 1964-66; mgr. profit planning Monroe, The Calculator Co. (divsn. Litton Industries), Orange, N.J., 1966-67, contr., 1967-68; v.p. fin. Bus. Sys. Group of Litton Industries, Beverly Hills, Calif., 1968-70; pres. Royal Typewriter Co. divsn., Hartford, Conn., 1970-73; exec. v.p., COO, treas., dir. Tenna Corp., Cleve., 1973-75, pres., dir., 1975-77; v.p. fin. Arby's, Inc., Youngstown, 1978-79; exec. v.p., dir. Roxbury Am., Inc., 1979-81; v.p. fin., treas. Royal Crown Cos., Inc., Atlanta and Miami Beach, Fla., 1981-86, TDS Healthcare Sys. Corp., Atlanta, 1987-88; v.p. Corp. Fin. Assocs., 1988-90; prin. The Janelle Co., 1991—. Vice chmn. Ga. Mental Health, Mental Retardation, Substance Abuse Regional Bd. #6, 1994-2002, chmn. leadership coun., 1999-2000; v.p. and dir. Ga. Alliance for Mentally Ill, 1997—; instr. acctg. Wharton Sch. U. Pa., 1952-53, instr. industry, 1953-54. Deacon area United Ch. of Christ. Lt. USNR, 1954-57. Mem. Am. Mgmt. Assn., Inst. Mgmt. Accts., Nat. Assn. Corp. Dirs., Fin. Execs. Internat., Acacia, Masons, Rotary. Office: The Janelle Co 2362 Kingsgate Ct Atlanta GA 30338-5931 E-mail: rlwcfo@mindspring.com.

WHITE, RONNIE L. state supreme court justice; AA, St. Louis C.C., 1977; BA, St. Louis U., 1979; JD, U. Mo., Kansas City, 1983. Bar: Mo. Law intern Jackson County Prosecutors Office; legal asst. U.S. Def. Mapping Agy.; trial atty. Office of Pub. Defender; mem. Mo. Ho. of Reps., 1989-93; judge Mo. Ct. Appeals, 1994; spl. judge Mo. Supreme Ct., 1994-95, justice, 1994-95, assoc. justice, 1995—. Adj. faculty Washington U. Sch. Law, 1997—. Office: PO Box 150 Jefferson City MO 65102-0150*

WHITE, ROY BERNARD, theater executive; b. Cin. s. Maurice and Anna (Rudin) W.; m. Sally Lee Ostrom, June 17, 1951; children: Maurice Ostrom, Barbara Dee, Daniel Robert. BA, U. Cin., 1949. Formerly mem. sales staff Twentieth Century Fox Films, Cin.; now pres. Mid-States Theatres; dir. Nat. Assn. Theatre Owners, nat. pres., exec. com., chmn. bd. Mem. film adv. panel Ohio Arts Coun.; bd. dirs. Will Rogers Meml. Fund, Found. Motion Picture Pioneers, Inc.; mem. media arts panel Nat. Endowment for Arts. Served with USAAF, 1944-45. Named Exhibitor of Year Internat. Film Importers and Distbrs. Am. Mem. Nat. Assn. Theater Owners (pres.), Am. Film Inst. (trustee 1972-75, exec. com. 1972-75), Fedn. Motion Picture Pioneers (v.p.), Masons, Queen City Racquet, Amberley Village (Ohio) Tennis Club (pres. 1972-73), Bankers Club, Quail Creek Country Club, Bay Colony Country Club, Bay Colony Golf Club. Home: 1274 Waggle Way Naples FL 34108-1994

WHITE, SARAH JOWILLIARD, counselor; b. Oxford, N.C., Sept. 1, 1921; d. John Hiriam and Emma (Redfern) Isham; m. Hamilton B. Carson, Sept. 20, 1945 (div. 1968); 1 child, Lynne Denise. Student, Bennett Coll., 1939-42, Cornell U., 1979-82; BA, CCNY, 1973. Clk. N.Y. Dept. Law, N.Y.C., 1948-53; auditor U.S. Fed. Govt. Svc., 1955-62; postal clk. U.S. Govt., Mt. Vernon, N.Y., 1963-66; prin. N.Y. State Dept. Labor, 1966-88, ret., 1988; youth organizer N.Y. State Careerists Soc., Inc., N.Y.C., 1989—. Youth and employment counselor Women in Community Svc., Nat. Coun. Negro Women, Manhattan sect., N.Y.C., 1983—. Vol. Advanced Vocation Edn. Day, Albany, N.Y., 1988; vol., coord. Decade of the Youth, N.Y.C., 1989-90; corres. sec. Lower East Side United Neighbors, N.Y.C., 1989. Recipient Youth award, 1987, Recognition award, 1987, Internat. Assn. Pers. Employees Youth award, Plaque for Women in Cmty. Svcs., Outstanding Vol. Svc. award Gov. Mario Cuomo, 1994, Outstanding Vol. award, 1991-92, Outstanding Vol. award Women in Cmty. Svc., 1994, Cert. Appreciation, 1995, Appreciation award South Bronx Job Alumni chpt., 1995, Nat. Coun. Negro Women Recognition award, 1996; named one of N.Y.'s Finest Vols. Women in Cmty. Svcs. Mag., 1994, Woman on the Move, Cable TV, 1994, Outstanding Recognition award Women in Cmty. Svcs., 1996, Joint Action in Cmty. Svc. award, 1996, Nat. N.E. Regional award Women in Cmty. Svcs., 1997, Youth Recognition award Yale U., New Haven, 1997, award Joint Action in Cmty. Svc., 1997, N.E. Regional Pres. Vol. award, 1998, JAC Recognition award, 1998, Horthers Regional award, 1998, Nat. Coun. Negro Women Pres.'s award, 1998, 99, Cert., Women in Cmty. Svc. Northeast Regional Pres. award, 1998, Nat. Coun. Negro Women Pres. award, 1998, Joint Action Cmty. Svc. award, 1998, 99, Nat. Pres.'s award Women in Cmty. Svc., 1999, Samuel and May Rudin Cmty. Svc. award NYU, 1999. Mem. NAFE, N.Y. Careerists Soc. (sec., Merit award 1988), Assn. U.S. Govt. Job Corps. (alumni recognition award 1995), Nat. Coun. Negro Women (chairperson, Achievement award 1988-90), Internat. Assn. Pers. Employees, Black Alumni CCNY (pub. rels. com., outstanding award 1989). Democrat. 7th Day Sabbath Keeper House of God. Avocations: reading, writing, music.

WHITE, SHANON KATHLEEN, accountant, consultant; b. Hackensack, NJ, July 25, 1953; d. Patrick William Carr, Trudy McFarland; m. Chester Haines White, II; children: Tiffany. Associate of Arts in Accounting, Community College of Aurora, Aurora, Colorado, 1982—84. Acct. Denver Cascade, Inc, Denver, 1984—86, MDC, Inc, Denver, 1986—86; owner Jacqueline, Too, 1986—86; contr. Michael's Constrn. Co., Kansas City, Kans., 1987—87; acctg. mgr., system mgr. Walton Constrn. Co, Inc, Mo., 1987—93; owner Profit Enhancement Profls., Olathe, Kans., 1993—98; acctg. mgr. Mark One Electric Co, Inc, Kansas City, Mo., 1998—99; owner Shanon White Cons., 1999—2002. Selection Committee Kansas City Fairness in Construction Board, Kansas City, MO, 1991—92; Board President Greater Kansas City NAWIC Scholarship Foundation, Kansas City, MO, 1992—95. Treasurer Romanelli West Homes Association, Kansas City, MO, 1999—2002. Mem.: Nat. Assn. of Women in Constrn. (pres. 1991—92), Greater Kansas City Timberline Users Group (organizer, local coord. 2001—02). Avocation: Traveling, Dining, Reading. Office: Shanon White Consulting 10500 Meadow Ln Leawood KS 66206 Business E-Mail: scarrwhite@earthlink.net.

WHITE, SIDNEY HOWARD, English educator; b. Bangor, Maine, Aug. 29, 1923; s. Benjamin and Sadie (Sedoff) W.; m. Phyllis Evelyn Siegel, June 4, 1950 (div. Apr. 1982); children: Michael, Benjamin, Susan, Deborah; m. Pauline Elaine Allen, Oct. 22, 1982. BS, Loyola U., 1950; MA, U. So. Calif., 1951, PhD, 1962. Assoc. prof. English Marymount Coll., L.A., 1953-66; prof. English UCLA, 1962-66, U. R.I., Kingston, 1966-93. Vis. prof. English U. Victoria, B.C., 1965. Author: Critical Study of The Scarlet Letter, 1967, Critical Study of The Great Gatsby, 1968, Arthur Miller, 1970, Sidney Howard, 1977, Alan Ayckbourn, 1984; editor, reviewer books; advisor Norton Anthology of American Literature, 3d edit.; contbr. articles to profl. jours. Fundraiser March of Dimes, L.A., 1951-61. With U.S. Army, 1942-46, USAF, 1950. Mem. MLA. Republican. Avocations: music, gardening, tennis. Home: 34 Terrace Dr East Greenwich RI 02818-2527

WHITE, STANLEY ARCHIBALD, research electrical engineer; b. Providence, Sept. 25, 1931; s. Clarence Archibald White and Lou Ella (Givens) Arford; m. Edda María Castaño-Benítez, June 6, 1956; children: Dianne, Stanley Jr., Paul, John. BSEE, Purdue U., 1957, MSEE, 1959, PhD, 1965. Registered profl. engr., Ind., Calif. Engr. Rockwell Internat., Anaheim, Calif., 1959-68, mgr., 1968-84, sr. scientist, 1984-90; pres. Signal Processing and Controls Engring. Corp., 1990-99; ind. cons., 2000—. Adj. prof. elec. engring. U. Calif., 1984-97; cons. and lectr. in field; bd. dirs. Asilomar Signals, Systems and Computers Conf. Corp. Contbr. chpts. to books; articles to profl. jours.; patentee in field. With USAF, 1951-55. N.Am. Aviation Sci. Engring. fellow, 1963-65; recipient Disting. Lectr. award Nat. Electronics Conf., Chgo., 1973, Engr. of Yr. award Orange County (Calif.) Engring. Coun., 1984, Engr. of Yr. award Rockwell Internat., 1985, Leonardo da Vinci Medallion, 1986, Sci. Achievement award, 1987, Disting. Engring. Alumnus award Purdue U., 1988, Meritorious Inventor's award Rockwell Internat. Corp., 1989, Outstanding Elec. Engr. award Purdue U., 1992, Boeing N. Am. Aviation Top Inventor award, 1998. Fellow AAAS (life), AIAA, IEEE (life, Centennial medalist Millenium medalist, chair of ICASSP and ISCAS, Signal Processing Soc. disting. lect. and founding chmn. L.A. coun. chpt., Circuits and Sys. Soc. Tech. Achievement award 1996, Golden Jubilee medal 1999), Inst. for Advancement Engring., N.Y. Acad. Scis. (life); mem. VFW (life), Air Force Assn. (life), Am. Legion (life), Sigma Xi (life, founding pres. Orange County chpt., pres. 1988-2000), Eta Kappa Nu (disting. fellow, internat. dir. emeritus), Tau Beta Pi. Avocation: choral music. Home: 433 E Avenida Cordoba San Clemente CA 92672-2350 E-mail: stan.white@ieee.org.

WHITE, STEPHEN HALLEY, biophysicist, educator; b. Wewoka, Okla., May 14, 1940; s. James Halley and Gertrude June (Wyatt) W.; m. Buff Ertl, Aug. 20, 1961 (div. 1982); children: Saill, Shell, Storn, Sharr, Skye, Sunde; m. Jackie Marie Dooley, Apr. 14, 1984. BS in Physics, U. Colo., 1963; MS in Physics, U. Wash., 1965, PhD in Physiology and Biophysics, 1969. USPHS postdoctoral fellow biochemistry U. Va., Charlottesville, 1971-72; asst. prof. physiology and biophysics U. Calif., Irvine, 1972-75, assoc. prof. physiology and biophysics, 1975-78, prof. physiology and biophysics, 1978—, vice chmn. physiology and biophysics, 1974-75, chmn. physiology and biophysics, 1977-89. Guest biophysicist Brookhaven Nat. Lab., Upton, L.I., N.Y., 1977-99. Contbr. numerous articles to profl. jours. Served to capt. USAR, 1969-71. Recipient Research Career Devel. award USPHS, 1975-80, Kaiser-Permanente Tchg. award, 1975, 92; fellow Biophysical Soc., 2002; grantee NIH, 1971—, NSF, 1971—. Mem. NSF (adv. panel for molecular biology 1982-85, mem. nat. steering com. advanced neutron source 1992-95), Internat. Union Pure and Applied Biophysics (U.S. nat. com. 1997—, chmn. 2000—), Fedn. Am. Soc. for Exptl. Biology (bd. dirs. 1998-2002), Biophys. Soc. (chmn. membrane biophysics subgroup 1977-78, acting sec., treas. 1979-80, coun. 1981-84, exec. bd. 1981-83, program chmn. 1985, ann. meeting sec. 1987-95, pres. 1996-97, Disting. Svc. award 1999), Am. Physiol. Soc. (editl. bd. 1981-93, membership com. 1985-86, publ. com. 1987-91), Assn. Chmn. Depts. Physiology (rep. to coun. acad. socs. 1981-82, councilor 1982-83, pres. 1986-87), Soc. Gen. Physiologists (treas. 1985-88), The Protein Soc. (electronic pub. coord. 1993—). Avocations: skiing, cooking, travel. Office: U Calif Dept Physiology & Biophysics Med Sci I-D346 Irvine CA 92697-4560

WHITE, SUSAN ROCHELLE, psychologist, real estate investor; b. Highland Park, Mich., Jan. 23, 1957; d. John Tyree and Jayne Rochelle White. BA, U. Mich., 1979; MS, Ea. Mich. U., 1990. Lic. psychologist, Mich. Disability examiner State of Mich. - Dept. Social Svcs., Southfield, Mich., 1980-88, group leader Whitmore Lake, 1988-92; case mgr. State of Mich. - Dept. Mental Health, Mt. Clements, 1992-93; group leader State of Mich. Family Ind. Agy., Whitmore Lake, 1993-94, psychologist, 1994—. Rschr.: Aggression Replacement Training, 1998. Mem. APA (assoc.), Mich. Women Psychologists. Avocations: guitar, racquetball, biking, animal training, rental property renovation. Office: Family Ind Agy PO Box 349 Whitmore Lake MI 48189-0349 E-mail: WhiteS3@State.MI.US.

WHITE, SUSIE MAE, school psychologist; b. Madison, Fla., Mar. 5, 1914; d. John Anderson and Lucy (Crawford) Williams; m. Daniel Elijah White, Oct. 20, 1958 (dec. Sept. 29, 1968). BS, Fla. Meml. Coll., St. Augustine, 1948; MEd, U. Md., 1953; postgrad., Mich. State U., 1955, Santa Fe Community Coll., 1988; Cert. Child Care Supervision, W.T. Loften Edn. Ctr., Gainesville, Fla., 1994. Elem. tchr. Grove Park (Fla.) Elem. Sch., 1943; tchr. Douglas High Sch., High Springs, Fla., 1944-55; sch. psychologist Alachua County Sch. Bd., Gainesville, 1956-69, coord. social svcs., 1970; owner, dir. Mother Dear's Child Care Ctr., 1988—. Author: Determined--in spite of...Autobiography of Susie Mae Williams White, 1998, Lord, Fix Me Inspirational Poems, 2000. Del. Bapt. World Alliance, Bapt. Conv. Fla., Tokyo, 1970; state dir. leadership Fla. Bapt. Gen. Conv., 1971-85. Recipient Cert. of Appreciation, Fla. State Dept. Edn., 1971, Appreciation for Disting. Svc. award, Fla. Gen. Bapt. Conv., 1979, Hall of Fame award, Martin Luther King Jr. Hall of Fame, 1994, Cert. Appreciation for Outstanding Svc. & Leadership, Mt. Sinai Woman's Conv., 1997, The Susie Mae White scholarship fund established, Mt. Sinai Congress Christian Edn., 1995, Cert. Appreciation, Friendship Bapt. Ch., 2000, Deloris Keith Meml. Good Neighbor award, East Gainesville Devel. Task Force, Inc., 1999, Trophy for Being Inspiration to Young Women, Alachua Pratical Academic Cultural Edn. Ctr. for Girls, Inc., 2001, Plaque for Appreciation of 60 Yrs. of Svc., Friendship Baptist Ch., 2001, Plaque for Appreciation of Leadership & Dedication to Cmty., Faith Tabernacle of Praise Mins., Inc., 2001. Mem. Nat. Ret. Tchrs. Assn., Alachua County Tchrs. Assn., Fla. Meml. Coll. Nat. Alumni Assn., AAUW, Heroines of Jerico, Masons. Democrat. Avocations: gardening, speaking, working with police on crime prevention. Office: Child Care Ctr 811 NW 4th Pl Gainesville FL 32601-5049

WHITE, TERRENCE HAROLD, academic administrator, sociologist; b. Ottawa, Ont., Canada, Mar. 31, 1943; s. William Harold and Shirley Margaret (Ballantine) W.; m. Susan Elizabeth Hornaday; children: Christine Susan, Julie Pamela. PhD, U. Toronto, 1972. Head dept. sociology and anthropology U. Windsor, Ont., Can., 1973-75; prof., chmn. dept. sociology U. Alta., Edmonton, 1975-80, dean faculty of arts, 1980-88; pres. T.H. White Orgn. Research Services Ltd., 1975—, Brock U., St. Catharines, Ont., 1988-96, U. Calgary, Alta., 1996—; dir. Labatt's Brewing Alta., Edmonton, 1981-88. Author: Power or Pawns: Boards of Directors, 1978, Human Resource Management, 1979; editor: Introduction to Work Science, 1981, QWL in Canada: Case Studies, 1983. Bd. dirs. Progressive Conservative Assn., Edmonton South, 1976-81, 1st v.p., 1981-85, pres., 1985-87; bd. dirs. Tri-Bach Festival Found., Edmonton, 1981-88, Alta. Ballet Co., 1985-88, Edmonton Conv. and Tourism Authority, Arch Enterprises, 1984-88, Niagara Symphony Soc., YMCA, St. Catharines, 1988-92; chair United Way Campaign St. Catharines, 1992, Fox Found., 1990-96, Canada Summer Games 2001 Bid Com.; bd. dirs. Edmonton Symphony Soc., v.p., 1986-88; bd. govs. U. Alta., 1984-88, Brock U., 1988-96, Ridley Coll., 1990—, Alberta Heritage Found. for Med. Rsch.; mem. Calgary R&D Authority, 1997; divsn. chair Calgary United Way Campaign, Calgary Econ. Devel. Authority, 1997—. Recipient Can. 125 Commemorative medal, Govt. of Can. Mem. Calgary Petroleum Club, Ranchmen's Club, Rotary (pres. Edmonton South 1981-82), Delta Tau Kappa, Alpha Kappa Delta Home: Box 68028 28 Crowfoot Terr NW Calgary AB Canada T3G 3N8 Office: U Calgary 2500 University Dr NW Calgary AB Canada T2N 1N4

WHITE, TERRY JOE, writer, editor; b. Kansas City, Kans., June 3, 1953; s. Delmar Alonso and Joan Lorraine (Crystal) White; m. Susan Jane Kuntz, June 23, 1979; 1 child Claire Lorraine. BS in Journalism, U. Kans., 1975; MA in Journalism, U. Md., 1980. Editor Forte, Inc., Alexandria, Va., 1976-78; pub.

info. dir.Dept. Health, Mental Retardation City of Alexandria, 1978-80; pub. rels. acct. exec. Henry J. Kaufman & Assocs., Washington, 1980-83; pres. T&S White Co., Burke, Va., 1982—. Author: (book) Newspapers and Real Estate- The New Realities, 1996, Make the Right Moves, 1997; editor: (book) Keep 'Em Coming Back, 1997. Recipient Grad. Rsch. assistantship U. Md., 1980, Best Feature article, Profl. Ins. Comm. of Am., 1984, Best Ann. report Am. Soc. Assn. Execs., 1998. Mem. Washington Ind. Writers. Democrat. Avocations: reading, hiking, swimming, tennis. Office: T&S White Co 9104 Blue Jug Lndg Burke VA 22015-2107 E-mail: twhite-writer@att.net.

WHITE, THOMAS DAVID, II, academic administrator; b. Pittsburg, Kans., Sept. 19, 1946; s. Thomas David and Audrey Marie (Parrish) White; m. Jacquelyn Lee Trone; children from previous marriage: Thomas David III(dec.) , Phillip Edward. AA, Valley Forge Mil. Coll., 1967; BA, North Ga. Coll., 1969; postgrad., Pa. State U., 1978-82. Cert. adminstr., vol. svcs. Assn. Vol. Adminstrs. Dist. scout exec. Boy Scouts Am., Phila., 1969-72; vol. resource coord. Norristown (Pa.) State Hosp., 1972-74; assoc. dir. vol. resources Pennhurst Ctr., Spring City, 1974-79; dir. vol. resources Embreeville State Hosp., Coatesville, 1979-81; dir. alumni affairs and constituent rels. Valley Forge Mil. Acad., Wayne, 1981-85; assoc. univ. dir. alumni rels. Rutgers U., Newark, 1985-90; exec. dir. alumni rels. George Washington U., Washington, 1990-93; exec. dir. Nat. Assn. for Artisans and Craftsmen, Audubon, Pa., 1993-97; dean continuing edn. Montgomery County C.C., West Campus, 1997-2001; dir. alumni rels. Albright Coll., 2001—. Adj. faculty Pa. State U., 1975—76; sr. cons., co-founder Cons. Cmty., Phila., 1976—82; founder, pres. AADM Assocs., Wayne, Pa., 1983—90; prin. ptnr. Colonial Yard, 1984—. Contbr. articles to profl. publs.; author: profl. manuals; designer 18th and 19th century garden design, Early Am. Homes Mag., 1997. Sec. Roboda Cmty. Assn., Royersford, Pa., 1981—83; mem. Lower Providence Twp. Planning Commn., 1998—2002; chmn. Lower Providence Twp. Traffic Impact Com., 1999—2001; exec. com., v.p. Cornerstone of the Arts, Inc., Pottstown, Pa., 1997—99; bd. dirs. Women's Ctr. Montgomery County, 1998—2001. Mem.: Assn. Voluntary Action Scholars, Nat. Assn. Ind. Schs., Assn. Vol. Adminstrs., Coun. Advancement and Support Edn., VFMA Soc. Golden Sword (knight), Valley Forge Mil. Acad. Alumni Assn. (bd. dirs. exec. com. 1982—90), Rutgers Club (trustee 1985—90). Republican. Avocations: American antiques, woodcarving, 19th Century landscaping, folk art, antique weapons. Home: 500 S Park Ave Audubon PA 19403-1921 Office: Albright Coll Alumni Rels PO Box 15234 Reading PA 19612-5234 E-mail: twhite@alb.edu.

WHITE, THOMAS E. federal agency administrator; Degree in ops. rsch., Naval Postgrad. Sch., Monterey, Calif., 1974; postgrad., U.S. Army War Coll., 1984; grad., U.S. Mil. Acad., 1967. Commd. 2d lt. U.S. Army, 1967, advanced through grades to brigadier gen., 1990, ret., 1990; various sr. exec. positions Enron, 1990—2001; sec. of Army Dept. Def., Washington, 2001—. Office: US Dept Def Sec of Army 101 Army Pentagon Washington DC 20310-0101*

WHITE, THOMAS EDWARD, lawyer; b. N.Y.C., July 11, 1933; s. Thomas Aubrey and Gladys Mary (Piper) W.; m. Joan Carolyn Olsen, Dec. 2, 1967 (dec.); children: Charles Garret, Nancy Carolyn, Linda Marie, Penelope Lindsay, Elizabeth Ann. AB, Princeton U., 1955; LLB, Columbia U., 1960; BA summa cum laude, SUNY-Purchase Coll., 2002; student, NYU Inst. Fine Arts, 2002—. Bar: N.Y. 1961. Atty. Seward & Kissel, N.Y.C., 1960-69; gen. counsel Howmet Corp., 1969-70; v.p., gen. counsel, sec. Howmedica, Inc., 1970-74, sr. v.p., dir., 1974-83; pvt. practice N.Y.C., 1983-97. Ptnr. Westmed Venture Ptnrs. (formerly Integrated Med. Venture Ptnrs.), N.Y.C., 1987-99; chmn. Shoreside Cons. Ltd., Miami, Fla., 1987-98. Mem. Mamaroneck Town Coun., 1971-75; mem. vestry Episcopalian Ch., 1987-90; mem. diocesan coun. Episcopal Ch. N.Y., 2001--. Served to 1st lt. U.S. Army, 1955-57. Mem.: Larchmont (N.Y.) Yacht; Princeton (N.Y.C.). Republican. Home: 260 Barnard Rd Larchmont NY 10538-1941

WHITE, THOMAS RAEBURN, III, law educator, consultant; b. Phila., Aug. 18, 1938; s. Thomas Raeburn Jr. and Charlotte (Gerhard) W.; m. Margaret Bardwell, Dec. 12, 1960 (div. June 1975); children: Elizabeth Krusenstjerna, Kathleen White, Thomas Ray IV; m. Maria Llanes, Oct. 19, 1975. BA, Williams Coll., 1960; LLB, U. Pa., 1963. Bar: Pa. 1964, Va. 1971. Assoc. White and Williams, Phila., 1963-65; atty.-advisor TLC U.S. Treasury Dept., Washington, 1965-67; assoc. prof. U. Va., Charlottesville, 1967-70, prof. law, 1970-96, John C. Stennis prof., 1996—. Legis. atty. Joint Com. on Tax U.S. Congress, Washington, 1973-75; cons. adminstrn. conf. IRS Project, Washington, 1975-76; vis. prof. NYU Law Sch., N.Y.C., 1978-79. Mem. ABA (com. chmn. tax sect. 1987-87, 96-98), Am. Coll. Tax Counsel, Va. Bar Assn., Va. State Bar Assn., Phila. Bar Assn., Charlottesville-Albemarle Bar Assn. Home: 12 Deer Path Charlottesville VA 22903-4707 Office: U Va Sch Law 580 Massie Rd Charlottesville VA 22903-1738 Office Fax: 434-982-2079. Business E-Mail: trw@virginia.edu. E-mail: bus.trw@virginia.edu.

WHITE, THOMAS S. lawyer; b. Sharon, Pa., Aug. 27, 1949; s. Herbert F. and Ruth J. W.; m. Linda K. Clark, May 12, 1973; children: Kimberly, Nicholas. BA, Case Western Reserve U., 1973; JD, Gonzaga U., 1976. Bar: Wash. 1980, U.S. Dist. Ct. (we. dist.) Wash. 1983, U.S. Dist. Ct. (we. dist.) Pa. 1983, U.S. Ct. Appeals (3rd cir.) 1983. Legal advisor Spokane Legal Svcs., Wash., 1977; revenue officer State of Wash., Everett, 1979-80; dep. pros. atty. Snohomish County, 1980; postal insp. U.S. Postal Svc., Pa., W.V., 1981-84, regional insp. atty., 1984-85, insp. atty., nat. money laundering advisor Washington, 1985-93, insp. atty. Seattle divsn. Seattle, 1993—2001; corp. investigator Amazon.com, 2002—. Active Spotsylvania County Boy Scouts, Fredericksburg, Va., 1988-89; trustee Peace United Meth. Ch., Fredricksburg, 1988-89. Recipient Meritorious Svc. honor award U.S. Postal Svc., 1988, 90-91, Spl. Achievement award, 1988, 93, 97, Dirs. award FBI, 2000, U.S. Attys. award, 2001. Mem. ABA (criminal justice sect.), Wash. State Bar Assn. Methodist. Avocations: gardening, fishing, camping. Office: Amazon.com PO Box 81226 1200 12th Ave South Seattle WA 98108-1226

WHITE, TIMOTHY PAUL, brokerage house executive; b. Ft. Sill, Okla., Jan. 9, 1963; s. Paul R. and Lucille (Mattison) White; m. Susan Gertrude Foreman, Dec. 29, 1984; children: Jessica Lynn, Rebecca Anne, Kathleen Marie. BS in Fin., Pa. State U., 1985. Cert. fin. planner Colo. Assoc. planner, agt. Pa. Fin. Group, Harrisburg, Pa., 1988-92; mgr. mktg. and sales Meridian Securities, Inc., Reading, 1992-96; v.p. products and sales mgr. Core States Securities Corp., 1996-98; regional sales mgr. First Union Brokerage Svcs. Inc., 1998-2001; fin. advisor First Union Securities Inc., 2001—; pres. Investors Ctrl. Comm. Inc.; mng. dir. Guidon, LLC, 2001—. Spkr. Nat. Mut. Fund Conf., 1995, Cmty. Bank Investment Program Symposium, 1996, Nat. Investment Products Conf., 1996. Contbg. editor: Bank Securities Jour.; contbr. articles to profl. jours. Program cons. Jr. Achievement, Lancaster, Pa., 1990—91; pres. Adamstown Recreation Bd., 1996. 1st lt. U.S. Army, 1985—88, with USAR, 1989—92. Decorated Commendation medal, Achievement medal; recipient George C. Marshal award, U.S. Army, 1985; scholar ROTC, 1980—84. Mem.: Ctrl. Pa. Soc. Inst. CFP (bd. dirs. 1996—, pres.-elect 1998, pres. 1999), U.S. Cav. Assn. (fundraising com. 1994—96), Inst. CFP. Republican. Lutheran. Avocations: military and political history, reading, gardening, woodworking. Office: Wachovia Securities Inc 12 E Market St York PA 17401

WHITE, TOM WILLINGHAM, private investor; b. McAllen, Tex., Feb. 16, 1943; s. Louis Thomas and Leota Faye (Grimm) W.; m. Lauryn G. Longwell, Mar. 8, 1968; children: Brad Edward, Parker Thomas, Landon Allen. BBA, U. Tex., 1965. Acct. Haskins & Sells, CPAs, Houston, 1965-67, Paul Veale, CPA, McAllen, Tex., 1967-68; pvt. practice acctg. Corpus Christi, 1969-79; chmn. White Capital Mgmt., Inc., Dallas. Wholesale beer/beverage distributor executive; b. McAllen, Tex., Feb. 16, 1943; s. Louis Thomas and Leota Faye (Grimm) W.; m. Lauryn G. Longwell, Mar. 8, 1968; children: Brad Edward, Parker Thomas, Landon Allen. BBA, U. Tex., 1965. Acct. Haskins & Sells, CPA's, Houston, 1965-67, Paul Veale, CPA, McAllen, Tex., 1967-68; pvt. practice acctg., Corpus Christi, Tex., 1969-79; chmn. White Capital Mgmt. LLC, Dallas; chmn. Tower Beverages of East. Tex. Inc., 1989-99. Mem. chancellor's coun. U. Tex. Sys.; mem. bd. trustees St. Marks Sch. Tex. Mem. Wholesale Beer Distbrs. Tex., U. Tex. Ex-Students Assn., Crescent Club, Brookhollow Golf Club. Mem. chancellor's coun. U. Tex. Sys.; ; mem. investment com. St. Mark's Sch. of Tex. Mem. U. Tex. Ex-Students Assn., World President's Orgn. Home: 10111 Strait Ln Dallas TX 75229 Office: 300 Crescent Ct Ste 1640 Dallas TX 75201-6926

WHITE, TOM MARTIN, playwright, music publisher; b. Pittsburg, Tex., June 20, 1951; s. Thomas R. and Georgia (Martin) W. BA, U. Tex., 1973. Pres. Prophecy Pub., Inc., Austin, Tex., 1982—, Black Coffee Music, Inc., Austin, 1982—. Author plays: Willie the Shake, 1978, Yes, No, and Yellow, 1973, N. York Ion, 1980, The Silo, 1981, Colonel Mustard, 1982, The Sun & Moon & Stars, 1983, 7:11 in Lebanon, 1986, The Trouble with Tofu, 1989, The Church Computer, 1999, Gym Short, 2001; pub.: (songs)(recorded by Brooks & Dunn) My Maria, 1996; (recorded by Lyle Lovett) Bears, 1998, I've Had Enough, 1998, All Through My Days (by Vince Bell), 1999, The Sun and Moon and Stars (performed by Trout Fishing in America), 1999, I'd Have to Be Crazy, 2001. Home: 1904 Sharon Ln Austin TX 78703-3032 E-mail: tarrytown8@aol.com.

WHITE, W. ROBIN, writer; b. Kodaikanal, Madras, India, July 12, 1928; came to U.S., 1944; s. Emmons Eaton and Ruth Esther (Parker) W.; m. Marian Lucille Biesterfield, Feb. 3, 1948 (dec. Mar. 1983); children: Christopher, Parker, Shelley. BA, Yale U., 1950; MA, Calif. State Poly. U., 1991. Instr. writers program UCLA, 1985-93; lectr. Calif. State Poly. U., Pomona, 1985-93. Exec. officer Calif. State Regional Ctrs., Ukiah, Calif., 1973-79. Author: Elephant Hill, 1959 (Harper prize), House of Many Rooms, 1958, Men and Angels, 1961, Foreign Soil, 1962, All in Favor Say No, 1964, His Own Kind, 1967, Be Not Afraid, 1972, The Special Child, 1978, The Troll of Crazy Mule Camp, 1979, Moses the Man, 1981, The Winning Writer: Studies in the Art of Self-Expression, 1997; anthologies include: Best American Stories, O. Henry Prize Stories, Best Modern Short Stories, Seventeen's Stories, others; contbr. numerous mags. including Harper's, The New Yorker, New York Times, L.A. Times, Harper's Bazaar, Saturday Evening Post, Ladies' Home Jour., Seventeen, Nat. Wildlife, Mademoiselle, The Reporter; author poetry (Poetry award 1993, 94, 95); editor-in-chief Per/Se Internat. Quar., 1965-69; fiction editor UCLA West/Word, 1989-90. Class rep. Kodai-Woodstock Found., 1986-2000; elder Presbyn. Session, Claremont, Calif., 1988-91; mem. libr. commn. Pasadena Presbyn. Ch., 1996-99. Recipient Disting. Achievement award Ednl. Press Assn., 1974, North Coast Regional Ctr., Ukiah, 1978, Harper prize Harper & Bros., 1959, O. Henry award Doubleday, 1960, New Century Writers award, 2000; Bread Loaf fellow Middlebury Coll., 1956, Stegner fellow Stanford U., 1956-57. Mem. Calif. State Poetry Soc., Authors Guild, Am. Acad. Poets. Democrat. Presbyterian. Avocations: backpacking, gardening, photography, birds. Home: 1940 Fletcher Ave South Pasadena CA 91030-4625 E-mail: romarwrite@aol.com.

WHITE, WARREN WURTELE, retired retailing executive; b. McKeesport, Pa., Feb. 29, 1932; s. Jay Leonard and Elizabeth Katherine (Fehr) W.; m. Marjorie Ada Shuman, Mar. 20, 1954; 1 dau., Laura Lynn. BS, Duquesne U., 1954; M.Retailing, U. Pitts., 1957. With Strawbridge & Clothier, Phila., 1957-97, buyer, 1960-67, budget store divisional mdse. mgr., 1968-70, Clover Div. gen. mdse. mgr., 1970-76, v.p. for mdse. and sales promotion, 1977-79, exec. v.p., 1979-96, also dir., 1981-97; gen. mgr. Strawbridge & Clothier (Clover Div.), 1979-96; pvt. retailing cons. Haddonfield, N.J., 1997-98, Naples, Fla., 1998—. Bd. dirs. Ea. Star Charity Found. N.J., 1978-83. Served to 1st lt. arty. U.S. Army, 1954-56. Mem. Internat. Mass Retail Assn. (officer 1987-93, bd. dirs. 1981-96, chmn. bd. 1991-93), South Jersey C. of C. (bd. dirs. 1991-96), Am. Lung Assn. (bd. dirs. Phila. chpt. 1991-94). Clubs: Kensington Golf and Country. Lodges: Masons. Republican. Presbyterian. Home and Office: 514 High Ct Naples FL 34105

WHITE, WILL WALTER, III, public relations consultant, writer; b. Glen Ridge, N.J., July 3, 1930; s. Will Walter and Miriam Chandler (Milburn) W.; m. Phyllis Marcia DuFlocq, Dec. 28, 1951 (div. 1971); children: Will Walter IV, Scott, Alan; m. Anne Elizabeth Levenson, Nov. 21, 1971 (div. 1992); children: Duncan, Christopher; stepchildren: Michael, Susan; m. Catherine Laur, Aug. 26, 1992. BA, Cornell U., 1952. Supr. Union Carbide Corp., N.Y.C., 1954-59; account exec. Ketchum, MacLeod & Grove, 1959-62; sr. v.p. Wilson, Haight & Welch, Hartford, Conn., 1962-72; chmn., chief exec. officer Lowengard & Brotherhood, 1972-83; pres., chief exec. officer Harland & Tine & White, 1983-87; chmn. Donahue Inc., 1987-89; ptnr. Laur White & White, Heathsville, Va., 1992—; owner Omega Cubed Press, 1996—. Exec. com. Conn. Dist. Export Council, 1979-88. Author: The Sunfish Book, 1983, 96; contbg. editor Mid-Gulf Sailing mag., 1994-95. Mem. exec. com. Hartford Stage Co., 1982-86; pres. Vis. Nurse Assn., Hartford, 1979; fin. chmn. Vis. Nurse and Home Care, Inc., Hartford and Waterbury, 1982-91; mem. pub. rels. com. Fairfield County Rep. Com., 1961; chmn. S.W. Fla. Regional Harbor Bd., 1995-2000. 1st lt. U.S. Army, 1952-54. Nat. champion Sunfish Racing Class, 1966, 68 Mem. Pub. Rels. Soc. Am. (accredited, chmn. investor rels. sect. 1983, charter mem. Hall of Fame 1990), Bus. Profl. Advt. Assn. (cert. bus. communicator), Nat. Investor Rels. Inst., U.S. Sunfish Class Assn. (pres. 1985-88, charter mem. Hall of Fame 1991), Boaters Action and Info. League (exec. v.p. 1992-2000), Hist. Soc. Sarasota County (bd. dirs. 1995-2000). Address: 1271 Island Point Rd Heathsville VA 22473-3731

WHITE, WILLIAM DEAKINS, economics educator; b. Phila., July 13, 1945; s. Gilbert F. and Anne (Underwood) W.;m. Olivia Peabody Murray, Aug. 24, 1985; children: Lydia Bayard, Gilbert Edward. BA, Haverford Coll., 1967; PhD, Harvard U., 1975. Asst. prof. econs. U. Ill., Chgo., 1975-82, assoc. prof. econs. and Inst. Govt. and Pub. Affairs, 1982-92, prof., 1992-98, assoc. dir. Inst. Govt. and Pub. Affairs, 1989-92; assoc. prof. Med. Sch. Yale U., New Haven, 1998—, head health mgmt. program, 1998—2001. Author: Public Health and Private Gain, 1979. Vis. Rsch. scholar Yale U., New Haven, 1979-80; recipient Health Care Rsch. award Nat. Inst. for Health Care Mgmt., 1998, Article of Yr. award Assn. for Health Svcs. Rsch., 1999, Faculty Publ. of Yr. award Am. Acad. Med. Adminstrs., 1999. Mem. Cosmos Club. Democrat. Office: Dept Epidemiology and Public Health Yale U Sch of Medicine 60 College St PO Box 208034 New Haven CT 06520-8034 E-mail: william.white@yale.edu.

WHITE, WILLIAM BLAINE, geochemist, educator; b. Huntingdon, Pa., Jan. 5, 1934; s. William Bruce and Eleanor Mae (Barr) W.; m. Elizabeth Loczi, Mar. 27, 1959; children: Nikki Elizabeth White Vezendi, William Brion (dec.). BS, Juniata Coll., 1954; PhD, Pa. State U., 1962. Rsch. assoc. Mellon Inst., Pitts., 1954-58; asst. prof. Pa. State U., University Park, 1963-67, asso. prof., 1967-72, prof. geochemistry, 1972—, chmn. grad. program in materials, 1990-93. Assoc. editor: Am. Mineralogist, 1972-75, Materials Rsch. Bull., 1979-93, Jour. Am. Ceramic Soc., 1985-93, Water Resources Bull., 1992-93; editor earth scis. Nat. Speleol. Soc. Bull., 1964-94; author: Geomorphology and Hydrology of Karst Terrains, 1988, (with Elizabeth L. White) Karst Hydrology: Concepts from the Mammoth Cave Area, 1989, (with Susan Barger) Daguerreotype: Nineteenth-Century Technology and Modern Science, 1991; contbr. articles to profl. jours. Home: Miller Rd RR 1 Box 527 Petersburg PA 16669-9211 Office: Pa State U Materials Rsch Lab University Park PA 16802

WHITE, WILLIAM CHARLES, physicist; b. May 12, 1922; married. BA in Astronomy and Physics, Ohio Wesleyan U., 1948; MS in Astrophysics and Physics, Ohio State U., 1950; postgrad., U. Utah, 1951-52; student in sculpture, Calif. State U., Sacramento. Physicist Naval Weapons Ctr., China Lake, Calif., 1950-71, project engr., 1971-73, ops. rsch. analysist, 1973-80, rsch. analysist, 1978-81. Bd. dirs. WSU Extension Beach Watchers, 1992—, Maxwelton Creek Restoration, 1992-97; mem. restoration-adv. bd. Naval Air Sta., Whidbey Island, Wash., 1996—; mem. tech. adv. com. Marine Resources Commn., Island County, Washington. Fellow U. Utah Naval Ordnance Test Sta., 1951-52. Mem. AAAS, Am. Inst. Physics, Nature Conservancy, Am. Astronomical Soc., Smithsonian Assn., N.Y. Acad. Sci., Sigma Xi. Methodist. Avocations: skiing, fishing, hiking, coins, stamps. E-mail: wwoth@Whidbey.com.

WHITE, WILLIAM DUDLEY, safety engineer; b. Birmingham, Mich., June 11, 1958; s. Paul Richard and Annetta Carole (Manhart) W.; m. Tamara Jean Wishon, Mar. 13, 1992; 1 child, Stacy Michelle; 1 stepchild, Royce Edward Vorel. BS cum laude, U. Ctrl. Okla., 1994. Chief maintenance engr. First Union Mgmt., Oklahoma City, 1984-89; safety rep., chmn. safety and suggestion coms. E-Systems, Inc., Greenville, Tex., 1994—. Creator curriculum for various safety programs, 1994, 96. Pack master Boy Scouts Am., Edmond, Okla., 1991-92; CPR instr., std. first aid instr. ARC, Hunt County, Tex., 1993—. Mem. Am. Soc. Safety Engrs., Alpha Chi. Roman Catholic. Achievements include development of safety certification/O-J-T checklist trng. program to meet OSHA, Air Force Occupational Safety and Health and Department of Defense standards regarding task proficiency for aircraft servicing, maintenance and daily ops. powered aircraft ground and mobile equipment; restructured indsl. hygiene program in accordance with American Conference of Governmental Industrial Hygienists guidelines. Home: 10203 Blanch Ln Edmond OK 73003-1107

WHITE, WILLIAM NELSON, lawyer; b. Balt., Sept. 8, 1938; s. Nelson Cardwell and Ellen Atwell (Zoller) W.; m. Mary Kathleen Bitzel, Sept. 2, 1960 (div. 1971); children: Craig William, Jeffrey Alan, Colin Christopher; m. Christine Lewin Hanna, July 8, 1978. LLB, U. Md., 1968, JD, 1969. Bar: Md. 1972, U.S. Ct. Appeals (4th cir.) 1975, U.S. Dist. Ct. Md. 1976, U.S. Supreme Ct. 1976. Asst. state's atty., Balt., 1972; assoc. Brooks & Turnbull, 1973-76; pvt. practice, 1977—. Counsel St. Andrews Soc. Balt., 1989—; counsel, bd. dirs. St. George's Soc. Former elder, pres. deacons, trustee Roland Park Presbyn. Ch.; former mem. worship, music and sacrament coun., former elder Second Presbyn. Ch. Mem. Md. Bar Assn., Baltimore County Bar Assn., U. Md. Alumni Assn. for Greater Balt. (pres. 1977), Supreme Ct. Hist. Soc., SAR (chancellor for Md. Soc.). Avocations: history, philosophy, classical music, tennis, sailing.

WHITE, WILLIAM NORTH, chemistry educator; b. Walton, N.Y., Sept. 16, 1925; s. George Fitch and Frances (Peck) W.; m. Hilda R. Sauter, Sept. 8, 1951; children: Carla Ann, Eric Jeffrey. AB, Cornell U., 1950; MA, Harvard U., 1951, PhD, 1953. NRC postdoctoral fellow Calif. Inst. Tech., Pasadena, 1953-54; asst. prof. Ohio State U., Columbus, 1954-59, asso. prof., 1959-63; prof. chemistry U. Vt., Burlington, 1963-76, 77-95, prof. emeritus, 1995—, chmn. dept., 1963-70, acting chmn. dept., 1975-76; prof. chemistry U. Tex. at Arlington, 1976-77, chmn. dept., 1976-77. NSF sr. postdoctoral fellow Brookhaven Nat. Lab., Upton, N.Y., 1963-64, Harvard U., 1965; vis. scholar Brandeis U., 1974-75; chmn. arrangements com. Nat. Organic Chemistry Symposium, 1965-67 Contbr. articles on organic chemistry profl. jours. Selectman Town of Shelburne, Vt., 1968-74, water commr., 1973-74, justice of the peace, 1981—, sewer commr., 1991-93; mem. Chittenden County Regional Planning Commn., 1983-91; mem. bd. suprs. Winooski (Vt.) Natural Resources Conservation Dist., 1999—. With AUS, 1943-46. Recipient Outstanding Forest Stewardship award Winooski Conservation Dist., 1997. Mem. Am. Chem. Soc. (chmn. Western Vt. sect. 1966-67), Royal Soc. Chemistry, New Eng. Assn. Chemistry Tchrs., AAAS, N.Y. Acad. Scis., Phi Beta Kappa, Sigma Xi, Phi Kappa Phi, Phi Lambda Upsilon. Home: Pierson Dr Shelburne VT 05482-7224 Office: U Vt Dept Chemistry Burlington VT 05405-0001

WHITE, WILLIAM SAMUEL, foundation executive; b. Cin., May 8, 1937; s. Nathaniel Ridgway and Mary (Lowndes) W.; m. Claire Mott, July 1, 1961; children: Tiffany Lowndes, Ridgway Harding. BA, Dartmouth Coll., 1959, MBA, 1960; LL.D. (hon.), Eastern Mich. U., 1975; hon. degree, GMI Engring. & Mgmt. Inst., 1996. With Barrett & Williams, N.Y.C., 1961-62; sr. assoc. Bruce Payne & Assos., 1962-71; v.p. C. S. Mott Found., Flint, Mich., 1971-75, pres., 1976—, trustee, 1971—, also chmn. bd. dirs. Bd. dirs. Am. Water Works; chmn. bd. dirs. U.S. Sugar Corp. Mem. exec. com. Daycroft Sch., Greenwich, Conn., 1966-70; bd. dirs. Flint Area Conf., 1971-84, Coun. on Founds., 1985-90, Independent Sector, 1994-99, European Found. Centre, 1994—, Civicus, 1995-2001; mem. citizens adv. task force U. Mich., Flint, 1974-79; chmn. Coun. of Mich. Founds., 1979-81, Flint Area Focus Coun., 1988—; mem. Pres.'s Task Force on Pvt. Sector Initiatives, 1982; trustee GMI Engring. and Mgmt. Inst., 1982-86. Served with U.S. Army, 1960-62. Office: C S Mott Foundation 1200 Mott Foundation Bldg Flint MI 48502-1807

WHITEAKER, RUTH CATHERINE, retired secondary education educator, counselor; b. Monte Vista, Colo., Mar. 3, 1907; d. Samuel sigel and Vina Catherine (Becraft) Heilman; m. George Henry Whiteaker, June 23, 1946. BA, U. Denver, 1930, MA, 1954; student, Columbia U., Ohio State, and others, 1933-66. cert. tchr. Tchr./drama coach Brighton (Colo.) High Sch., 1930-36; tchr. Meeker Jr. High Sch., Greeley, Colo., 1936-42, South High Sch., Denver, 1942-52, couselor, 1952-61; tchr. Thomas Jefferson High Sch., 1961-66. Organizer first career day Greeley High Sch., 1939, Future Tchrs. Am. in Colo. High Schs. Colo. Edn. Assn., 1949-55; co-organizer Wyo. Future Tchrs. Am. Wyo. Edn. Assn., 1951; com. mem. Nat. Future Tchrs. Am. Adv. Bd., 1954. Author: (English speech units) Colo. English Guide, 1939, Denver K-12 Program, 1951; editor: (guidebook) South High Syllabus, 1952-60. Chmn. 50th reunion U. Denver Class 1930, 1980. Recipient plaque Colo. Future Tchrs. Am., 1955, Student Nat. Edn. Assn., Colo., 1955, Lifetime's Dedication to Edn. Colo. medal South Denver H.S., 1998; Heroine of S.P. Meek's Rusty, 1938; named Citizen of Week, Greeley Kiwanis Club, 1939; grantee U.S. Dept. Edn. and Mexican Ministry Edn., 1945. Mem. Bus. and Profl. Women's Club (pres. 1933, 38), Colo. Bus. and Profl. Women's Club (v.p. 1944), Columbia U. Women's Club Colo. (pres. 1975-77), Rep. Ladies Roundtable, Colo. Symphony Guild, PEO Sisterhood, Meth. Women's Assn., Terr. Daus., Columbia U. Alumni Club, Alpha Gamma Delta (regional sec.-treas. 1934-36, pres. 1936-40), Delta Kappa Gamma (v.p. Colo. chpt. 1959, Cert. of Appreciation 2001). Methodist. Avocations: reading, travel, politics, lectures, theater. Home: 3455 S Corona St Apt 409 Englewood CO 80110-2871

WHITEHEAD, CLAY THOMAS, business executive; b. Neodesha, Kans., Nov. 13, 1938; s. Clay Bell and Helen (Hinton) W.; m. Margaret Mahon, May 19, 1973; children: Abigail Walton, Clay Cother. BS, Mass. Inst. Tech., 1960, MS in Elec. Engring, 1961, PhD in Mgmt, 1967. Cons. def. studies RAND Corp., 1961-63, economist, 1967-69; mem. Pres.-Elect's Task Force on Budget Policies, 1968-69; spl. asst. to Pres. Nixon, 1969-70; dir. U.S. Office Telecommunications Policy, 1970-74; organized Pres. Ford transition, 1974; fellow Harvard Inst. Politics Mass. Inst. Tech. Center for Internat. Studies, 1974-76; pres. Allison Tech. Services, Santa Monica, Calif., 1976-78, Hughes Communications Inc., Los Angeles, 1979-83; founder Data Satellite Sys., 1983-85; pres. Nat. Exch. Inc., 1985—, Clay Whitehead Assocs., McLean, 1988—. Served with AUS, 1963-65. Office: PO Box 8090 Mc Lean VA 22106-8090

WHITEHEAD, DAVID BARRY, lawyer; b. San Francisco, Oct. 14, 1946; s. Barry and Fritzi-Beth (Bowman) W.; m. René Dayan, May 26, 1990. AB in History, Stanford U., 1968, JD, 1971. Bar: Calif. 1972, U.S. Dist. Ct. (no. dist.) Calif. 1972, U.S. Ct. Appeals (9th cir.) 1972, U.S. Dist. Ct. (cen. dist.) Calif. 1974. Assoc. Cullinan Hancock Rothert & Burns, San Francisco, 1972-74, Cullinan Burns & Helmer, San Francisco, 1975-77, ptnr., 1977-78, Burns & Whitehead, San Francisco, 1979-85, Whitehead & Porter, San Francisco, 1986-97, Whitehead, Porter & Gordon LLP, San Francisco, 1998—. Bd. dirs. Rainbow Music, Inc., San Francisco, ITP, Inc., Sunnyvale, Calif.; founding dir. A. Lincoln High Sch. San Francisco, 1989—. Mem. San Francisco Rep. Steering Com., 1984-89; bd. dirs. Enterprise for High Sch. Students, San Francisco, 1982-86, San Francisco chpt. Easter Seal Soc., 1986-90, Opera West Found., San Francisco, 1986-90, Traveler's Aid Soc., San Francisco, 1989—, Hosp. de la Familia, 1995-2000, Gold Rush Trail Found., 1998—. 1st lt. USAR, 1968-71. Mem. ABA, Calif. Bar Assn., San Francisco Bar Assn., Calif. Scholarship Fedn. (life) Family Club San Francisco (bd. dirs. 1986-89, 93-95), World Trade Club, Abraham Lincoln High Sch. San Francisco Alumni Assn. (founding dir.). Roman Catholic. Avocations: tenor, writer, director, actor. Home: 1896 Pacific Ave Apt 502 San Francisco CA 94109-2302 Office: Whitehead Porter & Gordon LLP 220 Montgomery St Fl 18 San Francisco CA 94104-3402

WHITEHEAD, DAVID LOUIS, writer, educator; b. Barksdale AFB, La., Oct. 26, 1957; s. Judge and Dorothy Whitehead. BA in Polit. Sci., Southern U., Baton Rouge, La., 1980; MA in Polit. Sci., Howard U., Washington, D.C. Mem. U.S. CIA, Washington, 1983—90; part time sub. tchr. D.C. Pub. Schs., 1991—96; tchr. Prince Georges County Pub. Schs., 1996—2000; adj. instr. Strayer U., Va., 2001—. Lectr. to several orgs. in Washington area, 1989—2002. Author: (novels) The Big Bad Wolf vs Ms. Little Red Riding Hood-The Mike Tyson story, 1998, How Rebecca Zinani Madison Got Her Freak Off, 1998, Brains, Sex & Racism in the CIA & The Escape, also poetry and plays. Candidate for Senator D.C., 1990. Pvt. USAR, 1980—81, seaman USNR, 1981—82. Named to State All-Star Basketball Team in La., Airline H.S., Bossier, 1975. Home: 1101 Westfield Dr Oxon Hill MD 20745

WHITEHEAD, EDGAR DOUGLAS, urology educator; b. Galashiels, Scotland, Aug. 24, 1939; 1 child, Robin Stacey. BA, Vanderbilt U., 1961; MD, Ind. U., 1965; postgrad., U. London, 1972. Diplomate Am. Bd. Urology; med. lic. Ind., Ill., N.Y., Calif., N.J. Intern. surgery Mount Sinai Hosp., N.Y.C., 1965-66; resident in surgery Presbyn.-St. Luke's Hosp., Chgo., 1966-67; resident in urology N.Y.U. Med. Ctr., 1969-73; clin. assoc. urology Mount Sinai Sch. Medicine, N.Y.C., 1973-77, sr. clin. instr. urology, 1977-80, asst. clin. prof. urology, 1980-92; pvt. practice, 1973—; assoc. clin. prof. urology Mount Sinai Sch. Medicine, 1992-94, Albert Einstein Coll. of Medicine, 1994—; attending NYU Downtown Hosp. Assoc. attending Beth Israel Med. Ctr., N.Y.C.; mem. advisor Impotence Anonymous & Jr., Diabetes Self-Mgmt., 1983-85, Jour. Urol. Nursing; editl. adv. bd. The Female Patient, Med. Aspects of Human Sexuality; mem. med. adv. bd. Colostomy Soc., N.Y., Inc.; investigator Protocol 2560 (alfus) Alfuzosin study, 1998; cons. and speaker in field. Author: Viagra--The Wonder Drug for Peak Performance; editor: Current Operative Urology, 1975, 2d rev. edit., 1984, ann. edits., 1989-92, Mgmt. Impotence and Infertility, 1994, Sex Over Forty, 1990-2000, Atlas Surgical Techniques in Urology, 1997; contbr. articles to profl. jours.; patentee in field. Grantee U.S.P.H., Clin. Research Ctr. Fellow ACS, Clin. Soc. Am. Diabetes Assn., N.Y. Diabetes Affiliate; mem. AMA, AAAS, Am. Urol. Assn., Soc. Internat. Urology (diplomate), Soc. for the Study of Impotence, Sexual Medicine Soc. N.Am., Am. Assn. Clin. Urologists, N.Y. State Urol. Assn., Am. Acad. of Phalloplasty Surgeons (pres., bd. dirs.), Internat. Soc. for Artificial Organs, Am. So. Nephrology, Med. Soc. State N.Y., Med. Soc. County N.Y., Am. Assn. Sex Educators, Counselors and Therapists, Soc. for the Sci. Study of Sex, Soc. for Sex Therapy and Rsch., Sex Info. and Edn. Coun. of the U.S. Coalition on Sexuality and Disability, Am. Cancer Soc., Nat. Kidney Found., Am. Geriatric Soc., N.Y. Acad. Sci., N.Y. Acad. Medicine, N.Y. Urodynamic Soc., Internat. Continence Soc., Soc. Genitourinary Reconstructive Surgeons, Assn. Male Sexual Dysfunction (dir.), N.Y. Phalloplasty (dir.). Office: 24 E 12th St Ste 2-1 New York NY 10003-4403 E-mail: info@drwhitehead.com.

WHITEHEAD, GEORGE WILLIAM, retired mathematician; b. Bloomington, Ill., Aug. 2, 1918; s. George William and (Christine) Mary (Gutschlag) W.; m. Kathleen Ethelwyn Butcher, June 7, 1947. SB, U. Chgo., 1937, SM, 1938, PhD, 1941. Instr. math. Purdue U., West Lafayette, Ind., 1941-45, Princeton (N.J.) U., 1945-47; asst. prof. Brown U., Providence, 1947-48, assoc. prof., 1948-49; asst. prof. MIT, Cambridge, 1949-51, assoc. prof., 1951-57, prof., 1957-85, prof. emeritus, 1985—. Author: Homotopy Theory, 1966, Elements of Homotopy Theory, 1978, Recent Advances in Homotopy Theory, 1970. Fellow Guggenheim Found., 1955-56, sr. post-doctoral fellow NSF, 1965-66; Fulbright Rsch. scholar, 1955-56. Fellow Am. Acad. Arts & Scis.; mem. NAS, Am. Math. Soc. (v.p.), Math. Assn. Am. Avocations: archeology, bridge, genealogy. Home: Apt 706 53 Hill Rd Belmont MA 02478-4307 E-mail: whthd@math.mit.edu.

WHITEHEAD, J. RENNIE, science consultant; s. William and Beatrice Cora (Fenning) W.; m. Nesta Doone James, Jan. 11, 1944; children— Valerie Lesley (dec.), Michael James Rennie. B.Sc. in Physics, Manchester U., Lancashire, Eng., 1939; PhD in Phys. Chemistry, Cambridge U., Eng., 1949. Cert. profl. engr., Ont.; chartered engr., U.K. Sci. officer TRE (UK Radar), Eng., 1939-51; assoc. prof. McGill U., Montreal, P.Q., Can., 1951-55; dir. research RCA Victor Co Ltd., 1955-65; prin. sci. adviser Govt. of Can., Ottawa, Ont., 1965-75; sr. v.p. Philip A. Lapp Ltd., 1975-82; pvt. practice sci. cons., 1982-86. Bd. dirs. Hancock-Lapp Assocs., Ottawa, 1986-89; bd. dirs. Found. for Internat. Tng., Toronto, 1976-86. Author: Superregenerative Receivers, 1949 Fellow Royal Soc. Can., Inst. Physics, Instn. Elec. Engrs., Can. Aeronautics and Space Inst., Can. Assn. for Club of Rome (chmn. 1976-81, editor and pub. newsletter and procs. 1987-99). Anglican. Avocations: automobiles; philately; carpentry; computers. Home and Office: 1368 Chattaway Ave Ottawa ON Canada K1H 7S3 E-mail: drrennie@sympatico.ca.

WHITEHEAD, JAMES FRED , III, lawyer; b. Atlanta, July 3, 1946; s. James Fred Jr. and Jessie Mae (Turner) W.; m. Joanne Christina Mayo, June 21, 1969 (div. Feb. 1992); children: Matthew Nicholas, Rebecca Catherine; m. Nancy Karean Hatley, May 28, 1992; stepchildren: Brandon, Madison. AB with distinction, Stanford U., 1968; JD, U. Mich., 1975. Bar: Wash. 1975, U.S. Dist. Ct. (we. dist.) Wash. 1975, U.S. Ct. Appeals (9th cir.) 1975, U.S. Supreme Ct. 1976, U.S. Dist. Ct. (ea. dist.) Wash. 1994, Alaska 1995, U.S. Dist. Ct. Alaska 1995. Assoc. LeGros, Buchanan, Paul & Madden, Seattle, 1975-79; dir., officer LeGros, Buchanan, Paul & Whitehead, 1979-92; ptnr. McGee, Reno & Whitehead, 1993; of counsel Holmes Weddle & Barcott, 1993-97, shareholder, 1997—. Organizer, lectr. Pacific Northwest Admiralty Law Inst., Seattle, 1981—; chmn. Internat. Maritime Law Conf., Seattle, 1996. Assoc. editor Am. Maritime Cases, 1991—; contbr. articles to profl. jours. Mem. ABA, Maritime Law Assn. of U.S. (bd. dirs. 2000—). Avocations: tennis, golf, boating, birding. Office: Holmes Weddle & Barcott Wells Fargo Center Ste 2600 Seattle WA 98104 E-mail: jwhitehe@sea.hwb-law.com.

WHITEHEAD, JAMES MADISON, law librarian; b. Mobile, Ala., July 16, 1929; s. James Manikee and Fanny (Salmon) W.; m. Elena Hulings, June 11, 1955; children: James M.M., John Douglass, Kenneth Clark, Julia Harker. BA, U. Chgo., 1951; JD, Tulane U., 1959; MS, La. State U., 1963; PhD, U. Pitts., 1981. Bar: La. 1959. Acting head pub. svscs. La. State U., New Orleans, 1965; head sci. library U. Colo., Boulder, 1965-66; asst. prof. head dept. circulation Va. Poly. Inst., Blacksburg, 1967-70; adminstrv. asst. Va. Poly. Ins. and State U., 1970-71; asst. prof., assoc. prof., law librarian Coll. William and Mary, Williamsburg, Va., 1971-76; asst. prof. SUNY, Geneseo, 1978-80, Atlanta U., 1980-84; pvt. practice Stone Mountain, Ga., 1984-85; libr. IV U. Ga. Law Library, Athens, 1985-95; ret., 1995. Cons. ultra microfiche adv. group Ency. Britannica, Blacksburg, 1969. Author: Logos of Library and Information Science: Apperceptions on the Institutes of Bibematics with Commentaries on the General Humanistic Method and the Common Philosophy, 1981. Asst. cubmaster Webelos, leader Boy Scouts Am., Blacksburg, 1969-70, patrol dad, adviser, 1970-71. Cpl. USMC, 1952-54. Mem. La. Bar Assn., Masons, Beta Phi Mu. Republican. Christian Scientist. Avocations: fishing, dog and cat care, poetry and play writing, reading. Home: 104 Hurst St Williamsburg VA 23185-3305 E-mail: jimnickie@aol.com.

WHITEHEAD, JOHN, poet; b. Dec. 23, 1945; Student, U. Calif., Berkeley, 1970-74. Author of numerous poems published in jours. Home and Office: 8424 NW 56th St Miami FL 33166-3327 E-mail: jwethead@conexion.com.gt.

WHITEHEAD, JOHN CUNNINGHAM, bank executive, diplomat, philanthropist; b. Evanston, Ill., Apr. 2, 1922; s. Eugene C. and Winifred W.; m. Helene E. Shannon, Sept. 28, 1946 (div. Dec. 1971); children: Anne Elizabeth, John Gregory; m. Jaan W. Chartener, Oct. 22, 1972 (div. 1986); 1 child, Sarah; m. Nancy Dickerson, 1989 (dec. 1997). BA, Haverford Coll., 1943; MBA, Harvard U., 1947; LLD (hon.), Pace. U., Rutgers U., Haverford Coll., Harvard U., Amherst Coll., Seton Hall U. With Goldman, Sachs & Co., N.Y.C., 1947-84, ptnr., 1956-76, sr. ptnr., co-chmn., 1976-84; dep. sec. Dept. State, Washington, 1985-89; chmn. Lower Manhattan Devel. Corp., 2001—. Past chmn. Fed. Res. Bank of N.Y. Trustee Haverford Coll., Rockefeller U., Lincoln Ctr. Theater; past pres. bd. overseers Harvard U.; past chmn. trustees coun. Nat. Gallery Art; co-chmn. greater N.Y. coun. Boy Scouts Am.; past chmn. Internat. Rescue Com., UN Assn. U.S.A.; chmn. emeritus Internat. House, Brookings Inst., Youth for Understanding, Andrew Mellon Found. With USNR, 1943-46. Mem. Coun. on Fgn. Rels., Links Club, Univ. Club. Office: 65 E 55th St New York NY 10022-3219

WHITEHEAD, JOHN WAYNE, law educator, organization administrator, author; b. Pulaski, Tenn., July 14, 1946; s. John M. and Alatha (Wiser) W.; m. Virginia Carolyn Nichols, Aug. 26, 1967; children: Jayson Reau, Jonathan Mathew, Elisabeth Anne, Joel Christofer, Joshua Benjamen. BA, U. Ark., 1969, JD, 1974. Bar: Ark. 1974, U.S. Dist. Ct. (ea. and we. dists.) Ark. 1974, U.S. Supreme Ct. 1977, U.S. Ct. Appeals (9th cir.) 1980, Va. 1981, U.S. Ct. Appeals (7th cir.) 1981, U.S. Ct Appeals (4th and 5th cirs.). Spl. counsel Christian Legal Soc., Oak Park, Ill., 1977-78; assoc. Gibbs & Craze, Cleve., 1978-79; sole practice law Manassas, Va., 1979-82; pres. The Rutherford Inst., Charlottesville, 1982—, also bd. dirs. Frequent lectr. colls., law schs.; past adj. prof. O.W. Coburn Sch. Law. Author: Schools on Fire, 1980, The New Tyranny, 1982, The Second American Revolution, 1982, The Stealing of America, 1983, The Freedom of Religious Expression in Public High Schools, 1983, The End of Man, 1986, An American Dream, 1987, The Rights of Religious Persons in Public Education, 1991, Home Education: Rights and Reasons, 1993, Religious Apartheid, 1994, Slaying Dragons, 1999, Grasping For the Wind, 2001, others; writer, dir.: (video series) Grasping for the Wind (Silver World medal N.Y. Film Festival), 1998-99; contbr. articles to profl. jours., chpts. to books. 1st lt. U.S. Army, 1969-71. Named Christian Leader of Yr. Christian World Affairs Conf., Washington, 1986; recipient Bus. and Profl. award Religious Heritage Am., 1990, Hungarian Freedom medal, Budapest, 1991. Mem. ABA, Ark. Bar Assn., Va. Bar Assn. Office: The Rutherford Inst PO Box 7482 Charlottesville VA 22906-7482

WHITEHEAD, KARL PETER, construction executive, arbitrator, writer; b. Pittsburg, Calif., June 5, 1955; s. George Joseph Whitehead, Anita Kaspara Whitehead; m. Katherine Lee Steege; children: Christopher Duvall, Daniel Duvall. BA in Mgmt. with honors, St. Mary's Coll., Moraga, Calif., 1993. Cert. arbitrator 1992, lic. gen. contractor 1982, cert. constrn. industry expert Calif., 1990, Calif., 1997. Project mgr. Hafen Devel. Co., Walnut Creek, Calif., 1973—82; CEO Karl Whitehead, Gen. Contractor, Pleasant Hill, 1982—; pub. Whitehead Pub. Co., 2000—. Constrn. industry expert Calif. Contractors State Lic. Bd., Sacramento, 1990—; constrn. industry arbitrator Am. Arbitration Assn., San Francisco, 1992—2000. Author: (children's book) My Friend Jimmy, 2001, (biography) My Heart Is A Stone That Bleeds, 2001. Avocation: amatuer astronomy.

WHITEHEAD, KENNETH DEAN, author, translator, retired federal government official; b. Rupert, Idaho, Dec. 14, 1930; s. Clarence Christian and May Bell (Allen) W.; m. Margaret Mary O'Donohue, Aug. 2, 1958; children: Paul Daniel, Steven Francis, Matthew Patrick, David Joseph. BA in French, U. Utah, 1955; postgrad., U. Paris, 1956-57; cert. in Arabic and Middle East studies, Fgn. Service Inst., Beirut, 1962. Instr. English U. Utah, Salt Lake City, 1955-56; fgn. service officer Dept. State, Rome, Beirut and Tripoli, Libya, 1957-65; chief Arabic service Voice of Am., Washington, 1965-67; dep. dir. fgn. currency program Smithsonian Instn., 1967-72; exec. v.p. Caths. United for Faith Inc., New Rochelle, N.Y., 1972-81; dir. Ctr. for Internat. Edn. U.S. Dept. Edn., Washington, 1982-86, dep. asst. sec. for higher edn. programs, 1986-88, asst. sec. for postsecondary edn., 1988-89. Author: Respectable Killing: The New Abortion Imperative, 1972, Agenda for the Sexual Revolution, 1981, Catholic Colleges and Federal Funding, 1988, DOA: The Ambush of the Universal Catechism, 1993, Political Orphan? The Prolife Cause after 25 Years of Roe v. Wade, 1998, One, Holy, Catholic, and Apostolic: The Early Church Was the Catholic Church, 2000; co-author: The Pope, The Council and the Mass, 1981, Flawed Expectations: The Reception of the Catechism of the Catholic Church, 1996; sr. editor: World Almanac Book of Dates, 1982, Macmillan Concise Dictionary of World History, 1983; editor: Marriage and the Common Good, 2001, Pope John Paul II--Witness to Truth, 2001; co-editor: The Battle for the Catholic Mind, 2001; translator 22 books from French, German, Italian, 1980—. Bd. dirs. Notre Dame Inst. for Advanced Study, Arlington, Va., 1986-95, Philosophy Edn. Soc., 1995—, Christas Magister Found., 1997—. Fulbright scholar U.S. Dept. State, 1956-57. Mem. Fellowship Cath. Scholars (bd. dirs. 1990-2000), Brent Soc. Cath. Profls. (bd. dirs. 1992-98), Cath. League for Religious and Civil Rights (bd. dirs. 1992—), KC. Republican. Home: 809 Ridge Pl Falls Church VA 22046-3631 Fax: (703) 534-3015. E-mail: whiteheadz@msn.com.

WHITEHEAD, MICHAEL ANTHONY, chemistry educator; b. London, June 30, 1935; emigrated to Can., 1962; s. Francis Henry and Edith Downes (Rotherham) W.; 1 son, Christopher Mark. B.Sc. in Chemistry with honors, Queen Mary Coll., U. London, 1956, PhD, 1960, D.Sc., 1974. Asst. lectr. Queen Mary Coll., U. London, 1958-60; postdoctoral fellow U. Cin., 1960, asst. prof., 1961; asst. prof. theoretical chemistry McGill U., Montreal, Que., Can., 1962-66, asso. prof., 1966-74, prof., 1974-99, prof. emeritus, 1999—. Vis. prof. U. Cambridge, Eng., 1971-72, U. Oxford, Eng., 1972-74; vis. professorial fellow Univ. Coll. Wales, Aberystwyth, 1980, U. Oxford, 1990-91; invited prof. U. Geneva, 1983-84; life guest prof. Nat. U. Def. Tech., Changsha, People's Republic of China; vis. Erskine fellow chemistry dept. U. Canterbury, Christchurch, N.Z., co-chair history and advanced in quantum chemistry 84th conf., Montreal, 2001; mem. Internat. Com. on Nuclear Quadrupole Resonance.; co-chmn. 7th Internat. Symposium on Nuclear Quadrapole Resonance, Kingston, Ont., Can., 1983 Author more than 250 rsch. publs. in field of quantum chemistry and radio spectroscopy. Fellow Royal Chem. Soc., Chem. Inst. Can., Royal Soc. Arts; mem. Am. Chem. Soc., Am. Phys. Soc., James McGill Soc. (pres. 1993-95), Sigma Xi (pres. McGill chpt. 1971-72, 81-82, 92-95, 97-99, dir. Can. and internat. constituency group 2000—, chair awards com. 2001—, ad hoc mem. internat. com., 2001-), Phi Lambda Upsilon. Anglican. Office: McGill U Dept Chemistry 801 Sherbrooke St W Montreal QC Canada H3A 2K6 E-mail: tony.whitehead@mcgill.ca., tony@maw.chem.mcgill.ca. *My faith in God and belief in Christ.*

WHITEHEAD, NELSON PETER, foreign service officer; b. Washington, Sept. 12, 1960; s. Edwin Nelson and Marguerite (Janko) W. Degree, U. Grenoble, France, 1980; BA, BS, Washington and Lee U., 1984; M Engring., U. Va., 1991. Dir. testing def. meteorol. satellite program Westinghouse Space Div., Balt., 1985-86; joined Fgn. Svc. U.S. Dept. State, 1986, engr., 1986—; U.S. consulate Casablanca, Morocco, 1994-96; attache U.S. Embassy, Brussels, 1996-99; with Office of Insp. Gen., Vienna, 1999—, Photonics Engring., Viasystems, Richmond, 2001—. Mem. IEEE, SPIE, Internat. Soc. Optical Engring., Lasers and Electro-Optics Soc. Presbyterian.

WHITEHEAD, WENDY LEE, special education educator; b. Wabash, Ind., Mar. 1, 1955; d. John Francis and Virginia Mae (Ritzi) W. BS, Ball State U., 1977, MS, 1981; cert. in visually impaired edn., Ind. U., Ft. Wayne, 1987. Cert. spl. edn. tchr., Ind. Tchr. of multiply handicapped Sharp Creek Elem. Sch., Met. Sch. Dist., Wabash, Ind., 1977—. Active locla sch. dist. Assistive Tech. Team. Mem. Coun. for Exceptional Children (human rights com.). Republican. Roman Catholic. Avocations: reading, bowling, cross-stitch. Office: Sharp Creek Elem Sch 264 W 200 N Wabash IN 46992-9136

WHITEHEAD, ZELMA KAY, special education educator; b. Tupelo, Miss., Sept. 20, 1946; d. Henry Neal and Zelma Lee (Rye) W. BS in Spl. Edn., Miss. State Coll. for Women, Columbus, 1968; MEd in Spl. Edn., Miss. State U., Starkville, 1971, Edn. Specialist, 1975; postgrad., U. Miss., Oxford, 1978, 85, Miss. Coll., 1990-92. Cert. tchr. spl. edn., elem. edn., adult basic edn., spl. subject supervision, ednl. adminstrn., elem. principal, secondary principal, elem. supr. Tchr. spl. edn. Nettleton (Miss.) Elem. Sch., 1968-71; site monitor Appalachian Edn. Satellite Program Itawamba Jr. Coll., Tupelo, Miss., 1977-79, instr. spl. edn. Spl. Vocat. Edn. Ctr., 1971-85, supr. Spl. Vocat. Edn. Ctr., 1984-85, instr. adult basic edn., 1979-85; tchr. spl. prevocat. edn. Shannon (Miss.) High Sch., 1985; edn. specialist Miss. State Dept. Edn., Jackson, 1986, edn. specialist sr., 1986-90; acad. tchr. III Miss. State Hosp., Whitfield, 1990-93, coord. patient edn. and skill tng., 1993-95; adminstr. Lakeside Sch., 1995-2000, Millcreek of Pontotoc Sch., Inc., 2000—. Mem. Coun. Exceptional Children, Miss. Orgn. Spl. Edn. Suprs. Methodist. Avocations: softball, running, sailing. Home: 177 Little Cir Belden MS 38826-9368

WHITEHILL, ANGELA ELIZABETH, artistic director; b. Leeds, Yorkshire, Eng., Oct. 21, 1938; came to U.S., 1952, naturalized, 1995; d. Donald Paul and Audrey May (Clayforth) Warner; m. Norman James Whitehill, Dec. 23, 1959; children: Norman James III, Pamela Elizabeth; m. William Parker Noble, Dec. 27, 1998. Student, Arts Ednl. Sch., London, 1955-59. With corps de ballet Ballet Paris, 1958-59; dir. London Sch. Ballet, St. Thomas, V.I., 1960-63; asst. dir. Ocean County Ballet Co., Toms River, N.J., 1965-68; founder, dir. Shore Ballet Sch., 1968-76; artistic dir. Shore Ballet Co., 1971-76; artist in residence Castleton State Coll., Rutland, Vt., 1977-79; founder, artistic dir. Burklyn Ballet Theatre, Johnson, 1977—. Vis. prof. Colby Sawyer Coll., New London, N.H., 1978-79; resident designer Atlanta Ballet Co., 1982-83; designer, pub. relations N.J. Ballet Co., Orange, 1983-85; artistic dir. Vt. Ballet Theatre, Burlington, 1985-94; master tchr. 1st Congress Internat. de Ballet Classico Contemporaneo, Mex., 2000. Choreographer Arensky Dances, 1983, A Deux, 1984, 4 Plus 2, 1986, Twins From A Time Gone By, 1987; co-author: Parent's Book of Ballet, 1988, The Young Professional's Book of Ballet, 1990, The Dancer's Book of Ballet, 2000, Ballet Magic, The Burklyn Story, 2001. Dir. Vt. Ballet Theatre Found., Calledonia County, 1993-96. Recipient Francis Hopkins award Ocean County, N.J., 1976, Woman of Achievement award Vt. Woman, 1989, Author's award N.J. Inst. Tech., 1989. Mem. Vt. Council on the Arts, Regional Dance Am. Mem. Soc. Of Friends. Home: 218 Ocean Ave Island Heights NJ 08732 Home (Winter): PO Box 907 Island Heights NJ 08732-0907 Office: Burklyn Ballet Theatre PO Box 302 Johnson VT 05656-0302 E-mail: awhitehill@aol.com.

WHITEHORN, W. ELIZABETH RANDAZZO, accountant; b. New Orleans, May 15, 1954; d. Nick and Willa (Wileman) Randazzo; m. Richard S. Whitehorn, Nov. 21, 1976 (div. Sept. 1995). BA in History, U. New Orleans, 1976, BS in Acctg., 1980. CPA, La. Various bookkeeping and office mgr. positions for hotel and archtl. firm, New Orleans, 1976-78; staff acct. Parson-Gilbane, Lafayette, La., 1978-79; acct., tax practitioner, New Orleans, 1979-83; pvt. practice pub. acctg., Metairie, La., 1983—. Spkr. in field. Sec.-treas. Young Reps., U. New Orleans, 1975-76. Mem. AICPA, Am. Soc. Women Accts. (editl. staff New Orleans chpt. 1982), La. Soc. CPA's, DAR. Avocations: gourmet cooking for HIV/AIDS treatment, arts, crafts, playing piano and violin, theatrical dance.

WHITEHOUSE, DAVID BRYN, museum director; b. Worksop, Nottinghamshire, Eng., Oct. 15, 1941; came to U.S., 1984; s. Brindley Charles and Alice Margaret (Dobson) W.; m. Ruth Delamain Ainger, 1963; children: Sarah, Susan, Peter; m. Elizabeth-Anne Ollemans, 1975; children: Julia, Simon, Nicola. BA, Cambridge U., 1963, MA, 1965, PhD, 1967. Wainwright Fellow Oxford U., England, 1966-73; dir. Brit. Inst. Afghan Studies, Kabul, Afghanistan, 1973-74, Brit. Sch., Rome, 1974-84; chief curator Corning Mus. Glass, N.Y., 1984-87, dep. dir., 1988-92, dir., 1992-99, exec. dir., 1999—. Dir. Siraf expdn. Brit. Inst. Persian Studies, Tehran, Iran, 1966-73. Author: (with Ruth Whitehouse) Archaeological Atlas of the World, 1975, (with David Andrews and John Osborne) Aspects of Medieval Lazio, 1982, (with Donald B. Harden and others) Glass of the Caesars, 1987, Glass of the Roman Empire, 1988, (with Richard Hodges) Mohammed, Charlemagne and the Origins of Europe, 1983, Glass: A Pocket Dictionary, 1993, English Cameo Glass, 1994, Roman Glass in The Corning Museum of Glass, Vol. 1, 1997, Excavations at ed-Dur (Umm al-Qaiwan, UAE), Vol. 1, The Glass Vessels, 1998, The Corning Museum of Glass, A Decade of Glass Collecting, 1990-1999, 2000, (with Stefano Carboni) Glass of the Sultans, 2001, Roman Glass in the Corning Museum of Glass, vol. 2, 2001; contbr. numerous articles and revs. to profl. jours. Fellow Soc. Antiquaries (London), Royal Geog. Soc., Pontificia Accademia Romana di Archeologia; mem. Accademia Fiorentina delle Arti del Disegno, Accademia di Archeologia, Lettere e Belle Arti di Napoli, Deutsches Archaologisches Inst., Internat. Assn. for the History of Glass (pres. 1991-95), Athenaeum Club (London). Office: Corning Mus of Glass 1 Mus Way Corning NY 14830-2253

WHITEHOUSE, FRANK, JR. microbiologist, educator; b. Ann Arbor, Mich., Nov. 20, 1924; s. Frank and May Belle (McIntire) W.; m. Helen Alice Schimkat Whitehouse; children: Lynne, Beth Ann, Frank Scott, Kim Elaine. AB, U. Mich., Ann Arbor, 1953; MD, 1953. Faculty U. Mich. Med. Sch., Ann Arbor, 1954-95. Vis. scientist Queen Victoria Hosp., East Grinstead, Eng. Contbr. over 65 articles and abstracts to profl. jours.; secular and religious mus. compositions performed in concert and in church. Scoutmaster Boy Scouts Am. 1st Lt. USAF, 1942-46. Decorated Air medal, 1945; recipient Univ. Hopwood Literary award, Ann Arbor, 1947, Undergrad. & Med. Sch. Curriculum Devel. award; Sr. Fulbright lectr. Bahrain, 1979-80. Mem. Am. Soc. Microbiology, Nat. Assn. Advisors for the Health Professions (founder, first exec. dir.), Nat. Bd. Med. Examiners, Gilbert and Sullivan Soc. and Choral Union. Avocations: secular and religous musical compositions and their public presentations, philately. Home: 3411 Woodland Rd Ann Arbor MI 48104-4257 Office: U Mich PO Box 620 Ann Arbor MI 48106-0620 E-mail: frwh@umich.edu.

WHITEHOUSE, FRED WAITE, endocrinologist, researcher; b. Chgo., May 6, 1926; s. Fred Trafton Waite and Grace Caroline (Peters) W.; m. Iris Jean Dawson, June 6, 1953; children: Martha, Amy, Sarah. Student, Northwestern U., 1943-45; BS, U. Ill., Chgo., 1947, MD, 1949. Diplomate Am. Bd. Internal Medicine; cert. endocrinology and metabolism. Intern, then resident Henry Ford Hosp., Detroit, 1949-53, staff physician, 1955—, chief divsn. metabolism, 1962-88, chief divsn. endocrinology and metabolism, 1988-95; divsn. head emeritus, 1995—; fellow Joslin Clinic, Boston, 1954-55. Cons. FDA, Washington, 1980—; mem. Coalition on Diabetes Edn. and Minority Health, 1989-91. Contbr. articles to profl. jours. Bd. dirs. Wheat Ridge Found., 1984-93. Lt. USNR, 1951-53. Master ACP; mem. NIH (nat. diabetes adv. bd. 1984-88), Am. Diabetes Assn. (pres. 1978-79, Banting medal 1979, Outstanding Clinician award 1989, Outstanding Physician Educators award 1994), Detroit Med. Club (pres. 1976), Detroit Acad. Medicine (pres. 1991-92). Lutheran. Avocations: bicycling, gardening. Home: 1265 Blairmoor Ct Grosse Pointe Woods MI 48236-1230 Office: Henry Ford Hosp 2799 W Grand Blvd Detroit MI 48202-2689 Fax: (313) 916-8343. E-mail: fwhitehouse@msms.org.

WHITEHOUSE, GARY, industrial engineer, educator, university provost; b. Trenton, N.J., Aug. 13, 1938; s. Edward Ernest and Lorraine Lee Etta (Baker) W.; m. Marian Greenhalgh, Aug. 24, 1963; children: Gail W. DePuy, Glenn Alan. BS in Indsl. Engring., Lehigh U., 1960, MS in Indsl. Engring., 1962; PhD, Ariz. State U., 1966. Registered profl. engr., Fla. Instr. indsl. engring. Lehigh U., Bethlehem, Pa., 1962-63; instr. Ariz. State U., Tempe, 1963-65; asst. prof. Lehigh U., Bethlehem, 1965-69, assoc. prof., 1969-74, prof., 1974-78; dept. chmn. U. Cen. Fla., Orlando, 1978-83, prof., 1983-87, acting dean, 1987-88, dean, 1988-93; provost, v.p. acad. affairs, 1993—. Cons. Air Products and Chem., Allentown, Pa., 1965-78, Martin-Marietta, Orlando, 1986-92. Author: Analysis and Design of Systems using Network Techniques, 1973, Applied Operations Research, 1976, Practical Partners (Outstanding I.E. Publ. award), 1985; co-author: Computer Tools, Models and Techniques for Project Management, 1989; editor: Software for Engineers and Managers, 1984, Softcover Software-28 Programsfor the IE and Manager, 1985, Proceedings of the 7th Annual Computers and Industrial Engring Conf., 1985, Software for Engineers and Managers Volume II, 1987; co-editor: Proceedings of the 8th Annual Conference on Computers and Industrial Engineering, 1986, Proceedings of the 9th Annual Conference on Computers and Industrial Engineering, 1986; editor I.E. Micro column, 1980-92; assoc. editor Computers and I.E. jour., 1983-89; contbr. articles to profl. jours. Fellow Inst. Indsl. Engrs. (dir. 1976-78, H.B. Maynard award 1978, Computer and Info. Systems Div. award 1982), Am. Soc. Engring. Educators (Western Electric award 1976), Fla. Engring. Soc. (com. chmn.). Democrat. Avocations: biking, music, sports. Home: 1251 Hillsbrough Rd Geneva FL 32732-9612 Office: U Ctrl Fla Office Acad Affairs PO Box 160065 Orlando FL 32816-0065 E-mail: whitehse@mail.ucf.edu.

WHITEHOUSE, JOHN HARLAN, JR. systems software consultant, diagnostician; b. Lakewood, Ohio, Sept. 12, 1951; s. John Harlan and Frances Elizabeth (Nation) W.; divorced; 1 child, John Harlan III. BA magna cum laude, Ohio Wesleyan U., 1973; MBA, Cleve. State U., 1976; PhD, Columbia Pacific U., San Rafael, Calif., 1988; postgrad., U. Chgo., 1974, Vedic U. of Am., 1996—. Cert. computing profl.; cert. info. sys. auditor; cert. in Visual Basic. Programmer San Antonio Express-News, 1977; programming mgr. S.W. Info. Mgmt. Sys., San Antonio, 1977, Utility Data Corp., Houston, 1978; sr. data sys. auditor Nat. City Corp., Cleve., 1978-81; sys. programmer Standard Oil Co., 1981-84; adv. sys. engr. IBM, 1984-92; pres. Semiotica Corp., 1992—. Mem. exams. editl. coun. Inst. for Cert. Computer Profls., Des Plaines, 1990—, test deployment mgr., 1996-2001, dir. certification, 1999—. Author: CICS Problem Determination Workshop, 1990; co-author: ICCP Guidelines for Recertification, 1990, ICCP Official Study Guide, 1991-95; editor Clifton-Gaston Allen Light, 1994—; also numerous articles, columnist. Mem. Assn. for Computing Machinery (chmn. Greater Cleve. chpt. 1982-83, Svc. Recognition award 1984), Assn. of Inst. for Cert. Computer Profls. (regional dir. 1989-93, nominating com. 1991), Masons, Philalethes Soc., Phi Beta Kappa. Unitarian Universalist. Home: 22291 Berry Dr Rocky River OH 44116-2013 Office: Semiotica Corp PMB 241 25935 Detroit Rd Westlake OH 44145-2449 E-mail: consultx@ix.netcom.com.

WHITEHOUSE, SHELDON, state attorney general, lawyer; b. N.Y.C., Oct. 20, 1955; s. Charles Sheldon and Mary (Rand) Whitehouse; m. Sandra Christine Thornton, Sept. 20, 1986; 2 children. BA, Yale U., 1978; JD, U. Va., 1982. Bar: W.Va. 1982, R.I. 1983, U.S. Dist. Ct. R.I. 1984, U.S. Supreme Ct. 1986, U.S. Ct. Appeals (1st cir.) 1984. Atty., Providence, 1983—84; spl. asst. atty. gen., 1985—90; chief regulatory unit, 1988—90; asst. atty. gen.,

1989—90; exec. counsel Office of Gov., 1991, dir. gov. policy office, 1991—92; dir. Dept. Bus. Regulation, 1992—94; U.S. atty for dist. of R.I., 1994—98; atty. gen. State of R.I., 1999—.*

WHITEHURST, BROOKS MORRIS, chemical engineer; b. Apr. 9, 1930; s. David Brooks and Bessie Ann (Lowry) W.; m. Carolyn Sue Boyer, July 4, 1951; children: Garnett, Anita, Robert. BS, Va. Poly. Inst. and State U., 1951. Registered profl. engr., N.C. Sr. process engr. Am. Enka Corp., Lowland, Tenn., 1951-56; sr. process devel. engr. Va.-Carolina Chem. Corp., Richmond, Va., 1956-63; project engr. Texaco Inc., 1963-66; mgr. engring. svcs. Texasgulf, Inc., Aurora, N.C., 1967-80, mgr. spl. projects, long range planning, 1980-81; pres. Whitehurst Assocs., Inc., New Bern, 1981—. Instr., lectr., cons. alt. sources of energy comty. colls. and univs.; presenter paper Solar World Forum, Brighton, Eng., 1981. Co-chmn. N.C. state supt. task force on secondary edn., 1974—; mem. N.C. state adv. com. on trade and indsl. edn, 1971-77; chmn. Gov.'s Task Force Vols. in Workplace, 1981; chmn. State Adv. Coun. Career Edn., 1977—; gov.'s liaison for edn. and bus., 1978-79. Recipient commendation Pres. U.S., 1981. Mem. AIChE, Am. Inst. Chemists (cert., bd. dirs. 1980-84), N.C. Inst. Chemists (pres. 1975-77), Nat. Soc. Profl. Engrs., N.C. Soc. Profl. Engrs., Royal Soc. Chemistry. Achievements include patents and current work on biodegradable chelate systems, municipal yard waste disposal, micronutrients for agriculture, waste rubber recycling, conversion of industrial by-products containing manganese and phosphorous to useful non-toxic materials for use in agriculture for environmental clean-up; development of environmentally friendly products for forest fertilization. Home: 1983 Hoods Creek Rd New Bern NC 28562-9103 Office: PO Box 3335 New Bern NC 28564-3335

WHITEHURST, GROVER JAY, psychologist and educator; b. Washington, Sept. 28, 1944; s. Grover J. and Dixie (Daniel) W.; m. Janet E. Fischel, June 7, 1981; children: Owen E., Adam E. BA, East Carolina U., Greenville, 1966; MA, U. Ill., 1968, PhD, 1970. Lic. psychologist, N.Y. Asst. prof. SUNY, Stony Brook, 1970-74, assoc. prof., 1975-79, prof. psychology, 1981—, chair dept. psychology, 1998—; sr. lectr. U. N.S.W., Sydney, Australia, 1974-75; acad. v.p. Merrill-Palmer Inst., Detroit, 1979-81. Author: Child Behavior, 1977; editor Developmental Rev., 1981-2000; contbr. over 100 articles to profl. jours. Grantee NIH, 1985, Smith Richardson Found., 1990, Pew Charitable Trusts, 1992, U.S. Adminstrn. Children and Families, 1996, 2000. Fellow APA, Am. Assn. Profl. and Applied Psychology; Nat. Rsch. Coun. (commn. early childhood); Head Start, Nat. Adv. Bd. on Rsch. Avocations: sailing. Office: SUNY Dept Psychology Stony Brook NY 11794-2500*

WHITEHURST, MARY TARR, artist, poet, writer; b. Norfolk, Va., Nov. 20, 1923; d. Henry Bennitt and Martha Ida Tarr; m. Jerry Rutter Whitehurst, Dec. 24, 1943; children: Henry Armistead, Jeffrey Tarr, Martha W. Bryant. Student, Coll. William & Mary, 1940-42, Wytheville C.C., 1968, Sullins Coll., 1976-80, Va. Western C.C., 1988. Docent Mus. Fine Arts, Roanoke, Va., 1973-75. Dir., endowing mem. Fine Arts Ctr. of New River Valley, Pulaski, Va., 1980-93; charter, endowing mem. Bristol Mus. Fine Arts, Va./Tenn., 1975-80; benefactor, mem. Arts Found. Radford U., Va., 1991—. One-woman shows include Mus. Fine Arts, Roanoke, Va., 1977, Emory & Henry Coll., Emory, Va., 1982, Radford U. Art Gallery, Va., 1991, Ashland Area Art Galery, Ky., 1993, Va. Polytech. Inst. & State U., Blacksburg, 1985—, New River C.C. Found., 1985—, Coll. William & Mary, Williamsburg, 1995; endowment Poly. Inst. & State U., Blacksburg, Va., 1998; author: (poetry) Silent As Birds, 1997. Endowing mem. Va. Polytech. Inst. & State U., Blacksburg, 1985—, New River C.C. Found., 1985—, Coll. William & Mary, Williamsburg, 1995; mem. Va. Polytech. Found., Blacksburg, Va. Recipient Clement Gueenberg award of distinction Mus. Fine Arts, Roanoke, 1976, Grumbacher Gold medal Soc. Water Color Artists, 1995; art dept. named in honor New River C.C., Dublin, Va., 1994. Mem. Catharine Lorillard Wolfe Art Club (Joyce Williams water color award 1985), Midwest Transparent Water Color Soc. (signature mem.), Va. Water Color Soc. (dir. 1994), Ala. Water Color Soc., Blacksburg Regional Artists Assn., Allied Artists (assoc.), So. Water Color Soc. (two awards 1997, Blue Ribbon winner 2000). Avocations: travel abroad, art collection, history, philanthropy. Home: Painters Wood 2492 Forest Hill Dr Draper VA 24324-3224

WHITEHURST, WILLIAM WILFRED, JR. management consultant; b. Balt., Mar. 4, 1937; s. William Wilfred and Elizabeth (Hogg) W.; B.A., Princeton, 1958; M.S. with distinction, Carnegie Inst. Tech., 1963; m. Linda Joan Potter, July 1, 1961; children— Catherine Elizabeth, William Wilfred, III. Mathematician Nat. Security Agy., Fort George G. Meade, Md., 1961-63; mgmt. cons. McKinsey & Co., Inc., Washington, 1963-66; partner L.E. Peabody & Assos., Washington, 1966-69, exec. v.p., dir. L.E. Peabody & Assos., Inc., Lanham, Md., 1969-82, pres., dir., 1983-86, pres. W.W. Whitehurst & Assoc., Inc., Cockeysville, Md., 1986—. Contbr. to Code of Fed. Regulations 49 C.F.R. Sect. 1157. Served to comdr. USNR, 1958-65. Recipient Diploma De Honor 14th Pan Am. Rwy. Congress. Mem. Am. Railway Engring. Assn., Transportation Rsch. Forum, Assn. for Investment Mgmt. and Rsch., Washington Soc. Investment Analysts. Episcopalian. Clubs: University, Princeton (Washington); Princeton (N.J.) Quadrangle. Home and Office: 12421 Happy Hollow Rd Cockeysville Hunt Valley MD 21030-1711

WHITEKER, ROY ARCHIE, retired chemistry educator; b. Long Beach, Calif., Aug. 22, 1927; s. Ewing Harris and Mabel Mary (Williams) W.; m. Jean Fiske MacLean, June 3, 1960; 1 son, Scott MacLean. BS, UCLA, 1950, MS, 1952; PhD, Calif. Inst. Tech., 1956. Instr. chemistry M.I.T., 1955-57; asst. prof. Harvey Mudd Coll., Claremont, Calif., 1957-61, assoc. prof., 1961-67, prof. chemistry, 1967-73; assoc. dir. fellowships Nat. Acad. Scis., Washington, 1967-68; dep. exec. sec. Council Internat. Exchange Scholar, 1971-72; exec. sec. Com. on Internat. Exch. of Persons, 1972—75; dir. Coun. Internat. Exchange Scholar, 1975-76; prof. chemistry U. Pacific, Stockton, Calif., 1976-92, dean Coll. Pacific, 1976-89. Bd. dirs. Stockton Symphony Assn., 1978-80; dir. cmty. adv. bd. Sta. KUOP, 1981-89; bd. dirs. Stockton Chorale, 1989-97; pres. U. of the Pacific Emeriti Soc., 1992-94, 2000-02. With USNR, 1945-46. Recipient Dow Chem. Co. fellowship, 1953-54; DuPont Teaching fellowship, 1954-55; NSF Sci. Faculty fellowship Royal Inst. Tech., Stockholm, Sweden, 1963-64 Mem. Am. Chem. Soc., Alpha Chi Sigma, Phi Beta Kappa, Phi Kappa Phi, Sigma Xi. Home: 3734 Portsmouth Cir N Stockton CA 95219-3843 E-mail: rwhiteker@uop.edu.

WHITELAW, CHRISTINE CAPPELLE, pediatrician, educator; b. DePere, Wis., Mar. 18, 1960; d. Aloyiosus Jules and Audrey Mae (Jacques) Cappelle; m. Grady Lightfoot Whitelaw, Oct. 29, 1994; children: Conlon Arthur, Robert Dean, Hayden Keith. Student, Baylor U., 1978-79; BS in Biology, U. Notre Dame, 1982; MD, St. George's U., Grenada, West Indies, 1989. Diplomate Am. Bd. Pediatrics. Intern and resident in pediat. Pitt County Meml. Hosp. E. Carolina U., Greenville, N.C., 1989-91; resident in pediat. Children's Hosp. King's Dau. E. Va. Med. Sch., Norfolk, 1991-92; fellow in pediatric emergency medicine U. Louisville, 1992-94, clin. instr., 1994-95, asst. prof., 1995-99, clin. prof., 1999—. Contbr. articles to profl. jours. Mem. sci. coun. cardiopulmonary and critical care Am. Heart Assn.; camp physician Beber Camp, Mushwonaka, Wis., 1999. Alliant Cmty. Trust Fund grantee, 1997. Mem. European Resuscitation Coun., Am. Acad. Pediat., Jefferson County Med. Soc. Avocations: tennis, skiing, running. Home: 4000 Greenhaven Ln Goshen KY 40026 Office: U Louisville Dept Pediat 235 E Chestnut St Louisville KY 40292 E-mail: cgwhitelaw@email.msn.com.

WHITELAW, DOLORES FAHEY, artist; b. Bklyn., June 12, 1941; d. John Michael and Irene Marie (Bulger) Fahey; m. Bruce David Whitelaw, June 23, 1962; children: Erin Carolyn, Casey Bruce. Student, Newark Sch Fine & Indsl. Arts, 1959, 60, Art Student League, 1962, 63. One woman shows include E3 Gallery, N.Y.C., 1996, Les Malamut Art Gallery, Union, N.J., 1998; exhibited in group shows at Carole Franklin Gallery, Emerson, N.J., 1997, JCB Internat., N.Y.C., 1997, La MaMa La Galleria, N.Y.C., 1998, Westbeth Gallery, N.Y.C., 1998. Mem. Orgn. Ind. Artists, City Without Walls. Home: 362 Forest Dr Union NJ 07083-7942

WHITELAW, KEVIN JOHN, journalist; b. London, Mar. 28, 1973; s. John David and Susan (Johnson) W. B, Princeton U., 1995. Reporter bus. sect. U.S. News & World Report, Washington, 1995—96, assoc. editor world sect., 1996—2001, sr. editor world sect., 2001—. Contbr. numerous articles on world affairs. Office: US News and World Report 1050 Thomas Jefferson St NW Washington DC 20007-3837 E-mail: kwhitelaw@usnews.com.

WHITELEY, BENJAMIN ROBERT, retired insurance company executive; b. Des Moines, July 13, 1929; s. Hiram Everett and Martha Jane (Walker) W.; m. Elaine Marie Yunker, June 14, 1953; children— Stephen Robert, Benjamin Walker BS, Oreg. State U., 1951; MS, U. Mich., 1952; postgrad. advanced mgmt. program, Harvard U.; DHL (hon.), Pacific U., 2001. Clk. group dept. Standard Ins. Co., Portland, Oreg., 1956-59, asst. actuary group dept. then asst. actuary actuarial dept., 1959-63, asst. v.p., asst. actuary, 1963-64, asst. v.p., assoc. actuary, 1964-70, v.p. group ins. adminstrn., 1970-72, v.p. group ins. div., 1972-80, exec. v.p. group ins., 1980-81, exec. v.p., 1981-83, pres., CEO, 1983-92, chmn. bd. dirs., CEO, 1993-94, chmn. bd. dirs., 1994—98; ret., 2000. Bd. dirs. Gunderson, Inc., Portland, The Greenbrier Cos. Past pres. Columbia Pacific coun. Boy Scouts Am.; past chmn. bd., trustee Pacific U., Forest Grove, Oreg.; past chmn. Oreg. Health Scis. Found., Oreg. Trail Coordinating Coun., Portland Opera Assn.; trustee Oreg. Cmty. Found., 1998—; campaign chair, bd. mem. United Way Portland, 1994. 1st lt. USAF, 1952-55. Recipient Silver Beaver award Cascade Pacific coun. Boy Scouts Am., 1993, Harvey and Emiline Clark medal Pacific U., 1991, Alumni fellow award Oreg. State U., 1991, Aubrey R. Watzek award Lewis and Clark Coll., 1994, Lifetime Achievement award Bus. Youth Exch., Portland, Oreg., 1995. Fellow Soc. Actuaries; mem. Am. Acad. Actuaries (bd. dirs. 1984-86), Am. Council of Life Ins. (bd. dirs. 1986-89), Internat. Congress Actuaries, Portland C. of C. (bd. dirs. 1983-89). Clubs: Arlington (pres. 1991), Waverley Country, Multnomah Athletic (Portland, Oreg.). Republican. Methodist. E-mail: eorbwhiteley@earthlink.net.

WHITELEY, HAROLD LEE, director; b. Graham, Tex., Aug. 5, 1948; s. Arthur Wiley and Cecilia Elizabeth (Boisclair) W.; m. Linda Sue Day, Dec. 27, 1969; children: Michael Kevin, Jason Lee, Christopher Brian, Kristen Michelle BS, N. Tex. State U., 1970, MS, 1972; PhD, U. North Tex., 1995. Tchr. math., coach Newcastle (Tex.) Ind. Sch. Dist., 1970-71; tchr. biology, head football, basketball, track & field coach Munday (Tex.) Ind. Sch. Dist., 1971-73; asst. prin., athletic dir., head coach football, basketball and track, tchr. Argyle (Tex.) Rural H.S., 1973-77; mgr. S.E. & N.W. mktg. Turbo Refrigerating Co., Denton, Tex., 1977-82; pres., owner ICE Sys. Internat. Inc., Marietta, Ga., 1982-85, Whiteley & Assocs., Lewisville, Tex., 1983—; transp. rep. Spl. Programs for Assisting the Needy, Inc., 1992-97. Pres., owner So. Heritage Developers, Inc., Marietta, 1980-84, So. Heritage Assessments, Inc., Lewisville, 1984—; aerial crop photo technician Agrl. Stabilization and Conservation Svc. Denton, 1991—; instr. golf, tennis, raquetball U. North Tex., Denton, 1989-90; ind. rep. Destiny Telecom. Internat., Inc., 1997—, Hello World, Inc., 1997—, Telecom Resources, Internat., 1997—; lic. realtor, Tex., 1999—/ Inventor (game boards) Bass Classic, 1986, Golf Classic, 1986; developer Amateur Sports Network, 1991, Amateur Team Golf Assn., 1991; contbr. articles on HIV issues in athletics to profl. jours. Grantee Bertha Found., 1991. Mem. Nat. Athletic Trainers Assn., Nat. Assn. Acad. Advisors for Athletes, Am. Assn. Wellnes Edn. Counseling and Rsch., Nat. Assn. Coll. Dirs. of Athletics, Am. Med. Athletic Assn., Golden Key Honor Soc. Baptist. Avocations: tennis, softball, refinishing antiques, writing, recreational activities. Home and Office: 531 W Main St Ste 100 Lewisville TX 75057-3628 Fax: 972-221-0533. E-mail: Whiteleyphd@msn.com.

WHITELEY, HENRY HOWARD, religious studies educator, minister; b. Roswell, N.Mex., Oct. 31, 1928; s. Alford and Ruth Henrich Whiteley; m. Yvonna Margaret Cornell, Feb. 28, 1953; children: Emma Lachelle Whiteley Yoder, Lynn Howard. BS in Music Edn., John Brown U., Siloam Springs, Ark., 1961; postgrad., West Tex. State U., 1963. Tchr., band dir. K-12 Gravette Pub. Schs., Ark., 1960—62, Balko Pub. Schs., Okla., 1962—63; minister Galena, Kans., Hardesty, Okla., Logan, Baxter Springs, Kans.; prof. music, bibl. studies Apostolic Faith Bible Coll., 1965—68, 1984—88, 1995—, supt., 1977—78; pastor Pampa Chapel of Apostolic Faith, Tex., 1988—95. Founder, dir. Cantatas cmty. choir, 1965—70. Editor: Apostolic Faith Report, 1964—72. Dir. Ann. Nat. Ch. Camp, Baxter Springs, 1965—69, Laverne, Okla., 1973, 1975; pres. Ministerial Alliance, Pampa, 1990, sec. Baxter Springs, Kans., 1999—2000; dir. Ann. Youth Camp, 1965—69, Laverne, 1973—75; adv. bd. Salvation Army, Pampa, 1993—95; bd. dirs. Apostolic Faith Bible Coll., 1971—78. Cpl. U.S. Army, 1948—51. Trinity Apostolic Faith. Avocations: reading, music, travel. Mailing: 2353 Washington Baxter Springs KS 66713

WHITELEY, JAMES MORRIS, retired aerospace engineer; b. Bangs, Tex., Jan. 27, 1927; s. Charles David and Ruby May (Snead) W.; m. Oleta Wright Basham, Nov. 6, 1993. BS, Daniel Baker Coll., 1951; postgrad., U. Va., 1951-52, So. Meth. U., 1954-57. Rsch. scientist Nat. Adv. Com. for Aeronautics, Hampton, Va., 1951-52; engring. specialist Gen. Dynamics, Ft. Worth, 1952-91; ret., 1991. With USN, 1945-46, PTO. Assoc. fellow AIAA; mem. AARP, The Air Force Assn., Am. Legion. Home: PO Box 297 Bangs TX 76823-0297

WHITELEY, ROSE MARIE, city clerk, treasurer; b. Benkelman, Nebr., Mar. 26, 1942; d. Alvin James and Grace Rebecca (Alsbury) W. BS, Nebr. State U., Kearney, 1963; MS, Colo. State U., 1968. Cert. home cons./bus. secondary tchr. Home econs. instr. Deuel County H.S., Chappell, Nebr., 1963-66; adult ednl. cons. McCalls Patterns, N.Y.C., 1967-70; exec. dir. Nebr./Iowa chpt. Nat. Multiple Sclerosis Soc., Omaha, 1971-78; grant writer, fundraising dir. Omaha Theatre, 1978-94; city clk., treas. City of Benkelman, 1994—. Cons. Fundraising/Grantwriting, Omaha, 1982-94, 94—. Contbr.: The Harvest Gardener, 1992. Treas. Prevention Policy Bd., 1994—, Dundy County Resource Ctr., 1994-2001, pres., 2001--; mem. Benkelman Tree Bd., 1994—. Mem. S.W. Clks. Assn. (pres.), Nebr. Mcpl. Clks. Assn., Internat. Inst. of Mcpl. Clks., Kappa Omicron Phi. Avocations: gardening, gourmet cooking. Home: HC 64 Box 58 Benkelman NE 69021-9156 Office: City of Benkelman PO Box 347 Benkelman NE 69021-0347

WHITEMAN, DAVID NEIL, physicist; b. Washington, Apr. 6, 1956; s. Arley Blaine and Lois Katherine Whiteman; m. Iliana Maria Restrepo, June 6, 1998; children: Stephanie. PhD, U. Md., 2000. Physical scientist NASA Goddard Space Flight Ctr., Greenbelt, Md., 1979—. Pres. LFRA Flying Club, Washington, 1992—94. Mem.: Am. Meteor. Soc. (com.laser atmopsheric sensing 2001—), Am. Physical Soc., Am. Geophysical Union, Optical Soc. of Am. (Allen prize 2001). Avocations: hiking, travel, piano, flying. Office: NASA Goddard Space Flight Center Building 33 Room D404 Code 912 Greenbelt MD 20771 Fax: 301-614-5492. Business E-Mail: david.whiteman@gsfc.nasa.gov.

WHITEMAN, DOUGLAS E. publisher; b. Emporia, Kans., Mar. 4, 1961; s. Floyd E. and Phyllis E. (Troyer) W.; m. Susan R. Anderson, Sept. 14, 1985; 1 child, Aaron Anderson Douglas. BS in Bus. Administrn., U. Kans., 1983. With Putnam Pub. Group, Denver and N.Y.C., 1983—, dir. trade sales and mktg., internat. sales mgr. N.Y.C., 1987-89, v.p. sales and mktg., 1989-94; sr. v.p., pub. Putnam and Grosset Book Group, 1994-95, pres., pub., 1995-97; pres. Penguin Putnam Books for Young Readers, 1997—. Methodist. Avocations: literature, tennis, fantasy baseball. Office: Penguin Putnam Inc 345 Hudson St Fl 14 New York NY 10014-4592 E-mail: dwhiteman@penguinputnam.com.

WHITEMAN, JOSEPH DAVID, retired lawyer, manufacturing company executive; b. Sioux Falls, S.D., Sept. 12, 1933; s. Samuel D. and Margaret (Wallace) W.; m. Mary Kelly, Dec. 29, 1962; children: Anne Margaret, Mary Ellen, Joseph David, Sarah Kelly, Jane. BA, U. Mich., 1955, JD, 1960. Bar: D.C. 1960, Ohio 1976. Assoc. Cox, Langford, Stoddard & Cutler, Washington, 1959-64; sec., gen. counsel Studebaker group Studebaker Worthington, Inc., N.Y.C., 1964-71; asst. gen. counsel. United Telecommunications, Inc., Kansas City, Mo., 1971-74; v.p., gen. counsel, sec. Weatherhead Co., Cleve., 1974-77, Parker Hannifin Corp., Cleve., 1977-98; ret., 1998. Immediate past chmn. bd. dirs. St. Lukes Med. Ctr. Served as lt. USNR, 1955-57. Mem. ABA, Beta Theta Pi, Phi Delta Phi. Republican. Roman Catholic. Home and Office: 2508 Robinson Springs Rd Stowe VT 05672

WHITEMAN, RICHARD FRANK, architect; b. Mankato, Minn., Mar. 24, 1925; s. Lester Raymond and Mary Grace (Dawald) W.; m. Jean Frances Waite, June 20, 1948 (dec. May 1980); children: David, Sarah, Lynn, Ann, Carol, Frank, Marie, Steven; m. Mavis Patricia Knutsen, May 30, 1982. BArch, U. Minn., 1945; MArch, Harvard U., 1948. Registered architect, Minn. Designer Ellerbe Co., St. Paul, 1946; architect Thorshov and Cerny, Mpls., 1948-53; ptnr. Jyring and Whiteman, Hibbing, Minn., 1953-62; pres. AJWM Inc., Hibbing and Duluth, 1963-72, Architects Four, Duluth, 1972-83; owner Richard Whiteman, 1983-95; sr. architect U. Minn. Chmn. Architect Sect. Registration Bd., Minn., 1972-80. Prin. works include Washington Sch., Hibbing, 1957 (Minn. Soc. Architects Design award 1957), Whiteman Summer Home, Pengilly, Minn. (Minn. Soc. Architects Design award 1959), Bemidji State Coll. Phys. Edn. Bldg. (Minn. Soc. Architects Design award 1960), Whiteman Residence, Griggs Hall UMD, 1990. Pres. U. for Srs., 1993-94; mem. adv. com. Glensheen, U. Minn. Duluth; active Duluth Housing Authority, 2001—. Mem. Minn. Soc. Architects (pres. 1972), Northeast Minn. Architects (pres. 1962), Service Corps Retired Execs. (chmn. Northeast Minn. chpt. 1986), Minn. Designer Selection Bd. (chmn. 1990). Clubs: Kitchi Gammi (Duluth). Lodges: Kiwanis. Democrat. Roman Catholic. Avocations: photography, fishing, cross-country skiing, travel. Home: 3500 E 3rd St Duluth MN 55804-1812

WHITENER, CAROLYN RAYE, artist; b. Corpus Christi, Tex., Feb. 2, 1941; d. Rayburn N. and Alice G. Hamilton; m. Howard Dwain Whitener; children: Mark Dwain, Rynn Rayna. Student, U. Sci. and Arts Okla., 1981-85. Co-owner Honk'n'Holler's, Stillwater, Okla., 1962-75; owner Clynn's Designs, 1969—; co-owner W&W Cattle Ranch, Ninnekah, Okla., 1973—; comml. artist, co-owner Colorvision, Inc., Okla. and Tex., 1979—. Cons. Tele-Weight, Buena Vista, Colo., 1985-92, Craig Versus Boren, 1972-76; design cons. Rynn's Svcs., Oklahoma City, 1997—. Active Grady County Environ. Coalition, 1991-92. Recipient Outstanding Cmty. Svc. award, 1992, One Person Who Made a Difference LWVOK, 1997, Pres. Prestigious award Okla. State U., 1996, First Adv. award Okla. Commn. on Status of Women, 2001, Gov.'s Commendation award Gov. Frank Keating, 2001, State of Okla. Citation award Rep. Richard Phillips and Sen. Mike Fair, 2001; named Woman of Yr. Okla. City Coun. of Beta Sigma Phi, 1997-98, other awards. Mem. Okla. Assn. Family Cmty. and Edn., Grady County Ext. Homemakers, Oklahoma City Newcomer's Club, Beta Sigma Phi (Woman of Yr. award 1997-98, Outstanding Svc. award 1992, Evening Lions Homecoming Window Design awards, 1966-68). Democrat. Methodist. Avocations: art, sewing, cooking, travel, meeting new people. E-mial. Home: 10400 Mantle Dr Oklahoma City OK 73162-4522 E-mail: CrWhitener@aol.com.

WHITENER, LAWRENCE BRUCE, political consultant, consumer advocate, educator; b. Alexandria, Va., Mar. 5, 1952; s. Ralph Verly and Alice Lee W.; m. Deborah Susan Koons, Dec. 7, 1985; 1 foster child. BA in History and Polit. Sci., Va. Commonwealth U., 1975; diploma, Nat. Inst. Real Estate, 1986; AA in Sci., No. Va. C.C., Annandale, 1987, student, 1995—. Tchr. Fairfax (Va.) County Pub. Schs., 1975-96, Arlington (Va.) Pub. Schs., 1998—; wholesaler Consignment Auto, Falls Church, Va., 1975-77; coach Groveton High Sch. Wrestling Team, Alexandria, 1975-77; senate aide Va. Gen. Assembly, Richmond, 1978; pres. Whitener Cons., Springfield, Va., 1977-86, Real Estate Fin. Svcs., Springfield, 1986-90; U.S. Postal Svc., 1989-97; pres. Amicus Curiae, Springfield, 1992-99; mgr. Petco, 1999-2000, CVS Pharmacy, 2000—. Coach wrestling team Langley H.S., McLean, 1991-93, J.E.B. Stuart H.S., Falls Church, 1993-95, Mt. Vernon Wrestling Club, 1997-99; panelist Am. Arbitration Assn., Washington; automotive and banking specialist, 1994—. Author poetry, 1975, 76, 94, 97, screenplays Sorrow, 1993, Saro, 1996; photographer landscapes; subject of article in The Postal Record, 1996. Mem. Athletic Coun., Fairfax County, 1975-84; appointee Housing Assistance Adv. Com., Fairfax County, 1990; commr. Indsl. Devel. Authority, Fairfax County, 1985-93; candidate Fairfax County Bd. Suprs., Springfield Dist., 1991, Fairfax County Sch. Bd., 1995; chmn. vol. rev. com. Fairfax County Access Cable Ch. 10, 1994—; chmn. W.T. Woodson High Sch.'s Class of '70 25th Reunion, 1995, 30th Reunion, 2000; umpire Am. Softball Assn., 1996—; v.p. Newington Forest Cmty. Assn., 1989-90, bd. dirs., 1998-99; treas. No. Va. Wrestling Found., 1999-2002, commr., 2002-. Recipient Cert. of Appreciation, Fairfax County Bd. of Suprs., 1990, Cert. of Appreciation, Nat. Ctr. for Missing and Exploited Children, 1990. Mem. Mortgage Bankers Assn. (legis. com. 1985-90, edn. com. 1986-89), No. Va. Bd. Realtors (pub. rels. com. 1985-90, Cert. of Appreciation, Am. Home Week 1986, 90), No. Va. Wrestling Assn. (treas. 1999—). Avocations: Tae Kwon Do (Black Belt), scuba diving, skydiving, mountaineer, skiing.

WHITENER, PHILIP CHARLES, aeronautical engineer, consultant; b. Keokuk, Iowa, July 9, 1920; s. Henry Carroll and Katherine Ethel (Graham) W.; m. Joy Carrie Page, Oct. 9, 1943; children: David A., Barbara C., Wendy R., Dixie K. BSME, U. N.Mex., 1941. Ordained to elder Presbyn. Ch., 1956. Engr. Boeing Airplane Co., Seattle, 1941-47, supr. wind tunnel model design, 1947-57, project engr. B-52 flight test, 1957-62, engring. mgr. Fresh I hydrofoil, 1962-65, configurator supersonic transport, 1965-70, with preliminary design advanced concepts, 1970-83, ret., 1983; pres., chief engr. Alpha-Dyne Corp., Bainbridge Island, Wash., 1983-98; mgr. Advanced Marine Concepts, LLC, 1998—. Patentee in field. Organizer Trinity Ch., Burien, Wash., 1962, Highline Reformed Presbyn., Burien, 1970, Liberty Bay Presbyn., Poulsbo, Wash., 1978; pres. Whitener Family Found., Bainbridge Island, 1979; bd. dirs. Mcpl. League of Bainbridge, 1993—, v.p., 1994, pres., 1996—; pres. Mcpl. League Found., 1994-98, bd. dirs., 1998—. Republican. Avocations: designing, computers, boating. Home: 5955 NE Battle Point Dr Bainbridge Island WA 98110 E-mail: pwhitener1@email.msn.com.

WHITENER, WILLIAM GARNETT, dancer, choreographer; b. Seattle, Aug. 17, 1951; s. Warren G. and Virginia Louise (Garnett) W. Student, Cornish Sch. Allied Arts, Seattle, 1958-69. Dancer N.Y.C. Opera, 1969, Joffrey Ballet, N.Y.C., 1969-77, Twyla Tharp Dance, N.Y.C., 1978-87; asst. to choreographer Jerome Robbins for Robbins' Broadway, 1988; artistic dir. Les Ballets Jazz de Montréal, 1991-93, Royal Winnipeg Ballet, 1993-95, Kansas City Ballet, 1996—. Coord. dance dept. Concord Acad., Mass., 1988; vis. artist U. Wash., 1989-91; tchr. Harvard U. Summer Dance, 1989-90, NYU, 1985. Appeared in original Broadway cast Dancin', 1978; choreographer for Princeton Ballet, Joffrey II, John Curry Ice Theatre, Ballet Hispanico of N.Y., Boston Ballet Internat. Choreography Competition, Tommy Tune, Martine Van Hamel/Kevin McKenzie, Ann Reinking, Seattle Repertory Theatre, Am. Ballroom Theater, N.Y.C., Hartford (Conn.) Ballet, On the Boards, (with Bill Irwin) Alive From Off Center (PBS-TV), (opera ensemble of N.Y.) A Little Night Music, Pacific Northwest Ballet, (Seattle Opera) Rusalka, Aida; dancer (films) Amadeus, Zelig, (TV shows) The Catherine Wheel, Dance in America; performer Garden of Earthly Delights, 1988. Bd. trustees DanceUSA, 2000—. Ford Found. scholar, 1963-64. Mem. Actor's Equity, Am. Guild Mus. Artists. Office: Kansas City Ballet 1601 Broadway St Kansas City MO 64108-1207*

WHITE-PLUTZ, ELIZBETH ABBE, artist; b. Hartford, Conn., July 18, 1963; d. Susan Tyron W.; m. David Scott Pultz, May 22, 1993. BFA summa cum laude, Hunter Coll., 1993. Calligrapher Chase Manhattan Bank, N.Y.C., 1986-90; artist, calligrapher Ames & Rollinson, 1992—. Avocation: choral singing. Home: 47 E 3d St Apt 2 New York NY 10003

WHITESELL, DALE EDWARD, retired association executive, natural resources consultant; b. Miamisburg, Ohio, Oct. 12, 1925; s. Harry Parker and Carmen Lucille (Holtzman) W.; m. Alma Irene Wells, Mar. 24, 1945; children: Catherine Elizabeth, Kimberly Lynn. BS, Ohio State U., 1950, MS in Wildlife Mgmt., 1951. Game mgmt. supr. Ohio Div. Wildlife, Xenia, 1951-63, author farmer attitude survey, 1951-58, chief Columbus, 1963-65; sr. exec. v.p. Ducks Unltd., Inc., Long Grove, Ill., 1965-87, ret., 1987. Bd. dirs. Safari Club Internat. Conservation Found., Tucson, 1982-83 Served as 2d lt. USAAF, 1943-46. Fellow Ohio State U., 1950; recipient Conservation award Gulf Oil Co., 1985. Mem. Ohio Wildlife Mgmt. Assn. (pres.), Internat. Assn. Fish, Game and Conservation Commrs. Office: Ducks Unltd Inc 1 Waterfowl Way Memphis TN 38120-2351 *Natural resource conservation means wise use—anything more or less will be manifested in additional zoos, museums, junk yards and the bone yards of fertilizer plants.*

WHITESELL, JOHN EDWIN, motion picture company executive; b. DuBois, Pa., Feb. 23, 1938; s. Guy Roosevelt and Grace Ethlyn (Brisbin) W.; m. Amy H. Jacobs, June 12, 1960; 1 child, Scott Howard; m. Martha Kathlyn Hall, Sept. 3, 1975; m. Phyllis Doyle, May 8, 1993. BA, Pa. State U., 1962. Asst. mgr. non-theatrical div. Columbia Pictures Corp., N.Y.C., 1963-66; with Warner Bros., Inc., 1966—, nat. sales mgr. non-theatrical div. Calif., 1968-75, v.p., 1975-76; v.p. internat. sales adminstrn. Warner Bros. Internat. TV Distbn., 1976-2001, cons., 2001—. Bd. dirs. Mastermedia Internat. Inc.; past bd. dirs. Found. Entertainment Programming in Higher Edn.; mem. self-study com. Nat. Entertainment Conf., 1974-75. Served with USNR, 1956-58. Recipient

Alumni Fellow award Pa. State U., 2001, Outstanding Alumnus award Pa. State U. DuBois Campus, 1995, Founders award Nat. Entertainment Conf., 1975. Mem. Nat. Audio-Visual Assn. (motion picture coun. 1973-76, exec. com. film coun. 1969-76, ednl. materials producers coun. 1970-76), Acad. TV Arts and Scis., Nat. Assn. Media Educators (adv. com. 1973-76)

WHITESELL, STEPHEN ERNEST, parks and recreation director; BS in Environ. Resources, Calif. State U., Sacramento, 1973; M in Landscape Architecture, Harvard U., 1977. Landscape architect, planner Denver Svc. Ctr., Lakewood, Colo., 1977-80, Ind. Dunes Nat. Lakeshore, Porter, Ind., 1980-83; chief maintenance Apostle Islands Nat. Seashore, Bayfield, 1983-84; supt. Longfellow, John F. Kennedy, Frederick Law Olmsted Nat. Hist. Sites, Cambridge, Mass., 1984-87; supt. Sandy Hook Unit Gateway Nat. Recreation Area, Albuquerque, 1987-91; supt. Petroglyph Nat. Monument, San Antonio, 1991-95, San Antonio Missions Nat. Hist. Park, 1995—. Bd. dirs. Cultural Alliance of San Antonio Area Tourism Coun., City Year San Antonio. Recipient Award of Merit Boston Soc. Landscape Architects, 1985, U.S. Dept. Interior Superior Svc. Honor award, 1998. Mem. Boy Scouts Am., Rotary Club San Antonio, South San Antonio C. of C. (adv. dir.), Los Compadres de San Antonio Missions (adv. bd.), San Antonio Tourism Coun. (bd. dirs.). Avocations: golf, fishing, gardening. Office: San Antonio Missions Nat Hist Park 2202 Roosevelt Ave San Antonio TX 78210-4919 Fax: 210-534-1106.

WHITESIDE, CAROL GORDON, foundation executive; b. Chgo., Dec. 15, 1942; d. Paul George and Helen Louise (Barre) G.; m. John Gregory Whiteside, Aug. 15, 1964; children: Brian Paul, Derek James. BA, U. Calif., Davis, 1964. Pers. mgr. Emporium Capwell Co., Santa Rosa, 1964-67; pers. asst. Levi Strauss & Co., San Francisco, 1967-69; project leader Interdatum, 1983-88; with City Coun. Modesto, 1983-87; mayor City of Modesto, 1987-91; asst. sec. for intergovtl. rels. The Resources Agy., State of Calif., Sacramento, 1991-93; dir. intergovtl. affairs Gov.'s Office, 1993-97; pres. Great Valley Ctr., Modesto, Calif., 1997—. Trustee Modesto City Schs., 1979-83; nat. pres. Rep. Mayors and Local Ofcls., 1990. Named Outstanding Woman of Yr. Women's Commn., Stanislaus County, Calif., 1988, Woman of Yr., 27th Assembly Dist., 1991; Toll fellow Coun. of State Govts., 1996. Republican. Lutheran. Office: Great Valley Ctr 911 13th St Modesto CA 95354-0903 E-mail: carol@greatvalley.org.

WHITESIDE, CHARLES B., III, investment company executive; b. Ft. Smith, Ark., Mar. 17, 1941; s. Charles B. Jr. and R. Evelyn Cindy Whiteside; m. Catherine Ware, Jan. 29, 1966; children: Carrie H., Charles B. IV. BSBA, U. Ark., 1963. 1st v.p. Merrill Lynch & Co., Little Rock, 1965—. Trustee Ark. Children's Hosp., 1974—, chmn., treas., 1983-88; trustee Ark. Children's Rsch. Inst., 1989—, chmn., 1990-99; trustee, treas. Lyon Coll., Batesville, Ark., 1992—; bd. dirs. U. Ark. Nat. Devel. Coun., Fayetteville, 1997—; vice chmn. bd. dirs. Ark. Children's Hosp. Found., 1983—. 1st Lt. U.S. Army, 1963-65. Recipient Outstanding Vol. Fundraiser award for State of Ark., Nat. Soc. Fund Raising Execs., 2000. Mem. Kappa Sigma Alumni Assn. (pres. bd. dirs. 1974—) Episcopalian. Avocations: hunting, fishing. Office: Merrill Lynch 2200 Rodney Parham Ste 300 Little Rock AR 72212

WHITESIDE, DUNCAN, disability and child welfare foundation executive; b. Boston, Nov. 30, 1935; s. Frederick Shattuck and Caroline Freeman (Lawrence) W.; m. Elena Scott, June 11, 1960 (div. 1975); children: Nicholas, Michael, Sylvia; m. Sandra Gates, 1976; stepchildren: Todd, Tim, Keith, Wendy. AB, Harvard U., 1961; MBA, NYU, 1971; cert. in non-profit mgmt., Columbia U. Russian specialist U.S. Army Security Agy., 1956-58; with Am. Nat. Exhbn., Moscow, 1959, Chase Manhattan Bank, N.Y.C. and Frankfurt, Germany, 1960-72; chair East West Trade Consultants, 1972-75; adminstrv. dir. Transitional Svcs. N.Y., N.Y.C., 1975-77; dir. tech. assistance, pres. One to One Found., 1977-82; dir. Resource Ctr. for Devel. Disabilities, 1983-90; pres. Maidstone Found., 1984—. Vice chair N.Y. State Devel. Disabilities Planning Coun., 1985—; bd. dirs. Mertz Fund, Lakeside Family and Children's Svc., Coun. on Adoptable Children, Inst. for Families and Children, Touch, Inc.; mem. emeritus bd. New Alternatives for Children; adv. bd. Ind. Residenc, Inc., Ecuadorian Muscular Distrophy Assn. Bd. dirs. Unitarian Universalist UN Office, 1991-97, Internat. Com. Fundacion Gen. Ecuatoriana, Quito, Unitarian Universalist Veatch Found., 1989-95, chair, 1992-93; pres. Internat. Assn. Religious Freedom-USA, 1993-96. Recipient Merit award U.S. Info. Agy., 1959; named Chase Manhattan Citizen of Yr., 1972; named Adv. of Yr. N.Y. Asns. Community Residence, 1983, Advs. for Svcs. for Blind Multihandicapped, 1985, Independence Residences, 1993. Mem. Assn. for People with Severe Handicaps, Soviet Am. Sail Found., Includsion Internat., Am. Assn. Mental Retardation. Office: Maidstone Found 1225 Broadway Fl 9 New York NY 10001-4309 E-mail: Whitesideds@Juno.com.

WHITESIDE, GLENN G. aircraft design engineer; b. Long Beach, Calif., Aug. 1, 1961; s. William A. and Helga A. (Herzog) W.; Monica A. Garcia, Dec. 17, 1988. AAS in Automotive Tech., Glendale (Ariz.) C.C., 1987; BS in Mfg. Engring. Tech summa cum laude, Ariz. State U., 1992. Tooling engr. Cessna Aircraft Co., Wichita, Kans., 1993-98, aircraft sys. design engr., 1998-99, landing gear design engr., 1999-2001; mfg. engr. Koch-Glitsch Inc., 2001—. Author: How Products Are Made, Volume 1, 1994, How Products Are Made, Volume 2, 1996 (Libr. Reference Book Award), (with others) Gale Encyclopedia of Science, 1996. Recipient citation of merit Cessna Aircraft Co., 1994, Cert. of Appreciation NASA Tech. Briefs, 1995. AIAA, Nat. Space Soc., Soc. Automotive Engrs. Avocations: space and science fiction, rapid prototyping research. Home: 609 W 2nd St Andover KS 67002-9255 E-mail: siderwhite@att.net.

WHITESIDE, LOWELL STANLEY, seismologist; b. Trinidad, Colo., Jan. 7, 1946; s. Paul Edward and Carrie Belle (Burgess) W. BS, Hamline U., 1968; postgrad., Oswego State U. of N.Y., 1970-72; MS, U. Nebr., 1985; postgrad., Ga. Inst. of Tech., 1986-88; PhD, U. Colo., 1999. Instr. U.S. Peace Corps, Mhlume, Swaziland, 1968-71; rsch. assoc. CIRES, U. Colo., Boulder, 1988-90; geophysicist in charge of internat. earthquake data base NOAA, Nat. Geophys. Data Ctr., 1990-99, natural hazards data dir., 1999—. Vis. rschr. Nuclear and Geol. Scis. Inst., Wellington, New Zealand, 1997; gen. ssec. UN Workshop on Forecasting Nat. Disasters by Geomagnetic Methods, Beijing, 1998, on Geomagnetic Methods, Beijing, 1998; co-chair Internat. Workshop on Statis. Earthquake Prediction, Hangzhou, China, 1998. Scoutmaster Boy Scouts Am., St. Paul, Lincoln, Nebr., 1968-80, camp counselor, 1968-76. Recipient Eagle Scout award Boy Scouts Am., 1968, NGDC/NOAA Customer Svc. award, 1995. Mem. AAAS (chmn. 1986-87, vice chmn. 1985-86, Geology-Geography, Rocky Mountain sect., Outstanding Articles Referee 1992, Best Student Paper award 1984, 85), Seismol. Soc. of Am., Am. Geophys. Union, Sierra Club, Planetary Soc. Presbyterian. Avocations: hiking, camping, music, biking, running. Home: PO Box 3141 Eldorado Springs CO 80025-3141 Office: NOAA/NGDC/NESOIS 325 Broadway St Boulder CO 80305-3337

WHITESIDE, NANCY DARROW, social worker, consultant, therapist, educator; b. N.Y.C., Feb. 12, 1950; d. Robert Morton and Maureen (Sullivan) Darrow; m. David Edward Whiteside, June 14, 1986; 1 child, Daniel Orion. BA, Oberlin Coll., 1972; MSW, Boston U., 1975. lic. clin. social worker, Maine. Med. and pediatric social worker Waltham (Mass.) Hosp., 1975-76; clin. social worker Worcester (Mass.) Youth Guidance Ctr., 1976-78, clin. supr., 1978-85, adminstr. outpatient svcs., 1985-88; pvt. practice Portland, Maine, 1991, Brunswick, 1991—. Mem. adj. faculty U. So. Maine, Gorham and Lewiston, 1989-91; cons. Human Svcs. Devel. Inst., Portland, 1990. Mem. NASW, Acad. Cert. Social Work. Democrat. Avocations: art, reading, film, hiking, swimming. Office: 39 Baribeau Dr Brunswick ME 04011-3242

WHITESIDE, PATRICIA LEE, fine art antique and personal property appraiser; b. Keokuk, Iowa, Dec. 29, 1957; d. Francis Lee and Ruby Elaine (Higbee) W. AA, Merced Coll., 1980; Cert. Appraisal Studies, NYU, 1997, 99. Proprietor estate specialist Lexington Ave. Antiques, Magnolia, Mass., 1984-88; pub., editor, dir. The Art and Antique Tour Guide, 1988—; art advisor, pres. Fine Art and Antique Tour Assocs., 1988—; estate specialist East Coast region, 1981—, New Eng. Appraisers Assn., Palm Beach, Fla., 1988—. Contbr. articles to profl. publs. and newspapers. Active Palm Beach Civic Assn., 1995—, Palm Beach C. of C., 1990—, Children's Mus., Boca Raton, Fla., others. Recipient award Mass. Hist. Assn., Harvard U., 1987, others. Mem. New Eng. Appraisers Assn. (S. Fla. regional dir.), Soc. for the Preservation of New Eng. Antiquities, Compass Inc. Charities, Palm Beach Hist. Soc., Epilepsy Assn., Nat. Assn. Profl. Appraisers, others. Democrat. Avocations: painting, hist. preservation, writing children's books, sailing, travel. Office: PO Box 2101 Palm Beach FL 33480-2101

WHITESIDE, WILLIAM ANTHONY, JR. retired lawyer; b. Phila., Feb. 23, 1929; s. William Anthony and Ellen T. (Hensler) W.; m. Eileen Ann Ferrick, Feb. 27, 1954; children: William Anthony III, Michael P., Eileen A., Richard F., Christopher J., Mary P. BS, Notre Dame U., 1951; LLB, U. Pa., 1954. Bar: Pa. 1955. Assoc. Speiser, Satinsky, Gilliland & Packel, Phila., 1956-58, ptnr., 1958-61, Fox, Rothschild, O'Brien & Frankel, Phila., 1961—2001; ret., 2001. Trustee Am. Coll. Mgmt. and Tech., Dubrovnik, Croatia; chmn. emeritus bd. trustees and exec. com., emeritus trustee, Rochester Inst. of Tech.; mem. pres. adv. coun. U. Notre Dame; bd. dirs. PAL, mem. exec. com.; emeritus trustee Germantown Acad., past pres. 1st lt. USAF, 1954-56. Named Man of Yr. Notre Dame club Phila, 1967. Mem. ABA, Pa. Bar Assn., Phila. Bar Assn., N.Y. Union League Club, Pyramid Club, Wissahickon Skating Club, Pa Soc. Republican. Roman Catholic. Home: 7808 Cobden Rd Glenside PA 19038-7256 also: 901 Gardens Plz Ocean City NJ 08226-4719 Office: Fox Rothschild O'Brien & Frankel 2000 Market St Ste 10 Philadelphia PA 19103-3231

WHITESIDES, GEORGE MCCLELLAND, chemistry educator; b. Louisville, Aug. 3, 1939; m. Barbara Breasted; children: George Thomas, Benjamin Haile. AB, Harvard U., 1960; PhD, Calif. Inst. Tech., 1964. Asst. prof. dept. chemistry MIT, Cambridge, 1963—69, assoc. prof., 1969—71, prof., 1971—75, Arthur C. Cope prof., 1975—80, Haslam and Dewey prof., 1980—82; prof. dept. chemistry Harvard U., 1982—86, Mallinckrodt prof., 1986—. Recipient Pure Chemistry award, Am. Chem. Soc., 1975, Harrison Howe award, Rochester sect., 1979, Arthur C. Cope award, 1995, James Flack Norris award, 1994, Remsen award, 1983, Arthur C. Cope Scholar award, 1989, Disting. Alumni award, Calif. Inst. Tech., 1980, Def. Advanced Rsch. Projects Agy. award, 1996, Madison Marshall award, Am. Chem. Soc., 1996, Nat. Medal of Sci., 1998, von Hippel award, Material Rsch. Soc., 2000; fellow Alfred P. Sloan fellow, 1968. Fellow: AAAS; mem.: Am. Philos. Soc., Am. Acad. Arts and Scis., NAS. Office: Harvard U Dept of Chemistry 12 Oxford St Cambridge MA 02138-2902 E-mail: gwhitesides@gmwgroup.harvard.edu.

WHITESIDES, JOHN LINDSEY, JR. aerospace engineering educator, researcher; b. San Antonio, Feb. 27, 1943; s. John Lindsey and Florene Lyndelle (Wheelis) W.; m. Sheila LaVerne Beadle, May 30, 1964 (div. 1975); children: Lisa Diane, John Gregory; m. Andrea Martina Chavez Lewis, Mar. 26, 1994. BS in Aerospace Engring., U. Tex., 1965, PhD, 1968. Asst. prof. George Washington U., Hampton, Va., 1968-74, assoc. prof., 1974-80, prof., 1980—; assoc. dir. Joint Inst. for Advancement of Flight Scis., 1986—. Contbr. articles to profl. jours. Mem. Sigma Series Lectures, Hampton, 1990-2000. Recipient disting. pub. svc. medal NASA, 1993, Malina medal Internat. Astronautical Fedn., 1995. Fellow AIAA (dir. 1987-93, nat. faculty advisor 1989, v.p. mem. svcs. 1999-2002); mem. Am. Soc. Engring. Edn., Soc. Engring. Sci. (organizing com. 1975, 76, 77), Tau Beta Pi, Phi Eta Sigma, Sigma Gamma Tau. Avocations: sports, art. Home: 218 Cheadle Loop Rd Seaford VA 23696-2428 Office: George Washington U-JIAFS Ms 335 Nasa Lrc Hampton VA 23665 E-mail: j.l.whitesides@seas.gwu.edu.

WHITESIDES, LAWSON EWING, JR. investment management executive; b. Cin., Dec. 31, 1946; s. Lawson Ewing and Elizabeth Igler Whitesides; m. Jane Grissom Whitesides, Sept. 29, 1973; children: Lawson Ewing III, Ellen Elizabeth, Margaret Mary. BSE, Princeton U., 1968; SM in Chem. Engring., MIT, 1971; MBA, Harvard U., 1973. Chartered fin. analyst. Assoc. Stein Roe & Farnham, Chgo., 1973-80, ptnr., 1981-86; 1st v.p. Stein Roe & Farnham, Inc., 1986-87, sr. v.p., 1988-95; v.p., chief investment officer Miami Corp., 1995-98, exec. v.p., chief investment officer, 1999-2000, pres., 2001—, also bd. dirs. Bd. dirs. Cutler Oil & Gas Corp., Chgo., 2000—. Mem. Soc. Colonial Wars (Ill.), Assn. for Investment Mgmt. and Rsch., Investment Analyst Soc. Chgo., The Casino, Indian Hill Club, Chgo. Club, Tau Beta Pi, Sigma Xi. Episcopalian. Office: Miami Corp 410 N Michigan Ave Chicago IL 60611

WHITE-THOMSON, IAN LEONARD, retired mining executive; b. Halstead, Eng., May 3, 1936; came to U.S., 1969; s. Walter Norman and Leonore (Turney) W-T.; m. Barbara Montgomery, Nov. 24, 1971. BA with 1st class honors, New Coll., Oxford U., 1960, MA, 1969. Mgmt. trainee Borax Consol. Ltd., London, 1960-61, asst. to sales mgr., 1961-64, asst. to sales dir., 1964; comml. dir. Hardman & Holden Ltd., Manchester, Eng., 1965-67, joint mng. dir., 1967-69; v.p. mktg. dept. U.S. Borax Inc., Los Angeles, 1969-73, exec. v.p. mktg., 1973-88, pres., 1988-98, also dir., chmn., 1996-99; group exec. Pa. Glass Sand Corp., Ottawa Silica Co., U.S. Silica Co., 1985-87; exec. dir. L.A. Opera, 2000—01; dir. LA Master Chorale, 2001—, Colburn Sch. Performing Arts, 2000—. Bd. dirs. Canpotex Ltd., chmn. bd., 1974-76. Bd. dirs. L.A. Mastor Chorale, Colburn Sch., Amb. Hall. Served with Brit. Army, 1954—56. Named Mfr. of Yr., Calif. Mfrs. Assn., 1997. Mem. Can. Potash Prodrs. Assn. (v.p. 1976-77, dir. 1972-77), Chem. Industry Coun. of Calif. (bd. dirs. 1982-85, chmn. 1984), Am. Mining Congress (bd. dirs. 1989), RTZ Borax and Minerals (bd. dirs. 1992, chief exec. 1995-99), Kerr-McGee Corp. (bd. dirs. 1999—), Calif. Club, Valley Hunt Club, Naval and Mil. Club (London). Home: 851 Lyndon St South Pasadena CA 91030-3712

WHITE-WHITFIELD, LISA DENISE, social worker, career consultant; b. L.A., June 11, 1968; d. Charles L. White and Martha White Jackson, Burrell Jackson (Stepfather); m. Ervin L. Whitfield, Apr. 25, 1992 (div. Oct. 1, 1995); children: Alexis Ximara. BS in Bus. Adminstrn., Calif. State U., Long Beach, 1992; postgrad., Calif. State U., Carson. Tchg. credential Calif. Bank teller Wells Fargo Bank, Lakewood, Calif., 1987—88; proof operator Bank of Am., Long Beach, 1988—89; spl. edn. tchrs. asst. Inglewood (Calif.) Unifield Sch. Dist., 1989—91; adminstrv. asst. Remax Realtors, Carson, 1991—92; substitute tchr. Compton (Calif.) Unified Sch. Dist., 1992—93; acctg. clk. United Airlines, El Segundo, 1993—94; social worker LA County Dept. Pub. Social Svcs., 1994—. Mentor Welfare-to-Work Career Mentor Program, El Monte, CALIF., 2002—. Vol. March of Dimes, L.A., 1994—2000, TDC Dance Acad., L.A., 2002, Redeemer Christian Acad., L.A., 1999, West Angeles Ch. of God in Christ, L.A., 1996—2002. Scholar, Calif. Regional Purchasing Com., 1986. Mem.: ASPA, Dominguez Pub. Adminstrn. Assn., Assn. County Administrs., Calif. State U. Long Beach Alumni Assn. Avocations: marathon running, social research, volunteering, travel, hiking. Office: Los Angeles County Dept Social Svcs 10728 S Central Ave. Los Angeles CA 90059

WHITFIELD, ANDREA BILLINGSLEY, elementary school educator; b. Birmingham, Ala., June 11, 1954; d. Arthur Brooke Billingsley, Ollie Lee (Bolden) Billingsley; children: Andrenetta, April, Amber. BS, Ala. A&M U., 1976; MA, cert. elem. edn., U. Ala. Birmingham, 1978, cert. principalship, 1993. Tchr. reading Blessed Sacrament Sch., Birmingham, 1977—79; tchr. reading Title I Birmingham Bd. Edn., 1979—85, tchr. elem., 1985—. Author (poetry): The Essence of a Flower, 2001 (1st pl., 2001); choreographer praise dance I Believe I Can Fly, 1999 (cert., 2000); contbr. ; founder, dir. Melodies from Heaven Dance Acad. Named Outstanding Young Women Am., Poet of Yr., Inst. Poetry. Mem.: NEA (nat. black caucus 2001—), Birmingham Edn. Assn. (legis. contact team 2000—), Ala. Edn. Assn. (elections com. 2000—, SW minority leader 2000—), Birmingham West End Optimist Club (spkr. 2001—, Plaque 2001), Phi Delta Kappa, Delta Sigma Theta. Democrat. Baptist. Avocations: dancing, reading, writing, backgammon, billiards. Home: 620 McCary St SW Birmingham AL 35211

WHITFIELD, DANIEL, music educator; b. Hollywood, Fla., Jan. 2, 1956; s. Mary Louise Whitfield; m. Rhoda McGhee, Oct. 18, 1980; children: Arnica Danielle, Jarred Sean. BS, Fla. A&M Univ, Tallahassee, FL, 1980. Music tchr. Pineview Elem. Sch., Tallahassee, 1980—88; choral dir. Griffin Mid. Sch., 1988—93, Godby H.S., Tallahassee, 1993—2000, Griffin Mid. Sch., Tallahassee, 2000—; min. of music Phila. P B Ch., 1977—93, Tabernacle M B Ch., Tallahassee, 1993—. Gospel music cons. Trinity M B Ch., Honolulu, 2001—02, Fla. Free Will Bapt. Congress, Fla., 1993—. Mem.: Music Educators Conf., Fla. Vocal Assn, Alpha Phi Alpha Frat. (dean of pledges 1977—79). Democrat-Npl. Baptist. Achievements include founder of Fine Arts Institute (piano,drama,dance). Avocations: piano, basketball. Home: 7869 Maclean Rd Tallahassee FL 32312 Office: Whitfields Music Studio 1406 Hays St Ste S Tallahassee FL 32304 Personal E-mail: minofmusic06@yahoo.com.

WHITFIELD, EDWARD (WAYNE WHITFIELD), congressman; b. Hopkinsville, Ky., May 25, 1943; m. Constance Harriman; 1 child, Kate. BS in Bus., U. Ky., 1965; JD, U. Ky. Coll. of Law, 1969. Mem. Ky. Ho. of Reps., 1974-75; pvt. practice law, 1970-79; govt. affairs counsel Seaboard Sys. R.R. subs. CSX Corp., 1979-83, counsel to pres., 1983-85; v.p. state rels. CSX Corp., 1986-88, v.p. fed. r.r. affairs, 1988-91; legal counsel to chmn. Interstate Commerce Commn., 1991-93; mem. U.S. Congress from 1st Ky. dist., 1995—; mem. energy and commerce com. 1st lt. USAR. Republican. Office: US Ho of Reps 236 Cannon Hob Washington DC 20515-1701*

WHITFIELD, GRAHAM FRANK, orthopedic surgeon; b. Cheam, Surrey, Eng., Feb. 8, 1942; came to U.S., 1969, naturalized, 1975; s. Reginald Frank and Marjorie Joyce (Bennett) W. BSc, King's Coll., U. London, 1963; PhD, Queen Mary Coll., U. London, 1969; MD, N.Y. Med. Coll., 1976. Rsch. scientist Unilever Rsch. Lab., Eng., 1963-66; postdoctoral fellow dept. chemistry Temple U., 1969-71, instr., 1971-72, asst. prof., 1972-73; resident in surgery N.Y. Med. Coll. Affiliated Hosps., N.Y.C., 1976-78, resident in orthopedics, 1978-79, sr. resident in orthopedic surgery, 1979-80, chief resident, 1980-81; attending orthopedic surgeon Good Samaritan Hosp., West Palm Beach, Fla., 1981-87, JFK Med. Ctr., Lake Worth, 1981—, Palms Wellington Surg. Ctr., West Palm Beach, 1994-96, Wellington Regional Med. Ctr., West Palm Beach, 1996—, Bethesda Health City, Boynton Beach, 1996-2000, Palms West Hosp., Loxahatchee, 1997—, Columbia Hosp., West Palm Beach, 1997—2002. Instr. health professions divsn. Nova Southeastern U., North Miami, Fla., 1994-95, clin. asst. prof. dept. surgery, Coll. Osteo. Medicine, Nova Southeaster U., Ft. Lauderdale, Fla., 1995—. Author: (with Joseph Cohn and Louis Del Guercio) Critical Care Readings, 1981; editl. bd., contbg. editor Hosp. Physician, 1978-82; cons. editor Physician Asst. and Health Practitioner, 1979-82; orthopedic cons. Conv. Reporter, 1980-82; assoc. editor in chief Critical Care Monitor, 1980-82; editorl. bd. Complications in Orthopedics, 1986-96; practice panel cons. in orthopedic surgery Complications in Surgery, 1982-96. Recipient N.Y. Med. Coll. Surg. Soc. award, 1976. Fellow Internat. Coll. Surgeons; mem. AMA, Fla. Med. Assn., Palm Beach County Med. Soc., Royal Inst. Chemistry (Eng.), So. Orthopedic Assn., Fla. Orthopedic Soc., Brit. Schs. and Univs. Club, Soc. Sons of St. George (N.Y.C.), Explorer's Club (N.Y.C.), Rotary, Sigma Xi. Office: 2150 S Congress Ave West Palm Beach FL 33406-7604 Personal E-mail: grahamfwhitfield@aol.com. E-mail: gfw2150@aol.com.

WHITFIELD, KENNARD O. mayor, retired cartographer; b. St. Louis, May 28, 1933; s. Ossie and Nettie Whitfield; (stepmother) Irma Whitfield; m. Ettie Jean Phillips, Mar. 31, 1937; children: Stacy Ruff, Lorna Whitfield. BS, St. Louis U., 1958, MPA, 1963. Cartographer, supr. Def. Mapping Agy., St. Louis, 1958-93; ret. Mayor City of Rock Hill, Mo., 1973—. With U.S. Army, 1953-55. Recipient Govt. Achievement award East/West Gateway Coord. Coun., 1998, Disting. Svc. award Mo. Mcpl. League, 1999. Democrat. African Methodist Episcopal. Avocations: travel, reading, civic service. Home: 507 Hinsdale Ct Saint Louis MO 63119 Office: City of Rock Hill 9620 Manchester Rd Saint Louis MO 63119 Home Fax: (314) 961-4013; Office Fax: (314) 968-4843. E-mail: kenwhit@inlink.com.

WHITFORD, DENNIS JAMES, naval officer, meteorologist, oceanographer; BS, U.S. Naval Acad., 1972; MS, Naval Postgrad. Sch., 1979, PhD, 1988. Commd. ensign USN, 1972, advanced through grades to capt., 1994; officer-in-chg., staff oceanographer Naval Oceanography Cmd Detachment, Moffett Field, Calif., 1982-84; comdg. officer Oceanographic Unit Four aboard USNS Chauvenet, 1985; dir. numerical models dept. Fleet Numerical Oceanography Ctr., Monterey, Calif., 1988-89; comdg. officer Naval Oceanography Command Facility, San Diego, 1989-91; dir. Operational Oceanography Ctr., Stennis Space Ctr., Miss., 1991-93; exec. officer Naval Oceanographic Office, 1993-95; chmn. dept. oceanography U.S. Naval Acad., Annapolis, Md., 1995—, permanent mil. prof., 1998—2002, full prof., 2002—. Contbr. articles to profl. jours. Named to Outstanding Young Men of Am., 1982; Adm. Burke PhD fellow, 1972. Mem. Am. Geophys. Union, Sigma Xi. Office: US Naval Academy 572M Holloway Rd Annapolis MD 21402-1314

WHITHAM, GERALD BERESFORD, mathematics educator; b. Halifax, Eng., Dec. 13, 1927; came to U.S., 1956; s. Harry and Elizabeth (Howarth) W.; m. Nancy Lord, Sept. 1, 1951; children— Ruth H., Michael G., Susan C. BS, Manchester U., Eng., 1948, MS, 1949, PhD, 1953. Lectr. Manchester U., 1953-56; assoc. prof. NYU, N.Y.C., 1956-59; prof. math. MIT, Cambridge, 1959-62; prof. aeros. and math. Calif. Inst. Tech., Pasadena, 1962-67, prof. applied math., 1967-83, Charles Lee Powell prof. applied math., 1983-98, emeritus, 1998—. Author: Linear and Nonlinear Waves, 1974; also research papers on applied math. and fluid dynamics. Recipient Wiener prize in applied math., 1980 Fellow Royal Soc., Am. Acad. Arts and Scis. Office: Calif Inst Tech Applied Math 217-50 Pasadena CA 91125-0001 E-mail: Sheila@acm.caltech.edu.

WHITING, ALBERT NATHANIEL, former university chancellor; b. Jersey City, July 3, 1917; s. Hezekiah Oliver and Hildegarde Freida (Lyons) W.; m. Charlotte Luck, June 10, 1950; 1 dau., Brooke Elizabeth. AB, Amherst Coll., 1938; student, Columbia, summer 1938, U. Pitts., 1938-39; MA in Sociology, Fisk U., 1941, L.H.D. (hon.), 1980; PhD in Sociology, Am. U., 1952; LL.D., Amherst Coll., 1968, Western Mich. U., 1974, Duke, 1974, Kyung Hee U., Seoul, Korea; L.H.D., N.C. Central U., 1983. Research and teaching asst. Fisk U., 1939-41; instr. sociology, dir. rural community study Bennett Coll., Greensboro, N.C., 1941-43, 46-47; asst. prof. sociology Atlanta U., 1948-53; dean coll., prof. sociology Morris Brown Coll., Atlanta, 1953-57; asst. dean coll. Morgan State Coll., Balt., 1957-59, dean of college, 1960-67; pres. N.C. Central U., Durham, 1967-72, chancellor, 1972-83. Mem. bd. regents U. Md. Sys., 1988-95. Contbr. articles profl. jours. Bd. dirs. Am. Coun. Edn., Ednl. Testing Svc.; bd. dirs., past pres. Assn. State Colls. and Univs.; v.p. Internat. Assn. Univ. Pres.; bd. dirs. Research Triangle (N.C.) Inst.; mem. Md. Higher Edn. Commn., 1995-98. 1st lt. AUS, 1943-46. Episcopalian. Home: 11253B Slalom Ln Columbia MD 21044-2810

WHITING, ANTHONY, executive search consultant; b. Saigon, Indochina, Nov. 6, 1951; s. Dinty Warmington and Lorraine (Yarborough) W. BA summa cum laude, Tulane U., 1973; MA with honors, Columbia U., 1974, MPhil, 1977, PhD, 1984. V.p. Columbia Consulting Group, N.Y.C., 1987-92; partner Johnson, Smith, and Knisely, 1993-99; mng. dir. Illsley Bourbonnais, 1999-2000; mng. ptnr. The Waterman Group, LLC, 2000—. Vis. scholar Columbia U., 2001-2002. Author: The Never Resting Mind: Wallace Stevens' Romantic Irony, 1996, Edward Thomas, 1996. Mem. Soc. of Mayflower Descendants, Order of Crown of Charlemagne, Baronial Order of Magna Carta, Soc. of the Cinn., Hereditary Order of Descendants of Colonial Govs., Soc. of Order of Founders and Patriots of Am., Soc. of Descendants of Colonial Clergy, Sons of Am. Revolution, Phi Beta Kappa. Office: 489 5th Ave New York NY 10017-6105

WHITING, CHRISTINE LIGHT, art librarian; b. Mentor, Ohio, July 6, 1929; m. John Leland Whiting, 1954. BS, Simmons Coll., 1951; MLS, U. Mich., 1952; scholarship, Cooper Union Inst. Sch. Art, N.Y.C., 1963. Cert. Fla. Internat. U. Paralegal Program, Miami, 1990, Inst. Children's Lit., 1998. Asst. librarian Sch. Architecture U. Calif., Berkeley, 1952-54; librarian Kansas City (Mo.) Art Inst., 1958-59, Cleve. Inst. Art, 1959-60; asst. librarian Bklyn. Mus., 1960-61; co-editor N.Y. Arts Calendar, 1964-65, Art Collector's Guide, 1965; exec. asst. to dir. N.Y.C. Office Marlborough Fine Arts Gallery, London, 1966-68; sec./treas. European Svc. Patents, Inc., Miami, 1975-79; contract paralegal Miami, San Francisco law firms, 1990—. Author: Fantastic Green Apples, 2001; contbr. The Astral Journey, 1975. Avocations: writing, art, travel, riding, old movies, hiking. Home: 396 Pine Hill Rd Apt 3 Mill Valley CA 94941-3850

WHITING, GORDON JAMES, investment banker; b. Bronxville, N.Y., Nov. 17, 1965; s. William Gordon Whiting and Doris (Chubb) Whiting Simmons. BS, Cornell U., 1988; MBA, Columbia U., 1994. Sales and mktg. mgr. Epcot Ltd., Tsim Sha Tsui, Kowloon, Hong Kong, 1989-90; mng. dir. Stapenhurst Ltd., Victoria, Hong Kong, 1990-92; acquisitions assoc. W. P. Carey & Co. LLC, N.Y.C., 1993-94, 2d v.p., 1994-95, v.p., 1995-97, 1st v.p., 1997-98, sr. v.p., 1998-2000, dep. dir. of acquistions, 1999—, exec. dir., 2000—; exec. v.p. and portfolio mgr. Corp. Property Assocs.: 14 Inc., 1998-2000, pres. and portfolio mgr., 2000—. Local bd. mem. Selective Svc.

Sys., Eagle Scout. Mem. Profl. Assn. Diving Instrs., Bronxville Field Club, Constant Spring Golf Club (Jamaica), Holland Lodge No. 8 F&AM, Leander Club (U.K.), The Camp Fire Club Am., Mashomack Preserve Club (Pine Plains, N.Y.), The Order of St. John, The Pilgrims, Hon. Order Ky. Cols., Racquet and Tennis Club, Royal Hong Kong Yacht Club, Sigma Chi. Republican. Episcopalian. Avocations: fly fishing, golf, scuba diving, skiing, squash. Home: 136 E 55th St Apt 3P New York NY 10022-4518 Office: W P Carey & Co LLC 50 Rockefeller Plz New York NY 10020-1605 E-mail: gwhiting@wpcarey.com.

WHITING, HENRY H. state supreme court justice; LLB, Univ. Va., 1949. Former judge 26th Jud. Cir. of Va.; sr. justice Va. Supreme Ct., Richmond, 1987—. Office: Va Supreme Ct 100 N 9th St Fl 5 Richmond VA 23219*

WHITING, MARTHA COUNTEE, retired secondary education educator; b. Marshall, Tex., Mar. 24, 1912; d. Thomas and Nannie Selena (Yates) Countee; m. Samuel Whiting, June 8, 1937; children: Jacqueline Bostic, Sammie Ellis, Nan Broussard, Tommye Casey, Martha Goddard. BA in Sci., Bishop Coll., 1934; M of Secondary Edn., Tex. So. U., 1959, postgraduate, 1962; postgrad., U. Colo., 1963. Tchr., sci., math. Houston Ind. Sch. Dist., 1942-73; researcher, local history Houston, 1973—. Lectr. in field. Mem. exec. com. (life mem.) Houston YWCA, 1977; advisor Preservation 4th Ward, Houston, 1991—; trustee Antioch Missionary Bapt. Ch., Houston, 1977; instrumental in getting the Antioch Missionary Bapt. Ch. in Christ Inc. on the Nat. Register of Hist. Places, 1976; presented Queen Elizabeth II with miniature history of Antioch Missionary Bapt. Ch. in Christ, 1991; author nomination form for Tex. hist. marker Antioch Missionary Bapt. Ch. in Christ, 1994; presenter to Harris County Heritage Soc. of Jack Yates House, the only house built by a former slave to be maintain ed by a U.S. city, and chmn. Pathfinder presentation of achievements of 64 Negro pioneers in Harris County, 1966-1986. Named Woman Courage, Houston Radcliffe Club, 1985, Black Womens Hall Fame Mus. Africal Am. Life, Dallas, 1986; recipient Friend of the Soc. award Harris County Heritage Soc., 1994. Mem. Tex. Ret. Tchrs. Assn., Houston Mus. Fine Arts, Harris County Heritage Soc. (exec. com. 1984), Bluebonnet Garden Club (pres. 1968), Jack & Jill Am. (pres. Houston chpt. 1955-57), Smithsonian, Nationwide Trust for Historic Preservation. Avocations: writing, gardening, travel, sewing, singing. Home: 3446 Southmore Blvd Houston TX 77004-6349

WHITING, MEREDITH ARMSTRONG, public affairs executive; b. Cin., Nov. 28, 1937; d. Arthur Elmer and Laura Mae (Handley) W.; m. Raymond E. Armstrong, Jan. 20, 1956 (div. Aug. 1968); m. John D. Whiting, Sept. 7, 1985; children: Holly R. Wood, Lucinda Parker, Eric Armstrong, Robert Armstrong, India Leclef. BA, U. Cin., 1969. Pub. rels. dir. U. No. Ky., Alexandria, Ky., 1972-76, Cin. Symphony Orch., 1976-79; pub. affairs dir. Young & Rubicam Cin., 1979-80; dir. pub. liaison Dept. Commerce, Washington, 1980-81; dir. congl. and press affairs Office of V.P., 1980-85; pres. Whiting & Co., 1985—. Sr. fellow govt. affairs The Conf. Bd., N.Y.C., 1987—; mem. White House Working Group on Universal Basic Edn., Washington, 2000—. Author: Public/Private Partnerships, 1997, rev. edit., 2000. Chairwoman Goose Creek Assn., Middleburg, Va., 1999—. Republican. Home: 5423 Free State Rd Marshall VA 20115 Office: The Conf Bd 1255 34th St NW Washington DC 20007 E-mail: mwhiting@whitingcom.com.

WHITING, RICHARD ALBERT, lawyer; b. Cambridge, Mass., Dec. 2, 1922; s. Albert S. and Jessie (Coleman) W.; m. Marvelene Nash, Feb. 22, 1948 (div. 1984); children— Richard A. Jr., Stephen C., Jeffrey D., Gary S., Kimberly G.; m. Joanne Sherry, Oct. 14, 1984 AB, Dartmouth Coll., 1944; JD, Yale U., 1949. Bar: D.C. 1949. Assoc. Steptoe & Johnson, Washington, 1949-55, ptnr., 1956-86, of counsel, 1987—. Adj. prof. Vt. Law Sch., South Royalton, 1985-90; mem. exec. com. Yale Law Sch. Assn., New Haven, 1985-88; mem. adv. bd. The Antitrust Bull., N.Y.C., 1975-99. Contbr. articles to profl. jours. Trustee Colby-Sawyer Coll., 1987-97. 1st lt. U.S. Army, 1945-46. Mem. ABA (council mem. Antitrust Law sect. 1977-85, del. to Ho. Dels. 1982-83, chmn. 1984-85) Presbyterian. Home: PO Box 749 Grantham NH 03753-0749 Office: 1330 Connecticut Ave NW Washington DC 20036-1704 E-mail: whiting@srnet.com.

WHITING, STEPHEN CLYDE, lawyer; b. Arlington, Va., Mar. 20, 1952; s. Richard A. Whiting; m. Patrice Quinn, May 24, 1980; children: Kelsey, Daniel, Seth, Samuel. BA magna cum laude, Dartmouth Coll., 1974; JD, U. Va., 1978. Bar: Maine 1978, U.S. Dist. Ct. Maine 1978, U.S. Ct. Appeals (1st cir.) 1999. Ptnr. Douglas, Whiting, Denham & Rogers, Portland, Maine, 1978-98; founder The Whiting Law Firm, P.A., 1998—. Maine state dir. Am. Ctr. Law and Justice, 1998—. Co-author: Trying the Automobile Injury Case in Maine, 1993, Premises Liability: Preparation and Trial of a Difficult Case in Maine, 1994, Trying Soft Tissue Injury Cases in Maine, 1995, How to Litigate Your First Civil Trial in Maine, 2001. Mem. ATLA, Maine Bar Assn., Maine Trial Lawyers Assn., Phi Beta Kappa. Office: The Whiting Law Firm PA 75 Pearl St Ste 207 Portland ME 04101 E-mail: mail@whitinglawfirm.com.

WHITING, WALLACE BURTON, II, chemical engineer, educator; b. Hartford, Conn., Sept. 6, 1952; s. Harold Alan and Lillian Anne (Jones) W.; m. Patricia Rose Headington Moore, June 17, 1978; children: Sharon E. Moore, Cynthia L. Moore Restivo. BS, Rensselaer Polytechnic Inst., 1974; MSChemE, Polytechnic Inst. N.Y., 1976; PhD, U. Calif., Berkeley, 1982. Registered profl. engr., Calif., W.Va., Nev. Asst. mech. engr. Pratt & Whitney Aircraft Co., East Hartford, Conn., 1973; chem. process engr. Dorr-Oliver Inc., Stamford, 1974-76; rsch. assoc. Lawrence Berkeley Lab., Berkeley, Calif., 1976-82; prof. W.Va. U., Morgantown, 1982-96. Program dir. NSF, 1991, 94; vis. prof. UCLA, 1992; prof., chair U. Nev., Reno, 1996—. Co-author: Analysis, Synthesis and Design of Chemical Processes, 1997; editor Fluid Phase Equilibria Jour.; contbr. articles to profl. jours. Grantee NSF, U.S. Dept. Energy. Mem. AIChE (nat. program chair for edn. 1988—), Am. Soc. Engring. Edn. (bd. dirs. nat. projects 1990—, chair programming chem. engring. and edn. divsn. 1986-90, Dow Outstanding Faculty award 1986, Centennial Svc. award 1993), Am. Chem. Soc., Internat. Gesellschaft Fuer Ingenieurpaedagogik, Assn. Environ. Engring. Profs., Sigma Xi, Tau Beta Pi. Achievements include development of a new approach to mixing rules for equations of state for asymmetric mixtures, and a new approach to quantifying uncertainties in process design caused by thermodynamic uncertainties. Office: U Nev Engring Mailstop 170 Reno NV 89557-0001

WHITING-DOBSON, LISA LORRAINE, video production educator, producer, director; b. Lansing, Mich., July 22, 1959; d. Lowell Stanton and Ruth Lorraine (Gregory) Whiting. BS in Psychology, Mich. State U., 1981, BA in Telecommunication cum laude, 1984, MA in Telecommunication, 1988; AA in Dance magna cum laude, Lansing Community Coll., 1984. Video prodr., dir. Coll. of Comm. Arts, instr. dept. telecomm. Mich. State U., East Lansing, Mich., 1987—; producer, dir. Cath. Diocese Lansing, 1984—; instr. media tech. Lansing C.C., 1999—. Mem. Jr. League of Lansing. Office: Mich State U Dept Telecom 409 Communication Arts Bldg East Lansing MI 48824-1212 E-mail: whiting3@msu.edu.

WHITINGTON, PETER FRANK, pediatrics educator, pediatric hepatologist; b. Memphis, May 8, 1947; s. Frank Everett and Mary Lena (Hollingsworth) Whitington; m. Susan Maurine Hoagland, June 6, 1967; children: Helen Frances Josephic, Mary Louise, Katherine Daphne, Patrick M. BA in Econs., Tulane U., 1968; MD, U. Tenn., Memphis, 1971. Diplomate Am. Bd. Pediat., Am. Bd. Pediatric Gastroenterology. Resident in pediat., then chief resident U. Tenn. Ctr. for Health Scis., 1972—74, instr., 1975, asst. prof., 1978—81, assoc. prof., 1981—84, chief divsn. pediatric gastroenterology, 1978—84; rsch. fellow in gastroenterology Johns Hopkins Hosp., Balt., 1975—77; rsch. fellow in gastroenterology dept. pediatrics U. Wis., Madison, 1977—78; assoc. prof. dept. pediat. U. Chgo. Pritzker Sch. Medicine, 1984—87, assoc. prof. depts. pediat. and medicine, 1987—92, prof., 1992—97; prof. pediat. Northwestern U. Med. Sch., 1997—, Sally Burnett Searle prof. pediat. and transplantation; dir. divsn. gastroenterology, hepatology & nutrition Children's Meml. Hosp., Chgo., 1997—, dir. organ transplantation, Siragusa Transplantation Ctr., 1997—; co-dir. Northwestern U. Affiliated Transplant Ctrs., 1997—. Chief gastroenterology LeBonheur Children's Med. Ctr., Memphis, 1978—84; numerous invited lectures and guest spkr. at profl. meetings, workshops, symposia, hosps., confs.; mem. pediatric transplantation com. United Network for Organ Sharing, Nat. Organ Procurement and Transplantation Network, 1992—94; reviewer numerous med. jours. including New Eng. Jour. Medicine, Gastroenterology, Hepatology, Jour. Pediat., Digestive Diseases and Scis., Pediat., Transplant. Editl. bd. Jour. Pediatric Gastroenterology and Nutrition, 1991—96, Liver Transplantation, 1994—, Pediatric Transplantation, 1997—, sect. editor Birth Defects Compendium, 1987—90, contbr. numerous articles and abstracts to med. jours. Mem. sci. adv. bd. Mid-South chpt. Nat. Found. for Ileitis and Colitis, Memphis, 1983—84; chmn. med. adv. com. Ill. chpt. Am. Liver Found., 1996—, mem., med. adv. on bd. dirs., 1993—; med. dir. The Johnny Genna Found., Chgo., 1987—; bd. dirs. Parents for Ctrl. H.S. , Memphis, 1983—84, Liver/Organ Transplant Fund, Memphis, 1983—84. Recipient Cmty. Svc. award, NCCJ, Memphis, 1983; fellow postdoctoral rsch. NIH, 1977. Mem.: Am. Assn. Transplantation, N.A.m Soc. for Pediatric Gastroenterology and Nutrition, Soc. for Pediatric Rsch., Am. Gastroenterol. Assn., Gastroenterology Rsch. Group, Am. Assn. for Study of Liver Diseases. Avocations: making fine furniture, fly fishing. Home: 5490 S South Shore Dr Apt 8 Chicago IL 60615-5984 Office: Childrens Meml Hosp Box 57 2300 Childrens Plaza Chicago IL 60614-3394 E-mail: p-whitington@northwestern.edu.

WHITLAM, MICHAEL RICHARD, voluntary sector administrator; b. Normanton, Yorkshire, Eng., Mar. 25, 1947; s. Richard William and Mary Elizabeth (Land) W.; m. Anne Jane McCurley, Aug. 23, 1968; children: Rowena Cross, Kirsty Evans. Cert. in edn., U. Warwick, 1968; MPhil, Cranfield Inst. Tech., 1988. Biology tchr. North Yorks Dist., Ripon, 1968-69; asst. govt. HM Borstal Hollesley Bay and HM Prison, Brixton, 1969-74; dir. Hammersmith Teenage Project, London, 1974-78; dep. dir. U.K. ops. Save the Children Fund, 1978-86; chief exec. Royal Nat. Inst. Deaf, 1986-90; dir. gen. Brit. Red Cross Soc., 1990-99; chief exec. Mentor Found., 1999—. Bd. dirs. Charity Appointments, Ltd., Ret. Execs. Action Clearing House; chmn. Sound Advantage Plc, 1988-90; mem. exec. coun. Howard League, 1974-84; chmn. Prisoners Abroad, 1999—. Contbr. numerous articles to profl. jours. Mem. Cmty. Alternative Young Offenders Com., Nat. Assn. Care Resettlement Offenders, 1979-82; exec. coun. Nat. Children's Bur., 1980-86; chmn. London Intermediate Treatment Assn., 1980-83; companion Inst. Mgmt., 1997—. Decorated companion Brit. Empire. Fellow Royal Soc. Arts; mem. Nat. Vol. Orgns. (assoc. chief execs. 1988—), Ret. Execs. Action Clearing House (bd. dirs. 1997), New Cavendish Club, Inst. Mgmt. Mem. United Reform Ch. Avocations: painting, walking, family activities, voluntary organizations, politics, woodsculpting.

WHITLATCH, ELBERT EARL, JR. engineering educator, consultant; b. Braddock, Pa., Oct. 29, 1942; s. Elbert Earl and Wanda Louisa (Gibson) W.; m. Janet Kay Baker, June 15, 1974; children: Susan Elizabeth, Brian David. BS in Engring. magna cum laude, Geneva Coll., 1965; BSCE, Carnegie-Mellon U., 1965; MS in Environ. Engring., Johns Hopkins U., 1967, PhD in Environ. Sys. Engring., 1973. Asst. prof. Ohio State U., Columbus, 1973-79, assoc. prof., 1979—; dir. Ohio Water Resources Ctr., 1995—. Co-author: Civil and Environmental Systems Engineerng, 1997; contbr. articles to profl. jours. With U.S. Peace Corps., 1967-69. Johns Hopkins fellow, 1965-67, 69-73. Mem. ASCE (Edn. Rsch. award 1983), Am. Geophys. Union, Am. Water Resources Assn., Am. Water Works Assn., Internat. Water Resources Assn., Inst. for Mgmt. Sci., Water Mgmt. Assn. Ohio, Phi Kappa Phi. Avocations: reading, hiking, hunting, travel. Office: Ohio State Univ Dept Civil Environ Engring 2070 Neil Ave Columbus OH 43210-1226

WHITLEY, ARTHUR FRANCIS, retired international manufacturing company executive, engineer, lawyer; b. Bklyn., Apr. 14, 1927; s. John Boyd and Ellen (Walls) W.; m. Isabella Maria Passidomo, Apr. 9, 1950; children: Brent John, Scott Michael, Todd Joseph. B.E.E., Poly. Inst. N.Y., 1951; JD, Seton Hall U., 1955; LL.M., Bklyn. Law Sch., 1958. Bar: N.J. 1960, U.S. Customs Ct. 1967, U.S. Patent Office 1972. Sales engr., atty. Pub. Service E&G, Newark, 1951-60; mgmt. cons. Nelson Walker Assocs., N.Y.C., 1961; atty. assoc. gen. counsel Engelhard Industries, Iselin, N.J., 1962-75, v.p., group v.p., 1976-80, sr. v.p., 1981, exec. v.p., 1982-83; pres. Bro-Whit Assocs. Inc., 1983-89. Pres. World Trade Assn. N.J., 1965. Served with USN, 1945-46. Republican. Roman Catholic. Home: 4738 West Blvd Naples FL 34103-3051

WHITLEY, DAVID SCOTT, archaeologist; b. Williams AFB, Ariz., Mar. 5, 1953; s. Edgar Duer and Yvonne Roca (Wightman) W.; m. Tamara Katherine Koteles, Feb. 13, 1987; 1 child, Carmen. AB Anthro and Geography magna cum laude, U. Calif., 1976, MA in Geography, 1979, PhD in Anthropology, 1982. Soc. Profl. Archeology. Chief archeologist Inst. Archeology UCLA, L.A., 1983-87; rsch. fellow Archeology Dept. U. Witwatersrand, Johannesburg, 1987-89; pres. W&S Cons., Simi Valley, Calif., 1989—. U.S. rep. internat. com. rock art Internat. Coun. Monuments and Sites, 1992—, exec. com., 1997-99, mem. coun. dirs., 1997—. Author: A Guide to Rock Art Sites: Southern California and Southern Nevada, 1996, L'Art des chamanes: art rupestre en Californie, 1997, Handbook of Rock Art Research, 2001; editor: archeological monographs; contbr. articles to profl. jours. Prehistoric Archeologist, State of Calif. Hist. Resources Commn., 1986-87; mem. rsch. adv. com. Chauvet Cave, France, 1996—. Recipient Thomas F. King award for excellence in cultural resource mgmt., Soc. for Calif. Archaeology, 2001; fellow postdoctoral fellow, Assn. for Field Archeology, 1983; grantee tech. specialist grantee, U.S. AID, 1986. Fellow Am. Anthrop. Assn.; mem. Soc. Am. Archeology, SAR, Sons of the Indian Wars, Mayflower Soc. Home: 447 3d St Fillmore CA 93015-1413 Office: W&S Consultants 2422 Stinson St Simi Valley CA 93065

WHITLEY, JOE DALLY, lawyer; b. Atlanta, Nov. 12, 1950; s. Thomas Youngie and Mary Jo (Dally) W.; m. Kathleen Pinion, Sept. 27, 1975; children: Lauren Jacqueline, Thomas McMillan. BA, U. Ga., 1972, JD, 1975. Bar: Ga. 1975, U.S. Supreme Ct. 1989. Assoc. Kelly, Denney, Pease & Allison, Columbus, Ga., 1975-78; asst. dist. atty. Chattahoochee Jud. Cir., 1978-79; assoc. Hirsch, Beil & Partin, P.C., 1979-81; U.S. atty. Dept. Justice, Macon, Ga., 1981-87, dep. asst. atty. gen., Criminal Div. Washington, 1987-88, dep. assoc. atty. gen., 1988-89, acting assoc. atty. gen., 1989; ptnr. Smith, Gambrell & Russell, Atlanta, 1989-90; U.S. atty. Dept. of Justice, 1990-93; ptnr. Kilpatrick Stockton, 1993-97, Alston & Bird, Atlanta, 1997—. Mem. atty. gen.'s adv. com. Dept. Justice, Washington, 1982-85; chmn. organized crime and violent crime subcom. Atty. Gen.'s Adv. Com., 1990-93, mem. investigative subcom., chmn. white collar crime subcom., 1993-99. Treas. Muscogee County Young Reps., Columbus, 1979-80. Mem. Ga. Bar Assn., Macon Bar Assn., Young Lawyers Club (pres. Columbus chpt. 1980-81), Lawyers Club of Atlanta. Republican. Presbyterian. Office: Alston & Bird 1201 W Peachtree St NW Atlanta GA 30309-3424 E-mail: jwhitley@alston.com.

WHITLEY, JOHN QUENTION, JR. orthodontal educator, researcher; b. Burkesville, Ky., Jan. 24, 1955; s. John Quention Sr. and Pauline (Reid) W.; m. Daun Shearin Whitley, Aug. 9, 1980; children: Nicole Dominique, Zachary Cannon, Victoria Gabrielle. BS, Middle Tenn. State U., Murfreesboro, 1977; postgrad., U. N.C., 1977-78. Rsch. technician U. N.C., Chapel Hill, 1979—, lab. instr. orthodontics, 1988—, lab. instr. biomed. engring., 1989—. Cons. Enron Chem. Corp., Rolling Meadows, Ill., 1987, Ormco Corp., Unitek/3M, 1992. Contbr. numerous articles to profl. jours.; patentee in field. Mem. Am. Chem. Soc., N.Am. Thermal Analyis Soc., Am. Assn. Dental Rsch. Democrat. Baptist. Avocations: carpentry, electrical work, woodworking, fishing. Home: 9101 Greenbriar Sta Chapel Hill NC 27516-9747 Office: U NC Cb 7455 Rm 318drc Chapel Hill NC 27599-0001

WHITLEY, WALTER RALPH, educator; b. Mooresville, N.C., Oct. 2, 1943; s. Walter Ralph and Evelyn Elizabeth W. AA, Brevard Coll., 1963; AB, U. N.C., 1965; MA, Appalachian State U., 1968. Tchr. 7th grade social studies, English Randleman Elem. Sch., 1965-67; grad. asst. Appalachian State U., Boone, N.C., 1967-68; prof. Ctrl. Piedmont C.C., Charlotte, 1968—. Mem. Am. Hist. Assn. (life), N.C. Assn. Educators (life, pres. 1975-76), U. N.C. Alumni Assn. (life), Cabarrus Regional C. of C. Democrat. Methodist. Home: 1204 Ctrl Dr Kannapolis NC 28083

WHITLOCK, BENNETT CLARKE, JR. retired association executive; b. Charleston, S.C., June 10, 1927; s. Bennett C. and Isabel Price (Beckman) W.; m. Elizabeth Darley Marshall, July 18, 1959; children: Mary Elizabeth, Bennett C. III. AB, Presbyn. Coll., 1946; LL.B., U. S.C., 1949. With Am. Trucking Assns., Inc., Washington, 1949-89, asst. to mng. dir., 1961-70, asst. to pres., 1970-73, v.p., 1973-75, exec. v.p., chief oper. officer, 1975-76, pres., 1976-84, spl. adviser, pres., 1984-89; ret., 1989. Bd. dirs Braddock Road Boys Club, Mary Washington Coll. Found., 1998—; bd. visitors Mary Washington Coll., 1985-93, vice rector, 1986-88, rector, 1990-92 Mem. Hwy. Users Fedn. for Safety and Mobility (dir.), Country Club of Fairfax, Kiawah Island Govs. Club, Blue Key, Pi Kappa Alpha. Episcopalian.

WHITLOCK, BETTY, secondary education educator; b. Somerset, Ky., Mar. 17, 1942; d. Rual Robert and Hazel Ellen (Biers) Wilson; m. L. Craig Whitlock, June 12, 1962; children: Michael Craig, Jeffrey Robert, Katherine Elizabeth. BA, Georgetown Coll., 1964; MA, Miss. Coll., 1980, EdS, 1982; postgrad., U. So. Miss., 1986. Nat. bd. cert. tchr. Adolescence and Young Adulthood/English Lang. Arts. Tchr. kindegarten First Bapt. Ch. Kindergarten, Clinton, Miss., 1970-72, Northside Bapt. Ch. Kindegarten, Clinton, 1972-73; tchr. high sch. Miss. Bapt. High Sch., Jackson, 1973-75, Clinton High Sch., 1975—. Bd. dirs. Miss. Youth Congress, 1985—; chmn. com. Literary Map of Miss., 1985—; cons. Miss. High Sch. Activities Assn., 1991—. Co-author: Mississippi Writers: An Anthology, 1987, Mississippi Writers: Reflections on Childhood and Youth, 1988, (textbook) Dramatic Interpretation, 1994. Tchr. Sunday sch. First Bapt. Ch., Clinton, 1969—. Mem. Nat. Coun. Tchrs. English, Nat. Forensic League, Miss. Coun. Tchrs. English (chmn. maps 1975—, Outstanding Tchr, award 1992), Miss. Speech Communication Assn. (dir. congress 1973—), Miss. Profl. Educators, Miss. Forensic League (chmn. 1988-99), Jackson Cath. Forensic League (moderator 1991-93), Miss. Coll. Faculty Wives, Phi Delta Kappa. Republican. Baptist. Avocation: writing. Home: 100 Hannah Dr Clinton MS 39056-5107 Office: Clinton High Sch 401 Arrow Dr Clinton MS 39056-3108 E-mail: nanawhit@aol.com.

WHITLOCK, BRENT K. electrical engineer; b. Rockford, Ill., 1967; s. James Robert and Barbara Kay Whitlock; m. Ellen BS, U. Ill., 1990, MS, 1993, PhD, 1996. Co-op engr. IBM Fed. Systems Divsn., Manassas, Va., 1986, Sundstrand Corp., Rockford, Ill., 1987-89; summer intern engr. Motorola Comms. Sector, Schaumburg, 1990, Motorola Land Mobile Products, Schaumburg, 1991; tchg. asst. U. Ill., Urbana, 1990, rsch. asst., 1991-96; summer intern rschr. IBM Watson Rsch. Ctr., Yorktown Heights, N.Y., 1993; sr. CAD engr. Cypress Semiconductor, San Jose, Calif., 1996-98; v.p. optical sys. RSoft Design Group, Inc., Ossining, NY, 1998—2001, dir. link level rsch. & product develop., 2001—. Mem. com. and session chmn. for conf. in field. Author: (software) iFROST Fiber-Optics Simulator, 1996; contbr. articles to profl. jours.; reviewer jour. articles in field. Sec., co-founder U. Ill. studnet chpt. Optical Soc. Am., Urbana, 1994-95; chmn. U. Ill. Elec. and Computer Engring. Student Adv. Com., Urbana, 1992-94. Recipient fellowship NSF, 1991-94, univ. fellowship U. Ill., 1990-91. Mem. IEEE, Optical Soc. Am., U. Ill. Alumni Assn. Avocations: photography, piano, saxophone, bicycling, SCUBA diving. Office: RSoft Design Group Inc 200 Executive Blvd Ossining NY 10562-2560

WHITLOCK, CHARLES PRESTON, former university dean; b. Highland Park, N.J., June 19, 1919; s. Frank Boudinot and Rosena Craig (Foster) W.; m. Patricia Hamilton Hoey, Mar. 10, 1960; children: Carol Foster, Adam Hoey, Susan Boudinot, Matthew Fitzsimmons, Beth Brewer. BA, Rutgers U., 1941; MA, Harvard U., 1947. Assoc. dir. Bur. Study Counsel Harvard U., 1948-52, Allston Burr sr. tutor, 1952-58, lectr. social psychology, 1955-72, asst. to pres., 1958-70, assoc. dean of coll., 1970-72, dean of coll., 1972-76, assoc. dean faculty, 1976-82, master Dudley House, 1976-82. Dir. Cambridgeport Savs. Bank.; Mem. Mass. Higher Edn. Facilities Commn. Co-author: Harvard University Reading Films. Trustee Charity of Edward Hopkins, Lesley Coll.; bd. corporators New Eng. Deaconess Hosp.; treas. Annisquam Village Ch. Col. USAF. Decorated Silver Star, D.F.C., Air medal. Mem. Phi Beta Kappa. Home: 9 Barberry Heights Rd Gloucester MA 01930-1201 Office: Harvard U Cambridge MA 02138

WHITLOCK, DAVID C. retired military officer; b. Little Rock, Jan. 24, 1935; m. Rosemarie Binik (dec.); children: D. Patrick, David D.; m. Dagmar Gattung. B Bus., U. Nebr., 1962; grad., Squadron Officer Sch., 1965; MA Speech and Drama, U. Colo., 1966, PhD Communication, 1970; grad., Air Command and Staff Coll., 1978, Air War Coll., 1983. With USAF, 1952-62, tech. sgt., 1962, audiovisual tng. officer, 2d lt., 1st lt. Hdqs. N. Am. Air Defense Command Colo., 1962-67; from English, speech instr., asst., dir. forensics, capt. to prof., major USAF Acad., 1967-74, prof. English, Speech, dir. Forensics, lt. col., 1979, pres. Tenure Coun., 1981-82; dir. Disting. Visitors Bureau Hdqs. USAF, Ramstein AFB, Germany, 1982-84; assoc. dean Civilian Inst. programs, col. AF Inst. Tech., Ohio, 1984-86; base comdr. 26th Combat Support Group Zweibrucken AFB, Germany, 1986-88; dean Civilian Inst. Programs Wright Patterson AFB, Ohio, 1989, commandant emeritus AF Inst. Tech. Air U., 1992-93. Recipient Legion of Merit, Meritorious Svc. medal with four oak leaf clusters, Air Force Commendation medal with two oak leaf clusters. Achievements include qualified parachutist. Home and Office: 441 Green Vista Dr Enon OH 45323-1340

WHITLOCK, ELLEN DEAL, non-profit association administrator; b. High Point, N.C., May 8, 1955; d. Raymond Lester Jr. and Dorsey (Crumpler) Deal; m. David Evan Whitlock Sr.; children: David Evan, Jr., Dorsey Virginia, Leslie Ann, John Wilson. Student, Guilford Community Coll., High Point Coll. Small bus. owner, High Point, 1974—79; exec. dir. Mental Health Assn., 1982—95, Sr. Resources of Guilford, 1995—. Mem. program com. Guilford County Conf. on Youth, Greensboro, N.C., 1983—; mem. Guilford County Juvenile Delinquency Prevention Com., Greensboro, 1984-89; v.p. Jr. League of High Point, 1984-85, chairperson adv. planning com., 1987-88, pub. affairs 1989-90, pres.-elect, 1993-94, pres., 1994-95; rep. Inner Agy. Coun., High Point, 1985-92; chairperson sr. ctr. task force United Svcs. for Older Adults, Greensboro, 1985—; chmn. Guilford County Involvement Coun., Greensboro, 1986-90; co-chmn. Guilford County Commn. on Needs of Children, Greensboro, 1987-90; chairperson Sr. Ctr, Task Force USOA, 1985-88; sec. Big Bros. Big Sisters, 1986—; v.p. United Way of Greater High Pointfor Vol. Ctr., 1986; bd. dirs. YWCA, 1988; bd. dirs. Carousel Theatre, 1986—; bd.. dirs. High Point Alcoholism and Substance Abuse Coalition, 1993; mem. bd. visitors High Point U.; bd. dirs. Guilford Interfaith Hospitality Network; bd. dirs. The Deal Found. Mem. Assn. Mental Health Profls., Mental Health Assn. N.C. (exec. dir., rep. 1985-89, Spillman award 1986). Republican. Methodist. Avocations: needlework, traveling, reading.

WHITLOCK, JOHN JOSEPH, museum director; b. South Bend, Ind., Jan. 7, 1935; s. Joseph Mark and Helen Marcella (Cramer) W.; m. Sue Ann Kirkman, June 10, 1956; children— Kelly Ann, Michele Lynn, Mark. BS in Art, Ball State U., 1957, MA in Art, 1963; EdD, Ind. U., 1971. Tchr. art Union City (Ind.) Pub. Schs., 1957-59; tchr. art, art dir. Madison (Ind.) City Schs., 1959-64; prof. art, dir. gallery Hanover (Ind.) Coll., 1964-69; dir. Burpee Art Mus., Rockford, Ill., 1970-72; prof. arts and humanities Elgin (Ill.) Community Coll., 1970-72; dir. Brooks Meml. Art Gallery, Memphis, 1972-78; prof. mus. studies Southwestern Coll., 1973-78; adj. asst. prof. art and museology Memphis State U., 1976-78; dir. Univ. Mus., mem. grad. faculty So. Ill. U., Carbondale, 1978-2000, emeritus dir., 2000—, also dir. mus. studies, 1978-2000, adj. assoc. prof. anthropology, 1978-2000, adj. assoc. prof. polit. sci., 1988—, adj. assoc. prof. history, 1994—, dir. mus. studies, 1989—, mem. ROTC acad. avc. coun., 1988—, mem. president's coun., 1988-93, adj. assoc. prof. art Univ. Mus., 1978-99, vis. emeritus prof., 2000—. Chmn. bd. Nat. Coal Mus., 1983-85; mem. Newsfront adv. bd. NC Broadcast News, Washington, 1982-85; sr. cons. Marine Mil. Acad. Mus., 1988—, mem. bd. advisors, 1991-97. Mem. Rockford Human Rels. Commn., 1971-72; mem. pres.'s coun. Southwestern Coll., 1973-78; vol. Carbondale Police Dept., 2000—, com. resources, forensics records and acad.; bd. dirs. Carbondale Crime Stoppers, 2000—, DARE, 2000—; univ. club bd. So. Ill. U., 2000—, univ. mus. amb., 2000—. Mem. Am. Assn. Mus., Internat. Coun. Mus., Midwest Assn. Mus., Assn. Art Mus. Dirs., Marine Corps League (commandant Shawnee detachment 1994-96, 99-2001, comdr. USCG Aux. 1994-95), Dept. Ill. Marine Corps League (trustee rank and file 1994-99, judge advocate 1999—), Semper Fi Soc. (faculty adviser So. Ill. U. 1995—). Office: So Ill U 605 W Walnut St Carbondale IL 62901-2615

WHITLOCK, JOHN L. lawyer; b. New Orleans, Oct. 24, 1946; s. John Bert and Virginia Katherine (Marzolf) W.; m. Dorothy Florence Oeste, Sept. 13, 1969; children: Sarah Katherine, Thomas John. AB, Harvard U., 1968, JD, 1973. Bar: Mass. 1973, U.S. Dist. Ct. Mass. 1974, U.S. Ct. Appeals (1st cir.) 1975. Assoc. Herrick & Smith, Boston, 1973-80, ptnr., 1981-86, Palmer & Dodge LLP, Boston, 1986—. Mem. ethics rules adv. com. Mass. Supreme Jud.

Ct., 1996—. Bd. dirs., sec. Harvard-Radcliffe Collegiate Mus. Found., Inc., 1978—; treas. The Cecilia Soc., 1974-85, 98—, bd. dirs., 1974-86, 94—, pres., 1994-98 . With U.S. Army, 1968-70. Mem. Boston Bar Assn. (coun. 1996-97). Lutheran. Avocation: singing. Office: Palmer & Dodge LLP 111 Huntington Ave Boston MA 02199-7613 E-mail: jwhitlock@palmerdodge.com.

WHITLOCK, JULIE MARIE, lawyer; b. Omaha, May 28, 1968; d. Larry F. and Barbara E. Schucht; m. Kevin M. Whitlock, June 25, 1994. BA in Fgn. Affairs, U. Va., 1990; JD, U. Richmond, 1994. Bar: Va. 1994, U.S. Dist. Ct. (ea. dist.) Va. 1994, U.S. Ct. Appeals (4th cir.) 1995. Ptnr. Thorsen Marchant & Scher LLP, Richmond, Va., 1996-98; assoc. Thompson & McMullan, PC, 1998-2000; systems analyst, atty. Va. Dept. Motor Vehicles, 2000—. Mem. Chesterfield Jr. Woman's Club. Office: Tech Procurement PO Box 27412 Richmond VA 23269 E-mail: dmvjxw@dmv.state.va.us.

WHITLOCK, LAURA ALICE, research scientist; b. Birmingham, Ala., Feb. 23, 1959; d. Richard Gordon and Virginia Irene (Rowell) W. BS with honors, Southwestern at Memphis, 1981; PhD, U. Fla., 1989. Rsch. asst. Los Alamos (N.Mex.) Nat. Lab., 1984-88, collaborator space astronomy and astrophysics, 1989-92; rsch. scientist Nichols Rsch. Corp., Huntsville, Ala., 1989-92, Inst. for Space Sci. and Tech., Gainesville, Fla., 1990-93, Univ. Space Rsch. Assoc. Goddard Space Flight Ctr., Greenbelt, Md., 1992-99, Sonoma State U., Rohnert Park, Calif., 1999—. Contbr. articles to Astrophys. Jour., Astronomy and Astrophysics. Faculty scholar Southwestern at Memphis, 1977-81; faculty fellow U. Fla., 1981. Mem. Am. Astron. Soc., Soc. Photo-Optical Instr. Engrs., Internat. Acad. of Digital Arts and Scis., Nat. Sci. Tchrs. Assn., Nat. Coun. Tchrs. Math., Sigma Pi Sigma. Achievements include reorganization of the 10-year, all-sky Vela 5B X-ray satellite database for study of time variability in cosmic X-ray sources; development of system-level Monte Carlo simulation of IR sensor performance operating in a high-radiation environment; creation and development of several projects in high-energy astrophysics outreach and education. Office: Sonoma State U Dept Physics and Astronomy Rohnert Park CA 94928

WHITLOCK, PRENTICE EARLE, retired mathematics educator, clergyman; b. Pacolet Mills, S.C., Nov. 19, 1922; s. Carl French and Bertha Cleo Patra (Cook) W. BS, U.S. Mil. Acad., 1946; BA, Wofford Coll., 1950; MA, Columbia U., 1951, 65; PhD, Fordham U., 1974; MA, Princeton Theol. Sem., 1980; MDiv, Drew U., 1983, STM, 1992, postgrad., 1980; PhD, NYU, 1985; postgrad., Westminster Choir Coll. Ordained to ministry United Meth. Ch., 1983. Commd. 2d lt. U.S. Army, 1946; resigned, 1950; tchr. elem. schs., Spartanburg, S.C., jr. high sch., Teaneck, N.J., 1956-68, Dobbs Ferry, N.Y., 1958-61; prof. math. dept. N.J. City U., Jersey City, 1963-92, prof. emeritus, 1992—; min. music Hicksville (N.Y.) United Meth. Ch., 1983—. Mem. Nat. Math. Tchrs. Assn., N.J. Math. Assn., West Point Soc. N.Y., Organ Guild N.Y.C. and Nassau County, Univ. Club (N.Y.C.), N.Y. Athletic Club. Republican. Avocations: playing the organ. Home: 97 W Cherry St Hicksville NY 11801-3856

WHITLOCK, ROBERT H. veterinarian, educator; b. Easton, Pa., Feb. 28, 1941; s. Joseph Henry and Margaret Whitlock; m. Marion L. Whitlock; children: Karin Michelle, Christopher Robert, Craig Michael. DVM, Cornell U., Ithaca, NY, 1965, PhD, 1970; MS (hon.) , U. Pa, Philadelphia, PA, 1978. Asst. prof. Cornell U. Vet. Coll., Ithaca, NY, 1970—76; assoc. prof. U. Ga. Vet. Coll., Athens, Ga., 1976—78, U. Pa, Sch. Vet. Medicine, Philadelphia, Pa., 1978—. Co-chair Nat. Jofine's Working Group, 2002—. Advancement chmn. Boy Scouts Am., Unionville, Pa., 1978—84. Fellow NIH Spl. fellowship, NIH, 1969, NATO fellowship, NATO, 1972-1973. Mem.: Am. Coll. Veterinary Internal Medicine (diplomat 2002—02). Presbyterian. Office: University Pennsylvania 382 West Street Road Kennett Square PA 19340

WHITLOW, STACEY MATAXIS, English educator, university educator; b. Fort Beining, GA, Feb. 13, 1975; d. Theodore Christopher Mataxis, Kirby Jones Mataxis; m. Jeffrey Kenneth Whitlow. Master of Arts, North Carolina State University, Raleigh, North Carolina, 1999—2001; Bachelor of Arts, Universtiy of North Carolina-Greensboro, Greensboro, NC, 1993—96. English Instructor Durham Technical Community College, Durham, NC, 2001—; High School English Teacher Pinecrest High School, Southern Pines, 1996—99.

WHITLOW, WILLIAM LA FOND, minister, theology school planter; b. Mpls., Oct. 20, 1932; s. George Lester and Wanona Nadine (Ridgeway) W.; m. Donna Mae Magnuson, June 13, 1953; children: Debra, Cathleen, Lisa Mae. Ministerial diploma, Eugene (Oreg.) Bible Coll., 1953; postgrad., Seattle Pacific U., 1961; BTh, ThM, Internat. Sem., Orlando, Fla., 1981, ThD summa cum laude, 1986, DD (hon.), 1984; LittD, Evangel Christian U. Am., 1992. Ordained to ministry Open Bible Standard Chs., 1954, Biltmore Bible Ch., 1988. Asst. and pastor Oreg. chs., 1949-55; dean pers. Calif. Open Bible Inst., Pasadena, 1957-58; pres., island supt. Bible Inst., Montego Bay, Jamaica, 1958-59, San Fernando, Trinidad, 1960-65; sr. pastor Biltmore Bible Ch., Phoenix, 1967—; pres. Biltmore Bible Sch. Theology, 1982-86. Extension sch. rep. Internat. Sem., Orlando, 1984-91; adj. faculty mem. Evang. Theol. Sem., Dixon, Mo., 1989-91; affiliate prof. Vision Christian U., Ramona, Calif., 1991. Author, compiler: Basic Bible School Builder, 1986—; also numerous Bible tng. courses. Recipient Outstanding Acad. Achievement award Internat. Sem., 1987. Office: Biltmore Bible Christian Ctr 3330 E Camelback Rd Phoenix AZ 85018-2310

WHITMAN, BURKE WILLIAM, business executive; b. Newport, R.I., Feb. 26, 1956; s. Homer William and Anne (Sarran) W. BA cum laude, Dartmouth Coll., 1978; MBA, Harvard U., 1984. Project mgr. HCB Contractors/Barker Interests Ltd., Atlanta, Houston, 1979-85; investment banker Morgan Stanley & Co. Inc., N.Y.C., 1988-92; v.p. fin./devel. Almost Family Inc., Balt., 1992-94; pres., CFO Deerfield Healthcare Corp., 1994-99; CFO, Triad Hosps., Inc., Dallas, 1999—. Bd. dir. Fedn. of Am. Hosps., mem. audit com. Former bd. dirs. Outward Bound, Police Athletic League; bd. advisors Marine Corps U. Served with USMC, 1985—88, lt. col. USMCR, 1988—. Mem.: Fedn. Am. Hosps. (bd. dirs.), Piedmont Driving Club. Episcopalian. Avocations: hiking, bicycling, outdoor sports. Home: 3030 Mckinney Ave Dallas TX 75204-7482 Office: Triad Hosp Inc 13455 Noel Rd Fl 20 Dallas TX 75240-6620

WHITMAN, CHARLES S., III, lawyer; b. N.Y.C., Apr. 19, 1942; s. Charles S. Jr. and Janet (Russell) W; m. Christina L. Madden, Oct. 20, 1979; 1 child, Elizabeth R. AB, Harvard U., 1964, LLB, 1967; LLM, Cambridge U., 1989. BAr: N.Y. 1967, U.S. Supreme Ct. 1972. Asst. to chmn. U.S. SEC, Washington, 1971-74; gen. counsel Mitchell Hutchins Inc., N.Y.C., 1974; assoc. Davis Polk & Wardwell, 1968-71, 74-76, ptnr., 1977—. Bd. dirs. British Schs. and Univs. Found., Inc., 2000—. Mem. Am. Law Inst. Republican. Presbyterian. Office: Davis Polk & Wardwell 450 Lexington Ave Fl 18 New York NY 10017-3982

WHITMAN, CHRISTINE TODD, federal official, former governor; b. Sept. 26, 1946; d. Webster Bray and Eleanor Schley Todd; m. John Whitman, 1974; children: Kate, Taylor. BA in Govt., Wheaton Coll., 1968. Former freeholder Somerset County, N.J.; former pres. State Bd. Pub. Utilities; host radio talk show Sta. WKXW, Trenton, N.J.; gov. State of N.J., 1994-2001; adminstr. U.S. EPA, Washington, 2001—. Chmn. Com. for an Affordable N.J. Columnist newspapers. Bd. freeholders Somerset County, N.J., 1982-87; bd. pub. utilities, 1988-89; Rep. candidate for Senate State of N.J., 1990. Achievements include first female governor in N.J.; delivered Republican response to President Clinton's 1995 State of the Union address. Office: US EPA Ariel Rios Bldg 1101A 1200 Pennsylvania Ave NW Washington DC 20460*

WHITMAN, DALE ALAN, lawyer, law educator; b. Charleston, W. Va., Feb. 18, 1939; m. Marjorie Miller; 8 children. Student, Ohio State U., 1956-59; BES, Bringham Young U., 1963; LLB, Duke U., 1966. Bar: Calif. 1967, Utah 1971. Assoc. O'Melveny & Myers, Los Angeles, 1966-67; asst prof., then assoc prof. sch. law U. N.C., Chapel Hill, 1967-70; prof. law UCLA, 1970-71; dep. dir. Office Housing and Urban Affairs Fed. Home Loan Bank Bd., Washington, 1971-72; sr. program analyst FHA, HUD, 1972-73; prof. law Brigham Young U., 1973-78, 92-99; vis. prof. law U. Wash., 1978—82, U. Mo., Columbia, 1976; prof. law, assoc. dean U. Mo. Sch. Law, 1982-88, prof., 1988—91, 1998—. Cons., lectr. in field; reporter Am. law Inst. Co-author: Cases and Materials on Real Estate Finance and Development, 1976, Real Estate Finance Law, 1979, 4th edit., 2001, Cases and Materials on Real Estate Transfer, Finance and Development. 1981, 5th edit., 1998, Land Transactions and Finance, 1983, 3d edit., 1997, The Law of Property, 1984, 3d edit., 2000, Contemporary Property, 1996, 2d edit., 2002, Restatement of Property (Mortgages), 1997; contbr. articles to profl. jours. Fellow Am. Bar Found.; mem. Am. Law Inst., Am. Coll. Real Estate Lawyers, Assn. Am. Law Schs. (pres. 2002). Home and Office: 2505 Black Cherry Ct Columbia MO 65201-3539 E-mail: whitmand@missouri.edu.

WHITMAN, HOMER WILLIAM, JR. retired investment counseling company executive; b. Sarasota, Fla., , Jan. 8, 1932; s. Homer William and Phoebe (Corr) W.; m. Anne Virginia Sarran, May 8, 1954; children: Burke William, Michael Wayne. BA in Econs. optime merens, U. South, 1953; grad., U.S. Naval Officer Candidate Sch., 1953; postgrad., Emory U., 1969. Served to group v.p. 1st Nat. Bank Atlanta, 1956-72; pres., dir. Palmer 1st Nat. Bank & Trust Co., Sarasota, 1973-74, Hamilton Bank & Trust Co., Atlanta, 1974-76; v.p. Lionel D. Edie & Co., 1976-78, Mfrs. Hanover Trust Co., Atlanta, 1978-85; sr. v.p. Montag & Caldwell, Inc., 1985—. Dir. Asolo State Theatre. Trustee Selby Found., 1973-74, West Paces Ferry Hosp., Ringling Sch. Art, St. Stephen's Sch.; bd. vis. Emory U.; mem. Leadership Atlanta. Lt. j.g. USNR, 1953-56. Named Hon. French Consul, Atlanta, Atlanta's Outstanding Young Man of Yr., 1963. Mem. Govt. Fin. Officer's Assn., Gla. Govt. Fin. Officers Assn., Ga. Govt. Fin. Officers Assn., Assn. Investment Mgmt. Sales Execs., Atlanta Soc. Fin. Analysts, Healthcare Fin. Mgmt. Assn., Fla. Pub. Pension Trustees Assn., Assn. Pvt. Pension and Welfare Plans (regional chmn.), Am. Cancer Soc. (dir. Atlanta city unit), Newcomen Soc., 300 Club, Atlanta C. of C. (life mem.), Piedmont Driving Club, Peachtree Golf Club, Commerce Club, Buckhead Club (bd. govs.), Union League Club (N.Y.), Breakfast Club, Sarasota U. Club (bd. dirs.), Farmington Country Club, Rotary, Mid Ocean Club. Episcopalian. Home: 12 Mooregate Sq NW Atlanta GA 30327-1539 Office: Montag & Caldwell Inc Ste 500 3455 Peachtree Rd NE Atlanta GA 30326-3248 E-mail: annebowhit@aol.com.

WHITMAN, JEFFREY PAUL, philosophy educator; b. Scranton, Pa., Mar. 25, 1955; s. Paul Ralph and Arlene Ruth (Morris) W.; m. Susan Linn Shuler, June 10, 1978; children: Laura Linn, Kevin Paul. BS, U.S. Mil. Acad., 1977; MA, Brown U., 1987, PhD, 1991. Commd. 2d lt. U.S. Army, 1977, advanced through grades to maj., 1989; philosophy prof. U.S. Mil. Acad., West Point, N.Y., 1987-95, ret., 1995; philosophy prof. Susquehanna U., Selinsgrove, Pa., 1995—. Ethics cons. Geisinger Med. Ctr., Danville, Pa., 1996—. Author: Power and Value of Philosophical Skepticicsm, 1996; contbr. articles to profl. jours. Pres. Sharon Luth. Ch. Coun., Selinsgrove, 1997-99; sch. bd. dirs. Selinsgrove Sch. Dist., 1999—. Mem. Am. Philos. Assn., Am. Assn. of Philosophy Tchrs., Assn. Practical and Profl. Ethics, Joint Svcs. Conf. on Profl. Ethics, Ea. Paralyzed Vets. Assn. Lutheran. Avocations: wheelchair sports and recreation. Office: Susquehanna U 514 University Ave Selinsgrove PA 17870-1164 E-mail: Whitman@susqu.edu.

WHITMAN, KAREN, artist; b. NY, Feb. 22, 1953; d. Martin and Shirley W.; m. Richard Keith Pantell, Jul. 26, 1998. BFA Printmaking, SUNY, Buffalo, 1975; Certificate in Graphic Design, Parsons Sch. of Design, 1990; student, Art Students League, N.Y.C., Woodstock Sch. of Art. Represented artist The Old Print Shop, N.Y.C., 1995—. Lectr. Woodstock Sch. of Art, 1999. One-woman shows at Bird-In-Hand Gallery, Washington, 2001, Old Print Shop, N.Y.C., 2002; group exhbns. include: Woodstock Arts Assn., Woodstock, NY, 1993—, Arts Student League, N.Y.C., 1993, 94, Soc. Am. Graphic Artists Ann. Exhbn., 1994-, Market Theatre Gallery, Albany, NY, 1994, Northwest Print Coun., Portland, Or., 1994, McDermott, Will and Emery, N.Y.C., 1994, James Cox Gallery, Woodstock, NY, 1994, Walsh Art Gallery, Contemporary Am. Printmakers, Fairfield (Ct.) Univ., 1994, Firehouse Gallery, Nassau C.C., Garden City, NY, 1995, Lore Degenstein Gallery, Susquehanna U., Selinsgrove, Pa., 1995, Schenectady Mus., Print Club of Albany, 1995, 98, Gallery 479, N.Y.C., 1996, Fred Baker, Inc., Urban U.S.A. Portfolio Exhbn., Chgo., 1996, The Old Print Shop, Urban U.S.A. Portfolio Exhbn., N.Y.C., 1996, Kala Inst. Gallery, Berkeley, Calif., 1996, Seton Hall Univ., So. Orange, N.J., 1996, Olive Hyde Gallery, Fremont, Calif., 1996, Annex Gallery, East/West Print Exchange Exhbn., Santa Rosa, Calif., 1996, Coll. Art Gallery, Norwalk Cmty. Technical Coll., Norwalk, Conn., 1996, Rensselaerville (NY) Inst. Gallery, Print Club of Albany, 1997, Kleinert Art Gallery, Woodstock, NY, 1997, Cork Gallery, Lincoln Ctr., N.Y.C., 1997, SAGA Mems. Exhbn., Krasdale Galleries, White Plains, NY, 1998, Wagner Coll. Gallery, Staten Island, NY, 1998, The Old Print Shop, N.Y.C. Centennial Portfolio Exhbn., N.Y.C., 1998, Parkside Nat. Small Print Exhbn., U. Wisc., Kenosha, 1998, 99, Catharine Lorillard Wolfe Art Club, 2000, 2001, Nat. Arts Club, N.Y.C., (Medal of Honor for Graphics, Bronze medal 2001), Schoolhouse Galleries, Croton Falls, NY "Street Life" Exhbn, 1999, Woodstock Sch. of Art Instrs. and Lectrs. Exhbn, 1999, Prince St. Gallery, N.Y.C., 1999; printwork Barrett Art Ctr., Poughkeepsie, N.Y., 2000, The N.Y. Soc. of Etchers, Nat. Arts Club, 2000, Silvermine Guild 23rd Nat. Print Biennial, New Canaan, Conn., 2000, Audubon Artists Ann. Exhb., Salmagundi Club, N.Y.C., 200, 2001, Nat. Assn. Women Artists 112th Ann. Exbh., N.Y.C., 2001, Contemporary Pritnmaker, The Old Print Shop, N.Y.C., 2001, Pen and Brush Regional Juried Exhb., N.Y.C., 2001, NY Soc. Etchers, Nat. Arts Club, N.Y.C., 2000, Silvermine Guild 23d Nat. Print Biennial, New Canaan, Conn., 2000, Salmagundi Club, N.Y.C., 2000, 01; represented in permanent collections N.Y. Publ. Libr., Mus. City of NY, Hofstra Mus., British Museum, Portland Art Mus., Nat. Mus. of Printmaking of the Print Club of Albany, Mus. of N.Y., Hofstra Univ. Mus., Norwalk Comm. Tech. Coll.; featured in various publs. Recipient medal of honor, Catharine Lorillard Wolfe Art Club, Nat. Arts Club, N.Y.C., 1999, Anna Hyatt Huntington bronze medal, 2001, Rembrant Graphic Arts Printmaking award, Hunterdon Mus., Clinton, N.J., 2001, Yasuo Kuniyoshi Fund award, Woodstock, N.Y., 2001, Solo Exhbn. award, Pen and Brush, 2002, award, Elizabeth Morse Genius Found., 2002. Mem.: Catharine Lorillard Wolfe Art Club, Nat. Assn. Women Artists (medal of honor 2002), Woodstock Artists Assn. (honorable mention 1999), Print Club Albany, Soc. Am. Graphic Artists (coun. mem. 1994). Avocations: singing Eastern European folk music, folk dancing, playing violin, songwriting. Home: PO Box 550 Bearsville NY 12409

WHITMAN, KATHY VELMA ROSE (ELK WOMAN WHITMAN), artist, sculptor, art educator; b. Bismarck, N.D., Aug. 12, 1952; d. Carl Jr. and Edith Geneva (Lykken) W.; m. Robert Paul Luger, Feb. 21, 1971 (div. Jan. 1982); children: Shannon, Lakota, Cannupa, Palani; m. Dean P. Fox (div. 1985); 1 child, Otgadahe. Student, Standing Rock C.C., Ft. Yates, N.D., 1973-74, Sinte Gleska Coll., Rosebud, S.D., 1975-77, U. S.D., 1977, Ariz. State U., 1992-93. Instr. art Sinte Gleska Coll., 1975-77, Standing Rock C.C., 1977-78; co-mgr. Four Bears Motor Lodge, New Town, N.D., 1981-82; store owner Nux-Baga Lodge, 1982-85; jeweler, painter Phoenix. Artist-in-residence N.D. Coun. on Arts, Bismarck, 1983-84, bd. dirs., 1985; artist-in-residence Evanston Twp. H.S., Ill., 1996; cultural cons. movie prodn., Phoenix, Ariz., 1994. One woman shows include Mus. of Am. Indian, N.Y.C., 1983, Charleroi Internat. Fair, Belgium, 1984, Heard Mus., Phoenix, 1987-92, Phoenix Gallery, Nurnburg, Germany, 1990-96, Lovena Ohl Gallery, Phoenix, 1990-94, Phoenix Gallery, Coeur d'Alene, Idaho, 1992, Silver Sun Gallery, Santa Fe, N.Mex., 1992-96, Tribal Expessions Gallery, Arlington Heights, Ill., 1994-96, others; represented in permanent collections at Mus. of the Am. Indian, N.Y.C., Mesa (Ariz.) C.C. Bd. dirs. Ft. Berthold C.C., New Town, 1983-85; pres. Cannonball (N.D.) Pow-Wow Com., 1978; parent rep. Head Start, Ft. Yates, 1974. Recipient mentor for First Peoples Fund, 2001, 02, best craftsman spl. award Bullock's Indian Arts and Crafts, 1986, best of fine arts award No. Plains Tribal Arts, Sioux Falls, S.D., 1988, best of show award Pasadena Western Relic and Native Am. Show, 1991, 2 1st place awards Santa Fe Indian Market, 1993, 2 2nd place awards, 1994, 2 3rd place awards, 1994, 74th Ann. SWAIA Santa Fe Indian Mkt. 1st place award, 1995, 2d place award, 1995, 97, 2 3rd place awards, 1995, 2 Honorable Mentions in sculpture N.Mex. State Fair, 1996, Best of Show/Fine Arts, N.M. State Fair, 1999, 01. Mem. Indian Arts and Crafts Assn., S.W. Assn. on Indian Affairs (life, 1st and 2nd place awards Santa Fe Indian Market 1995, 2 3rd place awards 1995, 1st place and 2nd place awards Santa Fe Indian Market 1996). Avocations: native American crafts, furniture building, running and hiking, dancing, singing.

WHITMAN, MARINA VON NEUMANN, economist, educator; b. N.Y.C., Mar. 6, 1935; d. John and Mariette (Kovesi) von Neumann; m. Robert Freeman Whitman, June 23, 1956; children: Malcolm Russell, Laura Mariette. BA summa cum laude, Radcliffe Coll., 1956; MA, Columbia U., 1959, PhD, 1962; LHD (hon.), Russell Sage Coll., 1972; LLD (hon.), Cedar Crest Coll., 1973, Hobart and William Smith Coll., 1973; LHD (hon.), U. Mass., 1975, N.Y. Poly. Inst., 1975; LLD (hon.), Coe Coll., 1975, Marietta Coll., 1976. Mem. faculty U. Pitts., 1962-79, prof. econs., 1971-73, disting. pub. svc. prof. econs., 1973-79; v.p., chief economist Gen. Motors Corp., N.Y.C., 1979-85, group v.p. pub. affairs, 1985-92; disting. vis. prof. bus. adminstrn., pub. policy U. Mich., Ann Arbor, 1992-94, prof. bus. adminstrn., pub. policy, 1994—. Bd. dirs. JP Morgan Chase Corp., Alcoa, Procter & Gamble Co., Unocal; mem. Trilateral Commn., 1973-84, 88-95; mem. Pres. Adv. Com. on Trade Policy and Negotiations, 1987-93; mem. tech. assessment adv. coun. U.S. Congress Office of Tech. Assessment, 1990-95; mem. Consultative Group on Internat. Econs. and Monetary Affairs, 1979—; mem. U.S. Price Commn., 1971-72, Coun. Econ. Advisers, Exec. Office of Pres., 1972-73. Author: Government Risk-Sharing in Foreign Investment, 1965, International and Interregional Payments Adjustment, 1967, Economic Goals and Policy Instruments, 1970, Reflections of Interdependence: Issues for Economic Theory and U.S. Policy, 1979, New World, New Rules: The Changing Role of the American Corporation, 1999; bd. editors: Am. Econ. Rev., 1974-77; mem. editl. bd. Fgn. Policy; contbr. articles to profl. jours. Trustee Nat. Bur. Econ. Rsch., 1993—, Princeton U., 1980-90, Inst. Advanced Study, 1999—; bd. dirs. Inst. for Internat. Econs., 1986—, Salzburg Seminar, 1994—, Eurasia Found., 1992-95; bd. overseers Harvard U., 1972-78, mem. vis. com. Kennedy Sch., 1992-98. Fellow Earhart Found., 1959-60, AAUW, 1960-61, NSF, 1968-70, Social Security Rsch. Coun.; recipient Columbia medal for excellence, 1973, George Washington award Am. Hungarian Found., 1975. Mem. Am. Econ. Assn. (exec. com. 1977-80), Am. Acad. Arts and Scis., Coun. Fgn. Rels. (dir. 1977-87), Phi Beta Kappa. Office: U Mich Gerald Ford Sch Pub Policy 411 Lorch Hall Ann Arbor MI 48109-1220 E-mail: marinaw@umich.edu.

WHITMAN, MARLAND HAMILTON, JR. lawyer; b. Balt., Oct. 13, 1947; s. M. Hamilton and Josephine Lee (Chatard) W.; m. Susan Zimmerman, Mar. 21, 1976; children: Elizabeth Miles, Hannah Minor. AB, Princeton U., 1969; JD, U. Va., 1976. Bar: Md. 1976, U.S. Supreme Ct. 1982, U.S. Ct. Appeals (3d cir.) 1986, (4th cir.) 1979 , U. S. Ct. Internat. Trade 1985, U.S. Dist. Ct. Md. 1977. From assoc. to ptnr. Ober, Kaler, Grimes & Shriver, Balt., 1976-98, shareholder, 1998—. Contbr. chpt. (book) Construction Litigation: Strategies and Techniques, 1990. Lt. USN, 1969-73. Mem. ABA, Maritime Law Assn. of U.S. (proctor 1977—), Md. State Bar Assn., Bar Assn. of Balt. City, Propeller Club of U.S. Pt. of Balt. Office: Ober Kaler Grimes & Shriver 120 E Baltimore St Baltimore MD 21202-1643

WHITMAN, MEG, information technology executive; b. N.Y., 1957; m. Griffith R. Harsh IV. B in Econs., Princeton U., 1977; MBA, Harvard U., 1979. With Procter & Gamble, Bain & Co., Walt Disney, Stride Rite Shoes, Florists' Transworld Delivery (FTD), Hasbro; pres., CEO eBay, Inc., San Jose, Calif., 1998—. Office: eBay Inc 2145 Hamilton Ave San Jose CA 95125*

WHITMAN, ROBERT VAN DUYNE, civil engineer, educator; b. Pitts., Feb. 2, 1928; s. Edwin A. and Elsie (Van Duyne) W.; m. Elizabeth Cushman, June 19, 1954; children: Jill Martyne Whitman Marsee, Martha Allerton (dec.), Gweneth Giles Whitman Kaebnick. BS, Swarthmore Coll., 1948, DSc (hon.), 1990; SM, MIT, 1949, ScD, 1951. Faculty MIT, 1953—, prof. civil engring., 1963-93, head structural engring., 1970-74, head soil mechanics divsn., 1970-72; prof. emeritus, 1993—. Vis. scholar U. Cambridge, Eng., 1976-77; cons. to govt. and industry, 1953—; mem. adv. com. for nat. earthquake hazard reduction program Fed. Emergency Mgmt. Agy., 1991-94, mem. commn. engring. and tech. systems NRC, 1992-97. Author: (with T. W. Lambe) Soil Mechanics. Mem. Town Meeting Lexington, Mass., 1962-76, 85—, mem. permanent bldg. com., 1968-75, mem. bd. appeals, 1979-81, 84-2000. Lt. (j.g.) USNR, 1954-56. Recipient U.S. Scientist award Humboldt Found., 1984-90; Norwegian Geotech. Inst. Rsch. fellow, 1984. Mem. NAE, ASCE (Rsch. award 1962, Terzaghi Lecture 1981, Terzaghi award 1987, C. Martin Duke Lifeline Earthquake Engring. award 1992, James Croes medal 1994), Boston Soc. Civil Engrs. (Structural Sect. prize 1963, Desmond Fitzgerald medal 1973, Ralph W. Horne Fund award 1977), Internat. Soc. Soil Mechanics and Found. Engrs. (Nabor Carrillo lectr. 2000, hon. 2002), Mex. Soc. Soil Mechanics, Earthquake Engring. Rsch. Inst. (dir. 1978-81, 84-88, v.p. 1979-81, pres. 1985-87, Disting. lectr. 1994, hon. 1997—). Achievements include research in in soil mechanics, soil dynamics, earthquake engring. and earthquake loss estimation. Home: 5 Hancock Ave Lexington MA 02420-3412 Office: MIT Dept Civil & Environ Engring Cambridge MA 02139

WHITMAN, ROY ERIC, political activist, freelance writer; b. Scranton, Pa., May 1, 1964; s. Edward Eugene and Maj Barbro Hedvall W. BS, U. Scranton, 1986. Intern Pa. Dept. Revenue, Harrisburg, 1984, Pa. Dept. Agrl., Harrisburg, 1985, Woodrow Wilson Ctr., Washington, 1985, U.S. Dept. State, Washington, 1986; planning aide Econ. Devel. Coun., Pittston, Pa., 1990-91; monitor VMS, N.Y.C.; indexer Diversified Info. Techs., Scranton, Pa. Mem. Lackawanna County Rep. Com. Swiss Govt. grantee, 1986; Wolcott fellow, 1986, Finnegan fellow, 1984, 85. Mem. SAR, Internat. Soc. Poetry, Fulbright Assn. (life), Mulberry Poetry Writers Assn. (bd. dirs. 1998—), Lackawanna Hist. Soc., Alpha Sigma Nu. Avocations: travel, music, poetry, history, foreign affairs. Home: 906 N Rebecca Ave Scranton PA 18504-1144

WHITMAN, THOMAS, composer; b. N.Y.C., Aug. 8, 1960; s. Martin J. and Lois (Quick) Whitman; m. Mira Rabin, Aug. 18, 1991; children: Nathaniel, Raphael, Rosalie. BA, Swarthmore Coll., 1982; PhD, U. Pa., 1992. Asst. prof. Swarthmore (Pa.) Coll., 1990—; Luce scholar Acad. of Indonesian Performing Arts, Denpasar, Bali, Indonesia, 1986-87. Vis. asst. prof. Haverford Coll., Pa., 1994; vis. lectr. U. N.C., Chapel Hill, 1989—90. Composer (opera): The Black Swan, 1996; composer: (musical pieces) Romanza, 1994, Aubade, 1992, Deux Sonnets de Louise Labe, 1982 (ASCAP Found. grant, 1984), Afterimage, 1998, Ori, 2000, Fantasy Duo, 2000; composer: (opera) Sukey in the Dark, 2001. Named to artist residency, MacDowell Colony, Peterborough, N.H., 1990, Yaddo, Saratoga Springs, N.Y., 1988, 1989; fellow Mellon Grad., U. Pa., Phila., 1988—89, 1987—88; grantee Luce scholar, Luce Found., N.Y., 1986—87. Mem.: ASCAP, Soc. for Ethnomusicology, Phi Beta Kappa. Office: Swarthmore Coll/Music/Dance 500 College Ave Swarthmore PA 19081-1306 E-mail: twhitma1@swarthmore.edu.

WHITMER, FREDERICK LEE, lawyer; b. Terre Haute, Ind., Nov. 5, 1947; s. Lee Arthur and Ella (Diekhoff) W.; m. Valeri Cade; children: Caitlin Margaret, Meghan Connors, Christian Frederick. BA, Wabash Coll., 1969; JD, Columbia U., 1973. Bar: N.Y. 1975, U.S. Dist. Ct. (so. dist.) N.Y. 1975, N.J. 1976, U.S. Dist. Ct. N.J. 1976, U.S. Ct. Appeals (3d cir.) 1977, U.S. Ct. Appeals (fed. cir.) 1983, U.S. Ct. Appeals (2d cir.) 1987, U.S. Supreme Ct. 1988, U.S. Ct. Appeals (7th cir.) 1994. Assoc. Kaye, Scholer, Fierman, Hays & Handler, N.Y.C., 1973-76, Pitney, Hardin & Kipp, Morristown, N.J., 1976-78; ptnr. Pitney, Hardin, Kipp & Szuch, 1979—. Mem. ABA, N.J. Bar Assn., Phi Beta Kappa. Republican. Episcopalian. Home: 190 Hurlbutt St Wilton CT 06897-2706 Office: Pitney Hardin Kipp & Szuch PO Box 1945 Morristown NJ 07962-1945 E-mail: fwhitmer@phks.com.

WHITMER, GRETCHEN SUE, secondary school educator; b. Saginaw, Mich., Feb. 6, 1955; d. Ernest J. and Betty W. Fechter; m. Walter Glen Whitmer, June 16, 1979; children: Emily W., Harrison G. BA, Ctrl. Mich. U., 1977; MA in Edn., Mich. State U., 1984. Cert. tchr., Mich. Speech and phys. edn. tchr. Hillsdale (Mich.) H.S., 1978-79; phys. edn. tchr. St. Ann's Elem. Sch. Cadillac (Mich.) Area Pub. Sch. Dist., 1980-86, phys. edn. tchr. McKinley, Lincoln and Kenwood Schs., 1986—, speech tchr. Cadillac Jr. H.S., 1999—. Bd. dirs. Am. Heart Assn., Cadillac, 1990-99; mem. St. John's Luth. Ch., Lake City, 1979—; mem., founder Up North Investment Club, Lake City, 1998—. Mem. AAHPERD, Mich. Assn. Phys. Edn., Health, Recreation, and Dance, Mich. Edn. Assn. Avocations: sailing, snow and water skiing, gardening. Home: 7699 W White Birch Ave Lake City MI 49651-8502 Office: Cadillac Jr HS 500 Chestnut St Cadillac MI 49601 E-mail: WWhitmer@traverse.net.

WHITMER, J. A. lawyer; b. South Bend, Ind., Mar. 24, 1952; d. Charles Inman and Kathleen Louise Whitmer; m. John S. Frizzo, July 13, 1991; stepchildren: Jacinda Leigh Frizzo, Steven Richard Frizzo, Nathaniel Joseph Frizzo. BA magna cum laude, Hanover Coll., 1974; JD summa cum laude, U. Notre Dame Law Sch., 1982. Bar: Calif. 1982, U.S. Dist. Ct. (ctrl. dist.) Calif. 1982, Ind. 1983, U.S. Dist. Ct. (no. and so. dists.) Ind. 1983. Assoc. atty. Surr & Hellyer, San Bernardino, Calif., 1982-84, Barnes & Thornburg, South Bend,

Ind., 1984-85, Thorne, Grodnik, Elkhart, 1985-91; pvt. practice, 1992—. Ednowment chmn., trustee St. Paul's United Meth. Ch. Mem.: ABA, Elkhart City Bar Assn., Ind. State Bar Assn. (bd. govs. 2000—), Kiwanis Club of Elkhart (bd. dirs. 1995—98). Avocations: antiques, gardening, reading. Office: 219 S 4th St Elkhart IN 46516-2838 E-mail: whitmerlaw@juno.com.

WHITMER, LESLIE GAY, federal official; b. Lexington, Ky., July 31, 1941; s. Leslie Allen and Gaynelle Kimbrell (McPherson) W.; m. Patricia Ann Welch, July 5, 1969; 1 child, Mary Gay. BS, U. Ky., 1963, JD, 1965. Bar: Ky. 1966, U.S. Dist. Ct. Ky. 1972, U.S. Supreme Ct. 1972. Atty. advisor gen. Office of Gen. Counsel, U.S. Dept. Agr., Chgo., 1966-69; dir. bar counsel Ky. Bar Assn.; editor Ky. Bar Jour., 1974-83; registrar Supreme Ct. Ky., 1975-83; clk. U.S. Dist. Ct. (ea. dist.) Ky., 1983—, mem. civil justice reform act adv. group, 1992—. Adj. prof. law U. Ky. Coll. Law, 1980, 82; mem. Gov.'s Task Force on Office Pub. Advocacy, 1982; exec. dir. Ky. Bar Ctr., 1979-83; sec.-treas. Ky. Bar Title Ins. Agy. Inc., 1973-83; asst. sec.-treas. Ky. Bar Found., 1979-83; exec. dir. Ky. Fed. Jud. Selection Commn., 1978-83; bd. dirs., sec.-treas. Ky. Legal Services Plan, Inc., 1978-83. Contbr. articles to legal jours. Recipient Recognition of Merit award U. Ky. Coll. Law Alumni Assn., 1983. Mem. Nat. Soc. Arts and Letters, Ky. Bar Assn. (bd. dirs., bar counsel, treas. 1973-83, discipline com. 1987-98), Fed. Bar Assn. (bd. dirs. 1998—), Psi Chi, Phi Alpha Delta, Spindletop Hall Club. Office: Federal Courthouse Lexington KY 40507

WHITMER, RICHARD E. insurance company executive; JD, U. Mich. Law School, 1965. Sr. v.p., gen. counsel Blue Cross Blue Shield Mich., Detroit, 1977—87, pres., CEO, 1987—. Office: Blue Cross Blue Shield Mich 600 E Lafayette Blvd Detroit MI 48226-2927*

WHITMER, WALTER GLENN, band director; b. Hastings, Mich., Feb. 28, 1955; s. Webb Whitmer and Thelma J. Armentrout-Witmer; m. Gretchen S. Fechter, June 16, 1979; children: Emily W., Harrison G. BME, Ctrl. Mich. U., 1977, MA, 1987. Asst. dir. Tri-Country H.S., Howard City, Mich., 1978-79; dir. Manton (Mich.) Schs., 1979-82; dir. bands Cadillac (Mich.) Schs., 1982—; dir. band N.W. Mich. Coll., Traverse City, Mich., 1990-94. Assoc. condr. Mich. Ambassadors Bands, 1996, 98, 2000; drill design dir. marching bands various schs. Mem. St. John's Luth. Ch. Mem. NEA, Mich. Sch. Band and Orch. Soc. (pres. dist. 1 1997—), Mich. Edn. Assn., Cadillac Edn. Assn. Lutheran. Avocations: sailing, snow and water skiing, stain glass work. Home: 7699 W White Birch Ave Lake City MI 49651-8502 Office: Cadillac High Sch Bands 400 Linden St Cadillac MI 49601-1704 E-mail: wwhitmer@traverse.net.

WHITMER, WILLIAM EWARD, retired accountant; b. Ft. Wayne, Ind., May 6, 1933; s. Frank Edward and Helen (Eward) W.; m. Signa Charity Dukes, Apr. 11, 1958 (div. 1972); children: Charles Edward, Michael Lee; m. Judith Rehm, Feb. 11, 1984. BA in Econs., Denison U., 1954. CPA, Calif. Staff auditor Arthur Young & Co., San Francisco, 1957-61, audit mgr., 1961-66, audit principal, 1966, cons. prin., 1967, dir. mgmt. cons., 1968-71, office mng. ptnr. Sacramento, 1971-75, regional dir., mgmt. cons. Atlanta, 1975-81, regional dir., mng. ptnr. mgmt. cons., 1981-89; assoc. mng. dir. Ernst & Young, 1989-92; ret., 1992. Bd. dirs. Novoste Corp., Acalanes Union High Sch. Dist., LaFayette, Calif., 1965-71, pres. bd. 1969-70. Served with USAF, 1954-57. Mem. AICPA, Ga. Soc. CPA's, Atlanta Country Club, Sea Pines Country Club, Long Cove Club. Republican. Presbyterian. Avocations: flying, golf, reading. Office: 3232 Cobb Pkwy # 304 Atlanta GA 30339-3896

WHITMEYER, JOSEPH M. sociologist; b. Canastota, N.Y., Sept. 24, 1960; s. Rebecca K. Whitmeyer; m. Rosemary L. Hopcroft; children: Mark, Sophie. PhD, U. Wash., 1993. Asst. prof. U. N.C., Charlotte, assoc. prof., 1998—. Contbr. articles to profl. jours. Vol. U.S. Peace Corps, Ucchakot, Nepal, 1982—84. Recipient Sociology Program award, NSF, 1995, 1996, 1998, 2000. Mem.: Am. Sociol. Assn. Avocation: piano. Office: Dept Sociology U NC Charlotte Charlotte NC 28223 Office Fax: 704-687-3091. Business E-Mail: jwhitmey@email.uncc.edu.

WHITMIRE, KENTON HERBERT, chemist; b. Roanoke, Va., July 20, 1955; s. Davy St. Clair and Palmyra Theresa (Beckner) Whitmire; m. Debra Mary Ellis, May 2, 1981; children: Rachel Elisabeth, Anna Karina, Kenton-David Lee. BS, Roanoke Coll., 1977; MS, Northwestern U., 1978, PhD, 1982. Asst. prof. chemistry Rice U., Houston, 1982—88, assoc. prof. chemistry, 1988—94, prof. chemistry, 1994—, chmn. chemistry dept., 1999—. Assoc. editor Organometallics, Washington, 1996—. Contbr. articles to profl. jours. and conf. procs. Fellow NATO postdoctoral, Cambridge (Eng.) U., 1981—82, Alexander von Humboldt Rsch., Gottingen, Germany, 1987, 1989—90. Mem.: Am. Chem. Soc. (chair-elect Gtr. Houston chpt. 2001, chair 2002). Office: Rice U Dept Chemistry MS60 6100 Main St Houston TX 77005-1892

WHITMORE, DONALD CLARK, retired engineer; b. Seattle, Sept. 15, 1932; s. Floyd Robinson and Lois Mildred (Clark) W.; m. Alice Elinor Winter, Jan. 8, 1955; children: Catherine Ruth, William Owen, Matthew Clark, Nancy Lynn, Peggy Ann, Stuart John. BS, U. Wash., 1955. Prin. engr. The Boeing Co., Seattle, 1955-87, ret., 1987. Developer, owner mobile home pk., Auburn, Wash., 1979—. Author: Towards Security, 1983, (monograph) SDI Software Feasibility, 1990, Characterization of the Nuclear Proliferation Threat, 1993, Rationale for Nuclear Disarmament, 1995. Activist for arms control, Auburn, Wash., 1962—; chmn. Seattle Coun. Orgns. for Internat. Affairs, 1973, Auburn Citizens for Schs., 1975; v.p. Boeing Employees Good Neighbor Fund, Seattle, 1977, Spl. Svc. award, 1977; pres. Abe Keller Peace Edn. Fund, 1998—, v.p., 2000--; pres., founder Third Millennium Found., 1993-2000; founder abolishnukes.com. Recipient Human Rights award, Seattle chpt. UN Assn., 2001. Avocations: hiking, travel, collecting. Home and Office: 16202 SE Lake Moneysmith Rd Auburn WA 98092-5274 E-mail: 3rdm@gte.net.

WHITMORE, DOUGLAS MICHAEL, physician; b. Cambridge, Mass., Oct. 30, 1947; s. Donald Herbert and Marcela (Klein) W.; m. Ana Maria Lopez. BS, MS in Physics, U. Ill., Champaign Urbana, 1969; MS in Physics, Stanford U., 1970, PhD in Physics, 1975; MD, U. Miami, 1978. Diplomate Am. Bd. Internal Medicine, Am. Bd. Pulmonary Disease, Am. Bd. Critical Care Medicine, Am. Bd. Geriatric Medicine. Physician Holy Cross Hosp., Ft. Lauderdale, Fla., 1983—. Pres. med. staff Holy Cross Hosp., 1996-97, officer, med. staff, 1995-98. Trustee Holy Cross Hosp., 1995-98. Fellow Am. Coll. Physicians; mem. AMA, Am. Coll. Chest Physicians, 1983—, Caducean Med. Soc. (pres. 1996-97), Am. Thoracic Soc., Royal Soc. Medicine. Office: Medical Complex West 1930 NE 47th St Ste 205 Fort Lauderdale FL 33308-7728

WHITMORE, FRANK CLIFFORD, JR. geologist; b. Cambridge, Mass., Nov. 17, 1915; s. Frank Clifford and Marion Gertrude (Mason) W.; m. Martha Burling Kremers, June 24, 1939; children: Geoffrey, John, Katherine, Susan. BA, Amherst Coll., 1938; MS, Pa. State U., 1939; MA, Harvard U., 1941, PhD, 1942. Instr. geology R.I. State Coll., Kingston, 1942-44; geologist U.S. Geol. Survey, Washington, 1944-84, scientist emeritus, 1984—; mem. com. rsch. and exploration Nat. Geog. Soc., 1970-96, vice chmn., 1990-96, emeritus, 1997—; rsch. assoc. dept. palebiology Smithsonian Instn., Washington, 1967—97. Sci. cons. U.S. Army, Philippines, Japan, Korea, 1945-46; mem. adv. bd. Ctr. for Study of Early Man, U. Maine, Orono, 1985-90. Editor: Resources for 21st Century, 1982; contbr. articles to profl. jours. Bd. dirs. Prince Georges County Boys Clubs, Md., 1954-56; mem. program com. Nat. Capital coun. Girl Scouts U.S.A., Washington, 1967-69; pres. Thornton Soc., Washington, 1977-84. Recipient medal of Freedom, U.S. Army, 1946, spl. achievement award U.S. Geol. Survey, 1980, Meritorious Svc. award, U.S. Dept. Interior, 1981, Arnold Guyot Meml. award, Nat. Geographic Soc., 1993, Thomas Jefferson medal Va. Mus. Natural History, 2002; Tchg. fellow Harvard U., Cambridge, Mass., 1940-42. Fellow AAAS, Geol. Soc. Am.; mem. Soc. Vertebrate Paleontology (hon. life, exec. com. 1960-62), Midriver Club, Harvard Club. Democrat. Avocation: architectural history. Home: 20 Woodmoor Dr Silver Spring MD 20901-2447

WHITMORE, GEORGE MERLE, JR. management consulting company executive; b. Tarrytown, N.Y., Jan. 1, 1928; s. George Merle and Elizabeth Helen (Knodel) W.; m. Priscilla Elizabeth Norman, Mar. 30, 1963; children: Elizabeth Whitmore Lippincott, George Norman, Stephen Bradford. BE, Yale U., 1949; MBA, Harvard U., 1951. Test engr. Gen. Electric Co., Bridgeport, Conn., Erie, Pa., 1949; rsch. assoc. Harvard Bus. Sch., Boston, 1951-52; assoc. Cresap, McCormick and Paget Inc., N.Y.C., 1954-59, prin., 1959-61, ptnr., 1961-69, v.p., dir., 1969-79, mng. dir., CEO, 1979-81; mng. dir. Ayers, Whitmore & Co. Inc., 1981-88, Ayers, Whitmore divsn. A.T. Kearney, Inc., N.Y.C., 1988-90, Whitmore & Co., Greenwich, Conn., 1990—; chmn. bd. dirs. Philo Smith & Co., Inc., Stamford. Bd. dirs. Carroll Enterprises, Inc., Worcester, Mass. Hon. trustee, former bd. pres. Hackley Sch., Tarrytown; former trustee, chmn. bd. Greenwich Acad.; former trustee, treas. Salisbury (Conn.) Sch. With USAF, 1952-53. Mem. Inst. Mgmt. Cons. (founding mem.), Newcomen Soc., Stanwich Club (former dir.), Yale Club (N.Y.C.), Tau Beta Pi. Presbyterian. Home and Office: 4 Cedarwood Dr Greenwich CT 06830-3905 E-mail: whitpen@aol.com.

WHITMORE, MENANDRA M. librarian; b. Ancash, Peru; d. Rafael and Jacinta (Moreno) Mosquera; m. Jacob L. Whitmore III, Jan. 7, 1965; children: Jacqueline Grace, Michelle Jacinta. Degree in social work, U. Catolica del Peru, 1967; MLS, U. P.R., 1974, Catholic U. Am., 1984. Social worker Cornell U., Vicos, Peru, 1960-62, Servicio de Extension Agricola del Peru, 1962-63, Am. Friends Svc. Com., Mex. and Peru, 1963-65; libr. Colegio Maria Auxiliadora, P.R., 1971, Country Day Sch., San Jose, Costa Rica, 1974-76, Colegio San Ignacio, P.R., 1976-77; dir. libs. Am. Coll. P.R., 1977-80; libr. Lib. Gov. Printing Office, 1981-84; chief acquisitions sect., mgr. Hispanic employment program Pentagon Libr., Washington, 1984-99, chief tech. and stds. divsn., 1999—2002, acting dir., 2002—. Author: (all pub. under name Menandra Mosquera) Bibliography on Hypsipyla, 1976, Bibliography of Forestry of Puerto Rico, 1984, Useful Trees of Tropical North America, 1998. Recipient commendation Dept. Def., 1987-98. Mem. ALA, Soc. for Acquisition Latin Am. Libr. Materials, Reforma (treas. Washington chpt. 1988, pres. 1989-91, 95-99, nat. ways and means chair 1991-92).

WHITMORE, TERI A. city official; b. Rapid City, S.D., Feb. 13, 1969; d. Howard J. and Lori J. Adams; m. Michael J. Whitmore, Aug. 13, 1994. BA in Design and Planning, U. Wash., 1992, M Urban Planning, 1995; MBA, S.W. Mo. State U., 2000. Cert. Am. Inst. Cert. Planners. Rsch. asst. in growth mgmt. U. Wash., Seattle, 1992-93; planning asst. City of Sedro Woolley, Wash., 1993; planner Weslin Cons., Bellevue, 1993, Horry County Planning, Conway, S.C., 1994-96; sr. transp. planner City of Springfield (Mo.) Planning and Devel., 1996—. Mem. Transp. Com. Adv. Group, Springfield, 1996—; secondary hearing appeals officer City Utilities Paratransit Svc., Access Express, Springfield, 1998—. Big sister Big Bros. and Big Sisters Ozarks, Springfield, 1997—; coord. planning dept. United Way, Springfield, 1997-98, account exec. bus. and industry divsn., 1998, sect. chmn., 1999, co-chmn., 2000—. Named One of Top 40 under 40, Springfield Bus. Jour., 2000. Mem. Am. Planning Asn. (sec. Puget Sound sect. 1992-94, v.p. Ozarks sect. 1997-98, pres. 1998-99, conf. chmn. Mo. chpt. 1999), Toastmasters (v.p. pub. rels. Springfield 1997-98). Avocations: competitive swimming, rock climbing, travel, cooking, archery. Home: 1922 S Oak Grove Ave Springfield MO 65804 Fax: 417-864-1030. E-mail: teriadams@aol.com.

WHITMYER, ROBERT WAYNE, soil scientist, consultant, researcher; b. Elkhart, Ind., Feb. 5, 1957; s. Wayne Ellsworth and Janet Sue (Housour) W.; m. Mary Kathleen Cory, June 7, 1980; children: Sydney Michelle, Kellie Mairin, Steffani Marie, Emily Claire. Student, Mpls. Coll. Art and Design, 1975-76; BS in Natural Resources cum laude, Ball State U., 1980; MS in Soil Sci., U. Minn., St. Paul, 1984. Lic. individual sewage treatment system inspector, designer, site evaluator, soil scientist, Minn., designer engrng. pvt. sewage system, soil tester, soil scientist, Wis. Rsch. asst. soil physics Lab. U. Minn., St. Paul, 1980-84; soil scientist Hakanson Anderson Assocs., Anoka, 1984-85; code enforcement officer, sewage treatment sys. operator County of Washington, Stillwater, 1985—90; soil scientist Owen Ayres & Assocs., Madison, Wis., 1990-97, Duluth, Minn., 1997-99; pres. MATRIX Soils & Sys., 1999—. Tech. com. Iron Range Resources Rehab. Bd./No. Lights Tourism Alliance , 1999—; tech. adv. com. St. Louis County Onsite Sewage Treatment, 2000—; new tech. subcom. Minn. Individual Sewage Treatment Sys., 2000—01. Contbr. articles to profl. jours. Com. mem. Rice Creek Watershed Dist., Arden Hills, Minn., 1989, Shoreview (Minn.) Environ. Quality Com., 1988-90; mem. DeForest Student Effectiveness Coun., 1992-95; bd. dirs. DeForest Area Sch. Dist., 1995-97, St. John's Sch. Commn., 1998—; mem. Rice Lake Twp. Planning & Zoning Com., 2000—. Mem. Am. Registry Cert. Profl. in Agronomy, Crops and Soils, Soil Sci. Soc. Am., Minn. Assn. Profl. Soil Scientists, Wis. Assn. Profl. Soil Scientists. Achievements include development of menu based computer program for monitoring and reporting all aspects of small community wastewater collection/treatment system operation, of formula for evaluating actual water flow velocity in soil pores, research on and identification of on site sewage treatment systems effective in removal of nitrogen. Office: MATRIX Soils & Sys 3990 Fairview Rd Duluth MN 55803-2708 E-mail: matrixss@msn.com.

WHITNER, LILLIAN MADDOX (LILLIE WITNER), interior designer, consultant; b. Birmingham, Ala.; d. Milton udoxious and Harriette (Newell Coleman) Maddox; m. James Harrison Whitner II, Feb. 27, 1923 (div. 1942); children— Harriette, James Harrison III, Lillian II. Sweet Briar Coll., Owner, operator Mary Lewis Dress Shop, Charlotte, N.C., 1939-42; researcher Fortune mag., Charlotte, 1942-45, Nat. Research Ctr., Denver, 1942-45; artist's rep., Charlotte, 1946-48; prin. Lillian Whitner's Interiors, Charlotte, 1948— . Exhibited at Mint Mus. Art, Charlotte, 1955; decorator Queen's Sorority House, Charlotte, 1958; Davidson Coll. frat. (N.C.), 1958; asst. decorator Gov's home, Charlotte, 1958. Pres. Alumnae Orgn. Sweet Briar Coll., Charlotte, 1932; asst. Handicraft Div. Regional Art, Mint Mus. Art, 1938-39; radio worker Community Chest, Charlotte, 1939-40. Mem. Am. Soc. Interior Designers (cert.), Mint Mus. Art. Presbyterian. Clubs: Charlotte Country, Jr. League Charlotte (soc. editor 1929-30, corr. sec. 1931-32, chmn. ways and means com. 1933-34, editor-in-chief 1935-36, chmn. local advt. 1940-41), Jr. League U.S.

WHITNEY, CAROL MARIE, securities sales professional; b. Torrington, Conn., Mar. 31, 1946; d. Charles Lester and Emily Mae (Orr) W. BA in French, Wells Coll., 1968; 5th yr. cert., So. Conn. State Coll., 1971; postgrad., N.Y. Inst. Fin., 1976; MS in Mgmt., Rensselaer Poly. Inst., 1992, MBA in Internat. Mgmt., 1997. Trainee/investment exec. Blyth-Eastman Dillon, Hartford, Conn., 1976-77; licensee ins. fixed, variable, life and health, various cos., 1977—; account exec./registered rep. Bache Halsey-Stuart Shields, Hartford, Danbury, Conn., 1977-81, Advest, Inc., Hartford, 1981-88; registered securities rep. West Hartford, Conn., 1988-91; internat. fin. con., investment analyst, pres. Ask My Assoc., Collinsville, 1988—; v.p. registered rep. E.T. Andrews & Co. Inc., Hartford, 1991-92; v.p. Conn. Fin. Network, 1991-92; v.p., registered prin. Buell Securities Corp., Wethersfield, Conn., 1992—, br. mgr. Torrington office, 1993-95. Sec. Internat. Assn. for Fin. Planning, Hartford, 1982-83, pub. rels. Conn. chpt., Hartford, 1983-85, ethics chairperson Conn. chpt., Hartford, 1985-86. Exhibited 5 paintings in State Cultural Mus., Karelia, Russia, 1999, 16 paintings in The Cultural Mus., Petrozavodsky, Russia, 2000; solo exhibit Cultural Mus., Petrozarodsk, Russia, 2000; prodr. (CD) Guennady Vavilov, 1999; author: Global Corporate Derivatives, 1997. Performing mem. Farmington Valley chpt. Sweet Adelines, Simsbury, Conn., 1976-82; founder, exec. dir. Lydia Whitney Found Inc.; exec. dir. for classical composers concert, The Bushnell, Hartford, 1998—. Named for Effective Speaking and Human Rels., Dale Carnegie, West Hartford, 1985. Mem. DAR, Internat. Platform Assn. (3rd prize Washington 1995 Katyn Forest, World Tour 1997 for 5 paintings, 1st prize 1997), World Affairs. Republican. Episcopalian. Avocations: international travel, cooking and baking, writing, Russian language studies. Home: PO Box 462 Collinsville CT 06022-0462

WHITNEY, CRAIG RICHARD, journalist; b. Milford, Mass., Oct. 12, 1943; s. A. Gordon and Carol Alma (Kennison) W.; m. Heidi Witt, May 11, 1974; children: Alexandra Kennison, Stefan Robert. AB, Harvard, 1965. Reporter New York Times, Washington, 1965-66, N.Y.C., 1969-70, Saigon, Vietnam, 1971-72, Bonn, West Germany, 1973-77, Moscow, USSR, 1977-80, dep. fgn. editor, 1980-82, fgn. editor, 1982-83, asst. mng. editor, 1983-86, Washington Bur. chief, 1986-88, London bur. chief, 1988-92, European diplomatic corr., 1992-2000, asst. mng. editor, 2000—. Served with USNR, 1966-69. Mem. Coun. Fgn. Rels., Harvard Club (N.Y.C.). Home: 1 Pierrepont St Brooklyn NY 11201-3302 Office: The NY Times 229 W 43rd St New York NY 10036-3959 E-mail: whitney@nytimes.com.

WHITNEY, DAVID See MALICK, TERRENCE

WHITNEY, EDWARD BONNER, retired investment banker; b. Glen Cove, N.Y., June 6, 1945; s. Edward Farley and Millicent Bonner (Bowring) W.; m. Martha Congleton Howell, Aug. 17, 1974; children: William Howell, John Howell. BA, Harvard U., 1966, MBA, 1969. Systems engr. IBM, Cambridge, Mass., 1966-67; assoc. Dillon, Read & Co. Inc., N.Y.C., 1969-74, v.p., 1975-79, sr. v.p., 1980-83, mng. dir., 1984-97, also bd. dirs.; mng. dir. UBS Warburg, London, 1997—2002. Bd. dirs., vice-chair Investor Responsibility Rsch. Ctr., IRRC PubCo.; bd. dirs., Am. Rivers. Mem. Heights Casino Club (Bklyn.). Office: 299 Park Ave New York NY 10171-0002 E-mail: ned.whitney@aol.com.

WHITNEY, ENOCH JONATHAN, lawyer; b. Jacksonville, Fla., Oct. 7, 1945; s. Enoch Johnson and Iris Ida (Sperber) W.; m. Diane Marie Dupuy, Aug. 29, 1968; children: Elizabeth, William, Edward. BA, Fla. State U., 1967, JD, 1970; grad., FBI Nat. Law Inst., 1989. Bar: Fla. 1970, U.S. Dist. Ct. (no. dist.) Fla. 1970 U.S. Dist. Ct. (mid. dist.) Fla. 1982, U.S. Dist. Ct. (so. dist.) Fla. 1989, U.S. Ct. Appeals (5th cir.) 1971, U.S. Ct. Appeals (11th cir.) 1981, U.S. Supreme Ct. 1974. Rsch. asst. Fla. 1st Dist. Ct. Appeals, Tallahassee, 1971; asst. atty. gen. Fla. Dept. Legal Affairs, 1971-74; asst. gen. counsel Fla. Dept. Hwy. Safety & Motor Vehicles, 1974-79, gen. counsel, 1979-82, 86—. Gen. counsel Fla. Parole and Probation Commn., Tallahassee, 1982-85; instr. Fla. Hwy. Patrol Tng. Acad., Tallahassee, 1977-82, 86—. Named Able Toastmaster, Toastmasters Internat., 1977. Mem. ABA, Tallahassee Bar Assn. (ex officio dir. 1989-97), Fla. Govt. Bar Assn. (pres. 1977-78), Fla. Bar (bd. govs. 1989-97, charter mem. govt. law sect. 1991, appellate law sect. 1994, bd. cert. appellate lawyer 1994—, budget com. 1992-95, 96-99, appellate cert. com. 1998—, vice chair 2001-2002, chmn., 2002-), Fla. Coun. Bar Assn. Pres. (life), Fla. State U. Alumni Assn. (life), Fla. Gov. Gen. Counsels Assn. (pres. 1998-99), Fla. Assn. Women Lawyers, Tallahassee Assn. Women Lawyers, Fla. Supreme Ct. Hist. Soc., Supreme Ct. U.S. Hist. Soc., Atty. Gen.'s Hist. Soc. Fla., Fla. Sheriff's Assn., Govs. Club, Capital Tiger Bay Club, Fla. Assn. Police Attys., Kiwanis (pres. Tallahassee 1984-85, lt. gov. Fla. dist. 1986-87). Democrat. Roman Catholic. Avocations: antique collecting, reading. Home: 5001 Vernon Rd Tallahassee FL 32317-8534 Office: Fla Dept Hwy Safety & Motor Vehicles 2900 Apalachee Pky Tallahassee FL 32399-6552 E-mail: whitney.jon@hsmv.state.fl.us.

WHITNEY, GWIN RICHARD, brick distribution company executive; b. N.Y.C., Sept. 3, 1932; s. Gwin Allison and Charlotte (Wilson) W.; m. Marjorie Joan Turnbloom, Dec. 26, 1954; children: Gregg Richard, Laura Ann, Jane Louise, Eric Gwin. BA, Stanford U., 1954; postgrad., Brick Inst. Am., 1979. Asst. mgr. Whitney's, Duluth, Minn., 1958-70; adminstrn. mgr. Thomas and Vecchi Architects, 1970-75; owner, pres. Standard Brick and Supply Inc., 1975-89; gen. mgr. Standard Brick (div. Brock White), 1989-92; mem. exec. com. Brock White, St. Paul, 1992—, cons. Duluth, 1992—. Trustee Pilgrim Congl. Ch., Duluth, 1980-82; bd. dirs. Woodland Hills Juvenile Residential Treatment Home, 1993—, chair, 2000—; past bd. bldg. rev. City of Duluth. Mem. ASTM, Arrowhead Builder Assn. (bd. dirs. 1976-85), Nat. Assn. Brick Distbrs. (chmn. 1990-92, bd. dirs. 1982-93), Nat. Assn. Fleet Tng. Sailors, Duluth Builders Exch. (bd. dirs., pres. 1988-89), Minn. Brick Distbrs. (bd. dirs. 1980-2000, pres. 1993-95), Duluth C. of C., Sons of Union Vets., Rotary, Northland Club, Kitchi Gammi. Republican. Avocations: underwater archeology, cross country skiing. Office: Brock White Duluth PO Box 16507 4231 W 1st St Duluth MN 55807-2761

WHITNEY, JANE, foreign service officer; b. July 15, 1941; d. Robert F. and Mussette (Cary) W. BA, Beloit Coll., 1963; CD, U. Aix, Marseille, France, 1962. Joined Fgn. Svc., U.S. Dept. State, 1965; vice consul Saigon, Vietnam, 1966-68; career counselor, 1968-70; spl. asst. Office of Dir. Gen., 1970-72; consul Stuttgart, Fed. Rep. Germany, 1972-74, Ankara, Turkey, 1974-76; spl. asst. Office of Asst. Sec. for Consular Affairs, 1976-77; mem. Bd. Examiners Fgn. Svc., 1977-78, 79-81; consul Munich, Germany, 1978-79, Buenos Aires, Argentina, 1981-82; ethics officer Office of Legal Adviser, 1982-85; advisor Office of Asst. Sec. for Diplomatic Security, 1985-86; dep. prin. officer, consul Stuttgart, 1986-90; prin. officer, consul gen. Perth, Australia, 1990-91. Mem. Presbyterian Ch. Recipient awards U.S. Dept. State, 1968, 70, 81, 85, 87, 90.

WHITNEY, JOHN DENISON, English educator, writer; b. Pasadena, Calif., Sept. 23, 1940; s. John Keshishyan Whitney and Nathalie Adams Crane; children: Barbara, Joanne, Roger, David, Douglas, Suzanne, Michael. BA, U. Mich., 1962, MA, 1966. Prof. English U. Wis., Platteville, 1966-69, Wausau, 1969—. Coll. of Menominee Nation, Keshena, Wis., 1993-97. Author: (poems) The Nabisco Warehouse, 1971, Word of Mouth, 1986, sd, 1988, What Grandmother Says, 1995, 3d edit., 2001, sd and done, 1995. Writing fellow Wis. Arts Bd., 1976, Creative Writing fellow Nat. Endowment for Arts, 1994. Avocations: Tai Chi, motorcycling. Home: 829 E Thomas St Wausau WI 54403-6448 Office: U Wis Marathon County 518 S 7th Ave Wausau WI 54401-5362 E-mail: jdwhitne.@uwc.edu.

WHITNEY, LORI ANN, legislative staff member; b. Rhinelander, Wis., Feb. 20, 1968; d. Larry R. and Mary E. (Gaffney) W. BA in Spanish/Polit. Sci. cum laude, U. Wis., Eau Claire, 1990. Messenger Wis. State Assembly, Madison, 1991-95, postal clk. Assembly Post Office, 1995—. Fundraiser State Employees Combined Campaign, Madison, 1992—, mem. state coordinating com., 1996—; fundraiser Multiple Sclerosis Soc., 1993—; mem. Amnesty Internat., 1991—; fundraiser, vol. Am. Diabetes Assn.; monthly donor Planned Parenthood Nat. Leadership Coun.; vol., donor Planned Parenthood Advocates of Wis.; mem., donor YWCA; blood donor ARC; vol. Prevent Child Abuse Wis., 1994—; campaign vol. David Clarenbach and Tammy Baldwin, Madison, 1992, State Rep. Tammy Baldwin, 1994, 1996, 1998, Fred Risser, 1996, Russ Feingold, 1998, Tammy Baldwin and Al Gore, 2000. Recipient Hopebuilder Habitat for Humanity award, 1995, 9 SECC Fundraising awards, Cmty. Vol. award, United Way, 2002, Hannah Needham Rogers award, Planned Parenthood Advocates of Wis., 2002. Mem. NOW. Democrat. Avocations: reading, sports, rock music, movies (comedy), travel. Home: 15 N Hancock St Apt 102 Madison WI 53703-2839

WHITNEY, NATALIE WHITE, primary school educator; b. Pasadena, Calif., Mar. 26, 1917; d. Walter Patton and Natalie May (Brokaw) White; m. John Parker Whitney, Mar. 17, 1943 (dec. July 1969); children: John Parker, Jr., Sarah Carpenter. Student, Univ. Ariz., 1936-38, Claremont Coll., 1940-43; BA, Whittier Coll., 1940. Kindergarten primary tchr. credential, Calif. Asst. dir. M.B. Eyer Nursery Sch., Scripps Coll., Claremont, 1940-43; dir. kindergarten Westridge Sch. Girls, Pasadena, 1943-45; tchr. kindergarten Oak Grove Sch. Dist., San Jose, Calif., 1971-73, 73-86, primary tchr., 1973—. Author: Pumpkins, 1996 (also Spanish edit. Calabazas 1996), The Tiny Dot, 1996 (also Spanish edit. El puntito 1996). Gray Lady, ARC, Pasadena, 1943; sponsor Ford Country Day Sch., Los Altos, Calif., 1955-58, Children's Country Sch. (name now Hillbrook Sch.), Los Gatos, Calif., 1958-64, Youth Sci. Mus., San Jose, 1971-86; den mother Boy Scouts Am., Los Altos, 1956-58; mem. women's aux. San Jose Symphony, 1963; asst. gift shop Alexian Bros. Hosp. League, 1965. Recipient Merit award ARC, 1951. Mem. Mayflower Soc. (life), Valle Monte League (sustaining), Los Altos Hunt Club (resident), Kappa Kappa Gamma. Republican. Episcopalian. Avocations: reading, interior decorating, gourmet cuisine, gardening, hostessing. Home: 15785 Alta Vista Way San Jose CA 95127-1702

WHITNEY, PHYLLIS AYAME, author; b. Yokohama, Japan, Sept. 9, 1903; d. Charles J. and Lillian (Mandeville) W.; m. George A. Garner, July 2, 1925 (div. 1945); m. Lovell F. Jahnke, 1950 (dec. 1973). Grad., McKinley High Sch., Chgo., 1924. Instr. dancing, San Antonio, 1 yr; tchr. juvenile fiction writing Northwestern U., 1945; children's book editor Chgo. Sun, 1942-46, Phila. Inquirer, 1947, 48; instr. juvenile fiction writing N.Y.U., 1947-58; leader juvenile fiction workshop Writers Conf., U. Colo., 1952, 54, 56. Pres. exec. bd. 5th Ann. Writers Conf., Northwestern U., 1944. Author: A Place for Ann, 1941, A Star for Ginny, 1942, (vocat. fiction for teenage girls) A Window for Julie, 1943, (mystery novel for adults) Red Is for Murder, 1943, The Silver Inkwell, 1945, Willow Hill, 1947, Writing Juvenile Fiction, 1947, Ever After, 1948, Mystery of the Gulls, 1949, Linda's Homecoming, 1950, The Island of Dark Woods, 1951, Love Me, Love Me Not, 1952, Step to the Music, 1953, A Long Time Coming, 1954, Mystery of the Black Diamonds, 1954, The Quicksilver Pool, 1955, Mystery on the Isle of Skye, 1955, The Fire and The Gold (Jr. Lit. Guild), 1956, The Highest Dream (Jr. Lit. Guild), The Trembling Hills (Peoples Book Club), 1956, Skye Cameron, 1957, Mystery of the Green

Cat (Jr. Lit. Guild), 1957, Secret of the Samurai Sword (Jr. Lit. Guild), 1958, The Moonflower, 1958, Creole Holiday, 1959, Thunder Heights, 1960, Blue Fire, 1961, Mystery of the Haunted Pool, 1961 (Edgar award Mystery Writers Am.), Secret of the Tiger's Eye, 1961, Window on the Square, 1962, Mystery of the Golden Horn, 1962, Seven Tears for Apollo, 1963, Mystery of the Hidden Hand, 1963 (Edgar award Mystery Writers Am. 1964), Black Amber, 1964, Secret of the Emerald Star, 1964, Sea Jade, 1965, Mystery of the Angry Idol, 1965, Columbella, 1966, Secret of the Spotted Shell, 1967, Mystery of the Strange Traveler, 1967, Silverhill, 1967, Hunter's Green, 1968, Secret of Goblin Glen, 1968, Mystery of the Crimson Ghost, 1969, Winter People, 1969, Secret of the Missing Footprint, 1970, Lost Island, 1970, The Vanishing Scarecrow, 1971, Listen for the Whisperer, 1971, Nobody Likes Trina, 1972, Snowfire, 1973, Mystery of the Scowling Boy, 1973, The Turquoise Mask, 1974, Spindrift, 1975, Secret of Haunted Mesa, 1975, The Golden Unicorn, 1976, Secret of the Stone Face, 1977, The Stone Bull, 1977, The Glass Flame, 1978, Domino, 1979, Poinciana, 1980, Vermilion, 1981, Guide to Fiction Writing, 1982, Emerald, 1983, Rainsong, 1984, Dream of Orchids, 1985, Flaming Tree, 1986, Silversword, 1987, Feather on the Moon, 1988, Rainbow in the Mist, 1989, The Singing Stones, 1990, Woman Without a Past, 1991, The Ebony Swan, 1992, Star Flight, 1993, Daughter of the Stars, 1994, Amethyst Dreams, 1997; sold first story to Chgo. Daily News; later wrote for pulp mags., became specialist in juvenile writing, now writing entirely in adult field. Spent first 15 years of life in Japan, China and P.I. (father in shipping and hotel bus.). Recipient Friends of Lit. award for contbns. to children's lit., 1974; Reynal and Hitchcock prize in Youth Today contest for book Willow Hill; Today's Woman award Coun. Cerebral Palsy Auxs., 1983, Agatha award Malice Domestic, 1990, Rita award Romance Writers Am., 1990, Lifetime award Romance Writers Am., 1990, Midland Authors award for a lifetime of literary achievement, 1995. Mem. Mystery Writers Am. (pres. 1975, Grand-master award for lifetime achievement 1988), Am. Crime Writers League, Sisters in Crime, Authors League of Am., Authors Round Table (pres. 1943-44). Address: care McIntosh and Otis 353 Lexington Ave New York NY 10016-0941 *A learning period must be allowed for any talent. The accidental success is unfortunate because the person who achieves it doesn't really know how it happened. This does not mean that it ever becomes easy, even with learning. There is always work involved-long hours and dedication to that work-before a book is ready for publication. Any success demands a price, and the time and effort, and sometimes anguish a successful person gives to his work is that price. For me, the satisfactions have been worth it.*

WHITNEY, RALPH ROYAL, JR. financial executive; b. Phila., Dec. 10, 1934; s. Ralph Royal and Florence Elizabeth (Whitney) W.; m. Fay Wadsworth, Apr. 4, 1959; children: Lynn Marie, Paula Sue, Brian Ralph. BA, U. Rochester, 1957, MBA, 1972. Spl. agt. Prudential Ins. Co., Rochester, N.Y., 1958-59, divsn. mgr., 1959-63; gen. agt. Nat. Life Vt., Syracuse, 1963-64; contr. Wadsworth Mfg. Assocs. Inc., 1964-65, v.p., 1965-68, pres., 1968-71, Warren (Pa.) Components Corp., 1968-72; chmn. Hammond Kennedy Whitney & Co., N.Y.C., 1972—. Chmn. Reinhold Industries; chmn., CEO Grobet File Co.; bd. dirs. Baldwin Tech. Corp., First Tech., Ltd., M. Mossberg & Son, Inc., MedTek Inc., Wyo. Bus. Coun., Relm Wireless Comms. Inc., 1st Internet Bank, Horton Emergency Vehicles, Seneca Printing, Inc., Dura Automobile Sys. Inc., Polytwine Inc. Bd. trustees U. Rochester. Mem. N.Y. Yacht Club, Lotus Club (N.Y.C.), Century Club (Syracuse), Merion Cricket Club, Princeton Club. Episcopalian. Home: 3441 Highway 34 Wheatland WY 82201-8714 E-mail: rrw@hkwinc.com.

WHITNEY, RAY, hockey player; b. Saskatchewan, Alta., Can., May 8, 1972; s. Floyd and Wendy W. Stick boy Edmonton Oilers, 1986-87, 87-88, player, 1997, Spokane Chiefs, 1988-91, 90-91, San Jose Sharks, 1991—97, Edmonton Oilers, 1997—98, Fla. Panthers, 1998—2001, Columbus Blue Jackets, 2001—. Named most valuable player WHL, 1988-91, 90-91, Most Valuable Player All-Star Game IHL, 1992. Avocation: golf. Office: Columbus Blue Jackets JMAC Hockey 150 East Wilson Bridge Rd. Suite 230 Worthington OH 43085*

WHITNEY, RICHARD BUCKNER, lawyer; b. Corpus Christi, Tex., Mar. 1, 1948; s. Franklyn Loren and Betty Wolcott (Fish) Whitney; m. Chantal Marie Gindt, Aug. 18, 1972; children: Jennifer L, James R, Katherine E. BA in Polit. Sci., Union Coll., 1970; JD, Case Western Res. U., 1973. Bar: Ohio 1973, N.Y. 1998, US Ct Appeals (6th cir) 1974, US Ct Appeals (3d cir) 1987, US Dist Ct (so dist) NY 2000. From assoc. to ptnr. Jones, Day, Reavis & Pogue, Cleve., 1973—. Trustee Hospice of the We. Res., Fairmount Music Edn. Found. Mem.: Am Inns Cts, Legal Aid Soc Cleveland (trustee), Cleveland Bar Asn, Order of Coif. Roman Catholic. Home: 2750 Southington Rd Shaker Heights OH 44120-1603 Office: Jones Day Reavis & Pogue 901 Lakeside Ave Cleveland OH 44114-1190 E-mail: rbwhitney@jonesday.com.

WHITNEY, RICHARD WHEELER, artist, educator; b. Burlington, Vt., Jan. 22, 1946; s. Roland Allen and Harriet (Wheeler) W.; m. Susan Joyce Elliott, Feb. 3, 1968 (div.); children: Deborah Ellen, Emily Rose; m. Sandra H.A. Sherman, Nov. 23, 1999. BA, U. N.H., 1968. Artist-apprentice R.H. Ives Gammell Studios, Boston, 1965-71; painting instr. Sharon (N.H.) Arts Ctr., 1971-77, Cushing Acad., Ashburnham, Mass., 1971-80; founder, dir. Monadnock Studios, Marlborough, N.H., 1981-93; portrait painter Vose Galleries, Boston, 1976—, Portraits Inc., N.Y.C., 1981—, Grand Cen. Galleries, N.Y.C., 1982-94, Portraits S., Raleigh, and others, 1984—. Portrait & landscape demonstrator for several art orgns. 1979—. Artist: paintings in over 600 collections including the Newark Mus. Art, The Pentagon, Harvard U., U. of Chgo., Springville (Utah) Mus. of Art, and Anchorage Hist. and Fine Arts Mus.; author: booklet, Painting the Visual Impression, Minn. River Sch. Fine Art, 1995, (with others) book, Realism in Revolution, The Art of The Boston Sch., Taylor Publishing Co., Dallas, 1986. Mem. Memorial Tree Fund Com. Keene, N.H. 1987. Recipient of over 40 nat. awards and grants from various profl. orgns., including Silver medal, Soc. of Illustrators, 1987. Mem. Allied Artists Am. (Crescent Gallery award 1980), Guild of Boston Artists (Gold medal 1983), Copley Soc. (3 awards and Copley Master status 1984), Am. Artists Profl. League (Gold medal 1984, 91), Am. Soc. Portrait Artists Found. (chmn. adv. emeritus). Avocations: hiking, meditation, classical mus., pianist. Studio: Studios at Crescent Pond 100 Chalet Dr Stoddard NH 03464-4404 E-mail: studios@crescentpond.com.

WHITNEY, ROBERT MICHAEL, lawyer; b. Green Bay, Wis., Jan. 29, 1949; s. John Clarence and Helen (Mayer) W. Student, U. Wis., 1967-70, JD, 1974. Bar: Wis. 1974, U.S. Dist. Ct. (we. dist.) Wis. 1979, U.S. Ct. Appeals (7th cir.) 1980, U.S. Dist. Ct. (ea. dist.) Wis. 1984, U.S. Supreme Ct. 1990, U.S. Ct. Appeals (9th cir.) 1992. Legal counsel Wis. State Election Bd., Madison, 1976-78; ptnr. Walsh, Walsh, Sweeney & Whitney, S.C., 1979-86, Foley & Lardner, Madison, 1986-2000, Lawton & Cates SC, Madison, 2000—. Counsel Dane County Advocates for Battered Women; instr. torts I, U. Wis. Labor Sch., 1996; adj. prof. U. Wis. Law Sch., 1996-97. Contbr. articles to profl. jours. Bd. dirs. Community TV, Inc., Madison, 1984-87, Transitional/Homeless Shelters. Mem. Assn. Trial Lawyers Am., Wis. Acad. Trial Lawyers, Wis. Bar Assn., Dane County Bar Assn., Rugby Club of Madison. Office: Lawton & Cates 10 E Doty St Ste 400 Madison WI 53703-5103

WHITNEY, STEWART BOWMAN, social psychology educator and program director; b. Buffalo, Nov. 15, 1938; s. Stewart Badeau and Edythe Lillian (Walser) W.; m. Constance Dierks Whitney, May 25, 1971 (div. Nov. 1980); m. Joan Noel Conti, Apr. 23, 1988; children: Scott Boyd, Edythe-Louise, Belle Elizabeth, Constance, Stewart Bowman, Jr. BA, U. Buffalo, 1961; MA, SUNY, Buffalo, 1965, PhD, 1972. Cert. in family life edn., in family therapy, in sex therapy. Study dir. Sch. Medicine SUNY, Buffalo, 1962-65; asst. prof. Ithaca (N.Y.) Coll., 1965-69, SUNY, Buffalo, 1969-70, Antioch Coll., Yellow Springs, Ohio, 1970-72; assoc. prof. Niagara U., Lewiston, N.Y., 1973-77, prof., 1977-85, prof. emeritus, 1998—, chairperson, 1985—. Cons. SUNY, Buffalo, 1974-86; dir. space settlement studies project Niagara U., Lewiston, N.Y., 1977—; vis. lectr. U. Tubingen, Germany, 1972, U. Berne, Switzerland, 1977, 1993. Author: Anomie and Radicalization, 1990, Space Journal, 1983, Phenylketonuria Detection, 1964, Space Settlement, 1996, Socialization Digest, 1995, Stress Busters, 1998, Student Revolt, 1999; contbr. articles to profl. jours. Founding mem. Nat. Space Soc., Washington, 1987—; bd. dirs. Ctr. of the Black Family, Niagara Falls, N.Y., 1987—, Buffalo Philharm. Orch. Soc., 1977—. Acad. Rsch. grantee Niagara U., 1990, 91, 92, Faculty Rsch. grantee Niagara U., 1990, 91, 92, 93, 94, 95, 97, 98, 99, Whitney Found. grantee, 1981, Rsch. grantee U.S. Children's Bur., 1962, Rsch. grantee NAS, 1969. Fellow Am. Soc. Sexology (diplomate); mem. Am. Sociol. Assn., Nat. Coun. on Family Rels., Ea. Sociol. Soc., Soc. for the Sci. Study of Sex, World Future Soc. Episcopalian. Avocations: exploration, ethology, hiking, ethnography. Home: 73 Niagara Falls Blvd Buffalo NY 14214-1216 Office: Niagara U Timon Hall, Dept Sociology Niagara Dr Lewiston NY 14109 E-mail: swhitney@niagara.edu.

WHITNEY, WILLIAM CHOWNING, retired banker, financial consultant; b. Fullerton, Nebr., June 28, 1920; s. Barlow N. and Lena C. (Price) W.; m. Joan F. Whitney; children— William H., David M., Terri Lynn, Sherri Lee, Jonathan P., Laura Louise. BBA cum laude, Loyola U., Chgo., 1949. Asst. bank examiner Fed. Res. Bank, Chgo., 1938-41; asst. auditor South Side Bank and Trust Co., 1946-49; comptroller Peoples Nat. Bank, Bay City, Mich., 1949-52; asst. v.p., comptroller Tex. Bank and Trust Co., Dallas, 1952-54; with Old Kent Bank and Trust Co., Grand Rapids, Mich., 1954-86; sr. v.p., CFO, sec. bd., dir. Old Kent Fin. Corp., 1965-86. Cons. Amway Corp., 1986-96. Chmn. Met. Hosp., 1986-93, Met. Health Corp., 1987-95; treas. Keswick United Meth. Ch. Capt. AUS, 1941-46. Mem. Fin. Execs. Inst. (past pres.), Mich. Banks Assn., Bank Adminstrn. Inst., Grand Rapids C. of C., Rotary (treas.), Peninsular Club, Cascade County Club, Univ. Club, Ada Lodge, Masons, traverse City Econ. Club, VFW. Home: 742 N Apple Tree Dr Suttons Bay MI 49682-9778 E-mail: blwhit@aol.com.

WHITNEY, WILLIAM ELLIOT, JR. advertising agency executive; b. Albany, N.Y., Feb. 22, 1933; s. William Elliot and Louise E. (Goldsmith) W.; m. Nancy B. Bivings, Mar. 1, 1958; children— Susan, James, Douglas. BA cum laude, Amherst Coll., 1954; MBA, Harvard U., 1956. Account exec. McCann-Erickson, N.Y.C., 1956-58, Marschalk Co., N.Y.C., 1958-60; v.p., then sr. v.p. Ogilvy & Mather, 1960-80, sr. v.p., mng. dir. Chgo., 1980-85, exec. v.p., 1985-87, pres., 1987-89, chmn., 1990-91; cons. ptnr. Redirections, Inc., 1991-98. Lectr. U. Chgo. Grad. Sch. Bus., 1991-98. Bd. dirs., v.p. Chgo. Coun. Boy Scouts Am., 1978-81, 88—, Off-the-St. Club, Chgo., 1979—, pres., 1988-89; bd. dirs. Hinsdale (Ill.) Cmty. House, 1981, King-Bruwaert House, 1988—; v.p. civic adv. bd. Hinsdale Hosp., 1989-93; bd. dirs. Exec. Svc. Corps of Chgo., 1996—; trustee Village of Hinsdale, 1993-97, pres., 1997-2001; bd. dirs. Hinsdale Area United Way, 2001-. Mem. Chgo. Advt. Club (pres.), Econs. Club, Hinsdale Golf Club. Home: 736 S Park Ave Hinsdale IL 60521-4646

WHITSEL, RICHARD HARRY, biologist, entomologist; b. Denver, Feb. 23, 1931; s. Richard Elstun and Edith Muriel (Harry) W.; m. Laurie Pearson, May 25, 1997; children by previous marriages: Russell David, Robert Alan, Michael Dale, Steven Deane. BA, U. Calif., Berkeley, 1954; MA, San Jose State Coll., 1962. Sr. rsch. biologist San Mateo County Mosquito Abatement Dist., Burlingame, Calif., 1959-72; environ. program mgr., chief of watershed mgmt., chief of planning, chief of wetlands planning office Calif. Regional Water Quality Control Bd., Oakland, 1972-2000; ret. Trustee Alameda County Mosquito Abatement Dist., 1999-2001; mem. grad. faculty water resource mgmt. U. San Francisco, 1987-89. Served with Med. Svc. Corps, U.S. Army, 1954-56. Mem. Entomol. Soc. Am., Entomol. Soc. Wash., Am. Mosquito Control Assn., Calif. Alumni Assn., The Benjamin Ide Wheeler Soc., Nat. Parks and Conservation Assn. (life), Sierra Club. Democrat. Episcopalian. Home: 11552 Side Hill Cir Nevada City CA 95959 E-mail: rlwhitsel@yahoo.com.

WHITSELL, DORIS BENNER, retired educator; b. Poplar Grove, Ill., Mar. 17, 1923; d. Ralph Erwin and Sarah McKay (Mulligan) Wheeler; m. Robert M. Benner, Dec. 1945 (div. 1955); 1 child, Geoffrey Mark Benner (dec.); m. Eugene B. Whitsell, Feb. 1969 (dec. 1972). BS, No. Ill. U., 1944, MS in Secondary Edn., 1967; postgrad., Rockford Coll., 1964. Tchr. English and home econs. Lee (Ill.) High Sch., 1944-45; tchr. English Ashton (Ill.) Cmty. H.S., 1945-46; tchr. Morris Kennedy Sch., Rockford, Ill., 1952-55, William Nashold Sch., Rockford, 1955-56; tchr. English, drama Jefferson Jr. H.S., 1956-69; tchr. English Richwoods H.S., Peoria, Ill., 1969-71; tchr. Calvin Coolidge Sch., 1972-81. Mem. textbook selection com. Dist. 150, Peoria, 1973-75, curriculum planning com., 1974-75, tutor for homebound, 1982-83, cons. competency test seminar; cons. textbook divsn. Harcourt, Brace, Jovanovich, 1981-83; evaluator North Ctrl. Accreditation Team, Jefferson H.S., Rockford, 1980. Counselor Operation Sr. Security, Peoria, 1986-89; treas. Rockford Women's Club Fortnighty Dept., 1961-62; past deaconess 1st Federated Ch., Peoria; pres. Willow Heights Homeowner's Assn., Peoria, 1979-81; bldg. rep. Rockford Edn. Assn., 1954-56, 3d v.p., 1968-70; vol. Rockford Midway Village and Mus. Ctr., 1992, 95-96, 98, 99; bd. dirs. Forest Vale Estate Condominiums, Meadows Assn., Rockford, 1994-96, treas., 1995-97. Named for Significant Svc. to the Community, Ret. Sr. Vol. Program, Peoria, 1986. Mem.: AAUW (program v.p. 1988—89), Peoria Area Ret. Tchrs. Assn. (2d v.p. 1987—88, chmn. state bldg. fund. com. 1987—88, pres. 1989—90), Nat. Ret. Tchrs. Assn. (life), Ill. Ret. Tchrs. Assn. (life; sec. 1982—90, bd. dirs. Found. Inc. 1985—93, moderator conv. panel 1990), No. Ill. U. Alumni Assn., Delta Kappa Gamma (chmn. ins. com. Beta Gamma chpt. 1956—60, v.p. 1962—64, pres. 1964—66, mem. program com. Lambda state chpt. 1978—80, chmn. personal growth and svc. com. Nu chpt. 1988—90, mem. profl. affairs com. 1992—94, Winnebago County ret. tchrs. unit 1992—, mem. lit. com. 1996—98, mem. nominations com. 1999—2000, membership com. 2001—). Avocations: reading, traveling, interior decorating, theatre. Home: 1283 Aarons Ct Rockford IL 61108-1536

WHITSELL, JOHN CRAWFORD, II, general surgeon; b. St. Joseph, Mo., Dec. 21, 1929; s. Ora Earl and Lorena (Spratt) W. AB, Grinnell Coll., 1950; MD, Washington U., St. Louis, 1954. Diplomate Am. Bd. Surgery, Am. Bd. Thoracic Surgery. From instr. to clin. prof. surgery Cornell U. Med. Ctr., N.Y.C., 1963-70; from asst. attending to attending in surgery N.Y. Hosp., 1964-70; surg. dir. Rogosin Kidney Ctr. N.Y. Hosp.-Cornell Med. Ctr., 1973-75; attending in surgery N.Y. Hosp., 1970-98, hon. attending surgeon, 2001—; clin. prof. surgery Cornell Med. Coll., 1970-98, clin. prof. surgery emeritus, 1998. Surg. cons. Rogosin Kidney Ctr., 1975—, Sharon (Conn.) Hosp., 1976-2001; hon. attending surgeon, N.Y. Hosp., 2001—. Contbr. articles to profl. jours. Capt. USAF, 1961-63, Eng. Fellow ACS; mem. Transplantation Soc., N.Y. Surg. Soc., Am. Soc. Transplant Surgeons, N.Y. Soc. for Thoracic Surgery, Soc. Thoracic Surgeons, N.Y. Acad. Medicine, N.Y. Soc. Cardiovascular Surgery, Harvey Soc., Union Club of N.Y., Phi Beta Kappa. Avocations: golf, fishing, auto racing, antique cars.

WHITSETT, BRENDA LOUISE, non-profit organization executive; b. Ontario, Oreg., Sept. 17, 1939; d. Walter Charles and Thelma Louise White; m. David Thomas Pompel, Mar. 17, 196 (div. 1967); 1 child, David Charles; m. Donald Stewart Whitsett, June 17, 1972. BS, U. Oreg., 1961. Cert. Girl Scout exec. dir. Employment counselor State of Wash., Seattle, 1963-65; dir. cmty. resource devel. San Diego-Imperial coun. Girl Scouts U.S.A., San Diego, 1966-78; CEO, Girl Scouts Monterey Bay, Castroville, Calif., 1978—. Mem. Pub. Rels. Soc. Am. (accredited).

WHITSITT, MARJORIE RAE, artist, art educator; b. Superior, Wis., Dec. 3, 1922; d. Roy James and Emma Martha Emerson; m. William Harwood Whitsitt, Dec. 28, 1942 (div. 1962); children: William Harwood, Richard LeRoy, Lynne Marie. BS, U. Wis., Superior, 1964, MS in Tchg., 1966; PhD, U. Wis., Madison, 1975. Art tchr. Denfeld H.S., Duluth, Minn., 1964-66; art supr. McCaskill Lab. sch., instr. art edn. U. Wis., Superior, 1966-71, coord. art therapy program, prof. art, 1973-87, prof. emeritus, 1987—. Workshop leader Art Therapy - Creativity in Superior, 1977-87, Panama City, Fla., 1990-98; instr., lectr. Capstone House, 1990—. One-woman shows include Warwick Hotel Gallery, Trans-Atlantic Gallery, Houston, Tex., A Room of One's Own Gallery, Madison, Wis., Lakehead U., Thunder Bay, Can., Beijing Art Acad., Hangzhou, China, Visual Arts Ctr. N.W. Fla., Panama City, Fla.; exhbns. include: Nat. Watercolor Exhbns./Visual Arts Ctr. of N.W. Fla., Panama City, 1991-94, 96-99, Lake Superior Watercolor Soc., Tweed Gallery, U. Minn., Duluth, 1984-88, Beaux Arts Gallery, Pinellas Park, Fla., Cape May N.J. Art Ctr., St. Louis Mus., Duluth. Coord. Ann. Arts for Handicapped People U. Wis., Superior, 1980-87; vol. Visual Arts Ctr., Panama City, 1988—. Faculty Devel. and Rsch. grantee U. Wis., 1974, 80. Mem. Am. Assn. Artist-Therapists, Nature Conservancy, Nat. Mus. of Women in the Arts. Avocations: reading, swimming, traveling, psychic studies, painting. Home: 1522C Arthur Ave Panama City FL 32405-2610

WHITSON, ANGIE, artist; b. San Jose, Calif. d. Joseph and Francis (Chiaremonte) Noto; m. Claude Loren Whitson, May 11, 1932; children: Gregory, Jeffrey. Cert. art tchr. Cartoonist Warner Ctr. News, 1987—. Principle works include bronze busts sculptures of Ernie Kovacs, Joyce Hall, Leanard Goldenson for TV Arts and Scis.; exhibiter Art-A-Fair, Laguna Beach, Calif., 1976—. Mem. So. Calif. chpt. Mus. Women in Arts. Mem. Rotary Club Woodland Hills. Avocation: golf.

WHITSON, JAMES NORFLEET, JR. retired diversified company executive; b. Clinton, Okla., Mar. 14, 1935; s. James Norfleet and Georgia (Webb) W.; m. Lyda Lee Gibson, Apr. 19, 1956; 1 child, James Mark. BBA, Tex. Tech U., 1957. With LTV, Inc., Dallas, 1960-70; v.p. fin. Omega-Alpha, Inc., 1970-73; pres. Sammons Comm., Inc., Dallas, 1973-89; exec. v.p., coo Sammons Enterprises, Inc., 1989-98, also bd. dirs.; ret., 1998. Bd. dirs. C-Span, Seligman Group Investment Cos., CommScope, Inc. Mem. Alpha Tau Omega. Home: 6606 Forestshire Dr Dallas TX 75230-2856

WHITSON, LISH, lawyer; b. Washington, Oct. 13, 1942; s. I. Lish and Clytie B. (Collier) W.; m. Barbara Lee Sullivan, Sept. 16, 1965; children: L. Richard, Kimberly S. BA in Philosophy, Pa. State U., 1965; JD, U. Wash., 1972. Bar: Wash. 1973, U.S. Dist. Ct. (we. dist.) 1973, U.S. Dist. Ct. (ea. dist.) 1977, U.S. Supreme Ct. 1977. Assoc. Seattle-King County Pub. Defender Assn., 1972-76, Helsell, Fetterman, Martin, Todd & Hokanson, Seattle, 1976-81, ptnr., 1981-98; of counsel Badgley Mullins, 1998-2000, Lish Whitson PLLC, Seattle, 2000—. Bd. dirs., past chmn. Downtown Emergency Svc. Ctr., Seattle, 1981-97; bd. dirs. Allied Arts, 1988-96, pres., 1994-96; mem. Allied Arts Found., 1997—; trustee Seattle Youth Symphony Orch., bd. dirs., 1986-95; mem. alumni bd. U. Wash. Law Sch., 1993-2001, treas., 1997-99, pres., 1999-2001. Fellow Am. Bar Found., Am. Coll. Trial Lawyers; mem. ABA (young lawyers divsn. rep. to exec. coun. 1979, mem. standing com. on lawyer referral svc. 1990-96, chmn. 1992-96, commn. on women in the profn. 1998-2001), ATLA, Am. Bd. Trial Advocates (assoc.), Wash. State Bar Assn. (gov. 1995-98), King County Bar Found. (mem. pres. coun.), King County Bar Assn. (pro bono com. chmn. 1981-84, bd. dirs. 1988-91, young lawyers sect. 1977-79, chmn. 1979, Pro Bono Svc. award 1993, Atty. of Yr. 2000), Fed. Bar Assn., Am. Judicature Soc. (bd. dirs. 1981-86), Seattle Pub. Def. Assn. (bd. dirs. 1982-86), Wash. Athletic Club. Office: Lish Whitson Pllc Ste 3800 999 3d Ave Seattle WA 98104 E-mail: lwhitson@whitsonlaw.com.

WHITT, GREGORY SIDNEY, evolution educator; b. Detroit, June 13, 1938; s. Sidney Abram and Millicent (Ward) W.; m. Dixie Lee Dailey, Aug. 25, 1963. BS, Colo. State U., 1962, MS, 1965; PhD, Yale U., 1970. Asst. prof. zoology U. Ill., Urbana, 1969-72, asso. prof. genetics and devel., 1972-77, prof., 1977-87, prof. ecology, ethology and evolution, 1987-2000, prof. animal biology, 2000—. Affiliate Ill. Natural History Survey, 1981— ; mem. NIH study sect., 1975-76 Co-editor: Isozymes: Current Topics in Biological and Medical Research, 1977-87; editor: Isozyme Bull., 1978-81; mem. editl. bd. Biochem. Genetics, 1975—, Devel. Genetics, 1978-83, Jour. Molecular Evolution, 1979-2000, Molecular Biology and Evolution, 1983-93, Molecular Phylogenetics and Evolution, 1992-2000; contbr. articles to profl. jours. Fellow AAAS; mem. Am. Soc. for Microbiology, Soc. for Protection of Old Fishes, Internat. Soc. Molecular Evolution. Home: 1510 Trails Dr Urbana IL 61802-7052 Office: U Ill Dept Animal Biology 515 Morrill Hall 505 S Goodwin Ave Urbana IL 61801-3707

WHITT, LAURIE ANNE, philosophy educator; b. San Diego, Aug. 3, 1952; m. Alan William Clarke, Oct. 21, 1995. BA, Coll. of William and Mary, Williamsburg, Va., 1975; MA, Queen's U., London, Ont., 1976; PhD, U. Western Ont., London, 1985. Instr. philosophy U. Western Ont., London, 1981-83; vis. lectr. philosophy U. Ill., Urbana, 1983-84; asst. prof. philosophy So. Meth. U., Dallas, 1984-86, Mich. Technol. U., Houston, 1986-92, assoc. prof. philosophy, 1992—. Author: (poetry chapbook) A Long Dream of Difference, 2001, Words for Relocation, 2001 (1st place 2000 Norma O. Harrison Poetry Chapbook award). Howard Found. fellow George A. and Eliza Howard Found., 2000-2001, U. Auckland Found. visitorship, 1999, Humanities Rsch. Ctr. fellow Australian Nat. U., 1996, Va. Ctr. for Creative Arts fellow, 2001; Vt. Studio Ctr. Writer's grantee, 2000; Hedgebrook Poetry residency, 2001. Mem. Am. Philos. Assn., Law and Soc. Assn., Radical Philosophy Assn., Am. Indian Philos. Assn., Am. Indian and Alaska Native Professoriate, Soc. for Women in Philosophy, Nat. Lawyers' Guild, League of Can. Poets (assoc.). Home: PO Box 195 Chassell MI 49916 Office: Michigan Technol Univ Dept Humanities Houghton MI 49931 E-mail: lawhitt@mtu.edu.

WHITT, MARCUS CALVIN, marketing and communications executive; b. Paintsville, Ky., Feb. 5, 1960; s. Calvin Leo and Dora Sue (Spears) W.; m. Jennifer Marie McGuire, Jan. 4, 1986; children: Emily Marie, Elizabeth Anne, Jacob Robert. BA, Eastern Ky. U., 1982, MA, 1985. Intern, dir. student rels. dept. music Eastern Ky. U., Richmond, 1982-85; assoc. for ch. rels. Cumberland Coll., Williamsburg, Ky., 1985-87; dir. communications Conv. & Visitors Bur., Louisville, 1987; staff corr. The Western Recorder, 1987—; dir. pub. rels. Georgetown (Ky.) Coll., 1988-92; dir. pub. rels. and mktg. Campbellsville (Ky.) U., 1992-95, asst. to pres., 1995-97, v.p. advancement, 1997-2001, acting dir. Am. Civil War Inst., 1997—, v.p. comms. and mktg., 2001—. Bd. dirs. Coun. for Advancement and Support of Edn., Ky., 1990-96, pres.-elect, 1992, pres., 1993, 94, program co-chair, 1989-91, chair III pub. and promotion, 1994, mem. program com., 1997-98; mem. program com. Bapt. Pub. Rels. Assn., Louisville, 1987; program com. co-chair CASE III Conf., 1998, bd. dirs., 1999-2001; lectr. higher edn. instrl. advancement. Contbr. articles to profl. jours. Co-founder Assn. Communicators in Baptist Edn.; chair Ky. Heartland Civil War Trails Commn., 1997—; bd. dirs. Taylor County Tourism Commn., 1995-97, Campbellsville/Taylor County Adult Edn. Commn., 2001—; comm. chair Taylor County United; mem. tourism and econ. devel. adv. coun. U.S. 2d Congl. Dist. Ky., 2001—. Recipient Gold award for Instnl. Rels., Mktg. Higher Edn., 1991, Silver medal Coun. for Advancement and Support of Edn., 1991, award of excellence, 1992, 94, 95, Spl. Merit award, 1991, 94, 95, 2001, Grand award, 1991, 94, 2000, Silver medal, 1991, 92, Gold medal Image Improvement Mktg. Higher Edn., 1991, Gold award Outdoor Transit Billboard, Admissions Advt. awards, 1990, 91, Merit award in TV advt. Mem. Campbellsville/Taylor County C. of C. (bd. dirs. 1995-99, pres.-elect 1996-97, pres. 1997-98, program chair 1997-2001), Leadership Scott County (publicity 1990-92), Scott County Adult Lit., Scott County Cmty. Showcase (publicity chair 1989-92), Ky. Bapt. Communicators Forum (co-founder 1991), Mil. Order of the Stars and Bars (Ky. comdr. 1987). Republican. Baptist. Avocations: music, southern and Kentucky history, baseball, public speaking. Home: 109 Yorkshire Pl Campbellsville KY 42718-9552 Office: Campbellsville U Office of Comms and Mktg 1 University Dr Campbellsville KY 42718-2799 E-mail: marc@admin.campbellsvil.edu.

WHITT, MARY F. reading educator, consultant; b. Montgomery, Ala. d. Clarence D. Whitt Sr. and Georgia Arms. BS, Ala. State U., 1958; MEd, U. Ariz., 1971; EdD, U. Ala., 1980; postgrad., various colls. ongoing. Camp counselor N.Y.C. Mission Soc., Port Jervis, summer 1956; recreation counselor Dayton (Ohio) Parks and Recreation Dept., summer 1963; adminstrv. asst. Wiley Coll./NDEA Inst., Marshall, Tex., summer 1965; tchr. Montgomery (Ala.) County Schs., 1958-62; coordinator sci. and math. Dayton (Ohio) pub. schs., 1962-67; reading and spl. edn. tchr. Vacaville (Calif.) Unified Sch. Dist., 1967-70; coord. reading Dallas Pub. Schs., 1971-72; prof. reading Ala. State U., Montgomery, 1972-98; ret. prof. edn. Contbr. articles to profl. jurs. U.S. Office Edn. fellow, 1970, 76, 77, NSF fellow, 1961, 62, 64, 66. Mem. Internat. Reading Assn., Capstone Coll. of Edn. Soc., AAUW, Phi Delta Kappa, Kappa Delta Pi. Home: 717 Genetta Ct Montgomery AL 36104-5701

WHITT, RICHARD ERNEST, reporter; b. Greenup County, Ky., Dec. 15, 1944; s. Walter Charles and Irene (Hayes) W.; m. Terri Bellizzi; children: Hayes Chadwick, Emily Catherine, Christen Leigh McCollough. Student, Ashland (Ky.) Community Coll., 1966-68; BA in Journalism, U. Ky., 1970. Reporter Middlesboro (Ky.) Daily News, 1970-71; asst. state editor Waterloo (Iowa) Courier, 1971-72; city editor Kingsport (Tenn.) Times, 1972-76; No. Ky. bur. chief Courier-Jour., Louisville, 1977, Frankfort bur. chief, 1977-80, spl. projects reporter, 1980-89; investigative reporter Atlanta Jour. & Constn., 1989—. Served with USN, 1962-66. Decorated Air medal; recipient Pulitzer prize for coverage of Beverly Hills Supper Club fire, 1978; named Outstanding Ky. Journalist, 1978; recipient John Hancock award for excellence, 1983; named to U. Ky. Journalism Hall of Fame, 1995. Democrat. Office: Atlanta Jour & Constn 72 Marietta St NW Atlanta GA 30303-2804

WHITT, ROBERT AMPUDIA, III, advertising executive, marketing professional; b. San Antonio, Oct. 15, 1930; s. Robert and Alice (Whitt) Ampudia; m. Mary Jane Kothmann, June 2, 1951 (div.); children: April Whitt Horner, Robert IV, Roxanne Seaman; m. Patricia M. Gomar. BA in Internat. Trade, U. of the Ams., Mexico City, 1955, MBA, 1962; postgrad., Am. Grad. Sch. Internat. Mgmt., Phoenix, 1991-92. Sales mgr. Sinclair & Valentine Co., Cali, Colombia, 1956-59; CEO for L.Am. Vision, Inc., Mexico City, 1960-74; pres., CEO Tex. Parade, Inc., Austin, 1974-77; CEO world ops. Novedades Editores, Mexico City, 1977-82; chmn., CEO Mktg. Mercadeo Internat., San Antonio, 1982-96, Ampudia Whitt & Assocs., Inc., Dallas, 1996—. Bd. dirs. Robea, S.A., Mexico City, Poliform, S.A., Mexico City, Tex. Bus. Hall of Fame Found., Dallas; mem. Alliance for Progress Task Force, 1963-67; bd. dirs., dir. gen. Publicidad RD, Mexico City, 1996—; chmn. Legacy Ctr. for Rsch., 2002-02. Co-author: How to Market and Distribute in Mexico, 1995; editor (Spanish lang.) Dallas Cowboys mag., 1979-80, 91 (Best Content award), Bienestar mag., 1978 (Best Content award); contbr. articles to profl. jours. Sgt. U.S. Airborne, 1950-53. Recipient Nat. Winner award Silver Microphone, 1991, Nat. Finalist award, 1991, Addy award Am. Advt. Fedn., 1992, Nat. Winner award Telly awards (4), 1993, 95, Athletic and Acad. Achievement award U. of the Ams., 1995; named Speaker of the Year Toastmasters Internat., 1980. Mem. Fgn. Corr. Club, 11th Airborne Div. Assn. (life), Brookhaven Country Club (Dallas), Univ. Club (Dallas), Univ. Club (Mexico City), Dallas Ft. Worth Soc. Office: Quill/AWA Enterprises 1111 W Mockingbird Ln Ste 1300 Dallas TX 75247-5013 *Only oneself can truly measure one's achievements. My greatest achievement is that I have no regrets and wouldn't change a minute, day or year of my life...including the downtimes.*

WHITTAKER, BILL DOUGLAS, minister; b. Bowling Green, Ky., June 14, 1943; s. Ewing A. and Lois (Jenkins) W.; m. Rebecca Kaye Howard, June 18, 1966; children: John, Karen, Mary. BA, Western Ky. U., 1965; MDiv, So. Bapt. Theol. Sem., Louisville, 1969, D of Ministry, 1974. Ordained to ministry So. Bapt. Conv., 1964. Pastor 1st Bapt. Ch., Sturgis, Ky., 1969-76, Murray, 1976-82; missionary Internat. Mission Bd., So. Bapt. Conv., The Philippines, 1983-86; pastor Downtown Bapt. Ch., Orlando, Fla., 1986-88; pres. Clear Creek Bapt. Bible Coll., Pineville, Ky., 1988—. Author: Preparing to Preach, 1999; columnist Western Recorder newspaper, 1988—. Bd. dirs. Coalition for the Homeless, Cen. Fla. YMCA, Orlando, 1986-88. Mem. Assn. Bible Colls. (accredited, del. 1988—), Assn. So. Bapt. Colls. and Schs. (del. 1988—), So. Assn. Coll. and Schs. (del. 1999—), Ky. Bapt. Hist. Soc., Kiwanis (pres. Pineville chpt. 1994-95, dist. 6 lt. gov. 1997-98), Ky. Bapt. Conv. (pres. 1980). Home and Office: 300 Clear Creek Rd Pineville KY 40977-9752 E-mail: bwhittaker@ccbbc.edu.

WHITTAKER, DOUGLAS KIRKLAND, school system administrator; b. Westfield, N.J., July 14, 1949; s. Alfred Albert and Marion I. (Crocket) W.; m. Susan Kay Helsing, Aug. 9, 1969; children: Jessica Erin, Angela Gaye. BS, Taylor U., 1971; MA, Ball State U., 1975; EdD, Nova U., 1981. Cert. elem. educator, elem. and middle adminstrn. Tchr. Marion (Ind.) Community Schs., 1971-73, Lee County Schs., Ft. Myers, Fla., 1973-80, asst. prin., 1980-81, elem. prin., 1981-86, middle sch. prin., 1986-90, elem. prin., 1990-92, dir. curriculum svcs., 1993-95, exec. dir. curriculum and sch. improvement, 1995—2002, asst. supt. for tchg. and learning, 2002—. Adj. prof. Nova U., Ft. Lauderdale, Fla., 1983—; trainer in field. Contbr. articles to profl. jours. Mem. ASCD, NEA, Phi Delta Kappa. Republican. Avocations: golf, travel, reading, singing, flying. Home: 3931 Hidden Acres Cir Fort Myers FL 33903-7120 Office: Dr James A Adams Pub Edn Ctr 2055 Central Ave Fort Myers FL 33901-3916 E-mail: d.whittaker@worldnet.att.net, dougw@lee.k12.fl.us.

WHITTAKER, JEANNE EVANS, former newspaper columnist; b. Detroit, Jan. 1, 1934; d. Alfred Heacock and Margaret (Evans) W.; m. Charles Martin Hines Jr., Sept. 29, 1962 (div. Feb. 1970); children: Charles M. Hines III, Margaret Helen Whittaker Zimmerman. Student, Northwestern U., 1952-53; BS in History, U. Mich., 1956. Clubmobile worker UN forces ARC, Korea, 1956-58, staff programmer Evreux, France, 1958-61, dir. Bexar County chpt. youth San Antonio, 1961-62; staff writer/columnist Detroit Free Press, 1970-75; editor Mich. Social Register, 1975-77; Lifestyle editor Observer and Eccentric newspapers, Birmingham, Mich., 1977-87; staff writer, columnist Detroit News, 1987-91; cons. in field, 1992—. Contbr. articles to mags. Bd. dirs. Detroit chpt. ARC, 1989-92, Detroit Hist. Soc., Wayne State U. Press. Recipient Penney-Mo. award U. Mo., 1984; 1st place lifestyles/Family award Mich. Press Assn., 1982, 84, Gen. Excellence award 1982, 86; Gen. Excellence award Suburban Newspaper Assn., 1979. Mem. Detroit Hist. Soc. (bd. dirs. 1986-91), Southeastern Mich. Chpt. ARC (bd. dirs. 1987-93). Episcopalian. Avocations: writing, reading, travel. Home: 552 Cadieux Rd Grosse Pointe MI 48230-1508

WHITTAKER, SUE MCGHEE, music educator, pianist; b. Chgo., Feb. 17, 1942; d. Chester O. and Bevie Faye (Smith) McGhee; m. Jerry Roy Whittaker, Aug. 9, 1968; children: Judd, Eric, Holly. BME, Roosevelt U., Chgo., 1965, MM, 1966; DMA, U. Ariz., 1996. Faculty Lee Coll., Cleveland, Tenn., 1965-68; gen. music tchr. Madison Sch. Dist., Phoenix, 1969-72; faculty Ariz. Coll. of the Bible, 1983-92; founding dir. North Valley Sch. of the Arts, Scottsdale, Ariz., 1995—. Guest soloist (as part of 2-piano team Whittaker and Ross) Mesa Symphony, Scottsdale Symphony, Phoenix Symphony, others; accompanist Phoenix Little Theatre, Masterworks Chorale, Met. Opera auditions, Scottsdale Symphony Chorale. Named to Outstanding Young Women of Am., 1967. Mem. Music Educators Nat. Conf., Music Tchrs. Nat. Assn., Nat. Conf. Piano Pedagogy (mem. rsch. com. 1988—), Ariz. State Music Tchrs. Assn. (adjudicator 1980—). Republican. Avocations: antiques, reading, travel.

WHITTAKER, WILLIAM PAUL, financial analyst; b. Altoona, Pa., Sept. 4, 1967; s. William Franklin and Lovell Louise Whittaker; m. Barbara Katherine Cabral, May 12, 2001. BBs in Fin., Pa. State U., 1997. Equity rsch. analyst Trinity Investment Mgmt. Corp., Bellefonte, Pa., 1997—. With USN, 1988-93. Office: Trinity Investment Mgmt Corp 301 N Spring St Bellefonte PA 16823 Office Fax: 814-355-1060.

WHITTELL, POLLY KAYE (MARY WHITTELL), editor, journalist; b. Washington, Oct. 20; d. Alfred Whittell Jr. and Mary Halsey (Patchin) Hopper. BA in English, U. Calif., Berkeley; postgrad., Radcliffe Coll.; postgrad. in journalism, Columbia U. Rschr. Nat. Rev. Mag., N.Y.C., 1970-71; asst. to presdl. speech writer The White House, Washington, 1971-72; asst. editor TravelAge East Mag., Dun & Bradstreet Publs., N.Y.C., 1973-75; copy editor Ski Mag. Skier's Guides, Times Mirror Mags. and Am. Express, 1975-76; asst. editor to sr. editor Hearsts Mags., Motor Boating & Sailing Mag., 1977-2000; contbg. editor Powerboat Mag., Ventura, Calif., 2000—01, So. Boating Mag., 2002—. Contbg. author: (anthology) Against the Sea, 1998; contbg. editor Southern Boating Mag., Ft. Lauderdale, Fla., 2002-; contbr. articles to nat. and internat. consumer mags. Mem. charity benefit com. Youth Counseling League, N.Y.C., 1975-85, Am. Cancer Soc., 1998-99, and others; v.p. Knickerbocker Rep. Club, N.Y.C., 1979-80; elected mem. N.Y. Rep. County Com., N.Y.C., 1980-84. Mem. Boating Writers Internat. (award for environ. article 1995), Soc. Profl. Journalists, Princeton Club (N.Y.), SandBar Beach Club (v.p. membership 1980-82). Episcopalian. Avocations: photography, travel, boating, skiing. E-mail: pollywhitt@aol.com.

WHITTEMORE, EDWARD REED, II, poet, retired educator; b. New Haven, Sept. 11, 1919; s. Edward Reed and Margaret Eleanor (Carr) W.; m. Helen Lundeen, Oct. 3, 1952; children: Catherine Carr, Edward Reed III, John Lundeen (dec.), Margaret Goodhue. AB, Yale U., 1941; postgrad., Princeton U., 1945-46; Litt.D., Carleton Coll., 1971. Mem. faculty Carleton Coll., 1947-67, prof. English, 1962-67, chmn. dept., 1962-64; program assoc. Nat. Inst. Pub. Affairs, 1966-68; cons. in poetry Libr. of Congress, 1964-65, 84-85; Bain-Swiggett lectr. Princeton, 1967; prof. U. Md., 1968-84, prof. emeritus, 1984—; poet laureate State of Md., 1985-88. Lit. editor New Republic, 1969-74. Author: Heroes and Heroines, 1947, An American Takes a Walk, 1956, The Self-Made Man, 1959, The Boy From Iowa, 1962, The Fascination of the Abomination, 1963, Poems, New and Selected, 1967, From Zero to the Absolute, 1967, 50 Poems 50, 1970, The Mother's Breast and the Father's House, 1974, William Carlos Williams: Poet from Jersey, 1975, The Poet as Journalist, 1976, The Feel of Rock, 1982, Pure Lives, 1988, Whole Lives, 1989, The Past, the Future, the Present, 1990, Six Literary Lives, 1993; editor: Furioso, 1939-53, Browning, 1960, Carleton Miscellany, 1960-64, Delos mag., 1988-91. Capt. USAAF, 1941-45. Decorated Bronze star, 1945. Home: 4526 Albion Rd College Park MD 20740-3610

WHITTEMORE, LAURENCE FREDERICK, private banker; b. Bangor, Maine, Mar. 7, 1929; s. John Cambridge and Elizabeth Payson (Prentiss) Whittemore; m. Sarah Lee Arnold, Aug. 9, 1958; children: Arianna, Gioia, Lia, Nike. BA, Yale U., 1951; MBA, Harvard U., 1953; student, Balliol Coll., Oxford U., Eng., 1950. Account mgr. Brown Bros. Harriman, N.Y.C., 1956-72, gen. mgr., 1972-74; ptnr. Brown Bros. Harriman & Co., 1974—. Dir. Manhattan Life Ins. Co., N.Y.C., Albany Ins. Co., N.Y.C.; mem. investment adv. com. Union Investment GmbH, Frankfurt, Germany, 1973—2002; mem. Chgo. Stock Exch., 1975—. Trustee Sarah Lawrence Coll., 1988-2000, hon. trustee, 2001—; trustee Am. Inst. Contemporary German Studies, 1994—, Asia Soc., 1998—; mem. Nat. Com. on U.S. China Rels., N.Y.C., 1982—, Chgo. Coun. on Fgn. Rels., 1980—; del. Assn. Yale Alumni, New Haven, 1982-86; chmn. Yale 35th Reunion Gift Drive, 1983-86; gov. Opportunity Internat., 1996—; mem. Bus. Execs. for Nat. Security, 1996—, New Eng. Air Mus., 1999—. Mem.: Investment Analysts Soc. Chgo., N.Y. Soc. Security Analysts, Links, Yale, India House (N.Y.C.); Chicago. Republican. Episcopalian. Office: Brown Bros Harriman & Co 59 Wall St New York NY 10005-2808

WHITTEMORE, LINDA GENEVIEVE, clinical psychologist; b. Ft. Bragg, N.C., Nov. 1, 1948; d. James and Nancy (Caudill) White; children: Trevor Johnson, Dylan Lane. BA in Anthropology, East Carolina U., 1972, MA in Clin. Psychology, 1980. Rehab. svcs. coord. Social Center, Fairfax, Va., 1978-79; site coord. Mental Health Assn. of N. Va., Annandale, 1979-80; program asst. Alliance to Save Energy, Washington, 1981-82; ednl. psychology officer APA, 1984-88; exec. mktg. dir. I.D.N., Provo, Utah, 1989-93; supr. 24th Dist. Ct. Svcs. Unit, Lynchburg, Va., 1994-96; psychologist Ctrl. Va. Tng. Ctr., 1996—2001; clin. coord. children and family svc. City of Lynchburg, Va., 2001—. Prof. Benjamin Franklin U., Washington, 1986-87. Editor: Activities Handbook for the Teaching of Psychology, Vol. 2, 1987, Vol. 3, 1990. Mem. Noetic Soc., Assn. of Employee Assistance Counselors, Toastmasters Internat. Avocations: culinary arts, poetry, opera, travel, herb gardening. Home: Villa Mozart 517 Washington St Lynchburg VA 24504-2619

WHITTEMORE, PAUL BAXTER, psychologist; s. Harry Ballou and Margaret B. Whittemore; m. Jane Moore, Apr. 22, 1995. BA in Religion, Ea. Nazarene Coll., 1970; MDiv., Nazarene Theol. Sem., 1973; MA in Theology, Vanderbilt U., 1975, PhD in Theology, 1978; PhD in Clin. Psychology, U. Tenn., 1987. Cert. in clin. psychology Am. Bd. Profl. Psychology, lic. psychologists Calif. Asst. prof. philosophy and edn. Trevecca Nazarene Coll., Nashville, 1973-76; asst. prof. philosophy and theology Point Loma Coll., San Diego, 1976-80; asst. prof. philosophy Mid. Tenn. State U., Murfreesboro, 1980-83; clin. psychology intern. Los Angeles County/U. So. Calif. Med. Ctr., L.A., 1986-87; coord. behavior health ctr. Calif. Med. Ctr., 1987-88; clin. asst. prof. family medicine U. So. Calif. Sch. Medicine, 1988—; pvt. practice psychologist Newport Beach, Calif., 1989—. Mem. behavioral sci. faculty Glendale Adventist Family Practice Residency Program, Glendale, Calif., 1989—90; inpatient group therapist Ingleside Hosp., Rosemead, Calif., 1990—92; founder, pres. Date Coach, 1992—2000. Contbr. articles to profl. jours. Recipient Andrew W. Mellon Postdoctoral Faculty Devel. award, Vanderbilt U., 1981. Mem.: AAUP (chp. v.p. 1982—83), APA, Orange County Psychol. Assn. (bd. dirs. 1996—2001), Orange County Employee Assistance Profl. Assn. (bd. dirs. 1993—2001), Calif. Psychol. Assn. (media divsn. sec.-treas. 1997—98), Am. Philos. Assn., Am. Acad. Religion. Achievements include discovery of of link between phenylthiocarbamide tasting and depression. Office: 4750 Von Karman Ave Newport Beach CA 92660-2123

WHITTEMORE, RONALD PAUL, hospital administrator, retired army officer, nursing educator; b. Saco, Maine, Aug. 10, 1946; s. Ronald B. and Pauline L. (Larson) W.; m. Judy D. McDonald, Feb. 17, 1967; 1 child, Leicia Michelle. BGS, U. S.C., 1974, MEd, 1977; BSN, Med. Coll. Ga., 1975. Enlisted U.S. Army, 1968, advanced through ranks to maj., 1985, ret., 1991; adult/oncology nurse practitioner Martin Army Cmty. Hosp.; asst. head nurse SICU, infection control practitioner Moncrief Army Cmty. Hosp.; infection control practitioner U.S. Army Hosp., Seoul, Republic of Korea; chief nurse 2nd Combat Support Hosp., Ft. Benning, Ga.; cmty. health nurse Brooke Army Med. Ctr., Ft. Sam Houston, Tex.; cmty. health nurse Giessen (Germany) Mil. Cmty.; clin. instr. Eisenhower Army Med. Ctr., Ft. Gordon, Ga.; chief nursing adminstrn. E/N Frankfurt (Germany) Army Med. Ctr.; adminstr., dir. quality improvement Gracewood (Ga.) State Sch. and Hosp., 1995-97. Instr. Augusta (Ga.) Tech. Inst.; nurse epidemiologist Med. Coll. Ga., Augusta. Mem. ANA, Ga. ANA (3rd Dist. honoree, pres. 1983-85), Assn. Practitioners in Infection Control, Am. Holistic Nurses Assn., Nat. Assn. Health Care Quality Profls., Assn. for Profls. in Infection Control and Epidemiology, Sigma Theta Tau. Home: 310 Bon Air Dr Augusta GA 30907-4869 Office: Med Coll Ga Office Nurse Mgr/Infec Ctrl Augusta GA 30901-3196

WHITTEN, BEATRICE EHRENBERG, lawyer; b. Charleston, S.C., Oct. 19, 1959; d. David Owen and Susan Rush (Hills) W.; m. C. Patrick Leopold, Dec. 30, 1989; children: Jesse Lawrence, Susan Cameron. AS in Criminal Justice, Trident Tech. Coll., Charleston, 1980; BS in Criminal Justice, Charleston So. U., 1987; JD, U. S.C., 1990. Bar: S.C. 1990; cert. civil mediator. Assoc. Thomas W. Greene, Charleston, S.C., 1990-91; assoc./ptnr. Lucey & Whitten, PA, 1991-93; pvt. practice Mt. Pleasant, S.C., 1993—. Adj. faculty Trident Tech. Coll., Charleston, 1994—; instr. legal writing U. S.C., Columbia, 1988-90. Named Pro Bono Atty. of Yr., 2000. Mem. S.C. Bar Assn. (bar pro bono program 1990—). Avocations: canoeing, camping. Office: 745 A Johnnie Dodds Blvd Mount Pleasant SC 29464-3021

WHITTEN, C. G. lawyer; b. Abilene, Tex., Apr. 1, 1925; s. C.G. and Eugenia (St. Clair) W.; m. Alene Henley, Nov. 25, 1945; children: Julie, Jennifer, Blake; m. Carol Owen, Apr. 22, 1977. JD, U. Tex.-Austin, 1949. Bar: Tex. 1949, U.S. Dist. Ct. (no. dist.) Tex. 1950, U.S. Supreme Ct. 1955. Assoc. Grisham & King, Abilene, Tex., 1949-52; ptnr. Jameson & Whitten, 1952-54, Jameson, Whitten, Harrell & Wilcox, 1954-58, Whitten, Harrell, Erwin & Jameson, 1958-68, Whitten, Sprain, Wagner, Price & Edwards, 1968-79, Whitten, Haag, Cobb & Hacker, 1979-82; sr. ptnr. Whitten, Haag, Hacker, Hagin & Cutbirth, 1983-87; pres. Whitten, Hacker, Hagin, Anderson & Rucker, P.C., 1987-92; of counsel Whitten & Young, 1992—; gen. counsel Pittencrieff Comms., Inc., 1992-97, sr. v.p., dir., 1994-97; pres. Abilene Improvement Corp., 1994-2001. Mem. tax. increment funding dist., 1995—, mem. adv. coun. U. of Tex. Press, 1995-2001, chmn. 1998-2000. Mem. Abilene Ind. Sch. Dist. Bd. Edn., 1956-76, pres. 1972-76. Office: PO Box 208 Abilene TX 79604-0208

WHITTEN, CHARLES ALEXANDER, JR. physics educator; b. Harrisburg, Pa., Jan. 20, 1940; s. Charles Alexander and Helen (Shoop) W.; m. Joan Emann, Nov. 20, 1965; 1 son, Charles Alexander III. BS summa cum laude, Yale U., 1961; PhD in Physics, Princeton U., 1966. Research asso. A.W. Wright Nuclear Structure Lab., Yale U., 1966-68; asst. prof. physics UCLA, 1968-74, assoc. prof., 1974-80, prof., 1980—, vice chmn. physics dept., 1982-86. Vis. scientist Centre d'Etudes Nucléaires de Saclay-Moyenne Energie, 1980-81, 86-87. Contbr. articles to profl. jours. Mem. Am. Phys. Soc., Sigma Pi Sigma, Phi Beta Kappa. Home: 9844 Vicar St Los Angeles CA 90034-2719 E-mail: whitten@physics.ucla.edu.

WHITTEN, DAVID GEORGE, chemistry educator; b. Washington, Jan. 25, 1938; s. David Guy and Miriam Deland (Price) W.; m. Jo Wright, July 9, 1960; children: Jenifer Marie, Guy David. AB, Johns Hopkins U., 1959; MA, John Hopkins U., 1961, PhD, 1963. Asst. prof. chemistry U. N.C., Chapel Hill, 1966-70, assoc. prof., 1970-73, prof., 1973-80, M.A. Smith prof., 1980-83; C.E. Kenneth Mees prof. U. Rochester, N.Y., 1983-97, chair dept. chemistry, 1988-91, 95-97, dir. Ctr. for Photoinduced Charge Transfer, 1989-95; mem. tech. staff Los Alamos Nat. Lab., 1997-2000; co-founder, chief tech. officer QTL Biosystems, LLC, 2000—; prof. chemistry and biochemistry Ariz. State U., 2000—. Mem. adv. com. for chemistry NSF; cons. Eastman Kodak Co.; Rochester, N.Y. Editor-in-chief, Langmuir, 1998—. Alfred P. Sloan fellow, 1970; John van Geuns fellow, 1973; recipient special U.S. scientist award Alexander von Humboldt Found., 1975; Japan Soc. for Promotion of Sci. fellow, 1982 Mem. AAAS, Am. Chem. Soc. (award in colloid and surface chemistry 1992), Internat. Union of Pure and Applied Chemistry (commn. on photochemistry), Interam. Photochem. Soc. (award 1998). Democrat. Home: 811D W Manhattan Ave Santa Fe NM 87501-3786 Office: QTL Biosys LLC 2778 Agua Fria St Bldg C Santa Fe NM 87507 E-mail: whitten@qthbio.com.

WHITTEN, DAVID OWEN, economics educator; b. Beaver Falls, Pa., Nov. 30, 1940; s. Paul Harry and Bula (Owens) Ehrenbergh. BS, Coll. Charleston, 1962; MA, U. S.C., 1963; PhD, Tulane U., 1970. Instr. econs. and fin. U. New Orleans, 1965-68; asst. prof. econs. Auburn U., Ala., 1968-74, assoc. prof., 1974-82, prof., 1982—; cons. U.S. Army C.E., New Orleans, summers 1964, 65. Author: Andrew Durnford: A Black Sugar Planter in Antebellum Louisiana, 1981 (La. honor award 1982), Emergence of Giant Enterprise, 1983, A History of Economics and Business at Auburn University, 1992; co-author: Democracy in Desperation: The Depression of 1893, 1998 (Choice Outstanding Acad. Title 2000); editor: (with Bessie E. Whitten) Manufacturing: A Historiographical and Bibliographical Guide Vol. 1 Handbook of American Business History, 1990, Two-Hundred Years of Eli Whitney's Cotton Gin, 1994, Andrew Durnford: A Black Sugar Planter in the Antebellum South, 1995, Extractives, Manufacturing and Services, 1992, Infrastructure and Services, 2000; editor, Contbns. in Econ. and EEcon. History, 1980—, Wall St. Rev. of Books, 1981-89, Bus. Libr. Rev., 1990-2002; contbr. articles to profl. jours. Served with USMCR, 1957-63. Tulane Edn. Found. fellow, 1964, 65. Mem. Am. Econ. Assn. Agrl. History Soc., Soc. for History Early Am. Rep., Econ. History Assn., So. Econs. Assn., Bus. History Conf., Econ. and Bus. Hist. Soc. (v.p. 1988-91, pres. 1991-92, CEO 2000-01), Rexford G. Tugwell Internat. Inst. for Great Depression Era Studies (v.p., treas., dir. 1992—). Home: 102 Kimberly Dr Auburn AL 36832-6712 Office: Auburn U Dept Econs Bus Bldg 209 Auburn AL 36849 E-mail: DWhitten@Business.Auburn.edu.

WHITTEN, JERRY LYNN, chemistry educator; b. Bartow, Fla., Aug. 13, 1937; s. John Graves and Dorothy Iola (Jordan) W.; m. Mary Hill (div. Sept. 1977); 1 child, Jerrard John; m. Adela Chrzeszczyk, June 21, 1980; 1 child, Christina. BS in Chemistry, Ga. Inst. Tech., 1960, PhD, 1964. Cert. chemist. Rsch. assoc. to instr. Princeton (N.J.) U., 1963-65; asst. prof. chemistry Mich. State U., East Lansing, 1965-67, SUNY, Stony Brook, 1967-68, assoc. prof., 1968-73, prof., 1973-89, chmn. chemistry dept., 1985-89; prof. chemistry, dean Coll. Phys. and Math. Scis. N.C. State U., Raleigh, 1989-99. Vis. prof. Centre Européen de Calcul Atomique et Moléculaire, Orsay, France, 1974-75, Univ. Bonn and Wuppertal, Fed. Republic Germany, 1979-80, Eidgenossische Technische Hochschule, Zurich, Switzerland, 1984. Contbr. more than 160 articles to profl. jours. Bd. dirs. N.C. Sch. Sci. and Math Found., chair; bd. dirs. Burroughs Wellcome Fund. Recipient Alexander von Humboldt U.S. Sr. Scientist award, 1979; grantee Petroleum Rsch. Fund, 1966-67, 74-76, 77-81, NSF, 1967-72, U.S. Dept. Energy, 1977—; SDIO/ONR grantee, 1991-92; Alfred P. Sloan fellow, 1969-71. Mem. AAAS, Am. Phys. Soc., Am. Chem. Soc., N.Y. Acad. Scis., Sigma Xi (pres. N.C. chpt.), Phi Beta Kappa, Phi Kappa Phi. Democrat. Episcopalian. Avocations: boating, tennis, skiing. Office: NC State U Coll Dept Chemistry PO Box 8204 Raleigh NC 27695-0001 E-mail: j_whitten@nesu.edu.

WHITTEN, JOSEPH LEE, retired school librarian, elementary educator; b. Bryant, Ala., July 19, 1938; s. Jesse Nathan and Laura Lorene (Hawkins) W.; m. Gail Elaine McGeoch, May 21, 1971; 1 child, Miriam Elizabeth. BA, Bob Jones U., Greenville, S.C., 1960; M in Edn., U. Montevallo, Ala., 1977. Cert. tchr., Ala. English tchr. St. Clair Co. H.S., Odenville, Ala., 1961-70, Perry Christian Sch., Marion, 1970-71, Panama City Christian Sch., Fla., 1971-73; tchr., counselor St. Clair County H.S., Odenville, 1974-94; tchr., libr. Odenville Elem. Sch., 1994-2000. Contbr. articles to profl. jours. Bd. dirs. Ashville Mus. and Archives, 1995—, St. Clair Historical Commn., 1994-99, Cahaba Trace Commn., Montevallo, Ala., 1993-99, Nat. Endowment for Arts Continental Harmony Project: I Am A Song. Mem. NEA, Ala. Ednl. Assn., Ala. State Poetry Soc. (bd. dirs. 1998—, 2d v.p. 2000-2002, treas. 2001--, Ala. Poet of Yr. 2002), Ala. Writers Conclave. Republican. Baptist. Avocations: antiques, books, local history, writing. Home: PO Box 125 Odenville AL 35120-0125 Office: Odenville Elem Sch 400 Alabama St Odenville AL 35120-3047 E-mail: whitten93@alltel.net.

WHITTEN, LESLIE HUNTER, JR. author, newspaper reporter, poet; b. Jacksonville, Fla., Feb. 21, 1928; s. Leslie Hunter and Linnora (Harvey) W.; m. Phyllis Webber, Nov. 11, 1951; children: Leslie Hunter III, Andrew, Daniel, Deborah Wilson Gordon. BA in Journalism/English magna cum laude, Lehigh U., 1950, LHD, 1989. Newsman Radio Free Europe, 1952-57, I.N.S., 1957-58, U.P.I., 1958, Washington Post, 1958-63; with Hearst Newspapers, 1963-66, asst. bur. chief, 1966-69; sr. investigator Jack Anderson's Washington Merry-Go-Round, 1969-92; pres. Athanor Inc., 1977-93. Vis. assoc. prof. Lehigh U., 1967-69; adj. prof. So. Ill. U., 1984. Author: Progeny of the Adder, 1965, Moon of the Wolf, 1967, Pinion the Golden Eagle, 1968, The Abyss, 1970, F. Lee Bailey, 1971, The Alchemist, 1973, Conflict of Interest, 1976, Washington Cycle, 1979, Sometimes a Hero, 1979, A Killing Pace, 1983, A Day Without Sunshine, 1985, The Lost Disciple, 1989, The Fangs of Morning, 1994, Sad Madrigals, 1997, Moses, the Lost Book of the Bible, 1999; contbr. numerous poems to anthologies and other publs. Vol. Hospice, 1987—. Served with AUS, 1946-48. Recipient hon. mention pub. service Washington Newspaper Guild, 1963, Edgerton award ACLU, 1974 Home and Office: 114 Eastmoor Dr Silver Spring MD 20901-1507 E-mail: lhwhitjr@aol.com.

WHITTEN, NANCY BIMMERMAN, clinical social worker, marriage therapist; b. Wilmington, Del., Oct. 17, 1934; d. Harry Gordon and Marian Bimmerman; m. Robert Hunt Whitten, Jan. 2, 1960 (div. 1982); 1 child, Barbara Louise Whitten Debnam. BS in Biology, Bucknell U., 1956; postgrad., Stanford U., 1956-57, U. Del., 1957-59; M Social Svcs., Bryn Mawr Coll., 1995. Lic. clin. social worker, Del., Md. V.p. Robert Hunt Whitten Inc, Wilmington, 1960-81; br. mgr. Chase Manhattan Bank, 1985-88; realtor Patterson Schwartz Real Estate, 1988-95; clin. intern Penn Coun. for Relationships, Phila., 1995-96; med. social worker Chester River Home Care and Hospice, Chestertown, Md., 1997; clin. social worker S.O.A.R., Inc. (Survivors of Abuse in Recovery), Milford, Del., 1998—, bd. dirs., 1994-98; psychotherapist Nancy B. Whitten, LCSW, Easton, Md., 1997—, Possibilities LLC, Easton, 2002—. Crisis counselor Crime Victims Ctr., West Chester, Pa., 1992-95; condr. marriage seminars Mental Health Assn. Talbot County, Easton, Md., 1997-98, bd. dirs. 1996-99, pres.-elect 1998-99, pres., 2000—. Elks scholar Stanford U., 1956. Mem. NASW, Am. Assn. for Marriage and Family Therapy (clin. mem., cert.), Mortar Bd., Psi Chi, Phi Sigma. Unitarian Universalist. Avocations: sailing, fishing, tennis. Home and Office: 9660 Leeds Landing Cir Easton MD 21601-5562

WHITTEN, SUSAN ELIZABETH SMITH, artist; b. Memphis, Jan. 27, 1948; d. Mark Black and Mildred Elizabeth (Tinsley) Smith; m. William DeWitt Whitten, Feb. 14, 1970 (dec. Dec. 1990); 1 child, Christopher Mark. BFA in Painting, Memphis State U., 1971. Counselor Tenn. Dept. Human Svcs., Memphis, 1971-74, Nashville, 1980-81; interviewer Tenn. Dept. Employment Security, 1981-85; portrait artist, 1980—. Works represented in pvt. collections throughout U.S.; cover designer Letters for All Seasons, 1991. Pres. Rep. Career Women, Memphis, 1976; mem. exec. com. Shelby County Rep. Com., Memphis, 1978-80, mem. steering com., 1977-80; youth counselor Belmont United Meth. Ch., Nashville, 1985—. Named Miss. Tennessee Young Rep., Young Reps., 1969. Mem. Hort. Soc. Davidson County, Warner Park Garden Club, Alpha Phi. Avocations: golf, floral arranging, gourmet cooking, decorating, European travel. Home: 4400 Belmont Park Ter Apt 119 Nashville TN 37215-6267

WHITTERS, JAMES PAYTON, III, lawyer, university administrator; b. Boston, Oct. 23, 1939; s. James P. Jr. and Norene (Jones) W.; m. Elizabeth Robertson, July 19, 1969; children: James P. IV, Catharine A. BA in History, Trinity Coll., Hartford, Conn., 1962; JD, Boston Coll., 1969; MA in Am. Studies, U. Mass., Boston, 2002. Bar: Mass. 1969, U.S. Dist. Ct. Mass. 1970, U.S. Ct. Appeals (1st cir.) 1972. Assoc. Ely, Bartlett, Brown & Proctor, Boston, 1969-74, Gaston Snow & Ely Bartlett, Boston, 1974-79, ptnr., 1979-88, Gaston & Snow, Boston, 1988-91; of counsel Peabody & Brown,

1991-95; dir. Office Career Devel., Suffolk U. Law Sch., 1995—, adj. prof. Am. legal history, 1997—. Bd. dirs., sec. Robertson Factories, Inc., Taunton, Mass., 1979—; v.p. Alkalol Co., Taunton, 1976-97, sr. v.p., 1997—; vis. tchr. Groton (Mass.) Sch., 1993-94; mem. Mass. Conflict Intervention Mediation Team, 1995—. Bd. dirs. New Eng. com. NAACP Legal Def. Fund, 1982—, Beacon Hill Nursery Sch., 1976-78, Mass. Appleseed Ctr. Law and Justice, 1997—; chmn. Mass. Outdoor Advt. Bd., Boston, 1975-81; vice chmn. Mass. Jud. Nominating Coun., Boston, 1983-87; trustee Trinity Coll., 1983-95; trustee, sec. Hurricane Island Outward Bound Sch., 1977-87; bd. dirs. Mass. affiliate Am. Heart Assn., 1979-98, chmn., 1989-91; bd. dirs. Greater Boston Legal Svcs., 1982-84, 93-99, Mass. Assn. Mediation Programs and Practitioners, 1993-98; founder Beacon Hill Seminars, 2000-2001, bd. dirs., 2001—. Lt. (j.g.) USN, 1962-65. Recipient Alumni Excellence award Trinity Coll., 1987. Mem.: ABA, Boston Bar Assn. (standing com. on work-life balance, children's outreach task force, pub. svc. and criminal justice task force), Mass. Bar Assn., The Country Club (Brookline, Mass.). Democrat. Unitarian Universalist. Avocations: reading history, mountain climbing & jogging. Home: 44 Mount Vernon St Boston MA 02108-1302

WHITTIER, CHARLES TAYLOR, JR. consulting company executive, educational, management and scientific administrator; b. Cedar Falls, Iowa, Nov. 29, 1941; s. Charles Taylor and Sara Jane (Leckrone) W.; m. Wendi Lynn Walker, June 18, 1978; children: Megan Rose, Courtney Lynn, Karey Jean. Student, Montgomery Jr. Coll., 1959-62; BS, Morehead U., 1964; MBA, Temple U., 1968; postgrad., U. Okla., 1971-77. Cost analyst Philco-Ford Corp., Ft. Washington, Pa., 1967, programs adminstr., 1967-69, sr. salary adminstr., 1969-70, mgr. indsl. rels. for U.S. and Third Country nations Saigon, Vietnam, 1970, S.E. Asia liaison Phila., 1971; pres. Internat. Enterprises, Norman, Okla., 1971-76, Transnational Corp., Norman, 1977—, v.p., treas. mining co., 1977-81; pres. CTEC Inc., 1979-88, Transnational Energy Corp., 1983-92, Whittier Fin. Corp., 1979-92, Tech. Edn. & Devel. Svcs. Co., Norman, 1991—. Dir. Nat. Emergency Mgmt. Info. Ctr., Global Tech. Info. Centre, 1995—, Computer Advanced Security Inst., 1997—, Strategic Intelligence Dynamics, 1998—; past cons. to Okla. Aeronautical Commn.; past cons. and acting pres. Aviation FBO Co. Author: Economic Counter Espionage The 21st Century Challenge; co-editor: The Conduct of Business Overseas: An Oklahoma Perspective, 1974. Past mem., bd. advisers, nat. com. Internat. Assn. Students in Econs. and Commerce; ative 1st Presbyn. Ch. Mem. AAUP, AIESEC, Internat. Assn. for Fin. Planning, Aircraft Owners and Pilots Assn., Oklahoma City Internat. Trade Club, Licensing Exec. Soc. (chmn. Okla. chpt.), Soc. Competitive Intelligence, Alumni Soc. Home: 2104 Westwood Dr Norman OK 73069-6549 E-mail: whitct@tedsco.org.

WHITTIER, MONTE RAY, lawyer; b. Pocatello, Idaho, June 28, 1955; s. Raymond Max and Marjorie Lucille (Pea) W.; m. Denise Womack, May 29, 1982; children: Jason Dennis, Sarah Michelle, Sadie Mckenzie. BS in Acctg., U. Utah, 1976; JD, U. Idaho, 1978. Bar: U.S. Dist. Ct. Idaho, 1979, U.S. Supreme Ct. 1985, U.S. Tax Ct. 1989, U.S. Ct. Appeals (9th cir.) 1991, Idaho, 1979. Ptnr., shareholder Whittier & Souza, Pocatello, 1979-89; shareholder, mng. atty. Whittier, Souza & Naftz, 1989-97; asst. gen. counsel Melaleuca, Inc., Idaho Falls, 1997—. Vol. Internat. Spl. Olympics, South Bend, Ind., 1987, Mpls., 1991; mem. Magistrate Commn. 6th Jud. Dist., Pocatello, 1989-91; bd. dirs. Bannock Baseball, Inc., 1996-97; v.p. Idaho Falls Am. Legion Baseball, 2000—. Mem. ATLA, Idaho Trial Lawyers Assn. (bd. dirs. 6th Jud. Dist. Pro Bono award 1994), Civitan (pres. Bannock chpt. 1983-84, bd. dirs. 1981-87, 92-93, lt. gov. Intermountain chpt. 1986-87, Outstanding Pres. award 1984, Outstanding Svc. award 1982-83, 86-88, 91). Avocations: bicycling, skiing, golfing, Spl. Olympics vol. activities. Office: Melaleuca Inc 3910 S Yellowstone Hwy Idaho Falls ID 83402-6003 E-mail: mwhittier@melaleuca.com .

WHITTINGHAM, CHARLES ARTHUR, publisher, library administrator; b. Chgo., Feb. 11, 1930; s. Charles Arthur and Virginia (Hartke) W.; m. Jean Bragger Whittingham, June 4, 1955; children: Mary Elizabeth, Charles Arthur III, Philip Alexander, Leigh Ann. BS in English Lit. cum laude, Loyola U., Chgo., 1951. With McCall Corp., Chgo., 1956-59, Time, Inc., Chgo., 1959-62; pub.'s rep. Fortune mag., Time, Inc., N.Y.C., 1962-65, mgr. San Francisco, 1965-69; asst. to pub. Fortune, N.Y.C., 1969-70, asst. pub., 1970-78; pub. Life mag., 1978-88; sr. v.p. N.Y. Pub. Libr., 1989-92; exec. prodr. Kunhardt Prodns., Inc., 1995—. Lt. (j.g.) USNR, 1951-55. Named to Athletic Hall of Fame Loyola U., Loyola Acad. Mem. Century Assn., Brook Club, The Pilgrims. Home and Office: 11 Woodmill Rd Chappaqua NY 10514-1128 also: 5584 Bartram St Boca Raton FL 33433

WHITTINGHAM, HARRY EDWARD, JR. retired banker; b. Albany, N.Y., Dec. 25, 1918; s. Harry E. and Mary (Baer) W.; m. Gladys D. Willstaedt, Sept. 2, 1942; children: Jeffrey A., Neal E. Grad., Stonier Grad. Sch. Banking, 1961. With Schenectady Trust Co., 1947-84, pres., chief exec. officer, 1974-82, chmn., chief exec. officer, 1982-84. Author: (with Purdy, Schneider, Aldom) Automation in Banking, 1962. Vestryman Episcopal Ch. With AUS, 1941—46. Home: 6009 Addington Dr NW Acworth GA 30101-7148

WHITTINGHAM, M(ICHAEL) STANLEY, chemist; b. Nottingham, Eng., Dec. 22, 1941; came to U.S., 1968, naturalized, 1980; s. William Stanley and Dorothy Mary (Findlay) W.; m. Georgina Judith Andai, Mar. 23, 1969; children: Jenniffer Judith, Michael Stanley. BA in Chemistry, Oxford U., 1964, MA, DPhil, 1968. Rsch. assoc., head solid state electrochemistry group Materials Ctr., Stanford U., 1968-72; mem. staff Exxon Rsch. Co., Linden, N.J., 1972—; group head solid state chem. physics, 1975-78; dir. solid state scis., 1978-80; mgr. chem. engring. tech., 1980-84; dir. phys. scis. Schlumberger Co., Ridgefield, Conn., 1984-88; prof. chemistry, dir. The Inst. for Materials Rsch., SUNY, 1988—; vice provost for rsch. SUNY, 1994-2000; vice-chair bd. dirs. Rsch Found., 1995-2001. Cons., lectr. in field; JSPS fellow U. Tokyo. Author, editor papers in field; author 5 books. Recipient Gas Coun. scholarship, Oxford U., 1964-67. Mem. Electrochem. Soc. (Young Author award 1971, N.Y. chmn. 1980-81), Am. Chem. Soc. (chmn. solid state sect. 1987, chmn. Binghamton sect. 1991), Am. Phys. Soc., Materials Rsch. Soc. Achievements include patents in field; reversible (rechargeable) lithium batteries and methods for making intercalation batteries; method for making TiS2 mixed material cathodes, high briteness luminescent displays. Home: 396 Meeker Rd Vestal NY 13850-3230 Office: SUNY Dept Chemistry Binghamton NY 13902 E-mail: stanwhit@binghamton.edu.

WHITTINGTON, ANNE ELIZABETH, diabetes educator; b. Berea, Ohio, Apr. 4, 1957; d. Richard Murphy and Eleen Elizabeth (Cooney) Whittington. ADN, Sante Fe Coll., 1979; BSN, U. N.C., 1983; MSN, Med. Coll. Ga., 1990; MBA, Brenau U., 1997. Tchr. Nat. Cert. Bd. for Diabetes Educators; cert. water aerobics instr. Staff nurse U. Fla. Teaching Hosp., Gainesville, 1979-80, New Hanover Meml. Hosp., Wilmington, N.C., 1980-81, Cape Fear Meml. Hosp., Wilmington, 1983-84; home health nurse New Hanover Home Health Agy., 1984-85, Comprehensive Home Health Care, Augusta, Ga., 1985; coord. outreach edn. for Ga. Dept. of Human Resources Grant, 1990—2000; dir. diabetes programs Naval Med. Ctr., San Diego, 2001—. Docent Augusta Richmond County Mus., 1987-91; dir. Our Lady of Peace Choir, North Augusta, 1990—; co-founder Cen. Savannah River Area Arthritis Support Group, Augusta, 1991—; Cath. chaplaincy Augusta Correctional Instn., 1991—. Recipient Woman of Excellence award Cen. Savannah River Area, 1992; named Outstanding Diabetes Educator, GADE, 1992, Outstanding Alumnus, Med. Coll. Ga. Sch. Nursing, 1992, Outstanding Diabetes Educator, Am. Assn. Diabetes Edn., 1993; torchbearer Atlanta Olympics, 1996. Mem.: Arthritis Health Profl. Assn., Ga. Nurses Assn., U. N.C. Sch. Nursing Alumni Assn. (bd. dirs. 1989—93), Am. Diabetes Assn., Am. Assn. Diabetes Educator (sec. visual impaired preson speciality practice group 1994—97, chair visual impaired person speciality group 1997—2000, bd.dirs. 1999—2002), Greater Atlanta Diabetes Educators (chmn. profl. edn. 1991—2000, pres. 1995—97), ANA, Sigma Theta Tau (Grad. Student of Yr. 1991). Democrat. Roman Catholic. Avocations: music, water aerobics. Home: 34800 Bob Wilson Dr Ste 301 San Diego CA 92134-1301 E-mail: aewhittington@nmcsd.med.navy.mil.

WHITTINGTON, DENISE LYNN, music educator; b. Kansas City, Mo., Jan. 3, 1971; d. Dallas Deon and Judy Fay Bundy; m. Gregory Keith Whittington, June 12, 1998. MusB in Piano Performance, BS in Music Edn., U. Mo., 1994; M in Ch. Music, So. Seminary, 1997. Cert. music tchr., Mo., Ky. Organist Kenwood Bapt., Louisville, 1994-95; organist, choir dir. Va. Ave. Meth., 1995-97, Meadowview Presbyn., Louisville, 1997—; piano instr., 1999—; music educator St. Barnabas Cath. Sch., 1999—2002. Prof.'s asst. So. Seminary, Louisville, 1996-97. Coord. children's choir workshop Mo. Bapt. Conv., Boonville, 1992, 93; piano adjudicator Mo. Bapt. Conv. Keyboard Festival, 1992, 94; co-founder, accompanist Boonville (Mo.) Cmty. Worship Choir, 1993; accompanist Cmty. Ch. Men's Ensemble, Columbia, Mo., 1993. Mem. Am. Orff-Shulwerk Assn., Music Tchrs. Nat. Assn., Ky. Orff-Shulwerk Assn., Greater Louisville Music Tchrs. Assn. (co-chair Ensemble com. 1999-2000). Presbyterian. Avocation: reading and playing the piano. Home: 5345 Lost Trl Louisville KY 40214-3509

WHITTINGTON, FREDERICK BROWN, JR. business administration educator; b. Sept. 22, 1934; m. Marjorie Ann Babington; children: Frederick Brown III, Marjorie Ellen, Lisa Anne. SB, MIT, 1958; MBA, Tulane U., 1965; PhD, La. State U., 1969. Staff economist Miss. Rsch. Commn., Jackson, 1961-64; sr. assoc. econ. rsch. Gulf South Rsch. Inst., Baton Rouge, 1966-69; asst. prof. bus. adminstrn. Emory U., Atlanta, 1969-73, assoc. prof., 1973-79, prof., 1979-96, prof. emeritus, 1997—, dir. customer bus. devel. track, 1991-94. Bd. dirs. Gwinnett Industries, Inc.; mem. forecasting panel Fed. Res. Bank Atlanta; vis. prof. Johannes Kepler U., Linz, Austria, 1983, 84, 89, 95-2002; guest lectr. Austrian Univs., Linz, Vienna, Innsbruck and Klagenfurt; presenter workshops; cons. in field. Contbr. articles and reports to profl. jours. Mktg. plan, mgmt. audit State of Miss., Park Commn.; past chmn., bd. deacons Decatur Presbyn. Ch.; mem. adv. bd. DeKalb/Rockdale Svc. Ctr., ARC. Capt. USNR, ret., 1994. Recipient Badge of Hon., Austrian Marketing Rsch. Soc., 1996, recipient Trauner prize for ednl. innovation Upper Austrian Econ. Chamber, 1997; Sears Roebuck Found. fellow, 1965-66. Mem. Am. Mktg. Assn., Nat. Assn. Purchasing Mgmt., So. Mktg. Assn., Coun. for Logistics Mgmt., Warehousing Edn. and Rsch. Coun., Omicron Delta Kappa, Beta Gamma Sigma, Delta Tau Delta. Office: Emory U Goizueta Bus Sch Atlanta GA 30322-0001 E-mail: brown_whittington@bus.emory.edu.

WHITTINGTON, JAMES LELAND, finance educator; b. Stamford, Tex., Aug. 14, 1957; s. Leland Browning and Clara Ruth Whittington; m. Laura Anne Marsh, Nov. 24, 1978; children: Jennifer, Justin, Jordan, Janelle. BA, Austin Coll., 1979; MBA, U. Tex., 1981, PhD, 1997. Gen. mgr. Indsl. Air and Hydraulics, Arlington, Tex., 1987—94; prof. Tex. Wesleyan U., Ft. Worth, 1996—2000, U. Dallas Grad. Sch. Mgmt., Irving, 2000—. Pres. Bedford (Tex.) Consulting Group, 1994—. Contbr. Mem.: Acad. Mgmt. Home: 2620 Rollingshire Bedford TX 76021 Office: U Dallas Grad Sch Mgmt 1845 E Northgate Dr Irving TX 75062

WHITTINGTON, LORIN DALE, music educator; b. Balt., Nov. 1, 1951; s. Cicero Edward Whittington and Dorothy Virginia Peters. MusB, Appalachian State U., 1979. Cert. tchr. music k-12 N.C. Tchr. Hall Fletcher Mid. Sch., Asheville, NC, 1979—81, Hill St. Mid. Sch., Asheville, 1979—81, Owen H.S., Swannanoa. Chorus master Mid-Atlantic Opera Co., Asheville, 1985—86. Composer: (sound recording) Rochelle, 1972. Mem.: Music Educators Nat. Conf. Avocations: genealogy, art, computer graphics, guitar, travel. Home: 19 Clairmont Ave Asheville NC 28804 Office: Owen Mid Schl 730 Old US 70 Swannanoa NC 28778 Personal E-mail: vytiense@appleisp.net.

WHITTINGTON, ROBERT WALLACE, corporate professional; b. Birmingham, Ala., Sept. 25, 1967; s. Dorsey and Frances (Kohn) W.; m. Karen Smith, Dec. 10, 1967 (dec. 1984). BS, Auburn U., 1955; BA, U. Miami, Fla., 1956; MS, Cornell U., 1958. CEO Travel Ctrs., Inc., Chgo.; pres. Svc. Ctrs., Inc., Sarasota, Fla., 1970-88, Exotics S.A., 1988-89. Bd. dirs. Centro Cultural Costarricense N.Am., Eastern Airlines, Inc., 1974-76; chmn. U.S. Dept. Commerce "Visit USA", 1973-75. Lt. U.S. Intelligence, 1960-62, Korea. Mem. Fla. Hort. Soc., Am. Landscape Assn., Fly Fisherman Assn., Can. Salmonoid Assn., Fla. Turf Assn., Am. Soc. Travel Agts. (bd. dirs. 1961-63). Avocations: angling, cooking, photography, boating, bee keeping. Home and Office: PO Box 025292 Miami FL 33102-5292 E-mail: exotics@sol.rasca.co.cr.

WHITTINGTON, STEPHEN LUNN, museum director; b. Washington, Jan. 31, 1956; s. Charles Lunn and Alice Marie (Doyle) W.; m. Christine Ann Carlson, Aug. 18, 1979; children: Daniel, Joseph. AB in Anthropology, U. Chgo., 1977; MA, Pa. State U., 1981, PhD, 1989. Grad. asst. mus. anthropology Pa. State U., 1984—86, grad. teaching asst., 1986, mus. asst., 1986-87, part-time lectr., instr., 1987-88, adj. rsch. assoc., 1989-90, project coord. coll. health and human devel., 1990-91; dir. Proyecto Arqueologico Ostuman, Copan, Honduras, 1989; asst. curator collections Wyo. Hist. and Geol. Soc., Wilkes-Barre, Pa., 1989-90; cooperating assoc. prof. dept. anthropology U. Maine, 1991—2002; dir. U. Maine Hudson Mus., 1991—2002, dir. project arqueological, 2002—. Dir. iximche osteological project U. Maine, 1992—95; adj. assoc. prof. dept. anthropology Wake Forest U., dir. mus. anthropology. Editor: Bones of the Maya; contbr. articles to profl. jours. Active Maine State Mus. Commn., 1998—2002. Grantee Wenner-Gren Found. for Anthrop. Rsch., 1992-93, NSF, 1989, Inst. Internat. Edn., 1988, Found. for the Advancement of Mesoamerican Studies, 1995, 99, 2002, NEH, 1997. Mem. Am. Assn. Mus., Maine Archives and Mus., New England Mus. Assn., Soc. for Am. Archaeology. Avocations: racquetball, jogging, fencing. Home: 1307 Brookwood Dr Winston Salem NC 27106 Office: Wake Forest Univ Mus Anthropology PO Box 7267 Winston Salem NC 27109 E-mail: whittisl@wfu.edu.

WHITTINGTON-COUSE, MARYELLEN FRANCES, education administrator, not-for-profit developer, consultant; b. Waverly, N.Y., June 16, 1957; d. Philip John and Sheila (Dewey) Whittington; m. Daniel Couse, May 18, 1985; children: Kristen, Benjamin, Connor. BA, SUNY, Empire, 1983; M of Internat. Adminstrn., Sch. for Internat. Tng., Brattleboro, Vt., 1992. Adj. faculty Rockland C.C., 1983-85; cons. UN Non-Govtl. Liaison Svc., N.Y.C., 1987; adminstrv. asst. Manitoga Nature Ctr., Garrison, N.Y., 1987-88; coord. Intensive Tchr. Inst. Manhattanville and Coll. of New Rochelle Satellites, New Paltz, 1990-92; dir. Bilingual ESL Tech. Assistance Ctr. N.Y. State Edn. Dept., 1988-2000. Orgnl. devel. cons., personal coach, 2000—; assoc. prof. SUNY, New Paltz, 1994—; diversity specialist Cornell U., 2001—; co-chair PROSPAN; mem. Parent Edn. Adv. Coun., Ulster County, 1988—. Editor: (curriculum) Teacher's Guide and Content Activities for Limited English Proficient Students, 1992; co-author video script for N.Y. State Edn. Dept., 1992. Mem. Nat. Assn Bilingual Edn., N.Y. TESOL, TESOL Internat., N.Y. State Assn. Bilingual Edn. (conf. chair 1996), Nat. Assn. Multicultural Edn. Avocations: hiking, reading, gardening. Home and Office: 19 Quaker St Tillson NY 12486 E-mail: mwhit68421@aol.com.

WHITTLE, JOSEPH F., JR. engineering executive, consultant; BS in Geology, Rensselaer Poly. Inst., 1967; MSCE, Mass. Inst. Tech., 1974. Registered profl. engr., profl. geologist, environ. assessor, spl. bldg. inspector. Asst. geologist Dames & Moore, N.Y.C., 1967-68; sr. instr. U.S. Army Engr. Sch., Ft. Belvoir, Va., 1968-69; geologist Haley & Aldrich, Cambridge, Mass., 1970-74; geotech. engr. Law Engring., Tampa, Fla., 1974-81; sr. engr. PSI/Fla. Testing Labs., 1981-84; div. mgr. Profl. Svc. Industry, 1984-87, sr. div. mgr. Clearwater, Fla., 1987-90, br. mgr., sr. tech. cons. Lombard, Ill., 1990-97; engring. mgr. Robert B. Balter Co., 1997—. Author: Construction and Quarry Blasting, 1969, Consolidation Behavior of an Embankment, 1974. 1st Lt. U.S. Army, 1968-70. Decorated Bronze Star, U.S. Army, Vietnam, 1970; recipient Svc. award, Suffolk (N.Y.) Police Dept., 1970. Mem. ASCE, Assn. Engring. Geologists, Soc. Am. Mil. Engrs., Assn. Groundwater Scientists & Engrs., Phi Kappa Theta, Sigma Xi. Office: Robert B Balter Co 18 Music Fair Rd Owings Mills MD 21117-3603

WHITTLE, MACK IRA, JR. banking executive; b. Columbia, S.C., Nov. 5, 1948; s. Mack Ira and Eleanor (Howell) Whittle; m. Jennifer Ann Mooney, May 28, 2000; children from previous marriage: Quincy Nye, Patricia Cameron, Lee Forester. BS, U. S.C., 1971, MBA, 1975; grad. Banking Sch. South, La. State U., 1979. Trust officer Bankers Trust S.C. (formerly State Bank and Trust Co.), Greenville, from 1974, v.p. comml. bus. devel., to 1979, v.p. city exec. Myrtle Beach, 1979-82; sr. v.p., regional officer N.C. Nat. Bank (formerly Bankers Trust S.C.), Greenville, 1982-86; pres. & CEO Carolina First Corp., 1986—; also bd. dirs. Carolina First Bank, 1991—. Bd. dirs. Carolina First Corp., Carolina First Savs. Bank, R.L. Bryan & Co. Trustee U. S.C., Columbia, 1984; bd. dirs. campaign, cabinet Greenville United Way, 1984-85; bd. dirs. Community Found. Greater Greenville, Met. Arts Coun., Greenville Tech. Coll. Found., Carolina Piedmont Found., Inc.; trustee U. S.C.; bd. dirs., v.p., treas. Mus. Assn. Greenville/County Mus. Art; chmn. bd. dirs. Greenville Urban League; adv. bd. Peace Ctr.; chmn. Christ Ch. Endowment Corp., Greenville, 1989—; mem. ch. sch. bd. visitors Christ Episcopal Ch. Recipient Disting. Alumnus award U. S.C. Coll. Bus. Adminstrn., 1994; named Outstanding Young Banker S.C., 1988. Mem. S.C. Bankers Assn. (bd. dirs. 1989—, pres. 1993-94), Am. Bankers Assn., Ind. Banks S.C., Ind. Bankers Assn. Am., S.C. C. of C. (bd. dirs. 1989—), U. S.C. Alumni Assn. (past pres., Entrepreneur of Yr. in Fin. Industry 1993). Episcopalian. Avocations: running, reading. Office: Carolina First Bank PO Box 1029 Greenville SC 29602

WHITTLE, RANDOLPH GORDON, JR. retired city manager; b. Roanoke, Va., May 16, 1930; s. Randolph Gordon and Josephine Edmonds (Parrott) W.; m. Lucie Elizabeth Stevens, Dec. 2, 1967; children: Randolph Gordon III, Arthur Stevens, Lee Bolling, Lillian Elizabeth. AB, Washington and Lee U., 1952; MGA, U. Pa., 1955. Mgr. City of Bluefield, W.Va., 1958-66; asst. dir. Regional Planning Coun., Balt., 1966-72, Fla. State Planning Office, Tallahassee, 1972-75, dir., 1975-79; exec. dir. Greater Johnston Com., 1979-97; acting city mgr. Johnstown, Pa., 1997-98; ret., 1998. Mem. Cambria County Conservation and Recreation Commn., Ebensburg, Pa., 1995-98; bd. dirs. Allegheny Ridge Corp., Altoona, Pa., 1994-99; vice-chmn. Johnstown Planning commn., 1995—. Lt. (j.g.) U.S. Navy, 1954-58. Democrat. Episcopalian. Home: 1137 Confer Ave Johnstown PA 15905-4418 E-mail: whittle@surfshop.net.

WHITTLESEY, JOHN WILLIAMS, lawyer; b. Newton Upper Falls, Mass., Aug. 18, 1917; s. John Eddy and Dorothy (Williams) W.; m. Barbara Baur, June 13, 1942; children: J. Baur, Diana, Paul Woodman. BA, Harvard U., 1937, LLB, 1940; LLM, Columbia U., 1947. Bar: Mass. 1940, N.Y. 1953, U.S. Dist. Ct. (so. and ea. dists.) N.Y. 1972, U.S. Ct. Appeals (2d cir.) 1972, U.S. Supreme Ct. Labor atty. U.S. C. of C., Washington, 1946-51; asst. industry mem. Wage Stabilization Bd., 1951-52; counsel Fisher & Rudge, N.Y.C., 1952-53; chief labor counsel Union Carbide Corp., Danbury, Conn., 1953-82; pvt. practice Chappaqua, N.Y., 1982—; of counsel Wisehart & Koch, N.Y.C., 1984-2001, Keane & Beane, White Plains, N.Y., 1985-89. Adminstrv. law judge Office Hearings and Appeals Social Security Adminstrn., 1990-93; cons. in field; chmn. occupational safety and health com. N.Y. Bus. Coun., Albany, 1975-87; chmn. N.Y.C. Labor and Human Resources Com., 1987-89. Committeeman Westchester Rep. County Com., White Plains, 1957—, New Castle Rep. Town Com., Chappaqua, 1957—, chmn., 1969-73. Capt. U.S. Army, 1940-45, ETO. New Directions grantee OSHA, 1984-85. Mem. ABA, N.Y. State Bar Assn., Westchester County Bar Assn., N.Y.C. Bar Assn., Am. Arbitration Assn. Republican. Congregationalist. Avocations: sailing, philately. Home and Office: 310 Douglas Rd Chappaqua NY 10514-3100

WHITTLESEY, JUDITH HOLLOWAY, public relations executive; b. Bartlesville, Okla., Dec. 28, 1942; d. Harry Haynes and Suzanne (Arnote) Holloway; m. Dennis Jeffrey Whittlesey, Aug. 3, 1968; children: Kristin Arnote, Kevin Jeffrey. BA, U. Okla., 1964; postgrad., Tulsa U., 1965, U. Va., 1971-72. Staff aide Office of the V.P. of U.S., Washington, 1979-81, Com. for Future of Am., Washington, 1981-82; dep. dir. scheduling and advance Mondale-Ferraro Campaign, 1982-84; dir. media rels. Susan Davis Internat., 1986-87, v.p., 1987-88, exec. v.p., 1988—. Bd. dirs. Cultural Alliance of Greater Washington, 1983-93, Washington Project for the Arts, 1987-93, Levine Sch. Music, 1993-98, Food Rsch. and Action Ctr., 1993—; bd. dirs. Decatur House Suited For Change, Chevy Chase Presbyn. Ch., Washington. Avocations: art/contemporary and craft. Office: Susan Davis Internat 1000 Vermont Ave NW Washington DC 20005-4903

WHITWAM, DAVID RAY, appliance manufacturing company executive; b. Stanley, Wis., Jan. 30, 1942; s. Donald R. and Lorraine (Stoye) W.; m. Barbara Lynne Peterson, Apr. 13, 1963; children: Mark, Laura, Thomas BS, U. Wis., 1967. Gen. mgr. sales So. Calif. divsn. Whirlpool Corp., Los Angeles, 1975-77, mdse. mgr. ranges Benton Harbor, Mich., 1977-79, dir. builder mktg., 1979-80, v.p. builder mktg., 1980-83, v.p. whirlpool sales, 1983-85, vice-chmn., chief mktg. officer, 1985-87, chmn., pres., CEO, 1987-99, chmn., CEO, 1999—, also bd. dirs. Bd. dirs. Combustion Engring. Inc., Stamford, Conn. Pres. bd. dirs. The Soup Kitchen, Benton Harbor, 1980—; mem. Nat. Council Housing Industry, Washington. Capt. U.S. Army. Fellow Aspen Inst.; mem. Point O'Woods Club (Benton Harbor). Republican. Lutheran. Office: Whirlpool Corp 2000 N M 63 Benton Harbor MI 49022-2692*

WHITWORTH, HALL BAKER, forest products company executive; b. St. Paul, Feb. 15, 1919; s. A. Frederick and Maude Ethel (Baker) W.; m. Mary Margaret Mease, May 18, 1946; children: Hall Baker, Laura Ellen, David Allen. Student, Miss. So. Coll., 1942, U. N.C., 1957. With Champion Internat., Canton, N.C., 1936-62, mgr. materials, 1956-62, dir. materials packages div. Chgo., 1962-65, dir. purchase U.S. Plywood-Champion Papers, Inc. (now champion Internat. Corp.) Hamilton, Ohio, 1965-68, dep. dir. corporate materials services, 1966, v.p., dir. purchase, 1968-75, v.p. materials Stamford, Conn., 1975—, dir., 1975—, now ret.; v.p., dir. So. Agrl. Co., 1985—; pres., dir. H. Whitworth Enterprises, Cin., 1985—. Dir. Pathfork-Harlan Coal Co. Served with U.S. Army, 1942-46. Recipient Thomas award Carolina-Va. Purchasing Agts. Assn., 1963 Mem. Am. Paper Inst. (chmn. energy subcom.), Am. Mgmt. Assn. (v.p. purchasing, transp. and phys. distbn. div. council) Clubs: Canton Toastmakers (founder, 1st pres.). Lodges: Elks; Lions. Methodist. Home and Office: 3350 Brookwater Cir Orlando FL 32822-5800 E-mail: hall_whitworth@msn.com.

WHITWORTH, HORACE ALGERNON, mechanical engineer; b. Kingston, Jamaica, W.I., Mar. 24, 1953; came to U.S., 1967; s. Egbert Leopold and Violet Cecilia (Trouth) W. BSME, U. Mass., 1975; MS, George Washington U., 1977, DSc, 1983. Asst. prof. Howard U., Washington, 1983-89, dir. grad. studies dept. mech. engring., 1988-96, assoc. prof. mech. engring., 1989-99, prof. mech. engring., 1999—. Contbr. numerous articles to profl. publs. Bd. dirs. Jamaica Support Found., Washington, 1991-95. Recipient Sr. Fellows Found. award Pacific Telesis Found., 1988, Prof. Acad. award Honeywell Corp., 1992; rsch. grantee in field. Mem. ASME (bd. dirs. Washington chpt. 1994—, Instr. of Yr. student chpt. 1985-86, 87-89), Am. Soc. Metals, Soc. for Exptl. Mechanics. Democrat. Methodist. Achievements include development of mathematical models to evaluate fatigue damage development in fibrous composite materials. Avocations: chess, soccer, checkers. Office: Howard U 2300 6th St NW Washington DC 20001-2323 E-mail: hwhitworth@fac.howard.edu.

WHITWORTH, KATHRYNNE ANN, professional golfer; b. Monahans, Tex., Sept. 27, 1939; d. Morris Clark and Dama Ann (Robinson) W. Student, Odessa (Tex.) Jr. Coll., 1958. Joined tour Ladies Profl. Golf Assn., 1959—. Mem. adv. Square Two Golf Co. Named to Hall of Fame Ladies Profl. Golf Assn., Tex. Sports Hall of Fame, Tex. Golf Hall of Fame, World Golf Hall of Fame; Capt. of Solhiem Cup, 1990-92. Mem. Ladies Profl. Golf Assn. (sec. 1962-63, v.p. 1965, 73, 88, pres. 1967, 68, 71, 89, 1st mem. to win over $1,000,000). Office: care Ladies Profl Golf Assn 2570 Volusia Ave Daytona Beach FL 32114-8144

WHITWORTH, WILLIAM A. magazine editor; b. Hot Springs, Ark., Feb. 13, 1937; s. William C. and Lois Virginia (McNabb) W.; m. Carolyn Hubbard, Dec. 27, 1969; children— Matthew, Katherine. BA, U. Okla., 1960. Reporter Ark. Gazette, Little Rock, 1960-63; reporter N.Y. Herald Tribune, 1963-65; staff writer The New Yorker, 1966-72, assoc. editor, 1973-80; editor-in-chief The Atlantic Monthly, Boston, 1981-99, editor emeritus, 1999—; editor The American Scholar, Washington, 2002—. Office: Atlantic Monthly 77 N Washington St Ste 500 Boston MA 02114-1916

WHOLEBEN, BRENT EDWARD, educator; b. Olean, N.Y., July 7, 1946; s. Bernard Edward and Mildred Florence (Camp) W.; B.S. in Mathematics, St. Bonaventure U., 1968; M.Ed. in Psychology, U. Hawaii, 1972, M.Ed. in Adminstrn., 1974; Ph.D. in Ednl. Adminstrn. U. Wis., 1979; m. Judith Ann Braun, June 22, 1968; children: Melissa Anne, Kevin Patrick, Timothy Colin. Cert. emergency med. technician, Wash., Tex. Tchr. mathematics, coordinator student activities, dir. guidance services Hawaii Dept. Edn., 1970-75; family psychotherapist, vocat. guidance specialist interim dept. supr. Family Tng. Center, Glasgow, Mont., 1975-77; project asst., research cons. U. Wis., Madison, 1977-79, teaching asst. computer applications in edn., 1978-79; systems evaluation cons. to sch. dists., 1978-79; asst. prof. ednl. adminstrn., assoc. dir. Research Bur., U. Wash., 1979-82; assoc. prof. ednl. adminstrn. and supervision U. Tex., El Paso, 1982— ; prin. cons. computer edn. Young People's U., 1983-85; prin. Ysleta Project on Computer Edn., 1986-87; sr. mem. grad. faculty, 1983— ; also cons. UNESCO, 1985—. Served with arty. U.S. Army, 1968-70; Vietnam. Mem. Am. Ednl. Research Assn., Assn. Ednl. Data Systems, Am. Assn. Colls. Tchr. Edn., Assn. Tchr. Educators, Internat. Soc. Ednl. Planners, Phi Delta Kappa. Republican. Roman Catholic. Club: K.C. Author articles in field; manuscript and publs. reviewer N.W. Regional Ednl. Labs., Jour. Tchr. Edn.; author 5 books; instrnl. computing, mgmt. info. systems for schs. Home: 6700 Southwind Dr El Paso TX 79912-3239

WHORISKEY, ROBERT DONALD, lawyer; b. Cambridge, Mass., May 9, 1929; s. John Joseph and Katherine Euphemia (MacDonald) W.; m. Martha Beebe Poutas, Apr. 16, 1966; children: Alexandra, Jonathan, Eliza. AB, Harvard U., 1952; JD, Boston Coll., 1958; LLM, NYU, 1960. Bar: Mass. 1958, N.Y. 1963, U.S. Tax Ct. 1961, U.S. Claims Ct. 1969, U.S. Dist. Ct. (so. dist.) N.Y. 1969, U.S. Ct. Customs 1971, U.S. Ct. Appeals (2d cir.) 1972, U.S. Ct. Appeals (3d cir.) 1983, U.S. Ct. Appeals (D.C. cir.) 1991, U.S. Supreme Ct. 1974. Sr. trial atty. Office Chief Counsel, IRS, N.Y.C., 1960-67; assoc. Curtis, Mallet-Prevost, Colt & Mosle, 1967-70, ptnr., 1970-2000, of counsel, 2001—, exec. com., 1978-82, chmn. tax dept., 1982-87. Bd. dirs. Internat. Tax Inst., v.p., lectr., 1980-84, chmn. bd., pres., lectr., 1985-87; lectr. Practicing Law Inst., World Trade Inst., Tax Execs. Inst., Am. Mgmt. Assn., Coun. for Internat. Tax Edn.; bd. dirs. Life Ins. Co. of Boston and N.Y., Inc. Author: Foreign Trusts, 1977, Annual Institute on International Taxation, 1966, 80, 81, (with Sidney Pine, Ralph Seligman) Tax and Business Benefits of the Bahamas, 1986; contbg. author: International Boycotts, CCH Federal Tax Service, 1988, CCH Smart Tax CD-ROM: Third Party Information, John Wiley and Sons, Inc.'s Transfer Pricing, 1993, Transfer Pricing Under IRC & 482: Overview and Planning, Part I, 1996, Accuracy Related Penalty Regulations for Transfer Pricing, Part II, 1997, Third Party Information, Part III, 1997, U.S. Taxation of International Operations, Warren, Gorham Lamont, 1998; mem. editl. adv. bd. Corp. Bus. Taxation Monthly, 2000—. Trustee, treas. Montessori Sch. Westchester, 1974-77; mem. bd. ethics Village of Larchmont, N.Y., 1988—. With U.S. Army, 1952-54. Mem. ABA (com. on alternative tax sys. tax sect. 1994—, com. on ct. procedure tax sec. 1997—), N.Y. State Bar Assn. (com. on practice and procedure tax sect. 1990—), Assn. of the Bar of the City of N.Y., Harvard Club, Larchmont Yacht Club. Democrat. Roman Catholic. Office: Curtis Mallet-Prevost Colt & Mosle 101 Park Ave 35th Fl New York NY 10178-0061 E-mail: rwhoriskey@cm-p.com.

WHORTON, M. DONALD, occupational and environmental health physician, epidemiologist; b. Las Vegas, N.Mex., Jan. 25, 1943; s. R. H. and Rachel (Siegal) Whorton; m. Diana L. Obrinsky, Apr. 9, 1972; children: Matthew Richard, Laura Elizabeth, Julie Hannah. Student, U.S. Naval Acad., 1961—62; B of Biology, N.Mex. Highlands U., 1964; MD, U. N.Mex., 1968; MPH, Johns Hopkins U., 1973. Intern Boston City Hosp., 1968—69; resident in pathology U. N.Mex., Albuquerque, 1969—71; instr., resident in medicine Balt. City Hosp., 1972—74; instr. Johns Hopkins U., Balt.; assoc. dir. divsn. emergency medicine Balt. City Hosps., 1974—75; clin. asst. prof. divsn. ambulatory and cmty. medicine U. Calif. Sch. Medicine, San Francisco, 1975—77; lectr. U. Calif. Sch. Pub. Health, 1975—79; med. dir. labor occup. health program Inst. Indsl. Rels., Ctr. for Labor Rsch. and Edn., 1975—79, assoc. clin. prof. occup. medicine, 1979—87; prin. Environ. Health Assocs., Inc., Oakland, 1978—88; v.p. ENSR Health Scis., 1988—94; pvt. practice Alameda, Calif., 1994—2001; with WorkCare, 2001—. Chmn. adv. com. for hazard evaluation svc. and info. system Indsl. Relations Dept., State of Calif., 1979—84; cons. in field; chmn. statewide adv. com. on occupl. and environ. health U. Calif. Ctrs., 1996—. Contbr. articles. Recipient Upjohn Achievement award, 1968; scholar, Robert Wood Johnson Found., 1972—74. Fellow: Am. Coll. Occupl. and Environ. Medicine, Am. Coll. Epidemiology; mem.: Inst. of Medicine of NAS, Calif. Med. Assn. (adv. panel on occupl. and environ. medicine), Soc. for Occupl. and Environ. Health, APHA, Alpha Omega Alpha. Office: 1320 Harbor Bay Pkwy # 115 Alameda CA 94502-6556 E-mail: dwhorton@workcare.com., whobrin@lmi.net.

WHOULEY, KATE, book industry consultant, writer; b. Key West, Fla., Oct. 10, 1958; d. Paul Francis and Anne Marie (Ford) W. BA magna cum laude in Philosophy, Lit. and Music, Baldwin Wallace Coll., 1980. Bookseller, asst. mgr., store mgr. Waldenbooks, Newport, R.I., Needham, Mass., 1980-83; book buyer, mgr. gen. books Boston U. Bookstore, 1983-86; mdse. and mktg. dir. Garland & Grace/dba Booksmith Musicsmith, West Barnstable, Mass., 1986-88; founder, owner, cons. Books in Common, Centerville, 1988—. V.p. Booksellers Pub. Inc. subs. Am. Bookseller Assn., Tarrytown, N.Y., 1994-98. Author: Customers and Service, 1997; series editor Open Learning Study Series, 1997—2000; editor, co-author: Manual on Bookselling, 5th edit., 1996, online edit., 2002. Prin. flute Cape Cod Conservatory Concert Band, 1993—. Recipient Grover award Baldwin Wallace Coll., 1980. Mem. Am. Booksellers Assn., New Eng. Booksellers Assn., AAUW, Coop. Am. Avocations: music, gardening, reading, holistic studies, middle eastern dance. Office: Books in Common 263 S Main St Centerville MA 02632-3536

WHYBARK, DAVID CLAY, business educator, researcher; b. Tacoma, Sept. 18, 1935; s. Clay Alfred and Irene (Stanton) W.; m. Neva Jo Richardson, July 6, 1957; children: Michael David, Suzanne Marie (dec.). BS, U. Washington, 1957; MBA, Cornell U., 1960; PhD, Stanford U., 1967. Rsch. assoc. Stanford (Calif.) U., 1962-67; asst. prof. Ariz. State U., Tempe, 1965-66; assoc. prof. Purdue U., West Lafayette, Ind., 1967-76; prof. Ind. U., Bloomington, 1976-90; Macon G. Patton disting. prof. U. N.C., Chapel Hill, 1990—. Vis. prof. Shanghai Inst. Mech. Engring., 1986-87, Chinese U. of the Hong Kong, 1996, Victoria U., New Zealand, 1996, Canterbury U., New Zealand, 1996; adj. prof. Inst. for Mgmt. Devel., Lausanne, Switzerland, 1981-82, 85-90; dir., founder Global Mfg. Rsch. Group, 1990—; cons. in field. Author: Master Production Scheduling: Theory and Practice, 1979, Manufacturing Planning Control Systems, 1984, 5th edit., 2002, International Operations Management, 1989, Integrated Production and Inventory Management, 1993, Why ERP?, 2000; editor: Internat. Jour. Prodn. Econs., 1991-95, Global Manufacturing Practices, 1993. Recipient Lilly Alumni MBA Teaching Excellence award, 1990, Disting. Rsch. award Kenan-Flagler Sch., 1998. Fellow Decision Scis. Inst. (past pres., disting. svc. award 1984), Pan Pacific Bus. Assn. (mem. coun.); mem. Ops. Mgmt. Assn. (pres. 1992-93), Am. Prodn. Inventory Control Soc., Internat. Soc. Inventory Rsch. (mem. coun., pres.). Avocations: travel, winemaking. Office: U NC Kenan-Flagler Sch Chapel Hill NC 27599-3490 E-mail: clay_whybark@unc.edu.

WHYBROW, JOHN WILLIAM, electronics company executive; b. Hatfield, Eng., Mar. 11, 1947; s. Charles Earnest James and Doris Beatrice (Abbott) W.; m. Pauline Miriam Hobart, Oct. 19, 1968; children; Mark Charles, Andrea Patricia. BSc (hons.), Imperial Coll., London, 1968; MBA, Manchester Bus. Sch., England, 1973. Plant dir. Philips Components, Eng., 1983-86, Philips SemiConductors, Eng., 1986-88; mng. dir. TDS Circuits PLC, Eng., 1988-90; tech. dir. Philips Components UK, Eng., 1990-93; chmn., mng. dir. Philips Elect. U.K., Eng., 1993-95; pres., CEO Philips Lighting Holding BV, The Netherlands, 1995—2001; v.p. Philips Electronics N.V., 1998—, mem. governing com. The Netherlands, 2001—. Dir. Teletext Holding, Eng., 1993-95; non-exec. dir. Wolseley Plc, 1997—; chmn. lumileds Lighting BV, 1997-99. Mem.: Inst. of Dirs., East India Club. Avocation: sailing. Home: Hill House Clapgate Ln Slinfold West Sussex RH13 7QU England Office: Royal Philips Electronics Breitner Tower 13th Fl PO Box 77900 1070 MX Amsterdam Netherlands E-mail: john.whybrow@philips.com.

WHYBROW, PETER CHARLES, psychiatrist, educator, author; b. Hertforshire, Eng., June 13, 1939; U.S. citizenship, 1975; s. Charles Ernest and Doris Beatrice (Abbott) W.; children: Katherine, Helen. Student, Univ. Coll., London, 1956-59; MB BS, Univ. Coll., 1962; diploma psychol. medicine, Conjoint Bd., London, 1968; MA (hon.), Dartmouth Coll., 1974, U. Pa., 1984. House officer endocrinology Univ. Coll. Hosp., 1962, sr. house physician psychiatry, 1963-64; house surgeon St. Helier Hosp., Surrey, Eng., 1963; house officer pediatrics Prince of Wales Hosp., London, 1964; resident psychiatry U. N.C. Hosp., 1965-67, instr., research fellow, 1967-68; mem. sci. staff neuropsychiat. research unit Charshalton, Surrey, 1968-69; dir. residency tng. psychiatry Dartmouth Med. Sch., Hanover, N.H., 1969-71, prof. psychiatry, 1970-84, chmn. dept., 1970-78, exec. dean, 1980-83; prof., chmn. dept. psychiatry U. Pa., Phila., 1984-96, Ruth Meltzer prof. psychiatry, 1992; psychiatrist-in-chief Hosp. U. Pa., 1984-96; prof. psychiatry and biobehavioral scis., chmn. dept. psychiatry Sch. Medicine UCLA, 1996—, dir. Neuropsychiatric Inst., 1996—, physician-in-chief Neuropsychiatric Hosp., 1996-99, Judson Braun Prof. of Psychiatry, 1999—. Dir. psychiatry Dartmouth Hitchcock Affiliated Hosp., 1970-78; vis. scientist NIMH, 1978-79; cons. VA, 1970—, NIMH, 1972—; chmn. test com. Nat. Bd. Med. Examiners, 1977-84; researcher psychoendrocrinology. Author: Mood Disorders: Toward a New Psychobiology, 1984, The Hibernation Response, 1988, A Mood Apart, 1997; editor: Psychosomatic Medicine, 1977; mem. editl. bd. Cmty. Psychiatry, Psychiat. Times, Directions in Psychiatry, Neuropsychopharmacology, Depression; contbr. articles to profl. jours. Recipient Anclote Manor award psychiat. rsch. U. N.C., 1967, Sr. Investigator award nat. Alliance for Rsch. into Schizophrenia and Depression, 1989; Josiah Macy Jr. Found. scholar, 1978-79; fellow Cen. for Advanced Studies in Behavioral Sci., Stanford, 1993-94; recipient Lifetime Investigator award NDMDA, 1996; decorated Knight of Merit, Sovereign Order of St. John of Jerusalem, 1993. Fellow AAAS, Am. Psychiat. Assn., Royal Coll. Psychiatrist (founding mem.), Am. Coll. Psychiatrists, Ctr. Advanced Study of Behavioral Scis. (hon.), Soc. Psychosomatic Rsch. London (hon.); mem. Am. Assn. Chmn. Depts. Psychiatry (pres. 1977-78), Royal Soc. Medicine, Am. Psychopath Assn., Am. Coll. Neuropsychopharmacology, Soc. Biol. Psychiatry, N.Y. Acad. Scis., Soc. Neurosci., Sigma Xi, Alpha Omega Alpha. Office: UCLA Sch Medicine Neuropsychiat Rsch Inst 760 Westwood Plz Los Angeles CA 90095-8353

WHYTE, BRUCE LINCOLN, management executive, marketing professional; b. N.Y.C., Mar. 13, 1941; s. Lincoln Dodge and Louise (Connor) W.; m. Judith McCarthy. BS, Fordham U., N.Y., 1962; MS, NYU, 1963. Editor corp. planning Am. Airlines, N.Y.C., 1963-65; sr. mktg. analyst Ea. Airlines, 1965-67; v.p. Deckcraft Corp., 1967-69; founder & pres. Original Print Collectors Group, 1972; chmn. bd. OPCG (Sub. Reader's Digest), 1980-84; pres. Bruce Whyte Enterprises, internat. fine arts bus., 1984-92. Cons. mktg. The Prudential Co., N.Y.C., 1986, Am. Express, N.Y.C., 1987; sr. mktg. cons. A.R.T. Corp., N.Y.C., 1988; bus. cons. Mystic Seaport Mus., 1990—; Am. Art liaison Doctors of the World, Paris, 1992; chmn. Bus. Incubator Group Corp. Kingston, N.Y., 1993—; gen. mgr. Sherpa's Pet Trading Co., N.Y.C., 1996; exec. v.p. Sanctuary, Inc., N.Y.C., 1996-99, chmn. nat. bd. advisors, 2000—; pres. Bruce Whyte Bus. Devel. Co., 1998—; cons. N.Y. State coun. on the Arts, 1996-97; registered expert witness Dept. Treas., 1983—; mng. dir. Venture Capital Forum, 1995-96; tech. assistance program cons. N.Y. State Govt., 1996—; pres. Bruce Whyte Cons., 1998—; trustee Integrity Global Asset Mgmt., 1999—; gen. devel. dir. First Alert, Rockville Centre, N.Y., 1998—; pres. disaster recovery plans and response devel. Disaster Recovery Experts, Inc., Rockville Centre, 1999—; trustee Dow Jones Internet Index Fund/Dow Jones, Global Biotech. Index Fund, Dow Jones Global Wireless Commn. Fund Index, Wakefield, R.I., 19992001. Editor: Art Newsletter OPCG Newsletter, 1972-84 (Best award in U.S.A. 1983-84). Sr. advisor U.S. Congl. Adv. Bd., Wash. 1981-83; chmn. Com. U.S. Senatorial Bus. Adv. Bd., Wash. 1981-83; advisor N.Y. Dept. State, 1993; trustee, v.p. Hist. Preservation Soc., N.Y.C. 1986-92, U.S. art liaison Found. Mitterand (The Universal Declaration of Human Rights) on behalf of Amnesty Internat., U.N., UNESCO, High Commn. on Refugees, Nat. Mus., Heads of State, Paris, N.Y.C., 1989.; consumer art protection legis. advisor, atty. gen. N.Y. State Senate and Assembly, 1981; pres. Ulster Arts Alliance, 1993-96; chmn. Kingston Carnegie Libr./Pub. Mus., 1993, Mus. Arts and Tech. Old City Hall, 1994-95; trustee Entrepreneurial Catalyst Forum, 1994-96; advisor Congl. Bus. Commn., 2002--; Conn. Congl. Com. voting del. to U.S. Congress, The White House and IRS, 2002--; mem. nat. adv. bd. Am. Security Coun., 1981-93. Recipient Best of Art Catalogues award, Sroge Colorado Springs, 1983, Gold medal Congress Majority Whip Tom DeLay, 2002; named to U.S. Congl. Bus. HOnor Roll., 2002, NRCE Congl. Spkrs. Cir., 2002; Artist fellow, 1988—. Mem. Fine Arts Publ. Assn. (bd. dirs. 1984—), The Nat. Arts Club (gov., treas. 1972-74, 86—), U.S. C. of C. Office: 331 Stratfield Rd Fairfield CT 06432-1874

WHYTE, GEORGE KENNETH, JR. lawyer; b. Waukegan, Ill., Oct. 10, 1936; s. George K. and Ella Margaret (Osgood) W.; m. Ann B. Challoner, June 20, 1964; children: Mary, Douglas. AB in Polit. Sci., Duke U., 1958; LLB, U. Wis., 1965. Bar: Wis. 1965. Law clk. to chief justice Wis. Supreme Ct., Madison, 1965-66; assoc. Quarles & Brady, Milw., 1966-73, ptnr., 1973—. Lt. USN, 1958—62. Mem. ABA (employment law sect.), Wis. Bar Assn. (former chmn. labor and employment law sect.), Rotary (pres. 2002--), The Town Club, Milw. Country Club. Congregationalist. Home: 1026 W Shaker Cir Mequon WI 53092-6034 Office: Quarles & Brady 411 E Wisconsin Ave Ste 2550 Milwaukee WI 53202-4497 E-mail: gkw@quarles.com.

WHYTE, JAMES PRIMROSE, JR. former law educator; b. Columbus, Miss., Aug. 25, 1921; s. James P. and Mary (Savage) W.; m. Martha Ann Jones, Sept. 11, 1948; children— James Jones, Stuart Ward, Wilson Scott. AB, Bucknell U., 1943; MA, Syracuse U., 1948; JD, U. Colo., 1951. Bar: Okla. 1951, Mo. 1957, Va. 1961. With firm Gordon & Whyte, McAlester, Okla., 1951-55; county atty. Pittsburg County, 1955-56; atty. Great Lakes Pipe Line Co., Kansas City, Mo., 1957; prof. law Coll. William and Mary, 1958-82, asst. dean, 1958-68, assoc. dean, 1969-70, dean, 1970-75. Ad hoc arbitrator Fed. Mediation and Conciliation Svc., Va. Dept. Labor, also industry and govt. panels. Contbr. profl. jours.; Mem. editorial adv. bd.: John Marshall Papers, 1966-77. Mem. Bd. Zoning Appeals, Williamsburg, 1971-77, chmn., 1977; trustee, pres. Williamsburg Regional Libr., 1965; trustee Williamsburg Area Meml. Community Ctr., 1963-68, pres., 1966-67. Served with USNR, 1943-46. Mem. Va. State Bar, Phi Beta Kappa, Tau Kappa Alpha, Sigma Tau Delta. Home and Office: 5626 Boatwright Cir Williamsburg VA 23185-3799

WHYTE, MICHAEL PETER, medicine, pediatrics and genetics educator, research director; b. N.Y.C., Dec. 19, 1946; s. Michael Paul and Sophie (Dziuk) W.; m. Gloria Frances Golenda, Oct. 26, 1974; 1 child, Catherine Alexandra. BA in Chemistry, NYU, 1968; MD, SUNY, Bklyn., 1972. Diplomate Am. Bd. Internal Medicine, Nat. Bd. Med. Examiners. Intern, 1st yr. resident dept. medicine NYU Sch. Medicine Bellevue Hosp., N.Y.C., 1972-74; clin. assoc. devel. and metabolic neurology br. Nat. Inst. Neurol. and Communicative Disorders and Stroke NIH, Bethesda, Md., 1974-76; fellow divsn. bone and mineral metabolism dept. medicine Wash. U. Sch. Medicine, 1976-79, instr. dept. medicine, 1979-80, asst. sci. dir. Clin. Rsch. Ctr., 1979—; asst. physician Barnes Hosp., 1979—; dir. Metabolism Clinic Shriners Hosp. Crippled Children, St. Louis, 1979—; staff physician St. Louis Children's Hosp., 1979—; NIH clin. assoc. physician Clin. Rsch. Ctr. Wash. U. Sch. Medicine, 1980-82, asst. prof. medicine dept. medicine, 1980-86, assoc. prof. medicine dept. medicine, 1986-91, asst. prof. pediatrics Edward Mallinckrodt dept. pediatrics, 1982-89, assoc. prof. pediatrics Edward Mallinckrodt dept. pediatrics, 1989-92, prof. medicine dept. medicine, 1991—, prof. pediatrics Edward Mallinckrodt dept. pediatrics, 1992—, prof. genetics James S. McDonell dept. genetics, 1997—; med. dir. Metabolic Rsch. Unit Shriners Hosp. Crippled Children, St. Louis, 1982-2000, mem. staff., 1983—; assoc. attending physician Jewish Hosp. St. Louis, 1983—. Staff cons. Shriners Hosp. Crippled Children, St. Louis, 1979-83, Mexico City, 1991—; editl. bd. Calcified Tissue Internat., 1995-2000, Jour. Bone and Mineral Rsch., 1994—; med. adv. bd. Osteogenesis Imperfecta Found., 1986—, med. adv. panel Paget's Disease Found., 1986—; chmn. med. adv. com., bd. dirs. Osteogenesis Found., 1995—; med.-scientific dir. Ctr. for Metabolic Bone Disease and Molecular Rsch. Shriners Hosp. Children, St. Louis, 2000—. Assoc. editor: Primer on Metabolic Bone Diseases and Disorders of Mineral Metabolism, 1990, 93, 96; assoc. editor Calcified Tissue Internat., 1989-2000; contbr. chpts. to books, articles to profl. jours. Lt. comdr. USPHS, 1974-76. Fellow Am. Coll. of Endocrinology; mem. Am. Soc. Cell Biology, Am. Soc. Clin. Investigation, Am. Coll. Physicians (assoc.), Am. Fedn. Clin. Rsch., Am. Soc. Advancement Sci., Am. Soc. Bone and Mineral Rsch. (ednl. com. 1987—, Fuller Albright award 1987, Young Investigator award 1983, Dr. Boy Frame award 1997), Am. Soc. Human Genetics, Endocrine Soc., Soc. Exptl. Biology and Medicine, Japanese Soc. Inherited Metabolic Disease (hon.). Office: Barnes-Jewish Hosp 216 S Kingshighway Blvd Saint Louis MO 63110-1026 Business E-Mail: mwhyte@shrinenet.org.

WHYTE, NANCY MARIE, performing arts educator; b. Myrtlepoint, Oreg., Mar. 12, 1948; d. Lawrence Edward and Carol Elizabeth (Johnson) Guderian; m. Anthony John Whyte, Aug. 7, 1967 (div. Sept. 1968); 1 child, Charles Lawrence; m. Douglas Brian Graff, June 27, 1971 (div. Oct. 1974); m. Lawrence Hanson, Mar. 12, 1976 (div. Aug. 1984); m. Joseph Paul Deacon, Aug. 10, 1985; 1 child, Nina Alexandra. Student, U. Wash., 1969-72, Am. Sch. Dance, 1972; BA, Evergreen State Coll., 1987. Owner, dir. Nancy Whyte Sch. Ballet, Bellingham, Wash., 1969—; artistic dir. Garden Street Dance Players, 1969-72, MT Baker Ballet, Bellingham, 1975—; co-dir. Exptl. Performance Workshop, 1975-77; instr. creative dance St. Paul's Primary Sch., 1993-97; facilitator dance workshop Allied Arts/Whatcom Co., 1995—. Guest lectr. Western Wash. U., Bellingham, 1976—83, Bellingham, 1996—; guest faculty Dance Theatre N.W., Tacoma, 1995—; liturgical dance cons. Assumption Cath. Sch., 2001—. Author: Memoirs of a Child of Theatre Street, 1993; soloist Raduga Folk Ballet/N.Y. Character Ballet, N.Y.C., 1978-79; choreographer numerous ballets, 1972—. Mem. Nat. Dance Assn., Regional Dance Am. (assoc.). Democrat. Avocations: voice, writing. Office: MT Baker Ballet 1412 Cornwall Ave PO Box 2393 Bellingham WA 98227-2393

WIANT, SARAH KIRSTEN, law library administrator, educator; b. Waverly, Iowa, Nov. 20, 1946; d. James Allen and Eva (Jorgensen) W.; m. Robert E. Akins. BA, Western State Coll., 1968; MLS, U. North Tex., 1970; JD, Washington & Lee U., 1978. Asst. law libr. Tex. Tech. U., 1970-72, 020, Washington & Lee U., Lexington, Va., 1972—, dir., 1978—, asst. prof. law, 1978-83, assoc. prof. law, 1984-92, prof. law, 1993—. Participant Conf. on Fair Use, NII, 1995-98. Co-author: Copyright Handbook, 1984, Libraries and Copyright: A Guide to Copyright Law in the 1990s, 1994, Legal Research in the District of Columbia, Maryland, and Virginia, 1995, 2d edit., 2000; contbr. chpts. to books; mem. adv. bd. Westlaw, 1990-93. Mem.: ABA (com. on librs. 1987—93), U.S. Trademark Assn., Maritime Law Assn., Spl. Librs. Assn. (chair copyright com. 1990—96, John Cotton Dana award 1997), Am. Law Sch. (chmn. sec. on librs. 1990—92, accreditation com. 1991—94), Am. Assn. Law Librs. (copyright office rep., mem. copyright com. 1990—93, mem. exec. bd. 1981—84, Pres.' award 2001, Spl. Dist. Svc. award Southeastern chpt. 1997). Office: Washington & Lee U Law Libr Lewis Hall Lexington VA 24450 E-mail: wiants@wlu.edu.

WIATER, RICHARD M. manufacturing executive; b. Green Bay, Wis., Jan. 21, 1936; s. Adam Frank and Evelyn Catherine (Griakowski) W.; m. Eleanor G. Wiater, Mar. 17, 1987. Acctg. degree, Xavier U., 1961. Acct. P&G, Cin., 1957-62, various, 1963-66; mgr. auditing Aircraft Engine Group-GE, Cin., 1967-70, mgr. mfg. fin. analysis resource planning, 1971-78, mgr. fin. analysis overseas mfg., 1978-85; dir. Tusas Engine Industries, Aircraft Engine-GE, Turkey, 1986-89; mgr. GE90 fin. and bus. planning Aircraft Engine Group-GE, Cin., 1990-95; bus. cons., 1996-98; pres. Tactical Vehicle Sys. divsn. Stewart & Stevenson Svc., Inc., Sealy, Tex., 1999-2000, COO Specialty Wheeled Vehicle divsn. Houston, 2001—. Mem. AUSA, NDIA. Avocations: history, woodworking.

WIATR, CHRISTOPHER LOUIS, microbiologist; b. Chgo., Jan. 5, 1948; s. Joseph Thomas and Beatrice Harriet (Kaminski) Wiatr; m. Jeanne Lynn Malecki, Oct. 20, 1978; children: Kelli Jean, Christopher Joseph, Kaycee Lynn, Kirby Ann, Nicholas Aloysius. BS, Ill. Benedictine Coll., 1969; MS, IIT, 1974; PhD, U. Ill., Chgo., 1985. Cert. tchr. Tchr., coach St. Rita High Sch., Chgo., 1969-74; rsch. microbiologist Swift & Co./Esmark/Beatrice Foods, 1974-75, lab. mgr., 1975-76, tech. dir. rsch. and quality assurance, 1976-79; sr. microbiologist Nalco Chem. Co. Water and Waste Treatment R & D, Naperville, 1985-87, sr. rsch. microbiologist, 1988, group leader water microbiology, 1989-91; group leader Pulp & Paper Chems. R & D, 1991-94; mgr. microbiology and biochemistry R&D Calgon Corp.-ECCI, Pitts., 1994-2000; mgr. tech. support formulator chem. divsn. Buckman Labs., Memphis, 2000—; assoc. Water Techs. Tech. Com., 2000-2001, assoc. water com., 2001—, assoc. presentations subcom., 2001—. Reviewer Nat. Assn. Corrosion Engrs; chmn. biocide and biofilms session Internat. Water Conf., 1996-98; conducted workshops Mont. State U., Bozeman, 1990, Ill. Inst. Tech., Chgo., 1993, U. Ga., Athens, 1995, SUNY, Farmington, 1999. Author: Microbially Influenced Corrosion, 2002; contbr. articles to profl. jours. Eagle scout, merit badge counselor Boy Scouts Am., 1963—; com. Maplebrook I Swim Club, Naperville, 1990-94; football coach St. Raphael, Naperville, 1993-94. Named Researcher of Yr., Nalco Chem. Co., 1987. Mem. TAPPI (microbiology and microbiol tech. and water quality com. 1993-98), Am. Chem. Soc., Nat. Assn. Corrosion Engrs., Soc. Indsl. Microbiology, Am. Soc. for Microbiology, Assn. Water Technologies, Sigma Xi (pres. Nalco chpt. 1991-92). Roman Catholic. Achievements include 15 patents; enzyme applications for controlling bacterial adhesion on equipment and surfaces; nontoxic biocontrol; recognition as expert on biofilms, microbiologically influenced corrosion and molecular biology. E-mail: clwiatr@buckman.com.

WIATR, JEANNE MALECKI, education educator, educator; b. Chgo., July 20, 1952; d. Aloysius John and Eugenia (Szumik) Malecki; m. Christopher Wiatr, Oct. 20, 1978; children: Kelli, C.J., Kaycee, Kirby, Nicholas. BA, Roosevelt U., 1974, MA, 1976; postgrad., No. Ill. U., 1990-95, U. Pitts., 1998. Cert. tchr., Ill. Head tchr. Chgo. Assn. for Retarded Citizens, 1974—78; children's program coord. Parklawn Sch., Oak Lawn, 1979—85; children's reference libr. Woodridge Libr., Woodridge, 1986—87; instr. Coll. of DuPage, Glen Ellyn, 1987—95, instr. kids on campus, 1989—95; art instr. Wesley Acad., 1996—97; supplemental instrn. specialist U. Pitts., 1997—2001, U. Memphis, 2001; student acad. support Rhodes Coll., 2001—. Homebound tutor Dist. 203, Naperville, Ill., 1988-94; tutor, cons. Ednl. Svcs. of Glen Ellyn, 1992-95; program specialist Monyough Cmty. Svcs., 1996; storyteller, lectr. Dist. 203/204 and pvt. groups, DuPage County, Ill. and McMurray, Pa.; coord. supplemental instrn. program U. Pitts., 2001—. Master catechist St. Raphael REACH Program, Naperville, 1987-95; catechist St. Benedict The Abbot, McMurray. Roman Catholic. Avocations: cartooning and drawing, travel, golf. Home: 2910 Oakleigh Ln Germantown TN 38138-7646 E-mail: jwiatr@pitt.edu.

WIATT, CAROL STULTZ, elementary education educator; b. Roanoke, Va., July 9, 1946; d. Hubert Grant and Irene Ella (Barbour) Stultz (dec.); m. Alexander Lloyd Wiatt, June 14, 1969 (div.); children: Alexander Todd II, Christopher Campbell. BS in Elem. Edn., Radford U., 1968; cert., Coll. of William and Mary, 1991. Cert. elem. and mid. sch. prin., geography and elem. grades tchr. Tchr. 4th grade Roanoke County Pub. Schs. Sys., 1968-70; tchr. 6th grade Richmond (Va.) Pub. Schs. Sys., 1970-73; tchr. 5th and 6th grades Newport News (Va.) Pub. Schs. Sys., 1974-91, staff devel. specialist, 1991-93, tchr. 5th grade, 1993-99, McIntosh Elem. Sch., 1993-99; tchr. 7th grade reading, language Staunton River Mid. Sch., Moneta, Va., 1999—; tchr. 7th grade Bedford County Pub. Sch., 1999. Adj. faculty, master tchr. Hampton (Va.) U., 1988—; adj. faculty Christopher Newport U., Newport News, 1988-93, prof., 1993-94; adj. faculty U. Va., 1999—; computer specialist Newport News Pub. Schs. Sys., 1987-91; prin. Hidewood Elem. Sch., summer 1994, Newport News Pub. Sch. Enrichment Summer Sch., 1996—; adv. com. on tech. NNPS, 1997-98. Author: DESIGNS, 1986; contbr. articles to profl. jours. and newspapers. Active Friends of Mariners' Mus., Newport News, 1987-99; chmn. cultural arts com. Newport News Coun. PTA, 1980-83, 1st v.p., 1981-83, treas., 1983-85; mem. hospitality com. Hidenwood Sch. PTA, 1985-86, chmn. membership com., 1986-88; bd. dirs. Hidenwood Recreational Assn., Newport News, 1988-92. Recipient Hon. Mention, Tchr. of Yr. awards The Consortium for Interactive Instrn., 1987, 90; fellow Old Dominion U. Coll. Edn.; named Elem. Tchr. of Yr. Daily Press and Cannon, 1991, Va. Tech. Tchr. of Yr., 1998. Mem. ASCD, NEA, ICCE, AAUW, Va. Assn. Curriculum and Devel., Va. Edn. Assn., Va. Edn. Math. Assn., Va. Tech. Edn. Assn., Va. Geography Soc., Va. State Reading Assn. (chmn. tech. and reading com. 1997-98), Newport News Edn. Assn., Peninsula Coun. Math. of Va. (v.p. 1987-88), Newport News Reading Coun, Kappa Delta Pi. Republican. Baptist. Home: 312 Ashley Ct Vinton VA 24179-1800 Office: Staunton River Mid Sch 1 Golden Eagle Dr Moneta VA 24121-9616

WIBERG, DONALD MARTIN, electrical engineering educator, consultant; b. Battle Creek, Mich., Sept. 20, 1936; s. Martin and Lina (Havstein) W.; children: Erik M., Kristin A., Kenneth C. BS, Calif. Inst. Tech., 1959, MS, 1960, PhD, 1965. Registered profl. engr., Calif. Sr. design engr. Convair, San Diego, 1964-65; asst. prof. elec. engring. UCLA, 1965-71, assoc. prof., 1971-77, prof., 1977-94, prof. anesthesiology, 1979-94, vice chmn. dept. elec. engring., 1985-86, prof. emeritus, 1994-2001, U. Calif., Santa Cruz, 2001—, rsch. prof. Ctr. for Adaptive Optics, 2002. Cons. in field; vis. prof. German Rsch. Orgn. for Air and Space Flight, Munich, 1969-70, dept. elec. engring.

and computer sci. U. Newcastle, Australia, 1989-90, Inst. for Systems Rsch., U. Md., College Park, 1994. Author: State Space and Linear Systems, 1971; co-editor: Regulation of Breathing, 1983. Mem. adv. bd. Parthenia Sch., Los Angeles, 1971-74. Sr. NATO research fellow KFZ Karlsruhe, W.Ger., 1973; sr. Fulbright fellow, Copenhagen, 1976-77, Trondheim, Norway, 1983-84 Fellow IEEE (applications assoc. editor Trans. on Automatic Control 1983, assoc.. editor-at-large 1987-89, 92-94, named Congl. fellow legis. asst. office Senator Tom Harkin, D-IA 1995), Am. Physiol. Soc. (assoc. editor Modelling Methodology Forum 1980-91), Sigma Xi. Home: 2395 Delaware Ave #153 Santa Cruz CA 95060-5716 E-mail: wiberg@ee.ucla.edu.

WIBERG, LARS-ERIK, occupational compatibility consultant; b. Wakefield, Mass., June 1, 1928; s. Sverker Claesson and Ingrid (Heurlin) W.; m. Elizabeth Margaret Allenbrook, Oct. 18, 1957; children: Kirsten, Margaret, Brenda. *Surname "Wiberg" (old Swedish "vi" means little holy place; and "berg" means mountain) has been adopted, historically, by several unconnected families in Sweden. Lars-Erik Wiberg's line derives from an ancestor, "Troells," born in Bjära in southern Sweden in 1509, whose descendants are documented in Bjäraslākten I ("släkten" means family), published in 1958. The Wiberg branch of this family adopted the surname in the early 1800s. Father Sverker brought the family's share of the name to America when he emigrated in 1909 (sponsored as a prize fighter). He mastered English, qualified as one of the first instructor pilots in WW I, and ultimately founded a still-flourishing millwork dealership.* BS in Geology, MIT, 1950; MA in Teaching, Harvard U., 1952. From engr. to dir. corp. communications EG&G Inc., Boston and Bedford, Mass., 1956-69; from asst. v.p. to v.p. compensation and orgnl. planning First Nat. Bank of Boston, 1969-81; cons. Rockport, Mass., 1981—. Lectr. human resources mgmt. Boston U., 1988-92; lectr. job search and career planning U. Karlstad, Sweden, 1992. *Lars-Erik Wiberg is the inventor of "WIST," a race and gender-neutral system that can be used by anyone having English fluency to describe and measure occupational compatibilities. Based on knowledge and perspectives of Carl Gustav Jung and Emanuel Swedenborg, it affords men and women the ability to determine for themselves which career directions will best emphasize their strengths and minimize their weaknesses. He also developed a unique structure for examining: preferred methods of learning; patterns of decision-making; styles of leadership; and personal values. "Most of us are well-motivated at heart. We really want to do good work. We are capable of strong, personal commitment. Nevertheless, indifferent motivation and weak commitment too often prevail. The main culprit is the wrong job!"* Author: It's Your Move, 1991; inventor in field; interviewed in Rockport Recollected. Mem. Gov. John A. Volpe's Mgmt. Engring. Task Force, 1965; mem. Planning Bd., Rockport, 1965-72, chmn., 1969-72; pres. ch. coun. Swedenborg Chapel, Cambridge, Mass., 1984—; dir. Mass. New Ch. Union, 1990—; mem. Zoning Bd. Appeals, Rockport, 1986—; mem. Site Rev. com., Rockport, 1999-2001. 1st lt. USAF, 1953-55. Mem. Affiliated New Eng. Cons. (founder Lexington, Mass. 1985), Life Ext. Found., Heritage Found., Swedenborg Sci. Assn. Avocations: church work, home repairs, music, cooking, reading. Home and Office: 90 South St Rockport MA 01966-1916

WIBRIGHT, EDDY ANN, secondary education educator; b. Ashland, Kans., July 8, 1953; d. Henry Edgar and Donna Marie (Largent) W. BS in Edn., Emporia (Kans.) State U., 1974, MLS, 1979. Cert. tchr., Kans. Tchr. lang. arts Greensburg (Kans.) H.S., 1975-78; libr. dir. Ida Long Goodman Meml. Libr., St. John, 1984-87; tchr. lang. arts Unified Sch. Dist. 350, Kans., 1979—, chmn. dept., 1987—. Pres. Profl. Devel. Coun., St. John, 1992-96. Mem. Nat. Coun. Tchrs. English, Kans. Edn. Assn., St. John Tchrs. Assn. (sec. 1979—). Avocations: reading, gardening, computing, birdwatching, music. Home: 711 N Main St Saint John KS 67576-1533 Office: St John HS 505 N Broadway St Saint John KS 67576-1644

WICE, DURAND COPPLE, security officer; b. Greenville, Ky., July 16, 1946; s. Durham Tate and Eva Jo Wice. BSBA, U. Mo., St. Louis, 1969. Prodn. supr. Chrysler Corp., St. Louis, 1973-74, 77-78; cons. Alexander Proudfoot Co., Chgo. and N.Y.C., 1975-76; productivity specialist Integrated Control Systems, Litchfield, Conn., 1979; security guard, 1988-95; security officer Burns Internat. Security Svcs., San Francisco, 1995—. Recipient Nat. Def. Svc. medal U.S. Army, 1969. Mem. Commonwealth Club, Buckminster Fuller Inst.

WICH, DONALD ANTHONY, JR. lawyer; b. Apr. 13, 1947; s. Donald Anthony and Margaret Louise (Blatz) W. BA with honors, Notre Dame U., Ind., 1969; JD, Notre Dame U., 1972. Bar: Fla. 1972, U.S. Dist. Ct. (so. dist.) Fla. 1972, U.S. Ct. Appeals (5th and 11th cirs.) 1982, U.S. Supreme Ct. 1976; cert. civil trial lawyer, 1983. Assoc. VISTA, Miami, Fla., 1972-74; atty. Legal Svcs., 1973-75; adj. prof. law U. Miami, 1974-75; ptnr. Wich, Wich & wich, P.A., Ft. Lauderdale, Fla., 1992—. Pres., dir. Legal Aid of Broward, Ft. Lauderdale, 1976-82; mem. 17th Cir. Jud. Nominating Commn., 1998-02; spl. prosecutor, grievance chmn. The Fla Bar, 1982-90; chmn. UPL Standing Com., 2001— Treas. St. Thomas More Sch. of So. Fla., 1989—. Mem. ABA, ATLA, Am. Arbitration Assn., North Broward Bar Assn. (pres. 1983-84), Acad. Fla. Trial Lawyers Assn. (sustaining mem.), Broward County Trial Lawyers Assn. (pres. 1988-89, sustaining mem.), Broward Bar Assn. (chmn. legis. com. 1984-85, exec. com. 1986-92, 94-98, chmn. bench-bar com. 1993-94, chmn. clk.-bar com. 1993-95, mem. 1998-99, pres. 1997-98), Tex. Trial Lawyers Assn., N.Y. Trial Lawyers Assn., Pompano Beach C. of C. (pres. 1989-90, dir. 1984-87, 92-95, govtl. affairs chmn. 1983-84, art show chmn. 1984-85, seafood festival chmn. 1986-90), Notre Dame Frederick Sorin Soc., Rotary (bd. dirs. 1987-91), Woodhouse (bd. dirs. 1990-91). Office: Wich Wich & Wich PA 2400 E Commercial Blvd Fort Lauderdale FL 33308-4030 E-mail: wich3@msn.com.

WICHERN, DEAN WILLIAM, business educator; b. Medford, Wis., Apr. 29, 1942; s. Arthur William and Rebecca Ann (Ambler) W.; m. Dorothy Jean Rutkowski, Dec. 7, 1968; children: Michael, Andrew. BS in Math., U. Wis., Madison, 1964, MS in Stats., 1965, PhD in Stats., 1969. Instr. Sch. Bus. U. Wis., Madison, 1967-69, asst. prof., 1969-72, assoc. prof., 1972-76, prof., 1976-84, chmn. quantitative analysis dept., 1975-78; prof. Coll. Bus. Adminstrn. Tex. A&M U., 1984—, head info. and ops. mgmt. dept., 1984-88, 97-98, assoc. dean, 1988-95, John E. Pearson prof. bus. adminstrn., 1985—. Vis. prof. Math. Rsch. Ctr., 1978-79. Co-author: Intermediate Business Statistics, 1977, Applied Multivariate Statistical Analysis, 5th edit., 2002, Business Statistics: Decision Making With Data, 1997, Business Forecasting, 7th edit., 2001; mem. editl. bd. Jour. Bus. and Econ. Stats., 1983—91. Mem. Royal Statis. Soc., Am. Statis. Assn., Inst. Oper. Rsch. and Mgmt. Sci., Internat. Inst. of Forecasters, Beta Gamma Sigma, Phi Kappa Phi. Home: 9217 Riverstone Ct College Station TX 77845-8333 Office: Tex A&M U Coll Bus Adminstrn Dept Info And Opers Mgmt College Station TX 77843-4217 E-mail: d-wichern@tamu.edu.

WICHINSKY, GLENN ELLIS, lawyer; b. Monticello, N.Y., Dec. 22, 1952; s. Michael A. Wichinsky and Ann (Pesekow) Kaplan; m. Lillian Carol Rindom, June 6, 1976; children: Laura, David. BA in Polit. Sci., U. Miami, 1974; JD, U. Pacific, 1982. Bar: Fla. 1982, Nev. 1983, U.S. Dist. Ct. Nev. 1984. Legis. asst. Calif. Assembly, Sacramento, 1978-80; legal advisor Community Legal Svcs., 1980-81; jud. clk. Sacramento County Superior Ct., 1981-82; assoc. Rogers, Monsey, Woodbury, Las Vegas, Nev., 1983; pvt. practice Las Vegas and Boca Raton, Fla., 1983—. Gaming law com. State Bar Nev., 1999; pres. Global Gaming and Tech., Inc., Boca Raton, 2000—; of counsel Sheridan and Carroll, LLP, Sacramento, 2000—. Chmn. transp. com. Palm Beach County (Fla.) Coop., 1987-89, Palm Beach County Task Force for Responsible Representation, 1989-91; mem. Palm Beach County Comprehensive Planning Adv. Com., 1988, Zoning Bd. Adjustment, 1991-2001, West Boca Action Com., Boca Raton, 1986-90; apptd. FAA Part 150 Noise Study Com. Boca Raton Mcpl. Airport, 1999-2000; mem., bd. dirs. Boca Raton Airport Action Group, 1999; mem. FAA Part 150 noise study com. Boca Raton Mcpl. Airport, 1999—. Music scholar U. Miami, 1970. Mem. ABA (com. on air and space law), Internat. Assn. Gaming Attorneys, Fla. Bar Assn. (aviation law com.), Palm Beach County Bar Assn., South Palm Beach County Bar Assn., Tau Epsilon Phi (pres. 1973-74). Democrat. Jewish. Avocations: skiing, travel, aviation, meteorology. Office: 1200 N Fed Hwy Ste 200 Boca Raton FL 33432 E-mail: gwichinsky@sheridancarroll.com., gwichinsky@aol.com.

WICHMAN, EDNA CAROL, media specialist, librarian; b. Dodge City, Kans., Jan. 11, 1945; d. Robert Lyle and Mabel Josephine (Woodka) Smith; m. Kenneth C. Wichman, Sept. 2, 1967; children: Lorie Jean, Curtis Clouse. BSEd, Emporia State U., 1967, MEd, 1971. Kindergarten, elem. libr. Sinai/Timmons Elem. Sch., Bonner Springs, Kans., 1967-69; with Head Start, summer 1968; tchr. 3d grade Osage City (Kans.) Elem., 1970-71, Black Lane Elem., Fairborn, Ohio, 1971-77; media specialist Cen. Jr. High Sch., 1977-81, Fairborn High Sch., 1981-96, Northridge Local Schs., Montgomery County, 1996-00, ret., 2000. Presenter Edn. Day Western Ohio, Fairborn, 1988-90, Tech. Fair Miami U., Middletown, 1990, Ohio Dept. Edn., Columbus, 1990, OELMA conf., 1998; prof. Sch. Edn., Wright State U.; faculty edn. leadership dept. U. Dayton Edn.; librn. Am. Rsch. Ctr. Egypt, 2001. Mem. bd. elections Greene County, Xenia, Ohio; treas. Greene County Dem. Party, 1982-88, chair, 1988-90; mem. Friends of Fairborn Libr.; chairperson Greene County Mental Health Drug and Alcohol Bd., 1994-95, Ea. Miami Valley ADMH Bd., 1995-96, bd. dirs., 1995—; mem. Bath Twp. Zoning Bd., 1998—. Named Keeper of Flame Sec. State of Ohio, Dayton, 1990, Media Specialist of Yr. Ohio Sch. Libr., 1991; named to Greene County Women's Hall of Fame, Fairborn, 1990. Mem. AAUW (pres. 1984-88, Woman of Yr. Fairborn br. 1992, v.p. membership Fairborn br.), NEA (chair congl. contact team 1980-90), ALA, Am. Assn. Sch. Librs., Ohio Edn. Assn. (EPAC chair 1975-89), Fairborn Edn. Assn. (pres. 1975-76, Tchr. Salute 1977), Southwestern Ohio Young Adult Material Rev. Group (pres. 1985-87), Ohio Ednl. Libr./Media Assn. (legis. chairperson state bd.), Phi Delta Kappa. Democrat. Lutheran. Avocations: reading, politics, gardening. Home: 1335 Yellow Springs Fairfield Rd Fairborn OH 45324 Office: Am Rsch Ctr in Egypt Garden City 2 Midan Simon Bolivar Cairo Egypt E-mail: cwichman@aol.com.

WICHMANN, HENRY, JR. accounting educator, researcher; b. Bemidji, Minn., Sept. 14, 1939; s. Henry and Bethel (Wells) W.; m. Nilda Oca, May 25, 1990; children: Holly Brittany, Henry William. BSBA in Mktg., U. Denver, 1962; MA in Bus. Edn., Colo. State Coll., 1965; PhD in Bus. Tchg., U. No. Colo., 1972. CPA, Wis. Asst. buyer May Co. Dept. Stores, Colo., 1962-63; distbritive edn. coord. Newburgh (N.Y.) Free Acad., 1963-64; instr. in bus. adminstrn. and mid-mgmt. Dawson Coll., Mont., 1964-68; tchg. asst. acctg. U. No. Colo., Greeley, 1969-71; instr. mid. mgmt. Casper (Wyo.) Coll., 1971-72; asst. prof. acctg. U. Wis., Eau Claire, 1972-77, U. Wyo., Laramie, 1977-80; assoc. prof. U. Alaska, Anchorage, 1980-85, prof. Fairbanks, 1986-96, head acctg. & info. sys. dept., 1996—. Advisor Mktg. Club, Glendive, Mont., 1964-68; advisor Christmas promotion Laramie C. of C., 1978-80; dir. small bus. inst. U. Alaska, Anchorage, 1980-85; manuscript dir. Nat. Acctg. Assn., Anchorage, 1980-85; bd. dirs. JW Trading Co., Taichung, Taiwan; presenter in field. Contbr. articles to profl. jours. Recipient Keller Trophy, Nat. Assn. Acctg., 1981-82, Pres.'s award Nat. Assn. Acctg., 1985-86, At-Large Achiever Rsch. award Assn. of Govt. Accts., 1991-92, Disting. Theoretical Paper award Inst. Decision Sci., 1982. Mem. AICPA, Am. Acctg. Assn., Nat. Soc. Pub. Accts., Wis. Soc. CPAs, Assn. Govt. Accts., Inst. Mgmt. Accts. (bd. dirs.), Beta Alpha Psi, Beta Gamma Sigma, Alpha Kappa Psi (historian, dist. dir. 1978-80). Baptist. Avocations: hunting, fishing, camping. Home: 1965 Weston Dr Fairbanks AK 99709-6535 Office: U Alaska Sch Mgmt PO Box 756080 Fairbanks AK 99775-6080 E-mail: FFHW@uaf.edu.

WICK, DOUGLAS, producer; m. Tracy Fisher; 3 children. Grad. cum laude, Yale U. Owner Red Wagon Prodns., Culver City, Calif. Assoc. prodr. Starting Over; prodr. Hush, The Craft, Wolf, Working Girl (six Acad. Award Nomiations, five Golden Globes including Best Picture), Stuart Little, Girl, Interrupted, Gladiator, The Hollow Man, Memoirs Of A Geisha. Office: Red Wagon Prodns 10202 Washington Blvd Culver City CA 90232-3119 Fax: 310-244-1480.*

WICK, HILTON ADDISON, lawyer; b. Mt. Pleasant, Pa., Feb. 11, 1920; m. Barbara G. Shaw; children: James H., William S., B. Jane, Ann W., Julia A. BA, Maryville Coll., 1942; JD, Harvard U., 1948. Bar: Vt. 1948. Practiced in, Burlington; ptnr. Wick, Dinse & Allen, 1949-72; CEO Chittenden Bank, Chittenden Corp., 1969—85; bd. dirs. Sentinel Funds, 1970—76; of counsel Dinse, Allen & Erdmann, Burlington, 1972-80; bd. dirs. Nat. Life Ins. Co., 1976—92; of counsel Wick & Maddocks, Burlington, 1980—; state senator Vt., 1989-91; COO Gifford Med. Ctr., Inc., Randolph, 1993-95. Bd. dirs. Blue Cross/Blue Shield Vt., Beach Properties, Inc., Vt. Pub. Radio, chmn., 1990-96. Trustee Middlebury Coll., 1969-85, Champlain Coll., 1974-94, Maryville Coll., 1981-86, Shelburne Mus., 1985-94, Ethan Allen Homestead, 1989-96, Vt. Assn. for Blind and Visually Impaired, 1992-2001; pres. Coll. St. Congl. Ch., 1996-98; bd. dirs. Vt. divsn. Am. Cancer Soc., 1979-93, Intervale Found.; pres. bd. trustees Vt. Law Sch., 1975-95; chmn. bd. trustees Vt. Cmty. Found., 1985-91; chancellor Vt. State Colls., 1984-85; chmn. bd. dirs. Middlebury Coll., 1981-84. Mem. ABA, Vt. Bar Assn. (pres. 1967-68), Chittenden County Bar Assn. (pres. 1963-64), Internat. Soc. Barristers, Am. Bankers Assn. (bd. dirs. 1975-76), Vt. Bankers Assn. (pres. 1973-74), Ethan Allen Club, Harvard Club (Boston and N.Y.C.), Phi Kappa Delta. Home: Two Appletree Point Ln Burlington VT 05401 Office: 308 College St Burlington VT 05401-8319 E-mail: hiltbarb@aol.com.

WICK, LAWRENCE SCOTT, lawyer; b. San Diego, Oct. 1, 1945; s. Kenneth Lawrence (dec.) and Lorrayne (Scott) W.; m. Beverly Ann DeRoss, Aug. 26, 1972 (div.); children: Ryan Scott, Andrew Taylor, Hayley Lauren. BA, Northwestern U., Evanston, Ill., 1967; JD, Columbia U., 1970. Atty. Leydig Voit & Mayer Ltd., Chgo., 1978-84, shareholder, 1984-98; equity ptnr. Wildman, Harrold, Allen & Dixon, 1998—2002; v.p., gen. counsel Lionheart Prodns., Ltd., 1995—; pvt. practice Lake Bluff, Ill., 2002—. V.p., gen. counsel Purple Nurple Prodns. Ltd., 2001—. Contbr. articles to profl. jours. Mem. ABA, Internat. Trademark Assn. (N.Y.), Internat. Trade Assn. (Chgo. chpt.), Assn. Internat. Protection de la Propriete Industrielle (Geneva), Pharm. Trade Marks Group (London), Am. Film Inst. (L.A.), Chgo. Bar Assn. (mem. fin. com.). Avocations: international travel, film, swimming, snorkeling, free diving. Home: 317 Rothbury Ct Lake Bluff IL 60044-1927 E-mail: lwicklb@aol.com.

WICK, ROBERT THOMAS, retired supermarket executive; b. St. Louis, Nov. 26, 1927; s. Robert Berninger and Katherine (Burke) W.; m. Virginia Rose Allen, Sept. 6, 1952; children: Susan, Patrick, Nancy, Robert J. BS, St. Louis U., 1955; cert. in food distbn., Mich. State U., 1956. Sales mgr. Nat. Tea Co., St. Louis, 1966-68, asst. div. mgr., 1968-69, div. mgr. Sioux City, Iowa, 1969-71, Milw., 1971-73, Chgo., 1973-74; v.p., gen. mgr. A&P Food Stores, Indpls., 1975-77; div. v.p. Colonial Food Stores- Grand Union, Norfolk, Va., 1977-79; pres., chief exec. officer Bonnie Be-Lo Markets, Inc., 1979-90, ret., 1990. Bd. dirs. Virginia Beach (Va.) Community Svcs. Bd., 1985-89; mem. adv. bd. Straight, Inc., Chesapeake, Va., 1987-91; dir. Community Alternatives, Inc., Virginia Beach, 1991-92. Tech. cpl. U.S. Army, 1946-48. Recipient Citizen of Yr. award St. Louis Argus Newspaper, 1968. Mem. Food Mktg. Inst. (bd. dirs. 1982-89), Va. Food Dealers Assn. (bd. dirs. 1981-87), Tidewater Retail Mchts. Assn. (pres., bd. dirs. 1981-91). Conservative. Roman Catholic. Avocations: travel, golf, cycling. Home: 801 Winthrope Dr Virginia Beach VA 23452-3940 E-mail: rwick@cox.net.

WICK, WILLIAM SHINN, clergyman, chaplain; b. West Chester, Pa. s. William R. and Barbara (Shinn) W.; m. Debra R. Smith, Apr. 1, 1989; 1 child, Christopher R. BA, Trinity Coll., Deerfield, Ill., 1975; MDiv, Trinity Evang. Div. Sch., Deerfield, 1978. Ordained to ministry Evang. Free Ch. Am., 1978. Pastor Bradford (Vt.) Evang. Free Ch., 1978-85, Evang. Free Ch. Newport, Vt., 1985-89, Grace Evang. Free Ch., Northfield, 1989-96; chaplain Norwich U., 1989—; interim pastor First Bapt. Ch., Barre, Vt., 2001—. Mem. bd. govs. Trinity Western U., Langley, B.C., Can., 1999—. Avocations: alpine skiing, racquetball, tennis, scuba diving, sailing. Home: 763 S Main St Northfield VT 05663-5601 Office: White Chapel Norwich U 158 Harmon Dr Northfield VT 05663-1000 E-mail: chaplain@norwich.edu., theskiingrev@hotmail.com.

WICKE, DALLAS CLYDE, retired aerospace engineer; b. Atwood, Kans., Nov. 18, 1940; s. Ernest William and Edith (Wimer) W. BS in Aerospace Engring., U. Kans., 1962; MS in Aerospace Engring., U. So. Calif., 1968. From assoc. engr. to sr. prin. engr. McDonnell Douglas Corp., Huntington Beach, Calif., 1962—97; sr. prin. engr. The Boeing Co., Anaheim, 1997—2001; ret., 2001. Patentee in field. Mem. AIAA (sr., adv. bd., sect. tech. com. for guidance, navigation, dynamics and control), U. Kans. Alumni Assn., U.S. Ski Assn., Tau Beta Pi, Sigma Tau, Sigma Gamma Tau.

WICKER, DENNIS A. lawyer; b. Sanford, N.C., 1952; s. J. Shelton and Clarice (Burns) W.; m. Alisa O'Quinn; children: Quinn Edward, Jackson Dennis, Harrison Lee. BA in Econs. with honors, U. N.C., 1974; JD, Wake Forest U., 1978. Atty. Love & Wicker, 1978-92; mem. N.C. Ho. of Reps., 1981-92; lt. gov. State of N.C., 1993—2001; attorney Helms, Mulliss & Wicker, PLLC, Raleigh, NC, 2001—. Chmn. law enforcement com., 1983, house com. cts. and adminstrn. justice, 1985, house jud. com., 1987; chmn. N.C. Small Bus. Coun., 1993—, N.C. State C.C. Bd., 1993—, N.C. State Health Purchasing Alliance Bd., 1993—, Gov.'s Task Force on Driving While Impaired, 1994—, N.C. Local Govt. Partnership Coun.; mem. N.C. Capitol Planning Com., 1993—, N.C. Coun. of State, 1993, N.C. Commn. on Bus. Laws and The Economy. Chmn. N.C. Local Govt. Partnership Coun.; chmn. Gov.'s Task Force on Driving While Impaired. Named Legis. of Yr., Children's Learning Disability Assn. N.C.; recipient Jane Alexander Pub. Svc. award MADD, 1993, Pres.'s award N.C. Assn. Educators, Legis. Leadership award Nat. Commn. Against Drunk Driving, 1994; listed among 10 most effective legis. N.C. Ctr. Pub. Policy Rsch. Mem. Phi Beta Kappa. Democrat. Methodist. Office: Helms, Mulliss & Wicker 2600 Two Hannover Sq Raleigh NC 27601*

WICKER, ELMUS ROGERS, economics educator; b. Lake Charles, La., Sept. 13, 1926; s. Elmus Rogers and Georgia Mary (Moss) Wicker; m. Carolyn Braswell, Sept. 18, 1948; children: Vanessa Louise, Roger Andrew. BA, La. State U., 1945, MA, 1948; MPhil, Oxford (Eng.) U., 1951; PhD, Duke U., 1956. Prof. econs. Ind. U., Bloomington, 1955-92, prof. emeritus, 1992—. Author: Federal Reserve Monetary Policy, 1966; co-author: Principles of Monetary Economics, 1975, The Banking Panics of the Great Depression, 1996, Banking Panics of the Gilded Age, 2000. With USN, 1945-46. Rhodes scholar, 1948. Mem. Am. Econ. Assn., Econ. History Assn. Home: 1315 S Nancy St Bloomington IN 47401-6041

WICKER, MARIE PEACHEE, civic worker; b. Detroit, July 9, 1925; d. Charles Andrew and Bessie Louise (Sullivan) Peachee; m. Warren Jake Wicker, July 31, 1948; children: Beth Wicker Walters, Jane Fields Wicker-Miurin, Thomas Alton. BA, Westhampton Coll., 1946; MA, U. N.C., 1950. Test technician N.C. Merit Sys. Coun., Durham, 1950-51; classification analyst N.C. Pers. Dept., Raleigh, 1951-52; engring. placement dir. N.C. State U., 1952-57. Author: You Can Make It Yourself, 1988, First Women of Orange County, N.C., 1994, 2nd edit., 1995, 3d edit., 1997, A History of the Chapel Hill Woman's Club, 1910-1995, 1995. Chmn. Chapel Hill Recreation Commn., 1961-62; legis. chmn. N.C. Congress Parents and Tchrs., 1972-73; mem. Chapel Hill-Carrboro Bd. Edn., 1973-75, Historic Hillsborough (N.C.) Commn., 1987-93, Orange County (N.C.) Commn. for Women, 1992-97; v.p. Friends of the Chapel Hill Sr. Ctr., 1999-2000, pres., 2000-2001, past pres., 2001-02. Recipient Dist. Conservation award N.C. Wildlife Resources Commn., 1987. Mem.: N.C. Coun. Women's Orgns. (bd. dirs. 1990, 1st v.p. 1992—93), N.C. Fedn. Women's Clubs (dist. pres. 1984—86, dist. chmn. conservation dept. 1992—94, state chmn. conservation dept. 1992—94, sec.-treas. past dist. pres. club 1992—94, Sallie Southall Cotten scholarship com. 1994—98), Chapel Hill Women's Club (pres. 1985—87, 1st v.p. 1996—98, bd. dirs. 1998—99, 1st v.p. 1998—2000, 2001—02, pres. 2002—). Democrat. Avocations: cooking, crafts, family history research. Home: 1024 Highland Woods Rd Chapel Hill NC 27517-4410

WICKER, R. DAVID, JR. lawyer; b. Greensboro, N.C., Apr. 11, 1960; s. Ralph D. and Judith (Wade) W.; m. Susan Medders, June 5, 1982; children: Whitney L., Colby D., Lance D. BA in History, U.N.C., Greensboro, 1982; JD, N.C. Ctrl. U., Durham, 1985. Pvt. practice, Durham, 1985-92; ptnr. Roberti, Wittenberg, Lauffer & Wicker, 1992—. Mem. Masons, Shriners. Office: Roberti Wittenberg Lauffer & Wicker 100 E Parrish St Ste 200 Durham NC 27701-3345 E-mail: dwicker@rwhl.com.

WICKER, RICHARD FENTON, JR. editor; b. Benton County, Miss., Mar. 27, 1929; s. Richard Fenton and Willie Thomas (Dunn) W.; m. Louise Zeller, Mar. 29, 1953; children: Richard Fenton III, Stephen Bryant, David William. BA, U. Miss., 1952; MDiv, So. Meth. U., 1955; D Min., McCormick Theol. Sem., Chgo., 1974. Enlisted man, naval aviator USN, 1949-50, commd. ensign, 1950, advanced through grades to capt., 1973, aviation VC-4/VC-33, 1948-51, chaplain, 1955-82; dir. tng. Tidewater Pastoral Coun., Norfolk, Va., 1982-90, dir. clin. svcs., 1990-95; editor Wicker Pub. Co., Virginia Beach, 1988—. Cons. Lee's Friends, Norfolk, 1985—, United Meth. Ch., Norfolk, 1982-95; instr. USN, VA Chaplain Residency, Norfolk, 1985—. Author: The Wicker/Whicker Family, 1989, The Allen Family, 1995, The New Wicker/Whicker Family, 1997; editor Navy Chaplains Jour., 1978. Decorated Legion of Merit, Meritorious Svc. Medal, Air medal with 2 gold stars. Fellow Am. Assn. Pastoral Counselors; mem. Assn. Naval Aviation, Flying Midshipman Assn., Tailhook Assn., U.S. Naval Inst., Lions (pres., dir. 1973—), The Chosin Few, Jamestowne Soc., Order of Descendants of Ancient Planters. Democrat. Methodist. Avocations: medieval history, medieval church music. Office: Wicker Pub Co 5136 Violet Bank Dr Virginia Beach VA 23464-5643

WICKER, ROGER F. congressman, lawyer; b. Pontotoc, Miss., July 5, 1951; m. Gayle Long; children: Margaret, Caroline, McDaniel. BA in Polit. Sci. and Journalism, U. Miss., 1973; JD, Ole Miss Law Sch., 1975. Judge advocate USAF, 1976—80; mem. staff rules com. Staff of U.S. Rep. Trent Lott, 1980-82; pvt. practice, 1982—; mem. Miss. State Senate, 1987—95, U.S. Congress from 1st Miss. dist., 1995—; mem.. house appropriation com, 1995; mem. House Task Force for a Drug Free America, Rep. Policy Com., 2001; mem. subcommittee on labor, health and human svcs. and edn., subcommittee on energy and water development, subcommittee on foreign operations. With USNR, 1980—. Republican. Office: US House Reps 206 Cannon Bldg Washington DC 20515-2401*

WICKER, THOMAS CAREY, JR. judge; b. New Orleans, Aug. 1, 1923; s. Thomas Carey and Mary (Taylor) W.; children: Thomas Carey III, Catherine Anne; m. Jane Anne Trepanier, Dec. 29, 1995. BBA, Tulane U., 1944, LLB, 1949, JD, 1969. Bar: La. 1949. Law clk. La. Supreme Ct., New Orleans, 1949-50; asst. U.S. Atty., 1950-53; practiced in New Orleans, 1953-72; mem. firm Simon, Wicker & Wiedemann, 1953-67; partner firm Wicker, Wiedemann & Fransen, 1967-72; dist. judge Jefferson Parish (La.), 1972-85, judge, Court of Appeal 5th cir., 1985-98, mem. faculty Nat. Jud. Coll., 1979-93, Tulane U. Sch. Law, 1978-83. Past bd. visitors Tulane U.; bd. dirs. La. Jud. Coll.; past pres. Sugar Bowl. Author: (with others) Judicial Ethics, 1982, (with others) Modern Judicial Ethics, 1992; editor Tulane Law Review, 1949. Lt. (j.g.), USNR, 1944-46. Mem. ABA (jud. div. council), La. (chmn. jr. bar sect. 1958-59, gov. 1958, mem. ho. of dels. 1960-72), Jefferson Parish, bar assns., Tulane U. Alumni Assn. (past pres.), Am. Judicature Soc., La. Dist. Judges Assn. (past pres.), Order of Coif, Beta Gamma Sigma, Pi Kappa Alpha. Episcopalian. Clubs: Rotary (pres. 1971-72), Metairie (La.) Country. Avocations: golf, photography, military history.

WICKER, THOMAS GREY, retired journalist; b. Hamlet, N.C., June 18, 1926; s. Delancey David and Esta (Cameron) W.; m. Neva Jewett McLean, Aug. 20, 1949 (div. 1973); children: Cameron McLean, Thomas Grey; m. Pamela Abel Hill, Mar. 9, 1974. AB in Journalism, U. N.C., 1948. Exec dir. Southern Pines (N.C.) C. of C., 1948-49; editor Sandhill Citizen, Aberdeen, N.C., 1949; mng. editor The Robesonian, Lumberton, 1949-50; pub. info. dir. N.C. Bd. Pub. Welfare, 1950-51; copy editor Winston-Salem (N.C.) Jour., 1951-52, sports editor, 1954-55, Sunday feature editor, 1955-56, Washington corr., 1957, editorial writer, city hall corr., 1958-59; assoc. editor Nashville Tennesseean, 1959-60; mem. staff Washington bur. N.Y. Times, 1960-71, chief bur., 1964-68; assoc. editor N.Y. Times, 1968-85, columnist, 1966-91. James K. Batten vis. prof. pub. policy Davidson Coll., 1977; vis. scholar First Amendment Ctr., Nashville, 1998; vis. prof. Journalism Middle Tenn. State U., 1999, U So. Calif., 1999. Author: (novels) The Kingpin, 1953, The Devil Must, 1957, The Judgment, 1961, Facing the Lions, 1973, Unto This Hour, 1984, Donovan's Wife, 1992, Easter Lilly, 1998, (non-fiction) Kennedy without Tears, 1964, JFK and LBJ: The Influence of Personality upon Politics, 1968, A Time to Die, 1975, On Press, 1978, One of Us: Richard Nixon and the American Dream, 1991, Tragic Failure: Racial Integration in America, 1996, Keeping the Record, 2001. Served to lt. (j.g.) USNR, 1952-54. Nieman fellow Harvard, 1957-58, fellow Joan Shorenstein Barone Ctr. on the Press, Politics and Pub. Policy Harvard, 1993. Mem. Soc. Nieman Fellows, Century Assn., Soc. Am. Historians, Writers guild of Am. East.

WICKERT, STEPHAN P. artist, musician; b. Giessen, Germany, Dec. 26, 1911; s. Anton and Maria C. (Klein) Wi.; m. Thilde Kellner, Aug. 3, 1937 (dec. July 1989); children: Max-Albrecht, Christine, Eva, Monika, Gabrielle. Student, Tech. U. Munich, 1935. Tchr. Ludinghausen H.S., Hermann-Lietz Sch., Spiekeroog; tchr. tech. drawing Messerschmitt, Augsburg, Germany, 1939-45; tchr. art Peutinger Gymnasium, 1946-52; draftsman Graflex, Rochester, N.Y., 1952-62, engring. designer, 1962-76. Translator 10 vols. of German folk songs, 2 vols. French folk songs, 1 vol. German Christmas songs, 1 vol. French Christmas songs. With German Army, 1944-45. Democrat. Roman Catholic. Avocations: music, cello, violin, viola. Home: 91 Westerloe Ave Rochester NY 14620

WICKES, GEORGE, English literature educator, writer; b. Antwerp, Belgium, Jan. 6, 1923; came to U.S., 1923; s. Francis Cogswell and Germaine (Attout) W.; m. Louise Westling, Nov. 8, 1975; children by previous marriage: Gregory, Geoffrey, Madeleine (dec.), Thomas, Jonathan. BA, U. Toronto, Ont., Can., 1944; MA, Columbia U., 1949; PhD, U. Calif., Berkeley, 1954. Asst. sec. Belgian Am. Ednl. Found., N.Y.C., 1947-49; exec. dir. U.S. Ednl. Found. in Belgium, 1952-54; instr. Duke U., Durham, N.C., 1954-57; from asst. prof. to prof. Harvey Mudd Coll. and Claremont Grad. Sch., Calif., 1957-70; prof. English and comparative lit. U. Oreg., Eugene, 1970—, dir. comparative lit., 1974-77, head English dept., 1976-83. Lectr. USIS, Europe, 1969, Africa, 1978, 79; vis. prof. U. Rouen, France, 1970, U. Tübingen, Germany, 1981, U. Heidelberg, Germany, 1996. Editor: Lawrence Durrell and Henry Miller Correspondence, 1963, Henry Miller, Letters to Emil, 1989, Henry Miller and James Laughlin: Selected Letters, 1995; Author: Henry Miller, 1966, Americans in Paris, 1969, The Amazon of Letters, 1976: translator: The Memoirs of Frederic Mistral, 1986. Served with U.S. Army, 1943-46. Fulbright lectr. France, 1962-63, 66, 78; sr. fellow Ctr. for Twentieth Century Studies, U. Wis.-Milw., Milwaukee, 1971, Creative Writing fellow Nat. Endowment Arts, 1973, Camargo fellow, 1991. Mem. PEN. Office: U Oreg English Dept Eugene OR 97403

WICKESBERG, ALBERT KLUMB, retired management educator; b. Neenah, Wis., Apr. 2, 1921; s. Albert Henry and Lydia (Klumb) W.; m. Dorothy Louise Ahrensfeld, Oct. 28, 1944; children— Robert, William, James. BA, Lawrence Coll., 1943; MBA, Stanford U., 1948; PhD, Ohio State U., 1955. Staff accountant S.C. Johnson & Son, Inc., Racine, Wis., 1948-50; asst. prof. Sacramento State Coll., 1950-51; prof. U. Minn., Mpls., 1953-86, prof. emeritus, 1987—, chmn. dept. bus. adminstrn., 1959-62, dir. grad. studies, 1963-66, chmn. dept. mgmt. and transp., 1971-77. Author: Management Organization, 1966. Served with AUS, 1943-46, 51-52. Soc. Advancement Mgmt. fellow, 1972 Mem. Acad. Mgmt., Soc. Advancement Mgmt. (pres. Twin Cities chpt. 1961-62). Congregationalist. Home: 4501 Roanoke Rd Minneapolis MN 55422-5268

WICKFIELD, ERIC NELSON, investment company executive; b. Bryn Mawr, Pa., Feb. 14, 1953; s. Paul Gilbert Jacobs and Patricia Ruth (Nelson) Davies; m. Kristine Margaret Erickson, June 21, 1974 (div. 1976); m. Sara Lou Datt, July 23, 1977 (div. 1990); 1 child, Eric N. Jr.; m. Leslie Walsh Willingham, June 8, 1990; 1 child, Douglas N. BS, Rochester Inst. Tech., 1974; MBA, Boston U., 1990. Project mgr. Flight Safety Internat., Wichita, Kans., 1976-82; v.p. Aufleger-Garrett, Stillwater, Okla., 1982-86; demonstration pilot citation div. Gen. Dynamics, Wichita, 1986-87; pres. Prompt Fin. Inc., Concord, Mass., 1987—, bd. dirs.; adj. faculty Boston U. Grad. Sch. Mgmt., 1997—. Bd. dirs. The Learning Express, Groton, Mass. Co-author: Sustaining High Performance, 1990; editor: 421 Pilot's Training Manual, 1981; author: Financial Users Network User's manual, 1997, Losing Situational awareness, 2001. Bd. dirs. Groton Ctr. for The Arts. Mem. Internat. Operator's Coun., Aircraft Owner's & Pilot's Assn., Aero Club New Eng. (bd. dirs.). Republican. Methodist. Avocation: snow skiing. Office: Prompt Fin Inc 30 Monument Sq Concord MA 01742-1858

WICKHAM, JOHN ADAMS, JR. retired army officer; b. Dobbs Ferry, N.Y., June 25, 1928; s. John Adams and Jean Gordon (Koch) W.; m. Ann Lindsley Prior, June 18, 1955; children: Lindsley, John Adams, Matthew. BS, U.S. Mil. Acad., 1950; MA, Harvard U., 1955, M.P.A., 1956; grad., Nat. War Coll., 1967. Commd. 2d lt. U.S. Army, 1950, advanced through grades to gen., 1979; asst. prof. social scis. U.S. Mil. Acad., 1956-60; bn. comdr. 1st Cavalry Div., Republic of Vietnam, 1967; brigade comdr., chief of staff 3d Inf. Div., Fed. Republic of Germany, 1969-70; army mem. chmn.'s staff group Office of Chmn. Joint Chiefs of Staff, Washington, 1970-71; dep. chief of staff for econ. affairs Mil. Assistance Command, Republic of Vietnam, 1971-73; dep. chief, negotiator U.S. del. Four Party Joint Mil. Commn., Republic of Vietnam, 1973; sr. mil. asst. to Sec. Def. Washington, 1973-76; comdr. 101st Airborne Div. (Air Assault), Ft. Campbell, Ky., 1976-78; dir. Joint Staff Orgn. Washington, 1978-79; comdr. in chief UN Command, Republic of Korea-U.S. Combined Forces Command, Korea, 1979-82; vice chief of staff U.S. Army, Washington, 1982-83, chief of staff, 1983-87, ret., 1987; pres., chief exec. officer Armed Forces Communications and Electronics Assn., Fairfax, Va., 1987-92. Bd. dirs. Cooper Inst. for Aerobic Rsch., Xsirius, Inc., Honeywell Fed. Sys., Advanced Photonics, Nortel Inc. Author: Korea on the Brink, 2000. Pres. Sun City Town Council, 1996—99; elder St. Andrews Presbn. Ch., 2001—. Decorated D.S.M. (8), Silver Star (2), Legion of Merit (4), Bronze Star with V device, Air medal (11), Purple Heart, Legion of Honor (France), Order of Mil. Merit (Rep. of Korea), Royal Order of Polar Star (Sweden). Mem. Assn. U.S. Army, 101st Airborne Assn., Retired Officers Assn. Home: 13590 N Fawnbrooke Dr Tucson AZ 85737

WICKHAM-ST. GERMAIN, MARGARET EDNA, mass spectrometrist, environmental engineer; b. Kansas City, Mo., June 7, 1956; d. Ronald Lee and Mary Ann (Nicholas) Wickham; m. Christopher Newman St. Germain, June 11, 1988; 1 child, Mark Anthony. BS in Chemistry, St. Mary Coll., Leavenworth, Kans., 1978; BS in Civil Engring., U. Mo., Kansas City, 2000, student, 1979-80, , 1994-2000. Lab. technician VA Hosp., Kansas City, 1977; jr. chemist Midwest Rsch. Inst., 1978-80, jr. mass spectrometrist, 1980-81, asst. mass spectrometrist, 1981-85, assoc. mass spectrometrist, 1985-86, mass spectrometrist, 1986-90, sr. mass spectrometrist, 1990-94; owner Wickham Sci. Svcs., 1994—; chemist EPA Region 7, Kansas City, Kans., 1994-98, environ. scientist/quality assurance specialist, 1998—2001, environ. engr., 2001—. Co-author: Priority Pollutants, 1983; author: Method Development for VOST Fractionator, 1994. Active Mid-Continent coun. Girl Scouts U.S., 1962—, St. Bernadette's Ch., Kansas City, 1986—. Mem. ASCE, Am. Chem. Soc. (nat. younger chemist com. 1988-91, chmn. memberships com. Kansas City chpt. 1979-80, sec. 1984, chmn.-elect 1985, chmn. 1986, past chmn. 1987, chmn. chemistry conf. 1989, counselor 1999--, founding mem. regional younger chemist com. 1990—, Chemagro Essay award 1977, 78), Am. Soc. for Mass Spectrometry, Soc. for Applied Spectroscopy, Air and Waste Mgmt. Assn., Tau Beta Pi, Kappa Gamma Pi (Excellence award 1978), Delta Epsilon Sigma (Excellence award 1978). Avocations: medicinal herbs, children's songs, gardening, horses, trail competition. Office: Wickham Sci Svcs 9102 E 50th Ter Kansas City MO 64133-2120 E-mail: stgermain.margie@epa.gov.

WICKIZER, CINDY LOUISE, retired elementary school educator; b. Pitts., Dec. 12, 1946; d. Charles and Gloria Geraldine (Cassidy) Zimmerman Sr.; m. Leon Leonard Wickizer, Mar. 20, 1971 (div.); 1 child Charlyn Michelle. BS, Oreg. State U., 1968. Tchr. Enumclaw (Wash.) Sch. Dist., 1968-99, ret., 1999. Mem. Wash. State Ret. Tchrs. Assn., Am. Rabbit Breeders Assn. (judge, chmn. scholarship found. 1986-87, pres. 1988-94, 96-98, dist. dir. 1994-96, Disting. Svc. award 1987, Hall of Fame 1998), Wash. State Rabbit Breeders Assn. (life, Pres.'s award 1983, 94, sec., dir., v.p. 1995-97), Vancouver Island Rabbit Breeders Assn., Wash. State Rabbit and Cavy Shows Inc. (sec. 1994—), Evergreen Rabbit Assn. (sec., v.p., pres.), Alpha Gamma Delta. Home: 20825 Star Rte 410 E PMB 196 Sumner WA 98390 E-mail: CindyWick@aol.com.

WICKIZER, MARY ALICE See BURGESS, MARY ALICE

WICKIZER, STEPHEN WESLEY, pharmacist; b. Oklahoma City, Mar. 1, 1952; s. James and Virginia (Harris) W.; m. Joyce Baugher, Nov. 12, 1980; children: Alison, Stephanie. BS, U. Tenn. Ctr. Health Scis., 1975; D in Pharmacy, U. Md., 1996. Staff pharmacist Dept. Vets. Affairs, 1975-77; clin. pharmacist NIH, Bethesda, 1977-80; from dept. chief pharmacy to staff pharmacist USPHS Indian Health Svc., Okla, N.C., 1980-87; from pharmacist to health programs com. FDA, Rockville, Md., 1987-91; adminstrv. officer Office of Surgeon Gen. Pub. Health Svc., 1991-92; dep. dir. Office of Drug Pricing HRSA, Bethesda, Md., 1992-98; health sci. adminstr. sci. rev. divsn. Agency HealthCare Rsch. and Quality, Rockville, 1998—2001; tech. transfer specialist NIH, NCI, TTB, Frederick, 2001—. Clin. instr. U. Md. Sch. Pharmacy, Balt., 1997—. Mem.: Commd. Officers Assn. of USPHS, Aircraft Owner's and Pilots Assn., Food and Drug Pharm. Sco., Am. Pharm. Assn., Expt. Aircraft Assn., Assn. Mil. Surgeons U.S., Fed. Health Care Execs. Inst. Methodist. Avocations: flying, diving, skiing, substance abuse prevention counseling. Office: NIH NCI Frederick Tech Transfer Br 1003 W 7th St Fairview Ctr Ste 502 Frederick MD 21701-1201 E-mail: wickizes@mail.nih.gov.

WICKLEIN, JOHN FREDERICK, journalist, educator; b. Reading, Pa., July 20, 1924; s. Raymond Roland and Parmilla Catherine (Miller) W.; m. Myra Jane Winchester, July 31, 1948; children: Elizabeth, Peter, Joanna. LittB, Rutgers U., 1947; MS in Journalism, Columbia, 1948. Reporter Newark (N.J.) Evening News, 1947-51; news mng. editor Elec. World (McGraw-Hill weekly), N.Y.C., 1951-54; reporter, editor N.Y. Times, 1954-62; news dir. Sta. WNET-TV, N.Y.C., 1962-64; exec. producer news Sta. WABC-TV, 1964-67; exec. producer Washington Bur. chief Pub. Broadcast Lab. (Nat. Ednl. TV), 1967-70; mng. news and pub. affairs broadcasts Sta. WCBS-TV, N.Y.C., 1970-71; gen. mgr. Sta. WRVR, 1971-74; prof. journalism and broadcasting Boston U., 1974-80; dean Sch. Public Communication Boston U., 1974-78; vis. prof. communication Meth. U., São Paulo, Brazil, 1979; program officer for news and pub. affairs programs Corp. for Pub. Broadcasting, 1980-84; Willard M. Kiplinger chair in pub. affairs reporting, dir. Kiplinger mid-career program for journalists Ohio State U., 1984-89; Fulbright rsch. scholar Charles Sturt Univ., Bathurst, NSW, Australia, 1990. Lectr., cons. to Rutgers U. Media Resources Ctr., Warsaw, Poland, 1992; Ayers vis. prof. journalism Jacksonville (Ala.) State U., 1992-93; prodr. news documentaries for pub. and comml. TV; ind. writing, reporting and editing coach for newspapers including Washington Post, Buffalo News, Memphis Comml. Appeal, 1994—; lectr., cons. in field; coord. Working Group for Pub. Broadcasting, 1987-89; spl. com. on regulation of media ACLU, 1988-92; adj. faculty, Poynter Inst. for Media Studies, 1988; adj. prof. journalism for rsch. Ohio State U., 1991-93; at-large mem., media ethics com. Nat. Coun. Chs., 1975-92; fellow Inst. Dem. Comm. Boston U., 1975-78; lectr. journalism Columbia Grad. Sch. Journalism, 1966-67; Danforth lectr. Barnard Coll., 1960-61; cons. dept. journalism Jagiellonian U., Krakow, Poland, 1994. Author: (with Monroe Price) Cable Television: A Guide for Citizen Action, 1972, Electronic Nightmare: The New Communications and Freedom, 1981; editor: Investigative Reporting: The Lessons of Watergate, 1975; contgb. editor The Washington Monthly, 1969-72; contbr. to Am. Journalism Review, The Progressive, TV Quar., Atlantic Monthly, Columbia Journalism Rev., Archeology, Quill, Australian Journalism Rev., others. Recipient George Polk award, 1963, documentary award Venice Film Festival, 1968, Dupont award, 1973, Brechner Freedom Info. prize, 1987. Mem. ACLU, Investigative Reporters and Editors, Amnesty Internat. U.S.A., Soc. Prof. Jours., Phi Beta Kappa Democrat. Home and Office: 23200 Wilderness Walk Ct Gaithersburg MD 20882-2732 E-mail: jfwicklein@erols.com.

WICKLIFFE, MARY, art historian, artist; b. 1928; AA, Sullins Coll., 1948; BA in Art History summa cum laude, Drew U., 1977, postgrad., 1977-81. Exhbn. curator N.J. Ctr. for Visual Arts, Summit, 1978—2000, also writer/designer 13 exhbn. catalogs, 1983-99. One-person shows Summit YWCA, The N.H. House, The Summit Playhouse, Brayton Sch., Union Counties Bank, Chatham Pub. Libr., Drew U., Summit Art Ctr., N.J. Ctr. for Visual Arts; group shows Lever House, N.Y.C., Fairleigh Dickenson U., Short Hills Mall Exhibn., Nabisco Hdqrs., Sandoz Corp., Schering Plough Hdqrs. Trustee Summit Art Ctr., 1962-70, pres., 1965-66; asst. dir. Art Caravan, New Jersey Ctr. Visual Arts, 1979-80.

WICKLINE, MARIAN ELIZABETH, former corporate librarian; b. St. Louis, Feb. 18, 1915; d. William Anderson and Grace B. (Gooding) W. BA, Mills Coll., 1935; postgrad., U. Calif., Berkeley, 1935-37. Tech. files asst. Shell Devel. Co., San Francisco, 1938-45; libr. western div. Dow Chem. Co., Pitts. and Walnut Creek, Calif., 1945-75; ret., 1975. Mem. Planning Commn., Danville, Calif., 1982—86, El Dorado County Libr. Commn., Placerville, 1989—92, mem. policy adv. com. gen. plan, 1989—92, mem. commn. on aging, 2000—02; bd. dirs. Greenstone Country Cmty. Svcs. Dist., 1994—98. Named Woman of Yr. San Ramon Valley C. of C., Danville, Calif., 1983. Mem. AAUW (Gift Honoree 1982, 84), Am. Chem. Soc., Spl. Libr. Assn. (pres. San Francisco Bay region chpt. 1973-74, chair chemistry divsn. 1970-71). Avocation: gardening. Home: 5474 Comstock Rd Placerville CA 95667-8712

WICKLUND, DAVID WAYNE, lawyer; b. St. Paul, Aug. 7, 1949; s. Wayne Glenwood and Elna Katherine (Buresh) W.; m. Susan Marie Bubenko, Nov. 17, 1973; children: David Jr., Kurt, Edward. BA cum laude, Williams Coll., 1971; JD cum laude, U. Toledo, 1974. Bar: Ohio 1974. Assoc. Shumaker, Loop & Kendrick, Toledo, 1974-80, ptnr., 1981—. Adj. instr. law, U. Toledo, 1988. Editor-in-chief U. Toledo Law Rev. 1973-74. Mem. ABA, Ohio State Bar Assn. (emeritus mem. bd. govs. antitrust sect. 1994-2001), Toledo Bar Assn., U. Toledo Coll. of Law Alumni Assn. (pres. 1999-2000), Inverness Club, Toledo Club. Office: Shumaker Loop & Kendrick N Courthouse Sq 1000 Jackson St Toledo OH 43624-1573 E-mail: dwicklund@slk-law.com.

WICKMAN, JOHN EDWARD, librarian, historian; b. Villa Park, Ill., May 24, 1929; s. John Edward and Elsie (Voss) W.; m. Shirley Jean Swanson, Mar. 17, 1951; children— Lisa Annette, Eric John. AB, Elmhurst Coll., 1953; A.M., Ind. U., 1958, PhD, 1964; LL.D., Lincoln Coll., 1973. Instr. history Hanover (Ind.) Coll., 1959-62, Southeast Campus, Ind. U., Jeffersonville, 1962; asst. prof. history Northwest Mo. State Coll., Maryville, 1962-64; asst. to Gov. William H. Avery of Kans., Topeka, 1964-65; asst. prof. history Regional Campus, Purdue U., Fort Wayne, Ind., 1965-66; dir. Dwight D. Eisenhower Libr., Abilene, Kans., 1966-89; ret., 1989. Contbr. articles on Am. West, archival mgmt., adminstrv. history, oral history to profl. publs. Served with U.S. Army, 1953-55. Nat. Ctr. for Edn. in Politics faculty fellow, 1964-65; Am. Polit. Sci. Assn. Congl. fellow, 1975-76 Mem. Oral History Assn. (v.p. 1971-72, pres. 1972-73), Western History Assn. (coun. 1972-75), Kans. Hist. Soc. (2d v.p. 1974-75, pres. 1976-77, dir.). Home: 411 W 4th St PO Box 325 Enterprise KS 67441-0325

WICKMAN, PETER M. sociologist, educator; b. Sault Ste Marie, Mich., Feb. 23, 1923; s. John Silas and Estelle (MacAdam) W.; m. Helen L. Colborne, Mar. 19, 1949 (div. 1964); 1 child, Stephen B.; m. Winona Moore Marsh, Sept. 1, 1984; 1 child, Matthew L. Marsh. BA in History, Greenville Coll., 1948; MA, Northwestern U., 1949; EdD, Mich. State U., 1960. Instr. soc. sci. John Wesley Coll., Owosso, Mich., 1950-54; asst., assoc. prof. Greenville (Ill.) Coll., 1954-60; asst. prof. U. Fla., Gainesville, 1960-63; assoc. prof. Nassau Comm. Coll., Garden City, N.Y., 1963-67; prof. in soc. and crim. SUNY, 1967-92, emeritus prof. sociology crim. and pub. policy; instr. Coll. Within Prison Walls, Colo., Ariz., 1992-94. Vis. prof. Troy (Ala.) State U., 1961, dir., cons. St. Law Regional, Canton N.Y., 1971-72, evaluation rschr. Assoc. Coll., Potsdam, N.Y., 1974-75, conf. organizer SUNY EEOP, 1969, Internat. White Collar Cr. 1980, rschr. UUP & SUNY Sabbatic, 1983-84; spkr. in field; adj. prof. sociology and criminology, SUNY Oswego and Canton, 1995-98; dir. rsch. Housing of Aging, N.Y., 1971, Regional Cmty. Corrections, Study, LEAA, 1971-72; evaluation field rschr. Kircshner Assocs., Albuquerque, 1973-80; rsch. of prisons reform in Nordic countries, 1974-75; participant in combind Congress of Japanesse Soc. Control of Internat. Social Assn., Hiroshima, 1976. Editor: Readings in Soc. Prob's , 1973-76, Soc. Prob's Con' Per's, 1977, co-editor: Readings in Criminology, 1978, White Collar Crime, 1982, Contemporary Perspectives on Social Problems, 1977, others; co-author: Criminology Perspect's, 1980, Perspectives on Crime: Readings in Criminology, 1979; USIA Symposium lectures Am. Justice Sys., Estonia Nat. Pub. Svc. Acad., Nov. 1993; contbr. articles to profl. jours. Mem. bd. dirs. Potsdam Food Co-op, 1977-79, St. Francis Acad., Lake Placid, 1985-92, Reach-Out Crisis Line, Potsdam, N.Y., 1986-89; WWII vet. Mem. Am. Soc. of Criminology. Episcopalian. Avocations: tennis, reading, hiking, mountain climbing, travel. Home: 4 Somerset Dr Potsdam NY 13676-1635

WICKRAMASEKERA, IAN EDWARD, psychophysiologist, psychology educator; b. Colombo, Ceylon, Oct. 23, 1938; s. Harry S. and Maude (Robinson) W.; m. Judy Wickram; children: Melissa, Ian Edward II. BA, Friend's U., Wichita, Kans., 1961; MA, Roosevelt U., Chgo., 1966; PhD, U. Ill., 1969. Diplomate Am. Bd. Profl. Psychology; diplomate in exptl. hypnosis Am. Bd. Psychol. Hypnosis. Assoc. prof. psychiatry Coll. Medicine U. Ill., 1974-80; prof. Ea. Va. Med. Sch., Norfolk, 1981-95, prof. family medicine, 1995—; clin. prof. psychiatry Med. Sch. Stanford (Calif.) U., 1995—; prof. psychology Saybrook Inst., San Francisco, 1995—. Author: Clinical Behavioral Medicine, 1988; editor: Biofeedback, Behavior Therapy and Hypnosis, 1976; contbr. over 100 articles to med. and sci. jours. Recipient Morton Prince award Am. Bd. Profl. Hypnosis, 1992. Mem. APA (pres. divsn. 30F hypnosis 1996-97), Assn. for Applied Psychophysiology (pres. 1998-99, Salvador Dali award 1991), Va. Hypnosis Soc. (pres. 1987-88). Roman Catholic. Home: PO Box 1110 Tracy CA 95378-1110 Office: Saybrook Inst 450 Pacific Ave San Francisco CA 94133-4640 E-mail: iwickram@saybrook.edu.

WICKS, CHARLES CARTER, lawyer; b. Goshen, Ind., May 28, 1945; s. Charles Sterling and Christine (Carter) W.; m. Penny Rae Krull, Oct. 31, 1970; children: Jay, Kristin, Scott. BA, Tulane U., 1967; JD, Ind. U., 1970. Bar: Ind. 1970, U.S. Ct. Mil. Appeals 1971, U.S. Supreme Ct. 1991. Ptnr. Matthews Petsche-Wicks, South Bend, Ind., 1974-78, Virgil, Cawley, Platt & Wicks, Elkhart, 1978; pvt. practice, 1979—; dep. pros. atty., 1978—; ptnr. Wicks & Rieff, 1988-89. Lectr. forensic medicine Goshen Coll. Sch. Nursing. Mem. vestry St. James Episcopal ch., 1977-79, 81-84, 86-88, sr. warden, 1989, diocesan coun. Episcopal Diocese No. Ind., 1988-89; mem. Rep. CTrl. Com., Goshen, 1978--, chmn., 2001--. Capt. USAF, 1970-74. Mem. ABA, ATLA, Ind. Bar Assn., Ind. Trial Lawyers Assn., Elkhart County Estate Planning Coun. (pres. 1982-83), Elkhart County Past Masters' Assn. (pres. 1984, 89), Elkhart C. of C., Goshen C. of C., Goshen County Past Masters Assn., Am. Legion, Masons (master 1980, trustee 1981-83, 2001-2003, comdr. in chief 1992-94, chmn. degree com. 1995-2000, Scottish Rite 1995-2001, dir. 24 degree 2001--, trustee 2001--), Shriners (pres. Goshen club 1983), Jesters, Red Cross of Constantine, Moose, Elkhart Kiwanis (bd. dirs. 1986-87, 97-99), Christiana Creek Country Club, Bent Oak Golf Club, Greater Elkhart Pachyderm Club (pres. 1989—), Nat. Pachyderm Club (bd. dirs. 1998-99). Home: 26207 Hilly Ln Elkhart IN 46517-2243 Office: 514 S Main St PO Box 1884 Elkhart IN 46515-1884 E-mail: wix6316@aol.com.

WICKS, DAVID O., JR. communications executive; b. Boston, May 17, 1941; s. David O. and Elizabeth L. Wicks; m. Joan Gagnebin, Sept. 7, 1963; children: Perrin, Sara. BA, Trinity Coll., Hartford, Conn., 1963; MBA, U. Va., 1968. With nat. divsn. Chem. Bank, 1963-66; specialist in venture capital and cable TV Warburg Paribas Becker, N.Y.C., 1968-83, mng. dir., 1979-83; gen. ptnr. Becker Venture Assocs., Becker Comms. Asocs. II; sr. ptng. Criterion Venture Ptnrs., Houston, 1983-88. Mng. dir. Criterion Investments, Inc., 1983-88; pres. Criterion Investments, Inc., 1985-88; v.p. Cablevision Sys. Corp., Bethpage, N.Y., 1996-2002; exec. NASA Mid Continent Tech. Transfer Ctr., 1992-95; bd. dirs. Matrix Enterprises Inc.; expert witness on cable TV, U.S. Congress and state regulatory bodies. Contbr. articles to profl. jours. Bd. dirs. Adult Literacy Media Alliance, Vis. Nurse Assn. N.Y., Cable Positive, Inc. Recipient Vanguard award Nat. Cable TV Assn., 1978. Mem.: Univ. Club (NYC).

WICKS, EUGENE CLAUDE, college president, art educator; b. Coleharbor, N.D., Oct. 7, 1931; s. Claude Edward and Grace Ann (Wilkinson) W.; m. Lavonne Maureen Yineman, June 21, 1953; children: Christopher Edwin, Louis Eugene, James Edward. B.F.A., U. Colo., 1957, M.F.A., 1959. Mem. faculty U. Ill., Urbana, 1959-94, assoc. head, 1961-76, head Sch. Art and Design, 1977-80, dir., 1981-89; also prof. art U. Ill. (Sch. Art and Design); pres. Burren Coll. Art, Newtown Castle, Ireland, 1994-99. Cons. in field Represented in permanent collections at, Phila. Print Club, Art Inst. Chgo., Am. Fed. Arts, others. Served with USN, 1951-54. U. Ill. research grantee, 1960, 61, 67, 68, 69, 74, 75; Fulbright grantee, 1988-89. Mem. Coll. Art Assn., Nat. Assn. Schs. Art and Design (dir. commn. on accreditation 1978-81, v.p. 1981-84, pres. 1984-87) Home: 1405 Old Farm Rd Champaign IL 61821-5949 E-mail: wicks@uiuc.edu.

WICKS, JOHN R. lawyer; b. Ottumwa, Iowa, Dec. 8, 1937; m. Nedra Morgan, Mar. 27, 1940; children: Catherine, John. BSC, U. Iowa, 1959, JD, 1964. Bar: Iowa 1964, Minn. 1966. Assoc. Dorsey & Whitney, Mpls., 1966-71; ptnr. Dorsey & Whitney LLP, Rochester, Minn., 1972-2000, of counsel Mpls., 2001—. Fellow: Am. Coll. Trusts and Estates Counsel; mem.: Minn. State Bar Assn. (probate and trusts law coun. 1989—92). Office: Dorsey & Whitney LLP 50 S 6th St Minneapolis MN 55402-1498 E-mail: wicks.john@dorseylaw.com.

WICKS, MONA NEWSOME, medical/surgical nurse, educator; b. Memphis, July 11, 1958; d. Eddie Lee and Edna Rhea (Tisdale) Newsome; m. Sammie James Wicks, June 26, 1984; 1 child, Sammie James II. ADN, Memphis State U., 1978, BSN, 1981; MSN, U. Tenn., 1987; PhD, Wayne State U., 1992. Staff nurse Bapt. Meml. Hosp., Memphis, 1978-87; instr. nursing U. Tenn., 1987-93, asst. prof., 1993—. Recipient Patricia Roberts Harris fellowship award Wayne State U., 1988-90. Mem. AACN (pres.-elect 1994), Tenn. Nurses Assn. (del. dist. 1 1992, 94), Sigma Theta Tau. Avocations: reading, writing, gardening, family activities. Office: U Tenn 877 Madison Ave Memphis TN 38103-3408

WICKS, WILLIAM WITHINGTON, retired public relations executive; b. Chgo., Dec. 20, 1923; s. William and Alice (Withington) W.; m. Frances M. Horner, Nov. 29, 1947; children: Barbara Anne, Christine Frances. BNS, U. Notre Dame, 1944, AB in Journalism magna cum laude, 1947. Staff corr. United Press Assn., Milw., 1947; pub. rels. mgr. Internat. Harvester Co., Louisville, 1948-58; mgr. field svcs. pub. rels. Standard Oil Co. (Ind.), Chgo., 1959-60; v.p. pub. rels. Griswold-Eshleman Co., 1961-68; dir. pub. rels. G. D. Searle & Co., 1968-74; dir. pub. rels./investor rels. Kimberly-Clark Corp., Neenah, Wis., 1974, staff v.p., 1974-80, v.p. Neenah (hdqrs. relocated to Dallas in 1985), 1980-89, v.p. and asst. to CEO, 1989-92. Chmn. pub. relations sect. Pharm. Mfrs. Assn., Washington, 1974. Pres. Jr. Achievement Neenah-Menasha, 1978-81; bd. mem. Friends of the Irving Pub. Libr., 1997-99. Served to lt. (j.g.) USNR, 1942-46, PTO. Recipient Silver Anvil award Pub. Rels. Soc. Am., 1963, 79. Mem. PRSA (founder, pres. Bluegrass chpt. 1957-58), Optimist (pres. South End Club in Louisville 1957), Publicity Club of Chgo. (pres. 1967-68), USN Meml. Found. (plank owner), Navy League U.S., Patrol Craft Sailors Assn. Republican. Roman Catholic. Home: 1312 Travis Cir S Irving TX 75038-6243

WICKSTROM, ERIC, biophysical chemist, educator; b. Chgo., Dec. 21, 1946; s. Eric Lester and Lillian (Partnoy) W.; m. Lois June Sinsheimer, July 1, 1967; children: Erica Lorraine, Eileen Anitra. BS in Biology with honors, Calif. Inst. Tech., 1968; PhD in Chemistry, U. Calif., Berkeley, 1972. Research assoc. U. Colo., Boulder, 1973-74; asst. prof. U. Denver, 1974-81; sr. research scientist So. Biotech, Tampa, Fla., 1981-82; vis. assoc. prof. U. South Fla., 1982-83, asst. prof., 1983-87, assoc. prof., 1987-91, prof., 1991-92, Thomas Jefferson U., Phila., 1992—. Mem. Inst. Biomolecular Sci., Tampa, 1984-92; guest rschr. Nat. Cancer Inst., Bethesda, Md., 1986, Max Planck Inst. Molecular Genetics, Berlin, 1986. Editor: (Book) Prospects for Antisense Nucleic Acid Therapy for Cancer and Aids, 1991, Clinical Trials of Genetic Therapy with Antisense DNA and DNA Vectors, 1998; Mem. editl. bd. (Antisense and Nucleic Acid Drug Devel.) Jour. Pharm Sci. Grantee, NSF, 1976—81, Nat. Inst. Gen. Med. Sci., 1976—89, Luekemia Soc. Am., 1986—87, U.S. Army, 1986—88, Nat. Cancer Inst., 1987—, Am. Found. AIDS Rsch., 1989—90, Fla. High Tech. Indsl. Coun., 1988—91, Genta, Inc., 1989, Am. Cancer Soc., 1990—99, Dept. of Energy, 2000—. Mem.: Internat. Soc. Nuclads, Nucleds and Nuclear Acids, Am. Assn. Cancer Rsch., Am. Soc. Biochem and Molecular Biology, Biophys. Soc., Am. Chem. Soc. Democrat. Jewish. Office: Thomas Jefferson U 233 S 10th St Rm 219 Philadelphia PA 19107-5541

WICKSTROM, JON ALAN, telecommunications executive, consultant; b. San Antonio, Apr. 17, 1949; s. Stanley Alan and Louise (MacMillan) W.; m. Mary Carmen Sparkman, Jan. 25, 1969 (div. Jan. 1978); children: Dana Marie, Jon Alan Jr.; m. Jane Bielbey Slawson, June 19, 1988. BS, Tex. Tech. U., 1975; MS, U. Tex., 1998. Ptnr. Hensley & Assocs., Albuquerque, 1976-78; dealer svcs. mgr. Gulf States Toyota, Houston, 1978-80; comms. mgr. Hughes Tool Co., 1980-85; network svcs. mgr. Tenneco Oil Co., 1986-89; comms. mgr. Clarke Am., San Antonio, 1989-94; info/technology planner USAA, 1994-96; sr. mgr. MMC Ernst & Young LLP, 1996-2000, Cap Gemini Ernst & Young,

2000—. Prin. Comm. Tech. Cons., Houston, 1980-89; cons. Comms. Consulting Group, Inc., San Antonio, 1989-96. Author: (reference) 1976 Population Estimates for Bernallio County, New Mex., 1976. Rep. precinct chmn. Bexar County, Tex., 1992-94; cons. Houston Symphony Orch., 1988. Mem. Alamo Area Telecomms. Assn. (bd. dirs 1990-94, pres., 1992-93), S.W. Comms. Assn. (bd. dirs. 1981-85, pres. 1982-84), Tex. Telecomms. Conf. (bd. dirs. 1982-84, chmn. 1983), Am. Mensa. Avocations: sailing, golf, music, investing. E-mail: jon.wickstrom@us.cgey.com.

WICKSTROM, KARL YOUNGERT, publishing company executive; b. Moline, Ill., Sept. 20, 1935; s. George Washington and Harriet L. (Youngert) W.; m. Patricia Pinkerton, 1959 (div.); children: Eric, Blair, Drew, Holly; m. Sheila Zehner, June 9, 1979. BSJ., U. Fla., 1957. Writer, editor Orlando (Fla.) Sentinel-Star, 1958-60; writer Miami (Fla.) Herald, 1960-67; adminstrv. asst. Fla. Senate, Tallahassee, 1968; founder, pres., publisher Wickstrom Pubs. Inc., mags., books, Miami, 1968—. Original pub.: Aloft Mag., for Nat. Airlines passengers, 1968-80; pub.: Fla. Sportsman, 1969— , Ryder World for Ryder System, Inc, 1980— . Bd. dirs. Nat. Coalition for Marine Conservation; v.p. Fla. Conservation Assn. Served with USAF, 1967-68. Recipient 1st Pl. award for pub. svc. Fla. AP, 1967; named Man of Yr., Am. Sportfishing Assn., 1995, Conservationist of Yr., Fla. Wildlife Fedn., 1995. Mem. Sigma Delta Chi (nat. 1st pl. award for investigative reporting Miami area crime, corruption 1967) Home: 1900 NW River Trl Stuart FL 34994-9474 Office: Florida Sportsman 2700 S Kanner Hwy Stuart FL 34994-9474

WICKWIRE, PATRICIA JOANNE NELLOR, psychologist, educator; d. William McKinley and Clara Rose (Pautsch) Nellor; m. Robert James Wickwire, Sept. 7, 1957; 1 child, William James. BA cum laude, U. No. Iowa, 1951; MA, U. Iowa, 1959; PhD, U. Tex., Austin, 1971; postgrad., U. So. Calif., 1951-66, UCLA, 1951-66, Calif. State U., Long Beach, 1951-66. Lic. ednl. psychologist, marriage, family and child counselor, Calif. Tchr. Ricketts Ind. Schs., Iowa, 1946-48; tchr., counselor Waverly-Shell Rock Ind. Schs., 1951-55; reading cons., head dormitory counselor U. Iowa, Iowa City, 1955-57; tchr., sch. psychologist, adminstr. S. Bay Union H.S. Dist., Redondo Beach, Calif., 1962-82, dir. student svcs. and spl. edn. Cons. mgmt. and edn.; pres. Nellor Wickwire Group, 1981—; mem. exec. bd. Calif. Interagy. Mental Health Coun., 1968-72, Beach Cities Symphony Assn., 1970-82; chmn. Friends of Dominguez Hills, Calif., 1981-85. Contbr. articles in field to profl. jours. Pres. Calif. Women's Caucus, 1993-95. Mem. APA, AAUW (exec. bd., chpt. pres. 1962-72), Nat. Career Devel. Assn. (media chair 1992-98), Am. Assn. Career Edn. (pres. 1991—), L.A. County Dirs. Pupil Svcs. (chmn. 1974-79), L.A. County Pers. and Guidance Assn. (pres. 1977-78), Assn. Calif. Sch. Adminstrs. (dir. 1977-81), L.A. County SW Bd. Dist. Adminstrs. for Spl. Edn. (chmn. 1976-81), Calif. Assn. Sch. Psychologists (bd. dirs. 1981-83), Am. Assn. Sch. Adminstrs., Calif. Assn. for Measurement and Evaluation in Guidance (dir. 1981, pres. 1984-85, 98-2000), ACA (chmn. Coun. Newsletter Editors 1989-91, mem. com. on women 1989-92, mem. com. on rsch. and knowledge 1994—, chmn. 1995—, mem. and chmn. bylaws com. 1998-2001, rep. to joint com. on testing practices 2001—), Assn. Measurement and Eval. in Guidance (Western regional editor 1985-87, conv. chair 1986, editor 1987-90, exec. bd. dirs. 1987-91), Calif. Assn. Counseling and Devel. (exec. bd. 1984—, pres. 1988-89, jour. editor 1990—), Internat. Career Assn. Network (chair 1985—), Pi Lambda Theta, Alpha Phi Gamma, Psi Chi, Kappa Delta Pi, Sigma Alpha Iota. Office: The Nellor Wickwire Group 2900 Amby Pl Hermosa Beach CA 90254-2216

WIDAMAN, GREGORY ALAN, financial executive, accountant; b. St. Louis, Oct. 4, 1955; s. Raymond Paul Sr. and Louise Agnes (Urschler) W. BS in Bus. and Econs. cum laude, Trinity U., 1978. CPA, Tex. Sr. auditor Arthur Andersen LLP, Houston, 1978-82; sr. cons. Price Waterhouse, 1983-85; fin. advisor to segment pres. Teledyne, Inc., Century City, Calif., 1985-95; sr. mgr. ops. planning for consumer products ABC Broadcasting/TV The Walt Disney Co., Burbank, 1995-97; v.p. internal audit and spl. projects Hilton Hotels Corp., Beverly Hills, 1997—. Cons. Arthur Andersen LLP, Price Waterhouse, Teledyne, Walt Disney Co., Hilton Hotels Corp. Mem. AICPAs, Calif. Soc. CPAs, Christian Bus. Mens com. of U.S.A., World Affairs Coun., MIT/Calif. Tech. Enterprise Forum. Republican. Avocations: white water rafting, water and snow skiing, camping, business, chess. Home: 1416 S Barrington Ave No 4 Los Angeles CA 90025-2363 Office: Hilton Hotels Corp World Hdqrs 9336 Civic Center Dr Beverly Hills CA 90210-3604

WIDDEL, JOHN EARL, JR. lawyer; b. Minot, N.D., Nov. 17, 1936; s. John Earl Sr. and Angela Victoria W.; m. Yvonne J. Haugen, Dec. 21, 1973; children: John P., James M., Susan N., Andrea K. B in Philosophy, BSBA, U. N.D., 1966, BSBA, 1971. Bar: N.D. 1971, U.S. Dist. Ct. N.D., 1971, U.S. Ct. Appeals (8th cir.) 1989. Ptnr. Thorsen & Widdel, Grand Forks, N.D., 1971-97; shareholder Law Offices ND, PC. Mcpl. judge City of Grand Forks, 1972—; ct. magistrate Grand Forks County, 1975. Mem. N.D. Foster Parent Program, 1974-87, Nat. Conf. of Bar Pres.; mem. bd. dirs. YMCA, Grand Forks, 1982; dist. chmn. Boy Scouts Am., 1987-88; corp. mem. ALTRU Hosp. With U.S. Army, 1960-62. Mem. Am. Acad. Estate Planning Attys., State Bar Assn. N.D. (bd. govs. 1983-88, pres. 1986-87), Greater Grand Forks County Bar Assn. (pres. 1982), N.E. Cen. Jud. Dist. (pres. 1983), Grand Forks Cemetery Assn. (bd. dirs. 1984-96, pres. 1989-94), Grand Forks Hist. Soc. (pres. 1983), Grand Forks Jaycees, Antique Automobile Club Am. (nat. bd. dirs. 1984-2000, v.p. 1985-98, sec.-treas. 1989, pres. N.D . region 1977-78, 83-84), Sertoma (bd. dirs. 1994-99, pres. 1997-98, dist. gov. 2001-02), Elks (exalted ruler 1985-86), Masonic Bodies (Kem Temple Potentate 1995), Nat. Assn. Estate Planning Coun. (accredited estate planner, 1994), N.D. Mcpl. Judges Assn. (dir. 1993—). Roman Catholic. Home: Box 5624 Grand Forks ND 58206-5624 Office: Law Offices North Dakota PC PO Box 5624 Grand Forks ND 58206-5624

WIDDICOMBE, RICHARD PALMER, librarian; b. Paterson, N.J., Apr. 12, 1941; s. Robert Lord and Elvira Barbara (Guttilla) W.; m. Martha Elizabeth Bruyn, Feb. 26, 1972 BA, Alfred U., 1963; MS L.S., Syracuse U., 1964. Asst. librarian Yonkers Pub. Library, N.Y., 1964-65; asst. librarian Cooper Union, N.Y.C., 1965-66, Stevens Inst., Hoboken, N.J., 1966-72, dir. library, 1973—. Trustee Alfred U., NY; trustee, chmn. bd. Hoboken Hist. Mus., 2002—. Episcopalian. Home: 1 Castle Point Ter S1342 Hoboken NJ 07030-5906 Office: SC Williams Libr Stevens Inst Hoboken NJ 07030

WIDDICOMBE, RICHARD TOBY, educator; b. Salisbury, England, Apr. 12, 1955; s. John G. and Kathleen W. W.; m. Jill D. BA, Cambridge U., Eng., 1977; MA, U. Calif., Irvine, 1979; MA (hon.), Cambridge U., 1981; PhD, U. Calif., Irvine, 1984. Lectr. U. Calif., Santa Barbara, 1984-89; asst. prof. N.Y. inst. Tech., Old Westbury, 1989-92, U. Alaska, Anchorage, 1992-95, assoc. prof., 1996-2000, prof., 2001—. Mem. steering com. Soc. Utopian Studies, 1992—. Author: Edward Bellamy: An Annotated Bibliography of Secondary Criticism, 1989, A Reader's Guide to Raymond Chandler, 2001, Simply Shakespeare, 2001. Office: U Alaska Dept English 3211 Providence Dr Anchorage AK 99508 Fax: 907-786-4383. E-mail: aftrw@uaa.alaska.edu.

WIDENER, HIRAM EMORY, JR. federal judge; b. Abingdon, Va., Apr. 30, 1923; s. Hiram Emory and Nita Douglas (Peck) Widener; children: Molly Berentd, Hiram Emory III. Student, Va. Poly. Inst., 1940—41; BS, U.S. Naval Acad., 1944; LLB, Washington and Lee U., 1953, LLD, 1977. Bar: Va. 1951. Pvt. practice, Bristol, Va., 1953—69; judge U.S. Dist. Ct. (we. dist.) Va., Abingdon, 1969—71, chief judge, 1971—72; judge U.S. Ct. of Appeals (4th cir.) , 1972—. U.S. commr. Western Dist. Va., 1963—66; mem. Va. Election Laws Study Commn., 1968—69. Chmn. Rep. 9th Dist. , Va., 1966—69; state exec. com. Va. Rep. State Ctrl. Com., 1966—69. Lt. (j.g.) USN, 1944—49, lt. USNR, 1951—52. Decorated Bronze Star with combat V. Mem.: Va. State Bar, Va. Bar Assn., Am. Law Inst., Phi Alpha Delta. Republican. Presbyterian. Home and Office: 180 E Main St Rm 123 Abingdon VA 24210-2839

WIDERA, GEORG ERNST OTTO, mechanical engineering educator, consultant; b. Dortmund, Germany, Feb. 16, 1938; arrived in U.S., 1950; s. Otto and Gertrude (Yzermann) Widera; m. Kristel Kornas, June 21, 1974; children: Erika, Nicholas. BS, U. Wis., 1960, MS, 1962, PhD, 1965. Asst. prof. then prof. dept. materials engring. U. Ill., Chgo., 1965-82, prof. mech. engring., 1982-91, head dept., 1983-91, acting head indsl. sys. engring. dept., 1985-86, dir off-campus engring. programs, 1987-88; prof., chmn. mech. and indsl. engring. dept. Marquette U., Milw., 1991-99, dir. Ctr. Indsl. Processes and Productivity, 1995—2002, interim dean Coll. Engring., 1998-99, assoc. dean Coll. Engring., 1999—2001, sr. assoc. dean Coll. Engring., 2001—. Gastdozent U. Stuttgart, Germany, 1968; vis. prof. U. Wis.-Milw., 1973—74, Marquette U., Milw., 1978—79; cons. Ladish Co., Cudahy, Wis., 1967—76, Howmedica, Inc., Chgo., 1972—75, Sargent & Lundy, 1970—88, Nat. Bur. Stds., 1980, bd. dirs.; cons. Engrs. and Scientists Milw., 1996—98; vis. scientist Argonne Nat. Lab., Ill., 1968. Editor: Procs. Innovations in Structural Engring., 1974, Pressure Vessel Design, 1982; assoc. editor: Pressure Vessel Tech., 1977—81, assoc. editor: Applied Mechanics Revs., 1987—94, assoc. editor: Mfg. Rev., 1991—95, mem. editl. adv. bd.: Acta Mechanica Sinica, 1990—, mem. editl. bd.: Pressure Vessels and Piping Design Technology, 1982, tech. editor: Jour. Pressure Vessel Tech., 1982—93; co-editor: SME Handbook of Metalforming, 1985, 1994, Design and Analysis of Plates and Shells, 1986. Fellow Std. Oil Co. Calif., 1961—63, NASA, 1966, von Humboldt, Fed. Republic Germany, 1968—69. Fellow: WRC (pressure vessel rsch. coun., chmn. subcom. design procedures for shell intersections 1983—87, chmn. com. reinforced openings and external loads 1987—91, vice chmn. com. polymer pressure components 1991—99, chmn. com. shells and ligaments 1994—97), ASCE (sec.-treas. structural divsn. Ill. sect. 1972—73, chmn. divsn. 1976—77, chmn. peer rev. com., tech. coun. rsch. 1984, coun. structural plastics), ASME (chmn. machine design div. Chgo. sect. 1967—68, exec. com. Chgo. sect. 1970—73, editor newsletter Chgo. sect. 1971—73, chmn. jr. awards com. applied mechanics divsn. 1973—76, chmn. design and analysis com. pressure vessel and piping divsn. 1980—83, chmn. pressure vessel rsch. com. 1982—87, bd. editors 1983—93, mem. exec. com. and program chmn. pressure vessel and piping divsn. 1985—89, vice-chmn., sec. pressure vessel and piping divsn. 1989—90, mem. bd. pressure tech. codes and stds. 1989—94, chmn. 1990—91, mem. materials and structures group 1990—91, historian, senate pressure vessel and piping divsn. 1992—93, honors and awards chmn. Milw. sect. 1992—95, mem. coun. engring. 1992—96, v.p. materials and structures group 1993—96, mem. tech. execs. com. 1993—96, soc. rep. Fedn. Materials Soc. 1994—95, Pressure Vessel and Piping award and medal 1995), Wis. Mfg. Curriculum Com. (vice-chmn. exec. com. 1998—), 2d China Nat. Stds. Com. Pressure Vessels (hon. cons. 1989—94), Internat. Coun. Pressure Vessel Tech. (chmn. Am. regional com. 1988—, internat. chmn. 1992—96), Gesellschaft für Angewandte Mathematik und Mechanik, French Pressure Vessel Assn., Am. Soc. Engring. Edn., Soc. Mfg. Engrs. (sr.). Achievements include research in in mechanics of composite materials, plate and shell structures, stress analysis (including FEM), pressure vessels, mechanics of deformation processing. Office: Marquette U Coll Engring PO Box 1881 Milwaukee WI 53201-1881 E-mail: geo.widera@marquette.edu.

WIDGOFF, MILDRED, physicist, educator; b. Buffalo, Aug. 24, 1924; d. Leo Widgoff and Rebecca Shulimson; children— Eve Widgoff Shapiro, Jonathan Bernard Widgoff Shapiro. BA, U. Buffalo, 1944; PhD, Cornell U., 1952. Rsch. assoc. Brookhaven Nat. Lab., Yaphank, N.Y., 1952-54; rsch. fellow Harvard U., Cambridge, Mass., 1955-58; asst. prof. rsch. Brown U., Providence, 1959-66, assoc. prof. rsch., 1966-74, prof. physics, 1974-95; prof. rsch., 1995—. Fellow Am. Phys. Soc.; mem. Sigma Xi, Phi Beta Kappa, Phi Kappa Phi. Office: Brown U Dept Physics PO Box 1843 Providence RI 02912-1843

WIDISS, ALAN I. lawyer, educator; b. L.A., Sept. 28, 1938; s. Al and Rose H. (Sobole) W.; m. Ellen Louise Magaziner, June 28, 1964; children: Benjamin L., Deborah Anne, Rebecca Elizabeth. BS, U. So. Calif., 1960, LLB, 1963; LLM, Harvard U., 1964. Bar: Calif. 1963. Teaching fellow Harvard U., 1964-65; asst. prof. law U. Iowa, Iowa City, 1965-68, asso. prof., 1968-69, prof., 1969-78, Josephine R. Witte prof., 1978—. Vis. prof. U. So. Calif., U. San Diego; dir. CLRS Mass. No-Fault Automobile Ins. Study, 1971-76. Author: A Guide to Uninsured Motorist Coverage, 1969; (with others) No-Fault Automobile Insurance in Action: The Experiences in Massachusetts, Florida, Delaware and New York, 1977, Uninsured and Underinsured Motorist Insurance (revised edit.), Vol. 1, 1991, Vol. 2, 1992, Vol. 3, 1995; author, editor: (with others) Arbitration: Commercial Disputes, Insurance and Tort Claims, 1979; (with Judge Robert E. Keeton) Insurance Law, 1988 and Course Supplement, 1988; Insurance: Materials on the General Principles, Legal Doctrines and Regulatory Acts, 1989; contbr. articles to law jours. Bd. fellows U. Iowa Sch. Religion, 1976, v.p., 1991-93, pres., 1993-95; chmn. Johnson County Citizens Adv. Com. for Regional Transp. Study, 1971-75; pres. Agudas Achim Synagogue, 1983-85, Iowa City Youth Orch., 1991-92. Mem. ABA, Am. Law Inst., Calif. Bar Assn., Assn. Am. Law Schs., Order of Coif, Phi Kappa Phi, Delta Sigma Rho. Avocations: tennis, theater. Home: Iowa City, Iowa. Died Feb. 28, 2001.

WIDLUND, OLOF BERTIL, computer science educator; b. Stockholm, Feb. 11, 1938; s. Sten O. and Dagmar W.; m. Nadine H. Taub, June 13, 1972. MS in Engring., Royal Inst. Tech., Stockholm, 1960, PhD, 1964; Sc.D., Uppsala U., Sweden, 1966. Asst. prof. NYU, N.Y.C., 1968-72, assoc. prof., 1972-75, prof. computer sci., 1975—, chmn. dept. computer sci., 1980-86. Author articles on the numerical solutions of partial differential equations. Office: NYU Courant Inst 251 Mercer St New York NY 10012-1110 E-mail: widlund@cs.nyu.edu.

WIDMAN, GARY LEE, lawyer, former government official; b. Fremont, Nebr., June 1, 1936; s. Benjamin H. and Alice C. (Negley) W.; m. Mary Margaret Donnelly, Mar. 5, 1972(div. 1988); children: Andrew Scott, Natalie Claire. BS, U. Nebr., 1957; JD, Hastings Coll. Law U. Calif., 1962; LLM, U. Mich., 1966. Bar: Calif. 1962, D.C. 1982. Assoc. Thelen, Marrin, Johnson & Bridges, San Francisco, 1962-65; assoc. prof. law U. Denver, 1966-69; prof., dir. resource and environ. law program Hastings Coll. Law, U. Calif., San Francisco, 1969-80; gen. counsel Coun. Environ. Quality, Exec. Office Pres., Washington, 1974-76; lectr. U. Calif. at Davis, 1978, Boalt Hall, 1977-79; assoc. solicitor Dept. Interior, Washington, 1980-81; of counsel Fulbright & Jaworski, 1981-85; dir. staff attys. U.S. Ct. of Appeals (9th cir.), San Francisco, 1985-87; atty. Bronson, Bronson & McKinnon, 1988-95; chief counsel State Dept. Parks and Recreation, Sacramento, 1995-96; prof. law Santa Clara (Calif.) U. Law Sch., 1998-99; sr. mediator Concur Inc., Berkeley, Calif., 2001—. Trustee Rocky Mountain Mineral Law Found., 1969-74, 77-80; apptd. by gov. P. Wilson to Bay-Delta Oversight Coun., 1993-95. Author and project dir.: Legal Study of Oil Shale on Public Lands, 1969. Bd. dirs. Sustainable Bus. Inst. Served with U.S. Army, 1957-59. Mem. ABA (coun. sect. natural resources 1975-77, spl. com. energy law 1977-82, coun. lawyers and scientists 1984-90), Fed. Bar Assn. (chmn. com. natural resources 1977), Calif. Bar Assn., Trout Unltd. Calif. (pres. 1986-90), Calif. Heritage Coun. (exec. v.p. 2001—). Home: 28 Marinero Cir Apt 31 Belvedere Tiburon CA 94920-1644 Business E-mail: gary@concurinc.net.

WIDMAN, PAUL JOSEPH, insurance agent; b. DeSmet, S.D., Dec. 18, 1936; s. Warren Clay and Lorraine (Coughlin) W.; m. Elizabeth Ann Healy, July 30, 1959; children: Cynthia, Susan, Shelly, Richard, Mark. BS, Dakota State Coll., Madison, 1959; M in Comm., S.D. State U., 1968. Tchr. Clark (S.D.) Pub. Sch., 1959-60, Henry (S.D.) Pub. Sch., 1960-64, Custer (S.D.) Pub. Sch., 1964-66; ins. agt. Horace Mann Ins., Mitchell, S.D., 1966-77, Universal Underwriters, Mitchell, 1980-87, NGM Ins. Assn., Mitchell, 1987-91, Reginald Martin Agy., Mitchell, 1991—; state rep. State of S.D., 1993—; gen. agt., ins. sales agt. Reginald Martin Agy., Mitchell, 1992—. City coun. mem. Mitchell City Coun., 1972-76; state legislator S.D. Ho. of Reps., 1993-94. Sgt. U.S. Army N.G., 1955-61. Mem. Elks, Mitchell Jaycees (pres., v.p. 1968-70, Outstanding Jaycee 1970), S.D. Jaycees (v.p., regional dir. 1969-70). Democrat. Roman Catholic. Avocations: golf, bowling, hunting. Office: Reginald Martin Agy 510 W Havens St Mitchell SD 57301-3935

WIDMANN, EDWARD HEALY, lawyer; b. Pasadena, Calif., July 28, 1940; s. Frederick Carpenter and Nancy (Healy) W.; m. Nancy Louise DuClos, Aug. 25, 1962; children: Brian E., Beth Louise, Devin Bok-Sun. BA, Claremont Men's Coll., 1962; JD, U. Denver, 1965. Bar: Colo. 1965, U.S. Dist. Ct. Colo. 1965, U.S. Ct. Appeals (10th cir.) 1965, U.S. Supreme Ct. 1981. Ptnr. Hall & Evans, Denver, 1965—. Mem. ABA, Colo. Bar Assn. (pres. litig. sect. 1980), Colo. Def. Bar Assn. Democrat. Bus. Home: 703 Ash St Denver CO 80220-4928 Office: Hall and Evans 1200 17th St Ste 1700 Denver CO 80202-5817 E-mail: widmane@hallevans.com.

WIDMANN, JOHN ANDREW, account administrator, musician; b. Chambersburg, Pa., Sept. 23, 1963; s. John Macklem Jr. and Nina Louise (Shade) W.; m. Diane Marie King, June 17, 1989; children: Hans Andreas, Martin Joseph. BS in Edn., Ind. U. Pa., 1985. Tchr. South Lewis Ctrl. Sch., Turin, N.Y., 1985-86, Washington County Pub. Schs., Hagerstown, Md., 1988-97; supr. Chevy Chase Fed. Savs. Bank, Frederick, 1988-97; sr. acct. mgr. Thomson Fin., Boston, 1997—. City carillonneur, City of Frederick, Md., 1992—. Mem. Guild Carillonneurs N.Am. (master carillonneur), Am. Guild Organists (Ctrl. Md. chpt. dean 1996-99). Republican. Roman Catholic. Home: 623 Magnolia Ave Frederick MD 21701-8505 Office: Thomson Fin 22 Thomson Pl Boston MA 02210-1212 Fax: 301-545-6251. E-mail: JAWidmann@juno.com.

WIDMANN, ROGER MAURICE, investment banker, lawyer; b. N.Y.C., Oct. 7, 1939; s. Marcus and Dina (Sander) W.; m. Judith Dolger, Aug. 4, 1963; children: Daniel, Emily, Kenneth. BA cum laude, Brown U., 1961; LLB, Columbia U., 1964. Bar: N.Y. 1965. Trial atty. U.S. SEC, N.Y.C., 1964-67; v.p. New Ct. Securities Corp., 1967-75; sr. v.p. Donaldson, Lufkin & Jenrette, 1975-81; pres. First Rec. Securities Corp., Greenwich, Conn., 1981-86; sr. mng. dir. head of corp. fin. Chem. Bank, 1986-95; ptnr. Castle, Harlan & Widmann Energy, N.Y.C., 1995-96; prin. Tanner & Co., Inc., 1997—. Bd. dirs., chmn. Lydall, Inc., Manchester, Conn.; sr. moderator exec. seminar Aspen (Colo.) Inst. Pres. March of Dimes Birth Defects Found., N.Y.C. Office: Tanner & Co Inc 650 Madison Ave New York NY 10022 ALSO: LYDALL,INC PO Box 151 Manchester CT 06045-0151 E-mail: rwidmann@tanner-ny.com.

WIDMAR, RUSSELL C. airport executive; V.p. airport svcs. Lockheed Air Terminal Inc., 1980-94; dir. Burbank-Glendale-Pasadena Airport, 1984; dir. ops. airport sys. divsn. Hughes Aircraft Co., Fullerton, Calif., 1994-96; exec. dir. aviation Salt Lake City Airport Authority, 1996-99; aviation dir. Kansas City Aviation Dept., 2000—. Office: Kansas City Aviation Dept PO Box 20047 Kansas City MO 64195-0047*

WIDMARK, RICHARD, actor; b. Sunrise, Minn., Dec. 26, 1914; s. Carl H. and Ethel Mae (Barr) W.; m. Ora Jean Hazlewood, Apr. 5, 1942; 1 dau., Anne Heath. BA, Lake Forest (Ill.) Coll., 1936, D.F.A. (hon.), 1973. Instr. drama dept. Lake Forest Coll., 1936-38; Pres. Heath Prodns., 1955—; v.p. Widmark Cattle Enterprises, 1957—. Actor various radio networks, N.Y.C., 1938-47; Broadway appearances include Kiss and Tell, 1943, Get Away Old Man, 1943, Trio, 1944, Kiss Them for Me, 1944, Dunnigan's Daughter, 1945, Dream Girl, 1946-47; summer stock appearances include The Bo Tree, 1939, Joan of Lorraine, 1947; motion picture appearances include Kiss of Death, 1947, Street with No Name, 1948, Yellow Sky, 1948, Roadhouse, 1948, Down to the Sea in Ships, 1949, Night and the City, 1949, No Way Out, 1949, Panic in the Streets, 1950, Slattery's Hurricane, 1949, Halls of Montezuma, 1950, The Frogmen, 1950, Price of Gold, 1954, Co Blue, 1954, Broken Lance, 1954, Backlash, 1955, St. Joan, 1956, Time Limit, 1957, Warlock, 1958, The Alamo, 1959, Judgement at Nuremberg, 1961, Flight from Ashiya, 1962, How the West Was Won, 1962, The Long Ships, 1963, Cheyenne Autumn, 1963, Bedford Incident, 1964, Alvarez Kelly, 1965, The Way West, 1966, Madigan, 1967, Patch, 1968, Talent for Loving, 1968, The Moonshine War, 1969, When the Legends Die, 1971, Murder on the Orient Express, 1974, The Sellout, 1975, To the Devil, A Daughter, 1975, The Twilight's Last Gleaming, 1976, The Domino Principle, 1976, Roller Coaster, 1976, Coma, 1978, The Swarm, 1977, Hanky Panky, 1982, The Final Option, 1983, Against All Odds, 1984, True Colors, 1990; NBC TV appearance in Vanished, 1971, TV series Madigan, 1972; TV appearance in Benjamin Franklin, 1974, Mr. Horn, 1979, Bear Island, 1979, All God's Children, 1980, A Whale for the Killing, 1981, Blackout, 1985, A Gathering of Old Men, 1986, Once Upon a Texas Train, 1987, Cold Sassy Tree, 1989. True Colors, 1990. Bd. dirs. Hope for Hearing. Named Comdr. of Arts and Letters (France), 1987. Mem. Century Club (N.Y.C.).

WIDMAYER, PATRICIA, management consultant; b. Buffalo, Jan. 21, 1943; d. C. Lane and Elizabeth M. (Gillgus) Ramsdell; m. Lawrence C. Widmayer, June 15, 1963; children: Carole Lane, Christopher Almon. BA, Mich. State U., 1966, MA, 1969, PhD, 1971. Instr. Oakland U., Rochester, Mich., 1971-72; rsch. assoc. Office of the Speaker, Lansing, Mich., 1973-75; dist. staff dir. Congressman Bob Carr, Washington, 1975-77; dir. legis. Mich. Dept. Edn., Lansing, 1977-82; dir. policy Office of Gov., Lansing, 1982-83; exec. dir. Gov.'s Commn. on Higher Edn., Lansing, 1983-85; pres. Widmayer and Assocs., Chgo., 1985—; trainer Nat. Women's Edn. Fund, Washington, 1982-89; spl. project dir. colo. Commn. on Higher Edn., Denver, 1985-89; cons. Borg-Warner Found., Chgo., 1985-89, MacAuthur Found. 1987, Sears Found. 1987, Donors Forum Chgo., 1986, Associated Colls. Ill., 1986—, Colo. Dept. Edn., 1986—, Nat. Assn. Bank Women, 1987—, DePaul U., 1986-87, Dept. of Agri., 1986—, Mich. Community Coll. Assn., 1987-88, Nebr. Legis. Coun., 1989-90. Author numerous govt. papers, reports, 1977—; editor report: Putting our minds together, 1984. Vol. cons. to local, state and nat. campaigns and issue coalitions; coord. Nat. Women's Polit. Caucus of Mich., 1975-80, Mich. Women's Assembly, 1976-84; bd. dirs. Econ. Devel. Corp., East Lansing, Mich., 1979-85. Inst. for Ednl. Leadership fellow George Washington U., Washington, 1978-79. Mem. Am. Assn. Higher Edn., Execs.' Club of Chgo., Delta Delta Delta (officer 1968-85). Home: 2327 Park Pl Evanston IL 60201-1430 Office: Widmayer and Assocs 1603 Orrington Ave Ste 900 Evanston IL 60201-3845

WIDMAYER, WARREN J. lawyer; b. Detroit, Mar. 20, 1956; s. Warren Widmayer; m. Elizabeth A. Widmayer, Sept. 3, 1982; children: David J., Katherine R., Christine J. BA with high distinction, U. Mich., 1978, JD, 1982. Bar: Mich. 1983, U.S. Dist. Ct. (ea. dist.) Mich. 1983. Atty. Dobson, Griffin & Westerman, P.C., Ann Arbor, Mich., 1983-85, Dobson, Griffin, Austin & Berman, P.C., Ann Arbor, 1985-86, Ellis, Talcott, Ohlgren & Ferguson, P.C., Ann Arbor, 1986-89, Joscelyn & Treat, P.C., Ann Arbor, 1989-91; atty., prin. Ferguson & Widmayer, P.C., 1991—. Contbr. articles to law jours. Mem. ABA (mem. labor and employment sect., forum on health law), State Bar of Mich. (mem. taxation sect.), Washtenaw County Bar Assn. (chmn. tax law sect. 1991-93, mem. labor and employment law sect.), Washtenaw County Estate Planning Coun. (mem., bd. dirs. 1986-87), Nat. Health Lawyer Assn. Avocations: musician, gardening. Office: Ferguson & Widmayer PC 538 N Division St Ann Arbor MI 48104-1136 E-mail: warren@fergusonwidmayer.com.

WIDMER, CHARLES GLENN, dentist, researcher; b. Daytona Beach, Fla., Jan. 8, 1955; s. Ernest Clyde and Martha Elizabeth (Hunter) W.; m. Alyson Lynn Byrd, Jul. 11, 1981; children: Kathryn Michelle, Elizabeth Ann. BS, Emory U., 1977, DDS, 1981; MS, SUNY, 1983. Asst. prof. Emory U. Sch. Dentistry, Atlanta, 1983-91; assoc. prof. U. Fla. Coll. Dentistry, Gainesville, 1991—; acting assoc. dean for rsch. U. Fla., 1996-97. Reviewer NIH, Washington, 1988-89, 93-94, NIH Reviewer's Res., 1995-99. Editl. bd. Cells Tissues Organs 1999—; contbr. articles to profl. jours. Active Atlanta Zoo, 1985-91. Recipient rsch. career Devel. award NIH, 1991-96; grantee NIH, 1986—. Mem. ADA, Internat. Assn. Dental Rsch. (sec., treas., v.p., then pres., councilor neurosci. group 1989-95), Assn. Univ. Temporomandibular Disorders and Orofacial Pain Programs (sec., treas., v.p., then pres. 1990-95), Soc. Neurosci., Internat. Brain Rsch. Orgn., Am. Assn. Dental Rsch. (bd. dirs. 1998-2000), N.Y. Acad. Scis. Office: U Fla Dept Orthodontics PO Box 100444 Gainesville FL 32610-0444 E-mail: widmer@dental.ufl.edu.

WIDMER, LAURA BETH, mass communication educator; b. Moberly, Mo., May 6, 1956; d. John Richard and Gertrude (Roling) Widmer. BS, Northwest Mo. State U., 1979; MS, Iowa State U., 1983. Media asst. Earle Palmer Brown Advt. Agy., Washington, 1980; photo lab instr. Iowa State U., Ames, 1981, instr. yearbook workshop, 1981—; publs. coord. Clinton (Mo.) Sch. Dist., 1981-83, founder, dir. yearbook workshop and Idea, 1987—; publs. dir., asst. prof. Northwest Mo. State U., Maryville, 1983—, dir. summer publs. workshop, 1978—; instr. yearbook workshop Drake U., Des Moines, 1983, U. Mo., 1984—, La. Tech. U., U. Nebr. Cons. journalism and yearbook programs Fla. State U., Tex. Tech U., U. So. Calif., Baker U., Coll. Charleston. Recipient Gov.'s award for Tchg. Excellence, 1996. Mem. Nat. Press Photographers Assn., Soc. Profl. Journalists, Mo. Press Women's Fedn., Coll. Media Advisers (pres. 1991-93, Outstanding Yearbook Adviser 1989, Outstanding Multimedia

Adviser 1998), Mo. Coll. Media Assn. (Adviser of Yr. 1996). Roman Catholic. Home: 206 S Alco Ave Maryville MO 64468-2032 Office: Northwest Mo State U 236 Wells Hall Maryville MO 64468

WIDNALL, SHEILA EVANS, aeronautical educator, former secretary of the airforce, former university official; b. Tacoma, July 13, 1938; d. Rolland John and Genievieve Alice (Krause) Evans; m. William Soule Widnall, June 11, 1960; children: William, Ann. BS in Aero. and Astronautics, MIT, 1960, MS in Aero. and Astronautics, 1961, DSc, 1964; PhD (hon.), New Eng. Coll., 1975, Lawrence U., 1987, Cedar Crest Coll., 1988, Smith Coll., 1990, Mt. Holyoke Coll., 1991, Ill. Inst. Tech., 1991, Columbia U., 1994, Simmons Coll., 1994, Suffolk U., 1994, Princeton U., 1994. Asst. prof. aeros. and astronautics MIT, Cambridge, 1964-70, assoc. prof., 1970-74, prof., 1974-93, head divsn. fluid mechanics, 1975-79; dir. Fluid Dynamics Rsch. Lab., MIT, 1979-90; chmn. faculty MIT, 1979-80, chair com. on acad. responsibility, 1991-92, assoc. provost, 1992-93; sec. USAF, 1993-97; Inst. prof. MIT, Cambridge, 1997—. Trustee Sloan Found., 1998—; bd. dirs. Gen. Corp., Chemfab Inc., Bennington, Vt., Aerospace Corp., L.A., Draper Labs., Cambridge, Gencorp; past trustee Carnegie Corp., 1984-92, Charles Stark Draper Lab. Inc.; mem. Carnegie Commn. Sci., Tech. and Govt. Contbr. articles to profl. jours.; patentee in field; assoc. editor AIAA Jour. Aircraft, 1972-75, Physics of Fluids, 1981-88, Jour. Applied Mechanics, 1983-87; mem. editorial bd. Sci., 1984-86. Bd. visitors USAF Acad., Colorado Springs, Colo., 1978-84, bd. chair, 1980-82; trustee Boston Mus. Sci., 1989-93. Recipient Washburn award Boston Mus. Sci., 1987. Fellow AAAS (bd. dirs. 1982-89, pres. 1987-88, chmn. 1988-89), AIAA (bd. dirs. 1975-77, Lawrence Sperry award 1972, Durand Lectureship for Pub. Svc. award 1996, pres. 2000-01), Am. Phys. Soc. (exec. com. 1979-82); mem. ASME (Applied Mechs. award 1995, Pres. award 1999), NAE (coun. 1992-93, v.p. 1998—), NAS (panel on sci. responsibility), Am. Acad. Arts and Scis., Soc. Women Engrs. (Outstanding Achievement award 1975), Internat. Acad. Astronautics, Seattle Mountaineers. Office: MIT Bldg 33-411 77 Massachussetts Ave Cambridge MA 02139

WIDNER, RALPH RANDOLPH, civic executive; b. Phila., Oct. 21, 1930; s. Ralph Litteer and Viola (Cunningham) W.; m. Joan Sundelius Ziegler, July 9, 1955; children: Jennifer Anne, Wendy Rowe Ducharme. BA, Duke U., 1952; postgrad., NYU, 1957, Georgetown U., 1958; DHL (hon.), Union Coll., Ky., 1970, Capital U., Columbus, Ohio, 1971. Journalist Paterson (N.J.) Evening News, 1955-56, N.Y. Times, 1956-58; Congressional fellow Am. Polit. Sci. Assn., 1958; dir. pub. affairs Pa. Dept. Forests and Waters, 1959-60; asst. dir. Pa. Planning Bd., 1960-62; legis. asst. to U.S. Senator Clark, 1962-65; exec. dir. Appalachian Regional Commn., 1965-71; pres. Acad. for State and Local Govt., 1971-82; adj. prof. pub. adminstrn. and city planning Ohio State U., 1971-82; pres. Nat. Tng. and Devel. Service for State and Local Govt., 1979-81; staff v.p. Urban Land Inst., 1982-83; exec. dir. Greater Phila. First Corp., 1983-88; chmn. Fairfax House Internat., Alexandria, Va., 1988—. Fellow Nat. Acad. Pub. Adminstrn. Democrat. Methodist. Home: 2210 Belle Haven Rd Alexandria VA 22307-1100 Office: PO Box 7517 Alexandria VA 22307-0517 E-mail: fxhouse@compuserve.com.

WIDOM, BENJAMIN, chemistry educator; b. Newark, Oct. 13, 1927; s. Morris and Rebecca (Hertz) W.; m. Joanne McCurdy, Dec. 21, 1953; children: Jonathan, Michael, Elisabeth. AB, Columbia U., 1949; PhD, Cornell U., 1953; DSc (hon.), U. Chgo., 1991; Doctor honoris causa, U. Utrecht, 1999. Rsch. assoc. U. N.C., Chapel Hill, 1952-54; instr. chemistry Cornell U., Ithaca, N.Y., 1954-55, asst. prof., 1955-59, assoc. prof., 1959-63, prof., 1963-83, Goldwin Smith prof., 1983—; van der Waals prof. U. Amsterdam, The Netherlands, 1972; vis. prof. Harvard U., Cambridge, Mass., 1975; IBM vis. prof. Oxford (Eng.) U., 1978. Lorentz prof. U. Leiden, The Netherlands, 1985; vis. prof. Kath. U. Leuven, Belgium, 1988, U. Aix Marseille, France, 1995; Kramers/Debye prof. U. Utrecht, 1999. Author: (with J.S. Rowlinson) Molecular Theory of Capillarity, 1982. With U.S. Army, 1946-47. Recipient Clark disting. tchg. award Cornell U., 1973, Dickson prize for sci. Carnegie-Mellon U., 1986, Hirschfelder Prize in Theoretical Chemistry U. Wis., 1991, Bakhuis Roozeboom medal Royal Netherlands Acad. Arts & Scis., 1994, Onsager medal U. Trondheim, Norway, 1994, Boltzmann medal Internat. Union of Pure and Applied Physics, Commn. on Statis. Physics, 1998. Fellow Am. Phys. Soc., Am. Acad. Arts and Scis., N.Y. Acad. Scis. (Boris Pregel award for chem. physics rsch. 1976); mem. NAS, Am. Philos. Soc., Am. Chem. Soc. (Langmuir award in chem. physics 1982, Hildebrand award in theoretical and exptl. chemistry of liquids 1992, Theoretical Chemistry award 1999). Home: 204 The Parkway Ithaca NY 14850-2247 Office: Cornell U Chemistry Dept Ithaca NY 14853 E-mail: bw24@cornell.edu.

WIDYOLAR, SHEILA GAYLE, dermatologist; b. Vancouver, B.C., Can., June 11, 1939; d. Walter Herbert and Olive Louise (O'Neal) Roberts; Kithi K. Widyolar, 1960 (div. 1979); 1 child, Keith. BS, Loma Linda U., 1962; MD, Howard U., 1972. Resident U. Calif., Irvine, 1973-76; dermatologist pvt. practice, Laguna Hills, Calif., 1976—. Clin. instr. U. Calif. Sch. Medicine, 1978-86. Chmn. bd. dirs. Opera Pacific, Costa Mesa, Calif., 1996-97. Fellow Am. Acad. Dermatology, Am. Soc. Dermatophthology; mem. AMA, Calif. Med. Assn., Dermatological Soc. Orange County (pres. 1983), Alpha Omega Alpha. Avocations: music, travel. Office: Ste 403 23911 Calle de Mag Dalena Laguna Hills CA 92653

WIEBE, LEONARD IRVING, radiopharmacist, educator; b. Swift Current, Sask., Can., Oct. 14, 1941; s. Cornelius C. and Margaret (Teichroeb) W.; m. Grace E. McIntyre, Sept. 5, 1964; children: Glenis, Kirsten, Megan BSP, U. Sask., 1963, MS, 1966; PhD, U. Sydney, Australia, 1970; D.Pharm.Sci (hon.) , Meiji Pharm. U., Japan, 2002. Pharmacist Swift Current Union Hosp., 1963-64; sessional lectr. U. Sask., Can., 1965-66; asst. prof. U. Alta., Can., 1970-73, assoc. prof. Can., 1973-78, prof. Can., 1978—, dir. Slowpoke Reactor Facility Can., 1975-89, 2001—, asst. dean rsch. Can., 1984-87, assoc. dean Can., 1990-99; prof. dept. exptl. oncology, 1999—; sessional lectr. U. Sydney, Australia, 1973; pres. Internat. Bionucleonics Cons. Lts., 1991—; dir. BMH, Australian Nuclear Sci. Tech. Orgn., 1990, Noujaim Inst. Pharm. Oncology, 1994-2000. Rsch. assoc. Cross Cancer Inst., Edmonton, 1978—, Med. Rsch. Coun. Can.; vis. prof. Royal P.A. Hosp., Sydney, 1983-84, Searle vis. profl., 1986; MRC vis. prof., Toronto, 1987; PMAC vis. prof., 1988; McCalla prof. U. Alta, 1993-94; radiopharmacy cons. Australian Atomic Energy Commn., Sydney, 1983-84; mem. MRC standing com. on sci. and rsch., 1995-98; hon. liason prof. Peoples U. Bangladesh. Editor: Liquid Scintillation: Science and Technology, 1976, Advances in Scintillation Counting, 1983; guest editor Jour. of Radioanalytical Chemistry, 1981; editor Internat. Jour. Applied Radiation Instrumentation Sect. A, 1988-90; regional editor Internat. Jour. Nuclear Biology and Medicine, 1992-95; mem. editl. bd. Jour. Pharmacy & Pharm. Sci., Jour. Applied Radiation Isotopes, 1995—. Recipient Janssen-Ortho Rsch. award, 1998; Commonwealth Univs. Exchange grantee, 1966; Alexander von Humboldt fellow, 1976-79, 82. Mem. Pharm. Bd. of New South Wales, Sask. Pharm. Assn., Soc. Nuclear Medicine, Assn. Faculties of Pharmacy of Can. (McNeil Rsch. award 1988), Can. Radiation Protection Assn., Can. Assn. Radiopharm. Scientists, Am. Pharm. Assn., Am. Assn. Pharm. Sci., Internat. Assn. Radiopharmacy (exec. sec. 1991-95), Can. Assn. Pharm. Scis. (founding), Univ. Club (Edmonton) (pres. 1985). Mem. Mennonite Ch.

WIEBENSON, DORA LOUISE, architectural historian, editor, author; b. Cleve., July 29, 1926; d. Edward Ralph and Jeannette (Rodier) W. BA, Vassar Coll., 1946; MArch, Harvard U., 1951; MA, NYU, 1958, PhD, 1964. Architect, N.Y., 1951-66; lectr. Columbia U., 1966-68; assoc. prof. U. Md., 1968-72, prof., 1972-77; vis. prof. Cornell U., 1974; prof. U. Va., Charlottesville, 1977-92, prof. emeritus, 1992—, chmn. div. archtl. history, 1977-79, assoc. fellow U. Va. Ctr. Advanced Studies, 1982-83; pres. Archtl. Publs., N.Y.C., 1982—; editor-in-chief Centropa, 2000—. Editor: Marsyas XI: 1962-64, 1965, Essays in Honor of Walter Friedlaender, 1965; Architectural Theory and Practice from Alberti to Ledoux, 1982, rev., 1983, Spanish transl., 1988; Guide to Graduate Degree Programs in Architectural History, 1982, rev., 1984, 86, 88, 90; co-editor: The Architecture of Historic Hungary, 1998, Hungarian transl., 1998; author: Sources of Greek Revival Architecture, 1969, Tony Garnier: The Cité Industrielle, 1969, Japanese transl., 1983, The Picturesque Garden in France, 1978, Mark J. Millard Architectural Collection, Vol. I: French Books: Sixteenth through Nineteenth Centuries, 1993; contbr. articles to profl. jours. Student fellow Inst. Fine Arts, 1961-62, 62-63; grantee Am. Philos. Soc., 1964-65, 70, Samuel H. Kress Found., 1966, 72-73, 98, Gen. Rsch. Fund, U. Md., 1969, 74, 76, NEH, 1972-73, Am. Coun. Learned Socs., 1976, 81, 85, Ctr. Advanced Studies, U. Va., 1980, 81, 97, Graham Found. Advanced Studies Fine Arts, 1982, 93, Archtl. History Found., 1996; fellow Yale Ctr. Brit. Art, 1983; sr. rsch. fellow NEH, 1986-87. Mem. Soc. Archtl. Historians (bd. dirs. 1974-77, 80-83, chair edn. com. 1976-90), Coll. Art Assn., Am. Soc. Eighteenth Century (mem. exec. bd. 1991-94).

WIEBERS, DAVID OWEN, physician; b. Mar. 26, 1951; MD, U. Nebr., 1975. Diplomate Am. Bd. Psychiatry and Neurology. Intern in medicine U. Minn., Mpls., 1975-76; resident in neurology Mayo Clinic, Rochester, Minn., 1976-80, chair divsn. cerebrovasc. diseases, 1994—, head sect. neurology, 1987-96, dir. Mayo Stroke Ctr., 1994—; prof. neurology Mayo Med. Sch., 1991—. Author: 2 books, 3 med. textbooks; co-author: 1 med. textbook; contbr. more than 280 articles to profl. jours. Chair, bd. dirs. Humane Soc. U.S., Washington, 1995-99, Human Soc. Internat. (bd. dirs. 1994—), Earth Voice Internat. (bd. dirs. 1995—). Mem. World Soc. for the Protection of Animals (London; bd. dirs. 1997—). Office: Mayo Clinic Dept Neurology 200 1st St SW Rochester MN 55905-0002

WIEBUSCH, JANICE MARIE, real estate broker; b. Broken Bow, Nebr., Apr. 20, 1946; d. George William and Corinna Jane (Beal) W. B in Music Edn., U. Nebr., 1968, MusM, 1970. Tchr. music Lincoln (Nebr.) Pub. Schs., 1970-71, Gibbon (Nebr.) Pub. Schs., 1971-73; real estate salesperson Gateway Realty, Kearney, Nebr., 1976-79; real estate broker, owner CBS Real Estate, 1979-83; real estate owner Midland Ptnrs., 1983-92; owner Century 21 Midlands, 1992—. Mem. Downtown Revitalization Task Force, Kearney, 1980—; chmn. fund drive Kearney State Coll. Found., 1986; bd. dirs. Community Concert Assn., Kearney, 1980—; mem. Kearney City Coun. Mem. Women's Coun. of Realtors, Nebr. Realtors Assn. (treas.), Kearney Tomorrow Forum, Kearney Area C. of C. (chmn.). Republican. Episcopalian. Avocations: reading, snow skiing, traveling, piano, singing. Home: 2712 Central Ave Kearney NE 68847-4505

WIECHA, JOSEPH AUGUSTINE, linguist, educator; b. Chorzów II, Poland, Sept. 20, 1926; came to U.S., 1955, naturalized, 1958; s. Karol and Gertruda (Rudzki) W.; m. Mary Ruth Moore, 1953; children: Joseph Damian, Charles Francis, John Moore. BA with honors, Nat. U. Ireland, 1950; PhD with distinction, NYU, 1963. Instr. fgn. langs. U.S. Third Air Force, London, 1951-55; instr. German and Spanish U. Md., 1951-55; tchr. Spanish and math. Bklyn. Friends Sch., 1955-56; instr. German NYU, N.Y.C., summer, 1958; lectr. German and humanities Harvard U., Boston, 1959-63; lectr. German lit. Colby Coll., summer 1963; prof. German SUNY, Oswego, 1963-69, chmn. dept. fgn. langs. and lit., 1963-69, chmn. dept. Germanic and Slavic langs. and lit., 1969-72, disting. teaching prof., 1973-92, disting. tchg. prof. emeritus, 1992—; chmn. SUNY Fgn. Studies Ctr., 1972-73. Lectr. and cons. methodology of tchg. fgn. langs., 1959—; condr. seminars tchg. methodology fgn. langs. Nat. U. Pedro Enriquez Ureña, Santo Domingo, 1973, U. Pisa, Italy, 1974, Moscow State Pedagogical Inst.; Fgn. Langs., USSR, 1976; vis. prof. U. Wroctaw, Poland, 1977. Developed Wiecha Progressive-Reflex method of teaching fgn. langs. Served as officer 2d Polish Corps Brit. VIII Army, 1944-47. Decorated Bronze medal Polish Army, Brit. Def. medal; French Star; Star of Italy; recipient diploma of spl. recognition U. Nat. Pedro Enriquez Ureña, 1973; Galileo medal U. Pisa, 1974; Ogden Butler fellow, 1958-59, Fels fellow, 1956-59, Kosciuszko Found. fellow, 1959. Mem. MLA, N.Y. State Assn. Fgn. Lang. Tchrs. (dir. 1975-78, Disting. Tchr. award 1975, Disting. Bd. Dirs. award 1978, Spl. Contbn. to Teaching Fgn. Langs. award 1979), Am. Assn. Tchrs. of German, Polish Inst. Arts and Scis. in Am., Nat. Spanish Honors Soc. (hon.), Am. Coun. on Edn. (nat. honor roll), Delta Phi Alpha (hon.), Dobro Slovo (hon.) Home: 710 Copa De Oro Marathon FL 33050-5406 also: 22 Bayside Rd Northport ME 04849-4435

WIECHELT, EARL L., JR. music educator; b. Homestead, Pa., Sept. 23, 1961; s. Earl L., Sr. and Sally J. Wiechelt; m. Diane Lynn Kennedy, June 17, 1989; children: Tiffany, William. BS in Music Edn., Edinboro Coll., 1983; MS in Edn., Duquesne U., 1990. HS choral dir. West Allegheny Sch. Dist., Imperial, Pa., 1983—. Master: Freemason; mem.: Music Educators Nat. Conf., Pa. Music Educators Assn. Democrat. Presbyterian. Avocations: travel, reading. Office: West Allegheny HS 205 West Allegheny Rd Imperial PA 15126

WIECHERT, ALLEN LEROY, educational planning consultant, architect; b. Independence, Kans., Oct. 25, 1938; s. Norman Henry and Serena Johanna (Steinke) W.; m. Sandra Swanson, Aug. 19, 1961; children: Kristin Nan, Brendan Swanson, Megan Ann. BArch, Kans. State U., 1962. Lic. arch., Kans.; cert. Nat. Coun. Archtl. Registration Bds. Arch. in tng. McVey, Peddie, Schmidt & Allen, Wichita, Kans., 1962-63; arch. Kivett & Myers, Kansas City, Mo., 1963-68; asst. to vice chancellor plant planning and devel. U. Kans., Lawrence, 1968-74, assoc. dir. facilities planning, 1974-78, univ. dir. facilities planning, 1978-92, univ. arch., 1993-95; campus planner Gould Evans Assocs., 1995-96; code enforcement officer City of Prairie Village, Kans., 1997-2001; ret. Mem. long range phys. planning com. Kans. Bd. Regents, 1971-95; designer, archtl. programmer edml. facilities; bd. dirs. Kans. U. Fed. Credit Union, 1972-81, pres. bd., 1974. Editor, contbr.: Physical Development Planning Work Book, 1973. Chmn. horizons com. Lawrence Bicentennial Commn.; designer Kaw River Trail, 1976; mem. Action 80 Com., 1980-81, Lawrence-Douglas County Horizon 2020 Task Group, 1993-95; mem. standing com. Kans. Episcopal Diocese, 1976-80, pres. com., 1981, mem. diocesan coun., 1982-84, chmn. coll. work com., 1982-84, commn. on ch. arch. and allied arts, 1986-99, long range planning com., 1988; sr. warden Trinity Episc. Ch., Lawrence, 1978-80, 2001—, mem. vestry, 1997-99; trustee Kans. Sch. Religion, 1973-80, 82-95, v.p., 1984-85, pres., 1986-92, trustee friends of the dept. of religious studies, 1995—; mem. adv. bd. Salvation Army, 1990—; bd. dirs. Trinity Group Care Home, 1973-79; advancement chmn. troop com. Boy Scouts Am., 1981-87, dist. com. Pelathe dist., 1984—, vice chmn., 1984, chmn., 1985-87; exec. bd. Heart of Am. Coun., 1985-87. 1st lt. Kans. Air N.G., 1961-67. Recipient Dist. Award of Merit, Boy Scouts Am., 1988, Silver Beaver award, 1991. Mem. AIA, Assn. Univ. Archs. (sec.-treas. 1986-87, v.p. 1987-88, pres. 1988-89), Nat. Hist. Trust, Kans. U. Endowment Assn. (sec. 1981-85, founder, exec. bd. Hist. Mt. Oread Fund divsn.), Nat. Cathedral Assn. (regional co-chairperson 1993—). Home: 813 Highland Dr Lawrence KS 66044-2431

WIECHMANN, ERIC WATT, lawyer; b. Schenectady, N.Y., June 12, 1948; s. Richard Jerdone and Ann (Watt) W.; m. Merrill Metzger, May 22, 1971. BA, Hamilton Coll., 1970; JD, Cornell U., 1974. Bar: Conn. 1975, U.S. Dist. Ct. (so. and ea. dists.) N.Y. 1975, U.S. Dist. Ct. Conn. 1975, U.S. Dist. Ct. D.C. 1981, U.S. Ct. Appeals (2nd cir.) 1975, U.S. Ct. Appeals (9th cir.) 1980, U.S. Ct. Appeals D.C. 1982, U.S. Ct. Appeals (5th cir.) 1986, U.S. Ct. Appeals (10th cir.) 1989, U.S. Supreme Ct. 1978. Assoc. Cummings & Lockwood, Stamford, Conn., 1974-82, ptnr., 1982—, mng. ptnr. Hartford office, bd. dirs. Hartford, 1996—. Spl. pretrial master U.S. Dist. Ct. Conn. 1984—; state atty. trial referee, 1986—, mem. evidence code oversight com.; civil task force, civil jury instrn. com. Conn. Superior Ct., 1996-2000, docket control com., 2001; comml. arbitrator Am. Arbitration Assn. Contbr. articles to profl. jours. Active Zoning Bd. Appeals, New Canaan, Conn., 1984-85; bd. dirs. Conn. Rivers coun. Boy Scouts Am., trustee, 2001—. Mem. ABA (vice-chmn. toxics and hazardous law com. TIPS sect.), Def. Rsch. Inst., Internat. Assn. Def. Counsel (mem. faculty Def. Trial Acad. 1996, chmn. toxic and hazardous substance com. 1998-99, chmn. CLE bd. 2000-01), Internat. Soc. Barristers, Conn. Bar Assn. (exec. com. antitrust sect. 1982—, ct. rules adv. com, chmn. 1991-93), Golf Club Avon. Republican. Episcopalian. Home: 10 Langley Park Farmington CT 06032-1541 E-mail: ewiech@yahoo.com., ewiech@cl-law.com.

WIECKOWSKI, ANDRZEJ, chemistry educator; b. Lodz, Poland, Feb. 22, 1945; came to U.S., 1983; s. Andrzej and Halina (Motylewska) W.; m. Teresa Prussak, Aug. 2, 1967; 1 child, Zuzanna. PhD, U. Warsaw, Poland, 1973, DSc, 1980; postgrad., U. Calif., Santa Barbara, 1983-85. From assoc. to dr. habil. U. Warsaw, 1973-84; prof. U. Ill., Urbana, 1985—, prin. investigator Fredrick Seitz Materials Lab., 1985—. Rschr., tchr. dept. chemistry U. Ill., Urbana, 1985—; lectr., spkr. in field. Author: The Analysis of Adsorption Processes on Platinum Electrode, 1984; editor: Interfacial Electrochemistry, Theory, Experiment, Application; contbr. numerous articles to profl. jours. and chpts. to books including Modern Aspects of Electrochemistry, Handbook of Surface Imaging and Visualization. Recipient Outstanding Sci. Accomplishment in Materials award U.S. Dept. Energy, 1992, Procter & Gamble Lectr. award, 1996, Invited Internat. Lectr. award, Japan and Brazil, 1996, hon. lectureship Govt. Taiwan, 1990. Mem. Internat. Soc. Electrochemistry (chmn. fundamental electrochemistry divsn. 1994—. Tacussel award 1997), Am. Chem. Soc., The Electrochem. Soc. (vice-chmn. phys. electrochemistry divsn.), Soc. for Electroanalytical Chemistry (sec. 1995—). Office: U Ill Dept Chemistry Box 56 600 S Mathews Ave Dept Urbana IL 61801-3602

WIECZOREK, PATRICIA CHRISTINE, medical/surgical nurse; b. Balt., Mar. 17, 1961; d. John and Florence (Polek) W. BSN, U. Md., 1983. Nursing asst. Jenkins Meml. Home, Balt., 1981-82; staff nurse ICU Harbor Hosp. Ctr., 1983-84; sr. clin. nurse gen. oper. rm., cardiac surgery Johns Hopkins Hosp., 1984-96, nurse mgr. cardiovasc. and transplant surgery, 1996—. Pub. spkr. nursing practice. Contbr. articles to profl. jours. Mem. Assn. Operating Rm. Nurses (cert.). Office: Johns Hopkins Hosp Gen Oper Rms Bla 7 Cardiac 600 N Wolfe St Baltimore MD 21287-0005 E-mail: pwieczor@jhmi.edu.

WIECZOREK, WILLIAM FREDERICK, medical researcher; b. Feb. 4, 1959; BA, SUNY, Buffalo, 1982, MA, 1984, PhD, 1988. Dir., prof. Buffalo State Coll., 1997—; sr. rsch. scientist Rsch. Inst. on Addictions, Buffalo, 1988-97; rsch. asst. prof. SUNY, 1999; vis. prof., dir. Inst. Behavioral Medicine Dalian Med. U., Dalian, China, 1999—. Principal investigator Nat. Inst. Health, Nat. Inst. Alcohol Abuse and Alcoholism, 1991—; bd. dirs. Rsch. Found. Mental Hygiene, Albany, N.Y., 1993-97. Editl. bd. Jour. of Studies on Alcohol, 1998—; contbr. articles to profl. jours. Cons. Erie Co. Life Saver Patrol Program, 1993-94. Office: Ctr Hlth/Social Rsch Buffalo State Coll HA203 1300 Elmwood Ave Buffalo NY 14222-1004 E-mail: wieczowf@bscmail.buffalostate.edu.

WIED, GEORGE LUDWIG, physician; b. Carlsbad, Czechoslovakia, Feb. 7, 1921; came to U.S., 1953, naturalized, 1960; s. Ernst George and Anna (Travnicek) W.; m. Daga M. Graaz, Mar. 19, 1949 (dec. Aug. 1977); m. Kayoko Y. Yamauchi, Nov. 1, 1990. MD, Charles U., Prague, 1945, Hon. Med. Degree, 1995. Intern County Hosp., Carlsbad, Czechoslovakia, 1945; intern U. Chgo. Hosps., 1955; resident in ob-gyn U. Munich, Fed. Republic Germany, 1946-48; practice medicine specializing in ob-gyn West Berlin, 1948-53; asst. ob-gyn Free U., 1948-52; assoc. chmn. dept. ob-gyn Moabit Hosp., Free U., 1953; asst. prof., dir. cytology U. Chgo., 1954-59, assoc. prof., 1959-65, prof., 1965-91, mem. bd. adult edn., 1964-68, prof. pathology, 1967-91, Blum-Riese prof. ob-gyn, 1968-91, acting chmn. dept. ob-gyn, 1974-75. Editor-in-chief Jour. Reproductive Medicine, Acta Cytologica, Analytical and Quantitative Cytology, Clinical Cytology; editor: Introduction to Quantitative Cytochemistry, Automated Cell Identification and Cell Sorting, Compendium on Clinical Cytology, Compendium on the Computerized Cytology and Histology Laboratory, Compendium on Quality Assurance in Clinical Cytology; sr. editor Gen. and Diagnostic Pathology. Hon. dir. Chgo. Cancer Prevention Ctr., 1959-83; chmn. jury Maurice Goldblatt Cytology award, 1963-92. Recipient Cert. of Merit, U.S. Surgeon Gen., 1952, Maurice Goldblatt Cytology award, 1961, George N. Papanicolaou Cytology award, 1970, Masubuchi Gold Medal award 13th Internat. Cytology Congress, 1998, Kazumsa Masubuchi Lifetime Achievement award, 1998. Mem. Am. Soc. Cytology (pres. 1965-66), Mex. Soc. Cytology (hon.), Spanish Soc. Cytology (hon.), Brazilian Soc. Cytology (fgn. corr.), Indian Acad. Cytology (hon., Lifetime Achievement award 1998), Latin-Am. Soc. Cytology (hon.), Japanese Soc. Cytology (hon.), Internat. Acad. Cytology (pres. 1977-80), German Soc. Cytology (hon.), Ctrl. Soc. Clin. Rsch., Chgo. Path. Soc., Chgo. Gynecol. Soc. (hon.), Am. Soc. Cell Biology, German Soc. Ob-Gyn, Bavarian Soc. Ob-Gyn, German Soc. Endocrinology, Russian Assn. Cytologists (hon.), Swedish Soc. Medicine (hon.), Austrian Soc. Clin. Cytology (hon.), Sigma Xi. iac.org. Home and Office: 1640 E 50th St Chicago IL 60615-3161 E-mail: wied@cytology.

WIEDEL, JEROME D. orthopedic surgeon; b. Orleans, Nebr., Dec. 3, 1938; s. Albert and Clara Wiedel; m. Nancy Rae Wiedel, Aug. 26, 1961 (div. 1992); children: Teresa, Bridget, Janine, Courtney; m. Mary Jo Wiedel, Nov. 13, 1994; children: Abigail, Maritza. MD, U. Nebr., 1964. Diplomate Am. Bd. Orthopedic Surgery. Prof., chmn. dept. orthopedics U. Colo. Health Scis. Ctr., Denver, 1986—2000. With USAF, 1965-67. Fellow Am. Acad. of Orthopedics Surgeons; mem. Am. Orthopedic Assn., Am. Orthopedic Soc. for Sports Medicine, The Knee Soc., Orthopedic Rsch. Soc. Office: PO Box 6510 Aurora CO 80045-0510

WIEDELMAN, ROBERT ERIC, investment banker; MBA, U. Chgo. Dir. Banc One Capital Markets, Chgo., 1995—. Office: Banc One Capital Markets Inc 1 Bank One Plz Chicago IL 60670

WIEDEMAN, JAMES E. surgeon; b. Feb. 27, 1955; BA, So. Ill. U., 1977, MD, 1980. Diplomate Am. Bd. Surgery. Resident gen. surgery Wilford Hall Med. Ctr., Lackland AFB, Tex., 1980-85; staff gen. surgeon USAF Hosp. Yokota, Yokota AFB, Japan, 1985-88; chief gen. surgery RAF Lakenheath Hosp., U.K., 1988-93; chief surg. svcs. David Grant Med. Ctr., Travis AFB, Calif., 1993—. Office: David Grant Med Ctr Dept Surgery Travis AFB CA 94535 E-mail: james.wiedeman@60mdg.travis.af.mil.

WIEDEMANN, CHARLES LOUIS, dentist; b. Belvidere, N.J., May 6, 1936; s. Charles and Clothilde Paulina (Fischer) W.; m. Jacqueline Burdzy, June 11, 1960; children: Lorraine Carol, Julie Patricia. BA, Rutgers U., 1957; DDS with honors, Fairleigh Dickinson U., 1962; grad., U.S. Army Med. Field Svc. Sch., 1962; postgrad. student, Inst. for Grad. Dentists, 1968-69, St. Clare's Hosp. Continuing Edn., N.J., 1972—, U. Pa., 1974-75, Boston U. Sch. Grad. Dentistry, 1991. Pvt. practice dentistry, Hackettstown, N.J., 1966—. Mem., founder dental sect. staff dept. surgery Hackettstown Cmty. Hosp., chief dentistry, 1973-75, 77-78, chief of staff dental sect. dept. surgery, 1974, 80, 85; dental health dir. Clarence W. Sickles Med. Ctr., Hackettstown, 1970-90; co-dir. Stargazer, Bd. of Ed, Online Mag. telecomms. sys., 1985-86; pres. Rexxcom Sys. Electronic Pub. and Computer Software, Co., 1990—; lectr. Morris County Coll., dental socs.; designer giant talking toothbrush, talking molar. Author: The Now Philosophy for Dentistry, 1972, Fantastic Facts About Dental Health, 1975, (computer software) The Format Machine, 1987, Autofont, 1990, Autofont, rev. edit., 1996, The Magic Font Machine (Magifont, Magivue, Magishow), 1990, News 1, 1991, Digipad, 1993, The Autofont Titler (for electronic books), 1994; co-author: Autodoc, 1990, Autodoc, rev. edit., 1993, Font Mania, 1991, Font Mania, rev. edit., 1996, XL100, 1993, XL2000, 1993, XL2001, 1994, XL2001, rev. edit. (the XL book edit.), 1995, E-Z Book, 1995, Autofont Titler, 1995; author, designer: electronic publishing software Rexxcom., 1987—, editl. adv. panel: Dental Econs. Jour., 1979—80; editor: DPA News, 1993—95; contbr. articles to profl. jours. and mags.; editor: electronic books, 1995—; columnist: Hackettstown Gazette, 1983—85. Chmn. Bd. of Health, Washington Twp., Morris County, N.J., 1975-78; co-dir. telecomm. sys. Hunterdon Ctrl. Regional H.S., 1989-98; presentations to Morris, Warren, and Sussex Counties, N.J. elem. schs. ann., 1966-93. Capt. Dental Corps., U.S. Army, 1962-65. Recipient cert. Stuart L. Isler Found. for Preventive Dentistry, 1986. Fellow Acad. Gen. Dentistry, Am. Endodontic Soc. (Harold Katz Meml. award 1983); mem. ADA (panel on quarterly survey of pvt. practitioners 1990-93), Digital Pub. Assn. (founding mem., bd. dirs.), Am. Analgesia Soc., Internat. Analgesia Soc., N.J. Dental Assn., Warren-Sussex Dental Soc., Tri-County Dental Soc. (tchr. dental practice adminstrn. 1970-71), Hackettstown Dental Study Group (co-founder 1974—), Found. for Motivation in Dentistry (founder, chmn., bd. dirs. 1973—), Digital Pub. Assn. (bd. dirs. 1993-95). Republican. Achievements include co-inventor Electronic Pub. and e-books, 1990; design of computer fonts, modules, graphics simulations; first to electronic publishing software; invention of Rexxcom character set, 1992. Office: 110 Mill St Hackettstown NJ 07840-2343

WIEDEMANN, HERBERT PFEIL, physician; b. New Haven, May 9, 1951; s. Herbert Paul and Henrietta (Pfeil) W.; m. Patricia Barz, Feb. 12, 1983; children: Sarah, Andrew. BS, Yale U., 1973; MD, Cornell U., 1977. Diplomate Am. Bd. Internal Medicine, Am. Bd. Pulmonary Disease, Am. Bd. Critical Care Medicine. Med. resident U. Wash., Seattle, 1977-80; chief med. resident Harborview Med. Ctr., 1980-81; postgrad. fellow in pulmonary and critical care medicine Yale U., New Haven, 1981-84; staff physician Cleve. Clinic Found., 1984—, chmn. dept. of pulmonary and critical care medicine, 1991—. Pres. med. staff Cleve. Clinic Hosp., 1995—96, bd. trustees, 1994—96, bd. govs., 2002—; prof. medicine Cleve. Clinic Found. Health Scis. Ctr. of Ohio State U., Cleve., 1993—. Editor-in-chief Cleveland Clinic Jour. of Medicine,

1993-96; editor: Ann. Rev. of Pulmonary and Critical Medicine, 7 edits., 1986-93. Grantee NIH, 1994—. Fellow ACP, Am. Coll. Chest Physicians, Am. Coll. of Critical Care Medicine; mem. Am. Thoracic Soc., Am. Bd. Pulmonary Disease, Alpha Omega Alpha. Achievements include rsch. on surfactants decrease release of cytokines from stimulated macrophages. Home: 18040 S Woodland Rd Shaker Heights OH 44120-1773 Office: Cleve Clinic Found 9500 Euclid Ave Cleveland OH 44195-0001 E-mail: wiedemh@ccf.org.

WIEDEMANN, RAMONA DIANE, occupational therapist; b. Topeka, Oct. 1, 1962; d. John Daniel Fay and Sue Ann Strotman; m. William Newell Wiedemann, Aug. 9, 1986; children: William Jr., Meaghan, Nathaniel, Emily, Daniel, Madeleine. BS in Occupl. Therapy, Tex. Woman's U., 1988. Occupl. therapist Healthcare Staff Resources, Dallas, 1988-91, Associated Rehab. Svcs., Greenville, Tex., 1991-96, 97-99, 1st Rehab., Ft. Worth, 1996, Cmty. Rehab. Svcs., Dallas, 1996-97. Mem. Am. Occupl. Therapy Assn. Republican. Methodist. Avocations: reading, travel, bicycling. Home: 1001 Caledonia Paris TN 38242-1114

WIEDER, BRUCE TERRILL, lawyer, electrical engineer; b. Cleve., Dec. 9, 1955; s. Ira J. and Judith M. (Marx) W. BSEE, Cornell U., 1978; MBA, U. Tex., 1980, JD with honors, 1988. Bar: Tex. 1988, U.S. Dist. Ct. (we. dist.) Tex. 1989, U.S. Patent and Trademark Office 1989, U.S. Ct. Appeals (fed. cir.) 1990, D.C. 1991, U.S. Supreme Ct. 1992, U.S. Dist. Ct. (no. dist.) Tex. 1995, Va. 1997, U.S. Dist. Ct. (ea. dist.) Va. 1997. Engr. Motorola, Inc., Austin, Tex., 1979-85; assoc. Arnold, White & Durkee, 1988-90; law clk. U.S. Ct. Appeals (Fed. cir.), Washington, 1990-91; assoc. Burns, Doane, Swecker & Mathis, Alexandria, Va., 1991-97, ptnr., 1998—. Adj. prof. Georgetown U. Law Ctr., 1998—. Mem. IEEE, ABA, Am. Intellectual Property Law Assn., Alpha Phi Omega (life), Beta Gamma Sigma (life). Office: Burns Doane Swecker & Mathis 1737 King St Ste 500 Alexandria VA 22314-2727

WIEDERHOLD, PIETER RIJK, instrument company executive; b. Malang, Indonesia, Jan. 24, 1928; came to U.S., 1953, naturalized, 1959; s. Frederick Wilhelm and Isabella (Winter) W.; divorced; children: Edward P., Robert P., Conrad N. MSEE, U. Delft, Netherlands, 1953. Project engr. GTE-Sylvania, Ipswich, Mass., 1953-61; R&D dir. Ion Physics Corp., Burlington, 1961-64; dept. mgr. Magnion, Inc., 1964-66; divsn. mgr. Comstock and Wescott, Inc., Cambridge, Mass., 1966-73; pres. Gen. Ea. Instruments Corp., Watertown, 1973-91, Wiederhold Assocs., Boston, 1991—. Interim mktg. v.p. Protimeter, Inc., Commack, N.Y., 1991-92; mktg. specialist EDO Barnes, Inc., Shelton, Conn., 1992-93; cons. in field. Author: Water Vapor Measurement, Methods and Instrumentation, 1997; contbr. articles to profl. jours. Mem. Sun Valley Assn. (pres. 1971-73, treas. 1969-71), World Affairs Coun., Boston Ctr. Internat. Visitors. Avocations: skiing, tennis, golf, classical music. Office: Wiederhold Assocs 603 White Cliff Dr Plymouth MA 02360-1484 E-mail: pwiederhold@aol.com.

WIEDERHORN, SHELDON MARTIN, materials scientist engineer; b. N.Y.C., May 4, 1933; s. Joseph and Estha (Wasinsky) W.; m. Nancy Irene Wanderman, Feb. 18, 1961; children: Jonathan David, Miriam Ruth. BSChemE, Columbia U., 1956; MSChemE, U. Ill., 1958, PhDChemE, 1960. Rsch. engr. E.I. duPont de Nemours & Co., Wilmington, Del., 1960-63; phys. chemist Nat. Bur. Standards, Gaithersburg, Md., 1963-66, rsch. chemist, 1966-68, supervisory rsch. chemist, 1968-78, chief div., 1978-81, group leader, 1981-88; sr. fellow Materials Sci. and Engring. Lab. Nat. Inst. Standards and Tech. (NIST), 1988—. Contbr. numerous articles to profl. jours. Recipient Silver medal Dept. Commerce, 1970, Gold medal, 1982. Fellow Am. Ceramic Soc. (disting. lifetime mem. 1998, chmn. basic sci. div. 1974-75, Morey award 1977, John Jeppson award 1994, editor jour. 1991-94); mem. NAE. Home: 5718 Huntington Pky Bethesda MD 20814-1135 Office: Nat Inst Stds and Tech Materials Sci And Lab Gaithersburg MD 20899-0001 E-mail: sheldon.wiederhorn@nist.gov.

WIEDLEA, JANE LEACH SMITH, civic worker; b. Battle Creek, Mich., Oct. 14, 1910; d. William Reynolds and Edith Pearl (Leach) Smith; A.B., Battle Creek Coll., 1933; postgrad. U. Mich., 1933; m. Clare Edgar Wiedlea, June 30, 1934; children— William Clare, Jane Reynolds, John Towle. Sch. librarian Willard Library, Battle Creek, 1927-29; desk librarian Battle Creek Coll., 1931-33, instr. history, 1933-35. Mem. Sturgis (Mich.) Public Library Bd., 1950-86, pres., 1955-60, 75-86; mem. Sturgis Hosp. Bd., 1969— , v.p., 1974-85, 87—, pres., 1985-87; pres. Sturgis Hosp. Aux., 1969-70, life mem., 1970— ; sec. S.W. Dist. Hosp. Aux. Bd., 1970-74; active St. John's Guild, St. John's Altar Guild; chmn. planning com. centennial yr. Episcopal Diocese of Western Mich., 1874-1974; bd. dirs. James Monroe Meml. Found., 1956-59. Named Citizen of Yr., 1970. Mem. DAR (Amos-Sturgis chpt. regent 1953-55, 73-75, nat. vice chmn. Am. History month 1955-58, citizens steering com. 1959-60, state regent Mich. 1961-64, hon. state regent for life), U.S. Daus. of 1812, Daus. Colonial Wars, Daus. Am. Colonists. Republican. Episcopalian. Club: Polit. Study. Home: 28537 Maystead Rd Sturgis MI 49091-9174

WIEDL-KRAMER, SHEILA COLLEEN, biologist; b. Buffalo, Feb. 19, 1950; d. Frank George and Corinne Ruth (Nuskay) W.; m. Warren J. Kramer, May 8, 1993; children: Colleen Bryce, Paul John. BS, Daemen Coll., 1972; MS, U. Notre Dame, 1974; PhD, SUNY-Buffalo, 1986. Instr. Holy Cross Jr. Coll., South Bend, Ind., 1973-74; rsch. tech. SUNY, Buffalo, 1975-78; entomol. asst. N.Y. State Health Dept., 1979-80; entomol. intern Ohio Dept. Health, 1981; prof. natural scis. Trocaire Coll., Buffalo, 1974-85; scientist Am. Cyanamid, Lederle Labs., Pearl River, N.Y., 1985-86, clin. rsch. assoc., 1986-89; assoc. mgr. CIBA Consumer Pharms., Edison, N.J., 1989-90; assoc. dir. clin. projects AKZO/Oraganon, Inc., West Orange, 1990-95; pres. C. Bryce & Assocs., Flemington, 1995—. Adj. prof. Ramapo Coll. of N.J., 1988-92, Rockland C.C., 1989-92. Contbr. articles to profl. jours. Mem. Assn. Gnotobiotics, N.Y. State Archeol. Assn., Notre Dame Alumni Club. Home and Office: C Bryce & Assocs 39 Winding Way Flemington NJ 08822-7039

WIEDMAN, TIMOTHY GERARD, management educator; b. Detroit; s. Charles Albert and Doris Gertude Wiedman. BA, Oakland U., 1976; MS, Ctrl. Mich. U., 1978; cert. profl. fin. planning, Old Dominion U., 1995. Gen. mgr. Burger Chef Sys., Inc., Detroit, 1969-75; area mgr. Fotomat Corp., Cleve., Columbus, Ohio, 1978-85; instr. bus. mgmt. Ctrl. Ohio Tech. Coll., Newark, 1986-88, Ohio U., Lancaster, 1988-92; asst. prof. Thomas Nelson C. C., Hampton, Va., 1992-95; assoc. prof. Thomas Nelson C.C., 1995—. Workshop leader Va. Quality Inst., Hampton, 1994—; quality trainer Quality Union of Bus., Industry and Cmty. Program, Lancaster, 1991-92; invited spkr. Svc. Corps. Ret. Execs., Newark, 1988, USCGR Tng. Ctr., Yorktown, Va., 1994, USMCR, Hampton, 1994, So. Assn. Coll. and Univ. Bus. Officers, Memphis, 1996. Contbg. author: Great Ideas for Teaching Marketing, 1992, Great Ideas for Teaching Introduction to Business, 1994; contbr. articles to profl. jours.; author: (newsletter) The Quality Management Forum, 1993, 98. Judge regional competition Future Bus. Leaders Am., Hampton, 1993—; judge team excellence competition Ohio Mfrs. Assn., Lancaster, 1991; county rep. UNICEF, Fairfield County, Ohio, 1988-91. Mem. AAUP (chpt. treas. 1998-2000), Am. Soc. for Quality (invited speaker 1993, cert. quality mgr. 1997, recert. 2000), Nat. Assn. Profl. Fin. Planners, Va. Educator's Quality Network. Avocations: photography, travel, skiing, swimming, sailing. Office: 99 Thomas Nelson Dr Hampton VA 23666-1433 E-mail: wiedmant@tncc.vccs.edu.

WIEDMANN, TIEN-WEN TAO, medical scientist, educator; b. Shanghai, China, Jan. 12, 1938; came to U.S., 1955; d. Pai-chuan and Su-chuin (Chang) T.; m. Walter Wiedmann, June 20, 1966; children: Christian, Ulrich. Student, Nat. Taiwan U., Republic of China, 1953-55; BS, U. Okla., 1957; PhD, Harvard U., 1963. Rsch. assoc. Harvard U., Boston, 1965-69; scientist Basel (Switzerland) Inst. for Immunology, 1970-74, Bioctr., Basel, 1975-80; sr. rsch. assoc. Stanford (Calif.) U., 1980-84, assoc. prof. nuclear medicine, 1984-91; founder, organizer Health Corps, 1990—; v.p., rsch. dir., bd. dirs. Pharmagenesis, Calif., 1991—. Contbr. articles to profl. jours. Office: Pharmagenesis 3183 Porter Dr Palo Alto CA 94304-1213

WIEDMER, TERRY LYNN, educational administration educator, consultant; b. Missoula, Mont., Feb. 15, 1951; d. James Alvin Boyer and Darlene P. (Wills) Vining; m. Raymond Otto Wiedmer, July 15, 1972 (div. Sept. 1987). BA in Elem. Edn., U. Mont., 1972, MA in Edn1. Adminstrn., 1975, EdD, 1983. Sales clk. W.T. Grant Co., Missoula, 1967-69; asst. purchasing agt. Intermountain Lumber Co., 1968-72; kindergarten and elem. tchr. Sch. Dist. 1, 1972-84, prin. Prescott Sch., 1985-87; postdoctoral rschr. U. Mont. Sch. Edn., 1984-85; dir. membership and pub. rels. Phi Delta Kappa Internat., Bloomington, Ind., 1987-92; prof. ednl. adminstrn. Ball State U. Tchrs. Coll., Muncie, 1992-99, prof. ednl. leadership and curriculum, 1999—, dir. Resource Ctr. for Ednl. Svcs., 1992-95. Exec. sec. study coun. Upper Wabash Valley Sch., Muncie, 1995—; CEO, Edn. & Tng. Cons., Muncie, 1996—; trainer, group leader Ivy Tech State Coll., 1997—; cons., presenter Nat. Tchrs. Hall of Fame, Emporia, Kans., 1996—; v.p. profl. affairs coun. Ball State U. Contbg. author: Public Relations in Educational Organizations, 1997; contbr. articles to profl. jours. Mem., facilitator Very Spl. Arts Ind., Indpls., 1993-96 Recipient Outstanding Tchr. proclamation Gov. of Nev., 1994, Outstanding Scholar of 20th Century award Internat. Biog. Ctr., Cambridge, Eng., 1999, Universal award of Accomplishment Internat. and Am. Biog. Ctr., Cambridge, 1999, 1000 Leaders of Influence award Internat. and Am. Biog. Ctr., Cambridge, 1999, Internat. Woman of Yr. award Internat. Biog. Ctr., 1999, Outstanding Intellectuals of 20th Century award Internat. Biog. Ctr., 1999, 2000 Notable Am. Women Am. Biog. Inst., 2002, 2000 Outstanding Scholars of 21st Century Internat. Biog. Ctr., 2002; named Woman of Yr. Am. Biog. Inst., 2002. Mem. ASCD (exec. com., exec. com. 1992-95), Nat. State Tchrs. of Yr. (hon., exec. dir. 1993-96), Ind. ASCD (exec. sec. 1992-95), Ind. Sch. Pub. Rels. Assn. (pres.-elect, bd. dirs. 1992-98), Ind. Assn. for Sex Equity (founding, exec. com. 1996-98), Phi Delta Kappa (life, various offices 1978—), Kappa Delta Pi (Svc. for Soc. award 1994). Avocations: landscaping, dogs, travel, professional reading and writing, home repair. Home: 1923 E Robinwood Dr Muncie IN 47304-2854 Office: Ball State U Tchrs Coll Rm 824 Muncie IN 47306-0610 E-mail: twiedmer@bsu.edu.

WIEDMYER, THERESA, writer; b. Chgo., Apr. 11, 1939; d. Onofrio and Josephine (Necci) Loconsole; married; 1 child. Author: Episodes of Chewy, 2000, Loves Own Destiny, 2001. Recipient Editor's award Poetry, 1999. Home: 2928 Woodside Dr Joliet IL 60431

WIEFELS, PAUL HAROLD, management consultant; b. Los Angeles, Jan. 20, 1954; s. Frank Leonard and Nancy Jean (Allen) W. BS, U. So. Calif., 1975, MBA, 1977. Assoc. product mgr. Nissan Motor Corp., Gardena, Calif., 1977-79; account exec. Foote, Cone and Belding, Los Angeles, 1979-80; account supr. SCC & B:Lintas, 1980-81, Ketchum Communications, San Francisco, 1981-82; advt. mgr. Apple Computer, Inc., Cupertino, Calif., 1982-85, group mgr. internat. mktg., 1985-88; dir. worldwide mktg. Ingres Corp., alameda, 1988-90; dir. mktg. consulting Landor Assocs., 1990-91; sr. ptnr., mng. dir. the Chasm Group, 1991—. Mem. Am. Mktg. Assn., Commerce Assocs., U. So. Calif. Office: 411 Borel Ave Ste 550 San Mateo CA 94402-3528

WIEGAND, SYLVIA MARGARET, mathematician, educator; b. Cape Town, South Africa, Mar. 8, 1945; came to U.S., 1949; d. Laurence Chisholm and Joan Elizabeth (Dunnett) Young; m. Roger Allan Wiegand, Aug. 27, 1966; children: David Chisholm, Andrea Elizabeth. AB, Bryn Mawr Coll., 1966; MA, U. Wash., 1967; PhD, U. Wis., Madison, 1972. Mem. faculty U. Nebr., Lincoln, 1967—, now prof. math. Vis. assoc. prof. U. Conn., Storrs, 1978-79, U. Wis., Madison, 1985-86; vis. prof. Purdue U., 1992-93, Spring 1998, Mich. State U., Fall 1997. Editor Communications in Math., 1990—, Rocky Mountain Jour. Math., 1991—; contbr. rsch. articles to profl. jours. Troop leader Lincoln area Girl Scouts U.S., 1988-92. Grantee NSF, 1985-88, 90-93, 94-96, 97—; Vis. Professorship for Women, 1992, Nat. Security Agy., 1995-97. Mem. AAUP, Assn. Women in Math (pres.-elect 1995-96, pres. 1997-99), London Math. Soc., Math. Assn. Am., Am. Math. Soc. (mem. coun. 1994-96, chmn. policy com. on meetings and confs. 1994-96, mem. nominating com. 1997—), Can. Math. Soc. (bd. mem. at large 1997—). Avocations: running, family activities. Office: U Nebr Dept Math Lincoln NE 68588-0323 E-mail: swiegand@math.unl.edu.

WIEGEL, ROBERT LOUIS, consulting engineering executive; b. San Francisco, Oct. 17, 1922; s. Louis Henry and Antionette L. (Decker) W.; m. Anne Pearce, Dec. 10, 1948; children: John M., Carol E., Diana L. BS, U. Calif. at Berkeley, 1943, MS, 1949. Mem. faculty U. Calif. at Berkeley, 1946—, prof. civil engring., 1963-87, prof. emeritus, 1987—, asst. dean Coll. Engring., 1963-72, acting dean, 1972-73; dir. state tech. svcs. program for Calif. U. Calif., 1965-68, sec. acad. senate, 1988-89; vis. prof. Nat. U. Mex., summer 1965, Polish Acad. Sci., 1976, 88, U. Cairo, 1978; sr. Queen's fellow in marine sci. Australia, 1977; cons. to govt. and industry, 1946—. Chmn. U.S. com. for internat. com. oceanic resources, mem. marine bd. Nat. Acad. Engring., 1975-81; pres. Internat. Engring. Com. on Oceanic Resources, 1972-75, hon. mem., 1988; mem. coastal engring. research bd. Dept. Army, 1974-85; mem. IDOE adv. panel NSF, 1974-77, Gov. Calif. Adv. Commn. Ocean Resources, 1967, Calif. Adv. Commn. on Marine and Coastal Resources, 1967-73, Tsunami Tech. Adv. Council, Hawaii, 1964-66; U.S. del. U.S.-Japan coop. sci. programs, 1964, 65 Author publs. in field; editor Shore and Beach jour., 1988-96; patentee in field. V.p., bd. dirs. Am. Shore and Beach Preservation Assn., 1988-95, dir. emeritus, 1995—; mem. Nat. Rsch. Coun. com. on Beach Nourishment and Protection, 1992-95. Recipient Outstanding Civilian Svc. medal Dept. Army, 1985, Berkeley citation U. Calif., 1987, Joe W. Johnson Outstanding Beach Preservation award Calif. Shore and Beach Preservation Assn., 1993, Coastal Zone Found. award, 1993, Morrough P. O'Brien award Am. Shore and Beach Preservation Assn., 1995; Robert L. Wiegel scholar, 2001—. Fellow AAAS; mem. NAE, ASCE (hon., chmn. exec. com. waterways, harbors, coastal engring. div. 1974-75, vice chmn. coastal engring. rsch. coun. 1964-78, chmn. 1978-92, chmn. task com. wave forces on structures 1960-67, chmn. com. on coastal engring. 1970-71, Rsch. prize 1962, Moffatt-Nichol Coastal Engring. award 1978, Internat. Coastal Engring. award 1985), Japan Soc. Civil Engrs. (hon.), Sigma Xi. Home: 1030 Keeler Ave Berkeley CA 94708-1404

WIEGENSTEIN, JOHN GERALD, physician; b. Fredericktown, Mo., June 22, 1930; s. John Joseph and Dorothy Faye (Mulkey) W.; m. Dorothy Iris Scifers, Dec. 27, 1952; children: Mark, Barbara, Paula, Cynthia. BS, U. Mich., 1956, MD, 1960. Intern Tripler Army Gen. Hosp., Honolulu, 1960-61; chmn. Emergency Medicine Ingham Regional Med. Ctr., Lansing, 1975-95; pres. profl. staff Mich. Capital Med. Ctr., 1996-98; prof. emergency medicine Mich. State U., 1982-97, prof. emeritus, 1997—; founder Internat. Rsch. Inst. for Emergency Medicine, pres., 1983-85; v.p. occupl. health Emergency Cons., Inc., 1997-99, pres., 1999—. Founder Am. Bd. Emergency Medicine, 1982-83; pres. Physician Assocs., P.C., 1976-96; chmn. bd. Occupl. Medicine Assocs., P.C., 1989-98; owner Health Care Info. Svcs., Inc., 1989-97. With USAF, 1951-53; M.C., U.S. Army, 1960-63. Mem. AMA (Disting. Svc. award 2001), Am. Coll. Emergency Physicians (founder, pres., chmn. bd. 1968-71, bd. dirs. 1968-76, John G. Wiegenstein Leadership award named in his honor), Mich. State Med. Soc. (award 1971, 82), Ingham County Med. Soc., Galens Hon. Med. Soc., Soc. Acad. Emergency Medicine (hon.). Home: 796 Wiggins Bay Dr Naples FL 34110-6023 E-mail: jwiegen@aol.com.

WIEGMAN, EUGENE WILLIAM, minister, former college administrator; b. Fort Wayne, Ind., Oct. 27, 1929; s. A. Henry and E. Catherine (McDonald) W.; m. Kathleen Wyatt, Apr. 26, 1952; children: Kathryn, Rose Marie, Mark, Jeanine, Gretchen, Matthew. BS, Concordia Coll., 1953; MS, U. Kans., 1956, EdD, 1962; grad., Pacific Luth. Theol. Sem., 1985. Tchr., coach Trinity Luth. Sch., Atchison, Kans., 1954-58; prin. Tchr. St. John's Coll., Winfield, 1958-61; prof. Concordia Coll., Seward, Nebr., 1961-65; adminstrv. asst. to Rep. Clair Callan, Lincoln, 1965-66; asst. to adminstr. fed. extension service Dept. Agr., Washington, 1966-67; dean community edn. Fed. City Coll., 1967-69; pres. Pacific Luth. U., Tacoma, 1969-75, Independent Colls. Wash., 1975-76; dir. Wash. Office Community Devel., 1977-78; commr. Dept. of Employment Security, 1978-81; exec. dir., pres., CEO emeritus Family Counseling Service of Tacoma and Pierce County, Wash., 1987-97; assoc. pastor Luther Meml. Ch., Tacoma, 1987-90; pastor Gethsemane Luth. Ch., 1990-98, Luther Meml. Ch., Tacoma, 1998—2002; dean clin. pastoral edn. Grad. Sch. of Korea, 1992—. Mem. Wash. State Employment and Tng. Council; mem. cabinet Gov. of Wash., 1977-81. Candidate for U.S. Congress from 6th dist. Wash., 1976; mem. Council on Washington's Future; exec. bd. dirs. Pacific Harbors Coun. Boy Scouts Am.; bd. dirs. Tacoma Area Urban Coalition; past chmn. Wash. Friends Higher Edn.; bd. dirs. Tacoma Urban League, Bellarmine Prep. Sch., Tacoma, Camp Brotherhood, Nativity House; trustee Tacoma Gen. Hosp., Pacific Sci. Center; mem. Commn. on Children, Youth and Families for Tacoma and Pierce County; mem. com. Faith Homes for Young Women; pres. Second City chamber of Tacoma. Recipient Disting. Teaching award City Winfield, Kans., 1960, Freedom Found. Teaching award, 1961, Disting. Eagle Scout award, 1982, Pres. award St. Martins Coll., 1980. Mem. Kiwanis, Phi Delta Kappa. Home: 405 N Stadium Way Tacoma WA 98403-3228

WIEGNER, ALLEN WALTER, biomedical engineering educator, researcher; b. Bethlehem, Pa., July 22, 1947; s. Howard Jay and Anna (Strouse) W.; m. Sandra A. Waddock, Aug. 26, 1978; 1 child, Benjamin Waddock. SB, SM, MIT, 1970, PhD, 1978. Rsch. assoc. Harvard U. Med. Sch., Boston, 1978-87, asst. prof. neurology (biomed. engring.), 1987—; asst. biomed. engr. Mass. Gen. Hosp., 1980—. Cons. rsch. svc. VA Med. Ctr., 1984—, biomed. engr., 1987-96, computer specialist, 1996—. Contbr. articles, book chpts. to profl. publs. Lt. USPHS, 1970-72. Mem. IEEE (sr.), Rehab. Engring. and Assistive Tech. Soc. N.Am., Soc. for Neurosci. Office: VA Med Ctr IRM Svc 940 Belmont St Brockton MA 02301-5596

WIEGNER, EDWARD ALEX, multi-industry executive; b. Waukesha, Wis., Dec. 13, 1939; s. Roy Edward and Margaret (Kuehnlein) W.; m. Cathryn J. Mullens, Oct. 16, 1970; children: Carlin, Ryan; 1 child from previous marriage, Christine. BBA, U. Wis., 1961, MS in Econs., 1965, PhD in Econs., 1969. Asst. prof. bus. adminstrn. Marquette U., Milw., 1965-71; assoc. prof U. Wis., Madison, 1972-73; sec. Wis. Dept. Revenue, 1971-74; sr. v.p. fin., bd. dirs. Wis. Power and Light Co., 1974-76, sr. v.p. consumer, pub. and fin. affairs, dir., 1976-80, exec. v.p., bd. dirs., 1980-82; sr. v.p., chief fin. officer, bd. dirs. Am. Natural Resources Co., 1982-85, exec. v.p., chief adminstrv. officer, bd. dirs., 1985-86; sr. v.p. Coastal Corp., 1985-86; sr. v.p., chief fin. officer Household Internat., Inc., 1986-88; exec. v.p., chief fin. officer The Progressive Corp., Mayfield Heights, Ohio, 1988-91, pres. fin. svcs. div., 1989-93; gen. ptnr. Aurora Ptnrs., 1994-96; vice chmn. 1st Am. Ins. Co., Kansas City, Mo., 1994-97; chmn., CEO First Am. Fin. Corp., 1997-98. Chmn. Ins. Distbn. Solutions, LLC, Jacksonville, Fla., 1999—. Contbr. articles to Northwestern Law Rev., others. Mem. Grand Harbor Country Club. Home and Office: 151 Shores Dr Indian River Shores FL 32963 E-mail: edward@wiegner.com.

WIEHL, LIS W. law educator; b. Seattle, Aug. 9, 1961; d. Richard Lloyd and Inga (Wolfsberg) W.; m. Robb London; children: Jacob, Danielle. JD, Harvard U., 1987; MA, U. Queensland, Brisbane, Australia, 1985; BA, Columbia U, 1983, U. Helsinki, Helsinki, Finland, 1978-79. Bar: Wash., U.S. Dist. Ct. Wash., U.S. Ct. Appeals (9th cir.). Assoc. Perkins Coie Law Firm, Seattle, 1987-90; fed. prosecutor U.S. Attys. Office, 1990-95; assoc. prof. Law Sch., dir. of trial advocacy program U. Wash., 1995—. Counsel Perkins Coie Law Firm, Seattle; exec. asst. U.S. atty., Seattle, summer 1998; prin. dep. chief investigative counsel to U.S. Ho. of Reps. Com. on Judiciary, 1998-99; legal commentator Nat. Pub. Radio, NBC News, 2000—, Sta. KRIO (CBS) News, 2001—. Contbr. to law rev, U. Wash., 1987, U. Mich., 1998; contbr. articles to New York Times, ABA Jour., Jour. Trial Advocacy, Harvard Blackletter Law Jour.; legal analyst Fox-TV News Channel, 2001--. Treas. Lawyers Students Engaged in Resolution, Seattle, 1995-99. Recipient Distinction in Teaching award Harvard U., 1987, Emil Gumpert award A. Coll. Trial Lawyers, Richardson S. Jacobson award for Excellence in Tchg. Trial Advocacy Roscoe Pound Inst., 2001. Mem. Fed. Bar Assn., Order of the Coif, Phi Beta Kappa.

WIELAND, DOLORES SYBILLE, accountant; b. Vienna, Austria, Nov. 15, 1942; came to U.S., 1952; d. Norbert Anton and Erika Ilse (Veit) W. BS, Ind. U. Purdue U. Ind., Indpls., 1976. Contr. Bösendorfer Klavierfab, Vienna, 1976-82; auditor Ind. Dept. Revenue, Indpls., 1983—. Lutheran. Avocations: physical fitness, reading, history, dance, tennis. Home: 1101 N Riley Ave Indianapolis IN 46201-2851 Office: Ind Dept Revenue 100 N Senate Ave Rm N248 Indianapolis IN 46204-2217

WIELAND, JOHN, real estate executive; m. Sue Wieland; 2 children. BA magna cum laude, Amherst Coll., 1958; MBA with high distinction, Harvard Bus. Sch., 1964; LHD (hon.), Amherst Coll., 1993. Chmn., CEO, John Wieland Homes and Neighborhoods, Inc., Atlanta, 1970—. Bd. dirs. Fed. Res. Bank Atlanta. Internat. bd. dirs. Habitat for Humanity; bd. dirs. Ga. Trust Fund for Homeless, Atlanta Neighborhood Devel. Partnership; former chmn. High Mus. Art; former vice chmn. Woodruff Arts Ctr.; chmn. Adv. Coun., Emory U. Ctr. Ethics in Pub. Policy. Mem. Nat. Assn. Home Builders (life bd. dirs.), Phi Beta Kappa. Office: 1950 Sullivan Rd Atlanta GA 30337-5706 E-mail: john.wieland@jwhomes.com.

WIELAND, PAUL OTTO, environmental control systems engineer; b. Louisville, Apr. 9, 1954; s. Otto George and Flora Carolyn (Wolf) W. BS in Botany, U. Louisville, 1982, BS in Applied Sci., 1985, M. in Engring., 1987. Lic. profl. engr., Ala., Va.; cert. indoor air quality profl. Assn. of Energy Engrs. Paper carrier Courier-Jour., Louisville, 1976-77; youth program dir. UNICORN, 1978; recreation worker Met. Parks Dept., 1978-80; retail sales clk. Lose Bros. Lawn and Garden, 1980-82; trainee engr. Sealand Svc., Inc., Elizabeth, N.J., 1982; engr. NASA Marshall Space Flight Ctr., Huntsville, Ala., 1983—; pres. Wiseland Svcs., 1996—. Author: Designing for Human Presence in Space: An Introduction to Environmental Control and Life Support Systems, 1994, Living Together in Space: The Design and Operation of the Life Support Systems on the International Space Station, 1996, rev. edit., 1998, A Guidebook to a Healthier House, 1999; contbr. articles to profl. jours. Vol. advocate R.A.P.E. Relief Ctr., Louisville, 1977-80; vol. tutor Adult Basic Edn. Program, Huntsville, 1988-89; vol. projectionist Film Co-op., Huntsville, 1990-91; vol. tech. advisor Am. Lung Assn. Health House '96, Huntsville. Mem. ASME, ASHRAE, AIAA (chmn. student chpt. 1984-85), NSPE (mathcounts vol. 1990-91), Inst. for Advanced Studies in Life Support (treas. 1990-92). Avocations: appreciation of nature, creating visual arts, dancing. Home: 4212 9th Ave SW Huntsville AL 35805-3408 Office: NASA/MSFC/FD21 Marshall Space Flight Ctr Huntsville AL 35812

WIELAND, WILLIAM DEAN, healthcare consulting executive; b. Peoria, Ill., Feb. 15, 1948; s. George William and Virginia Lee (Delicath) W.; m. Joyce Lumia; 1 child, William Michael. BBA, Bradley U., 1971. Asst. adminstr. Galesburg (Ill.) Cottage Hosp., 1973-74; v.p. Anton & Damian, Iowa City, 1975-76; mgr. Clifton, Gunderson & Co., Peoria, 1977-80; v.p. OHMS Health Mgmt. Services, Columbus, 1980-84; dir., cons. VHA Cons. Svcs., Tampa, Fla., 1984-88; divsn. mgr. VHA, Inc., 1988-95; sr. cons. mgr. Cost Sys. Group, Inc., 1995-96; prin. Medifax Assocs., 1997-98; managed care systems analyst U. Cmty. Hosp., 1998—. Small bus. cons. Clifton, Gunderson & Co., 1977-80; cons. OHMS Health Mgmt. Svcs., Columbus, 1980-84. Mem.: Healthcare Info. and Mgmt. Sys. Soc., Am. Bus. Club, Sigma Nu (Zeta Phi chpt.).

WIELECH, DENNIS DAVID, telecommunications company executive; b. Balt., Oct. 2, 1936; s. George Vitold Wielech and Sylvia Earlene (LaGue) Wielech Braithwaite; m. Victoria Teresa Grzymala, Sept. 8, 1962; children—Kathryn Denise, D. David. Student Balt. City Coll., 1952-55, Johns Hopkins U., 1964-67; cert. fin. planner Coll. for Fin. Planning, Denver, 1972. C.L.U. Fin. cons. Dennis D. Wielech & Assocs., Balt., 1966-82; v.p., dir. internat. mktg. Internat. Mobile Machines Corp., Phila., 1982-86; chmn. bd. Omnilink Internat. Corp., Glen Burnie, Md., 1986-93, pres., chief exec. officer, 1988-92; pres., CEO Advanced Superconductor Techs., Inc., Balt., 1987-89; pres. Micrologix, Inc., 1990-93, Spectrum Group, Ltd., 1992-94; pres., CEO Teleport Corp., 1994—, Mindset, Inc., 1996—, Microspace Tech. Corp., 1998—; bd. dirs. MIT Enterprise Forum of Washington, D.C.-Balt., Inc., 1985-91. Mem. Am. Soc. C.L.U.s (pres. Balt. chpt. 1974-75), Nat. Assn. Corp. Dirs. (founding-Metro Washington, D.C.-Balt. chpt.), Balt. Assn. Fin. Planners (pres. 1970-75), Md. Assn. Life Underwriters (pres. 1977), Md. Assn. Health Underwriters (pres. 1976, Man of Yr. 1976). Roman Catholic. Home: Guilford House 4001 Greenway Baltimore MD 21218-1103 Office: 5411 Old Frederick Rd Ste 1A Baltimore MD 21229-2126

WIELENBERG, ERIK JOSEPH, philosophy educator; b. Mpls., Mar. 11, 1972; s. Norbert Joseph Wielenberg and Peggy Lou Reinking. BA in Philosophy, Lawrence U., 1994; PhD in Philosophy, U. Mass., 2000. Asst. prof. philosophy DePauw U., Greencastle, Ind., 1999—. Vis. grad. student fellow, Ctr. Philosophy of Religion, U. Notre Dame, 1998-99. Contbr. articles to profl. jours. Mem. Am. Philos. Assn. Avocations: basketball, writing short stories. Office: DePauw U Dept Philosophy Greencastle IN 46135

WIELER, SCOTT ALAN, investment banker; b. N.Y.C., Mar. 10, 1958; s. Richard Joseph and Valerie Helen (Straight) W.; m. Mary McCord Baily, Aug. 24, 1985; children: Alexander Evans, James Baily. AB in Econs. magna cum laude, Boston Coll., 1981; MBA, U. Pa., 1987. Mng. dir. BT Securities Corp.,

N.Y.C., 1981—94, Alexander Brown & Sons. Inc., Balt., 1994—99; with Deutsche Bank Alex Brown, 1999—2002; pres., CEO Signal Hill Capital Group, LLC, 2002—. Mem. Rockaway Hunt Club, Lawrence Beach Club (bd. dirs. 1985—), Elkridge Hunt Club, Balt. Republican. Avocations: tennis, golf. Office: Signal Hill Capital Group LLC 6225 Smith Ave Baltimore MD 21209-3630

WIELGUS, CHARLES JOSEPH, information services company executive; b. Hadley, Mass., Jan. 2, 1923; s. Joseph John and Anna Mary (Armata) W.; m. Irene Helen Graham, Jan. 1, 1949; children: Charles, Paul, Martha Jane. BS summa cum laude in Bus. Adminstrn, Bryant Coll., 1947, D.S. in Bus. Adminstrn. (hon.), 1977. With Bigelow-Sanford Carpet Co., Enfield, Conn. and N.Y.C., 1947-56; with Reuben H. Donnelley Corp. (subs. Dun & Bradstreet Corp.), Chicago and N.Y.C., 1956-71; v.p. personnel Dun & Bradstreet, Inc. (subs.), 1971-73, Dun & Bradstreet Corp., 1973-76, sr. v.p. human resources, 1976-82, exec. v.p. human resources and communications, 1983-88, ret., 1988; nature photographer, 1989—. Adj. faculty New Sch. Social Research, 1977-88, mem. adv. com. Masters program in human resources, 1977-88, ret., 1988; mem. adv. council on mgmt. edn. N.Y.C. C. of C., 1975-80; mem. bus. edn. adv. com. N.Y.C. Bd. Edn., 1977-88; dir. Nat. Ctr. Career Life Planning, 1986—; mem. adv. council on human resources mgmt. Nat. Conf. Bd., 1987-88. Bd. dirs. United Cerebral Palsy Assn. Westchester, 1966-75; trustee Operation Hope, Inc., 1966-75, active local and state Republican orgns., 1965-75. Served in USAF, 1943-46. Mem. Am. Arbitration Assn. (arbitrator 1988-98), Nat. Alliance Bus. (dir., steering com.), Lions, K. of C. Clubs: Univ, Larchmont Shore. Home: 151 Rockingstone Ave Larchmont NY 10538-1512 also: 7 Hummingbird Ct Hilton Head Island SC 29926

WIEMAN, CARL E. physics educator; b. Corvallis, Oreg., Mar. 26, 1951; m. Sarah Gilbert. BS, MIT, 1973; PhD, Stanford U., 1977; DS (hon.), U. Chgo., 1997. Asst. rsch. physicist dept. physics U. Mich., Ann Arbor, 1977—79, asst. prof. physics, 1979—84; assoc. prof. physics U. Colo., Boulder, 1984—87, prof., 1987—97, disting. rsch. prof., 1997—; fellow Joint Inst. for Lab. Astrophysics, 1985—. Loeb lectr. Harvard U., 1990—91; Rosenthal Meml. lectr. Yale U., 1988, Columbia U., 1988; Cherwell-Simon Meml. lectr. Oxford U., 1999; vis. scholar Phi Beta Kappa, 1999—2000. Recipient Ernest Orlando Lawrence Meml. award, U.S. Dept. Energy, 1993, Einstein medal for laser sci., Soc. Optical and Quantum Electronics, 1995, Fritz London prize for low temperature physics, 1996, Newcomb Cleveland prize, AAAS, 1996, King Faisal Internat. prize for Sci., 1997, Sci. award, Bonfils Stanton Found., 1998, Lorentz medal, Netherlands Royal Acad. Sci., 1998, Benjamin Franklin Medal in Physics, 2000, The Nobel Prize in Physics, 2001, Nat. Sci. Found. Dir. Award for Dist. Teaching Scholars, 2001. Fellow: Guggenheim, 1990-1991, Hertz Found., 1973-1977, Am. Phys. Soc. (Davisson-Germer prize 1994, Schawlow prize in laser sci. 1998); mem.: NAS, 1995, Am. Physical Soc. (fellow, 1990), Am. Acad. Arts and Sci., 1998, Am. Assn. Physics Tchrs. (Richtmyer lectr. award 1996), Optical Soc. Am. (R.W. Wood prize 1999). Achievements include first to achieve Bose-Einstein condensation, 1995. Office: U Colo PO Box 390 Boulder CO 80309-0390*

WIEMAN, THOMAS JEFFERY, surgeon; b. Holdrege, Nebr., Sept. 25, 1947; MD, U. Louisville, 1974. Diplomate Am. Bd. Surgery. Intern U. Louisville Health Scis. Ctr., 1974-75, resident in surgery, 1975-79; fellow Middlesex/Roswell Pk. Meml. Hosp., 1984-85; staff U. Louisville Hosp., Norton Hosp., Louisville, Norton Healthcare Pavilion, Louisville, Jewish Hosp., Louisville, Humana Hosp. Audubon, Louisville; prof. surgery U. Louisville, 1993—; v.p. Norton Healthcare Oncology, Norton Healthcare, Louisville, 1994—. Mem. AMA, Am. Acad. Surgeons, Am. Soc. Gastrointestinal Endoscopy, Ky. Med. Assn., Southeastern Surg. Congress, So. Surg. Assn., Soc. Surg. Oncology. Office: U Louisville Dept Surgery Norton Healthcare Pav 315 E Broadway Louisville KY 40202-1703 E-mail: thomas.wieman@nortonhealthcare.org.

WIEMANN, MARION RUSSELL, JR. (BARON OF CAMSTER), biologist; b. Sept. 7, 1929; s. Marion Russell and Verda (Peek) W.; 1 child from previous marriage, Tamara Lee (Mrs. Donald D. Kelley). BS, Ind. U., 1959; PhD (hon.), World U. Roundtable, 1991; ScD (hon.), The London Inst. Applied Rsch., England, 1994, ScD (hon.), 1995, World Acad., Germany, 1995. Ordained hon. min., 1998; cert. hypnotist. Histo-rsch. technician U. Chgo., 1959, rsch. asst., 1959-62, rsch. technician, 1962-64; tchr. sci. Westchester Twp. Sch., Chesterton, Ind., 1964-66; with U. Chgo., 1965-79, sr. rsch. technician, 1967-70, rsch. technologist, 1970-79; prin. Marion Wiemann & Assocs., cons. R&D, Chesterton, Ind., 1979-89. Advisor Porter County Health Bd., 1989-91; mem. consultive faculty World U., 1991-99, SkyWarn, Nat. Weather Svc., 1993—. Author: Tooth Decay, Its Cause and Prevention Through Controlled Soil Composition, 1985, The Mechanism of Tooth Decay, 1985; contbr. articles to profl. jours. and newspapers. Vice-chmn. The Duneland 4th of July Com., 1987-91; v.p. State Microscopical Soc. Ill., 1969-70, pres., 1970-71. With USN, 1951-53. Recipient Disting. Tech. Communicator award Soc. for Tech. Communication, 1974, Internat. Order Merit (Eng.), 1991; ennobled Royal Coll. Heraldry, Australia, 1991, Highland Laird, Scotland, 1995; named Sagamore of the Wabash Gov. Ind., 1985; McCrone Rsch. Inst. scholar, 1968; named Prof. of Sci. Australian Inst. for Co-Ordinated Rsch., Australia, 1995, knight corps Diplomatique The Sovereign Military Templar Order, 1994; recipient Scouters Key award Boy Scouts Am., 1968, Arrowhead honor, 1968, Albert Einstein Silver medal, Huguenin, Le Locke, Switzerland, Henri Dunant Silver medal with silver bars, 1995, Henri Dunant Silver medal, 1995, medal of honor, England, 1996. Fellow: Australian Inst. Co-Ordinated Rsch., World Lit. Acad.; mem.: Akademie MIDI, Maison Internat. des Intellectuels, Internat. Graphoanalysis Soc., Order Internat. Fellowship, World Acad., Assn. Masters Universe, Internat. Soc. Soil Sci., Govs. Club, VFW (charter mem., bd. dirs., post judge adv. 1986—99, apptd. post adj. 1986—99, Cross of Malta 1986). Achievements include demonstration that radiation does not produce dental caries; proved that soil calcium, magnesium, potassium and phosphorous, with soil PH, controls population size and longevity of earthworms and humans and the incidence of dental caries; demonstrated that flouride neither reduces or prevents dental caries. Address: PO Box 1016 Chesterton IN 46304-0016 *Personal philosophy: Leadership founded upon trust, perpetuated by participation, example and instruction, dedicated to wise use, protection or improvement of health and environment. If you put in an hour of real work you get an hour of results. There is no other way to do it.*

WIEMER, DAVID ROBERT, plastic surgeon; b. Houston, Sept. 16, 1940; m. Beverly Wiemer, Feb. 20, 1966. BS in Natural Sci., Okla. State U., 1961; MD, Baylor U., 1965. Intern Ben Taub Gen. Hosp., Houston, 1965-66; resident in gen. surgery Baylor Univ. Coll. Medicine Affiliated Program, 1966-69, resident in plastic surgery, 1971-74; pvt. practice Wiemer Plastic Surgery, 1974—. Active staff Meth. Hosp., Houston, 1975—, dep. chief divsn. plastic surgery, 1977—, sec. med. staff, 1990-92, pres., 1994-96, bd. dir., 1990-96; bd. dirs. The Meth. Hosp. Sys., 1996-98; dep. chief divsn. plastic surgery VA Med. Ctr., 1977—. Contbr. articles to profl. jours., chpts. to books. Maj. U.S. Army, 1969-71. Mem. ACS, Am. Soc. Plastic and Reconstructive Surgeons, Am. Soc. Aesthetic Plastic Surgery, Assn. Acad. Chmn. and Plastic Surgeons, Am. Hosp. Assn. (ho. of dels. 1997—), Tex. Med. Assn., Tex. Soc. Plastic Surgeons, Houston Soc. Plastic Surgeons (sec., v.p., pres.), Houston Surg. Soc. (sec., pres.). Presbyterian. Office: Wiemer Plastic Surgery Inc 6560 Fannin St Ste 1760 Houston TX 77030-2735

WIEMER, ROBERT ERNEST, film and television producer, writer, director; b. Highland Park, Mich., Jan. 30, 1938; s. Carl Ernest and Marion (Israelian) W.; m. Rhea Dale McGeath, June 14, 1958; children: Robert Marshall, Rhea Whitney. BA, Ohio Wesleyan U., 1959. Ind. producer, 1956-60; dir. documentary ops. WCBS-TV, N.Y.C., 1964-67; ind. producer of television, theatrical and bus. films, 1967-72; exec. producer motion pictures and TV, ITT, 1973-84, pres. subs. Blue Marble Co., Inc., Telemontage, Inc., Alphaventure Music, Inc., Betaventure Music, Inc., 1973-84; founder, chmn., chief exec. officer Tigerfilm, Inc., 1984—; chmn., bd. dirs. Golden Tiger Pictures, Hollywood, Calif., 1988—; pres, CEO Tuxedo Pictures Corp., 1993—. Bd. dirs., v.p. prodn. Las Vegas Internat. Film Festival; v.p. prodn. Cinevegas. Writer, prodr., dir.: (feature films) My Seventeenth Summer, Witch's Sister, Do Me a Favor, Anna to the Infinite Power, Somewhere, Tomorrow, Night Train to Kathmandu; exec. prodr.: (children's TV series) Big Blue Marble (Emmy and Peabody awards); dir. (TV episodes) New York Undercover, seaQuest DSV, Star Trek: The Next Generation, Deep Space Nine, The Adventures of Superboy; composer (country-western ballad) Tell Me What To Do. Capt. USAF, 1960-64. Recipient CINE award, 1974, 76, 77, 79, 81, Emmy award, 1978. Mem. NATAS, ASCAP, Info. Film Producers Assn. (Outstanding Producer award), Nat. Assn. TV Programming Execs., Am. Women in Radio and TV, N.J. Broadcasters Assn., Dirs. Guild Am., v.p., bd. mem. CineVegas The Las Vegas Internat. Film Festival. Office: Golden Tiger Pictures 3896 Ruskin St Las Vegas NV 89147-1097

WIEMERSLAGE, LESLIE JOSEPH, biology educator; b. Evanston, Ill., Jan. 17, 1942; d. George Henry and Hazel L. (Packwood) W.; married, June 19, 1971; children: Kristin, Karen, Kathryn, Kevin. BS, Quincy U., 1964; MS, Ill. State U., 1967; PhD, U. Pa., 1972. Postdoctoral fellow U. Ill., Champaign, 1972-73, U. Tex. Health Ctr., Dallas, 1973-75; prof. biology Southwestern Ill. Coll. (formerly Belleville Area Coll.), Belleville, 1975—. Author student study guide and instr. manual: Mader's Inquiry Into Life, 1991, 94. Belleville Area Coll. Found. grantee, 1991, 92, 94, 97. Mem. Human Anatomy and Physiology Soc. Methodist. Avocation: developing biology computer software. Home: 122 El Cerrito Dr Belleville IL 62221-3105 Office: Southwestern Ill Coll 2500 Carlyle Ave Belleville IL 62221-5859 E-mail: ljwiemer@apci.net.

WIEN, STUART LEWIS, retired supermarket chain executive; b. Milw., Sept. 11, 1923; s. Julius and Mildred (Rosenberg) W.; m. Charlotte Jean Milgram, June 4, 1949; children: Steven, John, William, Thomas.; m. Sheila B. Davis, July 25, 1982; stepchildren: Andrew, Stephen, Laurence, Geoffrey. BS, UCLA, 1947. Chmn. bd. Milgram Food Stores, Inc., Kansas City, Mo., 1979-84. Bd. dirs. UMB Scout Funds. Bd. regents Rockhurst Coll. Mem. Oakwood Country Club. E-mail: finewien@ao.com.

WIENER, DAVID L. secondary education educator; b. Utica, N.Y., Oct. 23, 1954; s. David L. Sr. and Phyllis (Jarmula) W.; m. Linda J. Ciccarelli, Sept. 22, 1979. AS, Mohawk Valley Community Coll., Utica, 1974; BS, Syracuse U., 1976; MS, U. Rochester, 1987. Photometrics lab. technician Elec. Testing Labs., Cortland, N.Y., 1977-78; digital/analog process control engr. Honeywell Inc., Amherst, 1978-85; tchr. math. Penfield (N.Y.) High Sch., 1985, tchr. physics, 1986—. Reviewer N.Y. State Edn. Dept., albany, 1990; advisor Alfred U. Coll. Ceramic Engring. Young Scholars' Program, Penfield H.S. Chess Club; tchr. NSF Ctr., U. Rochester, summer 1993. Counselor Camp Good Days and Spl. Times, Rochester, 1985-92; instr. swimming and lifesaving ARC, Rochester, 1979-89; advisor Penfield H.S. Solar Car. Fellow U. Rochester, 1985, 86, 87, fellow N.Y. State, 1985, 86, 87; ESEA-Title II Dwight D. Eisenhower Math./Sci. Edn. grantee, 1991, Toyota/NSTA Tapestry grantee, 1992; named Outstanding Tchr. Monroe County VFW, 1991; recipient Excellence in Tchg. award U. Rochester, 1990. Mem. Am. Assn. Physics Tchrs., Jr. Engring. Tech. Soc. (advisor), Penfield High Sch. Juggling Club (advisor, founder), Rochester Juggling Club (v.p.), Internat. Star Class Yacht Racing Assn., Seneca Yacht Club, Kappa Delta Pi. Avocations: sailing, skiing, scuba diving, juggling, biking. Home: 28 Old Winding Ln Fairport NY 14450-1108

WIENER, HESH (HAROLD FREDERIC WIENER), publisher, editor, consultant; b. Bklyn., July 20, 1946; s. Jesse Leonard and Regina (Rappaport) W. BS in Polit. Sci., MIT, 1969; LLB with honors, Open U., London, 2002. Mem. staff systems devel. Data Gen. Corp., Southboro, Mass., 1969-70; dir. computer edn. project U. Calif., Berkeley, 1970-72; editor Computer Decisions Mag., Rochelle Park, N.J., 1973-78; editor, pub. Tech. News Am., N.Y.C., 1976-88; pres. Tech. News of Am. Co., Inc., 1982—; mng. dir. Tech. News Ltd., London, 1992—. Webmaster, tech-news.com, 1996—, primrosehill.com, 1998—, luminum.com, 2000—; pub. Computer and Comms. Buyer Newsletter, 1979-95, Mainstream Newsletter, 1980-82, Infoperspectives Newsletter, 1982—, Storage Tech. Monitor, 1984-87, Infoperspectives Internat. (U.K.), 1989—, (Mid. East), 1991—, The Four Hundred Newsletter (U.K.), 1990-97, The Four Hundred Newsletter (U.S.), 1990-97; editor Infoperspectives Internat. (Italy), 1991-98, The Four Hundred Newsletter (Italy), 1995—; pub. U.S. edit. Computergram Internat. Newsletter, 1985-90; corr. Processeurs mag., 1989-99; cons. Hewlett-Packard Co. (Paris), 1971-72, Xerox Corp., 1972-73; advisor NSF, 1975; columnist 451.com, 2000—. Author: Big Blue and You, The IBM Atlas, The Mainframe; corr. Computer Weekly, U.K., 1975-81, Computable, Amsterdam, 1976-87, Computing Can., 1977-78, Ordinateurs, Paris, 1977-89, Data News, Brussels, 1979-86, Informatics, U.K., 1981-85, Datanytt, Copenhagen, 1982-89, Mgmt. Tech. mag., 1983-85; editor BusinessWeek Newsletter for Info. Execs., 1987-90, Datamation Mag., 1983-90, Infoperspectives Internat. (Milan), 1991—; contbg. editor Bus. and Soc. Rev., 1978-85; contbr. N.Y. Times Syndicate, Los Angeles Times Syndicate, N.Am. Newspaper Alliance Wireservice, Newsday, Manhattan, Inc., Rom Mag., Informatique (Paris), The Economist (London), Dun's Bus. Month, Software News, Intermedia, Digital News, Data Communications, Bus. Week Newsletter for Info. Execs., Bus. Strategy Internat., Nikkei Watcher on IBM (Tokyo), 1989-96; contbg. editor Midrange Svc. Pubs., 2002—. Mem.: Overseas Press. Home: 246 6th Ave Brooklyn NY 11215-2103 Office: Tech News Am 123 7th Ave Brooklyn NY 11215-1383

WIENER, JACQUES LOEB, JR. federal judge; b. Shreveport, La., Oct. 2, 1934; s. Jacques L. and Betty (Eichenbaum) Wiener; m. Sandra Mills Feingerts; children: Patricia Wiener Shifke, Jacques L. III, Betty Ellen Wiener Spomer, Donald B. BA, Tulane U., 1956, JD, 1961. Bar: La. 1961, U.S. Dist. Ct. (we. dist.) La. 1961. Ptnr. Wiener, Weiss & Madison, Shreveport, 1961—90; judge U.S. Ct. Appeals (5th cir.), New Orleans, 1990—. Mem. coun. La. State Law Inst., 1963; master of the bench Am. Inn of Ct., 1990—98. Pres. United Way N.W. La., 1975, Shreveport Jewish Fedn., 1969—70. Fellow: La. Bar Found., Am. Bar Found., Am. Coll. Trust and Estates Counsel; mem.: ABA, Am. Law Inst., Shreveport Bar Assn. (pres. 1982), La. Bar Assn., Internat. Acad. Estate and Trust Law (academician). Avocations: fly fishing, upland game bird hunting, photography, travel. Office: Court of Appeals Building 600 Camp St Rm 244 New Orleans LA 70130-3425

WIENER, JERRY M. psychiatrist; b. Baytown, Tex., May 11, 1933; s. Isidore and Dora L. (Lerner) W.; m. Louise W. Weingarten, Apr. 12, 1964; children— Matthew, Ethan, Ross, Aaron. Student, Rice U., 1952; MD, Baylor U., 1956; tng. in psychoanalysis, Columbia U. Psychoanalytic Center, 1968. Resident in psychiatry Mayo Clinic, Rochester, Minn., 1957-61, Columbia U. Coll. Physicians and Surgeons, N.Y.C., 1961-62; dir. child and adolescent psychiatry St. Luke's Hosp., 1962-71; dir. child psychiatry Emory U., Atlanta, 1971-75; chmn. dept. psychiatry Children's Hosp., Washington, 1976-77; prof., chmn. dept. psychiatry George Washington U., 1977-98; prof. emeritus. Mem. faculty Washington Psychoanalytic Inst. Editor: Textbook of Child and Adolescent Psychiatry, 1991, 96, Psychopharmacology in Childhood and Adolescence, 1977, Diagnosis and Psychopharmacology in Childhood and Adolescence, 1996; contbr. articles to profl. jours., chpts. to books. Fellow Am. Psychiat. Assn. (past pres.), Am. Coll. Psychiatrists; mem. Am. Assn. Chmn. Depts. Psychiatry (past pres.), Am. Psychiat. Press, Inc. (chmn. bd. dirs.), Am. Acad. Child and Adolescent Psychiatry (past pres.). Office: George Washington Univ Dept Psychiatry 2150 Pennsylvania Ave NW Washington DC 20037-3201

WIENER, JON, history educator; b. St. Paul, May 16, 1944; s. Daniel N. and Gladys (Aronsohn) Spratt. BA, Princeton U., 1966; PhD, Harvard U., 1971. Acting asst. prof. UCLA, 1973-74; asst. prof. history U. Calif.-Irvine, 1974-83, prof., 1984—. Vis. prof. U. Calif.-Santa Cruz, 1973; plaintiff Freedom of Info. Lawsuit against FBI for John Lennon Files, 1983—. Author: Social Origins of the New South, 1979; Come Together: John Lennon in His Time, 1984, Professors, Politics, and Pop, 1991, Gimme Some Truth: The John Lennon FBI File, 2000; contbg. editor The Nation mag.; contbr. articles to profl. jours. including The New Republic and New York Times Book Rev. Rockefeller Found. fellow, 1979, Am. Coun. Learned Socs.- Ford Found. fellow, 1985. Mem. Am. Hist. Assn., Nat. Book Critics Circle, Orgn. Am. Historians, Nat. Writers' Union, Liberty Hill Found. (bd. dirs.). Office: U Calif Dept History Irvine CA 92697-3275 E-mail: wiener@uci.edu.

WIENER, JOSEPH, pathologist; b. Toronto, Sept. 21, 1927; arrived in U.S., 1949, naturalized, 1960; s. Louis and Minnie (Salem) W.; m. Judith Hesta Ross, June 20, 1954; children: Carolyn L., Adam L. MD, U. Toronto, 1953. Intern Detroit Receiving Hosp., 1953-54; resident to chief resident pathology Mallory Inst. Pathology, 1954-55, 57-60; from asst. to assoc. prof. pathology Columbia U., N.Y.C., 1960-68; prof. pathology N.Y. Med. Coll., 1968-78, Wayne State U., Detroit, 1978—, chmn. dept., 1978-90. Cons. NIH, 1970—. Served to capt. M.C. U.S. Army, 1955-57. Grantee: Heart, Lung and Blood Inst., 1971-93; named fellow Coun. for High Blood Pressure Rsch., 1982—. Fellow Am. Heart Assn.; mem. AAAS, Am. Soc. Investigative Pathology, Am. Soc. Cell Biology, Mich. Path. Soc., Internat. Acad. Pathology, Am. Heart Assn., U.S./Can. Acad. Pathology, Mich. Heart Assn. (dir.), Internat. Soc. Hypertension. Achievements include rsch. on cellular/molecular biology of experimental hypert ension. Office: 540 E Canfield St Detroit MI 48201-1928

WIENER, JOSHUA MARK, public health service officer, researcher; b. Washington, Apr. 29, 1949; s. Jack and Florence Wiener; m. Susan Frances Klinger, Oct. 20, 1978; children: Jeremy, Noah Klinger, Michael. BA, U. Chgo., 1971; PhhD, Harvard U., 1981. Program analyst NYC Dept. of Health, N.Y.C., 1973—74; staff project analyst N.Y. State Moreland Act Commn. on Nursing Homes and Residential Facilities, 1975; policy analyst U.S. Congl. Budget Office, Washington, 1976; coord. long-term care and fin. analysis Mass. Dept. of Pub. Health, Boston, 1976—79; program analyst Health Care Financing Adminstrn., Washington, 1980—84; sr. fellow The Brookings Instn., 1982—96; prin. rsch. assoc. The Urban Inst., 1996—. Chair adv. panel on health services rsch. Nat. Multiple Sclerosis Soc., N.Y.C., 1996; co-chair long-term care com. Mayor's Health Policy Coun., Washington, 1997—; mem. com. quality of care in long-term care Inst. Medicine, Washington, 1998—2000. Author: (book) Caring for the Disabled Elderly: Who Will Pay?, 1988, Sharing the Burden: Strategies for Public and Private Long-Term Care Insurance, 1994; editor: Rationing America's Medical Care: The Oregon Plan and Beyond, 1992, Persons with Disabilities: Issues in Health Care Financing and Service Delivery, 1995; mem. editl. bd.: The Gerontologist , 1992—2000. Co-chair long-term care com. Mayor's Health Policy Coun., Washington, DC, DC, 1997—2002; mem. Adv. Com. on Health Care, Washington, 1992—92. Mem.: APHA, Gerontol. Soc. Am., Nat. Acad. Social Ins. Home: 5419 41st St NW Washington DC 20015 Office: The Urban Inst 2100 M St NW Washington DC 20037 Office Fax: 202-223-1149. Business E-Mail: jwiener@ui.urban.org.

WIENER, LEO, physician, oncologist; b. Wiesbaden, Germany, Apr. 22, 1949; came to U.S., 1951; s. Irving and Rachel Wiener; m. Estelle S. Faber, June 30, 1970; children: Lauren, Aliza, Eytan. BA, Yeshiva U., 1971; MD, Georgetown U., 1975. Diplomate Am. Bd. Internal Medicine, Am. Bd. Medical Oncology. Intern Grad. Hosp. of U. Pa., 1975-76; resident Cabrini Med. Ctr. N.Y. Med. Coll., 1976-78; chief clin. fellow, dept. neoplastic diseases Mt. Sinai Hosp., N.Y.C., 1978-80; attending physician Winthrop U. Hosp., Mineola, N.Y., 1980—; private practice Garden City (N.Y.) Oncology, P.C., 1980—. Rsch. fellow Nat. Cancer Inst., Mt. Sinai Hosp., 1978-80. Mem. ACP, Am. Soc. Clin. Oncology, Am. Soc. Internal Medicine, N.Y. State Soc. Oncologists and Hematologists, N.Y. State Med. Soc., Cancer and Leukemia Group B (investigator), Nat. Surg. Adjuvant Breast and Bowel Project (investigator). Office: 520 Franklin Ave Garden City NY 11530-5801

WIENER, LEONARD, news journalist; b. N.Y.C., Sept. 23, 1940; s. Isidore and Ethel (Berkowitz) W.; m. Edith Herman, June 16, 1974. BA, U. Mich., 1962, MA, 1964. Reporter Milw. Jour., 1964-67; reporter bus. news Chgo. Daily News, 1967-71, Chgo. Tribune, 1971-79; assoc. editor U.S. News and World Report, Washington, 1979-88, sr. editor personal taxes, personal finance, 1988—. Home: 5501 Burling Ct Bethesda MD 20817-6309 Office: U S News and World Report 1050 Thomas Jefferson St NW Washington DC 20007-3837

WIENER, MALCOLM HEWITT, foundation executive; b. Tsingtao, China, July 3, 1935; (parents Am. citizens); s. Myron and Ethel (Zimmerman) W.; m. Carolyn Talbot Seely, June 8, 1990; children: Catherine Diktynna Talbot, Elizabeth Ariadne Seely. BA, Harvard U., 1957, JD, 1963; LittD (hon.), U. Sheffield, 1997; PhD (hon.), Eberhard-Karl U., Tübingen, Germany, 1998; Doctorate (hon.), U. Athens, Greece, 1998. Bar: N.Y. 1964. Atty., N.Y.C., 1963-71; pvt. practice investing, 1971-98; chmn. Millburn Corp., 1977-98, Millburn Ridgefield Corp., Ridgefield, Conn., 1982—, ShareInVest, Ridgefield, 1982—; chmn. bd. trustees Malcolm Hewitt Wiener Found., N.Y.C., 1984—. Lectr. in field; fellow faculty of govt., John F. Kennedy Sch. Govt., Harvard U., 1985; advisor U.S. Dept. State on Internat. Conv. on Illicit Traffic in Antiquities, 1970-75 Columnist Newsday; contbr. articles to profl. publs. Co-dir. Aegean Bronze Age Colloquium, NYU Inst. Fine Arts, 1975—; founder, exec. dir. Inst. Aegean Prehistory, 1982-89, pres., 1990—; trustee Am. Classical Studies in Athens; founder Wiener Lab. Am. Sch. Classical Studies, Athens; bd. trustees, co-chmn. vis. com. Dept. Egyptian Art, mem. vis. com. Dept. Painting Conservation, Prints and Drawings, Greek and Roman, chmn.'s coun.; vice chmn. bus. com. Met. Mus. Art; mem. adv. bd. Malcolm Wiener Ctr. for Social Policy, Kennedy Sch. Govt. Harvard U.; mem. vis. com., paintings Boston Mus. Fine Arts, 1985-91, drawings and prints Frick Collection; sponsor Malcolm and Carolyn Wiener Lab. for Aegean and Near East Dendochronology Cornell U. With USN, 1957-60. Fellow Archaeol. Inst. Am. (hon. life); mem. ABA, Coun. on Fgn. Rels. (ind. task force on non-lethal weapons). Office: Millburn Ridgefield Corp 1270 Avenue Of The Americas New York NY 10020-1700

WIENER, MARVIN S. rabbi, editor, executive; b. N.Y.C., Mar. 16, 1925; s. Max and Rebecca (Dodell) W.; m. Sylvia Bodek, Mar. 2, 1952; children: David Hillel, Judith Rachel. BS, CCNY, 1944, MS, 1945; B.H.L., Jewish Theol. Sem. Am., 1947, M.H.L., Rabbi, 1951, D.D. (hon.), 1977. Registrar, sec. faculty Rabbinical Sch., Jewish Theol. Sem. Am., 1951-57; cons. Frontiers of Faith TV Series, NBC, 1951-57; dir., instr. liturgy Cantors Inst.-Sem. Coll. Jewish Music, Jewish Theol. Sem. Am., 1954-58; faculty coordinator Sem. Sch. and Women's Inst., 1958-64; dir. Nat. Acad. for Adult Jewish Studies, United Synagogue Am., N.Y.C., 1958-78; editor Burning Bush Press, 1958-78, United Synagogue Rev., 1978-86; dir. com. congrl. standards United Synagogue Am., 1976-86, cons. community relations and social action, 1981-82, editor, exec. joint retirement bd., 1986—. Mem. Joint Commn. on Rabbinic Placement, 1951-57, Joint Prayer Book Commn., 1957-62; mem. exec. coun. Rabbinical Assembly, 1958-86; editl. cons. N.Y. Bd. Rabbis, 1987-89; trustee joint retirement bd. Jewish Theol. Sem. Am. Rabbinical Assembly and United Synagogue Am., 1959-86, sec. 1968-76, 84-85, vice chmn., 1976-82, 85-86, chmn. 1982, treas., 1983-84; co-chmn. Jewish Bible Assn., 1960-64; chmn. bd. rev. Nat. Coun. Jewish Audio-Visual Materials, 1968-69; mem. exec. com. Nat. Coun. Adult Jewish Edn., 1966—; mem. exec. bd., editl. adv. bd., v.p. Jewish Book Couns., 1976-96; chmn. Internat. Conf. Adult Jewish Edn., Jerusalem, 1972. Editor: Nat. Acad. Adult Jewish Studies Bull., 1958-78, The High Holy Days, Book I (Herman Kieval), 1959, The Jewish Dietary Laws (Samuel H. Dresner and Seymour Siegel), 1959, Past and Present: Selected Essays (Israel Friedlaender), 1961, Heart of Wisdom, Book I (Bernard S. Raskas), 1962, Book II, 1979, Judaism: Profile of a Faith (Ben Zion Bokser), 1963, The Wisdom of Solomon Schechter (Bernard Mandelbaum), 1963, Jewish Tract Series, 1964-78 (15 titles), Foundations of A Faith (Simon Greenberg), 1967, Judaism and the Christian Predicament (Ben Zion Bokser), 1967, The Maturing of the Conservative Movement (Bernard Mandelbaum), 1968, The Sabbath (Samuel L. Dresner), 1970, Adult Jewish Edn., 1958-78, Talmudic Law and the Modern State (Moshe Silberg), 1973, Self-Incrimination in Jewish Law (Aaron Kirschenbaum), 1970, Sex and the Family in the Jewish Tradition (Robert Gordis), 1970; contbr. articles to numerous periodicals. Mem. Am. Acad. Jewish Research, Assn. Jewish Studies, N.Y. Bd. Rabbis, Rabbinical Assembly. Home: 67-66 108th St Apt D-46 Forest Hills NY 11375-2974 Office: Joint Retirement Bd 7 Penn Plz Ste 720 New York NY 10001-3900

WIENER, PHYLLIS AMES, artist; b. Iowa City, Sept. 17, 1921; d. Charles Louis and Loretta A. (Tucker) Zager; m. Allen Downs, Dec. 26, 1939 (div. 1960); children: Gareth, Allison, Barbara Hodne, Amy; m. Daniel Norman Wiener, Dec. 9, 1971. Student, U. Iowa, 1940-41, U. Mo., 1945, U. Minn., 1951-52. Mem. panel of selection Minn. Artists Program Mpls. Art Inst., 1976-78; mem. adv. panel Minn. State Arts Bd., St. Paul, 1978-81; juror anniversary exhibition Minn. Artists Mpls. Art Inst., 1985. One-woman shows include Walker Art Ctr., Mpls., 1951, 1956, Mpls. Inst. Art, 1967, Nash Gallery U. Minn., Mpls., 1981, Tweed Mus. Art, Duluth, Minn., 1982, Pindar Gallery, N.Y.C., 1984, 1986, 1988, U. Wis. Gallery, La Crosse, 1983, Janet Wallace Fine Arts, Macalester Coll., St. Paul, 1993, Murphy Gallery at St. Catherine's Coll., 2001, exhibited in group shows at Am. Fedn. Arts, 1954—58, U.S. State Dept., European Embassies, 1962, Represented in permanent collections Mpls. Art Inst., Walker Art Ctr., Mpls., Frederick Weisman Art Mus, Mayo Clinic, Scottsdale, Ariz., Minn. State Hist. Soc., St. Paul, Total Petroleum Co., Denver, Northwestern Bell Telephone Co., Omaha, Mus. Kuopio, Finland, Am. Embassy, Papua New Guinea, Carlson Co., Mpls. Recipient Individual Artist Project grant Minn. State Arts Bd., 1980. Mem. Nat. Book Critics Cir. Home: 1225 La Salle # 801 Minneapolis MN 55403

WIENER, RUSSELL WARREN, environmental scientist, researcher; b. N.Y.C., June 23, 1952; s. Max and Rhoda (Bruntil) W.; m. Martha E. Smith, Sept. 5, 1982; children: Benjamin, Victoria. Student, Rensselaer Poly. Inst., 1970-71; BS in Biology, Emory U., 1974, MS in Environ. Sci., 1978; PhD in Environ. Health, U. Cin., 1987. Rsch. technician U. N.C., Chapel Hill, 1978-79; aerosol tech. GE, Cin., 1984-86; chief atmospheric methods and monitoring br. U.S. EPA, Research Triangle Park, NC, 1987—2002, project dir. Ctr. for Homeland Security, 2002—. Adj. asst. prof. U. N.C., Chapel Hill, 1989—, N.C. State U., Raleigh, 1994—. Mem. Am. Assn. for Aerosol Rsch. (chair indoor air 1988-94), Am. Indsl. Hygiene Assn. (chair aerosol tech. com. 1997), Am. Acad. Indsl. Hygiene. Avocations: swimming, tennis. E-mail: wiener.russell@epa.gov.

WIENER, SOLOMON, writer, consultant, former city official; b. N.Y.C., Mar. 5, 1915; s. Morris David and Anna (Pinchuk) W.; m. Gertrude Klings, Feb. 24, 1946; children: Marjorie Diane, Willa Kay Ehrlich. BS, Cornell, 1936; MPA, NYU, 1946. Exam. asst. N.Y.C. Dept. Pers., 1937-42, civil svc. examiner, 1946-55, asst. divsn. chief, 1955-59, divsn. chief, 1959-67, asst. dir. exams, 1967-70, dir. exams, 1970-72, asst. pers. dir. for exams., 1972-75; author, cons., 1975—. Tchr. Washington Irving Evening Adult Sch., N.Y.C., 1949-60, tchr.-in-charge, 1960-67. Author: A Handy Book of Commonly Used American Idioms, rev. edit., 1981, Manual de Modismos Americanos Más Comunes, rev. edit., 1981, A handy Guide to Irregular Verbs and the Use and Formation of Tenses, 1959, Guia Completa de Los Verbos Irregulares en Inglès yel uso y Formación de los Tiempos, 1959, Questions and Answers on American Citizenship, rev. edit., 1982, Clear and Simple Guide to Business Letter Writing, rev. edit., 1978, The College Graduate Guide for Scoring High on Employment Tests, 1981, The High School Graduate Guide for Scoring High on Civil Service Tests, 1981, How to Take and Pass Simple Tests for Civil Service Jobs, 1981, Officer Candidate Tests, 5th edit., 2000, Military Flight Aptitude Tests, 4th edit., 2000; co-author Practice for the Armed Forces Test, ASVAB, 16th edit., 1999, Practica para el Examen de las Fuerzas Armadas, ASVAB en Español, 1989; contbr. to ARCO ROTC Coll. Guide, 1988. Served with AUS, 1942-46, PTO. Decorated Bronze Star. Mem. Am. Soc. Pub. Adminstrn., Internat. Pers. Mgmt. Assn., Authors Guild, Res. Officers Assn., Ret. Officers Assn., Assn. of U.S. Army, Nat. Def. Indsl. Assn., Marines Meml. Assn. Home: 523 E 14th St Apt 4F New York NY 10009-2931

WIENER, THOMAS ELI, lawyer; b. Dallas, Nov. 29, 1940; s. Samson and Fan (Gardner) W.; m. Felice Gloria Goodwin, Jan. 24, 1970; children: Gary Allen, Debra Roslyn, Allison Beth, Todd David. BA, U. Tex., 1962, JD with honors, 1968. Bar: Tex. 1968, D.C. 1969, Pa. 1972, U.S. Supreme Ct. 1972. Atty.-advisor office chief counsel IRS, Washington, 1968-72; assoc. Pepper Hamilton & Scheetz, Phila., 1972-74, Abrahams & Loewenstein, Phila., 1974-76, Goodis, Greenfield, Henry & Edelstein, Phila., 1976-77, Mesirov, Gelman, Jaffe, Cramer & Jamieson, Phila., 1977-78; prin. Franklin, Margulies & Huntington, 1978-91, Riley & DeFalice, P.C., Phila., 1991-92, Wiener & Caplan, P.C., Phila., 1992-95; pvt. practice, Bala Cynwyd, Pa., 1995—. Bd dirs. Lufkin (Tex.) Industries, Inc. Author: (with others) Tax Problems of Fiduciaries, 1977. Trustee Golden Slipper Club; pres. Main Line Reform Temple, 1992-94, pres. brotherhood 1981-83; pres. Rotary Gundaker Found., 1986-87; 1st v.p. N. Am. Fedn. Temple Brotherhoods, 1999-2001, Phila. Fedn. Reform Synagogues, 1993-98; chmn. Synagogue Fedn. Coun. of Phila., 1994-97; trustee Union Am. Hebrew Congregations, 1995—, exec. com., 2001-, ARZA/World Union N.Am. Mem. D.C. Bar Assn., Pa. Bar Assn., Tex. Bar Assn., Phila. Bar Assn., Am. Law Inst., Order of Coif. Lodges: Masons (32 degree K.C.C.H., past master), Rotary (pres. chpt. 1985-86). Home: 1233 Remington Rd Wynnewood PA 19096-2329 Office: One Belmont Ave Ste 605 Bala Cynwyd PA 19004-1609 E-mail: twiener@aol.com.

WIENER, VALERIE, writer, educator, communications executive; b. Las Vegas, Nev., Oct. 30, 1948; d. Louis Isaac Wiener and Tui Ava Knight. BJ, U. Mo., 1971, MA, 1972, U. Ill., Springfield, 1974; postgrad., McGeorge Sch. Law, 1976-79. Producer Checkpoint Sta. KOMU-TV, Columbia, Mo., 1972-73; v.p., owner Broadcast Assocs., Inc., Las Vegas, 1972-86; pub. affairs dir. First Ill. Cable TV, Springfield, 1973-74; editor Ill. State Register, 1973-74; prodr. and talent Nevada Realities Sta. KLVX-TV, Las Vegas, 1974-75; account exec. Sta. KBMI (now KFMS), 1975-79; nat. traffic dir. six radio stas., Las Vegas, Albuquerque and El Paso, Tex., 1979-80; exec. v.p., gen. mgr. Stas. KXKS and KKJY, Albuquerque, 1980-81; exec. adminstr. Stas. KSET AM/FM, KVEG, KFMS and KKJY, 1981-83; press sec. U.S. Congressman Harry Reid, Washington, 1983-87; adminstrv. asst Friends for Harry Reid, Nev., 1986; press sec. U.S. Senator Harry Reid, Washington, 1987-88; owner Wiener Comm. Group, Las Vegas, 1988—; mem. Nev. Senate, Dist. 3 Clark County, 1996—; Senate Dem. Whip, 2001; owner PowerMark Pub., 1998—. Author: Power Communications: Positioning Yourself for High Visibility (Fortune Book Club main selection 1994, Money Book Club selection 1995), Gang Free: Friendship Choices for Today's Youth, 1995, 2d edit., 1996, The Nesting Syndrome: Grown Children Living at Home, 1997, Winning the War Against Youth Gangs, 1999, Power Positioning: Advancing Yourself as The Expert, 2000, Power Master Handbook Series, 2000; contbg. writer The Pacesetter, ASAE's Comm. News. Sponsor Futures for Children, Las Vegas, Albuquerque, El Paso, 1979—83; mem. El Paso Exec. Women's Coun., 1981—83; media chmn. Gov.'s Coun. Small Bus., 1989—93; mem. Clark Coun. Sch. Dist. and Bus. Cmty. PAYBAC Spkrs. and Partnership Programs, 1989—, chair legis. com. on juv. justice, 1999—2000; chair Commn. on Sch. Safety of Juv. Violence, 1999—2000; various state and nat. legis. commns. and coms.; vice chmn. Congl. Awards Coun., 1989—93, Gov.'s Commn. on Postsecondary Edn., 1992—96; mem. Nev. Technol. Crimes Task Force, 1999—, Nev. Anti-Bullying Task Force, 2001—, Nev. Drug Commn., 1999—, Nev. Commn. on Aging, 1997—, Govs. Task Force on Corrections, 2002; Senate Minority Whip, 2001; mem. VIP bd. Easter Seals, El Paso, 1982; med. dir. 1990 Conf. on Women, Gov. of Nev.; bd. dirs. BBB So. Nev., 1994—, Pub. Edn. Found., 1997—; mem. steering com. Youth Recovery Network, 2001—. Named Outstanding Vol., United Way, El Paso, 1983, SBA Nev. Small Bus. Media Adv. of Yr., 1992, Disting. Sr. Athlete in Nev., 2000; recipient Outstanding Achievement award, Nat. Fedn. Press Women, 1991, Disting. Leader award, Nat. Assn.Cmty. Leadership, 1993, Outstanding Women Adv. for Edn. award, Va. Commonwealth U., 2000, gold medal, Nev. Sr. Olympics in Fitness and Weightlifting, 1998, 1999, 2000, 2001, Internat. Cmty. Svc. award, Internat. New Thought Alliance, 2001. Mem. Nat. Assn. of Women Bus. Owners (media chmn., nat. rep. So. Nev. 1990-91, Nev. Adv. of Yr. award 1992), Nev. Press Women, Nat. Spkrs. Assn., Small Pubs. Assn. N.Am., Dem. Press Secs. Assn., El Paso Assn. Radio Stas., U.S. Senate Staff Club, Las Vegas C. of C. (Circle of Excellence award 1993), Soc. Profl. Journalists. Democrat. Avocations: reading, writing, fitness and weightlifting training and competition, pub. speaking, community involvement. Office: 1500 Foremaster Ln Ste 2 Las Vegas NV 89101-1150

WIENKE, BRUCE R. physicist, consultant; b. Chgo., Sept. 21, 1940; s. Albert J. Wienke and Angeline Slager. BS, U. Wis., 1963; MS, Marquette U., 1965; PhD, Northwestern U., 1970. Cert. profl. diving instr., profl. ski instr., prof. ski coach. Engring. physics/computing cons. Sq. D Co., Milw., 1962—69; computing cons. Mission Rsch. Corp., Santa Barbara, 1979—81; dir. computational testbed for industry Advanced Computing Lab., Los Alamos, 1994—96; decompression algorithms cons. SW Enterprises Inc., Santa Fe, 1986—; postdoctoral physicist Los Alamos (N.Mex.) Nat. Lab., 1970—71, theoretical particle physicist, 1971—79, computational weapons physicist, 1982—91, group leader computing scis., 1991—94, program coord. computational physics, 1997—2001, computational physicist, 1999—. Cons. decompression algorithms Diving Equipment Mfrs. Assn., San Francisco, 1986—; dir. Manage Indsl. Computing Ctr., 1994. Author: (book) Technical Diving In Depth, 2001 (Best Seller, 2002); dir.: (manage industrial computing center) , 1994; author: (book) Physics, Physiology, And Decompression Theory, 1998, Diving Above Sea Level, 1998, Basic Diving Physics And Applications, 1994, High Altitude Diving, 1991, Basic Decompression Theory And Applications, 1991; contbr. tech. papers to profl. jours. Outward Bound coord. Parks and Recreation, Santa Fe, 1985—97. Recipient Bausch-Lomb Sci. award, Milw. Sch. Dist., 1958, All Conf. Football and Basketball Team, Wis. High Athletics Conf., 1956—58, Dept. of Energy Tech. Transfer Excellence award, US Dept. of Energy, 1996. Master: Nat. Assn. Underwater Instrs. (trainer, course dir., BOD mem. 1974—2002, level III trainer 1986, Svc. award 1996), Tech. Diving Assns. (course dir., trainer 1974—2002); fellow: Am. Acad. Underwater Scis. (cons. 1986—2002); mem.: PA of Diving Instrs. (trainer, course dir. 1974—2002), Profl. Ski Instrs. Am. (trainer 1974—2002, master instr. 1978), Undersea and Hyperbaric Med. Soc., Am. Nuc. Soc. (tech. com. mem. 1972—2000), Am. Phys. Soc. Achievements include development of RGBM model. Avocation: ski racing. Home: #102 3101 Old Pecos Trail Santa Fe NM 87505 Office: Los Alamos Nat Lab Ms-D413 Los Alamos NM 87545 Home Fax: 505-665-5538; Office Fax: 505-665-5538. Personal E-mail: brw61435@aol.com. E-mail: brw@lanl.gov.

WIENS, ARTHUR NICHOLAI, psychology educator; b. McPherson, Kans., Sept. 7, 1926; s. Jacob T. and Helen E. (Kroeker) W.; m. Ruth Helen Avery, June 11, 1949; children: Barbara, Bradley, Donald. BA, U. Kans., 1948, MA, 1952; PhD, U. Portland, 1956. Diplomate: Am. Bd. Examiners Profl. Psychology. Clin. psychologist Topeka State Hosp., 1949-53; sr. psychologist outpatient dept. Oreg. State Hosp., Salem, 1954-58, chief psychologist, 1958-61, dir. clin. psychology internship program, 1958-61; clin. instr. U. Oreg. Med. Sch., Portland, 1958-61, asst. prof., 1961-65, assoc. prof., 1965-66, prof. med. psychology, 1966—; clin. assoc. prof. psychology U. Portland, 1959-61, prof. med. psychology, 1966—96, prof. emeritus med. psychology, 1997—. Field assessment officer Peace Corps, 1965; cons. psychologist Portland Ctr. for Hearing and Speech, 1964—67, Dammasch State Hosp., 1967—69, Raleigh Hills Hosp., 1968—84, Oreg. Vocat. Rehab. Divsn., 1973—2001, mem. state adv. com., 1976—93; cons. William Temple Rehab. House, Episcopal Laymen's Mission Soc., 1968—88; chmn. State Oreg. Bd. Social Protection, 1971—84, State of Oreg. Bd. Psychologist Examiners, 1963—66, 1974—77; v.p. bd. dirs. Raleigh Hills Rsch. Found., 1974—80. Contbr. articles to profl. jours. Fellow AAAS, APA (chmn. com. on vis. psychologist program 1972-76, chmn. accreditation com. 1978, mem. task force edn. and credentialing 1979-84); mem. Am. Assn. State Psychology Bds. (pres. 1978-79), Nat. Register Health Svc. Providers in Psychology (bd. dirs. 1985-92), Profl. Exam. Svc. (bd. dirs. 1982-88, 90-96, chmn. 1986-88), Sigma Xi. Home: 74 Condolea Way Lake Oswego OR 97035-1010 Office: Oreg Health Scis U Portland OR 97201 E-mail: wiensa@ohsu.edu.

WIENS, BEVERLY JO, educator; b. Oildale, Calif., Oct. 2, 1947; d. Ernest and Irene Josephine (Klassen) Bartel; m. Gary D. Wiens, Aug. 19, 1967; children: Nicole Marie Wiens Cook, Katie Lyn Wiens. BA, San Jose State U., 1969, MA, 1971, Santa Clara U., 1992; PhD, No. Calif. Grad. U., 2001. Lic. counselor, Calif. Tchr. West Valley Coll., Saratoga, Calif., 1971-76, San Jose (Calif.) City Coll., 1974-75, San Jose State U., 1978; marriage, family therapist Coalition of Counseling Centers, Los Gatos, Calif., 1982-86; assoc. prof. San Jose Bible Coll., 1982-87; prof., dept. chair, counseling psychology San Jose Christian Coll., 1988—. Lectr. in field. Mem. Am. Assn. Christian Counselors, Am. Counseling Assn., Assn. Religious Value in Counseling, Assn. Counselor Training, Supervision, Calif. Assn. Marital Family Therapists. Republican. Mem. Mennonite Brethren. Office: San Jose Christian Coll 790 S 12th St San Jose CA 95112-2304 E-mail: bwiens@sjchristian.edu.

WIER, DARA, poet, English language educator; b. New Orleans, Dec. 30, 1949; d. Arthur Joseph and Grace Cecile (Barrois) Dixon; children: Emily Caitlin, Guy Gerard. Student, La. State U., 1967-70; BS, Longwood Coll., 1971; MFA, Bowling Green U., 1974. Asst. prof. Hollins (Va.) Coll., 1975-80; assoc. prof. U. Ala., Tuscaloosa, 1980-85; assoc. prof. English, U. Mass., Amherst, 1985-87, prof., 1988—. Vis. poet U. Tex., Austin, 1982; Richard Hugo prof. U. Mont., Missoula, 1992. Author: (poem collections) The Book of Knowledge, 1988, Blue for the Plough, 1991, Our Master Plan, 1999, Voyages in English, 2001, Hat on a Pond, 2001. Fellow Nat. Endowment for Arts, 1980, Guggenheim Found., 1991-92, Mass. Cultural Coun., 2001. Mem. Acad. Am. Poets, Poetry Soc. Am., Assoc. Writing Programs (bd. dirs. 1977-81, pres. 1980). Office: U Mass Program for Poets and Writers Amherst MA 01003 E-mail: daraw@hfa.umass.edu.

WIER, PATRICIA ANN, publishing executive, consultant; b. Coal Hill, Ark., Nov. 10, 1937; d. Horace L. and Bridget B. (McMahon) Norton; m. Richard A. Wier, Feb. 24, 1962; 1 child, Rebecca Ann. BA, U. Mo., Kansas City, 1964; MBA, U. Chgo., 1978. Computer programmer AT&T, 1960-62; lead programmer City of Kansas City, Mo., 1963-65; with Playboy Enterprises, Chgo., 1965-71, mgr. systems and programming, 1971; with Ency. Britannica, Inc., Chgo., 1971—; v.p. mgmt. svcs. Ency. Britannica USA, 1975-83, exec. v.p. adminstrn., 1983-84; v.p. planning and devel. Ency. Britannica, Inc., 1985, pres. Compton's Learning Co. divsn., 1985; pres. Ency. Britannica (USA), 1986-91, Ency. Britannica N.A., 1991-92; exec. v.p. Ency. Britannica, Inc., 1986-94; pres. Ency. Britannica N.Am., 1991-94; mgmt. cons. pvt. practice, Chgo., 1994—. Cons. pvt. practice, Chgo., 1994—; bd. dirs. NICOR, Inc., Golden Rule Ins.; mem. coun. Northwestern U. Assocs. Life mem. coun. Grad. Sch. Bus., U. Chgo.; mem. bd. regents Lewis U.; chmn. bd. dirs. San Miguel Sch. Mem. Direct Selling Assn. (bd. dirs. 1984-93, chmn. 1987-88, named to Hall of Fame 1991), Women's Coun. U. Mo. Kansas City (hon. life) Com. 200, The Chgo. Network. Roman Catholic. Office: Patricia A Wier Inc 175 E Delaware Pl Apt 8305 Chicago IL 60611-7748 E-mail: wier@prodigy.net.

WIERMAN, JOHN CHARLES, mathematician, educator; b. Prosser, Wash., June 30, 1949; s. John Nathaniel and Edith Elizabeth (Ashley) W.; m. Susan Shelley Graupmann, Aug. 13, 1971; 1 child, Adam Christopher. BS in Math., U. Wash., 1971, PhD in Math., 1976. Asst. prof. math. U. Minn., Mpls., 1976-81; asst. prof. Johns Hopkins U., Balt., 1981-82, assoc. prof., 1982-87, prof., 1987—, chmn. math. scis. dept., 1988-2000, dir. entrepreneurship and mgmt. program, 1996—. Sr. rsch. fellow Inst. Math. and Its Applications, Mpls., 1987-88. Co-author: First-Passage Percolation on the Square Lattice, 1978; contbr. articles to profl. jours. Grad. fellow NSF, 1971-74; NSF rsch. grantee, 1976-93. Fellow Inst. Math. Stats. (organizer spl. session on percolation theory 1982, organizer spl. session on probability and math. stats. 1986); mem. Am. Soc. Quality, Inst. Math. Stats., Am. Math. Soc., Am. Statis. Assn., Math. Assn. Am., Sigma Xi, Phi Beta Kappa. Office: Johns Hopkins U Dept Math Scis 34th & Charles Sts Baltimore MD 21218 E-mail: wierman@jhu.edu.

WIERNAS, TERRY KIRKHAM, pharmaceutical company executive; b. Richmond, Va., Oct. 21, 1957; d. Walter Eugene and Josephine Barnes Kirkham; m. James Steven Wiernas, Sr., Sept. 15, 1981; children: Deborah Grace, James Steven Jr., Gregory Scott, Jennifer Marie. BS in Pharmacy, Med. Coll. Va., Richmond, 1981; MBA, Va. Commonwealth U., Richmond, 1986; PhD in Biomed. Scis., U. North Tex., Fort Worth, 1997. Registered pharmacist. Pharmacist biopharmaceutics rsch. A.H. Robins Co., Richmond, 1981-85, assoc. internat. regulatory affairs, 1985-86, mgr. internat. regulatory affairs, 1986-90; assoc. sr. regulatory affairs Whitby Rsch. Inc., 1990-91, mgr. regulatory submissions, 1991-92; asst. dir. regulatory affairs Alcon Labs., Fort Worth, 1992-95, assoc. dir. regulatory affairs, 1996-98, dir. regulatory affairs, 1999-2001, sr. dir. regulatory affairs, 2001—. Contbr. articles to profl. jours. Mem. Am. Pharmaceutical Assn. Avocations: coaching softball, basketball and soccer. Home: 3611 Lake Powell Dr Arlington TX 76016 Office: Alcon Labs Inc 6201 S Freeway Fort Worth TX 76134-2099

WIERNIK, PETER HARRIS, oncologist, educator; b. Crocket , Tex., June 16, 1939; s. Harris and Molly (Emmerman) W.; m. Roberta Joan Fuller, Sept. 6, 1961; children: Julie Anne, Lisa Britt, Peter Harrison. BA with distinction, U. Va., 1961, MD, 1965; Dr. h.c., U. of Republic, Montevideo, Uruguay, 1982. Diplomate Am. Bd. Internal Medicine, Am. Bd. Med. Oncology (mem. writing com. 1981-87). Intern Cleve. Met. Gen. Hosp., 1965-66, resident, 1969-70, Osler Svc. Johns Hopkins Hosp., Balt., 1970-71; sr. asst. surgeon USPHS, 1966, advanced through grades to med. dir., 1976; sr. staff assoc. Balt. Cancer Rsch. Ctr., 1966-71, chief sect. med. oncology, 1971-76, chief clin. oncology br., 1976-82, dir., 1976-82; assoc. dir. div. cancer treatment Nat. Cancer Inst., 1976-82; assoc. dir. Albert Einstein Cancer Ctr., Bronx, 1982-98, prof. medicine, 1983-98, prof. radiation oncology, 1996-98, head divsn. med. oncology. Asst. prof. medicine U. Md. Sch. Medicine, Balt., 1971-74, assoc. prof., 1974-76, prof., 1976-82; prof. medicine and radiation oncology N.Y. Med. Coll., 1998—; cons. hematology and med. oncology Union Meml. Hosp., Greater Balt. Med. Ctr., Franklin Sq. Hosp.; bd. dirs. Balt. City unit Am. Cancer Soc., 1971-78; chmn. patient care com., 1972-75, mem. profl. edn. and grants com., N.Y.C. divsn., 1983-90, mem. nat. clin. fellowship com., 1984-96; mem. med. adv. com. Nat. Leukemia Assn., 1976-88, chmn. med. adv. com., 1989—; chmn. adult leukemia com. Cancer and Leukemia Group B, 1976-83; prin. investigator Ea. Coop. Oncology Group, 1982-94, 96—; chmn. gynecol. oncology com., 1986-88, chmn. leukemia com., 1988-94; sci. cons. Vt. Regional Cancer Ctr., 1987—; dir. OLM Comprehensive Cancer Ctr., N.Y. Med. Coll., 1998—. Editor: Controversies in Oncology, 1982, Supportive Care of the Cancer Patient, 1983, Neoplastic Diseases of the Blood, 1985, Neoplastic Diseases of the Blood, 2d edit., 1991, Neoplastic Diseases of the Blood, 3d edit., 1996, (book) Adult Leukemias, 2001; editor: (assoc.) Medical Oncology and Tumor Pharmacotherapy, 1987—91; editor: (sr.), 1991—; editor: (assoc.) (jour.) Am. Jour. Therapeutics, 1994—; co-editor: Year Book of Hematology, 1986—98, Handbook of Hematologic and Oncologic Emergencies, 1988—98, Bone Marrow Transplantation (textbook), 1995, (jour.) Am. Jour. Med. Scis., 1976—81; editor (N. Am.): Jour. Cancer Rsch. and Clin. Oncology, 1986—89; mem. editl. bd.: jour. Cancer Treatment Reports, 1972—76, mem. editl. bd.: jour. Leukemia Rsch., 1977—86, mem. editl. bd.: jour., 1991—, mem. editl. bd.: jour. Leukemia, 1986—, mem. editl. bd.: jour. Cancer Clin. Trials, 1977—, mem. editl. bd.: jour. Jour. Therapeutic Rsch., 1994—, mem. editl. bd.: jour. Hosp. Practice, 1979—, mem. editl. bd.: jour. Jour. Clin. Oncology, 1989—91, mem. editl. bd.: jour. PDQ Nat. Cancer Inst., 1987—94; editor (sect. antineoplastic drugs): Jour. Clin. Pharmacology, 1985—; editor: (assoc.) Cancer Investigation, 1998—; contbr. articles to profl. jours., chapters to books. Recipient Z Soc. award U. Va., 1961, Byrd S. Leavell Hematology award U. Va. Sch. Medicine, 1965 Fellow AAAS, ACP, Am. Coll. Clin. Pharmacology (awards com. 1999—), Internat. Soc. Hematology, Royal Soc. Medicine (London), N.Y. Acad. Medicine; mem. Am. Soc. Clin. Investigation (instl. rep. 1997—), Am. Soc. Clin. Oncology (chmn. edn. and tng. com. 1976-79, 84, subcom. on clin. investigation 1980-82, program com. 1990, pub. issues com., 1990-95, com. on rsch. awards 1996-2000, com. on health svcs. rsch. 2000—), Am. Assn. Cancer Rsch., Am. Soc. Hematology, Am. Fedn. Clin. Rsch., Am. Acad. Clin. Toxicology, Internat. Soc. Exptl. Hematology, N.Y. Acad. Sci., Am. Soc. Hosp. Pharmacy, Am. Soc. Clin. Pharmacology and Therapeutics, Am. Radium Soc. (program com. 1987-93, exec. com. 1988-95, publ. com. 1988-92, sec. 1990-91, pres.-elect, 1992-93; pres. 1993-94, Janeway medalist, 1996), Polish Oncology Soc. (hon.), Harvey Soc., Uruguayan Hematology Soc. (hon.), Acad. Medicine Uruguay (corr.), European Assn. Cancer Rsch., European Soc. for Hematology, Phi Beta Kappa (assoc. 1991—), Sigma Xi, Alpha Omega Alpha, Phi Sigma (award 1961). Office: Comprehensive Cancer Ctr Our Lady Mercy Med Ctr 600 E 233rd St Bronx NY 10466-2604 E-mail: wiernik@jimmy.harvard.edu. *Always remember why you entered a profession in the first place. Leave the politics to those who have forgotten.*

WIERSBE, WARREN WENDELL, clergyman, author, lecturer; b. East Chicago, Ind., May 16, 1929; s. Fred and Gladys Anna (Forsberg) W.; m. Betty Lorraine Warren, June 20, 1953; children: David, Carolyn, Robert, Judy. B.Th., No. Baptist Sem., 1953; D.D. (hon.), Temple Sem., Chattanooga, 1965, Trinity Ev-Div. Sch., 1986; LittD (hon.), Cedarville Coll., 1987. Ordained to ministry, Bapt. Ch., 1951. Pastor Central Bapt. Ch., East Chicago, 1951-57; editl. dir. Youth for Christ Internat., Wheaton, Ill., 1957-61; pastor Calvary Bapt. Ch., Covington, Ky., 1961-71; sr. min. Moody Ch., Chgo., 1971-78; bd. dirs. Slavic Gospel Assn., Wheaton, 1973-87; columnist Moody Monthly, Chgo., 1971-77; author, conf. minister, 1978-80; pres. ScripTex, Inc., Lincoln, Nebr., 1982—. Vis. instr. pastoral theology Trinity Div. Sch., Deerfield, Ill.; gen. dir. Back to the Bible Radio Ministries, Lincoln, Nebr., 1984-89; writer-in-residence Cornerstone Coll., Grand Rapids, Mich.; disting. prof. preaching Grand Rapids Bapt. Sem. Author: over 150 books including William Culbertson, A Man of God, 1974, Live Like a King, 1976, Walking with the Giants, 1976, Be Right, 1977, (with David Wiersbe) Making Sense of the Ministry, 1983, Why Us? Why Bad Things Happen to God's People, 1984, Real Worship: It Can Transform Your Life, 1986, Be Compassionate, 1988, The Integrity Crisis, 1988, Be What You Are, 1988, The New Pilgrim's Progress, 1989, Be Courageous, 1989, Living With the Giants, 1993, Preaching and Teaching with Imagination, 1994, Be Myself, 1994, Be Authentic, 1997, Be Basic, 1998. Home and Office: 441 Lakewood Dr Lincoln NE 68510-2419

WIERSEMA, HAROLD LEROY, aerospace engineer; b. Erie, Ill., Sept. 17, 1919; s. Clarence John and Tena (Griede) W.; m. Joanne Kearney, Mar. 19, 1955; children: Roger Kent, Marilyn Tena. BS, U. Ill., 1949. Aerospace engr. Space Div. Rockwell Internat., Downey, Calif., 1953-78; sr. spl. engr. Boeing Mil. Airplane Co., Wichita, Kans., 1978-86; aerospace engr., avionics cons. Long Beach, Calif., 1986-94. Com. chmn. Boy Scouts Am., Lynwood, Calif., 1968-70; pres. Compton (Calif.) Pacific Little League, 1966-69; deacon Presbyn. Ch., Southgate, Calif., 1942-70. Col. USAF, World War II, Korea. Decorated D.F.C., Air medal (5); recipient Mach Buster award N.Am. Aviation, Edwards AFB, 1963, Order of Arrow, Boy Scouts Am., 1967. Mem. IEEE (life), U.S. Air Force Assn. (life), 388th Bomb Group/8th Air Force Assn. (life), Nat. Geog. Soc., UCLA Alumni Assn., Shriners. Democrat. Presbyterian. Home: 5451 Jonesboro Way Buena Park CA 90621-1615

WIERSMA, G. BRUCE, dean, forest resources educator; b. Paterson, N.J., Oct. 26, 1942; s. George and Marjorie (Zeedyk) W.; m. Ann Becker, Aug. 15, 1964; children: Heather, Robin, Jennifer, Joshua. BS, U. Maine, 1964; MF in Forestry, Yale U., 1965; PhD Coll. Environ. Sci. & Forestry, SUNY, 1968. Teaching asst., 1965-66; rsch. biologist Coll. Environ. Sci. and Forestry SUNY, 1968; combat devels. staff officer U.S. Army Inst. Land Combat, Alexandria, Va., 1968-70; head monitoring sect. EPA, Washington, 1970-72, chief ecol. monitoring branch, 1972-74, chief pollutant pathways br. Las Vegas, Nev., 1974-79, sr. ecologist, 1979-80; mgr. environ. earth scis. group, Idaho Nat. Engring. Lab. EG&G Idaho, Inc., 1980-87; instr. Idaho Falls Campus of Higher Edn. U. Idaho, 1981-90, affiliate grad. faculty Coll. Forestry Wildlife and Range Scis., 1988-90; mgr., dir. Ctr. Environ. Monitoring and Assesment Environ. Sci. and Tech. Group, 1989-90; dir. Ctr. Environ. Monitoring and Assesment Idaho Nat. Engring. Lab., EG&G Idaho, Inc., Idaho Falls, 1988-90; dean Coll. Forest Resources, assoc. dir. Maine Agrl. Experiment Sta., prof. Forest Resources U. Maine, Orono, 1991-93, dean Coll. Natural Scis., Forestry and Agr., dir. Maine Agrl. and Forest Exptl. Sta., 1993—. Dir. Ctr. Environ. Monitoring and Assessment, Idaho Falls, Idaho, 1980-90, mem. ad-hoc task force to plan global environ. monitoring sys., 1993-95; trustee Nature Conservancy, 1993-95; mem. UN ad hoc task force to plan global terrestrial observing sys., 1993-95; bd. dirs. Maine Forest Products Coun., 1993—; U.S. Nat. Com. on Data for Sci. and Tech., 1990-92; chmn. com. on databased NRC, 1990-94, mem. com. on marine monitoring, 1986-90; mem. forest resources adv. com. U.S. Sec. Agr., 1998—; mem. Gov. Maine's Com. on Sawmill Biomass Conversion, 1999. Contbr. chpts. to books, articles to profl. jours; editor, founder Jour. Environ. Monitoring and Assesment. Capt. U.S. Army, 1968-70. Recipient numerous rsch. grants from various orgns. Mem. NRC (chair com. on databases, 1990-94, com. on marine monitoring, 1986-90, Nat. Assn. Profl. Forestry Schs. (exec. com. 1993-98), Assn. Expt. Sta. Dirs. (exec. com. N.E. region 1996-2000, chmn. 1998-99, com. on policy 1997—). Avocations: jogging, swimming, cross country skiing, backpacking, mountain climbing. Home: 103 Wildwood Estates Dr Holden ME 04429-7344 Office: Univ of Maine/Coll Natural Scis Forestry and Agr 5782 Winslow Hall Orono ME 04469-5782

WIERWILLE, MARSHA LOUISE, elementary education educator; b. Springfield, Ohio, Mar. 19, 1951; d. Eugene Junior and Donna Catherine (Bodine) Randall; m. Bob Edward Wierwille, June 14, 1975; children: Benjamin Joseph Reuben, Jeremiah James Eugene, Samuel John Philip, Adam Joel David. BS, Ohio State U., 1973; MEd, Wright State U., 1976; postgrad., U. Dayton, Ohio, 1982, 84, 87, Coll. of Mt. St. Joseph, summer 1985, 86. Cert. elem. edn. tchr., curriculum supr., Ohio. Tchr. 1st grade New Bremen (Ohio) Sch., 1973-76, tchr. 2d grade, 1976—. Mem. NEA, Ohio Edn. Assn., Western Ohio Edn. Assn., New Bremen Tchrs. Assn. (pres. 1976-77), Ohio Coun. Tchrs. Math., Delta Kappa Gamma. Avocations: reading, walking, biking, family, travel. Office: New Bremen Sch 202 S Walnut St New Bremen OH 45869-1297

WIERZBICKI, JACEK GABRIEL, physicist, researcher; b. Lódz, Poland, Oct. 27, 1948; came to U.S., 1986; s. Gabriel Wiktor and Jadwiga Krystyna (Skarzynska) W.; m. Grazyna Maria Chawrona, Aug. 31, 1974; children: Grazyna, Przemystaw, Danuta, Kinga. MS in Physics, U. Lódz, 1971, MS in Math., 1973, PhD in Physics, 1981. Researcher U. Lódz, 1971-75; reseacher Joint Inst. for Nuclear Rsch., Dubna, USSR, 1975-79; med. physicist Oncological Ctr., Lódz, 1980-83; lectr. Fed. U. Tech., Bauchi, Nigeria, 1983-86; rsch. fellow Ohio U., Athens, 1986-88; asst. prof. U. Ky., Lexington, 1988-92; assoc. prof. Wayne State U., Detroit, 1993-98; chief physicist St. Mary's Med. Ctr., Saginaw, Mich., 1998—. Clin. assoc. prof. Mich. State U., East Lansing, 1998—. Contbr. over 200 articles to sci. jours. Mem. Am. Phys. Soc., Am. Assn. Physicists in Medicine, Radiation Rsch. Soc., Sigma Xi. Roman Catholic. Achievements include rsch. in interactions of neutrons with light nuclei, in devel. of radium treatment in gynecology and radiation protection in the hospital, in interactions of 24 MeV neutrons with nuclei and optical model analysis, in use of Cf-252 in therapy of cancer, clinical radiobiology; clinical use of intensity modulated radiotherapy, cardiovascular brachytherapy. Home: 3422 Shakespeare Dr Troy MI 48084-1489 Office: St Mary's Med Ctr Cancer Treatment Ctr Saginaw MI 48601 E-mail: jwierzbi@saintmarys-saginaw.org.

WIES, BARBARA, editor, publisher; b. Dec. 5, 1939; BA, U. Conn., 1961; student, New Sch. for Social Rsch., 1961-62. Product devel. Fearn Soya, Melrose Park, Ill., 1973-75; product devel. Modern Products, Milw., 1973-75; editor, pub. Bestways Mag., Carson City, Nev., 1977-89; pub. The Healthy Gourmet Newsletter, 1989-91, Fine Wine-Good Food Newsletter, 1991—; publicity dir. Nev. Artists Assn., 1994—; owner Gualala (Calif.) Galleries, 1989-90; assoc. pub., mgr. Edn. Range Mag., 1998—. Owner, operator cooking sch. Greensboro N.C. 1969-73; instr. Very Spl. Arts Nev., 1997. Author: Natural Cooking, 1968, Wok and Tempura, 1969, Japanese Home Cooking, 1970, The Wok, 1971, Super Soy, 1973, The Health Gourmet, 1981, International Healthy Gourmet, 1982; one-woman show paintings Dolphin Gallery, Gualala, Calif., 1990, River Gallery, Reno, 1994; 2 women show 1992, 94, 96, Dolphin Gallery, Calif., 1994, solo exhbn. Nev. Artists Assn. Gallery, 1993, 95, 96, 97; featured artist Nev. State Libr., 1996, Silver State Gallery, Reno, 1998, West Nev. C.C., 1996, art show judge, 1997; restaurant critic Reno Gazette Jour., 1995-2001. Performer Nev. Arts sponsored Tumblewords, 2000—. Grantee Nev. Arts Coun., 2002; recipient First Place adult fiction Nev. State Lit. Co., 1995, First Place fiction State Lit. Comp., 1998, 2d Place fiction Writers Block; Nev. Arts Coun. fellow, 1999-2000. Mem. Nat. League Am. Pen Women (chair 1st and 2d ann. lit. competition Reno br., chairperson 1st Nat. Lit. award), Inst. Food Technologists, Pastel Soc. of the West Coast, Inst. Am. Culinary Profls.

WIESCHAUS, ERIC F. molecular biologist, educator; b. June 8, 1947; BS, U. Notre Dame, 1969; PhD in Biology, Yale U., 1974. Rsch. fellow Zool. Inst., U. Zurich, Switzerland, 1975-78; group leader European Molecular Biol. Lab., Germany, 1978-81; from asst. prof. to assoc. prof. Princeton (N.J.) U., 1981-87, prof. molecular biology, 1987—. Fellow Lab. de Genetique Moleculaire, France, 1976; vis. rschr. Ctr. Pathobiology, U. Calif., Irvine, 1977; mem. sci. adv. coun. Damon Runyon-Walter Winchell Cancer Fund, 1987-92. Contbr. articles to profl. jours. Recipient Nobel Prize in Medicine, 1995. Fellow Am. Acad. Arts and Scis.; mem. NAS. Office: Princeton U MOF 435 Dept Molecular Biology Washington Rd Princeton NJ 08544-0001*

WIESCHENBERG, KLAUS, retired management consultant; b. Hannover, Germany, Mar. 2, 1932; came to U.S., 1959; s. Heinz and Ruth (Wilke) W.; m. Nona Bodareva, June 7, 1958; children: Michael, Axel, Natasha. BA, Fairleigh Dickinson U., Madison, N.J., 1974, MBA, 1977. Export/import corr. Deutsche Bank, Hannover, 1953; export corr. Hoechst AG, Frankfurt, Germany, 1954-55; various mktg. positions Am. Hoechst Corp., 1956-68; various fin. positions, 1969-78; v.p. planning corp. divsn. Somerville, N.J., 1978-85; v.p. Office of Pres. and Corp. Devel., 1985-87; v.p. corp. devel. Hoechst Celanese Corp., 1987-95; strategic mgmt. concepts, prin., 1995-2001; ret., 2001. Mem. editl. bd. Bus. 2000, 1990-91. Mem. Comml. Devel. Assn. (chmn. membership com. 1984-86), Am. Mgmt. Assn., Strategic Leadership Forum (internat. bd. dirs. 1990-97, exec. com. 1991-92, chmn. internat. com. 1990-95, chmn. res. & edn. found. 1995-97, v.p. N.Y. met. chpt. 1986-91), Somerset County C. of C. (bd. dirs. 1990-96). Republican. Eastern Orthodox. Home: 494 Steele Gap Rd Bridgewater NJ 08807-2339

WIESE, DANIEL EDWARD, marketing and communications researcher; b. Cedar Rapids, Iowa, June 16, 1936; s. Erwin Edward and Bernice Virginia (Cristy) W.; m. Mary Virginia Smith, Nov. 3, 1958 (div. 1982); children: Anne, John, Amy; m. JoBeth Kuehl, Aug. 6, 1982; children: Jamie, Jill, Eric. BS, Iowa State U., 1958. Rsch. assoc. Meredith Pub. Co., Des Moines, 1961-65; rsch. dir. Popular Sci. Pub. Co., N.Y.C., 1965-66; assoc. rsch. dir. Reader Digest Assn., 1966-67; rsch. dir. Successful Farming divsn. Meredith Corp., Des Moines, 1967-77; mgr. Agtrack divsn. Chilton Rsch. Svcs., Radnor, Pa., 1977-80; v.p., dir. rsch. svcs. Creswell, Munsell, Fulta & Zirbel, Inc., Cedar Rapids, Iowa, 1980-86; pres. Dan Wiese Mktg. Rsch., 1986—. Mem. editl. adv. bd. Agrimarketing mag., 1989. Bd. dirs. Plymouth Congl. Nursery Sch., Des Moines, 1975; mktg. com. Cedar Rapids Symphony, 1984; mem. adv. bd. Cedar Rapids Better Bus. Bur., Area Mktg. Task Force, Linn County I-Club Bd., 1991-92; bd. dirs., chmn. mktg. com. Witwer Sr. Ctr., 2001—. Capt. U.S. Army, 1959. Mem. Nat. Agri-Mktg. Assn. (chmn. mktg. rsch. com. 1982-83, Cornbelt chpt. bd. 1995-2001), Advt. Fedn. Cedar Rapids (1st v.p. 1988-89, pres. 1989-90, bd. dirs. 1987-90), Cedar Rapids C. of C. (agr.-bus. com.), Ag-Maizing Cedar Rapids (exec. com. 1998-99). Home and Office: 2108 Greenwood Dr SE Cedar Rapids IA 52403-2727 E-mail: danwiese@mchsi.com.

WIESE, KEVIN GLEN, entrepreneur; b. Ogden, Utah, Mar. 19, 1960; s. Glen James and Kay Jon (Mildon) W. BS in Fin. and Mktg., U. Utah, 1982; MBA, Golden State U., 1987; PhD in Internat. Bus., Columbia Pacific U., 1987. Fin. advisor Silverstein Fin., L.A., 1983-85; fin. cons. Christopher Weil & Co., Inc., 1985-87; chief exec. officer, pres. Internat. Venture Enterprises, 1988—, Internat. Venture Rsch., L.A., 1988—, Internat. Leadership Performance Advisors, L.A., 1988—, Internat. Wealth Group, Ltd., L.A., 1988—; chief oper. officer Albatross Sportcoear, Inc., Huntington Beach, Calif., 1990—. Adj. prof. Loyola Marymount U., Los Angeles, 1986-87, Coll. for Fin. Planning Denver, 1986-87; cons. United Industries, L.A., 1987-88, Rouse Fin. Network, Phoenix, 1989—; researcher Harvard U., Boston, 1987—, Oxford U., Eng., 1987—, Stanford U., Palo Alto, Calif., 1987—, Cambridge U., Eng., 1987—; cons. Concierge Mgmt. Group, 1990, Heuristics Search, Inc., 1990; resident bus. expert on Fin. News Network cable program The Am. Entrepreneur, 1990; pub. speaker in field. Pub. Trend Newsletter for Small Bus. Entrepreneurs, 1990—. Bus. liaison Mega-Cities Project L.A. Sect., 1988—; vol. Hugh O'Brian Youth Found., L.A., 1986-88, assoc. mem. community leadership, 1989—; mem. HOBY Assocs. Mem. Internat. Assn., for Fin. Planning (bd. dirs. L.A. chpt. 1985-86, sec., treas. 1984-85), Inst. Cert. Fin. Planning. Republican. Avocations: fencing, karate, skiing, romance langs., mus. instruments. Office: 288 Springridge Dr North Salt Lake UT 84054-3035

WIESE, NEVA, critical care nurse; b. Hunter, Kans., July 23, 1940; d. Amil H. and Minnie (Zemke) W. Diploma, Grace Hosp. Sch. Nursing, Hutchinson, Kans., 1962; BA in Social Sci., U. Denver, 1971; BSN, Met. State Coll., 1975; MS in Nursing, U. Colo., Denvr. 1978; postgrad., U. N.Mex., 1986; PhD, Kennedy Western U., 1999. RN, N.Mex.; CCRN. Cardiac ICU nurse U. N.Mex. Hosp., Albuquerque; coord. critical care edn. St. Vincent Hosp., Santa Fe, charge nurse CCU, clin. nurse III intensive and cardiac care. Recipient Mary Atherton Meml. award for clin. excellence St. Vincent Hosp., 1986. Mem. ANA (cert. med. surg. nurse), AACN (past pres., sec. N.Mex. chpt., Clin. Excellence award 1991, Lifetime Achievement award 1997), N.Mex. League Nursing (past v.p., bd. dirs., sec., membership com. 1992-97).

WIESE, THOMAS JOHN, biochemistry educator; b. LaCrosse, Wis., Jan. 9, 1964; s. Reuben henry and Arlene mae W.; married. BS, U. Wis., 1986; PhD, U. N.D., 1990. Post-doctoral rsch. assoc. Washington U., St. Louis, 1990-92, U. Iowa, Iowa City, 1992-96; asst. prof. chemistry Ft. Hays State U., Hays, Kans., 1996—. Contbr. articles to profl. jours. Mem. Am. Chem. Soc., AAAS, Sigma Xi (sec. 2000-02). Lutheran. Avocations: woodworking, fishing. Office: Fort Hays State Univ 600 Park St Hays KS 67601

WIESE, WOLFGANG LOTHAR, physicist, researcher; b. Tilsit, Germany, Apr. 21, 1931; came to U.S., 1957; naturalized, 1965; s. Werner Max and Charlotte (Donath) W.; m. Gesa Ladehoff, Oct. 12, 1957; children: Margrit, Cosima. BS, U. Kiel, Fed. Republic Germany, 1954, PhD, 1957, PhD (hon.), 1993. Rsch. assoc. U. Md., College Park, 1958-59; rsch. physicist Nat. Bur. Standards, Gaithersburg, Md., 1960-62, chief plasma spectrosc. sect., 1962-77, chief atomic and plasma radiation div., 1978-91, chief atomic physics div., 1991—. Lectr. U. Calif., 1963, 64. Author: Atomic Transition Probabilities, Vol. I., 1966, Vol. II, 1969, Vol. III, 1988, Vol. IV, 1988, Atomic Transition Probabilities for C, N, and O, 1996, Spectral Data for Highly Ionized Atoms, 2000. Recipient Silver Medal award Dept. Commerce, 1962, Gold Medal award, 1971, Humboldt award, 1986, A.S. Fleming award U.S. C. of C., 1971, Disting. Career in Sci. award Wash. Acad. Sci., 1992; Guggenheim fellow, 1966. Fellow Am. Phys. Soc., Optical Soc. Am., Wash. Acad. Sci.; mem. Internat. Astron. Union. Lutheran. Home: 8229 Stone Trail Dr Bethesda MD 20817-4555 E-mail: wolfgang.wiese@nist.gov.

WIESEL, ELIE, writer, educator; b. Sighet, Romania, Sept. 30, 1928; arrived in Paris, 1945; came to U.S., 1956, naturalized, 1963; s. Shlomo and Sarah (Feig) W.; m. Marion Erster, 1969; 1 child, Shlomo Elisha. Student, The Sorbonne, Paris, 1948-51; LittD (hon.), Jewish Theol. Sem., N.Y.C., 1967, Marquette U., 1975, Simmons Coll., 1976, Anna Maria Coll., 1980, Yale U., 1981, Wake Forest U., 1985, Haverford Coll., 1985, Capital U., 1986, L.I. U., 1986, U. Paris, 1987, U. Conn., 1988, U. Cen. Fla., 1988, Wittenberg U., 1989, Wheeling Jesuit Coll., 1989, Fairleigh Dickinson U., 1993; LHD (hon.), Hebrew Union Coll., 1968, Manhattanville Coll., 1972, Yeshiva U., 1973, Boston U., 1974, Coll. of St. Scholastica, 1978, Wesleyan U., 1979, Brandeis U., 1980, Kenyon Coll., 1982, Hobart/William Smith Coll., 1982, Emory U., 1983, Fla. Internat. U., 1983, Siena Heights Coll., 1983, Fairfield U., 1983, Dropsie Coll., 1983, Moravian Coll., 1983, Colgate U., 1984, SUNY, Binghamton, 1985, Lehigh U., 1985, Coll. of New Rochelle, 1986, Tufts U., 1986, Georgetown U., 1986, Hamilton Coll., 1986, Rockford Coll., 1986, Villanova U., 1987, Coll. of St. Thomas, 1987, U. Denver, 1987, Walsh Coll., 1987, Loyola Coll., 1987, Ohio U., 1988, Concordia Coll., 1990, N.Y.U., 1990, Fordham U., 1990, Conn. Coll., 1990, Upsala Coll., 1991, Duquesne U., 1991, Roosevelt U., 1991; PhD (hon.), Bar-Ilan U., 1973, U. Haifa, 1986, Ben Gurion U., 1988; LLD (hon.), Hofstra U., 1975, Talmudic U. Fla., 1979, U. Notre Dame, 1980, La Salle U., 1988, Bates Coll., 1995; HHD (hon.), U. Hartford, 1985, Lycoming Coll., 1987, U. Miami, 1988, Brigham Young U., 1989; D of Hebrew Letters, Spertus Coll. Judaica, 1973; DSc (hon.), U. Health Scis./Chgo. Med. Sch., 1989; ThD, U. Åbo Akadem, 1990; LHD (hon.), Hunter Coll., 1992, Susquehanna U., 1992, Am. U., 1992, Millersville U., 1993; hon. degree, U. Dayton, 1993, U. Mich., 1993; LHD (hon.), U. Bordeaux, 1993, Gustavus Adolphus Coll., 1994, McGill U., 1994, Mt. Sinai Med. Sch., 1994, Spelman Coll., 1995; Doctorat (hon.), U. Catholique de Louvain, 1995; LHD (hon.), Sacred Heart U., 1995; D (hon.), U. Buenos Aires, 1995; Docteur (hon.), U. de Picardie Jules Verne, Amiens, France, 1996, U. Paris, Sorbonne, 2001; LHD (hon.), Briar Cliff Coll., 1996, Clark U., 1996, Phila. Coll. Textiles, 1996, U. Mass., Dartmouth, 1997, U. South Fla., 1997, Fla. Atlantic U., 1997, U. R.I., 1997, U. Mass., Lowell, 1997; LLD (hon.), U. Guelph, 1997; LHD (hon.), De Paul U., 1997, Seton Hall U., 1998; LittD (hon.), St. John's U., 1998; LHD (hon.), Eckerd Coll., 1998, Appalachian State U., 1998, Merrimack U., 1998; D. in Pub. Svc. (hon.), Cedar Crest Coll., 1998; LHD (hon.), Gettysburg Coll., 1998, Loyola U., Chgo., 1999; HHD (hon.), Mich. State U., 1999; Doutor (hon.), U. do Estado do Rio de Janeiro, 1999; Docteur (hon.), U. Montreal, 1999; LHD (hon.), St. Norbert Coll., 1999, St. Joseph's U., 2000, U. Fla., 2000, Hebrew Coll., 2001; PhD (hon.), Hebrew U., 2000, U. Bologna, 2000; EdD (hon.), Regis U., 2001. Disting. prof. Judaic studies CCNY, 1972-76; prof. religious studies and univ. prof. Boston U., 1976—, prof. philosophy, 1988—, now prof. relig. studies, univ. prof., prof. philosophy, now Andrew W. Mellon prof. in the humanities. Disting. vis. prof. Henry Luce, 1982-83, Yale U.; lectr. Andrew W. Mellon Ann. Lecture Series Boston U., 92d St. YMHA, YWHA Ann. Lectr. Series, ann. radio broadcast series Eternal Light for Jewish Theol. Sem. Am., advisory bd. Rena Costa Ctr. for Yiddish Studies at Bar-Ilan U., 1994, advisory coun. Carnegie Commn. on Preventing Deadly Conflict, 1994; chmn. U.S. Pres.'s Commn. on the Holocaust, 1979-80, U.S. Holocaust Meml. Coun., 1980-86; hon. chmn. Holocaust Studies Ctr. of Bronx H.S. Sci., Nat. Jewish Resource Ctr., N.Y.C., 1983, Holocaust Meml. Commn., Vancouver Holocaust Ctr. Soc., 1992—, Ctr. Christian-Jewish Understanding, Sacred Heart U., Am. Friends of Ghetto Fighter's House; co-chmn. Children of Chernobyl/Children at Heart, 1995—; steering com. The Balkan Inst., 1996—; mem. Nat. hon. com. Darius Milhaud Soc.; mem. coun. Ethic Accord Project on Ethic Rels., (hon.) Am. Friends of Neve Shalom/Wahat al-Salam, 1996—; leadership coun. Tanenbsum Ctr. Interreligious Understanding, 1997—; founder Elie Wiesel Found. for Humanity, 1987; founding pres. Paris-based Universal Acad. Cultures, 1993; pres. Am. Friends Kiryat Ungvar-Jerusalem, 1990—; hon. pres. Comité Français Pour "Yad Vashem," Am. Gathering of Jewish Holocaust Survivors, 1985, Am. Kurdish Info. Network, 1997, adv. bd., 1997; v.p. Internat. Rescue Com., 1985—; adv. bd. The Raoul Wallenberg Commn. of U.S., 1981—, Friends of LeChambon, 1982, Boston U. Inst. for Philosophy & Religion, 1986, Boston U. Students for a Free Tibet, Nat. Inst. Against Prejudice & Violence, Internat. Ctr. in N.Y., 1986—, Friends of Akim USA, 1991, Sholom Aleichem Meml. Found., Nat. Jewish Law Students Assn., 1995—, Ameri-Cares, 1995, React Take Action Awards, 1996—, No Greater Love, 1996—, Inst. Study of Violence, 1996—, Global Lawyers and Physicians: Working Together for Human Rights, 1997; internat. adv. bd. Elmhurst Coll. Holocaust Edn. Project, 1996—; Am. bd. adv. The Moscow Ctr.; adv. coun. U.S. Com. Refugees, 1996—, Nat. Endowmet for Democracy, 1996—; Helsinki adv. com. Human Rights Watch; bd. govs. Haifa U., (mem. emeritus) Tel Aviv U. 1976—, Massuah - Inst. Study of Holocaust, Israel; bd. dirs. Nat. Com. on Am. Fgn. Policy, Elaine Kaufman Cultural Ctr., Humanitas, Am. Assocs. Ben-Gurion U. of the Negev, Mut. of Am., France Libertés; hon. dir. HIAS; bd. trustees Annenberg Rsch. Inst., 1983-89, Am. Jour. World Svc., 1985—, Haifa U., Tel-Aviv U., Yeshiva U., 1977—, Am. Jewish Heritage Ctr., Mus. Jewish Heritage, N.Y.; patron Internat. Peace U., Berlin, 1995—; colleague Cathedral St. John the Divine, 1975—; mem. jury Neustadt Internat. Prize Lit., 1984; mem. Task Force Apprehending Indicted War Criminals, 1998—. Author: Night, 1960, Dawn, 1961, The Accident, 1962, The Town Beyond the Wall, 1964, The Gates of the Forest, 1966, The Jews of Silence, 1966, Legends of Our Time, 1968, A Beggar in Jerusalem, 1970, One Generation After, 1970, Souls on Fire, 1972, The Oath, 1973, Ani Maamin, 1973, Zalmen, or the Madness of God, 1974, Messengers of God, 1976, A Jew Today, 1978, Four Hasidic Masters, 1978, The Trial of God, 1979, The Testament, 1980, Le Testament D'Un Poète Juif Assassiné (France's Prix Livre-Inter 1980, Bourse Goncourt, 1980, Prix des Bibliothécaires, 1981), 1985, Images from the Bible, 1980, Five Biblical Portraits, 1981, Somewhere A Master, 1982, Paroles d'Étranger, 1982, The Golem, 1983, The Fifth Son (Grand Prix de la Littérature, City of Paris), 1985, Signes d'Exode, 1985, Against Silence (3 vols., ed. Irving Abrahamson), 1985, Job ou Dieu dans la Tempête, 1986, A Song for Hope, 1987, The Nobel Address, 1987, Twilight, 1988; (essays) Silences et Mémoire d'hommes, 1989, L'Oublié, 1989, From the Kingdom of Memory, 1990, Célébration Talmudique, 1991, Sages and Dreamers, 1991, The Forgotten, 1992, (with John Cardinal O'Connor) A Journey of Faith, 1990, (with Albert Friedlander) The Six Days of Destruction, 1988, (dialogues with Philippe-Michaël Saint-Cheron) Evil and Exile, 1990, commentaries to A Passover Haggadah, 1993, All Rivers Run To The Sea (a memoir), 1995, (with Jorge Semprun) Setaire est Impossible, 1995, (with François Mitterand) Memoir in Two Voices, 1996, Et la Mer N'est Pas Remplie, Memoirs II, 1996, Célébration Prophétique, Portraits et Légendes, 1998, Les juges, 1999, King Solomon and His Magic Ring, 1999, And the Sea is Never Full (English transl. of Et la mer n'est pas remplie, Memoirs II 1999), The Judges, 2002, (dialogues with Michael de Saint Cheron) Le Mal et L'Exil/Dix ans après, 1999, (essays) D'où viens-tu? (pub. by Le Seuil), 2001, After the Darkness, 2002; editorial and adv. bds. Midstream, Religion and Lit. (U. Notre Dame), Sh'ma: Jour. of Responsibility, Hadassah Mag., Acad. of the Air for Jewish Studies, Holocaust and Genocide Studies: An Internat. Jour., Passages, Religion and the Arts; subject of 44 books; journalist Israeli, French and Am. newspapers. Chmn. adv. bd. World Union Jewish Students, 1985—; comité d'Honneur Ligue International Contre le Racisme et l'Antisemitisme, 1985—; founder Nat. Jewish Ctr. Learning and Leadership, 1974; mem. soc. fellows Ctr. Judaic Studies, U. Denver, 1980, bd. overseer Bar-Ilan U., 1970—. Recipient Prix Rivarol, 1963, Prix de l'Universite de la langue Francaise, 1963, Ingram Merrill award, 1964, Jewish Heritage award, Haifa U., 1975, Remembrance award, 1965, Prix du Souvenir, 1965, Nat. Jewish Book Council award, 1965, 73, Prix Médicis, 1968, Prix Bordin French Acad., 1972, Eleanor Roosevelt Meml. award, N.Y. United Jewish Appeal, 1972, Am. Liberties medallion Am. Jewish Com., 1972, Martin Luther King Jr. medallion, CCNY, 1973, Annual award for Disting. Service to Am. Jewry, Nat. Fedn. of Jewish Men's Clubs, 1973, Faculty Disting. Scholar award Hofstra U., 1974, Rambam award Am. Mizrachi Women, 1974, Meml. award N.Y. Soc. Clin. Psychologists, 1975, First Spertus Internat. award, 1976, Myrtle Wreath award Hadassah, 1977, King Solomon award, 1977, Liberty award HIAS, 1977, Jewish Heritage award, B'nai B'rith, 1966, Avodah award, Jewish Tchrs. Assn., 1972, Humanitarian award, B'rith Sholom, 1978, Joseph Prize for Human Rights, Anti-Defamation League, 1978, Zalman Shazar award State of Israel, 1979, Presdl. Citation, NYU, 1979, Inaugural award for Lit., Israel Bonds Prime Minister's Com., 1979, Jabotinsky medal, S.Y. Agnon medal, State of Israel, 1980, Rabbanit Sarah Herzog award Emunah Women of Am., 1981, Le Grand Prix Littéraire du Festival Internat. Deauville, 1983, Internat. Lit. prize for Peace, Royal Acad. Belgium, 1983, Lit. Lions award N.Y. Pub. Library, 1983, Jordan Davidson Humanitarian award Fla. Internat. U., 1983, Anatoly Scharansky Humanitarian award, 1983, Grand Officer, Legion of Honor, France, Congressional gold medal, 1985, Voice of Conscience award Am. Jewish Congress, 1985, Remembrance award, Israel Bonds, 1985, Anne Frank award, 1985, 4 Freedoms award FDR 4 Freedoms Found., 1985, Medal of Liberty award Statue of Liberty Presentation, 1986, Nobel Peace Prize, 1986, First Herzl Lit. award, First David Ben-Gurion award, Nat. UJA, Gov.'s award, Shaarei Tzedek, Internat. Kaplun Found. award Hebrew U. Jerusalem, Scopus award, 1974, Am.-Israeli Friendship award, Disting. Writers award Lincolnwood Library, 1984, First Chancellor Joseph H. Lookstein award Bar-Ilan U., 1984, Sam Levenson Meml. award Jewish Community Relations Council, 1985, Comenius award Moravian Coll., 1985, Henrietta Szold award Hadassah, 1985, Disting. Community Service award Mut. Am., 1985, Covenant Peace award Synagogue Council Am., 1985, Jacob Pat award World Congress Jewish Culture, 1985, Humanitarian award Internat. League Human Rights, 1985, Disting. Foreign-Born Am. award Internat. Ctr. N.Y., Inc., 1986, Freedom Cup award Women's League Israel, 1986, First Jacob Javits Humanitarian award UJA Young Leadership, 1986, Boston City Coun. Commendation, 1986, medal of Jerusalem, 1986, Freedom award Internat. Rescue Com., 1987, Achievement award Artist and Writers for Peace in the Middle East, 1987, La Grande Médaille de Vermeil de la Ville de Paris, 1987, La Médaille de la Chancellerie de l'Université de Paris, 1987, La Médaille de l'Université de Paris, 1987, First Eitinger Prize, U. Oslo, 1987, Lifetime Achievment award Present Tense mag., 1987, Spl. Christopher award The Christophers, 1987, Achievement award State Israel, 1987, Sem. medal Jewish Theol. Sem. Am., 1987, Metcalf Cup and Prize for Excellence in Teaching, Boston U., 1987, Spl. award Nat. Com. on Am. Fgn. Policy, 1987, Grã-Cruz da Ordem Nacional do Cruzeiro do Sul, Brazil's highest distinction, 1987, Profiles in Courage award B'nai B'rith, 1987, Centennial medal U. Scranton, 1987, Citation from Religious Edn. Assn., 1987, Golda Meir Sr. Humanitarian award, 1987, Spl. Christopher award The Christophers, 1987, Profiles in Courage award B'nai B'rith, 1987, Presdl. medal Hofstra U., 1988, Human Rights Law award Internat. Human Rights Law Group, 1988, Bicentennial medal Georgetown U., 1988, Hofstra U. Presdl. medal, 1988, Human Rights Law award Internat. Human Rights Law Group, 1988, Janus Korczak Humanitarian award INTERPHIL, 1989, Count Sforza award in Philanthropy Am. Hungarian Found., 1989, Lily Edelman award for Excellence in Continuing Jewish Edn. B'nai B'rith Internat., 1989, George Washington award NAHE, Kent State U., 1989, Bicentennial medal N.Y.U., 1989, Humanitarian award Human Rights Campaign Fund, 1989, Internat. Brotherhood award C.O.R.E., 1990, Frank Weil award for Disting. Contbn. to Adv. of N.Am. Jewish Culture Jewish Community Ctrs. Assn. N.Am., 1990, 1st Raoul Wallenberg medal U. Mich., 1990, Award of Highest Honor Soka U., 1991, Facing History and Ourselves Humanity award, 1991, La Médaille de la Ville de Toulouse, 1991, 5th Centennial Christopher Columbus medal City of Genoa, 1992, 1st Internat. Primo Levi award, 1992, Lit. Arts award Nat. Found. for Jewish Culture, 1992, Ellis Island Medal of Honor, 1992, Guardian of the Children award AKIM USA, 1992, Bishop Francis J. Mugavero award for religious and racial harmony Cath. Newman Ctr. Queens Coll., 1994, Golden Slipper Humanitarian award, 1994, Interfaith Coun. on the Holocaust Humanitarian award, 1994, Crystal award Davos World Economic Forum, 1995, First Niebuhr award, Elmhurst Coll., 1995, Mathilde Schecter award Women's League Conservative Judaism, 2000, Manhattan award Nat. Arts Club, 2000, Benediction medal The Delbarton Sch., 2001; named Humanitarian of the Century Coun. Jewish Orgns., Presdl. medal Freedom, 1992; Beth Hatefutsoth hon. fellow, 1988; honors established in his name: Elie Wiesel award for Holocaust Rsch., U. Haifa, Elie Wiesel Chair in Holocaust Studies, Bar-Ilan U., Elie Wiesel Endowment Fund for Jewish Culture, U. Denver, 1987, Elie Wiesel Disting. Svc. award, U. Fla., 1988, Elie Wiesel awards for Jewish Arts and Culture B'nai B'rith Hillel Founds., 1988, Elie Wiesel Chair in Judaic Studies Conn. Coll., 1990, Disting. Libery award N.Y.C. Refugee Employment Project, 1995, Freedom award Nat. Civil Rights Mus., 1995, Humanitarian award Queensborough Comty. Coll./Holocaust Resource Ctr. Archives, 1995, Socio Honorario de la Sociedad Hebrai ca Argentina, 1995, Pres. award Quinnipac Coll., 1996, Golden Plate award Am. Acad. Achievement, 1996, Lotos medal of Merit, The Lotos Club, 1996, Guardian of Zion award Ingeborg Rennert Ctr. Jerusalem Studies, Bar-Ilan U., 1997, Eisenhower Leadership prize Eisenhower World Affairs Inst. Gettysburg Coll., 1997, Canterbury medalist Becket Fund for Religious Liberty, 1998, ABA ann. award, 1998, Rabbi Marc H. Tanenbaum award for Advancement Interreligious Understanding, 1998, Yitzhak Rabin Peacemaker award Merrimack Coll., 1998, Aesop prize Children's Am. Folklore Soc. for King Solomon and His Magic Ring (Children's Folklore sect. 1999), Raoul Wallenberg Internat. Humanitarian award The Am. Jewish Joint Distbn. Com., 1999. Fellow Jewish Acad. Arts and Scis., Am. Acad. Arts and Letters (dept. lit.), Am. Acad. Arts & Scis., Modern Lang. Assn. Am. (hon.), Timothy Dwight Coll., Yale U.; mem. Fgn. Press Assn. (hon. life), Amnesty Internat., PEN (New England coun. 1993—), Writers & Artists for Peace in Middle East, Writers Guild of Am. East, The Author's Guild, Royal Norwegian Soc. Scis. and Letters, Soc. des auteurs Paris, European Acad. of Arts, Sci. and Humanities, Albert Einstein Soc. (hon., Phila.), Phi Beta Kappa (Assocs. award 1994). Office: Boston U Univ Profs Program 745 Commonwealth Ave Boston MA 02215-1401*

WIESEL, SAM W. dean, educator, department chairman; Exec. v.p. health scis., exec. dean Georgetown U. Med. Ctr.; dean, prof., chmn. dept. orthop. surgery Georgetown U. Sch. Medicine, Washington, 1997—. Office: Georgetown U Main Campus and Med Ctr 37th and O St NW Washington DC 20057 Business E-Mail: wiesels@georgetown.edu.*

WIESEL, TORSTEN NILS, neurobiologist, educator; b. Upsala, Sweden, June 3, 1924; arrived in U.S., 1955; s. Fritz Samuel and Anna-Lisa Elisabet (Bentzer) Wiesel; 1 child Sara Elisabet. MD, Karolinska Inst., Stockholm, 1954; D Medicine (hon.) , Karolinska Inst, Stockholm, 1989; AM (hon.) , Harvard U., 1967; ScD (hon.) , NYU, 1987, U. Bergen, 1987. Instr. physiology Karolinska Inst., 1954—55; asst. dept. child psychiatry Karolinska Hosp., 1954—55; fellow in ophthalmology Johns Hopkins U., 1955—58, asst. prof. ophthalmic physiology, 1958—59; assoc. in neurophysiology and neuropharmacology Harvard U. Med. Sch., Boston, 1959—60, asst. prof. neurophysiology and neuropharmacology, 1960—64, asst. prof. neurophysiology, dept. psychiatry, 1964—67, prof. physiology, 1967—68, prof. neurobiology, 1968—74, Robert Winthrop prof. neurobiology, 1974—83, chmn. dept. neurobiology, 1973—82; Vincent and Brooke Astor prof. neurobiology, head lab. Rockefeller U., N.Y.C., 1983—98, pres., 1991—98, pres. emeritus, 1998—, dir. Leon Levy and Shelby White Ctr. for Mind, Brain & Behavior, 1998—2000; sec. gen. Human Frontier Sci. Program, 2000—. Ferrier lectr. Royal Soc. London, 1972, NIH lectr., 75; Grass lectr. Soc. Neurosci., 1976; lectr. Coll. de France, 1977; Hitchcock prof. U. Calif.-Berkeley, 1980; Sharpey-Schafer lectr. Phys. Soc. London; George Cotzias lectr. Am. Acad. Neurology, 1983. Contbr. numerous articles to profl. jours. Recipient Jules Stein award, Trustees for Prevention of Blindness, 1971, Lewis S. Rosenstiel prize, Brandeis U., 1972, Friedenwald award, Assn. Rsch. in Vision and Ophthalmology, 1975, Karl Spancer Lashley prize, Am. Philos. Soc., 1977, Louisa Gross Horwitz prize, Columbia U., 1978, Dickson prize, U. Pitts., 1979, Nobel prize in physiology and medicine, 1981, W.H. Helmerich III award, 1989. Mem.: AAAS, Royal Soc. (fgn.), Soc. Neurosci. (pres. 1978—79), Swedish Physiol. Soc., Nat. Acad. Arts and Scis., Am. Acad. Arts and Scis., Am. Philos. Soc., Am. Physiol. Soc., Physiol. Soc. (Eng.) (hon.). Office: Rockefeller U 1230 York Ave New York NY 10021-6399 also: Internat Human Frontier Sci Program Orgn Bureaux Europe 20 place des Halles 67080 Strasbourg Cedex France E-mail: wiesel@mail.rockefeller.edu.*

WIESEN, DONALD GUY, retired diversified manufacturing company executive; b. N.Y.C., July 4, 1928; s. Benjamin and Grace (Heath) W.; m. Patricia Ann Elfers, Apr. 29, 1950; children: Mara, Caitlin, Elizabeth, Anne, Megan. BS, Columbia U., 1948, MS, 1954. C.P.A., N.Y. Sr. tax specialist Price Waterhouse & Co., N.Y.C., 1950-58; with Chesebrough-Pond's Inc., Greenwich, Conn., 1958-87, gen. mgr. ops. Europe, 1965-70, treas., 1970-72, group v.p., chief fin. officer, 1972-77, group v.p., internat., 1977-82, sr. group v.p., 1982-84, vice chmn., chief fin. officer, 1984-87, also dir., ret., 1987. Bd. dirs. Skandia Am. Corp., 1985-91. Trustee Greenwich Libr., 1974-80; bd. govs. St. Bernard Coll., Cullman, Ala., 1973-75; rep. Columbia U. Alumni, Geneva, 1968; bd. dirs. Inner-City Found. for Charity and Edn., Bridgeport, Conn., 1992-93. Capt. USMC, 1951-54. Mem. AICPA, Indian Harbor Yacht Club, Univ. Club (N.Y.). Roman Catholic.

WIESENBERG, JACQUELINE LEONARDI, lecturer; b. West Haven, Conn., May 04; d. Curzio and Filomena Olga (Turrinziani) Leonardi; m. Russel John Wiesenberg, Nov. 23; children: James Wynne, Deborann Donna. BA, SUNY, Buffalo, 1970; postgrad., 1970-73, 80—. Interviewer, examiner U.S. Dept. Labor, New Haven, 1948-52; sec. W.I. Clark Co., Hamden, Conn., 1952-55; acct. VA Hosp., West Haven, 1956-60; acct.-commissary USAF Missle Site, Niagara Falls, N.Y., 1961-62; tchr. Buffalo City Schs., 1970-73, 79; acct. Erie County Social Svcs., Buffalo, 1971-73; lectr., 1973—. Contbr. articles to CAP, USAF mag. Capt., Nat. Found. March of Dimes, 1969—, com. mem. telethon, 1983-86; vol. VA, 1973—; den mother Boy Scouts Am., 1961-68; chmn. Meals on Wheels, Town of Amherst, 1975-76; leader, travel chmn. Girl Scouts U.S., 1968-77; mem. Nat. Congress Parents and Tchrs., 1957—; heart fund vol. Heart Assn., 1960-86; rep. Am. Diabetes Assn., 1994—, vol. diabetes collection, 1994-95; mem. Humane Soc. U.S., ASPCA, N.Y. Srs. Coalition. Mem. AAUW, NAFE, Internat. Platform Assn., Nat. Pks. and Conservation Assn., Am. Astrol. Assn., Nat. Arbor Day Found., Western N.Y. Conf. Aging, Nat. Geog. Soc., Wilderness Soc., Nat. Wildlife Fedn., Nat. Trust for Hist. Preservation, Nature Conservancy, Ctr. for Marine Conservation, Internat. Funds Animal Welfare, North Shore Animal League, The Nature Conservancy, The Libr. Congress, U. Buffalo Found., Pvt. Land Conservancy-Nat. Park Trust, U. Buffalo Alumni Assn., Epsilon Delta Chi, Alpha Iota. Home: 14 Norman Pl Amherst NY 14226-4233

WIESENBERG, RUSSEL JOHN, statistician; b. Kaukauna, Wis., Apr. 9, 1924; s. Emil Martin and Josephine (Appelbaker) W.; m. Jacqueline Leonardi, Nov. 23; children: James Wynne, Deborann Donna. BS, U. Wis., 1951; postgrad. Cornell U., 1960-61, U. Mich., 1969, George Washington U., 1976. Analyst, Gen. Electric Co., West Lynn, Mass., 1951-56; specialist Internat. Gen. Electric Co., Rio de Janeiro, Brazil, 1956-59; statistician Gen. Motors Corp., Lockport, N.Y., 1959-65, sr. statistician, Harrison Radiator div., 1965-78, sr. reliability engr., 1978-82, sr. reliability statistician, 1982-87 . Auditor, Community Chest Fund, 1952-55; umpire Little League Baseball, 1962-65; committeeman Buffalo Area council Boy Scouts Am., 1962—, Cub Scout committeeman, 1962-64, Webelos cubmaster, 1963-64; mem. Nat. Congress Parents and Tchrs., 1963—; heart fund Vol. Heart Assn., 1968; tournament dir. Am. Legion Baseball, 1975; vol. United Way campaign, 1983, nat. teIethon March of Dimes, 1983-84. Served with AUS, 1943-46. Decorated Bronze Star. Mem. AAAS, Am. Statis. Assn., Nat. Register Sci. and Tech. Pers., U. Wis. Alumni Assn., Artus, Internat. Platform Assn., Phi Kappa Phi. Lutheran. com.). Contbr. articles to profl. jours. Home: 14 Norman Pl Buffalo NY 14226-4233

WIESENFARTH, JOSEPH JOHN, retired literature educator; b. Bklyn., Aug. 20, 1933; s. Charles Adam and Elizabeth Koechler Wiesenfarth; m. Louise Halpin Wiesenfarth, Aug. 21, 1971; 1 child Adam Joseph Halpin. BA, Cath. U. Am., 1956, PhD, 1962; MA, U. Detroit, 1959. Asst. prof. English LaSalle U., Phila., 1962—64, Manhattan Coll., Bronx, NY, 1964—67, assoc. prof. English, 1967—70, U. Wis., Madison, 1970—76, prof. English, 1976—2000, prof. emeritus, 2000—. Author: Henry James and the Dramatic Analogy, 1963, Errand of Form: Jane Austen's Art, 1967, George Eliot: A Writer's Notebook, 1981, George Eliot's Mythmaking, 1977, Gothic Manners and the Classic English Novel, 1988, Ford Madox Ford and the Arts, 1989. Fellow, NEH, 1967—68, Fulbright Found., 1981—82; grantee, Am. Philos. Soc., 1976. Home: 5401 Greening Ln Madison WI 53705

WIESENFELD, BESS G. interior designer, real estate developer; b. Elizabeth, N.J., May 6, 1915; d. Morris and Rebecca (Sokolov) Gazevitz; m. Benjamin Wiesenfeld, Oct. 23, 1938 (dec.); children: Myra Judith Wiesenfeld Lewis, Elaine Phyllis Wiesenfeld Livingston, Ira Bertram (dec.), Sarah Ann Wiesenfeld Wasserman. BFA, N.Y. Sch. Interior Design, N.Y.C., 1982. Pres. Anasarca Corp., 1958—; real estate devel. Colonia, N.J., 1961—; pres. Carolier Lns., Inc., 1986—, BGW LLC, Bess & Co. Patron Met. Opera; sustaining mem. N.J. Symphony Orch. Mem.: AAUW, Am. Soc. Interior Designers (allied mem.), Friends of Music at Princeton, Friends of Art Mus. of Princeton, N.J., Mus. Modern Art, Met. Mus. Art. Jewish. Avocations: tours, travel. Home: 374 New Dover Rd Colonia NJ 07067-2713 also: 2600 S Ocean Blvd Palm Beach FL 33480-5484

WIESENFELD, JOHN RICHARD, chemistry educator; b. N.Y.C., July 26, 1944; s. Walter and Trude (Rosenberg) W. Stokes fellow, Pembroke Coll., Cambridge, Eng., 1971-72; BS with honors, CCNY, 1965; PhD, Case Inst. Tech., Cleve., 1969; MA, U. Cambridge, Eng., 1970. Asst. prof. Cornell U., Ithaca, N.Y., 1972-77, assoc. prof., 1978-84, prof., 1984-95, chair dept. chemistry, 1985-88, dep. v.p. for rsch., 1988-90, v.p. for plan, 1990-94, v.p. academic programs and planning, 1994-95; prof.. Fla. Atlantic U., Boca Raton, 1995—, dean of sci., 1995-2001. Vis. scholar Stanford U. Calif., 1978-79, U. Wash., 1988; cons. E.I. DuPont, Wilmington, Del., 1975, Phys. Dynamics, La Jolla, Calif., 1980-82, U.S. Dept. Energy, Pitts., 1982, NIH, 1994; bd. dirs. Associated Univs., 1989-92. Contbr. more than 100 sci. articles to profl. jours. Sloan Found. research fellow, 1975; recipient Tchr.-Scholar award, Dreyfus Found., 1975. Fellow AAAS; mem. Am. Chem. Soc., Coun. Chem. Rsch. (governing bd. 1987-90). Home: 3011 Jasmine Ct Delray Beach FL 33483-4701 Office: Fla Atlantic U PO Box 3091 Boca Raton FL 33431-0991 E-mail: jwiesenf@fau.edu.

WIESENTHAL, ANDREW MICHAEL, physician; b. N.Y.C., Mar. 5, 1950; s. Jerome Mitchell and Gladys Hortense (Heilig) W.; m. Billie Sue Gunkel Wiesenthal, July 1, 1978. BA, Yale U., 1971; MD, SUNY Downstate Med. Ctr., 1975. Cert. Pediatrics and Pediatric Infectious Disease Am. Bd. Pediatrics. Internship, residency pediatrics U. Colo. Health Scis. Ctr., Denver, 1975-78; epidemic intelligence svc. officer Ctrs. for Disease Control, Atlanta, 1978-80; fellowship pediatric infectious diseases U. Colo. Health Scis. Ctr., Denver, 1980-83; pediatrician Colo. Permanente Med. Group, PC, 1983-2000, chief pediat. arapahoe med. office, 1986-89, physician dir. quality assurance, 1988-93, assoc. med. dir., 1994-2000; assoc. exec. dir. for clin. info. systems Fedn. Permanente Med. Groups, Oakland, Calif., 2000—. Bd. dirs. Colo. Permanente Med. Group, PC, Denver, 1988—93, chair, 1991—93; govs. hemophilia adv. coun. State of Colo., 1990—2000; bd. dirs. Nat. Com. for Quality Assurance, Washington, 1996—2001, Care Mgmt. Inst. Fedn. Permanente Med. Groups, Oakland, Calif.; clin. assoc. prof. U. Colo. Health Scis. Ctr., Denver, 1996—2000. Contbr. numerous articles to profl. jours. Vol. pediatric clinic Samaritan House Homeless Shelter, 1990—2000, Warren Village Single Parent Housing, 1995—2000. Fellow Am. Acad. Pediatrics; mem. Pediatric Infectious Disease Soc, Epidemic Intelligence Svc. Alumni Assn., No. Calif. Yale Assn., Infectious Disease Soc. Am., Healthcare Info. Mgmt. Svcs. Soc. Jewish. Avocations: running, biking, hiking, camping, crossword puzzles. Office: Fedn Permanente Med Group PC 1800 Harrison St Fl 22D Oakland CA 94612-3429

WIESEPAPE, BETTY HOLLAND, writing educator; b. Tex., Jan. 10, 1941; d. Hugh and Dois Miles Holland; m. Cordell Floyd Wiesepape, Sept. 2, 1961; children: Katherine Wiesepape Pownell, Paul Allen Wiesepape. BS in Home Econ., Sam Houston State U., 1962; MA, U. Tex. Dallas, 1991, PhD, 1998. Devel. reading tchr. Premont (Tex.) Pub. Schs., 1964-65, Richardson, Tex., 1965-76; curriculum writer, tchg. cons. BEL Pub. 1994 Enterprise, 1976-92; sr. lectr. dept. arts and humanities U. Tex. Dallas, 1998-2001, undergrad. assoc. dean, 2001—. Reviewer, presenter in field; contbr. articles to profl. jours. Co-organizer, chair arrangements, mem. exec. com., mem. author selection com. In-Person series Friends Richardson Pub. Libr., 1986-95, 97—, bd. dirs., 1993-95; mem. Tex. State Hist. Soc. Recipient 3rd Pl. award Pine Grove Press Literary Competition, 1994; Jordan scholar U. Tex. Dallas, 1992. Mem. MLA, Nat. Coun. Tchrs. English, S. Ctrl. MLA, Associated Writing Programs, Tex. Assn. Creative Writing Tchrs. (Grad. Fiction award 1993, state sec. 1995-98, chair reading panel annual meeting 1998, chair state conf. arrangements annual meeting 1998), Poets and Writers. Ch. of Christ. Avocations: painting, boating, reading. Home: 1706 Cheyenne Dr Richardson TX 75080-2903 Office: U Tex Dallas Richardson TX 75080 E-mail: Betwx@aol.com.

WIESER, SIEGFRIED, planetarium executive director; b. Linz, Austria, Oct. 30, 1933; came to Can., 1955; s. Florian Wieser and Michaela Josepha (Kaufmann) Wieser-Burgstaller; m. Joan Xaven Quick, Sept. 8, 1962; children: Leonard Franz, Bernard Sidney. BS in Physics, U. Calgary, Alta., Can., 1966. Lead chorus singer, dancer Landes Theatre, Linz, 1949-53; project engr. EBG, 1952-54; with Griffith Farms Ltd., Eng., 1954-55; seismic computer operator Shell Can., Calgary, 1956-61; GTA systems analyst U. Calgary, 1961-66; planetarium dir. Centennial Planetarium, Calgary, 1966-84, exec. dir., 1984-91; exec. dir. emeritus Alberta Sci. Ctr., 1991—. Cons. Electro Controls, Salt Lake City, 1978-79. Contbr. articles to profl. publs. Recipient Violet Taylor award U. Calgary, 1964, Immigrant of Distinction Arts and Culture award, 2002; Queen Elizabeth scholar Province Alta., 1961; Paul Harris fellow Rotary Internat. Mem. Calgary Region Arts Found. (pres. 1999-2000), Alberta Coll. of Art Alumni Assn. (pres. 1991-92). Anglican. Avocations: swimming, hiking, astronomy, lecturing. E-mail: sigwies@shaw.ca.

WIESLER, JAMES BALLARD, retired banker; b. San Diego, July 25, 1927; s. Harry J. and Della B. (Ballard) W.; m. Mary Jane Hall, Oct. 3, 1953; children: Tom, Ann, Larry. BS, U. Colo., 1949; postgrad., Stonier Sch. Banking, Rutgers U., 1962, Advanced Mgmt. Program, Harvard U., 1973. With Bank of Am., NT & SA, 1949-87; v.p., mgr. main office San Jose, Calif., 1964-69; regional v.p. Cen. Coast adminstrn., 1969-74; sr. v.p., head No. European Area office Frankfurt, Fed. Republic of Germany, 1974-78; exec. v.p., head Asia div. Tokyo, 1978-81; exec. v.p., head N.Am. div. Los Angeles, 1981-82; vice chmn., head retail banking San Francisco, 1982-87; ret., 1987. Bd. dirs. Visa USA, Visa Internat., Sci. Applications Internat. Corp.; bd. dirs., chmn. Bank Adminstrn. Inst., 1986-87. Pres. Santa Clara County United Fund, 1969, 70, San Jose C. of C., 1968; fin. chmn. Santa Clara County Reps., 1967-74; bd. dirs. San Diego Armed Svcs., YMCA, Sidney Kimmell Cancer Ctr.; trustee, chmn. bd. dirs. Sharp Meml. Hosp.; hon. consul-gen. for Japan, 1990-95. With USN, 1945-46. Mem. San Diego Hosp. Assn. (bd. dirs., treas.), San Diego Zool. Soc., Greater San Diego C. of C. (pres., CEO 1998-99), Bohemian Club, DeAnza Country Club, San Diego Yacht Club. Presbyterian. Home: 605 San Fernando St San Diego CA 92106-3312 Office: Bank Am Nat Trust & Savs 450 B St San Diego CA 92101-8001

WIESNER, DALLAS CHARLES, immunologist, researcher; b. Brookings, S.D., Mar. 19, 1959; s. Charles Howard Wiesner and Coleen Marie (Hendrickson) Bailey; m. Priscilla Anne Semon, 1992. BS in Microbiology with high honors, S.D. State U., 1982. HIV product devel. tech. Abbott Labs., Diagnostic Div., Abbott Park, Ill., 1985-87, HIV retrocell product mgr. North Chicago, 1987-88, sect. mgr. infectious disease and immunology Abbott Park, 1988-90; mgr. sexually transmitted diseases tech. product devel. Diagnostic div. Abbott Labs., 1990-91, sect. mgr. retrovirus tech. product devel., 1991-96; with hepatitis r&d diagnostic divsn. Abbott Labs, 1996—. Mem. Am. Biog. Inst. Rsch. Assn. (dep. gov.), Am. Soc. for Microbiology, Phi Kappa Phi. Republican. Lutheran. Avocations: fishing, camping, scuba diving, photography, amateur radio. Home: 8710 Lakeshore Dr Pleasant Prairie WI 53158-4721 Office: Abbott Labs 1 Abbott Park Rd North Chicago IL 60064-3500

WIESNER, LOUIS ARNOLD, social welfare organization consultant; b. Apr. 14, 1916; m. Elizabeth Quincy Phenix, June 3, 1950; children: Jonathan Louis, Elizabeth Quincy, Margaret Bolles, Andrew Christopher. BS, Mich. State Coll., 1937; AM, Harvard U., 1938, postgrad., 1938-42. Rsch. sec. Coun. on Fgn. Rels., N.Y.C., 1942-43; rsch. analyst Office of Strategic Svcs., Washington, 1943-44; fgn. svc. officer Dept. of State, 1944-75, dir. office refugee and migration affairs, 1973-75; counselor and adminstr. Internat. Rescue Com., 1975-84, bd. dirs., exec. com. N.Y.C., 1985-96, mem. of corp., 1996—. Dir. office of refugee and migration affairs Dept. of State, Washington, 1973-75. Author: Victims and Survivors: Displaced Persons and Other War Victims in Viet-Nam 1954-75, 1988. Home and Office: PO Box 76 Chocorua NH 03817-0076

WIESNET, DONALD RICHARD, retired hydrologist; b. Buffalo, Feb. 7, 1927; s. Charles Anthony Wiesnet and Rose Elizabeth Nee Hildenbrand; m. Evelyn Elaine Jordan, Dec. 27, 1952; children: Peter Christopher, Ellen Elaine, Andrew John, Elizabeth Ann. AS, Syracuse U., Syracuse, NY, 1946—47; BA Geology, State U. NY, Buffalo, NY, 1950, MA Geology, 1951. Teaching Certificate NY State Bd. Regents, 1952. Geologist US Geol. Survey, Washington, 1952—61, hydrogeological map editor, 1961—64; rsch. hydrologist US Naval Oceanog. Office, Suitland, Md., 1967—71; sr. rsch. hydrologist NOAA / Nat. Environ. Satellite Svc., Camp Springs, 1971—80; chief, land sciences br. NOAA / Nat. Environ. Satellite & Info. Svc., 1980—82; ceo Satellite Hydrology, Inc., Vienna, 1982—90. Author: (book) Satellite Hydrology; contbr. book. Del. White Ho. Conf. on Aging, Washington, 1995—95; silver rep. (11th, va) Nat. Silver Haired Congress, Alexandria, Va., 1996—2002. Capt. USNR - Ret., 1965—87, Us. Grantee Monetary Grant - Antarctic Mapmaking, NSF, 1978; scholar NY State Veterans' Scholarship, NY State, 1951, Govt. Employee Grad. Scholarship, US Geol. Survey, 1964. Fellow: Am. Soc. Photogrammetry & Remote Sensing, Geol. Soc. of Am.; mem.: Nat. Assn. Ret. Fed. Employees (pres. 1993—94). Roman Catholic. Achievements include first to Pioneered the application of remote-sensing techniques and satellite data to snow measurements, river basin parameters, flood mapping, ocean currents, and estuarine tidal flows. Avocation: ornithology. Home: 601 McKinley St NE Vienna VA 22180 Home Fax: 703-242-1251.

WIESSLER, DAVID ALBERT, news correspondent; b. Cambridge, Mass., July 20, 1942; s. Albert Francis and Vivian Mary Wiessler; m. Mary Judith Burton, Dec. 28, 1968. AB, Princeton U., 1964; MA, U. Tex., 1968. Editor UPI, Dallas, N.Y.C., Washington, 1966-82; assoc. editor U.S. News & World Report, Washington, 1982-84; Washington Bur. chief UPI, 1984-90, sr. polit. editor, 1990-93; news editor Bloomberg News Svc., 1994-95; editor nat. news Reuters, Washington, 1995-98, sr. Wash. corr., 1998—. Recipient Best Feature Writer award, Dallas Press Club, 1970. Mem.: Washington Gridiron Club. Avocations: reading, travel, cooking.

WIEST, DONALD EDWIN, secondary education educator; b. Ogallala, Nebr., Dec. 23, 1947; s. Donald Duane and Evelyn Lucille Wiest; m. Kathryn Ann Wiest, July 18, 1970; children: Ellen Ruth Shrauger, Emily Dawn Steele, Edwin James Wiest, Elisa Kay Wiest. BS in Edn., U. Nebr., 1970; MS, Kans. State U., 1975. Tchr. math. and sci. Ctrl. Cath. H.S., Elgin, Nebr., 1970-72, Paxton (Nebr.) Pub. Sch., 1972-73; tchr. math. and physics Bruning (Nebr.) Pub. Sch., 1973-86; tchr. math. Eastern Heights Pub. Sch., Agra, Kans., 1986-90; tchr. sci. Guide Rock (Nebr.) Pub. Sch., 1990-98; tchr. sci. and math. Mankato (Kans.) Pub. Sch., 1998—. Advisor, sponsor Nat. Honor Soc., Mankato, 1999—; mem. senate adv. team Nat. Republican Senatorial Com., Washington, 2001. Mem.: Mankato Assn. Profl. Educators (pres. 2000—). Avocation: astronomy. Office: Mankato HS 303 N West St Mankato KS 66956 E-mail: don_wiest@hotmail.com.

WIET, RICHARD JAMES, otolargynologist; b. Chgo., Oct. 6, 1945; s. John Florian and Othelia Catherine Wiet; m. Jamee Denise, Sept. 11, 1970; children: Elizabeth, Mark, Marie. MD, Loyola U., Chgo., 1971. Prof., chief otolaryngology Evanston Northwestern Healthcare, Evanston, Ill., 1997—. Surg. instrument designer; author books on surgery of the ear. Mem. ACS (gov.), Am. Otological Soc., Triological Soc., Am. Neurotology Soc. (past pres.). Office: Evanston Northwestern Healthcare Ste 610 1000 Central Evanston IL 60201

WIETING, GARY LEE, federal agency executive; b. Huron, S.D., Apr. 24, 1937; s. LeRoy Charles and Edna Lorraine (Crawley) W.; m. Nancy Lou Clark, July 9, 1961 (div. 1991); children: Kevin Clark, Brian David; m. Julia Gladys Eli, Dec. 31, 1998. BA, U. Ill., 1961; MBA, Lake Forest Sch. Mgmt., 1983; travel and tourism diploma, Heritage Coll., Las Vegas, Nev., 1997. Logistics mgr. U.S. Army, Vietnam, 1967-68, NATO/Shape Support Group, Belgium, 1968-72, 8th U.S. Army, Korea, 1972-73, U.S. Army Readiness Region, Ft. Sheridan, Ill., 1973-77, U.S. Army Recruiting Command, Ft. Sheridan, 1977-83; rsch. and devel. logistics mgr. Belvoir Rsch. and Devel. Ctr., Ft. Belvoir, Va., 1983-85, 88-90; personal svcs. logistics mgr. Hdqrs. Dept. of Army, Washington, 1985-88; logistics mgr., assoc. program mgr. for adv. automation FAA, 1990-94; ret., 1994. Travel counselor, 1997; mem. So. Nev. Area Mil. Retiree Coun., 1998. Capt. U.S. Army, 1957-77, ret. lt. col., 1986. Decorated Army Commendation medal, Bronze Star medal; recipient Comdr. Award for Civilian Svc., U.S. Army, 1988. Avocations: collecting art, U.S. and internat. travel, playing bridge. Home: 2421 Flower Spring St Las Vegas NV 89134-1822

WIETING, J. MICHAEL, physician, medical educator; b. Atlanta, June 18, 1955; s. David Lee and Roberta Jean (Hill) W.; m. Shelley Wynne Smith, Mar. 16, 1985. BA, Centenary Coll. of La., 1978; MEd, Ctrl. State U., 1986; DO, Okla. State U., 1990. Diplomate Am. Bd. Phys. Medicine and Rehab., Am. Osteo. Bd. Rehab. Medicine, Am. Bd. Forensic Medicine, Am. Osteo. Bd. Preventive Medicine. Asst. exec. dir. Open Ear, Inc., Shreveport, La., 1976-78; asst. dir. safety svcs. ARC, Atlanta, 1978-80, nat. safety specialist Oklahoma City, 1980-84; dir. BLS/ACLS edn. Okla. State U., Tulsa, 1988-90; intern Hillcrest Health Ctr., Oklahoma City, 1990-91; med. fellow specialist U. Minn., Mpls., 1991-94; instr. Mich. State U., East Lansing, 1994-95, asst. prof., 1995-98, assoc. prof., 1998—, dir. residency tng. in rehab. medicine, 1997—; med. dir. Med. Rehab. Ctr.; med. dir., co-chair critical care neurology task force Ingham Regional Med. Ctr. Cons. ARC, Oklahoma City, 1984-91, Am. Heart Assn., Oklahoma City, 1980-91, Ctrl. State U., Edmond, Okla., 1980-91, Haceteppe U., Ankara, Turkey, 1995—. Author: Guide for Medical Student Rotations in Physical Medicine and Rehabilitation, 1994, (with others) Essentials of Sports Medicine, 1995, Basic Standards for Residency Training in Rehabilitation Medicine, 1996, The Use of Manipulation in the Treatment of Chronic Pain, 1999. Vol. physician Spl. Olympics, Lansing, Mich., 1994—, Paralympic World Games, 1996; adult leader Boy Scouts Am., Ypsilanti, Mich., 1996—; program chmn. Am. Heart Assn., Oklahoma City, 1981-91. Recipient Cmty. Svc. award Okla. State U., 1987, Leadership award Minn. Aquatics Assn., 1994, Profl. Svc. award Okla. State U. Alumni Assn., 1990, award for achievement in internat. health Mich. State U., 1999. Mem.: AMA, Ingham Osteo. Assn. (pres.-elect 1997—99, pres. 1999—2001), Mich. Osteo. Assn. (edn. com. 1999—), Am. Osteo. Coll. Phys. Medicine and Rehab. (chmn. spl. awards com. 1995—, trustee 1997—, v.p. 2001—), Am. Osteo. Bd. Phys. Medicine and Rehab. (chmn. 1999—), Am. Osteo. Assn. (Bur. Osteo. Specialists stds. rev. com.), Am. Osteo Acad. Occupl. and Preventive Medicine (trustee 1999—), Am. Acad. Osteopathy, Am. Osteo. Acad. Sports Medicine, Internat. Soc. Phys. and Rehab. Medicine, Assn. Acad. Physiatrists (edn. com. 1998—), Am. Acad. Phys. Medicine and Rehab., Am. Coll. Sports Medicine. Democrat. Episcopalian. Avocations: sailing, canoeing, refinishing antique furniture. Home: 4520 Weswilmar Dr Holt MI 48842-1646 Office: Mich State U Dept PM & R B-401 W Fee Hall East Lansing MI 48824

WIETZKE, DONALD, industrial engineer; b. Berea, Ohio, Mar. 7, 1950; s. Robert Frank and Hazel May Wietzke; m. Julie Lee Wietzke, Dec. 29, 1973; children: Matthew, Allison, Meredith, Jessica. BSME, Purdue U., 1972. Registered profl. engr., Ohio. Svc. engr. Babcock & Wilcox, Barberton, Ohio, 1972-78, field coord., 1978-80, internat. svc. mgr., 1980-83, regional sales and svc. mgr., 1983-85; mgr. field svc. engr. Pyropower Corp., San Diego, 1985-92; mgr. design engring. Ahlstrom Pyropower Corp., 1992-97, Babcock & Wilcox, Barberton, Ohio, 1997-2000; dir. engring. Babcock & Wilcox Asia, Beijing, China, 2001—. Patentee fluid bed boiler system. Mem. Nat. Fire Protection Assn. (fluid bed boiler subcom. 1992—). Home: 7832 Quebrada Cir Carlsbad CA 92009 Office: Babcock & Wilcox 200 S Van Buren Ave Barberton OH 44203 E-mail: dlw7832@aol.com., dlwietzke@.babcock.com.

WIG, ROBERT CURTIS, retired music educator, conductor; b. Montevideo, Minn., Oct. 10, 1934; s. Emil Corneilius and Melda Dina Wig; m. Marilyn Ruth Berg, Nov. 9, 1935; children: Curtis, Karen, Kathleen. BS, St. Cloud State U., 1957, MS, 1963. Registered music educator Music Educators Nat. Conf., Washington, 1991. Music tchr. Dassel (Minn.) Pub. Sch., 1957—64, Milaca (Minn.) Pub. Sch., 1964—93, Pease (Minn.) Christian Sch., 1999—2000; ret. Mem., past condr. St. Cloud (Minn.) Mcpl. Band, 1957—; mem. Bell Choir, Trinity Luth., Milaca, 1977—; dir. Alleluia Singers, Milaca, 1993—. Recipient Commendation Mcpl. Band, City of St. Cloud, 1986. Mem.: NEA (life), Assn. Concert Bands, Ret. Edn. Assn. Minn. (life), Minn. Edn. Assn. (life), Windjammers Unlimited Inc., Lions Club (past pres.). Lutheran. Avocations: gardening, golf, bowling, music. Home: 525 2nd Ave SW Milaca MN 56353

WIGELL, RAYMOND GEORGE, lawyer; b. Chgo., Apr. 18, 1949; s. Raymond Carl and Amanda D. (Santiago) W.; m. Barbara E. Buettner, June 28, 1980; children: Katherine, Elizabeth, Charles. BA, U. Ill., Chgo., 1971; JD, John Marshall Law Sch., 1975; LLM in Taxation, DePaul U., 1991. Bar: Ill. 1975, U.S. Dist. Ct. (no. dist.) Ill. 1975, U.S. Ct. Appeals (7th cir.) 1978, U.S. Supreme Ct. 1979, U.S. Tax Ct. 1987. Pvt. practice law Raymond G. Wigell, Chgo., 1975-77; trial atty. Cook County Pub. Defender, 1977-78; pres., owner, atty. Wigell & Assocs., Chicago Heights, Ill., 1978—. Instr. MacCormac Jr. Coll., Chgo., 1976-77; lectr. in bus. law Oakton C.C., Des Plaines, Ill., 1976-84; adj. prof. Govs. State U., University Park, Ill., 1984-92. Commn. chair inquiry bd. Atty. Registration Disciplinary Commn. Supreme Ct. Ill., Chgo., 1985-90, commn. chair hearing bd., 1990-95. With USN, 1971-77. Mem. U. Ill. Alumni Assn. (life mem.). Roman Catholic. Office: Wigell & Assocs Atty at Law 4749 Lincoln Mall Dr Ste 505 Matteson IL 60443 E-mail: wgllaw@aol.com.

WIGERT, LEE ROY, psychology educator; b. Hastings, Nebr., Dec. 5, 1951; s. Robert Dale and Helen Mae (Krabel) W.; m. Diane Lynne Sackett, June 30, 1979; children: Benjamin, Nathan, Ashley. BA, Hastings Coll., 1974; MA in Psychology, U. Nebr., 1977; MDiv, Union Theol. Sem., 1980; D of Ministry, Drew U., 1982; PhD, U. Nebr., 2001. Pastor United Meth. Ch., Lincoln, Nebr., 1978—; family therapist Mary Lanning Eppley Treatment Ctr., Hasting, 1989-92; psychotherapist Counseling & Psychol. Svcs., 1991—; assoc. prof. psychology Hastings Coll., 1989—. Lectr. in field. Bd. dirs. Sanitary Improvement Dist., Adams County, Nebr., 1997—, Luth. Family Svcs., Hastings, 1997—. Mem. APA, AAUP, Nebr. Psychol. Assn. Democrat. Avocations: golf, tennis, fishing, walking, travel. Office: Hastings Coll 7th & Turner Hastings NE 68901 Home: 2615 S Deer Trl Hastings NE 68901-7496 E-mail: lwigert@hastings.edu.

WIGFIED-PHILLIP, RUTH GENIVEA, genealogist, author, researcher; b. Couer d' Alene, Idaho, Dec. 1, 1918; d. Arthur and Jenivea Caroline (Crisp) Wigfield; m. Milton Fred Phillip, May 14, 1942 (dec. Nov., 1984); children: Rochelle Ruth, Gloria Genivea, Nancy Lenore, Douglas Fred, Andrea Arleen. BA, U. Montana, Missoula, 1939; registered genealogist, Augustine Genealogy Sch., Torrance, Calif., 1985, Desc. of William the Conquerer, Desc. of Companion of William Conquerer, Augustine Genealogy Sch., Torrance, Calif., 1997. Med. technician Deaconess Hosp., Great Falls, Mont., 1939-42; social worker Mont. State Welfare Dept., Helena, 1944-46; musical instr. Mont. Music Tchrs. Assn., Great Falls, 1947-62, Missoula, 1962-72; genealogy rschr. Phillip Heritage House, 1962-66, writer, author, 1972—. Author, editor: (5 newsletters on genealogy) Wigfield Genealogy, 1972—, Crisp Genealogy, 1981—, Lipscomb Genealogy, 1981, Martin Genealogy, 1981, New Race, 1985—. Mem. Immanuel Luth. Ch., Sunday sch. supt., 1965-72; sec. Mont. State Music Tchrs. Union, 1969-71. Recipient music scholarship Harlowtown Music Dept., Harlowtown, Mont., 1932-35. Mem. DAR (regent Bitterroot chpt. 1973-75, state Indian chmn. 1976-90, 25 yr. h on. award Bitterroot chpt. 1997), Guild of St. Margaret of Scotland (grand dame Mont., 1986—), Eastern Star (organist), Rebecca Lodge (organist). Avocations: bridge, garden club, travel, fishing, golf. Home and Office: Phillip Genealogy Heritage House 605 Benton Ave Missoula MT 59801-8633

WIGGANS, THOMAS G. pharmaceutical executive; BS, U. Kans.; MBA, So. Meth. U. Various sales and mktg. positions Eli Lilly & Co.; various positions including pres. U.S. pharm. ops. and mng. dir. U.K. pharm. ops. Ares-Serono Group, 1980—92; pres., COO CytoTherapeutics, 1992—94; pres., CEO, dir. Connetics, 1994—. Dir., governing mem. emerging co. section Biotechnology Industry Orgn.; dir. Paladin Labs, Inc., DJ Pharma, Inc. Office: Connetics Corp 3290 West Bayshore Rd Palo Alto CA 94303*

WIGGIN, KENDALL FRENCH, state librarian; b. Manchester, N.H., Aug. 21, 1951; s. Ralph M. Jr. and Frances (Miltimore) W.; m. Elaine M. Elliott, June 2, 1973 (div. Jan. 1989); children: Sara, Douglas; m. Laura A. Larson, May 26, 1990; children: Lindsey, Tess. BA, U. N.H., 1974; MS in LS, Simmons Coll., 1975. Libr. Litchfield (N.H.) Pub. Libr., 1975; dir. Merrimack (N.H.) Pub. Libr., 1975-83; coord. tech. svcs. Manchester City Libr., 1983-90; state libr. N.H. State Libr., Concord, 1990-99, Conn. State Library, Hartford, 1999—. Mem. ALA,, New Eng. Libr. Assn., N.H. Libr. Assn., Chief Officers State Libr. Agys., Chief Officers State Libr. Agys. in N.E., N.H. Writers and Publishers Project. Republican. Presbyterian. Avocations: philately, gardening. Office: 231 Capitol Ave Hartford CT 06106*

WIGGINS, CHARLES HENRY, JR. lawyer; b. Balt., July 15, 1939; s. Charles Henry and Kathryn Wilson (Walker) W.; m. Wendy Jane Horn, June 20, 1964 (div. 1996); children: Charles Hunter, Rebecca Rae, Melinda Marie; m. Karen Ann Kowal, Apr. 26, 1997 (div. 2002). BSEE, U. Ill., Urbana, 1962; JD with honors, U. Ill., 1965. Bar: Ill. 1965, U.S. Dist. (no. dist.) Ill. 1970, U.S. Tax Ct. 1974, U.S. Ct. Appeals (7th cir.) 1983. Assoc. Vedder, Price, Kaufman & Kammholz, Chgo., 1969-73, ptnr., 1974—. Mem. zoning bd. appeals Village of Indian Head Pk., Ill., 1984-91. Capt. U.S. Army, 1965-68. Mem. Chgo. Bar Assn., University Club (Chgo.), Edgewood Valley Country Club (LaGrange, Ill., bd. dirs. 1991-98), SAR. Avocations: golf, tennis, bridge. Office: Vedder Price Kaufman & Kammholz 222 N La Salle St Fl 26 Chicago IL 60601-1003

WIGGINS, DEWAYNE LEE, financial executive; b. Stillwater, Okla., Jan. 6, 1949; s. Lloyd Lee Wiggins and Joyce Yvonne Blair; m. Susan Sochinski, Sept . 9, 1978. BS in Acctg., Okla. State U., 1972; MBA, Ind. U., 1984. Pilot Braniff Internat., Dallas, 1977-82; investment analyst Duff & Phelps, Inc., Chgo., 1984-86; portfolio mgr. Centerre Trust Co., St. Louis, 1986-88; pres. Lindbergh Capital Mgmt., Inc., 1988—; founder, pres. Lindbergh Signature Fund, 1999—. Capt. USAF, 1972-76. Mem. Ind. U. Alumni Assn., Beta Gamma Sigma. Roman Catholic. Avocations: reading, tennis, gardening. Office: Lindbergh Capital Mgmt Inc 5520 Telegraph Rd Ste 204 Saint Louis MO 63129-3570

WIGGINS, GLORIA, nonprofit organization administrator, television producer; b. N.Y.C., Jan. 17, 1933; d. John and Gladys (Jones) Pruden; m. Albert Wiggins, Jan. 15, 1954 (dec. Aug. 1982); children: Michael, Teresa. BA, Richmons Coll., Staten Island, N.Y.; MA, SUNY, Albany. Project dir. Suffolk County Black History Assn., Smithtown, N.Y., 1982; pres., chair, founder Zamanii Internat. Devel. Corp., Central Islip, 1983—; chair, founder Ikeda Mandela Uhuru Cultural Ctr., Inc., 1991—. Chair Univ. Sons & Daughters of Ethiopia, Deer Park, N.Y., 1990-91. Producer, artist: (pub. access TV) Celebration of Kwanzaa, 1993 (grant 1993); prodr.: (pub. access TV) Living Arts, 1994 (grant 1994), (exhibit) Adventure to the Homeland, 1995 (grant 1995), African Women/African Art, 1992 (grant 1992), 2d Roots Internat. Homecoming Festival, 1998, Women Achievers of 1998, Black History Celebration Senegal, 1999, We Sing America, 2000, International Poets, 2000, Postive Images, 2000, African American Couples in the Arts, 2000, Public Library Exhibits, 2000, TV Public Access, 2001, African Americans in West Africa, Celebration of Black History Month, 2001, (TV pub. access program of Senegalese in N.Y.) A Naming Ceremony, (pub. access TV) 10th Birthday Celebration Pow Wow, 2002, TV Pub. Access 100th Birthday Celebration, 2002, Smithsonian Township Art Exhibit, Sr. Citizen Art Exhibit; author (poem) Man of Two Worlds (prize 2001). Pres. Mariners Harbor Tenant Assn., Staten Island, 1968-70; vol. Peace Corps, 1980, Peace Corps, 1979. Recipient Internat. Libr. Photography editors choice award, 1998, Poet of the Yr. medallion and the Diamond Homer trophy Famous Poets Soc., 1999; grantee Suffolk County Office of Cultural Affairs, 1987-2001. Avocations: art, television production, swimming, writing, community service. Home: 248 Tree Ave Central Islip NY 11722-2745 E-mail: fatou@webtv.net.

WIGGINS, JAMES BRYAN, religion educator; b. Mexia, Tex., Aug. 24, 1935; m. Elizabeth R. Wiggins, May 28, 1995; children: Bryan, Karis. BA, Tex. Wesleyan U., 1957; BD, So. Meth. U., 1959; PhD, Drew U., 1963; postgrad., Tübingen U., Fed. Republic Germany, 1968-69. Ordained to ministry Meth. Ch., 1959. Instr. humanities Union Jr. Coll., Cranford, N.J., 1960-63; asst. prof. religion Syracuse (N.Y.) U., 1963-69, assoc. prof., 1969-75, prof., 1975—, dir. grad. studies, 1975-80, chair dept., 1980—, Eliphalet Remington prof. religion, 1999—; exec. dir. Am. Acad. Religion, 1983-91, dir., 1973-75, 83-91. Cons. in field; People to People del. leader to former Soviet Union, 1992. Author: The Embattled Saint, 1966, Foundations of Christianity, 1970; editor: Religion as Story, 1975, Christianity: A Cultural Perspective, 1987, In Praise of Religious Diversity, 1996; contbr. articles to profl. jours. Trustee Scholars Press, Atlanta, 1983-91, chmn., 1986-91; chair, bd. dirs. Onondaga Pastoral Counseling Ctr., 1997-99; bd. dirs. Inter-religious Coun. Ctrl. N.Y., 1997-2001. Rockefeller Found. fellow, 1962-63; Lilly Endowment rsch. grantee, 1992-93. Fellow Soc. for Arts (bd. dirs. 1976—), Religion and Culture; mem. AAUP, Am. Acad. Religion. Democrat. Avocations: golf, tennis, music, reading, travel. Office: Syracuse U Dept Religion 501 Hall Of Langs Syracuse NY 13244-0001 E-mail: jwiggins@twcny.rr.com.

WIGGINS, KIM DOUGLAS, artist, art dealer; b. Roswell, N.Mex., Apr. 8, 1959; s. Walton Wray Wiggins and Barbara Jo (Chesser) Ortega; m. Mary Allison Raney, Sept. 4, 1977 (div. May 1984); children: Rebekah, Mona; m. Maria C. Trujillo, June 17, 1995; children: Gianna Josiah, Elisha Douglas, Eden Renee. Student, Ea. N.Mex. U., Roswell, 1977, 83-84, San Antonio Coll., 1978-79, Ind. Bapt. Coll., Dallas, 1982-83, Santa Fe Inst. Fine Art, 1989, Rhema C.B.S., Tulsa, 1997. Dir. Clarke-Wiggins Fine Art, Palm Springs, Calif., 1986-89; owner, mgr. Wiggins Fine Art, Santa Fe, 1989-93, Wiggins Studio, Roswell, 1991—; owner Print & Promise, 1996—. Cons. Mus. N.Mex., Santa Fe, 1992—, Cline Fine Art, Santa Fe, 1993—; lectr. in field. One man shows at Altermann Morris Galleries, Houston, Dallas, Santa Fe, 1992-2002, Studio Gallery, Laguna Beach, San Diego, 1998; exhibited in group shows Pa. Acad. Fine Art, Phila., 1992-96, M.H. DeYoung Mus., San Francisco, 1993-96, Autry Mus. Western Heritage, L.A., 1999-2002, Desert Caballeros Wstern Mus., Wickenburg, Ariz., 2000, The Denver Art Mus., 2000, The Corcoran Gallery of Art, 2001; represented in permanent collections Mus. of N.Mex., Anschutz Collection, Autry Mus. Western Heritage, L.A., Denver, Staples Ctr., L.A., Autry Mus. Western Heritage, L.A.; editor: K. Douglas Wiggins: Sense of Spirit, 1993; pub., contbr.: Art of the American West, 1999, Painters and the American West, 2000. Mem. NRA, HOG, CMA, Internat. Platform Assn., Soc. Am. Impressionists, Coun. for Art of West, Gladney Ctr., Assurance Home, Other Side of the West. Republican. Avocations: printmaking, poetry, pottery, motorcycles, scuba diving. Home: 6 El Arco Iris Dr Roswell NM 88201-7711 Studio: Altermann Galleries 225 Canyon Rd Santa Fe NM 87501-2755

WIGGINS, MARY ANN WISE, small business owner, educator; b. Coushatta, La., Dec. 25, 1940; d. George Wilkinson and Maitland (Allums) Wise; m. Gerald D. Paul (div. Nov. 1977); children: John Barron, James Gordon, Brenda Michelle; m. Billy J. Wiggins, Oct. 3, 1981; children: Marshall Wade, Brian David, William Joshua, George Justin; stepchildren: Joseph James, Winona Gail. BA, Northwestern State U., Natchitoches, La., 1964, postgrad., 1994, Weaterford Coll., 1967, North Tex. State U., 1968. Lic. ins. agt., real estate agt., La., pvt. pilot. Tchr. U.S. Army Schs., Nuremberg, Germany, 1964—66, Mineral Wells Ind. Sch. Dist., 1967—70; bookkeeper Wise Dept. Store, Coushatta, La., 1966—67; amb. of good will Vietnam, 1971; owner, mgr. Mary Ann's Furniture & Hardware, Coushatta, 1977—97; tchr. Springville Mid. Sch., 1994—96, Red River Parish Alternative Sch., 1996—98, tchr. youth ctr., 1998—. Com. mem. Instrn. and Profl. Devel. Com. La. Assn. Educators, 1998-2000, vice chmn. 1999-2002; v.p. La. Juvenile Detention Tchrs. Assn., 1999—. Chmn. Am. Cancer Soc., Conway, Ark., 1972, Red River Parish United Way, Coushatta, 1985; treas., bd. dirs. Hall Summit United Meth. Ch.; pres. Red River Parish Assn. Educators Polit. Action Com. Recipient German-Am. hospitality award Orgn. German-Am. Women, Nuremberg, 1965. Mem. NEA, La. Assn. Educators (legis. com.), Red River Assn. Educators (v.p. 1994, pres. 1998-2001), U.S. C. of C., Coushatta-Red River C. of C. (charter), Pi Kappa Sigma, Sigma Kappa. Democrat. Methodist. Avocations: gardening/landscaping, swimming, horseback riding, computers, week-enders with family. Home: 2217 E Carrol St Coushatta LA 71019-8567

WIGGINS, NANCY BOWEN, real estate broker, market research consultant; b. Richmond, Va., Oct. 9, 1948; d. William Roy and Mary Virginia (Colson) Bowen; m. Samuel Spence Saunders, Aug. 16, 1969 (div. 1977); m. Edwin Lindsey Wiggins, Jr., Apr. 16, 1983 (div. 1999); children: Neal Bowen, Mark Edwin. AA, St. Mary's Coll., Raleigh, N.C., 1968; postgrad., Trinity U., 1968-69; BA, U.S. Internat. U., San Diego, 1970; MA, U. Tex., Arlington, 1975; postgrad., Tulane U., 1976-77. Cert. comml. investment mem. Bank teller Bank of Am., San Diego, 1971-72; lectr. U. Tex., Arlington, 1974-76; instr. Johnson C. Smith U., Charlotte, N.C., 1977-78; human svcs. planner Centralina Coun. of Govt., 1978-80; mktg. rsch. analyst First Union Nat. Bank, 1980-81; mktg. rep. Burroughs Corp., 1981-83; ptnr., mktg. researcher George Selden & Assocs., 1983-84; pres., broker Bowen Wiggins Co., 1984-92; pres. WRB, Inc. (merger Bowen Wiggins Co. and W. Roy Bowen Co., Inc.), 1992-96; mgr., prin. Nancy Wiggins, LLC, 1996—; ptnr. Buster & Wiggins Internat., Myrtle Beach, S.C. Instr. U. N.C., Charlotte, 1984-85, 87-90, Winthrop U., Rock Hill, S.C., 1985-86, 91-92; bd. dirs. Roy Bowen, Inc., Frogmore, S.C., v.p., sec., 1990. Contbr. articles to profl. jours. Vice chmn. United Cerebral Palsy Coun., Charlotte, 1984; chmn. bd. dirs. Carriage House Condominium Assn., Charlotte, 1980-82; mem. Charlotte Mayor's Budget Adv. Com., 1980-81, Charlotte-Mecklenburg Planning Commn., 1994-99, mem. planning com., 1994-95, zoning com., 1995-97, vice-chmn. zoning com., 1997, planning com. 1998, vice chmn. planning com. 1998—, exec. com., 1997—; pres. Mecklenburg Dem. Women's Club, 1990; mem. state exec. com. N.C. Dem. Party, 1991-95, 99-2000; mem. Mecklenburg County Solid Waste Adv. Bd., 1991-92, chmn. recycling com., 1991-94, 95-96; mem. Comml. Investment Real Estate Inst., 1997-98, bd. dirs. N.C. chpg., 1999. Mem. AAUW, Charlotte Region Comml. Bd. Realtors, N.C. Assn. Appraisers (bd. dirs., pres. 1989-90), Internat. Coun. Shopping Ctrs., Internat. Real Estate Fedn. (Paris, U.S. del. Retail Conf. at World Congress 1998, U.S. vice chair trade missions, sec.-gen. exch. com. 1999-2000), Am. Planning Assn., Charlotte C. of C. (bd. advisors 1997), Multimillion Dollar Club, Tournament Players Club Piper Glen, Rose Soc., Good Friends, Nat. Assn. Realtors, FIABCI, Paris, Internat. Trade Mission Com. (sec. gen. internat. exch. com.), N.C. Citizens for Bus. and Industry, NAR Charlotte (region comml. bd.), CCIM (N.C. chpt. bd. dirs.), Pi Sigma Alpha. Democrat. Episcopalian. Avocations: gardening, art collecting. Home: 6919 Seton House Ln Charlotte NC 28277-4517 Office: Ste 300 501 N Church St Charlotte NC 28202-2207

WIGGINS, NORMAN ADRIAN, university administrator, legal educator; b. Burlington, N.C., Feb. 6, 1924; s. Walter James and Margaret Ann (Chason) W.; m. Mildred Alice Harmon. AA, Campbell Coll., 1948; BA, Wake Forest Coll., 1950, LLB, 1952; LLM, Columbia U., 1956, JSD, 1964; Exec. Program, U. N.C., 1968-69; LLD, Gardner-Webb Coll., 1972. Deacon Wake Forest Baptist Ch., Winston-Salem, N.C., 1963-66, Buies Creek (N.C.) Bapt. Ch., 1973—; deacon, tchr. Sunday sch., 1952—; lay preacher, 1953—; pres. N.C. Found. of Ch.-Related Coll., 1969-70, Campbell U., Buies Creek, 1967—, prof. law, 1976—. Author: Wills and Administration of Estates in North Carolina, 1964— , (with Gilbert T. Stephenson) Estates and Trusts, 1973; Editor: N.C. Will Manual, 1958— , Trust Functions and Services, 1978; Contbr. articles to legal jours. Chmn. Gov.'s Task Force Com. on Adjudication of the Com. on Law and Order, 1969-71; mem. Com. on Drafting Interstate Succession Act for N.C., 1957-59; mem. Com. for Revision of the Laws Relating to the Adminstrn. of Descs.' Estates, 1959-67, chmn., 1964-67; trustee Sunday Sch. Bd., So. Bapt. Conv., 1975—, chmn. bd. trustees, 1978—, nominations com., 1988—; pres. Bapt. State Conv. N.C., 1983-85; bd. dirs. N.C. Cititzens for Bus. and Industry, 1982—. Recipient Outstanding Civilian Svc. award Dept. Army, 1985, Patriotic Civilian Svc. award U.S. Dept. Army, 1998, award for longest tenure as univ. pres. Coalition Christian Colls. and Univs., 1998, The Order of the Long Leaf Pine award, 1998, John J. Parker award, 1999; Campbell Law Sch. renamed in his honor the Norman Adrian Wiggins Sch. of Law, 1989; recognized for outstanding svc. to high edn. and legal edn. Newcomen Soc. U.S., 1993; Comdr.'s award for Pub. Svc., 1995, Internat. Freedom of Mobility award, 1995; named to List of 100 Influential Bapt. Leaders in 20th Century, 2000. Mem. ABA, Nat. Assn. Coll. and Univ. Attys. (pres. 1972-73, Disting. Svc. award 1991), Am. Assn. Presidents Ind. Colls. and Univs. (pres. 1981-83), N.C. Assn. Colls. and Univs. (exec. com. 1980— , pres. 1984-85), N.C. Assn. Ind. Colls. and Univs. (pres. 1970-72, exec. com. 1980-81), N.C. Bar Assn., Harnett County Bar Assn., Nat. Fellowship Baptist Men (pres. 1987-90), Jay Waugh Evang. Assn. (dir./pres. 1970-72), Dunn Area C. of C., Wake Forest Alumni Assn., Rotary (hon. mem. Dunn club), Phi Alpha Delta, Phi Kappa Phi, Omicron Delta Kappa. Office: Campbell U PO Box 127 Buies Creek NC 27506-0127 E-mail: matthews@mailcenter.campbell.edu.

WIGGINS, ROBERT RAY, criminal justice educator; b. Endicott, N.Y., Aug. 2, 1939; s. Robert C. and Evelyn Wiggins; m. Frances R. Wiggins; children: Robert R., Steven M. ThB, Bapt. Bible Sem., 1964; BA, Olivet Nazarene U., 1966; MS, Am. U., 1970; PhD, U. Tex., Arlington, 1987. Case worker, parole agt. State Pa., Phila., 1966-68; probation officer Superior Ct., Washington, 1968-70; various staff positions U.S. Parole Commn., Washington and Dallas, 1970-89; assoc. prof. Liberty U., Lynchburg, Va., 1989-92; prof. criminal justice and pub. adminstrn. Cedarville (Ohio) U., 1992—. Contbr. articles to profl. jours. Mem. ASPA, Am. Probation and Parole Assn., Am. Correctional Assn., Acad. Criminal Justice Scis., Midwestern Criminal Justice Assn., Ohio Coun. Criminal Justice Edn. (trustee, pres. 1998-99). Office: Cedarville U Dept Social Scis & History 251 N Main St Cedarville OH 45314 E-mail: wigginsr@cedarville.edu.

WIGGINS, ROBERT ROEBUCK, management consultant; b. Victoria, Tex., July 14, 1953; s. Frank LaRue and Merriam Roebuck Wiggins. AB, Vassar Coll., 1975; MBA, U. Tex., 1977, PhD, 1995. Asst. prof. Tulane U., New Orleans, 1995—; asst. instr. U. Tex., Austin, 1993—95; prin. cons. The Wiggins Group, Palo Alto, Calif., 1987—90; pres. Roebuck Wiggins Assocs., Inc., N.Y.C., 1982—86; contbg. editor MediaDirect CDROM Mag., Tokyo, 1993—95, WindowsUser Mag., N.Y.C., 1992—93, MacUser Mag., N.Y.C., 1986—91; sys. engr. IBM Corp., 1977—81. Dir. Ray West Warehouses, Inc., Corpus Christi, 1997—2002. Author: (book chpt.) Digital Marketing, 2001, (book) The Trail Guide to Compuserve, 1994. Mem.: INFORMS, Assn. for Info. Sys., So. Mgmt. Assn., Strategic Mgmt. Soc., Acad. Mgmt., Phi Kappa Phi. Office: Tulane U 7 McAlister Dr New Orleans LA 70118 Business E-Mail: robert.wiggins@tulane.edu.

WIGGINS, ROGER C. internist, educator, researcher; b. Tetbury, Eng., May 26, 1945; BA, Cambridge U., Eng., 1968; BChir, Middlesex Hosp. Med. Sch., London, 1971, MB, MA, 1972. House physician dept. medicine The Middlesex Hosp., London, 1971-72; house surgeon Ipswich (Eng.) and East Suffolk Hosps., 1972; sr. house officer Hammersmith Hosp., The Middlesex Hosp., Brompton Hosp., London, 1972-74; rsch. registrar The Middlesex Hosp. Med. Sch., 1975-76; postdoctoral fellow Scripps Clinic and Rsch. Found., La Jolla, Calif., 1976-78, rsch. assoc., 1978-79, asst. mem. 1, 1979-81; asst. prof. U. Mich., Ann Arbor, 1981-84, assoc. prof., 1984-90, prof., 1990—, chief nephrology, 1988—, dir. O'Brien Renal Ctr., 1988—, dir. NIH Nephrology Tng. Program, 1988-96. Lectr., speaker in field. Author chpts. to books; assoc. editor: Jour. Am. Soc. Nephrology, Clin. Sci.; contbr. articles to profl. jours. First Broderip scholar, 1971, Harold Boldero scholar, 1971, James McIntosh scholar, 1971, The Berkeley fellow Gonville and Caius Coll., 1976; recipient Leopold Hudson prize, 1971, The William Henry Rean prize, 1971, Disting. Rsch. Jerome W. Conn award, 1984. Fellow Royal Coll. Physicians (U.K.); mem. Am. Assn. Pathologists, Am. Assn. Immunologists, Am. Soc. Nephrology, Fedn. Clin. Rsch., Am. Soc. Clin. Investigation, Ctrl. Soc. Am. Fedn. Clin. Rsch., Assn. Am. Physicians. Office: U Mich Nephrology Div 3914 Taubman Ctr Ann Arbor MI 48109

WIGGINS, SAMUEL PAUL, education educator; b. Salisbury, N.C., Sept. 20, 1919; s. James Andrew and Mollie (Wilhelm) W.; m. Linda Jean Bessent, June 29, 1947; children: Stanley, David, Timothy, Mark. BS, Ga. Tchrs. Coll., 1940; M.Ed., Duke U., 1942; PhD, Peabody Coll., 1952. Teaching prin., Alma, Ga., 1939-40; dir. lab. sch. Ga. Southwestern Coll., 1940-42; dir. student teaching Emory U., 1947-53; prof., adminstr. Peabody Coll., 1953-67; dean Coll. Edn., Cleve. State U., 1967-75, prof., 1975-85, Norfolk State U., 1985-96, co-dir. project nat. bd. profl. tchg. stds., 1995-96. Chief advisor ICA (AID), Korea Tchr. Edn. Project, 1961-62; Fulbright lectr., Colombia, S.Am., 1966, Lisbon, Portugal, 1978; pres. Am. Assn. Colls. Tchr. Edn., 1974-75; mem. forum of leaders Nat. Ednl. Orgns. USOE, 1975-77. Author: Successful High School Teaching, 1958, Student Teacher in Action, 1957, Southern High Schools and Jobless Youth, 1961, The Desegregation Era in Higher Education, 1966, Higher Education in the South, 1966, Battlefields in Teacher Education, 1964, Educating Personnel for Urban Schools, 1972, Improving Education for the Youth of Portugal, 1980, Revolution in Teacher Education: A Review of Reform Reports, 1985; co-author: Equity and Excellence for Minorities in T.Ed. (A.T.E.), 1988, Served with USNR, 1942-47, comdr. Res. ret. Home: 5345 Marian Lane Manor Virginia Beach VA 23462

WIGGINS, STEPHEN EDWARD, family practice physician, medical administrator; b. Phila., May 7, 1951; s. Ralph Cannon and Bernice J. (Maslovitz) W.; m. Rebecca del Carmen, Oct. 3, 1992; children: Daniel Stephen, Elizabeth Rebekah. BA, Rutgers U., 1973; MD, Med. Coll. Va., 1977. Diplomate Am. Bd. Family Practice. Resident in family practice Riverside Hosp., Newport News, Va., 1977-80; staff emergency physician North Arundal Hosp., Glen Burnie, Md., 1980-81, So. Md. Hosp. Ctr., Clinton, 1982-84; med. dir. Convenient Health Care, Waldorf, Md., 1984—. Ptnr. Old Line Med. Partnership, Waldorf, 1990-97, Convenient Health Care Mgmt., Waldorf, 1989-97; instr. family practice Georgetown U. Sch. Medicine, Washington, 1995—; pres. 640 Old Line Ctr. L.P., 1997—; pres. Old Line Med. Svcs. P.C., 1997—. Vol. physician and citizen diplomat Gesundheit Inst., Russia, 1991; citizen diplomate U.S.-China Peoples Friendship Assn., China, 1988; vol. physician March of Dimes Walk-a-thon, Md., 1985-86. William Demarest scholar, Rutgers U., New Brunswick, N.J., 1969-73. Fellow Am. Acad. Family Physicians; mem. Med. and Chirurgical Faculty of the State of Md., Md. Acad. Family Physicians, Charles County Med. Soc. Avocation: scuba diving. Office: Convenient Health Care 12090 Old Line Ctr Waldorf MD 20602-2556

WIGGINTON, EUGENE H. retired publishing executive; b. Louisville, Mar. 4, 1935; m. Shirley Walter; children: Denise Wigginton Hamilton, Tressa Wigginton Treadway. BA, Cin. Christian Coll.; LLD (hon.), Milligan Coll. Sr. min. South Jefferson Christian Ch., Louisville, 1957-60; dir. pub. rels. Cin. Christian Coll., 1960-63; sr. min. Westside Christian Ch., Atlanta, 1963-71; exec. v.p. Milligan Coll. (Tenn.), 1971-82; v.p., pub., pres., CEO, Standard Pub., Cin., 1982-2000; ret., 2000. Bd. dirs. Evang. Christian Pubs. Assn. Trustee Milligan Coll., 1983—. Recipient Citizenship award DAR and Am. Legion, I Dare You award Danforth Found., Fide et Amore award Milligan Coll. Home: 612 Douglas Dr Johnson City TN 37604-1919 Office: Standard Pub Co 8121 Hamilton Ave Cincinnati OH 45231-2396

WIGGLESWORTH, DAVID CUNNINGHAM, business and management consultant; b. Passaic, N.J., Sept. 23, 1927; s. Walter Frederick and Janet (Cunningham) W.; m. Rita Dominguez, Mar. 15, 1956 (dec.); children: Mitchell Murray, Marc David, Miles Frederick, Janet Rose; m. Gayle Coates, Aug. 1, 1981; 1 child, Danielle. BA, Occidental Coll., 1950, MA, 1953; postgrad., U. de las Ams., 1954-56; PhD, U. East Fla., 1957; LHD (hon.), Arubaanse Handels Academie, 1969. Ordained minister Universal Life Ch., 1969. Dir. Spoken English Inst., Mexico City, 1954-56; also lectr. Mexico City Coll., 1954-56; headmaster Harding Acad., Glendale, Calif., 1956-58; also lectr. Citrus Jr. Coll., 1956-58; dir. Burma-Am. Inst., Rangoon, 1958-60; project dir. Washington Ednl. Rsch. Assocs., Washington, Conakry, Guinea, Benghazi, Libya, Carbondale,IL, 1960-64; mng. editor linguistics divsn. T. Y. Crowell Pub. Co., N.Y.C., 1964-66; dir. linguistic studies Behavioral Rsch. Labs., Palo Alto, Calif., 1966-67; pres. D.C.W. Rsch. Assocs. Internat., Foster City, 1967-98, now Kingwood, Tex., 1998—. Author: PI/LT-Programmed Instruction/Language Teaching, 1967, Career Education, 1976, ASTD in China, 1981, Resources for Workforce Diversity, 1993; contbr. articles to profl. publs., mem. editorial bd. Vision/Action; mem. editorial rev. bd. Human Resource Devel. Quar. Trustee City U. L.A.; bd. dirs. Cmty. Career Edn. Ctr., San Mateo, Calif., 1996—; mem. adv. bd. Martin Luther King Reading Acad., L.A., Internat. Ctr. Cultural Ergonomics, 1990—; mem. tng. systems design and prodn. program adv. bd. U. Calif.-Santa Cruz; U.S. rep. Internat. Com. Human Resources Devel., Kuwait, 1990—. Served with U.S. Army, 1945-46, 52-54. Mem. Am. Mgmt. Assn., Orgn. Devel. Network, ASTD (bd. dirs. internat. divsn., named Practitioner of Yr. 1988), Internat. Fedn. Tng. and Devel. Organs. (task force), Soc. Internat. Edn. Tng. and Rsch., 1st World Congress Internat. Orgn. Devel., Orgn. Devel. Forum, Peninsula Orgn. Devel. Support, Houston Soc. for Internat. Edn., Tng. and Rsch. (bd. dirs.), Mideast Am. Bus. Conf., World Future Soc., Peninsula Exec. Club (Los Altos), SEDUMEX (Mexico City), Benghazi Sailing Club, Orient Club (Rangoon), Arctic Brotherhood (Skagway, Alaska). Office: DCW Rsch Assocs Internat 2606 Parkdale Dr Kingwood TX 77339-2476 E-mail: dcwigg@aol.com.

WIGGS, KENNETH EARL, II, music educator; b. Charleston, S.C., Dec. 27, 1972; s. Kenneth Earl and Bessie Carol Wiggs; m. Kristen F. Kaldor; children: Wiggs Kendra, Wiggs Paul. BA in Music Edn., U. N.D., Grand Forks, 1995; MS in Ednl. Leadership, Minn. State U., 2001, cert., 2002. Cert. K-12 music edn. Minn., K-12 prin. Minn. Music specialist Canby (Minn.) Indep. Sch. Dist., 1996—98, ISD # 564, Thief River Falls, 1998—. Mem.: TRFEA (v.p. 2000—02).

WIGGS, SHIRLEY JOANN, retired secondary school educator; b. Johnston County, N.C., Nov. 6, 1940; d. William H. and Sallie P. (Barden) W. BA, Atlantic Christian Coll., 1963; postgrad., Duke U., 1966, East Carolina U., 1979-80; grad., Newspaper Inst. Am. Tchr. pub. schs., South Hill, Va., 1963-64; tchr. lang. arts and social studies Glendale Chapel H.S., Kenly, N.C., 1964-65, Benson (N.C.) H.S., 1965-69; tchr. advanced placement English, lang. arts, journalism South Johnston H.S., Four Oaks, N.C., 1969-96, chairperson dept. lang. arts, 1971-83; ret., 1996. Evaluator profl. books Allyn and Bacon, Inc., 1974, 79; yearbook judge Columbia Scholastic Press Assn., 1986-92, yearbook advisor, 1980-94. Sunday Sch. tchr. 1st Bapt. Ch., Smithfield, N.C., 1964-66, assoc. supt. young people's dept., 1964-67, scholarship chair, 1987-91, ch. libr., 1992—, Clothes' Closet, 2002, tutor, 2000; chmn. Keep Johnston County Beautiful, 1979-81. Named Woman of Yr., Atlantic Christian Coll., 1962; recipient Internat. Cheerleading Found. award 1972, Acad. Booster Club award, 1986. Mem. NEA, Nat. Coun. Tchrs. English, Assn. Supervision and Curriculum Devel., N.C. Assn. Educators), N.C. English Tchrs. Assn. (dir. dist. 12, 1980-85), Johnston County Assn. Educators (pres. 1979). Home: 102 E Sanders St Smithfield NC 27577-4211

WIGHT, DARLENE, retired speech educator, emerita educator; b. Andover, Kans., Jan. 5, 1926; d. Everett John and Claudia (Jennings) Van Biber; m. Lester Delin, Jan. 21, 1950; children: Lester Delin II, Claudia Leigh. AA, Graceland Coll., 1945; BA, U. Kans., 1948, MA, 1952. Permanent profl. cert., Iowa; life tchr.'s cert., Mo. Instr. U. Kans., Lawrence, 1949-50; instr. overseas program U. Md., Munich, 1954; speech pathologist Independence (Mo.) Pub. Sch. Dist., 1958-61; assoc. prof. Graceland Coll., Lamoni, Iowa, 1961-87, prof. emeritus. Cons. Quad-County Sch. Dist., Leon, Iowa, 1966-67, Mt. Ayr (Iowa) Cmty. Sch. Dist., 1967-70; cons. Head Start program SCIAP, Leon, 1972-75, MATURA, Bedford, Iowa, 1973-75. Co-author: Speech Communication Handbook, 1979. Mem. Common Cause, Friends of Art, Nelson-Atkins Mus. Art, U.S. English, Inc., Habitat for Humanity, Nat. Mus. Women in Arts, Am. Craft Coun. Recipient Award of Merit U. Kans., 1982, Award of Distinction U. Kans., 1947-48. Mem. AAUW, Am. Speech, Lang. and Hearing Assn. (speech pathology clin. competency), Coun. Exceptional Children, Archaeol. Inst. Am. Democrat. Mem. Community Of Christ Ch. Avocations: weaving/fibers, traveling, gardening, cooking. Office: Graceland Coll Speech Dept Lamoni IA 50140 E-mail: darlenewight@yahoo.com.

WIGHT, PATRICIA ANNE, neuroscience educator; b. Providence, June 10, 1955; d. Howard Morrison Jr. and Nancy Lee (Phillips) W.; m. Mark David Crew, Jan. 15, 1988; children: Joseph David, Kyle Douglas, Michael Patrick. BS, U. Calif., Irvine, 1978; PhD, U. Calif., Riverside, 1988. Rsch. asst., tchg. asst. U. Calif., Riverside, 1981-88; postdoctoral fellow UCLA, 1988-92; asst. prof. U. Ark. Med. Scis., Little Rock, 1992-99, assoc. prof., 1999—. Contbr.

articles to profl. jours. Mem. AAAS, Am. Soc. Neurochemistry, Am. Physiol. Soc., Soc. for Neurosci., Sigma Xi. Roman Catholic. Avocations: hiking, skiing, swimming. Office: U Ark Med Scis 4301 W Markham St # 750 Little Rock AR 72205-7101

WIGHTMAN, ALEC, lawyer; b. Cleve., Jan. 23, 1951; s. John and Betty Jane (Follis) W.; m. Kathleen A. Little, June 19, 1976; children: Nora, Emily. BA, Duke U., 1972; JD, Ohio State U., 1975. Bar: Ohio 1975, U.S. Tax Ct. 1982, U.S. Ct. Appeals (6th cir.) 1983. Assoc. Krupman, Fromson & Henson, Columbus, Ohio, 1975-77; ptnr. Krupman, Fromson, Bownas & Wightman, 1978-82; assoc. Baker & Hostetler, 1982-83, ptnr., 1984—. Bd. trustees The Arthur G. James Cancer Hosp., Richard J. Solove Rsch. Inst. Mem. ABA, Ohio Bar Assn., Columbus Bar Assn., Ohio Oil and Gas Assn. Avocation: tennis. Office: Baker & Hostetler 65 E State St Ste 2100 Columbus OH 43215-4260

WIGHTMAN, ARTHUR STRONG, physicist, educator; b. Rochester, N.Y., Mar. 30, 1922; s. Eugene Pinckney and Edith Victoria (Stephenson) W.; m. Anna-Greta Larsson, Apr. 28, 1945 (dec. Feb. 11, 1976); 1 child, Robin Letitia (dec. Mar. 2, 2001); m. Ludmilla Popova, Jan. 14, 1977. BA, Yale U., 1942; PhD, Princeton U., 1949; DSc, Swiss Fed. Inst. Tech., Zurich, 1968, Göttingen U., 1987. Instr. physics Yale, 1943-44; from instr. to asso. prof. physics Princeton, 1949-60, prof. math. physics, 1960-92; prof. emeritus, 1992—; Thomas D. Jones prof. math. physics Princeton, 1971-92. Vis. prof. Sorbonne, 1957, École Polytechnique, 1977-78. Served to lt. (j.g.) USNR, 1944-46. NRC postdoctoral fellow Inst. Teoretisk Fysik, Copenhagen, Denmark, 1951-52; NSF sr. postdoctoral fellow, 1956-57; recipient Dannie Heineman prize math. physics, 1969, Poincaré prize Internat. Assn. Math. Physics, 1997. Fellow Am. Acad. Arts and Scis., Royal Acad. Arts, Am. Phys. Soc.; mem. NAS, AAAS, Am. Math. Soc. Office: Princeton U 350 Jadwin Hl Princeton NJ 08544-0001

WIGHTMAN, DORIS STEPHENSON, library director, city collector; b. Bosworth, Mo., May 27, 1927; d. Frank Audsley and Junie Ethel (Patton) Stephenson; m. Buford Earl Wightman, June 18, 1951; children: John Buford, Nancy Jo. Student, Mo. State Libr. Summer Sch., Columbia, Mo., 1964, 65, 66. Dir. Norborne (Mo.) Pub. Libr., 1969—. Picture editor: (book) Centennial History of Norborne, 1968. Mem. PTA Norborne, 1958-72. Republican. Methodist. Avocations: needlepoint, stamp collecting, fishing. Office: Norborne Pub Libr 109 E 2nd St Norborne MO 64668-1301

WIGHTMAN, LUDMILLA G. POPOVA, language educator, foreign educator, translator; b. Sofia, Bulgaria, Sept. 29, 1933; came to U.S., 1977; d. Genko Mateev and Liliana (Kusseva) Popov; m. Ivan Todorov Todorov, Aug. 13, 1957 (div. 1976); 1 child, Todor; m. Arthur Strong Wightman, Jan. 14, 1977. MS, U. Sofia, 1956. Cons. Nat. Libr., Sofia, 1956-58; rsch. assoc. Joint Inst. for Nuclear Rsch., Moscow, 1958-65; lectr. Russian Rutgers U., New Brunswick, N.J., 1969-70; editor Bulgarian Ency., Sofia, 1973-77; tchr. lang. Princeton (N.J.) Lang. Group, 1977—2001. Libr. Firestone Libr., Princeton U., 1983-87. Translator: Introduction to Axiomatic Field Theory, 1975, New Eng. Rev., Bread Loaf Quar., 1987, Mr. Cogito, 1989, N.Y. Rev. Books, 1990, Poetry East, 1990-91, Literary Rev., 1992, US1 Worksheets, 1992-2000, Visions International, 1993-2000, Partisan Rev., 1996, Shifting Borders: East European Poetries of the Eighties, 1993, Internat. Quarterly, 1999, Cry of a Former Dog, 2000, Forbidden Sea, 2000, Frost Flowers, 2001, Scars, 2002. Avocations: bird watching, music, photography, travel. Home and Office: 16 Balsam Ln Princeton NJ 08540-5327

WIGHTMAN, THOMAS VALENTINE, rancher, researcher; b. Sacramento, Oct. 7, 1921; s. Thomas Valentine and Pearl Mae (Cutbirth) W.; m. Lan Do Wightman. Student, U. Calif., Berkeley, 1945-46; B of Animal Husbandry, U. Calif., Davis, 1949; student, Cal. Poly. Inst., 1949-50. Jr. aircraft mechanic SAD (War Dept.), Sacramento, 1940-42; rancher Wightman Ranch, Elk Grove, 1950-59; machinest Craig Ship-Bldg. Co., Long Beach, 1959-70; rancher Wightman Ranch, Austin, Nev., 1970-88; dir. Wightman Found., Sacramento, 1988—. Dir. med. rsch. Staff sgt. U.S. Army, 1942-45. Recipient scholarship U.S. Fed. Govt., 1945-50. Fellow NRA, VFW, U. Calif. Alumni Assn., U. Calif. Davis Alumni Assn., Bowles Hall Assn.; mem. Confederate Air Force, The Oxford Club. Republican. Avocations: antique automobiles and aircraft. Home and Office: Wightman Found 2130 51st St Apt 129 Sacramento CA 95817-1507

WIGINGTON, RONALD LEE, retired chemical information services executive; b. Topeka, May 11, 1932; s. Oscar and Virginia C. (Ritchie) W.; m. Margaret E. Willey, Aug. 17, 1951; children: Linda (dec.), Carol, David, Brian. BS in Engring. Physics, U. Kans., 1953; MEE, U. Md., 1959; PhD in Elec. Engring., U. Kans., 1964; postgrad., Harvard Bus. Sch., 1976-77. Tech. staff Bell Telephone Labs., Murray Hill, N.J., 1953-54; divsn. chief Dept. Def., Washington, 1956-68; dir. R & D Chem. Abstracts Svc., Am. Chem. Soc., Columbus, Ohio, 1968-84; dir. Washington ops. Am. Chem. Soc., 1984-86; CEO, dir. Chem. Abstracts Svc., Am. Chem. Soc., Columbus, 1986-91; dir. info. tech. Am. Chem. Soc., 1991-94. Chmn. bd. Online Computer Libr. Ctr., Dublin, Ohio, 1985-87, trustee, 1978-92. Contbr. articles to profl. jours. Pres., various positions PTA Prince George's County, Md., 1966-68; moderator, treas. Cmty. Assn. Upper Arlington (Ohio) Schs., 1970-74; mem. Upper Arlington Civic Orch., 1970-84, pres., 1973, 76; bd. dirs. Nat. Fedn. Abstracting and Info. Svcs., 1979-84, pres. 1982-83, hon. fellow 1995—; bd. dirs. Ohio Ctr. of Sci. and Industry, 1988-93; trustee Health Coalition of Ctrl. Ohio, Columbus, 1991-99, treas., 1994-99, vice-chmn., 1996-99. With U.S. Army, 1954-56. Summerfield scholar U. Kans., 1949; recipient Nat. Capital award D.C. Council Engring. and Archtl. Socs., 1967, Meritorious Civilian Service award Dept. Defense, 1967. Mem.: IEEE (sr.; Topeka H.S. Hall of Fame 2001, exec. bd. 1986—94, treas. 1992—94), Material Property Data Network (bd. dirs. 1987—94), Internat. Coun. Sci. and Tech. Info., Am. Chem. Soc., Sigma Xi. Avocations: gardening, music, genealogy. Home: 2470 Wimbledon Rd Columbus OH 43220-4212

WIGINTON, JAY SPENCER, sales executive; b. Lubbock, Tex., Sept. 21, 1941; s. Clarence Elbert and Faye (George) W.; m. Billye Kay Freitag, Nov. 28, 1968 (div. Feb. 1993); children: Lauren, Lindsay; m. Laverne Shook, June 18, 1993. BS, Tex. Tech. U., 1963, MS, 1968. Sales rep. West Tex. ter. Syntex Labs., Lubbock, 1968-70, regional sales rep., 1970-72, Far East regional mgr. Des Moines, 1972-73, dir. mtkg., 1973-74; regional sales mgr. Zoecon Corp., Dallas, 1974-76; nat. account mgr. Custom divsn., 1976-78; gen. mgr. V.A. Snell & Co. divsn. Gt. Plains Chem. Co., San Antonio, 1978-83, Southwest regional mgr., 1983-84, dir. field devel., 1984-85; dist. mgr. Agri-Sales Assocs., Inc., 1985-87; sales mgr. western region Allflex U.S.A., Inc., 1987-91; gen. mgr. Pro. Vet. S., 1991-93; equine sales specialist Merial Ltd., 1993—. With AUS, 1964-66, Vietnam. Mem. Tex. Grain and Feed Assn., Tex. Cattle Feeders Assn., Tex. Chem. Assn., Kappa Sigma. Mem. Christian Ch. (Disciples Of Christ).

WIGLER, ANDREW JEFFREY, lawyer; b. Bklyn., Aug. 11, 1965; s. Jerome L. and Florence (Hoffstein) W.; m. Nancy D. Wigler, Feb. 22, 1992. BA, Albany State U., 1987; JD, Yeshiva U., N.Y.C., 1990. Bar: N.J. 1990, U.S. Dist. Ct. N.J. 1990, N.Y. 1991, U.S. Dist. Ct. (so. and ea. dists.) N.Y. 1991, U.S. Ct. Appeals (2nd cir.) 1991, D.C. 1993. Legis. intern Hon. Thomas J. Bartosiewicz, Albany, N.Y., 1986; legis. aide Hon. Anthony J. Genovesi, 1987; assoc. Reisman, Peirez, Reisman & Calica, Garden City, N.Y., 1993-94, Berger & Ackman, P.C., N.Y.C., 1990-93, ptnr., 1994-95, Law Offices of Andrew J. Wigler, Esq., Great Neck, N.Y., 1995—; atty. in pvt. practice Advanced Mortgage Sys., L.L.C., 1995—. Bd. dirs. Advanced Mortgage Sys., LLC, N.Y.C., Advanced Informatics, Inc., CancerMD.com, Inc. Committeeman Queens County Dem. Com., 1993, Kings County Dem. Com., 1990, Nassau County Dem. Com., 2000—; mem. bd. zoning appeals Village of Great Neck Estates, 2001—. Recipient First Place Brief award Phillip C. Jessup Moot Ct. Competition, N.Y., 1989, Best Brief award Cardozo Advocacy Competition, N.Y.C., 1988. Mem. ABA, N.Y. State Women's Bar Assn., Nassau County Bar Assn., N.Y. State Bar Assn., N.Y. County Lawyers Assn., Washington Bar Assn. Democrat. E-mail: andrew516@aol.com.

WIGLESWORTH, MICHAEL BLAND, advertising executive; b. Balt., Apr. 13, 1949; s. Reginal A. and Janice (Peppler) W.; m. Barbara Atkinson, Aug. 5, 1972 (div. Apr. 1980); m. Shari Kulik, Dec. 7, 1997. BS, Va. Commonwealth U., 1975. Account exec. Richmond (Va.) Newspapers, 1973—75; v.p. mktg. Bunch & Laughon Advt., Richmond, 1975—76; pres. Collier & Wiglesworth, Inc., 1976—80; v.p. account svcs. Brand Edmonds Bolio, 1980—82; v.p. sales promotion Eisner & Assocs., Balt., 1983—85; dir. promotion J. Walter Thompson, L.A., 1985—87; mgmt. supr. Einson Freeman, Paramus, NJ, 1987—89; sr. v.p., mgmt. supr. SAI/Earle Palmer Brown Promotions, Phila., 1989—94; sr. v.p. acct. svc. Hadley, N.Y.C., 1994—96; ptnr. Allegis Mktg., 1996—2000; sr. v.p. acct. svcs. SAI Mktg., 1996—2000; v.p. promotional mktg. Marketsource, Cranbury, NJ, 2000—01; group dir., relationship mktg. Carlson Mktg. Group, Phila., 2001—. Pres. M & W Ventures, Richmond, 1977-83; ptnr. Recreation Unltd., Inc., Richmond, 1979-80. Recipient best in Show award Am. Newspaper Assn., N.Y.C., 1979, Maxi award Direct Mail Assn., 1992, Reggie award Promotional Marketers Assn. Am., 1993, Pro award Coun. of Sales Promotion Agencies, 1994. Mem. Am. Advt. Fedn. (Retail Advt. award 1979), Am. Mktg. Assn. (Effie award 1980, Spire award 1992), Phi Kappa Sigma. Republican. Avocations: jogging, skiing, scuba diving, travel, music. Home: 520 Station Ave Glenside PA 19038-1419 Office: Carlson Mktg Group Ste 237 111 Presidential Blvd Philadelphia PA 19004 E-mail: mwiglesworth@carlson.com., mswigs@earthlink.net.

WIGLEY-MORRISON, KAREN, accountant, travel consultant, paralegal, administrative assistant; b. Dallas, July 14, 1950; d. Willard Robert Jr. and Jerry (McDonald) Wigley; m. Jon Edwin Morrison, Jan. 20, 1982. Student, Dallas Bapt. Coll., 1968-69; BA, U. Okla., 1971; diploma, Exec. Secretarial Sch., Dallas, 1971. Profl. model Kim Dawson Model Agy., Dallas, 1962-72; legal sec. Gardere & Wynne, 1972-76; paralegal, sec. Geary, Brice Law Firm, 1983-84; v.p., sec.-treas. Astraea Co., 1984-90; paralegal, sec. Geary, Bryce Law Firm, 1983-84; paralegal Gardere & Wynne, 1972-76; corp. sec. X Part, Inc., 1987-90; pvt. cons., 1990—; acct., 1992—. Vol. I Have a Dream Found., Dallas, 1988—, exec. vol. coun., 1990—; vol. Texans' War on Drugs, Austin. Mem. NAFE, Am. Bus. Women's Assn., North Dallas Network Career Women, Dallas Summer Musicals Guild, Dallas Symphony Assn., Arboretum and Botanical Gardens, Phi Beta Lambda. Republican. Episcopalian. Avocations: foreign and domestic travel, legal workshops, cruise/travel seminars, horse-back riding and training, charitable work. Home: 6919 Deloache Ave Dallas TX 75225-2420

WIGMORE, BARRIE ATHERTON, investment banker; b. Moose Jaw, Sask., Can., Apr. 11, 1941; came to U.S., 1970; s. Fred Henry and Pauline Elizabeth (Atherton) W.; m. Deedee Dawson, Aug. 24, 1964 BEd, U. Sask., Can., 1962, BA, 1963; MA, U. Oreg., 1964; BA, Oxford U., Eng., 1966, MA, 1971; L.L.D. (hon.) , U. Saskatachwan, 2002. Investment banker Goldman Sachs Group Inc., N.Y.C., 1970—. Author: The Crash and Its Aftermath, A History of U.S. Securities Markets 1929-33, 1985, Securities Markets in the 1980s, 1997. Chmn. Am. Friends of Worcester Coll. (Oxford U.) Inc.; trustee Metropolitan Mus. Art. Hon. fellow Worcester Coll., Oxford. Avocations: financial history, golf. Home: 1 W 72nd St New York NY 10023-3486 Office: Goldman Sachs Inc 85 Broad St New York NY 10004-2456 E-mail: barrie.wigmore@gs.com.

WIGMORE, JOHN GRANT, lawyer; b. L.A., Mar. 14, 1928; s. George Theodore and Mary (Grant) W.; m. Dina Burnaby, July 27, 1968 (dec. 1994); children: Alexander Trueblood, Adam Trueblood, John G. Jr., Mary. BS in Geology, Stanford U., 1949; JD, UCLA, 1958. Geologist Western Geophys., Calif., Colo., Mo., 1953-55; assoc. Lawler, Felix & Hall, L.A., 1958-62, ptnr., 1963-86, Pillsbury, Madison & Sutro, L.A., 1986-90; ret. Lectr. in field. Contbr. articles to profl. jours. Trustee L.A. County Mus. Natural History, 1970—; participant various local & state election campaigns, 1965-80. Officer USN, 1950-53. Fellow Am. Coll. Trial Lawyers, Am. Bar Found.; mem. ABA (chair litigation com. antitrust sect. 1970-74), Calif. State Bar (L.A. County bar del. 1965-75), L.A. County Bar Assn. (exec. com. trial sect. 1965-68), L.A. County Bus. Trial Lawyers (exec. com. 1984-87), Barristers (exec. com. 1960-65). Home: 870 Neptune Ave Encinitas CA 92024-2062

WIGSTEN, PAUL BRADLEY, JR. computer and financial consultant; b. Elmira, N.Y., June 27, 1947; s. Paul B. and Josephine N. (Lyman) W.; children: Tracy A., Kelly L.; m. Bonnie L. Carpenter, May 11, 1968. BS, Cornell U., 1969; MBA, Syracuse U., 1986. Cert. info. systems auditor. Mgmt. training GTE Sylvania, Camillus and Batavia, N.Y., 1969-72, data systems supr. Smithfield, N.C., 1972-74; sr. auditor GTE Svc. Corp., Syracuse, N.Y., 1974-77; bus. systems analyst GTE Products Corp., Stamford, Conn., 1977-79; systems planning mgr. GTE Service Corp., 1979-80; project mgr. Philips ECG, Inc., Seneca Falls, N.Y., 1980-83, mgr. internal control, 1983-84, gen. mgr., 1984-86; mgr. new bus. Amperex Electronic Corp., Slatersville, R.I., 1987-88; dir. fin. and info. systems Consol. Electronics Industries Corp., Stamford, Conn., 1989-91; with Tall Oaks Cons., Trumbull, 1990-92; asst. v.p. info. svcs. div. N.Y.C. Transit Authority, Bklyn., 1993-94; v.p. info. svcs. Beth Abraham Health Svcs., Bronx, 1994—2002. Trustee, treas. Mynderse Library, Seneca Falls, 1982-87; v.p. Community Ctr., Seneca Falls, 1982-87; commr. Seneca Falls Parks & Recreation Commn. Served with USAR, 1970-76. Mem. Inst. Mgmt. Accts., EDP Auditors Assn., Inst. Mgmt. Cons. (v.p. Fairfield/Westchester County chpt.), Coll. Healthcare Info. Mgmt. Execs., Healthcare Info. and Mgmt. Systems Soc. Republican. Roman Catholic. Avocation: wood working.

WIGSTON, DAVID LAWRENCE, biologist, dean; b. London, Dec. 12, 1943; came to U.S., 1993; s. Frederic Roland Wigston and Joan Mavin; m. Patricia Anne Werner, May 25, 1991; 1 child, Alexa Joan Dobinson. BSc with 1st class honors, U. Exeter, Eng., 1965; PhD in Forest Ecology, U. Exeter, 1972. Lectr. in biology Exeter Coll., 1967-69; sr. lectr. biology Coventry (Eng.) U., 1970-74; reader environ. sci. Plymouth (Eng.) U., 1974-82; prof., chair dept. forestry Papua New Guinea U. Tech., Lae, 1982-86; prof. environ. sci. No. Territory U., Darwin, Australia, 1986-93, dean faculty of sci. Australia, 1986-92; rsch. prof. U. Fla., Gainesville, 1993-96; rsch. assoc. dean U. Mich., Flint, 1996—. Vis. fellow St. Cross Coll. Oxford (Eng.) U., 1980; cons. Swedish Biomass Energy Program, 1981-82; chief wildlife scientist No. Territory (Australia) Govt., 1992-93. Narrator (symphonic works) Peter & The Wolf, Jungle Book, Hassan, 1961—. Cons. Internat. Convention Biodiversity, Australia, 1992-93; pres., bd. dirs. Gainesville Symphony Orch., 1994-96. Fellow Australian Inst. Biology (sec. No. Territory br. 1987-93); mem. Ecol. Soc. Am., Soc. Human Ecology, Soc. Econ. Botany. Avocations: music, theater, art, literature. Office: U Mich 303 Kearsley St Flint MI 48502

WIGTON, CHESTER MAHLON, family physician; b. Pueblo, Colo., Jan. 12, 1928; s. Washington Irving and Bessie Marie (Ramsey) W.; m. Marjorie Chanak, Aug. 29, 1953 (dec. Jan. 1981); children: Robin, Renee, Kent, Lance, Bruce, Scott; m. Anita Kay Nelson, July 4, 1993; children: Sallie Michelle Short, Sadie Kay Short. BS cum laude, Colo. Coll., 1950; MD, U. Colo., Denver, 1954. Diplomate Am. Bd. Family Practice. Intern Swedish Hosp., Seattle, 1954-55; pvt. practice family medicine, Durango, Colo., 1957—; emeritus active Med. Mercy Hosp., 1990—, v.p. staff, 1970-73. Med. dir. Hacienda Nursing Home, Bloomfield, N.Mex., 1992-95. Pres. CAMP Inc., Durango, 1970, CEOW Inc., Durango, 1964; treas. Tamarron Owners Assn. Bd., Durango, 1986-95; sec. Durango Sch. Bd., 1969-73; dir. San Juan Devel., Durango, 1971. Lt. (j.g.) USPHS, 1955-57; sec. Cmty. Hosp. Bd., Durango, 1986-92. Fellow Am. Acad. Family Practice; mem. Durango C. of C. (pres. 1965-66), Durango Rotary Club (pres. 1968), Electra Lake Sporting Club (pres. 1982-85), Delta Epsilon, Sigma Nu, Nu Sigma Nu. Republican. Presbyterian. Avocations: skiing, tennis, golf, fishing, hunting. Home: 151 Riverview Dr Durango CO 81301-4349 Office: 3575 Main Ave Durango CO 81301-4028

WIIG, ELISABETH HEMMERSAM, speech language pathologist, educator; b. Esbjerg, Denmark, May 22, 1935; arrived in U.S., 1957, naturalized, 1967; d. Svend Frederick and Ingeborg (Hemmersam) Nielsen; m. Karl Martin Wiig, June 10, 1958; 1 child Charlotte E. BA, Statsseminariet Emdrupborg, 1956; MA, Western Res. U., 1960; PhD, Case Western Res. U., 1967; postgrad., U. Mich., 1967-68. Clin. audiologist Cleve. Hearing and Speech Center, 1959-60; instr. dept. phonetics Bergen (Norway) U., 1960-64; asst. prof., dir. aphasia rehab. program U. Mich., 1968-70; asst. prof. Boston U., 1970-73, asso. prof., chmn. dept., 1973-77, prof. dept. communication disorders, 1977-87, prof. emerita, 1987—; v.p. EDUCOM Assocs. Inc., 1992-93; pres. Knowledge Rsch. Inst., 1995—. Author: (book) Language Disabilities in Children and Adolescents, 1976, Language Assessment and Intervention for the Learning Disabled, 1980, 1984, CELF Screening Tests: Elementary and Secondary Levels, 1980, Clinical Evaluation of Language Fundamentals, rev. edit., 1987, Clinical Evaluation of Language Fundamentals 3, 1995, Test of Language Competence, 1985, Test of Language Competence, expanded edit., 1989, Test of Word Knowledge, 1992, Clinical Evaluation of Language Fundamentals Preschool, 1992, Bateria de Lenguaje Objectiva y Critical, 1998, Arabic Language Screening Tests, 1999, Map it Out! Visual Tools for Planning, Organizing and Communicating, 2000, Arabic Receptive-Expressive Vocabulary Test, 2000, Multilingual Continuous Naming Test, 2000, 2001, Quick Test for Assessment of Parietal-Lobe Dysfunction, 2002; co-author: Evaluació de llenguatje; editor: Human Communication Disorders: An Introduction, 1982, 1986, 1990, 1994, 1998; contbr. articles to profl. jours. Recipient Metcalf Cup and Prize for excellence in tchg., Boston U., 1967, Frank R. Kleffner Career award, Am. Speech and Hearing Found., 2001. Fellow: Am. Speech and Hearing Assn. (cert. clin. competence in speech pathology and audiology); mem.: Am. Psychol. Soc., Internat. Assn. Rsch. Learning Disabilities, Coun. Exception Children, Coun. for Learning Disabilities.

WIIG, KARL MARTIN, knowledge management expert and consultant; b. Karasjok, Norway, Feb. 8, 1934; came to U.S., 1957; s. Alf Kristian and Margarethe (Soylann) W.; Elisabeth Hemmersam Nielsen, June 10, 1958; children: Charlotte Elisabeth, Erik Daniel (dec.). BS, Case Inst. Tech., 1959, MS, 1964. Rschr. Chr. Michelsen Inst., Bergen, Norway, 1960-64; sys. engr. GE, Cleve., 1964-66; mgr. sys. engring. Dundee (Mich.) Cement Co., 1966-70; chmn. bd. Abacus Alpha, Inc., Newton, Mass., 1980-81; mgr. sys. and policy analysis Arthur D. Little, Inc., Cambridge, 1970-80, dir. artificial intelligence, 1981-87; ptnr. Coopers & Lybrand, Dallas, 1987-89; mng. ptnr. The Wiig Group, Arlington, Tex., 1989-95; chmn. bd., CEO Knowledge Rsch. Inst., Inc., 1995—. Presenter, cons. in field; co-founder Internat. Knowledge Mgmt. Network; spk. U.S. Info. Agy., Australia, 1998; lectr. U. Sao Paulo, Brazil, 1999, 2000, 2001; keynote spkr. Johannesburg, 1999, Prague, 2000, New Delhi, 2000, Taipei, 2000, Seoul, 2000, Atlanta, 2001, Washington, 2001, Venezuela, 2001, Taiwan, 2002, Can., 2002, Singapore, 2002, Taipei, 2002, Monterrey, Mex., 2002 Author: The Economics of Offshore Oil and Gas Supplies, 1977, Expert Systems: A Manager's Guide, 1990, Knowledge Management Foundations: Thinking About Thinking - How People and Organizations Create, Represent and Use Knowledge, 1993, Knowledge Management: The Central Management Focus for Intelligent-Acting Organizations, 1994, Knowledge Management Methods: Practical Approaches to Manage Knowledge, 1995, Approaching Knowledge Management in Practice, 1996, Leveraging Knowledge for Business Performance, 1997; (publs.) Managing Knowledge: Executive Perspectives, 1989, Knowledge-Based Systems and Issues of Integration, 1988, Management of Knowledge: A New Opportunity, 1988, Knowledge Management Goals at Different Levels of Society and the Enterprise, 1996, Knowledge Management: Where Did It Come From--and Where Will it Go?, 1997, Knowledge Management: An Introductory Perspective, 1998, What Future Knowledge Management Users May Expect, 1999, (with Elisabeth H. Wiig) On Conceptual Learning, 1999, Introducting Knowledge Management into the Enterprise, 1999, What Future Knowledge Management Users May Expect, 1999, Knowledge Management in Innovation and R&D, 2000, Application of Knowledge Management in Public Administration, 2000, Exploiting Knowledge for Productivity Gains, 2001, Knowledge Management: The Major Enabler of Enterprise Performance, 2002; contbr. 14 chpts. to books, over 65 articles to profl. publs. With Norwegian Army, 1953-54. Achievements include patent in variable ratio power steering. Home and Office: 7101 Lake Powell Dr Arlington TX 76016-3517 E-mail: kmwiig@krii.com.

WIITA, KATHRYN CARPENTER, public relations company executive; b. Casper, Wyo., Sept. 15, 1961; d. Hugh Lewis and Kathryn Estelle (Pepper) Carpenter; m. Thomas A. Wiita, Sept. 1, 1991. BS in Mass Communications, U. Utah, 1983. Mcht. rep. Tracy Collins Bank & Trust, Salt Lake City, 1983-84; communications specialist Arthur Young & Co., 1984-88; officer, dir. pub. rels. 1st Interstate Bank Utah, 1988-89; pres. KC Communications, Jackson, Wyo., 1989—. Cons. Mountain West Venture Group, Salt Lake City, 1984-87, Catheter Tech. Inc., Salt Lake City, 1986-89, Sta. KTVX, Salt Lake City, 1986, Inter Therapy, Inc., Costa Mesa, Calif., 1990, Stop Gap, Santa Ana, Calif., Jackson Peak Outfitters, 1992—, M W Med., 1990—, Jacksoh Hole Cowboy Ski Challenge, 1994; mktg. cons.Wines & Spirits, 1992—. Mem. Pub. Rels. Soc. Am. (accredited; officer 1988-89), Pub. Rels. Soc. Am. Counselors Acad., Women in Comms. (officer 1988-89), Jr. League Orange County, Calif. Inc. (pub. rels. coord. 1991-92, dir. pub. rels. c992—), Kappa Kappa Gamma. Avocations: travel, cooking, skiing, hiking, reading. Home and Office: 2620 SE Bella Vista Loop Vancouver WA 98683-7671

WIJNBERG, MARION H. social work educator; b. N.Y.C., Dec. 26, 1928; d. Ira H. and Florence (Stone) Holley; m. Louis Wijnberg (div. Jan. 1979); children: Deborah Lynn, Jonathan Leonard. BS, Cornell U., 1951; MSW, U. Buffalo, 1955; PhD, SUNY, Buffalo, 1974. Case worker Monroe County Dept. Social Svc., Rochester, 1951-53, Children's Aid & SPCC, Buffalo, 1955-58; sr. case worker Ch. Mission of Help, 1958-64; asst. prof. Sch. of Social Work, SUNY, 1964-70, assoc. prof., 1970-78; prof. Sch. Social Work, Western Mich. U., Kalamazoo, 1978—, coord. social treatment, 1978-82, 85—. Cons. Community Support Svcs., Lansing, Mich., 1986-88, Mich. State Extension div., Lansing, 1992, Employee Asst. Degree Program, 1991-92; vis. prof. York (Eng.) U., 1993. Author: (with others) Jossey Bass Superoisy and Performance, 1988. Bd. dirs. Kalamazoo Consultation Ctr., 1987-89; mem. Blue Ribbon Commn. Future Univ., 1983-85; chair rsch. and scholarship of strategic planning Coll. of Health and Human Svcs., Kalamazoo 1992. Mem. Coun. of social Work, Phi Lambda Theta, Phi Kappa Phi. Democrat. Jewish. Avocations: reading, literature, cross country skiing, tennis, hiking/walking. Office: Sch of Social Work Western Mich U Kalamazoo MI 49008

WIK, JEAN MARIE (JEAN MARIE BECK), librarian, media specialist; b. Aitkin, Minn., Feb. 10, 1938; d. Herman Otto Beck and Ferdina Mathilda (Petersen) Kalt; m. Richard Lyle Wik, Aug. 17, 1958; children: Steven L., Lori Jo. BS, No. State U., Aberdeen S.D., 1963; MA, U. Minn., 1972; cert. in media arts, Mankato State U., 1974. Elem. tchr. Howard Hedger Sch., Aberdeen, S.D., 1958-62; tchr. spl. edn. Westwood Sch., Bloomington, Minn., 1963-64; elem. tchr. Washburn Sch., 1964-71; media generalist elem. elem. and secondary schs., 1972-85; media generalist Kennedy High Sch., Bloomington, 1985-96; fashion coord. Weekender Casual Wear, 1993—2001. Dir. Annehurst Curriculum Classifications System project Bloomington Schs., 1976-85, dist. media leadership position, 1990-92. Chmn. Christian Women's Club, 1972-74, area rep., 1981-85. Mem. NEA, Minn. Edn. Assn., Minn. Ednl. Media Assn. Avocations: songwriting, singing, public speaking for Christian groups.

WIKANDER, LAWRENCE EINAR, librarian; b. Pitts., Dec. 16, 1915; s. Oscar Ragnar and Mary Edna (Gerdes) W.; m. Ethel Marie Whitlow, Nov. 23, 1940; children: Frederick Whitlow, Matthew Hays. BA, Williams Coll., 1937; BS in Library Sci, Columbia U., 1939; MA, U. Pa., 1949. Gen. asst. Carnegie Library, Pitts., 1939-40; supr. circulation Mt. Pleasant Br., D.C. Public Library, Washington, 1940-42; asst. librarian Temple U., Phila., 1946-50; librarian Forbes Library, Northampton, Mass., 1950-68, Williams Coll., Williamstown, 1968-82, librarian emeritus, from 182; curator Calvin Coolidge Meml. Room Forbes Library, Northampton, 1982-93. Author: Disposed to Learn, 1972, Completing a Century: History of the Northampton Social and Literary Club, 1962, Calvin Coolidge: A Chronological Summary, 1957; editor: The Hampshire History, 1962, The Northampton Book, 1954, A Guide to the Personal Files of Calvin Coolidge, 1986, (with Robert H. Ferrell) Grace Coolidge: An Autobiography, 1992; contbr. articles to profl. jours. Pres. Northampton Community Chest, 1958-60; bd. dirs. Civil Liberties Union Mass., Hampshire, 1957-68; trustee Calvin Coolidge Meml. Found., 1969-99, trustee emeritus, 1999—; dir. South Mountain Concert Assn., 1975— ; clk. Northampton Hist. Soc., 1955-68; dir. Hampshire Inter-Library Center, 1956-68. Served to capt. AUS, 1942-46; military intelligence in Africa, Italy, Austria. Mem. Am. Library Assn. (mem. council 1962-68), New Eng. Library Assn. (pres. 1967-68), Mass. Library Assn. (pres. 1960-61), Western Mass. Library Club (pres. 1953-55) Home: Williamstown, Mass. Died July 13, 2002.

WIKARSKI, NANCY SUSAN, information technology consultant; b. Chgo., Jan. 26, 1954; d. Walter Alexander and Emily Regina (Wejnerowski) W.; m. Michael F. Maciekowich, Dec. 5, 1976 (div. Feb. 1985). BA, Loyola U., Chgo., 1976, MA, 1978; PhD, U. Chgo., 1990. Paralegal Winston & Strawn,

Chgo., 1978-79; real estate analyst Continental Bank, 1979-84, systems analyst, 1984-88, ops. officer, 1988-89, automation cons., 1989-92; systems mgr. PNC Mortgage Co. of Am., Vernon Hills, Ill., 1992-94; ind. cons., 1994—. Book reviewer Murder Past Tense, 2000—. Author: German Expressionist Film, 1990, The Fall of White City, 2002. Fellow U. Chgo., 1987-90. Mem. Mystery Writers Am., Sisters in Crime (v.p. Mpls. chpt.), Mensa. Avocation: gardening.

WIKE, D. ELAINE, business executive; b. Ridgecrest, Calif., Sept. 26, 1954; d. Robert G. and Jimmie Mae (Sallee) Field; m. Mike Wike, Oct. 14, 1978; children: Mike II, Angelina Elaine, William V., Danielle Elizabeth, Edward Lawrence, Windy Gale. Student, U. Houston, 1975—77. Legal sec. Morgan, Lewis & Bockius, Washington, 1977—78; legal asst. Alfred C. Schlosser & Co., Houston, 1972—77, 1978—81, Jerry Sadler, atty., Houston, 1982—83; founder, owner DEW Profl. & Bus. Svcs., 1979—; office mgr. Law Offices Mike Wike, 1983—. Contbr. poetry to publs. including Internat. Libr. of Poetry. Treas. Wilhelm Schole Parents Orgn, 1981—82; mem. Free, Inc.; vol. campaign worker Ron Paul for Congress and Reagan for Pres., 1975, 1976. Recipient 3d place, Nassau Bay Tex. Christmas Boat Lane Parade First Ann. Photography Contest, 1990. Mem.: Nat. Paralegal Assn., Am. Soc. Notaries, Nat. Assn. Female Execs., Nat. Notary Assn., Young Ams. for Freedom. Republican. Libertarian. Mem. Christian Ch. Office: 2421 S Wayside Dr Houston TX 77023-5318

WIKMAN, MICHAEL RAYMOND, advertising executive; b. Mpls., Dec. 28, 1950; s. Charles Pierce and Jeanne Elizabeth W.; m. Carrie Brandt, Feb. 7, 1981; children: Caroline Celeste, Charles Michael. B in Elected Studies, U. Minn., 1973. Analyst, supr. media services Cambell-Mithun Advt., Mpls., 1973-77, account mgr., 1977-80; pres. MWA Direct, 1980—. Mem. Direct Mktg. Assn. (Echo award 1987), Midwest Direct Mktg. Assn. (Art, Response and Copy award 1987). Avocations: art collecting, downhill skiing, tennis, sailing. Home: 6929 Mark Terrace Cir Minneapolis MN 55439-1622 Office: MWA Direct 6465 Wayzata Blvd Ste 330 Saint Louis Park MN 55426-1789*

WIKSTEN, BARRY FRANK, communications executive; b. Seattle, June 23, 1935; s. Frank Alfred and Alice Gertrude (Ensor) W.; m. Madeleine Schmeil, Nov. 23, 1979; children: Karen Anne, Eric Marshal, Kurt Edward. BA, Miami U., Oxford, Ohio, 1960; MA, Fletcher Sch. Law and Diplomacy, 1961. Dir. econ. programs U.S. Council, Internat. C. of C., N.Y.C., 1962-63; with TWA, 1964-79, dir. fin. relations, 1972, v.p. pub. affairs, 1973, v.p. pub. rels., 1973-76, sr. v.p. pub. affairs, mem. airline policy bd., 1976-79; v.p. corp. adminstrn. Trans World Corp., 1979-82, also sec. corp. policy com., mem. consumer affairs com. and corp. compensation com.; sr. v.p. communications CIGNA Corp., Phila., 1982-84, sr. v.p. pub. affairs, 1984—. Served with USMC, 1954-57. Mem. Pub. Rels. Seminar, Wisemen, Union League Club (N.Y.), The Athenaeum (Phila.). Office: CIGNA Corp 1650 Market St OL55E 1 Liberty Pl Philadelphia PA 19192-0001

WIKTOR, PETER JAN, engineer; b. Astrida, Rwanda, Oct. 12, 1956; came to U.S., 1960; s. Tadeusze Jan and Anna (Krzyzanowska) W.; m. Deirdre Ruth Meldrum, Aug. 19, 1989. BS, U. Pa., 1978; MS, Rensselaer Polytech., 1984; PhD, Stanford U., 1992. Engr. McDonnell Douglas, Long Beach, Calif., 1978-80; design engr. Hughes Helicopter, L.A., 1982; rsch. asst. Rensselaer Polytech. Inst., Troy, N.Y., 1982-84; engr. GM Rsch. Lab., Detroit, 1983, Jet Propulsion Lab., Pasadena, Calif., 1984-87; rsch. asst. Stanford (Calif.) U., 1987-92; pres. Engring. Arts, 1992—; aux. faculty U. Wash., 1993—. Contbr. articles to profl. jours. Mem. Am. Soc. Mech. Engrs., Am. Astron. Soc., Sigma Xi. Achievements include briefing of NASA on reactionless precision pointing actuator, rotating transformer equations, thruster systems for liquid helium cooled spacecraft and patents for liguid handling systems using peizo-electric ink-jet dispensers. E-mail: www.engineering-arts.com. Home: 7236 91st Ave SE Mercer Island WA 98040-5802

WILAND, GEORGE WILLIAM, JR. legislative staff member, consultant; b. Balt., Apr. 10, 1947; s. George William Wiland Sr. and Anna Ferguson; m. Linda Lois Scantling, June 11, 1966; children: Jody Lynn Streck, Joel David, George W. (Billy) III. BA in History, Oral Roberts U., 1974; AA in Bus., Tulsa C.C., 1993; MS in Mgmt., So. Nazarene U., Bethany, Okla., 1995. Address info. sys. specialist U.S. Postal Svc., Tulsa, 1984-88, directory analysis specialist, 1988-92; program rep. Oklahoma City U., 1997—2002; constituent rep. Congressman John Sullivan, 2002—. Postmaster's customer adv. coun. U.S. Postal Svc., Tulsa, 1999—; dep. voter registrar Tulsa County Election Bd., 1984-. Exec. com. Tulsa County Reps., 1994—; exec. com., sec. Heartland Mission Fest, 1995—; presdl. elector 54th Meeting Electoral Coll., Oklahoma City, 2000; study group leader Salvation Army, Tulsa, 2000—. Mem. Reaching Hands Inc. (bd. dirs.), Delta Mu Delta. Avocations: genealogy, orthography, numismatics. Home: 7927 E 77th Pl Tulsa OK 74133-3655 Office: Congressman John Sullivan 2424 E 21st St # 510 Tulsa OK 74114-1723 E-mail: george.wiland@mail.house.gov.

WILBANKS, JAN JOSEPH, retired philosopher; b. Lynchburg, Ohio, Dec. 17, 1928; s. James Odell and Bernice Elizabeth (Daugherty) W.; m. Alice Ramona Pacheco, Nov. 14, 1953; children— Elise, Anita, Jennifer. BS, Cin. Coll. Pharmacy, 1951; PhD in Philosophy, Ohio State U., 1964. Instr. philosophy Purdue U., 1961-64; mem. faculty Marietta (Ohio) Coll., 1964-89, prof. philosophy, 1973-89. Author: Hume's Theory of Imagination, 1968, also articles. With AUS, 1951-53. Home: 122 High St Marietta OH 45750-2636

WILBANKS, MARY, artist; b. Lexington, Ky., Aug. 31, 1940; d. Marino Francis and Louise Traynor Peyrefitte; m. Robery Leroy Wilbanks, May 7, 1959; children: Ann Wilbanks Scardaville, Ken. Student, Glassel Sch. of Art, Houston, 1975-80. Painting tchr. Phoenix Art Mus., 1980-84, Fine Arts Ctr.-Bemis Sch., Colorado Springs, 1984-87, Juvenile Detention Ctr., Houston, 1989-94; collage painting tchr. various locations, 1994—, Art League of Houston, 1994—. Exhibited works at Goldesberry Gallery, Gallery 5, Rock Hill, S.C., Art-Art-Bobart Gallery, Taos, N.Mex., ; represented in books including Best of Watercolor II, 1999, Best of Watercolor-Painting Texture, 1998, Collage Techniques, 1997, (on cover) Art and Healing, 1999. Active Big Bros.-Big Sisters, 1996—2002, Art League of Houston, 1994—. Recipient 1st award Rocky Mountain Nat., 1997, 30 awards nat. shows, 1990-99. Mem. Nat. Watercolor Soc., Watercolor USA Honor Soc., Watercolor Art Soc. Houston, Art League of Houston (faculty), Soc. of Layerists. Democrat. Roman Catholic. Avocations: studying Spanish, traveling, sailing, yoga, hiking. Home and Office: 18307 Champion Forest Dr Spring TX 77379-3973

WILBER, CLARE MARIE, musician, educator; b. Denver, Mar. 21, 1928; d. Thomas A. and Kathleen M. (Brennan) O'Keefe; m. Charles Grady Wilber, June 14, 1952 (dec. 1998); children: Maureen, Charles, Michael, Thomas (dec.), Kathleen, Aileen, John Joseph. AB, Loretto Heights Coll., 1948; MS, Fordham U., 1950; MM, Colo. State U., 1972. Instr. biology and music various colls. and univs., 1951-83; mgr. Ft. Collins (Colo.) Symphony, 1969-81, exec. dir., 1981-85, exec. dir. emerita, 1985—; pvt. music instr. Ft. Collins, 1973—. Trustee Ft. Collins Symphony, 1986—, mem. young artist competition com., 1985—. Composer Fantasie Romantique, 1972, Mass in D, 1980, Seascapes for Suzanne, 1988, Panoramas for Polly, 1990, Journeys for Jennifer, 1994, Augustine's Lament, 1996, Collage for Cynthia, 1997, Daydreams for Drew, 2001. Mem. adv. coun. Ft. Collins H.S., 1972—74; mem. adv. bd. Children's Sch. of Sci., Woods Hole, Mass., 1965—95. Recipient AT&T Crystal Clef award, 1982, Clare Wilber award named in her honor, Ft. Collins Symphony, 1992. Mem. Ft. Collins Music Tchrs. Assn. (treas. 1984-90), Colo. State Music Tchrs. Assn., Music Tchrs. Nat. Assn. (cert. music tchr. 1978—), Marine Biol. Lab. Assocs., Cosmos Club (assoc.), Sigma Xi (assoc.), Delta Omicron (local chpt. pres. 1970-72, sec. 1988—, Spl. Svc. award 1974, Star of Delta Omicron award 1995). Republican. Roman Catholic. Home and Office: 900 Edwards St Fort Collins CO 80524-3824

WILBER, DAVID JAMES, cardiologist; b. Wis., Apr. 1, 1951; s. Howard Spencer and Leona (Von Reuden) W.; m. Sandra Irene Reynertson, June 28, 1992. BS, U. Wis., 1973; MD, Northwestern U., 1977. Intern medicine Northwestern Meml. Hosps., 1977-80; fellow cardiology U. Mich., 1982-84; fellow electrophysiology Mass. Gen. Hosp., Boston, 1984-86; asst. prof. medicine Loyola U., Maywood, Ill., 1986-90, assoc. prof. medicine, 1990-94; prof. medicine U. Chgo., 1994—. Fellow Am. Coll. Cardiology, Am. Heart Assn. Office: Loyola U Chgo Divsn Cardiology 2160 S First Ave Maywood IL 60153-

WILBER, ROBERT EDWIN, corporate executive; b. Boston, Dec. 15, 1932; s. Charles Edwin and Mary Charles (Gay) W.; m. Bonnie Marilyn Jones; children: Debra, Kathleen, Robert Jr., Thomas, Jeffrey, Mark, Matthew. BSBA in Acctg., Bowling Green State U., 1954. CPA, Mass., Tex. Sr. acct. Peat, Marwick, Mitchell and Co., Boston, 1954-58; gen. mgr. Door Controls Inc., 1958-59; asst. controller MKM Knitting Mills Inc., Manchester, N.H., 1959-63; internal audit supr. Raytheon Co., Lexington, Mass., 1963; asst. treas. Glens Falls (N.Y.) Ins. Co., 1963-66; controller Pnobscott Co., Boston, 1966-67; v.p. fin. and adminstrn. S.S. Pierce Co., 1967-73; v.p. Samson Ocean Systems Inc., 1973-78; v.p., chief acctg. officer Enserch Corp., Dallas, 1978-88; pres. Trade U.S.A., 1990—. Mem. AICPAs, Nat. Assn. Trade Exchanges, Mass. Soc. CPAs, Fin. Execs. Inst., BANC, Pres.'s Club (Bowling Green, Ohio). Home: 5804 Goliad Ave Dallas TX 75206-6818 Office: 5019 McKinney Ave Ste 110 Dallas TX 75205

WILBERGER, JAMES E. neurosurgeon; b. Richmond, Va., May 5, 1955; s. James E. and Florence C. Wilberger; children: Matthew, Adam. MD, Med. Coll. Va., 1978. Cert. Am. Bd. Neurol. Surgery. Dept. chmn., neurosurgery Allegheny Gen. Hosp., Pitts., 1998—. Program dir., neurosurgery resident Allegheny Gen. Hosp., Pitts., 1995—. Author: (textbook) Neurotrauma, 1998. Cir. bd. dirs. Pitts. Cultural Trust, 2002. Recipient Wakeman award in the neurosci., Duke U., 1990. Mem.: Allegheny Country Club. Conservative. Roman Catholic. Avocations: writing, golf, travel. Office: Allegheny Gen Hosp Dept Neurosurgery Ste 302 E North Ave Pittsburgh PA 15212 Personal E-mail: jwilberg@wpahs.org. E-mail: jwilberg@wpahs.org.

WILBON, ANTHONY D. technology educator; b. Flint, Mich., May 20, 1963; s. Jessie and Lizzie M. Wilbon; m. Rhonda Wells-Wilbon, July 23, 1988; children: Azaan, Jabari. BSEE, Mich. State U., 1986; MBA, Howard U., 1990; PhD, George Washington U., 1999. Mfg. engr. Westinghouse Electric Corp., Balt., 1986-88; sr. cons. Booz Allen & Hamilton, Bethesda, Md., 1988-90; project leader Am. Mgmt. Systems, Fairfax, Va., 1990-94; sr. tech. analyst Fed. Res. Bd., Washington, 1994-99; asst. prof. Morgan State U., Balt., 1999—. Contbr. articles to profl. jours. Mem. Acad. Mgmt., INFORMS, Beta Gamma Sigma. Office: Morgan State U 1700 E Cold Spring W Baltimore MD 21251 E-mail: awilbon@morgan.edu.

WILBUR, ANDREW CLAYTON, radiologist, educator; b. Phila., May 30, 1952; s. Richard Sloan and Betty Lou (Fannin) W.; m. Debra Jean Jones, June 29, 1996; children: Curtis Richard, Clayton Samuel. AB in Human Biology, Stanford U., 1974; MD, George Washington U., 1978. Diplomate Am. Bd. Radiology. Extern in diagnostic radiology Palo Alto (Calif.) Med. Found., 1978-79; resident in diagnostic radiology U. Ill. Hosp., Chgo., 1979-83, fellow in body imaging, 1983-84; asst. prof. radiology U. Ill. Coll. Medicine, 1984-90, assoc. prof., 1990—, dir. body imaging dept. radiology, 1988—, dir. radiology residency program, 1989—. Contbr. articles to profl. jours. Mem. Radiol. Soc. N.Am., Am. Coll. Radiology, Am. Roentgen Ray Soc., Chgo. Radiol. Soc. (trustee 1996-2000). Office: Univ of Illinois Hosp M/C 931 1740 W Taylor St Chicago IL 60612-7232

WILBUR, BARBARA MARIE, elementary education educator; b. Homer City, Pa., Dec. 1, 1945; d. Nicholas and Ann (Bender) Hrebik; m. Samuel Scime, Nov. 21, 1970 (div. Jan. 1974); m. Frederick Layton Wilbur, June 21, 1986 (dec. June 1989). BS in Elem. Edn., SUNY, Buffalo, 1967, EdM in Guidance Counseling, 1971; postgrad., Harvard U., 1969; grad., John Robert Powers Modeling Sch., Buffalo, 1974. Cert. permanent elem. sch. tchr., N.Y. Elem. tchr. Buffalo Pub. Schs., 1967-70, 94—. Diocese of Ft. Lauderdale, Fla., 1971-72, Diocese of Buffalo, 1973-94. Mem. Internat. Platform Assn., State U. Buffalo Alumni Assn., State U. Coll. Buffalo Alumni Assn. (Outstanding Svc. award 1982), Buffalo State Coll. Alumni Assn. (bd. dirs. 1980-87, active various coms.). Republican. Roman Catholic. Avocations: modeling, volleyball, ice skating, tennis. Home: 20 Schimwood Ct Amherst NY 14068 Office: Buffalo Pub Schs Sch # 40 89 Clare St Buffalo NY 14206-2020

WILBUR, COLBURN SLOAN, foundation consultant and trustee, former executive; b. Palo Alto, Calif., Jan. 20, 1935; s. Blake Colburn and Mary (Sloan) W.; m. Maria Grace Verburg, Sept. 1, 1961; children: Marguerite Louise, Anne Noelle. BA in Polit. Sci., Stanford U., 1956, MBA, 1960. Asst. cashier United Calif. Bank, San Francisco, 1960-65; v.p. Standata, 1965-68; adminstrv. mgr. Tab Products, 1968-69; exec. dir. Sierra Club Found., 1969-76, David and Lucile Packard Found., Los Altos, Calif., 1976—. Bd. dirs. Colo. Coll., Colorado Springs; sr. fellow Coun. on Founds., Washington. Bd. dirs. Philanthropic Ventures Found.; former bd. dirs., mem. adv bd. Global Fund Women, Palo Alto, Calif.; past bd. dirs. Big Bros. San Francisco, Calif. Confederation Arts, Peninsula Grantmakers, Women's Fund Santa Clara; former bd. dirs., pres. Big Bros. Peninsula, North Fork Assn., Peninsula Conservation Ctr.; past bd. dirs., chmn. No. Calif. Grantmakers; bd. dirs., mem. adv. bd. Sierra Club Found., Stanford Theater Found., Palo Alto, U. San Francisco/Inst. Nonprofit Orgn. Mgmt. With U.S. Army, 1957-58. Mem. Commonwealth Club (bd. advisors). Office: David & Lucile Packard Found 300 2nd St Los Altos CA 94022-3694 E-mail: c.wilbur@packfound.org.

WILBUR, E. PACKER, investment company executive; b. Bridgeport, Conn., Sept. 9, 1936; s. E. Packer and Elizabeth (Wells) W.; m. Laura Mary Ferrier, Sept. 17, 1965; children— Alison Mary, Andrew Packer, Gillian Elizabeth. BA, Yale U., 1959; MBA, Harvard U., 1965. Cons. McKinsey & Co. Inc., N.Y.C., 1964-67; dir. corp. planning Am. Express Co., 1967-69; v.p. Van Alstyne Noel & Co., 1969-70; exec. v.p., dir., mem. exec. com. Newburger Loeb & Co. Inc., 1970-73; pres. E.P. Wilbur & Co., Inc., Southport, Conn., 1973—, Southport Fin. Corp., 1986—. Chmn. bd. Criterion Mgmt., Inc., Lafayette, Ind., Trend Mgmt., Inc., Tampa, Fla., Fairfield Advisors, Inc., Southport, EPW Securities, Inc., Southport; gen. ptnr. Grandland Realty Assos., Embankment Properties Ltd., London, Autumn Woods Assos., others; former allied mem. N.Y. Stock Exchange. Contbr. articles to fin. jours. Bd. dirs. Mus. Art, Sci., Industry, Bridgeport, Wakeman Meml. Boys'/Girls' Club, Southport, Greater Bridgeport Jr. Hockey League, Pequot Library, Southport, Bridgeport U., Northfield-Mt. Hermon Sch.; mem. dean's coun. John F. Kennedy Sch. of Govt. at Harvard U. Served AUS, 1959-60. Mem.: Pequot Yacht (Southport), Pequot Running (Southport) (chmn.); Country Club of Fairfield; Yale (N.Y.C.). Office: 2507 Post Rd Southport CT 06490-1259 Home: PO Box 669 Southport CT 06490-0669

WILBUR, FRANKLIN PIERCE, education educator; b. Middleboro, Mass., Nov. 2, 1947; s. Franklin Pierce and Lillian Taylor (Arthur) W.; m. Cheryl Lynn Boyer; children: Jeffrey Taylor, Timothy Blake. BS in Elem. Edn., Bridgewater (Mass.) State Coll, 1969; MS in Instructional Tech., Syracuse U., 1970, PhD, 1976. Assoc. instrn. tech. Ctr. Instructional Devel., Syracuse U., 1972-78, dir. Project Advance, 1978—, assoc. prof. Sch. Edn., 1976—, assoc. v.p. undergrad. studies, 1990; exec. dir. Ctr. Support Tchg. and Learning Syracuse U., 1997—. Rsch. fellow Am. Assn. Higher Edn.; cons. in field. Author: Linking America's Schools and Colleges, 1994, 2d edit., 1995; contbr. papers, revs., reports in field. Mem. Am. Assn. Higher Edn., European Coun. Insternat. Schs., Internat. Learning Coop, Am. Ednl. Rsch. Assn., Am. Coun. Edn., Assn. Ednl. Comm. and Tech., Profl. and Orgnl. Network in Higher Edn., Phi Delta Kappa. Office: 400 Ostrom Ave Syracuse NY 13210-3250

WILBUR, JANIS A, financial consultant, sales professional; b. Canadian, Tex., June 18, 1940; d. Harry Samuel Jr. and Margaret Hervey Wilbur; m. Martin Alfred Wasserman, Oct. 18, 1969 (div. Dec. 1981); 1 child, Paul Scott Wasserman. Student, U. Hawaii, 1958; BS in Commerce, Tex. Christian U., 1962. Cert. sr. advisor. Exec. asst. First Nat. Bank, Dallas, 1962-65, So. Union Gas, Dallas, 1965-69; adminstrv. sec. IBM, Armonk, N.Y., 1969-72; owner Leisure Sports Sys., Dallas, 1972-79; sec. to econometrics prof. So. Meth. U., 1989-95; part time sales assoc. Neiman Marcus, 1989—; registered rep., cert. sr. advisor Oxford Fin. Group, 2000—. Pub. (quarterly newsletter) The Fin. News RE-View, 1999. Vol. Am. Cancer Soc., Am. Diabetes Assn., Dallas Crippled Children Soc., Am. Heart Assn., Dallas Ct. Apptd. Spl. Advs.; mem. women's coun. Dallas Arboretum and Bot. Garden, 2000; organizer ann. golf tournament benefiting Parkinson Disease; vol. Buckner Orphans Home, 2000—01, Planned Giving Program Bd., 2002. Mem.: DAR (nat. com. chmn. on Americanism and manual for citizenship 1999, Literacy Challenge chmn. 2001—02, chaplain 2002—, Michael Stoner chpt.), NAFE, Internat. Exec. Guild, First Dallas Alumni Club (charter), Park Cities Bapt. Ch. Women's Bible Study, Water Skiing Club, Dallas Skiing Club, Kappa Alpha Theta Alumni (v.p. 1989—99, pres. 2000—01, advisor 2002—). Republican. Baptist. Avocations: tennis, bridge, snow skiing, cooking, water rafting, hiking. Home: 9563 Windy Knoll Dr Dallas TX 75243-7561 Office: Oxford Fin Group 9563 Windy Knoll Dallas TX 75243 E-mail: janiswilbur@sbcglobal.net.

WILBUR, LESLIE CLIFFORD, mechanical engineering educator; b. Johnston, R.I., May 12, 1924; s. Clifford Elwood and Isabel (Winsor) W.; m. Gertrude Monica Widmer, Sept. 9, 1950; children— Clifford Leslie, Kenneth Charles, Ted Winsor, Christopher Francis. BS in Mech. Engring, U. R.I., 1948; MS, Stevens Inst. Tech., 1949. Registered profl. engr., Mass. Instr., then asst. prof. Duke, 1949-57; mem. faculty Worcester Poly. Inst., 1957—, prof. mech. engring., 1961—, dir. nuclear reactor facility, 1959-86, prof. emeritus, 1987—. Mem. N.E. adv. council Atomic Indsl. Forum, 1972— Editor-in-chief: Handbook of Energy Systems. Served with AUS, 1943-46, ETO. Mem. Am. Nuclear Soc. (mem. at large exec. com. Northeastern sect. 1961-62, 66-67, chmn. Northeastern sect. 1968-69), ASME (vice chmn. Eastern N.C. sect. 1956-57), Am. Soc. Engring. Edn., AAAS, Sigma Xi, Tau Beta Pi, Phi Kappa Phi, Pi Tau Sigma. Baptist (deacon 1962-65). Home: 94 Parkway N Brewer ME 04412-1235 Office: Worcester Poly Inst Dept Mech Engring Ed Worcester MA 01609

WILBUR, RICHARD SLOAN, physician, executive; b. Boston, Apr. 8, 1924; s. Blake Colburn and Mary Caldwell (Sloan) Wilbur; m. Betty Lou Fannin, Jan. 20, 1951; children: Andrew, Peter, Thomas. BA, Stanford U., 1943, MD, 1946; JD, John Marshall, 1990. Intern San Francisco County Hosp., 1946—47; resident Stanford Hosp., 1949—51, U. Pa. Hosp., 1951—52; postgrad. tng. U. Mich. Hosp., 1957, Karolinska Sjukhuset, Stockholm, 1960; staff Palo Alto (Calif.) Med. Clinic, 1952—69; dep. exec. v.p. AMA, Chgo., 1969—71, 1973—74; asst. sec. for health and environment dept. def., 1971—73; sr. v.p. Baxter Labs., Inc., Deerfield, Ill., 1974—76; exec. v.p. Council Med. Splty. Socs., 1976—91, sec. accreditation coun. for continuing med. edn., 1979—91; assoc. prof. medicine Georgetown U. Med. Sch., 1971—77, Stanford Med. Sch., 1952—69; pres. Nat. Resident Matching Plan, 1991—92. Chmn. bd., CEO Inst. for Clin. Info., 1994—99; sr. v.p. healthcare Buckeye Corp. Pte, Ltd., Singapore, 1997—2000; CEO Medic Alert, 1992—94; pres. Am. Bd. Med. Mgmt., 1992; mem. Am. Bd. Electrodiagnostic Medicine, 1993—98; chmn. med. adv. bd. Med. City, Bangalore, India, 1997—2000; bd. vis. Drew U. Postgrad. Med. Sch. Contbr. articles to profl. jours. Bd. govs. ARC; chmn. Mid-Am. Blood Svcs. Bd., Lifesource Blood Bank, 1996—98; Vice-chmn. Rep. Cen. Com. Santa Clara County, Calif., 1966—89; bd. dirs. Nat. Adv. Cancer Coun., Nat. Health Coun., 1993—95; chmn. bd. dirs. Medic Alert Found.; chmn. bd. Calif. Med. Assn., 1968—69, Calif. Blue Shield, 1966—68, Am. Medico-Legal Found., 1987—; pres. Royal Soc. Medicine Found., 1998—. With USNR, 1942—49. Recipient Disting. Svc. medal, Dept. Def., 1973, Scroll of merit, Nat. Med. Assn., 1971. Fellow: ACP, Am. Coll. Physician Execs. (bd. regents 1985—89, pres.-elect 1987, pres. 1988—89), Am. Coll. Legal Medicine (bd. dirs.), Internat. Coll. Dentistry (hon.); mem.: Am. Soc. Internal Medicine, Am. Gastroent. Assn., Santa Clara County Med. Soc. (hon.), Lake County Med. Soc., Ill. Med. Assn., Inst. Medicine, Union League Phila., Cedars Club, Pacific Interurban Clin. Club, Alpha Omega Alpha, Phi Beta Kappa. Home: 985 Hawthorne Pl Lake Forest IL 60045-2217 Office: APT Management Inc 207 E Westminster Rd # 201 Lake Forest IL 60045-1881 E-mail: aptmgmnt@aol.com.

WILBUR, RICHARD PURDY, writer, educator; b. N.Y.C., Mar. 1, 1921; s. Lawrence L. and Helen (Purdy) W.; m. Mary Charlotte Hayes Ward, June 20, 1942; children: Ellen Dickinson, Christopher Hayes, Nathan Lord, Aaron Hammond. AB, Amherst Coll., 1942, AM, 1952, DLitt (hon.), 1967; AM, Harvard U., 1947; LHD (hon.), Lawrence Coll., Washington U., Williams Coll., U. Rochester, SUNY, Potsdam, 1986, Skidmore Coll., 1987, U. Lowell, 1990; DLitt (hon.), Clark U., Am. Internat. Coll., Marquette U., Wesleyan U., Carnegie-Mellon U.; DLitt. (hon.), Lake Forest Coll., 1982, Smith Coll., 1996, Sewanee U., 1996; DD (hon.), St. Mary's Sem. and U., 2001. Jr. fellow Harvard U., Cambridge, Mass., 1947-50, Asst. prof. English, 1950-54; assoc. prof. Wellesley Coll., 1955-57; prof. Wesleyan U., 1957-77; writer in residence Smith Coll., 1977-86. Author: The Beautiful Changes, 1947, Ceremony, 1950, A Bestiary, 1955, reprint, 1993, Things of This World, 1956, Poems 1943-56, 1957, Advice to a Prophet, 1961, Poems of Richard Wilbur, 1963, Walking to Sleep, 1969, The Mind-Reader, 1976, Seven Poems, 1981, The Whale, 1982, New and Collected Poems, 1988 (Pulitzer prize for poetry, 1989), Bone Key and Other Poems, 1998, Mayflies: New Poems and Translations, 2000, (children's books) Loudmouse, 1963, Opposites, 1973, More Opposites, 1991, A Game of Catch, 1994, Runaway Opposites, 1995, The Disappearing Alphabet, 1998, Opposites, More Opposites and Some Differences, 2000, The Pig in the Spigot, 2000, (criticism) Responses, 1976, expanded edit., 2000, (prose pieces) The Catbird's Song, 1997; co-author (with Lillian Hellman): (comic opera) Candide, 1957; co-author: (with William Schuman) (cantata) On Freedom's Ground, 1986; translator (Moliere): The Misanthrope, 1955, Tartuffe, 1963 (co-recipient Bollingen Translation prize , 1963), The School for Wives, 1971, The Learned Ladies, 1978, Four Comedies, 1982; translator: (Racine) Andromache, 1982, Phaedra, 1986, The Suitors, 2001; translator: Moliere's The School for Husbands, 1992, Imaginary Cuckold, 1993, Molière's Amphitryon, 1995, Don Juan, 1998, Molière's The Bungler, 2000; editor: Complete Poems of Poe, 1959, Poems of Shakespeare, 1966, Selected Poems of Witter Bynner, 1978. Decorated chevalier Ordre des Palmes Academiques; recipient Harriet Monroe prize Poetry mag., 1948, Oscar Blumenthal prize, 1950, Prix de Rome, Am. Acad. Arts and Letters, 1954, Edna St. Vincent Millay Meml. award, 1957, Nat. Book award, 1957, Pulitzer prize, 1957, Sarah Josepha Hale award, 1968, Bollingen prize, 1971, Brandeis U. Creative Arts award, 1971, Prix Henri Desfeuilles, 1971, Shelley Meml. award, 1973, Harriet Monroe Poetry award, 1978, St. Botolph's Club Found. award, 1983, Drama Desk award, 1983, Aiken-Taylor award, 1988, Bunn award, 1988, Washington Coll. Lit. award, 1988, St. Louis Lit. award, 1989, Grand Master award Birmingham-So. Coll., 1989, Gold Medal for Poetry, Am. Acad. Inst. Arts and Letters, 1991, Edward MacDowell medal, 1992, Nat. Arts Club Medal of Honor for Lit., 1994, PEN/Manheim Medal for Translation, 1994, Milton Ctr. prize, 1995, Acad. Am. Achievement award, 1995, Robert Frost medal Poetry Soc. of Am., 1996, T.S. Eliot award, 1996; Guggenheim fellow, 1952-53, 63, Ford fellow, 1960-61, Camargo Found. fellow, 1985; named U.S. Poet Laureate, Libr. Congress, 1987, Nat. Medal of the Arts, 1994. Fellow MLA (hon.); mem. AAAL (pres. 1974-76, chancellor 1976-78, 80-81), ASCAP, PEN (Transl. award 1983), Am. Acad. Arts and Scis., Acad. Am. Poets (chancellor emeritus), Dramatists Guild, Century Club. Home: 87 Dodwells Rd Cummington MA 01026-9705 also: 87 Dodwells Rd Cummington MA 01026-9705

WILBUR, STEPHEN, internist, oncologist, hematologist, pathologist; b. Cheyenne, Wyo., Dec. 6, 1954; MD, U. Kans., 1980. Diplomate Am. Bd. Internal Medicine, Am. Bd. Oncology, Am. Bd. Hematology, Am. Bd. Pathology, Am. Bd. Anatomic Pathology, Am. Bd. Clin. Pathology. Resident in internal medicine St. Francis Hosp., Wichita, Kans., 1980-81; resident in pathology U. Kans. Sch. Medicine, Kansas City, 1981-85, resident in internal medicine, 1985-87, fellow in hematol. oncology, 1987-89, 89-90; mem. staff Royal C. Johnson VA Hosp., Sioux Falls, S.D. Mem. Am. Soc. Clin. Oncology, Am. Soc. Hematology.

WILBURN, MARY NELSON, retired lawyer, translator, poet; b. Balt., Feb. 18, 1932; d. David Alfred and Phoebe Blanche (Novotny) Nelson; m. Adolph Yarbrough Wilburn, Mar. 5, 1957; children: Adolph II, Jason David. AB cum laude, Howard U., 1952; MA, U. Wis., 1955, JD, 1975; cert. in translation, Georgetown U., 1997. Bar: Wis. 1975, U.S. Supreme Ct. 1981. Commr. Nat. Coun. of Negro Women Commn. on Edn., 1986—2001; English lang. officer U.S Dept. of State, Washington, 1999—. Vol. One Ch. One Addict, 1995—, bd. dirs., 1997—; mem. bd. Office Employee Appeals, D.C., 1997—2001; vol. Black Revolutionary War Patriots' Found., 1998—; judge NAACP ACT-SO Competition, 1994—, Leadership Am., 1991—; mem. bd. edn. Cath. Archdiocese of Washington, 1995—2000. Mem. Internat. Fedn. Women Lawyers (exec. coun. 1996—), Am. Translators Assn., Links, Inc., Leadership Greater Washington (bd. dirs. 1992-94, v.p. 1995-96).

WILCHER, LARRY K. lawyer; b. Lebanon, Ky., July 19, 1950; s. Dwain LaRue and Juanita (Tungate) W.; m. Mary Jo Hayden, Aug. 21, 1971; children: Emily Jane, Joseph Keith. BS in Pharmacy, St. Louis Coll. Pharmacy, 1973; JD, No. Ky. U., 1984; program of instrn. for lawyers, Harvard U., 1987, 91,

94. Dir. real esate SuperX Drugs Corp., Cin., 1975-84; dir. real estate, real estate counsel Dollar Gen. Corp., Goodlettsville, Tenn., 1984-85, gen. counsel, 1985—2002; dir. U.S. Bank, 1995—; pres. Nations Title Co., Inc., 1999—2002; ptnr. Wyatt, Tarrant & Combs, 2002—. Contbr. to book: Kentucky Business Organizations, 1989. Sec., dir. Scottsville-Allen County Leasing Corp., 1992—, Scottsville-Allen County Indsl. Devel. Authority, Inc., 1991—; dir. Leadership Ky., 1994—2000, mem. exec. com., 1997—2000; dir. Bowling Green-Western Ky. U. Symphony Orch., 1998—2000; chmn. Warren County Young Reps, Bowling Green, Ky., 1979, Scottsville-Allen County Planning Commn., 1997—. Named to Hon. Order Ky. Cols., 1968, One of Outstanding Young Men of Am., U.S. Jaycees, 1978; recipient Johnson & Johnson award St. Louis Coll. Pharmacy, 1973, Thurston B. Morton Leadership award Ky. Young Rep. Fedn., 1979. Mem. ABA, Nat. Assn. Corp. Dirs., Ky. Bar Assn. (recognition award 1987), Tenn. Bar Assn., Def. Rsch. Inst. Republican. Baptist. Office: Wyatt Tarrant & Combs 918 State St Bowling Green KY 42101

WILCHINS, HOWARD MARTIN, lawyer; b. Paterson, N.J., Mar. 6, 1945; s. Philip Aaron and Esther (Blake) Wilchins; m. Margaret Mandon, Sept. 6, 1970 (dec. July 2001); children: Julie, Daniel. AB, Mich. State U., 1966; JD, U. Chgo., 1969. BAR: D.C. 1969, U.S. Supreme Ct. 1975. Trial atty. FPC, Washington, 1969-70; spl. asst. to N.Y. Public Service Commn., Albany, 1970-72; dep. sect. chief AEC, Washington, 1972-75; dep. gen. counsel-litigation U.S. Ry. Assn., 1975-81, gen. counsel, 1981-84; dep. chief enforcement div. FCC Common Carrier Bur., 1984-90; v.p. Arnold S. Tesh Advisors, 1990-92; sr. litigation atty. Office Nuclear Safety Enforcement, U.S. Dept. Energy, 1992—. Mem. faculty Trial Practice Inst., U.S. CSC, 1977-79 Bd. dirs. United Jewish Appeal Greater Washington, 1984-90, 92-96; bd. dirs. Charles E. Smith Jewish Day Sch., 1983—, v.p., 1986-88, pres., 1988-90; mem. Hillel of Greater Washington, 1990—, v.p., 1992-94, pres., 1994-96; bd. dirs., mem. Capital Camps, 1990-96; bd. dir. Jewish Edn. Svc. N.Am., 1996—, asst. treas., 2000—; bd. dirs. Tikvat Israel Congregation, Rockville, Md., 2000—. Mem. ABA, D.C. Bar Assn., Fed. Comm. Bar Assn. (co-chmn. com. on arbitration and mediation 1991-94), Am. Arbitration Assn. Home: 5 Feather Rock Pl Rockville MD 20850-3114 Office: US Dept Energy Office Nuclear Safety Enforc Washington DC 20585-0001 E-mail: howard.wilchins@hq.doe.gov.

WILCHINS, SIDNEY A. gynecologist; b. Paterson, N.J., Feb. 2, 1940; s. Philip Aaron and Esther (Blake) W.; m. Carole Diane Brill, June 23, 1963, (div. Mar. 1985); children: Joan Helen, Edward Victor; m. Estelle Angel, Mar. 15, 1985; children: Jacqueline, Susan. BA in Biol. Scis., Rutgers U., 1961; MD, Georgetown U., 1965. Diplomate Am. Bd. Ob Gyn. Clin. instr. N.J. Med. Sch., Newark, 1971-73, clin. asst. prof., 1973-78, clin. assoc. prof., 1978—; med. dir. Cryosurgical Systems, 1999—. Adj. rsch. prof. N.J. Inst. Tech., Newark, 1978—; assoc. dir. Pilgrim Med. Ctr., Montclair, N.J., 1982-93; med. dir. Ultrasound Diagnostic Sch., Union, N.J., 1989-91, N.J. Menopause Found., 1992-98; gynecol. cons. Organon/Akzo, 1991—; med. dir. Gynchoices of Cen. Jersey, 1994—; pres. Soc. of Forensic Obstetricians & Gynecologists, 1994-96; bd. dirs. N.Y. Met. MSO Physicians Network, 1996-99 Author, editor: Cryosurgery and Medicine, 1990; contbr. articles to profl. jours. Lt. USNR, 1965-69. Fellow ACOG, ACS, N.Y. Acad. Medicine; mem. Assn. Trial Lawyers Am., N.Y. Acad. Scis., Forensic Soc. Ob-Gyn. (pres. 1994-95), Peer Rev. Orgn. N.J., Colonia Country Club. Achievements include patent pending on Intraperitoneal Hyperthermia Device, pregnancy conducto for labor software copyright; application of chaost level to analysis of labor physiology. Home: 154 Devon Rd Colonia NJ 07067-3205 Office: Union County Ob-Gyn 236 E Westfield Ave Roselle Park NJ 07204-2084 E-mail: guynee@aol.com.

WILCOX, BENSON REID, cardiothoracic surgeon, educator; b. Charlotte, N.C., May 26, 1932; s. James Simpson and Louisa (Reid) W.; m. Lucinda Holderness, July 25, 1959; children: Adelaide, Alexandra, Melissa, Reid. BA, U. N.C., 1953, MD, 1957. Diplomate Am. Bd. Surgery, Am. Bd. Thoracic Surgery (chmn. 1991-93). Resident Barnes Hosp., St. Louis, 1958-59, N.C. Meml. Hosp., Chapel Hill, 1959-60, 62-64; clin. assoc. Nat. Heart Inst., Bethesda, Md., 1960-62; instr. U. N.C., Chapel Hill, 1963-65, asst. prof., 1965-68, assoc. prof., 1968-71, chief divsn. of cardiothoracic surgery, 1969-98, chief emeritus, 1998—, prof. of surgery, 1971—. Cons. NIH Grant Com., Bethesda, 1986—89; pres. Atlantic Coast Conf., Greensboro, NC, 1980—81; dir. Am. Bd. Thoracic Surgery, 1983—93, chmn., 1991—93; mem. coun. for grad. edn., 1993—; bd. dirs. Nat. Residency Matching Program, 1998—, pres., 2001—02, res. rev. com. for thoracic surgery, 1999—. Contbr. articles to profl. jours.; author (with others): Atlas of the Heart, 1988, Surgical Anatomy of the Heart, 1992. Recipient Samaritan's Purse award, 1999; Markle scholar John and Mary Markle Found., 1967; recipient Hadassah Myrtle Wreath award, 1979, Disting. Alumnus award Darlington Sch., Rome, Ga., 1997. Mem.: ACS (mem. adv. coun. cardiothoracic surgery 1992—, chmn. 1998—2002), Grad. Med. Edn. (coun. 1993—), Womack Soc. (pres. 1991—93), Thoracic Surgery Dirs. Assn. (pres. 1985—87), So. Surg. Assn., Soc. Univ. Surgeons, Soc. Thoracic Surgeons (treas. 1980—86, pres. 1994—95), Am. Surg. Assn., Am. Assn. Thoracic Surgery, CTS Net Corp. (bd. dirs. 1999—). Democrat. Presbyterian. Avocations: medical history, golf, hiking. Office: U NC Med Sch Div Cardiothoracic Surgery 108 Burnett-Womack CB 7065 Chapel Hill NC 27599-0001 E-mail: benson@med.unc.edu.

WILCOX, BRUCE GORDON, publisher; b. Boston, Sept. 3, 1947; s. Edward Teed and Maud (Eckert) W.; m. Greta Green, Apr. 7, 1974; children: Sarah M., Thor E., Hilary A. BA, Harvard U., 1969; postgrad., Peace Corps, Senegal, 1969-70. Asst. sales mgr. U. Wash. Press, Seattle, 1970-71, editor, 1975-82; program officer Franklin Book Programs, N.Y.C. and Dacca, Bangladesh, 1972-75; dir. U. Mass. Press, Amherst, 1983—. Cons. NEH, Washington, 1983, 85, NEA, Washington, 1991. Mem. editl. adv. bd. Jour. Scholarly Publ., 1992—. Bd. dirs. Mass. Rev., 1987—. Mem. Assn. Am. Univ. Presses (del. to USSR and Ea. Europe 1977, to China 1985, to Estonia and CSFR 1992, to Colombia, 1997, bd. dirs. 1990-96, pres. 1994-95). Home: 191 Lincoln Ave Amherst MA 01002-2009 E-mail: wilcox@umpress.umass.edu.

WILCOX, CHARLES JULIAN, geneticist, educator; b. Harrisburg, Pa., Mar. 28, 1930; s. Charles John and Gertrude May (Hill) W.; m. Eileen Louise Armstrong, Aug. 27, 1955; children: Marsha Lou, Douglas Edward. BS, U. Vt., 1950; MS, Rutgers U., 1955, PhD, 1959. Registered animal scientist. Dairy farm owner, operator, Charlotte, Vt., 1955-56; prof. U. Fla., Gainesville, 1959-95; prof. emeritus, 1995—. Cons. in internat. animal agrl. Gt. Britain, France, Sudan, Pakistan, Can., Mex., El Salvador, Ecuador, Brazil, Bolivia, Peru, Colombia, Venezuela, Dominican Republic, Saudi Arabia, Sweden, Norway, 1965. Mem. editl. bd.: Genetics and Molecular Biology, 1979—; editor: Large Dairy Herd Management, 1978, 1993; author (with others): Animal Agriculture, 1973, Animal Agriculture, 2d edit., 1980, Improvement of Milk Production in Tropics, 1990—. 1st Lt. U.S. Army, 1951—53, Korea. Decorated Combat Infantryman badge, 3 Korean Campaign medals, Korean War medal; recipient Disting. Svc. award, Fla. Purebred Dairy Cattle Assn., 1986, Jr. Faculty award, 1968, Internat. award for Disting. Svc. for Agr., Gamma Sigma Delta, 1987, Sr. Rsch. Scientist award, Sigma Xi, 1994, Sr. Faculty award, 1984. Mem.: Fla. Hostein Assn. (pres. 1979), Am. Registry Profls. Animal Sci. (examining bd. 1987—95), Am. Soc. Animal Sci., Am. Dairy Sci. Assn. (mem. editl. bd. 1999—), Fla. Gurensey Cattle Club. (pres. 1974—76), Fla. Jersey Cattle Club (bd. dir.). Republican. Avocations: spectator sports, baseball, football, basketball, tennis. Office: Univ Fla Animal Sci Dept Gainesville FL 32611-0920 E-mail: cjwgenetic@aol.com.

WILCOX, DAVID ERIC, electrical engineer, educational consultant; b. Cortland, N.Y., Sept. 4, 1939; s. James A. and Lucille (Fiske) C.; m. Phyllipa Ann Wilcox, Jan. 23, 1977; children: Terri L., Cinda A., Jana L. 0postgrad., Syracuse U., 1965; BSEE, U. Buffalo, 1961; 0postgrad., Marist Coll., Rutgers U.; MS, U. Bridgeport, 1977. Registered profl. engr., N.Y. Rsch. engring. mgr. input/output devices Rome (N.Y.) Air Devel. Ctr., 1966-70; dir. sales Mercom Inc., Winsooki, Vt., 1970-73, dir., 1972-98; ores, Wilcox Tng. Sys., Newburgh, N.Y., 1973—. Exec. dep. dir., Nat. Skill Stds. Bd.; prin. Exec. Effectiveness, Inc., N.Y.C.; instr. Dale Carnegie courses. Author: Information System Sciences, 1965; contbr. articles to profl. jours.; patentee in field. Pres. N.Y. State Jaycees, 1972-73, chmn., 1973-74; dir. U.S. Jaycees, 1970-71; bd. dirs., v.p. N.Y. State Spl. Olympics, 1972-73; bd. dirs., treas. Family Counseling Svc., Inc.; mem. Orange County Pvt. Industry Coun., N.Y. State Excelsior Examiner, 1995. Lt. USAF, 1961-65. Mem. IEEE, Soc. Info. Display, N.Y. State Soc. Profl. Engrs., Internat. Transactional Analysis Assn., Internat. Platform Assn., Am. Soc. Quality Control. Methodist. Home: 528 Tobacco Quay Alexandria VA 22314 also: 30 W 60th St New York NY 10023-7902 Address: 528 Tobacco Quay Alexandria VA 22314-2042

WILCOX, DIANE MARIE, educational psychologist, software designer; b. Cin., June 26, 1957; d. Herbert Arthur and Doris Ann Beard; m. Thomas Minshull Wilcox, Sept. 18, 1982; children: Alexandra Frances, Annika Marie. BBA in Bus. Mgmt., Coll. William and Mary, 1979; MA in Ednl. Psychology, U. N.C., 1994, PhD in Ednl. Psychology, 1997. Sales and tech. support corr. Tax Mgmt., Inc., Washington, 1980-82; dist. rep. Bur. Nat. Affairs, Inc., 1982-86; freelance computer graphic designer, editor Diane Wilcox & Assocs., San Rafael, Calif., 1986-91; instr. psychology King's Coll., Charlotte, N.C., 1995; pres. Mindforge, Inc., Burlington, 1996-98, Wilcox Instrnl. Media, LLC, Hillsborough, 1998—; instnl. design mgr. Autodesk, Inc., San Rafael, 2000—. Designer ednl. CD-ROM Mindforge Fractons, 1998. Cons. for gifted and talented programs River Mill Charter Sch., Saxapahaw, N.C., 1999-2000; vol. art instr. Grady Brown ELem. Sch., Hillsborough, N.C., 1997-98. Mem. APA, Am. Ednl. Rsch. Assn., Internat. Soc. for Performance Improvement. Avocations: art, music, dance. E-mail: drwilcox@wilcoxmedia.com.

WILCOX, DONALD ALAN, lawyer; b. Grantsburg, Wis., July 18, 1951; s. John Charles and Lois Margaret (Finch) W.; m. Rachel Ann Johnson, Dec. 28, 1973; children: Benjamin Ray, Joseph Charles (dec.), Sara Johanna. BS, USAF Acad., 1973; JD, Georgetown U., 1979. Bar: Minn. 1979. Commd. 2d lt. USAF, 1973, advanced through grades to capt., resigned, 1979; assoc Holmquist & Holmquist, Benson, Minn., 1979-81; ptnr. Holmquist & Wilcox, 1981-90; shareholder Wilcox, Erhardt & Spates, P.A., Benson, 1990-91; pvt. practice, 1991—. Gen. counsel Swift County-Benson Hosp., 1981—. Farmers Mut. Coop., Bellingham, Minn., 1986—, Agralite Coop., Benson, 1986—, Kandiyohi Electric Coop., 1995—; atty. City of Benson, 1985—; examiner of titles, Swift County, Benson, 1986—, Federated Tel. Coop., Chokio, Minn., 1988—; bd. dirs. State Bank Danvers. Mem. Benson Planning Commn., 1979—; pres. Our Redeemer's Luth. Ch., Benson, 1985-86, 93-94; pres., bd. dirs. Swift County Homes, Inc., Benson, 1984-92. Recipient Lawyers Coop. Pub. award Lawyers Coop. Pub. Co., 1979. Mem. Minn. Bar Assn., Twelfth Dist. Bar Assn. (pres. 1995-96), Benson C. of C. (bd. dirs. 1981-84), Kiwanis (treas. Benson 1982-84, pres. 1999-00). Avocations: reading, golf, skiing. Home: 604 13th St S Benson MN 56215-2017 Office: 1150 Wisconsin Ave Benson MN 56215-1841 E-mail: dwilcox@willmar.com.

WILCOX, GREGORY B. lawyer; b. Des Moines, Sept. 22, 1954; s. Lawrence R. and Mary T. Wilcox; m. Melinda S. Vande Lune, Sept. 4, 1976; children: Andrew, Austin, Morgan. BBA, U. Iowa, 1976; JD, Drake U., 1982. Bar: Iowa, 1982. V.p. Wilcox Enterprises, Inc., West Des Moines, Iowa, 1976-79; atty. Nyemaster Law Firm, Des Moines, 1982—, shareholder, dir., 1987—. Mem. bd. couns. Drake U. Law Sch., 1990-96, chair admissions com., 1992-93, exec. com., 1992-93. Assoc. articles editor Drake Law Sch., 1981-82; contbr. articles to profl. jours. Dir. Iowa State Chpt. March Dimes, Des Moines, 1993—; dir., sec. Iowa Sports Found., Des Moines, 1996—. Mem. ABA, Iowa State Bar Assn. (chair forms com. 1988-91, chair profl. corp. com. 1993-95), Polk County Bar Assn., Order of the Coif. Office: Nyemaster Law Firm 700 Walnut St Ste 1600 Des Moines IA 50309-3899

WILCOX, HARRY HAMMOND, retired medical educator; b. Canton, Ohio, May 31, 1918; s. Harry Hammond and Hattie Estelle (Richner) W.; m. D. June Freed., June 21, 1941; children: Joyce L. Wilcox Graff, Margaret J. (Mrs. Grayson S. Smith), James Hammond. BS, U. Mich., 1939, MS, 1940, PhD, 1948. Asso. prof. biology Morningside Coll., Sioux City, Iowa, 1947-48; asso. in anatomy U. Pa., 1948-52; mem. faculty U. Tenn. Center for Health Scis., 1952-83, Goodman prof. anatomy, 1966-83, emeritus prof. anatomy, 1983—. Assoc. editor: Anat. Record, 1968-83. Served with AUS, 1945-46. Mem.: AAAS, Soc. for Integrative and Comparative Biology, Am.Assn. Anatomists, Sigma Xi. Home: 1031 Marcia Rd Memphis TN 38117-5513

WILCOX, HARRY WILBUR, JR. retired corporate executive; b. Phila., Feb. 13, 1925; s. Harry Wilbur and Justine Elizabeth (Doolittle) W.; m. Colleen Ann Cerra, Apr. 6, 1946; children: Justine, Harry Wilbur III. BS, Yale U., 1949. With Gen. Electric Co., N.Y.C., 1949-50; mfg. supt. Sylvania Electric Products, 1951-67; v.p., gen. mgr. Granger Assocs. (electronics), Palo Alto, Calif., 1967-70; gen. mgr. ITT-Cannon Electric Co., Phoenix, 1970-72; pres. Hills McCanna Co., Carpentersville, Ill., 1972-75, VSI, and group v.p. IU Internat. Corp., 1975-78; exec. v.p. ITT-Grinnell, 1978-85; pres. ITT Indsl. and Constrn. Divsn., Lancaster, Pa., 1985-88. Dir. Meyer Industries, Nat. Temperature Control Centers, Paul N. Howard Co.; former chmn. VSI, VSI-UK. Patentee in electroluminescence. Mem. adv. com. Town of Sherborn, Mass. Served with U.S. Army, 1943-46. Decorated Bronze star. Mem. Yale Club of Treasure Coast, Grand Harbor Golf and Beach Club (Vero Beach). Home: 31 Sea Breeze Ln Bristol RI 02809-1520 also: 31 Sea Breeze Ln Bristol RI 02809-1520 E-mail: hwwilcoxjr@aol.com.

WILCOX, HARVEY JOHN, lawyer; b. Elyria, Ohio, Nov. 1, 1937; s. Hubbard Clyde and Sylvia (Wahter) W.; m. Leslie Louise Coleman, Apr. 11, 1970. BA cum laude, Amherst Coll., 1959; LLB, Yale U., 1962. Bar: Ohio 1962, Va. 1994. Mem. firm Wilcox & Wilcox, 1962-78; with office gen. counsel Dept. Navy, Washington, 1966-94, asst. to gen. counsel, 1969-72, counsel Naval Air Systems Command, 1972-76, Navy dep. gen. counsel, 1976-94, cons. atty., arbitrator, 1994—. Guest lectr. U.S. Army Logistics Mgmt. Center; mem. Navy Contract Adjustment Bd., 1968-72 Designed Arlington County (Va.) flag, 1983. Bd. dirs. Navy Fed. Credit Union, 1974-77, sec.-treas., 1974-75, 2d v.p., 1975-77; mem. Def. Adv. Panel on Streamlining Acquisition Laws, 1991-92. Lt. USNR, 1963-66. Recipient Meritorious Exec. rank 1980, Disting Exec. rank, 1981, 89, Navy Disting. Civilian Svc. award, 1989, Defense Disting. Civilian Svc. award, 1994. Mem. Ohio Bar Assn., Va. State Bar, Charlottesville-Albemarle Bar Assn., Nat. Trust Hist. Preservation, Nature Conservancy, Piedmont Environ. Coun. Home: PO Box 338 Turner Mountain Rd Ivy VA 22945-0338

WILCOX, JAMES PETER, language educator, writer; b. Hammond, La., Apr. 4, 1949; s. James Henry and Marie Agnes W. BA, Yale U., 1971. Editl. asst., asst. editor, assoc. editor Random House, N.Y.C., 1971-77; freelance writer, 1978-98; spkr. writing resource Radcliffe Pub. Course, Cambridge, Mass., 1989-2000; vis. prof. English dept. Miss. State U., 1998-2001; asst. prof. dept. English La. State U., 2001—. Assoc. editor Doubleday & Co., N.Y.C., 1977-78; writer in residence Writers Cmty., N.Y.C., 1991; faculty MFA program for writers Warren Wilson Coll., 1992; adj. tchr. Rutgers U., Camden, N.J., 1996. Author: (novel) Modern Baptists, 1983, North Gladiola, 1985, Miss Undine's Living Room, 1987, Sort of Rich, 1989, Polite Sex, 1991, Guest of a Sinner, 1993, Plain and Normal, 1998. Guggenheim fellow, 1986. Avocations: piano.

WILCOX, JOHN CAVEN, lawyer, corporate consultant; b. N.Y.C., Nov. 12, 1942; s. Daniel A. and Jessie Alexandra (Caven) W.; m. Vanessa Guerrini-Maraldi, Sept. 30, 1983; children Daniel D.G., William G.M., Julia G.M. BA magna cum laude, Harvard U., 1964; MA, U. Calif., Berkeley, 1965; JD, Harvard U., 1968; LLM, NYU, 1981. Bar: N.Y. 1973. Account exec. Georgeson & Co. Inc., N.Y.C., 1973-79, mng. dir., 1979-90, chmn., 1990; trustee Family Dynamics, Inc., 1979-96, Georgeson Shareholder Comm., Inc., 1999—. Dir. ACTV, Inc., GSC Proxitalia S.p.A.; chair cross-border voting practices com. Internat. Corp. Governance Network. Trustee Woodrow Wilson Nat. Fellowship Found., 1996, vice chmn., 1996—; trustee Bennington Coll., 1998—. With U.S. Army, 1968-70, Vietnam. Woodrow Wilson fellow. Mem. ABA, NYSE (mem. shareholders comm. com. 1989-95), Am. Soc. Corp. Secs., Nat. Assn. Security Dealers (mem. issuer affairs com 1990—), Downtown Assn., Harvard Club (N.Y.C.), Phi Beta Kappa. Democrat. Home: 580 West End Ave New York NY 10024-1723 E-mail: jwilcox@georgeson.com.

WILCOX, JOHN GREGOR, military analyst; b. Atchison, Kans., June 15, 1940; s. Robert Elbart and Ruth Wilcox; m. Darlene Illena MedBerry; children: Leslie Estrella, Paul. BS, U.S. Mil. Acad., West Point, N.Y., 1962; MA in Polit. Sci., U. Colo., 1971. Sr. systems analyst SRI Internat., Arlington, Va., 1984—97, mgr. engring. ops. for Washington, 1997—. Dir. The Mil. Conflict Inst., Springfield, Va., 2000—. Author: (anthology) Spirit, Blood, and Treasure: The American Cost of Battle in the 21st Century, 2001. Lt. col. U.S. Army, 1962—84. Recipient Bronze Star Medal, 1969. Fellow: Armed Forces and Soc. Home: 8335 Terra Grande Ave Springfield VA 22153 Office: SRI International 1611 N Kent St Arlington VA 22209 Office Fax: 703-537-3087. Business E-Mail: wilcox@wdc.sri.com.

WILCOX, JON P. state supreme court justice; b. Berlin, Sept. 5, 1936; m. Jane Ann; children: Jeffrey, Jennifer. AB in Polit. Sci., Ripon Coll., 1958; JD, U. Wis., 1965. Pvt. practice Steele, Smyth, Klos and Flynn, LaCrosse, Wis., 1965-66, Hacker and Wilcox, Wautoma, 1966-69, Wilcox, Rudolph, Kubasta & Rathjen, Wautoma, 1969-79; elected judge Waushara County Cir. Ct., 1979-92; apptd. justice Wis. Supreme Ct., 1992-97, elected justice 10-yr. term, 1997. Commr. Family Ct., Waushara County, 1977-79; Wis. state legislator, 1969-75; del. Wis. Conservation Congress, 1975-80; vice chmn., chmn. Wis. Sentencing Commn., 1984-92; chief judge 6th Jud. Dist., 1985-92; mem. State-Fed. Jud. Coun., 1992-99, Jud. Coun. Wis., 1993-98; mem. Prison Overcrowding Task Force, 1988-90; mem. numerous coms. Wis. Judiciary; mem. faculty Wis. Jud. Coll., 1986-97; chmn. Wis. Chief Judges Com., 1990-92; co-chair comm. on judiciary as co-equal br. of govt. Wis. State Bar, 1995-97; lectr. in field. Contbr. (with others): Wisconsin News Reporters Legal Handbook: Wisconsin Courts and Court Procedures, 1987. Bd. visitors U. Wis. Law Sch., 1970—76; with Wis. State Legis., 1969—75; del. wis. Conservation Congress, 1975—80. Lt. U.S. Army, 1959—61. Named Outstanding Jaycee Wautoma, 1974; recipient Disting. Alumni award Ripon Coll., 1993. Fellow Am. Bar Found.; mem. ABA (com. on continuing appellate edn.), Wis. Bar Assn. (bench bar com.), Wis. Law Found. (bd. dirs.), Tri-County Bar Assn., Dane County Bar Assn., Trout Unltd., Ruffed Grouse Soc., Ducks Unltd., Rotary, Phi Alpha Delta. Office: Supreme Court State Capitol PO Box 1688 Madison WI 53701-1688

WILCOX, LAIRD MAURICE, researcher, writer, carpenter; b. San Francisco, Nov. 28, 1942; s. Laird and AuDeene Helen (Stromer) Wilcox; m. Eileen Maddocks, 1962 (div. 1967); children: Laird Anthony IV, Elizabeth Leone; m. Diana Brown, 1978; 1 child Carrie Lynn. Student, Washburn U., 1961—62, U. Kans., 1963—65. Cert. storm spotter, lic. radio operator. With Fluor Corp., Ltd., 1960—62; editor Kans. Free Press, 1963—66; owner, operator Maury Wilcox Constrn. Co., Kansas City, Mo., 1967—70; carpenter foreman various employers, 1974—87; semi-profl. genealogist, 1975—78; chief investigator Editl. Rsch. Svc., Kansas City, Mo., 1977—. Assoc. faculty Baker U., 1986—; lectr. various fields. Author: Guide to the American Left, 1970, 1991, Guide to the American Right, 1970, 1991, Psychological Uses of Genealogy, 1976, Directory of the Occult and Paranormal, 1981, Nazis, Communists, Klansmen, and Others on the Fringe, 1992; editor: Wilcox Report, 1979—, Civil Liberties Rev., 1986—, Master Bibliography on Terrorism, Assassination, Espionage and Propaganda, 1988, What is Political Extremism?, 1989, Be Reasonable: Selected Quotations for Inquiring Minds, 1993, Crying Wolf, 1994, The Watchdogs, 1997, The Writer's Rights, 2002. Spl. dep. sheriff Shawnee County, Kans., 1966; dep. sheriff Wyandotte County, 1971—75; founder Wilcox Collection on Contemporary Polit. Movements, U. Kans. Librs.; benefactor Kans. U. Friends of Libr. Recipient award, Kansas City Archivists Assn., 1989, Meyer Ctr. Human Rights award, 1993, Intellectual Freedom award, Kans. Libr. Assn., 1994. Fellow: Acad. Police Sci., Augustan Soc.; mem.: Internat. Legion of Intelligence, Am. Radio Relay League, Nat. Assn. Investigative Specialists, Internat. Brotherhood of Carpenters and Joiners of Am. (officer 1975—82, condr. carpenter's local 61 1971—82), Bertrand Russell Soc., St. Andrew Soc., Nat. Soc. Old Plymouth Colony Descs., Mil. Order Loyal Legion of U.S., Soc. Mayflower Descs., SAR, Free Press Assn., Nat. Coalition Against Censorship, Amnesty Internat., ACLUL, Mensa, NRA. Home and Office: PO Box 2047 Olathe KS 66051-2047

WILCOX, LANCE ELLIOTT, English literature educator; b. Phila., Nov. 9, 1953; s. Lawrence F. and Madeline Eichholz Wilcox; m. Linda Celeste Roberts, Aug. 1, 1981; children: Nathan, David. BA in Psychology, U. Tex., Austin, 1974; MA in Psychology, U. Minn., 1979, PhD in English, 1989. Asst. prof. English Elmhurst (Ill.) Coll., 1989-95, assoc. prof. English, 1996-2000, prof. English, 2000—. Co-author: Writing in Context, 1988, A Field Guide to Writing, 1992; author (full-length plays): Dostoyevsky's Gamble, 1996, Saving Nineveh, 1992. Mem.: Am. Soc. 18th Century Studies (v.p. Midwestern sect. 2002). Democrat. Mem. Soc. Of Friends. Avocations: reading, theater, canoeing, travel, history. Office: Elmhurst Coll Box 66 190 Prospect Elmhurst IL 60126-3296 E-mail: lancew@elmhurst.edu., lancewilcox@earthlink.net.

WILCOX, MARK DEAN, lawyer; b. May 25, 1952; s. Fabian Joseph and Zeryle Lucille (Tase) W.; m. Catherine J. Wertjes, Mar. 12, 1983; children: Glenna Lynn, Joanna Tessie, Andrew Fabian Joseph. BBA, U. Notre Dame, 1973; JD, Northwestern U., 1976; CLU, Am. Coll., 1979, ChFC, 1992. Bar: Ill. 1976, U.S. Dist. Ct. (no. dist.) Ill. 1976, Trial Bar 1982, U.S. Ct. Appeals (7th cir.) 1987, U.S. Supreme Ct. 1989. Staff asst. Nat. Dist. Attys. Assn., Chgo., 1974-75; trial asst. Cook County States Atty., 1975; intern U.S. Atty. No. Dist. Ill., 1975-76; assoc. Lord, Bissell & Brook, 1976-85, ptnr., 1986—. Bd. mgrs. YMCA Met. Chgo., Internat. Spl. Olympics; trustee Trinity United Meth. Ch., No Bats Baseball Club. Mem. ABA (tort and ins. practice sect.), Am. Soc. CLU and ChFC, Chgo. Bar Assn. (ins. law com.), Nat. Assn. Ins. and Fin. Advisors, Def. Rsch. Inst., Soc. Fin. Svc. Profls., Trial Lawyers Club Chgo., Notre Dame Nat. Monogram Club, Union League Club, Chgo. Lions Rugby Football Club, Beta Gamma Sigma. Office: Lord Bissell & Brook 115 S La Salle St Chicago IL 60603-3902

WILCOX, MARTHA ANNE, lawyer; b. Miami, Fla., Jan. 13, 1948; m. Ralph Ogden, Jan. 31, 1981; children: Helen, Chris. BA in Philosophy, Speech summa cum laude, Ind.-Purdue U., 1976; JD, Ind. U., 1976. Bar: Ind. 1976, Colo. 1984, U.S. Dist. Ct. (so. dist.) Ind. 1976, U.S. Dist. Ct. (no. dist.) Ind. 1980, U.S. Dist. Ct. Colo. 1984, U.S. Ct. Appeals (7th cir.) 1976, U.S. Ct. Appeals (10th cir.) 1983, U.S. Supreme Ct. 1984. Pub. defender Marion County Criminal Ct., 1977-74; adj. prof. appellate advocacy, practice Ind. U., 1976-77; pvt. practice Indpls., 1977-78; spl. judge civil and criminal divs. Marion County Superior Ct., 1975-80, appellate pub. defender, 1982-83; ptnr. Wilcox, Ogden & DuMond, Indpls., 1979-83, Wilcox & Ogden, Denver, 1983—. Editor-in-Chief Genesis Lit. and Philos. Jour. Mem. of com. on character and fitness Ind. Supreme Ct., 1982-84; pres., vice pres. Student Govt.; mem., capt., coach varsity debate team; student rep. to Faculty Senate and Univ. Budget Com.; state chmn. Older Hoosiers Law Day, 1979; founding mem., mem. bd. dirs. Network of Women in Bus., Inc., 1976-81; speakers bur. Ind. U., 1976-84, search, screen com. for dean of the Sch. of Liberal Arts, 1982; bd. dirs. YWCA of Met., Indpls.; team mem. on brief, oral argument Nat. Moot Ct., bd. dirs, coach. Recipient Disting. Alumni award Ind.-Purdue U., 1981. Fellow Ind. Bar Found. (charter mem. 1980); mem. ABA (faculty mem. ann. conf. on atty. discipline 1982), Assn. Trial Lawyers Am., Ind. State Bar Assn. (litigation sect., co-chmn. of Nat. Moot Ct. Com. 1978, judge 1980), Am. Arbitration Assn. (panel mem. 1981—), Colo. Bar Assn., Denver Bar Assn., Indpls. Bar Assn. (legal ethics com. 1979-84), Alpha Tau Alpha, Sigma Tau Delta. Office: Wilcox & Ogden PC 1750 Gilpin St Denver CO 80218-1206 E-mail: wilcox1750@aol.com.

WILCOX, MARY MARKS, Christian education consultant, educator; b. Madison, Wis., Apr. 23, 1921; d. Roy and Mary Celia (Leary) Marks; m. Ray Everett Wilcox, Nov. 28, 1942; children: Peter, Anne, Susan, Steven. BA, U. Wis., 1942; MRE, Iliff Sch. Theology, Denver, 1968. Cert. Christian educator. Cons. local chs., Lakewood, Littleton, Wheat Ridge, Colo., 1963-74; instr., leader numerous seminars throughout U.S. and Can., 1963—; interim parish cons. 1st Presbyn. Ch., Lakewood, 1988-90, profl. assoc. for faith devel. Colo., 1993-97; adj. prof. Iliff Sch. Theology, 1970—. Author: Developmental Journey, 1979; co-author: Viewpoints, 1998; contbr. articles to various publs., chpts. to books. Trustee, mem. exec. bd. Nat. Ghost Ranch Found., Abiquiu, N. Mex., 1983-93. Recipient award Iliff Alumni Assn., 1989. Mem.: Moral Edn. Assn., Assn. Presbyn. Christian Educators (past mem. exec. bd.), Religious Edn. Assn. Democrat. Presbyterian. Home: 3590 Estes St Wheat Ridge CO 80033-5933 E-mail: marywilcox@aol.com.

WILCOX, MAUD, editor; b. N.Y.C., Feb. 14, 1923; d. Thor Fredrik and Gerda (Ysberg) Eckert; m. Edward T. Wilcox, Feb. 9, 1944; children: Thor (dec.), Bruce, Eric, Karen. AB summa cum laude, Smith Coll., 1944; A.M., Harvard U., 1945. Teaching fellow Harvard U., 1945-46, 48-51; instr. English

Smith Coll., Northampton, Mass., 1947-48, Wellesley Coll., 1951-52; exec. editor Harvard U. Press, 1958-66, humanities editor, 1966-73, editor-in-chief, 1973—89; freelance editorial cons. Cambridge, 1989—; ret. Cons., panelist NEH, Washington, 1974-76, 82-84; cons. Radcliffe Pub. Course, 1991. Mem. MLA (com. scholarly edits. 1982-86), Assn. Am. Univ. Presses (chair com. admissions and standards 1976-77, v.p. 1978-79, chair program com. 1981-82), Phi Beta Kappa. Democrat. Episcopalian. Home and Office: 63 Francis Ave Cambridge MA 02138-1911

WILCOX, MICHAEL JOHN, vision systems researcher, medical educator; b. Detroit, Mar. 20, 1948; s. Fred Edwin and LaVergne Elizabeth (Anderson) W.; m. Claudie Nicole Zamet, June 26, 1980; children: Christopher, Marc. BS, Purdue U., 1971, MS, 1976, PhD, 1980. Teaching asst. Purdue U., West Lafayette, Ind., 1972-74, rsch. assoc., 1974-80; postdoctoral fellow Fogarty Internat. Ctr., Bethesda, Md., 1980-82; chercheur associé Centre Nat. de la Recherche Scientifique, Marseille, France, 1982-83; chercheur boursié Fondation de la Recherche Medicale, Paris, 1983-84, Delduca Found., Marseille, 1984-85; asst. prof. U. P.R., Mayaguez, 1984-86, U. So. Calif., L.A., 1987-89; staff scientist Doheny Eye Inst., 1986-89. Rsch. asst. prof. U. N.Mex., Albuquerque, 1989-96, assoc. prof., 1996—; cons. Allergan Pharms., Irvine, Calif., 1986-89, Kirtland AFB, Albuquerque, 1990—; co-founder Interdisciplinary Computational Sys. Group, Albuquerque, 1993-95; pres. Hyperacuity Sys.; dir. Sensory Systems Rsch. AFB Acad., Colorado Springs, Colo., adj. prof. biology, 1997 Author chpts. and articles. Leader Boy Scouts Am., Albuquerque, 1989-92. NIH grantee, 1985-90; Office of Naval Rsch. grantee, 1989—. Mem. AAAS, IEEE, Assn. for Rsch. in Vision and Ophthalmology, N.Y. Acad. Scis., Am. Soc. for Cell Biology, Internat. Neural Network Soc. Avocations: model building, sports, weight lifting, hiking, motorcycles. Home: 6555 Delmonico Dr Apt 212 Colorado Springs CO 80919-4014

WILCOX, RICHARD HOAG, information scientist; b. Wooster, Ohio, Sept. 23, 1927; s. Raymond Bourman and Hazel (Hoag) W.; m. Jean Balderston, May 13, 1950; children: Linda, Kathryn. BSEE, Lafayette Coll., Easton, Pa., 1951, Elec. Engr., 1955; M in Engring. Adminstrn., George Washington U., Washington, 1964. Enlisted USN, 1945-47; commd. ensign USNR, 1951, advanced through grades to comdr., 1969, ret., 1979; electronic scientist, ops. rsch. analyst U.S. Naval Rsch. Lab., Washington, 1951-58; ops. rsch. analyst, electronic engr. Office Naval Rsch., 1958-62, head info. systems br., acting dir. math. scis. divsn., 1962-68; dep. head resource evaluation divsn. Exec. Office of Pres., Office Emergency Preparedness, 1968-69, head info. systems divsn., 1969-74; from chief mil. affairs divsn. to sr. scientist U.S. Arms Control and Disarmament Agy., 1974-93; cons. Info. Systems Mgmt. Sci., Ft. Washington, Md., 1993—. Commr., dir. Commn. on Profls. in Sci. and Tech., Washington, 1967-92; asst. dir. computers and comm. Fed. Emergency Mgmt. Agy., Washington, 1981; vis. scholar Ctr. for Strategic and Internat. Studies, Georgetown U., Washington, 1983-84; diplomatic courier, 1990. Co-editor: Redundancy Techniques for Computing Systems, 1962, Computer and Information Sciences, 1964, Research Program Effectiveness, 1965; contbr. articles to profl. jours, chpts. to books; subject of nationally distributed documentary video about prostate cancer, 1998. Bd. dirs. Broad Creek Citizens Assn., 1997—; pres. Riverview Cmty. Assn., 1998—; mem. regional adv. coun. Kaiser Permanente, 1999—. Recipient Superior Civilian Svc. award Office Naval Rsch., 1966, Citation Pres. U.S., 1973, Superior Honor award U.S. Arms Control and Disarmament Agy., 1993. Mem. AAAS, Herrington Harbour Sailing Assn., Master Chorale of Washington (formerly Paul Hill Chorale), Sigma Xi, Tau Beta Pi. Achievements include patent for microwave multiplier device; devising info.-theoretic measure of randomness of human performance; mgmt. devel. and operation of first operational computer conferencing system; creation a variety of novel info. systems. Home: 1218 W Riverview Rd Fort Washington MD 20744-5837 *The only decision available to us is what we are actually going to do in the circumstances presented to us in life. Not deciding actively or simply reacting to others, is a decision by default. Evaluating life's circumstances honestly requires a sense of humor, and acting so as to be at peace with our memories provides a good guide.*

WILCOX, ROBERT KALLEEN, journalist; b. Indpls., July 21, 1943; s. Jacob Guire and Agnes Louise (Kalleen) W.; m. Begoña de Amezola, June 1, 1970; children: Robert, Amaya Begoña. BS in Journalism, U. Fla., 1966. Reporter, editor Miami (Fla.) News, 1967-72; freelance author, 1972—. Author: The Mysterious Deaths at Ann Arbor, 1977, Shroud, 1977, Fatal Glimpse, 1981, Japan's Secret War, 1985, 2d edit., 1995, Scream of Eagles: The True Story of Top Gun, 1990, paperback edit., 1991, Wings of Fury, 1997, paperback edit., 1998, Black Aces High, 2002; (film, TV) Simon and Simon, 1985, God's Order, 1986, Frank's Place, 1987, Legend, 1994; writer TV pilots; staff story editor Famous Teddy Z, 1988-89, The New WKRP in Cin., 1990-93; sr. editor eStar, 1999—; contbr. to numerous mags. With USAF, 1967-72. Recipient William Randolph Hearst award Gainesville Sun, 1967, Cine Golden Eagle award, 1981, 82, Gold medal Venice Internat. Film Festival, 1982, Supple Meml. award Religious Newswriters Assn., 1970. Mem. Author's Guild, Writer's Guild Am. West. Avocations: history, sports. E-mail: robkwilcox@aol.com.

WILCOX, ROBERTA MOAT, music educator; b. Santa Monica, Oct. 20, 1933; d. John Edlington and Ethel Dorothy (Bautz) M.; m. Omer Divers, June 1, 1964; 1 child, Timothy Divers; m. David Henry Smith Wilcox, Dec. 16, 1973. BA in Music, UCLA, 1959; MA in Music Edn., Calif. State U., Los Angeles, 1963. Cert. in secondary music edn., Calif. Freelance violinist Dunes Hotel, Las Vegas, 1963-66; violinist Pasadena (Calif.) Symphony Orch., 1963-73; music tchr. Eldorado Sch. for Gifted, Orange, Calif., 1970-79; strolling violinist The Strolling Two, Pasadena, 1970—; pvt. violin, viola tchr., 1958—; violin, viola tchr. Pasadena City Coll., 1972-77; music tchr. Pasadena Unified Schs., 1986—. Founder, mgr. Pasadena Summer Youth Chamber Orch., Pasadena, 1986—; dir. Music to Go chamber music, 1989; mgr. Pasadena Young Musicians Orch., 1994—. Mem. Music Educators Nat. Conf., So. Calif. Sch. Band and Orch. Assn., The Tuesday Musicale (pres. 1980-82, Gold Crown award for Art in Edn. 1995), Mu Phi Epsilon. Republican. Christian Sci. Avocations: collecting antiques, musical instruments, statues and stuffed animals. Home: 734 N Wilson Ave Pasadena CA 91104-4652

WILCOX, RONALD BRUCE, biochemistry educator, researcher; b. Seattle, Sept. 23, 1934; s. Howard Bruce and Edna Jane (McKeown) W.; m. Susan Lenore Folkenberg, May 15, 1937; children: Deanna Marie, Lisa Suzanne. BS, Pacific Union Coll., 1957; PhD, U. Utah, 1962. Research fellow Harvard Med. Sch., Boston, 1962-65; asst. prof. Loma Linda U., Calif., 1965-70, assoc. prof., 1970-73, prof., 1973—, chmn. dept. biochemistry, 1973-83. Mem. gen. plan rev. com. City of Loma Linda, 1981-92; bd. dirs. East Valley United Way, 1990-97. Fellow Danforth Found., St. Louis, 1957; fellow Bank Am. Giannini Found. San Francisco, 1965 Mem. Am. Thyroid Assn., Endocrine Soc. Democrat. Seventh-day Adventist. Home: 25516 Lomas Verdes St Loma Linda CA 92354-2417 Office: Loma Linda U Dept Biochemistry Loma Linda CA 92350-0001 E-mail: bwilcox@som.llu.edu.

WILCOX, SHIRLEY JEAN LANGDON, genealogist; b. Arcata, Calif., Dec. 10, 1942; d. Elmore Harold and Alberta May (Starkey) Langdon; m. Wayne Kent Wilcox, June 22, 1963; 1 child, Harold Bonner. BS, U. Md., 1964. Cert. Bd. for Certification of Genealogists. Tchr. Prince George's County (Md.) Sch. System, 1964-67, substitute tchr., 1968-73; profl. genealogist Lanham, Md., Arlington, Va., 1973—; genealogy tchr. Fairfax County Pub. Schs., 1995-99. Level II coord. Mid-Atlantic Genealogy and History Inst., George Mason U., Fairfax, Va., 1986; trustee bd. for Certification of Genealogists, 2000—. Editor: A Bibliography of Published Genealogical Source Records, Prince George's County, Maryland, 1975, Prince George's County Land Records, Vol. A, 1696-1702, 1976, 1850 Census Prince George's County, Maryland, 1978, 1828 Tax List Prince George's County, Maryland, 1985. Elder Presbyn. Ch., 1970-73, 95-98. Fellow Nat. Geneal. Soc. (chmn. conf. program subcom. 1990, 2d v.p. 1990-94, councilor 1994-96, pres. 1996-2000); mem. DAR (libr. Belle Air chpt. 1985—, Outstanding Jr. Mem. award 1979), Assn. Profl. Genealogists (pres. 1991-93, pres. Nat. Capital area chpt. 1994-96, Grahame Thomas Smallwood Jr. award of merit 1995), Va. Geneal. Soc. (gov. 2001—), Prince George's County Geneal. Soc. (pres. 1973, 75-76, book rev. editor 1976-96, Jane Roush McCafferty award of excellence 1985), Fairfax Geneal. Soc. (pres. 1986-89), Soc. Mayflower Descs. in D.C., Paperweight Collectors Assn. (pres. Md.-D.C.-Va. chpt. 1988-90), numerous others. Avocation: collecting paperweights. Home: 1500 23rd St S Arlington VA 22202-1523

WILCOX, STEVEN A. public relations executive; b. Belvidere, Ill., July 18, 1957; s. Walter William and Lois Jeanette (Hulke) W.; 1 child, Connor David. AA, McHenry C.C., Crystal Lake, Ill., 1980; BA, Ea. Ill. U., 1981; MA, No. Ill. U., 1983. Pub. rels. assoc. Haworth, Inc., Holland, Mich., 1984-87; pub. rels. mgr. Coachmen Industries, Elkhart, Ind., 1987-88, Furnas Electric Co., Batavia, Ill., 1988-94; account supr. Golin-Harris Com., Chgo., 1994-96; account dir. Ogilvy Pub. Rels., 1996-2000; mng. dir. Hill and Knowlton, 2000—; pub. rels. dir. Brady Mktg. Group, Menomonee Falls, Wis. Sgt. USAF, 1975-79. Mem. Internat. Assn. Bus. Communicators (accredited mem., job referral network dir. 1993-94). Avocations: bicycling, basketball. Office: Brady Mktg Group N80 W 12878 Fond du Lac Ave Menomonee Falls WI 53051

WILCOX, VICTORIA LYNN, nurse; b. Circleville, Ohio, Mar. 27, 1955; d. Kenneth L. and Patricia Lou (Miller) Tomlinson; m. James M. Wilcox, Mar. 11, 1988; 1 child, Amanda. Diploma, Holzer Sch. Nursing, 1976. RN; cert. oncology. Staff nurse Holzer Medical Ctr., Gallipolis, Ohio, 1976-82, IV therapist, 1982-87; oncology nurse Holzer Clinic, 1987—. Active Simpson Chapel United Meth. Ch., Rio Grande, Ohio. Mem. Oncology Nursing Soc., DAR, Ohio Eastern Star. Home: 2598 White Oak Rd Bidwell OH 45614-9681 Office: Holzer Clinic 90 Jackson Pike Gallipolis OH 45631-1543

WILCOX, WINTON WILFRED, JR. communications specialist, consultant; b. Independence, Mo., Aug. 24, 1945; s. Winton Wilfred Wilcox and LaPreal (Adams) Craig; children: Steven Michael, Jake Anders. BS, U. Nev., 1973. Nat. product dir. Am. Photography Corp., N.Y.C., 1974-77; gen. mgr. Golden Valley (Minn.) Coffee, 1977-80; div. mgr. Cable Data, Sacramento, 1981-84; v.p., chief fin. officer Cultch Enterprises, Inc., 1980-86; v.p. mktg. div. Parallex, Winston-Salem, N.C., 1985-88; owner IK & Cons., Sacramento, 1990-94; pres. Broadcast Comm. Sys. Inc., New Glarus, Wis., 1995-96; owner ComTrain, Monroe, 1996—. Instr. Heald Bus. Coll., 1990-94, Blackhawk Tech. Coll., 1996—. Author: How to Create Computer Entertainment, 1985, Tower Climbing Safety & Rescue, 1997, Basic Tower Technology, 1999; contbg. author: Apple Fun & Games, 1986. Mem. Nate, Nat. Safety Coun. Entelec. With USAF, 1966-70. Mem. Cable TV Adminstrn. and Mktg. (pay view com. Washington chpt. 1985-87, SE chpt. formation com. Tampa, Fla. chpt. 1986-87). Republican. Avocations: skiing, model railroads. Office: 1511 13th Ave Monroe WI 53566-2422 E-mail: comtrain@comtrainusa.com. *Personal philosophy: The main goal of any job is to keep learning and applying that knowledge.*

WILCOXEN, JOAN HEEREN, fitness company executive; b. Flushing, N.Y., May 30, 1948; d. Paul Arnold and Helena Catherina (Laskowski) Heeren; m. Eddie Dean Wilcoxen, Dec. 31, 1981. BA, Long Island U., 1971; grad., Radford U. Karate Coll., 1994. Cert. referee AAU. Real estate broker Heeren Agy., Riverhead, N.Y., 1970-72; 2d v.p. Levitt House, Inc., Medford, 1972-78; radio broadcaster Sta. KWHW Radio, Altus, Okla., 1979-84; exec. dir. Ironworks Family Gym and Heartland Health Club, 1984-94, Wilcoxen's Acad. of the Martial Arts, Altus, 1994—. Lectr. martial arts; lectr. Shortgrass Arts and Humanities Coun., Altus, 1988—. Vol. United Way of Jackson County, Altus, 1989—, project co-chair, 1994; fundraiser Muscular Dystrophy Assn., Wichita Falls, Tex., 1987—; mem. Shortgrass Arts and Humanities Coun., 1988-93, Nat. Bd. Realtors, 1978-79; state coord., co-chair Sooner State Games Karate, Oklahoma City, 1989-93; bd. dirs. Am. Heart Assn. 1993-95; mem. Altus 2000 edn. task force. Named for civic leadership Okla. State U. Coop. Extension Svc., Altus, 1988, S.W. Bell Tel. Co., Altus, 1989, Rotary Club and March of Dimes, Altus, 1989, Jackson County Free Fair, Altus, 1988, 89; Okla. State AAU karate champion, 1990, black belt, Nat. AAU women's karate (sparring) champion, 1995. Mem. AAUW (v.p. Altus chpt. 1990, pres. 1992-93), Altus C. of C. (amb. 1989-90), Am. Bus. Women's Assn., Biz Tips Women's Assn. (v.p. 1989-90, pres. 1991-92), Am. Heart Assn. (bd. dirs. Altus chpt. 1994, pres. Jackson County divsn. 1996), Altus C. of C., Air Force Assn. Cmty. Ptnrs., Am. Ind. Karate Instrs. Assn. (instr. Christiansburg, Va. chpt. 1986—). Avocations: multimedia art, horseback riding, hiking, gardening. Home: 1112 N Main St Altus OK 73521-3122 Office: Wilcoxen's Acad Martial Art Altus Plz Shopping Ctr 1100 N Main St # C5B Altus OK 73521-3122 E-mail: wilcoxens@blackbeltclub.com.

WILCOXSON, ROY DELL, plant pathology educator and researcher; b. Columbia, Utah, Jan. 12, 1926; m. Iva Wall, 1949; children: Bonnie, Paul, Karren, John. BS, Utah State U., 1953; MS, U. Minn., 1955, PhD in Plant Pathlogy, 1957. Asst. prof., 1957-66; prof. plant pathology U. Minn., St. Paul, 1966-91, prof. emeritus, 1991—. Spl. staff mem. Rockefeller Found.; vis. prof. Indian Agrl. Rsch. Inst., New Delhi; dir. Morocco project U. Minn., 1983-87; adj. prof. Inst. Agronomy and Vet. Medicine, Hassan II, Rabat, Morocco, 1985—. Fellow Am. Phytopath Soc., Indian NAS, Indian Phytopath Soc., AAAS. Achievements include research in diseases of forage crops and cereal crops; cereal rust diseases. Office: 1669 County Road 8230 West Plains MO 65775-5766 Address: Dept Plant Path U Minn Saint Paul MN 55101

WILCUTT, TERENCE W. astronaut; b. Russellville, Ky., Oct. 31, 1949; BA in Math., Western Ky. U., 1974; grad. with distinction, U.S. Naval Test Pilot Sch., 1986. Math. tchr., 1974—76; commd. 2d lt. USMC, 1976, advanced through grades to col.; with VMFAT-101, VMFA-235, Kaneohe, Hawaii; F/A-18 fighter weapons and air combat maneuvering instr. VFA-125, Lemoore, Calif.; test pilot/project officer Strike Aircraft Test Directorate, Naval Aircraft Test Ctr., Patuxent River, Md.; astronaut NASA, Houston, 1990—, mem. astronaut support personnel team Kennedy Space Ctr., with Astronaut Office Ops. Devel. Br., dir. ops. Yuri Gagarin Cosmonaut Tng. Ctr., Star City, Russia, chief Astronaut Office Shuttle Ops. Br. Decorated DFC, Navy Commendation medal. Mem.: Soc. Exptl. Test Pilots. Achievements include logged over 4,400 flight hours in over 30 different aircraft; logged over 1,007 hours in space; pilot STS-68 (1994), STS-79 (1996); mission comdr. STS-89 (1998), STS-106 (2000). Avocations: flying, running, weightlifting, woodworking. Office: Astronaut Office/CB NASA Johnson Space Ctr Houston TX 77058*

WILCZYNSKI, JANUSZ S. packaging technology executive, retired physicist; b. Warsaw, Poland, May 12, 1929; came to U.S., 1962; m. Brahna Lauger. Diploma in Indsl. Mechanics, Mining Acad., Cracow, Poland, 1954; MSc in Physics, Jagellonian U., Cracow, Poland, 1957; PhD in Physics and Optics, Imperial Coll. U. London, 1961. Physicist Watson, Ltd., London, 1961-62; research staff mem. T.J. Watson Research Ctr., IBM, Yorktown Heights, N.Y., 1962-63, mgr. tech. optics, 1963-83, 2d level mgr., 1983-84, sr. mgr., 1984-86, dir., 1986-93; gen. ptnr. Wilc Instruments LLP, 1995. Contbr. over 60 articles to profl. jours. Recipient 13 Invention awards, 1966-98, 7 Outstanding Innovation awards IBM, 1968-91; IBM fellow, 1981. Fellow Optical Soc. Am. (Richardson medal 1988); mem. NAE. Avocation: astron. optics. Home: 11 Rue du Soleil Sandia Park NM 87047-9337 Fax: 505-286-8273. E-mail: wilczyn@swcp.com.

WILD, DIRK JONATHAN, accountant; b. Metairie, La., Sept. 15, 1967; s. Karcher Charles Jr. and Betty Ann (Crowley) W.; m. Kathryn Leigh Gates, Aug. 10, 1991. BS in Acctg., La. Tech. U., 1989; M Profl. Acctg., U. Tex., 1990. CPA, La. Experienced mgr. Arthur Andersen, New Orleans, 1990—. Mem. AICPA. Office: Arthur Andersen 201 Saint Charles Ave Ste 4500 New Orleans LA 70170-4500

WILD, JAMES ROBERT, biochemistry and genetics educator; b. Sedalia, Mo., Nov. 24, 1945; s. Robert Lee and Frances Elleta (Wheeler) W.; m. Ann Lynn Brenner, Aug. 1, 1973; 1 child, Kalli Ann. BA in Zoology, U. Calif., Davis, 1967; PhD in Cell Biology, U. Calif., Riverside, 1971, post doctoral fellow, 1972. From asst. to assoc. prof. genetics and biochemistry Tex. A&M U., Coll. Sta., Tex., 1975-84, prof., chair genetics faculty, 1984-87, prof. biochemistry & genetics, 1984—2000, head biochemistry and biophysics dept., 1986-90; exec. assoc. dean Coll. Agriculture & Life Scs., Tex. A&M U., 1987-92, prof., head dept. biochemistry and biophysics, 1994-2000. Fellow faculty Tex. Agrl. Experiment Sta., 1999. With USN, 1972-75. Recipient So. Regional award for excellence in coll. anduniv. tchg. in food and agrl. scis., Higher Edn. program USDA, 1992. Fellow AAAS. Methodist. Office: Tex A&M U 2128 Biochemistry Bldg Rm 332 College Station TX 77843-2128 E-mail: j-wild@tamu.edu.

WILD, JOHN JULIAN, surgeon, director medical research institute; b. Sydenham, Kent, Eng., Aug. 11, 1914; came to U.S., 1946; s. Ovid Frederick and Ellen Louise (Cuttance) W.; m. Nancy Wallace, Nov. 14, 1949 (div. 1966); children: John O., Douglas J.; m. Valerie Claudia Grosenick, Aug. 9, 1968; 1 child, Ellen Louise. BA, U. Cambridge, Eng., 1936, MA, 1940, MD, 1942, PhD, 1971. Intern, resident U. Coll. Hosp., London, 1938-42; intern U. College Hosp., 1938-42; staff surgeon Miller Gen., St. Charles and North Middlesex Hosps., 1942-44; venereologist Royal Army Med. Corps, 1944-45; rsch. fellow, instr. depts. surgery and elec. engring., prin. investigator U. Minn., Mpls., 1946-51; dir. rsch. Medico.-Technol. Rsch. Dept. St. Barnabas Hosp., 1953-60; dir. Medico-Technol. Rsch. Unit Minn. Found., St. Paul, 1960-63; pvt. practice Mpls., 1966—; dir. Medico-Technol. Rsch. Inst. Mpls., St. Louis Park, Minn., 1965—. Lectr. in field of medical instruments, ultrasound. Contbr. articles to profl. jours. Recipient Japan prize in Medical Imaging, Sci. and Tech. Found. Japan, 1991, 1st Frank Annunzio award Christopher Columbus Fellowship Found., 1998, lifetime achievement award U. Minn. Med. Sch., 2000, Ian Donald Tech. Achievement aard ISUOG, 2000. Fellow Am. Inst. Ultrasound in Medicine (Pioneer award 1978); mem. AMA, World Fedn. Ultrasound in Medicine and Biology, Minn. State Med. Assn., Hennepin County Med. Soc., N.Am. Alvis Owners Club; hon. mem. Brit. Inst. Radiology, Japan Soc. of Ultrasound in Medicine. Achievements include patents in field; origination of ultrasonic medical imaging instruments and diagnostic techniques; origination of the field of pulse-echo ultrasonic diagnostic medicine. Avocations: automobile restoration, antique collecting and restoration. Home and Office: Medico-Technol Rsch Inst 4262 Alabama Ave S Minneapolis MN 55416-3105

WILD, NELSON HOPKINS, lawyer; b. Milw., July 16, 1933; s. Henry Goetseels and Virginia Douglas (Weller) W.; m. Joan Ruth Miles, Apr. 12, 1969; children: Mark, Eric. AB, Princeton U., 1955; LL.B., U. Wis., 1961. Bar: Wis. 1962, Calif. 1967; cert. specialist in probate, estate planning and trust law State Bar of Calif. Research assoc. Wis. Legis. Council, Madison, 1955-56; assoc. Whyte, Hirschboeck, Minahan, Harding & Harland, Milw., 1961-67, Thelen, Marin, Johnson & Bridges, San Francisco, 1967-70; sole practice law, 1970—. Mem. State Bar Calif. Client Trust Fund Commn., 1983, mem. exec. com. conf. dels., 1985-88. Contbr. articles to legal jours. Bd. dirs. Neighborhood Legal Assistance Found., San Francisco, 1974-85, chmn. bd., 1978-81. Served with USAF, 1956-58. Mem. ABA, Calif. Bar Assn., San Francisco Bar Assn., Am. Bar Found., Lawyers of San Francisco Club (gov. 1975, treas. 1981, v.p. 1982, pres.-elect 1983, pres. 1984), Calif. Tennis Club (bd. dirs. 1995-97, pres. 1997). Office: 332 Pine St Ste 710 San Francisco CA 94104-3230

WILD, RICHARD P. lawyer; b. N.Y.C., Aug. 13, 1947; s. Alfred P. and Harriet C. (Hoffman) W.; m. Deirdre L. Felbin, June 15, 1969; children: Nicholas B., Daniel M. AB, Columbia U., 1968; JD, Yale U., 1971. Bar: Pa. 1971, U.S. Dist. Ct. (ea. dist.) Pa. 1971, U.S. Tax Ct. 1973, U.S. Claims Ct. 1977. Assoc. Dechert Price & Rhoads, Phila., 1971-78, ptnr., 1978—. Mem. Phila. Bar Assn. (tax sect.). Office: Dechert Price & Rhoads 4000 Bell Atlantic Tower 1717 Arch St Philadelphia PA 19103-2793

WILD, ROBERT ANTHONY, university president; b. Chgo., Mar. 30, 1940; s. John Hopkins and Mary Dorothy (Colnon) W. BA in Latin, Loyola U. Chgo., 1962, MA in Classical Lang., 1967; STL, Jesuit Sch. Theology, Chgo., 1970; PhD in Study of Religion, Harvard U., 1977. Joined S.J., Roman Cath. Ch., 1957, ordained priest, 1970. From asst. to assoc. prof. Marquette U., Milw., 1975-83; vis. prof. Pont. Istituto Biblico, Rome, 1983-84; dir. Jesuit philosophate program Loyola U. Chgo., 1984-85, assoc. prof. theology, 1985-92; provincial superior Chgo. Province S.J., Chgo., 1985-91; pres. Weston Jesuit Sch. Theology, Cambridge, Mass., 1992-96, Marquette U., Milw., 1996—. Trustee Jesuit Sch. Theology, Berkeley, Calif., 1985-90, Weston Sch. Theology, Cambridge, Mass., 1985-96, Marquette U., 1990—, St. Louis U., 1994-2002, Wis. Assn. Ind. Colls. and Univs., 1996-, chmn., 2001-; trustee Milw. Rsch. Park, 2002-. Author: Water in the Cultic Worship of Isis and Sarapis, 1981; co-editor: Sentences of Sextus, 1981; contbr. articles to profl. jours. Mem. Soc. Bibl. Lit., Cath. Bibl. Soc., Wis. Assn. Ind. Colls. and Univs. (chmn. 2001-). Office: Marquette Univ O'Hara Hall PO Box 1881 Milwaukee WI 53201-1881

WILD, ROBERT LEE, physics educator; b. Sedalia, Mo., Oct. 9, 1921; s. Alwin Bernard and Nellie Marie (Nowlin) W.; m. Frances Elleta Wheeler, Oct. 7, 1943; children: James Robert, Janet Gayle, Margaret Nell. BS, Central Mo. State U., 1943; MA, U. Mo., 1948, PhD, 1950. Asst. prof. physics U. N.D., Grand Forks, 1950-52; prof. U. Calif., Riverside, 1953-88, prof. emeritus, 1988. Fulbright lectr. U. Philippines, 1981-82; mem. adv. com. Calif. Sci. Project, 1988—. Contbr. articles profl. jours. Served with AUS, 1943-45. NSF fellow, 1959-60; recipient Disting. Teaching award U. Calif., Riverside, 1973, Faculty of the Yr. award U. Calif.-Riverside Alumni, 1993. Pub. Svc. award Citizens U. Com., 1994; named most honored Alumni Smith Cotton H.S. Hall of Fame class of 1939. Mem. Am. Phys. Soc., Am. Assn. Physics Tchrs. (v.p. sect. 1983-84, pres. So. Calif. sect. 1985-86, pres., 1986-87, award 1966), Sigma Xi. Baptist. Home: Riverside, Calif. Died Feb. 6, 2001.

WILD, STEPHEN KENT, securities broker, dealer; b. Omaha, Nov. 18, 1948; s. Roger Charles and Marguerite Mae W.; m. Cheryl Katherine Sparano, June 5, 1971; children: Deric Justine, Drew Ian. Student, Ottawa U., 1967-68, U. Nebr., Omaha, 1968-71. Internal auditor Kirkpatrick, Pettis, Smith and Polian, Omaha, 1971-75; fin. planner First Fin. Planning Group, 1975-80; mng. gen. agt. E.F. Hutton Life Ins. Co., 1980-81; chmn. bd. Fin. Dynamics, 1981-98, Securities Am., Inc., 1984—. Bd. dirs. Am. Express Fin. Advisors, 1998; chmn. bd. Quantum Alliance, 1998—. Trustee U. Nebr. Found.; bd. dirs. Child Saving Inst., U. Nebr., Omaha, Neb. Children & Families Found.; mem. hockey orgnl. com.; councillor Knights of Ak-Sar-Ben Found. Recipient Outstanding Alumni award U. Nebr. at Omaha, 1994, Omaha Family of Yr. award Family Svcs., 1998. Mem. Internat. Assn. Fin. Planners, Securities Industry Assn. (ind. firms com.). Baptist. Home: 14025 Lafayette Cir Omaha NE 68154-5118 Office: One Valmont Plz 4th Fl Omaha NE 68154-5203

WILD, VICTOR ALLYN, lawyer, educator; b. Logansport, Ind., May 7, 1946; s. Clifford Otto and Mary E. (Helvey) W.; 1 child, Rachel. BS in Pub. Adminstrn., U.Ariz., 1968, JD, 1974. Bar: Ariz. 1975, U.S. Dist. Ct. Ariz. 1975, Mass. 1984, U.S. Dist. Ct. Mass. 1984, U.S. Ct. Appeals (1st cir.) 1985, U.S. Ct. Appeals (9th cir.). Chief escrow officer Lawyers Title Co., Denver, 1971-72, escrow officer Tucson, 1970-71; law clk. Pima County Atty., 1973-75, dep. county atty., 1975-81, chief criminal dep., 1981-84; asst. U.S. Atty. Dist. of Mass., Boston, 1984—. Civef gen. crimes unit U.S. Atty.'s Office, Boston, 1986-89; seminar instr. Mass. Continuing Legal Edn., Internat. Assn. Law Enforcement Investment Analysts, Dept. of Justice Office Internat. Affairs, Dept. of Labor, FBI, U.S. Postal Svc., Internat. Assn. Fin. Crims Investigators, Secret Svc., State Bar Ariz., Tucson and Phoenix, 1981-84; instr. U. Ariz., Tucson, 1981-84, Pima C.C., Tucson, 1981-84. Mem. editl. bd. Episcopal Times, Diocese of Mass., 1988—. Mem. vestry St. Michael's Episc. Ch., Marblehead, Mass., 1986-90, lay Eucharistic min., 1988—, parish warden, 1992-96; mem. Boston Ctr. for Internat. Visitors, 1989—; bd. dirs. Crime Resistors, Inc., Tucson, 1983, CODAC, Tucson, 1983, 88-Crime, Inc., Tucson, 1983, Marblehead Seaport Trust, 1987-89, Old ahd Historic Oversight Com., 1999-2000; chmn. Marblehead Capital Planning Commn., 1989—; bd. dirs. Marblehead Citizen Scholarship Found., 1997—, Marblehead Sch. Master Plan. Com., 2000—; mem. PhD rev. com. Law Policy and Soc. Northeastern U., 1997-00; bd. dirs. Davenport House Child Enrichment Ctr., Marblehead, 1986-89. With USAF, 1968-70. Recipient Commendation awards Dept. Labor, Dept. State, USCG, USIA, U.S. Postal Svc., Dept. Treasury, EOUSA Rev., Software Pub. Assn., Mass. Ins. Fraud Bur.; named Prosecutor of Yr., Office Insp. Gen., U.S. Dept. Labor, 1986, DOJ Spec. Achievement Award, 1993, 95, 96. Master Boston Inn of Ct.; mem. Ariz. Bar Assn., Mass. Bar Assn., Tau Kappa Epsilon, Delta Sigma Pi, Phi Kappa Delta. Office: US Attys Office Ste 9200 US Courthouse One Courthouse Way Boston MA 02210

WILDASIN, DAVID E(ARL), economics educator; b. Willimantic, Conn., Dec. 2, 1950; m. Kathleen Ann Preslin, Aug. 10, 1973. BA in Econs., U. Va., 1972; PhD Econs., U. Iowa, 1976. Asst. prof. U. Ill., Chgo., 1976-79, Ind. U., Bloomington, 1979-82, assoc. prof., 1982-86, prof. econs., 1986-93, prof. West European studies, 1993; prof. econs. Vanderbilt U., Nashville, 1993—2000; endowed prof. pub. fin. Martin Sch. Pub. Policy and Adminstrn., prof. econs. U. Ky., Lexington, 2000—. Cons. World Bank, 1992—, long-term cons. policy rsch. dept. pub. econs. divsn., 1995-96; vis. assoc. prof. Queen's U., Kingston, Ont., Can., 1982-83; vis. prof. U. Cath. Louvain, Louvain-la-Neuve, Belgium, 1986-87, Sch. of Higher Studies in Social Scis., Marseille, France, 1995; summer fellow U. Bonn, Germany, 1990; vis. scholar Interuniv. Ctr. for Econ. Studies, Gadjah Mada U., Indonesia, 1990, Ctr. for Econ. Studies U. Munich, 1991, U. B.C., Can., 1992; lectr. Helsinki (Finland) U., 1993, Norwegian Sch. Econs. and Bus. Adminstrn., 1994; lectr. summer sch. European Econ. Assn., San Domenico di Fiesole, Italy, 1995; econ. policy rsch. unit Copenhagen Bus. Sch., 1996; lectr. Nordic doctoral program in econs. Uppsala U., 1997; cons. Dept. Fin., Can., 1990, Midwest U., Consortium for Internat. Activities, 1990. Author: Urban Public Finance, 1986; co-author: Public Sector Economics, 1984; editor Fiscal Aspects of Evolving Federations, 1997; assoc. editor Regional Sci. and Urban Econs., 1987—, Jour. Regional Sci., 1989—, Jour. Urban Econs., 1991—, Internat. Tax and Pub. Fin., 1993—. Rev. Internat. Econs., 1994-, Nat. Tax Jour., 1998-, Jour. Pub. Econ. Theory, 1999-, Jour. Pub. Econs., 1999-, Papers and Rsch. Sci., 1999-2001, German Econ. Rev., 2000-, Finanzarchiv, 2000—; referee profl. jours.; contbr. over 80 articles to Am. Econ. Rev., Econ. Jour., others. Ameritech fellow Ind. U., 1988-89; Rsch. fellow Ctr. for Ops. Rsch. and Econometrics U. Cath. de Louvain, Belgium, 1986-87, U. Bonn, Germany, 1990, U. Munich, 1999, Inst. for Study of Labor, U. Bonn, Germany, 2000-; grantee NSF, 1978-81. Mem. Am. Econ. Assn., Econometric Soc., European Econ. Assn., Nat. Tax Assn., Tax Inst. Am., Regional Sci. Assn. Office: U Ky Martin Sch Pub Policy Lexington KY 40506-0027

WILDAUER, ANITA JEAN, company executive; b. St. Louis, May 24, 1955; d. Harry and Dorthy Jo Wildauer. BA in Speech Pathology, Fontbonne Coll., 1977, MS in Speech Pathology, 1979. Corp. cons. Irwin Lehroff & Assocs., L.A., Rehab. Care Corp., St. Louis; v.p. profl. svcs. Advanced Rehab. Resources Inc.-STL, Charlotte, NC; asst. adminstr., v.p. Charlotte (N.C.) Inst. Rehab.; corp. rehab. dir. Integrated Health Care, Charlotte; v.p. profl. svcs., dir. mktg. Transitional Care Inc. Mem. Commn. on Accreditation Nat. Surveys, Tucson.

WILDE, ALAN CONRAD, mathematician; b. Balt., Mar. 30, 1946; s. Walter Samuel and Mary Katherine (Koehler) W. BS, U. Mich., 1970, MA in Math., 1973. Ind. study tchr. Extension Svc. U. Mich., 1972-87; pvt. practice Ann Arbor, Mich., 1992—. Contbr. articles to profl. jours. including Am. Math. Monthly, Jour. of Undergrad. Math., Notre Dame Jour. of Formal Logic, Procs. of the Am. Math. Soc. Co-chair com. Aid Disabled Students, U. Mich., 1972-73, chair disabled student svcs. program policy bd., 1973; mem. Homeless Action Com., Ann Arbor, 1990-97. Mem. AAAS, Am. Chem. Soc. (affiliate), N.Y. Acad. Sci. Home: 601 Pearl Ypsilanti MI 48197-2616 Office: U Mich Dept Math Ann Arbor MI 48109

WILDE, CARLTON D. lawyer, director; b. Houston, Apr. 11, 1935; s. Henry Dayton and Louise (Key) W.; m. Martha Cloyes, July 26, 1958; children: Carlton D. Jr., Jennifer. Student, Coll. of William and Mary, 1953-55; BA, U. Tex., 1957, JD, 1959. Assoc. Bracewell & Patterson, Houston, 1959-62, ptnr., 1962-67, 85—, mng. ptnr., 1967-85. Trustee Presbyn. Sch. Fellow Am. Bar Found., Tex. Bar Found., Houston Bar Found.; mem. ABA, State Bar Tex., River Oaks Country Club, Coronado Club (Houston), Biltmore Forest Country Club (Asheville, N.C.). Republican. Home: 3105 Reba Dr Houston TX 77019-6209 Office: Bracewell & Patterson 2900 S Tower Pennzoil Pl 711 Louisiana St Ste 2900 Houston TX 77002-2781 E-mail: cwilde@bracepatt.com.

WILDE, DANIEL UNDERWOOD, computer engineering educator; b. Wilmington, Ohio, Dec. 27, 1937; s. Arthur John and Ruby Dale (Underwood) W. BSEE, U. Ill., 1960; MS, M.I.T., 1962, PhD, 1966. Research instr. medicine Boston U. Med. Sch., 1964-66; asst. prof. info. adminstrn. U. Conn., 1966-69, assoc. prof., 1970-75, prof., 1976-85; assoc. dir. New Eng. Rsch. Application Ctr., Storrs, Conn., 1966-72, dir., 1973-85, NASA Indsl. Application Ctr., 1972-91; pres. NERAC, Inc., Tolland, Conn., 1985-99. Cons. NERAC Inc., 1999—; trustee Engring. Index, Inc.; cons. Am. Soc. Metals, 1973-76; bd. dirs. Internat. Coun. Sci. Info. Author: Introduction to Computing: Problem Solving, Algorithms and Data Structures, 1973; contbr. articles to profl. jours. Served with USAF. Recipient NASA Public Service award, 1975 Fellow Nat. Fedn. Abstracting and Indexing Svcs. (hon.), Internat. Coun. Sci. Info.; mem. IEEE, Am. Soc. Info. Sci., Assn. Computing Machinery, Assn. Info. and Dissemination Centers (sec.-treas. 1976-79, pres. 1979-81). Home: 45 B East Battery Charleston SC 29401

WILDE, EDWIN FREDERICK, retired mathematics educator; b. Lombard, Ill., Jan. 14, 1931; s. Edwin Frederick and Carrie Belle (Hammond) W.; m. Connie Mae Rawlings, Aug. 23, 1952; children— Brad Alan, Bruce Ramon, Elizabeth Lynn. BS, Ill. State U., 1952, MS, 1953; MA, U. Ill., 1955, PhD, 1959; postgrad., U. Wis., part time, 1955-58, Stanford U., 1964-65. With Beloit (Wis.) Coll., 1955-76, prof. math., dean faculty, 1969-71, v.p. for planning, 1971-75; dean Roger Williams Coll., Bristol, R.I., 1976-80; provost, dean of faculty U. Tampa, Fla., 1980-86; vice chancellor U. S.C., Spartanburg, 1986-91, prof. math., 1991-99; ret., 1999. Cons. AID insts., India, 1964, Insts. Internat. Edn., East Pakistan, 1969 NSF Sr. Sci. Faculty fellow, 1964-65 Mem. Math. Assn. Am. (bd. govs. 1968-69, 72-75). Home: 275 James Rd Gaffney SC 29341-4013 E-mail: edwilde@teleplex.net.

WILDE, HAROLD RICHARD, college president; b. Wauwatosa, Wis., May 14, 1945; s. Harold Richard and Winifred (Wiley) W.; m. Benna Brecher, Feb. 4, 1970; children: Anna, Henry, Elizabeth Ty. BA, Amherst Coll., 1967; MA, PhD, Harvard U., Cambridge, Mass., 1973. Spl. asst. to gov. Office of Gov., State of Wis., Madison, 1972-75; ins. commr. Office of Commr. of Ins., State of Wis., 1975-79; spl. asst. to pres. U. Wis. System, 1979-81; v.p. for external affairs Beloit (Wis.) Coll., 1981-91; pres. North Ctrl. Coll., Naperville, Ill., 1991—. Bd. dirs. Ctr. for Pub. Representation, Inc., Madison, 1981-87, Beloit Community Found., 1988-91, Budget Funding Corp., 1993-99, Naperville Devel. Partnership, 1996—. Mem. Phi Beta Kappa. Home: 329 S Brainard St Naperville IL 60540-5401 Office: North Ctrl Coll 30 N Brainard St Naperville IL 60540-4607 E-mail: hrw@noctrl.edu.

WILDE, JAMES ALFRED, pediatrician, educator; b. Ithaca, N.Y., Oct. 29, 1958; s. John Wirth and Doreen Ellen Wilde; m. Paula Jo Wilde, Aug. 18, 1990; children: Rebecca Maria, Anthony James. BA, Duke U., 1980; MD, Ind. U., 1984. Diplomate Am. Bd. Pediatrics, Pediatric Emergency Medicine. Resident in pediatrics Med. Coll. Va., Richmond, 1984-87; fellow pediatric infectious disease Johns Hopkins U., Balt., 1987-91, fellow pediatric emergency medicine, 1992-94; asst. prof. pediatrics Case We. Reserve U., Cleve., 1994-98; asst. prof. emergency medicine and pediatrics Med. Coll. Ga., Augusta, 1998—. Republican. Roman Catholic. Office: Med Coll Ga 1120 15th St AF 2031 Augusta GA 30912

WILDE, JOHN, artist, educator; b. Milw., Dec. 12, 1919; s. Emil F. and Mathilda (Lotz) W.; m. Helen Ashman, July 1943 (dec. Dec. 1966); children: Jonathan, Phoebe; m. Shirley Miller, 1969. BS, U. Wis., 1942, MS, 1948. Mem. faculty U. Wis., 1948—, prof. art, 1960—, chmn. dept. art, 1960-62, Alfred Sessler Distinguished prof. art, 1969-82, prof. emeritus, 1982—. Elected mem. Nat. Acad. Design, 1994. Works exhibited Met. Mus. Art, Mus. Modern Art, Whitney Mus. Am. Art, Corcoran Mus. Art, Mpls. Art Mus., San Francisco Mus. Art, Whitney Mus. Am. Art, 1978-80, Nat. Portrait Gallery, Smithsonian Instn., 1980, Nat. Gallery, Washington, 1988; drawing retrospective Elvehjem Mus. Art, U. Wis., 1984-85; 3-man retrospective (with Curry and Bohrod), Milw. Art Mus., 1982, 55 Yr. Retrospective Eluehjem Mus. of Art, U. Wis., Madison drawings and paintings, 1999-2000, others; represented in permanent collections, Pa. Acad. Art, Detroit Inst. Fine Art, Worcester Art Mus., Wadsworth Atheneum, Whitney Mus. Am. Art, Carnegie Inst., Nat. Collection Art, Smithsonian Instn., Yale U. Art Gallery, Butler Inst. Am. Art, Art Inst. Chgo., Sheldon Meml. Art Gallery, U. Nebr., Zimmerli Mus. Art, Rutgers U., N. Brunswick, N.J., Mus. Contemporary Art, Chgo., others, also extensive exhbns. abroad; subject of book WildeWorld, The Art of John Wilde, 1999. Recipient numerous awards for painting and drawing in regional and nat. exhbns. including, Childe Hassam purchase award Am. Acad. and Inst. Arts and Letters, 1968, 81, 87, Richard Florsheim Art Purchase award, 1994, Henry LeGrand Cannon prize Nat. Acad. Design, 2001; E.D. Found. grantee, 1995.

WILDE, NORMAN TAYLOR, JR. investment banking company executive; b. Phila., Sept. 13, 1930; s. Norman Taylor and Elizabeth (Duthie) W.; m. Ruth Nancy Osterndorf, Sept. 26, 1959; children: Karen, Suzanne, Norman Taylor III. BS, U. Pa., 1953. Vice pres. Janney, Montgomery, Scott, Inc., Phila., 1966-69; pres. Janney, Montgomery, Scott, Inc., 1969-99, co-chmn., 2000—. Chmn. NASDAQ Stock Market, 1984. Bd. dirs. Montgomery County C.C., 2000—, Abington Meml. Hosp. Served to lt. USN, 1953-55. Mem.: Securities Industries Assn. (gov. 1979—82), Nat. Assn. Security Dealers (chmn. 1983—), Phila. C. of C. (bd. dirs. 1998—), Sunnybrook Golf Club, Phila. Cricket Club, Pine Valley Golf Club. Office: Janney Montgomery Scott Inc 1801 Market St Lbby 11 Philadelphia PA 19103-1602

WILDE, PATRICIA, retired artistic director; b. Ottawa, Ont., Can., July 16, 1928; m. George Bardyguine; children: Anya, Youri. Dancer Am. Concert Ballet, Marquis de Cuevas Ballet Internat., N.Y.C., 1944-45, Ballet Russe de Monte Carlo, N.Y.C., 1945-49, Roland Petit's Ballet Paris, Met. Ballet Britain, London, 1949-50; prin. ballerina N.Y.C. Ballet, 1950-65; dir. Harkness Sch. Ballet, N.Y.C., 1965-67; ballet mistress, tchr. Am. Ballet Theatre, 1969-77; dir. Am. Ballet Theatre Sch., 1977-82; artistic dir. Pitts. Ballet Theatre, 1982-97, artistic adviser, master tchr., 1997—. Tchr. Am. Ballet Theatre, 1969-77, Joffrey scholarship program, N.Y.C. Ballet, 1968-69; established Sch. of Grand Theatre of Geneva, 1968-69; adjudicator Regional Ballet in Am. S.E. and S.W., 1969-82; choreographer N.Y. Philharmonic; guest tchr. various ballet cos. and colls.; trustee Dance U.S.A.; panelist Nat. Choreographic Project. Recipient Leadership award in Arts and Letters YWCA, 1990, Pitts. Woman of Yr. in Arts award, 1993, Cultural award for outstanding contbns. to cultural climate of region Pitts. Ctr. for Arts, 1997, History Makers award in arts and letters Sen. John Heinz History Ctr. and the Hist. Soc. Western Pa., 1999. Office: Pitts Ballet Theatre 2900 Liberty Ave Pittsburgh PA 15201-1511

WILDE, PATRICK JOSEPH, administrator; b. Decatur, Tex., July 21, 1959; s. Joseph Leroy and Alice Jean (Pennartz) W.; m. Donna Sue Stephenson, Mar. 28, 1981; children: Michael Patrick, Nicholas Everad, Gregory Allen, Johnathan Paul. BS in Physics, U. North Tex., 1983. Physics lab. trainer North Tex. State U., Denton, 1977-82; rsch. tech. InkJet Tech. (Xerox Corp.), Dallas, 1979-82; process engr. Tex. Instruments, 1984-88, product mgr., 1989—. Patentee in field. Dir. religious edn. Wise & Jack County Cath. Chs., Decatur, Tex., 1984—. Republican. Roman Catholic. Avocations: hiking, welding, fishing, computers. Home: 1600 N Business 81/287 Decatur TX 76234 Office: Raytheon TI Systems 13510 N Central Expy Dallas TX 75243-1108 E-mail: p-wilde@raytheon.com.

WILDE, WILLIAM KEY, lawyer; b. Houston, May 3, 1933; s. Henry Dayton and Louise (Key) W.; m. Ann Jeannine Austin, Aug. 3, 1957; children— William Key, Austin, Adrienne, Michael AB, Coll. William and Mary, Williamsburg, Va., 1955; JD, U. Tex., Austin, 1958. Bar: Tex. 1958. Assoc. Bracewell & Patterson, Houston, 1958-61, ptnr., 1961—. Bd. dirs. Goodwill Industries Houston, 1972—; elder 1st Presbyn. Ch.; trustee Presbyn. Found. U.S.A., Ky., 1983-91; chmn. bd. trustees Schriener Coll., 1991—. Fellow ABA, Am. Bar Found., Am. Coll. Trial Lawyers; mem. Tex. Bar Assn. (bd. dirs. 1984-87), Houston Bar Assn. (pres. 1982-83), Houston Club (pres. 1981-82), Houston Country Club (bd. dirs., pres. 1989-90). Republican. Avocations: golf, skiing, scuba diving. Home: 6206 Woods Bridge Way Houston TX 77007-7041 Office: Bracewell & Patterson 2900 S Tower Pennzoil Place Houston TX 77002

WILDE, WILLIAM RICHARD, lawyer; b. Markesan, Wis., Mar. 1, 1953; s. Leslie Maurice and Elaine Margaret (Schweder) W.; m. Carolyn Margaret Zieman, July 17, 1981 (div. 1987); 1 child, Leah Marie; m. Barbara Joan Rohlf, Jan. 6, 1990. BA, U. Wis., Milw., 1975; JD, Marquette U., 1980. Bar: Wis. 1980, U.S. Dist. Ct. (ea. and we. dists.) Wis. 1980. Dist. atty. Green Lake County, Green Lake, Wis., 1980—83, corp. counsel, 1981; ptnr. Curtis, Wilde and Neal, Oshkosh, 1983—97, Wilde Law Offices, LLC, Oshkosh, 1997—. Mem. ATLA, Wis. Bar Assn., Wis. Acad. Trial Lawyers (Amicus Curiae Brief com. 1987-92, bd. dirs., assoc. editor The Verdict, treas. 1993, sec. 1994, v.p. 1995, pres.-elect 1996, pres. 1997), Winnebago County Bar Assn., Green Lake County Bar Assn. Office: Wilde Law Offices LLC 1901 S Washburn PO Box 3422 Oshkosh WI 54903-3422 also: PO Box 282 Markesan WI 53946-0282 E-mail: wildelaw@expc.com.

WILDE, WILSON, insurance company executive; b. Hartford, Conn., Sept. 24, 1927; s. Philip Alden and Alice Augusta (Wilson) W.; m. Joanne Gerta Menzel, June 19, 1953; children— Stephen W., David W., Elisabeth L., Richard A. Student, Swarthmore Coll., 1945-46; BA, Williams Coll., 1949. Sales agt. Conn. Gen. Life Ins. Co., Hartford, 1949-53; with Hartford Steam Boiler Inspection & Ins. Co., 1953-70, exec. v.p., 1970-71, pres., CEO, 1971—, from chmn., CEO to chmn. emeritus, 1993-98, chmn. emeritus, 1998—. Corporator Inst. Living, Hartford; hon. bd. dirs. Hartford Stage Co., 1973—, Jr. Achievement, Old State House Assn., 1976—; trustee Loomis-Chaffee Sch., 1974—, chmn. bd., 1988-98. With USNR, 1945-47, 51-53. Mem.: Hartford (pres. 1974). Office: PO Box 5024 Hartford CT 06102-5024

WILDENTHAL, BRYAN HOBSON, university administrator; b. San Marcos, Tex., Nov. 4, 1937; s. Bryan and Doris (Kellam) W.; m. Joyce Lockhart; children: Rebecca, Bryan, Lora; m. Adele Sutton; children: Kerry, Andrea. BA, Sul Ross State Coll., 1958; PhD, U. Kans., 1964. Rsch. assoc. Rice U., Houston, 1964-66; AEC postdoctoral fellow Oak Ridge (Tenn.) Nat. Lab., 1966-68; asst. prof. physics Tex. A&M U., College Station, 1968-69; assoc. prof. physics Mich. State U., East Lansing, 1969-72, prof. physics, 1972-83; head physics and atmospheric sci. Drexel U., Phila., 1983-87; dean arts and scis. U. N.Mex., Albuquerque, 1987-92; v.p. acad. affairs U. Tex., Dallas, 1992-94, provost, v.p. acad. affairs, 1994-99, exec. v.p., provost, 1999—. Cons. Los Alamos (N.Mex.) Nat. Lab., 1987-92; sr. U.S. prof. Humboldt Found., Germany, 1973. Fellow J.S. Guggenheim Found., 1977. Mem. Phi Beta Kappa. Home: 3002 Cross Timbers Ln Garland TX 75044-2008 Office: U Tex Office Academic Affairs Richardson TX 75083

WILDENTHAL, C(LAUD) KERN, physician, educator; b. San Marcos, Tex., July 1, 1941; s. Bryan and Doris (Kellam) W.; m. Margaret Dehlinger, Oct. 15, 1964; children: Pamela, Catharine. BA, Sul Ross Coll., 1960; MD, U. Tex. Southwestern Med. Ctr., Dallas, 1964; PhD, U. Cambridge, Eng., 1970. Intern Bellevue Hosp., N.Y.C., 1964-65; resident in medicine, fellow cardiology Parkland Hosp., Dallas, 1965-67; research fellow Nat. Heart Inst., Bethesda, Md., 1967-68; vis. research fellow Strangeways Research Lab., Cambridge, 1968-70; asst. prof. to prof. internal medicine and physiology U. Tex. Southwestern Med. Ctr., Dallas, 1970-76, prof., dean grad. sch., 1976-80, prof., dean Southwestern Med. Sch., 1980-86, prof., pres., 1986—. Hon. fellow Hughes Hall, U. Cambridge, 1994—. Author: Regulation of Cardiac Metabolism, 1976, Degradative Processes in Heart and Skeletal Muscle, 1980; contbr. articles to profl. jours. Bd. dirs. Dallas Symphony, Dallas Opera, Dallas Mus. Art, S.W. Mus. Sci. and Tech., Dallas Citizen's Coun., Am. Friends Cambridge U. Recipient rsch. career devel. award NIH, 1972; spl. rsch. fellow USPHS, 1968-70; Guggenheim fellow, 1975-76. Mem. AMA, Inst. Medicine/NAS, Am. Soc. Clin. Investigation, Am. Coll. Cardiology, Royal Soc. Medicine Gt. Britain, Am. Physiol. Soc., Internat. Soc. Heart Rsch. (past pres. Am. sect.), Am. Fedn. Clin. Rsch., Assn. Am. Med Colls., Assn. Am. Physicians, Am. Heart Assn. (past chmn. sci. policy com.), Assn. Acad. Health Ctrs. (past chmn. sci. policy com.), British N.Am. Com. Home: 4001 Hanover Ave Dallas TX 75225-7010 Office: U Tex Southwestern Med Ctr 5323 Harry Hines Blvd Dallas TX 75390-7208

WILDER, ALMA ANN, English educator, consultant; b. Savannah, Ga., Jan. 19, 1947; d. Pelham Jr. and Alma Sterly (Lebey) W. BA, Agnes Scott Coll., 1968; MA, U. N.C., 1971. English tchr. Carrington Jr. High, Durham, N.C., 1972-74, Chewning Jr. High, Durham, 1974-88, So. H.S., Durham, 1988-2001. Writing instr. talent identification program Duke U., Durham, summers, 1982-84, Duke Young Writers Camp, Durham, summers, 1986-97. Co-author: Reel Conversations, 1997; contbr. articles to profl. jours. Active Jr. League, Durham County, Orange County, N.C. Named Tchr. of Yr. Durham County Schs., 1983, Outstanding Young Educator, Jaycees, Durham, 1983. Mem. Nat. Coun. Tchrs. English, N.C. English Tchrs. Assn. (bd. dirs. 1987-91), Assembly Lit. for Adolescents (bd. dirs. 1994-97), Assembly on Media Arts, Phi Delta Kappa (sec., newsletter editor), Delta Kappa Gamma.

WILDER, DAVID RANDOLPH, materials engineer, consultant; b. Lorimor, Iowa, June 11, 1929; s. Rex Marshall and Ethel Marie (Busch) W.; m. Donna Jean Moore, June 17, 1951; children: Susan, Michael, Margaret, Bruce. BS, Iowa State U., 1951, MS, 1952, PhD, 1958. Registered profl. engr., Iowa (inactive). Engr. Ames Lab., 1951-81; faculty mem. dept. materials sci. and engring. Iowa State U., Ames, 1955—, prof. engring., chmn. dept., 1961-89, prof. engring., 1989-91, prof. emeritus, 1991—; cons. to various industries, fed. agys, 1955—. Contbr. numerous tech. paper to profl. lit.; patentee in field. Fellow Am. Ceramic Soc., Accreditation Bd. for Engring. and Tech.; mem. Nat. Inst. Ceramic Engrs., Am. Soc. for Engring. Edn., Keramos. Home: 1214 Ridgewood Ave Ames IA 50010-5208

WILDER, DOROTHY MAY, artist, educator, librarian; b. Castalia, N.C. d. David Lee and Leila Pleasant (May) W.; m. Frederick Howell Fornoff (div.). BA, U. N.C., 1981; MFA, Carnegie Mellon U., 1983; MLS, SUNY, Albany, 1997; ArtsD, NYU, N.Y.C., 2001. Lectr. in art, dir. ceramics studio U. Pitts., Johnstown, Pa., 1975-79; asst. prof. art Rensselaer Poly. Inst., Troy, N.Y., 1983-90; assoc. prof. art Ea. Wash. U., Cheney, 1991-95, Hartwick Coll., Oneonta, N.Y., 1995; adj. faculty art The New Sch./Parsons Sch. Design, N.Y.C., 1995-98; mus. libr. 20th Century Art Libr. Met. Mus. Art, 1997-98; libr. Louisburg (N.C.) Pub. Libr., 1998—. Archival/artistic cons. Nat. Mus. Dance, Saratoga Springs, N.Y.; lectr., presenter in field. One woman shows at U. Pitts., Johnstown, 1985, 86, 88, Rensselaer County Coun. Arts, Troy, N.Y., 1985, Shelnutt Gallery, Troy, 1986, Louisburg (N.C.) Coll. Fine Arts Ctr. Gallery, 1987, Chatham Coll., Pitts., 1990, SOHO 20, N.Y.C., 2002; installation at Cedar Rock, N.C., 1995, Fulton St. Gallery, Troy, 1998; exhibited at numerous group exhbns., including Greene Gallery, Rensselaer Poly. Inst., Troy, 1985, Albany (N.Y.) Inst. History and Art, 1986, Russell Sage Coll. Gallery, Troy, 1987, Green Gables Mountain Playhouse, Jennerstown, Pa., 1988, Cooperstown (N.Y.) Art Assn. Exhbn., 1988, U. N.C., Chapel Hill, 1989, Three-Rivers Arts Festivals, Pitts., 1979, 81, 82, 85, 88, 89, Rice Gallery, Albany Inst. History and Art, 1989, 91, Schenectady (N.Y.) Mus., 1990, Campo San Giacomo dell'Orio, Venice, Italy, 1990, 92, 93, Ea. Wash. U., Cheney, 1992, Casa Italiana Zerelli-Marimó, N.Y.C., 1995, Carolina Club at George Watts Alumni Ctr., U. N.C., 1995, Parson's Sch. Design, N.Y.C., 1998, FultonSt. Gallery, Troy, 1998, others. Recipient Paul Beer Trust mini grant Rensselaer Poly. Inst., Troy, 1985, 86, 87; Faculty Rsch. grantee Ea. Wash. U., Cheney, 1993. Avocations: tree farming, gardening. Home: 5568 NC 56 Hwy East Castalia NC 27816

WILDER, DWIGHT SAFFORD, academic administrator; b. Plainfield, N.J., Dec. 24, 1946; s. Glenn Safford and Marion Seaver (Fiske) W.; children: Thomas, Douglas; m. Margaret Ruth Holland, Sept. 9, 1995. BA, Johns Hopkins U., 1969; postgrad., Harvard U., 1969-70; MBA, So. N.H. Coll., 1981. Mem. faculty Hebron (Maine) Acad., 1969-70; assoc. dir. continuing edn. N.H. Coll., Manchester, 1975-78, seminar adminstr., 1978-80, asst. to dean, 1980-84; program design specialist N.H. Job Tng. Council, Concord, 1984-89; apprentice program mgr. Portsmouth Naval Shipyard, 1989-92; coord. Seacoast Tech. Prep. Consortium, 1992-96; sch.-to-career coord. Timberlane Sch. Dist., Plaistow, N.H., 1996—. Mng. editor Jour. Ednl. Computing Research, 1983-84. Treas. St. Paul's United Meth. Ch., 1988-90; mem. Cold River Camp Com., 1999—; v.p. Chatham Trails Assn., 2000—. Mem. Am. Soc. Tng. and Devel., Appalachian Mountain Club (vol. educator and cons., 1975—, sec. North Country bd. 1980-87), N.H. Personnel and Guidance Assn., Navy Brunswick Toastmasters (pres. chpt. 1973-74), Toastmasters of Manchester (pres. 1982-83) Avocations: hiking, backpacking, painting. Home: 15 Pinecrest Dr Somersworth NH 03878 Office: Timberlane Sch Dist 36 Greenough Rd Plaistow NH 03865 E-mail: kiknshoes@attbi.com.

WILDER, ELEANOR MARIE (NORA ROBERTS WILDER), writer; b. Washington, Oct. 10, 1950; d. Bernard Edward Robertson and Eleanor Margaret Harris; m. Ronald Eugene Aufdem-Brinke, Aug. 17, 1968 (div. 1985); children: Daniel, Jason; m. Bruce Allen Wilder, July 6, 1985. Grad. high sch., Silver Spring, Md.; writer, 1979—. Author: Homeport, 1998, The Reef, 1998, River's End, 1999, Carolina Moon, 2000, others; (writing as J.D. Robb) Judgement in Death, 1990, Conspiracy in Death, 1999, Witness in Death, 2000. First inductee Romance Writers of Am. Hall of Fame, 1986; recipient Waldenbooks award, 1985, 86, 88, 91, 92, 94, B. Dalton award, 1990, 91, 92, Centennial award, Waldenbooks Lifetime Achievement award. Mem. Washington Romance Writers, Romance Writers Am. (Lifetime Achievement award), Mystery Writers Am. Democrat. Roman Catholic. Avocations: dancing, reading, films.

WILDER, JAMES D. geology and mining administrator; b. Wheelersburg, Ohio, June 25, 1935; s. Theodore Roosevelt and Gladys (Crabtree) W.; children: Jaymie Deanna, Julie Lynne. Graduated high sch., Wheelersburg. Lic. real estate agt., Ohio. Real estate agt., Portsmouth, Ohio; mgr. comml. pilots, fixed base operator Scioto County Airport; mgr. and part owner sporting goods store, Portsmouth; cons. geologist Paradise, Calif., 1973-81; pres. Mining Cons., Inc., 1981-84; dir. geology and devel. Para-Butte Mining, Inc., 1984-88, pres., 1988-90, pres., chief exec. officer, 1990—. Served with U.S. Army, 1956-57. Avocations: hunting, fishing, camping. Home and Office: Para Butte Mining Inc PO Box 564 Paradise CA 95967-0564

WILDER, JAMES EDWARD, resident manager; b. Washington, Dec. 28, 1948; s. Nathaniel Everett and Marie Inez Wilder; m. Barbara Anne Tracey, Aug. 13, 1973; 1 child, Huan. B of Ministry magna cum laude with high honors, Andersonville Bapt. Sem., Camilla, Ga., 1999. Cert. resident mgr. RM801484, D.C. Dept. Consumer and Regulatory Affairs, Occupl. and Profl. Licensing Adminstrn., Real Estate Commn.; lic. minister, 1994. Mgr. hardware dept. Gaylord's Dept. Store, New Castle, Pa., 1970-72; sales rep. Gumpert Printing Co., Silver Spring, Md., 1980-82; shipping/receiving mgr. Bradlees, Annandale, VA., 1982-84; warehouse mgr. Juhl Pacific Corp., Landover, Md., 1984-86; resident mgr. William C. Smith Co., Washington, 1989—. Pres. Altar of Ed Ministry, Washington, 1994—. Editor: (newsletter) Breach Repairer News, 1997—; creator: (Web site) Altar of Ed Ministry, 1999; host (radio program) Sta. KYTX, Beeville, Tex., 2001. Bd. dirs. Cmty. Coun. for the Homeless at Friendship Pl., Washington, 1994-96; pres. Student Govt. Assn., Prince George's C.C., 1981-82; advisor Triple C Jaycees, 1979-80; founder, pres. Centennial Slammer Jaycees, 1977-78, advisor, past pres., 1978-79. Specialist 4/E4 U.S. Army, 1966-69, Vietnam. Recipient Keyman award Centennial Slammer Jaycees, 1978-79, Keyman award Triple C Jaycees, 1979-80; named one of 25 Outstanding Jaycees Pres. in U.S., 1977-78. Mem. VFW (life), DAV (life), Internat. Critical Incident Stress Found., Am. Numismatic Assn., Am. Assn. Christian Counselors (charter), Baptist. Avocations: post-prison ministry, eagle collectibles, collecting coins. Office: Altar of Ed Ministry Ste 506 2800 Ontario Rd NW Apt 506 Washington DC 20009-2227 Fax: (202) 319-7704. E-mail: altaredmin@aol.com.

WILDER, JOHN SHELTON SHELTON, state official, lieutenant governor, former state legislator; b. Fayette City, Tenn., June 3, 1921; s. John Chamblee and Martha (Shelton) W.; m. Marcelle Morton, Dec. 31, 1941; children: John Shelton Wilder, II, David Morton. Student, U. Tenn.; LLB, U. Memphis, 1957. Bar: Tenn. 1957. Engaged in farming, Longtown, Tenn., 1943—; supr. mgmt. Longtown Supply Co.; judge Fayette County Ct.; mem. Tenn. Senate, 1959—; mem. senate 81st, 85th, 86th through 102nd Gen. Assemblies; lt. gov., spkr. senate State of Tenn. for Dist. 26 , Chester, Crockett, Fayette, Hardeman, Hardin, others, 1971—; pres. senate State of Tenn., 1971—. Past pres. Nat. Assn. Soil Conservation Dists., Tenn. Soil Conservation Assn., Tenn. Agrl. Council; exec. com. So. Legis. Conf., Conf. Lt. Govs.; dir. Bank Tenn., Cumberland Bank; chmn. Cumberland BanCorp, Inc. Served with U.S. Army, 1942-43. Mem. Tenn. Cotton Ginners Assn. (past pres.), Shriner, Scottish Rite, Mason, Delta Theta Phi. Clubs: Shriners. Democrat. Methodist. Office: Legislative Plz Ste 1 Nashville TN 37243-0026*

WILDER, LAWRENCE DOUGLAS, former governor; b. Richmond, Va., Jan. 17, 1931; children: Lynn, Larry, Loren. BS, Va. Union U., 1951; JD, Howard U., 1959. Bar: Va. 1959. Mem. Va. Senate, 1969-85; lt. gov. State of Va., 1986-89, gov., 1989-93; Al Douglas Wilder Distinging. prof. Va. Commonwealth U., Richmond, 1998—. Del. Democratic Nat. Conv., 1980; agt. NAACP Legal

Def. Fund. Bd. dirs. United Givers Fund; chmn. bd. Red Shield Boys' Club. Served with U.S. Army, 1952-53 Decorated Bronze Star. Mem. ABA, Va. Bar Assn., Nat. Bar Assn., Am. Judicature Soc., C. of C., Urban League (bd. dirs. Richmond), Omega Psi Phi. Clubs: Masons; Shriners. Office: Virginia Commonwealth Univ 923 W Franklin St PO Box 842028 Richmond VA 23284-2028

WILDER, ROBERT GEORGE, advertising and public relations executive; b. Hornell, N.Y., Mar. 27, 1920; s. George Reuben and Laura (Nolan) W.; m. Annabel D. Heritage, Feb. 21, 1953; children: Loraine Wilder Powell, Gordon Heritage. BA, Coll. Wooster, 1942. Propr. Robert G. Wilder & Co., Inc. (public relations), Phila., 1945-50; dir. public relations Lewis & Gilman (advt.-public relations), 1950-55, v.p., 1955-59, exec. v.p., 1959-64, pres., from 1964; chmn. Lewis, Gilman & Kynett ((merger with Foote, Cone & Belding)), 1983-90, chmn. emeritus, 1990—. Bd. dirs. Rittenhouse Trust Co.; dir. Pa. Acad. Fine Arts. Trustee emeritus Franklin Inst., Lankenau Hosp., Phila.; life trustee emeritus Coll. of Wooster, Ohio. Served to lt. comdr. USNR, 1942-46. Recipient award Charles M. Price Sch., 1971, Bus. and Industry award Opportunities Industrialization Ctr., 1971, Disting. Alumni award Coll. Wooster, 1971, Area Council Econ. Edn. Enterprise award, 1980, Gold Liberty Bell award TV, Radio & Advt. Club Phila., 1982, Vol. of Yr. award Leukemia Soc. Eastern Pa., 1983, Silver medal Phila. Club of Advt. Women, 1984, ann. achievers award Wheels, 1985, Good Scout award Phila. coun. Boy Scouts Am., 1986, Heart of Phila. award Am. Heart Assn., 1989, Great Am. award Poor Richard Club Phila., 1990; named to Bus./Profl. Advt. Assn. Hall of Fame, 1988; inducted into First Annual Hall of Fame of Broadcast Pioneers, Phila. chpt., 1992. Mem. Res. Officers Assn. (past pres. Pa.), Greater Phila. C. of C. (past chmn., bd. dirs., William Penn award 1991); Clubs: Union League (past pres.), Penn, Bachelors Barge (chmn.), Phila. Country, Merion Cricket, Sunday Breakfast. Home: Grays Ln House 100 Grays Ln Haverford PA 19041-1727 Office: Tierney Comms 200 S Broad St Philadelphia PA 19102-3803

WILDER, ROLAND PERCIVAL, JR. lawyer; b. Malden, Mass., June 21, 1940; s. Roland Percival and Clarissa (Hunting) W.; m. Susan McAra Randell, Sept. 3, 1965; children: Roland Percival III, William Randell. BA, Washington and Jefferson Coll., 1963; JD, Vanderbilt U., 1966. Bar: D.C. 1967, U.S. Dist. Ct. D.C. 1967, U.S. Dist. Ct. Md. 1994, U.S. Dist. Ct. Colo. 1997, U.S. Dist. Ct. (ea. dist.) Mich. 1999, U.S. Ct. Appeals (D.C. cir.) 1967, U.S. Ct. Appeals (4th, 5th and 6th cirs.) 1976, U.S. Ct. Appeals (8th and 9th cirs.) 1977, U.S. Ct. Appeals (2d cir.) 1978, U.S. Ct. Appeals (11th cir.) 1981, U.S. Ct. Appeals (3d cir.) 1997, U.S. Ct. Appeals (7th cir.) 2002, U.S. Supreme Ct. 1972. Atty. Office of Solicitor U.S. Dept. Labor, Washington, 1967-69; asst. counsel civil rights office of solicitor U.S. Dept. Labor, 1969-70, counsel civil rights office of solicitor, 1970-71; supr. atty. office gen. counsel NLRB, 1972-74; assoc. gen. counsel Internat. Brotherhood Teamsters, 1974-85; sr. mem. Baptiste & Wilder P.C., 1985—. Lectr. numerous continuing legal edn. programs various states, 1970—. Mng. editor Vanderbilt U. Law Rev., 1965-66; contbr. articles to profl. jours. V.p. Arlington (Va.) Cubs Youth Club, Inc., 1975-81; coach Fairfax (Va.) Hockey Club, 1979-83. Mem. ABA, D.C. Bar Assn., Assn. Trial Lawyers Am., Phi Delta Phi, Pi Sigma Alpha, Phi Alpha Theta, Roosevelt Soc., Joint Council Flight Attendant Unions (hon. flight attendant 1985). Democrat. Avocations: history, tennis, skiing. Office: Baptiste & Wilder PC 1150 Connecticut Ave NW Ste 500 Washington DC 20036-4194 E-mail: rpwilderjr@bapwild.com.

WILDER, RONALD PARKER, economics educator; b. Freeport, Tex., Jan. 15, 1941; s. J. Barton and Lois (Parker) W.; m. Charlotte D. Pearson, Sept. 4, 1965; children: Erika, Rachel, David. BA, Rice U., 1963, MA, 1964; PhD, Vanderbilt U., 1969. Asst. prof. econs. U. S.C., Columbia, 1970-75, assoc. prof., 1975-80, prof., 1980—, chmn. dept. econs., 1987—. Co-author: Stock Life Insurance Profitability, 1986; mem. editorial bd. So. Econ. J., 1978-80; contbr. articles to profl. jours. Capt. U.S. Army, 1968-70. Fellow Ford Found., Vanderbilt U., 1964-65. Mem. Am. Econ. Assn., So. Econ. Assn., Omicron Delta Epsilon. United Methodist. Avocations: hiking, canoeing. Office: U of SC Dept Of Econs Columbia SC 29208-0001

WILDER, SUSAN SHERN, medical educator, family physician; b. Milw., Jan. 2, 1962; d. John Edward and Mary (Steeves) Shern; m. Robert Evan Wilder, Aug. 8, 1987; children: Nicole K., Jessica M., Danielle M. BA in Biology and Psychology, Washington U., 1984; MD, George Washington U., 1988. Diplomate Am. Bd. Family Practice, cert. of added qualification in sports medicine. Asst. prof. family practice Uniformed Svc. U., Bethesda, Md., 1991-95, George Washington U., Washington, 1995-96, Mayo Med. Sch., Rochester, N.Y., 1996—. Intern and resident Malcolm Grow USAF MEd. Ctr., Andrews AFB, Md., family practice faculty, 1991—95, asst. chair dept. family medicine, 1994—95; residency dir. Mayo Scottsdale (Ariz.) Family Medicine, 1996—2000; mem. edn. and managed care com. Mayo Clinic, Scottsdale, 1996—; spkr. in field. Author: Family Practice Guide, 1990, 92, 94, 96. Maj. USAF, 1988-95. Faculty devel. fellow U. N.C., Chapel Hill. Mem.: Ariz. Acad. Family Practice, Soc. Tchrs. Family Medicine, Am. Acad. Family Practice, Am. Acad. Family Practice (Tar Wars campaign educator 1996—, com. to promote the splty. 1997—, del. 1999—). Avocations: gardening, biking. Office: Mayo Clinic Scottsdale 13737 N 92nd St Scottsdale AZ 85260-7438 E-mail: wilder.susan@mayo.edu.

WILDER, WALTER LLEWELLYN, allergist, immunologist, pediatrician; b. Ann Arbor, Mich., May 23, 1926; MD, Harvard U., 1950. Diplomate Am. Bd. Allergy and Immunology, Am. Bd. Pediatrics. Rotating intern Cleveland City Hosp., 1950-51; resident in pediatrics U. Hosps. Cleveland, 1951-52, U. Minn. Hosps., Mpls., 1954-55; pvt. practice Edina, Minn.; clin. assoc. prof. U. Minn.; staff Mpls. Children's Hosp., Fairview Southdale, Edina; courtesy staff Meth. Hosp., St. Louis Park, Minn., Abbott Northwestern, Mpls. Mem. AMA, Am. Acad. Environ. Medicine, Am. Acad. Pediatrics, Am. Coll. Allergy, Asthma and Immunology. Home: 4905 Payton Ct Edina MN 55435-1544 Office: 6525 Drew Ave S Edina MN 55435-2103

WILDEROTTER, PETER THOMAS, non-profit executive; b. Newark, May 24, 1954; s. Arthur W. and Dorothy (King) T.; m. Nancy Ann Lanza, Apr. 27, 1985; children: Peter Arthur, Lindsey Marie, Michael John, David Charles. BA in English, Marist Coll., 1976. Area dir. Am. Cancer Soc. N.J. Div., North Brunswick, 1976-86; v.p. resources Planned Parenthood Fedn. Am., N.Y.C., 1987-90; dir. devel. NAACP Legal Defense Fund, 1991-94; v.p. devel. Planned Parenthood of N.Y.C., 1994-2000, WNYC Radio, N.Y.C., 2000—. Bd. dirs. Cath.'s for Choice, Washington, Nat. Unified Svc. Agys.; govt. rels. com. Ind. Sector, Washington, 1990. Chair America's Charities; bd. dirs. Rattlestick Theatre Co. Mem. Nat. Soc. Fund Raising Execs. Mem. Ctrl. Jersey Road Runner's Club (treas.). Democrat. Roman Catholic. Home: 41 Elizabeth Ct New Providence NJ 07974-1625

WILDHABER, MICHAEL RENE, accountant; b. Jefferson City, Mo., Aug. 4, 1952; s. Rainey A. and Velma W.; m. Paula M. Wildhaber, Sept. 28, 1974; 1 child, Wendy. AA, Florissant Valley Coll., 1972; BS, U. Mo., 1974. CPA, Mo.; cert. info. sys. auditor, cert. internal auditor, cert. tax preparer, assoc. ins. acctg. and fin., enrolled agt. Sr. auditor, enrolled agt. I.T.T. Fin., St. Louis, 1974-79; audit mgr. Navco, 1980-85; contr. Millers mutual, Alton, Ill., 1985-88; pres. R&M Tax and Acctg., St. Louis, 1988—. Tchr. Jr. Achievement, St. Louis, 1993-94; vol. Olympic Festival, St. Louis, 1994, 100 Neediest Cases, St. Louis, 1990-94, Old News Boy, St. Louis, 1992-94. Mem. AICPA, Mo. Soc. CPAs, Inst. Internal Auditors, Habitat for Humanity (pres.). Office: R&M Tax and Acctg 3805 S Kingshighway Blvd Saint Louis MO 63109-1818

WILDHACK, WILLIAM AUGUST, JR. lawyer; b. Takoma Park, Md., Nov. 28, 1935; s. William August and Martha Elizabeth (Parks) W.; m. Martha Moore Allston, Aug. 1, 1959; children: William A. III, Elizabeth L. BS, Miami U., Oxford, Ohio, 1957; JD, George Washington U., 1963. Bar: Va. 1963, D.C. 1965, Md. 1983, U.S. Supreme Ct. 1967. Agt. IRS, No. Va., 1957-65; pvt. prac. Washington, 1965—69; v.p., corp. counsel B.F. Saul Co. and affiliates, Chevy Chase, Md., 1969-87, Chevy Chase Bank, F.S.B. and affiliates, 1987-90; atty. pvt. practice, Arlington, Va., 1990—. Sec. B.F. Saul Real Estate Investment Trust, Chevy Chase, 1972-87. Chmn. Arlington Tenant Landlord Commn., 1975-91. Mem. ABA, Md. Bar Assn., D.C. Bar, Va. Bar, Arlington County Bar Assn., Nat. Acad. Elder Law Attys., Am. Soc. Corp. Secs. Presbyterian.

WILDING, DIANE, marketing, financial and information systems executive; b. Chicago Heights, Ill., Nov. 7, 1942; d. Michael Edward and Katherine Surian; m. Manfred Georg Wilding, May 7, 1975 (div. 1980). BSBA in Acctg. magna cum laude, No. Ill. U., 1963; postgrad., U. Chgo., 1972-74; cert. in German lang., Goethe Inst., Rothenburg, Germany, 1984; cert. in internat. bus. German, Goethe Inst., Atlanta, 1994; cert. in Web page design, Kennesaw State U., 2000. Lic. cosmetologist. Systems engr. IBM, Chgo., 1963-68; data processing mgr. Am. Res. Corp., 1969-72; system R & D project mgr. Continental Bank, 1972-75; fin. industry mktg. rep. IBM Can., Ltd., Toronto, Ont., 1976-79; regional telecom. mktg. exec. Control Data Corp., Atlanta, 1980-84; gen. mgr. The Plant Plant, 1985-92; SAP cons. IBM, 1993—. Pioneer installer on-line Automatic Teller Machines, Pos Equipment. Author: The Canadian Payment System: An International Perspective, 1977. Mem. Chgo. Coun. on Fgn. Rels.; bd. dirs. Easter House Adoption Agy., Chgo., 1974-76. Mem. Internat. Brass Soc., Goethe Inst., Mensa. Clubs: Ponte Verde (Fla.); Royal Ont. Yacht, Libertyville Racquet. Avocations: horticulture, travel, dancing, gourmet cooking, foreign languages. Home: PO Box 723055 Atlanta GA 31139-0055 Office: IBM 1600 Riveredge Pkwy NW Atlanta GA 30328-4697 E-mail: wilding@usa.com.

WILDING, LAWRENCE PAUL, pedology educator, soil science consultant; b. Winner, S.D., Oct. 1, 1934; s. William Kasper and Ruth Inez (Root) W.; m. Gladys Dora Milne, Nov. 25, 1956; children: Linda Kay, Doris Bertha, Charles William, David Lawrence. BSc, S.D. State U., 1956, MSc, 1959; PhD, U. Ill., 1962. Asst. in agronomy S.D. State U., Brookings, 1956-59; rsch. fellow U. Ill., Urbana, 1959-62; prof. agronomy Ohio State U., Columbus, 1962-76; prof. pedology Tex. A&M U., College Station, 1976—. Vis. prof. U. Guelph, Ont. Can., 1971-72; mem. NATO Advanced Rsch. Workshop on Expansive Soils, Cornell U., 1990-91; mem. U.S. Nat. Com. on Soil Sci.; mem. NRC-NAS, 1998-2000; mem. exec. com. Am. Geol. Inst. Coun., 1998-2001. Author or/and editor 4 books; assoc. editor Catena Verlag, 1989, Geoderma, 1988-92; contbr. over 130 articles to profl. jours., chpts. to books. Sgt. S.D. N.G., 1956-59. Recipient Mem. award Sigma XI, 1988, Superior Svc. Group award sci. rsch. USDA, 1993; Campbell Soup fellow, 1959-62, Faculty fellow Tex. A&M U.; grantee USDA, AID, 1986—. Fellow AAAS, Am. Soc. Agronomy (cert.), Soil Sci. Soc. Am. (Soil Sci. Rsch. award 1987, opportunities in soil sci. com., chmn. subcommn. B 1989-92, chmn. divsn. S-5, bd. dirs. rep., mem. steering com. 1990-91, pres. elect 1992-93, pres. 1993-94, pst pres. 1994-95), Am. Inst. Chemists; mem. Soil Scientists Assn. Tex., Soil and Water Conservation Soc. Am., Tex. A&M Faculty Club, Gamma Sigma Delta. Democrat. Presbyterian. Avocations: golf, woodworking, travelling, sports, antiques. Office: Texas A&M U Dept Soil And Crop Scis College Station TX 77843-0001

WILDMAN, GARY CECIL, chemist, researcher; b. Middlefield, Ohio, Nov. 25, 1942; s. Gerald Robert and Frances Jane (Swager) W.; m. Linda Bufkin, Mar. 27, 1999; children: Debbie, Eric. AB in Chemistry, Thiel Coll., 1964; PhD in Chemistry, Duke U., 1970. Research asst. B.F. Goodrich Research, Brecksville, Ohio, summer 1964; instr. Duke U., 1966-67; research chemist Hercules Research Center, Wilmington, Del., 1968-71; asso. prof. polymer sci. U. So. Miss., Hattiesburg, 1971-76, prof., 1976-83, chmn. dept., 1971-76, dean Coll. Sci. and Tech., 1976-83; v.p. research and devel. Schering Plough, Memphis, 1983—. Mem. Am. Chem. Soc., So. Soc. Coatings Tech., Soc. Plastics Engrs., Am. Crystallographic Assn., Phi Beta Kappa, Sigma Xi, Phi Lambda Upsilon, Sigma Pi Sigma, Omicron Delta Kappa. Clubs: Rotary. Republican. Methodist. Home: 2140 Johnson Rd Germantown TN 38139-3500 Office: PO Box 377 Memphis TN 38151-0002

WILDMAN, MAX EDWARD, lawyer, director; b. Terre Haute, Ind., Dec. 4, 1919; s. Roscoe Ellsworth and Lena (Shaw) W.; m. Joyce Lenore Smith, Sept. 25, 1948; children: Leslie, William. BS, Butler U., 1941; JD, U. Mich., 1947; MBA, U. Chgo., 1952. Bar: Ill., Ind. Ptnr. Kirkland & Ellis, Chgo., 1947-67; mng. ptnr. Wildman, Harrold, Allen & Dixon, 1967-89. Dir. Colt Industries, N.Y., Nat. Blvd. Bank, Ill. Contbr. articles to profl. jours. Trustee Butler U., Indpls., Lake Forest Hosp., Ill., Lake Bluff Library Bd., Ill.; chmn. Lake Bluff Zoning Bd. Served to lt. col. USAF, 1943-46; PTO Fellow Am. Coll. Trial Lawyers; mem. Soc. Trial Lawyers, Law Club, Legal Club, Trial Lawyers Club of Chgo. Clubs: Anglers (Chgo.), Pere Marquette Rod and Gun (Baldwin, Mich.), Shoreacres (Lake Bluff), Univ. of Chgo. Presbyterian. Office: Wildman Harrold Allen & Dixon 225 W Wacker Dr Chicago IL 60606-1224

WILDNAUER, RICHARD HARRY, pharmaceutical company executive; b. New Kensington, Pa., Feb. 14, 1940; s. Richard Michael and Rosemary Elizabeth (Moore) W.; BS in Chemistry, St. Vincent Coll., 1962; PhD in Biochemistry, W.Va. U., 1966; postgrad. (NSF fellow) U. Kans., 1967; MBA in Mgmt., Rider Coll., 1974; m. Sharon Ann Novick, Jan. 22, 1966; 1 dau., Tara Lynne. NIH trainee W.Va. U., 1963-66; sr. rsch. assoc. in skin biology, exploratory rsch. divsn. Johnson and Johnson Domestic Operating Co., New Brunswick, N.J., 1975, assoc. mgr. tech. planning, exploratory rsch. divsn., 1975-77; sr. project coord., new products, pharm. divsn. McNeil Labs., Ft. Washington, Pa., 1977-79; dir. new product devel. Janssen Pharmaceutica Inc., New Brunswick, N.J., 1979-82, v.p. research and devel., 1982-88; v.p. tech. and bus. devel., Johnson & Johnson Corp., New Brunswick, N.J., 1988-92; pres. Baker Cummins Dermatologicals, Inc., Lakewood, N.J., 1992-95; pres., CEO NeoStrata Co., Inc., Princeton, N.J., 1995—. Trustee, bd. dirs. United Way Cen. N.J., 1988-95, pres. 1991-93. Mem. N.Y. Acad. Scis., Soc. Investigative Dermatology, Am. Mgmt. Assn., Med. Mycology Soc., Am. Acad. Dermatology, Pharm. Advt. Club, Soc. Cos. Chemists, Sigma Xi. Roman Catholic. Contbr. articles to profl. jours. Office: NeoStrata Co Inc 4 Research Way Princeton NJ 08540-6618

WILDRICK, KENYON JONES, minister; b. Rahway, N.J., June 14, 1933; s. Stanley B. and Adele (Jones) W.; BA, Trinity Coll., Hartford, Conn., 1955, BD, Princeton U., 1958, ThM, 1962, DD, Trinity Coll., Conn., 1985; m. Nancy Ruth Mersfelder, Aug. 23, 1958; children: Catherine Ruth, Margaret Jeanne, Kenyon Douglas. Ordained to ministry Presbyterian Ch., 1958; asst. minister Community Congregational Ch., Short Hills, N.J., 1958-61, assoc. minister, 1961-67, sr. minister, 1967-93, min. emeritus, 1993—; sr. min. Pilgrim Congregational Ch., Warren, N.J., 1993—; campus ministry Middle Atlantic Conf., 1962-65. Bd. dirs. Milburn-Short Hills chpt. ARC, 1963-64; ch. and ministry com. N.J. Assn., 1965— ; trustee Ctr. Theol. Inquiry, Princeton, N.J., 1985—; pres. bd. trustees Overlook Protestant Chaplaincy Program, 1973—; trustee investment com. Fellowship Conn. Congregational Chs., 1996—; trustee, vice-chmn. Presbyn. Homes N.J., 1981—. Mem. Millburn Clergy Assn. (chmn. 1987—), Rotary (dir. Milburn Club 1973), Delta Phi. Home: 214 Preston Dr Gillette NJ 07933-1439 Office: 105 Mountainview Rd Warren NJ 07059-5020

WILDS, BONNIE, author, community volunteer; b. Phila. m. Walter Warren Wilds; children: Stephanie Wilds Shea Blackhurst, Eugenia Wilds Ardrey, Vanessa Wilds Cunningham Wassenar, Pamela Wilds Cole. BA, Sarah Lawrence Coll.; MA, PhD, U. Pitts. Desk officer Dept. State, Washington, economist. Author: A Critical Edition of El Animal Profeta by Antonio Mira de Amescua, 1979. Mem. women's com. Carnegie Mus. Art, Pitts.; mem. social svc. bd. dirs. Shadyside Hosp.; pres. women's aux. bd. dirs. Magee Women's Hosp., Pitts; pres. bd. dirs., v.p. Bethany Lenox Hill Day Care Ctr., N.Y.C.; pres.bd. dirs., v.p. Mary Walton Children's Ctr.; pres., bd. dirs. Musicians Emergency Fund.; pres., hon. dir., mem. Hospitality Com. for UN Dels.; resource coordinator Inst. of Internat. Edn. Recipient Pub. Svc. citation City of Pitts. Fellow: Frick Collection, Pierpont Morgan Libr.; mem.: MLA, The New Eng. Soc., St. George's Soc., The Pilgrims, Rolling Rock Club (Ligonier, Pa.), Colony Club (N.Y.). Republican. Episcopalian. Avocations: community service, travel, reading. Home: 20 E 68th St New York NY 10021-5837

WILDS, KAREN R. housing authority executive; b. Newport News, Va. BS Govtl. Adminstrn., Christopher Newport U., 1976; M of Urban Studies, Old Dominion U., 1983. Cmty. devel. dir. Newport News (Va.) Redevel. and Housing Authority, 1985—99, exec. dir., 1999—. Mem. VA Gen. Assembly Housing Study Commn. Com. on Eminent Domain, Richmond, 1999—. Vice dhmn., bd. dirs. Office of Human Affairs, Newport News, 2000—02. Mem.: Nat. Assn. Housing and Cmty. Devel. Ofcls. (mem. cmty. revitalization and devel. com. 2001—).

WILE, JOAN, composer, lyricist, singer; b. Rochester, N.Y., July 17, 1931; d. Louis and Janet Louise (Wile) Meltzer; children: Ron Wasserman, Diana Wasserman McCloskey. BA, U. Chgo., 1952. Freelance composer, lyricist, singer, mus. book writer. Rec. artist Vanguard Records, 1954; singer Storyville, 1954, The Crystal Palace, 1957; mem. vocal-revue act The Neighbors performances include The Village Vanguard, Le Ruban Bleu, The Bon Soir and The Living Room ; singer, lyricist feature film The Happy Hooker, 1974; singer radio and TV jingles, movie sound tracks, supper clubs, hotels, TV music spls. and variety shows; lyricist, composer mus. Tobacco Road, 1974, Seven Ages of Woman, 1987 (named most promising new musical); writer, producer When They Turned on the Tap at the Watergate, The Truth Come Pourin' Out; lyricist songs for Romper Room, 1983; lyricist, composer, writer People is People, 1983; lyricist, composer script for children's albums for Golden and Peter Pan Records, others; lyricist, composer material in Julius Monk's Upstairs at the Downstairs, 1958; lyricist, composer, performer Nancy's Economic Plan, 1980; lyricist, composer Mothers and Daughters, 1984; lyricist, composer, author The Symposium, 1987; lyricist, composer From There to Here, 1987; writer Rhyme, Women and Song; lyricist, librettist, composer Museum of Natural Sex History, 1992; composer Women Walking, 1997. Organizer Women in Def. Eleanor Roosevelt, N.Y.C., 1989—; founder, organizer Revolt Against the Tax Refund, 2001; bd. dirs. Soc. Singers, 2002. Runner-up Am. Song Festival, 1976. Mem.: ASCAP (Popular award 1970—2001), AFTRA, SAG, Theatre Artists Workshop, Dramatists Guild. Avocation: political and musical activities. Home and Office: 263 West End Ave Apt 4B New York NY 10023-2613 E-mail: jwile@prodigy.net.

WILE, JULIUS, former corporate executive, educator; b. N.Y.C., Apr. 17, 1915; s. Irwin and Harriet (Brussel) W.; m. Ruth Miller, June 26, 1941 (dec. Feb. 3, 1992); children: Barbara Miller Wile Schwarz, Andrew Brussel. BS in Mech. Engring. and Aeronautics, NYU, 1936; DFA (hon.), Culinary Inst. Am., 1994. With Julius Wile Sons & Co. Inc., N.Y.C., 1936-41, 45-76, v.p., 1955-66, sr. v.p., 1967-76; prodn. engr. Brewster Aero. Corp., L.I City, N.Y., 1942-44, Greer Hydraulics Inc., Bklyn., 1944-45; trustee Culinary Inst. Am., Hyde Park, N.Y., 1970-79, 81-90, chmn. bd. trustees, 1981-83, chmn. emeritus, 1983—. Vis. lectr. Sch. Hotel Adminstrn. Cornell U., Ithaca, N.Y., 1953-82; wines and spirits lectr.; v.p. New Eng. Distillers Inc., Teterboro, N.J., 1955-72 Contbr. Brit. Book of Yr, 1957-75; editor: Frank Schoonmaker's Encyclopedia of Wine, 7th edit., 1978. V.p. Spain-U.S. C. of C., N.Y.C., 1972; bd. dirs. Scarsdale Family Counseling Service, N.Y., 1973-79; chmn. ann. drive ARC, Scarsdale, 1976. Decorated Ordre de l'Economie Nationale France, Ordre National du Merite France, Membre d'Honneur Academie du Vin de Bordeaux. Mem. Commanderie de Bordeaux (founding, gov. 1959—, dep. grand maitre 1978-88, grand chancelier 1988-2000), Soc. Wine Educators (bd. dirs. 1980—, treas. 1986-93), Wine and Food Soc. N.Y. (bd. dirs. 1971-73, 77-83), Nat. Assn. Beverage Importers (chmn. table wine com. 1954-60, 65-76), Explorers Club, Quaker Ridge Golf Club (Scarsdale). Democrat. Jewish. Home and Office: 27 Grand Park Ave Scarsdale NY 10583-7611 Fax: (914) 723-4257. E-mail: j.wile@att.net. *Fifteen years of Prohibition led to public ignorance of fine wines and spirits. Education of myself, employees, the trade and the public has been an important part of my career. It was and still is both a duty and a pleasure to pass on what I have learned and enjoyed. My tenet is that 'there is no premium for good taste.'.*

WILE, PHILIP HODGES, law educator; b. Cleve., Dec. 2, 1930; s. Ralph H. and Elizabeth (Mower) W.; m. Nancy D. Wile, Oct. 26, 1952 (dec. Jan. 1992); children: James, Elizabeth Wile Meyerowitz, Janet Wile Melikian; m. JoAnne Steninger, May 29, 1993. AB, Stanford U., 1952, JD, 1957. Bar: Calif. 1957. Assoc. Kimble, Thomas, Snell, Jamison & Russell, Fresno, Calif., 1957-61; asst. prof. law Stanford (Calif.) Sch. Law, 1961-62; ptnr., shareholder Thomas, Snell, Jamison, Russell & Asperger, Fresno, 1962-87; prof. law, dir. tax programs U. Pacific McGeorge Sch. Law, Sacramento, 1987—. Author: Federal Income Tax—A Case Book on the Basics, 1995; contbr. articles to law jours. Pres. Sacramento Traditional Jazz Soc. Found., 1996-99. Mem. ABA, Order of Coif. Office: U Pacific McGeorge Sch Law 3200 5th Ave Sacramento CA 95817-2705 E-mail: pwile@UOP.Edu.

WILENSKY, GAIL ROGGIN, economist, researcher; b. Detroit, June 14, 1943; d. Albert Alan and Sophia (Blitz) Roggin; m. Robert Joel Wilensky, Aug. 4, 1963; children: Peter Benjamin, Sara Elizabeth. AG with honors, U. Mich., 1964, MA in Econs., 1965, PhD in Econs., 1968; hon. degree, Hahnemann U., 1993, Rush U., 1997, U. of Scis., Phila., 2002. Economist President's Commn. on Income Maintenance Programs; exec. dir. Md. Council of Econ. Advs., 1969-71; sr. researcher Urban Inst., Washington, 1971-73; assoc. research scientist, public policy and pub. health U. Mich., Ann Arbor, 1973-75, vis. asst. prof. econs., 1973-75; sr. research mgr. Nat Center for Health Services Research, Hyattsville, Md., 1975-83; assoc. profl. lectr. George Washington U., 1976-78; v.p. div. health affairs Project HOPE, Millwood, Va., 1983-90; adminstr. Health Care Fin. Adminstrn., Washington, 1990-92; dep. asst. to the pres. for policy devel. White House, 1992-93; sr. fellow Project HOPE, Bethesda, Md., 1993—, chair phys. payment rev. com., 1995-97; chmn. Medicare Payment Adv. Commn., 1997-2001; co-chair Pres.'s Task Force to Improve Healthcare Delivery for Vets., 2001—. Contbr. 100 articles in field to profl. jours. Vol. Am. Heart Assn., 1980-85; mem. health adv. com. Compt. Gen. U.S., 1987-90; bd. dirs. United Healthcare Corp., Adv. Tiss Sci., Syncor Internat., ManorCare, Gentiva Health Svcs., Inc., Quest Diagnostics; mem. vis. com. med. sch. U. Mich., 1993-97; trustee United Mine Workers Am. Retirement Fund, 1993—. Flinn Found. disting. scholar, 1985; recipient Dean Conley award Am. Coll. Healthcare Execs., 1989. Mem. NAS (mem. inst. medicine 1989—), Am. Econ. Assn. (women's com. 1982-84), Fedn. Orgns. of Profl. Women (chmn. econ. task force 1981-83), Am. Statis. Assn., Nat. Tax Assn., Washington Women Economists, Assn. Health Svcs. Rsch. (dir. 1984-87), Found. Health Svcs. Rsch. (bd. dirs. 1987-90), Cosmos Club (Washington). Home: 2807 Battery Pl NW Washington DC 20016-3439

WILENSKY, HAROLD L. political science and industrial relations educator; b. New Rochelle, N.Y., Mar. 3, 1923; s. Joseph and Mary Jane (Wainsten) W.; children: Stephen David, Michael Alan, Daniel Lewis Student, Goddard Coll., 1940-42; AB, Antioch Coll., 1947; MA, U. Chgo., 1949, PhD, 1955. Asst. prof. sociology U. Chgo., 1951-53, asst. prof. indsl. relations, 1953-54; asst. prof. sociology U. Mich., Ann Arbor, 1954-57, assoc. prof., 1957-61, prof., 1961-62, U. Calif., Berkeley, 1963-82, prof. polit. sci., 1982—, research sociologist Inst. Indsl. Relations, 1963—, project dir. Inst. Internat. Studies, 1970-90; project dir. Ctr. for German and European Studies, 1994-96, Inst. Govtl. Studies, 1996—. Mem. rsch. career awards com. Nat. Inst. Mental Health, 1964—67; cons. in field. Author: Industrial Relations: A Guide to Reading and Research, 1954, Intellectuals in Labor Unions: Organizational Pressures on Professional Roles, 1956, Organizational Intelligence: Knowledge and Policy in Government and Industry, 1967, The Welfare State and Equality: Structural and Ideological Roots of Public Expenditures, 1975, The New Corporatism, Centralization, and the Welfare State, 1976, Rich Democracies: Political Economy, Public Policy, and Performance, 2002, (with C.N. Lebeaux) Industrial Society and Social Welfare, 1965, (with others) Comparative Social Policy, 1985, (with L. Turner) Democratic Corporatism and Policy Linkages, 1987; editor: (with C. Arensberg and others) Research in Industrial Human Relations, 1957, (with P.F. Lazarsfeld and W. H. Sewell) The Uses of Sociology, 1967; contbr. articles to profl. jours. Recipient aux. award Social Sci. Rsch. Coun., 1962, Book award McKinsey Found., 1967; fellow Ctr. for Advanced Study in Behavioral Scis., 1956-57, 62-63, German Marshall Fund, 1978-79; Harry A. Millis rsch. awardee U. Chgo., 1950-51. Fellow AAAS; mem. AAUP, Internat. Sociol. Assn., Internat. Polit. Sci. Assn., Indsl. Relations Research Assn. (exec. com. 1965-68), Soc. for Study Social Problems (chmn. editorial com.), Am. Polit. Sci. Assn., Am. Sociol. Assn. (exec. council 1969-72, chmn. com. on info. tech. and privacy 1970-72), Council European Studies (steering com. 1980-83). Democrat. Jewish. Avocations: music, trumpet, skiing. Office: U Calif Dept Polit Sci 210 Barrows Hall Berkeley CA 94720-1902 E-mail: hwilensk@socrates.berkeley.edu.

WILENSKY, JULIUS M. publishing company executive; b. Stamford, Conn., Oct. 10, 1916; s. Joseph and Mary (Wainstein) W.; m. Dorothy T. Jobrack, July 2, 1939 (dec. 1998); children— Joseph L. (dec.), Nancy L. Jamie, Martha J. Hansen; m. Jennifer Meinert Wilensky, Aug. 13, 2000. Student, Rensselaer Poly. Inst., 1934-36. Methods engr. Yale & Towne Mfg. Co., Stamford, 1939-49, prodn. mgr., 1953-57; dir. purchasing lock and hardware div. Eaton Yale & Towne, Rye, N.Y., 1957-67; mayor of Stamford,

1969-73; dir. materials, arms operations Winchester div. Olin Corp., New Haven, 1973-78; pres. Wescott Cove Pub. Co., 1978—. Lectr. in field. Author guide books on cruising L.I. Sound, Cape Cod, Windward Islands, Bay Islands of Honduras and Abacos; contbr. articles to boating mags. and newspapers; comtbg. editor: Rudder, 1970-77; author cruising columns Ea. and So. edits. Sea mag., 1978-80, Rudder mag., 1981-83; editor cruising guides to Tahiti, French Soc. Islands, Maine (2 vols.), Turkey, Belize, Mexico's Caribbean Coast, I Don't Do Portholes, Lights and Legends, Beachcombing and Beachcrafting, Pacific Wanderer, Irma Quarterdeck Reports, Inside American Paradise, Beachcruising and Coastal Camping, Circumnagivation: Sail the Trade Winds (2 vols.), First Time Around, Chesapeake Bay Cruising Guide-Vol. I, Upper Bay, Florida Keys and Everglades Cruising Guide. Bd. dirs. Stamford Ctr. for Arts, 1981-90; treas. Lifeline, 1983-85; first v.p. Met. Regional Coun., 1973; mem. Tri-State Regional Planning Commn., 1971-73, Stamford Bd. Fin., 1965-69, Stamford Planning Bd., 1963-65; chmn. Coun. Rep. Clubs, Stamford, 1961-62. With USAAF, 1943-46. Named Republican of Yr. Stamford Reps., 1962 Mem. Am. Mgmt. Assn., Stamford Power Squadron, Stamford Good Govt. Assn. (dir., treas. 1949-57), Stamford Chamber Residences (pres. 1953-55) Home: Apt 54 202 Soundview Ave Stamford CT 06902-7046 Fax: (203)383-8143. *To be productive in fields or enterprises which are useful to other people has been my aspiration, and it's a high one. It's important to set goals early in life, then follow a plan to obtain the education and experience required to achieve these goals. Courage, honesty, objectivity, determination, hard work, and consideration for others will enable one to become outstanding in any field.*

WILENSKY, ROBERT J. plastic surgeon, historian; b. N.Y.C., Oct. 2, 1941; s. Thomas and Gertrude Wilensky; m. Gail S. Roggin Aug. 4, 1963; children: Peter, Sara. BA, U. Mich., 1962, MD, 1966; PhD in History, Am. U., 2000. Diplomate Am. Bd. Surgery, Am. Bd. Plastic Surgery. Resident in gen. surgery U. Md., Balt., 1969-73; resident in plastic surgery U. Mich., Ann Arbor, 1973-75; pvt. practice, Washington, 1975-99; historian Am. U., 2000—, George Mason U., Va., 2000—. Chmn. sect. plastic surgery Columbia Hosp. for Women, Washington, 1983-93. Contbr. articles to med. jours., including Am. Jour. Ob-Gyn., Jour. Plastic and Reconstructive Surgery, Clin. Procs. Children's Hosp.; also chpts. to books. Capt. M.C., U.S. Army, 1967-69, Vietnam. Decorated Bronze Star. Fellow ACS; mem. Am. Soc. Plastic Surgery, Am. Soc. Aesthetic Surgery, Nat. Capital Soc. Plastic Surgery (pres. 1992), Washington Soc. History Medicine (pres. elect). Jewish. Avocations: biking, skiing, photography. Home and Office: 2807 Battery Pl NW Washington DC 20016-3439 E-mail: robertjwilensky@erols.com.

WILENSKY, ROBERT L. cardiologist, educator; b. Amsterdam, The Netherlands, Aug. 21, 1954; m. Emily Pollard. BA, U. Colo., 1976; MD with distinction, U. Amsterdam, The Netherlands, 1985. Diplomate Am. Bd. Internal Medicine, Am. Bd. Cardiology, Am. Bd. Interventional Cardiology. Intern, resident in internal medicine Georgetown U. Med. Ctr./VA Med. Ctr., Washington, 1985-88; fellow in cardiovascular diseases Krannert Inst. Cardiology Ind. U. Med. Ctr., 1988-91; lectr. dept. medicine Ind. U. Sch. Medicine, 1988-91, asst. prof. medicine, 1991-96, assoc. prof. medicine, 1996; asst. prof. medicine U. Pa., Phlia., 1996, assoc. prof. medicine, 1998; dir. cardiac catheterization lab. Presbyn. Med. Ctr., U. Pa. Health Sys., Phila., 1996-99, dir. coronary care unit, 1997-99, dir. interventional cardiology rsch., 1999—. Rsch. assoc. Krannert Inst. Cardiology Ind. U. Med. Ctr., 1991-96, head cardiac catheterization lab Wishard Meml. Hosp., 1992-96. interim chief cardiovascular sect. presbyn. Med. Ctr., U. Pa. Health Sys., 1997; session chmn. numerous meetings and symposia; lectr. in field; chmn. Data Safety and Monitoring Bd., 1997; manuscript reviewer for med. jours. Contbr. articles to profl. jours. Recipient Quality award USPHS, 1999. Fellow Am. Coll. Cardiology, Am. Fedn. Clin. Rsch.; mem. Am. Heart Assn. (mem. coun. on clin. cardiology). Office: Hosp of U Pa 3400 Spruce St Philadelphia PA 19104-4206

WILES, BETTY JANE, accountant; b. Scott County, Ark., Dec. 21, 1940; d. Edd and Nellie Margaret (Richey) Staggs; m. Ralph A. Wiles, July 18, 1959; children: Ralph A. Jr., Penny Margaret. BBA magna cum laude, Henderson State Coll., 1983. CPA, Ark. Sec. Royalty Holding Co., Oklahoma City, 1959-65, Rector & Eubanks, Mena, Ark., 1966-69; paralegal Shaw & Shaw Attys., 1969-83; pvt. practice acctg., 1984—. Cons. adv. bd. Mena H.S., 1985-86; cons. adv. bd. St. John Libr., Rich Mountain C.C., 1987-90, mem. svc. adv. com., 1988-90; trustee Mena Hosp. Com., 1991—. Mem. AAUW (pres. Mena br. 1993-95), Ark. Soc. CPAs (emergency assistance com., govt. acct. and auditing com. 1993-95), Ouachita Chpt. CPAs (v.p. 1996-97, pres. 199798—), Mena Lioness, Ouachita Writer's Guild. Clubs: Mena Lioness. Baptist. Avocation: writing poetry. Home: PO Box 522 Mena AR 71953-0522 Office: 513 Mena St Mena AR 71953-3337

WILES, CHARLES PRESTON, minister; b. Frederick, Md., Aug. 5, 1918; s. Charles Wesley and Nellie (Burgess) W.; m. Mary McCallum; children: Mary Margaret, Charles Preston, Wade Burgess. AB, Washington Coll., 1939; postgrad., U. Va., 1940; MA, Duke U., 1945, PhD (Univ. fellow 1947-51, Kearns Honor fellow 1949-50), 1951; B.D., Va. Theol. Sem., 1947. Ordained to ministry Episc. Ch., 1947. Priest-in-charge St. Joseph's Ch., Durham, N.C., 1947-51; rector St. Mary's Episcopal Ch., Burlington, N.J., 1951-64; pres., trustee Burlington Coll., 1951-64, faculty cons., 1956-64; mem. faculty Phila. Div. Sch., 1959-62, lectr. ch. history, 1960-62; dean St. Matthew's Episcopal Cathedral, Dallas, 1964-87, dean emeritus, 1989; assoc. priest St. Luke's, 1987—. Faculty U.S. Army War Coll., Carlisle, Pa., 1964; dep. gen. Conv. from Diocese Dallas, 1967, 69, 70, 73, 76, 79; del. Provincial Synod from Diocese Dallas, 1966, 69, 72, 75, 78; mem. exec. council Diocese Dallas, 1967-77, 84-86, pres. mem. standing com., 1970-73, pres., 1971-73, mem. bd. missions, 1967-69, chmn. dept. coll. work, 1965-71, mem. bd. examing chaplains, 1965-71; mem. standing liturgical commn.; dean, warden Cathedral Center for Continuing Edn. and Pastoral Concern, 1971-87, Commn. Ministry, 1971-76; dean Dallas Deanery, 1965-69, 84-86, Bicentennial preacher, 1975; pres. convocation and clericus Diocese of N.J., 1961-64; examining chaplain, mem. bd. missions, mem. bd. Christina edn., dean Burlington-Trenton convocation; instr., dean Drew Conf. for Adults in N.J., 1952-56; retreat conductor St. Martin's House, Bernardsville, N.J., St. John Bapt. Convent, Mendhan, N.J.; dean Diocesan Sch. Religion, N.J., 1962-63, Anglican Sch. Theology, 1971-75; parish life lab. and weekend conductor Nat. Dept. Christian Edn., 1962; co-founder, dean Princeton (N.J.) Conf., 1956-64; mem. Goals for Dallas Com.; co-chmn. N.Am. Cathedral Deans' Conf., 1980-81 Author: Sacrament and Sacrifice, 2d edit., 1973, Lancelot Andrews, Caroline Divine, 1951, Lift Up Your Hearts, 1956, A Manual of Prayers, 1975, The Holy Eucharist: Word and Sacrament, 1993, The Gate of Heaven, 1993, A Centennial Narrative History of the Episcopal Diocese of Dallas, 1995, Troubadours of God, 1998, Windows for Faith, 2000. Trustee Gen. Theol. Sem., 1968-80; bd. dirs. Evergreen Home for Aging, St. Philip's Community Center, Overseas Mission Soc. Named Priest of Yr., 1969 Mem. Navy League, Ch. Hist. Soc. (dir. 1960-68), Kiwanian Club (Disting. Svc. award 1951, Disting. Citizen award Brunswick, Md. 1986), Dallas Athletic club, Chaparral, Vesper (Phila.) Club, Burlington Country Club. Home: 7023 Northwood Rd Dallas TX 75225-2439 E-mail: deanwdallastexas@mymail.com.

WILES, DAVID MCKEEN, chemist; b. Springhill, N.S., Can., Dec. 28, 1932; s. Roy McKeen and Olwen Gertrude (Jones) W.; m. Valerie Joan Rowlands, June 8, 1957; children: Gordon Stuart, Sandra Lorraine. B.Sc. with honors, McMaster U., 1954, M.Sc., 1955; PhD in Chemistry, McGill U., 1957. Research officer chemistry div. Nat. Research Council of Can., Ottawa, 1959-66, head textile chemistry sect. chemistry div., 1966-75, dir. chemistry div., 1975-90; pres. Plastichem Cons., Victoria, B.C., Can., 1990—. Bd. dirs. MLB Industries, Malahat Sys. Corp.; chmn. Can. High Polymer Forum, 1967-69; v.p. N.Am. Chem. Congress, Mexico City, 1975 Contbr. articles to profl. jours.; mem. editl. adv. bd. numerous profl. jours.; patentee in field. Can. Ramsay Meml. fellow, 1957-59 Fellow Chem. Inst. Can. (chmn. bd. dirs. 1972-74, pres. 1975-76, Dunlop Lectr. award 1981), Royal Soc. Chem. London, Royal Soc. Can.; mem. Am. Chem. Soc. (Polymer Chem. div.). Home and Office: 3965 Juan Fuca Terr Victoria BC Canada V8N 5W9 E-mail: dmwiles@telus.net.

WILES, JON W(HITNEY), education educator, consultant; b. Mineola, N.Y., Sept. 22, 1944; s. Kimball and Hilda (Long) W.; m. Margaret Alison, Dec. 28, 1966 (div. 2001); children: Amy Kathryn, Michael Whitney; m. Michele Tillier, Nov. 20, 2001. BA in Edn., U. Fla., 1966, MEd, 1967, EdD, 1972. Classroom tchr. Broward County Schs., Ft. Lauderdale, Fla., 1967-68; asst. prof. George Peabody Coll., Vanderbilt U., Nashville, 1972-75; chair dept. edn. U. Tex., Arlington, 1975-77; assoc. dean, acting dean U. Mont., Missoula, 1977-81; prof. edn. U. South Fla., Tampa, 1981-98; prof. U. North Fla., 1998—. Dir. Civil Engr. Corps Officers Sch., 1970; rsch. project dir. U. Fla., 1971; field svcs. assoc. dir. George Peabody Coll., Vanderbilt U., 1972-75; dir. Learning Webs, Inc., 2000—. Author: (with G. Hass and J. Bondi) Curriculum Planning : A New Approach, 1974, Planning Guidelines for Middle School Education, 1976, (with D. Wiles and J. Bondi) Practical Politics for School Administrators, 1981, (with J. Bondi) Principles of School Administrators, 1981, (with J. Bondi) The School Board Primer, 1985, (with J. Bondi) Making Middle Schools Work, 1986, (J. Wiles) The Essentials of Teaching, 1990, (with J. Bondi) The Essential Middle School, 2nd edit., 1993, Promoting Change in Schools, 1993, (with J. Bondi) Supervision: A Guide to Practice, 5th edit., 1999, (with J. Bondi) Curriculum Development: A Guide to Practice, 5th edit., 1998, Curriculum Essentials, 1999, The New America Middle School, 2000, Learning Webs: Curriculum Journeys on the Internet, 2001; contbr. articles to profl. jours. Lt. USN, 1968-70. Mem. Phi Delta Kappa. Home: 7840 AIA S Saint Augustine FL 32080 Office: U North Fla 4567 Saint Johns Bluff Rd S Jacksonville FL 32224-2646

WILES, MARILYN MCCALL, communications consultant; b. Miami, Fla., Aug. 21, 1944; d. Alexander Charles and Dorothy (Peeples) McC.; m. David Kimball Wiles, Jan. 31, 1964; children: Corey, Matthew. BS, Fla. State U., 1966; MEd, U. Fla., 1968; D. of Edn., Va. Poly. Inst., 1974; Postdoctoral Assoc. (hon.), Scripps Found. Gerontology Ctr., 1977. Tchr. Ft. Knox (Ky.) High Sch., 1966-67, Westwood Jr. High Sch., Gainesville, Fla., 1967-69; asst prof. Miami U., Oxford, Ohio, 1975-77; sr. policy analyst N.Y. State Senate, Albany, 1978-83; coord. profl. svcs. NEA, 1983-84; pres. The Alliance for Lobbying, Evaluation, Rsch. and Tng., 1984—. Evaluation specialist Ctr. for Mgmt. Devel., FAA; cons. in field. Columnist Capital Dist. Bus. Review, Albany, 1990-98; author: Connections, 1998, (policy reports) Old Age and Ruralism, 1980, Energy Conservation and Schs., 1982; (instr. manual) The Social Problems of Aging, 1978; pub. The Directory of Successful Enterprising Women of New York; contbr. articles to profl. jours. and newsletters. Cons. Kettering (Ohio) Found., 1974-77; former bd. dirs. YWCA, 1985-87, Am. Heart Assn., Albany Symphony, 1992—; pres. bd. Sr. Citizens Found., Albany, v.p.; pres. bd. Jr. Achievement; mem. St. Johns County Health Improvement Partnership Chair; mem. adv. coun. Hudson Valley Girl Scouts U.S.; mem. Friends of Matanzas; bd. dirs. YWCA Maternal Infant Network; bd. dirs. Gift of Life Found., Inc.; bd. dirs. Sr. Svcs. Albany Found., pres.; mmem. St. Johns County Econ. Devel. Com.; mem. Fla. Export Trade Coun.; mem. South Anastasia Cmtys. Assn. Named to U.S. Dept. Labor for Bus. Hall of Fame; named Small Bus. Adv., U.S. Small Bus. Adminstrn., Leadership Am., 1998. Mem. AAUW, U.S.-China Friendship Assn., Women's Bus. Devel. Ctr. (founder, chmn. bd. dirs. 1985-89, chmn. bd. 1998—), New Scotland Hist. Assn., Am. Soc. Assn. Execs., Internat. Platform Assn., Internat. Trade Assn. (cert. trade specialist), Enterprising Women's Leadership Inst. (founder, pres., chmn. bd. dirs.), Rotary Internat. (dist. chair pub. rels. com., Paul Harris fellow), Albany-Colonie C. of C. (Capital Leadership 1978), St. Augustine/St. Johns County C. of C., Zeta Tau Alpha, Phi Kappa Phi. Avocations: swimming, bicycle riding, gardening, reading. Home: 8220 A1A S Saint Augustine FL 32080-8307 Office: EWLI PO Box 840021 Saint Augustine FL 32080-0021

WILES, PATRICIA DIANE, writer; b. Owensboro, Ky., May 6, 1963; d. Jimmie Gale and Barbara Sue Daniel; m. Timothy Dale Wiles; children: Ami, Jessica, Aaron. AA, Madisonville C.C., Madisonville, Ky., 1998. Author: (novels) A Year At The Buzzard Bait Motel , 2001; author: (author, essayist, commentator) (Radio Commentaries) WKMS-FM, NPR affiliate, 1997; contbr. essays to profl. jours. Mem. Lds Ch. Home: 1825 Forest Acres Dr Madisonville KY 42431

WILES, WILLIAM PATRICK, English language educator; b. Portland, Maine, Sept. 14, 1950; s. Earle Lawrence and Marion Katherine (Keenan) W.; m. Nancy Lee Biathrow, Dec. 29, 1979; children: Andrew, Caitlin. BA, Assumption Coll., 1972; MA, Middlebury Coll., 1996. Correctional instr. Vt. Dept. Corrections, Rutland, 1998—. Adj. prof. C.C. Vt., Rutland, 1981—; adj. instr. Champlain Coll., Vt., North Country C.C., N.Y., Johnson State Coll., Vt. Episcopalian. Avocations: music, crime fiction, Boston Red Sox. E-mails: (personal) (bus.). Home: 1342 Meadow Lake Dr Rutland VT 05701-9325 Office: PO Box 175 Rutland VT 05702-0175 E-mail: bwilesvt@adelphia.net., bwiles@doc.state.vt.us.

WILES, WILLIAM WHARTON, retired federal government official; b. Knoxville, Tenn., June 9, 1931; s. James H. and Sally May (Wharton) W.; m. Lessley K. Decker, Aug., 1961; 1 child, Kenneth W. BA, Murray State U., 1953; MBA, U. Ky., 1959; PhD, U. Wis., 1973. Instr. U. Ky., 1959-61; with Fed. Res. Sys., Washington, 1964-98, sec. of bd., 1981-98. With U.S. Army, 1954-56. Home: 4001 N Woodstock St Arlington VA 22207-2943 E-mail: Lessleyva@aol.com.

WILETS, LAWRENCE, physics educator; b. Oconomowoc, Wis., Jan. 4, 1927; s. Edward and Sophia (Finger) W.; m. Dulcy Elaine Margoles, Dec. 21, 1947; children: Ileen Sue, Edward E., James D.; m. Vivian C. Wolf, Feb. 8, 1976. BS, U. Wis., 1948; MA, Princeton, 1950, PhD, 1952. Research asso. Project Matterhorn, Princeton, N.J., 1951-53, U. Calif. Radiation Lab., Livermore, 1953; NSF postdoctoral fellow Inst. Theoretical Physics, Copenhagen, Denmark, 1953-55; staff mem. Los Alamos Sci. Lab., 1955-58; mem. Inst. Advanced Study, Princeton, 1957-58; mem. faculty U. Wash., Seattle, 1958—, prof. physics, 1962-95, prof. emeritus, 1995—. Cons. to pvt. and govt. labs.; vis. prof. Princeton, 1969, Calif. Inst. Tech., 1971 Author: Theories of Nuclear Fission, 1964, Nontopological Solitons, 1989; contbr. over 180 articles to profl. jours. Del. Dem. Nat. Conv., 1968. NSF sr. fellow Weizmann Inst. Sci., Rehovot, Israel, 1961-62; Nordita prof. and Guggenheim fellow Lund (Sweden) U., also Weizmann Inst., 1976—; Sir Thomas Lyle rsch. fellow U. Melbourne, Australia, 1989; recipient Alexander von Humboldt sr. U.S. scientist award, 1983 Fellow Am. Phys. Soc., AAAS; mem. Fedn. Am. Scientists, AAUP (pres. chpt. 1969-70, 73-75, pres. state conf. 1975-76), Phi Beta Kappa (chpt. pres. 1996-97), Sigma Xi. Clubs: Explorers. Achievements include research on theory of nuclear structure and reactions, nuclear fission, atomic structure, atomic collisions, many body problems, subnuclear structure and elementary particles. Office: U Wash Dept Physics PO Box 351560 Seattle WA 98195-1560 E-mail: wilets@u.washington.edu.

WILEY, ALBERT LEE, JR. physician, engineer, educator; b. Forest City, N.C., June 9, 1936; s. Albert Lee and Mary Louise (Davis) W.; m. Janet Lee Pratt, June 18, 1960; children: Allison Lee, Susan Caroline, Mary Catherine, Heather Elizabeth. B in Nuclear Engring., N.C. State U., 1958, postgrad., 1958-59; MD, U. Rochester, 1963; PhD, U. Wis., 1972. Diplomate Am. Bd. Nuclear Medicine, Am. Bd. Radiology, Am. Bd. Med. Physics, Am. Bd. Sci. in Nuclear Medicine. Nuclear engr. Lockheed Corp., Marietta, Ga., 1958; intern in surgery-medicine U. Va. Med. Sch., Charlottesville, 1963-64; resident in radiation therapy Sanford U., Palo Alto, Calif., 1964-65; resident, postdoctoral trainee U. Wis. Hosp., Madison, 1965-68; med. dir. USN Radiol. Def. Lab., San Francisco, 1968-69; nuclear safety instr. Navy Nuclear Weapons Training Ctr. North Is. Air Sta., 1968-70; staff physician Balboa Hosp., USN, San Diego, 1969-70; asst. prof. radiotherapy M.D. Anderson Hosp. U. Tex., Houston, 1972-73; assoc. dir., clin. dir. radiation oncology U. Wis., Madison, prof. radiology, human oncology, med. physics, nuclear safety ctr., 1970-88; vis. prof. U. Helsinki Hosp., Finland, 1979, The Norwegian Radium Hosp., Montebello, Norway, 1979; adj. prof. physics, chmn./prof. radiation, oncology, interim dir. cancer ctr. East Carolina U. Med. Sch., Greenville, N.C., 1988-93, prof. NC, 2001—; clin. prof. Cancer Ctr. East Carolina U., 2001—; prof. emeritus human oncology and radiology U. Wis., Madison, 2000—; cons. radiation medicine Watson Clinic, Lakeland, Fla., 1994—. Navy rep. to meetings on radiation accidents Internat. Atomic Energy Agy., U.S. Embassy, Vienna, Austria, 1969; nuclear safety instr. Nuclear Tng. Ctr.; sr. med. officer USN Radiol. Def. Lab. Radiation Accident Team, 1968-70; cons. Los Alamos Meson Therapy Project, 1971-73, U.S. NRC, adv. com. on Nuclear Reactor Safeguards, 1981-82, Nat. Cancer Inst., VA, 1989-2000, Dept. Vet. Affairs; completed bus. adminstrv. program in med. mgmt. U. N.C.-Chapel Hill, Sch. of Bus., 1999; advisor, cons. numerous univs., govt. agys. and biotech. corps.; gov. apptd. mem. Wis. State Radioactive Waste Bd., Wis. Gov.'s Coun. on Biotech., Gov.'s Com. on UN. Author more than 150 articles and abstracts on med. physics, med. and environ. health physics, neutron radiobiology, nuclear medicine, radiation biology and treatment of pancreatic, prostate, and head/neck cancer; assoc. editor Jour. Med. Physics. Rep. candidate for U.S. Congress for 2d Wis. dist., 1982, 84; rep. primary candidate for gov., State of Wis., 1986; mem. Greenville Mayor's Drug Task Force, 1989-93; bd. dirs. Greenville Salvation Army, 1989-94; Rep. primary candidate N.C. 1st Dist. U.S. Congress, 2000; Dem. primary candidate U.S. Senate, 2002; Dem. primary candidate for U.S. Senate from N.C., 2002. Lt. comdr. USNR, 1959-89, ret. Oak Ridge Inst. Nuclear Studies fellow N.C. State U., 1958-59; Phillips Acad. Andover scholar, 1953. Fellow: N.C. Inst. Polit. Leadership, Am. Coll. Nuclear Medicine, Am. Coll. Radiology, Am. Coll. Preventive Medicine; mem.: AMA, AAUP, Fla. Vols. in Medicine, N.C. Med. Soc., Am. Acad. Health Physics, Am. Bd. Sci. Nuc. Medicine (sec.-treas.), Am. Coll. Occupl.-Environ. Medicine, N.C. Assn. Physics Tchrs., Am. Soc. Therapeutic Radiation Oncologists, Am. Assn. Physicists in Medicine, Am. Nuc. Soc., Am. Legion, U.S. Navy Inst., Am. Cancer Soc. (N.C. bd.dirs. 1989—93, pres. Polk Count, Fla. 1995), VFW, Vietnam Vets. Am., Scottish Rite, Masons, N.C. Rotary, IEEE (sr.), Tau Beta Pi, Phi Eta Sigma, Sigma Phi Epsilon, Phi Kappa Phi, Sigma Xi. Avocations: fishing, politics, painting, languages, hiking. Home: PO Box 588 Salter Path Rd Salter Path NC 28575-0588 E-mail: aljanwiley@aol.com.

WILEY, CARL ROSS, timber company executive; b. Astoria, Oreg., Apr. 17, 1930; s. Hamilton Ross and Ada Ellen (Smith) W.; m. Dolores Eileen Brice, Dec. 19, 1953; children: Susan, Steven, Kenneth. BS in Indsl. Engring., Oreg. State U., 1958; grad. exec. tng. program, MIT, 1974. Quality control engr. Oreg. Metall. Corp., 1958-59; indsl. engr. Osborne Electronics Corp., Portland, Oreg., 1959-62; v.p. timber and mfg. Boise Cascade Corp., Idaho, 1962-80; exec. v.p. Roseburg (Oreg.) Lumber Co., 1980-85; chief exec. officer Puget Sound Plywood, Tacoma, 1986-93; pres., CEO Lane Plywood, Eugene, Oreg., 1993-96; retired, 1996. Bd. dirs. Boise YMCA, 1975-78. With AUS, 1951-53. Mem. Am. Plywood Assn. (trustee), Western Wood Products Assn. (bd. dirs., chmn. econ. svcs. 1974-80). Lutheran. E-mail: wileycd@juno.com.

WILEY, CATHERINE ANNE, literature educator; b. Goshen, Ny, Sept. 26, 1965; d. John P. Wiley, Jr. and Barbara Teresa Wiley. BA, Reed Coll., Portland, OR, 1989; MA, Temple Univ., Philadelphia, PA, 1995, PhD, 2001. Asst. prof. Temple Univ., Philadelphia, Pa., 2001—. Contbr. articles to profl. jours. Mem.: Modern Lang. Assoc. Home: 1036 Montgomery Ave Narberth PA 19072-1606 Office: Temple University English Dept 1114 W Berks Street 10th Fl Philadelphia PA 19122

WILEY, DAVID COLE, producer; b. Long Beach, Calif., Sept. 12, 1948; s. Norman Cole and Bettigene Rosamond W. Ind. prodr., 1987—. Prodr.: Abduction-the UFO Soap, 1987, Speak-Out, 1988-89, Coal Canyon BMX, 1989, PC 101-Computer Repair, 1989, Young Lives, 1990, A Slice of Life, 1990, 91, Hidden Talents, 1992, Rock Talk, 1992—, History of the Santa Ana Canyon, 1994-2001, Buena Park Journal, 1994-2001, Avenging Angel, 2001; (documentaries) In Search of the Butterfield Trail, 1990, George Key Ranch - Centennial Celebration, 1993, Visitors from Catalan, 1996, History of the Santa Ana River, 1997, The Steam Kalliope, 1998, Plan 10 from Outer Space, 1998, Avenging Angel, 2001, History of Orange County, 2002. Vice-pres. Santa Ana Canyon Hist. Coun., 1995-2001. Recipient Western Access Video Excellence award Nat. Fedn. Local Cable Programmers, 1992, CABY Comcast Cablevision, 1996. Mem. Alliance Cmty. Media. Address: PO Box 6481 Fullerton CA 92834-6481

WILEY, DIANNE, aeronautical engineer; PhD in Applied Mechanics, UCLA; student, Def. Systems Mgmt. Coll., 1996. With Northrop Grumman, mgr. airframe tech., sr. tech. specialist on B-2 program; program mgr. Boeing Phantom Wks., Seal Beach, Calif. Office: Boeing Phantom Works PO Box 2515 Seal Beach CA 90740*

WILEY, EDWIN PACKARD, retired lawyer; b. Chgo., Dec. 10, 1929; s. Edwin Garnet and Marjorie Chastina (Packard) W.; m. Barbara Jean Miller, May 21, 1949; children: Edwin Miller, Clayton Alexander, Stephen Packard. BA, U. Chgo., 1949, JD, 1952. Bar: Wis. 1952, Ill. 1952, U.S. Dist. Ct. (ea. dist.) Wis. 1953, U.S. Supreme Ct. 1978. Assoc. Foley & Lardner, Milw., 1952-60, ptnr., 1960-98; ret. Bd. dirs. Genetic Testing Inst., Inc., other corps. and founds. Co-author: Bank Holding Companies: A Practical Guide to Bank Acquisitions and Mergers, 1988, Wisconsin Uniform Commercial Code Handbook, 1971; author: Promotional Arrangements: Discrimination in Advertising and Promotional Allowances, 1976; editor in chief U. Chgo. Law Rev., 1952. Bd. dirs. Blood Ctr. of Southeastern Wis., pres., 1978-82; pres. Blood Ctr. Rsch. Found., Inc., 1983-87; v.p. Friends of Schlitz Audubon Ctr., Inc., 1975-87; active United Performing Arts Fund of Milw.; pres. Wis. Conservatory ofMusic, 1968-73; pres. First Unitarian Soc. Milw., 1961-63; v.p. Mid-Am. Ballet Co., 1971-73, Milw. Ballet Co., 1973-74; pres. Florentine Opera Co., 1983-86; bd. dirs. Milw. Symphony Orch., pres., 1993-95; bd. dirs. Milw. Pub. Mus., Inc., sec., 1992—; bd. dirs. Wis. History Found., v.p., 1998—; bd. dirs. Preserve Our Parks, Inc., 1999—; mem. Wis. Gov.'s Commn. on Historic Sites, 2002--. Mem. ABA, State Bar of Wis., Milw. Bar Assn., Am. Law Inst., Order of Coif, Univ. Club, Phi Beta Kappa (pres. Greater Milw. assn. 1962-63). Home: 929 N Astor St Unit 2101 Milwaukee WI 53202-3488 E-mail: epwiley@execpc.com., eqiley@foleylaw.com.

WILEY, GREGORY ROBERT, publisher; b. Sept. 21, 1951; s. William Joseph and Terese (Kunz) W.; children: Kathleen, Mary Glennon. BA in Pers. Adminstrn., U. Kans., 1974. Dist. sales mgr. Reader's Digest, St. Loius, 1976-80, regional sales dir. Chgo., 1980-82; nat. sales mgr. retail divsn. Rand McNally & Co., 1982-83, nat. sales mgr. premium incentive divsn., 1983-86, nat. sales mgr. bookstore and mass market sales, 1986-88; book pub. The Sporting News, St. Louis, 1988-90; v.p. mktg. Marketmakers Internat., 1990-93, Sofsource Inc., St. Louis, 1993—. Mem. Nat. Premium Sales Execs., Promotional Mktg. Assn. Am. Roman Catholic. Avocations: private pilot, historic restoration, golf. Office: Sofsource Inc Ste 120 14615 Manchester Rd Saint Louis MO 63131 Home: Apt 1B 4309 Maryland Ave Saint Louis MO 63108-2748

WILEY, HELEN BERNADETTE, interior designer; b. Herrin, Ill., May 15, 1944; d. Sidney and Marguerite Bernadette (Mathews) Jenkins; m. James Boyd Wiley, June 25, 1966; 1 child, Karen Bernadette. B.S., Bradley U., 1966. Interior designer C.S. Wo & Co., Honolulu, 1968-75; comml. rep. Sherwin-Williams Co., Honolulu, 1975-76; interior designer Very Spl. Environments, Honolulu, 1976-79; residential designer Midwest Furniture Corp., Denver, 1979-80; interior designer, owner Welcome Homes Interiors, Springfield, Ohio, 1980-86; pres. design firm The Focal Point, Inc., Springfield and Cin., 1986— . Active S. Fountain Ave. Preservation Assn. Mem. Nat. Assn. Female Execs., Abilities Unlimited (sec.-treas. 1986), Springfield/Clark County C. of C. Republican. Episcopalian. Avocations: art and sculpture collecting; equestrian riding. Office: The Focal Point Inc 345 Upper Valley Pik Springfield OH 45504

WILEY, JASON LARUE, JR. neurosurgeon; b. Canandaigua, N.Y., Dec. 2, 1917; s. Jason LaRue and Eva Althea (Moore) W.; m. Alma Williams, Jan. 4, 1944 (div. Feb. 1956); children: Robert W., Richard L.; m. Ann Valentine Gerrish, Apr. 14, 1956 (div. July 1979); children: Martha V., Pamela M., Catherine A. Student, Antioch Coll., 1934-37; MD, Harvard U., 1941. Diplomate Am. Bd. Surgery, Am. Bd. Neurol. Surgery. Intern Kings County Hosp., Bklyn., 1941-42; asst. resident surgery Ellis Hosp., Schenectady, N.Y., 1948-49; from asst. to assoc. resident surgery Rochester (N.Y.) Gen. Hosp., 1949-51; from asst. to assoc. to chief resident neurosurgery Yale U. and Hartford Hosp., New Haven and Hartford Conn., 1951-54; practice medicine specializing in neurosurgery Kansa City, Mo., 1954-56, Rochester, 1956—. Chief neurosurgery Rochester Gen. Hosp., 1959-71, emeritus neurosurgeon, 1989—; clin. asst. prof. neurosurgery U. Rochester, 1961-88. Mem. Bd. for Profl. Med. Conduct, N.Y. State Dept. Health, Albany, N.Y., 1985—. Served to lt. comdr. USN, 1942-47, PTO. Mem. Med. Soc. County Monroe, Med. Soc. State N.Y., N.Y. State Neurosurg. Soc., Congress Neurol. Surgeons, Am. Assn. Neurol. Surgeons, Canandaigua Yacht Club. Republican. Episcopalian. Avocations: sailing, skiing, fishing, genealogy. Office: 1445 Portland Ave Rochester NY 14621-3036

WILEY, JEROLD WAYNE, environmental services executive, retired air force officer; b. Urbana, Ill., Jan. 7, 1944; s. Jesse Scott and Eula Eileen (Deffenbaugh) W.; m. Gloria J. USelton, May 6, 1982; children: Jackson Scott, Justin Wayne. BS, So. Ill. U., 1967; MS, U. N.D., 1973. Registered laundry and linen dir. 2001, Am. Laundry and Linen Coll. Commd. 2d lt. USAF, 1968, advanced through grades to maj., 1982; minuteman II launch officer 321 Strategic Missile Wing, Grand Forks AFB, N.D., 1969-73; minuteman II initial qualification instr. 4315 Combat Crew Tng. Squadron, Vandenberg AFB, Calif., 1973-76; asst. prof. aerospace studies Coll. St. Thomas, St. Paul, 1976-79; dir. trng. and devel. 325 Fighter Weapons Wing, Ops. Tng. Devel. Team, Tyndall AFB, Fla., 1979-83; chief internat tng. Joint U.S. Mil. Mission for Aid to Turkey, Ankara, 1983-85; comdr. 3743 Basic Mil. Tng. Squadron, Lackland AFB, Tex., 1985-87; chief acads. br. Hdqrs. Basic Mil. Tng. Sch., 1987-88; retired USAF, 1988; asst. dir. environ. svcs. North Miss. Med. Ctr., Tupelo, 1989-90; dir. environ. svcs. Bapt. Hosp., Miami, Fla., 1990-91; dir. housekeeping Great Oaks Nursing Home, Roswell, Ga., 1992-93; dir. environ. svcs. St. Francis Hosp., Columbus, 1993-94, ARAMARK svc. master, 1995—; asst. dir. environ. svcs. Baptist Med. Ctr., Montgomery, Ala., 1995—, U. Va. Med. Ctr., Charlottesville, Va., 1995-97; dir. environ. svcs. Palm Shores Retirement Ctr., St. Petersburg, Fla., 1997-98; dir. environ. svcs., safety dir. Madison County Hosp., London, 1998—. Contbr. articles to profl. jours. Pres. Madison County Habitat for Humanity; mem. London Bd. Zoning Appeals, Madison County Local Emergency Planning Com. Decorated Meritorious Svc. medal with 1 oak leaf cluster, Combat Readiness medal, Air Force Commendation medal with 2 oak leaf clusters, Humanitarian Svc. medal, Def. Meritorious Svc. medal. Mem. Am. Soc. Tng. & Devel., Am. Mgmt. Assn., Am. Assn. Cmty. & Jr. Colls., Nat. Cmty. Edn. Assn., Soc. Am. Foresters, Air Force Assn. (life), USTA (cert. umpire), Am. Soc. Healthcare Environ. Svcs., So. Ill. U. Alumni Assn. (life), Ret. Officers Assn. (life), Nat. Fire Protection Assn., Nat. Assn. Instl. Linen Mgmt., Am. Legion, Amvets, Exch. Club. Republican. Home: 194 N Main St London OH 43140-1156 E-mail: jwwiley@aol.com.

WILEY, MILLICENT YODER, retired secondary school educator, realtor; b. Mercedes, Tex., June 7, 1923; d. Frank and Grace Yoder; m. William Gregory Wiley, Mar. 25, 1946; children: Sandra Kay Wiley, Patti Gayle Wiley Stickle. BS, Tex. State Coll. Women, 1949; postgrad., U. Houston, 1950-53. Choral dir., music tchr. schs. in Tex. and La., 1945-60; tchr. Kingsville (Tex.) Ind. Sch. Dist., 1960-80, trustee, 1981-87, v.p., 1986-87; choral dir. H.M. King H.S., 1964-80; ret., 1980. Choral adjudication, Tex., 1960—; clinician for area choirs, 1965—86; area admissions advisor, adminstr. Pacific Am. Inst., 1976—80; state dir. South Tex. for Am. Internat. Edn. and Tng., 1980—83; Tex. rep. Internat. Travel Study, Inc., 1983—90; adminstr. Travel Selections, 1990—96, 2000; pianist Tex. State Fedn. Women's Clubs, 1994—96. Ch. organist various Meth. Ch., Tex. and La., 1935-65; bd. dirs. Kingsville chpt. Am. Heart Assn., 1973-78, Cmty. Concerts Assn., 1994-96, Helen Kleberg Cmty. Ctr., 1994-96, Kingsville Action Com.; adjudicator Tex. Choral Contests, 1960-96; mem. Tex. All-State Alumni Bd., 1995, 2000; active Mayor's City Com., Mayor's Future Com., 1993-96, Rep. Task Force. Recipient various certs. appreciation. Mem.: NEA, Tex. Assn. Sch. Bds. (trustee 1981—87, Kingsville ISD v.p. 1986—87), Kingsville Ret. Tchrs., Tri-City Ret. Tchrs., Fgn. Study League (counselor 1970—76, adminstr. 1971—76, advisor, prin.), Nat. Bd. Realtors, Multiple Listing Svc. Kingsville, Tex. Assn. Realtors, Kingsville Bd. Realtors (bd. dirs. 1994—95), Tex. Music Adjudicators Assn., Tex. State Tchrs. Assn., Tex. Choral Dirs. Assn. (state clinic condr. 1977, accompanist for vocal scloists , instrumental soloists, choirs 1939—98, piano soloist 1940—46), Tex. Music Educators Assn. (bd. dirs. 1973—74), Music Educators Nat. Conf., Am. Choral Dirs. Assn., Am. Sch. Bd. Assn. (trustee 1980—87), 36th Divsn. Assn. (soloist for men's meetings and ceremonies 1980—, 1st v.p. nat. ladies aux. 1989—90, pres. 1990—91, 2nd v.p. 1999—2000), Kingsville C. of C. Navy League (bd. dirs. 1997—, nat. dir. 1998—), Gen. Women's Club Kingsville (parliamentarian 1992—94, pres. 1994—96), Duplicate Bridge Club, NAS Bridge Club, Kingsville Country Club, Monday Bridge Club, Exxon Bridge Club, Kiwanis (pianist Kingsville Club 1985—98), Rotary (pianist 1966—, first woman mem. 1987, chmn. membership devel. com. 1987—, fellowship chair 1997—98, mem. scholarship com. and social com. 2000—, fellowship chair 2001—02, past social chmn., program chmn. and membership chmn.), Exxon Annuitant Club (bd. dirs. 1992—94), Women's Club Kingsville (chmn. "As You Like It" dept. 1990, 1st vice chmn. 1992—94, gen. club parlimentarian 1992—94, pres. 1994—96), Music Club Kingsville (pres. 1982—84, 3d v.p. 1988—89, 1st v.p. 1989—91). Methodist. Home: 229 Helen Marie Ln Kingsville TX 78363-7305 Fax: 361-592-9300. E-mail: c21millicent@excite.com., millie@gcol.net.

WILEY, RICHARD ARTHUR, lawyer; b. Bklyn., July 18, 1928; s. Arthur Ross and Anna Thorsen (Holder) W.; m. Carole Jean Smith, Aug. 13, 1955; children: Kendra Elizabeth, Stewart Alan, Garett Smith. AB, Bowdoin Coll., Brunswick, Maine, 1948; BCL, Oxford (Eng.) U., 1951; LLM, Harvard U., 1959; LLD, Bowdoin Coll., 1994. Bar: Mass. 1954, U.S. Ct. Mil. Appeals 1954, U.S. Dist. Ct. Mass. 1962, U.S. Supreme Ct. 1985. Atty. John Hancock Mut. Life Ins. Co., Boston, 1956-58; from atty. to mng. ptnr. Bingham, Dana & Gould, 1959-76; gen. counsel, asst. sec. Dept. Def., 1976-77; v.p., counsel First Nat. Bank Boston, 1977-78, exec. v.p., 1978-85, Bank of Boston Corp., 1985; ptnr. Csaplar & Bok, Boston, 1986-90, mem. exec. com., 1987-90, chmn., 1989-90, of counsel, 1990, Gaston & Snow, Boston, 1990-91; dir. Powers and Hall P.C., 1991-94, of counsel, 1994-95, Hill & Barlow, Boston, 1995—. Bd. dirs., chmn. Automated Assemblies Corp., Mass. Higher Edn. Assistance Corp.; bd. dirs. Edn. Rsch. Inst., Nomadic Structures, Inc., Nypro, Inc., Carlo Gavazzi, Inc.; lectr. Boston U. Law Sch., 1961-64; past vice chmn. New Eng. Conf. on Doing Bus. Abroad; trustee New Eng. Legal Found., chmn., 1980-83; adj. prof. govt. and legal studies Bowdoin Coll., 1995—; adj. prof. law Boston Coll. Law Sch., 1998—. Author: Cases and Materials on Law of International Trade and Investment, 1961; contbr. articles to profl. jours. Bd. overseers Bowdoin Coll., 1966-81, pres., 1977-80, trustee, 1981-93, trustee emeritus, 1993—; mem. Mass. Edn. Financing Authority, 1986-91, chmn., 1987-91; mem. Wellesley (Mass.) Town Meeting, 1971-75, mem. fin. adv. com., 1973-74; chmn. Mass. Bd. Regents of Higher Edn., 1991; bd. regents Task Force on Student Fin. Aid, 1987; mem. Mass. Higher Edn. Coord. Coun., 1991-95, vice chmn., 1991-93, chmn., 1993-95; chmn. lawyers divsn. United Way Mass. Bay, 1975; mem. devel. com., trustees of donations Episcopal Diocese Mass., 1971-75; trustee, exec. com. North Conway Inst., mem., 1980-92, chmn., 1988-92; bd. trustees Internat. Coun. Trust, Boston; trustee, mem. exec. com., chmn. Mass. Taxpayers Found., 1989-92; chmn. bd. trustees World Peace Found., Boston, 1983-95; corporator Schepens Eye Rsch. Inst., 1991-95; dep. chmn. planning Mass. rep. state com., 1971, vice chmn. fin. com., 1971-72. Officer USAF, 1953-56. Decorated Air Force Commendation medal; recipient Dep. Def. Disting. Pub. Svc. medal, 1977; Rhodes scholar, 1949. Mem. ABA (vice chmn. fgn. and internat. bus. law com. 1967-69), Boston Bar Assn. (exec. com., antitrust com. 1965-68), Council on Fgn. Relations, Boston Com. on Fgn. Relations (mem. exec. com., chmn. 1980-83), Phi Beta Kappa.

WILEY, RICHARD EMERSON, lawyer; b. Peoria, Ill., July 20, 1934; s. Joseph Henry and Jean W. (Farrell) W.; m. Elizabeth J. Edwards, Aug. 6, 1960; children: Douglas S., Pamela L. BS with distinction, Northwestern U., 1955, JD, 1958; LLM, Georgetown U., 1962; LLD (hon.) , Cath. U. of Am., 1998. Bar: Ill. 1958, D.C. 1972. Pvt. practice, Chgo., 1962-70; gen. counsel FCC, Washington, 1970-72, mem., 1972-74, chmn., 1974-77, chmn. FCC's adv. com. on advanced TV svc., 1987-96; mng. ptnr. Wiley, Rein & Fielding, 1983—. Prof. law John Marshall Law Sch., U. Chgo., 1963-70. Chmn. adv. bd. Inst. for Tele-Info., Columbia U., 1989—. Capt. AUS, 1959-62. Recipient Emmy award Nat. Acad. Arts, 1997, Medal of Honor, Electronic Industries Am., 1996, Disting. Svc. award, Nat. Assn. Broadcasters. Fellow Am. Bar Found.; mem. ABA (mem. ho. of dels. 1969-71, 77-84, chmn. young lawyers sect., 1977-84, chmn. Forum com. on communications 1969, chmn. bd. editors ABA Jour. 1984-89, chmn. com. on scope and correlation of work 1989, chmn. adminstrv. law and regulatory practice 1993-94), Fed. Bar Assn. (pres. 1977), Fed. Communications Bar Assn. (pres. 1987), Ill. Bar Assn., Chgo. Bar Assn., Adminstrv. Conf. U.S. (coun., sr. fellow), Phi Delta Phi, Phi Delta Kappa. Methodist. Home: 3818 N Woodrow St Arlington VA 22207-4345 Office: Wiley Rein & Fielding 1776 K St NW Ste 1100 Washington DC 20006-2332 E-mail: rwiley@wrf.com.

WILEY, RICHARD GORDON, electrical engineer; b. Wind Ridge, Pa., Aug. 25, 1937; s. Asa Gordon and Mildred Louise (Fisher) W.; m. Jane Bradley Wilmes, Oct. 15, 1960; children: Richard Bradley, John Gordon, Laura Jane, Timothy Scott, Martha Anne, James Robert. BS, Carnegie-Mellon U., 1959, MS, 1960; PhD, Syracuse U., 1975. Rsch. engr. Syracuse (N.Y.) Rsch. Corp., 1960-67, staff cons. engr., 1975-86; asst. dir. applied rsch. Lab. Microwave Systems, Inc., Syracuse, 1967-75; v.p., chief scientist Rsch. Assocs. Syracuse, Inc., 1986—. Author: Electronic Intelligence: The Analysis of Radar Signals, 1982, 2d edit. 1993, Electronic Intelligence: The Interception of Radar Signals, 1985; co-author: Radar Vulnerability to Jamming, 1990; co-inventor pulse train analysis using personal computer, 1987. 1st lt. U.S. Army, 1961-63. Fellow IEEE; mem. Assn. Old Crows. Republican. Episcopalian. Office: Rsch Assocs Syracuse Inc 6280 Northern Blvd Ste 100 East Syracuse NY 13057 E-mail: dickwiley@aol.com.

WILEY, THOMAS MATHEW, physician; b. Kansas City, Kans., Apr. 16, 1959; s. Thomas A. and Ruby Wiley; children: Seth, Marissa. BS, U. Kans., 1982, MD, 1986. Diplomate Am. Bd. Ob-Gyn. Resident in ob-gyn U. Chgo., 1986-90; ob-gyn Storment Vail Health Care, Topeka, 1990—, St. Francis Med. Ctr., Topeka, 1990—. Mem. ACOG, AMA, Am. Soc. Colposcopy, Am. Cervical Pathology. Office: Cons in Gyn-Obs Cons in Gynecology/Obstets 823 SW Mulvane St Ste 280 Topeka KS 66606-1671

WILEY, WILLIAM DAVID, engineer, hydrologist; b. Phoenix, Nov. 4, 1954; s. Don M. and Ellen Louise (Martins) W.; m. Cheryl Renea Gentry, Mar 1, 1986; children: Megan, Lisa. BS in Physical Geography, Ariz. State U., 1976, MS in Civil Engring., 1991. Registered profl. engr., Ariz. Watershed program mgr. U. Bur. of Land Mgmt., Cedar City, Utah, 1979-83; hydrologist Ariz. Dept. Health Svcs., Phoenix, 1983-86; groundwater sect. mgr. Ariz Dept. Environ. Quality, 1986-91; dep. dir. Ariz. Dept. Environ., 1991-94; with Ariz. Pub. Svc., 1994-98, mgr. environ. health/safety govt. affairs and corp. rels., 1996—2001; dir. environtl. programs TRW Inflatable Restraint Systems N.Am., Mesa, 1998—; sr. EHS policy advisor Pinnacle West Cap Corp., 2002—. Co-author: Multimedia Environmental Management, 1999; contbr. articles to Environment and Total Quality Mgmt. Coach Little League, Cedar City, Utah, 1981. Recipient Merit award U.S. Dept. Interior, Cedar City, Utah, 1981; Gov.'s Quality award State of Ariz., Phoenix, 1994. Mem. NSPE, Am. Soc. for Quality, Air and Waste Mgmt. Assn., Phi Beta Kappa. Achievements include development of "On the Road" outreach program for Ariz. Dept. Environ. Quality to bring agency to rural Ariz. on a regular basis. Avocations: hiking, tennis, golf. Home: 4100 W Linda Ln Chandler AZ 85226-2185 Office: Pinnacle West Cap Corp PO Box 53999 MS 8376 Phoenix AZ 85072-3999

WILFERT, CATHERINE M. medical association administrator, medical educator; Asst. prof. pediatrics Duke U., 1969-80, prof. pediatrics and microbiology, chief pediatric infectious diseases, 1980-98, prof. emeritus; sci. dir. Elizabeth Glaser Pediat. AIDS Found., Santa Monica, Calif., 1997—. Mem. Inst. Medicine. Office: Elizabeth Glaser Pediatric AIDS Found 2950 31st St Ste 125 Santa Monica CA 90405-3092*

WILFONG, BRENDA ANN, telecommunications executive; b. Ashland, Ohio, Jan. 2, 1963; d. Edward Eugene and Barbara Ann (Butterfield) Bush; m. Duane Hubert Wilfong, Oct. 22, 1984 (dec. Sept. 1994); children: Jessie Leona, Christina Elizabeth. BBA, Kent State U., 1989, postgrad., 1998. Asst. editor Ohio dir. Harris Pub. Co., Twinsburg, Ohio, 1983-84; accounts payable clerk M. O'Neil's Co., Akron, 1984-85; network mgmt. asst. Alltel Corp., Hudson, 1985-86, treasury asst., 1986-87, assoc. analyst treasury, 1987-92, carrier svcs. coord., 1992-93, sr. staff asst. Twinsburg, 1993-95, adminstr. carrier svcs., 1995—, contracts adminstr. Hudson, Ohio, 1995—. Recipient Brownie Mother Vol. award Girl Scouts Am., Akron, 1994. Mem. Inst. Mgmt. Accts. (editor newsletter 1990-92, dir. ins. 1992-94). Brethren. Avocations: reading medical journals, weight lifting, aerobics, classical music. Office: 50 Executive Pkwy Hudson OH 44236-1605 E-mail: wilfongb@hotmail.com.

WILFORD, JOHN NOBLE, JR. science news correspondent; b. Murray, Ky., Oct. 4, 1933; s. John Noble and Pauline (Hendricks) W.; m. Nancy Everett Watts, Dec. 25, 1966; 1 child, Nona. Student, Lambuth Coll., 1951-52; BS, U. Tenn., 1955; MA, Syracuse U., 1956; Internat. Reporting fellow, Columbia, 1961-62; DHL (hon.), R.I. Coll., 1987; DSc (hon.), Middlebury Coll., 1991. Reporter Comml. Appeal, Memphis, summers 1954-55; reporter Wall St. Jour., N.Y.C., 1956, 59-61; contbg. editor Time mag., 1962-65; sci. reporter N.Y. Times, 1965-73, asst. nat. editor, 1973-75, dir. sci. news, 1975-79, sci. corr., 1979—. Vis. journalist Duke U., 1984; McGraw lectr. Princeton U., 1985; Disting. prof. journalism, U. Tenn., Knoxville, 1989-90; mem. Am. Mus.-Mongolian Gobi Expdn., 1991, Dir.'s Visitor, Inst. for Advanced Study, 1995. Author: We Reach The Moon, 1969, The Mapmakers, 1981, The Riddle of the Dinosaur, 1985, Mars Beckons, 1990, The Mysterious History of Columbus, 1991; co-author: The New York Times Guide to the Return of Halley's Comet, 1985, (with William Stockton) Spaceliner, 1981, Israel: The Historical Atlas, 1997; editor: Scientists at Work, 1979, Cosmic Dispatches, 2000. With CIC AUS, 1957-59. Recipient Book award Aviation/Space Writers, 1970, Writing award Aviation/Space Writers, 1983, G.M. Loeb Achievement award U. Conn, 1972, Press award Nat. Space Club , 1974, AAAS-Westinghouse Sci. Writing award, 1983, Ralph Coats Roe medal ASME, 1995, Pulitzer prize, 1984, N.Y. Times Pulitzer Prize Winning Team, 1987, N.Y.C. Mayor's award, 2001, Am. Geol. Inst. award, 2001, Sagan award Coun. Sci. Soc. Pres., 2001. Mem. Nat. Assn. Sci. Writers, Authors Guild, Soc. Profl. Journalists, Am. Geog. Soc. (councilor 1994—, sec. 2000—), Am. Acad. Arts and Scis., Century Assn., Sigma Chi, Phi Kappa Phi, Phi Beta Kappa. Home: 232 W 10th St New York NY 10014-2976 Office: 229 W 43rd St New York NY 10036-3913 E-mail: wilford@nytimes.com.

WILFORD, WILLIAM GUSTAAF, investment company executive; b. Antwerp, Belgium, Jan. 17, 1943; s. Charles and Julienne Wilford; m. Marie-Claire De Vos, Feb. 15, 1980; children: Dennis, Maureen, Fabienne Gross, Christophe Gross, Michael. Student, St. Lodewyk, Antwerp, Inst. Lefebvre, Brussels, Inst. Catholique, France, INSEAD, Fontainebleau, France. CEO ATAB, Antwerp, 1966-98, Ter Eiken, Antwerp, 1980—, Concordimo, Antwerp, 1983—, Erable Invest, Antwerp, 1992—, Helimo, Antwerp, 1994—, Noordzee Helikopters Vlaanderen, Ostend, Belgium, 1997—. Bd. dirs. Algovision PLC, London, Best of Internet, Brussels. Recipient award Ridder in de Kroonorde, Eredeken Vande Arbeid, 1998. Avocations: squash, water skiing, alpine skiing, sailing, surfing. Office: Concordimo NV d'Herbouvillekaai 80 B-2020 Antwerp Belgium Fax: +32.3.248.25.60. E-mail: william.wilford@concordimo.be.

WILHELM, FRANK LEO, publisher, writer; b. Kansas City, Mo., Apr. 9, 1926; s. Matilda Theresa Wilhelm; m. Deena L. Levin, Mar. 2, 1950 (div. Sept. 22, 1992); children: David Donne, Anita Sue, Laura Jean. BA in English, U. Ill., 1950, MS in Vocat. Counseling, 1951. Registered social worker, Ill. Tchr. English, Bd. Edn., Windsor and Clifton, Ill., 1951-53; personnel mgr. J.P. Smith Shoes, Chgo., 1953-55; outside sales Ency. Britannica, 1955-57; vocat. counselor, supr. tng. Cook County, Ill. and State of Ill., 1957-89; owner Books of Am., Evanston, Ill., 1998—. Author: (poetry) Poetry City, USA, 1997, (novels) Francis, 1998, republished as Orphan's Odyssey, 2002. Folk dancer Folk Dance Coun. Chgo. With USN, 1944-46. Avocations: bridge, chess, gardening, cooking, ancient Mid-East history. Home: 2940 W Sherwin Ave Chicago IL 60645-1210 Office: BOA Pub Co PO Box 6272 Evanston IL 60204-6272 E-mail: BOAPublish@aol.com., xopo@aol.com.

WILHELM, KATE (KATY GERTRUDE), author; b. Toledo, June 8, 1928; d. Jesse Thomas and Ann (McDowell) Meredith; m. Joseph B. Wilhelm, May 24, 1947 (div. 1962); children: Douglas, Richard; m. Damon Knight, Feb. 23, 1963; 1 child, Jonathan. PhD in Humanities (hon.), Mich. State U., 1996. Writer, 1956—. Co-dir. Milford Sci. Fiction Writers Conf., 1963-76; lectr. Clarion Fantasy Workshop Mich. State U., 1968-94. Author: More Bitter Than Death, 1962; (with Theodore L. Thomas) The Clone, 1965, The Nevermore Affair, 1966, The Killer Thing, 1967, Let the Fire Fall, 1969, The Year of the Cloud, 1970, Abyss: Two Novellas, 1971, Margaret and I, 1971, City of Cain, 1971, The Clewiston Test, 1976, Where Late the Sweet Birds Sang, 1976, Fault Lines, 1976, Somerset Dreams and Other Fictions, 1978, Juniper Time, 1979; (with Damon Knight) Better Than One, 1980, A Sense of Shadow, 1981, Listen, Listen, 1981, Oh! Susannah, 1982, Welcome Chaos, 1983, Huysman's Pets, 1986; (with R. Wilhelm) The Hills Are Dancing, 1986, The Hamlet Trap, 1987, Crazy Time, 1988, Dark Door, 1988, Smart House, 1989, Children of the Wind: Five Novellas, 1989, Cambio Bay, 1990, Sweet, Sweet Poison, 1990, Death Qualified, 1991, And the Angels Sing, 1992, Seven Kinds of Death, 1992, Naming the Flowers, 1992, Justice for Some, 1993, The Best Defense, 1994, A Flush of Shadows, 1995, Malice Prepense, 1996, The Good Children, 1998, Defense for the Devil, 1999, No Defense, 2000, The Deepest Water, 2000, Desperate Measures, 2001; (multimedia space fantasy) Axoltl, U. Oreg. Art Mus., 1979, (radio play) The Hindenburg Effect, 1985; editor: Nebula Award Stories #9, 1974, Clarion SF, 1976; contbr. articles to popular mags., profl. jours. Mem. Nat. Writers Union, Mystery Writers Am., Authors Guild. Address: 1645 Horn Ln Eugene OR 97404-2957 E-mail: kwilhelm@msn.net.

WILHELM, SISTER PHYLLIS, religious organization administrator, director; b. Toledo, Aug. 3, 1941; d. Edward John and Ellen Catherine (Sorg) W. BA, St. Francis Coll., 1964; MEd in Instruction, U. Wis., Superior, 1994. Cert. tchr., Wis., elem. tchr. spl. edn., Ill.; joined Sisters of St. Francis of Mary Immaculate, 1959. Tchr. primary St. Rita of Casica Sch., Aurora, Ill., 1963-65, St. Joseph Sch., Manhattan, 1965-74, Holy Family-St. Francis Sch., Bayfield, Wis., 1974-77, tchr., 1979-99, prin., 1979-99, peace edn. instr. K-6, 1989-99, pastoral assoc., 1999—, dir. religious edn., 2000—. Tchr. spl. edn. Guardian Agenl Sch., Joliet, Ill., 1977-79. Recipient Outstanding Prin. award Wis. Assn. Non-Pub. Schs., 1999, Sister Catherine McNamee award for leadership in promoting cultural and econ. diversity, 1999. Mem. Superior Diocesan Prin. Assn. (treas. 1981-83, 96-99, Educator of Yr. award 1991), Phi Delta Kappa. Avocations: crafts, gardening, cooking. Home: 88850 Church Rd RR 1 Box 92 Bayfield WI 54814-9724 E-mail: pwilhelm@ncis.net.

WILHELM, ROBERT OSCAR, lawyer, civil engineer, developer; b. Balt., July 7, 1918; s. Clarence Oscar and Agnes Virginia (Grimm) W.; m. Grace Sanborn Luckie, Apr. 4, 1959. BSCE, Ga. Tech. Inst., 1947, MSIM, 1948; JD, Stanford U., 1951. Bar: Calif. 1952, U.S. Supreme Ct. Mem. Wilhelm, Thompson, Wentholt and Gibbs, Redwood City, Calif., 1952—; gen. cousnel Bay Counties Gen. Contractors; pvt. practice civil engring., Redwood City, 1952. Pres. Bay Counties Builders Escrow, Inc., 1972-88. Author: The Manual of Procedures for the Construction Industry, 1971, Manual of Procedures and Form Book for Construction Industry, 9th edit., 1995, Construction Law for Contractors, Architects and Engineers; columnist Law and You in Daily Pacific Builder, 1955-2001. With C.E., AUS, 1942-46. Named to Wisdom Hall of Fame, 1999. Mem. Bay Counries Civil Engrs. (pres. 1957), Peninsula Builders Exch. (pres. 1958-71, dir.), Calif. State Builders Exch. (treas. 1971), Del Mesa Carmel Cmty. Assn. (bd. dirs. 1997-99), Masons, Odd Fellows, Eagles, Elks. Home: 134 Del Mesa Carmel Carmel CA 93923-7950 Office: 702 Marshall St Ste 510 Redwood City CA 94063-1826

WILHELM, WILLIAM JEAN, civil engineering educator; b. St. Louis, Oct. 5, 1935; s. Maurice Ferdinand and Winifred Eileen (McClintock) W.; m. Patricia Jane Zietz, Aug. 17, 1957; children: William, Robert, Andrew, Mary, David. BME, Auburn U., 1958, MS, 1963; PhD, N.C. State U., 1968. Lic. profl. engr., Kans. Structural engr. Palmer & Baker Engrs., Mobile, Ala., 1958-60; instr. engring. graphics Auburn U., 1960-64; asst. prof. civil engring. W.Va. U., Morgantown, 1967-72, assoc. prof., 1972-76, prof., 1976-79, chmn., 1974-79; dean engring., prof. Wichita State U., 1979-2000, dean, prof. emeritus, 2000—, dir. Ctr. for Productivity Enhancement, 1984-86, exec. dir. Ctr. for Tech. Application, 1988-91. Bd. dirs. Kans. Tech. Enterprise Corp., Orthopaedic Rsch. Inst. Via Christi Regional Med. Sys.; chair bd. dirs. Envision. Contbr. articles to profl. jours. Officer C.E. U.S. Army, 1959, 62. Recipient Recognition award Wichita State U. Alumni Assn., 1993, Engr. Svc. award Wichita Coun. Engring. Socs., 2000. Fellow NSPE, ASCE, Am. Soc. Engring. Edn. (George K. Wadlin award 1998, MidWest sect. Spl. Appreciation award 2001), Am. Concrete Inst. (Joe W. Kelley award 1986, Henry L. Kennedy award 1994); mem. Soc. Women Engrs. (sr., Rodney D. Chipp Meml. award 2000), Kans. Soc. Profl. Engrs. (pres. 1994-95, Outstanding Engr. of Yr. award 1989, Career Recognition award 2000), Order of the Engr., Sigma Xi, Phi Kappa Phi, Tau Beta Pi, Pi Tau Sigma, Chi Epsilon (chpt. hon. W.Va. U. 1979), Golden Key (hon.). Roman Catholic. Home: 7014 E 25th St N Wichita KS 67226-1734 E-mail: wilhelmwj@aol.com.

WILHELM-HASS, ELAINE, managed care administrator, consultant; b. San Francisco, Jan. 29, 1955; d. Roger Mathias and Dorothy Jane (Conway) Wilhelm; m. James Hass, Nov. 10, 1998. BSN, U. Wash., 1978; MN, La. State U., New Orleans, 1982; MBA, Averett Coll., Springfield, Va., 1992. RN; cert. profl. in healthcare quality. Maternal child health mgr. Merrimack Valley Mass.) Region, 1987-88; dir. oper. rn. and obstetrics Mary Washington Hosp., Fredericksburg, Va., 1989-92; perioperative dir. Bayshore Hosp., Holmdel, N.J., 1992-94; agy. mgr. Slidell (La.) Home Health, 1994-96; v.p. Health Sphere Cons., Baton Rouge, 1996-97; propr. Wilhelm-Hass Cons., Crownsville, Md., 1997-98; quality improvement dir. Sierra Mil./TRICARE-Region 1, Balt., 1998—2001; o.r. mgr. Napa Surgery Ctr., Napa, Calif., 2002—. Contbr. articles to profl. jours. Mem. Am. Soc. for Quality (exec. sec., bd. dirs. Balt. sect. 1999—), Nat. Assn. for Health Care Quality, Sigma Theta Tau. Home: 221 Sunset Dr Novato CA 94949 Office: 3444 Villa Verde Dr Napa CA 94558 E-mail: jim_elaine_h@msn.com.

WILHELMI, CYNTHIA JOY, information technology professional, consultant; b. Marshalltown, Iowa, Sept. 12, 1946; BA in Art and Edn., U. Iowa, 1969; MA in Comm., U. Nebr., Omaha, 1996. Master Artist-in-Residence Nebr. Arts Coun., Omaha, 1985—91; grad. tchg. asst., tchg. fellow U. Nebr., 1993—95; Family Friends of Eastern Nebr. program coord. Vis. Nurse Assn., 1996—97; instr. Midland Luth. Coll., Fremont, 1997—99; info. tech. cons., project mgr., test engr., bus. analyst Bass & Assocs., Omaha, 1999—2000; info. tech. cons. Robert Half Internat. Cons., 2000, Maxim Group/TEKSystems, 2000. Bus. analyst, sr. test engr., project mgmt., third party vendor interface mgmt., CD installation testing, tech. documentation. Editor, pub., contbg. author Salaam mag., 1985-86. Mem. adv. coun. Foster Grandparents, Omaha, 1999—; bd. dirs., pub. rels./publicity chair U. Nebr. Friends of Art, Omaha, 1997-99. Named Outstanding Grad. Tchg. Asst., U. Nebr., Omaha, 1995, Adm. in the Gt. Navy of Nebr., 1990. Mem. AAUW, Soc. for Tech. Comm. (bd. dirs., chair pub. rels. 1999), Nebr. Adms. Assn., Soc. for Collegiate Journalists (hon.), Phi Delta Gamma. Republican. Address: 13516 Redwood St Omaha NE 68138-6205 E-mail: cwi813@earthlink.net.

WILHELMI, MARY CHARLOTTE, education educator, college official; b. Williamsburg, Iowa, Oct. 2, 1928; d. Charles E. and Loretto (Judge) Harris; m. Sylvester Lee Wilhelmi, May 26, 1951; children: Theresa Ann, Sylvia Marie, Thomas Lee, Kathryn Lyn, Nancy Louise. BS, Iowa State U., 1950; MA in Edn., Va. Poly. Inst. and State U., 1973, cert. advanced grad. studies, 1978. Edn. coord. Nova Ctr. U. Va., Falls Church, 1969-73; asst. adminstr. Consortium for Continuing Higher Edn. George Mason U., Fairfax, Va., 1973-78, adminstr., asst. prof., 1978-83; dir. coll. mktg., pub. affairs, assoc. prof. No. Va. C.C., Annandale, 1983—. Bd. dirs. No. Va. C.C. Edn!. Found., Inc., No. Va. C.C. Real Estate Found.; v.p. audience devel. Fairfax (Va.) Symphony, 1995—; chmn. Health Systems Agy. No. Va., Fairfax; mem. George Mason U. Inst. for Ednl. Transformation. Mem. Editl. bd. Va. Forum, 1990-93; contbr. articles to profl. jours. Bd. dirs. Fairfax County chpt. ARC, 1981-86, Va. Inst. Polit. Leadership, 1995—, Fairfax Com. of 100, 1986-88, 90—, Arts Coun. Fairfax County, 1989—, Fairfax Spotlight on the Arts, Inc., 2002—; bd. dirs. Hospice No. Va., 1983-88, mem. devel. bd., 1997-2000; mem. steering com. Hurrah for Hospice Gala, 1999, Nat. Capital Region Hospices Gala, 2002, No. Va. Mental Health Inst., Fairfax County, 1978-81, Fairfax Profl. Women's Network, 1981; vice chair Va. Commonwealth U. Ctr. on Aging, Richmond, 1978—; mem. supt.'s adv. coun. Fairfax County Pub. Schs., 1974-86, No. Va. Press Club, 1978—; mktg. chair, mem. exec. com. Internat. Childrens Festival, 1997—; pres. Fairfax Ext. Leadership Coun., 1995; mem. Leadership Fairfax Class of 1992, Commonwealth Va. Combined campaign, State Adv. Coun., 1999, 2000, 01. Named Woman of Distinction, Soroptomists, Fairfax, 1988, Bus. Woman of Yr., Falls Church Bus. and Profl. Women's Group, 1993; fellow Va. Inst. Polit. Leadership, 1995. Mem. State Coun. Higher Edn. Va. (pub. affairs adv. com. 1985—), Greater Washington Bd. Trade, Fairfax County C. of C. (legis. affairs com. 1984—, millenium steering com. 1999) Va. Women Lobbyists, 1991—, No. Va. Bus. Roundtable, Internat. Platform Assn., Phi Delta Kappa (20-Yr. Continuous Svc. award 2001), Kappa Delta Alumni No. Va., Psi Chi, Phi Kappa Phi. Roman Catholic.

Avocations: piano, organ, reading, hiking. Home: 4902 Ravensworth Rd Annandale VA 22003-5552 Office: No Va CC 4001 Wakefield Chapel Rd Annandale VA 22003-3796 E-mail: mcwilhelmi@nvcc.edu.

WILHELMSEN, HAROLD JOHN, accountant, operations controller; b. Kansas City, Mo., July 13, 1928; s. Karl John and Cora Irene (Reynolds) W.; m. Audrey Loraine Woodard, Oct. 14, 1950. BBA, U. Wis., 1950. CPA, Wis. With S.C. Johnson & Son Inc., Racine, Wis., 1953-90, dir. fin. South Pacific, 1970-72, mgr. overseas fin. svcs., 1972-76, contr. U.S. ops., 1976-78, v.p., contr. internat. ops., 1978-90, ret., 1990. Pres. Racine Symphony Orch. Assn., 1957-60; trustee Carthage Coll., Kenosha, Wis., 1984-91, dir., sec. Pinnacle Peak Country Club Estates, 1992-95; dir., 1993-97, pres. Pinnacle Peak Country Club, 1996-97; treas. Christ the Lord Luth. Ch. Served with U.S. Army, 1950-52. Mem.: Pinnacle Peak Country (Scottsdale, Ariz.); Am. Nat. (Sydney, Australia). Republican. Lutheran. Avocations: golf, squash, bridge, reading, music. E-mail: hjw-az@att.net.

WILHELMY, ODIN, JR. insurance agent; b. New Kensington, Pa., Oct. 9, 1920; s. Odin and May (Hazeltine) W.; m. Betty M. Rollins, Nov. 23, 1945; children: Ann Leslie, Margaret Linn, Janet Lee. BA with honors, U. Cin., 1941; PhD, Cornell U., 1950. CLU, ChFC. Asst. prof. Cornell U., Ithaca, N.Y., 1949-52; div. chief Battelle Meml. Inst., Columbus, Ohio, 1952-70; sr. agt. Prin. Mut. Life Ins. Co., 1970—. Scoutmaster Boy Scouts Am., Ithaca, N.Y., Columbus, Ohio, 1946-74. Sgt. U.S. Army, 1942-46, Aleutian Islands. Recipient Silver Beaver award Boy Scouts Am. Mem. Phi Beta Kappa, Phi Kappa Phi, Pi Kappa Alpha, Omicron Delta Kappa. Presbyterian. Avocations: church work, scouting, gardening. Home: 2942 N Star Rd Columbus OH 43221-2961

WILHITE, JEFFREY MARK, librarian, educator; b. Shreveport, La., Nov. 9, 1968; s. Tom R. and Donna Odom Wilhite. M in Librr. and Info. Sci., U. Okla., 1993. Govt. documents reference libr. U. Okla., Norman , 1993—. Cons. Okla. Dept. Justice, Oklahoma City, 1999; mem. adv. coun. Okla. Publs. Clearinghouse, 1996. Author: (book) International Biographical Directory of National Archivists, Documentalists, and Librarians, 2nd edit., 2000; contbr. chapters to books, articles to profl. jours. Mem.: ALA, Okla. Libr. Assn. (chair govt. documents roundtable 1997—98). Avocations: play writing, reading, theater . Home: 316 Chauatauqua Norman OK 73069 Office: Univ Okla 401 W Brooks Norman OK 73019 Office Fax: 405-325-1841. Business E-Mail: jwilhite@ou.edu.

WILHJELM, CHRISTIAN, conductor, artist; b. Long Branch, Nj, Nov. 6, 1949; s. Carl and Alice Wilhjelm; children: Carl, Hannah. PhD Edn., Teacher's Coll. at Columbia U., New York, New York, 1998; MA Edn., Coll. of NJ, Trenton, New Jersey, 1978; BA Music, The New Eng. Conservatory, Boston, Massachusetts, 1972. Musician - french horn Richmond Symphony, Richmond, Va., 1972—76; band dir. Ridgewood H.S., Ridgewood, NJ, 1979—82, Rye H.S., Rye, NY, 1982—84; music dir. Ridgewood Concert Band, Ridgewood, NJ, 1983—; band dir. Pascach Hills H.S., Montvale, 1984—; artist Montclair State U., Montclair, 1996—; condr./music dir. The Goldman Band, New York, NY, 2000—02. Bd. of directors Classical NJ, Westfield, NJ, 1998, Bergen Youth Orch., Engelwood, NJ, 2001—. Contbr. book. Recipient Sudler Award of Merit, John Philip Sousa Found., 1998; fellow Paul Harris Fellowship, Rotary Internat., 1992. Mem.: Music Educator's Nat. Conf., Coll. Band Dir. Nat. Assn., Am. Fedn. of Musicians. Office: The Goldman Memorial Band 80 Eighth Avenue Suite 1107 New York NY 10011 E-mail: cwilhjelm@msn.com.

WILHOIT, CAROL DIANE, retired special education educator; b. Rockford, Ill., June 2, 1950; d. Iris May (Zeigler) Cleeton; m. Jerry Dean Wilhoit, Aug. 15, 1971; children: David, Heather, Hilary, Erin. BSE, N.E. Mo. State U., 1972; MS in Edn., 1991. Cert. spl. edn. tchr., Mo. Tchr. emotionally handicapped Clarence Cannon Elem., Elsberry, Mo., 1972-73; EMH tchr. Bowling Green (Mo.) Elem., 1973-77, Clopton High Sch., Clarksville, Mo., 1979-82; tchr. learning disabilities Eugene Field Elem., Hannibal, 1982—2002; ret., 2002. Active Accelerated Sch., chair curriculum cadre, intervention cadre, steering com., 1992-93, mem. parent involvement com., 1994; del. Northeast Dist. Tchrs. Assn. Assembly, 1994. Mem. state due process subcom., 1994; PL-94-142 adv. com., 1992—. Mem. Coun. Exceptional Children (pres. 1986-88, bd. dirs. Mo. chpt. 1986, 1988-91, organizer local chpt. 1988, awards chmn., chair profl. devel. subcom., chair registration com. 1991-92, chair membership com. Mark Twain chpt. 1991—, spring conf. session leader, del. to internat. coun. assembly 1992-93, spring conf. chair 1994, del. to internat. conf. 1995), Mo. State Tchrs. Assn. (del. to state assembly 1989-90, superintendent's com. 1989-91, dist. prof. devel. com. 1990—, mentor tchr. 1990-92, state spl. edn. monitoring com. 1991-92), Hannibal Cmty. Tchrs. Assn. (bldg. rep. exec. com. 1987—, v.p. 1988, pres. 1989), Learning Disabilities Assn. Avocations: reading, crafts, sewing. Office: Eugene Field Elem 1405 Pearl St Hannibal MO 63401-4151

WILHOIT, DARREL LOEL, chemical engineer; b. Portland, Oreg., May 8, 1938; s. D. Irvan and Vivian Eloise (Piepgrass) W.; m. Lana Reneè Carpenter, Sept. 10, 1963; children: Michele, Reneè, April, Ryan. BS, Brigham Young U., 1965; PhD, Wash. State U., 1990. Project leader pioneering R & D Crown Zellerbach, Camas, Wash., 1965-81; mgr. nonwoven R & D Am. Hosp. Supply, Evanston, Ill., 1981-82; cons. nonwoven products and processes Estech Corp., Neenah, Wis., 1982-87; sr. rsch. engr. Viskase Corp., Chgo., 1987-96; exploratory R&D leader Tredegar Film Products, Terre Haute, Ind., 1996—. Author: Improvements in Design and Control of the Drying Process in French Fry Manufacturing. Sch. bd. dir. Washougal (Wash.) Sch. Dist., 1975-77; county planning commr. Skamania (Wash.) County, 1979-81. Mem. AIChE, Instrument Soc. Am., Tech. Assn. Pulp and Paper Industry, Soc. Plastics Engrs. Achievements include patents for New Paper Making Headbox, Paper Softening Method, Splice for Cellulosic Food Casing, Antimicrobial Treatment for Food Surfaces, Biaxially Oriented Shrinkable Film, Cook-in Plastic Casing; conception and commercial implementation of advanced heat transfer methods in the manufacture of biaxially oriented polythylene film; developed commercial processes for making short fibers from PE and for making dry formed paper, unique algorithm for optimal control of cellulose substrate during drying operation, advanced process for adhering short fibers to apertured films. Home and Office: Columbia Plymer and Processing Inc 692 Buhman Rd Washougal WA 98671 E-mail: dl.wilhoit@mstar2.net.

WILHOIT, G. CLEVELAND, journalism educator; b. Albemarle, N.C., Aug. 4, 1939; s. Grover and Ruth Alberta (Hopkins) W.; m. Frances Goins, Aug. 31, 1963; children: Hannah Ruth, Peter Francis. BA, U. N.C., 1961, MA, 1963, PhD, 1967. Prof. journalism Ind. U., Bloomington, 1967—, dir. grad. study Sch. of Journalism, 1967-73, assoc. dir. Inst. for Advanced Study, 1988-93, dir. bur. media rsch. Sch. of Journalism, 1993-96. Vis. rsch. fellow Netherlands Broadcasting Corp., Hilversum, 1975. Co-author: (book) The American Journalist in the 1990s, 1996, The American Journalist, 1986, (rev.), 1991, Newsroom Guide to Polls and Surveys, 1990; editor: (book) Mass Communication Review Yearbook, 1980, 81; co-author: (monograph) News Media Coverage of U.S. Senators, 1953-74, 1980, Editorial Writers on American Newspapers: A Twenty Year Portrait, 1991. With USAF and Air Nat. Guard, 1962-68. Named NSF fellow Polit. Comm. Rsch. Inst., Ohio U., 1970, fellow Ctr. for Media Studies, Columbia U., 1991; recipient Disting. Svc. award Am. Newspaper Pubs. Assn., 1984. Mem. Assn. for Edn. in Journalism and Mass Comm. (divsn. head 1980-81), Soc. Profl. Journalists Sigma Delta Chi (Disting. Svc. award for Rsch. 1986, 97), Kappa Tau Alpha. Democrat. Mem. Christian Ch. (Disciples Of Christ). Avocation: cycling. E-mail: wilhoitc@indiana.edu.

WILK, BARBARA, artist, educator; b. N.Y.C., Mar. 27, 1923; d. Irvin and Edith (Mittelman) Balensweig; m. Max Zalk Wilk, Oct. 28, 1949; children: David, Richard, Frances. BA, Smith Coll., Northampton, Mass., 1944; MS, U. Bridgeport, Conn., 19758. Women's editor UP Radio, N.Y.C., 1944-48; instr. Housatonic C.C., Bridgeport, 1975-78, Norwalk (Conn.) C.C., 1978-81, Fairfield (Conn.) U., 1980; art cons. Tchrs. Ctr., Fairfield, 1980-83; master tchg. artist Conn. Commn. on Arts, Hartford, 1995—. Adminstr. CETA Arts Program, Westport, 1979-81; pres. Westport-Weston Arts Coun., 1977-80. Filmmaker 5 animated films shown on pub. TV (Cine Gold Eagle award, 1st prize Filmex); exhbns. in groups shows include Crafts of the Ams., Washington, 1975, Conn. Women Artists, New Haven, 1975-78, Elements Gallery, Greenwich, N.Y.C., 1979-80, Smithsonian Traveling Crafts Show, 1975-77, U. Rochester, N.Y., 1981, Art of the N.E., Silvermine, Conn., 1989-95, Stamford (Conn.) Mus., 1988-92, Conn. allery, 1989-90, Women in the Visual Arts, New Haven, Conn., 1990-95, Ariel Gallery, N.Y.C., 1990, Discovery Mus., Bridgeport, Conn., 1991, Rachel Adler Gallery, N.Y.C., 1996-97, Seven Arts Festival, Pitts., 1999, Greer Gallery, Northport, N.Y., 1999—, Phoenix Gallery, N.Y., 1999, Paintings Direct.com, 1999—; one-woman shows include U. Conn., Storrs, 1988, Conn. Commn. on the Arts, Hartford, 1987, Silo Gallery, Milford, Conn., 1987, Satmford Mus., 1995, Discovery Mus., Bridgeport, Conn., 1995, Silvermine Guild of Artists, 1978, 87, 91, 94, 97, City Spirit Artists, New Haven, Conn., 1997, Westport (Conn.) Art Ctr., 1996, 99, Jean Cocteau Gallery, Santa Fe, 2000. Bd. mem. Westport-Weston Arts Ctr., 1984-87, Silvermine Guild Arts Ctr., 1979-82, Cultural Survival, Cambridge, 1998—; observer UN, N.Y.C., 1998—; mem. adv. bd. Helen Keller, N.Y.C., 1999—; dir. Eyes on the Future, 1996; organizer 1st Grandmother's Circle Gathering, Westport, Conn., 2002. Recipient Guggenheim Found. fellowship, N.Y.C., 1995, Pres. Vol. Action award U.S. Pres., 1993. Mem. Soc. Am. Graphic Artists (award 1999), Silvermine Guild Arts Ctr., Soc. Layerists, Artists Equity, Women's Caucus for Arts. Democrat. Avocations: tennis, aerobics. Home: 29 Surf Rd Westport CT 06880-6734 E-mail: bwilk@attglobal.net.

WILK, RONALD, physician; b. N.Y.C., Nov. 27, 1944; BA, L.I. U., Bklyn., 1966; MD, U. Bologna, Italy, 1972. Diplomate Am. Acad. Neurology, 1980. Intern, resident Mt. Sinai Hosp., N.Y.C., chief resident, 1977. Mem. stroke coun. Am. Heart Assn. Fellow Royal Soc. Medicine, Am. Acad. Neurology.

WILKAS, JAMES ALAN, music educator; b. Waterbury CT, Sept. 25, 1957; s. James Albert and Patricia Eleanor Wilkas; m. Maureen Ellen Norris, July 18, 1997. BS Music Edn., Western Conn. State U., Danbury, CT, 1975—79; MS Ednl. Tech., Ctrl. Conn. State U., New Britain, CT, 1998—2002. Dir. of instrumental music Naugatuck Bd. of Edn., Naugatuck, Conn., 1979—81; gen. mgr. Zinno Music, Waterbury, 1982—93; gen. music tchr. Newtown Mid. Sch., Newtown, 1994—94; dir. of instrumental music West Side Mid. Sch., Waterbury, 1995—. Musician Various Local Bands, Waterbury, Conn., 1975—2001. Mem.: Conn. Educators Assn., Conn. Music Educators Assn., Music Educators Nat. Conf. Avocations: music composition, television & radio jingles, music production, educational software design, web design. Home: 143 Columbia Boulevard Waterbury CT 06710 Office: West Side Middle School 483 Chase Parkway Waterbury CT 06708 Personal E-mail: jimmididr@aol.com. E-mail: jimmididr@aol.com.

WILKE, ALLAN JOHN, family physician; b. Iron Mountain, Mich., Apr. 12, 1951; s. Albert Ernest and Shirley Anne (Ladwig) W.; m. Bonnie Jean Smith, Mar. 21, 1975; children: Meredith Leigh, Gillian Anne, Ethan Aaron. BS, Mich. State U., 1973, MA, 1974, MD, 1980. Diplomate Am. Bd. Family Practice. Tchr. Lake Fenton (Mich.) Cmty. Schs., 1974-76; resident St. Joseph Hosp., Flint, Mich., 1980-83; staff physician Sparta (Mich.) Health Ctr., 1983-85; asst. program dir. Cedar Rapids (Iowa) Family Practice, 1985-89, assoc. program dir., 1989-90; program dir. Family Physicians Assn., Sylvania, Ohio, 1990-94, St. Cloud (Minn.) Hosp./Mayo Family Practice Residency, 1994-98, Med. Coll. Ohio Family Practice, 1998—. Mem. adv. faculty Advanced Life Support in Obstetrics, Kansas City, Mo., 1994—. Reviewer Jour. of Family Practice, E. Norwalk, Ct., 1990—, Joint AAFP/F-AAFP Grant Awards Program, Kansas City, Mo., 1994—. Fellow: Am. Acad. Family Physicians (Mead Johnson award for grad. edn. in family practice 1982); mem.: Soc. Tchrs. Family Medicine, Assn. Family Practice Residency Dirs. Democrat. Avocations: personal computing, cooking, bicycling. Office: Med Coll of Ohio Dept Family Medicine 1015 Garden Lake Pkwy Toledo OH 43614-2798 E-mail: awilke@mco.edu.

WILKE, CHET, real estate broker; b. Chgo., Dec. 10, 1942; m. Beverly J. Galuska, July 31, 1981; children: Lisa Michelle, Rebecca Ann, Christa Leann. BA in Comm., Columbia Coll., L.A., 1970; Grad., Realtor Inst. Cert. Residential Broker Mgr., Residential Specialist, Accredited Buyer Rep. Sta. mgr., dir. TV news, personality Armed Forces Radio & TV, 1965-69; acct. exec. Sta. KALI, L.A., 1969-72; sr. acct. exec. HR/Stone Radio Reps., 1972-75; gen. sales mgr. Sta. KYXY-FM, San Diego, 1975-77; pres., founder Wilke Enterprises Inc., San Diego and Houston, 1977-81; gen. sales mgr. Sta. KEYH, Houston, 1982; gen. sales mgr., acting mgr. Sta. KYST, 1982-85; mgr., mktg./creative dir. Advt. Concepts Inc., 1985-88; exec. v.p. First Hanover Real Estate/Mortgage, Houston and Sugar Land, 1988-89; pres., real estate broker AmeriStar Group Corp., Plano, 1989—, AmeriStar Realty, Inc., 1995—, AmerStar Comml., 1996—; broker host Your Real Estate Advisor, TXCN, Tex. Cable News (TV 38), Dallas, 2001. With USAF, 1964—69. Mem. Nat. Assn. Realtors, Tex. Assn. Realtors, Collin County Assn. Realtors, Womens Coun. Realtors, Lions. Republican. Methodist. Home: 2312 Cardinal Dr Plano TX 75023-1470 Office: AmeriStar Group Corp 4949 Hedgcoxe # 130 Plano TX 75024 E-mail: chet@cwilke.com.

WILKE, LEROY, church administrator; Exec. dir. dist. and congl. svcs. Luth. Ch.-Mo. Synod, St. Louis. Office: 1333 S Kirkwood Rd Saint Louis MO 63122-7226

WILKE MONTEMAYOR, JOANNE MARIE, nursing administrator; b. Jerome, Ariz., Sept. 10, 1941; d. Karl Nickolas and Anna Linda (Worgt) Wilke; m. Casimiro L. Montemayor, Oct. 8, 1978. BS in Nursing, U. Colo., 1965; M in Nursing, U. Washington, 1974. Patient care coord. Vesper Hospice, San Leandro, Calif., 1989-93, RN case mgr., 1993-95, Summit Med. Ctr., 1995—. With USNR, 1959-79. Mem. Nat. Hospice Orgn. Democrat. Methodist. Avocations: music, gardening, cooking, silk flower arranging.

WILKEN, CAROLINE DOANE, critical care, emergency, recovery room, and medical/surgical nurse; b. Watseka, Ill., Jan. 4, 1962; d. Robert Charles and Barbara Jane (Perkinson) W. BSN, Rush U., Chgo., 1984. RN, Ill., Calif., Del., Mass., Md., N.J., Ariz., Conn., Va., Ga., Nev., U.K.; cert. ACLS, PALS, trauma nurse corp. course. Travel nurse AMN, San Diego, Nurses Across Am., Boynton Beach, Fla., HSSI, Ft. Lauderdale; staff nurse Rush-Presbyn.-St. Luke's Med. Ctr., Chgo., UCLA Med. Ctr.; travel nurse CrossCountry Travcorps, Malden, Mass.; staff nurse Riverside Med. Ctr., Kankakee, Ill. Mem. Emergency Nurses Assn. Home: PO Box 51 Onarga IL 60955-0051 E-mail: Cardwil@aol.com.

WILKEN, CLAUDIA, judge; b. Mpls., Aug. 17, 1949; BA with honors, Stanford U., 1971; JD, U. Calif., Berkeley, 1975. Bar: Calif. 1975, U.S. Dist. Ct. (no. dist.) Calif. 1975, U.S. Ct. Appeals (9th cir.) 1976, U.S. Supreme Ct. 1981. Asst. fed. pub. defender U.S. Dist. Ct. (no. dist.) Calif., San Francisco, 1975-78, U.S. magistrate judge, 1983-93, dist. judge, 1993—; ptnr. Wilken & Leverett, Berkeley, Calif., 1978-84. Adj. prof. U. Calif., Berkeley, 1978-84; prof. New Coll. Sch. Law, 1980-85; mem. jud. br. com. Jud. Conf. U.S.; past mem. edn. com. Fed. Jud. Ctr.; chair 9th cir. Magistrates Conf., 1987-88. Mem. ABA (mem. jud. adminstrn. divsn.), Alameda County Bar Assn. (judge's membership), Nat. Assn. Women Judges, Order of Coif, Phi Beta Kappa. Office: US Dist Ct No Dist 1301 Clay St # 2 Oakland CA 94612-5217

WILKENING, LAUREL LYNN, academic administrator, planetary scientist; b. Richland, Wash., Nov. 23, 1944; d. Marvin Hubert and Ruby Alma Wilkening; m. Godfrey Theodore Sill, May 18, 1974 BA, Reed Coll., Portland, Oreg., 1966; PhD, U. Calif., San Diego, 1970; DSc (hon.), U. Ariz., 1996. From asst. prof. to assoc. prof. U. Ariz., Tucson, 1973—80, dir. Lunar and Planetary Lab., head planetary scis., 1981—83, vice provost, prof. planetary scis., 1983—85, v.p. rsch., dean Grad. Coll., 1985—88; divsn. scientist NASA Hdqrs., Washington, 1980; prof. geol scis., adj. prof. astronomy, provost U. Washington, Seattle, 1988—93; prof. earth system sci., chancellor U. Calif., Irvine, 1993—98. Dir. Rsch. Corp., 1991—, Seagate Tech., Inc., 1993-2000, Empire Ranch Found., 1998—; vice chmn. Nat. Commn. on Space, Washington, 1984-86, Adv. Com. on the Future of U.S. Space Program, 1990-91; chair Space Policy Adv. Bd., Nat. Space Coun., 1991-92; co-chmn. primitive bodies mission study team NASA/European Space Agy., 1984-85; chmn. com. rendezvous sci. working group NASA, 1983-85; mem. panel on internat. cooperation and competition in space Congl. Office Tech. Assessment, 1982-83; trustee NASULGC, 1994-97, UCAR, 1988-89, 97-98, Reed Coll., 1992-2002. Editor: Comets, 1982. Trustee UCAR, 1997—98. U. Calif. Regents fellow, 1966-67; NASA trainee, 1967-70. Fellow Meteoritical Soc. (councilor 1976-80), Am. Assn. Advanced Sci.; mem. Am. Astron. Soc. (chmn. div. planetary scis. 1984-85), Am. Geophys. Union, AAAS, Planetary Soc. (dir. 1994-2000, v.p. 1997-2000), Phi Beta Kappa. Democrat. Avocations: gardening, camping, swimming.

WILKERSON, JAMES NEILL, retired lawyer; b. Tyler, Tex., Dec. 17, 1939; s. Hubert Cecil and Vida (Alexander) W.; m. Cal Cantrell; children: Cody, Ike. AA, Tyler Jr. Coll., 1960; BBA, U. Tex., 1966, JD, 1968. Bar: Tex. 1968, U.S. Supreme Ct. 1973, U.S. Dist. Ct. (wc. dist.) Tex. 1974. Pvt. practice, Georgetown and Mason, Tex., 1977-2001; ret., 2001. Instr. Cen. Tex. Coll., Copperaas Cove, Tex., 1973-74; asst prof. law U.S. Mil. Acad., West Point, N.Y., 1971-73; pres. C&N Bus. Developers, 19925. Pres. Beautify Georgetown Assn., 1977-80, 81-82; pres. U. Tex. Young Reps., 1964-65; co-chmn. Bush for Pres., 1988, Reagan-Bush campaign, 1980; mem. Williamson County Rep. Com., 1977-81; chmn. Hist. Preservation Com., 1979-85; trustee 1st United Meth. Ch., 19945, chmn. bd. trustees, 1996-99; vol. Mason Lions Club, Steady Steps After Sch. Homework Helper; substitute tchr. Mason Schs. Col. USAR, 19685, trial judge JAGC, 1975-91, appellate judge Army Ct. Mil. Rev., 1991-93. Decorated Legion of Merit, Bronze Star, Air medal. Mem. Tex. State Bar Coll., Williamson County Bar Assn., Sertoma (v.p. 1981-83, 87, sec. 1988-89, pres. 1992-93), Lions (pres. 1982-83), Vietnam War Vets. Address: PO Box 1807 Mason TX 76856-1807

WILKERSON, MATHA ANN, oil company executive; b. Mill Creek, Okla., Sept. 1, 1937; d. Frank and Lottie Evelyn (Cordell) Stie; m. Ronald Gene Wilkerson, Dec. 22, 1956; 1 child, Mitchell Linn. BS in Edn., East Cen. U., 1966. Elem. sch. tchr. Moore (Okla.) Pub. Schs., 1966-74; office mgr. S. S. Sanbar, M.D., Oklahoma City, 1974-78; ops. mgr., acct. John A. Taylor Oil Co., 1978-84; office mgr., controller Lance Ruffel Oil & Gas Corp., 1984—. Mem. Coun. of Petroleum Accounts Soc. (com. mem. 1979—). Baptist. Avocations: handicrafts, reading. theatre, cooking. Office: Lance Ruffel Oil & Gas 210 Park Ave Ste 2150 Oklahoma City OK 73102-5632

WILKERSON, RITA LYNN, special education educator, consultant; b. Crescent, Okla., Apr. 22; BA, Cen. State U., Edmond, Okla., 1963; MEd, Cen. State U., 1969; postgrad., U. Okla., 1975, Kans. State U. Elem. tchr. music Hillsdale (Okla.) Pub. Sch., 1963-64; jr. high sch. music and spl. edn. Okarche (Okla.) Pub. Sch., 1965-71; cons. Title III Project, Woodward, Okla., 1971-72; dir. Regional Edn. Svc. Ctr., Guymon, 1972-81; dir., psychologist Project W.O.R.K., 1981-90; tchr. behavioral disorders Unified Sch. Dist. 480, Liberal, Kans., 1990—; sch. psychologist Hardesty (Okla.) Schs., 1994. Cons. Optima (Okla.) Pub. Schs., 1990, Felt (Okla.) Pub. Schs., 1990, Texhoma (Okla.) Schs., 1994, Balko (Okla.) Pub. Schs., 1996; spl. edn. cons. Optima Pub. Schs., 1992—, Goodwell (Okla.) Pub. Schs., 1992—; diagnostician Tyrone, Okla. Pub. Schs., 1992-95; home svcs. provider Dept. Human Svcs., Guymon, 1990; active Kans. Dept. Social and Rehab. Svcs., 1993—; adj. tchr. Seward County C.C., 1994—. Grantee Cen. State U., 1968-69, Oklahoma City Dept. Edn., 1988-89. Mem. ASCD, NAFE, NEA (liberal Kans. chpt.), AAUW, Coun. Exceptional Children, Okla. Assn. Retarded Citizens, Okla. Assn. for Children with Learning Disabilities, Phi Delta Kappa. Republican. Avocation: crafts. Home: 616 N Crumley St Guymon OK 73942-4341 Office: Unified Sch Dist 480 7th And Western Liberal KS 67901

WILKERSON, WILLIAM HOLTON, banker; b. Greenville, N.C., Feb. 16, 1947; s. Edwin Cisco and Agnes Holton (Gaskins) W.; m. Ellen Logan Tomskey, Oct. 27, 1973; 1 child, William Holton Jr. AB in Econs., U. N.C., 1970. Asst. v.p. 1st Union Nat. Bank, Greensboro, N.C., 1972-77; v.p. Peoples Bank & Trust Co., Rocky Mount, 1977-79, exec. v.p., 1987-89, pres., 1989-90; sr. v.p. Hibernia Nat. Bank, New Orleans, 1979-86; group exec. officer, vice chmn. bd. dirs. Centura Banks, Inc., Rocky Mount, 1990-97, pres., 1998—2001, Wilkerson Co., Inc., Greenville, NC, 2001—. Bd. visitors U. N.C., Chapel Hill, 1999—. Mem. Rocky Mount C. of C. (bd. dirs. 1989-96, vice chmn. 1992-94, chmn.-elect 1994, chmn. 1995), Omicron Delta Epsilon, Chi Beta Phi, Phi Sigma Pi. Republican. Home: 407 Rutledge Rd Greenville NC 27858 Office: PO Box 2095 Greenville NC 27836-0095 E-mail: wwilkerson@ec.rr.com.

WILKERSON, WILLIAM S. philosopher; b. Orange, Calif., Mar. 23, 1968; s. William D. Wilkerson and Jo W. Stanford; life ptnr. Keith Wilkerson. PhD, Purdue U., 1997. Asst. prof. philosophy dept. philosophy U. Ala., Huntsville, 1997—; clin. asst. prof. U. Birmingham Med. Sch., 2001—. Editor: (Book) New Critical Theory: Essays on Liberation, 2001; contbr. ; author: (essay in book) Reclaiming Identity, 2000 (Outstanding Liberal Arts Tchr., 2000). Pres. bd. dirs. Aids Action Coalition, Huntsville, 2002—04. Fellow Andrews fellow, Purdue U., 1992—94; grantee Mini-Research grantee, U. Ala., Huntsville, 1998, NEH Summer Seminar, NEH, 1999. Business E-Mail: wilkerw@email.uah.edu.

WILKES, ANGELA BIGGS, mental health consultant; b. Reynolds, Ga., Nov. 6, 1952; d. George William and Biease Annetta (Grice) Biggs; m. Linster Bryant Jr., Feb. 22, 1979 (div. Mar. 1983); m. Gary M. Wilkes, June 25, 1983; children: Stephen Alexander, David Alan. BA, Clark Atlanta U., 1974; MA, U. Cin., 1980. Program coord. Alice Paul House battered women's shelter, Cin., 1977-80; dir. cmty. svcs. Mental Health Svcs. N.W., 1981-82; dir. devel. Community Guidance, Inc., Cleve., 1983-84; mktg. and cmty. svcs. cons. CIT Mental Health Svcs., University Heights, Ohio, 1984-88; v.p., dir. tng. Wilkes Mental Health Cons., Shaker Heights, 1985—. Guest lectr. Mendel Sch. Applied Social Scis., 1996—. Trustee Citizens Mental Health Assembly, Cleve., 1989-90, Women Together, Inc., Cleve., 1986-87, League Park Ctr., Cleve., 1984-86; mem. Action Ohio-Battered Women, Columbus, Ohio, 1979-84; dep. registrar Cuyahoga County Bd. Elections, Cleve., 1988-89; mem. Guild of St. Dominic, Shaker Heights, 1982—; tchr. parish sch. religion St. Dominic Cath. Ch., 1992—; trustee Orange Schs. Found., 2000—, Ursuline Sophia Ctr., 1999—; mem. Ohio State Med. Assn. Aux., 1990-96, bd. dirs., 1992-94. Recipient Vol. award Whitney Young Sch., 1987, cert. of recognition State of Ohio Voter Registration Program, 1988, Disting. Alumni Citation of Yr. Clark Atlanta U. Mem. Acad. Medicine Cleve. Aux. (pres. 1993-94, bd. dirs. 1987-88, 90-97), AMA Aux., NAACP, Nat. Assn. Equal Opportunity in Higher Edn., Diabetes Assn. Gtr. Cleve. (bd. dirs. 1993—, Trustee of Yr. 1999), Clark Atlanta U. Alumni Assn., Zonta Internat. Democrat. Roman Catholic. Avocations: collecting china, Black folk art. Office: Wilkes Mental Health Cons Ste 170 23811 Chagrin Blvd Beachwood OH 44122 Fax: 216-765-0448.

WILKES, BRENT AMES, management consultant; b. Melrose, Mass., Sept. 30, 1952; s. Gordon Borthwick and Frances (Ames) W.; 1 child, Erin; m. Linda Dadourian, Oct. 18, 1998. Bachelor, U. Mass., 1974; M of Pub. Affairs, U. Conn., 1977. Cert. assn. exec., 1998, assoc. risk mgmt., 1998. Adminstrv. asst. Town of Tolland, Conn., 1975-76; mgmt. specialist Mass. Dept. Community Affairs, Boston, 1976-79; adminstrv.. asst. to mayor City of Gloucester, 1979-80; assoc. dir., dir. of field svcs. Mass. Mcpl. Assn., Boston, 1980-89; v.p., treas. Mass. Interlocal Ins. Assn., 1984-89; pres. MMA Consulting Group, Inc., 1989-94, MMA Mgmt. Svcs. Inc., Boston, 1995-98, N.E. Pub. Risk, Inc., Boston, 1998, Northeast Assn. Mgmt., Inc., Boston, 1999—; v.p., treas. Pub. Employer Risk Mgmt. Assn., Albany, NY, 1989—97, pres. N.Y., 1997—; bd. dirs. NLC Mut. Ins. Co., 1994—2000. Bd. dirs. Assn. Govt. Risk Pub.; adj. prof. Suffolk U. Grad. Sch. Mgmt., Boston, 1980—82; lectr. numerous regional and nat. trade assns. Author and editor: Managing Small Towns, 1986; contbr. articles to profl. jours. Mem. fin. com. Town of Acton, Mass., 1977-79; mem. town meeting Town of Reading, Mass., 1987-89; pres. Unitarian Universalist Ch. of Reading, 1990-93. Mem. Am. Soc. Assn. Execs., Internat. City Mgmt. Assn. (cert. in mgmt.), Mass. Mcpl. Mgmt. Assn. Democrat. Unitarian Universalist. Avocations: golf, tennis, volleyball, reading, boating. Office: Northeast Assn Mgmt Inc 100 Conifer Hill Dr Ste 307 Danvers MA 01923-1168 E-mail: bwilkes@neami.com.

WILKES, CHRISTOPHER COMAS, judge; b. Annapolis, Md., Apr. 12, 1956; s. Gilbert III and Elizabeth S. (Lewis) W.; m. Patricia Ann Skelly, June 9, 1984; children: Catherine Ann, Lauren Elizabeth. BA, W.Va. U., 1980; JD, Ohio No. U., 1982; postgrad., Nat. Jud. Coll., 1994. Bar: W.Va. 1983, U.S. Dist. Ct. (so. dist.) W.Va. 1983, U.S. Surpeme Ct. 1985, U.S. Dist. Ct. (no. dist.) W.Va. 1986. Ptnr. Wilkes & Wilkes Legal Corp., Martinsburg, W.Va., 1983-93; judge Mcpl. Ct., 1985-93, Ranson, W.Va., 1985-93, 23rd Jud. Cir., 1993—, chief judge, 1995, 1998, 2001. Mem. Am. Judges Assn., W.Va. Jud. Assn., Am. Inns of Ct., Phi Kappa Phi. Republican. Office: 23rd Jud Ct 110 W King St Martinsburg WV 25401-3287

WILKES, CLEM CABELL, JR. stockbroker; b. Johnson City, Tenn., Apr. 5, 1953; s. Clem Cabell Sr. and Dorothy Jane (Miller) W.; m. Tonya Jean McCall, July 20, 1974; children: Elizabeth Layne, Clem Cabell III. BS, East Tenn. State U., 1975; postgrad., Med. Coll. Pa., 1978, Owen Sch. Mgmt., Nashville, 1984. Salesman Beecham Labs., Bristol, Tenn., 1975-78, Smith Kline & French Labs., Phila., 1978-81; stockbroker J.C. Bradford & Co., Johnson City, 1981-85; stockbroker, ptnr. Raymond James Fin. Svcs., Inc., 1985-99; dir. Johnson City Med. Ctr. Hosp., 1997—; fin. advisor, v.p. Citizens Investment Svcs. Inc., 1999—, vice chmn., 1999-2000. Vice chmn. bd. dirs. Mountain States Health Alliance, vice chmn., bd. dirs. Mem. com. Am. Cancer Soc., Johnson City, 1986—87, 2d v.p., 1989—; treas. Johnson City Ties for the Blind Found., 1998—; mem. Johnson City Parks and Recreation Bd., Johnson City Pub. Bldg. Authority, 2001—02; v.p. Citizens Investment Svcs., 1999—; vice chmn. Mountain States Health Alliance, 1999—2000, treas., 2000—02, chmn., 2002—; vestry mem. St. John's Episcopal Ch., 1986—89, treas., 1986—, sr. warden, 1989. Recipient award, Johnson City Ties for the Blind Found., 1989. Mem. Johnson City C. of C. (membership chmn. 1987), Robert Thomas Securities Pres. Club, Raymond James Fin. Svcs. Leaders Coun., Lions (v.p. Johnson City 1986-88, pres. 1989-90, Lion of Yr. award 1985, Lion of Decade award 1992, Melvin Jones fellow 1989), Johnson City Parks and Recreation Bd., Kappa Alpha. Office: Citizens Investment Svcs Inc 901 N Roan St Johnson City TN 37601-4604

WILKES, DAVID ROSS, therapist; b. Springfield, Ohio, Sept. 4, 1951; s. Carol Monroe and Margaret (Perdi) W.; m. Donna Marie Roach, Apr. 11, 1987; children: Andrew David, Lauren Rose. AAS in Community Mental Health Tech., Borough Manhattan C.C., 1980; BA in Psychology, Queens Coll., 1985; postgrad., Ctr. Modern Psychoanalytic Studies, 1986-89; PhD in Clin. Psychology, Union Inst., 1999. Admission interviewer, referral counselor Westside Social Setting/Manhattan Bowery Project, N.Y.C., 1978—79; with dept. psychiatry City Hosp. Elmhurst, 1980—83; behavioral counselor Assn. Children with Retarded Mental Devel., 1985—87; therapist, social worker West Lawrence Care Ctr., 1987—90; case mgr. Nassau Case Mgmt. Program Nassau County Dept. Mental Health, Hempstead, NY, 1990—2000; psychologist St. Vincent's Svcs., 2001—. Recipient Note of Commendation from Commr. Nassau County Dept. Mental Health and Devel. Disabilities, 1992. Mem. Am. Counseling Assn., Am. Psychol. Assn., Nat. Psychology Adv. Assn., Nat. Assn. Advancement of Psychoanalysis (assoc.), Phi Theta Kappa. Avocations: history of jazz, jazz musician. Office: 415 Degraw St Brooklyn NY 11217-2903 E-mail: dwilkes@suffolk.lib.ny.us.

WILKES, DEBORAH ANN, neonatal intensive care nurse; b. Balt., May 21, 1954; d. Elbert D. and Elizabeth Erna (Hess) White; m. John Lindsey Wilkes II, June 21, 1975 (div.); children: Jennifer Lauren, John Lindsey III. AA, Prince Georges Community Coll., 1975. RN, Md.; cert. low risk neonatal nurse, neonatal resuscitation provider. Staff nurse newborn nursery Prince Georges Hosp. Ctr., Cheverly, Md., 1976-77, 85-87, asst. head nurse newborn nursery, 1977-81, 82-85, acting head nurse newborn nursery, 1981-82, staff nurse spl. care nursery, 1987-91, staff nurse, clin. nurse III, neonatal ICU, 1991—, chair neonatal ICU practice com. Mem. Am. Legion Aux. Mem. AACN, Assn. Women's Health, Obstetric and Neonatal Nurses, Nat. Assn. Neonatal Nurses, Washington Met. Assn. Neonatal Nurses, Profl. Staff Nurses Assn. Md. Local 1998 Svc. Employees Internat. Union (sec. PSNA, collective bargaining coun., v.p. local chpt., negotiating team, Membership award 1991-95, Nurse of Yr. 1993). Home: 10526 Apple Ridge Rd Gaithersburg MD 20886-1010 Office: Prince George's Hosp Ctr 3001 Hospital Dr Cheverly MD 20785-1189 E-mail: wilkes3@erols.com.

WILKES, DELANO ANGUS, architect; b. Panama City, Fla., Jan. 25, 1935; s. Burnice Angus and Flora Mae (Scott) W.; m. Dona Jean Murren, June 25, 1960. BArch, U. Fla., 1958. Cert. Nat. Coun. Archtl.; registration bds. cert. personal trainer, older adult specialty cert. Am. Coun. on Exercise. Designer Perkins & Will Partnership, Chgo., 1960-63; designer, job capt. Harry Weese, Ltd., 1963-66; project arch. Fitch Larocca Carrington, 1967-69; arch. Mittelbusher & Tourtelot, 1970-71; assoc. Bank Bldg. Corp., 1972-75; sr. assoc. Charles Edward Stade & Assocs., Park Ridge, Ill., 1975-77; sr. arch. Consoer Morgan Arch., Chgo., 1977-83, mktg. coord., 1980-83; design cons. Chamlin & Assocs., Peru and Morris, Ill., 1969-82, dir. arch., 1983-86, v.p. arch., 1986-2000. Archtl. cons. Sweet's divsn. McGraw Hill, Inc., Chgo., 1984-90; ptnr. Deri Wilkes Assocs., 1990-95; trainer Fitness Barn, 1995-96, Q Sports Club, 1997-98, Alpha Fitness, 1999—. Author: Colonel Ebenezer Folsom, 1778-1789, North Carolina Patriot and Tory Scourge, 1975; editor Folsom Bull., 1977-80; prodr. documentary film The Angry Minority, Menninger Found., 1978. Mem. coord. com. Dune Acres Plan Commn. (Ind.), 1983-91; bldg. commr. City of Dune Acres, 1984-89, Arch. Rev. Bd. Marsh Creek Country Club, St. Augustine, Fla., 1988—; chmn. Ind. party Dune Acres, 1987; elected trustee Dune Acres Town Bd., 1988-91, pres., 1988-89; mem. Dune Acres Civic Improvement Found., 1988-91 (leadership recognition for drive to restore Dune Acres Clubhouse); cons. Inst. of Crippled and Disabled, N.Y.C., 1978-83; guest lectr. field trip guide Coll. DuPage, Glen Ellyn, Ill., 1968-76; guest arch. med. adv. com. to Pres.'s Com. for Handicapped, 1977, 78; vice chmn. Westchester County Dem. Precinct, Porter County, Ind., 1986; chmn. selection com. Dem. Hdqrs., Porter County, 1986; treas. Com. to Elect Kovach to Coun., Porter County, 1986; vice chmn. Duneland Dems., 1988-92; pres. Ocean House Condominium Assn., St. Augustine, Fla., 1993-94; mem. architectural Rev. Bd. Marsh Creek, 1998—, chair natural landscape com., 2001—. Mem.: Putnam County Hist. Soc., New Eng. Hist. Geneal. Soc., N.C. Geneal. Soc., Am. Soc. Interior Design (coord. Info. Fair 1979), Chgo. Assn. Commerce and Industry (display dir. 1979 mtg.), Art Inst. Chgo., Chgo. AIA (chmn. design awards display com. 1978-79, prodr. New Mem. Show 1979, chmn. pub. rels. com. 1980), AIA, Folsom Family Assn. Am. (pres. 1978-82, v.p. 1982-, nominating chmn. 1983, host ann. meeting, Chgo. 1981), Businessmen for Pub. Interest, Marsh Creek Country Club (chmn. Fla. landscape com.), German Shorthaired Pointer Club North Fla., Gargoyle, Soc. Colonial Wars, Cook County Hist. Soc., chgo. Lyric Opera Guild. Democrat. Unitarian Universalist. Home: 332 Marsh Point Cir Saint Augustine FL 32080-5858 E-mail: dwdw@aug.com.

WILKES, E.M., III, judge; b. Hazlehurst, Ga., Mar. 27, 1946; s. E.M. Jr. and Beatrice McDuffie Wilkes; m. Patricia Elyse Edwards, Aug. 30, 1967; children: Thomas McLangton, Andrew McLean. BS in Gen. Mgmt., Ga. Inst. Tech., 1972; JD, Mercer U., 1975. Bar: Ga. 1975. Atty., pres. Wilkes, Johnson, Smith & Knox, P.A., Hazlehurst, 1975-93; judge Mcpl. Ct. City Hazlehurst, 1977-84, city atty., 1984-87; judge Juvenile Ct. Jeff Davis County State Ga., Hazlehurst, 1979-93, judge State Ct. Jeff Davis County, 1984-93, judge Superior Cts. Ga., Brunswick Jud. Cir., 1993—. Bd. dirs. Jeff Davis Hosp., Hazlehurst, Bank Hazlehurst. Pres. Lions Club, Hazlehurst, 1977-78, Jeff Davis Athletic Booster Club, Hazlehurst, 1990-92; dir., sec. Jeff Davis Athletic Assn., Inc., Hazlehurst, 1977—. 1st lt. U.S. Army, 1967-70. Named Profl. of the Yr., Hazlehurst-Jeff Davis C. of C., 1978. Mem. ABA, State Bar Ga., Coun. Superior Ct. Judges Ga., Hazlehurst-Baxley Bar Assn. (pres.). Methodist. Avocations: hunting, fishing, golfing, gardening. Office: Jeff Davis Superior Ct Jeff Davis Cty Courthouse PO Box 1540 Hazlehurst GA 31539-1540 Fax: 912-375-6634. E-mail: wilkesem@altamaha.net.

WILKES, GARTH L. educator, researcher; s. Paul H. Wilkes, Florence Wilkes; m. Barbara Wilkes. BS, NY State Coll. Forestry, 1964, Masters Degree, 1966, U. Mass., 1968—68, PhD, 1969. Univ. disting. prof. Va. Tech. U., Blacksburg, 1999—. Recipient Young Engring. Faculty award, Princeton U., 1974, Turner Alfrey Vis. Professorship, Mich. Molecular Inst. & Dow Chem. Co., 1993, Frank Giblin Meml. award in Polymer Analysis, Netzsch Instruments, 1998, EPSDIV ANTEC 2001 Best Paper award, Soc. Plastics Engrs., 2002. Mem.: Polymer Materials Sci. and Engring., Soc. Rheology, Am. Chem. Soc. (polymer divsn., rubber divsn., Best Paper award rubber divsn. 1985, Creative Polymer Chemistry award polymer divsn. 1987). Office: Virginia Tech Dept Chem Engring Blacksburg VA 24061

WILKES, GEORGE GARDNER, JR. landscape architect; b. Baton Rouge, Dec. 5, 1927; s. George Gardner and Irene Ola (Sowar) W.; m. Betty Jay Stokes Partinhimer, July 6, 1949 (div. Nov. 1976); children: George Gardner III, Rebecca Wilkes Yarbrough; m. Royetta Brown, Feb. 19, 1977. BS in Landscape Arch., La. State U., Baton Rouge, 1952, postgrad., 1953. Registered landscape architect, La., Calif., Md., Va., Ga. Landscape architect Lamberts, Shreveport, La., 1953-55, chief landscape architect, 1955-60; owner George G. Wilkes Assocs., 1960-66; land planner U.S. VA, Atlanta, 1966-70, asst. chief appraiser, 1970-72, chief appraiser, 1972-76, land planner Washington, 1976-81; owner George G. Wilkes L.A., Atlanta, 1981—. With USN, 1945-46. Mem. Am. Soc. Landscape Architects (emeritus mem.), Masons, Shriner. Republican. Presbyterian. Avocations: fishing, reading. Home and Office: 10 Westminster Close Dr NW Atlanta GA 30327-1604 E-mail: biggeorge3@juno.com.

WILKES, JOSEPH ALLEN, architect; b. N.Y.C., Aug. 14, 1919; s. Abraham P. and Rose W.; m. Margaret Wilcoxson, Dec. 7, 1946; children— Jeffrey, Roger BA, Dartmouth Coll., 1941; M.Arch., Columbia U., 1949. Registered architect, N.Y., Fla., Md., D.C., Va. Assoc. prof. architecture U. Fla., Gainesville, 1952-59; project dir. Bldg. Research Adv. Bd. Nat. Acad. Sci., Washington, 1959-62; assoc. architect Keyes, Lethbridge & Condon, 1962-66; ptnr. Wilkes & Faulkner, 1966-82, Wilkes Faulkner Jenkins & Bass, Washington, 1983-90. Lectr. architecture U. Md., 1971-85 Editor: Ency. of Architecture, 5 vols., 1988-89: chmn. editorial rev. bd.: Architectural Graphic Standards, 7th edit., 1980; archtl. works include: bldgs. Nat. Zool. Park; (bldg. renovation) Fed. Res. Bd. Bldg., Washington. Pres. Nat. Ctr. for a Barrier Free Environment, Washington, 1978; mem. profl. adv. council Nat. Easter Seals Soc. for Crippled Children, 1977-80; mem. Pres. Com. for Employment of Handicapped, Washington, 1976-82. Served to capt. AC U.S. Army, 1942-45; ETO Fellow AIA; mem. Alpha Rho Chi Home: 1720 Winchester Rd Annapolis MD 21401-5851

WILKES, SHAR (JOAN CHARLENE WILKES), elementary education educator; b. Chgo., July 15, 1951; d. Marcus and Hattie (Ehrich) Wexman; 1 child, McKinnon. Student, U. Okla., 1973, U. Wyo., 1975—. Rsch. dirs., exhibit designer Nicolaysen Art Mus.-Children's Ctr., Casper, Wyo., 1984-85; tchr. Natrona County Sch. Dist. 1, 1974-2001, spelling bee coord.; reading specialist Southridge Elem. Sch., 1995—. Enrichment coord. Paradise Valley Elem. Sch., 1993-94; co-coord. Children's Health Fair/Body Works Healthfair, Ptnrs. in Edn., Paradise Valley Elem. Sch./Wyo. Med. Ctr. and Blue Envelope, 1994; developer Fossil Trunk, Tate Museum Ednl. Program, 1999—; cofounder, dir. Ink Link, Sunday page Casper Star Tribune; spkr. Schs. to Careers Confs., S.D., Wyo. Author: Fantastic Phonics Food Factory, children's edit., 2000, parent/teacher edit., 2000. Dem. candidate Wyo. State Legis., 1986, 88; edn. chair United Way, Casper, 1988; chairperson Very Spl. Arts Festival, 1988, March of Dimes, 1989; grants person Casper Symphony, 1990; NCSD coord. Bear Trap Meadow Blue Grass Festival, 1995—. Recipient 3d Pl. Newspaper Across Am., 2000. Mem. NEA, Nat. Coun. Edn. Assn., Internat. Reading Assn. (lectr. Colo. coun. 2000—), Wyo. Edn. Assn., Soroptimist (charter), Phi Delta Kappa (exec. bd. 1988-98), Delta Kappa Gamma. Home: 4353 Coffman Ct Casper WY 82604-5145 Office: Natrona County Sch Dist # 1 Casper WY 82604

WILKEY, ELMIRA SMITH, illustrator, artist, publisher, author, educator; b. Kankakee, Ill., Dec. 13, 1936; d. Edmond Anthony Dorothy Agnes (Schilling) Smith; m. Lowell Gene Wilkey; children: A. Shelley, Eric, Martin, Barry, Tad, Jeremy. BA cum laude, Loretto Heights Coll. (now Regis U.), 1958. Mgr. Duncan Assocs., Champaign, Ill., 1960-61; English/drama speech tchr. Kankakee Sch. Dist., 1958-60; substitute tchr. Kankakee County, 1965-80; art instr. Kankakee C.C., 1988, 2000; behavior couns. Nutri-Sys., Bourbonnais, Ill., 1987-91; English tchr. Bishop McNamara H.S., Kankakee, 1994-2000; founder, co-owner, printer Studio Sans Serif Divsn., Bronte Press, Manteno, Kankakee, Bourbonnais, 1977—. Textbook art cons. DSP, Boston, 1965-74; art adj. Olivet Coll., Bourbonnais, 1993-94; writer, art presenter W.C. Workshops Oliver Coll., Kankakee Art League, 1980-90; lectr. in field. Artist-illustrator several books including Come Spring, History of Rockville, Hoofbeats, 2001; involved with Children's Book Program, cable TV, Manteno, Ill., 1996-99; author newspaper column Pat's Meanders, 1992—; one woman shows include Invitational: Ill. Women in Art Prairie State Coll., Galesburg, 1980; contbr. art Tall Grass Art Assn., Children's Art Sch. Benefit. Mem. cmty. arts. coun. Kankakee; cmty. art adv. bd. Kankakee C.C.; donated artwork for benefit auctions Hospice, Catholic Charities, United Way. Recipient numerous local, regional awards in art; Straw Series Signature art technique, V.I.P. Mem. Nat. League Am. Penwomen (Ill. state pres, Chgo. br. v.p. 1979—, treas. 2002), Ill. State Poetry Soc. (charter), Midwest Watercolor Soc., Nat. Mus. Women in Arts, Great Books (charter, pres. 1980-85), Miniature Book Soc., Christians in Visual Arts. Republican. Roman Catholic. Avocations: walking, herb/plant identification, singing, piano, camping. Home and Office: Studio Sans Serif Divsn The Bronte Press 4136 W 6940N Rd Bourbonnais IL 60914-4208 Fax: 815-936-9913. Personal E-mail: miraswilkey@yahoo.com.

WILKEY, MALCOLM RICHARD, retired ambassador, former federal judge; b. Murfreesboro, Tenn., Dec. 6, 1918; s. Malcolm Newton and Elizabeth (Gilbert) W.; m. Emma Secul Depolo, Dec. 21, 1959. AB magna cum laude, Harvard U., 1940, LLB, 1948; LLD (hon.), Rose-Hulman Inst. Tech., 1984. Bar: Tex. 1948, N.Y. 1963, U.S. Supreme Ct. 1952, D.C. 1970. U.S. atty. So. Dist. Tex., 1954-58; asst. atty. gen. U.S., 1958-61; ptnr. Butler Binion Rice & Cook, 1961-63; gen. counsel, sec. Kennecott Copper Corp., 1963-70; judge U.S. Ct. Appeals D.C. Circuit, 1970-85; U.S. amb. to Uruguay, 1985-90. Official in charge fed. forces at Little Rock Sch. Crisis, Dept. Justice, 1958; mem. U.S.-Chile Arbitration Commn., 1991-97; lectr. internat. constl. and adminstrv. law London Poly., 1979, 80; lectr. Tulane U. Law Summer Sch., Grenoble, France, 1981, 83, San Diego Law Summer Sch., Oxford, Eng., 1983, Brigham Young Law Sch., 1984, 93; vis. fellow Wolfson Coll., Cambridge U., 1985; chmn. Pres.'s Commn. on Revision Fed. Ethics Laws, 1989; spl. counsel to Atty. Gen. for inquiry into the House Banking Facility, 1992. Author: Is It Time For A Second Constitutional Convention, 1995, As the Twig Is Bent, 2003. Del. Republican Nat. Conv., 1960. Served from 2d lt. to lt. col. AUS, 1941-45. Hon. fellow Wolfson Coll., Cambridge. Fellow Am. Bar Found.; mem. Am. Law Inst. (adv. com. restatement fgn. rels. law of U.S.), Jud. Conf. U.S. (com. on standards for admission to fed. cts. 1976-79), Phi Beta Kappa, Delta Sigma Rho, Phi Delta Phi (hon.). Address: Av El Bosque 379 Providencia Santiago Chile

WILKEY, MARY HUFF, investor, writer, publisher; b. Dayton, Ohio, Sept. 30, 1940; d. Charles Joseph and Frances Rose (Wintersteen) Huff; divorced; children: Christopher Tyson, Charles Cory, Jennifer Jo. Student, Sinclair C.C., Dayton, 1979—85. Pvt. sec. Dare, Inc., Troy, Ohio, 1962-63; legal sec. Smith & Schnacke, Dayton, 1963-68; adminstrv. asst. U.S. Magistrate, 1971-74; legal technician Coolidge, Wall, Womsley & Lombard Co., L.P.A., 1968-75, 81-85, Lair & Owen, Dayton, 1979-81; owner, operator Village Mill Country Store, Tipp City, Ohio, 1987-88; owner, mgr. Happy Days Residence, Franklin, 1989—; pres., owner 'elf Expressions, 1988—. Author, pub. (directory) Your Personal Guide, 1988, 89, 'elf Expressions Ezine, 2001—. Phone support vol. Operation Golden Ring, Dayton, 1984-85; vol. Sta. WPTD Pub. TV, Dayton, 1983-85. Mem. NAFE, Mensa, Internat. Platform Assn., Greater Dayton Real Estate Investor Assn. Avocations: Bible study, creative writing, natural health, real estate, internet marketing. Office: PO Box 854 Franklin OH 45005-0854 E-mail: elfbutter@erinet.com.

WILKIE, BRIAN F. English educator; b. Bklyn., Mar. 30, 1929; s. James William and Mary Ellen (Devine) W.; m. Ann Allen Johnson, Aug. 8, 1957; children: John Michael, Brian Scott, Neil Thomas. BA, Columbia U., 1951; MA, U. Rochester, 1952; PhD, U. Wis., 1959. Asst. prof. English Dartmouth Coll., Hanover, N.H., 1959-63; assoc. prof. English U. Ill., Urbana, 1963-70, prof. English, 1970-85; U. Ark., Fayetteville, 1985—. Author: Romantic Poets and Epic Tradition, 1965, Blake's Thel and Oothoon, 1990; co-author: Blakes Four Zoas The Design of a Dream, 1978, (anthology) Literature of the Western World, 1984, 88, 92, 97, 2001. Cpl. U.S. Army, 1952-54. Mem. MLA (mem. exec. com. English Romantics div. 1973-78, del. assembly 1974-76). Avocations: piano, music, book collecting. Home: 1012 E Oaks Manor Dr Fayetteville AR 72703 Office: U Ark Dept English 333 Kimpel Hall Fayetteville AR 72701 E-mail: bfwilkie@aol.com.

WILKIE, CHARLES A. chemistry educator; b. Detroit, Nov. 21, 1941; s. Elmer A. and Marion I. Wilkie; m. Nancy B. Wilkie, Sept. 5, 1964; children: Christine Cotey, Stephen, Richard. BS, U. Detroit, 1963; PhD, Wayne State U., 1967. Contbr. articles to profl. jours.; editor: 2 books on polymer additives, 2000, 2 books on fire retardancy, 2000. Office: Marquette U PO Box 1881 Milwaukee WI 53201

WILKIE, DONALD WALTER, biologist, aquarium museum director; b. Vancouver, B.C., Can., June 20, 1931; s. Otway James Henry and Jessie Margaret (McLeod) W.; m. Patricia Ann Archer, May 18, 1980; children: Linda, Douglas, Susanne. BA, U. B.C., 1960, M.Sc., 1966. Curator Vancouver Pub. Aquarium, 1961-63, Phila. Aquarama, 1963-65; exec. dir. aquarium-mus. Scripps Instn. Oceanography, La Jolla, Calif., 1965-93, exec. dir. emeritus, 1993—. Cons. aquarium design, rschg. exhibit content; sci. writer and editor naturalist-marine edn. programs. Author books on aquaria and marine ednl. materials; contbr. numerous articles to profl. jours. Bd. mem. Miramar Trip & Skeet Club. Mem. Am. Soc. Ichthyologists and Herpetologists, San Diego Zool. Soc., Home: 4548 Cather Ave San Diego CA 92122-2632 Office: U Calif San Diego Scripps Instn Oceanography Libr 9500 Gilman Dr La Jolla CA 92093-5004 E-mail: dwilkie@ussd.edu., donaqua27@aol.com. *As a biologist and teacher my major goal has been to increase public interest in learning about our environment and promoting proper use of the earth's resources.*

WILKIE, NANCY CLAUSEN, classics and archaeology educator; b. Milw., Dec. 27, 1942; d. Harry H. and Teresa (D.) Clausen; m. Robert J. D. Wilkie, May 9, 1964 (div. 1974); m. Craig H. Anderson, Sept. 27, 1975. AB, Stanford U., 1964; MA, U. Minn., 1967, PhD, 1975. Instr. Macalester Coll., St. Paul, 1972-75, Carleton Coll., Northfield, Minn., 1974-75, from asst. prof. to assoc. prof., 1975-93, prof., 1993—, chair dept. classical langs., 1991-96. Parker vis. scholar Brown U., Providence, 1983; Fulbright lectr. Tribhuvan U., Kathmandu, Nepal, 1988; trustee Archaeol. Inst. Am., Boston, 1989-94, 1st v.p., 1994-98, pres., 1998—; mem. exec. com. Ctr. for Ancient Studies, U. Minn., Mpls., 1990-93; mem. exec. bd. Soc. Profl. Archaeologists, Fresno, Calif., 1991-93, 95-98. Editor: Contributions to Aegean Archaeology, 1985, The Great Isthmus Corridor Route, Vol. I, 1991; author, editor: Excavations at Nichoria in SW Greece, Vol. II, 1992. Mem. Assn. Ancient Historians, Am. Philol. Assn., Soc. for Am. Archaeology, Women's Classical Caucus. Avocations: sailing, cross country skiing. Home: 1515 Waters Edge Ln Northfield MN 55057-4899 Office: Dept Classical Lang Carleton College Northfield MN 55057 E-mail: nwilkie@carleton.edu.

WILKIN, RICHARD EDWIN, clergyman, religious organization executive; b. nr. Paulding, Ohio, Nov. 3, 1930; s. Gaylord D. and Beulah E. (Tarlton) W.; m. Barbara A. Zehender, Aug. 10, 1952; children— Richard Edward, James Lee, Deborah Ann. Student, Giffin Jr. Coll., 1948-49; BS, Findlay Coll., 1952, D.D., 1975; postgrad., Ind. U., 1959-60. Ordained to ministry Churches of God Gen. Conf., 1953; pastor Neptune Ch. of God, Celina, Ohio, 1952-59, Wharton (Ohio) Ch. of God, 1959-64, Anthony Wayne Ch. of God, Ft. Wayne, Ind., 1964-70; adminstr., chief exec. Chs. of God Gen. Conf., Findlay, Ohio, 1970-87; supr. mission work India, Bangladesh, Haiti, 1970-85; dir. field edn. and Inst. for Biblical Studies, faculty mem. Winebrenner Theol. Sem., Findlay, 1987-92, adj. facult O.T., 1993-97; interim sr. pastor Coll. 1st Ch. of God, 1992-93. Dir. summer youth camps, sec., mem. exec. com. Ohio Conf., 1952-59, state clk., pres., 1959-64; chmn. Commn. on Edn., mem. exec. com. Ind. Conf., 1964-70; adv. com. Am. Bible Soc.; steering com. U.S. Ch. Leaders, 1979; pres. Ft. Wayne Ministerial Assn.; bd. dirs. Associated Chs. of Ft. Wayne and Allen County, 1966-70; tchr. Center Twp. Jr. High Sch., Celina, Mendon (Ohio) Union High Sch., Van Del High Sch., Van Wert, Ohio, 1954-59; interim pastor Shawnee First Ch. of God, Lima, Ohio, 1987-88, ch. cons., 1987-98. Vice pres. bd. trustees Winebrenner Haven, mem. adv. com. in race relations regarding sch. reorgn. and busing, Ft. Wayne, 1967-69; trustee Winebrenner Theol. Sem., 1980-87, sec. bd. trustees; trustee U. Findlay, 1985—, chmn. of com. on trustees of bd. of trustees; sec. Bd. of Pensions of Ch. of God, Gen. Conf., 1986-99; trustee Found. Ohio Conf. Chs. of God, 1998—, chmn. bd. dirs., chmn. adminstr.'s adv. com., 1997—. Recipient Outstanding Tchr. award, 1958; Disting. Alumnus award Findlay Coll., 1973, Outstanding Leadership award Ohio Conf. Chs. of God, 1986, Disting. Assoc. award U. Findlay, 1992; named Hon. Alumnus Winebrenner Theol. Sem., 1978. Home: 1806 Greendale Ave Findlay OH 45840-6918

WILKIN, WILLIAM EDMUND, lawyer; b. Rochester, N.Y., Dec. 3, 1950; s. William James and Mary Jo (Nollet) W. BA, Canisius Coll., 1972, MS, 1977; MA, U. Notre Dame, 1980; JD, Catholic U., 1985. Bar: Md. 1985, D.C. 1998, U.S. Ct. Appeals (4th cir.) 1986, U.S. Ct. Appeals (3d cir.) 1988., U.S. Dist. Ct. Md. 1986., U.S. Ct. Appeals (1st cir.) 1994, U.S. Supreme Ct. 1999. Tchr. Aquinas High Sch., Augusta, Ga., 1976-82; trial atty. Office of Gen. Counsel, U.S. Dept. Health and Human Svcs., Balt., 1986-88; fgn. svc. officer U.S. Dept. State, Washington, 1988-93. Alt. del. Dem. Nat. Conv., 1972. 2nd lt. U.S. Army, 1972-74. Recipient Meritorious Hon. award Dept. State, 1993. Mem. Federalist Soc., Am. Legion. Republican. Roman Catholic. Office: The Normandy Group Ltd PO Box 5099 Herndon VA 20172-1966 E-mail: normandy@biztech.net.

WILKINS, ANN THOMAS, classics educator; b. Portsmouth, N.H., Jan. 23, 1944; d. George R. and Naomi W. Thomas; m. David George Wilkins, June 25, 1966; children: Rebecca, Katherine. BA, Wellesley Coll., 1966; MA, U. Pitts., 1975, PhD, 1990. Tchr. asst., tchg. fellow, part-time instr. classics dept. U. Pitts., 1973-77, lectr. classics dept., 1986-94, mem. faculty humanities dept. Greensburg campus, 1991-92; instr. dept. classics Vassar Coll., Poughkeepsie, N.Y., 1978-79; mem. faculty fgn. lang. dept. Winchester-Thurston Sch., Pitts., 1980-87; lectr. classics dept. Duquesne U., 1992-94, asst. prof. classics, 1994-2000, assoc. prof. classics, 2000—. Flute instr. Anna Perlow Sch. music, 1979-93; pvt. flute instr., 1980—; presenter in field; adminstr. Pitts. Chamber Music Project Workshop for Young Musicians, 1984-86. Author: Villain or Hero: Sallust's Portrayal of Catiline, 1994; contbr. articles to profl. jours. Hunkele grantee Duquesne U., 1995, NEH grantee, 1996, 2002, Noble K. Dick Faculty Devel. grantee, 1997; Presdl. scholar, 1998. Mem. Am. Philol. Assn., Am. Inst. Archaeology, Classical Assn. Atlantic States, Classical Assn. Mid. West and South, Pa. Classical Assn., Classical Assn. Pitts. and Vicinity, Internat. Soc. Classical Tradition, Renaissance Soc. Am., Coll. Art Assn. Office: Duquesne U Dept Classics Forbes Ave Pittsburgh PA 15282-0001

WILKINS, ARTHUR NORMAN, retired college administrator; b. Kansas City, Sept. 24, 1925; s. Arthur Miller and Jean (DeWitt) W. AA, Jr. Coll. Kansas City, 1947; MA, U. Chgo., 1950; PhD, Washington U., St. Louis, 1953. Grad. asst. Washington U., St. Louis, 1950-52; instr. English La. State U., Baton Rouge, 1953-56, Jr. Coll. Kansas City, 1956-64, chmn. dept. English, 1961-64; instr. English Met. Jr. Coll., Kansas City, 1964-69, chmn. dept. English, 1964-68, chmn. divsn. humanities, 1968-69; instr. English, chmn. dept. humanities Longview C.C., Lee's Summit, Mo., 1969-70, dean instrn., 1970-84; dir. acad. affairs Met. C.C.s, Kansas City, 1984-90. Author: Mortal Taste, 1965, High Seriusness, 1971, The Lenore Overtures, 1975, Attic Salt, 1984, Dirt Behind Our Ears, 1995; contbr. articles to profl. jours. Mem. Mo. State Libr. Planning com., 1980-83. With U.S. Army, 1943-46. Washington U. fellow, 1952-53. Mem. Bookmark Soc., Phoenix Soc., U. Chgo. Libr. Soc. Home: 210 W 100th Ter Apt 202 Kansas City MO 64114-4431

WILKINS, BARRATT (GEORGE WILKINS), librarian; b. Atlanta, Nov. 6, 1943; s. George Barratt and Mabel Blanche (Brooks) W. BA, Emory U., 1965; MA, Ga. State U., 1968, U. Wis., 1969. Reference libr. S.C. State Libr., Columbia, 1969-71; instl. libr. cons. Mo. State Libr., Jefferson City, 1971-73; asst. state libr. State Libr. Fla., Tallahassee, 1973-77, state libr., 1977—; dir. div. Libr. and Info. Svcs. State of Fla., Tallahassee, 1986—; acting asst. sec. state Fla. Dept. of State, 1987. Abstractor Hist. Abstracts, 1967-71; dir. survey project Nat. Ctr. Edn. Statistics, 1976-77; del. The White House Conf. on Libr. and Info. Svcs., 1991, The White House Conf. on Sch. Librs., 2002; mem. planning com. Fla. Gov.'s Conf. on Libraries and Info. Svcs.; bd. dirs. Southeastern Libr. Network, Inc., 1979-82, treas., 1980-81, vice chmn., 1981-82; mem. adv. coun. U.S. Pub. Printer, 1983-86, Southeastern/Atlantic Regional Med. Libr. Svcs. 1986-89; mem. planning com., Fla. Automated Edn. Commn., 1989-94; mem. adv. coun. Fla. State Bd. INd. Colls. and Univs., 1995-98; mem. steering com. and state libr. surveys Nat. Ctr. Edn. Stats., 1992—; mem. privacy and tech. task force State of Fla., 2000—; bd. dirs. First Am. Found., Inc., Fla. Distance Learning Network, Inc.; mem. adv. coun. Fla. State U. Sch. Info. Studies, 1999—; mem. libr. stats. revision com. Nat. Info. Stds. Orgn., 2001—; cons. in field. Contbr. articles to profl. jours. Mem. adv. com. statewide jail project Mo. Assn. Social Welfare, 1971-73, bd. dirs. central div., 1971-73; mem. State Univ. System Interinstl. Library Com., 1977— ; bd. dirs. Fla. Ctr. Libr. Automation, 1984— , Fla. Ctr. for the Book, 1984—, Fla. Coll. Ctr. for Libr. Automation, 1990—, Coun. for Fla. Librs., 1981—. Recipient Exceptional Achievement award Assn. Specialized and Coop. Libr.

Agys., 1991, Outstanding Pub. Svc. award Gov. of Fla., 1991, Keppel award and Lorenz award Nat. Ctr. Edn. Stats., 1995—; U. Wis. fellow, 1969. Mem. ALA (coun. 1981-85, legis. com. 1982-86, com. on orgn. 1988-90, planning com., 1993-95, standards, 1996-98, legis. honor roll 1996), Assn. State Libr. Agys. (pres. 1976-77), Assn. Hosp. Instl. Librs. (bd. dirs. 1973-74), Am. Correctional Assn. (chair instn. libr. com. 1975-80), Southeastern Libr. Assn. (pres. 1982-84), Assn. Specialized and Coop. Libr. Agys. (bd. dirs. 1981-85, 87-89, stds. rev. 1997—), Fla. Libr. Assn. (hon. life mem.), Libr. Adminstrn. and Mgmt. Assn. (chair govt. affair com. 1984-86), Chief Officers of State Libr. Agys. (bd. dirs. 1980-82, pres. 1990-92, chair legis. com. 1992-96, chair rsch. & stats. com. 1998—), Univ. Club, Gov.'s Club, Beta Phi Mu, Phi Alpha Theta. Democrat. Episcopalian. Office: Dept State Divsn Libr Svcs RA Gray Bldg Tallahassee FL 32399-0250 E-mail: bwilkins@mail.dos.state.fl.us.

WILKINS, BURLEIGH TAYLOR, philosophy educator; b. Bridgetown, Va., July 1, 1932; s. Burleigh and Helen Marie (Taylor) W.; children: Brita Taylor, Carla Cowgill, Burleigh William. BA summa cum laude, Duke U., 1952; MA, Harvard U., 1954, Princeton U., 1963, PhD, 1965. Instr. MIT, Cambridge, 1957-60, Princeton U., 1960-61, 63; asst. prof. Rice U., Houston, 1965-66, assoc. prof., 1966-67, U. Calif., Santa Barbara, 1967-68, prof., 1968—. Author: Carl Becker, 1961, The Problem of Burke's Political Philosophy, 1967, Hegel's Philosophy of History, 1974, Has History Any Meaning?, 1978, Terrorism and Collective Responsibility, 1992. Mem. Phi Beta Kappa. Office: U Calif Dept Philosophy Santa Barbara CA 93106

WILKINS, CAROLINE HANKE, consumer agency administrator, political worker; b. Corpus Christi, Tex., May 12, 1937; d. Louis Allen and Jean Guckian Hanke; m. B. Hughel Wilkins, 1957; 1 child, Brian Hughel. Student, Tex. Coll. Arts and Industries, 1956-57, Tex. Tech. U., 1957-58; BA, U. Tex., 1961; MA magna cum laude, U. Ams., 1964. Instr. history Oreg. State U., 1967-68; adminstr. Consumer Svcs. divsn. State of Oreg., 1977-80, Wilkins Assoc., 1980—. Mem. PFMC Salmon Adv. subpanel, 1982-86. Author: (with B. H. Wilkins) Implications of the U.S.-Mexican Water Treaty for Interregional Water Transfer, 1968. Dem. precinct committeewoman, Benton County, Oreg., 1964-90; publicity chmn. Benton County Gen. Election, 1964; chmn. Get-Out-the-Vote Com., Benton County, 1966; vice chmn. Benton County Dem. Ctrl. Com., 1966-70; vice chmn. 1st Congl. Dist., Oreg., 1966-67, chmn., 1967-68; vice chmn. Dem. Party of Oreg., 1968-69, chmn., 1969-74; mem. exec. com. Western States Dem. Conf., 1970-72; vice chmn. Dem. Nat. Com., 1972-77, mem. arrangements com., 1972, 76, mem. Dem. Charter Commn., 1973-74; mem. Dem. Nat. Com., 1972-77, 85-89, mem. size and composition com., 1987-89, rules com., 1988; mem. Oreg. Govt. Ethics Commn., 1974-76; del., mem. rules com. Dem. Nat. Conv., 1988; 1st v.p. Nat. Fedn. Dem. Women, 1983-85, pres., 1985-87, parliamentarian, 1993-95, 99-2001, chair Pres.'s coun., 2001—; mem. Kerr Libr. bd. Oreg. State U., 1989-95, pres., 1994-95; mem. Corvallis-Benton County Libr. Found., 1991-2001, sec., 1993, v.p., 1994, pres., 1995, mission and goals com. chair 2000-01; bd. dirs. Oreg. chpt. U.S. Lighthouse Soc., pres., 1997-98; bd. dirs. Oreg. State U.-Corvallis Symphony, 1998-2001, v.p. 1999-2000, resources com.; pres. Oreg. Fedn. Dem. Women, 1997-2001. Oreg. State-Corvallis chpt., UNIFEM, 1998-2002. Named Outstanding Mem., Nat. Fedn. Dem. Women, 1992, Woman of Achievement, Oreg. State U. Women's Ctr., 1998. Mem.: Soc. Consumer Affairs Profls., Nat. Assn. Consumer Agy. Adminstrs., Oreg. State U. Folk Club (pres. faculty wives 1989—90, scholarship chair 2000—01), Zonta Internat. (vice area bd. dirs. dist. 8 1992—94, bd. dist. 8 1994—96, by laws and resolutions chair 1997—98, internat. rels. coord. dist. 8 2000—02, area dir.). Office: 3311 NW Roosevelt Dr Corvallis OR 97330-1169

WILKINS, CHARLES L. chemistry educator; b. Los Angeles, Calif., Aug. 14, 1938; s. Richard and Lenore M. W.; m. Ingrid Fritsch, 1997; children: Mark R., Connor W. Fritsch. BS, Chapman Coll., 1961; PhD, U. Oreg., 1966. Prof. chemistry U. Nebr., Lincoln, 1967-81; prof. U. Calif., Riverside, 1981-98; disting. prof. U. Ark., Fayetteville, 1998—. Recipient Frank H. Field and Joe L. Franklin award for Outstanding Achievement in mass spectrometry Am. Chem. Soc., 1997, Ea. Analytical Symposium award in the field of Analytical Chemistry, 2002. Office: U Ark Dept Chem & Biochem Fayetteville AR 72701 E-mail: cwilkins@mail.uark.edu.

WILKINS, CHRISTOPHER PUTNAM, conductor; b. Boston, May 28, 1957; s. Herbert Putnam and Angela (Middleton) W. BA, Harvard U., 1978; MusM, Yale U., 1981. Condr.-in-residence SUNY, Purchase, 1981-82; assoc. condr. Oreg. Symphony, Portland, 1982-83, Cleve. Orch., 1983-86; assoc. condr. Utah Symphony, Salt Lake City, from 1986; condr. Colo. Springs Symphony Orch., 1989-96, artistic advisor, 1998—; music dir. San Antonio Symphony, 1992—. Condr. Exxon Arts Endowment, 1982-86. Home: 168 Nashawtuc Rd Concord MA 01742-1617 Office: San Antonio Symphony Orch 222 E Houston St Ste 200 San Antonio TX 78205-1808*

WILKINS, DAVID GEORGE, fine arts educator; b. Battle Creek, Mich., Sept. 12, 1939; s. George Henry and Marjorie Ewing (Pierce) Wilkins; m. Ann Thomas, June 25, 1966; children: Rebecca Louise, Katherine May. BA, Oberlin Coll., 1961; MA, U. Mich., 1963, PhD, 1969. Instr. U. N.H., Durham, 1963-64; prof. dept. history of art and arch. U. Pitts., 1967—, chair, 1989-92, 98—, dir. univ. art gallery, 1976-92. Faculty mem summer sessions Sarah Lawrence Col-Univ Mich, Florence, Italy, 1975—81. Author (with Bernard Schultz and Katheryn M Linduff): (book) Art Past/Art Present, 4th ed, 2001; author: (with Bonnie A Bennet) Donatello, 1984, Maso di Banco, 1985; author: (with K J Arbitman) The Illustrated Bartsch, Vol 53, Pre-Rembrandt Etchers, 1985, The Art of the Duquesne Club, 2002; author: (with Mark M Brown and Lu Donnelly) The History of the Duquesne Club, 1989; editor (revising ed): Hartt History of Italian Renaissance Art, 4th ed, 1994; editor: (with Rebecca L Wilkins) The Search for a Patron in the Middle Ages and the Renaissance, 1996; editor: (with Sheryl Reiss) Beyond Isabella: Secular Women Patrons of Art in the Italian Renaissance, 2001. Mem Humanities Coun, 1984—88; mus adv panel Pa Coun Arts, 1985—87; bd dirs Pittsburgh Ctr Arts, 1979—98; Mendelssohn Choir Pittsburgh, 1979—84. Recipient Chancellor's Distinguishing Teaching Award, Univ Pittsburgh, 1987; fellow William E Suida, Kress Found, Kunsthistorisches Inst, Florence, 1966—67. Mem.: Renaissance Soc Am, Italian Art Soc, Col Art Asn. Democrat. Home: 1217 Shady Ave Pittsburgh PA 15232-2811 Office: U Pitts Dept History Art & Arch 104 Frick Fine Arts Pittsburgh PA 15260-7601

WILKINS, DAVID HORTON, state legislator; b. Oct. 12, 1946; m. Susan Clary; children: James, Robert. BA with honors, Clemson U.; JD, U. S.C.; hon. degree, Med. U. S.C., The Citadel. Bar: S.C. Atty. in pvt.practice, 1970s—; mem. S.C. Ho. of Reps., 1980—, chmn. judiciary com., 1986—, speaker pro tem, 1992-95, speaker, 1995—. Recipient Friend of the Taxpayer award S.C. Assn. Taxpayers, others; named Outstanding Legislator of Yr. by S.C. C. of C., Dept. Probation of Parole, S.C. Sch. Bds. Assn., S.C. Troopers Assn., others, Nat. Republican Legislator of Yr. Nat. Rep. Legis. Assn. Baptist. Office: 508 Blatt Bldg. Columbia SC 29201*

WILKINS, ELIZABETH ANN, training and development manager; b. Honolulu, June 12, 1964; d. William Ralph and Susan May (Bower) W.; 1 child, Ashley Elizabeth Wilkins Hummell. BA in History, Wash. State U., 1988; MS in Instrnl. Leadership/Curr. Devel. with distinction honors, Nat. U., San Diego, 1994. Ops. mgr. Video Unltd., Inc., Spokane, Wash., 1983-86, Koala Blue, Inc., Van Nuys, Calif., 1989-90, dir. corp. stores, cons. ops. and leadership, 1990-91; sr. sales mgr. TMC/Crazy Shirts, Inc., San Diego, 1991-92; ops. cons. Hummell Chiropractic, 1993-94; tng. and devel. mgr. CSR-West, Everett, Wash., 1995—. Practicum facilitator Wash. State U., Pullman, 1987-88. Vol. Am. Cancer Soc., San Diego, 1993; student rep. Nat. U., San Diego, 1992-94; vol. donations Women's Resource Ctr., San Diego, 1994; alumni mem. Gonzaga Prep. Sch. Bldg. Found., 1987—. Leadership scholar Nat. U., 1993. Mem. ASCD, Assn. Tng. and Devel., Nat. Assn. Hist. Preservation, Assn. Early Childhood Devel., Kappa Alpha Theta (adv. bd. Zeta Rho chpt. 1994—, chmn/historian 75 yr. reunion 1987-88, sr. of yr. 1988). Republican. Avocations: spending time with daughter, historical research, classical ballet, traveling, country line dancing. Home: 12211 N Nevada Ct Spokane WA 99218-1714

WILKINS, FLOYD, JR. retired lawyer, consultant; b. Fowler, Calif., Sept. 8, 1925; s. Floyd and Kathryn (Springborg) W.; m. Holly Blee, June 18, 1949 (div. Jan. 1964); children: Douglas B., Janet H., Steven B., Kevin D.; m. Sybil Ann Perrault, Feb. 22, 1964. BS, U. Calif., Berkeley, 1946; LLB, Harvard U., 1952. Bar: N.Y. 1953, Calif. 1959. Assoc. Dwight, Royall, Harris, Koegel & Caskey, N.Y.C., 1952-58; v.p., trust officer San Diego Trust & Savs. Bank, 1958-63; assoc., then ptnr., prin. Seltzer Caplan Wilkins & McMahon, P.C. and predecessors, San Diego, 1963-91. Lectr. U. So. Calif. Tax Inst., L.A., 1975, Title Ins. and Trust Co., L.A. and Santa Ana, Calif., 1973, 78, 83, Trust Svcs. of Am. Tax Forum, San Diego, U. Calif. Continuing Edn. of Bar, San Diego, 1977-91. Bd. dirs., pres. San Diego County Citizens Scholarship Found. Served with USNR, 1944-46. Mem. ABA, State Bar Calif., San Diego County Bar Assn. Republican. Avocations: travel, photography, wine, gardening. Home: 2005 Soledad Ave La Jolla CA 92037-3904

WILKINS, GUY (IRA WILKINS), painter, art teacher; b. Seaview, Va., Jan. 7, 1927; s. Ira Guy and Margaret Grace (Nottingham) W.; children: Sarah Gay, Elizabeth, Kate, Johnny. Student, Coll. William and Mary, Norfolk, Va., 1946, U. Va., 1947, 48. Reporter Birmingham (Ala.) News, 1949-51, Greenville (S.C.) Piedmont, 1951-52, Norfolk Virginian Pilot, 1952-54; dir. info. Norfolk Port Authority, 1954-56; press liaison Norfolk Mus. (now Chrysler Mus.), 1963-65; painter, art tchr. Wachapreague, Va., 1975—. Gallery dir. Norfolk Mus.'s Gallery Va. Artists, 1964, 65. Author: (poetry) Day Moon, 1986; one-man shows include Regional Libr., Williamsburg, Va., 1987, Eso Art Ctr., Belle Haven, Va., 1994, Art Ctr., Carrboro, N.C., 2002; exhbns. include Irene Leach Biennial, 1960's; represented by Smiling Dolphin Gallery, Nassawaddox, Va., Stage Door Gallery, Cape Charles, Va., collections in China, Australia. Recipient Glidden Painting prize Tidewater Artist Assn., 1963, A.B. Jackson award Ghent Arts Festival, 1983, 1st place award for feature writing Va. Press Assn., 1963, Best Oil Tidewater Regional Exhibn., others. Mem. Eastern Shore Art League (bd. dirs. 1980-91). Presbyterian. Home: 4 Center St Wachapreague VA 23480 Office: Seaside Studio Main St Wachapreague VA 23480

WILKINS, J. ERNEST, JR. mathematician, educator; b. Chgo., Nov. 27, 1923; s. J. Ernest and Lucille B. (Robinson) W.; m. Gloria Louise Stewart, June 22, 1947 (dec.); children: Sharon Wilkins Hill, J. Ernest III; m. Maxine G. Malone, June 2, 1984 (dec.). BS, U. Chgo., 1940, MS, 1941, PhD, 1942; BME, NYU, 1957, MME, 1960. Mathematician Am. Optical Co., Buffalo, 1946-50; mgr. R&D United Nuclear Corp., White Plains, N.Y., 1950-60; assoc. dir. lab. Gen. Atomic Co., San Diego, 1960-70; Disting. prof. applied math. physics Howard U., Washington, 1970-77; vis. scientist Argonne (Ill.) Nat. Lab., 1976-77, fellow, 1984-85; v.p., dep. gen. mgr. EG & G Idaho, Idaho Falls, 1977-84; Disting. prof. Clark Atlanta U., 1990—. Chmn. Army Sci. Bd. Dept. Army, 1978-81; mem. Adv. Com. on Reactor Safeguards, Washington, 1990-94, chmn., 1993-94. Contbr. articles to profl. jours. With AUS, 1946-47. Recipient Outstanding Civilian Svc. medal U.S. Army, 1980. Mem. NAE, Am. Nuclear Soc. (pres. 1974-75, cons. 1987-90), Am. Math. Soc., Math. Assn. Am., Oak Ridge Assn. Univs. (coun. 1990—). Office: PO Box 348 Atlanta GA 30301-0348

WILKINS, JOHN WARREN, physics educator; b. Des Moines, Mar. 11, 1936; s. Carl Daniel and Ruth Elizabeth (Warren) W. BS in Engring, Northwestern U., 1959; MS, U. Ill., 1960, PhD, 1963; DTech (hon.), Chalmers Tekniska Hogskola, Göteborg, 1990. NSF fellow U. Cambridge, Eng., 1963-64; asst. prof. physics Cornell U., 1964-68, assoc. prof., 1968-74, prof., 1974-88; eminent scholar, prof. physics Ohio State U., 1988—. Vis. prof. H.C. Ørsted Inst., Copenhagen, 1968, Nordita, Copenhagen, 1972-73, 75-76, 79-81; cons. Los Alamos Nat. Lab., 1984—, Lawrence Livermore Nat. Lab., 1997—; adv. com. U. Chgo. Sci. and Tech., 1990—. Assoc. editor Physica Scripta, 1977-85, Phys. Rev. Letters, 1982-85, Rev. Modern Physics, 1983-95; mem. editorial bd. Phys. Rev. B, 1991-94; coord. Comments on Condensed Matter Physics, 1985-90. Sloan fellow, 1966; Guggenheim fellow, 1985. Fellow AAAS, Am. Phys. Soc. (publs. oversight com. 1995-97, chmn. 1995-96, councillor divsn. condensed matter physics 1989-93, exec. com. divsn. biol. physics 1973-77, vice-chair through past chair divsn. condensed matter physics 2001—); mem. European Phys. Soc. Office: Ohio State U Dept Physics 174 W 18th Ave Columbus OH 43210-1106

WILKINS, LUCIEN SANDERS, gastroenterologist; b. Sanford, N.C., Mar. 30, 1942; s. Alexander Betts and Olive Elizabeth (Pittman) Wilkins; m. Freda Barry Hartness, July 16, 1966; children: Lucien Sanders Wilkins Jr., Elise Perryman. BA, Duke U., 1963; MD, Med. Coll. Va., 1967. Diplomate Am. Bd. Internal Medicine. Intern Medical Coll. Va., Richmond, 1967-68, resident in internal medicine, 1970-72, gastroenterology fellow, 1972-73; clin. gastroenterologist Wilmington (N.C.) Health Assoc., 1973—99; pres. Lucien Wilkins Cons., 2000—; pres., med. dir. Am. Physician Ptnrs. Assn., 2002—. Vis. physician Hopital St. Croix, Leogane, Haiti, 1979—84, founder Divsn. Gastrointestinal Endoscopy, 1984; 1st Endoscopic Ambulatory Surgery Facility State of N.C., 1990; chmn. dept. medicine New Hanover Regional Med. Ctr., Wilmington, NC, 1990—92; asst. prof. clin. medicine U. N.C., Chapel Hill, 1974—; bd. dirs. Br. Banking and Trust, Wilmington; physician adv. Nat. Found. Ileitis and Colitis, 1976—78. Author: Progeny, 1994. Bd. dirs. Cape Fear Coun. for Arts, Wilmington, 1976—77, New Hanover Regional Med. Ctr. Found., Wilmington, 1993—95, exec. com., 1994—95; bd. dirs. Com. of 100, 1992—95. Lt. comdr. M.C.1970 USN, 1968. Recipient winner GTP-LAI Holbert Meml. Race, Sebring, Fla., 1995; fellow D. Williams rsch. fellow, 1965, Paul Harris fellow, Rotary, 1986. Mem.: ACP, New Hanover-Pender County Med. Soc. (pres. 1980), Wrightsville Beach Ocean Racing Assn. (commodore), Figure Eight Island Yacht Club (charter), Hist. Stock Car Racing Group, Surf Club, Cape Fear Country Club. Presbyterian. Avocation: Avocations: vintage automobile racing, tennis, sailing, skiing, outdoor activities. Home: 2215 Lynnwood Dr Wilmington NC 28403-8026 Office: 2215 Lynwood Dr Wilmington NC 28403 E-mail: lucienwilkins@msn.com. *Being a true physician means continually learning from your patients, about your patients, and on behalf of your patients.*

WILKINS, MARGARET NELL STAMPER, music educator, musician; b. Mayfield, Ky., Apr. 6, 1943; d. Raleigh E. and Alberta Frances (Boren) Stamper; m. Thomas Humphrey Wilkins, June 7, 1964; children: Michael, Shannon. BA, Murray (Ky.) State U., 1964; MS in Zoology, U. Ky., 1966. Registered Suzuki piano tchr. Ch. organist Meml. Bapt. Ch., Murray, 1966-90; pvt. music tchr., 1967—; ch. organist First Bapt. Ch., 1991—. Adj. biology tchr. Murray State U., 1968-69, 83-84. Pres., mem. Woman's Missionary Union, 1968-90, Louella Beddoe Mission Group, FBC, 1993-94, 98-99; Sunday sch. tchr. Meml. Bapt. Ch., Murray, 1968-88. Mem.: Murray Music Tchrs. Assn. (pres. 1985—), Ky. Music Tchrs. Assn. (elem. workshop chmn. 1980—84), Suzuki Assn. of The Ams., Music Tchrs. Nat. Assn. (elem. workshop chmn. 1977—80), Nat. Guild Piano Tchrs., Delta Lambda Alpha, Alpha Omicron Pi (treas. 1962—64). Baptist. Avocations: bird watching, hiking, crossword puzzles, reading, all stitching crafts. Home: 1703 Plainview Ave Murray KY 42071-2838

WILKINS, MELINDA ANN, director university program, educator; b. Tulia, Tex., Sept. 21, 1960; d. Don Kelly and Clara Ann (Neves) Jennings; children: Amber Lane, Michael Steven Heaton, Brett Allen Wilkins. BS in Med. Record Adminstrn., Southwestern Okla. State U., Weatherford, 1983, MEd, 1988. Registered health info. adminstr. Office mgr. Dr. Gary Lawrence, Weatherford, 1983-84; dir. med. record dept. Southwestern Meml. Hosp., 1984-88; program dir., health info. mgmt. program, assoc. prof. Ark. Tech. U., Russellville, 1988—. Pres. ad. com. Med. Record Program, Southwestern Okla. State U., 1984-88; pres. Employee Assn. Southwestern Meml. Hosp., 1985-86. Chairperson Christian Women's Fellowship-Lydia Circle, Weatherford, 1988; co-moderator long range planning Ctr. Presbyn. Ch., Russellville, 1993. Mem. Am. Health Info. Mgmt. Assn. (mem. coun. on cert. 1996-97, chair 1998), Okla. Med. Record Assn., Ark. Health Info. Mgmt. Assn. (ctrl. office coord. 1989—, co-chmn. edn. com. 1989-90, sec. 1991-92, pres. 1993-94, 1st yr. dir. 1994-95, mem. assembly on edn. 1988—). Democrat. Avocations: needlework, sewing. Home: RR 3 Box 1475 Dardanelle AR 72834-9671

WILKINS, ROBERT HENRY, neurosurgeon, editor; b. Pitts., Aug. 18, 1934; s. George H. and Mary M. (Lemon) W.; m. Gloria A. Kohl, Dec. 28, 1957; children: Michael I., Jeffrey K., Elizabeth A. BS, U. Pitts., 1955, MD, 1959. Diplomate Am. Bd. Neurol. Surgery. Intern, resident gen. surgery Duke U. Med. Ctr., Durham, N.C., 1959-61, resident in neurosurgery, 1963-68, asst. prof. neurosurgery, 1968-72, prof. neurosurgery, 1976—, chief divsn. neurosurgery, 1976-96; clin. assoc. surgery br. Nat. Cancer Inst., Bethesda, Md., 1961-63; chmn. dept. neurosurgery Scott and White Clinic, Temple, Tex., 1972-75; assoc. prof. neurosurgery U. Pitts., 1975-76. Lectr. Cook County Grad. Sch. Medicine, Chgo., 1976-96; attending neurosurgeon Durham VA Hosp., 1968-72, 78-98; mem. Nat. Adv. Coun. Nat. Inst. Neurol. Disorders and Stroke, 1989-92. Co-editor: Neurosurgery, 2d edit., 3 vols., 1996, Neurosurgery Updates I and II, 1990, 91, Neurosurgical Operative Atlas, 1991—, Principles of Neurosurgery, 1994; editor Clin. Neurosurgery, 1972-75; assoc. editor Surg. Neurology, 1975-76; founding editor Neurosurgery, 1977-82, mem. editl. rev. bd., 1997-2001; mem. editl. bd. Jour. Neurosurgery, 1987-96, chmn., 1996-97, mem. adv. bd., 1997—; neurosurgery editor Key Neurology and Neurosurgery, 1993-96, Yr. Book of Neurology and Neurosurgery, 1994-97. Recipient Travel award Copenhagen, Nat. Inst. Neurol. Diseases and Blindness, 1965, Royal Australasian Coll. Surgeons, Found. lectr. Adelaide 1986. Fellow ACS (gov. 1996); mem. Congress Neurol. Surgeons (pres. 1979-80), Am. Assn. Neurol. Surgeons (treas. 1989-92), So. Neurosurg. Soc. (sec. 1988-91, pres. 1992-93), Soc. Neurol. Surgeons (v.p. 1995-96), Am. Bd. Neurol. Surgery (dir. 1991-97, chmn. 1996-97), Phi Beta Kappa, Alpha Omega Alpha. Democrat. Avocations: medical writing and editing. Office: Duke U Med Ctr PO Box 3807 Durham NC 27710-0001 E-mail: rhwilkins@aol.com.

WILKINS, ROBERT PEARCE, lawyer; b. Jesup, Ga., Sept. 10, 1933; s. Ransom Little and Sarah (Pearce) W.; m. Rose Truesdale, Jan. 7, 1956; children: Robert Pearce, Chisolm Wallace (dec.), Sarah Ruth Weiss, Rose Anne Brooks. BA, U. S.C., 1953, JD, 1954; LL.M., Georgetown U., 1957. Bar: S.C. 1954; cert. mediator and arbitrator, S.C. Atty. Office Gen. Counsel, Sec. Army, Washington, 1956; trust officer First Nat. Bank S.C., Columbia, 1957-60; practice law, 1960-64; ptnr. McLain, Sherrill & Wilkins, 1964-68, McKay, Sherrill, Walker, Townsend & Wilkins, Columbia, 1969-75; sole practice law Columbia and Lexington, S.C., 1975-88; of counsel Nelson, Mullins, Riley & Scarborough, Lexington, 1988—. Pres. Sandlapper Press, Inc., 1967-72, pub. Sandlapper Mag. S.C., 1968-72; editor Sandlapper Mag. S.C., 1968-69, 89—; editor, pub. S.C. History Illustrated, 1970; pres. R.P.W. Pub. Corp.; mem., chmn. S.C. Splty. Adv. Bd. Estate Planning and Probate, 1982-85; lectr. in law U. S.C., 1971-78. Author: Draftin Wills and Trust Agreements in South Carolina, 1971, Drafting Wills and Trust Agreements in Michigan, 1978, Wills and Trust System (Arkansas), 1978, Drafting Wills and Trust Agreements: A Systems Approach, 1998, 3d edit., 1999, software edit.; (with others) Word Processing for a Law Office, 1979, also articles; editor: The Lawyer's Microcomputer, 1982-85, The Lawyer's PC, 1983-97, What a Lawyer Needs to Know to Buy and Use a Computer, 1984, The Perfect Lawyer, 1990-97, The Lawyers' Word, 1991, Shepard's Elder Care/Law Newsletter, 1991-95, Hot docs Toolbox, 1996-97, Drafting Wills and Trust Agreements Newsletter, 1997. Del., Spl. Liaison Tax Com. Southeastern Region, 1967-70; exec. com. Richland County Rep. Com., 1960-64; sec.-treas. Richland County Rep. Club, 1960; bd. dirs. Ctrl. Tb-RD Assn.; trustee Sch. Dist. 1, Lexington County, S.C., 1971-78, sec., 1972-75, chmn., 1975-78; mem. S.C. Commn. on Higher Edn., 1978-80, S.C. Commn. on Lawyer Competence, 1980-82; bd. dirs. Crime Stoppers of the Midlands, 1983-85, RPW Learning Ctr., 1987-94, Mt. Hope Cemetary, 1991—, also v.p., 1992—; v.p. 11th cir. Alumni Coun. U. S.C., 1993-95, mem. awards com., 1995-97; mem. commn. Riverbanks Zoo, 1986—, sec., 1991-95, chmn., 1995-96, 97—, vice-chmn., 1996-97. With AUS, 1954-55. Recipient Compleat Lawyer award Law Sch. U. S.C., 1997, Diamond Circle award U. S.C. Coll. Journalism and Mass Comms., 1998. Fellow Am. Bar Found., Am. Coll. Trust and Estate Counsel (publs. com. 1984-87, bd. regents 1986-87, mem. tech. com. 1989-98), Am. Coll. Tax Counsel, Coll. Law Practice Mgmt. (charter, trustee 1994-98), S.C. Bar (tax coordinating com. 1968-70, chmn. legal econs. com. 1973-75, ho. of dels. 1978-80, editor S.C. Lawyer 1989-91, mem. alternative dispute resolution sect. 1993—), S.C. Bar Found. (life, bd. dirs. 1984-88, v.p. 1986-87, pres. 1987-88); mem. ABA (ho. of dels. 1986-87, chmn. valuation subcom., estate and gift tax com., taxation sect. 1967-73, vice chmn. svc. and assistance to law student div. com. gen. practice sect. 1971-72, vice chmn. corp. counsel com. gen. practice sect. 1972-74, editor econs. of law practice sect. legal econs. 1974-78, sec. 1977-78, vice chmn. 1978-79, chmn. 1980-81, mem. standing com. assn. comm. 1981-84, real property, probate and trust law, mem. publs. com. 1985-89, editor Probate and Property, 1986-89), Richland County Bar Assn. (chmn. probate sect. 1973-74, unauthorized practice of law com. 1976), Lexington County Bar (chmn. mediation com. 1994—), Columbia Jaycees (sec.-treas. 1958-59), Columbia Estate Planning Coun. (pres. 1964-65), Am. Y-Flyer Yacht Racing Assn. (area v.p. 1971, internat. dir. 1972-73), Omicron Delta Kappa, Sigma Chi Clubs: Columbia Sailing (dir. 1968-71), Columbia Tip Off (dir. 1968-73), Columbia (pres. 1971-72). Home: 124 Lake Murray Ct Lexington SC 29072-9104 Office: 955 Old Cherokee Rd Lexington SC 29072-9042

WILKINS, SHEILA SCANLON, management consultant; b. Oakland, Calif., Sept. 23, 1936; d. Michael Joseph and Joan (Daly) Scanlon; m. Thomas Wayne Wilkins, Aug. 14, 1965; children: Mary, John, Kathleen. BMusic, AB Liberal Arts maxima cum laude, Holy Names Coll., Oakland, 1958, MA in Music, 1972; MA in Ednl. Adminstrn., St. Mary's Coll., Moraga, Calif., 1983. Cert. tchr., Calif.; cert. in human resources mgmt., human resources tng. and devel. Tchr., dir. student activities Vallejo (Calif.) Unified Sch. Dist., 1962-63; tchr. Berkeley (Calif.) Unified Sch. Dist., 1963-66; pub. rels. asst. Alta Bates Hosp., Berkeley, 1973-74; tchr. Walnut Creek (Calif.) Sch. Dist., 1974-80; dist. tchg. Moraga Sch. Dist., 1980-83; tech. tng. adminstr. Crocker Nat. Bank, Walnut Creek, Calif., 1984-85; tng. officer Wells Fargo Bank, Concord, 1985-86; tng. mgr. Fab 3 Intel Corp, Livermore, 1986-91, orgn. cons. CIS ops. Folsom, 1991-92, mgr. profl. devel. corp. edn. Santa Clara, 1992-94; prin. The Wilkins Group, Walnut Creek, 1994—. Contbr. articles to profl. jours. Chair parent com. Boy Scouts Am., Concord, 1977-80; pres. Parents Club of St. Francis Sch., Concord, 1978-79; v.p. Parents Club of Carondelet High Sch., Concord, 1983-84. Mem. Internat. Soc. for Performance Improvement (v.p. fin. 1988-89, pres. 1989-91 Bay area chpt.), Internat. Fedn. Tng. and Devel. Orgns. Home: 2182 Gill Port Ln Walnut Creek CA 94598-1150 Office: 2182 Gill Port Ln Walnut Creek CA 94598-1150 E-mail: sheila@wilkinsgroup.com.

WILKINS, WILLIAM WALTER, JR. federal judge; b. Anderson, S.C., Mar. 29, 1942; s. William Walter Wilkins and Evelyn Louise (Horton); m. Carolyn Louise Adams, Aug. 16, 1964; children: Lauren, Lyn, Walt. BA, Davidson Coll., 1964; JD, U. S.C., 1967. Bar: S.C. 1967, U.S. Dist. Ct. S.C. 1967, U.S. Ct. Appeals (4th cir.) 1969, U.S. Supreme Ct. 1970. Law clk. to Hon. Clement F. Haynesworth Jr. U.S. Ct. Appeals (4th cir.), 1969—70; legal asst. to U.S. Senator Strom Thurmond, 1970—71; ptnr. Wilkins & Wilkins, Greenville, SC, 1971—78; solicitor 13th Jud. Cir., 1974—81; judge U.S. Dist. Ct., Greenville, 1981—86, U.S. Ct. Appeals (4th cir.), 1986—. Lectr. Greenville Tech. Coll., 1973—97; chmn. U.S. Sentencing Commn., 1985—94. Editor-in-chief : S.C. Law Rev., 1967; contbr. articles to profl. jours. With U.S. Army, 1967—69, with USAR, 1969—83. Mem.: S.C. Bar Assn., Wig and Robe. Republican. Baptist. Office: US Cir Ct 4th Ct PO Box 10857 Greenville SC 29603-0857*

WILKINSON, ALAN HERBERT, nephrologist, medical educator; b. Johannesburg, So. Africa, July 11, 1948; came to U.S., 1985; s. Raymond C. and Nonie (Levick) W.; m. Angelika A. E. Adami, Dec. 22, 1973; one child: Rebecca Kate Adami. BS in Physiology, Biochem., Philosophy, U. Witwatersrand, So. Africa, 1969, BS with honors in Biochemistry, 1970, MB, BCh, 1975; cert. health care mgmt., U. Calif., Irvine, 1998. Fellow Royal Coll. Physicians (U.K.), specialist in clin. hypertension. Visiting assoc. Dept. Internal Medicine U. Iowa, Iowa City, 1987-88; assoc. prof. of medicine UCLA Sch. Med., L.A., 1988-95, prof. med., 1995—; dir. clin. nephrology UCLA Dept. Med., 1988-93, dir. kidney and pancreas transplantation, 1993—. Bd. dirs. UCLA Ctr. Health Schs., 1994-97. Contbr. articles to profl. jours. Mem. Nat. Kidney Fdn. Steering Comm., U.S. Transplant Games, L.A., 1992. Recipient Exceptional Svc. award, Nat. Kidney Fdn, S.C., 1992. Fellow Nat. Kidney Rsch.; mem. Am. Soc. Transplant Physicians, Internat. Nephrology Soc., Am. Soc. Nephrology. Avocations: ornithology, gardening. Office: UCLA Dept Med 200 Medical Plz Box 951693 Los Angeles CA 90095-1693

WILKINSON, ALBERT MIMS, JR. lawyer; b. Nashville, June 29, 1925; s. Albert Mims and Mary Nelle (Derryberry) W.; m. Edythe Bush, Mar. 27, 1953 (div.); children: William Terry, Elizabeth Ann, David Bush; m. Dolores Jean Attard, Oct. 22, 1971 (div.); 1 child, Mary Dolores. Student, Emory U., 1942-43; JD, U. Ga., 1949. Bar: Ga. 1948. Pvt. practice law, Atlanta, 1950-85; gen. counsel GEC-Marconi Avionics Inc., 1985-98; hon. legal adviser to Brit.

Consul Gen. at Atlanta. Author: The Winning of the Revolutionary War in the South, 1976, The Rights of Unsecured Creditors-The Law in Georgia, 1979. Mem. DeKalb County Bd. Elections, 1966-72; chmn. 4th Congl. Dist. Republican Exec. Com., 1968-70, Ga. State Rep. Exec. Com., 1968-74; 1st vice chmn. Ga. Rep. Party, 1972-74, asst. gen. counsel, 1974-75; vice chmn., trustee Atlanta Counseling Center, Inc., 1960-83. Served with USCGR, 1943-46. Decorated Order Brit. Empire. Fellow Comml. Law Found.; mem. BA, Ga. Bar Assn., Atlanta Bar Assn., Ga. Soc. (pres. 1962-63), SAR, Southeastern Mem.'s Assn. (pres. 1960-61), Comml. Law League Am., Ga. Soc. Colonial Wars, Old Guard of Gate City Guard (comdt. 1986), N.C. Soc. of Cincinnati, Sphinx Club, Gridiron Club, Commerce Club, Civitan, Masons, Blue Key, Omicron Delta Kappa. Baptist. Home and Office: 66 Demorest Ln # 333 Sky Valley GA 30537-2581 E-mail: amims@HEMC.net. *By precept and example my parents pointed out the upward way in life, on a foundation of religious faith. "To do justly, to love mercy, to walk humbly with thy God." Later a beloved teacher taught the lines from Ulysses as he prepared to set sail, "To strive, to seek, to find and never yield." Their inspiration has continued throughout my life.*

WILKINSON, CLAUDE HENRY, writer, artist, English literature educator; b. Memphis, Dec. 17, 1959; s. Henry Bridgforth and Lula (Moncrief) W. BSc, U. Miss., 1981; cert. d'excellence, Alliance Française, Memphis, 1991; MA, U. Memphis, 1992. Instr. English McNeese State U., Lake Charles, La., 1990-91, U. Memphis, 1991-92, Lane Coll., Jackson, Tenn., 1992-94, LeMoyne-Owen Coll., Memphis, 1998-99; owner Claude Wilkinson Fine Art Studio, Nesbit, Miss., 1984—. Editor River City Mag., Memphis, 1991; John and Renée Grisham So. writer in residence U. Miss., 2000. Author: Reading the Earth, 1998 (Naomi Long Madgett Poetry award 1998); author poetry; contbr. articles to profl. jours. Recipient New Poets award, Ursus Press, 1984, Grand prize, Miss. Poetry Soc., 1985, W.M. Whittington Jr. Purchase award, Cottonlandia Mus. Juried Exhbn., 1993, 1st prize in painting, Carnegie Ctr. for Arts and History, 1994, Pioneer Br. Poetry award, Ark. Writers' Conf., 1995, Kenneth Beaudoin Meml. award, Mid-South Poetry Festival, 1995, Paul Laurence Dunbar Poetry award, Detroit Black Writers Guild, 1998, Whiting Writer's award, Mrs. Giles Whiting Found., 2000; fellow Walter E. Dakin, Sewanee Writers' Conf., 1999. Avocations: music, mythology, nature study.

WILKINSON, CLIFFORD STEVEN, civil engineer; b. Orange, N.J., Mar. 18, 1953; s. Clifford James and Elizabeth Adelade (Fairbanks) W.; m. Judith Anne Simon, Oct. 6, 1979; children: Brian Steven, David James, Caitlin Elizabeth. BCE, N.J. Inst. Tech., 1975, MCE, 1986. Registered profl. engr., N.J. Sr. assoc. Killam Assocs., Millburn, N.J., 1975-92, Paulus Sokolowski and Sartor, Warren, NJ, 1992—99; sr. v.p. Killam Assocs., 1999—. Coach Little League, youth soccer, hockey, Bridgewater, N.J., 1991—; leader Cub Scouts, Boy Scouts Am.; com. mem. North Br. Reformed Ch., Bridgewater. Mem. NSPE, N.J. Soc. Profl. Engrs., Water Environ. Fedn., Water Environ. Assn. Republican. Home: 520 Rolling Hills Rd Bridgewater NJ 08807-1932 Office: Killam Assocs PO Box 1008 27 Bleeker St Millburn NJ 07041

WILKINSON, DAVID TODD, physics educator; b. Hillsdale, Mich., May 13, 1935; s. Harold Arba and Thelma Ellen (Todd) W.; m. Sharon E. Harper, June 14, 1958 (div. June 1979); children: Wendy, Kenton; m. Eunice H. Dowell, Oct. 13, 1984. BS in Engring. Physics, U. Mich., 1957, MS in Nuclear Engring., 1959, PhD in Physics, 1962. Lectr. physics U. Mich., Ann Arbor, 1962-63; instr. Princeton U., N.J., 1963-65, asst. prof., 1965-68, assoc. prof., 1968-71, prof., 1971—, chmn. dept., 1987-90. Cons. NASA, mem. COBE satellite team, mem. MAP satellite team. Contbr. articles to profl. jours. Alfred P. Sloane fellow, 1965-67, John Simon Guggenheim fellow, 1977-78, James Craig Watson medal, 2001. Mem. NAS. Office: Princeton U Dept Physics Jadwin Hall PO Box 708 Princeton NJ 08544-0001

WILKINSON, DAVID STANLEY, pathologist, consultant, researcher; b. Richmond, Va., Feb. 2, 1945; s. Herbert Carroll and Hattie Mae (Vaughan) W.; m. Judith Farish Pace, June 16, 1967; children— Jill Marie, Julie Lynne, Virginia Ann. B.S. in Chemistry, Va. Mil. Inst., Lexington, 1967; Ph.D. in Exptl. Oncology and Pathology, U. Wis.-Madison, 1971; M.D., U. Miami, 1978. Diplomate: Am. Bd. Pathology. Commd. 2d lt. U.S. Army, 1967, advanced through grades to maj., 1982; fellow McArdle Lab. Cancer Research U. Wis., 1967-71; asst. prof. biochemistry U. South Fla., Tampa, 1972-76; resident in pathology Walter Reed Army Med. Ctr., Washington, 1978-82; instr. pathology Uniformed Services U. of Health Scis., Bethesda, 1979-82; chief clin. pathology Eisenhower Army Med. Ctr., Ft. Gordon, Ga., 1982-84; assoc. prof. pathology, 1984-92, dir. clin. pathology div. George Washington U. Med. Ctr., 1984-89, prof. pathology, 1989-93; med. dir. George Washington U. Hosp., 1992-93; prof. pathology, chmn. dept. pathology, Med. Coll. Va. Va. Commonwealth U., 1993—; instr. pathology Med. Coll. Ga. Augusta, 1982-84; lectr. in field. Editor: Clinical Laboratory Management Rev., Clinical Laboratory Management International; contbr. articles to profl. jours. Damon Runyon-Walter Winchell Cancer Fund grantee, 1973; Am. Cancer Soc. grantee, 1973; Nat. Cancer Inst. grantee, 1975. Fellow Am. Soc. Clin. Pathology, Coll. Am. Pathologists; mem. Am. Assn. Cancer Research, Soc. Exptl. Biology and Medicine, Am. Assn. Clin. Chemistry, Clin. Lab. Mgmt. Assn., Am. Med. Informatics Assn., Am. Assn. Blood Banks, Soc. for Analytical Cytology, Am. Soc. Investigative Pathology, U.S. and Canadian Acad. Pathology. Republican. Club: VMI Keydet (Lexington, Va.). Office: Med Coll Va PO Box 980662 Richmond VA 23298-0662

WILKINSON, DORIS, medical sociology educator; b. Lexington, Ky., June 13, 1936; d. Howard Thomas and Regina Wilkinson. BA, U. Ky., 1958; MA, Case Western Res. U., 1960, PhD, 1968; MPH, Johns Hopkins U., 1985; postgrad., Harvard U., summer 1991. Asst. prof. U. Ky., Lexington, 1968-70; assoc. prof., then prof. Macalester Coll., St. Paul, 1970-77; exec. assoc. Am. Sociol. Assn., Washington, 1977-80; prof. med. sociology Howard U., 1980-84; vis. prof. U. Va., 1984-85; prof. sociology U. Ky., Lexington, 1985—. Chmn. panel women in sci. program NSF, Washington, 1976; rev. panelist Nat. Inst. Drug Abuse, Washington, 1978—79; mem. bd. sci. counselors Nat. Cancer Inst., Bethesda, Md., 1980—84; vis. scholar Harvard U., Cambridge, Mass., 1989—90, vis. prof. (summers), 1992, 93, 94, 97; Rapoport vis. prof. social theory (summers) Smith Coll., 1995, 96; bd. dirs. Nat. Conf. for Cmty. Justice, 1992—96; dir. Heritage Project, 2000—. Author: Wookbook for Introductory Sociology, 1968; editor: Black Revolt: Strategies of Protest, 1969; co-editor: The Black Male in America, 1977, Alternative Health Maintenance and Healing Systems, 1987, Race, Gender and the Life Cycle, 1991, Race, Class and Gender, 1996; social history photographic exhbn. "The African American Presence in Medicine" Harvard Med. Libr., 1991, Pearson Mus.- So. Ill. U. Med. Sch., 1992, N.J. Coll. Medicine and Dentistry, 1993, Louisville Mus. History and Sci., 1994, U. Cin. Med. Sch. Libr., 1994, Albert Einstein Coll. of Medicine, 1995, Midway Coll., 1996; contbr. articles to profl. jours. Bd. overseers Case Western Res. U., Cleve., 1982-87; apptd. Ky. Commn. on Women, 1993-96. Recipient Pub. Humanities award U. Ky., 1990, Midway Coll. Women's History Month award, 1991, Gt. Tchr. award Nat. Alumni Assn. U. Ky., 1992, Disting. Scholar award Assn. Black Sociologists, 1993; inducted into Hall of Disting. Alumni, U. Ky., 1989; fellow Woodrow Wilson Found., 1959-61, Ford Found., 1989-90; grantee Social Sci. Rsch. Coun., 1975, Nat. Inst. Edn., 1978-80, Nat. Cancer Inst., 1986-88, Ky. Humanities Coun., 1988, 2001, Am. Coun. Learned Soc., 1989-90, NEH, 1991; Disting. Prof. in Coll. Arts and Scis., U. Ky., 1992-93, Coll. of Social Work Hall of Fame, U. Ky., 1999; Disting. Professorship named in hon., 2000. Mem.: Ea. Sociol. Soc. (v.p. 1983—84, pres. 1992—93, I. Peter Gellman award 1987), Soc. for Study of Social Problems (v.p. 1984—85, pres. 1987—88), D.C. Sociol. Soc. (pres. 1982—83), So. Sociol. Soc. (honors com. 1993—94), Am. Sociol. Assn. (exec. assoc. 1977—80, budget com. 1985—88, v.p. 1991—92, mem. coun. 1994—97, Dubois-Johnson-Frazier award 1988), Phi Beta Kappa.

WILKINSON, EDWARD ANDERSON, JR. retired naval officer, business executive; b. Selma, Ala., Sept. 21, 1933; s. Edward Anderson and Alice Margaret (Moorer) W.; m. Barbara Anne Parker, June 4, 1955 (dec. June 1991); children: Daryl Edward, Daniel Bryan, Edward Anderson III, David Park; m. Sondra Marie Moore, Oct. 2, 1994. BS, U.S. Naval Acad., 1955; MS in Mech. Engring., 1964; grad., Nat. War Coll., 1972. Commd. ensign U.S. Navy, 1955, advanced through grades to rear adm., 1979; dir. Anti-Submarine Warfare Systems Program Office, Washington, 1978-79; dep. dir. Def. Mapping Agy., 1979-81; cmdr. Patrol Wings, U.S. Atlanta Fleet, Brunswick, Maine, 1981-83; dir. Def. Mapping Agy., Washington, 1983-85; ret., 1985; exec. v.p. Internat. Fed. Systems Intergraph Corp., Reston, Va. Decorated Legion of Merit, D.S.M. (Dept. Def.) Methodist. Home: 1555 Regatta Ln Reston VA 20194-1219 E-mail: awilkins@ingr.com.

WILKINSON, EUGENE PARKS, nuclear engineer, director; b. Long Beach, Calif., Aug. 10, 1918; s. Dennis William and Daisy Amelia (Parks) W.; m. Janice Edith Thuli, Mar. 28, 1942; children: Dennis Eugene, Stephen James, Marian Lynn, Rodney David. AB in Chemistry, San Diego State U., 1938. Instr. chemistry San Diego State U., 1938-39; commd. ensign U.S. Navy, 1940, advanced through grades to vice adm., 1970; served various locations including 1st comdg. officer USS Nautilus (1st nuclear-powered submarine), 1953-57; 1st comdg. officer USS Long Beach, 1959-63, 1st nuclear-powered surface ship; ret., 1974; exec. v.p. Data Design Labs., Cucamonga, Calif., 1977-80; pres., chief exec. officer Inst. Nuclear Power Ops., Atlanta, 1980-84, pres. emeritus, 1984—. Chmn. bd. dirs. MDM Svcs. Corp., Laguna Niguel, Calif. Decorated Legion of Merit, Silver Star, D.S.M. with three oak leaf clusters, others, Second Order Sacred Treasure Japan; recipient George Westinghouse Gold medal ASME, 1983, Oliver Townsend medal Atomic Indsl. Forum, 1984, Gold medal Uranium Inst., 1989. Mem. Am. Soc. Naval Engrs., Am. Nuclear Soc. (Henry DeWolf Smyth Nuclear Statesman medal 1994, Walter Zinn award 1998), Navy League, Submarine League, Nat. Acad. Engring. Avocations: tennis, bridge. Home: 1449 Crest Rd Del Mar CA 92014-2530

WILKINSON, FRANCES CATHERINE, librarian, educator; b. Lake Charles, La., July 20, 1955; d. Derrell Fred and Catherine Frances (O'Toole) W.; div.; 1 child, Katrina Frances. BA in Communication with distinction, U. N.Mex., 1982, MPA, 1987; MLS, U. Ariz., 1990. Mktg. rsch. auditor Mktg. Rsch. N.Mex., Albuquerque, 1973-78; freelance photographer, 1974-75; from libr. supr. gen. libr. to dep. dean libr. svcs. U. N.Mex., Albuquerque, 1978—2001, interim dean libr. svcs., 2001—. Cons., trainer ergonomics univs. and govt. agys. across U.S., 1986—; bd. dirs. Friends of U. N.Mex. Librs., Aubuquerque, 1991-94; mediator Mediation Alliance, 1991-94, U. N.Mex. Faculty Dispute Resolution, 1999—; mediation coach U. N.Mex., 1999-2000. Author, editor books; editor jour. columns; contbr. articles to profl. jours. Counselor, advocate Albuquerque Rape Crisis Ctr., 1981-84. Mem.: ALA (mem. com. 1990—2000), N.Mex. Assn. Rsch. Librs., N.Mex. Preservation Alliance (vice chair 1995—96), N.Mex. Libr. Assn., N.Am. Serials Interest Group (mem. com. 1994—97, 2001—, mem. exec. bd. 1997—2001), Pi Alpha Alpha, Phi Kappa Phi (chpt. treas. 1991—92, chpt. pres. 1992—94). Home: PO Box 8102 Albuquerque NM 87198-8102 Office: U N Mex Dean's Adminstrv Offices Albuquerque NM 87131-1466 E-mail: fwilkins@unm.edu.

WILKINSON, GRANT ROBERT, pharmacology educator; b. Derby, U.K., Aug. 27, 1941; came to U.S., 1966; s. Arthur Henry and Gwendoline Mary (Fox) W.; m. Margaret Kay Fletcher, Aug. 8, 1964 (div. Apr. 1978); children: Grant Russell, Nicole Estelle; m. June Zoe Dass, July 12, 1978 (div. Jan. 1995); children: Tracey Allyson, Erika Lynne; m. Merrily Anne Bossart, Jan. 18, 2000. BSc in Pharmacy, U. Manchester, 1963; PhD, U. London, 1966; DSc, U. Manchester, 2002. Postdoctoral fellow U. Calif., San Francisco, 1966-68; asst. prof. U. Ky., Lexington, 1968-71, Vanderbilt U., Nashville, 1971-73, assoc. prof., 1973-78, prof. of pharmacology, 1978—. Cons. NIH, Bethesda, Md., 1972—, NRC, NAS, Washington, 1986-87, 92-94, also pharm. industry: assoc. editor. Clin. Pharmacology and Therapeutics; mem. editorial adv. bd. various jours. in field. Author: Drug Metabolism and Disposition: Considerations in Clinical Pharmacology, 1985; contbr. articles more than 250 articles and revs. to profl. publs.; assoc. editor: Clin. Pharmacology and Therapeutics. Recipient NIH Merit award, 1991. Fellow AAAS (sect. chmn. 1986-87), Am. Assn. Pharm. Sci.; mem. Am. Soc. for Pharmacology and Exptl. Therapeutics, Am. Soc. Clin. Pharmacology and Therapeutics (Rawls-Palmer Progress in Medicine award 1996), Am. Assn. Pharm. Sci. (Rsch. Achievement award 2000). Achievements include research on drug metabolism in humans, effects of disease-states, pharmacokinetics, clinical pharmacology. Business E-Mail: grant.wilkinson@vanderbilt.edu.

WILKINSON, HARRY EDWARD, management educator and consultant; b. Richmond Heights, Mo., June 30, 1930; s. Harry Edward and Virginia Flo (Shelton) W.; m. Sara Beth Kikendall, Aug. 30, 1958; children: Linda Beth, Cheryl Susan. BA in Physics, Princeton U., 1952; MBA, Washington U., St. Louis, 1957; D Bus. Adminstrn., Harvard U., 1960. Lic. psychologist, Mass. Staff engr. Southwestern Bell Tel. Co., St. Louis, 1954-57; traffic engr. New Eng. Tel. & Telegraph Co., Boston, 1957-60; sr. mgmt. cons. Harbridge House Inc., 1961-65; dean bus. adminstrn., dir. Mgmt. Inst., Northeastern U., 1965-67; pres., chmn. bd. Univ. Affiliates Inc., North Port, Fla., 1967-2000; vis. prof. mgmt. Rice U., Houston, 1990-94, 97-2000, dir. office of exec. devel., 1993-97. Cons. to various industries and govt., 1961—. Author: Influencing People in Organizations, 1993; contbr. articles to mgmt. jours. Lt. (j.g.) USNR, 1952-54, Korea. Mem. APA, Acad. Mgmt., N.Am. Case Rsch. Assn., Harvard Bus. Sch. Assn. E-mail: wilkinso@rice.edu.

WILKINSON, JAMES ALLAN, lawyer, healthcare executive; b. Cumberland, Md., Feb. 10, 1945; s. John Robinson and Dorothy Jane (Kelley) W.; m. Elizabeth Susanne Quinlan, Apr. 14, 1973; 1 child, Kathryn Barrett. BS in Fgn. Svc., Georgetown U., 1967; JD, Duquesne U., 1978; MA, U Pitts., 2001. Bar: Pa., U.S. Dist. Ct. (we. dist.) Pa. Legis. analyst Office of Mgmt. and Budget, Washington, 1972-73; dep. exec. sec. Cost of Living Coun., 1973-74; sr. fin. analyst U.S. Steel Corp., Pitts., 1974-82; ptnr. Buchanan Ingersoll, 1982-88; exec. v.p., gen. counsel Meritcare, 1988—; sr. v.p. Culwell Health Inc., 1991—2001. Adj. prof. U. Pitts. Sch. Law, 1988-91. Author: Financing and Refinancing Under Prospective Payment, 1985, Family Caregivers' Guide Planning and Decision Making for the Elderly, 1998; contbr. articles to profl. jours. Chmn. Oversight Com. on Organ Transplantation, Pitts., 1986--; sec.-treas. bd. dirs. Pitts. Symphony Soc., 1986-98, exec. com. bd. dirs., 1999—; bd. dirs. Western Pa. Com. of Prevention of Child Abuse, 1987-90, Comprehensive Safety Compliance, 1988-91, Buchanan Ingersoll Profl. corp., 1988-90, Parental Stress Ctr., 1990-94; sec. Ross Mountain Club, 1995-98, 99—, v.p., 1999-2001, pres., 2001—; bd. dirs. Carnegie Inst., 1997—, Carnegie Mus. Natural History, 1997—, Andy Warhol Mus., 1998—, Soc. for Contemporary Crafts, 1999—, treas., 2000-01, v.p., 2001—. Mem. Am. Health Lawyers Assn., Audubon Soc. Southwestern Pa. (treas. 1996-2000), Duquesne Club. Republican. Episcopalian. Home: 1005 Elmhurst Rd Pittsburgh PA 15215-1819 Office: Meritcare Inc 625 Stanwix St Ste 1220 Pittsburgh PA 15222-1415 E-mail: wilkinso@bellatlantic.net.

WILKINSON, JAMES HARVIE, III, federal judge; b. N.Y.C., Sept. 29, 1944; s. James Harvie and Letitia (Nelson) W.; m. Lossie Grist Noell, June 30, 1973; children: James Nelson, Porter Noell. BA, Yale U., 1963-67; JD, U. Va., 1972; JD (hon.), U. Richmond, 1997, U. S.C., 1998. Bar: Va. 1972. Law clk. to U.S. Supreme Ct. Justice Lewis F. Powell, Jr., Washington, 1972-73; asst. prof. law U. Va., 1973-75, assoc. prof., 1975-78; editor Norfolk (Va.) Virginian-Pilot, 1978-81; prof. law U. Va., 1981-82, 83-84; dep. asst. atty. gen. Civil Rights div. Dept. Justice, 1982-83; judge U.S. Ct. Appeals (4th cir.), 1984—, chief judge, 1996—. Author: Harry Byrd and the Changing Face of Virginia Politics, 1968, Serving Justice: A Supreme Court Clerk's View, 1974, From Brown to Bakke: The Supreme Court and School Integration, 1979, One Nation Indivisible: How Ethnic Separatism Threatens America, 1997. Bd. Visitors U. Va., 1970-73; Republican candidate for Congress from 3d Dist. V a., 1970; bd. dirs. Fed. Jud. Ctr., 1992-96. Served with U.S. Army, 1968-69. Mem. Va. State Bar, Va. Bar Assn., Am. Law Inst. Episcopalian. Home: 1713 Yorktown Dr Charlottesville VA 22901-3035 Office: US Ct Appeals 255 W Main St Ste 230 Charlottesville VA 22902-5058

WILKINSON, JEFFREY DAVID, engineer; b. Washington, Nov. 28, 1958; s. William Mckain and Marlis Phyllis (Osnes) W.; m. Wendy Carpenter, May 31, 1980; children: Rebecca Lynne, Grace Marie. BA, St. Olaf Coll., 1980. Systems mgr. St. Olaf Coll., Northfield, Minn., 1977-80; project engr. GCA/ParSystems, St.Paul, 1980-83; sr. engr. Medtronic, Inc., Mpls., 1983-89, prin. engr., 1989—. Mem. tech. adv. bd. Midwest Electronics Expn. Mem. IEEE, Assn. Computing Machinery. Home: 459 Colleen Dr Saint Paul MN 55127-7087 Office: Medtronic Inc 7000 Central Ave NE Minneapolis MN 55432-3576

WILKINSON, JOAN KRISTINE, nurse, pediatric clinical specialist; b. Rochester, Minn., June 15, 1953; d. A. Ray and Ruth Audrey (Wegwart) Kubly; m. Robert Morris Wilkinson, June 14, 1975; children: Michael Robert, Kathryn Ann. BS in Nursing, U. Wis., 1975; MS, U. Colo., 1986. RN, clin. nurse specialist. Team leader Mendota Mental Health Inst., Madison, Wis., 1975-76; care leader Boulder (Colo.) Psychiat. Inst., 1976-78; pub. health nurse, head nurse Rocky Mountain Poison Ctr., Denver, 1978-83; research teaching asst. U. Colo. Health Scis. Ctr., 1986-87. Disaster nurse ARC, Boulder, 1976—; participant community service United Way, Denver, 1981-84; vol. nurse Channel 9 Health Fair, Boulder, 1983. Fellow U. Colo. Health Scis. Ctr., 1986; recipient Recognition cert. ARC, Madison, 1978, Gold award United Way, Denver, 1981, Outstanding Citizen award Boulder, 1990, Torch award for outstanding leader Girl Scouts, 1995, Torch award Girl Scouts Am., 1999. Mem. Colo. Nurses Assn. (dist. 12 scholar 1983-86), Am. Nurses Assn., World Health Assn., Sigma Tau Theta. Lutheran. Home: 1195 Hancock Dr Boulder CO 80303-1101 Office: Denver Vis Nurse Assn 390 Grant St Denver CO 80203-4022

WILKINSON, JOHN HART, lawyer; b. Newton, Mass., Dec. 31, 1940; s. Roger Melvin and Margaret (Carter) W.; children: Heather, Carter. BA, Williams Coll., 1962; LLB, Fordham U., 1965. Bar: N.Y. 1965, U.S. Dist. Ct. (so. and ea. dists.) 1968, U.S. Ct. Appeals (2d cir.) 1981, U.S. Ct. Appeals (11th cir.) 1982, U.S. Ct. Appeals (3d cir.) 1984, U.S. Ct. Appeals (5th cir.) 1987. Assoc. Donovan, Leisure, Newton & Irvine, N.Y.C., 1965, 67-73, ptnr., 1973-98, editor, contbg. author to firm's ADR Practice Book, 1990; law clk. to presiding justice U.S. Dist. Ct. N.Y. (so. dist.), 1967-68; of counsel Fulton, Rowe, Hart & Coon, N.Y.C., 1998—. Spkr. in field. Contbr. articles to profl. jours. Bd. dirs., pres. Childfind of Am., Inc., 1993-94; v.p. bd. dirs. Pelham (N.Y. Family Svc., 1982-85; vol. learning disabled children Chelsea Neighborhood, N.Y.C., 1965-67; bd. dirs. Catskill Ctr. for Conservation and Devel., 1993—. Recipient Am. Jurisprudence award Fordham U. Mem. ABA (alt. dispute resolution com. 1989-93), N.Y. State Bar Assn. (alt. dispute resolution com. 1989-93), Fed. Bar Coun., Assn. Bar City N.Y. (profl. responsibility com. 1987-89, pub. assistance com. 1991-94). Avocation: woodworking, flyfishing, biking, camping. Office: Fulton Rowe Hart & Coon One Rockefeller Plz New York NY 10020

WILKINSON, KENTON TODD, communications educator; b. June 3, 1961; BA, U. Colo., 1986; MA, U. Calif., Berkeley, 1991; PhD, U. Tex., Austin, 1995. Asst. prof. Monterrey Tech., Mex., 1994-96; asst. prof. comm. U. Tex., San Antonio, 1996—2001, assoc. prof. comm., 2001—. Office: U Tex Dept Comm 6900 N Loop 1604 W San Antonio TX 78249-1130 E-mail: kwilkinson@utsa.edu.

WILKINSON, LOUISE CHERRY, psychology educator, dean; b. Phila., May 15, 1948; BA magna cum laude with honors, Oberlin Coll., 1970; EdM, EdD, Harvard U., 1974. Prof., chmn. dept. ednl. psychology U. Wis., Madison, 1976-85; prof., exec. officer Grad. Sch. Ph.D. Program CUNY, N.Y.C., 1984-86; disting. prof., dean Grad. Sch. Edn. Rutgers U., 1986—. Chairperson ednl. strategic planning Rutgers U.; mem. nat. rev. bd. Nat. Inst. Edn., 1977, 85, 87; cons. Nat. Ctr. for Bilingual Rsch., 1982, 84, U.S. Dept. Edn., 1995-96; adv. bd. Nat. Reading Rsch. Ctr., 1992-98. Co-author: Communicating for Learning, 1991; editor: Communicating in Classroom, 1982, Social Context of Instruction, 1984, Gender Influences in the Classroom, 2002; co-editor: Literacy and Language Learning, 2002; mem. editl. bds.: ; contbr. articles to profl. jours. Fellow: APA, Am. Assn. for Applied and Preventive Psychology, Am. Psychol. Soc.; mem.: NJ Coun. Acad. Policy Advisors, Am. Ednl. Rsch. Assn. (v.p. 1990—92, program chair 1997).

WILKINSON, RALPH RUSSELL, biochemistry educator, toxicologist; b. Portland, Oreg., Feb. 20, 1930; s. Tracy Chandler and Lavern (Russell) W.; m. Evelyn Marie Wickman, Aug. 5, 1956. BA, Reed Coll., 1953; PhD, U. Oreg., 1962; MBA, U. Mo., Kansas City, 1974. Rsch. chemist VA Hosp., Kansas City, Mo., 1973-74; sr. rsch. chemist Midwest Rsch. Inst., 1975-84; prof. Rockhurst Coll., 1985-86, Cleve. Chiropractic Coll., Kansas City, 1987-99, prof. emeritus, 1999—. Cons. in biochemistry, toxicology, environ. impact, tech. assessment, Kansas City, 1984—. Author: (book) Neurotoxins and Neurobiological Function, 1987; contbr. articles to profl. jours. Mem. Southtown Coun., Kansas City, Mo., 1989—, Spina Bifida Assn. Am., Kansas City, 1989—. Recipient NSF fellowship, 1959-60. Mem. Am. Chem. Soc., Sigma Xi. Avocations: travel, history, biography, music, antiques. Home: 7911 Charlotte St Kansas City MO 64131-2175

WILKINSON, RANDEL, county official; b. Sikeston, Mo., July 25, 1953; s. Elvis Lee and Virginia (Lee) W.; 1 child, Evan Randel. BA in Psychology, Carsen Newman Coll., Jefferson City, Tenn., 1975; MRE, So. Bapt. Theol. Sem., Louisville, 1979, MDiv, 1981; MA in Libr. and Info. Sci., U. South Fla., 1989. Rsch. libr. Lakeland (Fla.) Pub. Libr., 1984-88; news and sports corr. The News Chief, Winter Haven, Fla., 1983-95; libr. dir. Harden County Pub. Libr., Wauchula, 1988-95; real estate salesperson CDC Properties, Lakeland, 1998—; commr. Polk County Bd. Commrs., Bartow, Fla., 1998—. Youth min. Gateway Bapt. Ch., Lakeland, 1983-88, Lake Garfield Bapt. Ch., 1983-88; mem. Polk County Sch. Bd., 1994-98; mem. Future Fla. Found., Tallahassee, 1998—. Mem. James Madison Inst., Fla. Assn. County Commrs. Republican. Baptist. Avocations: travel, skiing, reading. Home: 1350 N Wilson #202 Bartow FL 33830 Office: Polk County Board County Commrs 330 W Church St Bartow FL 33830 E-mail: randywilkinson@polk-county.net.

WILKINSON, RICHARD K. lawyer; b. Burlington, Vt., June 4, 1957; s. Earl J. and Marcia E. (Learned) W.; m. Debbie Kay Draper, Oct. 27, 1979; children: Emily Kim, David Mack, Ethan Allen. BA, James Madison U., Harrisonburg, Va., 1979; JD, Coll. William and Mary, 1983. Bar: Va. 1983, U.S. Dist. Ct. (we. dist.) Va. 1983, Bankruptcy Ct. (we. dist.) Va. 1984. Assoc. Wolfe & Farmer, Norton, Va., 1983-86, Shackelford & Honenberger, Orange, 1987-89; pvt. practice Gordonsville, 1989-94; assoc. Somerville, Wilkinson & Wheeler, Ltd., Orange, 1994-95, atty., 1995—. Town atty., Gordonsville, 1995-99; mem. Orange County Bd. Suprs., 2000—; chmn. Orange County Nursing Home Commn., 2001—. Dir. Community Diversion Incentive Prog., Culpeper, Va., 1987-95, Gordonsville Housing Alliance, Va., 1988-90. Mem. Va. State Bar Assn., Piedmont Bar Assn., Gordonsville Lions Club (pres. 1992-93). Home: 305 Cadmus Cir Gordonsville VA 22942-9103 Office: Bank of Am Bldg 113 W Main St Fl 3 Orange VA 22960-1524 E-mail: lawrickwilk@aol.com.

WILKINSON, ROBERT E. management consultant, educator; b. Burlington, N.J., Mar. 19, 1925; s. Milton Ernest and Gladys Mae (Estilow) W.; m. Cecilia Elizabeth Chew, Apr. 8, 1950; children: Robert H., Miriam S., Jeffrey S., John K. AB, Syracuse U., 1951; MS in Mgmt., Fla. State U., 1967, DBA in Mgmt., 1974. Asst. prof. mgmt., coord. bus. programs Brevard Ctr. Fla. Tech. U., Orlando, 1971-77; rsch. assoc., asst. dir. Fla. Bd. Regents, Tallahassee, 1974-75; assoc. prof. mgmt. W.Va. Coll. Grad. Studies, Charleston, 1977-78; Fulbright prof. mgmt. Istanbul (Turkey) U., 1978-79, 99; prof. emeritus mgmt., dean Sch. bus., chmn. pers. mgmt. Troy State U. Sys., Ala., 1979-90; pvt. practice mgmt. cons. Satellite Beach, Fla., 1990—. Vis. prof. Crummer Grad. Sch. Bus., Rollins Coll., 1990-93; adj. prof. Webster U., 1993-96; prof., internat. MBA dir., presdl. advisor Estonian Bus. Sch., Tallinn, 1994-98; vis. prof. Shanghai U. Fin. and Econs./Webster U., 1997; arbitrator Fla. Bd. Regents Arbitration Panel; cons. in field; adviser W.Va. Commr. Labor, 1977-78; mem. policy com. MIS Devel. Project, Dothan, Ala., 1983-84. Contbr. articles to profl. publs. Spl. master Fla. Pub. Employee Rels. Commn. With AUS, 1943-45. Fulbright scholar, 1978-79, NDEA fellow, 1969-70. Mem. Am. Soc. Pers. Adminstrn. (diplomate), Acad. Mgmt., So. Regional Indsl. Rels. Rsch. Assn., Acad. Academic Pers. Adminstrs., Fla. Pub. Pers. Assn., Internat. Pers. Mgmt. Assn., Indsl. Rels. Rsch. Assn., W.Va. Indsl. Rels. Rsch. Assn. (pres.-elect), Soc. Profls. in Dispute Resolution, Brevard County Pers. Coun. (chmn.), Am. Arbitration Assn. (arbitrator), Sigma Iota Epsilon. Avocation: genealogy. Home: 260 Magnolia St Melbourne FL 32937-3011

WILKINSON, RONALD EUGENE, aircraft engines engineer; b. Citronelle, Ala., Dec. 7, 1945; s. Emmett Eugene and Faye Cecile (Tanner) W.; m. Peggy Lee Hergesheimer, Dec. 30, 1966; children: Rhonda Denise, Damon Eugene. BS in Aero. Engring., Auburn U., 1968. Design engr. Pratt & Whitney, West Palm Beach, Fla., 1969-72; with Aircraft Products Teledyne Continental Motors, Mobile, Ala., 1972—, devel. engr., project engr., sr. project engr., mgr. advanced programs to program mgr., dir. bus. devel., 1990, dir. engring.,

1990-91, v.p. engring., 1991-94; dir. advanced programs, 1994—; chmn. GAMA ad hoc AVGAS com., 1992—; mem. exec. coun. NASA AGATE, 1995—. Recipient SAE Manly award 1987 Best Tech. Paper on Aero Engines, SAE Excellence in Presentation award, 1987, 89, Teledyne Pacific Group Excellence in Mgmt. award, 1987; named Outstanding Aerospace Engring. Alumni, Auburn U., 1986. Mem. AAIA, Soc. Automotive Engrs., Assn. Unmanned Vehicle Systems, Am. Mgmt. Assn. Republican. Methodist. Achievements include patent for liquid cooled engine which powered the voyager aircraft on its nonstop, non-refueled flight around the world; devel. and design of the engine and turbochargers which powered the Boeing Condor-an experimental high-altitude long-endurance aircraft which set a world altitude record of 66980 feet for piston engine-powered aircraft; holder six patents relating to aircraft piston engine technology. Home: 6804 Hunters Ct Mobile AL 36695-2705 Office: Teledyne Continental Motors PO Box 90 Mobile AL 36601-0090

WILKINSON, RONALD STERNE, science administrator, environmentalist, historian; b. Chgo., Feb. 16, 1934; s. Maurice Sterne and Florence Marie (Colby) W.; m. Mary Morgan Springer, May 18, 1963 (div. 1967); m. Karen Ensinger, June 14, 1969 (div. 1976). BA, Mich. State U., 1960, PhD, 1969. Chemist Berry Bros., Detroit, 1955-57; mem. faculty Mich. State U., East Lansing, 1960-70; sci. specialist Libr. of Congress, Washington, 1970-90, sr. sci. specialist, 1990—; assoc. in bibliography Am. Mus. Nat. History, N.Y.C., 1976-82. Trustee William T. Hornaday Conservation Trust, La Jolla, Calif., 1989—; initiator 2d Nat. Forum on Biodiversity, Washington, 1997. Author: John Winthrop, Jr. and the Origins of American Chemistry, 1969, Benjamin Wilkes, The British Aurelian, 1982, Earth Decade Reading List series, 1990—; editor-in-chief The Mich. Entomologist (later The Great Lakes Entomologist), 1966-71; prodr., narrator ann. Earth Day environ. film festival, Washington, 1990—; contbr. more than 160 articles to sci. and history of sci. publs. Ryder scholar Mich. State U., U. London, 1960, Woodrow Wilson Found. fellow Harvard U., 1960-61, Fulbright scholar Univ. Coll., London, 1965-66. Fellow Linnean Soc. London, Geol. Soc. London, Royal Entomol. Soc. London; mem. Grolier Club (N.Y.C., asst. editor 1979-82). Democrat. Home: 228 9th St NE Washington DC 20002-6110 Office: Libr Of Congress Washington DC 20540-0001

WILKINSON, SIGNE, cartoonist; b. Wichita Falls, Tex. BA in English, 1972. Reporter West Chester (Pa.) Daily Local News, Academy of Natural Scis., Phila.; freelance cartoonist Phila. and N.Y. publs.; cartoonist San Jose (Calif.) Mercury News, 1982-85, Phila. Daily News, 1985—. Illustrator: Abortin Cartoons in Demand, 1992, You Bet Your Tomatoes, 2002; contbr. to Univ. Barge Club News, various mags. Bd. dirs. Fair Hill Burial Ground. Recipient Pulitzer Prize for editl. cartooning, 1992, Overseas Press Club award, 1997, 2001, Robert F. Kennedy award, 2002. Mem. Assn. Am. Editl. Cartoonists (pres. 1994-95). Avocations: gardening, rowing. Office: Phila Daily News PO Box 7788 400 N Broad St Philadelphia PA 19130-4015

WILKINSON, STANLEY RALPH, retired agronomist; b. West Amboy, N.Y., Mar. 28, 1931; s. Ralph Ward and Eva Goldie (Perkins) W.; m. Jean Saye; children: Rachael, Stanley Ralph., Augusta J. BS, Cornell U., 1954; MS, Purdue U., 1956, PhD, 1961. Soil scientist U.S. Regional Pasture Rsch. Lab., University Park, Pa., 1961-64, So. Piedmont Conservation Rsch. Ctr., Watkinsville, Ga., 1965-98, ret., 1998. Contbr. more than 15 chpts. to books, more than 140 articles to tech. jours. Past advance chmn. Boy Scouts Am. Served to capt. USAF, 1955-57. Recipient 3d prize Freedoms Found., 1956. Fellow Soil and Water Conservation Soc. Am., Am. Soc. Agronomy; mem. Soil Sci. Soc. Am. Methodist. E-mail: wilkson@negia.net.

WILKINSON, TOLBERT SIENER, plastic surgeon; b. Wake Forest, N.C., Dec. 28, 1937; s. Charles T. and Ursula B. (Bernstein) W.; m. Suzanne Tonetti; 4 children. BS, Wake Forest U., 1958; MD, Duke U., 1962. Diplomate Am. Bd. Surgery, Am. Bd. Plastic Surgery. Chief, divsn. plastic surgery U. Tex. Health Sci. Ctr., San Antonio, 1971—75; dir. Cosmetic Surgery Ctr. and Spa, 1975—. Lectr. Am. Soc. Aesthetic Plastic Surgery; speaker in field; editor Tech. Forum, 1977—. Author: Practical Procedures in Aesthetic Plastic Surgery, Tips and Traps, 1994, Circumareolar Techniques for Breast Surgery, 1996; contbr. articles to profl. jours. Maj. USAF, 1969-71. Fellow ACS. Avocations: polo, ranching. Office: Cosmetic Surgery Ctr & Spa 109 Gallery Cir #127 San Antonio TX 78258 E-mail: drt1901@aol.com.

WILKINSON, UNA MCCANN, artist; b. Redwood City, Calif., Feb. 15, 1913; d. Robert James and Maria Endicott (Chapin) McC.; widowed; 1 child, Catherine Marie Wilkinson Zerner. Student, Calif. Art Inst., 1932-37. Vis. artist painting Sch. Spl. Studies U. Calif., Santa Barbara, 1978; vis. artist U. Oreg. Sch. Architecture and Allied Arts, 1978. Exhbns. include Wheaton Coll., Norton, Mass., 1976, Benson Gallery, Bridgehampton, N.Y., 1976, Green Mountain Coll., N.Y.C., 1976, 78, Gallery East, East Hampton, N.Y., 1978, Blue Mountain Gallery, N.Y.C., 1980, 83, Noel Butcher Gallery, Phila., 1982, 20 Broad St., N.Y.C., 1985, Stanford U. Mus., 1986, Mus. Art U. Oreg., 1986; juried exhbns. include Parrish Art Mus., Southampton, N.Y., 1981, 82, Nat. Acad. Design, N.Y.C., 1982, A.M. Sachs Gallery, N.Y.C., 1983, One Penn Plaza, N.Y.C., 1983, 20 Broad St., N.Y.C., 1984. Recipient 1st prize Parrish Mus., 1981. Mem. Jimmy Ernst Art Alliance, Nat. Mus. Women in Arts, Group for South Fork. Democrat. Episcopalian. Avocation: environment. Office: La Maladrie Segre Maine et Loire 49500 France

WILKINSON, WARREN SCRIPPS, manufacturing company executive; b. Detroit, Feb. 2, 1920; s. Almadus DeGrasse and Harriet Gertrude (Whitcomb) W.; m. Joan Todd, June 14, 1941; m. Mireille De Bary, Dec. 17, 1966. Grad., Hotchkiss Sch., Lakeville, Conn., 1937; BS in Math, Harvard U., 1941; student, Calif. Inst. Tech., 1941-42. With U.S. Rubber Co., Detroit, 1942-43, Hanson Van Winkle-Munning Co., Matawan, N.J., 1946-64, pres., 1961-64; v.p., gen. mgr. Hanson-Van Winkle-Munning div. M & Chems. Inc., 1964-66; chmn. RPI Designs, Marlette, Mich., 1966—. Mem. Detroit Hist. Commn., 1994—; mem. overseer's com. on univ. resources Harvard U. John Harvard fellow, 1996. Home: 2 Woodland Pl Grosse Pointe MI 48230-1920

WILKINSON, WILLIAM C., III, foundation executive; b. Trenton, N.J., Dec. 2, 1946; s. William Clayton Wilkinson and Virginia Mary Corio; m. Janet K. Dale, Apr. 7, 1953; children: W. Clayton Wilkinson IV, Megan Maguire Moe. BA, George Mason U., 1978. Cert. planner, Washington. Cartographer U.S. Geology Survey, Washington, 1968-69; systems analyst Gen. Svcs. Adminstrn., 1969-70; park ranger Nat. Park Svc., 1970-73; planner Fairfax (Va.) County Park Authority, 1973-76; policy analyst U.S. Dept. Transp., Washington, 1976-80; program dir. Bicycle Mfrs. Assn. Am., 1980-83; exec. dir. Bicycle Fedn. Am., 1984—. Mem. bicycle com. Transp. Rsch. Bd., Washington, 1976-94, pedestrian com., 1994—; mem. steering com. Surface Transp. Policy Project, Washington, 1990—. Mem. Am. Inst. Cert. Planners. Avocation: amateur radio (extra class). Office: Nat Ctr Bicycling and Walking 1506 21st St NW Washington DC 20036-1006

WILKINSON, WILLIAM SHERWOOD, lawyer; b. Williston, N.D., Sept. 6, 1933; s. John Thomas and Evelyn (Landon) W.; m. Carol Ann Burns, Aug. 20, 1960; children— Leslie Ann, Richard Sherwood, Greta Diann. BS in Bus, U. Idaho, 1955; JD, U. Denver, 1960. Bar: Colo. bar 1960, Mich. bar 1966. Practiced in, Canon City, Colo., 1960-66; asst. dist. atty. 11th Jud. Dist., 1961-65; gen. counsel, sec. Mich. Farm Bur. Family Cos., Lansing, 1966-96. Lectr. Pre-Parole Release Center, Colo. State Penitentiary, 1961-65; instr. adult edn., Canon City, 1965; counsel Canon City Recreation Dist., 1964-65 Mem. lay adv. bd. St. Thomas More Hosp., Canon City, 1963-66; Del., county, dist. and congl. convs. Republican party, 1964. Served to capt. USAF, 1955-58. Recipient Cmty. Disting. Svc. award Canon City Jr. C. of C., 1964. Mem. ABA, Colo. Bar Assn., Mich. Bar Assn., Am. Judicature Soc., Am. Corp. Counsel Assn., Nat. Coun. Farmer Coops. (legal, tax and acctg. com.), Phi Delta Phi, Tau Kappa Epsilon. Methodist (lay leader, mem. ch. ofcl. bd.). Home: 1707 Foxcroft Rd East Lansing MI 48823-2131

WILKNISS, PETER E. foundation administrator, researcher; b. Berlin, Sept. 28, 1934; U.S. citizen. s. Fritz and Else (Stueber) W.; m. Edith P. Koester, May 25, 1963; children: Peter F., Sandra M. MS in Chemistry, Tech. U., Munich, Ger., 1958, PhD in Radio and Nuclear Chemistry, 1961. Rsch. chemist, radiological protection officer U.S. Naval Ordnance Sta., 1961-64, head nuclear chemistry branch, 1964-66; rsch. oceanographer U.S. Naval Rsch. Lab., 1966-70, head chemical oceanography branch, 1970-75; mgr. Nat. Ctr. Atmospheric Rsch. Program NSF, Washington, 1975-76, mgr. Internat. Phase of Ocean Drilling/Ocean Sediment Coring Program, 1976-80, mgr. Ocean Drilling Project Team, AAEO Directorate, 1980, dir. Ocean Drilling Programs, 1980-81, sr. sci. assoc. Office of Dir., 1981-82, dep. asst. dir. Sci, Tech., Internat. Affairs Directorate, 1982-84, dir. divsn. Polar Programs, 1984-93, sr. sci. assoc. Geoscis. Directorate, 1993-96; pres. Polar Kybernetes Internat. LLC, Fairbanks, Alaska, 1997—, Transnat. Arctic and Antarctic Inst., Fairbanks, 1997—. Liaison mem. NRC, NAS, Marine Bd., 1978-81, Polar Rsch. Bd., 1984-93; mem. atmospheric chemistry and radioactivity com. Am. Meteorological Soc., 1975-78; mem. interagy. com. atmospheric scis., 1975-76, space station adv. com., NASA, 1988-93. Ontbr. over 60 articles to sci., tech. jours., USN reports; over 100 formal presentations nat., internat. sci. confs., symposia, meetings; participant 16 nat., internat. workshops. Presdl. citation AIA, 1993; Wilkniss mountain Antarctic named in his honor Sec. Interior, U.S. Bd. Geographic Names, 1992. Mem. AAAS, Am. Geophys. Union, Assn. for Machine Translation in the Americas, Am. Polar Soc., Antarctican Soc. Episcopalian. Avocations: soccer, swimming, skiing. Office: Polar Kybernetes Internat 1305 W 7th Ave Anchorage AK 99501-3210 E-mail: pwilkniss@aol.com.

WILKS, DUFFY JEAN, counselor, educator; b. Spur, Tex., Feb. 15, 1936; d. Rube Lee Jay and Elizabeth Audeen (Simmons) Austin; children: Vicki Ratheal, Juli Ratheal, Randy Ratheal, Rodney Ratheal; m. W.B. Wilks, Oct. 22, 1986. BA in Psychology, Tex. Tech. U., 1981, MEd in Psychology, 1984, EdD in Ednl. Psychology, 1995. Cert. substance abuse counsleor; lic. profl. counselor, Tex.; lic. marriage and family therapist, Tex. Editor writer Floydada (Tex.) newspaper, 1972-80; probation officer Adult/Juvenile Probation, Lubbock, Tex., 1982-86; pvt. practice Horseshoe Bay, 1986—. Prof. Western Tex. Coll., Snyder. Mem. ACA (mem. editl. bd. ACA Jour. 1998—), Tex. Assn. Counseling and Devel. (editorial bd. jour. 1989-91, author revs., editor Disting. Svc. award 1991), Tex. Counseling Assn. (exec. editor Tex. Counseling Assn. Jour. 1998-2000), Tex. C.C. Tchrs. Assn., Internat. Assn. for Addictions and Offender Counselors. Avocations: playing piano, writing, researching.

WILKS, JACQUELIN HOLSOMBACK, educational association executive; b. Jan. 18, 1950; d. Jack and Ida Mae (Bass) Holsomback; m. Thomas M. Wilks, Jan. 28, 1972; children: David, Bryan. BS, La. Coll., 1972; MAT., Okla. City U., 1982; postgrad., So. Bapt. Theol. Sem., Louisville, 1974, Capella U.; S.E., Mo. State U., 1977; counseling cert., Cen. State Univ., 1983. Lic. realtor Mo. Sec. to adminstr. Allen Parish Hosp., Kinder, La., 1968-69; tchr. horseback riding, swimming Triple D Guest Ranche, Warren, Tex., 1969; singer, speaker Found. Singers, 1970-71; tchr. English Pine Bluff (Ark.) H.S., 1972-74; tchr. kindergarten Doyle Elem. Sch., East Prairie (Mo.) R-2, 1974-75; tchr. 1st grade Bertrand (Mo.) Elem. Sch., 1975-76; tchr. 6th grade sci. A.D. Simpson Sch., Charleston, Mo., 1976-78; dir. admissions and fin. adminstr. Control Data Inst., Control Data Corp., St. Louis, 1980-81. Bd. dirs. Computer Commn. Svcs. Inc., 1986—, dir. tutorial svcs., instr. tutorial methods Okla. Bapt. U., 1981-83, instr. horsemanship St. Gregory's Jr. Coll., 1981; counselor Gordon Cooper Area Vocat. Tech. Sch., 1982-83, Shawnee Jr. H.S. Okla.), 1983-85, Grove Sch., Shawnee, 1989—; dir. Resource Ctr., instr. English St. Gregory's Coll., Shawnee, Okla., 1985-89; counselor Spanish tchr. North Rock Creek Sch., Shawnee; translator med. grp. missions Dominican Rep. and Guatemala, 1995, 96, Cosecha 2000, Argentina, 1998, El Salvador, 1998, 99, Ecuador, 2000; bd. dirs. Computer Commn. Svcs. Inc., Tulsa; tutor for children under jurisdiction Juvenile Ct., Jefferson County, Ark., 1972-73; leader group counseling/therapy sessions, 1972; dir. devel. Nat. Insts. Devel. Delays, 2000. Choreographer First Bapt. Ch. Youth Choir, Pine Bluff; v.p. St. Gregory's Coll. Therapeutic Horsemanship Program, 1981-82; Rep. election judge. Recipient Kathryn Carpenter award La. Bapt. Conv., 1971, real Scope award Realty World, St. Louis, 1980, NEH grantee, 1993—. Mem. Univ. Alliance Okla. Bapt. U. Baptist. Home: 18 Woodcrest Shawnee OK 74804-9048 Office: North Rock Creek Nat Inst Devel Delays 42400 Garrett's Lake Rd Shawnee OK 74804

WILKS, LARRY DEAN, lawyer; b. Columbia, S.C., Jan. 8, 1955; s. Ray Dean and Jean (Garrett) W.; m. Jan Elizabeth McIllwain, May 2,1981; children: John Ray, Adam Garrett. BS, U. Tenn., 1977, JD, 1980. Bar: Tenn. 1981, U.S. Dist. Ct. (mid. dist.) Tenn. 1981, U.S. Supreme Ct. 1986, U.S. Ct. Appeals (6th cir.) 1993, U.S. Dist. Ct. (we. dist.) Tenn. 1996. Assoc. Mayo & Norris, Nashville, 1981-82; sole practice Springfield, Tenn., 1982-84; ptnr. Walton, Jones & Wilks, 1984, Jones & Wilks, 1984-89; pvt. practice Springfield, Tenn., 1989—. Chmn. Dem. Orgn. Robertson County Tenn., 1986-93. Fellow Tenn. Bar Found.; mem. ABA, ATLA, Tenn. Bar Assn. (assoc. gen. counsel 1991-94, gen. counsel 1994-99, bd. profl. responsibility 1993-98, bd. govs. 1991—, young lawyers divsn. lifetime fellow, asst. treas. 1999-2000, treas. 2000—), Tenn. Assn. Criminal Def. Lawyers, Tenn. Trial Lawyers Assn., Robertson County Bar Assn. (pres. 1993-96), Nat. Assn. Criminal Def. Laywers, Tenn. Young Lawyers Conf. (bd. dirs. 1987, editor quar. newsletter 1987-88, Mid. Tenn. v.p. 1988-89, v.p. 1989-90, pres.-elect 1990-91, pres. 1991-92). Methodist. Office: 509 W Court Sq Springfield TN 37172-2413

WILKS, THOMAS MILTON, religious studies educator, minister; b. Mansfield, La., Feb. 14, 1945; s. Milton E. and Bernice (Thompson) W.; m. Jacquelin Holsomback, Jan. 28, 1972; children: T. David, Bryan E. BA, La. Coll., Pineville, 1967; ThM, New Orleans Bapt. Theol. Sem., 1971; DMin, So. Bapt. Theol. Sem., Louisville, 1977. Lic. field traumatologist, in-svc. guidance dir. Youth min. First Bapt. Ch., Bastrop, La., 1968; pastor Magnolia Bapt. Ch., Vancleave, Miss., 1969-71; youth assoc., pastoral intern First Bapt. Ch., Pine Bluff, Ark., 1971-73, pastor Charleston, Mo., 1973-78; min. Bapt. Metro Campus, St. Louis, 1978-80; assoc. dean students for counseling, univ. chaplain Okla. Bapt. U., Shawnee, 1980-84, asst. prof. applied ministry, dir. in-svc. guidance, 1984-87, assoc. prof. applied ministry, dir. in-svc. guidance, 1987-93, prof. applied ministry, dir. in-svc. guidance, 1993-94, dir. off-campus programs and insvc. guidance, prof., 1994-96, prof. applied ministry, dir. in-svc. guidance, 1996-97, Jewell and Joe Huitt prof. religious edn., 1998—, dir. in-svc. guidance, 1998—. Adj. prof. psychology Oklahoma City U. Grad. Sch., 1983-84; adj. prof. pastoral leadership Southwestern Bapt. Theol Sem., 1996, 98; cons. family ministry Bapt. Gen. Conv. Okla., Oklahoma City, 1999—; mem. bd. Summit Youth Camps, Edmond, Okla., 1994—; mem. long-range planning co. So. Bapt. In-Svc. Guidance Conf., 1992-99, pres., 1991, bd. dirs., 1999—; mem. Youth Matrix Team, Lifeway Christian Resources, Nashville, 1996—; state cons. in family ministry Bapt. Gen. Conv. Okla., 1998—; mem. Nat. Task Force on Bi-Vocat. Ministry, 1992; spkr. various civic clubs and orgns., graduations and faculty devel. workshops for schs. and colls. Author: Blind Faith, 1995; writer youth ministry, local ch. and missions internship, preaching, pastoral care and pastoral ministry study guides. Pres. North Rock Creek Bd. Edn., Shawnee, 1989; treas. Shawnee H.S. Quarterback Club, 1994-95. Mem. Nat. Network Youth Ministries, In-Svc. Guidance Assn. (chmn. exec. com. 1996-99, bd. dirs. 1999—, chmn. bd. dirs. 2002), Assn. Theol. Field Educators. Republican. Avocations: coach, youth baseball, basketball, soccer, track. Home: 18 Woodcrest Shawnee OK 74804-9048 Office: Okla. Bapt. U. Box 61273 Shawnee OK 74804 E-mail: tom.wilks@mail.okbu.edu.

WILKS-OWENS, DIXIE RAE, conference and meeting planner, workforce preparation specialist; b. Oakland, Calif., Nov. 1, 1943; d. James D. Wilks and Pauline Ruth (Peoples) Biddulph; m. August Edward Slagle (div. 1974); children: Tonya Davina Slagle, Victor Scott Slagle; m. Howard Laverne Owens, Dec. 15, 1984. AA, Ohlone Coll., 1973; attended, U. Calif., Davis, 1993-94; cert. mgmt. effectiveness, U. So. Calif. Unemployment ins. specialist, employment and tng. generalist. Employment supr. Calif. Employment Devel. Dept., Sacramento, 1969-86, employment specialist, 1986-88, legis. analyst, 1988-90, legis. re-employment ctr. mgr., 1990-91, mktg. mgr., 1991-94, mgr. workforce preparation conf., 1994-98, dep. dir. pub. affairs, 1999—. Pres. Meeting Masters, Sacramento, 1996-99; state mgr. Dept. Labor's Nationwide One-Stop Career Ctr. Conf., 1997, 98. Bd. dirs., membership chair Sacramento Women's Campaign Fund, 1993-97. Mem. Internat. Assn. Pers. in Employment Security (mem. internat. rels. com. 1991, Calif. chpt. pres. 1992-94, bd. dirs. conf. planning bd. 1993-94, legis. chair 1995-98, internat. retiree chair 1999—), Soc. Govt. Meeting Profls., Nat. Coun. Sr. Citizens (life), Congress of Calif. Srs. (life). Democrat. Unitarian Universalist. Avocation: marketing. Office: Calif Employment Devel Dept MIC84 800 Capitol Mall Sacramento CA 95814-4807 also: State Job Tng Coord Coun 800 Capitol Mall # C67 Sacramento CA 95814-4807

WILL, CLIFFORD MARTIN, physicist, educator; b. Hamilton, Ont., Can., Nov. 13, 1946; m. Leslie Saxe, June 26, 1970; children: Elizabeth, Rosalie. BS, McMaster U., Hamilton, 1968; PhD, Calif. Inst. Tech., 1971. Enrico Fermi fellow U. Chgo., 1972-74; asst. prof. physics Stanford U., Palo Alto, Calif., 1974-81; assoc. prof. physics Washington U., St. Louis, 1981-85, prof. physics, 1985—, chmn. dept. physics, 1991—2002. Chmn. com. on time transfer in satellite systems Air Force Studies Bd., Washington, 1984-86; chmn. sci. adv. com. NASA Gravity Probe B, 1998—. Assoc. editor Physical Rev. Letters, 1989-92, Physical Rev. D, 1999-2001; author: Theory and Experiment in Gravitational Physics, 1981, rev. edit., 1993, Was Einstein Right?, 1986, rev. edit., 1993. Alfred P. Sloan Found. fellow, 1975-79, J.S. Guggenheim Found. fellow, 1996-97, J.W. Fulbright fellow, 1996-97; recipient Sci. Writing award Am. Inst. Physics, 1987, Disting. Alumni award, McMaster U., 1996. Fellow Am. Phys. Soc. (exec. com. astrophysics divsn. 1988-90, vice chair, chair elect, chair topical group on gravitation 1997-2001), Am. Acad. Arts and Scis.; mem. Am. Astron. Soc., Am. Assn. Physics Tchrs. (Richtmyer Meml. Lectr. 1987), Internat. Soc. Gen. Relativity and Gravitation. Office: Washington U Dept Physics Campus Box 1105 1 Brookings Dr Saint Louis MO 63130-4899

WILL, FREDERIC, university administrator, writer; b. New Haven, Dec. 4, 1928; s. Samuel F. and Constance B. Will; m. Julie Omotejohwo, July 27, 1995; children: Barbara, Alex, Chris, Carson, Kyle. BA, Ind. U., 1948; PhD, Yale U., 1952. Asst. prof. classics Dartmouth, Hanover, N.H., 1952-54, Pa. State U., University Park, 1955-60; prof. classics U. Tex., Austin, 1960-65; prof. comparative lit. U. Iowa, Iowa City, 1965-70, fellow Inst. Advanced Studies, 1985-92; prof. comparative lit. U. Mass., Amherst, 1971-84; pres. Mellen U., Mt. Vernon, Iowa, 1995—. Author: Intelligible Beauty in Aesthetic Thought, 1956, Mosaic and Other Poems, 1959, A Wedge of Words, 1963, The Twelve Words of the Gypsy, (trans.) 1964, Metaphrasis, 1964, Flumen Historicum, 1965, Hereditas, 1965, Literature Inside Out, 1966, The King's Flute (trans.), 1966, From A Year in Greece, 1967, Planets, 1968, Archilochos, 1969, Herondas, 1972, Brandy in the Snow, 1972, The Fact of Literature, 1973, The Knife in the Stone, 1973, The Jargon of Authenticity, (trans.) 1973, Guatemala, 1973, Botulism, 1975, The Generic Demands of Greek Literature, 1976, Belphagor, 1977, Epics of America, 1977, Selected Poems, 1980, Shamans in Turtlenecks, 1984, The Sliced Dog, 1984, The Fall and The Gods 3 vols., 1988-92, Entering the Open Hole, 1989, Big Rig Souls, 1992, Translation Theory and Practice, 1993, Literature as Sheltering the Human, 1993, Singing with Whitman's Thrush, 1993, Recoveries, 1993, Trips of the Psyche, 1993, Textures, Spaces, Wonders, 1993; lit. papers archived in Humanities Rsch. Ctr., U. Tex., Austin. Fulbright fellow, Germany, 1951, Greece, 1957, Tunisia, 1973, Congo, 1980, Ivory Coast, 2000-02; Bollingen Found. fellow, 1956, Am. Coun. Learned Socs. fellow, 1957, Nat. Endowment Arts fellow, 1960. Roman Catholic. Home: 617 7th St NW Mount Vernon IA 52314-1130

WILL, JERRIE ANN, psychologist; b. Hazleton, Pa., Apr. 6, 1950; d. Gordon John and Doris Griffiths (Brown) W.; m. Gene G. Kuehneman, June 26, 1982 (div. Oct. 1984). BA, Bucknell U., 1971; MA, W.Va. U., 1974, PhD, 1977. Lic. psychologist, Maine. Teaching fellow W.Va. U., Morgantown, 1974-76; clin. psychology intern U. Md. Hosp., Balt., 1976-77; sr. child psychologist Michael Reese Hosp., Chgo., 1977-82; cons. psychologist Ridgeway Psychiat. Hosp., 1982-83, Sanford Sch. Dept., Maine, 1983—; pvt. practice Sanford and Wells, 1984—. Team and child psychologist York County Counseling Svcs., Sanford, 1983-85; owner, mgr. Sanford Psychol. Assocs., 1987-95; panelist, reviewer NSF, 1976. Contbr. articles to profl. jours. NIMH Grantee, 1972-75. Mem. APA. Home: 314 Webhannet Dr Wells ME 04090-4225 Office: 828 Main St Sanford ME 04073-3523

WILL, JON NICHOLSON, small business owner, financial consultant; b. Washington, Apr. 26, 1940; s. Hubert Louis and Phyllis Fae (Nicholson) W.; m. Martha Cecilia Neira, Aug. 21, 1965 (div. Aug. 1980); children: David, Jonathan; m. Ada Mary Withington Gugenheim, July 1, 1983. BA, Parsons Coll., 1963; MA in Social Svc. Adminstrn., U. Chgo., 1968. Exec. dir. Near North Family Guidance Ctr., Chgo., 1971-73, Atty. Gen. Ill. Pub. Health Trust, Chgo., 1974-79; adminstrv. asst. Atty. Gen. Ill., 1979-83; pres., CEO Hyde Pk. Coop. Fed. Credit Union, 1983-89; br. mgr. Credit Union, 1989-91; pvt. practice cons., 1992-94; pres. Jon. N. Will & Assocs. Inc., 1995—. Pres. bd. dirs. Hyde Pk. Coop. Soc., Chgo., 1991-97. Vol. Peace Corps., Ecuador, 1963-65; treas., bd. dirs. Wendy Will Case Fund, Chgo., 1983—; bd. dirs. Ill. Humane Soc., Chgo., 1996—. Sgt. USAR, 1966-72. Mem. Kiwanis Club Hyde Pk. (treas. 1985—), Hyde Pk. C. of C. (v.p., bd. dirs. 1992-96). Avocations: swimming, water skiing. Home: 1359 E 52nd St Chicago IL 60615-4047 Office: Jon N Will & Assocs Inc 1525 E 53rd St Ste 526 Chicago IL 60615-4575 E-mail: JNWASSOC@interaccess.com.

WILL, ROBERT JOHN, lawyer; b. St. Louis, May 17, 1963; m. Stephanie Rutkoski, Aug. 8, 1987; children: Thomas, Rachel. BA, St. Louis U., 1984; JD, George Washington U., 1987. Bar: Mo. 1987, U.S. Dist. Ct. (ea. dist.) Mo., U.S. Dist. Ct. (we. dist.) Ill., 1988, U.S. Dist. Ct. (so. dist.) Ill. 1990, U.S. Ct. Appeals (7th and 8th cirs.) 1988. Mem. Lewis, Rice & Fingersh, St. Louis, 1987—. Mem. Vol. Lawyers Assn., St. Louis, 1987—. Nat. Merit scholar, 1981. Mem. ABA (vice chair tort and ins. practice sect., medicine and law com. 1999—), Mo. Bar Assn., Ill. Bar Assn., Order of Coif, Phi Beta Kappa. Roman Catholic. Home: 433 Hazelgreen Dr Saint Louis MO 63119-1319 Office: Lewis Rice & Fingersh LC 500 N Broadway Ste 2000 Saint Louis MO 63102-2147 E-mail: rwill@lewisrice.com.

WILL, ROLAND TRACY, II, writer, editor, journalist, publisher, actor; b. Schenectady, N.Y., May 18, 1954; s. Albert Roland and Constance Mary (Headley) W.; m. Gay Adair Strandemo, July 1, 1989; children: Roland Leigh Leonard, Glenn Tracy. BA, U. Wis., 1988. Pol. sci., comm. arts editor, pub., journalist Wis. Health Policy Report, Wis. Ind. News Svc., Madison, 1994—. Author: (Compass Am. Guide) Wisconsin, 1994, 2d edit., 1997; (plays) Packer Glory, 1984, Fatal Time to Final End, 1986; actor (plays) Bombs Away Enola Gay, 1983, Hans Brinker and Silver Skates: Rock Musical on Roller Skates, 1984, Light My Fire—Jim Morrison, 1985, The Cherry Orchard, 1985, The Hangwoman, 1986, The Phantom of Shoppko, 1987, Joe a Life: The Story of Joe McCarthy, 1988, Chain Reaction, 1996. Bus. mem. Dane County Hist. Soc., Madison, 1995; sec. bd. dirs. Broom St. Theater, Madison, 1984—; curator photography exhibit Wis. Hist. Mus. Episcopalian. Avocations: history, architectural renovation, travel. Office: Wis Health Policy Report Press Rm BW41 State Capitol Madison WI 53703

WILL, TREVOR JONATHAN, lawyer; b. Ashland, Wis., Aug. 11, 1953; s. William Taylor and Geraldine Sue (Trevor) W.; m. Margaret Ann Johnson, Aug. 28, 1976; children: Tyler William, Alexandra Marie, Jennifer Catherine. BA summa cum laude, Augustana Coll., 1975; JD cum laude, Harvard U., 1978. Bar: Wis. 1978, U.S. Dist. Ct. (ea. dist.) Wis. 1978, U.S. DIst. Ct. (we. dist.) Wis. 1980, U.S. Ct. Appeals (7th cir.) 1983, U.S. Supreme Ct. 1984, U.S. Dist. Ct. (ea. dist.) Mich. 1985. Assoc. Foley & Lardner, Milw., 1978-87, ptnr., 1987—. Adj. law prof. Marquette U. Law Sch., 1994—. Mem. ABA, State Bar Wis., Milw. Bar Assn., Def. Rsch. Inst. Home: 10011 N Waterleaf Dr Mequon WI 53092-6146 Office: Foley & Lardner 777 E Wisconsin Ave Ste 3800 Milwaukee WI 53202-5367 E-mail: twill@foleylaw.com., tajwill@aol.com.

WILLADSEN, MICHAEL CHRIS, marketing professional, sales executive; b. Cheboygan, Mich., Sept. 18, 1946; s. Chris Jens and Helen Margaret (Barr) W.; m. Kay Ann Brooks, Dec. 10, 1964, (div. Dec. 10, 1989); children: Michael Jr., Erik; m. Linda Sue Degroff, Apr. 4, 1992; children: Stephanie, Gretchen, Ross. Student, Delta Coll., 1964-66; A in Bus. Mgmt., Northwood Inst., 1968, BA in Bus. Mgmt., 1969. Mktg. rep. Detroit dist. Petemco, Inc., 1970-73, mktg. rep. Indpls. Dist., 1973-74; dist. mgr. Petemco Inc.-Ind. Ohio Mich., Ind., Ohio, Mich., 1974-76, Consolidated Stas. Marathon Oil, Oshkosh, Wis., 1976-79; sales mgr. Champaign (Ill.) Dist. Marathon Oil, 1981-82, supr. Credit Card Ctr. Ohio, 1982-84; wholesale mktg. profl. Marathon Brand Mktg./Ohio, Mich., Ky., 1982-84; jobber sales Marathon Oil/Ohio, Pa., W.Va., Ohio, Pa., W. Va., 1984-92, Marathon Oil/Ill., Wisc., Chgo., Chgo., 1992-2000, Marathon Ashland Petroleum, Atlanta, 2000—, N.C., S.C., Ala. Named to Nat. Assn. Intercollegiate Athletes Sml. Coll. All-State Football Team/Dist.

23, 1968. Mem. Cleve. Petroleum Club (v.p. 1988-91), Chgo. Oilmens. Republican. Presbyterian. Avocations: camping, softball, basketball, physical work out. Office: Marathon Ashland Petroleum PO Box 1007 Cumming GA 30028

WILLANS, JEAN STONE, bishop, religious organization executive; b. Hillsboro, Ohio, Oct. 3, 1924; d. Homer and Ella (Keyes) Hammond; m. Richard James Willans, Mar. 28, 1966; 1 dau., Suzanne Jeanne. Student, San Diego Jr. Coll.; DD (hon.), Am. Coll. Sems., 1996. Ordained archdeacon, 1996, ordained priest 1997, consecrated bishop 1998, Ch. of the East. Asst. to v.p. Family Loan Co., Miami, Fla., 1946-49; civilian supr. USAF, Washington, 1953-55; founder, dir. Blessed Trinity Soc.; editor Trinity mag., L.A., 1960-66; co-founder, exec. v.p., dir. Soc. of Stephen, Altadena, Calif., 1967—; exec. dir. Hong Kong, 1975-81. Lectr. in field. Author: The Acts of the Green Apples, 1974, rev. edit. 1995; co-editor: Charisma in Hong Kong, 1970, Spiritual Songs, 1970, The People Who Walked in Darkness, 1977, The People Who Walked in Darkness II, 1992, 2d edit., 2000. Recipient Achievement award Nat. Assn. Pentecostal Women, 1964; monument erected in her honor Kowloon Walled City Park, Hong Kong Govt., 1996. Republican. Office: Soc of Stephen PO Box 6225 Altadena CA 91003-6225

WILLANS, RICHARD JAMES, bishop, religious organization executive; b. Detroit, July 24, 1943; s. James Cyril and Georgie Agnes (Ray) W.; m. Jean Stone, Mar. 28, 1966; 1 child, Suzanne Jeanne. Student, Dartmouth Coll., 1960-63; BS in Orgnl. Behavior, U. San Francisco, 1984; DD (hon.), Am. Coll. Seminarians, Santa Cruz, Calif., 1996. Ordained priest Ch. of the East/St. Thomas Tradition, 1996, consecrated as bishop, 1997. Assoc. editor Trinity Mag., Van Nuys, Calif., 1963-66; co-founder, pres., chmn. Soc. of Stephen, Altadena, 1967—, missionary pastor Hong Kong, 1968-81; tchr. Hong Kong Christian Coll., Caineway English Coll., Hong Kong, 1968-71; ops. mgr. RCM Svcs., Hong Kong, 1972-74; dir. exec. selection Peat, Marwick, Mitchell & Co., Hong Kong, 1974-81; pers. dir. Gen. Bank, L.A., 1982-83; dir. human resources Calif. Commerce Bank, 1984-88; mgr. human resources info. ctr. Union Bank of Calif., Monterey Pk., 1988-96. Lectr. in field. Co-editor: (collection of personal stories) Charisma in Hong Kong, 1970, (song book) Spiritual Songs, 1970, (book series) The People Who Walked in Darkness, Vol. I, 1977, Vol. II, 1992, updated, 2000, (book) The Acts of the Green Apples, 1995. Monument in his honor for drug addict rehab. work Kowloon Walled City Pk., Hong Kong, 1996. Republican. Office: PO Box 6225 Altadena CA 91003-6225

WILLARD, GARCIA LOU, artist; b. Huntington, W.Va., Apr. 15, 1943; d. Harry Lee and Laura Lillian (Riley) Hall; m. Victor Percy Young, Sept. 2, 1972 (dec. Mar. 1980); m. Roger Lee Willard, Aug. 22, 1988. Student, Marshall U., 1978-83, W.Va. U., 1993, U. N.D., 1994-95. Owner, pres. Young's Fine Art, Huntington, 1975-85, Dyna Line, Wheeling, W.Va., 1980-85; instr. pastel and drawing Oglebay Mus.'s Stifel Fine Art Ctr., 1984-87; instr. pastel and portraiture Ohio U., Athens, 1987; owner, operator Outlines, Phoenix, 1988-91; contbg. artist Sonoran Gallery, 1993—. Mem. adv. bd. Profl. Art League, St. Clairsville, Ohio, 1984-85; lectr. and exhbn. juror various art orgns., Ohio, W.Va., Pa., 1987-88; art cons. Journey's End Designs, Wheeling, 1987. One woman shows include: Delf-Norona Mus., Moundsville, W. Va., Ariel Gallery, N.Y.C., Sonoran Gallery, Phoenix; Group shows include: Pen & Brush Club, N.Y.C., 1988, Hermitage Found. Mus., Va., 1988; contbr., illustrator: (book) Dr. Horton on African Art, 1985. Advisor Ariz. Fine Arts Commn., Phoenix, 1989-92. Recipient Best of Show award Delf-Norona Mus., 1985, Molly Guion award for graphics Catharine Lorillard Wolfe Art Club, 1988, Douglas Pickering Carnegie Mellon award, 1986. Fellow Am. Artists Profl. League (Pastel award 1988); mem. Pastel Soc. Am. (signature mem. artist mem., A & M design award, 1988), Acad. Artists Assn. (artist mem., award for pastel portrait 1989), Degas Pastel Soc. (artist mem., M. Grumbacher award for pastel excellence 1988), Nat. Drawing Assn., Art Assn. Harrisburg (artist mem.), Signature Mem. Pastel Soc. Am., N.Y.C. Republican. Avocations: archeology, astronomy, paper-making, attending symphonies, traveling. Office: Sonoran Gallery 8819 W Corrine Dr Peoria AZ 85381-8166 E-mail: rlwillard1@msn.com.

WILLARD, H(ARRISON) ROBERT, electrical engineer; b. Seattle, May 31, 1933; s. Harrison Eugene and Florence Linea (Chelquist) W. BSEE, U. Wash., 1955, MSEE, 1957, PhD, 1971. Lic. profl. engr., Wash. Staff assoc. Boeing Sci. Rsch. Labs., Seattle, 1959-64; rsch. assoc. U. Wash., 1968-72, sr. engr., rsch. prof. applied physics lab., 1972-81; sr. engr. Boeing Aerospace Co., Seattle, 1981-84; dir. instrumentation and engring. MetriCor Inc. (formerly Tech. Dynamics, Inc.), Woodinville, Wash., 1984-92; sr. engr. B.E. Meyers & Co., Inc., 1992—. Contbr. articles to profl. jours.; patentee in field. With AUS, 1957-59. Mem. IEEE, Am. Geophys. Union, Phi Beta Kappa, Sigma Xi, Tau Beta Pi. Office: 17525 NE 67th Ct Redmond WA 98052-4939

WILLARD, JOHN GERARD, consultant, author, lecturer; b. Pitts., Nov. 20, 1952; s. Cornelius Merle and May E. (Hinds) W.; m. Lorraine L. Franze, Sept. 2, 1978; children: Mary Elizabeth, Kristen Anne, Lisa Lorraine, Jessica Kathleen. BA in Journalism, Duquesne U., 1974. Producer, dir. air talent Sta. WDUQ-FM, Pitts., 1971-73; master control tech. dir. Sta. KDKA-TV, 1973; cons. comms. Better Bus. Bur., 1974; asst. account exec. Marc & Co. Advt., 1975; adminstr., employee benefit adminstrn. Rockwell Internat. Corp., 1975-80, adminstr. relocation and corp. personnel procedures, 1980-81, mgr. corp. policy, 1981-82; pres. John G. Willard Cons., 1982—. Contbr. articles to profl. jours. Mem. Am. Mensa Ltd., Internat. Platform Assn., Smithsonian Nat. Instn., NRA (marksmanship instr.), Stage 62, Kappa Tau Alpha, Alpha Tau Omega. Office: 360 Middlegate Dr Bethel Park PA 15102-1438 E-mail: jgw7@telerama.com.

WILLARD, KATHARINE STOCKTON, music educator; b. Nashville, Feb. 20, 1975; d. Robert Morgan Jr. and Corinne (Martin) Stockton; m. Mark Aaron Willard, Sept. 27, 1997. MusB, Samford U., 1997; MM, U. Ala., 2000. Piano tchr. First Bapt. Centerpoint, Birmingham, Ala., 1995-96; children's music dir. Covenant Presbyn. Ch., 1995-99; piano instr. Samford U., 1996-2000; centrifuge staff Bapt. Sunday Sch. Bd., Nashville, 1996-97; presch. choir dir. Hunter St. Bapt. Ch., 1999—; faculty piano Ga. Southwestern State U., 2000—. Performer City Stages, 1995. Winner ARIA award Samford U., 1995, 96. Mem. Music Tchrs. Nat. Assn., Hypatia Honors Soc., Omicron Delta Kappa, Phi Kappa Lambda. Avocations: running, writing, reading, hiking.

WILLARD, LOUIS CHARLES, librarian; b. Tallahassee, Sept. 28, 1937; s. Bert and Rose (De Milly) W.; m. Nancy Booth, June 22, 1963. BA, U. Fla., 1959; BD, Yale, 1965, MA, 1967, PhD, 1970. Tchr. Tripoli (Lebanon) Boys' Sch., 1959-62; ordained to ministry Presbyn. Ch., 1965; acting librarian Princeton Theol. Sem., 1968-69, librarian, 1969-86; librarian, mem. faculty Harvard Div. Sch., 1986-99; dir. accreditation and instnl. evaluation Assn. Theol. Schs., 1999—. Mem. A.L.A., Theol. Library Assn., Soc. Bibl. Lit., Am. Acad. Religion, Phi Beta Kappa, Chi Phi. Home: PO Box 569 136 Centennial Ave Apt 201 Sewickley PA 15143-1248 Office: Assn Theol Schs 10 Summit Park Dr Pittsburgh PA 15275-1103 Address: PO Box 569 Sewickley PA 15143-0569 E-mail: willard@ats.edu.

WILLARD, NANCY MARGARET, writer, educator; b. Ann Arbor, Mich. d. Hobart Hurd and Margaret (Sheppard) W.; m. Eric Lindbloom, Aug. 15, 1964; 1 child, James Anatole. BA, U. Mich., 1958, PhD, 1963; MA, Stanford U., 1960. Lectr. English Vassar Coll., Poughkeepsie, N.Y., 1965—. Author: (poems) In His Country: Poems, 1966; Skin of Grace, 1967; A New Herball: Poems, 1968, Testimony of the Invisible Man: William Carlos Williams, Francis Ponge, Rainer Maria Rilke, Pablo Neruda, 1970, Nineteen Masks for the Naked Poet: Poems, 1971, The Carpenter of the Sun: Poems, 1974, A Visit to William Blake's Inn: Poems for Innocent and Experienced Travelers, 1981 (Newbery Medal 1982), Household Tales of Moon and Water, 1983, Water Walker, 1989, The Ballad of Biddy Early, 1989; (short stories) The Lively Anatomy of God, 1968, Childhood of the Magician, 1973; (juveniles) Sailing to Cythera and Other Anatole Stories, 1974, All on a May Morning, 1975, The Snow Rabbit, 1975, Shoes Without Leather, 1976, T0e Well-Mannered Balloon, 1976, Night Story, 1986, Simple Pictures are Best, 1977, Stranger's Bread, 1977, The Highest Hit, 1978, Papa's Panda, 1979, The Island of the Grass King, 1979, The Marzipan Moon 1981, Uncle Terrible, 1982, (adult) Angel in the Parlor: Five Stories and Eight Essays, 1983, The Nightgown of the Sullen Moon, 1983, Night Story, 1986, The Voyage of the Ludgate Hill, 1987, The Mountains of Quilt, 1987, Firebrat, 1988; (novel) Things Invisible To See, 1984, Sister Water, 1993; (play) East of the Sun, West of the Moon, 1989, The High Rise Glorious Skittle Skat Roarious Sky Pie Angel Food Cake, 1991, A Nancy Willard Reader, 1991, Pish Posh said Hieronymus Bosch, 1991, Beauty and the Beast, 1992; illustrator: The Letter of John to James, Another Letter of John to James, 1982, The Octopus Who Wanted to Juggle (Robert Pack), 1990, (novel) Sister Water, 1993, (essays) Telling Time, 1993, (juvenile) A Starlit Somersault Downhill, 1993, (juvenile) The Sorcerer's Apprentice, 1993; author, illustrator: An Alphabet of Angels, 1994; (juvenile) Gutenberg's Gift, 1995, The Good Night Blessing Book, 1996, Cracked Corn and Snow Ice Cream, 1997, The Tortilla Cat, 1998; (poems, with Jane Yolen) Among Angels, 1995, Swimming Lessons, 1996, The Magic Cornfield, 1997; editor: (anthology of poems) Step Lightly: Poems for the Journey, 1998, The Tale I Told Sasha, 1999, (juvenile) Shadow Story, 1999, (juvenile) The Moon and Riddler Diner and the Sunny Side Cafe, 2001. Recipient Hopwood award, 1958, Devins Meml. award, 1967, John Newbery award, 1981, Empire State award, 1996; Woodrow Wilson fellow, 1960; NEA grantee, 1987. Mem. The Lewis Carroll Soc., The George MacDonald Soc., Movable Book Soc. Office: Vassar Coll Dept English Raymond Ave Poughkeepsie NY 12604-0001

WILLARD, RALPH LAWRENCE, surgery educator, physician, former college president; b. Manchester, Iowa, Apr. 6, 1922; s. Hosea B. and Ruth A. (Hazelrigg) W.; m. Norma L. Hattel, Nov. 12, 1943 (div. 1968); children: Laurie, Jane, Ann, H. Thomas; m. Margaret Dyer Dennis, Sept. 26, 1969. Student, Cornell Coll., 1940-42, Coe Coll., 1945; D.O., Kirksville Coll. Osteo. Medicine, 1949; EdD (hon.), U. North Tex., 1985; ScD (hon.), W.Va. Sch. Osteo. Medicine, 1993. Intern Kirksville Osteo. Hosp., 1949-50, resident in surgery, 1954-57; chmn. dept. surgery Davenport Osteo. Hosp., 1957-68; dean, prof. surgery Kirksville Coll. Osteo. Medicine, 1969-73; asso. dean acad. affairs, prof. surgery Mich. State U. Coll. Osteo. Medicine, 1974-75; dean Tex. Coll. Osteopathic Medicine, 1975-76, pres., 1981-85, prof. surgery, 1985-87; v.p. med. affairs North Tex. State U., Denton, 1976-81; assoc. dean W.Va. Sch. Osteo. Medicine, Lewisburg, 1988-91. Mem. Nat. Adv. Council Edn. for Health Professions, 1971-73, Iowa Gov.'s Council Hosps. and Health Related Facilities, 1965-68; chmn. council deans Am. Assn. Colls. Osteo. Medicine, 1970-73, pres., 1979-80 Served with USAAF, 1942-45; Served with USAF, 1952-53; col. USAFR, ret. Decorated D.F.C., Air medal with 4 oak leaf clusters, Meritorious Svc. medal, Legion of Merit; recipient Robert A. Kistner Educator award Am. Assn. Colls. Osteo. Medicine, 1989; named Disting. scholar Acad. Osteo. Medicine Nat. Acads. Practice, 2000. Fellow Am. Coll. Physician Execs., Am. Coll. Osteo. Surgeons; mem. Am. Osteo. Assn. (Disting. Svc. cert. 1992), Tex. Osteo. Assn., W.Va. Soc. Osteo. Medicine, Am. Acad. Osteopathy, Acad. Osteo. Dirs. Med. Edn., Quiet Birdmen, Davis-Monthan Officers Club, Masons, Shriners, Ft. Worth Rotary (Paul Harris fellow), Internat. Comanche Soc., Order of Daedalians. Democrat. Episcopalian. Address: PO Box 79267 Fort Worth TX 76179-0267 E-mail: willardrl@aol.com. *The wise man has faith, the fool is he who betrays that faith.*

WILLARD, RICHARD KENNON, lawyer; b. Houston, Sept. 1, 1948; s. Fair McDaniel Willard and Elsbeth Rowe (Kennon) Willard Armistead; m. Leslie Harral Hopkins, July 10, 1976; children: Stephen Hopkins, Lauren Suzanne. BA, Emory U., 1969; JD, Harvard U., 1975. Bar: D.C. 1988, Tex. 1978, Ga. 1975. Law clk. U.S. Ct. Appeals, San Francisco, 1975-76, U.S. Supreme Ct., Washington, 1976-77; atty. Baker & Botts, Houston, 1977-81; counsel for intelligence policy U.S. Dept. Justice, Washington, 1981-82; dep. asst. atty. gen. civil div., 1982-83, asst. atty. gen., 1983-88; ptnr. Steptoe & Johnson, 1988-99; sr. v.p., gen. counsel The Gillette Co., 1999—. Adj. prof. Georgetown U. Law Ctr., 1991-96. Note editor: Harvard U. Law Rev., 1974-75. Gen. counsel Republican Party of Tex., Austin, 1980-81. Served to 1st lt. U.S. Army, 1969-72. Mem. Met. Club. Epsicopalian. Office: Prudential Tower Bldg Boston MA 02199-8004

WILLARD, SHIRLEY ANN OGLE, museum director, editor; b. Morocco, Ind., Sept. 28, 1936; d. Charlie Ernest and Maye Elizabeth (Nicewander) Ogle; m. Willis D. Willard, June 5, 1964; children: Thomas Jefferson, Doyle Allen, William Joseph. BA, Manchester Coll., 1959; MA, Ball State U., 1966. Cert. tchr., Ind. Tchr. Rock Creek Sch., Bluffton, Ind., 1959-60, Kewanna (Ind.) H.S., 1960-67, 76-77, North Miami H.S., Denver, 1968-73; reporter, page editor Rochester (Ind.) Sentinel, 1975-76; mus. dir. Fulton County Hist. Soc., Rochester, 1978—2001, editor, pres., 1971—2001. Editor, author: Fulton County Folks, Vol. 1, 1974, Vol. 2, 1981; editor Fulton County FolkFinder, 1982—, Indian Awareness newsletter, 1983—. Sec. Indian Awareness Ctr., Rochester, 1982—; founder, dir. Trail of Courage Living History Festival, Rochester, 1976—; organizer, leader Trail of Death Commemorative Caravan, 1988, 93, 98; founder Trail of Death Regional Hist. Trail, Ind.-Kans., 1994—, editor, 1994—; mem. hist. marker com. Ind. Hist. Soc., 1989-96; rural preservation com. Hist. Landmarks Found. Ind., 1992—; founder Living History Village called Loyal, Rochester, Ind. Named Outstanding Young Woman Manchester Coll., 1982, Sagamore of the Wabash, State of Ind., 2001; recipient 20 Yrs. Leadership award Am. Assn. State and Local History, 1989, Cmty. Svc. award Rochester C. of C., 1986, Disting Svc. award Ind. Humanities Coun., 1994, Dorothy Riker awrad for innovation in field of history Ind. Hist. Soc., 2001. Mem. Nat. Coun. History Edn., Assn. Ind. Mus. Republican. Lutheran. Avocations: reading, writing, historic dancing, living history festivals. Home: 3063 S 425 E Rochester IN 46975-8233 Office: Fulton County Hist Soc 37 E 375 N Rochester IN 46975-8384 E-mail: wwillard@rtcol.com.

WILLARD, TIMOTHY J. higher education executive, consultant; b. Denver, June 24, 1943; m. Carmen A. McCanna, June 10, 1967; children: Anna, Adam, Elizabeth. BA, Regis Coll., Denver, 1965; MA, U. Colo., 1970, PhD, 1984; postgrad., Harvard U., 1995. Cert. fund raising exec. Instr. English Regis H.S., Denver, 1965-73, chmn. dept. English, 1973-74, asst. to prin., 1974-75, asst. to headmaster, 1975-77, dir. devel., 1977, Regis Coll., 1977-80, U. San Diego, 1980-86, capital campaign dir., 1986-92; v.p. univ. advancement Millikin U., Decatur, Ill., 1992-95; v.p. devel. and instl. advancement Fontbonne Coll., St. Louis, 1996-2001; v.p. devel. Ranken Tech. Coll., 2001—, 2001—. Cons. U. Dallas, 1994; mem. devel. com. Assoc. Colls. Ill., Chgo., 1995; speaker in field. Author articles. Chair pub. svc. and edn. United Way of Decatur and Macon County, Ill., 1994-95; bd. dirs. Gallery 510, Decatur, 1994-95, Family Svc. Assn., San Diego, 1984-92, ARC; mem. strategic planning com. Holy Family Sch.; mem. FOCUS St. Louis, 1996—, St. Louis Planned Giving Coun., 1997—. Recipient Bd. Trustees commendation U. San Diego, 1992, Outstanding Leadership award Kiwanis Club of San Diego Found., 1991. Mem. Coun. for Advancement and Support of Edn., Assn. Fundraising Profls. E-mail: tjwillard@ranken.org., twillard@peoplepc.com.

WILLAUER, GEORGE JACOB, English literature educator; b. Oct. 30, 1935; s. George Jacob and Mary Catherine (Eshleman) W.; m. Cynthia Cameron Thun, June 11, 1966; children: George Jacob III, Elizabeth Christian. BA, Wesleyan U., 1957; MA, U. Pa., 1959, PhD, 1965. Asst. instr. U. Pa., Phila., 1958-62; instr. Conn. Coll., New London, 1962-66, asst. prof., 1966-72, assoc. prof., 1972-78, prof., 1978—2002, chair dept. English, 1972—77, 1991—94, 2000—02. Charles J. MacCurdy prof. of Am. Studies, 1993-2002; coll. marshal, 1989-2002, dean of acad. programs, 1997-2000; instr. Williams Coll.-Mystic Seaport Program in Maritime Studies, 1986-88; vis. prof. lit. U. Dar es Salaam, Tanzania, 1995. Author: A Lyme Miscellany: 1776-1976, 1977; contbr. articles to profl. jours. Trustee Cmty. Found. Southeastern Conn., pres., Lyme Hist. Soc., Florence Griswold Mus., pres. 1983-88, Lymes Youth Svc. Bur., 1978-83, Lyme Land Conservation Trust, 1996-2002, Lyme Pub. Libr., Lyman Allyn Art Mus., MacCurdy-Salisbury Ednl. Found. English-Speaking Union fellow, 1969, 72. Mem. AAUP, MLA, Century Assn. Home: 55-1 Beaver Brook Rd Old Lyme CT 06371-3219 Office: Conn Coll New London CT 06320

WILLAUER, WHITING RUSSELL, consultant; b. Boston, May 24, 1931; s. Whiting Russell and Louise Knapp (Russell) Willauer; m. Julie Mackie McConine, Mar. 15, 2001; stepchildren: Frances Moran McConine, Marguerite Isabelle McConine; m. Julie Matheson Arnold, July 11, 1959 (div.); children: Whiting Russell, Jr., William Arnold. BS, Princeton U., 1955, MS, 1959; PhD, Georgetown U., 1964. Research assoc. joint research com. Dept. Def., 1951-52; ops. mgr. Civil Air Transport Airline Taiwan, 1952-53; scientist Analytic Services, Inc., 1958-61; asst. prof. astronomy Georgetown U., 1965-68; mgr. TRW Systems Group support to chief Naval ops., McLean, Va., 1968-73, TRW Antisubmarine projects, 1973-79, TRW Ship Acquisition project, 1979-85; advanced systems mgr. TRW Systems Integration Group, 1985-90, cost estimating mgr., 1990-95, sr. cons., 1995-99; sr. v.p., chief strategist K12Nation.net, 1999-2000. Cons. Nat. Geog. Soc., 1961-65, U. Tex., 1962, NSF, 1963, Booz-Allen & Hamilton, 1966-67 Mng. editor: Jour. Astronautical Scis, 1969-71; Designer: Orrery (planetarium) on permanent exhibit, New Explorers Hall, Nat. Geog. Soc. Asst. chief steward Alpine Venue XIII Olympic Winter Games, Lake Placid, 1980; mem. U.S. Olympic Com., bd. dirs., 1987-94, sec. nat. governing bodies, 1989-92, mem. membership svcs. com., 1988-92, mem. athletic devel. com., 1992-96; chef de mission Winter Pan Am. Games, Las Lenas, Argentina, 1990; asst. chief de mission XVI Winter Olympics, Albertville, France, 1992; U.S. Olympic Com. liaison to VI Paralympic Winter Games, Lillehammer, Norway, 1994. Research fellow Georgetown U., 1961-65 Fellow AAAS (coun.); mem. Am. Astronautical Soc. (v.p. fin.), Blue Ridge Ski Coun. (pres. 1976-78), U.S. Ski Assn. (pres. 1982-87, Julius Blegan award 1988, Mary and Bud Little award 1998), U.S. Ski and Snowboard Assn. (vice chmn. 1994-96, trustee emeritus 1997—), Internat. Ski Fedn. (chmn. U.S. del. 1983, 85, chmn. recreational skiing com. 1987-98, eligibility com. 1988-98), Ea. Ski Assn. (treas. 1980-82), Pan Am Sports Orgn. (winter games adv. com. 1988—), Sigma Xi, Chevy Chase Club (Md.), Nantucket Yacht Club (Mass.) (commodore 1981-83, bd. govs. 1957-59, 68—). E-mail: willauer@erols.com.

WILLBANKS, ROGER PAUL, publishing and book distributing company executive; b. Denver, Nov. 25, 1934; s. Edward James and Ada Gladys (Keller) W.; m. Beverly Rae Masters, June 16, 1957; children: Wendy Lee, Roger Craig. BS, U. Denver, 1957, MBA, 1965. Economist, bus. writer, bus. forecaster U.S. West, Denver, 1959-65; dir. pub. rels. Denver Bd. Water Commrs., 1967-70; pres. Royal Publs. Inc., Denver, 1971—, Nutri-Books Corp., Denver, 1971—, Inter-Sports Book and Video, Denver, 1986—. Editor Denver Water News, 1967-70, Mountain States Bus., 1962-66. Mem. Gov. of Colo.'s Revenue Forecasting Com., 1963-66. With U.S. Army, 1957-58. Recipient Pub. Rels. award Am. Water Works Assn., 1970, Leadership award Nat. Inst. Nutritional Edn., 1989, Medal of Freedom, U.S. Senate, 1994. Mem. Am. Booksellers Assn., Nat. Nutritional Foods Assn., Pub. Rels. Soc. Am. (charter mem. health sect.), Denver C. of C., SAR, Aspen Glen Club, Denver Press Club, Auburn Cord Duesenberg Club, Rolls Royce Owners Club, Classic Car of Am. Club, Denver U. Chancellor's Soc., Ferrari Owners Club. Republican. Lutheran. Address: Royal Publs Inc PO Box 5793 Denver CO 80217-5793

WILLCOCKS, HAROLD JOHN, retired project engineer; b. London, Mar. 27, 1920; came to U.S., 1968; s. William Lock and Lillian Harriet (Royston) W.; m. Anne Boyd Ringland, June 16, 1945; children: Rosemary Anne Glithero, Raymond Harold Willcocks. MS in Aerospace Propulsion, Cranfield Inst. Tech., Bedford, Eng., 1958. Enlisted RAF, 1936, advanced through grades to squadron leader, 1958, ret., 1968; sr. scientific officer Nat. Gas Turbine Establishment, Farnborough, Eng., 1958-62; engine installation mgr. F111 S.P.O. USAF, Dayton, Ohio, 1966-68; project engr. Pratt & Whitney Aircraft, East Hartford, Conn., 1968-76, West Palm Beach, Fla., 1976-86, ret., 1986. Cons. In-Flight Thrust Com., SAE, 1976-86; mem. Ground Test Com., AIAA, 1977-82; cons. Take-Off Monitor Com., 1982-86. Assoc. fellow Am. Inst. Aero and Astronautics (mem. Turbine Engine Test Group 1968—); mem. Masons, Shriners. Achievements include writing first requirement for electronic turbine engine controls, 1963. Avocations: golf, helping crippled and burned children through Shriners. Home: 9872 SE Little Club Way S Tequesta FL 33469-1368

WILLCOX, RODERICK HARRISON, lawyer; b. Columbus, Ohio, Jan. 10, 1934; s. Richard V. and Marcella A. (Rehl) W.; m. Rita Kay Click, July 2, 1955; children: Sharon Marie Willcox Hazlewood, Kathy Lynn, Patricia Ann Willcox Hanna, Roderick Harrison Jr. BA, Williams Coll., 1955; LLB, U. Mich., 1958. Ptnr. Chester, Willcox & Saxbe, Columbus, Ohio, 1971—. Office: Chester Willcox & Saxbe LLP 17 S High St Ste 900 Columbus OH 43215-3442 E-mail: rwillcox@cwslaw.com.

WILLE, KARIN L. lawyer; b. Northfield, Minn., Dec. 14, 1949; d. James Virginia Wille. BA summa cum laude, Macalester Coll., 1971; JD cum laude, U. Minn., 1974. Bar: Minn. 1974, U.S. Dist. Ct. Minn. 1974. Atty. Dresselhuis & Assoc., Mpls., 1974-75; assoc. Dorsey & Whitney, 1975-76; atty. Dayton-Hudson Corp., 1976-84; gen. counsel B. Dalton Booksellers, Edina, Minn., 1985-87; assoc. Briggs & Morgan, Mpls., 1987-88; shareholder Briggs and Briggs, 1988—. Co-chair Upper Midwest Employment Law Inst., 1983—. Named Leading Minn. Atty., Super Lawyer, Mpls.-St. Paul Mag., Twin Cities Bus. Monthly and Minn. Law and Politics; named one of Best Lawyers in Am. Mem. ABA, Minn. State Bar Assn. (labor and employment sect., corp. counsel sect., dir. 1989-91), Hennepin County Bar Assn. (labor and employment sect.), Minn. Women Lawyers, Phi Beta Kappa. Office: Briggs & Morgan 80 S 8th St Ste 2400 Minneapolis MN 55402-2157 E-mail: kwille@briggs.com.

WILLE, LOIS JEAN, retired newspaper editor; b. Chgo., Sept. 19, 1931; d. Walter and Adele S. (Taege) Kroeber; m. Wayne M. Wille, June 6, 1954. BS, Northwestern U., 1953, MS, 1954; Litt.D. (hon.), Columbia Coll., Chgo., 1980, Northwestern U., 1990, Rosary Coll., 1990. Reporter Chgo. Daily News, 1958-74, nat. corr., 1975-76, assoc. editor charge editorial page, 1977; assoc. editor charge editorial and opinion pages Chgo. Sun-Times, 1978-83; assoc. editor editorial page Chgo. Tribune, 1984-87, editor editorial page, 1987-91, ret., 1991. Author: Forever Open, Clear and Free: the Historic Struggle for Chicago's Lakefront, 1972, At Home in the Loop: How Clout and Community Built Chicago's Dearborn Park, 1997. Recipient Pulitzer prize for public svc., 1963, Pulitzer prize for editorial writing, 1989, William Allen White Found. award for excellence in editorial writing, 1978, numerous awards Chgo. Newspaper Guild, numerous awards Chgo. Headline Club, numerous awards Nat. Assn. Edn. Writers, numerous awards Ill. AP, numerous awards Ill. UPI. Home: 1530 S State St Apt 1011 Chicago IL 60605 E-mail: lowille@aol.com.

WILLE, ROSANNE LOUISE, higher education administrator; b. Hackensack, N.J., Aug. 4, 1941; d. Albert Wille and Rose Marie (Rock) Eberhardt; m. George B. Jacobs, Mar. 12, 1980; children: Leigh, Steven, Alexander, Jeffrey. M Pub. Adminstrn., Rutgers U., 1986; PhD, N.Y.U., 1980. Dept. chair Rutgers U., Newark, 1978-84, Lehman Coll., Bronx, NY, 1984-87, dean, 1987-92, provost, sr. v.p., 1992—2002; cons. for higher edn., 2002—. Contbr. articles to profl. jours. Bd. dirs. Family Support Svcs., Bronx, N.Y., 1994—, bd. dirs. South Bronx Overall Economic Devel., Inc., Bronx, 1991—. Recipient Vision award Family Support Svcs., Bronx, 1996, Thousand Points of Light award Pres. George Bush, Washington, 1991. Mem. N.Y. Acad. Scis., N.Y. Acad. Medicine, Am. Assn. Higher Edn. Avocations: aviation, golf. E-mail: rlwille@earthlink.net.

WILLE, WAYNE MARTIN, retired editor; b. Des Plaines, Ill., Nov. 17, 1930; s. Clarence Louis and Lois Naomi (Martin) W.; m. Lois Jean Kroeber, June 6, 1954. BSJ, Northwestern U., 1952, MSJ, 1953. Reporter Chgo. Sun Times, 1956-57; dir. press info. WBBM-TV and CBS-TV, Chgo., 1957-58; feature editor Sci. and Mechanics mag., 1958-60, mng. editor, 1960-62; news editor Nat. Safety Council, Chgo., 1962-64, asst. dir. pub. info., 1964-67; mng. editor World Book Year Book, 1967-69; exec. editor World Book Yr. Book, 1969-83; mng. editor World Book Yr. Book and Sci. Yr. and Health & Med. Ann., 1983-91. Served with AUS, 1953-55. Mem. Chgo. Headline Club (pres. 1967-68), Soc. Profl. Journalists, Art Inst. Chgo., Oriental Inst. Clubs: La Salle Street Rod and Gun.

WILLEMS, CONSTANCE CHARLES, lawyer; b. Zuilen, Utrecht, The Netherlands, Oct. 31, 1942; came to U.S., 1967, naturalized, 1977; d. Anton Henri and Maria (Van der Meys) Charles; m. Cornelis Franciscus Willems, May 25, 1965; 1 son, Maurice. BA in Sociology magna cum laude, U. New Orleans, 1974; JD with honors, Tulane U., 1977. Bar: La. 1977, U.S. Dist. Ct. (ea. dist.) La. 1977, U.S. Ct. Appeals (5th cir.) 1977, U.S. Dist. Ct. (mid. dist.) La. 1979, U.S. Supreme Ct. 1983, U.S. Dist. Ct. (we. dist.) La. 1997. Assoc. McGlinchey, Stafford, Mintz, Cellini and Lang, New Orleans, 1977-81, ptnr., 1982—, now McGlinchey Stafford, New Orleans. Instr. law office mgmt. Loyola U. Sch. Law, 1986—90; instr. European law Tulane U. Sch. Law, New Orleans, 1994, New Orleans, 96, New Orleans, 98; bd. mem. World Trade Ctr. New Orleans, 2001. Mem. task force on municipalization; hon. consul for The

Netherlands, 1989—; sec.-treas. Consular Corps.; bd. visitors Coll. Liberal Arts, U. New Orleans, 1995—, pres., 1999—; bd. dirs. United Way Agy. Rels. Com., 1987—91, Coun. Internat. Visitors, 1992—94, Com. of 21, 1994—, New Orleans Opera Assn., 1995—. Recipient Disting. alumni award U. New Orleans, 1989. Mem. ABA, La. Assn. Women Attys. (pres. 1983-85, 86-87), La. State Bar Assn. (mem. ho. dels. 1984-85, chair internat. law sect. 1994—), Dutch-Am. Bus. Coun. (founder), New Orleans Ballet Assn. (sec. 2000—). Office: McGlinchey Stafford 643 Magazine St New Orleans LA 70130-3477

WILLENBECHER, JOHN, artist; b. Macungie, Pa., May 5, 1936; s. John George and Geneva (Bacon) W. BA, Brown U., 1958; postgrad., N.Y. U., Inst. Fine Arts, 1958-61. Sculptor-mem. N.Y.C. Art Commn., 1980-92; mem. commn. for plaza and pavillion, Mpls. Inst. Arts, 1991. Exhibited in one-man shows including Hamilton Gallery Contemporary Art, N.Y.C., 1977, 80, U. Mass. Art Gallery, Amherst, 1977, Wright State U. Art Gallery, Dayton, Ohio, 1977, Jaffe-Friede Gallery, Dartmouth Coll., Hanover, N.H., 1977, Fine Arts Ctr. U. R.I., Kingston, 1978, Neuberger Mus., SUNY at Purchase, 1979, Allentown (Pa.) Art Mus., 1979, Mpls. Inst. Arts, 1993, U. N.Mex. Art Gallery, Albuquerque, 1996; exhibited in numerous group shoes including Albright-Knox Art Gallery, Buffalo, 1963, Whitney Mus. Am. Art, N.Y.C., 1964-68; represented in permanent collections including Solomon R. Guggenheim Mus., N.Y.C., Met. Mus., N.Y.C., Whitney Mus. Am. Art, Albright-Knox Art Gallery, Phila. Mus. Art, Centre d'Art et Culture Georges Pompidou, Paris, Hirshhorn Mus. and Sculpture Garden, Washington, Art Inst. Chgo. Nat. Endowment for Arts grantee, 1977, Esther and Adolph Gottlieb Found. grantee, 1994. Achievements include being subject of profl. articles and catalogues.

WILLENBRINK, ROSE ANN, lawyer; b. Louisville, Apr. 20, 1950; d. J.L. Jr. and Mary Margaret (Williams) W.; m. William I. Cornett Jr. Student, U. Chgo., 1968-70; BA in Anthropology with highest honors, U. Louisville, 1973, JD, 1975. Bar: Ky. 1976, Ind. 1976, U.S. Dist. Ct. (we. dist.) Ky. 1976, Ohio 1999. Atty. Mapother & Mapother, Louisville, 1976-79; v.p., counsel Nat. City Bank, 1980-99, v.p., sr. atty. Cleve., 1999—. Mem. ABA, Ohio Bar Assn., Ky. Bar Assn., Louisville Bar Assn., Conf. on Consumer Fin. Law, Corp. House Counsel Assn., Phi Kappa Phi. Home: 359 Glengarry Dr Aurora OH 44202-8584 Office: Nat City Bank 1900 E 9th St Cleveland OH 44114-3484 E-mail: Rose.Ann.Willenbrink@nationalcity.com.

WILLENZ, JUNE ADELE, writer, public affairs executive, playwright, screenwriter, writer, columnist, scholar, speaker; BS, U. Mich., 1945, MA, 1947; ABD, New Sch. for Social Rsch., 1951. Instr. English, Montgomery Coll., Md. Exec. dir. Am. Vets. Com., 1965—; chair standing com. on women World Vet. Fedn., 1983—; conf. organizer Women In and After War, Bellagio, Italy, Rape in Armed Conflicts, Istanbul; lectr. USIA; radio and TV guest appearances; honored guest internat. vets. assns.; del. White House Conf. on Youth, White House Conf. Aging; planning com. 5th and 6th legis. confs. World Vets. Fedn.; presenter UN; scholar in residence Am. U., 1997—; NGO rep. to UN; lectr. and spkr. on internat. women's veterans issues; social and polit. commentator; rep. for U.S. Internat. Seminar on Peace Keeping, Baeria, Norway, 2001. Author: Women Veterans: America's Forgotten Heroines, 1983; co-author: Gender Differences, 1991; editor, author: Dialogue on the Draft, 1967, Human Rights of the Man in Uniform, 1969; editor: AVC Bull.; presenter Am. Hist. Assn., Am. Polit. Sci. Assn.; columnist Stars and Stripes; advisor, commentator (documentary film) The GI Bill: The Law That Changed America, 1997; contbr. articles to profl. jours. Exec. com. 1st VA Adv. Com. Womens Vets., 1983—86, First Lady's Women's Conf. Cir., 1995; com. mem. UN Decade for Women, head of working group on refugee women and women in armed conflict; accredited non-govtl. orgn. rep. UN; organizer Workshops on Refugee Women, Armed Conflict, Gender Justice, and other issues at UN; pub. mem. 19th Fgn. Officer Selection Bd. USIA; chair Task Force on Vets. and Mil. Affairs for Leadership Com. on Civil Rights; spkr. Nat. Urban League, Ctr. for Policy Rsch., Nat. League of Cities Vets. Program; advisor; co-chair Coordinating Com. on Voluntary Nat. Svc.; organizer nat. conf. Dialogue on Nat. Svc., 1989, The Draft, 1966, Human Rights of Man in Uniform, 1968, 1970; spkr. NAACP, Ednl. Problems of Vietnam Vets., 1972; chair subcom. on disabled vets. Pres. Com. Employment of People with Disabilities, 1995—96; active Inter-Univ. Seminar Armed Forces & Soc.; adviser Vets. Brain Trust Conf., 1997; presenter UN Experts meetings, 1993, 1996. Recipient La Médaille de la Ville de Paris, Mayor of Paris, 2000, Human Rights award, UNA Nat. Capital, 2001, honored by Congl. Black Caucus, 1997, honored for outstanding leadership on behalf of disabled vets., U.S. Dept. Labor, 2002. Mem. Non-Govtl. Orgn. Com. on Status of Women (convener task force on women in armed conflict, convener working group on refugee women), Authors Guild.

WILLER, EDWARD HERMAN, real estate broker; b. Concord, N.C., June 12, 1941; s. Emil Francis and Mary (McKinley) W.; m. Cornelia Campbell, Nov. 30, 1963; children: Laura Campbell, Edward Groves. AB, Davidson Coll., 1963. V.p., sales mgr. Bacon & Co., Realtors, Raleigh, N.C., 1971-84; pres. residential div. York Properties, Inc., 1984—2001. Treas. N.C. Real Estate Ednl. Found., Greensboro, 1984, pres., 1988; bd. dirs. Rex Hosp. Found., Raleigh, 1988-89, Relo, The Internat. Referral Network, Inc., Chgo., dir., 1988-92, treas., 1992. Author: Real Estate Exam Ready Book, 1984; contbr. articles to profl. jours. Bd. dirs. Ea. N.C. Multiple Sclerosis Soc., Raleigh, 1982-85; campaign chair United Way of Wake County, 1996, bd. dirs., 1994-2000, mem. exec. com., 1996-97, treas., 2001—. 1st lt. U.S. Army, 1963-66, Vietnam. Named Realtor of the Year, 1984. Mem. Nat. Assn. Realtors (cert.), N.C. Assn. Realtors (bd. dirs. 1978-82), N.C. Real Estate Ednl. Found. (pres.), Raleigh Bd. Realtors (pres. 1979), Greater Raleigh C. of C. (bd. dirs. 1991-94), Quite Birdmen Club. Democrat. Presbyterian. Avocations: teaching, flying, woodworking. Home: 1512 Saint Mary's St Raleigh NC 27608-2217 Office: York Simpson Underwood 311 Oberlin Rd Raleigh NC 27605-3125

WILLERDING, MARGARET FRANCES, mathematician, educator; b. St. Louis, Apr. 26, 1919; d. Herman J. and Mildred F. (Icenhower) W. AB, Harris Tchrs. Coll., 1940; MA, St. Louis U., 1943, PhD, 1947. Tchr. (Pub. Schs.), St. Louis, 1940-46; instr. math. Washington U., 1947-48; asst. prof. Harris Tchrs. Coll., 1948-56; mem. faculty San Diego State Coll., 1956—, asso. prof., 1959-65, prof. math., 1966-76, prof. emeritus, 1976—. Author: Intermediate Algebra, 1969, Elementary Mathematics, 1971, College Algebra, 1971, College Algebra and Trigonometry, 1971, Arithmetic, 1968, Probability: The Science of Chance, 1969, Mathematics Around the Clock, 1969, Mathematical Concepts, 1967, From Fingers to Computers, 1969, Probability Primer, 1968, Mathematics: The Alphabet of Science, 1972, 74, 77, A First Course in College Mathematics, 1973, 77, 80, Mathematics Worktext, 1973, 77, Business and Consumer Mathematics for College Students, 1976, The Numbers Game, 1977. Mem. Nat. Council Tchrs. Math., Assn. Tchrs. Sci. and Math., Am. Math. Soc., Math. Assn. Am., Greater San Diego Math. Council (dir. 1963-65), Sigma Xi, Pi Mu Epsilon. Home: 10241 Vivera Dr La Mesa CA 91941-4370 Office: San Diego State Coll Dept Math San Diego CA 92085

WILLES, MARK HINCKLEY, media industry executive; b. Salt Lake City, July 16, 1941; s. Joseph Simmons and Ruth (Hinckley) W.; m. Laura Fayone, June 7, 1961; children: Wendy Anne, Susan Kay, Keith Mark, Stephen Joseph, Matthew Bryant. AB, Columbia Coll., 1963, PhD, 1967. Staff banking and currency com. Ho. of Reps., Washington, 1966-67; asst. prof. fin. Wharton Sch. U. Pa., Phila., 1967-69; economist Fed. Res. Bank, 1967, sr. economist, 1969-70, dir. rsch., 1970-71, v.p., dir. rsch., 1971, 1st v.p., 1971-77; pres. Fed. Res. Bank of Mpls., 1977-80; exec. v.p., chief fin. officer Gen. Mills, Inc., Mpls., 1980-85, pres., COO, 1985-92, vice-chmn., 1992-95; chmn., pres., CEO Times Mirror Co., L.A., 1995-2000; pub. L.A. Times, 1997-99. Pres. Hawaii Honolulu Mission Ch. of LDS, 2001. Office: Hawaii Honolulu Mission Ch of LDS 1500 S Beretania St #410 Honolulu HI 96826 E-mail: willes@byu.edu. *My success is based on adherence to principles I learned in the home, which is the most basic and important organizational unit in the world. Three of those principles stand out in my mind: Be just, honest and moral—do things not only because they are required, but because they are right. Have mercy—care enough about others to be fair and kind. Be humble—you can get more done effectively with the help of others than you can do on your own.*

WILLET, E(VERETT) CROSBY, artist; b. Phila., Jan. 8, 1929; s. Henry Lee and Katharine Muriel (Crosby) W.; m. Augusta Winter, Nov. 27, 1954; children: William, Nancy Lee, Katharine Crosby, Henry Lee II. BA, Lafayette Coll., 1950; DFA (hon.), Orthodox Cath. Archdiocese, Phila., 1982. Apprentice Blenko Glass Co., Milton, W.Va., 1950; craftsman Willet Stained Glass Studio Inc., Phila., 1950-54, v.p., 1954-64, pres., 1964—. Works include: Portsmouth Priory, R.I., 1956, Folger Bay Washington Cathedral, 1973, murals Assocs. Dining Room, Smithsonian Instn., 1976, 2d Bapt. Ch., Houston, 1985-86, Gethsemane Cathedral, Fargo, N.D., 1992-95, Peachtree Road United Methodist Church, Atlanta, 2001. Recipient George Washington Kidd award Lafayette Coll., 1985. Fellow Stained Glass Assn. Am. (exec. bd. 1958-78, 81, pres. 1964-66); mem. InterFaith Forum, Religion, Art and Architecture (exec. bd. 1979—), Am. Soc. Appraisers (sr. mem.), Nantucket Yacht Club. Republican. Presbyterian. Home: 721 Davidson Rd Philadelphia PA 19118-4301 Office: Willet Stained Glass Studio Inc 10 E Moreland Ave Philadelphia PA 19118-3539 E-mail: crosbyw@earthlink.net.

WILLETT, ANNA HART, composer; b. Bartlesville, Okla., June 18, 1931; d. Thomas Kellogg and Mary Kathryn (Feist) Willett Dalferes; m. Roger Garland Horn, Aug. 1956 (div. June 1962). B in Music Edn., Southwestern La. Inst., 1954; MA, La. State U., 1964, postgrad. in piano, voice majors, 1976-87. Lifetime tchr. cert., La. Pub. sch. vocal music tchr. Iberville Parish, Plaquemine, La., 1954-55, Orleans Parish, New Orleans, 1966-71; elem. music pedagogy tchr. St. Mary's Dominican Coll., 1972. Post-grad. rsch. history life scholar in late Medieval English Crown changes LSU. Composer: Dances for Solo Violin, 1981, Weaving Song, 1982, Entertainer's Song, (from the opera Omar), 1983, Hercules Piano Variations, 1986, En Ivrez Solo Song, 1989, Solo Songson Poems of Alfieri, 1996, 2000, Variations on a Southern Folk Hymn for piano, Memories of New Orleans, variations for piano, voice Recital at Fest For All, Baton Rouge, La., (operas) How to Murder Mother, Who Murdered Mother, Omar, 1982, Cellini the Opera, Lines on Wine, Caught, Druid Installation, 1997, Seven Gables, 1998, The Icey Road, 1999. Mem. ch. choir St. Albans Episcopalian chapel, 1976—. Scholar Loyola U. of the South, New Orleans, 1972-73. Mem. AAUW, Alpha Sigma Alpha, Sigma Alpha Iota. Episcopalian. Avocations: gardening, bridge, local archeology. Home: 2244 Ferndale Ave Baton Rouge LA 70808-2830

WILLETT, CHRIS GODWIN, securities company executive, consultant; b. Norfolk, Va., Dec. 24, 1955; s. Elbert Henry and Jean Daly (Lloyd) W.; m. Marian Potts, July 29, 1978 (div. June 1984); 1 child, Hellen Lloyd; m. Elizabeth Harley, Aug. 30, 1986; 1 child, Catherine Cahill. BA cum laude, Washington and Lee U., 1978; MA, Jacksonville (Ala.) State U., 1980. Account exec. Sta. WDNG, Anniston, Ala., 1978-79; tchr. Altamont Sch., Birmingham, 1980-82; account exec. E.F. Hutton Securities, Atlanta, 1982-88, coord. direct investments, 1984-88; v.p. investments, quantum portfolio mgr. Prudential Bache Securities, 1988-96; ptnr. J.C. Bradford & Co., 1996-2000; sr. v.p. Legg Mason Wood & Walker, 2000—. Retirement planning cons. Bd. dirs. Support to Employment Project, Atlanta, 1986—. Mem. Internat. Soc. Retirement Planners, Buckhead Fifty Club, Kiwanis (sec. Atlanta 1989-90, pres. 1993-94), Phi Alpha Theta (hon. historian 1979). Avocations: tennis, golf, running, reading. Home: 2396 Christophers Walk NW Atlanta GA 30327-1110 Office: Legg Mason Wood & Walker 3414 Peachtree Rd Ste 1100 Atlanta GA 30326

WILLETT, LANCE, orchestra executive; Exec. dir. Quad City Symphony Orch., Davenport, Iowa, 1982—. Office: Quad City Symphony Orch Assn PO Box 1144 Davenport IA 52805-1144*

WILLETT, ROSLYN LEONORE, public relations executive, food service consultant, writer; d. Edward and Celia (Stickler) Sternberg; m. Edward Willett (separated); 1 child, Jonathan Stanley. BA, Hunter Coll., N.Y.C.; postgrad., Columbia U., CUNY, NYU, New Sch. Dietitian YWCA, N.Y.C.; tech. and patents libr. Stein Hall & Co., food technologist in charge tech. svcs. and devel. dept.; editor McGraw-Hill, Inc., Harcourt Brace Jovanovich, Inc., N.Y.C.; pub. rels. writer Farley Manning Assocs.; cons. pub. rels. and food svc. Roslyn Willett Assocs., Inc., 1959—. Adj. prof. Hunter Coll., Poly U., Columbia U. Sch. Pub. Health; seminar presenter in field. Author: The Woman Executive in Woman in Sexist Society, 1971, short stories. V.p. North Shore Ams. for Dem. Action; ofcl. rapporteur Post-Assembly Tech. Sessions; WHO; juror Am. Film Festival, Arts and Scis. , 1962—88; chmn. Women's Polit. Caucus, Inc. NY, NJ, Conn, 1971—73; v.p. Mid Hudson Arts and Sci. Ctr., Poughkeepsie, NY; apptd. to regional adv. coun. Fed. SBA, 1976—78; bd. dirs. Small Bus. Task Force, Assn. for Small Bus. and Professions , 1981—85, Rhinebeck Chamber Music Soc., 1985—86, Will Inst., New Paltz, 1980—2001, Women Studies Abstracts , 1971—81; pres. Hunns Lake Assn., 1999—2001. Mem. Pub. Rels. Soc. Am. (accredited), Food Svc. Cons. Soc. Internat. (bd. dirs.1978-80), N.Y. Acad. Scis., Inst. Food Technologists, Paris Club. Avocations: writing, dance, art collecting, hiking, swimming. Home: 97 W Hunns Lake Rd Stanfordville NY 12581-5606 Office: 441 West End Ave New York NY 10024-5328

WILLETT, THOMAS EDWARD, lawyer; b. N.Y.C., Nov. 8, 1947; s. Oscar Edward and Alice (Fleming) W.; m. Marilyn Kenney, Dec. 28, 1969; children: Thomas Justin, Christopher Joseph. BS, USAF Acad., Colo., 1969; JD with distinction, Cornell U., 1972. Bar: N.Y. 1973, U.S. Ct. Claims 1973, U.S. Supreme Ct. 1977. Judge advocate USAF, Syracuse, N.Y., 1973-75, Kincheloe AFB, Mich., 1975-77, USAF Hdqs., Washington, 1977-79; assoc. Harris, Beach & Wilcox, Rochester, N.Y., 1979-84, ptnr., 1985—. Pres. Monroe County Legal Assistance Corp., Rochester, 1983-89. Capt. USAF, 1969-79. Mem. ABA, N.Y. State Bar Assn., Monroe County Bar Assn., Order of Coif. Office: Harris Beach LLP 99 Garnsey Rd Pittsford NY 14534 E-mail: twillett@harrisbeach.com.

WILLEY, JAMES LEE, dentist; b. Colorado Springs, Colo., Oct. 26, 1953; s. Elwood James and Dorothy Jean (Norton) W.; m. Catherine Margaret Whitmer, Aug. 23, 1975; children: Andrew James and David Lee (twins). BA, So. Ill. U., 1975; BS in Dentistry, U. Ill., Chgo., 1977, DDS, 1979; MBA, No. Ill. U., 1986. Pvt. practice, Elburn, Ill., 1979—; pres. Elburn Dental, P.C., 2000—. Lectr. Dental Arts Labs., Peoria, Ill., 1981-90. Asst. scoutmaster Boy Scouts Am., Elburn, 1995—2001; village trustee Village of Elburn, 1995—97, fin. com., 1995—97, police com., 1995—96, pub. works com., 1996—97, village mayor, 1997—; mem. Kane County Stormwater Mgmt. Com., 1999—, vice chmn., 2000—; mem. Kane County Bd. Health Adv. Commn., 1999—; mem. adminstrv. bd. United Meth. Ch., 1991—92; trustee Paul W. Clopper Meml. Found., 1989—97, chmn. fund raising com., 1991—97, treas., 1992—97; spokesperson Prevent Abuse and Neglect Through Dental Awareness, 1995—97. Recipient Cert. of Merit, Swissedent Found., Glendale, Calif., 1983, benefactor, Clopper Found., 1992, Bugles Across Am. citation and medal, 2002. Fellow Am. Endodontic Soc.; mem. ADA (Outstanding Young Dentist Leader award 1992), Ill. State Dental Soc. (alt. del. 1990, spokesperson 1990-97, del. 1991-92, dental edn. com. 1991-93, chmn. 1994-97, vice-spkr. ho. of dels. 1992-93), Fox River Valley Dental Soc. (bd. dirs. 1988-93, sec. 1989, treas. 1990, v.p. 1991, pres. 1992), The Dental PAC of Ill. (bd. dirs. 1988-97, exec. com. 1989-97, 2d v.p. 1991-93, 1st v.p. 1993-95, pres. 1995-97). Avocations: fishing, photography. Home: PO Box 190 711 N Third St Elburn IL 60119-0190 Office: PO Box 190 135 S Main St Elburn IL 60119-0190 E-mail: jlwilley@email.msn.com.

WILLEY, JOHN DOUGLAS, retired newspaper executive; b. Melrose, Mass., June 4, 1917; s. Arthur Peach and Lillian (Holden) W.; m. Marilynn Miller, July 3, 1943; children: Margery Lynn Willey Marshall (dec.), John Douglas, James Campbell, David Spencer, Peter Whitney. LLD (hon.), U. Toledo, 1972. Sec. Boston & Maine R.R., Boston, 1935-40, Jones & Lamson Machine Co., Springfield, Vt., 1940-41; reporter The Blade, Toledo, 1946-49, asst. to pub., 1949-51, city editor, 1952-54, asst. mng. editor, 1954-56, dir. pub. rels., 1956-58, treas., 1962-69, assoc. pub., 1965-81, pres., 1969-81, also bd. dirs. Pres. Clear Water, Inc., 1966-89; bd. dirs. Buckeye Cablevision, Inc., Monterey Peninsula Herald; v.p., dir. Lima Communications Corp., 1971-81, Red Bank Register, 1975-81; mem. Ohio adv. bd. Liberty Mut. Ins. Co., 1976-82. Mem. exec. com. of bd. trustees, treas. Toledo Area Med. Coll. and Edn. Found., 1960-75, hon. trustee, 1975—; mem. adv. bd. St. Vincent Hosp., 1961-75; trustee Maumee Valley Country Day Sch., 1974-77, Med. Coll. Ohio, 1982-91; treas. Amateur Athletic Union Task Force Com., 1976-82, Ohio chmn. U.S. Olympic Commn. 1979-80; mem. Inter-Univ. Coun., Ohio, 1988-91. Capt. A.C., U.S. Army, 1942-46. Recipient Disting. Citizen award Med. Coll. Ohio, 1994. Mem. Belmont Country Club, Med. Coll. Ohio Faculty Club, Sigma Delta Chi. Home: 3534 River Rd Toledo OH 43614-4326

WILLEY, MARGARET MARY, author, educator; b. Chgo., Nov. 5, 1950; d. Foster L. and Barbara R. W.; m. Richard I. Joanisse; 1 child, Chloe W. BA, Grand Valley State U., 1975; MFA in Fiction, Bowling Green State U., 1980. Faculty Grand Valley State U., Allendale, Mich., 1998—, Grand Rapids (Mich.) C.C., 1998—. Lectr., presenter schs. and librs., 1990—. Author 7 young adult novels, 2 children's picture books; contbr. 3 anthologies. Adv. bd. New Moon Network, 1999—; judging panel Mich. Arts Found., Detroit, 1996-97; mem., vol. Teen Pregnancy Forum, Ottawa County, Grand Haven, Mich., 1995-98. Recipient 6 book awards Am. Libr. Assn., Paterson prize Passaic County C.C., Disting. Alumni Grand Valley State U., 1995, Charlotte Zolotow award, 2002. Mem. Authors Guild.

WILLEY, STEPHEN DOUGLAS, lawyer, accountant, estate planner; b. Mt. Pleasant, Iowa, Apr. 30, 1950; s. Charles David Willey and Sally Ann (Hall) Stringer; m. Martha Frances Wood, June 3, 1978; children: Stephen David, John Brandon, Mark Charles, Andrew Joseph (twins). Student, U.S. Mil. Acad., 1969-70; BBA, U. Tex., Arlington, 1973; JD, U. Tex., 1978. Bar: Tex. 1978, U.S. Dist. Ct. (no. dist.) Tex. 1983, U.S. Tax Ct. 1985, U.S. Ct. Claims, 1988; cert. estate planning and probate law Tex. Bd. Legal Specialization; CPA, Tex. Acct. Ernst & Ernst CPAs, Ft. Worth, 1972-74; atty. Hilgers, Watkins, Ledbetter & Hays, Austin, Tex., 1976-78; acct. Rolater, Ducote & Belew, CPAs, Dallas, 1978-79; assoc. Hill, Heard & Oneal, Attys., Arlington, Tex., 1979-81; pvt. practice, 1981—. Adj. prof. Blaw, Tex. Wesleyan U.; lectr. in field. Pres. bd. Boys Clubs Arlington; mem. Northwest Arlington Homeowners Assn., YMCA Indian Guides, Meth. Men's club, Ch. choir; chmn. dist. com. Boy Scouts of Am., 1990-93; founding dir., v.p. Tex. Alliance of Boys and Girls Clubs, Inc., 2000--, Tex. Boys and Girls Clubs Found., 2002--. Mem. AICPA, Tex. Soc. CPAs, Am. Assn. Atty. CPAs, Arlington Bar Assn., (dir. 1997—), Dallas Bar Assn. (tax sect. real property, probate and trust sect.), Tex. State Bar (tax sect. real estate probate and trust law sect.), Coll. State Bar of Tex., Tex. Acad. Probate Counsel, Tarrant County Bar Assn., Tarrant County Debtor's Bar, Tex. Acad. Probate and Trust Lawyers, Fin. Planning Assn., Nat. Assn. Estate Planning Couns. (accredited estate planner), Mid-Cities Assn. CPAs (dir. 1997-99), Arlington C. of C., U. Tex.-Austin Alumni Assn. (dir. 1997—), Rotary. Office: Law Offices of Stephen D Willey #203 1414 W Randol Mill Rd Arlington TX 76012 Fax: 817-801-5418. E-mail: swilley@attorney-cpa.com.

WILLGING, GERALDINE MARY, pediatrics nurse, artist; b. Hampton, Va., Mar. 27, 1943; d. John Anthony Demonico and Jane Mary Demonaco; m. Richard Lawrence Willging, Oct. 27, 1978; m. Joseph John Pulvino, Sept. 19, 1964 (div.); children: Lisa Rose O'Keefe, Joseph John Pulvino. RN, Lawrence Gen. Hopsital Sch. of Nursing, Lawrence, MA, 1961—64; pediatric nurse, Bunker Hill Health Ctr., Boston, MA, 1971. Certification Aerobic Fitness Assn. and Am. Coun. of Exercise, 1984. Artist Self Employed, Hampton, Va., 1997—. Exhbn. dir. Nat. Acrylic Painter's Assn., Los Angeles, Calif., 1998—. Contbr. articles to profl. jour. Roman Catholic. Personal E-mail: gerrywillging@hotmail.com.

WILLHAM, RICHARD LEWIS, animal science educator; b. Hutchinson, Kans., May 4, 1932; s. Oliver S. and Susan E. (Hurt) W.; m. Esther B. Burkhart, June 1, 1954; children: Karen Nell, Oliver Lee. *Father Oliver S. was President of Oklahoma State University from 1953 to 1966. His wife received a BS from Iowa State IL In 1972 Oliver daughter; Karen received a BFA in dance, attending at South Meth University in 1980. Oliver son received a DDS in practice, at Des Moines, IA.* BS, Okla. State U., 1954; MS, Iowa State U., 1955, PhD, 1960. Asst. prof. Iowa State U., Ames, 1959-63, assoc. prof., 1966-71, prof. dept. animal sci., 1971-78, Disting. prof., 1978—; assoc. prof. Okla. State U., Stillwater, 1963-66. Cons. in field; tchr. livestock history; guest curator exhbn. Art About Livestock, 1990. *Richard Lewis William, Mentors were J.L. Lush and L.N. Hazel- Major Prof. For MS& PhD at Iowa State IL. D.F. Stephens taught me Beef Industry in 1963-1980 at Oklahoma State IL. Frank Baker leader of Beef Improvement Federation, worked with him from 1968-1973. Instigated his portrait handling in Saddle & Sirloin Club at Louisville, KY show in 1985. Together developed national breed wide sire evaluation for Beef Industry.* Author: A Heritage of Leadership - The First 100 Years of Animal Science at Iowa State University, 1996. Recipient Svc. award Beef Improvement Fedn., 1974, Edn. and Rsch. award Am. Polled Hereford Assn., 1979, Rsch. award Nat. Cattlemen's Assn., 1986, 91, Disting. Alumnus award Okla. State U., 1978, Regents Faculty Excellence award Iowa State U., 1993; named to Hall of Fame Am. Hereford Assn., 1982, Am. Angus Assn., 1988. Fellow Am. Soc. Animal Sci. (animal breeding and genetics award 1978, industry service award 1986). Home: 2316 Hamilton Dr Ames IA 50014-8201 Office: Iowa State U Dept Animal Sci Ames IA 50011-0001 E-mail: rwillham@iastate.edu.

WILLHITE, CALVIN CAMPBELL, toxicologist; b. Salt Lake City, Apr. 27, 1952; s. Jed Butler and Carol (Campbell) W. BS, Utah State U., 1974, MS, 1977; PhD, Dartmouth Coll., 1980. Toxicologist USDA, Berkeley, Calif., 1980-85, State of Calif., Berkeley, 1985—. Adj. assoc. prof. toxicol. Utah State U., 1984-94; mem. data safety rev. bds. Johns Hopkins Sch. Medicine, 1996; mem. Calif./OSHA Gen. Industry Safety Order PEL Adv. Bd., 1994, 96; mem. com. toxicology NAS, 1998—; mem. com. validation alternative methods Nat. Toxicology Program, 2000, rev. bd. NIEHS Ctr. Evaluation Risk Human Reproduction, 2001. : mem. editl. bd. Toxicology and Applied Pharmacology, 1989—; editor: N.Y. Acad. Scis., 1993—, Toxicology, 1996—, Jour. Toxicol. Environ. Health (B), 1997—, Toxicology Letters, 1998—2002, Reproductive Toxicol., 2001—; contbr. articles on birth defects to profl. jours. Mem. WHO IARC Cancer Prevention Work Group, 1999, European Union/OECD validation regulatory methods ENV/EHS, 2002; commr. City of Novato, Calif., 2000—. Nat. Inst. Child Health and Human Devel. grantee, 1985-92, March of Dimes Birth Defects Found. grantee, 1987-91, Hoffmann LaRoche grantee, 1992-94. Mem. NIH (Health Promotion/Disease Prevention Study sect. 1998), NSF (mem. health effects adv. bd. 1986—), Am. Conf. Govt. Indsl. Hygienists (mem. threshold limit values com. 1989-99), Soc. Toxicology (program com. 1995-99, Frank R. Blood award 1986), Teratology Soc. Home: 10 Altamira Ct Novato CA 94949-6154 Office: State Calif 700 Heinz Ave Berkeley CA 94710-2721 E-mail: calvinwillhite@hotmail.com.

WILLHOIT, JIM, minister; b. Springfield, Ill., June 25, 1943; s. Richard and Virginia (Hampton) W.; m. Karen Huddleston, June 19, 1966; children: Amy Lynn, Todd Christopher. BA, Lincoln Christian Coll., 1969; MDiv., Lincoln Christian Sem., 1974, MA, 1975. Ordained to ministry Ch. of Christ, 1971. Minister Salisbury (Ill.) Christian Ch., 1964-72, Walnut Grove Christian Ch., Arcola, Ill., 1972-81; sr. minister First Ch. Christ, Highland, Ind., 1981—. Mem. site com. Project 300, Lincoln, Ill., 1979-81; bd. dirs. Onesimus Ministries, 1978-81; chaplain Lake County Police Dept., Crown Point, Ind., 1982-83, Glenwood (Ill.) Police Dept., 1986—, Highland (Ind.) Police Dept., 1996—; mem. Highland Leadership Coun., 1994—; pres. Highland Mins. Fellowship, 1996—; instr. N.W. Ind. Law Enforcement Acad., 1997--. Mem. sch. bd. Unit Dist. 306, Arcola, 1978-81; chaplain South Suburban (Ill.) Emergency Response Team, 1992—. Mem. Internat. Conf. Police Chaplains (cert. Basic Chaplain), Soc. Bibl. Lit., Am. Sci. Affiliation (assoc.), Chgo. Dist. Minister's Assn. (sec.-treas. 1982—), Chgo. Dist. Evangelistic Assn. (dir. 1981—). Home: 8936 Schneider Ave Highland IN 46322-1841 Office: First Ch Christ 2420 Lincoln St Highland IN 46322-1876 E-mail: jimwillhoit@yahoo.com.

WILLHOIT-RUDT, MARILYN JEAN, medical resources company executive; b. Paterson, N.J., Aug. 9, 1947; d. Robert and Eleanor Jean (Lewis) Houston; m. Robert Norval Willhoit, Mar. 29, 1969 (div. 1978); m. Louis Lazare Rudt, Jan. 1, 1982. BA in Speech Correction, Trenton State Coll., 1968; MA in Audiology, U. Conn., 1970. Grad. fellow U. Conn., Storrs, 1968-69; audiologist Grove Hill Clinic, New Britain, Conn., 1968-77, Hartford Hearing League, West Hartford, 1969-71, Gaylord Hosp., Wallingford, 1971-77; ind. instr. Sch. for Tympanometry, 1977—, chmn. dept. speech and hearing, 1973-77; ednl. cons. Am. Electromedics Corp., Acton, Mass., 1978-79, nat. sales mgr., 1980-83; v.p. Micro Audiometrics Corp., Daytona Beach, Fla., 1983-86; pres. Med. Resources, Jacksonville, 1986-90; v.p. sales and mktg. K&A Med. Internat., Port Orange, Fla., 1990-91; v.p. Visions in Endosurgery,

1991—. Part-time prof. So. Conn. State Coll., 1976-77; cons. Blue Cross of Conn., 1973-77, Pfeizer Industries, North Haven, Conn., Conn. State Dept. Health, Phelps-Stokes Fund, Washington; profl. adv. Employees Ins. of Wausau, Conn.; public speaker in field; mem. adv. bd. Profl. Standards Rev. Orgn., Conn. Author: Guidelines for the Provision of Speech, Hearing and Language Services State of Conn., 1977. Mem. adv. com. Sch. of Nursing Daytona Beach C. C.; mem. adv. bd. Trees/Beatification City of Daytona Beach, Fla., 2000—; sec. Ocean Dunes Neighborhood Assn., Daytona Beach; bd. dirs. Rape Crisis Ctr. of Volusis and Flagler Counties, 1994—, Sch. Nursing U. Ctrl. Fla., 2001—. Mem. NAFE, Assn. for Advancement of Med. Instrumentation, Am. Speech and Hearing Assn. (cert., legis. del. Conn. 1981-82), Conn. Speech and Hearing Assn. (award for spl. contbn. 1977), Nat. Assn. Bus. Planners, Nat. Assn. Small Bus. Mgrs., Am. Mgmt. Assn., Nat. Hearing Conservation Assn., Computer Users in Speech and Hearing, Volusia Mfrs. Assn. Office: 1867 Spruce Creek Blvd Daytona Beach FL 32128-6742 Home: Rte 76 2051 Wheeler Ln Jacksonville FL 32259-9046 E-mail: vie@earthlink.net.

WILLI, STEVEN MATTHEW, physician, educator, researcher; b. Amityville, N.Y., Apr. 3, 1959; s. John Edward and Doris Mae (Smith) Willi; children: Matthew, Thomas; m. Maria Szpiech, July 27, 2002. BA cum laude, Johns Hopkins U., 1981, MD, 1985. Diplomate in pediatrics and pediatric endocrinology Am. Bd. Pediatrics. Resident in pediatrics Children's Hosp. of Phila., 1985-88; fellow in pediatric endocrinology Children's Hosp. Phila., 1988-91; instr. pediatrics U. Pa., Phila., 1991-92; asst. prof. pediatrics Med. U. S.C., Charleston, 1992-98, assoc. prof., 1998—. Contbr. chpts. to books, articles to profl. jours. Med. dir. Camp Adam Fisher for Children with Diabetes, Summerton, S.C., 1995—; bd. dirs. Juvenile Diabetes Found., 1995-99. Recipient Nat. Rsch. Svc. award NIH, 1990, Clin. Assoc. Physician award NIH, 1996; Healfman scholar, 1985. Fellow Am. Acad. Pediatrics; mem. Endocrine Soc., Lawson Wilkins Pediatric Endocrine Soc., Am. Diabetes Assn. (profl. sect., mem. youth svcs. com. 1993—), So. Med. Assn., Charleston County Med. Soc. Avocations: tennis, bicycling, photography, golf. Office: Med U SC Dept Pediatrics 171 Ashley Ave Charleston SC 29425-0001 E-mail: willis@musc.edu.

WILLIAM, DANIEL CHARLES, retired physician; b. Washington, Jan. 22, 1946; s. Milton Paul and Ray (Block) W. BA, NYU, 1967; MD, Med. Coll. Va., 1972. Intern then resident NYU Med. Ctr. and Manhattan Vets. Hosp., 1972-75; chief med. resident Manhattan Vets. Hosp., 1975-76; asst. clin. prof. medicine Columbia U., N.Y.C., 1982—; sr. attending physician St. Lukes-Roosevelt Hosp., 1986—. Recipient Achievement award Am. Venereal Disease Assn., 1982. Mem. AMA, N.Y. County Med. Soc. (speaker). Avocations: sci. and computers. Home: 161 W 15th St Apt 7I New York NY 10011-6769 E-mail: nyc_dcwilliam@hotmail.com.

WILLIAM, DAVID, director, actor; b. London, Eng., June 24, 1926; arrived in Can., 1986; s. Eric Hugh and Olwen (Roose) W. BA, U. Coll., Oxford, Eng., 1950. Artistic dir. Glasgow Citizen's Theatre, The Nottingham Playhouse, The New Shakespeare Co., London, The National Theatre of Israel, Stratford Festival, Can., 1989-93. Vis. prof. theater dept. De Paul U., Chgo., 1985-88; founder, 1st artistic dir. Ludlow Festival. Profl. debut as Rosencrantz to Richard Burton's Hamlet, Old Vic Theatre, London, 1953; theatre directing credits include: Bacchae, The Importance of Being Earnest, The Tempest, Entertaining Mr. Sloane, Love Letters, Treasure Island, Hamlet, Love for Love, The Shoemaker's Holiday, Murder in the Cathedral, Troilus and Cressida, The Winter's Tale, She Stoops to Conquer, Antigone, Separate Tables, Romeo and Juliet, Othello, King Lear, Volpone, Albert Herring, The Merry Wives of Windosr, Twelfth Night; directing world premiers of operas include: Therese, Royal Opera House Covent Garden, The Lighthouse, Edinburgh festival, Red Emma; other operas directed include Iphigenie en Tauride, The Fairy Queen, Lisbon, La Traviata, Scottish Opera, Il Re Pastore, Camden Festival, Albert Herring, Aldeburgh Festival, Cosi Fan Tutte, Opera St. Louis, Tosca, Can. Opera Co., Mrs. Mozart, Hartford Symphony Orch., 1999; appeared in Uncle Vanya as Serebryakov, As You Like It as Jaques, Twelfth Night as Malvolio; appeared in numerous TV prodns. most notably as Richard the Second in the BBC series An Age of Kings; compiled, directed and acted in My Shakespeare, Stratford Festival and CBC Radio; played A.E.H. in The Invention of Love, Guthrie Theatre, Mpls., 2000, Studio Theater, Washington, 2001. Home: 194 Langarth St E London ON Canada N6C 1Z5

WILLIAMES, LEE JOHN, university official, history educator; b. Phila., July 4, 1942; m. Frances Gray, Feb. 24, 1968; children: Elizabeth Jamerlan, Lee D., David. BA in Pre-Law and Liberal Arts, LaSalle U., 1964; MA in European History, ACS in Soviet Studies, Niagara U., 1966; PhD in History, SUNY, Binghamton, 1981. Prof., honors dir. Coll. Misericordia, Dallas, 1966-86; asst. provost, prof. U. Scranton, 1987-92; v.p. acad. affairs, prof. history U. St. Thomas, 1992-2000, now emeritus v.p. acad. affairs, 2000—; vis. prof. Mary Immaculate Coll., U. Limerick, Ireland, 2000. Sec. gen. internat. coun. U. St. Thomas, 1995-97. Author: Anton Chekov: Iconoclast, 1989; (curriculum exercises) Odyssey of the Mind, 1988-96. Cons. Penn's Woods coun. Girl Scouts U.S.A., 1986-90; commr. Northeastern Pa. coun. Boy Scouts Am., 1988-92, v.p., 1984-88; mem. water safety bd. ARC, N.E. Pa., 1988-91; chair steering com. St. Thomas/Shell Oil/Helms Collaboration, 1997—. Fellow Med. History Soc. Baylor U. Coll. Medicine, 1997; recipient Silver Beaver medal Boy Scouts Am., 1984, St. George medal Cath. Com. on Scouting, 1986, Jubalarian medal La Salle U., Phila., Centennial medal U. Scranton. Fellow Am. Coun. on Edn. (exec. com. coun. fellows 1989-92); mem. Mid. Atlantic Hist. Assn. of Cath. Colls. and Univs. (editor jour. 1985-92), Am. Assn. for Advancement of Slavic Studies. Roman Catholic. Avocations: swimming, canoeing, martial arts, stained glass, antique restoration. Office: U St Thomas 3800 Montrose Blvd Houston TX 77006-4626 E-mail: lwilliames@houston.rr.com., williames@stthom.edu.

WILLIAMS, ADAIR L. artist; b. Jackson, Tenn., Apr. 15, 1928; d. Horace Adair and Mary Elizabeth (Nelson) Lovin; m. Thomas Schuyler Williams Jr., June 13, 1950; children: Thomas Schuyler III, Elizabeth Leigh, Nelson Lovin. BA in art, Randolph Macon Women's Coll., 1950; postgrad., Atlanta Sch. of Art. Home studio art tchr., Atlanta, 1960s-70s. Co-op. owner Golden Easel Art Gallery, Atlanta; spkr. Emory U., Atlanta, 1978; demonstrator Roswell Fine Arts Assn., 2000; spkr. in field. One-woman shows include Ga. Tech. Student Ctr. Art Gallery, 1971, The Tea Room, Nashville, 1977, Kennesaw Coll. Art Gallery, 1984, Ch. of Atonement, 1970, 90, 96, Houston Lake Country Club, Perry, Ga., 1996, Barnes and Noble, North Point Mall, 1998; exhibited in group shows at DeKalb Fed, 1980s, Atlanta Artists Ctr. 1980s and 90s, Patron's Watercolor Gala, Okla., 1984, Winter Arts Festival, 1985 (MGAA award), Coker Creek Artists, Brasstown, N.C., 1987, Marietta Gallery, 1987, Albany Mus. Art, 1989, Roswell Fine Arts City Show, 1991-93, Valdosta State Fine Arts Gallery, 91, Roswell Visual Arts Ctr., 1993, 94, 99, Ctrl. South at Parthenon, Nashville, 1993 (Nations Bank award), Grandview Gallery, 1995, Gwinnett Fine Arts Ctr., 1996, Ga. Watercolor Soc., 1996, 98, Atlanta Bot. Gardens, 1996, North Fulton Invitational, 2000, Gov.'s office Ga. State Capitol, 2001, Work of Our Hands in Buckhead, Atlanta, others; represented in permanent collection Kennesaw State U. Mem. Atlanta Arts Coun., 1970s; art tchr. Meth. Settlement House, Atlanta, 1960s-70s; painter scenery Sandy Springs Players, North Springs H.S., Atlanta, 1960-70; vol. Girl Scouts U.S., Sr. Citizens, Northside Meth. Ch., Atlanta, 1960-70. Recipient Art of the Golden Generation award Kennesaw U., 2001. Mem. Ga. Watercolor Soc. (signature mem., bd. dirs.), So. Watercolor Soc. (signature mem.), Atlanta Arts Ctr. (pres.), Tenn. Art League, Atlanta Athletic Club (chmn.), Alpha Omicron Pi. Republican. Episcopalian.

WILLIAMS, ALAN HAROLD, economics educator; b. Birmingham, Eng., June 9, 1927; s. Harold George and Gladys May (Clarke) W.; m. June Frances Porter, Nov. 9, 1953; children: Mark Alan, Susan Heather, Paul Robert. B Commerce, U. Birmingham, Eng., 1951; DPhil (hon.), U. Lund, Sweden, 1977. Asst. lectr. Exeter (Eng.) U., 1954-57; vis. lectr. MIT, Cambridge, 1957-58; lectr. in econs. Exeter U., 1958-63; vis. fellow Princeton (N.J.) U., 1963-64; sr. lectr. econs. U. York, Eng., 1964-66, reader in econs., 1968-70, prof. econs., 1970—. Dir. econ. studies, Her Majesty's Treasury: Ctr. Adminstrv. Studies, London, 1966-68. Author: Public Finance and Budgetary Policy, Efficiency in the Social Services, Principles of Practical Cost-Benefit Analysis, Being Reasonable About the Economics of Health; contbr. articles to econs. publs. Mem. Royal Commn. on Nat. Health Svc., London, 1975-77. Cpl. RAF, 1945-48, Middle East. Mem. Royal Econ. Soc., Am. Econ. Assn., Health Economists Study Group. Avocations: music, walking. Office: U York Heslington York Y01 5DD England

WILLIAMS, ALAN KEISER, management consultant; b. Harrisburg, Pa., Dec. 19, 1928; s. Paul Rupp and Margaret Helen (Keiser) W.; m. Barbara Elaine Hanson, Aug. 7, 1952 (div. Aug. 1975); children: Margaret Vivian Williams Westfall, Bryn Barbara Williams Stuart, Andrew Hanson Williams; m. Peggie Lucille Tusinger, May 29, 1988. BA, U. No. Colo., 1952. Sr. rsch. mgr. Dow Chem. Co., Golden, 1952-74; v.p. Allied-Gen. Nuclear Svc., Barnwell, S.C., 1974-83; prin. engr., project mgr. Bechtel Nat. Inc., San Francisco, 1983-91; sr. program analyst Sci. Applications Internat. Co., Germantown, Md., 1991-95; pvt. cons. Hathaway Pines, Calif., 1995—. Contbr. articles to Jour. Electro Chem. Soc. Tech. co-chmn. ENC-3 Brussels, 1982. With U.S. Army, 1946-47. Fellow Am. Nuclear Soc. (chmn. Savannah River sect 1980, bd. dirs. 1982-85); mem. AAAS, Am. Chem. Soc. Achievements include research in processing and handling actinide elements, principally uranium, plutonium and americium. Home and Office: PO Box 12 Hathaway Pines CA 95233-0012

WILLIAMS, ALEXANDER HAZARD, III, health care executive, consultant; b. N.Y.C., Sept. 14, 1939; s. Alexander Hazard Jr. and Blanche Mildred (Evans) W.; m. Christine Vanderwarker, June 24, 1961 (div. June 1974); children: Alexander Hazard IV, Ashley, James; m. Caroline Lueloff, Feb. 12, 1977 (div. Jan. 1990); m. Monica Traut Dreuth, Nov. 17, 1990. BA, Williams Coll., 1961; MPA, Cornell U., 1963. Vol. Peace Corps, Monrovia, Liberia, 1963-65; asst. adminstr. Evanston (Ill.) Hosp., 1965-68; dir. planning Am. Hosp. Assn., Chgo., 1968-70, dir. N.Y. office, 1970-72; sr. v.p. Chgo., 1987-91; dir. Univ. Hosp. SUNY Downstate, Bklyn., 1972-76; assoc. dir. Univ. Hosp. U. Mich., Ann Arbor, 1976-77; exec. v.p. St. Lukes-Roosevelt Hosp., N.Y.C., 1977-81; exec. v.p., CEO Ch. Charity Found., Hempstead, N.Y., 1981-87; v.p. Witt Kieffer Ford Hadelman, N.Y.C., 1991—. Contbr. chpts. to books. Bd. dirs. Bklyn. YWCA, 1985-86, Nat. Fire Protection Assn., Quincy, Mass., 1990-96, Medic Alert Found., Turlock, Calif., 1990-96, East End Seaport Mus. Found., Greenport, N.Y., 1996—; chmn. bd. Ednl. Commn. Fgn. Med. Grads., Phila., 1991—, Ea. L.I. Hosp., 2000—. Mem. Williams Club N.Y., Cornell Club. Avocations: sailing. Home: 425 Cedar Point Dr PO Box 1337 Southold NY 11971-0937 Office: Witt/Kieffer Ford Hadelman & Lloyd 780 Third Ave New York NY 10017

WILLIAMS, ALFRED BLYTHE, management consultant, educator; b. Oakland City, Ind., Sept. 17, 1940; s. Ross Merl and Jesse Adell (Helsley) W. BS cum laude, Oakland City U., 1963; MS, Ind. U., 1964; PhD, Ga. State U., 1974. Tchr. Arlington H.S., Indpls., 1964-65, Oakland City (Ind.) U., 1965-69; editor Southwestern Pub. Co., Cin., 1969-72, cons., 1981-93; adj. prof. Ga. State U., Atlanta, 1972-74; prof. mgmt. and bus. comm. U. La., Lafayette, 1975—2002, chmn. dept., 1986-96; ret., 2002. Cons. John Wiley Pub. Co., N.Y., 1988-89, Irwin Pub., 1989. Author study guides; editor Info. Systems Bus. Comm. Jour., 1983, 93. Patron Lafayette Cmty. Concerts, 1984—; contbr. La. and Nat. Rep. parties, Baton Rouge, Washington, 1983—. Mem. AAUP, Assn. Bus. Communicators (bd. dirs. 1986-90, Francis W. Weeks Merit award 1984), La. Assn. Higher Edn., Sierra Club, Kiwanis, Phi Delta Kappa, Phi Kappa Phi, Delta Pi Epsilon, Beta Gamma Sigma. Methodist.

WILLIAMS, ALICE NOEL TUCKERMAN, foundation administrator; b. Bethesda, Md., Dec. 21, 1918; d. Walter Rupert and Edith (Abercrombie-Miller) Tuckerman; m. Robert Hugh Williams, June 21, 1939 (dec. 1983); children: Sarah Fenno Williams Lord, Edith Tuckerman Williams Ward. Mem. ladies bd. St. John's Child Devel. Ctr., Washington, 1960—69; pres. ladies bd. St. John's Devel. Ctr., 1969-72, v.p., trustee, 1970-72. Mem. Colonial Dames Am. (pres. Washington chpt. 1970-74), Sulgrave Club, The Investment Group (co-founder). Episcopalian. Avocations: volunteer work, reading.

WILLIAMS, ANN CLAIRE, federal judge; b. 1949; m. David J. Stewart. BS, Wayne State U., 1970; MA, U. Mich., 1972; JD, U. Notre Dame, 1975. Law clk. to Hon. Robert A. Sprecher, 1975-76; asst. U.S. atty. U.S. Dist. Ct. (no. dist.) Ill., Chgo., 1976-85; faculty Nat. Inst. for Trial Advocacy, 1979—, also bd. dirs.; judge U.S. Dist. Ct. (no. dist.) Ill., 1985-99, U.S. Ct. Appeals (7th cir.), Chgo., 1999—. Chief Organized Crime Drug Enforcement Task Force for North Ctrl. Region, 1983-85; mem. ct. adminstrn. and case mgmt. com. Jud. Conf. U.S., 1990-97, chair, 1993-97. Sec. bd. trustees U. Notre Dame; founder Minority Legal Resources, Inc. Mem. FBA, Fed. Judges Assn., Ill. State Bar Assn., Ill. Jud. Coun., Cook County Bar Asn., Women's Bar Assn. Ill., Black Women's Lawyers Assn. Greater Chgo. Office: US Ct Appeals 7th Circuit 219 S Dearborn St Ste 2612 Chicago IL 60604-1803*

WILLIAMS, ANN MEAGHER, retired hospital administrator; b. Hull, Mass., May 28, 1929; d. James Francis Meagher and Dorothy Frances (Meagher) Mullins; m. Joseph Arthur Williams, May 15, 1954; children: James G., Mara A., A. Scott (dec.), Gordon M., Mark J., Antoinette M., Andrea M. BS, Chestnut Hill Coll., 1950; MS, Boston Coll., 1952. Radioisotope biologist Air Force Cambridge Rsch. Ctr., Bedford, Mass., 1952-55; asst. mgr. Roxbury Businessmen's Exch., Boston, 1956-66; owner, operator Chatterlane, Osterville, Mass., 1961-66; realtor James E. Murphy Inc., Hyannis, 1968-77; dir. cmty. affairs Cape Cod Hosp., 1977-95; realtor James E. Murphy, Inc., Osterville, 1995—. Bd. dirs. Community Coun., Mid Cape, Mass., 1977-88, Cape Cod Mental Health Assn., 1977-82, Ctr. for Individual and Family Svcs., Mid Cape, 1982-87, Am. Cancer Soc., Mid Cape, 1981-96, Cape Cod C.C. Ednl. Found., 1998—; mem. sch. com. Cape Cod Regional Tech. High Sch., 1978—, United Way of Cape Cod, 1988-89; chmn. fin. com. City of Barnstable, Mass., 1969-77. Named Woman of Yr. Bus./Profl. Women's Club, 1982; recipient cert. of appreciation Am. Cancer Soc., 1983, 88, Pres. Recognition award United Way Cape Cod, 1989. Life Achievement award Mass. Assn. Sch. Cos., 2000. Mem.: Nat. Assn. Hosp. Devel., SE Mass. Hosp. Mktg. & Pub. Rels., New Eng. Hosp. Mktg. & Pub. Rels., Am. Soc. Hosp. Mktg. & Pub. Rels., Chestnut Hill Coll. Alumnae Assn., Rotary (bd. dir. Osterville 1993—98, pres. 1996—97, asst. gov. dist. 7950 1998—99, area rep. 1999—2000, gov. elect 2001—02, gov. 2002—), Hyannis Area C. of C. (bd. dir. 1993—98). Roman Catholic. Avocation: community theater. Home: 25 Wedgewood Dr Centerville MA 02632-3162 Office: James E Murphy Inc 971 Main St Ste A Osterville MA 02655-2018 E-mail: amwms@capecod.net.

WILLIAMS, ANNA M. social worker; b. Ft. Meade, Md., Sept. 5, 1956; d. William Arthur and Jacqueline Rae (Hull) W. BA in African Studies, BA in Social Work, U. Md., 1978; MSW, U. Pitts., 1981. Lic., cert. social worker. Investigator child abuse Dept. Social Svcs., Balt., 1978-80; counselor, program coord., supr. girls unit Ward Home for Children, Pitts., 1981-86; mental health therapist Pace Sch., 1986-89; program coord. Justice Resources Inc., Balt., 1989-94; therapist Union Meml. Hosp., 1993-94; v.p. resdl. svcs. Children's Home Wyoming Conf., Binghamton, N.Y., 1994-95; dir. Casey Family Svcs., Balt., 1995—; bus. owner Basket Magic, 1993—. Cons. Youth Advocacy Program, Balt., 1992-94. Bd. dirs. Ward Home for Children, Pitts., 1986-88, South Balt. Youth Ctr., 1993-94, Florence Crittenton, Balt., 1996—, v.p. bd., 2000-01, pres., 2002; spkr. Meth. Women; adv. bd. WSKG Pub. Broadcasting, 1994-96; cmty. adv. bd. Johns Hopkins Sch. Pub. Health, 1998—; active New Psalmist Bapt. Ch. Mem. NASW, Nat. Girls Caucus (charter), Md. Assn. Resources for Family and Youth (bd. dirs. 1997-2000, 2001-02, treas. 1999-2000), Kiwanis Internat., Alpha Kappa Alpha. Democrat. Avocations: reading, cooking, gardening, interior decorating. Office: Casey Family Svcs 25 N Caroline St Baltimore MD 21231 E-mail: basketmagic1@hotmail.com., amwilliams-01@msn.com.

WILLIAMS, ANNEMARIE HAUBER, secondary education educator; b. Schorndorf, Baden Württenberg, Germany, Mar. 6, 1946; came to U.S., 1951; d. William Carl and Hertha (Franze) Hauber; m. William C. Young, Nov. 23, 1972 (div.); 1 child, Niccole Anne Young; m. Evan J. Williams, Aug. 1, 1982. BA, U. S.C., 1968; postgrad., U. London Sch. Econs., 1969; MA, SUNY, New Paltz, 1974. Cert. social studies educator. Tchr. history Monticello (N.Y.) High Sch., 1968-70; tchr. history, coach male varsity and jr. varsity tennis, varsity basketball cheerleaders Yorktown (N.Y.) High Sch., 1970-71; tchr. history Hendrick Hudson High Sch., Montrose, N.Y., 1971—, coach male varsity tennis, 1971-73. Textbook rater in field. Mem. Dems. for Am., U. S.C., 1965-68. Recipient Outstanding Tchr. award U. Chgo., 1988, Inspirational Tchr. award Tufts U., 1996; Study grant U. Hawaii, 1969. Mem. ASCD, N.Y. State Coun. for Social Studies, Nat. Coun. for Social Studies. Republican. Lutheran. Avocations: tennis, gardening, reading, swimming, art collecting. Home: Box 365 336 Rock Hill Dr Rock Hill NY 12775-5019 E-mail: awilliams@in4web.com.

WILLIAMS, ANTHONY A. mayor; b. 1951; s. Lewis and Virginia W.; m. Diana Lynn Simmons; 1 child, Asantewa Foster. BA in Polit. Sci. magna cum laude, Yale U., 1982; JD, M of Pub. Policy, Harvard U., 1987. Law clk. to Hon. David Nelson U.S. Dist. Ct., Boston, 1987-88; asst. dir. Boston Redevel. Authority, 1988-89; exec. dir. Cmty. Devel. Agy., St. Louis, 1989-91; dep. comptr. State of Conn., Boston, 1991-93; exec. dir. Cmty. Devel. Agy., St. Louis, 1989-91; dept. contr. State of Conn., 1991-93; CFO Dept. Agr., Washington, 1993-98; mayor Washington D.C., 1999—. Adj. prof. pub. affairs Columbia U., N.Y.C., 1992-93. Pres. pro tempore, chmn. cmty. devel. com. Conn. Bd. Alderman, 1980-83; dir. comm. Conn. Spkr. House and Assembly Dem., 1983. Kellogg Found. Nat. fellow, 1991. Office: Office of the Mayor 1634 I Street NW Washington DC 20006*

WILLIAMS, ARLEEN ROLLING, pediatrics nurse; b. New Orleans, Dec. 8, 1943; d. Alfred Bonnabel and Marie Frances (Sutter) Rolling; divorced; children: Laura Roane, Keith Clayon. BSN, Northwestern State U. of La., 1965; postgrad., Am. U., 1966, Phoenix Coll., 1977. RN, Ariz.; cert. sch. nurse, rehab. nurse, case mgr. Acting supr., pub. health nurse II Children and Youth Project, St. Thomas, V.I.; rehab. and sch. nurse Gompers Rehab. Ctr., Phoenix; nurse mgr. Meridian Point Rehab. Hosp., Scottsdale, Ariz.; child health coord. Phoenix Health Plan; dir. nurses S.W. Human Devel., Phoenix, 1992-97; sch. nurse Casa Blanca Cmty. Schs., Inc., 1997-99; rehabilitation nurse, case mgr. Rehab Without Walls, Phoenix, 1999—. Recipient Vol. award ARC, 1983, 85. Mem. Assn. Rehab. Nurses (pres. com. 1987-88, del.nat. conf. 1984, 86, 87, 88, pres. Cen. Ariz. chpt. 1986-87, pres. 1988, editor, co-editor newsletter 1986-90), Nat. Assn. Sch. Nurses, Sch. Nurse Orgn. Ariz., Am. Sch. Health Assn., Ariz. Sch. Health Assn. Home: 15814 N 44th St Phoenix AZ 85032-4201 E-mail: rolling@flash.net.

WILLIAMS, ARTHUR BENJAMIN, JR. bishop; b. Providence, June 25, 1935; m. Lynette Rhodes, 1985. AB, Brown U., 1957; MDiv, Gen. Theol. Sem., 1964; MA, U. Mich., 1974; DD, Gen. Theol. Sem., 1986. Clarence Horner fellow Grace Ch., Providence, 1964-65; asst. St. Mark, Riverside, R.I., 1965-67; sub-dean St. John Cathedral, Providence, 1967-68; assoc. & interim rector Grace Ch., Detroit, 1968-70; asst. to bishop Diocese of Mich., 1970-77; archdeacon Ohio Cleve., 1977-85; suffragan bishop Episcopal Diocese of Ohio, 1986—; v.p. House of Bishops, 1995—. Chair Com. on Justice, Peace and Integrity of Creation, 1995-97; Epsicopal vis. Order of St. Benedict, 2000—. Chair editl. com. Lift Every Voice and Sing II, 1993. Office: Diocese of Ohio 2230 Euclid Ave Cleveland OH 44115-2499 E-mail: bishsuff@dohio.org.

WILLIAMS, ARTHUR ROSS, health service and public administrator; b. Dayton, Ohio, June 11, 1946; s. Russell W. Sr. and Violet Ross Williams; m. Phoebe Dauz, Aug. 10, 1972; children: Arthur, Diane, David. BA, Wright State U., 1968; MPA, U. Pitts., 1972; MA in Econ., U. Philippines, 1976; PhD, Cornell U., 1981. Asst. to mgr. City of Dayton, Ohio, 1968-70, Twp. of Mt. Lebanon, Pa., 1970-72; rsch. assoc. Cornell U., Ithaca, N.Y., 1976-80; prof. U. Philippines, Diliman, 1976-81; project dir. Robert Wood Johnson Found., Gainesville, Fla., 1982-84; prof. U. Fla., 1984-90, U. Mo., Kansas City, 1990—2002, Mayo Med. Sch., 2002—. Cons. U.S. Agy. for Internat. Devel., Manila, 1976-82, Rockefeller Found., Manila, 1974-78; cons., grant dir. Ford Found., Manila, 1976-80; methodology cons. U.S. Dept. of Health and Human Svcs., Washington, 1990-96. Author: Measuring Local Government Performance, 1981, (with others) Path Analysis, 1994; contbr. articles to profl. jours. Mem. Friends of Art, Kansas City, Ams. for Dem. Action, Washington; dir. health svcs. rsch. Mo. Assn. for Social Welfare, Jefferson City, Mo. Henry Luce Faculty fellow Luce Found., 1990, Andrew Mellon fellow U. Pitts., 1971-72, Fulbright Rsch. scholar, 2000-01; recipient De la Costa award Philippine-Am. Ednl. Found., 1981. Fellow Philippine Econ. Soc. (life), Am. Pub. Health Assn., Assn. for Health Svc. Rsch., Soc. for Epidemiologic Rsch., Am. Polit. Sci. Assn. (sect. chair), Am. Econ. Assn., Am. Soc. for Pub. Adminstrn. Avocations: chess, stamp collecting, reading, walking, swimming. Home: 8410 Cherokee Ln Leawood KS 66206-1414 Office: Divsn Hlealth Care Policy & Rsch Mayo Clin Rochester MN 55904 E-mail: artwill@aol.com.

WILLIAMS, ATHANASIA MARIA, perinatal nurse specialist; b. Englewood, N.J., Nov. 15, 1950; d. Nicholas P. and Stella Thespina (Zaharias) W. BSN, Duke U., 1972. Staff nurse Columbia Presbyn. Hosp., N.Y.C., 1972-75, asst. head nurse, 1975-87, clin. nurse III, 1987-2000; nurse specialist Specialty Home Health Care, Hawthorne, N.J., 2000—. Contbg. author: High Risk Pregancy, 1986; also articles. Greek Orthodox. Avocations: reading, crossword puzzles, travel. E-mail: amw@spiridon.org.

WILLIAMS, B. JOHN, JR. federal agency administrator, lawyer; b. Lancaster, Pa., Dec. 13, 1949; s. Bernard John and Sarah Elizabeth (Sykes) W.; m. Martha Caroline Roberts, Aug. 6, 1977; children: Robert, Sarah, Anne, Bernard. BA, George Washington U., 1971, JD, 1974. Bar: D.C., Pa., U.S. Tax Ct., U.S. Ct. Appeals (3rd, 9th and fed. cirs.), U.S. Supreme Ct. Law clk. to judge U.S. Tax Ct., Washington, 1974-76; assoc. Ballard, Spahr, Andrews & Ingersoll, Phila., 1976-81; spl. asst. to chief counsel IRS, Washington, 1981-83; dep. asst. atty. gen. Tax Div. Dept. Justice, 1983-84; ptnr. Morgan, Lewis & Bockius, 1984-85; judge U.S. Tax Ct., 1985-90; ptnr. Morgan, Lewis & Bockius, 1990-2000, Shearman & Sterling, Washington, 2000—02; chief counsel, IRS U.S. Dept. Treasury, 2002—. Mem. adv. com. U.S. Ct. Appeals, Fed. Cir. Fellow Am. Coll. Tax Counsel; mem. ABA, Am. Law Inst., Phi Beta Kappa, Omicron Delta Kappa. Republican. Office: US Dept Treasury Chief Counsel 1111 Constitution Ave NW Washington DC 20224 E-mail: BJWilliams@sherman.com.*

WILLIAMS, BARBARA ANNE, college president emerita; b. Camden, N.J., Oct. 14, 1938; d. Frank and Laura Dorothy (Szweda) W. BA cum laude, Georgian Court Coll., 1963; MLS, Rutgers U., 1965; MA, Manhattan Coll., 1973; postgrad., NYU, 1976-81, 93—. Cert. English tchr., N.J.; joined Sisters of Mercy, 1957. Sec. Camden Cath. High Sch., 1956-57; registrar Georgian Ct. Coll., Lakewood, N.J., 1960-66, dir. libr. svcs., 1966-74, dean acad. affairs, 1974-80, pres., 1980-2000, sci. and math. libr., 2000—, pres. emerita, 2000—. Bd. dirs. N.J. Natural Gas Co., 1986-91. Mem. editorial bd. N.J. Woman mag. Bd. dirs., mem. ednl. adv. coun. Diocese of Trenton, N.J., 1983-90; mem. adv. bd. Ocean County Ctr. for Arts, Lakewood, N.J., 1983-91; mem. Ocean County Pvt. Industry Coun., 1983-92; bd. dirs. Monmouth/Ocean Devel. Coun., 1981-84; mem. State of N.J. Student Assistance Bd., 1995-99; mem. Ocean County School-to-Career Com., 1996-2000; mem. art adv. coun. Nat. Mus. Cath. Art and History, 2000—. Named Outstanding Woman N.J. Assn. Women Bus. Owners, 1983; recipient Humanitarian award Monmouth/Ocean Devel. Coun., 1985, Salute to Policymakers award Exec. Women N.J., 1986, Woman in Leadership award Monmouth Coun. Girl Scouts, 1987, Citizen of Yr. Alcoholism & Drug Abuse Coun. Ocean County, 1993, Brotherhood/Sisterhood award Monmouth/Ocean chpts. NCCJ, 1994, Friend of Scouting award Boy Scouts Am. Jersey Shore Coun., 1999, Leadership award Mercy Higher Edn. Colloquium, 2000. Mem. Assn. of Mercy Colls. (pres. 1981-83, sec. 1996-98), Mercy Higher Edn. Colloquium (mem. exec. com. 1980-87), Ocean County Bus. Assn. (trustee 1982-84), Nat. Assn. Inc. Colls. and Univs. (secretariat 1981-83, 87-91), NAIA (coun. of pres. 1997-2000). Home and Office: Georgian Ct Coll 900 Lakewood Ave Lakewood NJ 08701-2600 E-mail: williamssb@georgian.edu.

WILLIAMS, BARBARA IVORY, educational researcher; b. Detroit, Apr. 28, 1936; d. Henry Oliver and Willa Mae (Frazier) I.; m. Alney Elliott Whitener, Jan. 1, 1987. BS, Wayne State U., 1957, MEd, 1960; PhD, U. Washington, 1973. Tchr. Detroit Pub. Schs., 1957-68; program assoc. Mich.-Ohio Regional Lab., Detroit, 1968-70; lectr. predoctoral U. Wash., Seattle, 1970-73; sr. program assoc. Far West Lab. for Ednl. Research and Devel., San Francisco, 1973-76; sr. cons. E.H. White & Co., 1976-77; sr. program assoc. Northwest Regional Lab., Portland, Oreg., 1977-84; area coord. Ednl. Testing Service, Washington, 1984-85; edn. group dir. Research and Evaluation Assocs., 1985-87; ind. cons., 1987-89; assoc. dir. edn. studies Westat, Rockville, Md., 1989—. Mem. Am. Ednl. Research Assn., Am. Psychol.

Assn., Nat. Assn. Black Sch. Educators, Phi Delta Kappa, Alpha Kappa Alpha (pres. Portland chpt. 1980-84). Democrat. Baptist. Avocations: desk top publishing, needle work. Home: 15320 Pine Orchard Dr Apt 2F Silver Spring MD 20906-8315

WILLIAMS, BARBARA STAMBAUGH, editor; b. Jenkins, Ky., Nov. 22, 1937; d. James Cosby and Jessie Kate (Bise) Stambaugh; m. Manning Williams, Sept. 11, 1963. BS in Journalism, U. Tenn., 1959. Polit. reporter News and Courier, Charleston, S.C., 1961-63, 67-76, asst. mng. editor, 1976-81; city hall reporter Camden (N.J.) Courier Post, 1963-67; editor The Evening Post, Charleston, S.C., 1981-90, The Evening Post and News Courier, Charleston, 1990-91, The Post and Courier, Charleston, 1991—. Pres. Nat. Conf. Editl. Writers, Rockville, Md., 1992. Bd. dirs. Charleston Sci. and Cultural Edn. Fund. Named Outstanding Newspaper Woman in S.C., S.C. Press Assn., 1962. Mem. Sigma Delta Chi (ByLiner award 1973). Office: The Post & Courier 134 Columbus St Charleston SC 29403-4800 E-mail: barbara@postandcourier.com.*

WILLIAMS, BETTY LOURENE, volunteer, manager, consultant; b. Topeka, Oct. 3, 1934; d. Jim and Catherine (Sears) Lewis; m. Herman Williams, Sept. 22, 1950; children: Herm Jr., Danny Clay, Iris Angela, John Joseph, Steve Arnold. AA, Compton Coll., 1988. Lic. real estate agt., Calif. Lumbleau Real Estate Sch. Kindergarten, music tchr. St. Catherine Cath. Mission Sch., Guthrie, Okla., 1956-57; real estate agt. Diamond Realty, Compton, Calif., 1964-65; office mgr. J & H Clin. Lab., Inglewood, 1967-71; exam clk. typist Fed. Office of Personnel Mgmt., L.A., 1981, consulting adminstrv. coord., designer of office ops. system, 1983; vol. Harbor Chpt. AAKP, Long Beach, Calif., 1979—. Office orgn., cons. Inglewood Chpt., 1989—; kidney peer patient counseling. Author: (book of poems) Expressions, 1988. Mem. NAACP, Compton, Calif. Br., 1992; mem. Congl. hearing com. Nat. Urologic and Kidney Diseases Adv. Bd. for West Coast, L.A., 1988; organizer Tng. Seminar for So. Calif. State Rehab. Dept., 1988. Recipient Shirley Berman Nat. Outstanding Vol. of Yr. award, 1992, Award for 20 Yrs. of Outstanding Svc., Am. Assn. for Kidney Patients; grantee McDonald Douglas to purchase van for patients, 1993. Mem. Am. Assn. Kidney Patients, Normal Bridge Club (sec. 1986-87), Am. Bridge Assn. (L.A. unit 1986—). Democrat. Avocations: piano playing, duplicate bridge, singing, collector of Black history, poetry writing, scenery painting.

WILLIAMS, BETTY OUTHIER, lawyer; b. Woodward, Okla., Sept. 11, 1947; d. Robert E. and Ethel M. (Castiller) Outhier; children: Amanda J., Emily Rebecca. BA, Oklahoma City U., 1969; JD, Vanderbilt U., 1972. Bar: Okla. 1972, U.S. Dist. Ct. (no. dist.) Okla. 1972, U.S. Dist. Ct. (ea. dist.) Okla. 1973, (U.S. Ct. Appeals (10th cir.) 1973, U.S. Supreme Ct. 1980, U.S. Dist. Ct. (we. dist.) Okla. 1988. Atty. Reginal Heber Smith Cmty. Lawyer Fellowship, Tulsa, 1972-73; asst. U.S. atty. Muskogee, Okla., 1973-81; U.S. atty., 1981-82; ptnr. Robinson, Locke, Gage, Fite & Williams, 1982-96, Robinson, Gage & Williams, Muskogee, 1996-97, Gage & Williams, Muskogee, 1997—. Chair local rules com. U.S. Bankruptcy Ct. Ea. Dist., Okla., 1994, U.S. Dist. Ct. Ea. Dist. Okla., 1995; adj. settlement judge U.S. Dist. Ct. Ea. Dis. Okla., 1998—. Mem. editl. bd. Okla. Law Enforcement Ops. Bull., 1993-94; editor Okla. Bar Jour., 1996-2002. Pres. Bus. and Profl. Women, Muskogee, 1975-77, 83; pres., bd. dirs. YWCA, Muskogee, 1975-82; bd. dirs. Green County Mental Health, Muskogee, 1986-88, WISH, 1990—; trustee Frontier Heritage Found., 1990-98; chmn. bd. commrs. Muskogee Housing Authority; adminstrv. bd. chmn., St. Paul United Meth. Ch., Muskogee, 1999-2001; state exec. com. Internat. Order the Rainbow for Girls. Named One of Outstanding Young Career Women, Bus. and Profl. Women, 1974. Fellow: Okla. Bar Found. (trustee 1989—, v.p. 1994, pres. 1996, gov. 2000—); mem.: Muskogee County Bar Assn. (pres. 1984—85), Okla. Bar Assn. (editl. bd. 1996—, bd. govs. 2000—), ABA, Soroptomists (pres. 1986—88), Order Eastern Star (Hope chpt.), Gamma Phi Beta (alumnae pres. 1993—). Republican. Methodist. Home: 4326 Oklahoma St Muskogee OK 74401-2351 Office: Gage & Williams PO Box 87 Muskogee OK 74402-0087 E-mail: bowlaw@swbglobal.net.

WILLIAMS, BILLIE JEAN, small business owner; b. Tarrytown, Ga. d. Willard and Sara (Beckworth) Burch; m. Randall Carroll; m. David Jones (div.); m. Robert F. Fortner, Jr., Sept. 20, 1981 (div.); children: Gina Sumner, Simone Dixon, Natalie Garner; m. Jack L. Williams, Aug. 2000. AA summa cum laude, Brewton Parker Coll., 1970; BS, Ga. So. Coll., 1972, MEd, 1975, EdS, 1977. Math & sci. tchr. Toombs County Schs., Lyons, Ga., 1971-76, gifted tchr., 1976-81, Montgomery County Schs., Mt. Vernon, 1985-88; ptnr. Rabbit's Quik Stop, Vidalia, 1985—, Rabbit's Cargo Inc., Vidalia, 1987—, Fortner Rentals, Vidalia, 1988—, Rabbit On the Strip, Vidalia, 1988—, Fortner Farms, Vidalia, 1989—; artist-in-residence, ptnr. F.C.F. Investments, 1992—; ptnr. Kipling B. Collins. Artist-in-residence, Vidalia, Ga. Troup leader Girl Scouts, Vidalia, 1972-76; block coord. Ga. Heart Assn., Vidalia, 1976. Mem. Phi Beta Kappa. Baptist. Home: 404 Slayton St Vidalia GA 30474-4436 Office: Rabbit's Quik Stop Hwy 292 W Vidalia GA 30474

WILLIAMS, BOBBY See EVERHART, ROBERT PHILLIP

WILLIAMS, BRADLEY ROBERT, pharmacy and gerontology educator, consultant; b. L.A., Sept. 22, 1953; s. Raymond Ewell and Frances Williams; m. Marilyn D. Williams, July 17, 1976; children: Sean, Shannon. PharmD, U. So. Calif., 1977. Lic. pharmacist, Calif. Pharmacist coord. Beverly Enterprises, Pasadena, Calif., 1978-79; resident in geriatric pharmacy U. So. Calif., L.A., 1977-78, asst. prof. pharmacy and gerontology, 1979-89, assoc. prof., 1989—. Mem. competency com. Calif. Bd. Pharmacy, Sacramento, 1988-99; dir. geriatric pharmacy Rancho Los Amigos Nat. Rehab. Hosp., Downey, Calif., 1991—; mem. med. and sci. adv. bd. Alzheimer's Assn., L.A., 1992-94; mem. Commn. for Cert. in Geriatric Pharmacy, Alexandria, Va., 1997—, chmn., 2000-01; rsch. subcontractor Archstone Found., L.A., 1999—. Author: Applied Therapeutics—The Clinical Use of Drugs, 1995, 2001; editor: Clinical Pharmacology and Nursing, 1996; contbr. articles to sci. jours. Merit badge counselor Boy Scouts Am., Lomita, Calif., 1999—. Rsch. grantee John A. Hartford Found., 1989, Adminstrn. on Aging, 1989. Fellow Am. Soc. Cons. Pharmacists; mem. Am. Soc. Health Sys. Pharmacists (geriatrics network liaison 1996-98), Am. Geriatrics Soc., Gerontol. Soc. Am. Democrat. Roman Catholic. Avocations: photography, hiking. Office: U So Calif 1985 Zonal Ave Los Angeles CA 90089-0121

WILLIAMS, BRIAN, news anchor, correspondent; m. Jane Stoddard; 2 children. Student, George Washington U., Cath. U. Am.; hon. doctorate, Elmira Coll. Corr. various stas., Phila., Washington; and Pittsburgh, Kans.; anchor, corr. Sta. WCBS-TV, N.Y.C.; anchor NBC Nightly News Sat., 1993—; chief White House corr. NBC, Washington, 1994-96; permanent substitute host Nightly News with Tom Brokaw, N.Y.C.; anchor mng. editor The News with Brian Williams, MSNBC. T.V. guest appearances include The Tonight Show with Jay Leno, Late Night with Conan O'Brien, and The Late Show with David Letterman. Recipient Emmy award, 1993; nominee Emmy award, 1994; named Father of Yr., Nat. Father's Day Com., 1996. Office: c/o MSNBC NBC/Microsoft Corp 1 Msnbc Blvd Secaucus NJ 07094-2419*

WILLIAMS, BROWN F, media services company executive; b. Evanston, Ill., Dec. 22, 1940; s. Jack Kermit Williams and Virginia Helen (Benjamin) Likar; m. Linda Francee Ludt, Sept. 1961 (div. 1968); 1 child, Eden Carol Williams McCarthy; m. Martha Amidon Powers, Sept. 1970 (div. 1974); m. Sandra Ann Matkowski, Jan. 1984 (wid. May, 2000); 1 child, Bronwyn Emily. AB in Math. and Physics, U. Calif., Riverside, 1962, MA in Physics, 1964, PhD in Physics, 1966. Mgr. Electro-Optics Lab., Princeton, N.J., 1969-75; dir. RCA Labs., 1976-82, v.p., 1982-87; pres. Williams Cons. Group, 1988-90. Chmn. Princeton Video Image, 1990—. Fellow IEEE; mem. AAAS, Am. Phys. Soc., Sigma Xi. Avocations: skiing, ocean sailing, horses. Office: 15 Princess Rd Lawrenceville NJ 08648-2301 E-mail: brown@pvimage.com.

WILLIAMS, BRYAN, university dean, medical educator; b. Longview, Tex., July 28; s. Lewis Bryan and Margaret Louise (Smart) W.; m. Frances Montgomery, Mar. 31, 1950; children: Harrison, Amy, Philip, Nickolas, Margaret, Lincoln. MD, Southwestern Med. Sch., 1947. Diplomate Am. Bd. Internal Medicine. Pvt. practice, Dallas, 1957-70; prof. internal medicine, assoc. dean student affairs Southwestern Med. Sch., 1970-90, prof. internal medicine emeritus, dean student affairs emeritus. Fellow ACP; mem. Inst. Medicine Nat. Acad. Scis. (charter). Home: 1215 Old Bethany Rd Allen TX 75013

WILLIAMS, CALVIN, librarian, consultant; b. Hogansville, Ga., Jan. 29, 1946; s. Azell and Lella (Mullins) W.; m. Delores Hayes, June 23, 1973; children: Sheniqua LaToya, Calvin Mikkel. BA, Morris Brown Coll., 1969; MS in Library Sci., Atlanta U., 1973; MSA, Cen. Mich. U., 1979. Librarian assoc. Atlanta Pub. Library, 1972-73, community analyst, 1973; head librarian Morris Brown Coll., Atlanta, 1971-73; br. librarian Saginaw (Mich.) Pub. Library, 1973-75; acad. librarian Saginaw Valley State Coll., University Center, Mich., 1975-87; librarian Oakland Community Coll., Auburn Hills, 1987—, dept. chmn., 1989—. Mem. Bridgeport (Mich.) Library Commn., 1981-88, pres. 1985-86; library cons. Saginaw County Mental Health Ctr., 1984-86. Editor Great Lakes and Finger Lakes newsletter, 1981-88, Bethel AME Ch. newsletter, 1989-90, 98—. Pres. Bridgeport (Mich.) Library Commn., 1985-88; trustee bd. Bethel AME Ch. and Credit Com., Bethel Fed. Credit Union, 1994—, asst. ch. treas., 1998—. Served to U.S. Army, 1969-71. Atlanta U. fellow, 1971-73; recipient Community Service awards Saginaw Pub. Schs., 1975-85. Mem. ALA, NAACP, Mich. Acad. Sci. and Arts, Atlanta U. Alumni Assn., Ctrl. Mich. U. Alumni Assn. (life), Saginaw Alumni Chpt. (treas. 1984-92), Kappa Alpha Psi (life, Outstanding Alumni 1982). Democrat. Methodist. Avocations: reading, bicycling, drawing, sports, writing basic programs. Home: 3286 Southfield Dr Saginaw MI 48601-5642 Office: Oakland Community Coll 2900 Featherstone Rd Auburn Hills MI 48326-2817 E-mail: cxwillia@yahoo.com., cwillia@oaklandcc.edu.

WILLIAMS, CALVIT HERNDON, environmental chemist; b. Houston, Dec. 28, 1936; s. Calvit Herndon and Julia Eloise (Tybor) W.; children: Sabina, Terence, Russel, Damon. BA in Chemistry, U. St. Thomas, Houston, 1958; PhD in Phys. Chemistry, Brown U., 1965. Cert. indsl. hygienist, safety profl.; qualified environ. profl. Postdoctoral fellow Rice U., Houston, 1964-66; rsch. scientist Sandia Labs., Albuquerque, 1966-70; prof. chemistry U. Estadual De Sao Paulo En Campinas, Brazil, 1971-76; lab. dir. Aer-Aqua Labs. Inc., Houston, 1976-77; prin. scientist URS/Radian Corp., Austin, Tex., 1977—. Author: Chlorinated Dioxins and Furans, 1985; contbg. author: Principles of Environmental Sampling, 1996. Fellow Am. Indsl. Hygiene Assn. (com. chair-elect 1994, chmn. 1995, bd. dirs. 1992-93, 94-99, chmn. bd. 1990-92), Am. Inst. Chemists; mem. Am. Chem. Soc. (chmn. ctrl. Tex. chpt. 1980-82), Austin C. of C. (Leadership Austin 1992-93), N.Y. Acad. Sci., Am. Soc. Safety Engrs., Sigma Xi, Delta Epsilon Sigma. Achievements include development of numerous strategies and methods for environmental health monitoring, especially for ambient, indoor and workplace air. Avocations: backpacking, racquetball, skiing, coffee, sailing. Office: URS/Radian Corp PO Box 201088 Austin TX 78720-1088

WILLIAMS, CARL CHANSON, insurance company executive; b. Cin., Oct. 16, 1937; s. Charles J. and Alcie (Brazile) W.; m. Claire Bathé, May 26, 1985; 1 child, Michelle. A.S., U. Cin., 1965; BS, SUNY-Brockport, 1974; MBA, U. Rochester, 1975. Mgr. fin. systems Xerox Corp., Rochester, N.Y., 1972-77; dir. info. mgmt. Am. Can Co., Greenwich, Conn., 1977-79, mng. dir. info. mgmt., 1979-80, mng. dir. ops. control, 1980-82; sr. v.p., dir. mgmt. info. systems DDB Needham Worldwide, N.Y.C., 1982-91; pres. The Intertechnology Group, Inc., 1990-91; v.p. infosystems and tech. Macmillan Pub. Co., 1991-93; gen. mgr. info. tech. Amoco Corp., Chgo., 1993-94, v.p. info. tech., 1994-97; sr. v.p., chief info. officer Principal Fin. Group, Des Moines, 1997—. Cons. Stamford (Conn.) Bd. Edn., 1981-82; lectr. U. Rochester, N.Y., 1975-77; adj. prof. Fordham U., 1991—. Exec. dir. Concerned Assn. Rochester, N.Y., 1971-75; bd. dirs. Stamford Cmty. Arts Coun., 1983-84; trustee Roosevelt U., 1995-97, U. Rochester, 1999—. Exec. Leadership Found., 2000—; mem. Exec. Leadership Coun. 1993—. Mem. Soc. Info. Mgmr. (exec. coun. 1980-83, pres. 1985, pres. coun. 1986—), Exec. Leadership Coun. (found. bd. trustees). Office: Principal Fin Group 711 High St Des Moines IA 50392-0002 E-mail: williams.carl@principal.com.

WILLIAMS, CARL HARWELL, utilities executive; b. Mansfield, Ga., Oct. 22, 1915; s. John Horace and Mary Ruby (Harwell) W.; m. Diane Barnes, June 25, 1967; children: Edward Vincent, Lesa Anne. Student, U. Fla., 1934-35; BS, Ga. Sch. Tech., 1939; postgrad., Harvard Advanced Mgmt. Program, U. Hawaii, 1956. Registered profl. engr., Hawaii. Engr. Fla. Power & Light Co., Miami, 1939-41; with Hawaiian Electric Co., Inc., Honolulu, 1945-80, mgr. engring., 1955-62, v.p., 1962-71, exec. v.p., 1971-72, pres., 1972-80, dir., 1970-85, chmn. exec. com., 1980-85. Chmn. bd., dir. Maui Electric Co. (subsidiary), 1972-80, Hawaii Electric Light Co. (subsidiary), 1972-80; dir. Bank of Hawaii., Hawaiian Electric Industries, Inc., Bancorp Hawaii, Inc. Bd. dirs. Aloha United Way, 1973-79; bd. dirs. Oahu Devel. Conf., 1972-81, chmn., 1979-80; bd. visitors Coll. Bus. Adminstrn., Hawaii, mem. adv. con. advanced mgmt. program, 1969-75, mem. adv. com. Hawaii geothermal project, 1973-78; mem. State Energy Policy Task Force, 1974-78, Hawaii Energy Conservation Council, 1978-80, Gov.'s Com. Alt. Energy Devel., 1978-80; bd. dirs. Am.-Samoa Power Authority, 1981-83. Served to lt. col., Signal Corps AUS, 1941-45. Decorated Legion of Merit. Fellow IEEE; mem. Hawaii C. of C., Engring. Assn. Hawaii, Nat. Soc. Profl. Engrs. (past dir.), Hawaii Soc. Profl. Engrs. (past dir., pres.), Pacific Coast Elec. Assn. (dir. 1972-81, pres. 1979-80), AIEE (past chmn. Hawaii sect.) Clubs: Pacific, Outrigger Canoe. Home: 2969 Kalakaua Ave Apt 501 Honolulu HI 96815-4620

WILLIAMS, CARLISLE M., JR. municipal official; b. Painter, Va., June 27, 1937; s. Carlisle M. and Evelyn Hickman Williams; m. Barbara Belle Schuyler, July 11, 1987; m. Dolly Evans Taylor, June 15, 1958 (div. Mar. 19, 1987); children: Carlisle M. III, Valerie Taylor. AA, Goldey-Beacom Coll., Wilmington, Del., 1958; BA, East Carolina U., 1959. County adminstr. County of Accomac, Va., County of Stafford, 1984—. Adminstrv. officer & sec./treas. George Washington Boyhood Home Found., Stafford, 1992—99; chmn. Fredericksburg Area Met. Planning Orgn., Va., 2001—, VACO Group Self Ins. Assn., Roanoke, Va., 2001—; pres. Va. Local Govt. Mgmt. Assn., Richmond, Va., 1981—82; sec./treas. Cedar Island Bridge and Beach Authority, Accomac, 1975—83. Pres. Ea. Shore Jaycees, Onancock, Va., 1967—68, Onancock Rotary Club, 1981—82. Recipient Jefferson Cup, Va. Assn. Counties, 2000. Methodist. Avocation: sailing. Home: 12 Aiken Rd Fredericksburg VA 22405-3340 Office: County of Stafford 1300 Courthouse Rd PO Box 339 Stafford VA 22555-0339 Office Fax: 540-658-7643. E-mail: cmwjr@co.stafford.va.us.

WILLIAMS, CAROL JORGENSEN, social work educator; b. New Brunswick, N.J., Aug. 12, 1944; d. Einar Arthur and Mildred Estelle (Clayton) Jorgensen; m. Oneal Alexander Williams, July 4, 1980. BA, Douglass Coll., 1966; MS in Computer Sci., Stevens Inst. Tech., 1986; MSW, Rutgers U., 1971, PhD in Social Policy, 1981. Child welfare worker Bur. Children's Svcs., Jersey City, 1966-67, Outagamie County Dept. Social Svcs., Appleton, Wis., 1967-69; supr. WIN N.J. Divsn. Youth and Family Svcs., New Brunswick, 1969-70; coord. Outreach Plainfield (N.J.) Pub. Libr., 1972-76; rsch. project dir. County and Mcpl. Govt. Study Commn., N.J. State Legislature, 1976-79; prof. social work Kean U., Union, 1979—, assessment liaison social work program, 1987-2000, dir. MSW program, 1995-2000. Chmn. faculty senate gen. edn. com. Kean U., N.J., 1990-94, chmn. faculty senate ad hoc com. for 5-yr. review of gen. edn. program, 1991-93, mem. retention and tenure com. Sch. of Liberal Arts, 1988-94, vice chmn., 1992-94; cons. N.J. div. Youth and Family Svcs., 1979-93, Assn. for Children N.J., 1985-88; cons., evaluator Thomas A. Edison Coll., 1977—, mem. acad. coun. and others. Mem. adv. coun. Outdoor World, 2000—. Named Grad. Tchr. of Yr., Kean U. social work grad. students, 2001. Mem.: NASW (chpt. com. on nominating and leadership identification 1990—92, co-chmn. 1991—92), NOW, Nat. Assn. Deans and Dirs. Sch. Social Work, Assn. Baccalaureate Program Dirs. (com. on info tech. and distance edn. 1995—, assoc. editor BPD Update 2000—), Coun. on Social Work Edn. (commn. on confs. and faculty devel., dir. APM Med. Tech. Ctr. 1999—2002, chair subcom. on abstract rev. 2000—02, chair electronic poster session 2002—), Kean U. Fedn. Tchrs., Outdoor World (adv. coun. 2000—), Good Sam Club. Democrat. Home: 32 Halstead Rd New Brunswick NJ 08901-1619 Office: Kean U Social Work Program Morris Ave Union NJ 07083-7117 E-mail: caroljwilliams@worldnet.att.net.

WILLIAMS, CAROL MARIE, secondary school educator; b. Kansas City, Kans., June 10, 1939; d. Leonard Cropley and Minnie Marie (Wass) Nicholson; m. Howard Dean Williams, Dec. 29, 1961; children: Jeffrey Allen, Gregory Scott AA, Kansas City (Mo.) Jr. Coll., 1959; BS in Edn., Ctrl. Mo. State U., 1962. English tchr. Raytown (Mo.) H.S., 1961-62; English tchr., coord. dist. lang. arts Ruskin H.S., Kansas City, Mo., 1964-66; English tchr. Hickman Mills H.S., 1969-70; tchr. English, debate, history, leadership comms., student govt. Andover (Kans.) H.S., 1982-95, dist. lang. arts coord., dept. chair, 1982-95; English tchr. Olathe South (Kans.) H.S., 1996—. Coord., debate and forensics coach Andover Sch. Dist., 1982-85, chair North Ctrl. Accreditation, 1983-84, supt., prin. adv. couns., 1983-95, dist. curriculum coun., 1983-95; coord. AP Lang. Exam. Prep. Workshop; new tchr. mentor. Publicity editor The Lamp mag., 1969 (Nat. Recognition award 1969); contbg. editor Topeka mag., 1977-79; co-editor Andover Rsch. jour., 1993. Recipient Outstanding Tchr. and Mentor Recognition award U. Kans., Outstanding H.S. Edn. Recognition award Kans. Newman Coll. Mem. NEA, Kans. Olathe-NEA, Nat. Coun. Tchrs. of English, Kans. Assn. Tchrs. of English. Republican. Episcopalian. Avocations: reading, music, tennis, travel, writing. Home: 1204 W 63d St Kansas City MO 64113 Office: Olathe South HS 1640 E 151st St Olathe KS 66062-2851

WILLIAMS, CAROLYN WOODWORTH, retired elementary education educator, consultant; b. Binghamton, N.Y., Aug. 29, 1937; d. Charles Byron Woodworth and Dorothy Louise (Wheeler) Krum; m. James C. Williams, Mar. 29, 1958; children: Christopher, Lizette Macaluso, Matthew (dec.). BS in Elem. Edn., SUNY, Cortland, 1958; postgrad., SUNY, Geneseo, 1973-74, U. Vt., 1988; MS in Edn., SUNY, Brockport, 1989. Cert. tchr. K-6, N.Y. Elem. tchr. grade 6 Whitney Point (N.Y.) Ctrl. Sch., 1959-69, Palmyra (N.Y.)-Macedon Ctrl. Sch., 1969-71, elem. tchr. grade 4, 1971-79, 84-95, elem. tchr. grade 1, 1979-84, ret., 1995. Author, editor booklets. Active Women's Rep. Club, Binghamton, N.Y., 1959-67. Recipient Bring Local History Live into Classroom award Griffiss-McLouth Fund, 1993. Mem. ASCD, AAUW, N.Y. State United Tchrs., N.Y. State Hist. Soc., Wayne County Hist. Soc. (bicentennial history fair coord. 1989), Ea. Star (sister). Methodist. Avocations: children's welfare, literacy, women's issues, history, technology. Home: 104 Florence Dr Shohola PA 18458-3511

WILLIAMS, CATHLENE ANN, association executive, researcher; b. Waterloo, Iowa, Apr. 17, 1945; d. Harold Stanley and Martha Elizabeth (Loonan) Nation; m. Jan Adrian DeYoung, June 10, 1967 (div. Feb. 20, 1976); 1 child: Laura Elizabeth; m. Clyde Roydon Williams, Jan. 3, 1977. BS, Iowa State U., 1967; MA, U. N. Iowa, 1971; PhD, George Washington U., 1995. Tchr. Oak Park (Ill.) Pub. Schs., 1967-69, Cedar Falls (Iowa) Pub. Schs., 1969-75; adminstrv. asst. Sys. Rsch. Inc./Ednl. Methods, Washington, 1975-77; adminstrv. asst. to exec. dir. Nat. Assn. State Bds. Edn., Alexandria, Va., 1985-86, project specialist, 1978-80, project dir., 1980-82, dir., 1985-86; communications mgr. Nat. Soc. Fund Raising Execs., 1987-89, dir. external affairs, 1989-91, dir. libr. and rsch. svcs., 1991-94, dir. edn. and rsch. programs, 1994—. Author: (with others) Manual on State Policies Related to Adolescent Parenthood, 1980, A Guide to Employment and Training Programs for Adolescent Parents, 1981; editor: The Journal, 1987-92, Nat. Soc. Fund Raising Execs. News, 1987-91, The State Bd. Connection, 1981-86. Vestry Ch. of the Resurrection Episcopal Ch. (register 1988, jr. warden 1989, 93, assoc. sr. warden 1990, lay ordination com. 1990, cmty. concerns com. 1993—, stewardship com.). Mem. Am. Soc. Assn. Execs., PRSA, Internat. Soc. for 3d Sector Rsch., AAUW (newsletter editor 1986-87, treas. 1986-87, v.p. mem. 1984-85, pres. Alexandria br. 1988-89), Assn. Rsch. on Nonprofit Orgns. and Voluntary Action, Phi Gamma Delta, Phi Upsilon Omicron, Omicron Nu. Office: Nat Soc Fund Raising Execs 1101 King St Ste 700 Alexandria VA 22314-2944

WILLIAMS, CATHY LYNN, nurse; b. Galion, Ohio, Nov. 22, 1947; d. Ernest LeRoy and Wilma Eleanor (Fauth) Denton; m. Michael Earl Williams, July 14, 1979 (div. July 1984). ADN, Lorain County C.C., 1971. RN Ohio, Calif. Staff nurse U. Hosp., Cleve., 1971-75; critical care nurse, med. ICU Cedars-Sinai Med. Ctr., L.A., 1975-76; critical care nurse, surg. ICU Santa Clara Valley Med. Ctr., San Jose, Calif., 1976-80, Ohio State U. Hosp., Columbus, 1980-88; nurse utilization rev. Peer Rev. Sys., 1988-91; case mgr. United Health Care of Ohio, 1991-99, risk mgr., 2000, cardiac disease state mgr., 2000—. Bd. dirs. Ctrl. Ohio Case Mgmt. Network, 2000—, co-chmn. membership com., 2000—02. Vol. Children's Immunization Clinic. Avocations: travel, reading. Home: 3417 Leighton Rd Upper Arlington OH 43221-1300 E-mail: cathywilliams@columbus.rr.com.

WILLIAMS, CECILIA LEE PURSEL, optometrist; b. Lewisburg, Pa., Nov. 15, 1948; d. Lee LaVerne and Geraldine May (Steininger) Pursel; m. Richard Lee Williams, May 17, 1975; 1 son, Kent Lee. Student, Lycoming Coll., 1966-68; BS, Pa. Coll. Optometry, 1970, OD, 1972. Lic. and/or cert. optometrist, D.C., Pa., N.Y., N.J., Va. Rsch. optometrist in soft lens materials Gumpelmayer Optik, Vienna, Austria, 1973; optometrist Sterling Optical Co. Contact Lens Ctr., Washington, 1974-79; pvt. practice optometry Springfield, Va., 1980—. Recipient Clin. Efficiency award Pa. Coll. Optometry, 1972; Women's Aux. of Pa. Optometrists scholar, 1968-70, 70-72; Pa. State grantee, 1968-70, 70-72. Mem. Optometric Ctr. of Nation's Capital (dir. 1977-80), Am. Optometric Assn., Va. Optometric Assn., No. Va. Optometric Soc., Nat. Honor Soc. for Optometry, Omega Delta. Home: 3600 Wilton Hall Ct Alexandria VA 22310-2176 Office: 7241 Commerce St Springfield VA 22150-3411

WILLIAMS, CEOLA C. quality assurance professional; b. Beatrice, Ala., July 12, 1936; d. Frank Mann and Flossie Mae (Stallworth) Webb; m. O.B. Williams, Apr. 16, 1955; children: Marilyn Gurnell, Frances Smith, O.B. Jr., Michael, Ronald, Greg, Jeffrey. BA, Martin U., 1993. Printed cir. clk. Radio Corp. Am., Indpls., 1966—77, selective video operator, 1981—83; machinist Chrysler Corp., 1977—79; engraver Herff Jones Jewelry, 1979—81; quality control staff F.P. Video, 1986—98; with Thomson Consumer Electronic, 1994—99; part-time assoc. Sears Hardware, 1995—2001; youth staff stopover Cmty. Ctrs. Indpls., Inc., 2001—. Student body staff Rethinking Prison Orgn., Indpls., 1992; asst. pres. Deaconess Bd., Indpls., 1995-96. Author: Myself 1990 (Plaque Libr. Congr. 1997); songwriter Jesus Is My Savior, 1997, Satisfied with Jesus, 1997, Johnny, 1998, There Were Twelve Disciples, 1998. Vol. asst. Pres. Election, Indpls., 1968. Recipient Indpls. Police League plaque, 1995-96. Democrat. Methodist. Home: 4018 N Bolton Ave Indianapolis IN 46226-4831

WILLIAMS, CHARLES EDWARD, engineer; b. Warsaw, July 9, 1939; s. Charles Dwight and Oletha (Davenport) W.; m. Grace Norma Robertson, June 30, 1965 (div. 1970); 1 child, Eric Charles; m. Virginia Vee Parker, May 3, 1980. BS in Ceramic Engring., Alfred U., 1961; MS in Phys. Metallurgy, Denver U., 1968. Ceramic engr. Rocky Flats plant Dow Chem., Golden, Colo., 1961-65; ceramic engr. Coors Porcelain Co., 1965-69; packaging engr. Fairchild Semiconductor, San Diego, 1969-71; sales engr., cons. Otto Jahnke and Assocs., 1971-72; plant engr. Tecate (Mex.) Internat., Baja California, 1972-73; prodn. engr. ceramic divsn. Buckbee Mears, San Diego, 1973-75; mem. group tech. staff Tex. Instruments, Dallas, 1975—. Contbr. articles to profl. jours.; 13 patents in field; performer (audiocassette) Up The Trail, 1993. Exec. v.p. Acad. We. Artists, Ft. Worth, 1995-99. Mem. IEEE, Internat. Microelectronic and Packaging Soc. Republican. Presbyterian. Avocations: cowboy poetry, professional storytelling, pottery. Home: 6245 Chesley Ln Dallas TX 75214-2118 Office: Tex Instruments m/s 8719 12500 TI Blvd Dallas TX 75243-4136 E-mail: c-williams7@ti.com.

WILLIAMS, CHARLES JUDSON, lawyer, writer; b. San Mateo, Calif., Nov. 23, 1930; s. John Augustus and Edith (Babcock) W.; children: Patrick, Victoria, Apphia. AB, U. Calif., Berkeley, 1952, LLB, 1955. Bar: Calif. 1955, U.S. Supreme Ct., 1970. Assoc. Kirkbride, Wilson, Harzfeld and Wallace, San Mateo County, Calif., 1956-59; sole practice Solano County, 1959-64, Martinez, 1964—, Benicia, 1981-88; city atty. Pleasant Hill, 1962-80, Yountville, 1965-68, Benicia, 1968-76, 80-82, Lafayette, Calif., 1968—, Moraga, 1974-92, Danville, 1982-88, Pittsburg, 1984-93, Orinda, 1985-97; of counsel Best Best and Krieger, Best, Best and Krieger, 2002—. Lectr. Calif. Continuing Edn. Bar 1964-65, U. Calif. Extension 1974-76, John F. Kennedy U. Sch. Law 1966-69; spl. counsel to various Calif. cities; legal advisor Alaska Legis. Council 1959-61; advisor Alaska sup. ct. 1960-61; advisor on revision Alaska statues 1960-62; atty. Pleasant Hill Redevel. Agy. 1978-82; sec., bd. dirs. Vintage Savs. & Loan Assn., Napa County, Calif., 1974-82; bd. dirs. 23d Agrl. Dist. Assn., Contra Costa County, 1968-70. Author: California Code Comments to West's Annotated California Codes, 3 vols., 1965, West' California Code Forms, Commercial, 2 vols., 1965, West's California Government Code Forms, 3 vols., 1971, Supplement to California Zoning Practice,

1978, 80, 82, 84, 85, 87, 89, 91, 94, 96, 98, 2000, 01; contbr. articles to legal jours. Mem. ABA, Calif. Bar Assn., Contra Costa County Bar Assn. Office: 1330 Arnold Dr Ste 149 Martinez CA 94553-6538 E-mail: chaslaw@aol.com.

WILLIAMS, C(HARLES) K(ENNETH), poet, literature and writing educator; b. Newark, Nov. 4, 1936; s. Paul Bernard and Dossie (Kasdin) W.; m. Sarah Dean Jones, June, 1966 (div. 1975); 1 child, Jessica Anne; m. Catherine Justine Mauger, Apr. 15, 1975; 1 child, Jed Mauger. BA, U. Pa., 1958. Vis. prof. lit. Beaver Coll., Jenkintown, Pa., 1975, Drexel U., Phila., 1976, U. Calif., Irvine, 1978, Boston U., 1979-80, Bklyn. Coll., 1982-83; Mellon vis. prof. lit. Franklin and Marshall Coll., Lancaster, Pa., 1977; prof. writing Columbia U., N.Y.C., 1981-85; prof. lit. George Mason U., Fairfax, Va., 1982-95. Halloway lectr. U. Calif., Berkeley, 1986, Princeton U., 1995—. Author: A Day for Anne Frank, 1968, Lies, 1969, I Am the Bitter Name, 1972, With Ignorance, 1977, The Lark, The Thrush, The Starling, 1983, Tar, 1983, Flesh and Blood, 1987, Poems, 1963-1983, 1988, The Bacchae of Euripides, 1990, Helen, 1991, A Dream of Mind: Poems, 1992, Selected Poems, 1994, The Vigil, 1997, Poetry and Consciousness, 1998, Repair, 1999, Misgivings, A Memoir, 2000; contbg. editor Am. Poetry Rev., 1972—; translator: Women of Trachis (Sophocles), 1978. Sponsor People's Fund, Phila., 1967—. Recipient Nat. Book Critics Circle award in poetry, 1987, Morton Dauwen Zabel prize, Am. Acad. of Arts and Letters, 1989, Lit. prize, 1999, Harriet Monroe prize, 1993, Berlin prize, Am. Acad. in Berlin, 1998, Pulitzer prize, 2000, Book award, L.A. Times, 2000, Weathertop prize, 2000, Pen Marth Albrand Memoir prize, 2001; fellow, Guggenheim Found., 1975, Nat. Endowment for Arts, 1985, 1993; grantee, Lila Wallace-Reader's Digest, 1993—95. Mem. PEN (Voelcker Career Achievement award 1998), Poetry Soc. Am., Am. Acad. Arts & Scis. Avocations: piano, guitar, drawing. Home: 82 Rue d'Hauteville 75010 Paris France

WILLIAMS, CHARLES LAVAL, JR. physician, international organization official; b. New Orleans, Jan. 19, 1916; s. Charles Laval and Lewise (McLaurine) W.; m. Ellen Clendenin Ustick, Dec. 14, 1946; children: Ellen Clendenin, Katherine McLaurine. Student, U. Va., 1933-35; MD, Tulane U., 1940; M.P.H., U. Mich., 1945. Diplomate: Am. Bd. Preventive Medicine and Pub. Health. Intern U.S. Marine Hosp., New Orleans, 1941; with USPHS, 1941-67; assigned N.C. State Health Dept., 1941-44, USPHS States Relations div., 1944, U. Mich., 1944-45, Am. Acad. Pediatrics Nat. Study Child Health Services, 1945-47; chief planning unit, asst. chief div. commd. officers, 1947-51; with US/AID Div. Pub. Health, 1951-62; chief pub. health adviser AID Mission to Peru, 1959-62; asso. dir. internat. relations Office Internat. Health, 1962-64; chief Office Internat. Research, NIH, Bethesda, Md., 1965-66; dep. dir., then dir. Office Internat. Health, Office Surgeon General, USPHS, Washington, 1966-67; dep. dir. Pan Am. Health Orgn., 1967-79; ret.; exec. v.p. Am. Assn. World Health, 1980-84. U.S. del./alt. or advisor to eight world health assemblies between 1955 and 1967, and to ten sessions of the Directing Coun. of the Pan Am. Health Orgn. between 1953 and 1966. Fellow Am. Pub. Health Assn.; mem. U.S.-Mexico Border Pub. Health Assn., Phi Kappa Phi, Delta Omega. Home: 5600 Wisconsin Ave Apt 1009 Chevy Chase MD 20815-4411

WILLIAMS, CHARLES VERNON, III, education administrator; b. York, Pa., May 26, 1940; s. Charles Vernon Jr. and Ruth Irene (Barton) W.; m. Marie Carmel Felix, Mar. 20, 1973; children: Joann C., Monique M., Michelle C. Diploma, Modern Sch. Photography, 1975; AAS in Religious Instn. Mgmt., C.C. of the Air Force, 1977; B in Gen. Studies in Bus., U. Nebr., 1974; MA in Logistics, Ctrl. Mich. U., 1977. Pvt. pilot cert. FAA. Served to rank of MSgt. USAF, to 1980, chapel mgmt. supt., 1958-80, chief budget and logistics; pers. mgr. Job Corps, Dayton, Ohio, 1984-85; pvt. practice cons., 1985-86; asst. mgr. purchasing Dayton Pub. Schs., 1986-97, dir. adminstrv. svcs., 1997-98, dir. logistical support svcs., 1998—. Part-time faculty Sinclair C.C., Dayton, 1977—, Capital U., Columbus, Ohio, 1979-84; exec. com. mem. Ednl. Purchasing Coun., Dayton, 1986—, chmn., 1994—; mem. adv. coun. Miami Valley Career Tech. Ctr., Dayton, 1989—; treas. Ohio Coun./Edn. Purchasing Consortia, 1990—. Mem. Optimist Internat. (pres. 1994, Royal Arch Mason (high priest 1989), 33rd Degree Mason (pres. 1974), Order of the Ea. Star (past patron 1970-73), Shrine Temple (potentiate 1984, Shriner of Yr.), Masonic Lodge (treas., worshipful master 1985, treas. 1986—). Baptist. Avocations: flying, photography. Office: Dayton Bd Edn 4280 N James H Mcgee Blvd Dayton OH 45427-3482 E-mail: cwilliam@dps.k12.oh.us.

WILLIAMS, CHARLES WESLEY, technical executive, researcher; b. Palestine, Ark. s. Fredrick Charles and Fannie Rochet (Southall) W.; m. Nancy Sue Rhea, Sept. 5, 1959; children: Brent L., Brian E. BSE.E., U. Tenn.-Knoxville, 1959, MS, 1963. Registered profl. engr., Ohio. Devel. engr. Mead Research Lab., Chillicothe, Ohio, 1959-60, Oak Ridge Nat. Lab., 1960-63; tech. mgr. EG & G Ortec, Oak Ridge, 1963-76, tech. dir. phys. and life sci., 1976-81; mgr. Assay Inst. EG & Ortec, 1981-85; pres. Autograffix Inc., Knoxville, Tenn., 1985—. Contbr. articles to tech. jours., chpt. to book. Fellow IEEE (v.p. Nuclear and Plasma Sci. Soc. 1979); mem. Tau Beta Pi, Eta Kappa Nu Baptist.

WILLIAMS, CHERYL A. secondary education educator; b. Neosho, Mo., July 7, 1957; d. Travestine Williams. BS in Math., Tex A&M U., 1978, postgrad., 1978-79, Rose State Coll., 1980-81, Sheppard Tech. Tng. Ctr., 1980-81; MS in Math., U. Tex., 1997. Computer scientist Tinker AFB, Oklahoma City, 1980-81, Defense Comm. Agy., Washington, 1986; tchr. Parent Child Inc., San Antonio, 1989; asst. sec. Antioch Bapt. Ch., 1989-92; substitute tchr. San Antonio Ind. Sch. Dist., 1990-93; instrnl. asst. Northside Ind. Sch. Dist., San Antonio, 1995-96, asst. tchr., 1994-95, North East Ind. Sch. Dist., San Antonio, 1996—2001; rep. West Telemarketing, 1998-99; math. tutor St. Philips Coll., 1998-99, instr. math., 1998—, Alamo C.C. Dist., 1998—; math. tutor Trave and G.G.'s Tutorial Svc., 1999—; instr. math. Guardian Angel Performing Arts Acad., 2002—. Asst. mgr. Fashion Pl., San Antonio, 1994—95; tax preparer H&R Block, 1994—95; distbr. Avon, 1999—2001; indep. beauty cons. Mary Kay Cosmetics, 1999—; scorer Harcourt Brace Corp., 2001, Randstad, 2001; rep. Express Svcs., 2001. Counselor YMCA, San Antonio, 1989-91; active Girl Scouts U.S., 1964-86; mem. choir, asst. sec. area ch., 1972, tutor, 1970—, tchr. Sunday Sch., 1973-86, asst. sec. Sunday Sch., 1973-86, 88—, asst. ch. sec., 1988-91; mem. Dorcas Circle, Lupus Found. Am., Biomed. Rsch. U. Tex., 1995—; mem. Epilepsy Found. Am., Tex. Head Injury Assn., Nat. Head Injury Assn., Smithsonian Instn. Mem. NEA, Tex. Edn. Assn., Mu. Alpha Theta. Avocations: jigsaw puzzles, bowling.

WILLIAMS, CHRISTINE HEWES, elementary education educator; b. Jersey City, May 18, 1951; d. John Libbey and Virginia (Pennell) Hewes; m. A. Wesley Williams Jr., June 9, 1973; children: Sarah, Robert Charles. BS in Edn., U. Maine, Machias, 1973; MEd, U. Maine, 1993; postgrad., U. Main, 1997—. Cert. tchr., Maine. Substitute tchr. Bucksport (Maine) Sch. Dept., 1973-74, 75-77, chpt. 1 aide, 1974-75, spl. edn. aide handicapped students, 1977-78, classroom tchr., 1978—; coop. tchr. for student tchrs., 1988, 90, 94; facilitator of K-8 sci. curriculum team, 1992-94; coord. chem. health programs Bucksport (Maine) Sch. Dept., 1988—, mem. sch. improvement team, 1986-89, coord. student assistance team, 1989—. Chair faculty coun. Jewett Sch., Bucksport, 1985-86, past team leader 5th grade. Sec. Substance Abuse Info. Team, Bucksport, 1985—. Mem. ASCD, NEA, Maine Tchrs. Assn., Maine Assn. Mid. Level Edn. (presenter fall conf. 1995, 1998, Exemplary Practices award 1996), New Eng. League Mid. Schs., Bucksport Tchr. Assn., Camp Laughing Loon YMCA Alumni Assn. (reunion chair 1985-90), Phi Kappa Phi. Democrat. Congregationalist. Avocations: walking, swimming, stamp collecting, reading. Office: GH Jewett Sch Bridge St Bucksport ME 04416

WILLIAMS, CHRISTINE WHALEY, county official, consultant; b. Magnolia, N.C., Oct. 28, 1915; d. Mack J. and Jeanette Thomas Whaley; m. Lehman Guy Williams, Dec. 23, 1937 (dec.); children: Guy Melvin, Joseph Glenn. Corr. course in bus., Southeastern U., Rock Hill, S.C., 1933; postgrad., Mt. Olive Coll., 1989. Office mgr. Duplin County Agr. Adjustment Adminstrn., Kenansville, NC, 1933—42, Turner & Turner Ins., Pink Hill; elected ofc. Duplin County Register of Deeds, Kenansville. Author: Chrysthine, 1998 (Duplin County Hall of Fame, 1998). Sec. Pink Hill Bus. and Profl., 1990—94; hospice vol., 1988—; Stephen min., 1998—. Named Tar Heel of Week, Raleigh News and Observer, 1962. Mem.: N.C. Assn. Registers of Deeds (state pres. 1962—63), Kinston Arts Study Club, Kenansville Garden Club (pres. 1990—92, 1996—97), Warsaw Garden Club (pres. 1992—94). Democrat. Presbyterian. Home: # 11 663 E NC Pink Hill NC 28572

WILLIAMS, CLARENCE, protective services official; b. Shreveport, La., Oct. 1, 1945; s. Leonard and Hearlean (Willis) W.; m. Mary K. Mannings, Nov. 30, 1974 (div. 1982); 1 child, Makala Deloris; m. Paulette Maria Guyton, Nov. 9, 1991; children: Kevin Michael, Maleah Requal. Student, So. U., 1963-64, Seattle C.C., 1968. Aerospace mechanic Boeing Aircraft Co., Seattle, 1965-68; fire fighter Seattle Fire Dept., 1968-76, engr., driver, 1976-82, emergency med. tech., 1976—, lt., 1982—. Accreditation inspector Nat. Fire Protection Assn., Quincy, Mass., 1990—; cons. Pryor McClendon Counts Investment Bankers, 1993. Chmn. bd. trustees Mt. Zion Bapt. Ch., Seattle, 1992—; active Leadership Tomorrow, Seattle, 1986—, N.W. Conf. Black Pub. Ofcls., Wash., 1980—. With Wash. NG, 1965-71. Named one of Outstanding Young Men Am., 1978, 81, Most Outstanding Fire Fighter in State of Wash. Wash. State Jaycees, 1979; recognized for furthering cause of human rights UN Assn. U.S.A., 1979. Mem. Internat. Assn. Black Profl. Fire Fighters (pres. 1984-88), NAACP (membership com. 1976), Seattle Urban League (scholarship com. 1978), Seattle Black Fire Fighters Assn. (pres. 1968), So. U. Alumni Assn. Democrat. Office: Internat Assn Black Profl Fire Fighters PO Box 22005 Seattle WA 98122-0005

WILLIAMS, CLAY RULE, lawyer; b. Milw., Sept. 25, 1935; s. George Laverne and Marguerite Mae (Rule) W.; m. Jeanne Lee Huber, Jan. 18, 1986; children: Gwynne, Amy, Daniel, Sarah. BA, Lawrence U., 1957; LLB, U. Mich., 1960. Bar: Wis. 1960, U.S. Dist. Ct. (ea. and we. dists.) Wis. 1964, U.S. Ct. Appeals (7th cir.) 1965, U.S. Ct. Mil. Appeals 1963, U.S. Supreme Ct. 1963. Assoc. Gibbs, Roper & Fifield, Milw., 1963-67; ptnr., shareholder Von Briesen & Roper, S.C., 1967-99, of counsel, 1999—. Mem. Gov.'s Task Force Creation Bus. Ct., 1994-99; instr. profl. seminars. Author: Berry, Davis, Deguire and Williams, Wisconsin Business Corporation Law, 1992; contbr. articles to profl. jours. Active Shorewood (Wis.) Sch. Bd., 1976-79. Capt. USAF, Judge Adv. Corps., 1960-63. Fellow Wis. Bar Found.; mem. ABA (sect. antitrust law, corp. counseling com.), Wis. Bar Assn. (co-chmn. com. to revise corp. laws 1986-90, chmn. standing com. on bus. corp. law 1990-97, Pres.'s Award of Excellence 1990, 97), Milw. Bar Assn. (probate and real property sect., joint bench-bar com. Ct. Appeals, 1986-88, long-range planning com. 1987), Am. Law Inst., Milw. Club, Univ. Club. Republican. Episcopalian. Avocations: hunting, fishing, skiing, reading. Office: von Briesen Purtell & Roper SC 735 N Water St Milwaukee WI 53202-4100 E-mail: cwilliam@vonbriesen.com.

WILLIAMS, CLIFFORD GLYN, economics educator; b. Pembrokeshire, Wales, Feb. 23, 1928; came to U.S., 1958, naturalized, 1967; s. Arthur J. and Annie M. Williams; m. Nancy K. Hammons, Mar. 24, 1977; children— Karen Jean, John Andrew. B.A., U.Wales, Aberystwyth, 1956; M.A., Victoria U., Manchester, Eng., 1958; Ph.D., U. Va., 1962. Asst. prof. econs. U. Alta., Edmonton, Can., 196-163, Ind. U.-Bloomington, 1963-66, Boston Coll., Chestnut Hill, Mass., 1966-69; assoc. prof. U. S.C., Columbia, 1969-73, prof., 1973— . Author: Labor Economics, 1970. Contbg. editor Wall St. Review of Books. Book rev. editor The Economics of Education Review. Contbr. articles to profl. publs. Mem. Am. Econ. Assn., Indsl. Relation Research Assn. Mem. Recovery Movement. Home: 201 Tyborne Cir Columbia SC 29210-4233 Office: U SC Dept Econs Columbia SC 29208-0001

WILLIAMS, CRAIG FOSTER, osteopathic emergency physician; b. Akron, Ohio, July 23, 1949; s. Robert Daniel and Jeanne Marie (Schulte) W.; m. Carol Giglia, May 6, 1978; children: Joy Caroline, Cara Jeanne, Eric James. BA, Notre Dame U., 1971; DO, Kansas City Coll. Osteo., 1977. Diplomate Am. Bd. Emergency Medicine. Intern Doctor's Hosp., Columbus, Ohio, 1977-78; resident in emergency medicine Wright State U., Dayton, 1978-80, mem. faculty, 1982—, asst. clin. prof. emergency medicine, 1983—; commd. officer USPHS Indian Health Svc., Phoenix, 1980-82. Staff emergency physician St. Elizabeth Med. Ctr., Dayton, 1982-95, Upper Valley Med. Ctr., Troy, Ohio, 1995—; dir. Fletcher (Ohio) Emergency Med. Svc., 1995—. Named Clin. Tchr. of Yr., Wright State U., 1985, 88, Miami County Physician of Yr., 1996, Ohio Emergency Physician of Yr., 1999. Fellow Am. Coll. Emergency Physicians; mem. AMA, Univ. Assn. Emergency Medicine, Am. Coll. Osteo. Emergency Physicians, Am. Osteo. Assn., Notre Dame Alumni Assn. Roman Catholic. Home: 6649 Stamford Pl Dayton OH 45459-3310 Office: Upper Valley Med Ctr Troy OH 45373

WILLIAMS, CURTIS CHANDLER, III, retired chemical engineer, consultant; b. N.Y.C., Sept. 30, 1926; s. Curtis Chandler Jr. and Margareathe (Cramer) W.; m. Barbara G. Williams; children: Richard Quimby, Susan Williams Darrow. B in Engring. with honors, Yale U., 1948; MS, MIT, 1950, DSc, 1953. Cert. profl. engr., Tex. Process engr. Emeryville Rsch. Ctr. Shell Oil Co., 1953-59, supr. Emeryville Rsch. Ctr., 1959-64, sr. engr. Mfg. Rsch. Devel., 1964-65, head petroleum processing dept. Emeryville Rsch. Ctr., 1965-67; chief technologist Wood River Refinery Shell Devel. Co., 1967-71; mgr. facilities Shell Oil Co., Houston, 1971-74, mgr. process engring.-refining, 1974-82, mgr. process engring.-separations, 1982-92, mgr. separations, 1992-93, cons., 1994—. Chmn. tech. data com. API, 1965-99; cons. Exec. Svc. Corps Houston, 1994—. Judge Houston Sci. Fair, 1983—; trustee Wilchester W. Homeowner's Assn., 1987-92; pres. Hosp. Presbiteriano de Mainero, Inc., 1999—. With U.S. Navy, 1945-46. Fellow AIChE (mem. continuing edn. com. 1992); mem. Am. Chem. Soc., Sigma Xi. Presbyterian. Home: 1249 Ripple Creek Dr Houston TX 77057-1764

WILLIAMS, CYRIL LABODÉ, mechanical engineer; b. Freetown, Sierra Leone, Mar. 8, 1963; came to U.S., 1985; s. Adebayo Samuel and Letitia Rosamond (Macauley) W.; m. Cheryl Denise Rodgers, Aug. 15, 1992 (div.); m. Sally Abionor Alhadi, Dec. 26, 1997. BS in Engring., U. Md., 1997, MS in Engring., 2000. Design engr. AMBEC, Owings Mills, Md., 1992-96, cons., 1996-2000; reliability engr. DuPont Engring., Belle, W.Va., 2000—. Cons. Black and Decker, Easton, Md., 1997-98, Am. Mech., Balt., 1996-98, UMBC, Balt., 1997-98. Mem. Pres. Student's Adv. Coun. U. Md., 1997. With USAF. Fellowship McNair Scholars Program, 1997-98. Mem. ASME, Soc. of Mfgs. Engrs. (assoc., scholarship 1998), Soc. Automotive Engrs., Sigma Xi. Avocations: ballistics, golf, tennis, computers. E-mail: l.williams@usa.dupont.com.

WILLIAMS, DANIEL BRYAN, obstetrician/gynecologist, educator; b. St. Louis, Dec. 13, 1961; MD, U. Mo. Kansas City, 1985. Diplomate Am. Bd. Ob-Gyn, Am. Bd. Reproductive Endocrinology. Intern, resident King-Drew Med. Ctr., L.A., 1985—89; fellow reproduction, endocrinology, infertility UCLA Cedars Sinai Med. Ctr., 1989—91; instr. dept. ob-gyn Washington U., St. Louis, 1991—93, asst. prof., 1993—96, assoc. prof., 1997—2002; assoc. prof. medicine U. Cin., 2002—. Office: Christ Hospital 2123 Auburn Ave #415 Cincinnati OH 45219

WILLIAMS, DANNY ROBERT, systems administrator, consultant; b. Phenix City, Ala., Aug. 24, 1960; s. Houston Lymul and Mary Alma Williams; m. Lou Ann Tucker, Mar. 2, 1961; children: Danny Jr., Joy Marye, Leslie DeAnn, Malcom Sean. AS in Electronics, Phillips Coll., 1985; AS in Computer Info. Sci., Chattahoochee Valley C.C., 2000; AAS in Data Processing , Chattahoochea Valley C.C., 2000; BS in Computer Tech., Tray State U., 2001. Equipment operator Crouch Constrn. Co., Columbus, Ga., 1978—79, Alexander Constrn. Co., Columbus, 1979—81, Taylor Logging Co., Seale, Ala., 1981—83; carpenter William L. Newman Co., Columbus, 1983—85; electric/engring. technican Techsonic Industry, Eufaula, Ala., 1985—90; assoc. engr. Hughes Aircraft Co., LaGrange, Ga., 1991—98; programmer analyst St. Francis Hosp., Columbus, 1998—. Avocation: swimming. Home: 1620 S Seale Rd Phenix City AL 36869

WILLIAMS, DARRYL MARLOWE, medical educator; b. Denver, Apr. 3, 1938; s. Archie Malvin and Dorothy Merle (Grapes) W.; m. Susan Arlene Moore, June 24, 1966; children: Carol Ruth, Peter Todd, Sarah Elizabeth. Student, U. Colo., 1956-58; BS, Colo. State U., 1993; MD, MS in Anatomy, Baylor U., 1964; MPH, U. Tex., 2001. Diplomate Am. Bd. Internal Medicine, Am. Bd. Hematology. Intern and resident Baylor Affiliated Hosps., Houston, 1964-66, 67-68; resident U. Utah, Salt Lake City, 1966-67, fellow in hematology, 1968-73, asst. prof., 1973-77; assoc. prof. La State U., Shreveport, 1977-81, prof., 1981-90, chief hematology sect., 1977-85, asst. dean/rsch., 1981-85, dean Sch. Medicine, 1985-90; prof. medicine, dean Sch. Medicine Tex. Tech U. Health Scis. Ctr., Lubbock, 1990-95; prof. medicine office border health and area health edn. Tex. Tech. Health Scis. Ctr., El Paso, 1995—, also bd. dirs., 1995—; dir. med. edn. Cmty. Partnership Tex. Tech. Health Sci. Ctr., 1995—2001. Mem. hemophilia adv. com. La. Legislature, Baton Rouge, 1977-83; vice chair La. Lung and Cancer Bd., New Orleans, 1984-90; pres. N.W. La. AIDS Task Force, Shreveport, 1987, pres. El Paso Unit Am. Cancer Soc. Mem. editl. bd. Tex. Jour. Rural Health, 1990—. Mem. Am. Heart Assn., Lubbock chpt., Shreveport Biracial Commn., 1988, Lubbock Indigent Health Care Coalition Task Force, 1991-92, Health Professions Edn. Adv. Com., Lubbock Friends of Pub. Radio; vice chair health profls. edn. adv. com. Tex. Coord. Bd. Higher Edn., 1992-95; sec. Health Edn. and Tng. Consortium of Tex., 1990-99, vice chmn., 1999-2002, chmn., 2002-; mem. steering com. Border Vision Fronteriza, 1995-2000; bd. dirs. El Paso Cancer Consortium; project dir. Hispanic Ctr. of Excellence, 2001—. Recipient award Nat. Ski Patrol System, Salt Lake City, 1975 Fellow ACP, Am. Coll. Nutrition; mem. AMA, Am. Soc. Hematology, Am. Inst. Nutrition, Am. Soc. Clin. Nutrition, Tex. Med. Assn. (physicians oncology edn. com.), Am. Cancer Soc. (bd. dir. El Paso unit, 1999—, pres., 2001—), Alpha Omega Alpha. Office: Tex Tech Health Sci Ctr at El Paso 4800 Alberta Ave El Paso TX 79905-2709

WILLIAMS, DAVE HARRELL, investment executive; b. Beaumont, Tex., Oct. 5, 1932; s. George Davis and Mary (Hardin) W.; m. Reba White, Mar. 15, 1975. BS in Chem. Engring, U. Tex., 1956; MBA (Baker scholar, Teagle fellow), Harvard U., 1961. Chartered fin. analyst. Chem. engr. Exxon Corp., Baton Rouge, 1959; security analyst deVegh & Co., N.Y.C., 1961—64; dir. research Waddell & Reed, Kansas City, Mo., 1964—67; exec. v.p. Mitchell Hutchins, Inc., N.Y.C., 1967—77; chmn. bd. Alliance Capital Mgmt. Corp., 1977—2001, chmn. emeritus, 2001—. Contbr.: articles to Fin. Analysts Jour. Trustee, chmn. bd. Fgn. Policy Assn.; trustee U.S.S. Intrepid Mus. Found. Served with USNR, 1956-59. Mem. Fin. Analysts Fedn. (past officer, dir.), N.Y. Soc. Security Analysts (past pres.), Bond Club N.Y., Econ. Club N.Y., Knickerbocker Club, Century Assn., Grolier Club. Presbyterian. Office: Alliance Capital Mgmt Corp Ste 31R 1345 Avenue Of The Americas New York NY 10105-0302

WILLIAMS, DAVID ALEXANDER, retired chief pilot; b. Helena, Mont., May 29, 1939; s. Daniel samuel and Dorothy (Alexander) W.; m. Jacquoline anders, Feb. 14, 1964 (div. Mar. 1988); children: Daniel Alexander, Darryl Jackson. BA, U. So. Calif., L.A., 1962. Lic. airline transport pilot, FAA. Commd. ensign USNR, 1963, advanced through grades to capt., 1985; tng. and test pilot McDonnel Douglas, Long Beach, Calif., 1980-87, chief pilot flight stds. and safety, 1987-97, Douglas Products divsn. Boeing, Long Beach, 1997-99; ret., 1999. Mem. internat. adv. com. Flight Safety Found., Washington, 1987-99; mem. windshear tng. aid task force FAA/industry, Washington, 1985-87; mem. CFIT tng. com. Flight Safety Found./FAA, 1992-96, joint safety analysis team FAA Industry, 1997-99. Author: Turbulence Education and Training Aid FAA/Industry, 1996-97. Mem. Naval Res. Assn., catalina Conservancy. Republican. Avocations: scuba diving, sailing. Home: 223 Mission Ln San Luis Obispo CA 93405

WILLIAMS, DAVID ALLAN, dentist, educator; b. Dayton, Ohio, June 30, 1949; s. Robert Eugene and Mary Ellen (Moore) W.; m. Diane Elizabeth Costello, Nov. 12, 1993. BS, Mich. State U., 1971; DDS, Case Western Res. U., 1975. Clin. assoc. prof. Northwestern U. Dental Sch., Chgo., 1978-98; gen. practice dentistry Northbrook, Ill., 1979—, Chgo., 1980-96. Pres. United Way of Northbrook, 1997-99. With USN, 1975-78. Armed Forces Health Profls. Scholar, 1972-75. Fellow: Acad. Gen. Dentistry; mem.: ADA (commn. on dental accreditation), Acad. Operative Dentistry, Chgo. Dental Soc., Ill. State Dental Soc., Delta Tau Delta. Lutheran. Avocations: sailing, skiing, cycling. Office: Ste 801 666 Dundee Rd Northbrook IL 60062-2734

WILLIAMS, DAVID C. federal agency administrator; Grad. degrees, U. Ill., 1975. Spl. agent U.S. Secret Svc., 1979; with Office of Inspector Gen. Office of Labor Racketeering U.S. Dept. Labor, spl. agent in charge, N.Y.C., with Pres. Reagan's Commn. on Organized Crime, field dir. Office of Labor Racketeering, dir. Office Spl. Investigations Gen. Acctg. Office; inspector gen. Nuclear Regulatory Commn., 1989—96, Social Security Adminstrn., 1996—98, Dept. of the Treasury, Washington, 1998—99, treasury inspector gen. for tax adminstrn., 1999—. Active mem. Treasury Task Force. Office: US Dept Treasury Tax Adminstrn 1125 15th St NW Washington DC 20005*

WILLIAMS, DAVID KEITH, technical trainer; b. Exeter, N.H., Mar. 4, 1965; s. Horace Robert and Arlene Emily (Locke) W. BS, U. N.H., 1987. Software engr. Micro-Integration, Newmarket, N.H., 1988-89, Alloy Computer Products, Marlboro, Mass., 1989-90; sr. software engr. Cabletron Systems, Inc., Rochester, N.H., 1990-95, tech. trainer, 1995-97; sr. tech. trainer Infinity-A SunGard Co., Mountain View, Calif., 1997-99, Art Tech. Group, Inc., Boston, 1999—. Cons. in computer software. Asst. scoutmaster Boy Scouts Am., Newton Junction, N.H., 1986-91; bd. dirs. Newton Junction Fireman's Assn., 1983-95. Mem. Amnesty Internat. Ptnrs. of Conscience. Baptist. Avocations: foreign languages, musical instruments, hiking, skiing, karate.

WILLIAMS, DAVID MICHAEL, manufacturing executive; b. Bklyn., Feb. 25, 1936; s. Robert Irving and Patricia Margaret (Flanagan) W.; m. Carol Bultmann, Nov. 13, 1965; children: Mark, Jennifer. Cert., NYU, Ctr. for Safety Engring., Manhattan, N.Y., 1960. Mgr. various mfrs., 1956-79; pres. D.M. Williams, Inc., Livermore, Calif., 1979—. Cons. various mfrs., 1979—. Candidate for Gov., Calif., 1990; candidate for Congress, Calif., 1986, 88, 89, 92, 94, 96, 98; active Rep. Ctrl. Com., Calif., 1987-88. Cole grantee NYU, 1960. Mem. Inst. Packaging Profls. (bd. dirs. no. Calif. chpt., 1982-85, chmn. 1985-86), ASTM, Mensa (founder interest group 1983-86). Roman Catholic. Avocation: politics. Office: 1560 Kingsport Ave Livermore CA 94550-6149

WILLIAMS, DAVID NEVILLE, physician; b. Carmarthen, Wales, Sept. 19, 1943; came to U.S., 1972; s. Goronwy Owen and Lillian Eirwen (Jones) W.; m. Patricia Ann Thorne, Apr. 10, 1971; children: Heloise, Megan, Nicholas. MB, ChB, Edinburgh (Scotland) U., 1967. Diplomate Am. Bd. Internal Medicine, Am. Bd. Infectious Diseases. Resident internal medicine U. Edinburgh, 1967-70; sr. resident U. Sheffield, Eng., 1970-72; fellow infectious diseases Harvard Med. Unit, Boston, 1972-74; asst. prof. dept. medicine U. Minn. Hosps., Mpls., 1974-76; staff physician Park Nicollet Med. Ctr., 1976-94; dir. med. edn. Meth. Hosp., 1986-94; vice-chmn. medicine Hennepin County Med. Ctr., 1994—. Chmn. devel. com. Mpls. Med. Rsch. Found., 1995-2000; prof. dept. medicine U. Minn. Med. Sch., 1996—. Contbr. articles to profl. jours. Recipient Amb. of Yr. award Mpls. Med. Rsch. Found., 1996. Fellow ACP, ACP/ASIM (gov.-elect Minn. chpt. 2002-), Royal Coll. Physicians (Edinburgh), Infectious Disease Soc. Am. (chmn. subcom. 1995-97, bd. dirs. No. Ctrl. chpt. 1990-96), Mpls. Soc. Internal Medicine (councilor 1992-99). Office: Hennepin County Med Ctr 701 Park Ave Minneapolis MN 55415-1623 E-mail: david.williams@co.hennepin.mn.us.

WILLIAMS, DAVID R. astronaut; b. Saskatoon, Saskatchewan, Can., May 16, 1954; s. William and Isobel Williams; m. Cathy Fraser; 2 children. BSc in Biology, McGill U., 1976, MSc, MD, CM, McGill U., 1983. Resident in family practice U. Ottawa Faculty Medicine, Canada, 1983—85; resident in emergency medicine U. Toronto, Canada, 1985—88; fellow in emergency medicine Royal Coll. Physicians & Surgeons, Canada, 1988; emergency physician Sunnybrook Health Sci. Ctr., 1988—89, Emergency Assoc. of Kitchener Waterloo, Canada, 1989—90; med. dir. Sunnybrook Health Sci. Ctr., 1990—92; with Can. Space Agy., 1992—95; astronaut NASA, Houston, 1995—. Lectr. dept. surgery U. Toronto, Canada, 1988; course dir. Can. Heart & Stroke Found., Am. Coll. Surgeons; asst. prof. U. Toronto, Canada, 1989—90; asst. prof. surgery McGill U.; mem. staff St. Mary's Hosp., Montreal Gen. Hosp.; mission specialist Neurolab, 1998; dir. space & life sci. directorate NASA, 1998—. Recipient Commonwealth cert. Thanks, 1973, Commonwealth Recognition award, 1975, A.S. Hill bursary, McGill U., 1980, Walter Hoare bursary, 1981, J.W. McConnell award, 1981—83, Psychiatry prize, Wood Gold Medal award. Mem.: Can. Aeronautics & Space Inst., Can. Soc. Aerospace Medicine, Aerospace Med. Assn., Can. Assn. Emergency Physicians, Royal Coll. Physicians & Surgeons Can., Coll. Family Physicians Can., Ontario Med. Assn., Coll. Physicians & Surgeons Ontario. Avocations: flying, scuba diving, hiking, sailing, kayaking. Office: Astronaut Office CB NASA Johnson Space Ctr Houston TX 77058*

WILLIAMS, DAVID RUSSELL, retired music educator; b. Indpls., Oct. 21, 1932; s. H. Russell and Mary Dean (Whitmer) W.; m. Elsa Bühlmann, Jan. 30, 1960. AB, Columbia U., 1954, MA, 1956; PhD, U. Rochester, 1965. Dir. music Windham Coll., Putney, Vt., 1959-62; opera coach Eastman Sch. Music, Rochester, N.Y., 1962-65, assoc. prof. theory, adminstr. of MusM program, 1965-80; prof., chmn. dept. music U. Memphis (formerly Memphis State U.), 1980-87, prof. music, 1980-98, prof. emeritus, 1998—. Bd. dirs. Memphis Youth Symphony, Memphis Symphony, 1984-90; mem. exec. bd. Opera Memphis, 1980-87, Salute to Memphis Music, 1980-87. Author: Bibliography of the History of Music Theory, 1971, Conversations with Howard Hanson, 1988, Music Theory from Zarlino to Schenker: A Bibliography and Guide, 1990; producer: Highwater Records album 8201 featuring John Stover, classical guitar, 1983; composer Suite for Oboe, Clarinet and Piano, 1968, Five States of Mind, 1970. Bd. dirs., sec. Rochester Philharm. Orch., 1976-78; v.p., bd. dirs. Rochester Chamber Orch., 1974-78; pres., bd. dirs. Opera Theatre of Rochester, 1973-74; bd. dirs., chmn. Am. Ritual Theatre, 1979-80; bd. sponsors Met. Opera Mid. South Region, Memphis, 1983—. Served as cpl. U.S. Army, 1957-59. Recipient Eastman Sch. Music Pub. award, 1970. Mem. NARAS (treas. Memphis chpt. 1984-86), Coll. Music Soc. (sec. 1973-83), Music Tchrs. Nat. Assn. Sci. (state chmn. 1971-74), Nat. Assn. Schs. of Music (chmn. region 8 1989-92), Tenn. Assn. Music Execs. in Colls. and Univs. (pres. 1986-87), Southeastern Composers League (composer mem.), Pi Kappa Lambda (pres. U. Memphis chpt. 1988-90), Phi Beta Kappa, Phi Mu Alpha (hon.), Sigma Alpha Iota (hon.). Clubs: Rochester, Univ., Summit. Avocations: language study, word puzzles. Home: 273 W Central Park St Apt 1 Memphis TN 38111-4570 E-mail: drwillrus@memphis.edu. *Having had a family background that was superior in so many ways has helped me to sharpen my purpose in life, in that it has made me realize to what an extent affirmative action is necessary in order to provide a milieu in which truly equal opportunity can exist. Many doors of opportunity have been held open for me; those of disadvantaged access are often not aware that these doors exist. The more individuals I can lead to these portals, the more I will have achieved in my lifetime.*

WILLIAMS, DEBBIE KAYE, optometrist; b. Benham, Ky., Mar. 13, 1960; d. Charles Hughes and Bernice (Knotts) W.; m. Gregory Allen Collins, July 2, 1983 (div. July 1989); re-married, Dec. 28, 1990; 1 child, Arianna Courtney, 1994. AS, U. Louisville, 1980-82, BS, 1985; OD, Ill. Coll. Optometry, 1989. Pvt. practice, Whitesburg, Ky., 1989—. Cons. LKLP Head Start, Whitesburg, 1991—; adj. faculty So. Coll. Optometry, 1999. Mem. Letcher County Bd. Health, 1993. Mem. Am. Optometric Assn., Ky. Optometric Assn., U. Louisville Alumni Assn., Ill. Coll. of Optometry Alumni Assn., Retinitis Pigmetosa Found. (Letcher county chpt. v.p. 1990-91), Beta Simga Kappa. Democrat. Baptist. Avocations: travel, walking, reading, painting. Home and Office: Dr DK Williams OD PSC 120 River Rd Whitesburg KY 41858-1178

WILLIAMS, DELWYN CHARLES, telephone company executive; b. Idaho Falls, Idaho, Apr. 27, 1936; s. Charles H. and Vonda (Wood) W.; m. Marlene Grace Nordland, Feb. 29, 1964; children— Stephen, Kirstin, Nicole. BS in Bus., U. Idaho, 1959. C.P.A., Calif. Accountant Peat, Marwick, Mitchell & Co. (C.P.A.s), San Francisco, 1960-65; treas. Dohrmann Instruments Co., Mountain View, 1965-68; with Continental Telephone Co. of Calif., Bakersfield, 1968-84, controller, 1969-70, v.p., treas., 1970-77, v.p., gen. mgr., 1977-79, pres., 1977-84, also dir.; pres. J.H. Evans, Inc., and subs., 1984-95, CEO, 1995—2001, Via Wireless LLC, 1996—2001. Home: 10052 Oak Branch Cir Carmel CA 93923-8000

WILLIAMS, DENNIS THOMAS, civil engineer; b. Washington, Aug. 22, 1925; s. Dennis Thomas and Margaret Madelene (Henley) W.; m. Jane Elizabeth Fisher (div. 1996); children: Roy Thomas, Laurence James, Laura Josephine, Eric; m. Keiko Kanda, 1999. Student, Howard U., 1943-46; ME, Pratt Inst., Bklyn, 1959; BCE, NYU, Bklyn., 1990-92; BS, Nyack Coll., 1993; SCE cert. in comm., NYU, 1991, SCE cert. in journalism, 1992; BS in Orgnl. Mgmt., Nyack Coll., 1993. Civil engr. N.Y.C. Dept. Pub. Works, 1952-58; supr. Bur. Water Pollution Control, N.Y.C., 1959-77; elec. engr. N.Y.C. Bur. Environ. Protective Agy., 1978-87. Tech. advisor North River Community Environ. Rev. Bd., N.Y.C., 1986—; cons. engr. N.Y. State D.E.C., 1991—. Author screen plays: Campaign, 1988, Napoleon, 1988. Fellow Profl. Engrs. Alumni Assn.; mem. Water Pollution Control Fedn., Artists for Mental Health Assn., Greenpeace, Greater Paterson C. of C., Kiwanis. Democrat. Mem. Lds Ch. Avocation: travel.

WILLIAMS, DEREK, JR. pharmaceutical professional; b. Ft. Rucker, Ala., June 25, 1958; s. Derek W. Sr. and Carol E. (Kaufman) W.; m. Penny L. Bradly, Apr. 22, 1991; children: Jason Brian, Courtney Elizabeth. AS, U. Nev., 1981; BA, U. Colo., 1984; MA, U. Nev., 1986; postgrad., Pepperdine U. Cert. Inst. Regulatory Affairs, 1997. Rsch. asst. U. Nev., Reno, 1984-86; surgical counselor St. Lukes Hosp., Denver, 1987-89; pub. health advisor Ctrs. for Disease Control, Atlanta, 1989-91; clin. rsch. assoc. Amgen, Inc., Thousand Oaks, Calif., 1991-92, regulatory affairs specialist, 1992-97; mgr. regulatory affairs SangStat Med. Corp., Menlo Park, 1997-98; assoc. dir. regulator affairs Nexell Therapeutics, Inc., Irvine, 1998-2000; assoc. dir. U.S. regulatory affairs Purdue Pharma, L.P., Stamford, Conn., 2000—. Named Outstanding Young Men of Am., 1989-90. Mem. Regulatory Affairs Profls. Soc., Brit. Inst. Regulatory Affairs., Am. Assn. Pharm. Scientists. Avocations: sports, history, literature. Office: Purdue Pharma LP 1 Stamford Forum Stamford CT 06901-3516 E-mail: derek.williams@pharma.com.

WILLIAMS, DEWAYNE ARTHUR, JR. artist, exhibit specialist; b. San Diego, Aug. 20, 1943; s. DeWayne Arthur Sr. and Mary Elizabeth (Cardell) W.; m. Suelynn Davison, Jan. 18, 1964; children: Regan Lane, Rani Chellane Garcia, DeWayne Arthur III. BA in Biol. Sci., Fla. State U., 1966; MA in Interdisciplinary Studies, Oreg. State U., 1974; postgrad., U. Idaho, 1997-99, Clayton Coll. Natural Health, 2000—. Aquatic biologist Oreg. Game Commn., Corvallis, 1966-72; biol. technician (plants) EPA, 1974-75; crafts shop dir., instr. U.S.Army, Ft. Gulick, Canal Zone, 1975-79; artist/mus. curator U. Mont., Missoula, 1980-88; artist, author, editor, photographer Artistwork, 1988-93; biol. technician (fish) Nat. Marine Fisheries Svc., Honolulu, 1994; exhibit specialist Nat. Pk. Svc., Homestead, Fla., 1994-96; environ. protection asst. U.S. Army Corps of Engrs., Boise, Idaho, 1996-2000; fish and wildlife biologist U.S. Fish and Wildlife Svc., Sacramento, 2000-2001; exhibit specialist Nat. Pk. Svc., Mammoth, Wyo., 2001—. Fine arts dir. student union Oreg. State U., Corvallis. Author, editor, photographer, pub.: Montana Tribute, 1990 (Mont. Offcl. Centennial book); contbg. photographer: Erotic Art by Living Artists, 1988, American Photographers, 1989, Living Artists in America, 1989, Photographic Possibilities, 1991, Who's Who in Photography, 1991, Center for Creative Photography, Mont. Hist. Soc., Idaho State U., Oreg. State U.; designed Missoula County seal, 1982; creator of the Correlative Composite Photograph. Boy Scout leader, 1967-93. Democrat. Episcopalian. Avocations: hunting, fishing, camping. Office: Nat Park Svc PO Box 168 Yellowstone WY 82190-0168 Home: PO Box 82 Yellowstone National Park WY 82190-0082 Fax: 307-344-2443. E-mail: dewaynearthur@hotmail.com.

WILLIAMS, DIANE, writer, editor; b. Chgo., Jan. 16, 1946; d. William Maurice and Mary Rosen Swartz; m. Paul Casey Williams, June 28, 1970 (div. 1993); children: Jacob, Alexander. BA in English Lit., U. Pa., 1968. Asst. editor J. G. Ferguson divsn. Doubleday, N.Y.C., 1969—71, Scott, Foresman Co., Glenview, Ill., 1971—73; assoc. editor Sci. Rsch. Assoc., Chgo., 1973—76; co-editor StoryQuarterly, Glenview, 1985—97; founding editor NOON, N.Y.C., 2000—. Vis. asst. prof. Syracuse (N.Y.) U., 1999; vis. assoc. prof. Bard Coll., Annandale-on-Hudson, NY, 2001. Co-editor: (anthology) The American Story: The Best of Story quarterly, 1990; author: (stories) This Is About the Body, the Mind, the Soul, the World, Time and Fate, 1990, Some Sexual Success Stories Plus Other Stories in Which God Might Choose to Appear, 1992, (stories and novella) The Stupefaction, 1996, Excitability: Selected Stories, 1998, Romancer Erector, 2001; contbr. stories to jours.; author: (stories) This Is About the Body, The Mind, The Soul, The World, Time and Fate, 1990. Recipient Pushcart prize, 1991, 1992, 2000. Office: NOON PMB 298 1369 Madison Ave New York NY 10128

WILLIAMS, DIANE ELIZABETH, architectural historian, photographer; b. Glendale, Calif., July 9, 1948; BA, Calif. State U., L.A., 1973; MA, UCLA, 1988. Cert. elem. tchr., Calif. Tchr. L.A. area schs., 1975-78; editorial asst. L.A. Times, 1978-80, copyeditor, feature writer, 1980-83; preservation planning cons. Sierra Madre, Calif., 1983-94; assoc. planner Environ. Planning Assocs., L.A., 1989; asst. planner City of Burbank, Calif., 1989-90; assoc. planner City of Claremont, 1990-91; planner City of Glendale, 1991-94; sr. archtl. historian Hardy Heck Moore & Assocs., Austin, Tex., 1994, ptnr., 1995; preservation planning cons., 1996—. Instr. Cerritos Community Coll., Norwalk, Calif., 1990-94. Bd. dirs. Pasadena Heritage, 1984-90, sec., 1985-86; mem. steering com. Pasadena Residents in Def. of the Environment, 1988-90; reader Henry E. Huntington Libr. and Art Gallery, 1985—; commr. Cultural Heritage Commn., City of Pasadena, 1990-93; mem. state bd. of rev. Tex. Hist. Commn., 1999—. Recipient Cecilia Steinfeldt fellowship for Rsch. in the Arts and Material Cutlure, 2002. Mem. Soc. Archtl. Historians (bd. dirs. So. Calif. chpt. 1989-94, v.p. 1991-92, bd. dirs. Tex. chpt. 1997—, founding editor SPECS 1997). Avocations: hiking, travel, study of Am. Indian cultures, photography. Office: Diane E Williams & Assocs PO Box 49921 Austin TX 78765-0921 E-mail: texashistory@juno.com.

WILLIAMS, DONALD CLYDE, lawyer; b. Oxnard, Calif., Oct. 12, 1939; s. Leslie Allen and Elizabeth Esther (Orton) W.; m. Miriam Arline, Oct. 5, 1966; children— Erin K., Nikki Dawn. BA in Gen. Bus, Fresno State Coll., 1963; JD, Willamette U., 1967. Bar: Oreg. 1967. Practice in, Grants Pass, 1967-70; ptnr. Myrick, Seagraves, Williams & Nealy, 1968-70, Carlsmith, Ball, Wichman, Murray & Ichiki, 1977—; asst. atty. gen. Am. Samoa, 1970-71, atty. gen., 1971-75; assoc. justice High Ct. Trust Ter. of Pacific Islands, 1975-77. Served with USCGR, 1958-59. Mem. ABA, Calif. Bar Assn., Oreg. Bar Assn., Am. Samoa Bar Assn., Guam Bar Assn., Hawaii Bar Assn., Commonwealth No. Mariana Islands Bar Assn., Fed. States of Micronesia Bar Assn., Guam C. of C. Office: Carlsmith Ball 444 S Flower St Fl 9 Los Angeles CA 90071-2901 E-mail: dwilliams@carlsmith.com.

WILLIAMS, DONALD EDWARD, endocrinologist; b. Oakland, Calif., May 21, 1942; s. Lyman Eugene and Janice (Powell) W.; m. Ann Elizabeth Gelardy, Nov. 25, 1967; children: Mark Andrew Williams, Jodi Lynn Williams. BS in Med. Sci., U. Calif., Berkeley, 1964; MD, U. Calif., San Francisco, 1967. Diplomate Am. Bd. Internal Medicine, Am. Bd. Endocrinology. Intern UCLA Med. Ctr., 1967-68, resident in internal medicine, 1968-69, 71-72, chief resident in internal medicine, 1972-73, fellow in endocrinology, 1973-75; pvt. practice Newport Beach, Calif., 1975—. Bd. dirs. Physicians' Care of Calif., Irvine, chmn. utilization mgmt., 1994—96; bd. dirs. Hoag Meml. Presbyn. Hosp., Newport Beach, Calif., 1998—2001, chmn. dept. medicine, Calif., 1979—81, chief of staff, Calif., 1984—85, chmn. credentials com., Calif., 1995. With USAF, 1969-71. Fellow ACP, Am. Coll. Endocrinology; mem. AMA, Calif. Med. Assn., Orange County Med. Assn. (del. to Calif. Med. Assn.), Am. Soc. Internal Medicine, Am. Assn. Clin. Endocrinologists. Office: Donald E Williams PC 1501 Superior Ave Ste 312 Newport Beach CA 92663-3641

WILLIAMS, DONALD HOWARD, chemist, educator, chemist, consultant; b. Ellwood City, Pa., Mar. 9, 1938; s. Howard John and Dorothy Olive (Devitt) W.; m. Susan Jane Bell, June 11, 1990; children: David Devitt, Brian Andrew. BS, Muskingum Coll., 1960; PhD, Ohio State U., 1964. Asst. prof. chemistry U. Ky., Lexington, 1964-69; assoc. prof. Hope Coll., Holland, Mich., 1969-73, prof., 1973—, chmn. dept. chemistry, 1979—82, dir. Inst. Environ. Quality; expert cons. U.S. Dept. of Energy, Washington, 1988-89, intermittent cons., 1989—. Chmn. dept. chemistry Hope Coll., 1979-82, dir. Inst. for Environ. Quality; chmn. bd. govs. Mich. Low-Level Radioactive Waste Authority, 1995—. Contbr. articles to profl. jours; patentor combined energy systems. Sec. Ottawa County (Mich.) Environ. Health Bd. of Appeals, 1978-89, 90—; mem. adv. com. minority outreach com. Mich. Dept. Edn., 1990—. Joyce Found. grantee, 1983—, GTE Lectureship Found. grantee, 1988-89. Mem. AAAS, Am. Chem. Soc., Am. Nuclear Soc., Nat. Sci. Tchrs. Assn., Rotary, Sigma Xi, Sigma Pi Sigma. Presbyterian. Avocations: photography, public speaking. Home: 732 Van Raalte Ave Holland MI 49423-6951 Office: Hope Coll Dept of Chemistry Holland MI 49422-9000

WILLIAMS, DONALD MACE, newswriter, educator; b. Abilene, Tex., Oct. 24, 1929; s. Robert H. and Betty Lou (Montgomery) W.; m. Nell Osborne, Oct. 22, 1956; children: Andrew Montgomery, Elizabeth. BA, Tex. Tech. U., 1969, MA, 1970; PhD, U. Tex., 1975. Asst. city editor Fort Worth Star-Telegram, 1956-63; city editor Amarillo (Tex.) Globe-News, 1965-68; assoc. prof. Baylor U., Waco, Tex., 1976-80; co-owner The Miami (Tex.) Chief, 1981-82; exec. editor Pine Bluff (Ark.) Comml., 1984-87; spl. writer Newsday, Melville, N.Y., 1987-89; writing coach The Wichita (Kans.) Eagle, 1989-98. Author: Interlude in Umbarger, 1992. Sgt. Army, 1948-49. Recipient 2nd place Ernie Pyle award Scripps-Howard Found., 1981. Presbyterian. Home: 2920 Mable Dr Canyon TX 79015-4808

WILLIAMS, DOYLE Z. university dean, educator; b. Shreveport, La., Dec. 18, 1939; s. Nuell O. and Lurline (Isbell) W.; m. Maynette Derr, Aug. 20, 1967; children: Zane Derr, Elizabeth Marie. BS, Northwestern State U., 1960; MS in Acctg., La. State U., 1962, PhD, 1965. CPA, Tex. Mgr. spl. edn. projects AICPA, N.Y.C., 1967-69; assoc. prof. Tex. Tech. U., Lubbock, 1969-71, prof. acctg., 1972-73, prof. area acctg., coord., 1973-78; prof. acctg. U. So. Calif., L.A., 1978-93, dean Sch. Acctg., 1979-87, interim dean Sch. Bus., 1986-88; dean Walton Coll. Bus. Adminstrn. U. Ark., Fayetteville, 1993—. Vis. prof. U. Hawaii, Honolulu, 1971-72. Author over 40 jour. articles and books. Chmn. Acctg. Edn. Change Commn., 1989-93. Named Mem. of Yr. N.Y. chpt. Nat. Assn. Accts., 1967, Outstanding Acctg. Educator Beta Alpha Psi, 1982; recipient Disting. Faculty award Calif. CPA Found., 1983, Nat. Leadership award Acad. Bus. Adminstrs., 1995, Lifetime Achievement award Ark. Soc. CPAs. Mem.: AICPA (coun. 1983—91, v.p. 1987—88, bd. dirs. 1987—91, Outstanding Educator award 1990), Assn. to Advance Coll. Schs. Bus. Internat. (chair acctg. accreditation com. 1995—97, 1999—2000, bus. accreditation com. 1995—97, bd. dirs. 1999—), S.W. Bus. Dean's Assn. (pres. 1998—99), Adminstrs. Acctg. Programs (pres. 1977—78), Fedn. Schs. Accountancy (pres. 1982, Faculty Merit award 1993), Am. Acctg. Assn. (dir. edn. 1973—75, pres. 1984—85, Outstanding Educator award 1996). Home: 2447 E Boston Mountain Vw Fayetteville AR 72701-2802 Office: U Ark Sam M Walton Coll Bus Fayetteville AR 72701

WILLIAMS, DREW DAVIS, surgeon; b. San Augustine, Tex., Jan. 18, 1935; s. Floyd Everett and Villamae (Morehead) W.; m. Marilyn Raus, June 27, 1958; children: Leslie, Cynthia, Matthew, Jennifer, Amelia. BS, Tex. A&M Coll., 1957; MD, U. Tex., 1960; grad., naval flight surgeon, U.S. Naval Sch. Aviation Medicine, 1963. Diplomate Am. Bd. Surgery, Am. Bd. Quality Assurance and Utilization Rev. Physicians. Intern USPHS Hosp., Seattle, 1960-61; resident in gen. surgery U. Tex. Med. Br., Galveston, 1961-62, 64-68; resident in pulmonary svc. M.D. Anderson Hosp., Houston, 1968; pvt. practice Baytown, Tex., 1968—. Active staff San Jacinto (Tex.) Meth. Hosp., 1968-95, chief of surgery, 1972, 73, pres. med. staff, 1976; mem. courtesy staff Bay Coast Hosp., Baytown, 1968-95; cons. staff Baytown Med. Ctr. Hosp., 1972-95; 1st chmn. dept. surgery in devel. of family practice residency program affiliated with Tex. Med. Sch., Houston, 1977; mem. Tex. State Bd. Med. Examiners, 1983-89, sec.-treas., 1984-88, pres., 1988-89; unit med. dir., clin. instr. dept. preventive medicine and cmty. health U. Tex. Med. Br., Galveston, 1995-99. Contbr. chpt. to book and articles to profl. jours. Flight surgeon USN, 1962-64; lt. comdr. USNR, ret., 1967. Am. Cancer Soc. Clin. fellow, 1966-67. Fellow: AMA (Physicians Recognition award), ACS, Tex. Med. Assn. (fed. peer rev. group); mem.: KT, SAR (past pres. local chpt.), Houston Surg. Soc. (past pres.), Baytown Surg. Soc., East Harris County Med. Soc. (pres. 1982), Harris County Med. Soc. (mem. exec. bd. 1994, chmn. coun. med. splty.), Singleton Surg. Soc. (past pres.), Tex. Surg. Soc., Tex. Med. Found., Sovereign Colonial Soc.-Am. of Royal Descent, Colonial Order of the Crown, Soc. Descendents of Colonial Clergy, Sons of Republic of Tex. (life; at large life), Sir William Osler Soc., Magna Carta Barons (Somerset chpt.), Am. Cancer Soc. (pres. Baytown chpt. 1970—71), Gideons Internat., Masons (32 degree), Shriners, Phi Beta Pi. Democrat. Mem. Ch. of Christ. Avocations: gardening, hunting, fishing, genealogy, golf. Home and Office: 1217 Kilgore Rd Baytown TX 77520-3912 E-mail: dwilliams95@houston.rr.com.

WILLIAMS, DUANE JEROME, JR. computer company executive, consultant, retired computer company executive; b. Huntington, Ind., Nov. 7, 1926; s. Duane Jerome Williams Sr. and Rose Mary Williams; m. Dolores Appolonia Drozd; 1 child Duane Jerome Williams III;1 child Daniel 1 child Dennis 1 child Thomas 1 child Timothy. Student, Mich. Coll. Mining and Tech., 1944—45, DePaul U., 1946—52. Sales rep. Addressograph-Multigraph Corp., Euclid, Ohio, 1957—65; pres. McCormack, Allen & Co., Chgo., 1967—70, Duane Williams & Assocs., Elmhurst, 1971—76; sales assoc. Agy. Records Control, Bryan, Tex., 1977—80; pres. Bus. Computers, Chgo. Cons. Advt. Age, Chgo., 1966—67. Editor: (Book) Civil War Diaries, 2002, author computerized zip coding sys. Adj. officer Am. Legion Glenn Maker Post, Chgo., 1963—64. Aviation cadet USAAF, 1945—45. Personal E-mail: duanwllms@netzero.net.

WILLIAMS, EARL PATRICK, JR. editor, freelance writer; b. Washington, May 14, 1950; s. Earl Patrick Sr. and Charlie Mae (Wright) W.; m. Susan Miller Day, July 20, 1985. BA, U. Md., 1973; postgrad., Cath. U., 1974. Duplication machine operator Applied Physics Lab. Johns Hopkins U., Silver Spring, Md., 1968-74; substitute tchr. Fairfax County Va. Schs., 1974-75; clk. U.S. Govt. Printing Office, Washington, 1975-76; editor U.S. GAO, 1976—. Freelance writer, Washington, 1974—. Author: Amtrak's Washington-New York Corridor, 1977, What You Should Know About the American Flag, 1987, What You Should Know About Flags of the Confederacy, 1993; contbr. articles to mags. and newspapers. Active in efforts to achieve recognition of Francis Hopkinson, the designer of first ofcl. U.S. flag; lectr. to sch. groups and civic orgns. on the history of the U.S. flag; discussed history of U.S. flag on radio and TV broadcasts nationwide; mem. N.J. Coun. for Social Studies. Recipient Cert. of Appreciation Mil. Order of World Wars, Bronze Good Citizenship medal Nat. Soc. of Sons of Am. Revolution. Mem.: N.Am. Vexillological Assn., Nat. Cathedral Assn., Star Bangled Banner Flag House Assn. Democrat. Methodist. Avocations: railroad buff, history buff, singing folk music. Home: 2323 40th Pl NW Apt 201 Washington DC 20007-1617

WILLIAMS, EARLE CARTER, retired professional services company executive; b. Selma, Ala., Oct. 15, 1929; s. Henry Earle and Nora Elizabeth (Carter) W.; m. June Esther Anson, Sept. 7, 1951; children: Gayle Marie, Carol Patrice, Sharon Elaine. B.E.E., Auburn U., 1951; postgrad., U. N.Mex., 1959-62; DSc (hon.), Auburn U., 1991. Registered profl. engr., N.Mex. (ret.). Utilities design engr. Standard Oil Co. Ind., Whiting, 1954-56; mem. tech. staff Sandia Corp., Albuquerque, 1956-62; sr. engr. BDM Internat., Inc., El Paso, Tex., 1962-64, spl. projects dir., 1964-66, dir. ops., 1966-68, v.p., gen. mgr. Vienna, 1968-72, pres., CEO, Vienna and McLean, 1972-92, bd. dirs., 1972-97; ret. as CEO, BDM Internat. Inc., 1992. Bd. dirs. GTS Duratek, Inc., Dimensions Internat., Inc.; chmn. Va. Forward, 1997—; mem. Naval Rsch. Adv. Com., 1984-90, chmn., 1986-90; dir. Am. Bus. Conf., 1985-88. Exec. com., steering com. El Paso C.C., 1968-69, trustee, 1969-70; commr. Fairfax County Econ. Devel. Authority, 1976-80, chmn., 1978-80; mem. Va. State Bd. for C.C., 1980-87; bd. dirs. Ctrl. Va. Ednl. TV Corp., 1978-87, Atlantic Coun. U.S., 1987-93; chmn. George Mason Inst. Indsl. Policy Bd., 1982-91; bd. dirs. Wolf Trap Found., 1984-92, 97—, vice chmn., 1985-87, chmn., 1988-90, emeritus dir., 1992-97; trustee Va. Found. for Ind. Colls., 1984-87, 90-94, Flint Hill Sch., Oakton, Va., 1990-95, George Mason U. Found., 1987-98, Auburn U. Found., 1991—; bd. dirs. Potomac KnowledgeWay Project, 1995-99; mem. Va. Bus. Higher Edn. Coun., 1995—;bd. dirs. Spl. Ops. Warrior Found., 1997—. With AUS, 1951-53. Recipient Engr. of Yr. award Va. Soc. Profl. Engrs., 1989, Superior Pub. Svc. award Dept. Navy, 1990; named to Ala. Engrng. Hall of Fame, 1994. Mem. NSPE, Profl. Svcs. Coun. (bd. dirs. 1974-92, emeritus bd. dirs. 1992—, pres. 1976-79), Armed Force Comm. and Electronics Assn. (bd. dirs. 1978-82, 86-87, permanent dir. 1990, internat. v.p. 1979-82, 84-85, chmn. 1988-90, Disting. Svc. award 1987), Fairfax County C. of C., City Club (D.C.), Met. Club (D.C.), Tower Club (Vienna, Va.), Bay Colony Club (Naples, Fla.), Eta Kappa Nu. Presbyterian.

WILLIAMS, EDDIE R. communications and information technology executive, consultant; b. Muskegon, Mich., June 9, 1950; s. Bessie Lee and Ira David Williams; m. Betty Ann Wright; children: Byron Wright; m. Karen Gaskins; 1 child Eddie Ray II. A, Prince George'S C.C., 1975; postgrad., Bowie State Coll., 1975—77; B in Mgmt., U. Redlands, 1981. Cert. project mgmt. profl. N.J. Sys. & procedures analyst, bus. adminstr. Bendix Field Engrng. Corp., Columbia, Md., 1972—79; contract, data and quality adminstr. space divsn. Rockwell Internat., Downey, Calif., 1979—81; rsch. engr., project mgr. Northrop Aircraft, Hawthorne, 1981—83; configuration mgmt. Ford Aerospace, Aeronutronics, Newport Beach, 1983—84; software quality assurance mgr. sys. divsn. Hughes Aircraft, Fullerton, 1984—85; divsn. adminstr., mgr. RCA/Gen. Electric, Camden, NJ, 1985—89; tech. & mgmt. cons. Independent Consultant, Phila., N.J., & Del., 1989—96; info. tech. program,project mgr. Omicron Cons., Phila., 1996—98; info. tech. program mgr. CoreTech Cons. Group, King Of Prussia, 1998—2001; pres., owner RayAnn Enterprise Pub., Burlington , NJ, 2001—. Adj. faculty mem. Temple U., Phila., 1988; tchr. Reeths Puffer/TriValley Acad., Muskegon, Mich., 1995—96. Author: (book) Software and Firmware Configuration Management, 2001. Chair tech. & computer cluster YMCA Black Achievers, Phila., 2000—02, chair program develop. com., 2001—02, mem. Phila. steering com., 2001—02. Sgt. U.S. Army, 1968—71. Recipient Cert. of Appreciation, Youth Motivation Task Force, 1980. Mem.: Electronic Industries Assn/, Black Data Processing Assoc., Project Mgmt. Inst., Burlington C. of C.

WILLIAMS, EDDIE NATHAN, research institution executive; b. Memphis, Aug. 18, 1932; s. Ed and Georgia Lee (Barr) W.; m. Jearline F. Reddick, July 18, 1981; children: Traci Lynne, Edward Lawrence, Terence Reddick. BS, U. Ill., 1954; postgrad., Atlanta U., 1957, Howard U., 1960; LLD, U. D.C., 1986; DHL, Bowie State Coll., 1980, Chgo. State U., 1994, Dillard U., 2001. Reporter Atlanta Daily World Newspaper, 1957-58; staff asst. U.S. Senate Com. on Fgn. Relations, Washington, 1959-60; fgn. service res. officer U.S. Dept. State, 1961-68; v.p. U. Chgo., 1968-72; pres. Joint Ctr. for Polit. and Econ. Studies, Washington, 1972—. Vice chmn. Black Leadership Forum, 1996; bd. dirs. Harrah's Entertainment, Inc., JCC Holding Co., The Riggs Nat. Corp. Editorial columnist: Chgo. Sun Times, 1970-72; contbr. articles to profl. jours. Am. Polit. Sci. Assn. fellow, 1958, MacArthur Found. fellow, 1988, Nat. Acad. Pub. Adminstrn. fellow, 1993, Am. Acad. Arts and Scis. fellow, 1998; recipient Adam Clayton Powell Award Congl. Black Caucus, 1981, Washingtonian of Yr. award Washingtonian Mag., 1991, Alumni of Yr. award U. Ill. Alumni Club of Greater Washington, 1994, Outstanding Leadership award Korean Am. Alliance, 1994. Mem. Coun. Fgn. Rels., Kappa Tau Alpha, Omega Psi Phi, Sigma Pi Phi. Office: Joint Ctr Polit & Econ Studies 1090 Vermont Ave NW Ste 1100 Washington DC 20005-4905 E-mail: ewilliams@jointcenter.org.

WILLIAMS, EDSON POE, retired automotive company executive; b. Mpls., July 31, 1923; s. Homer A. and Florence C. Williams; m. Irene Mae Streed, June 16, 1950; children: Thomas, Louise, Steven, Linnea, Elisa. BSM.E. cum laude, U. Minn., 1950. Spl. purpose machinery operator, 1946-50; mfg. mgr., project engr. Crestliner div. Bigelow Sanford Inc., 1950-53, v.p., mgr. mfg. and engrng., 1953-58, pres., 1958-63; with Ford Motor Co., 1963-87, mgr. customer svc. div., 1973; gen. mgr. Ford Motor Co. (Ford Mexico), 1973-75; pres. Ford Motor Co. (Ford Mid-East & Africa), 1975-79, Ford Motor Co. (Ford Asia-Pacific Inc.), 1979-87; v.p. Ford Motor Co., 1979-82, v.p.-gen. mgr. N.Am. truck ops., 1982-86, v.p. Ford Diversified Products ops., 1986-87. Served with USAAF, 1942-46. Mem. Naples Yacht and Sailing Club. Home: 688 21st Ave S Naples FL 34102-7610

WILLIAMS, EDWARD DAVID, consulting executive; b. Scranton, Pa., June 20, 1932; s. David Thomas and Mabel (Sims) W. m. Natalie Imnadze, Oct. 18, 1952; children: Denise, Claudia. BBA, Hofstra U., 1960; postgrad. in Bus. Adminstrn., Fairleigh Dickenson U., 1979. Cons. Cresap, McCormick and Paget, N.Y.C., 1964-65; sr. mgmt. cons. Union Carbide Corp., 1965-67; asst. contr. data processing Western Union, 1967-69; v.p. mgmt. info. systems ABC, Hackensack, N.J., 1970-86; v.p., chief info. officer Blue Cross Blue Shield of N.J., Newark, 1986-88; v.p. Chantico Pub. Co., Carrellton, Tex., 1989-90; pres. SMC-BIS Inc., Basking Ridge, N.J., 1990-93; pres., CEO Strategic Outsourcing Svcs. Inc., Mountain Lakes, 1993-97; sr. v.p. Computer Horizons Corp., 1997-99; exec. v.p. PRT Group Inc., Windsor, Conn., 1999-2000; sr. dir. ISI Profl. Svcs., Washington, 2000—. Spkr. in field. Mem. adv. bd. YMCA. With U.S. Army, 1948-52. Decorated Silver Star with oak leaf cluster, Bronze Star with V, Purple Heart with 2 oak leaf clusters. Mem. Soc. Mgmt. Info. Systems, N.J. C. of C., Profit Oriented Systems Planning Bd. (bd. dirs.), Masons. Republican. Office: ISI Profl Svcs 915 15th St NW Ste 200 Washington DC 20050 E-mail: Edward.D.Williams@att.net.

WILLIAMS, EDWARD EARL, JR. entrepreneur, educator; b. Houston, Aug. 21, 1945; s. Edward Earl and Doris Jewel (Jones) W.; m. Susan M. Warren, June 28, 1983; children: Laura Michelle, David Brian. BS, U. Pa., 1966; PhD, U. Tex., 1968. Asst. prof. econs. Rutgers U., New Brunswick, N.J., 1968-70; assoc. prof. fin. McGill U., Montreal, Que., 1970-73; v.p. Svc. Corp. Internat., Houston, 1973-77; prof. adminstrv. sci. Rice U., 1978-82, Henry Gardiner Symonds prof., 1982—, prof. stats., 1995—. Chmn. bd. dirs. Edward E. Williams & Co., Houston, 1976-92; chmn. bd., pres. Tex. Capital Investment Co., 1979-95; chmn. bd. First Tex. Venture Capital Corp., 1983-92; mng. dir. First Tex. Venture Capital, LLC, 1992-2000, Svc. Corp. Internat, EQUUS II, Inc.; adv. dir. Frost Nat. Bank. Author: Prospects for the Savings and Loan Industry, 1968, An Integrated Analysis for Managerial Finance, 1970, Investment Analysis, 1974, Business Planning for the Entrepreneur, 1983, The Economics of Production and Productivity: A Modeling Approach, 1996, Entrepreneurship and Productivity, 1998, The N.Y. Times Pocket MBA Series: Business Planning, 1999, Models for Investors in Real World Markets, 2002; contbr. articles to profl. jours. Benjamin Franklin scholar, Jesse Jones scholar U. Pa., 1966; fellow Tex. Savs. and Loan League, fellow NDEA U. Tex., 1968. Mem. Am. Statis. Assn., Coll. Innovation and Entrepreneurship, Fin. Mgmt. Assn., So. Pacific Hist. and Tech. Soc., Soc. on Econs. and Mgmt. in China, Raveneaux Country Club, Jewish Comm. North, Beta Gamma Sigma, Alpha Kappa Psi. Republican. Home: 7602 Wilton Park Dr Spring TX 77379-4672 Office: Rice U Jesse H Jones Grad Sch Mgmt Houston TX 77251 E-mail: jmkeynes@rice.edu.

WILLIAMS, EDWARD F(OSTER), III, environmental engineer; b. N.Y.C., Jan. 3, 1935; s. E. Foster Jr. and Ida Frances (Richards) W.; m. Sue Carol Osenbaugh, June 5, 1960; children: Cecile Elizabeth, Alexander Harmon. BS in Engring., Auburn U., 1956; MA in History, U. Memphis, 1974. Registered profl. engr., Tenn. Engr. Buckeye Cellulose Corp. (subs. of Procter & Gamble), Memphis, 1957, process safety engr., 1960, resident constrn. engr. Perry, Fla., 1960-61, staff engr. Memphis, 1961-70; chief engr., v.p. Enviro-trol, Inc., 1970-73; from v.p. to pres. Ramcon Environ. Corp., 1973-80; pres. E.F. Williams & Assocs., Inc., 1980-98; v.p. engring. Environ. Testing & Cons. of the Americas, Inc., 1998—2001, pres., 2001—. Chmn. bd. EFW Comml. Ventures, Inc., 1990—, Spiridon Press, Inc., 1998-99; bd. dirs. Mobile Process Tech. Inc., Memphis; v.p. Environ. Testing and Cons., Inc., Memphis, 1985-94; environ. coord. Shelby County, Tenn., 1995-96. Author: Fustest with the Mostest, 1968, Early Memphis and Its River Rivals, 1969, Great American Civil War Trivia Book, 1998; editor Environ. Control News for So. Industry, 1971—. State rep. Tenn. Gen. Assembly , 1970—78; mem. Shelby County Bd. Commrs., Memphis, 1978-94, chmn., 1987-88, 90-92, Shelby County Records Commn., 1978-, chmn., 1993-; Chickasaw Basin Authority, 1980-94, 98-, vice chmn., 1982-94; historian Shelby County , 1994—; environ. coord. Shelby County Mayor's staff , 1995—96; vice chmn. Shelby County Stormwater Steering Com., 1998—; trustee Bolton Coll., 1982-, chmn., 1987-88, 90-92; del. Rep. Nat. Conv., 1988, 92, 96Rep. state exec. com., 1994-; state chmn. Nat. Conf. Rep. County Ofcls., 1993—96; vice-chmn. Memphis-Shelby local Emergency Planning Com. , 1986—; bd. dirs. Better Bus. Bur. Memphis, 1995—; chmn. Shelby County Hist. Commn. , 1997—98; vice chmn. Shelby County Courthouse Hist. Preservation Commn., 2000—; pres. Christ United Presbyn. Ch. Corp., 1995—98. Capt. USAF, 1957—60. Named Tenn. Water Conservationist of Yr., Tenn. Conservation League, 1973, Tenn. Legis. Conservationist of Yr., Nat. Wildlife Fedn., 1974, Memphis Outstanding Engr., Memphis Joint Engrs. Coun., 1980; recipient Shelby County Environ. Improvement award, 1983, Tenn. Lifetime Environ. Stewardship award Tenn. Dept. Environ. and Conservation, 1995. Mem. NSPE, ASME, Am. Acad. Environ. Engrs. (diplomate), Environ. Assesment Assn., TSPE, Water Environ. Fedn., Am. Indsl. Hygiene Assn. (chpt. pres.), Am. Soc. Safety Engrs. (Outstanding Achievement award 1995-96), Air and Waste Mgmt. Assn., Engrs. Club Memphis (bd. dirs. 1979-80, 98—, pres. 2000-01), Rotary, C. of C. (environ. coun. chmn. 1988-2000, chmn. emeritus 2000—), Tenn. Hist. Soc. (v.p. 1972), Tenn. Hist. Commn. (vice-chmn. 1987-99), West Tenn. Hist. Soc. (pres. 1983-85), Am. Hist. Assn., Memphis-Shelby County Tenn. Bicentennial Commn. (chmn. 1994-96), Davies Manor Assn. (pres. 1999-2000), Miss. Historical Soc. Republican. Avocation: history. Home: 148 Perkins Ext Memphis TN 38117-3127 Office: ETC of the Americas Inc 751 E Brookhaven Cir Memphis TN 38117-4501 also: PO Box 241813 Memphis TN 38124-1813 also: Shelby Co Office 150 Washington Ave Rm 210 Memphis TN 38103 E-mail: efwilliams@etcamemphis.com. *It has been my observation that history does not repeat itself, but human nature does. Knowledge of this principle can be put to use in politics, business, and other endeavors if one knows history.*

WILLIAMS, EDWARD FRANK, poet, entertainment company executive; b. N.Y.C., Oct. 3, 1949; s. Frank and Maggie W.; m. B.L. Williams, 1980 (div. 1985). AAS, Kingsborough C.C., Bklyn., 1970. Instr. bd. edn. Cmty. Sch. Dist. # 13, Bklyn., 1971-99; FCC 3rd class permit FCC, 1980—; performance poet Poets and Writers Inc., N.Y.C., 1980—; CSAC State of N.Y., 1990—; CEO, pres. Libra Prodns./Entertainment Inc., Bklyn., 1998. Author: E.F. Williams, Urban Poet, 1985, (CD version), 1999. Avocations: lyricist, motivational speaker, educational consultant. Home: 1633 Sterling Pl Apt 4H Brooklyn NY 11233-4970

WILLIAMS, EDWARD GILMAN, retired banker; b. Ware, Mass., Apr. 11, 1926; s. Carl Emmons and Susan Helen (Gilman) W.; m. Barbara Thompson Russell, June 19, 1959; children: Thomas Clarke, Susan Gilman. BA, Trinity Coll., Conn., 1950. With Union Trust Co., New Haven, 1951-89; asst. trust officer Union & New Haven Trust Co., 1956-59, trust officer, 1959-64, v.p., 1964-65, v.p., sr. adminstrv. officer, 1965-69; sr. v.p. Union Trust Co., 1969-72, exec. v.p., 1972-89; v.p. Northeast Bancorp., Inc., 1972-89. Former treas. Leila Day Nurseries, Inc., New Haven; treas., pres. Ridge Rd. Sch. PTA, Hamden Hall Country Day Sch. Parents Assn.; bd. dirs. Vis. Nurse Assn., New Haven, 1963-86, pres., treas., 1970-75; trustee New Eng. Sch. Banking, 1971-74, 81-88, vice chmn., 1985-86, chmn. 1986-88; trustee Shubert Performing Arts Ctr., New Haven, 1985-90; bd. dirs. New Haven Colony Hist. Soc., 1987-89; trustee, deacon, chmn. music com. Ch. of Redeemer, New Haven; bd. dirs., treas. Edgerton Garden Ctr., 1992-99, asst. treas. 1999-2001, Friends of Grove St. Cemetery, treas., 1997—; bd. dirs. Easter Seals Goodwill Rehab. Ctr., New Haven, 1993-99, Whitney Ctr. Continuing Care Retirement Cmty., Hamden, 1998—. Mem. English-Speaking Union (treas. New Haven br. 1994—), New Haven Lawn Club (pres. 1979-82), Masons. Home: 900 Mix Ave Apt 17 Hamden CT 06514-5107 Office: 3074 Whitney Ave # 2-L Hamden CT 06518-2391

WILLIAMS, EDWARD JOSEPH, banker; b. Chgo., May 5, 1942; s. Joseph and Lillian (Watkins) W.; children: Elaine, Paul; m. Ana J. Ortiz, Apr. 20, 1996. BBA, Roosevelt U., 1973. Owner Mut. Home Delivery, Chgo., 1961-63; exec. v.p. Harris Trust and Savs. Bank, 1964—. Mem. Consumer Adv. Council, Washington, 1986—. Trustee, treas. Adler Planetarium, Chgo., 1982; trustee Roosevelt U., Chgo., Art Inst. of Chgo.; bd. dirs. Chapin-May Found., Chgo. Botanic Garden, Chgo. Capital Fund; trustee, treas. Chgo. Low Income Housing Trust Fund; dir. Leadership Coun. for Met. Open Communities; dir., former pres. Neighborhood Housing Svcs. of Chgo.; chmn. Provident Med. Ctr., Chgo., 1986; bd. dirs. Voices for Ill. Children, Chgo. Coun. on Urban Affairs; pres. Neighborhood Housing Svcs. Recipient Disting. Alumni award Clark Coll., Atlanta, 1985. Mem. Nat. Bankers Assn., Urban Bankers Forum (Pioneer award 1986, 97), Econ. Club. Chgo. Clubs: Metropolitan, Plaza (Chgo.). Office: Harris Trust & Savs Bank 111 W Monroe St Chicago IL 60603-4096

WILLIAMS, EDWARD MACON, poet; b. Rose Hill, N.C., Feb. 11, 1931; s. Samuel Paul and Laura Alethia (Murray) W. Author poems: Angels of Mercy, 1995, Beautiful Rose of Sharon, 1996, The Sacrificial Lamb, 1996, Heaven Rejoices, 1996, The Sweet Spirit of Yahweh, 1996, The Birth of Messiah, 1998, The Christ, 2000. Mem. Internat. Soc. Poets.

WILLIAMS, EDWARD VINSON, music history educator; b. Orlando, Fla., July 12, 1935; B.M., Fla. State U., 1957; M.M., Ind. U., 1962; MA, Yale U., 1966, PhD, 1968. Prof. music history dept. music U. Kans., Lawrence, 1969-90, chmn. dept. music history, 1975-84; assoc. dean rsch. and grad. studies Coll. Arts and Architecture, prof. music Pa. State U., University Park, Pa., 1990—. Author: The Bells of Russia: History and Technology, 1985 Served with U.S. Army, 1957-60 Recipient Chancellor's award for Excellence in Teaching, U. Kans., 1975; Kennan Inst. fellow Wilson Ctr., Washington, 1985; fellow Nat. Humanities Ctr., Research Triangle Park, N.C., 1980-81 Mem. Am. Musicological Soc., Am. Assn. for Advancement Slavic Studies, Assn. Bell Art (Moscow). Home: 330 Toftrees Ave Apt 149 State College PA 16803-2043 Office: Pa State U Coll Arts and Architecture 114 Arts Bldg University Park PA 16802-2900

WILLIAMS, ELEANOR CLAFLIN (CLAFFY WILLIAMS), artist; b. Brookline, Mass., Jan. 31, 1916; d. Thomas Mack and Alice Morton (Osborn) Claflin; m. Thomas Blake Williams, Jan. 26, 1940; children: Thomas B. Jr., Susan Williams Dickie, Eleanor Williams Wright, Sandra M. Williams Weiss. Student, Sweet Briar Coll. Art tchr.; lectr. on contemporary art. One woman shows include Pual Platt Libr., Cohasset, Mass., 1998, Cohasset Paul Pratt Meml. Libr., 1999; exhibited in various art shows including Copley Soc., Boston, 1974, 77, 98, 99, 2000, Chinese Cultural Inst., Boston, 1992, 98, 2000, South Shore Art Ctr., Cohasset, 1996, 97, 98, 2000, Modern Art D'unet, Tonniens, 1993, Chinese Cultural Inst., Boston, 1992, 96, Ariel Gallery, Soho, N.Y., 1990, Art Complex, Duxbury, Mass., 1982, 97; 3 paintings in book The Best in Acrylic Painting, 1996, Artexpo in N.Y.C. promoted by ARTREPS, 1998; 3 paintings in Creative Inspirations, 1997. Pres. bd. dirs. South Shore Art Ctr., Cohasset, Mass., 1985-87, mem. adv. bd., 1987—; dir. Prison Art Project, Boston, 1973-76; bd. dirs. Copley Soc., Boston, 1975-79. Recipient 1st prize for graphics North River Art Assn., Marshfield, Mass. Avocations: skiing, tennis, walking, reading, travel.

WILLIAMS, ELEANOR JOYCE, retired government air traffic control specialist; b. College Station, Tex., Dec. 21, 1936; d. Robert Ira and Viola (Ford) Toliver; m. Tollie Williams, Dec. 30, 1955 (div. July 1978); children: Rodrick, Viola Williams Smith, Darryl, Eric, Dana Williams Robinson, Sheila Williams Watkins, Kenneth. Student, Prairie View A&M Coll., 1955-56, Anchorage Community Coll., 1964-65, U. Alaska-Anchorage, 1976. Clk./stenographer FAA, Anchorage, 1965-66, adminstrv. clk., 1966-67, pers. staffing asst., 1967-68, air traffic control specialist, 1968-79, air traffic control supr. San Juan, P.R., 1979-80, Anchorage, 1983-85, airspace specialist Atlanta, 1980-83, with Washington, 1985-87; area mgr. Kansas City Air Rt. Traffic Control Ctr., Olathe, Kans., 1987-89, asst. mgr. Quality Assurance, 1989-91, supr. traffic mgmt., 1991, supr. system effectiveness section, 1991-93, asst. air traffic mgr., 1993-94; air traffic mgr. Cleve. Air Route Traffic Control Ctr., Oberlin, Ohio, 1994-97; acting mgr. sys. mgmt. br. Des Plains, Ill., 1995-96; mem. human resource reform team task force Washington, 1996—; acting regional exec. mgr. Great Lakes Region Des Plaines, Ill., 1996-97. Proprietor Williams Apts., Anchorage. Sec. Fairview Neighborhood Coun., Anchorage, 1967-69; mem. Anchorage Bicentennial Commn., 1975-76; bd. dirs. Mt. Patmos Youth Dept., Decatur, Ga., 1981-82; mem. NAACP; del. to USSR Women in Mgmt., 1990; v.p. A&M Consol. Lincoln H.S. Alumni Assn., 2000—; mem. citizens amb. program People to People Internat.; mem. adv. bd. Lincoln Recreation Ctr. Recipient Mary K. Goddard award Anchorage Fed. Exec. Assn. and Fed. Women's Program, 1985, Sec.'s award Dept. Transp., 1985, Pres. VIP award, 1988, C. Alfred Anderson award, 1991, Disting. Svc. award Nat. Black Coalition of Fed. Aviation Employees, 1991, Paul K. Bohr award FAA, 1994, Nat. Performance Rev. Hammer award from V.P. Al Gore, 1996, Regional Adminstrs. award for meritorious svc. Gt. Lakes Regional Adminstrn., 1997, Top Flight award for outstanding svc. FAA, 1997; A salute to Her Name in the Congl. Record 104th Congress, 1995, Execs. in Profile award for exemplary career performance Region Ten Blacks in Govt., 1998, Pres.'s award for outstanding svc. Lincoln Former Students Assn.; named Disting. Alumnus Lincoln H.S., 2000; inducted into Black Aviation Hall of Fame, Memphis, Tenn., 2001; named Youth Advocate Cmty. Champion State of Tex., Tex. Commn. Alcohol & Drug Abuse, 2001. Mem.: Women in Mgmt. (del. Soviet Union), Internat. Platform Assn., Fed. Mgrs. Assn., Air Traffic Contrs. Assn., Profl. Women Contrs. Orgn., Nat. Black Coalition of Fed. Aviation Employees (pres. cen. region chpt. 1987—92, Over Achievers award 1987, Disting. Svc. award 1988, Sojourner Truth award Great Lakes region 1997, inducted into Black Aviation Hall of Fame 2001), Blacks in Govt., Nat. Assn. Negro Bus. and Profl. Women USA Inc. (North to the Future club, charter pres. 1975—76), Gamma Phi Delta. Democrat. Baptist. Avocations: singing, sewing. Home: 7931 Old Seward Hwy Apt 8 Anchorage AK 99518-3265 E-mail: ejw4atc@aol.com., ejtwmsent@msn.com.

WILLIAMS, ELIZABETH ANNEGA, communications executive; b. Bainbridge, Ga., May 22, 1955; d. Jack and Bertha (Wynn) Williams. BS, Lane Coll., 1977; postgrad. Ind. U.-Indpls., 1980-82. Mgr. trainee McDonalds Restaurants, Indpls., 1978; account analyst Western Electric, Indpls., 1978-81, warehouse supr., 1981-82, bus. methods exec., 1982-83; customer service mgr. AT&T Consumer Products, Indpls., 1983-84; mktg. and sales exec. AT&T Technologies, Inc., Indpls., 1984-86; phone ctr. store mgr. AT&T Consumer Sales & Service, Jackson, Tenn., 1986—. Vol., Spl. Olympics, Indpls., 1983-85, Ind. Sch. for Blind, 1984. Mem. Am. Mgmt. Assn., Direct Mktg. Assn., Nat. Assn. Female Execs., NAACP, Alpha Kappa Mu, Zeta Phi Beta. Democrat. Mem. Methodist Episcopal Ch. Avocations: aerobics, jogging, photography, traveling. Home: 5 Fairfax Cv Jackson TN 38305-2205 Office: AT&T Consumer Sales and Svc 2021 N Highland Ave Jackson TN 38305-4903

WILLIAMS, ELIZABETH YAHN, writer, lecturer, lawyer; b. Columbus, Ohio, July 20, 1942; d. Wilbert Henry and Elizabeth Dulson (Brophy) Yahn. BA cum laude, Loyola Marymount U., 1964; secondary tchg. credential, UCLA, 1965; JD, Loyola U., 1971. Cert. tchr. h.s. and jr. coll. law, English and history. Writer, West Covina, Calif., 1964—; designer, 1966-68; tchr. jr./sr. h.s. L.A. City Schs., Santa Monica, Calif., 1964-65, La Puente (Calif.) H.S. Dist., 1965-67; legal intern, lawyer Garvey, Ingram, Baker & Uhler, Covina, Calif., 1969-72; lawyer, corp. counsel Avco Fin. Svcs., Inc., Newport Beach, 1972-74; sole practitioner and arbitrator Santa Ana, 1974-80, Newport Beach, 1980-87; writing scholar Episcopal Diocese of L.A., 1999. Mem. faculty continuing edn. State Bar of Calif., 1979; adj. prof. Western State U. Sch. Law, Fullerton, Calif., 1980; mem. fed. cts. com. Calif. State Bar, San Francisco, 1977-80. Author: (1-act plays) Acting-Out Acts, 1990, Grading Graciela, 1992, Boundaries in the Dirt, 1993; author: (lyricist) (1-act children's musical) Peter and the Worry Wrens, 1995; author: (lyricist, narrator) (musical narrative) Love in Our Midst, 2000; : A Medley of Cherry, 2000, Verses for Violins, 2001, Joy: Moments for Reflection, 2002; editor: The Music of Poetry, 1997, 1998; contbr. articles to profl. jours.; panelist (TV show) Action Now, 1971, interviewee Women, 1987; scriptwriter, dir.: TV show Four/Four, 1994; author: (3-act adaptation) Saved in Sedona, 1995; scriptwriter, prodr., host: TV show Guildelights to Success, 1996; developer board game Go With Your Goals!, 1995, 1999. Mem. alumni bd. Loyola-Marymount Coll., L.A., 1980-84; mem. adv. bd. Rancho Santiago Coll., Santa Ana, 1983-84; spkr. Commn. on Status on Women, Santa Ana, 1979. Recipient Telly award finalist, 1996, Unterberg/semi-dinalist, The Nation Discovery, 1997; grantee, Ford Found., 1964—65; scholar French scholar, Ohio State U., 1959, acad. scholar, Loyola-Marymount U., 1960—64, Book Expo 2000 scholar, Pubs. Mktg. Assn.-San Diego Pubs. Alliance Pub Mktg. U., 2000. Mem.: Nat. League Am. Pen Women, Magee Park Poets, Poetry Soc. Am., Orange County Bar Assn. (chmn. human and individual rights com. 1974—75, comml. law and bankruptcy com. 1978—79, corp. and bus. law sect. 1980—81, faculty Orange County Coll. Trial Advocacy 1982), Acad. Am. Poets, Calif. Women Lawyers (life; bd. dirs. 1975—76, co-founder), Phi Theta Kappa (life most disting. hon.). Avocation: directing and producing ensemble and liturgical dramas and musicals. Address: PO Box 233 San Luis Rey CA 92068-0233 E-mail: drbethwilliams@hotmail.com.

WILLIAMS, ELLEN C. political party official; m. Greg Williams; children: Sam, Joey. Grad., U. Ky. Staff asst. Congressman Larry Hopkins. Cons. Lexington/Bluegrass Bd. of Realtors; active Anderson County United Way Bd., Ch. of Lawrenceburg. Polit. dir. Dole/Kemp Ky.; dep. campaign mgr. Larry Forgy campaign for Gov.; exec. dir. Rep. Party of Ky., 1991-92; regional polit. dir. Nat. Rep. Com.; chmn. Ky. Republican Party, 1999-; exec. asst. Senator Bob Kasten; mem. Pres./Bush '84; exec. dir. Young Rep. Fedn. Office: Rep Party of Ky PO Box 1068 Frankfort KY 40602 E-mail: chair@rpk.org.*

WILLIAMS, EMMA, management executive; b. Cleveland, Ark., Feb. 8, 1928; d. James and Frazier (Byers) Wallace; m. Augusta Griggs, Mar. 20, 1954 (dec.); children: Judy A., Terri V.; m. John Williams. Grad. H.S., Chgo. Pres., CEO Burlington No. Inc., Inglewood, Calif., 1986—. Republican. Avocations: reading, gardening, housekeeping. Office: Burlington No Corp 2nd Fl 2650 Lou Menk Dr Fort Worth TX 76131-2830 E-mail: judygr7@aol.com.

WILLIAMS, EMMA CRAWFORD, business owner; b. Dillon, S.C., Aug. 16, 1945; d. Moses and Sallie Lee (McInnis) Crawford; m. Johnny Lee Williams, Nov. 25, 1967; 1 child, GiGi T. A in Bus. Adminstrn., Durham (N.C.) Bus. Coll., 1964; A in Acctg., Strayer Coll., Washington, 1969. From sec. to office mgr. Ferris & Co., Washington, 1965-68; exec. asst. mgr. Manpower Assistance Program, 1968-71; adminstrv. asst./office mgr. Appalachian Regional Com., 1971-81; adminstrv. sec. Home Owners Warranty Ins., 1981-82; office mgr. Hilton Internat. Hotels, 1986-89; pres., CEO, owner AHA Enterprises, Inc. (Added Hands Agy.), Ft. Washington, Md., 1989—. Mem. Fairfax County Commerce Dept.; motivational spkr. D.C. Treatment Facility; guest spkr. Julia Jackson's Other Office on Bus. and Fins., Va., 1996. Block capt. Ft. Washington Citizen Assn., 1975—; active Laura House Assn., Tex., 1992—; vol. office asst. nat. presdl. campaign, Washington, 1976. Mem. Am. Woman's Econ. Devel., Nat. Notary Assn., Dillionite, Inc. Democrat. Avocations: reading journals and self-help publications, collecting antiques, polo, fundraising campaigns. Home: 9108 Overlook Trl Fort Washington MD 20744-6882 Office: AHA Enterprises Inc Added Hands Agy 1800 Diagonal Rd Ste 600 Alexandria VA 22314-2840

WILLIAMS, EMMETT LEWIS, engineer, researcher, physicist, educator; b. Lynchburg, Va., June 6, 1933; s. Emmett Lewis Williams, Sr. and Essie Bernice Gibson; m. Mary Caroline Austin, June 17, 1957; children: Deborah, Robert, Mary Martha. BS, Va. Tech., 1956, MS, 1961; PhD, Clemson U., 1965. Engr. Atomic Energy Divsn. Babcock & Wilcox, Lynchburg, Va., 1957—59; asst. prof. Va. Tech., Blacksburg, 1959—63; rsch. asst. Clemson (S.C.) U., 1964—65; scientist Y-12 Plant, Oak Ridge, Tenn., 1965—66; prof. Bob Jones U., Greenville, SC, 1966—79; scientist Lockheed Aircraft, Marietta, Ga., 1981—90; various field projects, 1990—2000; ret., 2000. Cons. Electrotec Corp., Blacksburg, Va., 1950—63, Continental Telephone, Hickory, NC, 1970. Editor: Thermodynamics and the Development of Order, 1981; contbr. articles to profl. jours. With USMC, 1950—52. Fellow: Creation Rsch. Soc.; mem.: Sigma Xi. Avocations: reading, travel, philately. Home: PO Box 2006 Alpharetta GA 30023 Address: 10465 Stonefield Landing Duluth GA 30097

WILLIAMS, EMORY, former retail company executive, banker; b. Falco, Ala., Oct. 26, 1911; s. William Emory and Nelle (Turner) W.; m. Janet Hatcher Allcorn, May 15, 1943; children: Nelle (Mrs. Gilbert Brown), Janet (Mrs. Edwin Harrison), Bliss (Mrs. Howell Browne), Carol (Mrs. James Schroeder), Emory III. AB, Emory U., 1932. With Sears, Roebuck & Co., 1933-75; pres. Sears, Roebuck (S.A.), Brazil, 1958-60, Homart Devel. Co., 1960-67; treas. parent co., 1962-64; v.p., treas., 1964-75; chmn. bd., chief exec. officer Sears Bank & Trust Co., 1975-81, also dir. Chmn. bd. dirs., pres. Chgo. Milw. Corp., 1981-85; ptnr. Williams Realty Co.; chmn. Williams & Nichols Co., Sure-Block Co., Am. Investors in China. Div. chmn. Chgo. Crusade of Mercy, 1962-64, gen. chmn., 1966, pres, 1976-78; chmn. Ill. Health Edn. Commn., 1968-70; pres. Adler Planetarium, 1972-75, Ravinia Festival Assn., 1972-78; pres. bd. dirs. Community Fund, 1970-73; trustee Emory U., Chgo. Community Trust, Northwestern Meml. Hosps., Kellstadt Found.; chmn. Chgo. Chamber Musicians. Lt. col. C.E., U.S. Army, World War II, CBI. Mem. Piedmont Driving Club (Atlanta); Chgo. Club, Old Elm Club (Chgo.), Commercial Club; Indian Hill Club (Winnetka, Ill.), Loblolly Club (Hobe Sound, Fla.), Seminole Golf Club (North Palm Beach). Home: 1630 Sheridan Rd Wilmette IL 60091-1876 Also: 7760 SE Lake Shore Dr Hobe Sound FL 33455-3833 E-mail: emoryjanet@aol.com., ewilliams@bldgsolutions.com.

WILLIAMS, ENID JO, freelance/self-employed writer; b. Laverne, Okla., Feb. 6, 1920; d. Oliver John and Esther (Root) Bourgois; m. Edward L. Williams, Aug. 8, 1936; children: Loretta June Smith, Gary L. Student, Cerritos Adult Edn., 1978-80. Tchr. Sunday sch. Full Gospel, Bellflower, Calif., 1950-55; with Shady Acres, Redding and Ctrl. City, 1968-74; office mgr. Little Moe Zarellas, Long Beach, 1980—. Songwriter; contbg. poet: Best Poems of 1997, Best Poems of the 90's, Poetry in New Libr. of Congress; lyricist Hilltop Records, 1999. Named in top 2% of poets Nat. Libr. Poetry, 1997; recipient Golden Poet award, 1990, 91; named Top Song Writer, Chapel Recording Co., 1995. Mem. ASCAP, Am. Nat. Libr., Nat. Libr. Poetry (Golden Post award), Nat. Libr. Congress, Internat. Libr. Poets, Internat. Soc. Poets (life, Bronze medallion, Copper medallion 1997, Poet of Yr. 1999), Rebekah Lodge. Republican. Methodist. Avocations: reading, writing, flowers. Home: 1501 W Hickory St Deming NM 88030-4434

WILLIAMS, ERIC JOSEPH, transportation executive; b. Havana, Cuba, Nov. 15, 1945; came to U.S., 1961; s. Ereic and Frances (Waterhouse) W.; m. Maria Julia Williams, Mar. 30, 1984; children: Jason, Natasha. BS in Fgn. Svc., Georgetown U., 1968. With Emery Worldwide, 1970-88, regional mgr. S.Am., 1977-81, dist. mgr. L.Am.-Caribbean, 1984-86, dir. L.Am.-Caribbean sector, 1986-88, LEP Internat., Miami, 1988-90, dir. L.Am.-Caribbean region, 1988-90; mng. dir. sales L.Am. divsn. Fed. Express, 1990-96; sr. mgr. L.Am. sales Fritz Co., 1996-98; v.p. internat. Pilot Air, 1999—. Adult edn. tchr., Miami, 1973-75; chmn. Air Cargo Ams., 1999. Exec. bd. Hist. Mus. South Fla.; mem. mem. Miami Beacon Coun., 1995-97. 1st lt. U.S. Army, 1968-70. Mem. Soc. Ams., Coral Gables C. of C., Georgetown U. Alumni Assn. (com.), Coconut Grove Sailing Club (com. 1975-76). Episcopalian. Home: 501 Raven Ave Miami FL 33166-3950

WILLIAMS, ERIK GEORGE, professional football player; b. Phila., Sept. 7, 1968; Student, Ctrl. State U. Offensive tackle Dallas Cowboys, 1991—2000. Mem. Superbowl Championship team, 1993, 94. Named to Pro Bowl Team, 1993; named offensive tackle on The Sporting News NFL All-Pro Team, 1993; selected to Pro Bowl, 1996.*

WILLIAMS, ERVIN EUGENE, religious organization administrator; b. Corning, N.Y., Feb. 25, 1923; s. Douglas Lewis and Mina P. (Barnes) W.; m. Ruth Evelyn Snyder, June 12, 1945; children: Roger Eugene, Virginia Ruth. Student, Toccoa Falls (Ga.) Bible Coll., 1939, Cornell U., 1942; BA, Pa. State U., 1949; MA, Mich. State U., 1961, PhD in Communications, 1971. Ordained to ministry Ind. Bapt. Ch., 1950. Acad. dean Greensburg (Pa.) Bible Inst., 1949-51; min. Bapt. Ch., New Kensington, Pa., 1951-53; instr. Pa. State U., 1953-55; sr. min. East Lansing (Mich.) Trinity Ch., 1955-71; vis. prof. Trinity Evang. Div. Sch., Deerfield, Ill., 1968-71, prof. comm. and practical theology, 1971-77, dir. D Ministry program, 1975-76; gen. dir. Am. Missionary Fellowship, Villanova, Pa., 1977-92; exec. min. Ch. of the Apostles, Atlanta, 1993-95; ch. and instl. cons. Smyrna, Ga., 1995—; sr. pastor New Life Bible Ch., Abaco, The Bahamas, 1997-98. Chaplain Mich. State U., East Lansing, 1955-71; cons. Haggai Inst. for Advanced Leadership Tng., Atlanta, 1969-95; lectr. Calvary Bapt. Coll., Kansas City, Mo., 1962, Haggai Inst. Third World Leaders, Singapore, 1970-95; Staley lectr. Robert Wesleyan Coll., North Chili, N.Y., 1973, Judson Coll., Elgin, Ill., 1977-79; cons. to mission bds., 1967-76; assoc. dir. Camp of Woods, Speculator, N.Y., 1971-77. Author: 3 books; contbr. numerous articles to religious periodicals, also monographs. Trustee Dorothy H. Theis Meml. Found., Sierra Vista, Ariz., 1987-95, Gospel Vols., Speculator, N.Y., 1963-93; mem. bd. regents Owosso (Mich.) Coll., 1971-73. Pilot USAAF, 1942-45, prisoner of war, ETO, 1945. Decorated DFC, Air medal with two oak leaf clusters, POW medal, ETO Campaign medal with six clusters, Victory medal, Presdl. citation., Air medal with two oak leaf clusters. Mem. Nat. Sunday Sch. Assn., Christian Assn. Psychol. Studies, Mich. Acad. Arts and Scis., Aircraft Owners and Pilots Assn., Phi Beta Kappa, Pi Gamma Mu, Phi Kappa Phi, Alpha Kappa Delta. *It is much more difficult to conceal ignorance and prejudice than it is to acquire knowledge and fairness.*

WILLIAMS, EVELYN LOIS, chemical company executive, safety consultant; b. Richmond, Va., Sept. 20, 1954; d. Kenneth R. and Ardis M. (Paul) W. AB, Brown U., 1977. Engr. tech. svc. DuPont Co., Wilmington, Del., 1976-79, area engr. Gibbstown, N.J., 1979-83, sr. supr. Deepwater, 1983-85, prodn. asst. Wilmington, 1985-87, unit mgr. Memphis, 1987-88, plant mgr. Montague, Mich., 1988-92, Antioch, Calif., 1992-96; sr. cons., project mgr., sr. devel. cons., devel. mgr., client support assoc. DuPont Safety Resources Bus., Newark, 1996—. Dir. FMB-Lumberman's Bank, Muskegon, Mich., 1990-92. Campaign cabinet United Way, Muskegon, 1989-91, Concord, Calif., 1993-94; trustee Delta Meml. Hosp., Antioch, 1994-96. Named One of 100 Women to Watch in Corp. Am., Bus. Monthly Mag., 1989. Mem. AAAS, AAUW, ASM

Internat., Soc. Women Engrs. Home: 4 Barley Mill Dr Wilmington DE 19807-2218 Office: DuPont Safety Resources Christiana Exec Campus 121 Continental Ste 207-9 Newark DE 19713-4324 E-mail: elwilliams2229@prodigy.net., evelyn.l.williams@usa.dupont.com.

WILLIAMS, FORMAN ARTHUR, engineering science educator, combustion theorist; b. New Brunswick, N.J., Jan. 12, 1934; s. Forman J. and Alice (Pooley) W.; m. Elsie Vivian Kara, June 15, 1955 (div. 1978); children: F. Gary, Glen A., Nancy L., Susan D., Michael S., Michelle K.; m. Elizabeth Acevedo, Aug. 19, 1978. BSE, Princeton U., 1955; PhD, Calif. Inst. Tech., 1958. Asst. prof. Harvard U., Cambridge, Mass., 1958-64; prof. U. Calif.-San Diego, 1964-81; Robert H. Goddard prof. Princeton U., N.J., 1981-88; prof. dept. applied mechs. and engring. scis. U. Calif., San Diego, 1988—, predsidential chair in Energy and Combustion Rsch, 1994—. Author: Combustion Theory, 1965, 2d edit., 1985; contbr. articles to profl. jours. Fellow NSF, 1962; fellow Guggenheim Found., 1970; recipient U.S. Sr. Scientist award Alexander von Humboldt Found., 1982, Silver medal Combustion Inst., 1978, Bernard Lewis Gold medal Combustion Inst., 1990, Pendray Aerospace Literature award Am. Inst. of Aeronautics and Astronautics, 1993 Fellow AIAA ; mem. Am. Phys. Soc., Combustion Inst., Soc. for Indsl. and Applied Math., Nat. Acad. Engring., Nat. Acad. Engring Mex. (fgn. corr. mem.), Sigma Xi. Home: 8258 Caminito Maritimo La Jolla CA 92037-2204 Office: U Calif San Diego Ctr Energy Rsch 9500 Gilman Dr La Jolla CA 92093-5004 E-mail: faw@mae.ucsd.edu.

WILLIAMS, FRANCES ELIZABETH, secondary education educator; b. Eccles, W.Va., May 30, 1948; d. Decolious R. and Wilhelmina (Bell) W. BA, U. D.C., 1973; MAT, Trinity Coll., 1975, postgrad., 1976-85. From keypunch operator to computer operator GSA, Washington, 1966-72; with computer tape div. HHS, 1972-73; tchr. social studies H. D. Woodson Sr. High Sch., 1973—. Mem. U.S. Capitol Hist. Soc. Democrat. Baptist. Avocations: travel, reading, coin collector. Home: 1220 E West Hwy Apt 209 Silver Spring MD 20910-3269 Office: HD Woodson Sr H S 55th and Eads Sts NE Washington DC 20019

WILLIAMS, FRANK J. chief justice, historian, author; b. Providence, Aug. 24, 1940; s. Frank and Natalie L. (Corelli) W.; m. Virginia E. Miller, Aug. 24, 1966. BA, Boston U., 1962, JD, 1970; MS in Taxation, Bryant Coll., 1986; LHD, Lincoln Coll., 1987, So. New England Sch. Law, 2001. Bar: R.I. 1970, U.S. Dist. Ct. R.I. 1970, U.S. Supreme Ct. 1976. Assoc. Tillinghast, Collins & Graham, Providence, 1970-75, Leonard Decof Ltd., Providence, 1976-78; law clk. Graham, Reid, Ewing & Stapleton, 1969; law clk., adminstrv. asst. R.I. Atty. Gen., 1967-68; pres. Frank J. Williams Ltd., attys.-at-law, 1978-95; assoc. justice R.I. Superior Ct., 1995-2001; chief justice Supreme Ct. R.I., 2001—. Judge of probate Town of Hopkinton (R.I.), 1978-82, 84-90, solicitor, 1978-82, 84-87; judge of probate Town of West Greenwich, R.I., 1984-86, 92-95, solicitor, 1984-92, asst. solicitor, 1992—; dep. judge of probate, 1987-92; solicitor Town of Coventry, R.I., 1972-74, 76-78, Town of Barrington, R.I., 1993-95, Town of Bristol, R.I., 1995, Town of South Kingstown, R.I., 1995; past spl. counsel Towns of Westerly, Bristol, Hopkinton, South Kingstown, City of Providence; atty. Town of Smithfield Sewer Authority, 1974-90; legis. counsel R.I. Retail Fedn., 1975-93, Credit Info. Bur., R.I. Mortgage Bankers Assn., 1992-95; adj. prof. Roger Williams Sch. of Law, 1997—; lectr. bus. and legal practice R.I. Sch. Design, Providence, 1976-80; mem. panel of arbitrators Am. Arbitration Assn., panel of mediators R.I. Superior Ct., 1993-95; mem. R.I. Bd. Bar Examiners, 1987-95, chair, 1995; chair R.I. Housing and Mortgage Fin. Corp., 1995, The Lincoln Forum, 1996—. Pres. Lincoln Group of Boston, 1976—88, Abraham Lincoln Assn., Springfield, Ill., 1986—95, Ulysses S. Grant Assn., 1990—; elected del. R.I. Constnl. Conv., 1986; elected town moderator Richmond, RI, 1992—95; dist. moderator Chaniho Regional Sch. Dist., 1994; chmn. Lincoln adv. com. Brown U.; mem. Lincoln prize adv. com. Gettysburg Coll.; bd. dirs. John E. Fogarty Found. for Persons with Mental Retardation, 1975—, South County Hosp., 1995—, R.I. Com. for the Humanities, 2001—, Narraganset Coun. Boy Scouts Am., 1969—80, 1998—2001. Capt. U.S. Army, 1962—67, Vietnam. Decorated Bronze Star, Combat Infantryman's badge, Army Commendation medal, Air medal with 2 oak leaf clusters, Republic of Vietnam Gallantry Cross with silver star; recipient Disting. Svc. award, Mil. Order of Fgn. Wars, award of merit, Mil. and Fgn. Wars of the U.S.-RI Commandery. Fellow: ATLA (jud.); mem.: RI Bar Assn. (ho. of dels. 1986—93, chmn. new lawyers adv. com. 1976—87, chmn. mcpl. law com. 1993), Conf. Chief Justices, Am. Law Inst., Nat. Assn. for Ct. Mgmt., Am. Judges Assn., Am. Antiquarian Soc., Phi Alpha Delta, Alpha Phi Sigma, Phi Sigma Alpha. Roman Catholic. Office: 250 Benefit St Providence RI 02903

WILLIAMS, FRANKLIN CADMUS, JR. bibliographer; b. Palestine, Tex., July 30, 1941; s. Franklin Cadmus and Cathryn Lucille (Pessoney) W. BA, Baylor U., 1963; MA, Stephen F. Austin State U., 1965; PhD, U. Wis., 1975. Cert. in secondary edn. English and History. Teaching fellow Stephen F. Austin State U., Nacogdoches, Tex., 1964-65, U. Wis., Madison, 1965-68; instr. English Austin Peay State U., Clarksville, Tenn., 1970-71; adj. asst. prof. East Tex. State U., Commerce, 1975; asst. prof. English Jarvis Christian Coll., Hawkins, Tex., 1976-78, 79-81; ind. scholar Palestine, 1981—; owner, bibliographer Goldsmith Archive, 1981—. Cons. Diocese of Galveston-Houston, 1977-84, Tex. State Hist. Assn., Austin, 1988; speaker, editor Jarvis Christian Coll., Hawkins, Tex., 1976-78, 79-81; nat. teaching fellow Office Edn., Washington, 1976-77; del. to Baylor U., U. Wis. System, Madison, 1981. Author: Lone Star Bishops: The Roman Catholic Hierarchy in Texas, 1997; contbr. articles to profl. jours. Mem. Modern Lang. Assn., Tex. State Hist. Assn., Tex. Cath. Hist. Soc., Baylor Alumni Assn. (life), Wis. Alumni Assn. (life), Sigma Tau Delta. Avocations: reading, record collecting, historical genealogy, tennis, swimming. Office: PO Box 96 Palestine TX 75802-0096

WILLIAMS, FRANKLIN J. artist; b. Ogden, Utah, Feb. 5, 1940; s. Rulon and Ruth W. Williams; m. Carol Shaw Williams, Dec. 20, 1961; children: Spencer, Stuart. BFA, Calif. Coll. Arts and Crafts, 1964, MFA, 1966. Prof. painting Calif. Coll. Arts and Crafts, Oakland, 1969—. Prof. painting San Francisco Art Inst., 1966—99, Ruskin Sch. Drawing and Painting, Oxford, England, 1990, Cowent Coll. Higher Edn., Newport, Wales, 1990. Author: Soft as Cotton Centered and Hard, 1997. Named Spencer Mackey scholar, Calif. Coll. Arts and Crafts, Oakland, 1965—66; grantee, Ford Found., 1966, Nat. Endowment Arts, 1968. Home: 713 Elm Dr Petaluma CA 94952 Office: Lizabeth Oliveria Gallery 942 Clay St Oakland CA 94607

WILLIAMS, FREDA BERRY, administrative assistant; b. Petersburg, Va., June 9, 1956; d. William Lewis and Estella Virginia (Bouldin) Berry; m. LaMar Williams, Sr., Sept. 9, 1980 (div. Nov. 1992); children: LaMar Jr., Keana Trahearn, Genique Renee. Student, John Tyler C.C., Chester, Va., 1973-80; Diploma, United Truck Master, Clearwater, Fla., 1988. Lic. tractor trailer driver, reupholsterer, drafting technologist. Reupholstery worker Berry's Sewing Shop, Colonial Heights, Va., 1969-75; office asst. John Tyler C.C., 1975-76; domestic worker Ramada Inn, Richmond, Va., 1977-78; engr., drafter C.C. Towns & Assocs., Colonial Heights, 1979; owner, operator Williams Ind. and Assocs., 1981-88; sewing machine operator Crawford Mfg., Richmond, 1982-88; tractor trailer driver Capital Dist., Ashland, Va., 1988-91; transp. clk. Golden Capital Dist., 1991, transp. adminstrv. asst., 1991-95. Network mgr. Pegasus Female Execs., 1985—88; cons. Williams Enterprises and Assocs--Cyberspace and Catalog Svc., 2000—. County exec. Women's Congl. Congress 4th Dist., Richmond, 1988—89; spokesperson Safety Coun. Transp. Dept., 1991—94; mem. policy coun. Chesterfield Head Start, 1998—, treas., 1998—99, mem. sch. yr. health adv. com., 1990—2000, merchandiser, 1996—; head of women's fellowship ministry Pavilion of Joy, 2001—, primary Sunday sch. tchr., 2001—. Mem. Newbridge Book Club, NAFE. Baptist. Avocations: drawing, painting, arts and crafts.

WILLIAMS, GARY MURRAY, medical researcher, pathology educator; b. Regina, Sask., Can., May 7, 1940; s. Murray Austin and Selma Ruby (Domstad) W.; m. Julia Christine Lundberg; children: Walter, Jeffrey, Ingrid. BA, Washington and Jefferson Coll., 1963; MD, U. Pitts, 1967. Diplomate Am. Bd. Pathology, Am. Bd. Toxicology. Assoc. prof. pathology Temple U., Phila., 1971-75; mem. Fels Rsch. Inst., 1971-75; rsch. prof. N.Y. Med. Coll., Valhalla, 1975-98, prof. pathology, environ. pathology and toxicology, dir., 1999—. Mem. toxicology study sect. NIH, Bethesda, Md., 1985-87; mem. working groups Internat. Agy. Rsch. on Cancer, Lyon, France, 1976, 80, 82, 83, 85, 86, 87, 89, 91, 96, 97, 98, 99; mem. subcom. on upper limits of nutrients NRC, 1999—. Founding editor: Cell Biology and Toxicology, 1984—; mem. editl. bd. Archives of Toxicology, 1988—, European Jour. Cancer Prevention, 1991—, Drug and Chem. Toxicology, 1994—; contbr. over 465 articles to sci. jours.; editor or co-editor 8 books. Lt. comdr. USPHS, 1969-71. Recipient Sheard-Sanford award Am. Soc. Clin. Pathologists U. Pitts., 1967. Fellow Internat. Acad. Toxicol. Pathology (accreditation com.); mem. Am. Assn. Cancer Rsch., Soc. Toxicology (Arthur J. Lehman award 1982, Lectr. award 1996, Advancement Animal Welfare award 2002), Soc. Toxicol. Pathology, Soc. Toxicology (Mid-Atlantic chpt., amb. in toxicology 2001), Phi Beta Kappa, Alpha Omega Alpha. Home: 8 Elm Rd Scarsdale NY 10583-1410 Office: Dept Pathology NY Med Coll Valhalla NY 10595-1549 E-mail: Gary_Williams@NYMC.edu.

WILLIAMS, GAYLEN EUGENE, accountant; b. Marlow, Okla., June 24, 1940; s. Gaylen Lafayette and Myrtle Francis (Sage) W.; m. Janice Ladean Moore, July 19, 1958; children: Mark, Gayla, Leland, Charm. Assoc. degree, Cameron Coll., Lawton, Okla., 1960. With Whiteway Grocery, Marlow, 1950-60; store mgr. Pratt Foods, 1960-67; sales mgr. Jewel Co., Chgo., 1967-76; pvt. practice acct. Midwest City, Okla., 1976—.

WILLIAMS, GEORGE EARNEST, engineer, retired business executive; b. Bartow, Fla., Nov. 27, 1923; s. Earnest Roscoe and Ruby Barnett (Mathews) W.; m. Muriel Theodorsen, June 9, 1949. BS in Engring. with honors, USCG Acad., 1944; postgrad., Harvard U., 1945-46; SM in Mgmt., MIT, 1949. Registered profl. engr. 2 states. Project engr., bus. cons. Ebasco, N.Y.C.; design engr., prodn. supr. Minute Maid Corp., Orlando, Fla.; asst. contr., div. contr., group contr., corp. dir. fin. planning and analysis United Technologies Corp., Hartford, 1957-76, v.p., 1977-82; sr. v.p. Kensington Mgmt. Cons., 1982-84; sr. v.p. fin. Otis Elevator Co., N.Y.C., 1976-77. Mem. exec. com. Conn. Commn. Services and Expenditures, 1971, Under then Gov. Meskill. Contbr. articles to fin. jours., chpts. to books. Served with USCG, 1941-47, PTO and Atlantic. Mem. AIAA, Fin. Execs. Inst., Army and Navy Club (Washington), Naples Yacht Club, Port Royal Club. Achievements include originating pricing system purchase of Fla. oranges for concentrate mfg. Avocation: yachtsman. Home: 1325 7th St S Naples FL 34102-7354

WILLIAMS, GEORGE HOWARD, lawyer, association executive; b. Hempstead, N.Y., Feb. 12, 1918; s. George R. and Marcella (Hogan) W.; m. Mary Celeste Madden, Nov. 23, 1946; children— Mary Beth Williams Barritt, Stephen, Kevin, Jeanne Marie. AB, Hofstra Coll., 1939, LL.D. (hon.), 1969; JD, N.Y. U., 1946, LL.D. (hon.), 1969; postgrad., NYU, 1959. Bar: N.Y. 1946. Adminstrv. asst. to dean NYU Law Sch., N.Y.C., 1946-48, instr. law, 1948-50, asst. prof., 1950-52, assoc. prof., 1952-55, prof., 1956-62, v.p. univ. devel., 1962-66, exec. v.p. planning and devel., 1966-68; pres. Am. U., Washington, 1968-75; exec. v.p., dir. Am. Judicature Soc., Chgo., 1976-87. Author: (with A.T. Vanderbilt and L.L. Pelletier) Report on Liberal Adult Education, 1955; (with K. Sampson) Handbook for Judges, 1984 Bd. dirs. Nat. Ctr. Edn. Politics, 1948-58, trustee, 1958-65; trustee Hofstra U., 1961-64; chmn. bd. trustees Trinity Coll., Vt., 1978-86; bd. dirs. Ctr. for Conflict Resolution, 1988—, Univ. Support Svcs. Served to lt. col., inf. AUS, World War II. Decorated Legion of Merit, Silver Star. Mem. Am. Polit. Sci. Assn., ABA Assn. Bar City N.Y., Alpha Kappa Delta, Phi Delta Phi. Clubs: N.Y. U. (N.Y.C.); Nat. Lawyers (Washington). Home: 1322 Judson Ave Evanston IL 60201-4720 Office: Am Judicature Soc 180 N Michigan Ave Ste 600 Chicago IL 60601-7454

WILLIAMS, GEORGE LEO, historian, landmark preservationist, educator; b. N.Y.C., June 29, 1931; s. Leo Dominick and Cathryn Margaret (Schellderfer) W.; m. Adelia Gilda Musa, Feb. 26, 1958; children: Adelia, Marina, Gilda. BA, CUNY, 1953, MA, 1955; PhD, NYU, 1966. Tchr. Port Washington (N.Y.) Pub. Schs., 1953, chairperson integrated studies, 1960-65, coord. Amherst project, 1968-69, chairperson English dept., 1970-90; adminstrv. asst. secondary and higher edn. dept. NYU, N.Y.C., 1965-66. Adj. prof. NYU, 1966-74, Adelphi U., Garden City, N.Y. 1967-69, Hofstra U., Hempstead, N.Y., 1967-74; chmn. profl. growth and devel. com. Port Washington Pub. Schs., 1973-90, chmn. bicentennial com. 1989-90, mem. policy bd. Port Washington Tchr. Ctr., 1987-90; mem. alumni bd. Queens Coll. History Dept., 1996-2000. Co-author: (play) The Triumph of the Constitution, 1988; author: Fascist Thought and Totalitarianism in Italy's Secondary Schools: Theory and Practice, 1922-1943, 1993, Port Washington in the Twentieth Century: Places and People, 1995, Papal Genealogy: The Families and Descendants of the Popes, 1998, (play) Remembrances of the First Colonial Settlement, 1993; contbg. author: Erziehungsstaaten, 1998; editor Port Arrow Community Newsletter, 1973-84, Cow Neck Peninsula Hist. Soc. Newsletter, 1974-77, Cow Neck Peninsula Hist. Soc. Jour., 2001—; contbg. editor L.I. Forum, 1985—; author, prodr. (video) Port Washington into the 21st Century, 1996. Chairperson landmarks com. Cow Neck Peninsula Hist. Soc., Port Warhington, 1980—97, trustee, 1974—77; commr. landmarks com. Village of Port Washington North, 1983—; mem., chairperson Historical Landmark Preservation Commn., North Hempstead, NY, 1984—, chmn., 1991—; chairperson 1701 Roslyn Grist Mil Com., 1997—; mem. Port Washington Continuing Edn. Adv. Coun., 1988—97; co-chair Roslyn Clock Tower Com., 1994—96; mem. Preservation League of N.Y., Bigelow Soc., N.Y. Pub. Libr., W.A.R. Goodwin Soc.; grant writer Dodge House Restoration Com.; mem. orgnl. com. Landmark on Main St., 1984—90; mem. Cow Neck Peninsula Hist. Soc. Dodge House Restoration Com., 1992—; adv. bd. records Town of North Hempstead, 1994—; mem. 1998 ann. com. L.I.R.R. to Port Washington. Recipient environ. award Residents for a More Beautiful Port Washington, 1994, numerous Certs. of Appreciation, Civic award for Outstanding Cmty. Svc., Port Washington Rotary, 2001, Cert. of Appreciation, Port Washington Police Dist., 2001, Exec. Citation, Nassau County, 2001, citation N.Y. State Assembly, 2001, Legis. citation Nassau County, 2001. Mem.: ASDE, Pi Sigma Alpha, Friends of the Arts, Friends of Planting Fields, Nat. Trust Hist. Preservation, N.Y. State Mus. Assocs., Fulbright Assn., Am. Hist. Assn. (cert. recognition 1988), Port Washington Tchrs. Assn. (v.p. 1963—64, bd. dirs. 1966—74, founder and 1st pres. ret. tchrs. chpt. 1991, newsletter editor 1990—92), Soc. for Preservation L.I. Antiquities, Nat. Coun. Tchrs. English, North Hempstead Hist. Soc. (pres. 2001—), Residents for a More Beautiful PortWashington (Environ. award 1994), N.Y. Geneal./Bldg. Soc., Friends for L.I.'s Heritage, Roslyn Landmark Soc., N.Y. State Hist. Assn., Assn. Pub. Historicans of N.Y. State, Phi Alpha Theta, Phi Beta Kappa. Home: 84 Radcliff Ave Port Washington NY 11050-1600

WILLIAMS, GEORGE WALTON, English educator; b. Charleston, S.C., Oct. 10, 1922; s. Ellison Adger and Elizabeth Simonton (Dillingham) W.; m. Harriet Porcher Simons, Nov. 28, 1953; children: George Walton Jr., Ellison Adger II, Harriet Porcher Stoney. BA, Yale U., 1947; MA, U. Va., 1949, PhD, 1957. Asst. cashier Carolina Savs. Bank, Charleston, 1949-54; asst. prof. English, Duke U., 1957-63, asso. prof., 1963-67, prof., 1967, chmn. dept. English, 1982-86, prof. emeritus, 1993—. Dir. summer inst. Commn. on English, Coll. Entrance Exam. Bd., 1962; pres. Durham Savoyards, Ltd., 1966-68, 81-82; sr. fellow Coop. Program in Humanities, Duke-U. N.C., 1969; Historiographer, Diocese of S.C., 1960-78; vis. prof. U.S. Mil. Acad., 1982-83 Author: St. Michael's, Charleston, 1751-1951, 1951, rev. edit., 2001, Image and Symbol in the Sacred Poetry of Richard Crashaw, 1963, The Craft of Printing and the Publication of Shakespeare's Plays, 1985, 4 children's books; editor: Romeo and Juliet, 1964, Complete Poetry of Richard Crashaw, 1970, Jacob Eckhard's Choirmaster's Book, 1971, Shakespeare's Speech-Headings, 1997; contbg. editor Dramatic Works of Beaumont and Fletcher, 1966-96; assoc. gen. editor Arden Shakespeare, 1996—. Served with inf. U.S. Army, 1943-45, ETO. Decorated Combat Inf. badge; recipient Outstanding Civilian Service medal Dept. Army, 1983; Guggenheim Found. fellow, 1977-78; Huntington Library fellow, 1981 Mem. MLA (com. on new variorum 1980-92, chmn. Shakespeare divsn. 1990), South Atlantic MLA (pres. 1980-81, J.H. Fisher award 2001), Southeastern Renaissance Conf. (editor 1960-70, 91-95, pres. 1973), Bibliog. Soc., Royal Soc. Arts London, S.C. Hist. Soc., Carolina Yacht Club (Charleston), St. Cecilia Soc. (Charleston), Elizabethan Club Yale U., Phi Beta Kappa, Phi Kappa Phi. Home: 2701 Pickett Rd Apt 2007 Durham NC 27705-5648 Office: Duke U Dept English PO Box 90015 Durham NC 27708-0015

WILLIAMS, GILBERT THOMAS, systems engineer, consultant; b. New Bern, N.C., Dec. 29, 1956; s. Clayton Olan and Dawn Vernice (Hart) W. BS, Jacksonville State U., 1977; postgrad., Case Western Res. U., 1990—. Programmer Computer Sci. Corp., Huntsville, Ala., 1978-81; engr. Nat. Aeronautics & Space Adminstrn., 1981-83, Honeywell, Inc., Hopkins, Minn., 1983-86; systems engr. Westinghouse Electric Co., Cleve., 1986-95; founder 4C cons., Richmond Heights, Ohio, 1994—. Propr. Williams Oil and Gas, Richmond Heights, 1989—. Inventor in field; contvr. articles to profl. jours. Mem. Heritage Found., Wilderness Soc. Recipient Snoopy award NASA, Huntsville, 1980, cert. of appreciation NASA, 1983. Mem. IEEE, Am. Motorcycle Assn., Assn. for Computing Machinery. Avocations: playing in blues bands, motorcycling, fishing, golf. Office: 4C Cons 25101 Chardon Rd Richmond Heights OH 44143-1340

WILLIAMS, GLEN MORGAN, federal judge; b. Jonesville, Va., Feb. 17, 1920; s. Hughy May and Hattie Mae W.; m. Jane Slemp, Nov. 17, 1962; children: Susan, Judy, Rebecca, Melinda. AB magna cum laude, Milligan Coll., 1940; JD, U. Va., 1948. Bar: Va. 1947. Pvt. practice law, Jonesville, 1948-76; judge U.S. Dist. Ct. (we. dist.) Va., 1976-88, sr. judge, 1988—; commonwealth's atty. Lee County, Va., 1948-51; mem. Va. Senate, 1953-55. Mem. editorial bd.: Va. Law Rev, 1946-47. Mem. Lee County Sch. Bd., 1972-76; trustee, elder First Christian Ch., Pennington Gap, Va.; trustee Milligan Coll., 1990—, Appalachian Sch. of Law, 1995—. Lt. USN, 1942-46, MTO. Recipient Citation of Merit Va. Def. Lawyers Assn., Oustanding Alumnus award Milligan Coll., 1980, Svc. to Region award Emory & Henry Coll., 1996. Mem. ABA, Va. State Bar (citation of merit), Va. Bar Assn. (citation of merit), Fed. Bar Assn., Va. Trial Lawyers Assn. (Meritorious Svc. award 1986, Disting. Svc. award), Am. Legion, 40 and 8. Clubs: Lions, Masons, Shriners. E-mila. Office: US Dist Ct Fed Bldg PO Box 339 Abingdon VA 24212-0339 E-mail: glenw@vawd.uscourts.gov.

WILLIAMS, GLENDA CARLENE, writer; b. Jefferson County, Ala., Jan. 17, 1946; d. Wilmer and Lucy Iris (Crowley) W.; three children: Shawna Dawn White, Crystal Lee, Tomas Lee. Ballroom dance instr. Continental Dance Studio, Birmingham, Ala., 1968-70; receptionist, instr. Occupl. Rehab., 1970-74; exec. sec. Educators Investment, 1974-76; sec., county agt. County Extension Office, Rusk, Tex., 1976-78. Freelance tchr. spl. needs children, Ala., 1990—; counselor natural healing and nutrition, Ala., 1990—; founder, dir. Healing Hands Ministry, Birmingham, 1998—. Author: Nutrition and Attention Deficit Disorder, 1991, Beyond this Hill, 1995, And When You Wake, 1995; editor: Legends of the Owl, 1995. Mem. Concerned Women of Am., Washington, 1994; founding mem. United We Stand Am., Montgomery, Ala., 1995. Avocations: writing, reading, nutritional research, sewing, drawing. Home: PO Box 236 Elmore AL 36025-0236

WILLIAMS, GREGG, professional football coach; b. July 15, 1958; m. Leigh Ann Williams; children: Blake, Chase, Amy. BS, Truman State U.; MEd, Ctrl. Mo. State. Spl. team coach Oilers' linebackers, 1993, supr., 1994—96; coord. Titans, 1st quality control coach, 1990; def. coord. Tenn./Houston orgn., with; profl. football head coach Buffalo Bills, 2001—. Office: Ralph Wilson Stadium One Bills Dr Orchard Park NY 14127*

WILLIAMS, GREGORY CARL, SR. city official; b. New Orleans, May 2, 1967; s. Leo Gordan Williams, Jr. and Ethel Nuchurch McClinton; 1 child, Gregory Carl, Jr. EdB, So. U. New Orleans, 1998; student, U. New Orleans, 1999—. Enlisted man USN, 1985-93, dispatcher Conn., 1985-88, New Orleans, 1988-93; resigned, 1993; dispatcher Kenner Police Dept., 1989-95; comm. officer Kenner Fire Dept., 1995—. With USNR, 1988-93. USAA scholar, 1996—, Rhodes Family scholar, 1996. Mem. Alpha Sigma Lambda.

WILLIAMS, GREGORY KEITH, accountant; b. Elizabethtown, Ky., Mar. 20, 1958; s. James Marion and Shirley Catherine (Yates) W.; m. Diana Lynn McGuffin, May 26, 1979; 1 child, Kathryn May. BA in Pub. Mgmt., U. Ky., Lexington, 1985; BSBA, U. Louisville, 1987; MPA, Ball State U., 1996. Cert. mgmt. acct., info. sys. auditor, govt. fin. mgr. Supervisory staff acct. Fin. Acctg. Off., Fort Knox, Ky., 1983-85, internal auditor, 1985-89, sys. acct., 1989-93, Def. Fin. and Acctg. Svc. Indpls. Ctr., 1993-95, electronic commerce/data interchange coord., 1995-97; dep. project mgr. corp. database Def. Fin. and Acctg. Svc. Hdqrs., 1997-98, project mgr. corp. database, 1998-2000, program mgr. corp. database/warehouse, 2000—. Mem. Inst. Cert. Mgmt. Acct., Info. Sys. Audit and Control Assn., Am. Soc. Mil. Comptr., Assn. Govt. Acct., Phi Beta Kappa, Beta Gamma Sigma, Phi Kappa Phi. Home: 136 Lake Dr Greenwood IN 46142-9182 Office: Def Fin Acctg Svc 8899 E 56th St Indianapolis IN 46249-0002 Fax: 317-510-7250. E-mail: gkwdlw@msn.com.

WILLIAMS, HAROLD EUGENE, music educator; b. Kansas City, Mo., Sept. 3, 1957; s. Harold Eugene and Dorothy Ellen Williams; m. Mary Kay Williams, June 19, 1982. BA Music Ed., Univ. Kans., Lawrence, KS, 1981. Band educator Unified Sch. Districts 495, Larned, Kans., 1981—2002. Chmn. Kans. Music Educators Assn., Dodge City, Kans., 1996—97, clinician, Junction City, Kans., 199. Recipient Outstanding Music Educator, Kans. Music Educators Assn., 1998. Mem.: Music Educators Nat. Conf., Kans. Music Educators Assn., Phi Mu Alpha, Sinfonia. Achievements include composed band music for the city of Larned, March 1998. Home: RR1 Box 3 Garfield KS 67529-9702 Office: Larned Middle School 904 Corse Larned KS 67550

WILLIAMS, HAROLD ROGER, economist, educator; b. Arcade, N.Y., Aug. 22, 1935; s. Harry Alfred and Gertrude Anna (Scharf) W.; m. Lucia Dorothy Preuschoff, Apr. 23, 1955; children: Theresa Lynn, Mark Roger. BA, Harpur Coll., SUNY, Binghamton, 1961; MA, Pa. State U., 1963; PhD, U. Nebr., 1966; postgrad., Harvard U., 1969-70. Instr., Pa. State U., 1962-63; Instr. U. Nebr., 1965-66; mem. faculty Kent (Ohio) State U., 1966—, prof. econs. and internat. bus., 1972—, chmn. dept., 1974-81, dir. Internat. Bus. Program, Grad. Sch. Mgmt., 1980-86, chmn. faculty senate, 1988-89; assoc. dean Grad. Sch. Mgmt., 1994-96; program dir. Kent State-Geneva Program, Geneva, 1996-97. Econ. cons. and adv. to numerous govt., bus. and internat. orgns. Author over 100 books and articles in field. Served with AUS, 1954-57. Grantee NSF. Mem. Am. Econ. Assn., Internat. Econs. Assn., Acad. Internat. Bus., Midwest Econ. Assn. (v.p. 1969-70), So. Econ. Assn., Phi Gamma Mu, Omicron Delta Epsilon, Beta Gamma Sigma, Phi Beta Delta. Home: 415 Suzanne Dr Kent OH 44240-1933 Office: Dept Econs Kent State U Kent OH 44242-0001 E-mail: Hwilliam@BSA3.Kent.edu.

WILLIAMS, HARRIET CLARKE, retired academic administrator, artist; b. Bklyn., Sept. 5, 1922; d. Herbert Edward and Emma Clarke (Gibbs) W. AA, Bklyn. Coll., 1958; student, Art Career Sch., N.Y.C., 1960; cert., Hunter Coll., 1965, CPU Inst. Data Processing, 1967; student, Chineses Cultural Ctr., N.Y.C., 1973; hon. certs., St. Labre Sch./St. Joseph's, Ind. Sch., Mont., 1990. Adminstr. Baruch Coll., N.Y.C., 1959-85. Mktg. researcher 1st Presbyn. Arts and Crafts Shop, Jamaica, N.Y., 1986-96; tutor in art St. John's U., Jamaica, 1986-96; founder, curator Internat. Art Gallery, Queens, N.Y., 1991—. Exhibited in group shows at Union Carbide Art Exhibit, N.Y.C., 1975, Queens Day Exhbn., N.Y.C., 1980, 1st Presbyn. Arts and Crafts Shop, N.Y.C., 1986, others; contbr. articles to profl. publs. Vol. reading tchr. Mabel Dean Vocat. High Sch., N.Y.C., 1965-67; mem. polit. action com. dist. council 37, N.Y.C., 1973-77; mem. negotiating team adminstrv. contracts, N.Y.C., 1975-78; mem. Com. To Save CCNY, 1976-77, Statue Liberty Ellis Island Found., Woodrow Wilson Internat. Ctr. Scholars, Wilson Ctr. Assocs., Washington, St. Labre Indian Sch., Ashland, Mont. Appreciation award Dist. Coun. 37, 1979; recipient Plaque Appreciation Svcs., Baruch Coll., Key award St. Joseph's Indian Sch., 1990, Key award in Edn. and Art, 1990, others. Mem. NAFE, AAUW, Women in Mil. Svc., Assn. Am. Indian Affairs, Nat. Mus. of Am. Indian, Artist Equity Assn. N.Y., Lakota Devel. Coun., Am. Film Inst., Bklyn. Coll. Alumni, Nat. Geographic Soc., Nat. Mus. Woman in the Arts, Statue of Liberty Ellis Island Found., Inc., Alliance of Queens Artists, U.S. Naval Inst., El Museo Del Barrio, Am. Mus. Natural History, Internat. Ctr. for Scholars-Wilson Ctr. Assocs., Arrow Club-St. Labre Indian Sch., Mus. of Television and Radio, Women in Military Meml. Found., Nat. Mus. of Am. Indian, U.S. Holocaust Mus., Navy Meml. (adv. coun.). Roman Catholic. Avocations: aerobics, vol. work, world travel, music. Office: Baruch Coll 17 Lexington Ave New York NY 10010-5518

WILLIAMS, HARRIETTE FLOWERS, retired school system administrator, educational consultant; b. L.A., July 18, 1930; d. Orlando and Virginia (Carter) Flowers; m. Irvin F. Williams, Apr. 9, 1960; children: Lorin Finley, Lori Virginia. BS, UCLA, 1952, EdD (HEW fellow), 1973; MA, Calif. State U., L.A., 1956. Tchr. L.A. Unified Sch. Dist., 1952-59, counselor, 1954-59, psychometrist, 1958-62, faculty chmn., 1956-57, student activities coord., 1955-59, leader insts. and workshops, 1952-76, dir. counseling, 1960-65, supr. Title I programs Elem. Secondary Edn. Act, 1965-68, asst. prin., 1968-76, prin., 1976-82, dir. instrn. sr. high sch. divsn., 1982-85, adminstr. ops., 1985-92; field svc. rep. Assn. Calif. Sch. Adminstrs., Culver City, 1992-2000. Asst. dir. HEW project for high sch. adminstrn. UCLA, 1971-72; adj. prof. in Masters in Sch. Adminstrn. program Pepperdine U., L.A., 1974-78, U. LaVerne, 1999—; ednl. cons. Teach for Am., 1991-94; L.A. County commr. Children and Family Commn., 1996—. Recipient Sojourner Truth award Nat. Assn. Negro Bus. and Profl. Women's Clubs, L.A., 1968, Life Membership Svc. award L.A. PTA, 1972, 75, L.A. Mayor's Golden Apple award for ednl. excellence. Mem. Assn. of Adminstrs. of L.A. (pres. region 16), Assn. Calif. Sch. Adminstrs. (state chmn. urban affairs com. 1985-88, region pres. 1989-90), Nat. Assn. Secondary Sch. Prins., Sr. H.S. Asst. Prins. Assn. L.A. (bd. dirs. 1974-76, sponsor 1985-91), Sr. H.S. Prins. Orgn., Nat. Coun. Negro Women (life), Lullaby Guild Children's Home Soc. L.A. (pres. 1987-89), UCLA Gold Shield (vol. 1980—, 1st v.p. 1994-96, pres. 1998-2000), NAACP, Urban League, Inglewood-Pacific chpt. Links Inc. (sec. 1984-86, treas. 1987-89), Jack and Jill of Am. (pres. L.A. chpt. 1980-82), UCLA Alumni Assn. (bd. dirs. 1979-83, 2000-, v.p. 1992-94, donor rels. chmn. 1999—, chairperson support & honorary com. 2000—, Excellence in the Cmty. award 1996), Wilfandel (pres. 1994-97), Minerva Found. (CEO 2002—), Delta Sigma Theta (pres. L.A. chpt. 1964-66, regional dir. 1968-72, nat. committeewoman 1966-94), Pi Lambda Theta, Kappa Delta Pi, Delta Kappa Gamma (treas. 1991-94). Baptist. E-mail: royphd@sbcglobal.net.

WILLIAMS, HARRY EDWARD, management consultant; b. Oak Park, Ill., July 20, 1925; s. Harry E. and Mary E.; m. Jean Horner; 1 child, Jeanne. Student, West Coast U., Los Angeles, 1958-60; BS in Engring., Calif. Coast Coll., Santa Ana, 1975; MA, Calif. Coast Coll., 1975; PhD, Golden State U., Los Angeles, 1981. Registered profl. engr., Calif. Mgr. Parker Aircraft Co., Los Angeles, 1958-60, Leach Corp., Los Angeles, 1968-69, Litton, Data Systems, Van Nuys, Calif., 1969-72; dir. Electronic Memories, Hawthorne, 1972-78, Magnavox Co., Torrance, 1978-80; v.p. Stacoswitch Inc., Costa Mesa, 1981-87; mgmt. cons., Westminster, 1987—. Cons. in field. Contbr. articles to profl. jours. With USAF, 1943-46. Recipient Mgr. of the Yr. award Soc. for Advancement of Mgmt., 1984, Phil Carroll award for outstanding contbns. in field of ops. mgmt., 1985, Profl. Mgr. citation, 1984. Fellow Internat. Acad. Edn. Republican. Methodist. Avocation: target shooting. E-mail: heworg@aol.com.

WILLIAMS, HART JOSEPH, screenwriter; b. Grand Island, Nebr., Dec. 11, 1955; s. Josephus Hart Williams and Lela May (Cornelius) Claussen; m. Candice Joan Welch, June 1, 1974 (div. 1980); m. Cynthia Lee Gray, Nov. 14, 1985; 1 child, Dionna Gabrielle. Student, Tex. Christian U., 1973-76. Contbg. editor Knight Publs., Hollywood, Calif., 1978-87; driver Checker Cab, Eagle Rock, 1979; editor Hustler mag., Century City, 1979-80; ind. screenwriter Hollywood, 1984-86; pres. Hart Williams Films, 1986—. Novelist: Hideaway, 1983, Craving, 1984; screenwriter Trial of Blood, 1986; contbg. editor Oui mag., 1986-87; mng. editor Film World Reports, 1985; book reviewer: Los Angeles Herald Examiner, 1978-81, Orange County Register, 1987; film reviewer Hollywood Press, 1985-86; contbr. numerous articles, interviews, short stories to various publs. Recipient Nat. Merit Scholarship Tex. Christian U., 1973. Democrat. Buddhist. Office: 4655 Kingswell Ave Ste 213 Los Angeles CA 90027-4351

WILLIAMS, HELEN MARGARET, retired accountant; b. Fresno, Calif., Mar. 16, 1947; d. James Ray Jr. and Barbara (LaRue) Franklin; m. Phillip Dean Bangs, Apr. 16, 1977; children: Aluvia, Adevia, Rodney. AA in Home Economics, Sacramento City Coll., 1969, AA in Acctg., 1971; BS in Acctg. and Fin. cum laude, Calif. State U., Sacramento, 1988. Acct. tech. Sacramento Regional Transit Dist., 1974-87, revenue rm. contr., 1987-88, acct. I, 1988, acct. II, 1988-97. Editor employee newsletter Sacramento Regional Transit Dist., 1986-90. Past mother and worthy adv. Rainbow for Girls; past host parent Am. Field Svc., past chair host family selection com. Mem. Am. Soc. Women Accts. (chair scholarship com. 1992-94, chair pub. com. 1993-94, bd. dirs. 1993-96, 2000—, sec. 1994-95, 99-2000, 2002—, chair roster com. 1995-96, chair hospitality com. 1996-98, 2001—, chair publicity com. 1998-99, treas. 2000-02), Calif. State U.-Sacramento Alumni Assn., Capital Investors Investment Club (fin. ptnr., recording ptnr. 1998—), Order Ea. Star, Precious Moments Collectors Club (newsletter editor 1992—, treas. 1993—). Avocations: sewing, interior design, needlework, collectibles, geneology.

WILLIAMS, HENRY THOMAS, retired banker, real estate agent; b. Worton, Md., Mar. 27, 1932; s. Henry Thomas W. and Ivy Lorraine Urie; m. Laura Lynne Davis, Sept. 13, 1958; children: Lisa C. Ross, Henry Thomas III, Davis F. Student, Washington Coll., 1951-52; grad., ABA Nat. Installment Credit Sch. at U. Chgo., 1968, Va.-Md. Sch. Bank Mgmt. at U. Va., 1972. Grad. Realtors Inst. Teller Chestertown Bank Md., 1960-61, note teller, 1961-63, asst. cashier, 1963-68, mgr. installment loans, 1968-73, v.p., sr. loan officer, sec., 1973-85, v.p., br. mgr., 1985-88; now assoc. broker-realtor The Hogans Agy., Inc., Chestertown. Mem. Bay Area Assn. Realtors. Past dir. United Way Kent County, Chestertown; past vestryman, past chmn. budget com. St. Paul's Ch., Chestertown. Mem. Bank Adminstrn. Inst. (past sec., past chmn. Ea. Shore Chpt.), Md. Bankers Assn. (past v.p., past chmn. group 5), Md. Young Bankers Com., Chester River Yacht and Country Club, Lions (bd. dirs., past sec., past v.p.). Democrat. Home: 21139 Green Ln Rock Hall MD 21661-1634 Office: The Hogans Agy Inc PO Box 132 5770 Main St Rock Hall MD 21661 E-mail: Tomw@hogans.com.

WILLIAMS, HENRY WARD, JR. lawyer; b. Rochester, N.Y., Jan. 12, 1930; s. Henry Ward and Margaret Elizabeth (Simpson) W.; m. Christina M.; children: Edith Williams Linares, Margaret Williams Warren, Sarah Williams Farrand, Ann Williams Treacy, Elizabeth DeLancey, Victoria Maureen. AB, Dartmouth Coll., 1952; LLB, U.Va., 1958. Bar: N.Y. 1959, U.S. Dist. Ct. (we. dist.) N.Y. 1959, U.S. Dist. Ct. (so. dist.) Mich. 1982, U.S. Ct. Appeals (2d cir.) 1963, U.S. Tax Ct. 1960, U.S. Supreme Ct. 1968, D.C. 1978. Ptnr. Harris, Beach & Wilcox, Rochester, 1958-78, Robinson, Williams, Angeloff & Frank, Rochester, 1978-80, Weidman, Williams, Jordon, Angeloff & Frank, Rochester, 1980-82, The Williams Law Firm, Rochester, 1982—. Exec. editor Va. Law Rev., 1957-58. Chmn. Genesee Finger/Lakes Regional Planning Coun., 1973-89; majority leader Monroe County Legislature, 1967-73; councilman Town of Wheatland, N.Y., 2002--; mem. alumni coun. Dartmouth Coll., 1995-99; mem. no. 8020 Nat. Ski Patrol Sys. Lt. (j.g.) USN, 1952-55. Mem. ABA, N.Y. State Bar Assn., Monroe County Bar Assn. (trustee 1982-85), Rochester Yacht Club, Royal Can. Yacht Club, Lake Yacht Racing Assn. (pres. 1985-87, hon. pres. 1988-90), Royal Ocean Racing Club, Royal Nfld. Yacht Club, Raven Soc., Order of Coif, Omicron Delta Kappa. Office: The Williams Law Firm PO Box 8 Scottsville NY 14546-0008

WILLIAMS, HIBBARD EARL, medical educator, physician; b. Utica, N.Y., Sept. 28, 1932; s. Hibbard G. and Beatrice M. W.; m. Sharon Towne, Sept. 3, 1982; children: Robin, Hans. AB, Cornell U., 1954, MD, 1958. Diplomate Am. Bd. Internal Medicine. Intern Mass. Gen. Hosp., Boston, 1958-59, resident in medicine, 1959-60, 62-64, asst. physician, 1964-65; clin. assoc. Nat. Inst. Arthritis and Metabolic Diseases, NIH, Bethesda, MD, 1960-62; instr. medicine Harvard U., Boston, 1964-65; asst. prof. medicine U. Calif., San Francisco, 1965-68, assoc. prof., 1968-72, prof., 1972-78, chief divsn. med. genetics, 1968-70, vice chmn. dept. medicine, 1970-78; prof., chmn. dept. medicine Cornell U. Med. Coll., N.Y.C., 1978-80; physician-in-chief N.Y. Hosp.-Cornell Med. Ctr., 1978-80; dean Sch. Medicine U. Calif., Davis, 1980-92, prof. internal medicine, 1980-2000; prof. emeritus, 2000—. Mem. program project com. NIH, Nat. Inst. Arthritis and Metabolic Diseases, 1971-73 Editor med. staff confs. Calif. Medicine, 1966-70; mem. edtl. bd. Clin. Rsch., 1968-71, Am. Jour. Medicine, 1978-88; cons. editor Medicine, 1978-86; assoc. editor Metabolism, 1970-80; mem. adv. bd. physiology in medicine New Eng. Jour. Medicine, 1970-75; contbr. articles to med. jours. With USPHS, 1960—62. Recipient Career Devel. award USPHS, 1968; recipient award for excellence in teaching Kaiser Found., 1970, Disting. Faculty award U. Calif. Alumni-Faculty Assn., 1978; John and Mary R. Markle scholar in medicine, 1968 Fellow ACP; mem. AAAS, Am. Soc. Clin. Investigation (sec.-treas. 1974-77), Assn. Am. Physicians, Assn. Am. Med. Colls. (adminstrv. bd., coun. deans 1989-92, exec. coun. 1990-92), Calif. Acad. Medicine (pres. 1984), San Francisco Diabetes Assn. (bd. dirs. 1971-72), Western Assn. Physicians (v.p. 1977-78), Western Soc. Clin. Rsch., Calif. Med. Assn. (chmn. coun. sci. affairs 1990-95, bd. dirs. 1990-95), Calif. Med. Assn. Found. (chmn. bd. dirs. 1997-99), Gianinni Found. (sci. adv. bd. 1990-2000—), St. Francis Yacht Club, Alpha Omega Alph. Office: U Calif Sch Medicine TB150 Davis CA 95616

WILLIAMS, HIRAM DRAPER, artist, educator; b. Indpls., Feb. 11, 1917; s. Earl Boring and Inez Mary (Draper) W.; m. Avonell Baumunk, July 7, 1941; children— Curtis Earl, Kim Avonell. BS, Pa. State U., 1950, M.Ed., 1951. Tchr. art U. So. Calif., 1953-54, UCLA, summer 1959, U. Tex., 1954-60; mem. faculty and pres's. coun. U. Fla., Gainesville, 1960—, Disting. Service prof., until 1982, prof. emeritus, 1982. Mem. chancellor's council U. Tex. System. Exhibited, Pa. Acad. Fine Arts anns., Whitney Mus. Am. Art bi-anns., Corcoran Gallery Bi-anns., U. Ill. bi-anns., Mus. Modern Art exhbns., also Nordness Gallery, N.Y.C.; represented in permanent exhbns., Mus. Modern Art, Wilmington Art Center, Whitney Mus. of Am. Art, N.Y.C., Sheldon Meml. Art Mus., Milw. Art Center, Guggenheim Mus., Smithsonian Inst., Harn Art Mus., U. Fla., Yale; also pvt. collections.; author: Notes for a Young Painter, 1963, rev., 1985; contbr. articles to mags. Served to capt. C.E. U.S. Army, World War II, ETO. Tex. Rsch. grantee, 1958; Guggenheim fellow, 1962-63; inducted into Fla. Artists Hall of Fame, 1994. Address: 2804 NW 30th Ter Gainesville FL 32605-2727 *My desire as a painter is to animate material with imagery that strikes conjunctions of art and life.*

WILLIAMS, HOLLY THOMAS, retired business executive; b. Pitts., Dec. 24, 1931; d. Andrew Matthew and Elizabeth (Kuklinca) Thomas; m. Donald Evan Williams, May 14, 1961. AA cum laude, Keystone Jr. Coll., LaPlume, Pa., 1978; BS magna cum laude, U. Scranton, 1981. Dancer Arthur Murray Studios, Pitts., 1953-60, franchise owner Scranton, Pa., 1960-80; mgr. Nutri/System Weight Loss Ctr., 1984-85, franchise owner, 1985-2001. Fund raiser United Cerebral Palsy of Lackawanna County, Scranton, 1970-79, St. Joseph's Children's Hosp., Scranton, 1962-76; exec. sec. Foxhowe Assn., Buck Hill Falls, Pa., 1984-85. Mem. AAUW (bd. dirs. 1985-86, 94-2001, br. pres. 1999-2001), Scranton Club. Republican. Christian. Avocations: reading, golf, bridge, dancing, travel. Home: PO Box 151 Buck Hill Falls PA 18323-0151 also: 213 Karen Dr Scranton PA 18505-2207

WILLIAMS, HOWARD WALTER, aerospace engineer, executive; b. Evansville, Ind., Oct. 18, 1937; s. Walter Charles and Marie Louise (Bollinger) W.; m. Phyllis Ann Scofield, May 4, 1956 (div. Sept. 1970); m. Marilee Sharon Mulvane, Oct. 30, 1970; children: Deborah, Steven, Kevin, Glenn, Lori, Michele. AA, Pasadena City Coll., 1956; BSME, Calif. State U., Los Angeles, 1967; BSBA, U. San Francisco, 1978; PhD in Comml. Sci. (hon.), London Inst. Applied Rsch., 1992. Turbojet, rocket engr. Aerojet-Gen. Corp., Azusa, Calif., 1956-59, infrared sensor engr., 1959-60, rocket, torpedo engr., 1960-66, power, propulsion mgr. propulsion divsn. Sacramento, 1967-73, high speed ship systems mgr., 1974-78, combustion, power mgr., rocket engine and energy mktg. mgr., 1979-89, dir. strategic planning, 1989-94; strategic analyst, program mgr. Pratt & Whitney Space Propulsion, San Jose, Calif., 1995—. Author: (with others) Heat Exchangers, 1980, Industrial Heat Exchangers, 1985, History of Liquid Rocket Engine Development in the U.S., 1992, Aerojet: The Creative Company, 1997; co-inventor Closed Cycle Power System, 1969. Recipient Energy Innovation award U.S. Dept. Energy, 1985. Mem. AIAA (sr., Best Paper 1966), Am. Soc. Metals (organizing dir. indsl. heat exch. confs. 1985). Avocations: bicycling, grandchildren. *Personal philosophy: I hope to be as good a parent and grandparent as mine have been.*

WILLIAMS, HUGH ALEXANDER, JR. retired mechanical engineer, consultant; b. Spencer, N.C., Aug. 18, 1926; s. Hugh Alexander and Mattie Blanche (Megginson) W.; m. Ruth Ann Gray, Feb. 21, 1950; children: David Gray, Martha Blanche Williams Heidengren. BS in Mech. Engring., N.C. State U., 1948, MS in Diesel Engring., 1950; postgrad., Benedictine U. Inst. Mgmt., 1977. Registered profl. engr., Ill. Jr. engr.-field svc. engr. Baldwin-Lima Hamilton (Ohio) Corp., 1950-52, project engr., 1953-55, Electro-Motive divsn. Gen. Motors Corp., La Grange, Ill., 1955-58, sr. project engr., 1958-63, supr. product devel. engine design sect., 1963-86, staff engr. advanced mech. tech., 1986-87. Editor So. Engr., 1947-48; contbr. articles to profl. jours. Trustee Downers Grove (Ill.) San. Dist., 1965-92, pres., 1974-91, v.p., 1991-92; pres. Ill. Assn. San. Dists., 1976-77, bd. dirs., 1977-89; mem. statewide policy adv. com. Ill. EPA, 1977-79; mem. DuPage County Intergovtl. Task Force Com., 1988-92; elder Presbyn. Ch. Served with USAAC, 1945. Recipient Trustee Svc. award Ill. Assn. San. Dists., 1986, Citizens award Downers Grove Evening chpt. Kiwanis, 1991; Norfolk So. R.R. fellow, 1950. Fellow ASME (chmn. honors and awards com. 1993-96, Diesel and Gas Engine Power Divsn. Spkr. awards 1968, 84, Divsn. citation 1977, 97, Internal Combustion Engine award 1987, exec. com. Internal Combustion Engine divsn. 1981-87, 88-92, chmn. 1985-86, sec. 1988-92); mem. Soc. Automotive Engrs. (life), ASME (chmn. Soichiro Honda medal com. 1987-92, chmn. Internal Combustion Engine Award com. 1993-98), Ill. Assn. Wastewater Agys. (Outstanding Mem. award 1990, hon. mem. 1992), Raleigh Host Lions Club (pres. 1996-97), SAR (pres. Raleigh chpt. 2000-02), St. Andrew's Soc. N.C., Masons (32 degree), Sigma Pi. Republican. Achievements include patentee in field. Home: 2108 Weybridge Dr Raleigh NC 27615-5562

WILLIAMS, IAN GEORGE, writer; b. Liverpool, U.K., Sept. 21, 1949; s. Edward and Margaret (Cooper) W.; m. Nadia Hijab, Aug. 13, 1989; 1 child, Alexander James. BA with hons., Liverpool U., 1973. Columnist N.Y. Observer, 1991-95; writer London Indep., London Guardian, London, Telegraph, London, 1987—, The European, New Statesman, London, 1984—, Nation, N.Y., 1991—; author Reed Publ., London, 1992—. Speechwriter U.K. Labor Leader N. Kinnock, 1987. Author: The Alms Trade, 1989, The UN for Beginners, 1995; U.S. editor War Report, Investor Rels. Mag.; contbr. articles to N.Y. mag., Village Voice, Nation. Mem. U.N. Corrs. Assn. (pres.), Royal Inst. Internat. Affairs. Avocations: theatre, reading, cycling. Home: 235 E 49th St Apt 1A New York NY 10017-1556 E-mail: uswarreport@igc.org.

WILLIAMS, IDA JONES, consumer and home economics educator, writer; b. Coatesville, Pa., Dec. 1, 1911; d. William Oscar and Ida Ella (Ruth) Jones; m. Charles Nathaniel Williams, Mar. 17, 1940 (dec. July 1971). BS, Hampton Inst., 1935; MA, U. Conn., 1965; cert. recognition, Famous Writers Sch., Westport, Conn., 1976, 78. Cert. high sch. tchr., English, sci., home econs., Va., Pa. Sci. and home econs. tchr. Richmond County H.S., Ivondale, Va., 1935-36; English and home econs. tchr. Northampton County H.S., Chesapeake, 1936-40, consumer and home econs. tchr. Machipongo, 1940-71, Northampton Jr. H.S., Machipongo, 1971-76. Author: Starting Anew After Seventy, 1980 (plaque 1980), News and Views of Northampton County High Principals and Alumni, 1981, Great Grandmother, Leah's Legacy-Remember You're Free, 2000; co-author: The History of Virginia State Federation of Colored Women's Clubs, Inc., 1996; editor: Fifty Year Book 1935-1985 - Hampton Institute Class, 1985, Favorite Recipes of Ruth Family & Friends, 1986. V.p. Ea. Lit. Coun., Melfa, Va., 1987-89; mem. Ea. Shore Coll. Found., Inc., Melfa, 1988-2000; mem. Gov.'s Adv. Bd. on Aging, Richmond, Va., 1992-94; instr. Ladies Community Bible Class, 1976-80 (Plaque 1980); sec., treas., v.p. Hospice Support of Ea. Shore, 1980-94; mem. Northampton/Accomack Adv. Counc., 1992-94; marshall 28th anniv. commencement Ea. Shore Cmty. Coll., 1996; bd. dirs. Ea. Shore C.C. Found., 1997—. Named Home Econs. Tchr. of Yr., Am. Home Econs. Assn. and Family Cir., 1975, Woman of Yr., Prog. Women of E.S., 1997, Ida J. Williams scholarship fund named in her honor, Keller Ch. Christ, 1999; recipient Nat. Sojourner Truth Meritorious Svc. award, Negro Bus. and Profl. Women's Clubs, Gavel Ea. Shore Ret. Tchrs. Assn., 1994, Jefferson award, Am. Inst. Pub. Svc., Wavy-TV-Bell Atlantic and Mattress Discounters, 1991, Gov.'s award for vol. excellence, 1994, Contribution to Edn. award, Ea. Shore Coll. Found., 1997, Leadership award, 2001, trophy for outstanding and dedicated svc., 2001, plaque, Southeastern Assn. Colored Women's Clubs, Inc., 2001, award for dedicated svc., Nat. Assn. Colored Women's Club, Inc., 1998, E.S. C.C. Found., Inc. Svc. award, 2000, Exemplary Svc. award, Nat. Assn. Colored Women's Club, 2001, outstanding citizen award, Ea. Shore C. of C., 2002. Mem. AARP (Citation award 1996, Mem. of Yr. 1997, v.p. Northampton chpt. 1998-2000), Progressive Women of Ea. Shore (pres. 1985-93, Gold Necklace 1993, Woman of Yr. 1997), C. of C., Univ. Women (v.p. Portsmouth br. 1985-87), Ea. Shore Ret. Tchrs. (pres. 1977-84), Dist. L Ret. Tchrs. (pres. 1989-91, chmn. legis. com. 1998, 99, 2001), Va. State Fedn. Colored Women's Club (pres. 1990-94, editor history com. 1994-96), Am. Assn. Ret. Persons (Va. state legis. com. 1995-2001). Mem. Ch. of Christ. Avocations: crafts, travel, writing, lecturing. Home and Office: PO Box 236 14213 Lankford Hwy Eastville VA 23347-0236

WILLIAMS, IRVING LAURENCE, physics educator; b. Newport, R.I., Dec. 3, 1935; s. Leroy Payton and Alberta Helen (Troy) W.; m. Carrie Mae Graves, Aug. 26, 1967; children: Cheryl Anita, Carla Chantrase. EdB, R.I. Coll., 1957; MA in Teaching, Brown U., 1962; PhD, NYU, 1975. Cert. teaching, R.I. Classroom tchr. Newport (R.I.) Sch. Dept., 1962-63; prof. physics Morgan State U., Balt., 1963-67, Nassau Community Coll., Garden City, N.Y., 1967-97, prof. emeritus, 1998, asst. to pres. N.Y., 1980-85, prof. emeritus, 1998—. Adj. prof. Hofstra U., Hempstead, N.Y., 1980-87; adj. instr. physics Guilford Tech. C.C., Greensboro, N.C.; dist. clk. Roosevelt (N.Y.) Sch. Bd., 1989-91; instr. physics Guilford Tech. C.C., Greensboro, N.C., 1999—. Co-author: (lab. workbook) Meterology Lab. Exercises, 1975, 76. Treas. Econ. Opportunity Commn., Nassau County, N.Y., 1984; trustee Grace Lutheran Ch., Malverne, N.Y., 1987, Roosevelt Bd. Edn., 1988; active Roosevelt Rep. Club, 1989; mem. sch. bd. Grace Lutheran Sch., Malverne, 1991. With U.S. Army, 1957-60. Recipient Chancellor's award SUNY, 1975, Citzen's award EOC Nassau County, Hempstead, 1987, Roosevelt Educator's award, Roosevelt Coun., 1989; NSF Weather Svc. grantee, Washington, 1989. Mem. AAUP, Nat. Sci. Tchrs. Assn., Am. Assn. Physics Tchrs., Soc. Coll. Sci. Tchrs., N.Y. Acad. Sci., Am. Assn. Higher Edn., N.Y. Assn. Two Yr. Colls. Republican. Avocation: piano. Home: 2 Leeward Ct Greensboro NC 27455-0812 E-mail: IWill220@aol.com.

WILLIAMS, J. BRYAN, lawyer; b. Detroit, July 23, 1947; s. Walter J. and Maureen June (Kay) Williams; m. Jane Elizabeth Eisele, Aug. 24, 1974; children: Kyle Joseph, Ryan Patrick. AB, U. Notre Dame, 1969; JD, U. Mich., 1972. Bar: Mich. 1972, U.S. Dist. Ct. (ea. dist.) Mich. 1972. Atty. Dickinson, Wright, PLLC (and predecessor firm), Detroit, 1972—, CEO Bloomfield Hills, 1991-2000. Pres. U.S. Law Firm Group, Inc., 2002. Mem.: ABA, Detroit Legal News Co. (bd. dirs.), Econ. Club Detroit (bd. dirs. 1996—2001), Detroit Bar Assn., Mich. Bar Assn., Detroit Regional C. of C. (bd. dirs., vice chmn. 1998—2002), Nat. Club Assn. (bd. dirs., sec. 1995—97, treas. 1997—98, v.p. 1998—2002, chmn. 2002—), Oakland Hills Country Club, Notre Dame Club Detroit (pres. 1984). Roman Catholic. Home: 993 Suffield Ave Birmingham MI 48009-1242 Office: Dickinson Wright PLLC 38525 Woodward Ave Ste 2000 Bloomfield Hills MI 48304 E-mail: jwilliams@dickinson-wright.com.

WILLIAMS, J. LINDA, librarian; b. Bethesda, Md., June 30, 1945; d. Joseph Gordon and Annie Louise (Whitfield) DiMisa; m. Charles Edward Williams, Nov. 2, 1968. BS in Secondary Edn./English and History, Radford U., 1966; MLS, U. Md., 1977; cert. adminstrn., supr., Bowie (Md.) State Coll., 1987. Cert. tchr., librarian. Tchr. English, history Prince William County Pub. Schs., Woodbridge, Va., 1967-73; tchr. English Charles County Pub. Schs., LaPlata, Md., 1973-76; library media specialist St. Mary County Pub. Schs., Leonardtown, 1977-84; staff specialist Md. Dept. Edn., Balt., 1985-94; supr. media and instrnl. materials Prince George's County Pub. Schs., Landover, Md., 1994-99; dir. libr. media and instrnl. technology Anne Arundel County Pub. Schs., Annapolis, 1999—. Named Alumnus of Yr. Coll. Library and Info. Svcs., 1988 U. Md.; profl. devel. grantee 3M, 1981. Mem. ALA (various divs.), Md. Library Assn., Md. Edn. Media Assn. (pres. 1998-99), Beta Phi Mu. Home: 1726 Farmington Ct Crofton MD 21114-2307 Office: 188 Green St Annapolis MD 21401-2502 E-mail: lwilliams@aacps.org., jw177@aol.com.

WILLIAMS, J. MAXWELL, lawyer, arbitrator and mediator; b. Spartanburg, S.C., Aug. 11, 1943; BA, Vanderbilt U., 1965; JD, U. Fla., 1971. Bar: Fla. 1971, Tenn. 1980, U.S. Dist. Ct. (mid. dist.) Fla. 1973, U.S. Dist. Ct. (so. dist.) Fla. 1972, U.S. Dist. Ct. (we. dist.) Tenn. 1984, U.S. Ct. Appeals (5th and 11th cirs.) 1974, U.S. Supreme Ct. 1974; cert. mediator, Fla., Tenn. Atty. Kimbrell & Hamaan, Miami, Fla., 1971-73, State of Fla., Tampa, 1974-75; county atty. Hillsborough County, 1976-79; chief group counsel, asst. sec. W.R. Grace & Co., Memphis, 1980-98; v.p., gen. counsel, gov. rels. officer Memphis Light, Gas and Water, 1998—. Steering com. Shelby County Rep. Party, Memphis, 1991-95. With USMCR. Named Vol. of Yr., Memphis Legal Svcs., 1992, one of Outstanding Young Men in Am., 1980. Mem. Nat. Assn. Security Dealers (mediator, arbitrator 1996—), Memphis Bar Assn. (chair alt. dispute resolution com. 1996-98), Am. Arbitration Assn. (West Tenn. adv. coun. 1995—, mediator, arbitrator 1994—), Rotary. Baptist. Avocations: swimming, tennis, travel, weight training. org. Home: 7242 Neshoba Cir Germantown TN 38138-3749 Office: Memphis Light Gas and Water 220 S Main St Memphis TN 38103-3917 E-mail: jmwilliams@mlgw.org.

WILLIAMS, J. VERNON, lawyer; b. Honolulu, Apr. 26, 1921; s. Urban and W. Amelia (Olson) W.; m. Malvina H. Hitchcock, Oct. 4, 1947 (dec. May 1970); children— Carl H., Karin, Frances E., Scott S.; m. Mary McLellan, Sept. 6, 1980. Student, Phillips Andover Acad., 1937-39; BA cum laude, Amherst Coll., 1943; LL.B., Yale, 1948. Bar: Wash. 1948. Assoc. Riddell, Riddell & Hemphill, 1948-50, ptnr., 1950-95; sr. prin. emeritus Riddell Williams, P.S., Seattle, 1996—. Sec., dir. Airborne Freight Corp., 1968-79, gen. counsel, 1968-96. Chmn. March of Dimes, Seattle, 1954-55; Mem. Mayor's City Charter Rev. Com., 1968-69; chmn. Seattle Bd. Park Commrs., 1966-68; co-chmn. parks and open space com. Forward Thrust, 1966-69; dir. bd. and commrs. br. Nat. Recreation and Parks Assn., 1968-69; chmn. Gov.'s adv. com. Social and Health Services, 1972-75; Bd. dirs. Seattle Met. YMCA, 1965— , pres., 1976-79; trustee Lakeside Sch., 1971-79; mem. alumni council Phillps Andover Acad., 1970-73, Yale Law Sch., 1969-77; chancellor St. Mark's Cathedral, Seattle, 1964-2000. Served with USAAF, 1943-45. Mem. Univ. Club, Seattle Tennis Club, Birnam Wood Golf Club. Home: 1100 38th Ave E Seattle WA 98112-4434 Office: 4500 1001 4th Ave Plz Seattle WA 98154-1065

WILLIAMS, JACK JEFF, realtor, retired executive administrator; b. Cushing, Okla., July 28, 1936; s. Jeff Davis and Pauline Vera (Meyers) W.; m. Mary Ann Hill, June 1, 1957; children: Janet Lee Williams Charlin, Jeff Brian. BA in Econs., U. Calif., Dominguez Hills, 1974. Lic. real estate sales, Calif. Exec. adminstr. TRW Space & Electronics, Redondo Beach, Calif.; realtor Moore & Assocs. Hermosa Bch. (Top ten agent). Cons. Delta Airlines, Atlanta, Aerospace Corp., El Segundo, Calif., Amdahl Corp., Santa Clara, Calif., Continental Airlines, L.A. Author, editor: Meyers from Moyers, 1996. Mem. TRW Retirees Assn. (v.p. 1997, pres. 1998), Torrance Rose Float Assn. (bd. dirs. 1996—, v.p., 1997—), South Bay Genealogy Soc., Snow Valley Ski Club (coord.), Masons (sr. deacon 1993). Republican. Baptist. Avocation: genealogy research. Home: 5216 Emerald St Torrance CA 90503-2724 Office: Moore & Assocs Realtors 2615 Pacific Coast Hwy Ste 100 Hermosa Beach CA 90254-2278

WILLIAMS, JACK MARVIN, research chemist; b. Delta, Colo., Sept. 26, 1938; s. John Davis and Ruth Emma (Gallup) W. BS with honors, Lewis and Clark Coll., 1960; MS, Wash. State U., 1964, PhD, 1966. Postdoctoral fellow Argonne (Ill.), Nat. Lab., 1966-68, asst. chemist, 1968-70, assoc. chemist, 1970-72, chemist, 1972-77, sr. chemist, group leader, 1977—; vis. guest prof. U. Mo., Columbia, 1980, 81, 82, U. Copenhagen, 1980, 83, 85. Chair Gordon Rsch. Conf. (Inorganic Chemistry), 1980. Bd. editors: Inorganic Chemistry, 1979-96, assoc. editor, 1982-93. Crown-Zellerbach scholar, 1959-60; NDEA fellow, 1960-63; recipient Disting. Performance at Argonne Nat. Labs. award U. Chgo., 1987, Centennial Disting. Alumni award Wash. State U., 1990. Mem. AAAS, Am. Crystallographic Assn., Am. Chem. Soc. (treas. inorganic div. 1982-84), Am. Phys. Soc., Phi Beta Kappa. Office: Chemistry Div 9700 S Cass Ave Lemont IL 60439-4803

WILLIAMS, JACK RAYMOND, civil engineer; b. Barberton, Ohio, Mar. 14, 1923; s. Charles Baird and Mary Williams; m. Mary Berneice Jones, Mar. 5, 1947 (dec.); children: Jacqueline Rae, Drew Alan; m. Betty Ruth Scholfield, Nov. 9, 1990. Student, Colo. Sch. Mines, 1942043, Purdue U., 1944-45; BS, U. Colo., 1946. Gravity and seismograph engr. Carter Oil Co., Western U.S. and Venezuela, 1946-50; with Rock Island R.R., Chgo., 1950-80, structural designer, asst. to engr. bridges, asst. engr., 1980-82, engr. bridges system,

1963-80; sr. bridge engr. thomas K. Dyer Inc., 1980-82; v.p. Alfred Benesch & Co., 1982-96. Served with USMCR, 1943-45. Fellow ASCE (life); mem. Am. Concrete Inst., Am. Ry. Bridge and Bldg. Assn. (past pres.), Am. Ry. Engring. Assn. (hon. mem., past chmn. com. 8, Concrete and Foundations, past chmn. com. 10 concrete ties). Home: 293 Minocqua St Park Forest IL 60466-1942

WILLIAMS, JAMES ARTHUR, retired army officer, information systems company executive; b. Paterson, N.J., Mar. 29, 1932; s. Charles M. and Elsie (Kretszchmar) W.; m. Barbara Widnall, June 26, 1959; children: Steven, Karen. BS, U.S. Mil. Acad.; MA in Latin Am. Studies, U. N.Mex. Commd. 2d lt. U.S. Army, 1954, advanced through grades to lt. gen.; asst. army attache U.S. Def. Attache Office, Caracas, Venezuela, 1966-72; exch. officer State-Def. Exch. Program Office of Sec. Def., Washington, 1972-74; comdr. 650th MI Group, Shape, 1974-76; dep. dir. estimates Def. Intelligence Agy., Washington, 1977-80; dep. chief staff for intelligence U.S. Army, Europe, 1980-81; dir. Def. Intelligence Agy., Washington, 1981-85; ret., 1985; v.p. PSC Corp., 1986; pres. Direct Info. Access Corp., Annandale, Va., 1987—; chmn. bd. dirs. Info. Ops. Inc., 2000—. Decorated Legion of Merit, Bronze Star with oak leaf cluster, Air medals, D.S.M., Nat. Intelligence D.S.M.; Legion of Honor (France); named Disting. Mem. Mil. Intelligence Hall of Fame. Mem. Assn. U.S. Army, Nat. Mil. Intelligence Assn. (chmn. bd. 1986—). Methodist. Home: 8928 Maurice Ln Annandale VA 22003-3914 Office: Information Operations Inc 1298 Bay Dale Dr Ste 207 Arnold MD 21012-2815

WILLIAMS, JAMES BOUGHTON, artist, art educator; b. Bethlehem, Pa., Oct. 20, 1947; s. William Rendell and Rose Everall (Fisher) W.; m. Raisa Blanca Godin, Nov. 11, 1972; 1 child, Miguel Angel. BA in English, U. Va., 1969; MA in English, SUNY, Binghamton, 1972; MFA in Painting, U. Del., 1990. Tchr. English The Concept Sch., Westtown, Pa., 1978-80; lead tchr., therapist Ctr. for Early Childhood Svcs., Phila., 1983-85; adj. prof. art LaSalle U., 1985—. One-man shows include Rosemont Coll., Phila., 1995, Cabrini Coll., Phila., 1996, Widener U., Chester, Pa., 1997, Gross McCleaf Gallery, Phila., 1997, 99, LaSalle U. Art Mus., 1999; exhibited in group shows in Phila. and N.Y.C. including Knickerbocker Artists, 1991, Allied Artists Am., 1992. Recipient Morris Freed Meml. prize Woodmere Art Mus., Phila., 1990, Blumenthal Meml. award Cheltenham Art Ctr., Phila., 1995. Fellow Fellowship Pa. Acad. Fine Arts (Mary Butler Meml. purchase prize 1997), Coll. Art Assn. Avocations: music (guitar, harmonica, vocals), bicycling, rock climbing, skiing. Home: 6045 Daniel St Philadelphia PA 19144-3703 Office: LaSalle U 20th St and Olney Ave Philadelphia PA 19141

WILLIAMS, JAMES BRYAN, banker; b. Sewanee, Tenn., Mar. 21, 1933; s. Eugene G. and Ellen (Bryan) W.; m. Betty G. Williams, July 11, 1980; children: Ellen, Elizabeth, Bryan. AB, Emory U., 1955. Pres. Peachtree Bank & Trust Co., Chamblee, Ga.; chmn. bd. First Nat. Bank & Trust Co., Augusta; pres. Sun Banks, Inc., Orlando, Fla., Trust Co. of Ga., Atlanta; chmn. exec. com. SunTrust Banks, Inc., 1998—. Bd. dirs. The Coca-Cola Co., Atlanta, Genuine Parts Co., Atlanta, Rollins, Inc., Ga.-Pacific Corp., Atlanta, RPC, Inc., Atlanta, Genuine Parts Co., Atlanta. Trustee Emory U.; chmn. bd. trustees Robert W. Woodruff Health Scis. Ctr.; nat. trustee Boys & Girls Clubs Am.; trustee emeritus Westminster Schs., Atlanta. Lt. USAF, 1955-57. Mem.: Bankers Roundtable, Ga. C. of C. (dir. emeritus), Peachtree Golf Club, Augusta Country Club, Commerce Club, Capital City Club, Ocean Forest Golf Club, Piedmont Driving Club, Phi Beta Kappa, Omicron Delta Kappa. Office: SunTrust Banks Inc PO Box 4418 25 Park Pl NE Atlanta GA 30303-2900

WILLIAMS, JAMES CASE, metallurgist; b. Salina, Kans., Dec. 7, 1938; s. Luther Owen and Clarice (Case) W.; m. Joanne Rufener, Sept. 17, 1960; children: Teresa A., Patrick J. BS in Metall. Engring, U. Wash., 1962, MS, 1964, PhD, 1968. Rsch. engr., lead engr. Boeing Co., Seattle, 1961-67; tech. staff N.Am. Rockwell Corp., Thousand Oaks, Calif., 1968-74; mgr. interdivisional tech. program N.Am. Aerospace group, 1974, program devel. mgr. structural materials, 1974-75; prof. metallurgy, co-dir. Ctr. for Joining of Materials, Carnegie-Mellon U., Pitts., 1975-81; pres. Mellon Inst., 1981-83; dean Carnegie Inst. Tech., Carnegie-Mellon U., 1983-88; gen. mgr. materials dept. GE Aircraft Engines, 1988-99; Honda prof. Ohio State U., Columbus, 1999—, dean of engring., 2001—. Bd. dirs. com. on engring. and tech. systems NRC, 1996—; chmn. Nat. Materials Adv. Bd., 1988-95, materials and structures com. NASA Aero. Adv. Com. 1992-97; mem. NASA Propulsion Rsch. and Tech. Com., 1997-99; mem. Materials Sci. and Engring. Study, 1986-88; bd. govs. Inst. for Mechs. and Materials, U. Calif., San Diego, 1989-95; trustee Min. Math. Sci. and Engring., Cin., 1988-99; mem. sci. adv. bd. USAF, 1996-2001; mem. materials rsch. com. Def. Advanced Rsch. Projects Agy., 1981-2000; adv. com. Divsn. Engring. and Phys. Sci., NRC, 2001—. Co-editor: Scientific and Technological Aspects of Titanium and Titanium Alloys, 1976; contbr. numerous articles to tech. jours. Trustee Oreg. Grad. Inst. Sci. and Tech., 1988-94; cons. Cubmaster Boy Scouts Am., 1976-77. Recipient Ladd award Carnegie Inst. Tech.; Adams award Am. Welding Soc.; Boeing doctoral fellow. Fellow: TMS-AIME, Am. Soc. Metals (Disting. lectr. on materials and soc. 1997, Campbell lectr. 1999, Gold medal 1992); mem.: AIME (Leadership award 1993), NAE, ASM, Alpha Sigma Mu. Republican. Episcopalian. Home: 7711 Charlotte Hull Ct New Albany OH 43054-9680 Office: GE Aircraft Engines Gen Mgr Material Dept MD H85 Cincinnati OH 45215 E-mail: williams.1726@osu.edu.

WILLIAMS, JAMES EUGENE, management consultant; b. Macon, Ga., June 23, 1927; s. James Eugene and Margaret Elizabeth (Tinker) W.; m. Linda K. Magnuson, June 23, 1984; children: Paul David, Lisa Jane Williams Robertson, Philip Alan, Gail Ellen Williams Feeney, Amanda Allen Thompson, Jason Douglas Allen, Joel Winston Allen. BS in Aero. Engring., Iowa State Coll., 1950. Engr., Robins AFB, Ga., 1950-54, Hdqrs. USAF, Washington, 1954-61; dep. asst. sec. Office Asst. Sec. Air Force, 1961-85; dir. govt. bus. policy Northrop Corp., 1986-88; pvt. practice mgmt. cons. Tempe, Ariz., 1988—. Co-founder The Williams Inst. for Ethics and Mgmt., Tempe, 1993—. Recipient Presdl. Meritorious Exec. award, 1981, Presdl. Disting. Exec. award, 1982. Home: 3223 S College Ave Tempe AZ 85282-3773 E-mail: LJWMS@aol.com.

WILLIAMS, JAMES FRANCIS, professional baseball manager; b. Arroyo Grande, Calif., Oct. 4, 1943; m. Peggy Sallee, Feb. 19, 1977; children: Monica, Brady, Shawn, Jenna. BS, Fresno State U. Semi-profl. baseball player, shortstop Basin League, Sturgis, S.D., 1963-64; semi-profl. baseball player, shortstop Alaska Goldpanners, 1964; profl. baseball player, shortstop Waterloo, Midwest League, 1965, St. Louis Cardinals, Nat. League, 1966-68, Cin. Reds, 1968-69, Montreal Expos, 1969-71; mgr. Calif. Angels, 1974-78, 79, St. Louis Cardinals, 1978; 3d base and outfield coach Toronto Blue Jays, Ont., Can., 1980-82, 3d base and infield def. coach, 1982-86, mgr. Ont., Can., 1986-89; 3d base coach Atlanta Braves, 1990-96; mgr. Boston Red Sox, 1996—. Office: Boston Red Sox 4 Yawkey Way Boston MA 02215-3496*

WILLIAMS, JAMES FRANCIS, JR. religious organization administrator; b. Coffeyville, Kans., June 20, 1938; s. James Francis and Sarah Kathryn (Tavenner) W.; m. Alice Carol Kinney, June 1, 1963; children: James F. III, Todd Alexander, Leslie. BA, So. Meth. U., 1960; ThM, Dallas Theol. Sem., 1964; HHD, U. Tex., 1988. Campus dir. Campus Crusade for Christ, Dallas, 1961-64, area dir. various North Tex. locations, 1964-68; dir. music campus Crusade for Christ, Arrowhead, Calif., 1967-71; regional dir. Campus Crusade for Christ, Southwestern U.S., 1968-71, nat. dir. tng. U.S., 1971-72; founder, min. at large Probe Ministries, Internat., Dallas, 1973—, pres., 1973-97. Dir. music Campus Crusade for Christ, Arrowhead, Calif., 1967-71. Soloist, chorus Dallas Opera, 1982-84. Named one of Outstanding Young Men in Am. Dallas Jaycees, 1965. Evangelical Christian. Office: Probe Ministries 1900 Firman Dr Ste 100 Richardson TX 75081-6796

WILLIAMS, JAMES FRANKLIN , II, university dean, librarian; b. Montgomery, Ala., Jan. 22, 1944; s. James Franklin and Anne (Wester) W.; m. Madeline McClellan, Jan. 1966 (div. May 1988); 1 child, Madeline Marie; m. Nancy Allen, Aug. 1989; 1 child, Audrey Grace. BA, Morehouse Coll., 1966; MLS, Atlanta U., 1967. Reference libr. Wayne State U. Sci. Libr., Detroit, 1968-69; document delivery libr. Wayne State U. Med. Libr., 1969-70, head of reference, 1971-72, dir. med. libr. and regional med. libr. network, 1972-81, regional dir., 1975-82; assoc. dir. of librs. Wayne State U., 1981-88; dean librs. U. Colo., Boulder, 1988—. Bd. regents Nat. Libr. Medicine, Bethesda, Md., 1978-81; bd. dirs. Denver Art Mus., 1997—, pres. 1999—; bd. dirs. Ctr. Rsch. Librs., 1998—; pres. Big Twelve Plus Libr. Consortium, 2000; bd. dirs. Coun. on Librs. and Info. Resources. Mem. editl. bd. Portal: Libraries and the Academy; contbr. articles to profl. jours., chpts. to books; book editor and author. Bd. dirs. Educom, 1997-98, Boulder Cmty. Hosp., 2000—. Subject of feature interview in centennial issue Am. Librs. jour., 1976. Mem. ALA (Visionary Leader award 1988, Melvil Dewey medal 2002), Coll. and Rsch. Librs. (editl. bd.), Assn. Rsch. Librs. (bd. dirs. 1994-96), Boulder C. of C. (bd. dirs.). Avocations: cycling, travel, fishing. Office: U Colo Office Dean Librs PO Box 184 Boulder CO 80309-0184

WILLIAMS, JAMES HENRY, JR. mechanical engineer, educator, consultant; b. Newport News, Va., Apr. 4, 1941; s. James H. Williams and Margaret L. (Holt) Mitchell; children: James Henry III, Mariella Louisa. Student, Newport News Apprentice Sch., 1965; BS, MIT, 1967, MS, 1968; PhD, Cambridge U., 1970. Sr. design engr. Newport News (Va.) Shipyard, 1960-70; asst. prof. mech. engring. MIT, 1970-74, assoc. prof., 1974-81, prof., 1981—, duPont prof., 1973, Edgarton prof., 1974-76. Cons. engring. to numerous cos. Contbr. articles on stress analysis, materials and nondestructive testing to profl. jours. Recipient Charles F. Cailey Bronze medal, 1961, Silver medal, 1962, Gold medal, 1963, Baker award, 1973; named prof. teaching excellence Sch. Engring., 1991; C.F. Hopewell faculty fellow, 1993—. Mem. ASME, Am. Soc. Nondestructive Testing, Nat. Tech. Assn. Office: MIT Room 3-360 77 Massachusetts Ave Rm 3-360 Cambridge MA 02139-4307

WILLIAMS, JAMES LEE, financial industries executive; b. Tampa, Fla., Nov. 5, 1941; s. Donald Clark and Nell (Medlin) W.; m. Linda Taylor, Dec. 28, 1968; children: Donald Clark II, Taylor Lee. AA, St. Petersburg (Fla.) Jr. Coll., 1965; BS, Fla. State U., 1967. Mgmt. Ryder Truck Lines, Jacksonville, Fla., 1967-69; dist. mgr. underwriting div. U.S. Leasing Corp., Dallas, 1969-73; area v.p. Mfrs. Hanover Leasing Corp., Houston and London, 1973-79; v.p. corp. fin. Underwood Neuhause & Co. Inc., Houston, 1979-81; chmn., chief exec. officer 1st City Leasing Corp., 1981-85; mng. dir. capital markets 1st City Bancorp., 1985-89; mng. dir. fin. svcs. M.P.S.I. Systems Inc., Dallas, 1989-90; pres., chief exec. officer Strategic Decisions Holdings Corp., 1990-92; sr. mng. dir. Williams and Assocs., 1992; pres. Global Svcs. Capital Corp., Houston, 1993-96; v.p., dist. CFO Ikon Hov. Adminstrv. Svc. Ctr., 1997-98; CFO Insync Internet Svcs., 1998-99, Walkabout Software, 1999-2001; pres. BancLeasing, Inc., 2001—. Served with USN, 1959-62. Mem. Equipment Leasing Assn. (fed. govt. rels. com. 1984-88, 95—), Tex. Assn. Equipment Lessors (bd. dirs. 1985-89), Greater Houston Partnership (vice-chmn. Arabian horse com. Houston Livestock Show and Rodeo). Clubs: Houston Ctr. (bd. dirs. 1985-89), Lakeside Racquet (athletic com. 1986-89), Forum (Houston). Republican. Presbyterian. Avocations: golf, jogging, swimming. Office: BancLeasing Inc 1600 Redbud Blvd Mc Kinney TX 75069

WILLIAMS, JAMES ORRIN, university administrator, educator; b. New Orleans, Jan. 8, 1937; married, 1978; 5 children. BS, Auburn U., 1960, MEd, 1963, EdD, 1967; postgrad., Tchrs. Coll., Columbia U., summer 1964. Tchr. social sci., coach Columbus High Sch. Ga., 1960-61; tchr., coach Eufaula High Sch. Ala., 1961-63; prin. Troy Jr. High Sch., 1963-65; grad. asst. Sch. Edn. Auburn U., 1965-66, interim dir. field service, 1966-67; asst. prof. edn. adminstrn. U. Fla., 1967-68; asst. prof. Columbus Coll., 1968-69; assoc. prof., chmn. div. Auburn U., Montgomery, 1969-73, vice chancellor acad. affairs, 1973-80, chancellor, 1980-93; v.p. U. So. Miss.-Gulf Coast campus, Long Beach, 1993—. Contbr. articles to profl. jours. Phi Delta Kappa grantee, 1967. Mem. Am. Assn. State Colls. and Univs., Am. Assn. Coll. Tchr. Edn., Assn. Tchr. Edn., So. Regional Council Edn. Adminstrn., Phi Delta Kappa (v.p. 1965), Phi Kappa Phi. Office: U So Miss 730 E Beach Blvd Long Beach MS 39560-6259

WILLIAMS, JAMES RICHARD, human factors engineering psychologist; b. Chgo., Apr. 16, 1932; s. James Henry and Margaret Lucille (Keefer) W.; m. Jonetta Rae Gilbert, Dec. 19, 1959; children: Janise Rebecca, Jason Richard. BS in Psychology, Purdue U., 1958, MS in Human Factors/Indsl. Psychology, 1960; PhD in Edn., NYU, 1971. Bd. cert. in profl. ergonomics. Technical asst. Sci. Rsch. Assocs., Chgo., 1960-61; sr. systems cons. System Devel. Corp., Paramus, N.J., 1961-64; human factors engr. Kollsman Instrument Corp., Elmhurst, N.Y., 1964-66; project mgr. System Devel. Corp., Paramus, 1966-69; supr. tng. and standards Bell Labs., Piscataway, N.J., 1969-74; dist. mgr. AT&T, Basking Ridge, 1975-80; mem. technical staff Bell Labs., Piscataway, 1981-83; sr. performance technologist Telcordia Techs., 1984—2001; prin. ergonomist Synergetic Applications, Bloomsbury, NJ, 2002—. Cons. NYU, N.Y.C., 1968-70; chair U.S. Tech. Adv. Group, to internat. orgn. for standardization in ergonomics of human system interaction, 1988—; co-owner Del Vista Vineyards, 1982-92. Editor: International Standards for Menu Dialogues, Command Dialogues and Form-fill Dialogues with Computer Systems. Cub master Boy Scouts, Watchung, N.Y., 1973-74, asst. scout master, 1975-78. With USAF, 1951-55. Mem. Am. Psychol. Soc. (charter), Assn. for Computing Machinery (spl. interest group on computer-human interaction), Human Factors and Ergonomics Soc. (rep. 1986—), Delta Rho Kappa, Kappa Delta Pi. Avocations: astronomy, body building. Home: 16 Staats Rd Bloomsbury NJ 08804-3300 Office: Synergetic Applications 16 Staats Rd Bloomsbury NJ 08804-

WILLIAMS, JAMES THOMAS, physician, educator; b. Martinsville, Va., Nov. 10, 1933; s. Harry Pemberton and Ruth Ellen (Thomas) W.; m. Jacqueline Cecile Shepard, Apr. 21, 1962; children: Lawrence Dudley, Laurie Cecile. BS, Howard U., 1954, MD, 1958. Diplomate Am. Bd. Internal Medicine, Am. Bd. Endocrinology and Metabolism. Intern Phila. Gen. Hosp., 1958-59; resident in medicine D.C. Gen. Hosp., 1959-60, Freedmen's Hosp., Washington, 1960-62, 64-65; fellow in endocrinology Howard U., 1965-67, asst. prof. medicine, 1967-74, chief endocrine sect. dept. medicine, 1973-76, assoc. prof. medicine, 1974-85, prof. medicine, 1985—. Capt. U.S. Army, 1962-64. Fellow ACP, Am. Coll. Endocrinology; mem. Endocrine Soc., Am. Diabetes Assn., Nat. Med. Assn. Democrat. Home: 13414 Tamarack Rd Silver Spring MD 20904-1469 Office: Howard U Hosp 2041 Georgia Ave NW Washington DC 20060-0001

WILLIAMS, JANE MARIE, special education educator; b. Hagerstown, Md., May 23, 1949; d. George Ernest and Marie Gertrude (Magaha) Lambillotte. BA, Wittenberg U., 1971; MA, U. Iowa, 1973; PhD, U. Md., 1984. Tchr. learning disabilities Danville (Ky.) Bd. Edn., 1973-74; diagnostic and prescriptive tchr. Chelsea (Mass.) Sch. Com., 1974-76; coord. learning disabilities program Hudson (N.H.) Sch. Dist., 1976-78; coord. work study Charles County Bd. Edn., La Plata, Md., 1978; coord. learning ctr. program Montgomery County Pub. Schs., Rockville, 1978-79, tchr. spl. edn., 1979-81, 82-84, resource tchr. in spl. edn., 1984-92; edn. specialist, expert Office of Spl. Edn. Programs U.S. Dept. Edn., 1992-97; Ariz. State U. West, Phoenix, 1997-2000; assoc. dir. Ariz. K-12 Ctr., No. Ariz. U., 2000-01; asst. prof. U. Nev., Las Vegas, 2001—. Cons. So. N.H. Profl. Psychiat. Assn., Nashua, 1976-77, Lake Region Spl. Edn. Dist., Devil's Lake, N.D., 1990; asst. professorial lectr. George Washington U., Washington, spring 1989; presenter Internat. Spl. Edn. Congress, Cardiff, Wales, 1990. Author instrnl. materials. Ednl. cons., expert witness to atty., Rockville, 1988; reader small grant awards Found. for Exceptional Children, Reston, Va., 1985-91. Recipient Outstanding Spl. Educator award Montgomery Coun. Coun. PTA's, 1989. Mem. Coun. for Exceptional Children (sec. Md. fedn. 1982-91, gov. 1991-92, v.p. Montgomery County 1986-87, sec. 1986-87), Coun. for Learning Disabilities (sec. 1991-92), Learning Disabilities Assn. Am., Montgomery County Edn. Assn. (Broome award 1985). Avocations: running, swimming, reading. Home: 8243 Coyado St Las Vegas NV 89123-4320 Office: U Nev Las Vegas Dept Spl Edn Box 453014 4505 Maryland Pkwy Las Vegas NV 89154-3014 E-mail: janew@unlv.edu.

WILLIAMS, JANICE MACHELLE, managed care company official; b. New Haven, Oct. 14, 1968; d. Fred Alfred and Lucile (Hill) W. BA in Psychology/Sociology, Wesleyan U., Middletown, Conn., 1990; MBA in Health Care Mgmt., U. Pa., Phila., 1994. Fin. analyst N.Y. Hosp., N.Y.C., 1990-92; sr. healthcare cons. Deloitte & Touche Cons. Group, Parsippany, N.J., 1994-96; assoc. mgr. analytical svcs. Merck-Medco Managed Care LLC, Franklin Lakes, 1997-98, mgr. bus. analysis, 1998-2000, sr. mgr. bus. analysis, 2000—02; mgr. market analytics Pfizer, Inc., N.Y.C., 2002—. Mem. Nat. Black MBA Assn., Healthcare Fin. Mgmt. Assn. (managed care com. 1996-97), Delta Sigma Theta (North Manhattan Alumnae chpt. journalist 1998-2000). Democrat. Baptist. Avocations: gospel singing, African dance, rollerblading, the internet, exercising. Office: Pfizer Inc 235 E 42d St MS 219/36 New York NY 10017

WILLIAMS, JEFFREY N. astronaut; b. Superior, Wis., Jan. 18, 1958; s. Lloyd D. and Eunice A. Williams; m. Anna-Marie Moore; 2 children. BSc in Applied Sci. & Engring., U.S. Military Acad., 1980; MSc in Aero. Engring., U.S. Naval Postgraduate Sch., 1987; MA in Nat. Security & Strategic Studies, U.S. Naval War Coll., 1996. Commd. 2d lt. USN, 1980, advanced through grades to lt. col., aeroscout platoon leader Germany, 1981—84, various assignments, 1984—92; assigned to Edwards AFB, Calif., 1993—95, Naval War Coll., 1995—96; astronaut NASA, Houston, 1996—. Astronaut Space Shuttle Atlantis, 2000. Decorated Def. Superior Svc. medal USN, Legion of Merit, Meritorious Svc. medal; recipient William Adger Moffett award, Naval Postgraduate Sch., 1988. Mem.: USMA Assn. Graduates, Army Aviation Assn. Am., Am. Helicopter Soc., Soc. Exptl. Test Pilots, Assn. U.S. Army, Officer Christian Fellowship, Order of Daedalians. Avocations: running, fishing, camping, skiing, scuba diving. Office: Astronaut Office CB NASA Johnson Space Center Houston TX 77058*

WILLIAMS, JEFFREY P. investment banker; b. July 13, 1951; BArch, U. Cin., 1975; MBA, Harvard U., 1979. Mng. dir. Morgan Stanley, N.Y.C., 1979-96; exec. v.p. McGraw-Hill, 1996-98; ptnr. Greenhill & Co., LLC, 1998—. E-mail: jwilliams@greenhill-co.com.

WILLIAMS, JENNIFER MARGARET, freelance artist; b. Bridgeton, N.J., Oct. 22, 1967; d. Harold Stinson and Virginia Frances (Macera) W. Student, Moore Coll. Art, Phila., 1985-86; AA, Cumberland County Coll., Vineland, N.J., 1988; BFA, Rowan U., 1998. Printer Garden State Color Corp., Hammonton, NJ, 2001—. Part-time graphic artist The Daily Jour., Vineland, N.J., 1997. Contbr. poetry to Treasured Poems of Am., 1989, Am. Poetry Anthology, 1989; contbr. illustrations to Hawkfan, U.K., 1994; contbr. photos and article Weird N.J., 1999-2000. Thelma Parkinson Sharp scholar, 1986. Avocations: Medieval and Celtic art, pen and ink illustrations, fossil collection, Welsh language and culture, audiophile, writing. Home: 19 Preston Ave Bridgeton NJ 08302-1424

WILLIAMS, JERRY OWEN, music educator; b. Detroit, June 11, 1945; m. Rae Reece, Mar. 18, 1972; children: Jennifer. BA Music, Findlay Coll., Findlay, OH, 1974. Band dir./music educator Vanlue Local Sch., Vanlue, Ohio, 1974—78; band dir. Moore County Sch., Carthage, 1978—84, Pinecrest H.S., Southern Pines, 1984—. Pub. safety commr. Town of Pinebluff, Pinebluff, NC, 1998. Sargeant USAF, 1967—71, Korea. Mem.: NC Assn. of Educators, Music Educators Nat. Conf. Achievements include Private Pilots License, 1980. Avocation: flying. Home: 360 South Plum Street Pinebluff NC 28373-8044 Office: Pinecrest High School 100 Pinecrest Road Southern Pines NC 28387 Office Fax: 910-692-0606. E-mail: brassman@mindspring.com.

WILLIAMS, JIMMIE LEWIS, research chemist; b. Indianola, Miss., June 3, 1953; s. West and Lorene (Mayfield) W.; m. Patricia Ann Rodgers; 2 children. BS in Chemistry, Jackson (Miss.) State U., 1975; MS in Chemistry, Yale U., 1977; PhD in Inorganic Chemistry, U. Calif., Riverside, 1983. From sr. rsch. scientist to sr. rsch. assoc. Corning (N.Y.) Inc., 1983-97, project mgr. environ. product devel., 1997—; mgr. Materials Devel., Environ. Techs. Devel., Corning, NY, 2001. Speaker and presenter in field. Contbr. articles to profl. jours. Coach sport programs, Corning, 1983—; vol. Big Bro. Program, Corning, 1983-85. Named one of Outstanding Young Men in Am., 1980, 83. Fellow Am. Inst. Chemists; mem. Am. Chem. Soc. (pres. Corning chpt. 1998pres. Corning sect. 2002, Eguene S. Sullivan award), Am. Ceramic Soc., Air and Waste Mgmt. Assn., Soc. Automotive Engrs., Nat. Soc. Black Engrs. (Disting. Engr. of Yr. award 2001), NACCP (v.p. Elmira br. 1991—, President's award Elmira/Corning br. 1995), Sigma Xi (pres. local chpt. 1990-91). Achievements include patents in field; research on automotive and industrial emissions control. Office: Corning Inc SP-DV-2-1 Corning NY 14831 E-mail: williamsjl@corning.com.

WILLIAMS, JIMY, professional athletics manager; b. 1943; Mgr. Quad Cities affiliate Midwest League Angels, 1974; 3d base coach Blue Jays, 1986—89; mgr. Boston Red Sox, 1996—2001, Houston Astros, 2001—. Named Mgr. of Yr., Pacific Coast League, 1976, 1979, AL Mgr. of Yr., BBWAA, 1999. Office: Houston Astros PO Box 288 Houston TX 77001-0288*

WILLIAMS, JOANNE MERLE, volunteer hospice coordinator; b. Stewartville, Minn., Mar. 20, 1930; d. Eric Walter and Martha Dorothy Blomberg; m. Lowell Roy Williams, Sept. 29, 1973; children: Diane Collis Emmons, Julie Collis Davis, Cindy, David. Student, San Francisco Theol. Sem., 1980-81. Activity coord. Carmichael (Calif.) Convalescent Hosp., 1975-80; vol. coord. Hospice of Roseville, Calif., 1983-91; ret., 1991. Lectr. pvt. practice, Roseville, Calif., 1980—; video producer Cable Found., Sacramento, Calif., 1988; cons. Nat. Cert. Coun. Activity Profls., 1990—. Author: (book) Volunteers Are Special, 1980; columnist: Geriatric Exchange, 1984; contbr. numerous articles to profl. jours. and mags. Lt. rescue squad S. Placer Fire Dist., Roseville, Calif., 1977-88; vol. March for Hospice Rocklin, Calif., 1988—; facilitator grief recovery, Presbyn. Ch., Fair Oaks, Calif., 1990—. Recipient Dedicated Svc. Leadership award South Placer Fire Dept., Roseville, 1988, Outstanding Accomplishment award Fair Oaks Presbyn. Ch., 1988; scholarship named in honor of her Therapeutic Activity Social Coordination, Sacramento. Mem. Nat. Assn. of Activity Profls. (steering com. 1981, membership chmn. 1982-87, Dedicated Svc. award 1987, charter), No. Calif. Coun. Activity Coords. (Dedicated Svc. award 1985). Avocations: jewelry designing, traveling, arts and crafts, video prodn. Home: 350 E 1st S Saint Anthony ID 83445-2122 Office: Hospice of Roseville 333 Sunrise Ave Roseville CA 95661-3479

WILLIAMS, JOANNE MOLITOR, elementary education educator, retired; b. Medford, Wis., Oct. 25, 1935; d. Lawrence John and Marie Catherine Molitor; m. Jack Dean Williams, Dec. 30, 1953; children: Patricia Varma, Ralph (Skip), L. Bradley. BS in Elem. Edn., U. Wis., Whitewater, 1971, MS in Elem. Edn., 1980; postgrad., U. Va., U. Colo. Cert. tchr. in elem. edn. and geography, Wis. Tchr. grades 4, 5 and 6 Lakewood Sch., Twin Lakes, Ill., 1971-82, 83-98, tchr. 5th grade gifted, 1989-91; dir. Resources for Children, Milw., 1982-83. Mem. textbook selection com. for reading, social studies, sci., lang.; mem. Lakewood Blue Ribbon Com., 1991, Lakewood Discipline Com., 1990-94; mem. Educators Consortium-Parkside, Kenosha, Wis., 1988-98; co-developer Respect, Obedience, Attitude, Responsibility program for students with good behavior, 1990; mem. Social Studies Curriculum Com., 1990, Strategic Planning Com., 1994, Inservice Com., 1997-98; mem. Kohl Scholarship Selection Com., 1990, 93; mem. Blue Ribbon Task Force Dept. Pub. Instrn., 1993. Audubon editor Chat, 1975. Phone bank organizer Friends of Channel 10/36, Milw., 1987, chair Walworth County portion of Fund Dr., 1989; leader Badger coun. Girl Scouts U.S., 1960—82; mem. Friends of Lake Geneva Libr., 1986—, Friends of Twin Lake/Randall Pub. Libr., 1992—, Assn. Preservation of Va. Antiquitie, 1994—; participant Rediscover Jamestown Archaeology Field Sch., 1994, Colonial Williamsburg Tchr. Inst., 1995; mem. 1st Congl. Dist. Acad. Selection Bd., 1988—95; v.p. membership 1st Congl. Dist.; mem. Walworth County Dem. Party, 1972—, vice chair, 1988—91, sec., 1998—; host for congl. aide, 1988—93; program chair, 1997—; county organizer presdl. campaign, 1980; vol. coord. assembly campaign, 1992, 1994, 1996, 1998, 2000; Statutory Party pollworker of Lake Geneva, 1984—. Recipient Youth Leader award Am. Legion, 1976, award VA Bloomfield Twp., 1977, Nat. Girl Scout award for community svc., 1976; Herbert Kohl fellow, 1990. Mem.: NEA (congl. contact team 1986—93, legis. com. 1995—2000, 2002—, Twin Lakes del. to rep. assemblies), ACLU, Concerned Parents and Edn., Tchr. Place and Parent Resources, State and Nat. Coun. Social Studies (curriculum writing team 1991), Twin Lakes Edn. Assn. (local negotiator 1974—98), So. Lakes United Educators (pres. 1979—82, treas. 1982—84, v.p. 1998—99, pub. rels. chair 1986—, editor Membersheet 1987—), Wis. Edn. Assn. (regional pub. rels. com. 1990—92), So. Lakes United Educator-Ret. (pres. 1999—), Wis. Citizen Action, Lakeland Audubon Soc., Nat. Audubon Soc., Habitat for Humanity (Wal. county), People for the Am. Way, Crow Canyon Archaeology Ctr., Archael. Inst. Am., Sierra Club (coord. NEA Dump Watt campaign 1981, environ. Bill Rights campaign 1995). Democrat. Avocations: photography, gardening, reading. Home: 307 Water St Lake Geneva WI 53147-1521 E-mail: jowms@genevaonline.com.

WILLIAMS, JOCELYN JONES, reading educator; b. Greenville, N.C., Sept. 24, 1948; d. William Edward and Elinor Suejette (Albritton) Jones; m. Robert Alexander Simpkins Jr., Sept. 7, 1969 (div. May 1972); m. Oscar James Williams Jr., July 12, 1985 (div. Mar. 1989). BS, Bennett Coll., 1970; MEd, N.C. Cen. U., 1988; MS, N.C. Agrl. & Tech. State U., 1992. Kindergarten/1st grade tchr. Greenville City Schs., 1970-74; elem./reading tchr. Orange County Schs., Hillsborough, N.C., 1974-97; Reading Recovery tchr. leader Durham (N.C.) Pub. Schs., 1997—. Mem. N.C. Reading Recovery Adv. Bd., 1994—, Reading Recovery Coun. N.Am., 1994—. Mem. NEA, ASCD, Internat. Reading Assn., Nat. Assn. Edn. Young Children, N.C. Assn. Educators, Phi Delta Kappa, Alpha Kappa Alpha, Progressive Sertoma Club. Democrat. Baptist. Avocations: reading, singing, sewing, cooking. Home: 47 Celtic Dr Durham NC 27703-2833

WILLIAMS, JODY, political organization administrator; b. Rutland, Vt., Oct. 9, 1950; BA, U. Vt.; MA, Sch. Internat. Tng., Johns Hopkins Sch.; PhD (hon.), Briar Cliff Coll., Marlboro Coll., U. of Vermont, Williams Coll. Past English tchr., Washington, Mex.; former coord. Nicaragua-Honduras Edn. Project; assoc. dir. Children's Project Med. Aid El Salvador, L.A./El Salvador, 1986—92; founder Internat. Campaign to Ban Landmines Vietnam Vet. Found. Am., Washington, 1991—; amb. Internat. Campaign to Ban Landmines, Alexandria, Va., 1997—; founder Sponsor a Mine-Detection Dog program, 1998—. Spkr. in field. Contbr. articles to profl. jours, co-authored After the Guns Fall: The Enduring Legacy of Landmines. Past vol. El Salvadoran rescue group. Recipient Distinguished Peace Leadership award, Nuclear Age Peace Found., Fiat Lux award, Clark U., Nobel Peace Prize, 1997, Hollywood Humanitarian award, 2002. Office: ICBL 110 Maryland Ave NE # 6 Washington DC 20002-5626*

WILLIAMS, JOEL CASH, lawyer; b. Dacula, Ga., Dec. 19, 1942; s. Joel Cash and Cora Belle W.; m. M'Liss Gurneym Dec. 11, 1976 (div.); children: Laurel M'Liss, Morgan Delannoy. BA, Shorter Coll., 1964; LLB, Mercer U., 1967. Bar: Ga., 1966, Ga. (no. dist.), 1967, Ga. (mid. dist.), 1967. Intern Atty. Gen. Ga., Atlanta, 1966, deputy asst. atty. gen., 1967-68, asst. atty. gen., 1968-69; legal counsel U.S. Senator Richard Russell, Washington, 1970-71, U.S. Senator David Gambrell, Washington, 1971; asst. to pres. Savannah (Ga.) Foods & Industry, 1971-78, v.p. corp. affairs, 1978-97; ptnr. Powell, Goldstein, Frazer & Murphy, Atlanta, 1998—. Chmn. adv. bd. 1st Liberty Bank, Savannah, 1993-97. Editor-in-chief Mercer LAw Rev., 1966-67. Chmn. bd. dirs. Savannah C. of C., United Way, Savannah, 1987-88. Mem. State Bar Ga. (corp. coun.), Ga. C. of C. (bd. dirs. 1994—). Office: Powell Goldstein Frazer & Murphy 191 Peachtree St NE Ste 1600 Atlanta GA 30303-1700

WILLIAMS, JOEL MANN, polymer material scientist; b. Suffolk, Va., Apr. 6, 1940; s. Joel Mann and Mildred (Barlow) W.; m. Mary Carol Gregory, Sept. 1, 1962; children: Catherine Reine, Michael Gregory. BS, Coll. William and Mary, 1962; PhD, Northwestern U., 1966. Asst. prof. chemistry U. Minn., Mpls., 1967-68; research chemist E.I. DuPont de Nemours, Waynesboro, Va., 1968-72; mem. staff Los Alamos (N.Mex.) Nat. Lab., 1972-93. Contractor Ray Raskin Assocs., 1995-97; cons. JMC Williams Consultants, 1993—. Author: The Electronic Puzzle, 1994, The Delta State: Molecular Carpooling, 1995, Moles, Bits and Cubes, 1996, The MCAS Way, 1999, Modeling the MCAS Way, 2001; co-author: Advances in Physical Organic Chemistry, 1968, Analytical Chemistry of Liquid Fuel Sources, 1978, Coal Science and Chemistry, 1986. Fellow NIH, 1963-66, NSF, 1966-67. Mem. Sigma Xi. Clubs: Tennis (Los Alamos) (tres. 1984-86), Mountain Mixers Square Dance (treas. 1977-79), Barranca Mesa Pool Assn. (treas. 1975-76). Republican. Roman Catholic. Avocations: skiing, camping, tennis, gardening. Home: 51 Zuni St Los Alamos NM 87544-2647 E-mail: science@swcp.com.

WILLIAMS, JOHN ALAN, secondary education educator, coach; b. Watertown, N.Y., May 30, 1949; s. John F. and Doris (Fuess) W.; m. Ana Maria Delima Moniz, Feb. 22, 1977; children: Timothy John, Katherine Evelyn. BS in Oceanography, U.S. Naval Acad., 1971; MS in Sci. Edn., Syracuse U., 1978; postgrad., SUNY, Oswego, 1989-90. Sci. tchr., coach Liverpool (N.Y.) High Sch., 1977-80, sci. tchr., coach, dir. sci. and tech. fair, 1981—, advisor, coach Olympiad Team, 1987-98; application engr. Hoffman Air & Filtration, Syracuse, N.Y., 1980-81. Coach wrestling team Liverpool High Sch., 1982—, Liverpool Optimist Wrestling Club, 1999—; coach local Pee Wee wrestling team, 1982-96; bd. dirs. sci. fair com. Syracuse Discovery Ctr., 1986-97. Lt. USN, 1971-76, Vietnam. Named Ctrl. N.Y. Sci. Tchr. of Yr. Syracuse Discovery Ctr., 1986-87, Onondaga High Sch. League-North Wrestling Coach of Yr., 1984-85, 88-89, 92-93, 97-98, 2000-01. Mem. Nat. Earth Sci. Tchrs. Assn., United Liverpool Faculty Assn., N.Y. State Sci. Tchrs. Assn. (10 Yr. award 1990), Assn. Sci. Tech. Ctrs. (Honor Roll Tchrs. 1987), Syracuse Tech. Club (Outstanding Tchr. award 1990), NFL (Tchr. of Yr. 1990), Sigma Xi (Outstanding Sci. Tchr. award 1989). Home: 4320 Luna Crse Liverpool NY 13090-2050 Office: Liverpool High Sch 4338 Wetzel Rd Liverpool NY 13090-2098 E-mail: rocksminsandmore@aol.com.

WILLIAMS, JOHN ANDREW, physiology educator, consultant; b. Des Moines, Aug. 3, 1941; s. Harold Southall and Marjorie (Larsen) W.; m. Christa A. Smith, Dec. 26, 1965; children: Rachel Jo, Matthew Dallas. BA, Cen. Wash. State Coll., 1963; MD, PhD, U. Wash., Seattle, 1968. Staff fellow NIH, Bethesda, Md., 1969-71; research fellow U. Cambridge, Eng., 1971-72; from asst. to prof. physiology U. Calif., San Francisco, 1973-87; prof. physiology, chair dept. physiology, prof. internal medicine U. Mich., Ann Arbor, 1987—. Mem. gen. medicine study sect. NIH, Bethesda, 1985-88, NIDDK, DDK-C study sect., 1991-95. Contbr. numerous articles to profl. jours.; editor Am. Jour. Physiology: Gastrointestinal Physiology, 1985-91; assoc. editor Jour. Clin. Investigation, 1997-2001. Trustee Friends Sch. in Detroit, 1992—2000. NIH grantee, 1973—. Mem. Am. Physiol. Soc. (Hoffman LaRoche prize 1985, mem. coun. 1996-99, pres.-elect 2002), Am. Soc. Cell Biology, Am. Soc. Clin. Investigation, Am. Gastroenterology Assn., Am. Pancreatic Assn. (pres. 1985-86). Democrat. Home: 1115 Woodlawn Ave Ann Arbor MI 48104-3956 Office: Dept Physiology Univ of Mich Med Sch Ann Arbor MI 48109 E-mail: jawillms@umich.edu.

WILLIAMS, JOHN ANDREW, computer specialist; b. Upper Darby, Pa., June 26, 1964; s. Richard John and Charlotte Jean (Franklin) Williams. BS in Computer Sci., Pa. State U., 1986; MEd, Kutztown State U., 1989, MA in Math., 1990. Foreman R&R Christmas Trees, New Ringgold, Pa., 1979-86; programmer, analyst HHC Discom, Harrisburg, 1986-91; math specialist/tutor coord. Dept. Devel. Studies, Kutztown, 1986-90; commd. 2d lt. Pa. ANG, 1988; bn. chem. officer aviation Bn. Chem. Office/Aviation Bn., Ft. Indiantown Gap, Pa., 1991-94; computer specialist Navy Fleet Materials Support Office, Mechanicsburg, 1990-94; programmer Pottsville Rep., Pottsville, 1994—; platoon leader 128th Chem. Co., 1995—. Team author mil. publs. Grad. Coun. Kutztown State U., 1988-89; mem. softball team New Ringgold (Pa.) Ch. League, 1991—. Mem. New Ringgold Fire Co., New Visions Racquetball Club, New Ringgold Little League, Pa. Army Nat. Guard Assn. Republican. Baptist. Avocations: sports, camping, music. Home: RR 3 Box 17A New Ringgold PA 17960-9702

WILLIAMS, JOHN ANDREW, lawyer; b. Toccoa, Ga., Oct. 18, 1962; s. Sanford Herbert and Linda (Way) W.; m. Dawn Marie Alsop, Aug. 10, 1996; children, Jeannie, Katie. BA in Polit. Sci., U. Ga., 1984, MA in Polit. Sci., 1986; JD, NYU, 1993. Bar: S.C. 1993, N.C. 1997, Ga. 1999, U.S. Dist. Ct. S.C. 1993, U.S. Dist. Ct. (mid. dist.) N.C. 1997, U.S. Dist. Ct. (we. dist.) N.C. 1998, U.S. Ct. Appeals (4th cir.) 1996. Assoc. Nelson, Mullins, Riley & Scarborough, Greenville, S.C., 1993-95; pvt. practice, 1995-96; assoc. Edwards, Ballard, Clark, Barrett and Carlson, Winston-Salem, N.C., 1996-99, Hayes, O'Brien, O'Rourke, Hogan & Pickert, Atlanta, 2000—00, Rachelson & White, Atlanta, 2000—. Mem. NYU Ctr. for Labor and Employment Law, N.Y.C., 1996-99. Contbr. articles to profl. jours. Chmn. Upstate Young Reps., Greenville, 1995-96, Bob Dole for Pres., Greenville County, S.C., 1996. 1st lt. USAF, 1986-90. Mem. ABA, N.C. Bar Assn., S.C. Bar Assn. Republican. Methodist. Avocations: reading, jogging, politics. Home: 981 Memory Ln Lawrenceville GA 30044-2614 Office: Rachelson & White PC 5555 Glenridge Connector Ste 425 Atlanta GA 30342

WILLIAMS, JOHN CHARLES, II, data processing executive; b. Dayton, Ohio, Jan. 29, 1955; s. John Charles and Frances Jerline (McKean) W.; m. Diane Catherine Busch, Feb. 11, 1978; 1 child, Tabitha Anne. BSBA, postgrad., U. Phoenix, 2001—. Programmer Kino Starr, Tucson, 1977-78, City of Boise (Idaho), 1978; data processing mgr. Nat. Assn. Ind. Businesses, Inc., Boise, 1978-79; chief exec. officer Williams Rsch. Assoc., 1979-80, MRW Data Systems, Inc., Tucson, 1981-82, Computer Security, Tucson, 1983-86, Modern Magic, Tucson, 1986-88; tech. support dir. Program Sources, Inc., 1988-89; chief exec. officer Cactus Explosives Corp., 1989-90, Systems Cons. Assocs., Tucson, 1990-94; sr. systems analyst Desert Diamond Casino, 1994-97; program analyst Muscular Dystrophy Assn., Tuscon, 1997—. Area coord. Kolbe For Congress Campaign, Tucson, 1984; Ariz. Rep. State Committeeman, 1986—; mem. Ariz. Sonora Desert Mus., Tucson, 1983—. Republican. Avocations: leather crafting, horsemanship, numismatics.

WILLIAMS, JOHN EDWARD, lawyer; b. Atlanta, May 21, 1946; s. Edward Carl and Mary E. (Griffin) W.; m. Kristin Forsberg, May 22, 1976; children: Alexandra, Courtney, Charles. BA, Yale U., 1968; JD, U. Va., 1974; LLM in Taxation, Georgetown U., 1977. Bar: Va. 1974, D.C. 1975, U.S. Dist. Ct. D.C. 1975, U.S. Tax Ct. 1975, U.S. Ct. Appeals (D.C. cir.) 1975, U.S. Supreme Ct. 1977. Law clk. to Judge Charles R. Richey U.S. Dist. Ct. (D.C. dist.), 1974-75; assoc. Patton, Boggs & Blow, Washington, 1975-78, Cadwalader, Wickersham & Taft, Washington, 1978-81; asst. to the commr. IRS, 1981-84; tax counsel Ropes & Gray, 1984-86; ptnr. David & Hagner, P.C., 1986-90, Winston & Strawn, Washington, 1990-2000. Mem. Jud. Conf. of D.C. Circuit, 1978, 82, 85, 87, 92. With U.S. Army, 1968-74. Mem. ABA (tax sect., chmn. tech. subcom., adminstrv. practice com. 1986-88), Met., Yale N.Y.C., Heritage Hunt Club. Home: 4908A John Ticer Dr Alexandria VA 22304 Office: Ste One 407 N Washington St Alexandria VA 22314 E-mail: williamslawfirm@hotmail.com.

WILLIAMS, JOHN FRANKLIN, real estate broker; b. Durham, N.C., Apr. 23, 1959; m. Stacey Williams. BSBA, Appalachian State U., 1981; MBA, So. Ill. U., 1984. Cert. real estate brokerage mgr., residential specialist, relocation profl., real estate appraiser. Computer analyst McDonnell Douglas, St. Louis, 1981-86; real estate broker Christian Bros. Realty, Bridgeton, Mo., 1986-92, Re/Max Properties West, Chesterfield, 1992—. Mem. St. Louis Assn. of Realtors (multimillion dollar club 1989-91), Mo. Assn. of Realtors (life mem. million dollar club 1989). Avocation: karate. Office: Re/Max Properties West Ste 250 16100 Swingley Ridge Rd Chesterfield MO 63017-1788

WILLIAMS, JOHN FRANKLIN, anesthesiologist educator and administrator; b. N.Y.C., May 17, 1948; m. Delia DePaola; 1 child, Daniel Stephen. BA, Boston U., 1970; MSc in Health Care Adminstrn., The London Sch. Econs., 1973; MPH in Health Svcs. Adminstrn., Yale U., 1975; MD, The George Washington U., 1979, EdD in Human Resource Devel., 1996. Diplomate Am. Bd. Anesthesiology; MD, D.C., Md. Intern U.S. Office of Edn. Bur. of Higher Edn., Washington, 1970; asst. to dir. admissions Wheelock Coll., Boston, 1970-72, asst. to pres., 1971-72; rsch. coord. The Martin Luther King Jr. Afro-Am. Ctr., 1972-73; dir. health and employment The Nat. Vets. Frat., Inc., New Haven, 1973-75; intern in ob-gyn. The George Washington Univ. Med. Ctr., Washington, 1979-80, residency in anesthesiology, 1980-82, chief resident in anesthesiology, 1981-82, fellowship in critical care medicine, 1982-83; co-dir. Coronary/ICU The Capitol Hosp., 1983-84; asst. prof. anesthesiology, co-dir. ICU The George Washington Univ. Med. Ctr., 1984—; lt. commissioned corps, USPHS, dep. dir. anesthesia Gallup (N.Mex.) Indian Med. Ctr., 1984-85; asst. prof. anesthesiology, co-dir. ICU The George Washington U. Med. Ctr., Washington, 1985-89, assoc. prof. anesthesiology, co-dir. ICU, 1989—; assoc. dean for admissions The George Washington U. Sch. Medicine & Health Scis., 1993—99; dean, v.p. for health affairs Wash. U. Sch. of Med., 1999—. Internat. experience on behalf of the George Washington U. Med. Ctr., The Spl. Saudi MD Program, 1991—, Thailand Project for Undergrad. and Grad. Med. Edn., 1995—, Lill Found. Grad. Med. Edn. Program, 1995—, Operation Smile Internat., 1996—. Contbr. numerous articles to profl. jours. Mem. Found. for Critical Care, 1985—, chmn. waiting rm. brochure, 1985-86, chmn. family support program, 1985-90, chmn. profl. edn. com., 1989-90; coord. Disaster Drill for the D.C. Nat. Guard, 1985-87; mem. Mayor's Office of Drug Control Policy, 1989-90, D.C. Drug Control Policy Strategy Team, D.C. Police Chiefs Task Force on Youth Violence, 1991-93, bd. dirs. Superleaders, 1992—, adv. coun. Med. 1995—, Anesthesia, 1992—, bd. dirs. Internat. Med. Data Stds. Found., The George Washington Univ. Health Plan, 1996—; humanitarian med. missions Hosp. Canape Vere, Port Au Prince, Haiti, 1983-86, Kenyatta Gen. Hosp., Nairobi, Kenya, 1987-88, Hangzhous Plastic Surgery Hosp., 1990, Meizou Hosp., Peoples Republic of China, 1991, Shantou Hosp., Peoples Republic of China, 1993, United Arab Emirates, 1993. Recipient Lange Med. Book award, 1977, Mosby Med. Book award for scholastic excellence, 1979, Commendation for Implementation of Pathnet Lab. Info. System, 1987, The Am. Med. Student Assn. Golden Apple award for Outstanding Clin. Tchr. of Yr., 1988, Commendation for Drug Strategy Team Report, Mayor's Office of Drug Control Policy, 1990, The Disting. Alumni award for outstanding contbns. to cmty. and profession, 1990, The People's medal Mayor of Guang Zhou, 1991; grantee Pharmco/Wyeth Ayerst, 1990-93, Robert Wood Johnson, 1995—. Mem. APHA, AMA, N.Y. Acad. Scis., Am. Soc. Anesthesiologists, Soc. Critical Care Medicine. Democrat. Roman Catholic. Home: 5881 Nebraska Ave NW Washington DC 20015-1267 Office: The George Washington U Sch Medicine & Health Scis 2300 Eye St NW # 615 Washington DC 20037-2336*

WILLIAMS, JOHN HORTER, civil engineer, oil, gas, telecommunications and allied products distribution company executive; b. Havana, Cuba, Aug. 17, 1918; s. Charles P. and Alice Magruder (Dyer) W.; m. Emily Alice Ijams, June 6, 1942 (dec.); children: John H., Burch L, S. Miller; m. Joanne Harwell Simpson., Feb. 1, 1975. BS, Yale U., 1940. Registered profl. engr., Okla., Minn. With The Williams Cos. Inc., Tulsa, 1940-42, 46-50, pres., dir., 1950-70, chmn., chief exec. officer, 1971-78, now hon. dir. Bd. dirs. Apco Argentina, Inc., Unit Corp., Westwood Corp., Willbros Group, Inc. Served with USNR, 1942-46. Decorated Order of Condor of Andes (Bolivia); named Okla. Hall of Fame, 1977; recipient Outstanding Okla. Oil Man awad Okla.-Kans. Oil and Gas Assn., 1982, Disting. Svc. award Nat. Petroleum Hall of Fame, 1985; inducted into Okla. Commerce and Industry Hall of Honor, 1986, Tulsa Hall of Fame, 1993. Mem. ASCE, Yale Engring. Assn. Office: The Williams Cos Inc 10th Fl 1800 S Baltimore Ave Tulsa OK 74119-5210

WILLIAMS, JOHN HOWARD, retired architect; b. Littleton, N.C., Feb. 07; s. Ruffin Hampton and Emma Maude (Fitts) W.; m. Thelma Lorena McGuffin, June 9, 1944; children: Juan McGuffin and Jeffrey Howard. BS in Archtl. Engring. with honors, N.C. Agrl. and Tech. U., 1942; Diploma/Architects Rev., U. Va./No. Extension, Falls Church, 1958; postgrad., U. Minn., 1965. Registered architect. Draftsman, architect, asst. chief Tech. Svc. Section/Div. Hosp., Pub. Health Svc., Washington, 1947-67; chief facilities planning br., Fed. Health Programs Svcs. HHS, 1967-73, chief facilities planning and constrn., Indian Health Svc., 1973-84. Cons. health care facilities. Co-dir. hosp. systems studies, 1971, bed determination methodology, 1979; dir. health facilities planning manuels, 1980, cost estimating system, 1981. Vestryman Calvary Episcopal Ch., Washington, 1957; mem. Brotherhood of St. Andrew, Washington. Recipient Merrick medal for excellence in mechanic arts N.C. Agrl. and Tech. U., Greensboro, 1942, Outstanding Svc. and Dedication award Indian Health Svc., Health and Human Svcs.; established John H. Williams scholarship in archtl. engring. N.C. A&T State U., 1980. Mem. AIA (emeritus), Acad. of Architecture for Health, Forum for Health Care Planning, Nat. Soc. Archtl. Engrs., Alpha Kappa Mu, Kappa Alpha Psi. Avocations: tutoring, travel, golf, reading, TV.

WILLIAMS, JOHN JAMES, JR. architect; b. Denver, July 13, 1949; s. John James and Virginia Lee (Thompson) W.; m. Mary Serene Morck, July 29, 1972. BArch, U. Colo., 1974. Registered architect, Colo., Calif., Idaho, Va., Utah, Nev., N.Mex., Wyo., Ohio, Nebr. Project architect Gensler Assoc. Architects, Denver, 1976, Heinzman Assoc. Architects, Boulder, Colo., 1977, EZTH Architects, Boulder, 1978-79; prin. Knudson/Williams PC, 1980-82, Faber, Williams & Brown, Boulder, 1982-86, John Williams & Assocs., Denver, 1986-97; John Williams Architecture P.C., 1997—. Panel chmn. U. Colo. World Affairs Conf.; vis. faculty U. Colo. Sch. Architecture and Planning, Coll. Environ. Design, 1986-91; mem. dean's adv. bd. Coll. Arch. and Planning, 2000—. Author (with others) State of Colorado architect licensing law, 1986. Commr. Downtown Boulder Mall Commn., 1985-88; bd. dirs. U. Colo. Fairway Club, 1986-88; mem. Gov's. Natural Hazard Mitigation Coun., State of Colo., 1990. Recipient Teaching Honorarium, U. Colo. Coll. Architecture and Planning, 1977, 78, 79, 80, 88, Excellence in Design and Planning award City of Boulder, 1981, 82, Citation for Excellenc, WOOD Inc., 1982, 93, Disting. Profl. Svc. award Coll. Environ. Design U. Colo., 1988, James Sudler Svc. award AIA, Denver, 1998. Mem. AIA (sec. 1988, bd. dirs. Colo. North chpt. 1985-86, chair Colo. govtl. affairs com. 1995-98, Design award 1993, 2001, pres. 1990, sec. Colo. chpt. 1988, ednl. fund Fisher I traveling scholar 1988, state design conf. chair 1991, North chpt. Design award 1993, treas. Denver chpt. 1998, v.p. 1999, pres. edn. Colo. chpt. 2001, Disting. Svc. award Colo. chpt. 2001), Architects and Planners of Boulder (v.p. 1982), Nat. Coun. Architect Registration Bd., Nat. Golf Found. (sponsor), Kappa Sigma (chpt. pres. 1970). Avocations: golf, polit. history, fitness and health. Home: 1031 Turnberry Cir Louisville CO 80027-9594 Office: John Williams Architecture PC 3012 Huron St Ste 200 Denver CO 80202-1032

WILLIAMS, JOHN LEE, lawyer; b. Nashville, Dec. 23, 1942; s. Leslie Elwood and Gladys Mae (Ridings) W.; m. Norma Jean Givens, May 27, 1967; 1 child, Jacob Andrew. BA, Tenn. Technol. U., 1964; JD, U. Tenn., 1967. Bar: Tenn 1967. Ptnr. Porch, Peeler & Williams, Waverly, Tenn., 1967-78, Porch, Peeler, Williams Thomason, Waverly, 1978—; asst. dist. atty. 23d Jud. Cir. Ct. Tenn., 1972-74; judge Ct. Gen. Sessions of Humphreys County, Tenn., 1978-82. County atty. Humphreys County, 1968—72, 1982—86, 1994—; city atty. City of Waverly, 1978—, City of McEwen, Tenn., 1978—, City of Lobelville, Tenn., 1985—89; gen. counsel Meriwether Lewis Elec. Coop., Centerville, Tenn., 1980—. State legal counsel Tenn. Jaycees, 1970; treas., sec. Humphreys County Dem. Exec. Com., 1978-2001; chmn. Humphreys County Election Commn., 1968-72. Col. U.S. Army ret. Mem.: Humphreys County Bar Assn. (pres. 1978—), Tenn. Bar Assn. (ho. of dels.), Masons (master 1985, 1999). Home: 1739 Ogden Rd Mc Ewen TN 37101 E-mail: john.williams@porchpeeler.com.

WILLIAMS, JOHN MICHAEL, physical therapist, sports medicine educator; b. Columbus, Ohio, Oct. 19, 1951; s. James Hutchison and Helen Lucille (Knight) W.; m. Karen Sue Eaglen, June 23, 1973; children: Michelle Rene, Elizabeth Ann. BS in Phys. Therapy, Ohio State U., 1975, MS in Allied Medicine, 1983. Lic. phys. therapist, Ohio. Asst. dir. phys. therapy Licking Meml. Hosp., Newark, 1975-80; pvt. practice Westerville, 1977-80; asst. dir. rehab. St. Anthony Hosp., Columbus, 1980-88; from chief phys. therapist to dir. phys. and sports medicine St. Ann's Hosp., Westerville, 1988-95; mgr. Nova Care Rehab., 1995-97. Clin. instr. Ohio State U., Columbus, 1984—, faculty instr., 1997—; adj. faculty sports medicine Otterbein Coll., Westerville, 1989-96; cons. Licking County Arthritis Found., Newark, 1978-80; phys. therapy adv. bd. Ctrl. Ohio Tech. Coll., Newark, 1978-2001; bd. dirs. SAHCU Credit Union, Westerville; asst. prof. phys. and occupl. therapy programs U. Findlay, Ohio, 1996-2000. Author monograph. Med. team capt. Columbus Marathon, 1989—, U.S. Men's Olympic Marathon Trials, Columbus, 1992, U.S. Men's Nat. Marathon Championships, 1991, 92. Lt. col. USAR, 1969—; exec. and spl. ops. officer 914th Combat Support Hosp., 2000—. Decorated Army Commendation medal with 3 oak leaf clusters, Meritorious Svc. medal; recipient Mayor's award for vol. svc. City of Columbus, 1993. Mem. Am. Acad. Med. Adminstrs., Am. Phys. Therapy Assn. (rep. to state assembly 1987—, state of Ohio facutly liaison to state bd. dirs. 2000—). Episcopalian. Avocations: volleyball, golf, sailing. Home: 132 Ormsbee Ave Westerville OH 43081-1151

WILLIAMS, JOHN N. dean; DDS Dental-Gen. Practice, U. Louisville, 1980. Dean U. Louisville, 2001—. Office: 501 S Preston St #227 Louisville KY 40202*

WILLIAMS, JOHN RODMAN, theologian, educator; b. Clyde, N.C., Aug. 21, 1918; s. John Rodman and Odessa Lee (Medford) W.; m. Johanna SerVaas, Aug. 6, 1949; children: John, Lucinda Lee, David Bert. AB, Davidson Coll., 1939; BD, Union Theol. Sem., 1943, ThM, 1944; PhD, Columbia U., 1954. Ordained to ministry Presbyn. Ch., 1943. Chaplain USNR, 1944-46; chaplain, assoc. prof. philosophy Beloit Coll., 1949-52; pastor First Presbyn. Ch., Rockford, Ill., 1952-59; prof. systematic theology and philosophy of religion Austin Presbyn. Theol. Sem., 1959-72; prof. Christian doctrine, pres. Melodyland Sch. Theology, Anaheim, Calif., 1972-82; prof. Christian theology Regent U., Virginia Beach, Va., 1982—. Author: Contemporary Existentialism and Christian Faith, 1965, The Era of the Spirit, 1971, The Pentecostal Reality, 1972, Ten Teachings, 1974, The Gift of the Holy Spirit Today, 1980, Renewal Theology, Vol. 1. God, the World, and Redemption, Vol. 2, 1988, Salvation, the Holy Spirit and Christian Living, Vol. 3, 1990, The Church, the Kingdom, and Last Things, 1992, Renewal Theology, 3 vols. in one, 1996. Home: 608 Fleet Dr Virginia Beach VA 23454-7344 E-mail: rodmwil@regent.edu. *There is only one ultimate "Who", Jesus of Nazareth, in whose light all the rest of us are but dimly burning candles.*

WILLIAMS, JOHN TAYLOR, lawyer; b. Cambridge, Mass., June 19, 1938; s. Paul Merchant Taylor and Audrey Arlene Dowling; m. Leonora Hall; children: Caleb, Jared, Nathaniel. AB, Harvard U., 1960; LLB, U. Pa., 1965. Bar: Mass. 1965, U.S. Dist. Ct. Mass., U.S. Ct. Appeals (1st cir.), U.S. Supreme Ct. Corp. loans officer State St. Bank & Trust Co., Boston, 1960-62; from assoc. to ptnr. Haussermann, Davison & Shattuck, 1965-83; ptnr. Palmer & Dodge, 1983—. Bd. dirs. Blackwell Sci. Inc.; lectr. on 1st amendment, copyright, pub. and intellectual property law for Practicing Law Inst., Mass. CLE/New Eng. Law Inst., Nat. Assn. Archivists, Boston Patent Lawyers Assn., others; apptd. mem. U.S. Courthouse Arts Comm., U.S. Publ. Del. to China, 1993; mem. lit. panel Nat. Endowment for the Arts, 1990, 91, 94, mem. presentation and creation panel, 1996. Author: (screenplay) Rolf in the Woods, 1987, (screenplay) Toussaint L'Overture, 1999, (with E. Gabriel Perle) The Publishing Law Handbook, 2 vols. (revised annually); contbg. author: Legal Problems in Book Publishing, 1981, 84, 86; contbg. editor: Small Voices and Great Trumpets: Minorities and the Media, 1980. Bd. dirs. City of Cambridge Arts Coun., 1973-83, chmn., 1981-83; bd. dirs. Ploughshares Inc., 1988-89; trustee Arthur Fiedler Meml. Inc., 1983—, Boston Philharm. Orch., 1983-85, Petra Found., 1988—; trustee, gen. counsel Inst. Contemporary Art, 1970-92; mem. corp. Mass. Gen. Hosp., 1985—; mem. Patent and Tech Conflicts Coms., 1985-91; clk. John F. Kennedy Meml. Commn. Inc., 1986—; mem. adv. bd. Provincetown Fine Arts Work Ctr., 1992—. Mrm. ABA (sect. patent, trademark, copyright law, chmn. com. on authors 1978-81, communications and entertainment law forum coms.), Boston Bar Assn. (former chmn. com. on delivery of legal svcs. to indigent), Lawyers' Com. for Civil Rights under Law (chmn. steering com. 1988-91), Mass. Bar Assn. (bus. law and computer law sects.), Nat. Lawyers' Com. for Civil Rights (bd. dirs. 1989—), Tavern Club (Boston). Home: 9 Orchard St Cambridge MA 02140-1321 Office: Palmer & Dodge 1 Beacon St Ste 24 Boston MA 02108-3106

WILLIAMS, J(OHN) TILMAN, insurance executive, real estate broker, city official; b. Detroit, Feb. 26, 1925; s. Aubrey and Martha (Lou) W.; m. Sally Jane Robinson, Aug. 22, 1947; children: Leslie Ann, Martha Lou. BS in Agr, Mich. State U., 1951. Pres. Satellite Ins. Brokerage, Garden Grove, Calif., 1959—. Pres. Satellite Real Estate, Satellite Mortgage & Loan Co. Mayor Garden Grove, 1976-78, re-elected, 1987, mem. coun., 1980-92, apptd. vice mayor, 1989—; mem. Ad Hoc Com. on Property Tax to Limit Govt. Spending with Spirit of 13 Initiative; elected to Orange County Dem. Cen. Com., 68th Assembly Dist., 1996; past pres. Garden Grove High Sch. Band Boosters; trustee Garden Grove Unified Sch. Dist., 2000—. With USAAF, World War II, PTO. Mem. Bd. Realtors, Ind. Ins. Agts. Assn., Orange County Esperanto Assn. (pres. 1985—), Am. Legion, VFW. Clubs: Toastmasters (Anaheim, Calif.); Fifty-Plus Sr. Citizens of Garden Grove (pres. 1986—). Lodges: Lions, Elks. Democrat. Home: 11241 Chapman Ave Garden Grove CA 92840-3301 Office: 12311 Harbor Blvd Garden Grove CA 92840-3809 *Service to one's fellowman and community is the greatest avocation and pleasure one can follow.*

WILLIAMS, JOHN TROY, librarian, educator; b. Oak Park, Ill., Mar. 11, 1924; s. Michael Daniel and Donna Marie (Shaffer) W.; B.A., Central Mich. U., 1949; M.A. in Libr. Sci., U. Mich., 1951, M.A., 1954; Ph.D., Mich. State U., 1973. Reference libr. U. Mich., Ann Arbor, 1955-59; instr. Bowling Green (Ohio) State U., 1959-60; reference librarian Mich. State U., East Lansing, 1960-62; 1st asst. reference dept. Flint (Mich.) Pub. Library, 1962-65; head reference svcs., Purdue U., West Lafayette, Ind., 1965-72; head pub. svcs. No. Ill. U., Dekalb, 1972-75; asst. dean, asst. univ. libr. Wright State U., Dayton, Ohio, 1975-80; vis. scholar U. Mich., Ann Arbor, 1980— ; cons. in field. Served with U.S. Army, 1943-46. Mich. State fellow, 1963-64; HEW fellow, 1971-72. Mem. Am. Libr. Assn., Spl. Libraries Assn., Am. Soc. for Info. Scis., Am. Sociol. Assn., AAUP, Coun. on Fgn. Rels. Contbr. articles to profl. jours. Home: PO Box 7531 Ann Arbor MI 48107-7531

WILLIAMS, JOHN WESLEY, fine arts educator; b. Memphis, Feb. 25, 1928; s. Wesley Alfred and Anna Belle (Curtis) W.; m. Mary Ellen Schmidt, Dec. 26, 1955; children: Maxwell, Katherine, Sarah, Cyril, Elena, Amelia. Student, Duke U., 1948-50; BA, Yale U., 1952; MA, U. Mich., 1953, PhD, 1960. Instr., assoc. prof. Swarthmore Coll., Pa., 1960-72; prof. fine arts U. Pitts., 1972—, Disting. Svc. prof., 1993-2000. Dir. Internat. Center Medieval Art, N.Y.C., 1982-85 Author: Early Spanish Illum, 1977, Apocalypse in Spain, 1991, The Illustrated Beatus, 1994. Served with USMC, 1946-48. Guggenheim fellow, 1984-85, Inst. for Advanced Study member, 1991-92. Home: 749 S Linden Ave Pittsburgh PA 15208-2814

WILLIAMS, JOHN YOUNG, merchant banker; b. Cordele, Ga., Apr. 13, 1943; s. George Wilmer and Minnie Converse (Roberts) W.; m. Julian Perdue Boykin; m. Joyce, Isabel. BS in Indsl. Engrng., Ga. Inst. Tech., 1965; MBA in Fin., Harvard U., 1969. CFA, Ga. Assoc. Kuhn, Loeb & Co., N.Y.C., 1969-71; asst. v.p. Stone & Webster Securities Corp., 1971-74, Chem. Bank, N.Y.C., 1974-75; mng. dir. Dean Witter Reynolds, Inc., Atlanta, 1975-84; sr. v.p., ltd. ptnr. Bear Stearns & Co., 1984-85; mng. dir. Robinson Humphrey Co., 1985-87; mng. dir., co-founder Grubb & Williams, Ltd., 1987—, Equity South Ptnrs., 1995—. Bd. dirs. Tech Data Corp., Clearwater, Fla., Williams Group Internat., Inc., Atlanta, Carstar Automotive, Inc., Kansas City, Kans., Am. Screen Art, Inc., Knoxville. 1st lt. U.S. Army, 1965-67, Korea. Fellow Soc. Internat. Bus. Fellows (sec. 1988-89); mem. Assn. for Investment Mgmt. and Rsch., Assn. for Corp. Growth (pres. 1983-84), Harvard Bus. Sch. Club (pres. 1982-83), Phi Delta Theta (alumni pres. 1980-81). Episcopalian. Avocation: military history. Home: 750 Arden Close NW Atlanta GA 30327-1275 Office: Equity South Advisors LLC 3399 Peachtree Rd NE Ste 1790 Atlanta GA 30326-1151

WILLIAMS, JOHN ZIGLER, anesthesiologist; b. Washington, 1927; s. Paul Lyle Sr. and Beulah Rebecca (Zigler) Williams; m. Barbara Dorothy Krueger, Oct. 28, 1961; children: Karen Lynn, Lisa Carol. BS, U. Md., 1954, MD, 1956. Intern Harrisburg Hosp., 1956-57; resident St. Joseph Hosp., Joliet, Ill., 1957-59; with Copley Meml. Hosp., Aurora. Mem. AMA, Am. Soc. Anesthesiology, Am. Bd. Anesthesiology, Kane County Med. Soc. E-mail: jzwill@aol.com.

WILLIAMS, JOSEPH CLAUDE, physician assistant; b. Terre Haute, Ind., Dec. 16, 1948; s. Farrell and Doris Alma (McKean) W.; m. Sharon Lee Wilson, Oct. 21, 1978; children: Jennifer Lynn, Emily Ruth, Gabrielle Rose. BS, U. Ill., 1971; AS in Physician Assisting, Cin. Tech. Coll., 1978. Cert. Nat. Commn. for Cert. Phys. Assts. Orderly Casey (Ill.) Nursing Home, 1965-67, 71-73; clk. Wells Dept. Store, Waterloo, Iowa, 1973-74; surg. orderly Schoitz Meml. Hosp., 1974-75; tchr. sci. Crossville (Ill.) H.S., 1975-76; physician's asst. Casey Med. Ctr., 1978-83, U.S. Penitentiary, Terre Haute, 1983—. Mem. bd. deciding importance of duplication of med. svcs. in several ctrl. Ill. counties involving cert. of need determinations, Champaign, 1985-87. Elder Cmty. Christian Ch., Casey. Mem. Nat. Acad. Physician Assts. Home: 25 SE 8th St Casey IL 62420-2012 Office: US Penitentiary PO Box 33 4200 Bureau Rd N Terre Haute IN 47808

WILLIAMS, JOSEPH DALTON, pharmaceutical company executive; b. Washington, Aug. 15, 1926; s. Joseph Dalton and Jane (Day) W.; m. Mildred E. Bellaire, June 28, 1973; children: Terri, Daniel. BS in Pharmacy, U. Nebr., 1950; DSc (hon.), Union U., 1991, U. Nebr., 1989; LHD (hon.), Albany Coll. Pharmacy, Union U., 1980, Rutgers U., 1987, Long Island U., 1988; DSc (hon.), Phila. Coll. Pharmacy and Sci., 1988, Long Island U., 1988, Albany Coll. Pharmacy of Union U., 1991; D Human Svcs. (hon.), Caldwell Coll., 1989; LLD (hon.), Bethune-Cookman Coll., 1990, Coll. St. Elizabeth, 1990, Seton Hall U., 1990, U. Md., 1991, St. Augustine Coll., 1992. Pres. Parke-Davis Co., Detroit, 1973-76; pres. pharm. group Warner-Lambert Co., Morris Plains, N.J., 1976-77; pres. Internat. Group, 1977-79; pres., dir. Warner-Lambert Corp., 1979-80, pres., chief operating officer, 1980-84, chmn., CEO, 1985-91, chmn. exec. com., 1991-97; retired, 1997. Bd. dirs. AT&T, 1984-1997, J.C. Penny & Co., 1985-1998, Exxon Corp., 1985-1997, Rockefeller Fin. Svcs. Inc., Rockefeller and Co., Inc., 1992-1999, Eckerd Corp., 1997-2000. Trustee emeritus Columbia U. With USNR, 1943—46. Mem. Am. Pharm. Assn., Links Club, Pine Valley Golf Club, Baltusrol Golf Club, Mid Ocean Club. Office: Warner-Lambert Co 55 Madison Ave Morristown NJ 07960-7397

WILLIAMS, JOSEPH SCOTT, energy and natural resources company executive, city commissioner; b. Chgo., Nov. 10, 1951; s. Hagle Eugene and Helen Elizabeth (Mellon) W.; m. Tamalou Mitchell, June 10, 1972 (dec. Apr. 2000); children: Troy Scott, Ari Layne. Welding Cert., John A. Logan Coll., Carterville, Ill., 1971; Cert. in Mining Tech., Rend Lake Coll., Ina, Ill., 1975. Dealer S&S Motors, West Frankfort, Ill., 1970-74; coal mine laborer Peabody Coal Co., Freeburg, 1973; coal mine electrician Old Ben Coal Co., Sesser, 1973-76; alt. energy cons. Helios Devel. Co., West Frankfort, 1977-83; instr. Rend Lake Coll., Ina, 1979-82; coal mine repairman Freeman United Coal Co., Pittsburg, Ill., 1979-87; mgr. ops. Royal Talon Co., West Frankfort, 1989—, pres., 2000—, Egyptian Energies, Inc., West Frankfort, 1987—, Horn Dimond Coal Co., West Frankfort, 1991-99; commr. of public health and safety City of West Frankfort, Ill., 1999—. Mem. Ill. State Mining Bd., Springfield, 1993—, sec., 1996—; pres. United Mine Workers Labor Union 9878, West Frankfort, 1990—. Precinct committeeman Rep. Party, Franklin County, 1988-94; reg. coord. Citizens for Sue Suter, 1990, Citizens for Jim Ryan, 1994; transition adv. com. mem. Jim Ryan Ill. Atty. Gen., Chgo., 1995; advisor, dir. Ill. YMCA Youth and Govt., 1992—. Mem. Ill. Oil and Gas Assn., West Frankfort C. of C. (dir. 1988—), Moose, Masons (32 deg.), Shriner (Krazy Klown unit dir. 1997-99), Lions (pres. 1992-93). Avocations: motorcycling, collecting automobiles and memorabilia. Office: Egyptian Energies Inc 107 S Van Buren St PO Box 127 West Frankfort IL 62896-0127

WILLIAMS, JOYCE MARILYN, artist, business owner; b. Waterbury, Conn., Sept. 12, 1933; d. Carl Vosburgh and Arline Dorothy (Cummings) Miller; m. Ralph Gray, Apr. 8, 1949 (div. 1955); children: Diane Leslie, Jerri Joyce-Gray; m. Charles Edward Williams, July 24, 1958; 1 child, Carol Lea. Grad. h.s., San Mateo, Calif., 1950. Pres., owner JC Enterprises, Phoenix, 1993—. Art instr. Sta. KHIZ-TV, Victorville, Calif., 1995; judge fine art San Bernardino County Fair, Victorville, 1995. Author: (instrn. books) Painting Portraits, 1994, Painting Horses, 1995; author, artist: (videos) Painting Portraits, 1993, Painting Horses, Wildlife, 1995; numerous portrait commns., U.S. and Can.; commd. cover art for world's largest Arabian horse show. Recipient numerous 1st pl. awards various art shows, 1985-95. Mem. High Desert Art League, High Desert GD (editor newsletter 1992-95). Avocations: teaching art, giving demonstrations, painting for galleries, writing, selling paintings on ebay. Office: JC Enterprises 3405 N Sinton Rd #220 Colorado Springs CO 80907- E-mail: artvideos@aol.com.

WILLIAMS, JUANITA ROSALIE, artist; b. Zanesville, Ohio, Aug. 7, 1933; d. Joseph Russell and Gladys Lucille (Worden) Somers; m. Roy George Williams, Feb. 16, 1952 (div. 2002); children: Karin Sue Williams Brandi, Kenneth Roy. Grad. high sch., Zanesville. Juror Bexley (Ohio) Art Guild, Capital U., 1984. One-woman shows include Collector's Gallery Columbus Mus. Fine Art, Ohio, 1972, Pomerene Fine Arts Ctr., 1991, McDonough Gallery, Marietta Coll., 1991, Blue Sky Gallery, Columbus, 1992, exhibited in group shows at Zanesville Art Ctr., 1981, 1990, Franklin U., Columbus, Ohio, 1985, Marietta (Ohio) Coll., 1991, Pomerene Fine Arts Ctr., Coshocton, Ohio, 1991, No. Ariz. U., 1992, French Art Colony, Gallipolis, Ohio, 1992, Soc. Layerists in Multi-Media, San Miguel Allende, Mex., 1996, Marlborough, Eng., 1997, Sirius Gallery, Santa Fe, 2001, Represented in permanent collections Zanesville Art Ctr., Ohio, Soc. Bank Cleve., Edward Cherry Corp., Columbus, First Nat. Bank, Zanesville. Bd. dirs. Zanesville Art Ctr., 1986-90. 92-95. Recipient 1st award Rocky Mountain Nat., 1984, Elsie and David Wu-Ject Key award Am. Watercolor Soc., 1989, 4th award San Diego Watercolor Soc., 1993. Mem. Nat. Watercolor Soc., Soc. Layerists in Multi-Media, Ohio Watercolor Soc. (silver Buckeye award 1986), Southeastern Ohio Watercolor Soc. (co-founder, 1st pres. 1978-79). Avocations: gardening, interior decorating, reading, metaphyics, travel. Home: PO Box 26 Cerrillos NM 87010-0026

WILLIAMS, JULIA REBECCA KEYS, secondary school educator; b. Bristol, Va., July 13, 1922; d. Walter King and Eleanor Fell (Fickle) K.; m. Charles Edwin, Feb. 19, 1944; children: James Edwin, Eleanor Lynn. BA, Queens Coll., Charlotte, 1943; MA, Appalachian State U., Boone, N.C., 1969; EdS, Nova U., 1989. Fla. Tchr. Cert. in Bible, History, English. Tchr. Watauga County Sch. Bd., Blowing Rock, N.C., 1943-44; bank teller, mgr. The Northwestern Bank, Boone, Blowing Rock, 1944-51; owner, mgr. Yonahlossee Motel, Blowing Rock, 1952-65; tchr. Sarasota County Sch. Bd., Fla., 1965-89. English Dept. Chmn. McIntosh Jr. High Sarasota Fla. 1976-82; English Curriculum Coordinator McIntosh Middle Sch. 1982-87. Author Poems 1986 (Golden Poet award), Interdisciplinary Units for Middle Sch., Ch. History Bee Ridge Presbyn. Ch. (elder 1981). Mem. Elder Bee Ridge Presbyn. Ch., 1990—92, 1998—2001; mem. DAR. Mem. Sarasota English and Reading Coun. (pres. 1974-75), Nat. and Fla. Coun. of English Tchrs., Presbyn. Womens Club (Life Mem. award), DAR, Delta Kappa Gamma Soc. (pres. Beta Upsilon chpt. 1990-92), Alpha Delta Kappa (pres. 1972-74). Democrat. Presbyterian. Avocations: travel, sewing, reading, movies. Home: 4509 Beacon Dr Sarasota FL 34232-5215

WILLIAMS, JULIE BELLE, psychiatric social worker; b. Algona, Iowa, July 29, 1950; d. George Howard and Leta Maribelle (Durschmidt) W. BA, U. Iowa, 1972, MSW, 1973. Lic. psychologist, ind. clin. social worker, marriage and family therapist, Minn.; lic. ind. social worker, Iowa. Social worker Psychopathic Hosp., Iowa City, 1971-72; OEO counselor YOUR (Your Own United Resources), Webster City, Iowa, 1972; social worker Child Devel. Clinic, Iowa City, 1973; therapist Mid-Ea. Iowa Cmty. Mental Health Ctr., 1973; psychiat. social worker Mental Health Ctr. No. Iowa, Mason City, 1974-79, chief psychiat. social worker, 1979-80; asst. dir. Cmty. Counseling Ctr., White Bear Lake, Minn., 1980-85, dir., 1985—. Lectr., cons. in field. Grantee NIMH, 1972-73. Mem.: NOW, NASW (acad. cert. social workers, qualified clin. social worker, diplomate), Minn. Women in Psychology, Counselors and Therapists, Am. Assn. Sex Educators, Am. Orthopsychiat. Assn., Shoreview Human Rights Commn., Women in Psychology, Phi Beta Kappa. Democrat. Office: 1280 N Birch Lake Blvd Saint Paul MN 55110-6708

WILLIAMS, JULIE FORD, mutual fund officer; b. Long Beach, Calif., Aug. 7, 1948; d. Julious Hunter and Bessie May (Wood) Ford; m. Walter Edward Williams, Oct. 20, 1984; 1 child, Andrew Ford. BA in Econs., Occidental Coll., 1970. Legal sec. Kadison, Pfaelzer, Woodard, Quinn & Rossi, L.A., 1970-71, 74-77; legal sec. Fried, Frank, Harris, Shriver & Jacobson, N.Y.C., 1971-72, Pallot, Poppell, Goodman & Shapo, Miami, Fla., 1973-74; adminstrv. asst. Capital Research-Mgmt., Los Angeles, 1978-82; corp. officer Cash Mgmt. Trust Am., 1982—, Bond Fund Am., 1982—, Tax-Exempt Bond Fund Am., 1982—, AMCAP Fund, 1984-98, 2000—, Am. Funds Income Series, 1985—, Am. Funds Tax-Exempt Series II, 1986—, Capital World Bond Fund, 1987—, Am. High-Income Trust, 1987—, Intermediate Bond Fund Am., 1987—, Tax-Exempt Money Fund Am., 1989—, U.S. Treasury Money Fund Am., 1991—, Fundamental Investors, 1992-2000, Ltd. Term Tax-Exempt Bond Fund Am., 1993—, Am. High-Income Mcpl. Bond Fund, 1994—; v.p. fund bus. mgmt. group Capital Rsch. Mgmt., 1986—; sec. Growth Fund of Am., 1998-2000; Am. Mutual Fund, 2000—. Pres. Alumni Bd. Govs. Occidental Coll., 1997-98; bd. trustees Occidental Coll., 1999—. Democrat. Episcopalian. Office: Capital Rsch & Mgmt Co 333 S Hope St 55th Floor Los Angeles CA 90071-1452

WILLIAMS, JULIE LLOYD, lawyer; b. Washington, May 24, 1950; d. Walter Herbert and Jean (Grabill) W.; m. Don Scroggin, May 9, 1981; 1 child, Patrick Conner. BA, Goddard Coll., 1971; JD, Antioch Sch. Law, 1975. Bar: Va. 1975, D.C. 1976. Assoc. Fried, Frank, Harris, Shriver, Washington, 1975-83; assoc. gen. counsel Fed. Home Loan Bank Bd., 1983-86, dep. gen. counsel, 1986-89; dep. chief counsel Office of Thrift Supervision, 1989-91, sr. dep. chief counsel, 1991-93; dep. chief counsel Comptr. of the Currency, 1993-94, chief counsel, 1994-98, acting comptr., 1998-99, 1st sr. dep. comptr., chief counsel, 1999—. Co-author: (handbook) How to Incorporate: A Handbook for Entrepreneurs & Professionals, 1987; author: Savings Institutions: Mergers, Acquisitions & Conversions, 1988. Mem. ABA (banking law com.), Women in Housing and Fin. Home: 3064 Q St NW Washington DC 20007-3080 Office: Office Comptroller Currency 250 E St SW Washington DC 20024-3208

WILLIAMS, JUSTIN W. government official; b. N.Y.C., Jan. 4, 1942; s. Louis P. and Edith W. Williams. BA, Columbia U., 1963; LLB, U. Va., 1967. Bar: Va. 1967. Atty. Dept. Justice, 1967-68; asst. commonwealth atty. Arlington County, Va., 1968-70; asst. U.S. atty. Ea. Dist. Va., 1970-78, 1st asst. U.S. atty., 1978-79; U.S. atty. Alexandria, Va., 1979-81; asst. U.S. atty., 1981-86; U.S. atty. Ea. dist. Va., 1986, asst. U.S. atty., chief criminal divsn. Va., 1986—. Episcopalian. Office: US Atty's Office 2100 Jamieson Ave Alexandria VA 22314-5702

WILLIAMS, KAREN HASTIE, lawyer; b. Washington, Sept. 30, 1944; d. William Henry and Beryl (Lockhart) Hastie; m. Wesley S. Williams, Jr.; children: Amanda Pedersen, Wesley Hastie, Bailey Lockhart. Cert., U. Neuchatel, Switzerland, 1965; BA, Bates Coll., 1966; MA, Tufts U., 1967; JD, Cath. U. Am., 1973. Bar: D.C. 1973. Staff asst. internat. gov. relations dept. Mobil Oil Corp., N.Y.C., 1967-69; staff asst. com. Dist. Columbia U.S. Senate, 1970, chief counsel com. on the budget, 1977-80; law clk. to judge Spottswood Robinson III U.S. Ct. Appeals (D.C. Cir.), Washington, 1973-74; law clk. to assoc. justice Thurgood Marshall U.S. Supreme Ct., 1974-75; assoc. Fried, Frank, Harris, Shriver & Kampelman, 1975-77, 1975-77; adminstr. Office Mgmt. and Budget, 1980-81; of counsel Crowell & Moring, 1982, ptnr., 1982—. Bd. dirs. Chubb Corp., Gannett Co., Inc., Sun Trust Bank, Inc., Charles E. Smith Residential Realty, Washington Gas Light Co., Continental Airlines. Trustee Greater Washington Research Ctr., chair. Mem. ABA (pub. contract law sect., past chair), Nat. Bar Assn., Washington Bar Assn., Nat. Contract Mgmt. Assn., NAACP (legal def. fund, bd. dirs.). Office: Crowell & Moring Ste 1200W 1001 Pennsylvania Ave NW Washington DC 20004-2595

WILLIAMS, KAREN JOHNSON, federal judge; b. Orangeburg, S.C., Aug. 4, 1951; d. James G. Johnson and Marcia Johnson (Reynolds) Dantzler; m. Charles H. Williams, Dec. 27, 1968; children: Marian, Ashley, Charlie, David. BA, Columbia Coll., 1972; postgrad., U. S.C., 1973, JD cum laude, 1980. Bar: S.C. 1980, U.S. Dist. Ct. S.C. 1980, U.S. Ct. Appeals (4th cir.) 1981. Tchr. Irmo (S.C.) Mid. Sch., 1972—74, O-W H.S., Orangeburg, 1974—76; assoc. Charles H. Williams PA, 1980—92; judge U.S. Ct. Appeals (4th cir.), 1992—. Exec. bd. grievance commn. S.C. Supreme Ct., Columbia, 1983—92. Child devel. bd. First Bapt. Ch., Orangeburg; bd. dirs. Orangeburg County Mental Retardation Bd., 1986—94, Orangeburg-Calhoun Hosp. Found., Columbia Coll., 1988—92, Reg. Med. Ctr. Hosp. Found., 1988—92; adv. bd. Orangeburg-Calhoun Tech. Coll., SC, 1987—92. Mem.: ABA, Bus. and profl. Women Assn., S.C. Trial Lawyers Assn., Orangeburg County Bar Assn. (co-chair Law Day 1981), S.C. Bar Assn., Fed. Judges Assn., Am. Judicature Soc., Rotary, Order of Coif, Order of Wig and Robe. Home: 2503 Five Chop Rd Orangeburg SC 29115-8185 Office: Lewis F. Powell Jr US Courthouse Annex 1100 E Main St Ste 617 Richmond VA 23219-3517*

WILLIAMS, KAREN OLIVIA, nurse manager, maternal/child health nurse; b. Alexandria, La. d. Edward and Calian (Jacobs) W. AS, La. State U., Alexandria, 1980; BS with honors, Northwestern State U., 1991. RN, La.; cert. ACLS, BLS, neonatal resuscitation provider, PALS, TNCCP; cert. nurse oper. rm., cert. public mgr., 1998; health touch practitioner; Reiki practitioner. Nurse ob.-gyn. Huey P. Long Med. Ctr., Pineville, La., 1980-83, nurse labor and delivery, 1983-87, charge nurse oper. rm., 1987-91, emergency rm. supr., 1992-94; maternal child health mgr., 1994—. Nurse ARC, 1991. Mem. ANA, Assn. Women's Health Obstet. and Neonatal Nurses, La. Assn. Nurse Practitioners, La. Nurse Polit. Action Com., Emergency Nurse Assn., Assn. Oper. Rm. Nurses (cert., bd. dirs. 1991-92), La. State Nurses Assn. (polit. action com.), Alexandria Dist. Nurses Assn. (bd. dirs. 1992-93, pres. 1993-95), Sigma Theta Tau. Republican. Roman Catholic. Avocations: fishing, viewing television, gardening, horseback riding. Home: 107 Navajo Pl Pineville LA 71360-5931 Office: Huey P Long Med Ctr Hospital Blvd Pineville LA 71360 E-mail: karenowilliams@aol.com.

WILLIAMS, KARL, writer, musician; b. Balt., Sept. 4, 1949; s. Joseph Maria and Carlyn Mildred (Schmidt) Thaler; m. Nancy Regina Kuzma, Dec. 26, 1970; 1 child, Aaron Richards. BA in English, U. Scranton, 1971; MBA, U. Pa., 1981. Childcare worker Keystone Residence, Scranton, Pa., 1971-72, River Crest Ctr., Collegeville, Pa., 1972-74; house parent Ken Crest Ctrs., Phila., 1974-78. Composer, rec. artist: Living at the End of Time, 1984, Respect: Songs/Self-Advocacy Movement, 1998 (Grammy nomination 1998), From One Millennium to Another, 1999, Big Fish Little Fish, 2000; author: If Your Dreams Are Big Enough The Facts Don't Count: The Michael S. Long Story (as told to K.W.), 1999, Lost in a Desert World: The Autobiography of Roland Johnson (as told to K.W.), 1999. Performer self-advocacy songs for various state and nat. self-advocacy groups, 1987—. Office: Greene St Records PMB # 372 2033 Linglestown Rd Harrisburg PA 17110 E-mail: cannylark@aol.com.

WILLIAMS, KATHERINE, educational consultant, artist, poet; b. Tunapuna, Trinidad and Tobago, Sept. 7, 1941; came to U.S., 1976; d. Hugh Lionel Williams and Norma Delores (Balcon) Baird; 1 child, Garvin. EdM, Harvard U., 1984, EdD, 1987. Ops. officer The Workers' Bank of Trinidad and Tobago, 1971-75; cons. Smithsonian Instn., Washington, 1977-83; program mgr. N.Y. State Dept. Soc. Svcs., Albany, 1987-91; cons. Washington, 1992—. Mem. Sr. Fgn. Svc. Selection Bd., U.S. Dept. of State and USIA; mem. Sr. Review Bd., U.S. Dept. of State, Interagy. Selection Bd. One-woman shows include Gutman Libr., Harvard U., Cambridge, Mass., Johns Hopkins U., Balt., Nat. Ctr. Gallery, U.S. Geol. Survey, Reston, Va., Touchstone Gallery, Washington, NASA/Goddard Space Flight Ctr., Greenbelt, Md.; author: Fitting Them Together, Where Else but America?, Computers: Our Road to the Future. Mem. Pub. Mems. Assn. Fgn. Svc., Harvard Club of Washington. Home: 1440 N St NW Apt 616 Washington DC 20005-2819 E-mail: williams41@post.harvard.edu.

WILLIAMS, KATHRYN BLAKE, retired librarian; b. Lancaster, Pa., Mar. 20, 1923; d. Harry Leslie and Mary Kauffman (Strine) Blake; m. William George Williams Sr., June 1, 1945; children: Leslie Williams Aronson, William George Jr. BS in Edn., U. Pa., 1944; elem. cert., Shippensburg U., 1969, MLS, 1973. Home economist Pa. State Extension Svc., Carlisle, 1944-46; kindergarten tchr. Blind Assn. Harrisburg, Pa., 1955; asst. elem. tchr. Sweeney Day Sch., Harrisburg, 1955-57; week-day kindergarten tchr. Presbyn. Ch., Camp Hill, Pa., 1961-63; 1st grade tchr. West Shore Sch. System, Lemoyne, 1965-71; dir. Ralpho Twp. Pub. Libr., Elysburg, 1973-75; libr. Bloomsburg (Pa.) Univ. of Pa., 1979-80, Bloomsburg Hosp., 1980-81. Mem. adv. coun. North Cen. Region Job Tng. of Pa., Ridgeway, 1991-96; organizing dir. DuBois office, vista vol. Mid-State Literacy Coun., State College, Pa., 1987-88. Leader, day camp dir. Girl Scouts U.S., Harrisburg, 1957; field svc. coord. Am. Field Svc., Camp Hill, 1963-65; weekly radio panelist United Coun. of Chs., Harrisburg, 1963-65; vol. libr. DuBois (Pa.) Regional Med. Ctr., 1990—; story teller Bloomsburg Pub. Libr., 1974-83; commr. to gen. assembly Presbyn. Ch., 1983, elder, 1973—, deacon, 1994—, sec. of deacons, 1994-97; sec. Presbyn. Women Huntington, 1998—; grandparent vol. pub. sch. Mem. AAUW (v.p. 1987-89), Pa. State Edn. Assn. (life), Friends of DuBois Pub. Libr. (pres. 1984-86), Presbyn. Women (resource coord. 1975-85, mission coord. 1992-97). Avocations: golf, sewing, reading, quilting, public speaking. Home: 377 Treasure Lk Du Bois PA 15801-9008

WILLIAMS, KATHY MARGENE, real estate broker; b. Rinard Mills, Ohio, Oct. 16, 1940; d. Willis S. and Juanita B. (Gray) Dye; m. Paul D. Williams, June 21, 1959; children: Gregory, Christine. Grad., Realtors Inst., 1987. Cert. relocation profl., cert. residential specialist, accredited buyer's rep. Sales assoc. Jack Croy Realty, Findlay, Ohio, 1976-79, Bishop-Kandel Realty, Findlay, 1979-83, Geyer Assocs., Findlay, 1983-85; broker, owner Re/Max Realty, 1985—. Recipient Ohio award of distinction Ohio Assn. Realtors, Columbus, 1993, 94, 95, 96, 97, 98, 99, 2000, 2001. Mem. Employee Relocation Coun. (CRP), Residential Sales Coun., Findlay C. of C. (bd. dirs. 1993-95). Avocations: boating, gardening. Office: Re/Max Realty/Findlay 1621 Tiffin Ave Findlay OH 45840-6848 E-mail: KathyWilliams@remax.net.

WILLIAMS, KEITH ROY, museum director; b. Sunnyside, Wash., Sept. 5, 1958; s. Charles N. Williams and Ruth Arlene (Plank) Hicks; m. Nancy Maxson, 1980 (div. 1984); m. Deanna Lynn Murphy, Oct. 26, 1987; children: Steven, Jeremy. AA in Gen. Studies, Columbia Basin C.C., Pasco, Wash., 1979; BA in Anthropology, Wash. State U., 1981, MA in History/Pub. History, 1984, PhD in History, 1991. Interpretive ranger Nez Perce Nat. Hist. Pk. Nat. Pk. Svc., 1984, historian Alaska regional office, 1986; dir. Wenatchee Valley Mus. and Cultural Ctr., Wenatchee, 1987—. Cons. Office Archaeology and Hist. Preservation, 1985, Batelle N.W. DOSE Reconstruction Project, Hanford, 1987, 88; instr. Wenatchee Valley C.C., 1988, 93—; Wash. state adviser Smithsonian Instn. exhibit Barn Again, 2000-01; field assessor and surveyor Am. Assn. Museums Mus. Assessment program, 1996—; spkr. in field. Author: (video, booklet) The People and The Plow, 1987; contbr. articles to profl. jours. Active Wash. State Heritage Coun., Olympia, 1988-90, Wash. Centennial Com., Wenatchee, 1989; mem. design com. Wenatchee Downtown Assn., 1993-96; bd. dirs. Wash. Friends Humanities, Seattle, 1990—, Wenatchee Centennial Com., 1992, Wash. Commn. for the Humanities, 2001—. Grantee Assn. Humanities Idaho, Wash. Commn. Humanities, various other founds. Mem. Wash. Mus. Assn. (bd. dirs. 1988-90, 94-96), Kiwanis (bd. dirs. 1998-99, past pres.). Avocations: boating, gardening, hunting, camping, reading. Office: Wenatchee Valley Mus and Cultural Ctr 127 S Mission St Wenatchee WA 98801-3039 E-mail: kwilliams@cityofwenatchee.com.

WILLIAMS, KEN MICHAEL, logistics engineer; b. Charleston, W. Va., Mar. 7, 1944; s. R. Don and Ruth Norma (Berg) W.; children: Xali Khanh, Donn Christopher. BA, Ohio State U., 1968; MA, Mich. State U., 1977; AA, Cerritos Coll., 1987. Cert. bus. and indsl. mgmt. tchr., Calif. Commd. U.S. Army, 1968, ret., 1990; logistics specialist McDonnell Douglas, Long Beach, Calif., 1985; asst. material mgmt. officer U.S. Army, 1986-90; ret., 1990. Bd. dirs. TFW Scis., Long Beach; pres. Wms. Scis., Westminster, Calif., 1984-89; cons. Success Strategy Tng., Orange, Calif., 1985-89; logistics instr. Cerritos Coll., Norwalk, Calif., 1985—. Bd. dirs. Site Coun. Clegg Sch., Westminster, 1985-89. Recipient Community Svc. award Camp Zama, 1978; numerous awards U.S. Army, 1968-90. Mem. Soc. Logistics Engrs. (sr. mem., chmn. 1987-88, vice-chmn. ops. 1986-87, newsletter editor 1985-86, chpt. chmn. 1987-88, Award of Excellence 1986, 87, Internat. Logistics award 1987, Internat. Newsletter award 1987, Pres.' Honor Roll 1986, 87, Soc. Commendation 1987, Soc. Cert. of Achievement 1989), Am. Prodn. Inventory Control Soc., Retired Officers Assn., VFW. Republican. Baptist. Avocations: little league activities, coaching, cons. Office: Forsyth County Social Svcs PO Box 999 Winston Salem NC 27102-0999

WILLIAMS, KENNETH SCOTT, entertainment company executive; b. Tulsa, Okla., Dec. 31, 1955; s. David Vorhees Williams and Mary Louise (Newell) Rose; m. Jann Catherine Wolfe, May 20, 1989; children: Catherine Eloise, Michael Holbrook. BA, Harvard Coll., 1978; MS, Columbia U., 1985. Bank officer Chase Manhattan Bank, N.Y.C., 1978-82; asst. treas. Columbia Pictures Entertainment, 1982-84, v.p., treas., 1984-89, sr. v.p. fin. and adminstrn. Burbank, Calif., 1990-91; sr. v.p. corp. ops. Sony Pictures Entertainment, Culver City, 1991-95, exec. v.p., 1995-96; pres. Digital Studio divsn. Sony Pictures Entertainment, 1996-2000; pres., CEO Stan Lee Media, Inc., Encino, Calif., 2000—02; pres. Technicolor Digital Cinema, Burbank, 2002; COO Liberty Livewire Corp., Santa Monica, 2002—. Mem. Blue Hill Troupe, N.Y.C., 1979—; past pres., bd. dirs. L.A. Conservancy; bd. dirs. L.A. Music Ctr.; former chmn. Entertainment Tech. Ctr., U. So. Calif.; trustee the Buckley Sch., U. Calif. Riverside. Mem. N.Y. Soc. Securities Analysts, Fin. Execs. Inst. (v.p.), Harvard Club So. Calif. (bd. dirs.), Beta Gamma Sigma. Home: 457 Cuesta Way Los Angeles CA 90077-3434 Office: Liberty Livewire Corp 5th Fl 520 Broadway Santa Monica CA 90401 E-mail: kwilliams@libertylivewire.com.

WILLIAMS, KEVIN LEONARD, social worker, marriage and family therapist; b. Ashland, Oreg., Sept. 9, 1952; s. Leonard Milton and Yvonne Williams; m. Melissa Catherine Lansing, Dec. 15, 2001. BS in Psychology,

Regents Coll., 1997; MSW, Portland (Oreg.) State U., 2000. LCSW assoc. Oreg.; cert. therapist Wash. Grief counselor Winterspring Ctr., Medford, Oreg., 1996—98; clin. social worker Oreg. State Hosp., Portland, 1998—99; mental health therapist Kaiser Permanente, Vancouver, Wash., 1999—2000; addictions medicine fellow, psychiat. social worker VA/Seattle Med. Ctr., 2000—01; jail outreach therapist VA, 2000—01, psychiat. admissions coord. White City, Oreg., 2000—. Children's program counselor Dunn Ho. Shelter Battered Women & Children, Medford, 1995—97; group therapist Vet. Hosp., Seattle, 2000—01. Mem.: NASW. Democrat. Avocations: hiking, skiing, fishing, swimming, gym. Home: 251 Meadows Dr Ashland OR 97520 Office: Dept Vet Affairs 8495 Crater Lake Hwy White City OR 97503

WILLIAMS, LARRY ROSS, surgeon; b. Murphysboro, Ill., July 20, 1952; s. Laurel Ross and Mary Elizabeth (Blankenship) W.; m. Sarah Elizabeth Hecht, June 17, 1978; children: Gretchen Elizabeth, Noelle Louisa. BS, So. Ill. U., 1974; MD, U. Ill., Chgo., 1978, MS, 1982. Resident in surgery U. Ill., Chgo., 1978-83, fellow in surgery, 1983-84; fellow in vascular surgery Northwestern U., 1984-85; asst. prof. U. South Fla., Tampa, 1985-92, clin. asst. prof., 1992—. Chief vascular surgery Bay Pines VA Hosp., St. Petersburg, Fla., 1985-89; pvt. practice St. Anthony's Hosp., St. Petersburg, 1985—, chief of surgery, 1993-95, 2002–, pres. med. staff, 1996-97; bd. govs. Physician-Hosp. Orgn., 1994—. Contbr. articles to profl. jours. Active First United Meth. Ch., St. Petersburg, 1985—, Polywogs, St. Petersburg, 1989—. Fellow ACS; mem. Internat. Soc. Cardiovascular Surgery, Soc. Non-Invasive Vascular Technology, Pinellas County Med. Soc. (bd. govs. 1994-97), Fla. Med. Assn. (splty. soc. rep. 1994-96), Am. Inst. Ultrasound in Medicine, Fla. Assn. Gen. Surgeons, Peripheral Vascular Surg. Assn., Warren Cole Surg. Soc., So. Assn. for Vascular Surgery, Fla. Vascular Soc. (sec. 1991-94, pres. 1994-95), Fla. Surg. Soc., Acad. Med. Arts and Scis., Frederick A. Coller Surg. Soc., Soc. for Clin. Vascular Surgery, Fla. Assn. Cardiovascular and Pulmonary Rehab., Phi Eta Sigma, Phi Kappa Phi, Phi Beta Kappa. Avocations: family activities, golf, tennis. Office: 1111 7th Ave N Saint Petersburg FL 33705-1348

WILLIAMS, LAWRENCE SOPER, photographer; b. Balt., July 8, 1917; s. Lawrence S. and Ida (Exall) W.; m. Avilda Leyshon Williams, Nov. 21, 1940; children: Jay Stephen, Wendy Lauren. Student, Md. Inst. Wirephoto operator AP, Balt., 1937-38; news photographer Balt. Sun Papers, 1938-40, Harris and Ewing News Photos, Washington, 1940-41; war corr., photographer Bur. Info. U.S. War Dept., 1941-45; picture editor Holiday mag., Phila., 1945-48; freelance photographer Havertown, Pa., 1949-59; pres. Lawrence S. Williams, Inc., Upper Darby, 1959-83, chmn., 1983-93. Pres. Archtl. Photographers Assn., N.Y.C., 1968-70, Paoli (Pa.) Woods Homeowner's Assn., 1985-86. Recipient Gold medal Artist Guild of Phila., 1965, Silver medal Artist Guild of Pa., 1964, George W. Berry trophy Soc. Comml. Photographers Del. Valley, 1961, 66, 78, 79, 82, Best of Show trophy Am. Mus. Photography, Phila., 1966, 71, 77, 79, 82, Best Comml. Print trophy Guild of Profl. Photographers Del. Valley, 1971, 70, Award of Excellence Am. Advtg. Assn. Pa., 1978, Pres.'s Cup Profl. Photographers Assn. Pa., 1971, numerous archtl., comml., indsl., pictorial awards. Fellow Am. Soc. Photographers; mem. Soc. Comml. Photographers Del. Valley (life), Profl. Photographers Assn. Pa. (life), Profl. Photographers Am., Inc. (life, master photography degree 1966, craftsman photography degree 1968), Hershey's Mill Golf Club (West Chester, Pa.), Shriners. Republican. Lutheran. Avocation: travel. Home: 1268 Robynwood Ln West Chester PA 19380-5747 Office: PO Box 694 Kimberton PA 19442-0694 Fax: 610-344-7895. E-mail: larryvil@aol.com.

WILLIAMS, LAWRENCE D. surgeon; b. Mocksville, N.C., July 20, 1956; m. Karen Henderson; children: Bryan Dale, Wendy Karen, Megan Janell. BS in Biology, High Point (N.C.) Coll., 1978; MD, Wake Forest U., 1982. Diplomate Nat. Bd. Med. Examiners, Am. Bd. Surgery; registered vascular technologist. Resident in gen. surgery East Carolina U. Sch. Medicine/Pitt County Meml. Hosp., Greenville, N.C., 1982-87; Charles E. Culpepper Transplant fellow East Carolina U. Sch. Medicine, 1983-84; ptnr. Med. Ctr. Surgeons, Inc., 1987-93; employee physician Westwood Surg. Assocs., Inc., 1993-95; shareholder, surgeon Cornerstone Health Care, PA, 1995—; med. dir. Cornerstone Imaging Svcs., 1998—. Active med. staff High Point Regional Hosp., 1987—, chief of surgery, 1991-93; med. dir. Med. Ctr. Diagnostic Imaging, High Point, 1995-98; active med. staff High Point Surg. Ctr., 1989—, Lexington Meml. Hosp., 1999—. Contbr. articles to profl. jours. Mem. fin. com. Covenant United Meth. Ch., 1995-97; vol. physician Cmty. Clinic of High Point, 1993—. Recipient numerous fellowships and honors. Fellow ACS; mem AMA, Am. Soc. Gastrointestinal Endoscopists, Am. Registry Diagnostic Med. Sonographers, N.C. Med. Soc., High Point Med. Soc., Carolina Vascular Soc., Internat. Soc. for Endovascular Surgery, So. Med. Assn., N.C. Vascular Technologists, Old North State Club, High Point Country Club. Office: Cornerstone Health Care PA 611 Lindsay St Ste 100 High Point NC 27262-4305 E-mail: ldwbry@aol.com.

WILLIAMS, LAWRENCE FLOYD, conservation organization official; b. Eugene, Oreg., Mar. 26, 1937; s. Carroll Parven and Catherene (Dorris) W.; m. Patricia Ann Pride, Feb. 25, 1978. Student, Portland State U. Advt. staff asst. Omark Industries, Portland, Oreg., 1963-67; internat. advt. liaison Hyster Co., 1968; exec. dir. Oreg. Environ. Coun., 1969-78; policy analyst pub. land mgmt. White House Coun. on Environ. Quality, Washington, 1978-81; spl. cons. Sierra Club, Portland, 1969, Washington rep., 1981-85, dir. internat. program, 1985-98, coord. internat. spl. projects, 1998; ptnr. Kibale Forest Wild Coffel Project, Uganda. Former mem. dist. adv. bd. Bur. Land Mgmt.; former mem. Adv. Com. on Forest Mgmt. Policy; former cons. Coun. on Econ. Priorities; former mem. acv. com. Bonneville Power Adminstrn.; mgr. N.W. Workshops for Conservation Found. on Implementation Clean Air Act, 1972, Clean Water Act, 1975, U.S. Energy Policy, 1976; former mem. Western Forst Environ.-Industry Policy Discussion Group; environ. cons. Uganda Coffee Trade Fedn. Author: (with Raymond Mikesell) International Banks and the Environment, from Growth to Sustainability: An Unfinished Agenda, 1992; mng. editor: Bankrolling Disasters, International Development Banks and the Global Environment, 1986. Past mem. bd. dirs. Inst. for Transp. and Devel. Policy, N.W. Environ. Def. Ctr.; past chmn. Nat. Coalition for Clean Water, Pacific N.W. chpt. Sierra Club; founder, past 1st chmn. Portland Sierra Club; past v.p. Fedn. Western Outdoor Clubs; past pres. Trails Club Oreg.; past assembly pres. Inst. Ecology; organizer, past chmn. Com. for Volcanic Cascades Study, People Against Nerve Gas; organizer Oreg. League Conservation Voters; mem. steering com. Biodiversity Action Network, 1993; mem. adv. bd. Global Forest Policy Project, 1994. With USAF, 1956-70. Recipient Richard L. Neuberger award Oreg. Environ. Coun., 1988. Democrat. Home: 4607 Van Ness St NW Washington DC 20016-5631 E-mail: lfw11ams26@earthlink.net.

WILLIAMS, LEAFORD CLEMETSON, writer, political scientist; b. St. Elizabeth, Jamaica, Oct. 3, 1924; came to U.S., 1948; s. Jeremiah and Alice Williams; m. Bertha M. Bussey, May 19, 1950; children: Valerie, Kharl, Brenda. Student, Georgetown U., 1957-60; BA in Internat. Rels., Am. U., Washington, 1961, MA in Internat. Rels., 1972. Fgn. svc. officer USIA, Washington, 1961-67; pub. affairs officer U.S. Civil Svc. Dept. Transp., 1968-79; asst. to dir. White House Conf. on Small Bus., 1979-80. Chief mission, Taegu, Korea; cultural attache, Bombay, India; pub. affairs officer Am. Embassy, Seoul, Korea. Author: Rebirth of a Nation, 1954, Journey Into Diplomacy, 1996, Boys Without Dads: When Dads Abandon Homes, 2000. City Coun. candidate Dem. Party, Washington, 1974; chmn. Disciples Men Christian Ch., Washington, 1990; chmn. UN Assn., Washington, 1980-90; bd. mem. Immigration and Refugees Svcs., Washington, N.Y.C., 1992—. With USAF, 1950-56. Decorated Bronze Star. Mem. Thursday Luncheon Group Dept. State (program officer 1980-84). Avocations: golf, public speaking, writing. Home and Office: 1037 Crittenden St NE Washington DC 20017-2718 E-mail: fort@erols.com.

WILLIAMS, LENA HARDING, educational administrator; b. Portsmouth, Va., June 12, 1947; d. Arthur McKinley and Mildred (Smith) Harding; m. Leroy Stephen Williams, July 8, 1966; children: Michael LaMar, Darryl LaVon, Stephen LaSean. AB in English Edn. and Speech, Norfolk State U., 1969; postgrad., U. Va., 1972-73, Norfolk State U., 1987, Old Dominion U., 1973-88, MS in Ednl. Administrn., 1993. Cert. 7-12 English and speech tchr., mid. sch. and h.s. prin., postgrad. cert., Va.; cert. Nat. Bd. for Profl. Tchg. Stds. Tchr. English S.H. Clarke Sch. Portsmouth Schs., 1969-70, tchr. English W.E. Waters Sch., 1970-71, tchr. English Churchland Mid. Sch., 1971-74, chmn. English dept., 1974-86, 88-99, cons. coll. bd. English vertical teaming, 1997, adminstrv. intern in curriculum and instrn., 1999; asst. prin. Hunt-Mapp Mid. Sch., Portsmouth, 1999—. Fieldtester Va. Standards of Learning Lang. Arts; tchr./trainer Portsmouth Schs., 1986-88, lead mentor tchr., 1990—, cons. coll. bd.; presenter SAT prep. workshop, New-Tchr. Insvc., Writing Across the Curriculum, Reading to Learn, Technology in the Classroom. Active Hodges Manor Civic League, Portsmouth, 1985—, PTA; dir. Christian edn., summer camp youth adv., coord. vol. tutorial svc., mem. sr. choir, usher, coord. youth activities, mem. ch. coun., bd. dirs. kindergarten, Edna Hyke Corbett Achievement Award Found.; coord. Multiple Sclerosis Read-a-Thon, Back to Sch. Seminar; community campaign vol. Mother's March, Am. Cancer Soc., Muscular Dystrophy, Am. Heart Assn.; co-sponsor Cavalier Manor Deep Doubles Tennis Tournament. Named State Tchr. of Yr., State Bd. Edn., Richmond, Va., 1992, Outstanding Young Educator, Portsmouth Jaycees, 1978, Va. Secondary Reading Tchr. of Yr., Secondary Reading Coun. Va., 1999; recipient 25 svc. and honor awards from local orgns. Fellow Hampton Rds. Inst. for Advanced Study of Tchg.; mem. ASCD, NEA, NAACP, Va. Edn. Assn., Nat. State Tchrs. of Yr. Assn., Nat. Coun. Tchrs. of English, Internat. Reading Assn., Va. State Secondary Reading Assn., Va. Congress English Teachers, Va. Assn. Tchrs. of English (Foster B. Gresham award 1994), Portsmouth Edn. Assn., Portsmouth Reading Coun., Tidewater Assn. Tchrs. English, Delta Sigma Theta. Democrat. Avocations: singing, speaking, reading, collecting dolls. Home: 801 Nottingham Rd Portsmouth VA 23701-2118 Office: Hunt-Mapp Middle Sch 3701 Willett Dr Portsmouth VA 23707-1295 E-mail: LLWMS2@aol.com.

WILLIAMS, LEONA RAE, lingerie shop owner, consultant; b. Fairfield, Nebr., July 1, 1928; d. Melton M. and Helga D. (Sorensen) Brown; m. Eugene F. Williams, June 6, 1946; 1 child, Dennis D. Grad. high sch., Fairfield. Owner Alice Rae Apparel Shop, Tucson, 1953-96, second location, 1967-96, Green Valley, Ariz., 1976-93, Sun City, 1979-96; ret., 1996; owner Boutique on Wheels, 2001—, prin., 2001—. Cons. in field. Sponsor Distributive Edn. Program, 1978-82; coord. fashion shows Am. Cancer Soc., Tucson, 1987, 88, 89. Mem. Exec. Women's Internat. Assn. (chpt. pres. 1994), Mchts. Assn. (pres. 1987-89), Soroptomists, C. of C. Better Bus. Bur. Republican. Baptist. E-mail: leonagene@msn.com. *Personal philosophy: We can be what we want to be with dedicated hard work, time, determination working with professionalism at all times.*

WILLIAMS, LEWIS T. (RUSTY WILLIAMS), education educator; Pres. Chiron R&D, 1994—, chief scientific officer, 1999; adj. prof. medicine U. Calif., San Francisco.

WILLIAMS, LINDA HUNT, not-for-profit developer, consultant; b. New Orleans, Aug. 12, 1948; d. Abram Davis and May (Botsay) Hunt; m. W. Patrick Williams, Oct. 7, 1983; 1 child, Erica Bailey. BBA in Mgmt., Loyola U., New Orleans, 1986; MPA with honors, U. N.C., Charlotte, 1996. Mem. adj. faculty Ctrl. Piedmont C.C., Charlotte, N.C., 1988-94; staff dir. Charlotte Area Ednl. Consortium, 1994-96; mem. staff U.S. Senate, Charlotte, 1997-99; exec. dir. Children's Scholarship Fund-Charlotte, 1999—2001, ret., 2001. Treas. exec. bd. Mecklenburg County Republican Party, 1997-99, vice chmn. exec. bd., 1999-2001; mem. at large N.C. Exec. Com., 1997-2001, N.C. Mecklenburg County Exec. Com., 1997-2001, N.C. 9th Congl. Dist. Exec. Com., 1997—2001, N.C. State Exec. Com., 1999-2001; alt. del. Rep. Conv., 2000; 2d v.p. exec. bd. Substance Abuse Prevention Svcs. of the Carolinas, 1997-98. With USN, 1967-72. Fellow, Inst. of Polit. Leadership, UNC-W, 2002. Mem. Am. Soc. Pub. Adminstrs., Pi Alpha Alpha (v.p. 1996-97, pres. 1997-98), Rotary, Kiwanis (pres.-elect Holly Springs chpt.), Sunset Ridge Homeowners Assn. (v.p.). Roman Catholic. Avocations: family, reading, camping, fishing.

WILLIAMS, LISA ROCHELLE, logistics and transportation educator; b. Toledo, Feb. 11, 1964; d. Lionel and Mary Moore; divorced; 1 child, Matthew Malik. BS, Wright State U., 1985, MBA, 1988; MA, PhD, Ohio State U., 1992. Prof. Ctrl. State U., Wilberforce, Ohio, 1988-89, Pa. State U., University Park, 1992—; prof., Oren Harris chair in logistics U. Ark. Cons. CLSA, University Park, 1992—; owner, operator Collage, State College, Pa., 1994-96. Author: Evolution, Status and Future of the Corporate Transportation function, 1991; contbr. articles to profl. jours. Mem. Coun. of Logistics Mgmt. (chmn. com. 1997—), Am. Soc. Logistics and Transp., World Conf. on Transport Rsch. (chmn. track com. 1997-98), Alpha Kappa Alpha.

WILLIAMS, LISLE EDWARD, civil, planning and structural engineer; b. Indiana, Pa., Feb. 10, 1945; s. Lisle Edward and Marguerite Lighte (Roadarmel) Williams; m. Pamela Jayne Long, Aug. 12, 1972; children: April, Andrew, Amy. Assoc. Degree, Gateway Tech. Inst., Pitts., 1967; Cert., Carnegie-Mellon U., 1970, U. Pitts., 1974, Pa. State U., 1982. Registered profl. engr., Pa., profl. land surveyor, Pa., fallout shelter analysis lic., value engrng. specialist. Numerous managerial and tech. engrng. positions, engr. Dist 11-O, Pa. Dept. Transp., Pitts., 1964-90; program mgr. transp. HDR Engrng., Inc., 1991-92; asst. v.p. Parsons Brinckerhoff, Inc., 1992-93; dep. dir. ops. Buchart-Horn, Inc., 1993-97; dir. govt. affairs DMJM+ Harris, Inc., 1998—. Bd. dirs. TRB Bridge Deck com. (A3C06)(2), Washington, Planning & Design Dvisn. ARTBA, Washington; pres. Constrn. Legis. Coun., 1988, 2001. Aurthor, editor, editl. bd.: newsletter Cross-Sect., 1968—, aurthor, editor, editl. bd.: Pitts. Profl. Engr., 1974—; contbr. articles to profl. jours. Instnl. rep. Troop # 77 Boy Scouts Am., Pitts., 1980—90; mem. Plum Parent Tchr. Soccer Assn., Plum Area Soccer League, 1983—; mem. citizens adv. panel Southwestern Pa. Regional Planning Orgn./Met. Planning Orgn., 1996—2002; mem. Mon-Fayette Expy./So. Beltway Projects Alliance Group, 1996—, Pa. Hwy. info. Assn., 1990—; elder, deacon, trustee, chmn. Plum Creek Presbyn. Ch., Pitts., 1972—. Named a resolution in his honor, City of Pitts., 1995, clamation, Coutny of Allegheny, 1995; named Pitts. Outstanding Young Civil Engr. of the Yr., ASCE, 1983; recipient Svc. to People award, 1988, citation, Pa. Senate, 1991, Pa. Ho. Reps., 1991. Mem.: Western Pa. Conservancy, Internat. Bridge Conf. (gen. chmn. 1992—93, chmn. 1993), Pa. Engrng. Found. (trustee 1991—), Pa. Soc. Profl. Engrs. (v.p., pres.-elect, pres., bd. dirs. 1970—, Young Engr. of Yr. award 1980, L. W. Hornfeck award 1984, Pres.'s Four Star award 1986, Past Pres's plaque 1997, Dedicated Svc. award 1998), Am. Soc. Hwy. Engrs. (life; nat. bd. dirs. 1964—, pres. 1983—84, tesitmonial 1987, Pres.'s award 1983, 1984, 1998, Disting. Svc. award 1984), Greater Pitts. C. of C. (chmn. CEC/Pa. Trans. subcom. 1992—). Democrat. Home: 15 Plumcrest Dr Pittsburgh PA 15239-1503 Office: DMJM Harris Inc Ste 500 Four Gateway Ctr Pittsburgh PA 15222-1416 Fax: 412 395-8897. E-mail: lwilliams@dmjmharris.com.

WILLIAMS, LORAINE PLANT, civic worker; b. Savannah, Ga., Nov. 24, 1929; d. Lorne Lawrence and Janet (H.) P.; m. Thomas Rice Williams; children: Janet Williams Osborne, Susan Williams Tinsley, Thomas R. Jr. BA, U. Ga., 1951. With radio talk show WBTM, Danville, Va., 1950-52; with promotion dept. WNAC-TV, Boston, 1952-54. Author: Life on the Asa Zachry Plantation, 1983. Bd. visitors Emory U., Atlanta, 1989-93; bd. dirs. Atlanta Cerebral Palsy, 1979-98, Emory U. Art and Archaeol. Mus., Atlanta, 1989—, Ga. trust Hist. Preservation, 1974-83, Atlanta Symphony, 1976-85; past chmn. Ga. Heritage Trust; trustee Atlanta Hist. Soc., 1978-89, Forward Arts Found., Atlanta, 1975—, Madison-Morgan Cultural Ctr., Madison, Ga., 1982-89, 94-98; bd. adv. Shepherd Spinal Clinic. Mem. So. Ctr. for Internat. Studies, Centre Lit. Guild, Piedmont Garden Club (past pres.), Piedmont Driving Club, Capital City Club, Peachtree Golf Club, Highlands (N.C.) Country Club. Republican. Episcopalian. Avocations: travel, tennis, reading. Home: 3200 Arden Rd NW Atlanta GA 30305-1919 also: Lemon Tree Cottage PO Box 786 Boca Grande FL 33921-0786 also: High Hickory 120 Split Rail Row Highlands NC 28741

WILLIAMS, LORETTA DODSON, financial advisor, investment broker; b. Charleston, W.Va., Sept. 4, 1936; d. Theron Samuel and Dorothy (Roberts) Dodson; m. Joseph Milton Williams, Feb. 26, 1955; children: Vickie L., Karen Williams Hadley, Kim Williams Disse. CFP; registered investment advisor. Registered rep. A.G. Edwards & Sons, Inc., Richmond, Va., 1983-89; prin. Saunders, Shepherd, Cortright & Williams, 1990-91; br. mgr. Linsco-Pvt. Ledger, 1990—; owner, investment advisor Loretta D. Williams Co., 1991—. Author For Women Only investment seminars, 1984—. Mem. Nat. Assn. for Fin. Planning, Assn. Women Bus. Owners, Inst. Cert. Fin. Planners (bd. dirs. 1991-93), Nat. Fedn. Ind. Bus., Altrusa Internat., Inc., Better Bus. Bur. Richmond. Mem. Assembly of God Ch. Avocations: bowling, camping, hiking. Office: Loretta D Wiliams Co 8002 Discovery Dr Ste 214 Richmond VA 23229-8601

WILLIAMS, LOUIS CLAIR, JR. public relations executive; b. Huntington, Ind., Nov. 7, 1940; s. Louis Clair and Marian Eileen (Bowers) W.; children— Terri Lynn, L. Bradley, Lisa C.; m. Mary Clare Moster. B.A., Eastern Mich. U., 1963. Copywriter, Rochester (N.Y.) Gas and Electric Co., 1963-65, editor RG&E News, 1965-66; employee info. specialist Gen. Ry. Signal Co., Rochester, 1966-67, supr. employment and employee rels., 1967-69; supr. pub. rels. Heublein, Inc., Hartford, Conn., 1969-70; dir. corp. communications Jewel Cos., Inc., Chgo., 1970-71; account exec. Ruder & Finn of Mid-Am., Chgo., 1971-73, v.p., 1973-76, sr. v.p., 1976-78; cons. Towers, Perrin, Forster & Crosby, Los Angeles, 1978-79; exec. v.p., gen. mgr. Harshe-Rotman & Druck, Inc., Chgo., 1979, pres. midwest region, 1979-80; v.p. Hill & Knowlton, Inc., Chgo., 1980-81, sr. v.p., 1981-83; pres. Savlin Williams Assocs., Evanston, Ill., 1983-85, L.C. Williams & Assocs., Chgo., 1985—. Recipient Clarion award Women in Communications, 1978, award of Excellence, Internat. Coun. Indsl. Editors, 1969, Bronze Oscar-of-Ind., Fin. World, 1974. Mem. Internat. Assn. Bus. Communicators (pres. 1979-80), Chgo. Assn. Bus. Communicators (pres.), Publicity Club Chgo., Pub. Rels. Soc. Am.

WILLIAMS, LOWELL CRAIG, lawyer, employee relations executive; b. Tehachapi, Calif., Dec. 3, 1947; s. Lyndon Williams and Gertrude (White) Sievert; m. Marsha Mendelssohn; children: John S., Jeffrey A. Bescheinigungeschiedte, Georg August U., Germany, 1968; BA, U. Calif., Santa Barbara, 1969; JD, Columbia U., 1972. Bar: N.Y. 1973, U.S. Ct. Appeals (2nd cir.) 1974, U.S. Supreme Ct. 1974. Assoc. Sullivan & Cromwell, N.Y.C., 1972-75; sr. v.p. Elf Aquitaine, Inc., 1976-95; v.p. Compagnie des Machines Bull, 1995—, exec. v.p. group human resources, 1998-99; exec. dir. Exult Inc., 1999—2001; sr. advisor TPI Sourcing Inc., The Woodlands, Tex., 2002—. Past pres. Scarsdale Synagogue. Mem. Internat. Bar Assn., German Law Assn. (dir.). Office: TPI Sourcing Inc Ste 200 10055 Grogan's Mill Rd The Woodlands TX 77380-2552 E-mail: lowell.williamsl@tpi.net.

WILLIAMS, LUCINDA, country musician; b. Lake Charles, La., 1953; d. Miller W.; m. Greg Sowders (div.). Albums include: Ramblin' On My Mind, 1979, Happy Woman Blues, 1980, Lucinda Williams, 1988, Passionate Kisses, 1989 (Grammy award Best Country Song 1994), (EP, Sweet Old World, 1992; contbr. songs to: Sweet Relief, 1993, Born to Choose, 1993. Office: c/o Universal Music Group 1755 Broadway New York NY 10019*

WILLIAMS, LUTHER STEWARD, research scientist; b. Sawyerville, Ala., Aug. 19, 1940; s. Roosevelt and Mattie B. (Wallace) W.; m. Constance Marie Marion, Aug. 23, 1963; children: Mark Steward, Monique Marie. BA magna cum laude, Miles Coll., 1961; MS, Atlanta U., 1963; PhD, Purdue U., 1968, DSc (hon.), 1987, U. Louisville, 1992, Capitol Coll., 1996, Bowie State U., 1996, Tuskegee U., 1997, U. D.C., 1999. NSF lab. asst. Spelman Coll., 1961-62, Atlanta U., 1962-63, instr. biology, faculty rsch. grantee, 1963-64, asst. prof. biology, 1969-70, prof. biology, 1984-87, pres., 1984-87; grad. tchg. asst. Purdue U., West Lafayette, Ind., 1964-65, grad. rsch. asst., 1965-66, asst. prof. biology, 1970-73, assoc. prof., 1973-79, prof., 1979-80, NIH Career Devel. awardee, 1971-75, asst. provost, 1976-80; dean Grad. Sch., prof. biology Washington U., St. Louis, 1980-83; v.p. acad. affairs, dean Grad. Sch. U. Colo., Boulder, 1983-84; Am. Cancer Soc. postdoctoral fellow SUNY-Stony Brook, 1968-69; assoc. prof. biology MIT, 1973-74; spl. asst. to dir. Nat. Inst. Gen. Med. Scis., NIH, Bethesda, Md., 1987-88; dep. dir. Nat. Inst. Gen. Med. Scis. NIH, 1988-89; sr. sci. advisor to dir. NSF, Washington, 1989-90, asst. dir. for edn. and human resources, 1990-99; visiting scholar Payson Ctr. Internat. Devel./Tech., Arlington, Va., 1999-2000, edn. cons., 2000—. Educator, cons., 2000—; dir. edn., sr. advisor to dir. Mo. Bot. Garden, St. Louis, 2001–; chmn. rev. com. MARC Program, Nat. Inst. Gen. Med. Scis., NIH, 1972-76; grant reviewer NIH, 1971-73, 76, NSF, 1973, 76-80, Med. Rsch. Coun. of N.Z., 1976; mem. life scis. sreening com. recombinant DNA adv. com. HEW, 1979-81; mem. nat. adv. gen. med. sci. council NIH, 1980-85; mem. adv. com. Office Tech. Assessment, Washington, 1984-87; chmn. fellowship adv. com. NRC Ford Found., 1984-85; mem.-at-large Grad. Record Exam. Bd., 1981-85, chmn. minority grad. edn. com., 1983-85; mem. health, safety and environ. affairs. com. Nat. Labs., U. Calif., 1981-87; mem. adv. panel Office Tech. Assessment, U.S. Congress, 1985-86; mem. fed. task force on women, minorities and the handicapped in sci. and tech., 1987-91; mem. adv. panel to dir. sci. and tech. ctrs. devel. NSF, 1987-88; mem. nat. adv. com. White House Initiative on Historically Black Colls. and Univs. on Sci. and Tech., 1986-89; numerous other adv. bds. and coms. Contbr. sci. articles to profl. jours. Vice chmn. bd. advisors Atlanta Neighborhood Justice Ctr., 1984-87; bd. dirs. Met. Atlanta United Way, 1986-87, Butler St. YMCA, Atlanta, 1985-87; trustee Atlanta Zool. Assn., 1985-87, Miles Coll., 1984-87, Atlanta U., 1984-87, 90-96; mem. nominating com. Dana Found. NIH predoctoral fellow Purdue U., 1966-68, William A. Hinton Rsch. Trng. award, Am. Soc. Microbiology, 1998. Fellow Am. Acad. Microbiology; mem. Am. Soc. Microbiology, Am. Chem. Soc., Am. Soc. Biol. Chemists (mem. ednl. affairs com. 1979-82, com. on equal opportunities for minorities 1972-84). Home and Office: 11608 Split Rail Ct Rockville MD 20852-4423

WILLIAMS, MALISSA, guidance counselor; b. Scottsville, Ky., Feb. 27, 1963; d. Vernon Woodruff Jr. and Wilma Nell Frost; m. Mark Lee Williams, Aug. 29, 1981; children: Marideth, MacKenzie, Macey, Madison. BS in Elem. Edn., Western Ky. U., 1986, MA in Counseling, 1990. Cert. elem. thcr., sch. counselor 1-12. Teller, receptionist First Am. Bank, Nashville, 1981-83; tchr. Allen County Bd. of Edn., Scottsville, Ky., 1987-96, sch. counselor, 1996—. Chairperson Consolidated Planning, Scottsville, 1990—; com. mem. Jr. Achievement Bd., Scottsville, 1997-98; mem. Reality Store Com., Scottsville, 1997—; com. mem. Renaissance Club, Scottsville, 1993—. Named Tchr. of Yr. Campbellsville Coll., 1993. Mem. South Ctrl. Counseling Assn., Ky. Counseling Assn., Bapt. Women in Action, Emmaus Cmty. (table leader), Alpha Delta Nu (scrap book com. 1999). Avocations: reading, shopping, family. Home: 135 Red Oak Ln Scottsville KY 42164-6309 Office: J Bazzell Mid Sch 201 New Gallatin Rd Scottsville KY 42164-8836

WILLIAMS, MARCUS DOYLE, judge; b. Nashville, Oct. 24, 1952; s. John Freelander and Pansy (Doyle) W.; m. Carmen Myrie, May 21, 1983; children: Aaron Doyle, Adam Myrie. BA with honors, Fisk U., 1973; JD, Cath. U. of Am., 1977. Bar: Va. 1977, D.C. 1978. Asst. commonwealth's atty. County of Fairfax, Fairfax, Va., 1978-80, asst. county atty. Faifax, 1980-87; dist. ct. judge 19th Jud. Dist., 1987-90; judge 19th Jud. Cir., 1990—. Lectr. bus. legal studies George Mason U., Fairfax, 1980-95; instr. pvt. investigators North Va. Community Coll., Fairfax, 1979; mem. Fairfax Criminal Justice Adv. Bd., 1980-86; faculty advisor Nat. Jud. Coll., 1991, faculty, 1992—; Am. participant lectr. for USIA, 1990; lectr. George Mason U. Law Sch., 1987. Book reviewer for ABA Jour., 1981-84; contbr. articles to legal jours. Bd. visitors Cath. U. Law Sch., 1998—. Recipient cert. of appreciation for outstanding svc. Burke-Fairfax Jack & Jill, Cert. of Appreciation, Nat. Forum for Black Pub. Adminstrs. and Black Women United for Action, 1995; Thomas J. Watson Found. fellow, 1977, Otis Smith award BLSA of Cath. U. Law Sch. Mem. ABA (chair subcom. Victims of Crimes 1996-2000), Fairfax Bar Assn. (CLE com., vice chmn. 1986-87), Am. Bus. Law Assn., Am. Judges Assn., Phi Alpha Delta, Beta Kappa Chi, Omega Psi Phi. Methodist. Office: Cir Ct 4110 Chain Bridge Rd Fairfax VA 22030-4009

WILLIAMS, MARGARET LU WERTHA HIETT, nurse; b. Midland, Tex., Aug. 30, 1938; d. Cotter Craven and Mollie Jo (Tarter) Hiett; m. James Troy Lary, Nov. 16, 1960 (div. Jan. 1963); 1 child, James Cotter; m. Tuck Williams, Aug. 11, 1985. BS, Tex. Woman's U., 1960; MA, Tchrs. Coll., N.Y.C., 1964, EdM, 1974, postgrad., 1981, U. Tex., 1991-92, U. Wis.; cert. completion, U. Wis., Scotland. Cert. clin. nurse specialist, advanced practice nurse, psychiat./mental health nurse, nursing continuing edn. and staff devel., TNCC, PALS, ACLS, ENPC, neonatal resuscitation course. Nurse Midland Meml. Hosp., 1960-63; instr. Odessa (Tex.) Coll., 1963-67; dir. ADNP Laredo (Tex.) Jr. Coll., 1967-70; asst. prof. Pan Am. U., Edinburgh, Tex., 1970-72; rsch. asst. Tchrs. Coll., 1973-74; nursing practitioner St. Luke's Hosp., N.Y.C., 1975-79; sgt. Burns Security, Midland, 1979-81; with Area Builders, Odessa, 1981-83; field supr. We Care Home Health Agy., Midland, 1983-87; clin. educator, supr. Glenwood, A Psychiat. Hosp., 1987-92; dir. nursing Charter Healthcare

Systems, Corpus Christi, Tex., 1992-93; nurse III Brown Sch., San Marcos, 1993-97; owner MTW Nursing Consultation, Whitney, 1996—, Margaret Hiett Williams RN, CNS, Whitney, 1996—; clin. devel. specialist Heritage Health Svcs., L.C., 1997-99. Nurse emergency dept. Hill Regional Hosp., Hillsboro, Tex., 1999—; co-owner, operator MTW Med. Legal Cons.; adj. prof. Pace U., 1974-75, S.W. Tex. State U., 1995; reviewer in field. Mem. Gov. Richards' Exec. Leadership Coun., 1991-95, re-election steering com., 1994. Named to, Ladies 1st of Midland, 1974, Tex. Woman's U. Great 100 Nurses; recipient Isabelle Hampton-Robb award, Nat. League for Nursing, 1976, Achievement award, Cmty. Leaders of Am., 1989. Mem. NAFE, ANA, Tex. Nurses Assn. (pres. dist. 21 1962-65, dist. 32 1970-72), Am. Psychiat. Nurses Assn., Emergency Nurses Assn., Parkland Meml. Hosp. Nurses Alumnae Assn., Tex. Women's U. Alumnae Assn., Midland H.S. Alumni, Bus. and Profl. Women's Club, Mensa, Lockhart Breakfast Lions Club. Democrat. Avocations: songwriting, public speaking, singing, travel, writing. Office: PO Box 2509 Whitney TX 76692-5509 Fax: 254-694-6335. E-mail: mhiettwilliams@hotmail.com.

WILLIAMS, MARION LESTER, government official; b. Abilene, Tex., Dec. 1, 1933; s. Martin Lester and Eddie Faye (Wilson) W.; m. Johnnie Dell Ellinger, Dec. 14, 1957; children: Tammy Dawn Cole, Pamela DeAnn Ritterbush. BS, Tex. A&M U., 1956; MS, U. N.Mex., 1967; PhD, Okla. State U., 1971. Test engr. Sandia Nat. Labs., Albuquerque, 1959-61; weapons sys. engr. Naval Weapons Evaluation Facility, 1961-66; ops. rsch. analyst Joint Chiefs of Staff/Joint Task Force II, 1966-68; chief reliability div. Field Command DNA, 1969-71; prin. scientist SHAPE Tech. Ctr., The Hague, Netherlands, 1971-74; chief tech. advisor HQ AF Test & Evaluation Ctr., Albuquerque, 1974-81; chief scientist HQ AF Operational Test & Evaluation Ctr., 1981-89, tech. dir., 1989—. Vis. adv. com. Okla. State U., Stillwater, 1988—; adv. com. U. N.Mex., Albuquerque, 1985—. Editor T&E Tech. Jour., 1987—; contbr. articles to profl. jours. Sci. advisor N.Mex. Sci. & Tech. Oversigh Com., Albuquerque, 1988; bd. advisors U. N.Mex. Cancer Ctr., 1987—; bd. dirs. Contact Albuquerque, 1986-87. 1st lt. USAF 1956-59. Recipient Presdl. Rank award, 1987, 92. Fellow Mil. Ops. Rsch. Soc. (pres. 1982-83, bd. dirs. 1976-81, Wanner award 1991), Internat. Test & Evaluation Ctr. (bd. dirs. 1984-86, 88-90, v.p. 1990, pres. 1992-93), Ops. Rsch. Soc. Am., Tau Beta Pi, Phi Eta Sigma, Alpha Pi Mu, Sigma Tau, Kappa Mu Epsilon. Democrat. Baptist. Avocations: skiing, computers. Home: 1416 Stagecoach Ln SE Albuquerque NM 87123-4429 Office: HQ AF Operational Test Ctr Kirtland AFB Albuquerque NM 87117-0001 E-mail: williams505@flash.net.

WILLIAMS, MARK GRAYSON, artist; b. Palo Alto, Calif., 1960; BA, U. Calif., Santa Cruz, 1982; MFA, Art Inst. Chgo., 1988. Dir. exhibns., bd. dirs. SITE, L.A., 1992-94. Pub. books, audio tapes, video tapes, CD's; work included in pvt. collections in U.S., Europe; exhbns. include 1078 Gallery, Chico, Calif., 1998, The Crest Hardware Show, N.Y.C., 1996, San Diego Art Inst., 1993, Moving Arts solo show, L.A., 1993, Sch. of the Art Inst., Chgo., 1988, The Brewery, L.A., 1985, Triton Art Mus., Santa Clara, Calif., 1982. Home: Apt 2401 10993 Bluffside Dr Studio City CA 91604-4452 E-mail: markgrayson@homeburner.com.

WILLIAMS, MARK H. marketing communications executive; b. Omaha, Apr. 30, 1959; s. Perry T. and Donna M. (Hodges) W. BA in Comm. and Bus., Loyola U., Chgo., 1981. Account mgmt. Bozell & Jacobs, 1981—87; v.p. Bozell, Jacobs, Kenyon & Eckhardt, 1987—93; sr. v.p., dir. Bozell, Chgo., 1993—2001; sr. v.p. Campbell Mithun, 2001—. Bd. dirs., exec. v.p. Internat. Food Strategies; speaker Harvard Graduate Sch. Bus., Northwestern U., U. Nebr., Creighton U., Loyola U. Chgo., U. Ill., numerous confs. and seminars. Contbr. articles to profl. jours. Mem. numerous trade assns. Home: 57 E Delaware Chicago IL 60611-1476 Office: Campbell Mithun 676 N Saint Clair Chicago IL 60611

WILLIAMS, MARK SHELTON F. lawyer; b. Missoula, Mont., Oct. 12, 1964; s. Shelton C. and Donna L. (Finstad) W.; m. Susan E. Schild, Sept. 5, 1993. BA, Middlebury Coll., 1987; JD with honors, U. Mont., 1992. Bar: Mont. 1992, U.S. Dist. Ct. Mont. 1992, U.S. Ct. Appeals (9th and 10th cirs.) 1992. Acct. officer Chem. Bank, N.Y.C., 1987-89; law clk. U.S. Ct. Appeals 10th cir., Denver, 1992-93; atty. Williams & Ranney P.C., Missoula, 1993—. Editor-in-chief Mont. Law Rev., 1991. Mem. Leadership Missoula, 1994-95. Mem. ABA, Mont. Young Lawyers (pres. 1995-96), Montana Law Found. (bd. dirs.), Phi Delta Phi. Avocations: ski racing, sail boarding, mountain biking. Office: Williams & Ranney PC 235 E Pine St Missoula MT 59802-4512

WILLIAMS, MARSHA RHEA, computer scientist, educator, researcher, consultant; b. Memphis, Aug. 4, 1948; d. James Edward and Velma Lee (Jenkins) W. Cert., Schiller Coll., West Berlin, Germany, 1968; BS in Physics, Beloit Coll., 1969; MS in Physics, U. Mich., 1971; MS in Sys. and Info. Sci., Vanderbilt U., 1976, PhD in Computer Sci., 1982. Cert. data processor. Engring. coop. student Lockheed Missiles & Space Co., Sunnyvale, Calif., 1967-68; asst. transmission engr. Ind. Bell Tel. Co., Indpls., 1971-72; sys. analyst, instr. physics Memphis State U., 1972-74; computer-assisted instrn. project programmer Fisk U., 1974-76; mem. tech. staff Hughes Rsch. Labs., Malibu, Calif., 1976-78; assoc. sys. engr. IBM, Nashville, 1978-80; rsch. and tchg. asst. Vanderbilt U., 1980-82, spl. asst. to dean Grad. Sch., spring 1981, minority engr. advisor, 1975-76; cons. computer-assisted instrn. project Meharry Med. Coll., summer 1982; assoc. prof. computer sci. Tenn. State U., 1982-83, 84-90, full tenured prof., 1990—, univ. marshal, 1992-97. Assoc. prof. U. Miss., Oxford, 1983-84, faculty senator; assoc. program dir. Applications of Advanced Techs. Sci. and Engring. Edn., NSF, 1987-88, apptd. USRA Sci. and Engring. Edn. Coun., Advanced Design Program, 1992-94; cons. on minority scientists and engrs. Univ. Space Rsch. Assn., Washington, 1988; vis. scientist CSNET-Minority Instn. Networking Project Bolt, Beranek & Newman, Cambridge, Mass., 1989; mem. tech. staff Bell Comm. Rsch., Red Bank, N.J., 1990; presenter papers profl. meetings. Editor-in-chief newspaper Pilgrim Emanuel Bapt. Ch., 1975-76. Advisr Chi Rho Youth Fellowship, Temple Bapt. Ch., 1975-81, adv. com. Golden Outreach Sr. Citizens Fellowship, 1979-80, 86-87, 89-93, Women's Day spkr., 1979-81, Ebenezer Missionary Bapt. Ch., 1993; adviser Nat. Soc. Black Engring. Students, 1983-84; founder, coord. Tenn. State U. Assn. for Excellence in Computer Sci., Math. and Physics (AE-COMP), 1986-87, coord. Tech. Opportunities Fair, 1986, 87; dir. Tenn. State U. Minorities in Sci., Engring. and Tech. Rsch. Project-MISET, 1989—; child sponsor World Vision, 1981—; mem., newsletter staff Lake Providence Missionary Bapt. Ch. Recipient Disting. Instr. award, 1984, Disting. Svc. citation Beloit Coll. Alumni Assn., 1994; grantee Digital Equipment Corp., 1989-92; faculty rsch. grantee Tenn. State U., 1993, 94. Mem. AAUP, NAACP (nat. judge ACT-SO sci. olympics 1992), Assn. Computing Machinery, Assn. Info. Tech. Profls. (formerly Data Processing Mgmt. Assn.) (edn. chmn., bd. dirs. 1986), Tenn. Acad. Sci., Am. Assn. of Univ. Profs., Phi Kappa Phi. Achievements include research in developing a formally complete model information/support system (database, network and human-computer interfacing), for minority scientists, especially African American science students, and for providing/locating technical resources for developing countries. Home: PO Box 270545 Nashville TN 37227-0545 Office: PO Box 136 Nashville TN 37202-0136

WILLIAMS, MARSHALL HENRY, JR. physician, educator; b. New Haven, July 15, 1924; s. Marshall Henry and Henrietta (English) W.; m. Mary Butler, Aug. 27, 1948; children: Stuart, Patricia, Marshall, Frances, Richard. Grad., Pomfret Sch., 1942; BS, Yale, 1945, MD, 1947. Diplomate Nat. Bd. Med. Examiners, Am. Bd. Internal Medicine. Intern Presbyn. Hosp., N.Y.C., 1947-48, asst. resident medicine, 1948-49, New Haven Hosp., 1949-50, asst. in medicine, 1950; trainee Nat. Heart Inst., 1950; practice medicine, specializing in internal medicine Bronx, N.Y.; chief respiratory sect., dept. cardiorespiratory diseases Army Med. Service Grad. Sch., Walter Reed Army Med. Center, 1953-55; dir. cardiorespiratory lab. Grasslands Hosp., Valhalla, N.Y., 1955-59; dir. chest svc. Bronx Mcpl. Hosp. Ctr., 1959-94; vis. asst. prof. physiology Albert Einstein Coll. Medicine, Bronx, 1955-59, assoc. prof. medicine and physiology, 1959-66, prof. medicine, 1966-95, prof. emeritus, 1995—. Dir. pulmonary div. Montefiore Med. Ctr., Albert Einstein Coll. Medicine, 1981-94. Author: Clinical Applications of Cardiopulmonary Physiology, 1960, Essentials of Pulmonary Medicine, 1982, Consultation in Chest Medicine, 1985; contbr. articles to profl. jours. Served from 1st lt. to capt. U.S. Army, 1950-52. Mem. Am. Physiol. Soc., AAAS, Am. Heart Assn., Westchester Heart Assn (past pres.)., Am. Thoracic Soc., Am. Fedn. Clin. Research, N.Y. Acad. Sci., N.Y. Trudeau Soc. (past pres.), Am. Soc. Clin. Investigation, Soc. Urban Physicians (past pres.), N.Y. Tb. and Health Assn. (past dir.), Alpha Omega Alpha. Home: 103 Fox Meadow Rd Scarsdale NY 10583-2301 Office: Albert Einstein Coll Medicine Bronx NY 10461

WILLIAMS, MARTHA ETHELYN, information science educator; b. Chgo., Sept. 21, 1934; d. Harold Milton and Alice Rosemond (Fox) W. BA, Barat Coll., 1955; MA, Loyola U., 1957. With IIT Rsch.Inst., Chgo., 1957-72, mgr. info. scis., 1962-72, mgr. computer search ctr., 1968-72; adj. assoc. prof. sci. info. Ill. Inst. Tech., 1965-73, lectr. chemistry dept., 1968-70; rsch. prof. info. sci., coordinated sci. lab. Coll. Engring. U. Ill., Urbana, also dir. info. retrieval research lab., 1972—, prof. info. sci. grad. sch. of libr. info. sci., 1974—, affiliate, computer sci. dept., 1979—. Chair large data base conf. Nat. Acad. Sci./NRC, 1974, mem. ad hoc panel on info. storage and retrieval, 1977, numerical data adv. bd., 1979-82, computer sci. and tech. bd., nat. rsch. network rev. com., 1987-88, chair utility subcom., 1987-88, subcom. promoting access to sci. and tech. data for pub. interest; task force on sci. info. activities NSF, 1977; U.S. rep. review com. for project on broad system of ordering, UNESCO, Hague, Netherlands, 1974; vice-chair Gordon Rshc. Conf. on Sci. Info. Problems in Rsch., 1978, chair, 1980; mem. panel on intellectual property rights in age of electronics and info. U.S. Congress, Office of Tech. Assessment; program chmn. Nat. Online Meeting, 1980—; founder, pres. Info. Market Indicators, Inc., 1982—; cons. in field; invited lectr. Commn. European Communities, Industrial R&D adv. com., Brussels, 1992. Editor-in-chief: Computer-Readable Databases Directory and Data Sourcebook, 1976—89, founding editor: , 1989—92; editor: Ann. Rev. Info. Sci. and Tech., 1976—2001, Online Rev., 1979—92, Online and CD-ROM Rev., 1993—2000; mem. editl. adv. bd.: Database, 1978—88, mem. editl. bd.: Info. Processing and Mgmt., 1982—89, mem. editl. bd.: The Reference Libr., founding editor: Online Info. Rev., 2000—; contbr. Trustee Engirng. Info., Inc., 1974-87, bd. dirs., 1976-91, chmn. bd. dirs., 1982-91, v.p., 1978-79, pres., 1980-81; regent Nat. Libr. Medicine, 1978-82, chmn. bd. regents, 1981; mem. task force on sci. info. activities NSF, 1977-78; mem. nat. adv. com. ACCESS ERIC, 1989-91. Recipient best paper of year award H. W. Wilson Co., 1975; Travel grantee NSF, Luxembourg, 1972, Honolulu, 1973, Tokyo, 1973, Mexico City, 1975, Scotland, 1976 Fellow: AAAS (mem. nominating com. 1983, 1985), Nat. Fedn. Abstracting and Info. Svcs. (hon.), Inst. Info. Scis. (hon.); mem.: NAS (mem. joint com. with NRC on chem. info. 1971—73), Internat. Fedn. for Documentation (U.S. nat. com.), Assn. Sci. Info. Dissemination Ctrs. (v.p. 1971—73, pres. 1975—77), Assn. Computing Machinery (pub. bd. 1972—76), Am. Soc. Info. Sci. (councilor 1971—72, mem. publs. com. 1974—, pres. 1987—88, councilor 1987—89, contbg. editor bull. column 1974—78, award of merit 1984, Pioneer Info. Sci. award 1987, Watson Davis award 1995), Am. Chem. Soc. Home: 2134 Sandra Ln Monticello IL 61856-8036 Office: U Ill 1308 W Main St Urbana IL 61801-2307 E-mail: m-will13@uiuc.edu.

WILLIAMS, MARY ALICE BALDWIN, retired home economist, volunteer consultant; b. St. Louis, Mar. 24, 1928; d. Ulysses Grant and Irene (Jenkins) Gray; m. Earl Randolph Baldwin, June 28, 1952 (div. 1973); 1 child, Arlene Denise; m. Robert Williams Jr., Dec. 21, 1985. BS, Lincoln U., 1952; MA, Webster U., 1971; postgrad., Harris Stowe Tchrs. Coll., 1976-78, Cen. Mo. State U., 1979-80, U. Mo., 1981-82. Cert. home economist, Mo. Tchr. home econs. Cen. H.S., Hayti, Mo., 1952-53, Cleve. Pub. Schs., 1953-56; tchr. elem. sch. St. Louis Pub. Schs., 1958-67, tchr. home econs., 1968-83, curriculum supr. home econs., 1984-93, cons. home econs. and character edn., 1993; ret., 1993; vol. cons. Family & Consumer Sci. Fiber Art, 1993—. Presenter in field. Author curriculum materials in home econs. and character edn. Fund raising com. Annie Malone Children's Home, St. Louis, 1987-90; 75th anniversary com. YWCA Phylliss Wheatley, St. Louis, 1988. Mem. Nat. Assn. Univ. Women (del. 1992, Woman of Yr. 2001), Am. Home Econs. Assn. (ethics com. 1990-92, population com. 1990-91), Mo. Home Econs. Assn. (tchr. rep. 1988-90), Am. Vocat. Assn., Mo. Vocat. Assn. (legis. com.), St. Louis Home Econs. Tchrs. Assn. (founder, adviser), Lincoln Univ. Alumni Assn. (chair founders day), Delta Sigma Theta. Avocations: sewing, clothing design, music, reading, tennis, quilting. Home: 4910 Maffitt Pl Saint Louis MO 63113-1727

WILLIAMS, MARY BETH, lawyer; b. Marshfield, Wis., Aug. 8, 1948; d. Delos A. and Leona E. (Kademan) Kobs; m. Ernest F. Wittwer, July 15, 1967 (div. Jan. 1989); children: Jake, Freddie; m. Paul L. Williams, July 22, 1989. BBA, U. Wis., 1983, JD, 1986. Bar: Wis. 1986, U.S. Dist. Ct. (we. dist.) Wis. 1986, U.S. Dist. Ct. (ea. dist.) Wis. 1988. Assoc. Wickhem & Gage, S.C., Janesville, Wis., 1986-88, Brennan, Steil, Basting & MacDougall, S.C., Janesville, 1988-91; pvt. practice law, 1991-2000; atty. Hill, Glowacki, Jaeger, Reiley, Zimmer & Hughes, LLP, 2000-01, Mary B. Williams Law Office, S.C., 2001—. Mem. legal secs. program adv. com. Blackhawk Tech. Coll., Janesville, 1992—; mem. alcohol license adv. com. City of Janesville, 1994-2000. Mem. ABA, State Bar Wis., Rock County and Dane County Bar Assn. Avocations: reading, puzzle solving, piano playing, genealogy, historical restoration. Office: PO Box 8066 20 S Main St Ste 23 Janesville WI 53545-3959 E-mail: pmwilli@inwave.com.

WILLIAMS, MARY HICKMAN, social worker; b. Newton, Tex., July 09; d. Casey and Mattie (Allen) Hickman; m. Herman Williams, Aug. 25, 1984; children: Michael, Mitchell, Marcus. BSW, Prairie View A&M U., Tex., 1980; MSSW, U. Tex., Arlington, 1982. Cert. social worker, Tex.; lic. profl. counselor, Tex. Clin. social worker Rusk (Tex.) State Hosp., 1982, Deep East Tex. Mental Health/Mental Retardation, Lufkin, 1982-87, Lufkin State Sch., 1987—. Mem. NASW. Home: RR 3 Box 7620 Lufkin TX 75901-9170

WILLIAMS, MARY JANE, fundraiser; b. Phila., Dec. 4, 1943; d. Herbert S. and Constance (Clements) W. BA in History, U. Pa., 1965; MEd, Temple U., 1968, MBA in Mktg., 1981. Advt. prodn. asst. N.W. Ayer Inc., Phila., 1965-66; auto and personal liability claims adjuster Reliance Ins. Co., 1966-67; asst. dir. ann. giving U. Pa., 1967-71, dir. individual gifts, 1982-86, asst. v.p. devel. and alumni rels., 1986-88; assoc. dir. devel. Haverford (Pa.) Coll., 1971-73; dir. devel. Med. Coll. Pa., Phila., 1973-77; asst. v.p. devel. Temple U., 1977-80; v.p. devel. NYU Med. Ctr., N.Y.C., 1988-90. Mem. women's athletic bd. U. Pa.; mem. adv. bd. Fund-Raising Inst., 1981-94. Mem. Coun. Penn Women (assoc. trustee), Nat. Soc. Fund Raising Execs. (Fund Raising Exec. of Yr. 1993), Assn. for Healthcare Philanthropy, Cosmopolitan Club. Office: Schultz & Williams Inc 421 Chestnut St Ste 400 Philadelphia PA 19106-2415

WILLIAMS, MARY MARGARET, nurse administrator; b. Gloucester, Mass., Jan. 1, 1947; d. James Robert and Margaret Mary (Gillis) W. Dipl. in Nursing, Beth Israel Hosp., Boston, 1967; BSN, Salem State Coll., 1978; MSN, Boston Coll., 1981. Staff nurse Addison Gilbert Hosp., Gloucester, Mass., 1967; staff nurse gen. med. Beth Israel Deaconess Med. Ctr., Boston, 1967-68, asst. head nurse, 1968-70, staff nurse MICU, 1970-71, head nurse MICU, 1972, clin. advisor, 1973-82, nurse mgr., 1982—. Chair nursing rsch. rev. com. Beth Israel Deaconess Med. Ctr., 1984—2001, vice chmn. IRB, 1982—. Editor newsletter Nat. Gen. Clin. Rsch. Ctr. Nurse Mgrs., 1990-91. Mem. Am. Orgn. Nurse Execs. (com. on rsch. 1991-93), Nat. Assn. Gen. Clin. Rsch. Ctr., Nurse Mgrs. (treas. 1989-91, regional rep. 1991-93, pres. 1993-95, 96-97, bd. dirs. 1989-99), Sigma Theta Tau. Home: 401 Western Ave Gloucester MA 01930-4048 Office: Beth Israel Deaconess Med Ctr 330 Brookline Ave Boston MA 02215-5400

WILLIAMS, MARY PEARL, judge, lawyer; b. Brownsville, Tex., Jan. 12, 1928; d. Marvin Redman and Theo Mae (Kethley) Hall; m. Jerre Stockton Williams, May 28, 1950; children— Jerre Stockton, Shelley Hall, Stephanie Kethley. BA, U. Tex., 1948, JD, 1949. Bar: Tex. 1949, U.S. Supreme Ct. 1955, U.S. Dist. Ct. (we. dist.) Tex., 1987. Asst. atty. gen. State of Tex., Austin, 1949-50; relief judge Municipal Ct., summer 1964; asst. instr. dept. govt. U. Tex., 1966-67; atty. Office of Emergency Preparedness, Exec. Office of Pres., Washington, 1968-70; labor arbitrator, mem. arbitration panel Am. Arbitration Assn., 1972-73; judge County Ct. at Law 2, Travis County, Tex., 1973-80, 53d Judicial Dist. Ct., 1981-2000. Cons. Dept. HEW, 1966-67 Mem. adv. com. Juvenile Bd. of Travis County, 1964-67; trustee United Way, 1974-78. Named Outstanding Woman, Austin Am.-Statesman, 1974, Austin Citizen, 1978; named Woman of Yr., Austin Dist. Bus. and Profl. Women, 1977; elected to Austin H.S. Hall of Fame, 1996. Fellow ABA, Am. Bar Found.; mem. State Bar Tex., Coll. State Bar Tex., Travis County Bar Assn., Am. Law Inst., Am. Judicature Soc., Inst. Jud. Adminstrn., Jr. League Austin, Kappa Alpha Theta, Delta Kappa Gamma (hon.). Democrat. Methodist. Office: Travis County Courthouse PO Box 1748 Austin TX 78767-1748 E-mail: marypw@iopener.net.

WILLIAMS, MATT (MATTHEW DERRICK WILLIAMS), professional baseball player; b. Bishop, Calif., Nov. 28, 1965; Student, U. Nev., Las Vegas. With San Francisco Giants, 1987-96, Cleveland Indians, 1997, Ariz. Diamondbacks, 1998—. Player Nat. League All-Star Team, 1990, 94. Recipient Gold Glove award, 1991, 93, 94, Silver Slugger award, 1990, 93-94; named to Sporting News Nat. League All-Star team, 1990, 93-94, Coll. All-Am. team Sporting News, 1986; Nat. League RBI Leader, 1990. Office: Arizona Diamondbacks Bank One Ballpark 401 E Jefferson St Phoenix AZ 85004-2438*

WILLIAMS, MATT EUGENE, chiropractor, educator; b. Homestead, Fla., July 22, 1957; s. Matt Ransom Jr. and Cora Lee (Geanette) W.; m. Kari Lynne Poss, Dec. 12, 1998. BA in Biology, U. N.C., Greensboro, 1979; M of Ednl. ADminstrn., U. Ga., 1987; DChiropractic, Life U., Marietta, Ga., 1991. Lic. chiropractic physician, N.C., Ga.; cert. sports fitness chiropractor; cert. in chiropractic orthospinology. Assoc. prof. Life U., Marietta, 1992-95, head dept. diagnosis, 1995-97, chair clin. scis., 1997-2000. Mem. adv. bd. Nat. Bd. Chiropractic Examiners, Greeley, Colo., 1998-2001. Supporter, Atlanta Union Mission, 1997—, Run for Life, Marietta, 1992—, Dynamic Essentials, Marietta, 1992—, Vietnam Vets, Marietta, 1998—. Named to Outstanding Young Men of Am., 1996. Mem. Internat. Chiropractors Assn. (coun. on fitness and health sci.), Soc. Chiropractic Orthospinology, Nat. Upper Cervical Chiropractic Assn., Acad. Upper Cervical Chiropractic Orgns., Nat. Strength and Conditioning Assn. Baptist. Avocations: travel, photography. Home: PO Box 6816 Marietta GA 30065-0003 Office: Life U Clin Scis Divsn 1269 Barclay Cir SE Marietta GA 30060-2903

WILLIAMS, MELVIN DONALD, anthropologist, educator; b. Pitts., Feb. 3, 1933; s. Aaron and Gladys Virginia (Barnes) W.; m. Faye Wanda Strawder, June 20, 1958; children: Aaron Ellsworth, Steven Rodney, Craig Haywood. AB, U. Pitts., 1955, MA, 1969, PhD, 1973. Owner, operator Wholesale Periodical Distbn. Co., Pitts., 1955-66; instr. dept. sociology and anthropology Carlow Coll., 1969-71, asst. prof., 1971-75, chmn. dept. sociology and anthropology, 1973-75; assoc. prof. anthropology U. Pitts., 1976-79, adj. prof., 1979-82; prof. anthropology Purdue U., 1979-83, U. Md., College Park, 1983-88, U. Mich., Ann Arbor, 1988—. Olie B. O'Connor prof. Am. instns. Colgate U., 1976-77 Author: On the Street Where I Lived, Community in a Black Pentecostal Church, The Human Dilemma, The Black Middle Class, An Academic Village, Race for Theory; editor: Selected Readings in Afro-American Anthropology; contbr. articles to profl. publs. Co-chmn. project area com. Urban Redevel. Authority, Pitts., 1972—; co-dir. interdisciplinary family community project Western Psychiat. Inst. and Clinic, 1973-76; bd. dirs. Cath. Social Svc. of Allegheny County, Pa., 1973-76; coll. ombudsman, 1991-93, faculty senate, 1993-96. NSF field tng. fellow in anthropology, 1967; grantee, 1969-72; Community Action Pitts. grantee, 1969-71; Social Sci. Research Council grantee, 1974-75; Lilly Endowment grantee, 1980-83, 85-86; NDEA Title IV fellow, 1969. Fellow Am. Anthrop. Assn.; mem. African Studies Assn., AAAS, AAUP, Am. Sociol. Assn., Assn. Study Afro-Am. Life and History, Soc. for Psychol. Anthropology. Home: 520 W Washington St Ann Arbor MI 48103-4232 E-mail: mddoublu@umich.edu. *Personal philosophy: An abiding interest in people has stimulated me to discover more and more about humankind and has been an ever-present motivation to develop, grow and experience.*

WILLIAMS, MICHAEL ALAN, psychologist; b. Cin. , May 20, 1948; s. Chester and Gentry Mae (Canada) W.; m. Linda Ann Presswood, Aug. 8, 1970; children: Michael Alan II, Derrick Alexander. BA, U. Cin., 1970, MA, 1971, EdD, 1980. Instr. U. Cin., 1972-75; sch. psychologist Dayton Bd. Edn., Ohio, 1975-78; assoc. prof. Wright State U., Dayton, 1978-99, coord. spl. edn. program, 1992-99; prof. Montgomery County Children's Services, 1999—; clin. psychologist Profl. Psychol. Services, 1981—; psychol. services coordinator Montgomery County Children's Services, 1983-88. Psychol. cons. Diversion Alternative for Youth, Dayton, 1990—, Miami Valley Juvenile Rehab. Ctr., 2001—; program mgr. Head Start Supplementary Tng. Program, Cin., 1973-74; cons. Ohio Luth. Synod, Dayton, 1981-83, Blacks in Govt., Dayton, 1982-85, Montgomery County, Stillwater Health Ctr., Dayton, 1982-86. Co-editor (book): Teaching in a Multicultural Pluralistic Society, 1982, 2d edit., 1987. Treas. Dayton Free Clinic and Counseling Ctr., Dayton, 1983; bd. dirs. Planned Parenthood Assn., Dayton, 1983, Miami Valley Literacy Coun., Dayton, 1990-97, Dayton Mediation Ctr., 1995-98, S. Cmty., Inc., 1996, Choices in Cmty. Living, 2001—, Diamond Gems Spl. Need Ctr., 2001—. Recipient Faculty Excellence award Wright State U., 1997, Disting. Prof. award Wright State U., 1997; named Outstanding Young Man Am., Jaycees, 1984, Top Ten African-Am. Males, Dayton chpt. Urban League, 1995; McCall Scholarship, 1966-70. Mem. Am. Psychol. Assn., Nat. Assn. Black Psychologists, Nat. Assn. Sch. Psychologists, Dayton Assn. Black Psychologists (v.p. 1986-88, pres. 1988-89), Mental Health Assn. (bd. dirs. 1985), Assn. Tchr. Educators. Avocations: bible student, music, handiwork, writing. Home: 4830 Old Hickory Pl Dayton OH 45426-2149 Office: Profl Psychol Svcs 4130 Linden Ave Ste 309 Dayton OH 45432-3034 E-mail: ppsdocs@aol.com.

WILLIAMS, MICHAEL ANTHONY, lawyer; b. Mandan, N.D., Sept. 14, 1932; s. Melvin Douglas and Lucille Ann (Gavin) Williams; m. Marjorie Ann Harrer, Aug. 25, 1962 (div. 1989); children: Ann Margaret, Douglas Raymond, David Michael; m. Dorothy Ruth Hand, 1989. BA, Coll. of St. Thomas, 1954; LL.B., Harvard U., 1959. Bar: Colo. 1959, N.D. 1959, U.S. Dist. Ct. Colo. 1959, U.S. Ct. Appeals (10th cir.) 1959, U.S. Supreme Ct. 1967. Assoc. Sherman & Howard and predecessor Dawson, Nagel, Sherman & Howard, Denver, 1959—65, ptnr., 1965—91; pres. Williams, Youle & Koenigs, P.C., 1991—2002; prin. Michael A. Williams LLC, 2002—. Served as 1st lt. USAF, 1955—57. Mem.: ABA, Arapahoe County Bar Assn., Denver Bar Assn., Colo. Bar Assn., Am. Law Inst., Colo. Bar Found., Am. Bd. Trial Advs., Am. Coll. Trial Lawyers. Office: Michael A Williams LLC 950 17th St Ste 1700 Denver CO 80202-2811 E-mail: mwilliams@wyk.com.

WILLIAMS, MICHAEL EDWARD, lawyer; b. Ft. Worth, Aug. 10, 1955; s. Jerrol Evans and Helen Louise (Hoffner) W.; m. Jackie Ann Gordinier, Dec. 30, 1978; children: Margaret Eileen, James Andrew. BA, U. Calif., Riverside, 1977; JD, U. San Diego, 1980. Bar: Calif. 1980, U.S. Dist. Ct. (so. dist.) Calif. 1980, U.S. Tax Ct. 1981, U.S. Dist. Ct. (ea. and cen. dists.) Calif. 1982, U.S. Dist. Ct. (no. dist.) Calif. 1985. Assoc. Jamison & McFadden, Solana Beach, Calif., 1980-86, Dorazio, Barnhorst & Bonar, San Diego, 1986; sole practice Encinitas, Calif., 1987—. Pres. Casa de Amistad, Centro de Ensenaza, 2001—. Atty. pro bono Community Resource Ctr., Encinitas, Calif., 1984—; vice moderator San Diego Presbytery, Presbyn. Ch. U.S.A., 1998, moderator, 1999. Mem. Calif. State Bar Assn. (fee arbitrator 1992—), San Diego County Bar Assn. (client rels. com. 1990—, fee arbitration com. 1991—, ct. arbitrator). Democrat. Presbyterian. Office: 4405 Manchester Ave Ste 206 Encinitas CA 92024-7902

WILLIAMS, MILLER, poet, translator; b. Hoxie, Ark., Apr. 8, 1930; s. Ernest Burdette and Ann Jeanette (Miller) W.; m. Lucille Day, Dec. 29, 1951 (div.); m. Rebecca Jordan Hall, Apr. 11, 1969; children: Lucinda, Robert, Karyn. BS, Ark. State Coll., 1951; MS, U. Ark., 1952; postgrad., La. State U., 1951, U. Miss., 1957; HHD (hon.), Lander Coll., 1983; DHL, Hendrix Coll., 1995. Instr. in English La. State U., 1962-63, asst. prof., 1964-66; vis. prof. U. Chile, Santiago, 1963-64; assoc. prof. Loyola U., New Orleans, 1966-70; Fulbright prof. Nat. U. Mex., Mexico City, 1970; co-dir. grad. program in creative writing U. Ark., 1970-84, assoc. prof., 1971-73, prof. English and fgn. langs., dir. program in transl., 1973-87, univ. prof., 1987—, dir. poetry-in-the prisons programs div. continuing edn., 1974-79, chmn. program in comparative lit., 1978-80. Fellow Am. Acad. in Rome, 1976—, mem. adv. coun. Sch. Classical Studies, 1985-91; first U.S. del. Pan Am. Conf. Univ. Artists and Writers, Concepcion, Chile, 1964; invited del. Internat. Assembly Univ. Press Dirs., Guadalajara, Mex., 1991; mem. poetry staff Bread Loaf Writers Conf., 1967-72; founder, exec. dir. Ark. Poetry Cir., 1975; founding dir. U. Ark. Press, 1980-97; participant Assn. Am. Univ. Presses Soviet Mission, 1989. Author: (poems) A Circle of Stone, 1964, Recital, 1965, So Long At the Fair, 1968, The Only World There Is, 1971; (criticism) The Achievement of John

Ciardi, 1968, The Poetry of John Crowe Ransom, 1971; (with John Ciardi) (criticism) How Does a Poem Mean?, 1974; (poems) Halfway From Hoxie: New & Selected Poems, 1973, Why God Permits Evil, 1977, Distractions, 1981, The Boys on Their Bony Mules, 1983; translator: (poems) Poems & Antipoems (Nicanor Parra), 1967, Emergency Poems (Nicanor Parra), 1972, Sonnets of Giuseppe Belli, 1981; editor: (poems) 19 Poetas de Hoy en Los Estados Unidos, 1966, (with John William Corrington) Southern Writing in the Sixties: Poetry, 1967, Southern Writing in the Sixties: Fiction, 1966, Chile: An Anthology of New Writing, 1968, Contemporary Poetry in America, 1972, (with James A. McPherson) Railroad: Trains and Train People in American Culture, 1976, A Roman Collection: An Anthology of Writing about Rome and Italy, 1980, Ozark, Ozark: A Hillside Reader, 1981, (criticism) Patterns of Poetry, 1986, (poetry) Imperfect Love, 1986, Living on the Surface: New and Selected Poems, 1989, Adjusting to the Light, 1992, Points of Departure, 1995, The Ways We Touch, 1997, Some Jazz A While: The Collected Poems, 1999; poetry editor La. State U. Press, 1966-68; contbr. articles to profl. publs. Mem. ACLU. Recipient Henry Bellaman Poetry award, 1957, award in poetry Arts Fund, 1973, Prix de Rome, Am. Acad. Arts and Letters, 1976, Nat. Poets prize, 1990, Charity Randall citation Internat. Poetry Forum, 1993, John William Corrington award for excellence in lit., Centenary Coll., Shreveport, La., 1994, Acad. Lit. award AAAL, 1995, Presdl. Inaugural Poet, 1997; named Bread Loaf fellow in poetry, 1963. Mem. MLA, PEN, AAUP, South Ctrl. MLA, Am. Lit. Translators Assn. (v.p. 1978-79, pres. 1979-81), Authors' Guild, Soc. Benemerito dell'Assn. Centro Romanesco Trilussa (Rome). Home: 1111 Valley View Dr Fayetteville AR 72701-1603 E-mail: mwms1000@aol.com.

WILLIAMS, MILTON LAWRENCE, judge, educator; b. Nov. 14, 1932; s. Richard and Helen (Riley) W.; m. Rose King, Oct. 22, 1960; children: Milton Lawrence, Darrie T. BS, NYU, 1960; LLB, N.Y. Law Sch., 1963. Bar: N.Y. 1965, U.S. Dist. Ct. (so. and ea. dists.) N.Y. 1967, U.S. Supreme Ct. 1968, U.S. Customs Ct. 1971. Regional counsel SBA, N.Y.C., 1966-68; assoc. gen. counsel Knapp Commn., 1970-71; exec. dir. Mckay Commn., 1972; judge N.Y.C. Criminal Ct., 1977-84; acting justice N.Y. State Supreme Ct., 1978-84; adminstrv. judge criminal term N.Y. State Supreme Ct. 1st Jud. Dist., 1983-85, justice, 1985—. Dep. chief adminstrv. judge N.Y.C. Cts., 1985-93; assoc. justice appellate divsn. 1st Dept., 1994-2002, presiding justice, 2002--. Mem. N.Y. State Commn. on Sentencing Guidelines, N.Y.C., 1983-86; bd. trustees St. Patrick's Cathedral, Inner City Scholarship Fund, St. John's U. With USN, 1951-55. Mem. Assn. of Bar of City of N.Y., Sigma Pi Phi, Zeta Boule, Knight of Malta. Roman Catholic. Office: Presiding Justice Appellate Divsn First Dept 27 Madison Ave New York NY 10010-2201

WILLIAMS, MONTEL, television talk show host; Host The Montel Williams Show. Actor(TV films): Perry Mason: The Case of the Telltale Talk Show Host, 1993, Educating Matt Waters, 1996, (TV series): A Different World, The New Adventures of Robin Hood, JAG; co-author: Bodychange, 2001; author: A Dozen Ways to Sunday, 2001, Mountain Get Out of My Way. Office: 433 W 53rd St New York NY 10019-5603

WILLIAMS, MORGAN LLOYD, retired investment banker; b. N.Y.C., Mar. 30, 1935; s. John Lloyd and Adelaide Veronica (Patchell) W.; m. Margaret Patricia Rooney, May 13, 1961; children: Morgan Lloyd Jr., John Graham, Christine Joyce. BS in Econs., Wharton Sch., U. Pa., 1957; MBA, Columbia U., 1961. V.p., stockholder Kidder, Peabody & Co., N.Y.C., 1970-90, mng. dir., 1985-87. Trustee Inc. Village of Plandome, N.Y., 1982-86, mayor, 1986-87. Lt. USN, 1957-59. Mem. Nassau Country Club (Glen Cove, N.Y.). Republican. Roman Catholic. Home: 79 Long Ridge Rd Plandome NY 11030-1541

WILLIAMS, NANCY LOUISE, health care facilities evaluator; b. Fremont, Ohio, Sept. 6, 1947; d. Dale Ronald and Helen Myrtle (Peterson) Shedenhelm; m. Eddie Lewis Williams, Dec. 10, 1971; 1 child, Nicole Lynn. Diploma, Clara Maass Meml. Hosp., 1968. RN, N.J. Staff nurse Clara Maass Meml. Hosp., Belleville, N.J., 1968, 69-72; acting head nurse Johns Hopkins Hosp., Balt., 1968-69; charge nurse East Orange (N.J.) Gen. Hosp., 1972-73; asst. head nurse Meml. Gen. Hosp., Union, N.J., 1973-76; staff nurse Hosp. Ctr. Orange (N.J.), 1976-82, Meml. Hosp. Burlington County, Mt. Holly, N.J., 1982-85; health care facilities evaluator N.J. Dept. Health, Trenton, 1985—. Democrat. Methodist. Avocations: crocheting, reading, jazz. Home: 36 Eden Rock Ln Willingboro NJ 08046-2211 Office: NJ Dept Health 300 Whitehead Rd Trenton NJ 08619-3253

WILLIAMS, NATALIE, professional basketball player, restaurant executive; b. Utah , Nov. 30, 1970; d. Nate Williams; 1 adopted child Sydney 1 child Turasi. Profl. basketball player Portland Power ABL, 1997—99, Long Beach StringRays, 1998, Utah Starzz, 2000—; mem. U.S. Women's gold-medal winning basketball team , Sydney, Australia, 2000; owner Natalie's, Salt Lake City, 2002—. Named Female Athlete of Yr., USA Basketball, 1999, Winter Championship Team, 2002, Utah's Female Athlete of Century, 2nd Greatest Athlete Utah, Sports Illustrated . Office: 301 W South Temple Salt Lake City UT 84101*

WILLIAMS, NATHANIEL, JR. elementary education educator; b. Jacksonville, Fla., June 7, 1940; s. Nathaniel Sr. and Alice Elizabeth (Dusom) W.; m. Carol Ann Odom, Sept. 6, 1969; children: Monica C., Nathaniel Joshua. BS in Chemistry and Math., Bethune-Cookman Coll., Daytona Beach, Fla., 1965; M in Teaching Elem., U. Pitts., 1973. Chemist Pitts. Plate Glass Coating and Resin, Springdale, Pa., 1966-67; ins. agt. Can. Life Assurance Co., Pitts., 1967-70; tutorial tchr. Model Cities Program, 1968-69; employment adminstr. South Oakland Citizen Coun., 1969-70; substitute tchr. Bd. Edn., 1970-72; elem. tchr. Penn Hills (Pa.) Sch. Dist., 1973—. Dir. edn. Pitts. Challenge, Wilkinsburg, Pa., 1974-79; bd. dirs. East End Family Ctr., Pitts., 1982-84; elem. evaluator Pa. Dept. Edn., Harrisburg, 1992—. Editor newsletter Ethnic Minority News, 1989—; coord. sci. program Invent Am., 1993. Ch. trustee, deacon Lincoln Ave. Ch. of God, Pitts., 1980-90, 94, mem. scholarship com., 1990-94. Recipient 1st place Mural award WQED/MacDonald, Pitts., 1992, plaque Ethnic Minority Caucus, Gettysburg, Pa., 1993. Mem. NEA, Pa. State Edn. Assn. (Western region com. chair 1988-94, bd. dirs. 1989-91), Penn Hills Edn. Assn. (com. chair 1983-94). Democrat. Avocations: reading, science projects, plays. Home: 218 Hawkins Ave Braddock PA 15104-2117 Office: Dible Elem Sch 1079 Jefferson Rd Pittsburgh PA 15235-4723

WILLIAMS, NEIL, JR. lawyer; b. Charlotte, N.C., Mar. 22, 1936; s. Lyman Neil and Thelma (Peterson) W.; m. Sue Sigmon, Aug. 23, 1958; children: Fred R., Susan S. AB, Duke U., 1958, JD, 1961. Bar: Ga. 1962, U.S. Dist. Ct. (no. dist.) Ga. 1977, U.S. Ct. Appeals (11th cir.) 1977. Assoc. Alston & Bird (and predecessor firm), Atlanta, 1961—65, ptnr., 1966—99, mng. ptnr., 1984-96; gen. counsel, global ptnr. Amvescap PLC, 1999—. Bd. dirs. Nat. Data Corp., Atlanta, Printpack, Inc., Atlanta, Acuity Brands, Inc., Atlanta. Chmn. bd. trustees Duke U., 1983—88, trustee, 1980—93; chmn. bd. trustees Vasser Woolley Found., Atlanta, 1975—, Leadership Atlanta, 1976—80; trustee Brevard Music Ctr., 1977—86, 1991—2001, Presbyn. Ch. USA Found., Jeffersonville, Ind., 1983—90, Research Triangle Inst., 1983—88, The Duke Endowment, Charlotte, NC, 1997—; bd. dirs. Atlanta Symphony Orch., 1970—76, 1984—93, 1995—98, pres., 1988—90; bd. dirs. Woodruff Arts Ctr., 1987—98, 1999—, chmn., 2001—; bd. counsellors The Carter Ctr., Atlanta, 1987—96, Ctrl. Atlanta Progress, 1984—96; bd. dirs. Am. Symphony Orch. League, Washington, 1990—2000, chmn., 1995—99. Recipient Disting. Alumni award Duke U., 1991, Rhyne award, 1996. Mem. ABA, Am. Bar Found., State Bar Ga., Am. Law Inst., Atlanta C. of C. (bd. dirs. 1992-97, vice chmn. 1994-97), Piedmont Driving Club, Commerce Club (Atlanta), University Club (N.Y.C.), Phi Beta Kappa, Omicron Delta Kappa. Home: 3 Nacoochee Pl NW Atlanta GA 30305-4164 Office: Amvescap PLC 1315 Peachtree St NE Atlanta GA 30309-3503 E-mail: neil_williams@amvescap.com.

WILLIAMS, NEIL FRANKLIN, physical education educator; b. Bridgeport, Conn., Mar. 8, 1946; m. Sheron Rose Stokes, Aug. 25, 1968; 1 child, Adam. BS, Harpur Coll., Binghamton, N.Y., 1967; MS, Springfield (Mass.) Coll., 1972, PhD, 1975. Tchr. Vernon Verona Sherrill (N.Y.) Schs., 1968-71; grad. asst. Springfield (Mass.) Coll., 1972-75; tchr. Children's Study Home, Springfield, 1974-75, West Springfield (Mass.) Schs., 1975-81; lectr. Smith Coll., Northampton, Mass., 1981-82; prof. phys. edn. Eastern Conn. State U., Willimantic, 1983—. Cons. Spl. Olympics, Agawam, Mass., 1978-88, various sch. dists., N.Y., Conn., Mass., 1983—. Contbr. articles to profl. jours. Coach, Little League Baseball, Longmeadow, 1985—. Grantee Eastern Conn. State U. Faculty Devel. Orgn., Willimantic, Conn., 1988, Ctr. Ednl. Excellence, New Britain, 1989. Mem. AAHPER and Dance, Conn. Assn. Health, Phys. Edn., Recreation and Dance (membership chair 1983—). Avocations: antiques, sports. Office: Eastern Conn State U High St Willimantic CT 06226-2206

WILLIAMS, NELSON GARRETT, retired lawyer, mediator; b. Detroit, Feb. 16, 1926; s. Nelson Wallace and Sylvia Marie (Bowen) W.; m. Marian Pearl Stemme, May 29, 1948 (dec. 1972); children: Elizabeth, Margaret, Roberta. BA, Bowling Green State U., 1947; MA, U. Mich., 1950; MEd, U. South Fla., 1980; JD with honors, Fla. State U., 1987. Bar: Fla. 1987. Editor Huron County Tribune, Bad Axe, Mich., 1947-48; asst. prof. Keuka Coll., Keuka Park, N.Y., 1954-57, Ball State Tchrs. Coll., Muncie, Ind., 1957-63; lectr. Ind. U., Bloomington, 1963-65; assoc. prof. Dana Coll., Blair, Nebr., 1965-69, Sch. of Ozarks, Point Lookout, Mo., 1969-72; exec. dir Am. Cancer Soc., Gainesville, Fla., 1972-74; tchr. Sumter Correctional Inst., Bushnell, Fla, 1974-84; staff atty. Withlacoochee Area Legal Svcs., Floral City, Fla., 1987-89, ret., 1989. Author: Labor Journalism, 1963; contbr. articles to popular jours. Grad. fellow U. Fla., 1951-54, Fla. Bar Found. pub. svc. fellow, 1984-87; econs. fellow Case Inst. Tech., 1954, U. Wis., 1958. Mem. Fla. Bar Assn., AAUP (chpt. pres. 1968-69), AFSCME (local v.p., del. 1978-84), Assn. for Union Democracy, Soc. Profl. Journalists, Train Collectors Assn., Lionel Collectors Club, Toy Train Operating Soc., Sigma Delta Chi, Phi Alpha Theta, Pi Sigma Alpha, Pi Gamma Mu, Phi Kappa Phi. Democrat. Avocation: collecting and writing about antique electric toy trains. Home: 7589 S Grovewood Loop Floral City FL 34436-2915

WILLIAMS, NEVILLE, international solar energy corporation executive; b. Muncie, Ind., Mar. 28, 1943; s. Donald Charles and Rose Eileen (Boughton) W. Student, U. Colo., 1964-66, U. Neuchatel, Switzerland, 1967. Freelance corr., Vietnam, 1968-69; freelance journalist Montreal, Que., Can., 1970-71, London, 1971-73; writer, producer Sta. WNBC-TV News, N.Y.C., 1973-74; freelance writer Telluride, Colo., 1975-79; media liaison Office of Solar Energy U.S. Dept. Energy, Washington, 1979-80; dir. of mktg. Telluride Ski Resort, Inc., 1981-83; owner, operator Hist. Sheridan Opera Ho., Telluride, 1983-85; nat. media dir. Greenpeace U.S.A., Washington, 1987-89; chmn., pres. Solar Electric Light Fund, 1990-97; also, bd. dirs. Chmn., CEO, Solar Electric Light Co.; chmn. SELCO-India, SELCO-Vietnam, SELCO-Sri Lanka. Author: The New Exiles, 1971, (monograph) Great Telluride Strike, 1977; contbr. articles to N.Y. Times mag., Penthouse, Outside, New Times, The Nation, The New Republic, Nature, others. Apptd. mem. Adv. Com. for Commerce and Devel., State of Colo., 1980-85; apptd. mem. Gov.'s Motion Picture & TV Commn., 1981-85. Fellow Internat. Solar Energy Soc. Avocations: mountaineering, hiking, history, metaphysics. Office: Solar Electric Light Co 35 Wisconsin Cir Chevy Chase MD 20815-7015 E-mail: info@selco-intl.com.

WILLIAMS, OLIVER FRANKLIN, priest, educator; b. West Orange, N.J., Dec. 4, 1939; s. Justin James Williams and Ruth Amelda Flammer. BS in Chem. Engring., U. Notre Dame, 1961, MTh, 1969; PhD, Vanderbilt U., 1974. Prof. U. Notre Dame, Ind., 1973—, dir. Master of Divinity program, 1974—77, assoc. provost, 1987—94, dir. Ctr. for Ethics and Religious Values in Bus., 1994—. Chmn. bd. leadership devel. program (USSALEP), U.S. - South Africa, Washington, 1995—; mem. adv. coun. U.S. Cos. in South Africa (Sullivan Principles), N.Y.C., 1987—94; bd. trustees St. Augustine's U., Johannesburg, 1996—. Co-author: (Book) Economic Imperatives and Ethical Values, 2001; author: The Apartheid Crisis, 1986; Editor, contbr.: book Global Codes of Conduct: An Idea Whose Time Has Come. Bd. dirs. Edn. Africa, Johannesburg, 1993, Catholic Charities, Diocese of Fort Wayne, South Bend, 1986—92. Named Recommended by Coun. for Internat. Exch. of Scholars for a Fulbright in South Africa, 2002—03; recipient Charles C. Slater Meml. award, Jour. Macromarketing, 1992. Mem.: Assn. for Practical and Profl. Ethics, Soc. for Bus. Ethics, Acad. Mgmt. (social issues divsn.) (chairperson 1990—91). Roman Catholic. Avocations: hiking, travel, writing.

WILLIAMS, OWEN BRIAN, music educator; b. Thomson, Ga., Apr. 25, 1958; s. Owen and Ruth Williams; m. Jana Grace Baxley; children: Jeremy, Bethany. B in Music Edn., Ga. Coll., 1980; M in Music Edn., Ga. State U., 1989. T-5 TSS Ga. State Bd. Edn. Choral dir. Forest Pk. (Ga.) Jr. High, 1980—85, Mundy's Mill Jr. High, Jonesboro, 1985—89, Lovejoy (Ga.) H.S., 1989—99, Upson Lee H.S., Thomaston, 1999—. Named Tchr. of Yr., Mfrs.' Round Table, 2002. Mem.: Profl. Assn. Ga. Educators, Am. Choral Dirs. Assn., Ga. Music Educators Assn. (condr. All State Men's Chorus 1994, choral adjudicator 1988—), Music Educators Nat. Conf. Home: 466 Pates Lake Ct Hampton GA 30228 Personal E-mail: willib@mindspring.com. E-mail: brwilliams@upson.k12.ga.us.

WILLIAMS, PAT, former congressman; b. Helena, Mont., Oct. 30, 1937; m. Carol Griffith, 1965; children: Griff, Erin, Whitney. Student, U. Mont., 1956-57, William Jewell U.; BA, U. Denver, 1961; postgrad., Western Mont. Coll.; LLD (hon.), Carroll Coll., Montana Coll. of Mineral Sci. and Tech. Mem. Mont. Ho. of Reps., 1967, 69; exec. dir. Hubert Humphrey Presdl. campaign, Mont., 1968; exec. asst. to U.S. Rep. John Melcher, 1969-71; mem. Gov.'s Employment and Tng. Council, 1972-78, Mont. Legis. Reapportionment Commn., 1973; co-chmn. Jimmy Carter Presdl. campaign, Mont., 1976; mem. 96th-102nd Congresses from 1st Mont. dist., 1979-96; sr. fellow W. U. Mont., Missoula, 1996—. Ranking mem. postsecondary edn. subcom. Coordinator Mont. Family Edn. Program, 1971-78. Served with U.S. Army, 1960-61; Served with Army N.G., 1962-69. Mem. Mont. Fedn. Tchrs. Lodges: Elks. Democrat. Home: 3533 Lincoln Hills Pt Missoula MT 59802-3381 Office: U Montana O Connor Ctr Rocky Mtn W Milw Sta 2nd Fl Missoula MT 59812-0001

WILLIAMS, PATRICIA ANNE, philosopher, writer; b. Alexandria, Va., May 26, 1944; d. Samuel Leonard and Kay Cloaninger Williams. BA, Coll.of William and Mary, Williamsburg, Va., 1966; MA in English, U. Va., 1967, MA Philosophy, 1985; PhD, U. of Guelph, Ont., Can., 1989. Lectr. La Trobe U., Melbourne, Australia, 1968—71; asst. prof. Virginia State U., Petersburg, 1990—95. Del. Citizen Amb. People to People Program, China, 1993. Author: (book) Doing without Adam and Eve: Sociobiology and Original Sin, 2001, Where Christianity Went Wrong, When, and What You Can Do About It, 2001; editor: Evolution and Human Values, 1995; contbr. jours., encys. including. Mem. ACLU, 1973—; charter mem. U.S. Holocaust Meml. Mus., Washington, 1993—; mem. So. Poverty Law Ctr. Wall of Toleration, Montgomery. Fellow NEH fellow, 1989. Mem.: Inst. on Religion in an Age of Sci., Internat. Soc. for History, Philosophy, and Social Studies of Biology (program chmn. 1992—93), Philosophy of Sci. Assn., Am. Philos. Assn. Mem. Soc. Of Friends. Avocations: travel, hiking. Home: PO Box 69 Covesville VA 22931 Personal E-mail: theologyauthor@aol.com.

WILLIAMS, PATSY RUTH, poet, freelance/self-employed writer; b. Shreveport, La., Oct. 23, 1946; d. Frank and Ruth (Holmes) W. BA, Dillard U., 1969; MA, So. Meth. U., 1971. Instr. psychology So. U., Shreveport, 1969, Grambling (La.) State U., 1972-73. Author (poems) Red River Revel, 1979, World of Poetry, 1991, Listen With Your Heart, 1992; contbr. poems to profl. publs. including Se La Vie Writer's Jour., Winter's Gems, 1993, Living Jewels-A Treasury of Lyric Poetry, 1993, others. Democrat. Methodist. Avocations: art, recording & writing music. Home: 3333 Sidney St Shreveport LA 71107-4631 E-mail: pwilli94@bellsouth.net.

WILLIAMS, PAUL, retired federal agency administrator; b. Jacksonville, Ill., Aug. 6, 1929; s. Russell and Bernice (Wheeler) W.; m. Ora B. Mosby; 1 child, Reva Williams. BA, Ill. Coll., 1956, LHD, 1980. Dir. fin. City of Chgo., 1956-63; assoc. dir. fin. United Planning Orgn., Washington, 1964-65; internat. adminstrv. officer U.S. Dept. State, 1965-68; dir. of office mgmt. U.S. HUD, 1968-93, gen. deputy dept. fair housing and equal opportunity, 1993-94, dep. ops. and mgmt., 1994-97, ret., 1997. Cons. S.E. Econ. Devel. Corp., Nat. Exec. Svc. Corp., 1998; Buzan learning instr. for mind mapping, 2000-2002. Author: Questionnaire on Execution of Urban Renewal Programs, 1959. Pres. Bel Pre Civic Assn., Wheaton, Md., 1978, bd. dirs., 1971, 79; pres. Bel Pre PTA, Wheaton, 1973; bd. dirs. Habitat for Humanity Montgomery County, Md., 1998. Sgt. U.S. Army, 1948-52. Recipient letter of recognition for 36 yrs. fed. svc. U.S. Pres., letter of recognition for 36 yrs. govt. svc. Senators of Md., citation for 36 yrs. dedicated govt. svc. Gov. of Md., cert. of recognition Nat. Assn. Black and Minority C. of C., 1987. Baptist. Avocations: reading, jogging, golf, Tai Chi. Home: Unit 306 2900 N LeisureWorld Blvd Silver Spring MD 20906-2321 E-mail: e-owilli7738@aol.com.

WILLIAMS, PAUL ALAN, artist; b. Detroit, Sept. 10, 1934; s. Archie Theodore and Alva (Constance) W.; m. Sandi Oliver Simoni, May 2, 1982; children: John Mortimer Wilson, Melissa Anne Wilson, Philip Keith Wilson. Student, Chadsey Art Sch., Detroit, 1948-49, Meinzinger, 1950-51; BPA, Art Ctr., L.A., 1959. Illustrator self-employed, Weston, Conn., 1962-84; fine artist, oil painter self-employed, 1982—. Art tchr. Hampton, Va., 1960-61. Prin. works include 3 major internat. calendars Scot Paper Co., 1972-79 (Gold Medal); space coordinator artist for major promotions Nordon-Unit-Tech., 1982-85 (12 awards), Radio City Music Hall, 1980-83. With U.S. Army, 1959-61. Recipient Bravo Advt. award, Detroit Art Dirs., 1960—80, award of excellence, Soc. of Illustrators, 1967—71, Gold Medal Ccert., 1972—82, 1st prize, Braswell Galleries, 1987—98, Greenfield Hill Gallery, 1993, 1994, 1996, auction record (paintings), 1987—2001. Mem. Soc. Am. Impressionists, Allied Artists of Am. Inc., Am. Fedn. Artists, New Eng. Appraisers Assn., Soc. of Illustrators, Carriage Barn of Waverly Pk. Avocations: antique collecting, historian, gardening, mini-dashunds and bassets. Home: 11 Tubbs Spring Dr Weston CT 06883-1413 Office: Sandi Oliver Fine Art PO Box 1203 Weston CT 06883-0203

WILLIAMS, PAUL C(HESTER), consultant; b. Ironton, Ohio, Jan. 14, 1926; s. Paul Morton and Elsie Doreta (Venz) W.; m. Jeanne Ellen Potter, Jan. 22, 1955; children: Amber, Mark, Ross. BS in Marine Engring., U.S. Mcht. Marine Acad., Kings Point, N.Y., 1947; BS in Mech. Engring., Ohio State U., 1951; postgrad., Northeastern U., Boston, 1966. Test engr. Babcock Ann Wilcox Co., Alliance, Ohio, 1951-56; asst. to engring. mgr. Babcock and Wilcox Co., Barberton, 1957, engring. sect. mgr., 1957-59, gen. prodn. control mgr., 1959-61, purchasing agt., 1962-69; pres. Clifford Industries, Wadsworth, 1969-71; gen. mgr., v.p. Stock Equipment Co., Chagrin Falls, 1971-86; owner Paul Williams & Assocs., Medina, 1986—. Mem., pres. Drug Abuse Commn., Medina County, 1992-98. Lt. USN, 1944-47. Mem. ASME, Am. Nuclear Soc. (local sect. pres. 1962-98). Achievements include invention of sintering test, superheater slag test, 1954, container filling radioactive waste, 1981. Home and Office: 3364 E Smith Rd Medina OH 44256-8785 E-mail: pwa7230915@aol.com.

WILLIAMS, PAULINE M. psychiatric-mental and community health nurse; b. Mt. Pleasant, Mich., Feb. 26, 1942; d. George Francis and Eva May (Cotter) Campbell; m. Clyde H. Williams, Apr. 16, 1966 (dec.); 1 child Lynette M. Williams Disberry. Diploma, St. Mary's Hosp. Sch. Nursing, Saginaw, Mich., 1963; student, Cen. Mich. U. RN, Ind., Mich., Fla., N.C. Pub. health nurse Saginaw County Health Dept., Saginaw, 1972-80; staff nurse Mercy Wood Psych. Hosp., Ann Arbor, Mich., 1980-81; psych. staff nurse Meth. Hosp., Indpls., 1981-83; head nurse Meml. Hosp., South Bend, 1983-88; nursing supr. Ball Meml. Hosp., Muncie, 1988-90, Valley Inst. Psychiatry for Children and Adolescents, Owensboro, Ky., 1990-91; staff nurse Psychiat. Ctr., Tallahassee Meml. Hosp., 1991-92; staff nurse psychiatry Duke Med. Ctr. Duke U., Durham, N.C., 1992-2000; behavioral health resource nurse Meml. Hosp., South Bend, Ind., 2000—. Speaker on pub. health. Home: 23028 Montrose Cir Elkhart IN 46514 E-mail: PLWill219@aol.com.

WILLIAMS, PEARL See GOOD-BLACK, EDITH

WILLIAMS, PETER CHARLES, engineer; b. Chgo., July 14, 1949; s. Maurice Jaquetot and Betty Jane (Bath) W.; m. Ann Hazard Sawyer, Aug. 28, 1971; children: Marion, Joan, Joseph. BS in Chem. Engring., MSME, Tufts U., 1972. Registered profl. engr., Ohio. Environ. cons. Eli Bulba, Inc., Cambridge, Mass., 1973-74; ind. engring. cons. Gates Mills, Ohio, 1975-76; project engr. Whitey Co., Highland Heights, 1976-83, chief engr., 1983-91, Crawford Fitting Co., Solon, 1992—. Mem. ASME, Sigma Xi, Tau Beta Pi. Achievements include 28 U.S. patents and numerous foreign patents. Office: Crawford Fitting Co 29500 Solon Rd Solon OH 44139-3474

WILLIAMS, PETER MACLELLAN, nuclear engineer; b. N.Y.C., Aug. 30, 1931; s. Gilbert Harris and Evelyn (Buss) W.; m. Lois Crane, Oct. 6, 1956; children: Jane, Gilbert, Katherine, Anne, Louise, Robert. BChemE, Cornell U., 1954; MS in Nuclear Engring., MIT, 1957; PhD in Nuclear Engring., U. Md., 1971. Engr. DuPont Savannah River, Aiken, S.C., 1954-55; task engr. AGN, San Ramon, Calif., 1957-60; project mgr. Am. Machine & Fdry., Greenwich, Conn., 1960-62; research staff Princeton U., N.J., 1962-67; sr. project mgr., specialist in high temperature gas cooled reactors U.S. Nuclear Regulatory Commn., Washington, 1967-91; dir. div. high temperature gas cooled reactors U.S. Dept. of Energy, 1991-94; cons. Internat. Atomic Energy Agy., Vienna, 1994—; cons. nuclear engr., 1995—. Mem. Chernobyl Tracking Team, 1986; U.S. del. to gas-cooled reactors working group, Internat. Atomic Energy Agy., 1991; steering com. mem. U.S.-Japan Implementing Agreement on gas-cooled reactors, 1991. Contbr. articles to profl. jours.; author various reports. Scoutmaster Boy Scouts Am., Potomac, Md., 1972, cubmaster, 1983-86; pres. PTA Winston Churchill High Sch., Potomac, 1981. Assoc. fellow AIAA; mem. Am. Nuclear Soc., Sigma Xi. Democrat. Unitarian Universalist. Achievements include patent for liquid core nuclear rocket; patent pending for advanced helium turbine reactor. Home and Office: 9418 Thrush Ln Potomac MD 20854-3991 E-mail: peterwill@starpower.net.

WILLIAMS, PHILIP COPELAIN, gynecologist, obstetrician; b. Vicksburg, Miss., Dec. 9, 1917; s. John Oliver and Eva (Copelain) W.; B.S. magna cum laude, Morehouse Coll., 1937; M.D., U. Ill., 1941; m. Constance Shielda Rhetta, May 29, 1943; children— Philip, Susan Carol, Paul Rhetta. Intern, Cook County Hosp., Chgo., 1942-43, resident in ob-gyn, 1946-48; resident in gynecology U. Ill., 1948-49; practice medicine specializing in ob-gyn, Chgo., 1949— ; mem. staff St. Joseph Hosp., Ill. Masonic Hosp., Cook County Hosp., McGaw Hosp.; clin. prof. Med. Sch. Northwestern U., Chgo. Bd. dirs. Am. Cancer Soc. Chgo. unit and Ill. div. Served with U.S. Army, 1943-45. Recipient Civic award Loyola U., 1970; Edwin S. Hamilton Interstate Teaching award, 1984; diplomate Am. Bd. Ob-Gyn, Fellow ACS, Internat. Coll. Surgeons; mem. AMA, Chgo., Ill. med. socs., AMA, Chgo. Gynecol. Soc. (treas. 1975-78, pres. 1980-81), Am. Fertility Soc., Inst. Medicine, N.Y. Acad. Scis., AAAS. Presbyn. Clubs: Barclay, Carlton, Plaza. Contbr. articles to profl. jours. E-mail: pwill2oo@aol.com. Home: 1040 N Lake Shore Dr Chicago IL 60611-1165 E-mail: PWill200@aol.omc.

WILLIAMS, PHILIP LEE, b. Athens, Ga., Jan. 30, 1950; s. Marshall Woodson and Ruth Sisk Williams; m. Linda Rowley, Sept. 30, 1972; children: Brandon, Megan. AB in Journalism, U. Ga., 1972. Editor Clayton (Ga.) Tribune, 1972, Athens Observer, 1978-85; copy editor Madisonian, Madison, Ga., 1973-78; sci. writer U. Ga., Athens, 1985-92, dir. pub. info., 1997—. Editor, founder poetry mag. Ataraxia, 1974-77. Author: (fiction) The Heart of a Distant Forest, 1984, paperback edit., 1985, Brit. edit., 1986, Swedish translation, 1988, paperback trade edit., 1991 (Townsend prize for fiction 1986), Slow Dance in Autumn, 1988, paperback edit., 1989, Japanese translation, 1990, All the Western Stars, 1998, German translation, 1993, The Song of Daniel, 1989, softcover edit., 1990 (Georgia Author of Yr. award in Fiction), Perfect Timing, 1990, paperback edit., 1990 (Lit. Guild selection), Final Heat, 1992, French translation, 1994, German translation, 1998, Blue Crystal, 1993 (Lit. Guild selection), The True and Authentic History of Jenny Dorset, 1997, paperback edit., 2001; (nonfiction) The Silent Stars Go By, A True Christmas Story, 1998, large print edit., 2000, Crossing Wildcat Ridge, 1999; (poetry) New Seeds, 1972; (anthologies) Speak So I Shall Know Thee, 1989, You Haven't to Deserve, 1992, Georgia Voices: Nonfiction, 1994, The New Georgia Guide, 1996, Georgia Voices: Poetry, 2000; writer, co-prodr.: (documentaries) Oconee: Valley of the Chiefs, 1987, Eugene Odum: An Ecologist's Life, 1997 (Finalist's award N.Y. Film Festival, 1997, Hon. Mention award 1997), Hugh Kenner: A Modern Master, 1999-2000 (Hon. Mention Columbus Film Festival, Hon. Mention Communicator award); contbr. prose, essays, stories to lib. publs. Office: U Ga 300 New College Athens GA 30602 E-mail: phil@franklin.uga.edu.

WILLIAMS, PORTIA JEAN, educational organization executive, writer; b. Portsmouth, Ohio, Dec. 23, 1969; d. George Sisson and Betty Jean Reaves; m. Mark Andrew Williams, Apr. 25, 1993; children: Jori, Pajah, Micah. AA, Shawnee State U., 1995, BA in English and Humanities, 1996. Cert. tchr. Ohio. Resident mgr. RLJ Mgmt. Co., Portsmouth, 1994; substitute tchr.

Portsmouth City Schs., 1997—2000; prevention specialist Counseling Ctr., 2000—01; admission counselor Shawnee State U., 2001; pres., CEO Higher Heights Enterprises, 2001—. Spkr. in field.; mem. adv. planning team So. Ohio Mus., Portsmouth, 2000—, cons., 2002—; mem. 12th ann. leadership conf. U. Cin., 2000—01. Author: Soaring to New Heights, 2001; actor: (column) Portia's Perspective, 2002. Mem. com. Martin Luther King Jr. Com., Portsmouth, 2002—; bd. dirs. 14th St. Cmty. Ctr., 2001—, Habitat for Humanity, Portsmouth, 2001—. Mem.: Poetry & Praise Prodns., Inc., Bus. and Profl. Women (exec. dir. 2001—, Young Careerist award 2001). Avocations: poetry, volunteer work, walking, singing. Home: 1214 Coles Blvd Portsmouth OH 45662

WILLIAMS, PRESTON NOAH, theology educator; b. Alcolu, S.C., May 23, 1926; s. Anderson James and Bertha Bell (McRae) W.; m. Constance Marie Willard, June 4, 1956; children— Mark Gordon, David Bruce. AB, Washington and Jefferson Coll., 1947, MA, 1948; B.D., Johnson C. Smith U., 1950; S.T.M., Yale, 1954; PhD, Harvard, 1967. Ordained to ministry Presbyn. Ch., 1950. Martin Luther King. Jr. prof. social ethics Boston U. Sch. Theology, 1970-71; Houghton prof. theology and contemporary change Harvard U. Div. Sch., Cambridge, Mass., 1971—, acting dean, 1974-75; acting dir. W.E.B. DuBois Inst., 1975-77. Editor-at-large: Christian Century, 1972—; contbr. articles to profl. jours. Mem. Am. Acad. Religion (pres. 1975—), Am. Soc. Christian Ethics (dir., pres. 1974-75), Phi Beta Kappa. Home: 36 Fairmont St Belmont MA 02478-2919 Office: 45 Francis Ave Cambridge MA 02138-1911

WILLIAMS, QUENTIN CHRISTOPHER, geophysicist, educator; b. Wilmington, Del., Jan. 1, 1964; s. Ferd Elton and Anne Katherine W.; m. Elise Barbara Knittle, Dec. 19, 1987; children: Byron Frederick, Alanna Katherine, Lynette Barbara, Benjamin Ferd. AB, Princeton U., 1983; PhD, U. Calif., Berkeley, 1988. Rsch. geophysicist Inst. of Tectonics, U. Calif., Santa Cruz, 1988-91; asst. prof. dept. earth sci. U. Calif., 1991-95, assoc. prof. dept. earth sci., 1995-99, prof. dept. earth sci., 1999—. Contbr. articles to profl. jours. Presdl. Faculty fellow, 1993-98. Fellow Am. Geophys. Union (Macelwane medal 2000), Mineral. Soc. Am. (award 2000); mem. Am. Phys. Soc. Office: U Calif Santa Cruz Dept Earth Sciences Santa Cruz CA 95064 E-mail: qwilliams@emerald.ucsc.edu.

WILLIAMS, QUINN PATRICK, lawyer; b. Evergreen Park, Ill., May 6, 1949; s. William Albert and Jeanne Marie (Quinlan) W.; m. Ingrid E. Haas; children: Michael Ryan, Mark Reed, Kelly Elizabeth. BBA, U. Wis., 1972; JD, U. Ariz., 1974. Bar: Ariz. 1975, N.Y. 1984, U.S. Dist. Ct. Ariz. 1976. V.p., sec., gen. counsel Combined Comm. Corp., Phoenix, 1975-80; sr. v.p. legal and adminstrn. Swensen's Inc., 1980-86; of counsel Winston & Strawn, 1985-87, ptnr., 1987-89, Snell & Wilmer, Phoenix, 1989—. Chmn. Ariz. Tech. Incubator, 1993-94, Ariz. Venture Capital Conf., 1993-94; co-chmn. Gov.'s Small Bus. Advocate Exec. Coun., 1993—; chair, bd. dirs. Greater Phoenix Econ. Coun., 1996—, Scottsdale Area Chamber Partnership; vice-chair Gov. Regulatory Coun., 1995-97; sec. GSPED High Tech. Cluster, 1993—. With USAR, 1967-73. Mem. ABA, State Bar Ariz., Maricopa County Bar Assn., N.Y. Bar Assn., Internat. Franchise Assn., Scottsdale C. of C. (bd. dirs.), Paradise Valley Country Club, Scottsdale Charros. Republican. Roman Catholic. Home: 6201 E Horseshoe Rd Paradise Valley AZ 85253 Office: Snell & Wilmer One Arizona Ctr Phoenix AZ 85004 E-mail: qwilliams@msn.com.

WILLIAMS, R. SANDERS, dean, academic administrator, educator, researcher; Undergrad., Princeton U., 1970; MD, Duke U., 1974, fellow in cardiology, 1977; resident internal medicine, Mass. Gen. Hosp. Asst. prof. medicine, physiology, cell biology Duke U. , 1980, assoc. prof. medicine and microbiology, 1986; chief cardiology, prof. internal medicine, biochemistry, and molecular biology U. Tex. Southwestern Med. Ctr.; dean, vice chancellor acad. affairs Duke U. Sch. Medicine, 2001—. Rschr. in field; vis. prof. dept. biochemistry Oxford U. , 1984—85. Contbr. more than 150 scholarly articles to biomed. jours. , such as Cell, Nature, New Eng. Jour. Medicine , Proceedings of the Nat. Acad. Scis. Achievements include being the leader of the Dallas Heart Disease Prevention Project, an innovative program of research in the genetic epidemiology of cardiovascular disease. Office: Duke U Sch Medicine Box 2927 Durham NC 27710*

WILLIAMS, RALPH CHESTER, JR. physician, educator; b. Washington, Feb. 17, 1928; s. Ralph Chester and Annie (Perry) W.; m. Mary Elizabeth Adams, June 23, 1951; children— Cathy, Frederick, John (dec.), Michael, Ann. AB with distinction, Cornell U., 1950, MD, 1954; MD (hon.), U. Lund, Sweden, 1991. Diplomate Am. Bd. Internal Medicine. Intern Mass. Gen. Hosp., Boston, 1954-55, asst. resident in internal medicine, 1955-56; resident in internal medicine N.Y. Hosp., 1956-57; chief resident Mass. Gen. Hosp., Boston, 1959-60; guest investigator Rockefeller Inst., N.Y.C., 1961-63; physician in internal medicine and rheumatology, 1963—; assoc. prof. U. Minn., Mpls., 1963-68, prof., 1968-69; prof., chmn. dept. medicine U. N.Mex., Albuquerque, 1969-88; Schott prof. rheumatology and medicine U. Fla., Gainesville, 1988-98; with rheumatology dept. U. N.Mex. Sch. Medicine, Albuquerque, 1998, emeritus prof. medicine, 1998—. Diplomate Am. Bd. Internal Medicine. Assoc. editor: Jour. Lab. and Clin. Medicine, 1966-69; mem. editl. bd.: Arthritis and Rheumatism, 1968—; contbr. articles to profl. jours. Capt. USAF, 1957-59. Master Am. Coll. Rheumatology; fellow ACP; mem. Am. Assn. Immunology, Assn. Am. Physicians, Am. Fedn. Clin. Rsch., Am. Soc. Clin. Investigation, Ctrl. Soc. Clin. Rsch., Western Soc. Clin. Investigator, Phi Beta Kappa, Alpha Omega Alpha. Achievements include rsch. in immunologic processes and connective tissue diseases. Home: 624 E Alameda St Apt 13 Santa Fe NM 87501-2293 E-mail: coolypatch@msn.com.

WILLIAMS, RALPH WATSON, JR. retired securities company executive; b. Atlanta, July 2, 1933; s. Ralph Watson and Minnie Covington (Hicks) W.; m. Nancy Jo Morgan, Mar. 19, 1955 (dec. Dec. 1989); children: Ralph Watson III, Nancy Jane, John Martin Hicks; m. Almonese Brown Clifton, Nov. 24, 1990. Grad., Sewanee Mil. Acad., 1951; BBA, U. Ga., 1955. Trainee banking Trust Co. Ga., Atlanta, 1955; mcpl. sales staff Courts & Co., 1955-57; v.p., salesman securities First Southeastern Corp., 1957-60; br. mgr. Francis I. duPont & Co., 1960-69; spl. partner duPont Glore Forgan Inc., N.Y.C., 1969-70, gen. partner, 1970, exec. v.p., 1971—, sr. v.p., 1972—; also dir.; sr. v.p., dir., mem. exec. com. duPont-Walston Inc., 1973-74; sr. v.p. E.F. Hutton & Co. Inc., 1974-81; exec. v.p., dir. E.F. Hutton & Co., Inc., 1981-88; exec. v.p. Shearson Lehman Hutton Inc., Atlanta, 1988-89; ret., 1989. Bd. trustees St. Andrews Sewanee (Tenn.) Sch., chmn. fin. com. Mem. Nat. Assn. Security Dealers (chmn. dist. com. 7), Benedicts Atlanta, Phi Delta Theta. Clubs: Commerce (Atlanta), Capital City (Atlanta), Piedmont Driving (Atlanta). Presbyterian. Home: 3504 Dumbarton Rd NW Atlanta GA 30327-2614

WILLIAMS, RANDOLPH LEIGH, management consultant, rare book dealer; b. N.Y.C., Feb. 16, 1943; s. Thomas Leigh Williams and Louise Archer Clyde, Norman Browning (Stepfather); m. Karen Garvan Noble. BA, Harvard U., 1967; student, Columbia U. Rare Book Program, 1988—91. Tech. advisor Honeywell Info. Sys., N.Y.C., 1967—81; v.p., dir. tech. Am. Express Internat. Bank, 1981—87; owner Randolph Williams, Bookman, 1987—; v.p., client ptnr. Gartner, Inc., Stamford, Conn., 1993—2001; mgmt. cons. Williams Performance Consulting, N.Y.C., 2001—. Mem.: Trollope Soc. (pres., founder 1989), Harvard Club of N.Y., Grolier Club, Knickerbocker Club. Avocations: book collecting, travel, scuba diving, athletics. Home: 11 West 81st St New York NY 10024 Office: Williams Performance Mgmt 11 West 81st St New York NY 10024 Personal E-mail: randolph.williams@att.net.

WILLIAMS, RANDOLPH STUART, urban planner; b. St. Petersburg, Fla., Nov. 9, 1961; s. Kenneth Sterling and Mary Elizabeth (Lemmons) W. BS in Geography and Planning, Western Carolina U., Cullowhee, 1983; MS in Architecture, U. N.C., Charlotte, 1997. Planning technician City of Ft. Myers, Fla., 1984-85; jr. planner City of Sarasota, 1985-86; planner City of Lenoir, N.C., 1986-91; planning dir. City of Conover, 1991—. Coach youth soccer 1978 Catawba Valley Blast, Hickory, N.C., 1995, 1982 Catawba Valley Blast, Hickory, 1997; asst. soccer coach Lenoir Rhyne Coll., Hickory, 1998; mem. adv. bd. Caldwell County C. of C., Lenoir, 1987-91. Mem. Am. Inst. Cert. Planners, Am. Planning Assn. (N.C. chpt.), Urban and Regional Info. Systems Assn. (instr. 1988). Methodist. Avocations: soccer, baseball, travel. Office: City of Conover 101 1st St E Conover NC 28613-2155

WILLIAMS, RANDY G. community relations executive, communication professional; b. Independence, MO, Mar. 15, 1956; s. Harold L. Williams, A. Joan Williams; m. Penny S. Robinson; children: Bradley, Kristen. Bachelor of Science, Mass Communication and Public Relations, Central Missouri State University, Warrensburg, MO, 1974—78; Certificate in Corporate Community Relations, Boston College, Boston, MA, 2000—01. Community Relations Manager American Century Investments, Kansas City, MO, 1997—2002; Communications Specialist Twentieth Century Mutual Funds (now American Century), 1995—97; Senior Media Specialist AlliedSignal Inc., 1988—95; Senior Program Planner Bendix Corporation, 1978—88. Chapter President International Association of Business Communicators, Kansas City, MO, 1993—94. Prodr.: (Education curriculum) Tips for Kids, 2000 (IABC Gold Quill Award for Outstanding Community Relations Program, 2000). Kansas City Tomorrow Leadership Program Civic Council of Kansas City, Kansas City, MO, 2001—02; Vice President - Public Relations Jim Eisenreich Foundation for Children with Tourette Syndrome, 1996—2002; Board member Coterie Theater, 1999—2002; Nominating Committee Board Girl Scouts of Mid America, 1999—2001; Scoutmaster Boy Scout Troop 603, Blue Springs, 1997—2000. Mem.: Boston College Center for Corporate Citizenship, International Association of Business Communicators (Chapter President - Kansas City Chapter 1993—94). Methodist. Avocation: Water sports, Camping, SCUBA Diving, Community Service. Office: American Century Investments 4500 Main Street Kansas City MO 64111 Business E-Mail: rgw@americancentury.com.

WILLIAMS, REBA WHITE, financial executive, writer; m. Dave H. Williams. BA in Enlgish, Duke U.; MBA, Harvard U.; MA in Art History, Hunter Coll.; MA in Philosophy, PhD in Art History, CUNY. Rschr. McKinsey & Co., Inc.; securities analyst Mitchell Hutchins, Inc.; dir. spl. projects Alliance Capital Mgmt. Corp. Bd. dirs. Alliance Capital Mgmt., Austria Fund, Spain Fund, India Liberalization Fund, So. Africa Fund; vice chmn. White Williams Pvt. Equity Ptnrs., 2001—; lectr. in field. Mem. editl. bd. Print Quar.; contbr. articles to Am. Artist, Bus. and Soc., Chgo. Daily News, Fin. Analysts Jour., The Tamarind Papers, The Daily News, Jour. of the Print World, others; author catalog essays; appeared on TV. Mem. Manhattan Cmty. Bd. 8, 1999-2000; mem. Art Commn. City N.Y., 1995-98, pres., 1997-98; mem. N.Y. State Coun. on the Arts, 1996-99, vice chmn., 1999; hon. keeper of Am. prints The Fitzwilliam Mus., Cambridge, Eng. Decorated Polish Order of Merit, cavalier of grand cross Order of Poland 1st class; recipient Pacesetter award N.Y. City Coun., 1999, Disting. Cultural Leadership award N.Y. Rep. County Com., 1999, Augustus Graham medal Bklyn. Mus., 1998, others. Mem. Cosmopolitan Club. Office: Alliance Capital Mgmt LP Ste 31R 1345 Avenue Of The Americas New York NY 10105-0302

WILLIAMS, REBECCA LYNN, lawyer, nurse; b. LaGrange, Ill., Jan. 24, 1959; d. Richard Fowler and Anita (Albro) W. BSN magna cum laude, Duke U., 1981; JD, Loyola U., 1986. Bar: Ill. 1986, U.S. Dist. Ct. (no. dist.) Ill. 1986. Nurse Children's Meml. Hosp., Chgo., 1981-84, St. Jude's Hosp., Vieux Fort, St. Lucia, 1983; assoc. McDermott, Will & Emery, Chgo., 1986-88, Winston & Strawn, Chgo., 1988-93; ptnr. Sonnenschein Nath & Rosenthal, 1993-98, Davis Wright Tremaine LLP, Seattle, 1998—. Contbr. articles to profl. jours. Patron various civic, environ., charitable and polit. groups. Mem. ABA, ANA, Am. Health Lawyers Assn. Avocations: scuba diving, reading, hiking, photography. Office: Davis Wright Tremaine LLP 2600 Century Sq 1501 4th Ave Seattle WA 98101-1688 E-mail: beckywilliams@dwt.com.

WILLIAMS, REBECCA WALLS, non-profit organization executive; b. Dallas, Apr. 3, 1954; d. Henry Leon McBee and Sarah Elizabeth (Scudder) Tindle; m. Larry D. Walls, May 4, 1974 (div. 1982); children: Robert Glen Walls, Zachary James Walls; m. Keith D. Williams, Sept. 15, 1990. AA, Richland Coll., 1980; BSW, Tex. Woman's U., 1984; postgrad., U. Tex., Arlington, 1984-86. Cert. fundraising exec. Project mgr. South Dallas Cmty. Ctr., Dallas, 1970-72; graphic artist Blanks Engraving Co., 1973-77, Rabbit Reprodns., Dallas, 1977; dir. social svcs. Family Planning and Treatment Ctrs., 1978-81; dir. Soma Health Sys., 1981-84, Richardson (Tex.) YWCA, 1984-87; dir. program planning and analysis YWCA of Met. Dallas, 1988-89; asst. regional dir. S.W. regional office CARE, Internat. Relief and Devel., Dallas, 1989-94; regional dir. south ctrl. U.S. Soc. of St. Andrew, 1994-95; exec. dir. Stress Rsch. Fedn., 1995-96; dir. Dallas Nature Ctr., 1996—. Bd. dirs. YWCA of Met. Dallas; chair Richardson Outreach Project, Vol. Ctr. of Dallas, 1986; chair com. on adminstrn. Garland (Tex.) YWCA, 1990-91; bd. dirs. young profl. league Dallas World Salute; mem. fin. adv. com. Circle Ten Explorer Scouts divsn. Boy Scouts Am. Recipient Speaker's Bur. award United Way of Met. Dallas, 1984-89, Spl. Svc. award Assn. of Retarded Citizens, 1986, 10 Yrs. of Vol. Svc. award Dallas Ind. Sch. Dist., 1989, Gov.'s Humanitarian award for outstanding vol. svc. State of Tex., 1991. Mem. NASW (internat. task force), Nat. Soc. Fundraising Execs., Network Masters, The Women's Ctr. Dallas, Fedn. of Women's Clubs, Assn. of Dirs. of Vols. (advisor to bd. of dirs.). Avocations: sculptor/potter/jewelry design, swimming, dancing.

WILLIAMS, REDFORD BROWN, medical educator; b. Raleigh, N.C., Dec. 14, 1940; s. Redford Brown Sr. and Annie Virginia (Betts) W.; m. Virginia Carter Parrott, August 9, 1940; children: Jennifer Betts, Lloyd Carter. AB, Harvard U., 1963; MD, Yale U., 1967. Diplomate Am. Bd. Internal Medicine. Intern, then resident Yale-New Haven Med. Ctr., 1967-70; sr. surgeon USPHS, Bethesda, Md., 1970-72; asst. prof. Duke U. Med. Ctr., Durham, N.C., 1972, prof. psychiatry, 1977—, prof. psychology, 1990—, dir. behavioral medicine rsch. ctr., 1985—; CEO Williams LifeSkills, Inc., 1997—. Cons. NIH rev. coms., Bethesda, 1977—. Author: The Trusting Heart, 1989, Anger Kills, 1993, Lifeskills, 1998; contbr. articles to profl. jours. Dir. N.C. Heart Assn., Chapel Hill, 1980-83. Recipient Rsch. Scientist award NIMH, 1974—; NIH grantee, 1976—. Fellow Soc. Behavioral Medicine (pres. 1984-85, Upjohn Disting. Scientist award 1992), Acad. Behavioral Medicine Rsch. (pres. 1995—); mem. Am. Psychosomatic Soc. (bd. dirs. 1978-81, pres. 1992). Unitarian Universalist. Avocation: tennis. Office: Duke U Med Ctr PO Box 3926 Durham NC 27710-0001

WILLIAMS, RHYS, minister; b. San Francisco, Feb. 27, 1929; s. Albert Rhys and Lucita (Squier) W.; m. Eleanor Hoyle Barnhart, Sept. 22, 1956; children: Rhys Hoyle, Eleanor Pierce. AB, St. Lawrence U., 1951, BD, MDiv, 1953, DD, 1966; postgrad., Union Sem., summer 1956; LLD (hon.), Emerson Coll., 1962. Ordained to ministry Unitarian Ch., 1954. Min. Unitarian Ch., Charleston, S.C., 1953-60, 1st and 2d Ch., Boston, 1960-00, min. emeritus, 2000—. Mem. faculty, field edn. supr. Harvard U., 1969—; Russell lectr. Tufts U., 1965, Minns lectr., 1986. Pres. Edward Everett Hale House, 1987—, Soc. of Cincinnati, State of N.H., 1986-89; v.p. Franklin Inst., 1960-99, , sec., 1990-96, trustee, 1999—; v.p. Benevolent Frat. Unitarian Universalist Chs., 1982-93; pres. Unitarian Universalist Urban Ministry, 1991-99, pres. emeritus, 1999—; sec. bd. trustees Emerson Coll., 1961-94, trustee, 1994—; chaplain Gen. Soc. Cin., Washington, 1977—, Founders and Patriots of Mass., SR; chmn. Festival Fund, Inc., Am.-Soviet Cultural Exch., 1989-91; trustee Opera Co. Boston, 1970—; trustee Meadville Lombard Theol. Sch., Chgo., 1971-77, mem. ministerial fellowship com., 1961-69, chmn., 1968-69; fin. chmn. Ch. Larger Fellowship, 1968-86; bd. dirs. Peter Faneuil Housing Corp., AIDS Housing, 1995, clk. 1996—; trustee Franklin Square House, 1993—; chmn. Franklin Found., 1997; mem. pres. coun. U.U.A., 1999—, mem. adv. com. New Horizons - U.S.-Russia students. Mem. Unitarian Universalist Mins. Assn. (pres. 1968-70), Unitarian Hist. Soc. (pres. 1960-75), Evang. Missionary Soc. (pres. 1965-80, v.p. 1980—), Soc. for Propagation Gospel Among Indians and Others in N.Am. (v.p. 1975-99, pres. 1999—), Unitarian Svc. Pension Soc. (pres. 1973—), Soc. Ministerial Relief (pres. 1973—, mem. com. for ch. staff fin.), Mass. Hist. Soc., Colonial Soc. Mass., Union Club (Boston), Union Boat Club (Boston), Unitarian Universalist Assn., Beta Theta Pi (pres. New Eng. 1964-66). Office: Hale-Bannard 273 Clarendon St Boston MA 02116-1404 Home: 1 Avery St Apt 25A Boston MA 02111-1026

WILLIAMS, RHYS A. surgeon; b. Mexico, Mo., Jan. 2, 1929; MD, Washington U., 1953. Diplomate Am. Bd. Surgery. Intern Brooke Army Hosp., Ft. Sam Houston, Tex., 1953-54; resident surgery St. Louis City Hosp.-Washington U., 1955-59; cons., ret. part time. Cons. Ark. State Med. Bd., 1987-97. Fellow ACS, AMA. Office: 10 Maroon Dr Aspen CO 81611-1059 E-mail: rhrsa@msn.com.

WILLIAMS, RICHARD CHARLES, computer programmer, consultant; b. Boston, Dec. 25, 1955; s. Richard Clayton and Nancy Karolyn (Kerr) W. BA, SUNY, New Paltz, 1991. Cert. in software engring. Programmer/cons. Shared Ednl. Computing, Poughkeepsie, N.Y., 1976-78; systems programmer, comms. mgr. Cornell U. Med. Sch., N.Y.C., 1978-79; staff programmer IBM Corp. Hdqrs., White Plains, N.Y., 1979-84; systems programmer IBM Data. Systems Div., Poughkeepsie, 1984-86; adv. programmer IBM Network Systems, White Plains, 1986-89; open systems cons. IBM Large Systems, Kingston, N.Y., 1989-95; sr. R/3 basis architect, cert. SAP cons. IBM-SAP Competency Ctr., Phila., 1996-97, sr. architect, 1997—. Cons. IBM Hudson Valley Fed. Credit Union, Poughkeepsie, 1986—, C-Net, Broomfield, Colo., 1988-89, Toastmasters Bd. Dirs., Santa Ana, Calif., 1987, Landmark Edn., N.Y.C., 1989—. Author: Lasting Legacy, 1987; co-author: Migrating to TSO from VSPC, 1986; inventor, patentee. Bd. dirs. Hudson Valley FCU, 1995-2001, 2d vice chair, 1996-97, 1st vice-chair, 1997—; bd. dirs. SUNY Alumni Bd. Named one of Outstanding Young Men of Am., 1985, Vol. of Yr., NACUSAC, 1995. Mem. IEEE, ACM, SUNY Alumni Assn. (bd. dirs. 1994-99), Poughkeepsie Toastmasters Internat. (chpt. pres. 1982, dist. gov. 1985, Toastmaster of Yr. 1984), Open Online Transactional Programming Users Group (planning bd. 1995-97). Democrat. Methodist. Avocations: skiing, community organizing, travel. Home: 6040 Kennedy Blvd E Apt 29C West New York NJ 07093-3862 also: SAP Neurottstrasse 16 D-69190 Walldorf Germany

WILLIAMS, RICHARD CLARENCE, retired librarian; b. Guide Rock, Nebr., Apr. 9, 1923; s. Lyall Wesley and Elsie Marie (Guy) W. Student, Southwestern U., Georgetown, Tex., 1944-45; student, U. Tex., Austin, 1945-46; BA, U. Idaho, Moscow, 1948; BA in Librarianship, U. Wash., Seattle, 1949; MLS, U. Mich., Ann Arbor, 1952. Sec. Schaefer-Hitchcock Co., Sandpoint, Idaho, 1941-42; asst. librarian Willamette U. Library, Salem, Oreg., 1949-51; cataloger U. Mich. Library, Ann Arbor, 1951-59; serials cataloger N.Y.C. Pub. Library, 1959-66, asst. dir. for cataloging, 1967-88, Astor fellow for library research, 1988-89. Mem. subcom. on cataloging standards Research Libraries Group, Palo Alto, Calif., 1978-88. Contbr. poetry to coll. publs., 1944-48; bibliographer for Mexicon, 1986—. Bd. dirs. Eugene James Dance Co., N.Y.C., 1978—. Served with USN, 1943-46 Mem.: ALA, Pre-Columbian Art Rsch. Inst., Coun. on Bot. and Hort. Librs., John Bartram Assn., Am. Assn. Bot. Gardens and Arboreta, Archeol. Inst. Am., Am. Anthrop. Assn., Soc. Am. Archaeology, Phi Beta Kappa (U. Idaho chpt.). Avocations: New World archeology, Black studies, botany.

WILLIAMS, RICHARD DONALD, retired wholesale food company executive; b. Audubon, Iowa, Feb. 19, 1926; s. Walter Edward and Olga M. (Christensen) W.; m. Carol Francis, June 17, 1950; children: Gayle, Todd, Scott. BA, Ohio Wesleyan U., 1948; MBA, Northwestern U., 1949. Dir. indsl. and pub. rels. Gardner div. Diamond Nat. Corp., Middletown, Ohio, 1949-61; with Fleming Cos., Inc., 1961-89, v.p. pers., 1972-76, sr. v.p. human resources, 1976-80, exec. v.p. human resources, 1980-89, ret., 1989. Pres. Jr. Achievement, Topeka, Kans., 1972; v.p. Last Frontier council Boy Scouts Am., Oklahoma City, 1980; campaign chmn. United Way Greater Oklahoma City, 1980, pres., 1985-87; bd. dirs. Community Council Central Okla., Oklahoma City chpt. ARC, Support Ctr. Okla., Better Bus. Bur., Okla. City Beautiful. Served with USN, 1944-46. Mem. Am. Soc. Personnel Adminstrn., Soc. Advancement Mgmt., Am. Mgmt. Assn., Phi Gamma Delta. Clubs: Quail Creek Country (Oklahoma City), Petroleum (Oklahoma City); Baille 'd Oklahoma (hon.), La Chaine des Rotisseurs. Home: 2940 Brush Creek Rd Oklahoma City OK 73120-1858

WILLIAMS, RICHARD LEROY, federal judge; b. Morrisville, Va., Apr. 6, 1923; s. Wilcie Edward and Minnie Mae (Brinkley) W.; m. Eugenia Kellogg, Sept. 11, 1948; children: Nancy Williams Davies, R. Gregory, Walter L., Gwendolyn Mason. LLB, U. Va., 1951. Bar: Va. 1951. Ptnr. McGuire, Woods & Battle and predecessor firms, 1951-72; judge Cir. Ct. City of Richmond, 1972-76; ptnr. McGuire, Woods & Battle, 1976-80; dist. judge U.S. Dist. Ct., Richmond, Va., 1980—, sr. judge, 1992—. 2d lt. Air Corps., U.S. Army, 1940-45. Fellow Am. Coll. Trial Lawyers; mem. Va. State Bar, Va. Bar Assn., Richmond Bar Assn. Office: US Dist Ct/Lewis F Powell Ste 305 1000 E Main St Richmond VA 23219-3525 E-mail: barbarakreuter@uaed.uscourts.gov.

WILLIAMS, RICHARD LUCAS, III, electronics company executive, lawyer; b. Evanston, Ill., Oct. 30, 1940; s. Richard Lucas Jr. and Ellen Gene (Munster) W.; m. Karen Louise Carmody, Nov. 11, 1967 AB, Princeton U., 1962; LLB, U. Va., 1965. Bar: Ill. 1965, D.C. 1968, U.S. Supreme Ct. 1968. Assoc. Winston & Strawn, Chgo., 1968-74, ptnr., 1974-79; sr. v.p., gen. counsel Gould Inc., Rolling Meadows, Ill., 1979-81, sr. v.p., adminstrn., gen. counsel, 1981-90, also bd. dir., 1985-88; ptnr. Smith Williams and Lodge, Chgo., 1990-95, Vedder, Price, Kaufman & Kammholz, Chgo., 1995—. Bd. dirs. GNB Batteries, Inc., 1984-86, ULINE Inc., Waukegon, Ill. Bd. dirs., 1990—, Internat. Tennis Hall of Fame, Newport, R.I., 1993-97; v.p. Chgo. Dist. Tennis Assn., 1968-70; vice chmn. Am. Cancer Soc., Chgo., 1984; bd. dirs., pres. Lake Shore Found. for Animals, Chgo., 1990-94. With JAGC USNR, 1965-68. Mem. ABA, Ill. Bar Assn., Chgo. Bar Assn., Execs. Club Chgo. (co-chmn. Western Europe internat. com. 1990-97), The Lawyers Club (Chgo., 1997—), Meadow Club (Rolling Meadows, gov. 1979-90, chmn. 1985-90), Club Internat. Home: 1200 N Lake Shore Dr Chicago IL 60610-2370 Office: Vedder Price 222 N La Salle St Ste 2600 Chicago IL 60601-1104

WILLIAMS, RICHARD THOMAS, lawyer; b. Evergreen Park, Ill., Jan. 14, 1945; s. Raymond Theodore and Elizabeth Dorothy (Williams) W. AB with honors, Stanford U., 1967, MBA, JD, Stanford U., 1972. Bar: Calif. 1972, U.S. Supreme Ct. 1977. Assoc.,then ptnr. Kadison Pfaelzer Woodard Quinn & Rossi, L.A., 1972-87; ptnr. Whitman & Ransom, 1987-93, Whitman, Breed, Abbott & Morgan, L.A., 1993-2000, Holland & Knight, LLP, L.A., 2000—. Contbg. editor Oil and Gas Analyst, 1978-84. Mem. ABA, L.A. County Bar Assn. Office: Holland & Knight LLP 633 W 5th St Los Angeles CA 90071-2005

WILLIAMS, RICHMOND DEAN, library appraiser, consultant; b. Reading, Mass., Dec. 10, 1925; s. Theodore Ryder and Anabel Lee (Hutchison) W.; m. Eleanor Davidson Washbourne, Sept. 26, 1953; children— Richmond Lyttleton, Eleanor Davidson, Anne Ryder AB cum laude, Williams Coll., 1950; MA, U. Pa., 1952, PhD, 1959. Instr., asst. dean Williams Coll., Williamstown, Mass., 1954-56; dir. Wyo. Hist. and Geol. Soc., Wilkes-Barre, Pa., 1956-60; asst. dir. Am. Assn. State and Local History, Madison, Wis., 1960-61; dir. libraries Eleutherian Mills-Hagley Found., Wilmington, Del., 1962-87. Instr. Acad. Lifelong Learning U. Del., 1996—; cons. archivist M.S. Hershey Found., Pa., 1981—, Md. Dept. Housing and Community Devel., 1993-94; bd. dirs. Scholarly Resources Inc. Co-author: A Look at Ourselves, 1962; author: They Also Served, 1965; compiler: Directory of Historical Records in Delaware, 1995, (ann. series) Writing Haiku—, 1997—. Sec., U. Del. Library Assocs., Wilmington, 1972-86; mem. adv. bd. Del. Hist. Records, Dover, 1982-2002; mem. Del. Humanities Forum, Wilmington, 1984-91; trustee Conservation Ctr. Phila., 1984-86. Served to lt. AUS, 1943-47. Pennfield fellow U. Pa., 1953 Mem. Econ. History Assn (sec.-treas. 1975-88), Mid-Atlantic Regional Archives Com., Am. Assn. State and Local History (pres. 1974-76), Am. Antiquarian Soc., Libr. Co. Phila., Phi Beta Kappa. Avocations: golf, book collecting. Home and Office: 202 Brecks Ln Wilmington DE 19807-3011 E-mail: rdwms@udel.edu.

WILLIAMS, RICKY, professional football player; b. May 21, 1977; Running back/receiver New Orleans Saints, 1999—2002; running back Miami Dolphins, 2002—. Recipient Heisman Trophy, 1998. Mailing: Miami Dolphins Training Facility 7500 SW 30th St Davie FL 33314*

WILLIAMS, RITA CARROLL, language educator, poet; b. Norfolk, Va., Jan. 11, 1962; d. William Henry Carroll Jr. and Joyce Riddick Carroll; m. Stafford Clayton Williams Jr., Dec. 2, 1985; 1 child Thaddeus Clayton. BA in English, BS in Geology, Elizabeth City State U., 1985. Lang. arts tchr. Ctrl. Mid. Sch., Gates, NC, 1999—. Author: (poetry) Daily Inspirations: Daily Living With God, 2002. Mem.: N.C. Assn. Educators. Avocations: writing poetry, stamp collecting, coin collecting, sports card collecting. Home: 1468 Lambs Grove Rd Elizabeth City NC 27909-7502

WILLIAMS, RITA TUCKER, lawyer; b. Atlanta, Jan. 26, 1950; d. Claude Edward and Lillian Bernice (Barber) Tucker; m. Raymond Williams, Jr., Jan. 1, 1973; children: Monet Danielle, Brandon Raynard, Blake Hassan. BA, Spelman Coll., 1972; MA, U. Mich., 1976; JD, Emory U., 1987. Bar: Ga. 1987. Tchr. pub. schs., Suisun, Calif., 1977-82; assoc. Alston & Bird, Atlanta, 1987-89, Bernard & Assocs., Decatur, Ga., 1989-90; prin. Williams & Assocs., 1990—. Instr. seminar Nat. Inst. Trial Advocacy, Emory U., Atlanta, spring 1992-95, tutor 1st yr. law students, 1996. Named Outstanding Alumna, Emory U. Law Sch., 1996. Mem. ABA, State Bar Ga. Assn., Ga. Trial Lawyers Assn., Omicron Delta Kappa. Democrat. Office: 220 Church St Decatur GA 30030-3328 E-mail: ritw@atlonline.com.

WILLIAMS, ROBERT BRUCE, civil engineer, retired army officer; b. Reno, Nov. 29, 1937; s. John Francis and Mary Gertrude (Greiner) W.; m. Melanie Ann Treacy, July 22, 1960; children: Kenneth Bruce, Dougals John. BSCE, U. Utah, 1960; MSCE, Utah State U., 1966; grad., U.S. Command and Staff Coll., Ft. Leavenworth, Kans., 1971, U.S. War Coll., Carlisle, Pa., 1980. Commd. 2d lt. U.S. Army C.E., 1961, advanced through grades to col., 1981, ret., 1985; test group engr., dir. Def. Nuclear Agy., Albuquerque, 1971-75; staff engr. Dept. Army Ops., Washington, 1975-76, Asst. Chief Engrs., Washington, 1980-82; engr. bn. comdr. 7th Engr. Brigade, Stuttgart, Fed. Republic Germany, 1976-79; dist. engr. Walla Walla (Wash.) Engring. Dist., 1982-85; dir. correctional facilities planning and constrn. dept. Ariz. Dept. Adminstrn., 1985-87; dir. capital facilities planning and constrn. Ariz. Bd. Regents, 1987-90; sr. v.p. Chanen Constrn. Co., 1990-95; dir. Maricopa County Stadium Dist., 1995-98, Maricopa County Criminal Justice Facilities Devel. Dept., Phoenix, 1998—. Author: (with others) Engineer Professional Development Study, 1980. Decorated Legion of Merit (2), Bronze Star (2), Air medal (2); recipient Unsung Hero award Downtown Phoenix Revitalization, Downtown Phoenix Partnership, 1998. Mem. ASCE (v.p. Columbia sect. 1983-84, pres. 1984-85), Soc. Am. Mil. Engrs., Walla Walla Area C. of C. (bd. dirs. 1982-85). Presbyterian. Office: Maricopa County Criminal Justice Facilities Devel 411 N Central Ave Phoenix AZ 85004-2115

WILLIAMS, ROBERT CARL, architect; b. Chattanooga, May 21, 1931; s. Robert Carl Williams and Ethel Beaulah Ortimeier; m. Annabelle Westling Williams, Oct. 2, 1993; m. Lucy Jeanne Adams; children: Gregory Carl; m. Mariana Sundstrom; children: Tanya Yolanda. BS Civil Engring., U. Tenn., Knoxville, TN, 1954; BA Architecture, Grad. Sch. Design, Harvard U., Cambridge, MA, 1962. Registered Architect (VT, NY, NH, NJ, CT, MA), Nat. Coun. of Archtl. Registration Boards. Founder, pres., ceo Hawk Mountain Corp., Pittsfield, Vt., 1962—80, Robert Carl Williams Associates, Pittsfield, 1982—93; sr. ptnr., chmn. Robert Carl Williams Associates (Architects), 1993—. Author: (book of poetry) Low Sweet Notes. Capt. Air Force, 1955—59. Avocation: ocean sailing. Home: 810 Upper Michigan Rd Pittsfield VT 05762 Office: Robert Carl Williams Associates 810 Upper Michigan Rd Pittsfield VT 05762 Home Fax: 802-746-8903. Personal E-mail: rcwartects@aol.com.

WILLIAMS, ROBERT CHADWELL, history educator; b. Boston, Oct. 14, 1938; s. Charles Reagan and Dorothy (Chadwell) W.; m. Ann Bennett Kingman, Aug. 27, 1960; children: Peter, Margaret, Katharine. BA, Wesleyan U., 1960; A.M., Harvard U., 1962, PhD, 1966. Asst. prof. history Williams Coll., Williamstown, Mass., 1965-70; prof. history Washington U., St. Louis, 1970-86; dean of faculty, prof. history Davidson Coll., N.C., 1986-98, Vail prof. history, 2000—. Pres. Central Slavic Conf., 1971-72; v.p. History Assocs. Inc., Gaithersburg, Md., 1980— ; sr. research assoc. St. Antony's Coll., Oxford, 1985. Author: Culture in Exile, 1972, Artists in Revolution, 1976, Russian Art and American Money, 1980 (Pulitzer nominee), The Other Bolsheviks, 1986, Klaus Fuchs, Atom Spy, 1987, Russia Imagined, 1997, Ruling Russian Eurasia, 2000; co-author: Crisis Contained, 1982; mem. editorial bd.: Slavic Rev., 1979-82. Trustee Wesleyan U., 1996-99. Fellow Kennan Inst., 1976-77; fellow Am. Council Learned Socs., 1973-74, W. Wilson Found., 1960-61 Mem. Am. Assn. for Advancement of Slavic Studies, Phi Beta Kappa, Sigma Xi Presbyterian. Office: Davidson Coll Davidson NC 28036 E-mail: bowilliams@davidson.edu.

WILLIAMS, ROBERT HENRY, oil company executive; b. El Paso, Jan. 12, 1946; s. William Frederick and Mary (Page) W.; m. Joanne Marie Mudd, Oct. 22, 1967; children: Lara, Michael, Suzanne, Jennifer. BS in Physics, U. Tex., El Paso, 1968; PhD in Physics, U. Tex., Austin, 1973; MS in Physics, Va. Poly. Inst., 1971. Dir. Gulf Oil R&D, Houston, 1978-81; tech. mgr. Gulf Oil Internat., 1981-83; exploration mgr. Gulf Oil Co., 1983-85; mgr. geophys. rsch. Tenneco Oil Co., 1985-87, mgr., chief geophysicist, 1987-88; founder, mng. dir. Dover Energy, 1988—; exec. v.p. Tatham Offshore Inc, 1989-95, also bd. dirs.; chmn., CEO Dover Tech. Inc., 1989—. Cons. Tenneco Inc., Houston, 1989—; DeepTech Internat., 1992-95; Ukraine Acad. Sci., 1993; bd. dirs., exec. v.p. DeepTech Inc., 1991-95; founder, pres. Westway tech. Assocs., 1986—; co-founder, chmn. CEO Castaway Graphite Rods, Inc., 1990—; owner, CEO Team Tex. Inc., 1993—; Bulldog Lures, Inc., 1994—; founder, CEO Houston Books Inc., 1994—; founder, CEO, chmn. Dover Energy Exploration, 1995—; pres. Westway Interests; chmn., CEO, bd. dirs. W.B. Oil & Gas Inc., 1997-2001, Dover (Belize), 1996-2001; bd. dirs. Tatham Offshore, Swep, Inc.; CEO Norman Lures, 1997—; founder, bd. dirs., CEO Win Leisure Products, 1997—; dir./founder William Found., 1998—. Contbr. articles to profl. jours. Mem. coun. Boy Scouts Am., Houston, 1989—; patron Mus. Fine Arts, 1990—2002, Houston Zool. Soc., 1990—2002; leader Girl Scouts U.S., Houston, 1989—, life mem. Mem. Soc. Exploration Geophysics, Am. Assn. Petroleum Geologists, Am. Geophys. Union. Republican. Avocations: scuba diving, book collecting, fishing. Office: Dover Tech 11767 Katy Fwy Ste 1000 Houston TX 77079-1730

WILLIAMS, ROBERT JOSEPH, museum director, educator; b. Bennington, Vt., June 21, 1944; s. Joseph and Ruthe Allison (Moody) W. BS in Edn., U. Vt., 1970; MA in Interdisciplinary Social Sci., San Francisco State U., 1981. Tchr. adult edn. Mt. Anthony Union H.S., Bennington, Vt., 1972-74; columnist Bennington Banner, 1972-77; tchr. San Francisco State U., 1976-79; founder, dir. NORRAD Drug Rehab. Ctr., San Francisco, 1986-88; mus. curator Shaftsbury (Vt.) Historical Soc., 1989—. Founder, dir. Bennington Tutorial Ctr., 1971-74. Author: Toward Humanness in Education, 1981, Chalice of Leaves: Selected Essays and Poems, 1988, Modern Salvation: Guidelines from Cosmology, 1994; author: (with others) Intimacy, 1985. Recipient Edmunds Essay medal Vt. Historical Soc., Montpelier, 1961, award of the League of Vt. Writers, 1972, Golden Poet award World of Poetry, Sacramento, Calif., 1990. Democrat. Avocation: cosmology. Home: 102 Putnam St Bennington VT 05201-2348 Office: Shaftsbury Hist Soc PO Box 401 Shaftsbury VT 05262-0401 *I sought the truth, and sought to live by it.*

WILLIAMS, ROBERT JOSEPH, behavioral health services executive, psychologist; b. Durango, Colo., Feb. 14, 1948; s. Owen C. and Florence K. Williams; m. Kay Lynn Williams, Mar. 24, 1973; children: Robin, Matthew, Nicholas. BA, U. Colo., 1970; MA, U. No. Colo., 1976; PhD, U. Minn., 1979. Diplomate Am. Bd. Forensic Psychol. Specialties. Tchr. math. Jefferson County Schs., Lakewood, Colo., 1970-76; psychologist Pikes Peak Mental Health Ctr., Colorado Springs, 1979-82, clin. dir., 1982-83; dir. Inst. for Family and Personal Devel., 1983-86; mng. ptnr. Marriage and Family Treatment Ctr., 1986-90; COO Quinco Behavioral Health Systems, Columbus, Ind., 1990-92, pres., CEO, 1992—. Feedback cons. Ctr. for Creative Leadership, Colorado Springs and San Diego, 1986-96; facilitator Franklin Covey Ctr., Columbus, 1994-99; cons. Trustee Leadership Tng. Program, Indpls., 1991-98; adj. faculty U. Denver, U. Colo., Colorado Springs, 1981-90. Contbr. articles to profl. jours. Trustee Bartholomew Consol. Sch. Corp., Columbus, 1996-2001, pres., 1999-2000; past pres., moderator Leadership Bartholomew County. Served with USMCR, 1970-76. Boettcher Found. scholar, 1966-70; Regents scholar, 1966. Mem. Rotary Club, Masons. Democrat. Presbyn. Avocations: hiking, reading, motorcycling, weight training. Office: Quinco Behavioral Health Svcs 720 North Marr Rd Columbus IN 47201 E-mail: rjwilliams@quincoinc.com.

WILLIAMS, ROBERT L. principal; b. Jersey Shore, Pa., Oct. 19, 1958; s. Robert E. and Jo Ann Williams; m. Bonnie Marie Moorhouse, June 20, 1981; children: Tyler R., Maria R., Garret R. BA Music Ed/Vocal Performace, Milligan Coll., Milligan College, Tennessee, 1976—80; MEd Music, Penn State U., University Park, PA, 1982—84, MEd Ed. Adm., 1993—95. Music educator, grades k-6 Jersey Shore Area Sch. Dist., Jersey Shore, Pa., 1980—84, Montgomery Area Sch. Dist., Montgomery, 1984—96, music educator, grades 7-12, 1996—98; music educator, grades 7-9 Jersey Shore Sch. Dist., Jersey Shore, 1998—99; asst. m.s. prin. Williamsport Area Sch. Dist., Williamsport, 1999—. Mem. MENC/PMEA, Reston, Va., 1980—, PASSP/NASSP, Harrisburg, Pa., 1999—. Contbr. articles to profl. jours. Recipient PA Tchr. of the Yr. Nominee, Montgomery Sch. Dist., 1992, Musical Dedicated to Me, Shawnee Press-Gallina Composers, 1996. Home: 766 West Line Rd Linden PA 17744 Office: Lycoming Valley Middle School 1825 Hays Lane Williamsport PA 17701 Office Fax: 570-494-1706. E-mail: rwilliam@wasd.org.

WILLIAMS, ROBERT LEON, psychiatrist, neurologist, educator; b. Buffalo, July 22, 1922; s. Leon R. and L. Paulyne (Ingraham) W.; m. Shirley Glynn Miller, Feb. 5, 1949; Karen, Kevin BA, Alfred U., 1944; MD, Albany Med. Coll., Union U., 1946. Chief neurology and psychiatry Lackland AFB Hosp., USAF, San Antonio, 1952-55; cons. neurology and psychiatry to USAF Surgeon Gen., 1955-58; faculty Coll. Medicine, U. Fla., Gainesville, 1958-72, prof., chmn. dept. psychiatry, 1964-72; prof. psychiatry Baylor Coll. Medicine, Houston, 1972-92, chmn. dept., 1972-90, prof. neurology, 1976-92, acting chmn. dept., 1976-77, prof. emeritus psychiatry and neurology, 1992—. Mem. faculty various univs., part time 1949-58 including Albany Med. Coll. at Union U., Columbia Coll. Physicians and Surgeons, Boston U., U. Tex., Georgetown U. Author: (with W.B. Webb) Sleep Therapy: A. Bibliography and Commentary, 1966, (with others) EEG of Human Sleep: Clinical Applications, 1974; editor: (with Ismet Karacan and Carolyn J. Hursch) Psychopharmacology of Sleep, 1976, Sleep Disorders: Diagnosis and Treatment, 1978, 2d edit., 1988; (with others) Phenomenology and Treatment of Anxiety, 1979, of Alcoholism, 1980, of Psychophysiological Disorders, 1982, of Psychosexual Disorders, 1983, of Psychiatric Emergencies, 1984 Served from 1st lt. to lt. col. USAF, 1949-58; col. Res., ret. Recipient Cert. Profl. Achievement USAF Surgeon Gen., 1967 Mem. Am. Psychiat. Assn., Am. Electroencephalographic Soc., Am. Coll. Psychiatrists (pres. 1982-83), Am. Acad. Neurology, AMA, Group for Advancement of Psychiatry, Benjamin Rush Soc. (pres. 1986-88), Accreditation Coun. for grad. Med. Edn. (residency rev. com. for psychiatry 1985-93), Alpha Omega Alpha. Achievements include research and publs. on basic psychophysiology of human sleep. E-mail: RWilli3541@aol.com.

WILLIAMS, ROBERT LUTHER, city planning consultant; b. Porterville, Calif., June 24, 1923; s. Luther Esco and Mary (Lyon) W.; children: Jeffrey Robert, Derrick Paul, Gail Diane. Student, Utah State Coll., 1944; AB, U. Calif.-Berkeley, 1949, M.C.P., 1951. Asst. planning dir., Stockton, Calif., 1951-54; planning dir. Alameda, 1954-57, Alameda County, 1957-63; exec. dir. Am. Inst. Planners, Washington, 1963-69; v.p. Hill Devel. Corp., Middletown, Conn., 1969-71; dir. land mgmt. dept. Gulf Oil Corp., Reston, Va., 1971-74; pres. Coleman-Williams, Inc., Greenbrae, Calif., 1975-78, Robert Williams Assocs., Inc., San Rafael, 1978-87; mem. community affairs panel KQED-TV, San Francisco, 1991-94. Lectr. U. Calif. at Berkeley extension, 1956-59; tech. adviser regional planning Assn. Bay Area Govts., Calif., 1961-63; vis. prof. U. R.I., 1969-71; pres. G.I.F.T. Inst., Inc., 1991-94. Bd. dirs. Planning Found. Am., 1965-70, Communities Found., Inc., 1973-77. Served to 1st lt. AUS, 1943-46, 52, ETO. Named Young Man of Year Alameda, 1956 Mem. Am. Inst. Cert. Planners (pres. Calif. chpt. 1960), Am. Planning Assn., World Future Soc., Lambda Alpha, Lambda Chi Alpha. Presbyterian. Home: 93 N Cobbtown Rd Lincolnville ME 04849

WILLIAMS, ROBERT LYLE, corporate executive, consultant; b. Nowata, Okla., June 22, 1942; s. Clifford Lyle and Eula Mae (Barnes) W.; m. Lorene Linnet Dillahunty, June 12, 1965; 1 child, Eleanor Lynn BS, Okla. State U., 1964; MBA, Baylor U., 1965. Acctg. supr. Southwestern Bell Telephone Co., Houston, 1965-66; fin. exec. Ford Motor Co., Dearborn, Mich., 1969-80; treas. Ford Brazil, Sao Paulo, 1976-79, Agrico Chem. Co., Tulsa, 1980-82; v.p., chief fin. officer Texas City Refining, Inc., Tex., 1983-88; sr. v.p. Furnishings 2000, Inc., San Diego, 1988-89; pvt. cons. and investor Houston, 1990—. Chmn. Galveston County Taxpayers Research Council, 1987-88. Served to lt. USN, 1966-69 Republican. Presbyterian. Avocation: travel. Office: 2500 E T C Jester Blvd Ste 200 Houston TX 77008-1375

WILLIAMS, ROBERT RAYMOND, obstetrician and gynecologist; b. Willits, Calif., 1941; MD, McGill U., 1968. Diplomate Am. Bd. Ob-Gyn. Intern Chelsea (Mass.) Naval Hosp., 1968-69; resident in ob-gyn. Women and Infants Hosp., Providence, 1972-75, mem. staff, 1975—. Miriam Hosp., Providence, 1990—2000, R.I. Hosp., Providence, 1996—; clin. asst. prof. ob-gyn. Brown U. Fellow Am. Coll. Ob-Gyn, R.I. Med. Soc., Providence Med. Soc. Office: 120 Dudley St Ste 301 Providence RI 02905 also: 1050 Main St East Greenwich RI 02818

WILLIAMS, ROBERTA GAY, pediatric cardiologist, educator; b. Rocky Mount, N.C., Oct. 23, 1941; BS, Duke U., 1963; MD, U. N.C., 1968. Diplomate Am. Bd. Pediats. (mem. com. ofcl. examiners 1985—, bd. dirs. and rep. sub-bd. chmn. com. 1992—, mem. exec. com. 1993—), Am. Bd. Pediat. Cardiology (chmn. 1991-92, cons. 1993). Med.-pediat. intern N.C. Meml. Hosp., Chapel Hill, 1968-69; pediat. resident Columbia Presbyn. Med. Ctr., N.Y., 1969-70; fellow in cardiology Children's Hosp. Med. Ctr., Boston, 1970-73, from asst. in cardiology to assoc. in cardiology, 1973-75, sr. assoc. in cardiology, 1976-82; from instr. pediats. to asst. prof. pediats. Harvard Med. Sch.-Children's Hosp., 1973-82; assoc. prof. pediats. UCLA Med. Ctr., 1982-86, chief divsn. pediat. cardiology, 1982-95, prof. pediats., 1986-95; chmn. pediat. U. N.C. Sch. Medicine, Chapel Hill, 1995-2000, U. So. Calif., L.A., 2000—; v.p. pediat. and acad. affairs Children's Hosp. L.A., 2000—. Attending physician Cardiac Med. Svcs., Children's Hosp. Med. Ctr., Boston, 1974, cardiology cons. Cardiothoracic Surgery Svc., 1974, med. dir. Cardiovasc. Surgery ICU, 1974-79, dir. Cardiac Graphic Lab. and Cost Ctr., 1977-82, mem. com. neonatal ICU, 1978-79, v.p. med. staff, 1980-81; guest lectr., invited spkr., seminar leader in field; cons. FDA, 1998—; chmn. pediatric cardiac svcs. subcom. N.Y. State Cardiac Adv. Com., 1996—; mem. adv. com. Nat. Heart, Lung and Blood Inst., 1999—. Mem. editl. bd.: Pediat. Cardiology, 1979, Circulation, 1983-91, Am. Jour. Cardiology, 1984-91, Jour. Applied Cardiology, 1985, Clin. Cardiology, 1988, Internat. Jour. Cardiology, 1992-95, Archives of Pediats. and Adolescent Medicine, 1994—; editl. cons. Jour. of Am. Coll. of Cardiology, 1992-94. Mem. exec. coun. cardiovasc. disease in the young Am. Heart Assn., 1979-85, mem. subcom. congenital cardiac defects, 1980-82, subcom. nominating com., 1982-83; mem. Am. Heart Assn.-Greater L.A. affiliate, 1983—, exec. com. and rsch. com., 1984—, judge young investigator competition, 1984, mem. program com., 1986-90, v.p. med.-exec. com., 1991-92, pres.-elect, 1992-93, and numerous other coms.. Fellow Am. Coll. Cardiology (allied health profls. com. 1984-87, mem. physician workforce adv. com. 1988-94, mem. manpower adv. com. 1988—, mem. extramural continuing edn. com. Heart House 1990—, co-chmn. Bethesda conf. 1993, gov. So. Calif. chpt. 1994—, pres. Calif. chpt. 1994—, govt. rels. com., 1998—, trustee 2001—), Am. Acad. Pediats. (sec. exec. com. sect. on cardiology 1985-87, mem. com. on fetus and newborn 1985-88, mem. exec. com. sect. on cardiology 1985—, chmn. program com. 1988-89, mem. subcom. Am. Heart Assn. task force on assessment of diagnosis and therapeutic cardiovascular procedures 1989, chairperson sec. cardiology 1989, mem. mem. coun. on sects. mgmt. com. 1995—); mem. Soc. for Pediat. Rsch., Am. Pediat. Soc. (dept. chair 1995, exec. com. 1997), Am. Soc. Echocardiography (mem. exec. com. 1975-78, com. on guidelines for technician tng. 1975-78, bd. dirs. 1976-80, treas. exec. coun. com. 1981-83, steering com. Future of Pediatric Edn. Task Force, 1996-99, chmn. Future of Pediatric Subspeciality Workgroup, 1996-99). Avocations: photography, hiking. Office: Childrens Hosp La Ms 71 4050 W Sunset Blvd Los Angeles CA 90029-2106 E-mail: rwilliams@chla.usc.edu.

WILLIAMS, ROBIN, actor, comedian; b. Chgo., July 21, 1951; s. Mr. and Mrs. Robert W.; m. Valerie Velardi, June 4, 1978 (div.); 1 child, Zachary; m. Marsha Garces, Apr. 30, 1989; children: Zelda, Cody. Attended, Claremont Men's Coll., Marin Coll., Juilliard Sch., N.Y.C. Started as stand-up comedian in San Francisco clubs, including Holy City Zoo, The Boardinghouse; later became regular at Comedy Store, Los Angeles; appeared in TV series Laugh-In, The Richard Pryor Show, America 2-Night, Happy Days, Homicide: Life on the Streets, 1993 (Emmy nomination, Guest Actor - Drama Series, 1994); star of TV series Mork and Mindy, 1978-82 (People's Choice award), (cable) Robin Williams: An Evening at the Met, 1986 (Grammy award), host of HBO's Shakespeare: The Animated Tales, 1993 (CableAce Award, Best Entertainment Host); film appearances include: Popeye, 1980, The World According to Garp, 1982, The Survivors, 1983, Moscow on the Hudson, 1984, Club Paradise, 1986, Good Morning Vietnam, 1987 (Golden Globe award 1988, Acad. Award nominee for best actor), The Adventures of Baron Munchausen, 1989, Dead Poets Society, 1989 (Best Actor nomination Golden Globe award, 1994, nominated best actor Acad. award), Cadillac Man, 1990, The Fisher King, 1991 (Golden Globe award, Acad. award nominee for best actor 1991), Dead Again, 1991, Hook, 1991, Aladdin (voice) (Spl. Achievement award Hollywood Fgn. Press, Nat. Bd. Rev. 1992), 1992, Toys, 1992, Mrs. Doubtfire, 1993 (Best Picture, Best Actor in a Musical or Comedy, Golden Globe, 1994, Best Picture, Best Actor, People's Choice award), Nine Months, 1995, Jumanji, 1995, The Bird Cage, 1996, Jack, 1996, The Secret Agent, 1996, Hamlet, 1996, Deconstructing Harry, 1997, (tv series, voice) Great Minds Think for Themselves, 1997, Father's Day, 1997, Flubber, 1997, Good Will Hunting, 1997, What Dreams May Come, 1998, Patch Adams, 1998, In My Life, 1998, Get Bruce, 1999, Bicentennial Man, 1999, Jakob the Liar, 1999, The Interpreter, 2000; theatre: Waiting for Godot, 1988; recorded albums: Reality, What a Concept, 1979 (Grammy award), Throbbing Python of Love, A Night at the Met (Grammy award); host Comic Relief, 1986; appeared in TV variety programs, ABC Presents a Royal Gala, 1988 (Emmy award, 1988), Carol, Carl, Whoopi & Robin, 1987 (Emmy award). Recipient Golden Apple award Hollywood Women's Press Club; Golden Globe award; ACE award; Am. Comedy award, 1987, 88; Grammy award for best comedy rec., 1987; recipient Man of Yr. award Hasty Pudding Theatricals, 1989, People's Choice award Favorite Comedy Motion Picture Actor, 1994, ShoWest Conv. award Male Star of Yr., 1994.

WILLIAMS, ROGER COURTLAND, lawyer; b. Atlanta, June 11, 1944; s. Ralph Roger and Beatrice (Hill) W.; m. Jo Ann Davenport, June 9, 1968; children: Melissa, Kimberly, Courtland. BS, U. Ala., 1966, JD, 1969. Bar: Ala. 1969, U.S. Dist. Ct. (no. and mid. dists.) Ala. 1969, U.S. Supreme Ct. 1972. V.p. Williams, Williams & Williams, P.C., Tuscaloosa, Ala., 1969-90, pres., 1990—. Adj. prof. U. Ala. Sch. Law, 1999—. Mem. bd. trustees Tuscaloosa Acad., 1987—, pres., 1990-94; bd. dirs. Children's Hands On Mus., Tuscaloosa, 1986-97. 1st lt. U.S. Army, 1969-71. Mem. ABA, Ala. State Bar Assn. (vice chmn. ADR com. 1997-98), Assn. Trial Lawyers Am., Nat. Acad. Arbitrators, Am. Arbitration Assn., Jaycees (nat. assoc. legal counsel 1979-80, state pres. 1978-79, pres. Ala. Found. 1980-81, Internat. Senator), Tuscaloosa Toastmasters (pres. 1975), Kiwanis of Tuscaloosa (bd. dirs. 1974, 90, v.p. 1995-98, pres. 1998-99), Kiwanis of Ala. (dist. lt. gov. 2001-2002), Indian Hills Country Club (bd. dirs. 1996—). Methodist. Office: Williams Williams & Williams PC PO Box 2690 Tuscaloosa AL 35403-2690

WILLIAMS, ROGER LAWRENCE, historian, educator; b. Boulder, Colo., June 22, 1923; s. Raymond Ustick and Mabel (Woolf) W. BA, Colo. Coll., 1947; MA, U. Mich., 1948, PhD, 1951. Asst. prof. Minn. State Coll., Mankato, 1950-52, MIT, Cambridge, 1952-55; vis. prof. Mich. State U., East Lansing, 1955-56; assoc. prof. Antioch Coll., Yellow Springs, Ohio, 1956-65; prof. U. Calif., Santa Barbara, 1965-71, U. Wyo., Laramie, 1971-78, Disting. prof., 1978-88. Author: French Revolution of 1870-71, 1969, The Mortal Napoleon III, 1971, The Horror of Life, 1980, Aven Nelson of Wyoming, 1984, Gérard and Jaume: Two Neglected Figures in the History of the Jussiaean Classification, 1988, Napoleon III and the Stoffel Affair, 1993, The Letters of Dominique Chaix, Botanist-Curé, 1997, Botanophilia in 18th Century France: The Spirit of the Enlightenment, 2001; co-author: How Modernity Came to a Provençal Town, 1988, Handbook of Rocky Mountain Plants, 1992, A Guide to Rocky Mountain Plants, 2002; mem. editl. bd. Antioch Rev., 1958-64. Vol. Rocky Mountain Nat. Park, Estes Park, Colo., 1986-87. Mem. French Hist. Studies (life), History Sci. Soc. (life), Hist. Soc., Nat. Coun. for History Edn., N.Y. Bot. Soc., Denver Bot. Soc. Home: 1701 S 17th St Laramie WY 82070-5406

WILLIAMS, ROGER STEWART, physician; b. San Diego, Feb. 15, 1941; s. Manley Samuel and Ethelyn Mae W.; children: Roger S., Karen E., David G., Sarah E. MD cum laude, Emory U., 1966. Diplomate Am. Bd. Psychiatry and Neurology. Intern, Grady Hosp., Atlanta, 1966-67. Med. resident Emory U., Atlanta, 1966-68; resident neurology Mass. Gen. Hosp., Boston, 1970-73, assoc. neurologist, 1973-87; assoc. prof. neurology Harvard Med. Sch., Boston, 1977-87; neurologist Billings (Mont.) Clinic, 1987-97; adj. prof. Mont. State U., Bozeman. Contbr. articles to profl. jours. Served to lt. comdr. USN, 1968-70. Kennedy fellow Kennedy Found., Washington, 1973-75; NIMH grantee, Bethesda, Md., 1979-87. Fellow Am. Acad. Neurology; mem. AMA, Mont. Med. Assn., Alpha Omega Alpha.

WILLIAMS, RONALD DAVID, telecommunications executive; b. Marshall, Ark., Mar. 15, 1944; s. Noble Kentucky and Elizabeth (Karns) W.; m. Beth L. Williams, Nov. 1977; children: Stephanie Noble, Keith Michael. BA, Columbia U., 1966, BS, 1967, MBA, 1973. Process engr. DuPont, Deepwater, N.J., 1966; design engr. Combustion Engring. Co., Hartford, 1971; cons. Arthur Andersen & Co., N.Y.C., 1973-76; corp. planner Amax Inc., Greenwich, Conn., 1976-77, group planning adminstr., 1978-80, mgr. corp. planning and analysis, 1980-94, dir. fin. analysis, 1984-86; project mgr. Olin Corp., Stamford, 1977-78; mgr. ops. planning and analysis Savin Corp., 1986-88; dir. fin. Bandgap Tech. Corp., Broomfield, Colo., 1988-90, v.p. fin. and adminstrn., 1990-93; v.p., gen. mgr. Bandgap Chem. Corp., 1992-94; contr. Heraeus PMR, Inc., Alden, N.Y., 1994-95, v.p. fin. and adminstrn., 1995-96; gen. mgr. Acoustiflo, Boulder, Colo., 1996-97; sr. fin. staff analyst Energy Corp., New Orleans, 1998-99; mgr. fin. planning Energy Tech. Co., 1999—. Served with USN, 1967-70, Vietnam. NASA trainee, 1971; S.W. Mudd scholar, 1971. Mem. AAAS, Am. Chem. Soc., Am. Mgmt. Assn., Ark. Hist. Assn., Westport Hist. Soc., Colo. Hist. Soc., Appalachian Mountain Club, Boulder Road Runners, Checkers Running Club, Chalmette Track Club, Green Mountain Club, New Orleans Track Club, Gulf Coast Running Club, Pine Belt Pacers. Home: 7361 S Meadow Ct Boulder CO 80301-3951 Office: 639 Loyola Ave New Orleans LA 70113-3125

WILLIAMS, RONALD DEAN, minister, religious organization administrator; b. Decatur, Ill., Oct. 23, 1940; s. Henry Lawrence and Ella Loudica Williams; m. Carole Jeanette Lane, June 16, 1962; children: Scott Allan, Mark Lawrence, Derek James. BTh, LIFE Bible Coll., L.A., 1965; DD, Internat. Ch. Foursquare Gospel, L.A., 1992. Ordained to ministry Internat. Ch. Foursquare Gospel, 1966. Pastor Foursquare Gospel Ch., Surrey, B.C., Can., 1965-69, missionary Hong Kong, 1969-85; prof. LIFE Bible Coll., 1985-95; mng. editor Foursquare World ADVANCE, 1993—; comm. officer Internat. Ch. of Foursquare Gospel, 1988-2000. Bd. dirs. Foursquare Gospel Ch.; pres. exec. bd. Internat. Pentecostal Press Assn., Oklahoma City, 1990-98; comm. officer Pentecostal/Charismatic Chs. North Am., Memphis, 1994—; coord. E. Coun. Foursquare Miss., 1979-82. Editor: The Vine and The Branches, 1992; mng. editor Foursquare World ADVANCE mag., 1985. Coord. 19th Pentecostal World Conf., 2001. With USAF, 1958-61. Avocations: writing, golf, reading, music. Office: Internat Ch Foursquare Gospel 1910 W Sunset Blvd Ste 200 Los Angeles CA 90026-3295

WILLIAMS, RONALD DOHERTY, lawyer; b. New Haven, Apr. 6, 1927; s. Richard Hugh and Ethel W. (Nelson) w.; m. Laura Costarelli, Aug. 25, 1951; children: Craig F., Ronald D., Ellen A., Jane E. BA, U. Va., 1951; LLB, 1954. Bar: Conn. 1954. Assoc. Pullman, Comley, Bradley & Reeves, Bridgeport, Conn., 1954-60; ptnr., 1960-88, Williams, Cooney & Sheehy, 1989—. Mem. Fed. Jud. Com., 1988-91, com. unauthorized practice law, 1988-94, com. to study rules civil practice & procedure, 1984-86; atty. state trial referee, 1984-90. Selectman Town of Easton (Conn.), 1975-85, justice of the peace, 1977—, town atty., 1985-2000; mem. Bridgeport Area Found., 1971-90, adv. com. U. Bridgeport Law Sch., 1982-92; mem. statewide grievance com., 1985-91, chmn., 1989-91; mem. exec. bd. Sch. Law Quinnipiac Coll., 1994—. Served with U.S. Army, 1945-46. Fellow Am. Coll. Trial Lawyers; mem. ABA, Am. Bd. Trial Advs., Conn. Bar Assn. (bd. govs. 1975-78), Bridgeport Bar Assn. (pres. 1975), Conn. Def. Lawyers Assn. (pres. 1984-85), Trial Attys. Am. Republican. Roman Catholic. Home: 14 Newman Dr Easton CT 06612-1915 Office: 799 Silver Ln Trumbull CT 06611-0753 E-mail: WilCooShee@aol.com.

WILLIAMS, RONALD LEE, pharmacologist; b. Koleen, Ind., June 26, 1936; s. Marion Raymond and Doris May (Lynch) Williams; m. Sondra Sue Cobb, June 7, 1957; children: Robin Lee, Christopher P., David R., Jonathan V.; m. Eunice Symphrosa Lovato, Oct. 10, 2001. BS, Butler U., 1959, MS, 1961; PhD, Tulane U., 1964. Registered pharmacist, Colo. From instr. to assoc. prof. pharmacology La. State U., New Orleans, 1964-84, assoc. prof. medicine, 1978-84, ret., 1984; asst. dir. Dept. of Corrections Hosp. Pharmacy, Canon City, Colo., 1986-93; with Canon Pharmacy, 1994-95; lead clin. pharmacist VA Med. Ctr., Ft. Lyon, 1996—. Expert adv. panel renal drugs U.S. Pharmacopeia Drug Info., 1981-85; cons. in field. Mem. editl. bd. Pharmacology, 1979; reviewer Jour. Pharmaceutical Sci., 1976, Fed. Practitioner Jour. Health Care for VA, PHS and DOD, 1999; contbr. articles to profl. jours. Mayor Fort Lyon, Colo., 1998. La. Heart Assn. grantee, 1964, 66. Mem. Am. Soc. Pharmacology, N.Y. Acad. Sci., Fedn. Am. Soc. Exptl. Biology, So. Colo. Soc. Hosp. Pharm. Assn., Sigma Xi, Rho Chi. Republican. Baptist. Avocations: hiking, camping, back-packing, hunting, book collector.

WILLIAMS, RONALD OSCAR, systems engineer; b. Denver, May 10, 1940; s. Oscar H. and Evelyn (Johnson) W. BS in Applied Math. Coll. Engring., U. Colo., 1964; postgrad, U. Colo., U. Denver, George Washington U. Computer programmer Apollo Sys. dept. Missile and Space div. Gen. Electric Co., Kennedy Space Ctr., Fla., 1965-67, Manned Spacecraft Ctr., Houston, 1967-68; computer programmer U. Colo., Boulder, 1968-73; computer programmer analyst Def. Sys. divsn. Sys. Devel. Corp. for NORAD, Colo. Springs, 1974-75; engr. def. sys. and command-and-info. sys. Martin Marietta Aerospace, Denver, 1976-80; sys. engr. space and comm. group, def. info. sys. divsn. Hughes Aircraft Co., Aurora, Colo., 1980-89; rsch. analyst Math. Rsch. Ctr., Littleton, 1990—, dir., sr. rsch. mathematician, 1996—. Vol. fireman Clear Lake City (Tex.) Fire Dept., 1968; officer Boulder Emergency Squad, 1969-76, rescue squadman, 1969-76, liaison to cadets, 1971, pers. officer, 1971-76, exec. bd., 1971-76, award of merit, 1971, 72, emergency med. technician, 1973—; spl. police officer Boulder Police Dept., 1970-75; spl. dep. sheriff Boulder County Sheriff's Dept., 1970-71; mem. nat. adv. bd. Am. Security Coun., 1979-91, Coalition of Peace Through Strength, 1979-91. Served with USMCR, 1958-66. Decorated Organized Res. medal. Mem. AAAS, AIAA (sr.), Math. Assn. Am., Am. Math Soc., Soc. Indsl. and Applied Math., Math. Study Unit of Am. Topical Assn., Armed Forces Comm. and Electronics Assn., Assn. Old Crows, Nat. Def. Indsl. Assn., Marine Corps Assn., Air Force Assn., U.S. Naval Inst., Nat. Geog. Soc., Smithsonian Inst., Nat. Space Soc., Soc. Amateur Radio Astronomers, Met. Opera Guild, Colo. Hist. Soc., Hist. Denver Inc., Historic Boulder Inc., Hawaiian Hist Soc., Denver Bot. Gardens, Denver Mus. Nature and Sci., Denver Zool. Found. Inc., Mensa. Lutheran.

WILLIAMS, ROSS ARNOLD, application development architect; b. Canton, Ohio, Feb. 28, 1953; s. Nick P. Williams and Dolores M. (Gilson) Kobzowicz; m. Kimberly Ann Werner, June 25, 1983; children: Michael, Emily. Student, Ohio State U., 1970-73; BA, U. Akron, 1977, MS, 1980; MA, Kent State U., 1994. Cert. computing profl. Computer sys. analyst Goodyear Tire and Rubber Co., Akron, Ohio, 1979-92, sr. computer applications analyst, 1992-95, sys. engr., 1995—2001, application devel. architect, 2001—. Lectr. U. Akron, 1979-84; adj. prof. meth. Ashland U., 2002--. Mem. Kappa Kappa Psi, Pi Mu Epsilon. Lutheran. Avocations: reading, sports, chess, music. E-mail: rawilliams@goodyear.com.

WILLIAMS, ROY, airport terminal executive; Former dir. Dayton Internat. Airport , Ohio; aviation dir. New Orleans Internat. Airport, 2001—. Office: 900 Airline Hwy Kenner LA 70062*

WILLIAMS, ROY HENRY, software engineer; b. Pensacola, Fla., Jan. 19, 1936; s. Frank B. and Rebecca (Mullens) W.; m. Nancy Gail Truitt, May 31, 1958; children: Julie, Trudy, Roy Jr. BS in Engring. Physics, U. Tenn., 1959; MS in Advanced Tech., SUNY, Binghamton, 1988. Co-op. programmer Union Carbide Nuclear Co., Oak, Tenn., 1957-58; engr. programmer N.Am. Rockwell, L.A., 1959-62; sr. assoc. programmer IBM Corp., Houston, 1962-70, adv. programmer Morris Plains, N.J., 1970-74, Cape Canaveral, Fla., 1974-76, Owego, N.Y., 1976-85, Gaithersburg, Md., 1985-94, ret., 1994; adv. programmer Lockheed Martin Federal Systems, 1994-99, ret., 1999. Prof. computer sci. dept. Montgomery Coll., Rockville, Md., 1988-95. Mem. Internat. Soc. Parametric Analysts. Home: 5066 S Mesquite Hills Pl Tucson AZ 85746-8614

WILLIAMS, RUSS, marketing professional; Grad. summa cum laude, Christian Bros. U.; MBA with honors, U. Va. Pres., prin. Valent USA, Kraft Food Ingredients, Storage USA, CB Richard Ellis, The Conwood Co., Belz Factory Outlet World, Archer Malmo, 2002—. Named featured engr., Memphis Joint Engring. Coun., 1983, Top 40 Under 40, Memphis Bus. Jour., 2000. Office: 65 Union at Front Memphis TN 38103*

WILLIAMS, RUSSELL JOHN, government program executive; b. Whitehall, N.Y., Jan. 10, 1944; s. William John and Eleanora Aina (Engstrom) W.; m. Marsha Jean Nowicki, June 15, 1970; children: Amrys Orenda, Valian Orenda (dec. 1999). BS, SUNY, Plattsburgh, 1965; ArtsD, U. Albany, 1979. Cert. secondary English and social studies, N.Y. Faculty/residence officer World Campus Afloat, 1969; faculty dept. English SUNY, Plattsburgh, 1969-73; faculty, co-founder Miner Inst. for Man and His Environment, Chazy, Plattsburgh, N.Y., 1972-73; trade books merchandiser Dalton/Pickwick Bookseller, Torrance, Calif., 1974-75; tchr. lang. arts Ichabod Crane Middle Sch., Valatie, Kinderhook, N.Y., 1975-76; tchg. fellow U. Albany, 1977-79; dir. student programs N.Y. State Senate, Albany, 1979—. Vis. writer in poetry Breadloaf Writers Conf., Middlebury, Vt., 1964; secondary tutor N.Y. State Divsn. for Youth, N.Y.C., 1975; owner Greenmantle, Albany, 1979-98, Slingerlands, N.Y., 1998—. Writer of poetry and short stories. V.p. N.Y. State Rifle and Pistol Assn., Inc., Troy, N.Y., 1985-90; lay leader Calvary Ct./United Meth. Chs. in Albany, 1990— (now Emmaus United Meth. Ch.); trustee, 1990-99, pres. bd. trustees, 1998-99; chmn. City of Albany (N.Y.) Rep. Com./City Reps., Albany, 1991-94; Rep. challenger 21st Congl. Dist., 1994. Mem. NRA, U.S. Internat. Practical Shooters Assn. (life), N.Y. State Rifle and Pistol Assn., Inc. (life, dir. edn. and tng. 1998-99, v.p. 2000—), Calif. Rifle & Pistol Assn. (life), N.Y. State Outdoor Writers Assn., Poets and Writers, Inc., Empire State Wildlife Fedn. (co-founder), Soc. Pub. Adminstrs., N.Y. State Conservation Coun. (life). Avocations: skilled ethical outdoorsman, hunter/conservation philosopher-ethicist. Home: 12 S Helderberg Pkwy Slingerlands NY 12159-9262 Office: NY State Senate 90 S Swan St # 401 Albany NY 12210-2105 E-mail: lrpleader@aol.com.

WILLIAMS, RUTH ELIZABETH (BETTY WILLIAMS), retired secondary school educator; b. Newport News, Va., July 31, 1938; d. Lloyd Haynes and Erma Ruth (Goodrich) W. BA, Mary Washington Coll., 1960; cert. d'etudes, Converse Coll., 1961, Lycée Balzac, Tours, France, 1962. Cert. tchr., Va. French tchr. York High Sch., York County Pub. Schs., Yorktown, Va., 1960-65; French resource tchr. Newport News Pub. Schs., 1966-74, tchr. French and photography, 1974-81, tchr. French, Spanish, German and Latin, 1981-91, ret., 1991; founder, CEO Cresset Elder Care. Pres. Cresset Publs., Williamsburg, Va., 1977—; lectr. Sch. Edn., Coll. Williamand Mary, Williamsburg, 1962-65; French tchr., coord. fgn. langs. York County Pub. Schs., 1962-65; workshop leader dept. pub. instrn. State of Del., Dover, 1965; cons. Health de Rochemont Co., Boston, 1962-71; chmn. faculty senate Dozier Intermediate Sch., Newport News, 1977-79. Driver Meals on Wheels, Williamsburg, 1989-90; contbr. Va. Spl. Olympics, Richmond, 1987—; charter mem. Capitol Soc. Colonial Williamsburg Found., Inc., 1994; mem. Colonial Williamsburg Assembly, Colonial Williamsburg Found., Inc., Chesapeake Bay Found., 1996—, W.A.R. Goodwin Soc., 1996—, Assn. Preservation Va. Antiquities, 1998—, Williamsburg Hist. Records Soc., 1998—, Mortar Bd. Nat. Found., 1998—, Williamsburg Land Conservancy; mem. Altar Guild, Bruton Parish Ch., Williamsburg, 1960—. Grantee Nat. Def. Edn. Act, 1961, 1962. Mem. AAAU, Fgn. Lang. Assn. Va., AARP (ret. tchrs. divsn.), Heritage Soc., Mary Washington Coll. Alumni Assn., Va. Hist. Soc., Am. Assn. Tchrs. French, Mortar Bd., Women in the Arts, Mary Washington Coll. Alumni Assn. (class agt. 1995—), Alpha Phi Sigma, Phi Sigma Iota. Episcopalian. Avocations: photography, coin and stamp collecting, walking, sailing, archaeology and Virginia History. Home and Office: Apt D310 3800 Treyburn Dr Williamsburg VA 23185-6422

WILLIAMS, RUTH LEE, clinical social worker; b. Dallas, June 24, 1944; d. Carl Woodley and Nancy Ruth (Gardner) W. BA, So. Meth. U., 1966; M Sci.in Social Work, U. Tex., Austin, 1969. Milieu coordinator Starr Commonwealth, Albion, Mich., 1969-73; clin. social worker Katherine Hamilton Mental Health Care, Terre Haute, Ind., 1973-74; clin. social worker, supr. Pikes Peak Mental Health Ctr., Colorado Springs, Colo., 1974—2000; pvt. practice social work, 1978—2000; pres. Hearthstone Inn, Inc., 1978—; practitioner Jin Shin Jyutsu, 1978—2000; dir. cmty. rels. Walker Wear, 2001—. Pres., v.p. bd. dirs. Premier Care (formerly Colorado Springs Mental Health Care Providers Inc.), 1986-87, chmn. quality assurance com., 1987-89, v.p. bd. dirs., 1992-93; bd. dirs. Beth Haven, Inc., JAC Svcs. Author, editor: From the Kitchen of The Hearthstone Inn, 1981, 2d rev. edit., 1986, 3d rev. edit., 1992. Mem. Am. Bd. Examiners in Clin. Social Work (charter mem., cert.), Colo. Soc. Clin. Social Work (editor 1976), Nat. Assn. Soc. Workers (diplomate), Nat. Bd. Social Work Examiners (cert.), Nat. Assn. Ind. Innkeepers, So. Meth. U. Alumni Assn. (life). Avocations: gardening, hiking, sailing. Office: 11555 Howells Rd Colorado Springs CO 80908-3735

WILLIAMS, RUTH RUSSELL, artist; b. Townsville, N.C., Mar. 16, 1932; d. Sandy Terry and Sarah Virginia Dabney; m. Samuel Williams, Dec. 25, 1971; m. Odell Russell, 1946 (div.); children: Rick Russell, Matthew Russell, Robin Russell, Paula Russell Evans. Student, Henderson Inst., Apex Beauty Coll. Cosmetologist Ruth's Beauty World, Richmond, Va., 1951—2001, Henderson, NC, 1951—2001; folk artist, 1977—2001. Calendar. Recipient Key to the City, Office of the Mayor, 1993, plaque, Nat. Coalition of 100 Black Women, Phila., 1999. Mem.: N.C. Mus. Art Assn. (artist), Sigma Gamma Rho (hon. medallion 1998). Presbyterian. Avocations: painting, cooking, reading, traveling, music. Home: 45 Williams Ln Henderson NC 27537

WILLIAMS, SANDRA CASTALDO, elementary school educator; b. Rahway, N.J., Sept. 19, 1941; d. Neil and Loretta Margaret (Gleason) Castaldo; m. Arthur Williams III, 1962; children: Arthur IV, Melinda S., Thomas N. Student, Syracuse U., 1959-61; AB, Kean Coll., 1969, MA magna cum laude, 1978. Cert. tchr. K-8, early childhood, N.J. Preschool tchr. St. Andrew's Nursery & Kindergarten, New Providence, N.J., 1973-82; kindergarten tchr. Walnut Ave. Sch. Cranford (N.J.) Sch. Dist., 1978-79; adjunct prof. Farleigh Dickinson Coll., Rutherford, Teaneck, N.J., 1983-86; tchr. 4th grade The Peck Sch., Morristown, 1986-89; dir. Summit Child Care Ctr., 1990-91; tchr. 1st grade Oak Knoll Sch. of Holy Child Jesus, Summit, N.J., 1992—, tchr. Confraternity of Christian Doctrine, 1995—. Bd. dirs. Summit Child Care Ctr., 1970-71, cons., 1991; cert. instr. Jacki Sorensen Aerobic Dancing, Inc., Summit, 1990, Westfield, 1992-95. Co-chair United Way, Summit, 1991; Eucharistic min. St. Teresa's Ch., Summit, 1994—. Mem. ASCD, Internat. Reading Assn., Phi Kappa Phi, Alpha Sigma Lambda, Kappa Kappa Gamma. Republican. Roman Catholic. Avocations: needle work, gardening, church, physical fitness. Home: 8 Sunset Dr Summit NJ 07901-2323 Office: Oak Knoll Sch Holy Child Jesus 44 Blackburn Rd Summit NJ 07901-2499

WILLIAMS, SANKEY VAUGHAN, health services researcher, internist; b. San Antonio, Apr. 15, 1944; s. James Sankey and Helen (Long) W.; m. Constance Hess, June 27, 1972; children: Elizabeth Helen, Jennifer Lee. AB, Princeton U., 1966; MD, Harvard U., 1970. Diplomate Am. Bd. Internal Medicine. Intern Hosp. of U. Pa., 1970-71, jr. resident, 1971-72, chief med. resident, 1974-75; assoc. dir. clin. rsch. Ctr. for Study of Aging, U. Pa., 1982-86; assoc. dir. for med. affairs Leonard Davis Inst. for Health Econs., U. Pa., 1978-90; dir. clin. scholars program U. Pa., Phila., 1988-96; prof. health care systems Wharton Sch., U. Pa., 1989—; prof. medicine U. Pa., 1989—, chief div. gen. internal medicine, 1992—, Sol Katz prof. medicine, 1992—. Commr. Prospective Payment Assessment Commn., U.S. Congress, Washington, 1988-91; chairman health svcs. rsch. devel. grants study sect. Agy. for Health Care Policy and Rsch., 1991-94; counselor for med. affiars to the pres. U. Pa., 1990-92. Co-editor: The Physician's Practice, 1980; author 25 revs, chpt. or editorials; contbr. 48 articles to various sci. jours. Lt. comdr. USPHS, 1972-74. Recipient Career Devel. award Henry S. Kaiser Family Found., 1981-86. Mem. ACP (master, chmn. clin. privileges com. 1989-93, Am. Fedn. Clin. Rsch. (program chmn. health svcs. rsch. 1985), Soc. for Med. Decision Making (pres. 1985-86), Soc. for Gen. Internal Medicine (coun. 1979-84, editor Jour. Gen. Internal Medicine 1994-99, pres. 2000-01). Office: Hosp Univ of Pa Divsn Gen Internal Medicine 1220 Blockley Hall 423 Guardian Dr Philadelphia PA 19104-6021

WILLIAMS, SERENA, professional tennis player; b. Saginaw, Mich., Sept. 26, 1981; Defeated 6th seed in 1st round Australian Open, 2d seed Sudney, 1998; ranked # 27 WTA Tour, 1998, #6 in 1999; finalist Roland Garros Mixed Doubles, 1998; winner doubles, Oklahoma City, 1998, French Open (wth Venus Williams), 1999, Hannover (with Venus Williams), 1999; singles semifinalist, Sydney, 1997, Chgo., 1998; singles winner U.S. Open, 1999, Paris Indoors, 1999, Indian Wells, 1999, L.A., 1999, singles winner Australian Open, 2002, French Open, 2002, Wimbledon, 2002, U.S. Open, 2002. Office: c/o USTA 70 W Red Oak Ln White Plains NY 10604-3602 also: ATP Tour 201 Atp Tour Blvd Ponte Vedra Beach FL 32082-3211*

WILLIAMS, SHARON A. lawyer; b. Portland, Oreg., Nov. 8, 1960; BS in Polit. Sci. with honors, Portland State U., 1982; JD, Willamette U., 1985. Bar: Oreg. 1985, U.S. Dist. Ct. Oreg. Assoc. Birkland & Houze, Portland, 1985-87, Thompson, Adams, DeBast & Ray, Beaverton, Oreg., 1987-89, Sorensen-Jolink, Trubo, Koch & McIlhenny, Portland, 1989-93; ptnr. Sorensen-Jolink, Trubo, Williams, McIlhenny & Williams LLP, 1993—. Bd. dirs. Tualatin Valley Mental Health Ctr., Beaverton, Oreg., 1988-92. Mem. Oreg. State Bar Assn. (com. on balancing career and family 1992-94), Multnomah Bar Assn., Oreg. Acad. Family Law Practitioners, Wash. County Bar Assn. (mem. jud. selection com. 1998—). Avocations: travel, family, cooking. Office: Sorensen-Jolink Trubo Williams McIlhenny & Williams LLP 1020 SW Taylor St Ste 880 Portland OR 97205-2596

WILLIAMS, SHEILA A.T. elementary education educator, consultant; b. Columbus, Miss., Dec. 30, 1963; d. James Thurman and Lillian Augusta Thomas; divorced; children: Phillip James Thomas, Kristin Nicole Sims. BA in English, U. Miss., Oxford, 1986. Cert. in elem. edn. K-8, Miss. Tchr. Oxford City Schs., 1986-88; flight attendant Eastern Airlines, Miami, Fla., 1988-89; photographer Sears, Columbus, Miss., 1989-90; tchr. Cumberland County Schs., Fayetteville, N.C., 1994-95, Oktibbeha County Schs., Crawford, Miss., 1995-98, Lowndes County Schs., Columbus, 1990-94, 98—. Pres., founder S.H.A.K.E.R./Flight Buddies Aviation Program, Columbus, 1994—. Coord. Promote the Vote mock election, Crawford, 1996. Recipient Excellence in Tchg. award Nat. Coun. Negro Women, 1999; named Tchr. of Yr., Southview Mid. Sch., 1995. Fellow U.S. Space Found.; mem. AAUW, Air Force Assn. (Christa McAuliffe award 1998), Tuskegee Airmen (v.p. 1999—), Nat. Historic Preservation Soc. Democrat. Baptist. Avocations: flying, writing, swimming, hiking, reading. Home: 1377 N Booth St Dubuque IA 52001-6117

WILLIAMS, SHERRILYN RATLIFF, administrative assistant; b. Memphis, Dec. 23, 1957; d. Roosevelt Ratliff, Clithiel L. Ratliff; m. Alton Roosevelt Williams; 1 child Altronise 1 child Sheronda Williams 1 child Alton Jr.1 child Allison Williams 1 child Joy. B in Bus. Edn., U. Tenn., Martin, 1979. Cert. elem. tchr. grades 1-8, econs., typewriting, bus. English, office/clerical practice, gen. bus., shorthand, bus. arithmetic, bus. machines, consumer edn., secretarial practice. Bus. tchr. Miller Hawkins Bus. Coll., Memphis, 1980—83, Collierville (Tenn.) H.S., 1983—84; credit collections clk. Am. Airlines, Tulsa, Okla., 1988—90; tchr. Alcy Elem. Sch., Memphis, 1990—91; adminstrv. asst. World Overcomers Outreach Ministries Ch., 1997—. Counselor, min., motivational spkr., author, min. music women's ministry advisor World Overcomers Outreach Ministries, Memphis, 1992—. Named Miss Essence, Alpha Kappa Alpha, 1976, 1st Runner Up Miss Black Student Assn., Black Student Assn., 1977; recipient cert. Sch. Ministry, Rhema Bible Tng. Ctr., 1989, cert. Ordination, World Overcomers Outreach Ministries, 1995. Avocations: reading, piano, singing, jogging. Home: 4795 Windsong Park Dr Collierville TN 38017-9331 Office: Understanding For Life Ministries PO Box 1481 Collierville TN 38027-1481 Home Fax: 901-861-5041; Office Fax: 901-861-5041. Personal E-mail: SRWms1223@aol.com. Business E-Mail: SRWms1223@aol.com.

WILLIAMS, SHIRLEY J. daycare provider, educator, writer; b. Kansas City, Kans., Feb. 18, 1931; d. Anna Mae Oostenbrook; d. James Ralph and Florence (Snodgrass) Akers; m. Raymond Gale Williams, Feb. 17, 1949 (dec. 2000); children: David Ray, James Ronald, Vickie Sue, Richard Gene, Randy Wayne. Tchr., owner Su-Z-Lu Ceramics, Kansas City, 1957-70, 78, 79; sch. bus. driver Argentine Transit Lines, 1959-69; ceramic tchr., owner Su-Z-Lu Ceramics, Tonganoxie, Kans., 1972-78; tchr. Ft. Leavenworth Army Post, Leavenworth, 1979-85; pres. Wagonettes Extension Homemakers Club, Forsyth, Mo., 1987-88; ceramic tchr. Crystal's Creations and Ceramic Shop, Drexel, 1995-96; owner Classic Ceramics Studio, 1996-2001. Day-care provider for the elderly, 1990-93; founder, head Drexel Ceramic Show, 1996-2001. Contbr. articles to Popular Ceramics Trade Mag. Den mother Boy Scouts Am., Kansas City and Tonganoxie, 1955-66, instr., 1961; driver ARC, Kansas City, 1958-63, canteen chmn., campfire leader, 1961-64; contbr. Taney County Rep. newspaper, Forsyth, 1986-87, bd. dirs., 1987-91; mem. Univ.-Extension Coun. bd., 1988-91; vol., supt. ceramic divsn. Leavenworth County Fair, 1974-84; vol. tchr. Kester Found., 1956-57; program chmn. Sr. Citizen's Group of Drexel, Mo., 1996-97; pres. Drexel (Mo.) Sr. Citizens Assn., 1998-2000. Recipient 4-H Gold Clover, Taney County 4-H, 1987. Democrat. Avocations: photography, minatures, crafts, short stories, ceramics. Home: 7461 Edgehill Ave Kansas City KS 66111

WILLIAMS, SPENCER MORTIMER, federal judge; b. Reading, Mass., Feb. 24, 1922; s. Theodore Ryder and Anabel (Hutchison) W.; m. Kathryn Bramlage, Aug. 20, 1943; children: Carol Marcia (Mrs. James B. Garvey), Peter, Spencer, Clark, Janice, Diane (Mrs. Sean Quinn). AB, UCLA, 1943; postgrad., Hastings Coll. Law, 1946; JD, U. Calif., Berkeley, 1948. Bar: Calif. 1949, U.S. Supreme Ct. 1952. Assoc. Beresford & Adams, San Jose, Calif., 1949, Rankin, O'Neal, Center, Luckhardt, Bonney, Marlais & Lund, San Jose, Evans, Jackson & Kennedy, Sacramento; county counsel Santa Clara County, 1955-67; adminstr. Calif. Health and Welfare Agy., Sacramento, 1967-69; judge U.S. Dist. Ct. (no. dist.) Calif., San Francisco, from 1971, now sr. judge. County exec. pro tem, Santa Clara County; adminstr. Calif. Youth and Adult Corrections Agy., Sacramento; sec. Calif. Human Relations Agy., Sacramento, 1967-70 Chmn. San Jose Christmas Seals Drive, 1953, San Jose Muscular Dystrophy Drive, 1953, 54; team capt. fund raising drive San Jose YMCA, 1960; co-chmn. indsl. sect. fund raising drive Alexian Bros. Hosp., San Jose, 1964; team capt. fund raising drive San Jose Hosp.; mem. com. on youth and govt. YMCA, 1967-68; Candidate for Calif. Assembly, 1954, Calif. Atty. Gen., 1966, 70; Bd. dirs. San Jose Better Bus. Bur., 1955-66, Boys City Boys' Club, San Jose, 1965-67; pres. trustees Santa Clara County Law Library, 1955-66. Served with USNR, 1943-46; to lt. comdr. JAG Corps USNR, 1950-52, PTO. Named San Jose Man of Year, 1954 Mem. ABA, Calif. Bar Assn. (vice chmn. com. on publicly employed attys. 1962-63), Santa Clara County Bar Assn., Sacramento Bar Assn., Internat. Assn. Trial Judges (pres. 1995-96), Calif. Dist. Attys. Assn. (pres. 1963-64), Nat. Assn. County Civil Attys. (pres. 1963-64), 9th Cir. Dist. Judges Assn. (pres. 1981-83), Fed. Judges Assn. (pres. 1982-87), Kiwanis, Theta Delta Chi.

WILLIAMS, STEPHEN, anthropologist, educator; b. Mpls., Aug. 28, 1926; s. Clyde Garfield and Lois (Simmons) W.; m. Eunice Ford, Jan. 6, 1962; children: Stephen John, Timothy. BA, Yale U., 1949, PhD, 1954; MA, U. Mich., 1950; MA (hon.), Harvard, 1962. Asst. anthropology dept. Peabody Mus., Yale U., 1950-52; mem. faculty Harvard U., Cambridge, Mass., 1958—, prof. anthropology, 1967-72, Peabody prof., 1972-93, prof. emeritus, 1993—, chmn. dept., 1967-69; rsch. fellow Peabody Mus., Harvard U., 1954-57, mem. staff, 1954—, dir. mus., 1967-77. Curator N.Am. Archaeology, 1962-93, hon. curator 1993—; dir. rsch. of Peabody Mus.'s Lower Miss. Survey, 1958-93. Author books and articles on N.Am. archaeology, "Fantastic" archaeology and the history of Am. archaeology. Home: 1017 Foothills Trail Santa Fe NM 87505-4537 Office: PO Box 22354 Santa Fe NM 87502-2354 E-mail: williamsstephen@msn.com.

WILLIAMS, STEPHEN FAIN, federal judge; b. N.Y.C., N.Y., Sept. 23, 1936; s. Charles Dickerman and Virginia (Fain) Williams; m. Faith Morrow, June 11, 1966; children: Susan, Geoffrey Fain, Sarah Margot Nu, Timothy Dwight, Nicholas Morrow. BA, Yale U., 1958; JD, Harvard U., 1961. Bar: N.Y. 1962, Colo. 1977. Assoc. Debevoise, Plimpton, Lyons & Gates, N.Y.C., 1962—66; asst. atty. U.S. Dist. Ct. (so. dist.), 1966—69; asst. prof. law U. Colo., Boulder, 1969—77, prof., 1977—86; judge U.S. Ct. Appeals (D.C. cir.), Washington, 1986—. Vis. prof. UCLA, 1975—76; vis. prof., fellow in law and econs. U. Chgo., 1979—80; vis. William L. Hutchison prof. energy law So. Meth. U., 1983—84; cons. Adminstrv. Conf. U.S., 1974—76, FTC, 1983—85; mem. Boulder Area Growth Study Commn., 1972—73. Contbr. articles to profl. jours. and mags. With U.S. Army, 1961—62. Mem.: Am. Law Inst. Office: US Courthouse 3rd & Constitution Ave NW Washington DC 20001 E-mail: SFWilliams@cadc.uscourts.gov.

WILLIAMS, STEPHEN LAWRENCE, writer, consultant; b. Birmingham, Ala., Sept. 27, 1944; s. Percy James and Gladys (Harris) W. Student, Tuskege U., 1962-66; BS in Sociology, SUNY, Buffalo, 1971, postgrad., 1973-75. Lectr. SUNY, Buffalo, 1975-77; real estate law clk. City of Buffalo, 1976-77; investigator Erie County, Buffalo, 1977-78; CEO Starmaker Machinery, Erie County, N.Y., 1988-95. Author: Native Son - Natural Law, 1977—. With U.S. Army, 1967. Home and Office: 140 Niagara St Buffalo NY 14201 E-mail: sw0052@earthlink.net.

WILLIAMS, STEVEN A., JR. federal agency administrator; b. Bellows Falls, Vt. m. Beth Williams; 2 children. B in Environ. Resource Mgmt., D in Forest Resources, Pa. State U.; MS, U. N.D. Grad. tchg. asst. U. N.D., 1979—81, Pa. State U., 1981—85; wildlife biologist Mass. Divsn. Fisheries and Wildlife, 1985—89, asst. dir. for wildlife, 1989—92; dep. exec. dir. Pa. Game Commn., 1992—95; sec. Kans. Dept. Wildlife and Parks, 1995—; dir. Fish and Wildlife Svc. U.S. Dept. Interior, Washington, 2002—. Mem.: Wildlife Soc., Internat. Assn. Fish and Wildlife Agys. Office: US Dept Interior Fish and Wildlife Svc 1849 C St NW Washington DC 20240*

WILLIAMS, STEVEN ROBERT, lawyer; b. Columbus, Ohio, Oct. 10, 1962; s. Robert O. and Marjorie S. Williams; m. Amy McDaniel, May 26, 1990. BA, Coll. William & Mary, 1985; JD, Cornell Law Sch., 1988. Spl. asst. U.S. atty. So. Dist. Ga., Savannah, 1989-90; capt. U.S. Army, Saudi Arabia, Iraq, 1989-92; from assoc. ptnr. McGuire, Woods, Battle, & Boothe, LLP, Richmond, Va., 1993—. Capt. U.S. Army, 1989-92, Desert Storm. Decorated Meritorious Svc. medals U.S. Army, 1991, 92, S.W. Asian Campaign medal with 2 stars U.S. Army, 1991, Saudi Arabian Def. medal Kingdom of Saudi Arabia, 1991, Kuwait Liberation medal, Kuwait, 1994. Home: 1702 Park Ave Richmond VA 23220-2911 E-mail: srwillia@mwbb.com.

WILLIAMS, SUE DARDEN, library director; b. Miami, Fla., Aug. 13, 1943; d. Archie Yelverton and Bobbie (Jones) Eagles; m. Richard Williams, Sept. 30, 1989. BA, Barton Coll., Wilson, N.C., 1965; M.L.S., U. Tex., Austin, 1970. Cert. librarian, N.C., Va. Instr. Chowan Coll., Murfreesboro, N.C., 1966-68; libr.'s asst. Albemarle Regional Libr., Winston, 1968-69; br. libr. Multnomah County Pub. Libr., Portland, Oreg., 1971-72; asst. dir. Stanly County Pub. Libr., Albemarle, N.C., 1973-76, dir., 1976-80; asst. dir. Norfolk (Va.) Pub. Libr., 1980-83, dir., 1983-94, Rockingham County Pub. Libr., Eden, N.C., 1996—. Mem. ALA (coun. 1987-91, orientation com. 1990-92, chair 1991), Libr. Adminstrv. and Mgmt. Assn. (pub. rels. sec. 1985-87), Southeastern Libr. Assn. (staff devel. com. 1986-88, Rothrock award com. 1984-86, sec. pub. libr. sect. 1982-84), Va. Libr. Assn. (SELA rep. 1993-96, coun. 1984, 88-91, 93-96, ad hoc conf. guidelines com. 1985-86, chmn. conf. program 1984, awards and recognition com. 1983, mem. SELA outstanding libr. program award com. 2002-2002), Pub. Libr. Assn. (bd. dirs.-at-large Met. area 1986-89), Va. State Libr. (coop edn. com. 88-89), N.C. Libr. Assn. (scholarship com. 1999—, chair 2001-03). Home: 817A Carter St Eden NC 27288-5923 Office: Rockingham County Pub Libr 527 Boone Rd Eden NC 27288-4905 E-mail: swilliams@library.rcpl.org.

WILLIAMS, SUE M. corporate communications specialist, writer; b. Sumter, S.C., Aug. 20, 1942; d. Perry Harrington and Ida (Sumter) Taylor; m. Elwood E. Williams, Mar. 9, 1963 (div. 1969); 2 children. Diploma, cert., Comms. Inst. Am., 1968; BA, U. Colo., 1974; R. Sc. F., Ernest Holmes Coll. Ch. of Religious Sci., 1979; M in Mgmt. Sci., Regis U., Denver, 1999. Ordained to ministry. Long distance operator Mountain Bell/Penn Bell, Phila. & Colorado Springs, 1964-69; comml. teller Exch. Nat. Bank, Colorado Springs, 1969-74; ops. trainee Cen. Bank of Denver, 1974-75; legal specialist USAFR, Lowry AFB, Colo., 1975-77; asst. mgr. Western Airlines, L.A., 1974-87; supr. reservation sales Delta Air Lines, 1987-88; sr. sec., office mgr.

U. Colo., Denver, 1988-89; sales coord. Hewlett Packard Co., Englewood, Colo., 1989-90; supr. U.S. Sprint (United Telecom), Denver, 1990—. Contbr. articles to profl. jours. Mem. Vets. Club, Colorado Springs, 1973-74; various offices L.A. Election Dept., 1983-85; appointed vet. com. Calif. Reps., L.a., 1985; participant Hands Across Am., L.A., 1985, The Bolder Boulder, various walking races for local charity; charter mem. Women in Mil. Meml. Found., Washington, 1990. With USAF, 1961-63. Mem. Am. Legion, Coll. Devine Metaphysics Alumni Assn. (area v.p. 1982—). Office: US Sprint 1099 18th St Ste 1210 Denver CO 80202-1908

WILLIAMS, SUNITA L. astronaut; b. Euclid, Ohio, Sept. 19, 1965; d. Deepak N. and Ursaline B. Pandya; m. Michael J. Williams. BS in Physical Sci., U.S. Naval Acad., 1987; MS in Engring. Mgmt., Fla. Inst. Tech., 1995. Commn. ensign USN, 1987, advanced through grades to lt. comdr., various assignments, 1987—89, overseas combat, 1989—92; officer in charge Hurrican Andrew Relief Ops. USS Sylvania, 1992—93; various assignments USN, 1993—95; served on USS Saipan, Norfolk, Va., 1995—98; astronaut NASA, Houston, 1998—. Decorated Commendation medal USN, Achievement medal USN & USMC, Humanitarian Svc. medal USN. Mem.: Soc. Flight Test Engrs., Soc. Exptl. Test Pilots, Am. Helicopter Assn. Office: Astronaut Office CB NASA Johnson Space Center Houston TX 77058*

WILLIAMS, SUSAN EILEEN, urban planner; b. Chgo., Dec. 13, 1952; d. Joseph Andrew and Alice (Regnier) W.; 1 child, Ryan Joseph. AA in Polit. Sci., Coll. of Desert, Palm Desert, Calif., 1971; BA in Polit. Sci., U. Calif., Riverside, 1973; M of Pub. Adminstrn., Consortium Calif. State Colls. and Univs., 1982. Planning trainee City of Indio, Calif., 1975-79, assoc. planner, 1979-80, prin. planner, 1980-90, prin. planner redevel. agy., 1983-90; supervising planner J.F. Davidson Assocs., Inc., Palm Desert, 1990-94; dir. cmty. devel. City of Coachella, 1994—. Mem. Am. Planning Assn., Assn. Environ Profls., Ill. Geneal. Soc., Geneal. Club Am. Roman Catholic. Office: City of Coachella 1515 6th St Coachella CA 92236-1713 E-mail: swilliams@coachella.org.

WILLIAMS, SUZANNE, pediatric nurse practitioner; b. Murray, Ky., Sept. 23, 1961; d. Clifton Eugene and Mary Helen (Lee) W. Diploma, Bapt. Meml. Hosp. Sch. Nursing, 1982; BSN, U. Ky., 1985; MSN, Vanderbilt U., 1989; postgrad., U. N.C., 1997. RN Ky., Tenn., Fla., cert. pediat. nurse practitioner, case mgr. Staff nurse pediatric ICU U. Ky. Hosp., Lexington, 1982-86, divisional charge nurse pediatrics, 1988-89, pediatric clin. nurse specialist/case mgr., 1989-90; staff nurse pediatric ICU Vanderbilt U. Hosp., Nashville, 1986-87; pediatric cardiovascular case mgr. Med. U. of S.C., Charleston, 1990-94, clin. nurse V/nurse educator, 1994-96; clin. nurse pediat. ICU Duke U. Hosp., Durham, N.C., 1996-98; pediat. nurse practitioner Assocs. in Pediats., Ft. Meyers, Fla., 1998—. Mem.: ANA, AACN, Nat. Assn. Pediat. Nurses Assocs. and Practitioners, Sigma Theta Tau. Avocations: reading, needlecrafts, hiking. Home: 2319 Woodland Ter Fort Myers FL 33907-5818

WILLIAMS, SYLVESTER EMANUAL, III, educator, consultant; b. Chgo., Feb. 4, 1937; s. Sylvester Emanual and Carita (Brown) W.; children: Sylvia, Sylvester, Sydnee, Steven. BS, No. Ill. U., 1958; MA, Chgo. State U., 1968; PhD, U. S.C., 1992. Cert. tchr., S.C., N.C., Ill. From asst. to supt. Washington D.C. Pub. Schs., 1968-69; tchr. Chgo. Pub. Schs., 1958-68; program officer Dept. Edn., Washington, 1971-86; prof. Lander U., Greenwood, S.C., 1986-89, U. S.C., Akin, 1990-91; tchr., coach Charlotte (N.C.) Mecklenburg Pub. Schs., 1992-93; edn. devel. cons. South Shore Cmty. Ch., Chgo.; rsch. assoc. Houston Ctr., Clemson U., 1999-2000; devel. cons. Rose Garden Cmty. Svcs., Chgo., 1999-2000; cons. DHHS, 1994-2000; demographic rschr., 1992—. Bd. dirs. John de Home Sch., McCormick, S.C. Mem. Phi Delta Kappa. Republican. Baptist. Avocation: motion picture production. Home: 205 Briggs Ave Greenwood SC 29649-1603 E-mail: drsewiii@greenwood.net.

WILLIAMS, TED VAUGHNELL, physical education educator; b. Bronx, N.Y., Apr. 1, 1952; s. Joseph Alexander and Annie (Canady) W. BS, Springfield Coll., 1977. Cert. tchr., N.Y. Substitute tchr. Valhalla (N.Y.) High Sch., 1977; tchr. aide for handicapped children, tchr. spl. edn. Rye Lake Campus, Valhalla, 1978; supr. recreation activities Springfield (Mass.) Girl's Club Family Ctr., 1979; assoc. dir. boy's and men's phys. edn. dept. Trenton YMCA, 1979—; house supr. Cardinal McCloskey's Group Home, Tappan, N.Y., 1980-81; phys. edn. tchr. Our Lady of Refuge Sch., Bronx, 1982-83; tchr. phys. edn. various Cath. elem. schs. Yonkers, 1983—. With ops. dept. Hudson Valley Nat. Bank, 1990-92. Active Walk Am. for Healthier Babies, March of Dimes, 1990-93. Recipient Ed Steitz award Basketball Hall of Fame, 1975, Capitol award Nat. Leadership Coun., 1991. Mem. ASCD, AAHPERD, Am. Assn. Leisure and Recreation, Hudson Valley Leisure Svcs. Assn. Democrat. Baptist. Home: 49 Bradford Ave White Plains NY 10603-2143

WILLIAMS, TEMPLE WEATHERLY, JR. internist, educator; b. Wichita Falls, Tex., Apr. 19, 1934; s. Temple Weatherly and Dorothy (Coleman) W.; married; children: Holly Clare, Temple Weatherly III; m. Joan Loos, Apr. 6, 1991. Student, Midwestern U., 1951-53; BS, So. Meth. U., 1955; MD, Baylor U., 1959. Intern, resident in internal medicine Duke U. Hosp., Durham, N.C., 1959-60, 62-63; fellow in infectious disease Baylor U., 1960-62; clin. assoc. infectious disease NIH, Bethesda, Md., 1963—65; mem. faculty Baylor Coll. Medicine, 1965—, prof. medicine and microbiology-immunology, 1974—. Contbr. over 100 articles on infectious diseases to profl. jours., chpts. to books. Served with USPHS, 1963-65. Fellow ACP, Infectious Disease Soc. Am.; mem. AMA. Republican. Methodist. Office: 6565 Fannin St # Ms910 Houston TX 77030-2704

WILLIAMS, THEODORE EARLE, retired industrial distribution company executive; b. Cleve., May 9, 1920; s. Stanley S. and Blanche (Albaum) W.; m. Rita Cohen, Aug. 28, 1952; children: Lezlie, Richard Atlas, Shelley, William Atlas, Wayne, Marsha, Patti Blake, Jeff Blake. Student, Wayne U., 1937-38; BS in Engring, postgrad. in bus. adminstrn, U. Mich., 1942. Pres. Wayne Products Co., Detroit, 1942-43, L.A., 1947-49; pres. Williams Metal Products Co., Inglewood, Calif., 1950-69; chmn. bd. Bell Industries, L.A., 1970-2000; ret., 2000. Instr. U. Mich., 1942 Patentee in field. Served to 1st lt. AUS, 1943-46. Recipient Humanitarian award City of L.A., 1977. Democrat. Home: 435 N Layton Way Los Angeles CA 90049-2022 *It seems to me that many of our current problems in this world originate from the drift away from concern for other people to the emphasis on self. We are reluctant to get involved, and as this spaceship gets smaller, we become more interdependent all the time. If we don't learn to live together, I'm afraid we may all perish together.*

WILLIAMS, THEODORE JOSEPH, engineering educator; b. Black Lick, Pa., Sept. 2, 1923; s. Theodore Finley and Mary Ellen (Shields) W.; m. Isabel Annette McAnulty, July 18, 1946; children: Theodore Joseph, Mary Margaret, Charles Augustus, Elizabeth Ann. BSCh.E., Pa. State U., 1949, MSCh.E., 1950, PhD, 1955; MS in Elec. Engring., Ohio State U., 1956. Research fellow Pa. State U., University Park, 1947-51; asst. prof. Air Force Inst. Tech., 1953-56; technologist Monsanto Co., 1956-57, sr. engring. supr., 1957-65; prof. engring. Purdue U., Lafayette, Ind., 1965-94, prof. emeritus, 1995—, dir. control and info. systems lab., 1965-66; dir. Purdue Lab. Applied Indsl. Control, 1966-94, dir. emeritus, 1995—; cons., 1964—. Vis. prof. Washington U., St. Louis, 1962-65. Author: Systems Engineering for the Process Industries, 1961, Automatic Control of Chemical and Petroleum Processes, 1961, Progress in Direct Digital Control, 1969, Interfaces with the Process Control Computer, 1971, Modeling and Control of Kraft Production Systems, 1975, Modelling, Estimation and Control of the Soaking Pit, 1983, The Use of Digital Computers in Process Control, 1983, Analysis and Design of Hierarchical Control Systems - With Special Reference to Steel Plant Operations, 1985, A Reference Model for Computer Integrated Manufacturing (CIM) - A Description from the Viewpoint of Industrial Automation, 1989, The Purdue Enterprise Reference Architecture, 1992; editor: Computer Applications in Shipping and Shipbuilding, 6 vols., 1973-79, Proceedings Advanced Control Confs., 19 vols., 1974-93, Architectures for Enterprise Integration, 1996. Served to 1st lt. USAAF, 1942-45; to capt. USAF, 1951-56. Decorated Air medal with 2 oak leaf clusters. Fellow AAAS, AIChE, Instrument Soc. Am. (hon. mem., pres. 1968-69, Albert F. Sperry gold medal 1990, Lifetime Achievement award 1995), Am. Inst. Chemists, Inst. Measurement and Control (London, Sr. Harold Hartley silver medal 1975), Indsl. Computing Soc.; mem. IEEE (sr.), Internat. Fedn. for Info. Processing (Silver Core award 1978), Soc. for Computer Simulation (hon.), Am. Chem. Soc., Am. Automatic Control Coun. (pres. 1965-67), Am. Fedn. Info. Processing Socs. (pres. 1976-78), Sigma Xi, Tau Beta Pi, Phi Kappa Phi, Phi Lambda Upsilon. Home: 208 Chippewa St West Lafayette IN 47906-2123 Office: Purdue U Potter Rsch Ctr Inst Interdisciplinary Engring Studies West Lafayette IN 47907-1293 E-mail: tjwil@ecn.purdue.edu.

WILLIAMS, THEODORE JOSEPH, JR. lawyer; b. Pitts., July 23, 1947; s. Theodore Joseph and Isabel (McAnulty) W.; m. Sherri Lynne Foust, July 4, 1970; children: Kelley Shields, Jonathan Stewart, Jordan Fuller. BA, Purdue U., 1969; JD, U. Tulsa, 1974. Bar: Ill. 1975, Colo. 1996, U.S. Ct. Appeals (7th cir.) 1975, U.S. Dist. Ct. (no., so. and cen. dists.) Ill. 1975, Mo. 1978, U.S. Ct. Appeals (8th cir.) 1978, U.S. Dist. Ct. (ea. and we. dists.) Mo. 1978, U.S. Supreme Ct. 1978, D.C. 1981, U.S. Ct. Appeals (D.C. cir.) 1988, U.S. Dist. Ct. D.C 1988, U.S. Ct. Mil. Appeals 1991, U.S. Ct. Appeals (10 cir.) 1996, U.S. Dist. Ct. (no. dist.) Ind. 2000. Asst. city prosecutor City of Tulsa, 1974; trial atty., law dept. Chgo. and North Western R.R., Chgo., 1975-78; assoc. Thompson and Mitchell, St. Louis, 1978-81, Shepherd, Sandberg & Phoenix, P.C., St. Louis, 1981-84, ptnr., 1984-88; ptnr., chmn. transp. law dept. Armstrong, Teasdale, Schlafly & Davis, 1988-2001; ptnr. Williams, Venker & Sanders, LLC, 2001—. State Counsel for Mo. and Ill., Chgo. and North Western Transp. Co., 1981-95. Assoc. editor Law. Jour., U. Tulsa, 1974. Treas. sch. bd. Mary Queen of Peace Sch., Webster Groves, Mo., 1986, v.p., 1987. Capt. U.S. Army, 1969-72, lt. col. USAR, 1991—. Mem. ABA (vice chmn. rail and motor carrier law com., torts and ins. practice law sect. 1989-90, chair-elect 1990-91, chair 1991-92), Ill. Bar Assn., Mo. Bar Assn., Def. Rsch. Inst. (chair, railroad law commn. 1996), Nat. Assn. R.R. Trial Coun. (exec. com. 2002--), We. Conf. Ry. Coun., Assn. ICC Practitioners, Maritime Law Assn., Internat. Assn. Def. Coun., Transp. Lawyers Assn., Assn. Transp. Practitioners, D.C. Bar Assn., Colo. Bar Assn. Republican. Roman Catholic. Office: Williams Venker Sanders LLC Ste 1600 10 S Broadway St Saint Louis MO 63102 E-mail: Twilliams@wvslaw.com.

WILLIAMS, THOMAS FRANKLIN, physician, educator; b. Belmont, N.C., Nov. 26, 1921; s. T. F. and Mary L. (Deaton) Williams; m. Catharine Carter Catlett, Dec. 15, 1951; children: Mary Wright, Thomas Nelson. BS, U. N.C., 1942; MA, Columbia U., 1943; MD, Harvard U., 1950; DSc (hon.) , Med. Coll. Ohio, 1987, U. N.C., 1992. Intern Johns Hopkins, Balt., 1950—51, asst. resident physician, 1951—53; resident physician Boston VA Hosp., 1953—54; research fellow U. N.C., Chapel Hill, 1954—56, instr. dept. medicine and preventive medicine, 1956—57, asst. prof., 1957—61, assoc. prof., 1961—68, prof., 1968; attending physician Strong Meml. Hosp., Rochester, NY, 1968—; cons. physician Genesee Hosp., 1973—; prof. medicine, preventive medicine and cmty. health U. Rochester, 1968—92, prof. radiation biology and biophysics, 1968—91, on leave, 1983—91, prof. emeritus, 1992—; clin. prof. medicine U. Va., 1983—89; lectr. medicine Johns Hopkins U., 1983—89; clin. prof. depts. family medicine and medicine Georgetown U., 1983—89; dir. Nat. Inst. on Aging NIH, 1983—91; asst. surgeon gen. USPHS, 1983—91, ret., 1991; attending physician Monroe Cmty. Hosp., Rochester, 1991—, vice-chmn. cmty. coalition for long term care, 1991—; disting. physician VA Med. Ctr., Canandigua, NY, 1995—98. Adv. bd. U. Rochester Sch. Medicine and Dentistry, 1968—83; med. dir. Monroe Cmty. Hosp., Rochester, 1968—83; mem. rev. coms. Nat. Ctr. for Health Svcs. Rsch.; adv. bd. St. Ann's Home; mem. gov. bd. NRC, 1981—83; sci. dir. Am. Fedn. Aging Rsch., 1992—; cons. in field. Contbr. articles to profl. publs. With USNR, 1943—46. Recipient Civic award for health care, Rochester N.Y. C. of C., 1998; fellow, USPHS, 1966—67; scholar Markle scholar, 1957—61. Fellow: ACP, APHA; mem.: NAS (coun. 1980—83, governing bd. 1981—83, Gustav O. Lienhard award Inst. Medicine 1969), AAAS, Am. Clin. Climatol. Assn., N.C. Coun. for Human Rels. (chmn. 1963—66), Rochester Regional Diabetes Assn. (pres. 1977—79), Am. Gerontol. Soc., Am. Geriatrics Soc., Soc. Exptl. Biology and Medicine, Am. Fedn. Clin. Rsch., Am. Diabetes Assn. (bd. dirs. 1974—80), Monroe County Med. Soc., N.Y. State Med. Soc., Assn. Am. Physicians, Inst. Medicine. Episcopalian. Home: 287 Dartmouth St Rochester NY 14607-3202 Office: Monroe Community Hosp Office Med Dir Rochester NY 14620

WILLIAMS, THOMAS ALAN, elementary education educator, coach; b. Kingston, Pa., Dec. 15, 1961; s. Thomas Elwin and Lois Jean (Vanderhoff) W.; m. Jeanne Ann Sweinberg, July 10, 1993; children: Lindsay Nicole, Thomas Lee. BS in Edn., Bloomsburg (Pa.) U., 1983; MS in Counselor Edn., U. Scranton, Pa., 1987. Cert. secondary counselor, elem. counselor. Tchr. N.W. Sch. Dist., Shickshinny, Pa., 1983-84; tchr. grades 4-6 Lake-Lehman (Pa.) Sch. Dist., 1984-88, tchr. social studies grades 7-8, 1988-93, tchr. social studies grades 10-12, 1993-99, tchr. grades 4-6, 1999—, asst. athletic dir., 2001—. Wrestling coach Lake-Lehman Sch. Dist., 1984-99. Wrestling official Pa. Interscholastic Athletic Assn., Wilkes-Barre, 1981—. Named Pa. N.E. Regional Coach of Yr., Regional Wrestling Com., 1991, 95, Coach of Yr., Times-Leader, 1990, 91, 92, 94, 95, 96, 97. Mem. Nat. Wrestling Coaches Assn., Pa. State Athletic Dirs. Assn., Pa. Wrestling Coaches Assn., Dist 2 Pa. Interscholastic Athletic Assn., Wrestling Coaches Assn. (Coach of Yr. 1992, 95, Sportsmanship award 1995), Masons, Shriners, Caldwell Consistory. Republican. Methodist. Avocations: fishing, collectibles, photography, travel, gardening. Home: 1087 Mountain View Dr Dallas PA 18612-9539 Office: Lake-Lehman H S Lehman PA 18627 E-mail: TNJWilly@aol.com.

WILLIAMS, THOMAS ARTHUR, biomedical computing consultant, psychiatrist; b. Racine, Wis., May 11, 1936; s. Robert Klinkert and Marion Anne (Wisneski) Williams; m. Christine Frances Fannon, July 3, 1970; children: Jennifer, Thomas, Hailey, Renate, Alexa. BA, Harvard Coll., 1958; MD, Columbia U., 1963; postgrad., NIH, 1967-68. Diplomate Nat. Bd. Med. Examiners, Am. Bd. Psychiatry and Neurology. Intern in surgery Columbia Presbyn. Med. Ctr., N.Y.C., 1963-64; resident in psychiatry Columbia Presbyterian Med. Ctr., N.Y. State Psychiat. Inst., 1964-67; chief depression sect. NIMH, Bethesda, Rockville, Md., 1967-71; asst. prof. U. Pitts., 1969-70; assoc. prof. U. Utah, Salt Lake City, 1971-77; prof., chmn. dept. psychiatry Eastern Va. Med. Sch., Norfolk, Va., 1977-78; clin. dir. Sheppard & Enoch Pratt Hosp., Towson, Md., 1978-80; prof. U. South Fla., Tampa, 1980-83; practitioner psychiat. medicine, med. dir. St. Augustine (Fla.) Psychiat. Ctr., 1983-89, 89-90; prin. Williams & Assocs., Palm Harbor, Fla., 1990—. Dir., treas., pres. Klinkart Realty Co., Inc., Racine, Wis., 1960-85; dir., CEO Psych Systems, Inc., Norfolk, Va., 1977-78. Chief editor: Psychobiology of Depression, 1972, Mental Health in the 21st Century, 1979; contbr. numerous articles to profl. jours. and chpts. to books. Mem. Gov.'s Adv. Com. on Mental Health, Salt Lake City, 1971-77, Gov.'s Adv. Com. on Penal Code, Richmond, Va., 1978, Dist. Mental Health Bd., Tampa, 1980-83; mem. U.S. Govt. Mission on Psychiatry to USSR, 1974; sponsor, coach Forest Hills Little League Baseball, Tampa, 1980-83. Sr. surgeon USPHS, 1958-67. Recipient Predoctoral fellowship NIMH, 1960-61, Alumni Rsch. award N.Y. State Psychiat. Inst., 1964, Rush Bronze Medal award Am. Psychiat. Assn., 1973, Rsch. grants VA, 1971-77. Mem. AMA, Fla. Med. Assn., Hillsborough County Med. Assn., Columbia U. Alumni Club (dir. 1995—), Harvard Club of the West Coast of Fla. Avocations: personal computing, classical music, opera, profl. basketball. Home: 3844 Muirfield Ct Palm Harbor FL 34685 E-mail: tawmd@earthlink.net.

WILLIAMS, THOMAS BLAKE, natural resources consultant, educator; b. Joplin, Mo., June 12, 1948; s. Sherman Blake and Patricia Janet Williams; m. Elizabeth Anne Moler, Oct. 19, 1979; children: Blake, Eleanor. BA, Trinity U., San Antonio, 1970; MA, Wash. State U., 1973. Prof. staff mem. Senate Energy and Natural Resources Com., Washington, 1973-96, Dem. staff dir., 1997-99; pres. The Williams Group, McLean, Va., 1999—. Adj. faculty Am. U., Washington; fed. projects dir. The Conservation Fund; mem. Nat. Pk. Sys. Adv. Bd. 1st lt., U.S. Army Signal Corps, 1972, Ft. Gordon. Mem. Am. Polit. Sci. Assn. Home: 1537 Forest Ln Mc Lean VA 22101 Office: The Williams Group 1537 Forest Ln Mc Lean VA 22101

WILLIAMS, THOMAS EUGENE, pediatric hematologist-oncologist, pharmaceutical executive; b. Texarkana, Ark., May 13, 1936; s. Thomas Earle and Frankie Jo (Garner) W.; m. Peggy Jane O'Neill, May 31, 1958; children: Thomas Eugene, Elizabeth Anne, James David. BA, Yale U., 1958; MD, U. Tex. Southwestern Med. Sch., 1962. Diplomate Am. Bd. Pediat., Am. Bd. Pediat. Hematology and Oncology. Rotating intern Hermann Hosp., Houston, 1962-63; pediat. resident Children's Med. Ctr., Dallas, 1963-65; fellow pediat. hematology U. Va. Sch. Medicine, Charlottesville, 1967-68; rsch. assoc. Cancer Rsch. Lab., U. Va., 1968-69; asst. prof. pediat. and pathology U. Tex. Health Sci. Ctr., San Antonio, 1969-72, assoc. prof. pediat., asst. prof. pathology, 1972-73, assoc. prof. pediat. and pathology, 1973-79, assoc. prof. pediat., 1985-94. Med. dir. Santa Rosa Children's Hosp. Cancer Rsch. and Treatment Ctr., 1974—79, South Tex. Comprehensive Hemophilia Ctr., 1977—79, dir. pediat. bone marrow transplantation program, 1986—93; sr. clin. rsch. scientist Burroughs Wellcome Co., 1979—85; dir. new drug devel. Orphan Med., Inc., 1994—96; dir. med. affairs Ilex Oncology Svcs., Inc., 1997—98, ILEX Oncology Products, Inc., 1998—2000, 2001—02; exec. dir. Episcopal Med. Missions Found., 1997—; clin. assoc. prof. pediat. U. N.C. Sch. Medicine, 1979—85; clin. fellow bone marrow transplantation program Johns Hopkins U. Sch. Medicine, Balt., 1985. Contbr. articles to med. jours. Lt. comdr. USN, 1965-67. Recipient travel award Am. Soc. Pharmacology and Exptl. Therapeutics, 1968; Am. Cancer Soc. advanced clin. fellow, 1968-69, 70-72. Mem. Am. Soc. Clin. Oncology, Am. Soc. Hematology, Am. Assn. for Cancer Rsch. Episcopalian. Office: 4545 Horizon Hill Blvd San Antonio TX 78229-2263 E-mail: twilliams@ilexonc.com.

WILLIAMS, THOMAS FFRANCON, chemist, educator; b. Colwyn Bay, Wales, Jan. 30, 1928; came to U.S., 1961; s. David and Margaret (Williams) W.; m. Astra Silvia Birins, Jan. 31, 1959; children: Ifor Rainis, Gwyn David. BSc, U. Coll., London, 1949; PhD, U. London, 1960. Sci. officer U.K. Atomic Energy Authority, Harwell, Eng., 1949-55, sr. sci. officer Eng., 1955-61, prin. sci. officer Eng., 1961; rsch. scientist Ill. Inst. Tech. Research Inst., Chgo., 1961; asst. prof. chemistry U. Tenn., Knoxville, 1961-63, assoc. prof., 1963-67, prof., 1967-74, Alumni Distinguished Service prof., 1974—. Tchg. and rsch. assoc. Northwestern U., Evanston, Ill., 1957-58; NSF vis. scientist Kyoto (Japan) U., 1965-66; coord. U.S.-Japan Sci. Sem., Hakone, Japan, 1969; chmn. Gordon Rsch. Conf. on Radiation Chemistry, New Hampton, N.H., 1971, Gordon Rsch. Conf. Radical Ions, Wolfeboro, N.H., 1984; John Simon Guggenheim Meml. Found. fellow, Swedish Rsch. Coun. Lab., Studsvik, Nykoping, 1972-73; vis. scientist Royal Inst. Tech., Stockholm, Sweden, 1972-73; chmn. 10th Southeastern Magnetic Resonance Conf., 1978; mem. chemistry div. rev. com. Argonne (Ill.) Nat. Lab., 1988, 91, 95; cons. Pacific N.W. Nat. Lab., 1996-97. Contbg. author: Fundamental Processes in Radiation Chemistry, 1968, Radiation Chemistry of Macromolecules, 1972; mem. editl. bd. Radiation Rsch., 1993—, assoc. editor, 1993-97, cons. editor, 1997-2000; contbr. numerous articles on chem. effects of high energy radiation to profl. jours. AEC, ERDA, Dept. Energy grantee, 1962-99. Mem. Am. Chem. Soc. (program chmn. sect. 1968-69, exec. com. 1986-88), Brit. Chem. Soc., Radiation Rsch. Soc., Phi Beta Kappa (hon.), Sigma Xi (pres. U. Tenn. chpt. 1993-94). Home: 3117 Montlake Dr Knoxville TN 37920-2836 Office: U Tenn Dept Of Chemistry Knoxville TN 37996-1600 E-mail: ffwilliams@utk.edu.

WILLIAMS, THOMAS KENNON, retired surgeon; b. Fulton, Ky., Dec. 19, 1919; MD, Tulane U., 1944. Diplomate Am. Bd. Surgery. Intern So. Bapt. Hosp., New Orleans, 1944-45, resident in surgery, 1952-55; fellow in surgery Mahorner Clin., 1955-56, U. Miss. Med. Ctr., 1956-58, resident in thoracic surgery, 1956-58. Home: 4026 Cabell Ln Jackson MS 39206-6115

WILLIAMS, THOMAS LLOYD, psychiatrist; b. Mt. Carmel, Pa., May 8, 1925; s. Thomas Lloyd and Anna (Roberts) W.; m. Lucille H. Held, June 23, 1993; children: Scott, Michael, Thomas Held. BS, U. Pitts., 1949, MD, 1952. Diplomate Am. Bd. Neurology and Psychiatry. Intern Allegheny Gen. Hosp., Pitts., 1952-53; family practice Gilbert, Pa., 1953-59; resident Mental Health Hosp. affiliated with U. Iowa, Cherokee, 1959-62, mem. staff, 1962-63; pvt. practice, Bethlehem, Pa., 1963-97; ret., 1997; chief of psychiatry St. Lukes Hosp., Bethlehem, Pa., 1976-88, mem. staff emeritus, 1988—. 1st lt. navigator, U.S. Army Air Corps, 1943-45, ETO. Decorated DFC, Air medal with three oak leaf clusters, ETO Ribbon with seven battle stars. Fellow Am. Psychiat. Assn. (life). Republican. Avocations: hunting, fishing, carving.

WILLIAMS, THOMAS RHYS, anthropologist, educator; b. Martins Ferry, Ohio, June 13, 1928; s. Harold K. and Dorothy (Lehew) W.; m. Margaret Martin, July 12, 1952; children: Rhys M., Ian T., Tom R. BA, Miami U., Oxford, Ohio, 1951; MA, U. Ariz., 1956; PhD, Syracuse U., 1956. Asst. prof., asso. prof. anthropology Calif. State U., Sacramento, 1956-65; vis. asso. prof. anthropology U. Calif. Berkeley, 1962; vis. prof. anthropology Stanford U., 1976; prof. anthropology Ohio State U., Columbus, 1965-78, chmn. dept. 1967-71, mem. grad. council, 1969-72, mem. univ. athletic council, 1968-74, chmn. univ. athletic council, 1973-74, exec. com. Coll. Social and Behavior Scis., 1967-71; dean Grad. Sch. George Mason U., Fairfax, Va., 1978-81, prof. anthropology, 1981—, dir. Ctr. for Rsch. and Advanced Studies, 1978-81, fed. liaison officer, 1978-81, chmn. faculty adv. bd. grad. degree program in conflict resolution, 1980-86. Author: The Dusun: A North Borneo Society, 1965, Field Methods in the Study of Culture, 1967, A Borneo Childhood: Enculturation in Dusun Society, 1969, Introduction to Socialization: Human Culture Transmitted, 1972, Socialization, 1983; editor, contbg. author: Psychological Anthropology, 1975, Socialization and Communication in Primary Groups, 1975, Cultural Anthropology, 1990; contbr. articles to profl. jours. Mem. United Democrats for Humphrey, 1968, Citizens for Humphrey, 1968. Served with USN, 1946-48. Research grantee NSF, 1958, 62, Am. Council Learned Socs.-Social Sci. Research Council, 1959, 63; Ford Found. S.E. Asia, 1974, 76; recipient Disting. Faculty award Calif. State U., Sacramento, 1961, George Mason U., 1983; Disting. Teaching awards Ohio State U., 1968, 76 Fellow Am. Anthrop. Assn., Royal Anthrop. Inst. Gt. Britain; assoc. mem. Current Anthropology; mem. AAAS, Sigma Xi. Office: George Mason U Robinson Hall B-315 4400 University Dr Fairfax VA 22030-4444

WILLIAMS, TONDA, entrepreneur, consultant; b. N.Y.C., Nov. 21, 1949; d. William and Juanita (Rainey) W.; 1 child, Tywana. Student, Collegiate Inst., N.Y.C., 1975-78, C.W. Post Coll., 1981-83; BA in Bus. Mgmt., Am. Nat. U., Phoenix, 1983; grad., L.I. Bus. Inst., 1996. Notary pub. N.Y. Asst. controller Acad. Ednl. Devel., N.Y.C., 1971-81; mgr. office Chapman-Apex Constrn. Co., Bayshore, N.Y., 1982-84; specialist computer RGM Liquid Waste Removal, Deerpark, 1985-87; contr. LaMar Lighting Co., Freeport, 1987—; owner, pres. Omni-Star, Bklyn., 1981—; pres. Omni-Data Tech., Bayshore, N.Y., 1996—. Author: Tonda's Songs in Poetry, 1978, The Magic of Life, 1991; co-author: Computer Management of Liquid Waste Industry, 1986. Recipient Golden Poet award World of Poetry, 1992. Mem. Am. Mus. Natural History, Am. Soc. Notary Pubs. Avocations: bowling, chess, singing. Home: 74 Cedar Dr Bay Shore NY 11706-2419 Fax: 631-968-1016. E-mail: tonda@omnidatatech.com.

WILLIAMS, TREAT (RICHARD TREAT WILLIAMS), actor; b. Stamford, Conn., Dec. 1, 1951; s. Richard Norman and Marian (Andrew) W. BA, Franklin and Marshall Coll., 1973. Appeared in Broadway plays Over There, Grease; (repertory plays) Servant of Two Masters, Ohio, Claptrap, Cambridge, Mass., 1985, Pirates of Penzance at N.Y. Shakespeare Festival, Glass Menagerie, Long Wharf, New Haven, 1986, Bobby Gould in Hell, 1989; (films) Deadly Hero, Eagle Has Landed, Hair, 1941, 1978, Why Would I Lie, 1979, Pursuit, 1980, Prince of the City, 1980, Once Upon a Time in America, 1982, Flashpoint, 1984, Men's Club, 1985, Sweet Lies 1986, Smooth Talk, 1986, The Heart of Dixie, 1989, Russicum, 1989, Where the Rivers Run North, 1994, Parallel Lives, 1994, Handgun, 1994, Things to do When You're Dead, 1995, The Phantom, 1996, Mullholland Falls, 1996, The Devil's Own, 1997, Deep Rising, 1997, The Deep End of the Ocean, 1999, Skeletons in the Closet, 2000, Critical Mass, 2000, Crash Point Zero, 2000, Venemous, 2001, The Circle, 2001, Gale Force, 2002; TV movies Jack Dempsey Story, 1982, Streetcar Named Desire, 1983, Some Men Need Help, 1983, Hoover, Sweet Lies, 1986, Things To Do in Denver When You're Dead, 1995, In the Shadow of Evil, 1995, The Late Shift, 1996, Escape Human Cargo, 1998, Substitute 2: School's Out, 1998, 36 Hours to Die, 1999, The Substitute 3: Winner Takes All, 1999, Journey to the Center of the Earth, 1999, Guilty Hearts, 2002; TV appearances Faerie Tale Theatre, 1984, Men's Club, 1985, Third Degree Burn, 1989, Max and Helen, 1990, Drug Wars: The Enrico Camerena Story, 1990, Bonds of Love, 1993, Eddie Dodd, 1992; (TV series) Good Advice, 1993-94. Mem. AFTRA, SAG, Actors Equity Assn. Episcopalian.*

WILLIAMS, UNA JOYCE, psychiatric social worker; b. Youngstown, Ohio, June 24, 1934; d. Samuel Wilfred and Frances Josephine (Woods) Ellis; children: Wendy Louise, Christopher Ellis, Sharon Elizabeth. *Una Williams is descendant of the Ellis family of great-grandparents Thomas and Mary Ellis from Staffordshire, England. Mary came to America with her children after the* *death and burial of Thomas in Staffordshire. Her grandson, Sam Ellis, was an engineer with Saturn Rockets and her great grandson, Sam Ellis, was a professional baseball player. She is also descended from pioneering families Scott and Woods, who migrated via wagon train into North Georgia from Virginia and the Carolinas in late 1700s and early 1800's. These families were farmers of Scotch-Irish lineage, and both have members who served in the Revolutionary and Civil Wars as well as WWI, WWII and Vietnam.* BA, U. Ala., 1957; MSW, Adelphi U., 1963. Diplomate in profl. counseling Internat. Acad. Behavioral Medicine, Counseling and Psychotherapy. Dir. Huntington Program for Sr. Citizens; psychiat. social worker-supr. N.Y. State Dept. Mental Hygiene, Suffolk Psychiat. Hosp., Central Islip; info.-referral counselor Mental Health Assn. Nassau County, Hempstead, N.Y.; therapist Madonna Heights Family Clinic, Dix Hills; med. and psychiat. social worker Northport (N.Y.) VA Med. Ctr., psychiat. social worker acute psychiat. treatment svcs.; med. social worker dialysis svcs. Northport (N.Y.) Va. Med. Ctr. Cons. on programs for aging Luth. Social Svcs. met. N.Y., 1959, sr. citizens programs, Bd. Edn. Port Jefferson, N.Y., 1963. Chmn. Huntington Twp. Com. Human Rels., 1970; sec. bd. trustees Unitarian Universalist Fellowship Huntington, 1984. Mem. NASW (diplomate in social work), Am. Assn. Family Counselors and Mediators,Germany Philatelic Soc. (pres. chpt. 30, 1990, Mem. of Yr. 1987). Avocations: oil painting, stamp collecting, music (voice & piano), family genealogy. Home: 316 Lenox Rd Huntington Station NY 11746-2640

WILLIAMS, VENUS, professional tennis player; b. Lynwood, Calif., June 17, 1980; Profl. debut Bank of West Classic, Oakland, Calif., 1994; tennis player Bausch & Lomb Championships, 1996. Ranked No. 64 Am. tennis player, ranked 3d, 1999; winner 7 singles titles WTA Tour including Oklahome City, 1998, 99, Lipton, 1998, 99, Hamburg, 1999, Italian Open, 1999, Gland Slam Cup, 1998, 4 doubles titles, 1 doubles Grand Slam title, 2 mixed doubles; mixed doubles quarterfinalist Wimbledon, 1999; named TENNIS Mag. Most Improved Player, WTA Tour, 1998, Most Impressive Network Newcomer award, 1997; winner (with Serena Williams) French Open, 1999, Hannover, 1999, singles and doubles gold medal winner, Sydney Olympics, 2000, winner Bank of the West Classic, 2000, Acura Tennis Classic, 2000, recip. ESPY award for outstanding women's tennis player, 2001, doubles winner (with sister Serena) Grand Slam, 2001, winner Open Gaz de France, 2002, Gold Coast, 2002, Antwerp, 2002, Amelia Island, 2002. Office: US Tennis Assn 70 W Red Oak Ln White Plains NY 10604-3602*

WILLIAMS, VERONICA MYRES, psychologist, social worker, psychotherapist; b. Shreveport, La., May 11, 1947; d. McEura and Margie Virgina (Reagan) Myres; divorced; children: Nicole Leann, Jennifer Lyn, Erica Maria. BA, La. Tech. U., Ruston, 1969; MSW, U. Mich., Ann Arbor, 1977; PhD, So. Calif. U., 2001. Diplomate Am. Bd. Clin. Social Workers, Am. Psychotherapy Assn.; cert. social worker, Mich. Probation counselor Citizens Probation Authority, Flint, Mich., 1970-72; unit dir., therapist Svcs. to Overcome Drug Abuse Among Teenagers, 1972-74; psychiat. therapist Psycho-Therapeutic Treatment Clin., P.C., 1974-77; psychiat. social worker Hurley Med. Ctr., 1977-79; field instr. Sch. Social Work U. Mich., Ann Arbor, 1978-79, 86—; psychiat. social worker Inst. Mental Health, Flint, 1979-81, Psychotherapeutic Treatment Clinic, 1981-83; clin. social worker Flint Bd. Edn., 1979-83; pupil appraisal spl. edn. Caddo Parish Sch. Bd., Shreveport, La., 1983-85. Developer dropout prevention program Flint Bd. Edn., 1986-98; Beecher Sch. Dist., 1998—; psychiat. therapist Mott Children's Health Ctr., 1986-92, Oakland Psychol. Clinic, P.C., 1991-92; owner, dir. V. Williams, PhD, MSW, ACSW, BCD, PC, 1992—. Bd. dirs. Boys & Girls Club. Mem. NASW, ACSW, NEA, Mich. Edn. Assn. Democrat. Office: 225 E 5th St Ste 110 Flint MI 48502 E-mail: vwilliams000@ameritech.net.

WILLIAMS, VERONICA ANN, marketing and business consultant; b. Washington, Feb. 8, 1956; d. Vernon and Shirley Ann (Felton) W. BA in Econs. with honors, Brandeis U., 1977; MBA, Northwestern U., 1979. Systems mktg. rep. Control Data Corp., Chgo., 1979-81, mktg. rep., 1981-82; staff mgr. AT&T, Basking Ridge, N.J., 1982-84, nat. account exec. N.Y.C., 1984-86, mgr. bus. planning Berkeley Heights, N.J., 1986-87, product mgr. Morristown, 1987-88; dist. mgr. Unisoft Corp., N.Y.C., 1988-89; acct. mgr. Lotus Devel. Corp., 1989-90; dir. bus. devel., 1990-91, Software Corp. of Am., Stamford, Conn., 1990-91; founder, prin., mng. dir. ACT, Inc., South Orange, NJ, 1993—. Adv. bd. Fall COMDEX, 1994-96, 99, COMDEX/SCIB, 1996—, found./creator COMDEX/DISCOVER IT Wireless & Mobile Computing Showcase, Healthcare Forum, 1996—, Expo Commn., 1998; Consumer Electronics Show ExpoComm, 1998—; developer, presenter, moderator Enterprise Computing Solutions Conf., 1994-95, Wireless Datacomm, 1994-95, Mobile World, 1994-95, PDA Forum, 1996, Networld & Interop, 1996, Network World Unplugged, 1996, others; judge Windows World Open Contest spring COMDEX, 1996, 97, Apple Enterprise Awards PCEXPO, 1995; strategic mktg. and wireless computing advisor. Author: Wireless Computing Primer: A Comprehensive Guide to Wireless and Mobile Computing, 1996, Turning Technology Into Value: It's Not Just Sales and Promotion, 2002; featured in book, Women Who Mean Business, 1999; featured guest (TV show) Chgo. Tomorrow, 2001, Computer Chronicles, 1996; contbr. over 40 articles to profl. jours. Mem. South Orange Planning Bd., 1985-87, South Orange Citizens Budget Adv. Com., 1983-87. Named BMBA Alumni of Yr., Kellogg Grad. Sch. Bus., 2000. Mem. Nat. Black MBA Assn. (fin. chmn. Chgo. br. 1979-81, Performance award 1981). Avocations: swimming, scuba diving, skiing, music. Home: 541 Scotland Rd South Orange NJ 07079-3009 Office: ACT Inc PO Box 978 71 S Orange Ave Ste 440 South Orange NJ 07079

WILLIAMS, VIDA VERONICA, guidance counselor; b. Charleston, S.C., May 4, 1956; d. Timothy and Dotlee (Pendarvis) W. BA, Fisk U., 1978; MS in Edn., Queens Coll., 1986, postgrad., 1994-95, profl. diploma in adminstrn./supervision, 2001. Cert. sch. counselor, spl. edn. tchr., N.Y. Job counselor Trident Work Experience, Charleston, 1980; spl. edn. tchr. Jr. High Sch. 158, Bayside, N.Y., 1983-86, Pub. Sch. 214, Bklyn., 1986-90; guidance counselor I.S. 171, 364, Pub. Sch. 214, 1990-95, I.S. 302, Bklyn., 1995—; dir. Springfield Garden Meth. After Sch. Tutorial Program, Jamaica, N.Y. Co-dir. I.S. 302 Gospel Chorus, 1994-95; counselor Dist. 19 Bereavement, Bklyn., 1991-95; bd. dirs. Alpha Kappa Alpha Day Care Ctr., St. Albans, N.Y., 1992-94; dir. Springfield Gardens Meml. Ch. After-Sch. Tutorial Program, 1997-98. Vol. Voter Registration, Jamaica, 1992, Increase the Peace Corps, N.Y.C., 1992, Feeding of 5,000, Jamaica, 1993, Victim Svcs., Bklyn., 1994-95; chair activities Harlem Dowling Foster Care, Jamaica, N.Y., 1995; active Allen A.M.E. Ch. Gospel Choir, 1994-95, Voices of Victory, 1994-95. Named one of Outstanding Young Women Am., 1980. Mem. Alpha Kappa Alpha. Avocations: reading, singing, sewing, arts and crafts. Home: 11240 205th St Jamaica NY 11412-2214 Office: IS 302 350 Linwood St Brooklyn NY 11208-2199 E-mail: vivaciousvv@aol.com.

WILLIAMS, VIRGINIA PARROTT, writer, company executive; b. Nassawadox, Va., Aug. 9, 1940; d. Lloyd Pinckney and Elva Gray (Humphries) Parrott; m. Redford Brown Williams, Aug. 12, 1963; children: Jennifer Williams Phillips, Lloyd Carter. AB, Duke U., 1962; MA in Tchg., Brown U., 1963; MA, Duke U., 1973, PhD, 1980. Tchr. North Providence (R.I.) H.S., 1962, Amity Regional H.S., Woodbridge, Conn., 1963-68, tchr., dept. chair, 1966-68; part time tchr. Duke U., Durham, N.C., 1977-78; physician recruiter Kron Med., Chapel Hill, 1982-86; dir. recruiting Medstaff, Durham, 1986-90; writer, 1990—; pres. Williams Life Skills, Inc., 1996—. Author: Surrealism, Quantum Philosophy and World War I, 1987; co-author: Anger Kills, 1993, Lifeskills, 1997. Home: 5811 Buck Quarter Rd Hillsborough NC 27278-7867 E-mail: virginia@williamslifeskills.com.

WILLIAMS, VIVIAN LEWIE, college counselor; b. Columbia, S.C., Jan. 23, 1923; d. Lemuel Arthur Sr. and Ophelia V. (McDaniel) Lewie; m. Charles Warren Williams, Apr. 4, 1947 (div. 1967); children: Pamela Ann Williams-Coote, Charles Warren Jr. (dec.). BA, Allen U., 1942; MA in Psychology, U. Mich., 1946, postgrad., 1946, 48; MS, U. So. Calif., 1971, postgrad., 1971-72. Cert. marriage and family therapist, Calif.; cert. Calif. C.C. counselor. Asst. prof. psychology Tenn. State Agrl. and Indsl. U., Nashville, 1946-47; asst. prof. edn. Winston-Salem (N.C.) State U., 1947-50; asst. prof. edn., dir. tchr. edn. Allen U., Columbia, S.C., 1951-53; specialist reading, coord. lang. arts Charlotte (N.C.) Mecklenburg Schs., 1963-67, cons. comprehensive sch. improvement project, 1967-69; asst. prof. edn., psychology Johnson C. Smith U., Charlotte, 1967-69; counselor, team leader Centennial, U. So. Calif. Tchr. Corps, L.A., 1970-73; counselor Compton (Calif.) C.C., 1973—, adv. fgn. student, 1975-85. Co-developer Hyde Park Estates and The Moors, Charlotte, N.C., 1960-63. Pres. bd. dirs. Charlotte Day Nursery, 1956-59; bd. dirs. Taylor St. USO, Columbia, S.C., 1951-53; sec. southwest region Nat. Alliance Family Life, 1973-74; sec. bd. dirs. NCCJ, Charlotte, 1959-62. Recipient Faculty Audit Program award Ford/Carnegie Found., Harvard U., Cambridge, Mass., 1968, Pub. Svc. Achievement award WSOC Broadcasting Co.; fellow U. Mich., 1946. Mem. NAACP (life, Golden Heritage mem. 1992), AAUW (life), NEA (life), Am. Fedn. Tchrs., Faculty Assn. Calif. C.C., Nat. Acad. Counselors and Family Therapists (life, clin. mem., pres. S.W. region 1989), C.C. Counselors Assn., The Links, Inc. (Harbor area chpt. historian 1985-87, chaplain 1990-94, 96-98), Jack and Jill Am. (charter mem., organizer Charlotte chpt., pres. 1954-56), Women on Target, Calif. Tchrs. Assn., Delta Sigma Theta, Alpha Gamma Sigma (Golden Apple award 1981). Democrat. Methodist. Avocations: sewing, crafts, photography. Home: 6621 Caro St Paramount CA 90723-4755 Office: Compton Community Coll 1111 E Artesia Blvd Compton CA 90221-5314 E-mail: WilliamsV@www.ComptonCC.ca.us.

WILLIAMS, W. VAIL, psychologist; b. Denver, Apr. 13, 1940; s. Warren J. and Edna M. (Follen) W.; m. Sandra M. Eisenrich (div. 1972); 1 child, Jason; m. Linda Lou Fain, Dec. 27, 1975; children: Ken, Dan, Davis, Jeremiah. BS, Bradley U., 1963, MA, 1964; PhD, U. Okla., 1968. Lic. psychologist, S.D., Colo., Calif. Owner Social Systems Devel., 1970-78; sr. psychologist Ft. Logan Mental Health Ctr., Denver, 1968-74; sr. rsch. assoc. Mental Rsch. Inst., Palo Alto, Calif., 1974-78; assoc. prof. Med. Sch. U. S. D., Sioux Falls, 1978—; chmn. curriculum and evaluation com. Sch. Medicine U. S.D., 1989-92, mem. exec. com. dept. psychiatry Sch. Medicine, 1999—. Bd. dirs. Univ. Physicians, U. S.D. Sch. Medicine, 1997—; cons. Sioux Valley Behavioral Health, Sioux Falls, 1989-94, 99—, Woodfield Home, LSS, 1998—; clin. dir. Psychiatry Assocs., 1989—. Contbr. to books and articles to profl. jours. Bd. dirs. S.D. Jr. Football Assn., Sioux Falls, 1988-92, Citizens Against Rape and Violence, Sioux Falls, 1988-89, Post 15 Baseball Program, 1995-98. Fellow Am. Orthopsychiat. Assn.; mem. APA, AAAS, S.D. Psychol. Assn. (pres. Div. 1 1993-94), Woodlake Athletic Club, El Raid Shrine. Avocation: computers. Office: Psychiatry Assoc 1000 E 21st St Ste 4000 Sioux Falls SD 57105-1015 E-mail: wwilliam@usd.edu.

WILLIAMS, WALKER RICHARD, JR. social services administrator; b. Dayton, Ohio, July 11, 1928; s. Walker Richard Sr. and Addie Mary (Smith) W.; m. Eddora L. Saunders, Aug. 6, 1949 (dec. Sept. 1966); 1 child, Yvette R.; m. Emma Jean Griffin, Sept. 4, 1971; children: Timotny E., Walker R. III. Student, U. Dayton, 1946-48. Commd. 2d lt. U.S. Army, 1952; advanced through grades to capt. USAF, Wright Patterson AFB, Ohio, 1963, employee rels. specialist, pers. mgmt. specialist, 1966-71; EEO investigator and grievance examiner Army and Air N.G., 1971-88; retired USAR, 1988; program dir. Youth Svc. U.S.A.-Dayton, 1988-89; pvt. contractor Dayton, 1989—. Mem. Adjutant Gen. Ohio Minority Recruiting Adv. Com., 1988—; bd. dirs. Dayton Opportunities Industrialization Ctr., 1976—, Wright Patterson Domestic Action Programs, Inc., 1984—; pres. Jefferson Twp. Bd. Edn., 1980—; mem. Nat. Black Caucus of Black Sch. Bd. Mems., 1980—, Nat. Black Caucus Local Elected Officials, Gov.'s Com. to Preserve Statue of Liberty, 1987, Citywide Vocat. Ednl. Com., 1986—, adv. com. Dayton Bd. Edn., 1980—, Miami Valley Mil. Affairs Assn., Black Elected Democrats of Ohio. Recipient Air Force Civilian Svc. award, Dayton C. of C., Internat. Personnel Mgmt. Assn. Employee of the Yr., Blacks in Govt. Pres.'s award, Federally Employed Women's Supr. of the Yr. runner up, Hispanic Heritage Wk. Spl. award, NAACP Humanitarian award, Community Svc. award, Dayton Bd. Edn., James W. Cisco award , Vocat. Ednl. award Wilberforce U., Urban League Humanitarian award, Svc. to Youth award Girl Scouts U.S., Spl. award United Negro Coll. Fund, Jack & Jill, 7 Air Force Logistics Command Significant Achievement awards, AG of Ohio award, Ohio State U. award, Black Studies Group award, Russell Lyle award Wright Patterson AFB Quarter Century Club, Student Intervention Program Radcliff Sch., others; a day named in his honor, Dayton, 1987, 88, Svc. award Jefferson Township Bd. Edn. Mem. Miami Valley Pers. Assn., Internat. Pers. Mgmt. Assn., Retired Officers Assn., Air Force Assn., NAACP, Urban League, Blacks in Govt. (Medallion award), Dayton Intergovt. EEO Coun. (chmn., historian 1967—), Miami Valley Mil. Affairs Assn., Wright Patterson Quarter Century Club (past pres.). Democrat. Avocations: reading, photography. Home: 5050 Fortman Dr Dayton OH 45418-2233

WILLIAMS, WALTER DAVID, aerospace executive, consultant; b. Chgo., July 22, 1931; s. Walter William and Theresa Barbara (Gilman) W.; m. Joan Haven Armstrong, Oct. 22, 1960; children: Latham Lloyd, Clayton Chapell, William Haven. BS, Ohio U., 1951; MBA, Harvard U., 1955; MS, MIT, 1972. Supr. fin. policy and systems Hughes Aircraft Co., Culver City, Calif., 1955-57; staff mem. Rand Corp. and SDC, Santa Monica, 1957-60; mgr. adminstrn. and fin. Microwave Div. TRW Inc., Canoga Park, 1960-63; exec. asst. Space Labs. Northrop Corp., Hawthorne, 1963-66; fin. mgr. comml. group Aircraft Div. Northrop Corp., 1966-72; dir. internat. plans Northrop Corp., L.A., 1972-74, dir. internat. mkt. devel., 1974-77, exec. dir. internat., 1977-93; pres. Williams Internat. Assocs., 1994—. Export advisor U.S. Sec. Commerce, Washington, 1986-98. Author (study/lect. series) Internat. Def. Mktg., 1982. Dir. KCET Men's Coun., L.A., 1970; pres. Westwood Rep. Club, L.A., 1970; assoc. mem. Rep. State Ctrl. Com., Calif., 1968; div. chmn. Rep. Ctrl. Com., L.A. County, 1968, Team 100. Served to capt. U.S. Army, 1951-53. Recipient fellowship Alfred P. Sloan Found., 1971-72. Mem. AIAA, Soc. Sloan Fellows, MIT Club, Harvard Bus. Sch. Assn., Newcomen Soc., Chaine des Rotisseurs, L.A. Country Club, Harvard Club, Soc. Bacchus Am., Order of Malta, Delta Sigma Pi, Pi Kappa Alpha. Avocations: golf, tennis, paddle tennis. Office: Williams Internat Assocs PO Box 491178 Los Angeles CA 90049-9178

WILLIAMS, WALTER E. economics educator; BA in Econs., Calif. State U., L.A., 1965; MA in Econs., UCLA, 1967, PhD in Econs., 1972; DHL, Va. Union U., 1984; DHL honoris causa, Grove City Coll., 1992; LLD honoris causa, Washington & Jefferson Coll., Washington, Pa., 1994. Life-time std. teaching credential State Calif. Group supr. L.A. County Probation Dept., 1963-67; instr. econs. Angeles City Coll., L.A., 1967-69; asst. prof. econs. Calif. State U., 1967-71; rsch. staff Urban Inst., Washington, 1971-73; nat. fellow Hoover Instn. on War, Peace and Revolution, Stanford U., 1975-76; assoc. prof. econs. Temple U., Phila., 1973-80; dept. chmn. John M. Olin disting. prof. econs. George Mason U., Fairfax, Va., 1980—. Adj. scholar Cato Inst., HeritageFound.; assoc. scholar Ethics and Pub. Policy Ctr. Author: The State Against Blacks, 1982, America: A Minority Viewpoint, 1982, All It Takes Is Guts, 1987, South Africa's War Against Capitalism, 1989, revised edit., 1990; contbr. articles to profl. jours.; mem. editl. bd. Jour. Labor Rsch.; mem. editl. rev. bd. Current Mag.; numerous debates, lectures, TV and radio appearances including appearances on Milton Friedman's Free to Choose, WQLN's Star Spangled Spenders, WTBS Debate Series Counterpoint, William F. Buckley's Firing Line, ABC Nightline, CBS Nightwatch, Face The Nation, Crossfire, MacNeil/Lehrer News Hour, CNN's Larry King Show, C-Span, Inside Story; former commentator NPR Radio, All Things Considered; commentator PBS Nightly Business Report, 1991-93; nationally syndicated columnist Creators Syndicat, 1980—; past weekly columnist Phila. Tribune; frequent appearance on network and local TV and radio news. Mem. adv. bd. Abraham & Sarah Found., Alexis de Rocqueville Inst., Atlas Econ. Rsch. Found., Buckeye Ctr. Pub. Policy Solutions, Capitol Rsch. Ctr., Ctr. for Rebldg. America's Schs., Commonwealth of Va., Gov.'s Adv. Coun. on Self-Determination and Federalism, Consumer Alert, Contemporary Econs. and Bus. Assn., Destiny Mag., Drury Coll., Breech Sch. Bus. Adminstrn., The Dumont Inst., Family Security Found., Free Enterprise Edn. Ctr., Ind. Inst., Inst. Econ. Affairs, Jour. Inst. Socioecon. Studies, Landmark Legal Found. Ctr. Civil Rights, Libertarian Alliance, London, Lincoln Inst., Nat. Found. Teaching Entrepreneurship to Handicapped and Disadvantaged Youth, Inc., Nat. Tax Limitation Com., Nellie Thomas Inst. Learning, Rep. Nat. Com., Rev. Bd. Econ. Studies NSF, Taxpayer's Found., Young Americans for Freedom; bd. overseers Hoover Instn. on War, Peace and Revolution, Stanford U.; bd. dis. Citizens for a Sound Economy, Reason Found. UCLA grad. opportunity fellow, Ford Found. dissertation fellow, Hoover Inst. War, Revolution and Peace Nat. fellow, Heritage Found. disting. scholar, 1978-79, UCLA Inst. Govt. and Pub. Affairs fellow; recipient Honor award Freedoms Found. at Valley Forge, 1977, Ann. award Alpha Kappa Psi Found., 1978, Nat. Svc. award Inst. Socioecon. Studies, 1980, George Washington medal of honor Freedoms Found., 1983, Disting. Alumnus award Calif. State U., 1987, L.A. City Commendation award, 1987, Adam Smith award Assn. Pvt. Enterprise Edn., 1989, Wilson S. Johnson award Nat. Fedn. Ind. Businesses, 1991, Robert J. Courtney award LaSalle U., 1993, U.S. News Media award VFW, 1993, award Heartland Inst., 1994, Warren Brooks award Am. Legis. Exch. Coun., 1994. Mem. Mt. Pelerin Soc., Am. Econ. Assn. Office: George Mason U 4400 University Dr Fairfax VA 22030-4444

WILLIAMS, WALTER JOSEPH, lawyer; b. Detroit, Oct. 5, 1918; s. Joseph Louis and Emma Geraldine (Hewitt) W.; m. Maureen June Kay, Jan. 15, 1944; 1 child, John Bryan. Student, Bowling Green State U., 1935-36; BSBA, Ohio State U., 1940; JD, LL.B., U. Detroit, 1942. Bar: Mich. bar 1942. Title atty. Abstract & Title Guaranty Co., 1946-47; corp. atty. Ford Motor Co., 1947-51, Studebaker-Packard Corp., 1951-56; asst. sec., house counsel Am. Motors Corp., Am. Motors Sales Corp., Am. Motors Pan-Am. Corp., Evart Products Co., Ltd., 1956-65, corp. sec. house counsel, 1965-72; asst. corp. sec., dir. Am. Motors (Can.) Ltd.; dir. Evart Products Co., 1959-72; dir., corporate sec., house counsel Jeep Corp., Jeep Sales Corp., Jeep Internat. Corp., 1968-72; partner Gilman and Williams, Southfield, Mich., 1972-74; atty. Detroit Edison Co., 1974-75; asst. sec., sr. staff atty. Burroughs Corp. (and subsidiaries), 1975-84; pvt. practice, pres. Walter J. Williams P.C., Bloomfield Hills, Mich., 1984—. Charter commr., city of Dearborn Heights, Mich., 1960-63; dir. Detroit Met. Indsl. Devel. Corp., 1962-72, also asst. sec. Served to capt. U.S. Army, 1942-46. Mem. ABA, Detroit Bar Assn. (chmn. corp. gen. counsel com. 1965-68), Fed. Bar Assn., State Bar Mich., Ohio State U. Alumni Assn. (pres. Detroit 1961-63), U. Detroit Law Alumni, Delta Theta Phi. Clubs: Oakland Hills Country. Home and Office: 3644 Darcy Dr Bloomfield Hills MI 48301-2125

WILLIAMS, WALTER WAYLON, lawyer, pecan grower; b. Gause, Tex., Nov. 12, 1933; s. Jesse Nathaniel and Lola Fay (Matthews) W.; m. Velmalene Von Gonten, Mar. 6, 1953; children— Diana Lee, Virginia Marie. BBA with honors, U. Tex., 1959, JD with honors, 1960. Bar: Tex. bar 1960. Since practiced in, Houston; mem. firm Fulbright, Crooker, Freeman, Bates & Jaworski, 1960-63, Bates & Brock, 1964-66, Brock, Williams & Boyd, 1966-79, Williams & Boyd, 1979-88; pres. Nat. Pecan Growers Coun., 1976-78, Tex. Pecan Growers Assn., 1976-78. Served with AUS, 1953-55. Named Outstanding Soldier of Second Army, 1955 Mem. ABA, Houston Bar Assn., State Bar Tex., Tex. Trial Lawyers Assn. (dir. 1972-76), Houston Trial Lawyers Assn. (dir. 1969), Assn. Trial Lawyers Am., Chancellors, Beta Gamma Sigma, Phi Delta Phi. Home: 545 Williams Rd Yoakum TX 77995-5320

WILLIAMS, WAYNE FRANCIS, art educator, sculptor; b. Newark, July 22, 1937; s. Ashley E. and Pauline L. (Soliman) W.; m. Marlene G. DeBout, Nov. 7, 1963; children: Andrea M., Christine A. BFA, Syracuse U., 1958, MFA, 1962. Sculptor, Newark, 1958-68; prof. art Finger Lakes C.C., Canandaiqua, N.Y., 1968—. Dept. chair Finger Lakes C.C., 1975-80, gallery coord., 1980—; mem. bd. dirs. Wayne County Arts Coun., 1995. One-man shows include Maynard Walker Gallery, N.Y.C., 1960, 64, Frank Rehn Gallery, N.Y.C., 1974; prin works include statue The Graduate, North Rose (N.Y.) Wolcott High Sch., 1974, statue Portrait of Wm. Simon, U. Rochester (N.Y.), 1987, statue for Vietnam Meml., Rochester, N.Y., 1995, meml. sculpture Woodcliff Lodge, Rochester, 1998; represented by Oxford Gallery, Rochester. Recipient John Armstrong Chaloner fellowship Chaloner Found., 1958, 59, Louis Comfort Tiffany grant Tiffany Found., 1964. Mem. Wayne County Arts Coun., Ontario County Arts Coun., SUNY Gallery and Mus. Dirs. Assn. Avocations: sailing, fishing. Home: 1954 Gardner Rd Newark NY 14513-9009 Office: Finger Lakes CC Lakeshore Dr Canandaigua NY 14424

WILLIAMS, WESLEY SAMUEL, JR. lawyer; b. Phila., Nov. 13, 1942; s. Wesley Samuel and Bathrus Amanda (Bailey) W.; m. Karen Roberta Hastie, Aug. 17, 1968; children: Amanda Pedersen, Wesley Hastie, Bailey Lockhart. BA in French Lit. magna cum laude, Harvard U., 1963, JD, 1967; MA (Woodrow Wilson fellow), Fletcher Sch. Law and Diplomacy, 1964; LLM, Columbia U., 1969. Bar: D.C., U.S. Supreme Ct., N.Y. Spl. counsel D.C. City Council, 1967-69; assoc.-in-law Columbia U. Law Sch., 1968-69; legal counsel Com. on D.C. U.S. Senate, 1969-70; assoc. Covington & Burling, Washington, 1970-75, ptnr., 1975—. Trustee Penn Mut. Life Ins. Co., Phila., 1978—; bd. dirs. Broadcast Capital Cos., 1979-92, chmn., 1989-92, Carr Realty, Co., Inc., 1993—; mem. Pres.'s U.S. Circuit Judge Nominating Commn., 1977-80; gen. counsel D.C. Bar, 1979-81; adj. prof. Georgetown U. Law Sch., 1971-73; mem. exec. com. Washington Lawyers Com. Civil Rights Under Law, 1972—; mem. editorial bd. D.C. Real Estate Reporter; vice chmn., bd. dirs. Lockhart Cos., St. Thomas, U.S. Virgin Islands, 1987—, co-chief exec. officer, 1989—; vice chmn., bd. dirs. Blackstar Communications, Cos., 1987—. Author legal articles, texts. Pres. bd. trustee Nat. Child Rsch. Ctr., 1980-82; bd. overseers Harvard U., 1985-91, chmn. vis. com. Harvard U. Div. Sch., 1986-91; bd. dirs. World Affairs Coun. Washington, D.C., Inc., 1980—, Nat. Symphony Orch. Assn., 1977-92; bd. dirs. Family and Child Svcs. Washington, 1970—, pres., 1973-76; exec. com. community adv. com. Jr. League Washington, 1977-86; pres. standing com. Epsic. Diocese of Washington, 1983-88; sec. bd. trustees Protestant Episc. Cathedral Found., 1982-90; bd. regents Smithsonian Inst., 1993—. Fellow Am. Bar Found.; mem. ABA, Am. Law Inst., Nat. Bar Assn., Fed. Bar Assn., D.C. Bar Assn., Washington Bar Assn., Harvard Law Sch. Assn. (pres.), Order Hosp. St. John Jerusalem, Harvard Club, City Tavern Club, Met. Club, Chevy Chase Club, Univ. Club, Alpha Phi Alpha, Sigma Pi Phi. Office: Covington & Burling PO Box 7566 1201 Pennsylvania Ave NW Washington DC 20044

WILLIAMS, WILLIAM ARNOLD, agronomy educator; b. Johnson City, N.Y., Aug. 2, 1922; s. William Truesdall and Nellie Viola (Tompkins) W.; m. Madeline Patricia Moore, Nov. 27, 1943; children— David, Kathleen, Andrew BS, Cornell U., 1947, MS, 1948, PhD, 1951. Prof. emeritus U. Calif., Davis, 1993—. Editor agr. sect. McGraw-Hill Ency. Sci. & Tech.; contbr. articles to profl. jours. Mem. Nat. Alliance for Mentally Ill. Served to lt. U.S. Army, 1943-46 Grantee NSF, 1965-82, Kellogg Found., 1963-67; Fulbright scholar, Australia, 1960, Rockefeller Found. scholar, Costa Rica, 1966 Fellow AAAS, Am. Soc. Agronomy, Crop Sci. Soc. Am.; mem. Soil Sci. Soc. Am., Soc. Range Mgmt., Am. Statis. Assn., Assn. for Tropical Biology, Fedn. Am. Scientists. Democrat. Home: 1515 Shasta Dr Davis CA 95616 Office: U Calif Dept Agronomy & Range One Shields Ave Davis CA 95616-8515

WILLIAMS, WILLIAM COREY, theology educator, consultant; b. Wilkes-Barre, Pa., July 12, 1937; s. Edward Douglas and Elizabeth Irene (Schooley) W.; m. Alma Simmenroth Williams, June 27, 1959; 1 child, Linda. Diploma in Ministerial Studies, NE Bible Inst., 1962; BA in Bibl. Studies, Cen. Bible Coll., 1963, MA in Religion, 1964; MA in Hebrew and Near Ea. Studies, NYU, 1966, PhD in Hebrew Lang. and Lit., 1975; postgrad., Hebrew U., 1977-78, Inst. Holyland Studies, 1986. Ref. libr. Hebraic section Libr. of Congress, Washington, 1967-69; prof. Old Testament So. Calif. Coll./Vanguard U., Costa Mesa, 1969—; adj. prof. Old Testament Melodyland Sch. Theology, Anaheim, Calif., 1975-77; vis. prof. Old Testament Fuller Theol. Sem., Pasadena, 1978-81, 84, Asian Theol. Ctr. for Evangelism and Missions, Singapore and Sabah, E. Malaysia, 1985, Continental Bible Coll., Saint Pieters-Leeuw, Belgium, 1985, 2000-01, Mattersey Bible Coll., Eng., 1985, Inst. Holy Land Studies, Jerusalem, 1986, Regent U., 1994. Transl. cons. and reviser New Am. Std. Bible, 1969-94; transl. cons. The New Internat. Version, 1975-76, New Century Version, 1991, The New Living Translation, 1992-95, New Internat. Version, Reader's Version, 1993-94; transl. cons. and editor Internat. Children's Version, 1985-86. Author: (books, tapes) Hebrew I: A Study Guide, 1986, Hebrew II: A Study Guide, 1986; contbr. articles to International Standard Bible Encyclopedia, New International Dictionary of Old Testment Theology and Evangelical Dictionary of Biblical Theology; contbr. articles to profl. jours.; contbr. notes to Spirit Filled Life Study Bible. Nat. Def. Fgn. Lang. fellow NYU, 1964-67; Alumni scholar N.E. Bible Inst., 1960-61; NEH fellow, summer 1992; recipient Disting. Educator's award Assemblies of God, 1997. Mem. Soc. Bibl. Lit., Evang. Theol. Soc. (exec. office 1974-77), Inst. Bibl. Rsch., The Lockman Found. (hon. mem. bd. dirs. 1992-94, mem. editl. bd. 1974-94). Home: 1817 Peninsula Pl Costa Mesa CA 92627-4591 Office: Vanguard U 55 Fair Dr Costa Mesa CA 92626-6520

WILLIAMS, WILLIAM HARRISON, retired librarian; b. Seattle, Apr. 18, 1924; s. William E. and Letah M. (Hollenback) W.; m. Mary Helen Sims, Apr. 19, 1945; children: Linda Lee, Dee Ann. BS, Brigham Young U., 1969, M.L.S., 1970. Dir. Provo Pub. Library, Utah, 1969-70; Wyo. State Librarian, 1970-78; dir. Wyo. state Archives and Hist. dept., 1971-78; exec. sec. Wyo. Hist. Soc., 1971-78; sr. research analyst Wyo. Taxpayers Assn., 1978-84. Served to lt. col. USAAF, 1943-64. Decorated USAF commendation with oak leaf cluster. Mem. Masonic Order, Order of the Ea. Star, Order of the Amaranth, Beta Phi Mu, Phi Alpha Theta. Home: 21607 N 123rd Dr Sun City West AZ 85375-1950 E-mail: weewilli@juno.com.

WILLIAMS, WILLIAM HENRY, II, publisher; b. Birmingham, Ala., Oct. 21, 1931; s. Calvin Thomas and Lillian Elizabeth (Levey) W.; m. Lewis Mozelle Hensley, Feb. 28, 1959; 1 child, William Henry III. Student, Baylor U., 1952-55. Printer Waco (Tex.) Tribune-Herald, 1950-59; internat. rep. Internat. Typog. Union, Colorado Springs, Colo., 1960-68; editor, gen. mgr. Colorado Springs Free Press, 1969-70; dir. labor relations The Morning Telegraph, N.Y.C., 1970-72; gen. mgr. Daily Racing Form, Hightstown, N.J., 1972-89, nat. gen. mgr. for U.S. and Can., 1990-91, pub., 1991-92; ret., 1992; pub. Kerrville (Tex.) Mountain Sun, 1993-96. Mem. adv. council journalsim dept. Baylor U., Waco, 1970-72. Chmn. CentraState Med. Ctr., Freehold, N.J., 1982-83, CentraState Health Affiliates, Freehold, 1987-94; vice chmn. Ctr. for Aging, Inc., Freehold, 1985-90; dep. mayor Freehold Twp. Com., 1987, mayor, 1989-90, 93, committeeman, 1985-94; county commr. Kerr County, 1999—; chmn. Freehold Mayor's Task Force on Substance Abuse, 1987-91; mem. Upper Guadalupe River Authority, 1995-99, Kerr Econ. Devel. Found.; mem. devel. bd. Alamo Area Workforce, 1997-99. Named an Hon. Trustee Freehold Area Hosp., 1985—. Mem. Tex. Press Assn. (bd. dirs. 1995-96), NCCJ (Brotherhood award 1986), Exch. Club (Hightstown; carter pres.), Masons (32 deg.), Shriners, Optimists (charter mem. Freehold chpt.), Lions Club (host, pres. 1998-99). Republican. Lutheran (congregation pres. 1999-2000). Club: Optimists (charter mem. Freehold chpt.). Avocations: music, golf, football, skiing. Home and Office: 172 Saint Andrews Loop Kerrville TX 78028-6441 E-mail: williams@ktc.com.

WILLIAMS, WILLIAM HENRY, history educator, liberal arts coordinator; b. Port Jervis, N.Y., June 9, 1936; s. Henry and Esther Marcy (Crocker) W.; m. Helen Garrett, June 28, 1959; children: Dawn, Mark. BA, Drew U., 1958; MS in Edn., Yeshiva U., 1959; PhD, U. Del., 1971. Tchr. social studies Pawling (n.Y.) Cen. High Sch., 1959-63; instr. U. Del., Georgetown, 1967-71, asst. prof., 1971-77, assoc. prof., 1977-86, prof., 1986-2000, prof. emeritus, 2000—, Southern coord. MALS program, 1990-2000. Cons. Pa. Hosp., Phila., 1975; mem. bd. archives and history Peninsula Conf. United Meth. Ch., Dover, Del., 1988—; cons. Smith Island Project, State of Md., Annapolis, 1991-93 Author: America's First Hospital, 1976, Garden of American Methodism, 1984, The First State: An Illustrated History of Delaware, 1985, Slavery and Freedom in Delaware, 1996, The Delmarva Chicken Industry, 1998. Chair Del. Humanities Coun., Wilmington, 1976-77, Georgetown Bicentennial Com., 1975-76, Sussex County Magna Carta Com., Georgetown, 1986-87; cons. scholarship com. Del. Heritage Commn., Wilmington, 1985-87, mem. 2001-; trustee Del. Agrl. Mus. U. Del. fellow, 1976, 80, 90-91, Am. Philos. Soc. fellow, 1972, NEH fellow, 1973, 85; recipient Joseph P. del Tufo award Del. Humanities Forum, 1980. Mem. Hist. Soc. Del. (bd. editors 1988—), Soc. History of the Early Am. Rep. Methodist. Avocations: travel, sports. Home: 238 W Pine St Georgetown DE 19947-1830 E-mail: 25159@udel.edu.

WILLIAMS, WILLIAM JOHN, JR. lawyer; b. New Rochelle, N.Y., Feb. 6, 1937; s. William John and Jane (Gormley) W.; m. Barbara Reuter. BA, Holy Cross Coll., Worcester, Mass., 1958; LLB, NYU, 1961. Bar: N.Y. 1961. Practiced in, N.Y.C., 1962—; ptnr. firm Sullivan & Cromwell, 1969—. Trustee NYU Law Sch. Found., 1977—, Holy Cross Coll., 1988-96. Fellow Am. Bar Found.; mem. ABA, Am. Law Inst., N.Y. State Bar Assn., Assn. of Bar of City of N.Y., U.S. Golf Assn. (mem. exec. com. 1978-87, sec. 1980-81, v.p. 1982-85, pres. 1986-87). Democrat. Roman Catholic. E-mail: williamsw@sullcrom.com.

WILLIAMS, WILLIAM JOSEPH, physician, educator; b. Bridgeton, N.J., Dec. 8, 1926; s. Edward Carlaw and Mary Hood (English) W.; m. Margaret Myrick Lyman, Aug. 12, 1950 (dec. Aug., 1985) ; children: Susan Lyman, William Prescott, Sarah Robb; m. Karen A. Hughes, Feb. 18, 1989. Student, Bucknell U., 1943-45; MD, U. Pa., 1949. Diplomate: Am. Bd. Internal Medicine. (hematology com. 1976-80). Intern U. Pa., 1949-50, Am. Cancer Soc. research fellow in Biochemistry, 1950-52, resident medicine, 1954-55, from asst. to assoc. prof. medicine, 1955-58, assoc. prof. to prof. medicine, chief hematology, 1961-69; sr. instr. microbiology Case Western Res. U., 1952; asst. prof. medicine Washington U., St. Louis, 1959-60; research fellow Oxford U., Eng., 1960-61; mem. hematology tng. com. Nat. Inst. Arthritis and Metabolic Disease, 1964-68, research career program com., 1968-72; chmn. dept. medicine SUNY Health Sci. Ctr., Syracuse, N.Y., 1969-92, prof. medicine, 1969—, interim dean Coll. Medicine, 1991-92. Vis. scientist Walter and Eliza Hall Inst., Melbourne, Australia, 1980; vis. prof. Monash U., Melbourne, 1980; mem. thrombosis adv. com. Nat. Heart and Lung Inst., 1969-73, chmn., 1971-73; adv. coun. Nat. Arthritis, Metabolism and Digestive Diseases, 1975-79; mem. residency rev. com. internal medicine Accreditation Coun. Grad. Med. Edn., 1983-89, mem. bd. appeals panel for internal medicine, 1989-2000; mem. N.Y. State Coun. Grad. Med. Edn., 1987-89. Editor-in-chief: Hematology, 1972, 4th edit., 1989, Williams Hematology Companion Handbook, 1996; contbr. articles to med. lit. Trustee Everson Mus. Art, 1975-81, 83-89. With USNR, 1944-46, 52-54. Recipient Research Career Devel. award Nat. Heart Inst., 1963-68; Daland fellow Am. Philos. Soc., 1955-57; Markle scholar, 1957-62 Mem. ACP (gov. Upstate N.Y. 1976-81), Am. Soc. Biochemistry and Molecular Biologists, Am. Soc. Clin. Investigation, Assn. Am. Physicians, Am. Clin. and Climatol. Assn., Am. Soc. Hematology, Interurban Clin. Club (sec. 1964-70), Internat. Hematology Soc., Alpha Omega Alpha. Mem. Soc. Friends. Home: 5160 Peck Hill Rd Jamesville NY 13078-9724 Office: 750 E Adams St Syracuse NY 13210-2306 E-mail: williamw@upstate.edu.

WILLIAMS, WILLIAM LOUIS See AS-SALAAM, JAMAAL

WILLIAMS, WILLIAM MAGAVERN, headmaster; b. Niles, Mich., Dec. 22, 1931; s. Errol Edwin and Mary Elizabeth (Magavern) W.; m. Linda Carol Grush, June 15, 1958; children: Diana, William Jr., Sarah. BA, Williams Coll., 1953, LHD (hon.), 1984; postgrad. in Philosophy, Columbia U., 1954-58, MA in Ednl. Psychology, 1966. Tchr. elem. English, history, phys. edn. McTernan Sch., Waterbury, Conn., 1953-54; head guidance, boarding, and humanities depts., instr. English, coach varsity wrestling Riverdale Country Sch., Bronx, N.Y., 1955-66; headmaster Doane Acad., Burlington, N.J., 1966-70, Poly. Prep. Country Day Sch., Bklyn., 1970-00, headmaster emeritus, 2000—. Trustee Bklyn Inst. Arts and Scis., 1972-79, Bklyn. Ctrl. YMCA, 1974-78, Profl. Children's Sch., 1976-79, Bklyn. Children's Mus., 1979-82, Plymouth Ch. Pilgrims, 1979-86, N.Y. State Assn. Ind. Schs., 1980-86. Mem. Headmasters' Assn., Country Day Sch. Headmasters' Assn. (v.p. 1998-99, pres. 1999-2000), Cum Laude Soc. (regent dist. III 1971-87, dep. pres. gen. 1981-87, pres. gen. 1987-96, regent-at-large 1996—), Guild Ind. Schs. N.Y. (pres. 1986-88). Avocations: skiing, chess, travel, Civil War history. Home: PO Box 26 232 Justin Morrill Mem Hwy Strafford VT 05072-9730 E-mail: wmw232@aol.com.

WILLIAMS, WILLIE, JR. physicist, educator; b. Independence, La., Mar. 24, 1947; s. Willie Sr. and Lee Anner (Booker) W.; 1 child, Willie Williams III. BS, So. U., 1970; MS, Iowa State U., 1972, PhD, 1974. Mem. faculty Lincoln U., Lincoln University, Pa., 1974—, assoc. prof. physics, 1979-84, prof. physics, 1984—, chmn. dept., 1976-95, chmn. sci. and math. div., 1978-80, 83-88, founder, dir. Lincoln Advance Sci. and Engring. Reinforcement (LASER) Program, 1980-96, dir. pre-engring., 1976-96, dir., prin. investigator Early Alert-Young Scholars Program, 1992-96. Bd. dirs. women tech. program Lincoln U. Urban Ctr., Phila.; vis. prof. Ctr. for Teaching Innovation, Drexel U., 1975; liaison officer Nat. Assn. for Equal Opportunity in Higher Edn., Dept. Def. Program, 1987—; mem. steering com. NSF Comprehensive Ctr. for Minorities, Phila.; bd. dirs. Prime Inc., Phila. Contbr. articles to profl. jours. Chmn. Cheyney Lincoln Temple Cluster, 1974-78; pres. The Men Fedn., So. U., 1968-69. Recipient Lindback award for Outstanding Teaching, 1976, Outstanding Scientist award White House Initiative, 1988; named one of Outstanding Young Men of Am., 1979; fellow NASA, 1979, Mobil Oil Corp., 1977, Nat. Bur. Standards, 1979, Dept. Def., 1980-81, Navy fellow, 1982 Mem. AAAS, AAUP, Am. Assn. Physics, N.Y. Acad. Scis., Math. Assn. Am., Am. Phys. Soc., Nat. Soc. Black Physicists, Nat. Geog. Soc., Iowa State Alumna Assn., Sigma Xi, Sigma Pi Sigma. Baptist. Home: 448 W Baltimore Pike West Grove PA 19390-9201 Office: Lincoln U Dept Physics Lincoln University PA 19352 E-mail: wwillie2@aol.com. *Throughout my life I have always striven to achieve the very best and have held on to the belief that wherever possible improve upon today, so that everyone might have a better tomorrow! I have been guided by the the principle of being selective in my endeavors, having specific objectives, followed by detailed analysis, concise actions, and intense work with continous review.*

WILLIAMS, YVONNE G. corporate trainer; b. Waycross, Ga., Jan. 27; d. Alfred Hayward and Elizabeth Thomas; 1 child, Benjamin Nkrumah Williams. BA in Bus. Mgmt., Eckerd Coll., 1993; MA in Adult Edn., U. South Fla., 1995, PhD, 2000. Mktg. rep. Xerox, Tampa, Fla., 1987—90, account exec., 1990—92, document mgmt. tng. rep., 1992—96, edn. specialist, 1996—97; pres., CEO BYNTER Cons., Inc., St. Petersburg, 1997—. Adv. bd. PIMEG, St. Petersburg, Fla., 1995-97; bd. dirs. Happy Workers Daycare Ctr. Active First Bapt. Instnl. Ch., St. Petersburg; bd. dirs. Happy Workers Childcare Ctr. Mem. NAACP, ASTD, Assn. Voters Edn. Rsch. Com., Nat. Coun. Negro Women, South Ctrl. Rotary, Top Ladies of Distinction, St. Petersburg Urban League Guild, Phi Kappa Phi, Delta Sigma Theta. Home: Apt 210 7300 Sunshine Skyway Ln S Saint Petersburg FL 33711-4957

WILLIAMS-BARNARD, CAROL LOU, mental health nurse; b. New Britain, Conn., Feb. 20, 1950; d. Robert L. and Charlotte L. (Manon) W.; m. Theodore P. Barnard Jr., Aug. 10, 1974; children: Lauren, Kaetryn. AS in Nursing, Vt. Coll., 1970; BSN, Cath. U. Am., 1973, MS in Nursing, DNSc, 1979. Vis. nurse Vis. Nurse Assn., Washington, 1973; asst. prof. nursing U. N.H., Durham, 1978-83, assoc. prof. nursing, 1984—. Mem. ANA, AAUP, Nat. League for Nursing, N.H. Nurses Assn., Alliance for Mentally Ill, Sigma Theta Tau, Phi Theta Kappa.

WILLIAMSEN, DANNYE SUE, health facility administrator, personal development educator; b. Memphis, Mar. 26, 1949; d. Roy Fauntly and Arliss Wyleen Goodroe; m. Jon Charles Beckum, Dec. 23, 1969 (div. Mar. 1972); m. John Dean Williamsen, Dec. 24, 1986. BA cum laude, U. Memphis, 1995. Adminstr. Security Investments, Inc., Memphis, 1972-75; nightclub owner, investor, 1976-78; internat. tech. analyst ContiCommodity, Inc., 1977-80; owner, tech. analyst Commodity Cons., Inc., 1981; project mgr. B&P Devel. Co., Austin, Tex., 1982-84; asst. to pres. Memphis C. of C., 1984-86; owner, dental technician Williamsen Dental Lab., Memphis and Prophetstown, Ill., 1986—; ptnr., editor Personal Edn. Network, Prophetstown, 2001—. Bd. dir. Heartland Equine Assisted Therapeutic Ctr., Rock Falls, Ill. *In 30 years of management has successfully reorganized two companies bringing a construction company out of the red into a $250,000 quarterly cash flow and gaining a 100% increase in production for a dental laboratory. Taught analysis of commodities in Chicago, prepared seminars, wrote technical glossary, chosen to debate former financial advisor Of Ford Motor Corp. and fundamental analyst in a Dallas, Texas, seminar. Organized Personal Education Network to produce seminars, books, and tapes on personal development by her and her husband, John, a motivational speaker, and an interactive website(www.penetwork.org), which won a 2002 Golden Web Award.* Author: (novels) Illusions, 1998; editor(publisher): Creative Living-an evolving approach to business life, 2001. Mem. AAUW (pres. 1998-99), APA, NOW, Am. Bus. Women's Assn., Assn. for Humanistic Pscyhology, Small Pubs. Assn. N.Am., Pubs. Mktg. Assn., Psi Chi, Chi Beta Phi. Avocations: reading, philosophy. Office: Personal Edn Network 4343 16th St Moline IL 61265 E-mail: wmsen@essex1.com., dannyew@penetwork.org.

WILLIAMS JONES, ELIZABETH, financial planner, business consultant; b. San Francisco, Jan. 16, 1948; d. John and Myrtle Mary (Thierry) W.; children: Brian, Jonathan; m. Archie W. Jones Jr. Cert. in bus., U. Calif., 1979. Cert. computers loan processing. Manpower coord., fed. programs U.S. Govt., San Francisco; patient svc. rep. Health Care Svc., Oakland, Calif.; ins. and real estate cons.; pres. Investments Unlimited, Oakland, EWJ & Assocs. Mktg. Firm; leisure svcs. commr. City of Pitts.; CEO Ultimate Vacations Inc. Mem. NAACP, Contra Costa County Womens Commn.; bd. dirs. Coun. on Child Abuse. Recipient Pub. Speaking award; European Investment fellow. Mem. AAUW, NAFE, Nat. Real Estate Owners Assn., Nat. Notary Assn., Order Ea. Star, Heroines Jericho, Daus. Isis, Toastmistress Club, Beta Phi Sigma. Home: PO Box 523 Pittsburg CA 94565-0052

WILLIAMS-JONES, MICHAEL ROBERT, media company executive; b. Sussex, U.K., June 3, 1947; s. Erik H. Williams-Jones and Valerie L. (Lyons) Allan; m. Lynnete A. Raath, Oct. 6, 1969 (dec. 1993); m. Eve R. Foreman, Jan. 2, 1994; children: Allan, Clive; stepchildren: Jonathan and Amanda Foreman. Sales dir. United Artists, South Africa, 1969-71, mng. dir. Brazil, 1971-74, U.K., 1974-76, v.p. Europe divsn., 1976-78, sr. v.p. internat. divsn., 1978-81; pres., CEO United Internat. Pictures, London, 1981-96; owner, pres. Merlin Anglesey Ltd., 1996—. Recipient Lifetime Achievement award Locarno (Switzerland) Festival, 1989, Freedom of City award, Rio de Janeiro, 1973, Lifetime Achievement Cinema Expo award Motion Picture Industry, Amsterdam, 1994. Mem. Motion Picture Acad. Arts & Scis., British Film & TV Acad., Am. & British Film Insts., British Nat. Film & TV Sch. (bd. govs.). Avocations: reading, travel, films, music, painting. Office: Merlin Anglesey 49 C Princes Gate London SW7 2PG England

WILLIAMS MADDOX-BROWN, JANICE HELEN, nurse; b. Boston; d. Arthur Hamilton Wade and Edith Josephine (Weekes) Williams; m. Larry Maddox, May 21, 1977 (dec.); m. Richard Brown, Mar. 11, 2000. BS in Nursing, Boston U., 1957; MA, Atlanta U. Sch. Edn., 1971; MPH, Emory U., 1976; PhD, Union Inst., Cin., 1998. Staff nurse Beth Israel Hosp., Boston, 1958, N.Y. Hosp.-Cornell U. Med. Ctr., N.Y.C., 1958-59; ward supr. Jewish Meml. Hosp., Boston, 1959-61; staff and pvt. duty nurse Mass. Gen.Hosp., 1961-63; pub. health nurse Boston Health Dept., 1963-64; intravenous nurse Hughes Spalding Hosp., Atlanta, 1964-66; pub. health nurse Fulton County (Ga.) Health Dept., 1966-69; sr. tchr. Atlanta Southside Comprehensive Health Ctr., 1970-73, acting dir. edn., 1973-74, assoc. dir. clin. nursing, 1974-76; assoc. dir. mental health planning project So. Region Edn. Bd., Atlanta, 1976-78; nursing cons. Dept. Health and Human Svcs., 1978-81; head nurse VA Med. Ctr., 1982-85; br. mgr. Am. Home Health Care of Ga., Inc., Jonesboro, 1985-86; mem. staff Med. Emergency Clinic-Grady Meml. Hosp., 1986-91; project dir. Morehouse Sch. Medicine Initiative, W.K. Kellogg Found., 1991-95; assoc. prof. Ctrl. Mich. U., 2000—01. Evening coordinator, instr. for innovative practical nursing program for health para-profl. Atlanta Area Tech Sch., 1971-81; mem. admissions com. M. Pub. Health program Emory U. Sch. Medicine, 1979-91. Mem. coms., including Women's Day com. Ctrl. United Meth. Ch., Atlanta, Beh Hill United Meth. Ch. (mem.). Recipient spl. recognition Am. Cancer Soc., 1975.

WILLIAMS-MONEGAIN, LOUISE JOEL, retired science educator, ethnographer; b. Chgo., June 13, 1941; d. Sylvester Emanuel Jr. and Carita Bell (Brown) Williams; m. Martin Monegain, Aug. 19, 1961; children: Michael Martin, Martin Marion II. BS, Shaw U., 1975; JD, Antioch Sch. of Law, Washington, 1979; cert. adminstrn., Roosevelt U., 1988; PhD, U. Ill., 1994. Tchr. Chgo. Archdiocese, 1968-73; assoc. dir. pub. affairs Warren Regional Planning Commn., Soul City, N.C., 1973-74; comm. specialist Coun. of the Great City Schs., Washington, 1974-76; lawyer Equal Employment Opportunity Commn., 1979-80; tchr. Olive Harvey City Coll., Chgo., 1981-83; mgr. Joy Travel Agt., 1981-83; owner, pres. MJS Your Travel Agt., 1983-86; sci. tchr. Chgo. Pub. Schs., 1986-91; program leader, evaluator Argonne (Ill.) Nat. Lab., 1991-97; ethnographer Sch. Edn. and Sch. Policy Northwestern U., Evanston, Ill., 1997-98; pres. Monegain & Assocs. Program leader, evaluation rep. Nat. Cancer Program, Accra and Jumasi, Ghana, West Africa, 1995. Vol. Art Inst., Chgo., 1994; green team adv. bd. Lincoln Park Zool. Soc., Chgo., 1992—. Scholarship State of Ill., 1987. Mem. ASCD, Am. Edn. Rsch. Assn., Nat. Sci. Tchrs. Assn., Assn. for Coll. and Univ. Women, Phi Delta Kappa. Avocations: attending opera, dance performances, plays, galleries, swimming, traveling.

WILLIAMSON, ALAN BACHER, English literature educator, poet, writer; b. Chgo., Jan. 24, 1944; s. George and Jehanne (Bacher) W.; m. Anne Winters, Oct. 12, 1968 (div. Feb. 1988); 1 child, Elizabeth Kilner. BA, Haverford Coll., 1964; MA, Harvard U., 1965, PhD, 1969. Asst. prof. U. Va., Charlottesville, 1969-75; Briggs-Copeland lectr. Harvard U., Cambridge, Mass., 1977-80; Fannie Hurst lectr. Brandeis U., Waltham, 1980-82; prof. English, U. Calif., Davis, 1982—. Poetry panelist Nat. Endowment for Arts, 1989. Author: (criticism) Pity the Monsters, 1974, Introspection and Contemporary Poetry, 1984, Eloquence and Mere Life, 1994, Almost a Girl, 2001, (poetry) Presence, 1983, The Muse of Distance, 1988, Love and the Soul, 1995, Res Publica, 1998. Poetry fellow Nat. Endowment for Arts, 1973; Guggenheim fellow, 1991. Mem. MLA (exec. com. div. on poetry 1987-91). Democrat. Zen Buddhist. Office: U Calif Dept English Davis CA 95616 E-mail: abwilliamson@ucdavis.edu.

WILLIAMSON, BARBARA JO, retired community health nurse, educator; b. Hopkins County, Tex., July 13, 1931; d. Wallace G. and Ellie (Williams) Swindell; m. Billy W. Williamson, Nov. 5, 1952; children: Joellyn Brickhouse, Jan Boyett. Diploma, Dallas Meth. Hosp., 1951; BS, East Tex. State U., 1981. Cert. in vision and hearing, scoliosis screening, CPR instr. Dir. Sch. Vocat. Nursing Titus County Meml. Hosp., Mt. Pleasant, Tex.; dir. nursing and edn. Winnsboro (Tex.) Hosp. Inc.; sch. nurse Winnsboro Ind. Sch. Dist., Mesquite (Tex.) Ind. Sch. Dist., part-time mem. hearing screening team., 1996; ret. Mem. Tex. Assn. Sch. Nurses, Tex. Sch. Health Assn., Dallas Area Sch. Health Assn. (nomination com.). Home: 2233 Aloha Dr Mesquite TX 75150-3728

WILLIAMSON, BRIAN DAVID, information systems executive, consultant; b. Danbury, Conn., May 14, 1973; s. Robert Garth and Celeste Marie (D'Alessio) W. AA in Specialized Bus., Art Inst. Phila., 1993; BS in Gen. Studies, Teikyo Post U., 1994; postgrad. in Tech. Mgmt., Polytech. U., 1997. Asst. mgr. The New Milford (Conn.) Music Ctr., 1991-93; prodn. asst. Med. Broadcasting Co., Conshohocken, Pa., 1993; CIO Custom Designs, Inc., Danbury, Conn., 1991—; info. systems and telecomms. analyst Datahr Rehab. Inst., Brookfield, 1996-97; LAN adminstr. Praxair, Inc., Danbury, 1998—. Video technician Danbury Corp., Bethel, Conn., 1992-97. Author, writer (film script) The Senior, 1994. Republican. Roman Catholic. Avocations: tennis, computer graphics, movies, music, hiking. Home: 34 Lindencrest Dr Danbury CT 06811-4232 Office: Praxair Inc 39 Old Ridgebury Rd Ste 7 Danbury CT 06810-5109

WILLIAMSON, C. DEAN, university official; b. Abilene, Tex., Apr. 2, 1959; s. Troy Dean and Barbara Ann (Evans) W.; m. Sharla Elaine Coldewey, Dec. 11, 1983; children: Bradley Dean, Christopher Alan. Student, Hardin-Simmons U., Abilene, Tex., 1977-78, Western Tex. Coll., Snyder, 1978, 82, 89-91; BA, Sul Ross State U., Alpine, Tex., 1994, postgrad., 1994-95, Midwestern State U., Wichita Falls, Tex., 1996; MBA, Wayland Bapt. U., Plainview, Tex., 1998; postgrad., Regent U., 2000—. 2d class petty officer USN, Yokosuka, Japan, 1979-82; sales mgr. Williamson Auto Supply, Inc., Snyder, Tex., 1982-91; editor Colorado City (Tex.) Record, 1991-92; pub. Alpine (Tex.) Avalanche, 1992-95; staff writer Abilene Reporter-News, 1995-96, Vernon (Tex.) Daily Record, 1996; dir. pub. rels. Wayland Bapt. U., Plainview, 1997-99, Brewton-Parker Coll., Mt. Vernon, Ga., 1999—2002, exec. dir. for planning and instnl. rsch., 2002—, dir. sports info., editor ArchWay, campus newspaper, 2000—, also advisor to Fellowship Christian Athletes, 1999—. Corr. Abilene Reporter-News, 1991-92; advisor Traveler Yearbook, Plainview, 1997-99. Trail Blazer Newspaper, Plainview, 1997-98. Editor: (alumni mag.) Lamp; contbr. articles to newspapers, mags., jours. in field. Mem. Police Acad. Adv. Bd., Alpine, 1994, Conv. and Visitors Bur., Plainview, 1997-98; publicity com. 1st Bapt. Ch. Mt. Vernon, Ga., 2000—, usher, 2001—; messenger Ga. Bapt. Conv., 1999-; bus. ptnr. sch. coun. Montgomery County H.S., 2001-. Mem. Pub. Rels. Soc. Am., Bapt. Communicators Assn., Coll. Sports Info. Dirs. Assn., Assn. Instnl. Rsch., Toombs/Montgomery C. of C., Pi Sigma Alpha Avocation: golf. Home: PO Box 843 Mount Vernon GA 30445-0843 Office: Brewton Parker Coll Hwy 280 Box 2039 Mount Vernon GA 30445 E-mail: dwillia@bpc.edu.

WILLIAMSON, CARL AUGUSTUS, engineering executive; b. Newport News, Va., Sept. 7, 1950; s. Marvis Harrison Sr. and Annie Lucille (Amos) W.; m. Bonnie Bernel Mitchell, Sept. 21, 1973; 1 child, Carl Michael; 1 stepson, Leon Mitchell. BS, Norfolk State Coll., 1972; MBA, Northeastern U., 1982; DEng, MIT, 1987. Cert. secondary edn. tchr. Electrical estimator Stone & Webster, Boston, 1973-74; instr. D.C. Pub. Schs., Washington, 1974-76; sales engr. Westinghouse, Framingham, Mass., 1976-78; cost engr. Gilbert Commonwealth, Jackson, Mich., 1978-80; instr. Boston Pub. Schs., Boston, 1980-82; cons. Gilbert Commonwealth, Washington, 1983—. Col. U.S. Army, 1968-72. Mem. NRA, MBA Assn., Washington Tchrs. Union. Baptist. Avocations: sports, arts, dance. Home and Office: Apt 207 2700 Martin Luther King Jr Ave # A Washington DC 20032-2601

WILLIAMSON, CHARLES R. energy company executive; PhD in Geology, U. Tex., Austin, 1978. Rsch. assoc. Sci. and Tech. Divsn. Unocal Corp., Brea, Calif., 1977-83, chief exploration geologist U.K., 1983-86; exploration mgr., dir. Unocal Netherlands, The Hague, 1986-89; v.p. exploration Unocal Thailand, Bangkok, 1989-92; v.p. Energy Resources Divsn. Unocal, 1992-94, v.p. planning and info. svcs., 1994-95, v.p. corp. planning and econs., 1995-96, group v.p. internat. opers., 1996-97, group v.p. Asia Opers., 1997-99; exec. v.p. internat. energy ops. Unocal Corp., El Segundo, Calif., 1999—2001; CEO Unocal, 2001—, also bd. dirs. Mem. adv. bd. earth scis. dept. Stanford U. Mem. Am. Soc. Petroleum Geologists, Soc. Econ. Paleontologists and Mineralogists, Soc. Petroleum Engrs., Internat. Assn. Sedimentologists. Office: Unocal Corp 2141 Rosecrans Ave Ste 4000 El Segundo CA 90245-4746*

WILLIAMSON, DEBORAH DAYWOOD, lawyer; b. Greenville, S.C., Mar. 8, 1954; d. Narcief M. Daywood and Margaret Elizabeth (Guy) Robbins; m. George F. Williamson, Nov. 9, 1974; children: Christal Elizabeth, Victoria Whitney. BA, San Antonio Coll., 1973, S.W. Tex. U., 1974, U. Tex., El Paso, 1977; JD, U. Houston, 1981. Bar: Tex. 1982, U.S. Dist. Ct. (we. dist.) Tex. 1983, U.S. Dist. Ct. (so. dist.) Tex. 1986, U.S. Dist. Ct. (no. dist.) Tex. 1989, U.S. Dist. Ct. Ariz. 1991, U.S. Ct. Appeals (5th cir.) 1983. Atty. Cox & Smith Inc., San Antonio, 1982—. Author: (with others) Single Asset Real Estate Bankruptcies, 1996; columnist Am. Bankruptcy Inst. Jour., 1985—. Fellow Tex. Bar Found., Am. Coll. Bankruptcy, San Antonio Bar Found.; master Am. Inns of Ct., William Session; mem. Am. Bankruptcy Inst. (pres. 1998-99), San Antonio Bankruptcy Bar Assn. Office: Cox & Smith Inc 112 E Pecan St Ste 1800 San Antonio TX 78205-1521 E-mail: ddwillia@coxsmith.com.

WILLIAMSON, DEBORAH MCKIBBEN, social services administrator, educator; b. Cin., May 19, 1958; d. Herbert and Julia Irene McKibben; m. Stephen Ross Williamson, Dec. 5, 1986. BS, No. Ky. U., 1982; MA, U. Cin., 1985; PhD, U. Ky., 2000. Rsch. asst. U. Cin., 1983-86; intake officer juvenile svcs. Adminstrv. Office Cts., Newport, Ky., 1988-90, field supr. juvenile svcs. Frankfort, 1990-92, dir. law related edn., 1992-98, gen. mgr. juvenile svcs., 1998—. Adj. prof. U. Ky. State U., Lexington and Frankfort, 1997-2001. Editor: Law Related Education and Juvenile Justice, 1997; contbr. articles to profl. jours. Mem. Gov.'s Juvenile Justice Adv. Bd., 1999—. Recipient Outstanding Crime Prevention Practitioner award Ky. Crime Prevention Coun., 2000, Early Intervention Program award Ky. Cert. Bd. Prevention Profls., 2000; Adoptions Opportunities grantee HHS, 1997. Mem. Juvenile Justice Trainer's Assn., Nat. Youth Justice (coord. com. 2000), Civitas (Educator for Democracy com. Bosnia-Herzegovina 1997, Poland 2000). Democrat. Avocation: environmental preservation. Office: Adminstrv Office of Cts 100 Millcrek Pk Frankfort KY 40601 E-mail: deborahw@mail.aoc.state.ky.us.

WILLIAMSON, DIANA JEAN, nurse; b. Portland, Oreg., Dec. 21, 1956; d. Gerald George and Jean Elizabeth Musson; m. Bradley Alan Williamson, Dec. 12, 1981. Grad., Good Samaritan Hosp./Med. Ctr., 1977. RN, Oreg.; bd. cert. psychiat. and mental health nurse. Staff nurse Western Lane Hosp., Florence, Oreg., 1977-79; asst. head nurse Providence Portland Med. Ctr., Portland, 1979-99, staff nurse, 1999—. Activist Oreg. Wildlife Fedn./Witness Against Lawless Logging, Portland and Rhododendron, Oreg., 1996. Mem. ANA, Am. Inst. Archaeology, Oreg. Nurses Assn. (unit rep.), Oreg. Wildlife Fedn., Defenders of Wildlife. Democrat. Avocations: reading, music, wine. Home: PO Box 239 Rhododendron OR 97049-0239

WILLIAMSON, DONALD ELLIS, state official; b. Louisville, June 17, 1955; m. Anita Hudspeth; 1 child, Jonathan Stuart. Student, East Miss. Jr. Coll., 1972-73, Miss. State U., 1973-75; MD cum laude, U. Miss., 1979. Diplomate Am. Bd. Internal Medicine. Intern, resident in internal medicine U. Va. Hosp., Charlottesville, 1979-82; with East Miss. State Hosp., Meridian, 1979; state tb control oficer Miss. State Dept. Health, 1982-86; dir. divsn. disease control Ala. Dept. Pub. Health, 1986-88, dir. bur. preventive health svcs., 1988-92, state health officer, 1992—. Faculty mem. Injury Control Rsch. Ctr. U. Ala., Birmingham; clin. assoc. prof. dept. internal medicine U. South Ala.; presenter in field. Contbr. articles to profl. jours. Chmn. Ala. Pub. Health Care Authority, Ala. Radiation Adv. Bd. Health; mem. Ala. Commn. Aging, State Bldg. Commn., Statewide Health Coordinating Coun., Ala. Youth Svcs. Bd., Gov.'s Task Force Health Care, 1993, Ala. Child Abuse & Neglect Prevention Bd., Ala. Resource Devel. Com., Ala. Anatomical Bd., Planning and Adv. Coun. Devel. Disabilities, Ala. Bd. Med. Scholarship Awards, Pesticides Adv. Com., Gov.'s Interagy. Coordinating Coun., Ala. Juvenile Justice Coordinating Coun., Emergency Med. Svcs. Adv. Coun., 1986-92, Legis. Adv. Com. AIDS, 1988-90, Atty. Gen.'s Task Force Med.Waste, 1989, Water Resources Adv. Coun., exec. coun. Ala. Children's Svcs. Facilitation Team, 1993—; mem. med. adv. com. ARC. Recipient Mosby Book award, 1979, Dr. Robert Ramsey award, 1993; Pub. Health Leadership Inst. scholar, 1996. Mem. APHA, Assn. State and Territorial Health Ofcls. (exec. com. 1995-2000, pres. 1997-98), Am. Acad. of Pediatrics (Child Health Advocate of the Yr. award 1999), Pub. Health Found. (Theodore R. Ervin award 1999), Med. Assn. State Ala., Ala. Pub. Health Assn. (bd. dirs. 1991—, chmn. disease control and epidemiology sect. 1991-92, D.G. Gill award 1997), Pub. Health Found. (bd. dirs. 1995-99, treas. 1997—), Phi Theta Kappa, Phi Kappa Phi, Alpha Omega Alpha. Home: 8113 Lichfield Ct Montgomery AL 36117-5124 Office: Ala Dept Pub Health PO Box 303017 201 Monroe St Montgomery AL 36104-3735

WILLIAMSON, DONALD R. construction executive; b. Anacortes, Wash., May 30, 1940; s. Hans and Dagny R. (Hjelle) Williamson; m. Julie A. Wood; children: Pamela Anne, James Robert. BA in Econ., U. Wash., 1962, MBA, 1964. Analyst Ford Motor Co., Dearborn, Mich., 1964—68; v.p., CFO Aladdin Industries, Nashville, 1968—81; exec. v.p. Anvil Corp., 1981—82; mgmt. cons., 1982—83; exec. v.p. Symbion Inc., Salt Lake City, 1983—85; pres., CEO Rogers Group, Inc., Nashville, 1986—. Dir. NSSGA, Arlington, Va., 1998—, Pencil Found., Nashville, 1997—. Dir. Nashville Area C. of C., 1998—, Boys & Girls Club, Nashville, 1980—. Mem.: Fin. Execs. (pres. 1973—74), Moles. Home: 1137 Travelers Ridge Drive Nashville TN 37220-1438 Office: Rogers Group Inc 421 Great Circle Rd Nashville TN 37228 Fax: 615-780-5606. E-mail: dwilliams@rogersgroupinc.com.

WILLIAMSON, DONALD RAY, retired career Army officer; b. Amarillo, Tex., Oct. 13, 1943; s. Floy Edwin and Dorothy Lorene (Orr) W.; m. Beverly Ann Howard, Aug. 31, 1963; children: Rebecca Ann, Catherine Paige. BS in Econs., W. Tex. State U., 1966; MA in Bus., Cen. Mich. U., 1977; degree, Dept. Def. Program Mgrs., 1982, U.S. Army Command and Gen. Staff Coll., 1980. Commd. 2d lt. U.S. Army, 1966, advanced through grades to lt. col., 1982, retired, 1986, comdg. officer combat support co. Tex., 1973-74, comdg. officer 2d aviation co., 1974-75, dep. insp. gen. Ft. Leavenworth, Kans., 1975-78, comdg. officer 213th aviation co. Rep. of Korea, 1978-79, asst. program mgr. advanced scout helicopter program, 1981-86; owner Witan Group, Chesterfield, Mo., 1986-88; pres. Sys. Test Evaluation Inc., Huntsville, Ala., 1988-99; gen. mgr. LESCO, 1999-2000. Contbr. articles to profl. jours. Decorated Bronze Star, 37 Air medals with "V" device, D.F.C. with oak leaf cluster, Legion of Merit. Mem. Army Aviation Assn. Am., Assn. U.S. Army, Lansing Jaycees (past pres.), Mensa. Avocations: flying, reading, tennis. Home: 2110 Greenslope Trl NE Huntsville AL 35811-2608

WILLIAMSON, DOUGLAS FRANKLIN, JR. lawyer; b. Anniston, Ala., Mar. 23, 1930; s. Douglas Franklin and Elizabeth Louise (Connor) W.; m. Barbara Tuerk, Dec. 28, 1957; children: Mary Leyden, Douglas Franklin III, Bruce Reynolds. AB summa cum laude, Amherst Coll., 1952; LLB, Yale U., 1955. Bar: NY 1958, Fla. 1976. Assoc. Breed, Abbott & Morgan, N.Y.C., 1957-63, ptnr., 1963-72, Williamson & Hess and predecessor firm, N.Y.C., 1972-79; of counsel Winthrop, Stimson, Putnam & Roberts, 1979-81, ptnr., 1982-95, sr. counsel, 1996-2000, Pillbury Winthrop LLP, N.Y.C., 2001—. Bd. dirs. World Wildlife Fund, Washington, 1979-88, treas., 1986-88, mem. nat. coun., 1988—; bd. dirs. Conservation Found., Washington, 1985-88, treas., 1986-88; bd. dirs. Lower Hudson chpt. Nature Conservancy, Katonah, N.Y., 1976-87, 93-97, sec., 1976-87, hon. dir., 1987—, chmn., 1993-94; bd. dirs. Oblong Land Conservancy, Pawling, N.Y., 1990-98, chmn. 1996-98; bd. dirs. Quaker Hill Civic Assn., Pawling, 1974-2000, past pres.; chmn. Pawling Assessment Rev. Bd., 1976-2001. With U.S. Army, 1955-57. Fellow N.Y. State Bar Found.; mem. Assn. Bar City N.Y. (life), English Spkg. Union, Old Guard Soc. Palm Beach Golfers, Everglades Club, Quaker Hill Country Club (pres. 1980-81), Phi Beta Kappa, Phi Beta Kappa Soc. (sec. 1975-77, v.p. 1977-79). Office: Pillsbury Winthrop LLP One Battery Park Plz New York NY 10004

WILLIAMSON, EDWARD HENRY, chaplain, army officer; b. Jackson, Miss., Dec. 9, 1957; s. Oliver Frank and Edith Elise (Berch) W.; m. Jeanne Marie Lazio, May 28, 1988. BA in History, Miss. Coll., 1983; MDiv, Golden Gate Sem., 1988; DMin, Trinity Coll. and U., 1999; 5 units clin. pastoral edn., 2002. Ordained to ministry So. Bapt. Ch., 1988. Chaplain Letterman Army Med. Ctr. USAR, San Francisco, 1988-90; post chaplain U.S. Army, Camp Parks, Calif., 1990, chaplain 1-14th AV Ft. Rucker, Ala., 1991, chaplain 46th engr., 1992, chaplain 1-503rd rgt. Camp Casey, South Korea, 1993-94, chaplain 5-29th Field arty. Ft. Carson, Colo., 1994-96, chaplain 1-72 Armor, 1996-97, chaplain 68th corps support, 1997-99; ret. from active duty, 1999; dir. spirtual care Sangre de Cristo Hospice, Pueblo, Colo., 2000. Author: 20 Questions You Should Ask a Potential Spouse. Mem. Army Aviator Assn. Am., VFW (dist. 2 chaplain Colo.), Pi Gamma Mu, Phi Alpha Theta. Republican. Avocations: chess, model aircraft, computer programming, hiking, swimming. Home: 305 Rudd Ave Canon City CO 81212-3255

WILLIAMSON, EDWIN DARGAN, lawyer, former federal official; b. Florence, S.C., Sept. 23, 1939; s. Benjamin F. and Sara (Dargan) W.; m. Kathe Gates, July 12, 1969; children: Samuel Gates, Edwin Dargan Jr., Sara Elizabeth. BA cum laude, U. of the South, 1961, DCL (hon.), 1992; JD, NYU, 1964. Bar: N.Y. 1965, D.C. 1988. Assoc. Sullivan & Cromwell, N.Y.C., 1964-70, ptnr., 1971-76, London, 1976-79, N.Y.C., 1979-88, Washington, 1988-90, 93—; legal adviser U.S. Dept. State, 1990-93. Regent U. of the South, Sewanee, Tenn., 1981-87, chmn., 1985-87, coun. fgn. rels., 1995—; bd. dirs. Nat. Dance Inst., N.Y.C., 1984-88, Episcopal Ch. Found., N.Y.C., 1986-94; vestryman St. James Episcopal Ch., N.Y.C., 1984-88. Mem. U.S. Coun. Internat. Bus., Bus. and Industry Adv. Com. to OECD (vice chmn. com. on multinat. enterprise and investments 1993—, chmn. BIAC expert group on multilat agt. on investment 1996-99, vice-chmn. BIAC 1998—, mem. exec. com. USCIB 1999—), Internat. Rep. Inst. (rule of law adv. bd. 1993—), Racquet and Tennis Club (N.Y.C.), Met. Club. Republican. E-mail: williamsone@sullcrom.com.

WILLIAMSON, EDWIN LEE, wardrobe and costume consultant; b. Downey, Calif., Dec. 2, 1947; s. Cecil Earnest and Edwina Louise (Tedie) W. AA, L.A. City Coll., 1967-70; BA in Theater and Music Edn., 1971, MA in Theater and Music Edn., 1973; student, U. So. Calif., 1971-73. Wardrobe master Ice Capades, 1973-76; mem. wardrobe dept. Paramount Studios, 1976-78, Disney Studios, 1978-81; freelance wardrobe and costume cons., L.A., 1981—. Editor spl. events & theatre presentations Nightlife Mag. Appeared as Michael in original mus. Peter Pan Mem. adv. bd. Halfway House and AIDS Hospsice, Valley Presbyn. Hosp.; founder West Coast Singers L.A., Inner City Athletic Union L.A.; founding mem. Gay Mens Chorus, Gt. Am. Yankee Freedom Band L.A., L.A. Gay and Lesbian Community Ctr.; hon. mem. bd. dirs. U. So. Calif. Idylwild Sch. Music and Arts.; bd. dirs. One Christopher St. West; founding vol. Gay Community Svc. Ctr.; emperor Imperial Ct. of San Fernando Valley. Scholar U. So. Calif., 1971-73; nominee Tony award Best Supporting Actor in musical Happy Time. Mem. SAG, AFTRA, Wardrobe Union, Masons. Lutheran. Address: Nightlife Pubs 1800 N Highland Ave Ste 604 Hollywood CA 90028-4525

WILLIAMSON, FLETCHER PHILLIPS, real estate broker; b. Cambridge, Md., Dec. 16, 1923; s. William Fletcher and Florence M. (Phillips) Williamson; m. Betty June Stoker, Apr. 6, 1943 (div. 1972); 1 child Jeffrey Phillips ; m. Helen M. Stumberg, Aug. 28, 1972 (dec. Jan. 2002). Student, U. Md., 1941-42. Test engr. engring. lab. Glen Martin Co., 1942-43; salesman Corkran Ice Cream Co., Cambridge, 1946-50; real estate broker, 1950—. Chmn. bd. Williamson Real Estate, Dorchester Indsl. Devel. Corp., 1963—72; dir. Dorchester indsl. Devel. Corp.; vice-chmn. bd., dir. Nat. Bank Cambridge, 1979—; dir. Cam-Storage, Inc., Delmarva Bank Data Processing Ctr.; co-receiver White & Nelson, INc.; v.p. Delmarva Bank Shares. Bd. dirs. Delmarva coun. Boy Scouts Am., Dorchester County Pub. Libr.; past pres. Cambridge Hosp.; United Fund Dorchester County; bd. dirs., v.p. Game Conservation Internat., Del. Mus. Natural History. With AUS, 1943—46, ETO. Methodist. Home: 310 E Wilowood Dr San Antonio TX 78212

WILLIAMSON, FREDERICK BEASLEY, III, rubber company executive; b. Balt., June 21, 1918; s. Frederick Beasley and Virginia Ogden (Ranson) W.; m. Katherine Stryker, Apr. 19, 1941 (dec. Jan. 15, 1997); children— Katherine L., Frederick Beasley IV, Marsha R. Student, Princeton, 1937-40. With Goodall Rubber Co., Trenton, N.J., 1940-41, 46-88, pres., chmn. bd., 1957-85, dir., 1950-89. Bd. dirs. N.J. Nat. Bank. Bd. dirs. Mercer Med. Center, Trenton, N.J. 1965-89, New Jobs, 1962-91 ; campaign chmn. Delaware Valley United Way, 1964. Served to capt., 5th Armored Div. U.S. Army, 1942-46. Mem. Rubber Mfrs. Assn. (dir. 1958-86), Nat. Assn. Mfrs. (bd. dirs. 1981-82), N.J. Mfrs. Ins. Co. (bd. dirs. 1965-90, dir. emeritus 1990-2000, chmn. 1977-79), N.J. Bus. Industry Assn. (dir. emeritus 1990-2000). Clubs: Princeton (N.Y.C.); Trenton Country; Hartwood (Port Jervis, N.Y.); Pine Valley Golf. Home: 1265 Eagle Rd New Hope PA 18938-9221

WILLIAMSON, HUGH JACKSON, statistician; b. Dallas, Jan. 12, 1943; s. Hugh and Edna (Mays) W.; m. Sheri Lynn Wooten, Jan. 19, 1980; 1 child, Laura Elizabeth. BA in Math. with Honors, U. Tex., 1965, MA in Math., 1967, PhD in Mech. Engring., 1975. Engr., scientist Tracor, Inc. and subs., Austin, Tex., 1967-73; rsch. engr., scientist assoc. U. Tex., 1973-77; sr. scientist Radian Internat. LLC, 1977-85, sr. staff scientist, 1986-91, prin. scientist, 1992-2000, CACI Techs., Inc., Austin, 2000—. Contbr. articles, reports to profl. publs. Mem. Am. Statis. Assn., Sigma Xi, Phi Kappa Phi. Avocations: reading, gourmet cooking, music appreciation, golf. Home: 2401 Indian Trl Austin TX 78703-2337 E-mail: hwilliamson@caci.com.

WILLIAMSON, JACK (JOHN STEWART), writer; b. Bisbee, Ariz., Apr. 29, 1908; s. Asa Lee and Lucy Betty (Hunt) W.; m. Blanche Slaten Harp, Aug. 15, 1947 (dec. Jan. 1985); stepchildren: Keigh Harp (dec.), Adele Harp Lovorn. BA, MA, Eastern N.Mex. U., 1957, LHD (hon.), 1981; PhD, U. Colo., 1964. Prof. English Eastern N.Mex. U., Portales, 1960-77, prof. emeritus, 1977—. Author numerous sci. fiction books including The Legion of Space, 1947, Darker Than You Think, 1948, The Humanoids, 1949, The Green Girl, 1950, The Cometeers, 1950, One Against the Legion, 1950, Seetee Scock, 1950, Seetee Ship, 1950, Dragon's Island, 1951, The Legion of Time, 1952, (with Frederik Phhl) Star Bridge, 1955, Dome Around America, 1955, The Trial of Terra, 1962, Golden Blood, 1964, The Reign of Wizardry, 1965, Bright New Universe, 1967, Trapped in Space, 1968, The Pandora Effect, 1969, People Machines, 1971, The Moon Children, 1972, H.G. Wells: Critic of Progress, 1973, Teaching SF, 1975, The Early Williamson, 1975, The Power of Blackness, 1976, The Best of Jack Williamson, 1978, Brother to Demons, Brother To Gods, 1979, Teaching Science Fiction: Education for Tomorrow, 1980, The Alien Intelligence, 1980, The Humanoid Touch, 1980, Manseed, 1982, The Queen of a Legion, 1983, Wonder's Child: My Life in Science Fiction, 1984 (Hugo award 1985), Lifeburst, 1984, Firechild, 1986, Mazeway, 1990, Undersea Quest, 1954, Undersea Fleet, 1955, Undersea City, 1956, The Reefs of Sapce, 1964, Starchild, 1965, Rogue Star, 1969, The Farthest Star, 1975, Wall Around a Star, 1983, Land's End, 1988, Mazeway, 1990. (with Frederik Phol) The Singers Of Time, 1991, Beachhead, 1992, Demon Moon, 1994, The Black Sun, 1996, The Fortress of Utopia, 1998, The Silicon Dagger, 1999, The Stone from the Green Star, 1999, Terraforming Earth, 2001; (with Miles J. Breuer) The Birth of an New Republic, 1981. Served as staff sgt. USAAF, 1942-45. Mem. Sci. Fiction Writers Am. (pres. 1978-80, Grand Master Nebula award 1976), Sci. Fiction Research Assn. (Pilgrim award 1968), World Sci. Fiction, Planetary Soc. Avocations: travel, astronomy, photography. Home: PO Box 761 Portales NM 88130-0761 Office: Ea NMex U Golden Libr Portales NM 88130 E-mail: Jack.Williamson@enmu.edu.

WILLIAMSON, JAMES ROBERT, JR. lawyer; b. Morgantown, W.Va., Nov. 9, 1961; s. James Robert Williamson and Katheryn Williamson Kay; m. Elizabeth Anne Warlick, June 16, 1984; children: Lindsey, Molly, Anne. BS in Bus. Adminstrn., Vanderbilt U., 1983; JD, W.Va. U., 1986. Bar: Ga. 1986, W.Va. 1986, Fla. 1990. Assoc. King & Spalding, Atlanta, 1986-90, Stichter, Riedel, Blain & Prosser, Tampa, Fla., 1990-91, Bisbee, Rickertsen & Herzog, Atlanta, 1991-93; ptnr. Scroggins & Williamson, 1993—. Steptoe & Johnson scholar W. Va. U. Law Sch., 1984-86. Mem. Atlanta Bar Assn. (mem. bankruptcy sect.), Ga. State Bar Assn. (mem. bankruptcy sect., bd. dirs. 1998), Ansley Golf Club. Methodist. Office: 1500 Candler Bldg 127 Peachtree St NE Atlanta GA 30303-1810

WILLIAMSON, JOEL RUDOLPH, humanities educator; b. Anderson County, S.C., Oct. 27, 1929; s. James Henry and Carrie Mae (Swaney) W.; m. Marie Ahearn, Nov. 17, 1953 (div. May 1983); children: Joelle, William, Alethea; m. Anna Woodson, Oct. 18, 1986. AB, U. S.C., 1948, MA, 1951; PhD, U. Calif., 1964. Instr. dept. history U. N.C., Chapel Hill, 1960-64, asst. prof., 1964-66, assoc. prof., 1966-69, prof., 1969-85, Lineberger prof. in humanities, 1985—. Resident fellow Rockefeller Ctr., Bellagio, Italy, 1988; Eudora Welty prof. in so. studies Millsaps Coll., 1984; disting. vis. prof. Rhodes Coll., 1984; vis. prof. dept. history, assoc. Lowell House Harvard U., 1981-82. Author: After Slavery: The Negro in South Carolina During Reconstruction, 1861-1877, 1965, The Origins of Segregation, 1968, New People: Miscegenation and Mulattoes in the United States, 1980, The Crucible of Race, 1984 (Francis Parkman prize Soc. Am. Historians, Ralph Waldo Emerson award Phi Beta Kappa, Mayflower Cup, Frank L. and Harriet C. Owsley award 1985, Robert Francis Kennedy Book award, Pulitzer prize in History nomination 1985), A Rage for Order, 1986, William Faulkner and Southern History, 1993 (Pulitzer prize in History nomination 1994, Mayflower Cup), also articles. Lt. USN, 1951-55. Fellow Guggenheim Found., 1970-71, NEH, 1987-88, Ctr. for Advanced Study in Behavioral Scis., Stanford, Calif., 1977-78, summer 1979, 80, 81, So. fellow, 1961-62, Charles Warren Ctr., 1981-82. Mem. Soc. Am. Historians, Orgn. Am. Historians, Am. Hist. Assn., So. Hist. Assn., So. Assn. for Women Historians. Avocation: travel. Home: 211 Hillsborough St Chapel Hill NC 27514-3522 Office: U NC Dept History 567 Hamilton Chapel Hill NC 27599-3195 E-mail: william@email.unc.edu.

WILLIAMSON, JOHN, economist; b. Hereford, Eng., June 7, 1937; s. Harry and Eileen (Heap) W.; m. Denise Rausch de Souza, Mar. 30, 1974; children: Andre, Daniel, Theresa. BSc in Econs., London Sch. of Econ., 1958; PhD, Princeton U., 1963. Lectr. U. of York, Eng., 1963-68; cons. UK Treasury, London, 1968-70; prof. U. Warwick, Eng., 1970-77; advisor IMF, Washington, 1972-74; prof. Pontificia Universidade Catolica, Rio de Janeiro, Brazil, 1978-81; sr. fellow Inst. for Internat. Econs., Washington, 1981—. Specialist advisor House of Commons Select Com. on Treasury, London, 1982-83; chief economist South Asia region World Bank, 1996-99; project dir. UN High-Level Panel on Financing for Devel., 2001. Author: Failure of World Monetary Reform, 1977; Political Economy and International Money, 1987. Pres. U. London Liberal Fedn., London, 1957-58. Mem. Royal Econ. Soc. (coun. 1976-77), Am. Econ. Assn. Avocation: birding. Office: Inst for Internat Econ 1750 Massachusetts Ave NW Washington DC 20036-1903 E-mail: jwilliamson@iie.com.

WILLIAMSON, JOHN BUTLER, sociology educator; b. Gloversville, N.Y., Mar. 18, 1943; s. John William and Nancy (Butler) Chambers; m. Nancy Thomas, Mar. 22, 1968; m. Elizabeth Szwarc Johnson, July 7, 1987. BS in Philosophy and Physics, MIT, 1964; PhD in Social Psychology, Harvard U., 1969. Assoc. Inst. Human Scis., Boston Coll., Chestnut Hill, Mass., 1969-72, asst. prof. sociology, 1969-75, assoc. prof., 1975-83, prof., 1983—, asst. chmn. dept., 1977-83, chmn., 1985-88, dir. applied social rsch. sequence, 1979-81. Presenter numerous papers at profl. meetings; manuscript reviewer numerous profl. jours.; reviewer or editorial cons. numerous pub. cos. and univ. presses; cons. project on FCC's funeral rule Nat. Consumer Law Ctr., Boston, 1988; mem. externala rev. team dept. social and cultural scis. Marquette U., Milw., 1987; grant application reviewer NEH, 1980, NSF, 1999, 2001; cons. project on elder and child neglect Mass. Gen. Hosp., Boston, 1987; presider 28th Internat. Congrress Internat. Inst. Sociology, Portugal, 1986. Author: Strategies Against Poverty in America, 1975, (with others) Aging and Society, 1980, Growing Old, 1980, The Research Craft, 1977, 2d edit., 1982, The Politics of Aging: Power and Policy, 1982, Aging and Public Policy: Social Control or Social Justice?, 1985, Poverty and Public Policy, 1986, Poverty in the U.S., 1988, The Senior Movement, 1991, Age, Class, Politics and the Welfare State, 1989, Old-Age Security in Comparative Perspective, 1993, Death: Current Perspectives, 4th edit., 1995, The Senior Rights Movement, 1996, The Generational Equity Debate, 1999; also numerous articles, chpts. in books. Fellow USPHS, 1965-69; grantee NSF, summer 1970, Nat. Inst. on Aging, 1977, 83-86, U.S. Cmty. Svcs. Adminstrn., 1980, Boston Coll. Mellon Found., 1981-82, Am. Coun. Learned Socs., 1994. Mem. Am. Sociol. Assn. (chmn. com. sect. 1996-98, chmn. com. on rsch. groups sect. on aging 1993-96, sec.-treas. sect. on aging and the life course 1995-98), Gerontol. Soc. Am., Nat. Acad. Social Ins., Internat. Sociol. Assn. Home: 50 Paul St Newton MA 02459-2760 Office: Boston Coll Dept Sociology Chestnut Hill MA 02467 E-mail: jbw@bc.edu.

WILLIAMSON, JOHN PRITCHARD, utility executive; b. Cleve., Feb. 22, 1922; s. John and Jane (Pritchard) W.; m. Helen Morgan, Aug. 3, 1945; children: John Morgan, James Russell, Wayne Arthur. BBA, Kent State U., 1945; postgrad., U. Toledo, 1953-56, U. Mich., 1956. CPA, Ohio, ret. Sr. acct. Arthur Andersen & Co., Detroit and Cleve., 1945-51; dir. methods and procs. Toledo Edison Co., 1951-59, asst. treas., 1959-60, sec., 1960-62, sec.-treas., 1962-65, v.p. finance, 1965-68, sr. v.p., 1968-72, pres., chief exec. officer, 1972-79, chmn., chief exec. officer, 1979-86; chmn. Centerior Energy Corp., 1985-86. Chmn. emeritus Toledo Edison Co., Centerior Energy Corp. (now First Energy Corp.), 1986—; dir. emeritus, chmn. 1st Nat. Bank of Toledo, 1974-75; chmn. N.Am. Electric Reliability Coun., 1984-87; chmn. Nat. Electric Security Com., 1987-88. Pres. Ohio Electric Utility Inst., 1972; chmn. East Cen. Area Power Coordination Pool, 1971-72, mem. exec. com. Edison Electric Inst., 1981-85; trustee Assn. Edison Illuminating Cos., 1982-84; pres. Toledo C. of C., 1970; chmn. Ohio C. of C., 1979-81, life dir.; pres. Toledo Symphony Orch., 1985-86; hon. trustee Toledo Mus. Art, Toledo Hosp., Toledo Symphony; trustee U. Toledo Found., 1980-87; hon. trustee Kent State U. Found.; vice chmn. Greater Toledo Corp., 1984-86; trustee, treas. Rio Verde Cmty. Ch., 1989-92; elder Presbyn. Ch.; pres. Toledo Cmty. Chest, 1972; chmn. Greater Toledo Area United Way, 1971; dir. Rio Verde Cmty. Assn. Named Toledo Outstanding Citizen, 1976; recipient Kent State U. medallion, 1992;Williamson Alumni Ctr. named in his honor, 1991. Mem. Fin. Analysts Soc. Toledo (pres. 1968-69), Systems and Procs. Assn. (internat. treas. 1960), Inst. Pub. Utilities (chmn. exec. com. 1969-70), Toledo Boys Club (Echo award 1974), Kent State U. Alumni Assn. (pres. 1971-72, Outstanding Alumnus 1974), Belmont Country Club, Rio Verde Country Club, Inverness Club (gov., treas. 1967-76), Rio Verde Saddle Club (past pres.), Kiwanis (past pres. Toledo, Disting. Svc. award 1977), Blue Key, Delta Sigma Pi, Beta Alpha Psi, Delta Upsilon. Republican. Home: 10661 Cardiff Rd Perrysburg OH 43551-3404 also: 18524 E Poco Vista Rio Verde AZ 85263-7125 E-mail: williamsonjp@aol.com.

WILLIAMSON, JOHN THOMAS, SR. minerals company executive; b. Atlanta, Oct. 1, 1925; s. Walter Berry and Clare (Mathews) W.; m. Ava Gene Shealy, June 11, 1949; children: John Thomas, Ava Clare, Robin E., Leila Ann. Diploma, N. Ga. Coll., 1942-43; BS in Indsl. Engring., Ga. Inst. Tech., 1949. Registered profl. engr. and land surveyor, Ga. Chief engr. Thiele Kaolin Co., Sandersville, Ga., 1949-57; assoc. W.C. Davis and Assocs., Atlanta and Tallahassee, 1957-60; chief engr. So. Clays, Inc., Gordon, Ga., 1960-63; asst. gen. mgr. Freeport Kaolin Co., N.Y.C., 1972-77, v.p., gen. mgr., 1977-78, pres., 1978-85; cons., gen. mgr. Gordon ops. Engelhard Corp., N.J., 1985-86; pres. IMPEX Corp., Milledgeville, Brunswick, Ga., 1987—. Bd. dirs. Freeport Export Corp., Freeport Overseas Sales Co., 1978-83. Patentee on processing kaolins; contbr. articles to profl. jours. Mem. adv. bd. Ga. Coll., 1979-82, found. bd., 1983-98, emeritus, 1998—, vice chmn. found. bd., 1988-89, chmn., 1989-90; mem. nat. adv. bd. Ga. Tech. Inst., 1979-85, emeritus; adv. bd. sch. mgmt. U. Ga., 1979-80; mem. Ga. Mil. Coll. Found. Bd., 1993—, exec. com., 1995. With USNR, 1943-46. Recipient Robert Earll McConnell award AIME, 1996, GMC Hon. Alumni award, 2000. Mem. TAPPI, China Clay Prodrs., Ga. State Mining Assn., Ga. Soc. Profl. Engrs., Ga. Bus. and Industry Assn. (bd. dirs. 1978-83), Bus. Coun. Ga. (bd. dirs. 1983-88), Ga. Soc. Mining Engrs., Ga. C. of C., Jaycees, Lions (pres. 1957), Alpha Tau Omega. Baptist (deacon). Home: 1810 Tanglewood Rd Milledgeville GA 31061-2461 Office: PO Box 1028 Milledgeville GA 31059-1028 also: IMPEX Corp 157 Darien Hwy Brunswick GA 31525-2423 also: IMPEX Corp 2474 Kingsley Dr Macon GA 31204-1757 E-mail: impex@alltel.net.

WILLIAMSON, JUDY DARLENE GREENLEE, secondary school educator, librarian; b. Gallipolis, Ohio, Nov. 10, 1948; d. Byron Jr. and Margaret Mae Greenlee; m. Lannes Clay Williamson, Aug. 29, 1984. AB, Glenville State Coll., 1970; MA, Marshall U., 1973, postgrad., 1994. Librarian, tchr. Mason County Bd. Edn., Point Pleasant, W.Va., 1970—; acting dir. Mason County Pub. Library, 1986-87. Cons. Found. for Library Research, Point Pleasant, 1983—; adj. faculty Marshall U., Mid Ohio Valley Ctr. C.C., 1996-2000. Created the Automated Library System computer software; contbr. articles to profl. jours. Treas. Point Pleasant Emergency Med. Svcs., 1976-82; mem. chpt. 2 com. Mason County Bd. Edn., 1983—, mem. computer com., 1984—; mem. bicentennial steering com. City of Point Pleasant, 1987; chmn. Mason County Tech. com., 1993-2001, Point Pleasant H.S. Tech., 1993-2001. Grantee W.Va. Dept. Edn., 1981, 82, 97. Mem. W.Va. Libr. Assn., W.Va. Edn. Assn., Mason County Reading Coun., W.Va. Ednl. Media Assn., Alpha Delta Kappa, Delta Kappa Gamma. Republican. Methodist. Avocations: flowers, reading, travel. Home: 2764 Us Route 35 Southside WV 25187-9730 Office: Point Pleasant HS RR 1 Box 4 Point Pleasant WV 25550-9702 E-mail: jwilliam@access.K12.wv.us.

WILLIAMSON, KENNETH N. civilian military employee; b. Miss. BS, U. Ala. CEO U.S. Army Res. Command', Fort McPherson, Ga., 1998—; dep. dir. Dep. Chief of Staff Pers., 1996—98, Dep. Chief of Staff Engr. Recipient Meritorious Civilian Svc. award, Superior Civilian Svc. award (3). Mem.: Ret. Officers Assn., Assn. U.S. Army, Res. Officers Assn. (past state sec.), Atlanta Fed. Exec. Bd., Mid. Tenn. Fed. exec. Assn. (past pres./v.p.), Am. Soc. Mil. Comptr. (past pres. Greater Atlanta chpt.). Office: Army Reserve Command Fort Mcpherson GA 30330-1069*

WILLIAMSON, KEVIN, writer, producer, director; b. New Bern, N.C., Mar. 14, 1965; Exec. prodr. (TV series) Wasteland, 1999, Dawson's Creek, 1998, Glory Days, 2002; prodr. Scream 3, 1999; exec. prodr., writer Scream 2, 1997; writer The Faculty, 1998, I Know What You Did Last Summer, 1997, Scream, 1996 (Saturn award Acad. of Sci. Fiction, Horror and Fantasy Films); writer, dir. Teaching Mrs. Tingle, 1999; writer, co-exec. prodr. Halloween H20: Twenty Years Later, 1998; actor Dirty Money, 1994, (TV) Another World, 1990. Office: Geibelson Young & Co c/o Melody Young c/o Melody Young 16501 Ventura Blvd 304 Encino CA 91436*

WILLIAMSON, LAIRD, stage director, actor; b. Chgo., Dec. 13, 1937; s. Walter B. and Florence M. (Hemwell) W. BS in Speech, Northwestern U., 1960; MFA in Drama, U. Tex., 1965. Dir. Am. Conservatory Theatre, San Francisco, 1974-2002; stage dir. A Christmas Carol, 1976-81, The Matchmaker (tour of Soviet Union), 1976, A Month in the Country, 1978, The Visit, 1979, Pantagleize, 1980, Sunday in the Park, 1986, End of the World, 1988, Imaginary Invalid, 1990, Machinal, 1997, Long Day's Journey, 1999, Master Harold and the Boys, 2001, The Glass Menagerie, 2002; dir. Oreg. Shakespearean Festival, Ashland, 1972-2002, Western Opera Theatre, San Francisco, 1976-77, Theater Fest, Santa Maria, Calif., 1971-84, Denver Theater Ctr., 1981-2002, Bklyn. Acad. Music, 1981, Seattle Repertory Theatre, 1990, Old Globe Theatre, San Diego, 1977, 92, 94, 97; artistic dir. Theater Fest, Solvang, Calif., 1983-84, Intiman Theatre, 1986, 88, Berkeley Shakespeare Festival, 1990, Guthrie Theatre, 1991, 93, The Shakespeare Theatre, Washington, 1995, 96, 98; actor in Othello, 1973, Twelfth Night, 1974, Cyrano, 1974, Enrico IV, 1977, Judas, 1978, Hamlet, 1979, The Bacchae, 1981, Hamlet, 2000, Shrew, 2000. Mem. Soc. Stage Dirs. Actors Equity Assn., Screen Actors Guild.

WILLIAMSON, MARILYN LAMMERT, English educator, university administrator; b. Chgo., Sept. 6, 1927; d. Raymond Ferdinand and Edith Louise (Eisenbies) Lammert; m. Robert M. Williamson, Oct. 28, 1950 (div. Apr. 1973); 1 child, Timothy L.; m. James H. McKay, Aug. 15, 1974. BA, Vassar Coll., 1949; MA, U. Wis., 1950; PhD, Duke U., 1956. Lectr. Duke U., Durham, N.C., 1955-56, 58-59, N.C. State U., Raleigh, 1957-58, 61-62; asst. prof. Oakland U., Rochester, Mich., 1965-68, assoc. prof., 1968-72; prof. English Wayne State U., Detroit, 1972-90, Disting. prof. English, 1990-97, Disting. prof. emerita, 1997—, chmn. dept. English, 1972-74, 81-83, assoc. dean Coll. Liberal Arts, 1974-79, dir. women's studies, 1976-87, dep. provost, 1987-91, sr. v.p. for acad. affairs, provost, 1991-95, 98-200. Pres. Assn. Depts. English, 1976-77. Author: Infinite Variety, 1974, Patriarchy of Shakespeare's Comedies, 1986, British Women Writers 1650-1750, 1990; editor: Renaissance Studies, 1972, Female Poets of Great Britain, 1981; contbr. articles to profl. jours. Pres. LWV, Rochester, 1963-65. Recipient Detroit Disting. Svc. award, 1986, Faculty Recognition award Bd. Govs., Wayne State U., 1991; Bunting Inst. fellow, 1969-70, AAUW fellow, 1982-83, J.N. Keal fellow, 1985-86. Mem.: MLA (exec. coun. 1977—80, mem. editl. bd. 1992—94), Fed. State Humanities Coun. (bd. dirs. 1994—2001, chair 1997—99), Mich. Coun. Humanities (bd. dirs. 1988—2001, chair 1991—93), Shakespeare Assn. Am., Mich. Acad. (pres. 1978—79), Coll. English Assn., Renaissance Soc. Am. Democrat. Home: 2275 Oakway Dr West Bloomfield MI 48324-1855

WILLIAMSON, MARVEL, dean, sexologist, nursing administrator, author, speaker; b. Holton, Kans., Nov. 4, 1953; d. Thomas Arthur and Lois M. (Ihrig) Ansley; m. Paul Williamson, May 12, 1973; children: Marcus W., Sean W. BS in Nursing, Wichita State U., 1976; MS in Nursing, U. Ky., 1978; PhD, U. Iowa, 1987. Cert. sex educator. Prof. U. Iowa, Iowa City, 1980-89; dir. patient svcs. Ransom Meml. Hosp., Ottawa, Kans., 1989-91; dir. schs. nursing at Rolla, Sikeston and Kansas City Park Coll., Parkville, Mo., 1991-97; prof. Albany (Ga.) State U., 1997-99; sexologist Silver Spring, Md., 1999—2001; dean Kramer Sch. Nursing, Oklahoma City U., 2001—. Contbr. articles to profl. jours. Mem. ANA, Am. Assn. Sex Educators, Counselors and Therapists, Sigma Theta Tau. Address: 2501 N Blackwelder Oklahoma City OK 73106

WILLIAMSON, MICHAEL ALLEN, music educator; b. Davenport, Iowa, Oct. 20, 1940; s. Williford Taft and Anne Elizabeth Williamson; m. Judith Claire Sleeper, June 9, 1962; children: Michael James, Roy Allen. BS, Ithica Coll., Ithica, NY, 1958—63; masters music, S.U.N.Y. Stony Brook, Stony Brook, NY, 1970—71; Ph. D, NYU, New York. Music educator Vestal H.S., Vestal, NY, 1971—77, Connetguet H.S., Bohemia, 1978—96, Coll. of William and Mary, Williamsburg, Va., 1991—. Composer: (songs) (music) A Sweet For Brass, Speaking of Frank, A Minor Conspiracy. Recipient Best Band Dir., Sherburne Band Festival, 1973, Festivals of Music, 1996. Mem.: Internat. Assn. Jazz Edn., NYSSMA (all-state jazz chair 1994—95). Avocations: golf, sailing, reading. Home: 304 Reed Court Williamsburg VA 23185 Office: College of William and Mary Williamsburg VA 23183 Personal E-mail: michaelwilliamson6@juno.com.

WILLIAMSON, MICHAEL STANLEY, photojournalist, writer; b. Washington, June 8, 1957; s. Valerie Ann (Beatty) W.; m. Michelle Caroline Lambert, Mar. 14, 1992; children: Sophia Rose, Valerie Maria. Student, Am. River Coll., Sacramento, Calif., 1976, Contra Costa Coll., Richmond, Calif., 1977. Staff writer, photographer The West County Times, Pinole, Calif., 1975-77; staff photographer The Sacramento Bee, 1978-91; photojournalist-in-residence Western Ky. U., Bowling Green, 1991-92; staff photographer The Washington Post, 1993—. Documentary film prodr. ZDF, Mainz, Germany, 1984, 92; mem. bd. Who Cares mag., Washington, 1993—. Author: Journey to Nowhere, 1985, And Their Children After Them, 1989 (Pulitzer prize 1990), The Last Great American Hobo, 1993; freelance photographs pub. in various nat. and internat. mags., including Life, Rolling Stone, Nat. Geog. Soc., The Nation, Time, Newsweek, Sports Illustrated, Am. Photographer, Der Spiegel, others; over 100 appearances on TV and radio. Named Photographer of Yr., No. Short Course in Photography, 1995, 2001, So. Short Course in Photography, 1996, San Francisco Bay Area Press Photographers Assn., 1989; recipient Nikon World Understanding Spl. Recognition award, 1983, Pulitzer prize in feature photography for coverage of Kosovo conflict, 2000. Mem. Nat. Press Photographers Assn. (Kodak Crystal Eagle award 1994, Photographer of Yr. 1995), White House News Photographers Assn. (Photographer of Yr. 2000), Fgn. Corrs. Club. Democrat. Avocations: playing guitar, car travel, collecting Americana and books. Office: The Washington Post 1150 15th St NW Washington DC 20071-0002

WILLIAMSON, NORMA BETH, adult education educator; b. Hamilton, Tex., Nov. 2, 1939; d. Joseph Lawrence and Gladys (Wilkins) Drake; m. Stuart Williamson, Mar. 14, 1981. BA, Baylor U., 1962; MA, Tex. A&M U., 1969; postgrad., Tex. Tech. U., 1976-80, CIDOC, Cuernavaca, Mex., 1973, 75. Instr. English, Tex. Southmost Coll., Brownsville, 1969-81; sr. English tchr. The Woodlands McCulloch H.S., 1981-83; lectr. in English Sam Houston State U., 1983-85; coll. prep. tchr. Tex. Dept. Corrections, 1985-95; ret., 1995. Lectr. Spanish Sam Houston State U.; faculty advisor Circle K, Sam Houston State. Vol., reading mentor Big Bros./Big Sisters; pres. S.W. Dist. Unitarian Universalist Assn., 1982-86. Mem. AAUW (pres. Huntsville br. 1995-96), Huntsville Kiwanis (pres. 1999-2000), Walker County Geneal. Soc. (editor newsletter), Delta Kappa Gamma, Alpha Mu (pres. 1980-81), Upsilon (pres. 1994-96). Home: 794A Round Prairie Rd Bedias TX 77831-3238 E-mail: betwil@aol.com., fol.nbw@shsu.edu.

WILLIAMSON, OLIVER EATON, economics and law educator; b. Superior, Wis., Sept. 27, 1932; s. Scott Gilbert and Lucille S. (Dunn) W.; m. Dolores Jean Celeni, Sept. 28, 1957; children: Scott, Tamara, Karen, Oliver, Dean. SB, MIT, 1955; MBA, Stanford U., 1960; PhD, Carnegie-Mellon U., 1963; PhD (hon.), Norwegian Sch. Econs. and Bus. Adminstrn., 1986; PhD in Econ. Sci. (hon.), Hochschule St. Gallen, Switzerland, 1987, Groningen U., 1989, Turku Sch. Econs. & Bus. Admin, St. Petersburg, Russia, 1996, HEC, Paris, 1997, Copenhagen Bus. Sch., 2000, U. Chile, 2000. Project. engr. U.S. Govt., 1955-58; asst. prof. econs. U. Calif., Berkeley, 1963-65; assoc. prof. U. Pa., Phila., 1965-68, prof., 1968-83, Charles and William L. Day prof. econs. and social sci., 1977-83; Gordon B. Tweedy prof. econs. law and orgn. Yale U., 1983-88; Transam. prof. of bus., econs. and law U. Calif., Berkeley, 1988-94, Edgar F. Kaiser prof. bus. adminstrn., prof. econs. and law, 1994—. Spl. econ. asst. to asst. atty. gen. for antitrust Dept. Justice, 1966—67; dir. Ctr. for Study of Orgnl. Innovation, U. Pa., 1976—83; cons. in field. Author: The Economics of Discretionary Behavior, 1964, Corporate Control and Business Behavior, 1970, Markets and Hierarchies, 1975, The Economic Institutions of Capitalism, 1985, Economic Organization, 1986, Antitrust Economics, 1987, The Mechanisms of Governance, 1996; assoc. editor Bell. Jour. Econs., 1973-74, editor, 1975-82; co-editor Jour. Law, Econs. and Orgn., 1983—. Fellow Ctr. for Advanced Study in Behavioral Scis., 1977-78; Guggenheim fellow, 1977-78; Fulbright scholar, 1999; Am. Acad. Arts and Scis. fellow, 1983; recipient Alexander Henderson award Carnegie-Mellon U., 1962, Alexander von Humboldt Rsch. prize, 1987, Irwin award Acad. of Mgmt., 1988, John von Newmann prize, 1999. Fellow Econometric Soc., Am. Acad. Polit. and Social Sci.; mem. NAS, Internat. Soc. for New Instnl. Econs. (pres. 1999-2001), Am. Econ. Assn. (v.p. 2000-01), Am. Law and Econs. Assn. (pres. 1997-98), Western Econ. Assn. (pres. 1999-2000). Office: U Calif Dept Econs Berkeley CA 94720-0001

WILLIAMSON, PETER DAVID, lawyer; b. Houston, Oct. 13, 1944; s. Sam and Sophie Ann (Kaplan) W.; m. Patricia Golemon; children: Heather, Amber, Asia, Ginger. BA, U. Ill., 1966; JD, U. Tex., 1969. Bar: Tex. 1969, U.S. Supreme Ct. 1974, U.S. Ct. Appeals (4th, 5th, 6th, 8th, 9th, 10th, 11th and D.C. cirs.); lic. comml. pilot. Pvt. practice, Houston, 1971—. Founder IMMLAW, The Nat. Consortium of Immigration Law Firms. Mem. Am. Immigration Lawyers Assn. (pres. 1994-95). Home: 2417 Branard St Houston TX 77098-2213 Office: 500 Jefferson Ste 2040 Houston TX 77002 E-mail: pwilliamson@pdwlaw.com. *I do not believe in the existence of national boundaries. The philosophy of my practice of the law is to help my clients achieve the ability to pass freely through such artificial political barriers.*

WILLIAMSON, RAMONA DIANE, special education educator; b. Baton Rouge, Apr. 20, 1962; d. John Thomas and Virginia (Harmeyer) W. BA, Nicholls State U., 1983; MEd, U. New Orleans, 1994, postgrad., 1994, 2000. Mid/moderate spl. edn. tchr. St. Bernard Parish Pub. Schs., Chalmette, La., 1988-96; grad. asst. U. New Orleans, 1996-97. Mem. vis. com. So. Assn. Colls. and Schs., La., 1994-98; new tchr. mentor St. Bernard Parish Pub. Schs., 1997—; presenter internat. profl. confs., U.S., Australia. Contbr. articles to profl. jours. Vol. Algiers Point Assn., New Orleans, 1987—; guide Preservation Resource Ctr./Live in a Landmark Program, New Orleans, 1990-98; vol., neighborhood coord., runner, liaison Christmas in October, New Orleans, 1993—. Recipient Tchr. of Yr. award Wal-Mart Found., 1999; La. State Dept. Edn. grantee, 1991-2001, La. Fedn. Coun. Exceptional Children grantee. Mem. La. Fedn. Coun. for Exceptional Children, St. Bernard Coun. Internat. Reading Assn., Kappa Delta Pi. Republican. Presbyterian. Avocations: travel, gardening, cooking, reading. Home: 329 Alix St New Orleans LA 70114-2305 Office: CF Rowley Elem Sch 49 Madison Ave Chalmette LA 70043-4429 E-mail: ramonaw413@aol.com.

WILLIAMSON, RICHARD CARDINAL, physicist; b. Minocqua, Wis., Sept. 10, 1939; s. Lyman Olaf and Edna (Cardinal) W.; m. Christine Bauer, Sept. 2, 1961; children— Kari, Meagan, Heidi, Ryan BS in Physics, MIT, 1961, PhD in Physics, 1966. Staff physicist NASA Electronics Research Ctr., Cambridge, Mass., 1965-70; staff mem. and assoc. group leader MIT Lincoln Lab., Lexington, 1970-80, group leader applied physics, electrooptic device rsch., 1980-95, sr. staff electro-optical devices and materials group, 1995—. Contbr. articles to jours., chpts. to books; patentee in field Fellow IEEE (Centennial award 1984, Sonics and Ultrasonics Achievement award 1985); mem. IEEE, Am. Phys. Soc., Optical Soc. Am., Sigma Xi. Methodist. Home: 21 Pendleton Rd Sudbury MA 01776-1612 Office: 244 Wood St Rm C317 Lexington MA 02421-6426 E-mail: williamson@ll.mit.edu.

WILLIAMSON, RICHARD HALL, association executive; b. Canton, N.C., July 29, 1940; s. James Eustace and Gwendolyn (Nevada) H.; m. Julia Draper Brown, Nov. 7, 1965 (div. Jan. 1981); children: Shawn Nicol, Kevin Carson; m. Janie E. Shaheen, Nov. 18, 1998. BS in Physics, N.C. State U., 1962, MS in Nuclear Engring., 1970, postgrad., 1972. Instr. N.C. State U., Raleigh, 1968-72; chief, energy systems analysis AEC, Washington, 1972-75; asst. dir., energy analysis U.S. Energy R & D Adminstrn., 1975-77; dir., program analysis U.S. Dept. Energy, 1977-80, dir., policy devel., 1980-84, dep. asst. sec. for internat. affairs, 1984-94; dep. exec. dir. U.S. Energy Assn., 1995-99. Bd. dirs. Houston World Energy Congress Inc., 1994-99; chmn. Worth Assocs. Inc., Flint Hill, Va., 1998—. Author: A Group Strategy for Energy Research, Development and Demonstration, 1980; contbr. articles to jours. in field. Football ofcl. Atlantic Coast Conf., Greensboro, N.C., 1980—, Rose Bowl, Pasadena, Calif., 1995; treas. Sigma Alpha Mu Endowment Fund, 1994—, Sigma Alpha Mu Found., 1989—; treas. St. Simmons Island Newcomers Club, 2001—. 1st lt. U.S. Army, 1962-64; col. USAR, 1964-93. NSF fellow, 1964-65; AEC fellow, 1965-68; recipient Outstanding alumnus award IFC, N.C. State U., 1971, Presdl. Rank award U.S. Dept. Energy, 1990, Atlantic Coast Conf. Svc. to Football Officiating award, 2000. Mem. Sigma Alpha Mu (nat. pres. 1984-86), Tau Beta Pi, Phi Kappa Phi, Omicron Delta Kappa, Sigma Pi Sigma, Pi Mu Epsilon. Republican. Methodist. Avocations: stamp collecting, tennis, golf, skiing. Home: 906 Champney Saint Simons GA 31522-5464 Office: Worth Assocs PO Box 456 205 E Washington St Flint Hill VA 22627

WILLIAMSON, RICHARD SALISBURY, ambassador; b. Evanston, Ill., May 9, 1949; s. Donald G. and Marion (Salisbury) W.; m. Jane Thatcher, Aug. 25, 1973; children: Elizabeth Jean, Craig Salisbury, Richard Middleton. AB with honors, Princeton U., 1971; JD, U. Va., 1974. Bar: Ill. bar 1974, D.C. bar 1975. Legis. counsel, adminstrv. asst. to Congressman Philip M. Crane of Ill., 1974-76; assoc. firm Winston & Strawn, Washington, 1977-80, ptnr., 1980; asst. to Pres. for intergovtl. affairs, Washington, also assoc. dir. President's Task Force on Regulatory Relief, 1981-83; U.S. ambassador Vienna, 1983-85; sr. v.p., corp. and internat. relations Beatrice Cos., Inc., Chgo., 1985-86; ptnr. Mayer, Brown & Platt, 1986—2001; asst. sec. of state internat. orgn. affairs U.S. Dept. State, Washington, 1988-89; alt. repr. to the U.N. for special polit. affairs U.S. Dept. State , 2002—. Rep. UN Orgns., Vienna, 1983-85; dep. ref. with rank of ambassador IAEA. Editor: Trade & Economic Growth, 1993, United States Foreign Policy and the United Nations System, 1996; co-editor: (with Paul Laxalt) A Changing America: Conservatives View the 80's From the United States Senate, 1980; author: Reagan's Federalism: His Efforts to Decentralize Government, 1990, The United Nations: A Place of Promise and of Mischief, 1991, Disorder in the New World, 1997, Seeking Firm Footing: America in the World in the New Centur7, 2001. Chmn. Ill. Rep. Party, 1999-2002. Republican. Office: U.S. Mission to the U.N. 799 United Nations Plaza New York NY 10017-3505*

WILLIAMSON, ROBERT CLIFFORD, sociology educator; b. Los Angeles, Apr. 25, 1916; s. Bert Alfred and Mary Ellen (Kenyon) W.; m. Virginia Mabel Lorenzini, Apr. 11, 1953; children: Lawrence, Eric. BA, UCLA, 1938, MA, 1940; PhD, U. So. Calif., 1951. Prof. psychology and sociology Los Angeles City Coll., 1946-60; Fulbright prof. Nat. U. Colombia, Bogota, 1961-62; prof. sociology Lehigh U., Bethlehem, Pa., 1963-84; Fulbright prof. Cath. U. of Chile, Santiago, 1967-68; adj. prof. sociology Lehigh U., 1984—. Smith-Mundt prof. Nat. U. El Salvador, San Salvador, 1958-59; vis. assoc. prof. Haverford (Pa.) Coll., 1962-63; cons. Peace Corps, Washington, 1962-65. Author: Minority Languages and Bilingualism, 1991, Early Retirement Promises and Pitfalls, 1992, Latin American Societies in Transition, 1997, (with S. Sargent) Social Psychology, 1958, 2d edit., 1966, 3d edit., 1982, Marriage and Family Relations, 1966, 2d edit., 1972; editor: (with G. Seward) Sex Roles in Changing Society, 1970; contbr. articles to profl. jours. Mem. Latin-Am. Com., Population Com., Am. Friends Service Com., 1962-71; bd. advisors Family Cons. Ctr., Bethlehem, 1964-70; chmn. pub. affairs com. Planned Parenthood of Lehigh Valley, 1984-87. Served as sgt. USAF, 1942-45. Research grantee Social Sci. Research Council, 1960, Konrad Adenauer Found., 1976, Andrew Mellon Found., 1977, Rockefeller Found., 1984. Mem. Am. Sociol. Assn., Am. Psychol. Assn., Latin Am. Studies Assn., Sierra Club. Democrat. Mem. Unitarian Ch. Home: 218 E Market St Bethlehem PA 18018-6211 Office: Lehigh U Dept Sociology and Anthropology Bethlehem PA 18015 E-mail: RW01@lehigh.edu.

WILLIAMSON, ROBERT ELMORE, engineering educator; b. York County, S.C., Nov. 8, 1937; s. Charles Edward Jr. and Margaret Gladys (Elmore) W.; m. Eva Evelyn Simpson, June 27, 1964; children: Margaret Edye, Robert Elmore Jr. BS, Clemson U., 1959, MS, 1964; PhD, Miss. State U., 1972. Registered profl. engr., Ga. Rsch. assoc. Miss. State U., Starkville, 1966-71; asst. prof. agrl. engring. U. Ga., Tifton, 1971-78; assoc. prof. Clemson (S.C.) U., 1978-81, prof. biosys. engring., 1981—. Co-inventor bulb, root and leafy vegetable harvester, improved harvesting machinery, multi-purpose horticultural tractor; contbr., co-contbr. numerous articles to scholarly jours.; contbr., co-contbr. numerous articles to sci. jours. Asst. scoutmaster Clemson area Boy Scouts Am., 1972-78, 80—. 1st lt. USAF, 1959-62. Recipient Silver Beaver award Boy Scouts Am., 1999. Mem. Am. Soc. AGrl. Engrs., Phi Kappa Phi (Clemson chpt. pres. 1984-85), Gamma Sigma Delta, Alpha Zeta, Sigma Xi. Presbyterian. Avocations: hunting, camping, backpacking, woodworking, tennis. Home: 303 Princess Grace Ave Clemson SC 29631-1215 Office: Agrl & Biol Engring McAdams Hall Clemson U Clemson SC 29631

WILLIAMSON, ROBERT THOMAS, educational administrator; b. Detroit, Nov. 6, 1946; s. Robert Thomas and Sarah Jane (Simmons) W.; m. Jean Thompson Simmonds, Aug. 23, 1969; children: Robert Thomas III, Josephine Simmonds, Katherine Grace, Rebecca Jean. BA, Coll. Wooster, 1968; JD, U. Balt., 1975. Officer USN, 1968-70; coord. new products legal dept. McCormick & Co., Inc., Hunt Valley, Md., 1970-76; dir. econ. devel./tech. asst. ctr. SUNY, Plattsburgh, 1976-82; v.p. external rels. Clarkson U., Potsdam, N.Y., 1982-87, exec. v.p., 1987-97; pres. Westminster Coll., New Wilmington, Pa., 1997—. Bd. dirs. Jamison Hosp., New Castle, Pa., 1998—, Hoyt Inst., New Castle, 1997—. Avocations: golf, tennis, outdoor activities.

WILLIAMSON, RONALD THOMAS, lawyer; b. Paterson, N.J., Nov. 12, 1948; s. Thomas Sim and Jessie Carnegie (Sandilands) W.; m. Nancy Anne Hough, June 13, 1982; children: Kate Elizabeth, Brad Francis Thomas. BA, Rutgers U., 1970; JD cum laude, Widener U., 1975. Bar: Pa. 1976, U.S. Dist. Ct. (ea. dist.) Pa. 1976, U.S. Supreme Ct. 1979, U.S. Ct. Appeals (3d cir.) 1980. Assoc. Modell, Pincus, Hahn and Reich, Phila., 1976-77; asst. dist. atty., chief of appeals County of Montgomery, Norristown, Pa., 1977-85; sr. dep. atty. gen. appeals and legal svcs. sect. Pa. Atty. Gen., Harrisburg, 1997—, 1997—. Instr. search and seizure Southeastern Tng. Ctr., Pa. State Police, Worcester, 1979-85; legal instr. Montgomery County C.C., Whitpain, Pa., 1984. Contbr. to profl. publs. Bd. dirs. Denbigh Group Foster Home, Bridgeport, Pa., 1979-83, pres., 1984; mem. Cen. Montgomery Optimist Club, Norristown, 1980-81. Mem. Pa. Bar Assn., Montgomery County Bar Assn. (chmn. appellate ct. practice com., bd. dirs.). Republican. Presbyterian. Avocations: tennis, squash, sailing, triathlon, reading. Office: Pa Office Atty Gen 2490 Blvd of the Generals Norristown PA 19403-5234 E-mail: rwilliamson@attorneygeneral.gov.

WILLIAMSON, RUSHTON MAROT, JR. information technology project manager; b. Evanston, Ill., Aug. 4, 1948; s. Rushton Marot and Marjorie Adelaide (Woods) W.; m. Katherine Calvert Watson, Dec. 17, 1977; children: Marot Roelker, Alec Armstrong. BS, Utah State U., 1971; MS, U. So. Calif., 1982, Capital Coll., 1994. Project mgmt. profl., 1987, acquisition career field level III: comms.-computer sys. and program mgmt., CIO cert. Commd. 2d lt. USMCR, 1971, advanced to capt., 1976; mem. tech. staff Electrospace Systems Inc., Arlington, Va., 1982-86; project mgr. Def. Info. Systems Agy., Washington, 1986—. Editor: PMP Certification Workbook, 1989; contbr. articles to profl. jours. Vice chmn. Nat. Debutante Cotillion, Washington, 1976-77, mem. married com., 1980-85, chmn. married com., 1985-93, sponsor 1994—; mem. Boy Scouts Am., 1979-84, 95—, asst. scoutmaster, 1995-96, com. chmn., 1996-2000, scoutmaster, 2001—, dist. chmn. advancement, 1999-2002, staff nat. jamboree, 1997, 2001, mem. high coun. adventure com., 2000—; Traffic Action Com., Rockville, 1987-88, Armed Forces Inaugural Com., 1977; mem.-at-large Potomac Woods Citizens Assn., Rockville, Md., 1984-87, 90-92, v.p., 1988-89; leader Girl Scouts Am., 1996-98. Recipient Dist. award of merit Boy Scouts Am., 2001, God and Svc. award Boy Scouts Am., 2002. Mem. Project Mgmt. Inst. (Washington chpt. treas. 1984, v.p. 1985, pres. 1988-89, internat. chmn. cert. rev. com. 1988-91, cert. test com. 1988-90, adv. 1990-95, chpt. trustee 1996—, founding mem. Balt. chpt. 1995, chmn. mktg. com. 1990-91, advisor cert. bd. 1991-94, asst. v.p. mktg. gov. 1995-97, disting. contbn. award 1991), Nat. Coun. Acquisition Professionalism, Nat. Contract Mgmt. Assn. (project mgmt. com. 1993-94), Canoe Cruisers Assn. Washington, Blue Ridge Voyageurs (bd. dirs. 1988), Appalachian Trail Conf. Methodist. Avocations: canoeing, flat & whitewater canoeing instructing, camping, hiking. Home: 1583 Kimblewick Rd Rockville MD 20854-6152 E-mail: willia1r@ncr.disa.mil.

WILLIAMSON, SAMUEL RUTHVEN, JR. historian, emeritus university president; b. Bogalusa, La., Nov. 10, 1935; s. Samuel Ruthven and Frances Mitchell (Page) W.; m. Joan Chaffe Andress, Dec. 30, 1961; children: George Samuel, Treeby Andress, Thaddeus Miller. BA, Tulane U., 1958; AM, Harvard U., 1960, PhD, 1966, grad. advanced mgmt. program, 1986; hon. degree, Furman U., Va. Theol. Sem., Centre Coll. Asst. prof. U.S. Mil. Acad., 1963-66; instr. history Harvard U., 1966-68, asst. prof., 1968-72, Allston Burr sr. tutor, 1968-72, asst. to dean of Harvard Coll., 1969-70; rsch. assoc. Inst. Politics, faculty assoc. Ctr. for Internat. Affairs, 1971-72; mem. faculty J.F. Kennedy Sch. Govt., 1971-72; assoc. prof. history U. N.C., Chapel Hill, 1972-74, prof., 1974-88, dean Coll. Arts and Scis., 1977-85, provost univ., 1984-88; pres., vice chancellor U. of South, Sewanee, Tenn., 1988-2000, vice chancellor emeritus, prof. history, 2000—, Robert M. Ayres Jr. Disting. Univ. Prof., 2001—. Cons. Historian's Office, Office of Sec. Def., 1974-76; vis. fellow Churchill Coll., 1976-77; mem. vis. com. Harvard Coll., 1986-92; dir. Research Triangle Inst., 1984-88; trustee N.C. Sch. Sci. and Math., 1985-88, Day Found., 1990-93; mem. bd. visitors Air U., 1994—. Author: The Politics of Grand Strategy: Britain and France Prepare for War, 1904-1914, 1969, 2nd edit., 1990; co-author: The Origins of U.S. Nuclear Strategy, 1945-53, 1993; editor: The Origins of a Tragedy: July 1914, 1981; co-editor: Essays on World War I: Origins and Prisoners of War, 1983, Austria-Hungary and the Origins of the First World War, 1991; Am. editor: War and Soc. Newsletter, 1973-88. Mem. cen. com. Morehead Found., 1978-93; vice chmn. bd. visitors Air U., 1996-98, chmn. bd. visitors, 1998-2000. Capt. U.S. Army, 1963-66. Fulbright scholar U. Edinburgh, 1958-59, Woodrow Wilson Ctr. scholar, Washington, 2002; Woodrow Wilson fellow, 1958-63, Danforth fellow, 1958-63, Nat. Endowment Humanities fellow, 1976-77; Ford Found. grantee, 1976; fellow Nat. Humanities Ctr., 1983. Mem. Am. Hist. Assn. (George Louis Beer prize 1970), Internat. Inst. Strategic Studies, Nat. Assn. Colls. and Univs. (vice chmn., chmn. bd. dirs. 1993-95). Democrat. Episcopalian. Home: PO Box 837 Sewanee TN 37375-0837 Office: U of South duPont Libr Sewanee TN 37383-1000 E-mail: swilliam@sewanee.edu.

WILLIAMSON, STANLEY G. management consultant, educator; b. Shreveport, La., Feb. 5, 1950; s. Earl G. Williamson Jr. and Alice Cochran Williamson. BS, La. Tech U., Ruston, 1968—72; MS in Healthcare Adminstrn., Trinity U., San Antonio, Tex., 1973—75; PhD, U. No. Tex., Denton, 1988—90. Sales rep. Williamson Motors, Vivian, La., 1965—71; fishing guide Yellowstone Park Co., Gardner, Mont., 1972; v.p. Willis-Knighton Med. Ctr., Shreveport, La., 1975—87; adminstr. North Claiborne Hosp., Haynesville, 1987—88; assoc. prof. of mgmt. U. of La., Monroe, 1990—. Presenter U. of La. at Monroe Ctr. for Managerial and Profl. Devel., Monroe, 1993—2002. Co-author: Fundamentals of Strategic Planning for Healthcare Organizations, 1997. Named a Scott Endowed Prof. in Tchg. Excellence, U. of La. at Monroe, 1999—2002. Mem.: Tex. Hosp. Assn., Am. Hosp. Assn., SW Acad. Mgmt., The Acad. of Mgmt. Republican. Avocations: hunting, fishing, golf, travel, reading. Home: 126 Hillcrest Ave West Monroe LA 71291 Office: Univ of La at Monroe Dept Mgmt and Mktg Monroe LA 71209 Office Fax: 318-342-1209. Business E-Mail: mmwilliamson@ulm.edu.

WILLIAMSON, SUSAN, mathematician, educator; b. Boston, Dec. 29, 1936; d. Richard Phillip and Mary Elizabeth Williamson. AB, Radcliffe Coll., Cambridge, Mass., 1958; MA, PhD, Brandeis U., Waltham, Mass., 1963. Instr. Cardinal Cushing Coll., Brookline, Mass., 1962—63; asst. prof. Boston Coll., Chestnut Hill, 1963—64, Regis Coll., Weston, 1965—67, assoc. prof., 1967—71, acad. dean, 1973—75, prof., 1971—2002, prof. emerita, 2002—. Reviewer Math. Revs., Ann Arbor, 1968—. Contbr. articles to profl. jours. Mem.: AAUP, Math. Assn. Am., Am. Math. Soc. Avocation: Landscape drawing. Home: 37 Hagen Rd Newton Centre MA 02459 Personal E-mail: susanwilliamson@compuserve.com.

WILLIAMSON, THOMAS ARNOLD, publishing company executive; b. Sagamore, Pa., Oct. 4, 1939; s. Thomas and Mabel (Kennedy) W.; m. Kathryn Steiner White, Mar. 1, 1980; 1 child, Thomas J. Grad., Phillips Exeter Acad., 1957; AB, Harvard U., 1961. With Harcourt Brace & Co., N.Y.C., 1962-95, editor-in-chief coll. dept., 1971-76, dep. dir. coll. dept., 1976-77, sr. v.p. Academic Press, Inc., 1977-80, exec. v.p. Academic Press, Inc., 1981-82, v.p. Orlando, Fla., 1986-88, sr. v.p., 1988-95; pres. The Psychol. Corp., San Antonio, 1982-88; v.p. Holt Rinehart & Winston Harcourt Brace, 1989-95, pres. Sch. Pubs., 1989-93, pres. Ednl. Devel. Group, 1993-94; pres. The Learning Initiative, Austin, Tex., 1994—, T. Williamson Assocs., Inc., Austin, 1995—, Focused Learning, Ltd., Austin, 1998—2002. Co-chmn. vis. com. to psychology dept. U. Tex., Austin, 1986-89. Mem.: Town and Gown Club, Westwood Country Club, Harvard Club N.Y.C. Home: 5 Cheverly Ct Austin TX 78738-1511 Office: T Williamson Assoc Inc PO Box 340097 Austin TX 78734-0097

WILLIAMSON, THOMAS MICHAEL, pastor, civil servant; b. N.Y.C., Jan. 4, 1954; s. Hassan and Dorothy (Romlein) Abtahi. BA, Ill. Wesleyan U., 1974; ThM, Bethany Theol. Seminary, 1987, PhD, 1989. Civil servant U.S. Dept. Housing and Urban Devel., Chgo., 1979—. Editor Illinois-Indiana Missionary Baptist newspaper, 1995—; asst. pastor Metro. Bapt. Tabernacle, Chgo., 1997-2000. Author: Universal Church Theory, 1987, Waldenses Were Independent Baptists, 1996. Mem. Bapt. Missionary Assn. Ill. and Ind. (clk. 1995—), Bapt. Missionary Assn. Am. Home: 3131 S Archer Ave Chicago IL 60608-6223

WILLIAMSON, VIKKI LYN, university official, financial executive; b. Huntington, W.Va., June 30, 1956; d. Ernest E. and Wanda C. (Cole) W. BA in Secondary Edn., English, Temple U., 1978; postgrad. in Acctg. and Fin., U. Cin., 1984-86. CPA, Ohio; cert. tchr., Tenn., Ohio. Tchr. Springfield Christian Acad., Tenn., 1978-79; acctg. asst. Children's Hosp. Med. Ctr., Cin., 1979-84; asst. dir. fin. svcs. U. Cin. Med. Ctr., 1984-85, dir. fin. svcs., 1985-88, dir. fin. and adminstrn., 1988-91, dep. dir., CFO, 1991-2000; chief fin. adminstrv.

officer Antioch U McGregor, Yellow Springs, Ohi, 2000—. Bd. dirs. Contemporary Dance Theatre, 1987-90. Bd. dirs. Habitat for Humanity-Hamilton, 1991-94, v.p., 1991, pres., 1992; v.p. PTA, 1997-98, pres., 1989-99, treas. 1999—. Mem. AICPA, Healthcare Fin. Mgmt. Assn., Am. Assn. Blood Banks, Ohio Assn. Blood Banks (fin. com. 1986-90, treas. 1991-97), Am.'s Blood Ctrs. (fin. com. 1991-2000, alt. trustee 1991-2000), Assn. Women Adminstrs. (fin. com. 1987-90), Assn. Mid-Level Adminstrs. (bd. dirs. 1987-90), Alpha Epsilon Theta, Beta Gamma Sigma, Delta Mu Delta. Office: Antioch U McGregor 800 Livermore St Yellow Springs OH 45387-1608 E-mail: vwilliamson@mcgregor.edu.

WILLIAMSON, WILLIAM PAUL, JR. journalist; b. Des Moines, Mar. 30, 1929; s. William Paul and Florence Alice (Dawson) W.; m. Vania Torres Nogueira, Nov. 27, 1959; children— Mary Liz, Jon Thadeus, Margaret Ann (Mrs. Cesar Rocha). Student, Mex. City Coll., 1952, U. Havanna, 1955; BA, U. No. Iowa, 1953; MA, U. Iowa, 1954. Editor Brazilian Bus., Rio de Janeiro, 1958-60; mng. ptnr. Editora Mory Ltd., 1960-79; editor Brazil Herald, 1960-80; exec. dir. Inter Am. Press Assn., Miami, Fla., 1981-94, hon. life mem., mem. adv. coun., 1994—, dir., 1966-80, chmn. awards com., 1975-80. Solo navigator 1st passage Madeira Island, Portugal-Madeira Island, Brazil, 1994-95. Editor for Brazil, Fodor's South America, 1970-79; contbr. articles to various newspapers and mags. Pres. Am. Soc., Rio de Janeiro, 1968; bd. dirs. Instituto Brasil-Estados Unidos, Rio de Janeiro, 1977-80, Am. C. of C. for Brazil, Rio de Janeiro, 1964-68; pres. Seven Seas Cruising Assn., 1997-2000, rear commodore, 2000—. Served with USMC, 1946-48. Decorated Order of Rio Branco (Brazil); recipient Citizen of Rio de Janeiro award State Legislature, 1975; Hon. Carioca award O Globo Newspaper, Rio de Janeiro, 1972; Ralph Greenburg award Am. Soc. Rio de Janeiro, 1977; Outstanding Svc. to Freedom of Expression and Newspapers awards Internat. Fedn. of Newspaper Pubs. and Internat. Assn. of Broadcasting, 1994; Benemeritous Citizen award Mcpl. Legislature, Itaquai, Brazil, 1995. Mem. Am. Soc. Assn. Execs., South Fla. Soc. Assn. Execs. (pres. 1987), Soc. Profl. Journalists, Overseas Press Club Am., Rio Yacht Club, Ilha da Madeira Yacht Club, Kappa Tau Alpha. Home: 3051 NE 47th Ct Apt 204 Fort Lauderdale FL 33308-5304

WILLIAMSON, WILLIAM SIMPSON, military science educator; b. Rahway, N.J., Dec. 20, 1936; s. John Graham and Margaret (Simpson) W.; m. Barbara Sherer, Dec. 22, 1962; children: Scott Graham, Michael Cameron. BS, U.S. Naval Acad., 1962; MS, U. So. Calif., 1976; MPA, Nova Southeastern U., 1978, DPA, 1980; MA, Georgetown U., 1980. Commd. ensign USN, 1962, advanced through grades to capt., 1983, active, 1962—70, USNR, 1970—92; ret. USN, 1992; prodn. dir. Naval Sci. and Tech. Intelligence Ctr., Washington, 1970-74; staff officer Def. Intelligence Agy., 1974-76, chief naval warfare, 1980-91, staff dir., sci. adv. bd., 1992-95; prin. staff Office of Sec. of Navy, 1976-79; chmn. intelligence dept. Joint Mil. Intelligence Coll., 1995-2000, lectr. sci. and tech. intelligence, 2000—. Mem. Brit. Mensa. Republican. Avocations: distance running, diving. Office: Def Intelligency Agy ATTN OSI-5 Washington DC 20340-5100

WILLIAMS-TIMS, LILLIE ALTHEA, distribution administrator, genealogist, preservationist; b. Laurens, S.C., Aug. 17, 1951; d. Hunter Nathenial and Alma Sue Peal (hunter) W.; m. Benny Woodrow Tims, Sept. 1, 1973 (div. 1987); 1 child, Eltaro. Assoc. in Gen. Bus., Piedmont Tech. Coll., Greenwood, S.C., 1988. Cert. arbitrator. Weaver Delta Woodside Mills, Fountain Inn, S.C., 1981-87; seamstress, data entry clk. Josten's Cap and Gown, Laurens, 1987-88; supr. Wal-Mart Distbn. Ctr., 1988-2000. Bd. dirs. Main St. Laurens USA, Inc. Asst. supt. Flat Ruff Bapt. Ch. Sch., Laurens, 1989-91; pres. Young Woman Assn. for Flat Ruff Bapt. Ch., 1991-97; founder, pres. African-Am. Hist. Found., Laurens.; arbitrator 8th Jud. Cir. Juvenile Arbitration Program, Abbeville, Greenwood, Laurens and Newberry counties, S.C. Mem. Nat. Coun. Negro Women, Inc. (life), S.C. Geneal. Soc. (sec. Laurens chpt. 1992-95), S.C. African Am. Heritage Coun. (assoc.). Democrat. Avocations: reading poetry and adventure books, hiking. Home: 600 Anderson Dr Laurens SC 29360 E-mail: lillietims@aol.com.

WILLIAMS-WENNELL, KATHI, human resources consultant; b. Danville, Pa., Sept. 22, 1955; d. Raymond Gerald and Julia Dolores (Higgins) Williams; m. Mark Kevin Wennell, Apr. 3, 1982; children: Ryan Christopher, Lauren Ashley. BA, Immaculata Coll., 1977; MEd, Pa. State U., State College, 1978. Cert. rehabilitation counselor, Pa. From project dir. to coord. devel. activities Community Interactions, Blue Bell, Pa., 1978-83; from mgmt. trainee to coord. coll. recruiting and rels. Meridian Bancorp, Inc., Reading, 1983-86, mgmt. recruiter, 1986-88, compensation analyst, 1989-93, recruiter, spl. projects, 1993-96; cons. Chet Mosteller & Assocs., 1996—. Cons. Norristown (Pa.) Life Ctr., 1981; instr. Immaculata (Pa.) Coll., 1981-83, Alvernia Coll., Reading, 1988-89. Meridian campaign coord. United Way Berks County, Reading, 1985. Named Recruiter of Yr. LaSalle U., Phila., 1986; recipient Excellence in Programming award Nat. Assn. Bank Women, Pa., 1986. Mem. Soc. Human Resources Mgmt. Republican. Roman Catholic. Avocations: walking, golf, tennis, piano, reading. Home: 69 S Hampton Dr Wyomissing PA 19610-3108

WILLIE, CHARLES VERT, sociology educator; b. Dallas, Oct. 8, 1927; s. Louis James and Carrie (Sykes) W.; m. Mary Susannah Conklin, Mar. 31, 1962; children: Sarah Susannah, Martin Charles, James Theodore. BA, Morehouse Coll., 1948, DHL (hon.), 1983; MA, Atlanta U., 1949; PhD, Syracuse U., 1957, DHL (hon.), 1992; DD (hon.), Gen. Sem., 1974; DHL (hon.), Berkeley Div. Sch., Yale U., 1972, R.I. Coll., 1983, Johnson C. Smith U., Charlotte N.C., 1991; MA (hon.), Harvard U., 1974; DL (hon.), Framingham (Mass.) State Coll., 1992; DHL (hon.), Franklin Pierce Coll., Rindge, N.H., 1996, Haverford Coll., 2000; D of Engring. Tech. (hon.), Wentworth Inst. Tech., 1996. Instr. to asst. prof. sociology Syracuse (N.Y.) U., 1952-63, assoc. prof., 1964-67, prof., 1968-74, chmn. dept. sociology, 1967-71, v.p., 1972-74; prof. edn. and urban studies Grad. Sch. Edn. Harvard U., Cambridge, Mass., 1974-98, Charles William Eliot prof. edn. Grad. Sch. Edn., 1999-99, prof. emeritus Grad. Sch. Edn., 1999—. Instr. dept. preventive medicine SUNY Upstate Med. Center, Syracuse, 1955-60; research dir. Washington Action for Youth delinquency prevention project, Pres.' Com. on Juvenile Delinquency and Youth Crime, Washington, 1962-64; vis. lectr. Lab. Community Psychiatry, Harvard U. Med. Sch., Boston, Mass., 1966-67; vis. lectr. ch. and soc. Episcopal Div. Sch., Cambridge, Mass., 1966-67; commr. Pres.'s Commn. on Mental Health, 1977-78; mem. tech. adv. bd. Maurice Falk Med. Fund, 1968-99; bd. dirs. Social Sci. Rsch. Coun., 1969-75; master Boston Sch. Desegregation case, Fed. Dist. Ct., 1975; mem. nat. adv. com. Maxwell Sch. Syracuse U., 1992-2000, Hogg Found. for Mental Health, 1998-2002, Morehouse Rsch. Inst., 1997-2002; bd. overseers Boston Sci. Mus., 1997-2002, overseer emeritus, 2002—; corporator Emerson Hosp., Concord, Mass., 1998—; chmn. bd. dirs. Judge Baker Children's Ctr., 2001—. Author: Church Action in the World, 1969, Black Students at White Colleges, 1972, Race Mixing in the Public Schools, 1973, Oreo, 1975, A New Look at Black Families, 1976, 5th edit., 2002, The Sociology of Urban Education, 1978, The Caste and Class Controversy on Race and Poverty, 1979, 2d edit., 1989, The Ivory and Ebony Towers, 1981, Race, Ethnicity and Socioeconomic Status, 1983, School Desegregation Plans That Work, 1984, Black and White Families, 1985, Five Black Scholars, 1986, (with Michael Grady) Metropolitan School Desegregation, 1986, Effective Education, 1987, (with Michael Grady and Richard Hope) African-Americans and the Doctoral Experience, 1991, Theories of Human Social Action, 1994, (with Michael Alves) Controlled Choice, 1996, (with Ralph Edwards) Black Power/White Power in Public Education, 1998, (with Edwards and Alves) Student Diversity, Choice and School Improvement, 2002; editor: The Family Life of Black People, 1970, (with B. Brown and B. Kramer) Racism and Mental Health, 1973, Black/Brown/White Relations, 1977, (with R. Edmonds) Black Colleges in America, 1978, (with S. Greenblatt) Community Politics and Educational Change, 1981, (with Inabeth Miller) Social Goals and Educational Reforms, 1988, (with A. Garibaldi and W. Reed), The Education of African-Americans, 1991, (with P. Rieker, B. Kramer and B. Brown) Mental Health, Racism and Sexism, 1995. Hon. trustee Episcopal Div. Sch., Cambridge; mem. United Negro Coll. Fund, 1983-90, pres. assembly; mem. nat. exec. coun. Episcopal ch., 1967-74, v.p. gen. conv., 1970-74; host Inner City Beat nat. pub. affairs weekly TV program, monitor channel, 1991-92. Recipient faculty svc. award Nat. Univ. Ext. Assn., 1969, 50th Anniversary Distig. Alumnus award Syracuse U. Maxwell Sch., 1974; Lee-Founders award Soc. for Study Social Problems, 1983, Family Scholar award, 1986; Disting. Career Contbn. award com. on role and status minorities in ednl. R & D, Am. Ednl. Rsch. Assn., 1990, Benjamin E. Mays Svc. award Morehouse Coll., 1994, Father John LaFarge, S.J. award Fairfield U., 1995, Disting. Career award Assn. Black Sociologists, 1996, Outstanding Book award for mental health, racism and sexism Myers Ctr. for Study of Human Rights, 1996, Arents Alumni award Syracuse U., 2000. Mem. Am. Ednl. Rsch. Assn., Am. Sociol. Assn. (coun. 1980-83, 95-98, v.p. 1996-97, DuBois-Johnson-Frazier award 1994), Phi Beta Kappa, Alpha Phi Alpha. Episcopalian. Home: 41 Hillcrest Rd Concord MA 01742-4615 Office: Harvard U Grad Sch Edn 405 Gutman Libr 6 Appian Way Cambridge MA 02138-3704 E-mail: cvmswillie@aol.com.

WILLIFORD, DRURY FISHER, JR. historical researcher, writer, editor-in-chief; b. Memphis, Nov. 27, 1929; s. Drury Fisher and Irene Frances (Dawson) W.; m. Virginia Lucile Jackson, Dec. 1950 (div. Sept. 1971); children: Peggy Leigh, Virginia Fisher, Alan Lyle, Mark Edward; m. Shirley Ann Hagedorn, Aug. 1981. BA, W.Va. U., 1986. Cert. police firearms instr. Fed. Law Enforcement Tng. Ctr. Audit clk. Nat. Bank of Commerce, Memphis, 1953-54; patrolman Police Dept., 1954-55; patrol inspector U.S. Border Patrol, El Paso, Tex., Tucson, Buffalo, 1955-57; from inspector to operations officer U.S. Customs Svc., Toronto, Ont., Can., 1957-63, Buffalo, 1963-72, Washington, 1972-81; ret., 1981. Freelance photographer. Contbr. articles to profl. jours. Boys hockey coach Amherst (N.Y.) Hockey Assn., 1964-72, Wheaton (Md.) Hockey Club, 1972-73, Morgantown (W.Va.) Hockey Club, 1981-82; literacy vol. tutor, 1985-88. With USN, 1950-52. Named Marion County Tutor of Yr., 1987; elected to Hockey Hall of Fame, Amherst, N.Y., 1984; Judith Herndon fellow W.Va. Legislature, 1984. Democrat. Avocation: animal protection and conservation of natural habitat. Home: PO Box 734 Reedsville WV 26547-0734

WILLIFORD, LEX AKERS, educator; b. El Paso, Tex., Nov. 28, 1954; s. Don French and Teresa James W. BA in English, Stephen F. Austin State U., 1979, MA in English, 1984; MFA in Fiction Writing, U. Ark., 1987. Grad. asst. dept. English U. Ark., Fayetteville, 1984-87; instr. dept. English Auburn (Ala.) U., 1987-90; lectr. creative writing, dept. English So. Ill. U., Carbondale, 1990-94; asst. prof. fiction writing, dept. English U. Ala., Tuscaloosa, 1994-99; asst. prof. U. Texas, El Paso, Texas, 2000—. Editor: Scribner Anthology of Contemporary Short Fiction, 1999; author: (short stories) Macauley's Thumb, 1994 (Iowa Short Fiction award 1993). NEA fellow, 1993. Avocations: jazz/blues drums, watercolor & airbrush painting, digital photography. E-mail: lex@utep.edu.

WILLIG, KARL VICTOR, computer firm executive; b. Idaho Falls, Idaho, June 4, 1944; s. Louis Victor and Ethel (McCarty) W.; m. Julianne Erickson, June 10, 1972; 1 son, Ray. BA magna cum laude, Coll. of Idaho, 1968; MBA (Dean Donald Kirk David fellow), Harvard U., 1970. Pres. Ariz. Beef, Inc., Phoenix, 1971-73; group v.p. Ariz.-Colo. Land & Cattle Co., 1973-76; v.p. Rufenacht, Bromagen & Hertz, Inc., Chgo., 1976-77; pres. Sambo's Restaurants, Inc., Santa Barbara, Calif., 1977-79; ptnr. Santa Barbara Capital, 1979-85; pres. EURUSA Equities Corp., 1985-86; pres., chief exec. officer InfoGenesis, 1986—. Trustee Am. Bapt. Sem. of West, 1977-85; mem. Chgo. Merc. Exch., 1976-77, mem. audit com. and membership coms., 1976-77. Named one of Outstanding Young Men of Am., 1972; recipient Assn. of U.S. Army award, 1964.

WILLIG, ROBERT DANIEL, economics educator; b. Bklyn., Jan. 16, 1947; s. Jack David and Meg W.; m. Virginia Mason, July 8, 1973; children: Jared Mason, Scott Mason, Brent Mason, Alexandra Mason. BA, Harvard U., 1967; MS in Ops. Rsch., Stanford U., 1968, PhD in Econs, 1973. Lectr. Stanford U., Palo Alto, Calif., 1971-73; mem. tech. staff Bell Labs., Holmdel, N.J., 1973-77, supr. dept. econs. rsch., 1977-78; prof. econs. and pub. affairs Princeton U., 1978—; mem. Aspen Inst. Task Force on Future of Postal Svc., 1978-80; dep. asst. atty. gen. U.S. Dept. Justice, Washington, 1989-91. Cons. in field; rsch. fellow U. Warwick, Eng., 1977; mem. organizing com. Telecom Policy Rsch. Conf., 1977-78; mem. rsch. adv. bd. Am. Enterprise Inst., 1980-88; mem. N.J. Gov.'s Task Force on Market-Based Pricing of Electricity, 1987; bd. dirs. Consultants in Industry Econs., Inc., 1983—; mem. Def. Sci. Bd. Task Force on Antitrust for the Def. Industry, 1993-94, Transp. Rsch. Bd. Task Force, 1995-96; advisor Inter-Am. Devel. Bank, 1997—. Author: Welfare Analysis of Policies Affecting Prices and Products, 1973, Contestable Markets and the Theory of Industry Structure, 1982; editor: Handbook of Industrial Organization, 1986, Can Privatization Deliver: Infrastructure for Latin America, 1999; contbr. articles to profl. jours. mem. editorial bd.: M.I.T. Press Series on Govt. Regulation, 1978— , Am. Econ. Rev., 1980-83, Jour. Indsl. Econs., 1985-89, Utility Policy, 1989—. Mem. adv. bd. B'nai B'rith Hillel Found., Princeton U., 1978—. NSF grantee, 1979-85. Fellow Econometric Soc. (program com. 1978-81); mem. Am. Econ. Assn. (nominating com. 1980-81). Office: Princeton Univ Economics Dept Princeton NJ 08540

WILLIMAN, PAULINE, shorthand reporter, farm foundation administrator; b. Albany County, N.Y., Jan. 11, 1926; d. Harrison and Alta Allen (Hallenbeck) Salisbury; m. Raymond Williman, Jan. 11, 1947 (div. Oct. 1951). Grad., Albany Stenotype Secretarial, 1941-42. Cert. shorthand reporter. Staff reporter Empire Stenographers, Albany, 1942-46; exec. sec. Res. Officers Assn., Dept. of N.Y., 1947-49; ofcl. reporter N.Y. State Supreme Ct./Third Jud. Dist., 1958-64; ofcl. stenographer N.Y. State Senate, 1979-98; profl. shorthand reporter self employed, N.Y., 1949—. Mem. Cert. Shorthand Reporter Licensure Bd., Albany, 1992—; specialized in reporting tech. engring. rev. procs. involving water supply and waste water treatment facilities throughout N.Y. state, 1952-94; mem. edn. and small bus. coms. Bus. Coun. N.Y. State. Contbr. articles to profl. jours. Mem. RNSC Inner Circle, Washington, 1980-97; mem. Senatorial Bus. Adv. Bd., Washington, 1982-86. Recipient resolution and commendation for svc. N.Y. State Senate, 1998. Mem. Am. Water Works ASsn. (life), Nat. Ct. Reporters Assn., N.Y. State Ct. Reporters Assn., Kiwanis Internat. (club pres. 1997-99, award of excellence 1999). Republican. Mem. Dutch Reformed Ch. Avocations: golf, gardening, fitness, reading, music. Office: 447 Loudonville Rd Albany NY 12211-1499

WILLINGER, LOWELL DAVID, lawyer; b. Mar. 8, 1942; BA, Cornell U., 1964; LLB, Harvard U., 1967. Bar: N.Y. 1968. Assoc. Hofheimer, Gartlir, Gottlieb & Gross, N.Y.C., 1968-69, Goldstein, Gurfein, Shames & Hyde, N.Y.C., 1969-78, Carb, Luria, Glassner, Cook & Kufeld, N.Y.C., 1978-82; assoc., sr. counsel Proskauer, Rose, 1982—. Mem. Phi Beta Kappa. Office: Proskauer Rose 1585 Broadway Fl 25 New York NY 10036-8299 E-mail: lwillinger@proskauer.com.

WILLINGER, RHONDA ZWERN, optometrist; b. Bklyn., Apr. 26, 1962; d. Jerome Max and Jeanette (Zwern) Willinger; m. Wayne Ken Chan, Aug. 26, 1990; children: Jamie S. Chan, Jared Max. BS, U. Miami, 1983; OD with honors, New Eng. Coll. Optometry, 1987. Resident in optometry VA Med. Ctr., Bedford, Mass., 1987-88; pvt. practice, Burlington, 1988-89; pvt. practice specializing in contact lenses Framingham, 1989—. Scholar New Coll., U. South Fla., 1979-81; honors scholarship U. Miami, 1981-83. Mem. Am. Optometric Assn. (contact lens sect.), Mass. Soc. Optometrists. Avocation: violin. Home: 228 Lowell Ave Newton MA 02460-1830 Office: 659 Worcester Rd Framingham MA 01701-5204

WILLINGHAM, CLARK SUTTLES, lawyer; b. Houston, Nov. 29, 1944; s. Paul Suttles and Elsie Dell (Clark) W.; m. Jane Joyce Hitch, Aug. 16, 1969; children: Meredith Moores, James Barrett. BBA, Tex. Tech U., 1967; JD, So. Meth. U., 1971, LLM, 1984. Bar: Tex. 1971. Ptnr. Kasmir, Willingham & Krage, Dallas, 1972-86, Finley, Kumble et al, Dallas, 1986-87, Brice & Mankoff, Dallas, 1988-98, Moseley Martens, LLP, Dallas, 1999—. Contbr. articles to profl. jours. Exec. com. Dallas Summer Musicals, 1979-93, pres., 1994-95. Mem. ABA (chmn. agrl. com. tax sect. 1984-86), State Bar Tex. (chmn. agrl. tax com. 1985-87), Dallas Bar Assn., Am. Law Inst., Tex. Rangers Law Enforcement Assn.(bd. dirs. 2000—), Nat. Cattlemen's Beef Assn. (bd. dirs., pres. 1998), U.S. Meat Export Fedn. (exec. com. 1991-93), Beef Industry Coun. (exec. com. 1990-91, promotion chmn. 1992-94), Tex. Cattle Feeders Assn. (bd. dirs., pres. 1988), Tex. Bd. Vet. Med. Examiners (pres. 1994), Tex. Beef Coun. (bd. dirs., pres. 1989), Dallas Country Club. Republican. Episcopalian. Home: 3824 Shenandoah St Dallas TX 75205-1702 Office: Moseley Martens LLP 3878 Oak Lawn Ave Ste 400 Dallas TX 75219-4469

WILLINGHAM, DEBORAH N. information technology executive; BS in Indsl. and Systems Engring., Ga. Inst. Tech. Various sr. mgmt. pos. IBM Corp.; v.p., support, Enterprise Customer Unit Microsoft, Redmond, Wash., 1993—96, v.p., Enterprise Customer Unit, 1996—99, v.p., bus. and enterprise divsn. mktg., sr. v.p., human resources. Mem. Nat. Bd. Advisors Coll. Bus. and Pub. Adminstrn., U. Ariz.; mem. indsl. and systems engring. alumni adv. bd., pres.'s adv. bd. Ga. Inst. Tech. Office: One MIcrosoft Way Redmond WA 98052-6399*

WILLINGHAM, DOUGLAS BARTON, dentist; b. Mobile, Ala., Feb. 23, 1954; s. Welborn Kiefer and Mary Maxine (McCollum) W.; m. Michele Joy Saunders, Mar. 21, 1981 (div. 1997); 1 child, Sofia. BA, Tex. Tech. U., 1976; DDS, Baylor Coll. Dentistry, Dallas, 1980. Pvt. practice dentistry, Salado, Tex., 1981—. Editor Tex. Dental Jour., Austin, 1986-93. Mem. vestry St Luke's Episcopal Ch., Belton, Tex., 1998-2000, sr. warden, 1999; pres. Salado Hist. Soc., 1983, Railroad & Pioneer Mus., Temple, Tex. 1985-86, Bell County Hist. Commn., 1983-90; Tex. Coun. Advisors, Inst. for Humanities, Salado, 1985-92. Fellow Internat. Coll. Dentists (golden pen award 1988, 89, 91, ann. literary award 1991, golden scroll award 1980, 88), Am. Coll. Dentists, Pierre Fauchard Acad. (Disting. Svc. award 1993); mem. Am. Assn. Dental Editors, Tex. Dental Assn. (historian, editor, Pres.'s award 1993, award of merit 1993, Disting. Svc. award 1992), Baylor Dental Alumni Assn. (trustee 1989-92), Ctrl. Tex. Dental Soc. (Dentist of Yr. 1988). Republican. Episcopalian. Avocations: maritime history, historic preservation, geneaology, travel. Home: 9 N Church St Salado TX 76571-5690 E-mail: willingham@vvm.com.

WILLINGHAM, EDWARD BACON, JR. ecumenical minister, administrator; b. St. Louis, July 27, 1934; s. Edward and Harriet (Sharon) W.; m. Angeline Walton Pettit, June 14, 1957; children: Katie, Carol. BS in Physics, U. Richmond, 1956; postgrad., U. Rochester, 1958-59; MDiv., Colgate Rochester Div. Sch., 1960. Ordained to ministry Am. Bapt. Ch., 1960. Min. Christian edn. Delaware Ave. Bapt. Ch., Buffalo, 1960-62; dir. radio and TV Met. Detroit Coun. Chs., 1962-75; exec. dir. Christian Communication Coun. Met. Detroit Chs., 1976-98. Chmn. N.Am. Broadcast sect. World Assn. for Christian Comm., 1970-71, bus. mgr., 1972-98, archivist, 1999—; broadcast cons. Mich. Coun. Chs., 1965-75; guest cons. religious broadcasting Germany, 1968; mem. coord. com. Mich. Ecumenical Forum, 1986, 90-92, chmn., 1991-92. Bd. mgrs. Broadcasting and Film Commn., Nat. Coun. Chs., 1965-73; mem. Muslim-Christian-Jewish Leadership Forum, 1987—; bd. deacons 1st Bapt. Ch. Birmingham, chmn., 1994. Recipient Gabriel award Cath. Broadcasting Assn., 1972, 1st Ann. Ecumenical award Am. Bapt. Chs. of Mich., 1992, Race Rels. award Booker T. Washington Bus. Assn. of Detroit, 1983. Mem. Assn. Regional Religious Communicators (pres. 1969-71), World Assn. Christian Comm. (ctrl. com. 1973-78), Phi Gamma Delta, Sigma Pi Sigma. Office: 21440 Lathrup St Southfield MI 48075-4218

WILLINGHAM, EMAGENE EMANUEL, social worker; b. Bainbridge, Ga., June 1, 1937; d. Frank Wooten and Louie (Coburn) Emanuel; children: Tracy Coburn, Robert Wesley, Jeffrey Reeves. BA in Psychology and Sociology, Jacksonville U., 1959; MSW, U. N.C., 1984; postgrad., UNC-Duke Psychoanalytic Edn. Program. Diplomate in clin. social work. Personnel asst. Jacksonville (Fla.) Paper Co., 1959-60; social worker Dept. Social Svc., Raleigh, N.C., 1984-86, Wake County Alcohol Treatment Ctr., Raleigh, 1986-88; counselor Duke U., Durham, 1988—; psychotherapist pvt. practice, Chapel Hill, 1989—. Mem. NASW, Nat. Fedn. Soc. Clin. Social Work (com. on psychoanalysis), N.C. Soc. Clin. Social Work, Am. Psychoanalytic Assn., N.C. Psychoanalytic Soc., N.C. Psychoanalytic Found. Office: 727 Eastowne Dr Ste 300A Chapel Hill NC 27514-2209

WILLINGHAM, HELEN PITTARD, artist; b. Abbeville, S.C., July 10, 1921; d. Charles Edgar and Rachel Clifford (Pittard) Armour; m. Robert Marion Willingham, Nov. 25, 1945 (dec. Aug. 1994); 1 child, Robert Marion Jr. Student, U. Ga., 1939-40, LaGrange Coll., 1940-41. Tchr. art Washington (Ga.) H.S., 1952-69. Book illustrator Willingham Art Studio, Washington, Ga., 1948-85, heraldry artist, 1948—, portrait and still life painter, 1948—. Exhibited in group shows at Augusta, Ga., 1964, Lake Lanier, Ga., 1968, 69, Thomaston, Ga., 1970, City of Washington (Ga.) Pub. Libr., 1993; represented in permanent collection at Augusta (Ga.) Mus. Mem. Women in the Arts, Augusta Art Assn. Republican. Presbyterian. Avocations: collecting antiques, reading. Home: 102 Water St Washington GA 30673-1748

WILLINGHAM, JAMES EDWARD, youth development agency executive; b. Phila., June 15, 1948; s. Rubin and Ruth (Gibbs) W.; m. Dawn Michelle Carter, Dec. 31, 1995; children: Lynette, Lynone, Andrea, Tiffany, James Jr. A in Polit. Sci., Phila. C.C., 1973; student, Spring Garden Coll., 1974, Temple U., 1977; B in Profl. Studies, NYU, 1980. Mailing clk. U.S. Post Office, L.A., 1968-71; pre-profl. staff Boy Scouts Am., Phila., 1971-74, dist. exec., 1974-78, sr. dist. exec. N.Y.C., 1978-80, field dir., 1980-85, borough scout exec., 1985-89, dir. field svcs. Pitts., 1989-93, scout exec., CEO Hartford, Conn., 1993—. Mem. N.Y. Urban League, 1981-89; past pres., bd. dirs. Cmty. Health Svcs., Inc., 1992-96; bd. dirs. St. Francis Hosp., 1995-97; mem. adv. bd. Capital C.C., 1995-97; founder Ludlow Crusaders Athletic Assn.; former bd. mem. Martin Luther King Football Conf. Recipient Outstanding Man of Yr. award Congressman William H. Gray, Phila., Svc. to Youth award, Jewish Event Purim Com., Cmty. Svc. to Youth award N.Y. Urban League, Four Chaplains Legion of Honor award. Mem. Greater Hartford C. of C., Kappa Alpha Psi (officer 1990-97, chmn. guide right program com. Pitts. Alumni chpt., Achievement award 1991), Sigma Pi Phi (officer 1995-97). Democrat. Baptist. Avocations: reading, golfing, traveling. Home: 16 Cliffmount Dr Bloomfield CT 06002-2226 Office: Conn Rivers Coun Boy Scouts Am 60 Darlin St East Hartford CT 06108-3201

WILLINGHAM, MARY MAXINE, fashion retailer; b. Childress, Tex., Sept. 12, 1928; d. Charles Bryan and Mary (Bohannon) McCollum; m. Welborn Kiefer Willingham, Aug. 14, 1950; children: Sharon, Douglas, Sheila. BA, Tex. Tech U., 1949. Interviewer Univ. Placement Svc., Tex. Tech U., Lubbock, 1964-69; owner, mgr. buyer Maxine's Accent, 1969—. Speaker in field. Leader Campfire Girls, Lubbock, 1964-65; sec. Cmty. Theatre, Lubbock, 1962-64. Recipient Golden Sun award Dallas Market, 1985, Woman of Excellence award in Bus., YWCA, 2001; named Outstanding Mcht., Fashion Retailer Mag., 1971, also Outstanding Retailer. Mem. Lubbock Symphony Guild, Ranch and Heritage Ctr., Faculty Women's Club. Office: 16 Briercroft Shopping Ctr Lubbock TX 79412-3022

WILLINGHAM, WARREN WILLCOX, psychologist, testing service executive; b. Rome, Mar. 1, 1930; s. Calder Baynard and Eleanor (Willcox) W.; m. Anna Michal, Mar. 17, 1954; children: Sherry, Judith, Daniel. Student, Ga. Inst. Tech., 1952; PhD, U. Tenn., 1955. Rsch. assoc. World Book Co., N.Y.C., 1959-60; dir. evaluation studies Ga. Inst. Tech., Atlanta, 1960-64; dir. rsch. Coll. Bd., N.Y.C., 1964-68, dir. access rsch. office Palo Alto, Calif., 1968-72; asst. v.p., disting. rsch. scientist Ednl. Testing Svc., Princeton, N.J., 1972—. Vis. prof. U. Minn., 1988; mem. adv. bd. on ednl. requirements on Sec. Navy, 1968; leader Psychometric Seminar, Nat. Inst. Testing and Evaluation, Jerusalem, 1999; cons. to numerous schs., colls. U.S. Office Edn. Author: Free Access Higher Education, 1970, Source Book for Higher Education, 1973, College Placement and Exemption, 1974, Assessing Experimental Learning, 1977, Selective Admissions in Higher Education, 1977, Personal Qualities and College Admissions, 1982, Success in College, 1985, Testing Handicapped People, 1988, Predicting College Grades, 1990; Gender and Fair Assessment, 1997; editor: Measurement in Education, 1969-72; mem. editl. bd. Jour. Ednl. Measurement, 1971-75, Alternate Higher Edn., 1976-80, Am. Ednl. Rsch. Jour., 1968-71; contbr. articles, tech. reports to profl. jours. Served to lt. USNR, 1955-59. Recipient Ann. award So. Soc. Philosophy and Psychology, 1958 Fellow Am. Psychol. Assn., AAAS; mem. Nat. Council on Measurement in Edn. (dir.), Am. Ednl. Research Assn., Am. Psychol. Soc., CAEL (hon. life mem.), Sigma Xi. Office: 131 Bertrana Dr Princeton NJ 08540 Mailing: 131 Bertrand Dr Princeton NJ 08540

WILLINGHAM, WELBORN KIEFER, psychologist, educator; b. Rotan, Tex., Mar. 12, 1928; s. W.B. and Juanita Madge (Eason) W.; m. Mary Maxine McCollum, Aug. 14, 1950; children: Sharon, Douglas, Sheila. BA, Tex. Tech U., 1949; MEd, U. Tex., 1950; PhD, Tex. Tech U., 1964. Diplomate Am. Bd. Psychol. Specialties. Tchr., prin. elem. sch., Hale Center, Tex., 1951-53; edn. and tng. officer USAF, Brookley Air Force Base, Ala., 1953-55; tchr., coach Hutchinson Jr. High Sch., Lubbock, Tex., 1955-57; counselor Monterey High

Sch., 1957-60; asst. dean students Tex. Tech U., 1963-64; clin. psychologist South Plains Guidance Ctr., 1964-66; from asst. prof. to prof. emeritus Tex. Tech U., 1966—; clin. prof. neuropsychiatry and behavioral scis. Tex. Tech. U. Health Scis. Ctr., 1983—. Cons. psychologist Big Spring (Tex.) VA Med. Ctr., 1990—; mem. allied health staff psychology Meth. Hosp., Lubbock, 1990. Cons. editor Individual Psychology, 1989—; tech. reviewer Tex. Dental Jour., 1989—; contbr. articles to profl. jours. Lt. col. USAFR, 1949-77. Paul Harris fellow Rotary Internat., 1985. Fellow Am. Bd. Forensic Examiners (diplomate), Am. Bd. Forensic Medicine (diplomate); mem. N.Am. Soc. Adlerian Psychology (del. assembly 1983-89, chmn. publs. com. 1986-89). Avocations: travel, study, reading. Home: 1605 56th St Lubbock TX 79412-2803 Fax: 806-741-1776.

WILLIS, ALBERT LEE, broadcast technician; b. Syracuse, N.Y., June 6, 1960; s. James Edward Sr. and Pearl Mae W.; m. Deborah Anne Mathew, Dec. 16, 1947; 1 child Chelsea Antoinette J. Diploma, William Nottingham High Sch., Syracuse, N.Y., 1978. Commd. N.Y. Army Nat. Guard, 1985, ret., 2001, warehouse mgr. NY, 1984—2001; network cable tester Philips Broadband Networks, Inc., Manlius, 1994—. Author: poems, 2000. Mem. adv. coun. Onondaga County Commn. Human Rights, Syracuse, NY, 1997—99; bd. dirs. Syracuse Black Leadership Congress, 1996—2001, Syracuse Affiliate Black Leadership Commn. on AIDS, Syracuse, NY, 1998—2001. Decorated Army Achievement United States Army. Democrat. Christian Methodist Episcopal. Avocations: cooking, science fiction, poetry, jazz, singing gospel. Home: 243 W Matson Ave Syracuse NY 13205 Office: Philips Network Broadband 100 Fairground Blvd Manlius NY 13041 Home Fax: 315-469-6099. Personal E-mail: Alwillis38@juno.com. Business E-Mail: Alwillis38@juno.com.

WILLIS, ANDRÉ MAURICE, electrical engineer, computing service executive; b. Fairfield, Ala., Oct. 16, 1957; s. Lamar and Marie (Davis) W.; m. Selene Yvette Lowe, Mar. 4, 1958. BSEE, Tuskegee U., 1981; postgrad., Focus Automation, 1993-94. Cert. in elec. sys. FAA, network engr. Novell. Project engr. Arco, Port Arthur, Tex., 1980; sys. engr. Dictaphone Corp., Milford, Conn., 1982-86, project engr., 1986; mgr. avionic flight test McDonnell Douglas Corp., Long Beach, Calif., 1987-93; info. sys. cons. EDP, L.A., 1994, So. Calif. Presbyn. Homes, Glendale, Calif., 1994; network sys. analyst Weyerhauser Mortgage, Woodland Hills, 1995; sr. network engr. CB Comml. Real Estate, Torrance, 1995—, project mgr., 1997—; tech. customer adv. bd. Cheyenne divsn. Intel & Computer Assocs., 1998. Corp. mgr. tng. McDonnell Douglas, 1990; info. sys. cons. EDP/Contract Svcs., L.A., 1994-95; pres., owner Datronics, L.A., 1996—. Vol. Going to Coll. program UCLA, 1997-98. Tuskegee U. Sch. Engring. scholar, 1976-80; recipient CB Comml Real Estate Project award IT, 1997. Mem. IEEE, ASME. Avocations: tennis, swimming, reading, chess, camping.

WILLIS, ARNOLD JAY, urologic surgeon, educator; b. Phila., Feb. 12, 1949; s. Alexander and Rosaline May (Dortort) W.; m. Lilian Marie Mortensen, Aug. 29, 1981; children: Adam Mark, Simon Matt, Andreas Morton. BA, Franklin & Marshall U., 1970; MD, Thomas Jefferson Med. Ctr., 1974. Intern George Washington U. Hosp., Washington, 1974-75, resident in surgery, 1975-77, resident in urology, 1977-80; instr. in urology George Washington U. Med. Ctr., 1980-82, asst. clin. prof., 1982-88, assoc. clin. prof., 1988—. Founder, dir. Met. Ambulatory Urologic Inst.; mem. Del Marva Found. Med. care, Washingotn, 1985-90; mem. profl. adv. bd. Nat. Kidney Found., Washington, 1988-92; cons. Caremark Internat., Washington, 1990-93, Managed Care Options, Bethesda, Md., 1993-95; med. dir., founder Met. Ambulatory Urologic Inst.; med. dir., founder Continence Treatment Ctr. of Md.; urologic cons. Johnson & Johnson; expert on transgluteal brachytherapy for prostate cancer; med. dir., founder Met. Brachytherapy Assocs.; keynote spkr. 12th Copenhagen Urologic Symposium on Brachytherapy. Mem. editl. bd. Health Educator, 1995-96; contbr. articles to sci. jours.; inventor ultrasound guide. Founder profl. sports league/major league roller hockey; owner world champion Washington Power profl. hockey team. Clin. Oncology Tng. grantee NIH, 1974; named Tchr. of Yr., Georgetown Family Practice Residency, 1991. Fellow Internat. Coll. Surgeons (v.p. U.S. sect. 1986—, Washington regent); mem. Am. Urologic Assn., Am. Assn. Clin. Urologists, Washington Urol. Assn. (Resident's prize 1980). Jewish. Avocations: tennis, squash, skiing, fishing, sailing. Home: 2011 Whiteoaks Dr Alexandria VA 22306-2432 Office: 650 Pennsylvania Ave SE Ste 450 Washington DC 20003-4339

WILLIS, BARBARA FLORENCE, artist; b. Bronx, N.Y., Dec. 17, 1932; d. Gerard and Anna Barbara (Schelmeyer) Ossman; m. Sidney Frank Willis, 1955; children: Jerry Dale, Frank Larkworthy. Grad., Vesper George Sch. Art, 1955. Exhbns. include Jackson Weatherbee, Newburyport, Mass., 1986-87, Am. Artists Profl. League, 1987, 88, 89, 93, Audubon Soc., N.Y.C., 1988, Peel Gallery, Danby, Vt., 1988, Springfield (Mass.) Art League, 1989, Springfield Acad. Artists, 1989-90, 91, Pastel Soc. Am., N.Y.C., 1989, Copley Soc. Am., Boston, 1990, 94, R.H. Love Gallery, Chgo., 1990, Cape Cod Artists Assn., 1990, 91, Cuneo Mus. and Gardens, Vernon Hills, Ill., Conn. Pastel Soc., 1994, Wilson Gallery, Dennisport, Mass., 1994; joint one-man show Peel Gallery, 1992; exhibited in group show Copley Soc., 1996, Peel Gallery, 1997, Wilson Gallery, 1997, Acad. Artists Assn., Springfield, 1998, 99; group shows include Am. Artist Profl. League Salmagundy Club, N.Y.C., 1997 (Meml. award 1997), Salmagundi Club 22d Ann. Juried Art Exhbn., N.Y.C., 1999, Downeast Decoy Classical Collection, Irvington, N.Y., 1997; included in Ency. of Oil Painting Techniques, others. Recipient hon. mention Am. Artists Profl. League, 1987, Michael Werliaff Meml. award, 1996; hon. mention Springfield Acad. Artists, 1989, 90, Salamagundi Show, 1990, Cape Cod Artists Assn., 1991, Realistic Artists award Pastel Soc. Am., 1989, Catherine Larilard Wolfe Art Club award, 1995, N.Y.C. Master Pastelist Designation award, 1995; 1st Ann. Nat. Dick Blick award Conn. Pastel Soc., 1993, 98, Nat. Show honor award, 1995; 1st prize Winter Mem. Show, Copley Artists Soc., 1991, Spring Mems. Show Jurors award, 1991, award Acad. Artists Assn., 1992, Watson-Guptill award, 1996, Michael Werhoff Meml. award, 1996, Acad. Artists Assn. award, 1997, 98. Mem. Guild of Boston Artists. Home: 64 US Highway 202 Bennington NH 03442-4116

WILLIS, BEN, writer, artist; b. Racine, Wis., Dec. 4, 1930; s. Ben Sherlock Willis and Beryl Hester (Smith) Young; div. 1971. Attended, Phila. Coll. Art, 1953-54, Pa. Acad. Fine Arts, 1954-55, Academie Julian, Paris, 1955-57. Author: The Tao of Art, 1987, Internet reprint edit., 2001; collaborator: The Art of Oriental Embroidery, 1980; exhibited in group shows Salmagundi Club, N.Y.C., 1971-75, Am. Watercolor Soc., Nat. Acad. Design, N.Y.C., 1978, Cicchinelli Galleries, N.Y.C., 1980, Nat. Arts Club, N.Y.C., 1980, Salmagundi Club, 1980, Manasquan Group Artists, 1981, Pastel Soc., N.Y.C., 1982, Allied Artists Am., N.Y.C., 1982, Am. Artists Profl. League, N.Y.C., 1984; represented in numerous pvt. collections. Seaman 1st class, USN, 1948-52, Korea. Recipient 1st prize N.Y.C. Ctr., 1960, Manasquan Outdoor Art Show, 1981, Best in Show award Manasquan Group Artists, 1981, others. Fellow Alumni Fellowship Pa. Acad. Fine Art, Author's Guild. Episcopalian. Avocations: languages, music, reading, judo. Home: 10 C Bennington Ln Whiting NJ 08759-1621

WILLIS, BEVERLY ANN, architect; b. Tulsa, Feb. 17, 1928; d. Ralph William and Margaret Amanda (Porter) W. BFA, U. Hawaii, 1954; PhD in Fine Arts (hon.), Mt. Holyoke Coll., 1983. Registered architect, Calif. Prin. Willis Atelier, Honolulu, 1954-58, Willis & Assocs., Inc., San Francisco, 1958-88, Beverly Willis Architects, N.Y.C., 1988—. Pres., dir. Architecture Rsch. Inst., Inc., N.Y.C., 1993—; co-chair Rebuild Downtown Our Town Coalition, 2002; lectr. U. Hong Kong, 2000, Internat. Women's U., Kassel, Germany, 2000. Author: Invisible Images: The Silent Language of Architecture, 1997; prin. works include Union St. Stores (merit award San Francisco AIA, award of distinction State of Calif.), Nob Hill Cts. (merit award AIA), 1970, Margaret Hayward Park (grand and merit awards Pacific Coast Bldg. Con., Honor award Design Internat.), 1983, San Francisco Ballet Bldg., 1984, Manhattan Village Acad. H.S., N.Y.C., 1995; contbr. articles to profl. jours., chpts. to books. Founding trustee Nat. Bldg. Mus., Washington, 1976—; bldng. rsch. adv. bd. Nat. Acad. Sci., 1971-79, chair Fed. Construction Coun., 1976-79. Recipient Phoebe Hearst Gold Medal award, 1969. Fellow AIA (v.p. Calif. coun. 1979, pres. 1980); mem. Achievement Rewards for Coll. Scientists, Internat. Women's Forum, Villa Taverna Club, Lambda Alpha (pres. San Francisco chpt. 1981-82). Clubs: Villa Taverna (San Francisco). Avocations: poetry, sketching, tennis, walking. Office: 119 E 35th St New York NY 10016-3805 E-mail: bevwillis@architect.org.

WILLIS, BRUCE DONALD, judge; b. Mpls., Jan. 29, 1941; s. Donald Robert and Marie Evelyn (Edwards) W.; m. Elizabeth Ann Runsvold, July 17, 1971; children: Andrew John, Ellen Elizabeth. BA in English, Yale U., 1962; LLB, Harvard U., 1965. Bar: Minn., 1965, U.S. Dist. Ct. Minn. 1965, U.S. Ct. Fed. Claims 1989, U.S. Ct. Appeals (8th cir.) 1991, U.S. Supreme Ct. 1992. Assoc. Popham, Haik, Schnobrich & Kaufman, Ltd., Mpls., 1965-71, ptnr., 1971-95; judge Minn. Ct. Appeals, 1995—. Mem. jud. adv. bd. Law and Orgnl. Econs. Ctr., U. Kans., 1997—2001. Contbr. articles to profl. jours. Del. Rep. Nat. convs., 1976, 88; vice chmn. Ind.-Rep. Party Minn., 1979-81; mem. State Ethical Practices Bd., 1990-95, sec. 1990-91, vice chmn. 1991-92, chmn., 1992-93; mem. Minn. Commn. on Jud. Selection, 1991-94; mem. Minn. Bd. Jud. Stds., 1997—; mem. adv. com. on rules of civil appellate procedure Minn. Supreme Ct., 1997—. Named one of 1990's Lawyers of Yr., Minn. Jour. Law and Politics, 1991, one of Minn.'s Best Trial Lawyers, Minn. Lawyer, 1991. Mem.: ABA, Minn. Bar Assn. (professionalism com. 1998—). Mem. United Ch. of Christ. Home: 2940 Walnut Grove Ln N Plymouth MN 55447-1567 Office: Minn Jud Ctr 25 Constitution Ave Saint Paul MN 55155-1500 E-mail: bruce.willis@courts.state.mn.us.

WILLIS, CARL RAEBURN, JR. pharmaceutical executive; b. Madison, Wis., Apr. 5, 1939; s. Carl Raeburn and Annie Marie (Sjoblom) W.; m. Marilynn Lee Sheron, Oct. 15, 1960 (div. Mar. 1979); children: Bryan Keith, Alexandra Marie, Heather Anne, Shannon Leigh; m. Candace Jane Oldham, Apr. 26, 1980. PhD in Indsl. Pharmacy, Purdue U., 1966, BS in Pharmacy, 1961, MS in Indsl. Pharmacy, 1964. Sr. pharm. chemist Warren-Teed Pharms., Columbus, Ohio, 1966-69; mgr. CIBA/CIBA-Geigy, Summit, N.J., 1969-72; deputy dir. drug regulatory affairs Sterling Drug Inc., N.Y.C., 1972-78; dir. drug regulatory affairs Cooper Labs., Cedar Knolls, N.J., 1978-79, Berlex Labs. Inc., Cedar Knolls, 1979-83, sr. dir. R & D, 1983-84, v.p. ops. Wayne, N.J., 1984-96; v.p. Corp. Bus. devel., 1996—. Co-author: Drug & Cosmetic Industry, 1972; guest editorial Pharmaceutical engineering, 1987; contbr. articles to Jour. Pharmaceutical Sci., 1965, 68. Advisor Jr. Achievement, Columbus, 1968, bd. mem., Newark, N.J., 1984-88. Fellow NIMH, 1965-66; named Disting. Alumnus Purdue U., 1990. Mem. Morristown Airport Pilots Assn., Sigma Xi, Phi Lambda Upsilon, Rho Chi. Office: Berlex Labs Inc 340 Changebridge Rd PO Box 1000 Montville NJ 07045-1000

WILLIS, CLIFFORD LEON, geologist; b. Chanute, Kans., Feb. 20, 1913; s. Arthur Edward and Flossie Duckworth (Fouts) W.; m. Serreta Margaret Thiel, Aug. 21, 1947 (dec.); 1 child, David Gerard. BS in Mining Engring., U. Kans., 1939; PhD, U. Wash., 1950. Geophysicist The Carter Oil Co. (Exxon), Tulsa, 1939-42; instr. U. Wash., Seattle, 1946-50, asst. prof., 1950-54; cons. geologist Harza Engring. Co., Chgo., 1952-54, 80-82, chief geologist, 1954-57, assoc. and chief geologist, 1957-67, v.p., chief geologist, 1967-80; pvt. practice cons. geologist Tucson, 1982—. Cons. on major dam projects in Iran, Iraq, Pakistan, Greece, Turkey, Ethiopia, Argentina, Venezuela, Colombia, Honduras, El Salvador, Iceland, U.S. Lt. USCG, 1942-46. Recipient Haworth Disting. Alumnus award U. Kans., 1963. Fellow Geol. Soc. Am., Geol. Soc. London; mem. Am. Assn. Petroleum Geologists, Soc. Mining, Metallurgy and Exploration Inc., Assn. Engring. Geologists, Sigma Xi, Tau Beta Pi, Sigma Tau, Theta Tau. Republican. Roman Catholic. Avocations: travel, reading. Home: 4795 E Quail Creek Dr Tucson AZ 85718-2630

WILLIS, CONNIE (CONSTANCE E. WILLIS), author; b. 1945; Tchr. elem. and jr. H.S., Branford, Conn., 1967-69. Author: (novels) Letter from the Clearys (Nebula award, 1982, Hugo award, 1983), Lincoln's Dreams, 1987, Doomsday Book (Nebula award, 1992, Hugo award, 1993), Impossible Things, 1993, Unchartered Territory, 1994, Even the Queen (Nebula award, 1992, Hugo award, 1993), Fire Watch (Nebula award, 1982, Hugo award, 1983), The Last of the Winnebagos (Nebula award, 1988, Hugo award, 1989), Death on the Nile (Hugo award, 1994), The Soul Selects (Hugo award, 1997), Uncharted Territory, 1994, Remake, 1995, Bellwether, 1996, To Say Nothing of the Dog (Hugo award, 1999), Miracle, 1999, Water Witch, 1982, Light Raid, 1989, Promised Land, 1997, Miracle and other Christmas Stories, 1999, The Winds of Marble Arch (Hugo award, 2000), Passage, 2001. Named Best Sci. Fiction/Fantasy Author of Nineties Locus Mag. Address: 1716 13th Ave Greeley CO 80631-5418

WILLIS, CRAIG DEAN, academic administrator; b. Cambridge, Ohio, Mar. 21, 1935; s. John Russell and Glenna (Stevens) W.; m. Marilyn Elaine Foster, June 9, 1956; Mark Craig, Bruce Dean, Todd Laine, Garth John. BA, Ohio Wesleyan U, 1957; MA, Ohio State U., 1960, PhD, 1969. Registrar Ohio Wesleyan U., 1964-69; dir. admissions Wright State U., 1970-72, dean, 1971-77; v.p. acad. affairs Concord Coll., 1977-82; pres. Lock Haven U. Pa., 1982—. Chmn. internat. affairs com. Am. Assn. State Colls. and Univs.; A.C.E. pres.'s commn. on internat. edn.; vice chmn. Clinton region Mellon Bank Ctr., 1987, chmn., 88, also bd. dirs.; bd. dirs. Lock Haven U.; cons. Ellis Assocs., Princeton, W.Va., 1980—82. Chmn. bd. Kirkmont Preschool, Beavercreek, Ohio, 1974-77, Beavercreek Library, 1976-77, Regional Edn. Service Agy., Beckley, W.Va., 1978-82; mem. N.E.-Midwest leadership Coun., 1989—. Recipient Disting. Alumnus award dept. edn. Ohio Wesleyan U., 1991; scholar Sohio Oil, 1953, Govt. of France, Paris, 1964, Shell Oil Co, 1967. Mem. Commn. State Coll. and Univ. Pres., Assn. State Colls. annd Univs., Clinton County C. of C. (pres.), Rotary (v.p., pres. elect, Citizen of Yr. award Lock Haven 1989), Ohio Wesleyan U. Alumni Assn. (Disting. Sesquicentennial Alumnus of the Edn. 1992), Phi Kappa Phi, Kappa Kappa Psi, Phi Delta Kappa, Kappa Delta Pi. Presbyterian. Office: Lock Haven U North Fairview St Lock Haven PA 17745

WILLIS, DAWN LOUISE, paralegal, small business owner; b. Johnstown, Pa., Sept. 11, 1959; d. Kenneth William and Dawn Louise (Joseph) Hagins; m. Marc Anthony Ross, Nov. 30, 1984 (div.); m. Jerry Wayne Willis, Dec. 16, 1989 (div.). Grad. high sch., Sacramento, Calif. Legal sec. Wilcoxen & Callahan, Sacramento, 1979-87, paralegal asst., 1987-88; legal adminstr. Law Office Jack Vetter, 1989-99; owner, mgr. Your Girl Friday Secretarial and Legal Support Svcs., 1991—; legal asst. Foley & Lardner, 1999-2001; case mgr. Larry Lockshin, Esq. Law Corp., 2001—02; legal asst. Hunter, Richey, Di Benedetto & Eisenbeis, 2002—. Vol ARC, 1985, Spec Olympics, 1997—. Mem.: Sacramento Legal Secys Assn. Democrat. Avocations: water sports, camping, reading, cooking. Office: Hunter Richey DeBenegetto & Eisenbeis 801 K St 23d Fl Sacramento CA 95814 E-mail: dwillis@hrdb.com.

WILLIS, DOUGLAS MACARTHUR, secondary education educator, consultant; b. Ironton, Ohio, Oct. 11, 1945; s. Brady C. and Mary T. (Dodson) W.; m. Karen K. Cory, June 8, 1969; children:: Andrew M., Matthew D.. BS in Indsl. Arts, Morehead (Ky.) State U., 1968; MS in Indsl. Edn., Ctrl. Mo. State U., 1973. Cert. permanent K-12 tchr., Ohio. Tchr. indsl. arts Dawson-Bryant H.S., Coal Grove, Ohio, 1968-71, Little Miami H.S., Morrow, 1971-72; grad. asst. Ctrl. Mo. State U., Warrensburg, 1972-73; tchr. indsl. arts Ankeney Jr. H.S., Beavercreek, Ohio, 1973-75, tchr. unified arts, 1975-80, tchr. tech., dept. chmn., 1980-2000; ret., 2000. Mem. Greene County Tech. Edn. Curriculum Com., Xenia, Ohio, 1980—, Beavercreek Tech. Study Com., 1992—; western rep. State Stds. Task Force, Columbus, Ohio, 1991—. Mem. Xenia Twp. Vol. Fire Dept., 1974-89, pres., 1980-82. Recipient cert. of accomplishment Ohio Ho. of Reps., 1995. Mem. Internat. Tech. Edn. Assn., Ohio Tech. Edn. Assn., Western Ohio Tech. Edn. Assn., Ohio Tech. Edn. Leadership Coun. (pres. 1993-94). Avocation: custom woodworking. Home: 985 Jane Ave Xenia OH 45385-1517

WILLIS, DOUGLAS ALAN, lawyer; b. Taylorville, Ill., Feb. 22, 1963; s. Roy Willis and Sharon (Peel) Boaden. BA, Ill. Coll., 1985; JD, DePaul Coll. of Law, 1988. Bar: Ill. 1988, U.S. Dist. Ct. (no. dist.) Ill. 1988, U.S. Ct. Appeals (7th cir.) 1992, U.S. Supreme Ct. 2001. Intern BBC, Dallas, 1984, Ill. Dept. Registration/Edn., Springfield, 1983, Ill. State Senate Staff, Springfield, 1982, 84; rsch. asst. M.C. Bassiouni, Chgo., 1986-87; summer clk. Hon. Richard Mills, U.S. Dist. Judge, Springfield, 1987; asst. corp. sec. Profl. Svc. Industries, Inc., Lombard, Ill., 1991—, assoc. corp. counsel, 1989—. Intern U.S. House Minority Leader Robert Michel, Jacksonville, Ill., 1983. Named to Order of the Barrister, 1988, DePaul Exec. Moot Ct. Bd., 1988. Mem. Ill. State Bar Assn., Delta Theta Phi. Republican. Methodist. Home: 735 Blossom Ct Naperville IL 60540-1841 Office: Profl Svc Industries Inc 1901 S Meyers Rd Ste 400 Oakbrook Terrace IL 60181

WILLIS, DOYLE HENRY, state legislator, lawyer; b. Kaufman, Tex., Aug. 18, 1907; s. Alvin and Eliza Jane (Phillips) W.; m. Evelyn McDavid, 1942; children: Doyle Jr., Dan, Dina, Dale. BS, BA, U. Tex., 1934; LLB, Georgetown U., 1938. Bar: D.C. 1937, Tex. 1938, U.S. Supreme Ct. 1942. Mem. coun. City of Fort Worth, 1963-64; mem. Tex. Ho. of Reps., Austin, 1946-52, 69-96, Tex. State Senate, Austin, 1952-62. Tex. state comdr. VFW, 1958-59. Maj. USAF, 1941-46, PTO. Decorated Bronze Star, 4 battle stars, USAF; named Tex. Vet. of Yr., 1999. Mem. KP (life), Masons (life), Shriners (life), Ind. Order Odd Fellows., Lions Club, Sons Republic of Tex. Knights of the Order of San Jacinto. Democrat. Methodist. Avocations: golf, fishing, reading. Home: 3316 Browning Ct E Fort Worth TX 76111-5021 Office: 2019 N Riverside Dr Fort Worth TX 76111-2802

WILLIS, EDWARD OLIVER, management consultant, state official; b. St. Louis, Apr. 6, 1948; s. George Washington and Mary (Fantroy) W.; m. Jennifer Linnea Johnson, June 17, 1972 (div. Dec. 1991); children: Linnea, Eric; m. Linda Diane Clark, Aug. 8, 1992. AA, Am. River Coll., Sacramento, 1972; BS in BA, Calif. State U., Sacramento, 1974; MBA in Mgmt., Golden Gate U., San Francisco, 1978. Divsn. ops. supr., casualty claims investigator Allstate Ins. Co., Menlo Park, Sacramento, 1974-75; budget analyst Dept. Fin., State of Calif., Sacramento, 1975-77; assoc. govtl. program analyst Dept. Health, Medi-Cal Procurement Project, State of Calif., 1977-78; chief fiscal br. solid waste mgmt. bd. State of Calif., 1978-79, mgr. adminstrv. svcs. state lands commn., 1979-80, asst. to assoc. supt. pub. instrn. dept. edn., 1980-82, dep. dir. adminstrn. dept. fish and game, 1982-90, acting adminstr. office of oil spill prevention and response, 1990-92, dep. dir. adminstrn. dept. developmental svcs., 1992-93, dep. dir. adminstrv. svcs. program dept. toxic substances, 1993-94, asst. sec. policy devel. Calif. Environ. Protection Agy., 1994-95, chief dep. dir. Calif. Conservation Corps, 1995—; owner, prin. cons. WW Assocs., 1994—. Part-time instr. Cosumnes River Coll., Sacramento, 1980-83 Author: Business Employment Equity Plan, 1994. Vol. United Way Campaign, United Negro Coll. Fund, Sacramento Children's Home, YMCA; 1st v.p. Nat. Black Child Devel. Inst., Sacramento, 1981-82; chmn. Black Adv. Com. to State Pers. Bd., 1984-85; mem. St. Francis of Assisi Sch. Bd., Sacrammento, 1996—, pres., 1991-93; bd. trustees Black Advocates in State Svc., 1992; bd. dirs. Nat. Forum for Black Pub. Adminstrs., Washington, 1993—, pres., 1991-93, 1st v.p. 1990-91); Little League coach, 1996—. With USAF, 1966-70. Decorated Air medals (4). Mem. Nat. Forum for Black Pub. Adminstrs. (Sacramento chpt. bd. dirs. 1993—, 1st v.p. 1990-91, pres. 1991-93), Am. Soc. Pub. Adminstrn. (Pub. Adminstr. of the Yr.). Avocations: golf, softball. Home: 1065 Almaden Village Ln San Jose CA 95120-3361 Office: Conservation Corps State of California 1719 24th St Sacramento CA 95816-7114

WILLIS, ELLEN, communications educator; b. N.Y.C., Dec. 14, 1941; d. Miriam Weinberger and Melvin H. Willis; m. Stanley Aronowitz; children: Nona Willis-Aronowitz. AB, Barnard Coll., 1962. Staff Village Voice, N.Y.C., 1979—83, sr. editor, 1983—90; prof. journalism N.Y. U., 1990—. Author: (book) Beginning To See the Light, 1981, No More Nice Girls, 1992, Don't Think, Smile! Notes on a Decade of Denial, 1999. Mem.: AAUP (N.Y. U. chpt. pres. 2000—02), Authors Guild, Nat. Writers Union. Office: NYU Dept Journalism 10 Washington Pl New York NY 10003

WILLIS, ELLEN DEBORA, psychiatric nurse; b. Carbondale, Pa., Feb. 21, 1941; d. Niles John and Ruth Elizabeth (Farrell) Kiefer; m. Bernard J. Willis; 1 child, Edward John Enslin III. Diploma, Kings County Hosp., 1960; BS, St. Joseph's Coll., 1984; MS, U. Scranton, 1986, postgrad. RN; cert. psychiat. mental health nurse, nursing edn., staff devel. Staff nurse Kings County Hosp. Ctr., Bklyn., 1960-62; rsch. asst. dept. cardiology Downstate Med. Ctr., U. Bklyn., 1962-63; pvt. duty nurse N.Y.C., 1963; operating room nurse Scranton (Pa.) Gen. Hosp., 1963-64; asst. operating room supr. Carbondale (Pa.) Gen. Hosp., 1964-65, staff nurse, 1969-70; head nurse St. Joseph's Hosp., Carbondale, 1965-66, Horton Hosp., Middletown, N.Y., 1966-67, Middletown State Hosp., 1967-68; nursing supr. Fairview State Hosp., Waymart, Pa., 1970-74, patient care coord., 1974-84, dir. nursing edn. staff devel., 1994-95; dir. nursing edn. State Correctional Instn. at Waymart Psychiat. Forensic Unit, 1995-96; ret., 1996. Commr. Econ. & Gen. Welfare Commn.; truste Pa. Nurses Assn. Health and Welfare Fund. Mem. Nat. Nursing Staff Devel. Orgn., Sigma Theta Tau. E-mail. Home: 26 Old Gravity Rd Carbondale PA 18407-1453 E-mail: budwillis@aol.com.

WILLIS, FRANK EDWARD, retired air force officer; b. Clinton, Ill., June 19, 1939; s. William Edward and Bernardine (Saveley) W.; m. Clarice Marie Hull, June 7, 1961; children: Michael, Steven, William. BS in Engring., USAF Acad., Colorado Springs, Colo., 1961; MA in Bus. Mgmt., U. Nebr., 1973. Commd. 2d lt. USAF, 1961, advanced through grades to maj. gen., 1989; dep. comdr. 314th Tactical Airlift Group, Little Rock AFB, 1978-79, comdr., 1979-80; vice comdr. 374th Tactical Airlift Wing, Clark Air Base, The Philippines, 1980-81, comdr. The Philippines, 1981-83, 317th Tactical Airlift Wing, Pope AFB, N.C., 1983-84; vice comdr. Air Force Manpower and Pers. Ctr., Randolph AFB, Tex., 1984-85; comdt. Air Command and Staff Coll., Maxwell AFB, Ala., 1985-88; vice comdr. 22d Air Force, Travis AFB, Calif., 1988-89; dir. and dep. chief of staff for requirements Air Mobility and Mil. Airlift Command, Scott AFB, Ill., 1989-93; ret., 1993; co-owner retail hobby shop Tinker Town, Inc., St. Louis, 1994—. Decorated D.S.M. (2), Legion of Merit (2), Air medal (7), Meritorious Svc. medal (2). Presbyterian. Avocations: electronics, computers, model railroading. Home: 1901 Mistflower Glen Ct Chesterfield MO 63005-4713 E-mail: frank@willis.net.

WILLIS, GLADDEN WILLIAMS, pathologist; b. Minden, La., Mar. 26, 1939; s. John Stillmon and Virgie Williams Willis; m. Lydia Hall, May 14, 1966; children: Charles Austin, Loye Stillmon. BS, Centenary Coll., 1960; MD, Tulane U., 1964. Intern La. State U. Med. Ctr., Shreveport, 1964-65, resident, 1965-69; fellow Meml. Sloan-Kettering Med. Ctr., N.Y.C., 1969-71; pathologist St. Luke's Hosp., Houston, 1971-72, St. Mary's Hosp., Roswell, N.Mex., 1972-73, Ochsner Clinic Found., New Orleans, 1973-76, dir. anatomic pathology, 1976—, vice chmn. lab. medicine, 1996—. Contbr. numerous sci. papers to profl. jours., over 913 sci. photographs to encys., books in field. Past pres. Jefferson Performing Arts Soc., Metairie, La. Capt. USAF, 1966-72. Recipient George Washington Honor medal Valley Forge Found., 1996. Fellow Arthur Purdy Stout Soc., Royal Microscopical Soc.; mem. Assn. Dirs. of Anatomic Pathology, Internat. Acad. Pathology, Am. Soc. Media Photographers, N.Y. Acad. Scis. Republican. Methodist. Avocation: photography. Home: 62 Verde St Kenner LA 70065-1029 Office: Ochsner Clinic Found 1516 Jefferson Hwy New Orleans LA 70121-2429 E-mail: gwillis@ochsner.org.

WILLIS, HAROLD WENDT, SR. real estate developer; b. Marion, Ala., Mar. 7, 1927; s. Robert James and Della (Wendt) W.; m. Patsy Gay Bacon, Aug. 2, 1947 (div. Jan. 1975); children: Harold Wendt II, Timothy Gay, April Ann, Brian Tad, Suzanne Gail; m. Vernette Jacobson Osborne, Mar. 30, 1980 (div. 1984); m. Ofelia Alvarez, Sept. 23, 1984; children: Ryan Robert, Samantha Ofelia. Student, Loma Linda U., 1950, San Bernardino Valley Coll. Ptnr. Victoria Guernsey, San Bernardino, Calif., 1950-63, co-pres., 1963-74, pres., 1974—. Pres. Energy Delivery Sys., Food and Fuel, Inc. San Bernardino City water commr., 1964-98, pres. bd. water commrs., 1964-98; bd. councillors Loma Linda (Calif.) U., 1968-85, pres., 1971-74; mem. So. Calif. Strider's Relay Team (set indoor Am. and World record in 4x800 1992, sec distance medley relay U.S. and World record for 60 yr. old 1992); pres. So. Calif. Striders Track and Field Club, 2001-02. With U.S. Mcht. Marine, 1945-46. Mem. Calif. Dairy Industries Assn. (pres. 1963, 64), Liga Internat. (2d v.p. 1978, pres. 1982, 83), Social Striders Masters Track & Field Club (pres. 2001-02). Seventh-day Adventist (deacon 1950-67). Avocation: lic. pvt. pilot. Office: PO Box 5607 San Bernardino CA 92412-5607

WILLIS, ISAAC, dermatologist, educator; b. Albany, Ga., July 13, 1940; s. R.L. and Susie M. (Miller) W.; m. Alliene Horne, June 12, 1965; children: Isaac Horne, Alliric Isaac. BS, Morehouse Coll., 1961, DSc (hon.), 1989; MD, Howard U., 1965. Diplomate Am. Bd. Dermatology. Intern Phila. Gen. Hosp., 1965-66; fellow Howard U., Washington, 1966-67; resident, fellow U. Pa.,

Phila., 1967-69, assoc. in dermatology, 1969-70; mem. staff Phila. Gen. Hosp., 1969-70; instr. dept. dermatology U. Pa., Phila., 1970-72; mem. staff Moffit Hosp. U. Calif., San Francisco, 1970-72; asst. prof. Johns Hopkins U., Johns Hopkins Hosp., Balt., 1972-73; mem. staff Johns Hopkins Hosp., Balt. City Hosp., Good Samaritan Hosp., 1972-72; asst. prof. Emory U., Atlanta, 1973-77; mem. staff Crawford W. Long Meml. Hosp., 1974—, West Paces Ferry Hosp. , Atlanta, 1974-2000; assoc. prof. Emory U., 1977-82; prof. Morehouse Sch. Medicine, 1982—, chief dermatology, 1991—; mem. staff Piedmont Hosp., 2000—. Dep. commdr. of 3297th USA Hosp. (1000B), 1990—; mem. gen. medicine group IA study sect., NIH, 1985—; mem. grants review panel EPA, 1986—; adv. bd. Arthritis and Musculoskeletal and Skin Diseases, 1991—, U. Pa. Sch. Medicine, 1995—, Emory U., 1994—; chmn. inst. review bd., mem. pharmacy and therapeutic com.; bd. dirs. Comml. Bank Gwinnett, Heritage Bank, Landmark Bank Fla., Learning Framework, West Paces Med. Ctr., Lupus Specialists, Inc., InterVu, Inc., Lupus Erythematosus Found., Jacquelyn McClure Lupus Erythematrosus Clinic, Skin Cancer Found., World Network Solutions; bd. dirs., chmn. audit com. Comml. Bank of Ga., 2000—, Landmark Bank of Fla., 1999—; mem. med. staff Piedmont Hosp., 2000—; adv. bd. Enable, Inc.; mem. adv. coun. U. Calif. Jacobs Sch. Engring., San Dieto, 2001-; cons. in field. Author: Textbook of Dermatology, 1971; contbr. articles to profl. jours. Trustee Friendship Bapt. Ch., Atlanta, 1980-82; mem. gov.'s commn. on effectiveness and economy in govt. State of Ga. Human Resources Task Force, 1991—, Ga. State Bd. of worker's Compensation Med. subcom., 1997—; mem. nat. alumni coun. U. Pa., 1995—; mem. coun. of advisors U. Calif. San Diego Jacobs Sch. Engring., 2001--. Col. USAR, 1983-95. EPA grantee, 1980—. Fellow Am. Acad. Dermatology, Am. Dermtol. Assn.; mem. AAAS, AMA, Nat. Cancer Inst., Soc. Investigative Dermatology, Nat. Med. Assn., Internat. Soc. Tropical Dermatology, Pan Am. Med. Assn., Am. Fedn. Clin. Rsch., Am. Soc. Photobiology, U. Pa. Nat. Alumni Adv. Coun., State of Ga. Dermatology Found., Frontiers Internat., Sportsman Internat., Phi Beta Kappa, Omicron Delta Kappa. Achievements include a patent for the development of a shaving composition and method for preventing Pseudofolliohtip Barbae, 1999; subspecialties in the areas of dermatology and cancer research (medicine). Home: 1141 Regency Rd NW Atlanta GA 30327-2719 Office: NW Med Ctr 3280 Howell Mill Rd NW Ste 342 Atlanta GA 30327-4109 E-mail: iwmd@bellsouth.net.

WILLIS, JEAN LOUISE, information technology specialist; b. Harrisburg, Pa., Sept. 26, 1951; d. James L. and Mary K. (Gibbel) W. BA in English Lit., Muhlenberg Coll., 1973; MA in Libr./Info. Sci., U. Denver, 1975; advanced cert. in MIS, Drexel U., 1990. Chief law libr. Holland & Hart, Attys., Denver, 1975-78; dir. pub. svcs. U. Sydney (Australia) Law Sch. Libr., 1979-82; acting dir. Law Cts. Libr., Sydney, 1982-85; systems analyst, cons. Son Systems Internat., Phila., 1986-88; chief libr. 3d Cir. Ct. Appeals, 1988-91; MIS mgr. McCormick, Barstow et al, Fresno, Calif., 1991-97; assoc. dir. for info. sys. San Diego County Pub. Law Libr., San Diego, 1998—. Hike leader Sierra Club, Fresno, 1991-97; mem., organizer Because We Care, Fresno, 1995-97; cmty. support vol. Darlinghurst Cmty. Ctr., Sydney, 1981-84. U. Denver scholar, 1975. Mem.: ALA, San Diego Assn. Law Librs., No. Calif. Law Librs. Assn., So. Calif. Law Librs. Assn., Calif. Libr. Assn., Libr. and Info. Tech. Assn., Am. Assn. Law Librs., Sierra Club, Beta Phi Mu. Avocations: skiing, travel, hiking, yoga. Office: San Diego County Pub Law Libr 1105 Front St San Diego CA 92101-3904

WILLIS, JEFFREY SCOTT, mechanical engineer, consultant; b. New OrleanS, Apr. 18, 1962; s. John Ray and Jane Ann (Broome) W.; m. Linda Faye Sanders, July 30, 1988. BSME, U. Southwest La., 1983-87. Registered profl. engr. Engr. Balco, Boston, 1987-90, R.G. Vanderweil Engrs., Boston, 1990—99, Thompson prof. group, Houston, 1999—2000, PageSoutherland-Page, Houston, 2000—. Sunday sch. tchr. First Bapt. Ch., Melrose, Mass., 1990-93, bd. Christian edn., 1990-93, trustee property mgr., 1993-97, trustee, vice chair, 1998, trustee, chair, 1998; cub master pack 1199 Boy Scouts Am., 2001-. Mem. ASME (assoc. Boston sect., vice chmn. 1991-93, chmn. 1993-94, region I sect. ops. chair 1994-99, nat. nominating com. region I del. 1995-97, B31.9 com. mem.), Assn. Energy Engrs. (New Eng. chpt. v.p. 1991, pres. 1992), Internat. Soc. Pharm. Engrs. Home: 7730 Northwoods Dr Sugar Land TX 77479-6428 Office: PageSoutherlandPage Post Oak Tower 5051 Westheimer Ste 600 Houston TX 77056 Business E-Mail: jwillis@psp.com.

WILLIS, JOAN ELLEN, nurse; b. Wheaton, Kans., Sept. 6, 1931; d. Henry Michael and Nelle Gerva (Keating) Horgan; m. Bernard Edward Willis, Nov. 10, 1956; children: Patricia, Mary, Eileen, Maureen, Mike, Tim. Diploma in nursing, St. Francis Hosp., Topeka, 1953. Staff nurse St. Francis Hosp., Topeka, 1953-56; staff nurse RN, CPR instr. Community Hosp., Onaga, Kans., 1956-92. Recipient Nursing Heart of Healthcare award Kans. U. Med. Ctr., Kansas City, 1991, 93. Avocations: reading, gardening, spending time with family, traveling. Home: 216 Lincoln St Wheaton KS 66551-9210

WILLIS, JOHN ALEXANDER, lawyer; b. Queens, N.Y., Feb. 3, 1966; s. John Joseph Willis and Dorothy Elizabeth (Savides) White. BA, SUNY, Stony Brook, 1989; JD, Nova Southeastern Law Ctr., 1994. Bar: Fla. 1994, U.S. Ct. Appeals (11th cir.) 1994, N.Y. 1995, U.S. Dist. Ct. (so. dist.) Fla. 1995, U.S. Supreme Ct., 1999. Acct. coord. Met. Life Ins. Co., Hauppauge, NY, 1989—91; cert. legal intern Palm Beach County State's Atty Office, West Palm Beach, Fla., 1994; assoc. David & French, P.A., Boca Raton, 1994—2000, Baker & Zimmerman, P.A., Boca Raton, 2000—01; ptnr. Law Offices of John A. Willis, P.A., 2001—. Mem. ATLA, Acad. Fla. Trial Lawyers, South Palm Beach County Bar Assn. Avocations: golf, computers, softball. Office: Law Offices of John A Willis 5355 Town Center Rd #801 Boca Raton FL 33486 E-mail: jawillis@aol.com.

WILLIS, JOHN ALVIN, editor; b. Morristown, Tenn., Oct. 16, 1916; s. John Bradford and George Ann (Myers) W.; m. Claire Olivier, Sept. 25, 1960 (div.); m. Marina Sarda, Jan. 26, 1978 (div.) BA cum laude, Milligan Coll., 1938; MA, U. Tenn., 1941; postgrad., Ind U., Harvard U. Asst. editor Theatre World, N.Y.C., 1945-65, editor, 1965—; asst. editor Screen World, 1948-65, editor, 1965—; tchr. pub. high schs., 1950-76; editor Dance World, 1966-80; asst. editor Opera World, 1952-54, Great Stars of Am. Stage, 1952, Pictorial History of Silent Screen, 1953, Pictorial History of Opera in America, 1959, Pictorial History of the American Theatre, 1950, 60, 70, 80, 85. Mem. Tony Theatre Awards Com. Nat. bd. dirs. U. Tenn. Theatre; mem. com. to select recipients for Mus. Theatre Hall of Fame, NYU. Lt. USNR, 1943-45. Recipient Lucille Lortel Lifetime Achievement award, 1993, Drama Desk Lifetime Achievement award, 1994, Nat. Bd. Rev. Lifetime Achievement Film History award, 1999, Profl. Excellence award Milligan Coll., 1999, Tony award for excellence in theater, 2001; high sch. auditorium renamed John Willis Performing Arts Ctr. in his honor, Morristown, 1993. Mem. Actors Equity Assn., Nat. Bd. Rev. Motion Pictures (past bd. dirs.). Home and Office: 190 Riverside Dr New York NY 10024-1008

WILLIS, JOHN PATRICK, chemist; b. Albany, N.Y., Mar. 10, 1947; s. John James and Mary Catherine (Varden) W.; m. Tientje Jane Dirzuweit, July 22, 1972. BS, Iona Coll., 1969; MS, SUNY, Oswego, 1974; PhD, U. Conn., 1977. Assoc. prodn. chemist Winthrop Labs., Rensselaer, N.Y., 1970-72; rsch. chemist Uniroyal, Inc., Middlebury, Conn., 1977-79; postdoctoral rschr. U. Minn., Mpls., 1979-80; mgr. chem. rsch. Nova Biomed Corp., Newton, Mass., 1980-83; founder, chmn. Ilex Corp., Marlboro, 1983-87; med. cons., 1987-88; founder T.J. Assocs., Biomed. Cons., 1987-89; v.p., chief oper. officer Sharon Drive Corp., Westlake, Ohio, 1988-93; dir. rsch. Medisense, Inc., Waltham, Mass., 1993-97; v.p. R&D Marathon Med. Techs., Inc., Worcester, 1997-98; exec. v.p., chief tech. officer BioValve Techs., Inc., North Grafton, 1999-2000; pres., CEO Teknow Source Inc., Shirley, 2000—; chmn., CEO North Country Naturals, Inc., 2000—; tech. dir. biotech. Mohawk Innovative Tech, Inc., Albany, NY, 2001—. Mem. adv. bd. Clin. Lab. Practice, Mass. Dept. Pub. Health, 1986-87, 128 Entrepreneurs' Ctr., Waltham, Mass., 1986-88; mem. tech. adv. coun. Edison Biotech. Ctr., Cleve., 1988-90. U. Conn. Rsch. Found. fellow, 1976. Fellow Am. Inst. Chemists; mem. Am. Chem. Soc., Electrochem. Soc., Am. Assn. Clin. Chemistry, N.Y. Acad. Scis., Sigma Xi, Phi Kappa Phi, Phi Lambda Upsilon. Achievements include research in bioelectrochemistry, organic electrochemistry and biosensors; patents in field. Office: 1037 Watervleit-Shaker Rd Albany NY 12205 E-mail: jwillis@tiac.net.

WILLIS, JOHN T. Secretary of State; b. Nov. 1, 1946; m. Kathy S. Mangan; children: Karen M., James T. BA in Econs. cum laude, Bucknell U., 1968; JD, Harvard Law Sch., 1971. Clk. Army Ct. of Mil. Rev., 1971-74; legal assistance officer Aberdeen Proving Grounds, 1974-75; pvt. practice atty. Westminster, Balt. City, Md., 1975-90; chief of staff County Exec. of Prince George's County, 1990-94; apptd. sec. of state State of Md., 1995—. Adj. prof. Western Md. Coll., 1979—; chmn. Gov.'s Commn. on Md. Mil. Monuments; adv. bd. U. Balt.'s Schaefer Ctr. for Pub. Policy. Author: Presidential Elections in Maryland, 1984; contbg. author: Western Maryland: A Profile, 1980, Justice and the Military, 1972; contbr. articles to profl. jours.; editor: The Advocate, 1973-74. Vice-chmn. Md. Dem. Party, 1987-89, mem. various coms. and del. to Dem. Nat. Convs., 1976-96; chair Dem. Secs. of State, 1995—. Judge advocate gen. corps U.S. Army, 1968-75. Mem. Md. Bar Assn., Carroll County Bar Assn., Md. Hist. Soc., Carroll County Arts Coun. (past pres.). Office: Office of Sec of State State House Annapolis MD 21401 E-mail: mdsos@sos.state.md.us.*

WILLIS, MEREDITH SUE, writer, educator; b. Clarksburg, W.Va., May 31, 1946; d. Glenn Ernest and Lucille Meredith Willis; m. Andrew Bruce Weinberger, May 9, 1982; 1 child, Joel. BA, Barnard Coll., 1969; MFA, Columbia U., 1972. Writing cons. Tchrs. and Writers Collaborative, N.Y.C., 1972—; spl. lectr. NYU, 1983—. Author numerous books including Deep Revision, 1993, Trespassers, 1997, (short stories) In the Mountains of America, 1994, Personal Fiction Writing, 2000. Pres. Ethical Culture Soc. Essex County N.J., 1996-98; co-vice chair Cmty. Coalition on Race, South Orange-Maplewood, N.J., 1997-2000. Named Disting. Tchg. Artist, N.J. Arts Coun., 2000--; fellow NEA, 1978, N.J. Arts Coun., 1993. Avocation: organic gardening. Home and Office: 311 Prospect St South Orange NJ 07079-1806 E-mail: MSueWillis@aol.com.

WILLIS, NORMAN HUNT, new media writer, director, producer; b. Ft. Worth, Feb. 11, 1934; s. Ray Logan and Ima H. Willis; m. Andrea Marie Laurent, June 11, 1934 (div. Aug. 1981); children: Christi, Michelle, Leslie; m. Mary Theresa Ciociola, Feb. 19, 1945. Student, Tex. Christian U., 1951-52, San Diego State Coll., 1953, George Washington U., 1955-56. Audio-visual specialist The Asphalt Inst., College Park, Md., 1956-58; film specialist GE, Evendale, Ohio, 1958-60; scriptwriter Scripts by Oeveste Granducci, Washington, 1960-61; supr. med. films Wyeth Labs., Radnor, Pa., 1961-66; exec. prodr. H.G. Peters & Co., Primose, 1966-68; pres. Intermedica, Inc., Wayne, 1968-80, Intermedia Comms., Inc., Paoli, 1980-91; media cons., 1991-96; sr. med. writer Otsuka Am., 1997-2000; mgr. Quintiles Inc., 1997-2000; dir. clin. comm. Agouron/Pfizer La Jolla, 2000—. Author: (book) Basic Infant Nutrition, 1964; dir. (film) Drivin' and Drugs, 1968 (CINE Golden Eagle award); writer, dir., prodr. (video) Quinolones: Mechanisms of Action, 1986 (Silver medal N.Y. Internat. Film and TV Festival), (film) Sterilization Procedures for the Medical Office, 1963 (Golden Eagle award), Tracy, 1978 (Silver medal); dir. prodr. (film) Your Life and the Pill, 1975 (Silver medal, CINE Golden Eagle award). With USN, 1952-56, Korea. Mem. Internat. Interactive Comms. Soc., Am. Med. Writers Assn., Am. Mensa, Drug Info. Assn., Regulatory Affairs Profl. Soc. Avocations: tennis, noncommercial photography. Home: 11301 E San Raphael Dr San Diego CA 92130 E-mail: NormaHW@AOL.Com.

WILLIS, PARK WEED, III, cardiologist; b. Seattle, Nov. 18, 1925; s. Park Weed Jr. and Leota Geraldine (Snider) W.; m. Christine Boone Weaver, June 5, 1948; children: Park Weed IV, Carol Lee, Edwin Allen, Christine Elizabeth, Sarah Ann, Elizabeth Ann Baldwin. Student, U. Wash., 1942-44; MD, U. Pa., 1948. Diplomate Am. Bd. Internal Medicine, Am. Bd. Cardiovascular Disease. Intern Penn Hosp., Phila., 1948-50; resident in internal medicine U. Mich., Ann Arbor, 1952-54, fellow in cardiology, 1954-55; from instr. to prof. U. Mich. Hosp. and Med. Sch., 1955-79; prof. medicine Mich. State U. Coll. Human Medicine, East Lansing, 1979-96, prof. emeritus, 1996—. Chief sec. cardiology U. Mich., 1969-77; mem. med. staff Ingham Regional Med. Ctr., Lansing, 1979—, vice chair dept. cardiology, 1992-95; chief cardiology Mich. State U. Coll. Human Medicine, 1979-95. Contbr. over 100 articles to profl. jours., chpts. to books, abstracts in field. With USNR, 1943-86, Rear Adm., 1979, ret., 1986. Master: ACP; fellow: Am. Heart Assn., Am. Coll. Cardiology; mem.: Soc. Med. Cons. to the Armed Forces, Ctrl. Soc. Clin. Rsch., Assn. U. Cardiologists, Am. Fedn. Clin. Rsch. Episcopalian. Office: A205 Clin Ctr Mich State U East Lansing MI 48824 E-mail: park.willis@ht.msu.edu.

WILLIS, PAUL ALLEN, librarian; b. Floyd County, Ind., Oct. 1, 1941; s. Clarence Charles and Dorothy Jane (Harritt) W.; m. Barbara Marcum, June 15, 1963; children: Mark, Sally. AB, U. Ky., 1963, JD, 1969; MLS, U. Md., 1966. Cataloger Libr. of Congress, Washington, 1963; head descriptive cataloging br. Sci. and Tech. Info. Facility NASA, College Park, Md., 1963-66; law libr., prof. law U. Ky., Lexington, 1966-73, dir. librs., 1973—2002, acting dean Coll. Libr. Sci., 1975-76, 88; dean of libr. U. SC, Columbia, 2002—. Exec. sec. Ky. Jud. Retirement and Removal Commn., 1977-81; mem. adv. com. Ctr. for Jud. Conduct Orgns., Am. Judicature Soc., Chgo., 1979-81; bd. dirs. Southea. Libr. Network, Atlanta, 1980-83, 96-2000, chair, 1998-99; mem. exec. com. Ky. Hist. Soc., 1984-88; mem. Ky. Adv. Coun. on Librs., 1985—, adv. com. Online Computer Libr. Ctr., 1986-90; cons. S.E. Consortium for Internat. Devel., U. Sriwijaya, Palembang, Sumatera, Indonesia, 1987-88, Hanoi U. Tech., 1999, 2001, Vietnam Nat. U., Ho Chi Minh City, 1999. Sr. fellow UCLA, summer 1982 Mem. Assn. Southea. Rsch. Librs. (chair 1986-88). Home: 111 Dene Ct. Georgetown SC 29440-1095 Office: Thomas Cooper Library U SC 1322 Green St Columbia SC 29208-0001

WILLIS, RALPH HOUSTON, mathematics educator; b. McMinnville, Tenn., Dec. 26, 1942; s. Carl Houston and Carrie Lee (Hill) W.; m. Gayle Catherine Celestin, June 29, 1973 (div. Apr. 1985); m. Velma Inez Church, Aug. 10, 1985; stepdau., Bobbie Lynn White. BS in Math., Mid. Tenn. State U., 1964, MA in Math., 1966. Cert. secondary edn. Instr. depts. math. & computer sci. Western Carolina U., Cullowhee, N.C., 1968-73, asst. prof., 1973-83, assoc. prof., 1983—. Co-founder N.C. State Math. Contest & Contest Network, 1977-78, state maths. contest com., 1977-78, western regional rep. exec. steering com., 1978—, recording sec., 1978—; co-founder N.C. Math. League, 1981-82, mem. problem writing com., 1981-84. Editor: (newsletters) Abelian Grapevine-Secondary Math, 1970-88, The Child of Mathematics-Elementary-Middle Grade Math., 1972-78; mem. editl. bd. The Centroid, 1995-00; contbr. articles to profl. jours. Founder, dir., coord. High Sch. Math. Contest, Western Carolina U., 1970—, solicitor-coord. Math. Contest Scholarship Program, 1971-82, founder, coord. math dept. student awards program, 1970—, initiator-coord. math. dept.'s Vis. Speaker Program, 1974-77; founder, faculty sponsor N.C. Coun. Tchrs. Math. Student Affiliate, Cullowhee, 1988—; coord. state road paving project Univ. Heights Cmty. Devel. Orgn., 1974-76, chmn., founder cmty. watch., 1978-79, coord. public water sys. upgrade project, 1980-84; founder, coord., bd. dirs., trustee Hunerwadle Cmty. Cemetery Assn., Beersheba, Tenn., 1983—; co-founder N.C. State Math. Contest and Contest Network, 1977-78. Recipient Paul A. Reid Disting. Svc. award Western Carolina U., 1991, hon. mention N.C. Gov.'s Award for Excellence, 1991, Innovator award N.C. Coun. Tchrs. in Math., 1994, Exemplary Site award State Math. Contest Com., 1990, W.W. Rankin Meml. award for Excellence in Mathematics Edn., 2001. Mem. Nat. Coun. Tchrs. Math., N.C. Coun. Tchrs. Math. (historian 1993-98, Innovator award 1994. editl. bd. Centroid 1995-2000, W.W. Rankin award 2001), Phi Kappa Phi, Kappa Mu Epsilon. Avocations: genealogy, gardening, military history, model building, carpentry. Office: Western Carolina U Math Dept Stillwell Bldg Cullowhee NC 28723

WILLIS, RALPH WALKER, retired firefighter; b. Redondo Beach, Calif., Nov. 21, 1921; s. Achatius Walker and Elizabeth Margaret (Dehm) W.; m. Helen Elizabeth Willis, May 18, 1946; 1 child, Ron Lee. Grad. h.s., San Diego. Firefighter Richmond (Calif.) Fire Dept., 1946-67. Author: Sansei Banzai, 1986, War and Rememberance Revisted, 1988, The Eternal Regiment, 1995, My Life as a Jarhead, 1999 (The Ernie Pyle WWII Roundtable award), Truth or Consequences, 2002. Sgt. USMC, 1941-45. Mem.: VFW (life), Iwo Jima Survivors Assn. American Independent Party. Avocations: travel, painting, writing, gardening. Home: 866 Camino De Oro San Jacinto CA 92583-6807 E-mail: jarheadhandr@aol.com.

WILLIS, ROBERT ADDISON, dentist; b. Wichita, Kans., Apr. 27, 1949; s. Everett Clayton and Mary Ann (Rohlin) W.; m. Janet Sue Jones, Jan. 21, 1968 (div. Dec. 1986); children: Gregory, Jeffrey; m. Sherryl Ann Galloway, Apr. 26, 1991; children: Wes Misak, Wendy Misak. Student, Okaloosa Walton Jr. Coll., Niceville, Fla., 1970-71, Wichita State U., 1972-74; DDS, U. Mo., 1978. Dentist, Wellington, Kans., 1978—. Cons. Sumner County Regional Hosp., 1980—, Lakeside Lodge Nursing Home, Wellington, 1980—. Bd. dirs. Kans. Babe Ruth Leagues, Inc., dist. commr., 1990—; bd. of elders Calvary Luth. Ch., 1989-94. With USAF, 1968-71. Mem. ADA, Acad. Gen. Dentistry, So. Dist. Dental Soc. (pres. 1980), Kans. Dental Assn. (coun. on peer rev. 1988-89), Wellington Dental Soc. (treas. 1981—), Optimist CLub, Wellington Area C. of C. (com. on indsl. devel. 1992), Am. Legion, Xi Psi Psi. Republican. Avocations: golf, photography, jogging, collecting music records, woodworking. Home: 620 Circle Dr Wellington KS 67152-3206 Office: 204 E Lincoln Ave Wellington KS 67152-3061 E-mail: rwillis@idir.net.

WILLIS, RONI MAY LEWIS, library administrator; b. Springfield, Mass., Dec. 27, 1954; d. Ralph Mansfield and Ruth Harriet (Williamson) Lewis; m. Arnold Thomas Willis, Aug. 7, 1976; 1 child, Dana Rene. BS in Edn., Winthrop Coll., 1976, MEd, 1979; M of Librarianship, U. S.C., 1982. Cert. pub. libr., Ga. Media specialist Chesterfield County S.C. Schs., Pogeland, 1976-79, Lancaster County S.C. Schs., 1979-81; young adult and audiovisual libr. West Ga. Reg. Libr., Carrollton, 1983-84, asst. dir., 1984—. Chair-elect, chair North Ga. Associated Librs., 1988-90. Mem. Carroll County Cmty. Theatre; treas. Carroll County Heart unit Am. Heart Assn., 1994—, sec., 1992-94. Mem. ALA, Ga. Libr. Assn. (chair pub. rels. com. 1988-90), Pub. Libr. Assn., Carroll County C. of C., Pilot Club of Carrollton (pres. 1986-87). Republican. Baptist. Avocations: puppetry, storytelling, dramatic arts, cross stitch, gardening. Office: West Ga Reg Libr Carrollton GA 30117

WILLIS, RUSSELL EDWARD, academic administrator; b. Ft. Stockton, Tex., Mar. 29, 1955; s. Ben Edward and Billie Jo W.; m. Dawn Orlean Olmstead, July 18, 1981; children; Katherine, Benjamin. BS in Mgmt. Systems, So. Meth. U., 1976, BSEE, 1977, MS in Engring. Mgmt., 1979, M of Theology cum laude, 1982; PhD in Ethics and Soc., Emory U., 1990. Product mktg. engr. Tex. Instruments, Inc., Dallas, 1977-79; pastor Decker United Meth. Ch., Austin, 1984-86; instr. Iowa State U., Ames, 1988-90; asst. prof., instr. sociology Iowa Wesleyan U., Mt. Pleasant, 1990-95; asst. prof., assoc. prof. religon & sociology McMurry U., Abilene, Tex., 1995-2000; dir. info. systems & instructional tech. Dakota Wesleyan U., Mitchell, S.D., 2000—, v.p. acad. affairs, dean, 2000—01, prof. religion and philosophy, 2001—. Co-author: Cosmic Witness: Commentaries on Science-Technology Themes, 1996; contbg. author: Living Responsibility in Community, 1997. Bd. dirs. Friends of Mid. Border Mus., Mitchell, 2000—. Mem. Am. Acad. Religion, Soc. Christian Ethics, Ctr. Theology and the Natural Scis. Office: Dakota Wesleyan U 1200 W Univ Ave Mitchell SD 57301 E-mail: ruwillis@dwu.edu.

WILLIS, SIDNEY FRANK, artist, educator; b. Newark, Dec. 14, 1930; s. Frank Larkworthy and Venita Pearl (Dupree) W.; m. Barbara Florence Ossman; children: Jerry Dale, Frank Larkworthy II. Grad., Vesper George Sch. of Art, Boston, 1956; student, Atelier Robert Douglas Hunter, 1956-59. Tchr. Sharon Art Ctr., Sharon, N.H., 1965-81; painting instr. Franklin Pierce Coll., Rindge, 1972-73; tchr. Vesper George Sch. of Art, Boston, 1970-74. Contbr. pictures to N.Y. Graphic Soc. and Yankee Mag. Recipient four Gold Medals Jordan Show, Vayana Meml. Grand Prize Oqunquit Art Ctrs., Stillife Prize Ellsworth Gallery, Acrylic Prize Cape Cod Art Assn., Gold Medal Best In Show Boston Guild, Gold Medal Popular Prize Heritage Salon, R.H. Ives Gammel prize. Mem. Guild of Boston Artists, Pastel Soc. of Am., So. Vt. Art Assn., Copely Soc. Am. Artists Profl. League, New Am. Acad. of Art, N.H. Art Assn. Home: 64 State Route 202 Bennington NH 03442-4116 Office: Robert Wilson Gallery 34 Main St Nantucket MA 02554-3531

WILLIS, TERRI MELANIE, civil engineer; b. Manchester, Jamaica, Oct. 20, 1971; came to U.S., 1990; d. Terrence Michael and Hazel (Kennedy) Sherlock; m. Ricardo Olanzo Willis, July 8, 1995. BSCE, Prairie View (Tex.) A&M U., 1994. Intern engr. ALCAN, Manchester, 1993; field engr. Dowell Schlumberger Inc., Maurice, La., 1994-95, lead field engr., recruiter, 1995-97, mktg. engr., recruiter Sugar Land, Tex., 1997-99, sr. tech. engr., 1999—. Competition engr. supporting worldwide ops, 2000. Contbr. articles to profl. jours. Recipient Women of Color Tech. award U.S. Black Engr. and Info. Tech. mag. Mem. ASCE, Soc. Profl. Engrs., Soc. of Petroleum Engrs., Tau Beta Pi. Methodist. Avocations: swimming, hiking, riding bikes and horses, exercising. Home: 2611 Grants Lake Blvd # 215 Sugar Land TX 77479 Office: Schlumberger Well Svcs 110 Schlumberger Dr Rm 247 Sugar Land TX 77479

WILLIS, THORNTON WILSON, painter; b. Pensacola, Fla., May 25, 1936; s. Willard Wilson and Edna Mae (Hall) W.; m. Peggy Jean Whisenhant, June, 1960; 1 son, David Shaw.; m. Vered Lieb, 1983; 1 dau., Rachel Elizabeth. BS, U. So. Miss., 1962; MA, U. Ala., 1966. Vis. artist-in-residence La. State U., New Orleans, 1971-72 Represented in U.S. by Todd Selbert, N.Y.C., and André Zarre Gallery, N.Y.C., in Europe by Galerie Nordenhake, Stockholm.; assoc. editor: Re-View, 1978—; one-man exhbns. include: Henri Gallery, Washington, 1968, Paley and Lowe, N.Y.C., 1970, New Orleans Mus. Art, 1972, 55 Mercer St. Gallery, 1979, Galerie Nordenhake, Sweden, 1980, Oscarsson Hood Gallery, N.Y.C., 1980-84, Gloria Luria Gallery, Miami, 1985, Pensacola Mus. retrospective, 1988, Galerie Nordenhake retrospective, Stockholm, 1988, 89, Twining Gallery retrospective, 1990, André Zarre Gallery, N.Y.C., 1993; group exhbns. include: Phila. Civic Center, 1970, Whitney Mus., 1971, Contemporary Art Mus., Houston, 1980, 81, Sidney Janis Gallery, N.Y.C., 1980, 81, Johnson Mus., Ithaca, N.Y., 1981, Mus. Modern Art, N.Y.C., 1981, 84, 85-86, Galerie Arnesen, Copenhagen, 1981, ARS '83, Helsinki, André Emmerich Gallery, N.Y.C., 1992, Anita Shapolsky Gallery, N.Y.C., 1993, The Mobile Mus. of Art, 1995, Rider U., Lawrenceville, N.J, 1997; represented in permanent collections, Whitney Mus., N.Y.C., Mus. Modern Art, N.Y.C., New Orleans Mus. Art, Denver Mus. Fine Art, Rochester Meml. Gallery, Albright-Knox Mus., Phillips Collection, Washington, Herbert F. Johnson Mus., Cornell U., Chase Manhattan Collection, William Paley Collection, CBS, Power Collection, Sidney, Australia, Solomon R. Guggenheim Mus., N.Y.C., various collections, museums Europe, Scandanavia. With USMC, 1954-57. Recipient award, Adolph and Esther Gottlieb Found., 1991; grantee John Simon Guggenheim Found., 1978—79, Nat. Endowment Arts, 1980—81, The Pollock-Krasner Found., 2001—02. Mem. U.S. Golf Assn., Profl. Golf Tchrs. and Coaches of Am. (cert.). Avocation: golf. Home: 85 Mercer St New York NY 10012-4438 Office: 87 Mercer St New York NY 10012-4402

WILLIS, WILLIAM DARRELL, JR. neurophysiologist, educator; b. Dallas, July 19, 1934; s. William Darrell and Dorcas (Chamberlain) W.; m. Jean Colette Schini, May 28, 1960; 1 child, Thomas Darrell. BS, BA, Tex. A&M U., 1956; MD, U. Tex. Southwestern Med. Sch., 1960; PhD, Australian Nat. U., 1963. Postdoctoral research fellow Nat. Inst. Neurol. Diseases and Blindness, Australian Nat. U., 1960-62, Istituto di Fisiologia, U. Pisa, Italy, 1962-63; from asst. prof. to prof. anatomy, chmn. dept. U. Tex. Southwestern Med. Sch., Dallas, 1963-70; chief lab. comparative neurobiology Marine Biomed. Inst., prof. anatomy and physiology U. Tex. Med. Br., Galveston, 1970—, dir. Marine Biomed. Inst., 1978—, chmn. dept. anatomy and neurosci., 1986—, Ashbel Smith prof., 1986-95, Cecil and Ida Green prof., 1995—. Mem. neurology B study sect. NIH, 1968-72, chmn., 1970-72, mem. neurol. disorders Program Project rev. com., 1972-76, Nat. Adv. Neurol. and Communicative Disorders and Stroke Coun., 1987-90; tng. grant com. Nat. Inst. of Neurol. Disorders and Stroke, 1994-98. Mem. editl. bd. Neurosci., Exptl. Neurology, 1970-90, Archives Italiene Biologie, Neurosci. Letters, 1976-92; chief editor Jour. Neurophysiology, 1978-83, Pain, 1986-89; assoc. editor Jour. Neurosci., 1986-89, editor-in-chief, 1993-94; sect. editor Exptl. Brain Rsch., 1990-92, 95—. Mem. AAAS, Am. Assn. Anatomists (exec. com. 1980-86), Am. Pain Soc. (pres. 1982-83), Internat. Assn. Study Pain (coun. 1984-90), Am. Physiol. Soc., Soc. Exptl. Biol. Medicine, Soc. Neurosci. (pres. 1984-85), Internat. Brain Rsch. Orgn., Cajal Club, Sigma Xi, Alpha Omega Alpha. Home: 2925 Beluche Dr Galveston TX 77551-1511 Office: U Tex Med Br 301 University Blvd Galveston TX 77555-1069 E-mail: wdwillis@utmb.edu.

WILLIS, WILLIAM ERVIN, lawyer; b. Huntington, W.Va., Oct. 11, 1926; s. Asa Hannon and Mae (Davis) W.; m. Joyce Litteral, Sept. 1, 1949; children: Kathryn Cunningham, Anne Dresser, William. Student, Ind. U., 1944, NYU, 1945; AB, Marshall U., 1948; JD, Harvard, 1951; LHD (hon.), Marshall U., 1997. Bar: N.Y. 1952. Pvt. practice, N.Y.C., 1951—; ptnr. Sullivan & Cromwell, 1960-94, sr. counsel, 1994—. Lectr. Practising Law Inst., 1963—; trustee Fed. Bar Council, 1968-72; mem. 2d Circuit Commn. on Reduction Burdens and Costs Civil Litigation, 1977-82. Co-author Doing Business in America; contbr. Edn. Civil Practice Law Rev. Forms and Guidance for Lawyers, also articles to legal jours. Mem. panel arbitrators Pub. Resources; trustee Tenafly (N.J.) Nature Ctr., 1994—2001, pres., 1997—2001; dir. Soc. Yeager Scholars Marshall U., Huntington, 1995—, v.p., 2001—. With AUS, 1944—46. Fellow Am. Coll. Trial Lawyers, Am. Bar Found.; mem. ABA (standing com. on fed. judiciary 1987-95, chair 1992-93, 94-95), N.Y. Bar Assn. (chmn. antitrust sect. 1976-77, exec. com. 1976-83), Assn. Bar City of N.Y. (chmn. profl. discipline com. 1983-86, chmn. ethics 2000 com. 1999—, judicial conduct 2000—), Fed. Bar Coun. (trustee 1969-72), Am. Judicature Soc., Am. Arbitration Assn. (panel arbitrators), N.Y. Law Inst., N.Y. County Lawyers, Ins. Jud. Adminstrn., India House. Home: 190 Tekening Dr Tenafly NJ 07670-1219 Also: Otterhole Rd West Milford NJ 07480 Office: Sullivan & Cromwell 125 Broad St 28th Fl New York NY 10004-2489

WILLIS, WILLIAM GEORGE, retired civil engineer; b. Bklyn., Aug. 10, 1936; s. William Franklin and Hildegard (Haars) W.; m. Frances Annette Lynch, Nov. 16, 1962; children: Wendy Kirsten Willis Owens, Andrea Willis Rosillo, Karen Elena. BS in Geol. Engring., La. Poly. Inst., 1963. Registered profl. engr., Miss. Civil engr. (rsch.) U.S. Army Waterways Experiment Sta., Vicksburg, Miss., 1963—66; engring. geologist U.S. Army Engr. Dist., Okinawa, Japan, 1966—68, Japan, 1968—71, civil constrn. engr. Albuquerque, El Paso, Dodge City, Kans. and Trinidad, Colo., 1971—75, civil engr. (constrn.), 1975—77, 1977—78; civil engr. (contract mgmt.) U.S. Army Engr. Divsn. Europe, Nuernberg and Frankfurt, Germany, 1978—91, U.S. Army Engring. Dist. Albuquerque, Holloman AFB, N.Mex., 1991—95; ret., 1995. Mem. emergency planning com. for El Paso City of El Paso, 1985; Bd. dirs. Headstart Program, Vicksburg, Miss., 1968—69. With USAF, 1954—58. Avocation: travel. Home: 3004 Del Cerro Alamogordo NM 88310-3949

WILLITS, CRAIG JOSLYN, military officer, operations research specialist; b. Newark, Oct. 13, 1961; s. Gordon Prowell Willits and Jean Marie Leete; m. Sara Elizabeth Brown; children: Steven, David, Joseph. BA, Rutgers U., 1983; MS, Air Force Inst. Tech., 1994, PhD, 1997. Commd. USAF, 1983; advanced through grades to lt. col. Contbr. articles to profl. jours. Mem.: Inst. Ops. Rsch. and Mgmt. Scis., Mil. Order of World Wars (life).

WILLKE, THOMAS ALOYS, university official, statistics educator; b. Rome City, Ind., Apr. 22, 1932; s. Gerard Thomas and Marie Margaret (Wuennemann) W.; m. Geraldine Ann Page, Dec. 28, 1954; children: Richard, Susan, Donald, Jeanne, Mary, Kathleen. AB, Xavier U., 1954; MS, Ohio State U., 1956, PhD, 1960. Sr. engr. N.Am. Aviation, Columbus, Ohio, 1959-60; instr. math. Ohio State U., 1960-61, assoc. prof., 1966-70, assoc. prof. statistics, 1970-72, prof., 1972-73, dir. stats. lab., 1971-73, vice provost Arts and Scis., 1973-86, acting dean Univ. Coll., 1983-86, dean undergrad. studies Arts and Scis., 1986-87; prof. math. scis. Otterbein coll., Westerville, Ohio, 1987-97, chmn. dept. math. scis., 1988-96; rsch. mathematician U.S. Nat. Bur. Standards, Washington, 1961-66; asst. prof. math. U. Md., College Park, 1963-66; prof. statistics, undergrad. dean Ohio State U., 1987—; prof. math. scis. emeritus Otterbein Coll., 1997—. Contbr. articles on statis. non parametric methods and robustness to profl. jours. Mem. Am. Statis. Assn., Math. Assn. Am. Roman Catholic. Home: 4375 Mumford Dr Columbus OH 43220-4438

WILLKE, THOMAS JOHN, family physician; b. Cin., Nov. 2, 1950; s. Alois Henry and Anna Cecilia Willke; m. Lori Ann Allen, Mar. 19, 1994; children: Brittany, Adam, Adam, Andrew, Matthew(dec.). BS, U. Dayton, 1972; MD, U. Cin., 1976. Diplomate Am. Bd. Family Practice, Nat. Bd. Med. Examiners; cert. added qualification in geriatrics. Intern Blodgett Hosp., Grand Rapids, Mich., 1976-77; resident in family medicine St. Mary's Hosp., Evansville, Ind., 1977-79; family physician Wilmington (Ohio) Family Physicians, 1979-82, GCAP, Cin., 1997-98, Health Svcs., Lawrenceburg, Ind., 1998-99, Mercy Health Sys., Indian Springs, Ohio, 1999-2000; pvt. practice family medicine Chillicothe, 1982-97; pvt. practice Indian Springs Family Medicine, 2000—. Lectr., moderator symposiums in field. Internet site developer and asst. for KC, various ch. orgns.; mem. Nat. Right to Life; bd. dirs. Am. Cancer Soc., Chillicothe, 1984-86, Am. Heart Assn., Chillicothe, 1990; active Cath. Big Bros./Big Sisters, Cin., 1977-89; chmn. Freedom Festival Walkway Dance, Evansville, 1977; mem. parish coun. St. John the Bapt. Ch., 1999—. Fellow Am. Acad. Family Physicians; mem. Am. Acad. Family Practice, Ohio State Med. Assn., Ohio Acad. Family Physicians, Butler County Med. Soc., Hamilton-Fairield Area Acad. Medicine, Inc., KC (navigator 1996-97, Knight of Yr. 1997). Roman Catholic. Avocations: gardening, alpine skiing. Office: 4125 Hamilton Middletown Rd Hamilton OH 45011-2262 Fax: (513) 863-6478. E-mail: willkemd@fuse.net.

WILLKIE, WENDELL LEWIS, II, lawyer; b. Indpls., Oct. 29, 1951; s. Philip Herman Willkie and Rosalie (Heffelfinger) Hall; m. Carlotta Fendig; children: Alexandra Elizabeth, Diana Fendig, Caroline Heffelfinger. AB, Harvard U., 1973; BA, Oxford (Eng.) U., 1975, MA, 1983; JD, U. Chgo., 1978. Bar: N.Y. 1979. Assoc. Simpson Thacher and Bartlett, N.Y.C., 1978-82; gen. counsel NEH, Washington, 1982-84; assoc. counsel to Pres. The White House, 1984-85; chief of staff, counselor to Sec. U.S. Dept. Edn., 1985, gen. counsel, 1985-88; counsel Office of the Pres.-elect, 1988-89; gen. counsel Dept. of Commerce, 1989-93; v.p. Westvaco Corp., N.Y.C., 1995-96, sr. v.p., gen. counsel, 1996—. Vis. fellow Am. Enterprise Inst., Washington, 1993-94. Co-author, editor: (with J.R. Lilley) Beyond MFN: Trade with China and American Interests, 1994. Harvard U. scholar, 1969-73, Rhodes scholar, 1973-75. Republican. Episcopalian. Office: Westvaco Corp 1 High Ridge Park Stamford CT 06905

WILLMANN, DONNIE GLENN, safety executive; b. Waco, Tex., Aug. 25, 1955; s. Robert and Marie Louise (Schraeder) W.; m. Susan Lynn Martin, June 14, 1975. Student, Tarleton State U., 1973-75; BS in Indsl. Tech., Tex. A & M U., 1978. Cert. safety profl. Mfg. ops. devel. trainee Sii Drilco, Houston, 1978-80, loss control rep., 1980-81; safety mgr. Weatherford/Lamb U.S. Inc., 1981-83; corp. safety mgr. Weatherford Internat., 1983-86; loss control specialist CNA Ins., 1986-88; sr. safety adminstr. Enron Ops. Corp., 1988-96; mgr. safety/environ. Enron Internat., 1996-99, dir. environ. health and safety, 2000—. Mem. Am. Soc. Safety Engrs. (membership chmn. 1989-90, treas. 1990-91, v.p. membership 1991-92, program chmn. 1992-94, pres.-elect. 1994-95, pres. 1995-96, named Gulf Coast chpt. Safety Profl. of Yr. 1994-95, asst. v.p. region III 1995-96), Nat. Safety Mgmt. Soc. Lutheran. Avocations: fishing, hunting, raquetball, woodworking. Home: 258 Lago Trace Dr Huffman TX 77336-4681 Office: Enron Corp 1400 Smith St Houston TX 77002-7327

WILLMARTH, WILLIAM WALTER, aerospace engineering educator; b. Highland Park, Ill., Mar. 25, 1924; s. Sinclair Anson and Dorothy (Cox) W.; m. Nancy Robinson, Nov. 20, 1959; children— Robert, Deborah, Elizabeth, Kathleen. BS in Mech. Engring, Purdue U., 1949; MS in Aero. Engring, Calif. Inst. Tech., 1950, PhD, 1954. Research fellow, then sr. research fellow Calif. Inst. Tech., 1954-58; mem. faculty U. Mich., Ann Arbor, 1958—, prof. aerospace engring., 1961-90, prof. emeritus aerospace engring., 1990—. Cons. to industry, 1952— Author papers, reports. Served with AUS, 1943-46. Vis. fellow Joint Inst. Lab. Astrophysics, Boulder, Colo., 1963-64; fellow Max Planck Inst. für Stromungsforschung, Göttingen, Fed. Republic Germany, summer 1975 Fellow AIAA, Am. Phys. Soc. (Fluid Dynamics prize 1989); mem. AAUP, Sigma Xi, Tau Beta Pi, Tau Sigma. Home: 765 Country Club Rd Ann Arbor MI 48105-1034

WILLMORE, LUTHER JAMES, JR. neurologist, academic administrator, educator; b. Fredericktown, Mo., Dec. 2, 1941; s. Luther James and Eunice Marie (Burkett) W.; m. Carolyn Lois Gilda, Dec. 10, 1961; children: John Andrew, Sydney Rebecca, Theodore Martin, Charles Caleb. BS, St. Louis U., 1964, MD cum laude, 1968. Diploma Am. Bd. Psychiatry and Neurology and Clin. Neurophysiology. Intern in surgery St. Louis U. Hosps., 1968-69; med. officer Naval Acad. Hosp. USS Austin (LPD-4) USN, Norfolk, Va., Annapolis, Md., 1969-72; resident in neurology U. Va., Charlottesville, 1972-75; from asst. to assoc. prof. neurology and neurobiology U. Fla. Coll. Medicine, Gainesville, 1975-82; faculty U. Tex., Houston, 1982-99, prof. neurology, dir. Tex. Comprehensive Epilepsy program; assoc. dean admissions and student affairs Sch. Medicine St. Louis U., 1999—, prof. neurology and pharmacology and physiology, 1999—. Contbr. numerous articles to profl. jours., book chpts.; editor numerous monographs. Profl. adv. bd. Epilepsy Found. Am., 1979-87; chair profl. adv. bd. Epilepsy Found. SE Tex., 1996-98; pres. Fla. Epilepsy Found., 1978-80; gov.'s commn. advocacy for persons with devel. disabilities State Fla., 1980-82. Named Physician of Yr. Tex. Rehab. Commn., 1984-85. Fellow Am. Acad. Neurology; mem. Am. Epilepsy Soc., Am. Neurol. Assn., Soc. Neurosci., Jesuit Men's Hon. Soc. (John Horsley Meml. prize 1980). Achievements include creation of a model of epilepsy in animals, research contribution in neurochemistry and molecular biology of epilepsy, and clinical drug development. Avocations: skiing, backpacking. Office: St Louis U Sch Medicine Office of Admissions 1402 S Grand Blvd Saint Louis MO 63104-1004

WILLMORE, ROBERT LOUIS, lawyer; b. Ramstein AFB, Fed. Republic Germany, July 16, 1955; s. Wendell James and Theresia Willmore. BS in Econs., MIT, 1977; JD, Yale U., 1980. Bar: D.C. 1981, U.S. Ct. Appeals (D.C. cir.) 1985. Legis. asst. Senator Carl T. Curtis, Washington, 1977-78; law clk. to presiding judge U.S. Dist. Ct. (no. dist.) Tex., Dallas, 1980-81; assoc. Shaw, Pittman, Potts & Trowbridge, Washington, 1981-82; asst. gen. counsel Office of Mgmt. and Budget, Exec. Office of the Pres., 1982-85; dep. asst. atty. gen. civil div. U.S. Dept. Justice, 1985-88; of counsel Arent, Fox, Kintner, Plotkin & Kahn, 1988-93; ptnr. Crowell & Moring LLP, 1993—. Exec. sec. Cabinet Council Tort Policy Working Group, Washington, 1985-88; chmn. task force on liability ins. availability, Washington, 1985-88. Editor Yale Law Jour., 1979-80. Mem. ABA, D.C. Bar Assn. Republican. Roman Catholic. Home: 1120 Old Cedar Rd Mc Lean VA 22102-2437 Office: Crowell & Moring 1001 Pennsylvania Ave NW Fl 14 Washington DC 20004-2595 E-mail: rwillmore@crowell.com.

WILLNER, ALAN ELI, electrical engineer, educator; b. Bklyn., Nov. 16, 1962; s. Gerald and Sondra (Bernstein) W.; m. Michelle Frida Green, June 25, 1991. BA, Yeshiva U., 1982; MS, Columbia U., 1984, PhD, 1988. Summer tech. staff David Sarnoff Rsch. Ctr., Princeton, N.J., 1983, 84; grad. rsch. asst. dept. elec. engring. Columbia U., N.Y.C., 1984-88; postdoctoral mem. tech. staff AT&T Bell Labs., Holmdel, N.J., 1988-90; mem. tech. staff Bell Communications Rsch., Red Bank, 1990-91; prof. U. So. Calif., L.A., 1992—, assoc. dir. Ctr. Photonic Tech., 1994—. Head del. Harvard Model UN Yeshiva U., 1982; instr. Columbia U., 1987; rev. panel mem. NSF, Washington, 1992, Washington, 93, Washington, 94, invited optical comm. workshop, 94; chair panel on optical info. and comm., 94; program co-chair Conf. on Lasers and Electro-Optics; steering com. and tech. com. mem. Conf. Optical Fiber Comm. Author 1 book; contbr. articles to IEEE Photonics Tech. Letters, Jour Lightwave Tech., Jour. Optical Engring., Jour. Electrochem. Soc., Electronics Letters, Applied Physics Letters, Applied Optics; assoc. editor Jour. Lighwave Tech., editor-in-chief; editor-in-chief IEEE Jour. Selected Topics in Quantum Electronics. Mem. faculty adv. bd. U. So. Calif. Hillel Orgn., 1992. Recipient Disting. Lecturer award, IEEE Lasers and Electro-Optics Soc., Best Engring. Tchr. award, USC/TRW, Armstrong Found. prize, Columbia U., 1984, young investigator award, NSF, 1992; fellow, Semiconductor Rsch. Corp., 1986, Sci. and Engring., David and Lucile Packard Found., 1993, presdl. faculty, NSF, 1994, sr. scholar, Fulbright Found., 1997; grantee NSF, Advanced Rsch. Projects Agy., Packard Found., Powell Found., Ballistic Missile Def. Orgn. Fellow: Optical Soc. Am. (symposium organizer ann. mtg. 1992, panel organizer ann. mtg. 1993, symposium organizer ann. mtg. 1995, panel organizer ann. mtg. 1995, program com. for conf. on optical fiber commn. 1996, 1997, vice chair optical comm. group, tech. coun. chair photonics divsn., program co-chair ann. mtg., tech. council chair-photonics divsn., program co-chair of OSA Annual Mtg., co-chair sci. and engring. coun.); mem.: IEEE (sr.; editor-in-chief IEEE/OSA Jour. Lightwave Tech.), Soc. Photo-Instrumentation Engring. (program chair telecomm. engring. photonics west 1995, chmn. conf. on emerging techs. for all-optical networks photonics west 1995, program com. for conf. on Optical Fiber Comm. 1996, conf. program com. components for WDM), IEEE Lasers and Electro-Optics Soc. (chmn. optical comm. subcom. ann. mtg. 1994, v.p. tech. affairs, mem. optical comm. tech. com., bd. govs., chmn. optical commn. tech. com., mem. optical networks tech. com., various awards coms., elected mem. bd. govs., awards com. mem. Quantum Electronics, IEEE Fellow, elected bd. govs., Disting. Lectr. award), Sigma Xi. Achievements include patents for localized photochemical etching of multilayered semiconductor body, optical star coupler utilizing fiber amplifier technology, and one-to-many simultaneous optical WDM 2-dim. plane interconnections. Home: 9326 Sawyer St Los Angeles CA 90035-4102 Office: U So Calif Dept Elec Engring Eeb 538 Los Angeles CA 90089-0001

WILLNER, ANN RUTH, political scientist, educator; b. N.Y.C., Sept. 2, 1924; d. Norbert and Bella (Richman) W. BA cum laude, Hunter Coll., 1945; MA, Yale U., 1946; PhD, U. Chgo., 1961. Lectr. U. Chgo., 1946-47, research assoc. Ctr. for Econ. Devel. and Cultural Change, 1954-56, 61-62; advisor on orgn. and tng. Indonesian Ministry for Fgn. Affairs, Jakarta, 1952-53; expert for small scale indsl. planning Indonesian Nat. Planning Bur., 1953-54; fgn. affairs analyst Congl. Reference Service, Library of Congress, 1960; asst. prof. polit. sci. Harpur Coll., Binghamton, N.Y., 1962-63; postdoctoral fellow polit. sci. and Southeast Asian studies Yale U., New Haven, 1963-64; research assoc. Ctr. Internat. Studies, Princeton U., 1964-69; assoc. prof. polit. sci. U. Kans., Lawrence, 1969-70, prof., 1970-98. Vis. prof. polit. sci. CUNY, 1975; cons. govt. agys. and pvt. industry Polit. sci. editor: Ency. of the Social Scis., 1961; mem. editl. bd. Econ. Devel. and Cultural Change, 1954-57, Jour. Comparative Adminstrn., 1969-74, Comparative Politics, 1977— ; author: The Neotraditional Accomodation to Political Independence, 1966, Charismatic Political Leadership: A Theory, 1968, The Spellbinders, 1984; also monographs, jour. articles, book chpts., newspaper columns. Grantee Rockefeller Found., 1965, Social Sci. Rsch. and Am. Coun. Learned Socs., 1966 Mem. Am. Polit. Sci. Assn. (gov. council 1979-81) Home: # N 405 560 N St SW # N405 Washington DC 20024-4605

WILLNER, DOROTHY, anthropologist, educator; b. N.Y.C., Aug. 26, 1927; d. Norbert and Bella (Richman) W. Ph.B., U. Chgo., 1947, MA, 1953, PhD, 1961; postgrad., Ecole Pratique des Hautes Etudes, U. Paris, France, 1953-54. Anthropologist Jewish Agy., Israel, 1955-58; tech. asst., adminstrn. expert in community devel. UN, Mexico, 1958; asst. prof. dept. sociology and anthropology U. Iowa, Iowa City, 1959-60; research assoc. U. Chgo., 1961-62; asst. prof. dept. sociology and anthropology U. N.C., Chapel Hill, 1962-63, Hunter Coll., N.Y.C., 1964-65; assoc. prof. dept. anthropology U. Kans., Lawrence, 1967-70, prof., 1970-90; professorial lectr. Johns Hopkins U. Sch. Advanced Internat. Studies, 1992. Author: Community Leadership, 1960, Nation-Building and Community in Israel, 1969. Contbr. numerous articles to profl. publs. Fellow Am. Anthrop. Assn., Soc. Applied Anthropology, Royal Anthrop. Inst.; mem. Cen. States Anthrop. Soc. (past pres.), Assn. Polit. and Legal Anthropology (past pres.). Home: # N 407 560 N St SW Washington DC 20024-4605

WILLNER, EUGENE BURTON, food and liquor company executive; b. Chgo., July 27, 1934; s. Fred and Mae (Goodhartz) W.; m. Karen Nell Kate, Feb. 22, 1962; children: Tracy Fran, Kelly Kaye. BA, Northwestern U., 1956. Pres. World Wide Fisheries Inc., Chgo., 1956-60; merchandiser Edison Bros. Stores Inc., St. Louis, 1960-66; v.p. Mo. Supreme Life Ins. Co., 1966-67; exec. v.p. Exec. Agys., Inc., 1966-67; pres. Bluff Creek Industries, Inc., Ocean Springs, Miss., 1967-69, Purse String Stores, Inc., Miami, Fla., 1969-73, World Wide Fisheries, Miami, 1969-73, Renwill Seafoods, Inc., 1979—. Chmn. bd. Astral Liquors, Inc., Foxy Laidy Lounges, Prime Universal Seafood Corp., Miami, also Key West, Fla., Caracas, Venezuela, San Juan del Sur, Nicaragua, Quito, Ecuador; pres., chmn. bd. Common Markets, Inc., Miami, London and Moscow, 1980— Mem. Deering Bay Country Club, Turnberry Club, Grove Isle Club, Fisher Island Club, Palm Beach Country Club. Office: 29000 S Dixie Hwy Homestead FL 33033-2302 Address: PO Box 561944 Miami FL 33256-1944 E-mail: asiamoon@att.net.

WILLNER, JAY R. consulting company executive; b. Aurora, Ill., Sept. 22, 1924; s. Charles R. and Ida (Winer) W.; m. Suzanne Wehmann, July 17, 1958; 1 child, Adam. Student, UCLA, 1946-48; BS, MIT, 1950; MBA, Rutgers U., 1959. Researcher Andrew Brown Co., Los Angeles, 1950-52; tech. salesman Glidden Co., 1952-54; market researcher Roger Williams Inc., N.Y.C., 1954-59; sr. market analyst Calif. Chem. Co., San Francisco, 1959-63; mgr. planning chem. coatings div. Mobil Chem. Co., N.Y.C., 1963-68; pres. WEH Corp., San Francisco, 1968—. Lectr. U. Calif., Berkeley, 1962—; adj. faculty U. San Francisco, 1977—; U.S. corr. German mag. Farbe & Lack. Contbg. editor Jour. Protective Coatings and Linings; editor The WEH Report; author 2d Ann. Comprehensive Survey for Steel Structures Painting Coun. Supporter San Francisco Mus. of Modern Art. 2d lt. A.C., AUS, 1943-46. Mem. Am. Chem. Soc. (50-yr. mem.), Steel Structures Painting Coun., Mechs. Libr., Chemists Club (N.Y.C.), MIT Club No. Calif. Home: 700 Presidio Ave San Francisco CA 94115-2956 Office: WEH Corp PO Box 470038 San Francisco CA 94147-0038 E-mail: jrw@wehcorp.com.

WILLNER, LARRY ELLIOTT, telecommunications company executive, consultant; b. New Haven, May 16, 1932; s. Abraham Louis and Ann (Kaye) W.; m. Inga Katz, Oct. 28, 1956; children: Allan, Susan. BS in Engring., U.S. Mil. Acad., 1954; MBA in Fin., Stanford U., 1964; diploma with distinction, Nat. Def. U., 1975. Commd. 2d lt. U.S. Army, 1954, advanced through grades to Col., ret., 1980; from dir. to v.p., gen. mgr. Govt. Systems Divsn. Western Union Corp., McLean, Va., 1981-86; sr. v.p. Govt. Networks Divsn. Contel Corp., 1986-87; group v.p. Info. Systems and Networks Inc., Bethesda, Md., 1988-89; exec. v.p. INTACT Inc., Chantilly, Va., 1989-97; v.p. Sherikon Corp., 1997-99. Chmn. bd. dirs. Western Union Hawaii, Honolulu, 1985-86; cons. Identity Rsch. Inc., McLean, 1981-92, U.S. Sprint Corp., Herndon, Va., 1989-97, Ops. Rsch., Arlington, Va., 1981, GTE Corp., McLean, 1990-91, Computer Scis. Corp., Falls Church, Va., 1991-97, ARINC, Inc., 1991-92, Boeing Computer Svcs., 1992-94, Harris Corp., 1992, Grumman Corp., 1992, GSI/Infonet, 1993-95, Boeing Info. Svcs., 1994-95, AT&T, 1994-96, Andrulis Rsch. Corp., 1993-94, SRC Corp., 1994, DC Net, Inc., 1993-95, UNITEL Communication Corp., 1993-96, AT&T Canada, 1997, A.T. Kearney Corp., 1995-97, Sherikon Corp., 1996-97, 99-2000, Cable and Wireless Corp., 1997, USAA Ednl. Found., 1999-2000. Contbr. articles on telecommunications, fgn. policy, weapons systems acquisition, etc. to profl. jours. Decorated Disting. Svc. medal, Legion of Merit, Bronze Star; Disting. Rsch. fellow Nat. Def. U., 1975; named Hon. Prof. systems acquisitions Def. Systems Mgmt. Coll., 1974. Mem. IEEE, Armed Forces Communications-Electronics Assn. (internat. bd. 1986-90), Nat. Def. Exec. Res., Fed. Communications Commn. Nat. Industry Adv. Com., Stanford Grad. Sch. Bus. Alumni Assn. (chpt. bd. dirs. 1980-83), Masons, Scottish Rite. Republican. Jewish. Avocations: fishing, photography, collecting cameras. Home: 4160 Elizabeth Ln Annandale VA 22003-3648

WILLOCKS, ROBERT MAX, retired librarian; b. Maryville, Tenn., Oct. 1, 1924; s. Willis Lemuel and Hannah (Emert) W.; m. Neysa Nerene Ferguson, May 23, 1947; children— Margret Sharon, Samuel David, Mark Timothy, Robert Daniel, Kent Max. BA, Maryville Coll., 1949; B.D., Golden Gate Bapt. Theol. Sem., 1951, Th.M., 1962; MA in Library Sci, Peabody Coll., 1962. Ordained to ministry Bapt. Ch., 1950; pastor in Calif., 1950-56; missionary to Korea So. Bapt. Fgn. Mission Bd., Taejon, 1956- 65; asso. dir. library Heidelberg Coll., Tiffin, Ohio, 1965-67; dir. library Columbia (S.C.) Coll., 1967-70; asst. dir. libraries Syracuse (N.Y.) U., 1970-76; assoc. dir. libraries U. Fla., Gainesville, 1976-83, acting dir. libraries, 1983-84, dep. dir. libraries, 1984-89, ret., 1989; pastor Northwood Bapt. Ch., 1981-92; libr. Bapt. Theol. Sem., Lusaka, Zambia, 1994-97, Ghana Bapt. Sem., Kumasi, 1998—2002. Acting dir. Fla. Ctr. for Libr. Automation, 1984; cons. Choong Chung Nam Province Library Assn., Republic of Korea, 1962—65; dir. Korea Bapt. Press, 1959—61; prof. ch. history Korea Bapt. Sem., 1957—65, acting pres., 1958—59, librarian, 1959—65; vice chmn. Korea Bapt. Mission, 1962—64; del. Fla. Gov.'s Conf. on Libraries, 1978. Editor: Korean translations Thus it is Written, 1963, The Progress of Worldwide Missions, 1965. Chmn. trustees Wallace Meml. Bapt. Hosp., Pusan, Korea, 1964-65; pres. bd. dirs. Phoenix Homeowners Assn., 1980-88. With USNR, 1943-46. Mem. ALA (chmn. telefacsimile com. 1976-78, tech. com. 1980-84, chmn. standards com. 1985-88), Fla. Libr. Assn., Southeastern Library Assn., AAUP, Peabody Coll. Alumni Assn. (pres. S.C. 1968-69) Home: 1930 NW 12th Rd Gainesville FL 32605-5338

WILLOUGHBY, ANNE, health facility administrator, researcher, educator; Rschr. NICHD, 1984, leader pediat., adolescent, and maternal AIDS, educator HIV/AIDS in mothers and children; dir. Rsch. Mothers and Children's Ctr., 2002—. Office: 6100 Executive Bldg Rm 4B11 Bethesda MD 20892*

WILLOUGHBY, JOHN WALLACE, former college dean, provost; b. Brumanna, Lebanon, July 30, 1932; s. James Wallace and Ida Cecilia (Front) Willoughby; m. Joanne Arnoldt DeWitt, Sept. 2, 1959; children: James Wallace, David Frost. BA, Yale U., 1952; BA, MA, Oxford U., Eng., 1954; PhD, U. Rochester, 1959. Instr. English U. N.Mex., Albuquerque, 1959—60; instr. U. Chgo., 1960—63; from asst. prof. to prof., dean faculty Southampton Coll. Long Island, NY, 1963—73; v.p. for acad. affairs S.W. Minn. State Coll., Marshall, 1973—74, St. Francis Coll., Loretto, Pa., 1974—83; provost, dean of faculty, dir. continuing edn. Southwestern Coll., Winfield, Kans., 1983—92; distributor Success Motivation Inst., 1988—2001, dir. region VII (Kans., Mo., Iowa, Nebr.), 2000—01; distributor Leadership Mgmt., Inc., 2001—. Editor: English: Selected Readings, 1963; assoc. editor Brownings Correspondence Wedgestone Press, 1993-99; contbr. articles to profl. jours. Mem. com. on preparation for ministry South Kans. Presbytery, 1989—95, 1997—2002; treas. Cambria-Somerset Coun. for Health Edn., Johnstown, Pa., 1976—83; v.p. for scouting Penns Woods coun. Boy Scouts Am., 1978—82; pres. Winfield (Kans.) Lions Club, 1996—97. Rhodes scholar, Oxford, 1952-54 Mem. Am. Assn. Rhodes Scholars. Democrat. Presbyterian. Avocations: bicycling; camping; philately; gardening; singing. Home: 24 Braid Hills Dr Winfield KS 67156-6304 E-mail: jowill@hit.net.

WILLOUGHBY, ROBERT EARL, minister, writer; b. Detroit, Dec. 12, 1923; s. Earl Thomas Willoughby and Myrtle Irene Snider; m. Mary Barber, Dec. 18, 1945 (div. Apr. 1970); children: Barbara, Jeanne, Mary Ann, Robert; m. Elizabeth Darrow Eaman, June 10, 1970. BA in English, Duke U., 1945; MDiv, Yale U., 1948; MEd, Wayne State U., 1972. Ordained to ministry Meth. Ch., 1948. Min. Meth. Ch., Mich., 1948-68; tchr. Highland Park (Mich.) Schs., 1968-85; min. Unitarian Ch., Troy, Mich., 1969-80; writer Fithian Press, Santa Barbara, Calif., 1998—. Editl. advisor Lit. Cavalcade, 1975-77; author: Christian Mandates for a New Millennium, 2000, 21st Century Christianity: Dilemmas the Church Must Face or Die, 2001; editor Highland Park Tchr. Democrat. Home: 1001 Carpenters Way A323 Lakeland FL 33809-3928

WILLOUGHBY, STEPHEN SCHUYLER, mathematics educator; b. Madison, Wis., Sept. 27, 1932; s. Alfred and Elizabeth Frances (Cassell) W.; m. Helen Sali Shapiro, Aug. 29, 1954; children: Wendy Valentine (Mrs. Peter Gallen), Todd Alan. AB (scholar), Harvard U., 1953, AM in Teaching, 1955; EdD (Clifford Brewster Upton fellow), Columbia U., 1961. Tchr. Newton (Mass.) Pub. Schs., 1954-57, Greenwich (Conn.) Pub. Schs., 1957-59; instr. U. Wis., Madison, 1960-61, asst. prof. math. edn. and math., 1961-65; prof. math. edn. and math. NYU, 1965-87, dir. math. edn. dept., 1967-83, chmn. math., sci. and stats. edn. dept., 1970-80, 86-87, chmn. Univ. Faculty Council, 1981-82; prof. math. U. Ariz., Tucson, 1987—. Mem. nat. bd. advisor Sq. One TV, 1983-94, U.S. Commn. on Math. Instrn., 1984-95, chmn., 1991-95; math. adv. com. Nat. Tchr. Exam. Successor (Praxis), 1989-94; edn. panel New Am. Schs. Devel. Corp., 1991-97; U.S. Nat. rep. Internat. Commn. on Math. Instrn., 1991-95. Author: Contemporary Teaching of Secondary School Mathematics, 1967, Probability and Statistics, 1968, Teaching Mathematics: What Is Basic, 1981, Mathematics Education for a Changing World, 1990, Real Math, 1981, 85, 87, 91, Math: Explorations and Applications, 1998, College Mathematics Through Applications, 1999, The Other End of the Log: Memoirs of an Education Rebel, 2002; contbr. articles to profl. jours. and encys., chpts. to yearbooks and anthologies. Recipient Leadership in Math. Edn. Lifetime Achievement medal, 1995. Mem. Nat. Coun. Tchrs. Math. (dir. 1968-71, pres. 1982-84), Coun. Sci. Soc. Pres. (chmn. 1988). Home: 5435 E Gleneagles Dr Tucson AZ 85718-1805 Office: U Ariz Dept Math Tucson AZ 85721-0001

WILLOUGHBY, WILLIAM FRANKLIN, II, physician, researcher; b. Washington, Feb. 4, 1936; s. William Westel and Patricia (DeZychlinska) W.; m. Mary Scott Fishburne, 1963 (div. 1974); children: Westel Woodbury, William Franklin III, Laura Fishburne, Mary Scott; m. Judith Eleanor Barbaras, Oct. 25, 1975; 1 child, Robert Alexander Willoughby. AB, Johns Hopkins U., 1957, MD, PhD in Microbiology, Johns Hopkins U., 1965; grad. with distinction, USAF War Coll., 1985. Diplomate Am. Bd. Pathology. Intern then resident in pathology Johns Hopkins Hosp., 1965-67; asst. prof. depts. pathology and microbiology Case Western Res. U., Cleve.; dir. Virginia Mason Rsch. Ctr., Seattle, 1972-75; assoc. prof. dept. pathology Sch. Medicine, Johns Hopkins U., Balt., 1975-87; prof., chmn. dept. pathology Sch. Medicine, U. S.C., Columbia, 1987-92; dir. labs. Cook County Hosp., Chgo., 1992-98, interim med. dir., 1994-96. Cons. NIH, Bethesda, Md., 1979-98, mem. pathology A study sect., 1982-86; cons. NRC, Washington, 1981-84; mem. Res. Component Med. Coun., Dept. Def., Pentagon, 1991-93; dep. surgeon gen. for res. affairs USAF, Bolling AFB, D.C., 1993-95; asst. surg. gen. USAF, Operation Desert Storm/Desert Shield, 1990-91. Mem. editorial bd. Am. Rev. Respiratory Disease, 1978-84; contbr. articles to profl. jours., reviewer numerous sci. manuscripts. Vestryman Trinity Episcopal Ch., Long Green, Md., 1984-87; bd. dirs. Ctrl. S.C. chpt. ARC, Columbia, 1989-92; bd. fellow Norwich U., 1992-95. Maj. USAFR, 1975-95, advanced through grades to maj. gen., 1992-95. Decorated D.S.M., Legion of Merit, Meritorious Svc. medal; recipient Edwin E. Osgood prize Va. Mason Rsch. Ctr., 1973; Arthritis Found. fellow Scripps Clinic and Rsch. Found., 1967-69; Poncine scholar Poncine Found., 1972-74; NIH rsch. grantee, 1976-91. Fellow Coll. Am. Pathologists; mem. AAAS, Am. Soc. Investigative Pathology, Am. Assn. Immunologists, Am. Soc. Cell Biologists, Chgo. Coun. Fgn. Rels., Internat. Acad. Pathology, Assn. Pathology Chmns., Aerospace Med. Assn., Soc. USAF Flight Surgeons (bd. govs. 1993-96), Soc. Cons. to Armed Forces, Am. Thoracic Soc., Assn. Mil. Surgeons U.S., Army Navy Club (Washington), Air Force Assn., Midtown Tennis Club (Chgo.). Avocations: aviation, music, tennis, genealogy. Home: 1416A S Federal St Chicago IL 60605-2739 E-mail: wwilloughby@aol.com.

WILLOW, CHARLES CHANG, computer scientist, educator; b. Seoul, Republic of Korea, Jan. 9, 1966; s. Chul Hyun Willow and Kyung Soon Park; m. Saran Ran Sei Ran OH, May 30, 2001; children: Ocean. MS, Tex. A&M U., 1993; PhD, U. Calif., Berkeley, 1996, U. Houston, 1999. Registered profl. engr., Calif. Post-doctorate rsch. assoc. NASA/U. of Houston, 1997—99; assoc. prof. of computer info. sys. NY Inst. of Tech., Old Westbury, 2000—. Sr. tech. cons. Microsoft, Redmond, Wash., 1994—96. Author: (software development, nasa) Integrated System Design Methodology, 1999 (Best Rschr. Award, NASA, JSC, 1999); contbr. articles to profl. jours. Second lt., 1989—90, South Korea. Recipient Career award, NSF, 2001. Fellow: IEEE; mem.: Internat. Simultaneous Interpreters Soc., Inst. of Indsl. Engineers, Am. Computing Machinery. Office: NY Inst Tsch Sch Mgmt PO Box 8000 Old Westbury NY 11568-8000 Office Fax: 516-484-8328. E-mail: cwillow@nyit.edu.

WILLOW, JUDITH ANN LOYE, tax preparer; b. Harrisburg, Pa., Oct. 2, 1939; d. John Steve and Mary Grace (Bergstresser) Loye; m. Robert Glenn Willow, June 14, 1957; 1 child, Robert Allen. Grad. high sch., Harrisburg. Cert. tax preparation, Pa.; enrolled agent IRS, 1997. Legal sec. McNees, Wallace & Nurick, Harrisburg, 1957-58; tax preparer H&R Block, 1966—. Tax info. source TV interviews, Sta. WHP-TV 21, Harrisburg, 1982—, Sta. WHTM-TV 27, Harrisburg, 1988-89. Dir. Dauphin (Pa.) Recreation Assn., 1970-80; water safety instr. ARC, Harrisburg, 1970-80; v.p. PTA, Dauphin, 1966, sec., 1968. Mem. Nat. Honor Soc. Democrat. Mem. Lds Ch. Avocations: reading, swimming, travel. Home: 704 Charles Rd PO Box 171 Dauphin PA 17018-0171 Office: H&R Block Premium Olde Liberty Sq Harrisburg PA 17109 E-mail: judytaxldy@aol.com.

WILLOX, JAMES HUGH, realtor; b. Cheyenne, Wyo., Feb. 16, 1967; s. James Andrew and Susan Adell W.; m. Tione Marie Johnson, Apr. 8, 1995; children: Bolton, James. BS in Agrl. Econs., U. Wyo., 1989. Intern U.S. Rep. Craig Thomas, Washington, 1990; realtor--farm and ranch. Chmn. Convers County GOP, Douglas, 1993-98, dist. rep., 1997-98, state GOP vice chmn. 1999—; coach Little League Basketball, Douglas, 1991-92. Mem. Local, State, and Nat. Stockgrowers, U. Wyo. Alumni, Moose, Alpha Gamma Rho. Episcopalian. Avocations: politics, reading, basketball refereeing. Home and Office: 630 Poplar Douglas WY 82633

WILLRICH, MASON, energy industry executive; b. L.A., 1933; m. Patricia Rowe, June 11, 1960 (dec. July 1996); m. Wendy Webster, Aug. 30, 1997; children: Christopher, Stephen, Michael, Katharine. BA magna cum laude, Yale U., 1954; JD, U. Calif., Berkeley, 1960. Atty. Pillsbury Madison and Sutro, San Francisco, 1960-62; asst. gen. coun. U.S. Arms Control and Disarmament Agy., 1962-65; assoc. prof. law U. Va., 1965-68, prof. law, 1968-75, John Stennis prof. law, 1975-79; dir. internat. rels. Rockefeller Found., N.Y.C., 1976-79; v.p. Pacific Gas & Electric, San Francisco, 1979-84, sr. v.p., 1984-88, exec. v.p., 1988-89; CEO, pres. PG&E Enterprises, 1989-94; exec. Pacific Gas and Electric Co., 1979-94; chmn. EnergyWorks, 1995-98; prin. Nth Power Technologies, Inc., 1996-99, spl. ltd. ptnr., 1999—2002. Author: Non-Proliferation Treaty, 1969, Global Politics of Nuclear Energy, 1971, (with T.B. Taylor) Nuclear Theft, 1974, Energy and World Politics, 1975, Administration of Energy Shortages, 1976, (with R.K. Lester) Radioactive Waste Management and Regulation, 1977. Trustee, past chmn. World Affairs Coun. No. Calif.; trustee, past chmn. Midland Sch.; dir. Evergreen Solar, Inc., Winrock Internat., Atlantic Coun. Guggenheim Meml. fellow, 1973. Mem. Phi Beta Kappa, Order of Coif. Office: 38 Dudley Ct Piedmont CA 94611-3442 E-mail: willrichm@aol.com.

WILLS, BART FRANCIS, insurance company executive; b. Champaign, Ill., Jan. 22, 1955; s. Creed A. and Betty L. (Reifsteck) W. AAS, Parkland Coll., 1975; BS, So. Ill. U., 1977. Registered Health Underwriter, Am. Coll., Bryn Mawr, Pa. Coord. Program Runaway Youth U. Ill. (YMCA), Champaign, 1978; caseworker Survival Skills Program (YMCA), 1978-79, dir., 1979-80, Champaign County Youth Svcs., 1980-82; ins. agt., registered rep. Prudential Ins. Co., Champaign, 1982-95; with 1st Alliance Fin. Group, Inc., 1991—. Del. 2000 Congl. Small Bus. Summit, Nat. Fedn.Ind. Bus. Adv. bd. Ill. Children's Home and Aid Roundhouse Program, 1980; treas. Ill. Youth Svc. Bur., 1981-82; bd. dirs. Champaign County Mental Health, 1998-2002. Mem. Champaign Area Assn. Life Underwriters (chmn. legis. com. 1984-93, pub. rels. chmn. 1994-95, membership chmn. 1995-96, pres.-elect 1996-97, pres. 1997-98), Assn. Health Ins. Agts., Life Underwriters Polit. Action Com. (regional chmn. 1989-96), Ill. Life Underwriters Assn. (nat. quality award 1984-89, 91-92), Ill. Assn. Ins. and Fin. Advisors (regional v.p. 1999-2000), Ill. Movers and Warehousemen's Assn. (assoc.), Am. Oil Chemists Soc. Assn., Champaign County C. of C. (govt. affairs com. 1994-2000), Champaign C. of C. (legis. com. 1988-93, environ subcom. 1993-97), So. Ill. Alumni Assn., Heritage Found., Lincolnshire Fields Country Club, Stonecreek Golf Club, Fighting Illini Dugout Club (v.p. 2002--). Republican. Methodist. Avocations: golf, sports, softball, travel, investing. Home: 4202 Ironwood Ln Champaign IL 61822-9340 Office: 1st Alliance Fin Group Inc 206 N Randolph St Ste 400 Champaign IL 61820-3949 E-mail: bfw@first-alliance.com.

WILLS, CHARLES FRANCIS, former church executive, retired career officer; b. Avalon, N.J., July 26, 1914; s. Charles H. and Anna Margaret (Diemand) W.; m. Charlotte Emily Robson, Aug. 22, 1936; children: C. Frederic, Emily, Sally and Larry (twins). BS, Wheaton (Ill.) Coll., 1935; B.D., Eastern Bapt. Theol. Sem., 1938, Th.M., 1941; grad., Air War Coll., 1961. Commd. 1st lt. U.S. Army, 1941; advanced through grades to col. U.S. Air Force, 1963; chaplain AUS, 1941-49, U.S. Air Force, 1949-67; ret., 1967; exec. dir. chaplaincy services Am. Bapt. Chs., Valley Forge, Pa., 1969-75, exec. dir. profl. services, 1975-78; assoc. sec. Bapt. World Alliance, Washington, 1978-80, treas., 1980-81. Mem. Commn. on Doctrine and Interchurch Cooperation, 1980-90. Decorated Legion of Merit, Bronze Star, Purple Heart. Mem. Mil. Chaplains Assn., Mil. Order of Purple Heart.

WILLS, DAVID WOOD, minister, educator; b. Portland, Ind., Jan. 25, 1942; s. Theodore Oscar Mitchell and Elizabeth Lochore (Wood) W.; m. Carolyn Reynolds Montgomery, Aug. 22, 1964; children: John Brookings, Theodore Worcester, Thomas Churchill. BA, Yale U., 1962; BD, Princeton Theol. Sem., 1966; PhD, Harvard U., 1975. Ordained to ministry Presbyn. Ch., 1970. Asst. prof. Sch. of Religion, U. So. Calif., 1970-72; asst. prof. dept. of religion Amherst Coll., Mass., 1972-78, assoc. prof., 1978-83, prof., 1983-90, prof. religion and Black studies, 1990-94, Winthrop H. Smith '16 prof. Am. history and Am. studies, dept. religion and Black studies, 1994—, also dir. Luce Program in Comparative Religious Ethics 1978-88. Editor (with Richard Newman) Black Apostles at Home and Abroad, 1982, (with Albert Raboteau) Afro-American Religion: A Documentary History Project, 1987—. Kent fellow Danforth Found., 1966-70, 75, Ford Found. fellow, 1972, Inst. for Ecumenical and Cultural Rsch. fellow, 1972, Nat. Humanities Ctr. fellow, 1980-81, 94, NEH fellow for Coll. Tchrs., 1988-89, W. E. B. DuBois Inst. for Afro-Am. Rsch. fellow, 1989-91. Mem. Am. Acad. Religion (chair Afro-Am. religious history group 1975-78), Am. Hist. Assn., Am. Soc. Ch. History, Am. Studies Assn., Orgn. Am. Historians, So. Hist. Assn., Phi Beta Kappa. Home: 47 Stagecoach Rd Amherst MA 01002-3527 Office: Amherst Coll Dept Religion Amherst MA 01002 E-mail: dwwills@amherst.edu.

WILLS, EDWARD MICHAEL, medical and sports video producer; b. Phila., Dec. 12, 1958; s. Edward William and Elizabeth Rosa (Maida) W.; m. Susan Lynn Shaughessy, June 19, 1982; children: Ryan Michael, Eric Matthew, Patrick Thomas, Cory Jonathan. BS in Telecommunications, Kutztown U., 1982. Dir. ops.-teleproduction Cable Mgmt. Assocs. Inc., Hershey, Pa., 1983-86; producer, writer, editor U. Pitts., 1986—. Supervising instr. Milton S. Hershey Sch., Hershey, 1984-85. Producer, editor (sport TV program) Highlights of the Lady Keystone Open, 1984 (CMA Outstanding Achievement award 1984); producer, dir. (sports TV programs) Big Five Basketball, 1984, Big Five Football, 1984; producer, editor (ednl. videos) Magnetic Ressonance Imaging, 1990, Nutrition After Your Liver Transplant, 1990; videographer About Your Heart Surgery, 1988, Partnership for Med. Renaissance, 1987, ACL Treatment Options, 1989; videographer, editor Facial Prosthesis, CNBC, 1990; prodr. over 450 med. and ednl. programs for UPMC. Communications dir. Candlelighters of Pitts., 1988; active Boy Scouts Am. Mem. Internat. TV Assn., Internat. Learning Forum, Health Scis. Comm. Assn., Planetary Soc. Republican. Presbyterian. Avocations: motorsports, skiing, model building. Office: U Pitts Med Ctr Divsn Creative Svcs 200 Lothrop St Pittsburgh PA 15213-2546

WILLS, GARRY, journalist, educator; b. Atlanta, May 22, 1934; s. John and Mayno (Collins) W.; m. Natalie Cavallo, May 30, 1959; children: John, Garry, Lydia. BA, St. Louis U., 1957; MA, Xavier U., Cin., 1958, Yale U., 1959, PhD, 1961; LittD (hon.) , Coll. Holy Cross, 1982, Columbia Coll., 1982, Beloit Coll., 1988, Xavier U., 1993, St. Xavier U., 1993, Union Coll., 1993, Macalester Coll., 1995, Bates Coll., 1995, St. Ambrose, 1997, George Washington U., 1999, Spring Hill Coll., 2000, Siena Heights U., 2001, Gettysburg Coll., 2002. Fellow Center Hellenic Studies, 1961-62; assoc. prof. classics Johns Hopkins U. , 1962-67, adj. prof., 1968-80; Henry R. Luce prof. Am. culture and public policy Northwestern U., 1980-88, adj. prof., 1988—; newspaper columnist Universal Press Syndicate, 1970—. Mem. adv. com. Internat. Ctr. Jefferson Studies; mem. Historians' adv. bd., Mt. Vernon. Author: Chesterton, 1961, Politics and Catholic Freedom, 1964, Roman Culture, 1966, Jack Ruby, 1967, Second Civil War, 1968, Nixon Agonistes, 1970, Bare Ruined Choirs, 1972, Inventing America, 1978, At Button's, 1979, Confessions of a Conservative, 1979, Explaining America, 1980, The Kennedy Imprisonment, 1982, Lead Time, 1983, Cincinnatus, 1984, Reagan's America, 1987, Under God, 1990, Lincoln at Gettysburg, 1992 (Pulitzer Prize for gen. non-fiction 1993), Certain Trumpets: The Call of Leaders, 1994, Witches and Jesuits: Shakespeare's Macbeth, 1994, John Wayne's America, 1997, St. Augustine, 1999, A Necessary Evil, 1999, Papal Sin, 2000, Venice, Lion City, 2001, Augustine's Childhood, 2001, James Madison, 2002, Why Am I a Catholic, 2002, Augustine's Memory, 2002. Recipient Pulitzer prize, 1993, Merle Curti award Orgn. Am. Historians, Nat. Book Critics Circle award (2), Wilbur Cross medal Yale U., Peabody award, NEH Presdl. Medal, 1998, John Hope Franklin award. Mem.: AAAL, Am. Antiquarian Soc., Am. Acad. Arts and Scis., Mass. Hist. Soc. Roman Catholic. Office: Northwestern U Dept History Evanston IL 60201

WILLS, IRENE YOUNG, accountant; b. Wellington, Tex., Aug. 9, 1950; d. William Tiffin and Edith Irene Young; m. James Randolph Ward, Aug. 22, 1970 (div. 1987); m. Donald Eugene Wills, June 17, 1988; children: James Tiffin Ward, Lindsey DeAnne Ward. BA, Tex. Christian U., 1972; MBA, Angelo State U., 1992. Cert. cash mgr. Sr. acct. Grogan & Dane, CPAs, San Angelo, Tex., 1985-91, GTE, San Angelo, 1991-93; cash mgr. USAA Buying Svc., San Antonio, 1993-96; dir. shared svcs. H.E. Butt Grocery Co., 1997—2000; dir. disbursements 7-Eleven, Inc., 2000—02; dir. employee adminstrv. svcs. Flowserve Corp., Irving, 2002—. Mem. supervisory com. 1st Cmty. Fed., San Angelo, 1988-89, bd. dirs., 1989-91, chmn. bd. dirs., 1991. Pres. Shannon Med. Aux., San Angelo, 1982; bd. dirs. Tom Green County Child Welfare Bd., San Angelo, 1980-83, San Angelo Cultural Affairs Coun., 1983-89; chmn. Regional Child Welfare Coun., San Angelo, 1983. Mem. San Antonio Treasury Mgmt. Assn. (bd. dirs. 1997), Treasury Mgmt. Assn. (cert. cash mgr.), Jr. League San Angelo. Office: 222 W Las Colinas Blvd Irving TX 75039

WILLS, J. ROBERT, academic administrator, drama educator, writer; b. Akron, Ohio, May 5, 1940; s. J. Robert and Helen Elizabeth (Lapham) W.; m. Barbara T. Salisbury, Aug. 4, 1984 (dec. 1998); m. Jeanne Hokin, June 2002. BA, Coll. of Wooster, 1962; MA, U. Ill., 1963; PhD, Case-Western Res. U., 1971; cert. in arts adminstrn, Harvard U., 1976. Instr. to asst. prof., dir. theatre Wittenberg U., Springfield, Ohio, 1963-72; assoc. prof., dir. grad. studies, chmn. dept. theatre U. Ky., Lexington, 1972-77, prof. theatre, dean Coll. Fine Arts, 1977-81; prof. drama, dean Coll. Fine Arts U. Tex., Austin, 1981-89, Effie Marie Cain Regents chair in Fine Arts, 1986-89; provost, prof. theatre Pacific Luth. U., Tacoma, 1989-94; prof. theatre, dean coll. fine arts Ariz. State U., Tempe, 1994—. Cons. colls., univs., arts orgns., govt. agencies Author: The Director in a Changing Theatre, 1976, Directing in the Theatre: A Casebook, 1980, rev. edit., 1994; dir. 92 plays; contbr. articles to profl. jours. Bd. dirs. various art orgns., Ky., Tex., Wash., Ariz. Recipient grants public and pvt. agencies. Mem. Nat. Assn. State Univs. and Land-Grant Colls.(chmn. commn. on arts 1981-83), Coun. Fine Arts Deans (exec. com. 1984-89, sec./treas. 1986-89), Univ. and Coll. Theatre Assn. (pres. 1981-82), Assn. for Communication Adminstrn. (pres. 1986-87), Ky. Theatre Assn. (pres. 1976). Office: Ariz State U Coll Fine Arts Tempe AZ 85287-2101 E-mail: bob.wills@asu.edu.

WILLS, JOHN ARTHUR, computer programmer, analyst; b. Newport, Wales, Sept. 18, 1946; came to U.S., 1977; s. Gordon Henry and Jean Fances (Maley) W.; m. Sharlene Kuhnheim, May 18, 1972 (div. 1990). BA (1st hons.), Open U., Milton Keynes, Eng., 1974; BA (hon.), Open U., 1995. Libr., programmer Tylin Mgmt., Pangbourne, Eng., 1970-71; programmer Teknotalk, Ltd., London, 1971, City of Berlin, Fed. Republic of Germany, 1972-77; sr. systems programmer Burroughs Corp., Pasadena, Calif., 1977-79; programmer analyst Stationers Corp., L.A., 1979-80; programmer/analyst Pasadena City Coll., 1980-91. Mem. Assn. Computing Machinery. Roman Catholic. Home: 1169 Market St Apt 144 San Francisco CA 94103-1538

WILLS, JOHN ELLIOT, JR. history educator, writer; b. Urbana, Ill., Aug. 8, 1936; s. John Elliot and George Anne (Hicks) W.; m. Carolin Connell, July 19, 1958; children: Catherine, Christopher John, Jeffrey David, Joanne, Lucinda. BA in Philosophy, U. Ill., 1956; MA in East Asian Studies, Harvard U., 1960, PhD in History and Far Ea. Langs., 1967. History instr. Stanford (Calif.) U., 1964-65, U. So. Calif., L.A., 1965-67, asst. prof., 1967-72, assoc. prof., 1972-84, prof., 1984—, acting chair East Asian Langs. and Cultures, 1987-89; dir. East Asian Studies Ctr. USC-UCLA Joint East Asian Studies Ctr., 1990-94. Rsch. abroad in The Netherlands, Taiwan, China, Japan, Macao, Philippines, Indonesia, India, Italy, Spain, Portugal, Eng. Author: Pepper, Guns, and Parleys: The Dutch East India Company and China, 1662-1681, 1974, Embassies and Illusions: Dutch and Portuguese Envoys to K'ang-hsi, 1666-1687, 1984, Mountain of Fame: Portraits in Chinese History, 1994, 1688: A Global History, 2001; co-editor: (with Jonathan D. Spence) From Ming to Ch'ing: Conquest, Region, and Continuity in Seventeenth-Century China, 1979; contbr. articles to profl. jours. Grantee Nat. Acad. Scis., 1985, Am. Coun. Learned Soc., 1979-80; Younger Humanist fellow NEH, 1972-73. Mem. Assn. for Asian Studies, Am. Hist. Assn., Phi Beta Kappa, Phi Kappa Phi (recognition award 1986, 95). Avocation: travel. Office: U So Calif Dept History Los Angeles CA 90089-0034 E-mail: jwills@usc.edu.

WILLS, MICHAEL RALPH, medical educator; b. Bath, Somerset, Eng., May 4, 1931; came to U.S., 1977; s. Ralph Herbert and Una Read (Hearse) W.; m. Margaret Christine Lewis, Sept. 12, 1955; children: Matthew, Catherine, Sarah, Benjamin, Thomas. M.B., Ch.B., U. Bristol, Eng., 1954, MD, 1964, PhD, 1978. Intern Bristol Royal Infirmary, 1954-55, fellow, resident, 1957-64; sr. lectr. Royal Free Hosp. and Med. Sch., London, 1964-70, reader, 1970-74, prof., 1974-77; prof. pathology and internal medicine U. Va., Charlottesville, 1977-97, prof. emeritus, 1997. Author books, films; contbr. articles to profl. jours. Lt. comdr. Royal Naval Res., Eng. NIH rsch. fellow, 1967-68. Fellow ACP, Royal Coll. Physicians, Royal Coll. Pathologists. Roman Catholic. Avocations: reading, wood carving, gardening, military modelling, African art and scrimshaw. Home: 236 Rookwood Dr Charlottesville VA 22903-4644

WILLS, RITCHIE JEAN, hospital administrator; b. Belleville, Ill., July 28, 1928; d. Richard and Viola L. (Davis) Grossner; m. Richard R. Wills, Jan. 23, 1948; children: Valann M. Kampf, Sheila L.; m. Lawrence G. Wetherwax, June 29, 1974 (div. Oct. 1988). AA, Crafton Hills Coll., 1977; BA, Redlands U., 1977. Lic. nursing home adminstr., residential care facility for elderly adminstr. Patient svcs. rep. Loma Linda U. Hosp., 1968-72; office mgr. Canyon Crest Convalescent Hosp., Colton, Calif., 1972-74, Highland House Healthcare (Calif.), 1974-76; adminstr. Beverly Manor Convalescent Hosp., Riverside, Calif., 1977-79, Terracina Healthcare Ctr., Redlands, 1979-94; dir. cmty. rels. ARDAN Residential Care, Inc., Irvine, 1995-98; mktg. profl. HomeCare USA (divsn. of Accent Care), Palm Desert, 1999-2000; adminstr. Braswell's Yucaipa Valley Convalescent Hosp., Yucaipa, 2000—02. Co-dir. for your network Loma Linda/Redlands Connection; pres. bd. San Jacinto Day Care Ctr. Fellow Am. Coll. Health Care Adminstrs.; mem. NAFE, Calif. Assn. Health Facilities (v.p. region V), Redlands C. of C. (amb.), Order Ea. Star, Redlands Noon Soroptimists. Republican.

WILLS, ROBERT HAMILTON, retired newspaper executive; b. Colfax, Ill., June 21, 1926; s. Robert Orson and Ressie Mae (Hamilton) W.; m. Sherilyn Lou Niersheimer, Jan. 16, 1949; children: Robert L., Michael H., Kendall J. BS, MS, Northwestern U., 1950. Reporter Duluth (Minn.) Herald & News-Tribune, 1950-51; reporter Milw. Jour., 1951-59, asst. city editor, 1959-62; city editor Milw. Sentinel, 1962-75, editor, 1975-91; exec. v.p. Jour./Sentinel, Inc., Milw., 1991-92, pres., 1992-93; vice-chmn., 1993; also bd. dirs. Jour./Sentinel, Inc., Milw.; pub. Milw. Jour. Sr. v.p., bd. dirs. Jour. Communications; pres. Wis. Freedom of Info. Council, 1979-86, charter mem., 1979; Pulitzer Prize juror, 1982, 83, 90. Mem. media-law rels. com. State Bar Wis., 1969-99; vice chmn. privacy coun. Wis. Pub. Svc. Commn., 1996-97; mem. Wis. Privacy Coun., 1994-95. Recipient Leadership award Women's Ct. and Civic Conf. Greater Milw., 1987; inducted into Journalism Hall of Achievement Medill Sch. Northwestern U., 1997, Wis. Newspaper Assn. Found. Hall of Fame, 2001. Mem. Wis. Newspaper Assn. (pres. 1985-86, Disting. Svc. award 1992), Wis. AP (pres. 1975-76, Dion Henderson award Svc. 1993), Am. Soc. Newspaper Editors, Internat. Press Inst., Milw. Press Club (Media Hall Fame 1993), Soc. Profl. Journalists (pres. Milw. chpt. 1979-80, nat. pres. 1986-87), Sigma Delta Chi Found. (bd. dirs. 1993-96, Wis. Newsman of Yr. 1973, Freedom of Info. award Milw. chpt. 1988). Home: 2064 Tiger Links Dr Henderson NV 89012-6111 E-mail: wills2064@juno.com.

WILLS, WILLIAM RIDLEY, II, former insurance company executive, historian; b. Nashville, June 19, 1934; s. Jesse Ely and Ellen (Buckner) W.; m. Irene Weaver Jackson, July 21, 1962; children: William Ridley III, Morgan Jackson, Thomas Weaver. BA, Vanderbilt U., 1956. Agt., staff mgr. Nat. Life & Accident Ins. Co., Nashville, 1958-62, supr., 1962-64, asst. sec., 1964-67, asst. v.p., 1967-70, 2d v.p., 1970-75, v.p., 1975-81, sr. v.p., 1981-83, Am. General Services Co., 1982-83; dir. Nat. Life & Accident Ins. Co., Nashville, 1976-83; pres. Tenn. Hist. Soc., 1985-87; bd. dirs. Nat. Trust for Hist. Preservation, 1988-91. Author: History of Belle Meade: Mansion, Plantation and Stud, 1991, Old Enough to Die, 1996, Touring Tennessee: A Post Card Panorama, 1989-1955, 1996, Tennessee Governors at Home, 1999, Belle Meade Country Club: The First One Hundred Years, 2001. Nat. chmn. Living Endowment Drive Vanderbilt U., 1974; pres. Cumberland Mus. and Sci. Ctr., Nashville, 1977; gen. chmn. campaign United Way, Nashville and Mid. Tenn., 1978; pres. YMCA of Met. Nashville, 1984; trustee Ladies Hermitage Assn., 1981—90; mem. Tenn. Hist. Commn.; chmn. YMCA Found. Mid. Tenn., 1998—; chmn. bd. Montgomery Bell Acad., 1988—97, gen. chmn. $43 million capital campaign, 1999—2000; mem. adv. bd. Pub. Libr. of Nashville and Davidson County, 2002—; pres. Monteagle Sundy Sch. Assembly, 2002—; bd. dirs. Vanderbilt U., 1988—. Lt. USN, 1956—58. Recipient awards YMCA, 1977, 1983, United Way De Tocqueville award, 1989, Tenn. History Book award Tenn. Lib. Assn. and Tenn. Hist. Comm., 1991, Disting. Alumnus award Montgomery Bell Acad., 1996. Fellow Life Office Mgmt. Assn.; mem. Assn. Preservation Tenn. Antiquities (pres. Nashville chpt. 1987-89), Belle Meade Country Club, Coffee House Club, Round Table Literary Club. Presbyterian.

WILLSE, JAMES PATRICK, newspaper editor; b. N.Y.C., Mar. 17, 1944; s. Sherman Stokes and Katherine (Mackey) W.; m. Sharon Margaret Stack, Sept. 15, 1973; 1 child, Elizabeth Ruth. BA, Hamilton Coll., 1967; MS, Columbia U., 1968. Nat. editor AP, N.Y.C., 1969-74, news editor San Francisco, 1975-78; city editor San Francisco Examiner, 1978-82, mng. editor, 1982-84, N.Y. Daily News, 1984-89, editor, pub., 1989-95; editor Star Ledger, Newark, 1995—. Fellow Stanford U., 1975. Mem. Am. Soc. Newspaper Editors, AP Mng. Editors. Office: Star Ledger 1 Star Ledger Plz Newark NJ 07102-1291*

WILLSIE, SANDRA K. dean, physician, medical educator; BS in Med. Tech., Pittsburg (Kans.) State U., 1975; DO, U. Health Sci.-Coll. Osteo., Kansas City, Mo., 1983. Diplomate in internal medicine, pulmonary disease and critical care medicine Am. Bd. Internal Medicine. Rotating intern Univ. Hosp., Kansas City, Mo., 1983-84; resident in internal medicine U. Mo.-Kansas City Affiliated Hosps., 1984-87; fellow in pulmonary diseases Truman Med. Ctr.-West, Kansas City, Mo., 1987-89; instr. medicine U. Mo.-Kansas City Sch. Medicine, 1984-89; med. dir. pulmonary clinic Truman Med. Ctr., 1991-2000; asst. prof. medicine U. Mo. Kansas City Sch. Medicine, 1989-94, assoc. prof. medicine, 1994-99, asst. dean, 1997-2000, prof. medicine, 1999-2000, U. Health Scis., Kansas City, Mo., 2000—, vice dean acad. affairs, adminstrn., med. affairs, 2000—02, v.p. acad. affairs, dean, 2002—. Contbr. articles to profl. jours. Fellow ACP, Am. Coll. Chest Physicians; mem. Am. Thoracic Soc., Mo. Thoracic Soc., Soc. Critical Care Medicine, Met. Med. Assn., Am. Osteo. Assn. Office: U Health Scis 1750 Independence Ave Kansas City MO 64106-1453

WILLSON, C. GRANT, chemistry educator, engineering educator; b. Vallejo, Calif., Mar. 30, 1939; s. Carlton P. and Margaret Ann (Cosner) W.; m. Deborah Jeanne Merritt, Dec. 13, 1975; children: William, Andrew. BS in Chemistry, U. Calif., Berkeley, 1962, PhD in Organic Chemistry, 1973; MS in Organic Chemistry, San Diego State U., 1969. With propellent rsch. Aeroject Gen. Corp., Sacramento, 1962-64; tchr., coach Fairfax H.S., L.A., 1964-67; prof. Calif. State U., Long Beach, 1973-74, U. Calif., San Diego, 1974-78; mgr. polymer sci. and tech. IBM Almaden Rsch. Ctr., San Jose, Calif., 1978-93; prof. chemistry, chem. engring. U. Tex., Austin, 1993—. Contbr. articles to profl. jours.; patentee in field. Recipient Kosar award Soc. Imaging Sci. and Tech., 1998, Aristotle award Semicondr. Rsch. Corp. Mem. NAE, AAAS, Soc. Photog. and Instrumentation Engrs., Am. Phys. Soc., Am. Chem. Soc. (Arthur K. Doolittle award 1986, award Chemistry of Materials 1991, Carouthers award 1992, Coop. Rsch. award in Polymer Sci. 1993), NAS (award for chem. in svc. to soc. 1999), Coun. for Chem. Rsch. (Malcom Pruitt award 1997), St. Francis Yacht Club, Sigma Xi. Avocations: sailing, skiing. Office: U Tex Dept Chem and Chem Engring Austin TX 78712

WILLSON, CLYDE D. biologist, educator; b. Omaha, May 7, 1935; s. Paul Gallup and Elise Willson; m. Greta Jean Olsen, July 17, 1954; children: Ian, Bjorn, Scott, Gillian. BA in Biochemistry, U. Calif., Berkeley, 1956, PhD in Chemistry, 1960. Postdoctoral fellow Pasteur Inst. (NIH), Paris, 1960—62; asst. prof. biology U. Calif., Berkeley, 1962—67, Miller fellow, 1967—69; prof. biology and chemistry Laney Coll., Oakland, 1969—. Chair biology dept. Laney Coll., 1975—77, 1995—, rep. Acad. Senate, 1990—. Contbr. articles to profl. jours. Natural scis. docent Oakland Mus., 1969—72. Mem.:

AAUP (sec.-treas., U. Calif. at Berkeley 1963—64), No. Calif. Parasitologists, West Coast Bacterial Physiologists. Avocation: keyboard performance. Home: 136 International Blvd Oakland CA 94606 Office: Laney College 900 Fallon St Oakland CA 94607

WILLSON, DAVID ALLEN, reference librarian, writer; b. Seattle, June 30, 1942; s. Robert Richard and Alice Hansine (Aspen) W.; m. Penelope Poeschl, Dec. 13, 1972 (div. Mar. 1986); children: Mungo Park, Darcy Monroe; m. Michele Geraldine DeBruyne, Mar. 8, 1986; children: Joaquin Sandoval, Alice Maria. BA, U. Wash., 1964, MLS, 1970. Reference libr. Green River C.C., Auburn, Wash., 1970—. Archivist Joe Hooper Collection of Vietnam War Lit. at Green River C.C., 1987—. Author: (novels) REMF Diary, 1988, The REMF Returns, 1992, In the Army Now, 1995; co-editor: (bibliography) Vietnam War Literature, 1996, Viet Nam War Jour., 2000—. With U.S. Army, 1966-67. Recipient Disting. Faculty award Puget Power, 1996, Vietnam Vets. Am. Contbn. to Am. Culture award, 1997. Mem. Popular Culture Assn., Vietnam Vets. Am. Democrat. Lutheran. Avocations: movies; listening to the blues, especially Fred McDowell. Home: 23630 201st Ave SE Maple Valley WA 98038-8633 Office: Green River CC 12401 SE 320th St Auburn WA 98092-3622 E-mail: dawillson@earthlink.net.

WILLSON, JAMES DOUGLAS, aerospace executive; b. Edinburgh, Scotland, May 24, 1915; came to U.S., 1921; s. George William and Margaret (Douglas) W.; m. Genevieve Best, Nov. 11, 1939; children: James Douglas, Stephen J., Wendy. BS with honors, Ohio State U., 1937, MBA, 1938. C.P.A., N.Y. Sr. auditor Arthur Andersen & Co. (C.P.A.'s), N.Y.C., 1938-42; controller Stinson div. Consol. Vultee Aircraft Corp., 1946-48, Plaskon div. Libbey-Ownes-Ford Glass Co., 1948-53; treas. Affiliated Gas Equipment Co., Cleve., 1953; v.p. finance, treas. Norris-Thermador Corp., Los Angeles, 1957-59; controller, mgr. finance Tidewater Oil Co., 1959-60, v.p. finance, 1960-66, Northrop Corp., Los Angeles, 1966-70, sr. v.p. finance, treas., 1970-80, also dir. Author: Controllership, 1952, 63, 81, 90, 95, Business Budgeting and Control, 1956, 57, Internal Auditing Manual, 1983, 89, Budgeting and Profit Planning, 1983, 89, 92, Financial Information Systems, 1986. Served to lt. comdr. USNR, 1942-46. Mem. Nat. Assn. Accts. (Lybrand Gold medal 1960), Am. Inst. C.P.A.s, Controllers Inst. Am. Home: 1715 Chevy Chase Dr Beverly Hills CA 90210-2709

WILLSON, JOHN MICHAEL, retired mining company executive; b. Sheffield, England, Feb. 21, 1940; s. Jack Desmond and Cicely Rosamond (Long Price) W.; m. Susan Mary Partridge, Aug. 26, 1942; children: Marcus J., Carolyn A. BSc in Mining Engring. with honors, Imperial Coll., London, 1962, MSc in Mining Engring., 1985. With Cominco Ltd., 1966-74, v.p. No. Group B.C., Can., 1981-84; pres. Garaventa (Canada) Ltd., 1974-81; pres., CEO Western Can. Steel Ltd., 1985-88, Pegasus Gold Inc., Spokane, Wash., 1989-92, Placer Dome, Inc., Vancouver, B.C., Can., 1993-2000; ret., 2000. Bd. dirs. Nexen Inc., Finning Internat. Ltd., Garaventa (Can.) Ltd. Pres. N.W.T. Chamber Mines, Yellowknife, Can., 1982-84; chmn. bd. dirs. Western States Pub. Lands Coalition, Pueblo, Colo., 1990-91; bd. dirs. World Gold Coun. Mem. AIME, Can. Inst. Mining and Metallurgy, Inst. Mining and Metallurgy (London), Assn. Profl. Engrs. and Geologists N.W.T., N.W. Mining Assn. (bd. dirs. Corp. Leadership award 1991), World Gold Coun. (chmn. 1999-2001). Avocations: cycling, tennis, squash, sailing, skiing. Home: 4722 Drummond Dr Vancouver BC Canada V6T 1B4 Fax: 604-228-9664.

WILLSON, MARY FRANCES, ecology researcher, educator; b. Madison, Wis., July 28, 1938; d. Gordon L. and Sarah (Loomans) W.; m. R.A. von Neumann, May 29, 1972 (dec.). BA with honors, Grinnell Coll., 1960; PhD, U. Wash., 1964. Asst. prof. U. Ill., Urbana, 1965-71, assoc. prof., 1971-76, prof. ecology, 1976-90; rsch. ecologist Forestry Scis. Lab., Juneau, Alaska, 1989-99; sci. dir. Great Lakes program Nature Conservancy, 1999-2000. Prin. rsch. scientist, affiliate prof. biology, Inst. Arctic Biology and Sch. Fisheries and Ocean Scis., U. Alaska, Fairbanks-Juneau. Author: Plant Reproductive Ecology, 1983, Vertebrate Natural History, 1984; co-author: Mate Choice in Plants, 1983. Fellow AAAS, Am. Ornithologists Union; mem. Soc. for Study Evolution, Am. Soc. Naturalists (hon. mem.), Ecol. Soc. Am., Brit. Ecol. Soc. E-mail: mwillson@gci.net.

WILLSON, PARKER O. non-profit organization administrator; b. Dallas, Oct. 14, 1945; s. Parker Otwell and Lovie Viola (Orren) W.; m. Sarah Chase Conklin, Apr. 16, 1982 (div. 1989); 1 child, Nikkoli Robin Chase Willson; life ptnr., John Cameron Orr. BFA, U. Okla., 1967, MFA, 1969; cert. in non-profit mgmt., Baylor U., 2000. Lic. neuro linguistic programming practitioner Marzalek & Assocs. Box office mgr. Fox Theatre, Atlanta, 1984-85; spl. project dir. City Rep. Office, Phila., 1985-86; cons. Enterainment Consultants, Inc., 1986-88; exec. dir. Teen Aid of Tex., Inc., Richardson, 1987-92; dir. support svcs. Life Ptnrs., Inc., Waco, Tex., 1993-94; interim exec. dir. Nat. Viatical Assn., 1994; exec. dir. Keep McLennan County Beautiful, 1996—. Dir. plays, Waco Civic Theatre, 2000, Tin Bldg. Theater, Clifton. Bd. dirs., McLennan County HIV/AIDS Resources and Edn. Svcs., Waco, 1992—; co-chair, Names Project Waco, 1993-95, Names Project AIDS Meml. Quilt Display, Waco, 1993-94. Mem. Royal, Sovereign and Imperial Ct. of Ctrl. Tex. Empiare (pres. 1998—, sec.-treas. 1996-98, Emperor VII 2000-01. Emperor VIII 2001-02). Avocations: directing, singing, environmental concerns, human rights.

WILLSON, PRENTISS, JR. lawyer; b. Durham, N.C., Sept. 20, 1943; s. Prentiss and Lucille (Giles) W. AB, Occidental Coll., 1965; JD, Harvard U., 1968. Bar: Calif. 1969, U.S. Dist. Ct. (no. dist.) Calif. 1971, U.S. Ct. Appeals (9th cir.) 1971, U.S. Tax Ct. 1971, U.S. Supreme Ct. 1975. Instr. law Miles Coll., Birmingham, Ala., 1968-70; ptnr. Morrison & Foerster, San Francisco, 1970-98, Ernst & Young, Walnut Creek, Calif., 1998—. Prof. Golden Gate U., 1971-84; lectr. Stanford U. Sch. Law, 1985-88. Contbr. articles to profl. jours. Mem. ABA, Calif. Bar Assn. Democrat. Office: Ernst & Young 1331 N California Blvd Walnut Creek CA 94596 E-mail: prentiss.willson@ey.com.

WILLUMSON, GLENN GARDNER, curator, art historian; b. Glendale, Calif., June 22, 1949; s. Donald Herbert and Aileen Ann (Gardner) W.; m. Margaret Julia Moore, June 20, 1970; children: Erik Ryan, Ashley Aileen. BA, St. Mary's Coll., 1971; MA, U. Calif., Davis, 1984; PhD in Art History, U. Calif., Santa Barbara, 1988. Asst. curator Nelson Art Gallery, Davis, Calif., 1982-83; curator Getty Rsch. Inst., L.A., 1988-92; sr. curator Palmer Mus. of Art Pa. State U., University Park, Pa., 1992-2001; assoc. prof. art history, dir. mus. studies U. Fla., 2001—. Fellow Nat. Writing Project, 1987; vis. prof. U. Calif., Irvine, 1990; affiliate prof. art history Pa. State U., University Park, 1994-2001. Author: W. Eugene Smith and the Photo-Essay, 1992 (grantee J. Paul Getty Trust 1991), Collecting With a Passion, 1993; mem. editl. bd. History of Photography mag., London, 1991-94, Cambridge Univ. Press., N.Y.C., 1993-97. Haynes fellow Huntington Libr., 1995-96, Univ. Tchr.'s fellow NEH, 1997-98. Mem. Am. Studies Assn. (Annette K. Baxter prize 1987), Coll. Art Assn., Soc. Photog. Edn. (mem. governing bd. Mid-Atlantic region 1993-97), Assn. Historians Am. Art, Am. Assn. Mus. Office: Coll Fine Arts U Fla PO Box 115801 Gainesville FL 32611

WILLY, THOMAS RALPH, lawyer; b. Phila., Sept. 30, 1943; s. Albert Ralph and Dorothy Rose (Driver) W.; m. Kay Harris, Jan. 12, 1968; children: Elyn Alexandria, Jon Charles. BA in History, U. Mo.-Kansas City, 1966, JD with distinction, 1974. Bar: Mo. 1974, U.S. Tax Ct. 1982. Assoc. Deacy & Deacy, Kansas City, 1974-75, Logan, Hentzen, Haitbrink & Moore, Kansas City, 1975; ptnr. Hentzen, Haitbrink & Moore, 1976-78, Hentzen, Moore & Willy, Kansas City, 1978-80, Moore & Willy Profl. Corp., Kansas City, 1980-87, pres., dir., 1987-94; shareholder, dir., v.p. Van Osdol, Magruder, Erickson & Redmond, P.C., 1994—. Cons. Ctr. for Mgmt. Assistance, Kansas City; presenter living will project, Midwest Bioethics Ctr. Pres. Kansas City Swiss Soc., 1989-91, bd. dirs. 1993-96; bd. dirs. Greater Kansas City People to People, 1995-98, 2000—; active Greater Kansas City Coun. Philanthropy, Mid-Am. Planned Giving Coun., Nat. Com. on Planned Giving, Friends of Art, Kansas City, Kansas City Consensus, Hist. Kansas City Found. Capt. USAF, 1966-70. Mem. ABA (sect. intellectual property law, sect. bus. law), Mo. Bar Assn., Lions (bd. dirs. Leawood 1986-88, 90-92, sec. 1988-90, v.p. 1996-97. Home: 10314 Lee Blvd Shawnee Mission KS 66206-2629 Office: 2400 Commerce Tower 911 Main St Kansas City MO 64105-2009 E-mail: twilly@vomer.com.

WILMARTH, ARTHUR EDWARD, JR. law educator; b. Olean, N.Y., Feb. 16, 1951; s. Arthur Edward and Helen Mae (Sinon) W.; m. Ellen Kay Whetham, Oct. 15, 1983. BA, Yale U., 1972; JD, Harvard U., 1975. Bar: D.C. 1976, U.S. Supreme Ct. 1984, Pa. 1992. Assoc. Arent, Fox, Kintner, Plotkin & Kahn, Washington, 1975-79, Jones, Day, Reavis & Pogue, Washington, 1979-84, ptnr., 1985-86, Barley, Snyder, Senft & Cohen, Lancaster, Pa., 1992-94; assoc. prof. law George Washington U., Washington, 1986-2001, prof. law, 2001—. Exch. lawyer Kenneth, Brown, Baker & Baker, London, 1977-78; legal cons. Conf. State Bank Suprs., Washington, 1979—; adv. bd. state and local legal ctr. Acad. State and Local Govt., 1992—. Office: George Washington U Law Sch 720 20th St NW Washington DC 20052-0001 E-mail: awilmarth@main.nlc.gwu.edu.

WILMARTH, RICHARD, poet; b. Fall River, Mass., Dec. 24, 1949; s. Richard Borden and Helen Marie (Kelley) W. BA, MA in English, U. R.I.; MFA in Writing and Poetics, Naropa Inst., 1994. Prin., owner Dead Metaphor Press, Boulder, Colo., 1991—. Author: (poems) Voices in the Room, 1993, The Henry Miller Acrostics, 1996, Alphabetical Order, 1998, Trying to Make Sense Out of the Absurd, 2001. Office: Dead Metaphor Press PO Box 2076 Boulder CO 80306-2076 E-mail: richardwilmarth@hotmail.com.

WILMER, HARRY ARON, psychiatrist, educator; b. New Orleans, Mar. 5, 1917; s. Harry Aron and Leona (Schlenker) W.; m. Jane Harris, Oct. 31, 1944; children: Harry, John, Thomas, James, Mary. BS, U. Minn., 1938, MB, MS, U. Minn., 1940, MD, 1941, PhD, 1944. Intern Gorgas Hosp., Ancon, C.Z., 1940-41; resident in neurology and psychiatry Mayo Clin., Rochester, Minn., 1945-49, cons. in psychiatry, 1957-58; physician Palo Alto (Calif.) Clinic, 1949-51; pvt. practice medicine, Palo Alto, 1951-55, 58-64; prof. psychiatry U. Calif. Med. Sch., San Francisco, 1964-69; sr. psychiatrist Scott & White Clin., Temple, Tex., 1969-74; emeritus prof. pscyhiatry U. Tex. Health Sci. Ctr., San Antonio, 1974-87; staff mem.(part-time) Audie Murphy VA Hosp., 1974-82; founder, dir. Internat. Film Festivals on Culture and Psychiatry, U. Tex. Health and Sci. Ctr., 1972-80; founder, emeritus pres., dir. Inst. Humanities, Salado, TX, 1980—; pvt. practice, 1980—. Author: Huber the Tuber, 1942, Corky the Killer, 1945, This is Your World, 1952, Social Psychiatry in Action, 1958, First Book for the Mind, 1963, Vietnam in remission, 1985, Practical Jung, 1987, Closeness: A Dictionary of Ideas, Vol. I, 1989, Father Mother, 1999; (film) People Need People, 1961, Facing Evil, 1988, Evil, 1989, Creativity, 1990, Creativity Paradoxes and Reflections, 1991, Closeness: Personal and Professional Relations, 1992, Understandable Jung, 1994, How Dreams Help, 1999, Quest for Silence, 2000. Served to capt. M.C., USNR, 1955-57; Guggenheim fell., Zurich, 1969-70; NRC fell., Johns Hopkins Hosp., 1944-45. Fell. Am. Pscyhiatry Assn. (life, emeritus), Am. Coll. Psychiatrists, Am. Acad. Psychoanalysis; mem. AAAS, Internat. Assn. Analytical Pscyhology. Home: 1202 S Ridge Rd Mill Creek PO Box 528 Salado TX 76571-0528 E-mail: hawilmer@aol.com.

WILMER, MARY CHARLES, artist; b. Atlanta, Aug. 25, 1930; d. William Knox and Harriott Creighton (Thomas) Fitzpatrick; m. John Grant Wilmer, Dec. 28, 1950; children: John Grant, Knox Randolph, Charles Inman, Mary Catherine; m. Olin Grigsby Shivers, May 18, 1982. AB, Agnes Scott Coll., 1970; BFA, Coll. of Art, 1974. Co-pres. St. Elizabeth's Guild, Cathedral of Saint Philip. Exhibited in one-woman shows at Image South Gallery, 1974, Aronson GAllery, 1977, 79, Heath Gallery, 1982-, Coach House Gallery, 1983, 89; group shows include Colony Square, 1975, Coach House Gallery, 1999; portrait painter, 1974—. Bd. dirs. Hillside Cottages, 1963-65, Atlanta Child Svcs., 1965-68, Atlanta Coll. Art, 1965-85, Atlanta Puppetry Arts, 1982-87, Atlanta Med. Heritage, 1999-2000; co-chmn. Ga. Comm. Nat. Mus. of Women in the Arts, (pres.) 1985-87. Mem. Piedmont Driving Club, Jr. League, Piedmont Garden Club. Episcopalian. Address: 1 Vernon Rd NW Atlanta GA 30305-2964

WILMERDING, JOHN, art history educator, museum curator; b. Boston, Apr. 28, 1938; s. John Currie and Lila Vanderbilt (Webb) W. AB, Harvard U., 1960, AM, 1961, PhD, 1965. Asst. prof. art Dartmouth Coll., 1965-68, asso. prof., 1968-73, Leon E. Williams prof., 1973-77, chmn. dept. art, 1968-72, chmn. humanities divsn., 1971-72; sr. curator Am. art Nat. Gallery of Art, 1977-83, dep. dir., 1983-88; Sarofim prof. Am. art Princeton (N.J.) U., 1988—, chmn. dept. art and archeology, 1992-99. Vis. lectr. history of art Yale U., 1972; vis. prof. fine arts Harvard U., 1976; vis. prof. art U. Md., 1979; vis. prof. art history U. Del., 1982; hon. curator painting Peabody Mus., Salem, Mass.; vis. curator Met. Mus., 1988—. Author: Fitz Hugh Lane, American Marine Painter, 1964, A History of American Marine Painting, 1968, Pittura Americana dell' Ottocento, 1969, Robert Salmon, Painter of Ship and Shore, 1971, Fitz Hugh Lane, 1971, Winslow Homer, 1972, Audubon, Homer, Whistler and 19th Century America, 1972, The Genius of American Painting, 1973, American Art, 1976, American Light, The Luminist Movement, 1980, American Masterpieces from the National Gallery of Art, 1980, An American Perspective, 1981, Important Information Inside, 1982, Andrew Wyeth, The Helga Pictures, 1987, American Marine Paintings, 2d edit., 1987, Paintings by Fitz Hugh Lane, 1988; American Views: Essays on American Art, 1991, The Artist's Mount Desert: American Painters on the Maine Coast, 1994, Compass and Clock: Defining Moments in American Culture, 1999. Trustee Coll. of the Atlantic, Bar Harbor, Maine, Guggenheim Mus., N.Y.C., N.E. Harbor Libr., Maine, Wendell Gilley Mus., S.W. Harbor, Maine, Wyeth Endowment for Am. Art, Wilmington, Del.; trustee emeritus Shelburne Mus., Vt.; mem. trustees' coun. Nat. Gallery Art, Washington. Guggenheim fellow, 1973-74. Fellow Phila. Atheneum (hon.); Mem. Coll. Art Assn., Am. Studies Assn. Office: Princeton U Dept Art and Archaeology 105 Mccormick Hl Princeton NJ 08544-1018

WILMERING, KATHARINE JEAN, social worker, clinical nurse specialist; b. St. Louis, Sept. 17, 1958; d. Thomas H. and Jean (Dahm) W. BS in Nursing, St. Louis U., 1981, MSW, 1988; cert. in family therapy, Montlake Inst., Seattle, 1990. Cert. mental health counselor, clin. nurse specialist in Psychiatric Nursing. Nurse Cardinal Glennon Meml. Hosp., St. Louis, 1980-82; lead therapist, nurse Comprehensive Mental Health Ctr., Tacoma, 1982-86; counsellor Youth Emergency Svcs., St. Louis, 1986-87; nurse Harborview Med. Ctr., Seattle, 1987-93; therapist, community organizer Family Svcs., 1988-91; implementer family rsch. program Harborview Mental Health Ctr., 1989—; pvt. practice therapist. Adj. faculty Antioch U., 1992-95; presenter mental health workshops, 1990—. Mem. Homeless Network Bd., St. Louis, 1986-88, Ford Cmty. Group, St. Louis, 1987-88; mem. task force on housing and homelessness Ch. Coun. Greater Seattle, 1988-91; co-chmn. High Point Svc. Coalition, Seattle, 1989; chmn. pairing project Tacoma Speaker's Bur., 1984-85; vol. nurse Neighborhood Clinic, Tacoma, 1983, Family Care Ctr., St. Louis, 1982; bd. dirs. Presbyn. Coun. Svcs. Marriage and Family Tng. Clinic. Named Ursuline Acad. Alumna of Yr., 1995. Mem. NASW, N.W. Assn. Advanced Practice Psychiat. Nurses, Multiple Sclerosis Soc. (accessibility com. 1993-95), Mountaineers faculty liaison northwest environ. issues course 1994-96), Toastmasters (pres. Seattle 1991-92). Avocations: camping, hiking, reading, music, travel. Office: 1900 N Northlake Way Ste 127 Seattle WA 98103-9051

WILMERS, ROBERT GEORGE, banker; b. N.Y.C., Apr. 20, 1934; s. Charles K. and Cecilia (Eitingon) W.; m. Elisabeth Roche de la Rigodiere; children: Robert George, Christopher C. BA, Harvard U., 1956; postgrad., Harvard Bus. Sch., 1958-59. Dep. fin. adminstr. City of N.Y., 1966-70; v.p. Morgan Guaranty Trust Co., N.Y.C. and Belgium, 1970-80; chmn., chief exec. officer, dir. M&T Bank Corp., Buffalo, 1982—, chmn. bd., chief exec. officer, dir., 1983—. Vis. com. John F. Kennedy Sch. Govt., Harvard U.; bd. dirs. The Bus. Coun. N.Y. State, Buffalo Niagara Partnership; chmn. N.Y. State Bankers Assn. Decorated officer de l'Ordre de la Couronne (Belgium). Mem.: NY State Bankers Assn. (chmn.), Coun. Fgn. Rels., Fin. Svcs. Roundtable. Home: 800 W Ferry St Buffalo NY 14222-1660 also: 1 W 64th St New York NY 10023-6734 Office: M&T Bank 1 M&T Plz Buffalo NY 14203 E-mail: rwilmers@mandtbank.com.

WILMORE, DOUGLAS WAYNE, surgeon, educator; b. Newton, Kans., July 22, 1938; s. Waldo Wayne and Hilda Gard (Adrian) W.; m. Judith Kay Shabert; 1 child, Carol Kristann. BA, Washburn U., 1960; MD, Kans. U., 1964; MS (hon.), Harvard U., 1979; PhD (hon.), Washburn U., 1995. Diplomate Am. Bd. Surgery. Intern Hosp. U. Pa., Phila., 1964-65, resident, fellow, 1965-71; chief clin. rsch. and staff surgeon U.S. Army Inst. Surg. Rsch., Ft. Sam Houston, 1971-79; staff surgeon Brigham and Women's Hosp., Boston, 1979—; Frank Sawyer prof. surgery Harvard Med. Sch., 1989—. Editor Scientific American Surgery, 1988, ACS Surgery, 2001—. Mem. Inst. Medicine, 1999. Lt. Col. U.S. Army, 1971-74. Achievements include development of safe modern techniques for providing parenteral nutrition to critically-ill patients, use of the amino acid L-glutamine in clinical nutrition.

WILMOT, CLARE JULIA MAY, surgeon; b. 1954; MD, U. Bristol, 1977. Diplomate Am. Bd. Surgery. Intern St. Elizabeth Hosp., Boston, 1977-78, resident in gen. surgery, 1978-82; staff Littleton (N.H.) Regional Hosp. Office: Littleton Regional Hosp 580 St Johnsbury Rd Littleton NH 03561 E-mail: cwilmot@littlehospital.org.

WILMOT, ELIZABETH C. business owner; b. Norwalk, Conn., June 9, 1961; d. John A. and Janet I. Campbell; divorced; children: Paul C., Lauren G. BA magna cum laude, Duke U., 1983. Market rschr. Hahn Co., San Diego, 1983-85; leasing agt. Koll Co., 1986-87, Kaplan Group Inc., Newton, Mass., 1987-91, Wilmorite Inc., Rochester, N.Y., 1992-98; pres. Lebell Corp. Mktg. and Strategy Co., Pittsford, NY and Severn Park, Md., 1995—98; sr. v.p. mktg. Citifinancial, Balt., 2001—. Mktg. and strategy cons., Severna Park, Md., 1998—2001. Inventor glove design and shoe design. Bd. dirs. Writers and Books, Rochester, 1997-98, Arts and Cultural Coun., Rochester, 1994-97. Republican. Episcopalian. Avocations: running, tennis, reading, gardening, computers. Home: 47 Snellings Ct Severna Park MD 21146-4827 E-mail: elizabethwilmot@yahoo.com.

WILMOT, IRVIN GORSAGE, former hospital administrator, educator, consultant; b. Nanking, China, June 30, 1922; s. Frank Alonzo and Ethel (Ranney) W.; m. Dorothy Agnes Mohlfeld, Feb. 6, 1943; children: Marcia Beth, David Michael. BS, Northwestern U., 1955; MBA, U. Chgo., 1957. With Internat. Register Co., Chgo., 1946-47; buyer U. Chgo., 1947-49; adminstrv. asst., then asst. supt. U. Chgo. Clinics, 1949-61; adminstr. NYU Med. Center-Univ. Hosp., 1961-68, exec. v.p., 1968-81, Blue Cross-Blue Shield Greater N.Y., 1981-83, dir., 1977-81; exec. v.p., chief operating officer Montefiore Hosp. and Med. Ctr., N.Y.C., 1984-85; healthcare cons., 1985—. Instr. then asst. prof. U. Chgo., 1957-61; asso. prof. NYU, 1961-68; prof., 1968—; assoc. dir. U. Chgo. Grad. Program Hosp. Adminstrn., 1959-61; mem. hosp. rev. and planning council State of N.Y., 1979-87. Bd. dirs. N.Y. Blood Center, 1978-81. With USN, 1940-46. Fellow Am. Coll. Hosp. Adminstrs. (chmn. central. com. insts. 1959-65, regent N.Y. State and P.R. 1974—); mem. Assn. U. Programs Hosp. Adminstrs. (exec. sec. 1959-61), Am. Hosp. Assn. (mem. council research and planning 1965-68, council on mgmt. 1979-80, council on fin. 1981-84, trustee 1979-81), Assn. Am. Med. Colls. (chmn. council teaching hosps. 1970-71), Greater N.Y. Hosp. Assn. (bd. govs., pres. 1973-74), Hosp. Assn. N.Y. State (trustee, chmn. 1976-77). Home: 34 Helen Ave Rye NY 10580-2447

WILMOT, THOMAS RAY, medical entomologist, educator; b. Great Falls, Mont., Sept. 9, 1953; s. Donald D. and Jeanne M. W.; m. Gail A. Ballard, June 26, 1976; children: Lacey A., Eric T. BS in Entomology, Mont. State U., 1975; MS in Entomology, Oreg. State U., 1978; MPH, UCLA, 1984, PhD in Epidemiology, 1986. Inspector Cacade County Pesticide Program, Great Falls, Mont., 1970-75; mgr. Yakima County Mosquito Control, Wash., 1978-80; dir., entomologist Midland County Mosquito Control, Sanford, Mich., 1984—. Adj. instr. Saginaw Valley State U., University Center, Mich., 1988—; vector control cons., Midland, Mich., 1988—. Contbr. articles to profl. jours. Mem. Local Emergency Plan Com., Midland, Mich., 1990—; spkr. Dow Corning Spkrs. Bur., Midland, 1992-96. Pub. Health traineeship USPHS, 1980-84; recipient Achievement award Nat. Assn. Counties, 1994. Mem. Am. Mosquito Control Assn. (mem. editl. bd. 1989-92), Entomol. Soc. Am., Soc. for Vector Ecology (regional dir. 1990-99), Mich. Mosquito Control Assn. (pres. 1989, Disting. Svc. award 1994), Phi Kappa Phi. Avocation: coaching youth athletics. Office: Midland County Mosquito Control 2180 N Meridian Rd Sanford MI 48657-9200 E-mail: wilmotg@mindnet.com.

WILMOTH, WILLIAM DAVID, lawyer; b. Elkins, W.Va., July 11, 1950; s. Stark Amasa and Goldie (Johnson) W.; m. Rebecca Weaver, Aug. 21, 1971; children: Charles, Anne, Samuel, Peter. BS in Fin. cum laude, W.Va. U., 1972, JD, 1975. Bar: W.Va. 1975, U.S. Dist. Ct. (so. dist.) W.Va. 1975, U.S. Dist. Ct. (no. dist.) W.Va. 1976, U.S. Ct. Appeals (4th cir.) 1977, U.S. Supreme Ct. 1981, Pa. 1986. Law clk. to presiding judge U.S. Dist. Ct. (no. dist.) W.Va., Elkins, 1975-76; assoc. Bachmann, Hess, Bachmann & Garden, Wheeling, W.Va., 1976-77; asst. U.S. atty. U.S. Dept. Justice, 1977-80; ptnr. Schrader, Byrd, Byrum & Companion, 1980-93; U.S. atty. U.S. Dist. Ct. (no. dist.) W.Va., W.Va., 1993-99; ptnr. Steptoe & Johnson, 1999—. Past pres., chmn. bd. dirs. nat. trail coun. Boy Scouts Am., Wheeling; chmn. bd. dirs. Wheeling Nat. Heritage Area Corp., Wheeling YMCA, State Coll. Sys. W.Va., past chmn. Mem. ABA, Def. Research Inst., Def. Trial Counsel W.Va., Rotary Club Wheeling (past pres.). Democrat. Home: RR 4 Box 106 Wheeling WV 26003-9314 Office: Steptoe & Johnson PO Box 150 Wheeling WV 26003-0020 E-mail: wilmotw@steptoe-johnson.com.

WILMOUTH, ROBERT K. commodities executive; b. Worcester, Mass., Nov. 9, 1928; s. Alfred F. and Aileen E. (Kearney) W.; m. Ellen M. Boyle, Sept. 10, 1955; children: Robert J., John J., James P., Thomas G., Anne Marie. BA, Holy Cross Coll., 1949; MA, U. Notre Dame, 1950, LLD, 1984. Exec. v.p., dir. 1st Nat. Bank Chgo., 1972-75; pres., chief adminstrv. officer Crocker Nat. Bank, San Francisco, 1975-77; pres., chief exec. officer Chgo. Bd. Trade, 1977-82; chmn. LaSalle Nat. Bank, 1982-99. Pres., chief exec. officer Nat. Futures Assn.; chmn. consultative com. Internat. Orgn. Securities Commns. Life trustee U. Notre Dame; mem. adv. coun. Kellogg Grad. Sch. Mgmt., Northwestern U. Mem. Chgo. Club, Barrington Hill Country Club, Econ. Club. Office: Nat Futures Assn 200 W Madison St Ste 1600 Chicago IL 60606-3415

WILNER, JOSHUA DAVID, literature educator; b. Levittown, N.Y., July 22, 1948; s. Gabriel and Roslyn Wilner; m. Marsha Lou Hill, Aug. 11, 1973; children: Carrie Hill, Joseph Hill. PhD, Yale U., 1980. Chair dept. English CCNY, N.Y.C., 1991-94, dir. Simon H. Rifkind Ctr. for Humanities and Arts, 1996-2000; prof. English and comparative lit. CCNY and Grad. Ctr., CUNY, 2000—. Author: (book) Feeding on Infinity: Readings in the Romantic Rhetoric of Internalization, 2000 (Jean-Pierre Barricelli prize of Am. Conf. on Romanticism 2000); transl.: (book) Shibboleth: for Paul Celan (Jacques Derrida), 1994. Allon fellow Israeli Nat. Coun. for Higher Edn., 1983-85; Telluride scholar Telluride Assn., 1965-69. Democrat. Jewish. Avocations: guitar, cycling. Home: Apt 4A 1641 3d Ave New York NY 10128 Office: CCNY 138th St and Convent Ave New York NY 10031 Office Fax: 212-650-5410. E-mail: jowcc@cunyvm.cuny.edu.

WILNER, THOMAS BERNARD, lawyer; b. Toronto, Ont., Can., July 7, 1944; came to U.S., 1944; s. Morton H. and Zelda (Dunkelman) W.; m. Jane Ten Broeck; children: Amanda, Adam, David. BA, Yale U., 1966; LLB, U. Pa., 1969. Clk. to Chief Judge William Hastie U.S. Ct. Appeals, Phila., 1969-70; assoc. Debevoise Plimpton, N.Y.C., 1970-72; counsel Amtrak, Washington, 1972-73; ptnr. Arnold & Porter, 1973-89, Shearman & Sterling, Washington and Tokyo, 1989—. Office: 801 Pennsylvania Ave NW Washington DC 20004-2615

WILOCH, THOMAS, writer, editor; b. Detroit, Feb. 3, 1953; s. Joseph and Jane W.; m. Denise Gottis, Oct. 10, 1981. BA, Wayne State U., 1978. Rsch. asst. Wayne State U., Detroit, 1976; editl. asst. The Gale Group, Farmington Hills, Mich., 1977-78, asst. editor, 1978-81; sr. asst. editor The Gale Gp., Detroit, 1981-85, sr. writer, 1985-89, assoc. editor, 1989—. Prose poem collections include: Stigmata Junction, 1985, Paper Mask, 1988, The Mannikin Cypher, 1989, Tales of Lord Shantih, 1989, Mr. Templeton's Toyshop, 1995; cut-up haiku: Night Rain, 1991, Decoded Factories of the Heart, 1991, Narcotic Signature, 1992, Lyrical Brandy, 1993, Neon Trance, 1997; editor: (with Leonard Kniffel) Directory of Michigan Literary Publishers, 1982, Contemporary Authors, New Revision Series (asst. editor) Vols 1-5, 1982-85, (sr. asst. editor) Vols. 6-15, 1982-85, (sr. writer) Vols. 16-27, 1986-89, (assoc. editor) Vols. 28-90, 1989-2000; editor Grimopire mag., 1982-85; contbr. to over 200 periodicals including Publishers' Weekly, Bloomsbury Rev., Fiction

Rev., Small Press Rev., Factsheet 5, Kayak, Asylum, Wormwood Rev. and others. Mem. Assn. Literary Scholars and Critics. Office: The Gale Group 27500 Drake Rd Farmington Hills MI 48331-3535 E-mail: mssunltd@postmark.net.

WILPON, FRED, professional baseball team executive, real estate developer; b. Bklyn., Nov. 22, 1936; s. Nathan and Frances (Altman) W.; m. Judith Anne Kessler, Sept. 27, 1958; children: Jeffrey Scott, Robin Lynn, Bruce Nathan. BA, U. Mich., 1958. Vice pres. Hanover Equities Corp., N.Y.C., 1959-69, Peter Sharp & Co., N.Y.C., 1969-71; chmn. bd. Sterling Equities, Inc., Manhasset, N.Y., 1971—13; pres. N.Y. Mets Profl. Baseball Team, 1980—, now also chief exec. officer, 1980—. Mem. Vol. Urban Cons. Group, Mayor N.Y.C. Housing Task Force; trustee Jewish Inst. Geriatric Care, New Hyde Park, N.Y., 1976— , Green Vale Sch., Glen Head, N.Y., 1977— . Served with USAF, 1959. Mem. Young Pres. Orgn. Clubs: KP.*

WILSDON, THOMAS ARTHUR, product development engineer, administrator; b. Waterbury, Conn., Aug. 18, 1942; s. Arthur and Ruth (Wellington) W.; m. Yvonne Jeanne Pettit, June 19, 1964 (div. Apr. 1986); children: Thomas Charles, Beth Jeanne; m. Sharon Diann Culbertson, Feb. 14, 1988; children: Vandee Hyder, Jacklynn Hyder. BSEE, U. Conn., 1964; MBA, SUNY, Buffalo, 1978. Product design engr. Westinghouse Gen. Control Divsn., Buffalo, 1964-78; mgr. product devel. Westinghouse Control Divsn., Asheville, N.C., 1978-87; mgr. Advantage engring. Westinghouse Elec. Components Divsn., 1987-94; mgr. control products devel. engring. Eaton/Cutler Hammer, Milw., 1994—. Mem. IEEE, NSPE, Am. Mgmt. Assn. Methodist. Achievements include development of low voltage AC and DC motor starters, Ampgard 7200V motor starter components, solid state controlled Advantage motor starters, PLC, DCI, sensor development, pushbuttons, limit switch, electronic product engineering. Home: PO Box 250 Pewaukee WI 53072-0250 Office: Eaton/Cutler Hammer 4201 N 27th St Milwaukee WI 53216-1897 E-mail: wilsdsd@cs.com.

WILSEY, PHILIP ARTHUR, computer science educator; b. Kewanee, Ill., Sept. 24, 1958; s. George A. and Mary Lee (Smith) W.; m. Marilyn L. Hargis, Jan. 2, 1982; children: Patrick A., Zackary E., Alexis L. BS in Math., Ill. State U., 1981; MS in Computer Sci., U. La., Lafayette, 1985, PhD in Computer Sci., 1987. Computer programmer Union Ins. Group, Bloomington, Ill., 1980-81, Bob White Computing & Software, Bloomington, 1981-82; rsch. asst. U. La., Lafayette, 1983-87; asst. prof. U. Cin., 1987-2000, assoc. prof., 2000—; pres. Clifton Labs., Inc., 1997—; ptnr. Bubu Soft, LLC, 1998—. Cons. MTL, Dayton, 1992-99; mem. editorial bd. VLSI Design, 1993—. Assoc. editor: Potentials Mag., 1992-98, editor-in-chief, 1999—; contbr. articles to profl. jours. Mem. IEEE (sr.), Assn. Computing Machinery. Home: 3678 Fawnrun Dr Cincinnati OH 45241-3834 Office: Exptl Computing Lab Design Lab Dept ECECS PO Box 210030 Cincinnati OH 45221-0030 E-mail: philip.wilsey@ieee.org.

WILSON, AARON MARTIN, religious studies educator, college executive; b. Bazette, Tex., Sept. 30, 1926; s. John Albert and Myrtle (Hulsey) W.; m. Marthel Shoults, Jan. 31, 1947 (dec. Apr. 2001); children: Gloria Dallis, John Bert. BA, So. Bible Coll., 1963, DD (hon.), 1980; MA, Pitts. State U., 1972; PhD, Valley Christian U., 1980. Pastor various chs., 1947-58, Pentecostal Ch. of God, Houston, 1958-64, Modesto, Calif., 1985-88, nat. dir. Christian edn. Joplin, Mo., 1964-79, 88-93; pres. Evang. Christian Coll., Fresno, Calif., 1979-85; v.p. devel. Messenger Coll., Joplin, 1993-95; editor The Pentecostal Messenger, 1995-99, coordinating editor, 1999—. Treas. Evang. Curriculum Commn., 1988-93; prof. So. Bible Coll., Houston, 1962-64. Author: Basic Bible Truth, 1988, Studies on Stewardship, 1989, My Church Can Grow, 1996, Our Story, 2001. Republican. Home: 323 E 33rd St Joplin MO 64804-3809 Office: Messenger Publ House PO Box 850 Joplin MO 64802-0850 E-mail: aaronw@pcg.org.

WILSON, ADDISON GRAVES (JOE WILSON), senator, lawyer; b. Charleston, S.C., July 31, 1947; s. Hugh deVeaux And Wray Smart (Graves) W.; m. Roxanne Dusenbury McCrory, Dec. 30, 1977; children: Michael Alan, Addison Graves, Julian Dusenbury, Hunter Taylor. BA, Washington and Lee U., 1969; JD, U. S.C., Columbia, 1972. Bar: S.C. 1972. Staff mem. Sen. Strom Thurmond, Washington, 1967, Congressman Floyd Spence, Columbia, S.C., 1970-72; ptnr. Wilson, Moore, Taylor & Thomas, West Columbia, 1972—2001. Dep. gen. counsel U.S. Energy Sec. Jim Edwards, Washington, 1981-82; bd. dirs. Bank Am., Lexington, S.C.; senator State of S.C., Columbia, 1984-2001; presdl. appointee to Intergovtl. Adv. Coun. on Edn., 1990-91; mem. Internat. Observation Del. for 1990 Bulgarian parliamentary election. Campaing mgr. Congressman Floyd Spence, Columbia, 1974, 78, 80, 82, 98; dist. campaign mgr. Gov. Carroll Campbell, 1986; vice chmn. S.C. Rep. Party, 1972-74. Col. USNG, 1975—. Mem. Rotary, Masons, Shriners. Presbyterian. Office: 2405 Rayburn Office Bldg Washington DC 20515 also: PO Box 7168 Columbia SC 29201 Home: Apt 202 10401 Montrose Ave Bethesda MD 20814-4159

WILSON, ALICE BLAND, sales manager; b. Rainelle, W.Va., Apr. 1, 1938; d. Brady Floyd and Mildred Martha (George) Bland; m. Louis William Groves, Jr., Apr. 20, 1957 (div. 1981); children: Martha Rachel, Leonora Jayne; m. Glen Parten Wilson, Dec. 11, 1982 (div. 1996). AB, W.Va. U., 1959, postgrad. in microbiology, 1975-78. Contract adminstr. Washington Plate Glass Co., Washington, 1979-80; mem. acctg. staff Forbes Co., Washington, 1981; customer relations rep. Stern's Co., Washington, 1982; real estate assoc. Prudential Preferred Properties, Washington, 1985—. Contbr. articles to Jour. Parasitology. Vol. coord. John Glenn for Pres. campaign, Washington, 1983-84; co-chmn. hospitality com. Women's Nat. Dem. Club, Washington, 1985—; mem. internat. adv. coun. ARC, Washington, 1985—; mem. exec. com. Nat. Symphony Orch., 1990—. Mem. Washington Assn. Realtors (mem. residential sales com. 1985—), Leading Edge Soc., Million Dollar Club. Avocations: flying, aerobatics, nature study. Home: 641 1/2 E Capitol St SE Washington DC 20003-1234 Office: Antique & Contemporary Leasing & Sales Inc 709 12th St SE Washington DC 20003-2962

WILSON, ALICE MCATEER, secondary education educator; b. S.I., N.Y., July 28, 1947; d. Charles Francis Jr. and Clorinda)Mardus) McAteer; m. Van Ray Wilson, 1979; 1 child, Corinna Ann. BA in Math., Wells Coll., 1969; MS in Secondary Math. Edn. with honor, CUNY, 1971. Pemanent tchr. cert., N.Y. State; cert. tchr., N.Y.C. Tchr. math. Tottenville H.S., S.I., 1970—. Mem. alumnae coun. Wells Coll., Aurora, N.Y., 1992—. Mem. Phi Beta Kappa. Avocations: piano, sewing, swimming, sailing. Home: 599 Oakland Ave Staten Island NY 10310

WILSON, ALMON CHAPMAN, surgeon, physician, retired naval officer; b. Hudson Falls, N.Y., July 13, 1924; s. Almon Chapman and Edith May (Truesdale) W.; m. Sofia M. "Kit" Bogdons, Jan. 24, 1945; 1 child, Geoffrey Peter. BA, Union Coll., Schenectady, 1946; MD, Albany Med. Coll., 1952; MS, George Washington U., 1969; student, Naval War Coll., Newport, R.I., 1968-69. Diplomate: Am. Bd. Surgery. Served as enlisted man and officer U.S. Navy, 1943-46, lt. j.g., M.C., 1952, advanced through grades to rear adm., 1976; intern U.S. Naval Hosp., Bremerton, Wash., 1952-53; resident VA Hosp., Salt Lake City, 1954-58; chief of surgery Sta. Hosp. Naval Sta., Subic Bay, Philippines, 1959-61; staff surgeon Naval Hosp., San Diego, 1961-64, asst. chief surgery Chelsea, Mass., 1964-65; comdg. officer 3d Med. Bn., 3d Marine Div. Fleet Marine Force, Pacific, Vietnam, 1965-66; chief surgery Naval Hosp., Yososuka, Japan, 1966-68; assigned Naval War Coll., 1968-69; fleet med. officer, comdr. in chief U.S. Naval Forces, Europe; sr. med. officer Naval Activities London, 1969-71; dep. dir. planning div. Bur. Medicine and Surgery Navy Dept., Washington, 1971-72, dir. planning div., 1972-74; with additional duty as med. adv. to dep. chief naval ops. (logistics) and personal physician to chmn. Joint Chiefs of Staff, 1972-74; comdg. officer Naval Hosp., Great Lakes, Ill., 1974-76; asst. chief for material resources Bur. Medicine and Surgery Navy Dept., Washington, 1976-79; comdg. officer (Navy Health Scis. Edn. and Tng. Command), 1979-80; the med. officer U.S. Marine Corps., 1980-81, project mgr. Fleet Hosp. Programs, 1981-82; dir. Resources Div., 1982-83; dep. dir. naval medicine, dep. surgeon gen. Dept. Navy, 1983-84; ret., 1984. Mem. grad. med. edn. adv. com. Dept. Def. Decorated Legion of Merit with gold V (2 stars), Meritorious Service medal, Joint Service Commendation medal. Fellow ACS (gov.); mem. Assn. Mil. Surgeons U.S.

WILSON, ALPHUS DAN, plant pathologist, researcher; b. Ft. Worth, Sept. 27, 1958; s. Alphus James and Essie Morris (Nugent) W.; m. Lisa Beth Forse, July 11, 1992; 1 child, Jon Colter. BS in Bioenviron. Sci., Tex. A&M U., 1981, MS in Plant Pathology, 1983; PhD in Plant Pathology, Wash. State U., 1988. Grad. rsch. asst. Tex. A&M U., College Station, 1981-83, Wash. State U., Pullman, 1984-88; plant pathologist USDA-Agrl. Rsch. Svc., 1989-90, rsch. plant pathologist, 1990-91, USDA-Forest Svc., Stoneville, Miss., 1991-95, prin. rsch. pathologist, 1996—. Tech. cons. Tex. Oak Wilt Suppression Adv. Bd., Austin, 1992—, Tex. Forest Svc. Strategic Plan Team, Austin, 1994—. Author: (chpt.) Systematics, Ecology, and Evolution of Endophytic Fungi in Grasses and Woody Plants, 1996; contbr. articles to profl. jours. Project judge Delta Regional Sci. Fair, Greenville, Miss., 1992; sci. demonstrator Delta Schs. Sci. Awareness Day, Stoneville, 1993. Rsch. fellow Chevron Chem. Corp., 1981-83, Wash. State U., 1984-88. Mem. AAAS, N.Y. Acad. Scis., Am. Phytopathological Soc., Mycol. Soc. Am., Soc. Am. Foresters, Alpha Zeta. Republican. Achievements include discovery of genetic system controlling mating incompatibility in the Indian paint fungus E. tinctorium, endosymbiotic Acremonium (Neotyphodium) endophytes in wild Hordeum cereal grass species; genetic system controlling sexual incompatibility in the chickpea blight fungas, D. rabiei; development of Giemsa protocol for permanent nuclear staining of fungi, new algorithms and methodologies for mapping geographic positions of trees in forest stands; new applications of electronic aromascan analysis for the identification of plant pathogenic microbes and diagnosis of plant diseases; identified new fungal symbionts (wood decay fungi) of siricoid wood wasps in North America. Avocations: fly fishing, backpacking, exploring wilderness areas, snow skiing, photography. Home: 2202 Highway 1 N Greenville MS 38703-9471 Office: USDA Forest Svc So Hardwoods Lab PO Box 227 Stoneville MS 38776-0227

WILSON, ANGELA SABURN, nursing educator; b. Norfolk, Va., May 24, 1961; d. Richard Ruben and Rose Faye (Mobley) Saburn; m. Robert Walker Wilson, Mar. 4, 1989. Diploma, Norfolk Gen. Hosp. Sch. Nsg., 1987; BSN, Old Dominion U., 1989, MSN, 1993; PhD in Nursing, U. Va., 2001. RN, Va.; cert. pediatric nurse. Staff nurse Children's Hosp. of King's Daus., Norfolk, 1987-90, staff devel. coord., 1990-94, nurse educator, 1994-95; nursing instr. DePaul Hosp., 1995-96, Christopher Newport U., 1996—2001, asst. prof., dept. chair, 2001—. Mem.: Va. Nurses Assn., Phi Kappa Phi, Alpha Chi, Sigma Theta Tau (past pres. Epsilon chpt., Region 13 coord.), Golden Key Honor Soc. Home: 301 Faulk Rd Norfolk VA 23502-5329 E-mail: wilsona@cnu.edu.

WILSON, ARCHIE FREDRIC, medical educator; b. L.A., May 7, 1931; s. Louis H. and Ruth (Kert) W.; m. Tamar Braverman, Feb. 11, 1937; children: Lee A., Daniel B. BA, UCLA, 1953, PhD, 1967; MD, U. Calif., San Francisco, 1957. Intern L.A. County Gen. Hosp., 1957-58; resident U. Calif., San Francisco, 1958-61; fellow in chest disease dept. medicine UCLA, 1966-67, asst. prof., 1967-70, U. Calif., Irvine, 1970-73, assoc. prof., 1973-79, prof., 1979—. Editor: Pulmonary Function Test: Interpretation, 1986; contbr. articles to profl. jours. Bd. mem. Am. Lung Assn., Orange County, 1970-90, Am. Heart Assn., Calif., 1990—. Capt. USMC, 1961-63. Mem. Am. Fedn. Clin. Rsch., Western Soc. Clin. Investigation, best Dr.'s in U.S. 1991—, top Dr.'s in U.S. 2001—. Office: U Calif 101 The City Dr S Orange CA 92868-3201

WILSON, ARMIN, chemist, retired; b. Sapulpa, Okla., Dec. 13, 1916; s. Joseph Bartholomew and Amelia (Heller) W.; m. Evelyn Hodes, June 8, 1943; children: Jonathan, Robert. BA, Rice U., 1939, MA, 1941; AM, PhD, Harvard U., 1945. Sr. chemist Merck Labs., Rahway, N.J., 1945-53; dept. head Bristol Myers, Hillside, 1953-68; prof. Rutgers U., New Brunswick, 1968-78. Contbr. articles to profl. jours. Fellow N.Y. Acad. Scis.; mem. Phi Beta Kappa, Sigma Xi. Avocation: writing poetry. Home: 112 Crosslands Dr Kennett Square PA 19348-2014

WILSON, ARTHUR JESS, psychologist, educator; b. Yonkers, N.Y., Oct. 25, 1910; s. Samuel Louis and Anna (Gilbert) W.; m. Lillian Moss, Sept. 16, 1941; children: Warren David, Anton Francis. BS, NYU, 1935, MA, 1949, PhD, 1961; LLB, St. Lawrence U., 1940; JD, Bklyn. Law Sch., 1967. Tchr. Yonkers Pub. Schs, 1935-40; dir. adult edn. Yonkers, 1940-42; supr. vocat. rehab. N.Y. State Dept. Edn., 1942-44; personnel exec. Abraham & Straus, Blkyn., 1946-47; rehab. field sec. N.Y. Tb and Health Assn., 1947-48; dir. rehab. Westchester County Med. Center, Valhalla, N.Y., 1948-67; dir. Manhattan Narcotic Rehab. Center N.Y. State Drug Abuse Control Commn., 1967-68; clin. psychologist VA Hosp., Montrose, N.Y., 1968-73; pvt. practice clin. psychology Yonkers, 1973—. Cons. N.Y. State Dept. Edn., HEW; spl. lectr. Sch. Pub. Health and Adminstrv. Medicine, Columbia U. and Grad. Sch., N.Y. U.; instr. Westchester Community Coll., Valhalla, N.Y.; selected participant Clin. Study Tour of China, 1980. *In 1950, Dr. Wilson was contacted by Eleanor Roosevelt. She was preparing her address to be given before the National Rehabilitation Association. At that time, Dr. Wilson was Director of Rehabilitation at Grasslands Hospital, which is now the Westchester County Medical Center. He had just published a book on rehabilitation, entitled The Emotional Life of the Ill and Injured. He met with Eleanor Roosevelt at her residence in New York City where they reviewed a proposed draft of her planned remarks. He found Mrs. Roosevelt a most gracious, knowledgeable, and highly intelligent person.* Author: The Emotional Life of the Ill and Injured, 1950; A Guide to the Genius of Cardozo, 1939; The Wilson Teaching Inventory, 1941; also articles. Honored as Westchester Author, Westchester County Hist. Soc., 1957. With USN, 1944-46. Recipient Founders Day award NYU, 1961. Mem. APA, Internat. Mark Twain Soc. (hon.), N.Y. Acad. Scis., N.Y. State Psychol. Assn., Internat. Platform Assn. (selected mem.), Kappa Delta Pi, Phi Delta Kappa, Epsilon Pi Tau. Home and Office: 4121 NW 88th Ave Apt 204 Pompano Beach FL 33065-1880 also: 487 Park Ave Yonkers NY 10703-2121

WILSON, ARTHUR THEODORE, education consultant; b. Newark, July 2, 1945; s. Elmer and Dorothy May (Outlaw-Sloan) W. BA in Humanities, New Sch., 1971, MA in Philosophy, 1974; PhD in Program History, NYU, 1980. Cert. tchr., N.Y., N.J. Rschr. African Studies, N.Y.C., 1972; tchr. Teaneck Alternative High Sch., N.J., 1979-80, Hunter Coll., N.Y.C., 1980-81; gifted and talented program curriculum cons. Bd. Cooperative Ednl. Svcs., SUNY, Farmingdale, 1983—. Apptd. arts & edn. acad. artist N.J. Performing Arts Ctr., Newark, 1996—; advisor, tutor Master's Degree Program in Acting, New Actors Workshop, Antioch U., N.Y., 1995—; workshop leader Young Playwright's Festival, N.Y.C., 1981—; adj. prof. drama Drew U., Madison, N.J.; co-founder, workshop leader N.J. Young Playwrights Festival, 1983; project dir., playwright Am. Folk Theater Young Co.'s exch. program, London, 1984-85; theater workshop cons. Milneck Sch. for Deaf, L.I., 1984; literature workshop cons. Orion Gifted and Talented Program, Lindenhurst, N.Y., 1984—; artistic dir. exch. program Manhattan Empire and Tukak Theater, Denmark; dir. playwriting in sch. project N.Y. Shakespeare Festival, 1986—; instr. N.Y. Lit. Assn., N.Y.C., 1984—; poetry reading and workshop with Poet Laureate Gwendolyn Brooks, Union Coll., 1985, guest poet for Mother Hale of Hale House, 1987; dir. playwriting in edn. dept. schs. N.Y. Shakespeare Festival, dir./prodr. Live! (radio edn. program), cons. arts edn. New Dance Group Ctr., N.Y., 1987—. Editor, writer, publisher Dance Giant Steps, Inc., Bklyn., 1981—; author: (play) The Extended Family, 1987; dir. Daddy Say, 1987, Children of Dahomey and Spirit Ensemble, 1986; dance editor; Feet Mag., 1969-72, Blacj Creations Mag., 1970-72; editor, pub.: Attitude: The Dancers' Monthly, 1982; contbr. poetry to Open Mag., Other Countries, New Rain, A Taste of Salt; producer: (plays) Life Sea Treasures, 1989-90, Guns Like Candy, 1991, Red High Heels Snap Back, 1995. Workshop leader N.J. Teen Program, 1983-84; advisor, workshop leader, founder N.J. Young Playwrights Festival, 1964-68; rsch. asst. Weeksville Project, Bjlyn., 1969-70; theater dir. local orgns. Recipient numerous scholars, 1970-79; grantee Bklyn. Art and Cultural Assn., 1983, N.Y. Dept. Cultural Affairs, 1983-84, N.Y. State Coun. on Arts, 1982-84, BECA Capezio Found., Heart grant Union County Bd. Freeholders, 1998-00; N.J. State Coun. Arts fellow, 1985-86. Mem. Black Writers Union, Dramatists Guild, Inc., ASSITEJ, Internat. Assn. Children's Theater Professionals. Office: Dance Giant Steps Inc 1040 Park Place Ste 5C Brooklyn NY 11213

WILSON, BARY WALLACE, neuroendocrinologist; b. Moscow, Dec. 12, 1945; s. Arlin Chadwick and June (Rawlings) W.; m. Martha Ericka Ruf, Aug. 21, 1967; children: Melanie, Mark, Meaghan, Miranda, Brandon, Benjiman. BS, U. Wash., Seattle, 1972; PhD, U. London, 1977; post doctoral assoc., MIT, 1977-78. Engr. Varian Mat, Bremen, Germany, 1973-74; biochemist St. Bartholomew's Med. Sch., London, 1974-76; sr. rsch. scientist, staff scientist Battelle Northwest, Richland, Wash., 1978—; founder, prin. Tecna Corp., San Bernardino, Calif., 1983—; founder Columbia Magnetics Inc., Kennewick, Wash., 1993—; founder, chief scientist Gulf Tech. Ctr., Abu Dhabi, U.A.E., 1994—. Cons. SCA Assocs., McLean, Va., 1990-93, Univ. Petroleum & Minerals RI, Dhahran, Saudi Arabia, 1986-87; mem. EPA sci. adv. bd. NIEMF com., Washington, 1990—; bd. dirs. Bioelectromagnetics Soc., Falls Church, Md. Author, editor Extremely LF EMF: The Question of Cancer, 1990; patentee: Microbial Solubilization of Coal, 1990, Methods and Treatment of NIDDM, 1989; contbr. articles to profl. jours. Sgt. USMCR, 1965-72. Recipient Mentor award Internat. Sci. and Engring. Fair, 1991. Avocations: snow skiing, writing. Office: Pacific Northwest Lab 617 Battelle Blvd Richland WA 99352

WILSON, BENNIE JAMES, III, business educator; b. San Antonio, Aug. 5, 1943; s. Bennie James Jr. and Claressa (Deary) W.; m. Karen Inez Wanda Paul, Aug. 8, 1981; children: Benét Jenene, Claressa Delores. BS, San Jose (Calif.) State Coll., 1965; MBA, U. Rochester, N.Y., 1969; EdD, Auburn (Ala.) U., 1979. Sr. profl. in human resources Soc. for Human Resource Mgmt.; chief adminstrv. officer credentials C.C. State of Calif. Sr. rsch. fellow Nat. Def. U., Washington, 1982-83; dep. base comdr., dir. pers. Edwards (Calif.) AFB, 1983-86; vice comdr., dir. testing U.S. Mil. Entrance Processing Command, Gt. Lakes, Ill., 1986-90; asst. chief of staff for pers. and adminstrn. U.S. Forces, Seoul, Republic of Korea, 1990-92; interim comdr., vice commandant Air Force Inst. of Tech., Dayton, Ohio, 1992-95; dir. human resource devel. San Antonio State Hosp., 1996-97; gen. mgr. Lucent Techs. Svcs. Co., Inc., 1997-98; asst. dean Coll. of Bus. U. Tex., San Antonio, 1998—. Bd. dirs. Hidea Innovative Products, LLC, San Antonio. Editor: The Guard and Reserve in the Total Force: The First Decade, 1983. Trustee City of San Antonio Housing Trust Fund, San Antonio, 1998; mem. City of San Antonio Citizen Adv. Action Bd., 1998, Greater San Antonio C. of C., 1998; sec., bd. dirs. The Estates at Champions Run Homeowners Assn. Col. USAF, 1965-95. Mem. Am. Legion, Mensa, Phi Delta Kappa, Omega Psi Phi. Avocation: golf. Home: 73 Champions Run San Antonio TX 78258-7704 Office: U of Tex at San Antonio Coll of Bus 6900 N Loop 1604 W San Antonio TX 78249-1130 E-mail: bjwilson@utsa.edu.

WILSON, BLAKE SHAW, electrical engineer, researcher; b. Orlando, Fla., Mar. 7, 1948; s. Joseph Richard Hoyle and Jacqueline Lucy (Jones) W.; m. Doris Jane Rouse, Jan. 6, 1974; children: Nadia Jacqueline, Blair Elizabeth. BSEE, Duke U., 1974. Rsch. engr. Rsch. Triangle Inst., Research Triangle Park, N.C., 1974-78, sr. rsch. engr., 1978-83, sr. rsch. scientist, 1979-83, head neurosci. program, 1983-94, dir. Ctr. for Auditory Prosthesis Rsch., 1994—. Guest scientist Coleman Meml. Lab., U. Calif., San Francisco, 1983-86; adj. asst. prof. otolaryngology Duke U. Med. Ctr., 1984-94, assoc. prof., 1994—; oversight com. cochlear implants Kresge Hearing Rsch. Inst., U. Mich., 1987—, U. Iowa, 1994—; sci. adv. coun. House Ear Inst., L.A., 1990; gen. chair Conf. Implantable Auditory Prostheses, Pacific Grove, Calif., 1991; spl. panel hearing aids NIDCD, 1992, ad hoc adv. com. hearing aid R & D, 1993—; guest of honor Internat. Workshop on Cochlear Implants, Vienna, 1996; reviewer grant applications NIH, NSF, VA and Med. Rsch. Coun., Can.; cons. cochlear implants NIH; mem. faculty various continuing edn. courses; prin. investigator numerous projects; presenter numerous confs., symposia. Reviewer chpts. for books, papers and jours.; contbr. numerous articles to profl. jours. Recipient Discover award for tech. innovation, 1996, Presdl. citation for "major contbns. to restoration of hearing in profoundly deaf persons", 130th Ann. Mtg. of Am. Otologic Soc. Home: 2410 Wrightwood Ave Durham NC 27705-5802 Office: Rsch Triangle Inst PO Box 12194 Durham NC 27709-2194

WILSON, BLENDA JACQUELINE, foundation administrator; b. Woodbridge, N.J., Jan. 28, 1941; d. Horace and Margaret (Brogsdale) Wilson; m. Louis Fair Jr. AB, Cedar Crest Coll., 1962; AM, Seton Hall U., 1965; PhD, Boston Coll., 1979; DHL (hon.) , Cedar Crest Coll., 1987, Loretto Heights Coll., 1988, Colo. Tech. Coll., 1988, U. Detroit, 1989; LLD (hon.) , Rutgers U., 1989, Ea. Mich. U., 1990, Cambridge Coll., 1991, Schoolcraft Coll., 1992; DHL (hon.) , Cambridge Coll., 2001, Antioch U., 1999, Salve Regina U., 2002; DPublic Svc. (hon.) , U. Mass., 2002; DHL (hon.) , Merrimack Coll., 2001. Tchr. Woodbridge Twp. Pub. Schs., 1962-66; exec. dir. Middlesex County Econ. Opportunity Corp., New Brunswick, N.J., 1966-69; exec. asst. to pres. Rutgers U., 1969-72; sr. assoc. dean Grad. Sch. Edn. Harvard U., Cambridge, Mass., 1972-82; v.p. effective sector mgmt. Ind. Sector, Washington, 1982-84; exec. dir. Colo. Commn. Higher Edn., Denver, 1984-88; chancellor and prof. pub. adminstrn. & edn. U. Mich., Dearborn, 1988-92; pres. Calif. State U., Northridge, 1992-99, Nellie Mae Found., Braintree, Mass., 1999—. Am. del. U.S./U.K. Dialogue About Quality Judgments in Higher Edn.; adv. bd. Mich. Consolidated Gas Co., Stanford Inst. Higher Edn. Rsch., U. So. Col. Dist. 60 Nat. Alliance, Nat. Ctr. for Rsch. to Improve Postsecondary Teaching and Learning, 1988-90; bd. dirs. Alpha Capital Mgmt.; mem. higher edn. colloquium Am. Coun. Edn., vis. com. Divsn. Continuing Edn. in Faculty of Arts & Scis., Harvard Coll., Pew Forum on K-12 Edn. Reform in U.S., The Coll. Bd., Federated Dorchester Neighborhood Ho., Fed. Res. Bank of Boston. Dir. U. Detroit Jesuit High Sch., Northridge Hosp. Med. Ctr., 1993-99, Arab Cmty. Ctr. for Econ. and Social Svcs., Union Bank, J. Paul Getty Trust, James Irvine Found., 1996-99, Internat. Found. Edn. and Self-Help, Achievement Coun., L.A.; dir., vice chair Met. Affairs Corp.; exec. bd. Detroit area coun. Boy Scouts Am.; bd. dirs. Commonwealth Fund, Henry Ford Hosp.-Fairlane Ctr., Henry Ford Health System, Met. Ctr. for High Tech., United Way Southeastern Mich.; mem. Nat. Coalition 100 Black Women, Detroit, Race Rels. Coun. Met. Detroit, Women & Founds., Greater Detroit Interfaith Round Table NCCJ, Adv. Bd. Valley Cultural Ctr., Woodland Hills; trustee assoc. Boston Coll.; trustee emeritus Cambridge Coll.; trustee emeritus, bd. dirs. Found. Ctr.; trustee Henry Ford Mus. & Greenfield Village, Sammy Davis Jr. Nat. Liver Inst. Mem. AAUW, Assn. Governing Bds. (adv. coun. of pres.'s), Edn. Commn. of the States (student minority task force), Am. Assn. Higher Edn. (chair-elect), Am. Assn. State Colls. & Univs. (com. on policies & purposes, acad. leadership fellows selection com.), Assn. Black Profls. and Adminstrs., Assn. Black Women in Higher Edn., Women Execs. State Govt., Internat. Women's Forum, Mich. Women's Forum, Women's Econ. Club Detroit, Econ. Club, Rotary. Office: Nellie Mae Edn Found 1250 Hancock St 205N Quincy MA 02169-4331

WILSON, BRADLEY EVANS, philosophy educator; b. Detroit, July 1, 1961; s. Robert Franklin and Joan Diane Wilson; m. Jean Grace Jones, Oct. 10, 1997. BA, Purdue U., 1982; MA, U. N.C., 1984, PhD, 1991. Instr. U. N.C., Chapel Hill, 1989-91, N.C. State U., Raleigh, 1989-91; vis. asst. prof. U. Pitts., 1991-96; asst. prof. Slippery Rock (Pa.) U., 1997—. Ethics cons. Shadyside Hosp., Pitts., 1993-96. Contbr. articles to profl. jours. Mem. Am. Philos. Assn., Philosophy of Sci. Assn. Avocations: birding, gardening, camping. Home: 203 Linda Ln Meadville PA 16335 Office: Slippery Rock U Dept Philosophy Slippery Rock PA 16057 E-mail: bradley.wilson@sru.edu.

WILSON, BRIAN EUGENE, computer scientist; b. Dayton, Ohio, Dec. 19, 1963; s. Homer Eugene and Shirley Ann (Orth) W.; m. Donna Wimmer, Feb. 18, 1989; children: Lyndsey Marie, Brandy Lee. Student, Sinclair C.C., Dayton, 1982-85, Sage Evening Coll., Albany, N.Y. IBM cert. OS/2 Warp V4 Engr., AIX Specialist-Sys. Adminstrn., MQ series integrator V2 specialist, MQ series integrator V2 solutions expert. Programmer Sinclair C.C., Dayton, 1983-85; editor-in-chief, writer, v.p. Advanced Computer Enterprises, Englewood, Ohio, 1985-86; computer operator Albany (N.Y.) Savs. Bank, 1986-88; sr. computer programmer, analyst N.Y. State Dept. Tax and Fin., Albany, 1988-89, sys. programmer, 1990-94, database programmer/analyst, 1994-97, mgr. Internet technologies, 1997-2000; sr. info. tech. specialist IBM, 2000—. Computer programmer Pub. Domain, Inc., West Milton, Ohio, 1984-86, Ledex, Inc., Vandalia, Ohio, 1984-86; cons. WKB Software, Union, Ohio, 1982-85; cons., owner Wilson Software and Solutions, Rensselaer, N.Y., 1992—; v.p. Advanced Computer Enterprises Ltd. Partnership, Englewood, 1995-96. Author: Using Model 204, 1990; editor Commodore Users Bull. Jour., 1985-86, contbr.; editor-in-chief, writer, v.p. Commodore Users Bull. Coach Westland Hills Little League, Albany, 1990-94, Rensselaer Little League, 1995—; vol. Hudson Valley coun. Girl Scouts U.S.; trombonist Capitaland Bigband. Mem. Internat. Model 204 Users Group (libr. 1989—), Nat. Fedn. Interscholastic Ofcls. Assn., Northeast Model 204 Users Group (bd.

dirs.), N.Y. Assn. Cert. Football Ofcls. (Capital dist. chpt.), Pub. Employees Fedn. Methodist. Avocations: music, computers, woodworking, model railroading. Home: 1244 2nd St Rensselaer NY 12144-1816 Office: IBM 80 State St Ste 17 Albany NY 12207-2588 E-mail: bwilson@nycap.rr.com., brianwil@us.ibm.com.

WILSON, BRUCE BRIGHTON, retired transportation executive, lawyer; b. Boston, Feb. 6, 1936; s. Robert Lee and Jane (Schlotterer) W.; m. Elizabeth Ann MacFarland, Dec. 31, 1958; children: Mabeth, Mary, Bruce Robert, Caroline Daly. AB, Princeton U., 1958; LLB, U. Pa., 1961. Bar: Pa. 1962. Assoc. Montgomery, McCracken, Walker & Rhoads, Phila., 1962-69; atty. U.S. Dept. Justice, Washington, 1969-79, dep. asst. atty. gen. antitrust div., 1971-76; spl. counsel Consol. Rail Corp., Phila., 1979-81, gen. counsel litigation and antitrust, 1981-82, v.p., gen. counsel, 1982-84, v.p. law, 1984-87, sr. v.p. law, 1987-97, sr. v.p. merger, 1997. Bd. dirs. Phila. Indsl. Devel. Corp.; mem. mgmt. com. Concord Resources Group, 1989-91. Chmn. Radnor Twp. Cable Commn. Coun., 1993—2000, mem., 2002—, Radnor Twp. Ethics Commn., 2000—01. Fellow Salzburg Seminar in Am. Studies (Austria), 1965; fellow Felz Inst. State and Local Govt., 1967 Mem. ABA, Phila. Bar Assn., Corinthian Yacht Club, Beach Club Cape May. Home: 224 Chamounix Rd Wayne PA 19087-3606 E-mail: bbwils24@erols.com.

WILSON, BRUCE KEITH, men's health nurse; b. Alton, Ill., Aug. 18, 1946; s. Lewis Philip and Ruth Caroline Wilson; m. Karen Loughrey, Aug. 14, 1977; children: Sarah Ann, Andrew James. BSN, U. Tex., San Antonio, 1975, MSN, 1977; PhD, North Tex. State U., Denton, 1987. Coord. Pan Am. U., Edinburg, Tex., 1982-83; house supr. HCA Rio Grande Regional Hosp., McAllen, 1986-87; program dir. Tex. Southmost Coll., Brownsville, 1983-86; mem. faculty U. Tex.-Pan Am., Edinburg, 1986—. Author: Logical Nursing Math., 1987; contbr. chpts. to books, numerous articles to profl. jours. With U.S. Army, 1966-68. Mem. Am. Assembly for Men in Nursing (bd. dirs. 1997-2001), Tex. League for Nursing (bd. dirs. 1993-97). Avocations: photography, computer. Home: 1702 Ivy Ln Edinburg TX 78539-5367 Office: U Tex-Pan Am Dept Nursing Edinburg TX 78539 E-mail: wilson@hiline.net.

WILSON, C. DANIEL, JR. library director; b. Middletown, Conn., Nov. 8, 1941; s. Clyde D. and Dorothy M. (Neal) W.; m. M. April Jackson, Apr. 1986; children: Christine, Cindy, Clyde, Ben. BA, Elmhurst Coll., 1967; MA, Dominican U., 1968; MPA, U. New Orleans, 1995. Trainee Chgo. Pub. Libr., 1967-68; instr. U. Ill., 1968-70; asst. dir. Perrot Meml. Libr., Greenwich, Conn., 1970-76; dir. Wilton Pub. Libr., Wilton, 1976-79; assoc. dir. Birmingham Pub. Libr., Birmingham, Ala., 1979-83; dir. Davenport (Iowa) Pub. Libr., 1983-85, New Orleans Pub. Libr., 1985-97, St. Louis County Libr., 1997—. With USMC, 1962-65. Mem. ALA, Internat. Assn. Met. Librs. (pres. 1998—), Mo. Libr. Assn., Am. Soc. Pub. Adminstrs., Rotary, Pi Gamma Mu. Episcopalian. E-mail: dwilson@slcl.lib.mo.us.

WILSON, CARL WELDON, JR. construction company executive, civil engineer; b. Norfolk, Va., Sept. 4, 1933; s. Carl Weldon and Janie Marie (Ludford) W.; m. Jean Roberts, Feb. 13, 1960; children: Lisa Ann, Carl Weldon III. BCE, Tex. A&M U., 1954. Registered profl. engr., Tex. Engr. Magnolia Petroleum Co., Morgan City, La., 1954-55, Brown & Root, Houston, 1957-60; project mgr. Claude Everett Constrn. Co., 1960-62; pres. Falcon Constrn. Co., 1962-63; pres., owner Wilson Engrng. and Constrn. Co., 1963-68; v.p. Divcon, Inc., 1968-71, Wilson Industries, Inc., Houston, 1971-81; pres., prin. owner BS&B Engrng. Co., Inc., 1981-86; chmn., majority shareholder Task Internat., Inc., 1986—. Served to 1st lt. U.S. Army, 1955-57. Republican. Episcopalian. Avocations: tennis, running, painting. Home: 750 Bison Dr Houston TX 77079-4401 Office: Task Internat Inc PO Box 940121 Houston TX 77094-7121 E-mail: cwilson@silverfox.org.

WILSON, CAROL ANN, office manager; b. Camp Mackall, N.C., Dec. 22, 1943; d. Hinkle Melvin Starr and Katie Ruth Holcombe-Starr; m. Neil Elmo Rizzotto, Jan. 12, 1967 (div. Mar. 1972); children: Tab Anthoney, Tammy Ann, Scotti Ivan, Kimberly Kay Johnson-Rizzotto-Grace; m. James Edward Wilson, May 14, 1988. Cert., Rehab. Sch., San Francisco; student, Lake Chabot Jr. Coll., Hayward, Calif.; Cert., Heald Bus. Coll., Walnut Creek, Calif. Sec., clk. AAA Auto Dismantlers, Hayward; telephone repairer Western Electric, San Leandro, Calif.; clk. Naval Supply Ctr., Oakland; sec., office mgr. Baca & Sons Painting/Decorating, San Francisco; office mgr. Wil-Compute, Gastonia, N.C. Rschr., pub. rels. profl. Adults and Children Mental Health, San Leandro. Writer So. Backroads Mag., 2001. Rschr. Gaston/Lincolton Soc. Genealogy, 1994-99, The Amonsoquath Tribe of Cherokee; historian Nature Am. Indian the Five Civilized Tribes. Mem. Libr. of Congress, Beta Sigma Phi. Democrat. Seventh Day Adventist. Avocations: art, history, Native Am. rsch., geneal. rsch. Home: 233 Bright Ave Bessemer City NC 28016-8513 E-mail: carolann@caroline.rr.com.

WILSON, CAROLYN TAYLOR, librarian; b. Cookeville, Tenn., June 10, 1936; d. Herman Wilson and Flo (Donaldson) Taylor; m. Larry Kittrell Wilson, June 14, 1957 (dec.); children: Jennifer Wilson Rust, Elissa Anne Wilson. BA, David Lipscomb Coll., 1957; MLS, George Peabody Coll., 1976. Tchr. English Fulton County Sch. System, Atlanta, 1957-59; serials cataloger Vanderbilt U. Libr., Nashville, 1974-77; asst. libr. United Meth. Pub. House, 1978-80; collection devel. libr. David Lipscomb U., 1980—, acting dir. Beaman Libr., 1998, dir. Beaman Libr., 1999—. Cons. and rschr. in field; project dir. Tenn.'s Lit. Legacy for Tenn. Humanities Coun., 1994—, ALA grant, Frontier in Am. Culture, 1996-98; project dir. Tenn. Humanities Coun. grant, 1998—; rep. Tenn. Avd. Coun. Librs., Acad. Librs., 1999—. Rsch. asst. Handbook of Tennessee Labor History, 1987-89. Adv. bd. So. Festival of Books, Nashville, 1988-90, 90—, vol. coord., 1989, 90—; project dir. Women's Words (summer grant program) for Tenn. Humanities Coun., Tenn.'s Literary Legacy (summer grant program), 1994-96, Growing Up Southern (summer grant), 1996—, ALA grant The Frontier in Am. Culture, 1996—. Recipient Nat. Honor Soc. award Phi Alpha Theta, 1956, Internat. Honor Soc. award Beta Phi Mu, 1980, Frances Neel Cheney award Tenn. Libr. Assn., 1992; nominee Athena award, 1992; Growing Up Southern summer grantee, 1996—. Mem. ALA, Tenn. Hist. Soc., Tenn. Libr. Assn. (Frances Neel Cheney award 1992), Southeastern Libr. Assn. (chmn. outstanding S.E. author award com. 1991-92, chmn. So. Books competition 1992-94, sec. exec. bd. 1997—), Women's Nat. Book Assn. (pres., v.p., treas., awards chmn. 1980—), Tenn. Writers Alliance (bd. dirs. 1995—). Democrat. Avocations: reading, cooking, jogging, sailing. Office: David Lipscomb U Beaman Libr # 310 Nashville TN 37204 E-mail: carolyn.wilson@lipscomb.edu.

WILSON, CATHERINE ANN, critical care nurse, educator, health policy analyst; b. Portsmouth, Va., Dec. 26, 1957; d. John Louis and Mary Catherine (Bernat) Hostinsky; m. Don D. Wilson, Mar. 19, 1988; children: Bronwyn, Dewayne. BSN, The Cath. U. Am., 1979; MS in Mgmt., Golden State U., 1988; MS in Nursing, U. Md., 1990; Cert. in Legis. Studies, Georgetown U., 2001. Cert. in managed care. With USN, from 1979, advanced through grades to capt., staff nurse ICU Md., 1979-84, charge nurse surg. Phila., 1984-87, asst. charge nurse, educator Guantanamo Bay, Cuba, 1987-88; with Bur. Medicine and Surgery, Washington, 1988-94; sr. health policy analyst The Pentagon, 1994-96; regional health promotion dir. TRICARE Midatlantic, Norfolk, Va., 1996-98, dir. regional ops., 1998-99; Congl. detail with Senator Inoyue, Washington, 1999-2001; dep. dir. TRICARE MidAtlantic, 2001—02; dir. family medicine Naval Med. Ctr., Portsmouth, Va., 2002—. Named Outstanding Young Woman of Am. Mem. AACN, Navy Corps Assn., Soc. Trauma Nurses, Assn. Neurosci. Nursing, Sigma Theta Tau. Home: 3252 Wingfield Lake Rd Williamsburg VA 23185-7519 E-mail: northstar@widomaker.com.

WILSON, CATHERINE COOPER (KITTY WILSON), communications executive, writer; b. Dallas, Sept. 17, 1955; d. William Edward and Suzanne (Blessington) Cooper; m. James Alan Wilson, Oct.17, 1981; children: Nicholas James, Gregory Cooper. BA in Journalism, Tex. Tech U., 1977. Pub. rels. asst. Dallas Market Ctr., 1972-75, 77; pub. rels. coord. Herman Blum Engrs., Dallas, 1977-80, coord. new bus. devel., 1980; acct. exec. Helen Holmes & Assoc., 1980; mktg. and pub. rels. coord. EDI Architects, 1980-82; pres. Catherine Wilson Comm., 1982—; owner, v.p. Wilson Creative, Inc., 1988—. Craft of Writing conf. chair U. North Tex. and Greater Dallas Writers' Assn., 1997-99. Contbr. articles to trade mags. Mem. membership com. North Tex. Commn., Dallas, 1979-81; mem. pub. rels. com., bldg. com. St. Rita Cath. Ch., Dallas, 1984-87. Mem. Greater Dallas Writers Assn. Roman Catholic. Avocations: travel, reading, music, walking. Home and Office: 6435 Sudbury Dr Dallas TX 75214-2435

WILSON, CHARLES BANKS, artist; b. Springdale, Ark., Aug. 6, 1918; s. Charles Bertram and Bertha Juanita (Banks) W.; children— Geoffrey Banks, Carrie Vee. Student, Art Inst. Chgo., 1936-41. Mag. and book illustrator, 1943-60; head art dept. N.E. Okla. A. & M. Coll., Miami, Okla., 1947-61; painter, printmaker. Executed mural, Okla. State Capitol, 1975; represented in permanent collections Met. Mus., N.Y.C., Library of Congress, Washington, U.S. Capitol Bldg., D.C. Corcoran Gallery, Smithsonian Inst., Will Rogers Meml. Mus., Philbrook Art Center, Tulsa, Nat. Cowbow Hall of Fame, Oklahoma City.; illustrator numerous books. Bd. dirs. Thomas Gilcrease Mus. History and Art, Tulsa, 1957-61; chmn. Pub. Libr. Bd., Miami, Okla., 1954-59. Named to Okla. Hall of Fame, Okla. Historians Hall of Fame, 2001, an Okla. Treasure, State of Okla. Arts Commn., 2001; recipient Western Heritage award Cowboy Hall of Fame, D.S.C., U. Okla.; subject of books The Lithographs of Charles Banks Wilson, 1989, Search for the North American Purebloods, 2000, An Oklahoma Portrait, 1989. Mem. Internat. Inst. Arts and Letters (Geneva). Office: 1611 E Mission Blvd Fayetteville AR 72703-3043 E-mail: cvwilson@mail.uark.edu.

WILSON, CHARLES B. neurosurgeon, educator; b. Neosho, Mo., Aug. 31, 1929; married; 3 children. BS, Tulane U., 1951, MD, 1954. Resident pathologist Tulane U., 1955-56, instr. neurosurgery, 1960-61; resident Ochsner Clinic, 1956-60; instr. La. State U., 1961-63; from asst. prof. to prof. U. Ky., 1963-68; prof. neurosurgery U. Calif., San Francisco, 1968—, dir., Brain Tumor Research Ctr., 1972—97; dir. Inst. for the Future, Menlo Park, 1997—. Mem. Am. Assn. Neurol. Surgery, Soc. Neurol. Surgery, Inst. Medicine. Achievements include research in brain and pituitary tumors. Office: U Calif 125 Sch Medicine Box 0350 San Francisco CA 94143 also: Inst. for the Future 118 2nd St., 5th flr San Francisco CA 94105*

WILSON, CHARLES FRANK, lawyer, law educator; b. Scranton, Pa., July 11, 1943; s. Victor Peter and Rose (Sposito) W.; m. Diane P. Cardoni, June 30, 1973 (dec. 1979); m. Kathleen Geary, Sept. 16, 1983; children: Nicole, Lisa. BS in Edn., Villanova U., 1965; JD, Dickinson U., 1969. Bar: U.S. Dist. Ct. (mid. dist.) Pa. 1969, U.S. Ct. Appeals (3d cir.) 1975. Assoc. Laster, Strohl, Kane, Mattes & McDonald, Scranton, Pa., 1969-71, Epstein, O'Neill & Utan, Scranton, 1971-83; asst. dist. atty. Dist. Attys. Office, 1974-80; ptnr. Epstein, Utan, Wilson & Marsili, 1983—. Instr. bus. law Pa. State U., 1971. Contbr. articles to profl. jours. Mem. ABA, Lackawanna County Bar Assn., Pa. Bar Assn., Pa. Trial Lawyers Assn., Scranton Lions Club. Republican. Roman Catholic. Avocations: fishing, boating, snorkeling. Office: Epstein Utan Wilson & Marsili 800 Penn Security Bank Bldg 142 N Washington Ave Scranton PA 18503-2200

WILSON, CHARLES HAVEN, lawyer; b. Waltham, Mass., July 27, 1936; s. Charles Haven Sr. and Kathryn (Sullivan) W.; children: Kathryn Wilson Self, Charles H. Jr. AB in Govt. magna cum laude, Tufts U., 1958; MS in Journalism, Columbia U., 1959; JD, U. Calif., Berkeley, 1967. Bar: D.C. 1968, U.S. Supreme Ct. 1972. Sr. law clk. to Chief Justice Earl Warren, 1967-68; from assoc. to counsel Williams & Connolly, Washington, 1968-90; sr. counsel ACLU of Nat. Capital Area, 1992-98; sr. staff atty. Bazelon Ctr. for Mental Health Law, 1998-99. Adj. prof. constitutional law Georgetown U. Law Ctr., 1971, 72. With U.S. Army, 1959-62. Mem. ABA (litigation sect. coun. 1976-79, dir publs. 1975-90, founding editor jour. Litigation 1974, bd. editors ABA Jour. 1985-91), Order of Coif. Democrat. Roman Catholic. Avocation: reading.

WILSON, CHARLES LINDSAY, research scientist; b. Bristol, Va., Apr. 9, 1932; s. Crawford L. and Nannie R. (Rollins) W.; m. Miriam Janet Williams, Dec. 18, 1973; children: Barrie, Rebecca, Charles, Cathy, Nancy, Patrick. BA in Biology, U. Va., 1953; MS in Plant Pathology, W.Va. U., 1956, PhD in Plant Pathology, 1958. Prof. U. Ark., Fayetteville, 1958-68; investigations leader USDA, Delaware, Ohio, 1968-72, rsch. plant pathologist Wooster, 1972-80, ARS/USDA, Kearneysville, W.Va., 1980—. Adj. prof. Ohio State U., Wooster, 1972-80. Editor: Exotic Plant Pests and North American Agriculture, 1980, Biological Control of Postharvest Diseases, 1994, Microbial Food Contamination, 2001; author: Gardener's Hint Book, 1978, World of Terrariums, 1979; contbr. over 180 sci. articles to profl. jours. Recipient U. Ark. Disting. Svc. award, 1968, USDA/ARS Scientist of the Yr. award, 1988. Fellow Am. Phytopathology Soc., Washington Acad. Sci. (Disting. Svc. award 1984). Achievements include 14 patents on the use of biologically-based methods to control plant diseases. Avocation: sports, gardening. Home: PO Box 1194 Shepherdstown WV 25443-1194 Office: USDA ARS 45 Wiltshire Rd Kearneysville WV 25430-9425

WILSON, CHARLES REGINALD, federal judge; b. Pensacola, FL, 1954; BS, U. Notre Dame, 1976, JD, 1979. Bar: Fla. 1979. Law clk. to Hon. Joseph W. Hatchett U.S. Ct. Appeal for 11th Cir., 1979—80; asst. county atty. Hillsborough county, Fla., 1980—81; county judge 13th Jud. Cir. of Fla., 1986—90; pvt. practice Fla., 1981—86; U.S. magistrate judge U.S. Dist. Ct. (mid. dist.) Fla., 1990—94, U.S. atty., 1994—99; U.S. cir. judge U.S. Ct. Appeals 11th Cir., Tampa, Fla., 1999—. Mem.: Hillsborough County Bar Assn. (pres. young lawyers sect., Most Productive Young Lawyer award 1990), Fla. Bar Assn. (bd. govs. young lawyers sect.). Office: 11th Cir Ct Appeals 801 N Florida Ave Ste 14B Tampa FL 33602-3849*

WILSON, CHARLES ROBERT, port captain, harbor master; b. Biloxi, Miss., Aug. 28, 1947; s. William Clayborne, Sr. and Lyna Lowe Wilson; m. Bonnie Atwater, June 12, 1990 (div. Feb. 1995); 1 child, Michael Robert. PhB, State U. West Ga., 1975. Electronic engr. Rockwell, San Francisco, Atlanta, 1975-79; Alaskan bush pilot Anchorage, 1990-95; port capt., harbor master Midway Phoenix Corp., Midway Atoll, Hawaii, 1995—. Cons. Rockwell and subs. cos., Atlanta, 1969-79; ocean sailboat racer, 1979-90. Mem. U.S. Parachute Assn. (pres. 1969, Star Crest 187 award 1971, Night Star Crest 187 award 1973). Avocations: skydiving, sport flying, whitewater activities, sailing. Home and Office: Midway Phoenix Corp PO Box 29460 Honolulu HI 96820-1860 E-mail: bwilson@midwayisland.net.

WILSON, CHARLES STEPHEN, cardiologist, educator; b. Geneva, June 14, 1938; s. Robert Butler and Naoma Luella (Norgren) Wilson; m. Linda Stern Walt, Aug. 21, 1960; children: Michael Scott, Amy Lynn, Cynthia Lee. BA cum laude, U. Nebr., 1960; MD, Northwestern U., 1964. Diplomate Am. Bd. Internal Medicine subsplty. bd. cardiovascular disease, Nat. Bd. Med. Examiners. Intern Fitzsimons Gen. Hosp., Denver, 1964-65; fellow in internal medicine and cardiology Mayo Grad. Sch. Medicine, Rochester, Minn., 1968-72; practice medicine specializing in cardiology Lincoln, Nebr., 1972—; attending staff Bryan Meml. Hosp., 1972—, chmn. cardiology, 1976-79; attending staff Lincoln Gen. Hosp., 1978—; clin. prof. medicine and cardiology U. Nebr. Med. Ctr., Omaha; med. dir. Lifescan Preventative Imaging, Lincoln, 2001—. Mem. Mayor's Coun. on Emergency Med. Svcs., Lincoln, 1974-78; founder, chmn. Nebr. State Hypertension Screening Program; med. dir. Lincoln Mobile Heart Team, 1977-80, Lincoln Cardiac Rehab. Program, 1978-79; co-founder, pres. Nebr. Heart Inst., 1987; co-founder Lincoln Cardiac Transplant Program, 1987. Contbr. articles to profl. jours.; editorl. cons. Chest, 1975-76; assoc. editor Nebr. Med. Jour., 1981-88. Trustee U. Nebr. Found., 1983—, chmn. Nebr. Coordinating Commn. for Postsecondary Edn., 1984-88; mem. bd. regents U. Nebr., 1991—, chmn. 1994, 2001; mem. Gov.'s Exec. Coun., 1983-87. Served as maj., M.C., USAR, 1963-68. Gen. Motors Nat. scholar, 1956-60, Nat. Found. Med. scholar, 1960-64, Mead Johnson scholar ACP, 1968-71. Fellow ACP, Am. Coll. Cardiology (bd. govs. 1990-93, pres. Nebr. affiliate 1992-93), Am. Coll. Chest Physicans, Am. Heart Assn. (dir. Nebr. affilate 1973-80, pres. 1976-77); mem. Mayo Cardiovascular Soc., Nebr. Cardiovascular Soc. (pres. 1989-90), Nebr. Coun. on Pub. Higher Edn. (steering com. 1991—), Lincoln Heart Assn. (dir. 1972-75, pres. 1974-75), AMA, Nebr. Med. Assn. Lancaster County Med. Soc., Am. Soc. Internal Medicine, Lincoln Found., U. Nebr. Chancellor's Club, Lincoln U. Club (dir. 1981-84), U. Nebr. Pres. Club, Phi Beta Kappa, Sigma Xi, Alpha Omega Alpha, Phi Delta Theta (pres. Nebr. Alpha chpt. 1959-60). Home: 7430 N Hampton Rd Lincoln NE 68506-1624 Office: Lifescan Preventive Imaging 2930 Pine Lake Rd Ste 111 Lincoln NE 68516

WILSON, CHARLES VINCENT, human resources executive; b. Rockledge, Fla., May 7, 1949; s. Phillip J. and Etta R. (Talley) W.; m. Priscilla A. Johnson, Mar. 22, 1976; children: Stephanie Brooke, Rachel Marie. BSBA, Pa. State U., 1971. Dir. human resources Kendall Co., Boston, 1971-84; zone E.R. mgr. Frito-Lay, Dallas, 1984-86, group human resources mgr.-sales, 1986-87, group human resources mgr.-hdqrs., 1987-89; dir. mgmt. planning & devel. Pearle, Inc., 1989; v.p. cultural diversity & pers. devel. Grand Met. Food Sector, Mpls., 1989-91, v.p., dir. human resources tech., 1991-94; v.p. for human resources U. Md. Med. Sys., Balt., 1994-96; sr. v.p. human resources Clarian Health Ptnrs., Inc., Indpls., 1996—2001. Mem. tech. adv. coun. Olympus Corp., Inc., 1993; chmn. Univ. Med. System/Frederick Douglas H.S. Partnership Steering Com., 1994-96; mem. Univ. Hosp. Consortium Human Resources Officers Coun., 1994-01; bd. dirs. Indpls. Opera Co. Bd. dirs. Big Bros.-Big Sisters Ctrl. Md., 1996, Big Sisters Ctrl. Ind., 1998-2001; mem. human resources officers coun. Vol. Hosps. Am., 1997-2001. Recipient Black Achiever award Chgo. YMCA, 1975; Nat. Merit scholar, 1967. Mem. Nat. Black Human Resources Soc., Soc. for Human Resource Mgmt. Democrat. Baptist. Avocations: fitness workouts, golf, reading, travel, music. E-mail: cwilson@indy.rr.com.

WILSON, CHRISTIAN BURHENN, lawyer; b. Balt., Feb. 24, 1946; s. Christian Columbus and Ruth Louise Frieda (Burhenn) W.; m. Kay Spencer Lewis, June 20, 1974. BA, Towson State U., 1968; JD, U. Balt., 1975. Bar: Md. 1976, U.S. Dist. Ct. Md. 1976, U.S. Supreme Ct. 1980. Staff atty. Monumental Properties, Inc., Balt., 1977-79; counsel Mall Mgmt. Assocs., 1979-85; sole practice Bel Air, 1986—. Sr. lectr. Towson (Md.) State U., 1982-91. Served to 2d lt., Md. N.G., 1969-70. Mem. Md. State Bar Assn., Harford County Bar Assn., Sigma Delta Kappa. Republican. Lutheran. Home: 257 Victory Ln Bel Air MD 21014-5431 Office: 139 N Main St # 306 Bel Air MD 21014-8808

WILSON, CHRISTOPHER MONTGOMERY, historian, educator; b. Iowa City, Dec. 23, 1953; s. Martin Lucien and Joanne Marie (Hauser) Wilson; m. Kathryn Ann Williams, May 20, 1952; 1 child Lucian Banks. BA, Yale U., 1974; MA, U. N.Mex., 1981. Cons. historian, freelance writer, Albuquerque, 1981—98; adj. prof. U. N.Mex., 1985—98, J.B. Jackson prof., 1998—; Hubert chair Colo. Coll., Colorado Springs, 1997. Author: The Myth of Santa Fe: Creating a Modern Regional Tradition, 1997 (Cummings award Vernacular Arch. Forum, 1999), Facing Southwest: Life and Houses of J.G. Meem, 2001; co-author: Tierra Amarilla: Its History, Architecture and Cultural Landscape, 1992. Office: U NMex Sch Arch and Planning Albuquerque NM 87131 Office Fax: 505-277-0076 . E-mail: chwilson@unm.edu.

WILSON, CLARENCE SYLVESTER, JR. lawyer, educator; b. Bklyn., Oct. 22, 1945; s. Clarence Sylvester and Thelma Louise (Richards) W.; m. Helena Chapellin Iribarren, Jan. 26, 1972. BA, Williams Coll., 1967; JD, Northwestern U., 1974. Bar: Ill., 1975; U.S. Supreme Ct., 1985, U.S. Tax Ct. 1985, U.S. Ct. Appeals (7th cir.) 1985. Fgn. Svc. Res. officer U.S. Dept. of State, 1968-74; vice consul 3d sec. Am. Embassy, Caracas, Venezuela, 1969-71; adj. prof. law Kent Coll. of Law, Ill. Inst. Tech., Chgo., 1981-94; lecturer, Columbia Coll., Chgo., 1996-2000; mem. vis. com. music dept., visual arts, U. Chgo., 1991—; mem. bd. govs. Sch. of Art Inst. of Chgo., 1994—; vice chmn. Jazz Mus. of Chgo., 1994-97; adj. prof. The John Marshall Law Sch., 1999-2000. Trustee Chgo. Symphony Orch., 1987-96, Art Inst. Chgo., 1990—; mem. adv. bd. Chgo. Dept. Cultural Affairs, 1988-97; bd. dirs. Arts Midwest, Mpls., 1985-89, Harold Washington Found., Chgo., 1989-91; mem. MERIT Music Program, 1991-96, Ill. Arts Coun., 1984-89; project mgr. Dept. Justice Task Force. The Pres.'s Pvt. Sector Survey on Cost Control in the Fed. Govt. (Grace Commn.), 1982-84. Mem. com. to establish regional arts instns. Ill. Arts Coun., 1998—2001; mem. planned giving task force Diocese of Chgo. Mem. Lawyers for the Creative Arts (pres. 1987-88). Republican. Episcopalian. Avocations: music, art collecting. Home: 1130 S Michigan Ave #4303 Chicago IL 60605-2325 Fax: 312-583-0646. E-mail: hcwilson@ix.netcom.com.

WILSON, CLAUDE RAYMOND, JR. lawyer; b. Dallas, Feb. 22, 1933; s. Claude Raymond and Lottie (Watts) W.; m. Emilynn Wilson; children: Deidra Wilson Graves, Melissa Woodard Utley, Michele Woodard Dunn. BBA, So. Meth. U., 1954, JD, 1956. Bar: Tex. 1956; CPA, Calif., Tex. Assoc. firm Cervin & Melton, Dallas, 1956-58; atty. Tex. & Pacific R.R. Co., 1958-60; atty. office regional counsel IRS, San Francisco, 1960-63, sr. trial atty. office chief counsel Washington, 1963-65; ptnr. Wilson & White, Dallas, 1965-98, Vial, Hamilton, Koch & Knox LLP, Dallas, 1998—. Chmn., Dallas dist. dir. IRS Adv. Commn., 1990-91. Chmn. Dallas Hist. Soc., 2000-01. Mem.: AICPA (coun. 1989—93, tax exec. com. 1998—2001), ABA, Tex. Soc. CPAs (pres. 1989—90, pres. Dallas chpt. 1983—84), Dallas Bar Assn. (pres. sect. taxation 1969—70), State Bar Tex., Greater Dallas C. of C. (chmn. appropriations and tax com. 1990—91), Dallas Petroleum Club, Montaigne Club, Masons, Delta Theta Phi., Delta Sigma Phi. Republican. Episcopalian. Office: Vial Hamilton Koch & Knox 4400 Bank One Ctr 1717 Main St Dallas TX 75201-7388 E-mail: cwilson@vialaw.com.

WILSON, COLIN HENRY, writer; b. Leicester, Eng., June 26, 1931; s. Arthur and Anetta W.; m. Joy Stewart; children: Sally, Damon, Rowan; 1 child from previous marriage, Roderick. Writer in residence Hollins (Va.) Coll., 1966-67; vis. prof. U. Wash., Seattle, 1967, Rutgers U., New Brunswick, N.J., 1974. Author (numerous books including novels): The Outsider, 1956, The Glass Cage, 1967, The Occult, 1971, The Black Room, 1971, The Space Vampires, 1975, Mysteries, 1978; 6 critical studies in the Outsider series; non-fiction: Access to Inner Worlds, 1982, A Criminal History of Mankind, 1983, (with Donald Seaman) Modern Encyclopedia of Murder, 1983, The Essential Colin Wilson, 1984, The Personality Surgeon, 1986, (with Damon Wilson) Encyclopedia of Unsolved Mysteries, 1987, Spider World, 1987, The Misfits, 1988, Beyond The Occult, 1988, Written in Blood, 1989, (with Donald Seaman) The Serial Killers, 1990; (play) Mozart's Journey to Prague, 1991, Spider World: The Magician, 1992, The Strange Life of P.D. Ouspensky, 1993, Unsolved Mysteries Past and Present (with Damon Wilson), 1993, From Atlantis To The Sphinx, 1996, Atlas of Holy Places and Sacred Sites, 1996, Alien Dawn, 1998, The Books in My Life, 1998, The Devil's Party, 2000; (with Rand Fle'math) Atlantis Blueprint, 2000, Spider World: The Magician, 2002, Spiderworld: Shadowland, 2002. Mem.: Savage.

WILSON, DANIEL DONALD, engineering executive; b. Pitts., Oct. 28, 1958; s. Howard Raymond and Eleanor Hinsdale (Clark) Wilson. BS in Math., U. Vt., 1979; MS in Ops. Rsch., Stanford U., 1988. Systems analyst Raytheon System Design Lab., Bedford, Mass., 1979-83; software engr. Raytheon Svc. Co., Huntsville, Ala., 1983-85; sr. engr. Raytheon System Design Lab., Bedford, 1986-88, mgr. analytical models Tewksbury, Mass., 1988-95; sr. design engr. Raytheon Electronic Systems Lab., 1995-99, prin. engr., 1999-2000, sr. prin. engr., 2000—02; prin. engr.sr. Lockheed Martin NE&SS-SS, Burlington, Mass., 2002—. Mem. AIAA (sr., treas. 1990-92, sec. 1992-93, N.E. coun. 1993-95), Inst. for Ops. Rsch. and Mgmt. Scis. Home: 21 Symmes Rd Winchester MA 01890-3014 Office: Lockheed Martin NE&SS-SS One New England Pl Burlington MA 01803

WILSON, DAVID, artist; BA, Kalamazoo Coll., 1969; student, Calif. Inst. Arts. With L.A. Film Oasis collective; artist, designer, curator, founder Mus. Jurassic Tech., Culver City, Calif., 1984—. Office: Mus Jurassic Tech 9341 Venice Blvd Culver City CA 90232*

WILSON, DELANO DEE, consultant; b. Great Falls, Mont., Apr. 15, 1934; s. William McKinley and Alvina Henrietta (Beck) W.; m. Marilyn Ann Harant, Nov. 14, 1959; children: Robin David, Leslie Ann Wilson, Christian William. BSEE, Mont. State U., 1959. Analytical engr. GE, Schenectady, N.Y., 1960-69, sr. engr., 1964-69, mgr. alternating current studies, 1969-72, mgr. engrng. projects Phila., 1972-74; prin. engr. Power Techs., Inc., Schenectady, 1974-82; v.p., prin. engr. Power Techs., Inc.-Tech. Assessment Group, 1980-85; pres., CEO Power Techs. Inc., 1986-95, chmn. bd. dirs., 1989-95. Expert witness, cons. Internat. Conf. on High Voltage Systems, Paris, 1974-90. U.S. rep., 1986-92. Author, co-author 6 books; contbr. numerous tech. papers to profl. jours.; patentee in field. Bd. dirs. Ellis Hosp., Schenectady, 1987—; trustee Capital Dist. YMCA, 1989-98. With U.S. Army, 1954-56. Fellow IEEE (life, mem. transp. and dist. com., exec. bd. Power Engring. Soc. 1988-94, Disting. Svc. award 1988, Third Millennium medal 2000). Avocations: fishing, amateur auto rebuilding. Office: Power Techs Inc 1482 Erie Blvd PO Box 1058 Schenectady NY 12301-1058

WILSON, DENISE See EARLY, TERI WILSON

WILSON, DIANE DOERGE, consulting company executive; b. Cleve., Feb. 4, 1948; d. John O. Doerge and Martha Thompson Seelbach; m. Alvin J. Silk, Aug. 10, 1991. BA, Conn. Coll., 1970; MA, U. Denver, 1978; EdD, Harvard U., 1985. Prin. rsch. assoc. MIT, Cambridge, 1984-89; pres. D.D. Wilson & Assocs., Boston, 1980-95; ptnr. Andersen Cons., 1995—. Vis. prof. Hochschule St. Gallen, Switzerland, 1987—. Contbr. articles to profl. jours. Bd. dirs. Cathedral Assn., Seattle, 1980; chair childrens task force Seattles City Fair, Seattle, 1981; trustee Mktg. Scis. Inst. Fellow Harvard Club. Avocations: photography, French culture.

WILSON, DONALD EDWARD, dean, medical educator, physician; b. Worcester, Mass., Aug. 28, 1936; s. Rivers Rivo and Licine (Bradshaw) Wilson; m. Patricia C. Littell, Aug. 27, 1977; children: Jeffrey D.E., Sean D., Monique, Sheila L. AB, Harvard U., 1958; MD, Tufts U., 1962. Diplomate Am. Bd. Internal Medicine. Intern St. Elizabeth Hosp., Boston, 1962—63; resident in medicine, research fellow in gastroenterology VA Hosp. and Lemuel Shattuck Hosp., 1963—66; assoc. chief gastroenterology Bklyn. Hosp., 1968—71; instr. medicine SUNY Downstate Med. Center, Bklyn., 1968—71; asst. prof. medicine U. Ill., Chgo., 1971—73, asso. prof., 1973—75, prof., 1975—80, acting head dept. medicine, 1976—77; dir. divsn. gastroenterology U. Ill. Hosp., Chgo., 1971—78, chief of gastroenterology, 1973—80, physician-in-chief, 1976—77; prof., chmn. dept. medicine SUNY Downstate Med. Center, Bklyn., 1980—91; physician-in-chief State U. and Kings County Hosp., 1980—91; dean U. Md.Sch. Medicine, Balt., 1991—; v.p. of med. affairs U. Md. Sch. Medicine, 1999—. Vis. prof. medicine U. London, Kings Coll. Med. Sch., 1977—78; mem. gastrointestingal drugs adv. bd. FDA, 1985—87, chmn., 1986—87; mem. Part II test com. Nat. Bd. Med. Examiners, 1985—88; mem. nat. digestive adv. bd. NIH, 1985—87, chmn., 1986—87, mem. gen. clin. rsch. ctrs. com., 1987—; mem. nat. adv. com. Agy. for Health CAre Policy and Rsch., Dept. HHS, 1991—, chmn., 1992—; mem. residency rev. com. for internal medicine Acque, 1993—; mem. nat. com. fgn. med. edn. and accreditation U.S. Dept. Edn., 1994—; mem. nat. adv. rsch. resources com. NIH, 1997—2000. Contbr. articles to med. jours. Bd. vis. Harvard Sch. Pub. Health, 1992—94. Capt. M.C. USAF, 1966—68. Recipient Rsch. award, HEW, 1971, 1974, John A. Hartford Found., Inc., 1972—79, Distilled Spirits Coun. U.S., 1972—74, VA, 1974. Master: ACP; mem.: AAAS, NAS, Inst. of Medicine, Assn. Profs. Medicine (sec.-treas. 1990—91), Am. Clin. and Climatol. Assn., Nat. Med. Assn., Assn. for Acad. Minority Physicians (sec./treas. 1986—), Assn. Am. Physicians, Chgo. Soc. Gastrointestinal Endoscopy (pres. 1979—80), N.Y. Soc. Gastroenterology, N.Y. Acad. Medicine, N.Y. Acad. Scis., Soc. Exptl. Biology and Medicine, Midwest Gut Club, Digestive Disease Found., Chgo. Soc. Gastroenterology (pres. 1978—79), Ctrl. Rsch. Club, Ctrl. Soc. Clin. Rsch., Accreditation Coun. Grad. Med. Edn. (rev. com. internal medicine), Am. Assn. Study Liver Disease, Am. Fedn. Clin. Rsch., Am. Gastroent. Assn., The Ctr. Club (Balt.), Med. Club Bklyn., 14 West Hamilton St. Club (Balt.), Harvard Club (Chgo., N.Y.C.), Sigma Pi Phi (grand boule). Office: U Md Sch Medicine 655 W Baltimore St Rm 14029 Baltimore MD 21201-1509*

WILSON, DONALD GREY, management consultant; b. Bridgeport, Conn., Sept. 20, 1917; s. William Gray and Jeannetta McAvoy (Kerr) W.; m. Elizabeth Jean Lanning, Apr. 24, 1943 (div. Mar. 1971); children: Kirk Lanning, Craig Gardner, William Grey. BSEE, Rensselaer Poly. Inst., 1938; SM, Harvard U., 1939, MES, 1947, PhD, 1948. Mgr. automatic fire alarm divsn. Sealand Corp., Bridgeport, Conn., 1939-40; instr. elec. engring. Rensselaer Poly. Inst., 1940-42; staff mem. Radiation Lab. MIT, 1942-45; prof. elec. engring. U. Kan., Lawrence, 1947-55, chmn. dept., 1948-55; dir. Phila. Brass & Bronze, 1962-64, Mallory-Xerox Corp., 1964-65. Cons. U.S. Naval Ordance Test Sta., China Lake, Calif., 1953-54; assoc. dir. rsch. dept. Stromberg-Carlson Co., San Diego, 1955-59, gen. mgr., 1959, asst. v.p., 1959-60; v.p. rsch. P.R. Mallory & Co., Indpls., 1960, v.p. rsch. and engring., 1961-71, v.p. rsch., engring. and environ. affairs, 1971-75; alt. dir. Mallory Metal. Products, Eng., 1967; pres. Contemporary Custom Cabinets, San Diego, 1975-76; v.p. Continental Resources and Minerals Corp., Dayton, Ohio, 1978-79; sr. v.p. Tanzi Mergers/Acquisitions, San Diego, 1983-86; mgmt. cons., 1976—; sr. lectr. U. Rochester, 1956-57; lectr. dept. elec. engring. San Diego State U., 1981-92; asst. dean coll. engring., 1987, prof. emeritus, 1992—; mng. dir., exec. bd. Nat. Bur. Cert. Cons., 1988-94, sr. adv. counsel, 1994-2001. Contbr. articles to profl. jours. Bd. dirs. Speech and Hearing Clinic, Indpls., 1960-66, Washington Twp. Sch. Dist., 1964-68, pres., 1966-67. Recipient Outstanding Acad. Advisor award San Diego State U., 1992. Fellow AAAS; mem. IEEE (sr. life, exec. com. San Diego sect. 1992—, chmn. S.W. area region 6 1999-2000, sec. region 6 2001—, ethics and mem. conduct com. 2002—, Third Millennium medal), Affiliation Profl. Cons. Orgns. (chmn. bd. govs. 1991-93, Internat. IEEE Outstanding Br. Counselor award 1992, San Diego Engring. Coun. Outstanding Svc. award 2000), Intertel, Sigma Xi, Sigma Phi Epsilon, Tau Beta Pi, Eta Kappa Nu. Home: 3110 Levante St Carlsbad CA 92009-8332 E-mail: don.wilson@ieee.org.

WILSON, DONALD HURST, III, biopharmaceutical industry executive; b. Balt., Mar. 1, 1946; s. Donald H. Jr. and Winifred Arnold (Leist) W.; m. Beverly Lee Wright, Oct. 3, 1975 (div. 1998); children: Beverly Callaway, Sarah Elizabeth; m. Constance Fisher Neely, Sept. 23, 2000. AB, Yale U., 1968; MBA, JD, Harvard U., 1976. Bar: Mass. 1977. Cons. Boston Cons. Group, 1976-78; dir. mktg. I/C divsn. Black & Decker, Hampstead, Md., 1978-83; pres. MWI Tng. Svcs., Inc., Hunt Valley, 1983-96; v.p. Innoversity Edn. Ctrs., Global Knowledge Network, Inc., 1996-97; pres., COO Endacea, Inc. (formerly Link Tech., Inc.), Raleigh, 1997-98, pres., CEO, 1998-2000, also bd. dirs., v.p., COO, 2001—. Mem. vestry St. John's Episcopal Ch., 1993-96, lay eucharistic min., 1995-98; dir. The Bishop Claggett Ctr., 1995-97. Mem. Assn. Microcomputer Distbrs. (bd. dirs. 1988-90), Archaeol. Soc. Md. (trustee 1994-98). Republican. Avocations: Bible study, archaeology, golf. Home: 1112 Baslow Brook Ct Raleigh NC 27614-8866 Office: Endacea Inc PO Box 12076 2 Davis Dr Research Triangle Park NC 27709-2076 E-mail: dhwilson@msn.com.

WILSON, DONALD KENNETH, JR. lawyer, publisher; b. Lancaster, Pa., Mar. 5, 1954; s. Donald Kenneth and Gloria (Payne) W.; m. Lauren Elaine O'Connor, Sept. 3, 1977; children: Donald, Tameka, Veronica, Matthew. BA, U. So. Calif., 1976; JD, N.Y. Law Sch., 1979. Bar: Calif. 1979, U.S. Ct. Appeals (9th cir.) 1979, U.S. Ct. Appeals (ea. dist.) Mich., 1996, U.S. Ct. Appeals, Colo. 1997. Ptnr. Law Office, L.A., 1987-92; pres., chief operating officer Quincy Jones Productions, 1983-86; assoc. Garey, Mason & Sloane, 1979-82; pres., CEO 4 Kids Music, 1989—, Dotevema Music, L.A., 1989—; of counsel Law Offices Johnnie L. Cochran Jr., 1992—2000; pvt. practice Law Offices of Donald K. Wilson, 2000—. Producer: (video documentary) Frank Sinatra, 1984 (Vira award 1985, Grammy nomination 1985); contb. articles to newspapers. Trustee First African Meth. Episc. Ch., 1989-97; mem. NAACP, L.A., 1990. Recipient Citizenship award, Am. Legion, 1972; named Outstanding Young Men of Am., 1982, 83, Outstanding Contbr. to Community, Entertainment Civic Orgn., 1986. Avocations: tennis, reading, walking, fishing. Office: Law Offices Donald K Wilson Jr 4322 Wilshire Blvd Ste 300 Los Angeles CA 90010-3825

WILSON, DONALD MALCOLM, publishing executive; b. Glen Ridge, N.J., June 27, 1925; s. Robert and Adelaide (Streubel) Wilson; m. Susan M Neuberger, Apr. 6, 1957; children: Dwight Malcolm, Katherine Loudon, Penelope. Grad., Deerfield (Mass.) Acad., 1943; BA, Yale U., 1948. Reporter Life mag., 1949-53, chief Far Ea. corr., 1953-56, chief Washington corr., 1956-60, asso. pub., 1968-69; gen. mgr. Time- Life Internat., 1965-68; v.p. corporate and pub. affairs Time, Inc., 1969-81, corp. v.p. pub. affairs, 1981-89; pu. Business News N.J., New Brunswick, 1989—; dep. dir. USIA, 1961-65. Mem adv coun Edward R Murrow Ctr, Tufts Univ, Nat Coun La Raza, 1985—89; mem Pub Broadcasting Authority NJ, 1969—73, 1976—79. Trustee Vassar Col, 1971—79, Brearley Sch, 1977—86; bd dirs Solomon R Guggenheim Mus, 1985—89, Schumann Fund NJ, 1990—95. Decorated Air Medal. Mem.: Coun Foreign Relations, Century Asn (New York City). Home: 4574 Province Line Rd Princeton NJ 08540-2212 Office: Business News NJ 104 Church St New Brunswick NJ 08901-2002 E-mail: donaldmwilson@cs.com.

WILSON, DONNA MAE, administrator, foreign language educator; b. Columbus, Ohio, Feb. 25, 1947; d. Everett John and Hazel Margaret (Bruck) Palmer; m. Steven L. Wilson, Nov. 16, 1968. BA, Ohio State U., 1973, MA, 1976; postgrad studies, U. Wash., Seattle Pacific U., U. Mass., 1980-93; cert., U. Salamanca, Spain, 1985. Tchg. assoc. Ohio State U., Columbus, 1974-76; lectr. U. Wash., Seattle, 1977-78; grants officer Seattle U., 1978-82; adj. prof. Shoreline Coll., Seattle, 1982-84; coord. fgn. langs., prof. Spanish Bellevue (Wash.) Coll., 1984-87; prof. Spanish Highline Coll., Des Moines, 1987-98, chair fgn. lang. dept., 1990-94, chair arts and humanities, 1994-98; assoc. dean acad. affairs Greenfield (Mass.) Coll., 1998—. Spkr. at lang. orgns., confs. regional and nat., 1985—. Editor: (book) Fronteras: En Contacto, 1992-93; (jours.) Modern Lang. Jour., 1991, 92, 94, 96, 97, Hispania, 1993, 95; text editor D. C. Heath and Co., Harcourt, Brace and Jovanovich, Houghton Mifflin, Prentice Hall; contbr. articles to profl. jours., chpt. to English of Science and Technology Learning, 2000. Mem. Mass. Bd. Higher Edn. Exit Assessment; pres. Mass. Coun. Acad. Deans, 2000-2001; assoc. deans think tank New England Resource Ctr. Higher Edn. Recipient cert. of excellence Phi Theta Kappa, 1990, Pathfinder award Phi Beta Kappa, 1995; fellowship grant Coun. Internat. Edn. Exchange, Santiago, Chile, 1992. Mem. Nat. Coun. Instr. Adminstrns., Am. Assn. Tchrs. of Spanish (v.p. Wash.), Am. Coun. Tchrs. of Fgn. Langs. (cert. oral proficiency), Assn. Dept of Fgn. Langs. (exec. bd. 1994-97), Pacific N.W. Coun. Fgn. Langs., 1986-98, Nat. Assn. Fgn. Lang. Suprs., Sigma Delta Mu. (nat. exec. sec. 1992-98), Women in Highter Edn. Avocations: travel, assessment rsch. on 2d lang., outdoors. Office: Greenfield Coll 1 College Dr Greenfield MA 01301-9755 E-mail: wilsond@gcc.mass.edu.

WILSON, DORIS FANUZZI, learning disabilities consultant, educator; b. N.Y.C., Oct. 17, 1935; d. Vitoantonio and Rose (Colavito) Panzarino; children: James Douglas Fanuzzi, Robert Alan Fanuzzi; m. Richard Gerard Wilson, Aug. 21, 1977 (div. 1987). BA cum laude, Hunter Coll., 1956; MA, Montclair State U., 1978, supr. cert., 1996. With Tri-County Ednl. Vocat. High Sch., Totowa, N.J., 1979-80; learning disabilities tchr., cons. Fairlawn (N.J.) Bd. Edn., 1980-82, Somerville (N.J.) Bd. Edn., 1982-83, Regional Child Study Team, Franklin, N.J., 1983-84; cons. curriculum and instrn. divsn. devel. disabilities N.J. Dept. Human Svcs., Trenton, 1984-91; program dir. The ARC/Mercer, 1993; learning cons. Highlands (N.J.) Bd. Edn., 1993-94, Trenton (N.J.) Bd. Edn., 1994-96, Bergen County Spl. Svcs. Sch. Dist., 1996-97, Piscataway Bd. Edn., 1998—. Apptd. by gov. audiology and speech-lang. pathology adv. com. Active Nat. Women's Polit. Caucus; co-founder, exec. advisor Capital Caucus (Md., DC, Va.); vice chmn. Rep. Task Force. Mem. AAUW, Assn. Learning Cons., Pub. Rels. Soc. Am. (co-chmn. internat. com.), Learning Disabilities Assn., Internat. Platform Assn., Friends of Decatur House, Capitol Hill Club. Avocations: tennis, reading, ballroom dancing, foreign travel.

WILSON, DORIS H. volunteer; b. Akron, Ohio, Jan. 26, 1921; d. Charles Peter and Emma Clara (Howald) Huff; m. Angus Francis Wilson, June 14, 1952; children: Ann Wilson Lambertus, Lea Wilson MacInnis. BS, U. Akron, 1945; postgrad., Framingham State Coll., 1965, Salem State Coll., 1968. Adminstrv. asst. divsn. comml. engr. Ohio Bell Telephone Co., Akron, 1941-52; adminstr. Framingham Ctr. Kindergarten and Nursery Sch., 1965-68. Author: A History of Great Neck, Ipswich, 1984, 96. Vol. nurse's aide ARC, Akron, 1940s; mem. Gov.'s Coun. Civilian Def., Boston, 1960-66; co-founder, charter mem. Hospice at Home, Wayland, Weston, Natick, Sudbury, Mass., 1978; chmn. West Suburban Area Boston Symphony Orch. Coun. of Friends, 1978-81; docent The Great House at Castle Hill, Ipswich, 1984—, The Whipple House, Ipswich, 1985—; treas. Nuclear Freeze Coun., Ipswich, 1986-87; charter mem., bd. dirs. Aplastic Anemia Found. of Am. New Eng. region, Brookline, Mass., 1987-92; vol. office asst. Habitat for Humanity, St. Petersburg, Fla., 1988. Recipient Election Poll Officer citation Gov. of Mass., 1980, 1st Place in Ann. Short Story Contest, Gen. Fedn. Women's Clubs, 2002. Mem. AAUW (charter mem., pres. Framingham-Wellesley Br., North Shore Br., grantee 1974), Boston Symphony Assn. of Vols., Peace Action, Ipswich Hist. Soc., Ipswich Woman's Club, Ipswich Bay Yacht Club (dir. 1981-82), Friends of Glen Magna (Danvers, Mass. dir. 1991-93), Wayland Woman's Club (hon. mem., pres.). Democrat. Roman Catholic. Home: 8 Bowdoin Rd Ipswich MA 01938-2807

WILSON, DOUGLAS COOK, academic administrator; b. Providence, Dec. 18, 1940; s. William Edward and Ellen Janet (Cameron) W.; m. Cheryl Lee Bailey, Oct. 8, 1966; children: Jay Bailey, Emily Cameron, Samuel Bradford. BA, Amherst Coll., 1962; MA in Law and Diplomacy, Fletcher Sch. Law and Diplomacy, 1964. Reporter Providence Jour., 1962-69, Washington corr., 1969-75; assoc. sec. pub. affairs Amherst (Mass.) Coll., 1975-77, sec. pub. affairs, 1977-98, coll. editor, 1998—. Co-editor: Lost Amherst, 1980, Teaching What We Do, 1991, The College on the Hill, 1996; editor Amherst Mag., 1977—. Chmn. Amherst Hist. Commn., 1979-81, Western Mass. Broadcasting Coun., Amherst, 1980-82, Amherst Conservation Commn., Amherst, 1990-91. Recipient Merriman Smith award White House Corrs. Assn., 1975, W.M. Whitehill History prize Colonial Soc. Mass., 1986. Mem. Coun. Advancement and Support of Edn. Democrat. Presbyterian. Avocations: historical research, writing. Home: 136 Pomeroy Ln Amherst MA 01002-2909 Office: Amherst Coll PO Box 2202 Amherst MA 01004-2202 E-mail: dcwilson@amherst.edu.

WILSON, DWIGHT LISTON, former military officer, investment advisor; b. Hereford, Tex., Oct. 30, 1931; s. Liston Oscar and Pauline (Smart) W.; m. Barbara Ann Alderman, Sept. 4, 1955; children: Terri Ann, Ron Alan, Diana Kay. BA in Govt., Okla. U., 1953; MA in Public Adminstrn., Shippensburg (Pa.) U., 1973. Commd. 2d lt. U.S. Army, 1953, advanced through grades to maj. gen., 1980; service in Vietnam, W.Ger.; dir. force mgmt. (Hdqrs. Dept. Army), Washington, 1979-80; ret., 1980. Fin. cons., resident mgr. Merrill Lynch, Pierce, Fenner and Smith, Punta Gorda, Fla., 1981-95. Decorated D.S.M., Legion of Merit, Bronze Star, Meritorious Service medal, Army Commendation medal (3), Air medal (10). Mem. Assn. U.S. Army. Methodist. E-mail: tawa@milx.net.

WILSON, E. DOTSON, legislative staff member; b. Jan. 2, 1954; s. Edward James and Sheila Frances Wilson; m. Jacqueline R. Wilson, Apr. 3, 1993; 1 child, Nicole. BA, UCLA, 1976; JD, U. Calif., San Francisco, 1979. Floor mgr. Calif. Assembly, 1984-88, dep. chief of staff, Speaker Willie L. Brown, Jr., 1988-91, chief clk., parliamentarian, 1992—. Acitve Assembly Fellowship Jr.; former bd. dirs. Women's Civic Improvement Club. Named one of 100 Black Men of Sacramento. Address: State Capitol Bldg Rm 3196 Sacramento CA 95814

WILSON, E.B. business executive; b. Albany, N.Y., May 13, 1931; s. Harold Edgar and Marie Elizabeth (Brush) W.; m. Mary Beth Weilbacher, Aug. 2, 1956. BA , St. Lawrence U., 1953, PhD (hon.) , 2002; MBA , Harvard U., 1955. Mkt. dir. Richardson-Vicks, Inc., N.Y.C., Paris, Manila, 1957-64; CEO Japan Kimberly-Clark Corp., Neenah, Wis., 1964-68, France, 1968-71; pres., CEO French ops. Kimberly-Clark, Corp., Neenah, Wis., 1968—73; v.p. internat. div., gen. mgr. Pillsbury Co., Mpls., 1971-76; exec. v.p. Shaklee Corp., San Francisco, 1976-79; pres., CEO Almay Cosmetics, Inc., N.Y.C., 1979-84, Hathaway Group of Warnaco, N.Y.C., 1984—89; chmn. Global Brands, Inc., 1989—; found., pres. EBI, Inc., Chatham, Mass., 1995—. Chmn., chief exec. officer Sero Co., Branford, Conn., Mortin Jonap, Ltd., Hauppauge, N.Y.; bd. dirs. William Schneider, Inc., Miami, HMI, Inc., Norwood, Mass. Author: The Committee on Trustees, 2001; contbr. to columns. Trustee St. Lawrence U., Canton, N.Y., 1986-2001, chmn. bd. trustees, 1995-2001, Boston Conservatory, 2000-, San Francisco Ballet, 1978, New Horizons Project, Cambridge, Mass., 2001-; devel. dir. Cen. Park Conservancy, N.Y.C., 1983-89. With USAR, 1955-57. Mem. Eastward Ho Club (v.p., gov., 1985-91), Hardvard Club N.Y., Harvard Club Boston. Republican. Avocations: cooking, running, golf, reading, international travel. Home and Office: 1114 Orleans Rd North Chatham MA 02650 Fax: 508-945-9661. E-mail: ebi@cape.com.

WILSON, EDWARD CONVERSE, JR. oil and natural gas production company executive; b. Cambridge, Mass., Jan. 1, 1928; s. Edward Converse and Jean (McLean) W.; m. Patricia Ann Cairns, Sept. 10, 1953; children—Amy Cairns, Sarah Converse. AB, Harvard U., 1949. Brokerage trainee Estabrook & Co., Boston, 1951; Midwest Stock Exchange clk. Paul H. Davis & Co., Chgo., 1951-52; mem. Chgo. Bd. Trade, 1952-78, dir., 1966-67, chmn., 1970-71; partner Nolan & Wilson Co. (specialists on Midwest Stock Exchange), 1965-72; sr. partner Wilson Prodn. Co., Ft. Smith, Ark., 1972-74. Dir. Rutledge Assocs., Wakefield, Mass., 1965-74, Paul H. Robinson Inc., Chgo., 1972-81 Mem. devel. com. Chgo. chpt. Nat. Multiple Sclerosis Soc., 1970; mem. vis. com. on univ. resources Harvard, 1971-74, 76-81; Bd. dirs. Franklin Blvd. Community Hosp., 1970-74. Served with USAAF, 1946-47. Mem. Racquet Club (Chgo.). Home: 11114 Wickwood Dr Houston TX 77024-7523 Office: 1770 Saint James Pl Houston TX 77056-3471

WILSON, EDWARD NATHAN, mathematician, educator; b. Warsaw, Dec. 2, 1941; s. Hugh Monroe and Margaret Jane (Northrup) W.; m. Mary Katherine Schooling, Aug. 19, 1976; children: Nathan Edward, Emily Katherine. BA, Cornell U., 1963; MS, Stanford U., 1965; PhD, Washington U., St. Louis, 1971. Instr. Ft. Valley (Ga.) State Coll., 1965-67, Washington U., St. Louis, 1968-69, U. Calif., Irvine, 1970-71, Brandeis U., Waltham, Mass., 1971-73; asst. prof. Washington U., St. Louis, 1973-77, assoc. prof., 1977-87, dean grad. sch., 1983-93, dean univ. coll., 1986-88, prof., 1987—, chair dept. math., 1995-99. Mem. Grad. Record Exams. Bd., Princeton, N.J., 1986-90; sec.-treas. Assn. Grad. Schs. Contbr. articles to profl. jours. Mem. Brentwood Sch. Bd., Mo., 1984. Woodrow Wilson fellow, 1963; NSF fellow, 1963-65; NDEA fellow, 1967-70. Mem. Am. Math. Soc., Math. Assn. of Am. Democrat. Office: Washington U Campus Box 1146 1 Brookings Dr Saint Louis MO 63130-4899 E-mail: enwilson@math.wustl.edu.

WILSON, EDWARD OSBORNE, biologist, educator, writer; b. Birmingham, Ala., June 10, 1929; s. Edward Osborne and Inez (Freeman) W.; m. Irene Kelley, Oct. 30, 1955; 1 child Catherine Irene. BS, U. Ala., 1949, MS, 1950, LHD (hon.) , 1980; PhD, Harvard U., 1955; DPhil, Uppsala (Sweden) U.; DS (hon.) , Duke U., 1978; DS (hon.) , Grinnell Coll., 1978, U. West Fla., 1979, Lawrence U., 1979, Fitchburg State Coll., 1989, Macalester Coll., 1990, U. Mass., 1990, Oxford U., 1993, Ripon Coll., 1994, U. Conn., 1995, Ohio U., 1996, Bates Coll., 1996, Coll. Wooster, 1997; DS (hon.) , U. Guelph, 1997; DS (hon.) , U. Portland, 1997; LHD (hon.) , Hofstra U., 1986, Muhlenburg Coll., 1998, Yale U., 1998, Pa. State U., Bradford Coll., 1997, Conn. Coll., 2000; DHC, U. Madrid Complutense, 1995, Conn. Coll., 2000; LLD, Simon Fraser U.; Drernat, U. Würzburg, 2000; DS (hon.) , Kenyon Coll., 2002. Jr. fellow Soc. Fellows, Harvard U., 1953—56, mem. faculty, 1956—, Baird prof. sci., 1976—94, Pellegrino U. prof., 1994—97, univ. rsch. prof., 1997—2002, curator entomology, 1971—97, hon. curator entomology, 1997—. Mem. selection com. Guggenheim Found., 1982—89; bd. dirs. World Wildlife Fund, 1983—94, Orgn. Tropical Studies, 1984—91, N.Y. Bot. Garden, 1991—95, Am. Mus. Natural History, 1992, Am. Acad. Liberal Edn., 1993—, Nature Conservancy, 1994—, Conservation Internat., 1997—. Author: The Insect Societies, 1971, Sociobiology: The New Synthesis, 1975, On Human Nature, 1978 (Pulitzer prize for non-fiction , 1979); author: (with C.J. Lumsden)) Genes, Mind and Culture, 1981; author: Promethean Fire, 1983, Biophilia, 1984; author: (with Bert Holldobler)) The Ants, 1990 (Pulitzer prize for non-fiction , 1991); author: Success and Dominance in Ecosystems, 1990, The Diversity of Life, 1992 (Nat. Wildlife Assn. award, Deutsche Umweltstiftung Book award, Sir Peter Kent Conservation prize); author: (with Bert Holldobler)) Journey to the Ants, 1994 (Phi Beta Kappa prize sci. , 1995); author: Naturalist, 1994 (L.A. Times Book prize sci. , 1995), In Search of Nature, 1996, Consilience: The Unity of Knowledge, 1998 (Forkosch award Internat. Acad. Humanism , 2000), Biological Diversity: The Oldest Human Heritage, 1999, The Future of Life, 2002, Pheidole in the New World: A Dominant, Hyperdiverse Ant Genus, 2002, (book) The Future of Life, 2002. Recipient Cleve.-AAAS rsch. prize, 1967, Nat. Medal Sci., 1976, Leidy medal, Acad. Natural Sci., Phila., 1979, Disting. Svc. award, Am. Inst. Biol. Scis., 1976, Mercer award, Ecol. Soc. Am., 1971, Archie Carr medal, U. Fla., 1978, Silver medal, Nat. Zool. Park, German Ecol. Inst. prize, 1987, Weaver award scholarly letters, Ingersoll Found., 1989, Crafoord prize, Royal Swedish Acad. Scis., 1990, Prix di'Inst. de la Vie, Paris, 1990, Revelle medal, 1990, Gold medal, Worldwide Fund for Nature, 1990, Achievement award, Nat. Wildlife Fedn., 1992, Shaw medal, Mo. Bot. Garden, 1993, Internat. prize biology, Govt. of Japan, 1993, Eminent Ecologist award, 1994, Audubon award, Audubon Soc., 1995, Pub. Understanding Sci. award, AAAS, 1995, John Hay award, Orion Soc., 1995, Schubert prize, Germany, 1996, Washburn award, Mus. Sci., 1996, Hutchinson medal, Garden Club Am., 1997, Stone award, New Eng. Aquarium, 1999, Nonino prize, Letters and Sci., Italy, 2000, King Faisal Internat. prize for sci., 2000, Kistler prize, Found. for the Future, 2000, Phillips Meml. medal, World Conservation Union, 2000, Lewis Thomas prize, Rockefeller U., 2001, Nierenberg prize, Scripps Oceanographic Inst., 2001, Thoreau medal, Thoreau Soc., 2001, Lifetime Achievement award, Time, 2001, Global Environment Citizens award, Harvard U., 2001, others; fellow Guggenheim Found., 1978. Fellow: Deutsche Akad. Naturforsch, Am. Philos. Soc. (Franklin medal 1998), Am. Acad. Arts and Scis.; mem.: NAS, others, Royal Soc. Sci. Uppsala (Sweden), Russian Acad. Nat. Sci., Royal Entomol. Soc. (hon. life), Finnish Acad. Sci. and Letters, Royal Soc. London, Netherlands Entomol. Soc. (hon. life), Assn. Tropical Biology (hon. life), Acad. Humanism (hon. life), Am. Humanist Assn. (Disting. Svc. award 1982, Tyler ecology prize 1984, hon. life, Humanist of Yr.), Zool. Soc. London (hon. life), Entomol. Soc. Am. (Founders Meml. award 1972, L.O. Howard award 1985, hon. life), Brit. Ecol. Soc. (hon. life), Am. Genetics Assn. (hon. life). Home: 9 Foster Rd Lexington MA 02421-5505 Office: Harvard U Mus Comparative Zoology Cambridge MA 02138 E-mail: ewilson@oeb.harvard.edu.

WILSON, ELAINE LOUISE, learning resources educator/administrator; b. Bridgeport, Conn., Aug. 25, 1949; d. John Herbert and Helen Esther (Wold) Lewis; m. Richard Henry Wilson, Jr., June 7, 1975; children: Jessica Hope, Eric Samuel. BA, Smith Coll., 1971; MEd, Boston U., 1978; DEd. U. Mass., Boston, 2000. Lectr. ESL Boston Coll., Chestnut Hill, Mass., 1978-84, Harvard U., Cambridge, 1986-90; coord. resource devel. for spl. acad. svcs. U. Mass., Lowell, 1984-85; prof., coord. ESL Massachusetts Bay C.C., Wellesley, Mass., 1987-99, dir. learning programs and skills devel., 1999—2001; dir. grants devel. Bunker Hill C.C., Boston, 2002—. Contbr. articles to profl. jours. Recipient Excellence in Tchg. award Nat. Inst. Staff and Orgnl. Devel., 1993; scholar-in-residence Massachusetts Bay C.C., 1989. Mem. TESOL (presenter convs. Atlanta 1993, Balt. 1994), Am. Assn. Higher Edn., Am. Edn. Rsch Assn., Women in Devel., Phi Theta Kappa. Buddhist. Office: Bunker Hill CC 250 New Rutherford Ave Boston MA 02129 E-mail: ewilson@bhcc.mass.edu.

WILSON, ELDON RAY, minister; b. Tieton, Wash., Apr. 16, 1931; s. Frank Madison and Beatrice Jane (Snider) W.; m. LouCelle Charlotte Seward, Aug. 3, 1957; children: Randall Wayne, Gary Ray. BTh, Internat. Bible Coll., San Antonio, 1967; PhD, Sussex Coll., Hayward's Heath, Eng., 1972. Ordained to ministry Emmanuel Ch., 1956. Founder, pastor Emmanuel Tabernacle, Port Arthur, Tex., 1958-63; evangelist U.S., Can., 1963-65; founder, pastor Gospel Tabernacle, Ilion, N.Y., 1965-70; pastor Full Gospel Ch., Halifax, N.S., Can., 1970-72; missionary Europe, Africa, 1972-77; founder, pastor New Covenant Ch., Columbus, Ohio, 1977-84; missionary New Covenant Ministries, 1984-97; acad. dean City Bible Coll., Utica, N.Y., 1998-2001. Bd. dirs. Good News Mission, Bogota, Colombia, 1985—; trustee Team Missions, Internat., Elkton, Md., 1989—. Author: The New Creation, 1975. Bd. dirs. Kuyahoora Valley Libr., Newport, N.Y., 1985—; overseer Shekinah Ministries, Amsterdam, The Netherlands, Bread of Life Ministries, Bastogne, Belgium. With USN, 1951-55. Republican. Home: 7417 West St Newport NY 13416 E-mail: loucelle.wilson@juno.com.

WILSON, ELEANOR MCELROY, county official; b. Lancaster, Pa., Sept. 10, 1938; d. Hartford Ford and Jane Ann (Bowken) McElroy; m. Frank Eugene Wilson, July 17, 1976 (dec. Jan. 1980). AA, Monterey Peninsula Jr. Coll., Monterey, Calif., 1959; BA in Edn., San Jose State U., 1963; MA in Bus. Adminstrn./Mgmt., Webster U., St. Louis, 1981; MA in Internat. Rels., Salve Regina Coll., Newport, R.I., 1990; MA in Nat. Security/Strategic Studies, Naval War Coll., Newport, 1991. Sec. Geo. Dovolis Real Estate, Monterey, 1957-59; legal sec. Thompson & Thompson Attys., 1959-61; legal asst., supr. Thomson J. Hudson, Atty., 1963-68, legal asst., 1972-74. Mem. Orange County Grand Jury Superior Ct., Santa Ana, Calif., 1982—83; citizen mem.

Orange County Parole Bd., 1993—96, 1999—2001; mem. Orange County Juvenile Justice Commn., Orange, 1992—2000, chair, 1995; bd. advisors Flying Leatherneck Hist. Found., 2000—. Col. USMCR, 1968—98. Decorated Legion of Merit. Mem.: Sloan Found. (bd. dirs. 1996—98), Marine Corps Aviation Assn. (bd. dirs. 1980—94, bd. advisers 1994—), Marine Corps Heritage Found. (bd. dirs. 1992—98). Republican. Episcopalian. Avocations: reading, golf, tennis, travel. Home: 22476 Alcudia Mission Viejo CA 92692-1157

WILSON, EMERY ALLEN, university dean, obstetrician-gynecologist, educator; b. Frankfort, Ky., Apr. 8, 1942; s. Emery Lee and Mary Catheryne (Cooper) W.; m. Clara Bullock, June 18, 1966; children: Emily, Bryan. BA, Emory U., 1964; MD, U. Ky., 1968. Diplomate Am. Bd. Ob-Gyn (examiner 1979-89), Am. Bd. Reproductive Endocrinology. Intern, resident U. Ky., 1968-72; instr. Harvard U. Med. Sch., Boston, 1974-76; asst. prof. ob-gyn U. Ky. Coll. Medicine, Lexington, 1976-79, assoc. prof., 1979-81, prof., 1981—, dir. Ctr. for Reproductive Medicine, 1983-87; vice chancellor for clin. svcs., dean Coll. Medicine U. Ky., 1987—. Cons. Nat. Inst. Occupational Safety and Health, Cin., 1980-82; dir. Florence Crittendon House, Lexington, 1986-89. Editor: Nutrition in Pregnancy, 1980, Endometriosis, 1987, Professional Management and Practice Management, 1989; author over 100 articles, book chpts., abstracts; reviewer several profl. jours. Maj. USAF, 1972-74. Recipient Acad. Tng. award Ortho Pharms., 1972. Fellow Am. Coll. Obstetricians and Gynecologists; mem. Am. Fertility Soc., Soc. Gynecologic Investigation, Alpha Omega Alpha, Omicron Delta Kappa. Mem. Christian Ch. (Disciples Of Christ). Home: 967 Edgewater Dr Lexington KY 40502-3011 Office: U Ky Coll Medicine 800 Rose St Lexington KY 40536-0001*

WILSON, ESTHER ELINORE, technical college educator; b. Uehling, Nebr., Nov. 4, 1921; d. Lorenz John and Dorothea Emma Rosena (Schmidt) Paulsen; m. Billy LeRoy Wilson, Nov. 14, 1919; 1 child, Frances Ann Wilson Dellar. BS, Morningside Coll., 1950; postgrad., U. Nebr., 1947-80, U. S.D., 1954-83; MS, U. Minn., 1963. Cert. postsecondary tchr., Iowa. Tchr. Irvington (Nebr.) Pub. Schs., 1942-44, Immanuel Luth. Schs., Wichita, Kans., 1944-45, Winnebago (Nebr.) Pub. Schs., 1946-50, Nat. Bus. Coll., Sioux City, Iowa, 1950-51; tchr., asst. prin. Liberty Consol. Sch., Merrill, 1951-55; mktg. tchr. coord. South Sioux City (Nebr.) Community Schs., 1955-86; adj. faculty prof. adult basic edn. Western Iowa Tech. Coll., Sioux City, 1989-94; mgr. rental properties, 1950-2000. Real estate assoc. State Nat., Dakota City, Nebr., 1988-92, Century 21 Marketplace, Sioux City, 1987-88; advt. sales mgr. Auto Hotline, South Sioux City, 1986-87. Author: I Said I Would, 1995; contbg. author: Siouxland Anthology, 1995, Capturing Our Heritage, 1996, The Lutheran Message, 1999. Vol. tchr. N.E. Nebr. C.C., South Sioux City, 1987-90; supt. St. Paul's Luth. Sunday Sch., Sioux City, 1972-76; treas. Hope Luth. Ch., 1989-95, historian 1995-97, nursing home lamplighter 1987-92, 1995-2000; co-pres. Friends of Libr., South Sioux City, 1986-88; fundraiser South Sioux City Pub. Libr., 1984-85; pres. Am. Cancer Soc., Dakota County, Nebr., 1979-88; sponsor South Sioux City Distributive Club of Am., 1956-86; state pres. Nebr. Bus. Edn. Assn., 1979, Distributive Edn. Tchrs. Assn., 1980; pres. Luth. Svc. Aux., 2000-2001. Recipient Outstanding Svc. to State Orgns., Nebr. Vocat. Edn. Assn., 1976, Woman of the Yr. Am. Bus. Women Assn., 1972. Mem. Nebr. State Edn. Assn. (sec., treas., v.p., pres., Dedicated Svc. award 1986, Women of Excellence awards 1997), South Sioux City Chamberettes (sec., v.p., pres. 1972-89, 1st v.p. 1996-97, pres. 1998-99), Am. Federated Women's Club (sec. 1998, v.p., pres.), Svc. Corps Ret. Execs. (historian 1995-2002, sec. 1997-98, sec.-treas. 1998-2000), Am. Bus. Women's Assn. (sec. 1999-2001, Sr. SOOS 1998-2002). Avocations: reading, political and economic studies, internet, gardening, evangelism. Home and Office: 435 Dixon Path South Sioux City NE 68776-5300 E-mail: estherwls@aol.com.

WILSON, EVELYN L. legal educator; b. Parkersburg, W.Va., July 7, 1949; m. Charles A. Shropshire, Oct. 15, 1983; children: Charles A. II, Jeremy D. AB, Oberlin Coll., 1971; MS, U. Utah, 1975; JD, Paul M. Hebert Law Ctr., Baton Rouge, La., 1983. Bar: La. 1983. Sr. budget examiner N.Y. Dept. Budget, Albany, 1977-80; jud. law clk. Supreme Ct. La., New Orleans, 1983-84; atty. Losavio & Weinstein, Baton Rouge, 1984-86; prof. law So. U. Law Ctr., 1986—. Author: Louis Berry--A Man Among Men, 1993; contbr. chpt. to book, articles to profl. jours. Bd. dirs. Capital Area Legal Svcs. Coun., Baton Rouge, 1984-88; legal advisor Woodland Cmty. Ctr., Inc., Clinton, La., 1985—. Mem. Feliciana Bar Assn. (pres. 1993-94). Office: So U Law Ctr PO Box 9294 Baton Rouge LA 70813-9294 E-mail: Ewilson@sulc.edu.

WILSON, EWEN MACLELLAN, economist; b. Nairobi, Kenya, July 29, 1944; came to U.S., 1969; s. Walter Maclellan and Barbara (Gange) Maclellan W.; m. Kay Stephens, May 31, 1969; children: Libby, Cindy, Riana. BS, U. London, 1965; MS, W.Va. U., 1970; PhD, N.C. State U., 1973. With conservation and extension dept. Ministry of Agrl., Banket, Rhodesia, 1965-68; research fellow U. Rhodesia, Salisbury, 1973-74; asst. prof. Va. Tech., Blacksburg, 1975-77; dir. econs. and stats. Am. Meat Inst., Arlington, Va., 1977-83, v.p., 1983-85; apptd. dep. asst. sec. U.S. Dept. Agrl., Washington, 1985-87, asst. sec., 1987-89; pres. Wilson Agribus. Analysis, 1989-90; exec. dir. Commodity Futures Trading Comm., Washington, 1990-94; chief agriculture and fin. statistics div. U.S. Census Bur., 1994-98, chief co. stats. divsn., 1998—. Bd. dirs. Nat. Cooperative Bank, 1988-90, Commodity Credit Corp, 1987-89. Mem. Am. Agrl. Econs. Assn. Republican. Episcopalian. Office: US Census Bur Csd Rm 1182 Fb 3 Washington DC 20233-0001 E-mail: ewen.m.wilson@census.gov.

WILSON, FRANCES C. career military officer; BS, Mich. State U.; MEd, Pepperdine U.; MA in Psychology, U. No. Colo.; MS in Bus. Mgmt., Salve Regina Coll.; D in Edn., U. So. Calif. Commd. 2d lt. USMC, 1972, advanced through grades to brigadier gen.; air traffic control officer Marine Corps Air Sta., Yuma, Ariz., Kaneohe, Hawaii, 1975; tchr. instrnl. mgmt. Marine Corps Devel. & Edn. Ctr., Quantico, Va.; staff sec. 3d Marine Divsn., Okinawa, Japan, 1980-81; asst. prof., co. officer brigade of midshipmen U.S. Naval Acad., Annapolis, Md.; mgmt. analyst HQ USMC, Washington; spl. asst. for gen. and flag officer matters Joint Staff, Pentagon, exec. asst. to vice dir., 1987; comdr. 4th Recruit Tng. Battalion, Parris Island, S.C., 1988-90, Camp H.M. Smith, Svc. Battalion Marine Corps Pacific; sec. Joint Staff, until 1997; commanding gen. Marine Corps Base, Quantico, 1997-99, Third Force Svc. Support Group, Okinawa, Japan, 1999—.

WILSON, FRANCES EDNA, protective services official; b. Keokuk, Iowa, Aug. 4, 1955; d. David Eugene and Anna Bell (Hootman) W. BA, St. Ambrose Coll., 1982; MA, Western Ill., 1990; cert. massage therapist, Shocks Ctr. Edn., Moline, Ill., 1993. Lic. massage therapist, Iowa; cert. Rape Aggression Def. Systems instr.; 2d degree black belt Tai Ho Jujitsu. Trainer, defensive tactics Davenport (Iowa) Police, 1990—, police corporal, 1985-94, police sgt., 1994—; apptd. recs. bur. comdr. Iowa Assn. Women Police, 1996-98, pres., 1989-92, patrol supr., coord. comm. training operator, 1998—2001, CTO coord., 1999—2001, sr. sgt. day shift patrol, 2001—. Cons., def. tactics Scott C.C., Bettendorf, Iowa, 1993—; owner Wilson Enterprises Ltd., Davenport, 1995—; spkr. workshops; guest spkr. Genesis Employee Assistance Program, 1996—; training com. Davenport Police Dept., 1996-2001, recruitment com., 2001—; rape aggression def. instr., 1997—; instr. Rape Aggression Def. Kids, 1999—; with Davenport Cmty. Adult Edn., 2002.. Bd. dirs. Scott County Family YMCA, Davenport, 1990-95, instr., 1989—, The Family Connection, Ltd.; instr. Davenport Cmty. Adult Edn., 1991-94; mem. Iowa SAFE KIDS Coalition, 1992—; mem. First Presbyn. Ch., Davenport, 1986—, bd. deacons, 1995; vol. asst. Davenport Police Dept.'s Sgts. Planning Com. on Tng., 1991, K-9 Unit, 1990-94; apptd. adminstv. sgt. 2nd sr. sgt., 2001. Recipient Law Enforcement award Davenport Optimist Club, 1997. Mem. Am. Soc. Law Enforcement Trainers, Law Enforcement Alliance Am., Am. Women Self Def. Assn., Nat. Ctr. for Women and Policing, Iowa Assn. Women Police (pres. 1989-92, Officer of Yr. 1995), Iowa State Police Assn., Iowa Assn. Chiefs of Police and Peace Officers, Internat. Assn. Women Police. Avocations: photography, reading, education, massage therapy, enjoying life. Office: Davenport Police Dept 420 N Harrison St Davenport IA 52801-1304 E-mail: frankie_wilson@juno.com.

WILSON, FRANK HENRY, retired electrical engineer; b. Dinuba, Calif., Dec. 4, 1935; s. Frank Henry and Lurene (Copley) W.; m. Carol B. Greening, Mar. 28, 1964; children: Frank, Scott E. BS, Oreg. State U., 1957. Electronic engr. Varian Assoc., Palo Alto, Calif., 1960-61, Stanford U. Med. Sch., Palo Alto, 1961-68, U. Calif. Med. Sch., Davis, 1968-77, Litronix, Cupertino, Calif., 1978-81, Quantel, Santa Clara, 1981-87, Heraeus Lasersonics, Milpitas, 1987-91, Continuum Electro-Optics, Santa Clara, 1992-96, Laserscope, San Jose, 1997-98. 1st lt. Signal Corps U.S. Army, 1958-60. Mem. IEEE. Home: 69 Lakeshore Dr Hammonds Plains NS Canada B4B 1X1 E-mail: fhcb.wilson@ns.sympatico.ca.

WILSON, FRANKLIN D. sociology educator; b. Birmingham, Ala., Sept. 3, 1942; s. Ernest and Ollie Lee (Carter) W.; m. Marion F. Brown; children: Rachel, Chareese BA, Miles Coll., 1964; postgrad., Atlanta U., 1964-65; MA, Wash. State U., 1971, PhD, 1973. Instr. Grambling U., La., 1965-66; William H. Sewell-Bascom prof. sociology U. Wis.-Madison, 1973—, chmn. dept. Afro-Am. studies, 1984-87, chmn. dept. sociology, 1988-91, dir. Ctr. for Demography and Ecology, 1994-99. Author: Residential Consumption, Economic Opportunities and Race, 1979; deputy editor Demography, 1995-98; co-editor Am. Sociol. Rev. Bd. of Census adv. com. Profl. Assns., 1993-99. Served with U.S. Army, 1966-69; Vietnam Decorated Purple Heart, Silver Star, Vietnam medal of Valor; Census fellow Am. Statis. Assn., NSF, 1991-92, Population Coun. fellow, 1971-72. Mem. Population Assn. Am., Sociol. Rsch. Assn., Assn. Black Sociologists. Unitarian Universalist. Avocation: swimming, reading. Office: U Wis Ctr for Demography and Ecology Social Sci Bldg Madison WI 53713 E-mail: wilson@ssc.wisc.edu.

WILSON, FRED M., II, ophthalmologist, educator; b. Indpls., Dec. 10, 1940; s. Fred Madison and Elizabeth (Fredrick) W.; m. Karen Joy Lyman, Sept. 10, 1959 (div. June 1962); 1 child, Teresa Wilson Kulick; m. Claytonia Leigh Pemberton, Aug. 28, 1964; children: Yvonne Wilson Hacker, Jennifer Wilson DeLong, Benjamin James. AB in Med. Scis., Ind. U., 1962, MD, 1965. Cert. Am. Bd. Ophthalmology. Intern Sacred Heart Hosp., Spokane, Wash., 1965-66; resident in ophthalmology Ind. U., Indpls., 1968-71, fellow in ophthalmology, 1971-72, F.I. Proctor Found., San Francisco, 1972-73; from asst. prof. to assoc. prof. ophthalmology Ind. U., Indpls., 1972-76, prof. ophthalmology, 1981—. Med. dir. Ind. Lions Eye Bank, Inc., Indpls., 1973-99; cons. surgeon Ind. U., Indpls., 1973—. Author or editor numerous sci. articles, book chpts. and books on ophthalmology. Lt. comdr. USNR, 1966-68, PTO. Mem. Am. Acad. Ophthalmology (assoc. sec. 1988-93, Sr. Teaching award 1989), Assn. Proctor Fellows, Soc. Heed Fellows, Am. Ophthalmol. Soc., Am. Bd. Ophthalmology (bd. dirs. 1993-2000), Ill. Soc. Ophthalmology (hon.), Mont. Acad. Ophthalmology (hon.), Pacific-Coast Ophthalmol. Soc. (hon.). Republican. Avocations: photography, guitar, history, language, natural history. Home: 12262 Crestwood Dr Carmel IN 46033-4323 Office: Ind U Sch Medicine Dept Ophthalmolgy 702 Rotary Cir Indianapolis IN 46202-5133

WILSON, FREDERIC SANDFORD, pharmaceutical company executive; b. Schenectady, NY, Mar. 28, 1944; s. Robert Omer and Isabel May (Sandford) W.; children: Amy Kathleen, Adrienne Ann; m. Judith Ann Goettsche, Feb. 7, 1973; children: Marla Ann, Brian Bennett, Jessica Lea, Jennifer Lynn. BS, Syracuse U., 1968. Acct. exec. Mastropaul Design Inc., Syracuse, N.Y., 1969-70; copy editor Norwich Eaton Pharms., Norwich, 1970-72, sales rep. Gary, Ind., 1972-73, asst. product mgr. Norwich, 1974-75, mktg. svcs. mgr., 1975-76, product mgr., 1977-81, bus. devel. mgr., 1981-83, sr. product mgr., 1983-85, mgr. med. foods, 1986-89; assoc. mktg. mgr. P&G Pharms., 1989-92; dir. profl. rels. P & G Pharms., Cin., 1993-96; mgr. mktg. svcs. P&G, 1997-98; mgr. CME P&G, 1998—. Cons. Sandoz Nutrition Corp., Mpls., 1992. Inventor Jejunostomy Kit, 1981, Vivonex T.E.N. med. food, 1983, Tolerex med. food, 1987. Bd. dirs. Syracuse U. Minority Access Program, 1989-91; bd. dirs., v.p. Am. Osteo. Found.; bd. dirs. Alliance for Continuing Med. Edn.; mem. Nat. Task Force on CME Provider/Industry Collaboration. Mem.: Global Allaince Med. Edn. (bd. dirs., sec.). Office: Procter & Gamble Box 2075 8700 Mason-Montgomery Rd Mason OH 45040-9462 E-mail: wilsonfs@pg.com.

WILSON, FREDERICK ALLEN, medical educator, medical center administrator, gastroenterologist; b. Winchester, Mass., Aug. 22, 1937; s. Warren Archibald and Alice Jane (Springall) W.; m. Lynne Stewart Cantley, Feb. 24, 1962; children: Douglas, Victoria. AB, Colgate U., 1959; MD, Albany Med. Coll., 1963. Intern Hartford Hosp., Conn., 1963-64, resident in medicine, 1964-66; fellow in gastroenterology Albany Med. Coll., N.Y., 1966-67; USPHS postdoctoral fellow in gastroenterology U. Tex. Southwestern Med. Sch., Dallas, 1969-72; asst. prof. medicine Vanderbilt U. Sch. Medicine, Nashville, 1972-76, assoc. prof., 1976-82, mem. adv. com. clin. research ctr., 1978-81; prof. medicine, chief div. gastroenterology Milton S. Hershey Med. Ctr., Pa. State U., Hershey, 1982-90; prof. medicine, dir. div. gastroenterology Med. U. S.C., Charleston, 1990-94, dir. fellowship tng. program in gastroenterology & hepatolog, 1990—, chmn. sci. adv. com. gen. clin. rsch. ctr., 1997-98. Mem. ACP Med. Knowledge Self-Assessment Program VI, 1980-81; mem. gastroenterology and clin. nutrition rev. group Nat. Inst. ARthritis, Diabetes, Digestive and Kidney Disease, NIH, Bethesda, Md., 1985-89; pre=reviewer Am. Coun. Grad. Med. Edn., 1994-95. Contbr. numerous articles, abstracts, chpts. to profl. pubs.; reviewer for sci. jours. Served to maj. M.C., U.S. Army, 1967-69. Recipient Clin. Investigator award VA Med. Ctr., Nashville, 1972-75; recipient Investigator award Howard Hughes Med. Inst., Vanderbilt U., 1975-78; NIH Fogarty Internat. Ctr. sr. internat. fellow Max Planck Inst. for Biophysics, Frankfurt, W.Ger., 1979-80 Mem. Am. Fedn. Clin. Research, Central Soc. Clin. Research, Am. Gastroenterology Assn., Am. Assn. Study Liver Diseases, Am. Soc. Clin. Investigation, N.Y. Acad. Scis., So. Car. Med. Assn., Eastern Gut Club, Pa. Soc. Gastroenterology. Office: Med U SC Div Gastroenterology 96 Jonathan Lucas St/# 210 Charleston SC 29425-0001

WILSON, GAHAN, cartoonist, author; b. Evanston, Ill., Feb. 18, 1930; s. Allen Barnum and Marion (Gahan) W.; m. Nancy Dee Midyette ((Nancy Winters)), Dec. 30, 1966; stepchildren— Randy Winters, Paul Winters. Graduate, Art Inst. Chgo., 1952. Commentator, Nat. Public Radio. Collections include Gahan Wilson's Graveyard Manner, 1965, The Man In the Cannibal Pot, 1967, I Paint What I See, 1971, Weird World of Gahan Wilson, 1975, Gahan Wilson's Cracked Cosmos, 1975, First World Fantasy Collection Anthology, 1977, Gahan Wilson's Favorite Tales of Horror, 1977, And Then We'll Get Him, 1978, Nuts, 1979, Chog: A Gothic Fable, 1980, Is Nothing Sacred, 1982, Wilson's America, 1985, Eddy Deco's First Case, 1987, Playboy's Gahan Wilson, 1980, Eddy Deco's Last Caper, 1989, Still Weird, 1994; juvenile works: Harry, The Fat Bear Spy, 1973, The Bang Bang Family, 1974, Harry and the Sea Serpent, 1976, Harry and the Snow Melting Ray, 1978; editor: First World Fantasy Awards, 1977, The Raven & Other Poems, 1990; illustrator: Matthew Looney & the Space Pirates, 1972, Catch Your Breath: A Book of Shivery Poems, 1973, Granny's Fish Story, 1975, Maria Looney & The Cosmic Circus, 1978, Maria Looney & The Remarkable Robot, 1979, Bob Fulton's Amazing Soda-Pop Stretcher, 1982, Plots & Pans, 1989, How To Be A Guilty Parent, Murder For Christmas, Passport to World Band Radio, 1992, The Keep of Two Moons, 1992, The Keep of Two Moons, 1992, A Night in the Lonesome October, 1993, Credo!: The Game of Dueling Dogmas, 1993, A Night in the Lonesome October, 1993, Spooky Stories For A Dark & Stormy Night, 1994; co-editor: Animals, Animals, Animals, 1979; co-author: The Upside-Down Man, 1977, Hairticklers, 1989, The Devil's Dictionary & Other Works; author: Everybody's Favorite Duck, 1989; animator (movie): Gahan Wilson's Diner, 1993; contbr. to Nat. Lampoon, New Yorker, Collier's, Look, Playboy, Punch, Esquire, Fantasy and Sci. Fiction, Paris Match, Pardon. Mem. Mystery Writers Am., Sci. Fiction Writers Am., Soc. Illustrators, Wolfe Pack, Cartoonists Assn. Commentator, Horror Writers Am. (Life Achievement award 1992), Writers Guild East, Authors Guild, Nat. Public Radio. Office: HMH Pubs care Readers Svc 919 N Michigan Ave Chicago IL 60611-1681

WILSON, GARY DEAN, lawyer; b. Wichita, Kans., June 7, 1943; s. Glenn E. and Roe Zella (Mills) W.; m. Diane Kay Williams, Dec. 29, 1965; children: Mark R., Matthew C., Christopher G. BA, Stanford U., 1965, LLB, 1968. Bar: D.C. 1970, U.S. Dist. Ct. D.C. 1970, U.S. Ct. Appeals (D.C. cir.) 1972, U.S. Ct. Appeals (7th cir.) 1979, U.S. Ct. Appeals (2d cir.) 1983. Law clk. U.S. Ct. Appeals, 2d cir., N.Y.C., 1968-69, U.S. Supreme Ct., Washington, 1969-70; assoc. Wilmer, Cutler & Pickering, 1970-75, ptnr., 1976—. Acting prof. law Stanford (Calif.) Law Sch., 1981-82. Bd. visitors Stanford Law Sch., 1990-92, 2000—. Democrat. Home: 4636 30th St NW Washington DC 20008-2127 Office: Wilmer Cutler & Pickering 2445 M St NW Ste 900 Washington DC 20037-1435 E-mail: gwilson@wilmer.com., dwilson1@erols.com.

WILSON, GARY PAUL, music educator; b. Waco, Tex., Dec. 15, 1959; s. Harold Leon and Shelba Jean Wilson; m. Cheryl Ann Arnold, June 24, 1989; children: Amy, Scott. BA, Harding U., 1983; MusM, Baylor U., 1985. Tchr. Ctrl. Ark. Christian Sch., North Little Rock; asst. prof. York (Nebr.) Coll., 1998—. Clinician, adjudicator. Mem. York Area Arts Coun., 1998—2002. Mem.: Music Educators Nat. Conf., Am. Choral Dirs. Assn. Home: 1423 Ohio York NE 68467 Office: York Coll 1125 E 8th York NE 68467 Office Fax: 402-363-5713. E-mail: gpwilson@york.edu.

WILSON, GARY THOMAS, engineering executive; b. Pitts., Sept. 26, 1961; s. Charles Zachary and Doris Jean (Thomas) W.; m. Georgiann E. Wilson, Dec. 31, 1994. AB, Dartmouth Coll., 1983, BEEE, 1984; MSEE, Calif. State U., Long Beach, 1992; postgrad., UCLA, 1992-99. Elec. engr. AiResearch, Man., Garrett, Torrance, Calif., 1983; sr. mem. tech. staff TRW Space & Electronics Group, Redondo Beach, 1984-93; v.p. of R&D CZAND Assocs., L.A., 1993—; rsch. asst. UCLA Flight System Rsch. Ctr., Westwood, Calif., 1994-96; sr. scientist payload sys. Hughes Space & Comms., 1996-2000; sr. project mgr. Boeing Satellite Systems, 2000—01; dir. advanced systems Mission Rsch. Corp., 2001—. Cons. CZAND Assocs., L.A., 1985-93; instr. electronics UCLA Smarts Program. Tutor math. and sci. TRW Bootstrap, Redondo Beach, 1991-93. Recipient Meritorious Svc. award United Negro Coll. Fund, 1989; TRW master's fellow, doctoral incentive fellow Calif. State U., 1993. Mem. IEEE, Nat. Soc. Black Engrs. (pres. Dartmouth chpt. 1982-83), Dartmouth Soc. Engrs. Avocations: tennis, golf, chess, basketball, cycling. E-mail: wilson@mrcsb.com.

WILSON, GAYLE ANN, civic worker; b. Phoenix, Nov. 24, 1942; d. Clarence Arthur and Charlotte Evelyn (Davison) Edlund; m. Theodore William Graham, Sept. 14, 1963 (div. May 1983); children: Todd Chandler, Philip Edlund; m. Pete Wilson, May 29, 1983. BA, Stanford U., 1965; postgrad., U. San Diego, 1982. First lady State of Calif., Sacramento, 1991-99; bd. directors ARCO, Los Angeles, CA, 1999—. Adv. for early childhood health and improved math. and sci. edn.; bd. dirs. Ctr. for Excellence in Edn., McLean, Va., 1985—, also former chmn.; mem. Jr. League San Diego, 1968—, also past pres.; bd. dirs. Calif. Inst. Tech., Pasadena, 1995—, Children's Inst. Internat., Phoenix House; former spokesperson Access for Infants and Mothers (AIM), Calif. Breast Cancer Initiative, Never Shake a Baby Campaign, Partnership for Responsible Parenting; mem. Calif. Sesquicentennial Commn.; hon. chmn. Calif. Sci. Fair, Calif. 4-H Found., Calif. Perinatal Outreach-BabyCal, Calif. Commn. on Improving Life Through Svc., Keep Calif. Beautiful; hon. co-chmn. Calif. Mentor Initiative; mem. adv. coun. Ct. Apptd. Spl. Advs.; mem. adv. coun. computers in schs. program Detweiler Found.; hon. chmn. bd. dirs. Leland Stanford Mansion Restoration Found.; founding mem. Achievement Rewards for Coll. Scientists; mem. San Diego Park and Recreation Commn., 1980-83; regent Children's Hosp. L.A. Found., 1998—; bd. dirs. Center Theatre Group, L.A., 1998—, ARCO. Recipient Guardian Angel award L.A. ChildShare, 1995, lifetime achievemecnt award Jr. League L.A., 1996. Mem. Phi Beta Kappa. Republican. Avocations: lyric writing, singing, performing, watercolors. Office: 2132 Century Park Ln Apt 301 Los Angeles CA 90067-3320

WILSON, GENEVIEVE ADKINS, artist; b. Somerset, Ky., Apr. 18, 1935; d. Sylvester Adkins and Grace Mae Burkett; m. Cosby Dallo Wilson, July 4, 1951 (dec. Aug. 1978); children: A. Keith, David Neal, Teresa Ann, Kenneth Dale, Mellisa Grace. BS, Campbellsville Coll., 1971; MA, Western U., Bowling Green, Ky., 1982. Tchr. Russell Springs (Ky.) Elem., 1971-73, Russell County H.S., Russell Springs, 1973-88; painter Ky. Folk Art Ctr., Morehead, 1991—, VSA Arts Ky., Frankfort, 1998—. Exhibited in group shows at Cumberland Art League, Somerset, 1991, Transylvania U., Lexington, Ky., 1992, Folk Art Ctr., Morehead, 1993, Star Theator, Russell Springs, 1995-96, Riverstone Gallery, Somerset, 1998, VSA Arts Ky., Frankfort, 1998, Livings Arts & Sci. Ctr., Lexington, 1998, Bandy-Carroll-Heleige, Louisville, 2000, Ky. Fair Expo. Ctr., Louisville, 2002, Vance Burg Depot Mus., 2002, Maysville, Ky, 2002, others. Mem. Kiwanis (bd. dirs. 2000-01). Avocations: writing stories and poetry, reading, music, art. Home: 1020 Pattie Ridge Rd Russell Springs KY 42642-9711

WILSON, GEORGE DAVID, school administrator; b. Glen Ridge, N.J., Aug. 12, 1949; s. Howard Haldane and Bette Louise (Pierson) W.; m. Nancy Kathleen Miele, Aug. 22, 1970; children: Jennifer Leigh, Jody Lynn, James David. BA, Westminster Coll., 1971; MS, SUNY, Brockport, 1979; EdD, W.Va. U., 1990. Tchr. English Watertown (N.Y.) City Sch. Dist., 1971-78, chmn. dept. English, 1978-82; supr. secondary edn. Mt. Lebanon Sch. Dist., Pitts., 1982-91, dir. secondary edn., 1991-98, asst. supt., 1998—. Contbr. articles to profl. jours. Ruling elder United Ch. of Sackets harbor, N.Y., 1974-78, First Presbyn. Ch. Watertown, 1979-82. Mem. Assn. Supervision and Curriculum Devel., Nat. Coun. Tchrs. English, Pa. Sch. Bds. Assn. Republican. Presbyterian. Avocations: running, golf, photography, fishing. Home: 5772 Scenic View Dr Bethel Park PA 15102-2639 Office: Mt Lebanon Sch dist 7 Horsman Dr Pittsburgh PA 15228-1107

WILSON, GEORGE PETER, international organization executive; b. Perth, Scotland, July 6, 1935; came to U.S., 1985; s. Alan Johnson and Doris L. (Allan) W.; m. Sandra Graham, Feb. 6, 1960 (div. 1984); 1 child, Iain; m. Robbyn Dee LaCroix, Nov. 17, 1984; 1 stepchild, Orion. Diploma in Hotel Mgmt., Scottish Coll. Commerce, Glasgow, 1954. Chartered acct., 1965, cert. internal auditor, 1985. Hotel mgr., auditor Can. Nat. Rys., Ottawa and Montreal, 1956-65; fin. officer Treasury Bd. Can., asst. sec. to Cabinet, dir. Pub. Service Commn., counsellor external affairs Govt. of Can., Ottawa, Geneva, 1965-78; dir. gen. audit UN, N.Y.C., 1978-80; dep. auditor gen. of Can. Govt. of Can., Ottawa, 1980-85; pres. Inst. Internal Auditors, Orlando, Fla., 1985-92; dir. audit FAO UN, Rome, 1992-97, insp. gen., 1997—. Contbr. articles to profl. jours. Mem. Can. Inst. Chartered Accts. (com. mem.), Inst. Internal Auditors (com. mem.), Can. Comprehensive Audit Found. (gov. 1985-88), Internat. Consortium on Govt. Fin. Mgmt. (bd. dirs. 1983-92), Inst. for Fin. Crime Prevention. Home: Via Giulia 98 # 9 00186 Rome Italy Office: FAO Viale delle Terme di Caracalla 00100 Rome Italy E-mail: peter.wilson@fao.org.

WILSON, GLEN PARTEN, professional society administrator; b. Waco, Tex., Dec. 10, 1922; s. Glen P. and Hazel (Parnell) W. BS in Aero. Engring., U. Tex., Austin, 1943, MA in Psychology, 1948, PhD in Psychology, 1952. Engr. Lockheed Aircraft Co., Burbank, Calif., 1943-44; teaching fellow, rsch. asst., instr. U. Tex., Austin, 1946-52; rsch. psychologist USAF, Lackland AFB, Tex., 1952-53; gen. mgr. Tex. Ednl. Devices Co., Austin, 1953-54; asst. to Senator Lyndon B. Johnson Washington, 1955-57; staff Senate Preparedness Investigating Subcom. and Senate Spl. Com. on Space and Astronautics, 1957-59; chief clk., profl. staff mem. Senate Com. on Aero. and Space Scis., 1959-77; cons., 1977-79; spl. asst. for student activities NASA, 1979-80, acting dir. acad. affairs div., 1980-82; pres. Marie D. and Glen P. Wilson Found., 1982-87; exec. dir. Nat. Space Soc., 1984-88, exec. dir. emeritus, 1988—. Lectr. on aero. and space programs, Senate orgn., sci. policy, tech. assessment, student activities, space activism. Participant as staff passage of Nat. Aeros. and Space Act, 1958, Communications Satellite Act, 1962, NASA Authorization Acts, 1958-77; editor Policy Planning for Aeronautical Rsch. and Devel., Senate Document 90, 89th Congress, 1966; developer NASA shuttle student involvement program, 1980, space edn. orgn., 1984—. With USN, 1944-46. Recipient Exceptional Svc. medal NASA, 1981; named Disting. Engring. Grad., U. Tex. Coll. Engring., Austin, 2000; Nat. Space Soc. Hdqrs. renamed The Glen P. Wilson Internat. Space Ctr., 1988. Mem. AIAA (spl. presdl. citation 1976), AAAS, Nat. Space Soc., Internat. Acad. of Astronautics, Sigma Xi, Nat. Space Club, Cosmos Club.

WILSON, GLENN, economist, educator; b. East St. Louis, Ill., Feb. 4, 1929; s. Herschel and Regina (Hayes) W.; m. Helen Janice O'Dell, Jan. 28, 1951; children— David, Thomas, Ann. BA, U. Okla., 1951; MA, 1952. Adminstr., Welfare and Retirement Fund United Mine Workers, Pitts., Knoxville, Tenn., 1952-58; dir. med. care research Nationwide Ins. Co., Columbus, 1958-62; exec. dir. Community Health Found., Cleve., 1962-68; exec. v.p. Kaiser Community Health Found., 1968-69; assoc. dean U. N.C. Med. Sch., Chapel Hill, 1970-88, prof. dept. social medicine, 1977—, chmn. dept., 1977-89.

Cons. Sault Ste. Marie and Dist. Group Health Assn.; health adv. Mayor Stokes, Cleve., 1967-69 Contbr. articles to profl. jours. Home: 214 Glandon Dr Chapel Hill NC 27514-3816 Office: U NC Med Sc Dept Social Medicine Chapel Hill NC 27514

WILSON, GREGORY SCOTT, kinesiology educator, coach; b. Apr. 6, 1960; BEd, U. Evansville, 1983; MS in Phys. Edn., Ind. U., 1987, D of Phys. Edn., 1993. Cert. tchr., Ind., instr. CPR, ofcl. track and field, TAC level I coach. Tchr., head coach jr. high football, track and field St. Benedict Grade Sch., Evansville, Ind., 1984-85; tchr., asst. coach football, track and field Evansville Meml. High Sch., 1985-87; assoc. instr. motor devel. and phys. edn. Ind. U., Bloomington, 1987-91, grad. asst. coach track and field, cross country, 1988-91, lectr. kinesiology, 1991-94; instr. physiology, sport psychology, exercise, 1994-96; asst. coach track and field Ind. U., Bloomington, 1991-97; asst. prof., phys. and exercise studies Lander U., Greenwood, S.C., 1997-98; asst. prof. dept. human kinetics and sports studies U. Evansville, Ind., 1999—. Presenter in field; chmn. Ind. USA Youth Track and Field Assn.; rsch. in Anxiety and Acad./Athletic Performance publs.; vis. asst. prof. dept. kinesiology, Ind. U., 1996-98; nat. faculty U.S. Sports Acad., 1996; asst. dir. Indpls. Youth Sport and Fitness Network; coord. personal fitness Ind. U.; jour. reviewer for medicine and sci. in sports and exercise, rsch. quar. for exercise and sports, jour. of swimming rsch.; co-dir. Spl. Olympics Spring Games, 1999. Contbr. chpts. to books and articles to profl. jours. Mem. AAHPERD, ACSM, APA, Nat. Assn. Sport and Phys. Edn. (exec. com., coaches coun.), Am. Coll. Sports Medicine, Assn. Rsch., N.Am. Soc. for Psychology of Sport and Phys. Activity, Adminstrn. and Profl. Couns. and Socs., U.S. Olympic Ednl. Acad., Ind. Alliance Health, Phys. Edn., Recreation and Dance, Motor Devel. Acad., Rsch. Consortium. Office: Univ Evansville Dept Human Kinetics Evansville IN 47722-0001

WILSON, H. DAVID, dean; b. West Frankfort, Ill., Sept. 13, 1939; m. Jeannette Wilson; children: Jennifer, Jacqueline, Mary Jeanne. AB in Zoology, Wabash Coll., 1961; MD, St. Louis Sch. Medicine, 1966. Diplomate Nat. Bd. Med. Examiners, Am. Bd. Pediatrics. Intern pediatrics Cardinal Glennon Meml. Hosp. for Children, St. Louis U., 1966—67; resident dept. pediatrics U. Ky. Med. Ctr., Lexington, 1967—68, chief resident, 1968—69; NIH rsch. fellow U. Tex. Health Scis. Ctr., Dallas, 1971—73; fellowship Am. Coun. on Edn., 1988—89; dir. admissions Coll. of Medicine, U. Ky., 1986—88; assoc. dean for acad. affairs, prof. Coll. Medicine, U. Ky., 1989—95; dean, prof. U. N.D. Sch. of Medicine, Grand Forks, 1995—. Author: (TV series) For Kids Sake, 1987-88; dir. pediatric infectious diseases U. Ky. Med. Ctr., Lexington, 1973-95, dir. cystic fibrosis care and tchg. ctr., 1975-80, med. dir., clin. virology lab., 1982-95; staff United Hosp., Grand Forks, 1995—; elected univ. senate U. Ky., 1993-96, bd. trustees Gluck Equine Rsch. Found., 1991-95, rules and elections univ. senate standing com., 1991-92, steering com. for U.K. self-study, 1990-95, co-chmn. steering com., 1990-95, chmn. review and search com. for chmn. dept. obstetrics and gynecology, 1990, chmn. curriculum com. Coll. of Medicine, 1989-95; elected acad. coun. of med. ctr. U. Ky. Med. Ctr., 1989-92; lectr. in field. Contbr. numerous articles to profl. jours. Fellow Pediatric Infectious Dieseases Soc.; mem. AMA, Am. Soc. of Microbiology, Am. Thoracic Soc., Am. Acad. Pediatrics, Pan Am. Group for Rapid Viral Diagnosis. Home: 10 Shadyridge Estates Grand Forks ND 58201 Office: U ND Sch Medicine & Health Scis 501 North Columbia Rd Grand Forks ND 58202-9037*

WILSON, H(AROLD) FRED(ERICK), chemist, research scientist; b. Columbiana, Ohio, Aug. 15, 1922; s. Lloyd Ralph and Erma Rebecca (Frederick) W.; m. Alice Marjorie Steer, Aug. 20, 1949; children: Janice, Deborah, James, Kathleen. BA, Oberlin Coll., 1947; PhD, U. Rochester, 1950. With Rohm & Haas Co., Phila., 1950-83, beginning as rsch. scientist, successively lab. head, rsch. supr., asst. dir., assoc. dir., dir. rsch., 1950-74, v.p., 1974-83, chief sci. officer, from 1981; now with Wilson Assocs., Cape May, N.J. Mem. U.S. nat. com. IUPAC, 1977-84, vice chmn., 1980-82, chmn., 1982-84, fin. com., 1979-89, chmn., 1981-89; chmn. I.R.I. Research Corp., 1980-82, dir., 1979-82 Patentee in field. Served to 1st lt. USAAF, 1942-46. Decorated Air Medal. Mem. Am. Chem. Soc., AAAS, Soc. Chem. Industry, Dirs. Indsl. Research. Home: 24 Congress St Cape May NJ 08204 E-mail: hwilson44@snip.net.

WILSON, HARRY RANDOLPH, retired obstetrician, gynecologist; b. Pitts., 1920; married; 3 children. BS, Grove City (Pa.) Coll., 1942; MD, U. Pitts., 1945. Diplomate Am. Bd. Ob-Gyn. Intern Mercy Hosp., Pitts., 1945-46; resident in ob-gyn. Magee-Womens Hosp., 1954-57; ob-gyn. group practice U. Pitts., 1957—66; pvt. practice, 1966-78; gynecologist Hertzler Clinic, Kans., 1978-90; locum tenens U.S. Army Madigan Hosp., 1991—92; with Group Health Permanente, 1992-93, locum tenens, 1994-98; ret., 1998. Courtesy staff gynecology surgery St. Joseph Hosp., Tacoma. Mem. ACOG (life). Home: 3918 47th Ave NE Tacoma WA 98422-2446

WILSON, HEATHER ANN, congresswoman; b. Keene, N.H., Dec. 30, 1960; d. George Douglas Wilson and Martha Lou Wilson-Kernozicky. BS, USAF Acad., 1982; M. Philosophy, Oxford U., 1984, PhD, 1985. U.S. mission NATO, Brussels, 1987-89, Nat. Security Coun., Washington, 1989-91; pres. Keystone Internat., Inc., Albuquerque, 1991-95; cabinet sec. N.Mex. Dept. Children, Youth and Families, Santa Fe, 1995-98; mem. U.S. Congress from 1st N.Mex. Dist., Washington, 1998—; mem. armes svcs. com., energy and commerce com. Adj. prof. U. N.Mex.; mem. Def. Adv. Com. on Women in the Svcs. Contbr. articles to profl. jours. Capt. USAF, 1982-89. Rhodes scholar, 1982. Republican. Avocations: parenting, hiking, skiing. Office: 318 Cannon House Office Blg Washington DC 20515*

WILSON, HENRY ARTHUR, JR. management consultant; b. Detroit, June 12, 1939; s. Henry Arthur and Ruth (Scott) W.; m. Mildred Rendell, June 17, 1961; 1 child, Suzanne. BS, Mich. Luth. Coll., 1968; MA, U. Detroit, 1976. Police officer Grosse Pointe Park Police Dept., Mich., 1960-68; v.p. Uniflight, Inc., St. Clare Shore, 1968-73; coord. Criminal Justice Inst., Detroit, 1973-76; ptnr. Grant Thorton (formerly Alexander Grant & Co.), 1976-92; pres., owner Thunderboat Racing, Inc., 1998. Grand sec., CEO Grand Lodge F & A.M., Mich.; CEO Mich. Masonic Home; pres., CEO, Mich. Masonic Home Charitably Found., 1996-97. Author: Masonic Etiquette and Protocol, 1985. Sr. warden St. Columba Episcopal Ch., Detroit, 1976—; bd. dirs. Grosse Pointe Yacht Club, 1997-99. Served with USAF, 1957-60. Mem. Cert. Data Processing Auditors Assn., Masons (grand master Mich. 1984-85). Republican. Avocation: boating. Office: 3516 Cadleux Rd Detroit MI 48226

WILSON, HUGH STEVEN, lawyer; b. Paducah, Ky., Nov. 27, 1947; s. Hugh Gipson and Rebekah (Dunn) W.; m. Clare Maloney, Apr. 28, 1973; children: Zachary Hunter, Samuel Gipson. BS, Ind. U., 1968; JD, U. Chgo., 1971; LLM, Harvard U., 1972. Bar: Calif. 1972, U.S. Dist. Ct. (cen. dist.) Calif. 1972, U.S. Dist. Ct. (so. dist.) Calif. 1973, U.S. Ct. Appeals (9th cir.) 1975, U.S. Dist. Ct. (no. dist.) Calif. 1977, U.S. Supreme Ct. 1978, U.S. Dist. Ct. (ea. dist.) 1980. Assoc. Latham & Watkins, L.A., 1972-78, ptnr., 1978—. Recipient Jerome N. Frank prize U. Chgo. Law Sch., 1971. Mem. Calif. Club., Coronado Yacht Club, Order of Coif. Republican. Avocations: lit., zoology. E-mail: steve.wilson@lw.com.

WILSON, IAN EDWIN, cultural organization administrator, archivist; b. Montreal, Que., Can., Apr. 2, 1943; s. Andrew and Marion (Mundy) W.; m. Ruth Dyck, Mar. 24, 1979. BA, Queen's U., Kingston, Ont., 1968, MA History, 1974; DLitt York U. (hon.) , 2001. Archivist Queen's U., Kingston, Ont., Can., 1966-76; provincial archivist Sask. (Can.) Archives, 1976-86; archivist of Ont. Ont. Govt., Toronto, 1986-99; dir. gen. info. resource mgmt. divsn. Ministry Culture, Tourism and Recreation, 1990-93; nat. archivist Can., 1999—; v.p. Internat. Coun. on Archives, 2000—. Sec. Kingston Hist. Soc., 1967-72, v.p., 1972-76; chair cons. group Social Sci. and Humanities Rsch. Coun. Can., Ottawa, 1979-80; adj. prof. Faculty Info. Studies U. Toronto, 1993-2002; spkr. in field. Author: (with J. Douglas Stewart) Heritage Kingston, 1973; editor: Kingston City Hall, 1975; producer: (with J. William Brennan) Regina Before Yesterday, 1978; contbr. articles to profl. jours. Chmn. congregation Mennonite Ch., Regina, 1981-84; mem. Sask. award merit selection com., 1985-86; chair Sask. Heritage adv. bd., 1978-83, mem., 1983-86; Ont. dir. Forum for Young Canadians, 1995-99. Recipient Queen Elizabeth II silver jubilee medal, 1977, W.G. Leland cert. commendation Soc. Am. Archivists, 1981, W. Kaye Lamb prize Assn. Can. Archivists, 1983; Woodrow Wilson hon. fellow, 1967. Mem. Assn. Can. Archivists (various coms., editl. bd. 1986-88), Ont. Hist. Soc. (exec. coun. 1970-73, v.p. 1973-75, pres. 1975-76), Can. Hist. Assn. (past chmn., vice chmn., pres. archives sect. 1972-74), Champlain Soc. (bd. dirs., v.p. 1989-95, pres. 1995—). Home: 10 Bayport Priv Ottawa ON Canada K1V 0Z3 Office: Nat Archives of Canada 395 Wellington St Ottawa ON Canada K1A 0N3 E-mail: iwilson@archives.com.

WILSON, IAN HOLROYDE, management consultant, futurist; b. Harrow, Eng., June 16, 1925; came to U.S., 1954; s. William Brash and Dorothy (Holroyde) W.; m. Page Tuttle Hedden, Mar. 17, 1951 (div. Dec. 1983); children: Rebecca, Dorothy, Ellen, Holly, Alexandra; m. Adrianne Marcus, July 12, 1992. MA, Oxford U., 1948. Orgn. cons. Imperial Chem. Industries, London, 1948-54; various staff exec. positions in strategic planning, mgmt. devel. Gen. Electric Co., Fairfield, Conn., 1954-80; sr. cons. to maj. U.S. and internat. cos. SRI Internat., Menlo Park, Calif., 1980-93; prin. Wolf Enterprises, San Rafael, 1993—. Exec. in residence Va. Commonwealth U., Richmond, 1976; fellow Va. Ctr. for Creative Arts, 1994, 98, 2000. Author: Planning for Major Change, 1976, The Power of Strategic Vision, 1991, Rewriting the Corporate Social Charter, 1992, Managing Strategically in the 1990s, 1993, Executive Leadership, 1995, The New Rules of Corporate Conduct, 2000, The Subtle Art of Strategy, 2002; contbg. editor: Learning from the Future, 1998; mem. editl. bd. Planning Rev., 1973—81; Am. editor: Long Range Planning Jour., 1981—89; sr. editor, mem. editl. bd. Strategy and Leadership, 1993—. Mem. adv. bd. Technol. Forecasting and Social Change, 1989—99; chmn. Citizen's Long Range Ednl. Goals Com., Westport, Conn., 1967—70; mem. strategic process com. United Way of Am., Alexandria, Va., 1985—94. Capt. Brit. Army, 1943—45, ETO. Mem. AAAS, Assn. for Strategic Planning, World Future Soc. Unitarian Universalist. Avocations: travel, writing, photography. Home and Office: 79 Twin Oaks Ave San Rafael CA 94901-1915 E-mail: jason415xx@aol.com.

WILSON, JACK, aeronautical engineer; b. Sheffield, Yorkshire, Eng., Jan. 5, 1933; came to U.S., 1956; s. George and Nellie (Place) W.; m. Marjorie Reynolds, June 3, 1961 (div. Jan. 1991); children: Tanya Ruth, Cara; m. Carol Blixen, Jan. 3, 1997. BS in Engring., Imperial Coll., London, 1954; MS in Aero. Engring., Cornell U., 1958, PhD in Aero. Engring., 1962. Sr. scientific officer Royal Aircraft Establishment, Farnborough, Eng., 1962-63; prin. rsch. sci. Avco-Everett Rsch. Lab., Everett, Mass., 1963-72; vis. prof. Inst. Mecanique des Fluides, Marseille, France, 1972-73; sr. scientist U. Rochester, N.Y., 1973-80; sr. rsch. assoc. Sohio/BP Am., Cleve., 1980-90; sr. engring. specialist Sverdrup Tech. Inc., 1990-93, NYMA, Brook Park, 1994-98, DYNACS Engring. Co., Inc., Brook Park, 1998-2001, QSS Group Inc., Fairview Park, Ohio, 2001—. Author: (chpt.) "Gas Lasers" of Applied Optics in Engineering VI, 1980, "Laser Sources" of Techniques in Chemistry XVII, 1982; contbr. articles to profl. jours. Co-recipient Manley Meml. award Soc. Automotive Engrs., 1995; recipient Soaring gold Badge award Fedn. Aero. Internat., Paris, 1998. Fellow AIAA (assoc.; tech. com. 1991-92). Achievements include first to demonstrate gas-dynamic laser, measurement of air ionization rate at high speeds; patents in application of high speed flow to gas laser media, devel. of antimony dopant sources. Office: QSS Group Inc 21000 Brookpark Rd Cleveland OH 44135-3127 E-mail: jack.wilson@lerc.nasa.gov., wilson.blixen@juno.com.

WILSON, JACK FREDRICK, retired federal government official; b. Salt Lake City, Apr. 2, 1920; s. John Lorimer and Mayme J. (James) W.; m. Gwendolyn Gwynn, Nov. 20, 1947; children— Wendy, Elaine, Barbara Ann, Laurel, John F. Jr., James C. BS, Brigham Young U., 1942; postgrad., Mont. State U., 1962, Pa. State U., 1965. Range conservationist Bur. Land Mgmt., Rawlins, Wyo., 1949-57, dist. mgr. Burley, Idaho, 1957-67, dist. and land office mgr. Riverside, Calif., 1967-72; dir. Boise Interagy. Fire Ctr., Idaho, 1972-81; dir. Office Aircraft Services U.S. Dept. Interior, Boise, 1981-87; dir. Boise Interagy. Fire Ctr., 1987-92; ret., 1992. Contbr. articles to profl. jours. Dir. county disaster com. ARC, 1982-88. Maj. USAF, 1942-47 Recipient Meritorious award U.S. Dept. Interior, 1976, Disting. Service award, 1981, EEO Performance award, 1985; Outstanding Contbn. to Fire Mgmt. award U.S. Dept. Agr. Forest Service, 1976 Mem. Soc. Am. Foresters (chmn. fire com. 1980-82), Am. Soc. Range Mgmt. (sec. pres. 1967), So. Calif. Assn. Foresters and Fire Wardens, Lions (sec. 1954-57), Rotary. Mem. Ch. of Jesus Christ of Latter-day Saints. Avocations: long range weather forecasting, genealogy, reading, golf. Home: 1820 Sunrise Rim Rd Boise ID 83705-5138

WILSON, JACQUELYN, writer; b. Springfield, Ill., Apr. 8, 1952; d. Edward and Joanne (Ashby) W. BA in English, Nasson Coll., Springvale, Maine, 1973; postgrad., U. Salzburg, Austria, 1973-74; A.Comml. Art, Utah Tech. Coll., Salt Lake City, 1981-83, 85. Author 64 poems in anthologies, mags. Recipient Internat. Poet of Merit award Internat. Soc. Poets, 1993. Mem. Internat. Women's Writing Guild, Wis. Fellowship of Poets, Nature Conservancy, Madison Audubon Soc., Dragonfly Soc. Am., Mind's Eye Audio Prodns. Avocations: ceramics, bicycle riding, collecting dragonfly art. Home: 245 S Park St Apt 811 Madison WI 53715-1567 E-mail: jackieq@chorus.net.

WILSON, JAMES ALEXANDER, biologist; b. Mission Hills, Calif., Oct. 14, 1969; s. Jay Norton Wilson and Julie Ann Harness. BA, Calif. State U., Fullerton, 1994, MA, 1998; PhD, Okla. State U., Stillwater, 2002. Tchg. asst. Calif. State U., Fullerton, Calif., 1995—98; naturalist Oak Canyon Nature Ctr., Anaheim, 1997—98; adj. faculty Orange Coast Coll., Costa Mesa, 1998—98; grad. asst. Okla. State U., Stillwater, Okla., 1998—2002. Contbr. articles to profl. jours.; author: (book) Enviornmental Contamination in Terrestrial Vertebrates. Recipient Outstanding Tchr. Award, Calif. State U., 1999, Anna M. Jackson Award, Am. Soc. of Mammalogists, 2002; fellow Scottish Rite Fellowship, McAlester Scottish Rite, 2000. Mem.: The Wildlife Soc., Am. Soc. of Mammalogists. Achievements include Published nine scientific articles or book chapters; Presented ten scientific talks at national /international conferences. Avocations: banjo, evolution, evolution.

WILSON, JAMES CHARLES, JR. lawyer; b. Birmingham, Ala., Sept. 13, 1947; s. James C. and Angelina (Serio) W.; m. Ann Bullock, Mar. 1, 1975; children: Brent Trammell, Lucy Bullock. BA, Tulane U., 1969, JD, 1972; MBA, Samford U., 1995. Ptnr. Bradley, Arant, Rose & White, Birmingham, 1972-90, Lange, Simpson, Robinson & Somerville, Birmingham, 1990-93, Sirote & Permutt, P.C., Birmingham, 1993-96; v.p. and gen. counsel Shop-A-Snak Food Mart, Inc., 1996; pres. Lucent Holdings, Inc., Golden, Miss., 1997-98; ptnr. Baker, Johnston & Wilson LLP, Birmingham, Ala., 1999—. Adj. prof. internat. bus. transactions and internat. law U. Ala., Tuscaloosa, 1983-85, 89-96; internat. bus. transactions Cumberland Sch. Law, 1990-95, adj. prof. corp. fin., 2001—. Author: Alabama Business Corporation Law, 1980; co-author: Corporate Law for the Healthcare Provider: Organization, Operation, Merger and Bankruptcy, 1993, Alabama Business Corporation Law Guide, 1995. Adv. bd. Jr. League of Birmingham, 1984; bd. dirs. Ala. chpt. Am. Liver Found., 1993-97, sec., 1994-95; trustee The Altamont Sch., 1995-2001, v.p., 1996-98, pres., 1998-2000. With U.S. Army, 1972-76. Mem. ABA (sect. internat. law, tax and corp., banking and bus. law), Am. Law Inst., Ala. Bar Assn., Birmingham Bar Assn. (chmn. pub. rels. com. 1990, chmn. spl. projects com. 2002), Birmingham Golf Assn. (pres., v.p., treas. 1982-84). Lodges: Rotary (pres. Birmingham-Sunrise club 1986-87). Office: 2501 20th Pl S Birmingham AL 35223

WILSON, JAMES HARGROVE, JR. lawyer; b. Oliver, Ga., Nov. 26, 1920; s. James Hargrove and Louise (Sealy) W.; m. Frances Audra Schaffer, Dec. 24, 1942 (dec. Nov. 1990); children: Susan Frances, James Hargrove. AB with honors, Emory U., 1940; LL.B. summa cum laude, Harvard U., 1947. Bar: Ga. 1947, D.C. 1951. Assoc. firm Sutherland, Tuttle & Brennan (now Sutherland, Asbill & Brennan LLP), Atlanta and Washington, 1947-53, ptnr., 1953—. Lectr. Emory U., 1959, chmn. bd. visitors, 1967-68; trustee The Northwestern Mut. Life Ins. Co., Milw., 1972-91; mem. advisory group Commr. of Internal Revenue, 1963-64 Pres.: Harvard Law Review, 1946-47. Chmn. bd. trustees Met. Atlanta Crime Commn., 1970-71; mem. Harvard U. Overseers Com. to Visit Law Sch., 1959-65; trustee Emory U., 1983-90, trustee emeritus, 1990—. Served to lt. comdr. USNR, 1942-46. Fellow Am. Bar Found., Am. Coll. Tax Counsel; mem. ABA, State Bar Ga., D.C. Bar, Atlanta Bar Assn., Am. Law Inst. (coun. 1974—), Lawyers Club Atlanta (pres. 1960-61), Am. Judicature Soc., Harvard Law Sch. Assn. (coun. 1981-85), Emory U. Alumni Assn. (pres. 1966-67), Capital City Club, Piedmont Driving Club, Peachtree Club, Phi Beta Kappa, Omicron Delta Kappa, Kappa Alpha. Methodist. Home: 3171 Marne Dr NW Atlanta GA 30305-1931 Office: Sutherland Asbill & Brennan LLP 999 Peachtree St NE Ste 2300 Atlanta GA 30309-3996

WILSON, JAMES HARVEY, artist; b. Hollywood, Calif., Aug. 24, 1942; m. Linda Edwards, June 1, 1967; children: Mark B., Shane D., Ryan G., Heather, Nicole, Sarah. BS, MA, Brigham Young U., Provo, UT, 1968. Prin. works include Landscapes. Church Of Jesus Christ Of Latter-Day Saints.

WILSON, JAMES J. public administration consultant; b. Rahway, N.J., Jan. 29, 1962; s. James William and Sonia Eleanor (Hutchinson) W.; m. Pamela Ann Wilson, June 21, 1989; children: Kandace, Nicole. BA in Computer Sci., The Citadel, 1984; MS in Mgmt., Troy State U., 1992; MA in Econs., U. Ctrl. Fla., 1995; PhD in pub. policy, Fla. State U., 2000. Munitions specialist USAF, Eglin AFB, Fla., 1984-88; systems engr. Sverdrup Tech., Inc., 1988-94; exec. dir. Ctr. for Internat. Pub. Mgmt., Tallahassee, 1995-98. Discussant World Bank, Ohrid, Macedonia, 1996; project dir. Fla. Dept. Environ. Protection, Tallahassee, 1996-98. Contbr. articles to profl. jours.; pres. Fla. State Polich and Social Sci. Rev., 1997. Head coach Pee Wee Tackle Football, Tallahassee, 1997, mem. Big Bros./Big Sisters, Tallahassee, 1995; mentor One-on-One Program, Tallahassee, 1996, mentor/tutor Nims Mid. Sch., Tallahassee, 1996; dir. facilities/transp. Hugh O'Brien Youth Leadership. McKnight doctoral fellow, Fla. Edn. Fund, 1995, grad. rsch. fellow U. Ctrl. Fla., DeVoe L. Moore Dissertation fellow; rsch. grantee Fla. Dept. Cmty. Affairs, 1996. Mem. ASPA, Cmty. Devel. Soc., Omicron Delta Epsilon. Avocations: old movies, bowling, travel, parlor games, nutrition. Home: 640 Elmcroft Blvd Apt 1412 Rockville MD 20850-5641

WILSON, JAMES LAWRENCE, retired chemical company executive; b. Rosedale, Miss., Mar. 2, 1936; s. James Lawrence and Mary Margaret (Klingman) W.; m. Barbara Louise Burroughs, Aug. 30, 1958; children: Lawrence Burroughs, Alexander Elliott. B.Mech. Engring., Vanderbilt U., 1958; MBA, Harvard, 1963. Vice pres. Nyala Properties, Inc., Phila., 1963-65; staff assoc. Rohm & Haas Co., 1965-67, exec. asst. to pres., 1971-72, treas., 1972-74, regional dir. Europe, 1974-77, group v.p., 1977-86, vice-chmn., 1986-88, chmn., CEO, 1988-99; ret., 1999. Treas. Warren-Teed Pharms., Inc., Columbus, Ohio, 1967-68, v.p., 1969; pres. Consol. Biomed. Labs., Inc., Dublin, Ohio, 1970-71; bd. dirs. Vanguard Group Investment Cos., Cummins Inc., MeadWestvaco Corp., AmeriSourceBergen Corp. Trustee Vanderbilt U., 1987—, Culver Ednl. Found., 1988—; chmn. Phila. High Sch. Acads., 1989-99. Mem. Chem. Mfrs. Assn. (bd. dirs. 1988-99, chmn. 1996). Office: 175 Strafford Ave Ste 1 Wayne PA 19087-3331

WILSON, JAMES LAWRENCE, Internal Revenue Service special agent; b. El Paso, Tex., Dec. 23, 1955; s. Bobby James and Alice Rhoen (Taylor) Wilson; m. Jennifer Nancy Roland, June 17, 1978 (div. Aug. 15, 1981); m. Martha Hernandez, Mar. 6, 1983; children: Justine Marie, Katarina Lynann. Student, UCLA, 1985—88. Cert. fraud examiner. From enlisted man to officer U.S. Army, 1973—81; merchandise mgr. Cloth World, Oxnard, Calif., 1980; asst. mgr. Drug King, Ventura, 1980—81; mgr., owner Action Rent-All, Oxnard, 1981—85; construction contractor Self Employed, 1985—86; acctg. mgr. La. Pacific, 1986—87; resident spl. agt. IRS/C.I., 1987—. Resiident spl. agt. IRS/CI, San Luis Obispo, Calif., 1997—. Capt. USAR, 1973—81. Named Spl. Agt. of Yr., Fed. Bar Assn., L.A., 1993; recipient Recognition award, U.S. Atty.'s Office, 2001. Mem.: IRS Spl. Agts. Former, Fed. Criminal Investigator Assn. (pres. L.A. Divsn. Employee Assn.), Fed. Law Enforcement Officers Assn. Avocations: exercise, investing, golf. Office: IRS/CI 3220 S Higuera San Luis Obispo CA 93401

WILSON, JAMES LEE, retired geology educator, consultant; b. Waxahachie, Tex., Dec. 1, 1920; s. James Burney and Hallie Christine (Hawkins) W.; m. Della I. Moore, May 8, 1944; children: James Lee Jr., Burney Grant, Dale Ross (dec.). Student, Rice U., 1938-40; BA, U. Tex., 1942, MA, 1944; PhD, Yale U., 1949. Geologist Carter Oil Co., Tulsa, 1943-44; asst. and assoc. prof. U. Tex., Austin, 1949-52; rsch. geologist Shell Devel. Co., Houston, 1952-66; prof. Rice U., 1966-79, U. Mich., Ann Arbor, 1979-86; geol. cons. New Braunfels, Tex., 1986—. Cons. Erico Corp., London, 1985-88, Masera Corp., Tulsa, 1988—, Coyote Geol. Svcs., Boulder, Col., 1990—; adj. prof. Rice U., 1986—. Author: Carbonate Facies in Geologic History, 1975; contbr. articles to tech. jours. With C.E., U.S. Army, 1944-46, Italy. Grantee NSF. Fellow: Geol. Soc. Am.; mem.: Con. Soc. Petroleum Geologists, South Tex. Geol. Soc., West. Tex. Geol. Soc., Am. Assn. Petroleum Geologists (hon. Disting. Educator award), Paleontological Soc., Soc. Econ. Paleontology and Mineralogy (pres. 1972—73, field trip guide books 1989, Twenhofel award, Hedberg award, Sidney Powers Meml. award 2002), Internat. Sedimentological Soc. Avocations: piano, languages. Home and Office: 1316 Patio Dr New Braunfels TX 78130-8505 E-mail: mrgrey@nbtx.com.

WILSON, JAMES MILLER, IV, cardiovascular surgeon, educator; b. Atlanta, Mar. 11, 1946; s. James Miller Wilson III and Sara Sharp; m. Lisa VanLandingham; children: James Miller V, Robert Paul, Michael Simpson, Sara Ann. Student, Emory U.; MD, Duke U., 1971. Diplomate Am. Bd. Surgery, Am. Bd. Thoracic Surgery. Intern N.Y. Hosp., 1971-72; resident N.Y. Hosp.-Cornell Med. Ctr., 1972-73, U. Calif., San Francisco, 1975-80; attending staff Christ Hosp., Cin., 1980—, Bethesda Hosp., Cin., 1980—, Jewish Hosp., Cin., 1980—, Univ. Hosp., Cin., 1982—, Deaconess Hosp. Cin., 1982—; chmn. dept. cardiovasc. surgery Deaconess Hosp., 1985—; attending staff VA Med Ctr., 1983—, Children's Hosp., Cin., 1984—, Good Samaritan Hosp., Cin., 1994—; assoc. prof. clin. surgery U. Cin. Coll. Med., 1985—. Open heart surgery adv. com., Ohio, 1995—; dir. cardia surgery Mercy Hosp., 2001; mem. Thoracic Surgery Found.; lectr. in field. Contbr. articles to profl. jours. Lt. Comdr. submarine svc. USN, 1973-75. Fellow ACS, Am. Coll. Cardiology; mem. AMA, U.S. Naval Submarine League, UDT/SEAL Assn., U.S. Submarine Vets., Inc., Am. Assn. Thoracic Surgery, Assn. Acad. Surgery, Soc. Thoracic Surgeons, Am. Heart Assn. (mem. cardiovasc. coun.), Ohio State Med. Assn., Cin. Acad. Medicine, Howard C. Nafziger Soc. Avocations: music, diving, hiking, skiing, horses. Office: 311 Straight St Cincinnati OH 45219-1018

WILSON, JAMES RAY, international business educator; b. Mar. 7, 1930; s. Ray Crawford and Ruth Lee (Walthers) W.; m. Carolyn Dempsey, Feb. 1, 1952; children: Robin E., Victoria, Mark, Jamie. BA (U.S. Navy Coll. Tng. Program scholar), Miami U., Oxford, Ohio, 1952; postgrad., Miami U., 1967-68; MA, Ohio State U., 1956; PhD, U. Minn., 1984. Grad. asst. Ohio State U., 1955-56; grain mcht. Cargill Inc., Balt., 1956-58; pres. Granexport Corp., Manilla, Philipinnes, 1959-66; mng. dir. Tradax Graanhandel B.V., Amsterdam, 1966-67; instr. dept. geography Miami U., 1967-68; pres. Cargill Agricola S.A., Sao Paulo, Brazil, 1968-78; dir. indsl. div. Tradax Geneve S.A., Geneva, 1978-80; corp. v.p. Cargill Inc., Mpls., 1980-83; pres. Cargill S.E. Asia, Ltd., Singapore, 1984-88; internat. bus. prof. Miami U. of Ohio, Oxford, Ohio, 1988-92, prof. mgmt., 1994-98; chmn. Cargill Tech. Svcs., Ltd., Thame, Eng., 1992-94; proprietor Antiquarian Bookstore, 1998—. Served with USN, 1952-55. Fellow Royal Geog. Soc. Congregationalist. Home: 6533 Buckley Rd Oxford OH 45056-9727 Office: Books in Shandon 4795 Cincinnati-Brookville PO Box 8 Shandon OH 45063

WILSON, JAMES REID, JR. publishing executive; b. Phila., Aug. 5, 1934; s. James Reid Wilson and Florence Dunn; m. Eve-Ann Jones; children: Suzanne Winters, Diantha Curtis. BS in Econs., U. Pa., 1956. Assoc. dir. western hemisphere promotion The N.Y. Times, N.Y.C., 1966-69, mgr. indsl. advt., 1969-74; mgr. corp. advt. U.S. News & World Report, 1974-79, advt. mgr., 1979-85, mktg. mgr., 1985-86; sr. v.p. Newspaper Advt. Bur., 1986-93; dir. Izvestia/Hearst, WeMbl, N.Y.C. and Moscow, 1993-94; pres. Media Ptnr., N.Y.C., 1995-97; ad sales dir. Forbes SIP, 1997-2000, v.p., 2000—. Pres. Pa. Assn. Retarded Citizens, 1969-71; sr. v.p. Assn. Retarded Citizens U.S., Arlington, Tex., 1975-77, pres. 1977-79. Mem. St. Nicholas Soc., Union League, Scarsdale Golf Club, Penn Club, N.Y. Sons of the Revolution. Republican. Presbyterian. Office: Forbes SIP 28 W 23rd St New York NY 10010-5204

WILSON, JAMES ROBERT, lawyer; b. Meade, Kans., Dec. 3, 1927; s. Robert J. and Bess O. (Osborne) W.; m. Marguerite Jean Reiter, Nov. 27, 1960; 1 son, John Ramsey. BA, Kans. U., 1950, LL.B., 1953. Bar: Kans. 1953, Nebr. 1961, Colo. 1981. Pvt. practice, Meade, Kans., 1953-57, Lakewood, Colo., 1989-93; county atty. Meade County, 1954-57; city atty. Meade, 1954-57; asst.

gen. counsel Kans. Corp. Commn., 1957-59, gen. counsel, 1959-61, mem., 1961; atty. KN Energy, Inc., 1961-75, personnel dir., 1964-67, v.p., treas., 1968-75, exec. v.p., 1975-78, pres., chief operating officer, 1978-82, pres., chief exec. officer, 1982-85, chmn., pres., chief exec. officer, 1985-88, chmn., 1988-89. Dir. emeritus Farmers Alliance Mut. Ins. Co. With USNR, 1945-46. Mem. Phi Kappa Sigma. Home: 2431 S Xenon Way Lakewood CO 80228-4992 E-mail: jrwilson77@aol.com.

WILSON, JAMES RODNEY, air equipment company executive; b. Kalamazoo, Oct. 5, 1937; s. Orton James and F. Magdalene (Critchelow) W. BA in Psychology, Kalamazoo Coll., 1960. Musician, Kalamazoo, 1955-60; music tchr., 1958-60; capt. U.S. Army, 1960-68; sales rep. Wilson Air Equipment Co., Kalamazoo, 1962-70, v.p. mktg., 1970-91, pres., 1991-2000, chmn., 2001—. Cons. in field. Co-founder Rep. Presdl. Task Force, Washington, 1981—, life mem., 1990—; vol. probation officer Kalamazoo County Juv. Ct., Kalamazoo, 1971—; big bro. Mich. Dept. Social Svcs., Kalamazoo, 1987—; mem. steering com. U.S. Senatorial Bus. Adv. Bd., Washington, 1981-88; bd. dirs. Glowing Embers Coun. Girl Scouts Am., 1994-2000, Kalamazoo Pub. Edn. Found., 1995—, v.p.; bd. dirs. Justus House, 1998—. Recipient Presdl. citation Vols. in Juvenile and Criminal Justice, 1984, Cert. of Merit, Mich. Dept. Social Svcs., 1988, Points of Light award Pres. Bush, 1992, Disting. Svc. award Kalamazoo Coll., 1989. Mem. Chief Engrs. Club Kalamazoo, Kalamazoo Coll. Alumni Assn. (pres. 1984-86), Cathedral Canyon Country Club (Palm Springs, Calif., pres., bd. dirs. 1994—). Republican. Roman Catholic. Avocations: boating, swimming, skiing, exotic auto collecting. Office: Wilson Air Equipment Co PO Box 2620 Kalamazoo MI 49003-2620

WILSON, JAMES ROSS, communications educator, broadcasting executive; b. Petaluma, Calif., Nov. 25, 1939; s. Stanley Thomas and Billie (Ross) W.; m. Elizabeth Ann Buckleman, Dec. 29, 1964 (div. 1982); children: Greg, Tom. BA, Fresno State Coll., 1961; MA, Calif State U., Fresno, 1976. Radio and TV instr. Dept. Def. Info. Sch., Ft. Slocum, N.Y., 1962-65; news dir. Sta. KVON, Napa, Calif., 1965, Sta. KTIM, San Rafael, 1966; news reporter Sta. KMJ, Fresno, 1966-67, news dir., 1967-71; program dir. Sta. KMJ/KNAX-FM, 1971-78, v.p., gen. mgr., 1978-82; news assignment editor Sta. KFSN-TV, 1982-83; prof. mass comm., gen. mgr., faculty advisor KFSR-FM Calif. State U., 1983—; jazz disk jockey Sta. KVPR, Valley Pub. Radio, 1984-90; weekend news anchor KMPH-FM News Radio, 1994-96. Co-author: Mass Media/Mass Culture, 4th edit., 1997, 5th edit., 2000. Recipient Best Newscast award Calif. AP-TV-Radio Assn., 1971, Best News Documentary award Calif. AP-TV-Radio Assn., 1973-74, Broadcast Excellence award Billboard mag., 1976; Calif. State U. grantee, 1987. Mem. Broadcast Edn. Assn., Cen. Calif. Broadcasters Assn. (treas., bd. dirs. 1980-83), Assn. for Edn. in Journalism and Mass Communication, Soc. Profl. Journalists, Alpha Epsilon Rho, Phi Kappa Phi. Home: 4747 E Holland Ave Fresno CA 93726-2914 Office: Calif State U Dept Mass Comm Journalism Fresno CA 93740-0001 E-mail: james_wilson@csufresno.edu.

WILSON, JANE, artist; b. Seymour, Iowa, Apr. 29, 1924; d. Wayne and Cleone (Marquis) W.; m. John Gruen, Mar. 28, 1948; 1 child, Julia. BA, U. Iowa, 1945, MA, 1947. Mem. fine arts faculty Parsons Sch. Design, 1973-83, 89-90. Vis. artist U. Iowa, 1974; adj. assoc. prof. painting and drawing Columbia U., 1975-85, assoc. prof., 1985-86, prof., 1986-88, acting chair, 1986-88; Andrew Mellon vis. prof. painting Cooper Union, 1977-78 One-woman shows include Hansa Gallery, N.Y.C., 1953, 55, 57, Stuttman Gallery, N.Y.C., 1958, 59, Tibor de Nagy Gallery, N.Y.C., annually, 1960-66, Graham Gallery, N.Y.C., 1968, 69, 71, 73, 75, Fischbach Gallery, N.Y.C., 1978, 81, 84, 88, 90, 91, 93, 95, 97, D.C. Moore Gallery, N.Y.C., 1999, 2001, Munson-Williams-Proctor Inst., Utica, N.Y., 1980, Cornell U., Ithaca, N.Y., 1982, Compass Rose Gallery, Chgo, 1988, Am. U., Washington, 1989, U. Richmond, Va., 1990, Earl McGrath Gallery, L.A., 1990-91, 93, Dartmouth Coll., Hanover, N.H., 1991, Arnot Mus., Elmira, N.Y., 1993-94, Parrish Mus., Southampton, N.Y., 1996, Glenn Horowitz Gallery, East Hampton, N.Y., 1996, Heckscher Mus., Huntington, N.Y., 2001; represented in permanent collections Met. Mus., Mus. Modern Art, Whitney Mus., Wadsworth Athenaeum, Heron Art Mus., NYU Rockefeller Inst., Vassar Coll., Pa. Acad. Fine Arts, Hirsch Horn Mus., Washington, Nelson-Atkins Mus., Kansas City, Mo., San Francisco Mus. Modern Art. Recipient Purchase prize Childe Hassam Fund, 1971, 73, 81, Ranger Fund Purchase prize 1977; Ingram-Merrill grantee, 1963, Louis Comfort Tiffany grantee, 1967, Eloise Spaeth award The Guild Hall, East Hampton, N.Y., 1988. Lifetime Achievement award The Guild Hall, 2001. Mem. Am. Acad. Arts and Letters (Award in Art 1985), Nat. Acad. Design (pres. 1992-94), Phi Beta Kappa.

WILSON, JEAN DONALD, endocrinologist, educator; b. Wellington, Tex., Aug. 26, 1932; s. J. D. and Maggie E. (Hill) Wilson. BA in Chemistry, U. Tex., 1951, MD, 1955. Diplomate Am. Bd. Internal Medicine. Intern, then resident in internal medicine Parkland Meml. Hosp., Dallas, 1955—58; clin. assoc. Nat. Heart Inst., Bethesda, Md., 1958—60; instr. internal medicine U. Tex. Southwestern Med. Sch., Dallas, 1960—61, prof., 1968—. Editor: Jour. Clin. Investigation, 1972—77. Sr. asst. surgeon USPHS, 1958—60. Recipient Amory prize, Am. Acad. Arts and Scis., 1977, Fuller prize, Am. Urol. Assn., 1983, Lita Annenberg Hazen award, 1986, Dale medal, Soc. for Endocrinology, 1991, Pincus medal, Worchester Found., 1992. Fellow: Royal Coll. Physicians; mem.: NAS, Endocrine Soc. (Oppenheimer award 1972, Koch award 1993), Am. Soc. Biochemistry and Molecular Biology, Soc. Exptl. Biology and Medicine, Am. Philos. Soc., Assn. Am. Physicians (Kober medal 1999), Am. Soc. Clin. Investigation, Inst. Medicine, Am. Acad. Arts and Scis. (Amory prize 1977). Office: U Tex Southwestern Med Ctr Dept Internal Medicine 5323 Harry Hines Blvd Dallas TX 75390-8857 Fax: 214-648-8917. E-mail: jwils1@mednet.swmed.edu.

WILSON, JEAN MARIE HALEY, civic worker; b. Dallas, Oct. 16, 1921; d. William Eldred and Helen Marie (Littlepage) Haley; m. Edward Lewis Wilson, Jr., Mar. 19, 1943; children: Edward Lewis III, William Haley, Sarah. BA, So. Meth. U., 1943. Bd. dirs. Dallas Symphony Orch. League, 1963-89, sec., 1964-68, 1st v.p., 1968-72, vice chmn. spl. projects, 1977-78, rec. sec., 1984-85, 7th v.p., 1985-86, trustee, 1976-88, showhouse chmn., 1987, corr. sec., 1987-88, seating com. for Youth Concerts; v.p. activities, bd. dirs. Allegro Dallas, Inc., 1986-90; precinct chmn. Dallas Dem. Com., 1952-62; mem. Dallas County Dem. Exec. Com., 1952-62; bd. dirs. TACA (Com. for Fund Raising of Arts), 1975-88; mem. Southwestern hospitality bd. Met. Opera, 1965-70; charter mem., bd. dirs. North Tex. Herb Club, 1974-78; mem. Grand Heritage Ball com. Old City Park, exec. com., 1992-94; mem. exec. com. Les Femmes du Monde fundraising arm Dallas Coun. on World Affairs, 1992-95; docent for tours Dallas Mus. Art, 1997-2000. Mem. Dallas Mus. Art/League, Decorative Arts Guild North Tex., Herb Soc. Am. (life), Am. Hort. Soc., Pewter Collectors Club Am., Royal Hort. Soc., Le Circle Francaise of Dallas (hon. chmn. 1989-95), Mary K. Craig Class, Kappa Alpha Theta. Methodist. Home: 6342 Annapolis Ln Dallas TX 75214-2105 Office: 2909 Maple Ave Dallas TX 75201-1443

WILSON, JIM HAROLD, musician; b. Greenville, S.C., Aug. 18, 1955; s. James Wilson and Lillian (Cotnoir) Doyle; 1 child, Jason Ihbe. Owner L.A. Piano Svcs., Sherman Oaks, Calif., 1978—; recording artist Angel/EMI Classics, N.Y.C., 1998—; owner Willow Bay Music, Sherman Oaks, 1997—. Devel. cons. midi-adaptor for acoustic piano Forte Midi-Mod, 1984. Composer, artist (CD) Northern Seascape, 1998, (CD) Cape of Good Hope, 2001. Founder Our Children's World Found., Hollywood, 1990. Mem. NARAS (chpt. bd. govs. 1997-99). Avocations: freestyle skiing, scuba diving, hiking, travelling. Office: Willow Bay Music 5152 Sepulveda Blvd Ste 123 Sherman Oaks CA 91403-1154

WILSON, JIM LESTER, physician, medical educator; b. Hurley, Mo., Jan. 12, 1944; s. Marvin Lester and Maxine Springer Wilson; m. Margery Ann Peach, May 5, 1973; children: Peter, Matthew, Nathan, Mark. AB, Washington U., 1966; MD, U. Mo., 1970. Diplomate Nat. Bd. Med. Examiners, Coll. Family Physicians Can., Am. Bd. Family Practice, cert. added qualifications in geriat. medicine. Clin. asst. U. Nebr., Omaha, 1974-76; asst. prof. U. Iowa Coll. Medicine, Iowa City, 1976-79; assoc. prof. U. South Ala., Mobile, 1979-86, prof., 1986-89, prof., chmn., 1989-95, East Tenn. State U., Johnson City, 1995—. Item writer Am. Bd. Family Practice, 1983-87; v.p. bd. dirs. Ala. Rural Health, 1991-95; gov. apptd. mem. Ala. Rural Health Care Com., 1991-92, Ala. Commn. on Aging, 1994; mem. peer rev. com. Health Resources and Svcs. Adminstrn., 1993, 94, 95, 97, 99. Assoc. editor: Yearbook of Family Practice, 1977-80; contbr. chpts. to books and articles to profl. jours. Active Diocesan Commns., Episcopal Ch., Central Gulf Coast, 1983-85, 89-92, vestry mem., Mobile, 1988-91, 93-94, Elizabethton, Tenn., 1995-2000; sch. bd. mem. St. Lukes Episcopal Sch., Mobile, 1985-88, 94; bd. dirs. L'Arche, Mobile, 1991-94. Lt. comdr. USN, 1974-76. Recipient Pres. award Ala. Primary Care Assn., 1993; Family Medicine Tng. grantee Health Resources and Svcs. Adminstrn., 1981, 84, 88, 90, 94, 94, 97, 98, 98, 2000, Devel. grantee Ala. Rural Health Bd., 1991, 92, 93, 94, Ednl. Devel. grantee Ala. State Health Planning and Devel. Agy., 1994, 95, Area Health Edn. Ctr. grantee Health Resources and Svcs. Adminstrn., 1995. Fellow Am. Acad. Family Physicians; mem. AMA, AAFP, Am. Geriat. Soc., Soc. Tchrs. Family Medicine. Avocations: gardening, genealogy. Office: East Tenn State Univ PO Box 70621 Johnson City TN 37614-1709 E-mail: wilsonj@etsu.edu.

WILSON, JOANNE M. federal agency administrator; bachelor's, master's, Iowa State U. Tchr. grades 2 and 4, Ames, Iowa; continuing edn. instr. Braille and mobility for blind students La. Tech. U.; founder, dir. La. Ctr. Blind; commr. rehab. svcs. adminstrn. Dept. Edn., Washington, 2001—. Cons. Conn. Bd. Edn. and Svcs. for the Blind, N.J. Orientation and Adjustment Ctr. for the Blind, N.Y. Commn. for the Blind; founder, chair La. Rehab. Svcs. Coun. Office: Dept Edn Rehab Svcs Adminstrn 300 C St SW Washington DC 20202-2531*

WILSON, JOHN ALLEN, neurosurgeon; b. Sharon, Pa., May 16, 1959; s. John Allen and Patricia Ann W.; m. Marian Luise, July 13, 1991; children: Jacob, Megan. BS, Pa. State U., 1980; MD, Jefferson Med. Coll., 1982. Diplomate Am. Bd. Neurol. Surgery. Resident Allegheny Gen. Hosp., Pitts., 1982-85; resident in neurosurgery NYU Hosp., 1985-86, New Eng. Med. Ctr., Boston, 1986-90; staff surgeon Allegheny Gen. Hosp., 1990-93; assoc. prof. neurosurgery Wake Forest U., Winston-Salem, NC, 1993—. Fellow: ACS; mem.: N.C. Neurosurg. Soc. (sec.-treas.), Am. Assn. Neurol. Surgeons, So. Neurol. Assn., Congress of Neurol. Surgeons, Am. Assn. Neurol. Surgeons (advisor to AMA). Office: Wake Forest U Med Ctr Blvd Winston Salem NC 27157-0001

WILSON, JOHN PASLEY, law educator; b. Newark, Apr. 7, 1933; s. Richard Henry and Susan Agnes (Pasley) W.; m. Elizabeth Ann Reed, Sept. 10, 1955 (div.); children: David Cables, John Pasley, Cicely Reed. AB, Princeton U., 1955; LLB, Harvard U., 1962. Bar: N.J. 1962, Mass. 1963, U.S. Dist. Ct. N.J. 1962, U.S. Dist. Ct. Mass. 1963. Budget examiner Exec. Office of Pres., Bur. of the Budget, Washington, 1955-56; assoc. Riker, Danzig, Scherer & Brown, Newark, 1962-63; asst. dean Harvard U. Law Sch., Cambridge, Mass., 1963-67; assoc. dean Boston U. Law Sch., 1968-82; dean Golden Gate U. Sch. Law, San Francisco, 1982-88, prof., 1988—. Vis. prof. dept. health policy and mgmt. Harvard U., 1988; cons. Nat. Commn. for the Protection of Human Subjects of Biomed. and Behavioral Rsch.; mem. Mass. Gov's. Commn. on Civil and Legal Rights of Developmentally Disabled; former chmn. adv. com. Ctr for Cmty. Legal Edn., San Francisco. Author: The Rights of Adolescents in the Mental Health System; contbr. chpts. to books, articles to profl. jours. Bd. dirs. Greater Boston Legal Svcs., Chewonki Found.; mem. Health Facilities Appeals Bd., Commonwealth of Mass.; assoc. mem. Dem. Town Com., Concord; chmn. Bd. Assessors, Concord; bd. overseers Boston Hosp. for Women, past chmn. med. affairs com.; past mem. instl. rev. bd. Calif. Pacific Hosp., San Francisco. Served to lt. (j.g.) USNR, 1956-59. NIMH grantee, 1973. Mem. Nat. Assn. Securities Dealers (arbitrator). Office: Golden Gate U Sch Law 536 Mission St San Francisco CA 94105-2967 E-mail: jwilson@ggu.edu., jwlsn@earthlink.net.

WILSON, JOHN ROBERT, JR. pharmaceutical and chemical company executive; b. Key West, Fla., Mar. 16, 1951; s. John R. and Norma Ruth Wilson; m. Betty Elaine Whitten, Oct. 2, 1982; children: Gregory L., Jason L. BS, Centenary Coll. La., 1974; MA, Rice U., 1990, PhD, 1992; MPH, Columbia U., 2000. Sales rep. Reed & Carnrick Pharms. Inc., Little Rock, 1975-78, Boehringer Ingelheim Pharms. Inc., Little Rock, 1978-82, clin. rsch. assoc. Houston, 1982-89, mgr. Ridgefield, Conn., 1989-91, assoc. dir., 1991-94, dir., 1994-98, Boehringer Ingelheim Chems. Inc., Petersburg, Va., 1998-99, v.p., 1999—. Lectr. N.Y. Med. Coll., Valhalla, 1995-98. Mem. Am. Soc. Quality, Drug Info. Assn., Regulatory Affairs Profl. Soc. Avocations: baseball, philosophy. Home: 12121 Ashton Park Dr Glen Allen VA 23059-7126 Office: Boehringer Ingelheim Chems Inc 2820 Normandy Dr Petersburg VA 23805-9372 Fax: (804) 504-8869. E-mail: jwilson@bichemicals.com.

WILSON, JOHNNIE LOU, social work educator, retired; b. Moscow, Sept. 27, 1928; d. John Wesley and Hattie Idelle (Mitchell) Sprayberry; m. William Hayden Greene Wilson Sr., Apr. 23, 1950 (div.); children: William H. Greene Wilson Jr., John Beverly Greene Wilson, Lynn Greene Wilson Goodrum, David Greene Wilson, Diane Greene Wilson Hawk. AA in Bus. Adminstrn., Lee Coll., 1948; BA, Tex. Woman's U., 1980. Sec. Exxon-Humble, Baytown, Tex., 1947-50; social work lab. supr. Tex. Woman's U., Denton, 1974-94, ret., 1994. Owner Abbey Demo Svcs., Bowie, Tex., 1998—. Author poetry. Mem. Cancer Soc. Denton, 1990-94, Cystic Fibrosis, Denton, 1990-94, Heart Assn., Denton, 1990-94, Mimbres Arts Coun., Silver City, N.Mex., 1996-99, Cmty. Concert Assn., Silver City, 1996-99; sec.-treas. Daus. of King, Denton, 1990—; mem. altar guild St. Barnabas Episcopal Ch., 1990—, fellowship com., 1990-95, vestry, 1992-94, chair food com., 1994-99; mem. Environ. Com., Silver City, 1995-99. Recognition award Famous Poet for 1995, 1995, Editor's Choice award Nat. Libr. Poetry, 1996. Mem. Internat. Soc. Poets (Disting. Mem. award 1996). Democrat. Avocations: poetry, physical fitness, community help projects, church related activities. Home: PO Box 890 503 Malachite Ave Tyrone NM 88065 E-mail: Johnn88062@Juno.com.

WILSON, JOHNNY LEE, publishing executive; b. Santa Maria, Calif., Oct. 20, 1950; s. John Henry and Bobbie Lou (Henson) W.; m. Susan Lynne Leaville, Aug. 28, 1970 (div. 1998); children: Jennifer Lynne, Jonathan Lee; m. Wai Lam Chu, May 21, 1999; children: William Chu, Talyn Chu. BA, Calif. Bapt. Coll., Riverside, 1972; MDiv, Golden Gate Bapt. Seminary, Mill Valley, Calif., 1975; ThM, So. Bapt. Theol. Seminary, Louisville, 1978, PhD, 1981. Pastor Rollingwood Bapt. Ch., San Pablo, Calif., 1974-75, Temple Bapt. Ch., Sacramento, 1975-77, Hermosa-Redondo Beach (Calif.) Ministries, 1981-82, Immanuel. Bapt. Ch., La Puente, Calif., 1982-86; asst. editor Computer Gaming World, Anaheim, 1986-89, editor, 1989-93, editor-in-chief San Francisco, 1993-99; group pub. Wizards of the Coast, Renton, Wash., 1999—2002; pres. and prof. of Old Testament Calif. Korean Bapt. Sem., Walnut, 1990-93; pub., pres. Paizo Pub., LLC, Bellevue, Wash., 2002—. Adj. prof. O.T. studies So. Calif. Ctr., Garden Grove, Calif., 1981-86; mem. com. Software Pub. Assn. Ratings Group, Washington, 1994; mem. adv. coun. Recreation Software Adv. Coun., 1995; bd. govs. Acad. Interactive Arts and Scis., 1995; bd. dirs. Turbine Entertainment. Author: The Sim City Planning Commission Handbook, 1990, The Sim Earth Bible, 1991; co-author: The Mercer Dictionary of Bible, 1990, Holman Bible Dictionary, 1991, Sid Meier's Civilization: Rome on 640K A Day, 1992, Civilization: Call to Power Official Strategy Guide, 1999, Civilization: Call to Power 2 Strategy Guide, 2000, High Score: The First 30 Years of Video Games, 2002. Named to Outstanding Young Men of Am., Jaycees, Ala., 1977, Best Software Reviewer, Software Pubs. Assn., Washington, 1990. Mem. Sci. Fiction and Fantasy Writers Am. (assoc.). Avocations: drama, miniatures gaming, writing. Home: 4664 144th Pl SE Bellevue WA 98006-3158 Office: Paizo Pub LLC 3245 146th Pl SE Ste 101 Bellevue WA 98007 E-mail: johnny.wilson@paizopublishing.com.

WILSON, JOSEPH CHARLES, IV, ambassador; b. Bridgeport, Conn., Nov. 6, 1949; s. Joseph Charles III and Phyllis (Finnell) W.; m. Susan Dale Otchis, Apr. 27, 1973 (div. 1986); m. Valerie Elise Plame, Apr. 3, 1998; children: Sabrina Cecile, Joseph Charles, Trevor Rolph, Samantha Finnell Diana. BA in History, U. Calif., Santa Barbara, 1972. Fgn. svc. officer Dept. of State, Washington, 1976-98; congl. fellow Am. Polit. Sci. Assn., 1985-86; dep. chief of mission Am. Embassy, Bujumbura, Burundi, 1982-85, Brazzaville, Congo, 1986-88, Baghdad, Iraq, 1988-91; amb. Gabon, Sao Tome and Principe, 1992-95; polit. adv. to Commdr. in Chief U.S. Armed Forces Europe, 1995-97; spl. asst. to pres., sr. dir. for African affairs Nat. Security Coun., Washington, 1997-98; pres. JC Wilson Internat. Ventures, 1998—. Recipient Disting. Alumni award U. Calif. Santa Barbara, 1991, Comdr. Order of Equatorial Star govt. Gabon award, 1995, Disting. Def. Dept. Civilian award, 1997; named hon. adm. County Commr., El Paso, Tex., 1991. Mem. Am. Polit. Sci. Assn., Am. Fgn. Svc. Assn. (William R. Rivkin award 1987), U. Calif. Santa Barbara Alumni Assn., San Onofre Surfing Club. Avocations: golf, bicycling, fitness. Office: Ste #300 1717 Pennsylvania Ave NW Washington DC 20006-4619 E-mail: joewilson@rockcreekcorp.com.

WILSON, JOSEPH MORRIS, III, lawyer; b. Milw., July 26, 1945; s. Joseph Morris Jr. and Phyllis Elizabeth (Cresson) W.; children: Elizabeth J., Eric M.; m. Dixie Lee Brock, Mar. 23, 1984. BA, Calif. State U., Chico, 1967; MA, U. Washington, 1968; JD summa cum laude, Ohio State U., 1976. Bar: Alaska 1976, U.S. Dist. Ct. Alaska 1976, U.S. Ct. Appeals (9th cir.) 1986. Recruiter and vol. U.S. Peace Corps, Republic of Benin, 1969-73; legal intern U.S. Ho. of Reps., Washington, 1975; ptnr. Guess & Rudd P.C., Anchorage, 1976-88, chmn. comml. dept., 1981-82, ptnr. compensation com., 1982-84; mgr. Alaska taxes, sr. tax atty. BP Exploration Inc., Alaska, 1990-99. Bus. law instr. U. Alaska, Anchorage, 1977-78. Mem. Alaska Bar Assn., World Affairs Coun. Democrat. Avocations: music, sports, travel. Home and Office: 2556 Palmera Cir Las Vegas NV 89121-4016 E-mail: jsphwlsn@aol.com.

WILSON, JUDITH FALTYSEK, development executive; b. Oak Park, Ill., Jan. 22, 1945; d. Paul Holmes and Mary Jane (Ward) Faltysek; m. Anthony Parks Wilson, Aug. 20, 1966; children: Catherine Holmes, Christopher Ward. BS, Northwestern U., 1967. Tchr. Ewing Twp. Schs., Trenton, N.J., 1967-70; cons. Bensinger, DuPont & Assoc., Chgo., 1981-90; assoc. dir. devel. Lawrenceville (N.J.) Sch., 1990-94; dir. of devel. Out-of-Door Acad., Sarasota, Calif., 1995. Bd. dirs., chmn. Jr. League of Chgo., 1976-81; bd. dirs., benefit chmn. Infant Welfare Soc. Chgo., 1978-86; mem. founders group Women in Devel., Princeton, N.J., 1992-95. Named Vol. of Yr. for drug edn. of parents Chgo. Mag., 1983. Mem. Nat. Soc. Fundraising Execs., Jr. League of San Francisco. Episcopalian. Home: 2900 Pacific Ave Apt 101 San Francisco CA 94115-1065

WILSON, JULIA ANN YOTHER, lawyer; b. Dallas, Sept. 6, 1958; d. Julian White and Mary Ann (Estes) Yother. BA, East Ctrl. U., Ada, Okla., 1980; JD, U. Okla., 1983. Bar: Okla. 1990, Calif. 1993, D.C. 1995; U.S. Ct. Appeals (9th cir.) Calif. 1993, U.S. Supreme Ct. 1993, U.S. Dist. Ct. (ctrl. dist.) Calif. 1993, U.S. Dist. Ct. (we. dist.) Okla., 1997. Assoc. Law Office of George Rodda Jr., Newport Beach, Calif., 1984-96; sole practice law Oklahoma City, 1996-97; assoc. Coldiron, Wilson & Assocs., 1997—. Served to 1st lt. USAR, 1980-86. Mem. ABA, D.C. Bar Assn., Calif. Bar Assn., Oklahoma County Bar Assn., Okla. Bar Assn. (litigation sect.), Orange County Bar Assn. Office: Coldiron Wilson & Assocs 1800 E Memorial Rd Ste 106 Oklahoma City OK 73131-1827

WILSON, KAREN LEE, museum director; b. Somerville, N.J., Apr. 2, 1949; d. Jon Milton and Laura Virginia (Van Dyke) W.; m. Paul Ernest Walker, 1980; 1 child, Jeremy Nathaniel. AB, Harvard U., 1971; MA, NYU, 1973, PhD, 1985. Rsch. assoc., dir. excavation at Mendes, Egypt Inst. Fine Arts, NYU, 1979-81; coord. exhbn. The Jewish Mus., N.Y.C., 1981-82, adminstrv. cataloguer, 1982-83, coord. curatorial affairs, 1984-86; curator Oriental Inst. Mus. U. Chgo., 1988-96, mus. dir., 1996—. Author, editor: Mendes, 1982; contbr. articles to profl. jours. Mem.: Coll. Art Assn., Am. Oriental Soc. E-mail: k_wilson@uchicago.edu.

WILSON, KAREN LEROHL, lawyer; b. Albuquerque, Sept. 15, 1950; d. John Kenneth Sr. and Ann Castleman (Lawrence) LeRohl; children: Teddy, Tommy. BA, William & Mary U., 1972; JD, Am. U., 1978; LLM, George Washington U., 1982. Bar: Va. 1979, Calif. 1984, U.S. Claims Ct. 1980, U.S. Ct. Appeals (4th cir.) 1981, U.S. Supreme Ct. 1982. Supr. law dept. Prudential Ins. Co., Washington, 1972-74; law clk. Arnold & Porter, 1975-78; atty., advisor Def. Logistics Agy., Alexandria, Va., 1978-80, Office Sec. Def., Washington, 1980-84; counsel TRW Corp., Redondo Beach, Calif., 1984-87; asst. group counsel Hughes Aircraft Co., El Segundo, 1987-92; group contr., dir. govt. rels. and compliance Allied Signal Inc., Torrance, 1992-94, v.p. bus. ethics and govt. compliance, 1994-97, v.p. govt. fin. and process excellence, 1998-2000; trustee Def. Acquisition U.; v.p. govt. bus. & fin. Allied Signal Inc., Torrance, Calif., 2000—. Mem. adv. bd.: Fed. Contracts Report; contbr. articles to profl. jours. Recipient Presdl. Sports award Pres. Carter, Washington, 1980; Disting. Youth award U.S. Army, 1976. Mem. ABA (dep. chmn. 1980), Fed. Bar Assn., Va. Bar Assn., Calif. Bar Assn., Nat. Contract Mgmt. Assn. (nat. advisor, trustee), Fin. Execs. Inst. (past chmn. govt. bus. com., exec. coun.), Ethics Officers Assn., Inst. Mgmt. Accts., Inst. Internal Auditors, William and Mary Coll. Alumni Assn. (v.p. greater L.A. 1987-88), Am. Corp. Counsel Assocs., Aerospace Industries Assn. (past chmn. procurement and fin. exec. com.), Inst. Noetic Scis., Internat. Alliance Holistic Lawyers, Cameron Sta. Tennis Club (pres. 1980), Michelob Light Tennis Club (capt. 1983). Republican. Office: Allied Signal Aerospace M/S Torr-38-1-01422 2525 W 190th St Torrance CA 90504-6002

WILSON, KAREN WILKERSON, paralegal; b. Reidsville, N.C., June 28, 1957; d. William Henry and Jean Gloria (Tiller) W.; married. Student, N.C. State U., 1975-77, Western Carolina U., Cullowhee, N.C., 1978-80; diploma, Profl. Ctr. Paralegal Studies, Columbia, S.C., 1988. Paralegal Ken H. Lester, Esquire, Columbia, 1989—, Lester & Jones, Columbia. Spkr. Alumni Profl. Ctr. Paralegal Studies, Columbia, 1988-95. Mem. ATLA, S.C. Trial Lawyers Assn. (paralegal rep. 1993-96). Democrat. Presbyterian. Office: Lester & Jones 1716 Main St Columbia SC 29201-2820

WILSON, KEITH B. medical educator; b. Spartanburg, S.C., Feb. 19, 1962; s. George and Helen Annette Wilson; m. Beverly Jean Gaither, June 13, 1992; 1 child Aliya Imani. BA, Wilberforce U.; MEd, Kent State U., 1985; PhD, Ohio State U., 1997. Cert. rehab. counselor. Case mgr. Ohio Bur. Vocat. Rehab., Canton, 1985; counseling coord. Savannah (Ga.) State U., 1986—89; dir. counseling svc. Brewton-Parker Coll., Mt. Vernon, 1989—94; grad. program asst. Ohio State U., Columbus, 1994—95, tchg. asst., 1995—97; asst. prof. Pa. State U., State College, 1997—. Cons. Brewton-Parker Coll., Mt. Vernon, 1993; mem. adv. bd. Pa. Office Vocat. Rehab., Harrisburg, 1998—; cons. Indiana U. Pa., 2000. Author: (newsletter) Mosaic, 2001; co-editor: Rehab. Counseling Bull., 2002. Judge Pa. State Grad. Exhbn., State College, 2001; vice chairperson Multicultural Ad. Com., Harrisburg, 2001; bd. dirs. Inst. Sci. Advancement, 2001. Recipient Bobbie Atkins Rsch. award, Nat. Assn. Multicultural, 2001. Mem.: Pa. Counseling Assn. (Named Outstanding Rschr. 2000), Pa. Rehab. Assn., Phi Beta Kappa. Home: 109 Berwick Dr Boalsburg PA 16827 Office: Pa State U Counselor Edn 308 Cedar Bldg State College PA 16802-3110 Office Fax: 814-863-7750. Business E-Mail: kbw4@psu.edu.

WILSON, KEITH CHARLES, retired English educator, poet, short story writer; b. Clovis, N. Mex., Dec. 26, 1927; s. Earl Charles and Marjorie Valentine (Edwards) W.; m. Lorna Heloise Brigham, Feb. 15, 1958; children: Lorna Kathleen, Kristin Mavournin, Kevin O'Keith, Kerrin Noel. BS in Engring., U.S. Naval Acad., 1950; MA in English, U. N. Mex., 1958. Staff mem. Sandia Corp., Albuquerque, 1958-60; instr. English U. Ariz., Tucson, 1960-65; from asst. prof. to full prof. N. Mex. State U., Las Cruces, 1965-86. Vis. poet U. Kansas, Utah State U., U. Sibiu, Romania, Cluj-Napoca, Romania; vis. dir. workshops U. N. Mex., Bowling Green State U., SUNY, Cortland, Utah State U., Banff Art Ctr., Can. and others; cons. to Coordinating Coun. for Literary Mags., 1972-74, for NEA to Voice of Am., 1975; master poet N. Mex. Poetry in the Schs. Program; disting. vis. writer U.S. Naval Acad., 1998. Author: (books of poetry) Sketches for a New Mexico Hill Town, 1967, II Sequences, 1967, The Old Car, 1967, Graves Registry and Other Poems, 1969 (Lamont prize runner-up), Homestead, 1969, Rocks, 1971, The Shadow of Our Bones, 1971, The Old Man and Others: Some Faces for America, 1971, Psalms for Various Voices, Midwatch, Thantog: Songs of a Jaguar Priest, 1977, The Shaman Deer, 1977, While Dancing Feet Shatter the Earth, 1977 (Nat. Book award nominee), Desert Cenote, 1978, The Streets of San Miguel, 1979, Retablos, 1981, Stone Roses: Poems from Transylvania, 1983, Lovesongs and Mandalas, 1984, Lion's Gate: Selected Poems, 1963-86, 1988, The Winds of Pentecost, 1991, Graves Registry, 1992 (nominated for Nat. Book award, Critics Circle award, Western States Art Found. Book award, P.E.N., West Book award), The Way of the Dove, 1994, Warrior's Song and Other Poems, 1996, Etudes, 1998, Bosque Redondo, 2000; poems have been translated into Spanish, Polish, Japanese, Romanian, Hungarian, German and Indonesian. Lt. USN, 1950-54, Korea. Recipient Lifetime Achievement award Border Book Festival; D.H. Lawrence fellowship U. N. Mex., 1971,

Creative Writing fellowship Nat. Endowment for the Arts, Washington, 1974-75, Fulbright-Hays fellowship, Romania, 1974-75; grantee P.E.N., Am. Ctr., N.Y.C., 1971. Mem. Rio Grande Inst. Democrat. Episcopalian. Avocation: pen collector. Home: 1500 S Locust St Las Cruces NM 88001-5356 E-mail: kewilson@ivmsu.edu.

WILSON, KEITH DUDLEY, retired media and music educator, consultant; b. Windermere, July 13, 1936; s. Charles Alexander and Fanny (Shaw) W.; 1 child, Nicholas. BA with honors, Kings Coll., Cambridge, 1957, MA, 1960; LittD (hon.), U. Salford, 2000. Lectr. Brit. Coun./Zagreb Univ., Croatia, 1957-58; assoc. prof., dir. TV Brit. Coun. Tehran U., Iran, 1958-64; reader Brit. Coun. Osmania U., Hyderabad, India, 1964-66; head of liberal edn. Salford Coll. of Tech., U.K., 1967-72, head of humanities U.K., 1972-85; head of performing arts and media U. Coll. Salford, 1985-90; dir. ctr. for media performance and comm. U. Salford, 1990-96, founding chief exec. internat. media ctr., 1993-99; dean faculty of media, music and performance Salford U., 1996-99. Tutor, counsellor Open U., 1972-90; dir. TVUK, Adelphi Prodns., Salford, 1988-99, Channel M, 1997-2000; chair PRS John Lennon awards, 1990-93; co-chair NYNEX Cable TV, Manchester, 1993-95; vis. acad. The Brit. Coun., Korea, 1992; founder over 30 higher edn. courses in music, media, drama, recording, entertainment orgns., media and science, new media; European edn. advisor/cons. media, music and rec. industries, 2000—. Contbr. articles to profl. jours. and nat. papers; concert tours to Brazil, Belgium, Holland, Iceland, Norway, Denmark, Greece, Ecuador, Russia and Hungary; residencies at Edinburgh Internat. Festival, broadcasts and recordings, 1986-97. Mem. U. Salford Centenary Com., 1994-96, City of Salford LS Lowry Centenary, 1988, The Lowry, The Nat. Landmark Millennium Project for the Arts, The Digital World Ctr.; founder Salford U. Brass Band, Wind Band, Big Band, Soundworks, Jazz Ensembles, Groove Machine, Aspects Theatre; mem. City Pride Initiative, Manchester, 1993-97, Fellowship Gt. Britain Sasakawa Found., Japan, 1991. Fellow Royal Soc. of Arts; mem. Royal TV Soc., British Film Inst., British Acad. of Film and TV., Prodrs. Assn. Cinema and TV. Avocations: nordic lands and culture, wines of the world, walking. Home and Office: 60 Central Rd Didsbury Manchester M204 ZA England

WILSON, KEITH MARK, health services administrator; b. Carbondale, Ill., Jan. 1, 1971; s. Scott and Doreen Wilson. BBA in Mgmt., State U. West Ga., 1994. Employed in healthcare industry Beverly Enterprises, Douglasville, Ga., 1987—; adminstr. Mariner Health Care, Austell, 1997—. Mem. Am. Coll. Health Care Adminstrs. Home: 8628 Wood Springs Ct Douglasville GA 30135-1686 E-mail: Killerwilson@hotmail.com., A11135@marinerhealthcare.com.

WILSON, KELLY G. psychologist, educator; b. Olympia, Wash., Sept. 22, 1954; s. Gary Wilson and Barbara J. Blencoe, James O. Blencoe (Stepfather); m. Dianna M. Linder; children: Chelsea May, Emma Jane, Sarah Rose. AA, Spokane Falls C.C., 1987; BA summa cum laude, Gonzaga U., 1989; PhD, U. of Nev., Reno, 1998. Assoc. dir. of the ctr. for contextual psychology U. of Nev., Reno, 1997—2000; asst. prof. U. of Miss., University, Miss., 2000—; dir. of the ctr. for contextual psychology U. of Nev., 2001—. Author: Acceptance and Commitment Therapy: An Experiential Approach to Behavior Change, 1999; contbr. chapters to books. Recipient Outstanding Svc. Award, Spokane County Assn. for Retarded Citizens, 1988, Regent's Outstanding Student award, U. of Nev., 1994; scholar Gonzaga Academic scholar, Gonzaga U., 1987—89, Gonzaga Alumni Class of 1969 scholar, 1987—89, Father Irwin Toner, S.J. scholar, 1987—89, Father Cliff Caroll, S.J. scholar, 1987—89, Mr. and Mrs. F. Linzie scholar, 1987—89, Wilson scholar, U. of Nev., 1989—91, Grad. Student Assn. scholar, 1995—96. Mem.: Soc. for a Sci. of Clin. Psychology, Assn. for the Advancement of Behavior Therapy, Assn. for Behavior Analysis (chmn. of the clin. spl. interest group 1997—99), Am. Psychol. Soc. Office: Psychology 203 Peabody University of Mississippi Rochester NH 03867 Office Fax: 662-915-5398. Business E-Mail: kwilson@olemiss.edu.

WILSON, KENNETH JAY, writer; b. Oklahoma City, Aug. 25, 1944; s. Kenneth J. and Betty Wallace (Bleakmore) W. BA magna cum laude, Yale U., 1966, M.Phil., 1969; postgrad. Queen's Coll., Oxford U., Eng., 1969-70; PhD, Yale U., 1974. From instr. to assoc. prof. English U. Rochester, N.Y., 1970-83; assoc. Clare Hall, Cambridge U., Eng., 1977; vis. assoc. prof. English Coll. William and Mary, Williamsburg, Va., 1983; editor in chief Peter Lang Pub., N.Y.C., 1983-87; dir. of rights and permissions Princeton U. Press, 1987-88; commissioning editor polit. sci. and psychology Routledge, N.Y.C., 1988-90; adminstrv. dir. HIV Clin. Rsch. Ctr. Mt. Zion Med. Ctr./U. Calif., San Francisco, 1994-95. Cons. USIA, 1985 Editor: Letters of Sir Thomas Elyot, 1976, English Works of Thomas More, 1978; author: Incomplete Fictions, 1985, Pope John Paul II, 1992; contbr. essays, book revs. and short fiction to mags. and profl. jours. Woodrow Wilson fellow, 1966, 83; sr. fellow Folger Shakespeare Library, Washington, 1976; Am. Philos. Soc. grantee, 1976; Am. Council Learned Soc. fellow, 1977 Mem. Mory's Club, Elizabethan Club (New Haven), Yale Club (N.Y.C.), Palm-Aire Country Club, Phi Beta Kappa. Democrat. Roman Catholic. Home: 5570 Country Club Way Sarasota FL 34243-3759 E-mail: nuboy@comcast.net.

WILSON, KENNETH GEDDES, physics research administrator; b. Waltham, Mass., June 8, 1936; s. E. Bright and Emily Fisher (Buckingham) Wilson; m. Alison Brown, 1982. AB, Harvard U., 1956, DSc (hon.), 1981; PhD, Calif. Tech. Inst., 1961, U. Chgo., 1976. From asst. prof. to prof. physics Cornell U., Ithaca, NY, 1963—88, James A. Weeks prof. in phys. sci., 1974—87; Hazel C. Youngberg Trustees Disting prof. The Ohio State U., Columbus, 1988—. Co-author: Redesigning Education, 1974. Recipient Nobel prize in Physics, 1982, Dannie Heinemann prize, 1973, Boltzmann medal, 1975, Wolf prize, 1980, A.C. Eringen medal, 1984, Franklin medal, 1982, Aneesur Rahman prize, 1993. Mem.: NAS, Am. Acad. Arts and Scis., Am. Phys. Soc., Am. Philos. Soc.

WILSON, LANFORD, playwright; b. Lebanon, Mo., Apr. 13, 1937; s. Ralph E(ugene) and Violetta (Tate) W. Student, San Diego State Coll., 1955-56; PhD in Humanities (hon.), U. Mo., 1985, Grinnell Coll., 1994; PhD in Lit. (hon.), Southampton Coll., 1995. Playwright, 1962—; resident playwright, dir., co-founder Circle Repertory Co., N.Y.C., 1969-95. Author: (plays) So Long at the Fair, 1963, Home Free!, 1964, No Trespassing, 1964, The Sandcastle, 1964, The Madness of Lady Bright, 1964, Ludlow Fair, 1965, Balm in Gilead, 1965, This is the Rill Speaking, 1965, Days Ahead, 1965, Sex is Between Two People, 1965, The Gingham Dog, 1966, The Rimers of Eldritch, 1966, Wandering, 1966, Lemon Sky, 1969, Serenading Louie, 1970, The Great Nebula in Orion, 1970, The Hot L Baltimore, 1972, The Family Continues, 1972, The Mound Builders, 1975, Fifth of July, 1978, Brontasaurus, 1978, Talley's Folly, 1979, A Tale Told, 1981, Angels Fall, 1983, A Betrothal, 1984, Talley & Son, 1985, Burn This, 1987, A Poster of the Cosmos, 1987, The Moonshot Tape, 1990, Redwood Curtain, 1991, Trinity, 1993, I'm Not the Ocean, 1995, Sympathetic Magic, 1996, A Sense of Place (or Virgil is Still the Frogboy), 1997, Your Everyday Ghost Story, 1997, Book of Days, 1998, Rain Dance, 1999; translator Three Sisters, 1984, Ghosts, 2002; author: (books) Balm in Gilead and Other Plays, 1966, The Rimers of Eldritch and Other Plays, 1968, The Gingham Dog, 1969, Lemon Sky, 1970, The Hot L Baltimore, 1973, The Mound Builders, 1976, Fifth of July, 1979, Talley's Folly, 1980, Angels Fall, 1983, Serenading Louie, 1985, Talley & Son, 1986, Burn This, 1988, Redwood Curtain, 1992, 21 Short Plays, 1994, By the Sea, 1996, Collected Plays, Vol. I, 1997, Vol. II, 1999, Vol. III, 1999, A Sense of Place, 1999, Sympathetic Magic, 1999, Book of Days, 2001. ABC Yale fellow, 1969; Rockefeller grantee, 1967, 73, Guggenheim grantee, 1970, NEA grantee, 1990; recipient Vernon Rice award, 1966-67, Inst. Arts and Letters award, 1970, Obie award, 1972, 75, 84, 97, Outer Critics Circle award, 1973, Drama Critics Circle award, 1973, 80, Pulitzer prize, 1980, Brandeis award, 1981, John Steinbeck award, 1990, Edward Albee Last Frontier award, 1994, Am. Acad. of Achievement award, 1995, Am. Assn. Theatre Critics Best Play award, 1998, Guild Hall Lifetime Achievement award, 2000, William Inge Lifetime Achievement award, 2001; inducted into Theater Hall of Fame, 1996, Mo. Writers Hall of Fame, 1998; recipient Lucille Lortel's Edith Oliver award for Sustained Excellence, 2001. Mem. Dramatists Guild Am. Council.

WILSON, LANNA J. writer, writer; b. San Jose, Calif., May 10, 1974; d. Richard W. and Carroll J. Carter; m. Brian R. Wilson; 1 child Porter D. BA in Print Journalism, Brigham Young U., 1996. Assoc. editor Internat. Mag Liahona, Salt Lake City, 1998—99; promotions editor Bill Good Mktg., South Jordan, 1999—2001; mgr. Rema, Salt Lake City, 2000—01; editor Intermountain Contractor, 2001. Contbr. articles to profl. jours. Key vol. coord. U.S. Marine Corps., Salt Lake City, 2000—. Recipient 2d pl. music competition, Rotary, 1992; scholar, San Bernadino County Music Educator Assn., 1988—92. Avocations: piano, writing, travel. Home: 6729 S 615 E #B Midvale UT 84047

WILSON, LAVERNE, nursing administrator; b. Fontaine, Ark., July 27, 1931; d. James Gordon and Sophronia (Scott) Nutt; m. John Bruce Wilson, June 30, 1950 (div. 1971); children: Deborah French, Emily Wilson-Godinet, Valerie Keating, John B. Jr., B.G. Scott Wilson. AA, Ark. State U., 1974. Cert. health facility surveyor. Charge nurse Ark. Methodist Hosp., Paragould, 1975-78; instr. Delta Vo-Tech, Marked Tree, Ark., 1978-81; clin. nurse educator VA Hosp., North Little Rock, 1981-83; adminstrv. coordi. Ark. Methodist Hosp., Paragould, 1983—, in-svc. coord., 1983-88; coord. inspection of care rev. Ark. Found. for Med. Care, Ft. Smith, 1988-90; nursing home insp. and utilization rev. nurse Office of Long Term Care, Dept. Human Svcs., State of Ark., 1990—; pres. J.G.N., Inc. Mem. Ark. Bus. and Profl. Women's Orgn., Alpha Gamma Delta. Democrat. Baptist. Avocations: travel, boating. Home: 4905 Burrow Dr North Little Rock AR 72116-7019

WILSON, LAWRENCE WOODROW, retired air force officer, family physician; b. Mpls., Oct. 25, 1945; s. Henry Woodrow and Bonnie Laurette (Carlson) W.; m. Patricia Joanne Keenan, June 24, 1979; children: Patricia Kathleen, Scott Woodrow. BS, USAF Acad., 1967; MD, U. N.D., 1978; MBA, U. Phoenix, 2001. Diplomate Am. Bd. Family Practice. Intern Hennepin County Med. Ctr., Mpls., 1978-79; resident U. N.D., Bismarck, 1979-81; commd. 2d lt. USAF, 1967, advanced through grades to col., 1994; spl. agt. USAF Office of Spl. Investigation, 1981—89; family practice physician USAF, various cities, 1981-99, ret., 1999; med. dir. utilization mgmt. Blue Cross Blue Shield/HMO of N.Mex., 2000—. Fellow Am. Acad. Family Practice. E-mail: lwilson628@aol.com.

WILSON, LEIGH ANN, writer, educator; b. Florence, Ala., Sept. 5, 1971; d. Gerald Lee and Jimmie Lou (Allen) W.; 1 child, Matthew. BA, U. North Ala., 1993; MS, Kans. State U., 1995; postgrad., U. Tex., El Paso, 1998-99, U. Memphis, 2001—. Asst. editor Learning Resources Network, Manhattan, Kans., 1994; grad. tchg. asst. Kans. State U., 1995; freelance writer, Kans., 1993-96, Sanford, N.C., 1996-98, El Paso, Tex., 1993, 98-2000; instr. English as a Second Lang. El Paso C.C., 1999-2000; dir. continuing profl. edn. Dyersburg (Tenn.) State C.C., 2000—. Comms. dir. Jonesboro United Meth. Ch., Sanford, 1996-98, newsletter editor, 1996- 98; instr. GED prep. Am. Inst. of English, El Paso, 1998-99. Author: (geneal. rsch.) The Wilsons: A Study of..., 1996, The American Dream, 1997; co-author: Demographics of Tabloid Journalists, 1995. Reader's Digest Ednl. Found. grantee, 1995. Mem. Am. Assn. Women in C.C. (program chair 2001-02), U. North Ala. Alumni Assn., Kans. State U. Alumni Assn., Exch. Club of Dyer County (chair child abuse prevention 2002), Omega Phi Alpha (2d v.p. 1992, Individual Achievement Svc. award 1992). Avocations: reading, writing, sports, wine collecting, travel. Home: 533 Troy Ave Apt 4A Dyersburg TN 38024 E-mail: wilson@dscc.edu, leighann_w@hotmail.com.

WILSON, LELAND EARL, petroleum engineering consultant; b. Ft. Recovery, Ohio, Oct. 28, 1925; s. John Huffman and Matilda Caroline (Sunderhaus) W.; m. Marian Ruthetta Trygstad, Nov. 27, 1948; children: Kathleen Ann, Linda Kay, Mary Lee, John Russell. BS in Petroleum Engring., Tulsa U., 1950. Registered profl. engr., Alaska, Tex. Drilling engr. Atlantic Refining Co., Tex., Ark., and La., 1950-56, drilling supr. La., Tex., 1956-65; drilling supt. Atlantic Richfield, Anchorage, 1965-67, prodn. and drilling supt., 1967-72; ops. mgr. ARCO Oil Prodn. Co., London, 1972-75; resident mgr. ARCO Greenland, Copenhagen, 1975-78; pres. ARCO Indonesia, Inc., Jakarta, 1978-82; v.p. ARCO China, Hong Kong, 1982-85; petroleum cons. Lindale, Tex., 1985—. Bd. dirs. Houma Oil Treaters, Inc. Author family history Dear John, 1989; contbr. articles to profl. jours.; inventor in field. Aviation cadet AAF, 1943-45. Mem. NSPE, Tex. Soc. Profl. Engrs., Soc. Petroleum Engrs., Petroleum Club (pres. Anchorage 1971-72), Indonesian Petroleum Assn. (pres. 1981-82). Republican. Roman Catholic. Avocations: geneaology, golf, travel. Home: PO Box 893 428 Lone Star Ln Lindale TX 75771-5230 Office: PO Box 893 2715 S Main St Lindale TX 75771-7724

WILSON, LEONARD GILCHRIST, history of medicine educator; b. Orillia, Ont., Can., June 11, 1928; s. George Edward and Mary Agnes (MacPhee) W.; m. Adelia Katherine Hans, June 7, 1969; 1 child, George Edward Hans. BA, U. Toronto, Can., 1949; M.Sc., U. London, 1955; PhD, U. Wis., Madison, 1958. Lectr. Mount Allison U., Sackville, N.B., Can., 1950-53; vis. instr. U. Calif., Berkeley, 1958-59; asst. prof. Cornell U., Ithaca, N.Y., 1959-60, Yale U., New Haven, 1960-65, assoc. prof., 1965-67; prof., head dept. history of medicine U. Minn., Mpls., 1967-98, prof. emeritus, 1998—. Author: Charles Lyell: The Years to 1841: The Revolution in Geology, 1972, Medical Revolution in Minnesota, 1989, Lyell in America: The Trans Atlantic Years, 1841-1853, 1998; editor: Benjamin Silliman and His Circle, 1979, Sir Charles Lyell's Scientific Journals on the Species Question, 1971; editor Jour. History Medicine and Allied Scis., 1973-82; co-editor: Readings in History of Physiology, 1966; mem. bd. mgrs. Jour. Hist. Medicine, 1962— . Fellow AAAS; mem. Am. Assn. History of Medicine, Am. Hist. Assn., History of Sci. Soc., Minn. Acad. Medicine (pres. 1984-85, sec.-treas. 1989-98), Brit. Soc. for the History of Sci., Soc. for the History of natural History. Home: 797 Goodrich Ave Saint Paul MN 55105-3344 E-mail: wilso004@maroon.tc.umn.edu.

WILSON, LESLIE, biochemist, cell biologist, biology educator; b. Boston, June 29, 1941; s. Samuel Paul Wilson and Lee (Melnicker) Kamerling; m. Carla Helena Van Wingerden, Sept. 9, 1989; children from previous marriage: Sebastian A. Michael, Naomi Beth. BS, Mass. Coll. Pharmacy and Allied Health Scis., 1963; PhD, Tufts U., 1967; postdoctoral study, U. Calif. at Berkeley, 1967-69; doctorate honoris causa, U. de la Méditerranée, Marseille, France, 1998. Asst. prof. dept. pharmacology Stanford U. Sch. Medicine, 1969-74; assoc. prof. dept. biol. scis. U. Calif., Santa Barbara, 1975-78, prof. biochemistry, 1979—, chmn. dept. biol. scis., 1987-91, head divsn. molecular, cellular, devel. biol., 1992-93. Sci. adv. panel mem. cell and devel. biology Am. Cancer Soc., Atlanta, 1984-88; cons. Eli Lilly & Co., Indpls., 1980—, Tularik Corp., San Francisco, Amgen Corp., Thousand Oaks, Calif.; scientific adv. bd. Mycogenetics, 1990-92, Panphytica, Inc., 2001-, Genyous Life Scis., 2001-; co-organizer Internat. Colloquium on the Cytoskeleton and human dis., Marseille, France, 2001. Editor: Methods in Cell Biology, 1987—; assoc. editor: Biochemistry, 1992—. Bd. dirs. Cancer Ctr., Santa Barbara. Rsch. grantee NIH, 1970—, Am. Cancer Soc., 1986-97, Lilly Rsch. Labs., 1990—2001, Phone-Poulenc-Rover, France, 1998—2001, Pierre Fabre Medicament, Castres, France, 1998-. Mem. AAAS, Am. Soc. Cell Biology (chmn. sci. program 1977), Am. Soc. Biol. Chemistry and Molecular Biology, Am. Soc. Pharmacology and Exptl. Therapeutics, Am. Chem. Soc. Democrat. Office: U Calif Dept Molecular Cellular & Devel Biology Santa Barbara CA 93106 E-mail: wilson@lifesci.ucsb.edu.

WILSON, LESTER ARNAULD, III, lawyer; BA, U. Va., 1970; JD, Emory U., 1973. Bar: Va. 1973, U.S. Dist. Ct. (ea. dist.) Va. 1973. Asst. city atty. City of Norfolk, Va., 1973-75; pvt. practice Charlottesville, 1975-78, 92—; asst. commonwealth atty. Conty of Albemarle, 1978-82, dep. commonwealth atty., 1982-90, commonwealth atty., 1990-92; dir. student legals svcs. U. Va., 1998—. Bd. dirs. Community Diversion Incentive Program, Charlottesville, 1990-92, Jefferson Area Crime Stoppers, Charlottesville, 1988-92. Mem. Va. State Bar, Va. Bar Assn., Charlottesville-Albemarle Bar Assn. Episcopalian. Avocation: canoeing. Office: 204 University Way Charlottesville VA 22903-1822

WILSON, LEVON EDWARD, law educator, lawyer; b. Charlotte, N.C., Apr. 2, 1954; s. James A. and Thomasina Wilson. BSBA, Western Carolina U., 1976; JD, N.C. Ctrl. U., 1979; Ed D, 2001. Bar: N.C. 1981, U.S. Dist. Ct. (mid. dist.) N.C. 1981, U.S. Tax Ct. 1981, U.S. Ct. Appeals (4th cir.) 1982, U.S. Supreme Ct. 1984; lic. real estate broker, N.C.; cert. mediator N.C. Alternative Dispute Resolution Commn., arbitrator BBB. Pvt. practice, Greensboro, N.C., 1981-85; asst. county atty. Guilford County, 1985-88; asst. prof. N.C. Agrl. & Tech. State U., 1988-91, Western Carolina U., Cullowhee, NC, 1991-96, prof., head dept. bus. adminstrn., law and mktg., 1996—2002; pres. Integrated Mgmt. Resources, Inc., 2000—. Pres. Trade Brokers Cons.; legal counsel, bd. dirs. Rhodes Assocs., Inc., Greensboro, 1982—; legal counsel Guilford County Sheriff's Dept., Greensboro, 1985-88; bd. dirs. Webster Enterprises, Inc. Contbr. articles to profl. jours. Bd. dirs. Post Advocacy Detention Program; active mem. Prison Litigation Study Task Force, Adminstrn. Justice Study Com. Recipient Svc. award Blacks in Mgmt., 1980, Excellence in Tchg. award Jay I. Kneedler Found. of Western Carolina U., 1994-95; Student in Free Enterprise fellow. Mem. ABA, N.C. Bar Assn., Acad. Legal Studies in Bus., Southeastern Acad. Legal Studies in Bus. (former editor-in-chief Jour. of Legal Studies in Bus., mng. editor), N.C. Assn. Police Attys., N.C. Real Estate Educators Assn., So. Acad. Legal Studies in Bus., Phi Delta Phi, Beta Gamma Sigma. Democrat. Methodist. Home: PO Box 620 Cullowhee NC 28723-0620 Office: Western Carolina U Coll of Bus Cullowhee NC 28723 Personal E-mail: levonwilson@msn.com. Business E-Mail: lwilson@wcu.edu.

WILSON, LEWIS LANSING, insurance executive; b. Cobleskill, N.Y., Jan. 26, 1932; s. Clarence A. and Ordella (Walker) W.; m. Barbara Jane Kathan, June 7, 1952; children: Susan W. Coleman, Joan, Peter L. (dec.). Grad. high sch., Cobleskill. Cert. profl. ins. agt., ins. cons. Mgr. claims Sterling Ins. Co., Cobleskill, 1950-57; ins. agt. State Farm Ins. Co., 1957-59; pres. Lewis L. Wilson, Inc., 1959-91, Fire Mark Ins. Agy., Inc., Cobleskill, 1991—. Owner Wilson Travel Agy., 1978—, Wilson Tel. Exch., Cobleskill, 1978-86, Wilson Security, Inc., Cobleskill, 1981-86; rep. N.Y. Mapp Program, 1985-88. Town chmn. Cobleskill Rep. Party, 1978-83; chmn. Schoharie County Rep. Com., N.Y., 1983—, Cobleskill SUNY Found. Fund Drive; commr. Schoharie County Bd. Elections, 1983—; pres. Cobleskill Cen. Sch. Bd., Community Hosp. Schoharie County, Cobleskill; dir. Schoharie Colonial Heritage; pres. Pont Pleasant Owners Assn.; past chmn. Nat. PIA PAC (chmn. nat. gov. affairs, 1st v.p.); pres. Cobbleskill Cemetery Assn., 1999—; chmn. Two Million One Hundred Thousand Rescue Fund. Mem. Profl. Ins. Agts. (pres. 1989, bd. dirs. 1984—, v.p. 1987, 1st v.p. 1988, pres. 1989-90, nat. v.p., Ins. Agt. of Yr. 1986), N.Y. Ind. Ins. Agts. (regional v.p.), N.Y. Life Underwriters, Rotary (pres. Cobleskill chpt., gov. dist. 719 1982, Paul Harris fellow 1985-86), Elks (exalted ruler, hon. founder nat. found. 1980), Nat. Assn. of Profl. Ins. Agts. (v.p. 2000—, Person of the Yr. 1997). Republican. Methodist. Home: 31 Grandview Dr Cobleskill NY 12043-1321 Office: PO Box 39 Cobleskill NY 12043-0039

WILSON, LINDA, librarian; b. Rochester, Minn., Nov. 17, 1945; d. Eunice Gloria Irene Wilson. BA, U. Minn., Morris, 1967; MA, U. Minn., 1968. Libr. rsch. svcs. U. Calif., Riverside, 1968-69, head dept. phys. scis. catalog, 1969-71; city libr. Belle Glade (Fla). Mcpl. Libr., 1972-74; instr. part-time Palm Beach Jr. Coll., Belle Glade, 1973; head adult-young adult ext. Kern County Libr. Sys., Bakersfield, Calif., 1974-80; dir. dist. libr. Lake Agassiz Regional Libr. System, Crookston, Minn., 1980-85; supervising libr. San Diego County Libr., 1985-87; county libr. Merced (Calif.) County Libr., 1987-93; learning network mgr. Merced Coll., 1994-95; city libr. Monterey Park (Calif.) Bruggemeyer Meml. Libr., 1995—. Mem. Leadership Merced, 1987-88, East Site Based Coordinating Coun., Merced, 1990-92, Merced Gen. Plan Citizens Adv. Com., 1992-95, Sister City Com., Merced, 1992-95. Recipient Libr. award Eagles Aux., 1984, Woman of Achievement award Commn. on the Status of Women, 1990, Libr. award Calif. Libr. Trustees and Commrs., 1990, Woman of Yr. award Merced Bus. and Profl. Women, 1987. Mem. ALA (sec. pub. libr. sys. sect. 1988-89), Met. Coop. Library Sys. (pres. 1999-2000), Calif. Libr. Assn. (sec. govt. rels. com. 1991-92, continuing edn. com. 1993-96, pub. rels. 1997-2000, nominations com. 2000-01), Minn. Libr. Assn. (pres. pub. libr. divsn. 1985), Merced County Mgmt. Coun. (pres. 1989), Merced Bus. and Profl. Women (Woman of Yr. 1987, pres. 1988-89), East L.A.-Montebello Bus. and Profl. Women (v.p. 1998-2002, pres. 2002-), Rotary (pres. Monterey Park chpt. 1999-2000). Democrat. Lutheran. Avocations: travel, walking, reading, swimming, stamp collecting. Home: 1000 E Newmark Ave Apt 22 Monterey Park CA 91755-3129 E-mail: lindalwilson@juno.com.

WILSON, LINDA SMITH, academic administrator; b. Washington, Nov. 10, 1936; d. Fred M. and Virginia D. (Thompson) Smith; 1 child Helen K. Whatley ; m. Paul A. Wilson, Jan. 22, 1970; 1 stepchild Beth A. BA, Tulane U., 1957, HLD (hon.) , 1993; PhD, U. Wis., 1962; DLitt (hon.) , U. Md., 1993. Rsch. assoc. U. Md., College Park, 1962—64, rsch. asst. prof., 1964—67; vis. asst. prof. U. Mo., St. Louis, 1967—68; asst. to vice chancellor for rsch., asst. vice chancellor for rsch., assoc. vice chancellor for rsch. Washington U., 1968—75; assoc. vice chancellor for rsch. U. Ill., Urbana, 1975—85; assoc. dean U. Ill. Grad. Coll., 1978—85; v.p. for rsch. U. Mich., Ann Arbor, 1985—89; pres. Radcliffe Coll., Cambridge, Mass., 1989—99, pres. emeritus, 1999; sr. lectr. Harvard Grad. Sch. Edn., 1989—. Chmn. adv. com. office sci. and engring. pers. NRC, 1990—96; dir.'s adv. coun. NSF, Washington, 1980—89, adv. com. edn. and human resources, 1990—95; mem. Nat. Commn. on Rsch., Washington, 1978—80; com. on govt.-univ. relationships NAS, 1981—83, govt.-univ.-industry rsch. roundtable, 1984—89, coord. coun. for edn., 1991—93; rsch. resources adv. coun. NIH, Bethesda, Mass., 1978—82; energy rsch. adv. bd. Dept. of Energy, 1987—90; sci., tech. and states task force Carnegie Commn. on Sci., Tech. and Govt., 1991—92; overser Mus. Sci., Boston, 1992—2001; bd. dirs. Inacom Corp., Myriad Genetics, Inc., Internet Corp. Assignment Names and Numbers, U. Wis. Coll. Letters and Sci.; deans adv. coun. Newcomb Coll., 1998—; mem. bd. visitors Tulane U. Contbr. articles to profl. jours. Adv. bd. Nat. Coalition for Sci. and Tech., Washington, 1983—87; bd. govs. YMCA, Champaign, Ill., 1980—83; trustee Mass. Gen. Hosp., 1992—99, hon. trustee, 1999—; trustee Com. on Econ. Devel., 1995—. Named One of 100 Emerging Leaders, Am. Coun. Edn. and Change, 1978; recipient Centennial award, Newcomb Coll., 1986, Disting. Alumni award, U. Wis., 1997, Radcliffe medal, 1999. Fellow: AAAS (bd. dirs. 1984—88); mem.: Am. Coun. Edn. (commn. on women in higher edn. 1991—93, chair 1993), Inst. Medicine (coun. mem. 1986—89), Assn. for Biomed. Rsch. (bd. dirs. 1983—86), Nat. Coun. Univ. Rsch. Adminstrs., Soc. Rsch. Adminstrs. (Disting. Contbn. to Rsch. Adminstrn. award 1984), Am. Chem. Soc. (bd. coun. com. on chemistry and pub. affairs 1978—80), Phi Kappa Phi, Phi Delta Kappa, Alpha Lambda Delta, Sigma Xi, Phi Beta Kappa. Home: 47 Keene Neck Rd Bremen ME 04551

WILSON, LINDA ANN, renal dialysis nurse; b. Johnson City, Tenn., Feb. 22, 1947; d. Andrew Jackson and Dorothy (Pate) Robertson; m. William Eugene Wilson, Feb. 17, 1968. Student, U. Tenn., 1969. Cert. nephrology nurse. Nurse Johnson City (Tenn.) Med. Ctr., 1969-73, head nurse renal dialysis, 1973—. Vol. nurse Red Cross. Mem. NAFE, Internat. Platform Assn., Am. Nephrology Nurses Assn., Assn. Nurses Endorsing Transplantation.

WILSON, LINDA B. education specialist, medical association administrator; b. Kingston, Pa., Apr. 15, 1962; MSN in Critical Care and Trauma, Thomas Jefferson U., 1985. RN, Pa., N.J.; cert. ambulatory perianesthesia nurse, post anesthesia nurse, nursing continuing and staff devel. Resident N.J./Bermuda Perianesthesia Nurses, 1994-98; dir. edn. Thomas Jefferson U. Hosp., Phila., 1998—, ASPAN, 1999—. Cert. post anesthesia nurse, ambulatory perianesthesia nurse, nursing continuing edn. and staff devel. Mem. Am. Soc. Perianesthesia Nurses (co-chair nat. conf. 1998).

WILSON, LINDA LEE, financial company executive, president; b. Lakewood, Ohio, Nov. 9, 1943; d. Jon E. and Virginia L. (Weaver) Brown; m. Curtis Wilson, July 30, 1983 (div. 1991); children: Catherine, Laura. BA in English, UCLA, 1970. Lic. ins. agt. Pres. Americorp Fin. Group, Inc., Bellevue, Wash., 1984—. Co-founder panel discussion Women in Transition. Mem. AAUW (bd. dirs.), Internat. Assn. Fin. Planners (bd. dirs. Wash. chpt.), Soroptimist Internat., Toastmasters Internat. Avocation: equestrian.

WILSON, LISA MARIE, English educator; b. Syracuse, N.Y., Feb. 17, 1968; d. David Gilmore and Constance (Clark) W. BA, U. Rochester, 1990; PhD, U. Buffalo, 1999. Vis. asst. prof. English Murray (Ky.) State U., 1999-2000; instr. English Winona (Minn.) State U., 2000—. Contbr. articles to profl. jours. Mem. MLA, N.Am. Soc. Study of Romanticism, Internat. Gothic Assn., Phi Beta Kappa. Home: 119 Kansas Winona MN 55987 E-mail: LWilson17@aol.com.

WILSON, LLOYD LEE, organization administrator; b. Elkton, Md., Sept. 14, 1947; s. Clifton Laws and Betty Raye (Bare) W.; m. Susan Sieg Wilson, 1992; children: Asa, Ryan, Morgan, Daniel. BS in Mgmt., MIT, 1969, MS in

Mgmt., 1977. Bus. mgr. med. clinics Mass. Gen. Hosp., Boston, 1970-73; ptnr. Willow Co., mgmt. cons., Cambridge, Mass., 1974-77; dir. community relations Wilson Neuropsychiat. Hosp., Charlottesville, Va., 1977-78; exec. dir. Jefferson Area United Transp. Inc., 1978-80, Va. Mountain Housing Inc., Blacksburg, 1980-82; gen. sec. Friends Gen. Conf. Religious Soc. Friends, Phila., 1982-85; dir. rsch. and devel. Va. Mountain Housing, Inc., Christiansburg, 1985-88, dir. multifamily housing, 1989-91, regional dir., 1991-92; pres. Friendly Mgmt. Svcs. Corp., Norfolk, Va., 1992-95, Not-for-Profit Mgmt., Inc., Norfolk, 1995—. Dir. instnl. rsch. Chowan Coll., Murfreesboro, N.C., 2000—; pres., dir. Va. Housing Coalition, Inc., 1981-82; treas., bd. dirs. Fiddle Hill Farm, Inc., Barboursville, Va., 1982-89; bd. mgrs. Bible Assn. Friends in Am., Phila., 1983-85; mem. com. rec. ministers Balt. Yearly Meeting Friends, Sandy Spring, Md., 1984-86; asst. sec.-treas. Friends Meeting House Fund, Inc., Phila., 1984-85; asst. presiding clk. Communications Commn. of Friends United Meeting, Richmond, Ind., 1987-88; recorded minister of the gospel, Soc. of Friends, 1989— (presiding clk. Va. Beach monthly meeting 1990-92); dir. coordinating cabinet Va. Coun. Chs., 1988; presiding clk. N.C. Yearly Meeting of Friends, 1991-92. Author: Essays on the Quaker Vision of Gospel Order, 1993; contbr. articles to profl. jours. Treas., bd. dirs. Norfolk (Va.) Quaker House, Inc., 1995—; bd. dirs. New Dominion Housing, Inc., Norfolk, 1992-94; vice chmn. Montgomery County Cmty. Svc. Commn., Christianburg, Va., 1980-82; mem. ednl. coun. MIT, 19777-89; bd. dirs. Am. Friends Svc. Com., Inc., Phila., 1980-83; bd. dirs. Interfaith Housing Corp. Cambridge, Inc., 1975-77, treas., 1976-77, also numerous others. Home: PO Box 647 Woodland NC 27897-0647 E-mail: llwilson@alum.mit.edu.

WILSON, LOIS M. minister; b. Winnipeg, Man., Can., Apr. 8, 1927; d. Edwin Gardiner Dunn and Ada Minnie (Davis) Freeman; m. Roy F. Wilson, June 9, 1950; children: Ruth, Jean, Neil, Bruce BA, United Coll., Winnipeg, 1947, BDiv, 1969; Diploma in TV prodn., Ryerson Tech. Inst., 1974; DDiv (hon.), Victoria U., Toronto, 1978, United Theol. Coll., Montreal, 1978, Wycliff Coll., 1983, Queens U., Kingston, 1984, U. Winnipeg, 1986, Mt. Allison U., 1988; LLD (hon.), LLD (hon.), Dalhousie U., 1989, Ripon Coll., Wis., 1992; DCL (hon.), Acadia U., 1984; DHuml (hon.), Mt. St. Vincent, Halifax, 1984. Ordained to ministry United Church of Can., 1965. Minister, Thunder Bay, 1965-69, Hamilton, 1969-78, Kingston, 1978-80; moderator United Church of Can., 1980-82, McGeachy sr. scholar, 1989-91; pres. Can. Council of Chs., Toronto, Ont., 1976-79; co-dir. Ecumenical Forum Can., 1983-89; pres. World Council of Chs., Geneva, 1983-91; chancellor Lakehead U., Thurder Bay, Ont., 1990-2000; chmn. contemporary theology Lafayette-Orinda (Calif.) Presbyn. Ch., 1995; ind. senator Senate of Can., 1998—2002. Mem. adv. coun. internt. devel. studies U. Toronto, 1987-93; spokesperson Project Ploughshares, 1st and 2d UN Conf. on Disarmament, N.Y.C., 1978-82; lectr. Vancouver Sch. Theology, 1980, Queens Theol. Coll., 1982-83, 92, Chancellor's lectr., 1992; officer Human Rights Commn., Ont., 1973; mem. bd. regents Victoria U., 1990—; chief Can. Fact finding Mission to Sri Lanka, 1992; team mem. Ctrl. Am. Monitoring Group to El Salvador and Guatemala, 1993; spl. envoy of Can. to The Sudan, 1999—. Author: Like a Mighty River, 1980, Turning the World Upside Down, 1989, Miriam, Mary and Me, 1992, Telling Her Story, 1992, Stories Seldom Told, 1997, Nuclear Waste, 2000; mem. adv. bd.: Can. Woman Studies Jour., York U., 1993—; contbr. articles. Apptd. Can. Senator, 1998; pres. Social Planning Coun., Thunder Bay, 1967—68, Can. Com. for Scientists and Scholars, Toronto, 1982; mem. Refugee Status Adv. Com., 1985—89; chmn. Urban Rural Mission, Can., 1990—96; mem. environ. assessment panel Can. Nuclear Fuel Waste Mgmt. and Disposal Concept, 1989—96; bd. dirs. Elizabeth Fry Soc., Hamilton, 1976—79, Amnesty Internat., 1978—90, Can. Inst. for Internat. Peace and Security, 1984—88, Energy Probe, 1981—86, Internat. Ctr. Human Rights and Dem. Devel., 1997—98, Can. Univ. Svc. Overseas, 1983—85; trustee Nelson Mandela Fund, 1990—92. Decorated Order of Can., 1984, Order of Ont., 1991; recipient Queens Jubilee medal, Commemorative medal for 125th Anniversary of Confederation of Can., 1992, World Federalist Peace award, 1985, Pearson Peace medal UN Assn. of Can., 1985; named hon. pres. Student Christian Movement of Can., Toronto, 1976. Mem. CAW (pub. rev. bd. 1986—), Can. Assn. Adult Edn. (bd. dirs. 1986-90), Friends Can. Broadcasting (bd. dirs. 1986—, v.p.), Civil Liberties Assn. (v.p. 1986—), UNIFEM (nat. v.p. 1993-95, mem. CCIC team to monitor El Salvador election 1994), World Federalists (pres. Can. chpt. 1996-2000, v.p. World Federalist Movement 1998—), Parliament of World's Religions (del. 1993), Christian-Jewish Dialogue Jerusalem (keynote speaker 1994).

WILSON, LORRAINE M. medical and surgical nurse, nursing educator; b. Mich., Nov. 18, 1931; d. Bert and Frances Fern (White) McCarty; m. Harold A. Wilson, June 9, 1953; children: David Scott, Ann Elizabeth. Diploma in Nursing, Bronson Meth. Sch. Nursing, Kalamazoo, Mich., 1953; BS in Chemistry, Siena Heights Coll., 1969; MSN, U. Mich., 1972; PhD, Wayne State U., Detroit, 1985. RN, Mich. Staff nurse U. Mich. Med. Ctr., Ann Arbor, 1953-54, Herrick Meml. Hosp., Tecumseh, Mich., 1954-69; asst. prof. nursing U. Mich., Ann Arbor, 1972-78, Wayne State U., Detroit, 1978-79; assoc. prof. nursing Sch. of Nursing Oakland U., Rochester, Mich., 1986-89; prof. nursing Ea. Mich. U., Ypsilanti, 1989—. Researcher in field; bd. advs. Profl. Fitness Systems, Warren, Mich., 1986—; cons. wellness and exercise program General Motors CPC Hdqs., Warren, 1986; cons.,faculty liaison nurse extern program in critical care, MSN program dir. Ea. Mich. U. Catherine McAuley Health Ctr., 1989—. Author: (with S. Price and L. Wilson) Pathophysiology, 5th edit., 1997, (with Sylvia Price) Pathophysiology: Clinical Concepts of Disease-Processes, 5th edit., 1997; contbr. articles to profl. jours. Vol. Community Health Screening Drives, Tecumseh, 1960-70, leader Girl Scouts U.S., Tecumseh, 1960; sunday sch. tchr. Gloria Dei Luth. Ch., Tecumseh, 1960; mem. PTA. Grantee Mich. Heart Assn., 1984, 88, R.C. Mahon Found., 1988. Mem. ANA (various offices and com. chairs), Midwest Nursing Rsch. Soc. (v.p., sec.-treas., bd. dirs.), Mich. Nurses Assn. (del.), Nat. League Nursing, Nat. Orgn. Women, Sigma Theta Tau. Lutheran. Avocations: traveling, theatre, jogging. Home: 1010 Red Mill Dr Tecumseh MI 49286-1145 Office: Ea Mich U 53 W Michigan Ave Ypsilanti MI 48197-5436

WILSON, LYNTON RONALD, retired telecommunications company executive; b. Port Colborne, Ont., Can., Apr. 3, 1940; s. Ronald Alfred and Blanche Evelyn (Matthews) W.; m. Brenda Jean Black, Dec. 23, 1968; children: Edward Ronald, Margot Jean, Jennifer Lyn. BA, McMaster U., 1962, LLD, 1995; MA, Cornell U., 1967; D honoris causa, U. Montreal, 1995; D in Civil Law, Bishop's U., Lennoxville, Que., Can., 1997; LLD, Univ. Coll. Cape Breton, 1998, Mount Allison U., 2000. Dep. minister Ministry Industry and Tourism, Ont., 1978-81; pres., CEO Redpath Industries, Ltd., Toronto, 1981-88; mng. dir. N.Am. Tate & Lyle, PLC, 1986-89; chmn. bd. Redpath Industries, Ltd., 1988-89; vice chmn. Bank of N.S., Toronto, 1989-90; pres., chief operating officer BCE, Inc., Montreal, 1990-92; pres., CEO BCE Inc., 1992-93, chmn., pres. CEO, 1993-96, chmn., CEO, 1996-98, chmn. bd. dirs., 1998-2000. Chmn. bd. dirs. CAE Inc., Nortel Networks Corp., Daimler Chrysler Can. Inc.; chmn. bd. dirs., mem. supervisory bd. and chmn.'s coun. Daimler Chrysler AG; mem. internat. coun. J.P. Morgan Chase and Co., N.Y.C. Founding co-chmn. HISTORICA Found. Can. Decorated officer Order of Can. Mem. The Mount Royal Club of Montreal, York Club, Toronto Club, Toronto Golf Club, Rideau Club, Mount Bruno Country Club. Home: 2038 Lakeshore Rd East Oakville ON Canada L6J 1M3 Office: North Tower 483 Bay Ste 7th Fl Toronto ON Canada M5G 2C9

WILSON, LYNTON R. educational association administrator; b. Port Colborne, Ont. m. Brenda Jean Black; 3 children. BA honors, McMaster U., 1962; MA, Cornell U., 1967; D (hon.), McMaster U., Bishop's U., U. Coll. of Cape Breton, Mount Allison U. Dep. men. Industry and Tourism Govt. Ont., 1978—81; pres., CEO Redpath Industries Ltd., Toronto, 1981—88, chmn. bd., 1988—89; chmn. Historica Found. Can., 2001—. Chmn. bd. CAE, Inc., Oakville, Ont., Canada, 1999—; chmn. Nortel Networks Corp., Ontario, 2001—; vice-chmn. Bank of Nova Scotia, Montreal; pres., COO BCE Inc.; bd. dirs. DaimlerChrysler, Imperial Oil, Ontario Power Generation; mng. dir. N.Am., Tate & Lyle PLC. Mem. Trilateral Commn., Internat. Coun., J.P. Morgan & Co. Recipient Fellowship award, Inst. Corp. Dirs. Office: Historica Found Canada 60 Spadino Ave 2d Fl Toronto On M5V 2HB Canada Address: Nortel Networks Corp 8200 Dixie Rd Ste 100 Brampton On L6T 4P6 Canada also: CAE Inc Royal Bank Plz 200 Bay St Ste 3060 Toronto On Canada*

WILSON, MABLE JEAN, paralegal; b. Pine Bluff, Ark. d. James Arthur and Ruthia Mae (Dansby) Watson; children: Dana Eileen, Dana Kent, Carlos Alexander Fuller. BS, cert. in paralegal studies, U. So. Calif., 1982-86. Dep. sheriff L.A. County, 1971-80; ind. paralegal Wilson's Divorce Clinic, L.A., 1980—. Participant Dist. Atty. Victim Witness Program, L.A., 1991; active Brotherhood Crusade, 1992; mem. adv. bd. West L.A. Coll.-Paralegal Studies. Recipient Merit award L.A. County Bar Assn., 1993, Merit cert. City of L.A., County of L.A., Calif. Senate, U.S. Congress, Gov. State of Calif. Mem. Assn. Family and Conciliation Cts., Folk Power Inc. (bd. dirs. 1993—), Alpha Svc. Co. (v.p. 1993—, profl. women's adv. bd., Women's Inner Circle of Achievement), adv. bd on Paralegal Studies, W. L.A. Coll. Avocations: interior decorating, making stained glass windows, ceramics, painting, writing poetry. Office: 3860 Crenshaw Blvd Ste 201 Los Angeles CA 90008-1816

WILSON, MAGGIE ISABELLE LOVELL, art educator, English educator; b. Branchville, Ala., Jan. 26; d. Winston Porter and Ruth Kate (Buckner) Lovell. AB, Samford U., Birmingham, Ala., 1971; MA, EdS, U. Ala., 1978; MFA, Loyola U., 1979; PhD, Sussex (Eng.) U., 1981. Cert. elem./secondary tchr. Tchr. Engilsh Birmingham Pub. Schs., 1972-92; tchr. English secondary edn. Terrell County Schs., Dawson, Ga., 1992-93. Author, illustrator: Carousel of Creative Communication, 1976, Leeds, Her Story, 1979; author: Creative Expressions, 1980, Into Our Third Century, 1984, From Brush Arbor Days to the Twentieth Century, 1992. Historian Leeds (Ala.) First United Meth. Ch., 1990-99; docent Birmingham Mus. Art, 1970-80. Recipient numerous awards Ala. Watercolor Soc., Birmingham, 1970—, Pres. award Kappa Pi, Samford U., Birmingham, 1971, Art of Distinction Salon Des Nations, Paris, 1984. Mem. AAUW, Internat. Biog. Assn., Ala. Coun. Tchrs. English (bd. mem. 1976—), Leeds Art Coun., Leeds Hist. Soc., Birmingham Art Assn., Internat. Soc. Artists, Leeds Bus. and Profl. Women (pres. 1971-76, 86, 88—, Woman of Yr. 1996-97), Leeds United Meth. Women (pres. 1972-76, 84—), La. Watercolor Soc. (awards 1986-99), So. Watercolor Soc., Kappa Delta Epsilon, Phi Gamma Mu. Home: 610 Montevallo Rd SW Leeds AL 35094-1926

WILSON, MARC BURT, engineer; b. Queens, N.Y., Nov. 7, 1950; s. Henry and Ethel (Rudich) W.; m. Laura Greer Nagle Wilson, Dec. 9, 1973; children: Tammy Ann, Shana Alexis. BS in Nuclear, SUNY, Maritime, 1973; MSME, Naval Postgrad. Sch., Monterey, Calif., 1982; DSc, George Washington U., 1993. Cert. profl. ergnomist, N.Y. Commd. officer USCG, 1973, lt. commdr., 1993, marine inspector, 1978-80, chief engr. Portsmouth, Va., 1982-84, sect. chief tech. New Orleans, 1984-86, sr. marine inspector N.Y.C., 1986-87, resident inspector bremen, 1987-88; tech. advisor safety USCG Hdqs., Washington, 1988-93; asst. prof. Dowling Coll., Oakdale, N.Y., 1994-96; assoc. prof. U. Md. Ea. Shore, 1997-99; dir. Sch. Aviation and Visitors Svcs., Miami Dade C.C., 1999—2000; sr. engr., owner Ames Cons., Inc., Seminole, Fla. Cons. in field; initiated and implemented the Human Factors minor. Contbr. articles to jours. including U.S. Naval Inst., Am. Soc. Engring. Mgmt., Transp. Rsch. Forum, Jour. Air Transport World Wide. Decorated Commendation medal, Joint Svcs. Achievement medal, Achievement medal. Mem. Am. Soc. Engring. Mgmt., Am. Soc. Naval Engring., Human Factors and Ergonomic, Soc. Naval Arch and Maritime Engring. Home and Office: 9996 Indian Key Trl Seminole FL 33776-1074

WILSON, MARCIA SANDMEYER, artist; b. Rochester, Ny, Feb. 6, 1937; d. Earl Cranston and Katharine Margaret (Hubler) Sandmeyer; children: Diana Slote, Thomas, Rebecca. AB, Vassar, Poughkeepsie, N.Y., 1958. Painting, woodcarving, etching, batik (fellowship woodcarving, N.J. State Coun. Arts, 1982), exhibitions include two person exhibit Stories and Dreams, Noyes Mus., 2002. Home: 259 Leonia Ave Leonia NJ 07605 Personal E-mail: mwilson@infi.net.

WILSON, MARGARET BUSH, lawyer, civil rights leader; b. St. Louis, Jan. 30, 1919; married; 1 child, Robert Edmund. BA cum laude, Talladega Coll., 1940; LL.B., Lincoln U., 1943. Ptnr. Wilson & Wilson, St. Louis, 1947-65; now with firm Wilson & Assocs. Asst. dir. St. Louis Lawyers for Housing, 1969-72; asst. atty. gen. Mo., 1961-62; atty. Rural Electrification Adminstrn., Dept. Agr., St. Louis, 1943-45; instr. civil procedure St. Louis U. Sch. Law, 1971; chmn. St. Louis Land Reutilization Authority, 1975-76; mem. Mo. Coun. Criminal Justice, 1972—; chmn. Intergroup Corp., 1985-87; bd. dirs. Mut. of N.Y. Mem. gen. adv. com. ACDA, 1978-81; trustee emeritus Washington U., St. Louis; chmn. bd. trustees Talladega Coll., Ala., 1988-92; nat. bd. dirs. ARC, 1975-81, United Way, 1978-84, Police Found., 1976-93; treas. NAACP Nat. Housing Corp., 1971-84, chmn. nat. bd., 1975-84; dep. dir./acting dir. St. Louis Model City Agy., 1968-69; adminstr. Mo. Commn. Svc. and Continuing Edn., 1967-68. Recipient Bishop's award Episcopal Diocese Mo., 1962; Juliette Derricotte fellow, 1939-40, Disting. Lawyer award Bar Assn. Metro St. Louis, 1997. Mem. ABA (chmn. youth edn. for citizenship 1991-94, chmn. Nat. Law Day 1998-2000), Nat. Bar Assn., Mo. Bar Assn., Mound City Bar Assn., St. Louis Bar Assn., Alpha Kappa Alpha. Office: Wilson & Assocs 4054 Lindell Blvd Saint Louis MO 63108-3202

WILSON, MARGARET EILEEN, retired physical education educator; b. Kansas City, Mo., Aug. 4, 1925; d. Edward Leslie and Bertha Mae (Coe) W. BS in Edn., U. Ark., 1944, MS, 1949; PhD, U. Iowa, 1960. Cert. secondary tchr., Ark. Recreation dir. Pine Bluff (Ark.) Arsenal, 1944-45; instr. Ctrl. High Sch., Muskogee, Okla., 1945-48; grad. asst. U. Ark., Fayetteville, 1948-49; instr. Fayetteville High Sch., 1949-52; from instr. to asst. prof. Ark. Poly. Coll., Russellville, 1952-57, assoc. prof., 1959-65; grad. asst. U. Iowa, Iowa City, 1957-59; prof. Tex. Tech. U., Lubbock, 1965-90, dept. chair health, phys. edn. and recreation for women, 1967-76, prof. emerita, 1990—. Mem. Tex. Tech. Faculty Senate, 1978-90, pres., 1978-79, 85-86. Active Lubbock County Dem. Com., 1993, 94, 96. Recipient AMOCO Found. Disting. Tchg. award, 1978, Disting. Faculty award in Tex. Tech. Moms and Dads Assn., 1987. Mem. AAHPERD (life), Tex. Assn. for Health, Phys. Edn., Recreation and Dance (Honor award 1979, David K. Bruce award 1992), Tex. Tech. Faculty Legal Action Assn. (pres. 1990-96), Lubbock Ret. Tchrs. Assn. (cmty. svc. chair 1994-96, co-treas. 1996-99), Double T Connection (chair membership 1991-94), Delta Gamma (house corp. treas. 1982-91, Cable award 1978), Delta Kappa Gamma (chpt. pres. 1972-74, Chpt. Achievement award 1976, state corr. sec. 1979-81, state conv. chair 1979-80, state nominations com. 1985-87, state pers. com. 1987-89, State Achievement award 1987, state necrology com. 1993-95, state fin. com. 1995-96). Presbyterian. Avocations: gardening, needlepoint, reading. Home: 5411 46th St Lubbock TX 79414-1513 Office: Tex Tech U Womens Gymnasium Lubbock TX 79409

WILSON, MARGARET ELIZABETH, educator; b. New Haven, Apr. 11, 1935; d. Burriss Gahan and Margaret Henrietta (Shove) W. BS, Syracuse U., 1958, MS in Sci. Edn., 1962; MA in Biology, Hofstra U., 1973. Biology tchr. Homer (N.Y.) Ctrl. H.S., 1958-60; gen. sci. tchr. Manhassett (N.Y.) Jr. H.S., 1960-61; biology tchr. Bellmore-Merrick (N.Y.) Ctrl. H.S. Dist., 1961-90, ret., 1990. Cons. Wilson Ednl. Svcs., Inc., 1998-2001. Vol. marine ecology divsn Nassau Co. Health Dept., Mineola, NY, 1984—89; vol. N.Y. Aquarium, Bklyn., 1971—90; mem. curriculum writing team, 1989; sec. PTA J.F. Kennedy H.S., 1967—90; mem. Town of Ledyard Dist. Historic Commn., 1998—. NSF scholar, 1969. Fellow: Conn. Sci. Tchrs. Assn. (bd. dirs. 1992—98), Sci. Tchrs. Assn. N.Y. State (bd. of dirs. 1962—); mem.: Conn. Outdoor Edn. Assn., Am. Inst. Biol. Sci., N.Y. State Marine Edn. Assn. (bd. dirs. 1978—90). Avocation: photography. Home: 6 Eagle Ridge Dr Gales Ferry CT 06335-1904

WILSON, MARGARET SCARBROUGH, retail executive; b. Aug. 7, 1930; Student, Smith Coll., 1948-50; BA, U. Tex., 1952. Mem. staff Bayway Refinery Exxon Corp., N.J., 1960-61; mem. staff psychiat. ward VA Hosp., Houston, 1962; from mem. staff to chmn. Scarbroughs, Austin, 1952—74, chmn. bd., CEO, 1974—. Past mem., bd. dirs. audit and contbns. coms. R.J. Reynolds Industries, 1978-85; dir. Internat. Longevity Ctr., N.Y.C., 1994-97, hon. bd., 1997—; dir. Austin Nat. Bank, 1971-73, Scarbrough Devel. Corp. 1993—, Nat. Retail Fedn., 1991-2002, Am. Productivity & Quality Ctr., 1991—; dir. Fed. Res. Bank Dallas, San Antonio br., 1974-76, chmn. San Antonio br., 1975-76; trustee Nat. Policy Assn., 1997-98; pres., treas. Scarbrough Ventures LLC, 2001-, MSW-NSG Mgmt. LLC, 2000-, MSW-NSG Enterprises Ltd., 2000-, MSW-NSG Real Estate Ventures Ltd., 2001-. Trustee Com. Econ. Devel., 1973—, Cooper Inst. for Aerobics Rsch., Dallas, 1980-93, St. Stephen's Sch., Austin, 1979-83; mem. Nat. Com. U.S.-China Rels., 1976—, dir. 1980-94; mem. U.S. Council Internat. Bus., 1977—, mem. exec. com., 1978—, trustee, 1978—; bd. vistors Babcock Grad. Sch. Mgmt.-Wake Forest U., Winston-Salem, N.C., 1983-86; mem. bus. adv. council S.W. Tex. State U., 1983-86; mem. deptl. vis. com. dept. home econs. U. Tex.-Austin, 1983-84, pres.'s assocs., 1992—; mem. univ. council Rockefeller U., N.Y.C., 1982-86; mem. chancellor's coun. U. Tex. Sys., 1994—; mem. Tex. Research League, 1977—, dir. audit com. 1986—, Friends of L.B.J. Libr., 1980— ; assoc. mem. George Bush Presdl. Libr., 1995—; bd. dirs. World Bus. Coun., 1980-89; mem. adv. council Coll. Bus. Adminstrn., U. Tex.-Austin, 1964-68, Dean's Assocs. Coll. Fine Arts, 1985-87, Friends of Free Enterprise com. Coll. Engring., 1985-87; mem. India-U.S. Bus. Council, 1976-82, dir., 1978-82; mem. Pres.'s Commn. on Personnel Interchange, 1972-73, UN Day Com., 1971-74; mem. Mayor's Bus. Roundtable, Austin, 1985-87; mem. Houston Com. Foreign Rels., 1994—, Dallas Com. Foreign Rels., 1997—, SRI Internat. Assocs. Program, 1998—99; mem. Conf. Bd. Mem. Alliance Francaise, Asia Soc. (adv. bd. Houston chpt., 1991-94, mem. N.Y. chpt.), Houston World Affairs Coun., Austin World Affairs Coun., English Speaking Union, Fgn. Policy Assn., Tex. Assn. Taxpayers, Retail Industry Trade Action Coalition (trustee 1984), Nat. Planning Assn. (trustee 1985-97), Am. Enterprise Inst. Am. Mgmt. Assn. (dir. 1969-72), Internat. C. of C., British Am. Bus. Inc., U.S. C. of C. (bd. dirs. 1980-82), Tex. Asian C. of C. (mem. adv. coun. 1997—), Tex. State Soc. Wash., World Econ. Devel. Congress (mem. adv. bd. 1993), Internat. Indsl. Conf. (mem. adv. coun. 1996-97), Coun. Fgn. Rels., World Econ. Forum, Bus. Coun. Internat. Understanding, Ctr. Strategic and Internat. Studies (Washington Round Table 1998—), Am. Enterprise Inst., Pacific Coun. on Internat. Policy, World Pres.'s Orgn. (internat. chpt., met. chpt., Dallas chpt., Houston chpt., Cen. Tex. chpt.), Pres.'s Cir. Nat. Acad. Scis., Inst. of Medicine and Inst. Engrs., Houston Forum, Brookings Instn., Bretton Woods Com., Brit.-N.A. Com., Tarry House, The University Club N.Y., Met. Club (Washington), Headliners Club, Tex. Breakfast Club of Washington, Nat. Policy Assn. (trustee 1997-98), Kappa Kappa Gamma, numerous other local and nat. orgns. Office: 517 W 39th St Austin TX 78751-4904 E-mail: Margaret.Wilson@Scarbroughs.com.

WILSON, MARGARET SULLIVAN, retired executive dean, consultant; b. Norwich, Conn., Mar. 21, 1924; d. John Joseph and Margaret Ellen (Connelly) Sullivan; BS, Eastern Conn. State U., 1944; MA, U. Conn., 1949; m. William Robert Wilson, July 20, 1950 (dec.); children: Margaret Ellen, William Robert. Reading cons. Greenwich (Conn.) Pub. Schs., 1948-50; asst. prof. early childhood, chmn. dept. early childhood Eastern Conn. State U., Willimantic, 1967-77, exec. asst. to pres., 1977-78, v.p. adminstrv. affairs, 1978-80, exec. dean, 1980-89, emeritus dean, 1989—; commr. Nat. Commn. Prevention Infant Mortality, 1986-93, chair Norwich Econ. Devel. Commn., 1988-91, Southeastern Connecticut regional Planning Comm., 1999-2001(mem. 1993—); dir. Rose City Community Land Trust Housing, Com. on City Plan, 1992—; del. White House Conf. on Children, 1970, 80, White House Conf. on Travel and Tourism, 1995; corporator Chelsea Groton Savs. Bank, Norwich, Conn. Mem. Com. Mental Health Bd., 1979-83; mem. adv. bd. Norwich Hosp.; chmn. rev. com. Conn. Health Coordinating Council; mem. Eastern Regional Mental Health Bd., 1976-83, chmn., 1979-81; mem. Norwich Bd. Edn., 1954-69, 80-83, adv. coun. head start and day care programs, 1986-91; mem. Conn. Dem. Cen. Com., 1966-82, Dem. Town Com., 1964-82, 86-90; chmn. Blue Ribbon Commn. To Establish Goals for U. Conn. Health Ctr., 1975-76; sr. warden Ch. of Resurrection, Norwich., 1988-91, Dio Com on Ministry Higher Edn. Named Citizen of Yr., C. of C., 1970; recipient Disting. Alumni award Eastern Conn. State U., 1972, Mental Health Bell award Conn. Mental Health Assn., 1972, Valiant Women award Council Ch. Women, 1976, Woman of Yr. award Bus. and Profl. Women, 1978, Jefferson award Inst. Pub. Service, 1982, pres. Norwich Mus. Trust, Inc., 1992—; mem., vice chair Southeastern Conn. Regional Planning Commn., 1993—; dir. Family Svc. Southeastern Conn., 1995—, Southeastern Conn. Enterprise Region, Norwich Comm. and Tech. Learning Ctr.; past-pres. Eastern Conn. Cmty. Found.; del. White House Conf. on Aging, 1995. Mem. Norwich Area C. of C. (dir. 1979-81), Greater Willimantic C. of C. (edn. com. 1980-88), United Ch. Women Conn. (bd. dirs.). Democrat. Home: 27 Canterbury Tpke Norwich CT 06360-1812 Office: 83 Windham St Willimantic CT 06226-2211

WILSON, MARK RONALD, education educator; b. Melbourne, Australia, Aug. 23, 1954; s. Arthur Ronald and Mollie Eileen Wilson; m. Janet Susan Williams, July 5, 1985; 2 children. BS, U. Melbourne, Australia, 1975; MEd, U. Melbourne, 1981; PhD, U. Chgo., 1984. Tchr. Victorian Edn. Dept., Melbourne, 1977—79; rsch. officer Australian Coun. for Ednl. Rsch., 1979—81, sr. rsch. officer, 1984—85; asst. prof. La. State U., Baton Rouge, 1986; asst. to assoc. prof. U. Calif., Berkeley, 1986—94, prof., 1995—. Panel mem. Calif. H.S. Exit Exam, 1998—2001; rep. joint com. on stds. for edn. and evaluation, 1999—; com. mem. Nat. Rsch. Coun., Washington, 1998—2001; vis. prof. Katholieke U., Leuven, Belgium, 2001. Editor: (book) Objective measurement, Vols. I-V, 1992—2000, (jour.) Measurement, 2002—. Adv. com. mem. Nat. Bd. Osteopathic Med. Examiners, Chgo., 1999—2001; working group mem. Nat. Cancer Inst., Bethesda, Md., 2000—; adv. com. mem. Ga. Dept. Edn., Atlanta, 1997—. Recipient Galler prize, U. Chgo., 1985; fellow Nat. Acad. Edn., Spencer Found., Chgo., 1990. Office: U Calif Berkeley Tolman Hall Berkeley CA 94720

WILSON, MARY ALICE, violinist, music teacher; b. Nov. 2, 1939; MusB, Northwe. U., 1961. Orch. band dir., pvt. tchr. Lutheran Schs., Deerfield Pub. Schs., 1961-64; pvt. tchr. violin and piano Cleveland, 1964-77; dir. Suzuki Program, violin tchr. West Va. U., 1977—; founder, leader Seneca String Quartet, Morgantown, W.Va., 1986—. Accompanist. Ch. vol. Teaching and Music, Cleveland, Chgo., Morgantown, 1960—. Mem.: Am. String Tchrs. Assn. (co-developer, chmn. 3rd yr. state solo competition), W.Va. Music Tchrs. Assn. (dist. chmn. of strings 1977—, state officer pub. 1989—, State Outstanding Tchr. Yr. 1996), Music Tchrs. Nat. Assn. Home: 237 Poplar Dr Morgantown WV 26505-2519 E-mail: cwilson4@wvu.edu.

WILSON, MARY ELIZABETH, geriatrics nurse; b. Cin., Jan. 22, 1931; d. William S. and Mary E. (Arundel) Ferguson; m. Robert E. Wilson, Dec. 1, 1984; children: Maribeth, Deborah, Michael, Christina. Diploma, Christ Hosp. Sch. Nursing, Cin., 1952; BSN, U. Cin., 1955; postgrad., Xavier U. Instr. Christ Hosp. Sch. Nursing, 1952-56, 73-77; staff devel. coord. Deaconess Hosp., Cin., 1966-72; adminstrv. asst. health svcs. Twin Towers Retirement Home, 1977-84; staff devel. Good Samaritan Village Health Care Ctr., Kissimmee, Fla., 1985-87, DON, 1987-96; quality assurance/infection control coord., 1996—2002. Health educator Comty. Coord. Child Care; former mem. adv. coun. LPN program and health occupations Tech. Edn. Ctr., Kissimmee, 1996—2002. Mem. Nat. League Nursing, Nat. Assn. Dirs. Nursing Adminstrn./Long Term Care, Fla. Assn. Dirs. Nursing Adminstrn./Long-Term Care (past regional coord., past com. chmn., past sec.), Assn. Practitioners in Infection Control (past sec.), Fla. Bd. Nursing (past mem. ad hoc com.).

WILSON, MATTHEW FREDERICK, former newspaper editor; b. San Francisco, May 10, 1956; s. Kenneth E. and Verna Lee (Hunter) W. BA in Philosophy, U. Calif., Berkeley, 1978. Copy person San Francisco Chronicle, summers 1975, 76, 77, copy editor, 1978-82, editorial systems coord., 1982-84; budget analyst San Francisco Newspaper Agy., 1984085; asst. news editor San Francisco Chronicle, 1985-87, asst. to exec. editor, 1987-88, mng. editor, 1988-95, exec. editor, 1995—2001. Mem. Am. Soc. Newspaper Editors, AP Mng. Editors, Calif. Soc. Newspaper Editors.*

WILSON, MELFORD ALONZO, JR. secondary education educator; b. Columbia, S.C., Nov. 30, 1939; s. Melford Alonzo and Daisy Marion (Holler) W.; m. Janet Lytle Riggle, July 2, 1966; children: Marion Eveland, Melford Alonzo, III, John Lytle. BA, Wofford Coll., 1963; MA, Am. U., 1965, PhD, 1969. Tchr. Gulberg Internat. H.S., Lahore, Pakistan, 1960-61; dir. resident counselors Am. Univ., Washington, 1964-67; prof. Winthrop U., Rock Hill, S.C., 1967—, chair dept., 1970-75, 79-85, dir. internat. ctr., 1989-96, v.p. acad. affairs, 1996—. Rsch., staff asst. U.S. Ho. of Reps., Washington, 1975. Author: A Guide to International Relations, 1986; author, editor: Understanding International Relations, 1987; co-author: The Meaning of the Constitution, 1987. Mem. City Coun., Rock Hill, 1978-84; mem. econ. devel. bd., Rock Hill, 1978—; bd. dirs. labor rels. com. Nat. League Cities, 1979-82. Fulbright scholar, 1976, 85-86. Mem. Rock Hill C. of C., Rotary (sr.), Phi Beta Kappa, Phi Kappa Phi. Methodist. Office: Winthrop U 115 Tillman Rock Hill SC 29733-0001 E-mail: wilsonm@winthrop.edu.

WILSON, MELISSA ANNE, sculptor; b. New Rochelle, N.Y., July 9, 1968; d. Alan Williams and Sandra Oliver Simoni. Degree in art, Silvermine Sch. Art, 1989, Wooster Art Ctr., 1990. Art asst. Sandi Oliver, Weston, Conn., 1987—. (1st in show), (1st in show), (1st in show). Mem. Internat. Sculpture Assn., Stanley Bleifeld Assn. Fairfield (asst. sculptor). Avocations: acting, singing, tennis, running, walking. Home: 11 Tubbs Spring Dr # 1203 Weston CT 06883-1413 Office: Sandi Oliver Fine Art PO Box 1203 Weston CT 06883-0203

WILSON, MELISSA ELIZABETH, artist, educator; b. Norfolk, Va., Jan. 27, 1957; d. Joseph Robert and Jeanne Suzanne (Smith) W.; 1 child, Amelia Rose Nordmann. BA, U. Louisville, 1981; MFA, U. Cin., 1983. Decorative artist and designer, Louisville, 1983—. Part-time instr. various univs., pub. schs., pvt. art schs., Louisville, 1983—; visual arts coord., bd. dirs. Artswatch, Louisville, 1993-95; mentor Ky. Found. for Women with Kentuckiana Girl Scouts Art Mentoring Project, 1997-98. One person exhibit Huff Gallery, Spaulding U., Louisville, 1996; group shows include Birmingham Mus. Art, Columbia (S.C.) Mus. Art, La. Arts and Sci.. Ctr.; other prin. works include murals, faux finishes, canvas floor cloths, painted furniture for residential and commercial properties, full size art Nouveau style swinging carousel for theme park, Qingdao, China, eighteen hole miniature golf travelling ednl. exhibit, Natural History Mus. Phila. Selected awards include art residency and fellow Va. Ctr. for Creative Arts, 1994; Ky. Found. for Women Visual Arts grantee, 1988, 94, Ky. Arts Coun. Profl. Devel. grantee, 1990; scholar Ky. Art & Crafts Early Times, 1999.

WILSON, MELVIN EDMOND, civil engineer; b. Bremerton, Wash., Aug. 3, 1935; s. Edmond Curt and Madeline Rose (Deal) W.; m. Deanna May Stevens, Nov. 22, 1957 (div. Mar. 1971); children: Kathleen, Debra Wilson Frank. BSCE, U. Wash., 1957, MSCE, 1958. Registered profl. engr., Wash. Asst. civil engr. City of Seattle, 1958-60, assoc. civil engr., 1960-64, sr. civil engr., 1964-66, supervising civil engr., 1966-75, sr. civil engr., 1975-77, mgr. X, 1977-88; owner Wilson Cons. Svcs., Seattle, 1988-89; transp. sys. dir. City of Renton, Wash., 1989-96, ret., 1996. Owner Mel Wilson Photographer, Seattle, 1975-84. Contbr. reports to profl. jours. Rep. Renton transp. work group King County (Wash.) Growth Mgmt. Policy Com.; rep. Renton tech. adv. com. South County Area Transp. Bd., King County, 1992-96, developer svc. policy (adopted by Puget Sound Govtl. Conf.) to encourage travel by transit. successfuly led effort to make Renton first suburban city to receive direct transit svc. under Met. King County Plan, 1994; vol. personal trainer, 1988—; vol. trainer for medical patients, 1988—. Mem. ASCE, Am. Pub. Works Assn., Inst. Transp. Engrs., Tau Beta Pi, Sigma Xi. Avocations: photography, weight lifting, hiking.

WILSON, MELVIN NOBLE, JR. retired aeronautical and mechanical engineer; b. San Diego, Nov. 7, 1924; s. Melvin N. and Frances C. Wilson; m. Adina Marie Wagner, July 17, 1949; children: Cynthia G., Andrew N. BSME, Calif. Inst. Tech., 1945, MSAE, 1946. Registered profl. engr., Calif. Project aerodynamist Ryan Aero, San Diego, 1946-49; cons. engr. So. Pacific Co., San Francisco, 1949-52; design engr. Nat. Steel and Shipbuilding, San Diego, 1949; designer, planner, tech. facilities project mgr. Jet Propulsion Lab., Pasadena, Calif., 1953-94; pvt. cons., La Cañada, 1994—. Recipient Exceptional Svc. medal NASA, 1994. Mem. Masonic Lodge (past master), La Canada Kiwanis Club. Avocations: computers, fishing, shooting. Home and Office: 2125 Sunnybank Dr La Canada Flintridge CA 91011-1358

WILSON, MICHAEL HOLCOMBE, investment banker, former Canadian government official; b. Toronto, Ont., Can., Nov. 4, 1937; s. Harry Holcombe and Constance L. (Davies) W.; m. Margaret Catherine Smellie, Oct. 17, 1964; children: Cameron (dec.), Geoffrey, Lara. Student, Upper Can. Coll.; B. Comm., U. Toronto, 1959. With Harris & Partners Ltd., Toronto, 1961-63, 65-73, v.p., 1972; exec. v.p. following merger with Dominion Securities Ltd., 1973-79; mem. Can. Ho. of Commons, Ottawa, 1979-93; minister of state for internat. trade Govt. Can., 1979-80, minister of fin., 1984-91, min. of industry, sci. & tech., min. internat. trade, 1991-93; bus. advisor Michael Wilson Internat., Toronto, 1993—; vice chmn. RBC Dominion Securities Inc., 1995-2000; pres., CEO UBS Global Asset Mgmt. (Can.) Co. (formerly Brinson Can. Co.), 2000—. Mem. bd., campaign chmn. Ctr. for Addiction and Mental Health Found., 2000, Comty. Found. for Greater Toronto; bd. dirs. BP PLC, Manulife Fin.; chmn. Neurosci. Can. Found., Can. Coun. for Pub.-Pvt. Partnership. Mem. Toronto Club, Toronto Golf, Badminton and Racquet Club, Osler Bluff Ski Club, Mad River Golf Club, Kappa Alpha. Progressive Conservative. Anglican. Office: UBS Global Asset Mgmt Co 77 King St W PO Box 85 Toronto ON Canada M5K 1G8

WILSON, MICHAEL E. lawyer; b. Rantoul, Ill., Oct. 28, 1951; BA cum laude, Washington U., 1973, JD, 1977. Bar: Mo. 1977. Principal Greensfelder, Hemker & Gale, P.C., St. Louis. Instr. legal writing Washington U. Sch. Law, 1979-82; mem. nat. panel constrn. industry arbitrators and co-chmn. St. Louis Constrn. Adv. Com., 1987-97. Mem. ABA, The Mo. Bar (contbr. jour.), Bar Assn. Metro. St. Louis (contbr. jour.), Order Coif. Office: Greensfelder Hemker & Gale PC 2000 Equitable Bldg 10 S Broadway Saint Louis MO 63102-1712

WILSON, MICHAEL JOHN, biologist, educator; b. Iowa City, June 3, 1942; s. James H. and Doris E. (Lackender) W.; m. Martha J. Swartzwelter, June 7, 1969; 1 child, Matthew. AA, Divine Word Coll., 1962; BA, St. Ambrose Coll., 1964; MS, U. Iowa, 1967, PhD, 1971. Rsch. fellow Harvard Med. Sch. Boston, 1971-73; rsch. assoc. U. Minn., Mpls., 1973-75, asst. prof., 1975-82, assoc. prof., 1982-2000, prof., 2000—. Mem. regional adv. bd. Inst. Disability Studies, 1989-93; rsch. biochemist Mpls. VA Med. Ctr., 1976-2000, career rsch. scientist, 2000—. Mem. editl. bd. Jour. of Andrology, 1998—; contbr. articles to profl. jours. Chmn. spl. edn. coun. St. Paul Pub. Schs., Minn., 1982-85; bd. dirs. United Cerebral Palsy Minn., 1985-96; mem. devel. disabilities com. Ramsey County Citizens Adv. Coun., 1997—; mem. assistive tech. bd. Courage Ctr., 2001—. Mem. Am. Soc. Study Cell Biology, Soc. for Study Reprodn., Am. Soc. Andrology, Soc. Basic Urologic Rsch. Democrat. Roman Catholic. Home: 2053 Dayton Ave Saint Paul MN 55104-5732 E-mail: wilso042@tc.umn.edu.

WILSON, MICHAEL MOUREAU, lawyer, physician; b. Cheverly, Md., Dec. 30, 1952; s. Kenneth Moureau and Helen (Rice) Smith. BS, MIT, 1974; JD, Georgetown U., 1977, MD, 1986. Bar: D.C. 1977, N.Y. 1980, U.S. Dist. Ct. D.C. 1980, U.S. Dist. Ct. Md. 1992, U.S. Ct. Appeals (D.C. cir.) 1980, U.S. Supreme Ct. 1981. Law clk. Hon. John B. Hannum U.S. Dist. Ct., Phila., 1977-78; assoc. Cravath Swaine & Moore, N.Y.C., 1978-79; asst. to gen. counsel NSF, Washington, 1979-82; resident in psychiatry St. Elizabeth Hosp., 1986-89; pvt. practice med. malpractice litigation, 1989—. Notes editor Am. Criminal Law Rev., 1976-77. Mem. ABA, Assn. Trial Lawyers Am., D.C. Trial Lawyers Assn., Phi Beta Kappa. Office: 1700 K St NW Ste 1007 Washington DC 20006-3815 E-mail: wilson@wilsonlaw.com.

WILSON, MICHAEL WILLIAM, language educator; b. Camp Gordon, Ga., Nov. 18, 1953; s. William Woodrow Wilson, Roberta Ellen Burke; m. Harriet Dick Sperr, Oct. 9, 1999; stepchildren: Harriet Cazenove Haltermann, Mary Bryan Haltermann, Julia Speer Haltermann. BA in History, German and French, U. Ga., 1977, MA in German, 1981; PhD in Germanic Langs. and Lits., U. Calif.-Santa Barbara, 1992. Tchg. asst. U. Ga., Athens, 1978, 1979—80; lehrbeauftragter U. Erlangen, Germany, 1978—79; tchg. asst. U. Calif., Santa Barbara, 1981—84; tchr. English Tubman Mid. Sch., Augusta, Ga., 1985—88; tchr. history and English Aquinas H.S., 1988—2000; instr. history Augusta State U., 1995—2000; adj. prof. German and French Coll. of Charleston, SC, 2001—. Vis. instr. German and French Western Ky. U., Bowling Green, 2000—01. Grantee Exchange grantee, DAAD, 1978—79; scholar Fulbright-Hays scholar, Fulbright Com., 1982—83. Democrat. Roman Catholic. Home: 2114 Richmond Ave Augusta GA 30904 Office: College of Charleston Dept of Classics and German 66 George St Charleston SC 29242

WILSON, MICHELINE, small business owner; b. Villotte-Sur-Aire, Meuse, France, Dec. 7, 1945; came to U.S., 1967; d. Jean Roger Clausse and Mauricette Marie Bohin; m. Steven Owen Wilson, June 1, 1976 (div. 1984). Bachelor's, Lycee de Jeunes Filles, Metz, Moselle, France, 1964. Lic. cosmetology. Hairstylist Mr. John's Beauty Salon, Augusta, Ga., 1968-70, Laurens, S.C., 1970-72; hairstylist, owner Micheline Hair Salon, Lakeland, Fla., 1973—. One-woman show Burdines, 1996. Recipient awards Lakeland Art Guild, 1990, 92, 95, Ridge Art Assn., Winterhaven, Fla., 1994, Fla. Strawberry Festival, Plant City, 1993, Salon Today mag. and Chgo. Cosmetologists, 2000, one of Top 200 Fastest Growing Salons in the Nation Three Yrs. in a Row, Best Philanthropic Program for Salons of Its Size in the Nation, Small Bus. award Lakeland Area C. of C., 2001. Mem. The Salon Assn., Nat. Assn. Women Bus. Owners. Avocations: painting, world beat music, yoga, reading. Office: Micheline Salonspa 5035 S Lakeland Dr Lakeland FL 33813-2558

WILSON, MINTER LOWTHER, JR. retired officers association executive; b. Morgantown, W.Va., Aug. 19, 1925; s. Minter Lowther and Mary Mildred (Friend) W.; m. Helen Hope Sauerwein, June 18, 1946; children— Mary Florence, Barbara Ann, Karen Lee, Stephen David BS in Mil. Sci. and Engring., U.S. Mil. Acad., 1946; MS in Journalism, U. Wis., Madison, 1963; diploma, NATO Def. Coll., Rome, 1969, U.S. Army War Coll., 1971. Commd. officer U.S. Army, 1946, advanced through grades to col., comdg. officer 1st Brigade, 1st Armored Div., 1968-69; chief of pub. info. Supreme Hdqrs. Allied Powers, Europe, 1969-72; editor Ret. Officer Mag., Alexandria, Va., 1972-88. Dir. communications Ret. Officers Assn., Alexandria, 1972-88. Contbr. articles to profl. jours. Chmn. bd. deacons Ch. of the Covenant, Arlington, 1974-77, elder, 1977-80, 88-93, 98-2001, clk. of session, 1991-94, chmn. bd. trustees, 1982-86; mem. troop com. Boy Scouts Am., 1972-78. Decorated Commendation medal, Legion of Merit (2); recipient George Washington Honor medal Freedoms Found., 1975, 76, 77, George Washington Honor medal encased Freedoms Found., 1979, Honor cert. Freedoms Found., 1973, 74, 78 Mem. West Point Soc. of D.C. (life, bd. govs. 1978-81), Army Distaff Found. (bd. dirs. 1980-83), Assn. U.S. Army, Ret. Officers Assn. (life). Clubs: Army Navy Country. Presbyterian. Avocations: photography; golf; skiing; tennis; racquetball. Home: 3116 N Thomas St Arlington VA 22207-4120

WILSON, MIRIAM JANET WILLIAMS, publishing executive; b. London, Can., July 13, 1939; d. Ralph George and Lillian Conn Williams; m. Carson Winnette, Nov. 20, 1960 (div. 1971); children: Barrie Carson Winnette, Rebecca Lynn Winnette; m. Charles Lindsay Wilson, Dec. 14, 1973; 1 child, Charles William Wilson; stepchildren: Kenneth M., Carol Ann, Catherine S., Nancy L., Patrick L. Diploma in nursing, Glendale (Calif.) Sanitarium & Hosp., 1960. RN, Calif., Va., Ohio, Md., W.Va. Head nurse emergency and med. fls. Glendale Sanitarium and Hosp., 1960-65; psychometrist Harding Hosp., Worthington, Ohio, 1969-73; biofeedback specialist in assn. Dr. Randolph P. Johnston, Winchester, Va., 1980-84; dir. Stress Ctr. for Children and Adults, Shepherdstown, W.Va., 1985-87; pres. Rocky River Pubs. LLC, 1987—. Lectr. ednl., profl. and civic groups, 1984—. Author: Help For Children, 6 edits., 1987-95, Stress Stoppers, 2 edits., 1987-89; contbr. articles to profl. publs. Active Shepherdstown Women's Club, 1986-2000. Mem. NAFE, Internat. Platform Assn., Am. Booksellers Assn., N.Y. Acad. Scis. Avocations: gardening, music, reading. Office: Rocky River Pubs LLC PO Box 1679 Shepherdstown WV 25443-1679

WILSON, MITCHELL B. fraternal organization administrator; b. Berea, Ky., Jan. 27, 1956; s. William Paul and Shirley Ann (Rose) W.; m. Joan Gentry, May 25, 1985; 1 child, Theodore Mitchell. BA, U. Ky., Lexington, 1980. Chpt. cons. Kappa Sigma Frat., Charlottsville, Va., 1980-82, exec. asst., 1982-83, dir. chpt. ops., 1983-85, dir. pub. rels., 1985-87, exec. dir., 1987—. Editor: The Caducens Mag., 1987—. Mem. Am. Soc. Assoc. Execs., Frat. Execs. Assn. Home: 506 Nottingham Rd Charlottesville VA 22901-1239 Office: Kappa Sigma PO Box 5066 Charlottesville VA 22905-5066

WILSON, MORROW, theater producer, writer, actor; b. N.Y.C., N.Y., Jan. 11, 1940; m. Rue McClanahan, 1997. Graduate, The Putney Sch., 1957; BA in English, Columbia Coll. Creative group supr. Compton Advt., N.Y.C., 1966—70; copywriter BBDO, 1972—73; dir. broadcasting ACLU, Newark, 1978—79; dir. theatrical advt. J. Walter Thompson, N.Y.C., 1980—81; prodn. chief CBS Cable, 1981—82; dir. mktg. Herald Ctr., 1985—88; prodr. Broadway, 1988—; actor various, 1988—. Author: M.I.M., 1974; editor: Rural America, Drugs in American Life; contbr. columns in newspapers; performer: All N.Y. C. TV, radio stations in N.Y. and N.J.; prodr.: David Susskind's talk show, 1961; author: (plays) A Temporary Condition, 1998; actor: (TV series) The Adams Chronicles, 1975; (plays) more than 60 N.Y. prodns.; (films) State of Grace, As Strange As They Come, The Secretary; (TV series) Safe Harbor, As The World Turns, Guiding Light, Ryan's Hope, Somerset, The Edge of Night, All My Children. Nominee CLIO award; recipient Best Read award, STARCH, award, Time-Life Group. Mem.: Screen Actors Guild, Am. Fedn. TV & Radio Artists, Actors Equity Assn., Authors League Am., Dramatists Guild, The Players Club. Home: 248 E 31st St Apt 6d New York NY 10016-9715

WILSON, MYRON ROBERT, JR. retired psychiatrist; b. Helena, Mont., Sept. 21, 1932; s. Myron Robert Sr. and Constance Ernestine (Bultman) W. *Member of Sons of the American Revolution. Direct descendant of William Wilson, who emigrated to New York from England in 1740. Third generation Montanan, whose family owned and operated hardware jobbing and retail operation in Helena from 1866-1966. Maternal grandfather, D.G.F. Bultman, emigrated from Germany to Sumter, South Carolina in 1890, where he owned and operated dry goods and grocery stores, cotton farms. Sister, Josephine Wilson Boyington married World War II marine flying ace, "Pappy" Boyington.* BA, Stanford U., 1954, MD, 1957. Diplomate Am. Bd. Psychiatry and Neurology. Dir. adolescent psychiatry Mayo Clinc, Rochester, Minn., 1965-71; pres. and psychiatrist in chief Wilson Ctr., Faribault, 1971-86; ret., 1986; chmn. Wilson Ctr., 1986-90; ret., 1990. Assoc. clin. prof. psychiatry UCLA, 1985-99. *Among the first American psychiatrists to limit practice to the new sub-specialty of adolescent psychiatry; developed and directed the adolescent psychiatry program at the Mayo Clinic, including an 18 bed in-patient unit for the long term treatment of (mostly psychotic) adolescents from 1965-71. Acquired the St. James School campus in Faribault, MN where he established the C.B. Wilson Center for adolescents in 1971, as the first facility of its kind in the country. It combined a national referral hospital for teens whose prior treatments had been unsuccessful with an accredited private secondary school for patients and a two- year, master's degree training institute for adolescent psychotherapists.* Contbr. articles to profl. jours. Chmn., CEO C.B. Wilson Found., L.A., 1972—; mem. bd. dirs. Pasadena Symphony Orchestra Assn., Calif., 1987; vestryman, treas. St. Thomas' Parish, L.A., 1993-96. Lt. comdr., 1958-60. Fellow Mayo Grad. Sch. Medicine, Rochester, 1960-65. Fellow Am. Psychiat. Assn., Am. Soc. for Adolescent Psychiatry, Internat. Soc. for Adolescent Psychiatry (founder, treas. 1985-88, sec. 1985-88, treas. 1988-92); mem. Soc. Sigma Xi (Mayo Found. chpt.). Episcopalian. Office: Wilson Found 2565 Zorada Dr Los Angeles CA 90046-1747 E-mail: rwilso4488@aol.com.

WILSON, NANCY JEANNE, laboratory consultant, medical technologist; b. Neptune, N.J., Apr. 17, 1951; d. Harry E. Sr. and Kathryn E. (O'Shea) W. BS, Monmouth Coll., 1975; MPA, Fairleigh Dickinson U., 1988. Clin. intern med. tech., staff med. technologist Riverview Med. Ctr., 1975; staff med. technologist Rush Clin. Labs., Red Bank, N.J., 1975, Kimball Med. Ctr., Lakewood, 1975-76, clin. lab. supr., 1976-86; infection control practice Jersey Shore Med. Ctr., Neptune, 1990; dir. lab. and diagnostic svcs. Carrier Clinic, Belle Meade, NJ, 1991—2002, lab. and infection control cons., 2002—. Mem. Am. Soc. Clin. Pathologists (diplomate lab. mgmt.), Am. Assn. Clin. Chemistry, Am. Soc. Microbiology, Clin. Lab. Mgmt. Assn., Am. Soc. Clinics Lab. Sci., Pi Alpha Alpha. Avocations: golf, walking, relaxing. Home: 42 Monument St Freehold NJ 07728-1721

WILSON, NORMAN GLENN, church administrator, writer; b. Rensselaer, N.Y., Nov. 3, 1936; s. Lawrence Wilbur and Wilhelmena Augusta (Knapp) W.; m. Nancy Ann Deyo, Nov. 17, 1956; children: Beth, Lawrence, Jonathan. BRE in Religious Edn., United Wesleyan Coll., 1958, DD (hon.), 1986; MA in Biblical Studies, Winona Lake Sch. Theology, 1968. Pastor The Wesleyan Ch., 1958-76, Gloversville, N.Y., 1963-66, North Lakeport, Mich., 1966-70, Owosso, 1970-76, dir. comm. Indpls., 1992—. Program prodr., speaker The Wesleyan Hour, Indpls., 1975—; mem. gen. bd. adminstrn. The Wesleyan Ch., Indpls., 1992—; disting. lectr. Staley Found., 1986. Author: How to Have a Happy Home, 1976, Christianity in Shoe Leather, 1978, The Constitution of the Kingdom, 1989, People Just Like Us, 1994, Follow the Leader, A Daily Spiritual Journey, 1996; editor, contbr.: Journey Into Holiness, 2000; The Call to Contentment, 2002; editor The Wesleyan Advocate, 1992—. Mem. Nat. Religious Broadcasters (bd. dirs. 1984—, Merit award 1984). Avocations: oil painting, antique cars. Home: 304 Scarborough Way Noblesville IN 46060-3881 E-mail: wilsonn@wesleyan.org.

WILSON, ORPHA HILDRED, writer; b. Glenwood, Minn., Mar. 19, 1920; d. Martin Nelson and Helga Halvorson; m. Dale Wilson (dec. Apr. 1987); children: Bruce, Rodney, Richard, Mary, Marva (dec.), Maureen, Bradley, Dale Jr. GED, Southwestern Tech., 1988. Author: (children's books as Orpha Nelson Wilson) Twinky and Friends, 1995, Mittens, Peanut, Robbie and Friends, 1998, (short stories) Christmas Stories, 1991, 92; contbr. articles, short stories to profl. jours., mags., newspapers. Lutheran. Avocations: reading, writing, sewing stuffed animals, baking. Home: 550 W Schlieman Ave Appleton MN 56208-1234

WILSON, OWEN MEREDITH, JR. lawyer; b. Oakland, Calif., Dec. 22, 1939; s. O. Meredith and Marian Wilson; m. Sandra A. Wilson (div.); children: Ann, Melissa, Jennifer; m. Teddi Anne Wilson; children: Amanda, Lisa. Student, U. Utah, 1957-59; AB, Harvard U., 1961; LLB, U. Minn., 1965. Bar: Oreg. 1965, Wash. 1985. Ptnr. Lane Powell Spears Lubersky, Portland, Oreg., 1969—. Mem. mediation panel U.S. Dist. Ct., 1986—. Mem. bd. visitors Law Sch. U. Minn., 1990-96. Mem. ABA, Oreg. State Bar Assn., Wash. State Bar, Multnomah Bar Assn. Office: 601 SW 2nd Ave Ste 2100 Portland OR 97204-3158 E-mail: wilsonm@lanepowell.com.

WILSON, PATRICIA POTTER, library science and reading educator, educational and library consultant; b. Jennings, La., May 3, 1946; d. Ralph Harold and Wilda Ruth (Smith) Potter; m. Wendell Merlin Wilson, Aug. 24, 1968. BS, La. State U., 1967; MS, U. Houston-Clear Lake, 1979; EdD, U. Houston, 1985. Cert. tchr., learning resources specialist (libr.), Tex. Tchr. England AFB (La.) Elem. Sch., 1967-68, Edward White Elem. Sch./Clear Creek Ind. Schs., Seabrook, Tex., 1972-77; libr. C.D. Landolt Elem. Sch., Friendswood, 1979-81; instr./lectr. children's lit. U. Houston, 1983-86; with U. Houston/Clear Lake, 1984-87, asst. prof. libr. sci. and reading, 1988-94, assoc. prof. learning resources and reading edn., 1994—2001, assoc. prof. emeritus, 2001—, faculty devel. com. chair, 1995-97, mem faculty senate, 1992-93, reading search com. chair, tchg. task force, 1997-98, reading and libr. sci. program chair, 1997-98, Piper award com., 1996—, U. Faculty award com., 1997, U. learning assessment task force, 1997-98, promotion and tenure com. chair, 1999. Cons. Hermann Hosp., Baywood Hosp., 1986-87, Bedford Meadows Hosp., 1989-90, Wetcher Clinic, 1989; co-owner, v.p. Potter Farms, Inc., 1994—. Editor: A Review Sampler, 1985—86, 1989—90; author: Happenings: Developing Successful Programs for School Libraries, 1987, The Professional Collection for Elementary Educators, 1996, Premiere Events: Library Programs That Inspire Elementary Patrons, 2001, Leadership for Today's School Library, 2001, Igniting the Spark: Library Programs that Inspire High School Patrons, 2001, Center Stage: Library Programs That Inspire Middle School Patrons, 2002; contbg. editor: Tex. Libr. Jour., 1988—94; contbr. articles to profl. jours. Trustee Freeman Meml. Libr., Houston, 1982—87, v.p., 1985—86, pres., 1986—87; trustee Evelyn Meador Libr., 1993—94, adv. bd., 1994—; mem. Bay Area Houston Symphony League, Assistance League of the Bay Area, 1997—; founder Friends of Neumann Libr., 1998; chmn. hospitality com. Lunar Rendevous Festival, 1998—2001; gen. chmn. Lunar Rendezvous Festival, 2002; mem. adv. bd. Bay Area Soc. Prevention Cruelty Animals, 1994—98, Bay Area Turning Point, 1998—; bd. dirs. Sta. KUHT-TV, 1984—87, Friends of Neumann Libr., 1998—99, Clear Lake Met. Ballet, 2001—; dir. Learning Resources Book Rev. Ctr., 1989—90; bd. dirs. UHCL Alumni Assn., 1998—2001, v.p. adminstrn., 2000, anniversary hon. com., 1999—2000, mem. 25th anniversary com., 1999, alumni ball com., 1999; mem. Armand Bayou Nature Ctr., Houston, 1980, bd. dirs., 1989—94. Named Outstanding Vol. of Yr., Houston's Nat. Philanthropy Day, 1999; named one of 10 Men and Women of Heart, Bay Area Turning Point, 2001; recipient Rsch. award, Tex. State Reading Assn., 1993, Pres. award, Tex. Coun. Tchrs. English, Disting. Tchg. award, Enron Corp., 1996, Disting. Alumni award, U. Houston-Clear Lake, 1998, Disting. Alumna award, U. Houston-Main Campus, Coll. Edn., 2002, award, Minnie Piper Tchg., 1996; grantee, Tex. Libr. Assn., 1993. Mem. ALA, Am. Assn. Sch. Librs., Internat. Reading Assn., Nat. Coun. Tchrs. English (Books for You rev. com. 1985-88, 97—, Your Reading rev. com. 1993-96), Tex. Coun. Tchrs. English, Antarctican Soc., Alumni Assn. U. Houston-Clear Lake (bd. dirs. 1998-2000), Bay Oaks Country Club, Phi Delta Kappa, Phi Kappa Phi (sec. 1997-98, pres. 1998-99). Methodist.

WILSON, PAUL, baseball player; b. Orlando, Fla., Mar. 28, 1973; Baseball player Tampa Bay Devil Rays , 2000—. Office: Tampa Bay Devil Rays One Tropicana Dr Saint Petersburg FL 33705*

WILSON, PAUL HOLLIDAY, JR. lawyer; b. Schenectady, N.Y., Sept. 4, 1942; s. Paul H. and Sarah Elizabeth (MacLean) W.; m. Elaine Hawley Griffin, May 30, 1964; children: Hollace, Paul, Kirsten, Katherine. AB, Brown U., 1964; LLB, MBA, Columbia U., 1967. Bar: N.Y. 1967, U.S. Dist. Ct. (so. dist.) 1968. Law clk. U.S. Dist. Ct. (so. dist.) N.Y., N.Y.C., 1967-68; assoc. Debevoise & Plimpton, 1968-75, ptnr., 1976—, fin. ptnr., 1980-88, 91-93, 2001—, dep. presiding ptnr., 1993-98. Vice-chmn., trustee St. Michael's Montessori Sch., N.Y.C., 1977-79, chmn. bd. trustees, 1979-81. Mem. ABA, Assn. Bar City N.Y. (mem. commn. on securities regulations 1985-88). Clubs: Vineyard Haven Yacht (Mass.) (vice-commodore 1985, commodore 1986-87). Avocations: sailing, reading, music. Office: Debevoise & Plimpton 919 Third Ave New York NY 10022-6225 E-mail: phwilson@debevoise.com.

WILSON, PAUL W., JR. lawyer, entrepreneur; b. Salt Lake City, 1948; s. Paul W. and Helen June (Jackson) W.; m. Ann Stevens, 1971; children: Paul III, Laura, Jenny, Jane, Lisa, Mary. BA cum laude high honors with distinction, Brigham Young U., 1972; JD, U. Minn., 1975. Bar: Minn. 1975. Pres. LW Enterprises, Mpls., 1972-89, Sights on Svc., Inc., Mpls., 1989—. Bd. dirs. Am. Harvest, Chaska, Minn. Commr. Viking coun. Boy Scouts Am., Mpls., 1988—90; adv. bd., coach Plymouth, 1981—2001; mem. Brigham Young U. Alumni Bd., Provo, Utah, 1987—91, NHCP, 1987—95, pres., 1991—93. Recipient Silver Beaver Boy Scouts Am., 1988, Award of Merit Boy Scouts Am., 1984; Hinckley scholar, 1971-72, Univ. scholar, 1972. Mem. Ch. of Jesus Christ of Latter Day Saints. Avocations: reading, water skiing, basketball, scouting, youth activities.

WILSON, PAUL WAYNE, retired real estate developer; b. Kokomo, Ind., June 13, 1933; s. Floyd Wayne Wilson and Stella (Dugan) Emry; m. Dixie Lee Cooprider, Feb. 23, 1952; children: Michael Wayne, Susan Jo Wilson-Broadus, Marci Ann, Paul Wayne II. Student, Ind. Bus. Coll., 1957-59. Cert. environ. inspector, environ. specialist,. constrn. inspector. Salesperson Kothe, Wells & Bauer, Indpls., 1956-60; owner, founder Pickin Chicken, Kokomo, 1958-60; broker Wayne Wilson Realty, Inc., 1963-98; owner Wayne Wilson Constrn. Co., 1960-78; apartment developer, 1998-2000; retired, 2000. V.p. Pyramid Inc., Kokomo, 1967-72, Mi-Su-Mar, Inc., Kokomo, 1967-78; founder, pres. Able Alarm Co., Inc., Kokomo, 1976-83; mgr. Honeywell Protection Svcs., Kokomo, 1983-97, ret.; pres., founder Midwest Organics, Inc., Kokomo, 1989—. Sch. bd. Taylor Community Schs., Center, Ind., 1963-73, pres., 1971; del. Dem. State Conv., Indpls., 1972; pres. Ind. Burglar & Fire Alarm Assn., 1982. Staff sgt. USAF, 1951-55. Recipient Beautification award Kokomo C. of C., 1979. Mem. Elks, Rotary. Roman Catholic. Avocations: flying, organic gardening. Home: 3400 Tally Ho Dr Kokomo IN 46902-3961 E-mail: earthwomb@aol.com.

WILSON, PAUL WAYNE, economics educator, consultant; b. Memphis, Sept. 9, 1958; s. Claude Wayne and Anna Marie (Simmons) W. BA in Econs., Rice U., 1980; AM in Econs., Brown U., 1982, PhD in Econs., 1986. Asst. prof. econs. U. Ga., Athens, 1985-90, U. Tex., Austin, 1990-94, assoc. prof. econs., 1994—. Rsch. VA, Boston, 1990—; vis. scholar Fed. Res. Bank of St. Louis, 1993—, l'Inst. de Statistique Univ. Catholique de Louvain, Louvain-la-Neuve, Belgium, 1995-96. Contbr. articles to profl. jours. Grantee IBM, 1988, NSF, 1993-96. Mem. Am. Econ. Assn., Econometric Soc., Inst. for Math. Stats., Western Econ. Assn., Inst. for Ops. Rsch. and Mgmt. Scis. Office: U Tex Dept Econs Austin TX 78712

WILSON, PETER MASON, computer programmer; b. N.Y.C., Mar. 14, 1934; s. Kenneth Mason and Priscilla (Nickerson) W.; m. Lois S., July 13, 1957; children: Katherine Rose, Kenneth Mason II. BS, Ga. Tech., 1960; MS,

Fla. State U., 1965, PhD, 1975. Asst. prof. Fla. A&M U., Tallahassee, 1966-77; sys. analyst U. Fla., 1977-79; instrnl. designer Control Data Corp., Rockville, Md., 1979-85, Booze, Allen & Hamilton, Rockville, 1985-88, Pace Enterprises, Falls Church, Md., 1989-91; sr. tech. trainer Arbitron, Laurel, 1991-94; project mgr., instrnl. designer Bell Atlantic, Balt., 1994—. Chair computer usage in pub. schs. Fairfax (Va.) Bd. of Edn., 1985-88; cons. evaluation spl. edn. Howard County Bd. of Edn., Ellicott City, Md., 1991-93. Active vestry Holy Comforter, Vienna, Va., 1985-89, demographics com. St. John's Ch., Ellicott City, 1992-93. Nat. Urban League fellow, 1969, Atomic Energy Commn. fellow, 1972; recipient Howard County Bd. of Edn. commendation, 1993. Mem. AERA (session chair), SALT (presenter), Math. Assn. Am. (presenter), Theta Chi. Episcopalian. Home: 7409 Barrister Ct Spotsylvania VA 22553-2577 Office: Bell Atlantic 1 E Pratt St Ste 1 Baltimore MD 21202-1129

WILSON, PETER WYMAN, internist, cardiovascular metabolic epidemiologist; b. New Haven, Oct. 13, 1948; m. Peggy Susan Lindsey. BS, Yale U., 1970; MD, U. Tex., 1974. Diplomate Am. Bd. Internal Medicine, Am. Bd. Endocrinology. Resident Duke U., Durham, N.C., 1974-78; med. officer Nat. Heart, Lung and Blood Inst./NIH, Bethesda, Md., 1978-98; dir. labs. Framingham Heart Study, 1983—; prof. medicine Boston U. Med. Sch., 2000—. Contbr. over 250 articles to profl. jours. Office: BU Sch of Medicine 715 Albany St Evans 204 Boston MA 02118 E-mail: pwilson@bu.edu.

WILSON, PHILIP KEVIN, science and medical historian; b. Wichita, Kans., July 13, 1961; s. Robert Louis and Margaret Lilian (Guyot) W.; m. Janice C. Franklin, May 20, 1989; children: James Collier, Douglas Lawrence. B Gen. Studies with distinction, U. Kans., 1983; postgrad., U. Kans., Kansas City, 1983-85, 87; MA in Med. History, Johns Hopkins U., 1988; PhD in Sci. History, Univ. Coll., London, 1992. Historian of sci. Truman State U., Kirksville, Mo., 1994-99, Shimer Coll, Waukegan, Ill., 1999-2000; med. editor Encyclopedia Britannica, Chgo., 2000—; med. historian Pa. State Coll. of Medicine, 2000—. Dictionary salesman Southwestern Co., Bakersfield, Calif., 1980; lab. rschr. U. Kans. Pharmacology Dept., Lawrence, 1980-83; med. history rschr. U. Kans. Med. Ctr., Kansas City, 1984-85; oral history (Polio) rschr. Woods Hole (Mass.) Rsch. Labs, 1986; lectr. U. Hawaii, 1992-93; rsch. affiliate Yale U., 1993-94. Author: Surgery, Skin and Syphilis: Daniel Turner's London, 1999; editor: Childbirth History, 1996; contbr. articles to profl. jours. Student pres. Quivira Coun. Explorer Scouts, 1978, 79. Logan Clendening fellow U. Kans. Med. Ctr., 1984; Owsei Temkin fellow Johns Hopkins U., 1985-87; Folger Shakespeare Libr. fellow, Washington, 1987; Wellcome Trust fellow, London, 1989-92; Mellon fellow Am. Philos. Soc., 2001. Mem. Am. Assn. for History of Medicine, History of Sci. Soc., Brit. Soc. for History of Sci., Arthur Conan Doyle Soc., Soc. Psychical Rsch., Am. Hist. Assn., Am. Soc. for Eighteenth Century Studies, Alpha Chi Sigma (Master Alchemist 1982-83), Phi Kappa Phi (pres. chpt. 1997-98). Republican. Avocations: clarinetist, antiquarian, Sherlock Holmes/Conan Doyle enthusiast. Home: 1080 Shadywood Dr Hummelstown PA 17036 Office: Pa State Coll Medicine Dept Humanities H134 500 University Dr Hershey PA 17033-2390 E-mail: pwilson@psu.edu.

WILSON, PHILLIP DAVID, scriptwriter, educator; b. Fategarh, India, Apr. 16, 1931; arrived in U.S., 1967; s. George Cuthbert Wilson and Emily Norma Wagstaff; m. Maud Tomlin Wilson, Apr. 25, 1961; children: Dean Phillip, Dawn Elizabeth. Assoc., Royal Acad. Dramatic Arts, London, 1954; BS, U. Rochester, 1976; MA, SUNY, Brockport, 1986. Viceman fitter Guest, Keenwilliams & Co., Calcutta, India; merchant marine Norway; machinist Hoffman & Co., Chelmsford, England, 1962—67; quality insp. Mobil Chem., Macedon, NY, 1968—71; assembler Dollinger Corp., Henrietta, 1972; quality control insp. Ritter Co., Rochester, 1972—81, Tool-Tec, Inc., Rochester, 1981—82; machinist Macinnes Tool Co., 1983—96; quality control insp. Superior Tech., 1996—98, Gillette Machine and Tool Co., Rochester, 1998—. Sub. tchr. N.Y. Bd. Edn.; screenplay writer. Author: (screenplay) The Golden Lore, 1988, The Black Messiah, 1998, In Ages Past, 2000. Avocations: writing screenplays, reading, movies, Karom. Home: 3613 Haskell Rd Cuba NY 14727

WILSON, R. DALE, marketing educator, consultant; b. Ironton, Ohio, July 16, 1949; s. Robert J. and Treva L. (Shively) W.; m. Emily J. Ray, June 19, 1971; 1 child, Travis Ray. BBA cum laude, Ohio U., 1971; MBA, U. Toledo, 1972; PhD, U. Iowa, 1977. Asst. prof. mktg. Pa. State U., University Park, 1976-80; v.p., dir. mktg. scis. Batten, Barton, Durstine & Osborn, Inc., N.Y.C., 1980-83; vis. prof. Cornell U., Ithaca, N.Y., 1983-84; assoc. prof. Mich. State U., East Lansing, 1984-87, prof., 1987—. Cons. in field. Contbr. articles to profl. jours. Youth baseball and basketball coach, East Lansing, 1989-98. Faculty Rsch. grantee Pa. State U., Mich. State U. Mem. Am. Acad. Advt., Am. Mktg. Assn., Inst. Ops. Rsch. and Mgmt. Scis. (assoc. editor Interfaces, cert. recognition 1983), Product Devel. and Mgmt. Assn., Beta Gamma Sigma. Home: 859 Audubon Rd East Lansing MI 48823-3003 Office: Mich State U Eli Broad Grad Sch Mgmt Dept Mktg/Supply Chain Mgmt N322 N Business Complex East Lansing MI 48824-1122 E-mail: wilsonrr@msu.edu.

WILSON, RALPH COOKERLY, JR. professional football team executive; b. Columbus, Ohio, Oct. 17, 1918; s. Ralph Cookerly and and Edith (Cole) W.; children: Christy Cole, Linda Brown, Edith Denise. AB, U. Va., 1940; postgrad., U. Mich., 1940-41. Pres. Ralph C. Wilson Jr. Enterprises (privately owned family bus.); engaged in profl. football, roadbuilding Detroit, 1946—; pres., owner Buffalo Bills Profl. Football Club, 1959—. With USNR, 1941-46. Decorated Commendation medal. Mem. Ocean Club of Fla., Country Club of Detroit, Grosse Pointe (Mich.) Club, Buffalo Country Club, Shriners. Presbyterian.

WILSON, RAMON B. educator; b. Ogden, Utah, Sept. 22, 1922; s. Benjamin Andrew and Hannah Josephine (Browning) W.; m. Ruth G. Worlton, July 27, 1945; children: Lynn, William Scott, Bruce Ramon, JoAnne, Kathleen. BS, Utah State U., 1947; MS, Purdue U., 1948, PhD, 1950; postgrad., Georgetown U., 1976. Extension economist Utah State U., Logan, 1950-53; mktg. economist Calif. Dept. Agr., Sacramento, 1953-55; asst. prof. Purdue U., West Lafayette, Ind., 1955-57, assoc. prof., 1957-63, prof. agrl. econs., 1963-78, prof. emeritus, 1978—, market service dir., 1960-68; asst. dir. Ind. Coop. Extension Service, 1963-74; assoc. dir. agrl. expt. sta., asst. to dean agr. Purdue U., 1968-74; from asst. to assoc. dir. Benson Agrl. Food Inst. Brigham Young U., Provo, Utah, 1979-82. Asst. to sec. U.S. Dept. Agr., Washington, 1974-76; cons., lectr. in field. Served with U.S. Army, 1942-46. Home: 435 E 2200 N Provo UT 84604-1725

WILSON, RANDOLPH PRESTON, lawyer, businessman; b. Indpls., Sept. 22, 1945; s. Hobson and Elizabeth (Preston) W.; s. Rae Lathrop, June 11, 1966; children: Timothy, Whitney, Bradley, Spencer, Todd, Jamison. BA, Ind. U., 1967; JD, U. Denver, 1972. Bar: Ind. 1972. Ptnr. Krieg De Vault Alexander & Capehart, Indpls., 1972-86; v.p. devel., bd. dirs. METS, Inc., 1987-89; counsel to vice pres. Office of V.P., Washington, 1989-90; vice chmn. bd. Mchts. Nat. Corp., Indpls., 1990-92; pub. policy advisor Ipalco Enterprises, Inc., 1994-95. Bd. dirs. Happy Hollow Camp, Indpls., 1983—, Indpls. Pks. Found., 1993—, Greater Indpls. Progress Com., 1984-96, Jr. Achievement Ctrl. Ind., Indpls., 1990-92; prin. Coun. for Excellence in Govt., Washington, 1990—. Capt. USMC, 1967-70. Republican. Presbyterian. Avocations: fishing, hunting, scuba diving, boating, snow skiing. Home: 13504 Brentwood Ln Carmel IN 46033-9488

WILSON, RHYS THADDEUS, lawyer; b. Albany, Ga., May 9, 1955; s. Joseph Farr Jr. and Betty Ann (Wilkins) W.; m. Carolyn Reid Saffold, June 2, 1984. AB, Duke U., 1976; JD, U. Ga., 1979; LLM, Emory U., 1985. Bar: Ga. 1979. Pvt. practice law, Atlanta, 1979-89; sr. v.p., gen. counsel Monarch Capital Group, Inc., 1989-92, Jackson & Coker, Inc., Atlanta, 1992-93; pres. Jackson & Coker Locum Tenens, Inc., 1993-95; ptnr. Robins, Kaplan, Miller & Ciresi, 1995—. Spkr. continuing legal edn. seminars. Contbr. articles to profl. jours. Mem. ABA, Ga. Bar Assn. (chmn. internat. law sect. 1987-88, exec. com. corp. and banking law sect. 1987-89, editl. bd. Ga. State Bar Jour. 1986-89), Atlanta Bar Assn. (editor newsletter 1984-86, Outstanding Svc. award 1986), Assn. for Corp. Growth, Atlanta Network Alliance, Atlanta Tech. Angels, The Exec. Com. TEC, Atlanta Venture Forum, Capital City Club. Episcopalian.

WILSON, RICHARD ALLAN, landscape architect; b. Chgo., Feb. 5, 1927; s. Edgar Allan and Lois Helena (Hearn) W.; m. Lisabet Julie Horchler, May 31, 1958; children: Gary Allan, Carl Bruce. BS, U. Calif., Berkeley, 1952. Engring. draftsman Freeland Evanson & Christenson, San Diego, 1952-53; designer, estimator Blue Pacific Nursery & Landscape Co., 1955-59; prin. Richard A. Wilson, FASLA and Assocs., 1959—. Sec. Calif. Coun. Landscape Architects, 1982-85; expert witness for law firms, 1983—. Designer Phil Swing Meml. Fountain, 1967. Mem. landscape com. Clairemont Town Coun., San Diego, 1955. With U.S. Army, 1944-46, Korea. Recipient First Pl. award for landscape So. Calif. Expdn., Del Mar, 1963. Fellow Am. Soc. Landscape Architects (del. coun. 1982-85), Am. Inst. Landscape Architects (treas. 1970, 2d v.p. 1971). Republican. Home and Office: 2570 Tokalon Ct San Diego CA 92110-2232

WILSON, RICHARD CHRISTIAN, engineering firm executive; b. Bethlehem, Pa., July 17, 1921; s. Christian and Laura Barrows (Langham) W.; m. Jean M. Avis, July 16, 1949; children— Richard A., Christy. BS, Carnegie-Mellon U., 1943; MS, Lehigh U., 1947; PhD, U. Mich., 1961. Mfg. engr. Westinghouse Electric Corp., East Pittsburgh, 1943; instr. mech. engring. Carnegie-Mellon U., Pitts., 1943-44; vacuum test engr. Kellex Corp., N.Y.C., 1944; area supr. Carbide & Carbon Chem. Co., Oak Ridge, 1945-46; apparatus engr. Westinghouse Electric Corp., Jackson, Mich., 1947-55; instr. indsl. and operation engring. U. Mich., 1955-61, asst. prof., 1961-63, assoc. prof., 1963-66, prof., 1966-85, chmn. dept., 1973-77, assoc. dean Coll. Engring., 1968-72; pres. Techware, Inc., 1985-86, ret., 1986. Dir. Cascade Data Corp., 1969-72 Contbr. articles to profl. jours. Bd. dirs. Ecumenical Assn. Internat. Understanding, 1970-87, pres., 1975-76, 86-87. Mem. IEEE, Inst. Mgmt. Sci., Am. Inst. Indsl. Engrs., Ops. Research Soc. Am., Sigma Xi, Beta Theta Pi, Phi Kappa Phi. Clubs: Rotary. Home: 805 Mount Pleasant Ave Ann Arbor MI 48103-4776 Office: U Mich Dept Indsl Engring Ann Arbor MI 48109

WILSON, RICHARD EDWARD, composer, pianist, music educator; b. Cleve., May 15, 1941; s. James F. and Edith Ann (Zingler) Wilson; m. Adene Stevenson Green, May 15, 1971; children: Katherine Blanca, James Graham. AB magna cum laude, Harvard U., 1963; MA, Rutgers U., 1966. Asst. prof. music Vassar Coll., Poughkeepsie, N.Y., 1966-70, assoc. prof. music, 1970-76, prof. music, 1976—, chmn. dept. music, 1979-82, 85-88, 95-98, Mary Conover Mellon Chair, 1988—. Composer-in-residence Am. Symphony Orch., 1992—. Composer: Music for Violin and Violoncello, 1969; composer: (four string quartets) , ; composer: Eclogue for Piano Solo, 1974 (Burge prize, 1979), Figuration , 1980, Two Symphonies, 1984, 1987, Agitations, 1994, Pamietam, 1995, Five Love Songs, 1995, Transfigured Goat, 1996, A Child's London, 1997, Triple concerto for horn, bass clarinet, marimba and orch., 1998 (Koussevitzky commn.), Intimations for Piano and Orch., 2000; composer: (opera) Aethelred the Unready, 1994. Recipient Walter Henrichsen award, Am. Acad. Inst. Arts and Letters, 1986, Cleve. Arts prize, 1988, Exec.'s award Dutchess County, 1989, Stoeger prize, Chamber Music Soc. Lincoln Ctr., 1994; fellow, Guggenheim, 1992. Mem.: ASCAP, Am. Music Ctr., Harvard Club, Phi Beta Kappa. Home: 27 Vassar Lake Dr Poughkeepsie NY 12603-3120 Office: Vassar Coll Dept Music PO Box 18 Poughkeepsie NY 12604-0001

WILSON, RICHARD GEORGE, journalism educator; b. Towanda, Pa., June 11, 1937; s. Vernon E. and Pearl Lena Wilson; m. Deborah Lee Weimar, June 14, 1964; children: Peter, Geoffrey. BS, U. Ky., 1966. Reporter Lexington (Ky.) Leader, 1963, State-Journal, Frankfort, Ky., 1963-64; info. officer U. Ky., Lexington, 1964-67; reporter, bur. chief Louisville Courier-Jour., 1967-99; adj. prof. Ky. State U., Frankfort, 1999—. With U.S. Army, 1958-61. Named to Hon. Order Ky. Cols., 1999, Ky. Journalism Hall of Fame, 1999. Mem. U. Ky. Alumni Assn. Avocations: reading, travel.

WILSON, RICHARD HAROLD, government official; b. Waterloo, Iowa, July 15, 1930; s. Clarence Hough and Mary (Dillon) W.; m. Elaine Elizabeth Aniol., June 14, 1957; children: Elizabeth Aniol Wilson Adams, Andrew Edward. BA, U. Ill., 1952; MPA, U. Kans., 1958; AAS in Hotel-Motel Mgmt. and Food Svc. Adminstrn., Harold Washington Coll., Chgo., 1999. Lic. real estate broker, Tex.; cert. econs. devel. specialist Nat. Devel. Coun. Adminstrv. asst. to city mgr., San Antonio, 1956-58; budget analyst Kansas City, Mo., 1959; research asso. Internat. Union Local Authorities, The Hague, 1959-60; city mgr. Nevada, Mo., 1960-65; asst. to city mgr. Ft. Worth, 1965-67; asst. city mgr. Albuquerque, 1967-68; city mgr., 1968-72; dir. housing and urban rehab. Dallas, 1972-82; sr. v.p. Metroplex R&D Cons., 1982-83; regional dir. comty. planning and devel. HUD Region V, Chgo., 1983-94; CPD program advisor HUD, 1995—97, cmty. builder, 1998—. Lectr. real estate U. Tex.-Arlington; instr. govt. Dallas County Community Coll. Dist.; exec. v.p. Designs for Worship, Inc., Dallas, 1982-83 Bd. dirs. Neighborhood Housing Svcs. Am., Inc., 1974-82; chmn. Housing Tax Force of North Cen. Tex. Coun. Govts., 1974-80, chmn. human resources com., 1981-82; active Boy Scouts Am.; docent Prairie Ave. House Mus., 1990—; bd. dirs. Marina Towers Condominium Assn., 1991-96. Active USN, 1952-55, intelligence specialist USNR, 1955-82, comdr. ret. Fulbright fellow Leiden (The Netherlands) U., 1959-60, Kennedy Sch., Harvard U., 1981, 98, Fed. Exec. Inst., 1995, NEH, U. Calif., Santa Barbara, 1978, Urban Execs. Exch. Program, Internat. City-County Mgmt. Assn., 1979-80. Mem. Nat. Assn. Housing and Redevel. Ofcls. (v.p. Tex. chpt. 1975-80, mem. S.W. regional coun. 1975-82), Internat. City-Coun. Mgmt. Assn., Am. Soc. Pub. Adminstrn. (pres. N.Mex. 1968-69, v.p. North Tex. 1976-77, pres. North Tex. 1977-78, mem. nat. coun. 1979-82, Greater Chgo. chpt. coun. 1987-93, 95-96), Naval Res. Assn., Chgo. Arch. Found. (docent 1990—), Fed. Exec. Inst. Alumni Assn., Phi Gamma Delta, Pi Sigma Alpha, Alpha Phi Omega. Clubs: Rotary (Chicago). Episcopalian. Home: 300 N State St Apt 2833 Chicago IL 60610-5627 Office: HUD 77 W Jackson Blvd 26th Floor Chicago IL 60604-3507 E-mail: aniolwilson@aol.com., Richard_H._Wilson@hud.gov.

WILSON, RICHARD LEE, political science educator; b. Worthington, Minn., Dec. 20, 1944; s. G. Roy and Dorothy Eileen (Johnson) W.; m. Carolyn Ann Dirks, Aug. 24, 1968 (div.); 1 child, Kevin Richard. BA, U. Chgo., 1966, postgrad., 1966-67; PhD, Johns Hopkins U., 1971; postgrad., Columbia U., 1988, Stanford U., 1992. Congl. aide 4th Congl. Dist. Md., 1971; asst. prof. polit. sci. U. Tenn., Chattanooga, 1971-76, assoc. prof., 1976-87, prof., 1988—. Registrar-at-large Hamilton County Election Commn., 1977-84; lectr. Robert A. Taft Inst. Govt., U. Tenn., Nashville, 1978, 79, 81; supr. state legis. and met. internship program U. Chattanooga, 1972-86; vis. prof. Govt. Fgn. Affairs Coll., Beijing, 1986-87; Fulbright prof. govt. Beijing U., 1988-89, Samford U., Birmingham, Ala., 1991-93. Author: Tennessee Politics, 1976, American Government, 1993, 2d edit., 1995, Biographical Dictionary of American Political Leaders, 2001; editor: Encyclopedia of American Government, 2001; co-editor: Ready Reference: Censorship, 1997 (named Outstanding Ref. Source 1998 ALA), Encyclopedia of the Supreme Court, 2000 (named OUtstanding Ref. Scouce 2002 ALA); contbr. chpts. to books. Chmn. Hamilton County Health Planning Adv. Council, 1975-79; bd. dirs. Ga.-Tenn. Regional Health Commn., 1978-82; active Tenn. State Health Coordinating Council, 1977-81; exec. com. State Health Coordinating Council, 1979-81. Named Outstanding Educator of Yr., Signal Mountain (Tenn.) Jaycees, 1973, Outstanding Prof. of Yr., SGA, 1985-86, Oustanding Reference Source ALa, 2002; recipient Polit. Edn. award NAACP, 1980, Excellent Prof. award Fgn. Affairs Coll., Beijing, 1987, UTC Exceptional Merit award, 1990, 94; NEH grantee, 1988, 92. Mem. So. Polit. Sci. Assn., Midwest Polit. Sci. Assn., Am. Polit. Sci. Assn. (nat. rsch. grant 1995), Nat. Soc. Internships and Exptl. Edn., SAR, China People's Friendship Assn., Aircraft Owners and Pilots Assn. Methodist. Office: Univ of Tenn Dept Political Sci Fletcher Hall 417 Chattanooga TN 37403

WILSON, RICHARD RANDOLPH, lawyer; b. Pasadena, Calif., Apr. 14, 1950; s. Robert James and Phyllis Jean (Blackman) W.; m. Catherine Goodhugh Stevens, Oct. 11, 1980; children: Thomas Randolph, Charles Stevens. BA cum laude, Yale U., 1971; JD, U. Wash., 1976. Bar: Wash. 1976, U.S. Dist. Ct. (we. dist.) Wash. 1976, U.S. Ct. Appeals (9th cir.) 1977. Assoc. Hillis, Phillips, Cairncross, Clark & Martin, Seattle, 1976-81, ptnr., 1981-84, Hillis, Cairncross, Clark & Martin, Seattle, 1984-87, Hillis Clark Martin & Peterson, Seattle, 1987—, mem. mgmt. com., 1991—. Pres. Plymouth Housing Group, Seattle, 1998—2000, trustee, 1994—2001; bd. dirs. Plymouth Housing Properties, Seattle, 2001—, Quality Child Care Svcs., Inc., Seattle; lectr. various bar assns., 1980—. Contbr. articles to profl. jours. Chmn. class agts. Yale U. Alumni Fund, New Haven, 1985—87, class agt., 1971—2001, mem. class coun., 1991—96, mem. Western Wash. exec. com. Yale capital campaign, 1992—97, vice chmn. leadership gifts com. Yale 25th reunion, 1995—96, 30th reunion, 2000—01; mem., vice chmn. Medina (Wash.) Planning Commn., 1990—92; moderator, pres. ch. coun. Plymouth Congl. Ch., Seattle, 1998—2000; trustee, performer Gilbert & Sullivan Soc., 1984—91. Mem. ABA, Wash. State Bar Assn. (dir. environ. and land use law sect. 1985-88), Seattle-King County Bar Assn., Kingsley Trust Assn. (pres. 1996-98), Yale Assn. of Western Wash. Congregationalist. Avocations: acting, singing, rare book collecting. Home: 2305 86th Ave NE Bellevue WA 98004-2416 Office: Hillis Clark Martin & Peterson 1221 2nd Ave Ste 500 Seattle WA 98101-2925 *Notable cases include: Barrie vs. Kitsap County, 1980; Sore vs. Snohomish County, 1983; Conv. Ctr. Coalition vs. City of Seattle, 1986; Orion Corp. vs. State, 1987, Cougar Mountain Assocs. vs. King County, 1988; King County vs. Central Puget Sound Growth Management Hearings Board, 1998, 1999.*

WILSON, ROBERT ALBERT, communications consultant; b. Jamestown, N.Y., Dec. 20, 1936; s. Albert C. and Minnie M. (Leroy) W.; m. Marcia K. Milton, Aug. 22, 1959; children: Jonathan, Kathryn. BA magna cum laude, Colgate U., 1959; diploma, Sch. Advanced Internat Studies, Bologna, Italy, 1960; MA, Johns Hopkins, 1961. News editor/announcer Sta. WJOC, Jamestown, 1953-57; staff reporter Post-Jour., 1958-61; intelligence research specialist U.S. Info. Agy., Washington, 1963-66, sr. editor, 1966-72; sr. assoc. pub. affairs Pfizer, Inc., N.Y.C., 1972-78, assoc. dir. pub. affairs, 1978-81, v.p. pub. affairs, 1981-96. Pres. Pfizer Found., Inc., N.Y.C., 1981-95; dir. Nat. Health Coun., 1987-94; chmn. pub. affairs sect. Pharm. Rsch. and Mfrs. Am., 1982-83. Chmn. Religion in Am. Life, N.Y.C., 1988—; chmn. bd. dirs. Conn. Grand Opera & Orch., 1994—. Mem. Riverside Yacht Club, Phi Beta Kappa. Avocations: sailing, skiing. Office: Conn Grand Opera and Orch 4 Landmark Sq Stamford CT 06901-2502

WILSON, ROBERT ALLEN, religion educator; b. Geff, Ill., Oct. 7, 1936; s. Perry Arthur and Eva Mae (Dye) W.; m. Patsy Ann Jarrett, June 1, 1957; children: Elizabeth Ann, Angela Dawn, Christine Joy. AB, Lincoln (Ill.) Christian Coll., 1958, Hanover Coll., 1961; MRE, So. Bapt. Seminary, 1965, EdD, 1972. Ordained to ministry Ch. of Christ, 1958. Minister Fowler (Ind.) Christian Ch., 1955-59, Zoah Christian Ch., Scottsburg, Ind., 1959-64; minister of edn. and youth Shively Christian Ch., Louisville, 1964-69; prof. Christian edn. and family life Lincoln (Ill.) Christian Seminary, 1969—. Pres. Christian Marriage and Family Enrichment Services, Lincoln, 1980—. Contbr. articles to profl. jours. Mem. Nat. Assn. Profs. Christian Edn. (editor newsletter 1975-79, pres. 1979-80), Religious Edn. Assn. Lodges: Rotary (bd. dirs. Lincoln chpt. 1988—, pres. 1993-94). Home: 330 Campus View Dr Lincoln IL 62656-2106 Office: Lincoln Christian Coll & Seminary 100 Campus View Dr # 178 Lincoln IL 62656-2111 E-mail: rwilson@lccs.edu., drbob99@msn.com.

WILSON, ROBERT BRYAN, judge; b. San Mateo, Calif., Aug. 14, 1958; s. Robert Darrel and Helen Ann (Zidek) W.; m. Jacqueline A. Hallinan, Aug. 19, 1989. BS, No. Mich. U., 1980; JD, W.Va. Coll. Law, 1986. Bar: U.S. Dist. Ct. (no. and so. dists.) W.Va. 1986, U.S. Ct. Appeals (4th cir.) 1996, U.S. Supreme Ct. 1998. Atty. W.Va. Dept. Tax and Revenue, Charleston, 1986-92; pvt. practice, 1992-93, 95; assoc. Forman & Crane, L.C., 1993-95; pvt. Erisa practice, 1992—. Counsel ednl. com. W.Va. Senate, Charleston, 1991-92; adminstrv. law judge W.Va. Human Rights Commn., Charleston, 1995—. Avocations: cross country skiing, white water canoeing, traveling. Home: 1120 Swan Rd Charleston WV 25314-1426

WILSON, ROBERT FOSTER, lawyer; b. Windsor, Colo., Apr. 6, 1926; s. Foster W. and Anne Lucille (Svedman) W.; m. Mary Elizabeth Clark, Mar. 4, 1951 (div. Feb. 1972); children: Robert F., Katharine A.; m. Sally Anne Nemec, June 8, 1982. BA in Econs., U. Iowa, 1950, JD, 1951. Bar: Iowa 1951, U.S. Dist. Ct. (no. and so. dists.) Iowa 1956, U.S. Ct. Appeals (8th cir.) 1967. Atty. FTC, Chgo., 1951-55; pvt. practice, Cedar Rapids, Iowa, 1955—. Pres. Lawyer Forms, Inc.; dir. Lawyers Forms, Inc.; mem. Iowa Reapportionment Com., 1968; del. to U.S. and Japan Bilateral Session on Legal and Econ. Rels. Conf., Tokyo, 1988, Moscow Conf. on Law and Bilateral Rels., Moscow, 1990; U.S. del. to Moscow Conf. on Legal and Econ. Rels., 1990. Mem. Iowa Ho. of Reps., 1959-60; pres. Linn County Day Care, Cedar Rapids, 1968-70. Sgt. U.S. Army, 1944-46. Mem. ATLA, Am. Arbitration Assn. (panel arbitrators), Iowa Bar Assn., Iowa Trial Lawyers Assn., Linn County Bar Assn., Am. Legion (judge adv. 1970-75, 87-93), Cedar View Country Club, Elks, Eagles, Delta Theta Phi. Democrat. Home: 2179 Blake Blvd SE Cedar Rapids IA 52403-1128 Office: 810 Dows Bldg Cedar Rapids IA 52403-7010 E-mail: RWilsonlaw@aol.com.

WILSON, ROBERT GODFREY, radiologist; b. Montgomery, Ala., Mar. 18, 1937; s. Robert Woodridge and Lucille (Godfrey) W.; m. Dorothy June Waters, Aug. 31, 1957; children: Amy Lucille, Robert Darwin, Robert Woodridge II, Lucy Elizabeth. BA, Huntingdon Coll., 1957; MD, Med. Coll. Ala., 1961. Diplomate Nat. Bd. Med. Examiners, Am. Bd. Radiology, Am. Bd. Nuclear Medicine. Intern Letterman Gen. Hosp., San Francisco, 1961-62; resident in radiology U. Okla. Med. Center, Oklahoma City, 1965-68, clin. instr. in radiology, 1968—; practice medicine specializing in diagnostic and therapeutic radiology, nuclear medicine Shawnee, Okla., 1968—; mem. med. staff Shawnee Med. Center, Mission Hill Meml. Hosp., Shawnee, 1968—. Served to capt. M.C., USAF, 1960-65. Mem. AMA, Okla., Pottawatomie County med. socs., Okla., Greater Oklahoma City radiol. socs., Am. Coll. Radiology, Soc. Nuclear Medicine, Radiol. Soc. N.Am. Methodist. Home: 26 Sequoyah Blvd Shawnee OK 74801-5570 Office: 5606 Aquarius Shawnee OK 74804-9387

WILSON, ROBERT GORDON, investment banker; b. Mt. Vernon, N.Y., Dec. 16, 1933; s. Gerald and Ella Baxter (Close) W.; m. Valerie Ann Wilson, Apr. 25, 1966 (div. 1986); children: Jennifer Lynn, Kimberly Ann; m. Anne Marie Henriquez, Sept. 27, 1986; 1 child, Anthony H. Crotti. BA, Haverford Coll., 1955; MBA, Columbia U., 1957. Gen. ptnr. Goldman Sachs & Co., N.Y.C., 1967-80, ltd. ptnr., 1981-89; pres. Goldman Sachs Internat., London, 1977-80; chmn., pres. Ecologic Waste Svcs., Inc., Miami, Fla., 1990-94; vice chmn. Carter Kaplan & Co., Richmond, Va., 1993-94; chmn., pres. Ziani Internat. Capital, Inc., Miami, 1995—; dir., founder, CEO LendingTree, Inc., Charlotte, N.C., 1997-99, cons., 1999—. Bd. dirs. Phoenix Home Life Ins. Co., Hartford, Conn.; founder quoteship.com, 1999-2000, cons., 2000-. Former chmn. bd. trustees YMCA Greater N.Y., N.Y.C., 1985. Republican. Avocations: golf, wines, travel. Home: 151 Crandon Blvd Apt 1127 Key Biscayne FL 33149-1596 Office: Ziani Internat Capital Inc 151 Crandon Blvd Apt 1127 Key Biscayne FL 33149-1596 E-mail: rgw.55@hotmail.com.

WILSON, ROBERT GORDON, civil and mechanical engineer; b. Covina, Calif., Jan. 27, 1946; s. Robert Kenneth and Margaret Ellen (Gordon) W.; m. Barbara Ann Poole, June 15, 1968; children: Mark Gordon, Kristen Leigh. BS in Civil Engring., San Jose (Calif.) State U., 1968; AA in Bus. Adminstrn., Saddleback C.C., Mission Viejo, Calif., 1979; MBA, Calif. State U., Fullerton, 1983. Registered profl. engr., Calif. Constrn. field engr. Bechtel Power Corp., Calvert County, Md., 1968-72, asst. project mgr. Norwalk, Calif., 1972-73, nuclear engr. supr. Madrid, 1973-76, site engr. supr. San Onofre, Calif., 1976-78, constrn. supt., 1978-85; maintenance supr. So. Calif. Edison, 1985-94, project mgr., 1994—. Consulting engr. Wilson Engring., Dana Point, Calif., 1976—. Democrat. Avocations: sports, genealogy, computers. robert_g_wilson@yahoo.com. Home: 24361 Timothy Dr Dana Point CA 92629-1070 Office: So Calif Edison PO Box 128 San Clemente CA 92674-0128 E-mail: wilsonr@songs.sce.com.

WILSON, ROBERT JAMES MONTGOMERY, investment company executive; b. Millbrook, N.Y., Feb. 8, 1920; s. Albert James Montgomery and Charlotte (Kaye) W.; m. Yvette Laneres, May 10, 1952; children— Robert James Montgomery, Olivia Laneres Wilson Welbourn, Geoffrey Laneres. Grad., Choate Sch., 1938; AB, Yale U., 1942. Securities analyst buying dept. Union Securities Corp., N.Y.C., 1946-49; securities analyst Union Service Corp., 1949-59, v.p., 1959-62; pres., dir. Surveyor Fund, Inc. (formerly Gen. Public Service Corp.), N.Y.C., 1962-71; with Rockefeller Family and Assos., 1972-75; pres. Adams Express Co., N.Y.C., 1975-86, also bd. dirs., 1975—; pres. Petroleum & Resources Corp. (formerly Petroleum Corp. Am.), 1975-86, also bd. dirs., 1975—. Mem. adv. investment com. Md. State Retirement Systems, 1979-82; bd. dirs. Assn. Publicly Traded Investment Cos., 1968-71, chmn., 1969-71. Mem. 1940 Fahnestock Expdn. of Am. Mus. Natural History to South Seas. Served to capt. AUS, World War II. Mem. Md. Club. Office: 5680 N AIA Ste 312 Vero Beach FL 32963

WILSON, ROBERT M. business executive; b. St. Louis, Aug. 10, 1952; s. William H. and Mary E. (Sacksteder) W.; m. Joli S. Schneeberger, Oct. 7, 1978; 1 child, William Wilcox. BS, Miami U., Oxford, Ohio, 1974; JD, Cleve. State U., 1977. Bar: Ohio; CPA, Ohio. Ptnr. Touche Ross & Co., Dayton, Ohio, 1972-88, Roberds, Inc., Dayton, 1988-2000, pres., 1998—2000; exec. v.p. Wealthport, Inc., 2000—01; COO CCA Global Ptnrs. Inc., 2001—. Chmn. Dayton Ballet Assn., 1979-91; trustee Carillon Park, 1988-94, City-Wide Devel. Corp., 1991-2000, Cath. Social Svcs., 1995-2000; assoc. bd. Dayton Art Inst., 1989-95. Mem. ABA (com. chmn. 1990-92), Ohio Soc. CPAs (pres. 1985-86). Republican. Roman Catholic.

WILSON, ROBERT NATHAN, health care company executive; b. Covington, Ky., Aug. 7, 1940; s. Robert Thomas and Ruth (Pearce) W.; m. Anne Wright, Mar. 29, 1969; children: Julie Anne, Jonathan Robert. BA in Bus., Georgetown (Ky.) Coll., 1962; grad. exec. program Grad. Sch. Bus. Adminstrn., Columbia U., 1975; LLD (hon.), Phila. Coll. Pharmacy and Sci., 1991; DHL Georgetown Coll. (hon.) , 1998. Sales rep. Ortho Pharm. Corp., Raritan, N.J., 1964; various exec. and mgr. positions, 1964-77; pres. Johnson & Johnson Dental Products Co., East Windsor, N.J., 1977-79; co. group chmn. Johnson & Johnson, New Brunswick, 1981-83, mem. exec. com. NJ, 1983—2002, apptd. vice chmn. exec. com., 1994—2002, vice chmn., bd. dirs. N.J., 1989—, sr. vice chmn., bd. dirs. NJ, 2001—. Pres. Ortho Pharm. Corp., Raritan, N.J., 1979-83; chmn. Ortho Pharm. Ltd. Can., 1979-83; bd. dirs. U.S. Trust Corp. 1991—, James Black Found., London, Amerada Hess Corp. Nat. coun. World Wildlife Fund, 1995—; trutsee Mus. Am. Folk Art, N.Y.C., 1981—95; mem. Georgetown Coll. Found., World Bus. Coun. for Sustainable Devel., Pharm. Rsch. and Mfrs. Am. Found., 1994—, Trilateral Commn., 1993—99; chmn., bd. dirs. Healthcare Inst. N.J., 1966—99. Recipient Alumni Achievement award Georgetown Coll., 1987. Mem. Pharm. Rsch. and Mfrs. Am. (bd. dirs. 1984-2002, exec. com. 1988-2002, chmn. 2000-01). Presbyterian. Office: Johnson & Johnson 1 Johnson And Johnson Plz New Brunswick NJ 08933-0002

WILSON, ROBERT NEAL, sociologist, educator; b. Syracuse, N.Y., Nov. 15, 1924; s. Robert Marchant and May Eloise (Neal) W.; m. Arleene Eleanor Smith, Aug. 21, 1948 (div. 1973); children— Lynda Lee, Deborah Eloise; m. Joan Wallace, Aug. 1, 1973 BA, Union Coll., 1948; PhD, Harvard U., 1952. Research assoc. Cornell U., Ithaca, N.Y., 1951-53; staff Social Sci. Research Council, Washington, 1953-56; lectr. Harvard U., Cambridge, Mass., 1957-60; assoc. prof. Yale U., New Haven, 1960-63; prof. sociology U. N.C., Chapel Hill., 1963—. Trustee Easter Seal Research Found., Chgo., 1966-72; cons. NIMH, Washington, 1968-72, Nat. Inst. Child Health and Human Devel., Washington, 1970-77; reviewer NEH, Washington, 1977— Author: Man Made Plain, 1958, Sociology of Health, 1970, The Writer as Social Seer, 1979, Experiencing Creativity, 1986; author, editor: The Arts in Soc., 1964. Served to sgt. U.S. Army, 1943-46, ETO Ctr. for Advanced Study Behavioral Scis. fellow, 1956-57; Fulbright scholar, 1975 Fellow Am. Sociol. Assn., Am. Pub. Health Assn., So. Sociol. Soc. Democrat. Episcopalian. Avocation: poetry. Home: 103 Springvalley Rd Carrboro NC 27510-1246 Office: Univ NC Chapel Hill NC 27514

WILSON, ROBERT RUTHERFORD, religious studies educator; b. Louisville, Mar. 29, 1942; s. Ralph Elmer and Dorothy May (Rutherford) W.; m. Sharyn Elaine Beck, July 28, 1967. AB, Transylvania U., 1964; BD, Yale U., 1967, MA, 1969, PhD, 1972. Ordained to ministry Disciples of Christ, 1967. Instr. old testament Union Theol. Sem., N.Y.C., 1971-72; asst. prof. old testament Yale Univ., New Haven, 1972-76, assoc. prof. old testament, 1976-83, prof. old testament, 1983—, Hoober prof. religious studies, 1991—; chair dept. religious studies, 1986-92, 95-96. Author: Genealogy and History in the Biblical World, 1977, Prophecy and Society in Ancient Israel, 1980, Sociological Approaches to the Old Testament, 1984; editor (book): Canon, Theology, and Old Testament Interpretation, 1988. Mem. Civic Orch. of New Haven, 1975—. Dir. summer seminar for coll. tchrs. NEH, Washington, 1981; Danforth Grad. fellow Danforth Found., St. Louis, 1964; fellow Am. Coun. Learned Socs., Wash., 1975. Mem. Soc. Bibl. Lit. (coun. mem. 1977-79), Columbia Univ. Seminar Study Hebrew Bible (chair 1978-81), Am. Acad. Religion, Am. Oriental Soc., Am. Soc. for Study Religion, Am. Schs. Oriental Rsch. Avocations: music. Office: Yale Univ 409 Prospect St New Haven CT 06511-2167 E-mail: robert.wilson@yale.edu.

WILSON, ROBERT SPENCER, magazine editor; b. Bolling Field, D.C., Feb. 21, 1951; s. Joseph Griswold and Helen (Hodnett) W.; m. Martha Elaine Ritchie, Oct. 19, 1974; children: Matthew Spencer, Cole Ritchie, Robert Samuel. BA, Washington and Lee U., 1973; MA, U. Va., 1977. Lectr. U. Va., Charlottesville, 1977-80; asst. editor Washington Post, 1977-83; book editor, book columnist USA Today, Washington, 1983-94; lit. editor Civilization mag., 1994-95; editor Preservation mag., 1996—. Winner Nat. Mag. award for gen. excellence, 1998. Home and Office: 9301 Grant Ave Manassas VA 20110-5040

WILSON, ROBERT WARNE, philanthropist, investor; b. Detroit, Nov. 3, 1926; s. Clarence Warne Wilson and Margaret Ballantyne; m. Marillyn Buelow Wilson, Apr. 1957 (div. 1977). BA in Econs. magna cum laude, Amherst (Mass.) Coll., 1946; MA in Econs., U. Mich., 1947; postgrad., Mich. Law Sch., 1948-49. Trainee First Boston Corp., N.Y.C., 1949-50, 52-53; securities analyst Nat. Bank of Detroit, 1953-58; securities analyst to v.p. Gen. Am. Inv., N.Y.C., 1958-62; securities analyst A.G. Becker & Co., 1962-68; investor, 1968—. Bd. dirs. Bklyn. Mus., 1974-88, Bklyn. Botanic Garden, 1974-88, N.Y.C. Opera, 1977-98, chmn. 1981-93; adv. bd. Met. Opera, 1979-81; trustee Environtl. Def., 1986—, Lyric Opera of Chgo. Nat. Bd., 1995-2001, Manhattan Inst., 1986-2002, Whitney Mus. of Am. Art, 1978—, World Monuments Fund, 1990—, Deafness Rsch. Found., 1998-2001. With U.S. Army, 1951-52. Mem. Phi Beta Kappa. Republican. Avocations: opera, museums, theatre, movies, sightseeing. Office: 520 83rd St Brooklyn NY 11209-4520

WILSON, ROBERT WOODROW, radio astronomer; b. Houston, Jan. 10, 1936; s. Ralph Woodrow and Fannie May (Willis) W.; m. Elizabeth Rhaods Sawin, Sept. 4, 1958; children: Philip Garrett, Suzanne Katherine, Randal Woodrow. BA with honors in Physics, Rice U., 1957; PhD, Calif. Inst. Tech., 1962. Research fellow Calif. Inst. Tech., Pasadena, 1962-63; mem. tech. staff AT&T Bell Labs., Holmdel, N.J., 1963-76, head wireless tech. rsch. dept., 1976-94; sr. sci. Harvard-Smithsonian Ctr. for Astrophysics, Cambridge, Mass., 1994—. Discoverer 3 deg. k microwave background radiation, 1965, CO and other molecules in interstellar space using their millimeter wavelength radiation;. Named Fairchild Disting. scholar, Caltech., 1987; recipient Henry Draper medal, Royal Astron. Soc., London, 1977, Nobel prize in physics, 1978; fellow NSF fellow, 1958—61, Cole fellow, 1957—58. Mem.: NAS (Herschel medal 1977), Internat. Sci. Radio Union, Am. Phys. Soc., Internat. Astron. Union, Am. Astron. Soc., Sigma Xi, Phi Beta Kappa. Office: Harvard-Smithsonian Ctr Astrophysics 60 Garden St Cambridge MA 02138-2306*

WILSON, ROBIN SCOTT, university president, writer; b. Columbus, Ohio, Sept. 19, 1928; s. John Harold and Helen Louise (Walker) W.; m. Patricia Ann Van Kirk, Jan. 20, 1951; children: Kelpie, Leslie, Kari, Andrew. BA, Ohio State U., 1950; MA, U. Ill., 1951, PhD, 1959. Fgn. intelligence officer CIA, Washington, 1959-67; prof. English Clarion State Coll., (Pa.), 1967-70; assoc. dir. Com. Instnl. Cooperation, Evanston, Ill., 1970-77; assoc. provost instrn. Ohio State U., Columbus, 1977-80; univ. pres. Calif. State U., Chico, 1980-93, pres. emeritus, 1993—. Author: Those Who Can, 1973, Death By Degrees, 1995, Paragons, 1996; short stories, criticism, articles on edn. Lt. USN, 1953-57. Mem. AAAS, Phi Kappa Phi E-mail: wilson@redshift.com.

WILSON, ROBLEY CONANT, JR. English educator, editor, author; b. Brunswick, Maine, June 15, 1930; s. Robley Conant and Dorothy May (Stimpson) W.; m. Charlotte A. Lehon, Aug. 20, 1955 (div. 1991); children: Stephen, Philip; m. Susan Hubbard, June 17, 1995. BA, Bowdoin Coll., 1957, D.Litt (hon.), 1987; M.F.A., U. Iowa, 1968. Reporter Raymondville Chronicle, Tex., 1950-1951; asst. publicity dir. N.Y. State Fair Syracuse, 1956; instr. Valparaiso U., Ind., 1958-63; asst. prof. English U. No. Iowa, Cedar Falls, 1963-69, assoc. prof., 1969-75, prof., 1975-2000, prof. emeritus, 2000—, editor N.Am. Rev., 1969-2000. Author: The Pleasures of Manhood, 1977, Living Alone, 1978, Dancing for Men, 1983 (Drue Heinz Lit. prize , 1982), Kingdoms of the Ordinary (Agnes Lynch Starrett award , 1986), Terrible Kisses, 1989, A Pleasure Tree, 1990 (Soc. Midland Authors Poetry award, 1990), The Victim's Daughter, 1991, A Walk Through the Human Heart, 1996, Everything Paid For, 1999, The Book of Lost Fathers, 2001; co-editor: 100% Pure Florida Fiction, 2000. Bd. dirs. Associated Writing Programs, Norfolk, Va., 1983-86; pres. Iowa Woman Endeavors, Inc., 1986-90. With USAF, 1951-55. Guggenheim fellow, 1983-84, Nicholl Screenwriting fellow, 1996. Mem.: PEN, Am. Acad. Poets, Authors' Guild, Am. Soc. Mag. Editors. Home: PO Box 4009 Winter Park FL 32793-4009 E-mail: robley.wilson@uni.edu.

WILSON, ROGER BYRON, former governor, school administrator; b. Columbia, Mo., Oct. 10, 1948; m. Patricia O' Brien; children: Erin, Drew. BA, Ctrl. Methodist Coll.; MA in Edn., U. Mo.; grad., Harvard U., 1990. Asst. prin. Russell Blvd. Elem. Sch., Columbia, Mo.; real estate broker; collector Boone County, Mo., 1976-79; mem. Mo. State Senate from Dist. 19, 1979-92; lt. gov. State of Mo., 1993-2000, gov., 2000. Chmn. senate appropriations com., apportionment com., chmn. tourism commn.; mem. Mo. bus. and edn. partnership commn., transportation devel. commn., gov.'s adv. coun. phys. fitness. Bd. dirs. United Way, Columbia; mem. Mo. Assn. Cmty. Arts Agys., Boone County Hist. Soc.; mem. com. Mo. Parents as Tchrs. Recipient Everett award Mo. State Tchr.'s Assn., Outstanding Legislator of Yr. award, 1991, Boss of Yr. award Am. Businesswomen's Assn., Disting. Legislator award Nat. Conf. of State Legislatures, Horace Mann award Mo. Nat. Edn. Assn., Pub. Ofcl. of Yr. award Mo. Assn. Homes for Aging, M.U. Alumni award, 1991, Kirkpatrick award Northwest Mo. Press Assn., 1997. Mem. Columbia C. of C., Cosmopolitan Internat.*

WILSON, ROGER GOODWIN, lawyer; b. Evanston, Ill., Sept. 3, 1950; s. G. Turner Jr. and Lois (Shay) W.; m. Giovinella Gonthier, Mar. 7, 1975. AB, Dartmouth Coll., 1972; JD, Harvard U., 1975. Bar: Ill. 1975, U.S. Dist. Ct. (no. dist.) Ill. 1976, U.S. Ct. Appeals (7th cir.) 1977, U.S. Dist. Ct. (no. dist.) Ind. 1985. Assoc. Kirkland & Ellis, Chgo., 1975-81, ptnr., 1981-86; sr. v.p., gen. counsel, corp. sec. Blue Cross/Blue Shield, 1986—. Speaker Nat. Healthcare Inst., U. Mich., 1987-93, Am. Law Inst.-ABA Conf. on Mng. and Resolving Domestic and Internat. Bus. Disputes, N.Y.C., 1988, Washington, 1990; cert. health cons. program Purdue U., 1993-94, Inst. for Bus. Strategy Devel., Northwestern U., 1993-94, The Health Care Antitrust Forum, Chgo., 1995, Am. Health Lawyers Assn Managed Care Law Inst., 1995, Am. Health Lawyers Assn. Conf. on Tax Issues in Healthcare Orgns., 1996. Contbg. editor Health Care Fraud and Abuse Newsletter, 1998—. Advisor Constl. Rights Found., Chgo., 1982-87; mem. So. Poverty Law Ctr., Montgomery, Ala., 1981—. Mem. ABA, Am. Health Lawyers Assn. (spkr. 1984, 96), Legal Assistance Found. of Chgo. (bd. dirs. 1998—), Chgo. Coun. Lawyers (bd. govs. 1988-92), Coun. Chief Legal Officers (conf. bd. 1995—), Coun. Corp. Governance (conf. bd. 1998-00), Dartmouth Lawyers Assn., Sinfonietta (bd. dirs. 1987—), Univ. Club, Mid-Am. Club, Phi Beta Kappa. Home: 330 N Jefferson Ct Unit2004 Chicago IL 60661 Office: Blue Cross/Blue Shield 225 N Michigan Ave Ste 200 Chicago IL 60601-7601 E-mail: roger.wilson@bcbsa.com.

WILSON, ROGER STANLEY, physician, anesthesiologist; b. Bronx, N.Y., Aug. 30, 1939; s. Floyd Newton and Margaret (Stanley) Wilson; m. Donna Feldmann; children: Susan, Mark. BS cum laude, Trinity Coll., Conn., 1962; MD, N.J. Coll. Medicine, 1966. Diplomate Am. Bd. Anesthesiology, Am. Bd. Critical Care Medicine, Nat. Bd. Med. Examiners; lic. physician, N.Y., Mass. Intern Hackensack (N.J.) Hosp., 1966-67; resident in anesthesiology Columbia-Presbyn. Med. Ctr., N.Y.C., 1967-69; vis. fellow in anesthesiology Columbia U., 1969-70; from asst. in anesthesia to anesthetist Mass. Gen. Hosp., Boston, 1970-91; from instr. anesthesia to assoc. prof. Harvard Med. Sch., 1970-91; attending, chmn. dept. anesthesiology and critical care Meml. Hosp. for Cancer and Allied Diseases, N.Y.C., 1991—; mem. Meml. Sloan-Kettering Cancer Ctr., 1991—; prof. anesthesiology Cornell U. Med. Coll., 1991—. Assoc. examiner Am. Bd. Anesthesiology, 1978—; chmn. institutional reveiw bd. Meml. Sloan-Kettering Cancer Ctr., 1995—. Assoc. editor Jour. Cardiothoracic and Vascular Anesthesia, 1986—, Critical Care Medicine, 1990-93; contbr. numerous articles to profl. books; editor, author numerous book chpts. Recipient Henry K. Beecher Clin. Tchr. award Mass. Gen. Hosp., 1977, 84, Albert H. Andrews award Nat. Bd. Respiratory Care Inc., 1997. Mem. Am. Soc. Anesthesiologists, Soc. Critical Care Medicine, Internat. Anesthesia Rsch. Soc., Am. Thoracic Soc., Assn. Univ. Anesthetists, Am. Soc. Critical Care Anesthesiologists, Soc. Cardiovascular Anesthesiologists, N.Y. State Soc. Anesthesiologists, N.Y. State Thoracic Soc., Am. Heart Assn. (coun. on cardiothoracic and vascular surgery). Office: Meml Sloan-Kettering Cancer Ctr 1275 York Ave New York NY 10021-6094

WILSON, RONALD ALFRED JAMES, accountant; b. Bklyn., July 23, 1944; s. James Adams and Marion Ernessa (Werhan) W.; m. Barbara Jane Zaleski, Mar. 30, 1968; children— Matthew James, Jonathan Stanley. B.A., Harvard U., 1966; M.S. in Acctg., NYU, 1972. C.P.A., Mass., N.Y. Mem. Staff Peat, Marwick Mitchell & Co., N.Y.C., 1971-75, supr., Paris, 1975-78, ptnr., Boston, 1978-86 , nat. dir. high tech. tax services, 1984-86 , ptnr.-in-charge tax dept., Balt., 1986— . Served to capt. USMC, 1966-70, Vietnam. Mem. Am. Inst. C.P.A.s, Md. Soc. of CPA's, Combined Health Agys. (dir., exec. com. mem.) Club: Lake Sunapee Yacht (N.H.), Ctr. Office: Peat Marwick Main & Co 111 S Calvert St Ste 1800 Baltimore MD 21202-6135

WILSON, RUBY LEILA, nurse, educator; b. Punxsutawney, Pa., May 29, 1931; d. Clark H. and Alda E. (Armstrong) Wilson. BS in Nursing Edn., U. Pitts., 1954; MSN, Case Western Res. U., 1959; EdD, Duke U., 1969. Staff nurse, asst. head nurse Allegheny Gen. Hosp., Pitts., 1951—52, night clin. instr., adminstrv. supr., 1951—55; staff nurse, asst. head nurse Fort Miley VA Hosp., San Francisco, 1957—58; instr. nursing Duke U. Sch. Nursing, Durham, NC, 1955—57, asst. prof. med. surg. nursing, 1959—66, assoc. in medicine, 1963—66, prof. nursing, 1971—, dean sch. nursing., 1971—84, asst. to chancellor for health affairs, 1984—; asst. prof. dept. community and family medicine Duke U. Sch. Medicine, 1971—; cons., vis. prof. Rockefeller Found., Thailand, 1968—71; vis. prof. Case Western Res. U., 1982—84. Mem. Gov.'s Commn. on Health Care Reform in N.C., 1994—96. Contbr. articles. Active N.C. Med. Care Commn., N.C. Ctr. for Nursing, 1990—; adv. bd. Duke U. Cancer Ctr., 1986—. Fellow: Inst. Medicine, Am. Acad. Nursing; mem.: N.C. Found. for Nursing (pres. 1990—94), Women's Forum N.C. (bd. dirs. 1984—88, 1995—), Assn. for Acad. Health Ctrs. (mem. inst. planning com.), Nat. League Nursing, Am. Assn. Higher Edn., Am. Assn. Colls. Nursing, ANA, Sigma Theta Tau. Office: Duke U Med Ctr PO Box 3243 Durham NC 27715-3243

WILSON, SAL, computer systems analyst, business executive; b. Cedar Rapids, Iowa, May 9, 1947; d. Joseph John and Alma (Klouda) Nemec; m. Robert Foster Wilson, Oct. 1982. BS in Computer Sci., Mt. Mercy Coll., 1985. Cert. netware engr. Systems analyst State of Iowa Dept. Human Rights, Des Moines, 1987-97; exec. v.p. Lawyer Forms Inc., Cedar Rapids, Iowa, 1992—; client/server developer State of Iowa Dept. Human Svcs., Des Moines, 1997—. Home: 2179 Blake Blvd SE Cedar Rapids IA 52403- Office: State of Iowa Dept Human Svcs Hoover Bldg 1st St Fl N Des Moines IA 50319-0001 E-mail: mrspkhead@hotmail.com.

WILSON, SAMUEL ERIC, vascular and general surgeon; b. Lisburn, County Antrim, Ireland, Oct. 17, 1941; m. Sandra Wilson; children: Andrea, Brian Alexander. Student, Henry Ford Coll., 1958-59; BA, Wayne State U., 1963, MD, 1965. Diplomate Nat. Bd. Med. Examiners, Am. Bd. Surgery, Am. Bd. Gen. Vascular Surgery. Intern U. So. Calif., L.A., 1965-66; resident in surgery UCLA/Wadsworth VA Med. Ctr., 1966-70; chief and attending surgeon vascular sect. VA Med. Ctr., L.A., 1972-92, asst. chief surg. svc., 1978-82; asst. prof. surgery UCLA Sch. Medicine, 1972-76, assoc. prof. surgery, 1976-81, attending staff mem., 1972-92, prof. surgery, 1981-92; chmn. dept. surgery Harbor-UCLA Med. Ctr., Torrance, 1982-92; attending staff VA Med. Ctr., Long Beach, Calif., 1992—; prof. surgery U. Calif., Irvine, 1992—; chmn. dept. surgery U. Calif.-Irvine Med. Ctr., Orange, 1992—. McIlrath guest prof. Royal Prince Alfred Hosp., U. Sydney, Australia, 1991; 25th anniversary guest prof. Japanese Soc. for Vascular Surgery, 1993; Ira M. Teicher meml. lectr., vis. prof. Albert Einstein Coll. Medicine, L.I. Jewish Med. Ctr., 1994; lectr., cons. in field. Editor (12 textbooks) ; mem. editl. bd.: Jours. Host/Pathogen News, 1984—85, mem. editl. bd.: Jours. Infectious Disease Alert, 1989—91, mem. editl. bd.: Jours. Internat. Vascular Surgery, 1991—93, mem. editl. bd.: Jours. Postgrad. Medicine, mem. editl. bd.: Jours. Dialysis and Transplantation, 1988—94, mem. editl. bd.: Jours. Vascular Forum, 1993—94, mem. editl. bd.: Jours. Advances in Therapy, 1990—, mem. editl. bd.: Jours. Postgrad. Gen. Surgery, 1991—97, mem. editl. bd.: Jours. Surgical Infection Index and Revs., 1993—98, mem. editl. bd.: Jours. Antibiotics for the Clinician, 1996—, mem. editl. bd.: Jours. Surg. Infections, 1998—, reviwer: various jours; contbr. articles to profl. jours. Bd. govs. L.A. Transplant Found., 1974-75 Recipient Hon. Mention award AMA, 1975, Shed the Light on Cancer award Am. Cancer Soc., 1982, Disting. Alumni award Wayne State U. Sch. Medicine, 1990. Fellow: ACS (young surg. del. 1977, standing com. on operating rm. environ. 1981—90, chmn. exec. com. 1986—87, bd. govs. 1996—99, mem. gov.'s com. on surg. practice in hosps. 1998—99); mem.: Western Vascular Soc., Surg. Infection Soc., Southwestern Surg. Congress (councilor 1992—97, progam com. 1995—96, exec. com. 1996—97, nominating com. 1996—97), So. Calif. Vascular Surg. Soc. (pres. 1994), Soc. Vascular Surgery, Soc. Univ. Surgeons, Pacific Coast Surg. Soc. (program chmn. 1997), L.A. Surg. Soc. (pres. 1988), Internat. Cardiovascular Soc., Assn. VA Surgeons, Am. Surg. Assn., Soc. for Clin. Vascular Surg., Halsted Soc. Office: U Calif Irvine Dept Surgery Med Ctr 101 City Dr Orange CA 92868 E-mail: sewilson@uci.edu.

WILSON, SAMUEL MAYHEW, surgeon; b. Phila., June 26, 1950; m. Dorothy Hay Barrus, June 9, 1990; children: Elisabeth, Mary. BA, Swarthmore Coll., 1972; MS, Drexel U., 1975; MD, Temple U., 1979. Diplomate Am. Bd. Surgery. Resident in surgery Temple U. Hosp., Phila., 1979-84; fellow in vascular surgery Presbyn.-U. Pa. Med. Ctr., 1984-86; attending surgeon Evang. Cmty. Hosp., Lewisburg, Pa., 1986-88, Albert Einstein Med. Ctr., Phila., 1988-95. Attending surgeon Elkins Park (Pa.) Hosp., 1988-95, Frankford Hosp., Phila., 1988-95, JFK Meml. Hosp., Phila., 1988-95; staff surgeon Bayhealth Med. Ctr.-Kent Gen. Hosp., Dover, 1996—; asst. clin. instr. surgery U. Pa. Med. Sch., Phila., 1984-85, assoc. clin. instr., 1985-86; clin. instr. surgery Temple U. Sch. Medicine, Phila., 1988-95. Contbr. articles to profl. jours. Active Christ Episcopal Ch., Dover, 1996—. Corp. USMCR, 1972-78. Fellow ACS, Southeastern Surg. Congress; mem. AMA (Physician Recognition award), Med. Soc. Del., Kent County Med. Soc., Delaware Valley Vascular Soc., Ea. Vascular Soc. Avocations: sailing, skiing, hiking, photography, reading. Office: 540 S Governors Ave Ste 100A Dover DE 19904-3523

WILSON, SANDRA JEAN, educational administrator; b. California, Mo., Apr. 23, 1947; d. Thomas Israel and Erma Jean (Johnston) Garber; m. George Dee Wilson, Jr., Aug. 24, 1968; children: Justin, Nathan, Kyle, Cara. BA, Blackburn Coll., 1969; MS, So. Ill. U., 1971, Specialist, 1990. Tchr. Bethalto (Ill.) Unit #8, 1969—92, prin., 1992—99, dir. sch. improvement, 1999—. Mem. Bea Credit Union Bd., Bethalto, 1992-97, chmn. of bd., 1997—. Co-author: (book) Student Based Objectives, 1973, Visual Perceptual Development. Vol. I, Auditory Perceptual Development, Vol. 2, 1973; contbg. author: Metro East Kindergarten Position Statement, 1987. Mem. edn. com. Bethalto Spirit, 1990—. Recipient Outstanding Tchr. award Bethalto Unit #8, 1978, Award of excellence Ill. State Bd. of Edn., 1996. Mem. Ill. Women Adminstrs., Ill. Prin.'s Assn. (Nat. Disting. Prin. 1997), Southwestern Ill. Assn. Supervision & Curriculum Devel. (sec./treas. 1991—). Roman Catholic. Avocations: reading jogging, listening to music. Office: Central Office 322 Central Ave Bethalto IL 62010

WILSON, SCOTT NUMO, psychiatrist; b. N.Y.C., May 27, 1955; s. Charles Philip and Christine (Bagaloff) Wilson; m. Anne Elizabeth Allan, June 25, 1983; children: Eric, Julia. AB in Biology, Princeton U., 1977; MD, Columbia U., 1981. Intern in internal medicine Salem (Mass.) Hosp., 1981-82; resident in psychiatry Mass. Gen. Hosp. and Harvard Med. Sch., Boston, 1982-85; chief resident Eric Lindemann Mental Health Ctr., 1984-85; fellowship in psychotherapy Mass. Gen. Hosp., 1985-86; med. dir. Revere (Mass.) Counseling Ctr., 1987-91; assoc. med. dir. Freedom Trail Clinic, Boston, 1991—; faculty psychotherapy fellowship Mass. Gen. Hosp., 1990—, faculty Ctr. Psychoanalytic Studies Harvard Med. Sch.; pvt. practice, 1985—. Psychotherapy lectr., supr. Mass. Gen. Hosp. and Harvard Med. Sch., Boston, 1986—; instr. in psychiatry Harvard Med. Sch., 1990—; psychiatrist Mass. Gen. Hosp., 1999—. Author: (with others) Autognosis, 1988; contbr. articles to profl. jours. Laughlin fellowship Am. Coll. Psychiatrists, 1985. Mem. Am. Psychiat. Assn., Boston Psychoanalytic Inst. Office: 5 Longfellow Pl Ste 213 Boston MA 02114-2839

WILSON, SHERRI DIANE, shopping center official; b. Flushing, N.Y., Sept. 24, 1959; d. Richard Erik and Sheila Harriet (Finkelstein) Peterson; m. Ian Scott Wilson, May 19, 1990 (div. Jan. 1998). d. Richard Eric and Sheila Harriet (Finkelstein) Peterson; m. Ian Scott Wilson, May 19, 1990 (div. Jan. 1998). Notary pub., N.Y. Contract adminstr. Home Mktg. Am., Hartford, Conn., 1980-82, N.Y.C., 1982-84; mgr. shopping ctr. properties Related Properties Corp., 1984—; ptnr. KGM Ptnrs., L.L.C. Mem. Internat. Coun. Shopping Ctrs. (cert. shopping ctr. mgr.). Republican. Mem. Dutch Reformed Ch. Avocations: golf, travel, bowling, decorating. Home: 100 Chateau Ln Apt 25 Hawthorne NY 10532-1740 Office: Related Properties Corp 2 Manhattanville Rd Purchase NY 10577-2113 Fax: 914-694-5732. E-mail: swilson@relatedproperties.com.

WILSON, SLOAN, writer, educator; b. Norwalk, Conn., May 8, 1920; s. Albert F. and Ruth (Danenhower) Wilson; m. Elise Pickhardt, Feb. 4, 1941 (div.); children: Lisa, Rebecca, David Sloan; m. Betty Stephens; 1 child Jessica. Grad., Fla. Adirondack Sch., 1938; AB, Harvard, 1942; LHD (hon.) , Rollins Coll., 1982. Writer, contbr. New Yorker and other mags.; with Providence Jour., 1946-47, Time, Inc., 1947-49, Nat. Citizens Commn. for Pub. Schs., 1949-53; dir. info. svcs., asst. prof. English Buffalo U., 1953-55; asst. dir. White House Conf. on Edn., 1955-56; Disting. writer-in-residence Rollins Coll., Winter Park, Fla., 1981-82; dir. Winter Park Artists Workshop, 1983-85; cons. Philip Crosby Assocs., 1984-87. Lectr. Va. Commonwealth U., 1990. Author: (novels) Voyage To Somewhere, 1946, The Man in the Gray Flannel Suit, 1955, A Summer Place, 1958, A Sense of Values, 1960, Georgie Winthrop, 1962, Janus Island, 1966, Away From It All, 1969, All The Best People, 1970, What Shall We Wear to This Party?, 1976, Small Town, 1978, Ice Brothers, 1979, Greatest Crime, 1980, Pacific Interlude, 1982, The Man in the Gray Flannel Suit II, 1983. Served to lt. USCGR, World War II. E-mail: s.wilson.b@3n.net. *Although some of my books have been widely read, I of course am not as successful as a writer as I would like to be. Almost all writers, after all, must, if they are honest, suspect that their triumphs are temporary. This is no cause for lament, for the same happens to almost everybody in all walks of life. I am lucky to have a wife who makes my private life a joy and three daughters and a son who with my ten grandchildren and one great grandchild give me a kind of immortality. Much like the characters in most of my books, I find my family the only part of my life which does not disappoint. My children and my wife always give me excellent reviews which never yellow in a scrapbook. I sometimes lecture on the topic of "Success." Nowadays that word seems to me to be much more complex than it did when I was young. As I grow old I love life more and more.*

WILSON, SONJA MARY, secondary education educator, consultant, poet, legal agent; b. Lake Charles, La., Mar. 28, 1938; d. Albert Ronald and Annelia (DeVille) Molless; m. Willie McKinley Williams, Apr. 28, 1956 (div. May 1969); children: William P., Dwayne L., Rachelle A., Devon A., Lisa M., Ricardo Soto; m. Howard Brooks Wilson, Nov. 12, 1982 (div. Dec. 1999); stepchildren: Howard N. Wilson, Yvonne Wilson. AA in Social and Behavioral Scis., Mt. St. Jacinto Jr. Coll., 1992; designated subjects credential, U. Calif., San Bernardino, 1983; student, Calif. State Poly. U., 1986; M in Adminstrn., Laverne U., 1985; BS in Edn. Methodologies, So. Ill. U., 1995; student, Riverside (Calif.) City Coll., 1988-89, 94. Prin.'s sec. Elsinore (Calif.) H.S., Elsinore Jr. H.S., 1974-83, tchr. bus. and adult vocat. edn. coord., 1979-88, notary pub., 1981-85, class adviser, 1983-88. Long-term substitute tchr. Perris H.S. Dist., 1991-94; spkr. in field. Clk. Lake Elsinore Unified Sch. Dist. Bd., 1988, pres., 1988, 98, 2002; clk., mem. Lake Elsinore Elem. Sch. Bd., 1979-88; pres., sec. treas., v.p. Riverside County Sch. Bds. Assn., 1979-98; assoc. sponsor, advisor Black Student Union/Future Leaders of Am., 1984-90; svc. unit rep., leader Girl Scouts U.S.A., bd. dirs. San Gorgonio coun., 1995, mem. nominating com., 1998, 99; den mother Boy Scouts Am.; mem. Ctrl.

Dem. Com., 1989-91; del. PTSA, 1991-93. Tribute in her honor Black Student Union/Future Leaders Am., 1989; recipient Excellence in Edn. award Hilltop Community Ctr. Club, 1989, Leadership award Black Art and Social Club, 1989, Svc. award Sojourner Truth Media Network, 1989, Proclamation award City of Elsinore, 1989, County of Riverside, 1984; named Outstanding Poet, Nat. Libr. of Congress, 1994, 95; recipient Golden Leaf award PTSA. Mem. NAACP (charter mem. Lake Elsinore affiliate; treas. 1998-2000, pres. 2000-01, plaque), Calif. Sch. Bds. Assn. (regional dir. 1988-92, conf. planning com. 1989, legis. com. 1981-97, nominations com. 1988, media com., dir. at large black 1993-95, audit com. 1993, dir./del. trainer 1993, alt. del., sgt. at arms 1994, 95, Fed. Rels. Network del. 1992, 95), Calif. Elected Women Ofcls. Assn., Calif. Sch. Employees Assn. (pres., treas., regional rep. asst., state negotiation com., del. to conf.), Internat. Soc. Poets, Lake Elsinore C. of C., Calif. Coalition Black Sch. Bd. Mems. (v.p. 1989, pres. 1990, program liaison 1989), Nat. Sch. Bds. Assn. (alt. del. 1994, 95), Nat. Coalition Black Sch. Bd. Mems. (dir. 1989-94, v.p. 1995-2000, sec.-treas. 1998—), Nat. Coun. Negro Women (charter, Willa Mae Taylor sect.), Black Art and Social Club, Lake Elsinore Black Art Culture Club (treas. 1997-2002, Vol. of Yr. 1999-2000, RTA com.), Hilltop Cmty. Club (plaque), Eta Phi Beta (all offices Gamma Alpha chpt., pres. 1992-94, Western region dir. 1997-2001, Resurrection choir 1996—, plaque, Vol. of Yr. award 2000). Avocations: travel, writing poetry, gardening, childcare, dancing. Home: 30402 Jernigan St Lake Elsinore CA 92530-5045 E-mail: sonjawilson@msn.com., Sonja.Wilson@leusd.k12.ca.us.

WILSON, STANLEY LEIF, small business owner; b. Zanesville, Ohio, Jan. 13, 1961; s. Jack Clarence and Janet W.; m. Dana Venable, July 5, 1996; children: Alica Nicle Venable. AAS in Pre-Engring., Muskingum Area Jt. Tech. Coll., Zanesville, 1979; AAS, U. Tex., 1981, BS in Geology, 1983. Cert. legal asst., Profl. Paralegal Inst. Ga. Geologist/data analyst Tex. Electro-Seise, Ft. Worth, 1979-84; co-owner Wilson Collision & Coatings Techs., Zanesville, 1984-86; adminstr. Auto Collision Specialist Inc., Ft. Worth, 1987-91; founder, CEO Ft. Worth Body & Paint Works Corp., 1992—. Founder, chmn., dir. The Faith Found., Dallas, 1997—; owner Dawson Exploration, Dallas, 1997—. Contbr. articles to profl. jours.; patentee in field. Lic. min. Assn. of Evangel. Gospel Assemblies, Monroe, La., 1999—; founder, dir. The Internat. Drinking Water for Children, Dallas, 1998—. Mem. The Nature Conservancy, The Planetary Soc., Am. Bible Soc., I Car USA. Avocations: flying, racing, scuba diving, photography, reading. Home: 501 Texas St Daisetta TX 77533 E-mail: stansbodyandpaintworks@yahoo.com.

WILSON, STANLEY PATTERSON, retired lawyer; b. Hamlin, Tex., Sept. 1, 1922; s. Milton Young and Ethel M. (Patterson) W.; m. Claudie Park, Sept. 23, 1944; children: Stanley P., Russell Park, Marianne. BS, U. North Tex., Denton, 1943; LLB, U. Tex., Austin, 1948. Bar: Tex. 1948. Ptnr. McMahon, Smart, Wilson, Surovik & Suttle, Abilene, Tex., 1948-81; sr. v.p., gen. counsel Central and S.W. Corp., Dallas, 1981-86, exec. v.p., gen. counsel, 1986-88, ret., 1988. Lt. (j.g.) USN, 1943-46, PTO. Mem. ABA, State Bar Tex., Am. Coll. Trial Lawyers, Internat. Assn. Def. Counsel, Abilene Bar Assn., Abilene Country Club. Methodist. Home: 1921 Elmwood Dr Abilene TX 79605-4802 Office: Ste 800 First Nat Bank Bldg Abilene TX 79601 E-mail: swilson@mcmahonlawtx.com.

WILSON, STEPHANIE D. astronaut; b. Boston, 1966; m. Julius B.J. McCurdy. BS in Engring., Harvard U., 1988; MS in Aerospace Engring., U. Tex., 1992. Loads and dynamic engr. astronautics group Martin Marietta, Denver, 1988—90; mem. attitude and articulation control subsys. for Galileo spacecraft Jet Propulsion Lab., Pasadena, Calif., 1992—96; astronaut NASA, Johnson Space Ctr., Houston, 1996—. Mem.: AIAA. Achievements include research in control and modeling of large, flexible space structures. Avocations: snow skiing, music, astronomy, stamp collecting, travel. Office: Astronaut Office/CB NASA Johnson Space Ctr Houston TX 77058*

WILSON, STEPHEN EDWARD, technical services company executive; b. Ellensburg, Wash., May 12, 1945; s. Edward and Marjorie Louise (Tucker) W.; m. Mary Lynne Halwas, Aug. 28, 1966; children: Troy, Aubree-Anna. BA in English, Cen. Wash. State Coll., 1967; MA in Guidance Counseling, Wayne State U., 1973. Commd. USAF, 1967, advanced through grades to lt. col., 1983, chief intelligence career mgmt. USAF Mil. Pers. Ctr. Tex., 1976-80, br. chief Intelligence Ctr. Pacific Camp Smith, Hawaii, 1980-81, Commdr. in Chief Pacific Staff, 1981-83, dir. Alert Ctr. Hdqrs. Electronic Security Command Kelly AFB, Tex., 1983-84, dir. tng., 1984-85, commdr. 6981 Electronic Security Squadron Elmendorf AFB, Alaska, 1985-88; ret., 1988; v.p. logistics and tech. svcs. Operational Tech. Corp., San Antonio, 1989—, mgr. quality assurance, 1989—; free lance writer Psychol. Corp., 1989—. Mem. USAF Intelligence Career Field Study Group, Washington, 1978-84, Dept. Def. Intelligence Career Devel. Panel, Washington, 1976-80; chmn. Computer Intelligence Officer Study Group, Washington, 1979-80, Pacific Target Actions Group, Honolulu, 1981-83 Author: North Vietnamese Use of Inland Waterways, 1970, Petroleum Pipelines in the Laotian Panhandle, 1971; contbr. editor: DOD Armed Services Vocational Aptitude Battery (ASVAB) Manual, 1990. Founding mem. San Antonio Council of Adoptable Children, 1976-80; charter mem. Hosanna! Luth. Ch., San Antonio, 1983-85; mem. Friends of Luth. Social Services Tex., San Antonio, 1976-80. Decorated Bronze Star. Mem. Air Force Assn., Am. Soc. Quality Control, Am. Soc. Safety Engrs., Nat. Contract Mgmt. Assn., Am. Def. Preparedness Assn., Assn. Old Crows. Home: 19506 Wittenburg San Antonio TX 78256-2026 Office: 4100 NW Loop 410 Ste 230 San Antonio TX 78229-4253

WILSON, STEVEN MICHAEL, English educator, poet; b. Ft. Sill, Okla., Mar. 30, 1960; s. George William Wilson and Elizabeth Charlene Simonds; m. Nancy Ann Effinger, July 31, 1982; children: Samuel Nathan, Connor Patrick. BA in Letters, U. Okla., 1982; MA, Tex. Christian U., 1984; MFA, Wichita (Kans.) State U., 1987. Prof. English S.W. Tex. State U., San Marcos, 1987—. Author: Allegory Dance, 1991, The Singapore Express, 1994; contbr. articles to profl. publs., including Christian Sci. Monitor, Am., High Plains Lit. Rev., Commonweal, Yankee; editor: The Anatomy of Water, 1992. Bd. dirs. Rhetoric Soc. of Am., 1983-85. Grantee Nat. Endowment for the Arts, Washington, 1992-93; named sr. Fulbright lectr., Coun. for the Internat. Exch. of Scholars, Washington, 1994-95, 2002. Mem. Associated Writing Programs, Fulbright Assn., Tex. Assn. Creative Writing Tchrs. (bd. dirs. 1992-94), Poets & Writers. Avocation: travel. Home: 610 Clyde Ct San Marcos TX 78666-2840 Office: SW Tex State U Dept English San Marcos TX 78666 E-mail: sw13@swt.edu.

WILSON, TAMMY SUE, obstetrics nurse; b. Elkins, W.Va., June 15, 1969; d. Foster Gay and Bonnie Sue (Collins) Williams; divorced; 1 child, Ciara Nicole. ADN, Davis and Elkins Coll., 1993. RN, W.Va.; cert. in neonatal resuscitation. Staff nurse obstetrics unit Davis Meml. Hosp., Elkins, 1993—96; staff nurse pediat. United Hosp. Ctr., Clarksburg, W.Va., 1997—2001; staff nurse labor and delivery Mongahelia Gen. Univ. Hosp., Morgantown, 1997—2001, Stonewall Jackson Hosp., Weston, 2001—; pediat. staff nurse Ruby Meml. Hosp., 2001—. Mem. Nazarene Ch. Avocations: playing with daughter, helping friends. Home: PO Box 526 Belington WV 26250-0526 E-mail: cnw@bcnetmail.org.

WILSON, TAMRA MCELROY, writer; b. Pana, Ill., Aug. 14, 1954; d. Lynn and Enid (McKinley) McElroy: m. Tym Turner Wilson, May 26, 1979; 1 child, Lantz McKinley. Student, Ill. State U., 1972-74, Brighton (Eng.) Coll. Edn., 1974; BJ, U. Mo., 1976. Reporter Daily Union, Shelbyville, Ill., 1976-77; staff writer The Country Cos., Bloomington, 1978-79; account exec. Inform, Inc., Hickory, N.C., 1979-81; pub. rels. assoc. Centel, 1981-84; conf. coord. J. H. Heafner Co., Lincolnton, N.C., 1985-86; comms. specialist Meredith/Burda, Newton, NC, 1987—92; mktg. dir. Catawba Valley Area Girl Scout Coun., Hickory, 1992; dir. pub. rels. Lenoir-Rhyne Coll., 1992—98; pub. info. officer Catawba County Schs., Newton, NC, 1998—2001. Instr. Catawba Valley C.C., Hickory, 1992-94. Editor: (book) USS Cabot, 1986; editor The Register, 1987-92 (rate excellent 3 times by The Ragan Report), Profile, 1993—. Mem. steering com. March of Dimes, 1991-97; Sister Cities del. to Altenburg, Germany, 1995; bd. dirs. Ea. Catawba Coop. Christian Ministry, 2002—; v.p. Friends of Catawba County Libr., 2002—. Mem. DAR (John Hoyle chpt., bd. dirs.), Coll. News Assn. of the Carolinas, Western Piedmont Pub. Rels. Assn., Blumenthal Writers and Reders Series, NC Writers Network, Catawba County C. of C. (Leadership grad. 1993, chmn. 1996), Charlotte Writers Club, Catawba Valley Rotary Club (pres. 2000-01), Alpha Phi Women's Fraternity.

WILSON, TERESA ANN, neonatal/perinatal nurse practitioner; b. Iowa City, Sept. 1, 1950; d. Robert Reginald and Patricia Mary (McMahon) W. B of Gen. Studies, U. Iowa, 1972, BSN, 1983; MS in Maternal Newborn Nursing, U. Ariz., 1990. RN, Ariz., Iowa. Staff nurse maternity unit U. Iowa Hosps./Clinics, Iowa City, 1983-85; nurse level III Carondelet St. Joseph's Hosp., Tucson, 1985-94; clin. mgr. labor delivery recovery postpartum Carondelet St. Mary's Hosp., 1994-96, nurse level III, 1996-99, nurse level IV, 1999—2001, nurse level V, 2001—02, Carondelet St. Joseph's Hosp., Tucson, 2002—. Instr. childbirth and parenting Carondelet St. Joseph's Hosp., Tucson, 1986-93; project dir., rsch. specialist U. Ariz. Coll. Nursing, Tucson, 1991-92, clin. instr., 1993, 96, adj. clin. asst. prof., 1999—; nurse level III, Tucson Med. Ctr., 1992-94; cons. Ariz. Dept. Health Svcs., Office of Women & Children's Health, 1996-97; perinatal nurse care mgr. Carondelet Health Network, 1997-99; co-primary investigator Extended Length of Stay for Postpartum Women, 1997-2000; mem. Tucson-Almaty Health Care Coalition, 1994-99, Tucson Domestic Violence Healthcare Coalition, 1998—. Mem. cmty. svcs. com. So. Ariz. March of Dimes, 1990-96, cmty. adv. bd. The Parent Connection Inc., 1992-96; health educator El Rio Health Ctr., Tucson, 1992-98; adv. bd. trainer Woman to Woman Cmty. Prenatal Action Team, 1994-96. Mem. Pima County Health Mothers Health Babies Coalition (sec. 1991-96, co-chair 2001—), Assn. Women's Health, Obstetrics and Neonatal Nursing (chpt. coord. 1991-94), Ariz. Coalition Against Domestic Violence, Sigma Theta Tau. Avocations: running, swimming, gardening, reading, genealogy. Office: Carondelet St Josephs Hosp 350 N Wilmot Rd Tucson AZ 85711- Fax: 520-323-7536. E-mail: teresa6@mindspring.com.

WILSON, TERRY DOUGLAS, pharmaceutical manager; b. Waukesha, Wis., Sept. 19, 1942; s. Marvin and Georgia W.; divorced; children: Matthew, Kelly. BS, U. Wis., 1963; MNS, U. Idaho, 1971; PhD, U. Conn., 1978. Asst. prof. chemistry Annhurst Coll., Woodstock, Conn., 1970-79; sr. scientist Vicks Rsch., Mt. Vernon, N.Y., 1979-80, Sterling Rsch. Group, Rensselaer, 1985-90, group leader, 1985-90; assoc. dir., product devel. Bristol Myers Squibb, Evansville, Ind., 1990-94; dir. quality control BioPharm, Ft. Washington, Pa., 1994-95; rsch. fellow Cygnus, Redwood City, Calif., 1995-96; dir. tech. svcs. Theratech, Salt Lake City, 1996-97; dir. quality control, tech. devel. Patho Genesis/Chiron, Annandale, NJ, 1997—2001; sr. dir. quality assurance Chiron, 2001—. Assoc. editor: Jour. Pharm. Biomedical Analysis, 1988-92; patentee in field. Mem. Am. Assn. Pharm. Sci., Regulatory Affairs Profls. Soc. Avocation: tech. theater. Office: Chiron 1545 Route 22 E Annandale NJ 08801-3096 E-mail: terry_wilson@chiron.com.

WILSON, THEODORE HENRY, retired electronics company executive, aerospace engineer; b. Eufaula, Okla., Apr. 23, 1940; s. Theodore V. and Maggie E. (Buie) W.; m. Barbara Ann Tassara, May 16, 1958 (div. 1982); children: Debbie Marie, Nita Leigh, Wilson Axten, Pamela Ann, Brenda Louise, Theodore Henry II, Thomas John, Margaret Mariana; m. Colleen Fagan, Jan. 1, 1983 (div. 1987); m. Karen L. Lerohl, Sept. 26, 1987 (div. 1997); m. Sandra Rivadeneira, Mar. 27, 1997. BSME, U. Calif., Berkeley, 1962; MSME, U. So. Calif., 1964, MBA, 1970, MSBA, 1971. Sr. rsch. engr. N.Am. Aviation Co. div. Rockwell Internat., Downey, Calif., 1962-65; propulsion analyst, supr. div. applied tech. TRW, Redondo Beach, 1965-67, mem. devel. staff systems group, 1967-71, sr. fin. analyst worldwide automotive dept. Cleve., 1971-72, contr. systems and energy group Redondo Beach, 1972-79, dir. fin. control equipment group Cleve., 1979-82, v.p. fin. control indsl. and energy group, 1982-85, mem. space and def. group Redondo Beach, 1985-93, ret., 1993. Lectr., mem. com. acctg. curriculum UCLA Extension, 1974-79. Mem. Fin. Execs. Inst. (com. govt. bus.), Machinery and Allied Products Inst. (govt. contracts coun.), Nat. Contract Mgmt. Assn. (bd. advisors), Aerospace Industries Assn. (procurement and fin. coun.), UCLA Chancellors Assocs., Tau Beta Pi, Beta Gamma Sigma, Pi Tau Sigma. Republican. Avocations: golf, bridge. Home: 3617 Via La Selva Palos Verdes Peninsula CA 90274-1115

WILSON, THOMAS, museum director; Dir. Mus. of N.Mex, Santa Fe. Office: Mus of NMex 107 W Palace Ave Santa Fe NM 87501-2014*

WILSON, THOMAS LEON, physicist, researcher; b. Alpine, Tex., May 21, 1942; s. Homer Marvin and Ogarita Maude (Bailey) W.; m. Joyce Ann Krevosky, May 7, 1978; children: Kenneth Edward Byron, Bailey Elizabeth Victoria. BA, Rice U., 1964, BS, 1965, MA, 1974, PhD, 1976. With NASA, Houston, 1965—, astronaut instr., 1965-74, high-energy theoretical physicist, 1969—. Author: of two books on cosmic dust and astrophysics; contbr. articles in field to profl. jours. including Phys. Rev. Recipient Hugo Gernsback award IEEE, 1964; NASA fellow, 1969-76. Mem. AAAS, Am. Phys. Soc., N.Y. Acad. Scis., Am. Assn. Physicists in Medicine. Achievements include research on grand unified field theory, relativistic quantum field theory, quantum chromodynamics, quantum probability theory, supergravity, quantum cosmology, astrophysics, deep inelastic scattering, neutrino astronomy, neutrino tomography; discoverer classical uncertainity principle; subspeciality: relativity and gravitation; patentee in field; contributor to design of NASA's proposed lunar base; originator olive branch as symbol of man's 1st landing on moon (on Susan B. Anthony and Eisenhower dollars); and manual Saturn takeover for Apollo moon program. Home: 206 Woodcombe Dr Houston TX 77062-2538 Office: NASA Johnson Space Ctr Houston TX 77058 E-mail: twilson@ems.jsc.nasa.gov.

WILSON, THOMAS ARTHUR, economics educator; b. Vancouver, B.C., Canada, Aug. 5, 1935; s. Victor and Edith Christina Wilson; m. Julia Ann Dillon, Feb. 8, 1958; children: Christine Diana, Arthur Dillon. BA, U. B.C., 1957; PhD, Harvard U., 1961. Instr. Harvard U., 1961-62, asst. prof., 1962-67; assoc. prof. U. Toronto, 1967-68, prof., 1968—2001, dir. Inst. for Policy Analysis, 1969-75, dir. econs., 1979-82, chmn. econs. dept., 1982-85, dir. policy and econ. analysis program, 1987—2002, area coord. bus. econs. Rotmen Sch. Mgmt., 1989—, prof. emeritus, 2001—. Sr. advisor Inst. for Policy Analysis, 2002—; cons. various govtl. depts. Author: Advertising and Market Power, 1974, Canadian Competition Policy, 1979, Fiscal Policy in Canada, 1993, The Future of Telecommunications Policy in Canada, 1995, The Electronic Village, 1998, Rationality in Public Policy, 1999. Fellow Royal Soc. Can.; mem. Am. Econs. Assn., Canadian Econ. Assn. (pres. 1984-85) Office: 140 St George St Toronto ON Canada M5S 3G6 E-mail: twilson@chass.utoronto.ca.

WILSON, THOMAS DOUGLAS, JR. lawyer; b. Winston-Salem, N.C., Aug. 26, 1946; s. Thomas Douglas Wilson and Beatrice Burcham Chapman; m. Betsey Page Bent, Aug. 22, 1984; 1 child, Elizabeth. BA in Econs., U. N.C., Chapel Hill, 1968, JD, 1973. Bar: N.C. 1973, Ga. 1974; cert. arbitrator, mediator Ga., arbitrator N.C. Trial atty. FTC, Atlanta, 1973-78; pvt. practice, 1978-81; atty. Ga. Legal Svcs. Corp., Gainesville, 1981-84; mng. ptnr. Wilson, Cobb, Lichstenstein & Lao, Atlanta, 1984-93; pres. Ga. Emission Testing Co., Inc., 1993-95; assoc. McGuire, Wood & Bissette PA, Asheville, N.C., 1995-98, mng. ptnr., 1999—. Vol. atty. Pisgah Legal Svcs., Asheville, 1996—, also bd. dirs. Author: (manual) Social Security Disability Claims, 1984; co-author: (manual) North Carolina Construction Law: Rights and Remedies, 1998. Chmn. bd. dirs. RiverLink, Asheville, 1997-99; vice chmn. bd. dirs. Regional Waterh Authority Task Force, Asheville, 1996-99; mem. Asheville Econ. Devel. Task Force, 1999-2000; mem. Asheville Econ. Devel. Commn., 1997-99; youth basketball coach YMCA, Asheville Recreation League, 1997-2001. Mem. ABA, ATLA, Ga. Bar Assn., N.C. Bar Assn. (bd. dirs., constrn. law coun 2000—), N.C. Acad. Trial Lawyers. Home: 172 Marlborough Rd Asheville NC 28804 Office: 48 Patton Ave Asheville NC 28801-3321 Fax: (828) 252-2437. E-mail: t.d.wilson@home.com., tdwilson@mwbavl.com.

WILSON, THOMAS HENRY HENRY, museum director; b. L.A., Calif., May 6, 1948; s. James L. W. and Jane S. (Egbert) Jones; m. Rowan Lindley, Apr. 23, 1983; children: Manda, James. BA in Anthropology, U. N.Mex., 1970; MA in Anthropology, U. Calif., Berkeley, 1972, PhD in Anthropology, 1976; JD, U. Md., 1989. Lectr., asst. prof. archaeology U. Nairobi, 1975-77; rsch. assoc. Internat. Louis Leakey Meml. Inst. African Prehistory, 1977-80; coast archaeologist Nat. Mus. Kenya, 1977-82, sr. rsch. assoc., 1982-83; program officer mus. program NEH, 1985-90; deputy dir. The Ctr. African Art, 1990-92; exec. dir. Southwest Mus., 1992—. Adj. prof. anthropology U. So. Calif., 1992—; researcher in field. Contbr. chpts. to books and articles to profl. jours.; mem. editorial bd. Mus. Anthropology, 1992—, Native Peoples, 1992—. Bd. dirs. Ethnic Arts Coun. L.A., 1992—. Vis. fellow Johns Hopkins U. Dept. History, 1983-84. Mem. Am. Anthropol. Assn., Am. Assn. Mus., Soc. Am. Archaeology, African Studies Assn., British Inst. Eastern Africa, Sonali Studies Internat. Assn., Internat. Coun. Mus., Coun. Mus. Anthropology (pres. 1990-92), Soc. Africanist Archaeologists, Phi Beta Kappa, Phi Kappa Phi, Blue Key Honor Nat. Soc. Office: Southwest Museum PO Box 41558 Los Angeles CA 90041-0558

WILSON, THOMAS MATTHEW, III, lawyer; b. Ware, Mass., Feb. 22, 1936; s. Thomas Matthew Jr. and Ann Veronica (Shea) W.; m. Deborah Ord Lockhart, Feb. 10, 1962; children: Deborah Veronica, Leslie Lockhart, Thomas Matthew IV. BA, Brown U., 1958; JD, U. Md., 1971. Bar: Md. 1972, U.S. Ct. Appeals (4th cir.) 1976, U.S. Supreme Ct. 1977. Sales mgr. Mid-Ea. Box Mfg. Co., Balt., 1966-74; asst. atty. gen., chief antitrust divsn. State of Md., 1974-79; ptnr. Tydings & Rosenberg, LLP, 1979—. Author: Defending an Antitrust Action Brought by a State, 1987, The Spectre of Double Recovery in Antitrust Federalism, 1989; co-author: Reciprocity and the Private Plaintiff, 1972; mem. editl. adv. bd.: Bur. of Nat. Affairs Antitrust and Trade Regulation Report, 1979—. Mem. ABA (sect. on antitrust law 1974—, chmn. state antitrust enforcement com. 1986-89, antitrust sect. coun. 1990-93, coord. com. on legal edn. 1993—), Md. Bar Assn. (antitrust subcom. 1975-78), Internat. Bar Assn. (sect. on bus. law, antitrust law and monopolies com. 1983—), Churchwarden's Chess Club, Annapolis Yacht Club. Republican. Achievements include patents for nail cartons. Home: Baobab Farm Hampstead MD 21074 Office: Tydings & Rosenberg LLP 100 E Pratt St Baltimore MD 21202-1009

WILSON, THOMAS STRONG, JR. (TAM WILSON), judge; b. Portland, Oreg., Aug. 13, 1944; s. Thomas Strong and Ruth (Isherwood) W. BA, Dickinson Coll., 1967; JD, U. Miami, 1971. Bar: Fla. 1971, D.C. 1972, U.S. Dist. Ct. (so. dist.) Fla., U.S. Ct. Appeals (5th cir.). Rsch. aide to Justice James Adkins Fla. Supreme Ct., Tallahassee, 1971-72; assoc. Preddy, Haddad, Kutner & Hardy, 1973, John R. Farrell, PA., 1973; asst. pub. defender Pub. Defender's Office, Dade County, Fla., 1974-77; sole practice, 1978-84; asst. state's atty. State's Atty.'s Office, 1984-87, gen. master Family Divsn., 1987-90; judge Circuit Ct., 1990. Served to ensign USNR, 1968-69. Mem. Iron Arrow, Skull and Key. Roman Catholic. Office: Dade County Courthouse 73 W Flagler St Ste 524 Miami FL 33130-1707

WILSON, THOMAS WOODROW, III, research scientist, consultant; b. Greensboro, N.C., Mar. 29, 1956; s. Thomas Woodrow Jr. and Ruth Hanes (Friddle) W. BS in Textile Chemistry with honors, N.C. State U., 1978, MS in Textile Chemistry, 1981, PhD in Fiber and Polymer Sci., 1986. Registered patent agent. Polymer scientist Rsch. Triangle Inst., Research Triangle Park, N.C., 1989-91; rsch. scientist Family Health Internat., 1991-93, sr. rsch. scientist, 1993-94, assoc. dir., 1994-95; mgr. intellectual property and regulatory affairs Mayer Labs., Oakland, Calif., 1996-97; materials rschr. Nike, Beaverton, Oreg., 1997-99, advanced chemistry rsch. mgr. Taichung, Taiwan, 1999—. Cons. IPAS, Carrboro, N.C., 1991-94. Patentee med. devices; contbr. articles to profl. jours. Grantee USDA, NASA, NIH/Nat. Inst. Dental Rsch., 1986. Mem. AAAS, Am. Chem. Soc. (polymeric materials sci. and engring. divsn., polymer divsn., rubber divsn., chemistry and law divsn.), ASTM, Toastmasters (Taichang, Taiwan chpt.), Sigma Xi. Avocations: leatherworking, woodworking, writing fiction. Office: Nike 447 Wen Hsin Rd 28th Fl Taichung ROC Taiwan E-mail: Tom.Wilson@Nike.com.

WILSON, TIMOTHY WAYNE, music educator, musician; b. Pensacola, Fla., Sept. 3, 1961; s. Frank Melvin and Dannie Estelle Wilson; m. Stacie Celeste Lands, Nov. 21, 1998; children: Tabitha Dawn Hill, Tiffany Nicholle Hill. BME, Montevallo, Montevallo, IA, 1984; MA Ed., Univ. North Ala., Florence, AL, 1995. Class A Teachers Certificate State of Ala. Band dir. Moore County H.S., Lynchburg, Tenn., 1984—86, Falkville H.S., Falkville, 1986—99, Stone Mid. Sch., Huntsville, 1999—. Pres. Decatur Cmty. Band, Decatur, Ala., 1992—93; adjudicator Baldwin County Band Co., Bay Menette, Ala., 1999, Bay Menette, 2001. Recipient Kappa Delta Pi Honor Soc., Univ. North Ala., 1995. Mem.: Ala. Bandmasters Assn., Nat. Edn. Assn., Music Educators Nat. Conf. Methodist. Achievements include Orchestrator, Musical Production, 1984; development of responsible for creating a highly rated marching and concert band at Falkville School, AL. Avocations: playing billiards, golfing. Office: Stone Middle School 2620 Clinton Ave Huntsville AL 35805 E-mail: timwilson@teacher.com.

WILSON, VETA EMILY, community health nurse; b. Kingston, Jamaica, West Indies, Mar. 6, 1934; d. Norman Ivan and Gladys Gwendolyn Panton; children: Michael Bruce, Marlene Dawn. BS in Health Sci., Bklyn. Coll., 1974; MS in Cmty. Health, L.I. U., Bklyn., 1977, BSN, 1979; MPH, Columbia U., 1985; MDiv, N.Y. Theol. Sem., 1999. RN, N.Y.; cert. paralegal, correctional health profl. Coord. insvc. edn. N.Y.C. Correctional Health Svcs., 1989—. Mem. Queens Inst. Dist. Nurses. Home: 5036 Lost Dutchman Dr Lithonia GA 30038-3801

WILSON, VICTORIA JANE SIMPSON, farmer, nurse; b. Floresville, Tex., Nov. 30, 1952; d. Joseph Eugene and Eva Gertrude (Ferguson) Simpson; m. Richard Royce Wilson, May 15, 1976; children: Sarah Beth, Nathan Lawrence. BSN, U. Cen. Ark., 1977; MS in Nursing, Northwestern State U., 1981. Charge nurse surg. St. Vincent Infirmary, Little Rock; staff nurse ICU La. State U. Med. Ctr., Shreveport, La.; patient edn. coord. White River Med. Ctr., Batesville, Ark.; co-owner, CEO Health Plus, Stuttgart; co-owner Wilson Enterprises, Humphrey, 1992—98; staff nurse St. Vincent Health Sys., 2000—01; mem. faculty Southeast Ark. Coll., 2000, Jefferson Sch. Nursing, Pine Bluff, 2001—. Mem.: Ark. Nurse Assn., Am. Nurse Assn., Sigma Theta Tau. Home: 51 Wilson Ln Humphrey AR 72073-9097 E-mail: wilsonv@jrmc.org.

WILSON, VIRGIL JAMES, III, lawyer; b. San Jose, Calif., July 25, 1953; s. Virgil James Wilson Jr. and Phyllis Emily (Mothorn) Brasser; children: Gabriel James Hekili, Alexander Robert Kaimoku, Hayley Noelani, Maia E. Kailani. BA with honors, U. Calif., Santa Cruz, 1975; JD cum laude, U. Santa Clara, 1981. Bar: Calif. 1981, U.S. Dist. Ct. (no. dist.) Calif. 1981, Hawaii 1982, U.S. Dist. Ct. Hawaii 1982, U.S. Ct. Appeals (9th cir.) 1987, U.S. Supreme Ct. 1987, Oreg. 1990, U.S. Dist. Ct. Oreg. 1998, U.S. Ct. Fed. Claims 1999; lic. pvt. investigator, Hawaii. Atty. James Krueger P.C., Wailuku, Maui, 1981-83; resident counsel Sterns & Ingram, Honolulu, 1983-89; pvt. practice Kailua, 1989—; assoc. Thorp, Purdy, Jewett, Urness & Wilkinson, P.C., Springfield, Oreg., 1998-99; of counsel Law Offices of Ian L. Mattoch, 1993-96, Gaydos, Churnside & Balthrop PC, Eugene, Oreg. Owner Wilson Investigations, Santa Cruz, 1978-81, Honolulu, 1981—. Mem. Hawaii Bar Assn., Calif. State Bar Assn., Oreg. Bar Assn. Avocation: profl. magician. Fax: 541-607-6565. E-mail: VJWILSONiii@msn.com.

WILSON, WALTER CLINTON, retired gas and oil industry executive; b. Brownwood, Tex., Sept. 21, 1942; s. Henry Eliga and Lottie Mae (Palmore) W.; m. Debra M. Thompson, Aug. 26, 1965; children: Walter Scott, Aimée Renee. BS cum laude, Howard Payne U., 1965. CPA, Tex. Fin. mgmt. Exxon Co. USA, Kingsville, Corpus Christi, Houston, Tex., 1965-81; asst. contr. The Superior Oil Co., Houston, 1982-85, fin. cons., 1985-87; contr. Enron Oil and Gas Co., 1987-88, sr. v.p., CFO, 1988-2000; mem. bd. advisors A.S. Grace & Co., 2001—. Adv. bd. H.S. Grace & Co. Consulting, Inc., Houston. Chmn. deacons First Bapt. Ch., Houston, 1994-96, chmn. pers. com., 1985-87; trustee Fin. Exec. Rsch. Found., 1998-2001; bd. trustees Howard Payne U., Brownwood, Tex., 1999—. Lt. USNR, 1966-69, Vietnam. Mem. AICPA, Fin. Execs. Internat., Tex. Soc. CPAs (Houston chpt.), Club Corp. Am.-Houston Soc., Kingwood Country Club. Republican. E-mail: wwilson2@houston.rr.com.

WILSON, WANDA LEE DAVIS, entertainment promotions professional, casting director; b. Pitts., May 15, 1950; d. James A. Davis, Jr. and Dorothy (Love) Davis Anselmi; m. Kirby L. Wilson Sr., Apr. 23, 1976 (div. July 1984); children: Le Chon Kirb, Lia Shawnyea. Student, Connelly Tech. Sch., Pitts., 1968-71, Allegheny Community Coll., 1968-71, U. Pitts., 1984, 86. Stand-in co-host The Together Show Sta. KDKA-TV, CBS, Pitts., 1971; adminstrv. sec. GE, 1971-78; sec., notary public Sta. WPCB-TV, Wall, Pa., 1979-80; producer, host The Wanda Wilson Show Am. Cablevision Co., Monroeville, 1981-84, Warner Cable Co. and Pitts. Telecommunications, Inc., 1984-87; mktg. mgr. The Informer newspaper Homewood Brushton Revitalization and Devel., Pitts., 1984-87; pres. local, nat. internat. pub. rels. W-W

Prodns./Wanda Wilson Enterprises, 1984—; sr. clk./chemical monitor Gencorp Aerojet Tech. Systems, Rancho Cordova, Calif., 1987-90; publicist, cons. Easy Internat., Pitts., 1990—; studio camera operator Sta. WPXI-TV, 1990-92; casting dir. for commls., film, print media-theatre Wanda Wilson Enterprises, 1992—. Scout Modelsearch Am.; occasional writer, copywriter, announcer local radio shows, Pitts., 1972-85; radio show co-host, announcer Internat. People's Radio and TV, Sacramento, 1987; promoter concerts, screenplays, sound tracke Wan Mar Prodns., 1991—. Author (poetry) Love Traces on My Mind, 1972, (songs lyrics) The First Time I Saw You, 1982; performer poetry recitals, Pitts., 1973, (TV movies) $10,000,000 Getaway, 1990, Bump in the Night, 1990, Dead and Alive, 1991, (feature film) Lorenzo's Oil, 1991, Roommates, 1993; producer, hostess WanMar Info. and Talent Showcase Cable TV, Pitts., 1991—; line prodr., casting dir. With Abandon, 1999; casting dir. The Family Tree, 1999. Active Citizen Action for Reduction of Toxic Chems. in Product Packaging, 1990; organizer civic and community events, energy conservation, 1984-87; mem. Pitts. History and Landmarks Found., Smithsonian Assocs., 1991. Mem. AFTRA, NAFE, Pitts. Film Workers Assn., bd. dirs., Pittsburgh Film Workers Assn., Pitts. Models Assn., Pitts. Media Fedn. (bd. dirs.), Smithsonian Assocs. Democrat. Avocations: swimming, photography, art, interior decorating. Office: PO Box 100061 Pittsburgh PA 15202

WILSON, WENDY MELGARD, kindergarten and special education educator; b. Fargo, N.D., Jan. 13, 1952; d. Howard A. Melgard and Grace B. (Alphson) Watkins; m. Henry Milton Wilson II, July 31, 1982; children: Andrew J., Aaron C. BA/BS in Edn., U. N.D., 1972-77; postgrad., Drake U., 1984-86, Simpson Coll., 1992-94, U. No. Iowa, 1998—. Secondary spl. edn. tchr. Ctrl. Decatur Community Schs., Leon, Iowa, 1978-80; work experience instr. Green Valley AEA, Creston, 1980-82; elem. spl. edn. tchr. Stuart (Iowa) Menlo Community Schs., 1983-86, Greenfield (Iowa) Community Schs., 1986-93, kindergarten tchr., 1993-98; elem. spl. edn. tchr. Spirit Lake (Iowa) Sch. Dist., 1998-99; kindergarten tchr. Spirit Lake (Iowa) Cmty. Schs., 1999—. Pres., bd. dirs. Little Lambs Presch., Greenfield, 1991-92; sec., v.p. bd. Sunshine Daycare Ctr., Greenfield, 1987-90; co-chairperson S.W. Iowa Very Spl. Art Festival, Creston, 1981; innkeeper, co-owner Wilson Home Bed & Breakfast, 1986-95; team mem. New Iowa Schs. Devel. Corp., 1996-98; mem. Spirit Laek Sch. Dist. Bldg. and Dist. Improvement Teams, 2001--. Com. mem. Greenfield Tourism Com., 1988-94; mem. Greenfield Mother's Club, 1987-98, sec., 1991; mem. Adair County Meml. Hosp. Aux., 1987-98, Greenfield Elem. PTA, Grace Luth. Ch., Spirit Lake. Mem. NEA, PEO, Iowa State Edn. Assn., Greenfield Edn. Assn. (pres., v.p., com. ch. 1989-98), Nat. Assn. for Educating Young Children, Iowa Bed and Breakfast Innkeepers Assn. (sec. 1990-92), Spirit Lake Edn. Assn. (v.p. 1999-2000, pres. 2000-01), Greenfield C. of C., Winterset C. of C., Greenfield Bus. Women, Iowa Aviation Preservation Soc. Home: 13926 Hwy 276 Spirit Lake IA 51360-7048 E-mail: wwilson@spirit-lake.k12.ia.us.

WILSON, WESLEY M. retired lawyer, writer; b. Mangum, Okla., June 21, 1927; s. Frank Henry and Fern (McCool) W.; m. Marjorie Helen Montague, Sept. 7, 1957; children: Larry Arthur, Bruce Alan. BS, Ill. Inst. Tech., Chgo., 1952; MBA, U. Chgo., 1954; JD, U. Wash., 1960. Bar: Wash., 1960. With AT&T Long Lines, Chgo., 1948-50; equipment engr. Western Elec. Co., 1952-54; pers. asst., pers. dir. West Coast Telephone Co., Everett, Wash., 1954-57; atty. NLRB, Seattle, 1960-69; labor rels. atty. Wilson & Lofland, Yakima, Wash., 1970-85. Part-time mgmt. cons. Donworth & Assocs., Seattle, 1957-58; instr. pers. rels. U. Wash., Seattle, 1958; instr. labor rels. City U., Yakima, 1980-84. Author: Labor Law Handbook and 10 supplements, 1963, 68-85, The Labor Relations Primer, 1973, Know Your Job Rights, 1976, Countries and Cultures of the World, Then and Now, (3 vols.), 1997, Five Languages Made Simpler, French, Italian, English, Spanish, German, 1997, Curious Customs and Bizarre Beliefs Around the World, 1999. With U.S. Merchant Marines, 1945-46, U.S. Army, 1946-48. Mem. Wash. State Bar Assn., Yakima County Bar Assn. (pres. 1984-85). Avocations: travel, history, economics, languages, backpacking. Home: 3300 Carpenter Rd SE Apt 113 Olympia WA 98503-4012 E-mail: weswilson5@attbi.com.

WILSON, WESLEY WARREN, economics educator; b. Fargo, N.D., Feb. 7, 1958; children: Kelsey Gray, Regina Gray. BSBA, U. N.D., 1980; postgrad., N.D. State U., 1980-81; MA, Washington State U., 1984, PhD, 1986. Rsch. asst./assoc. Upper Great Plains Inst., N.D. State U., Fargo, 1980-81; rsch./teaching asst. dept. econs. Washington State U., Pullman, 1981-86, asst. prof. dept. agrl. econs., 1986-89; asst. prof. dept. econs. U. Oreg., Eugene, 1989-94, assoc. prof. dept. econs., 1995-2000, prof., 2000—. Cons. Upper Great Plains Transp. Inst., 1982; presenter in field. Contbr. articles to profl. jours. Grantee Washington State U., 1989, USDA Agrl. coop. Svc., 1988-90, USDA Office Transp., 1987, Washington State U., 1985. Mem. Am. Agrl. Econs. Assn., Western Agrl. Econs. Assn., Am. Econ. Assn. (pres. TRPN and pub. utility group), Econometrics Soc., Indsl. Orgn. Soc., World Conf. on Transp. Rsch., Ctr. for Asian and Pacific Studies, Transp. Rsch. Forum (pres. agrl. and rural transp. chpt.). Democrat. Methodist. Avocations: golf, tennis, backpacking. Home: 4820 Larkwood St Eugene OR 97405-4014 Office: U Oreg Dept Econs Eugene OR 97405

WILSON, WILLIAM CAMPBELL MCFARLAND, gastroenterologist; b. Pitts., June 8, 1953; s. George Lincoln and Nancy Adair (Lytle) W.; m. Marlis Howland, June 25, 1977; children: Sarah, Stephen, Corrie. BS in Biology, Va. Tech, 1975; MD, Hahnemann U., 1979. Intern, residency R.I. Hosp., Providence, 1978-82; staff internist USAF Med. Ctr., Wright-Patterson AFB, Ohio, 1982-86; fellowship Hahnemann U., Phila., 1986-88; with Digestive Care, Dayton, Ohio, 1988—. Chmn. planning com. Dayton Gastroenterology Symposium, 1990—; com. patient edn. Miami Valley Hosp., Dayton, 1990—94, quality assurance com., 1992—, vice chmn. dept. medicine, 1994—96, chmn. dept. medicine, 1996—98, chief of staff-elect, 2002—. Bd. dirs. Fairhaven Ch., Dayton, 1990—94, 2001—, Dayton Christian Schs., Inc., 1995—, physician, 1993—; bd. dirs., physician In His Name Ministries, 2000—02. Physician USAF, 1979—86. Fellow ACP; Mem. AMA, Am. Gastroenterological Assn., Am. Coll. Gastroenterology, Am. Soc. Gastrointestinal Endoscopy, Montgomory County Med. Assn., Alpha Omega Alpha. Avocations: tennis, computer, wood working, bicycling, photography. Office: 75 Sylvania Dr Dayton OH 45440-3237 E-mail: wcmw@aol.com.

WILSON, WILLIAM BERRY, lawyer; b. Cape Girardeau, Mo., June 17, 1947; s. Charles F. and Anita (Bartlum) Wilson; m. Suzanne T. Wilson; children: Matthew James, Sarah Talbot. BA summa cum laude, Westminster Coll., 1969; JD, U. Mich., 1972. Bar: Fla. 1972, U.S. Dist. Ct. (mid. dist.) Fla. 1972, U.S. Ct. Appeals (11th cir.) 1972, U.S. Supreme Ct. 1976, cert.: Civil Trial Lawyer Bd. 1983. Ptnr. Maguire, Voorhis & Wells P.A., Orlando, Fla., 1977-98, pres., 1984-97, chmn., 1997-98; ptnr. Holland & Knight LLP, 1998—, dir., 1999—. Mem. exec. com., trust com., bd. dirs. SunTrust Bank Ctrl. Fla., 1990—. Bd. overseers Crummer Sch. Bus., Rollins Coll., 1994—2002; chmn. Fla. Residential Property & Casualty Joint Underwriting Assn., 1995—2001; mem. Fla. Fed. Jud. Nominating Commn., 2001—; bd. dirs. Econ. Devel. Authority, Orlando, 1992—97, chmn., 1994—95, subcom. chmn. Project 2000 Orlando, 1985—87; bd. dirs. Fla. Symphony, Orlando1985; Fla. TaxWatch, Inc., 1992—98; bd. dirs. U. Ctrl. Fla. Found., 1996—, Jr. Achievement, 1998—; trustee Orlando Mus. Art, 1993—, pres., 1997—99. Mem.: Orlando Regional C. of C. (bd. dirs. 1997—, vice chmn. tech. 1999—, chair-elect 2001—), Greater Orlando C. of C. (bd. dirs., exec. com. 1997—), Am. Bd. Trial Advocacy, Orange County Bar Assn. (chmn. fed. and state practice sect. 1982—84, mem. jud. rels. com. 1984—, chmn. 1987—98, chmn. professionalism com. 1997—99), Fla. Bar Assn. (mem. exec. coun. trial lawyers sect. 1987—98, chmn. 1996—97, code and rules of evidence com. 1982—88, chmn. 1986—88), ABA, Citrus Club (bd. dirs. 1994—, chmn. 1998—), Country Club of Orlando (bd. dirs.), Rotary (bd. dirs.). Republican. Presbyterian. Avocation: Avocations: tennis, scuba diving. Office: Holland & Knight LLP PO Box 1526 200 S Orange Ave Ste 2600 Orlando FL 32801-3453 E-mail: bwilson@hklaw.com.

WILSON, W(ILLIAM) DANIEL, language professional, educator; b. Sedalia, Mo., Dec. 3, 1950; m. Christina von Hodenberg; children: Adrian, Marguerite, Martin. AB, Shimer Coll., 1973; MA, Cornell U., 1976, PhD, 1978. Asst. prof. U. Toronto, Can., 1978-79; asst. prof., postdoctoral rschr. McGill U., Montreal, Que., Can., 1979-83; asst. prof., assoc. prof. dept. German U. Calif. Berkeley, 1983-93, prof., 1993—, chair, 1997-2001. Author: Narrative Strategy of Wieland's Don Sylvio, 1981, Humanitaet und Kreuzzugsideologie, 1983, Geheimraete gegen Geheimbuende, 1991, Interirdische Gaenge, 1999, Das Goethe-Tabu, 1999; co-editor: Impure Reason: Dialectic of Enlightenment, 1993; mem. editl. bd. German Quar., 1998—. Mem. MLA (exec. com. divsn. 18th century German lit. 1993-98), Am. Assn. Tchrs. German, Am. Soc. 18th Century Studies, Goethe Soc. Weimar, Goethe Soc. N.Am., German Soc. 18th Century Studies, German Studies Assn., Lessing Soc. (Siberach prize 1979, mem. editl. bd. 1986—). Office: Dept German Univ Calif Berkeley CA 94720-3243 E-mail: danw@socrates.berkeley.edu.

WILSON, WILLIAM J. English language educator; b. Oxford, Ind., Sept. 18, 1932; s. William Woodward Wilson and Esta Ella (Burton) Dilley; m. Edith Lucille McElhaney, June 1, 1955 (dec. Mar. 1969); children: Susan Wilson Siener, Maura A., Kyle A. BS summa cum laude, Ill. State U., 1959; MA, Peabody-Vanderbilt U., Nashville, 1968; EdD, Nova U., Ft. Lauderdale, Fla., 1983. Tchr. Manteno (Ill.) High Sch., 1959-60; teaching asst. U. Ill., Urbana, 1960-61; tchr. Wheaton (Ill.) Central High Sch., 1961-67; editor Laidlaw Pubs., Chgo., 1968-69; asst. prof. Ball State U., Muncie, Ind., 1969-70; assoc. prof. English Palm Beach C.C., Lake Worth, Fla., 1970—. Test reader Ednl. Testing Svc., Princeton, N.J., 1965-96; pres. Am. Lang. Rsch. Found., Lake Worth, 1976—. Editor: New Approaches to Language and Composition, 1969; author children's mus. Winter Comes to Florida, 1974, children's mus. play A Cruise on the S.S. Eternal, 1975, Arnold's Answering Apparatus, 1976. Bd. dirs. Village Green Condominiums, Palm Springs, 1985-86. With USN, 1951-55. No. Ill. U. fellow in linguistics, DeKalb, 1965-66, humanities fellow Peabody-Vanderbilt U., Nashville, 1967. Mem. VFW, NEA, Am. Legion, Nat. Assn. Tchrs. English., Kappa Delta Pi, Sigma Tau Delta. Democrat. Episcopalian. Avocations: Kairos prison ministry, sports, square dancing, travel, collecting timepieces. Home: 2100 Springdale Blvd Apt 216Y Palm Springs FL 33461-6366 Office: Palm Beach C C 4200 Congress Ave Lake Worth FL 33461-4705 E-mail: barktree@bellsouth.net.

WILSON, WILLIAM JAMES, healthcare executive; b. Racine, Wis., Oct. 9, 1948; s. William Henry and Eileen (Tate) W.; m. Deborah Ann Leon, Nov. 14, 1987; children: Jacob Leon, James Tate. Degree in adminstrn. of justice summa cum laude, Am. U., 1972. Asst. dir. promotions Jerry Lewis Telthon, Richmond, Va., 1975; dir. mktg. Mile High Publs., N.Y.C., 1975-76; dir. bur. Travel Communicatiions, Honolulu, 1976-78; founder Hawaii 800, 1979—; v.p. mktg. Video Vacations, N.Y.C., 1982-84; founder Infovision, Los Angeles, 1984-87; chmn. bd. Visitor Cable Network, Honolulu, 1978—; pres. Comcor, 1976—; pres. bus. devel. 3HO Superhealth Hollistic Treatment Ctr., Tucson, 1990-93; pres. Educational Discovery, 1993-94; CEO Advanced Learning Inst., 1994—; mng. dir. Vet. Inst. Integrated Medicine, 1996—; founder, CEO Inst. Labs., 2001—. Founder Japan Am. News Network. Avocations: skiing, rugby. Home: 1109 Quince Ave Boulder CO 80304-0785 Office: PO Box 88377 Honolulu HI 96830-8377

WILSON, WILLIAM JAMES, marketing professional; b. Mpls., May 8, 1936; s. Elmo C. Wilson and Harriett (Ellis) Russo; m. Julie Steers, Sept. 24, 1960 (div. 1983); children: Amanda Jane, Heather May; m. Gabi Coatsworth, Aug. 4, 1983. AB, Yale U., 1958; MA, Cambridge U., Eng., 1964; postgrad., U. Vienna, summer 1964. Internat. advt. devel. mgr. Reader's Digest, London, 1964-67; exec. v.p., dir. Internat. Rsch. Assn., N.Y.C., 1968-71; chair, chief exec. officer Roper Starch Worldwide, Harrison, N.Y., 1971—. Bd. dirs. Roper Ctr. Storrs Ct.; U.S. rep. ESOMAR, The Netherlands 1982-88; chmn. Coun. of Am. Survey Rsch. Orgn., 1994, Coun. for Mktg. and Opinion Rsch., 1996—; past dir. Market Rsch. Coun; mem. bd. advisors MSMR program U. Tex., Arlington, A.C. Nielsen Ctr. for Market Rsch. U. Wis., Madison, Baruch Coll., N.Y.C.; mem. bd. dirs. Intersections Inc. Contbr. articles to profl. jours. Mem. Am. Mktg. Assn., Internat. Advt. Assn., Am. Assn. Pub. Opinion Rsch., World Assn. Pub. Opinion Rsch., European Soc. Opinion & Mktg. Rsch. Avocations: gardening, golfing, reading, walking. Office: Roper Starch Worldwide Inc 500 Mamaroneck Ave Ste 103 Harrison NY 10528-1608

WILSON, WILLIAM JULIUS, sociologist, educator; b. Derry Twp., Pa., Dec. 20, 1935; s. Esco and Pauline (Bracy) W.; m. Mildred Marie Hood, Aug. 31, 1957; children: Colleen, Lisa; m. Beverly Ann Huebner, Aug. 30, 1970; children: Carter, Paula. BA, Wilberforce U., 1958; MA, Bowling Green State U., 1961; PhD, Wash. State U., 1966; LHD (hon.), U. Mass., 1982, L.I. U., 1982, Columbia Coll., Santa Clara U., Loyola Coll., 1988, De Paul U., 1989; LLD (hon.), Marquette U., Mt. Holyoke Coll., 1989; LHD (hon.), New Sch. for Social Rsch., 1991, Bard Coll., 1992, John Jay Sch. Criminal Justice, 1992, U. Pa., 1993, So. Ill. U., 1993, Northwestern U., 1993, Bowling Green State U., 1994, SUNY, Binghamton, 1994, Princeton U., 1995, Columbia U., Rutgers U., Haverford Coll., 1996, Johns Hopkins U., Morehouse Coll., Niagara U., 1997, Dartmouth Coll., 1997, U. Amsterdam, 1998, Clarion U., 1999, Colgate U., 1999, Clark U., 1999, Bates Coll., 1999; D (hon.), Northeastern U., 1999, Macalester Coll. Ohio State U., 2001; DHL (hon.), Occidental Coll., 2001, Rensselaer Poly. Inst., 2001, Lawrence U., 2001, U Miami, 2002. Asst. prof. U. Mass., Amherst, 1965-69, assoc. prof., 1969-71; vis. asso. prof. U. Chgo., 1971-72, assoc. prof. dept. sociology, 1972-75, prof., 1975—, chmn. dept. sociology, 1978—, Lucy Flower prof. urban sociology, 1980-84, Lucy Flower disting. service prof., 1984—; Lucy Flower Univ. prof., 1990-96; Malcolm Wiener Prof. of social policy Harvard U., 1996-98, Lewis P. and Linda L. Geyser Univ. Prof., 1998—. Mem. bd. univ. publs. U. Chgo. Press, 1975-79; bd. dirs. Ctr. for Nat. Policy, 1987-92, Ctr. Budget and Policy Priorities, 1987—, Ctr. for Advanced Study of Behavioral Scis., 1988—, Twentieth Century Fund (now called Century Found., 1992—, Jerome Levy Inst., 1992—, Manpower Demonstration Rsch. Corp., 1993—; mem. domestic strategy group Aspen Inst., 1992—; bd. dirs. Pub./Private Ventures, Phila; elected mem., Inst. of Medicine, 2000. Author: Power, Racism and Privilege, 1973, Through Different Eyes, 1973, The Declining Significance of Race, 1978, The Truly Disadvantaged, 1987, The Ghetto Underclass, 1993, Sociology and the Public Agenda, 1993, When Work Disappears, 1996 (award Sidney Hillman Found. 1997), The Bridge Over the Racial Divide, 1999. Bd. dirs. Social Sci. Rsch. Coun., 1979-84, Chgo. Urban League, 1983-97, Spencer Found., 1987-97, George M. Pullman Found., 1986-93, Russell Sage Found., 1989-98, Ctr. for the Advanced Study of the Behaviorial Scis., 1989—, Nat. Humanities Ctr., 1990-95; mem. Com. on Sci., Engring. and Pub. Policy, NAS, 1995—; nat. bd. dirs. A. Philip Randolph Inst., Inst. Rsch. on Poverty, 1983—; trustee Spelman Coll., 1989-98; mem. Pres. Commn. on White House Fellowships, 1994-2001; mem. Pres. Com. Nat. Medal Sci., 1994-98; trustee Wilberforce U.; bd. advisors Frederick D. Patterson Rsch. Inst., United Negro Coll. Fund, 1996—. With U.S. Army, 1958-60. Recipient Disting. Tchr. of Year award U. Mass., Amherst, 1970, Regents Disting. Alumnus award Wash. State U., 1988, Burton Gordon Feldman award Brandeis U., 1991, Frank E. Seidman Disting. award in polit. econ., 1994, Martin Luther King Jr. Nat. award, 1998, Nat. Medal of Sci. 1998; MacArthur Prize fellow, 1987. Fellow AAAS, Am. Acad. Polit. and Social Sci., Am. Acad. Arts and Scis.; mem. NAS, Nat. Acad. Edn., Am. Philos. Soc., Inst. of Medicine, Am. Sociol. Assn. (pres. 1989-90, com. for pub. understanding of sociology award 1998, Sydney M. Spivack award 1977, DuBois, Johnson, Frazier award 1990, Lester F. Ward Disting. Contbns. to Applied Sociology award 1998), Soc. for Study Social Problems (C. Wright Mills award 1988), Sociol. Rsch. Assn. (pres. 1987-88), Consortium of Social Sci. Assn. (pres. 1993-94), Internat. Sociol. Assn., Chgo. Urban League (Beautiful People award 1979) Democrat. Home: 75 Cambridge Pkwy Unit E406 Cambridge MA 02142-1229 Office: John F Kennedy Sch Govt Harvard Univ 79 John F Kennedy St Cambridge MA 02138-5801*

WILSON, WILLIAM LEIGH, lawyer, educator; b. South Bend, Ind., May 23, 1966; s. William Lee and Dianne Marie (Duffy) W.; m. Catherine Maryjane McCarren. BA, U. Notre Dame, 1988; JD, Ind. U., 1991. Bar: Ind. 1991, U.S. Dist. . (no. and so. dists.) Ind. 1991, U.S. Dist. t. (no. dist.) Ill. 1994, U.S. Ct. Appeals (7th cir.) 1992, U.S. Supreme Ct. 1995. Atty. Hahn, Walz and Knepp, South Bend, 1991-2000, Anderson, Agostino & Keller P.C., South Bend, 2000—. Adj. asst. prof. U. Notre Dame, Ind., 1996—; instr. Ind. U., South Bend, 1996—. Dir. Ind. Civil Liberties Union, Indpls., 1993—, pres., bd. dirs., 1997-98. Mem. ABA, Robert A. Grant Inn Ct., Ind. Bar Assn., St. Joseph County Bar Assn. Roman Catholic. Avocation: Disneyana. Office: Anderson Agostino and Keller 131 S Taylor St South Bend IN 46601

WILSON, WILLIAM PRESTON, psychiatrist, emeritus educator; b. Fayetteville, N.C., Nov. 6, 1922; s. Preston Puckett and Rosa Mae (VanHook) W.; m. Dorothy Elizabeth Taylor, Aug. 21, 1950; children: William Preston, Benjamin V., Karen E., Tammy E., Robert E. BS, Duke U., 1943, MD, 1947. Diplomate: Am. Bd. Psychiatry and Neurology (examiner). Intern Gorgas Hosp., Ancon, C.Z.; then resident psychiatry Duke U. Med. Center, later resident neurology, 1949-54; asst. prof. psychiatry Duke U. Med. Sch., 1955-58; asso. prof. psychiatry, dir. psychiat. research U. Tex. Med. Br., Galveston, 1958-60; asso. prof. psychiatry Duke U. Med. Center, 1961-64, head div. clin. neurophysiology, 1961-83, prof. psychiatry, head div. biol. psychiatry, 1964-84, emeritus prof. psychiatry, 1985—; dir. Inst. Christian Growth, Burlington, N.C., 1985—; disting. prof. pastoral counseling Houston Grad Sch. Theology, High Point, 1996—. Chief neurophysiol. labs. VA Hosp., Durham, N.C., 1961-76; sec. Am. Bd. Qualification in Electroencephalography, 1971-77; mem. N.C. Gov.'s Task force on Diagnosis and Treatment; mem. med. adv. com. N.C. Found. Mental Health Rsch.; bd. dirs. nat. div. Contact Teleminstry USA, also mem. internat. commn. healing; cons. numerous area hosps.; Finch lectr. Fuller Theol. Sem., Pasadena, Calif., 1974; vis. prof. psychiatry Marshall U. Sch. Medicine, Huntington, W.Va., 1985-89. Co-author: The Grace to Grow; editor: Applications of Electroencephalography in Psychiatry; co-editor: EEG and Evoked Potentials in Psychiatry and Behavioral Neurology; Contbr. med. jours. Mem. ofcl. bd. Asbury United Methodist Ch., Durham; mem. program and curriculum com. United Meth. Ch., 1973-81; trustee Meth. Retirement Home, Durham, N.C.; pres. United Meth. Renewal Services, Inc., 1978-82. Served with AUS, 1943-46. Recipient Ephraim McDowell award Christian Med. Found., 1982, Pioneer in Christian Psychiatry award Congress on Christian Counseling, 1988; named Educator of Yr., Christian Med. and Dental Soc., 1996; EEG Montreal Neurol. Inst. fellow, 1954-55, postdoctoral fellow NIMH. Mem. Am. Psychiatric Assn., So. Psychiatric Assn. (pres. 1977-78), AMA, So. Med. Assn. (chmn. sect. neurology and psychiatry 1970), Med. Soc. N.C., Durham-Orange County Med. Soc. (chmn. student recruitment com. 1965), Soc. Biol. Psychiatry, Am. EEG Soc. (councillor), So. EEG Soc. (pres. 1964), Assn. Research Nervous and Mental Diseases, Am. Epilepsy Soc., AAAS, Am. Acad. Neurology, Sigma Xi, Alpha Omega Alpha. Clubs: U.S. Power Squadron (comdr. Durham 1971). Republican. Home: 1209 Virginia Ave Durham NC 27705-3263 Office: PO Box 2347 Burlington NC 27216-2347 E-mail: wpwilson@netpath.net.

WILSON, WILLIAM ROBERTS, JR. (BOB WILSON), lawyer, apparel executive; b. Rosedale, Miss., July 6, 1941; s. William Roberts Wilson Sr. and Mary Elizabeth (Boatner) W.; m. Elizabeth Ann Smith; children: William Roberts Wilson III, Elizabeth Ann, Augusta Elliott. Student, Vanderbilt U., Tenn., 1964; JD, U. Miss., 1969. Pvt. practice, Jackson, Miss.; chmn. bd., owner Dunn's Mid.-South Sporting Goods Co. Chmn. founder The Charitable Food Bank. Miss. Sportsman Against Hunger; active mem. Rep. Nat. Com. Team 100, Newcomen Soc. of U.S., Am. Intertrade Group, Presdl. Round Table, Rep. Senatorial Inner Circle. Mem. NRA (life mem.), Ala. State Bar Assn., Miss. Bar Assn., Miss. Trial Lawyers Assn. (life mem.), Assn. Trial Lawyers of Am. (sustaining mem.), Roscoe Pound Found. (fellow), Miss. State Bar Assn. (former commr.), Nat. Col. Advocacy, United Conservation Alliance (founding bd. mem.), Congressional Sportsmen Found. (bd. dirs.), Quail Unlimited (life mem., life sponsor), Miss. Wildlife Fedn. (life mem.), Ducks Unlimited (sponsoring mem.), Waterfowl, U.S.A., Delta Wildlife Found. (sponsoring founder), British Field Sport Soc. (life mem.), Catfish Point Hunting Club (gen. ptnr.), Athelstan Club, Country Club of Jackson Miss., Delta Kappa Epsilon (bd. dirs. R.O.A.R.), Delta Theta Phi. Office: 2506 Lakeland Dr Ste 500 Jackson MS 39232-7651

WILSON, WILLIAM STANLEY, oceanographer; b. Alexander City, Ala., June 5, 1938; s. Norman W. and Helen C. (Hackemack) W.; m. Anne M. Stout; children: Lauren, Jonathan (dec.). BS, William & Mary Coll., 1959, MA, 1965; PhD, Johns Hopkins U., 1972. Marine biol. collector Va. Inst. Marine Sci., Gloucester Point, 1959-62, computer systems analyst, 1964-65, Chesapeake Bay Inst., Balt., 1965-66; phys. oceanography program mgr. Office of Naval Rsch., Washington, 1972-78; chief oceanic processes program NASA, 1979-89, program scientist earth observing system, 1989-92; asst. adminstr. for ocean svcs. and coastal zone mgmt. NOAA, 1992-97, deputy chief scientist, 1997—2002; sr. scientist Nat. Environ. Satellite Data and Info. Svc., 2002—. Recipient Antarctica Svc. medal NSF, 1961, Superior Civilian Svc. award USN, 1979, Exceptional Sci. Achievement medal NASA, 1981, Disting. Achievement award MTS and Compass Publs., 1989, award Remote Sensing Soc., 1992, medal French Space Agy., 1994, Portuguese Naval Cross, 1997, Australian Antarctic Divsn. medal, Group Achievement award NASA, 2000. Mem. Am. Meteorol. Soc., Am. Geophys. Union (Ocean Scis. award 1984), Oceanography Soc. (com. chmn. 1989-92), Sigma Xi, Omicron Delta Kappa. Avocations: bicycling, scuba diving. Home: 219 Tunbridge Rd Baltimore MD 21212-3423 Office: NOAA/NESDIS 1325 E-W Hwy Silver Spring MD 20910 E-mail: stan.wilson@noaa.gov.

WILSON-COKER, PATRICIA ANNE, lawyer, social service administrator, educator; b. Willimantic, Conn., Aug. 26, 1950; d. Bertram W. and Mary Evelyn (Spurlock) Wilson; m. Edward H. Coker (div. 1973). BA, U. Conn., 1977, MSW, JD, 1981. Bar: Conn. 1981. Asst. prof. social work, dir. Ctr. for Child Welfare Studies St. Joseph Coll., West Hartford, Conn., 1981-86, assoc. prof. social work, chair social work & child welfare, 1986-88; exec. asst. to commr., statewide dir. divsn. children protective svcs. Conn. Dept. Children and Youth Svcs., Hartford, 1988-91, mediation panelist, Juan F. consent decree, 1990-91; monitoring panelist dept. children and youth svcs. Fed. Dist. Ct., New Haven, 1991-92; dir. social svc. planning & interdisciplinary program devel. Dept. Social Svcs., Hartford, Conn., 1992-93, dir. adminstrv. hearings and appeals Middletown, 1993-95, regional adminstr. north ctrl. region, 1995-99, commr., 1999—. Instr. U. Conn., Storrs, summer 1977, social rsch. asst. philosophy dept., summer 1978; legal social work intern juvenile unit Hartford (Conn.) Legal Aid Soc., 1978-79, legal rschr. juvenile unit, summer 1979, legal rschr., fall 1979; instr. Ea. Conn. State U., Willimantic, spring 1980; cons. New Eng. Clin. Assocs., West Hartford, 1985-86, Office of Policy & Mgmt., State Conn., Hartford, 1988, Perisky and Daniels, Hartford, 1988; apptd. Juvenile Justice Adv. Com. to the Office of Policy and Mgmt., State Conn., 1983-89, Conn. Task Force on Family Violence, 1985-86, Criminal Sanctions Task Force, 1987, Child Support Task Force, 1987-88, Conn. Children's Commn., 1988-91; assoc. prof. St. Joseph Coll., West Hartford, 1981-88, So. Conn. State Coll., New Haven, 1990—; trustee ednl. policies St. Joseph Coll., 1980-97, chair, 1997; lectr. and presenter in field. Contbr. articles to profl. jours. Recipient Judge Thomas Gill award Conn. Children in Placement Program, 1991, Annual award Conn. Coun. on Adoption, 1991, Disting. Alumna award U. Conn., 2001; named Educator of Yr., Conn. Girl Scout Coun., 1987. Fellow Conn. Bar Found. Office: Dept Social Svcs 25 Sigourney St Hartford CT 06106-5001 E-mail: PWCoker@aol.com., wilson-coker@po.state.ct.us.

WILSON-HOPKINS, DEBORAH DANA, research assistant, food technology consultant; b. Portsmouth, Va., Aug. 16, 1955; d. Bernice Audrey (Copeland) Wilson; m. Frederick Sherman Hopkins III, Dec. 29, 1986. BS, Iowa State U., 1978, MS, 1980; postgrad., Lancaster (Pa.) Theol. Sem., 1986-87, Howard U., 1988. Research asst. USDA Nat. Animal Disease, Ames, Iowa, 1980-81; agrl. cons. U.S. Peace Corps, Wash., 1981-83; premium fulfillment prayer counselor Christian Broadcasting Network, Va. Beach, 1984-85; repairperson, mdse. asst. Stewart Sandwiches Internat., Norfolk, Va., 1985-87; cashier Roy Rogers-Marriott, Annapolis, Md., 1987; sales assoc. Home Port Property, 1988; field aide Md. Dept. Agr., Annapolis, 1988; lab asst. Md. Fuels Testing Lab., Jessup, 1989—. Textiles artisan: Storm at Sea, 1988 (award of Merit, Wildflower tapestry judges award, 1990, 1st pl. award, 1990). Vol. Hugger Md. Spl. Olympics, Yowson, 1988; chmn. Broadneck Muscular Dystrophy. Recipient awards for textiles. Mem. Inst. Food Technology, MIT Enterprise Forum Tex., Broadneck Peninsula Jaycees (sec. canister coin campaign 1988-89, distbr. Christmas food baskets and toys 1988). Avocations: textile handicrafts and design, reading, traveling, ethnic foods. Home: 1423 Cape St Claire Rd Annapolis MD 21401-5697

WILSON-MCKEE, MARIE, museum director; Dir. Wyo. State Mus., Cheyenne. Office: Wyo State Mus Barrett Bldg 2301 Central Ave Cheyenne WY 82001-3173*

WILSON-PLEINESS, CHRISTINE JOYCE, writer, poet, columnist, real estate developer; b. Chgo., July 27, 1951; d. Peter Joseph Thelen and Edna (Milewski) Dombrowski; m. Douglas A. Wilson, July 7, 1973 (div. Oct. 1986); children: Amy Kathleen, Lauri Ellyn; m. Glenn B. Pleiness, Dec. 5, 1998. BS in Edn., No. Ill. U., 1973; postgrad., Spalding U. Asst. store mgr. County Seat Co., Joliet, Ill., 1981-83; cash applicator Aurora (Ill.) Pump Co., 1984-85, accounts payable clk., 1986-89; accounts payable technician Horizon Sportswear, Inc., Madison Heights, Mich., 1989-90; accounts payable rep. Crain Comm., Inc., Detroit, 1990-95; accounts payable specialist Philip Svcs. Corp., 1995-96, ORACLE project team, 1996, accounts payable team leader, 1996-97; accounts payable and expense supr. Superior Cons. Co., Inc., Southfield, 1997-98; accounts payable auditor The Profit Recovery Group Internat. Inc., Clawson, 1998-99; accounts payable supr. ACN Inc., Farmington Hills, 1999-2000; accts. supr. Roush Industries, Livonia, 2000—02. Owner/operator part-time comml. cleaning bus., Sterling Heights, Mich., 1997-98. Mem., bd. dirs. Somerset Square Condominium Assn., Sterling Heights, 1996, 97; rec. sec. Troy Cmty. Chorus, 1999-2000. Recipient Tchr. Edn. scholarship State of Ill., 1969. Mem. Parents Without Ptnrs. (treas. chpt. 761, 1996-98, Appreciation award 1997, 98, 99), Monday Night Writing Group (founding, facilitator 1997—), Beta Sigma Phi (Woman of Yr. award 1989, 98, Order of the Rose 2000). Avocations: writing, reading, dancing, attending the theatre, singing. Home: 8280 Crestview Dr Apt 1 Sterling Heights MI 48312-6081 E-mail: tinaw51@yahoo.com.

WILSON-WEBB, NANCY LOU, education administration consultant, rancher; b. Maypearl, Tex., Jan. 20, 1932; d. Madison Grady Wise and Mary Nancy Pearson-Bedford (Haney) Wilson; m. John Crawford Webb, July 29, 1972. BS magna cum laude, Abilene (Tex.) Christian U., 1953; MEd with high honors, Tex. Christian U., 1985. Cert. tchr., mid-mgmt., sch. adminstr., Tex. Tchr. elem. grades Ft. Worth Ind. Sch. Dist., 1953-67, adult edn. tchr., 1967-73; dir. adult edn. consortium for 38 sch. dists. Tex. Edn. Agy., 1973-2000. Pres. Nat. Commn. on Adult Basic Edn., 1994-95; pres. Tex. Adult Edn. Adminstrn., 1994; apptd. mem. Tex. State Literacy Coun., 1987-94, Tex. State Sch. Bd. Commn., 1994-99; exec. bd. Tex. Coun. Co-op Dirs., 1989-2001, pres., 1994—; apptd. to Gov. Ann Richard's Task Force for Edn.; owner, mgr. of ranch, 1998-2001. Cons. to textbooks, 1994-98; editor textbooks, 1999. Pres. Jr. Womans Club, Ft. Worth, 1969, Fine Arts Guild, Tex. Christian U., Ft. Worth, 1970-72, Ft. Worth Womens Civic Club Coun., 1970; active Exec. Libr. Bd., Ft. Worth, 1990—, Jewel Charity Ball, 1988-2002; apptd. bd. dirs. Literacy Plus in North Tex., 1988-99, pres., 2001—; apptd. bd. dirs. Greater Ft. Worth Literacy Coun., 1976-88, pres., 2001-02; commr. Ed-16 Task Forces Tex. Edn. Agy., 1985-94; literacy bd. dirs. Friends of Libr., 1967-2001, Opera Guild Bd. Ft. Worth, 1965-85, Fort Worth Ballet Guild, Johnson County (Tex.) Corrs. Bd., 1990-2000; bd. dirs. Salvation Army, 1991-2002, Ft. Worth Libr.; mem. Tarrant County Bd. on Aging, 1997-98; mem. Commn. Status of Women, Ft. Worth, 1973-99; mem. Southside Ch. of Christ. Recipient Bevy award Jr. Womans Club, 1968, Proclamation Commrs. Ct. Outstanding 43 Yr. Literacy Svc. to Tarrant County Com. Ctr., 1994, Tarrant County Woman of Yr. award, Fort Worth Star Telegram, 1995, Outstanding Leadership award Ft. Worth ISD Sch. Bd., 1985, 95; named one of Most Outstanding Educators in U.S. Nat. Assn. Adult Edn., 1983, Most Outstanding Woman Edn., City of Ft. Worth, 1991, others; nominated to Tex. Hall of Fame for Women, 1991; named to Ft. Worth Hall of Fame, 1992; scholar Germany, 1983. Mem. NEA, DAR (Mary Isham Keith chpt. 1985-2002, Nat. Most Outstanding Literacy award 1992, Leadership Literacy award 1985-87, 89, 94), AAUW, Am. Assn. Adult and Cont. Edn. (v.p. 1987-89, chair 1993 internat. conv. 1992, Nat. Adminstr. of Yr. in Adult Edn. 1998, Most Outstanding Adminstr. Adult Edn. in U.S. 1999), Tex. Assn. Adult and Cont. Edn. (pres. 1985-86, Most Outstanding Adult Adminstr. in Tex. 1984), Tex. Coun. Adult Edn. Dirs. (pres.), Coun. World Affairs (bd. dirs. 1980-2002), Am. Bus. Women's Assn., Ft. Worth C. of C., Lecture Found., Internat. Reading Assn. (Literacy Challenge award 1991), Ft. Worth Adminstrv. Assn., Zonta, Tanglewood Garden Club, Ft. Worth Garden Club (exec. bd. dirs. 2000-02), Woman's Club, Ft. Worth Petroleum Club, Carousel Dance Club, Met. Dinner Dance Club, Ridglea Country Club, Girls Svc. League, Aquarius (pres. 2000-01), Crescent Club (Dallas), Aquarius Woman's Club (pres. 2001), Alpha Delta Kappa (Nat. Literacy award 1992), Greater Ft. Worth Literacy Coun. (pres. 2000-03), Friendss of Libr. Bd., 1992-2002, Phi Delta Kappa. Home: 3716 Fox Hollow St Fort Worth TX 76109-2616

WILSTED, JOY, elementary education educator, reading specialist, parenting consultant; b. St. Marys, Pa., Aug. 12, 1935; d. Wayne and Carrie (Neiger) Furman; m. Richard William Wilsted, Feb. 14, 1982; 2 children. BA, Fla. Atlantic U., 1970; MS in Edn., Old Dominion U., Norfolk, Va., 1975. Cert. reading specialist, elem. tchr., Mo.; cert. permanent tchr., N.Y. Tchr. creative dramatics Hillsboro Country Day Sch., Pompano Beach, Fla., 1966-68; tchr. PTA Kindergarten, Boca Raton, 1968-69; tchr. creative dramatics Wee-Wisdom Montessori Sch., Delray Beach, 1969-70; elem. tchr. Birmingham (Mich.) Pub. Schs., 1970-72; classroom and reading resource tchr. Chesapeake (Va.) Pub. Schs., 1972-79; reading coord. Harrisonville (Mo.) Pub. Schs., 1979-81; Chpt. I reading tchr., reading improvement tchr. North Kansas City Pub. Schs., Kansas City, Mo., 1981-96. Instr. continuing edn. U. Mo., Kansas City, 1980-87, Ottawa U., Overland Park, Kans., 1990—; cons. Young Authors' Conf., Oakland U., Rochester, Mich., 1971; coord. fine arts Alpha Phi Alpha Tutorial Project, Chesapeake, 1973-75; presenter Chpt. I Summer Inst., Tech. Asistance Ctr., Mo., 1984; cons. on parenting Reading Success Unltd., Gallatin, Mo., 1987—; mem. adv. bd. Parents & Children Together, Ind. U. Family Literacy Ctr., Bloomington, 1990-93; keynote speaker ann conf. Nat. Coalition of Chapter I Parents. Author: Dramatics for Self-Expression, 1967, Now Johnny CAN Learn to Read, 1987, Reading Songs and Poems of Joy, 1987, Character-Building Poems for Young People. Mem. Internat. Reading Assn. (mem. coun., pres. local coun. 1986-88, state chmn. parents and reading com. 1988-89, mem. nat. parents and reading com. 1989-92, keynote spkr. IRA Conf. Inst. 1990, local coun., Literacy award 1989). Office: Reading SUCCESS Unltd PO Box 215 Gallatin MO 64640-0215

WILT, JEFFREY LYNN, pulmonary and critical care physician, educator; b. Fairmont, W.Va., Nov. 15, 1963; s. Paul Lynn and Linda (Amos) W. BA, U. Mich., 1986, MD, 1988. Diplomate Am. Bd. Internal Medicine, Am. Bd. Pulmonary Diseases, Am. Bd. Critical Care Medicine, Am. Bd. Med. Examiners, Am. Bd. Nutrition Support; cert. ACLS instr. Fellow sect. pulmonary and critical care medicine W.Va. U., Morgantown, 1992-95; resident in internal medicine Blodgett-St. Mary's Hosp., Grand Rapids, Mich., 1988-91, chief med. resident in internal medicine, 1990-91; asst. dir. internal medicine residency St. Mary's Hosp., 1991-92; pvt. practice, 1995—. Asst. dir. med. ICU, Blodgett Meml. Med. Ctr., co-dir. transitional residency, 1997-98, COO internal medicine residency, 1998, program dir., 1998-99; assoc. program dir. internal medicine residency Mich. State U., Grand Rapids, 1999—, asst. prof. medicine, 1999—. Fellow ACP (Nat. Clin. Vignette winner 1991), Am. Coll. Chest Physicians (Young Investigators award 1993); mem. AMA, Am. Thoracic Soc., Soc. Crit. Care Medicine. Republican. Avocations: bicycling, karate, magic, reading, chess. Home: 4995 Sequoia Dr SE Grand Rapids MI 49512-9622 Office: 1900 Wealthy St SE Ste 150 Grand Rapids MI 49506-2969

WILT, VALERIE RAE, lawyer; b. Springfield, Ohio, June 8, 1963; m. Gregory L. Wilt, July 11, 1987; children: Arianne Rae, Samantha Moore. BA, Miami U., Oxford, Ohio, 1985; JD cum laude, U. Dayton, 1988. Bar: Ohio 1988, U.S. Dist. Ct. (so. and we. dists.) Ohio 1988, U.S. Ct. Appeals (6th cir.) 1994. Assoc. Bieser, Greer & Landis, Dayton, Ohio, 1988-90; ptnr. Juergens & Wilt, Springfield, 1991-99, Juergens, Wilt & Strileckyj, Springfield, 1999—. Spkr. on risk mgmt. for vol. workshops; spkr. to Springfield Legal Secs. Assn. on Case Mgmt. Mem. Rep. Nat. Com., 1994—98; vol. spkr. career day United Way; PTO; soccer and softball coach. Named Lawyer of Yr. Greater Dayton Area Lawyers Vol. Projects, 1989. Mem. Ohio State Bar Assn., Clark County Bar Assn. (chair domestic/juvenile com. 1997—), Springfield Law Libr. Assn., Springfield-Clark County C. of C. Republican. Roman Catholic. Avocations: reading, athletics, speaking. Office: Juergens Wilt & Strileckyj 200 N Fountain Ave Springfield OH 45504-2596

WILTENBURG, ROBERT EDWARD, university dean; b. Evanston, Ill., Aug. 31, 1947; s. Robert Edward and Florence (Fellows) W.; m. Candace O'Connor, Sept. 6, 1970; children: Mary Norton, Katherine Welch. BA in English, Cornell U., 1968; MA in English, U. Rochester, 1974, PhD in English, 1982. Dir. expository writing Washington U., St. Louis, 1982-94, dir. summer sch., 1994-96, dean, 1996—. Trustee Jewish Hosp. Nursing, 1998—. Author: Ben Jonson & Self-Love, 1990; co-editor: Collective Wisdom, 1990. Mem.: Univ. Cont. Edn. Assn., Assn. Cont. Higher Edn., John Donne Soc., Milton Soc., Renaissance Soc. Avocations: music, bicycling, stamps. Home: 6157 Kingsbury Ave Saint Louis MO 63112 Office: Washington U Lindell and Skinker Blvds Saint Louis MO 63130 E-mail: rewilten@artsci.wustl.edu.

WILTROUT, ANN ELIZABETH, foreign language educator; b. Elkhart, Ind., Aug. 3, 1939; d. F. LeRoy and Margaret Elizabeth (Williams) W. BA, Hanover Coll., 1961; MA, Ind. U., 1964, PhD, 1968. Vis. asst. prof. Ind. U., Bloomington, 1968-69; asst. prof. Miss. State U., Mississippi State, 1969-71, assoc. prof., 1971-87, prof., 1987—. NEH fellow in residence Duke U., 1977-78. Author: A Patron and a Playwright in Renaissance Spain, 1987; contbr. articles to profl. publs. Recipient Disting. Svc. cert. Inst. Internat. Edn., 1986; named Humanities Tchr. of Yr., 1998. Mem. AAUP, MLA (del. to assembly 1975-78), Assn. Internat. Hispanistas, Cervantes Soc. Am., Am. Assn. Tchrs. of Spanish and Portuguese, Assn. Hispanic Classical Theater, Soc. Scholars in Arts and Scis., Phi Kappa Phi, Sigma Delta Pi. Avocations: Shakespeare, travel, reading, roses. Office: Miss State U Dept Fgn Langs Drawer FL Mississippi State MS 39762 E-mail: wiltrout@ra.msstate.edu.

WILTSE, JAMES CLARK, civil engineer; b. Dearborn, Mich., Apr. 14, 1927; s. Cecil C. and Mary G. (Brashear) W.; m. Marlyn R. Glatus, Feb. 14, 1953; children: Richard, Mary, Michael. BSCE, U. Mich., 1953. Registered profl. engr., Mass. Civil engr. U.S. Army C.E., Detroit, 1954-67; project engr. USAF Civil Engring., London, 1968-72; civil engr. USN Facilities Engring. Command, Norfolk, Va., 1973-75; chief engr. USN Resident Office, Keflavik, Iceland, 1976-81; staff civil engr. USAF Electronic Systems Div., Kaiserslautern, Germany, 1982-91; spl. asst. ROICC Norfolk, Lantnavfac Eng Com, Norfolk, Va., 1992-93; quality assurance engr. HQ Lantnavfac, 1993-94; ret., 1994. Sgt. U.S. Army, 1946-47, Japan. Fellow ASCE (life); mem. Soc. Am. Mil. Engrs. Home: 8555 Lawson Ave Norfolk VA 23503-5220 E-mail: JCWILTSE@aol.com.

WILTSE, RICHARD ALLAN, association executive; b. Grand Rapids, Mich., May 10, 1951; s. Eugene William and Ardath Aileen (Johnson) W.; m. Stephanie Ann Wolf, June 7, 1975; children: Jacob Vaughan, Joseph Robert. BS in Edn., Cen. Mich. U., 1973; Masters in Librarianship, Western Mich. U., 1979, postgrad., 1979—. Cert. secondary edn. Media specialist Allegan (Mich.) High Sch., 1974-81; media dir. Northview High Schs., Grand Rapids, Mich., 1981-92; dir. tech. East Grand Rapids Pub. Schs., 1992-98; exec. dir. Mich. Assn. for Computer Users in Learning, 1999—. Mem., sect. leader Grand Rapids Chamber Choir, 1984—; chmn. Festival of Music , Grand Rapids, 1985. Recipient Outstanding Tchr. award Northview High Sch., Grand Rapids, 1983, 84, 87, 89, 90, 92, Bus. Week Mag. award for Instructional Innovation, 1990. Mem. Internat. Soc. for Tech. in Edn., Mich. Assn. Media in Edn. (Outstanding Meritorious Svc. award 1997, Pub. Rels. award), Mich. Assn. Computer Users in Learning (columnist, pres. 1997-98), Beta Phi Mu. Methodist. Avocations: music, reading, computers, golf. Home: 1046 San Juan Dr SE Grand Rapids MI 49506-3453 Office: PO Box 518 Holt MI 48842-0518 E-mail: rwiltse@macul.org.

WILTSHIRE, WILLIAM HARRISON FLICK, lawyer; b. Martinsburg, W.Va., Dec. 29, 1930; s. Harrison Flick and Virginia Faulkner (White) W.; m. Edith Hayward, Nov. 13, 1954; children: Ashley Wiltshire Spotswood, Winn Wiltshire Crockard, William Harrison Flick Jr., Ashton Hayward. BA, Shepherd Coll., 1952; JD, U. Fla., 1960. Bar: Fla. 1960, U.S. Ct. Appeals (5th cir.) 1960, U.S. Dist. Ct. (no. dist.) Fla. 1960, U.S. Dist. Ct. (so. dist.) La. 1975, U.S. Dist. Ct. (so. dist.) Ala. 1978, U.S. Dist. Ct. (so. dist.) Fla. 1980, U.S. Dist. Ct. (so. dist.) Calif., 2000, U.S. Ct. Appeals (11th cir.) 1982, U.S. Supreme Ct. 1987, U.S. Ct. of Claims, 2001; cert. in civil trial Nat. Bd. Trial Advocacy and Fla. Bar Assn. With Jones & Harrell, Pensacola, Fla., 1960-62; ptnr. Harrell, Wiltshire, Stone, Swearingen, Wilson & Harrell and predecessor firms, 1962—. Pres. Bayou Tex. Assn., 1967-71; dir. Fiesta Five Flags, 1968-82, pres. 1976-77. Contbr. articles to profl. jours. and textbooks. Trustee, gen. counsel Naval Aviation Mus. Found., 1989—; trustee Episcopal Day Sch., 1965-69; bd. dirs. Pensacola Acad. Arts and Scis., 1970-75, pres. 1973-74; bd. dirs. Gul Goast Coun. Boy Scouts Am., 1982—. Served with USN, 1952-57. Fellow Am. Coll. Trial Lawyers, Nat. Bd. Trial Advocacy; mem. ABA, Fla. Bar Assn., Am. Trial Lawyers Assn., Acad. Fla. Trial Lawyers, State Bar Fla. (chmn. trial lawyers sect. 1973-74, chmn. appellate rules com. 1974-78), Def. Rsch. Inst., Am. Judicature Soc., Rotary Club. Republican. Address: PO Box 1832 Pensacola FL 32598-1832 Fax: (850) 432-7727. E-mail: whfw@aol.com.

WILZIG, SIGGI BERT, banker; b. Krojanke, Germany, Mar. 11, 1926; came to U.S., 1947, naturalized, 1956; s. Isidor and Sophie (Sommerfeld) W.; m. Naomi Barbara Sisselman, Dec. 31, 1953; children: Ivan, Sherry, Alan. Student high sch., Berlin; LL.D. (hon.), Hofstra U., 1983. Unskilled worker, salesman, 1947-54; gen. mgr. Nieswand & Son, Newark, 1954-58; dir., exec. v.p. Bronze & Granite Memorials, Inc., Clifton, N.J., 1958-65; pres., chief exec. officer Wilshire Oil Co., Tex., N.Y.C., 1965-80; dir. Trust Co. N.J., Jersey City, 1968—, vice chmn., 1970-71, chmn. bd., chief exec. officer, 1971—, pres., 1974—. Lectr. U.S. Mil. Acad., 1975; Mem. Jersey City Fiscal Adv. Bd., 1974 Mem. nat. campaign cabinet State of Israel Bonds; chmn. banking div. No. N.J. region; trustee Daus. of Miriam Center for Aged, Clifton; dir. trustees, fellow N. Cardozo Sch. Law Yeshiva U.; bd. dirs. Jewish Hosp. and Rehab. Center of N.J., L.I. Heart Inst., N.J. Banking Adv. Bd., Passaic County Econ. Devel. Commn.; mem. adv. bd. President's Commn. on Holocaust, 1978; mem. U. S. Holocaust Meml. Council, 1980—; Nazi forced laborer 1941-42; in Auschwitz concentration camp, 1943-45, Mauthausen concentration camp, 1945 Recipient Prime Minister's medal State of Israel, 1975; Disting. Service award Yeshiva U., 1977; Hadassah Myrtle Wreath award, 1981; Univ. medal Hofstra U., 1985, Medal of Honor Ellis Island, 1998; established Siggi B. Wilzig Disting. professorship, also Ctr. of Banking Law, Hofstra U. Sch. Law, 1985 Mem. Passaic C. of C. (dir.), Jersey City C. of C., dir.), B'nai B'rith., Odd Fellow. Jewish (trustee congregation). Club: Marco Polo (N.Y.C.). Office: Trust Co of NJ 35 Journal Sq Ste 1100 Jersey City NJ 07306-4089 *Free men do not deserve a bright future if they forget their bitter past.*

WIMBERLY, BEADIE RENEAU (LEIGH WIMBERLY), financial services executive; b. Fouke, Ark., Apr. 18, 1937; d. Woodrow Wilson and Grace B. (Winkley) Reneau; m. Benjamin Leon Price, 1954 (div. 1955); m. Elbert William Wimberly, Dec. 16, 1956; children: Stephanie Elaine Wimberly Davis, Jeffrey Scott, Lael Wimberly Carter Alston. Student, Coll. William and Mary, 1964-65, U. Md., Ludwigsburg/Stuttgart, 1966-68, Northwestern State U. La., 1973-75, Cornell U., 1979, Leonard Sch., 1983. Cert. ins. agt.; registered gen. securities rep. and registered investment advisor SEC. Internat. trainer of trainers North Atlantic coun. Girl Scouts U.S., Fed. Republic of Germany, 1965-69, 76-78; inventory master The Myers Co., Inc., El Paso, Tex., 1970; abstract asst. Vernon Abstract Co., Inc., Leesville, La., 1970-71; sec. to chief utilities and pollution control Dept. Army, U.S. Civil Svc., Ft. Polk, 1971-72, asst. to post safety officer, 1972-73, adminstr. tech. Adj. Gen.'s Office, 1973-75, sr. libr. technician post librs., 1975, pers. staffing specialist Stuttgart, Fed. Republic Germany, 1976-79, voucher examiner Fin. and Acct. Office Ft. Polk, 1980-81; CEO, Fin. Strategies, Inc., Leesville, La., 1981-91, stockbroker, 1984-93, ins. agt., 1983-94, corp. exec., 1983—, mktg exec., 1983—, investment advisor, 1984-93; tax assoc. H&R Block, 2001—. Investment advisor, 1984-93; fashion cons., 1993—; master gardener, 1995—; tax assoc. H&R Block, 2001-02; labor cons. AFL/CIO, Ft. Polk, 1981—; br. office mgr. Anchor Nat. Fin. Svcs. Inc., 1981-91; dir., treas. Wimberly Enterprises, Inc.; charter mem. Sundown Vol. Fire Dept. Bd. dirs. Calcasieu Parish coun. Boy Scouts Am., 1982-83; treas. Vernon Parish Hist./Geneal. Soc., 1986—; mpres. Vernon Parish Helpline/Lifeline, 1985; charter mem. Nat. Mus. Women in the Arts; mem. Vernon Parish Arts Coun.; mem. La. Supreme Ct. Task Force on Women in the Cts. of La. Mem. Pilot Internat., Nat. Assn. Govt. Employees (v.p. chpt. 1980-81), C. of C., Assn. U.S. Army, Am. Assn. Fin. Profls., Nat. Women's Polit. Caucus, Am. Soc. Mil. Comptrs., LWV (state bd. dirs. 1986-87, treas. Leesville chpt. 1982-87, La. chpt.), NOW, Toastmasters Club (Competent Toastmaster 1979), Rotary (bd. mem.-at-large Leesville club 1988—, treas. 1991—, v.p.), Leesville Pilot Club. Office: Cable Loop Ste 142 Leesville LA 71446

WIMBS, CASSANDRA MEROE, journalist, researcher; d. Brister Ross and Hazel Bernice Wimbs. BS, Howard U., 1973, MS in Human Ecology, 1977; cert. in Cinema Ethnographique, Sorbonne, Paris, 1986; MA, U. Calif., 1987. Cert. tchr. yoga. Instr./radio prodr. CUNY, Bklyn., 1977—80; host prodr. KPFA-FM, Berkeley, Calif., 1983—89; founding dir. R.O.O.T.S. Inst. for African Diaspora Folklife Studies, Jamaica, NY, 1984—; host/prodr. Paris Voice Newspaper, Paris, 1985—86; instr. ESL Brit. Lang. Inst., Cairo, 1988—89; host/prodr. WHRC-FM 90.3, N.Y.C., 1997—. Registered local organizer UN world health day WHO, Jamaica, 2002—; del. N.Y.C. area Nat. Dance Week, Jamaica, 2002—; assoc. mem. UN Corr. Assn., N.Y.C., 2002—; bd. dirs. African Am. Wax and History Mus., N.Y.C. Author: (anthology) Proclamations Book/Audio Line, 2001; editor: (book/conf. procs.) Traditional Healing Systems of the African Diaspora, 1985 (Mayoral Proclamation from the City of Berkeley, 1985); prodr.: (audio rec.) Blacks in Paris, 1986, (audio documentary) Back to Egypt, 1990, (interviewer/prodr.) (live broadcast rec.) The Egyptian Woman, The Cairo Women's Club and the Friendship Force in Egypt, 1990. Co-founding pres. Internat. African Vegetarian Network and Friends, Jamaica, 1999—2002; vol. Harlem 5K Heritage Run, N.Y.C., 2000—02; mem. UN Assn. of USA, 2000—02; citizen amb. Friendship Force Internat., Jamaica, 1997—2002. Recipient 3 Mayoral Proclamations for R.O.O.T.S., City of Berkeley, 1985—88. Mem.: Friendship Force Internat. (citizen amb. 1996—2002), Lambda Kappa Mu, Delta Sigma Theta. Liberal. Avocations: black heritage stamp collecting, health and fitness, windsurfing, travel, writing. Personal E-mail: cmwimbs@ccny.cuny.edu. E-mail: cmwimbs@ccny.cuny.

WIMMER, MAUREEN KATHRYN, chemical engineer; b. Quakertown, Pa., Oct. 25, 1969; d. Ronald Homer and Jane (Astheimer) W. BSChemE, Lehigh U., 1992. Engring. intern Gen. Chem., Claymont, Del., 1991; process control engr. Johnson Matthey CSD, Wayne, Pa., 1992-94, washcoat engr., 1994-97; process engr. Ashland Chem. Co., Easton, 1997-2001, GEO Splty. Chem. Co., Allentown, 2001—. Mem. AIChE. Republican. Lutheran. Avocations: music, movies. Home: Apt 1 1439 Center St Bethlehem PA 18018-1358 Office: 2409 N Cedar Crest Blvd Allentown PA 18104 E-mail: maureen.wimmer@verizon.net.

WIMMER, SCOTT, race car driver; Race car drive ASA ACDelco Challenge Series, Busch Series. Office: c/o Bill Davis Racing 302 Old Thomasville Rd High Point NC 27260*

WIMPFHEIMER, MICHAEL CLARK, lawyer; b. N.Y.C., July 9, 1944; s. Henry and Ruth (Rapp) W.; m. Susanne Rabner, June 11, 1968; children: Jan Steven, Barry Scott, Luba Rachel. BA, Columbia U., 1964; JD, Harvard U., 1967. Bar: N.Y. 1967, U.S. Dist. Ct. (ea. and so. dists.) N.Y. 1974, U.S. Ct. Appeals (2d cir.) 1974, U.S. Ct. Mil. Appeals 1979, U.S. Claims Ct., 1992. Ptnr. Wimpfheimer & Wimpfheimer, N.Y.C., 1970—. V.p. Union of Orthodox Jewish Congregations of Am., N.Y.C., 1978—. Comdr. JAGC USNR, ret. Mem. ABA, N.Y. State Bar Assn., Bronx County Bar Assn. Jewish. Home: 2756 Arlington Ave Riverdale Bronx NY 10463-4807 Office: Wimpfheimer & Wimpfheimer 330 W 58th St Ste 600 New York NY 10019-1818 Fax: 212-247-8196.

WIMPFHEIMER, STEVEN, lawyer; b. N.Y.C., Dec. 5, 1941; s. Kurt and Ruth (Prochnik) W.; m. Ruth L. Feigenbaum, June 26, 1966; children: Robert, Debra, Amy. BS, Syracuse U., 1963; LLB, Bklyn. Law Sch., 1966. Bar: N.Y. 1966, U.S. Supreme Ct. 1974, U.S. Dist. Ct. (so. and ea. dists.) N.Y. 1976. Assoc. Borden, Skidell, Fleck, Hunter Esquires, Jamaica, N.Y., 1968-69; law asst. Supreme Ct., Queens County, 1969-71, confidential law clk. to justice, 1971-75; assoc. Lippe, Ruskin, Schlissel, Esquires, Mineola, N.Y., 1975-79; ptnr. Wimpfheimer & Sherman, Esquires, Garden City, 1979-93; pvt. practice Garden City, Gt. Neck, 1993—. Adj. assoc. prof. Adelphi U., Garden City, 1979-86; bd. advisors Adelphi U. Lawyers' Asst. Program, Garden City, 1986-93; arbitrator Am. Arbitration Assn., Garden City, 1984—. Contbr. articles to profl. jours. Pres. Lake Success (N.Y.) Jewish Ctr., 1987-88, Royal Ranch Club, Floral Park, N.Y., 1978-79, Jamaica lodge B'nai B'rith, 1973-75. Capt. U.S. Army, 1967-68, Vietnam. Recipient Torch of Liberty, B'nai B'rith Anti-Defamation League, Queens, N.Y., 1979. Mem. N.Y. State Bar Assn. (Ho. of Dels. 2000—), Queens County Bar Assn. (bd. mgrs. 1989—, treas. 1995-97, v.p. 1997-99, pres. 1999-2000), Nassau County Bar Assn., Real Estate Tax Rev. Bar Assn. Avocations: tennis, cycling, photography. Office: 8 Bond St Great Neck NY 11021-2438 E-mail: wimpf@worldnet.att.net.

WIMPRESS, GORDON DUNCAN, JR. corporate consultant, foundation executive; b. Riverside, Calif., Apr. 10, 1922; s. Gordon Duncan and Maude A. (Waldo) W.; m. Jean Margaret Skerry, Nov. 30, 1946; children: Wendy Jo, Victoria Jean, Gordon Duncan III BA, U. Oreg., Eugene, 1946, MA, 1951; PhD, U. Denver, 1958; LLD, Monmouth Coll., Ill., 1970; LHD, Tusculum Coll., Greenville, Tenn., 1971. Lic. comml. pilot. Dir. pub. relations, instr. journalism Whittier (Calif.) Coll., 1946-51; asst. to pres. Colo. Sch. Mines, Golden, 1951-59; pres. Monticello Coll., Alton, Ill., 1959-64, Monmouth Coll., 1964-70, Trinity U., San Antonio, 1970-77; vice chmn. S.W. Found. for Biomed. Rsch., 1977-82, pres., 1982-92, also bd. govs.; pres. Duncan Wimpress & Assocs., Inc., 1992—. Chmn. Valero Energy Corp. scholarship commn.; bd. dirs. Southwest Rsch. Inst. Author: American Journalism Comes of Age, 1950 Mem. adv. bd. Alamo Area chpt. Am. Diabetes Assn.; ruling elder United Presbyn. Ch., U.S.A.; bd. dirs. ARC, Am. Heart Assn.; trustee San Antonio Med. Found. 1st lt. AUS, 1942—45, ETO. Decorated Bronze Star Mem. Aircraft Owners and Pilots Assn., Am. Acad. Polit. and Social Sci., Am. Assn. Higher Edn., MENSA, Nat. Pilots Assn., Pilots Internat. Assn., Inc., Quiet Birdmen, Greater San Antonio C. of C., North San Antonio C. of C., Assn. Former Intelligence Officers, Confederate Air Force, Pi Gamma Mu, Sigma Delta Chi, Sigma Delta Pi, Sigma Phi Epsilon (trustee found.), Sigma Upsilon, Newcomen Soc. N.Am., Argyle Club, San Antonio Country Club, The Dominion Club, Plz. Club, San Antonio Golf Assn., Rotary (dist. gov. San Antonio club 1983-84). Avocations: golf, skiing, flying. Office: PO Box 780818 San Antonio TX 78278-0818 E-mail: dunc@texas.net.

WIN, TAY ZA, business analyst, web designer; b. Rangoon, Burma, Feb. 11, 1967; came to U.S., 1995; s. Hla Than Win and Daw Than Khin. BS, Rangoon U., 1987; MBA, Cleve. State U., 1999. Project engr. Kiso-Jiban Cons., Singapore, 1990-95; bus. analyst Nexgenix, Irvine, Calif., 2000—. Adj. faculty Coast Line C.C., Calif. Vol. web designer Progressive Buddhist Assn., Azusa, Calif., 1999—. Mem. Am. Prodn. Inventory Control, Project Mgmt. Inst. Avocations: travelling, reading, basketball. Home: 16224 San Jacinto Cir Fountain Valley CA 92708

WINAKUR, JANE, artist; b. Dallas, Nov. 23, 1941; d. Osborne Samuel and Marjorie Faye (Moore) Edwards; m. Carl Frederick Shrawder, June 15, 1963 (div. Feb. 1975); children: Carl Eugene Shrawder, Susan Lee Klement; m. Howard Morton Winakur, Sept. 7, 1975 (dec. July 1997). BFA, Ohio State U., 1965. Artist, Calif., 1992—. Group shows: Ross Watkins Gallery, (Palm Desert, Calif., Maui Hawaii, Las Vegas, Nevada), McCarthy Fine Art, Newport Beach, Calif., Neiman Hayden Gallery, Scottsdale, Az., Art Connection, Los Angeles. Home: 78977 Lavender Cir Palm Desert CA 92211-1874

WINANS, ANNA JANE, dietitian; b. Freeport, Ill., June 13, 1939; d. Leo Dale and Gwendolyn Jane White; m. Roger Eugene Winans, Aug. 26, 1967; children: Robert, Jonathan. BS in Dietetics, Iowa State U., 1962. Registered dietitian. Clin. dietitian VA Hosp., Madison, Wis., 1963-67; coord. U. Wis. Hosp., 1967-69; instr. nutrition Madison Gen. Hosp., 1969-75, Madison Area Coll., 1976-81; nutritionist Women, Infants and Children Nutrition Program, USDA, Fremont, Nebr., 1981—. Nutrition cons. area health care facilities, Wis., 1976-81, Nebr., 1985—. Sec. Chapel Hill Pool Bd., Elkhorn, Nebr., 1987-89; bd. dirs. Homeowner's Assn., Elkhorn, 1989-93; active Elkhorn Woman's Club, 1982—, Elkhorn Libr. Found., 1999-2000; mem. Elkhorn Libr. Bd., 1985—, pres., 1989-91, 94. Mem. Am. Dietetic Assn. (registered), Nebr. Dietetic Assn., Omaha Dietetic Assn., PEO (pres. 1999), Omicron Nu, Psi Chi. Methodist. Avocations: travel, reading, nature activities. Home: 910 S 218th St Elkhorn NE 68022-1952 Office: WIC 626 N D St Fremont NE 68025-5054

WINAWER, SIDNEY JEROME, physician, clinical investigator, educator; b. N.Y.C. s. Nathan and Sally Winawer; children: Daniel, Jonathan, Joanna. BA, NYU, 1952; MD, SUNY, N.Y.C., 1956. Asst. in medicine Harvard Med. Sch., Boston, 1962-66; asst. physician Harvard Med. Svc. Boston City Hosp.,

1964-66; with Meml. Sloan-Kettering Cancer Ctr., N.Y.C., 1968—, chief gastroent. and nutrition svc., 1978-98, mem. with tenure of title, 1988—, Paul Sherlock chair, 1991—; prof. medicine Cornell U. Coll. Medicine, 1980—, dir. integrative oncology program, 1997-98. Head Ctr Prevention Cancer WHO, Geneva, 1985—2000; liaison rep Nat Cancer Adv Bd, Washington, 1984—89; mem adv comt cancer prevention Am Cancer Soc, 1988—90; mem sci adv bd ICRF; consult varios rev comts Nat Cancer Inst, Washington. Editor: (book) Prevention Colorectal Cancer, 1980, Basic and Clinical Perspectives of Colorectal Polyps and Cancer, 1988, Lar Bowel Cancers: Policy, Prevention, Research and Treatment, 1991, Management of Gastrointestinal Disease, 1992, Gastrointestinal Cancer, 1992, Cancer of the Colon, Rectum and Anus, 1994, Cancer Free, 1995, Healing Lessons, 1998; contbr. chapters to books, articles to profl jours. Capt USAF, 1959—61. Grantee Nat Cancer Inst, 1974, 1977, 1980, 1985, 1988, 1990, 1993, 1999. Master: Am Col Gastroenterology (pres 1979—80, Bker Predl lectr 1992, Distinguished Sci Achiement Award 1982, Clin Achievement Award 1997); fellow: ACP; mem.: NY Soc Gastrointestinal Endoscopy (founder, pres 1978—79, ann lectr 1985), Am Asn Cancer Research, Am Soc Clin Oncology (Am Cancer Soc Award 2001), Am Gastroentrological Asn (nat chmn cancer sect 1989—91, Joseph B Kirsner Award 1999), Am Soc Gastrointestinal Endoscopy (bd dirs 1974—78, distinguished lectr 1985, Schradler award 1994). Jewish. Avocations: opera, chorale, cross-country skiing, sailing, dancing. Office: Meml Sloan-Kettering Cancer Ctr 1275 York Ave New York NY 10021-6094

WINBURY, MARTIN MAURICE, pharmaceutical executive, educator; b. N.Y.C., Aug. 4, 1918; s. Ervin and Helen (Stein) W.; m. Blanche Mary Simons, July 11, 1942; children: Nancy Ellen, Gail Elizabeth. BS, L.I. U., 1940; MS, U. Md., 1942; PhD, NYU, 1951. Rsch. fellow U. Md., College Park, 1940-42, U.S. Bur. of Mines, College Park, 1942-44; scientist Merck Inst. Therapy Rsch., Rahway, N.J., 1944-47; pharmacologist G. D. Searle, Skokie, Ill., 1947-55; dir. pharmacology Schering Corp., Bloomfield, N.J., 1955-61, Warner Lambert, Morris Plains, 1961-80, dir. sci. devel. Ann Arbor, Mich., 1980-86, ret., 1986; pres. InterPharm, 1986—. Mem. faculty U. Mich. Med. Sch., Ann Arbor, 1986—. Contbr. articles to profl. jours. Fellow AAAS, Am Coll. Cardiology, N.Y. Acad. Scis.; mem. Am. Soc. Pharmacology and Exptl. Therapy, Am. Heart Assn., Gordon Rsch. Conf. (chmn.). Achievements include findings in mechanism of nitroglycerin action-redistribution of coronary blood flow. Home: 6 Southwick Ct Ann Arbor MI 48105-1410 Office: InterPharm PO Box 8335 Ann Arbor MI 48107-8335

WINCHELL, GEORGE WILLIAM, curriculum and technology educator; b. Coldwater, Mich., Nov. 12, 1948; s. Elwood F. and Ethel L. (DeBray) W.; m. Marcia A. Hersh, June 7, 1969 (dec.); 1 child, Paul Michael. BA, Mich. State U., 1969; diploma, Leningrad (USSR) State U., 1967; MA, Mich. State U., 1973; EdS, Cen. Mich. U., 1982. Cert. elem., secondary, Russian, lang. arts and social sci. tchr.; cert. adminstr., supt., elem. prin. Elem. tchr. Silverton (Colo.) Pub. Schs.; tech. edn. cons. Stanton, Mich.; off-campus instr. Cen. Mich. U., Mt. Pleasant; life-long learning instr. Mich. State U.; profl. devel. coord., facilitator strategic planning, dir. instrnl. tech. Montcalm Area Intermediate Sch. Dist., Stanton, 1997-99; dir. tech. edn. Cen. Montcalm Pub. Sch., 1969—99; grants coord., v.p. Crystal Automation Sys., Inc.; master online instr. Mich. Virtual H.S., 1999—. Master online tchr. Mich. Virtual H.S. Mem. ASCD, Internat. Soc. Tech. Edn., Am. Soc. Distance Learning, Am. Soc. Quality, Mich. Assn. Computer Users in Learning, Nat. Staff Devel. Coun. Office: Crystal Automation Sys Inc 617 E Lake St Stanton MI 48888-8902

WINCHESTER, ELIZABETH YOUNG, interior designer, consultant, space planner; b. Elgin, Ill., Dec. 7, 1934; m. Charles A. Winchester (div. Mar. 1996); 1 child, Susan. BA, Northwestern U., 1957; cert., N.Y. Sch. Interior Design, 1974; student Grad. Sch. Design, Harvard U., 1976. Exec. in fashion, cosmetics, design, promotion various orgns., N.Y.C., 1957-73; prin. Winchester Design, 1974—. Mem.: The Archtl. League, The Fashion Group, Inc., Apawamis Club (Rye, N.Y.). Avocations: travel, golf. Home and Office: Winchester Design 400 E 55th St New York NY 10022-5133

WINCHESTER, JESSE GREGORY, commercial real estate company executive; b. Charlotte, N.C., Mar. 2, 1957; s. Dewey Reece and Ruby Lee (Aldridge) W.; m. Jan Partain, May 14, 1983; children: Dustin, Mary-Elsye, Caleb, Sarah-Anne, Asa, Rebecca-Joy. BSBA, U. N.C., 1979; founds. diploma, Am. Inst. Banking, 1979; advanced mgmt. program, Fuqua Sch. Bus., Duke U. Asst. v.p. 1st Nat. Bank Atlanta, 1979-83; exec. v.p. Lomas Mgmt. Inc., Dallas, 1983-96; mng. dir. real estate fin. Hatfield Philips, Inc., Atlanta, 1996—. Campaign vol. United Way, Atlanta, 1982-83; participant Opportunity Dallas, 1985, Habitat for Humanity, Dallas and Atlanta, People Helping People, Dallas; treas. Coppell (Tex.) Rep. Club, 1986; Awana leader; leader Cub Scouts; scoutmaster Boy Scouts Am., Eagle Scout (God and Country award). Named Hon. Citizen Charlotte, N.C. Mem. CMSA, Internat. Coun. Shopping Ctrs., Nature Conservancy, U. N.C. Alumni Assn., Beta Gamma Sigma, Alpha Phi Omega. Avocations: running, skiing, camping, white-water rafting, golf. Home: Meadowbrook Farm 16035 Westbrook Rd Alpharetta GA 30004-2887 Office: Hatfield Philips Inc 285 Peachtree Center Ave NE Atlanta GA 30303-1229

WINCKLER, SUSAN MARIE, elementary school educator; b. L.I., N.Y., May 27, 1968; d. William Arthur and Sheila Dorothy (Pomilio) Winckler. BMus cum laude, Va. Commonwealth U., 1990. Music tchr. Va. Run Elem. Sch., Fairfax County, Va., 1991—92; band dir. Stonewall Jackson Mid. Sch., Hanover County, 1992—93; music tchr. Henry Clay Elem. Sch., 1993—. Pvt. music instr., flute/alto sax, Richmond, 1991—. EMT Ashcake Vol. Rescue Squad, Hanover County, 1993—95; dir. Ashland (Va.) Variety Show Children's Choir, 1998—. Avocations: running, swimming, softball, music, photography.

WINCOR, MICHAEL Z. psychopharmacology educator, clinician, researcher; b. Chgo., Feb. 9, 1946; s. Emanuel and Rose (Kershner) W.; m. Emily E.M. Smythe; children: Meghan Heather, Katherine Rose. SB in Zoology, U. Chgo., 1966; PharmD, U. So. Calif., 1978. Rsch. project specialist U. Chgo. Sleep Lab., 1968-75; psychiat. pharmacist Brotman Med. Ctr., Culver City, Calif., 1979-83; asst. prof. U. So. Calif., L.A., 1983-97, assoc. prof., 1997—, interim chair dept. phramacy, 2001—02. Cons. Fed. Bur. Prisons Drug Abuse Program, Terminal Island, Calif., 1978-81, Nat. Inst. Drug Abuse, Bethesda, Md., 1981, The Upjohn Co., Kalamazoo, 1982-87, 91-92, Area XXIV Profl. Stds. Rev. Orgn., L.A., 1983, Brotman Med. Ctr., Culver City, Calif., 1983-88, SmithKline Beecham Pharms., Phila., 1990-93, Tokyo Coll. of Pharmacy, 1991, G.D. Searle & Co., Chgo., 1992-97, 99-2001, Pfizer, N.Y., 1998—, Wyeth-Ayerst, Phila., 1999-2001, Novartis, East Hanover, NJ, 2002—, AstraZeneca, Wilmington, Del., 2002—. Contbr. more than 75 articles to profl. jours., chpts. to books, papers presented at nat. and internat. meetings and reviewer. Mem. adv. coun. Franklin Avenue Sch., 1986-89; bd. dirs. K.I. Children's Ctr., 1988-89; trustee Sequoyah Sch., 1992-93; mem. tech. com. Ivanhoe Sch., 1993-96. Recipient Cert. Appreciation, Mayor of L.A., 1981, Bristol Labs Award, 1978, DuPont Pharma Innovative Pharmacy Practice award, 1995, Pharmacy Coun. Mental Health award, 1996; Faculty scholar U. So. Calif. Sch. Pharmacy, 1978. Mem. Am. Coll. Clin. Pharmacy (chmn. constn. and bylaws com. 1983-84, mem. credentials com. 1991-93, 95-97, ednl. affairs com. 1994, constn. and bylaws com. 1999-00), Am. Assn. Colls. Pharmacy (focus group on liberalization profl. curriculum 1990-92, mem. pharmacy practice planning commn. 1996-97, chmn. pharmacy practice awards com. 1998-2000, mem. bylaws and policy devel. com. 2001-02, mem. computer tech. in edn. task force 2001-02, chmn. coun. of faculties strategic planning and resolutions com. 2001-02), Am. Soc. Health-Sys. Pharmacists (chmn. edn. and tng. adv. working group 1985-88, chmn. com. on academia 1996-97), Am. Pharm. Assn. (del. ann. meeting ho. of dels. 1989, 1998), Sleep Rsch. Soc., Am. Acad. Sleep Medicine, Calif. Pharmacists Assn. (trustee 1997-2001, chmn. editl. rev. com. 1998--), U. So. Calif. Sch. Pharmacy Alumni Assn. (bd. dirs. 1979—, pres. 1998—), Rho Chi. Avocation: photography. Office: 1985 Zonal Ave Los Angeles CA 90089-0105 E-mail: mwincor@usc.edu.

WINDEBANK, ANTHONY J. dean; BA Oxford U., 1970, MA Oxford U., 1973, BMBCh Oxford U., 1974. Dean Mayo Med. Sch. Mayo Found., Rochester, Minn., 1998—; also prof. of neurology and cellular neurobiology Mayo Med. Sch., dir., molecular neuroscience prgm. Office: Mayo Medical School 200 1st St SW Rochester MN 55905-0001*

WINDEKNECHT, MARGARET BRAKE, artist; b. Alma, Mich., June 27, 1936; d. Donald Potter and Ellen Hope (Noble) Brake; m. Thomas George Windeknecht, Aug. 30, 1958; children: Laura W. Grills, John F., Beth W. Haverkamp. BS in Design, U. Mich., 1958; M of Adult Edn., Memphis State U., 1976. Instr. weaving Birmingham (Mich.) Bloomfield Art Assn., 1981-83. Vis. artist-in-residence Rhodes Coll., Memphis, 1976-81. Author: Creative Monk's Belt, 1977, Creative Overshot, 1978, The Rosepath Motif, 1987, Point Twill, 1988, The Pinwheel, 1992, Color and Weave II, 1994, (cd-rom) Color and Weave, 2000; co-author: Color and Weave, 1981. Recipient Purchase award Tenn. Artists Craftsman Assn., 1976, Ark. Art Ctr., 1976, 77, Tenn Bicentennial-Tenn. StateMus., 1976, Best of Show award Mich. League Handweavers, 1997, 99. Mem. Handweavers Guild Am. (editor Mich. League Handweavers newsletter 1994-2000). Home: 9272 Seneca Dr Clarkston MI 48348-3169

WINDELS, PAUL, JR. lawyer; b. Bklyn., Nov. 13, 1921; s. Paul and Louise E. (Gross) W.; m. Patricia Ripley, Sept. 10, 1955 (dec. 1995); children: Paul III, Mary H., James H.R., Patrick D. AB, Princeton U., 1943; LLB, Harvard U., 1948. Bar: N.Y. 1949. Spl. asst. counsel N.Y. State Crime Commn., 1951; asst. U.S. atty. Ea. Dist. N.Y., 1953-56; N.Y. regional adminstr. SEC, 1956-61, also spl. asst. U.S. atty. for prosecution securities frauds, 1956-58; lectr. law Am. Inst. Banking, 1950-57; mem. Windels, Marx, Lane & Mittendorf and predecessor firms, 1961-88, of counsel, 1988—. Author: Our Securities Markets-Some SEC Problems and Techniques, 1962. Trustee, chmn. Bklyn. Law Sch.; trustee Knox Sch., Lexington Sch. for the Deaf, Gerta Charitable trust; past pres. Fed. Bar Coun. Capt. F.A., AUS, 1943-46, ETO; maj. USAR. Recipient Flemming award for fed. svc.; decorated chevalier Order French Acad. Palms; officer Nat. Order Merit France. Fellow Am. Bar Found.; mem. ABA, N.Y. State Bar Assn., Assn. of Bar of City of N.Y. Republican. Presbyterian. Office: Windels Marx Lane & Mittendorf 156 W 56th St Fl 23 New York NY 10019-3867

WINDER, ALVIN ELIOT, public health educator, clinical psychologist; b. N.Y.C., Feb. 17, 1923; s. Martin Winder and Frances (Erdrick) Isaacson; m. Barbara Ina Dietz, July 19, 1949; children: Mark, Joshua, Sarah, Susan; m. Doris M. Raphael, Aug. 18, 2001. BA, CUNY, 1947; MS, U. Ill., 1948; PhD, U. Chgo., 1952; MPH, U. Calif., Berkeley, 1980. Lic. clin. psychologist, Mass. Chief psychologist VA Hosp., Downey, Ill., 1953-56; rsch. asst., asst. prof. Clark U., Worcester, Mass., 1956-58; chief psychologist VA Clinic, Springfield, 1958-61; assoc. prof. psychology Springfield Coll., 1961-63; chmn. psychology dept. Westfield (Mass.) State Coll., 1963-65; assoc. prof. counseling edn. Sch. Edn., U. Mass., Amherst, 1965-69, prof., dir. grad. program div. nursing, 1969-78, prof. Sch. Pub. Health, 1978-93; dir. planning, cons. Springfield (Mass.) Pub. Health Dept., 1993-95. Adj. prof. Sch. Pub. Health, Boston U., 1995—; assoc. to exec. sec. Asian Pacific Assn. for Control of Tobacco, 1988—; cons. Mass. Dept. Pub. Health, 1998—. Author: Introduction to Health Education, 1984, Solid Waste Education Recycling Directory, 1989; editor: Adolescence Contemporary Studies, 1974; guest editor Jour. Applied Behavior, 1970; co-editor: Internat. Quar. of Cmty. Health Edn., 1992-96. Sr. selectman Town of Leverett, Mass., 1988-90; Lilly Found. mentor U. Mass., 1989. Grantee U.S. Childrens Bur., 1966, 67, Dexter Found., 1969, NIMH, 1974, Mass. Cancer Soc., 1997, Nat. Cancer Inst., 1986-91. Mem. APHA, APA, Mass. Assn. Older Ams. (v.p. 2002). Avocation: tennis. Home and Office: 84 Booth Rd Dedham MA 02026-5702 E-mail: march1931@aol.com.

WINDER, ANTHONY FREDERICK, biochemistry educator; b. London, Mar. 7, 1938; s. Fred and Ida Winifred (Ellis) W.; m. Sylvia Margaret Campbell, Aug. 3, 1963; children: Christopher Philip, Clare Elizabeth Jane, Charles David. BA, U. Oxford, 1959, MSc, 1962, MA, BMBch, U. Oxford, 1963; PhD, U. London, 1971; DM, U. Oxford, 1982. Med. diplomate. Lectr., sr. lectr. Guys Hosp. Med. Sch., London, 1964-73; sr. lectr., cons. Inst. Ophthalmology, 1973-82; cons., reader Leicester Health Auth. and Med. Sch., 1982-88; prof., hon. cons. U. London at the Royal Free and U. Coll. London Sch. of Medicine, 1988—. Chmn. ethics com. Royal Free Hosp. and Med. Sch., London, 1992-94; hon. cons. S. Thames Regional Health and Auth. and Hastings, 1991—; mem. Trent R.H.A. Rsch. Ctr., 1983-88. Contbr. articles to profl. jours. Mem. Enfield Health Authority, 1990-92; med. dir. Family Heart Assn., 1992-95, chmn., 1999—. Recipient Geoffrey Holt award BMA, 1995. Fellow Royal Coll. Pathologists, Royal Coll. Physicians; mem. Assn. Clin. Pathology (pres. 1996, sci. meeting sec., postgrad edn. sec.), Royal Soc. Medicine (chmn. forum lipids in clin. medicine 1996-99), European Atherosclerosis Soc. Avocations: swimming, playing and listening to jazz, clarinet, saxophone. Home: Burtons Wood Burtons Ln Chalfont St Giles HP8 4BA England Office: Royal Free Hosp Sch Med Pond St London NW3 2QG England

WINDER, CLARENCE LELAND, psychologist, educator; b. Osborne County, Kans., June 16, 1921; s. Clarence McKinley and Edna (Ikenberry) W.; m. Elizabeth Jane Jacobs, Aug. 14, 1943; children: David William, Christina Louise. Student, Santa Barbara State Coll., 1941; AB with honors, U. Calif. at Los Angeles, 1943; MA, Stanford U., 1946, PhD, 1949. From instr. to assoc. prof. Stanford U., 1949-61; dir. Psychol. Clinic, 1953-61; prof., dir. Psychol. Clinic, Mich. State U., 1961-62, prof. psychology, 1961-91, prof. emeritus, 1991—, chmn. dept., 1963-67; dean Coll. Social Sci. Mich. State U., 1967-74, assoc. provost, 1974-77, provost, 1977-86, provost emeritus, 1991—; prof., dir. Psychol. Svcs. Ctr., U. So. Calif., 1962-63. Spl. rsch. psychol. aspects schizophrenia, parent-child rels., personality devel., and higher edn. adminstrn. 1st lt. USAAF, 1943-45. Decorated Air medal with 7 clusters, D.F.C. Fellow APA, AAAS; mem. Sigma Xi. Home: 1776 Hitching Post Rd East Lansing MI 48823-2144

WINDER, RICHARD EARNEST, legal foundation administrator, writer, consultant; b. Vernal, Utah, Sept. 23, 1950; s. William Wallace and Winnifred (Jenkins) W.; m. Janice Fay Walker, Apr. 19, 1975; children: Scott Christian, Eric John, Brian Geoffrey, Laura Jeanne, Amy Elizabeth. BA magna cum laude, Brigham Young U., 1974, JD cum laude, 1978; MBA with honors, U. Michigan, Flint, 1988. Lic. life ins. agt. Mich.; bar: Utah 1978, U.S. Dist. Ct. Utah 1978, Mich. 1979, U.S. Dist. Ct. (ea. and we. dists.) Mich. 1979; lic. securities rep. series 6 and 63 NASD, Mich., first mortgage lic. Mich. Tchg. asst., grad. instr. Brigham Young U., Provo, Utah, 1976-78; law clk. Willingham & Coté, E. Lansing, Mich., 1978-79, atty., 1979-87; exec. v.p. Mgmt. Leasing, Inc., Battle Creek, 1987-88, Mgmt. Options, Inc., Lansing, 1988-91; fin. mgr. Mich. State Bar Found., 1991-94, dep. dir., fin. mgr., 1994—. Panelist 9th Nat. Legis. Conf. Small Bus., San Antonio, 1987; adj. prof. Davenport Coll. Bus., Lansing, 1990-92, mgmt. adv. com., 1993-96; mem. founding steering com. Capital Quality Initiative, Lansing, 1992-96; liaison State Bar Mich. Long Range Planning Process, 1996-97; co-founder, rsch. prin. Quality Dynamics Rsch. Inst., Haslett, Mich., 1994-97; rsch. prin. Leadership Dynamics Rsch. Inst., Haslett, 1998—; sr. rep. Primerica Fin. Svcs., 2001—. Author: (with others) Value Sharing: Value Building, 1990, Corporate Orienteering, 1995; contbr., bd. editors: Summary of Utah Real Property Law, 1978. Vol. leader Boy Scouts Am., Chief Okemos Coun., Lansing, 1978—. Fellow Mich. State Bar Found.; mem. ABA, Am. Soc. Quality (chmn. Lansing-Jackson sect. 1994-95, spkr. and writer 1992—), Mich. Bar Assn., Utah Bar Assn., Lansing Regional C. of C. (small bus. coun., MBA task force Bus. and Edn. com. 1988-92, recipient Chmn.'s award 1992), Beta Gamma Sigma. Republican. Mem. Lds Ch. Avocations: writing, speaking, computer technology, research, teaching. Office: Mich State Bar Found 306 Townsend St Lansing MI 48933-2012

WINDER, ROBERT OWEN, mathematician, computer engineer, geophysicist; b. Boston, Oct. 9, 1934; s. Claude V. and Harriet O. W.; m. Kathleen C. Winder; children by previous marriage: Katherine, Amy. AB, U. Chgo., 1954; BS, U. Mich., 1956; MS, Princeton U., 1958, PhD, 1962; MS, Ariz. State U., 2000. With RCA, 1957-78, group head N.J., 1969-75, dir. microprocessors, 1975-77, dir. systems, 1977-78; mgr. workstation devel. Exxon Enterprises, Inc., Princeton, 1978-85; v.p. Syntex Computer Systems Inc., Bordentown, N.J., 1985-88; mgr. product engring., Princeton Operation, Intel Corp., 1988-93; mgr. engring. ops. video products div., Intel, Chandler, Ariz., 1993-95. Vis. scholar dept. geol. scis., Ariz. State U., Tempe, 2001—. Contbr. articles to profl. jours.; patentee in field. NSF fellow, 1956-57; Recipient David Sarnoff award RCA, 1975. Fellow IEEE. E-mail: winder@asu.edu.

WINDHAGER, ERICH ERNST, physiologist, educator; b. Vienna, Austria, Nov. 4, 1928; came to U.S., 1954; s. Maximilian and Bertha (Feitzinger) W.; m. Helga A. Rapant, June 18, 1956; children: Evelyn Ann, Karen Alice. MD, U. Vienna, 1954. Research fellow in biophysics Harvard Med. Sch., Boston, 1956-58; instr. in physiology Cornell U. Med. Coll., N.Y.C., 1958-61; vis. scientist U. Copenhagen, 1961-63; asst. to prof. physiology Cornell U. Med. Coll., N.Y.C., 1963—. Maxwell M. Upson prof. physiology and biophysics, 1978—, chmn. dept. physiology, 1973—2002, acting chmn. dept. cell biology, 1998—2002. Recipient Homer W. Smith award N.Y. Heart Assn., 1978, Berliner-Abbott award Am. Physiol. Soc., 1999. Office: Weill Med Coll Cornell U Dept Physiology 1300 York Ave New York NY 10021-4805

WINDHAM, JOHN FRANKLIN, lawyer, educator; b. Fayette, Ala., Jan. 21, 1948; s. Grover B. Windham Jr. and Nancy Katherine (McAdams) Haynie; 1 child, John Franklin Jr.; m. Denise Roche McNair, Apr. 6, 1999; 1 stepchild, Brittany Danielle McNair. BA, U. West Fla., 1970; JD, U. N.C., 1975. Bar: Fla. 1975, U.S. Dist. Ct. (no. dist.) Fla. 1976, U.S. Ct. Appeals (11th cir.) 1983, U.S. Supreme Ct. 1984. Acctg. supr. Monsanto Co., Research Triangle Park, N.C., 1970-72; law clk. to U.S. Atty Pensacola, Fla., 1974; assoc. Beggs & Lane, 1975-79, ptnr., 1979—. Adj. asst. prof. bus. law Troy State U., Pensacola, 1983-90. Mem. exec. com. Fla. divsn. Am. Cancer Soc., 1982-93, 95-2000, chmn. bd. 1998-99, chmn. elect bd. 1997-98; chmn. legis. and planned giving, 1986-88, chmn. inc. devel., 1989-91, chmn. ad hoc adv. com., 1991—, legal advisor, 1992—, bd. dirs., 1982—, mem. scholarship com., 1995-98, mem. Winn Dixie adv. com., 1996-99, chmn. dist. VII steering com., 1995-96. v.p, 1996-97, chmn. field ops. com., 1996-98; chmn. bd. Escambia Christian Sch., Pensacola, 1976-86; deacon Ch. of Christ, 1985-95, 99—; mem. adv. bd. Interim Healthcare, 1993-96, Panhandle Rehab. Injury Mgmt. and Evaluation, 1993-96; mem. found. bd. East Hill Christian Sch., 1995-97; bd. govs. Pensacola chpt. Order Granaderos e Dames de Galvez, 1990-98, pres. 1995-98; mem. U. West Fla. Found., 1983-85. Mem. Fla. Bar (workers compensation rules com., 1995—, drafting subcom., 2000—), Fla. Def. Lawyers Assn., Fla. Workers Compensation Inst., Southeastern Admiralty Law Inst. (bd. dirs. 1986-89), Northwest Fla. Blook Ctr. Found. (treas. 2002-), U. West Fla. Nat. Alumni Assn. (bd. dirs.), Kiwanis (pres. Pensacola 1978-79, 88-89). Republican. Avocations: church activities. Office: Beggs & Lane PO Box 12950 Pensacola FL 32576-2950

WINDHAM, NANCY QUINTERO, obstetrician, gynecologist; b. Maracaibo, Venezuela, May 18, 1961; came to U.S., 1976; d. George Albert and Jean Louise (Gimbert) Quintero; 1 child, Kathleen Jean. BS, Tulane U., 1982, MD, 1986. Intern Baylor Coll. Medicine, Houston, 1986-87, resident in ob-gyn., 1987-90; pvt. practice ob-gyn. Florence and Darlington, S.C., 1990-91, La Grange, Ga., 1992, Florence, 1993—. Fellow Am. Coll. Obstetricians and Gynecologists (bd. cert.); mem. AMA, S.C. Med. Soc. Office: 901 E Cheves St Ste 360 Florence SC 29506-2769

WINDHAM, VELMA LEE AINSWORTH, writer, poet; b. Taylorsville, Miss., Dec. 11, 1919; d. Joseph Robert and Lou Tishie (Nichols) Ainsworth; widowed; children: Lex Randal, Donald Patrick, Sandra Lynn, James Enrique (dec.). Grad. h.s., Taylorsville High, Taylorsville, 1939. Author: Down Memory Lane, 1970s, Treasury of Wildflowers, 1980s, over 1000 poems; news columnist two newspapers. Recipient numerous poetry awards, including 8 certs. of merit World Poetry, 4 golden Poet awards World Poetry, 2 Silver Poet awrads World Poetry, Recognition award Famous Poets Soc., Cert. of Recognition, Follow That Dream Song Writers Assn. Home: 6780 Hwy 531 Taylorsville MS 39168

WINDHORST, JOHN WILLIAM, JR. lawyer; b. Mpls., July 6, 1940; s. John William and Ardus Ruth (Bottge) W.; divorced; 1 child, Diana Elizabeth. AB, Harvard U., 1962; LLB, U. Minn., 1965. Bar: Minn. 1965, U.S. Tax Ct., U.S. Ct. Appeals (8th cir.) 1965, U.S. Dist. Ct. Minn. 1967, U.S. Supreme Ct. 1975. Law clk. to Hon. H.A. Blackmun U.S. Cir. Ct., Rochester, Minn., 1965-66; assoc. Dorsey & Whitney, Mpls., 1966-70; with office of Revisor of Statutes State of Minn., 1967, 69; ptnr. Dorsey & Whitney, 1971-96, of counsel, 1997—. Bd. dirs. St. Paul Chamber Orch., 1980-86, Harry A. Blackmun Scholarship Found., 1996—, Minn. Taxpayers Assn., 1999—. Mem. ABA (com. on state and local taxes), Minn. Bar Assn., Hennepin County Bar Assn., Harvard Club of Minn. (pres. 1977-78). Home: 1235 Yale Pl Apt 1102 Minneapolis MN 55403-1946 E-mail: windhorst.john@dorseylaw.com.

WINDLE, PAMELA EVELYN, surgical nurse; b. Dumaguete City, Negros, The Philippines, Aug. 03; came to U.S., 1975; d. Lorenzo Sr. and Mary (Kho) Yang; m. David A. Windle, Jan. 12, 1980; children: Cynthia Ann, Michael Adam. BSN, Silliman U., Dumaguete City, 1973; MS in Nursing Adminstrn., Tex. Womans U., 1991. Cert. nursing adminstrn., post anesthesia nurse, ambulatory peri-anesthesia nurse. Staff nurse, charge nurse to asst. head nurse med.-surg. ICU Med. Ctr. Hosp., Tyler, Tex., 1975-81; staff nurse, unit tchr., nurse mgr. cardiovascular recovery room to nurse mgr. post-anesthesia care unit St. Luke's Episcopal Hosp., Houston, 1981-91; nurse mgr. day/ambulatory surgery, post-anesthesia care unit St. Luke's Med. Towers, 1991—, nurse mgr. day surgery/PACU/surg. observation, 2002—. Mem.: AACN (chair edn. com. 1994—95), Philippine Assn. Met. Houston (v.p. 1986, bd. dirs. 1994—), Houston Orgn. Nurse Execs., Tex. Nurses Assn. (chair dist. 9 nominating com. 1995—96, bd. dirs. 1996—, del. 1999—, 2001—, chair dist. 9 nominating com. 1999), Tex. Assn. Post Anesthesia Nurses (state sec. 1994—95, membership com. 1994—95, govtl. affairs com. 1994—95, chair bylaws and Outstanding Dist. award com. 1995—96, pres. 1996—97, immediate past pres. 1997—98, chair strategic planning com. 1997—98, nominating com. 1997—98), Am. Post Anethesia Nurses (regional dir., rsch. com. edn., provider com. 1994—98, stds. of care com. 1996—97, clin. practice com. 1997—98, Recruiter of Yr. 1995—98), Sigma Theta Tau (TNA Dist. 9 award 1992). Roman Catholic. Home: 5421 Valerie St Bellaire TX 77401-4708 Office: St Lukes Episcopal Hosp PO Box 20269 Houston TX 77225-0269

WINDMAN, ARNOLD LEWIS, retired mechanical engineer; b. N.Y.C., Oct. 17, 1926; s. Raphael and Anna (Wexler) W.; m. Patricia Foley, Dec. 13, 1967; children— Richard, Marjorie, Kevin, Colleen, Sean, JoAnn, Brian, William. B.M.E., Coll. City N.Y., 1947. Bar: registered profl. engr., N.Y., 13 other states. Project engr. F.E. Sutton, N.Y.C., 1947-50; with Syska & Hennessy, Inc., 1950-90, pres., 1976-86, vice chmn., 1986-90, also bd. dirs. Pres. Am. Cons. Engrs. Coun., 1985-86; chmn. N.Y. State Bd. Engring. and Land Surveying, 1982-84; bd. dirs., v.p. Sea Pines Plantation, 1997-2000. Bd. dirs. Phelps Meml. Hosp., Tarrytown, N.Y., 1974-82; chmn. planning commn. Hilton Head Island, 2000. Mem. Am. Soc. Heating, Refrigerating and Air Conditioning Engrs., chpt. pres. (1965), N.Y. Assn. Cons. Engrs. (pres. 1981-82, dir. 1977), ASME, Tau Beta Pi, Pi Tau Sigma. Democrat. Jewish. Home: 1919 S Beach Club Vl Hilton Head Island SC 29928-4068 *Professional integrity, enthusiasm, and a continuing effort to train younger people for advancement are three key ingredients of a successful career.*

WINDOM, HERBERT LYNN, oceanographer, environmental scientist; b. Macon, Ga., Apr. 23, 1941; m. Patricia Woodruff, 1963; children: Kevin, Elizabeth. BS, Fla. State U., 1963; MS, U. Calif., San Diego, 1965, PhD in Earth Sci., 1968. Prof. oceanography Skidaway Inst. Oceanography, Savannah, Ga., 1968—, acting dir., 1994-2001. Mem. Am. Soc. Limnol. and Oceanography, Am. Geophys. Union, Oceanography Soc. Office: Skidaway Inst of Oceanography 10 Ocean Science Cir Savannah GA 31411-1011 E-mail: herb@skio.peachnet.edu.

WINDOM, STEPHEN RALPH, lt gov, lawyer; b. Florence, S.C., Nov. 6, 1949; s. Ralph and Connie (Hinds) W.; children: Robert Stephen, Thomas Patrick. BS, U. Ala., 1971, JD, 1974. Bar: Ala. 1974, U.S. Supreme Ct. 1980. Assoc. McDermott, Slepian, Kittrell & Fleming, Mobile, Ala., 1974-77; ptnr. McDermott, Slepian, Windom & Reed, 1974-86, Sirote & Permutt, P.C., 1984—; mem. Ala. State Senate, 1989-99; lt. gov. State of Ala., 1998—. Lectr. in field, 1985—. Pres. Greater Gulf State Fair, Mobile, 1981, Cystic Fibrosis Found., Mobile, 1981. Capt. USAFR, 1971-82. Mem. Ala. State Bar Assn.,

Mobile Bar Assn., Am. Bankruptcy Inst., Comml. Law League, Jaycees, Shriners, Masons, Phi Delta Phi. Republican. Avocations: hunting, water sports. Office: Lt Govs Office 11 S Union St Ste 725 Montgomery AL 36130-2103*

WINDOM, WILLIAM, actor; b. N.Y.C., Sept. 28, 1923; s. Paul and Isobel Wells (Peckham) W.; m. Patricia Veronica Tunder, Dec. 31, 1975; children: Rachel, Heather Juliet, Hope, Rebel Russell. Student, Williams Coll., 1942, The Citadel, 1943, Antioch Coll., 1943, U. Ky., 1943, Biarritz Am. U., 1945, Fordham U., 1946. Actor: (Army) Richard III, 1945—46, (Broadway appearances) Mlle. Colombe, 1954, Fallen Angels, 1956, USA, 1958, Androdes and the Lion, Alice in Wonderland, Time Remembered, Viva Madison Avenue, The World of Suzie Wong, Double in Hearts, Come Blow Your Horn; (films) To Kill a Mockingbird, 1962, For Love or Money, 1963, Cattle King, 1963, One Man's Way, 1964, The Americanization of Emily, 1964, Hour of the Gun, 1967, The Detective, 1968, The Angry Breed, 1969, The Gypsy Moths, 1969, Brewster McCloud, 1970, Echoes of a Summer, 1974, Sommersby, 1993, Attack of the 50 ft. Woman, 1993, Children of the Corn: The Gatherine, 1996; (TV series, leading role) The Farmer's Daughter, 1962—65, My World and Welcome to It, 1969—70 (Emmy award, 1970), (one-man theatrical presentation) Thurber I, 1972, Thurber II, 1975, Ernie Pyle I, 1976, Ernie Pyle II, 1979; (TV series) Murder She Wrote, Parenthood, 1990, (appearances in numerous TV movies including) A Great American Tragedy, The Day the Earth Moved, Guilty or Innocent: The Sam Sheppard Murder Case, Seventh Avenue, Blind Ambition, Portrait of a Rebel: Margaret Sanger, Desperate Lives, The Rules of Marriage, Miracle on 34th St., 1994, Fugitive X: Innocent Target, 1996, The Thundering 8th, 1998, Early Bird Special, 1998, True Crime, 1999; actor, actor: others; (mem.): Am. Repertory Theatre, 1946—47. Served with 508th parachute inf. AUS, 1943-46. Mem. Catboat Assn., Actors Equity Assn.

WINDORSKI, AMY J. writer; BA with honors, U. Wis., Eau Claire, 1999. Cons., editl. asst. Hayden & Assoc., Mpls., 1999—2000; tech. comm. assoc. Guidant Corp., St. Paul, 2000—02, tech. svc. cons., 2002—. Vol. Spl. Olympics, 1999—2002. Mem.: Am. Med. Writers Assn. Avocations: gymnastics, volleyball, softball. Office: Guidant Corp 4100 Hamline Ave N F219 Saint Paul MN 55112 E-mail: amy.windorski@guidant.com.

WINDSOR, LAURENCE CHARLES, JR. publishing executive, writer; b. Bronxville, N.Y., July 4, 1935; s. Laurence Charles and Margaret (Phalen) W.; m. Ruth Ester Lindstrom, 1977. Disting. grad., St. John's Mil. Acad., 1953; student, Grinnell Coll., 1953-55, U.S. Mil. Acad., 1957-58. V.p., dir. promotion Conover-Mast, 1960-67; assoc. promotion dir. Life mag., N.Y.C., 1967-70, merchandising dir., 1970—. V.p., dir. advt. and pub. rels. Sterling Comms. subs. Time-Life; exec. v.p. Calderhead, Jackson, Inc., 1974-78; sr. v.p., dir. promotion Young and Rubicam Army Group, N.Y.C., 1978-2000; mng. dir. mktg. and comms. The Nat. Vets. Bus. Devel. Corp., 2002--; pub. rels. cons. Penobscot Charitable Trust, 1966.; spl. asst. to postmaster gen. U.S., 1972-74. Featured role in motion picture The D.I., 1957. Mem. pub. edn. com. N.Y. Gov.'s Conf. on Alcohol Problems; mem. coun. Episcopal Ch. Found., pres.'s coun. Phoenix House; mem. adv. bd. Army ROTC, Friend of West Point, 2000. With USMC, 1955-61. Decorated Commemorative War Cross Royal Yugoslav Army; recipient citation of merit Wis. Res. Officers Assn., Am. Spirit Honor medal Citizen's Com. for Army, Navy, and Air Force, Inc., 1956, award for pub. svc. Dept. of Army Comdrs., 2000. Mem. U.S. Sales Promotion Exec. Assn. (dir., named Promotion Exec. of Yr. 1969), Marine Corps Combat Corr. Assn. (sec.), West Point Soc. N.Y. (gov. 1967—), Publicity Club N.Y., Publicity Club Chgo., Nat. Acad. TV Arts and Scis., Internat. Radio and TV Soc., Am. Inst. Plant Engrs., Order Vet. Corps Arty. (lt. col., aide-de-camp, comdg. gen., coun. of adminstrn., Disting. Expert pistol award, 1st Provincial Regtl. medal, Order Centennial Legion), 7th Regt. Rifle Club, Marine Corps Pub. Affairs Unit, U.S. Darting Assn., Nat. Sci. Tchrs. Assn., Assn. U.S. Army (v.p. N.Y. chpt.), Am. Def. Preparedness Assn., Kosciuszko Assn., Navy League, Marine Corps League, Employer Support of the Guard and Res. (N.Y. State Exec. Com.), Army-Navy Union, NRA, Conn. AAU of U.S., Nat. Jogging Assn., New Eng. Soc., Ends of Earth Assn. (chaplain, hon. asst. sec.), English Speaking Union, Sovereign Mil. Order of the Temple of Jerusalem, Time-Life Alumni Soc., Nat. Com. for Responsible Patriotism, St. Georges Soc., Nat. Eagle Scout Assn., Old Boys Assn., Nat. Fedn. Breeders of Giant Flemish Rabbits, Soc. Colonial Wars, Soc. Colonial Clergy, Order Descs. Colonial Govs., Friends of St. George Order Colonial Acorn, SAR, Soc. Descs. Founders of Hartford, Order of St. Vincent, Soc. of 1812, Order Crown of Charlemagne in U.S.A., Order Lafayette, Sons and Daus. of Pilgrims, The Pilgrims (hon. sec., exec. com.), Sons of Colonial New England, N.Y. Geneal. and Biog. Soc., Met. Squash Racquets Assn., Church Club N.Y., Union League (v.p., bd. govs., chmn. pub. and mil. affairs), Manhattan Club, Bedford Bicycle Polo Club, Bombay Bicycle Club, Squadron A Club, Soldiers, Sailors and Airmens Club (bd. advisors), Mashomack Preserve Club, Road Runners Club, Alpha Phi Omega. Republican. Episcopalian (vestryman, lay reader, min. of communion). Home: 152 Millertown Rd Bedford NY 10506-1302 E-mail: windsorchuck@aol.com.

WINDSOR, PATRICIA (KATONAH SUMMERTREE), author, educator, lecturer; b. N.Y.C., Sept. 21, 1938; d. Bernhard Edward and Antoinette (Gaus) Seelinger; m. Laurence Charles Windsor, Jr., Apr. 3, 1959 (div. 1978); children: Patience Wells, Laurence Edward; m. Stephen E. Altman, Sept. 21, 1986 (div. 1989). Student, Bennington Coll., 1956-58, Westchester Community Coll.; AA, NYU. V.p. Windsor-Morehead Assocs., N.Y.C., 1960—63; info. mgr. Family Planning Assn., London, 1974-76; faculty mem. Inst. Children's Lit., Redding Ridge, Conn., 1976-94, 99—; editor-in-chief AT&T, Washington, 1978-80; instr. U. Md. Writers Inst., Open Univ., 1980-82; creative developer, faculty mem. Long Ridge Writer's Group, Danbury, Conn., 1988-2000; dir. Summertree Studios, Savannah, Ga., 1992—. Dir. Wordspring Lit. Cons., 1989—, Wordworks Writing Cons., 1999—; dir. Devel. Writing Workshops, Katonah, N.Y., 1976-78; judge Internat. Assn. Bus. Communicators, Washington, 1979, 89; lectr. L.I. U., Jersey City State Coll., Skidmore Coll., others, 1987—; instr. Coastal Ga. Ctr. for Continuing Edn., 1996—, Armstrong Atlantic U. Continuing Edn., 1997-2000, Anne Arundel (Md.) C.C., 2000—, workshop coord., 2000—. Author: The Summer Before, 1973 (ALA Best Book award 1973, transl. 1980 Austrian State prize 1980, also Brit., Norwegian, German edits.), Something's Waiting for You, Baker D, 1974 (starred selection Libr. Jour., Brit., Japanese edits.), Home Is Where Your Feet Are Standing, 1975, Diving for Roses, 1976 (N.Y. Times Outstanding Book for Young Adults award, starred selection Libr. Jour.), Mad Martin, 1976, Killing Time, 1980, Demon Tree, 1983 (pen name Colin Daniel), The Sandman's Eyes, 1985 (Edgar Allan Poe Best Juvenile Mystery award Mystery Writers Am.), How a Weirdo and a Ghost Can Change Your Life, 1986, The Hero, 1988 (highest rating Voice of Youth Advocate), Just Like the Movies, 1990, The Christmas Killer, 1991 (Edgar nominee, Brit., Danish, French edits.), Two Weirdos and a Ghost, 1991, A Weird and Moogly Christmas, 1991, The Blooding, 1996 (YALSA pick for reluctant readers), The House of Death, 1996; columnist The Blood Rev., 1990-92, Savannah Parent, 1990-92; columnist Coastal Senior, 1997-99; also short stories in anthologies and mags.; actress: The Haunting of Hill House, City Lights Theatre Co., 1991. Mem. City Lights Theatre Co., Savannah, Ga., 1991. Mem. Children's Book Guild, Authors Guild, Poetry Soc. Ga., Savannah Storytellers. Avocations: skiing, painting, modern dance. Office: Wordworks PO Box 799 Severna Park MD 21146

WINDSOR, WILLIAM EARL, consulting engineer, sales representative; b. Evansville, Ind., Jan. 24, 1927; s. Charles H. and Lora E. (Archey) W.; divorced; children: Kim, William, Robert. Student, Purdue U., 1946-50. Field engr. Philco Corp., Phila., 1950-53, Europe, Africa, Arabia; studio ops. engr. Sta. WFBM, Indpls., 1953-55; field engr. RCA Svc. Co., Cherry Hill, N.J., 1955-56; audio facilities engr. ABC, N.Y.C., 1956-62; rsch. engr. Fine Recording, Inc., 1962-66; chief engr. A & R Recording, Inc., 1966-68; chief engr., corp. sec. DB Audio Corp., 1968-70; pres. Studio Cons., Inc., 1970-72; sr. v.p., v.p., gen. mgr. Quad Eight Electronics-Quad Eight/Westrex, San Fernando, Calif., 1972-85; sr. mktg. exec. Mitsubishi Pro Audio Group, 1985-89. Pres., CEO Quad Eight Electronics, Inc., Valencia, Calif., 1989-90; ind. cons., Valencia, 1991—. Inventor monitor mixer for multitrack audio consoles, 1967, update function for audio console automation, 1973; designer of new architecture for film scoring and film re-recording sound mixing consoles, 1974 (Acad. award 1974). Served with USNR, 1945-50. Fellow: Audio Engring. Soc. (chmn. NY sect. 1970). Avocations: photography, foreign travel, art collecting. Home and Office: 23112 Yvette Ln Valencia CA 91355-3060

WINE, L. MARK, lawyer; b. Norfolk, Va., Apr. 16, 1945; s. Melvin Leon and Mildred Sylvia (Weiss) W.; m. Blanche Weintraub, June 8, 1969; children: Kim, Lara, Dana. BA with high honors, U. Va., 1967; JD, U. Chgo., 1970. Bar: D.C. 1970, U.S. Supreme Ct. 1977. Assoc. Kirkland & Ellis, Washington, 1970-72, ptnr., 1978—; trial atty. land and natural resources divsn. Dept. of Justice, 1972-78. Lawyer; b. Norfolk, Va., Apr. 16, 1945; s. Melvin Leon and Mildred Sylvia (Weiss) W.; m. Blanche Weintraub, June 8, 1969; children— Kim, Lara, Dana. B.A. with high honors, U. Va., 1967; J.D., U. Chgo., 1970. Bar: D.C. 1970, U.S. Supreme Ct. 1977. Assoc., Kirkland & Ellis, Washington, 1970-72; trial atty. land and natural resources div. Dept. of Justice, Washington, 1972-78; ptnr. Kirkland & Ellis, Washington, 1978— . Mem. ABA. Mem. ABA. E-mail: mark. Office: Kirkland & Ellis 655 15th St NW Ste 1200 Washington DC 20005-5793 E-mail: mark_wine@dc.kirkland.com.

WINE, MARK PHILIP, lawyer; b. Iowa City, Jan. 6, 1949; s. Donald Arthur and Mary Lepha (Schneider) W.; children: Kathryn Bouquet, Nicholas Cox, Meredith Kathryn. AB, Princeton U., 1971; JD, U. Iowa, 1974. Bar: Iowa 1974, Minn. 1976, Calif. 1997, U.S. Dist. Ct. Minn. 1976, U.S. Ct. Appeals (8th cir.) 1976, U.S. Supreme Ct. 1984, U.S. Ct. Appeals (4th cir.) 1985, U.S. Ct. Appeals (7th and Fed. cirs.) 1992, U.S. Ct. Appeals (9th cir.) 1997, U.S. Dist. Ct. (so., no. and ctrl. dists.) Calif. 1997. Law clk. to judge U.S. Ct. Appeals (8th cir.), St. Louis, 1974-76; ptnr. Oppenheimer Wolff & Donnelly LLP, Mpls., 1976—. Mem. ABA, Internat. Assn. Def. Counsel (chair spl. com. on intellectual property), Princeton Club of Southern Calif., Calif. Bar Assn., L.A. Bar Assn. Democrat. Avocations: cooking, reading, biking, golf. Home: 1420 Peerless Pl # 214 Los Angeles CA 90035 Office: Apt 214 1420 Peerless Pl Los Angeles CA 90035-2869 E-mail: mwine@oppenheimer.com.

WINE, SHERWIN THEODORE, rabbi; b. Detroit, Jan. 25, 1928; s. William Harry and Tillie (Israel) W. BA, U. Mich., 1950, A.M., 1952; B.H.L., Hebrew Union Coll., Cin., M.H.L., rabbi, Hebrew Union Coll., Cin., 1956. Rabbi Temple Beth El, Detroit, 1956-60, Windsor, Ont., Can., 1960-64, Birmingham (Mich.) Temple, 1964—. Cons. editor Humanistic Judaism, 1966— Author: A Philosophy of Humanistic Judaism, 1965, Meditation Services for Humanistic Judaism, 1977, Humanistic Judaism-What Is It?, 1977, Humanist Haggadah, 1980, High Holidays for Humanists, 1980, Judaism Beyond God, 1985, Celebration, 1988, Staying Sane in a Crazy World, 1996. Founder Ctr. for New Thinking, Birmingham, 1977—; founder Soc. Humanistic Judaism, 1969; pres. N.Am. Com. for Humanism, 1982-93. Chaplain U.S. Army, 1956-58. Mem. Conf. Liberal Religion (chmn. 1985-96), Leadership Conf. Secular and Humanistic Jews (chmn. 1983-93), Internat. Inst. Secular Humanistic Judaism (co-chmn. 1986—), Internat. Assn. Humanist Educators, Counselors and Leaders (pres. 1988-93), Internat. Fedn. Secular Humanistic Jews (co-chmn. 1993—). Home: 362 Southfield Rd Birmingham MI 48009-3739 Office: 28611 W 12 Mile Rd Farmington MI 48334-4225 E-mail: bhamtmpl@speedlink.net.

WINE-BANKS, JILL SUSAN, lawyer; b. Chgo., May 5, 1943; d. Bert S. and Sylvia Dawn (Simon) Wine; m. Ian David Volner, Aug. 21, 1965; m. Michael A. Banks, Jan. 12, 1980. BS, U. Ill., Champaign, Urbana, 1964; JD, Columbia U., 1968; LLD (hon.), Hood Coll., 1975. Bar: N.Y. 1969, U.S. Ct. Appeals (2d, 4th, 5th, 6th, 7th and 9th cirs.), U.S. Supreme Ct. 1974, D.C. 1976, Ill. 1980. Asst. press. and pub. rels. dir. Assembly of Captive European Nations, N.Y.C., 1965-66; trial atty. criminal divsn. organized crime & racketeering U.S. Dept. Justice, 1969-73; asst. spl. prosecutor Watergate Spl. Prosecutor's Office, 1973-75; lectr. law sem. in trial practice Columbia U. Sch. Law, N.Y.C., 1975-77; assoc. Fried, Frank, Harris, Shriver & Kampelman, Washington, 1975-77; gen. counsel Dept. Army, Pentagon, 1977-79; ptnr. Jenner & Block, Chgo., 1980-84; solicitor gen. State of Ill. Office of Atty. Gen., 1984-86, dep. atty. gen., 1986-87; exec. v.p., chief oper., officer ABA, Chgo., 1987-90; atty. pvt. practice, 1990-92; v.p., dir. transaction and govt. rels. Motorola Internat. Network Ventures, 1992-97; dir. strategic alliances Motorola Cellular Infrastructure Group, 1997—99; v.p. alliance mgmt. Maytag Corp., 1999-2001; CEO Winning Workplaces, Evanston, Ill., 2001—. Mem. EEC disting. vis. program European Parliament, 1987; chmn. bd. dirs. St. Petersburg Telecom., Russia, 1994-97, Omni Capital Ptnrs., Inc., 1994-97. Recipient Spl. Achievement award U.S. Dept. Justice, 1972, Meritorious award, 1973, Cert. Outstanding Svc., 1975; decorated Disting. Civilian Svc. Dept. Army, 1979; named Disting. Vis. to European Econ. Cmty. Mem.: The Chgo. Network, Internat. Women's Forum, Exec. Club (bd. dirs. 1999—2001), Econ. Club. Address: 1724 Asbury Ave Evanston IL 60201 E-mail: jwinebanks@winningworkplaces.org.

WINEBERG, RONNA I. writer, lawyer; b. Chgo., Jan. 12, 1949; d. Bernard B. and Loretta (Davis) W.; m. Martin Jack Blaser, Sept. 3, 1979; children: Daniel Benjamin, Genia Helene, Simone Beth. BA with honors, U. Mich., 1971; JD, U. Denver, 1975. Bar: Colo. 1975, Tenn. 1993; cert. mediator, Tenn. Supreme Ct. Occupl. therapist Fairview Psychiat. Hosp., Chgo., 1970; editl. asst. Sci. Rsch. Assocs., 1971-72; law clk. Judge James Flannigan Denver Dist. Ct., 1973-74; student coord. criminal def. advocacy U. Denver Coll. Law, 1974; rsch. clk. Joe Branney, Esq., Denver, 1974-75; atty. Colo. Rural Legal Svcs., 1975-76; dep. state pub. defender Littleton, 1976-79; lega. cons. Legal Svcs. Corp., Atlanta, 1980; pvt. practice Denver, 1981-89; pres., treas. Enteric Rsch. Labs., Inc., Nashville, 1988—; writer, mem. editl. team Daughters, 1999—2001; lectr. McGhee Sch. Profl. and Continuing Edn. NYU, 2001. Spkr. Colo. Rural Legal Svcs., 1975, Western Social Scis. Assn., Denver, 1982, Hunters Lane H.S., 1993, Hillwood H.S., Hume Fog H.S., 1998, Nashville Psychotherapy Inst., 1998, So. Festival of Books, 1996; tchr. creative writing U. Sch. Nashville, 1996-2000, Readers Forming Writing Group, 1997, pvt. students, 1996—. Contbr. articles to profl. jours. including Denver Law Jour., Ethics in Criminal Justice, Colo. Rev., Midstream, Writers Forum, among others; editor Bellevue Lit. Rev., 2000—. Chairperson Colo. Colfax Coalition, Denver, 1985-89; sec. U. Sch. Nashville Parent Network, 1993-99. Reginald Heber Smith fellow, 1975; Ragdale Found. fellow, 1997-2001. Mem. ABA, Colo. Bar Assn., Nashville Bar Assn., N.Y. Bar Assn., Mediation Assn. Tenn., Nashville Writers Alliance, Tenn. Writers Alliance (bd. dirs. 1995-2000, pres., bd. dirs. 1996-98, chairperson bd. dirs. 1998-99), Mag. Cir. Book Club. Office: 7-13 Washington Sq N #46B New York NY 10003

WINEBRENNER, SUSAN KAY, writer, educational consultant; b. Milw., Mar. 11, 1939; d. Samuel Bernard and Lillian (Ginsberg) Schuckit; m. Neil T. Winebrenner, Feb. 11, 1981 (dec.); children: Stacy Lynne Naimon, Kari Beth Naimon. BS, U. Wis., 1956; MS, U. Wis., Milw., 1979. Cert. tchr., Ill., Wis. Tchr. Shorewood (Wis.) Pub. Sch., 1961-81, River Forest (Ill.) Sch. Dist. 90, 1981-83; gifted coord. Forest Park (Ill.) Sch. Dist. 91, Ill., 1983-86; cons. Self-Edn. Cons. Svcs., San Marcos, Calif., 1986—. Author: Super Sentences Activity Book, 1987, Cluster Grouping Fact Sheet, 1996, Teaching Gifted Kids in the Regular Classroom, 2nd edit., 2000, Teaching Kids with Learning Difficulties in the Regular Classroom, 1996; contbr. numerous articles on differentiating instruction for atypical learners. Recipient Outstanding Tchr. award Joint Coun. on Econ. Edn., Wis., 1979. Mem. ASCD (presenter), Nat. Assn. Gifted Children (presenter). Home and Office: 1450 LaLoma Dr San Marcos CA 92069 E-mail: ecsfirst@aol.com.

WINEBRENNER, WILLIAM PATRICK, writer; b. West Columbia, W.Va., Sept. 26, 1933; s. Richard Arthur Winebrenner and Lucy Ethel Riley; children: Rita Jean Hreha, William Patrick II, Tonya Michelle Noel. Grad. h.s., Mason, W.Va. Journeyman Internat. Brotherhood Elec. Workers, Toledo, 1968-95; ret. Mem. adv. bd. Muskingum Area Tech. Coll., Zanesville, Ohio, 1998; owner Valley Enterprises Pub., Stockport, Ohio, 1993-98. Author: (books) The Woodwalkers, 1993, Smoke in the Valley, 1995, Narrowbackin', 1997, From Out of the Forest, 1998, A Place of Evil, 1999. Mem. Elec. Workers Retirement. Democrat. Avocations: hunting, fishing, writing and promoting books. Home: 2300 State Route 376 Stockport OH 43787-9570

WINEGAR, ALBERT LEE, computer systems company executive; b. Beloit, Wis., Apr. 23, 1931; s. Albert Richard and Theo Rayneta (Hubbell) W.; m. Phyllis M. Everill, June 21, 1953; children: Bradford, Steven, Kristine, Kathleen. BBA, U. Wis., 1954; Stanford Sloan Exec. fellow, Stanford U., 1970. With IBM Corp., 1956-79, div. dir. mgmt. services, 1977-79; v.p. corp. planning, then group v.p. field ops. Olivetti Corp., Tarrytown, N.Y., 1979-80, pres., 1980-81; v.p. field ops. NBI Inc., Boulder, Colo., 1981-84; pres., chief exec. officer Sensory, Inc., Santa Clara, Calif., 1984-85, VICOM Systems, Inc., Fremont, 1985-91, ret., 1991. Bd. dirs. JRL Systems, Inc., Advanced Sys. Integration Group, Acad. Software Inc.; pres. Barton Creek Water Supply Corp. V.p. bd. trustees Valley Hosp., Ridgewood, N.J., 1978-81; pres. N.J. Bus. Arts Found., 1977-78, Estates of Barton Creek Homeowners Assn., 1992-94. Capt. AUS, 1954-56. Mem. Computer and Bus. Equipment Mfrs. Assn. (dir. 1980-81), Barton Creek Country Club, Beta Theta Pi. Republican. Home: 8401 Hickory Creek Dr Austin TX 78735-1530

WINEGAR, ANTHONY C. health care worker; b. Jefferson City, Mo., Oct. 22, 1961; s. Alvon C. and Betty A. Winegar. Vocat. cert., Columbia, Mo., 1983. Data entry operator I Mo. Dept. Revenue, Jefferson City, 1985; data entry clk. Jefferson City Credit Bur., 1985, 87; automation clk. Lincoln U., Jefferson City, 1987-95; clk. St. Marys Health Ctr., 1996—. Author (poetry book) A Walk Through History, 1998, Inspirational Figures in Song, 2000. Recipient Editors Choice award Nat. Libr. Poetry, 1996. Republican. Roman Catholic. Home: 3108 W Truman Blvd Apt 100 Jefferson City MO 65109-4916

WINEGARDNER, KAREN ELIZABETH, management consultant; b. Danville, Pa., Sept. 8, 1946; d. Russell Lambert and Alta Marie (Engle) W.; 1 child, Russell William Logan. BA, Dickinson Coll., 1968; MA, Bowie State U., 1987; postgrad., Capella U. Cert. intelligence analyst and editor/writer U.S. Dept. of Def., Sr. Profl. Human Resources, HR Cert. Inst. Career devel. program dir. U.S. Dept. of Def., Ft. George G. Meade, Md., 1982-85, br. mgr., 1986-88, staff chief, 1988-89, dep. dir. corp. svcs., 1989-92, divsn. mgr., 1992-94, asst. inspector gen., 1994-96; sr. human resources specialist Vector Rsch., Rockville, Md., 1996; sr. mgmt. cons. EDS Corp/E. solutions Strategy and Consulting, Herndon, Va., 1996—. Mem. intelligence analyst career panel U.S. Dept. of Def., Ft. George G. Meade, 1994-95. Recipient Meritorious Civilian Svc. award Nat. Security Agy., 1985. Mem. NAFE, Soc. for Human Resource Mgmt. Avocations: reading, traveling, gardening, interior decorating. Home: 14509 Briercrest Rd Bowie MD 20720-4838 E-mail: Karen.winegardner@eds.com.

WINEGARDNER, ROSE MARY, special education educator; b. Granite City, Ill., Feb. 4, 1933; d. Arthur Udell and Margaret Helen (Brown) Barco; m. Carl Norman Winegardner, July 23, 1954; children: Laura Helen, Thelma Rose Winegardner Gordon, Jacob Harrison (dec.). BS in Edn., Mo. U., Columbia, 1954; MA in Ednl. Adminstrn., Wyo. U., 1977; edn. specialist, Nebr. U., 1988. Cert. tchr., Nebr., Iowa, Mo. Tchr. Elem. Sch. Grandview & Belton, Mo., 1957-64; tchr. mid. sch. Schleswig (Iowa) Community Schs., 1978-82; spl. edn. resource tchr. Ednl. Svc. Unit #4, Auburn, Nebr., 1982-94, Kans. U. Inst. Rsch. Learning trainer strategy implementation model, 1989—; spl. edn. resource tchr. Dawson-Verdon Consol. Schs., 1990—. Grantee Nebr. Dept. Edn., 1990-93. Mem. Internat. Reading Assn., Coun. for Exceptional Children (v.p. S.E. Nebr. chpt. 1990-92, pres. 1992-94, 94-96), DAR, Phi Delta Kappa, Zeta Tau Alpha. Lutheran. Home: 2100 23rd St Auburn NE 68305-2400

WINEMILLER, JAMES D. accountant; b. Sullivan, Ind., July 22, 1944; s. Floyd Maurice and Doris Marie (Lone) W.; m. Nancy Kay Walters, Aug. 10, 1963; 1 child, Nancy Marie. AS, Vincennes U., 1964; BS, Ind. U., 1966; MBA, 1967. CPA, Ind. With Peat, Marwick, Mitchell & Co., CPA's, Honolulu, 1967-71, Blue & Co., CPA's, Indpls., 1971-93, ptnr.-in-charge, 1974-92, mng. ptnr., 1976-93; grad. tchg. asst. dept. acctg. Ind. U., Bloomington, 1966-67; instr. acctg. Coll. Gen. Studies U. Hawaii, 1968-69; membership dir. Intercontinental Acctg. Assocs., Amsterdam, 1993—96; fin. cons., 1996—2001. Vis. prof. Ind. U., 1993; dir. Poland State Bank (Ind.), 1974-75; mem. bd. mgmt. Intercontinental Acctg. Assocs., 1990-93. Bd. dirs. Vincennes U. Found., 1992—, chair fin & investment com., 2001—; dir. Marion County Health Care Ctr, 1988-95; life mem., dir. Ind. CPA Ednl. Found., 1997-2000. Fellow Vincennes U. Found.; recipient Elizah Watt Sells Nat. Honorable Mention award 1966, faculty citation as disting. alumnus Vincennes U., 1996. Mem. AICPA (mem. com. 1985-2000, mem. coun. 1985-89), Inst. Mgt. Accts., Ind. CPA Soc. (dir. 1980-86, treas. 1981-82, mem. exec. com. 1983-86, pres. 1985-86, Outstanding Svc. award 1994), Continental Assn. CPA Firms (dir. 1978-92, v.p. 1982-83, pres. 1983-84), Ind. U. Well House Soc., Ind U. Bus. Sch. Deans Assocs. (sr.), Ind. U. Alumni Assn. (life), Ind U. Varsity-Hoosier Hundred, Vincennes U. Alumni Assn. (life, dir. 1991-99, pres. 1996-98, Pres. award 1994), Rotary (dir. 1973-75, 84-87, pres. 1974-75, 87-88, v.p. 1984-86, Paul Harris fellow). Home: 8084 River Bay Dr W Indianapolis IN 46240-2988 Office: 11460 N Meridian St PO Box 80069 Indianapolis IN 46280-0069

WINER, JESSICA DARYL, artist; b. N.Y.C., Aug. 29, 1962; d. Nahum J. and Toba (Brill) W. BA, Swarthmore Coll., 1984; postgrad., Nat. Acad. Sch. Fine Arts, 1987-89. One woman shows include Saks 5th Ave., N.Y.C., 1991, Westport (Conn.) Artists Gallery, 1992, Art Insights Gallery, N.Y.C., 1993, Lincoln Ctr. Gallery, N.Y.C, 1994, 95, Nat. Arts Club, N.Y.C., 1997, The Silo Gallery, New Milford, Ct., 1999, Times Square visitors Ctr., N.Y.C., 2002, Embassy Theatre, N.Y.C., 2002; group shows include List Gallery, Swarthmore (Pa.) Coll., 1994,, Cannondale Gallery (Conn.), 1996, 99, William Doyle Russian Tea Rm Auction, N.Y.C., 1996, Christies Benefit, N.Y.C., 1992, 94, 95; executed murals at White Barn Theatre, 1984, Times Square Visitors Ctr./Embassy Theatre, N.Y.C., 1998; permanent collections at Mus. of the City of N.Y.; set designer The Little Foxes at WCT Theatre, 1990; designer boxed sets cards, poster, T-shirts for Met. Opera, 1993-94, book covers for Simon & Schuster, 1995, 96; portrait illustrator New Yorker Mag., 1995-96. Mem. Nat. Arts Club, Artists Equity. Studio: 1199 Park Ave New York NY 10128-1711

WINER, WARD OTIS, mechanical engineer, educator; b. Grand Rapids, Mich., June 27, 1936; s. Mervin Augustus and Ina Katherine (Wood) W.; m. Mary Jo Wielinga, June 15, 1957; children: Mathew Owen, James Edward, Paul Andrew, Mary Margaret. Asso., Grand Rapids Jr. Coll., 1956; BS, U. Mich., 1958, MS, 1959, PhD, 1961; PhD (Cavendish Lab. fellow), Cambridge (Eng.) U., 1961-63. Asst. prof. dept. mech. engring. U. Mich., Ann Arbor, 1963-66, assoc. prof., 1966-69; assoc. prof. mech. engring. Ga. Inst. Tech., 1969-71, prof., 1971-84, Regents' prof., 1984—, mem. exec. bd., 1983-88, chmn., 1984-86, Eugene C. Gwaltney Jr. chair George W. Woodruff Sch. Mech. Engring., 2001. Chmn. Gordon Research Conf. on Friction, Lubrication and Wear, 1980; mem. NRC, 1980-88; chmn. Com. on Recommendations for U.S. Army Basic Sci. Research, 1985-87; mem. div. mech., structural, materials engring. adv. bd. NSF Engring. Directorate, 1984-89. Co-editor: Wear Control Handbook, 1980; tech. editor: Jour. Lubrication Tech., 1980-84, Jour. of Tribology, 1984-87; contbr. articles to profl. jours. Democratic precinct chmn., 1967-68; Mem. exec. bd. Horace H. Rackham Sch. Grad. Studies, U. Mich., 1968. Recipient Disting. Faculty Svc. award Coll. Engring. U. Mich., 1967, Alumni Merit award, 1998, Cert. Recognition, NASA, 1977, Clarence E. Earle Meml. award Nat. Grease Lubricating Inst., 1979, Disting. Prof. award Ga. Inst. Tech., 1987. Fellow AAAS, ASME (bd. comms. 1987-91, v.p. rsch. 1989-93, Melville medal 1975, Centennial medallion 1980, Mayor D. Hersey award 1986, Charles Russ Richards Meml. award 1988), Soc. Tribologists and Lubrication Engrs. (bd. dirs. 1983-86, Internat. award 1997), Brit. Tribology Trust (gold medal 1987); mem. Am. Soc. Engring. Educators (Benjamin Garver Lamme award 1995, Donald Marlowe award 1996), NAE, Metro Atlanta Engring. Soc. (Engr. of Yr. 1989), Am. Acad. Mechanics, Soc. Rheology, Soc. Engring. Sci. (dir. 1980-84), AAUP (pres. Ga. Tech. chpt. 1972-74, v.p. state conf. 1973-75), Sigma Xi (chpt. pres. 1982-83, Sustained Rsch. in Engring. award 1975), Tau Beta Pi, Pi Tau Sigma, Phi Kappa Phi. Home: 1025 Mountain Creek Trl NW Atlanta GA 30328-3535 E-mail: ward.winer@me.gatech.edu.

WINES, LAWRENCE EUGENE, lawyer, corporate executive, financial consultant; b. St. Louis, Jan. 17, 1957; s. Frank Peter and Audrey Margret (Murphy) W. BA, U. Mo., 1984; JD, St. Louis U., 1987; MBA, Columbia State U., 1996, PhD, 1998. Bar: Mo., U.S. Dist. Ct. (we. dist.) Mo.; registered fin. planner; registered rep. Cardinal Brokerage Fin., Inc. Mem. staff Gephardt for Pres., Washington, 1987—88; sole practice Ferguson, Mo., 1989—90; ptnr. Progressive Consulting, 1988—93, Wines & Stein attys., P.C., Ferguson, 1990—95, Wines Law Office, L.C., 1995—; pres. Wines Properties, Inc., Wines Enterprises, Inc.; prin. Wines Law Offices, L.C., 1995—, Stuart & Assocs., 1999—2002, Johnson Fin. Group, 2002—. Cons. fundraising Missourians for Mike Wolff, St. Louis, 1988—92, John Shear Election Com., St. Louis, 1988—95, Congresswoman Joan Kelly Horn, St. Louis, 1990—92, Quinn for Sec. State, St. Louis, 1991—92; mem. Ferguson com. St. Louis County Dem. Com., 1987—92; vol. Congressman Richard Gephardt, St. Louis and Washington, 1984—; chair alliance bd. U. Mo. Alumni Alliance, 2000—02. Recipient: Presdl. Svc. award U. Mo. St. Louis Alumni Assn., 1989-90, Disting. Svc. award Disabled Student Union, 1991, Disting. Vol. award U. Mo. St. Louis, 1987; named Outstanding Male Young Dem. Mo. Young Dems., 1986. Mem. ABA, ATLA, Mo. Bar Assn., Mo. Assn. Trial Attys., Bar Assn. Met. St. Louis, St. Louis County Bar Assn., Lincoln County Bar Assn., St. Louis Rams Quarterback Club. Roman Catholic. Avocations: weighlifting, shooting, archery. Office: 905 S Florissant Rd Saint Louis MO 63135-3254

WINET, HOWARD, medical educator; b. Chgo., Sept. 13, 1937; s. Maurice Winet and Lillian Silver; m. Carol Katherine Kasper; children: Evan Darwin, Wendy Lynn. BS in Zoology, U. Ill., 1959; MA in Zoology, UCLA, 1962, PhD in Zoology, 1969. Cert. tchr. secondary edn., Calif. Tchr. secondary sch. sci. L.A. City Schools, 1962—66; postdoctoral fellow engring. sci. Calif. Inst. Tech., Pasadena, 1970—74, rsch. engr., 1974—77; assoc. prof. physiology So. Ill. U., Carbondale, 1977—80; assoc. prof. rsch. orthopaedics U. So. Calif., L.A., 1980—98, assoc. prof. rsch. biomed. engring., 1996—98; assoc. rschr. orthopaedics U. Calif., 1998—2002, lectr. biomed. engring., 1998—, assoc. prof. orthopaedics in residence, 2002—. Cons. Commonwealth Sci. & Indsl. Rsch. Orgn., Canberra, Australia, 1979; vis. assoc. prof. math. U. Wis., Madison, 1982; fogarty internat. fellow orthopaedics Gothenburg U., Sweden, 1984; sr. assoc. U.S. Army M.C., Walter Reed Hosp., Washington, 1990—92. Contbr. chapters to books. Grantee Rsch. grant, NIH, 1978—81, 1986—89, 1994—97. Mem.: Soc. Biomaterials (vice chair spl. interest groups 2002). Avocation: fly fishing. Office: Orthopaedic Hosp UCLA 2400 Flower St Los Angeles CA 90007 Business E-Mail: hwinet@ucla.edu.

WINEY, KAREN I. engineering educator; b. Abington, Pa., Aug. 1, 1963; d. Donald A. and Patricia A. Winey; m. Russlel J. Composto, July 11, 1987; children: Jordana, Rebecca. BS, Cornell U., 1985; MS, U. Mass., 1989, PhD, 1991. Postdoctoral fellow AT&T Bell Labs., Murray Hill, N.J., 1991-92; asst. prof. dept. materials sci. and engring. and dept. chem. and biomolecular engrng. U. Pa., Phila., 1992-2000, assoc. prof., 2000—. Cons. Dow Chem., Midland, Mich., 1999—, Rhodia, Inc., Cranberry, N.J., 2000—; presenter in field. Mem. editl. bd.: Macromolecules, 2001—, mem. editl. bd.: Jour. Polymer Sci., 2000—; contbr. more than 55 articles to profl. jours. Recipient Young Investigator award, NSF, 1994—99, Cosslett award, Microscopy and Microanalysis Meeting, 2000; grantee, Office Naval Rsch., NSF, Petroleum Rsch. Found., Dow Chem. Mem.: Am. Chem. Soc., Materials Rsch. Soc., Am. Physics Soc. (mem.-at-large divsn. polymers 2001—). Office: U Pa 3231 Walnut St Philadelphia PA 19104-6272

WINFIELD, BETTY HOUCHIN, communications educator; b. Little Rock, Nov. 4, 1939; d. Rex O. and Mildred R. (Bock) Houchin; m. John Leonard Winfield, June 5, 1960 (div. June 1985); children: Sidonie Karen, Sharon Rebecca. BS, U. Ark., 1959; MA, U. Mich., 1965; PhD, U. Wash., 1978. Tchr. gifted programs Ann Arbor (Mich.) Pub. Schs., 1961-65; tchr. U.S. Army, Okinawa, Japan, 1965-67; tchr. Am. culture fgn. studies program U. Wash., Seattle, 1969-73, instr. comm., 1974-77; reporter KUOW Nat. Pub. Radio, 1978-79; asst., assoc. prof. Wash. State U., Pullman, 1979-90; prof. journalism U. Mo., Columbia, 1990—. Vis. scholar comm. U. Wash., Seattle, 1984-85, 96—; adj. prof. polit. sci. U. Mo., Columbia, 1995—. Author: The Edward R. Murrow Heritage, 1986, FDR & the News Media, 1990, 2nd edit., 1994, (monograph) Two Commanders-in-Chief, 1992, Bleep! Censoring Rock And Rap Music, 1998; columnist, editor Mercer Island Reporter, 1974-78, Bleep! Censoring Rock and Rap Music, 1998. Freedom Forum fellow Columbia U., N.Y.C., 1988-89, Shorenstein fellow Harvard U., Cambridge, 1991. Mem. Internat. Comm. Assn., Am. Polit. Sci. Assn., Assn. Edn. Journalism Mass Comm. (chair history divsn. 1989-90, chair tchg. standards com. 1990-91), Am. Culture Assn., Am. Hist. Assn. Avocations: skiing, mountain hiking, running, canoeing, cycling. Home: 12 E Clarkson Rd Columbia MO 65203-3520 Office: Mo Sch Journalism U Mo 113A Walter Williams Hall Columbia MO 65211-1200

WINFIELD, CYNTHIA LEES, middle school educator; b. Boston, Jan. 26, 1960; d. Wayne Lowry and Evelyn Elizabeth (Spencer) Lees; m. John Bayard Blinn, 1982 (div. 1999); m. Phyllis Winfield, 2000. BS in Edn., Lesley Coll., Cambridge, Mass., 1992; MFA in Creative Writing, Emerson Coll., Boston, 1999. Lic. tchr., Mass. Ednl./writing program cons. Mass. Dept. Corrections, 1993-96; freelance writer/editor Am. Correctional Assn., Lanham, Md., 1995-97; gifted/talented program asst., writing tchr. Ottoson Mid. Sch., Arlington, Mass., 1993-96, 8th grade English lang. arts tchr., 1997—; book reviewer Voice of Youth Advocates Mag., Lanham, Md., 1994—. Tchr. cons. Boston Writing Project, 1996—; ednl. tour cons. EF Ednl. Tours, Cambridge, Mass., 1995-98. Author: ABLE MINDS: Using Literature to Transform Behavior, 1995, rev., 1998; editor: Maternal Ties: A Selection of Programs for Female Offenders, 1997; contbr. articles to profl. jours. Vol. writer, fundraiser AIDS Action Com., Boston, 1985-95; vol. literacy tutor Harvard Adult Lit. Initiative, Greater Boston area, 1988-92, Laubach Lit. Internat., 1983-85; host family for inner city youth The Fresh Air Fund, N.Y.C., 1995-96, rep. Mass. Tchrs. Assn., 1997—; vol. mentor Just A Start House, 1998-2000. Boston Writing Project grantee, 1996. Mem. NEA, NCTE(Nat. Coun. Tchr. English) Correctional Ednl. Assn., Educators for Social Responsibility, Nat. Writers Union, Am. Correctional Assn., Mass. Tchrs. Assn. Home: 27 Bryant St Woburn MA 01801-5621 Office: Ottoson Middle Sch 63 Acton St Arlington MA 02476-6012

WINFIELD, JOHN BUCKNER, rheumatologist, educator; b. Kentfield, Calif., Mar. 19, 1942; s. R. Buckner and Margaret G. (Katterfelt) W.; m. Patricia Nichols (div. 1968); 1 child, Ann Gibson; m. Teresa Lee McGrath, 1969 (div. 2000); children: John Buckner III, Virginia Lee; m. Leigh Fleming Callahan, 2001. BA, Williams Coll., 1964; MD, Cornell U., 1968. Diplomate Am. Bd. Internal Medicine. Intern in medicine N.Y. Hosp., N.Y.C., 1968-69; staff assoc. LI/Nat. Inst. Allergy and Infectious Diseases NIH, Bethesda, Md., 1969-71; resident in medicine, fellow in rheumatology U. Va. Sch. Medicine, Charlottesville, 1971-73; fellow in immunology Rockefeller U., N.Y.C., 1973-75; asst. prof. medicine U. Va. Sch. Medicine, Charlottesville, 1975-76, assoc. prof. medicine, 1976-78, U. N.C., Chapel Hill, 1978-81, prof. medicine, 1981—, chief div. rheumatology and immunology, 1978-99; dir. Thurston Arthritis Rsch. Ctr. U. N.C. Sch. Medicine, 1982—2001; Smith prof. medicine U. N.C. Sch. Med., 1987—. Adv. coun. Nat. Inst. Arthritis and Musculoskeletal and Skin Diseases, NIH, 1988-92; chmn. edn. com. Am. Rheumatism Assn., Atlanta, 1980-84; immunol. scis. study sect. NIH, 1979-83, Arthritis Musculoskeletal and Skin study sect., 1992-96; vice-chair fellowship com. Arthritis Found., 1982; med. coun. Lupus Found. Am., 1987-96. Author more than 100 med. and sci. articles in peer reviewer rheumatology and immunology jours.; mem. editl. bd. Arthritis and Rheumatism, Bull. Rheumatic Diseases, Rheumatology Internat., Clin. Exptl. Rheumatology, Am. Jour. Medicine. Sr. asst. surgeon with USPHS, NIH, Bethesda, Md., 1968-71. Recipient Borden prize Cornell U. Med. Coll., 1964, numerous rsch. grants NIH and Arthritis Found., 1975—, Sr. Investigator award Arthritis Found., 1976-79, Kenan award U. N.C., 1985, NIH merit award, 1992. Fellow ACP; mem. Am. Assn. Immunologists, Am. Coll. Rheumatology, Am. Fedn. Clin. Rsch., Am. Soc. Clin. Investigation, Assn. Am. Physicians, Am. Clin. Climatol. Assn., Nat. Soc. Clin. Rheumatologists (treas. 1997—), Henry Kunkel Soc. (councilor 2000—), Chapel Hill Country Club. Republican. Episcopalian. Avocations: golf, off-road motorcycling, scuba diving instructor, skiing. Home: 102 Greenwood Ln Chapel Hill NC 27514-5957 E-mail: john_winfield@med.unc.edu.

WINFREE, ARTHUR TAYLOR, biologist, educator; b. St. Petersburg, Fla., May 15, 1942; s. Charles Van and Dorothy Rose (Scheb) W.; m. Ji-Yun Yang, June 18, 1983; children: Rachael, Erik from previous marriage. B of Engring. Physics, Cornell U., 1965; PhD in Biology, Princeton U., 1970. Lic. pvt. pilot. Asst. prof. theoretical biology U. Chgo., 1969-72; assoc. prof. biology Purdue U., West Lafayette, Ind., 1972-79, prof., 1979-86; prof. ecology and evolutionary biology U. Ariz., Tucson, 1986-88, Regents' prof., 1989—. Pres., dir. rsch. Inst. Natural Philosophy, Inc., 1979-88; Aisenstadt chair applied math. U. Montreal, 2000. Author: The Geometry of Biological Time, 1980, 2d ed., 2001, When Time Breaks Down, 1986, The Timing of Biological Clocks, 1987. Recipient Career Devel. award NIH, 1973-78, The Einthoven award Einthoven Found. and Netherlands Royal Acad. Scis., 1989, Norbert Wiener prize Am. Math. Soc. and Soc. Ind. Applied Maths., 2000-2004; NSF grantee, 1966—; MacArthur fellow, 1984-89, John Simon Guggenheim Meml. fellow, 1982. Home: 1210 E Placita De Graciela Tucson AZ 85718-2834 Office: U Ariz 326 BSW Tucson AZ 85721-0001 E-mail: winfree@email.arizona.edu.

WINFREE, LATHAM THOMAS, law educator; b. Wytheville, Va., Dec. 2, 1946; s. Latham Thomas Sr. and Adelaide (Cole) W.; m. Eileen Jeffery, July 12, 1969; 1 child, Matthew Ryan. BA, U. Richmond, 1968; MS, Va. Commonwealth U., 1974; PhD, U. Mont., 1976. Asst. prof. East Tex. State U., Commerce, 1976-79; from asst. to assoc. prof. La. State U., Baton Rouge, 1979-87; from assoc. prof. to prof. N.Mex. State U., Las Cruces, 1987—. Vis. instr. U. N.Mex., Albuquerque, 1975-76; cons. in field. Co-author: Treating the Offender: Problems and Issues, 1977, Juvenile Delinquency: Little Brother Grows Up, 1977, Legality, Morality and Ethics in Criminal Justice, 1979, Expert Witness, 1987, American Jails, 1991, Crime and Justice, 1992, Understanding Crime, 1996, Gang: A Criminal Justice Approach, 1996, Contemporary Corrections, 1998, Juvenile Justice, 2000; contbr. numerous chpts. to books, more than 70 articles to profl. jours. Sgt. U.S. Army, 1968-70. Grantee Nat. Inst. Justice, 1996, Office Juvenile Justice and Delinquency Prevention, 1988. Fellow NIMH; mem. Am. Soc. Criminology, Acad. Criminal Justice Scis. Democrat. Roman Catholic. Avocations: sailing, carpentry, reading. Home: 4939 Chippewa Trail Las Cruces NM 88011 Office: New Mexico State Univ Dept Criminal Justice Las Cruces NM 88003

WINFREY, CAREY WELLS, journalist, magazine editor; b. N.Y.C., Aug. 1, 1941; s. William Colin and Mary (Robinson) W.; m. Jane Elizabeth Keeney, Feb. 13, 1982; children: Graham William, Wells Millar. AB, Columbia U., 1963, MS in Journalism, 1967. Assoc. editor Time Inc., N.Y.C., 1968-71; exec. producer Ednl. Broadcast Corp., 1971-77; reporter, fgn. corr. for Africa N.Y. Times, 1977-80; mag. editor CBS Mags., 1981-90, editor Cuisine mag., 1983-84, v.p., editorial dir., 1985-87; founding editor-in-chief Memories mag. Diamandis Comm., Inc. (formerly mag. divsn. CBS), 1987-90; editor-in-chief Am. Health mag. Reader's Digest Publs., 1990-96; dir. Delacorte Ctr. for Mag. Journalism, Columbia U., 1996-98; asst. mng. editor People Mag., 1996—2001; editor-in-chief Smithsonian Mag., 2001—. Author: Starts and Finishes, 1975; exec. producer: (TV) Behind the Lines, 1971-75 (Emmy award 1973-74, NYU Don Hollenback award 1974), Assignment America, 1975, WNET Reports, 1976-77; columnist: "Eye on Books" for Book of the Month Club News, 1980, Parenting mag., 1986-89; producer Mixed Bag, video arts mag. for CBS Cable; editor-in-chief: Smithsonian Mag., 2001—; contbr. articles to publs. including The N.Y. Times Mag., Harpers, N.Y. Mag. Capt. USMC, 1963-66. Pulitzer Travelling fellow, 1967; recipient Meyer Berger award for Disting. Reporting Columbia U., 1978. Home: 3808 Reno Rd NW Washington DC 20008 Office: Smithsonian Mag MRC 951, PO Box 37012 Washington DC 20013-7012

WINFREY, JOHN CRAWFORD, economist, educator; b. Somerville, Tenn., July 2, 1935; s. Arthur Peter and Frances (Crawford) W.; m. Barbara Ann Strickland, July 20, 1957; 1 child, Mae Millicent. AB, Davidson Coll., 1957; PhD, Duke U., 1965. Asst. dir. data processing Hanes Hosiery, Winston Salem, N.C., 1959-62; research asst. in econs. Duke U., Durham, 1963-64; asst. prof. econs. Washington and Lee U., Lexington, Va., 1965-68, assoc. prof., 1969-73, prof., 1974—. Vis. prof. Vanderbilt U., Nashville, 1966, Tufts U., Boston, 1975, UCLA, 1978, U. Ill., 1982, U. Va., 1986, Duke U., 1989, 95, U. Calif., Berkeley, 1993, U. Utrecht, The Netherlands, 1995. Co-author: The Motion Commotion, 1972; author: Public Finance, Public Choice and the Public Sector, 1973, Social Issues, The Ethics and Economics of Taxes and Public Programs, 1997. Bd. dirs. Lexington Tennis Clinic, Va., 1968-72, Rockridge Area Conservation Council, 1982-84; pres. Rockbridge Arts Guild, 1986-88, 2001-02. Recipient Comunity Svc. Lexington Jaycees, 1971; NEH fellow, 1975, 78, 82, 86, 89, 93; vis. fellow U. Coll. Oxford U., Eng., 1979, 95. Fellow Soc. for Values in Higher Edn.; mem. Am. Econ. Assn., So. Econ. Assn., History of Econs. Soc., Eastern Econ. Assn. Clubs: High Wheelers (Lexington). Democrat. Presbyterian. Home: 628 Stonewall St Lexington VA 24450-1933 Office: Washington and Lee U Dept Econs Lexington VA 24450 E-mail: winfreyj@wlu.edu.

WINFREY, MARION LEE, retired television critic; b. Knoxville, Tenn., July 7, 1932; s. Charles Houston and Norma Elsa (Wesenberg) W.; m. Mary Anne Hight, Sept. 5, 1958 (div. 1977); 1 son, David Dylan; m. Kiki Olson, Aug. 24, 1978 (div. 1982). *Marion L. Winfrey is the first Winfrey in America. William Winfrey emigrated from England to Virginia in 1636.* BS, U. Tenn., 1966; M.F.A., U. Iowa, 1968. Reporter Nashville Tennessean, 1957-58, Knoxville News-Sentinel, 1958-60, Miami bur. UPI, 1960-62, Miami Herald, 1962-63, Washington bur. Knight Newspapers, 1963-66, Detroit Free Press, 1968-71; reporter Phila. Inquirer, 1972-74, TV critic, 1974-2001; ret., 2001. Instr. journalism U. Iowa, 1966-68; Bernard Kilgore journalism counselor DePauw U., 1971 Author: Kent State Report, The President's Commission on Campus Unrest, 1970; included in Best Sports Stories (edited by Marsh and Ehre), 1963. Served with U.S. Army, 1954-56. Nieman fellow Harvard U., 1971-72 Mem. TV Critics Assn. (founding pres. 1978-79), Sigma Delta Chi, Phi Gamma Delta. Clubs: Harvard (Phila.); Pen and Pencil; Nat. Press (Washington). Baptist. Home: 117 N 15th St Philadelphia PA 19102-1516

WINFREY, OPRAH, television talk show host, actress, producer; b. Kosciusko, Miss., Jan. 29, 1954; d. Vernon Winfrey and Vernita Lee. BA in Speech and Drama, Tenn. State U. News reporter Sta. WVOL Radio, Nashville, 1971-72; reporter, news anchorperson Sta. WTVF-TV, 1973-76; news anchorperson Sta. WJZ-TV, Balt., 1976-77, host morning talk show People Are Talking, 1977-83; host talk show A.M. Chgo. Sta. WLS-TV, 1984; host The Oprah Winfrey Show, Chgo., 1985—; nationally syndicated, 1986—; host series of celebrity interview spls. Oprah: Behind the Scenes, 1992—; owner, prodr., chmn., CEO Harpo Prodns., 1986—. Ptnr. in Oxygen Media, an Internet and cable TV co., 2000—; founder, editl. dir. O. The Oprah Magazine in conjunction with Hearst Mags., 2000—. Appeared in films The Color Purple, 1985 (nominated Acad. award and Golden Globe award), Native Son, 1986, Listen Up: The Lives of Quincy Jones, 1990, Beloved, 1998 (exec. prodr.); actress: About Us: The Dignity of Children, 1997 (TV), Before Women Had Wings, 1997 (TV; also exec. prodr. ABC series Oprah Winfrey presents); prodr., actress ABC-TV mini-series The Women of Brewster Place, 1989, also series Brewster Place, 1990, movie There Are No Children Here, 1993; exec. prodr. (ABC Movie of the Week) Overexposed, 1992; host, supervising prodr. celebrity interview series Oprah: Behind the Scenes, 1992, ABC Aftersch. Spls., 1991-93; host, exec. prodr. Michael Jackson Talks...to Oprah-90 Prime-Time Minutes with the King of Pop, 1993; exec. prodr. miniseries: Oprah Winfrey Presents: The Wedding, 1998, Oprah Winfrey Presents: David and Lisa, 1998, Oprah Winfrey Presents: Tuesdays with Morrie, 1999 (TV). Recipient Woman of Achievement award NOW, 1986, Emmy award for Best Daytime Talk Show Host, 1987, 91, 92, 94, 95, 97, Nat. Book Found's 50th Anniversary gold medal, 1999, America's Hope award, 1990, Industry Achievement award Broadcast Promotion Mktg. Execs./Broadcast Design Assn., 1991, Image awards NAACP, 1989, 91, 92, 94, Entertainer of the Yr. award NAACP, 1989, CEBA awards, 1989, 90, 91, George Foster Peabody's Individual Achievement award, 1996, Gold Medal award IRTS, 1996, Lifetime Achievement award NATAS, 1998, People's Choice award, 1997, 98, Horatio Alger award, 1993; named Broadcaster of Yr. Internat. Radio and TV Soc., 1988; recognized as one of America's 25 Most Influential People, Time mag.; inducted to Television Hall of Fame, 1994, Bob Hope Humanitarian Award, 2002. Office: Harpo Prodns 110 N Carpenter St Chicago IL 60607-2145*

WING, ADRIEN KATHERINE, law educator; b. Aug. 7, 1956; d. John Ellison and Katherine (Pruitt) Wing; children: Che-Cabral, Nolan Felipe. AB magna cum laude, Princeton U., 1978; MA, UCLA, 1979; JD, Stanford, 1982. Bar: N.Y. 1983, U.S. Dist. Ct. (so. and ea. dists.) N.Y. 1983, U.S. Ct. Appeals (5th and 9th cirs.). Assoc. Curtis, Mallet-Prevost, Colt & Mosle, N.Y.C., 1982-86, Rabinowitz, Boudin, Standard, Krinsky & Lieberman, 1986-87; assoc. prof. law U. Iowa, Iowa City, 1987-93, prof., 1993—, disting. prof. law, 2001—. Mem. alumni council Princeton U., 1983-85, 96-2000, trustee Class of '78 Alumni Found., 1984-87, 93—, v.p. Princeton Class of 1978 Alumni, 1993-98, trustee Princeton U. 1995; mem. bd. visitors Stanford Law Sch., 1993-96. Mem. bd. editors Am. J. Comp. Law, 1993—. Mem. Iowa Commn. on African Ams. in Prisons, 1999—. Mem.: ABA (exec. com. young lawyers sect. 1985—87), Am. Assn. of Law Schs. (minority sect. bd. 1996—, chair 2002), Am. Friends Svc. Com. (bd. dirs. Mid. East 1998—), Am. Soc. Internat. Law (exec. coun. 1986—89, 1996—99, exec. com. 1988—99, group chair S. Africa 1993—95, nominating com. 1991, 1993, membership com. 1994—95), Internat. Assn. Dem. Lawyers (UN rep. 1984—87), Nat. Conf. Black Lawyers (UN rep., chmn. internat. affairs sect. 1982—95), Internat. Third World Legal Studies Assn. (bd. dirs. 1996—, nominating trustee Princeton com. 1997—2000), Coun. on Fgn. Rels., Iowa Peace Inst. (bd. dirs. 1993—95), Iowa City Fgn. Rels. Coun. (bd. dirs. 1989—94), Transafrica Scholars Forum Coun. (bd. dirs. 1993—95), Black Alumni of Princeton U. (bd. dirs. 1982—87). Democrat. Avocations: photography, jogging, writing, poetry. Office: U Iowa Sch Law Boyd Law Bldg Iowa City IA 52242 E-mail: adrien-wing@uiowa.edu.

WING, CAROL, marketing professional, writer; b. N.Y.C., Nov. 6, 1963; d. Claude P. and Josephine Winge. BS, NYU, 1985. Mktg. mgr. Agfa Corp., Wilmington, Mass., 1989-96; mktg. dir. Number Nine Visual Tech., Lexington, 1996-98; vol. resource devel. staff Heifer Project Nepal, Kathmandu, 1998-99; mktg. dir. Chancellor Beacon Acads., Westboro, Mass., 2000—. Author: Sangai Jaane, 2000. Designer, fund raiser Downey Side Families for Youth, N.Y.C., 1984—; vol. Heifer Project Internat., Little Rock, 1998—, pub. spkr., Mass., 2000—. Mem. Aerobics and Fitness Assn. Am. (trainer), Appalachian Mountain Club. Avocations: reading, fitness, backpacking, textile design, cooking. Home: 33 Meadow Ln Westford MA 01886

WING, JOHN RUSSELL, lawyer; b. Mt. Vernon, N.Y., Jan. 20, 1937; s. John R. and Elinore (Smith) W.; m. Mary Zeller, Aug. 24, 1963 (div. June 1975); children: Ethan Lincoln, Catherine Dorothy; m. Audrey Strauss, Aug. 12, 1979; children: Carlin Elinore, Matthew Lawrence. BA, Yale U., 1960; JD, U. Chgo., 1963. Bar: N.Y. 1964. Assoc. Sherman & Sterling, N.Y.C., 1963-66; asst. U.S. atty. So. Dist. N.Y., 1966-78; chief fraud unit U.S. Dist. Atty. So. Dist. N.Y., 1971-78; ptnr. Weil, Gotshal & Manges, N.Y.C., 1978—. Contbr. articles to profl. jours. Fellow Am. Coll. Trial Lawyers; mem. ABA (white collar crime com. criminal justice sect. 1978—, environ. task force com. 1983-85), Assn. Bar of City of N.Y. (criminal advocacy com. 1985-88), Fed. Bar Coun. (2d cir. cts. com. 1982-84), N.Y. Coun. Def. Lawyers (bd. dirs. 1986-90). Republican. Episcopalian. Avocation: sailing. Home: 52 Livingston St Brooklyn NY 11201-4813 Office: Weil Gotshal & Manges 767 5th Ave Fl Concl New York NY 10153-0119

WING, KENNARD THOMPSON, educational organization official; b. Mobile, Ala., May 27, 1956; s. Kennard Loren and Phyllis Ellen (Thompson) W.; m. Cara Maureen McMenamin, Dec. 27, 1986; children: Thomas, Sara, James. BS, Brown U., 1978; MS, U. Pa., 1989. Cert. mgmt. acct. Statis. mgr. Gimbels, Phila., 1978-80; programmer, analyst Chase Econometrics, Bala Cynwyd, Pa., 1980-82; product mgr. Wharton Econometrics, Phila., 1982-84, acct. mgr., 1985-87; v.p. Thompson-Mayer, 1984-85; project dir. Interact, Bala Cynwyd, 1987-93; lectr. U. Pa., Phila., 1990-95; owner Kennard T. Wing & Co., Havertown, Pa., 1993-98; project dir. OMG Ctr. for Collaborative Learning, Phila., 1998—. Adv. bd. Weston Inst., West Chester, Pa., 1988—89; adj. prof. Immaculuta Coll., 2000. Contbr. articles to profl. jours. Co-founder Township Green, Haverford, Pa., 1990; vol. West Chester Small Bus. Devel. Ctr., Exton, Pa., 1991; pres. Haverford Twp. Adult Sch., 1994-95. Mem. Inst. Mgmt. Accts. Office: 1528 Walnut St Ste 805 Philadelphia PA 19102

WING, MICHAEL JAMES, telecommunications executive; b. Tucson, July 1, 1959; s. James and Bess (Acton) W.; m. Pamela Constantz Wing, May 18, 1980; children: Lindsay Leann, Jacqueline McKenna, Broderick James. BA in Internat. Affairs/Internat. Bus., U. Colo., 1981; MBA in Mktg./Fin., Denver U., 1986; M Pub. Policy, Georgetown U., 1988; M in Political Sci., U. Houston, PhD, 2000; JD, S. Tex. U., 1999. Head baseball coach U. Colo., Boulder, 1980-81; area rep. Kansas City Fellowship Christian Athletes, Denver, 1982; divsn. mgr., ops. mgr. Boyd Distbn. Co., Inc., 1982-84; pres. U.S. ops. Soft Am., Inc., 1984-88; pres. Lundby of Sweden U.S.A., Inc., N.Y.C. and Tucson, Ariz., 1985-90, InfoPlan, Inc./Info Plan Internat. Inc., Houston, 1987-96; spl. asst. to sec. Dept. Interior, 1993; spl. asst. to chmn. FCC, 1992-93; pres., CEO U.S. Space and Rocket Ctr., 1998-99; pres. Opencon Comm. Sys., Inc., Piscataway, N.J., 1999—. Pub. speaker to profl. sports teams, collegiate teams, luncheons, banquets, others. Author: Talking With Your Customers, 1993, 96. Bd. dirs. Young Life and Fellowship Christian Athletes; mem. Leadership Fairfax, Va., Leadership Tucson. White House fellow, Washington, 1992-93. Mem. C.of C. (legis. affairs com.). Republican. Baptist. Avocations: racquetball, tennis, hiking, bicycling, fishing. Home: 12921 Enchanted Dr Cypress TX 77429-2267 Office: 377 Hoes Ln Piscataway NJ 08854-4138

WING, ROGER, management consultant; b. N.Y.C., May 26, 1945; s. John A. and Norma M. (LeBlanc) W.; m. Judith A. King, June 7, 1963 (div. 1980); m. Peggy J. McFall, Aug. 27, 1983; children: Roger, Karin, Nicole, Sean, Nathan, Alexandra. BBA, Cleve. State U., 1972, MBA, 1975. Supr. Am. Greetings Co., Brooklyn, Ohio, 1969-74; dir. Revco D.S. Inc., Twinsburg, 1974-78; mgr. Hughes Aircraft Co., Los Angeles, 1978-79; sr. dir., v.p. Continental Airlines, 1979-81; dir., practice leader Coopers & LyBrand, 1981-83; pres. Huntington Cons. Group, Huntington Beach, Calif., 1983-98; assoc. pastor Calvary Chapel of Costa Mesa, Calif., 1998—. Prof. Cleve. State U., 1977-78. Named Systems Man of Yr., Assn. Systems Mgmt., 1978. Avocations: tennis, skiing, photography, travel, Christian ministry. Office: The Huntington Cons Group 8531 Topside Cir Huntington Beach CA 92646-2117 E-mail: Rogerwing@calvarychapel.com.

WING, VANETTE, sales executive, consultant; b. L.A., Feb. 21, 1947; d. Bennett Germaine and Anna Mae W.; children: John Hunt, Valorie Brinker. BA in Philosophy, Calif. State U., Fullerton, 1977. Account exec. Knoll Pharm. Co., Mount Olive, N.J., 1993-99; managed care account mgr. Biovail Pharms. Inc., Morriville, N.C., 2000—. Lobbyist HDS Med., Honolulu, 1994. Health care lobbyist, activist Coalition Health Care Prov., Honolulu, 1994. Recipient fellowship U. Calif., Riverside, 1978, 79. Republican. Presbyterian. Avocations: archery, gardening, reading, cooking. Office: Biovail Pharms Inc 808 Aviation Pkwy Morrisville NC 27560 Home: Apt 205 1001 Matthew Ln Braintree MA 02184-6638 Fax: 926-630-5493. E-mail: wingitv@pacbell.net.

WINGATE, BETTYE FAYE, librarian, educator; b. Hillsboro, Tex., Oct. 31, 1950; d. Warren Randolph and Faye (Gilmore) W. BA summa cum laude, Baylor U., 1971, MA, 1975; MLS, Tex. Womans U., 1985. Cert. prov. sec., learning resources endorsement. English tchr. Mexia (Tex.) H.S.; reading tchr. Connally Ind. Sch. Dist., Waco, Tex.; reading tchr., libr. Grapevine-Colleyville Ind. Sch. Dist., Grapevine; libr. Crockett Mid. Sch., Irving. Mem. librs. coms., Campus Action Planning Com., 1989-93, Irving Ind. Sch. Dist. Site Based Decision-Making Com., 1992-94, mem. staff devel. coun., 1994-96, chair media fair com., 1996—; rev. Linworth Pub.; spkr., presenter in field. Founding sponsor Challenger Ctr., Air Force Meml. Found. Recipient Tex. Media awards, 1988, 89, 94. Mem. ALA, NEA, Am. Assn. Sch. Librs. (vol. libr. Kids Connect), Tex. State Tchrs. Assn. (assn. rep.), Tex. Libr. Assn. (chmn. state media awards com. 1989-91), Tex. Assn. Edn. Tech., Tex. Computer Edn. and Tech., Assn. Ednl. Comm. and Tech., Planetary Soc., Nat. Space Soc., Nat. Parks & Conservation Assn., Baylor Alumni Assn. (life), Wilderness Soc., Sierra Club, Beta Phi Mu, Delta Kappa Gamma (scholar 1985). E-mail: bettyew@flash.net., bwingate@irvingisd.net.

WINGATE, C. KEITH, law educator; b. Darlington, S.C., May 12, 1953; s. Clarence L. and Lilly W.; m. Gloria Farley; stepchildren: Brenda, Marvin, Terry and Oliver Champion. BA in Polit. Sci., U. Ill., 1974, JD cum laude, 1978. Bar: Calif., 1978. Assoc. litigation dept. Morrison & Foerster, San Francisco, 1978-80; from asst. to assoc. prof. law U. Calif.-Hastings, 1980-86, prof., 1986—. Dir. Coun. Legal Edn. Opportunity Region I Inst., 1989; vis. prof. law Stanford Law Sch., fall 1990, 94, spring 1998; chair Minority Law Tchrs.' Conf. Com., 1990; mem. acad. assistance work group, 1991; trustee Law Sch. Admission Coun., 1997-2001. Author: (with David I. Levine and William R. Slomanson) Cases and Materials on California Civil Procedure, 1991, (with William R. Slomanson) California Civil Procedure in a Nutshell, 1992, (with Donald L. Doernberg) Federal Courts, Federalism and Separation of Powers, 1994, 2nd edit., 2000. Bd. dirs. Cmty. Housing Devel. Corp., North Richmond, 1990-99. Recipient 10 Outstanding Persons award U. Ill. Black

Alumni Assn., 1980; Harno fellow U. Ill., Coll. of Law, 1976. Mem. Assn. Am. Law Schs. (chair sect. minority groups 1990, exec. com. mem. sect. civil procedure 1991), Charles Houston Bar Assn., Phi Sigma Alpha. Office: U Calif Hastings Coll Law 200 Mcallister St San Francisco CA 94102-4707

WINGATE, CONSTANCE BLANDY, librarian; b. Woodbury, N.J., Mar. 7, 1935; d. John Chase and Josephine Spond (Black) Blandy; m. Len B. Cooke Jr., Jan. 7, 1978 (div. 1987); m. John B. Wingate, Mar. 12, 1999. BA, U. Pa., 1956; MA, U. Denver, 1957. Adult cons. Onondaga Library System, Syracuse, N.Y., 1965-66; asst. dir. Mt. Vernon (N.Y.) Public Library, 1966-75; dep. dir. Queens Borough Public Library, Jamaica, N.Y., 1975-79, dir., 1980-94. Founder pres. Literacy Vols. Mt. Vernon, 1972-74 Trustee METRO, 1980-81, v.p., 1985-88, pres., 1988-91; mem. N.Y. State Libr. Svcs. and Constrn. Act Adv. Coun., 1982-88, chmn., 1986-87; bd. dirs. Queens Coun. on the Arts, 1988-94, v.p., 1989-93; bd. dirs. Queens Mus. of Art, 1988-98, v.p., 1994-96, pres. 1996-98; bd. dirs. Queens Libr. Found., 1996—. Mem.: ALA, Circumnavigators Club (sec. 2002—). Republican. Episcopalian. Home: Apt 10D 166-25 Powells Cove Blvd Beechhurst NY 11357

WINGATE, ROBERT LEE, JR. internist; b. Columbia, S.C., May 28, 1936; s. Robert Lee and Helen (Owen) W.; m. Ritanne Cooper, Apr. 19, 1962 (div. 1965); 1 child, Elizabeth Anne Butterfield-Wingate; m. Jeannette DeLatte, Mar. 27, 1968 (div. 1980); children: Laura Owen Wingate, Charlotte Cramer; m. Ann Phyfer, Apr. 1, 1999; 1 child, Jeff Stamm. BS, U. S.C., 1957; MD, Med. Coll. S.C., 1961. Intern Cin. Gen. Hosp., 1961-62, jr. resident internal medicine, 1964-65; asst. resident in internal medicine Med. Coll. of Va., Richmond, 1965-66; resident in internal medicine Charity Hosp. of La., New Orleans, 1966-67, resident in neurology, 1967-68; pvt. practice Columbia, 1968-78; PruCare physician Memphis, 1983-85; med. dir. M. Lowennstein and Celanese Corps., Rock Hill, S.C., 1978-80; med. dir. nursing home care unit Dorn VA Hosp., Columbia, 1980-82; med. cons. disability determination div. Vocat. Rehab. S.C., 1982-83; cons. Student Health Ctr. U. S.C., 1985-86; cons. Urgent Care Ctrs. S.C., 1986-87; pvt. practice Pelion, S.C., 1987-92; staff internist, chief of staff, cons. internal medicine Western Mental Health Inst., Western Institute, Tenn., 1992-2000; with Memphis Mental Health Inst., 2000—. Med. dir. Forest Hills Nursing Ctr., Columbia, 1968-78; med. cons. S.C. Commn. for Blind, Columbia, 1970-78, Mid-Carolina Coun. on Alcoholism, Columbia, 1970-74; instr. internal medicine U. S.C. Sch. Medicine, 1980-82; cons. internal medicine and urgent care Pelion Cmty. Care Ctr., 1989-92; instr. Sch. Nursing, Med. Coll. S.C., Winthrop divsn., 1978-80; lectr. in field; mem. adv. bd. Vector Med. Techs. and Nutrition Superstores; cardiology cons. Western Mental Health Inst., 2000—. Contbr. articles to newspapers; reviewer Annal of Internal Medicine. Ofcl. physician Peanut Party S.C., 1990-92. Lt. comdr. M.C., USNR, 1958-66. Grantee Burroughs-Wellcome Co., 1958, Med. Coll. S.C., 1960, Congress of U.S.. 1987. Fellow ACP; mem. AMA (life mem., Physician's Recognition award 1969, 74, 79, 85, 86, 94-96, 96-99, 99-2002), Am. Soc. Internal Medicine, Am. Occupational Med. Assn., So. Med. Assn., West Tenn. Consolidated Med. Assembly, Soc. of 1824, State of Tenn. Med. Assn.Consol. Med. Assembly of West Tenn. Avocations: chess, hunting, fishing, gardening, billiards. Office: Memphis Mental Health Inst Memphis TN 38174-0966

WINGER, RALPH O. lawyer; b. Keokuk, Iowa, July 8, 1919; s. Ralph O. and Mary Ellen (Lee) W.; m. Irene L. Sutton, Apr. 5, 1941 (dec.); children: Ralph O. (dec.), Allen, Louise, Robert. BA, State U. Iowa, 1940; LLB, Harvard U., 1947. Bar: N.Y. 1948. Assoc. Cahill Gordon & Reindel and predecessor firms, N.Y.C., 1947-60, ptnr., 1960-91, sr. counsel, 1992—. Lt. USNR, 1942-46, PTO. Mem. ABA, N.Y. State Bar Assn. (chmn. tax sect. 1973-74, ho. of dels. 1974-75), Bay Terrace Country Club (N.Y.). Republican. Home: 20908 28th Rd Flushing NY 11360-2413 Office: Cahill Gordon & Reindel 80 Pine St Fl 17 New York NY 10005-1790

WINGER, ROGER ELSON, retired church administrator; b. Fisherville, Ont., Can., Dec. 25, 1933; s. Elson Clare and Bertha Caroline (Schweyer) W.; m. Della Bertha Lebien, June 7, 1958; children: Jeffrey, Karen Mohr, David, Thomas, Susan. AA, Concordia Jr. Coll., Ft. Wayne, Ind., 1953; BA, Concordia Sem., St. Louis, 1955, theol. diploma, 1958; DD (hon.), Concordia Luth. Sem., Edmonton, Alta., Can., 1991. Ordained to ministry, Luth. Ch., 1958. Pastor Holy Trinity Luth. Ch., London, 1958-64, Good Shepherd Luth. Ch., Coventry, Eng., 1964-69, Luth. Mission, Liverpool, Eng., 1969-72, Faith Luth. Ch., Dunnville, Ont., 1972-78, St. Matthew Luth. Ch., Smithville, 1972-78, St. Paul's Luth. Ch., Kitchener, 1978-91; pres. ea. dist. Luth. Ch.-Can., 1991-2000; ret., 2000. V.p. Ont. dist. Luth. Ch.-Can., 1982-88; sec. Luth. Ch.-Can., Winnipeg, Man., 1988-91; mem. bd. regents Concordia Luth. Sem., Edmonton, Alta., 1984-88, Concordia Luth. Sem., St. Catharines Ont., 1991-2000. Avocations: photography, golf, woodworking. Home: 76 Deerwood Crescent Kitchener ON Canada N2N 1R3 E-mail: rogerdella@aol.com.

WINGERSON, RICHARD CORTIS, renewable fuel company executive, researcher; b. Wichita, Kans., June 2, 1929; s. Cortis Leroy and Marie Clements W.; m. Patricia June Palmer, June 7, 1952 (div. Oct. 1965); children: Sharon Lee, Marcus Richard, James Cortis. BS, MIT, 1952; MS, AF Inst. of Tech., 1959; DSc, MIT, 1962. Ind. cons., Crested Butte, Colo., 1975-98; chief scientist Pure Vision Tech., Inc., Fort Lupton, 1999—. Inventor in field. Co-founder, dir. High County Citizens Alliance, Crested Butte, 1978-92; chmn. Gunnison County Planning Commn., 1978-91; chmn. Crested Butte Fire Protection Dist., 1980-90. Col. USAF, 1952-74. Democrat. Avocations: hiking, skiing, bridge, dancing, woodworking. Home: PO Box 168 Crested Butte CO 81224 Office: Pure Vision Tech Inc 511 N McKinley Ave Fort Lupton CO 80621 E-mail: dwingerson@aol.com.

WINGERT, HANNELORE CHRISTIANE, real estate agent, chemical company executive; b. Karlsbad, Czechoslavakia; came to U.S., 1962, naturalized, 1967; d. Andreas and Gisela Maria (Ciharz) Zwickel; m. Rudolf Wingert, Feb. 9, 1963; children: Angela Helene, Christopher Rudolf. I.BA, Stadt. Berufsschule, Germany, 1961; postgrad. in mgmt., Bergen Community Coll., 1983. Lic. real estate, N.J., Calif. Clk. various cos., N.J., 1963, bilingual sec., 1963-78; exec. sec., adminstrv. asst. Lurgi Corp., Hasbrouck Heights, 1978-81; sr. exec. sec. Degussa Corp., Teterboro, 1981-83, asst. product mgr. silica, 1983-85, asst. product mgr. H202, 1985-87, sales promotion coord., 1987; sales assoc. Schlott Realtors, Kinnelon, 1987-90; Caldwell Banker, 1990—. Million dollar club, 1988, multi-million dollar club, 1990—, Nat. Assn. Realtors Million Dollar Club, 1992, 98. Author real estate newsletter, 1992—, community newsletter, 1977-79. Mem. Garden State Multiple Listing Svc.; chmn. master planning com. High Crest Lake, West Milford, N.J., 1974-75; advisor Jr. Woman's Club Kinnelon-Butler (N.J.), 1973-74; techr. computer classes Bd. Realtors, Passaic County, 1989-92. Mem. Nat. Assn. Realtors, North San Diego County Assn. Realtors, N.J. Fed. of Woman's Clubs (past pres.), High Crest Lake Woman's Club (pres. 1972-73) (West Milford, N.J.). Republican. Roman Catholic. Home: 743 Atwood Pl San Marcos CA 92069 E-mail: HCWintert@cox.net.

WINGERTER, JOHN PARKER, artist, photographer; b. N.Y.C., July 27, 1940; s. William and Catherine (Parker) W. Student, Columbia U., 1958-61; LLB, LaSalle U., 1968; postgrad., Arts Student League, 1970-72. Dir. Noho Gallery, N.Y.C., 1982-84. One man shows include Nomo Gallery, 1978, 79, 80, 81, 82, 83, 84, 85, 86, 87, 88; exhibitions in group shows at Adelphi U., 1983, LeSalon Des Nations Centre for Contemporary Arts, 1984, Smithtownship Arts Coun. Artist Forum-Mill Pond House, 1996-97, Northeastern Brack Ch., 2000, Town Hall and Huntington Enrichment Ctr., N.Y. Grantee Suffolk County Decentralization, 1999, Spl. Opportunity Stipend grant East End Arts coun., 2000; recipient Proclamation for quality of work Huntington Town Hall. Home: 58 Meadow Glen Rd Northport NY 11768-2711 Studio: Main St Huntington NY 11743-6903

WINGERTER, JOHN RAYMOND, lawyer; b. Erie, Pa., June 30, 1942; s. Raymond J. and Magdalene (Pfeil) W.; m. Susan Tracy Smith, Aug. 5, 1967; children: Julie, Kara, Lori, Darcie, Daryle. BA, Norwich U., 1964; JD, U. Notre Dame, 1968. Bar: Pa. 1967, U.S. Dist. Ct. (we. dist.) Pa. 1967, U.S. Ct. Appeals (3d cir.) 1971, U.S. Supreme Ct. 1973. Assoc. Carney, Palmisano & Walsh, Erie, Pa., 1967-69; ptnr. Carney & Good, 1969—. Trustee Gannon U. Mem. ABA, Pa. Bar Assn. (ho. dels. 1983—), Erie Bar Assn. (exec. com.), Assn. Trial Lawyers Am., Pa. Trial Lawyers Assn. Clubs: Erie Yacht, Lake View Country Club. Republican. Roman Catholic. Home: 1540 S Shore Dr Erie PA 16505-2438 Office: Carney & Good 254 W 6th St Erie PA 16507-1398

WINGET, WALTER WINFIELD, lawyer; b. Peoria, Ill., Sept. 12, 1936; s. Walter W. Winget and Arabella (Robinson) Richardson; m. Alice B. Winget, Sept. 23, 1993; children: Marie, Marshall. AB cum laude, Princeton U., 1958; JD, U. Mich., 1961. Bar: R.I. 1962, Ill. 1962, U.S. Supreme Ct. 1971; cert. civil trial advocate Nat. Bd. Trial Advocacy. Assoc. Edwards & Angell, Providence, 1961-64; ptnr. Winget & Winget, 1964—69; sole practice Peoria, 1969—77; ptnr. Winget & Kane, 1977-2000, of counsel, 2000—. Asst. pub. defender Peoria, 1969-70; bd. dirs. various corps. Atty., bd. dirs. Better Bus. Bur. Cen. Ill., Inc. 1973-92, chmn., 1979-81; mem. Schs. Com., 1985–. Served to sgt. U.S. Army, 1961-62. Mem. Ill. Bar Assn., Peoria County Bar Assn. (pres. 1991-92), Peoria Country Club, Princeton Club Chgo. (mem. schs. com. 1980—), Safari Club, Oakland Hall Club. Republican. Episcopalian. Avocations: competitive target shooting, big game and duck hunting, farm management. Home: 6712 N Post Oak Rd Peoria IL 61615-2347 Office: Winget & Kane 416 Main St Ste 807 Peoria IL 61602-1177

WINGFIELD, THOMAS CHRISTOPHER, lawyer; b. N.Y.C., July 29, 1962; s. Samuel Griffin III and Maryann Margaret (Frost) W. BA, Ga. State U., 1987; JD, Georgetown U., 1996, LLM, 1999. Bar: Ga. 1996, D.C. 1997. Commd. officer USN, 1987, advanced through grades to lt., 1991; squadron intelligence officer USS Midway, Atsugi, Japan, 1988-90; desk officer Office of Naval Intelligence, Suitland, Md., 1990-93; intelligence officer Ctr. for Naval Analysis, Alexandria, Va., 1993-97; resigned USN, 1997; counsel, prin. nat. security analyst Aegis Rsch. Corp., Falls Church, Va., 1997—. Author: The Law of Information Conflict: National Security Law in Cyberspace, 2000. Lt. comdr. USNR, 1997-2001. Republican. Roman Cath. Home: 4702 English Ct Suitland MD 20746-3783 Office: Aegis Rsch Corp Ste 1000 North 7799 Leesburg Pike Falls Church VA 22043 E-mail: wingtom@worldnet.att.net.

WINGHAM, ERMA DORIS, secondary education educator; b. Hanover, Ind., Oct. 11, 1913; d. Raymond and Mable Irene (Driggs) Kyle; m. Raymond Wingham, Jan. 9, 1933 (dec. Dec. 1996); children: Barbara, Janet, Kenneth. AB, Hanover Coll., 1959; MA, Ind. U., 1964, cert. lang. arts tchr., 1976. Educator lang. arts, Madison, Ind., 1959-76; instr. fgn. studies Ea. Ind., 1966-76; dir., writer h.s. Madison, 1959-76. Author: Harvest of a Hundred Years, 1990; (poetry booklets) Theme Songs, 1985, 86, 87; writer, dir. 11 plays including Purple Palace, 2001; author numerous poems. Active voter enrollment Dem. Party, Ind., 1960; mentor Old Town Elem. Sch., 2000-01; chair coun. ministries Meth. Ch., Seminole, Fla. Poetry featured in Best Poetry of 20th Century, Internat. Libr. Poetry. Mem. PEO (v.p. 1996-97), Order of Ea. Star (Worthy Matron lodge 525 1936), Delta Kappa Gamma (pres. 1967-69). Democrat. United Methodist. Avocations: oil painting, singing, teaching Sunday school, gymnastics.

WINHAM, GEORGE KEETH, retired mental health nurse; b. Plain Dealing, La., Nov. 25, 1934; s. Henderson and Lula Mae (Kelly) W.; m. Patricia Annie Weise, Nov. 7, 1959; children: Adrian Keeth, George Kevin, Karla Ann. ADN, La. State U., 1974; BS in Health Care, Carolina Christian U., 1986. Cert. chem. dependency nurse specialist; RN, La.; cert. addictions nurse. Staff nurse preceptor ward 10 VAMC, Shreveport, La., 1992-96, staff nurse ward 10, 1976-88, 96; ret. Overton Brooks VA Med. Ctr., 1996. With USAFR, 1982-95. Mem.: DAV, VFW, Air Force Sgts. Assn., Nat. Fedn. Fed. Employees (local treas. 1956, nurse of yr. 1989), Masons, Am. Legion. Baptist. Avocations: repairing antique furniture, framing pictures. Home: 106 Lancashire Dr Bossier City LA 71111-2023

WINICK, MYRON, educator, physician; b. N.Y.C., May 4, 1929; s. Charles B. and Ruth E. (Gesser) W.; m. Elaine L. Lasky, Sept. 19, 1964; children: Jonathan, Stephen. AB, Columbia U., 1951; MS, U. Ill., 1952; MD, SUNY, 1956. Intern U. Pa., Phila., 1956-57; asst. resident pediatrics Cornell U. Med. Coll., N.Y.C., 1957-59, chief resident, 1959-60; attending pediatrician Stanford U. Hosp., 1963-64; asst. prof. pediatrics Cornell U. Med. Coll., N.Y.C., 1964-68, assoc. prof. pediatrics and nutrition, 1968-70, prof., 1970-71; dir. Inst. Human Nutrition Columbia U. Inst. Human Nutrition, 1972-87, prof. pediatrics, 1972-89, R.R. Williams prof. nutrition, 1973-89, R.R. Williams prof. emeritus, 1990—; pres. U. Health Scis./Chgo. Med. Sch., North Chgo., Ill., 1990-93; dir. Ctr. for Nutrition, Genetics and Human Devel., 1975-87. Vis. prof. pediatrics U. Chile, Santiago, 1967; asst. attending pediatrician N.Y. Hosp., N.Y.C., 1964-68, asso. attending pediatrician, 1968-70, attending pediatrician, 1970-71; attending pediatrician Presbyn. Hosp., N.Y.C., 1972-89; cons. Pan Am. Health Orgn., 1966—. Author: Malnutrition and Brain Development, 1976; textbook Nutrition in Health and Disease, 1980; Growing Up Healthy; A Parent's Guide to Good Nutrition, 1982; For Mothers and Daughters: A Guide to Good Nutrition for Women, 1983; Your Personalized Health Profile: Choosing the Diet That's Right for You, 1985; Nutrition, Pregnancy and Early Infancy, 1989; The Fiber Prescription, 1992; editor: textbook Current Concepts in Nutrition, 1972— , Nutrition: Pre- and Postnatal Development, Vol. I, Human Nutrition: A Comprehensive Treatise, 1979, Columbia Ency. of Nutrition, 1988; contbg. editor Nutrition Revs., 1969-76; mem. editorial bd. Jour. Nutrition, 1972-76, 82-86, The Year in Metabolism (now Contemporary Metabolism), 1975— ; assoc. editor Growth, 1984—; nutrition editor Cancer Prevention, 1994—. Trustee Found. for Internat. Child Health; mem. nutrition interdisciplinary cluster Pres.' Biomed. Research Panel, 1975; mem. panel on infants and children Pres.' Commn. on Mental Health, 1977; cons. Office of Tech. Assessment, U.S. Congress, 1976-78; mem. Food and Nutrition Bd. NRC, 1982-88. With USNR, 1960-62. Bank of Am.-Gianini Found. fellow Stanford, 1962; NIH Spl. fellow, 1963; recipient NIH Career Devel. award, 1968-71; E. Mead Johnson award pediatric research, 1970; Osborne and Mendel award Am. Inst. Nutrition, 1976; Agnes Higgins award March of Dimes Found., 1983 Fellow Royal Soc. Health, Am. Acad. Pediatrics; mem. AAAS, Am. Soc. Cell Biology, Soc. Developmental Biology, Harvey Soc., Soc. Pediatric Research, Royal Soc. Medicine, Brit. Nutrition Soc., Am. Inst. Nutrition, Am. Soc. Clin. Nutrition, N.Y. Acad. Scis., N.Y. Acad. Medicine, (cons.), Soc. for Exptl. Biology and Medicine, Soc. for Neurosci., Internat. Soc. for Devel. Neurosci. Home: 112 Lakeshore Dr Putnam Valley NY 10579-1312 Office: Columbia U Inst Human Nutrition New York NY 10027

WINICOV, ILGA BUTELIS, biochemist, educator; b. Riga, Latvia, May 16, 1935; d. Arturs and Zenta (Gutmanis) Butelis; m. Herbert B. Winicov, Aug. 30, 1958; children: Eric, Mark; m. Rodney E. Harrington, Jan. 26, 1979. AB, U. Pa., 1956, PhD, 1971; MS, U. Wis., 1958. Postdoctoral fellow Inst. for Cancer Rsch., Phila., 1972-74, rsch. assoc., 1974-76; rsch. asst. prof. biochemistry Fels Rsch. Inst., Temple U., 1976-78; asst. prof. biochemistry U. Nev. Sch. Medicine, Reno, 1979-85, assoc. prof. biochemistry, 1985-95, assoc. prof. microbiology, 1987-95, prof. biochemistry and microbiology, 1995-99; rsch. prof. plant biology Ariz. State U., Tempe, 1999—. Cons. in biochemistry of nucleic acids and molecular biology and plant biotech. Contbr. articles to profl. jours. Mem. Am. Soc. Biol. Chemists, Am. Soc. Microbiology, Am. Assn. Cancer Rsch., Internat. Soc. Plant Molecular Biology, Soc. Plant Physiology. Office: Ariz Sate U Plant Biology Tempe AZ 85257-1601 E-mail: winicov@asu.edu.

WINIK, JAY B. writer, political scientist, consultant; b. New Haven, Feb. 8, 1957; s. Herbert Edward Winik and Marilyn Joan (Fishman) Abrams; m. Lyric Wallwork, Nov. 17, 1991. BA in Psychology cum laude, Yale U., 1980, PhD in Polit. Sci., 1993; MS in Internat. Rels. with distinction, London Sch. Econs., 1981. Arms control cons. Rand Corp., Santa Monica, Calif., 1983; chief speechwriter Ambassador Benjamin Netanyahu, N.Y.C., 1984; sr. profl. staff mem. House Com. on Armed Svcs., Washington, 1985-88; vis. fellow Ctr. for Strategic and Internat. Studies, 1988; dep. exec. dir. Def. Sec.'s Commn. on Base Realignment and Closure, 1988; legis. asst. for def. and fgn. policy Office of Sen. Charls S. Robb & Senate Com. on Fgn. Rels., 1989-91; sr. fellow Sch. Pub. Affairs U. Md., College Park, 1991—; sr. fellow Hudson Inst., 2000—. Advisor to Sec. Defense, 1993; prin. advisor for def. and fgn. policy, 1986 policy commn. Dem. Nat. Com.; assoc. staff mem. select com to investigate covert arms transactions with Iran, 1987. Author: On the Brink, 1996, April 1865: The Month That Saved America, 2001 (New York Times bestseller); editl. contbr. Wall Street Jour., N.Y. Times, Washington Post, The Washingtonian, others pubs., 1981—. Grantee U.S. Inst. Peace, 1987; fellow Bradley Found. Fellow Ctr. for Strategic and Internat. Studies (adj.); mem. Coun. on Fgn. Rels. Jewish. Avocation: tennis. Home: 30 Grafton St Chevy Chase MD 20815-3428 Office: U Md CISSM Sch Pub Affairs College Park MD 20740

WININGS, KATHY, religion educator; b. Indpls., Apr. 4, 1953; d. James Russell and Isabelle (Watkins) W.; m. James Warren Garland, July 1, 1982 (div. Dec. 1988). BA, Fordham U., 1982; MDiv, MRE, Unification Theol. Sem., 1987; EdD, Columbia U., 1996. Cert. tchr., N.Y. Designer, dir. Sun. Sch./Weekly Edn., N.Y.C., 1979-82; pvt. tutor, Demarest, N.J., 1980-83; lectr. Interdenominational Conf. for Clergy, N.Y.C., 1987-89; unification campus minister Columbia U., 1989—; adj. Coll. of New Rochelle-Rosa Parks, 1990-91; lectr. religious edn. Unification Theol. Sem., Tarrytown, NY, 1990—96, dir. DMin. program, asst. prof., 1997—2002, asst. acad. dean N.Y., 1992-94; cons., advisor Unification Sunday Sch. Program, N.Y.C., 1992—; dir. nat. youth ministry Unification Campus Ministry Assn., Tarrytown, 1991-96; dean Unification Theol. Sem. Ext. Ctr., N.Y.C., 2000—, assoc. prof., 2002—. Scholar Internat. Conf. on Unity of Scis., N.Y.C., 1991—; cons. for edn. Women's Fedn. for World Peace, N.Y.C., 1992—, nat. bd. dirs., 1997-2000; exec. dir. Internat. Relief Friendship Found., also v.p. bd. dirs.; conf. spkr. on svc. learning, edn., devel., character, tchg., and youth issues. Author: Building Character through Service Learning, 2002; editor: American Christian Tradition, 1986; contbr. articles to profl. jours. Recipient Women's Essay prize Tchrs. Coll., 1991. Mem. Nat. Coun. for Religion and Pub. Edn., Religious Edn. Assn., Assn. for Profs. and Researchers of Religious Edn., Nat. Campus Ministry Assn., Campus Ministry Women, Am. Acad. Religion, Assn. Dir. D of Min. Edn., Kappa Delta Pi. Avocations: professional musician, tennis, swimming, reading. Home and Office: 177 White Plains Rd Apt 50F Tarrytown NY 10591-5509 E-mail: irffint@aol.com.

WINK, DOREEN MUSTO, interior designer; b. Rochester, N.Y., Oct. 18, 1945; d. Nunzio Edward and Ann (Iaculli) Musto; m. Douglas L. Wink; 1 child Douglass III 1 stepchild Melissa Lynn. AAS in Psychology cum laude, Monroe C.C., 1973; BSW cum laude, SUNY, Brockport, 1975. Social worker, dir. mental health Cobbs Hill Nursing Home, Ohio and N.Y., 1975-78; social worker Ohio, 1980-89; interior designer for retail stores Washington, 1989-91; CEO Three-D-Wink Inc., 1991—. Bd. dirs. Md. Design, Space Planning and Interior Props.; decorator offices of White Ho. staff, Washington, 1994—; mem Lowe's Gardening Panel, 2001. Mem. spl. publs. bd.: Home & Garden. Mem. Peerless Rockville (Md.) Hist. Soc.; judge, mem. 4-H Orgn., 1985—; organizer, pres. Rockshire New Comers Club, Rockville; chmn. Rockshire Arch. Com.; active nat., local politics; head art dept. Young Reps. Club, Rochester, 1967—69. Named Hon. Citizen of Civil War, Town of Sharpsburg, 1999. Mem.: NOW, Design to Make-Over Rm. Assn., Md. Design, space Planning and Props Soc. (founder, dir.), James Buchanan Soc., James Monroe Hist. Soc. (pres.), Smithsonian Instn., Tex. State Soc. (inaugural ball com. 1985—94), Decorative Arts Trust (cons.), Nat. Trust Hist. Preservation, White Ho. Hist. Soc., Nat. Must. Women in Arts (charter), Nat. Italian Am. Found., Woodrow Wilson Hist. Assn., Rockshire Assn. (bd. dirs.), USPHS Womens Club, Rockville Garden Club Rockshire. Avocations: painting, bicycling, crocheting, walking, reading.

WINK, JOHN JOSEPH, project manager; b. Rockville Centre, N.Y., Mar. 11, 1951; s. Joseph M. and Jessie N. (Hatzel) W.; m. Barbara Aland, Sept. 18, 1976; children: Jeffrey J., Brian L. BS in Computer Sci., Pa. State U., 1973; diploma in advanced acctg., Duquesne U., 1987. Cert. info. systems auditor; cert. in data processing; project mgmt. profl. Programmer, analyst Halls Motor Transit, Mechanicsburg, Pa., 1973-74, Babcock & Wilco, Beaver Falls, 1974-76; customer analyst Dresser Industries, Pitts., 1976-77; pres. Keynote Sys., Inc., 1977-81; asst. v.p. Mellon Bank, 1981-96; dir. human resources County Allegheny, 1996-98; asst. v.p. Mellon Bank, 1998—. Contbr. articles to profl. jours. Bd. dirs. Moon Twp. (Pa.) Mcpl. Authority, 1990—, pres., 1991—; bd. suprs. Moon Twp., 1997-99; sec., bd. dirs. Northwest 911, 1997-99. Republican. Roman Catholic. Home: 260 Burch Dr Moon Township PA 15108-3153 Office: Three Mellon Bank Ctr Rm 153-1015 3 Mellon Bank Ctr Pittsburgh PA 15259-0001 E-mail: waterwink@aol.com., wink.jj@mellon.com.

WINKEL, ERWIN CHARLES, II, retired urologist; b. Houston, July 7, 1934; s. Erwin Charles and Annie (Walther) W.; m. Jacquelyn Yvonne Watson, Sept. 3, 1960; children: Erwin Charles III, Carolyn, Todd. BA, Taylor U., 1956, MD, 1959. Diplomate Am. Bd. Urology. Intern Hermann Hosp., Houston, 1959-60, resident in urology, 1960-62, 64-66, now mem. staff; pvt. practice specializing in urology, 1996—. A founder North Central Gen. Hosp., Houston, 1974, chief of staff, 1974-75; a founder Houston Northwest Med. Center Hosp., 1973, chief of staff, 1977-78; clin. assoc. in urology U. Tex. Med. Sch., Houston, 1967-96. Committeeman Troop 9, Boy Scouts Am., 1952-82, instl. rep., 1960-66, merit badge counselor, 1967-71; mem. adv. bd. Vols. of Am., 1968-76. With U.S. Army, 1962-64. Fellow ACS, Internat. Coll. Surgeons; mem. AMA (Physicians Recognition awards), Am. Urol. Assn. (continuing edn.), Tex. Urologists Assn., Tex. Med. Assn., Am. Fertility Soc., Am. Geriatrics Soc., Harris County Med. Soc., Houston Urol. Soc., Houston Acad. Medicine. Republican. Methodist. Home: 64 Champions Bend Cir Houston TX 77069-1800

WINKEL, R. DENNIS, family practice physician; b. Des Moines, Aug. 10, 1948; s. Don and Evelyn W.; m. M. Patricia Stewart, Sept. 1, 1973; children: Todd, Kevin. BA, U. Colo., 1970; MD, Creighton U. Sch. Medicine, 1974. Diplomate Am. Bd. Family Practice. Resident Creighton U. Dept. Family Practice, Omaha, 1974-77; pvt. practice Kalispell, Mont., 1977—; chief staff Kalispell Regional Hosp., 1993; also bd. dirs. Bd. dirs. N.W. Healthcare. Mem. Mont. Med. Soc., Flathead Med. Soc. (pres. 1991-93). Avocations: whitewater rafting, downhill skiing, golfing, tennis. Office: 1250 Burns Way Ste 1 Kalispell MT 59901-3140

WINKEL, RAYMOND NORMAN, aerospace industry consultant, avionics manufacturing executive; b. Flint, Mich., Dec. 8, 1928; s. Norman Martin and Evelyn Matilda (Hylen) W.; m. Ellen Stefula, Dec. 29, 1955; children: Raymond Norman, Ann, Maryellen. BS, U.S. Naval Postgrad. Sch., Monterey, Calif., 1964; MS, Villanova (Pa.) U., 1967; grad. advanced mgmt. program, Harvard U., 1973. Enlisted in USN, 1948, commd. ensign, designated naval aviator, 1951, advanced through grades to rear adm., 1979; service in Far East; comdg. officer Naval Electronics Systems Test and Evaluation Facility St. Inigoes, Md., 1969-71; dir. avionics U.S. Navy, 1973-76; project mgr. Navy/Marine Corps heavy lift helicopter, 1976-78; gen. mgr. Navy/industry team to develop new ship/aircraft weapon system for anti-submarine warfare LAMPS Mark III, 1978-81; ret. USN, 1981; v.p. Washington ops. Telephonics Corp., Huntington, N.Y., 1981-82; v.p. programs and contracts Astronautics Corp. Am., Milw., 1982-94; aerospace industry cons. Heathsville, Va., 1994-95. Decorated Legion of Merit, Air medal, Navy Achievement medal. Mem. Exptl. Aircraft Assn., U.S. Naval Inst., Assn. Naval Aviation, Ret. Officers Assn., Kiwanis, Indian Creek Yacht and Country Club, U.S. Power Squadron. Republican. Roman Catholic. Home: 1860 Island Point Rd Heathsville VA 22473-3729 Fax: 804-580-4158. E-mail: rwinkel@crosslink.net.

WINKELMAN, JAMES WARREN, hospital administrator, pathology educator; b. Bklyn., Oct. 29, 1935; s. Charles Winkelman and Augusta Spiselman; m. Sidra Levi, Sept. 1, 1957 (div. Sept. 1972); children: Elizabeth, Claudia, Recha; m. Rina Lavie, Sept. 20, 1977; 1 child, Zev. AB, U. Chgo., 1955; MD, Johns Hopkins U., 1959; MA (hon.), Harvard U., 1990. Diplomate Am. Bd. Pathology. Intern in medicine Johns Hopkins Hosp., 1959-60; resident in pathology NYU Hosp., Bellevue Hosp., 1962-65; asst. prof. pathology NYU, 1965-67; assoc. clin. prof. UCLA, 1969-80; asst. dir. Bio-Sci. Labs., Van Nuys, Calif., 1967-70, v.p., 1970-72, pres., 1972-77, bd. dirs., 1970-77; exec. v.p. Nat. Health Labs., La Jolla, 1977-80; prof. pathology SUNY Health Sci. Ctr., Syracuse, 1980-86, Harvard U. Med. Sch., Boston, 1986—; v.p., dir. clin. labs. Brigham and Women's Hosp., 1986—. Cons. to numerous govt. agys. and industry; vis. prof. Soroka Med. Ctr., Beersheva, Israel, 1982. Author: Clinical Chemistry, 1974; contbr. more than 150 articles to profl. pubs.; patentee in field lab. sci. Capt. USPHS, 1960-62. Mem. Coll. Am. Pathologists, Acad. Clin. Lab. Scientists, Am. Soc. Clin. Pathology, Clin. Lab. Mgmt. Assn., Alpha Omega Alpha. Republican. Jewish. Avocations: tennis, golf, travel, classical music. Office: Brigham and Women's Hosp 75 Francis St Boston MA 02115-6106 E-mail: jwinkelman@partners.org.

WINKELMAN, JOHNNY MARTIN, lawyer, real estate development consultant and indian gaming consultant; b. Bell, Calif., Nov. 17, 1946; s. Roy Hugh and Phyllis Lorrane (Jansen) W.; m. Brenda Jean Scott, July 4, 1979; children; Brian, Jennifer, Kristina, Diana. AA, Southwestern Coll., 1974; LLB,

Western State U., 1976, JD, 1979. Bar: Calif. 1979, U.S. Dist. Ct. (so. dist.) Calif. 1979. Carpenter Local 1492, Los Angeles, 1969-70; constrn. mgr. Winkelman Constrn., Whittier, Calif., 1970-71; bldg. insp. City of Chula Vista, 1971-76; sr. bldg. insp. City of Nat. City, 1976-79; law practice San Diego, 1979—. Cons., instr. Southwestern Coll., 1979-85; corp. counsel Palm Homes, Inc., Chula Vista, 1979-88; tribal councilor Viejas Band Mission Indians, Alpine, Calif., 1985-91; advisor Bd. Appeals City of Chula Vista, 1981-88; CEO Viejas Casino & Turf, Club, 1991-99; bd. dirs. Multimedia Games, Inc., Austin, tex. Served with U.S. Army, 1966-68. Mem. Calif. State Bar, Kiwanis. Baptist. Avocations: skiing, travel, boating. E-mail: johncwinkelman.ws@CTS.COM.

WINKELMAN, LOIS ANAYA, womens health nurse; b. Chgo., Jan. 9, 1961; d. Jose Matias and Rosemary (Rocha) Anaya; m. Randy E. Winkelman, May 31, 1986; 1 child, Amanda Maria. BS, Rush U., 1984, MS, 1988. Staff nurse Rush Presbyn. St. Lukes, Chgo., 1984-88, clin. nurse specialist, 1988—. Author: (with others) Women & Cancer, 1997. Mem. Soc. Gynecol. Nurse Oncologists (sec.-treas. 1991-95, pres. 1996-98). Roman Catholic. Office: Rush Presbyn St Lukes Med Ctr 1750 W Harrison St Ste 720 Chicago IL 60612-3824

WINKELSTEIN, WARREN, JR. physician, educator; b. Syracuse, N.Y., July 1, 1922; s. Warren and Evelyn (Neiman) W.; children: Rebecca Winkelstein Yamin, Joshua, Shoshana; m. Veva Kerrigan, Feb. 14, 1976. BA, U. N.C., 1942; MD cum laude, Syracuse U., 1947; MPH, Columbia U., 1950. Diplomate Am. Bd. Preventive Medicine. Intern Charity Hosp., New Orleans, 1947-48; with ICA (Vietnam), 1951-53; from dir. div. communicable disease control to 1st dep. comdr. local, environ. health svcs. Erie County Health Dept., 1953-62; from assoc. prof. to prof. SUNY, Buffalo, 1962-68; prof. epidemiology, dean pub. health U. Calif., Berkeley, 1972-96, prof. emeritus, 1996. Dir. Internat. Environ. Epidemiology Inst., 1997. Author: Basic Readings in Epidemiology, 1972; contbr. articles profl. jours. With AUS, 1944-46. Mem. APHA, AAAS, Internat. Am. Epidemiol. Socs., Am. Heart Assn. Address: Dept Epidemiol Univ Calif Sch Pub Health Berkeley CA 94720-7360

WINKENWERDER, WILLIAM, JR. federal agency administrator; b. Apr. 27, 1954; BS, Davidson Coll., 1976; MD, U. N.C., 1981; MBA, U. Pa., 1986; postgrad., Stanford U., 1991. Resident internal medicine N.C. Meml. Hosp. U. N.C., 1981-84; instr. dept. medicine Sch. Medicine U. Pa., 1984-87; spl. asst. to adminstr. Health Care Financing Adminstrn. U.S. Dept. Health and Human Svcs., 1987-88; dir. quality assurance and utilization mgmt. Southeast Permanente Med. Group, Kaiser Permanente, Atlanta, 1988-90, assoc. med. dir., 1990-92; v.p. CMO so. ops. Prudential Health Care, 1992-95; v.p. primary care svcs. Emory Health Care, 1996-98; assoc. v.p. health affairs Robert Woodruff Health Scis. Ctr. Emory U., 1996-98; exec. v.p. health care svcs., vice chmn. Blue Cross Blue Shield Mass., Boston, 1998—; asst. secy. hlth. affairs U.S. Dept. Defense, Washington, 2001—. Mem. exec. com. Emory Healthcare, Emory Clinic, 1996-98; chmn. CMO com. Prudential Healthcare, 1992-95; bd. dirs. Care Sci. Corp., Wharton Sch. Bus. Health Care Alumni, Fed. Employees Program-Blue Cross Blue Shield Assn., The Reed and Barton Co.; founder HCFA Effectiveness Initiative, U.S. Dept. Health and Human Svcs., participant Task Forces on Health and Human Svcs. AIDS and Minority Health, 1987-88, U.S. Pub. Health Risk Assessment and Quality Assurance, Sec.'s Minority Health, Sec.'s Catastophic Illness; rep. Prudential on Med. Dirs. Com. on Group Health Assn. Am.; spkr. in field. Contbr. articles to profl. pubs. Kaiser Family Found. fellow, 1984-86, 87-88, Kellogg Pub. Health Policy fellow U. Pa., 1986, Wharton Washington fellow U. Pa., 1986. Mem. AMA, Am. Coll. Physicians, Am. Coll. Physician Execs., Am. Assn. Health Plans (bd. dirs.), Health Care Forum's Physican Leader Network, Davidson Coll. Alumni Assn. Office: US Dept Defense Hlth Affairs 1200 Defense Pentagon Washington DC 20301-1200 Office Fax: 703-697-4197.*

WINKLEMAN, JOHN SANDLER, public relations executive; b. Phila., June 25, 1955; s. Harris and Ruth Elizabeth (Sandler) W.; m. Katherine Lee Knapp, May 6, 1984; 1 child, Pendray Gregory. BA, Clark U., Worcester, Mass., 1977; postgrad., NYU, 1978-79; grad. Inst. Not-for-Profit Mgmt., Columbia U., 1997. Dir. Greenwich House Music Sch., N.Y.C., 1979-81; exec. asst. to pres., asst. sec. bd. trustees Clark U., Worcester, Mass., 1981-85; sr. account exec. Hill and Knowlton, N.Y.C., 1985-87; account supr., client svcs. mgr. Dorf and Stanton, 1987-88; v.p. Ruder Finn, 1988-90; founder, ptnr. Winkleman Co. LLC, 1990—. Adj. faculty Columbia U. Bus. Sch. Inst. for Not-for Profit Mgmt., N.Y.C., 1997—; spkr. pub. and pvt. elem. schs., N.Y. and Pa., 1994—; spkr. pub. rels., mktg. and crisis comms., not-for-profit and assns., 1998—. Illustrator (children's books) Firehouse, 1994, 96, Police Patrol, 1996; one-man shows include Tiffany & Co., 1980, 90, Clark U., 1993, U. Mass. Med. Sch., 1983. Mem., vice chairperson cmty. bd. Mt. Sinai Med. Ctr., N.Y.C., 1992—; trustee Mt. Sinai Hosp., 1998—; bd. dirs. Civitas, N.Y.C., 1995—; past trustee New Eng. Sci. Mus.; bd. dirs. Worcester Conv. and Visitors Bur., Worcester Heritage and Preservation Soc.; mem. Worcester Cultural Commn.; co-chmn. N.Y.C. Nat. Philanthropy Day, 2002-. Mem. Assn. Fundraising Profls. (bd. dirs. Greater N.Y. chpt. 2001—, co-chair Nat. Philanthopy Day NYC 2001, 02). Jewish. Home: 340 E 93d St Ste 18M New York NY 10128-5557 Office: 318 E 93 Ste 1C New York NY 10128

WINKLER, ALLEN WARREN, lawyer, educator; b. Chgo., Dec. 11, 1954; s. Maurice A. and Florence (Klein) W.; m. Bett C. Gibson, Nov. 1, 1986. BS, No. Ill. U., 1977; JD, Tulane U., 1981. Bar: La. 1982, Ill. 1982, U.S. Dist. Ct. (ea. dist.) La. 1982, U.S. Dist. Ct. (mid. dist.) La. 1987. Atty. La. Legal Clinic, New Orleans, 1982-84; pvt. practice law, 1984-85; staff atty. Oak Tree Savs. Bank, S.S.B., 1985-87, sr. atty., asst. v.p., 1987-90; atty. FDIC/Resolution Trust Corp., Baton Rouge, 1991-92, sr. atty. Atlanta, 1992-95; sr. corp. counsel Fleet Fin., Inc., 1996-97; pres. Legal Ease Inc., 1996—; corp. counsel Prudential Bank, 1997; gen. counsel, v.p. NCS Mortgage Svcs., Norcross, Ga., 1998-2000, gen. counsel, 1999-2000; exec. v.p., COO Companion Servicing Co., LLC, 1999-2000; corp. counsel Provident Bank, Atlanta, 2000-2001; sr. atty., v.p. SunTrust Bank, 2001—. Mem. faculty Franklin Coll. Ct. Reporting, Metairie, La., 1981-88; cons., guest lectr. paralegal studies Tulane U., New Orleans, 1982-90; guest lectr. U. New Orleans, 1988-90. Vol. Hawkins for Judge campaign, New Orleans. Mem. La. Bar Assn., Ill. Bar Assn. Home: 4754 Forest Glen Court Marietta GA 30066 Office: SunTrust Bank 2950 SunTrust Plz 303 Peachtree St NE Atlanta GA 30308 E-mail: allen.winkler@suntrust.com.

WINKLER, CHARLES HOWARD, lawyer, investment management company executive; b. N.Y.C., Aug. 4, 1954; s. Joseph Conrad and Geraldine Miriam (Borok) W.; m. Joni S. Taylor, Aug. 28, 1993. BBA with highest distinction, Emory U., 1976; JD, Northwestern U., 1979. Bar: Ill. 1979, U.S. Dist. Ct (no. dist.) Ill. 1979. Assoc. Levenfeld & Kanter, Chgo., 1979-80, Kanter & Eisenberg, Chgo., 1980-84, ptnr., 1985-86, Neal Gerber & Eisenberg, Chgo., 1986-96; sr. mng. dir., COO Citadel Investment Group, LLC, 1996—2001; sr. mng. dir. Citadel Trading Group, 1996—2000, Aragon Investments Ltd., Chgo., 1996—2000. Bd. dirs. Kensington Global Strategies Fund, Ltd., Antaeus Internat. Investments, Ltd., Jackson Investment Fund Ltd., Citadel Investment Group (Europe) Ltd., chief oper. officer, and sr. mng. dir. Amaranth Advisors, LLC, 2001—. Author: (with others) Basic Tax Shelters, 1982, Limited Liability Companies: The Entity of Choice, 1995; mng. editor Northwestern Jour. Internat. Law and Bus., 1979. Mem. ABA (mem. sect. on taxation), Beta Gamma Sigma. Office: Citadel Investment Group LLC 225 W Washington St Fl 9 Chicago IL 60606-2418 Home: 10 Taconic Rd Greenwich CT 06830-3428

WINKLER, DANA JOHN, lawyer; b. Wichita, Kans., Jan. 2, 1944; s. Donald Emil and Hazel Claire (Schmitter) W.; m. Mary Ann Seiwert, Oct. 14, 1967; 1 child, Jonathan. BA, Wichita State U., 1967; JD, Washburn Law Sch., 1971. Staff writer Wichita (Kans.) Eagle & Beacon, 1961-67; ptnr. Davis, Bruce, Davis & Winkler, Wichita, 1972-77; asst. city atty. City of Wichita, 1977-99; dir. Wichita Mcpl. Fed. Credit Union, 1980—, pres., 1982, 99-2000, sec.-treas., 1994-98, v.p., 1998-99. Dir. Deaf and Hard of Hearing Counseling Svc., 1979-80. Vol. Sedgwick County United Way, Wichita, 1973-74; vice-chmn. Wichita Pub. Schs. Spl. Edn. Adv. Coun., 1987-89. 1st lt. U.S. Army, 1967-69. Mem. Kans. Bar Assn., Wichita Bar Assn., Masons. Republican. Roman Catholic. Home and Office: 1621 Harlan St Wichita KS 67212-1842 E-mail: djwinkler@aol.com.

WINKLER, DOLORES EUGENIA, retired health facility administrator; b. Milw., Aug. 10, 1929; d. Charles Peter and Eugeneia Anne (Zamka) Kowalski; m. Donald James Winkler, Aug. 18, 1951; 1 child David John. Grad., Milw. Bus. Inst., 1949. Acct. Curative Rehab. Ctr., Milw., 1949-60; staff acct. West Allis (Wis.) Meml. Hosp., 1968-70, chief acct., 1970-78, reimbursement analyst, 1978-85, dir. budgets and reimbursement, 1985-95; ret., 1995. Mem. adv. coun., fin. com. Tau Home Health Care Agy., Milw., 1981—83. Mem.: Inst. Mgmt. Accts. (pres. 1983—84, nat. dir. 1986—88, pres. Mid Am. Regional Coun. 1988—89, award of excellence 1989), Healthcare Fin. Mgmt. Assn. (pres. 1989—90, Follmer Bronze award 1980, Reeves Silver award 1986, Muncie Gold award 1989, medal of honor 1993), Beta Chi Rho (pres. 1948). Avocations: travel, photography, golf. Home: 12805 W Honey Ln New Berlin WI 53151-2652

WINKLER, GAIL CASKEY, design historian, writer, educator; b. Chgo., Aug. 5, 1942; d. Robert E. and Ethel (Barquist) Caskey; m. Robert H. Winkler, Jan. 22, 1964 (div. 1976); m. Roger W. Moss, July 19, 1981. BA, Beloit (Wis.) Coll., 1964; MA, U. Wis., 1971, MS, 1977, PhD, 1988. Instr. U. Wis., Madison, 1976-81; sr. ptnr. LCA Assocs., Phila., 1982—; adj. faculty U. Pa., 1986—; asst. prof. U. Del., 1991-93. Author: Victorian Interior Decoration, 1986, Victorian Exterior Decoration, 1987, Floor Coverings for Historic Buildings, 1988, The Well-Appointed Bath, 1989, An Analysis of Drapery, 1993; (museum installations include), William Conner House, Conner Prairie, Fishers, Ind., Lanier Mansion, Madison, Ind., Tudor Hall in Pamplin Park, Petersburg, Va., Fairlawn Mansion, Superior, Wis., Adams House Mus., Deadwood, S.D., Villa Louis, Prairie du Chien, Wis., Hixon House, LaCrosse, Wis., Campbell House Mus., St. Louis, Dr. Richard Eells House, Quincy, Ill., (projects include) studies of the historic finishes and furnishings of the U.S. Senate and House , Chambers , City Hall, Phila., Capitol of the Commonwealth Pa., Rutherford B. Hayes house, Fremont, Ohio , Buchanan house, U.S. Naval Acad. , Anderson Cottage (summer White House Abraham Lincoln), Washington , D.C. , Wright Bros.' Printing Shop, Dayton, Ohio. Fellow Am. Soc. Interior Designers (bd. dirs. Pa. East chap. 1983-88, 2001—, Athena award 1989, Medallist award 1995), Found. Interior Design Edn. and Rsch. (rsch. com. 1986-96). Office: 604 S Washington Sq Philadelphia PA 19106-4118

WINKLER, GUNTHER, biotechnology executive, drug development expert; b. Laa Thaya, Noe, Austria, Aug. 20, 1957; came to U.S., 1986; s. Kurt and Irmgard W.; m. Maria, Sept. 11, 1979; children: Claudia, Marc. MS in Biochemistry, U. Vienna, Austria, 1983, PhD in Biochemistry, 1986. Rsch. assoc. Inst. Virology U. Vienna, 1982-86; postdoctoral fellow U. Medicine and Dentistry of N.J., Piscataway, 1986-88; rsch. scientist Biogen, Inc., Cambridge, Mass., 1988-91, dir. med. ops., 1991-97, program exec., 1995—2000, sr. dir. drug devel., 2001—02, v.p. strategic initiatives, 2002—. Contbr. to over 100 sci. confs.; expert presentations and articles on drug devel. strategies and mgmt. of clin. studies, chair clin. confs. Contbr. more than 30 articles to profl. jours. Recipient Outstanding Achievement award Austrian Soc. Microbiology, 1986. Achievements include research in vriology dealing with structure function relationship of proteins, vaccine development, flaviviruses, HIV; industrial research in immunology CD4, CD4-toxins, complement proteins; international clinical development of Angiomax and Beta-Interferon from phase I to phase III in cardiovascular indications, infectious diseases, and multiple sclerosis; preparations for FDA and international market approvals; registration of AVONEX, postmarketing studies; development of anti-inflammatory drug AMEVIVE & filing with FDA & EMEA in other countries, indications include psoriasis & psoriatric arthritis, rheumatoid arthritis, scleroderma & other autoimmune disorders; established drug development program in Japan. Home: 2 Davey Ln Winchester MA 01890-3170 Office: Biogen Inc 14 Cambridge Ctr Cambridge MA 02142-1481

WINKLER, HENRY RALPH, retired academic administrator, historian; b. Waterbury, Conn., Oct. 27, 1916; s. Jacob and Ethel (Rieger) W.; m. Clare Sapadin, Aug. 18, 1940; children— Allan Michael, Karen Jean; m. Beatrice Ross, Jan. 28, 1973. AB, U. Cin., 1938, MA, 1940; PhD, U. Chgo., 1947; hon. degrees, Lehigh U., 1974, Rutgers U., 1977, No. Ky. U., 1978, St. Thomas Inst., 1979, Hebrew Union Coll., 1980, Xavier U., 1981, U. Akron, 1984, U. Cin., 1987, Thomas More Coll., 1989. Instr. U. Cin., 1939-40; asst. prof. Roosevelt Coll., 1946-47; mem. faculty Rutgers U., 1947-77, prof. history, 1958-77, chmn. dept., 1960-64; dean Faculty Liberal Arts, 1967, vice provost, 1968-70, acting provost, 1970, v.p. for acad. affairs, 1970-72, sr. v.p. for acad. affairs, 1972-76, exec. v.p., 1976-77, U. Cin., 1977, pres., 1977-84, pres. emeritus, 1984—, Univ. prof. history, 1977-86, prof. emeritus, 1986—. Mng. editor Am. Hist. Rev., 1964-68; vis. prof. Bryn Mawr Coll., 1959-60, Harvard, summer 1964, Columbia, summer 1967; faculty John Hay Fellows Inst. Humanities, 1960-65; bd. overseers Hebrew Union Coll., 1984—. Author: The League of Nations Movement in Great Britain, 1914-19, 1952, Great Britain in the Twentieth Century, 1960, 2d edit., 1966; editor: (with K.M. Setton) Great Problems in European Civilization, 1954, 2d edit., 1966, Twentieth-Century Britain, 1977, Paths Not Taken: British Labour and International Policy in the Nineteen Twenties, 1994; mem. editorial bd. Historian, 1958-64, Liberal Edn., 1986—; mem. adv. bd. Partisan Rev., 1972-79; contbr. articles to jours., revs. Nat. chmn. European history advanced placement com. Coll. Entrance Exam. Bd., 1960-64; mem. Nat. Commn. on Humanities in Schs., 1967-68, Am. specialist Eastern Asia, 1968; exec. com. Conf. on Brit. Studies, 1968-75; chmn. bd. Nat. Humanities Faculty, 1970-73; chmn. adv. com. on history Coll. Entrance Exam. Bd., 1977-80; mem. council on acad. affairs, mem. bd. trustees, chmn., 1982-84; pres. Highland Park (N.J.). Bd. Edn., 1962-63; mem. exec. com. Nat. Assn. State Univs. and Land-Grant Colls., 1978-81, mem. Cin. Lit. Club, 1978—, pres., 1993—; bd. dirs. Am. Council on Edn., 1979-81; trustee Seasongood Good Govt. Found., 1979—, pres., 1991-93; trustee Thomas More Coll., 1986-93; mem. Ohio Indsl. Tech. and Enterprise Bd., 1983-89; bd. dirs. Nat. Civic League, 1986—, Planning Accreditation Bd., 1988—; mem. adv coun. U. Va.'s Coll at Wise, Ohio Regional Ctr. for Biotech., 1989. Fellow Am. Hist. Assn. Nat. Hist. Assn. Recipient Lifetime Humanities Coun., 1994— With USNR, 1943-46. Recipient Lifetime Achievement award N.Am. Conf. on Brit. Studies, 1995, Bishop William Hughes award for disting. svc. to Cath. higher edn. Thomas More Coll., 1997. Mem. Am. Hist. Assn., Phi Beta Kappa, Tau Kappa Alpha, Phi Alpha Theta. Clubs: Comml., Bankers, Cin., Lit. Office: U Cin 571 Langsam Library Cincinnati OH 45221-0001 E-mail: Henry.Winkler@uc.edu.

WINKLER, IRA SAMUEL, information security consultant, educator, author; b. Bklyn., Dec. 31, 1962; s. Seymour and Sheila (Kaplan) W.; m. Molly Ann Wray, Sept. 3, 1989; children: Matthew Ray, Jason Benjamin. BA, Syracuse U., 1984; MS, Bowie State U., 1989; PhD, U. Md., Balt., 1997. Computer sys. analyst Nat. Security Agy., Ft. Meade, Md., 1984-90; computer scientist Computer Scis. Corp., Hanover, 1990-92; sr. software engr. BTG, Inc., Vienna, 1992-93; faculty assoc. Johns Hopkins U., Balt., 1994—; project mgr. Sci. Applications Internat. Corp., Annapolis, Md., 1993-96; dir. technology Nat. Computer Security Assn., Carlisle, Pa., 1996—; pres. Argo Prodns., Las Vegas, Nev., 1997—. U.S. adv. group Internat. Stds. Orgsn. Com. on Ergonomics, 1993—; mem. ANSI 200 Com. for Human Computer Interaction, 1993—; adj. faculty Anne Arundel C.C., Arnold, Md., 1990-92; adj. asst. prof. U. Md., College Park, 1992—; presenter in field. Author: Corporate Espionage, 1997; co-author: Through the Eyes of the Enemy, 1997; co-author: People Before Technology, 1991, The Official Internetworld Internet Security Handbook, 1995, The Internet and Internetworking Security Handbook, 1997; editl. asst. Sigchi Bull., 1994—; reviewer MIS Quar., 1992—; contbg. editor: Internetwork, 1996—; contbr. articles to profl. jours. Mem. Assn. for Computing Machinery, Info. Sys. Security Assn., Nat. Computer Security Assn. (cons. 1995—), Soc. for Competitive Intelligence Profls., Armed Forces Comm. and Electronics Assn. (scholarship com. 1990), Chesapeake Bay Country Wanderers (club rep. 1995-96), Mensa, Intertel, Phi Kappa Phi. Avocations: volksmarching, karate. Home: 35 Sunset Dr Severna Park MD 21146-3229 Office: Nat Computer Security Assn 1200 Walnut Bottom Rd Carlisle PA 17013-7635

WINKLER, IRWIN, motion picture producer; b. N.Y.C., May 28, 1934; s. Sol and Anna Winkler. BA, NYU, 1955. Mailroom messenger William Morris Agy., N.Y.C., 1955-62; motion picture producer, owner Winkler Films, Culver City, Calif., 1982—. Pres., Chartoff-Winkler Prodns., 1966—. Producer: Rocky, 1976 (10 Acad. award nominations, winner 3 including Best Picture, Los Angeles Film Critics award for best picture), They Shoot Horses Don't They, 1969 (9 Acad. award nominations), Nickelodeon, 1976, The Gambler, 1974, Up the Sandbox, 1972, The New Centurions, 1972, Point Blank, 1967, Double Trouble, 1967, Leo the Last, 1970 (Best Dir. award Cannes Film Festival, Belgrade Film Festival), The Strawberry Statement, 1970 (Jury prize Cannes Film Festival), The Split, 1968, Breakout, 1975, Believe in Me, 1971, The Gang That Couldn't Shoot Straight, 1971, The Mechanic, 1972, Busting, 1974, S.P.Y.S, 1974, Peeper, 1975, New York, New York, 1977, Valentino, 1977, Uncle Joe Shannon, 1978, Comes a Horseman, 1978, Rocky II, 1979, Raging Bull, 1980 (8 Acad. award nominations, winner 2, Los Angeles Film Critics award for best picture), Rocky III, 1981, True Confessions, 1981, Author, Author, 1982, The Right Stuff, 1983 (8 Acad. award nominations), Rocky IV, 1984, Revolution, 1985, 'Round Midnight, 1986 (2 Acad. award nomiations, Acad. award Best Original Score), Betrayed, 1988 (Chgo. Film Festival Lifetime Irwin Achievement award 1987), Goodfellas, 1990 (6 Acad. award nominationThe Net, 1995, The Juror, 1996, Life as a House, 2001, The Shipping News, 2001, Enough, 2002; dir, writer: The Net, 1995, Guilty by Suspicion,1991.s, winner 1, Brit. Acad. award Best Picture, N.Y. Film Critics Best Picture, L.A. Film Critics Best Picture), Rocky V, 1990, Music Box, 1990 (Golden Bear award for best film Berlin Film Festival); writer/dir.: Guilty by Suspicion, 1991 (U.S. selection Cannes Film Festival); producer/dir.: Night and the City, 1992 (N.Y. Film Festival, London Film Festival), The Net, 1995, The Juror, 1997, First Sight, 1998; retrospectives Brit. Film Inst., 1989, Chgo. Film Festival, 1989, Mus. Modern Art, N.Y.C., 1990, L.A. County Mus. Art, 1992. Served with U.S. Army, 1951-53. Named Commander d'Artes et de Lettres, French Govt. Minister of Culture, 1985. Mem. Am. Film Inst. (bd. govs.), Prodrs. Guild Am. (bd. dirs.). Office: Winkler Films 211 S Beverly Dr Ste 200 Beverly Hills CA 90212-3882*

WINKLER, JOANN MARY, secondary school educator; b. Savanna, Ill., Dec. 17, 1955; d. Donald Edgar and Genevieve Eleanor (Withhart) Winkler; m. Russell Arthur Ehlers, May 25, 1990; 1 child, Genevieve Rose Winkler Ehlers. BS in Art Edn., No. Ill. U., 1979; MA in Art Edn., N.E. Mo. State U., 1984. Tchr. art, chmn. dept. art Clinton (Iowa) H.S., 1979—. Coll. for Kids instr. Area Edn. Agy. #9, Clinton, summers, 1986—, Davenport, summers, 1987—; instr. St. Ambrose U., Clinton, 1990, Mt. St. Clare Coll., Clinton, 1993-98. Costume designer Utah Mus. Theatre, "Two by Two," 1987; exhibited in group shows at Clinton Art Assn., 1990-93. Judge Art in the Park, Clinton, 1988, 93; co. mgr. Utah Mus. Theager, Ogden, 1987; founding bd. dirs. Art's Alive, Clinton, 1985-86; bd. dirs. Gateway Contemporary Ballet, Clinton, 1987-89; founding com. mem. Louis Sullivan's Van Allen Bldg. Jr. Mus., Clinton, 1991-93. Recipient Gold Key Group award Clinton Sch. Bd., 1990, Gold Key Individual award, 1989; R.I. Sch. Design scholar, 1989, Alliance for Ind. Colls. of Art scholar, summers 1988. Mem. NEA, Ill. Art Edn. Assn., Chgo. Art Inst., Clinton Art Assn., Art Educators of Iowa, Nat. Art Edn. Assn., PEO. Avocations: swimming, travel, theater. Home: 722 Melrose Ct Clinton IA 52732-5508 Office: Clinton High Sch 817 8th Ave S Clinton IA 52732-5698

WINKLER, JOHN CHARLES, information administrator; b. Washington, June 15, 1961; s. John William and Suzanne W.; m. Gloria Frida Mallma, Mar. 7, 1996. BS in Internat. Studies, Norwich U., 1984. Commd. ensign U.S Army, 1984, advanced through grades to capt., 1998; proposal devel. mgr. AC Tech., Fairfax, Va., 1998-2000; bus. devel. coor. Subsys. Tech., Arlington, 1999-2000; program analyst Future Tech., McLean, 2000; mil. analyst Emergent Info. Tech., Vienna, 2000—. Cons. foreign affairs U.S. Army. Republican. Roman Catholic. Avocations: ancient histroy, political and constitutional development, international affairs. Home: PO Box 10812 Alesandria VA 22310

WINKLER, JOSEPH CONRAD, former recreational products manufacturing executive; b. Newark, May 20, 1916; s. Charles and Mollie (Abrams) W.; m. Geraldine M. Borok, Sept. 20, 1953; children: Charles H., David J. BS, NYU, 1941. Gen. mgr. Indsl. Washing Machine Corp., New Brunswick, N.J., 1941-48; controller Mojud Corp., N.Y.C., 1948-52; controller, asst. treas. Barbizon Corp., 1952-57; controller Ideal Toy Corp., 1957-58, dir. fin. and adminstrn., 1960-62, v.p. fin., 1962-68, sr. v.p. fin., 1968-78, exec. v.p., COO, dir., 1978-81, pres., dir., 1981-83; controller McGregor-Doniger, Inc., 1958-59; exec. in residence, bus. adv. coun. Sch. Bus. Adminstrn., Montclair (N.J.) State U., 1983-90. Dir. Ideal of Australia Ltd., Melbourne, 1963-82, Ideal of Canada Ltd., Toronto, 1963-82, Ideal of Japan Ltd., Tokyo and Kiowa, 1963-80, Ideal Toy Co. Ltd., High Wycombe and Wokingham, Eng., 1966-82, Arxon Spiel & Freizeit GmBH, Rotgau, Germany, 1968-82, Perfekta Ltd. and Hollis Industries Ltd., Hong Kong, 1970-74, Ideal Loisirs S.A., Paris, 1972-82. Mem. editl. bd. Issues in Internat. Bus., 1985-92. Committeeman, troop treas. Boy Scouts Am., Tenafly, N.J., 1965-71; bd. dirs. N.Y. League Hard of Hearing, 1982-88; active Nat. Roster Sci. and Splized. Pers., War Manpower Commn., 1941-46. Served with Office Statis. Control USAAF, 1945. Mem. Fin. Execs. Inst. Home: 3546 S Ocean Blvd Apt 605 Palm Beach FL 33480-5720 E-mail: chada@worldnet.att.net.

WINKLER, KATHERINE MAURINE, management consultant, educator; b. Louisville, Nov. 29, 1940; d. Myrick and Maurine (Holland) W. Cert. in foreign studies, Inst. for Am. Univs., 1961; BA, Transylvania U., 1963. Market rsch. field supr. Procter & Gamble, Cin., 1963-65; Eng. tchr. Louisville Ky. Sch. System, 1967-68; mgmt. and staff positions in sales, mktg., human resources, total quality mgmt. and edn. IBM, Louisville, Lexington, Ky., Mpls., Cin., and Westchester, N.Y., 1968-93; pvt. practice N.Y.C., 1993—, Richmond, Va., 1993—. Adj. prof. NYU. Author: Leadership, 1982, Across the Board, Executive Excellence, Westchester Historian, The Scarsdale Inquirer; contbr. articles to publs. Com. mem. Mpls. Cultural Affairs Com., 1970, Village of Tarrytown (N.Y.) Main St. com., 1981—82; bd. dirs., chair trustee affairs com. Westchester County Hist. Soc., Elmsford, NY, 1989—99; mem. mgmt., bus., econs. study group NYU, 1995—97; vol. cons. White Plains Hosp. Ctr., 1998—2000; bd. dirs. Fan Dist. Assn. , Richmond, 2002. Named Outstanding Young Woman of Am., 1972. Mem. ASTD, Human Resource Planning Soc., Ky. Col., Soc. for Human Resource Mgmt., New Directions Human Resource Consultants Roundtable, Fan Woman's Club (bd. dirs. 2002--). Home: 1423 Grove Ave Richmond VA 23220-4601 E-mail: kittywink@ATTGlobal.net.

WINKLER, LEE B. business consultant; b. Buffalo; s. Jack W. and Caroline (Marienthal) W.; 1 child, James; m. Maria Mal Verde. BS cum laude, NYU, 1945, MS cum laude, 1947. Pres. LBW, Inc. (formerly Winkler Assocs. Ltd.), N.Y.C., Beverly Hills, Calif., 1948—, Winkler Assocs. Ltd., Beverly Hills, Calif., and N.Y.C., 1958—; exec. dir. Global Bus. Mgmt. Inc., 1967—. V.p. Bayly Martin & Fay Inc., N.Y.C., 1965-68, John C. Paige & Co., N.Y.C., 1968-71; cons. Albert G. Ruben Co., Beverly Hills, 1971— Served with AUS, 1943-45. Decorated chevalier comdr. Order Holy Cross Jerusalem, also spl. exec. asst., charge d'affaires, 1970; chevalier comdr. Sovereign Order Cyprus, 1970 Mem. Nat. Acad. TV Arts and Scis., Nat. Acad. Recording Arts and Scis., Beverly Hills C. of C., Phi Beta Kappa, Beta Gamma Sigma, Mu Gamma Tau, Psi Chi Omega. Office: 15250 Ventura Blvd Sherman Oaks CA 91403-3201 *In the final analysis, the bottom line, if you will— the only thing that truly matters in life are those friends and family that hold you dear to them. Success, and its attendant monies, rise and fall like the tides, and even vanish at times, but earned love is as constant as the earth's rotation is independent of the tides.*

WINKLER, PAUL FRANK, JR. astrophysicist, educator; b. Nashville, Nov. 10, 1942; s. Paul Frank and Estelle (Pye) W.; m. Geraldine Huck, Aug. 20, 1966 (div. 1979); children: Katharine Estelle, Johanna Pye; m. Janet Pippitt Beers, June 25, 1983; stepchildren: Sarah Creighton Beers, Nathan Pippitt Beers. BS, Calif. Inst. Tech., 1964; A.M., Harvard U., 1965, PhD, 1970. From instr. to prof. physics Middlebury Coll., Vt., 1969—, chmn. dept., 1980-88, William R. Kenan Jr. prof. physics, 1984-87, chmn. nat. scis. div., 1988-93, asst. to pres. for sci. planning, 1993-96, Gamaliel Painter Bicentennial prof. physics, 1997—. Vis. scientist MIT, Cambridge, 1973-74, 78-80; sr. vis. fellow Inst. Astronomy, U. Cambridge, 1985-86; vis. resident astronomer Cerro Tololo InterAm. Observatory, La Serena, Chile, 1990-91, 96-97; vis. fellow Joint Inst. for Laboratory Astrophysics, U. Colo., Boulder, 1991. Contbr. articles to profl. jours. NSF fellow, 1965-69, Alfred P. Sloan Found. fellow, 1976-80 Mem. Am. Phys. Soc., Am. Astron. Soc., Internat. Astron. Union, Coun. on Undergrad. Rsch., Sigma Xi. Office: Middlebury Coll Dept Physics Middlebury VT 05753

WINKLER, PENELOPE KELLOGG, foundation executive; b. Queens, Aug. 15, 1956; d. Frank David and Phyllis Laurine (Kellogg) W.; m. Ross Vann Waldrop, 1987. BA in English, Atlantic Union Coll., 1978; MA in English, Loma Linda U., 1983. Med. editor Loma Linda (Calif.) U., 1981-83; assoc. editor Spectrum, Assn. Adventist Forums, Takoma Park, Md., 1983-85; devel. assoc. World Wildlife Fund/Conservation Found., Washington, 1985—. Instr. Columbia Union Coll., Takoma Park, 1983-85. Home: 609 Ritchie Ave Silver Spring MD 20910-5240 Office: World Wildlife Fund Conservation Found 1250 24th St NW Fl 6 Washington DC 20037-1193

WINKLER, PETER ALEXANDER, plastic surgeon; b. May 1, 1950; MD, Semmelweis Med. U., 1979. Pres. Seacoast Plastic Surgeons PA, Dover, N.H., 1989—. Office: 660 Central Ave Dover NH 03820

WINKLER, SHELDON, dentist, educator; b. N.Y.C., Jan. 25, 1932; s. Ben and Lillian (Barsh) W.; m. Sandra M. Cohen, Aug. 13, 1961; children: Mitchell, Lori. BA, Washington Sq. Coll., 1953; DDS, NYU, 1956. Asst. prof. denture prosthesis NYU Coll. Dentistry, N.Y.C., 1958-61, 66-68, rsch. asst. prof., 1962-63; dir. materials rsch. Consol. Metal Products Industries Inc., Albany, N.Y., 1963-65, cons. materials rsch., 1966-68; asst. prof. removable prosthodontics sch. dentistry SUNY, Buffalo, 1968-70, assoc. prof., 1970-79; prof., chmn. dept. prosthodontics Temple U. Sch. Dentistry, Phila., 1979-86, 94-96, asst. dean for advanced studies, continuing edn./rsch., 1987-89, acting asst. dean, 1993-95, prof. restorative dentistry, 1996—. Asst. dir. dental dept. NYU Med. Ctr. Goldwater Meml. Hosp., NYC, 1966—68, vis. dentist dental dept., 1966—68; attending in prosthodontics E.J. Meyer Meml. Hosp., Buffalo, 1975—79; postgrad instr. First Dist. Dental Soc. NY, NYC, 1963—; cons. Coe Labs., Chgo., 1967—87, Harkness Ctr., Buffalo, Rosa Coplon Home & Infirmary, Buffalo, 1970—79, Erie C.C., Buffalo, 1979—, Lever Bros. Co., NYC, 1981—, VA Hosp., Phila., 1989—, Ivoclar N. Am., Amherst, NY, 2000—; lectr. dept. dental hygiene NYC C.C., 1967—68; hon. prof. Pierre Fauchard Sch. Dentistry, Asuncion, Paraguay, 1999—. Author: (with A. Davidoff and M.H.M. Lee) Dentistry for the Special Patient: The Aged, Chronically Ill and Handicapped, 1972, Essentials of Complete Denture Prosthodontics, 1979, 2d edit., 1988; editor: Resins in Dentistry, 1975, Complete Dentures, 1977, Removable Prosthodontics, 1984, Jour. Implant Dentistry, 1990-97; sr. editor Jour. Oral Implantology, 2000—; contbr. articles to profl. lit.; co-designer McGowan-Winkler complete denture trays. Served as capt. AUS, 1956-58, 61-62. Recipient Outstanding Layman award Vocat. Tech. Alumni and Student Assn., SUNY, Buffalo, 1974, Internat. Edn. award Internat. Congress Oral Implantologists, 1992, journalism award Internat. Coll. Dentists, 1993, Academic Devotion award Chulalongkorn U., Bangkok, 1995. Fellow Am. Coll. Dentists, Greater N.Y. Acad. Prosthodontics; mem. ADA, Internat. Assn. Dental Rsch., Am. Assn. Dental Schs., Am. Acad. Implant Prosthodontics (pres.-elect), Sci. Rsch. Soc. Am., Acad. Plastics Rsch., Am. Prosthodontic Soc., Am. Soc. Geriatric Dentistry, Internat. Congress of Oral Implantologists, Sigma Xi, Sigma Epsilon Delta, Omicron Kappa Upsilon. Home: 1224 Liberty Bell Dr Cherry Hill NJ 08003-2759 Office: Sch Dentistry Temple U Philadelphia PA 19140 E-mail: swinkdent@aol.com.

WINKLER, STEVEN ROBERT, hospital administrator; b. Chattanooga, Dec. 4, 1953; s. David Wilfred and Margaret (Tepper) W.; m. Monica Sue Nijoka, July 11, 1987; children: Megan Leigh, Sara Elizabeth, Alyssa Lauren. BA, Vanderbilt U., 1976; M in Health Adminstrn., Duke U., 1978. Cert. healthcare risk mgr. CPHRM. Asst. adminstr. Tepper Hosp. and Clinic, Chattanooga, 1978-79, adminstr., 1979-80; assoc. exec. dir. Humana Hosp.-Brandon (Fla.), 1981-83, Humana Hosp.-Bennett, 1983-84; v.p. ops. Baton Rouge Gen. Med. Ctr., 1984-86, v.p. mktg., 1986-88; v.p. risk mgmt. Gen. Health Systems, Baton Rouge, 1988-2001, v.p. patient svcs., 2001—. V.p. Beth Shalom Synagogue, 1990-93, pres., 1993-95, treas., 1997-2000, first v.p., 2000—; active Am. Diabetes Assn. (Baton Rouge, state chpts.), Arthritis Found., United Way of Baton Rouge, 1989, Crisis Intervention Ctr. Fellow Am. Soc. Healthcare Risk Mgmt. (cert. profl. healthcare risk mgmt., pres. midsouth region 1990); mem. Am. Coll. Healthcare Execs. (diplomat), Am. Hosp. Assn., Jewish Fedn. Greater Baton Rouge (v.p. 1990, pres. 1992-93), Tipmasters (pres., Tipmaster of Yr. 1989). Office: Baton Rouge Gen Med Ctr 3600 Florida Blvd Baton Rouge LA 70806 E-mail: steve_winkler@generalhealth.org.

WINKLER, VERA CORTADA (NINA WINKLER), retired government executive; b. Washington, Mar. 12, 1949; m. Edward Petty Winkler, May 25, 1974. BA, Lynchburg Coll., 1971; MPA, George Washington U., 1981; MBA, Harvard U., 1983. Emergency mgmt. specialist Fed. Emergency Mgmt. Agy., Washington, 1976-83; assoc. ICF Inc., 1983-84; policy analyst Office Mgmt. Budget, 1984-86; deputy dir. planning & evaluation svc. U.S. Dept. Edn., 1987-91, dir. guarantor and lender oversight staff, 1992-94, dir. policy tng. and analysis svc., office of student fin. assistance, 1995-99, ret., 2000. Dir. Y2K project U.S. Dept. Edn., 1998. Legis fellow U.S. Congress, Washington, 1994-95. Methodist.

WINKS, ROBIN WILLIAM, history educator; b. West Lafayette, Ind., Dec. 5, 1930; s. Evert McKinley and Jewell (Sampson) W.; m. Avril Flockton, Sept. 27, 1952; children: Honor Leigh, Eliot Myles. BA magna cum laude, U. Colo., 1952, MA, 1953; PhD with distinction, Johns Hopkins U., 1957; MA (hon.), Yale U., 1967; DLitt (hon.), U. Nebr., 1976, U. Colo., 1987; MA (hon.), Oxford U., 1992; DPhil, Westminster Coll., 1995. From instr. to Randolph W. Townsend prof. history Yale U., New Haven, 1957—, dir. office of spl. projects and founds., 1974-76, master Berkeley Coll., 1977-90, chair Can. studies, 1985-99. Eastman prof. Oxford U., 1992-93, chair studies in environment, 1993-96, Harmsworth prof. Oxford U., 1999-2000; chair dept. history Yale U., 1996-99. Author: Canada and the U.S., 1960, The Cold War, 1964, Historiography of the British Empire-Commonwealth, 1966, History of Malaysia, 1967, Age of Imperialism, 1969, Pastmasters, 1969; The Historian as Detective, 1969, A Forty-Year Minuet, 1970, The Blacks in Canada, 1971, Slavery, 1972, An American's Guide to Britain, 1977, Other Voices, Other Views, 1978, Relevance of Canadian History, 1979, Western Civilization, 1979, Detective Fiction, 1980, Modus Operandi, 1982, History of Civilization, 1984, Cloak and Gown, 1987, Asia in Western Fiction, 1990, Frederick Billings, 1991, The Imperial Revolution, 1994, Laurance S. Rockefeller, Catalyst for Conservation, 1997, Mystery and Suspense Writers, 1998, Oxford History British Empire: Historiography, 1999, To Stimulate to Some Action, 2001. Cultural attache U.S. Embassy, London, 1969-71; chair Nat. Park System Adv. Bd., Washington, 1981-83, bicentennial com. for Internat. Confs. of Americanists Dept. State, 1974-77. Smith-Mundt prof. U. Malaya, 1962; Inst. Commonwealth Studies at U. London fellow, 1966-67; Guggenheim fellow, 1976-77; grantee Social Sci. Rsch. Coun., 1959, 75; Resident scholar Sch. Am. Rsch., 1985, 91, 94. Fellow Royal Hist. Soc., Explorers Club; mem. Am. Hist. Assn., Can. Hist. Assn., Royal Commonwealth Soc. (life), Yale Club (N.Y.C.), Athenaeum, Spl. Forces Club. Office: Yale U Dept History PO Box 208324A New Haven CT 06520-8324

WINMILL, B. LYNN, judge; m. Judy Jones; 4 children. BA, Idaho State U., 1974; JD, Harvard U., 1977. Atty. Holland and Hart, Denver, 1977-79, Hawley, Troxell, Ennis and Hawley, Pocatello, Idaho, 1984-87; judge Idaho Sixth Jud. Dist. Ct., 1987-95; chief judge U.S. Dist. Ct. Idaho, Boise. Office: US Dist Ct Idaho US Courthouse 550 W Fort St 6th Fl Boise ID 83724-0001 Fax: (208) 334-9209.

WINN, ALBERT CURRY, clergyman; b. Ocala, Fla., Aug. 16, 1921; s. James Anderson and Elizabeth (Curry) W.; m. Grace Neely Walker, Aug. 29, 1944; children: Grace Walker (Mrs. Stewart E. Ellis), James Anderson, Albert Bruce Curry, Randolph Axson. AB, Davidson Coll., 1942, LLD, 1968; BD, Union Theol. Sem., Va., 1945, ThD, 1956; ThM, Princeton Theol. Sem., 1949; LLD, Stillman Coll., 1975. Ordained to ministry Presbyn. Ch., 1945; asst. prof. Davidson Coll., 1946-47; pastor Potomac Rural Parish, Va., 1948-53; prof. Bible Stillman Coll., 1953-60; prof. theology Louisville Presbyn. Theol. Sem., 1960-73, pres., 1966-73; pastor 2d Presbyn. Ch., Richmond, Va., 1974-81, N. Decatur Presbyn. Ch., Decatur, Ga., 1981-86. Moderator Presbyn. Synod Ala., 1958, Presbyn. Synod Ky., 1969, Gen. Assembly, Presbyn. Ch. in U.S., 1979; vis. prof. Union Theol. Sem. in Va., 1987, Columbia Theol. Sem., 1987, Louisville Presbyn. Theol. Sem., 1988; interim pastor Cen. Presbyn. Ch., Atlanta, 1989-90, St. Andrews Presbyn. Ch., Tucker, Ga., 1993-94; parish assoc. Trinity Prebyn. Ch., Winston-Salem, N.C., 1999—. Author: Layman's Bible Commentary on Acts, 1960, The Worry and Wonder of Being Human, 1966, Where Do I Go From Here, 1972, Proclamation Two: Epiphany, 1980, A Sense of Mission, 1981, Christ the Peacemaker, 1982, Plain Talk about the Apostles' Creed, 1985, The Christian Primer, 1990, Ain't Gonna Study War No More, 1993. Chmn. trustees Stillman Coll., 1965-70. Served as chaplain USNR, 1945-46. Mem. Phi Beta Kappa, Beta Theta Pi, Omicron Delta Kappa. Office: 212 Oakwood Ct Winston Salem NC 27103-1952

WINN, ANTHONY W. chess player, poet, screenwriter; b. Topeka, Aug. 14, 1958; s. Paul Winn and Ruby Green; m. Rhonda Guyle; 1 child, Samuel Harris. AA, St. Mary's Coll., Leavenworth, Kans., 1988. Owner Ind. World Chess Championships, Inc. Contbr. poetry to lit. publs. Vol. chess tchr. South Cen. Boys and Girls Club of Am. Recipient Golden Poet award, award of merit and hon. mention World of Poetry, 1990. Mem. Internat. Poetry Soc., U.S. Chess Fedn. (tournament dir. IWCCI), Wichita Chess Club (pres.). Home: PO Box 156 Hazelton KS 67061-0156

WINN, C(OLMAN) BYRON, former mechanical engineering educator; b. Canton, Mo., Nov. 21, 1933; s. Colman Kersey and Kiula Elmeda (Ingold) W.; m. Donna Sue Taylor, Aug. 25, 1957; children: Byron, Derek, Julie. BS in Aeronautics, U. Ill., 1958; MS in Aeronautics, Stanford U., 1960, PhD, 1967. Engr. Lockheed Missiles & Space Co., Palo Alto, Calif., 1958-60, sr. engr., 1962-64; rsch. scientist Martin-Marietta, Denver, 1960-62; lectr. Santa Clara (Calif.) U., 1963-65; assoc. prof. Colo. State U., Ft. Collins, 1966-74, prof. mech. engring., 1974—, prof., head dept., 1982-95, assoc. dean, 1995—. Cons. Space Rsch. Corp., North Troy, Vt., 1969-73; pres. Solar Environ. Engring. Co., 1973-85. Author: Controls in Solar Energy Systems, 1982, Controls in Solar Energy Systems, 1993; assoc. editor Jour. Solar Energy Engring., 1982-89, Passive Solar Jour., 1987, Advances in Solar Energy, 1996—. Loaned exec. United Way, Ft. Collins, 1992. With U.S. Army, 1953-55. Named Disting. Alumnus U. Ill., 1984, J.E. Cermak Adv. award, 1986, EPPEC award Platte River Power Authority, 1992, ABELL Svc. award, 1997. Fellow ASME; mem. AIAA (Energy Systems award 1991), Internat. Solar Energy Soc. (bd. dirs. 1980-89), Am. Solar Energy Soc. (bd. dirs. 1979-86, solar action com. 1991-93), Tau Beta Pi. Achievements include development of controllers for solar energy systems; design and development of the reconfigurable passive evaluation analysis and test facility; founding of the Energy Analysis and Diagnostic Center, The Waste Minimization Assessment Center, The Industrial Assessment Center and Manufacturing Excellence Center at Colo. State U. Office: Colo State U Dept Mech Engring Fort Collins CO 80523-0001

WINN, FRANCIS JOHN, JR. medical educator; b. Detroit, Aug. 12, 1946; s. Francis John and Margaret (Aubuchon) W.; m. Cathy Mannion, Aug. 24, 1974 (div. Dec. 1980); m. Gloria Elizabeth Morrow, Feb. 6, 1981; children: Francis John III, Paige Whitney. BS in Psychology, Mich. State U., 1968; MA in Physiol. Psychology, Cen. Mich. U., 1974; PhD in Psychology and Stats., Tex. Tech U., 1977. Commd. USPHS, 1978, advanced through grades to comdr., 1984, ret., 1997; chief mental health svcs. and Atlantic area psychiat. screening unit USCG Outpatient Clinic, Governor's Island, N.Y., 1978-83; staff rsch. psychologist, cons. to chief psychiatry br. USCG Tng. Ctr., Cape May, N.J., 1983-86; sr. scientist psychophysiology & biomechanics sect. Nat. Inst. Occupational Safety and Health, Cin., 1986-91; sr. rsch. support scientist officer Nat. Inst. Drug Abuse, 1991-92, Substance Abuse and Mental Health Svc. Adminstrn., 1992-95, sr. health statistician, 1995-97; clin. asst. prof. E. Carolina U., Greenville, N.C., 1997—. Cons. assoc. Duke U. Sch. Nursing, 1998—; program evaluation cons. New Bold Assocs., 1998—2001; asst. adj. prof. Med. Coll. Ga., 1995—; bd. collaborators N.C. Agro-Med. Inst., 1998—, exec. com., 2000—01; vis. asst. prof. dept. psychology U. Tex., El Paso, 1977—78; adj. assoc. prof. dept. human svcs., counseling St. John's U., Jamaica, NY, 1980—82; lectr. Stockton State Coll., Pomona, NJ, 1985—86, U. Cin., 1989—91; mem. adv. bd. Conf. Engring. and Aging, Stein Gerontol. Inst., Drexel U., 1990—91; mem. sci. program com. 2d Internat. Conf. on Aging and Work, Danish Working Environ. Fund, 1998; program chair tech. group on aging Triennial Congress of Internat. Ergonomics Assn., 2000; spkr. in field. Assoc. editor Exptl. Aging Rsch.; contbr. article to profl. jours. Mem. DAV, Res. Officers Assn. (v.p. Cin. Navy chpt. 1990, pres. 1991), Assn. Physician Assist Programs, Am. Psychol. Soc., Soc. for Exptl. Biology and Medicine, Gerontol. Soc. Am., Soc. Air Force Clin. Psychologists, Sigma Xi. Home: 3401 Cutler Ct Greenville NC 27834-7621 Office: E Carolina U W Rsch Campus 1157 V Site 'C' Rd Greenville NC 27834 E-mail: winnf@mail.ecu.edu.

WINN, H. RICHARD, surgeon; b. Chester, Pa., 1942; MD, U. Pa., 1968; BA, Princeton U., 1964. Diplomate Am Bd. Neurological Surgeons. Intern U. Hosp., Cleve., 1968-69, resident surgery, 1969-70; resident neurolog. surgery U. Hosp. Va., Charlottesville, 1970-74; neurol. surgeon U. Wash. Hosp., Seattle, 1983—; prof., chmn. neurol. surgery U. Wash., 1983—. Dir. Am. Bd. Neurol. Surgery. Founding editor Neurosurgical Clinics of North Amercia; mem. editl. bd. Jour. Neurosurgery, Am. Jour. Physiology, Am. Jour. Surgery. Fellow AAAS, ACS (gov.), Soc. Brit. Neurol. Surgeons (hon.); mem. AMA, Am. Assn. Neurol. Surgeons, Soc. Neurol. Surgeons, Congress of Neurol. Surgeons, Am. Bd. Neurol. Surgeons (vice chmn. 2000-01). Office: U Wash Dept Neurosurg 325 9th Ave # 359766 Seattle WA 98104-1834 Fax: 206-521-1881.

WINN, HUNG NGUYEN, obstetrician, gynecologist, maternal-fetal medicine physician; b. Thanh Hoa, Vietnam, Feb. 11, 1953; came to U.S., 1975; s. Su Cong Nguyen and Diep Thi Truong; m. Lee Nguyen Winn, Aug. 8, 1975; children: John, Jessica, Justin. BA in Biology and Chemistry, Greenville Coll., 1977; MD, U. Ill., Chgo., 1982. Resident in ob-gyn. U. Ill., Peoria, 1982-86, tchg. assoc. coll. medicine, 1983-86; fellow in maternal-fetal medicine Yale U. Sch. Medicine, New Haven, 1986-88, instr., 1986-88; asst. prof. ob-gyn Wash. U. Sch. Medicine, St. Louis, 1988-90; maternal-fetal medicine physician Barnes Hosp., 1988-90; dir. maternal-fetal medicine divsn. St. Louis U., 1990—, assoc. prof. ob-gyn., 1993-98, prof. ob-gyn., 1998—. Co-editor: (co-founder) Jour. of Maternal-Fetal Medicine, 1998; (textbook) Clinical Maternal-Fetal Medicine; assoc. editor Jour. of Perinatal Medicine; contbr. articles to profl. jours., chpts. to med. textbooks. Mem. ACOG, Soc. for Maternal-Fetal Medicine, Greater St. Louis Ob-gyn. Soc. (editor 1990-93, v.p. 1996-97, pres.-elect 1997-98, pres. 1998-99), Internat. Soc. of Fetus as a Patient (bd. dirs. 1999—). Roman Catholic. Avocations: tennis, swimming, reading, golf, travel. Office: St Louis U Sch Medicine St Mary's Health Ctr 6420 Clayton Rd Saint Louis MO 63117-1811 E-mail: winnh@slucare1.sluh.edu.

WINN, JAMES JULIUS, JR. lawyer; b. Colon, Panama, Nov. 7, 1941; came to U.S., 1941; s. James Julius and Molly (Brown) W.; m. Elizabeth Kokernot Lacy, Aug. 15, 1970; children: Mary Ann W. Burns, Elizabeth Lacy, James Julius VI. AB, Princeton U., 1964; JD cum laude, Washington and Lee U., 1970. Bar: Md. 1970, U.S. Dist. Ct. Md. 1971, U.S. Dist. Ct. D.C. 1982. Assoc. Piper Marbury Rudnick & Wolfe, LLP, Balt., 1970-78; ptnr. Piper Rudnick LLP, 1978—. Assoc. editor, contbr. author Washington & Lee U. Law Rev., 1968-70. Counselor St. John's Ch., Western Run Parish, Glyndon, Md., 1974—; mem. com. on canons and other bus., investment com. Episc. Diocese Md., 1986—; dir. Ctr. for Ethics and Corp. Policy, 1988-95, chmn., 1991-95; dir. Ctr. Stage, 1986—; dir. Oldfields Sch., 1991-96; v.p., dir. Ruxton Country Sch., 1988-91; dir. The Jemicy Sch., 1999—. Mem. ABA (chmn. subcoms. on publs. and govt. acctg. standards of com. on law and acctg. of sect. of bus. law), Md. State Bar Assn. (com. on corp. law of sect. of bus. law). Office: Piper Rudnick LLP 6225 Smith Ave Baltimore MD 21209-3600

WINN, MORRIS X. federal agency administrator; Grad., Prairie View A&M U. Divsn. dir. support svcs. Tex. Atty. Gen.'s Office, 1984—92, dir. employee rels., 1992—94; deputy commr. human resources Tex. Dept. Ins., 1994—99; divsn. mgr. human resources Tex. Comptroller Pub. Accts., 1999—2002; asst. adminstr. adminstrn. and resources mgmt. EPA, Washington, 2002—. Office: EPA 1200 Pennsylvanis Ave NW MC 301A Washington DC 20460*

WINN, ROBERT CHEEVER, rehabilitation services professional; b. N.Y.C., Apr. 11, 1939; s. Richard Wilkens and Ella Jane (Mackenzie) W.; m. Margery Ellen Irwin (div. Sept. 1983); children: Elizabeth Jane, Margaret Ruth, Nancy Louise; m. Susan Elizabeth Gengler, June 4, 1988. BA, U. Bridgeport, 1962; MA, Ball State U., 1975. Advanced through grades to maj. USAF, 1963-83; customer support rep. Boeing Mil. Airplanes, Wichita, Kans., 1983-89; counselor Wichita Counseling Ctr., 1988; vocat. rehab. counselor Kans. Rehab. Svcs., Wellington, 1989—. Mem. Sumner County ADA Accessibility Adv. Bd., 1994—; deacon Hillside Christian Ch., 1991-94, elder, 1995-97, 99-2001, chmn. ch. growth com., 2000. Named one of Outstanding Young Men of Am., 1974. Mem. Nat. Rehab. Assn., Kans. Rehab. Assn., Kans. Head Injury Assn., Lions (pres. 1994-95, zone chmn. 1991-92, 94-95), VFW (jr. vice comdr. Derby, Kans. chpt. 1989, adj. 1988), Kans. Rehab. Counselors Assn. (sec., treas. 1994-96), Kans. Rehab. Assn., Wellington C. of C. (bd. dirs. 1999-2001). Republican. Home: 924 Bristol Ter Wichita KS 67207-4306 Office: Kans Rehab Svcs 1116 W 8th St Wellington KS 67152-3423

WINN, STEVEN JAY, critic; b. Phila., Apr. 25, 1951; s. Willis Jay and Lois (Gengelbach) W.; m. Katharine Weber, Sept. 15, 1979 (div. Dec. 1985); m. Sally Ann Noble, July 22, 1989; 1 child, Phoebe Ann. BA, U. Pa., 1973; MA, U. Wash., 1975. Staff writer, editor Seattle Weekly, 1975-79; theater critic San Francisco Chronicle, 1960—2002, arts and culture critic, 2002—. Co-author: Ted Bundy: The Killer Next Door, 1980, Great Performances: A Celebration, 1997; contbr. articles to various publs. Wallace Stegner fellow Stanford U., 1979-80. Office: San Francisco Chronicle 901 Mission St San Francisco CA 94103-2905

WINN, WALTER GARNETT, JR. marketing strategist, advertising executive; b. Wilmington, N.C., Dec. 1, 1941; s. Walter Garnett and Pamela Weber (Bradham) W.; m. Linda Ann Irvin, July 1, 1964; children: Walter Welborn, Katie Hillary. BFA, U. Ga., 1966, MS with honors, 1968. Account exec. Sudler & Hennessey Advt., N.Y.C., 1968-69, Dean Burdick & Assocs. Inc., N.Y.C., 1969-70; v.p., creative dir. Buntin & Assocs. Inc., Nashville, 1970-72; pres. Smith & Winn Advt. Inc., Jacksonville, Fla., 1972-77; mktg. mgr. Standard Telephone Co., Cornelia, Ga., 1977-79; mktg., sales mgr. Commonwealth Telephone Co., Dallas, 1979-83; advt. dir. CTE Corp., Wilkes Barre, 1983-84; dir. mktg. North State Telephone Inc., High Point, N.C., 1984—. Creator, designer bus. strategy game Merchants and Movers, 1990, Air Mogul, 2000. Bd. dirs., chair com. High Point Area Arts Coun., 1989—96; bd. dirs. Back Mountain Arts Guild, Dallas, 1980, Misericordia Coll. Arts Endowment, 1982—84; apptd. mem. Gov. Hunt's N.C. Info. Hwy. Com., 1994—96; advisor Market Authority Bd., 2001—; pres. Civitan Found., 1998—2000; mem. adv. com. Furniture Market Bd., 2001—. Named Advt. Person of Yr. Am. Advt. Fedn., Northeastern Pa., 1983. Mem. N.C. Tel. Assn. (chmn. mktg. 1989-91, 95-97), Civitan (pres. High Point 1994-95, Civitan of Yr. 1996). Republican. Avocations: strategy games, model railroading, woodworking. Home: 203 Frontier Dr Lexington NC 27292-0203 Office: North State Comms 111 N Main St High Point NC 27260-5007 E-mail: wwinn@nscom.com.

WINN, WALTER TERRIS, JR. civil and environmental engineer; b. Houston, Aug. 26, 1949; s. Walter Terris and Sue (Colvard) W.; m. Phyllis Ann Hobart, May 22, 1971; children: Holly Kay, Walter Timothy. BS in Civil Engring., Tex. Tech. U., 1972, MS in Civil Engring., 1973. Registered profl. engr., Tex.; diplomate Am. Acad. Environ. Engrs. Design engr. Brown & Root, Inc., Houston, 1973-78; project mgr., v.p. KSA Engrs. Inc., Longview, Tex., 1978—. Mem. Tex. Tech. U. Civil Engring. adv. bd., 1995—. Adult tchr., leader 1st United Meth. Ch., Longview, 1986—; pres. Glenwood Water Supply Corp., Gilmer, Tex., 1988—. Named Young Engr. of Yr. Tex. Soc. Profl. Engrs., East Tex. chpt., 1980; named to Tex. Tech. U. Civil Engring. Acad., 1991. Fellow ASCE (br. pres. 1988-89, pres. Tex. sect. 2001-02); mem. Water Environ. Fedn. (sect. pres. 1992-93), Am. Water Works Assn. Achievements include projects in fields of civil & environ. engring. in water supply, water distbn., wastewater collection, wastewater treatment, water treatment, solid waste disposal, site remediation, roads, bridges, dams and air pollution control. Office: KSA Engrs Inc PO Box 1552 140 E Tyler St Ste 600 Longview TX 75601-7256

WINNER, KARIN E. editor; Editor San Diego Union-Tribune, 1995—. Office: San Diego Union-Tribune Pub Co 350 Camino De La Reina San Diego CA 92108-3003 E-mail: Karin.winner@uniontrib.com.

WINNER, MICHAEL ROBERT, film director, writer, producer; b. London, Oct. 30, 1935; s. George Joseph and Helen (Zloty) W. Degree in law and econs. with honors, Cambridge (Eng.) U., 1956. Writer Fleet St. (newspapers), London, 1956-58. Columnist London Sunday Times, 1990, London News of the World, 1995. Engaged in film prodn., 1956; dir. films Play it Cool, 1962, West 11, 1963, The Mechanic, 1972, Death Wish II, 1981; dir., writer The Cool Mikado, 1962, You Must be Joking, 1965, The Wicked Lady, 1982; producer, dir. The System, 1963, I'll Never Forget What's 'isname, 1967, The Games, 1969, Lawman, 1970, The Nightcomers, 1971, Chato's Land, 1971, Scorpio, 1972, The Stone Killer, 1973, Death Wish, 1974, Won Ton Ton The Dog Who Saved Hollywood, 1975, Firepower, 1978, Scream for Help, 1983, Death Wish III, 1985; producer, writer, dir. films The Jokers, 1966, Hannibal Brooks, 1968, The Sentinel, 1976, The Big Sleep, 1977, Appointment With Death, 1987, A Chorus of Disapproval, 1988, Bullseye!, 1989, Dirty Weekend, 1992, Parting Shots, 1997; producer plays Nights at the Comedy, Comedy Theatre, London, 1960, The Silence of St. Just, Gardner Centre, Brighton, 1971, The Tempest, Wyndhams Theatre, London, 1974, A Day in Hollywood, A Night in the Ukraine, Mayfair Theatre, London, 1978, (TV series London Weekend TV) Michael Winner's True Crimes, 1990, 91, 92, 93, 94; author: Winner's Dinners, 1999, rev. edit., 2000, Winner Guide, 2002; actor: (BBC film) For the Greater Good, 1990, Decadence, 1993, The Flump, 2000. Founder, chmn. Police Meml. Trust, 1984. Mem. Dirs. Guild Gt. Britain (coun., trustee, chief censorship officer 1983). Office: Scimitar Films Ltd 219 Kensington High St London W8 6BD England

WINNIE, GLENNA BARBARA, pediatric pulmonologist; b. Lansing, Mich., Oct. 14; d. Robert John and Irene (Fetchik) W.; m. Jeffrey Alan Cooper, Mar. 17, 1990; children: Robert Jefferson Cooper, David Jamison Cooper. BS, Mich. State U., 1973; MD, Vanderbilt U., 1977. Diplomate Am. Bd. Pediatrics, Am. Bd. Pediatric Pumonology. Resident in pediatrics Case Western Res. U./Babies and Childrens Hosp., Cleve., 1977-79, fellow in pediatric pulmonology, 1979-82; asst. prof. pediatrics Albany (N.Y.) Med. Coll., 1982-90, assoc. prof. pediatrcis, 1990-95, head pediatric pulmonology sect., 1982-95; adminstrv. dir. pulmonary divsn., co-dir. cystic fibrosis U. Pitts., 1995—. Dir. Albany Pediat. Pulmonary and Cystic Fibrosis Ctr., 1982—95; adminstrv. dir. pulmonary divsn. Children's Hosp. of Pitts., 1995—99; co-dir. Cystic Fibrosis Ctr., 1995—, dir. pulmonary divsn., 1999—, dir. pediatric sleep lab., 2001—, Children's Hosp. of Pitts., 2001—. Contbr. articles to profl. jours. Bd. dirs. Albany Ronald McDonald Ho., 1986-88, Cystic Fibrosis Found.-Western Pa. chpt., 1996—. Rsch. grantee Nat. Cystic Fibrosis Found., 1984-86, 88-90, 99-01, NIH, 1987-93. Mem.: Soc. Pediat. Rsch., Am. Acad. Sleep Medicine, Capital Dist. Pediatric Soc. (treas. 1985—90, pres. 1990—91), Am. Coll. Physician Execs., Am. Thoracic Soc. (rsch. fellowship review com. 1989—92), Am. Acad. Pediatrics (exec. com. chest sect. 1996—2001). Episcopalian. Achievements include description of role of Epstein Barr virus in pulmonary exacerbations in cystic fibrosis. Office: Childrens Hosp of Pitts 3705 5th Ave Pittsburgh PA 15213-2524

WINNOWSKI, THADDEUS RICHARD (TED WINNOWSKI), bank executive; b. Albany, N.Y., Feb. 20, 1942; s. Thaddeus Walter and Harriet Frances (Witko) W.; m. Sheila Margaret Neary, June 15, 1968; children: Dona, Paul. BS in Econs., Siena Coll., 1963; postgrad., Rensselaer Poly. Inst., 1968-72. Adminstrv. v.p. Key Bank N.A., Albany, N.Y., 1978-80; pres. Key Bank L.I., Sayville, 1980-85; pres., CEO Key Bank Oreg., Woodburn, 1985-86, chmn., CEO Portland, 1986-95, chmn., 1995-97; exec. v.p., group exec. N.W. region Key Corp., Seattle, 1995-97, chmn., CEO, 1996-97; pres., CEO Centennial Bank, Eugene, Oreg., 1998—. Chmn. Blue Cross/Blue Shield Oreg.; chmn. bd. regents U. Portland. 1st lt. U.S. Army, 1964-66. Mem. Oreg. Bankers Assn., Portland Met. C. of C. (hon. bd. dirs., former chmn.). Roman Catholic. E-mail: tedwinnowski@centennialbank.com.

WINOGRAD, NICHOLAS, chemist; b. New London, Conn., Dec. 27, 1945; s. Arthur Selig Winograd and Winifred (Schaefer) Winograd Mayes; m. Barbara J. Garrison. BS, Rensselaer Poly. Inst., 1967; PhD, Case Western Reserve U., 1970. Asst. prof. chemistry Purdue U., West Lafayette, Ind., 1970-75, assoc. prof. chemistry, 1975-79; prof. chemistry Pa. State U., University Park, 1979-85, Evan Pugh prof. chemistry, 1985—. Cons. Lawrence Livermore Lab., 1997—; mem. chemistry adv. bd. NSF, Washington, 1987-90, analytical chemistry adv. bd., 1986-89. Contbr. articles to profl. jours. A.P. Sloan Found. fellow, 1974; Guggenheim Found. fellow, 1977;

recipient Founder's prize Tex. Instruments Found., 1984, Faculty Scholar's Pa. State U., 1985, Bennedetti Pichler award Am. Microchem. Soc., 1991, Outstanding Alumnus award Case Western Res. U., 1991. Fellow AAAS (Sect. award); mem. Am. Chem. Soc. Home: 138 Chemistry Ln Spring Mills PA 16875-9703 Office: Pa State U Dept of Chemistry 152 Davey Lab University Park PA 16802-6300 E-mail: nxw@psu.edu.

WINOGRAD, SHMUEL, mathematician; b. Tel Aviv, Jan. 4, 1936; came to U.S., 1956, naturalized, 1965; s. Pinchas Mordechai and Rachel Winograd; m. Elaine Ruth Tates, Jan 5, 1958; children: Daniel H., Sharon A. BSEE, MSEE, MIT; PhD in Math., NYU, 1968. Mem. research staff IBM, Yorktown Heights, N.Y., 1961-70, dir. math. sci. dept., 1970-74, 81-94; IBM fellow, 1972—. Permanent vis. prof. Technion, Israel. Author: (with J.D. Cowan) Reliable Computations in the Presence of Noise; research on complexity of computations and algorithms for signal processing. Fellow IEEE (W. Wallace McDowell award 1974), Assn. Computing Machinery, N.Y. Acad. Scis.; mem. NAS, Am. Math. Soc., Math. Assn. Am., Am. Philos. Soc., Soc. Indsl. and Applied Math., Am. Acad. Arts & Scis. Home: 235 Glendale Rd Scarsdale NY 10583-1533 Office: IBM Research PO Box 218 Yorktown Heights NY 10598-0218

WINOGRADSKY, STEVEN, lawyer; b. N.Y.C., Sept. 22, 1949; s. Harry J. and Hazel (Sadoff) W.; m. Rosemary K. West, Dec. 8, 1985. BA in Polit. Sci., Calif. State U., Northridge, 1971; JD, U. San Fernando, 1977. Bar: Calif., 1977. V.p. bus. affairs Clearing House, Ltd., Hollywood, Calif., 1980-86; mng. dir. music, bus. and legal affairs MCA Home Entertainment and Universal Pictures and TV, Universal City, 1986-89; dir. music, bus. affairs Hanna-Barbera Prodns., Inc., L.A., 1989-91; pres. Winogradsky Co., Granada Hills, Calif., 1992—. Mem. Calif. State Bar, Calif. Copyright Conf. (bd. dirs. 1986-94, v.p. 1994-95, pres. 1995-97), Assn. Ind. Music Pubs. (bd. dirs. 1989-90, pres. 1991-94). Office: Winogradsky Co 11240 Magnolia Blvd Ste 104 North Hollywood CA 91601-3798 E-mail: steve@winogradsky.com.

WINOKUR, HARVEY JAY, rabbi; b. Bklyn., Aug. 16, 1950; s. Douglas Louis and Miriam (Weinberg) W.; m. Donnie Kanter, Nov. 22, 1997; children: Morasha, Iyal. BA in Sociology, SUNY, Buffalo, 1971; MA, Hebrew Union Coll., 1974; DD, Hebrew Union Coll.-Jewish Inst. Religion, 2001. Ordained rabbi, 1976. Rabbi The Temple, Atlanta, 1976-79, Temple Sinai, Atlanta, 1979-80, Balt. Hebrew Congregation, 1980-82, Temple Kehillat Chaim, Roswell, Ga., 1982—. Seminar dir. Prepare/Enrich, 1998—. Co-author: Lehava, 1979. Co-chmn. Ann. City-Wide Appeal To Address Homelessness, 1989-91; trustee N.W. Ga. coun. Girl Scouts U.S.A., 1983-86; officer Nat. Coalition Against Death Penalty, N.Y.C., 1982-86; mem. Atlanta-Fulton County Commn. on Children and Youth, Leadership Atlanta Class of 1992; bd. dirs. United Way Met. Atlanta, 1992-98. Mem. SEACCAR (pres. 1999-2001), Ctrl. Conf. Am. Rabbis (social action commn. 1987-89, bd. trustees 2000-2002), N.Am. Bd. World Union for Progressive Judaism, Atlanta Rabbinical Assn. (pres. 1988-90), Am. Jewish Com. (bd. dirs. Atlanta chpt. 1991-98, exec. com. 1998-2002), Interfaith Coalition Atlanta (co-chmn. 1994-96), Atlanta Jewish Bedn. (bd. dirs. 1988-91), Atlanta Black-Jewish Coalition (steering com.). Avocations: travel, nature photography, computers, music. Office: Temple Kehillat Chaim 1145 Green St Roswell GA 30075-3609 E-mail: hjwino@aol.com.

WINOKUR, NEIL, photographer; b. N.Y.C., June 28, 1945; s. Lewis and Sydell (Spector) W.; m. Anne Whiting Umland, Oct. 29, 1987; children: Lucy, Nick, Nathan; stepson, Nathan Bennett. BA, CUNY, 1967. Photographer: Everyday Things, 1994; one-man exhbns. include Mus. Art of Bahia, Brazil, 1985, Barbara Toll Fine Arts, N.Y.C., 1986-90, Janet Borden, Inc., N.Y.C., 1990, 93-2001, Cleve. Contemporary, 1993, Denver Mus. Art, 1993, 42d St Art Project, N.Y.C., 1994, Galerie du jour Agnes b, Paris, 1995, Janet Borden, inc. 1996-97, 2000; group exhbns. include Rheinisches Landesmuseum, Bonn, Germany, 1982, Grey Art Gallery, N.Y., 1982, Ritz Hotel, Washington, 1983, Castelli Graphics, N.Y., 1983, Taft Mus., Cin., 1983, Newcastle upon Tyne, 1983, Inst. for Art and Urban Resources, N.Y., 1984, Inst. Contemporary Art, Phila., 1984, Mus. Modern Art, N.Y., 1984, 87, Delahunty Gallery, Dallas, 1984, BBK Hahnentorburg, Cologne, West Germany, 1984, Walther Konig, Cologne, 1984, Schwan and Bode, Düsseldorf, Germany, 1984, White Columns Gallery, N.Y., 1985, Defactor Art Salon, N.Y., 1984, Steven Adams Gallery, N.Y., 1984, The Palladium, N.Y., 1985, Gallery Hirondelle, N.Y., 1985, U. Ill., Chgo., 1987, Balt. Mus. Art, 1987, Barbara Toll Fine Arts, N.Y., 1987, Internat. Ctr. for Photography, N.Y., 1987, Hoffman-Bormann Gallery, L.A., 1987, L.A. County Mus. Art, 1987, Jan Kesner Gallery, L.A., 1988, Vault Gallery, Boston, 1988, Queens Mus., Flushing, N.Y., 1988, Carlo Lamagna Gallery, N.Y., 1988, Lieberman and Saul Gallery, N.Y.C., 1988, Sewall Art Gallery, Houston, 1988, Laurence Miller Gallery, N.Y., 1989, George Eastman House, Rochester, 1989, Nat. Mus. Modern Art, Washington, 1989, Tatischeff Gallery, Santa Monica, Calif., 1989, Rutgers U., N.J., 1989, Herter Art Gallery, 1989, Phila. Art Alliance, 1990, Mus. Modern Art, N.Y.C., 1991, 93, Mus. Photographic Arts, San Diego, 1992, Internat. Ctr. Photography Midtown, N.Y.C., 1992, L.A. County Mus. Art, 1993, Nat. Mus. Photography, Film, and T.V., Bradford, Eng., 1995; represented in permanent collections Mus. Modern Art, N.Y.C., Met. Mus. Art, N.Y.C., Phila. Mus. Art, L.A. County Mus., Denver Mus. Art, Denver Mus. Art, Jewish Mus., N.Y.C., others. Recipient fellowship NEA, 1984, fellowship Art Matters, Inc., 1986, 88, fellowship John Simm Guggenheim Found., 1987. Democrat. Avocations: cooking, gardening, book collecting. E-mail: neilwinokur@earthlink.net.

WINSHIP, BLAINE H. lawyer; b. Ithaca, N.Y., Apr. 3, 1951; s. Hershell F. and June M. (Nickless) W.; m. Karin M. Byrne, Dec. 21, 1979. AB magna cum laude, Dartmouth Coll., 1973; JD, Cornell U., 1976. Bar: Ill. 1976, Fla. 1982. Assoc. Sonnenschein, Nath & Rosenthal, Chgo., 1976-82; ptnr. Winship & Byrne, Miami, Fla., 1983—. Contbg. author: ABA Criminal Antitrust Manual, 1982. Mem. bd. trustees StageWorks, Tampa, Fla., 1984-86, pres., 1986. Rufus Choate scholar Dartmouth Coll., 1972-73. Mem. Miami City Club, Fla. Bar Assn. (vice chmn., antitrust and trade regulation com., exec. com. bus. law sect.), Phi Beta Kappa. Office: Winship & Byrne 201 S Biscayne Blvd Ste 1950 Miami FL 33131-2329 Home: 4315 Des Plaines Dr Sarasota FL 34233-3605

WINSHIP, FREDERICK MOERY, journalist; b. Franklin, Ohio, Sept. 24, 1924; s. Wilbur William and Edna B. (Moery) W.; m. Joanne Tree Thompson, Aug. 29, 1967. AB, DePauw U., 1945; MS, Columbia, 1946. Corr. UPI, 1946—; assigned UN, 1947-49; editorial staff N.Y.C., 1950-60, cultural affairs editor, 1960-72, sr. editor, 1972-75, asst. mng. editor, 1975-80; sr. editor arts/theater N.Y.C., 1980-98; Broadway critic, 1985-98; arts critic at large, 2000—. Contbr. articles mags. Pres. Letters Abroad, Inc., 1962-83; chmn. Easter Seal Soc., N.Y.C., 1964-73, Oratorio Soc. N.Y., 1965-75, N.Y. Conf. Patriotic Socs., 1967-72; Bd. dirs. Odell House-Rochambeau Hdgrs., 1965-75, N.Y. State Easter Seal Soc., 1969-72, Mus. of City of N.Y., 1974—, Am. Philharm. Orch., 1981-82, Friends of the Am. Theater Wing, 1990—. Recipient Am. Legion Journalism award, 1955; Whitelaw Reid Journalism fellow India, 1958; Creative Club Journalism award, 1962 Mem. S.A.R. (sec. N.Y. chpt. 1963-68), St. Nicholas, Founders and Patriots, Mayflower Descs., Soc. Colonial Wars (bd. dirs.), S.R., Soc. Cincinnati, Sigma Delta Chi. Republican. Episcopalian. Home: 419 E 57th St New York NY 10022-3060

WINSKIE, RICHARD CLAY, retail executive, songwriter; b. Warrenton, Va., Sept. 19, 1962; s. Mark Walton and Norma Jean (Jolley) W.; m. Laynette Elaine Lykins, May 18, 1985; children: Crystal Brooke, Joshua Caleb, Rebekah Lynn. AS, Jacksonville Coll., 1983; postgrad., Stephen F. Austin U., 1983, U. Tex., 1984-85, 95-97, Bapt. Sem., 1984-85; BS, U. Tex., 1997, MA, 2001. Ordained to Gospel Ministry, 1990; lic. to Gospel Ministry, 1982. Minister of music Shady Grove Bapt. Ch., Purdon, Tex., 1979-81; guitarist, songwriter Calvary Boys Quartet, Teneha, 1984-89; music mgr. Better Books Christian Ctr., Tyler, 1984-89; minister of music Enterprise Bapt. Ch., Jacksonville, 1984-89; minister of music and youth 1st Bapt. Ch., Waldo, Ark., 1989-92; program dir. KSIZ and KBJS, Jacksonville, Tex., 1992-96; min. of music Enterprise Bapt. Ch., 1992-95; mgr. Life Discovery Store, 1995-96; music mgr. Better Books Christian Ctr., 1996-2001; asst. mgr. LifeWay Christian Store, 2001—. Choir mem. First Bapt. Ch., Jacksonville, 1995—, vocal ensemble mem., 1996—, praise band drummer and conga player, 1997—, Jr. Varsity Awana club dir., 1997—, asst. Sunday Sch. tchr., 1997-99, single adults Sunday Sch. tchr., 1999—. Songwriter: Appointment with the Lord, 1984, Is There Hope, 1992, He Arose, 1992, Don't Curse the Darkness, 1993, Nothing Compares (To the Love of God), 1994, Wait On the Lord, 1994, What A World It Would Be, 1994; contbr. articles to religion jours.; program dir., engr. syndicated gospel radio show So. Sonshine, 1986-87; columnist East Tex. Christian Monthly, 1995-96. Mem. Columbia County Right to Life, Magnolia, Ark., 1990-92; mem. Vol. Fire Dept., Waldo, 1989-92; co-dir. South Ark. Youth Choir Mission Singers Tour, 1992. Mem. Bapt. Missionary Assn. (del. 1985, 89, 90), Assn. Bapt. Students (truste 1988-89, 93-96), So. Gospel Songwriter's Assn., Broadcast Music. Home: RR 2 Box 2481 Bullard TX 75757-9469 Office: 3500 S Broadway Ave Tyler TX 75701-8729 *I am constantly amazed at the number of people who insist on separating life into "spiritual" and "secular". The Bible's instruction, "Do all to the glory of God," reminds me even the "secular" things are to be done with a purpose and are "spiritual" because of God's constant presence with me.*

WINSKILL, ROBERT WALLACE, manufacturing executive; b. Tacoma, Oct. 30, 1925; s. Edward Francis William and Margaret Eyre (Myers) W. BA, Coll. Puget Sound, Tacoma, 1947. Field rep. Ray Burner Co., San Francisco, 1954-57, nat. sales mgr., 1960-69; v.p. sales Western Boiler Co., L.A., 1957-60; gen. sales mgr. Ray Burner Co., San Francisco, 1973-82; v.p., chief exec. officer Orr & Sembower, Inc., Middletown, Pa., 1969-73; chmn. Combustion Systems Assocs., Inc., Mill Valley, Calif., 1982—. Bd. dirs. Sino-Am. Boiler Engring. Co., Shanghai, China, S. T. Johnson Co., Oakland, Calif. Contbr. articles to profl. jours.; columnist Marin Scope, Mill Valley Harold, Asia News, India, London, 1991—. With U.S. Army, 1943-44. Mem. ASME, Olympic Club (San Francisco), Rotary. Avocation: vineyard. Office: Combustion Sys Assocs Inc PO Box 749 Mill Valley CA 94942-0749 E-mail: comsai@aol.com.

WINSKUNAS, CANDACE A. management consultant; b. Chgo., Sept. 22, 1949; d. Albin H. and Ruth (Wilson) W. Diploma, St. Elizabeth's Hosp., 1970; BA, Calif. State U., Long Beach, 1982; MBA, U. Pitts., 1993. Cert. intravenous therapist. Nursing supr. Rush Presbyn.-St. Luke's Med. Ctr., Chgo., 1974-77; head nurse Cedars-Sinai Med. Ctr., L.A., 1978-83; nurse mgr. George Washington U. Health Plan, Washington, 1984-85; head nurse Foster Infusion Care, Pitts., 1986; mgr. Western Pa. Hosp., 1987-93; mgmt. cons. West Hudson & Co., L.A., 1994—. Mem. Intravenous Nurses Soc. (pres. Pitts. chpt.), League Intravenous Therapy Edn. (sec./treas. Pitts. chpt.), PONE. Home: 418 4th St Oakmont PA 15139-1629

WINSLADE, THOMAS EDWIN, lawyer; b. Omaha, May 30, 1952; s. George Edwin and H.I. (Lockhart) W. BA, Claremont Men's Coll., 1974; JD, Columbia U., 1976. Bar: N.Y. 1977, Pa. 1985. Assoc. Shearman & Sterling, N.Y.C., 1976-83; assoc. counsel Mellon Bank, Pitts., 1984-87; v.p., asst. resident counsel Morgan Guaranty Trust Co., N.Y.C., 1987-92; exec. dir. Emerging Markets Traders Assn., 1992-94; v.p., asst. gen. counsel J.P. Morgan Co., Singapore, 1994—. Office: care JP Morgan Co 60 Wall St New York NY 10260

WINSLET, KATE, actress; b. Reading, Berkshire, Eng., Oct. 5, 1975; Appeared in plays including Peter Pan, What the Butler Saw (Manchester Evening News award for Best Supporting Actress), A Game of Soldiers, (musical) Adrian Mole; appeared in TV shows including Anglo-Saxon Attitudes, Shrinks, Dark Season, Casualty, Get Back; appeared in films including Heavenly Creatures, 1994 (Best Fgn. Actress award New Zealand Film and TV Awards), Sense and Sensibility, 1995 (SAG award, Brit. Acad. of Film and TV award for Best Supporting Actress, Golden Globe nominee, Am. Acad. of Motion Picture Arts and Scis. nominee), A Kid in King Arthur's Court, 1995, Jude, 1996, Hamlet, 1996, Titanic, 1997 (nominated for Acad. award for Best Actress), Hideous Kinky, 1998, Plunge, 1999, Holy Smoke, 1999, Quills, 2000 (nominee Best Supporting Actress SAG award 2000), Faeries (voice), 2000, Iris: A Memoir of Iris Murdoch, 2001 (nominee Best Supporting Actress SAG award 2001, Brit. Acad. award 2001), Enigma, 2002; appeared in various TV commls. also: c/o Peters Fraser & Dunlop 503 The Chambers Chelsea Harbour SW14 CXF England Address: c/o Peter Fraser & Dunlop Drury House 34-43 Russell St London WC2B 5HA England*

WINSLETT, STONER, artistic director; b. Jacksonville, Fla., Aug. 17, 1958; m. Donald Paulding Irwin; children: Louise Gray Irwin, Elizabeth Irwin, Alexander Pankoff, Caroline Irwin. Student, Am. Ballet Theatre Sch., N.C. Sch. of the Arts; grad. summa cum laude, Smith Coll., 1980. Artistic dir. Richmond Ballet. Trustee John Butler Found. Mem. Phi Beta Kappa. Office: Richmond Ballet 407 E Canal St Richmond VA 23219-3811

WINSLOW, DONALD JAMES, retired English educator, archivist; b. Auburndale, Mass., Dec. 21, 1911; s. Guy Monroe and Clara Mellona (Austin) W.; m. Lois Ella Nelson, Aug. 23, 1941 (div. Apr. 1963); children: Paul Nelson, Sanford Austin; m. Charlotte Holt Lindgren, Aug. 11, 1978. BS, Tufts U., 1934, AM, 1935; PhD, Boston U., 1942. Tchr. social studies jr. high sch., East Greenwich, R.I., 1935-36; tchg. fellow in English, Boston U., 1936-39, instr., 1939-46, asst. prof., 1946-48, assoc. prof., 1949-52, prof., 1953-77, chmn. dept., 1952-62; ret., 1977. Archivist Lasell Coll., Auburndale, 1977—, trustee, 1959-89, trustee emeritus, 1989—. Author: (monographs) Life-Writing: A Glossary, 1980, 2d edit., 1995, Thomas Hardy's Sister Kate, 1982, Lasell: A History, 1987; contbr. numerous articles on Thomas Hardy to profl. jours. and revs. Staff sgt. USAAF, 1942-46. Recipient Lasell medal Lasell Coll., 1983, Lasell Bowl, 1986, archives named in his honor, 1998. Mem. MLA, Thomas Hardy Soc., London Johnson Soc., William Barnes Soc., Newton Hist. Soc., Orleans County Hist. Soc., Phi Beta Kappa, Delta Upsilon. Avocations: painting, book collecting, travel, genealogy. Home: 23 Maple St Auburndale MA 02466-2404

WINSLOW, F(RANCIS) DANA, state supreme court justice, record company owner; b. N.Y.C., Feb. 20, 1939; s. Francis Dana and Flora Brady (Garvan) W.; m. Beverly June Bell, Aug. 25, 1984; children by previous marriage: Francis Dana III, Michael, Jennifer. BA, Am. U., 1966; JD, Cath. U. Am., 1969. Bar: N.Y. 1970, U.S. Ct. Appeals (2d cir.) 1972, U.S. Supreme Ct. 1975. Assoc. Beekman & Bogue (Now Gaston & Snow, N.Y.C., 1969-73; spl. counsel Sutter, Moffatt, Vannelli & Zevin, Mineola, N.Y., 1973-78; pvt. law practice, 1978-89; pres., owner Winslow Prodsn. Ltd., 1983-96; ptnr. Schiavetti, Geiser, Corgan et al, various, N.Y., 1989-96; assoc. justice Village of Old Westbury, 1991-96; atty. Village of Centre Island, 1988-96; justice N.Y. State Supreme Ct., 1996—. Counsel World Tae Kwan Do championships, 1993; adj. prof. law sect. Grad. Bus. Law, St. John's U., 1998—2000. Judo instr. various univs. Washington met. area; instr. 2d Dan (Black Belt) Judo, 1963—, 5th Dan Tae Kwan Do, 1997; founding pres., chair Winslow Therapeutic Riding, Inc., 1974, bd. dirs., 1974—; founder, chmn. Helping Hand Horse Show, 1979-86; mem. N.Y. State Supreme Ct. Justice Task Force on N.Y. Ct. Reform, 1997—; chair judicial adv. com. of the Jud. Inst., 2000—; bd. dirs. N.Am. Riding for Handicapped Assn., 1983-87; chmn. publicity and pub. rels. Nat. Equestrian Sports Day; atty., legal counsel, advisor U.S. Tae Kwan Do Union, U.S. Olympic Com. for 1988 Olympics, 1984-89; co-organizer spl. song presentation for benefit Gift of Life program honoring Nancy Reagan, N.Y.C., 1984; appeared off-Broadway and cmty. prodns. musicals; pres. Glen Players, Glen Cove, N.Y., 1985-87, bd. dirs., 1986-90; trustee, police commr. Village of Old Wstbury, 1976-81, environ. commr., 19790-81. Spl. agt. M.I., U.S. Army, 1962-65, Korea. Recipient Outstanding Svc. award D.C. Bar Assn., 1968, citation of merit Uniformed Firefighters Assn., N.Y.C., 1983. Mem. Nassau County Bar Assn., Assn. N.Y. State Suprme Ct. Justices, Nassau County Magistrates Assn. (bd. dirs. 1995-96), The Creek Club (Locust Valley, N.Y.), Sigma Nu. Democrat. E-mail: judgewinslow@yahoo.com.

WINSLOW, JOHN FRANKLIN, lawyer; b. Houston, Nov. 15, 1933; s. Franklin Jarnigan and Jane (Shipley) W. BA, U. Tex., 1957, LLB, 1960. Bar: Tex. 1959, D.C. 1961. Atty., Hispanic law div. Library Congress, Washington, 1965-68; counsel, com. on the judiciary Ho. of Reps., 1968-71; atty., editor Matthew Bender & Co., 1973-79; atty. FERC, 1979-84; sole practice, 1984—. Researcher Hispanic Law Research, Washington, 1979—. Author: Conglomerates Unlimited: The Failure of Regulation, 1974; editor: Fed. Power Service, 1974-79; contbr. articles to Washington Monthly, Nation, 1975—. Mem. Tex. Bar Assn., D.C. Bar Assn. E-mail: jfwinslow@aol.com.

WINSLOW, JULIAN DALLAS, retired lawyer, historian, writer; b. Elizabeth City, N.C., Oct. 10, 1914; s. Joseph D. and Mary Anne (Cooper) W.; m. Jean Littell, Dec. 27, 1941; children: Julian Dallas, Mary P. Winslow Reddick, Helen L. BS in Commerce, U. N.C., 1935, JD, 1941; MA in History, U. Del., 1988. Bar: N.C. 1941, Del. 1949, U.S. Dist. Ct. Del. 1952, U.S. Ct. Appeals (3d cir.) 1982. Assoc. J.H. LeRoy Jr., Elizabeth City, 1941-42; pvt. practice, 1945-48, Wilmington, Del., 1949-89; ret., 1989; ptnr. Winslow Realty Co., 1974—. Solicitor Currituck County (N.C.) Ct. 1946-47; chief of enforcement heavy machinery and indsl. materials sect. Office Price Stablzn., Del. dist. 1952; arbitrator Am. Arbitration Assn. Author: Samuel Maxwell Harrington, A Pioneer Judge, 1994, Sussex Awakens to the Toot, 1999. Lt. USCG, 1942-45. Decorated Philippine Liberation medal. Mem. ABA (real estate, probate and trust, labor sects.), Del. State Bar Assn. (com. labor and employment law). Republican. Episcopalian.

WINSLOW, LILLIAN RUTH, nurse; b. Laconia, N.H., Oct. 23, 1930; d. James Edwin and Clemency (Anstey) Burbank; m. John Herrick Winslow, Apr. 25, 1964; children: Alice Faith Winslow Gay, Ruth Ellen Tenpenny. Diploma, Laconia (N.H.) Hosp. Sch. Nursing, 1951; BA, Providence Barrington Bible Coll., 1956; postgrad., Escuela de Idiomas, San Jose, Costa Rica, 1959. Sch. RN emotionally disturbed and handicapped Bedell Sch., Apache Junction, Ariz., 1977—79; sch. RN East Mesa (Ariz.) Christian Acad., 1982—83, Maranatha Christian Acad., 1980—81; nurse Mesa (Ariz.) Gen. Hosp. Med. Ctr., 1984—96; vis. RN Christian Home Health Svcs., Mesa, Ariz., 1994—99; pvt. duty nurse, 1999—. Missionary RN, World Radio Missionary Fellowship, Inc., Quito, Ecuador, 1959-63; camp RN, Camp Good News, 1971, Camp Pinnacle, N.H., 1968; mem., choir RN the Acapella Choir, Providence Barrington Bible Coll., 1954-57. Recipient Cert. of Appreciation for Devoted and Invaluable Svcs., Maranatha Christian Acad., 1980-81. Home: 1981 W 10th Ave Apache Junction AZ 85220-6933

WINSLOW, NORMA MAE, elementary education educator; b. Pawling, N.Y., Oct. 18, 1942; d. Franklin Norman and Florence (Chandler) Timpson; m. Donald Arthur Winslow, Aug. 5, 1961; children: Gregory Donald (dec.), Kevin Craig. AA in Liberal Arts, Adirondack Coll., 1970; BS in Edn. summa cum laude, Castleton State U., 1973; MS in Adminstrn. and Supervision, SUNY, Plattsburg, 1990; CAS, Plattsburgh State U., 1993. Cert. elem. and secondary tchr., N.Y., SAS and SDA in Adminstrn. Tchr. Ft. Ann (N.Y.) Cen. Sch., 1973-77, Corinth (N.Y.) Cen. Sch., 1977—, grade chair, 1984-89; Cert. of Advanced Study. Dir. music Corinth Theatre Guild, 1980—. Named Outstanding Tchr. of English, N.Y. State English Coun., 1981, One of 2000 Notable Women, 1995. Mem. Corinth Tchrs. Assn. (pres. 1980-86, 94-95), Rotary (pres. Corinth chpt. 1992, Paul Harris fellow), Delta Kappa Gamma (officer Beta Omega chpt. 1980—). Avocation: music. Home: 320 Center St Corinth NY 12822-1104 Office: Corinth Cen Sch 105 Oak St Corinth NY 12822-1203

WINSLOW, NORMAN ELDON, business executive; b. Oakland, Calif., Apr. 4, 1938; s. Merton Conrad and Roberta Eilene (Drennen) W.; m. Betty June Cady, Jan. 14, 1962 (div. Aug. 1971); 1 child, Todd Kenelm; m. Ilene Ruth Jackson, Feb. 3, 1979. BS, Fresno (Calif.) State U., 1959. Asst. mgr. Proctors Jewelers, Fresno, 1959-62; from agt. to dist. mgr. Allstate Ins. Co., 1962-69; ins. agt. Fidelity Union Life Ins., Dallas, 1969-71; dist. and zone mgr. The Southland Corp., 1971-78; owner Ser-Vis-Etc., Goleta, Calif., 1978—. Expert witness, cons. Am. Arbitration/Calif. Superior Cts. *Norman Winslow has been involved in the convenience store industry since 1971. His business since 1978 involves serving as a consultant to franchise owners of 7-Eleven Stores. He specializes in accounting issues, inventory and loss control, and the re-sale of stores, and has increased profits for his clients by $75 million. Serving as an advocate for 7-Eleven Franchisees, he has been a guest speaker at six National Franchise Conventions since 1987.* Pub./editor FranchiserviceNews; author: Hands in Your Pockets, 1992; contbr. numerous articles to profl. jours. With USAFNG, 1961-67. Mem. Nat. Coalition of Assn. of 7-11 Franchises (affiliate, mem. adv. bd. 1984-90). Republican. Methodist. Avocations: gardening, photography, traveling, model railroading. Home: 1179 N Patterson Ave Santa Barbara CA 93117-1813 Office: Ser-Vis-Etc PO Box 8276 Goleta CA 93118-8276 E-mail: serv-vis-etc@aol.com.

WINSLOW, PAUL DAVID, architect; b. Phoenix, June 12, 1941; s. Fred D. and Thelma E. (Ward) W.; 1 child, Kirk David. BArch, Ariz. State U., 1964. Lic. architect, Ariz., Calif., Nev. Ptnr. The Orcutt/Winslow Partnership, Phoenix, 1972—. Speaker solar energy workshops, Phoenix, 1986-89; adj. prof. Ariz. State U., 1991; mem. profl. adv. coun. Ariz. State U. Coll. Architecture, Tempe, 1970—, bd. dirs. Architecture Found., 1972-76; mem. adv. com. City of Phoenix Bldg. Safety Bd., 1981; mem. adv. bd. Herberger Ctr.; pres. Ariz. State U. Coll. Architecture, Coun. for Design Excellence; bd. dirs. Ctrl. Ariz. Project Assn., Phoenix, 1971-74, Ariz. Ctr. for Law in the Pub. Interest, Phoenix, 1979-86, Phoenix Cmty. Alliance; chmn. Encanto Village Planning Com., Phoenix, 1981-86; chmn. Indian Sch. Citizens adv. com. Ind. Sch. Land Use Planning Team; lectr. on planning Ariz. State U., 1989, city of Presott, Phoenix and Tempe, 1988-89; active Coun. Ednl. Facilities Planners Internat. Mem. Steering Com. on Re-inventing Neighborhoods Project; chmn. Central and Roosevelt Coalition, 1998-99; chmn. City of Phoenix Neighborhood Initiative Area Steering Com., 1998-99; pres. bd. dirs. Harrington House Internat. Ctr. for Universal Design, 1998-99; pres. bd. dirs. Maryvale Edn. Mall, 1998-99; exec. com. Phoenix Cmty. Alliance. Fellow AIA (bd. dirs. ctrl. Ariz. chpt., also sec., treas., pres.); mem. Ariz. Soc. Architects (bd. dirs. 1970-71, 78-82), Bldg. Owners and Mgrs. Assn. Greater Phoenix (pres. 1989-90, 90-91), Boar Valley Forward Assn. (exec. com. 1994-99), Ariz. Club (Phoenix). Methodist. Home: 5941 E Edgemont Ave Scottsdale AZ 85257 Office: The Orcutt/Winslow Partnership 1130 N 2nd St Phoenix AZ 85004-1896 E-mail: winslow.p@owp.com.

WINSLOW, WALTER WILLIAM, psychiatrist, educator; b. Lacombe, Alta., Can., Nov. 23, 1925; came to U.S., 1959, naturalized, 1964; s. Floyd Raymond and Lily Evangeline (Palmer) W.; m. Barbara Ann Spiker; children: Colleen Denise, Dwight Walter, Barbara Jean, Wendi Jae. BS, La Sierra Coll., 1949; MD, Loma Linda U., 1952. Diplomate: Am. Bd. Psychiatry and Neurology. Intern Vancouver Gen. Hosp., 1952; psychiat. resident Provincial Mental Hosp., Essondale, B.C., 1957-59, Harding Hosp., Worthington, Ohio, 1959-60; instr. dept. psychiatry and indsl. medicine U. Cin., 1960-66, dept. preventive medicine, 1964-66; asst. prof. psychiatry U. N.Mex., Albuquerque, 1966-68, assoc. prof. psychiatry, 1969-74, prof., chmn. dept. psychiatry, 1974-91, dir. mental health programs, 1976-91; med. dir. Charter Hosp. of Albuquerque, 1991-95, Charter-Heights BHS, Albuquerque, 1995—99. Assoc. prof. psychiatry Georgetown U., Washington, 1968-69; dir. bernalillo County Mental Health/Mental Retardation Ctr., 1970-78, 81-91. Contbr. articles to profl. jours. Recipient N.Mex. Gov.'s Commendation for 10 yrs. service in mental health, 1979 Fellow Am. Psychiat. Assn. (life, area VII rep. 1981-85, Assembly Speaker's award 1984), Am. Coll. of Psychiatrists, Am. Assn. Community Psychiatrists (hon.); mem. AMA, Am. Assn. Psychiatry and the Law, N.Mex. Psychiat. Assn. (pres. 1974-75) Republican. Office: 1625 Catron SE Albuquerque NM 87123-4255

WINSOR, DAVID JOHN, cost consultant; b. Duluth, Minn., May 27, 1947; s. Alphonse Joseph and Sylvia Mae (Petrich) W.; div. BA in Bus., U. Puget Sound, 1978; M of Mech. Engring., Pacific Western U., 1979. Jr. engr. J.P. Head Mech., Inc., Richland, Wash., 1965-67; estimator, project engr. Subs. of Howard S. Wright Co., Seattle, 1972-75; sr. estimator Massart Co., 1975-76; project mgr. Univ. Mechanical, Portland, Oreg., 1976; cons. Kent, Wash., 1976-79; owner Leasair, Federal Way, 1978-83; pres., owner Expertise Engring. & Cons., Inc., Bellevue, 1979-82, 90-95; cons. Winsor & Co., Walnut Creek, Calif., 1983—; estimator IDC, Portland, Oreg., 1996-99; cons., 1999—. Cons. NASA, Mountain View, Calif., 1986, Lockheed Missile & Space, Sunnyvale, Calif., 1984-87, The Boeing Co., Seattle, 1979-82. Author: (with others) Current Construction Costs, 1987, 88, 89, Construction Materials Inventory Systems, 1973, 74, Construction Inflation Trends, 1975, 76, 77, 78, 79, 80, 81, Construction Claims and Prevention, 1981, 82. Served to sgt. USAF, 1967-71. Mem. Jaycees (state dir. 1972-73, state chmn. 1973-74). Republican. Roman Catholic. Avocations: flying, golf, car and gun collecting.

WINSOR, ELEANOR WEBSTER, dispute resolution company executive; b. Champaign, Ill., Dec. 1, 1941; d. Chauncey Wilson and Eleanor (Litschauer) Webster; m. Curtin Winsor, May 6, 1972; 1 child, Ellen. AB, Hollins Coll., 1963; MA, U. Pa., 1966; DSc, Wilkes U., 1986. Mng. dir. Nat. and Hist. Resource Assn., Phila., 1967-74; exec. v.p. Pa. Environ. Coun., 1974-86, Pa. Environ. Rsch. Fedn., Phila., 1974-86; pres. Winsor Assocs., Ardmore, Pa., 1984—. Bd. dirs. Pa. Coun. Mediators, 1988-93, chairperson,

1989-90. Mem. citizens adv. coun. Pa. Dept. Environ. Resources, 1979-88, mem. environ. quality bd., 1980-83, 84-88; mem. Lower Merion Twp. Planning Commn., Ardmore, 1974-97, chairperson, 1990—; bd. dirs. Pa. Resources Coun., Media, 1969-86; chairperson Pa. Solid Waste Adv. Com., Harrisburg, 1984-86; chairperson bd. trustees West Hill Sch., Rosemont, Pa., 1985-91; trustee Agnes Irwin Sch., Rosemont, 1985-91. Recipient Conservationist of Yr., North Area Environ. Coun., 1984. Mem.: Internat. Assn. Facilitators, Nat. Assn. Dispute Resolution, Soc. for Profls. in Dispute Resolution (sec. Del. Valley chpt. 1993—96, chairperson 1996—2000), Am. Arbitration Assn. (mem. panel). Episcopalian. Office: Winsor Assocs 7534 Scottsville Rd Scottsville VA 24590

WINSTANLEY, DEREK, water resource executive; b. Wigan, England, May 19, 1945; s. Thomas and Bessie W.; m. Betty Lon, Jan. 30, 1982; children: Deborah Lon, Stuart Neil, Kay Dee. BA, Oxford Univ., England, 1966; MA, DPhil, Oxford Univ., 1970. Dir. Nat. Acid Precipitation Assessment Program, Washington, 1992-94; deputy chief scientist Nat. Oceanic and Atmospheric Adminstrn., 1994-97; chief Ill. State Water Survey, Champaign, Ill., 1997—. Adj. prof. geography U. Ill., Champaign, 1997—. Editor: The Scientific World; contbr. articles to profl. jours. Chair Ill. Global Climate Change Task Force, Springfield, Ill., 1999-2000; mem. sci. adv. com. Ill. River Coordination Coun., Springfield, 1999—. Mem. Am. Meterological Soc., Am. Geophysical Union. Avocations: wood sculpture, photography. Office: 2204 Griffith Dr Champaign IL 61820-7463 E-mail: dwinstan@uiuc.edu

WINSTEAD, DANIEL KEITH, psychiatrist; b. Cin., Dec. 30, 1944; s. Daniel Sebastian and Betty Jane (Kirsch) W.; m. Jennifer Reiner, June 15, 1968; children: Laura Suzanne, Nathaniel Scott. BA, U. Cin., 1966; MD, Vanderbilt U., 1970. Diplomate Am. Bd. Psychiatry and Neurology. Resident U. Cin., 1970-72, fellow, 1972-73; chief VA Med. Ctr. psychiat. svc. Tulane U., New Orleans, 1976-79, dir., consultation/liaison psychiat. tng., 1979-83, dir. psychiatric edn. and residency tng., 1983-87, assoc. prof., 1979-84, prof., 1984—, chmn. dept. psychiatry and neurology, 1987—; chief psychiat. svc. VA Med. Ctr., 1976-80; assoc. chief staff for edn. VA Med Ctr., 1979-87; staff psychiatrist VA Med. Ctr., 1987—. Med. dir. Jefferson Parish Substance Abuse Clinic, 1980-81; cons. E.R. Squibb and Sons, 1985-86; vis. physician psychiatry Charity Hosp., New Orleans, 1979-90. Contbr. articles to profl. jours. Maj. U.S. Army, 1973-76. Mem. AMA, Am. Coll. Psychiatrists, Am. Acad. Psychiatry and Law, Am. Psychiat. Assn., La. State Med. Soc., So. Assn. for Rsch. in Psychiatry, Acad. Psychosomatic Medicine (pres.), Am. Assn. Chairmen Depts. Psychiatry (pres.-elect), Am. Assn. Dirs. Psychiat. Residency Tng., Assn. Acad. Psychiatry, La. Psychiat. Assn. (pres. 1991-92), Soc. Biol. Psychiatry, New Orleans Area Psychiat. Assn., New Orleans Neurol. Soc., Orleans Parish Med. Soc. Republican. Presbyterian. Avocations: oenology, travel. Home: 5348 Bellaire Dr New Orleans LA 70124-1033 Office: Tulane Med Sch 1440 Canal St Ste 1000 New Orleans LA 70112-2703 E-mail: winstead@tulane.edu.

WINSTEAD, ELISABETH WEAVER, poet, writer, English language educator; b. Nashville, July 31, 1926; d. Charles Preston and Carrie Lawrence (Hadley) Weaver; m. George Alvis Winstead, July 18, 1942. BA, Vanderbilt U., 1946; MA, Peabody Coll. Vanderbilt U., 1947; postgrad., Vanderbilt U., 1980-83, Trevecca Nazarene, 1975-79. Cert. tchr. of lang. arts, bus. edn., social sci., English, Tenn., Va., Ind., Idaho, Ariz. Head bus. edn. dept. La Crosse (Ind.) High Sch., 1947-48, Franklin (Tenn.) High Sch., 1952-54, Belmont Coll., Nashville, 1954-56; with English dept. Boise (Idaho) High Sch., 1948-49; critical analyst Dept. Commerce, Washington, 1949-50; with bus. edn. dept. Averitt Coll., Danville, Va., 1950-52; elem. and high sch. tchr. Met. Nashville Schs., 1956-85. Cons. Model Tchr. Program, Nashville Met. Sch., 1958-68, mem. faculty adv. coun., 1970-79, mem. profl. devel. coun., 1980-84. Author: Social Studies Curriculum Guide, 1970, Metro Beautiful Programs, 1976, Metro PTA School History, 1980; contbr. poetry to anthologies and popular mags., including Ideals, New Hope Books, The Vanderbilt Review. Chmn. TB Seal Drive, Franklin, 1956-60, March of Dimes Fund Drive, Nashville, 1982-84, Red Cross Blood Drive, Nashville, 1984-86; capt. Heart Fund Drive, Nashville, 1979-81. Recipient Tchr. Appreciation awrd Sta. WKDA, 1970, Galaxy of Stars award Nashville Met. Schs., 1982, Ednl. Appreciation award City of Nashville, 1983, Commendation for pub. svc. Tenn. Legislature, 1994; named to Honorable Order of Ky. Cols., 1988. Mem. NEA, Am. Childhood Edn. Internat., Tenn. Hist. Soc., Wisdom Soc., Kappa Delta Pi (hon.), Pi Omega Pi (hon.), Pi Gamma Mu (hon.). Baptist. Avocations: camping, boating, gardening, reading, creative writing. Home: 3819 Gallatin Rd Nashville TN 37216-2609

WINSTEAD, GEORGE ALVIS, law librarian, biochemist, educator, consultant; b. Owensboro, Ky., Jan. 14, 1916; s. Robert Lee and Mary Oma (Dempsey) Winstead; m. Elisabeth Donelson Weaver, July 18, 1942. BS, We. Ky. U., 1938; MA, George Peabody Coll., 1940, MLS, 1957, MEd, 1958. Head chemistry and biology dept. Belmont Coll., Nashville, 1952-56; head chemistry dept. George Peabody Coll., Vanderbilt U., 1956-58; assoc. law librarian Vanderbilt U., 1958-76; dir. Tenn. State Supreme Ct. Law Libraries, 1976—. Law cons. Tenn. Youth Legis., Nashville, 1976—; cons. civic clubs, local colls., 1976—, Tenn. State Govt. Depts. Archives, Nashville, 1976—. Author: Tenn. State Law Library Progress Reports, 1975, Supreme Court Library Personnel Guide, 1981, Designing Future Law Libraries' Growth and Expansion, 1982, Problem Identification and Solutions in Law Libraries, Tenn. Supreme Courts, 1985; mem. editl. bd. A Dictionary of Chemical Equations, 1952—. Mem. Col. Tenn. Gov.'s staff, Nashville, 1978. With USAAF, 1943-46. Named to Gov.'s Staff of Ky. Cols., Lexington, 1988. Fellow Am. Inst. Chemists, SAR. Baptist. Avocations: camping, hiking, traveling, crafts, antique cars. Home: 3819 Gallatin Pike Nashville TN 37216-2609 Office: Tenn Supreme Ct Libr Nashville TN 37219

WINSTEAD, NASH NICKS, university administrator, phytopathologist; b. Durham County, N.C., June 12, 1925; s. Nash L. and Lizzy (Featherston) W.; m. Geraldine Larkin Kelly, Sept. 17, 1949; 1 dau., Karen Jewell. BS, N.C. State U., 1948, MS, 1951; PhD, U. Wis., 1953. Asst. prof. plant pathology, Raleigh, 1953-58; assoc. prof. N.C. State U., 1958-61, prof., 1961-90, prof. emeritus, 1991—, dir. inst. biol. scis., 1965-67, asst. dir. agrl. exptl. sta., 1965-67, asst. provost, 1967-73, assoc. provost, 1973-74, provost and vice chancellor, 1974-90, acting chancellor, 1981-82. Phillip Found. intern acad. adminstrn. Ind. U., 1965-66; bd. trustees N.C. Sch. Sci. and Math., 1985-90. Author: Home grown and Homemade, 1997, Mama's Book, 1998, The Provost's Office N.C. State U., An Informal History, 1955-93, 1999, The Civil War Campaigns Involving Corporal James Fletcher Winstead, 1999, Feathertson Memories, 2002; contbr. articles profl. jours. Mem. N.C. Council on Higher Edn. for Adults, 1967-75; inst. rep. So. Assn. for Colls. and Schs., 1967-74; mem. Cooperating Raleigh Colls., 1968-90, pres., 1971-73, 83-85; chmn. interaction between protoplasm and toxicants com. So. Regional Edn. Bd., 1964-65; Bd. dirs. N.C. State U. YMCA, 1963-65; trustee Meth. Home for Children, 1980-88, pres., 1983-84, N.C. Wesleyan Coll., 1987-97. Served with USAAF, 1943-46. Recipient Sigma Xi research award, 1960 Fellow AAAS; Mem. Am. Phytopath. Soc. (chmn. disease, pathogen physiology com.), Am. Inst. Biol. Scis., N.C. Assn. Colls. and Univs. (exec. com. 1974-80, pres. 1978-79); Nat. Assn. State Univs. and Land Grant Colls. (edn. telecommunications com. 1980-85, equal opportunity com. 1985-88), Acad. Deans for So. States, N.C. Assn. of Acad. Officers (exec. com. 1986-89, v.p., pres. 1987-88), Sigma Xi, Phi Kappa Phi, Omicron Delta Kappa. Clubs: Torch Internat. (sec.). Home: 1109 Glendale Dr Raleigh NC 27612-4709

WINSTEN, SAUL NATHAN, lawyer; b. Providence, Feb. 23, 1953; s. Harold H. and Anita E. Winsten; m. Patricia J. Miller, Aug. 7, 1977; children: David A., J. Benjamin, Jennifer M. BA, Beloit Coll., 1976; JD, Drake U., 1980. Ptnr. Michael, Best & Friedrich, Milw., 1988—. Contbr. articles to profl. jours. Co-chmn. Wis. Gov.'s Adv. Coun. on Internat. Trade, 1996-2000, mem., 1996—, Wis. Gov.'s Internat. Edn. Task Force, 1997-98. Mem. ABA (chmn. com. young lawyers divsn. 1989-90, governing coun., antitrust, bus. and internat. law sects.), Wis. Bar Assn., Internat. Bar Assn., Japan-Am. Soc. Wis. (pres. 1993-94, co-founder 1990, sec. 1990-92), Nat. Assn. Japan-Am. Socs. (bd. dirs. 1991-98, exec. com. 1993-97), Am. Soc. Assn. Execs. (legal sect.), Order of Barristers, Hessen-Wisconsin, Inc. (bd. dirs.). Office: Michael Best & Friedrich 100 E Wisconsin Ave Ste 3300 Milwaukee WI 53202-4108

WINSTON, EILEEN LYNN, rheumatologist; b. N.Y.C., Feb. 6, 1954; d. Leonard Winston and Muriel (Wiener) W.; m. Gary Alan Rosenberg, May 25, 1975; children: Kimberly Anne Rosenberg, Adam Winston Rosenberg. BS, SUNY, Stony Brook, 1974; MD, Boston U., 1978. Diplomate Nat. Bd. Med. Examiners, Am. Bd. Internal Medicine, Am. Bd. Rheumatology. Internship in internal medicine Boston City Hosp., 1978-79, jr. and sr. residency in internal medicine, 1979-81; fellowship in clin. immunology and rheumatology New Eng. Med. Ctr., Boston, 1981-83; assoc. staff Tufts-New Eng. Med. Ctr., 1983-85; practice in rheumatology Braintree (Mass.) Hosp., 1983-85; courtesy staff Leonard Morse Hosp. and Framingham (Mass.) Union Hosp., 1985-90; active vis. staff Metrowest Med. Ctr., 1990-91; staff physician rheumatology and internal medicine Medical East, Framingham, 1985-89; pvt. practice rheumatology, 1989—; courtesy staff U. Mass. Med. Sys. Marlborough Hosp., 1989—; active vis. staff Metrowest Med. Ctr., 1992—, Framingham Union. Recipient Sr. Fellowship award N.E. Regional Am. Rheumatism Assn., 1982. Mem. Mass. Med. Soc., New Eng. Rheumatism Soc.,Am. Coll. Rheumatology. Avocations: cooking, photography, skiing, hiking, swimming. Office: MetroWest Rheumatology PC 61 Lincoln St Ste 203 Framingham MA 01702 E-mail: ewmd@aol.com.

WINSTON, GEORGE, solo pianist, guitarist, harmonica player; b. Hart, Mich., 1949; Ind. musician, 1967—; founder Dancing Cat Productions, Santa Cruz, CA, 1983—. Eight solo piano albums, including Ballads and Blues, 1972, Autumn, 1980, Winter Into Spring, 1982, December, 1982, Summer, 1991, Forest, 1994, Linus & Lucy: The Music of Vince Guaraldi, 1996, Plains, 1999, Night Divides the Day--The music of the Doors, 2002; audiobook soundtracks: (with Meryl Streep) The Velveteen Rabbit, 1985, This is America Charley Brown--Birth of the Constitution, 1988, (with Liv Ullmann) Sadako and the Thousand Paper Cranes, 1995; prodr. 33 albums of the masters of traditional Hawaiian slack key (finger style) guitar. Office: c/o Dancing Cat Prodns PO Box 639 Santa Cruz CA 95061-0639 E-mail: ml@dancingcat.com.

WINSTON, HAROLD RONALD, lawyer; b. Atlantic, Iowa, Feb. 7, 1932; s. Louis D. and Leta B. (Carter) W.; m. Carol J. Sundeen, June 11, 1955; children: Leslie Winston Yannetti, Lisa Winston Shaw, Laura Winston Moritz. BA, U. Iowa, 1954, JD, 1958. Bar: Iowa 1958, U.S. Dist. Ct. (no. and so. dists.) Iowa 1962, U.S. Tax Ct. 1962, U.S. Ct. Appeals (8th cir.) 1970, U.S. Supreme Ct. 1969. Trust officer United Home Bank & Trust Co., Mason City, Iowa, 1958-59; mem. Breese & Cornwell, 1960-62, Breese, Cornwell, Winston & Reuber, Mason City, 1963-73, Winston, Schroeder & Reuber, Mason City, 1974-79, Winston, Reuber, Swanson & Byrne, P.C., Mason City, 1980-92, Winston, Reuber & Byrne, Mason City, 1992-96, Winston & Byrne, P.C., Mason City, 1996—. Police judge, Mason City, 1961-73. Contbr. articles to profl. jours. Past pres. Family YMCA, Mason City, Cerro Gordo County Estate Planning Coun.; active local charitable orgns. Capt. USAF, 1955-57. Fellow Am. Coll. Trust and Estate Counsel, Am. Bar Found. (life), Iowa Bar Found. (life); mem. ABA, ATLA, Iowa Bar Assn. (gov., lectr. ann. meeting 1977-79), 2d Jud. Dist. Bar Assn. (lectr. meeting 1981-82), Cerro Gordo County Bar Assn. (past pres.), Am. Judicature Soc., Mason City Country Club, Kiwanis, Masons. Republican. Presbyterian. Office: Winston & Byrne 119 2d St NW Mason City IA 50401-3105 E-mail: hwinston@netins.net.

WINSTON, JANET MARGARET, real estate agent, civic volunteer; b. Binghamton, N.Y., Sept. 30, 1937; d. Cornelius Adrian and Vera Helene (Strohman) Salie; m. Edmund Joseph Winston, Nov. 29, 1958 (dec. July 1981); children: Mark Edmund, Deborah Ann. Student, SUNY, 1955-57, Bliss Coll., 1978. Sales assoc. HER Realtors, Worthington, Ohio, 1979—. Dist. chair women's divsn. Cmty. Chest ARC, Kalamazoo, 1970; docent Indpls. Mus. Art, 1975, Columbus (Ohio) Mus. Art, 1976—, beaux art mem., 1976—87; docent Chinese Son of Heaven Exhibit, 1989, mus. fund drive, 1986—87, 1989—95; trustee Worthington Resource Ctr., 1979—84, v.p., 1984, chair youth employment svcs., 1980—83; trustee, sec. Worthington Hills Civil Assn., 1986—89; bd. dirs. Sessions Soc., 2001—02. Recipient Nat. Sales award The Dozen, 1996, TopHER award, 1980—. Mem.: Ohio Assn. Realtors, Nat. Assn. Realtors, Columbus Bd. Realtors (pub. rels. com. 1980, 1983, 1986, 1988, sales adv. com. 1987, svcs. task force 1989, 10 Million Dollar Club award), Worthington C. of C., Worthington Women's Club, Worthington Hills Garden Club (bd. dirs. 1989), Worthington Hills Women's Club. Republican. Episcopalian. Avocations: art, music, golf. Home: 8036 Golfview Ct Columbus OH 43235-1230 Office: HER Realtors 6902 N High St Worthington OH 43085-2555 E-mail: jane.winston@aol.com.

WINSTON, JUDITH ANN, lawyer; b. Atlantic City, Nov. 23, 1943; d. Edward Carlton and Margaret Ann (Goodman) Marianno; m. Michael Russell Winston, Aug. 10, 1963; children: Lisa Marie, Cynthia Eileen. BA magna cum laude, Howard U., Washington, 1966; JD, Georgetown U., 1977. Bar: DC 1977, US Supreme Ct. Dir. EEO project Coun. Great City Schs., Washington, 1971-74; legal asst. Lawyers Com. for Civil Rights Under Law, 1975-77; spl. asst. to dir. Office for Civil Rights, HEW, 1977-79; exec. asst., legal counsel to chair U.S. EEO Commn., 1979-80; asst. gen. counsel U.S. Dept. Edn., 1980-86; dep. dir. Lawyers Com. for Civil Rights Under Law, 1986-88; dep. dir. pub. policy Women's Legal Def. Fund, Washington, 1988-90, chair employment discrimination com., 1979-88, ednl. cons., 1974-77; asst. prof. law Washington Coll. Law of Am. U., 1990-93, assoc. prof. law, 1993-95, rsch. prof. law, 2001—; gen. counsel U.S. Dept. Edn., Washington, 1993-2001; exec. dir. Pres.'s Initiative on Race, 1997-98; undersec. U.S. Dept. Edn., 2000-01; research prof law Washington Col Law Am Univ, 2001—. Author: (book) Desegregating Schools in the Great Cities: Philadelphia, 1970, Chronicle of a Decade 1961-70, 1970, Desegregating Urban Schools: Educational Equality/Quality, 1970; contbr. articles to profl jours. Pres. bd. dirs. Higher Achievement Program; bd. dirs. Ptnrs. for Dem. Change, Nat. Pub. Radio, So. Edn. Found. Named Woman Lawyer of the Yr, Women's Bar Asn, 1997; recipient Margaret Brent, Am Bar Asn Comn Women in the Profession, 1998. Fellow: ABA Found; mem.: ACLU, Lawyers Comt Civil Rights Under Law, Nat Bar Asn, Washington Bar Asn, Washington Coun Lawyers, DC Bar Asn, Fed Bar Asn, Links Inc, Phi Beta Kappa, Delta Theta Phi, Alpha Kappa Alpha. Democrat. Episcopalian. Home: 1371 Kalmia Rd NW Washington DC 20012-1444 Office: Am U Law Sch 4801 Massachusetts AveNW Washington DC 20016-0001

WINSTON, KRISHNA, foreign language professional; b. Greenfield, Mass., June 7, 1944; d. Richard and Clara (Brussel) W.; 1 child, Danielle Billingsley. BA, Smith Coll., 1965; MPhil, Yale U., 1969, PhD, 1974. Instr. Wesleyan U., Middletown, Conn., 1970-74, asst. prof., 1974-77, assoc. prof., 1977-84, prof., 1984—, acting dean, 1993-94. Coord. Mellon Minority Undergrad. Program, 1993—. Author: O v. Horváth: Close Readings of Six Plays, 1975; translator: O. Schlemmer, Letters and Diaries, 1972, S. Lenz, The Heritage, 1981, G. Grass, Two States, One Nation, 1990, C. Hein, The Distant Lover, 1989, G. Mann, Reminiscences and Reflections, 1990, J. W. V. Goethe, Wilhelm Meister's Journeyman Years, 1989, C. v. Krockow, The Hour of the Women, 1991, E. Heller, With the Next Man Everything Will be Different, 1992, R. W. Fassbinder, The Anarchy of the Imagination, 1992, G. Reuth, Goebbels, 1994, E. Lappin, editor, Jewish Voices, German Words, 1994, P. Handke, Essay on the Jukebox, 1994, P. Handke, My Year in the No-Man's-Bay, 1998, G. Grass, Too Far Afield, 2000, P. Handke, On a Dark Night I Left My Silent House, 2000, G. Grass, Crabnik, 2003. Vol. Planned Parenthood, Middletown, 1972-77; mem. Recycling Task Force, Middletown, 1986-87; chmn. Resource Recycling Adv. Coun., Middletown, 1989—. Recipient Schlegel-Tieck prize for translation, 1994, 2001, Helen and Kurt Wolff prize for transl., 2001; German Acad. Exch. Svc. fellow. Mem. MLA, ALTA, Soc. for Exile Studies, Am. Assn. Tchrs. German, PEN, Phi Beta Kappa (pres. Wesleyan chpt. 1987-90). Home: 655 Bow Ln Middletown CT 06457-4808 Office: Wesleyan Univ German Studies Dept Middletown CT 06459-0040 E-mail: kwinston@wesleyan.edu.

WINSTON, MICHAEL RUSSELL, foundation executive, historian; b. N.Y.C., May 26, 1941; s. Charles Russell and Jocelyn Anita Prem Das Winston; m. Judith Ann Marianno, Aug. 10, 1963; children: Lisa Marie, Cynthia Eileen. BA magna cum laude, Howard U., 1962; MA, U. Calif.-Berkeley, 1964, PhD, 1974. Instr. dept. history Howard U., Washington, 1964-66, asst. dean Coll. Liberal Arts, 1968-69, asst. prof. dept. history, 1970-73, v.p. acad. affairs, 1983-90, prof. emeritus, 1990—; assoc. dir. Inst. Svcs. to Edn., 1966; fellow Haus. Hof-und Staatsarchiv, Vienna, Austria, 1969; dir. Moorland Spingarn Rsch. Ctr., 1973-83; v.p., bd. dirs. Alfred Harcourt Found., Silver Spring, Md., 1992-93, pres., 1993—. Cons. Smithsonian Instn., 1979—, nat. Inst. Edn., 1978-85, NSF, 1985—. Author: (with R.W. Logan) The Negro in the United States, 1970, The Howard University Department of History, 1913-73, 1973; editor: (with R.W. Logan) Dictionary of American Negro Biography, 1982, (with G.R. McNeil) Historical Judgements Reconsidered, 1988; mem. editl. bd. Washington History, 1993-97. Mem. exec. bd. Nat. Capital Area coun. Boy Scouts Am., 1988—90; trustee spl. contbn. fund NAACP, 1980—82; trustee D.C. Pub. Defender Svc., 1985—88; bd. trustees Woodrow Wilson Nat. Fellowship Found., 1997—; bd. mgrs. Hist. Soc. Washington; bd. dirs. Harcourt Brace Jovanovich, 1980—91, D.C. Pub. Libr. Found., 1994—2002, pres., 1995—99, Nat. Coun. for History Standards; mem. bd. overseers' com. to visit dept. history Harvard U., 1996—; mem. nat. adv. com. and coun. of scholars Libr. of Congress; nat. adv. bd. Protect Historic Am.; mem. Commn. on Coll. and Univ. Nonprofl. Studies ABA; mem. Nat. Ctr. for History in the Schs. UCLA/NEH. Moten fellow U. Edinburgh, 1962, Wilson fellow U. Calif., 1962, Ford fellow, 1969-70, Woodrow Wilson Internat. Ctr. Scholars fellow, 1979-80; sr. scholar, 2001—. Mem.: Nat. Coun. for History Standards, Coun. on Foreign Relations, Atlantic Coun. of U.S., Hist. Soc. Washington, Am. Antiquarian Soc., Orgn. Am. Historians, Am. Hist. Asn., Grolier Club (N.Y.C. chpt.), Century Assn., Cosmos Club (Washington), Phi Beta Kappa (Ralph Waldo Emerson prize com. 2000). Democrat. Presbyterian. Home: 1371 Kalmia Rd NW Washington DC 20012-1444 Office: Alfred Harcourt Found 8401 Colesville Rd Silver Spring MD 20910-3352 E-mail: mwinston@erols.com.

WINSTON, ROLAND, physicist, educator; b. Moscow, USSR, Feb. 12, 1936; s. Joseph and Claudia (Goretskaya) W.; m. Patricia Louise LeGette, June 10, 1957; children: Joseph, John, Gregory. AB, Shimer Coll., 1953; BS, U. Chgo., 1956, MS, 1957, PhD, 1963. Asst. prof. physics U. Pa., 1963-64; mem. faculty U. Chgo., 1964—, prof. physics, 1975—, chmn. physics dept., 1989-95. Recipient Kraus medal Franklin Inst., 1996, First Solar Personality of the Yr. award, Bangalore, India, 1999. Fellow: Am. Solar Energy Soc., Am. Optical Soc., Am. Phys. Soc., AAAS; mem.: Internat. Solar Energy Soc. ((Abbot award 1987, Farrington Daniels award 2001)), Franklin Inst. (hon.). Achievements include patent for ideal light collector for solar concentrators. Home: 5217 S University Ave Apt C Chicago IL 60615-4439 Office: Physics Dept U Chgo 5640 S Ellis Ave Chicago IL 60637-1433 E-mail: r-winston@uchicago.edu.

WINSTON, THOMAS GEORGE, engineering educator, consultant; b. Binghamton, N.Y., June 6, 1969; s. Leslie Francis and Mary Ann Winston; m. Moira B. Winston, Apr. 4, 1998. BA, SUNY, Albany, 1991, MS, 1995, Boston U., 2001. Sr. sys. engr. BBN Technologies, Cambridge, Mass., 1998—2000; WAN engr. Lucent Technologies, Marlboro, 2000; sr. network engr. Harvard-Net, Medford, 2001—. Security network cons. Boston U., 1999—. Co-author: Ideas for English Language Teacher Training, 1995. With U.S. Army until 1996. Mem. IEEE, Internet Engring. Task Force. Avocations: foreign languages, foreign travel, juggling, learning. E-mail: linguisttgw@yahoo.com.

WINT, DENNIS MICHAEL, museum director; b. Macon, Ga., Mar. 17, 1943; s. Paul Kenneth and Mary (McClure) W.; m. Patricia McLaughlin, Dec. 27, 1970; 1 child, Laurel Julia BS, U. Mich., 1965; tchr.'s cert., Lake Erie Coll., 1970; PhD, Case Western Res. U., 1977. Dir. environ. edn. Wiloughby Eastlake City Schs., 1968-70; dir. Ctr. Devel. Environment Curiculum, 1970-75; cons. Ohio Dept. Edn., 1975-77; dir. mus. and edn. Acad. Natural Scis., Phila., 1977-79, v.p., dir. natural history mus., 1979-82; dir. Cranbrook Inst. Sci., Bloomfield Hills, Mich., 1982-86; pres. St. Louis Sci. Ctr., 1986-95; pres., CEO The Franklin Inst., Phila., 1995—. Adj. asst. prof. Temple U.; past chmn. edn. and human resources adv. com. NSF, 1991-92; past pres. St. Louis Area Mus. Collaborative, 1991-92, mem. exec. com. Bd. govs. Greater Phila. 1st Partnership for Reform, 1995—98, mem. leadership com., 1995—98. Grantee in field Mem. Am. Assn. Mus., Assn. Sci.-Tech. Ctrs. (mem. nominating com., v.p. 1993-95, pres. 1995-97), Greater Phila. Cultural Alliance (bd. dirs. 1996—, v.p.). Home: 7128 Sheaff Ln Fort Washington PA 19034-2018 E-mail: dwint@fi.edu.

WINTER, ARCH REESE, retired architect; b. Mobile, Ala., Sept. 13, 1913; s. Augustus Reese and Winona (Battson). BArch, Auburn U., 1935; MArch, Cath. U. Am., 1937; postgrad., Cranbrook Acad. Art, Bloomfield Hills, Mich., 1939-41. Cons. Nat. Resources Planning Bd., Washington, 1941-43; prin. Arch R. Winter, Mobile, 1945-84; ret., 1984. Prin. works include city plans for Natchez and Gulfport, Miss., Shreveport and Monroe, La., Old Louisville, Ky.; restorations include YWCA Youth Center and Residence, Isle Dauphine Country Club, Dauphin Island (Gulf States region AIA Honor award, 1957). Cons. Mobile Planning Commn. Recipient Merit medal Tenn. Soc. Architects, 1971, Thomas Jefferson medal selection com U. Va. Sch. Architecture, 1976-79, cert. of commendation Mobile Historic Devel. Commn., 1981; named Ala. Disting. Arch. Ala. Archtl. Found., 1996. Fellow AIA (pres. Ala. chpt. 1955, nat. AIA engrs. joint coun. 1957-59, urban design com. 1959-64, chmn., del to commn. d'Urbanisme, 1962, design com. 1972-78, bd. dirs. 1968-71, chmn. Honor award, 1969, chmn. environ. commn. 1970-71, Citation for Excellence in Community Architecture 1965), Am. Inst. Cert. Planners; mem. Am. Planning Assn. (Disting Svc. Plaque Ala. chpt. 1984, Lifetime Achievement award 1998). Home: 9 Bienville Ave Mobile AL 36606-1463

WINTER, CHESTER CALDWELL, physician, surgery educator; b. Cazenovia, N.Y., June 2, 1922; s. Chester Caldwell and Cora Evelyn (Martin) W.; m. Mary Antonia Merullo, Oct. 22, 1983; children by previous marriage: Paul, Ann, Jane. BA, U. Iowa, 1943, MD, 1946. Diplomate: Am. Bd. Urology. Intern Meth. Hosp., Indpls., 1946-47; med. resident St. Luke's Hosp., Cedar Rapids, Iowa, 1947; resident gen. surgery VA Hosp., Los Angeles, 1952-53; resident urology VA Hosp.-U. Calif. at Los Angeles Med. Center, 1953-57; physician Calif., 1950-51; clin. asst. surgery UCLA, 1954-57, instr. surgery and urology, 1957-58, asst. prof. surgery and urology, 1958-59, asst. prof. Step II, 1959-60; prof. surgery and urology Ohio State U., 1960-88, prof. emeritus surgery and urology, 1988—, Louis Levy prof. urology, 1980-88. Dir. urology Ohio State U. Hosp., Columbus, 1960-78; cons. urology VA, Air Force hosps., Dayton, 1960-80. Author: Radioisotope Renography, 1963, Correctable Renal Hypertension, 1964, Nursing Care of Patients with Urologic Diseases, 4th edit, 1977, Practical Urology, 1969, Vesicoureteral Reflux, 1969, A Consice History of the U.S. and the States of Ohio, 2002; Editorial cons.: Exerpta Medica: Nuclear Medicine, Jour. AMA; editorial bd.: Andrology, Jour. Urology; Contbr. articles to med. jours. Served to capt. M.C. U.S. Army, 1943-46, 48-49. Fellow Am. Acad. Pediatricians, Am. Coll. Surgeons; mem. Am. Assn. Genitourinary Surgeons, Am. Urol. Assn., Soc. Univ. Surgeons, Soc. Pediatric Urology, Soc. Univ. Urologists, Internat. Soc. Urology, Urol. Investigators Forum, Ohio State Med. Assn., Columbus Surg. Soc., Central Ohio Urology Soc., Columbus Acad. Medicine, Ohio State U. Med. Soc. Home: 6425 Evening St Worthington OH 43085-3054 E-mail: cwinter3@ameritech.com.

WINTER, DARIUS GERJON, internist; b. Bucarest, Romania, Mar. 30, 1929; came to U.S., 1973; s. Alex Elek and Dora Winter; m. Jeanette Winter, Mar. 21, 1959; 1 child, Jacqueline. Bachelor's degree, Aurel Vlaicu, Bucarest, 1947; MD, Inst. Medicine and Pharmacy, Bucarest, 1953, PhD in Pharmacology, 1966. Bd. cert. diplomate in internal medicine. Pvt. practice, rschr., Romania, 1953-72; intern, resident in internal medicine Booth Meml. Med. Ctr., 1973-76; pvt. practice Rego Park, N.Y., 1976-98; group practice Mt. Sinai Med. Assoc., 1998—2002; pvt. practice, 2002—. Attending physician Parkway Hosp., Forest Hills., 1976—, N.Y. Hosp. Queens, 1976—, Mt. Sinai Hosp., N.Y.C., 1999, N. Shore U. Hosp. at Forest Hills, N.Y., 1999. Contbr. numerous papers to profl. jours. Fellow ACP; mem. AMA, Am. Soc. Internal Medicine, N.Y. State Med. Soc. Avocations: traveling, swimming. Office: 97-85 Queens Blvd Rego Park NY 11374 E-mail: darius.winter@smtplink.mssn.edu.

WINTER, DAVID FERDINAND, electrical engineering educator, consultant; b. St. Louis, Nov. 9, 1920; s. Ferdinand Conrad and Annie (Schaffer) W.; m. Bettie Jeanne Turner; children: Suzanne, Sharie Winter Chappeau. BSEE, Washington U., St.Louis, 1942; MSEE, MIT, 1948. Registered profl. engr., Mo. Staff mem. radiation lab. MIT, Cambridge, 1942-45, rsch. assoc. electronics lab., 1945-48; prof. elec. engring. Washington U., 1948-55, affiliate prof. elec. engring., 1955-67; v.p. engring. and rsch. Moloney Elec. Co., St. Louis, 1955-74; v.p. rsch. and engring. Blackburn div. IT&T, 1974-82, dir.

advanced tech. devel., 1982-86; pvt. practice cons., 1986—. Ct. recognized tech. expert on sources, mitigation, and effects of stray voltage on dairy cattle cons. Wis. Pub. Svc. Commn.; cons. Naval Ordanance Lab. of Ind., Indpls., 1950-53, other industries, St. Louis, 1979—. Contbr. articles to profl. jours.; holder 28 patents. Elder, pastor Maplewood Bible Chapel, St. Louis. Fellow IEEE (life), Inst. Radio Engrs.; mem. NSPE, Am. Soc. Agrl. Engrs., Mo. Soc. Profl. Engrs., Sigma Xi, Tau Beta Pi, Eta Kappa Nu. Avocations: cabinet maker, photography, music instruments. Home and Office: 735 Harvard Ave Saint Louis MO 63130-3135 E-mail: dfwinter@hotmail.com.

WINTER, DAVID LOUIS, systems engineer, human factors scientist, retired; b. Pitts., July 30, 1930; s. Louis A. and Gladys M. (Quinn) W.; m. Nancy L. Tear, July 1, 1952; children: Leeson, Blaise, Gregory, Lauren. BA, U. Pitts., 1952; MA, Columbia U., 1960; cert. computer sci., Northeastern U., 1971. Assoc. rsch. scientist Am. Insts. Rsch., Washington, 1961-66, sr. rsch. scientist Bedford, Mass., 1966-71, prin. rsch. scientist, 1976-94, retired, 1995; sr. systems analyst RCA Corp.-Sarnoff Labs., Princeton, N.J., 1971-73; mgr. systems engring. Codon Corp., Bedford, 1973-76. Computer systems cons. Mass. Dept. Mental Health, 1971-73. Pres. Mayo Peninsula Civic Assn., Edgewater, Md., 1964-65; v.p. Bedford Human Rels. Coun., 1992-94. Capt. USAF, 1952-64. Mem. Am. Acad. Polit. Sci., Human Factors Soc., Soc. Ednl. Tech. Democrat. Roman Catholic. Achievements include design and human factors test for 8 USAF electronic, intelligence and backscatter radar systems; design of 4 computer-assisted training systems for USAF E3 AWACS radar, computer displays, communications and navigation subsystems; cons. engr. for design and test of E6 Joint Stars battlefield surveillance system. Office: MicroVentures Ltd 27 Gould Rd Bedford MA 01730-1250

WINTER, DOUGLAS E. lawyer, writer; b. St. Louis, Oct. 30, 1950; s. William E. and Dorothy E. (Schuster) W.; m. Lynne G. Turner, July 9, 1977; step-children: John, Stephen. BS, U. Ill., 1971, MS, 1972; JD, Harvard U., 1975; postgrad., Judge Advocate Gen.'s Sch., 1977. Bar: Mo. 1975, Ill. 1976, D.C. 1976. Clk. to Hon. William H. Webster U.S. Ct. Appeals (8th cir.), St. Louis, 1975-76; assoc. Covington & Burling, Washington, 1976-84; ptnr. Bryan Cave LLP, 1985—. Vis. prof. U. Iowa, Iowa City, 1980-81. Author: Stephen King, 1982, Shadowings: The Reader's Guide to Horror Fiction, 1983, Stephen King: The Art of Darkness, 1984, Faces of Fear, 1985, Black Wine, 1986, Splatter: A Cautionary Tale, 1987, Prime Evil, 1988, Darkness Absolute, 1991, Black Sun, 1994, Millennium, 1997, Revelations, 1997, Run, 2000, Clive Barker: The Dark Fantastic, 2001; contbr. articles to popular mags. and nat. newspapers. Capt. U.S. Army, 1973-77. Recipient world fantasy award World Fantasy Conv., 1986, award Internat. Horror Critics Guild, 1995, 96, 98. Mem. Nat. Book Critics Circle, Horror Writers Assn. (chmn. grievance com. 1989—, trustee 1997—). Office: Bryan Cave LLP 700 13th St NW Fl 6 Washington DC 20005-3960 E-mail: dewinter@bryancave.com.

WINTER, EDWIN THOMAS, JR. accountant, treasurer; b. Darby, Pa., July 28, 1962; s. Edwin Thomas and Christa K. (Mang) W.; m. Patricia Anne Ott; children: Elizabeth Anne, Stephanie Marie, Edwin Thomas III, Matthew Dominic. BS in Acctg. and Fin., Drexel U., 1985, MBA in Fin. cum laude, 1993; M in Taxation, Villanova U., 1994. CPA, Pa. Auditor, rev. officer IRS, Phila., 1983, 84; acct. Cogen Sklar Levick, Bala Cynwyd, Pa., 1984-87, Shotz Miller & Glusman, Phila., 1987-88; acctg./office mgr. Bachmann Industries, Inc., 1988—; treas. Cyrax Fed. Credit Union, Upper Darby, Pa., 1996—. Tchr. Delaware County C.C. Bd. dirs., v.p. sch. bd. Upper Darby, 1996—; bd. dirs. Upper Darby Ednl. Cultural Found. Mem. Nat. Holy Name Soc. (exec. dir., treas. 1996—, fin. sec. 1995—), Phila. Archdiocesan Holy Name Union (exec. dir., pres. 1995-97). Republican. Roman Catholic. Avocations: reading, outdoor activities. Home: 347 Congress Ave Lansdowne PA 19050-1003 Office: E T Winter & Assocs PO Box 2266 Upper Darby PA 19082-0766 Fax: 610-394-2862.

WINTER, FREDERICK ELLIOT, fine arts educator; b. Barbados, W.I., June 19, 1922; s. Edward Elliot and Constance Mabel (Gill) W.; m. Joan Elizabeth Hay, June 9, 1951; children: Elizabeth, Penelope, Mary, Michael. BA, McGill U., 1945; PhD, U. Toronto, 1957. Instr. U. Toronto, 1947-49, 50-51, lectr., 1951-57, asst. prof., 1957-61, assoc. prof., 1961-68, prof., 1968-90, prof. emeritus, 1990—, chmn. dept. fine art, 1971-77, grad. coord. history of art, 1978-81, spl. lectr. history of art, 1990-98; chmn. U. Toronto Assn. Teaching Staff, 1968-69. Mem. mng. com. Am. Sch. Classical Studies, Athens, Greece, 1968-90, chair pers. com., 1975-77; mem. programme com. Can. Archaeol. Inst. at Athens, 1990-94; bd. dirs. Can. Acad. Inst., Athens. Author: (with G.S. Vickers, P.H. Brieger) Art and Man, Vol. I, 1963, Greek Fortifications, 1971; contbr. articles Jour. Classical Assn. Can., Am. Jour. of Archaeology, Echos du Monde Classique/Classical Views. Recipient Gold medal in classics McGill U., 1945; Flavelle fellow U. Toronto, 1947-48; White fellow Am. Sch., Athens, 1949-50; spl. research fellow, 1977-78, 87-88; sr. assoc. fellow, 1982, 83-84, 86, 91; Am. Philos. Soc. grantee, 1957; grantee Soc. Scis. Humanities Rsch. Coun. Can., 1962, 68, 71, 75, 77-78, 82, 83-84, 86, 87-88, 91; grantee U. Toronto Humanities and Social Scis. Rsch. Com., 1993. Mem. Classical Assn. Can., Archeol. Inst. Am. (editorial adv. bd. Am. Jour. Archaeology 1981-85) Home: 164 Highgate Ave Willowdale ON Canada M2N 5G8 Office: Dept Fine Art U Toronto Toronto ON Canada

WINTER, HARVEY JOHN, retired government official; b. New Albion, N.Y., Apr. 6, 1915; s. George J. and Irene (Harvey) W.; m. Virginia M. Shaw, Sept. 2, 1939; 1 child, Jeffrey S. BA magna cum laude, U. Buffalo, 1938, MA, 1939; teaching fellow, George Washington U., 1939-40. Historian U.S. Nat. Park Service, 1940-42; archivist U.S. Nat. Archives, 1942-43; with U.S. Office Alien Property Custodian, 1943-51, chief reports and stats. sect., 1948- 51; with State Dept., 1951—, chief internat. bus. practices div., 1959- 61, asst. chief, 1961-70, chief bus. practices div., 1970-71, dir. office bus. protection, 1971-73, dir. office bus. practices, 1973-90; dir. office intellectual property and competition, 1991-92; U.S. del. European Productivity Agy. cartel meetings, Paris, 1958-60; mem. U.S. del. diplomatic confs. Internat. Design Agreement, The Hague, 1960, 17th session GATT, Geneva, 1960; U.S. alt. rep. 5th session Intergovtl. Copyright Com., London, 1960, 6th session, Madrid, 1961, 7th session, New Delhi, 1963; U.S. alt. rep. Interunion Coordinating Com., Geneva, 1963-69; U.S. observer African Seminar on Indsl. Property, Brazzaville, Congo, 1963; U.S. alt. observer Latin Am. Indsl. Property Seminar, Bogota, Colombia, 1964, Asian Indsl. Property Seminar, Colombo, Ceylon, 1966, Com. of Experts on Inventors' Certificates, Geneva, 1965, Com. of Experts on Adminstrv. Agreement, Geneva, 1965, Intellectual Property Diplomatic Conf., Stockholm, 1967, Diplomatic Conf. on Agreement for Classification of Indsl. Designs, Locarno, Switzerland, 1968, Diplomatic Conf. on Patent Cooperation Treaty, Washington, 1970, Diplomatic Conf. on Agreement for Internat. Patent Classification, Strasbourg, France, 1971, Diplomatic Conf. on Universal Copyright Conv., Paris, 1971; U.S. alt. rep. Diplomatic Conf. on Phonogram Conv., Geneva, 1971, Diplomatic Conf. on Indsl. Property, Vienna, 1973; U.S. rep. Com. Experts on Type Face Agreement, Geneva, 1972, Com. Experts on Communications Satellites Problems, Nairobi, Kenya, 1973; U.S. del. Diplomatic Conf. on Communications Satellites Conv., Brussels, 1974, Diplomatic Conf. on Treaty for Deposit Microorganisms, Budapest, Hungary, 1977, Diplomatic Conf. on Plant Protection Conv., Geneva, 1978, World Intellectual Property Orgn. Governing Bodies, Geneva, 1979-82, alt. del., 1983-91; alt. U.S. del. Diplomatic Conf. on Revision of Paris Conv., Geneva, 1980, 82, 83, 84 Nairobi, 1981; ret., 1992. U.S. del. UNESCO Experts on Rental of Videograms, Paris, 1984, Com. Govtl. Experts on Audiovisual Works and Phonograms, Paris, 1986, Com. Govtl. Experts on Internat. Register of Audiovisual Works, Geneva, 1988, Diplomatic Conf. on Treaty for Internat. Registration of Audiovisual Works, Geneva, 1989, Com. Experts on Disputes Steelement Treaty on Intellectual Property, 1990; chmn. Internat. Patent Classification Assembly, 1992. Recipient Superior Honor award Dept. State, 1971, 75, 89, 92, 50-Yr. Svc. award, 1990, Jefferson medal, N.J. Patent Law Assn., 1982; honoree Copyright Soc. U.S.A., 1989. Mem. Phi Beta Kappa. Episcopalian (vestry). Home: 1019 22nd St S Arlington VA 22202-2137

WINTER, JANE, medical educator; b. N.Y.C., 1952; MD, U. Pa., 1977; intern, U. Chgo., 1977-78, resident int. medicine, 1978-80. Fellow in hematology and oncology Columbia P&S, N.Y.C., 1980-81, Northwestern U., 1981-83, prof., 1983—. Mem.: Ea. Coop. Oncology Group, Am. Soc. for Blood and Marrow Transplantation, Am. Assn. Cancer Rsch., Am. Fedn. for Clin. Rsch., Am. Soc. Clin. Oncology, Am. Soc. Hematology. Office: Divsn Hematology/Oncology 676 N St Clair St Ste 850 Chicago IL 60611-2978 E-mail: j-winter@northwestern.edu.

WINTER, JERRY ALAN, sociology educator; b. Bronx, July 23, 1937; s. Herman and Rose (Kavkewitz) W; m. GailDoreen Cameron, June 13, 1964; children: Wendy, Miriam. BA, NYU, 1958; MA, U. Mich., 1960, PhD, 1964. Asst. prof. Rutgers U., New Brunswick, N.J., 1965-68; dir. Rsch. on Tng. for Met. Ministry, Washington, 1967-69; asst. prof. sociology Temple U., Phila., 1968-70; assoc. prof. Conn. Coll., New London, 1970-77, prof. sociology, 1977-2000, Lucretia Allyn prof., 2000—02, prof. emeritus, 2002—. Author: Vital Problems for American Society, 1968, Clergy in Action Training, 1971, The Poor, 1971, Continuities in the Sociology of Religion: Creed, Congregation and Community, 1977, Jewish Choices, 1998. Mem. Ethics Com., Waterford, Conn., 1999—2002; chmn. United Way Campaign Com., Conn. Coll., 1987—88. Mem. AAUP, Am. Sociol. Assn., Religious Rsch. Assn., Assn. for Sociol. Study of Jewry (editor Contemporary Jewry Jour. 1992-97), Phi Beta Kappa, Psi Chi, Alpha Kappa Delta. Democrat. Jewish. Home: 43 Beacon Hill Dr Waterford CT 06385-4107 Office: Conn Coll Box 5302 270 Mohegan Ave New London CT 06320-4125 E-mail: jawin@conncoll.edu.

WINTER, JOAN ELIZABETH, psychotherapist; b. Aiken, S.C., Feb. 24, 1947; d. John S. and Mary Elizabeth (Caldwell) Winter. BS, Ariz. State U., 1970; MSW, Va. Commonwealth U., 1977; EdS, Coll. William and Mary, 1989, EdD, 1993. Lic. marriage and family therapist; lic. clin. social worker, Va.; diplomate Nat. Assn. Social Workers. Counselor Child Psychiatry Hosp., Phoenix, 1969-70, Ariz. Job Coll., Casa Grande, 1970-71; dir. Halfway House, Richmond, Va., 1971-73; state supr. resdl. treatment, 1973-75; psychotherapist Med. Coll. Va., 1975-76, Va. Commonwealth U., 1976-77; adj. prof., exec. dir. Family Rsch. Project Coll. William and Mary, Richmond, Va., 1979—; dir. Family Inst. Va., 1980—. Examiner, approved supr. Bd. Behavioral Scis., Commonwealth of Va., 1982—; faculty dept. psychiatry Med. Coll. Va., Commonwealth U.; mem. adj. faculty dept. psychology Coll. William & Mary, Med. Coll. Va.; mem. Avanta Network, Exec. Coun. and Faculty, Nat. Inst. of Drug Abuse, Rsch. Adv. Com. Author: The Phenomenon of Incest, 1977, The Use of Self in Therapy: The Person and Practice of the Therapist, 1987, Family Life of Psychotherapists, 1987, Enhancing to Marital Relationship: Virginia Satir's Parts Party, 1990, Enhancing the Marital Relationship: Virginia Satir's Parts Party, Satir Theory, 1991, Family Therapy Research Outcomes: Bowen, Haley and Satir; editor Jour. Couple Therapy; contbr. articles to profl. jours. Mem. Am. Soc. Cert. Social Workers, Am. Family Therapy Assn., Am. Assn. Marriage and Family Therapy (approved supr.), Avanta Network Faculty. Address: 2910 Monument Ave Richmond VA 23221-1404 E-mail: fiv1@erols.com.

WINTER, JOHN ALEXANDER, realtor, real estate appraiser; b. Cin., July 2, 1935; s. George Edward and Mary Alma (McAuliffe) W. BS, Georgetown U., 1957; grad., Annapolis Sailing Sch. Ptnr. Winter & Winter, Cleve., 1957-76; residential salesman Moreland Hills Co., Chagrin Falls, Ohio, 1976-77; residential appraiser Kiebler, Smith & Co., Chardon, 1977-91; founder, pres., CEO Cert. Appraisal Svc. Co., Shaker Heights, 1985—; v.p., dir. The Gas Pipe Co., Chagrin Falls, 1973—; part owner Cleve. Indians, 1998-2000. Contbr. articles to profl. jours. Rep. precinct committeeman Shaker Heights, 1996—; pres. New Engl. Soc. of Cleve. and Western Res., 1976—77, 1983—84, 2002—, treas., 1987—2002; pres. Shaker Heights Rep. Club, 1977—84; v.p., trustee Shaker Hist. Soc., 1985—91; trustee Dunham Tavern Mus., 2000—, docent, 1998—; mem. exec. com. Cuyahoga County Rep. Orgn., 1994—. Recipient Svc. award Pres. Ronald Reagan, 1984, New Eng. Heritage award New Eng. Soc., 1984. Mem. Cleve. Independence Day Assn. (v.p., trustee 1957—, Treharne award 1984), Am. Assn. Cert. Appraisers (v.p. No. Ohio chpt.), Nat. Assn. Ind. Fee Appraisers (cert. mem.), Ohio Assn. Realtors, Nat. Assn. Realtors (Ben Franklin award 1983), Grad. Realtors Inst., Cleve. Bar Assn. (grievance com. 1997—), Cathedral Latin Alumni Assn. (trustee 1965-2002, exec. com. 1988-2002, v.p. 1988-92, pres. 1992-94, Golden Alumni award 1996), Georgetown Club (pres. 1966-67), Cleve. of Washington Club (trustee 1984—). Roman Catholic. Avocations: tennis, sailing, sports collectibles. Home and Office: Cert Appraisal Svc Co 19271 Shaker Blvd Shaker Heights OH 44122-2547

WINTER, JOHN DAWSON, III, blues guitarist, singer; b. Beaumont, Tex., Feb. 23, 1944; s. John Dawson II and Edwina (Holland) W. Grad. high sch. Organizer, performer numerous rock and blues bands, rec. artist, CBS Records, Inc., 1969— , TV and concert appearances through, U.S. and Europe, 1969— ; albums include Johnny Winter, 1969, Second Winter, 1969, Johnny Winter-And, 1970, Live, 1971 (Gold Record award 1974), Still Alive and Well, 1973, Saints and Sinners, 1974, John Dawson Winter III, 1974, Captured Live, 1976, Nothin' But the Blues, 1977, White Hot and Blue, 1978, The Johnny Winter Story, 1980, Raisin' Cain, Serious Business, 1985 (Grammy nominee), 3rd Degree, 1986, The Winter of '88, 1988, Winter Scene, 1990, Let Me In, 1991, Hey Where's Your Brother, 1992, Scorchin' Blues, 1992, A Rock n' Roll Collection, 1994, Johnny Winter Live in New York City 1997, 1997; producer recs. by Muddy Waters: albums include Still Hard (Artist of Yr., Rolling Stone mag. 1969), Hard Again, 1977 (Grammy award), I'm Ready, 1978 (Grammy award), Muddy Mississippi Waters Live, 1979 (Grammy award), King Bee, 1980. Mem. Broadcast Music Inc., Musicians Union. Office: Slatus Mgmt 35 Hayward Ave Colchester CT 06415-1221 E-mail: cpwrecds@aol.com.

WINTER, KENNETH J. federal agency administrator; BA in Econs., U. New Hampshire, 1970—74; MBA, Suffolk U., 1975—78; student, No. Va. C.C., 1979—81. CPA Va., DC. Auditor, evaluator, mgmt. analyst U.S Gen. Acctg. Office, 1974—86; computer specialist U.S. Dept. Def., Office Sec. Def., 1986—89; dep. chief fin. officer U.S. Dept. Treasury, U.S. Mint, 1989—94, Office of Chief Fin. Officer. Mem.: AICPA, Assn. Govt. Accts. Office: NASA Hdqrs Mail Code B 300 E St SW Washington DC 20546*

WINTER, KENNETH MICHAEL, newspaper editor, publisher; b. Lansing, Mich., Aug. 7, 1950; s. Richard G. and Beverly (Radcliff) W.; 1 child, Michael. Student, Adrian Coll., 1968-69, Am. U., 1970; BA, Mich. State U., 1972; fellow in journalism, U. Mich., 1979. Youth beat writer Lansing State Jour., 1964-72, reporter, 1972-73, pub. svc. dir., 1973; editor Charlevoix (Mich.) Courier, 1974-76; reporter Petoskey (Mich.) News-Rev., 1973-74, asst. gen. mgr., spl. projects editor, 1976-79, editor, gen. mgr., 1979-2001, editor, publisher, 2001—. Sec., bd. dirs. Otsego Herald Times Inc., Gaylor, MIch., Rev. Dirs. Inc., Petoskey; v.p. No. Mich. Rev. Inc., Petoskey, 1994—. Author: (chpt. in book) Historical Glimpses - Petoskey, 1986; editor: Million Dollar Memories-A 125 Year Pictorial Recollection of Little Traverse Bay, 2000.; contbr. articles to profl. jours. Pres. Little Traverse Hist. Soc., Petoskey, 1977-82, United Way Emmet County, Petoskey, 1982; trustee Hist. Soc. Mich., 1979-85; trustee, chair Little Traverse Conservancy, Harbor Springs, Mich., 1982-98; v.p. Crooked Tree Arts Coun., Petoskey, 1979-86; bd. dirs. North Ctrl. Mich. Coll. Found., 1999—. No. Cmty. Mediation, 2000-. Nat. journalism fellow U. Mich., 1978-79; numerous journalism awards Nat. Newspaper Assn. Mem. Mich. Press Assn. (bd. dirs. 1992—, numerous journalism awards, pres.-elect 2000, pres. 2001-02), Mich.AP Edit. Assn. (bd. dirs. 1992-98, pres. 1995-96), Am. Soc. Newspaper Editors, Kiwanis (pres. Petoskey chpt. 1983-84). Home: 1004 Lockwood Ave Petoskey MI 49770-3156 Office: Petoskey News-Rev PO Box 528 319 State St Petoskey MI 49770-0528 E-mail: kwint@freeway.net.

WINTER, LARRY EUGENE, accountant; b. Williamsport, Pa., Jan. 17, 1950; s. Robert Schrader and Betty Irene (Foresman) W.; m. Constance Dianne Snyder, June 2, 1973; children: John, Matthew, Noël, James. A in Bus. Adminstrn., Palm Beach Jr. Coll., 1969; BSBA, U. Fla., 1971; cert. bus., U. Pa., 1977. Cert. valuation analyst, cert. fraud examiner, CPA, Fla., Ga.; accredited fin. planning specialist. Audit supr. Touche Ross & Co., Atlanta, 1971-74; chief. fin. officer Hawthorne Industries, Dalton, Ga., 1974-79; pvt. practice acctg., 1979-89; mng. ptnr. Winter & Harris, CPAs, 1990—. Mem. White House Conf. Small Bus., Atlanta, 1979; instr. West Ga. Coll., Carollton, 1985, Ea. European Bus. Coll., Budapest, Hungary, 1995; acct. in residence Ga. Coll., Milledgeville, Ga., 1989; cons. Christian Businessman, Chattanooga, 1986—. Author: The American Free Enterprise System and the Ethics that Make it Work, 1991. Trustee Dalton Jr. Coll. Found.; chair Whitfield County/Dalton Day Care Ctrs., 1987—92; vice chair NW Ga. Healthcare Partnership, 1996—; mem. Downtown Dalten Devel. Authority, 2001—; mem. adv. coun. Ga. State Bd. Workers Compensation, 1991—; mem. fee arbitration panel State Bar Ga., 1987—; elder Fellowship Bible Ch., 1985—. Hixson fellow Kiwanis, 2000. Mem. AICPA, Assn. Cert. Fraud Examiners, Nat. Assn. Cert. Valuation Analysts, Ga. Soc. CPAs (pres. 1983-84), Fla. Inst. CPAs (recipient), Ga. Sheriff's Assn. (Disting. Humanitarian award), Dalton-Whitfield C. of C. (Leadership 1990-91, treas. 1992-94), Walden Club, Kiwanis (life, pres. 1978-79, lt. gov. 1981-84, George Hixon fellow 2000), SAR. Avocations: cooking, credit and fin. counseling. Office: PO Box 2644 Dalton GA 30722-2644

WINTER, MICHAEL ALEX, federal agency administrator; b. Chgo. m. Atsuko Kuwana; 1 child. BA in Philosophy, So. Ill. U., 1974; postgrad. studies in Bus. Adminstrn., U. San Francisco, 1986. Dep. dir. Ctr. for Ind. Living, Berkeley, Calif., 1977-81; exec. dir. Hawaii Ctr. for Ind. Living, Honolulu, 1981-82; CEO Ctr. for Ind. Living, Berkeley, 1982-94; spl. asst. to assoc. dep. sec. U.S. Dept. Transportation, Washington, 1994-98, assoc. adminstr. for budget and policy, 1998—2001; dir. Office of Civil Rights, 2001—. Chair disability caucus Calif. Dem. Orgn., 1984-93; bd. dirs. Alameda-Contra Costa County Transit Dist., 1988-94, chair fin. com., govt. rels. com.; pres., exec. dir. Nat. Coun. on Ind. Living, 1989-91; chair disability com. Dianne Feinstein for Gov., Calif., 1990. Office: Dept Transp 400 7th St SW Washington DC 20590-0003

WINTER, MIRIAM THERESE (GLORIA FRANCES WINTER), nun, religious education educator; b. Passaic, N.J., June 14, 1938; d. Mathias William and Irene Theresa (Marton) W. BMus, Cath. U. Am., 1964; M in Religious Edn., McMaster Divinity Coll., Hamilton, Ont., Can., 1976; PhD in Liturgical Studies, Princeton Theol. Sem., 1983; LHD (hon.), Albertus Magnus Coll., 1991, St. Joseph Coll., 1993. Joined Med. Mission Sisters, Roman Cath. Ch., 1955. Dir. liturgy and liturgical music Med. Mission Sisters, Phila., 1960-76, pub. rels. dir., coord., 1963-72; assoc. prof. liturgy, worship and spirituality Hartford (Conn.) Sem., 1980-85, prof., 1985—, prof. liturgy, worship, spirituality, and feminist studies, 1994—. Mem. faculty St. Therese's Inst., Phila., 1964-68, acad. dir., 1968-72, Immaculate Conception Sem. Summer Program, Mo., 1969, Cath. U. Summer Grad. Program, Washington, 1970, Hope Ecumenical Inst., Jerusalem, summer 1974, 75, 76, McMaster Divinity Coll. Grad. Program, 1976, Continuing Edn. Program, 1976, N.Y. Archdiocesan Sch. Liturgical Music, summer 1980, 82, Vancouver Sch. Theology, summer 1982, USN Chaplains through Auburn Theol. Sem., 1990; mem. adj. faculty Union Inst., Cin., 1992-94; with emergency relief work Internat. Rescue Com., Cambodia, 1979-80, Malteser-Hilfsdienst Auslandsdienst, Germany, 1984, Med. Mission Sisters, Ethiopia, 1985; lectr., instr., performer, worship leader, song leader for various groups by invitation, nat. and internat., 1967—. Author: Preparing the Way of the Lord, 1978, God-With-Us: Resources for Prayer and Praise, 1979, An Anthology of Scripture Songs, 1982, Why Sing? Toward a Theology of Catholic Church Music, 1984, WomanPrayer, WomanSong: Resources for Ritual, 1987, WomanWord: A Feminist Lectionary and Psalter, 1990, WomanWisdom: A Feminist Lectionary and Psalter, Women of the Hebrew Scriptures, Part I, 1992 (First Place award for books on liturgy Cath. Press Assn. 1992), WomanWitness: A Feminist Lectionary and Psalter, Women of the Hebrew Scriptures, Part II, 1992 (First Place award for books on liturgy Cath. Press Assn. 1993), The Gospel According to Mary: A New Testament for Women, 1993; co-author: Defecting in Place: Women Claiming Responsibility for Their Own Spiritual Lives, 1994, (Second place award for books on gender studies Cath. Press Assn. 1995;), The Chronicles of Noah and Her Sisters: Genesis and Exodus According to Women, 1995 (2d place award for books on gender studies Cath. Press Assn. 1996); Songlines: Hymns, Songs, Rounds, and Refrains, 1996, The Singer and the Song: An Autobiography of the Spirit, 1999, Out of the Depths, The Story of Ludmila Javorova, Ordained Roman Catholic Priest, 2001; author numerous songs included in albums Hymns-ReImagined, SpiritSong, EarthSong, WomanSong, Remember Me, Sandstone, Songs of Promise, RSVP: Let Us Pray, Gold, Incense and Myrrh, In Love, Seasons (Christian Oscar award Nat. Evang. Film Found. 1971), Knock, Knock, Praise the Lord in Many Voices (live recording of Mass of A Pilgrim People premiered at Carnegie Hall, 1967), I Know the Secret, Joy is Like the Rain (Gold album in USA and Australia); contbr. articles to profl. jours. Bd. dirs. Capitol Region Conf. Chs., 1984-91, v.p., 1986-88. pres. bd. dirs., 1988-90, past pres., 1990-91, Archdiocesan Office Urban Affairs, 1986-95; mem. Christian Conf. ann. event WINFEST, 1986, 87; mem. small christian communities design team Archdiocese of Hartford, 1987-91; mem. major events design team RENEW, 1986; subcommn. chair Archdiocesan Office of Synod, 1991; mem. New Eng. team Ministry of Money, 1984-90, 93; mem. The New Century Hymnal editl. com. United Ch. of Christ, 1993-95; active Ho. of Bread, Pediats. AIDS Unit Yale-New Haven Hosp., Covenant to Care, Voices of Joy Gospel Choir women imprisioned at Niantic. Grantee Lilly Endowment, 1989-90, 91-93; recipient Ho. of Reps. citation Commonwealth of Pa., 1968, Women in Leadership Edn. award YWCA Conn., 1989, Convenant to Care award for ministry to children, 1993; named to McMaster U. Alumni Gallery, 1982, Celebration of 120 Women in Leadership, 1987, Bayley-Ellard H.S. Hall of Fame, 1993, Conn. Women's Hall of Fame, 2002. Mem. ASCAP (Popular Awards list 1968—), AAUW (Excellence in Equity award Conn. chpt. 1995), Nat. Assn. Pastoral Musicians, N.Am. Acad. of Liturgy, Societas Liturgica. Avocations: photography, calligraphy. Office: Hartford Sem 77 Sherman St Hartford CT 06105-2260 E-mail: mtwinter@hartsem.edu.

WINTER, PETER MICHAEL, anesthesiologist, educator; b. Sverdlovsk, Russia, Aug. 5, 1934; arrived in U.S., 1938, naturalized, 1944; s. George and Anne Winter; m. Michelle Yakopec, Dec. 28, 1991; children: Karin Anne, Christopher George, Lia Lynn, Tori Anne. BA, Cornell U., 1958; MD, U. Rochester, 1962. Diplomate Am. Bd. Anesthesiology. Intern U. Utah, Salt Lake City, 1962-63; resident in anesthesiology, pharmacology and respiratory physiology Mass. Gen. Hosp., Boston, 1963-65; USPHS fellow Harvard U. Med. Sch., 1964-66; Buswell fellow dept. physiology, asst. prof. SUNY, Buffalo, 1966-69; assoc. prof. dept. anesthesiology Sch. Medicine, U. Wash., Seattle, 1969-74, prof., 1974-79; prof., chmn. dept. anesthesiology and critical care medicine U. Pitts. Sch. Medicine, 1979-96, Peter and Eva Safar prof. anesthesiology/critical care med., 1987—96, prof. emeritus, dir. faculty devel., 1996—. Anesthesiologist in chief Univ. Health Ctr. Hosps., Pitts., 1979—96. Editl. cons.: Anesthesiology CCMJ; contbr. chapters to books, papers and abstracts to pubs. With U.S. Army, 1953—56. Recipient Career Devel. award, NIH, 1971. Mem.: AMA, Assn. univ. Anesthetists, Internat. Anesthesia Rsch. Soc., Undersea Med. Soc., Soc. Critical Care Medicine, N.Y. Acad. Scis., Royal Soc. Medicine, Am. Soc. Anesthesiologists, Am. Coll. Chest Physicians, Morton Soc., Am. Alpine Club. Office: 3471 5th Ave Ste 910 Pittsburgh PA 15213-3221

WINTER, RICHARD LAWRENCE, financial and health care company executive; b. St. Louis, Dec. 17, 1945; s. Melvin Lawrence and Kathleen Jane (O'Leary) W.; children from previous marriage: Leigh Ellen, Jessica Marie, George Bradford; m. Kathryn Ann Geppert, Dec. 4, 1993. BS in Math., St. Louis U., 1967, MS in Math. (fellow), 1969; MBA, U. Mo., St. Louis, 1976. Rsch. analyst Mo. Pacific R.R., St. Louis, 1971-73; dir. fin. rels. Linclay Corp., 1973-74; asst. v.p. 1st Nat. Bank in St. Louis (now Centerre Bank, NA) subs. Boatmen's Nat. Bank, 1974-79; v.p. fin. UDE Corp., St. Louis, 1979-81; pres. Health Care Investments, Ltd., 1981—, Larus Corp., St. Louis, 1981—, Garden View Care Ctr., Inc., O'Fallon, Mo., 1987—. Exec. bd. Duchesne Bank, St. Peters, Mo., 1989-97; lectr. math. U. Mo., St. Louis, 1972-74, St. Louis U., 1982-90. Bd. dirs. Dance St. Louis, 1998—; exec. adv. bd. St. Louis U. Coll. Arts and Sci., 2000—; fundraising staff St. Louis Symphony, Jr. Achievement, United Way St. Louis, Arts and Edn. Fund, St. Louis, 1974—79. With U.S. Army, 1969—71. Mem. Nat. Health Lawyers Assn., Mo. Athletic Club (St. Louis), Pi Mu Epsilon. Roman Catholic. Home: 725 S Skinker Blvd Unit 9N Saint Louis MO 63105 Office: Ste 170 12444 Powerscourt Dr Saint Louis MO 63131-3659

WINTER, RICHARD SAMUEL, JR. computer training company owner, writer; b. Denver, Mar. 17, 1958; s. Richard Samuel and Jerryl Dene (Gano) W.; m. Karen Annette Hansen, May 27, 1989. Student, Griffith U., Brisbane, Australia, 1979; BA in Internat. Environment, Colo. Coll., 1981; MA in Pub. Adminstrn., U. Colo., Denver, 1989. Range aide U.S. Forest Svc., Desert Exptl. Station, Utah, 1976-77; pub. health investigator, lab. technician Denver

Health Dept., 1982-84; projects mgr. Colo. Statesman, Denver, 1984-85; editor Mile Hi Prep, 1985; fin. analyst Pan Am. World Airways, N.Y.C., 1985-88; sr. ptnr., owner PRW, Denver, 1988—; tng. mgr. Qwest, 2000-01; tchr. Denver Pub. Schs., 2001—. Pres. info. systems Trainers, Denver, 1994. Co-author, revisor: MicroRef Quick Reference Bd. Lotus 1-2-3 Rel. 3.0, 1990, MicroRef Quick Reference Gd. Lotus 1-2-3 Rel. 2.2, 1990, Que Q&A QueCards, 1991, Que 123 Release 2.3 QuickStart, 1991, Que 123 Release 2.4 QuickStart, 1992, Que Look Your Best with Excel, 1992, Que Excel for Windows Sure Steps, 1993, Que Using Lotus 123 Release 4, 1994, Que Using Excel 5, 1994, Que Using Microsoft Office, 1994, Que Using Microsoft Office 95, 1995, Que Special Edition Using Microsoft Office Professional for Windows 95, 1996, Que Special Edition Using Microsoft Office 97 Professional, 1997, Que Microsoft Access 97 Quick Reference Guide, 1997, Que Using Microsoft Office 95, 1998, Que Microsoft Office 97 User Manual, 1998, Que Microsoft Excel 2000, Cheat Sheet, 1999, DDC Learning Office 2000, 1999, DDC Learning Access 2000, 1999, DDC One Day Office, Excel, Access, Word, Power Point (1999-00), Rising Moon, Dirty Bird Feet, 2000. Chmn. N.Y. Victims for Victims, N.Y.C., 1986-87; bd. dirs. Colo. Common Cause, Denver, 1984-85; steering com. Voter Registration "Motor Voter" Amendment, Denver, 1983-84; pres. Broadway Commons Homeowners Assn., Denver, 1982-84; pres. Info. Systems Trainers, 1994, bd. dirs. 1990-96; Dist. Accountability Adv. Com. budget chair Clear Creek Sch. Dist., 1996-98; chair Clear Creek Imagine Ednl. Excellence, 1997-98, Citizens for Improved Edn., 1999-2000, Clear Creek Sch. Bd., 2000—. Recipient Vigil Honor, Order of the Arrow, 1976, Disting. Svc. award Info. Sys. Trainers, 1996. Mem. Phi Beta Kappa, Alpha Lambda Delta.

WINTER, ROGER, artist; b. Denison, Tex., Aug. 17, 1934; s. Gordon Fillmore and Etta Mae Winter; m. Jeanette Winter, Apr. 16, 1960; children: Jonah, Max. BFA, U. Tex., 1956; MFA, U. Iowa, 1960. Instr. painting and drawing Dallas Mus. Art, 1969-69; mem. faculty fine arts So. Meth. U., 1963-89. Guest artist Washington U., St. Louis, 1989, U. Pa., Phila., 1990, Drury Coll., Springfield, Mo., 1990, San Antonio Art INst., 1990, Bklyn. Coll., 1991, Vt. Studio Ctr., Johnson, 1990, 92, 95, 2000, Ind. U., Bloomington, 1995; guest artist Ill. State U., Normal, 1995. One-man shows include Atelier Chapman Kelly, Dallas, 1963, Haydon Calhoun Gallery, Dallas, 1965, Witte Meml. Mus., San Antonio, 1967, Delgado Mus. Art, New Orleans, 1968, Owens Fine Arts Ctr., So. Meth. U., Dallas, 1968, Smither Gallery, Dallas, 1973, Longview (Tex.) Mus. and Art Ctr., 1976, Delahunty Gallery, Dallas, 1977, 81, Waco (Tex.) Art Ctr., 1978, Univ. Gallery, So. Meth. U., 1979, Fischbach Gallery, N.Y.C., 1984, 86, 89, 98, Eugene Binder Gallery, Dallas, 1992, Baxter Gallery, Maine Coll. Art, Portland, 1996, Maine Coast Artists, Rockport, 1996, Greenville (S.C.) County Mus. Art, 1996, El Paso (Tex.) Mus. Art, 1996, The McKinney Ave. Contemporary, Dallas, 1996, Art Gallery U. Tex. San Antonio, 1997, Edith Baker Gallery, Dallas, 1998, 2000, Artists Gallery, San Antonio, 2000; exhibited in group shows Mus. Art, Oklahoma City, 1961, 62, Ft. Worth Art Ctr., 1962, Dallas Mus. Art, 1963, 64, 66, 72, 75, 76, 84, 92, So. Meth. U., 1970, 71, 75, Elmira (N.Y.) Coll., 1977, Waco Arts Ctr., 1979, 82, 83, Contemporary Arts Mus., Houston, 1979, Navy Pier, Chgo., 1980-82, Delahunty Gallery, 1982, Peregrine Gallery, Dallas, 1984, 88, 89, Adams-Middleton Gallery, Dallas, 1984, Fischbach Gallery, 1985, 86, 92, Eugene Binder Gallery, 1986, Mus. Fine Arts, Houston, 1986, Frito-Lay, Inc., Plano, Tex., 1987, Haggar Gallery U. Dallas, 1988, Tex. Commerce Tower, Dallas, 1988, The Crescent Gallery, Dallas, 1988, City Place, Dallas, 1988, Tex. Christian U., Ft. Worth, 1989, Nelson Atkins Mus., Kansas City, Mo., 1989, Art Mus. at Fla. Internat. U., Miami, 1990, Flushing (N.Y.) Coun. on Culture and the Arts, 1994, Animals, Animals,Anita Shapolsky Gallery, N.Y.C., 1995, Gallery Artists Select artists, Mangel Gallery, Phila., 1998, Main Light, Am. Embassy, Santiago, Chile, 1998, Summer Invitational Show, The Ralls Collection, Washington, 1999, Outward Bound: American Art at the Brink of the 20th Century, 1900-2000, Meridian Internat. Ctr., Washington, Museum of Fine Arts, Hanoi, Vietnam, Ho Chi Minh City, Vietnam, The Painting Inst., Shangai, China, The Working People's Cultural Palace, Beijing, China, The Singapore Museum of Art, The CIPTA Gallery, Jakarta Arts Ctr., Indonesia; represented in permanent collections, Dallas Museum of Art, El Paso Museum of Art, Tex., Ill. State U., Normal, Longview Museum of Art, Tex., Museum of Fine Arts, Oklahoma, Owens Fine Arts Ctr., Southern Methodist U., Dallas, Portland Museum of Art, Maine, Atlantic Richfield Co., L.A., Barrow, Hanley, Mc Whinney and Strauss, Inc., Belo Corp., Crescent Collection, Ensearch Corp., Frito-Lay, Haynes and Boone, J.C. Penney Nat. Hdqs., Mostek Corp., Oak Cliff Savings and Loan, Southland Life Corp., Southland Trust, Southwest Med. Ctr. U. Tex., Texas Commerce Bank, U.S. Trust, WFAA, Dallas, Leede Explorations, Wilson Industries, Houston, Reader's Digest, N.Y.C., Southwestern Bell Corp., St. Louis, Tulsa Bank of Commerce, C-M Corp., Mobil Oil Corp., The Western Co., Fort Worth; author: Introduction to Drawing, 1982, On Drawing, 1991, rev. edition 1997. With U.S. Army, 1956-58. Recipient top award Mus. Art, Oklahoma City, 1962, award Ft. Worth Art Ctr., 1962, top award Dallas Mus. Art, 1964, 72, Artists of the S.E. and Tex., New Orleans, 1967, Longview (Tex.) Invitational, 1967; Max Beckmann Meml. scholar Bklyn. Mus., 1960; fellow Mid-Am. Arts Alliance/Nat. Endowment for the Arts, 1988. Home: 35 W 92d St Apt 9D New York NY 10025 E-mail: rodgersleewinter@cs.com.

WINTER, ROGER PAUL, federal agency administrator; b. Hartford, Conn., July 13, 1942; s. Raymond Gustav and Marion Nellie (Stafford) W.; m. Delorise Allen, Aug. 22, 1966; children: Jonathan, Raymond Todd, Nicole. BA in Psychology, Wheaton Coll., 1964; LLD (hon.), Holy Family Coll., 1993. Asst. sec. Md. Dept. Human Resources, Balt., 1970-79, Md. Dept. Budget and Fiscal Planning, Annapolis, 1979-80; dir. Office of Refugee Resettlement, HHS, Washington, 1980-81, U.S. Com. for Refugees, Washington, 1981-2001; exec. dir. Immigration and Refugee Svcs. Am., 1994-2001; dir. Office U.S. Fgn. Disaster Assistance, 2001—02; asst. adminr. USAID, 2002—. Cons. on refugee affairs Women's Refugee Project, Washington, 1981-84; adv. bd. Refugee Policy Group, 1981-86; mem. bd. Refugee Voices, 1988-96; mem. exec. com. Coun. Washington Reps. on UN, 1989-91. Recipient Disting. Service Cambodian Assn. Am., 1982, Disting. Service award Indochina Resource Action Ctr., 1988. Mem. Nat. Ry. Hist. Soc.-Balt., Sudan Relief and Rehab. Assn. (bd. dirs., sec. 1991-93). Lodges: Eagles. Office: USAID Bur for Humanitarian Response RRB 1300 Pennsylvania Ave NW Washington DC 20523 Office Fax: 202-216-3397. E-mail: rwinter@irsa-uscr.org.*

WINTER, RUTH GROSMAN (MRS. ARTHUR WINTER), journalist; b. Newark, May 29, 1930; d. Robert Delmas and Rose (Rich) Grosman; m. Arthur Winter, June 16, 1955; children: Robin, Craig, Grant. BA, Upsala Coll., 1951; MS, Pace U., 1989. With Houston Press, 1955-56; gen. assignment Newark Star Ledger, 1951-55, sci. editor, 1956-69; columnist L.A. Times Syndicate, 1973-78, Register and Tribune, syndicate, 1981-85, isyndicate-.com, 1999-2001. Columnist myskinMD.com, 2000-01; contbr. to consumer mags.; instr. St. Peters Coll., Jersey City.; vis. lectr. mag. writing Rutgers U. Author: Poisons in Your Food, rev. edits., 1971, 91, 99, How to Reduce Your Medical Bills, 1970, A Consumer's Dictionary of Food Additives, 1972, rev. edit., 1999, Vitamin E, The Miracle Worker, 1972, So You Have Sinus Trouble, 1973, Ageless Aging, 1973, So You Have a Pain in the Neck, 1974, rev. edit., 2000, A Consumer's Dictionary of Cosmetic Ingredients, 1974, 4th rev. edit., 1994, 5th rev. edit., 1999, Don't Panic, 1975, The Fragile Bond: Marriage in the 70's, 1976, Triumph Over Tension, 1976 (N.J. Press Women's Book award), Scent Talks Among Animals, 1977, Cancer Causing Agents: A Preventive Guide, 1979, The Great Self-Improvement Sourcebook, 1980, The Scientific Case Against Smoking, 1980, People's Guide to Allergies and Allergens, 1984, A Consumer's Guide to Medicines in Food, 1995; co-author: The Lean Line One Month Lighter Program, 1985, Thin Kids Program, 1985, Build Your Brain Power, 1986, Eat Right: Be Bright, 1988, A Consumer's Dictionary of Medicines: Prescription, Over-the-Counter and Herbal, 1994, 97, Super Soy,: The Miracle Bean, 1996, rev. edit., 2000, Pain in the Neck, 1997, rev. edit., 2000, Anti Aging Hormones, 1997, Brain Workout, 1997, Vitamin E: Your Protection Against Exercise Fatigue, Weakened Immunity, Heart Disease, Cancer, Aging, Diabetic Damage, Environmental Toxins, 1998, Smart Food, 1999. Recipient award of merit ADA, 1966, Cecil award Arthritis Found., 1967, Am. Soc. Anesthesiologists award, 1969, Arthritis Found. award, 1978; named Alumnus of Year Upsala Coll., 1971, Woman of Year N.J. Daily Newspaper Women, 1971, Woman of Achievement Millburn Short Hills Profl. and Bus. Women's Assn., 1991, Golden Triangle award Am. Dermatol. Assn., 1998. Mem. Soc. Mag. Writers, Authors League, Nat. Assn. Sci. Writers, Am. Med. Writers Assn. (Eric Martin Meml. award), N.J. Daily Newspaper Women (awards news series 1958, 70, named Woman of Achievement 1971, 83), Am. Soc. Journalists and Authors (pres. 1977-78, spl. service award 1983), N.J. Press Women (pres. 1982-84) Home and Office: 44 Holly Dr Short Hills NJ 07078-1318

WINTER, STEVEN, internist, cardiologist; b. Bklyn., July 25, 1950; s. Nathan Harold and Magda (Markowitz) W.; m. Florence Stein, Aug. 20, 1972; children: Amy R., Daniel. BA, Yeshiva U., 1972; MD, U. Med./Dentistry of N.J., 1976. Diplomate Am. Bd. Internal Medicine with subspecialty in cardiovascular disease. Intern North Shore Univ. Hosp., Manhasset, N.Y., 1976-77; resident in medicine North Shore Univ. Hosp. 1976-79, Meml. Sloan Kettering Cancer Ctr., Cornell Cooper Tng. Hosp., 1977-79; fellow in cardiology R.I. Hosp.-Brown U., Providence, 1979-81; pvt. practice S.I., N.Y.; attending in medicine and cardiology S.I. U. Hosp., 1981—, St. Vincent's Med. Ctr., Richmond, 1985—; asst. clin. prof. SUNY, Bklyn., 1985—. Fellow ACP, Am. Coll. Cardiology; mem. AMA, Am. Heart Assn. Office: 2627B Hylan Blvd Staten Island NY 10306-4353

WINTER, THOMAS SWANSON, editor, newspaper executive; b. Teaneck, N.J., Dec. 28, 1937; s. Frank J. and Beulah (Swanson) W.; m. Dawne Cina, Mar. 28, 1978; children: Victoria Ruth, Abigail Swanson. AB, Harvard U., 1959, MBA, 1961. Asst. editor Human Events newspaper Human Events, Inc., Washington, 1961-64, editor, 1964—, co-owner, pres., 1966-99, pres., editor-in-chief, 1999—; pres. Fund for Objective News Reporting. Treas. Conservative Victory Fund, Washington, 1975—; 1st vice-chmn. Am. Conservative Union, 1972—. Mem.: Nat. Press, Capitol Hill. Lutheran. Home: 16 4th St SE Washington DC 20003-3804 Office: Human Events 1 Massachusetts Ave NW Washington DC 20001-1401 E-mail: twinter@eaglepub.com.

WINTER, WILLIAM EARL, retired beverage company executive; b. Granite City, Ill., Sept. 21, 1920; s. William M. and Ada M. (Compton) W.; m. Dorothy E. Schuster, Feb. 20, 1944 (dec. 1976); children: William C., Douglas E.; m. Mildred E. Stiebel, Mar. 18, 1977. AB, U. Ill., 1942. With Seven-Up Co., St. Louis, 1946-81, v.p., dir. mktg., 1969-71, exec. v.p., 1971-74, pres., chief operating officer, 1974-76, pres., chief exec. officer, 1976-79, chmn. bd., 1979-81, also former dir., cons.; chmn. emeritus, 1996—; cons. Cadbury Beverages/Seven-Up, chmn. emeritus, 1996. Bd. dirs. YMCA Greater St. Louis, U. Ill. Found.; mem. exec. bd. St. Louis Area coun. Boy Scouts Am. Capt. U.S. Army, 1942-46. Named to Promotion Mktg. Hall of Fame, 1979, Beverage World Hall of Fame, 1986 Mem. Am. Mktg. Assn., Sales and Mktg. Execs. St. Louis, Promotion Mktg. Assn. Am. (chmn. bd. 1971-72), Phi Beta Kappa, Phi Eta Sigma, Omicron Delta Gamma. Home: 14112 Baywood Villages Dr Chesterfield MO 63017-3421 Office: Dr Pepper/Seven Up Cos Inc 8900 Page Ave Saint Louis MO 63114-6108

WINTER, WILLIAM FORREST, former governor, lawyer; b. Grenada, Miss., Feb. 21, 1923; s. William Aylmer and Inez (Parker) W.; m. Elise Varner, Oct. 10, 1950; children: Anne, Elise, Eleanor. BA, U. Miss., 1943, LLB, 1949; LLD, William Carey Coll., 1980, Millsaps Coll., 1983, Troy State U., 1988, Davidson Coll., 1996, Miss. U. for Women, 2000. Bar: Miss. 1949. Practice in Grenada, 1949-58; practice in Jackson, Miss., 1968—; ptnr. Watkins, Pyle, Ludlam, Winter and Stennis, 1968-80; sr. ptnr. Watkins Ludlam Winter & Stennis, 1985—; mem. Miss. Ho. of Reps., 1948-56; state tax collector, 1956-64; state treas., 1964-68; lt. gov. State of Miss., 1972-76; gov., 1980-84. Eudora Welty prof. So. studies Millsaps Coll., 1989; Jamie Whitten prof. law U. Miss., 1989; prof. pub. policy Miss. Valley State U., 2001—02; chmn. So. Growth Policies Bd., 1981, So. Regional Edn. Bd., 1982, MDC, Inc.; mem. Pres.'s Adv. Bd. on Race, 1997—99; chmn. Adv. Commn. on Intergovtl. Rels., 1993—97. Pres. bd. trustees Miss. Dept. Archives and History; chmn. Kettering Found., 1990-93, Appalachian Regional Commn., 1983, Commn. on Future of South, 1986, Nat. Civic League, 1987-88, Nat. Commn. on State and Local Pub. Svc., Stennis Ctr. for Pub. Svc., Found. for the Mid South. With AUS, 1943-46, 51. Harvard U. Inst. Politics fellow, 1985. Mem. Am., Miss., Hinds County bar assns., U. Miss. Alumni Assn. (pres. 1979), Phi Delta Phi, Omicron Delta Kappa, Phi Delta Theta. Clubs: Univ. (Jackson). Democrat. Presbyterian. Office: 633 N State St Jackson MS 39202-3306

WINTER, WILLIAM PAUL, JR. ministry director; b. Arkansas City, Kans., Apr. 27, 1942; s. Paul William and Dessie Marie (Francis) W.; m. Sharon Ruth Fells, Dec. 26, 1964; children: Todd William, Heidi Reneé. BA, Ashland (Ohio) Coll., 1965; Cert. Electronics Cirs. and Systems Program, RCA Inst., N.Y.C., 1970; MDiv, Ashland Theol. Sem., 1986. Chief engr. radio/TV dept. Ashland Coll., 1967-72; electronic technician CAVEA Studio, Buenos Aires, 1972-74, tech. dir., 1974-93; exec. dir. Open Arms Ministry, Denver, 1998—. Exec. bd. dirs. Evang. Found. of Argentina, Buenos Aires, 1979-93; tech. cons. various evang. orgns. in Argentina, Paraguay, Uruguay; bd. dirs. Trans World Radio, Buenos Aires, Interdenominational Theol. Sem., Buenos Aires. Contbr. articles to profl. jours. Baptist. Avocations: travel, camping, car restoration, amateur radio, photography. Home: 10817 Livingston Dr Northglenn CO 80234

WINTER, WINTON ALLEN, JR. lawyer, state senator; b. Ft. Knox, Ky., Apr. 19, 1953; s. Winton A. and Nancy (Morsbach) W.; m. Mary Boyd, July 28, 1978; children: Katie, Molly, Elizabeth. BA, U. Kans., 1975, JD, 1978. Bar: Kans. 1978. Ptnr. law firm Stevens & Brand, LLP, Lawrence, Kans., 1978—; v.p., gen. counsel Peoples, Inc., 2000-; pres. Corp. for Change; mem. Kans. Senate, 1982-92. Bd. dirs. Lawrence United Fund, Boys Club of Lawrence. Mem. ABA, Kans. Bar Assn., Douglas County Bar Assn. Kans. U. Law Soc., Rotary. Republican. Roman Catholic. Note and comment editor Kans. Law Rev., 1977-78. Office: PO Box 1795 4831 W 6th St Lawrence KS 66049

WINTERER, BARBARA JEAN, designer, author; b. Manchester, N.H., Apr. 1, 1938; d. John Edward and Elizabeth Virginia Grace; m. Allen George Winterer, Mar. 30, 1959 (div. 1977); children: Audrey Lyn Winterer-Chavez, Amy Jo Winterer DeNoble. AA, Mesa (Ariz.) C.C., 1980; BS summa cum laude, U. Md., Heidelberg, Germany, 1996. Art designer Morningstar Art Design Studio, Pagosa Springs, Colo., 1988—. Interpreter Colo. State Park; U.S. rail ranger Durango-Sivlerton R.R.; master gardener Colo. State U.; bd. dirs. Southwest Cmty. Resources. Contbr. articles to newspapers and jours. Ofcl. U.S. reporter at World Eskimo Indian Olympics, Faribanks, Alaska, 1994; asst. dir. Ariz. Myasthenia Gravis Found., 1977-80; mem. ARC Disaster Response Team, Pagosa Springs, ARC Durango chpt.; bd. mem., chmn. pub. rels. com. Habitat for Humanity, Pagosa Springs, Colo; interpreter Chimney Rock Hist. Archeol. Site. Recipient Humanitarian award Phila. Inst. Human Potential, 1972, Chancellor of Germany award for acad. achievement, 1986, Citation of Meritorious Achievement award in the arts and humanitarianism Internat. Biograph. Ctr., 1997. Mem. AAUW, Libr. of Congress (assoc.), Alpha Sigma Lambda, Phi Theta Kappa. Avocations: gardening, gourmet cooking. Office: Morningstar Art Design Studio 247 Davis Cup Dr Unit 4212 Pagosa Springs CO 81147-8338 E-mail: inuit@pagosa.net.

WINTERER, PHILIP STEELE, lawyer; b. San Francisco, July 8, 1931; s. Steele Leland and Esther (Hardy) W.; m. Patricia Dowling, June 15, 1955; children: Edward J., Amey W. Marrella. BA, Amherst Coll., 1953; LLB, Harvard U., 1956. Bar: N.Y. 1957, Republic of Korea 1958. Assoc., then ptnr. Debevoise & Plimpton, N.Y.C., 1956-93, ret. ptnr., 1993, of counsel, 1994-96. Dir. Am. Savs. Bank, 1972-92. Contbr. articles to profl. publs. Past pres. Am. Italy Soc.; trustee Amherst Coll., Adelphi U.; chmn. emeritus Sch. of Am. Ballet; chmn. exec. com. Phipps Houses; hon. trustee N.Y. State Bd. Nature Conservancy; trustee, past chmn. Austen Riggs Ctr.; mem. Com. on the Folger Shakespeare Libr.; bd. dirs., v.p. Adirondack Trail Improvement Soc. Recipient Amherst Coll. medal for Eminent Svc., 1980. Fellow: Phi Beta Kappa Soc. (bd. dirs.); mem.: Am. Coll. Tax Counsel, Tax Forum, N.Y. Acad. Scis., Citizens Housing and Planning Coun. N.Y., Am. Law Inst., Coun. on Fgn. Rels., Ausable Club (trustee, v.p.). Home: East Hill Rd Keene NY 12942 also: 1165 5th Ave New York NY 10029-6931 Office: Debevoise & Plimpton 919 3rd Ave New York NY 10022 E-mail: winterhill95@aol.com.

WINTERER, VICTORIA THOMPSON, hospitality executive; b. Chgo., May 4, 1943; d. Henry Lawrence and Charlotte (Mather) Thompson; m. William George Winterer, Sept. 2, 1967; children: William G. Jr., Andrew H., Britton T., Mark L. Cert., Emma Willard Sch., Troy, N.Y., 1961; BA, Vassar Coll., 1965. Picture rschr. Time, Inc., N.Y.C., 1965-72; pres. bd. trustees Conn. River Mus., Essex, 1983-86; dir. Rockfall Found., Middletown, Conn., 1986-92; chairwoman Campaign for Emma Willard, Troy, 1992-97; v.p., trustee Emma Willard Sch., 1986-2000; owner, exec. Griswold Inn, Inc., Essex, 1972-96. Bd. dirs. Conn. River Valley and Shoreline Visitors' Coun., Middletown, 1994-96; sec. Essex Twp. Bd. Trade, Essex, 1990-96; mem. Essex Rep. Town Com., 1976-84; trustee (life) Conn. River Mus. Recipient Disting. Alumnae award for Svc. to Emma Willard Sch., 1996, Tangeman medal, 1997; named Disting. Citizen of Yr., Middlesex County C. of C., 1996. Home: Snail's Pace Useppa Island PO Box 640 Bokeelia FL 33922-0640 also: Turtle Bay 93 River Rd Essex CT 06426-1307 E-mail: WWinterer@aol.com.

WINTERER, WILLIAM G. hotel executive, director; b. St. Louis, July 7, 1934; s. Herbert O. and Dorothy (Sprengnether) W.; m. Victoria Thompson, Sept. 2, 1967; children: William, Andrew, Britton, Mark. BA, U. Fla., 1956; MBA, Harvard U., 1962. Mgr. corp. fin. dept., ptnr. Goodbody & Co., 1966-69; pres. Fla. Capital Corp., Greenwich, Conn., 1969-72; owner Griswold INn, Essex, 1972—, Town Farms Inn, Middletown, 1978-85, Dock N' Dine at Saybrook Point, Old Saybrook, 1981-86. Mem. adv. bd. United Bank and Trust, 1972-89. Life trustee, founding pres. Conn. River Found. at Steamboat Dock, chmn. bd. trustees; trustee Ivoryton Playhouse Found., 1979-82, Useppa Island (Fla.) Hist. Soc. and Mus.; corporator Middlesex Hosp.; trustee Nat. Maritime Hist. Soc.; mem. bd. advisors Goodspeed Opera; mem. Conn. Hist. Commn., 1979-82; mem. bd. advisors USS Constitution Mus.; mem. selection panel America's Cup Hall of Fame; bd. dirs. Gov.'s Vacation Travel Coun., 1976-79. Officer USCGR. Named Conn. Disting. Citizen of Yr., 1996. Mem. Conn. Restaurant Assn. (bd. dirs. 1973-77), English Speaking Union, N.Y. Yacht Club, Seawanhaka Corinthian Yacht Club, Essex Yacht Club (bd. govs.), Pettipaug Yacht Club, Ocean Cruising Club, Harvard Club, Williams Club, Hartford Club, Old Lyme Beach Club, Poly. Club, Old Lyme Country Club, Essex Platform Tennis Club, Useppa Island Club, St. George's Soc., Royal Palm Yacht Club. Republican. Roman Catholic. Address: Snail's Pace Useppa Island PO Box 640 Bokeelia FL 33922-0640 E-mail: wwinterer@aol.com.

WINTERGERST, ANN CHARLOTTE, language educator; b. Memmingen, Bavaria, Germany, Mar. 11, 1950; came to U.S., 1958; d. Martin and Charlotte Frieda (Denk) W. BA summa cum laude, St. John's U., 1972; MA, Columbia U., 1978, EdM, 1981, EdD, 1989. Teaching fellow U. Pa., Phila., 1972-73; lang. arts tchr. Our Lady Miraculous Medal Sch., Ridgewood, N.Y., 1973-81; assoc. tchr. Columbia U., N.Y.C., 1978-82; asst. prof. St. John's U., Queens, N.Y., 1981-86, 92-93, dir. ESL, 1986-91, assoc. prof., 1993—. Cons. Ednl. Testing Svc., Oakland, Calif., 1989-99, Bd. Regents N.Y. State, Albany, 1992-95, St. Martin's Press, N.Y.C., 1993-95, UN, N.Y.C., 1994-95, 96-97. Author: Second-Language Classroom Interaction, 1994; editor: Focus on Self-Study, 1995; contbr. articles to profl. jours. Mem. Dem. Nat. Com., Washington, 1990—. Recipient N.Y. State TESOL's James A. Lydon Disting. Svc. award, 1998, Recognition award Nat. Assn. Bilingual Edn. Coun. for World Langs. and Cultures, 2000. Mem. N.Y. State TESOL (officer, 1st v.p. 1994-95, pres. 1995-96, immediate past pres. 1996-97), N.Y. State Coun. Langs. (officer, pres. 1988-90), Internat. TESOL (higher edn. chair 1993-94, officer). Democrat. Roman Catholic. Avocations: soprano in Diocesan choir, German folkdancer, traveling, bowling, skiing. Home: 70-15 71st Pl Glendale NY 11385-7326 Office: St Johns Univ Dept Fgn Langs Jamaica NY 11439-0001 E-mail: winterga@stjohns.edu.

WINTERHALTER, DOLORES AUGUST (DEE WINTERHALTER), art educator; b. Pitts., Mar. 22, 1928; d. Joseph Peter and Helen August; m. Paul Joseph Winterhalter, June 21, 1947 (dec.); children: Noreen, Audrey, Mark; m. Marvin Bernard Hoeing, Mar. 26, 1988 (div. Dec. 1994). Student, Yokohama, Japan, 1963-64, Paris, 1968-70, La Romita Sch. Art, Terni, Italy, 2001. Cert. tchr. Japanese Flower Arranging, Kamakuri Wood Carving. Tchr. YWCA, Greenwich, Conn., 1978-84, Friends of the Arts and Scis., Sarasota, Fla., 1992—. Lectr. Sarasota Art Assn, 1984—; tchr., workshop presenter, Bangkok, 1971; mem. staff Hilton Leech Art Studio and Gallery, Sarasota; events chmn. State of Fla. Watercolor Exhbn., Sarasota, 1995; cultural exch. tchr. univs., fine arts acads., China; mem., tchr. Venice Art Ctr., Sarasota, 1996—2002, Art Ctr., Sarasota, 1999—2002; Hilton Leech Tchr., Sarasota, 1996—99; mem. Women's Caucus of Arts in Am., 1996—98; selected demonstrator Fine Arts of Sarasota, 1995—98; paper cons. D'Arches Watercolor Paper Co., Paris, 1983—2000; tchr., lectr., judge Sumie Inks; demonstrator Fla. Watercolor Conv., Ocala, 2000; presenter workshop. Exhbns. Xiam, China, 1994, Creators Tour of Fine Arts Soc. Sarasota, 1994-2001; numerous works in watercolor, ink, oriental brushwork; paintings in numerous corp. collections. Pres., Am. Women's Club, Genoa, Italy, 1962; participant to help raise money for scholarships Collectors and Creators Tour of Fine Arts Soc. of Sarasota, 1994. Recipient numerous awards Old Greenwich (Conn.) Art Assn., 1971-84, Sarasota, 1985, Collectors and Creators Tour award Fine Arts Soc. Sarasota, 1994, Pat Buckman award, 2000; named Artist of Yr., Fine Arts Soc. Sarasota, 1994, Venice Art Ctr., 2000. Mem. Suncoast Fla. Watercolor Soc. (life), Fla. Watercolor Soc., Long Boat Key Art Assn., Sarasota Art Assn., Sumi-e Soc. Am., Nat. League Am. PEN Women (pres. 1994-96, scholarship bd. 1996-98), Internat. Soc. Marine Printers, Venice Art Ctr., Art Sarasota, Womens Contemporary Arts Soc. (tchr.). Democrat. Roman Catholic. Avocations: wood carving, travel, bridge, creative design in crochet and fashion. Home and Office: 4027 Westbourne Cir Sarasota FL 34238-3249

WINTERLING, ANN, artist; BA, Chatham Coll., 1954. Tchr. numerous classes and workshops; demonstrator in field. Exhbns. include N.H. Farm Mus., Milton, 1988, Found. Gallery of League of N.H. Craftsmen, 1988, 93, 2000, 2001, Thorne Sagendorph Gallery, 1992, Hopkinton (N.H.) Antiquarian Soc., 1992, 95, Newport (R.I.) Arts Ctr. Show, 1993, Cahoon Mus. Am. Art, Cotuit, Mass., 1993-94, 2001, N.H. Hist. Soc., 1994, Worcester (Mass.) Ctr. Crafts, 1994, Currier Gallery Art, Manchester, N.H., 1995, Wenham (Mass.) Mus., 1998; contbr. articles to profl. jours. Mem. League of N.H. Craftsmen, Nat. Assn. Traditional Rug Hooking Artists, Woolen Magic - Hooked Fiber Art Guild, Green Mountain Hooking Craft Guild (Vt.), The Internat. Guild of Handhooking Rug Makers (sec. 1997-2000). Studio: 61 Mountain Rd Concord NH 03301

WINTERLING, GEORGE ALFRED, meteorologist, broadcaster; b. Pine Beach, N.J., Sept. 1, 1931; s. Otto Gustav and Ruth (Cranmer) W.; m. Virginia Carter, June 25, 1955; children: George Franklin, Stephen Alan, Wendy. Student, Okla. State U., 1951-52, Jacksonville U., 1954-55; BS in Meteorology, Fla. State U., 1957. Weather observer, forecaster USAF, 1950-53; weather forecaster Nat. Weather Service, Jacksonville, Fla., 1957-62; Meteorologist Sta. WJXT-TV, 1962—. Adj. prof. Jacksonville U., 1975-94. Recipient Disting. Alumni award Jacksonville U., 1990. Fellow Am. Meteorol. Soc. (Outstanding Broadcast Meteorologist award for devel. of animation for TV weathercasts 1984).

WINTER-NEIGHBORS, GWEN CAROLE, special education/art educator, consultant; b. Greenville, S.C., July 14, 1938; d. James Edward and Evelyn (Lee) Walters (dec. 1998); m. David M. Winter Jr., Aug., 1963 (dec. Feb. 1982); children: Robin Carole Winter, Charles G. McCuen, Dustin Winter TeBrugge; m. Thomas Frederick Neighbors, Mar. 24, 1989. BA in Edn. and Art, Furman U., 1960, MA in Psychology, 1967; cert. in guidance/pers., Clemson U., 1981; EdD in Youth and Mid. Childhood Edn., Nova Southeastern U., 1988; postgrad., U. S.C., Spartanburg, 1981-89; cert. clear specialist instrn., Calif. State U., Northridge, 1991; art edn. cert., Calif. State U., L.A., 1991; JD, Glendale U., 1999. Cert. tchr. art, elem. edn., psychology, secondary guidance, S.C. Tchr. 7th grade Greenville Jr. H.S., 1960-63; art tchr. Wade Hampton H.S., Greenville, 1963-67; prin. adult edn. Woodmont H.S., Piedmont, S.C., 1983-85, Mauldin H.S., Greenville and Mauldin, 1981; tchr. ednl. psychology edn. dept. Allen U., Columbia, 1969; activity therapist edn. dept. S.C. Dept. of Corrections, 1973-76; art specialist gifted edn. Westcliffe Elem. Sch., Greenville, 1976-89; tchr. self-contained spl. day class Elysian Heights Elem. Sch., Echo Park and L.A., Calif., 1989-91; art tchr. medh. drawing Sch. Dist. Greenville County Blue Ridge Mid. Sch., Greer, 1991-95; tchr./asst. head edn. dept. N. Greenville Coll., 2001—02. Participant nat. conf. U.S. Dept. Edn./So. Bell, Columbia, 1989; com. mem. nat. exec. com. Nova Southeastern U., 1988—89; asst. chmn., tchr. edn. dept. North Greenville coll., 2001; adm., staff North Greenville Coll., 2001, U. S.C., Spartanburg, adj., student tchr., supr., 2002; adv. bd. S.C. Gov. Sch. for Arts & Humanities; parent/tchr. adv. bd. Spl. Edn.; adj. prof USCS Spartanburg, 2002—. Illustrator: Mozart Book,

1988; author: (drama) Let's Sing a Song About America, 1988 (1st pl. Nat. Music award 1990). Life mem. Rep. Presdl. Task Force , 1970—; mem. voter registration com. Lexington County Rep. Party , 1970—80; grand jury participant 13th Jud. Ct. Sys., Greenville, 1986—88, guardian ad litem, 1988—2002; mem. arts educators adv. task force S.C. Gov. Sch. Arts and Humanities, 2002—; mem. spl. edn. parent adv. bd. representing Sue Cleveland Elem. Sch. G'ville Co. Sch. Dist., Spl. Edn. Topics and Trends; poll manager Greenville Co. Tchr. Incentive grantee Sch. Dist. Greenville County, 1986-88, Project Earth grantee Bell South, 1988-89, 94-95, Edn. Improvement Act/Nat. Dissimination Network grantee S.C. State Dept. Edn., 1987-88, Targett 2,000 Arts in Curricular grantee S.C. Dept. Edn., 1994-95, Alliance grantee Bus. Cmty. Greenville, 1992-95, Greer Art Rsch. grantee, 1993-94, S.C. Govs. Sch. Study grantee, 1994, Edn. Improvement Act Competitive Tchr. grantee S.C. Dept. Edn., 1994-95, Alliance Grand grant, 1995-96; recipient Am. Jurisprudence Bancroft-Whitney award Glendale U. Sch. Law, 1997, 98, Excellence Recognition in Real Property award Glendale Law Faculty, 1997, Excellence in Art of Appellate Advocacy, Glendale U. Sch. Law, 1998, Am. Jurisprudence Bancroft-Whitney award Constl. Law I, 1998. Mem.: Nat. Art Edn. Assn., ABA, NEA, Palmetto State Tchr. Assn., S.C. Art Edn. Assn., S.C. Arts Alliance, Nat. Mus. Women in Arts, Phi Delta Kappa. Baptist Avocations: computers, art, writing, music composition, law. Home: 26 Charterhouse Ave Piedmont SC 29673-9139 E-mail: lawneighbors@aol.com.

WINTEROWD, WALTER ROSS, English educator; b. Salt Lake City, Jan. 24, 1930; s. Harold Ross and Henrietta Ethel (Fike) W.; m. Norma Graham, Aug. 2, 1952; children: Geoffrey Ross, Anthony Gordon. BS, Utah State U., 1952; PhD, U. Utah, 1962. Asst. prof. U. Mont., Missoula, 1962-66; assoc. prof. U. So. Calif., Los Angeles, 1966-71, prof. English, 1971-79, McElderry prof. English, 1979-97, prof. emeritus, 1997—. Author: Rhetoric: A Synthesis, 1967, Contemporary Rhetoric, 1975, The Contemporary Writer, 1975, Composition/Rhetoric: A Synthesis, 1986, The Culture and Politics of Literacy, 1989, The Rhetoric of the "Other" Literature, 1990, (with Geoffrey Winterowd) The Critical Reader, Thinker, and Writer, 1992, The English Department: A Personal and Institutional History, 1998. Served with U.S. Army, 1953-55. Mem. Nat. Council Tchrs. English, AAUP Democrat. Home: 17551 San Roque Ln Huntington Beach CA 92647-6641

WINTERS, ALICE GRAHAM BUTLER (MRS. CARL S. WINTERS), civic worker; b. Linton, Ind., July 5, 1907; d. William Austin and Mary (Inman) Butler; A.B., Franklin Coll., 1932; spl. student U. Rochester, 1929-30, Colgate-Rochester Div. Sch., 1929-30; m. Carl S. Winters, May 23, 1925; children— Barbara (Mrs. Robert Kane), Janet (Mrs. Ralph Kuzmic), Linda (Mrs. Allen F. Jones). Minister junior ch., Jackson, Mich., 1931-39, 1st Bapt. Ch. Oak Park, Ill., 1939-59; lectr. Adult Edn. Council Chgo.; also freelance writer. Organizer, pres. Jackson (Mich.) Peace Council, 1933-35; pres. Jackson County LWV, 1935, Chgo. Drama League, 1948-50, Chgo. Mission Union, 1956-60; treas. Art Assocs. Oak Park, 1961-64; pres. Infant Welfare Soc., 1960-62; mem. Com. of 100, Nat. Council of Chs., 1963— ; bd. dirs. Woman's Bd. Salvation Army, Chgo., 1960— , pres. bd., 1969— ; bd. dirs. Women's Bd. Mental Health Assn., Chgo.; bd. dirs. Maywood (Ill.) Home and Hosp., 1940-62, v.p. bd., 1958-62; mem. woman's bd. Christian U. of Tokyo, 1963— . Recipient Outstanding Woman award Chgo. Assn. Commerce and Industry, 1976; citation for outstanding contbns. to humanity Franklin Coll., 1978; Disting. Service award Salvation Army Internat., 1980; Cert. of Recognition for outstanding service Comprehensive Community Services of Chgo., 1980; citation for achievement and influence Chautauqua Instn., 1982, Alice and Carl Winters Park named in their honor, 1985. Mem. Delta Zeta, Beta Sigma Phi, Kappa Delta. Clubs: Conference Club Presidents (bd. dirs. 1962— , chmn. pub. relations, sec.); 19th Century Woman's; Garden; Chautauqua (N.Y.) Women's; Oak Park Country; Zonta. Home: 4130 Verdant Ln West Lafayette IN 47906-4673 also: Packard Manor Chautauqua NY 14722

WINTERS, BARBARA JO, musician; b. Salt Lake City; d. Louis McClain and Gwendolyn (Bradley) W. AB cum laude, UCLA, 1960, postgrad., 1961, Yale, 1960. Mem. oboe sect. L.A. Philharm., 1961-94, prin. oboist, 1972-94; ret. Clinician oboe, English horn, Oboe d'amore. Recs. movie, TV sound tracks. Avocation: painting in oils and mixed media. Home: 3529 Coldwater Canyon Ave Studio City CA 91604-4060 Office: 135 N Grand Ave Los Angeles CA 90012-3013

WINTERS, DARCY LAFOUNTAIN, medical management company executive; b. Middletown, N.J., Aug. 27, 1955; d. Donald Mark LaFountain and Suzanne (Gilman) LaFountain Westergard; m. Leland Monte McNabb, July 4, 1981 (div. Feb. 1989); 1 child, Leland Monte Jr.; m. Stephen H. Winters, May 30, 1997. BBA in Internat. Fin. cum laude, U. Miami, 1977. Real estate agent, Grad. Realtor's Inst. Market rsch. asst. Burger King Corp., Miami, Fla., 1975-77, regional mktg. supr. Huntington Beach, Calif., 1977-78; mgr., restaurant planning Holiday Inns, Inc., Memphis, 1978-79, mgr., nat. promotions, 1979-83; dir., lodging and travel planning Holiday Corp., 1983-86; affiliate broker The Hobson Co., Realtors, 1986-88, Crye Leike, Memphis, 1988-92; sr. v.p. comm. and planning Medshares Mgmt. Group, Inc., 1991-2000. Founder, Lunch for Two, LLC, 2001—. Active Friends Pink Palace Mus., Memphis, 1987-91, Family Link/Runaway, Memphis, 1980-88; chmn. Foster Care Rev. Bd., Memphis, 1988-98; bd. dirs. Bethany Home, Memphis, 1989—, pres., 1995, treas., 1998; bd. dirs. Am. Cancer Soc., 1994—, v.p. 2000, Univ. Club of Memphis, 2000—; mktg. com. Health Industry Coun., 1994-95. Named Profl. Vol. of Yr., Friends of Pink Palace Mus., Memphis, 1989, 93, U.S. Masters Swimming All-Am., 1993, 94; grad. Leadership Memphis, 1995; named Cmty. Hero for Olympic Torch Relay, 1996, named One of Fifty Women Who Make a Differnce in 1998, Women's News, Mertie Buckman Empowerment award, 1999. Mem. Le Bonheur Club, Memphis Runners Track Club, Univ. Club (bd. dirs. 2000—). Republican. Episcopalian. Avocations: competitive long distance running, tennis, swimming. Home: 1004 Murray Hill Ln Memphis TN 38120-2674 Office: Lunch for Two LLC 4745 Poplar Ave #303 Memphis TN 38117

WINTERS, DAVID JOHN, securities analyst; b. Orange, N.J., Apr. 6, 1962; s. Martin D. Winters. BA, Cornell U., 1984. Chartered Fin. Analyst, 1990. With KMS Investment Advisers, Seattle, 1985-87; jr. analyst dept. railroad & bankruptcy Herzog, Heine, Geduld, N.Y.C., 1987-88; securities analyst Heine Securities (now Franklin Mutual Advisors, Inc.), Short Hills, N.J., 1988—; v.p. Franklin Mutual Advisers, NJ, 1997-98, sr. v.p., 1998—2000. Co-portfolio mgr. Franklin Mut. Beacon, 1999—; portfolio mgr. Mutual Discovery, 2000—; dir. Rsch. Mutual Series Fund Inc., 2000—, Mut. Shares, 2001; co-portfolio mgr. Mut. European, 2001, chief investment officer, 2001, CEO, pres., 2002 Featured in Outstanding Investors Digest, 1996. Mem. Inst. Chartered Fin. Analysts (cert. of achievement 1994-95), N.Y. Soc. Security Analysts. Office: Franklin Mutual Adv 51 John F Kennedy Pkwy Short Hills NJ 07078-2702

WINTERS, HAROLD FRANKLIN, physicist; b. Renton, Wash., May 19, 1932; s. Walter Wade and Ruth Elizabeth (Meyer) W.; m. Marjorie Ann Neiswender, June 9, 1956; children: Kathie Moe, David Winters, John Winters, Janice Assadi, Judy Ahlquist. Attended, Biola Coll., 1950-51; BS, Whitworth Coll., 1958; PhD, Washington State U., 1963. Rsch. staff mem. IBM Almaden Rsch. Ctr., San Jose, Calif., 1963-93, emeritus, 1993—. Vis. prof. Odense U., Denmark, 1979-80; past N.Am. rep. Subcom. on Plasma Chemistry, Internat. Union Pure and Applied Chemistry; past trustee Am. Vacuum Soc.; past lectr. numerous major nat. and internat. confs. throughout the world. Past mem. editl. bd. Plasma Materials Interactions, Jour. Nuc. Instruments and Methods; contbr. numerous articles to sci. jours. Corp. U.S. Army, 1952-54. Recipient (with John Coburn) Thinkers award Tegal Corp., 1983, Disting. Alumni Achievement award Wash. State U., 1992. Fellow Am. Vacuum Soc. (John A. Thornton Meml. award and lectr. 1993, plasma sci. divsn. named grad. student award in honor of John Coburn and Harold Winters 1994); mem. AAAS, Am. Sci. Affiliation. Achievements include patents for plasma processing, ion sources and ion pumps; scientific contributions in the fields of plasma science, surface science, thin films, ion bombardment of solids, dissociation of gases by electron impact. Home: 632 Lanfair Dr San Jose CA 95136-1947 E-mail: hfmwinters@aol.com. *My conversion to evangelical Christianity in high school led to a change in my attitude, lifesyle, behavior, and study habits. I changed from a poor student with a bad attitude to an excellent student with a great love for science. These changes led to a successful and enjoyable scientific career. I find no contradiction or conflict between science and my Christian faith; on the contrary science has increased my respect for God.*

WINTERS, J. OTIS, oil industry consultant; b. Tulsa, Nov. 6, 1932; s. John McAfee, Jr. and Marian Dunn (McClintock) W.; m. Ann Allene Varnadow, Oct. 18, 1958; children: John, Richard, David, Paul. MS in Petroleum Engring., Stanford U., 1955; MBA, Harvard U., 1962. Registered profl. engr., Okla. V.p. Warren Am. Oil Co., Tulsa, 1962-65; pres. Ednl. Devel. Corp., 1965-73; exec. v.p., dir. Williams Cos., 1973-77, First Nat. Bank of Tulsa, 1978-79; pres. Avanti Energy Corp., Tulsa, 1980-87, Zephyr Corp., Tulsa, 1980-90; chmn. PWS Group, Inc., 1990—. Bd. dirs. Dynegy, Inc., Triton Energy Corp., AMX Corp. Chmn. bd. First United Meth. Ch., 1977-79; pres. Downtown Tulsa Unltd., 1977; former vice chmn. bd. Oral Roberts U.; bd. dirs. Jr. Achievement; commr. Tulsa Urban Renewal Authority; 1st v.p. Ark. Basin Devel. Assn. Served as 1st lt., C.E. U.S. Army, 1955-57. Recipient various pub. service awards. Mem. Tulsa C. of C. (bd. dirs.), So. Hills Country Club (Tulsa), Pine Valley Golf Club, Augusta Nat. Golf Club, Cypress Point Club, Royal and Ancient Club, St. Andrews. Home: 5956 Sherry Ln Dallas TX 75225 Office: PWS Group Inc 5956 Sherry Ln Ste 2001 Dallas TX 75225-8301

WINTERS, J. SAM, lawyer; b. Amarillo, Tex., July 7, 1922; m. Dorothy Jean Rushing, Dec. 21, 1947; 1 child, Leila Winters Mischer. BA, U. Tex., 1944, JD, 1948. Bar: Tex. 1948. Briefing atty. Supreme Ct. Tex., Austin, 1948-49; chief Charter div. Sec. of State, State of Tex., 1949-50; ptnr. Bagby & Winters, 1950-57; shareholder Clark, Thomas, & Winters, 1957—; bd. govs. U.S. Postal Svc., Washington, 1991-2000, chmn. bd. govs., 1994-96, 97-98, vice chair, 1996-97. Mem. devel. bd. U. Tex., Austin, 1988—, mem. Pres.'s Assocs., 1981—; mem. chancellor's coun. U. Tex. Sys., 1983—; mem. symposium planning com. Lyndon B. Johnson Sch. Pub. Affairs, Austin, 1987—. Named Disting. Alumnus of Amarillo Coll., 1996. Mem. ABA (chair sect. pub. utility, comms. and transp. law 1995-96), Am. Law Inst. (life), State Bar Tex. (past pres.), Travis County Bar Assn., Tex. Bar Found., Internat. Assn. Def. Counsel, Tex. Assn. Def. Counsel, Fedn. Ins. and Corp. Counsel, Tex. Rsch. League (past chair), Panhandle Plains Hist. Soc., SAR, Order of St. John. Democrat. Episcopalian. Office: Clark Thomas & Winters PO Box 1148 Austin TX 78767-1148

WINTERS, KAY LANNING, writer; b. Trenton, N.J., Oct. 5, 1936; d. Robert Dinsmore and Luella H. Lanning; m. Earl Dallas Winters, Sept. 27, 1960; 1 child, Linda Lee Winters Taback. BS, Beaver Coll., 1958; MS, Wheelock Coll., Boston, 1960. Cert. elem. tchr. Tchr. Newton (Mass.) Pub. Schs., 1960-63; tchr., elem. supr. Palisades Sch. Dist., Kintnersville, Pa., 1965-91. Adj. instr. Lehigh U., Bethlehem, Pa., 1963-64; reading lang. arts cons. various Am. overseas schs., Nepal, India, Egypt, Jordan, Greece, Italy, 1976-80. Author: (books) Did You See What I Saw? Poems About School, 1996, Teeny Tiny Ghost, 1997 (Children's Book of Month Club), Wolf Watch, 1997 (Pick of the List), Where are the Bears, 1998, How Will the Easter Bunny Know, 1998, Whooo's Haunting the Teeny Tiny Ghost (Children's Choice Internat. Reading Assn.), Tiger Trail (Best Books of 2000 Internat. Reading Assn. Spl. Interest Group), But Mom, Everybody Else Does, Abe Lincoln the Boy Who Loved Books (Book of Month Club Jr. Libr. Guild). Mem. Soc. Children's Book Writers and Illustrators, Toastmasters, Author's Guild. Recipient Leadership and Excellence award Bucks County Assn. Supervision and Curriculum Devel., 1981, 91, Golden Disc award Arcadia U., 2001. Avocations: reading, walking. Home: PO Box 339 Richlandtown PA 18955

WINTERS, PETER LEE, dermatologist; b. Lockport, N.Y., Dec. 19, 1938; s. Earl Lloyd and Ruby Josephine (Gilmer) W.; m. Judith Barbara Amenta, June 17, 1965 (div. June 1974); children: Christopher Lee, Jonathan Bright; m. Diana Louise bucher, Nov. 27, 1993. BS, Allegheny Coll., Meadville, Pa., 1960; MD, Temple U., 1965. Diplomate Am. Bd. Dermatology, Nat. Bd. Med. Examiners. Intern Meth. Dist. Hosp., Indpls., 1965-66, resident in family medicine, 1966-68; fellow in dermatology Skin and Cancer Hosp./Temple U., Phila., 1968-71; mem. med. staff St. Vincent Hosp., Indpls., Meth. Hosp., Indpls.; pvt. practice dermatology, 1971—. Lt. USNR, 1966-68. Fellow Am. Soc. Dermatology (pres. 1992-93), Am. Assn. Dermatology (mem. adv. bd.); mem. AMA (alt. del. 1998—), Ind. State Med. Soc. (chmn. bd. 1991-92, spkr. ho. of dels. 1993-96, pres. 1997-98), Indpls. Med. Soc. (pres. 1989-90), Meth. Hosp. Alumni (pres. 1992-94), Ind. Dermatol. Soc. (pres. 1989-90), Highland Country Club, Columbia Club. Republican. Methodist. Avocations: tennis, wine collecting, reading mystery novels. Home: 1591 Preston Trl Carmel IN 46032-8970 Office: 8402 Harcourt Rd Ste 620 Indianapolis IN 46260-2055 E-mail: poredoc@concentric.net.

WINTERS, RICHARD ALLEN, mineral economist; b. Butte, Mont., Feb. 19, 1963; s. Allen S. and Doris Ellen (Taylor) W. BS in Fin. and Econs., U. Mont., 1986; MS in Mineral Econs., Colo. Sch. Mines, 1990, postgrad., 1991-93. Office engr. Morrison Knudsen Engrs., Richland, Wash., 1986-88, project acct., 1987-88; ops. analyst Echo Bay Mines, Denver, 1989; instr. Colo. Sch. Mines, Golden, Colo., 1991-92; cons. Coors Brewing Co., 1991-92; sr. rsch. engr. Phelps Dodge Mining Co., Morenci, Ariz., 1992-94; gold analyst Robertson, Stephens and Co., San Francisco, 1994-95; v.p. corp. devel. Golden Star Resources Ltd., Denver, 1995-99; v.p. RMB Resources, 2000—. Pres. Mineral Econ. Grad. Student Assn., 1989-90. Mem. Soc. Mining, Metallurgy and Exploration, Assn. Environ. Resource Economists, Mineral, Econs. and Mgmt. Soc. Avocations: outdoors, jewelry craft. Office: 303 E 17th Ave Ste 700 Denver CO 80203-1260

WINTERS, ROBERT WAYNE, medical educator, pediatrician, healthcare executive; b. Evansville, Ind., May 23, 1926; s. Frank and Clara (Flentke) W.; m. Madoris Seiler, Sept. 5, 1948 (div. Feb. 1972); children: Henry N., R. George; m. Agnete Thomsen, Feb. 11, 1976; children: Charlotte, Anne. AB summa cum laude, Indiana U., 1948; MD cum laude, Yale U., 1952. Diplomate Am. Bd. Pediatrics. Intern, resident, and fellow U. N.C., Chapel Hill, 1954-58; asst. prof. U. Pa., Phila., 1959-61; prof. Columbia U., N.Y.C., 1962-81; CEO HNS-Healthdyne, Parsippany, N.J., 1985-89; chmn. Nat. Alliance Infusion Therapy, Washington, 1990-92; pres. Winters Assocs., Inc., Jersey City, 1989—. Contbr. to profl. jour.; author 5 books. 2nd lt. cav. U.S. Army, 1944-46. Recipient Mead Johnson award Am. Acad. Pediatrics, 1966, Borden award, 1972. Address: 11 E 87th St Apt 5C New York NY 10128

WINTERS, SHEILA, family nurse practitioner; b. U.S.A., Nov. 7, 1939; d. Edward and Katherine (Burke) Volwieder; m. Dan C. Winters, Sept. 1, 1962; children: Lance, Dan, Kaylee. BS in Edn., SUNY, Plattsburgh, 1961; MEd, Columbia U., 1978. Cert. family nurse practitioner, ANCC. Nurse practitioner VA Med. Ctr., Denver. Fed. Nurse trainee. Mem.: NOVA, ANA (treas. Colo. Nurses Assn. 1996—98, past pres. Dist. Nurses Assn. 12), Colo. Nurses Found. (treas. 1996—98, v.p. 1999—), Am. Assn. Nurse Practitioners, Phi Delta Kappa, Pi Lambda Theta, Sigma Theta Tau.

WINTERS, STANLEY B. history educator, writer, civic activist; b. N.Y.C., June 5, 1924; m. Helen Plavner, Sept. 12, 1948 (div. Dec. 1969); children: Jenifer O'Neill, Neal Winters; m. Zdenka Müllerová, Jan. 9, 1970. AB, NYU, 1948; AM, Columbia U., 1950; PhD, Rutgers U., 1966. Cert. secondary social studies educator, N.J. Artist, draftsman Art Glass Co., N.Y.C., 1942-43; instr. history NYU, 1949-50; dir., co-propr. Clinton Hill Day Sch., Newark, 1950-56; tchr. social studies Livingston (N.J.) H.S., 1956-57; disting. prof. history Newark Coll. Engring./N.J. Inst. Tech., 1957-91; disting. prof. emeritus history N.J. Inst. Tech., Newark, 1991—. Adj. prof. history Rutgers U., Newark, 1980-91, rsch. assoc. Urban Studies Ctr., New Brunswick, 1961-62; cons., columnist Office of Info., Newark, 1972-80. Author: Karel Kramář's Early Political Career, 1966, From Riot to Recovery: Newark After Ten Years, 1979, T.G. Masaryk, 1850-1937: Thinker and Politician, 1990; co-author, editor: Intellectual and Social Developments in the Habsburg Empire, 1975, Great Britain, the USA and the Bohemian Lands 1848-1938 1991; editor: Dynasty, Politics and Culture, 1991, East Ctrl. Europe jour., 1975-91; mem. editl. bd. Bohemia-Zeitschrift, Munich, 1985—; columnist (pseudonymous weekly) N.J. Afro-Am. newspaper, 1958-64; contbr. more than 200 articles to profl. jours. and publs. Pres., co-founder Clinton Hill Neighborhood Coun., Newark, 1955-61; chmn. edn. com. br. office NAACP, Newark, 1960-64; candidate city coun., Newark, 1962; N.J. senator, 1965; trustee Preservation and Landmarks Com., Newark, 1980-93; pres. Czechoslovak History Conf., Chapel Hill, N.C., 1988-90. Staff sgt. U.S. Army, 1943-46, ETO. Recipient Szendzimir award Polish Inst. Arts and Scis., N.Y.C., 1971, N.J. Inst. Tech. Pub. Svc. award, 1982, Josef Hlávka Meml. medal Czechoslovak Acad. Scis., Prague, 1991, Disting. Svc. award Czechoslovak History Conf., 1995; grantee NEH, 1967, N.J. Com. for Humanities, Trenton, 1976-77, 85. Mem. Am. Hist. Assn. (life, nominated first Czech historian as hon. fgn. mem.), Organization Am. Historians, Am. Assn. Advancement Slavic Studies, Collegium Carolinum, Josef Pekař Hist. Soc. (hon.), Hist. Assn. of Czech Republic (hon.), Phi Beta Kappa. Avocations: chess, travel, walking, correspondence, pre-contemporary music. Home: 22365 Queens Ave Port Charlotte FL 33952 Fax: 941-624-3247.

WINTERSHEIMER, DONALD CARL, state supreme court justice; b. Covington, Ky., Apr. 21, 1932; s. Carl E. and Marie A. (Kohl) W.; m. Alice T. Rabe, June 24, 1961; children: Mark D., Lisa Ann, Craig P., Amy T., Blaise Q. BA, Thomas More Coll., 1953; MA, Xavier U., 1956; JD, U. Cin., 1959; LHD (hon.), No. Ky. U., 1999. Bar: Ky. 1960, Ohio 1960. Pvt. practice, Covington, Ky., 1960-76; city solicitor City of Covington, 1962-76; judge Ky. Ct. Appeals, Frankfort, 1976-83; justice Ky. Supreme Ct., 1983—, chmn. criminal rules com., 1988-94, chmn. continuing jud. edn. com., 1983—, chmn. rules com., 1994—. Del. Foster Parent Rev. Bd., 1985-2002; mem. adv. bd. Sta. WNKU-FM, 1984-94, Am. Soc. Writers on Legal Subjects. Trustee Sta. WNKU-FM. Recipient Cmty. Svc. award Thomas More Coll., 1968; recipient Disting. Alumnus award Thomas More Coll., 1982, Disting. Alumni award Coll. Law/U.Cin., 1998; named Disting. Jurist Chase Coll. Law, 1983, Outstanding Jurist Phi Alpha Delta Law Frat., 1990. Mem. ABA, Am. Judicature Soc., Ky. Bar Assn., Ohio Bar Assn., Cin. Bar Assn., Inst. Jud. Adminstrn., Am. Inss of Ct. (founder Chase chpt.). Democrat. Roman Catholic. Home: 224 Adams Ave Covington KY 41014-1712 Office: Ky Supreme Ct Capitol Building Room 235 700 Capitol Ave Frankfort KY 40601-3410

WINTERSTEIN, JAMES FREDRICK, academic administrator; b. Copperas Cove, Tex., Apr. 8, 1943; s. Arno Fredrick Herman and Ada Amanda Johanna (Wagnr) W.; m. Diane Marie Bochmann, July 13, 1963; children: Russell, Lisa, Steven, Amy. Student, U. N.M., 1962; D of Chiropractic cum laude, Nat. Coll. Chiropractic, 1968; cert., Harvard Inst. for Ednl. Mgmt., 1988. Diplomate Am. Chiropractic Bd. Radiology; lic. chiropractic, Ill., Fla., S.D., Md. Night supr. x-ray dept. DuPage Meml. Hosp., Elmhurst, Ill., 1964-66; x-ray technologist Lombard (Ill.) Chiropractic Clinic, 1966-68, asst. dir., 1968-71; chmn. dept. diagnostic imaging Nat. Coll. Chiropractic, Lombard, Ill., 1971-73, chief of staff, 1985-86; pres. Nat. U. Health Scis., 1986—; pvt. practice West Chicago, 1968-73, Fla., 1973-85. Faculty Nat. Lincoln Coll. Post-Profl., Grad. and Continuing Edn., 1967—; chmn. x-ray test com. Nat. Bd. Chiropractic Examiners, 1971-73; govs. adv. panel on coal worker's pneumoconiosis and chiropractic State of Pa., 1979; v.p. Am. Chiropractic Coll. Radiology, 1981-83; mem. adv. coun. on radiation protection Dept. Health and Rehabilitative Svcs. State of Fla., 1984-85; cons. to bd. examiners State of S.C., 1983-84, State of Fla., 1980-85; cons. to peer review bd. State of Fla., 1980-84; trustee Chiropractic Centennial Found., 1989-90; mem. adv. com. Aids Alternative Health Ptnrs., 1996-2000, Consortial Ctr. for Chiropractic Rsch., 1998—; bd. dirs. Fedn. Ill. Ind. Colls. and Univs., 1995—; bd. dirs. Alternative Medicine, Inc., 1999—; spkr. in field. Pub. Outreach (Nat. Univ. Health Scis. monthly); author numerous monographs on chiropractic edn. and practice; co-inventor composite shielding and mounting means for x-ray machines; contbr. articles to profl. jours. Chmn., bd. dirs. Trinity Luth. Ch., West Chgo., 1970-72, Luth. High Sch., Pinellas County, Fla., 1979-82, St. John Luth. Ch., Lombard, 1988; chmn. bd. edn. First Luth. Sch., 1975-79; chmn. First Luth. Congregation, Clearwater, Fla., 1979-82; chmn. bldg. planning com. Grace Luth. Ch. and Sch., St. Petersburg, Fla., 1984-85; bldg. planning com. ch. expansion, new elem. sch., First Luth. Sch., 1975-79; stewardship adv. coun. Fla./Ga. dist. Luth. Ch. Mo. Synod, 1983-85; trustee West Suburban Regional Acad. Consortium, 1993-99. With U.S. Army, 1961-64. Recipient Cert. Meritorious Svc. Am. Chiropractic Registry of Radiologic Technologists, Cert. Recognition for Inspiration, Guidance, and Support Delta Tau Alpha, 1989, Cert. Appreciation Chiropractic Assn. South Africa, 1988, 1st pl. Fund Raiser Ride for Kids award Pediat. Brain Tumor Found. U.S., 1997, Cert. Appreciation Ill. Chiropractic Soc., 1997, Hope and Support award Alternative Health Ptnrs., 1998, Chiropractor of Yr., Ill. Chiropractic Soc., 2000. Mem. APHA, Am. Chiropractic Assn., Am. Chiropractic Coll. Radiology (pres. 1983-85, exec. com. 1985-86), Am. Chiropractic Coun. on Diagnostic Imaging, Am. Chiropractic Coun. on Diagnosis and Internal Disorders, Am. Chiropractic Coun. on Nutrition, Nat. Univ. Alumni Assn., Am. Acad. Chiropractic Physicians (sec.), Assn. Chiropractic Colls. (sec.-treas. 1986-91), Coun. Chiropractic Edn. (sec.-treas. 1988-90, v.p. 1990-92, pres. 1992-94, immediate past pres. 1994-96), Fla. Chiropractic Assn. (chmn. radiol. health com. 1977-85, Disting. Svc. award 1999). Republican. Lutheran. Avocations: reading, automobile rehabilitation, Harley-Davidson motorcycles, fishing.

WINTERTON, JOSEPH HENRY, computer software executive; b. Oneida, N.Y., July 22, 1948; s. Stewart Grant and Margaret (Durant) W.; m. Susan Marie Briggs, May 29, 1971; children: Tamara Leigh, Danielle Marie, Derek James. AAS, Canton (N.Y.) Coll., 1968; BA, SUNY, Potsdam, 1970. Adv. programmer IBM Corp., Poughkeepsie, N.Y., 1970-81; mgr. R & D Candle Corp., L.A., 1981-83, dir. R & D White Plains, N.Y., 1983-96, sr. dir. R&D, 1996—. Coach Yorktown (N.Y.) Athletic Club, 1988—; treas. Hudson Valley Christian Acad., Mahopac, NY, 1986—87, Yorktown Theatre Workshop, Yorktown Heights, 1989—92; trustee Calvary Bapt. Ch., Ossining, 1986, midnight run vol., 1993—; bd. dirs. Yorktown Theatre Co. Served with U.S. Army, 1970—76, N.G. Republican. Mem. Christian Ch. Avocations: photography, teaching Sunday sch., coaching youth sports, golf. Home: 1521 Hanover St Yorktown Heights NY 10598-4709 Office: Candle Corp 701 Westchester Ave Ste 200E White Plains NY 10604-3078 E-mail: joe_winterton@candle.com., jowintertn@aol.com.

WINTHROP, JOHN, wines and spirits company executive; b. Salt Lake City, Apr. 20, 1947; children: Grant Gordon, Clayton Hanford. AB cum laude, Yale U., 1969; JD magna cum laude, U. Tex., 1972. Bar: Calif. 1972. Law clk. 9th cir. U.S. Ct. Appeals, L.A., 1972-73; conseil juridique Coudert Freres, Paris, 1973-75; v.p. gen. counsel MacDonald Group, Ltd., L.A., 1976-82; pres., CEO MacDonald Mgmt. Corp. and MacDonald Group Ltd., 1982-86; pres., chief exec. officer MacDonald Corp. (gen. contractors), 1982-86; chmn., CEO Comstock Mgmt. Co., 1986—; pres., CEO Winthrop Investment Properties, Los Angeles, 1986—; CEO Veritas Imports, L.A., 1995—. Bd. dirs. Plus Prods., Tiger's Milk Prods., Irvine, Calif., 1977-80. Contbr. articles to profl. jours. Bd. dirs., sec. L.A. Sheriff's Dept. Found.; bd. dirs. L.A. Opera. Mem. Nat. Eagle Scout Assn. (life), French-Am. C. of C. (bd. dirs. 1982-87), Urban Land Inst., Yale Club N.Y., Calif. Club, The Beach Club, Elizabethan Club, Order of the Coif, Beta Theta Pi. Republican. Office: Veritas Imports Penthouse 9460 Wilshire Blvd Beverly Hills CA 90212-2720 E-mail: jwinthrop@veritaswine.com.

WINTHROP, KENNETH RAY, insurance executive; b. N.Y.C., Dec. 29, 1950; s. Ralph and Lore (Bruck) W.; m. Sharon Swinnich, 1976 (div. 1978); m. Diane Louise Denney, June 27, 1981; children: Alyssa Louise, Matthew Lawrence, Andrew Lee. BA in English, SUNY, Buffalo, 1972. CLU. Agt. Northwestern Mut. Life Ins., Woodland Hills, Calif., 1975-78, Nat. Life of Vermont, L.A., 1978-93; mgr. Mass Mut., 1993-97, agt., 1997—. Referee Am. Youth Soccer Orgn., L.A., 1996—. Mem. Million Dollar Round Table (life). Avocations: racquetball, snow skiing, trout fishing, gardening. Home: 1404 5th St Manhattan Beach CA 90266-6338 Office: 2401 Pacific Coast Hwy 201 Hermosa Beach CA 90254 E-mail: kwinthrop@finsvcs.com.

WINTHROP, LAWRENCE FREDRICK, lawyer; b. Apr. 18, 1952; s. Murray and Vauneta (Cardwell) W. BA with honors, Whittier Coll., 1974; JD magna cum laude, Calif. Western Sch., 1977. Bar: Ariz. 1977, Calif. 1977, U.S. Dist. Ct. Ariz. 1977, U.S. Dist. Ct. (so. dist.) Calif. 1981, U.S. Ct. Appeals (9th cir.) 1981, U.S. Dist. Ct. (cen. dist.) Calif. 1983, U.S. Supreme Ct. 1983. Assoc. Snell and Wilmer, Phoenix, 1977-83, ptnr., 1984-93, Doyle, Winthrop, P.C., Phoenix, 1993—. Judge pro tem Maricopa County Superior Ct., 1987-97, Ariz. Ct. Appeals, 1992—; lectr. Ariz. personal injury law and practice and state and local tax law Tax Exec. Inst., Nat. Bus. Inst., Profl. Edn. Systems, Inc., Ariz. Trial Lawyers Assn.,Am. Bd. Trial Advs., Maricopa County Bar

Assn.; bd. dirs. Valley of the Sun Sch., 1989-97, chmn., 1994-96; mem. Vol. Lawyers Program, Phoenix, 1980—. Editor-in-chief: Calif. Western Law Rev., 1976-77. Fellow Ariz. Bar Found., Maricopa Bar Found.; mem. ABA, Calif. Bar Assn., Ariz. Bar Assn. (mem. com. on exam. 1995—), Ariz. Tax Rsch. Assn. (bd. dirs. 1989-93), Maricopa County Bar Assn., Ariz. Assn. Def. Counsel (bd. dirs., pres. 1988-89, chmn. med.-malpractice com. 1993-95), Aspen Valley Club, LaMancha Racquet Club. Republican. Methodist. Avocations: music, golf, tennis. Home: 6031 N 2nd St Phoenix AZ 85012-1210 Office: Doyle and Winthrop PC 3300 N Central Ave Ste 1600 Phoenix AZ 85012 E-mail: lwinthrop@doylewinthrop.com.

WINTHROP, SHERMAN, lawyer; b. Duluth, Minn., Feb. 3, 1931; s. George E. and Mary (Tesler) W.; m. Barbara Cowan, Dec. 16, 1956; children: Susan Winthrop Crist, Bradley T., Douglas A. BBA, U. Minn., 1952; JD, Harvard U., 1955. Bar: Minn. 1955, U.S. Dist. Ct. Minn. 1955, U.S. Tax Ct. Law clk. to chief justice Minn. Supreme Ct., St. Paul, 1955-56; ptnr. Oppenheimer, Wolff & Donnelly, 1956-79; shareholder Winthrop & Weinstine P.A., 1979—. Bd. dirs. Bremer Fin. Corp., St. Paul, Minn., Capital City Partnership; bd. dirs., sec. St. Paul Progress Corp. Mem. ABA, Minn. Bar Assn. (chair exec. coun., bus. law sect. 1992-93), Ramsey County Bar Assn. Avocations: tennis, travel, family. Home: 1672 Pinehurst Ave Saint Paul MN 55116-2158 Office: Winthrop & Weinstine PA 3200 Minn World Trade Ctr 30 7th St E Saint Paul MN 55101-4914 E-mail: swinthrop@winthrop.com.

WINTLE, ROSEMARIE, biomedical electronics engineer; b. Brigham City, Utah, Sept. 13, 1951; d. DeVere and Kathleen (Layton) W. Student, Weber State U., 1972-76, Brigham Young U., 1978-79, U. Utah, 1980-87, ITT Electronic Tech. Inst., 1986-88, Utah State U., 1991-92. Engr. Morton Internat., Brigham City, Utah; computer technician Salt Lake City; engr. Nuclear Med., Mesa, Ariz., 1976-77, U. Utah Hosp. Lab., Salt Lake City, 1980-87; electronic engr. Varian Assocs., Inc., 1987-88; electronic bio-med. experiment and rsch. engr. Clin. Rsch. Assocs., Provo, Utah, 1988-89. Contbr. articles to profl. jours. Engr., builder Honeyville (Utah) town playground equipment; designer, mgr. Honeyville town water system. Recipient grant Brigham City. Mem. IEEE (pres.), NSPE, Inst. for Sci. Info., Am. Statis. Assn., Sci. Am. Libr., Computer Club, Amnesty Internat., Libr. of Science, Newbridge Book Club. Mem. Lds Ch. Avocations: chess, sports, computers.

WINTON, CALHOUN, literature educator; b. Ft. Benning, Ga., Jan. 21, 1927; s. George Peterson and Dorothy (Calhoun) W.; m. Elizabeth Jefferys Myers, June 30, 1948; children: Jefferys Hobart, William Calhoun. Student, Ga. Inst. Tech., 1944-46; BA, U. of the South, 1948; MA, Vanderbilt U., 1950, Princeton U., 1954, PhD, 1955. Instr. Dartmouth Coll., Hanover, N.H., 1954-57; asst. prof. U. Va., Charlottesville, 1957-60; asst. prof. then assoc. prof., asst. dean Grad. Sch. U. Del., 1960-67; prof. dept. English U. S.C., Columbia, 1967-75, chmn. dept., 1970-73; prof. U. Md., College Park, 1975-97, dir. Rsch. Ctr. for Humanities, 1988-90, prof. emeritus, 1997—. Del. Jt. Nat. Com. on Langs., Washington, 1986-90, 95-99. Author: (biography) Captain Steele, 1964, Sir Richard Steele, 1970; editor: Plays of Aaron Hill, 1981, John Gay and the London Theatre, 1993; author (with others) Colonial Book in the Atlantic World, 2000; contbr. entriesDictionary of National Biography. Pres. faculty guild U. Md., 1986-89; bd. dirs. Md. Fedn. Tchrs., Balt., 1986-89. Capt. USN, 1944-47, 50-52. Am. Philos. Soc. grantee, 1960; Guggenheim Found. fellow, 1965-66, Folger Shakespeare Libr. fellow, Washington, 1970, John Carter Brown Libr. fellow, Providence, 1995; Fulbright Commn. lectureship, Ankara, Turkey, 1979-80. Mem. MLA (exec. com. South Atlantic chpt. 1977-80), Am. Soc. 18th-Century Studies (founder 1970—), East Cen. Soc. 18th Century Studies (pres. 1987), Assn. Princeton Grad. Alumni (exec. bd. 1986-90), Cosmos Club Washington, Princeton Club (N.Y. and Washington), Am. Antiquarian Soc., Literary Soc. Washington. Democrat. Episcopalian. Avocations: swimming, book collecting. Home: 8201 16th St Apt 1025 Silver Spring MD 20910-3252 Office: U Md Dept English College Park MD 20742-0001 E-mail: cw41@umail.umd.edu.

WINTON, HAROLD RAYMOND, historian; b. Ft. Benning, Ga., Oct. 12, 1942; s. Walter Farrell and Wilma Patricia W.; m. Barbara Elizabeth Strydio, June 5, 1964; children: Eric, Douglas, Daniel, Mark. BS, U.S. Mil. Acad., 1964; MA, Stanford U., 1971, PhD, 1977. Commd. 2d lt. U.S. Army, 1964, advanced through grades to lt. col., 1979, ret., 1989; prof. mil. art and sci. Sch. Advanced Mil. Studies, Ft. Leavenworth, Kans., 1989-90; prof. mil. history and theory Sch. Advanced Airpower Studies, Maxwell AFB, Ala., 1990—. Deputy dir. Sch. Advanced Mil. Studies, 1985-89. Home: 656 Wiltshire Dr Montgomery AL 36117 Office: Sch Advanced Airpower Studies 600 Chennault Cir Maxwell AFB AL 36112-6424 Fax: 334-953-3015. E-mail: harold.winton@maxwell.af.mil.

WINTON, HOWARD PHILLIP, retired optometrist; b. Springfield, Mo., June 23, 1925; s. George Lecoumpt and Emma Pearl (Schoonover) W.; m. Frances Jeanne Zellweger, June 29, 1946; children: Susan, James, Stephen, Gary, Carolyn. Student, Northern Ill. Coll. of Optometry, Midwest Sch. of Optics; LHD, Ill. Coll. of Optometry, 1965. Diplomate Am. Bd. Optometry. Pvt. practice optometry, Melbourne, Fla. Nat. cons. to Surgeon Gen. USAF, 1979. Pres. Melbourne C. of C.; pres., chmn. bd. dirs. Brevard Econ. Devel. Coun., Brevard County, 1970-79. With USN, 1943-46, PTO. Named Optometrist of the Yr., Fla. Optometric Assn., 1972. Fellow Am. Acad. Optometry; mem. Fla. Optometric Assn. (pres. 1965), Am. Optometric Assn. (pres. 1975-76, mem. coun.), So. Coun. Optometrics (pres. 1968), Brevard Optometric Assn. (founder, pres. 1973), Rotary (founder 1st Interact Club 1962, pres. Melbourne 1962). Office: 3358 Cutty Sark Way Indialantic FL 32903

WINTRODE, RALPH CHARLES, lawyer; b. Hollywood, Calif., Dec. 21, 1942; s. Ralph Osborne and Maureen (Kavanagh) W.; m. Leslie Ann O'Rourke, July 2, 1966 (div. Feb. 1994); children: R. Christopher, Patrick L., Ryan B. BS in Acctg., U. So. Calif., 1966, JD, 1967. Bar: Calif. 1967, N.Y. 1984, Japan 1989, Washington 1990. From assoc. to ptnr. to of counsel Gibson, Dunn & Crutcher, Tokyo, L.A., Newport Beach and Irvine, Calif., 1967—. Sec. Music Ctr. Los Angeles County, 1986-88; bd. dirs. Coro Found., L.A. County, 1986-87. Mem. Newport Harbor Club, Am. Club Tokyo. Avocations: sailboat racing, car racing, flying. Office: Gibson Dunn & Crutcher 4 Park Plz Ste 1400 Irvine CA 92614-8557 also: 333 S Grand Ave Ste 4400 Los Angeles CA 90071-1548

WINTROL, JOHN PATRICK, lawyer; b. Wichita, Kans., Feb. 13, 1941; s. Clarence Joseph and Margaret (Gill) W.; m. Janet Lee Mitchell; children: John Howard, Joanna Lee. BA cum laude, Rockhurst Coll., 1963; JD, Georgetown U., 1969. Bar. D.C. 1969, U.S. Ct. Appeals (4th, 5th, 11th and D.C. cirs.) 1981, U.S. Dist. Ct. Md. 1984. Law clk. to Hon. Howard Corcoran U.S. Dist. Ct., Washington, 1969-71; assoc. Howrey & Simon, 1971-77; mng. ptnr. Perito, Duerk & Pinco, 1978-85; ptnr. Finley Kumble, 1985-87, Laxalt, Washington, Perito & Dubuc, Washington, 1988-91, McDermott, Will & Emery, Washington, 1991—. Mem. jud. conf. U.S. Ct. Appeals (D.C. cir.). Vol. Peace Corps, Turkey, 1963-65; bd. trustees Holton Arms Sch. Mem. ABA. Roman Catholic. Office: McDermott Will & Emery 600 13th St NW Washington DC 20005-3096 E-mail: jwintrol@mwe.com.

WINWOOD, STEPHEN LAWRENCE, musician, composer; b. Birmingham, Eng., May 12, 1948; s. Lawrence Samuel and Lillian Mary (Saunders) W.; m. Eugenia Crafton, Jan. 17, 1987; children: Mary Clare, Elizabeth Dawn, Stephen Calhoun, Lillian Eugenia. Rec. artist Spencer Davis Group, 1964-67, Blind Faith, 1970, Traffic, 1967-74; solo artist N.Y.C. and in England, 1974—. Dir. F.S. Ltd. Albums include: Arc of a Diver, 1980, Talking Back to the Night, 1982, Back in the High Life, 1986, Roll With It, 1988 (Grammy 1989), Chronicles, Refugees of the Heart, 1991, Traffic: Far From Home, 1994, Junction 7, 1997. Recipient 14 Gold Record awards, 4 Platinum Record awards, 2 Grammy awards.

WINZELER, JUDITH KAY, foundation administrator; b. Canton, Ohio, Dec. 17, 1942; d. Charles and Pauline Doris (Werstler) Wenzlawski; m. Robert Lee Winzeler, Nov. 4, 1961; children: Elizabeth Ann Wenzeler Williams, Alice Louise Wenzeler Smith. BA, U. Nev., 1971, MA, 1981. Instr. anthropology Western Nev. C.C., Reno, 1976-77; program developer Nev. Humanities Com., 1977-78, asst. dir., 1978-80, assoc. dir., 1980-84, exec. dir., 1984—. Panelist NEH, 1991; mem. Hilliard Found. Com., Reno, 1984—; mem. program com. Fedn. of State Humanities Couns., Washington, 1989; mem. selections com. Grace A. Griffen Chair in History, Reno, 1992. Mem. Nev. Commn. on Bicentennial of U.S. Constn., 1985—91; ad hoc mem. Adv. Com. Participatory Democracy, 1997—; pres. Luth. Ch. of Good Shepherd, Reno, 1987—89; mem. nominating com. Evang. Luth. Ch. Am., Sierra Synod, Oakland, Calif., 1991—94; bd. dirs., officer Reno/Sparks Metro Min., Reno, 1987—2002; adv. bd. Nev. Ctr. for the Book, 1998—; cmty. adv. bd. KNPB Pub. TV, 1999—; active Nev. Hist. Soc., Nev. State Mus.; Nev. Mus. Art; Western Folklife Ctr.; Friends of Washoe County Libr. Mem. Reno Rotary Club (Paul Harris fellow). Avocation: travel. Home: 1579 Belford Rd Reno NV 89509-3907 Office: Nev Humanities Com 1034 N Sierra St Reno NV 89503-3721 E-mail: winzeler@unr.nevada.edu.

WINZENREID, JAMES ERNEST, lawyer, entrepreneur; b. Wheeling, W.Va., June 9, 1951; s. Ernest Christian and Dorothy Emma (Wolf) W.; m. Rebecca Lee Rice, Aug. 11, 1979; children: Diana Lee, Lauren Rice. AB, W. Liberty State Coll., 1973; MBA, W.Va. U., 1979; JD, Duquesne U., 1987; LLM, Wayne State U., 1989. Bar: Pa. 1987, U.S. Dist. Ct. (we. dist.) Pa. 1987. Staff asst. Wheeling Pitts. Steel Corp., Wheeling, 1974—78, supr. indsl. rels., 1978; mgr. profl. planning and devel. Copperweld Corp., Pitts., 1978—79, mgr. human resources Glassport, 1979—81, plant mgr., 1981—83, group mgr. human resources Pitts., 1984—85, market program mgr., 1986—87; with lab. and employment dept. Eckert, Seamans, Cherin & Mellott, 1986—87; corp. staff rep. Tecumseh (Mich.) Products Co., 1987—89; v.p. human resources devel. Lafarge (Va.) Corp., 1989—94; v.p. human resources western region Lafarge Constrn. Materials, Calgary, Canada, 1994—96, Lafarge Can. Inc., Calgary, Canada, 1996—99; mgr. union rels. GE, Bloomington, Ind., 2000—01; dir. labor rels. and compliance Metaldyne Corp., Plymouth, Mich., 2002—. Mng. editor Juris mag., 1986. Bd. dirs. Wheeling Symphony Soc., 1977-86, Wheeling Jaycees, 1976-78; mem. adv. bd. Jr. Achievement Southwestern Pa., 1981-83. Named Outstanding Young Men Am. U.S. Jaycees, 1979. Mem. ABA, Pa. Bar Assn., Allegheny Bar Assn., Am. Soc. Human Resources Mgmt., Human Resource Planning Soc., Phi Alpha Delta. Republican. Lutheran. Avocations: golf, reading. Home: 4647 Fox Moor Ln Greenwood IN 46143-9279 Office: Metaldyne Corp 47603 Halyard Dr Plymouth MI 48170-2429

WINZER, P.J. lawyer; b. Shreveport, La., June 7, 1947; d. C.W. Winzer and Pearlene Hall Winzer Tobin. BA in Polit. Sci., So. U., Baton Rouge, 1968; JD, UCLA, 1971. Bar: Bar: Calif. 1972, U.S. Supreme Ct. 1986. Staff atty. Office of Gen. Counsel, U.S. HEW, Washington, 1971-80; asst. spl. counsel U.S. Office of Spl. Counsel Merit Systems Protection Bd., Dallas, 1980-82; regional dir. U.S. Merit Systems Protection Bd., Alexandria, Va., 1982—. Mem. Calif. Bar Assn., Fed. Cir. Bar Assn., Delta Sigma Theta. Office: US Merit System Protection 1800 Diagnol Rd Ste 205 Alexandria VA 22314-2840

WIONS, STEVEN PAUL, small business owner; b. Silver Spring, Md., May 19, 1971; s. David Joseph Wions, Karyn Dale Smith, and Ronald Gilbert Smith (stepfather); m. Michelle Alisa Ascher, Dec. 23, 1995; 1 child, Samantha Ariel. BS in Comm., SUNY, Brockport, 1994. Field cons. Jackson Hewitt Inc., Rochester, N.Y., 1994-95, dist. dir. Laurel, Md., 1995-98; owner franchise Jackson Hewitt Tax Svc., Balt., 1998—; pres. It Makes Cents Inc., 1998—. Office: Jackson Hewitt Tax Svc 2622G Annapolis Rd Severn MD 21144-1626 E-mail: jh.bgb@jhnet.com.

WIORKOWSKI, GABRIELLE KAY, data base consultant; b. Tulsa, Nov. 10, 1943; d. Marshall Frank and Iva Ann (Johnson) Patterson; m. John J. Wiorskowski, June 4, 1966; 1 child, Fleur. BA summa cum laude, St. Mary's U., 1971; MS, U. Tex., Dallas, 1979. Adminstrv. asst. Stritch Sch. Med. Loyola U., Chgo., 1963-67; sr. programmer Corn Products Co., 1967-68; mgr. data communications Jewel Co., 1971-74; ind. data processing cons. Dallas, 1975—. Lectr. U. Tex., Dallas, 1980—; mgr. data base mgmt. systems Sun Co. Inc., Dallas, 1981-83; DBA systems supr. Tex. Instruments, Inc., Dallas, 1983-85; sr. DB2 cons., founder Gabrielle & Assocs. (subs. Codd & Date Internat.), Dallas, 1985—, pres. DB2 Forum, 1988—. Author: (books) DBS: Design Development Guide, 1988, 3d edit., 1992, DB2 for z/OS and OS/390 Development for Performance, 2002; contbr. chapters to books, articles. Mem. Richardson Assn. Gifted and Talented (treas. 1979-80), Assn. Computing Machinery, Nat. Computer Conf. (publs. chmn., steering com., 1977), Delta Epsilon Sigman, Pi Gamma Mu. Home and Office: 9922 Lincolnshire Ct Rockwall TX 75087-4509 Fax: 972-412-8867.

WIOT, JEROME FRANCIS, radiologist; b. Cin., Aug. 24, 1927; s. Daniel and Elvera (Weisgerber) W.; m. Andrea Kockritz, July 29, 1972; children— J. Geoffrey, Jason. MD, U. Cin., 1953. Diplomate: Am. Bd. Radiology (trustee, pres.). Intern Cin. Gen. Hosp., 1953-54, resident, 1954-55, 58-59; gen. practice medicine Wyoming, Ohio, 1955-57; mem. faculty U. Cin., 1959-67, 68—, prof., chmn. radiology, 1973-93, acting sr. v.p., provost for med. affairs, 1985-86, prof. emeritus, 1998—; practice medicine specializing in radiology Tampa, Fla., 1967-68. Contbr. articles to med. jours. Bd. dirs. Ruth Lyons Fund, U. Cin. Found., 1997—. Served with USN, 1945-46. Fellow Am. Coll. Radiology (pres. 1983-84, chmn. commn. on diagnostic radiology); mem. Radiol. Soc. N.Am., Am. Roentgen Ray Soc. (pres. 1986-87), Am. Bd. Radiology (pres. 1982-84), Ohio Med. Assn., Cin. Acad. Medicine, Radiol. Soc. Greater Cin., Ohio Radiol. Soc., Am. Thoracic Soc., Ohio Thoracic Soc., Fleischner Soc., Soc. Gastrointestinal Radiologists. Office: U Cin Med Ctr Dept Radiology 234 Goodman St Cincinnati OH 45267-1000

WIPKE, W. TODD, chemistry educator; b. Dec. 16, 1940; BS, U. Mo., Columbia, 1962; PhD, U. Calif., Berkeley, 1965. Rsch. chemist Esso Rsch. and Engrng. Co., Baton Rouge, 1962; postdoctoral rsch. fellow Harvard U., 1967-69; asst. prof. Princeton U., 1969-75; assoc. prof. chemistry U. Calif., Santa Cruz, 1975-81, prof. chemistry, 1981—. Founder, cons. Molecular Design Ltd., San Leandro, Calif., 1978-91, Ciba-Geigy, Basle, Switzerland, 1978-82, BASF, Ludwigshafen, Fed. Republic Germany, 1974-78, Squibb, Princeton, N.J., 1976-81; adv. EPA, 1984—. Editor: Computer Representation and Manipulation of Chemical Information, 1973, Computer-Assisted Organic Synthesis, 1977; editor-in-chief: (jour.) Tetrahedron Computer Methodology, 1987-92; editor: Tetrahedron and Tetrahedron Letters, 1987-92; contbr. articles to profl. jours. Capt. U.S. Army, 1966-67. Recipient Eastman Kodak Rsch. award, 1964, Texaco Outstanding Rsch. award, 1962, Alexander von Humboldt Sr. Scientist award, 1987; Merck Career Devel. grantee, 1970; NIH fellow, 1964-65. Mem. NAS, Am. Chem. Soc. (assoc., Computers in Chemistry award 1987, St. Charles Found. Alumni award 1996), Assn. Computing Machinery, Chem. Soc., Am. Assn. Artificial Intelligence (charter), Chem. Structure Assn. (charter), Internat. Soc. Study Xenobiotics. Office: U Calif Dept Chemistry Santa Cruz CA 95064

WIPPEL, JOHN FRANCIS, philosophy educator; b. Pomeroy, Ohio, Aug. 21, 1933; s. Joseph Edward and Mary Josephine (Andrews) W. BA in Philosophy, Cath. U. Am., 1955, MA in Philosophy, 1956, STL in Theology, 1960; PhD in Philosophy, Louvain, Belgium, 1965; Maitre agrégé in Philosophy, Louvain, 1981. Ordained priest Roman Cath. Ch., 1960. Instr. philosophy Cath. U., Washington, 1960-61, 63-65, asst. prof. philosophy, 1965-67, assoc. prof. philosophy, 1967-72, ord. prof. philosophy, 1972—, acad. v.p., 1989-96, provost, 1996-97, Theodore Basselin prof. philosophy, 2001—. Vis. assoc. prof. U. Calif., San Diego, 1969 Assoc. editor Yale Libr. of Medieval Philosophy; author: Metaphysical Thought of Godfrey of Fontaines, 1981 (Mercier prize 1981), Metaphysical Themes in Thomas Aquinas, 1984, Boethius of Dacia, 1987, Mediaeval Reactions to the Encounter between Faith and Reason, 1995, The Metaphysical Thought of Thomas Aquinas: From Finite Being to Uncreated Being, 2000; co-author: Medieval Philosophy, 1969, Les questions disputées et les questions quodlibétiques dans les facultés de théologie, de droit et de médécine, 1985; editor: Studies in Medieval Philosophy, 1987; contbr. numerous articles to profl. jours., chpts. to books. Recipient Distinguished Alumni award for Scholarship Cath. U. Am., 2001, John Findlay award Metaphysicial Soc. Am., 2002; Basselin scholar, 1953-56, Penfield fellow, 1961-63; NEH fellow, 1970-71, 84-85. Mem. Am. Philos. Assn.; Medieval Acad. Am., Metaphys. Soc. Am., Am. Cath. Philos. Assn. (pres. 1986-87, Aquinas Medalist 1999), Soc. Medieval and Renaissance Philosophy (pres. 1982-84), Soc. internat. pour l'étude de la philosophie médiévale. Office: Cath Univ of Am 620 Michigan Ave NE Washington DC 20064-0001 E-mail: wippel@cua.edu.

WIPPOLD, FRANZ JOSEPH, II, medical educator; b. St. Louis, Mar. 31, 1951; s. Franz J. and Nelda C. (Cordes) W.; m. Carol Ann Krentz, May 27, 1977; children: Rachel K., Aaron C., Rebecca T. BA, Westminster Coll., 1973; MD, St. Louis U., 1977. adj. prof. radiology and nuclear medicine F. Edward Hébert Sch. Medicine, Uniformed Svcs. U. Health Scis., Bethesda, Md., 2000—. Intern in neurology Walter Reed Army Med. Ctr., Washington, 1977-78, resident in neurology, 1978-79, resident in radiology, 1979-82; fellow in neuroradiology Mallinckrodt Inst. Radiology, 1982-83; dir. MRI Christian Hosp. Northeast, St. Louis, 1986-89; assoc. prof. Mallinckrodt Inst., Washington U. Sch. Medicine, 1989—, chief neuroradiology, 2000—. Author: Practical MRI, 1996. Lt. col. U.S. Army, 1977—86. Fellow Am. Coll. Angiology, Am. Coll. Radiology; mem. Am. Soc. Neuroradiology (sr.), Am. Roentgen Soc., Radiol. Soc. N.Am., Soc. Magnetic Resonance Imaging, Soc. Magnetic Resonance, Christian Med. Soc., Am. Assn. Univ. Radiologists. Lutheran. Avocation: model railroading. Office: Mallinckrodt Inst Radiology 510 S Kingshighway Blvd Saint Louis MO 63110-1076

WIRE, GARY LEE, metallurgist; b. Freeport, Ill., May 29, 1943; s. John Raymond and Grace Florence W.; m. Janet Marie, Jun. 10, 1967; children: Cynthia, Jacqueline. BS in Engring., Northwestern U., 1966; PhD in Physics, U. Ill., 1972. Mgr. mech. rsch. Westinghouse Hanford, Richland, Wash., 1973-82; mgr. materials properties rsch. IIT Rsch. Inst., Chgo., 1982-85; mgr. materials Bettis Atomic Power Lab., West Mifflin, Pa., 1985-96, adv. engr., 1996—. Contbr. articles to profl. jours. Mem. ASME (Robert J. McGrattan award 1997). Avocations: woodwork, bridge. Home: 236 Hays Rd Upper Saint Clair PA 15241 E-mail: glwire@bettis.gov.

WIRE, WILLIAM SHIDAKER, II, retired apparel and footwear manufacturing company executive; b. Cin., Jan. 5, 1932; s. William Shidaker and Gladys (Buckmaster) W.; m. Alice Dumas Jones, Aug. 31, 1957; children: Alice Wire Freeman, Deborah Wire Suber. Student, U. of South, 1950; AB, U. Ala., 1954, JD, 1956; LLM, NYU, 1957. Bar: Ala. 1956. Atty. Hamilton, Denniston, Butler & Riddick, Mobile, 1959-60; with Talladega Ins. Agy., Ala., 1961-62, Genesco, Inc., Nashville, 1962-94, former chmn. and CEO. Bd. dirs. Genesco Inc., Dollar Gen. Corp., Am. Endoscopy Svcs., Inc. Mem.: Burnt Pine Golf Club (Destin, Fla.), Golf Club Tenn., Univ. Club (NY), Belle Meade Country Club (Nashville), Kappa Alpha. Presbyterian. Home: 6119 Stonehaven Dr Nashville TN 37215-5613

WIRKEN, JAMES CHARLES, lawyer; b. Lansing, Mich., July 3, 1944; s. Frank and Mary (Brosnahan) W.; m. Mary Morse, June 12, 1971; children: Christopher, Erika, Kurt, Gretchen, Jeffrey, Matthew. BA in English, Rockhurst Coll., 1967; JD, St. Louis U., 1970. Bar: Mo. 1970, U.S. Dist. Ct. (we. dist.) Mo. 1970. Asst. prosecuter Jackson County, Kansas City, Mo., 1970-72; assoc. Morris, Larson, King, Stamper & Bold, 1972-75; dir. Spradley, Wirken, Reismeyer & King, 1976-88, Wirken & King, Kansas City, 1988-93; pres. The Wirken Law Group, 1993—. Adj. prof. law U. Mo., Kansas City, 1984-89, 2001—. Author: Managing a Practice and Avoiding Malpractice, 1983; co-author Missouri Civil Procedure Form Book, 1984--; mem. editl. bd. Mo. Law Weekly, 1989—, Lender Liability News, 1990—, Emerging Trends and Theories of Lender Liability, 1991; host. Wirken on the Law, KMBZ Radio, 1998—. Mem. ABA (exec. coun.), Nat. Conf. Bar Pres. (coun. 1992-96), Nat. Caucus of Met. Bar Leaders (exec. coun., pres. 1988-94), Am. Trial Lawyers Assn., L.P. Gas Group (founder, chair 1986-90, founder, chair lender liability group 1987-96), Mo. Bar Assn. (bd. govs. 1977-78, chmn. econs. and methods practice com. 1982-84, quality and methods of practice com. 1989-91, vice chmn. young lawyers sect. 1976-78), Mo. Assn. Trial Attys. (bd. govs. 1983-85), Kansas City Met. Bar Assn. (pres. young lawyers sect. 1975, chair legal assistance com. 1977-78, chair tort law com. 1982, pres. 1990). Home: 47 W 53rd Kansas City MO 64112 Office: The Wirken Law Group PC 2600 Grand Blvd Ste 440 Kansas City MO 64108-4628

WIRKKALA, JOHN LESTER, cable company executive; b. Wadena, Minn., Sept. 25, 1947; s. Ruben Richard and Virginia Grace (Plank) W.; m. Connie Lee Cardarelle (div.); children: Scott, Todd; m. Lynn Diane Braund, Feb. 14, 1984; children: Scott, Seth, Shawn. AS in Electronic Tech., Brown Inst., 1982. Acct. La Maur Inc., Mpls., 1969-72, regional sales mgr., 1976-78; controller Nat. Beauty Supply, 1972-76; store mgr. Schaak Electronics, 1980-82; divsn. mgr. Mktg. Link, Denver, 1982-85; owner, operator Computer Systems Cons., Aurora, Colo., 1985-87; v.p. sales and mktg. Mgmt. Info. Support, Lakewood, 1987-89; sales mgr. Foothills Software Inc., Littleton, 1989-93; ops. mgr. Data Packaging Corp., Denver, 1993-96; pres. Practical Bus. Concepts, Aurora, Colo., 1996; v.p. affiliate rels. Across Media Networks, Golden, 1996—. Contbr. articles to profl. jours. and mags.; speaker at seimnars and industry trade shows. With U.S. Army, 1966-69, Vietnam. Mem. VFW (quartermaster post # 6331 1993-94). Home and Office: 11211 Winona Ct Westminster CO 80031-7811 E-mail: jwirkkala@hotmail.com.

WIRKLER, NORMAN EDWARD, architectural, engineering, construction management firm executive; b. Garnavillo, Iowa, Apr. 1, 1937; s. Herbert J. and Irene (Kregel) W.; m. Margaret Anne Gift, Oct. 16, 1959; children: Chris Edward, Scott Norman, Elizabeth Anne. BArch, Iowa State U., 1959. Designer The Durrant Group Inc., Dubuque, Iowa, 1959-64, assoc., 1964-67, prin., 1967-82, pres. Denver, 1982-98; bd. dirs. The Durrant Group, 1998—; co-owner Wirkler Property Mgmt., Snowmass, 1993; bd. dirs. Foresite Capital Facilities Corp., Denver County, 1993—. Commr., mem. exec. com. Commn. on Accreditation on Corrections, 1985-91; archtl. cons. to Am. Correctional Assn. Standards Program; mem. Am. Correctional Assn. Standards Com., 1992-98; v.p. Garnavillo (Iowa) Bank Corp. Co-author: Design Guide for Secure Adult Correctional Facilities, 1983 Bd. dirs. United Way, Dubuque, 1984. Fellow AIA (pres. Iowa chpt. 1977; mem. nat. com. on arch. for justice 1974—, chmn. 1979; chmn. AIA Ins. Trust 1985-87, mem. Colo. chpt. 1987—); mem. ASTM (detention component standards com. 1982-84), Dubuque C. of C. (legis. com. 1978-83, chmn. 1979; v.p. 1984, exec. com. 1982-85), Iowa State U. Devel. Coun. Club. Republican. Avocations: flying, skiing, jogging, golf, hunting. Office: 3773 Cherry Creek North Dr Ste 1000 Denver CO 80209-3804 E-mail: nwirkler@durrant.com.

WIRSCHING, CHARLES PHILIPP, JR. retired brokerage house executive, private investor; b. Chgo., Oct. 26, 1935; s. Charles Philipp and Mamie Ethel (York) W.; m. Beverly Ann Bryan, May 28, 1966. *In 1630, the Wirsching family established a winery in Iphofen, Germany which continues today. The Hans Wirsching Winery produces award winning Franken wine. In 1729, Charles VI of the Holy Roman Empire bestowed the Wirsching family with a hereditary title of nobility. Grandfather, Philipp, received a mathematics degree from the University of Wurzburg, Germany and in 1886 left Germany and settled in Salem, Ohio. He founded the Wirsching Organ Company in 1887, manufacturing church and theatre organs for worldwide sales. Father, Charles, was vice president and director of Adams-Millis Corporation, a textile manufacturer in High Point, North Carolina.* BA, U. N.C., 1957. Sales rep. Adams-Millis Corp., Chgo., 1963-67; ptnr. Schwartz-Wirsching, 1968-70; sec., dir. Edwin H. Mann, Inc., 1971-74; stockbroker Paine Webber, Inc., 1975-85, account v.p., 1986-95; ret., 1995. Cons. Paine Webber, Inc. Chgo., 1996-99. Adv. coun. John Nuveen & Co., Inc., 1993-95; trustee Wirsching Charitable Trust, 1987—. Republican. Episcopalian. Avocation: foreign travel. Home and Office: 434 Clinton Pl River Forest IL 60305-2249

WIRSHING, HERMAN, protective services official; b. San Juan, P.R., July 24, 1941; s. Herman and Antonia W.; m. Rose Elizabeth Pinkler, Nov. 23, 1967; 3 children. BBA, U. P.R., 1964. V.p. Abarca Enterprises, 1967-71, Garcia Comml., 1971-80, Garcia Centro, 1971-80; gen. mgr., recruiting mgr. Sun Container Corp., Caribbean Processing, 1981-82; U.S. marshal Hato Rey, P.R., 1985—. Maj. U.S. Army, 1982-85; lt. col. USNG Mil. Police. Honor grad. Command and Gen. Staff Coll. Mem. Phi Sigma Alpha. Avocations: salt water fishing, golf, carpentry, photography, horse breeding. Office: US Marshals Svc 200 Fed Bldg 150 Chardon Ave Hato Rey PR 00918-1703 E-mail: hwirshing@hotmail.com.

WIRSIG, WOODROW, magazine editor, trade organization executive, business executive; b. Spokane, Wash., June 28, 1916; s. Otto Alan and Beulah Juliet (Marohn) W.; m. Jane Barbara Dealy, Dec. 11, 1942; children: Alan Robert, Guy Rodney, Paul Harold. *Mother's grandfather General McClure, served on General George Washinton's staff during the Revolutionary War. Granddaughter Juliet McClure left teaching in New York State and traveled alone to Lead, S.D. Father Otto was born in a sod house on a farm near Taylor, Nebraska. Worked his way through high school, college as advance man for Chataugua. Continued education for M.S. under Kirkpatrick at Columbia University, learning genuine progressive education which he* *introduced to his schools as superintendent in Brock and Kearney, Nebraska. Continued work toward Ph.D. at Stanford and U.S.C., appointed Dean, School of Education at U.S.C. just before he died in 1933.* Student, Kearney (Nebr.) State Tchrs. Coll., Los Angeles City Coll., UCLA, 1933-39; BA, Occidental Coll., 1941; MS, Columbia Grad. Sch. Journalism, 1942. Dir. Occidental Coll. News Bur., 1939-41; radio newswriter WQXR, N.Y.C., 1941-42; news writer, propaganda analyst CBS, 1942-43; rewrite man Los Angeles Times, 1943-44; asst. editor This Week mag., 1944-45; staff writer Look mag., 1946, asst. mng. editor, 1946-49, exec. editor, 1950-52; mng. editor Quick mag., 1949-50; asso. editor Newsweek mag., Ladies' Home Jour., 1952; editor Woman's Home Companion, 1952-56; editorial cons. Ednl. Testing Service, Princeton, 1957-67; TV cons. NBC-TV, ABC-TV; creator Nat. Daytime Radio Programs, 1957-60; radio documentary Companion; pres. communications firm Wirsig, Gordon and O'Connor, Inc., 1956-58; editor Printers' Ink mag., N.Y.C., 1958-65, Salesweek mag., 1959-60; editorial dir. Overseas Press Club ann. mag. Dateline, 1961, 62; creator, editorial dir. Calif. Life mag.; pres. Better Bus. Bur. Met. N.Y., Inc., 1966-77; also pres. Edn. Research Found.; pres. Bus. Advocacy Center, Inc., 1977—. Creator Corp. Social Accountability Audit and Customer Services/Consumer Affairs Audit.; Cons. to Office Sec. HEW, 1965-66 *Pioneered consumer/business arbitration and use of social audit techniques in consumer affairs for Better Business Bureaus. Created Business Advocacy Center to audit corporations' customer services. While editor of LOOK and Woman's Home Companion magazines he was most successful in developing problem-solving articles. While editor of Woman's Home Companion, he recieved Gold Medal Benjamin Franklin Magazine Award for Public Service. As consultant to NBC-TV he helped develop formats for TODAY show, also consulted for ABC-TV. He wrote for most major magazines and wrote syndicated business column for the Los Angeles Times and other papers. He continues writing and lecturing from home in Mt.San Antonio Gardens,Pomera,CA 91767* Author: I Love You, Too., 1990; editor, contbr.: Your Diabetes (Dr. Herbert Pollack), 1951; editor: Advertising: Today-Yesterday-Tomorrow; New Products Marketing; cons. editor: Principles of Advertising; contbr. nat. mags.; lectr.; syndicated columnist: other newspapers L.A. Times, 1964-65. Recipient gold medal Benjamin Franklin Mag. Awards, 1956 Mem. Soc. Consumer Affairs Profls. (pres. 1983), Newcomen Soc., Archons, Players Club, Overseas Press Club, Nat. Press Club, N.Y. Advt. Club, N.Y.C. Club, Springdale Country Club, Evergreen Country Club (v.p.), Nassau Club, Century Assn., Families for Alzheimers Rights Assn. (pres. 1994—), Univ. Club, Sigma Delta Chi, Phi Gamma Delta, Gamma Delta Upsilon. Democrat. Presbyterian. Home and Office: Mount San Antonio Gardens B-39 900 East Harrison Ave Pomona CA 91767

WIRSZUP, IZAAK, mathematician, educator; b. Wilno, Poland, Jan. 5, 1915; came to U.S., 1949, naturalized, 1955; s. Samuel and Pera (Golomb) W.; m. Pola Ofman, July 19, 1940 (dec. 1943); 1 son, Vladimir (dec. 1943); m. Pera Poswianska, Apr. 23, 1949; 1 dau., Marina (Mrs. Arnold M. Tatar). *Izaak Wirszup and his wife Pera (Poswianska Deull) are both survivors of the Nazi-Holocaust. Izaak's entire family, including: his (first) wife Pola (Ofman), their 2 year old son Vladimir, both of Izaak's parents Samuel and Pera (Golomb) Wirszup, Izaak's brother Naum and sister Golda, and their families, all were killed by the Nazis. From September 1941 Izaak Wirszup was imprisoned first in the Ghetto Wilno, then in several Nazi concentration camps in Estonia and in Germany. He was liberated by the American Army on April 30, 1945 from camp Allach-Dachau (near Munich, Germany).* Magister of Philosophy in Math, U. Wilno, 1939; PhD in Math, U. Chgo., 1955. Lectr. math. Tech. Inst. Wilno, 1939-41; dir. Bur. d'Études et de Statistiques Spéciales, Société Centrale d'Achat-Société Anonyme des Monoprix, Paris, 1946-49; mem. faculty U. Chgo., 1949—, prof. math., 1965-85, prof. math. emeritus, 1985—, prin. investigator U. Chgo. Sch. Math. Project (sponsored by Amoco Found., also dir. resource devel. component), 1983—, dir. Internat. Math. Edn. Resource Ctr., 1988—. Dir. NSF Survey Applied Soviet Rsch. in Math. Edn., 1985-91; cons. Ford Found., Colombia, Peru, 1965-66, Sch. Math Study Group, 1960, 61, 66-68; participant, writer tchr. tng. material African Math. Program, Entebbe, Uganda, summer 1964, Mombasa, Kenya, summers 1965-66; assoc. dir. Survey Recent Ea. European Math. Lit., 1956-68, dir., 1968-84; dir. NSF program application computers to mgmt., 1976-83; cons. NSF-AID Sci. Edn. Program, India, 1969; mem. U.S. Commn. on Math. Instn., 1969-73; co-prin. investigator U. Chgo.-Polk Bros. Found. Program for the Devel. of Math. Tchrs. in Chgo. Pub. Schs., 1999—. *A December 1979 comparative studies report by Izaak Wirszup to the National Science Foundation which revealed a crisis in mathematics and science education in the U.S., came to the attention of President Jimmy Carter. The President ordered a review of U.S. science and engineering education policies. Wirszup was subsequently invited to testify six times before the U.S. Senate. With an 8.4 million dollar grant from the Amoco Foundation, Wirszup founded the University of Chicago School Mathematics Project in 1983. More than three million students and teachers are now using UCSMP texts.* Contbr. articles to profl. jours.; Editor Math. books, transls., adaptions from Russian.; Adviser math.: Ency. Brit., 1971—. Recipient Lewellyn John and Harriet Manchester Quantrell award U. Chgo., 1958, Univ. Alumni Svc. medal, U. Chgo., 1994; resident master Woodward Ct., U. Chgo., 1971-85; endowed Wirszup Lecture Series, U. Chgo., 1986. Mem. N.Y. Acad. Scis., Am. Math. Soc., Math. Assn. Am., AAAS, Nat. Council Tchrs. Math. (chmn. com. internat. math. edn. 1967-69, Lifetime Achievement medal for Leadership, Tchg., and Svc. in Math. Edn. 1996) Home: 5750 S Kenwood Ave Chicago IL 60637-1744 Office: U Chgo Dept Math 5734 S University Ave Chicago IL 60637-1514

WIRT, FREDERICK MARSHALL, retired political scientist, educator; b. Radford, Va., July 27, 1924; s. Harry Johnson, Sr. and Goldie (Turpin) W.; m. Elizabeth Cook, Sept. 6, 1947; children: Leslie Lee, Sandra Sue, Wendy Ann. BA, DePauw U., 1948; MA, Ohio State U., 1949, PhD, 1956. Instr. to prof. polit. sci. Denison U., Granville, Ohio, 1952-66; vis. prof., lectr. U. Calif., Berkeley, 1966-68, 69-72; dir. policy scis. grad. program U. Md. Balt. County, 1972-75; prof. polit. sci. U. Ill., Urbana, 1975-2000; ret., 2000. Dir. Inst. for Desegregation Problems, U. Calif.-Berkeley, 1970-72; cons. Motion Picture Assn. Am., Rand Corp., Nat. Inst. Edn., SUNY Sch. Edn. Albany; vis. prof. U. Rochester, Nova U., U. Melbourne; acad. visitor London Sch. Econs. Author: Politics of Southern Equality, 1970 (honorable mention for best book 1972), Power in the City, 1974; (with others) The Polity of the School, 1975, Political Science and School Politics, 1977, Education, Recession, and the World Village, 1986, (with others) Culture and Education Policy in the American States, 1992, Aint' What We Was: Civil Rights in the New South, 1997 (Best Book on So. Politics award So. Polit. Sci. Assn., 1998), The Political Dynamics of American Education, 1997, 2d edit., 2001. Mem. Granville City Charter Commn., 1964. Grantee Am. Philos. Soc., Denison Rsch. Assn., U. Ill. Rsch. Bd., NEH, Ford Found., Ctr. Advanced Studies; fellow U. Ill., Dept. Edn., Spencer Found.; recipient Lifetime Achievement awards Am. Ednl. Rsch. Assn., 1995, Am. Polit. Sci. Assn., 1994. Mem. Am. Polit. Sci. Assn. (nat. council, Midwestern Polit. Sci. Assn., Am. Ednl. Rsch. Assn., Policy Studies Orgn. Home: 2007B Eagle Ridge Ct Urbana IL 61802-8617 Office: U Ill Dept of Polit Sci Urbana IL 61801 E-mail: f-wirt@uiuc.edu.

WIRT, MICHAEL JAMES, library director; b. Sault Ste. Marie, Mich., Mar. 21, 1947; s. Arthur James and Blanche Marian (Carruth) W.; m. Barbara Ann Hallesy, Aug. 12, 1972; 1 child, Brendan. BA, Mich. State U., 1969; MLS, U. Mich., 1971; postgrad., U. Wash., 1990. Cert. libr., Wash. Acting libr. U. Mich. Ctr. for Rsch. on Econ. Devel., Ann Arbor, 1971-72; instnl. svcs. libr. Spokane County (Wash.) Libr. Dist., 1972-76, asst. dir., 1976-79, acting dir., 1979, dir., 1980—. Mem. adv. com. Partnership for Rural Improvement, Spokane, 1982-85, Wash. State Libr. Planning and Devel. Com., 1984-85, Ea. Wash. U. Young Writers Project Adv. Bd., 1988-89; mem. issues selection com. Citizens League of Greater Spokane, 1991-93, City of Spokane Indian Trail Specific Plan Task force, 1992-95; mem. comm. com. United Way Spokane County, 1994, campaign chair local govt. divsn., 1996. Mem. Wash. Libr. Assn. (2d v.p. 1984-86, Merit award 1984, dir. 1989-91, legis. planning com., 1991—, pub. rels. com. 1993-2001, coord. comm. 1996-98, 2001 conf. local arrangements chair 1999-2001, Pres. award 1998), Wash. Libr. Network (rep. Computer Svc. Coun. 1983-86, v.p., treas. State Users Group 1986-87), Am. Libr. Assn. (Pub. Libr. Affiliates Network 1990-93, PLA Bus. Coun. 1990-94, chmn. 1991-94), Spokane Valley C. of C. (local govt. affairs com. 1987-2000, co-chair 1996-98, pub. policy com. 2000—), Spokane Area C. of C. (inland n.w. legis. coalition, 2002, local govt. com. 1990-94, human svcs. com. 1990-92, chmn. 1991-92, govt. reorgn. task force 1995), Spokane Civic Theatre (bd. dirs. 1996—, v.p. 1997-98, sec. 1998-2000, v.p. 2000), Inland N.W. Legis. Coalition, Momentum (local govt. strategy com. 1992-94), New Century (govt. collaboration com. 1997-98), Inland N.W. Coun. Librs. (bd. dirs. 1979—, chmn. 1997-98). Office: Spokane Ct Libr Dist 4322 N Argonne Rd Spokane WA 99212-1853 E-mail: mwirt@scld.lib.wa.us.

WIRT, SHERWOOD ELIOT, minister, writer; b. Oakland, Calif., Mar. 12, 1911; s. Loyal Lincoln and Harriet Eliot (Benton) W.; m. Helen Winola Wells, July 2, 1940 (dec. Sept. 1986); 1 child, Alexander Wells; m. Ruth Evelyn Love, Aug. 29, 1987. BA, U. Calif., Berkeley, 1932; BD, Pacific Sch. Religion, Berkeley, 1943; PhD, Edinburgh (Scotland) U., 1951. Ordained to ministry, 1943. Pastor 1st Congl. Ch., Collinsville, Conn., 1943-44, Knox Presbyn Ch., Berkeley, 1951-55, Hillside Presbyn. Ch., Oakland, Calif., 1955-59; editor Decision mag. Billy Graham Evangelistic Assn., 1959-76; min. to students U. Wash., 1946-49. Chmn. San Diego Jesus 2000. Author 28 books including Crusade at the Golden Gate, 1959, Not Me, God, 1966, Social Conscience of the Evangelical, 1968, Translation, Confessions of Augustine, 1971, Jesus Power, 1972, Topical Encyclopedia of Living Quotations, 1974, Afterglow, 1975, A Thirst for God, 1980, The Doomsday Connection, 1986, The Making of a Writer, 1987, The Book of Joy, 1994, Billy, 1997, Spiritual Awakening, 1987 (Gold Medallion Book award Evang. Christian Pub. Assn.), Jesus, Man of Joy, 1999, The God Who Smiles, 2001; editor 7 books. Pres. San Diego Gilbert and Sullivan Soc., 1980-81; scoutmaster Boy Scouts Am., 1936. Capt. USAAF, 1944-46. Recipient Freedom of Valley Forge Found. award, 1968; named Hon. Col., State of Tenn. Mem. Associated Ch. Press (life), Evang. Press Assn. (life, pres. 1969-71), San Diego County Christian Writers Guild (founder/convener 1977-96), Theta Chi, Sigma Delta Chi. Republican. Avocations: hiking, swimming, golf. Home: 813 226th St SE Bothell WA 98021

WIRTH, DAVID EUGENE, software designer, consultant; b. Norfolk, Va., Oct. 20, 1951; s. Eugene Ross and Darlene (Worley) W. BA, Luther Coll., 1975. Systems analyst ASI Computer Systems, Cedar Falls, Iowa, 1974-87, v.p. ops., 1987-2001, pres., COO, 2001—. Avocations: basketball, softball, fishing, hunting. Office: ASI Computer Systems Inc PO Box 338 Cedar Falls IA 50613-0338

WIRTH, FREMONT PHILIP, JR. neurosurgeon, educator; b. Nashville, July 23, 1940; s. Fremont P. and Willa (Dean) W.; children: Fremont Philip III, Andrew Simpson, Carolyn Howe. BA with honors in History, Williams Coll., 1962; MD, Vanderbilt U., 1966. Diplomate Am. Bd. Neurol. Surgery (guest examiner 1989, bd. dirs. 1992-98, vice chmn. 1997-98), Nat. Bd. Med. Examiners; cert. advanced trauma life support ACS. Surg. intern Johns Hopkins Hosp., Balt., 1966-67, resident and fellow in surgery, 1967-68; asst. resident in neurosurgery Barnes Hosp., Washington U., St. Louis, 1970-72, fellow in neurosurgery, 1972-74; pvt. practice, Savannah, Ga., 1974—. Asst. clin. prof. neurosurgery Med. Coll. Ga., Augusta, 1991—, vis. prof., 1978, 79, 86, 87; mem. staff, neurosurg. ICU, St. Joseph's Hosp., 1974—, dir. neurosurg. ICU, 1978—; mem. staff Meml. Med. Ctr., 1974-75, dir. rehab., 1983; mem. staff Candler Gen. Hosp., 1974—; med. dir. Head and Spinal Cord Injury Prevention Project for Ga., 1984—; presenter in field, 1970—; vis. prof. U. Md., Balt., 1981, Tufts New Eng. Med. Ctr., Boston, 1982. Series editor (with R.A. Ratcheson) Concepts in Neurosurgery, 1986-93; editor: (with Ratcheson) Neurosurgical Critical Care, Concepts in Neurological Surgery, Vol. 1, 1987, Ruptured Cerebral Aneurysms, Concepts in Neurological Surgery, Vol. 6, 1994; contbr. articles and book revs. to med. jours., chpts. to books. Elder Skidaway Island Presbyn. Ch., 1981-83; mem. pack 57 com. Cub Scouts Am., Savannah, 1979-84; mem. troop 57 com. Boy Scouts Am., Savannah, 1980-85, mem. fin. com. Coastal Empire coun., 1987-90, mem. adv. bd., 1990-96; chmn. physicians' solicitation United Way Coastal Empire, 1987; bd. dirs. Think First Found., 1990-95. With USPHS, 1968-70. Fellow ACS (bd. govs. 1984-90, sr. mem. trauma com. 1991-93); mem. AMA (physician's recognition award 1973-76, 77-79, 80-82, 83-85, 88-91, 91-94, 95-98, 98—), Congress Neurol. Surgeons (profl. conduct com. 1989-93, v.p. 1985-86, Disting. Svc. award 1989), Am. Acad. Neurol. Surgeons, Neurosurg. Soc. Am., Am. Assn. Neurologic Surgeons (nominating com. 1994-96, bd. dirs. 1998-2001), Brain Surgery Soc., Ga. Med. Soc. (pres. 1995, bd. trustees 1996-2001, chmn. 2000-2001), Med. Assn. Ga. (editl. bd. 1987-93), pres. 1995, Ga. Neurosurg. Soc. (exec. com. 1981-88, pres. 1988-89), So. Neurosurg. Soc. (exec. com. 1982-91, pres. 1988-89, Semmes lectr. 1997), N.Am. Skull Base Soc., Am. Heart Assn. (fellow stroke coun.). Avocations: golf, fly fishing, hunting. Office: Neurol Inst Savannah 4 E Jackson Blvd Savannah GA 31405-5810

WIRTH, JOHN DAVIS, Latin American studies educator, academic administrator; b. Dawson, N.Mex., June 17, 1936; s. Cecil W. and Virginia M. Davis; m. Nancy Meem; 3 children. BA magna cum laude, Harvard U., 1958; postgrad. interdisciplinary subjects, Columbia U., 1963-64; PhD in Latin Am. History, Stanford U., 1966. Tchr. history Putney (Vt.) Sch., 1959-61; asst. prof. Stanford (Calif.) U., 1965-72, assoc. prof., 1972-78, prof., 1978—, Gildred prof. Latin Am. studies, 1990—, vice chmn. dept. history, 1972-74, dir. Ctr. for Latin Am. Studies, 1975-82, chmn. dept. Spanish and Portuguese, 1987-88, vice provost for acad. planning and devel., 1988—. Mem. adv. bd. Can. studies program U. Calif., Berkeley. Author: The Politics of Brazilian Development, 1930-54, 1970 (Conf. on Latin Am. History Bolton Meml. prize 1971, Pacific Coast Council on Latin Am. Studies prize 1971), Minas Gerais in the Brazilian Federation, 1889-1937, 1977; editor: Latin American Oil Companies and the Politics of Energy, 1985, State and Society in Brazil, Continuity and Change, 1987; (with Robert L. Jones) Manchester and Sao Paulo: Problems of Rapid Urban Growth, 1978; bd. editors: Hispanic Am. Hist. Rev., Latin Am. Research Rev. Vice chmn. bd. visitors and govs. St. John's Coll., 1988—; trustee Putney Sch., 1989—; bd. dirs. Pan Am. Soc. San Francisco, 1979—. Served with U.S. Army, 1958-59. Ella Moore Shiel fellow Stanford U., 1962-63, Fgn. Area fellow Stanford U., 1963-65, Fulbright-HEW Ctr. faculty fellow, 1967; Social Sci. Research Council grantee, 1968-70, summer 1972, Ctr. for Research in Internat. Studies grantee Stanford U., 1969-70; Fulbright scholar, Brazil, 1980. Mem. Conf. Latin Am. History (sec., chmn. com. on Brazilian history 1975), Latin Am. Studies Assn. (exec. council 1979-80). Home: 37 Park Dr Menlo Park CA 94027-4011 Office: Stanford U Dept History Stanford CA 94305

WIRTH, MICHAEL ALAN, orthopaedic surgeon; b. Corvallis, Oreg., Jan. 25, 1957; m. Kathleen Logan; children: Peter, Jenny. BS, Portland State U., 1980; MD cum laude, Oreg. Health Scis. U., Portland, 1985. Diplomate Am. Bd. Orthopaedic Surgery; lic. physician, Tex. Shoulder fellow dept. orthopaedics U. Tex., San Antonio, 1990-91, orthopaedic resident, 1985-90, instr. orthopaedics, 1990-91, asst. prof. orthopaedics, 1992-95, assoc. prof., 1995—; chief orthopaedic shoulder svc. Audie Murphy VA Hosp., 1990—; cons., shoulder and upper extremity Wilford Hall USAF Med. Ctr., Lackland AFB, Tex., 1992—. Contbr. numerous articles to profl. jours., chpts. to books; presenter in field; developed videos: (with Charles A. Rockwood Jr.) Global Total Shoulder Arthroplasty, Parts I and II, 1991 (1992 Am. Acad. Orthopaedic Surgeons Individual Orthopaedic Instrn. Video award), Plaster Cast and Splint Technique, 1991, (with Charles A. Rockwood Jr. and Carl Basamania) Modular Hemiarthroplasty for Fractures of the Proximal Humerus, 1993, (with Charles A. Rockwood Jr.) Surgical Treatment of a Traumatic Posterior Sternoclavicular Disloaction, 1994, (with Charles A. Rockwood Jr. and Kirk L. Jensen) Techniques of Global Shoulder Hemiarthroplasty: Emphasis on the Exposure; reviewer Am. Jour. Sports Medicine, 1993—, Jour. Arthroscopy, 1993—, Clin. Orthopaedics and Related Rsch., 1993—, Orthopaedic Update, 1993—, Jour. Bone and Joint Surgery, 1992—; guest editor Operative Techniques in Sports Medicine, 1997; co-editor The Shoulder, 2d edit., 1998; contbg. author Fractures, 4th edit., 1998. Am. Shoulder and Elbow Surgeons Traveling European fellow, 1995; recipient Traveling Resident award in sports medicine, Mid Am. Orthopaedic Assn., Memphis, 1989; Leukemia fellow, Oreg. Health Scis. Ctr., 1979; ABC Exchange fellow, 1997. Fellow Internat. Coll. Surgeons (jr.); mem. AMA, Am. Shoulder and Elbow Surgeons Ednl. Subcom., Orthopaedic Rsch. and Edn. Found., So. Orthopaedic Soc., We. Orthopaedic Assocs., Tex. Med. Assn., Tex. Orthopaedic Assn., Bexar County Med. Soc., Alamo Orthopaedic Soc., Venezuela Orthopaedic Soc. (hon.), Ecuadorean Orthopaedic Soc (hon.), Phi Beta Kappa, Alpha Omega Alpha. Office: UTHSCSA Dept Orthopaedics 7703 Floyd Curl Dr San Antonio TX 78284-6200

WIRTH, RUSSELL D. L., JR. investment and merchant banker; b. Milw., June 30, 1930; s. Russell and Mary (McMahon) W.; m. Alice Guion Ardrey, Jan. 4, 1958 (div. Jan. 1971); children: Mary Elizabeth, Russell III. BA summa cum laude, Yale U., 1951; MA honors with distinction, Sch. Advanced Internat. Studies, Johns Hopkins U., 1954; postgrad., N.Y.U. Grad. Sch. Bus. Adminstrn., 1957-59; grad. with honors, Airborne Sch. and Spl. Forces Officers Sch., 1980. Mem. staff U.S. Senate Fgn. Relations Com., Washington; personal aide to chmn. Senate Fgn. Rels. Com. Alexander Wiley, coord. with Pres. Eisenhower The White House, 1954-55; personal asst. to mng. ptnr. corp. underwriting dept. Blyth & Co., Inc., Wall Street, 1957-59; U.S. loan officer for Latin Am., U.S. Devel. Loan Fund, Washington, 1960-61; co-founder, pres. Saint-Phalle, Spalding & Wirth, Inc., Buenos Aires, 1962-63; exec. v.p. Internat. Investment Co., Washington, 1963-64; investment officer Chase Internat. Investment Co., 1965-67; asst. to pres. David Rockefeller, Chase Manhattan Bank, 1965-67; co-founder, pres. Puerto Rican Fin. Group (PRFG), San Juan, 1968-92; co-founder, dir., stockholder jointly with Sun Oil Co. in Hemisphere Oil Co., 1978-93, also bd. exec. com., 1978-93; founder and ltd. ptnr. in devel. with Tishman Realty and Constrn. Co., Concord Centre Complex, Concord, Calif., 1980-84; co-founder, mng. dir. Wirth and Co. Internat. Investment Bankers, 1989—. Rep. candidate Congress 5th dist. Milw., 1956. 2d lt.-capt. USMCR, Korea, 1951-53; maj. U.S. Army Spl. Forces (Airborne), Res. and N.G., 1977-84. Decorated Silver Star, Bronze Star, Purple Heart, UN medal with 4 battle stars, Disting. Svc. medal Gov. U.S. V.I.; named Scholar of the House, Yale U. Mem. Phi Beta Kappa. Episcopalian. Achievements include World and U.S. ranked amateur athlete, 1985-95: U.S. Nat. champion, sprint triathlon; 2x U.S. All-Am. in U.S. Triathlon; 4x Fla. State champion, sprint triathlon; Fla. State half-marathon champion; 4th in world in Iron Man World Triathlon Championship; qualified and completed Boston, N.Y.C., San Francisco, Miami marathons; mem. U.S. Nat. Triathlon Team USA which won World Triathlon Championship, Cancun, Mex., 1995.

WIRTSCHAFTER, IRENE NEROVE, tax consultant; b. Elgin, Ill., Aug. 5, 1918; d. David A. and Ethel G. Nerove; m. Burton Wirtschafter, June 2, 1945 (dec. 1966). BCS, Columbus U., 1942. Cert. tax profl.; enrolled agt. IRS. Commd. ensign Supply Corps, USN, 1944, advanced through grades to capt., 1975; comdg. officer Res. Supply Unit, 1974-75; ret., 1976; agt. Office Internat. Ops., IRS, 1967-75; internat. banking specialist; real estate profl., appraiser, 1976-80; now pvt. practice tax cons., Cocoa Beach, Fla. Hon. sec. agr., La., 1975; sr. intern program U.S. Senate, 1981; mem. Sec. Navy's Adv. Com. Ret. Pers., 1984-86, VA Adv. Com. for Women Vets., 1987-90. Past troop leader Girl Scouts U.S.A.; lt. col. and mission pilot CAP, 21 air races; comml. instrument pilot land and sea; Navy liaison officer Commd.'s Retiree Coun., Patrick AFB, 1985—89; mem. Nat. Com. Internat. Forest of Friendship, Atchison, Kans., 1976—; elected silver rep. Nat. Silver Haired Congress, 1977—2001; trustee Internat. Women's Air and Space Mus., 1993—, bd. dirs., 1999—; state rep. Nat. Soc. to Preserve Social Security and Medicare, 1999; bd. dirs., treas. Honor Am., 2001—02; sec. Navy League, 2000; cons. Jr. Achievement, 1989—94; founder sr. action com. Brevard County, 1981; chmn. College Park Airport Johnny Horizon Day, 1975; elected dir. Fla. Space Coast Philharm., 1985—, treas., 1986—92; bd. dirs., adv. mgr. Cocoa Beach Citizen's League, 1990—92; co-chmn. Internat. Women's Yr. Take Off Dinner, Washington, 1976; 1st v.p. Friends of Cocoa Beach Libr., 1988—90, pres., 1990—92, bd. dirs., 1993—; apptd. to Cocoa Beach Libr. Br., 1996—; mem. Cocoa Beach Bus. Improvement Coun.; elected senator Silver Haired Legislature, Fla., 1985—; vol., founding mem. Brevard Zoo; chmn. Cocoa Beach Code Enforcement Bd., 1989—96; mem., co-chmn. sr. adv. com. Cape Canaveral Hosp., 1994—. Named hon. citizen of Winnipeg, Man., Can., 1966, Atchison, 1989, New Orleans, 1988; hon. dep. state fire marshal, Fla., 1987; cert. of appreciation Cocoa Beach Women's Club, 2000; recipient Svc. Above Self award Rotary, 1998; named Ky. col., La. col. Mem.: RMGS, TROA, AAUW, Navy League (sec. 2001), WAVES Nat. (bd. dirs. chpt. 75 1989—), Cocoa Beach Area C. of C., Assn. Enrolled Agts., Banana River Squadron (founder, comptr. 1984—), Assn. Naval Aviation (nat. trustee 1988—), Naval Order U.S. (treas. nat. capitol commandry), Naval Res. Assn. (nat. treas. 1975—77, nat. adv. com. 1985—, Nat. award of Merit 1992), Internat. Platform Assn. (life), Ninety Nines (past chpt. sect. and nat. officer, 99 achievement awards), Jazz Soc. Brevard, Patrick Women's Golf Assn. (treas. 1996—), Silver Wings (bd. dirs. 1990—, nat. sec. 1986, nat. v.p. 2001, Woman of Yr. award 1985), Tailhook Assn. (life), Rotary. Achievements include being first female Navy Supply Corps officer to be assigned sea duty, 1956. Avocations: aviation, golf, music. Home: 1825 Minutemen Cswy Apt 301 Cocoa Beach FL 32931-2033 Fax: 321-783-4899. E-mail: irenwirt@juno.com.

WIRTZ, WILLEM KINDLER, garden and lighting designer, public relations consultant; b. N.Y.C., Jan. 8, 1912; s. Carel Augustus Marie and Wilhelmina Johanetta (Kindler) W. Ed., Ethical Culture Sch., N.Y.C., also Inst. Musical Art. Dir. exhibits svc. Pa. Art Program, 1937-42, pub. rels. dir., 1937-42; ptnr. Campbell-Wirtz Assos., Phila., 1942-51; pres. Willem Wirtz Assos., 1952—. Founder, 1961, since pres. Willem Wirtz Garden Assos., Inc., and Willem Wirtz Assocs., mfrs. of Ribbonlite; design assoc. Am. Soc. Interior Decorators; dir. Am. Jour. Nursing Co.; also chmn. Pa. bull. award com., 1964; guest lectr. Charles Morris Price Sch., Phila.; pres. Phila. chpt. Am. Pub. Relations Assn., 1954-56, nat. sec., 1955-57, Eastern v.p., 1960 Inventor (with Isaiah Roossine): Ribbonlite. Mem. Nat. Assn. Pub. Rels. Counsel (dir.), Pub. Rels. Soc. Am. (v.p. 1961, assembly del. 1961-63), Pa. Hort. Soc., Phila. Art Alliance, Zool. Soc. Palm Beaches (sec. 1971), Netherlands-Am. Soc., Poinciana Club (Palm Beach, Fla.). Office: 228 Phipps Plz Palm Beach FL 33480-4241 E-mail: wim2000@webtv.net.

WIRTZ, WILLIAM WADSWORTH, real estate executive, professional sports team executive; b. Chgo., Oct. 5, 1929; s. Arthur Michael and Virginia (Wadsworth) Wirtz; m. Joan Roney, Dec. 15, 1950 (dec. May 1983); children: William R., Gail W., Karen K., Peter R., Alison M.; m. Alice Pirie Hargrave, Dec. 1, 1987. AB, Brown U., 1950. Pres. Chgo. Blackhawk Hockey Team, Inc., 1966—, Chgo. Stadium Corp., 1966—, Consol. Enterprises, Inc., Chgo., 1966—, Forman Realty Corp., Chgo., 1965—, 333 Bldg. Corp., Chgo., 1966—, Wirtz Corp., Chgo., 1964—. Chmn. bd. govs. Nat. Hockey League. Named to NHL Hall of Fame, 1976; recipient Lester Patrick trophy, 1978. Mem.: Sunset Ridge Country Club (Northbrook, Ill.), Fin and Feather Club (Elgin, Ill.), Mid-America Club (Chgo.), Racquet Club (Chgo.), Saddle and Cycle Club (Chgo.). Office: Wirtz 680 N Lake Shore Dr Fl 19 Chicago IL 60611-3495 also: United Ctr 1901 W Madison St Chicago IL 60612-2459 also: Nat Hockey League 1155 Metcalfe St Ste 960 Montreal QC Canada H3B 2W2*

WIRTZ, WILLIAM WILLARD, lawyer; b. DeKalb, Ill., Mar. 14, 1912; s. William Wilbur and Alfa Belle (White) W.; m. Mary Jane Quisenberry, Sept. 8, 1936; children— Richard, Philip. Ed., No. Ill. State Teachers Coll., DeKalb, Ill., 1928-30, U. Calif. at Berkeley, 1930-31; AB, Beloit Coll., 1933; LL.B., Harvard, 1937. Instr. Kewanee (Ill.) High Sch., 1933-34; asst. prof. U. Iowa Sch. Law, 1937-39, Northwestern U. Sch. Law, 1939-42; asst. gen. counsel Bd. Econ. Warfare, 1942-43, with War Labor Bd., 1943-45, gen. counsel and pub. mem., 1945; chmn. Nat. Wage Stblzn. Bd., 1946; prof. law Northwestern U., 1946-54; engaged law practice, 1955-61; sec. of labor Dept. Labor, 1962-69. Prof. law U. San Diego, 0986-98. Mem. Ill. Liquor Control Commn., 1949-53. Mem. Am., D.C., Ill. bar assns., Phi Beta Kappa, Beta Theta Pi, Delta Sigma Rho.

WIRZ, PASCAL FRANCOIS, trust company executive; b. Paris, Dec. 26, 1943; came to U.S., 1971; s. Boris and Armande (Martini) W.;m. Sharon T. Oller, Aug. 16, 1968; children: Matthieu, Benoit, Colette, Severin. BA in Econs., U. Paris, 1966; MBA in Bus., Hautes Etudes Commerciales, Paris, 1965; MBA in Fin., Lehigh U., 1968. Audit traine Peat Marwick & Mitchell, N.Y.C., 1968-69; tchr. auditing CESA (HEC), Jouy en Josas, France, 1969-71; security analyst European-Am. Econ. Corp., N.Y.C., 1971-82; sr. v.p. Fiduciary Trust Internat., 1982—. Trustee Corlette Glorney Found. Served with French Air Force, 1969-70. Mem. India House, Paris-Am. Club.

WIRZBA, NORMAN R. philosophy educator; b. Lethbridge, Alta., CAn., Feb. 7, 1964; s. Alex and Ingrid Wirzba; m. Gretchen E. Ziegenhals, Dec. 30, 1989; children: Emily, Anna, Benjamin, Luke. BA, U. Lethbridge, 1986; MA in Religion, Yale U., 1988; MA, Loyola U., 1992, PhD, 1994. Asst. prof. St. Thomas More Coll., Saskatoon, Sask., Can., 1993-95; asst. prof. philosophy Georgetown (Ky.) Coll., 1995-2000, assoc. prof., 2000—. Contbr. articles to profl. jours. Christian Faith and Life Sabbatical grantee Louisville Inst., 2000-2001. Mem. Am. Philos. Assn., Soc. for Continental Philosophy and Theology (exec. bd. dirs. 1997—). Avocations: music, woodworking, hiking, sports. E-mail: norman_wirzba@georgetowncollege.edu.

WISBAUM, WAYNE DAVID, lawyer; b. Niagara Falls, N.Y., May 29, 1935; s. Franklin C. and Elizabeth (Boff) W.; m. Janet Katz, July 3, 1960; children— Karen, Wendy, Deborah. BA, Cornell U., 1956; LL.B., Harvard U., 1959. Bar: N.Y. 1960. Assoc. Kavinoky & Cook, Buffalo, 1960-66, sr. ptnr., 1966—. Mem. adv. com. Ticor Title Co.; bd. dirs., pres., chmn. bd. Kleinhans Music Hall Mgmt. Inc., 1990-2000. Pres. Buffalo Coun. on World Affairs, 1968-70; mem. Young Leadership Cabinet Nat. United Jewish Appeal, 1967-73; mem. com. on leadership devel. Nat. Coun. Jewish Fedn. and Welfare Funds, 1967—; mem. Mayor's Com. on Youth Opportunity; bd. dirs. Anti-Defamation League; mem. Coun. Internat. Studies, SUNY, Buffalo; chmn. Buffalo chpt. Am. Jewish Com.; pres., chmn. bd. dirs. Buffalo Found. Jewish Philanthropies, 2001--; bd. govs. United Jewish Fedn., Buffalo; chmn. bd. dirs. Buffalo Philharm. Orch. Soc.; bd. dirs., mem. exec. com. Burchfield Art Ctr.; bd. dirs., pres. Jewish Family Service of Erie County; vice chmn., bd. dirs. Artpark, Irish Classical Theatre; trustee Buffalo and Erie County Park Libr. Served to capt. U.S. Army, 1964. Recipient United Jewish Fedn. Buffalo Leadership award, 1967, Community Relations award Am. Jewish Com., 1985, Abram Pugash award Jewish Family Service, 1985, Cmty. Leadership award Israel Bond, 2001; named Harvard Alumnus of Yr., 1990. Mem. ABA, N.Y. State Bar Assn. (chmn. com. lawyers title guaranty funds), Erie County Bar Assn., Am. Law Inst., Harvard Law Sch. Assn. Western N.Y. (sec.), Zool. Soc. Buffalo (dir., mem. exec. com.), Harvard Club (pres. Buffalo chpt., mem. N.Y.C. chpt.), Buffalo Club, Cornell Club (N.Y.C. chpt.), Zeta Beta Tau. Home: 180 Greenaway Rd Buffalo NY 14226-4166 Office: Kavinoky & Cook 120 Delaware Ave Rm 600 Buffalo NY 14202-2793

WISCH, DAVID JOHN, structural engineer; b. Jefferson City, Mo., Dec. 6, 1953; s. Theodore A. and Josephine (Lauf) W.; m. Leslie Babin, Oct. 24, 1981; 1 child, Christine. BSCE, U. Mo., Rolla, 1975, MSCE, 1977. Registered profl. engr., La., Calif. Civil engr. Texaco-Ctrl. Offshore Engring., New Orleans, 1977-81, advanced civil engr., 1981-86, sr. project engr., 1986-92, specialist Bellaire, Tex., 1992-96, sr. specialist, 1997, fellow, 1997—, chair fellows, 1999—, tech. leader, 1998-99, chmn. Tex. fellows, 1999—; tech. leader Texaco Upstream Tech., 1999—. Chmn. fixed systems subcom. Am. Petroleum Inst., Dallas, Washington, 1991-93, mem. adv. bd. offshore standardization com., 1991-94, chmn., 1993-94, mem. exec. com. on standardization, 1994-98, chmn. offshore and subsea com., 1994-98, head U.S. Delegation Internat. Orgn. Stds. Tech. Com. 1967/Subcom 7, 1993—, mem. Tech. Com. 67/Subcom. 7/AG1, 1993—, convener Tech. Com. 67/Subcom 7/WG3-Fixed Steel Structures, 1993—; mem. structure subcom. Oil Soc. Internat. Exploration and Prodn. Forum, London, 1993-93; mem. spl. com. on offshore facilities Am. Bur. Shipping, 1996—, mem. marine bd., 1999—. Author numerous papers/presentations, 1984—. Mem. Am. Bur. Shipping (spl. com. on offshore structures), ASCE (program. subcom. for Offshore Tech. Conf. 1993—), Sigma Xi, Phi Kappa Phi, Tau Beta Pi, Chi Epsilon (chpt. pres. 1975-76). Office: Texaco Offshore Engring Dept 4800 Fournace Pl Bellaire TX 77401-2389 E-mail: wischdj@texaco.com.

WISCHNOWSKI, CHRISTOPHER, pathologists' assistant, consultant; b. Sacramento, June 7, 1968; s. James Wischnowski and June Chance; m. Ellen Wischnowski; children: John. BS, U. Calif., Davis, 1994; M in Health Sci., Quinnipiac U., 2002. Pathologist asst. Diagnostic Pathology Med. Group, Sacramento, 1994—2000. Recipient Nat. Collegiate Med. Professions award, U.S. Achievement Acad., 2001. Mem.: Am. Soc. Clin. Lab. Sci., Am. Assn. Pathologists' Assistants.

WISCOMBE, WARREN JACKMAN, research scientist; b. St. Louis, Feb. 4, 1943; s. Warren Seth Jackman and June (Narowetz) Wiscombe; m. Helenka Novak, June 8, 1984; m. Janet Tarwater, June 10, 1967 (div. Mar. 1, 1982); children: Juliet, Thomas. PhD, Caltech, Pasadena, Calif., 1970, MS, 1966; BS, M.I.T., Cambridge, Mass., 1964. Phys. scientist NASA Goddard Space Flight Ctr., Md., 1984—; assoc. prof. NYU, 1981—84; support scientist Nat. Ctr. Atmos Rsch., Boulder, Colo., 1974—80; staff scientist Sys. Sci. & Software, Inc., Calif., 1969—74. Fellow: Am. Meteorological Soc.; mem.: Am. Geophysical Union. Avocations: skiing, hiking. Office: NASA Goddard Code 913 Greenbelt MD 20771 E-mail: wiscombe@gsfc.nasa.gov.

WISDOM, BARRY LEE, academic administrator, educator; b. Little Rock, Jan. 1, 1953; s. William Harold and Evelyn Verwell Wisdom; m. Jeanie Kattan, Dec. 14, 1994 (div. Mar. 12, 1993); 1 child Hilary Ann ; m. Vickie Lynn Vanzant, May 20, 1995; 1 stepchild Brittany Leigh. BA in Psychology, U. Ark., 1975, MEd in Counseling, 1977, PhD in Mgmt., 1981. Counselor, testing officer U. Ark., Fayetteville, 1975—77, tchg. asst., instr., 1977—81; asst. prof. James Madison U., Harrisonburg, Va., 1981—87; assoc. prof. S.W. Mo. State U., Springfield, Mo., 1987—92, dept. head mgmt., 1992—, prof., 1993—. Mem. editl. bd. The Learning Orgn., England, 1996—. Co-author: (textbook) Organizational Behavior: Creating Quality and Value in the Workplace, 1995; contbr. Mem.: Acad. Mgmt. Methodist. Avocations: guitar, fishing, golf. Office: S W Mo State U 901 S National Springfield MO 65804 Office Fax: 417-836-3004. E-mail: blw355f@smsu.edu.

WISDOM, PEGGY JEAN, neurologist; b. OKeene, OKla., Nov. 4, 1947; d. Clarence W. and Grace V. Wisdom. BS in Biology/Chemistry, Northwestern State Coll., 1968; MD, U. Okla., 1972. Diplomate Am. Bd. Psychiatry and Neurology. Resident in neurology U. Fla., 1972-76; asst. prof. neurology U. Okla., Oklahoma City, 1976-90, assoc. prof. neurology, 1990—2002, prof. neurology, 2002—, vice chair dept. neurology, 1981—; med. dir. neurologic rehab. O'Donoghue Rehab. Inst., 1981-89, chief of staff, 1986-90; chief neurology VA Med. Ctr., 1994-97, chief neurology/rehab., 1997—. Cons. Commn. on Accreditation of Rehab. Facilities, Tuscon, 1990—, Okla. Dept. Rehab. Svcs., Oklahoma City, 1993-96. Sci. adv. bd. Omniplex Mus., Oklahoma City, 1994—. Mem. Am. Acad. Neurology, Am. Acad. Neurology (chmn. women issues in neurology sect. 1999-2001), Assn. of VA Neurologists, Am. Epilepsy Soc. Republican. Presbyterian. Office: U Okla Health Scis Ctr # 215 711 Stanton L Young Blvd Oklahoma City OK 73104-5021 E-mail: peggy-wisdom@ouhsc.edu.

WISDOM, WILLIAM RUSSELL, radiologist; b. Bedford, Iowa, 1922; s. Franklin Dale and Chloe (Huey) W.; m. Veronica Morrissey, Jan. 9, 1948; children: Deborah, William R. Jr., Franklin D. II, Stephanie, Sarah. MD, U. Iowa, 1947. Diplomate Am. Bd. Radiology. Intern St. Vincent's Hosp., L.A., 1947-48; resident in radiology Groover-Christie-Merritt, Washington, 1949-50; with U.S. Naval Hosp., Phila., 1950-51, USN Dept. Dispensary, Washington, 1951-52, U.S. Naval Hosp., San Diego, 1952-53; fellow in radiation oncology Soiland Cancer Found., L.A., 1953-54. Staff physician L.A. Tumor Inst., 1954-55; head radiation oncology St. Mary Hosp., Long Beach, Calif., 1955-62; head dept. radiology Little Company of Mary Hosp., Torrance, Calif., 1962-77; asst. clin. prof. U. Calif. Irvine Coll. Medicine, 1963-67. Lt. USNR, 1951-53. Fellow Royal Med. Soc., Am. Coll. Radiology; mem. AMA, Am. Roentgen Ray Soc., Radiol. Soc. N.Am. Republican. Roman Catholic. Home: 1637 Via Arriba Palos Verdes Estates CA 90274

WISE, AARON NOAH, lawyer; b. Hartford, Conn., Feb. 14, 1940; s. Joseph J. and Ethel (Sklar) W.; m. Genevieve Ehrlich, Dec. 17. 1966; children: Haywood Martin, Paul Russell, Renee Alicia. AB, Boston U., 1962; JD, Boston Coll., 1965; LLM in Comparative/Internat. Law, NYU, 1971; certificat de Doctorat, d' Université en Droit, U. Paris Law Sch., 1970. Bar: N.Y., U.S. Dist. Ct. (so. dist.) N.Y. Internat. atty. Schering-Plough, Kenilworth, N.J., 1969-74; ptnr. Conboy Hewitt O'Brien & Boardman, N.Y.C., 1974-80, Wise Lerman & Katz P.C. (formerly Rosenbaum Wise Lerman & Katz), N.Y.C., 1981-95, Klepner & Cayea, N.Y.C., 1995-98, Brand, Cayea & Brand, LLC, 1998-2000, Siller Wilk LLP, N.Y.C., 2000—02, Gallet, Dreyer & Berkey, LLP, N.Y.C., 2000—. Lectr. bus. and legal groups U.S., Europe, Latin Am. Author: International Sports Law and Business (Kluwer Law Internat., 1997, 3 vols.), Foreign Businessman's Guide to U.S. Law-Practice-Taxation; contbr. articles to pubs. in U.S. and Europe. Mem. ABA, N.Y. State Bar Assn. Avocations: multi-lingual including French, Spanish, Portuguese, Italian, Russian, Japanese and German. Home: 38 Cummings Cir West Orange NJ 07052-2264 Office: Gallet Dreyer & Berkey LLP 845 Third Ave New York NY 10022-6601 E-mail: awise@sillerwilk.com.

WISE, CARL STAMPS, accounting educator; b. Brunswick, Ga., Sept. 2, 1955; s. George Lewis Jr. and Alice (Andrews) W. AA, SUNY, Albany, 1983; BS in Occupl. Edn., So. Ill. U., 1984; MPA, Ga. So. U., 1997, postgrad. in Edn., 1998—. Lic. mobile comm. technician. Enlisted USN, 1975, electronics technician, 1975-85; adj. prof. electronics tech. Fla. Jr. Coll., Jacksonville, 1983-84; comm. electronics technician Hasty's Comm. East, Brunswick, Ga., 1985-94; primary care give maternal grandmother, 1994-95; electronics technician/purchase mgr./accounts receivable Thompson Comm., Savannah, 1996-97; adj. prof. acctg. Savannah Tech. Inst., Hinesville, 1997—; adj. prof. gen. studies Ctrl. Tex. Coll., Ft. Stewart and Hunter Army Airbase, 1998—. Computer upgrade/maintenance Ctrl. Tex. Coll. and Savannah Tech. Inst., Hinesville, 1998—. Recipient Sea Svc. Deployment ribbon, 1978, 79, 80. Mem. ASPA (East Ga. chpt. sec. 1998—), Personal Comm. Industry Assn. Republican. Episcopalian. Avocations: landscape painting, swimming, fishing, cooking. Office: Savannah Tech Inst 501 W General Screven Way Hinesville GA 31313-3059 E-mail: jandrews@infoave.net.

WISE, CAROL LEWIS, occupational therapist; b. Arlington, Mass., May 15, 1962; d. Robert Clayton and Phyllis June (Crowley) Lewis; m. Gary Allen Wise, Sept. 30, 1989; children: Evan Robert, Logan James. BA in Psychology, Manhattanville Coll., Purchase, N.Y., 1984; MS in OccupL. Therapy, Boston U., 1987. Diplomate in pediatric occupl. therapy Am. Occupl. Therapy Assn.; lic. and registered occupl. therapist; cert. early intervention splst. Mass. Dept. Pub. Health. Occupl. therapist St. Joseph's Hosp. & Med. Ctr., Phoenix, 1987-88; sr. occupl. therapist Spaulding Rehab. Hosp., Boston, 1988-92; occupl. therapy supr., pediat. program dir. Healthsouth/Braintree Rehab. Clinic, Plymouth, 1992-96; occupl. therapist Step One Early Intervention Program, Quincy, 1996—. Cons. Kennedy Donovan Ctr., Plymouth, Mass., 1993-94, StepOne Regional Cons. Program, Quincy, 2001-. Vol. Spl. Olympics, Westchester County, N.Y., 1983-84; vol. fundraising drive March of Dimes, Mass. chpt., 1994; baptism preparation team St. Paul's Ch., Hingham, Mass., 1997—, religious educator, 2001-; mem. Plymouth River Sch. PTO, Hingham, Mass., 1999—; coach Hingham Youth Soccer, 2002--. Mem. Am. Occupl. Therapy Assn., Mass. Occupl. Therapy Assn. Democrat. Roman Catholic. Avocations: reading, seashell collecting, walking, golf. Home: 30 Woodlock Rd Hingham MA 02043-3026 Office: Step One Early Intervention 6 Fort St Quincy MA 02169-4959 E-mail: cwise@gawise.com.

WISE, CHARLES DAVIDSON, science educator; b. Huntington, W. Va., June 13, 1926; s. Fred Eugene Wise and Maggie M. Harshbarger; m. Juanita Irene Meadows, Mar. 22, 1947; 1 child, Sandra. AB, MS, W. Va. U., 1950; PhD, U. N.Mex., 1962. Cert. tchr. N.Mex., W. Va., Tex. Tchr. St. Albans (W. Va.) High Sch., 1951-53; lab. assst. Marshall U., 1950-51; grad. fellow U. N.Mex., Albuquerque, 1953-55, grad. asst., 1960-61; rsch. scientist U. Tex., Port Aransas, Tex., 1958-60; prof. Ball State U., Muncie, Ind., 1961-91; rep. Ind. State Legislature, Indpls., 1967-69; senator Ind. State Senate, 1969-73. Contbr. articles to profl. jours., 1958—. Bd. dirs. Mental Health Svc. East Cen. Ind., 1974-77; pres. Muncie Bicentennial Festival Com., 1975-77. With U.S. Army, 1944-46. Recipient fellowship U. Ind., 1957, U. Tex., 1957-58, Marshall U. Alumni Community Achievement award, 1993; named Alumnus of Yr., East Bank High Sch., W.Va., 1977. Fellow Ind. Acad. Sci.; mem. Nat. Assn. State Legislators (life mem.), Nat. Audubon Soc., Ind. Audubon Soc. (past pres., conservation award 1977), E. Cen. Ind. Audubon Soc. (pres. 1988-90, conservation award 1984), Sigma Xi Rsch. Soc. (pres. Ball State U. chpt., bd. dir. Hoosier Environ. coun. 1990-93). Republican. Presbyterian. Avocations: birding, travel, languages, genealogy, history. Home: 1032 Brickyard Ave Milton WV 25541 Office: Ball State Univ Muncie IN 47306-0001

WISE, CHRISTOPHER MURRAY, internist, rheumatologist; b. Van Wert, Ohio, Feb. 20, 1951; s. George G. and Sallie (Wheeler) W.; m. Roxanne Grossman; children: Jacob, David. BS in Zoology, U. N.C., 1973, MD, 1977. Diplomate Am. Bd. Internal Medicine. Intern and resident in internal medicine Med. Coll. Va./Va. Commonwealth U., Richmond, 1977-80; fellow in rheumatology Med. Coll. Va., 1980-82, assoc. prof., 1992—, Bowman Gray Sch. Medicine, Winston-Salem, N.C., 1982-92. Fellow ACP (W. Robert Irby assoc. professorship 1997—); mem. Am. Coll. Rheumatology, Va. Soc. Rheumatologists (v.p., pres. 1992—). Office: Med Coll Va Va Commonwealth U PO Box 980647 Richmond VA 23298-0647

WISE, EDMUND JOSEPH, physician assistant, industrial hygienist; b. Pitts., June 18, 1947; s. Edmund Joseph and Marian Elizabeth (Burdelski) W. BA in Biology, Washington and Jefferson Coll., 1969; B of Health Scis., Duke U., 1974, cert. occupl. and environ. medicine, 2000; MPH, U. Tenn., 1990. Clin. care tech. II Duke U. Med. Ctr., Durham, N.C., 1971-72; physician asst. Oak Ridge (Tenn.) Nat. Lab., 1974—. Mem. toxic substance control act task team Lockheed Martin Energy Sys., Oak Ridge, 1995-97; mem. hazardous waste com. Oak Ridge Nat. Lab., 1993—, ergonomics com., 1994—, hearing conservation com., 1984—. Author: History Medical Activities 1/12 Infantry, 1970; co-author: AAPA Guidelines Continuing Medical Education, 1977, ORNL Hazwoper Program Manual, 1993; co-author: (chpt.) Tennessee Academy Constitution and Bylaws, 1976. Mem. malpractice review bd. Tenn. Dept. Pub. Health, Nashville, 1981—. Capt. U.S. Army, 1969-75, Vietnam. Decorated Bronze Star, Combat Med. badge, Army commendation medal; recipient Gold cert. of Appreciation, Am. Heart Assn., 1983. Fellow Am. Acad. Physician Assts. (house del. 1979, 86, profl. and continuing med. edn. com. 1975-80), Tenn. Acad. Physician Assts. (co-founder, v.p. 1975, pres. 1977); mem. Am. Coll. Occupl. and Environ. Medicine (charter affiliate), Am. Acad. Physician Assts. in Occupl. Medicine (charter), Tenn. Heart Assn. (cert. BCLS, affiliate faculty 1978-2000), East Tenn. Region Heart Assn. (CPR-Emergency Cardiac Care com. 1980-99), Duke U. Alumni Assn., Nat. 4th Infantry Divsn. Assn., Washington and Jefferson Alumni Assn. Roman Catholic. Avocations: model railroading, stamp collecting, gardening, tennis. Home: 1238 Venido Dr Knoxville TN 37932-2598 Office: Oak Ridge Nat Lab Health Divsn PO Box 2008 Oak Ridge TN 37831-6220 E-mail: wiseej@ornl.gov.

WISE, GEORGE EDWARD, lawyer; b. Chgo., Feb. 26, 1924; s. George E. and Helen L. (Gray) W.; m. Patricia E. Finn, Aug. 3, 1945; children: Erich, Peter, Abbe, Raoul, John. JD, U. Chgo. Bar: Calif. 1949, U.S. Dist. Ct. (no. dist.) Calif. 1948, U.S. Ct. Appeals (9th cir.) 1948, U.S. Dist. Ct. (cen. dist.) 1950, U.S. Supreme Ct. 1955. Law clk. Calif. Supreme Ct., 1948-49; sr. ptnr. Wise, Wiezorek, Timmons & Wise, Long Beach, 1949—; of counsel Wise Pearce Yocis & Smith. With USNR, 1943-45. Fellow Am. Coll. Trial Lawyers; mem. ABA, Los Angeles County Bar Assn., Long Beach Bar Assn. (pres. 1970, Atty. of Yr. 1990), Calif. State Bar. Home: 5401 E El Cedral St Long Beach CA 90815-4112 Office: Wise Pearce Yocis & Smith 249 E Ocean Blvd Ste 440 Long Beach CA 90802-4806

WISE, JOHN AUGUSTUS, lawyer, director; b. Detroit, Mar. 30, 1938; s. John Augustus and Mary Blanche (Parent) W.; m. Helga M. Bessin, Nov. 27, 1965; children: Monique Elizabeth, John Eric. Student, U. Vienna, 1957-58; AB cum laude, Coll. Holy Cross, 1959; JD, U. Mich., 1962; postgrad., U. Munich, 1962-63. Bar: Mich. 1963, D.C. 1966. Assoc. Dykema, Gossett, Detroit, 1962-64; asst. to pres. Internat. Econ. Policy Assn., Washington, 1964-66; assoc. Parsons, Tennent, Hammond, Hardig & Ziegelman, Detroit, 1967-70; pres. Wise & Marsac P.C., 1970-2001; sr. ptnr. Williams, Mullen, Clark & Dobbins, PLLC. Dir. Peltzer & Ehlers Am. Corp., 1975-80, Colombian Am. Friends Inc., 1974-89. Mem. Detroit Com. on Fgn. Rels.; bd. dirs. Hyde Park Coop., 1974-77; trustee Friends Sch., Detroit, 1977-81, Brighton Health Svcs. Corp., 1991-94, Providence Hosp., 2001—; chmn. bd. dirs. Brighton Hosp., 1995—. Ford Found. grantee U. Munich, 1962-63. Mem. ABA, Mich. Bar Assn., Detroit Bar Assn., Internat. Bar Assn., Detroit Athletic Club, Detroit Econ. Club. Roman Catholic. Home: 1221 Yorkshire Rd Grosse Pointe Park MI 48230-1105 Office: Buhl Bldg 11t Fl 535 Griswold St Detroit MI 48226-3604 E-mail: jwise@williamsmullen.com.

WISE, KELLY, private school educator, photographer, critic; b. New Castle, Ind., Dec. 1, 1932; s. John Kenneth W. and Geraldine (Kelly) Edwards Wise; m. Sybil Anahid Zulalian, Aug. 15, 1959; children: Jocelyn Anne, Adam Kelly, Lydia Louise. BS, Purdue U., 1955; MA, Columbia U., 1959. Instr. English Mt. Hermon Sch., Gill, Mass., 1960-66, Phillips Acad., Andover, 1966—, chmn. dept., 1978-82, acting dean faculty, 1982-83, dean faculty, 1985-90; founder, dir. Inst. for Recruitment of Tchrs., 1989—; photography critic The Boston Globe, 1982-93; art commentator Nat. Pub. Radio, 1987-89. Photography and English cons. Nat. Humanities Faculty, Concord, Mass., 1970-83; mem. Pub. Art Adv. Bd. of Mass. Coun.; cons. editor Addison House Pubs., Danbury, N.J., 1974-79. Author: (with Kalkstein and Regan) English Competence Handbook, 1972; editor: The Photographers' Choice, 1975, Lotte Jacobi, 1978, Portrait: Theory, 1981, Photo Facts and Opinions, 1981; author, photographer: Still Points, 1977, A Church, A People, 1979; editor photographer: City Limits, 1987; assoc. editor: Views, Jour. Photography, 1980-81; works included in anthologies, one-man shows, Portland Museum Art, Maine, 1974, Silver Image Gallery, Columbus, Ohio, 1975, Canon Photo Gallery, Amsterdam, Holland, 1977, Focus Gallery, San Francisco, 1977, Art Mus., U. Mass., Amherst, 1978, Neikrug Gallery, N.Y.C., 1979, Sheldon Gallery, U. Nebr., Lincoln, 1980, Yuen Lui Gallery, Seattle, 1980, Rose Art Mus., Brandeis U., Waltham, Mass., 1981, Blixt Gallery, Ann Arbor, Mich., 1981, Snite Art Gallery, U. Notre Dame, 1981, Jeb Gallery, Providence, 1981, Currier Gallery Art, Manchester, N.H., 1985, Addison Gallery Am. Art, Andover, Mass., 1985, Art Ctr., DePauw U., 1986, Art Gallery, Conn. Coll., 1986, Yuen Lui Gallery, Seattle, 1986, Kresge Art Mus., Mich. State U., 1987, Brockton Art Mus., 1987; group shows include Inst. Contemporary Art, Boston, 1972, Mus. Fine Arts, Boston, 1974, Fogg Art Mus., Cambridge, 1976, Sidney Janis Gallery, N.Y.C., 1977, The Photographer's Gallery, London, 1979, Il Diaframma, Milan, Italy, 1979, Iisalmen Kamera, Helsinki, Finland, 1984, Archive Gallery, N.Y., 1987, Mass. Coll. Art, 1988, Martin Schweig Gallery, St. Louis, 1988, Satellite Gallery, Cultural Affairs Dept., Los Angeles; works included in book Flesh and Blood: Photographers' Images of Their Own Families. Served with USN, 1955-57, PTO. Recipient Disting. Alumnus award Purdue U., 1996. Office: Phillips Academy Andover MA 01810-4161

WISE, LAWRENCE GEORGE, human resources executive; b. St. Petersburg, Fla., June 20, 1946; s. Lawrence George and Janet Mary (Butler) W.; m. Bonita Mary Stockler, June 21, 1967; children: Stephanie Mary, Lawrence George III. BA in Bus., U. South Fla., 1967. Cert. bus. tchr., Fla.; lic. in real estate sales, Fla. Underwriting specialist State Farm Ins. Cos., Winter Haven, Fla., 1967-87, credit union pres., 1987-88, credit union treas., mgr., human resources supr., 1988—. Bd. dirs. Citrus Community Fed. Credit Union, 1990. Mem. Citrus County Gifted Orgn., Fla.; coord. projects Citrus County Aquatic Control Bd., Lecanto; bd. dirs. Lake Buckeye Condominium Assn., Winter Haven, Fla., 1978-80; mem. adv. bd. Citrus High Sch., 1987-90. Mem. Lambda Chi Alpha Alumni Assn. (treas. 1966). Clubs: Inverness Golf and Country (Fla.). Republican. Methodist. Avocations: financial reading, fishing, tennis. Home: 8133 S Clarkwise Pt Floral City FL 34436-3422 E-mail: georgewise@yahoo.com.

WISE, PATRICIA, lyric coloratura; b. Wichita, Kans. d. Melvin R. and Genevieve F. (Dotson) W.; 1 child, Jennifer. B. Music Edn., U. Kans., Lawrence, 1966. Prof. voice Ind. U. Sch. Music, Bloomington, 1995—. Debut as Susanna in Marriage of Figaro, Kansas City, 1966; prin. roles include Lucia, Gilda, Micaela, Juliette, Zerbinetta, Pamina, Musetta, Lulu, Violetta, Nedda, others; appeared with leading Am. opera cos. including, Chgo., Santa Fe, N.Y.C., San Francisco, Houston, San Diego, Miami, Balt., Phila., Pitts.; European appearances, 1971-76, London Royal Opera, Glyndebourne Festival, Vienna Volksoper, Geneva Opera; guest artist with Vienna, Hamburg, Munich, Cologne, Frankfurt, and Berlin State Operas; guest appearances in Madrid, Barcelona, Rome, La Scala Milan, Nice, Paris Chatelet, Zurich, Dresden, Salzburg Festival, Theatro Colon, Buenos Aires; appeared with orchs. including, Chgo. Symphony Orch., Los Angeles Symphony Orch., N.Y. Handel Soc., Israel Philharm. Orch., Vienna Philharm. Orch., N.Y. Philharm., Cleve. Orch., Berlin Symphonic Orch., BBC Orch., Nat. Orch. France; Angel Recordings; internat. TV, film appearances. Recipient Morton Baum award N.Y.C. Ctr., 1971, Dealey Meml. award Dallas Symphony, 1966, Naftzger young Artist award Wichita Symphony, 1966, Midland Young Artist award Midland (Tex.) Symphony Orch., 1966; M.B. Rockefeller Fund grantee, 1967-70; Sullivan Found. grantee, 1967-68; named Kammersänger Vienna Staatsoper, 1989.

WISE, PAUL SCHUYLER, insurance company executive; b. Pratt, Kans., July 16, 1920; s. George Warren and Bess Grace (Cossairt) W.; m. Frances H. Christie, Oct. 26, 1975; children by previous marriage: Schuyler, David, Betsy Student, U. Kans., 1938-40; BA, Washburn U., 1942, JD, 1947; student, U. Mich., 1945-46. Bar: Kans. Atty. Kans. Ins. Dept., 1947, asst. commr. ins., 1948-51, commr. workmen's compensation, 1951-52; atty.-ins. legislation Alliance of Am. Insurers, Chgo., 1952-56, mgr. legis. bur., 1956-61, asst. mgr., 1961-62, gen. mgr., 1962-68, pres., chief exec. officer, 1968-84, chmn. bd., 1984-85. Dir. Ins. Inst. for Hwy. Safety, Coll. of Ins.; bd. overseers Inst. for Civil Justice; lectr. in field. Contbr. articles to profl. jours. Co-founder, bd. dirs. Hospice of North Shore; bd. dirs. Sr. Net. Lt. USN. Recipient Man of Yr. award Fedn. Ins. Counsel, 1982; inducted into Hall of Fame, Kans. Ins. Ednl. Found., 1983. Home: Unit 417 7501 E Thompson Peak Pkwy Scottsdale AZ 85255-4537

WISE, RICHARD EVANS, corporate executive; b. Lancaster, Pa., Sept. 24, 1947; s. William Edmund and Dorothy Christelle (Evans) W.; m. Kathrine Suzanne Keller, Jan. 2, 1971; 1 child, Thomas Edmund. BS, West Chester (Pa.) U., 1970; MEd, Pa. State U., 1976, PhD, 1980. Project adminstrn. mgr. Hartford Ins. Group, 1977-80; v.p., tng. mgr. Conn. Nat. Bank, 1980-83; corp. tng. and devel. dir. Travelers Corp., Hartford, 1983-89, dir. corp. strategy and rsch., 1989-93; pres. ValueNet Internat., Inc., Hartford, 1993—. Adj. prof. Hartford Grad. Ctr.; pres. Am. Inst. Banking; bd. dirs. Admiral Farragut Corp., Human Tech. Partnership, Greenfield, Mass. Mem. editl. bd. Internat. Jour. Instrnl. Media; contbr. articles to profl. jours.; designer Travelers Mgmt. Devel. Continuum, 1984-86. Mem. Hartford mgmt. devel. adv. bd. Greater Hartford Arts Coun.; vice chmn. Windsor Govt. Study Commn., 1992-93; bd. dirs., v.p. Better Bus. Bur., Inc. Hartford; chmn. Grand Destiny capital campaign Pa. State U. Coll. Edn., 1997—; bd. dirs. Summer Wind Performing Arts Ctr., 2002—. Named Outstanding Alumnus Pa. State U., 1987; Chapter of Excellence Am. Inst. of Banking, 1983. Mem. Assn. for Ednl. Communications and Tech. (cert. of Merit, 1986, 88, Outstanding Practice award, 1983, div. coun. pres. 1990—), Am. Soc. for Tng. and Devel., Phi Delta Kappa. Independent. Methodist. Lodge: Masons. Avocations: sailing, skiing, music, golf, photography. Home: 8 Cobblestone Way Windsor CT 06095-2224 Office: ValueNet Internat Inc 237 Hopmeadow St Weatogue CT 06089-9763 E-mail: rewise@valuenet-intl.com.

WISE, ROBERT POWELL, lawyer; b. Jackson, Miss., Nov. 13, 1951; s. Sherwood Willing and Elizabeth (Powell) W. AB, Colgate U., 1973; MA, U. Va., 1975; JD, Washington & Lee U., 1979. Bar: Miss. 1979, U.S. Dist. Ct. Miss. 1979, U.S. Ct. Appeals (5th cir.) 1988. Ptnr. Wise, Carter, Child & Caraway, Jackson, 1979—. Lic. lay reader, chalice bearer St. Andrews Episc. Cathedral, Jackson, 1984—; pres. Caledonian Soc. Miss., Jackson, 1987, bd. dirs., 1985-90; bd. dirs. Belhaven Improvement Assn., 1991—, pres., 1994-97, v.p., 1999—, English Speaking Union of Miss., Jackson, 1985-92, Nat. Kidney Found. Miss., 1987—, v.p., 1988-92, pres. 1993-94; pres. Belhaven Security Assn., 1992-93. Mem. ABA (forums on constrn. and comm. law), Fed. Comm. Bar Assn., Miss. Bar Assn. Home: 1336 Olive St Jackson MS 39202-1809 Office: 600 Heritage Bldg PO Box 651 Jackson MS 39205-0651 E-mail: rpw@wisecarter.com.

WISE, ROBERT ELLSWORTH, JR. (BOB ELLSWORTH), governor, former congressman; b. Washington, Jan. 6, 1948; m. Sandy Casber; children: Robert, Alexandra. BA, Duke U., 1970; JD, Tulane U., 1975. Bar: W.Va. 1985. Sole practice, Charleston, W.Va., 1975—80; atty., legis. coun. for judiciary com. W.Va. Ho. of Dels., 1977—78; mem. W.Va. Senate, 1980—82, 97th-106th Congresses from 2nd W.Va. dist., Washington, 1983—2001; whip at large, 1986—2001; mem. govt. reform and oversight com., transp. and infrastructure com.; gov. State of W.Va., W.Va., 2001—. Dir. West Virginians for Fair and Equitable Assessment of Taxes, Inc. Mem.: ABA, W.Va. State Bar Assn. Democrat. Avocations: physical fitness, bluegrass music. Office: Gov's Office WVa State Capitol Charleston WV 25305-0370 Business E-Mail: gov@wvgov.org.*

WISE, SANDRA CASBER, lawyer; BA, Macalester Coll., 1969; JD, U. Minn., 1972. Bar: Minn. 1972, D.C., 1986, W.Va., 1987. Legis asst. to Rep. Martha Keys, Washington, 1977-78; asst. to asst. to the pres. for women's issues Sara Weddington, The White Ho., 1979; staff sub-com. on pub.

assistance Ho. Com. on Ways and Means, 1980, staff sub-com. on health, 1981-85; atty. White, Fine and Verville, 1986; staff dir. sub-com. on social security Ho. Com. on Ways and Means, Washington, 1987-94, minority counsel subcom. on social security, 1995-2000; first lady State of W.Va., 2001—.

WISE, SARAJANE GOERS, community education nurse; b. Clinton, Iowa, Apr. 5, 1946; d. Charles Maurice and Sarah Mardelle (Nichols) Cavanagh; m. Donald Fred Goers, Sept. 22, 1972 (dec. Mar. 1991); children: Christine M., Sarah E., Donald E.; m. Keith Eugene Wise, May 21, 1999. Diploma, Mercy Sch. Nursing, Iowa City, 1966; student, U. Iowa, 1969-71. RN, Ill., Iowa. Staff Mercy Hosp., Clinton, 1964-66, staff, nursing relief supr., 1966-68, U. Iowa Hosp. Clinics, Iowa City, 1968-69, head nurse, 1969-71; with surg. intensive care Rockford (Ill.) Meml. Hosp., 1971-74, head nurse, 1974-77; patient edn./nursing supr. Freeport (Ill.) Meml. Hosp., 1977-90, RN community edn./svc., 1990—. Advisor Stephenson County Sr. Ctr., Freeport, 1991—; coord. Arthritis Support Groups, Carroll and Stephenson counties, Alzheimers Support Groups, Carroll and Stephenson counties. Mem. Am. Lung Assn. (bd. dirs. 1988—), Am. Cancer Soc. (bd. dirs., prevention early detection chair, reach/recovery trainer 1980—), Am. Bus. Woman's Assn. (sec. 1987-90, pres. 1993, Woman of Yr. 1992, 97), Am. Ostomy Assn., Am. Diabetes Assn. Avocations: family activities, reading, swimming, walking, yard work. Home: 1934 W Mesa Dr Freeport IL 61032-7205 Office: Freeport Meml Hosp 1045 W Stephenson St Freeport IL 61032-4899

WISE, STEVEN LANIER, lawyer, clergyman; b. Eufaula, Ala., Oct. 3, 1956; s. Edward Lanier and Cathryn (Ryals) W.; m. Eloise Massey, July 30, 1983. BA in English, U. Ala., 1978, MA in Counselling, 1979, JD, 1982; MDiv, New Orleans Bapt. Theol. Sem., 1993. Bar: Ala. 1982, U.S. Dist. Ct. (no. dist.) Ala. 1982. Staff atty. Ala. Ct. Civil Appeals, Montgomery, 1982-83; ptnr. Hardin & Wise, Tuscaloosa, Ala., 1983-88; pvt. practice, 1988-94; assoc. pastor 1st Bapt. Ch., Honea Path, S.C., 1994-98; assoc. N.Am. Mission Bd. SBC, 1998-2001; min. to singles 1st Bapt. Ch., Spartanburg, S.C., 2001—. Sec., bd. editors The Ala. Lawyer, Montgomery, 1983-88. Sponsor Ctrl. H.S. Key Club, Tuscaloosa, 1984-94, Belton-Honea Path H.S. Jr. Civitan Club, 1994-99; judge citizen lock-up March of Dimes, Tuscaloosa, 1986; mem. S.C. Youth and Recreation Min.'s Assn., 1995— (editor newsletter). Mem. ABA, Farrah Law Soc., Civitans, Kappa Delta Pi, Pi Tau Chi. Avocations: woodworking, golf, softball, music. Home: 400 Grayson Dr Moore SC 29369 Office: 250 E Main St Spartanburg SC 29306-5128 E-mail: notamagi@charter.net.

WISE, STEVEN M. lawyer; b. Balt., Dec. 19, 1950; s. Sidney and Seluma Rosen W.; m. Debra Slator; children: Roma, Siena, Christopher. BS, Coll. William and Mary, 1972; JD, Boston U., 1976. Pres. Fraser & Wise, P.C., Boston, 1977-95, Wise & Slater-Wise, P.C., Boston, 1995—. Pres. Ctr. Expansion of Fundamental Rights, Inc., Boston, 1995—. Author: Rattling the Cage, 2000. Office: 55 Maple St Needham MA 02492 E-mail: wiseboston@aol.com.

WISE, SUSAN TAMSBERG, management and communications consultant, speaker; b. Memphis, Nov. 16, 1945; d. Joseph Lane and Mable Rosa (Koth) Tamsberg; m. Roy Thomas Wise, June 29, 1968; children: Kristin Rebecca, Mary Catherine. BA in Math., Columbia (S.C.) Coll., 1967; M in Edn., Ga. State U., Atlanta, 1986. Tchr. high sch. math. various pub. schs., N.C., S.C., and Ga., 1967-73; instr. Cen. Piedmont Community Coll., Charlotte, N.C., 1979; devel. dir. Classique, Inc., Kannapolis, 1979-81; asst. v.p. First Nat. Bank of Atlanta, 1981-87; Ga. dir. The Exec. Speaker, Inc., Atlanta, 1987-90; pres. TrimTime, Inc., 1988—, Wise Consulting Inc., Atlanta, 1990—. Speaker Girl Scouts USA, Jr. League, numerous med. assns., Atlanta and S.E. area, 1985—; affiliate Exec. Coaching Network, Inc. Tng. cons. Jr. League of Atlanta, 1988-89; bd. dirs. Incarnation Luth. Ch., Atlanta, 1984; mem. ch. coun., bd. dirs, Luth. Ch. of the Redeemer, 1994. Mem. ASTD (v.p., bd. dirs., Leadership award 1987), Kappa Delta Pi. Republican. Avocations: international traveling, antiques, needlework.

WISE, SYBIL ZULALIAN, retired educator; b. Malden, Mass., Apr. 15, 1935; d. Badrig Barsam and Elmon (Jivelekian) Zulalian; m. Kenneth Kelly Wise, Aug. 15, 1959; children: Jocelyn Anne, Adam Kelly, Lydia Louise. BS in Early Childhood Edn, Wheelock Coll., Boston, 1957. Tchr. The Pike Sch., Andover, Mass., 1980-99; ret., 1999. Mem. Kindergarten Curriculum Adv. Com. for Highreach Learning. Avocations: travel, horticulture, antiques.

WISE, THOMAS NATHAN, psychiatrist; b. Reno, Dec. 10, 1943; s. Charles Samuel and Irene Ruth (Bernstein) W.; m. Karen Dalinsky, Feb. 10, 1979; children: Catherine Sara, Elizabeth Anne. BA, Dartmouth Coll., 1965; MD, Duke U., 1969. Diplomate Am. Bd. Psychiatry and Neurology. Dir. psychiatry cons. svc. Johns Hopkins Hosp., Balt., 1974-76, assoc. prof. psychiatry, 1990-99, prof. psychiatry, 1999—; chmn. dept. psychiatry Fairfax Hosp., Falls Church, Va., 1976—; pvt. practice psychiatry Falls church, 1976—; prof. psychiatry Georgetown U., Washington, 1984—, vice chmn. dept. psychiatry, 1992—; med. dir. behavioral svcs. Inova Health Systems, Falls Church, 1996—. Author: Anxiety and Depression in Medical Diseases, 1980; editor: Psychiatry for Primary Care Physicians, 1998, Diagnosis and Management of Sexual Disorders, 1992; editor-in-chief Advances in Psychosomatic Medicine, 1984—; editor Psychosomatics, 1986; cons. editor Gen. Hosp. Psychiatry, 1984-98. Bd. dirs. Krasnow Inst., Fairfax, 1997; med. advisor Com. to Combat Huntington's Disease, Fairfax, 1995—. Recipient Disting. Svc. award Soc. for Liaison Psychiatry, 1996; Am. Psychiat. Assn. Rsch. awardee, 1989. Fellow Am. Coll. Psychiatrists; mem. Am. Psychosomatic Soc. (pres. 1994-96), Acad. Psychosomatic Medicine (pres. 1995-96, Disting. Svc. award 1993), Am. Assn. Gen. Hosp. Psychiatrists, Cosmos Club, Hidden Creek Country Club, Yale Club of N.Y.C. Avocations: history of medicine, social history of U.S., golf. Office: Inova Fairfax Hospital 3300 Gallows Rd Falls Church VA 22042-3300

WISE, WILLIAM ALFRED, writer; b. N.Y.C., July 21, 1923; s. Alfred Leo Wise, Nina Wolf. BA, Yale U. Author (poetry collection): Jonathan Blake, 1956; author: Silversmith of Old New York: Myer Myers, 1958, Albert Einstein, Citizen of the World, 1960, The House With the Red Roof, 1961, The Cowboy Surprise, 1961, Alexander Hamilton, 1963 (Jr. Lit. Guild selection), The Story of Mulberry Bend, 1963, In the Time of the Dinosaurs, 1964, Detective Pinkerton and Mr. Lincoln, 1964, The Two Reigns of Tutankhamen, 1964 (Merit award, Boys Clubs Am.), The World of Giant Mammals, 1965, The Spy and General Washington, 1965, Franklin D. Roosevelt, 1967, Monsters of Today and Yesterday, 1967, When the Saboteurs Came, 1967, Sir Howard, the Coward, 1967, Killer Smog, 1968, Monsters of the Ancient Seas, 1968, Aaron Burr, 1968, Secret Mission to the Philippines, 1969, Booker T. Washington, 1968, Nanette: The Hungry Pelican, 1969, Giant Birds and Monsters of the Air, 1969 (Jr. Lit. Guild selection), The Terrible Trumpet, 1969, The Amazing Animals of Latin America, 1969, The Amazing Animals of Australia, 1970 (Jr. Lit. Guild selection), The Lazy Young Duke of Dundee, 1970, Fresh as a Daisy, Neat as a Pin, 1970, From Scrolls to Satellites, 1970, Giant Snakes and Other Amazing Reptiles, 1970, Charles A. Lindbergh: Aviation Pioneer, 1970, Monsters of the Middle Ages, 1971 (Weekly Reader Book Club selection), Amazing Animals of North America, 1971, All on a Summer's Day, 1971, Off We Go!, 1972, Leaders, Laws and Citizens, 1973, Cities Old and New, 1973, The Strange World of Sea Mammals, 1973, Monsters of the Deep, 1975, American Freedom and the Bill of Rights, 1975, Massacre at Mountain Meadows, 1976, Monsters From Outer Space?, 1978 (Weekly Reader Book Club selection), Monsters of North America, 1978, Animal Rescue, 1978, The Amazon Factor, 1980, The Black Falcon, 1989, Ten Sly Piranhas, 1993, Perfect Pancakes If You Please, 1997, Nell of Branford Hall, 1999, Dinosaurs Forever!, 2000; contbr. Sgt. U.S. Army, 1942—46, ETO. Mem.: Authors Guild, Elizabethan Club of Yale Univ. Home: 307 E 44th St Apt 610N New York NY 10017-4409

WISE, WILLIAM ALLAN, energy company executive; b. Davenport, Iowa, July 10, 1945; s. A. Walter and Mary Virginia (Kuhl) W.; m. Marie Figge, Sept. 27, 1969; children: Vivian Marie, Genevieve Marie, Mary Elizabeth BA, Vanderbilt U.; JD, U. Colo. Bar: Colo. 1970. Prin. counsel El Paso Natural Gas, Tex., 1970-80, sr. v.p. mktg., 1985-87, exec. v.p. mktg., 1987-89, pres., chief oper. officer, 1989-90, pres., chief exec. officer, 1990-93, chmn, pres. & CEO, 1994-96; asst. gen. counsel in Houston The El Paso Co., 1980-82, v.p., gen. counsel, 1983, sr. v.p., gen. counsel and sec., 1983-85; chmn., pres. & CEO El Paso Natural Gas Co. dba El Paso Energy Corp., 1996—; also bd. dirs. El Paso Energy Corp. Bd. dirs. Tex. Commerce Bank, El Paso, Tex. Commerce Bancshres, Inc., Houston, Interstate Natural Gas Assn. Am., Washington: mem. N.Y. Merc. Exch., Tri-Regional Com. Contbr. articles to profl. jours. Bd. dirs. Battle Mountain Gold Co., U. Colo. Found., Boulder, Gas Industry Stds., Natural Gas Coun., Tex. Gov.'s Bus. Coun.; mem. bus. adv. coun. and devel. bd. U. Tex., El Paso; bd. visitors M.D. Anderson Cancer Ctr. Mem. Nat. Petroleum Coun. (bd. dirs.), Colo. Bar Assn., El Paso County Club, George Town Club (Washington), River Oaks Country Club (Houston), Old Baldy Club (Saratoga, Wyo.). Republican. Roman Catholic. Avocations: golf, running. Home: 2121 Kirby Dr Unit 50 Houston TX 77019-6065 Office: El Paso Corp 1001 Louisiana St Houston TX 77002-5083*

WISE, WILLIAM HARVEY, IV, human service executive; b. Alexandria, Va., Apr. 28, 1948; s. William Harvey III and Emily Virginia (Miller) W.; m. Susana Andrea Joublanc, July 28, 1973; children: Adam J., Andrea Susana, Virginia Elizabeth. BS, Washington & Lee U., 1970; postgrad, George Washington U., 1972. Acct. Arthur Andersen & Co., Washington, 1970-71; contr. Joint Action in Community Svc., Inc., 1971-79, dep. dir., 1979-87, exec. dir., 1987—. Mem. Ind. Sector, Washington, 1987—, Nat. Assembly of Nat. Voluntary Health and Social Welfare Orgns., Washington, 1989—. V.p. Whittier Woods Civic Assn., Bethesda, Md., 1983-86; cubmaster Boy Scouts Am., Bethesda, 1984-85; fin. com. chmn. Concord-St.-Andrew's United Meth. Ch., Bethesda, 1983-86, chmn. adminstrv. bd., 1995-2000, bd, trustees, 2000—; bd. dirs. Ridgeleigh Homes Assn., Potomac, Md., 1988-99, Pax World Svc., 1995-2001, treas., 1996-2000, chmn., 2000-2001; del. Balt. Ann. Conf. United Meth. Ch., 1996-99; bd. ambs. Mercy Corps, 2000—. Mem. Mensa, Kenwood Golf and Country Club. Avocations: tennis, gardening, genealogy. Home: 8229 Gainsborough Ct W Potomac MD 20854-4273 Office: Joint Action Community Svc 5225 Wisconsin Ave NW Washington DC 20015-2014

WISE, WILLIAM JERRARD, lawyer; b. Chgo., May 27, 1934; s. Gerald Paul and Harriet Muriel (Rosenblum) W.; m. Peggy Spero, Sept. 3, 1959; children: Deborah, Stephen, Betsy, Lynne. BBA, U. Mich., 1955, MBA, JD with distinction, U. Mich., 1958. Bar: Ill. 1959. Spl. atty. Office Regional Counsel, IRS, Milw., 1959-63; with firm McDermott, Will & Emery, Chgo., 1963-70, Coles & Wise, Ltd., Chgo., 1971-81, Wise & Stracks, Ltd., Chgo., 1982-2000, Querrey & Harrow Ltd., Chgo., 2000—. Lectr., contbr. Ill. Inst. Continuing Legal Edn.; arbitrator Cir. Ct. Cook County Ill., 1990—. Mem. Village of Winnetka (Ill.) Caucus, 1974-75; Bd. dirs. Blind Service Assn., Chgo., 1964-74; dir., treas. Suzuki Orff Sch. for Young Musicians, Chgo., 1981-91. Served with AUS, 1958-59. Mem. Chgo. Bar Assn. Home: 1401 Tower Rd Winnetka IL 60093-1628 Office: Querrey & Harrow Ltd 175 W Jackson Blvd Ste 1600 Chicago IL 60604-2827 E-mail: dididoe@yahoo.com. *I believe that one succeeds best in our society if one gives as little thought as possible to one's personal well being.*

WISE, WILLIAM R. engineering educator; b. Texas City, Tex. s. Kenneth V. and Patricia A. Wise. BS, Rice U., Houston, 1983; MS in Engring., U. Tex., Austin, 1985, PhD, 1989. Registered profl. engr., Fla. Postdoctoral rsch. asst. Rice U., Houston, 1989-90; asst. prof. Auburn (Ala.) U., 1990-95; assoc. prof. engring. U. Fla., Gainesville, 1995—. Contbr. articles to profl. jours. Named Outstanding Prof., Auburn Panhellenic Coun., 1995; Oak Ridge Assoc. U. fellow in radioactive waste mgmt., 1985-89; Trigg and Fannie E. Twichell Centennial Endowed Presdl. scholar in civil engring. U. Tex., 1986-87. Mem. ASCE (com. on probablistic methods in subsurface transport 1995-99, com. on hydrologic monitoring of wetlands 2000—), Am. Geophys. Union, Am. Soc. for Engring. Edn., Assn. of Ground Water Scientists and Engrs., Tau Beta Pi, Phi Kappa Phi, Sigma Pi Sigma. Avocations: physical conditioning, kayaking. Office: Univ of Florida Environ Engring Scis Gainesville FL 32611-6450

WISE, WOODROW WILSON, JR. retired small business owner; b. Alexandria, Va., Mar. 9, 1938; s. Woodrow Wilson Sr. and Helen (Peverill) W.; m. Barbara Jean Hatton, Oct. 6, 1956 (div. 1975); m. Sandra Kay Habitz, Dec. 17, 1983; children: Anthony P., Laura J. Gen. mgr. Alexandria (Va.) Amusement Corp., 1956-73; curator Harold Lloyd Estate, Beverly Hills, Calif., 1973-75; pres. Discount Video Tapes, Inc./Hollywood's Attic, Burbank, 1975-2000; ret., 2000. Office: Discount Video Tapes Inc PO Box 7122 833A N Hollywood Way Burbank CA 91505-2814

WISECUP, BARBARA JEAN, retired medical and surgical nurse; b. Missouri Valley, Iowa, Apr. 7, 1933; d. Charles Arthur and Agnes Viola (Tollefson) W. Diploma, Meth. Hosp. Sch. Nursing, Sioux City, Iowa, 1955; postgrad., Morningside Coll., Sioux City, Sacred Heart Dominion Coll., Houston, Houston C.C. RN, Tex.; cert. CNOR. Staff nurse surg. floor U. Minn. Hosps., Mpls., 1955-57; staff nurse oper. rms. Hermann Hosp., Houston, 1957-63, nurse mgr. oper. rm. staff devel., 1963-97, ret., 1997. Mem. Assn. Operating Room Nurses. Home: 12037 Bob White Dr Houston TX 77035-3928

WISEHART, ARTHUR MCKEE, lawyer; b. Evanston, Ill., July 3, 1928; s. Arthur J. and Dorothy H. (Rice) W.; m. Mary Elizabeth Dodson, 1953; children: William, Ellen, Arthur, Charles. BA, Miami U., Oxford, Ohio, 1950; M.P.A., Wayne State U., 1953; JD, U. Mich., 1954. Bar: N.Y. 1955. With firm Chadbourne, Parke, Whiteside & Wolff, N.Y.C., 1954-59; with Am. Airlines, Inc., 1959-69, corp. sec., asst. gen. counsel, 1968-69; sr. v.p., gen. counsel, sec. REA Express, 1969-74; dir., sec. REA Holding Corp., 1969-74; sr. partner Law Offices of Arthur M. Wisehart, 1974-75, Wisehart & Koch, 1975-2001. Dir. Hoover Co., 1975-76 Author articles. Mem. ABA, Assn. of Bar of City of N.Y., Order of Coif, Delta Chi. Clubs: Princeton. Presbyterian.

WISEHART, MARY RUTH, retired religious organization executive; b. Myrtle, Mo., Nov. 2, 1932; d. William Henry and Ora (Harbison) W. BA, Free Will Bapt. Bible Coll., 1955, George Peabody Coll. Tchrs., 1959, MA, 1960, PhD, 1976. Tchr. Free Will Bapt. Bible Coll., Nashville, 1956-60, chmn. English dept., 1961-85; exec. sec.-treas. Free Will Bapt. Women Nat. Active for Christ, 1985-98. Author: Sparks Into Flame, 1985, Beyond the Gate, 1998; contbr. poetry to jours. Mem. Nat. Coun. Tchrs. English, Scribbler's Club. Avocations: photography, music, drama. E-mail: wisemrw@aol.com.

WISEHEART, MALCOLM BOYD, JR. lawyer; b. Miami, Fla., Sept. 18, 1942; s. Malcolm B. and Dorothy E. (Allen) W.; m. Michele I. Romanens, Dec. 11, 1976. BA, Yale U., 1965; MA in English Jurisprudence, Cambridge U., 1973; JD with honors, U. Fla., 1970. Bar: Fla. 1970, Eng. and Wales 1970, Jamaica 1970, Trinidad and Tobago, 1971, D.C. 1980; barrister Gray's Inn of Ct., London. Assoc. Helliwell, Melrose & DeWolf, Miami, 1970-72; sr. ptnr. Malcolm B. Wiseheart, Jr., P.A., 1973-86, 87-01, Wiseheart & Joyce, P.A., Miami, 1986-88. Sec., gen. counsel Wiseheart Found.; spl. master Dade County Property Appraisal Adjustment Bd., 1977—90; pres. Fla. Law Inst., 1980—2002, Wiseheart Found., 1985—2002; dir. Yale Alumni Schs. Com. S. Fla., 2001—02; trustee, mem. exec. com. Players State Theater, 1982—84; bd. dirs. Sta. WLRN Pub. Radio, 1982, Coun. Internat. Visitors; trustee Ransom Everglades Sch., 1995—97. Named Most Outstanding, U. Fla. Law Rev. Alumnus, 1981. Mem. Fla. Bar (chmn. grievance com. 1978-81), Dade County Bar Assn. (dir. 1971-74, 86-89, treas. 1974-75, sec. 1975-77), Order of Coif; Yale Club (Miami pres. 1976-77), United Oxford and Cambridge Univs. Club (London). Office: Wiseheart Bldg 2840 SW 3rd Ave Miami FL 33129-2317 E-mail: mbwjr@bellsouth.net.

WISEMAN, ALAN M(ITCHELL), lawyer; b. Long Branch, N.J., July 6, 1944; s. Lincoln B. and Gertrude (Gorcey) W.; m. Paula Wiseman, July 8, 1965; children: Steven, David, Julie. BA, Johns Hopkins U., 1965; JD, Georgetown U., 1968. Bar: Md. 1968, Ill. 1970, D.C. 1973. Law clk. to Hon. William J. McWilliams, Md. Ct. Appeals, 1968-69; assoc. Schiff, Hardin & Waite, Chgo., 1970-74; ptnr. Howrey Simon Arnold White, LLP, Washington, 1976—. Editor Georgetown Law Jour., 1967-68. Mem. U.S. C. of C. (coun. on antitrust policy). Office: 1299 Pennsylvania Ave NW Washington DC 20004-2400 E-mail: wisemana@howrey.com.

WISEMAN, CARTER STERLING, editor, author; b. N.Y.C., Oct. 8, 1945; s. Mark Huntington Wiseman and Eleanor Carter Wood; m. Eileen Condon, Oct. 19, 1985; children: Emma, Owen, Damian. BA, Yale U., 1968; MA, Columbia U., 1972. Newsman Associated Press, N.Y.C., 1972-74; assoc. editor Newsweek Mag., 1974-77; sr. editor Horizon Mag., 1977-79; mng. editor Portfolio Mag., 1979-80; archtl. critic N.Y. Mag., 1980-96; editor Yale Alumni Mag., New Haven, 1986—. Bd. dirs. MacDowell Colony, Peterborough, N.H., pres., 1999—. Author: Twentieth Century American Architecture, 2000, I.M. Pei, 2001; mem. editl. bd.: On Earth Mag., 2000—, contbg. editor: ARTnews, 1996—. Co-chair Loeb Fellowship Assn. Harvard U., 1986-95. With U.S. Army, 1968-71. Loeb Fellow Harvard U., 1985; Recipient Special Citation award Am. Inst. Archs., N.Y.C., 1984, Interpretive Writing award Soc. Silurians, N.Y.C., 1985, Inst. Honor award Am. Inst. Archs., N.Y.C., 1987, Roger Starr award Citizens Housing and Planning Coun., N.Y.C., 1987, 90. Mem. Century Assn., Yale Club of N.Y. Office: Yale Alumni Magazine PO Box 1905 New Haven CT 06509-1905 E-mail: carter.wiseman@yale.edu.

WISEMAN, CYNTHIA SUE, language educator; b. New Albany, Miss., Sept. 8, 1952; d. Paul W. and Betty J. (Gore) W.; m. Ivan A. Tardio, Jan. 25, 1983 (div. Dec. 1997); children: E. Alexandra, Robert Paul. BA in English Lit., U. Miss., 1974; postgrad., La Sorbonne, Paris, 1978-79; MA in Tchg., Sch. for Internat. Tng., 1982; postgrad., Columbia U. With Peace Corps, Senegal, 1975-77; editor Guita Rev., N.Y.C., 1983-86; coord. evening program Hunter Coll., CUNY, 1992-95; dir. Queensborough Adult Learning Ctr., CUNY, 1991-92; adj. instr. ESL Am. lang. program Columbia U.., 1989-91; adj. instr. ESL, LaGuardia C.C., CUNY., 1987—; adj. prof. dept. culture and comm. NYU, N.Y.C., 1995—. Adj. prof. John Jay Coll. Criminal Justice, CUNY, 1995-98, instr. Internat. English Lang. Inst., 1989—; co-chmn. part-timers caucus TESOL, Alexandria, Va., 1996-99, mem.-at-large HEIS, TESOL, 1999—; chair signage TESOL, 1999; mem. exec. bd. CUNY ESL Coun., 1997-99. Active AIDS orgns., N.Y.C., 1990—. Mem. N.Y. State Tchs. English to Speakers of Other langs. (pres. 2001, v.p. 2000, exec. bd., chmn. sociopolit. com. 1995-97). Democrat. Avocations: cycling, rollerblading. Home: 300 Cathedral Pky Apt 1E New York NY 10026-4051 Office: CUNY Hunter Coll 10th Fl East Bldg 695 Park Ave New York NY 10021-5024

WISEMAN, DENNIS GENE, academic administrator; b. Anderson, Ind., Sept. 25, 1947; s. Harold Leslie and Lillian Loetta (Woods) W.; m. Susan Jean Reidenbach, June 10, 1971; children: Matthew Benjamin, Andrew Joseph. BA, U. Indpls., 1969; MA, U. Ill., 1970, PhD, 1974; postgrad., Ind. U., 1970-71. Tchr. Indpls. Pub. Schs., 1970-71; rsch. asst. U. Ill., Urbana, 1971-74, clinician, supr., 1972-74, coord. Office for Profl. Svc., 1973-74; dir., tchr. Champaign (Ill.) pub. schs., 1972-73; asst. prof. U. S.C. Coastal Carolina Coll., Conway, 1974-77, assoc. prof., 1977-84, prof., 1982—, dean Sch. Edn., 1982-2000; assoc. provost, spl. asst. to pres. Coastal Caroline U., 2000—. Field disseminator Social Sci. Edn. Consortium, Boulder, Colo., 1979-81; reviewer Ethnic Heritage Studies Program, U.S. Office Edn., Washington, 1980-81; cons. S.C. State Dept. Edn., Columbia, 1986—; dir. Oxford program U. S.C. Coastal Carolina Coll., summer, 1990; evaluator So. Assn. Colls. and Schs., Atlanta, 1991; folio reviewer for Nat. Coun. for Social Studies, Nat. Coun. for Accreditation of Tchr. Edn., 1994—; field reader U.S. Dept. Edn., Higher Edn. Program, 1999—; spl. asst. to pres. U./Schs. Collaboration, 2001—. Co-author: Effective Teaching, 1984, 3d edit., 1999, Wondering about Thinking, 1998, The Middle Level Teachers' Handbook: Becoming a Reflective Practitioner, 1998, Best Practice in Motivation and Management in the Classroom, 2001; contbr. articles to profl. jours. Mem. Horry County Human Rels. Coun., Conway, 1990-93; mem. curriculum frameworks rev. panel S.C. Dept. Edn., 1993—. Named Tchr. of Yr., U. S.C. Coastal Carolina Coll., 1980; S.C. Com. for the Humanities grantee, 1984, S.C. Com. on Higher Edn. grantee, 1985, 86; Japan Study Program scholar U.S. Office Edn., 1980. Mem. S.C. Assn. Colls. for Tchr. Edn. (pres. elect 1989, pres. 1989-91, treas. 1997-2001), Coun. Edn. Deans (pres. 1986-90, pres. 1996-2000), Nat. Coun. for the Social Studies, Am. Assn. Colls. for Tchr. Edn. (instl. rep. 1980—), Assn. Tchr. Educators, Phi Delta Kappa (pres. Coastal Carolina chpt. 1984-85). Methodist. Avocations: reading, travel, writing. Office: Coastal Carolina U PO Box 261954 Conway SC 29528-6054 E-mail: dwiseman@coastal.edu.

WISEMAN, DOUGLAS CARL, education educator, department chairman; b. Nashua, N.H., Feb. 28, 1935; s. Howard W. and Ruth D. (Aiken) W.; m. Donna Wiseman; children: Mark, Cynthia, Lori, Alan, Kathleen, Steve. BEd, Plymouth (N.H.) State Coll., 1961; MS, Ind. U., 1962, PED, 1970. Cert. tchr. health, math., phys. edn., sci. Tchr., track coach Nashua (N.H.) Pub. Schs., 1960-61, tchr., baseball coach, 1962-63; tchg. asst. Ind. U., Bloomington, 1961-62; tchr. high sch., wrestling coach Portage (Mich.) High Sch., 1963-64; instr., asst. prof., soccer, wrestling and tennis coach Plymouth (N.H.) State Coll., 1964-69; asst. prof. Northeastern U., Boston, 1969-71; dir. athletics, chmn. phys. edn. dept. Plymouth State Coll., 1971-80, assoc. dean, dir. undergrad. studies, 1993-96, prof., accreditation coord., 1996-98, ret., 1998, prof. emeritus, 1998—; prof., chair dept. edn. Univ. Sys. of N.H. , 1980—. Aquatics cons. Am./Nat. Red Cross, Laconia, N.H., 1971-98, State Dept. Edn., Concord, 1980-98. Author, contbg. editor: Adapted Physical Education, 1982, Practical Research, 1989, Quantitative Research, 1992, Physical Education for Exceptional Students, 1994, Introduction to Educational Research, 1995, Educational Research, 1996, Research Strategies for Education, 1999; contbr. more than 50 articles to profl. jours. Cert. police officer Ashland, N.H., 1992-98; chair sch. bd. Plymouth Regional Sch. Dist., 1989-91; divsn. staff officer-pub. edn., flotilla career counseling officer USCG Aux., 2001-2002. AAHPERD Ea. Dist. scholar, 1990-91. Republican. Avocations: reading, hiking, boating. E-mail: d.wiseman@mchsi.com.

WISEMAN, JAMES ANTHONY, theology studies educator; b. Louisville, Feb. 19, 1942; s. James Vachel Wiseman, Virginia Marie (Brown) Wiseman. BA, Georgetown U., 1963; MA, Cath. U. Am., 1970, STD, 1979. Prof. theology Cath. U. Am., Washington, 1985—. Abbot St. Anselm's Abbey, Washington, 1975—83, prior, 1990—. Author: Theology and Modern Science, 2002; co-editor: Light From Light: An Anthology of Christian Mysticism, 2001, The Gethsemani Encounter, 1997. Recipient Course Devel. award, John Templeton Found., 1999, Alumni Achievement award, Cath. U. Am., 1999. Mem.: Ctr. for Theology and Natural Scis., Am. Acad. Religion, Cath. Theol. Soc. Am. Avocations: backpacking, theater . Home: 4501 S Dakota Ave NE Washington DC 20017 Office: Cath Univ Am Theology Dept 620 Michigan Ave NE Washington DC 20064

WISEMAN, JAMES RICHARD, classicist, archaeologist, educator; b. North Little Rock, Ark., Aug. 29, 1934; s. James Morgan and Bertie Lou (Sullivan) W.; m. Margaret Lucille Mayhue, Aug. 20, 1954; children: James Alexander, Stephen Michael. BA, U. Mo., Columbia, 1957; MA, U. Chgo., 1960, PhD, 1966; postgrad., Am. Sch. Classical Studies, Athens, Greece, 1959-60. Instr. U. Tex., Austin, 1960-64, asst. prof. classics, 1964-66, assoc. prof., 1966-70, prof., 1970-73; dir. archaeol. excavations at Ancient Corinth, Greece, 1965-72; chmn. archaeol. studies program, 1969-73; prof. classics Boston U., 1973—, prof. art history, 1975—, prof. archaeology, 1980—, chmn. dept. classical studies, 1974-82, chmn. dept. archaeology, 1982-96, dir. archaeol. studies program, 1975-76, 79-82, dir. Ctr. Archeol. Studies, 1980—; dir. summer program Greece, 1976-77, 81, 91-94. Vis. assoc. prof. classics U. Colo., Boulder, 1970; Am. prin. investigator, co-dir. Am.-Yugoslav Archaeol. Excavations at Stobi, Yugoslavia, 1970-81; project supr. Boston U. Archaeol. Excavations in Temple, N.H., 1975-76; vis. rsch. prof. Am. Sch. Classical Studies, Athens, 1978-79; cons. archaeology; chmn. exec. com. Ctr. Remote Sensing; dir. Boston U. Nikopolis Project in N.W. Greece, 1991-; vis. fellow Clare Hall and McDonald Inst. for Archaeol. Rsch., Cambridge, 1997; life mem. Clare Hall, Cambridge, 1997—; co-dir. Boston U. Archaeol. Project, Menorca, Spain, 2001-2002. Author: Stobi, A Guide to the Excavations, 1973, The Land of the Ancient Corinthians, 1978, (with Thomas Sever) Remote Sensing and Archaeology: Potential for the Future, 1985; contbr. numerous articles on ancient history, epigraphy, classical studies, archaeology to profl. jours.; editor, contbg. author: Studies in the Antiquities of Stobi 1, 1973, II, 1975, III, 1981; founding editor: Jour. Field Archaeology, 1974—; contbg. editor Archaeology Mag., 1995-2002. Trustee Am. Ctr. Oriental Rsch., 1996—, Am. Schs. Oriental Rsch., 1985-89. Served with USN, 1952-55. Recipient Bromberg award U. Tex., 1964, Bronze Plaque award City of Titov Veles, SR Makedonija, Yugoslavia; disting. alumnus award Coll. Arts and Sci. U. Mo. Columbia, 1989; Am. Council Learned Socs. fellow, 1967-68, 78-79, 90-91; Guggenheim fellow, 1971-72; U. Tex. Research Inst. grantee, summers 1961, 66, 67, and 1967-68, 71-72; NEH grantee, 1968, 69, 76-80; Ford Found. grantee, 1968-72; Smithsonian Instn. grantee, 1970-75, 79-81; Dumbarton Oaks fellow, 1983-84; NGS grantee, 1984, 92; NASA grantee, 1984, 91; W.M. Keck Found. grantee, 1985, 86, 88, 92; J.M. Kaplan Fund grantee, 1997-99;

NEH fellow, 1990; Mellon fellow Inst. Advanced Study, Princeton U., 1990-91. Fellow Soc. Antiquaries of London, Explorers Club; mem. Archaeol. Inst. Am. (nat. pres. 1985-88, exec. com. 1973-77, 81-92, trustee 1993—, pres. Ctrl. Tex. Soc. 1962-64, pres. Boston Soc. 1979-81, Gold Seal award 1989, Charles Eliot Norton lectr., Joukowsky Disting. Svc. award 1999), Am. Philol. Assn., Am. Sch. Classical Studies at Athens (exec. com. 1973-76), Am. Acad. at Rome, Assn. Ancient Historians, Assn. Field Archaeology (exec. com. 1970-85), Am. Inst. Nautical Archaeology, Internat. Assn. Archaeology, Ctr. Materials Rsch. in Archaeology and Ethnology (exec. com. 1975-78, 79-83), Soc. Am. Archaeology, Am. Coun. Learned Soc. (del. 1985-89), German Archeol. Inst. (corr.). Democrat. Office: Boston U Dept Archaeology 675 Commonwealth Ave Boston MA 02215-1406

WISEMAN, JAY DONALD, photographer, mechanical designer and contractor, developer, writer; b. Salt Lake City, Dec. 23, 1952; s. Donald Thomas and Reva (Stewart) W.; m. Barbara Helen Taylor, June 25, 1977; children: Jill Reva, Steve Jay. Ed, Utah State U., Logan, U. Utah, Salt Lake City. Cert. profl. photographer. Pvt. practice; owner, pres. JB&W Corp. Judge Utah State Fair, 1988, 91, 93, 95-97, 99, 2000. Represented in (permanent collections) Salt Lake City Internat. Airport, traveling loans collections, U.S. and Europe, 1988, loan collection Epcot Ctr., 1988—91, photographs published in profl. jours., inventor (traffic signal lights for the color blind), developer (indsl. subdivsn.) Pinnacle Park. Named Photographic Hall Fame, 1989, among World's Best, Walt Disney World and Profl. Photographers Assn., 1988; named one of World's Greatest, Kodak, 1987—88; recipient Grand prize, Utah State Fair, 1986, Kodak Crystal for Photographic Excellence, 1986, 1987, Master of Photography degree, 1989, Best of Show award, 1991—92, 2 prints tied for Masters Best of Show award, RMPA Regional contest, 1991—92, Master Photographer of Yr., Gold Medallion award Best in Show (worldwide). Mem. Profl. Photographers Assn. Am. (one of top 10 scores internat. photo contest), Rocky Mountain Profl. Photographers (Best of Show, highest score ever 1987, Master Photographer of Yr. 1991, Ct. of Honour 1981-91), Inter-Mountain Profl. Photographers Assn. (Master's Trophy Best of Show 1982, 86, 88, Photographer of Yr. award 1986, Ct. of Honour 1981-91), Photographers Soc. Am. (Best of Show award Utah chpt. 1986). Latter Day Saints.

WISEMAN, LAURENCE DONALD, foundation executive; b. Washington, Feb. 24, 1947; s. Leon Robert and Marion (Wiseman; m. Robin Lynn Jeweler, May 29, 1978; children: Justin J., David B. AB with highest distinction, Dartmouth Coll., 1969; M in Pub. Affairs, Princeton U., 1971. Exec. producer Sta. WQED-TV (pub. broadcasting), Pitts., 1971-75; prin. Moses, Epstein and Wiseman, Washington, 1975-78; v.p. Yankelovich, Skelly and White, N.Y.C., 1978-81, Am. Forest Council, Washington, 1981-84, pres., 1984—. Pres. Am. Forest Coun., 1984-92, Am. Forest Found., 1993—. Author: Coalition Building, 1977. Bd. dirs. Cystic Fibrosis Found., N.Y.C., 1979-80, Urban Philharmonic, Washington, 1980-83, Sasha Bruce House, Washington, 1980-82; adv. com. Soc. for Profl. Journalists, Washington, 1984; hon. trustee Nat. Arbor Day Found., Nebraska City, Nebr., 1984—; chairperson Nat. Coun. on Pvt. Forests, 1997-98, Inst. for Journalism and Natural Resources, 1998—. Mem. Am. Forestry Assn., Soc. Am. Foresters, Pub. Rels. Soc. Am. Home: 10621 Democracy Ln Potomac MD 20854-4016 Office: Am Forest Found 1111 19th St NW Washington DC 20036-3603 E-mail: lwiseman@affoundation.org.

WISEMAN, RANDALL, real estate broker; b. Dayton, Ohio, Jan. 19, 1950; married. Lic. real estate broker Fla. Real estate broker, Mount Dora, Fla., 1985—. Home: PO Box 528 Mount Dora FL 32756 Personal E-mail: rwiseman@realestateprofessional.net.

WISEMAN, RANDOLPH CARSON, lawyer; b. Staunton, Va., Jan. 25, 1946; s. Malcolm Bell Wiseman and Alberta Elizabeth (Forbus) Marshall; m. Patty Joanne Gray, June 28, 1969; 1 child, Michael Randolph. BS, East Tenn. State U., Johnson City, 1968; JD, Capital U., Columbus, Ohio, 1974. Bar: Ohio 1974, U.S. Dist. Ct. (so. dist.) Ohio 1974, U.S. Supreme Ct. 1977. Assoc. Tyack, Scott & Colley, Columbus, 1974-77; ptnr. Tyack, Scott, Grossman & Wiseman, 1977-79, Tyack, Scott & Wiseman, Columbus, 1979-81, Bricker & Eckler, Columbus, 1981—. Contbr.: Evidence in America: The Federal Rules in the States, 1987; contbr. law articles to profl. jours. Bd. trustees Nat. Multiple Sclerosis Soc., Columbus, 1987—, chmn. 1991-93, Big Bros. Assn., Columbus, 1976-78; bd. dirs. Lifecare Alliance, Ohio Hunger Task Force. Mem.: ABA, Fed. Bar. Assn. (treas. Columbus Chpt. 1995-99, sec. 1999-00, v.p. 2000-01, pres. 2001-02)., Franklin County Trial Lawyers Assn. (pres.), Columbus Bar Assn., Ohio State Bar Assn. Republican. Avocations: running, reading, auto racing. Office: Brickler & Eckler 100 S 3rd St Columbus OH 43215-4291 E-mail: rwiseman@bricker.com.

WISEMAN, ROBERT SWERN, engineering executive; b. Robinson, Ill., Feb. 27, 1924; s. W. Paul Wiseman and Mary Jean Swern; m. Norma Woodard, Feb. 1, 1947; children: Marnie. BSEE with high honors, U. Ill., 1948, MSEE in Illumination, 1950, PhD in Elec. Engring., 1954. Assoc. prof. Miss. State Coll., Starkville, 1948—51; chief rsch. and photometric sect. Army Engr. R&D Labs., Ft. Belvoir, Va., 1954—58, chief warfare vision br., 1958—65; dir. night vision and combat surveillance labs. Army Electronics Command, Ft. Monmouth, NJ, 1965—68, dir. labs., 1968—78; tech. dir. Army material labs. Army Devel. & Readiness Command, Alexandria, Va., 1979—81; dep. dir. rsch. and tech. Martin Marietta Electronics Sys. Group, Orlando, Fla., 1981—84, dir. engrg. electro-optics and image signal processing, 1984—87, dir. engrng. ops., 1987—91; spl. asst. for electro-optics Martin Marietta Electronics & Missile Group, 1991—93; exec. v.p. MK Rsch., Inc., Atlanta, 1993—98. With USAF, 1943—46, Iwo Jima, Saipan, and Guam. Named Disting. Elec. Engring. Alumni, Dept. Elec. Engring., U. of Ill., 1980; recipient Disting. Exec. award, Pres. of U.S., 1980, All Engring. Alumni Honor award, Coll. of Engring., U. Ill., 1987. Fellow: IEEE (Fellow 1970). Home: 8451 Bay Hill Blvd Orlando FL 32819-4932 Personal E-mail: rswiseman@aol.com.

WISEMAN, SUSAN J. English educator; b. Dodge City, Kans., May 16, 1951; d. D.A. and Jane Ann (Edwards) Bartlett; m. Niles Wiseman, Oct. 16, 1971; children: Amber, Matthew. AA, Dodge City (Kans.) C.C., 1991; BA, St. Mary of the Plains Coll., 1993. Tchr. English Bucklin (Kans.) H.S., 1993-98, Cimarron (Kans.) H.S., 1998—. Recipient Nat. Collegiate Edn. award, 1991, Nat. Collegiate Computer Sci. award, 1991. Mem. Nat. Coun. Tchrs. English, Kans. Assn. Tchrs. English (exec. bd. 1996-99), PTA (life). Methodist. Home: 11105 Primrose Rd Dodge City KS 67801-6685 Office: Cimarron High Sch 400 N 5th St Cimarron KS 67835

WISEMAN, TAMARA WYNESE, writer, director; b. Miami, Oct. 7, 1975; d. Annie Ree Wiseman - Patterson and William Patterson(Stepfather); children: Justus Woods. BSJ, Emory U., 1998. Second dir. Tornado Films, Atlanta, 1997—97; asst. dir. TV 57, 1997—2000. Writer Agape Internat., Atlanta, 2001—02. Dir.: (screenplay) Proud Mary, 1996. Founder W.T.S., Atlanta, 1999—2002. Avocation: basketball, tennis, camping,cooking. Personal E-mail: Wynese@yahoo.com. Business E-Mail: Wynese@yahoo.com.

WISEMAN, THOMAS ANDERTON, JR. federal judge; b. Tullahoma, Tenn., Nov. 3, 1930; s. Thomas Anderton and Vera Seleta (Poe) W.; m. Emily Barbara Matlack, Mar. 30, 1957; children: Thomas Anderton III, Mary Alice, Sarah Emily. BA, Vanderbilt U., 1952, LL.B., 1954; LLM, U. Va., 1990. Bar: Tenn. Pvt. practice, Tullahoma, 1956-63; ptnr. Haynes, Wiseman & Hull, Tullahoma and Winchester, Tenn., 1963-71; treas. State of Tenn., 1971-74; ptnr. Chambers & Wiseman, 1974-78; judge U.S. Dist. Ct. (mid. dist.) Tenn., Nashville, 1978—, chief judge, 1984-91, sr. judge, 1995—; 6th cir. rep. Jud. Conf. of the U.S., 1996—2001, chair dist. judges conf., 1998-99. Mem. Tenn. Ho. of Reps., 1964-68; adj. prof. law Vanderbilt U. Sch. Law. Asso. editor: Vanderbilt Law Rev, 1953-54. Democratic candidate for gov., Tenn., 1974; Chmn. Tenn. Heart Fund, 1973, Middle Tenn. Heart Fund, 1972. Served with U.S. Army, 1954-56. Fellow Tenn. Bar Found.; mem. Fed. Judges Assn. (bd. dirs. 1982-87, v.p. 1982-91, 87-91), Masons (33 deg.), Shriners, Amateur Chefs Soc. Presbyterian. Office: US Dist Ct 777 US Courthouse 801 Broadway Nashville TN 37203-3816

WISH, JAY BARRY, nephrologist, specialist; b. Hartford, Mar. 30, 1950; s. Martin and Evelyn Lillian (Lassman) W.; m. Linda Kristina Hansen, June 29, 1971; (div. 1980); children: Allen Jeremy, Robin Lindsey; m. Diane Elizabeth Perkins, June 5, 1983; children: Jeffrey Bryan, David Phillip. BA, Wesleyan U., 1970; MD, Tufts U., 1974. Diplomate Am. Bd. Internal Medicine, Am. Bd. Nephrology. Resident in medicine New England Med. Ctr., Boston, 1974-79; instr. in medicine Tufts U., 1978-79; lectr. in health sci. Northeastern U., 1978-79; asst. prof. of medicine Case Western Res. U., Cleve., 1979-85, assoc. prof. of medicine, 1985-96, prof. medicine, 1996—; dir. hemodialysis U. Hosps. of Cleve., 1980—, dir. continuing edn., 1987-95. Chmn. Med. Adv. Bd. Kidney Found. of Ohio, Cleve., 1985-88. Author: Renal Disease and Hypertension, 1982, Disorders of Potassium, 1984, Metabolic Diseases, 1986, Rheumatic Diseases of the Kidney, 1993, Acid-Base and Electrolyte Disorders in the Critically Ill Patient, 1993, Assuring Quality of Care in Dialysis Patients, 1994, Adequacy of Hemodialysis, 1998, Algorithms and Care Paths for Quality Improvement, 2000; contbr. articles to med. jours. Chmn. med. rev. bd. End-Stage Renal Disease Network #22, Pitts., 1982-87, End-State Renal Disease Network #9, Indpls., 1992-2000, pres., 2001—; mem. exec. com. Forum of End-Stage Renal Disease Networks, 1992—, v.p., 1996-98, pres., 1998-2001; bd. dirs. Renal Phys. Assn., 1993-99, sec. 1996-97, treas., 1997-98; mem. Nat. Kidney Found. Fellow Am. Coll. of Physicians; mem. Cleve. Restoration Soc., Am. Soc. of Nephrology, Internat. Soc. of Nephrology, Alpha Omega Alpha. Democrat. Jewish. Avocation: performing arts. Office: U Hosps Cleve 11100 Euclid Ave Cleveland OH 44106-1736

WISHARD, DELLA MAE, former newspaper editor; b. Bison, S.D., Oct. 21, 1934; d. Ervin E. and Alma J. (Albertson) Preszler; m. Glenn L. Wishard, Oct. 18, 1953; children: Glenda Lee, Pamela A., Glen Ervin. Grad. high sch., Bison. Mem. S.D. Ho. of Reps., Pierre, 1984-96; pub., editor Bison (S.D.) Courier, 1996-2000. Columnist County Farm Bur., 1970-96. Committeewoman state Rep. Cen. Com., Perkins County, S.D., 1980-84, 98-01, Rep. Chairman, 2001—. Mem. Am. Legis. Exch. Coun. (state coord. 1985-91, state chmn. 1991-96), Fed. Rep. Women (chmn. Perkins County chpt. 1978-84), S.D. Farm Bur. (state officer 1982), Perkins County Rep. (chmn. 2000-). Lutheran. Avocations: writing, gardening. Home: 16707 134th St Prairie City SD 57649-9714

WISHARD, GORDON DAVIS, lawyer; b. Indpls., Jan. 7, 1945; s. William Niles Jr. and Caroline (Davis) W.; m. Anne Emison; children: Claire Wishard Hoppenworth, Gordon Davis Jr. BA, Williams Coll., 1966; JD, Ind. U., 1969. Bar: Ind. 1969, U.S. Dist. Ct. (so. dist.) Ind. 1969, U.S. Ct. Appeals (7th cir.) 1976, U.S. Supreme Ct. 1980, U.S. Tax Ct. 1983. Ptnr. Ice Miller, Indpls. Mem. Am. Coll. Trust and Estate Coun. (Ind. chmn. 1990-95). Avocations: hunting, fishing. Office: Ice Miller 1 American Sq Indianapolis IN 46282-0020

WISHART, BETTY R. musician; b. Lumberton, N.C., Sept. 22, 1947; d. Francis Eli and Hallie Elizabeth (Freeman) W. BMus, Queens Coll., Charlotte, N.C., 1969; MMus, U. N.C., 1975. Cert. tchr. Am. Coll. Musicians. Owner, tchr. Kohinoor Studio, Chapel Hill and N.Y.C., 1971-80; v.p. Final Copy, Stamford, Conn., 1981-85; owner Wishart Studio, Coral Springs, Fla., 1984-98; instr. piano U. N.C., Chapel Hill, 1998—. Mem. faculty Am. Coll. Musicians, Austin, Tex., 1989—; entertainment coord. Pompano Sq., Pompano Beach, Fla., 1995-98; mem. rsch. bd. advisors Internat. Biographical Ctr.; mem. rsch. bd. Am. Biographical Inst. Composer works for piano, organ, violins and percussion, work for string quartet, flute, clarinet, violin and cello. Sponsor Nat. Jr. Music Club, Coral Springs, 1987—; co-chmn., founder Pompano Beach Piano Competition, 1994-97. Recipient 2d Pl. Music for Children award Composers Guild, 1995, Hon. Mention Instrumental award Composers Guild, 1995, 99, 1st Pl. Composition award Broward County Music Assn., 1994, Hon. Mention award Nat. Piano Guild, 1995, Honorable Mention Music for Children award Composers Guild, 1997, 98, 1st Pl. Internat. Guild of Piano Tchrs. Composition, 1999, 1st Pl. Am. Coll. Musicians Composition contest, 1999. Mem. ASCAP (Standard award 1996-2001), Coral Springs Philharm. Soc. (v.p. 1990-98), Broward Music Tchrs. Assn. (pres., bd. dirs. 1989-95), Southeastern Composer's League (sec., 2001-03) Soc. Composers Inc. Baptist. Home: 6205 Farrington Rd Apt F4 Chapel Hill NC 27517-7851 E-mail: bwishart@mindspring.com.

WISHART, LEONARD PLUMER, III, army officer; b. Newark, Sept. 24, 1934; s. Leonard Plumer and Mabel Dorothea (Womsley) W.; m. Sandra Frances De Vito, Apr. 12, 1958; children: Leonard Plumer IV, Scott Brian. Student, Va. Mil. Inst., 1952-53; BS in Engring., U.S. Mil. Acad., 1957; MS in Nuclear Physics, U. Va., 1966. Commd. 2d lt. U.S. Army, 1957, advanced through grades to lt. gen., 1988; served in Germany and Vietnam; tactical officer U.S. Mil. Acad., West Point, N.Y., 1971-73; sr. mil. asst. to Sec. of Army, 1975-76; comdr. 1st Brigade, 24th Inf. Div., Ft. Stewart, Ga., 1977-78; chief of staff 24th Inf. Div., 1979, VII Corps in Germany, 1979-81; asst. div. comdr. 1st Armored Div., 1981-83; dep. comdr. CACDA, Ft. Leavenworth, Kans., 1983-86; comdr. 1st Inf. Div., Ft. Riley, 1986-88, Combined Arms Command, Ft. Leavenworth, 1988-91; dep. comdr. TRADOC, 1988-91, ret., 1991; assoc. Burdeshaw Assocs. Ltd., Bethesda, Md., 1991-92. Apptd. 1st dir. non-legis. and fin. svcs. U.S. Ho. of Reps., Washington, 1992—94, resigned., 1994; assoc. Burdeshaw Assocs., Ltd., Bethesda, Md., 1994—; mgr. ind. study Army N.G. INNOLOG, McLean, Va., 1996—98. Active in cmty. activities; pres. Army Distaff Found., Washington, 1997-99, chmn., bd. govs. 5th Cavalry Regiment Assn., 1998—. Decorated Disting. Service Medal (2), Legion of Merit (2), D.F.C., Bronze Star medal (2), Army Commendation medal, Air medals. Mem. Assn. U.S. Army, Assn. Grads. U.S. Mil. Acad., Alumni Assn. U. Va., VFW, Soc. of the First Divsn., First Cavalry Divsn. Assn. Methodist. Office: Burdeshaw Assocs Ltd 4701 Sangamore Rd Bethesda MD 20816-2508

WISHART, RONALD SINCLAIR, retired chemical company executive; b. Bklyn., Mar. 1, 1925; s. Ronald Sinclair and Elizabeth Lathrop (Phillips) W.; m. Betty B. Burnup, Sept. 14, 1951 (dec. Dec. 1973); children: Michael Sinclair, James Ronald; m. Eleanor Dorothy Parrish Dooley, Jan. 11, 1975; stepchildren: Donna Dooley Willix, Arthur D. Dooley. BChemE, Rensselaer Poly. Inst., 1948. Engr., chemist Linde air div. Union Carbide Corp., Tonawanda, N.Y., 1948-51; sales rep. Chgo., Cleve., 1951-56; region mgr. Chgo., 1956-57; product mgr., mktg. mgr. Silicones div. N.Y.C., 1957-64; gen. mgr., pres., 1964-66; pres. devel. and coating materials divs., 1966-71; corp. dir. energy and transp. policy, 1972-82; v.p. fed. govt. regulations, 1983-85; v.p. pub. affairs Danbury, Conn., 1985-90; chief of staff to chmn. of corp. Union Carbide, N.Y.C., 1984-85. Mem. adv. coun. Gas Rsch. Inst., Energy Modeling Ctr., Stanford U., 1979-83, Environ. and Energy Policy Ctr., John F. Kennedy Sch. Pub. Policy, Harvard U., 1980-87; energy com. Aspen Inst., 1976-88; chmn., exec. dir. Electricity Consumers Resource Coun., Washington, 1976-79. Author: The Marketing Factor, 1966; contbr. chpts. to books and articles to profl. jours.; patentee silicone formulas. Vol. Am. Field Svc., Burma, 1944-45; pres., trustee, elder White Plains (N.Y.) Presbyn. Ch., 1987-90; elder Palm City Presbyn. Ch., 1996—; treas., bd. dirs. St. Christopher's Jenni Clarkson Home, 1968-91; mem. exec. bd. Westchester Putnam coun. Boy Scouts Am., White Plains, 1985-91; v.p. Carbide Retiree Corps.; v.p. Hospice Martin and St. Lucie, Inc., 1994-99, pres. 2000—; pres. Lancewood Assn., 1997. Mem. NAM (mem. energy com.), Am. Mgmt. Assn. (v.p. 1966-69), Chem. Mfrs. Assn. (chmn. energy com. 1974-78), Nat. Petroleum Refiners Assn. (v.p. 1972-76, chmn. issues com. 1985-89), Internat. Fedn. Ind. Energy Users (chmn. 1978), Am. Chem. Soc., Soc. Chem. Industry, U.S. C. of C. (mem. energy com.), Met. Club Washington, Harbor Ridge Yacht and Country Club. Republican. Presbyterian. Avocations: golf, skiing, reading. Home: 1329 Lancewood Ter Palm City FL 34990

WISHEK, MICHAEL BRADLEY, lawyer; b. Pasadena, Calif., June 25, 1959; s. Homer Cedric and Donna Jean (Arnold) W.; m. Shari Patrice Rubin, June 7, 1981 (div. Feb. 1986); m. Dorothea Jean Palo, Feb. 12, 1988; children: Kirstin Alyce, Lauren Ashley. BS in Polit. Sci and Philosophy, Claremont Men's Coll., 1981; JD, U. Calif., Davis, 1985. Bar: Calif. 1986, U.S. Dist. Ct. (ea. dist.) Calif. 1986. Assoc. Michael S. Sands, Inc., Sacramento, 1986-91; ptnr. Rothschild & Wishek, 1991-96, Rothschild, Wishek & Sands, Sacramento, 1996—. Mem. Milton L. Schwartz Am. Inn of Ct., 2000—; adj. instr. trial practice U. Calif., Sch. Law, Davis. Mem. ABA, Calif. Bar Assn., Sacramento County Bar Assn. (co-chmn. criminal law sect. 1988-90), Calif. Attys. for Criminal Justice. Office: 901 F St Ste 200 Sacramento CA 95814-0733

WISHENGRAD, MARCIA H. lawyer; b. Hudson, N.Y., Feb. 10, 1936; d. Joseph and Jessie (Diamond) W.; m. Robert J. Metzger, Sept. 3, 1961; 1 child, Jocelyn M. BA, Cornell U., 1957, JD, 1960. Bar: N.Y. 1960, U.S. Dist. Ct. (so. and ea. dists.) N.Y. 1962, U.S. Supreme Ct. 1964. Atty. Monroe County Family Court, Rochester, N.Y., 1963-65, Monroe County Legal Aid Soc., Rochester, 1965-67; sr. urban renewal atty. City of Rochester, 1971-74; dep. county atty. Monroe County, Rochester, 1974-93; pvt. practice, 1963—. Bd. visitors State Sch. Industry, Rochester, 1983-98, pres., 1991-98; pres. Arc of Monroe County, 1991-93; v.p. Arc Found. of Monroe, 1990-99. Mem. N.Y. State Bar Assn., Monroe County Bar Assn., Greater Rochester Assn. of Women Attys. (judiciary com.). Republican. Jewish. Avocations: boating, tennis, reading. Office: 36 W Main St Ste 312 Rochester NY 14614-1701

WISHERT, JO ANN CHAPPELL, music educator, elementary and secondary education educator; b. Carroll County, Va., July 10, 1951; d. Joseph Lenox and Helen Alata (Wagoner) Chappell; m. Clarence Hinnant Wishert, Jr., June l0, 1987; 1 child, Kelly Marie. BA, Oral Roberts U., 1974; MS, Radford U., 1977; degree in advanced postgrad studies, Va. Poly. Inst. and State U., 198l; postgrad., U. S.C., Spartanburg, 1990, Winthrop U., 1995, 96, U. S.C., Columbia, 1995, The Citadel, 1996. Cert. elem. music supr., Va., elem. and secondary music tchr., S.C., music tchr., ednl. specialist, N.C. Head start tchr. Rooftop of Va., Galax, 1975; elem. music tchr. Carroll County Pub. Schs., Hillsville, 1975-78; grad. asst., supr., course advisor Coll. Edn., Va. Poly. Inst. and State U., Blacksburg, 1975-81, pregrad. interviewer placement svcs., 198l-83; music dir. Heritage Acad., Charlotte, N.C., 1984-85, fine arts specialist, 1985-86; choral dir. Chester County Schs., Chester, 1986—2002; music tchr. Old Pointe Elem./Rock Hill Sch. Dist. #3, 2002—. Fine arts chairperson Chester H.S., 1995-96, adept evaluator, 1996—, chmn.; guest condr. workshop Patrick County Schs., Stuart, Va., 1980; liaison for Chester County Schs. to S.C. Gov.'s Sch. for Arts, 1990-91; faculty mem., sponsor Tri-M Music Honor Soc. Soloist PTL TV Network, Charlotte, 1984-85. Guest spkr. on battered women and marital abuse to chs. and workshops; entertainer; co-dir. Chester City Schs. Choral Festival; active Arts Coun. Chester County, 1988—, S.C. Arts Alliance and Arts Advocacy, Winthrop Consortium for the Arts; sponsor Tri-M Music honor society, 1991—, Beta Club. Named Tchr. of the Yr., Chester Sr. H.S., 1989, Chester County Schs., 1991, Educator of Yr., Chester County C. of C., 1992, Tchr. of the Week, The Herald, 1995. Mem. ASCD, AAUW (mem. bylaws com. Chester br. 1987—, sec. 1988-89, fine arts chmn. 1995—), Music Educators Nat. Conf., S.C. Music Educators Assn. (del. pub. rels. network Chester County Schs. 1991), S.C. Edn. Assn., Palmetto State Tchrs. Assn., Am. Ednl. Rsch. Assn., Am. Assn. Choral Dirs., Chester County Edn. Assn., Nat. Assn. Secondary Music Edn. (team evaluator divsn. tchr. edn. cert. 1989, 91—), State So. Assn. Schs. and Colls. (mem. evaluation team, mem. steering com.), All U.S.A. Chorus Student Group (alumni), Tri-M Music Honor Soc. (sponsor), 4-H Club (life), Phi Delta Kappa. Republican. Baptist. Avocations: reading, cross stitch, needlepoint, music. Home: 1922 Virginia Dare Dr Rock Hill SC 29730-9669 E-mail: jwishert@rock-hill.k12.sc.us.

WISHNER, MAYNARD IRA, retired finance company executive, lawyer; b. Chgo., Sept. 17, 1923; s. Hyman L. and Frances (Fisher) W.; m. Elaine Loewenberg, July 4, 1954; children: Ellen Kenemore, Jane Wishner, Miriam Segel. BA, U. Chgo., 1944, JD, 1947; LHD honoris causa, Spertus Inst., 1998, Hebrew Union Coll., 2001. Bar: Ill. 1947. Exec. dir. Chgo. Commn. on Human Relations, 1947-52; chief ordinance enforcement div. Law Dept., City of Chgo., 1952-55; mem. law firm Cole, Wishner, Epstein & Manilow, Chgo., 1955-63; with Walter E. Heller & Co., 1963-86, pres., 1974-86; of counsel Rosenthal and Schanfield, 1986-95. Dir. Walter E. Heller Internat. Corp., Am. Nat. Bank & Trust Co., and br. cos., Chgo. Pres. Jewish Fedn. Met. Chgo., 1987-89; chair Nat. Jewish Community Rels., 1992-94, pres. Coun. Jewish Fedn., 1993-96; chmn. bd. govs. Am. Jewish Com., 1977-80, nat. pres. 1980-83, hon. pres., recipient Human Rights medallion, 1975; bd. dirs. Nat. Found. for Jewish Culture; chmn. Ill. Humanities Coun.; commr. Nat. Hillel Found.; mem. vis. com. U. Chgo. Sch. Social Svc. Adminstrn. and Divsn. of the Humanities; chair Ill. Humanities Coun., 1991-93; bd. govs. Jewish Agy. for Israel. Recipient Rosenwald award Jewish Fedn. Met. Chgo., Officers medal of merit Republic of Poland, United Hellenic Leadership Coun. Frisis award, Civic Achievement award U. Chgo. Home: 1410 Sheridan Rd Wilmette IL 60091-1895 E-mail: maynwish@aol.com.

WISHNIA, KENNETH J.A. writer, translator, educator; b. Hanover, N.H., Aug. 20, 1960; s. Arnold and Judith (Passoff) W.; m. Mercedes Peña, Aug. 7, 1986; children: Leah Victoria, Jeremiah Angelo. BA, Brown U., 1982; PhD, SUNY, 1996. Sound designer, technician various theaters, N.Y.C., 1983-85; prodn. editor Plenum Press, Ecuador, 1985-86; theater instr. Casa de la Cultura Ecuatoriana, Cuenca, Ecuador, 1986-88; office mgr. World Hunger Yr., N.Y.C., 1988-89; adj. asst. prof. SUNY, Stony Brook, 1996-98, Queens Coll.-CUNY, Flushing, 1996-98; instr. Suffolk County C.C., 2000—. Judge Edgar Allan Poe Awards, 2000. Author: Las Paredes Tienen La Palabra (The Walls Have the Floor), 1994, Flat Rate and Other Tales, 1997, 98, 23 Shades of Black, 1997 (finalist for Edgar Allan Poe award 1998, Anthony award 1998), Soft Money, 1999, The Glass Factory, 2000, Red House, 2001, Blood Lake, 2002; 20th century Ecuadorian narrative, 1999; transl.: Alicia Yánez-Cossio, Bruna and Her Sisters in the Sleeping City, 1999; contbr. articles to profl. jours., short stories and articles to periodicals. Sholem Aleichem Fund scholar Nat. Yiddish Book Ctr., 1993, 95-96; Vivian L. Hort fellow Yivo Inst. Jewish Rsch., 1996; recipient Tableau d'Honneur Lycée Henri IV, 1974. Mem. Am. Lit. Translators Assn. (David Kornbacker scholarship 1994), Am. Assn. Profs. of Yiddish, Assn. Ecuatorianistas, Nat. Writers Union, Mystery Writers of Am. (bd. dirs. N.Y. chpt. 1999-01), Internat. Assn. Crime Writers, Sisters in Crime. Jewish. Avocations: photography, translating from Spanish and Yiddish.

WISHNICK, MARCIA MARGOLIS, pediatrician, geneticist, educator; b. N.Y.C., Oct. 10, 1938; d. Hyman and Tillie (Stoller) Margolis; m. Stanley Wishnick, June 12, 1960; 1 child, Elizabeth Anne. BA, Barnard Coll., 1960; PhD, NYU, 1970, MD, 1974. Diplomate Am. Bd. Pediatrics, Nat. Bd. Med. Examiners. Rsch. technician Lederle Labs./Am. Cyanamid, Pearl River, N.Y., 1960-66; postdoctoral fellow N.Y. Pub. Health Lab., N.Y.C., 1970-71; resident in pediatrics NYU-Bellevue Med. Ctr., 1974-77, asst. prof. pediatrics, 1977-82; clin. assoc. prof. pediatrics Bellevue Med. Ctr. NYU Med. Ctr., 1982-87; clin. prof. pediatrics NYU-Bellevue Med. Ctr., 1987—; pvt. practice, 1977—. Contbr. articles to profl. jours. Fellow Am. Acad. Pediatrics; mem. AMA, N.Y. Pediatric Soc., N.Y. Med. Soc. Office: 157 E 81st St New York NY 10028-1844 E-mail: wishpeds@earthlink.net.

WISLER, DARLA LEE, pastor; b. Balt., May 14, 1940; d. Hugh Charles Douglas and Angela Rita (Poffel) Mayer; m. Norman Marvin Wisler, Dec. 26, 1960; children: David Paul, Diane Lynn. A in Biblical Studies, Christian Internat. U., 1982, BTh, 1984, MDiv, 1990, D in Ministry, 1993. Asst. pastor Anderson Christian Assembly, 1978-80; founder, sr. pastor Living Water Ch., Anderson, 1981—. Mid-week devotion min. NHC Healthcare of Anderson, 1980—, pres. adv. bd., 1988—; dean Living Water Bible Coll., Anderson, 1982—; prin. Living Water Christian Sch., Anderson, 1983-88; regular co-host Dove Broadcasting TV-16, Greenville, S.C., 1984—; coord. Christian Internat. Network of Chs. Mid-East Region, 1994-96. Author: Basic Christian Teaching Made Plain and Clear, 1994, Advanced Christian Teaching Made Plain and Clear, 1995. Pres. clergy staff exec. com. Anderson Area Med. Ctr., 1993-94; sec. Anderson County Sheriff's Dept. Chaplaincy, Anderson, 1996-98; chaplain Anderson County Sheriff's Dept., 1996—, bd. dirs., 1996—, vice chairperson bd. dirs., 2001-02, chairperson, 2002—. Republican. Avocations: walking, reading, crocheting, cooking. Office: Living Water Ch PO Box 1823 Anderson SC 29622-1823

WISLER, WILLARD EUGENE, retired health care management executive; b. Cliffside Park, N.J., May 31, 1933; s. Willard Walter and Doris Alice (McGlone) W.; m. Carol M. Askey, Aug. 19, 1966; children: Diana Marie, Jennifer Lee. BBA, U. Fla., 1955; MBA, The George Washington U., 1963. Asst. adminstr. Halifax Dist. Hosp., Daytona Beach, Fla., 1963-64; CFO Waterman Meml. Hosp., Eustis, 1964-67, COO, 1967-72, Suburban Hosp., Louisville, 1972—73; exec. dir. Gen. Hosp. of Fort Walton Beach, Fla., 1973-77; pres. Winter Pk. (Fla.) Meml. Hosp., 1977-91, Park Health Corp., Winter Pk., 1985-91, The Tampa Bay Hosp. Assn., St. Petersburg, Fla., 1993-97. Bd. dirs. Village on the Green, Longwood, Fla., 1983-88; mem. ho. of dels. Am. Hsp. Assn., Chgo., 1985-88; regent State of Fla. Am. Coll. Healthcare Execs., Chgo., 1988-93. Advc. council mem. Hamilton Holt Sch., Rollins Coll., Winter Pk., 1986-89, Orlando Bus. Jour., 1989, Pioneer Savings Bank, Winter Pk., 1986-88; sec.-treas. bd. dirs. Albin Polasek Found., Winter

Park. Sgt. U.S. Army, 1955-59. Fellow Am. Coll. Healthcare Execs., Citrus Club, Winter Park Racquet, Interlachen Country. Democrat. Home: 665 Balmoral Rd Winter Park FL 32789-5204 E-mail: wwisler@juno.com.

WISMAR, GREGORY JUST, minister; b. Jersey City, Jan. 9, 1946; s. Adolph Harold and Norma Adela (Just) W.; m. Priscilla Emily Ames, June 7, 1969; children: Eric Andrew, Sarah Emily, Elizabeth Victoria, Jessica Eve. BA, Concordia Sr. Coll., Ft. Wayne, Ind., 1967; MDiv, Concordia Sem., St. Louis, 1971; MS, So. Conn. State U., 1977; D of Ministry, Hartford Sem., 1990. Ordained to ministry Luth. Ch.-Mo. Synod, 1971. Asst. pastor Immanuel Luth. Ch., Danbury, Conn., 1971-72; pastor St. Paul's Luth. Ch., Naugatuck, 1972-78, Redeemer Luth. Ch., Cape Elizabeth, Maine, 1978-83, Messiah Luth. Ch., Lynnfield, Mass., 1983-87, Christ the King Luth. Ch., Newtown, Conn., 1987—. V. p. New Eng. Dist. Luth.-Mo. Synod, Springfield, Mass., 1979—83; mem. nominations com. , St. Louis, 1985—86; archivist New Eng. dist., 1989—; mem. commn. on worship , St. Louis, 1990—95, St. Louis, 2001—; rsch. fellow Yale Inst. Sacred Music, Liturgy and Arts, 1991. Author: A Parish Portrait, 1990, Saints and Angels All Around, 1995; editor: Prayers for Worship, 1993. Chmn. Lynnfield Arts Commn. , 1985—87; sec. bd. regents Concordia Coll. , Bronxville, NY, 1998—2001; guest chaplain U.S. Ho. of Reps., Washington, 1977, U.S. Senate, Washington, 1982; CT-5 congl. adv. bd. Waterbury, Conn., 1975—79; Ft. Williams com. Cape Elizabeth, 1981—83; congl. adv. bd. Newton Family Life Ctr., 1988—90. Recipient Svc. award NED Youth Commn., 1987, award Kodak Internat., 1988, Lillyl Endowment Grant award 2000. Mem. New Eng. Luth. Hist. Soc. (v.p. 1999—). Home: 81 Mount Pleasant Rd Newtown CT 06470-1545 Office: Christ the King Luth Ch 85 Mount Pleasant Rd Newtown CT 06470-1535 E-mail: wismar@prodigy.net., ctkingchrch@snet.net. *There are many opportunities for enjoyment in our lives and days—enjoyment of God and of the people in our circles of relationship. Celebrations stemming from our perceptions of faith and life strengthen the self, build family bonds and enrich the communities of which we are part.*

WISMER, PATRICIA ANN, retired secondary education educator; b. York, Pa., Mar. 23, 1936; d. John Bernhardt and Frances Elizabeth Loreen Marie (Fry) Feiser; m. Lawrence Howard Wismer, Aug. 4, 1961. BA in English, Mt. Holyoke Coll., 1958; MA in Speech/Drama, U. Wis., 1960; postgrad., U. Oreg., 1962, Calif. State U., Chico, 1963-64, U. So. Calif., 1973-74. Tchr., co-dir. drama program William Penn Sr. High Sch., York, 1960-61; instr. English, dir. drama York Jr. Coll., 1961-62; assoc. church editor San Francisco Examiner, 1962-63; reporter, publicist News Bur. Calif. State U., Chico, 1963-64; chmn. English Dept. Chico Sr. H.S., 1966-96; mentor tchr. Chico Sr. High Sch., Chico Unified Sch. Dist., 1983-93. Judge writing awards Nat. Coun. Tchr. English, 1970—; cons. No. Calif. Writing Project, 1977—; curriculum cons., freelance writer and photographer, 1996—. Author: My Life with Vanessa: A Journal of the Plagued Years, 1998, 40 Year Photo Retrospective, 2002; newsletter editor Chico Cat Coalition, 1999—. Mem. Educators for Social Responsibility, Planetary Soc., Upper Calif. Coun. Tchrs. English (bd. dirs. 1966-85, pres. 1970-71), Calif. Assn. Tchrs. English, Nat. Coun. Tchrs. English, NEA, Calif. Tchrs. Assn., Chico Unified Tchrs. Assn. Democrat. Lutheran. Avocations: photography, play prodn., video prodn. Home: 623 Arcadian Ave Chico CA 95926-4504 Office: PO Box 1250 Cannon Beach OR 97110-1250 E-mail: pwismer@aol.com.

WISNER, CYNTHIA FICKE, lawyer, law educator; b. Cin., Aug. 17, 1957; d. Howard William and Verna Lee (Schriever) Ficke; m. Neal R. Wisner, Jan. 5, 1980; children: April Leigh, Shelbi Lynn. BS, Kent State U., 1978; JD, U. Mich., 1981. Bar: Mich. 1981, U.S. Dist. Ct. (ea. dist.) Mich. 1981, U.S. Tax Ct. 1982. Assoc. Jaffe, Snider, Raitt and Heuer, Detroit, 1981-83, Honigman Miller Schwartz and Cohn, Detroit, 1983-86, ptnr., 1987-93, Howard & Howard Attys., P.C., Bloomfield Hills, 1993-94; gen. counsel The Detroit Med. Ctr., 1994-99, Mercy Health Plans, 2000—01; asst. gen. counsel Trinity Health, Novi, Mich., 2001—. Adj. prof. U. Detroit Mercy, 1987-94; presenter at profl. confs. Co-editor Health Law Focus newsletter, 1991-93. Mem. ABA (health law forum), State Bar Mich., Mich. Soc. Hosp. Attys., Am. Health Lawyers Assn., Acctg. Aid Soc., Kent State U. Alumni Assn., U. Mich. Alumni Assn. Avocations: fishing, reading, teaching. Office: Trinity Health 27870 Cabot Dr Novi MI 48377

WISNER, FRANK GEORGE, insurance company executive, former ambassador; b. N.Y.C., July 2, 1938; s. Frank Gardiner W. and Mary Knowles (Fritchey) W.; m. Genevieve de Virel, July, 1969 (dec. 1974); 1 dau., Sabrina; m. Christine de Ganay, June, 1976; 1 son, David; stepchildren: Caroline Sarkozy, Olivier Sarkozy. BA, Princeton U., 1961. With Fgn. Svc. Dept. Dept. State, Algiers, Morocco, 1962-64; from dep. ambassador's staff aide to sr. advisor Vietnamese province Tuyen Duc Agy. Internat. Devel., Vietnam, 1964-68; officer-in-charge Tunisian affairs Dept. State, Washington, 1968-71; chief econ.-comml. sect. Am. Embassy, Tunis, Tunisia, 1971-73, chief polit. sect. Dacca, Bangladesh, 1973-74; dir. plans and mgmt. Bur. Pub. Affairs, Washington, 1974-75; spl. asst. to dir., then dep. dir. Pres.' Interagy. Task Force Refugee Resettlement, 1975; spl. asst. to undersec. polit. affairs, 1975-76; dir. office So. African affairs Dept. State, Washington, 1976-77, dep. exec. sec., 1977-79; U.S. amb. to Zambia Lusaka, 1977-82; dep. asst. sec. African affairs Dept. State, Washington, 1982-86; U.S. amb. to Egypt Cairo, 1986-91; U.S. amb. to Philippines Manila, 1991-92; under sec. of state for internat. security affairs Washington, 1992-93; under sec. of def. for policy Dept. Def., 1993-94; U.S. amb. to India, 1994-97; now vice chmn. external affairs Am. Internat. Group Inc., N.Y.C. Bd. dirs. Exxon Oil and Gas; trustee Am. U. of Beirut, Am. U. Cairo; mem. bd. bus. Coun. Internat. Understanding; bd. U.S.-India Bus. Coun.; bd. refugees Internat., United Svcs. Orgn. Recipient meritorious honor award Dept. State, 1973, superior honor award, 1992; recipient Mil. Medal of Honor Govt. Vietnam, 1968, Social Welfare medal of honor, 1968. Mem. Council on Fgn. Relations, Metropolitan Club (Washington), Ivy Club (Princeton, N.J.), Knickerbocker Club (N.Y.). Episcopalian. Office: Am Internat Group Inc 18th Flr 70 Pine St New York NY 10270-0002

WISNESKI, SHARON MARIE, critical care nurse, educator; b. Phila., June 22, 1952; d. Charles Edward and Hilda Marie (Riley) Ashley. AS, Wesley Coll., 1979, BS, 1985; MSN, Widener U., 1991, cert. in nursing edn., 1993, postgrad., 1994—. ACLS. Charge nurse, med.-surg. ICU Milford (Del.) Meml. Hosp.; clin. instr. Wesley Coll., Dover, Del. Tech. and CC, Dover; critical care per-diem nurse Med. Ctr. Del., Newark; instr. nursing Del. State U., Dover, 1991-95, asst. prof., 1995—. Part-time staff nurse med. ICU Med. Ctr. of Del., Newark; apptd. rev. bd. Del. Medicaid Drug Utilization Rev. Bd., 1993—; mem. Del. Bd. Nursing Practice Adv. Com., 1994—. Contbr. chpt. to book. Recipient Young Publisher of Yr. award ABNF, Inc., 1999, Dissertation award ABNF, Inc., 2001; named Faculty Mem. of Yr., Del. Student Nurse Assn., 1999, Young Pub. of Yr., Assn. Black Nursing Faculty, 1999. Mem.: AAUW, AACCN (southeastern Pa. chpt.), ANA (mem. nurse strategic action team 1993—, rev. panelist ANA continuing edn. ind. study 1995—97), Nat. Assn. Black Nurses Inc., Inst. Constituent Mems. in Nursing Practice, Ea. Nurses Rsch. Soc., Del. Nurses Assn. (chmn. nursing practice com. 1992, Del. Nurse of Yr. 1993), Assn. Black Nursing Faculty (Young Pub. of Yr. 1999, Pres. award 2000, Dissertation award), Chi Eta Phi, Sigma Theta Tau. Home: 336 Pine Valley Rd Dover DE 19904-7113 E-mail: pinevalley@earthlink.net.

WISNICKI, JEFFREY LEONARD, plastic surgeon; b. N.Y.C., May 15, 1957; s. Joseph and Lorraine (Justman) Wisnicki; m. Rebecca Lynn O'Shields, Feb. 2, 1997; children: Justin Robert, Brandon Lawrence. BS summa cum laude, Rensselaer Poly. Inst., 1976; MD cum laude with honors, Union U., 1980. Diplomate Am. Bd. Plastic Surgery. Intern in surgery Stanford (Calif.) U. Med. Ctr., 1980-81, resident in gen., plastic and reconstructive surgery, 1981-84, chief resident in plastic and reconstructive surgery, 1985-86; fellow in plastic and reconstructive surgery Dartmouth-Hitchcock Med. Ctr., Hanover, N.H., 1984; active staff Good Samaritan Hosp., West Palm Beach, Fla., 1986—, Wellington Regional Hosp., West Palm Beach, 1986—; chief divsn. plastic surgery John F. Kennedy Meml. Hosp., 1990-93; chmn. dept. surgery Palms West Hosp., 1991-93, chief med. staff, 1994-97, chmn. bd. trustees, 1997—; chief divsn. of plastic surgery Good Samaritan and St. Mary's Hosp., 1997—. Clin. instr. surgery U. Calif., San Francisco, 1985; bd. dirs. Interplast, 1985-86, clin. faculty, 1986—; presenter in field. Contbr. chpts. to books and articles to profl. jours. Fellow ACS; mem. Am. Soc. Plastic & Reconstructive Surgeons, Alpha Omega Alpha. Office: 2047 Palm Beach Lakes Blvd West Palm Beach FL 33409-6501

WISNIEWSKI, HELENA STASIA, telecommunications and information systems company executive, mathematician; b. Englewood, N.J., Dec. 8, 1949; d. Julius George and Katherine Rose (Godlewski) W.; m. Phillip B. Chesson, Jan. 1, 1978; 1 child, Alexis Wisniewski-Chesson. BS in Maths., William Patterson Coll., 1971; MS in Maths., Stevens Inst. Tech., 1973; PhD in Maths., CUNY, 1980. Cert. secondary tchr., N.J. Prof. computer and decision scis. Seton Hall U., South Orange, N.J., 1980-81, dept. chair, 1981-82, dir. div. rsch., 1983-84; prof. maths. Rochester (N.Y.) Inst. Tech., 1982-83; project officer CIA, Washington, 1984-85; founding dir. maths. program Def. Advanced Rsch. Projects Agy., 1985-88; corp. dir.hdqrs. Lockheed Corp., Calabasas, Calif., 1988-92; v.p. VITA, Arlington, Va., 1992-93; dir. advanced program devel. Titan Corp., Reston, 1993-94, v.p. advanced programs, 1995—. Rev. panel Computational Fluid Dynamics Office of the Under Sec. Def., Washington, 1987-88; chair adv. bd. So. Ill. U. Neuro-Engr. Rsch. Ctr., Carbondale, Ill., 1990—; founding bd. dirs. Calif. Coalition for Maths., 1991—. Founding editor: Technology Acceleration, 1991—; editl. bd. Jour. Applied Numerical Maths., 1987-91; co-chair Lockheed Horizons editl. bd., 1991-92; editor SPIE Proceedings, Springer Verlag, vol. 1771; contbr. articles to jour. SPIE, Visiual Info. Processing, Chaoes & Comm., NATO ASI Series-Springer Verlag, Transactions of the Am. Math. Soc., Internat. Symposium Dynamical Systems, Proceedings Rio de Janiero, Springer Verlag. Sci. fair judge Westlake High Sch., Westlake Village, Calif., 1990; organizer career exploration program Calabasas High Sch., 1990; mem. math. coun. L.A. Ednl. Partnership, 1991. Recipient Teaching Excellence award Va. Poly. Inst. and State U., 1976, Spl. Achievement award, CIA 1986, Spl. Recognition award DARPA, 1988, Dedicated Svc. award George Washington U. Adv. Bd., 1995. Mem. AIAA (sr.), N.Y. Acad. Scis., Soc. Indsl. and Applied Maths., Security Affairs Support Assn., Armed Forces Comm. & Electronics Assn., Lockheed Mgmt. Assn. (v.p. 1989-90, pres. 1990-91, adv. bd. George Washington U. 1995—, Recognition of Extraordinary Leadership, Mgmt. & Svc. Honor award 1992), Pi Mu Epsilon, Kappa Delta Pi. Office: Titan Corp 1900 Campus Commons Dr Ste 400 Reston VA 20191-1535

WISNIEWSKI, MARK STEVEN, writer, editor; b. Milw., Sept. 26, 1958; s. Thaddeus Louis and Rita Marie Wisniewski. BA, Creighton U., 1980; JD, Georgetown U., 1984; MA in English, U. Calif., Davis, 1991. Cert. English tchr., Tex. Author: Writing and Revising Your Fiction, (novel) Confessions of a Polish Used Car Salesman, 1997, (chapbook) The Dialogue on the Other Side of the Door, 2000, (short stories) All Weekend with the Lights On, 2001. Recipient Pushcart prize Pushcart Press, 1999. Home: PO Box 202 Lake Peekskill NY 10537

WISNIEWSKI, THOMAS JOSEPH, music educator; b. Chgo., Sept. 17, 1926; s. George Wisniewski and Rose (Jelewski) W.; children: Dieter, Lisa Ann, Ericka (dec.). B.Mus., Am. Conservatory of Music, Chgo., 1948; M.Mus., No. Ill. U., 1964. Instr. string instrument Sch. Dist. 89, Maywood, Ill., 1950-55; orch. dir. Sch. Dist. 44, Lombard, 1955-67; dir. orchs. Glenbard East High Sch., 1959-67; prof. music U. Ill., Urbana, 1967-94, emeritus prof., 1994—, chair music edn. div., 1988-92. Music cons. Webster Internat. Illustrated Dictionary, 1993. Prodr. films Playing the String Bass, 1967, Playing the Cello, 1968; developer (with Rodney Mueller) computer software program Visualized Vibrato, 1995, version 2.0, 1998. Author: Learning Unlimited String Program, Vol. 1, 1975, Vol. 2, 1976; editor Orch. Publs., 1990; music editor Webster International Illustrated Dictionary, 1994. Mem. Am. String Tchrs. Assn. Assn. (Disting. Svc. award Ill. unit 1991, Disting. Svc. award Tenn. unit 1993), Ill. Music Educators Assn. (Pres.'s award 1996), Music Educators Nat. Conf., Ill. String Tchrs. Assn. (editor 1967, 87, pres. 1970), Nat. Jazz Educators Assn. (nat. orch. chmn. 1976), Pi Kappa Lambda, Phi Mu Alpha.

WISNOSKY, THOMAS R. television director; b. Ocean City, N.J., Jan. 25, 1955; s. Peter and Elizabeth Y. Wisnosky; m. Ellen Marion, Mar. 1, 1986; 1 child, Michael. BSEd in Music magna cum laude, U. Bridgeport, 1978. Audio engr. ABC Network, N.Y.C., 1987-88; TV dir. NJN, Trenton, N.J., 1985-94, Sta. WPHL, Phila., 1994-97, Sta. WPVI, Phila., 1996-97, Fox Phila., 1997-2000, Sta. WPIX, N.Y.C., 2000—. Dir.: (morning news/entertainment TV show) WB 11 Morning News, 2000 (N.Y. Emmy as Best Morning Show 2001), Good Day Phladelphia, Fox Morning News, 1997, (evening newscast) WB16 News At Ten, 1996, (arts mag. show) State of the Arts, 1994 (Emmy award for outstanding prodn. design 1994); prodr.: (entertainment mag. show) Meadowlands Marquee, 1993, (pub. svc. announcement) Atlantic Electric, 1992 (Best Comml. award 1992). Borough councilman Morrisville (Pa.) Borough, 2000—01, mayor, 2002—. Recipient Regional Emmy awards NATAS. Mem. Dirs. Guild Am. Republican. Methodist. Avocations: home restoration, boating, skiing, music, running. Office: WPIX 220 E 42d St New York NY 10017 E-mail: trwiz@aol.com.

WISOFF, HUGH SOLOMON, neurosurgeon; b. Bklyn., July 12, 1927; s. Percy and Esther (Seewald) W.; m. Irene Lutzky, Dec. 24, 1951; children: Jeffrey, Marshall, Andrew, Janice. BS, Union Coll., 1949; MD, Albany Med. Coll., 1953. Diplomate Am. Bd. Neurol. Surgery. Attending neurosurgeon Montefiore Med. Ctr., Bronx, N.Y., 1960—; acting chmn. dept. neurol. surgery Montefiore and Albert Einstein Coll. Medicine, 1981-86. Contbr. numerous articles to profl. jours., chpts. to books. Fellow ACS; mem. Am. Assn. Neurol. Surgeons, Congress Neurol. Surgeons. Jewish. Avocations: tennis, gardening. E-mail: artandbrain@aol.com.

WISS, MARCIA A. lawyer; b. Columbus, Ohio, May 15, 1947; d. John William and Margaret Ann (Cook) W.; m. Donald Gordon MacDonald, Nov. 18, 1921; children: Christopher C. Wiss, Joan Merle. BS in Fgn. Svc., Georgetown U., 1969, JD, 1972. Bar: D.C. 1972. Econ. analyst World Bank, Washington, 1969; atty. U.S. Dept. Justice, 1972-73; atty. office gen. counsel Overseas Pvt. Investment Corp., 1973-78; gen counsel-designate Inst. for Sci. and Tech. Cooperation, 1979; ptnr. Kaplan Russin & Vecchi, 1987-92, Whitman & Ransom, 1992-93, Whitman, Breed, Abbott & Morgan, Washington, 1993-96, Wilmer, Cutler & Pickering, Washington, 1996-2000, Hogan & Hartson, Washington, 2000—. Gen. counsel Washington chpt., Soc. Internat. Devel., 1980-2001; gen. counsel, Assn. for Women in Devel., 1982—; bd. advisers, Procedural Aspects of Internat. Law Inst., 1985—; gen. counsel internat. policy coun. agr., adj. prof. of law Georgetown U. Law Ctr., 1984—, Johns Hopkins Sch. of Advanced Internat. Studies, 2001—. Editor Georgetown Law Ctr. Jour. Law and Policy in Internat. Bus., 1971-72. Chairperson Holy Trinity Parish Coun., Washington, 1976; mem. bd. advisers Trees for Life, Wichita, Kans., 1984—. Mem. Am. Fedn. Govt. Employees (chmn. 1975-76), D.C. Bar (steering com. divsn. 12, 1985-88, co-chmn. fin. and banking com. 1985), Am. Soc. Internat. Law (v.p. 1991-94, coun. 1987-90), Washington Fgn. Law Soc. (pres. 1983-84). Roman Catholic. Office: Hogan & Hartson 555 13th St NW Washington DC 20004

WISSE, BILLY, writer; b. Montreal, Que., Can., Dec. 19, 1962; arrived in U.S., 1989; s. Leonard H. and Ruth (Roskies) W. BA, McGill U., Montreal, 1984, MA, 1994. Assoc. mgr. Bibliophile Bookstore, Montreal, 1985-88; proofreader Reader's Digest, 1985-88; editor BB Comm., Santa Monica, Calif., 1989; proofreader The Workbook, L.A., 1989-90; rschr. Jeopardy!, 1990-96, writer Culver City, Calif., 1996—. Author: Defrosting, 1996, Poems from the Archive of the Pearl Roth Institute, 1999; co-prodr. Rev. Kirk Prodns., 1990-91; grip Gen. Frolic Prodns., 1990-92. Recipient Emmy award Acad. TV Arts and Scis., 1997. Mem. Writers Guild Am. West, Tea Club. Jewish. Office: Jeopardy! 10202 Washington Blvd Culver City CA 90232-3119 E-mail: billywisse@aol.com.

WISSEMANN-WIDRIG, NANCY, artist; b. Jamestown, N.Y., Mar. 19, 1929; d. Ross Frank and Gertrude (Peck) Widrig; m. John Joseph Wissemann, 1953; children: Melanie, Christopher, Timothy. BFA, Syracuse U., 1951; MFA, Ohio U., 1952. Art tchr. Oysterponds Sch., Orient, N.Y., 1970-85; founding mem. adv. bd. East End Arts and Humanities Coun., Riverhead, N.Y., 1970-80; demonstrating artist Arts in Southold Town, 1997. One-woman shows include Tibor de Nagy Gallery, N.Y.C., 1974-87, Maine Coast Artists, Rockport, 1974-98, Southampton (N.Y.) Coll., 1974, Tatistcheff Gallery, N.Y.C., 1987-2000, Caldbeck Gallery, Rockland, Maine, 1987—, LeVa Tout Gallery, Waldoboro, Maine, 1994, Gleason Gallery, Boothbay Harbor, Maine, 1996—; exhibited in group shows at Lizan-Tops Gallery, Easthampton, N.Y., 1995-97, Heckscher Mus., Huntington, N.Y., 1996, C.W. Post-L.I. U., Brookville, N.Y., 1997; represented in permanent collections Canton (Ohio) Art Inst., U. Kans. Mus. Art, MONY Corp. N.Y., Port Authority of N.Y., U. Tulsa, Farnsworth Mus. Art, Rockland, others. Recipient Outstanding Realist award Western N.Y. Artists, 1964, Purchase award Childe Hassam Fund Am. Acad. Arts and Letters, 1969. Avocation: travel. Home: PO Box 524 Southold NY 11971-0624 also: 87 Bird Point Rd Cushing ME 04563 E-mail: njwiss@aol.com.

WISSLER, ROBERT WILLIAM, physician, cardiovascular pathologist, educator; b. Richmond, Ind., Mar. 1, 1917; s. William Oscar and Muriel (Thomas) W.; m. Elizabeth Anne Polk, Jan. 9, 1940; children: Barbara Anne Wissler-Mayers, Mary Linda Wissler Graham, David William, John Polk. AB, Earlham Coll., Richmond, 1939, DSc (hon.), 1959; MS, U. Chgo., 1943, PhD, 1946, MD with honors, 1948; MD (hon.), Heidelberg (Germany) U., 1973, U. Siena, Italy, 1982; DSc (hon.), UMDNJ, Newark, 1982, Ohio State U., 1990. From instr. to assoc. prof. U. Chgo., 1943-57, prof. McLean Inst., 1953-80, prof. dept. pathology, 1957-82, prof. in the Coll., 1965-80, chmn. dept. pathology, 1957-72, Donald N. Pritzker prof. pathology, 1972-87, Disting. Svc. prof. pathology, 1977-87, emeritus prof., 1987—. Vis. scientist Theodor Kocher Inst., U. Berne, Switzerland, 1963, Baker Inst. for Med. Rsch., Melbourne, Australia, 1985; vis. prof. pathology Nihon U. Sch. Medicine, Tokyo, 1974; mem. faculty Given Inst. Pathology, Aspen, Colo., 1964, 71-73, 78-81; dir. U. Chgo. Spl. Ctr. Rsch. Atherosclerosis, 1972-82., program dir. Pathobiol. Determinates Atherosclerosis Youth, 1985-96. Editor, co-editor monographs; contbr. chpts. to books, more than 300 articles to profl. jours. Scout leader Boy Scouts Am., Chgo., 1951-56, 61-67; trustee First Unitarian Ch., Chgo., 1960-64, chmn. bd., 1962-64; trustee Earlham Coll., 1968-71, 75-85, chmn. edn. com., 1977-85; mem. Hyde Park-Kenwood Cmty. Conf., Chgo., 1960—. Recipient award of merit Am. Heart Assn., Dallas, 1971, Disting. Achievement award Modern Medicine, 1977, Joseph B. Goldberger award AMA, 1979, Coeur d'Or award Chgo. Heart Assn., 1982, Gold Headed Cane award, Am. Assn. Pathologists, 1983, U. Chgo. Gold Key award, 1984, Career Achievement award Internat. Atherosclerosis So., 1994, Rising Sun award Emperor of Japan, 1995. Mem. Am. Soc. Exptl. Pathology (pres. 1961-62), Am. Heart Assn. (chmn. coun. on arteriosclerosis 1965-66), Assn. Pathology Chairmen (pres. 1967-68), Coll. Am. Pathologists (chmn. edn. com. 1985-95), Univ. Assocs. for Rsch. and Edn. in Pathology (bd. dirs., pres. 1969-71), Am. Assn. Pathologists and Bacteriologists, 1952-90 (pres. 1968), others. Avocations: gardening, photography, playing clarinet. Home: 5550 S South Shore Dr Apt 515 Chicago IL 60637-5053 Office: U Chgo Med Ctr MC 3083 5841 S Maryland Ave Chicago IL 60637-1463

WISSLER-THOMAS, CARRIE, professional society administrator, artist; b. Ephrata, Pa., Nov. 2, 1946; d. Robert Uibel and Grace Urbane (Nicholas) Wissler; m. James Richard Gamber, June 12, 1968 (div. 1972); m. Scott Kerry Thomas, Mar. 3, 1972; 1 child, Dylan Crayton Llewellyn. BA, Hood Coll., 1968; MS, Temple U., 1986. Copywriter WGSA Radio, Ephrata, Pa., 1970-71, William Assocs., Harrisburg, 1977; correspondent Art Matters of Phila., 1984-86; art columnist Pennsylvania Beacon, 1983-85; writer Strictly Business, 1985-86; painting instr. Art Assn. of Harrisburg, 1980-86; freelance artist Harrisburg, 1968—; exec. dir., pres. Art Assn. of Harrisburg, 1986—. Mem. exhbn. panel Harrisburg City Govt. Ctr., 1983-89; mem. art adv. panel Harrisburg Area C.C., 1985—; mem. gallery com. Univ. Ctr. at Harrisburg, 1988—; chmn. Easter Seals Art Show by Disabled Artists, Harrisburg, 1983-86; trustee Pa. Sch. Art and Design, 1989—; mem. Harrisburg Multi-Cultural Coalition, 1992-94; chmn. Harrisburg Gallery Walk, 1989—; bd. dirs. Historic Harrisburg Assn., Better Bus. Bur.; pres. Allied Arts Affiliates Coun., 1993-95; mem. Dauphin Co. commn. on status of women, 2000-01. Prin. work includes Brandywine Babies oil painting, 1982 (Grumbacher Gold Medallion 1982); over 30 solo exhibitions. Mem. Hist. Soc. Cocalico Valley, Ephrata, 1982—, Dauphin County Hist. Soc., Harrisburg, 1986—; minority inspector Paxtang Election Bd., Harrisburg, 1977-79; mem. ACLU, Pa., 1988-91; bd. dirs. Hist. Harrisburg Assn., 1992-98. Recipient Women Who Work award Communications and the Arts Pomeroy's, 1985, Disting. Svc. to Arts award Harrisburg Community Theatre, 1991. Mem. Am. Coun. on Arts, Art Assn. Harrisburg (pres. 1980-84), Rotary. Democrat. Anglican. Avocations: reading, biographies, visiting museums/galleries, gardening. Home: 2721 N 2nd St Harrisburg PA 17110-1205 Office: Art Assn of Harrisburg 21 N Front St Harrisburg PA 17101-1606

WISSMANN, CAROL RENEÉ, sales executive; b. Berkeley, Calif., July 9, 1946; d. Conrad Clayton and Carol Elizabeth (Ward) W. BA, Whittier Coll., 1968; Montessori Diploma, Coll. Notre Dame, Belmont, 1970. Dist. mgr. U.S. C. of C., Washington; divsn. mgr. Classified Yellow Pages Inc., Cookeville, Tenn., 1986; pres. The BelleMann Corp., Gig Harbor, Wash., 1988—. Cons., writer, spkr. Republican. Avocations: horseback riding, ballroom dancing. Home and Office: PMB 305 5114-E Point Fosdick Dr NW Gig Harbor WA 98335-1733 E-mail: BelleMann@hotmail.com.

WISWALL, DOROTHY ROLLER, humanities educator; b. Alpirsbach, Germany, Aug. 6, 1947; d. Albert Roller; m. Thomas S. Wiswall, June 5, 1976; children: James, Karen. AB, Cornell Univ., Ithaca, NY, 1971; AM, Univ. Mich., Ann Arbor, MI, 1972, PhD, 1979. Instr. Sch. for Internat. Tng., Brattleboro, Vt., 1971—71; tchg. fellow Univ. Mich., Ann Arbor, 1971—75; adj. prof. Niagara Univ., Niagara University, 1981—91, Canisius Coll., Buffalo, 1991—, Buffalo State Coll., Buffalo, 2001—. Workshop presenter BOCES, Buffalo, 1998—99; vice pres. Am. Assn. of Teachers of German, Buffalo, 1998—2002. Author: (book) A Comparison of Selected Poetic and Scientific Works of Albrecht von Haller. Coun. mem. St. Timothy Luth. Ch., Grand Island, NY, 1999; bd. pres. STLCC Child Care Ctr., 1995—99. Recipient Nat. Merit Scholar, 1966, Phi Sigma Lota, Fgn. Lang. Honor Soc., 1981; grantee Travel Stipend, Univ. Bern, Switzerland, 1977. Mem.: Am. Assn. of Teachers of German (vice pres. 1998—2002). Independent. Lutheran. Avocations: swimming, playing violin, stamp collecting, sewing.

WISWALL, FRANK LAWRENCE, JR. lawyer, educator; b. Albany, N.Y., Sept. 21, 1939; s. Frank Lawrence and Clara Elizabeth (Chapman) W.; m. Elizabeth Curtiss Nelson, Aug. 9, 1975; children by previous marriage: Anne W. Kowalski, Frank Lawrence III. BA, Colby Coll., 1962; JD, Cornell U., 1965; PhD in Law, Cambridge U., 1967. Bar: Maine 1965, N.Y. 1968, U.S. Supreme Ct. 1968, D.C. 1975; lic. master near coastal steam and motor vessels, 1960—. Assoc. Burlingham, Underwood, Barron, Wright & White, N.Y.C., 1967-73; maritime legal adviser Rep. of Liberia, 1968-88; v.p. Com. Maritime Internat., 1997—; prof. (ad honorem) internat. maritime law Internat. Maritime Law Inst., 1999. Mem. legal com. Internat. Maritime Orgn., London, 1972-74, vice chmn. 1974-79, chmn., 1980-84; tutorial supr. internat. law Clare Coll., Cambridge, Eng., 1966-67; vis. lectr. Cornell Law Sch., 1969-76, 82; lectr. U. Va. Law Sch. and Ctr. for Oceans Law and Policy, 1978-82; prof. law Cornell U., 1984; Johnsen prof. maritime law Tulane U., 1985; vis. prof. law World Maritime U., Malmo, Sweden, 1986—; prof. Internat. Maritime Law Inst., Malta, 1991—, mem. governing bd., 1992—; prof. admiralty law Maine Maritime Acad., 1993-94; del. Internat. Conf. Marine Pollution, London, 1973; del., chmn. drafting com. Internat. Conf. Carriage of Passengers and Luggage by Sea, Athens, 1974; del. Internat. Conf. on Safety of Life at Sea, London, 1974, 3d UN Conf. on Law of Sea, Caracas, Venezuela, 1974, 3d UN Conf. on Law of Sea (all subsequent sessions); del., chmn. com. final clauses Internat. Conf. on Limitation of Liability for Maritime Claims, London, 1976; del. UN Conf. Carriage of Goods by Sea, Hamburg, 1978, XIII Diplomatic Conf. on Maritime Law, Brussels, 1979; chmn. com. of the whole Internat. Conf. Carriage of Hazardous Substances by Sea, 1984; del. internat. conf. on Maritime Terrorism, Rome, 1988; counsel various marine casualty bds. of investigation, 1970-90, harbormaster, Port of Castine, 1960-62; chmn. Joint Internat. Working Group on Acts of Piracy and Maritime Violence, 1998-2001. Author: The Development of Admiralty Jurisdiction and Practice Since 1800, 1970; editor-in-chief Benedict on Admiralty, Vols. 6, 6A-6F (Internat. Maritime Law), 1992—; contbr. articles to profl. jours. Ofcl. prin. Diocese of Mid-Atlantic States, 1988—, Diocese of the U.K., 1997—, Anglican Cath. Ch.; chancellor Missionary Diocese of N.E., 1993—, Diocese Australia, 1998—; spkr. assembly laity Anglican Cath. Ch., 1995—. Recipient Yorke prize U. Cambridge, 1968-69 Fellow Royal Hist. Soc.; mem. Nat. Lawyers Assn., Comité Maritime Internat. (exec. councillor 1989-96, v.p. 1997—), Maritime Law Assn. U.S. (chmn. com. on intergovtl. orgns. 1983-87, chmn. com. on CMI 1987-95), Ecclesiastical Law Soc., Selden Soc., Am. Soc. Legal History, U.K. Assn. Average Adjusters, U.S.

Assn. Average Adjusters, Maine Bar Assn., U.S. Navy League (pres. Penobscot coun. 1997), Oxford and Cambridge Club (London), Century Assn., Alpha Delta Phi, Phi Delta Phi. Office: PO Box 201 Castine ME 04421-0201

WISZ, JOSEPH A., JR. management consultant; b. Hamtramck, Mich., Apr. 2, 1928; s. Joseph John and Marcella Catherine (Miazga-Misko) W.; m. Josephine Diane Nowicki, May 5, 1951; children: Paula Ann, Claudia Mary, Christopher Joseph, William A. BA, BS, Lawrence Tech. U., 1950; MBA, U. Detroit, 1960; postgrad., U. Mich., 1998—. V.p., owner med. evaluation clinic; adminstr. nursing home Wisz & Assocs. Ltd., Warren, Mich. Aeronautical instr., adj. prof. Embry-Riddle U., Daytona, Fla.; mgmt. instr. Macomb C.C., Warren, Mich. Contbr. articles to profl. jours. With U.S. Army, 1951-53, Korea. Mem. numerous profl. orgns. Roman Catholic. Office: PO Box 1064 Warren MI 48090-1064

WIT, DAVID EDMUND, software company executive; b. N.Y.C., Feb. 25, 1962; s. Harold Maurice W. and Joan Leta (Rosenthal) Sovern; m. Kathleen Mary Bentley, Sept. 9, 1989. BA summa cum laude, Hamilton Coll., 1985. Rsch. assoc. E.M. Warburg Pincus and Co., N.Y.C., 1985-86; CEO Logicat Inc. Mem. N.Y. Software Industry Assn., Phi Beta Kappa. Avocation: exercise. Home: 3 Stratford Rd Larchmont NY 10538-1341 Office: Logicat Inc 201 E 16th St New York NY 10003-3706

WIT, HAROLD MAURICE, investment banker, lawyer, investor; b. Boston, Sept. 6, 1928; s. Maurice and Martha (Bassist) W.; children from previous marriage: David Edmund, Hannah Edna; 1 stepchild, Simon; m. Susan King, Sept. 16, 1999. AB magna cum laude, Harvard, 1949; JD (editor law jour.), Yale, 1954. Bar: N.Y. 1954. Assoc. Cravath, Swaine & Moore, N.Y.C., 1954-58; asst. sec. One William St. Fund, Inc., 1958-59, v.p., sec., 1959-60; assoc. Allen & Co., 1960-70; assoc Allen & Co., Inc., 1965—, v.p., 1965-70, exec. v.p., 1970-98, mng. dir., mem. exec. com. Mgr. Allen Investments II LLC. Former trustee South Folk-Shelter Island chpt. Nature Conservancy, 1993-2000; co-founder Group for South Fork; pres. South Fork Watchdogs, Inc.; mem. Panel on Future of Govt. in N.Y., 1979-80; mem. vis. com. Harvard U. Div. Sch., 1990-97. With Mass. N.G., 1947-50; lt. (j.g.) USNR, 1951-53, Korea. Mem. VFW, Am. Legion, Korean War Vets. Assn., University Club (N.Y.C.), Harvard Club (N.Y.C.), Phi Beta Kappa, Phi Delta Phi. Home: 150 E 69th St New York NY 10021-5704 also: 57 Cross Hwy PO Box 348 East Hampton NY 11937-0348 Office: Allen & Co Inc 711 5th Ave New York NY 10022-3111

WITAJEWSKI, ROBERT M. diplomat; b. Saginaw, Mich., Nov. 17, 1946; s. Marvin H. and Angeline J. (Smokoska) W. AB, U. Mich., 1968; MA, U. Calif., Berkeley, 1969; MPP, Princeton U., 1998. Case officer Social Security Adminstrn., Washington, 1979-80; vice-consul, polit. officer U.S. Embassy, Caracas, 1981-83, polit. officer Guatemala, 1983-85; watch officer, exec. secretariat ops. ctr. Dept. of State, Washington, 1986-89, sr. country affairs officer for Nicaragua, 1987-89; prin. officer, U.S. consul Hermosillo, Mex., 1989-92; head polit.-econ. affairs for U.S. interests sect. Embassy of Switzerland, Havana, 1994-97, dep. dir. Cuban affairs, 1998-2000; acting dir. for Argentina, Brazil, Chile, Paraguay and Uruguay, 2000—02; mem. Sr. Fgn. Svc., 2001—; counselor for polit. affairs U.S. Embassy, Brasilia, Brazil, 2002—. Contbr. articles to profl. jours., book. Spl. Career fellow Ford Found., 1969-72; recipient Superior Honor award Dept. of State, 1989, 94, 99, Spl. Achievement award Sonora-Ariz. Commn., 1992. Mem. Am. Fgn. Svc. Assn. Avocations: photography, running, diving. Office: Office Brazilian and Southern Cone Affairs Dept State Washington DC 20520-0001 E-mail: witajewskirm@state.gov.

WITANOWSKI, MICHAEL FRANK, surgeon; b. Warsaw, Poland, July 24, 1920; s. Matthew and Anna (Umbras) W.; m. Betty, Sept. 8, 1963. BS magna cum laude, Loyola U., 1940; MD cum laude, U. Ill. Med. Sch., 1944. Cert. Am. Bd. Surgery, 1953. Intern Ill. Rsch. Edn. Hosps., Chgo., 1944-45; resident in surgery Hines VA Hosp., 1948-51; surgeon pvt. practice. Mem. AMA, Internat. Coll. Surgeons, Am. Coll. Angiology. Home: 1104 W Downer Pl Aurora IL 60506-4822

WITCHER, DANIEL DOUGHERTY, retired pharmaceutical company executive; b. Atlanta, May 17, 1924; s. Julius Gordon and Myrtice Eleanor (Daniel) W.; divorced; children: Beth S., Daniel Dougherty Jr., J. Wright, Benjamin G.; m. Betty Lou Middaugh, Oct. 30, 1982. Student, Mercer U., 1946-47, Am. Grad. Sch. Internat. Mgmt., 1949-50. Regional dir. Sterling Drug Co., Rio de Janeiro and Sao Paulo, Brazil, 1951-56; gen. mgr. Mead Johnson & Co., Sao Paulo, 1956-60; area mgr. Upjohn Internat., Inc., 1960-64, v.p. Kalamazoo, 1964-70, group v.p., 1970-73; pres., gen. mgr. Upjohn Internat., 1973-86; v.p. Upjohn Co., 1973-86, sr. v.p., 1986-89, asst. to pres., 1988-89; chmn. Upjohn Healthcare Svcs., 1982-87; ret., 1989. Bd. dirs. Upjohn Co.; trustee Am. Grad. Sch. Internat. Mgmt., 1981—. With USNR, 1943-46. Mem. Pharm. Mfrs. Assn. (chmn. internat. sect. 1981-82, 85-86), Am. Grad. Sch. Internat. Mgmt. Alumni Assn. (pres. 1989-91). Republican. Episcopalian. Avocations: tennis, golf.

WITCHER, GARY ROYAL, minister, educator; b. Clinton, Okla., July 4, 1950; s. Alton Gale and Frances Loraine (Royal) W.; m. Victoria Amy Waddington, June 6, 1970; children: Jessica, Toni, Monica. BA in Art, Southwestern Okla. State U., 1973, BA in Art Edn., 1975, MEd in Art, 1978. Minister, 1979. Tchr. Window Rock Sch. Dist., Ft. Defiance, Ariz., 1973-76, Western Heights (Okla.) Sch. Dist., Oklahoma City, 1976-77, Mustang (Okla.) Sch. Dist., 1977-79; minister Ch. of Christ, Cervignano, Italy, 1979-86, Watertown, S.D., 1986—; instr. Mount Marty Coll., 1987—. Part-time tchr. Watertown Sch. Dist., 1987—; bd. dirs. East River Bible Camp, 1988-97. Recipient 1st Place Slide Program Competition prize Am. Fedn. Mineralogical Socs., 1993, 95. Mem. Coteau des Plains Gem and Mineral Soc. (pres. 1991-92, 95). Republican. Avocations: photography, car restoration, collecting rocks, coins and stamps. Home: PO Box 1622 1105 4th St NE Watertown SD 57201-1202 Office: Ch of Christ 1103 4th St NE Watertown SD 57201-1202

WITCHER, RANDOLPH SCOTT, minister; b. Chatham, Va., Nov. 3, 1950; s. Scott Witcher, Pearl Shelton; m. Yvette Tarpley Witcher, Dec. 23, 1983 (div. July 1993); 1 child Corinthian Scott. Cert. FCM, DC Bible Inst., 2000. Sr. pastor-bishop Tried Stone Ch., Sterling, Va., 1992—. Test technician E.I.T., Sterling, Va., 1996—2001; inspector quality control Star Technologies, Sterling, 1984—96; lab. technician Dan River Milk, Inc., Danville, Va., 1972—84. Author: Scandal on Goldmine Road, 2002; composer (song collection): The Prayer The Praise The Presence, 2001. Pres. R.S. Witcher Gospel Music Workshop, Sterling, 1982—; moderator Leadership Conf., 2000—. Democrat. Avocations: bowling, fishing, travel, coin collecting. Home: 43211 Center St Fairfax VA 20152 Office: Tried Stone Church 45529 W Church Rd Ste 110 Sterling VA 20164

WITCHER, ROBERT CAMPBELL, bishop; b. New Orleans, Oct. 5, 1926; s. Charles Swanson and Lily Sebastian (Campbell) W.; m. Elisabeth Alice Cole, June 4, 1957; 2 children. BA, Tulane U., 1949; MDiv, Seabury-Western Theol. Sem., 1952, DD, 1974; MA, La. State U., 1960, PhD, 1968; DCL (hon.), Nashotah House, 1989. Ordained priest Episc. Ch., 1953; consecrated bishop, 1975. Priest-in-charge St. Andrew Ch., Linton, La. and St. Patrick Ch., Zachary, La., 1953-56, St. Augustine Ch., Baton Rouge, 1953-54, rector, 1954-61; canon pastor Christ Ch. Cathedral, New Orleans, 1961-62; rector St. James Ch., Baton Rouge, 1962-75; coadjutor bishop L.I., 1975-77; bishop, 1977-91; prof. ch. history Mercer Sch. Theology, 1975-91; interim bishop of Armed Forces, 1989-90; bishop in residence Baton Rouge, New Orleans, 1991-92. Pres. Mercer Scholarship Fund; trustee Ch. Pension Fund, 1991-92; pres. bd. trustees estate belonging to Diocese of L.I., 1975-91; pres. Anglican Soc. N.Am., 1980-83; chmn. pastoral com. House of Bishops, 1980-90, Com. to Revise Title III, 1980-90; chmn. Com. on Developing Guidelines for Theol. Edn.; cons. Episc. Health Fund L.I.; historiographer Diocese of La. Author: The Episcopal Church in Louisiana, 1801-1861. Trustee U. of South, 1963-69, Seabury-Western Theol. Sem., 1963-82, Gen. Theol. Sem., 1979-88, Ch. Pension Fund, 1985-91, Bch. Reins. Corp., Killough Charitable Trust, Gen. Health Med. Ctr., Gen. Health Found.; pres. Episc. Health Svcs.; bd. dirs. Nat. Coun. Alcoholism, L.I. Coun. Alcoholism, Alcohol and Drug Abuse Coun., Baton Rouge, St. Mary's Hosp. for Children, Baton Rouge Green, La. Urban Forestry Coun., United Way, Gen. Health Sys., GHS Found.; bd. dirs., trustee St. James Place; active NCCJ (Baton Rouge chpt.). Capt. USNR, ret. Mem. N.Y. State Coun. Chs., L.I. Coun. Chs. (com. social justice), Am. Legion, Mil. Order of World Wars, Naval Res. Assn., Res. Officers Assn. Address: 1934 Steele Blvd Baton Rouge LA 70808-1673

WITCOFF, SHELDON WILLIAM, lawyer; b. Washington, July 10, 1925; s. Joseph and Zina (Ceppos) W.; m. Margot Gail Hoffner, Sept. 6, 1953; children: Lauren Jill, David Lawrence, Lisa Ann, Julie Beth. BS in Elec. Engring, U. Md., 1949; JD, George Washington U., 1953. Bar: D.C. 1953, N.Y. 1955, Ill. 1956. Patent examiner Patent Office, Dept. Commerce, 1949-53; patent lawyer Bell Telephone Labs., Murray Hill, N.J., 1953-55; ptnr. Bair, Freeman & Molinare, Chgo., 1955-69, Allegretti, Newitt, Witcoff & McAndrews, Chgo., 1970-88, Allegretti & Witcoff, LTD, Chgo., 1988-95, Banner & Witcoff Ltd., Chgo., 1995—. V.p. Art Splty. Co., Chgo., 1967—; v.p. Caspian Fur Trading Co., N.Y.C.; dir. Child Abuse Unit for Studies, Edn. and Svcs., Chgo. Fire and police commr., Skokie, Ill., 1960-63. Served with USNR, 1943-46. Mem. Am. Bar Assn., Intellectual Property Assn. of Chgo., Order of Coif, Tau Epsilon Phi, Phi Delta Phi., B'nai B'rith. Home: 2180 Kipling Ln Highland Park IL 60035- Office: 10 S Wacker Dr Chicago IL 60606-7407 E-mail: witcoff@bannerwitcoff.com.

WITCOVER, JULES JOSEPH, newspaper columnist, author; b. Union City, N.J., July 16, 1927; s. Samuel and Sarah (Carpenter) W.; m. Marian Laverty, June 14, 1952 (div. Oct. 1990); children: Paul, Amy, Julie, Peter; m. Marion Elizabeth Rodgers, June 21, 1997. AB, Columbia Coll., 1949; MS, Columbia Grad Sch. Journalism, 1951. Reporter Hackensack (N.J.) Star-Telegram, 1949-50, Providence Jour., 1951-52, Newark Star-Ledger, 1953, Washington br. Newhouse Newspapers, 1954-69, L.A. Times, Washington, 1970-72, Washington Post, 1973-76; columnist Washington Star, 1977—81, Balt. Sun, Washington, 1981—, Tribune Media Svcs., 1977—. Author: 85 Days: The Last Campaign of Robert Kennedy, 1969, The Resurrection of Richard Nixon, 1970, White Knight: The Rise of Spiro Agnew, 1972, (with Richard M. Cohen) A Heartbeat Away: The Investigation and Resignation of Vice President Spiro T. Agnew, 1974, Marathon: The Pursuit of the Presidency, 1972-76, 1977, (novel) The Main Chance, 1978, (with Jack W. Germond) Blue Smoke and Mirrors: How Reagan Won and Why Carter Lost the Election of 1980, 1981, (with Germond) Wake Us When It's Over: Presidential Politics of 1984, 1985, (with Germond) Whose Broad Stripes and Bright Stars?: The Trivial Pursuit of the Presidency 1988, 1989, Sabotage at Black Tom: Imperial Germany's Secret War in America, 1914-1917, 1989, Crapshoot: Rolling the Dice on the Vice Presidency, 1992, (with Germond) Mad as Hell: Revolt at the Ballot Box 1992, 1993, The Year the Dream Died: Revisiting 1968 in America, 1997, No Way to Pick a President: How Money and Hired Guns Haved Debased American Elections, 1999. With USN, 1945-46. Recipient Washington Corr. award Sigma Delta Chi, 1963, Alumni award Columbia Grad. Sch. Journalism, 1972; Reid Found. fellow, Europe, 1958. Roman Catholic. Home: 3042 Q St NW Washington DC 20007-3080 Office: Washington Bur Balt Sun 1627 K St NW Washington DC 20006-1702

WITECK, JOHN JOSEPH, labor union representative, educator; b. Washington, Feb. 18, 1945; s. John Matthew and Evelyn Ruth Forester (Langvardt) Witeck; m. Lucille Kimiyo Hashizume, Sept. 6, 1969; children: Matthew Iwakazu Berrigan, Lia Tamberlyn Harumi. BA Govt./Fgn. Affairs with high honors, U. Va., 1967; MA in Polit. Sci., U. Hawaii, 1995, P.D. (prof. diploma) in Secondary Edn., Social Stud., 1996. Cert. secondary edn. Coord. Youth Action, Inc., Honolulu, 1969-72, Hawaii People's Fund, Honolulu, 1971-90; asst. dir. Oahu divsn. United Pub. Workers AFSCME, AFL-CIO, 1972-98; student tchr. Hawaii Dept. Edn., 1996-98; nat. coord. Philippine Workers Support Com., 1983—. Editor Hawaii AFL-CIO, Honolulu, 1975-77, personnel mgmt. specialist, City and Cty. of Honolulu, Dept. of Environ. Svcs., 1998-99, tng. specialist, 1999—; tchr. Aiea H.S., 1998-99. Editor: (bull.) Philippine Labor Alert, 1984-98, (newsletter) Modern Times, 1977-83, Bus. Agent. Neighborhood bd. rep. Liliha-Kapalama Bd., Honolulu, 1990, 1995—96, 1998—; trustee Hawaii State Health Fund, 1994—98, 1998—99; bd. govs. People's Fund, 2001; bd. dirs. Vol. Legal Svcs. Hawaii, Honolulu, 1995—2001. Echols scholar U. Va., 1963-67, Nat. Merit scholar U. Va., 1963-64; recipient Jose W. Diokno Solidatarity award Alliance Philippine Concerns, 1991. Mem. Hawaii People's Fund (founder, sec. 1994), Honolulu Media Council (bd. dirs. 1995), Hawaii State Tchrs. Assn., 1998-99, Hawaii Govt. Employees Assn. (affiliate of Am. Fedn. State, County and Mcpl. Employees), Crisis Prevention Inst. (cert. trainer), Phi Beta Kappa. Labor Party. Avocations: stamp collecting, photography, saxophone, dancing, fund raising. Home: 2252 Puna St Honolulu HI 96817-1539 Office: Philippine Workers Support Com 2252 Puna St Honolulu HI 96817-1539 E-mail: jwiteck@co.honolulu.hi.us.

WITEK, JAMES EUGENE, retired public relations executive; b. LaPorte, Ind., Sept. 14, 1932; s. Stanley and Victoria (Peret) W.; m. Mary Carolyn Hood, June 18, 1955; children: James Jay, Janet Marie, Jeffrey Patrick, Jean Theresa. AB, Ind. U., 1954; MA, U. Mo., 1970. Joined U.S. Army, 1954, commd. 2d lt., 1954, advanced through grades to lt. col., 1968; editor, pub. Infantry Mag., Fort Benning, Ga., 1968-70; advisor to Vietnamese Mil. Region IV Ranger Comdr., 1970-71; plans officer CINCPAC, Hawaii, 1971-75; exec. editor Soldiers, Washington, 1975-77, editor in chief, 1977-79; dir. public affairs Nat. Com. for Employer Support Guard and Res., Arlington, Va., 1979-82, ret., 1982; dep. dir. pub. relations Am. Legion, Washington, 1982-86; mgr. pub. rels. Dowty Aerospace, Sterling, Va., 1986-99; ret. Decorated Legion of Merit, Bronze Star, Air Medal, Purple Heart, Vietnamese Cross of Gallantry with Silver Star. Mem. Am. Legion, Ret. Officers Assn., Disabled Am. Vets., Phi Beta Kappa, Tau Kappa Alpha, Pi Kappa Phi. Roman Catholic. Home: 3240 Atlanta St Fairfax VA 22030-2128

WITHERELL, NANCY LOUISE, education educator; b. Bridgewater, Mass., Aug. 1, 1952; d. Anthony and Bertha Eunice (Smith) Kopcych; m. Peter Walker Witherell, Aug. 27, 1973; children: Paul William, Jonathan Lewis, Thomas Clayton. BA in Sociology, U. Mass., Dartmouth, 1974; EdM in Elem. Sch. Adminstrn., U. Md., 1979; EdD in Lang. Arts and Literacy, U. Mass., Lowell, 1993. Cert. tchr., Mass. Elem. tchr. Prince Georges County Pub. Sch., Hyattsville, Md., 1974-80, Norton (Mass.) Pub. Schs., 1980-81; tchrs. asst. U. Mass., Lowell, summer 1992; vis. lectr. Bridgewater (Mass.) State Coll., 1985-93, assoc. prof., 1993—, sec. media literacy task force, 1995—. Cons., 1993—. Great Books coord., bd. dirs. Raynham (Mass.) Vol. Edn., 1986—; chairperson, bd. edn. Pilgrim Congl. Ch., Taunton, Mass., 1987—. Mem. ASCD, Mass. Reading Assn. (Sylvia D. Brown scholarship 1993, com. parent-child comm. com. 1993-94, tech. com. 1996—), Southeastern Regional Reading Coun. (pres.), Internat. Reading Assn., Assn. of Colls. U. Reading Educators (pres-elect), Internat. Reading Assn. (publ. proposal reviewer), Nat. Coun. Tchrs. English, Pi Lambda Theta (Virginia B. Biggy scholarship 1992). Avocations: reading, skiing, sailing. Home: 345 Elm St Raynham MA 02767 Office: Bridgewater State Coll Hart Hall Dept Elem Edn Bridgewater MA 02324 E-mail: nwitherell@bridgew.edu.

WITHERINGTON, MELISSA (MARTHA MELISSA WITHERINGTON), special education educator, music teacher; b. Fordyce, Ark., Oct. 9, 1937; d. Tracy Enoch and Mina Estelle (Wardlaw) W.; children: Martha Ellen Bachus Schmidt, Scott Thomas Bachus. BME, Ctrl. Mo. State U., Warrensburg, 1974, MS in Edn., 1978, EdS, 1985; student, Ouachita Baptist U., U. Ark., U. South Ark. Tech., U. Mo., Moberly Area C.C., Mo. Cert. spl. edn. learning disabled, educable and severely mentally retarded, behaviorally disordered tchr., sch. psychol. examiner, prin., Ark., Mo. Tchr. vocal and instrumental music Grain Valley (Mo.) Schs., 1974-76; cross categorical tchr. Drexel (Mo.) Schs., 1976-78; tchr. educable mentally retarded Harrisonville (Mo.) Jr. H.S., 1978-79; tchr. spl. edn., sch. psychol. examiner Kansas City (Mo.) Schs., 1979-90; tchr. spl. edn. Fairview/Camden (Ark.) Schs., 1990-92; ednl. examiner Chrysalis Assocs., Little Rock, 1992-93; supr. ind. study in assessment East Tex. State U., 1992; sch. psychol. examiner Franklin County Spl. Edn. Coop., St. Clair, Mo., 1993-95; tchr. spl. edn., sch. psychol. examiner Crawford County R-2, Bourbon, 1995-96; cross categorical tchr. Fulton (Mo.) Schs., 1996-97; tchr. spl. edn., sch. psychol. examiner Moberly (Mo.) H.S., 1997-98. Site coord. re-norming project Am. Guidance Soc., Bourbon, 1995-96; job developer Youth Opportunities Unltd., Henderson State U., Arkadelphia, Ark., 1993; part-time vocal and instrumental music instr. Holliday (Mo.) C-2 Sch., 1998-99, private piano and organ instr., ch. musician, 1955—; ind. contractor Sch. Psychometrist, 1998-99; freelance writer, 1999—. Editor newsletters, 1996—. Vol. hosp., cmty. orgns., nursing home, Christian orgns. Mem. Mo. Ret. Tchrs. Assn. (sr. cir.), Nat. Assn. Sch. Psychologists, Coun. for Exceptional Children, Coun. Diagnostic Svcs., Coun. Spl. Edn. Pioneers. Avocations: reading, gardening, bird watching, spectator sports, music. Home: 19 Broadway Village Dr Apt D Columbia MO 65201-8686

WITHEROW, CATHERINE SASLAWSKY, secondary school educator; b. West Islip, N.Y., Nov. 20, 1949; d. Sidney and Marjorie Leigh (Watson) Saslawsky; m. Stephen Michael Witherow, July 11, 1970; children: Jennifer, Eric, Alan, Scott. BA in English and Speech Edn., SUNY, Geneseo, 1971; MS in English, Elmira (N.Y.) Coll., 1978. Tchr. English R.L. Thomas H.S., Webster, N.Y., 1971-72, Canaseraga (N.Y.) Ctrl. Sch., 1977-79, Andover (N.Y.) Ctrl. Sch., 1981—, drama dir., 1981-84, 96. Mem. NEA, Nat. Coun. Tchrs. English, N.Y. State English Coun., N.Y. Edn. Assn., Andover tchrs. Assn. (pres. 1990-94, sec. 1995—). Office: Andover Central School 31 Elm St Andover NY 14806

WITHEROW, JIMMIE DAVID, secondary school educator; b. Dalton, Ga., Nov. 13, 1961; s. Jimmie W. and Jimmie Lou (Nixon) W. BA in English, Emory U., 1983; MEd in Secondary Edn., Ga. State U., 1989, PhD in Communicative Arts Edn., 1999. Cert. English tchr., Ga. Tchr. SE Whitfield High Sch., Whitfield County Bd. Edn., Dalton, 1983-92, Murray County High Sch., Chatsworth, Ga., 1992—. Contbr. article to profl. jour. Mem. NEA, Nat. Coun. Tchrs. English, Ga. Edn. Assn., Ga. Coun. Tchrs. English, Kappa Delta Pi. Home: PO Box 891 Chatsworth GA 30705-0891

WITHERS, ARLENE FALK, human resources professional, executive coach, lawyer; b. Stamford, Conn., Jan. 28, 1951; d. Leo and Ruth Joan (Levkin) Falk; m. David Withers, Sept. 19, 1981 (div.); children: Zachary Alexander, Hannah Blythe. BA, U. Conn., Storrs, 1972; JD, UCLA Sch. Law, L.A., 1978. Bar: Calif. 1978. Atty. Paul, Hastings, Janofsky & Walker, L.A., 1978-83; adjunct prof. UCLA Sch. Law, 1982-83; sr. counsel MGM/UA Entertainment Co., Culver City, Calif., 1983-85; v.p., assoc. gen. counsel Transamerica Life Cos., L.A., 1985-89, sr. v.p. human resources, 1989-93, pres. living benefits divsn., 1993-95; cons. bus. reengineering. PCF Assocs., Inc., 1996-97; v.p. human resources Cath. Healthcare West, Pasadena, Calif., 1997-98; cons. human resources Withers & Assocs., L.A., 1998-2000; chief adminstrv. officer, chief legal officer Motion Picture Industry Pension and Health Plans, Studio City, Calif., 2000—. Mediator, 1996—, adv. coun., 1997 EEOC, L.A.; work and family coun. Conf. Bd. N.Y.C., 1989-93; women in the law com. Calif. State Bar appointee, Calif., 1984-85; bd. mem. Nat. Alliance of Bus. Western Region, L.A., 1991-93. Mem. adv. bd. Sojourn Svcs. for Battered Women, Santa Monica, Calif., 1984-94; bd. dirs. Alliance of Bus. for Childcare Devel., 1989-93, Vis. Nurse Assn. L.A., 1980-89, 96-97, Ptnrs. in Care Found., L.A., 2000—, Orgn. of Women Execs., 2001—; vol. mediator L.A. Superior Ct., 1996. Mem. Calif. State Bar Assn., Women Lawyers Assn. L.A., Soc. for Human Resource Mgmt., Calif. Women Lawyers, L.A. County Bar Assn., Profl. Coaches and Mentors Assn., Human Resource Planning Soc., So. Calif. Mediation Assn. Avocations: cooking, reading, travel. Office: Motion Picture Industry Pension and Health Plans 11365 Ventura Blvd Studio City CA 91604-3148 Fax: 626-449-4049.

WITHERS, CARL RAYMOND, lawyer; b. Reading, Pa., Jan. 26, 1924; s. Stuart Snable Withers and Edith Garman; m. Jenny Constance Cory, Sept. 2, 1950; children: Wren, Jill, Bradford. AB, Wittenberg U., 1950; JD, U. Mich., 1953. Bar: Ohio 1954. Pvt. practice, Cleve., 1954—. Former pres. mus. Shaker Hist. Soc., Shaker Heights, Ohio, 1970—; former trustee, treas. N.E. Inter Mus. Coun., Cleve., 1980—; exec. com. Cuyahoga County Rep. Party, Cleve., 1984-94, Fairmount Presbyn. Ch. (former deacon and trustee), Cleve. Soldiers' and Sailors' Monument bd. trustees and sec. Mem. Ohio State Bar Assn. (former coun. of dels. 1955), Cleve. Bar Assn., Am. Legion (Army-Navy Shaker post 54, former commander, adjutant), Gt. Lakes Curling Assn. (treas., pres. 1985-96), Cleve. Grays, Estate Planning Coun. of Cleve., Cleve. Rotary Club (trustee), Cleve. City Club, Cleve. Skating Club (former trustee), Shaker Heights Republican Club, Beta Theta Pi (former pres.), Delta Theta Phi. Republican. Presbyterian. Avocation: curling, genealogy, American lithographs. Home: 3419 Courtland Rd Pepper Pike OH 44122-4280 Office: Van Aken Withers & Webster 629 Euclid Ave Cleveland OH 44114-3003

WITHERS, HUBERT RODNEY, radiotherapist, radiobiologist, educator; b. Queensland, Australia, Sept. 21, 1932; came to the U.S., 1966; s. Hubert and Gertrude Ethel (Tremayne) W.; m. Janet Macfie, Oct. 9, 1959; 1 child, Genevieve. MB BS, U. Queensland, Brisbane, Australia, 1956; PhD, U. London, 1965, DSc, 1982. Bd. cert. Ednl. Coun. for Fgn. Med. Grads. Intern Royal Brisbane and Associated Hosps., 1957; resident in radiotherapy and pathology Queensland Radium Inst. and Royal Brisbane Hosp., 1958-63; Univ. Queensland Gaggin fellow Gray Lab., Mt. Vernon Hosp., Northwood, Middlesex, Eng., 1963-65, Royal Brisbane Hosp., 1966; radiotherapist Prince of Wales Hosp., Randwick, Sydney, Australia, 1966; vis. rsch. scientist lab. physiology Nat. Cancer Inst., Bethesda, Md., 1966-68; assoc. prof. radiotherapy sect. exptl. radiotherapy U. Tex. Sys. Cancer Ctr. M.D. Anderson Hosp. & Tumor Inst., Houston, 1968-71, prof. radiotherapy, chief sect. sect. exptl. radiotherapy, 1971-80; prof. dir. exptl. radiation oncology dept. radiation oncology UCLA, 1980-89, prof., vice-chair dir. exptl. radiation oncology dept. radiation oncology, 1991-94, Am. Cancer Soc. Clin. Rsch. prof. dept. radiation oncology, 1992—, interim dir. Jonsson Comprehensive Cancer Ctr., 1994-95, chmn. radiation oncology, 1994—. Assoc. grad. faculty U. Tex., Grad. Sch. Biomed. Scis, Houston, 1969-73, mem. grad. faculty, 1973-80; prof. dept. radiotherapy Med. Sch., U. Tex. Health Sci. Ctr., Houston, U. Tex. Med. Sch., Houston, 1975-80; prof., dir. Inst. Oncology, The Prince of Wales Hosp., U. NSW, Sydney, Australia, 1989-91; mem. com. mortality mil. pers. present-at-atmosphere tests of nuclear weapons Inst. Medicine, 1993-94; mem. radiation effects rsch. bd. NRC, 1993—; mem. com. neutron dose reporting Internat. Commn. Radiation Units and Measurements, 1982—, mem. report com. clin. dosimetry for neutrons, 1993—; mem. task force non-stochastic effects radiation Internat. Com. Radiation Protection, 1980-84, mem. com. 1, 1993—; mem. radiobiology com. Radiation Therapy Oncology Group, 1979—, mem. dose-time com., 1980-89, mem. gastroenterology com., 1982-89; mem. edn. bd. Royal Australian Coll. Radiology, 1989-91; mem. cancer rsch. coord. com. U. Calif., 1991-97, mem. standing curriculum com. UCLA biomed. physics grad. program, 1993—; cons. exptl. radiotherapy U. Tex. System Cancer Ctr., 1980—. Mem. Am. editl. bd.: Internat. Jour. Radiat. Oncol. Biol. Phys., 1982-89, 91—, internat. editl. bd., 1989-91; cons. editor: The European Jour. Cancer, 1990-95; editl. bd. dirs.: Endocurietherapy/Hyperthermia Oncology, 1991—2001, Radiation Oncology Investigations, 1992—; assoc. editor: Cancer Rsch., 1993-94, editl. bd. 1995-97. Mem. Kettering selection com. Gen. Motors Cancer Rsch. Found., 1988-89, chmn., 1989, awards assembly, 1990-94. Decorated officer Order of Australia, 1998; recipient Medicine prize Polish Acad. Sci., 1989, Second H.S. Kaplan Disting. Scientist award Internat. Assn. for Radiation Rsch., 1991, Gray medal Internat. Commn. Radiation Units, 1995, U.S. Dept. Energy Fermi award 1997, Am. Radium Soc. Janeway medal, 1994, Am. Soc. Therapeutic Radiology, Oncology Gold medal, 1991, Radiation Rsch. Soc. Failla award, 1988, Gold Medal Australasia Coll. Radiology, 1997, Kettering prize GM Cancer Rsch. Found., 1998; named Gilbert H. Fletcher lectr. U. Tex. Sys. Cancer Ctr., 1989, Clifford Ash lectr. Ont. Cancer Inst., Princess Margaret Hosp., 1987, Erskine lectr. Radiol. Soc. N.Am., 1988, Ruvelson lectr. U. Minn., 1988, Milford Schultz lectr. Mass. Gen. Hosp., 1989, Del Regato Found. lectr. Hahnemann U., 1990, Bruce Cain Meml. lectr. New Zealand Soc. Oncology, 1990,Regard lectr., European Soc. Therapeutic Radiology and Oncology,others. Fellow Royal Australasian Coll. Radiologists (bd. cert., Gold medal 1997), Am. Coll. Radiology (bd. cert. therapeutic radiology, adv. com. patterns of care study 1988—, radiation oncology advisory group 1993-97, others), Am. Radium Soc. (mem. and credential c om. 1986-89, 93-94, treas. 1993-94, pres.-elect 1995-96, pres. 1996-97, others), Am. Soc. Therapeutic Radiology and Oncology (awards com. 1993, publs. com. 1993-97, vice-chair Publs. Commn., 1996-98, keynote address 1990); mem. Nat. Cancer Inst. (ad-hoc rev. coms. 1970—, radiation sudy sect. 1971-75, cons. U.S.-Japan Coop. Study high LET Radiotherapy 1975-77, cancer rsch. emphasis grant rev. com. 1976, clin. cancer ctr. rev. com. 1976-79, toxicology working group 1977-78, reviewer outstanding investigator grants 1984-93, bd. sci. counselors, 1986-88), Nat. Cancer Inst. Can. (adv. com. rsch. 1992-95), Pacific N.W. Radiol. Soc. (hon.), Tex. Radiol. Soc. (hon.), So. Calif. Radiation Oncology Soc. (sec., treas., 1992-94, pres. 1996-97), European Soc. Therapeutic

Radiology and Oncology (hon.; Regaud lectr. 2000), Polish Oncology Soc. (hon.) Austrian Radiation Oncology Soc. (hon.), Phila. Roentgen Ray Soc. (hon.), Radiation Rsch. Soc. (pres. 1982-83, honors and awards com. 1984-88, ad hoc com. funds utilization 1987-89, adv. com. Radiation Rsch. Jour. 1988-96). Office: UCLA Med Ctr 10833 Le Conte Ave Los Angeles CA 90095-3075 E-mail: withers@radone.ucla.edu.

WITHERS, RAMSEY MUIR, b. Toronto, Ont., Can., July 28, 1930; s. William Muir and Alice Smith Hope (Hannah) W.; m. Jean Alison Saunders, May 8, 1954; children— James Scott, Leslie Susan, Deidre Ann BSc, Royal Mil. Coll. Can., Kingston, Ont., 1952, DEng (hon.), 1994; BSc in Elec. Engring., Queen's U., Kingston, 1954; D Mil. Sci. honoris causa, Royal Roads Mil. Coll., Victoria, B.C., 1992. Registered profl. engr., Ont. Commd. officer Can. Army, 1948, advanced through grades to gen., 1980; sta. in Can., Republic of Korea, Fed. Republic of Germany and U.K., 1952-76; comdr. Can. Forces Europe, Fed. Republic of Germany, 1976-77; vice chief def. staff Can. Forces, 1977-80, chief def. staff, 1980-83, ret., 1983; dep. minister transport Dept. of Transp., Ottawa, Ont., 1983-88; pres., chief oper. officer Govt. Cons. Internat., 1988-93; dir. Can. Inst. Strategic Studies, 1990-96, ATS Aerospace Inc., 1993-97; chmn. Industry Govt. Rels. Group Inc. (IGRG Inc.), Ottawa, 1993-98—. V.p., sec. nat. coun. Boy Scouts Can., 1977-84, internat. commr., 1985-90, hon. v.p., 1990—; chmn. Can. War Mus. Com., 1988-95; trustee Can. Mus. Civilization, 1990-95; elected mem. Queen's U. Coun., Kingston, 1997—. Decorated comdr. Order of Mil. Merit, comdr. Order of St. John, Can. Forces Decoration with two bars; Georgian Coll. fellow, 1987; recipient Outstanding Achievement Pub. Svc. award, 1986, Silver Wolf award Boy Scouts Can., 1990, Alumni Achievement award Queen's U., Kingston, 1995. Mem. Assn. Profl. Engrs. Ont., Royal Mil. Colls. Club Can. (hon. pres. 1997—). Avocations: boating; cycling. Home: 150 Waverly St Apt 2C Ottawa ON Canada K2P OV4 E-mail: withers1809@rogers.com.

WITHERS, RICHARD ALLEN, JR. security firm executive, consultant; b. Kansas City, Mo., Oct. 8, 1957; s. Richard Allen and Edith Ethel (McLaughlan) W. BS criminal sci., criminology, Univ. Md., 1994; MA in security mgmt., Webster Univ., 1996, MA computer resources, 1997. Pvt. to gunnery sergeant U.S. Marine Corps, 1976-84, chief warrant officer, 1985-89, limited duty officer, 1990-97; owner/pres. Tech. Security & Countermeasures Cons., Carlsbad, Calif., 1997-00; corp. security mgr. ANACOMP, Inc., Poway, 1999-00; chief security officer eCharge Corp., Seattle, 2000—. Cons. U.S. Govt., 1997-00. Capt. U.S. Marine Corp, 1976-97. Mem. Am. Soc. Industrial Security, Internat. Computer Security Assn., Nat. Tech. Investigators Assn., Marine Corps Counterintelligence Assn., Marine Mustang Assn. Office: 500 Union St Ste 1000 Seattle WA 98101-2396

WITHERS, SYDNOR TERRY, SR. retired dermatologist; b. Abingdon, Va., Feb. 9, 1922; s. Henry Wilson and Natalie Sue (Terry) W.; m. Ruth Reynolds Moss, Mar. 21, 1943; children: Ruth Francis, Sydnor Terry Jr., Ann Katherine, James Nelson. MD, Med. Coll. Va., 1945. Diplomate Am. Bd. Dermatology. Intern U.S. Naval Hosp., Norfolk, Va., 1945-46, resident, 1947-50, N.Y. Skin and Cancer Hosp., 1948-49; commd. ensign USN, 1945, advanced through grades to comdr., 1982, resigned, 1955; pvt. practice dermatology Kinston, N.C., 1955-96; ret., 1996. Mem. AMA (life), Am. Acad. Dermatology (life), N.C. Med. Soc., Kinston Med. Soc. Avocations: fishing, motor boating. Home: PO Box 1929 Kinston NC 28503-1929

WITHERS, W. RUSSELL, JR. broadcast executive; b. Cape Girardeau, Mo., Dec. 10, 1936; s. Waldo Russell Sr. and Dorothy Ruth (Harrelson) W.; 1 child, Dana Ruth. BA, S.E. Mo. State U., 1958. Disc jockey Sta. KGMO Radio, Cape Girardeau, 1955-58; account exec. Sta. WGGH Radio, Marion, Ill., 1961-62; v.p. LIN Broadcasting Corp., Nashville, 1962-69; exec. v.p., dir. Laser Link Corp., Woodbury, N.Y., 1970-72; owner Withers Broadcasting of Hawaii, 1975-79, Withers Broadcasting of Minn., 1974-79, Withers Broadcasting Cos., Iowa, 1981—, Mood Music Ill., Mt. Vernon, 1973—, Mood Music, Inc., Cape Girardeau, 1972—, Royal Hawaiian Radio Co., Inc., others. Owner various radio and TV stas. including KREX-TV, Grand Junction, Colo., KREY-TV, Montrose, Colo., KREG-TV, Glenwood Springs, Colo., Page Ins. and Real Estate, Mt. Vernon, Ill.; chmn. bd., CEO Withers Beverage Corp., Mobile, Ala., 1973—79; chmn. adv. bd. Mut. Network; bd. dirs. Theatrevision, Inc., Turneffe Island Lodge, Ltd., Belize, Sta. WDTV, Clarksburg, W.Va., WMIX-AM-TV, Mt. Vernon, KGMO-KAPE, Cape Girardeau, KOKX AM-FM, Keokuk, Iowa, KTRC, Santa Fe, KRHW and KBXB, Sikeston, Mo., WKIB Anna, Cape Girardeau, WMOK, WREZ and WZZL, Paducah, Ky., WSDR-WSSQ, WZZL, Sterling Rock Falls, Ill., WILY, WRXX (FM), Centralia, Ill.; pres. Ill. Pub. Airports Assn.; co-chmn. TARPAC. Bd. dirs., chmn. bd. Mt. Vernon Tourism and Conv. Bur.; chmn. Mt. Vernon Airport Authority; bd. regents Lincoln Acad.; past pres. IPAA; past chmn. Conv. & Visitors, Airport Authority. With U.S. Army, 1957-58. Mem. Mt. Vernon C. of C. (bd. dirs.), Nat. Assn. Broadcasters, Ill. Broadcasters Assn., Stadium Club, Mo. Athletic Club, Elks, Moose, AmVets, Masons, Shriners, Sigma Chi. Christian Scientist. Home: 1 Sleepy Hollow Ln Mount Vernon IL 62864-2852 Office: PO Box 1508 Mount Vernon IL 62864-0030

WITHERSPOON, CAROLYN BRACK, lawyer; b. Little Rock, Mar. 29, 1950; d. Gordon Paisley and Mildred Louise (Lemon) Brack; m. Joseph Roger Armbrust, July 25, 1970 (div. 1976); 1 child, Catherine Paisley; m. John Leslie Witherspoon, June 15, 1979. Student, U. Ark., 1968-70, So. Meth. U., 1970; BA, U. Ark., 1974, JD with honors, 1978. Bar: Ark. 1978, U.S. Dist. Ct. (ea. and we. dists) Ark. 1978, U.S. Ct. Appeals (8th cir.) 1979, U.S. Supreme Ct. 1981. Asst. atty. City of Little Rock, 1978, chief dep. atty., acting city atty., 1984-85; assoc. House, Wallace & Jewell, Little Rock, 1985-87, ptnr., 1987-90; dir. McGlinchey Stafford Lang, 1990-97, Cross, Gunter, Witherspoon & Galchus, 1997—. Mem. com. Fed. Ct. Practice, 1988-91, Ark. Supreme Ct. Civil Practice Com., 1989-97; chair adv. com. Civil Justice Reform Act, 1993-95; mem. Continuing Legal Edn. Bd., Ark. Supreme Ct., 1998-2001; mem. State Bd. Bar Examiners, 2001—. Contbr. articles to profl. jours. Commr. Ark. Real Estate Commn., 1978-81; past chmn. Little Rock Housing Authority Bd. of Comm., past pres., bd. dirs. Advs. for Battered Women; past bd. dirs., pub. rels. chmn. LWV; past pres. Ark. Women's History Inst. Recipient Am. Jurisprudence labor law award, 1977. Fellow Am. Bar Found. (Ark. sec.-treas.); mem. ABA (EEO com., ho. of dels. 1997—), Am. Law Inst., Am. Jur Soc., Nat. Conf. Bar Pres. (mem. exec. coun. 1996-99), Transp. Lawyers Assn. (mem. exec. com. 1997-99), Ark. Bar Assn. (pres. 1995-96, Golden Gavel award 1989, 93, Ark. Inst. for Cont. Legal Edn. award 1991), Ark. Assn. Women Lawyers (pres. 1982-83), Pulaski County Bar Assn. (pres. 1989-90), Nat. Inst. Mcpl. Law Officers (state chmn. 1985-87, v.p. 1987-89), William R. Overton Inn of Ct. (pres. 1992-93). Avocations: hunting, fishing, reading, traveling. Office: Cross Gunter Witherspoon & Galchus 500 E Markham St Ste 200 Little Rock AR 72201-1747 E-mail: cspoon@cgwg.com.

WITHERSPOON, HILDA, artist, cable television producer; b. Istanbul, Turkey, Oct. 4, 1935; came to U.S., 1974, naturalized; d. Hagop and Mari (Avakian) Ekmekciyan; m. Robert Witherspoon, Jan. 2, 1967; 1 child, Eric Bentley. Diploma, Notre Dame de Sion, Istanbul, 1957, U. Paris, 1967; postgrad., Corcoran Sch. of Art, 1990. Armenian tchr. St. Mary's Cultural Ctr., 1968-78; pres. Hilda's Right, Washington, 1982—, Studio Gallery, Washington, 1989; French tchr. St. Albans Sch., 1991-92; art tchr. Sacred Heart Sch., 1991-92, Zagorsk (Russia) Elem. Sch., 1992; TV prodr. The Art of Living program Fairfax County Access Cable, Fairfax, Va., 1995—. Represented by Alla Rogers Gallery, Georgetown. One-woman shows include Armenian Cultural Ctr., Washington, 1987, Studio Gallery, Washington, 1988, 89, Gensler and Assocs., Washington, 1990, 91, Alla Rogers Gallery, 1990, 91, Astrea, Washington, 1991, Tula (Russia) Art Mus., 1992, Ctrl. Artists House, Moscow, 1992, Armenian Libr. and Mus. of Am., Watertown, Mass., 1993, World Bank, Washington, 1995, Roche Bobois, 1994, Embassy of France, Washington, 1995; exhibited in group shows at Fairfax County Art Show, 1982, Touchstone Gallery, Washington, 1986, Arts Club of Washington, 1986, Foundry Gallery, Washington, 1986, 88, 91, Whitewalls Gallery, Corcoran Sch. of Art, Washington, 1987, 1988, Arts Club of Washington, 1987, Inst. Policy Studies, Washington, 1987, R St. Gallery, Washington, 1987, Omni Hotel, Washington, 1987, Park Place Cafe, Washington, 1987, Arnold and Porter, Washington, 1987, Studio Gallery, Washington, 1987, 88, 89, United Meth. Ch., Washington, 1987, Corcoran Sch. of Art, Washington, 1987, 88, Stables Art Ctr., Washington, 1988, Gt. Falls Arts Ctr., Va., 1988, Martin Luther King Libr., Washington, 1988, Art Barn, Washington, 1989, Katchadourian Gallery, Saddlebrook, N.J., 1990, Corcoran Connection Gallery, Washington, 1991, Mayor's Art Gallery, Washington, 1991, Carnegie Libr., Washington, 1991, No. Va. C.C., Annandale, 1992, Congl. Offices, Washington, 1992, 93, New Eng. Fine Arts Inst. Exhibit, Woburn, Mass., 1993, Dante Alighieri Soc. Mass., Cambridge, 1993, Open Studio, Washington, 1993, 1054 Galleries, Washington, 1993, NIH, Bethesda, Md., 1993, Universal North, Washington, many others. Recipient Cmty. Residences award, 1996, Cmty. Edn. award, 1996. Armenian Apostolic. Avocations: tennis, photography, swimming, gourmet cooking. Home: 2101 Connecticut Ave NW Apt 5 Washington DC 20008-1752

WITHERSPOON, JAMES DONALD, biology educator; b. Springfield, Mo., Dec. 19, 1933; s. Harry H. and Lucy Catherine (Applegate) W.; m. Rebecca Jane Hutto, Jan. 24, 1958; children: Sarah Jane, John Edward. BS, Purdue U., 1955, MS, 1960, PhD, 1963. From instr. to asst. prof. biology Western Md. Coll., Westminster, 1960-68; assoc. prof. Southwestern at Memphis Coll., 1968-76; free-lance writer Phoenix, 1976-82; adj. prof. Grand Canyon Coll., 1982-84, prof., 1984—, chmn. dept. scis., 1985-92, acting chmn. dept. math. and computer scis., 1988-89; coord. allied health Grand Canyon U. (formerly Grand Canyon Coll.), 1992-94, assoc. dean Coll. Sci. and Allied Health, 1994-98. Cons. Doubleday & Co., Garden City, N.Y., 1960-62, Narco Bio-Sys., Houston, 1972-76; assoc. coord. med. edn. S.W. Kirksville Coll. Osteo. Medicine, 1990-94; leader Am. tchr.: Eszterhazy Karoly Tchrs. Tng. Coll., Hungary, summers 1991-93, 2000, Vilnius Pedagogical Univ., Lithuania, summers 1995-97, 99, 2001-02. Author: The Functions of Life, 1970, Human Physiology, 1984, From Field to Lab, 1993, Science and Health on the Internet, 1997, 98, 99, 2000, 01, 02, Guide to the Internet, 1999, 2000, 2001; co-author: The Living Laboratory, 1960; co-author numerous tapes and computer programs, 1973-87. Grantee Grass Found., 1962-72, Ariz. Commn. for Postsecondary Edn., 1985-87. Mem. Ariz. Alliance for Sci., Maths. and Tech. Edn. (bd. dirs. 1986-88), Sigma Xi. Republican. Presbyterian. Achievements include rsch. on relation of hypoxia to body temperature, innovative methods for biological education. Home: 17122 E Grande Blvd Fountain Hills AZ 85268-3224 Office: Grand Canyon U 3300 W Camelback Rd Phoenix AZ 85017-1097 E-mail: jwitherspoon@qwest.net.

WITHERSPOON, JOHN THOMAS, water resources consultant; b. Springfield, Mo., June 25, 1947; s. Warren Thomas and Kathryn (Corbus) w.; m. C. Frances Teter, June 12, 1971. BS, S.W. Mo. State U., 1969, MA, 1971; PhD, U. Mont., 1975. Water control inspector City of Springfield, Mo., 1976-78; dir. labs. City Utilities, Springfield, 1978-91, mgr. water treatment and supply, 1991—2001. Mem. safe drinking water commn. Mo. State Dept. Natural Resources, Jefferson City, 1992—, now chair; bd. dirs. James River Basin Partnership, Nixa, Mo., 1996; tech. advisor Watershed Com. of the Ozarks, Springfield, 1983—. Pres. Univ. Club Springfield, 1989. Mem. Am. Water Works Assn. (chair, Boyd Utility Mgr. award 1996, Fuller award 1999), Kiwanis. Avocations: golf, reading, guitar, travel. Home: 1927 E Lark St Springfield MO 65804-4345 Office: City Utilities PO Box 551 Springfield MO 65801-0551 E-mail: jtwithersp@aol.com.

WITHERSPOON, REESE (LAURA JEAN WITHERSPOON), actress; b. Nashville, Mar. 22, 1976; m. Ryan Phillippe. Motion picture and T.V. actress. Film appearances include The Man in the Moon, 1991, Jack the Bear, 1993, Freeway, 1996, Pleasantville, 1998, Twilight, 1998, Best Laid Plans, 1999, , Cruel Intentions, 1999, Election, 1999, Am. Psycho, 2000, Legally Blonde, 2001, The Importance of Being Earnest, 2002, Sweet Home Alabama, 2002, others; appeared in TV series Friends, 2000, (T.V. films) Wildflower, 1991, Desperate Choices: To Save My Child, 1992. Recipient Catalan Internat. Film Festival Award Best Actress, 1997, Movieline Young Hollywood Award for Breakthrough Performance (Female), 1999, Online Film Critics Soc. Award for Best Actress, 1999, National Soc. of Film Critics Award for Best Actress, 1999. Office: c/o Steve Dontanville William Morris 151 El Camino Dr Beverly Hills CA 90212-2412 also: c/o Blymel O'Neill 8912 Burton Way Beverly Hills CA 90211-1707*

WITHERSPOON, WALTER PENNINGTON, JR. orthodontist, philanthropist; b. Sept. 3, 1938; s. Walter P. and Florence Evelyn (Jones) W.; m. Joyce Ann Smith, Sept. 6, 1970; 1 child, Annie Melissa. BS, U. S.C., 1960; DDS, U. N.C., 1964, MSO, 1969. Bd. qualified Am. Bd. Orthodontics. Pvt. practice, Columbia, 1969—. Med. staff Bapt. Med. Ctr., Columbia, 1970—, Lexington County Hosp., West Columbia, 1974—. Host Nite Line Broadcasting Co. Adv. bd. 1st Palmetto Bank and Trust, West Columbia, 1982; mem. adv. bd. 1st Citizens Bank; candidate S.C. Ho. of Reps., 1994; del. S.C. Rep. Com., 1989—; mem. platform com. S.C. Rep. Party Conv., poll com., 1992; del. Rep. Nat. Conv., Houston, 1992, rules com., task force on edn.; Rep. nat. committeeman, 1996-2000, rules com., rep. nat. com.; pres. Rep. Electoral Coll., 1996, 2000; bd. dirs. Southeastern Coll. Assemblies of God, Lakeland, Fla., 1984, Brookland Plantation Home for Boys, Orangeburg, S.C.; pres. Friends of Irmo Libr.; bd. dirs. Irmo-St. Andrew's Coalition of Neighborhood Home Owners' Assns.; chmn. Lexington County Rep. Party; commr. Richland/Lexington Counties Commn. for Tech. Edn., S.C. Commn. on Alcohol and Drug Abuse; bd. dirs. Centerplace for Homeless; mem. Presdl. Visit-Ticket Com.; amb. Irmo C. of C.; vol. lockup telethon Muscular Dystrophy Assn. Lt. USN, 1964-66. Recipient Century Mem. award Boy Scouts Am., 1984. Mem. ADA, Greater Columbia Dental Assn. (pres. 1975-76), U. N.C. Dental Alumni Assn. (bd. dirs.), S.C. Dental Assn. (ho. of dels. 1971-73, 91-96, legis. com. 1993), S.C. Orthodontic Assn. (cen. dist. dir.), Am. Assn. Orthodontists, Sertoma (pres. 1975-76), Am. Legion (mem. baseball com.), So. Assn. Orthodontists, Cen. Dist. Dental Soc. Home: 250 Lancer Dr Columbia SC 29212-1216 Office: 205 Med Cir W Columbia SC 29169

WITHERSPOON, WILLIAM, investment economist; b. St. Louis, Nov. 21, 1909; s. William Conner and Mary Louise (Houston) W.; m. Margaret Telford Johanson, June 25, 1938; children: James Tomlin, Jane Telford, Elizabeth Witherspoon Vodra. Student, Washington U. Evening Sch., 1928-47. Chartered fin. analyst; registered investment advisor. Rsch. dept. A. G. Edwards & Sons, 1928-31; pres. Witherspoon Investment Co., 1931-34; head rsch. dept. Newhard Cook & Co., 1934-43, 45-53; ltd. ptnr. St. Louis Ordnance Dist., 1943-45; economist, investment analyst Newhard Cook & Co., 1965-68; chief price analysis St. Louis Ordnance Dist., 1943-45; owner Witherspoon Investment Counsel, 1953-64; v.p. rsch. Stifel, Nicolaus & Co., 1968-81; registered investment advisor St. Louis, 1981—. Lectr. on investments Washington U., 1948-67. Contbr. articles to profl. jours. Mem. Clayton Bd. Edn., 1955-68, treas., 1956-68, pres., 1966-67; mem. Clayton Park and Recreation Commn., 1959-60; trustee Ednl. TV, KETC, 1963-64; mem. investment com. Gen. Assembly Mission Bd. Presbyn. Ch. (USA), Atlanta, 1976-79, mem. permanent com. ordination exams, 1979-85; cons. to investment com. Ctr. Theol. Inquiry, Princeton, N.J., 1995-97. Served as civilian Ordnance Dept., AUS, 1943-45. Mem. St. Louis soc. Fin. Analysts (pres. 1949-50), Mo. Athletic (St. Louis). Home: 6401 Ellenwood Ave Saint Louis MO 63105-2228 E-mail: wwspoon@att.net. *Many of the current social and ethical problems of today might be partially resolved if theology would be influenced by the 4th dimension of spacetime plus the 5th dimension of the mind, the 6th dimension of the spirit and the 7th dimension of God the Father.*

WITHERSPOON, WILLIAM TOM, company executive; b. Dallas, Feb. 1, 1949; s. Vernon Howard and Mary Ruth (Coffee) W.; m. Sandra Stein, June 10, 1970; children: Mary Jacqueline, Stephen Thomas. BS in Civil Engring., So. Meth. U., 1971; MS in Mgmt. and Adminstrv. Sci., U. Tex., Dallas, 1979; postgrad., So. Meth. U., 1979-81. Registered profl. engr., Tex.; lic. irrigator, Tex.; registered surveyor, Tex., sanitarian, Tex. Field engr. Robert E. McKee Constrn. Co., Dallas, 1971-73; supt. Batson Cook Co., 1973-77; project mgr. Rucker Constrn. Co., 1977-81; v.p. Wynn Oil Co., 1981-85; pres. Sandco Petroleum Corp., 1985-87, S&W Found. Contractors, Richardson, Tex., 1986—. Pres. U.S. Weightlifting-North Tex., Dallas, 1975-95; bd. dirs. Internat. Assn. Found. Drilling, Dallas; pres. Found. Repair Assn. Tex., 1997-2000. Author: Residential Found. Performance, 1999; patentee in field. With USN, 1971-80. State champion U.S. Weightlifting, 1984, 87, 89, 90, 94; recipient Contractor of Yr. award Internat. Assn. Found. Drilling, 1997. Mem. Am. Assn. Civil Engrs., Am. Assn. Petroleum Engrs., Am. Assn. Petroleum Geologists, Nat. Assn. Waterproofers and Structural Repair Contractors (dir.), Am. Weightlifting Assn., Richardson C. of C. Republican. Avocations: weightlifting, golf, writing, ranching. Office: S&W Found Contractors 1030 E Belt Line Rd Richardson TX 75081-3703 E-mail: tomw5@ix.netcom.com.

WITHERWAX, CHARLES HALSEY, lawyer, arbitrator, mediator; b. Schroon Lake, N.Y., July 24, 1934; s. Halsey Jerome and Elizabeth Daisy (Bingham) W.; m. Marianne Jehander, June 24, 1980. BS in Marine Transp., N.Y. State Maritime Coll., 1956; LLB, Union U., 1959. Bar: N.Y. 1962, U.S. Dist. Ct. (so. dist.) N.Y. 1962, U.S. Supreme Ct. 1968, Hawaii 1971, U.S. Dist. Ct. Hawaii 1971, U.S. Ct. Appeals (9th cir.) 1984, U.S. Tax Ct. 1984, Nev. 1991, D.C. 1993, U.S. Ct. Appeals (2d cir.) 1995. Assoc. prof. N.Y. State Maritime Coll., Fort Schuyler, N.Y., 1963-64; asst. v.p., bond claims atty. Chubb Ins. Group, N.Y.C., 1961-70; v.p., gen. counsel Hawaiian Ins. Group, Honolulu, 1970-74; ptnr. Davis, Witherwax, Playdon & Gerson, 1974-78; prin. atty. Witherwax, Pottenger & Nishioka, 1978-91; of counsel D'Amato & Lynch, N.Y.C., 1992—. Author: (manual) Hawaii Construction Law, Mechanics Liens and Bond Claims, 1985, co-author, 1987. Bronx county chmn. N.Y. State Conservative Party, 1962-67; state sec. N.Y. State Conservative Party, 1967-70. Lt. comdr. USNR, 1959-79. Mem. ABA (vice chair fidelity and surety com. 1978-83), Internat. Assn. Def. Counsel. Roman Catholic. Avocations: sailing, travel, golf. Office: D'Amato & Lynch 70 Pine St 37th Fl New York NY 10270-0002 E-mail: www.simpnas2@aol.com.

WITHROW, LUCILLE MONNOT, nursing home administrator; b. Alliance, Ohio, July 28, 1923; d. Charles Edward Monnot and Freda Aldine (Guy) Monnot Cameron; m. Alvin Robert Withrow, June 6, 1945 (dec. 1984); children: Cindi Withrow Johnson, Nancy Withrow Townley, Sharon Withrow Hodgkins, Wendel Alvin. AA in Health Adminstrn., Eastfield Coll., 1976. Lic. nursing home adminstr., Tex.; cert. nursing home ombudsman. Held various clerical positions, Dallas, 1950-72; office mgr., asst. adminstr. Christian Care Ctr. Nursing Home, Mesquite, Tex., 1972-76; head adminstr. Christian Care Ctr. Nursing Home and Retirement Complex, 1976-91; nursing home ombudsman Tex. Dept. Aging and Tex. Dept. Health, Dallas, 1991-93; legal asst. Law Offices of Wendel A. Withrow, Carrollton, Tex., 1993—. Mem. con. on geriatric curriculum devel. Eastfield Coll., Mesquite, 1979, 87; mem. ombudsman adv. com. Sr. Citizens Greater Dallas; nursing home cons.; notary pub., 1995—. Vol. Dallas Arboretum and Bot. Soc., Dallas Summer Musicals Guild; mem. Ombudsman adv. com. Sr. Citizens of Greater Dallas, Health Svcs. Speakers Bur.; charter mem. Stage Show Prodns. Recipient Volunteerism awards Tex. Atty. Gen., 1987, Tex. Gov., 1992. Mem. Tex. Assn. Homes for Aging, Am. Assn. Homes for Aging, Health Svcs. Speakers Bur., White Rock Kiwanis. Mem. Ch. of Christ. Avocations: reading, travel, theater. Home: 11344 Lippitt Ave Dallas TX 75218-1922 Office: Law Office of W A Withrow 1120 Metrocrest Dr Ste 200 Carrollton TX 75006-5872

WITHROW, SHERRIE ANNE, financial specialist; b. Sacramento, Mar. 10, 1960; d. Jim and Ilene (James) Withrow. Student, Diablo Valley C.C., Pleasant Hill, Calif., 1977-81, Tarrant County Jr. Coll., Ft. Worth, 1982-83, Coll. of Marin, Kentfield, Calif., 1988, Merritt Coll., Oakland, Calif., 1990; AA in Bus. Adminstrn. and Mgmt., St. Louis C.C., Florissant, Mo., 1981. Internal cashier AAA Automobile Club Mo., St. Louis, 1977-79; receiving clk. Dayton-Hudson Target Stores, Florissant and Ft. Worth, 1979-81; supr. credit and collection World Svc. Life Ins. Co., Ft. Worth, 1982-83; bank br. balancer, data processing divsn. Tex. Am. Bank Svcs., Inc., 1984-85; asst. to contr. Positive Video-Post Prodn., Orinda, Calif., 1985-87; with contractor's desk adminstrn. dept. Shell Oil Co., Martinez, 1987-88; asst. to CFO J.T. Thorpe & Son, Inc., Richmond, 1988-89; founder, gen. ptnr. HomeVisions Constrn. Svcs., El Sobrante, 1989-99, AudioVisions Sound and Lighting Co., El Sobrante, 1990-2000; corp. acctg. and investments Liquidity Fund Mgmt., Inc., 1990-92; founder, gen. ptnr. AV Electric, El Sobrante, 1994-2000; tax and payroll benefits specialist, founder Roll 'em!, 2001—. Audio engr., cons. and project fin. cons. Contbr. (poetry) The Brilliance of Night, Internat. Libr. of Poetry Compilation, 2000, The Best Poems and Poets of 2001, 2001, The Silence Within, 2001, Nature's Echoes, 2001, Internat. Libr. poetry; audio recs.: The Sound of Poetry, 2001. Fundraiser Sr. Citizen Subsidized Housing Complex, Martinez, 1987-88. David L. Underwood scholar Florissant Valley (St. Louis) C.C., 1980-81. Mem. Internat. Platform Assn., Phi Theta Kappa. Democrat. Office: Roll 'em! PO Box 20368 El Sobrante CA 94820-0368 E-mail: sher@sherbear.com.

WITHUHN, WILLIAM LAWRENCE, museum curator, railroad economics and management consultant; b. Portland, Oreg., Aug. 12, 1941; s. Vernon Lawrence and Ruth Eleanor (Ferguson) W.; m. Gail Joy Hartman, Nov. 22, 1964; children: James, Thomas, Harold. BA, U. Calif.-Berkeley, 1963; MBA with distinction, Cornell U., 1977, MA, 1980. Commd. regular 2d lt. USAF, 1963, advanced through grades to capt., 1967; indsl. engr., asst. dir. manpower and orgn. USAF at Western Transport Air Force, 1964-65; global, polar, tactical, and instr. navigator worldwide USAF, 1965-72, spl. ops. navigator Vietnam, 1969—70, select lead navigator Mil. Airlift Command, 1970-72; ret., 1972; intern, then staff asst. U.S. Ho. of Reps., 1973-74; v.p. Va. & Md. R.R. Co., Cape Charles, Va., 1977-81, Md. & Del. R.R., Federalsburg, Md., 1977-81; sr. v.p. Ont. Midland R.R., Ont. Cent. R.R., Sodus, N.Y., 1979-83; v.p. Rail Mgmt. Svcs., Inc., Syracuse, 1979-83, RSA Leasing Co., Syracuse, 1980-83; exec. v.p. Am. Coal Enterprises, Inc., Akron, Ohio, 1980-82; v.p., gen. mgr. Allegheny So. Ry., Martinsburg, Pa., 1982-83; acting dir. R.R. Mus. of Pa., 1982-83; curator transp. Nat. Mus. Am. History Smithsonian Inst., Washington, 1983—, dep. chmn. dept. sci. and tech., 1984-91, spl. asst. to dir., 1990-94. Bd. dirs., chmn. The Waring Group Inc., Transp. Cons., Salisbury, Md., 1983-89; cons. Nat. Pk. Svc., Pa. Hist. & Mus. Commn., Expo 2000 (Germany), Fed. Railroad Admnstrn., Nat. Transp. Safety Bd.; apptd. Garrett Morgan Transp. Futures Program steering com. U.S. Dept. Transp.; apptd. founding mem., history com., Transp. Rsch. Bd. Nat. Rsch. Coun.; apptd. mem., task force on transp. Nat. Parks and Pub. Lands, Transp. Rsch. Bd. Nat. Rsch. Coun. Author: Spirit of Steam, 1995; editor, co-author: Rails Across America, 1993; contbr. articles to profl. jours. Decorated D.F.C. with oak leaf cluster, Bronze Star, Air medal with 12 clusters, Antarctic Svc. medal; De Karman fellow, 1979-80, Smithsonian fellow, 1980-81; recipient Gold Apple award Nat. Ednl. Film Festival, 1995. Mem. Am. Inst. Indsl. Engrs., Lexington Group in Transp. History, Nat. Parks Conservation Assn., Air Commando Assn., Disting. Flying Cross Soc., Internat. Assn. Ry. Operating Officers, Brotherhood of Locomotive Engrs., Cornell Club Washington, Theta Chi. Office: Nat Mus Am History Smithsonian Inst Rm 5010 Washington DC 20560-0628

WITKE, DAVID RODNEY, newspaper editor; b. Council Bluffs, Iowa, Mar. 24, 1937; s. Arnold and Rosamond Louise (Storer) W.; m. Priscilla Bill Smith, Oct. 8, 1960; 1 son, Carl. BS in Journalism, Northwestern U., 1959. Reporter, editor The Courier, Champaign-Urbana, Ill., 1962-66; copy editor The Register, Des Moines, 1966-70, city editor, 1970-73, asst. mng. editor adminstrn., 1973-74, asst. mng. editor electronics, 1974-75, mng. editor, 1975-83, dir. ops., 1983-85, dep. editor, omsbudsman, 1985-87, exec. sports editor, 1987-98, sr. editor, 1998—. Rep. Iowa Freedom of Info. Coun., Des Moines, 1973—, pres., 1986-88; vis. lectr. Drake U., 1986—, Iowa State U., 1990—; juror Pulitzer Prize, 1989-91. Served to lt. (j.g.) USN, 1959-62, PTO. Mem. Assoc. Press Mng. Editors Assn., Mid-Am. Newspaper Assn., AP Sports Editors Assn., Iowa Newspaper Found., The Prairie Club, Sigma Delta Chi Unitarian Universalist. Achievements include early lectures on electronic applications to large newspaper production. Home: 2521 48th Pl Des Moines IA 50310-2506 Office: Des Moines Register and Tribune Co 715 Locust St Des Moines IA 50309-3767

WITKIN, ERIC DOUGLAS, lawyer; b. Trenton, N.J., May 14, 1948; s. Nathan and Norma Shirley (Stein) W.; m. Regina Ann Bilotta, June 8, 1980; children: Daniel Robert, Sarah Ann. AB magna cum laude, Columbia U., 1969; JD, Harvard U., 1972. Bar: N.Y. 1973, D.C. 1989, U.S. Dist. Ct. (so. and ea. dists.) N.Y. 1974, U.S. Dist. Ct. (we. dist.) N.Y. 2001, U.S. Ct. Appeals (2d and D.C. cirs.) 1974, U.S. Supreme Ct. 1977, U.S. Dist. Ct. D.C. 1989. Assoc. Poletti, Freidin, Prashker & Gartner, N.Y.C., 1972-80, ptnr., 1980-85; sr. atty. labor Kaye, Scholer, Fierman, Hays & Handler, 1985-88; of counsel Akin, Gump, Strauss, Hauer & Feld, Washington, 1988-90; counsel Benetar, Bernstein, Schair & Stein, N.Y.C., 1990-99; ptnr. Roberts & Finger, LLP, 1999-2001, Greble & Finger, LLP, N.Y.C., 2001; counsel Brown, Raysman, Millstein, Felder, & Steiner LLP, 2001—. Treas., founder Property Owners Against Unfair Taxation, N.Y.C., 1983-90; trustee Congregation Emanu-El of

Westchester, 1996—, pres., 2002--. Lawrence Chamberlain scholar Columbia U., N.Y.C., 1968; recipient Alumni medal Alumni Fedn. Columbia U., 1982. Mem. ABA (labor and employment law sect.), N.Y. State Bar Assn. (labor and employment law sect., com. on equal employment opportunity law), Assn. of Bar of City of N.Y. (spl. com. on sex and law 1975-82, com. on labor and employment law 1982-85, 92-94), Westchester County Bar Assn., Columbia Coll. Alumni Assn. (pres. 1988-90, bd. dirs. 1974—, Robert Lincoln Carey prize, Alumni prize 1969, Lions award 1990), Alumni Fedn. Columbia U. (alumni trustee nominating com. 1990-97, pres. 1997-99), Am. Soc. Pers. Adminstrn. (contbr. monthly newsletter 1986-88), Soc. Human Resource Mgmt., Soc. Columbia Grads. (bd. dirs. 1994-97), Human Resources Assn. N.Y., Phi Beta Kappa. Clubs: Harvard (N.Y.C.). Avocations: piano, sailing. Home: 103 Wendover Rd Rye NY 10580-1939 Office: Brown Raysman Millstein Felder & Steiner 900 3rd Ave Fl 23 New York NY 10022 E-mail: ewitkin@brownraysman.com., ericwitkin@aol.com.

WITKIN, EVELYN MAISEL, retired geneticist; b. N.Y.C., Mar. 9, 1921; d. Joseph and Mary (Levin) Maisel; m. Herman A. Witkin, July 9, 1943 (dec. July 1979); children— Joseph, Andrew. AB, NYU, 1941; MA, Columbia U., 1943, PhD, 1947; DSc honoris causa, N.Y. Med. Coll., 1978, Rutgers U., 1995. Mem. staff genetics dept. Carnegie Inst., Washington, 1950-55; mem. faculty State U. N.Y. Downstate Med. Center, Bklyn., 1955-71, prof. medicine, 1968-71; prof. biol. scis. Douglass Coll., Rutgers U., 1971-79, Barbara McClintock prof. genetics, 1979-83, Waksman Inst. Microbiology, 1983-91; Barbara McClintock prof. emerita Waksman Inst. Microbiology, Rutgers U., 1991—. Author articles; mem. editorial bds. profl. jours. Postdoctoral fellow Am. Cancer Soc., 1947-49; fellow Carnegie Instn., 1957; Selman A. Waksman lectr., 1960; Phi Beta Kappa vis. scholar, 1980-81; grantee NIH, 1956-89; recipient Prix Charles Leopold Mayer French Acad. Scis., 1977, Lindback award, 1979 Fellow AAAS, Am. Acad. Microbiology; mem. NAS, Am. Acad. Arts and Scis., Environ. Mutagen Soc., Am. Genetics Soc. (Thomas Hunt Morgan medal, 2000), Am. Soc. Microbiology. Home: 1 Firestone Ct Princeton NJ 08540-5220 E-mail: ewitkin@aol.com.

WITKIN, JOEL-PETER, photographer; b. Bklyn., Sept. 13, 1939; s. Max and Mary (Pellegrino) W.; 1 child, Kersen Ahanu. B.F.A., Cooper Union, 1974; M.F.A., U. N.Mex., 1986; student (fellow), Columbia U., 1973-74. Artist in residence Zerybthia Rome, Italy, summer 1996; represented by Ricco/Maresca Gallery, NYC, Fraenkel Gallery, San Francisco, Galerie Baudoin Lebon, Paris; artist in residence Berlin, fall 1998, Paris, winter 1998. Lectr. Am. Acad. Rome, 1996, Camera Work, Berlin, El Escorial, Spain, 1998, Yale U., 2001, Soc. Photographic Edn., 1999. Exhibited in Projects Studio One, N.Y.C., 1980, Galerie Texbraun, Paris, 1982, Baudoin Lebon, Paris, 1982, 86, 90, 97, 2000, 02, Kansas Ctiy Art Inst., 1983, Stedelijk Mus., Amsterdam, 1983, Fraenkel Gallery, 1983-84, 87, 91, 93, 95, 97, Pace WildenStein MacGill Gallery, N.Y.C., 1983, 84, 87, 89, 91, 93, 95, 97, Pace Wildenstein, L.A., 1998, San Francisco Mus. Modern Art, 1985, Bklyn. Mus., 1986, Galerie Baudoin Lebon, Paris, 1987, 89, 91, 95, 97, 2000, Centro de Arte Reina Sofia Mus., Madrid, 1988, Palais de Tokyo, Paris, 1989, Fahey/Klein Gallery, L.A., 1987, 89, 91, 97, 98, Mus. Modern Art, Haifa, Israel, 1991, Photo Picture Space Gallery, Osaka, Japan, 1993, Guggenheim Mus., N.Y.C., 1995, Interkamera, Prague, 1995, Il Castello de Rivoli Mus., Turin, 1995, Encontros de Fotografia, Colombia, Portugal, 1996, Rencontres de la Photographie, Arles, France, 1996, Taipei Photo Gallery, Taiwan, 1994, 96, 98, Mus. of Fine Arts, Santa Fe, 1998, Wildenstein Gallery, Tokyo, 1998, Sternburg Mus., Prague, 1999, Sternburg Mus., Prague, 1999, Mesiac Fotographie, Slovakia, 1999, Hotel De Sully, Paris, 2000, Catherine Edelman Gallery, Chgo., 2000, Athens Sch. Fine Art, 2000, Ctr. Contemporary Art, Honolulu, 2000, Etherton Gallery, Tuscon, 2001, Stadt Mus., Jena, 2002, Picture Photo Space, Osaka, 2002, Infinito Gallery, Turin, 2002; group shows: Mus. Modern Art, N.Y.C., 1959, San Francisco Mus. Moder Art, 1981, Whitney Biennial, 1985, Palais de Tokyo, Paris, 1986, La Photographie Contemporaine en France, 1996, Foto Masson, Goteberg, Sweden, 1997, Hanlin Museum, So. Korea, 1997, Bogardenkapel, Bruges, 1998, Hayward Gallery, London, 1997, Strasborg Mus. d'Art Moderne et Contemporaine, 1998, The Ansel Adams Ctr., San Francisco, 1999, Camera Work, San Francisco, 1999, The Louvre, Paris, 2000, Museé Bourdelle, Paris, 2000, John Gibson Gallery, N.Y.C., 2000, The High Mus. Art, Ga., 2000, The Fotografie Forum, Frankfort, 2001, The Nat. Gallery of Can., 2002, Hotel de Sully, Paris, 2002, The Israel Mus., Jerusalem, 2002; represented in permanent collections, Mus. Modern Art, N.Y.C., San Francisco Mus. Modern Art, 1980, Nat. Gallery Art, Washington, Victoria and Albert Mus., London, George Eastman House, N.Y., The Getty Collection, Moder Museet, Stockholm, Sweden, Whitney Mus., N.Y.C., The Guggenheim Mus., N.Y.C., Tokyo Met. Mus. Photography, Nat. Gallery Can.; subject of monographs: Joel-Peter Witkin, 1985, 88-89, 91, 93, 95-96, 98, 99, 2000, 01, 02; editor: Masterpieces of Medical Photography, 1987, Harms Way, 1994; visual editor: Songs of Experience, 2002; artist residency, Rome, 1996, Berlin, 1998, Paris, 1998, 2000. Served with U.S. Army, 1961-64. Decorated Commandeur des Arts et de Lettres (France), 2000, The Augustus Saint Gaudens medal The Cooper Union, 1996; recipient Disting. Alumni award The Cooper Union, 1986, Internat. Ctr. Photography award, 1988, award for N.Y. Times "The Plague Yr.," Soc. Publ. Designers, 2000; Ford Found. grantee, 1977, 78, Nat. Endowment in Photography grantee, 1980, 81, 86, 92. Address: 1707 Five Points Rd SW Albuquerque NM 87105-3017 *My need is to understand existence. That need becomes art when it reaches into the extreme limit of the possible.*

WITKIN, MILDRED HOPE FISHER, psychotherapist, educator; b. N.Y.C. d. Samuel and Sadie (Goldschmidt) Fisher; m. Jorge Radovic, Aug. 26, 1983; children: Georgia Hope, Roy Thomas, Laurie Philips, Kimberly Hope, Nicole Sue, Scott Benjamin, Joshua William, Jennifer Ivy, Jacob Glen. AB, Hunter Coll.; MA, Columbia U., 1968; PhD, NYU, 1973. Diplomate Am. Bd. Sexology, Am. Bd. Sexuality. Head counselor Camp White Lake, Camp Emanuel, Long Beach, N.J.; tchr. econs., polit. sci. Hunter Coll. H.S.; dir., group leader follow-up program Jewish Vacation Assn., N.Y.C.; investigator N.Y.C. Housing Authority; psychol. counselor Montclair State Coll., Upper Montclair, N.J., 1967-68; mem., lectr. Creative Problem-Solving Inst., U. Buffalo, 1968; psychol. counselor Fairleigh Dickinson U., Teaneck, N.J., 1968; dir. Counseling Ctr., 1969-74; pvt. practice psychotherapy N.Y.C., also Westport, Conn.; sr. faculty supr., family therapist and psychotherapist Payne Whitney Psychiat. Clinic, N.Y. Presbyn. Hosp., Cornell Med. Ctr., 1973—; clin. asst. prof. dept. psychiatry Cornell U. Med. Coll., 1974—; assoc. dir. sex therapy and edn. program N.Y. Presbyn. Hosp. and Weill Med. Coll., Cornell U., 1974—. Cons. counselor edn. tng. programs N.Y.C. Bd. Edn., 1971—75; cons. Health Info. Sys., 1972—79; supr. master's and doctoral candidates NYU, 1975—82; sr. cons. Kaplan Inst. Evaluation and Treatment of Sexual Disorders, 1981—96; chmn. sci. com. 1st Internat. Symposium Female Sexuality , Buenos Aires, 1984; pvt. practice psychotherapy and sex therapy, N.Y.C., Westport, Conn.; vis. prof. numerous colls. and univs.; lectr. internat. and nat. workshops, radio and TV. Author: (book) 45-And Single Again, 1985, Single Again, 1994; contbr. articles to profl. jours., chpts. to textbooks. Chmn. edn. legislation com. PTA, Yonkers, 1955; Scarsdale chmn. mothers com. Boy Scouts Am., 1961—64; mem. Morrow Assn. Correction N.J., 1969—91; bd. dirs. Girl Scouts Am.; publicity chmn. United Jewish Appeal, Scarsdale, 1959—65. Recipient Bronze medal for svcs., Hunter Coll., plaque, United Jewish Appeal, 1962, Founders Day award, NYU, 1973, citation, N.Y. Hosp.-Cornell U. Med. Ctr., 1990. Fellow: Am. Acad. Clin. Sexologists, Internat. Coun. Sex Edn. and Parenthood of Am. U.; mem.: LWV, ACA, AAUW, APA, Conn. Assn. Marriage and Family Therapy, Am. Assn. Sexology (diplomate), Nat. coun. Women in Medicine, Am. Women's Med. Assn., Am. Assn. Counseling and Devel., Profl. Women's Caucus, Assn. Counselor Supervision and Edn., Am. Assn. Higher Edn., Creative Edn. Found., N.J. Psychol. Assn., N.Y. Psychol. Assn., Am. Pers. and Guidance Assn., Ackerman Family Inst., N.J. Assn. Marriage and Family Counselors, Am. Assn. Marriage and Family Counselors, Eastern Assn. Sex Therapists, Soc. Sci. Study Sex Therapy and Rsch., Argentine Soc. Human Sexuality (hon.), Am. Assn. Sex Educators, Counselors and Therapists (regional bd., nat. accreditation bd., cert. internat. supr.), Nat. Assn. Women Deans and Counselors, Am. Coll. Pers. Assn. (nat. mem. commn. II 1973—76), N.Y. Acad. Sci., Women's Med. Assn. N.Y.C., Am. Coll. Sexuality (cert.), Internat. Assn. Marriage and Family Counselors, Assn. Counseling Supervision, Alpha Chi Alpha, Kappa Delta Pi, Pi Lambda Theta. Home: 9 Sturges Commons Westport CT 06880-2832 Office: NY Presbyn Hosp Cornell Med Ctr 35 Park Ave New York NY 10016-3838 Business E-Mail: mwitkin903@aol.com.

WITKOP, BERNHARD, chemist; b. Freiburg, Baden, Germany, May 9, 1917; came to U.S., 1947, naturalized, 1953; s. Philipp W. and Hedwig M. (Hirschhorn) W.; m. Marlene Prinz, Aug. 8, 1945; children: Cornelia Johanna, Phyllis, Thomas. Diploma, U. Munich, 1938, PhD, 1940, Golden Dr. Diploma, 1990; ScD, Privat-Dozent, 1947. Matthew T. Mellon research fellow Harvard U., 1947-48, mem. faculty, 1948-50; spl. USPHS fellow Nat. Heart Inst., NIH, 1950-52; vis. scientist Nat. Inst. Arthritis and Metabolic Diseases, 1953, chemist, 1954-55, chief sect. metabolites, 1956-87, chief lab. chemistry, 1957-87, scholar, 1987-92, hon. scholar emeritus, 1993; vis. prof. U. Kyoto, Japan, 1961, U. Freiburg, Fed. Repubic Germany, 1962; adj. prof. U. Md. Med. Sch., Balt.; Nobel symposium lectr. Stockholm-Karlskoga, 1981. Mem. bd. Internat. Sci. Exchange, 1974; mem. exec. com. NRC, 1975; mem. Com. Internat. Exchange, 1977, Paul Ehrlich Award Com., Frankfurt, 1980-97. Editor: Fedn. European Biochem. Soc. Letters, 1979-90. Bd. dirs. Leo Baeck Inst., N.Y., 1996—. Recipient Superior Service award USPHS, 1967; Paul Karrer gold medal U. Zurich, 1971; Kun-ni-to (medal of sci. and culture 2d class) Emperor of Japan, 1975; Alexander von Humboldt award for sr. U.S. scientists, 1978 Mem. NAS, Am. Chem. Soc. (Hillebrand award 1958, Golden Membership 1997), Am. Acad. Arts and Sci., Am. Philos. Soc., Acad. Leopoldina (fgn.), Pharm. Soc. Japan (hon.), Chem. Soc. Japan (hon.), Japanese Biochem. Soc. (hon.), Acad. Scientarium et Artium Europaea, Rheinisch-Westfälische Akademie der Wissenschaften. Office: NIH-Dept Health Edn & Welfare 2A 27 Bldg 8 Bethesda MD 20892-0001 *A career between two worlds and two wars, spanning 50 years of research aims changing from structural to dynamic aspects, may be considered epigonal in the sense that my teacher H. Wieland (Nobel Prize 1928) always considered biochemistry as a neglected area of organic chemistry. In a small way I tried to follow his example and interests, such as oxidation mechanisms, natural products and highly active toxins.*

WITMAN, EDWARD PAUL, philosophy educator; b. Baldwin, N.Y., Jan. 27, 1945; m. Arlene Marie Rustmann, June 7, 1969; children: Christopher Paul, Michael Harrison. AB, Georgetown U., 1967; MA, PhD, Fordham U., 1978. Prof. Georgian Court Coll., Lakewood, NJ, 1972—, chmn. philosophy, history & gepgraphy, 2000—. Vis. lectr. Cathedral Coll., Dougleston, N.Y., 1971-72; ethics cons. Shoreline Behavioral Health, Toms River, N.J., 1994-96, Cmty. Med. Ctr., Toms River, 1992—. Trustee Citizens Com. Biomed. Ethics, N.J., 1988-93, Cath. Charities Ocean County, N.J., 1983-93. Mem. AAUP (chpt. pres. 1996-97), Am. Soc. Bioethics and Humanities, Assn. Practical and Profl. Ethics. Republican. Roman Catholic. Avocations: woodworking, rowing/sculling. Home: 108 Ridge Dr Toms River NJ 08753 Office: Georgian Court Coll 900 Lakewood Ave Lakewood NJ 08701 E-mail: witman@georgian.edu.

WITMAN, GEORGE BODO, III, cell biologist, researcher; b. Upland, Calif., July 19, 1945; s. George Bodo Jr. and Alwilda Marion (Cochran) W.; m. Rita Louise Ricciuti, June 14, 1969; children: George B., Anthony R., Andrew J. BA, U. Calif., Riverside, 1967; PhD, Yale U., 1972. Postdoctoral fellow U. Chgo., 1972-73, U. Wis., Madison, 1973-74; asst. prof. Princeton (N.J.) U., 1974-81; staff scientist Worcester Found. for Exptl. Biology, Shrewsbury, Mass., 1981-82, sr. scientist, 1983-90, prin. scientist, 1990-97, dir. male fertility program, 1985-97; dir. electron microscopy facility, 1981-97. Adj. assoc. prof. dept. cell biology U. Mass. Med. Sch., Worcester, 1985-93, adj. prof., 1993-97, prof., 1997—; George F. Booth chair of Basic Sci., 1998—; dir. U. Mass. MEd. Sch. Electron Microscopy Facility, 1997—. Mem. editl. bd. Cell Motility and the Cytoskeleton, 1986—; contbr. articles to profl. jours. Mem. AAAS, Am. Soc. for Cell Biology, Am. Soc. for Biochemistry and Molecular Biology, Genetics Soc. Am., Protein Soc., Microscopy Soc. Am., Soc. for Study of Reprodn. Office: Univ Mass Med Sch Dept Cell Biology 55 Lake Ave N Worcester MA 01655-0002

WITMAN, LAURA KATHLEEN, writer, security professional; b. Pottstown, Pa., Mar. 4, 1957; d. William Tedford and Kathleen (Nieman) W. Student, San Bernardino Valley Coll., 1976-79; Degree in Actg. magna cum laude, Adelphi Bus. Coll., San Bernardino, Calif., 1985. Cert. acctg. bookkeeper. Silent alarm monitor, payroll acct. Comml. Security Alliance, San Bernardino, Calif., 1985—. Author: The Sun, 1994; (poetry) World of Poetry, 1990, National Library of Poetry, 1992, 94, 95, 96, 98, Sparrowgrass, 1993; (short story) Antivivesection Soc., 1993, Animal Voice, 1994, Paws Newsletter, 1993, 94, 96, A Dogs Day Newsletter, 1994, House Rabbit Soc., 1994, 95, songs. Mem. Gay and Lesbian Cmty. Ctr. Inland Empire, Heartland Christian Fellowship Met. Cmty. Ch., Inland Empire Pride Coun. Mem. People for Ethical Treatment of Animals, House Rabbit Soc. Democrat. Home: 7877 Willow Ave Riverside CA 92504-2624

WITMAN, PHILIP ALAN, pharmaceutical researcher, epidemiologist; b. N.Y.C., Apr. 7, 1956; s. Seymour and Ruth Witman; m. Nancy Judith Kahn, Sept. 1, 1985 (dec. Apr. 1994); m. D. Bonnie Perlmutter, Mar. 24, 1996; children: Jonathan Krigel, Anna Krigel, Rebecca Kahn-Witman. BA, Yale Coll., 1978; MPH, Yale U., 1980, MPhil, 1986. Rsch. asst. Nicholas Inst. Sports Medicine and Athletic Trauma, N.Y.C., 1977-80; group leader internal medicine Ayerst Labs., 1981-84; sr. clin. rsch. assoc. Biogen Rsch. Corp., Cambridge, Mass., 1984-87; clin. team leader Centocor, Inc., Malvern, Pa., 1987-90; dir. clin. ops. HEM Pharm. Corp., Phila., 1993-94; mgr. clin. sci. affairs U.S. Bioscience, Inc., West Conshohocken, 1997-98; dir. clin. devel. Protarga, Inc., King of Prussia, 1998—2001; assoc. dir. supportive care group, oncology GlaxoSmithKline, Collegeville, 2001—. Cons. Covalent Rsch. Alliance, Wayne, Pa., 1994. Contbr. articles to profl. jours. Pub. Health Tng. grantee DHHS, 1978-80, Specialized Tng. grantee U. Pa., 1992-94, Rsch. grantee USPHS, 1993-94. Mem. Am. Assn. Cancer Rsch. (assoc. mem. coun. 1996-97), Assn. Clin. Rsch. Profls., Am. Soc. Clin. Oncology. Avocations: downhill skiing, cross country skiing, bicycling, hiking, reading. Home: 8210 Fairview Rd Elkins Park PA 19027-2119 Office: GlaxoSmithKline PO Box 5089 1250 S Collegeville Rd Collegeville PA 19426-0989

WITMER, DIANE F. communications educator; b. Pasadena, Calif., Jan. 20, 1945; d. Stanley Lamar and Mary Evelyn Witmer; 1 child, David William Penkoff. AA, Golden West Coll., Huntington Beach, Calif., 1977; BS in BA, U. LaVerne (Calif.), 1980; MS in Sys. Mgmt., U. So. Calif., L.A., 1989; MA in Communication Arts, U. So. Calif., 1993, PhD in Orgnl. Comm., 1994. Dir. pub. rels. Weight Watchers, Santa Ana, Calif., 1980-84; dir. comm. March of Dimes, Costa Mesa, 1986-90; prin. Penkoff Comm. Resources, L.A., 1990-92; instr. Calif. State U., Fullerton, 1990-94; asst. lectr. comm. arts and scis. U. So. Calif., University Park, 1991-94; asst. prof. Purdue U., West Lafayette, Ind., 1994-97; assoc. prof. Calif. State U., Fullerton, 1997—. Editor, The Paper Weight, 1981-84. Chmn. award com. March of Dimes, Costa Mesa, nat. vol., 1980—; pub. info. officer in disaster Orange County chpt. ARC, Santa Ana, Calif. Mem. Pub. Rels. Soc. Am. (accredited mem.), U. So. Calif. Alumni Assn., Pacific Chorale. Avocations: choral singing.

WITMER, G. ROBERT, retired state supreme court justice; b. Webster, N.Y., Dec. 26, 1904; s. George H. and Lillian (Woodhull) W.; m. Marian P. Costello, June 27, 1936; children: George Robert, John R., Thomas W., Sylvia Witmer Bissell. AB, U. Rochester, N.Y., 1926; LL.B., Harvard U., 1929. Bar: N.Y. 1929. Pvt. practice, Rochester, 1929-45; ptnr. Easton & Witmer, 1931-45; surrogate Monroe County, 1946-53; justice N.Y. State Supreme Ct., 1954-81, assoc. justice appellate div. 1st dept., 1963-67, appellate div. 4th dept., 1968-81; jud. adminstrv. officer, appellate div. N.Y. State Supreme Ct. (4th dept.), 1981-94; adminstrv. judge N.Y. State Supreme Ct. (7th Jud. Dist.), 1962-68; ret., 1994. Town atty., Webster, 1934-35; served on N.Y. State Ct. Appeals, 1974. Co-author: N.Y. Pattern Jury Instructions-Civil, Vol. 1, 1965, rev. edit., 1974, Vol. 11, 1968; co-chmn. pub. com. Practitioner's Handbook for Appeals Appellate Divs. N.Y., 1979, Practitioner's Handbook for Appeals to the Court of Appeals of New York, 1981. Supr. Town of Webster and County of Monroe, 1936-45; chmn. Webster Republican Com., 1933-45, mem. exec. com. of Monroe County Republican Com., 1933-45. Mem. Am., N.Y. State, Monroe County Bar Assns., Am. Law Inst., Webster Grange, Univ. Club (Rochester), Masons, Theta Chi. Home: 45 Corning Park Webster NY 14580-3503

WITMER, GEORGE ROBERT, JR. lawyer; b. Rochester, N.Y., Mar. 23, 1937; s. George Robert and Marian Pauline (Costello) W.; m. Nancy Rosetta Wenner, Dec. 28, 1968; children: Wendy Lynn, Heidi Dawn, George Robert, III, Frank David. AB, U. Rochester, 1959; LL.B., Harvard U., 1962. Bar: N.Y. 1962, U.S. Dist. Ct. (we. dist.) N.Y. 1963, U.S. Supreme Ct. 1967, U.S. Dist. Ct. (no. dist.) N.Y. 1977, U.S. Ct. Appeals (2d cir.) 1998. Assoc. Nixon, Hargrave, Devans & Doyle, Rochester, 1962-70, ptnr., 1970-99, Nixon Peabody, Rochester, 1999—. Instr. in bus. law U. Rochester, 1965-66; mem. com. to advise and cons. Jud. Conf. State N.Y. on Civil Practice Law and Rules, 1970-77; mem. N.Y. State Jud. Inst. on Professionalism in the Law, 1999—; mem. Adv. Group to N.Y. State and Fed. Jud. Coun., 1999—. Mem. N.Y. State Rep. Com., 1976-93; trustee Eastman Dental Ctr. Rochester, 1977-97, pres. bd. trustees, 1989-90; trustee U. Rochester, 1979—, chmn. exec. com., 1992—; trustee Eastman Dental Ctr. Found., 1997—. Fellow N.Y. Bar Found. (dir. 1991-96), ABA Found.; mem. ABA, Monroe County (N.Y.) Bar Assn., N.Y. State Bar Assn. (ho. of dels. 1978—, v.p. 1984-88, sec. 1989-90, pres.-elect 1993-94, pres. 1994-95, exec. com. environ. law sect. 1981-96, environ. law sect. Disting. Svc. award), Am. Law Inst., Rochester Rotary Club (dir. local club 1977-79, pres. local club 2001-02), Masons (master 1971), Phi Beta Kappa. Republican. Lutheran. Home: 892 Lake Rd Webster NY 14580-9008 Office: Nixon Peabody LLP PO Box 31051 Clinton Sq Rochester NY 14604-1729 E-mail: grwitmer@nixonpeabody.com.

WITMER, JOHN HARPER, JR. lawyer; b. Phila., May 5, 1940; s. John Harper and Jane Carolyn (Lentz) Witmer; m. Arlene Marie Rosipal, June 9, 1962; 1 dau., Tara Leah. BA, Pa. State U., 1962; JD, George Washington U., 1969. Bar: Md. 1969, D.C. 1970, Ill. 1979. Mgmt. analyst Nat. Security Agy., Ft. Meade, Md., 1963-66; mem. Sidley & Austin, Washington, 1969-78; sr. v.p., gen. counsel DEKALB Energy Co., 1978-95, DEKALB Genetics Corp., 1978-99; ret., 1999. Mem. Ill. State Bar Assn., Md. State Bar Assn., D.C. Bar Assn. Home: 2575 Greenwood Acres Dr Dekalb IL 60115-4916

WITMER, JOHN RICHARD, librarian; b. Dallas, Dec. 26, 1949; s. John Albert and Doris May (Ferry) W.; m. Joyce Ann Pelzl, Nov. 25, 1972; 1 child, Katherine Anne. Student, Wheaton (Ill.) Coll., 1967-70; BS, West Tex. State U., 1971; MSLS, East Tex. State U., 1974; postgrad., Dallas Theol. Sem., 1978-81. Cert. secondary tchr., driving instr., learning resources specialist, Tex. Learning resources specialist Sherman (Tex.) Ind. Sch. Dist., 1974-76, Ector County Ind. Sch. Dist., Odessa, Tex., 1978-80; acting head libr. Calvary Bible Coll., Kansas City, Mo., 1976-77; head libr. Am. Christian Coll., Tulsa, 1977-78; tech. svcs. libr. Odessa Coll., 1980-82; tchr. county youth ctr. Ector County Ind. Sch. Dist., Odessa, Tex., 1985; reader svcs. libr. Wayland Bapt. U., Plainview, 1986-87; vis. tchr. Lubbock (Tex.) Ind. Sch. Dist., 1987-88; learning resources specialist Dallas Ind. Sch. Dist., 1988-90, 94-99; head libr. San Elizario Ind. Sch. Dist., El Paso, Tex., 1991-94; audio visual libr. Klein Ind. Sch. Dist., Houston, 1999—. Deacon Scofield Meml. Ch., Dallas, 1971-74, Odessa Bible Ch., 1981-86; mem. cast, crew mem. Permian Playhouse, Odessa, 1979-82. Capt. U.S. Army, 1972-85. Mem. Tex. Libr. Assn. (life), Classroom Tchrs. Dallas (bldg. rep. 1989-90), Odessa Profl. Educators (sec., v.p., pres. state dist. rep. 1978-81), Odessa Univ. Kiwanis (v.p., pres. 1984-85). Republican. Avocations: collecting books and trivia, church work, contests, travel. Home: 15114 Runbell Pl Houston TX 77095-3228

WITMEYER, JOHN JACOB, III, lawyer; b. New Orleans, Dec. 18, 1946; s. John J. and Thais Audrey (Dolese) W. BS, Tulane U., 1968; JD with distinction, Duke U., 1971. Bar: N.Y. Assoc. Mudge Rose Guthrie & Alexander, N.Y.C., 1971-76; ptnr. Ford Marrin Esposito & Wittmeyer (now Ford, Marrin, Esposito, Witmeyer & Gleser LLP), 1976—. Bd. trustees Gregorian U. Found., 1999—; adv. coun. Paul Tulane Coll., Tulane U., 1998—; bd. dirs. Tulane Assocs., Tulane U., 2001—. Col. U.S. Army. Mem.: Order of the Holy Sepulchre (knight). Office: Ford Marrin Esposito Witmeyer & Gleser LLP Wall St Plz New York NY 10005-1875

WITROD, SISTER MARY ROSALITA, nursing home administrator; b. Chgo., Oct. 17, 1920; d. Anthony and Agatha (Kolodziejczyk) W. Grad., Holy Family Hosp. Sch. Nursing, 1945; BS, Marquette U., 1960, M in Nursing Edn., 1961. Joined Congregation of Felician Sisters, Roman Cath. Ch., 1939; lic. nursing home adminstr. Dir. nursing St. Mary's Hosp., Centralia, Ill., 1947-51; staff nurse Community Hosp., Bastrop, La., 1951-54; ICU instr. St. Mary Sch. Nursing, Chgo., 1977-81; quality assurance coord. St. Frances Hosp., Milw., 1981-84; long term care adminstr. St. Andrew Home, Niles, Ill., 1984-91; coord. nusing edn. program Polish Am. Assn. (formerly Polish Welfare Assn.), Chgo., 1991—. Program coord., developer Basic Nurse Asst. Program approved by Dept. Pub. Health to certify nurse assts., Job Tng. Program through Office of Mayor, Chgo.; developer Phys. Rehab. Aide Program approved by Dept. Long Term Care-Pub. Aid. Recipient Spl. Achievement award Polish Am. Assn., 1999; grantee Dept. Cmty. Affairs, Job Tng. and Econ. Devel., 2001; received funding to train students in basic nurse asst. program Job Tng. and Econ. Devel. Program, 2001, funding to train students in basic nurse asst. program from pvt. hosp., 2001. Mem. Am. Coll. Nursing Home Adminstrs., Ill. Assn. Nursing Home Adminstrs. Home: 3800 W Peterson Ave Chicago IL 60659-3116

WITSELL, ETHEL HOLDEN HOWARD, artist; b. Columbus, Ga., Jan. 3, 1941; d. William and Ethel (Holden) Howard; m. Edward Leigh Witsell, Nov. 1, 1963; children: William, Alice. BA, Columbus Coll. Exhibits include: Rankin Exec. Gallery, Columbus, 1990—, Columbus Coll. Fine Art Hall, 1980—, 3d Army Headquarters War Room, Atlanta; pvt. collections. Mem. Nat. League Am. Pen Women, Jr. League Columbus. Republican. Episcopal. Home: 3201 Turkey Ln Phenix City AL 36869-3326

WITT, ALAN MICHAEL, lawyer, accountant; b. Chgo., Apr. 13, 1952; m. Pamela Beth Ander, Dec. 29, 1976; children: Caryn, Kenneth, Amy. BS in Acctg., U. Ill., 1974, JD. Bar: Ill. 1977. Tax and audit cons. Weisbard, Strauss & Snider, Chgo., 1977-81; sole practice Wheeling, Ill., 1977—; tax mgr. Laventhol & Horwath, Chgo., 1981-83; tax ptnr. Ostrow, Reisin, Berk & Abrams, Ltd., 1983—; mng. dir., 1992-95. Lectr. law Lewis Coll. Law, Glen Ellyn, Ill., 1980, Kent Coll. Law, Chgo., 1981—. Co-author: Year End Tax Planning, 1982, 3rd rev. edit., 1986; editor: The Tax Advisor Tax Clinic, 1990-96; co-editor: Callaghan's Legal Checklists, 1985-96; contbg. editor: Hanbook for Tax Advisors, 1990—. Dir. Chgo. Estate Planning Coun.; chmn. profl. adv. com. Jewish Fedn. Mem. ABA, AICPAs (accredited personal fin. splst.), Ill. State Bar Assn., Chgo. Bar Assn., Ill. CPAs Soc., Beta Gamma Sigma, Tau Kappa Epsilon. Home: 1155 Wayne Ave Deerfield IL 60015-2824 Office: Ste 2600 455 N Cityfront Plaza Dr Chicago IL 60611-5506

WITT, CATHERINE LEWIS, neonatal nurse practitioner, writer; b. Burlington, Iowa, Nov. 21, 1957; d. Rodney Darrell and Neola Ann (Wharton) Lewis; m. John Robert Witt, Mar. 31, 1984; children: Jeffrey Lewis, Jennifer Diane. BSN, U. No. Colo., 1980; MSN, U. Colo., 1987. Cert. neonatal nurse practitioner. Staff nurse St. Joseph's Hosp., Denver, 1980-85; neonatal nurse practitioner Denver Children's Hosp., 1986-88; coord. neonatal nurse practitioner and neonatal transport Presbyn.-St. Luke's Med. Ctr., Denver, 1988—. Contbr. chpts. to books. Troop leader Girl Scouts U.S.; children's Bible tchr., altar guild Episcopal Ch. Mem. Nat. Assn. Neonatal Nurses (co-chair program com. 1992-94, bd. dirs., dir.-at-large 1997-99, sec. 1999-2000, pres.-elect 2001—), Nat. Cert. Corp. (test. com. 1994-96). Democrat. Episcopalian. Avocations: reading, sewing, dance. Home: 17586 E Dickenson Pl Aurora CO 80013-4180 Office: Presbyn-St Luke's Med Ctr 1719 E 19th Ave Denver CO 80218-1235 E-mail: 70044.2401@compuserve.com.

WITT, DAVID L. curator, writer; b. Kansas City, Mo., Nov. 3, 1951; s. Lloyd Vernon and Dean Witt. BS in Polit. Sci., Kans. State U., 1974; M Liberal Studies, U. Okla., 2000. Naturalist Naish Nature Ctr., Edwardsville, Kans., summers 1967-70; asst. curator Seton Mus., Cimarron, N.Mex., summers 1972-74; curatorial asst. Riley County Hist. Mus., Manhattan, Kans., 1973-74; mus. asst. Millicent Rogers Mus., Taos, N.Mex., 1976-77; curator The Gaspard House Mus., 1978-79, The Harwood Found., Taos, 1979—. Author: The Taos Artists, 1984, Taos Moderns: Art of the New, 1992 (Southwest Book award Border Regional Libr. Assn. 1993); co-author: Spirit Ascendant: The Art and Life of Patrociño Barela, 1996 (Southwest Book award Border Regional Libr. Assn. 1997); contbr. Taos Artists and Their Patrons, 1898-1950; contbr. articles to profl. jours. Organizer first N.Mex. Art History Conf., 1986;

founder S.W. Art Hist. Coun., 1990. Mem. PEN, Am. Assn. Mus., N.Mex. Assn. Mus. (pres. 1986-88). Democrat. Home: PO Box 317 Taos NM 87571-0317 Office: 4081 NDCBU Taos NM 87571-6004 E-mail: dlw@laplaza.org.

WITT, DENNIS RUPPERT, secondary school mathematics educator; b. Buffalo, Apr. 25, 1954; s. Carlton Albert and Elinor Marie (Ruppert) W.; m. Donna Violet Endres, July 9, 1983; 1 child Ashley Endres Witt. BS in Math., SUNY, Fredonia, 1976; cert. in Cobol programming, Erie C.C., 1979; MS in Edn., Canisius Coll., 1981, MS in Ednl. Adminstrn., 1993. Cert. math. tchr. and sch. dist. adminstr., N.Y. Tchr. jr. high math. Frontier Ctrl. Sch., Hamburg, N.Y., 1977-90, tchr. sr. high math., 1988-2001, tchr. middle sch. math., 2001—. Cons. spl. computer projects Goldome Realty Credit Corp., Amherst, N.Y., 1985-87, Chevrolet/GMC Saginaw divsn., Buffalo, 1988, Faulring's Cabinet Making, North Collins, N.Y., 1989, Avanti Corp., 1987, Gen. Mills, 1975-77; adminstrv. asst, prin.. Frontier Summer Sch., 1993-96; curriculum cons. in field. Named Girls Cross-Country Coach of Yr., Channel 7 TV, Buffalo, 1987. Avocations: coaching, running. Office: Frontier Ctrl Sch 2751 Amsdell Rd Hamburg NY 14075-1335

WITT, GERHARDT MEYER, hydrogeologist; b. New Haven, Sept. 28, 1953; s. Governor Martin and Florence Elizabeth (Meyer) W.; 1 chld, George Michael. BA in Geology, Furman U., 1976. Registered profl. geologist, Fla., N.C., Ind., Tenn., Alaska. Hydrogeologist Geraghty & Miller, Inc., West Palm Beach, Fla., 1976-82; sr. hydrogeologist, group mgr. water resource Camp Dresser & McKee Inc., Fort Lauderdale, 1982-90; mgr. spl. svcs. Versar, Inc., 1990; area mgr., supervising hydrogeologist, corp. geologist Parsons Brinckerhoff Gore & Storrie, West Palm Beach, 1990-93; pres., prin. hydrogeologist Gerhardt M. Witt and Assocs., Inc., 1993—. Contbg. author: Reverse Osmosis: Membrane Technology, Water Chemistry, and Industrial Applications, 1993; contbr. papers to profl. publs. Mem. Am. Inst. Profl. Geologists, Geol. Soc. of Am., Nat. Water Well Assn. Presbyterian. Home: 68 Paxford Ln Boynton Beach FL 33426-7627 Office: Gerhardt M Witt & Assocs Inc 1495 Forest Hill Blvd Ste F West Palm Beach FL 33406-6073

WITT, HUGH ERNEST, technology consultant; b. Winchester, Ky., Nov. 18, 1921; s. Hugh E. and Louella (Milliken) W.; m. Janie Bryan (dec. Oct. 1990); m. Evelyn Chapman, Apr. 22, 1993. Student, Transylvania U., 1941-43; BS, U. Ky., 1945; MS, MIT, 1957. Asst. to dep. asst. sec. Dept. of Air Force, Washington, 1954-61, dep. asst. sec., 1961-70, Dept. of Navy, Washington, 1970-73; prin. dep. asst. Sec. of Def., 1973-74; fed. procurement policy adminstr. Office Mgmt. and Budget, 1974-77; dir., govt. liaison United Techs. Corp., 1977-81, v.p., govt. liaison, 1981-87, cons. to United Techs. Corp., 1987—. Pres. Old Town Civic Assn., Alexandria, Va., 1961-63; bd. dirs. Alexandria Hist. Found.; mem. Alexandria Bd. Archtl. Rev., 1964-77; trustee Alexandria Hosp. Found., 1992-94. Alfred P. Sloan fellow MIT, Cambridge, Mass., 1956-57. Fellow Nat. Contract Mgmt. Assn.; mem. Aerospace Industries Assn., Nat. Security Indsl. Assn., MIT Alumni Assn., Soc. Sloan Fellows, Kappa Alpha.

WITT, JEFFREY R. cardiologist; b. Dec. 20, 1949; BS, U. Wis., 1972; MD, Abraham Lincoln Sch. Medicine, 1976. Clin. instr. medicine U. Ill., Chgo., 1978-81; pres. Suncoast Med. Clinic, St. Petersburg, Fla., 1986-90; med. dir. ICU Sun Bay Med. Ctr., 1981-92, chmn. dept. medicine, 1988-92; ptnr., joint practice Heart and Vascular Inst. Fla., Petersburg, 1993—. Dir. adult echocardiography Bayfront Med. Ctr., St. Petersburg, 1994—; asst. clin. prof. medicine dept. family practice, U. S. Fla., Tampa, 1984—. Office: Heart and Vascular Inst Fla 603 7th St S Saint Petersburg FL 33701-4719

WITT, JIM, editor; Asst. mng. editor, news Star-Telegram Arlington, 1986—92, editor, 1992—95; publ. Star Telegram Northeast Tarrant County Ed., 1995—95; editor Ft. Worth Star-Telegram Knight-Ridder, Inc., Ft. Worth, 1996—. Office: Knight-Ridder Inc 400 W 7th St Fort Worth TX 76102-4701*

WITT, MELVIN SYLVAN, periodical editor, publisher; b. Stockton, Calif., Dec. 25, 1925; s. Arnold and Sarah (Peletz) W.; m. Dorothy Halling, June 17, 1949; children: Ann, Mallory. BS, U. Calif., Berkeley, 1948; JD, U. Calif., San Francisco, 1951. Bar: Calif. 1952. Trial atty. State Compensation Ins. Fund, L.A., 1954-57; appellate atty. Calif. Indsl. Accident Commn., San Francisco, 1957-60, trial referee, 1961-64; pvt. practice Berkeley, 1966-68; rsch. atty. Calif. Continuing Edn. of Bar, 1969-75; sec., dep. commr. Calif. Workers' Compensation Appeals Bd., San Francisco, 1964-66, chmn., 1975-80, Calif. Workers' Compensation Adv. Commn. to Calif. State Bar, 1974-75; founder, editor, pub. Calif. Workers' Compensation Reporter, Berkeley, 1973—. Adj. prof. law Golden Gate U. Law Sch., San Francisco, 1971—75, 1981, McGeorge Law Sch., U. of Pacific, Sacramento, 1973—75. Editor, co-author: California Workers' Compensation Practice, 2nd edit., 1973. With inf., U.S. Army, 1944-46, ETO. Named Pub. Ofcl. of Yr., Calif. Applicants' Attys. Assn., Sacramento, 1980; recipient commendation by resolution Calif. State Legislature, Sacramento, 1981; CAAA scholar, 1999. Mem. 78th Inf. Divsn. Vets. Assn. Democrat. Avocations: WWII history, travel. Bus. Office: Calif Workers Compensation Reporter PO Box 975 Berkeley CA 94701-0975 E-mail: editor@cwcr.com.

WITT, MICHAEL JOHN, history educator, priest; b. St. Louis, July 2, 1948; s. Michael Joseph Witt and Ethel Florence Lang. BA, Christian Bros. Coll., Memphis, 1970; PhD summa cum laude, St. Louis U., 1980; MDiv summa cum laude, Kenrick-Glennon Sem., Shrewsbury, Mo., 1991. Ordained June 16, 1990. History instr. Bishop Kelley H.S., Tulsa, Okla., 1970-75, CBC Mil. Inst., Clayton, Mo., 1975-79; assoc. prof. Christian Bros. Coll., Memphis, 1981-87; assoc. pastor St. Monica Ch., Creve Coeur, Mo., 1990-92, Ste. Genevieve (Mo.) Ch., 1992-94; pastor Most Blessed Sacrament, St. Louis, 1994-2000; assoc. prof. Kenrick Sem., Shrewsbury, Mo., 1999—. V.p. student svcs. Christian Bros. Coll., 1985-86; mem. Continuing Formation, St. Louis, 1992—, Campaign for Human Devel., St. Louis, 1998-2000; retreat master Cenacle Retreat Ctrs., St. Louis, Memphis, New Orleans, 1996—; mem. Cath. Charities bd., Archdiocese Coun. Priests, Archdiocese Curia, DTR Continuing Formation. Author: Devolution of CBC, 1981, I Phil, 1987. Active City Coun. Task Force, Memphis, 1986, Build-up Ste. Genevieve Flood Relief, 1993-94, Kings Area Neighborhood Assn., St. Louis, 1994-2000; founder USA Youth Wrestling Club, Ste. Genevieve, 1992-94. Mem. KC, Pi Kapa Phi (chpt. founder 1986—), Alpha Sigma Nu. Roman Catholic. Avocations: sailing, gardening, coach wrestling, cooking, foreign travel. Home: 11917 Sioux Point Dr Sainte Genevieve MO 63670-7114 Office: Kenrich-Glennon Sem 6500 Glennon Dr Saint Louis MO 63119

WITT, NANCY CAMDEN, artist; b. Richmond, Va., Oct. 24, 1930; d. Roland Parker and Lucy Catherine (Haydon) Riddick; m. Robert Roy Camden, 1951 (div. 1960); children: John Bradley, Matthew David; m. John Temple Witt, Apr. 2, 1966 (div. June 1990); 1 child, Jeremy Temple. BA, Old Dominion U., 1965; MFA, Va. Commonwealth U., 1967; DFA (hon.), Randolph-Macon Coll., 1997. Comml. artist, 1952-60; chmn. art dept. Richard Bland Coll., Petersburg, Va., 1960-63; studio artist Ashland, 1965—; owner Cross Mill Gallery. One woman shows include Sharon Bennett Gallery, Atlanta, 1973, Asheville (N.C.) Mus. of Fine Arts, 1976, Longwood Coll., Farmville, Va., 1974, 77, Randolph-Macon Woman's Coll., Lynchburg, Va., 1974, 79, Phillip Morris, Inc., Richmond, 1978, VMI, Lexington, 1965, 79, Touchstone Gallery, N.Y.C., 1974, Roanoke Coll., Salem, 1979, 20th Century Gallery, Williamsburg, Va. 1974, 82, 93, Randolph-Macon Coll., Ashland, Va., 1974, 79, 84, SECCA, Winston-Salem, 1980, U. Ill., Chgo., 1989, Portsmouth (Va.) Mus., 1984, Cudahy's, Richmond, Va., 1990, 92, 94, 96, 98, 2000, 2002, Between the Muse Gallery, Camden, Maine, 1996, Nancy Moore Fine Art, N.Y.C., 1996, 98, others; exhibited in group shows at Valentine Mus. Biennial, Richmond, 1962, Mint Mus., Charlotte, 1971, Miss. Mus. Art, 1979, Chrysler Mus., Norfolk, 1983, Touchstone Gallery, N.Y.C., 1986, Huntington (W.Va.) Mus. Art, 1992, Ridderhof Martin Gallery, Mary Washington Coll, Fredericksburg, Va., 2001; represented in permanent collections Markel Corp., Richmond, David Rockefeller Collection, Phillip Morris Co., Fed. Res. Bank, U. Va., Charlottesville, Va., Norfolk, Ethyl Corp., Richmond, CSX Corp., Richmond, Wheat First, Richmond, others; author: On Alternate Days: The Paintings of Nancy Witt, 1995, (film) Vanishing Point, 1973. Named Va. Artist of Yr., Woman's Caucus for Art, Va., 1993. Mem. Jungian Venture (co-founder, convener 1984-86). E-mail: wittn@rcn.com.

WITT, RONALD G. educator; b. Wayne, Mich., Dec. 23, 1932; s. Elmer M. Witt and Iris I. Palmer; m. Mary Ann Frese, June 13, 1965; children: Eric Frese, Martha I. Witt-Santa Lucia, Daria C. BA, U. Mich., 1954; PhD, Harvard U., 1965. Asst prof. history Harvard U., Cambridge, Mass., 1964-71; assoc. prof. history Duke U., Durham, N.C., 1971-80, prof. history, 1980—. Author: Hercules at the Crossroads, 1983, In the Footsteps of the Ancients, 2000; co-author: Cultural Roots and Continuities, 2000. Mem. Internat. Soc. Rhetoric, Renaisance Soc. Am. (v.p. 2000—), Medieval Acad. Am., Italian Hist. Soc. Avocation: dance. Office: Duke Univ Carr Bldg Durham NC 27708 E-mail: rwitt@duke.edu.

WITT, SUSAN CARREER, environmental educator, society administrator; b. Hartford, Conn., Sept. 23, 1946; d. Irving Gordon and Elma DeBrune C.; m. Curt John Witt, Aug. 13, 1965 (div. June 1972); life ptnr. Robert Scott Swann. BA in English, Boston U., 1970; MA in English, U. N.H., 1972; cert., Emerson Coll., 1973. Chair English High Mowing Sch., Wilton, 1973-77; adminstrv. asst. Inst. for Cmty. Econs., Boston, 1977-80; founder, adminstr. Cmty. Land Trust in the So. Berkshires, Great Barrington, Mass., 1980—; exec. dir. E.F. Schumacher Soc., 1980—. Author (with others): Poeple, Land and Community: Collected E.F. Schumacher iety Lectures, 1997; author: Small is Beautiful: Economics as if People Mattered, 1999, A Forest of Voices: Conversations in Ecology, 2000, Environmental Activists, 2000, Rooted in the Land: Essays on Community and Place, 1996. Founder, dir. Self Help Assn. for a Regional Economy, Great Barrington, 1981-2000, Land Conservancy, Great Barrington, 1990—, Fund for Affordable Housing, Great Barrington, 1990-97; adv. bd. Legacy Banks, Pittsfield, Mass., 1992—; cmty. adv. bd. WAMC Pub. Radio, Albany, 1993—; dir. Main St. Action Assn., Great Barrington, 1994-97; dir. Cmty. Ctr. in the So. Berkshires, 1990-95. Mem. The Orion Soc. (adv. bd. 1995—), Great Barrington Rotary Club (pres. 1992-93, Paul Harris fellow 1997). Avocations: gardening, reading, walking, travel. Office: EF Schumacher Soc 140 Jug End Rd Great Barrington MA 01230 E-mail: efssociety@aol.com.

WITT, THOMAS ROY, surgeon; b. Bryn Mawr, Pa., Jan. 7, 1950; BA in Psychology, Duke U., 1971; MD, Northwestern U., 1975. Intern Rush-Presbyn.-St. Lukes Hosp., Chgo., 1975-76, resident surgery, 1976-80; fellow surg. oncology Sloan-Kettering Cancer Ctr., N.Y.C., 1980-82; assoc. attending dept. gen. surgery Rush-Presbyn. St. Luke's Hosp., Chgo., 1986; assoc. prof. surgery Rush Med. Coll., 1988. Mem. ACS, AMA, Am. Soc. Clin. Oncology, Soc. Surg. Oncology, Soc. Head and Neck Surgeons. Office: 1725 W Harrison St Ste 409 Chicago IL 60612-3836 E-mail: trwitt50@aol.com.

WITT, TOM, economics researcher, educator; b. Borger, Tex., Apr. 22, 1944; s. Eugene Thomason and Helen C. (Hathaway) W.; m. Grethe A. Myles, Mar. 4, 1976. BA, Okla. State U., 1966; MA, Washington U., St. Louis, 1968, PhD, 1974. Asst. prof. dept. econs. W.Va. U., Morgantown, 1970-75, assoc. prof. dept. econs., 1975-80, acting asst. dean Grad. Sch., 1977-78, exec. dir. Bur. Bus. Rsch., 1985—, dir. Ctr. Econs. Rsch., 1985—, acting assoc. dean Coll. Bus. and Econs., 1985-86, assoc. dean rsch. and outreach Coll. Bus. and Econs., 1994—. Cons. Nat. Regulatory Rsch. Inst., Columbia, Ohio, 1980-81, Am. Electric Power, 1995—, Allegheny Power, 1997—, exec. legis. br. Govt. W.Va., 1985—; cons., expert witness W.Va. Human Rights Commn., Charleston, 1984; expert witness W.Va. Atty. Gen., 1987-88, Ashland Oil, 1992-93. Author: Power from the Appalachians, 1989, also monographs; co-editor: West Virginia in the Nineties: Policies for Econ. Progress; contbr. articles to profl. jours. Pres. Cheat Canyon Park Homeowners, Morgantown, 1979-87, Monongalia Arts Ctr., 1980-81; bd. dirs., treas. Friends of W.Va. Pub. Radio, Charleston, 1985-93, chmn., 1989-91; sec.-treas. Cheat Neck Pub. Svc. Dist., 1989-95, Main Street Morgantown, 1994—; mem. Monongalia County Econ. Devel. Authority, 1994—. Mem. Am. Econ. Assn., Am. Statis. Assn., Regional Sci. Assn., So. Econ. Assn., Assn. for Univ. Bus. and Econ. Rsch. (pres. 2000-2001). Home: 3202 Deerfield Ct Morgantown WV 26508-8612 Office: Bureau of Bus & Econ Rsch WV U PO Box 6025 Morgantown WV 26506-6025 E-mail: twitt@wvu.edu.

WITT, WALTER FRANCIS, JR. lawyer; b. Richmond, Va., Feb. 18, 1933; s. Walter Francis and Evelyn Virginia (Riggleman) W.; m. Rosemary Winter, Sept. 5, 1964; children: Leslie Anne Millman, Walter Francis III. BS, U. Richmond, 1954, JD, 1966. Bar: Va. 1966, D.C. 1974. Assoc. Hunton and Williams, Richmond, 1966-74, ptnr., 1974—. Contbr. articles to profl. jours. 1st lt. U.S. Army, 1955-57. Mem. ABA (chmn. real property com. sect. gen. practice 1995-2000, Va. Bar Assn., Richmond Bar Assn., D.C. Bar Assn., Phi Beta Kappa, Phi Delta Phi. Home: 8901 Tresco Rd Richmond VA 23229-7725 Office: Riverfront Plaza East Twr 451 E Byrd St Richmond VA 23219-3833

WITTBRODT, EDWIN STANLEY, consultant, former bank executive, former air force officer; b. Flint, Mich., Aug. 13, 1918; s. Stanley Frank and Marie (Ross) W.; m. Joan Helen Miller, Apr. 22, 1950; children: Stephanie Rita, Candace Lee, Edwin Stanley. Student, Gen. Motors Inst. Tech., 1936-38, Grad. Sch. Dept. Agr., 1950-51, Indsl. Coll. Armed Forces, 1961-62, George Washington U., 1962, U. So. Calif., 1963-64. Joined U.S. Army, 1941, commd. 2d lt., 1942; advanced through grades to brig. gen. USAF, 1968; various assignments U.S., 1941-49; budget officer Hdqrs. USAF, 1949-53, 56-61; dir. budget and acctg. Hdqrs. N.E. Air Command, Nfld., 1953-56; comptroller space systems div. Los Angeles, 1962-64; comptroller aero., systems div. Wright-Patterson AFB, 1964-66; asst. comptroller USAF, 1966-67; dir. acctg. and fin. Hdqrs. USAF, 1967-68; asst. comptroller air force for acctg. and fin., comdr. Air Force Acctg. and Fin. Ctr., Denver, 1968-71; v.p. systems Cen. Bank Denver, 1971-81, v.p. info. resources mgmt., 1981-84. Dir. Computer Congenerics Corp. Colo., Hasa Corp. Co-chmn. Combined Fed. Campaign, Denver, 1968-87; Hon. dir. USO, Denver, 1968-71, mem. council, 1971-87 . Decorated D.S.M., Legion of Merit, Soldier's medal, Commendation medal with oak leaf cluster; recipient Gen. Jimmy Doolittle Disting. Fellow award, Flint No. Alumni Assn. Disting. Fellow award, 1990, Treas. Dept. Pioneer in Elec. Commerce award, 1995. Mem. Am. Soc. Mil. Comptrollers (past pres. Washington chpt., nat. v.p. 1968-70, pres. Denver chpt. 1971-72), Assn. Govt. Accountants, Assn. Mil. Banks (dir. 1974-84), Am. Inst. Banking, Denver C. of C. (chmn. mil. affairs com. 1979-82), Aurora C. of C. (def. coun. 1987—), Air Force Assn. (v.p. N. Colo. 1971-72, pres. Silver and Gold chpt. 1972-73, state treas. 1976-83, pres. Mile High chpt. 1987-88) Clubs: Columbine Country. Home: 10 Niblick Ln Columbine Valley CO 80123 *I have adopted two attitudes that I believe assisted me in all of my undertakings: (1)— that of being what I call a "responsible non-conformist" and (2)— "no problems— just opportunities".*

WITTBRODT, FREDERICK JOSEPH, JR. automotive designer; s. Frederick Joseph Sr. and Hilda Lottie (Neubert) W.; children: Robin Lynn, Daniel Joseph. Grad., Philpot Sch. Automotive Body Drafting, Royal Oak, Mich., 1977, Entech. Engring., Troy, Mich., 1984; grad. SDRC Basic, Advanced and Assembly Modeling Tng., Henry Ford C.C., 2001. Completed C3P: Basic Part Modeling, 2000, C3P: Advanced Part Modeling, 2001. Automotive designer Modern Engring Co., Troy, Mich., 1976—77, Detroit Indsl. engring., Troy, 1977—78, Entech. Engring., Troy, 1978—80, Engring. Tech Ltd., Troy, 1980—86, Pioneer Engring., Dearborn, 1986—88, APD, Harrison Twp., 1988-89, Mega-Tech. Engring., Warren, 1989-90, Uni-Tech, Madison Heights, 1990-91, Harmon Auto at Harvard, Southfield, 1991, Lincoln Tech. at Schlegel, Madison Heights, 1991-92, Resource Techs. at Harvard Industries, Farmington Hills, Mich., 1992-95, Schefenacker Mfg. Ctr. (formerly Britax Vision Sys., Inc.), Marysville, 1995—2001. Mem. NRA, Internat. Platform Soc. Avocations: furniture design, landscape design, astronomy, home remodeling. Home: 2722 Dashwood Troy MI 48083 Office: 1855 Busha Hwy Marysville MI 48040-1892 E-mail: dpwittbrodt@msn.com.

WITTCOFF, HAROLD AARON, chemist; b. Marion, Ind., July 3, 1918; s. Morris and Bessie (Pruss) W.; m. Dorothy Brochin, 1946; 2 sons AB magna cum laude, DePauw U., 1940; PhD, Northwestern U., 1943; grad., Advanced Mgmt. Program, Harvard U., 1964. From mem. staff to v.p., dir. chem. R&D Gen. Mills, Inc., Mpls., 1943—69, v.p., dir. corp. rsch., 1969—79; dir. R & D Koor Chems., Beer Sheva, Israel, 1979-82; dir. process evaluation and rsch. planning Chem Systems, Tarrytown, N.Y., 1982-85; sci. adviser NEXANT/Chem Systems , White Plains, NY, 1985—; adj. prof. chemistry U. Minn., 1973-82. Vis. prof. Chulalongkorn U., Thailand, 1995—, Weizmann Inst., Israel, 1979—. Author: The Phosphatides, 1951, Industrial Organic Chemistry: A Perspective 2 vols. 1980; Pharmaceutical Chemicals in Perspective, 1989, Industrial Organic Chemicals, 1996; patentee in field. Recipient Minn. award Am. Chem. Soc., 1976 Mem. Phi Beta Kappa, Sigma Xi, Phi Eta Sigma. Home: Box 307 Apt 46-I Scarborough Manor Scarborough NY 10510 E-mail: hawittcoff@yahoo.com.

WITTE, ANN DRYDEN, economics educator; b. Oceanside, N.Y., Aug. 28, 1942; d. Harry Clifford and Frances Elizabeth (Ferguson) Dryden; 1 child, Jeffrey Dryden. BA in Polit. Sci. and History with highest honors, U. Fla., 1963; MA in Econs., Columbia U., 1965; PhD in Econs. and Oceanography, N.C. State U., 1971. Econ. analyst U.S. Govt., Washington, 1963-66, systems analyst, 1966-67; instr. econs. Tougaloo (Miss.) Coll., 1967-68, N.C. State U., Raleigh, 1970-72; vis. asst. prof. U. N.C., Chapel Hill, 1972-74, asst. prof. econs., 1974-79, assoc. prof., 1979-83, prof., 1983-85; rsch. assoc. Nat. Bur. Econ. Rsch., 1984—; prof. Wellesley (Mass.) Coll., 1985—, Fla. Internat. U., Miami, 1992—2000. Cons. to subcom. on oversight House Ways and Means Com., 1979; Fulbright lectr. Fed. U. Pernumburo, Recife, Brazil, 1981, Fed. U. Ceará, Fortaleza, Brazil, 1984 Cen. Sch. of Planning and Statis., Warsaw, 1987, Victoria U., Wellington, N.Z., 1988; lectr. testimony joint econ. com. U.S. Congress, Washington, 1980, coms. U.S. Ho. of Reps., Washington, 1982; resident scholar Rockefeller Found. Study and Conf. Ctr., Bellagio, Italy, 1983; rsch. assoc. Nat. Bur. Econ. Rsch., Cambridge, Mass., 1984—; mem. adv. group Internal Revenue, 1989; mem. com. on status of women in econs. profession, 1993-96; speaker, presenter in field. Author: Work Release in North Carolina: The Program and the Process, 1973, Work Release in North Carolina: An Evaluation of Its Post Release Effects, 1975, (with others) Basic Issue in Corrections Performance, 1982, (with Carl Simon) Beating the System; The Underground Economy, 1982, (with Peter Schmidt) An Economic Analysis of Crime and Justice: Theory, Methods and Applications, 1984; editor: (with V. Kerry Smith) Advances in Applied Micro-Economics, Vol. 3, 1984; (with Peter Schmidt) Predicting Recidivism Using Survival Models, 1988, (with Jeffrey Roth and John Scholz) Tax Compliance: An Agenda for Research; adv. editor Evaluation Rev., 1982—; mem. adv. bd. Criminological Research: Advances In Quantitative Method and Application, 1983-84; mem. editiorial bd. Rev. Regional Studies, 1976-79, Law and Soc. Rev., 1985-89, Jour. Quantitative Criminology, 1988-2001, Policy Studies Rev., 1988-94; referee Am. Econ. Rev., Demography, Econometrica, Land Econs., Jour. Polit. Econ., Quar. Jour. Econs., numerous others; contbr. numerous articles to profl. jours. Mem. rsch. and adv. com. N.C. Dept. Correction, 1974-76; advisor criminal justice planning N.C. Gov.'s Office, 1977; mem. spl. com. correctional programs N.C. Employment and Tng. Coun., 1982-85, spl. com. on social expts. MacArthur Found., 1984; bd. dirs. Police Found., Washington, 1984-91; mem. committee on Fgn. Tax Matters, 1991—95 tech. expert group Nat. Evaluation Project Pregnant & Substance Abusing Women & Infants HHS, 1991-95; mem. econs. adv. panel NSF, 1992-94. Rsch. grantee Nat. Inst. Justice, Washington, 1978-92, Nat. Inst. Child Health and Devel., Washington, 1981-83, NIMH, Washington, 1981-85, NSF, Washington, 1982-90, 93-96, U.S. Dept. HHS, 1995-; Woodrow Wilson fellow, Harvard Law Sch. fellow, Cambridge, 1987-88. Fellow Am. Soc. Criminology, Am. Statis. Assn., Royal Statis. Soc.; mem. Am. Tax Policy Inst. (bd. trustees 1990—, subcom. on internat. taxation), Nat. Acad. Scis. (panel on research and rehabilitative techniques 1977-80, ad hoc com. future of justice research 1982, com. on research on law enforcement and adminstrn. of justice 1980-84, ex-officio mem. 1984-88, chair panel for research on taxpayer compliance 1984-88), Am. Econ. Assn. (census adv. com. 1979-85, chair 1981, com. status of women in econs. profession 1993-95), Am. Statis. Assn. (com. on law and justice statistics 1982-84, cons. 1981), Law and Soc. Assn. (trustee 1981-82, 87-90, program com. 1984, Kalven prize com. 1990-91), Nat. Tax Assn./Tax Inst. Am. (program com. 1985, 91, bd. dirs. 1990-94), Ea. Econ. Assn. (program com. 1985-86), Inst. Law and Social Policy (adv. com. on criminal justice 1983-86), Phi Beta Kappa. Avocations: swimming, hiking, modern chamber music, travelling, reading.

WITTE, ARLINE (LYN WITTE), author/poet; BA summa cum laude, Ravenscroft U., Calif.; postgrad., NYU; student, N.Y. Inst. Advt., N.Y. Sch. Interior Design. Interviewer, writer NBC-TV, N.Y.C.; exec. asst. Geffen-Dunn Pub.; pub. rels. writer Westinghouse, CBS-TV, N.Y.C. and Calif.; advt. copywriter Esquire Mag., N.Y.C.; editor-in-chief Esquire's Profit Maker Mag.; author/poet Status Publishers, Conn. Author: Passion, Power and Prophecy: Based On Actual Events, 1996, Archangel: Secrets of the Cosmic Dawn, 1997, Song of the Soul: Poetry for the New Millennium, 1998, In Pursuit of Perfection: The Divine Imperative, 2000. Recipient Poet of Yr. award Magnum Opus Fine Arts Soc., 1996, 97, 98, Excellence in Latin award N.Y. Classical Club, Best Costume Design award NBC Dramatic Workshop, Refinement and Culture award Elite Etiquette Group, Scholastic Achievement award Arista Honor Soc., N.Y.C. Avocations: ballet, music, photography, astronomy.

WITTE, MARLYS HEARST, internist, educator; b. N.Y.C., 1934; MD, NYU Sch. Medicine, 1960. Intern N.C. Meml. Hosp., Chapel Hill, 1960-61; resident Bellevue Hosp. Ctr., N.Y.C., 1961-63; fellow NYU Hosp., St. Louis, 1965-69; instr. Washington U., 1965-69; prof. surgery U. Ariz., 1969—; attending internist Ariz. Health Sci. Ctr., Tucson, 1965-69, 69—. Mem. AAAS, AMA, Alpha Omega Alpha. Office: U Ariz Coll Medicine PO Box 245063 1501 N Campbell Ave Tucson AZ 85724-0001

WITTE, MERLIN MICHAEL, oil company executive; b. Los Angeles, Mar. 28, 1926; s. Anthony A. and Julia (Macke) W.; m. Donna Patricia Hurth, Jan. 22, 1949; children: James Anthony, Daniel Michael, Catherine Ann, Michael Leon, Robert Joseph, Joseph William, Anne Marie, William Benson, Janet Mary. BA, Loyola U., Los Angeles, 1949. With IRS, U.S. Treasury Dept., 1949-51; investment, tax mgr. McCulloch Motors Corp., also Robert P. McCulloch, 1951-55; pres., gen. mgr., dir. McCulloch Oil Corp., Los Angeles, 1956-80; pres., dir. Merlin Assocs., Inc., 1980—, M.M. Witte & Assocs., Inc., Los Angeles, 1980—; mgr., chief exec. United Oil Producers, 1984-86. Bd. dirs. Kent Fin. Svcs., Inc., Search Exploration, Inc.; bd. dirs., chmn. McCulloch Energy, Inc., 1991-95; co-chmn. The Am. Drilling Co., L.L.C., 1995-98; dir., CEO South Coast Oil Corp., 1996—. Mem. bd. regents Loyola Marymount U., L.A., 1991-97. Served with USAAF, 1944-45. Mem. Ind. Oil and Gas Producers Assn., Ind. Petroleum Assn., Western, West Cen. Tex. oil and gas assns., Town Hall, Bel-Air Country Club (pres. 1990-91), PGA West Golf Club.

WITTELS, BARNABY CAESAR, lawyer, writer; b. Phila., Mar. 28, 1948; s. David G. and Beatrice Tanya (Graitcr) W.; m. Heidi Jo Linsk, Sept. 8, 1974 (div. Aug. 1997); children: Kate Sophie, William David; m. Mary M. Labaree, Sept. 20, 1998. BA cum laude, Temple U., 1970; MA in Pol. Sci., Boston U., 1972, JD, 1975. Bar: Pa. 1975, U.S. Dist. Ct. (ea. dist.) Pa. 1985, U.S. Ct. Appeals (2d, 3d and 4th cir.) 1986. Asst. defender Defender Assn. of Phila., 1975-80; law clk. to Hon. Stanley Kubacki Ct. Common Pleas Phila. County, 1980-84; ptnr. Wittels, Newman & Bornstein, Phila., 1980-82; assoc. LaCheen & Alva, 1982-86; ptnr. LaCheen & Assoc., 1986—. Contbr. column to newspapers. Chair Northwest Victim Svcs., Phila., 1981-84, mem. counsel, 1984-90, mem. bd. dirs., 1983-90, chair, 1997— (outstanding svc. & leadership 1990), founding mem.; com. man 21st Divsn. Dem. Party, Phila., 1985-90, various polit. and jud. campaigns, 1980—; baseball coach Chestnut Hill Fathers Club, 1985-98, commr. 1991-93, 92-98; mem. exec. com. Northwest Interfaith Movement, 1985-86. Mem. NACDL, Pa. Assn. Criminal Def. Lawyers, Phila. Bar Assn. (fee dispute com. 1996—, mem. com. to elect good judges 1987-88, Pa. Bar Assn., Phila. Bar Found. (Apothaker award 1983). Democratic. Jewish. Avocations: writing, baseball, football, reading, woodworking. Office: LaCheen & Assoc 3100 Lewis Tower Bldg Philadelphia PA 19102 Fax: 215 735-4649. E-mail: barnabyw@aol.com.

WITTEN, DAVID MELVIN, radiology educator; b. Trenton, Mo., Aug. 16, 1926; s. Buford Isom and Mary Louise (Melvin) W.; m. Netta Lee Watkins, Dec. 23, 1950; children— David Melvin, II, Michael Lee. Student, Trenton Jr. Coll., 1943-44, 46-47; AB, Washington U., St. Louis, 1950, MD, 1954; MS in Radiology, U. Minn., 1960. Diplomate: Am. Bd. Radiology. Intern Virginia Mason Hosp., Seattle, 1954-55; practice medicine specializing in family medicine Trenton, Mo., 1955-57; fellow in radiology Mayo Clinic/Mayo Found., Rochester, Minn., 1957-60; cons. in diagnostic roentgenology Mayo Clinic, 1960-70; instr. Mayo Grad. Sch. Medicine, Rochester, 1960-66, asst. prof. radiology, 1966-70; pvt. practice medicine specializing in radiology Aberdeen, Wash., 1970-71; clin. assoc. prof. U. Wash., 1970-71; prof.

diagnostic radiology, chmn. dept. diagnostic radiology U. Ala., Birmingham, 1971-82; diagnostic radiologist in chief Univ. Hosp., 1971-82; prof., chmn. dept. radiology U. Mo., Columbia, 1982-87, prof. emeritus, 1987—, interim chmn. dept. radiology, 1998-99. Pres. U. Ala. Health Services Found., 1973-75 Author: Atlas of Tumor Radiology-The Breast, 1969, Clinical Urography, 1970, 77; contbr. articles on radiology of breast cancer, urologic and gastrointestinal disease to profl. jours.; mem. editorial bd. Am. Jour. Roentgenology, 1976-87, Applied Radiology, 1978-87, Urologic Radiology, 1979-87, Radiographics, 1983-87. Served with USNR, 1944-46. Fellow Am. Coll. Radiology; mem. AAAS, AMA, Radiol. Soc. N.Am., Am. Roentgen Ray Soc., Soc. Genitourinary Radiology (pres. 1981-82), Assn. Univ. Radiologists, Mo. Radiol. Soc. (pres. 1988-89), Mo. State Med. Assn., Can. Assn. Radiologists (hon.), Audubon Soc. (editor The Bluebird (Mo.) chpt. 1990-98). Home: 601 W Covered Bridge Rd Columbia MO 65203-9562 Office: Univ Mo Health Scis Ctr 1 Hospital Dr Columbia MO 65201-5276 E-mail: dmw@tranquility.net.

WITTEN, LOUIS, physics educator; b. Balt., Apr. 13, 1921; s. Abraham and Bessie (Perman) W.; m. Lorraine Wollach, Mar. 27, 1949 (dec. 1987); children: Edward, Celia, Matthew, Jesse; m. Francis L. White, Jan. 2, 1992. B.E., Johns Hopkins U., 1941, PhD, 1951; BS, NYU, 1944. Research assoc. Princeton U., N.J., 1951-53; research assoc. U. Md., College Park, 1953-54; staff scientist Lincoln Lab., MIT, 1954-55; assoc. dir. Martin Marietta Research Lab., Balt., 1955-68; prof. physics U. Cin., 1968-91, prof. emeritus, 1991—. Trustee Gravity Research Found. Editor: Gravitation: An Introduction to Current Research, 1962, Relativity: Procs. of Relative Conf. in Midwest of 1969, Symposium on Asymptotic Structure of Space-Time, 1976; patentee in field; contbr. numerous articles to sci. jours. Served to 1st lt. USAF, 1942-46 Fulbright lectr. Weismann Inst. Scis., Rehovot, Israel, 1963-64 Fellow Am. Phys. Soc.; mem. Am. Math. Soc., Internat. Astron. Union, AAAS. Office: Univ Cincinnati Dept Physics Cincinnati OH 45221-0011 E-mail: witten@physics.uc.edu.

WITTENBRINK, BONIFACE LEO, priest; b. Evansville, Ill., June 30, 1914; s. Max C. and Catherine Rose (Pautler) W. PhL, Gregorian U., Rome, 1939; STL, Ottawa (Can.) U., 1943; MA, Cath. U. Am., 1947. Ordained priest Oblates of Mary Immaculate, Roman Cath. Ch., 1941. Instr. Latin, logic, history and religion St. Henry's Coll., Belleville, Ill., 1943-48; instr., registrar, prin. high sch. dept. Coll. of Our Lady of the Ozarks, Carthage, Mo., 1948-52; founding dir. King's House of Retreats, Buffalo, 1952-53; mission procurator Roman Cath. Ch., St. Paul, 1955-56, 59-62; prin. Alemany High Sch. for Boys, Oblate Western Province, San Fernando, Calif., 1956-59; permanent sec. Conf. Maj. Superiors of Men, Washington, 1963-69; exec. dir., sec. Found. for Community Creativity, 1970-71; founder, dir., then dir. devel. Radio Info. Svc. for Blind and Handicapped, Belleville, 1972-84; pres., then local dir. Friends of Eye Rsch., Boston, 1983-87; exec. v.p. Citizens for Eye Rsch., Belleville, 1987—. Pres. Oblate Ednl. Assn., St. Paul, 1961-62; sci. adv. bd. Nat. Acad. Child Devel., 1984-86; mem. com. Eye Experience St. Louis, 1984; adv. bd. Welfare of the Blind, Inc., 1984—; adv. coun. svcs. for print-handicapped Nat. Pub. Radio, 1976-77; active Internat. Christian Leadership, 1968-72; bd. dirs. LOGOS Translators; ptnr. CBMI. Bd. dirs. Technoserve, 1968-72, Internat. Book Svc., 1969-72; vol. Ill. Literacy Project, 1989-90; founding charter mem., bd. dirs. Washington Workshops Found. Recipient RPI Internat. Vision award, 27th Annual Vision Awards, Agrama Harmony Gold and Light award, 2000, Beverly Hills, Calif. Mem. Madison County Assn. Blind, Mo. Coun. Blind, Am. Coun. of Blind (ednl. radio com. 1974-76), Am. Found. for Blind (radio talking book com. 1973-76), Inst. for Study of Econ. Systems (bd. dirs. 1971-72), Ednl. Communications Assn., Coun. for Dept. of Peace, Wycliffe Bible Translators Assn., Vols. for Internat. Tech. Assistance, Ill. Radio Info. Svc., Soc. Internat. Devel., UN Assn., Rotary Internat. (Paul Harris fellow), Belleville Econ. Progress, Eagles, KC, Press Club St. Louis, Am. Assn. Ret. Persons. Avocations: reading, travel. Home: 200 N 60th St Belleville IL 62223-3951

WITTENBRINK, JEFFREY SCOTT, lawyer; b. Cairo, May 24, 1960; s. Howard Samuel and Cherie Ellen (Martin) W.; m. Tamara Inez Parker, Aug. 5, 1989; children: Charlotte Jane, Jeffrey Scott Jr. BA, La. State U., 1984, JD, 1987. Bar: La. 1988, U.S. Dist. Ct. (ea. and mid. dists.) La. 1988, U.S. Dist. Ct. (we. dist.) La. 1989, U.S. Ct. Appeals (5th cir.) 1989, U.S. Supreme Ct. 1996. Law clk. to Judge William H. Brown, 19th Jud. Dist. Ct., Baton Rouge, 1987-88; assoc. Roy, Kiesel, Aaron & Tucker, 1988-91, Winston G. DeCuir & Assocs., Baton Rouge, 1991-93; pvt. practice Wittenbrink Law Firm, 1993—. Arbitrator Baton Rouge City Ct., 1993—; instr. CPCU's, Baton Rouge, 1991, Office Emergency Planning State of La., 1993. Contbr. articles to Around the Bar legal newsletter, 1987—. Coach debate team Cath. H.S., Baton Rouge, 1987-91, mock trial team Baton Rouge H.S., 1989-93; treas. Ingleside United Meth. Ch., Baton Rouge, 1991-92, trustee, bd. dirs., 1991—, chair pastor-parish com., 1992-2000, lay leader, 2001; mem., lectr. La. Vol. Lawyers for Arts, Baton Rouge, 1988—; bd. dirs. La. Crafts Coun., Baton Rouge, 1990—. Mem. ABA, ATLA, La. Bar Assn., Baton Rouge Bar Assn. (mem. newsletter com. 1987—, vol. indigent panel 1992—, chair CLE 1992—, chmn. membership com. 1993, chair Law Expo com. 1998, Pres.'s award 1993, Triple Century award 2001), Dean Henry George McMahon Am. Inn of Ct. (barrister, reporter 1993-95), Cortana Kiwanis (bd. dirs. 1994-97, pres. 1998-99, Lt. Gov. 2001-2002, Kiwanis Internat., La.-Miss.-W.Tenn. Dist. Divn. 8-B). Avocations: photography, fencing, writing. Office: 533 Europe St Baton Rouge LA 70802-6408 E-mail: jwbrink@aol.com.

WITTENSTEIN, MICHAEL DAVID, marketing professional; b. Orlando, Fla., Dec. 29, 1958; s. Sheldon and Patsy Ruth (Printz) W.; m. Lois Ilene Green, Apr. 3, 1990; 1 child, Isaac David. BA with high honors, U. Fla., 1980; M in Internat. Mgmt., Am. Grad. Sch. Internat. Mgmt., Glendale, Ariz., 1985. Market analyst Cushman & Wakefield, Atlanta, 1986-87; info. sys. cons. Wittenstein & Assocs., 1987-90; co-pres., dir. mktg. strategies GALILEO Inc., 1991—. CEO SupportWare, software pubs., 1991-92; cons. Apple Computer, Inc., The Nutrasweet Co., Xerox; spkr. on implication of photo CD in digital imaging; internat. spkr. including Comdex, Am. Mktg. Assn., Gergia Tech, Brazilian Mktg. Assn., Image World, Interactive TV Assn., Bus. OnLine, Internat. Assn. Bus. Communicators, Media/Options, Electronic Advt. Strategies, Interactive Multimedia, Internet/Intranet, others. Author: Managing Change: A Guide to Automation, (software) Business Presentation on PC, 1989, Help Service for PC, 1990, What Can Multimedia Do for Your Company?, Principles of Knowledge Navigation; developer: (interactive products) Talking Business Card, Laptop Sales System; contbr. articles to profl. jours.; prodr. 150 interactive multimedia projects and websites including AT&T, CNN, Coca-Cola, Delta Airlines, IBM, MCI Telecom., Turner Broadcasting, Goodwill Games, others; inventor of various electronic advertising delivery and measurement programs. Cons. ARC, The Ga. Shakespeare Festival, Atlanta, 1990—, Jewish Family Svcs., Atlanta, 1988—, Chabad of Cobb. Mem. Internat. Interactive Comm. Assn., Bus. and Tech. Alliance, Southeastern Software Assn., Am. Mktg. Assn., Sales & Mktg. Execs. Tech. Execs. Roundtable, Phi Beta Kappa, Omicron Delta Kappa. Avocations: racquetball, hiking, travel. Home: 1862 Wilkenson Crossing Marietta GA 30066 E-mail: mikewitt@galileoinc.com.

WITTHUHN, BURTON ORRIN, university official; b. Allentown, Pa., Aug. 22, 1934; s. Ray Arthur and Mae Marcella (Kline) W.; m. Patricia King, June 24, 1961; children: Jonathan, Andrew. BS, Kutztown (Pa.) U., 1956; MEd, Pa. State U., 1962, PhD, 1968. Tchr. Allentown (Pa.) Pub. Schs., 1956-63; teaching asst., assoc. Pa. State U., University Park, 1963-66, rsch. asst., 1965-66; asst. prof. Ohio State U., Columbus, 1967-70; prof., chmn. dept. geography Edinboro (Pa.) State Coll., 1970-79, assoc. v.p. acad. affairs, 1980-83; provost, v.p. acad. affairs Edinboro Univ. of Pa., 1984-88, Western Ill. U., Macomb, 1988-93, acting pres., 1993, provost, v.p. acad. affairs, 1994—2002. Vis. rsch. prof. Nat. Taiwan Normal U., 1978; cons. Project Africa/Carnegie-Mellon U., Pitts., 1967-70, 92, 87, 95; mem. mid. states periodic rev. team, Phila., 1986—; mem. mid. states evaluation team in conjunction with Am. Optometric Assn. , 1987; mem. evaluation team Pa. Dept. Edn., 1988; mem. accreditation team Am. Optometric, 1990—; evaluator Higher Learning Commn. North Cen. Assn., 1994—; examiner Lincoln Found. for Bus. Excellence, 1996—; vice-chmn. Quad Cities Grad. Ctr., 1991-2000; mem. nat. screening com. for Africa, Inst. of Internat. Edn., 1994-96. Co-author: Discovery in Geography, 1976; co-author: So You Want to Go to College: 50 Questions to Ponder, Strategies for Timely Degree Completion: Connecting the Parts, Strategies for Timely Degree Completion: Myths and Realities, Technology: Bridge or Barrier To More Timely Degree Completion?, 1998; ; mem. editl. bd. Pa. Geographer, Chronicle of CQI; contbr. chpts. to books. Mem. Edinboro Planning & Zoning Commn., 1973-77. Recipient Disting. Alumnus award Kutztown U., 1990; Fulbright Hays fellow, Ethiopia, Kenya, Uganda, 1965. Mem. Nat. Coun. Geog. Edn. (exec. bd. 1977-80, mem. award com. for region IV 1981), Pa. Coun. Geog. Edn. (exec. sec. 1976-79, pres. 1975-76, Outstanding Prof. award 1978), Macomb Club (pres. 1998-99), Rotary (pres. Edinboro club 1972-73). Methodist. Avocations: reading, golf, photography, model constrn. Home: 1106 Bayberry Ln Macomb IL 61455-3518 Office: Western Ill U Sherman Hall 1 Circle Dr Macomb IL 61455

WITTICH, JOHN JACOB, retired college president, corporation consultant; b. Huntley, Ill., Nov. 13, 1921; s. John and Eva (Karl) W.; m. Leah Elliott, Apr. 2, 1944; children: Karen Ann Zvonar, Jane Ellen Tock, John Elliott. BA, DePauw U., 1943, LLD (hon.), 1971; MA, U. N.Mex., 1949; PhD, Stanford U., 1952; LHD (hon.), Ill. Coll., 1979; DPS (hon.), MacMurray Coll., 1980. Tchr. Albuquerque H.S., 1948-49; tchg. asst. Stanford, 1949-51; asst. prof. psychology Coll. of Pacific, Stockton, Calif., 1951-52; dean of admissions, dir. scholarships, assoc. prof. DePauw U., Greencastle, Ind., 1952-61; exec. dir. Coll. Center of Finger Lakes, Corning, N.Y., 1961-63, Coll. Student Personnel Inst., Claremont, Calif., 1963-68; dir. grad. studies in student pers. Claremont Grad. Sch., 1963-68; pres. MacMurray Coll., Jacksonville, Ill., 1968-80; program dir. Fla. Assn. Colls. and Univs., 1980-84; dir. higher edn. program Stetson U., 1981-88; v.p. Capital Formation Counselors, Inc., Belleaire Bluffs, Fla., 1983—. Contbr. articles to profl. jours. Exec. com. Divsn. Higher Edn., Ctrl. Ill. Conf. of United Meth. Ch., 1968-80; exec. com. Fedn. Independent Ill. Colls. and Univs. and Assoc. Colls. Ill.; mem. non-pub. adv. com. Ill. Bd. Higher Edn., 1972-78; mem. Nat. Merit Scholarship Selection Com., 1956, 61; cons. Calif. Gov.'s Conf. on Edn., 1965, on Youth, 1966; trustee Fla. Endowment for Humanities, 1982-85; presdl. counsellor Stetson U., 1987—; bd. dirs. DeLand House Next Door, 1990-94; citizens adv. com. West Volusia Hosp. Authority, 1992—, vice-chmn., 2001-02. With USMC, 1943-46, PTO. Recipient De Pauw Achievement award, 1969, Alumni citation DePauw U., 1994; Rockefeller fellow Aspen Inst. for Humanistic Studies, 1979. Mem. APA, Am. Coll. Pers. Assn. (commn. chmn.), Nat. Assn. Coll. Admissions Counselors (exec. bd. 1955-58), Cen. States Coll. Assn. (exec. com. 1969-77, sec.-treas. 1970-77), 4th Marine Divsn. Assn., Sigma Chi. E-mail: jwittich@totcom.com.

WITTIG, RAYMOND SHAFFER, lawyer, technology management advisor; b. Allentown, Pa., Dec. 13, 1944; s. Raymond Battie and Alice (Shaffer) W.; m. Beth Glover, June 21, 1975; children: Meaghan G., Allison G. BA, Pa. State U., 1966, MEd, 1968; JD, Dickinson Sch. Law, 1974. Bar: Pa. 1974, U.S. Ct. Appeals (D.C. cir.) 1978. Rsch. psychologist Intext Corp., Scranton, Pa., 1968; minority counsel Small Bus. Com., U.S. Ho. Reps., Washington, 1975-84; pvt. practice, 1984-92; tech. mgmt. group leader Geo-Ctrs., Inc., Newton Ctr., Mass., 1992—. Capt. U.S. Army, 1969-71. Mem. AAAS, ABA, Nat. Order Barristers, Fed. Lab. Consortium, Am. Intellectual Property Law Assn. E-mail: wittigsall@aol.com.

WITTING, CHRIS J. electrical manufacturing executive; b. Cranford, N.J., Apr. 7, 1915; s. Nicholas and Anne (Begasse) W.; B.S., N.Y. U., 1941; grad. Am. Inst. Banking; student Fordham Law Sch.; D.Eng. (hon.), Clarkson Coll. Tech.; m. Grace Orrok, Oct. 8, 1938 (dec. 1993); children— Leland James, Anne Kristin, Nancy Jane, Chris J.; m. Marshia K. Pullman, Nov. 15, 1997. Exec. asst. Guaranty Trust Co., 1933-36, N.Y. Trust Co., 1936-39; mgr. Price Waterhouse & Co., 1939-41; comptroller, treas. U.S.O. Camp Shows, Inc., 1941-46; mng. dir. Allen B. DuMont Labs., Inc., 1946-53; pres. Westinghouse Broadcasting Co., 1953-54, group v.p. and gen. mgr. consumer products group, Westinghouse Electric Corp., 1954-64; v.p. exec. asst. to chmn. and pres. Internat. Tel.& Tel. Corp., 1964-65; pres., chief exec. officer, dir. Crouse-Hinds Co., Syracuse, N.Y., 1965-75, chmn., chief exec. officer, 1975-82; vice chmn. bd. Cooper Industries Inc., Houston. Chmn. Pub. Auditorium Authority of Pitts. and Allegheny County, 1963-64; chmn. bd. trustees Syracuse U., 1975-93. Mem. Nat. Electric Mfrs. Assn. (chmn. bd. govs., bd. dirs.), Electronic Industries Assn. (bd. govs. 1961-62, dir. 1960-63), Nat. Planning Assn. (nat. council), Am. Mgmt. Assn. (mem. mktg. planning council), Elec. Mfrs. Club, Met. Devel. Assn. Syracuse and Onondaga County, N.Y. (dir.). Clubs: Athletic, Union League, Century, Onondaga Country, Athletic (Syracuse). Office: 518 Bradford Pky Syracuse NY 13224-1804

WITTLICH, GARY EUGENE, music theory educator, college administrator; b. Belleville, Ill., Dec. 3, 1934; s. Marvin Oscar and Erma Carrie (Garlich) Jackson Wittlich; m. Barbara L. Casey, Jan. 4, 1958 (div. Feb. 1969); children: M. Kent (d. 1999), Kristi L.; m. Mildred Elizabeth Read, Mar. 17, 1971. BM in Edn., So. Ill. U., 1957, MMus, 1959; PhD, U. Iowa, 1969. Asst. prof. music Upper Iowa U., Fayette, 1959-63; prof. music, grad. studies in music theory Ind. U., Bloomington, 1965-97; disting. tech. cons. Univ. Info. Tech. Svc., 1999—; assoc. dean faculty, ext. liaison, office v.p. info. tech. Ind. U., Bloomington, 1995-98, dir. of computing Sch. of Music, 1989-95; Meadows disting. vis. prof. music So. Meth. U., Dallas, 1982-83; vis. prof. U. Mich., Ann Arbor, 1974; dir. Ctr. for Profl. Devel. in Music Tech., CMS/ATMI, 1995-97. Dir. Ameritech Fellows program, 2001—2002, hon. emeritus fellow, 2002; cons. U. Del. Music Videodisc Series, NEH, 1982-85; mem. vis. performing arts com. U. Del., 1996-98; mem. music test com. Ednl. Testing Svc., Princeton, N.J., 1983-85, chmn., 1986-90. Author: (with C. Lee Humphries) Ear Training: An Approach Through Music Literature, 1974, (with others) Aspects of Twentieth-Century Music, 1975, (with J. Schaffer and L. Babb) Microcomputers and Music, 1986, (with D. Martin) Tonal Harmony for the Keyboard, 1988. Served with U.S. Army, 1957, 61-62. NSF grantee Ind. U., 1970, 2000-2004; fellow Inst. for Acad. Tech., 1992. Mem. Assn. for Tech. in Music Instrn. (founding), Coll. Music Soc. (bd. mem. for theory 1987-89), Soc. Music Theory (exec. bd. 1982-85, pres. 1988-91). Home: 3213 Coppertree Drive Bloomington IN 47401-9397 E-mail: wittlich@indiana.edu.

WITTLIFF, DANNY JOE, environmental engineer; b. Corpus Christi, Tex., Nov. 24, 1949; s. Joe Charles and Sarah Mary (Mitchell) W.; m. Donna Kay Covington, June 23, 1973 (div. 1991); children: Matthew Daniel, Juliana Prell; m. Manda Lee Rash, Jan. 24, 1998. BSME, So. Meth. U., 1972; MBA, U. Okla., 1975. Lic. profl. engr., Tex.; registered environ. mgr., environ. profl. Results engr. West Tex. Utilities, Abilene, 1981-85, plant engring. supr. Oklaunion Power Sta., 1985-90, environ. svcs. mgr. Abilene, 1991-95; chief engr. Tex. Natural Resource Conservation Commn., Austin, 1995—. Chair WTU United Way Campaign, Abilene, 1994-95. Col. USAFR, 1981—, with USAF, 1972-81. Mem. Tex. Soc. Profl. Engrs. (state water com. 1995—, Chpt. Young Engr. of Yr. 1985, past chpt. pres. 1994-95, Travis County Engr. of Yr. 1998), Soc. Am. Mil. Engrs., Armed Forces Com. Elec. Assn., Electric Reliability Coun. Tex. (chair waste task force 1992-95), Tex. Alliance for Minorities in Engring. (bd. dirs. 1996—). Methodist. Avocations: writing poetry, golf, basketball, fishing. Home: 12410 Deer Trak Austin TX 78727-5744 Office: Tex Natural Resource Conservation Com MC110 PO Box 13087 Austin TX 78711-3087

WITTLINGER, TIMOTHY DAVID, lawyer; b. Dayton, Ohio, Oct. 12, 1940; s. Charles Frederick and Dorothy Elizabeth (Golden) W.; m. Diane Cleo Dominy, May 20, 1967; children: Kristine Elizabeth, David Matthew. BS in Math., Purdue U., 1962; JD with distinction, U. Mich., 1965. Bar: Mich. 1966, U.S. Dist. Ct. (ea. dist.) Mich. 1966, U.S. Ct. Appeals (6th cir.) 1968, U.S. Supreme Ct. 1971. Assoc. Clark Hill (formerly Hill Lewis), Detroit, 1965-72, ptnr., 1973—, head litigation dept., 1976-91, gen. counsel, 1997—. Mem. profl. assistance com. U.S. Dist. Ct. (ea. dist.) Mich., 1981-82; mem. Mich. Supreme Ct. Com. to Evaluate Mediation Ct. Rule, 1997-98; author, lectr. Ctr. for Internat. Legal Studies, 1999—. Mem. ho. of deps. Episc. Ch., N.Y.C., 1979—; vice chmn. Robert Whitaker Sch. Theology, 1983-87; sec. bd. trustees Episc. Ch., Diocese of Mich., Detroit, 1983—, sec. conv. Episc. Diocese of Mich., 1990—, ch. atty., 1997—, mem., sec. Episc. nat. econ. justice implementation com., 1988-95, mem. Episc. nat. exec. coun., 1991-97, mem. nat. audit com.; mem. Nat. Standing Commn. on Ministry Devel., 2000—; active Nat. Episc. Jubilee Ministry Com., Nat. Episc. Coalition for Social Witness and Justice, Fifth Province Episc. Ecclesiastical Ct. Appeal; mem. nat. audit com. Episcopal Ch.; bd. dirs. Episc. Student Found., U. Mich., 1990-93, 2000-2002; chair Grubb Inst. Behavioral Studies Ltd., Washington, 1986—; bd. dirs. Birmingham Village Playhouse, 2000—. Mem. ABA, State Bar Mich., Nat. Bd. Trial Advocacy (cert.), Engring. Soc. Detroit. Home: 736 N Glenhurst Dr Birmingham MI 48009-1143 Office: Clark Hill 500 Woodward Ave Ste 3500 Detroit MI 48226-3435

WITTMAN, ALLAN HENRY, publishing executive; b. Bklyn., Feb. 22, 1933; s. William and Evelyn (Erdman) W.; m. Ruth Miller, Dec. 24, 1952; children: Michael, Robert. Student, MIT, 1949-51; BA, Bklyn. Coll., 1958. Advt. dir. Sci. Am., N.Y.C., 1951-71; pres. G. Schirmer, Inc., 1972-74; gen. mgr. periodicals divsn. John Wiley & Sons, Inc., 1974-82; sr. v.p. Macmillan Pub. Co., 1982-87, pres. profl. pub. divsn., 1982-87; ptnr. Wittman Assocs., 1988—. Trustee bd. edn. Hewlett (N.Y.)-Woodmere Sch. Dist., 1973-76; trustee Am. Found. for the Blind, N.Y.C., 1996-2000; bd. dirs. Oscar Dystel Fellowship in Pub., NYU, N.Y.C., 1987-99; trustee, mem. adv. coun. Engring. Info., Inc., N.Y.C., 1980-90; mem. edn. coun. MIT, Cambridge, Mass., 1971-76. Mem. N.Y. Acad. Scis. (chmn. publ. com. 1988-97), Assn. Am. Pubs. (chmn. copyright com. 1978-86, chmn. jours. com. 1975-78). Office: Wittman Assocs 160 Broadway New York NY 10038 E-mail: allanwittman@juno.com.

WITTMAN, CONNIE SUSAN, oncology clinical nurse specialist; b. Hays, Kans., June 30, 1956; d. Vernon M. and Armella M. (Herl) Wittman. BSN, Ft. Hays State U., Hays, Kans., 1978; M in Nursing, U. Kans., Kansas City, 1984; M in Health Adminstrn., U. Mo., 1997. RN, Nebr.; cert. advanced oncology nurse. Staff nurse, charge nurse Hays Med. Ctr., 1978-81, oncology clin. nurse specialist, 1983-99, dir. cancer program, 1991-99; adminstrv. dir. oncology svcs. Good Samaritan Health Sys., Kearney, Nebr., 1999—. Adj. prof. nursing Ft. Hays State U., 1986-99. Pres. Cancer Coun. Ellis County, Hays, 1986-92. Recipient Heart of Gold award Edward D. Jones Co., Hays, 1987, Alumni award Ft. Hays State U., 1988. Mem. ANA, Oncology Nursing Soc. Avocations: antiques, crafts, gardening. Home: 1211 W 13th St Kearney NE 68845-6517 E-mail: conniewittman@chi-midwest.org., cwittman@nebi.com.

WITTMANN, DIETMAR H. surgery educator; b. Duisburg, Rhine, Germany, June 16, 1940; s. Harry E. Wittmann and Elisabeth (Moik) Le Danois; m. Heide-Marie Heitmann, 1997; children: Mark-Matthias, Annemarei. MD, Hamburg (Germany) U., 1970; PhD, Dusseldorf (Germany) U., 1972. Asst. prof. Hamburg (Germany) U., 1975-82, assoc. prof. surgery, 1982-88, Med. Coll. Wis., Milw., 1988-92, prof. surgery, 1992—2000. Contbr. articles to profl. jours., chpts. to books. Mem. ACS, Am. Assn. Surgery of Trauma, Internat. Surg. Soc., German Surg. Assn., Surg. Infection Soc. Europe (founder, Disting. Svc. award Indonesian 1994), Columbian Surg. Assn. (hon.), Brazilian Coll. Diestin Surgery (hon.). Roman Catholic. E-mail: dhw@colonna.net.

WITTMER, JAMES FREDERICK, preventive medicine physician, educator; b. Carlinville, Ill., Dec. 30, 1932; s. Franklin Benjamin and Eva Caroline (Zihlman) W.; m. Juanita Lou Wilkey, June 29, 1962; children: Ellen, Carol, Nancy. MD, Washington U., St. Louis, 1957; MPH, Harvard U., 1961. Diplomate Am. Bd. Preventive Medicine. Intern U. Va. Hosp., Charlottesville, 1857-58; commd. capt. USAF, 1958, advanced through grades to col., 1971; ret., 1979; dean allied health U. Tex. Health Sci. Ctr., San Antonio, 1979-80; asst. med. dir. Conoco Oil Co., Ponca City, Okla., 1980-81; assoc. med. dir. Mobil Oil Corp., N.Y.C., 1981-83; dir. health, environ. and safety ITT, 1983-95, corp. v.p., 1990-95. Clin. prof. medicine Cornell U. Med. Coll., N.Y.C., 1984—; lectr. environ. medicine NYU, N.Y.C., 1984—; adj. prof. U. Tex. Sch. Pub. Health, Houston, 1987—, prof. occupl. health, 1996-97; nat. coord. com. on clin. preventive svcs. USPHS, 1994-97; cons. office hearings and appeals U.S. Social Security Adminstrn., 1997—, Met. Health Dist., San Antonio, Tex., 2002-. Mem. Pres.'s Com. on Employment People with Disabilities, Washington, 1986-2000, chmn. med. and ins. com., 1986-90. Fellow ACP, Am. Coll. Occupational and Environ. Medicine (bd. dirs. 1990-97, sec. 1992-94), Am. Coll. Preventive Medicine, Aerospace Med. Assn., N.Y. Acad. Medicine; mem. AMA, Tex. Occupational Med. Assn. Home and Office: 159 Sabine Rd Boerne TX 78006-6217 E-mail: wittmer@gvtc.com.

WITTMEYER, RICHARD ARTHUR, management consulting company executive; b. Trenton, N.J., Oct. 23, 1947; s. Arthur A. and Martha (Rhoads) W.; children: Megan Elizabeth, Richard Arthur, Jr. BA in Psychology and Philosophy, Norwich U., 1969; postgrad., Assumption Coll., 1969-70; MBA in Human Resources Mgmt., Century U., 1986, PhD in Orgnl. Behavior and Mgmt., 1988. Dir. orgnl. devel. and human resources Gen. Tire & Rubber Co., Akron, Ohio, 1972-75; chmn. Wittmeyer & Assocs. Internat. Cons., 1975—; pres. Ctr. for Strategic Mgmt., 1998—. Lectr. Am. Mgmt. Assn., Advanced Mgmt. Rsch. Internat., N.Y.C., 1971-87, Dow Leadership Ctr., Mich., 1976-78; cons. Wittmeyer & Assoc., Mt. Vernon, Ill., 1975—, Ctr. for Strategic Mgmt., 1998—; spl. appearences on TV/60 Minutes, 1972, PBS TV, 1973, others. Author: The Supervisor as a Conference Leader, 1974, Effective Supervision, 1974, Management Effectiveness in the Corporate Structure, 1975, (audiotape series) Assert Yourself, Develop Your Winning Edge, 1984; co-author: Facts Concerning Drug Use and Abuse, 1972. Active Rep. Presdl. Inner Circle, Washington, 1988-90, Rep. Presdl. Task Force, 1991-95; v.p. Prince of Peace Luth. Ch., Mt. Vernon, 1976; bd. dirs. Jefferson Meml. Hosp., Mt. Vernon, 1973-74, Jefferson County Regional Mental Health Ctr., Mt. Vernon, 1974. Recipient Gov. Legion of Merit award Vt. State Legis., 1969; named Internat. Man of Yr., Cambridge, Eng., 1993, Presdl. Legion of Merit award Washington, 1993, others; fellow Heidelburg U. Sch. Behavioral Sci., Germany, 1971. Mem. ASTD, AMA Presidents Assn., Am. Soc. Personnel Adminstrs., Am. Legion, Elks, Hon. Order Ky. Cols. Avocations: boating, swimming, tennis, sailing. Office: Wittmeyer & Assocs PO Box 1594 Mount Vernon IL 62864-0031

WITTNER, LAWRENCE STEPHEN, history educator; b. N.Y.C., May 5, 1941; s. Jacob and Rose (Barnett) W.; m. Patricia Ellen Sheinblatt (div. May 1981); 1 child, Julia; m. Dorothy Tristman, Aug. 31, 1999. AB, Columbia U., 1962, PhD, 1967; MA, U. Wis., 1963. Asst. prof. history Hampton (Va.) Inst., 1967-68, Vassar Coll., Poughkeepsie, N.Y., 1968-73; Fulbright sr. lectr. Fulbright-Hays Ednl. Exch. Program, Tokyo and Kyoto, Japan, 1973-74; lectr. history SUNY, Albany, 1974-76, asst. prof., 1976-77, assoc. prof., 1977-83, prof., 1983—. Pres. Conf. on Peace Rsch. in History (now Peace History Soc.), 1977-79; mem. exec. com. Albany chpt. United Univ. Professions, 1980—. Author: Rebels Against War: The American Peace Movement, 1941-60, 1969, rev. edit. Rebels Against War: The American Peace Movement, 1933-1983, 1984, Cold War America: From Hiroshima to Watergate, 1974, rev. edit., 1978, American Intervention in Greece, 1943-1949, 1982, One World or None: A History of the World Nuclear Disarmament Movement through 1953, Vol. 1 of The Struggle Against the Bomb, 1993 (Warren Kuehl prize Soc. for Historians Am. Fgn. Rels. 1995), Vol. 2, Resisting the Bomb: A History of the World Nuclear Disarmament Movement, 1954-70, 1997; co-exec. editor Peace and Change: Jour. Peace Rsch., 1984-87. Co-chmn. Capital Dist. Labor-Religion Coalition, Albany, 1982-84; treas. Solidarity Com. of Capital Dist., Albany, 1986—. Recipient Charles DeBenedetti prize Conf. on Peace Rsch. in History, 1989, excellence award N.Y. State and United Univ. Professions, 1990; fellow NEH, 1980-81, Am. Coun. Learned Socs. and Ford Found., 1987-88, U.S. Inst. Peace, 2002; rsch. grantee Nonprofit Sector Rsch. Fund, Aspen Inst., Washington, 1998-99, John D. and Catherine T. MacArthur Found., 2002. Mem. Internat. Peace Rsch. Assn. (chmn. Peace History Commn. 1998-2001), Peace History Soc. (N.Am. bd. 1990-94, 97-2000). Democrat. Avocation: music. Office: SUNY History Dept 1400 Washington Ave Albany NY 12222-0100 Fax: 518-442-3477. E-mail: wittner@albany.edu.

WITTREICH, WARREN JAMES, psychologist, consultant; b. Weehawken, N.J., Aug. 18, 1929; s. Andrew Otto and Muriel Viola (Wilson) Wittreich; m. Mary Shirley Wells, Sept. 10, 1951 (div. Sept. 1959); children: Michael(dec.) , Peter; m. Lois Vivian Llewellyn, Sept. 8, 1959 (div. July 1996); children: Benjamin, Debra, Susie(dec.) , Andrea; m. Eileen Burke, Aug. 20, 1996 (div. Sept. 1998); m. Diane L. Altif-Meyer, Jan. 8, 2000. AB in Psychology summa cum laude, Princeton U., 1951, MA in Psychology, 1953, PhD in Psychology, 1954; PhD in Clin. Psychology, Cath. U., Washington, 1958. Lic. psychologist, Pa. Guest scientist Naval Med. Rsch. Inst., Bethesda, Md., 1953-54; postdoctoral trainee VA, East Orange, N.J., 1954-55; clin. psychologist Lancaster and Phila., Pa., 1955—; exec. v.p. Nat. Analysts, Inc., Phila., 1959-64; pres. Daniel Yankelovich of Pa., 1964-67; pres., CEO Crossroads

Career Planning Corp., 1967-85; adj. prof., rsch. cons. U. Pa., 1968-73; CEO Focus Group Assocs. Ltd., Bethlehem, Pa., 1995—. Advisor to Sec. of Transp., U.S. Dept. Transp., Washington, 1968-72; expert witness FTC, Washington, 1957, U.S. Congress, Washington, 1959, N.Y. State Supreme Ct., N.Y.C., 1963. Exhibited in 4 one-man shows; 2 commd. paintings; contbr. articles to profl. jours. Worker Robert F. Kennedy Campaign Com., Washington, 1967; mem. Citizens Adv. Com. on Transp. Quality, U.S. Dept. Transp., Washington, 1968-74. Recipient fellowship NSF, 1952-53. Fellow Pa. Psychol. Assn.; mem. APA, Phi Beta Kappa, Sigma Xi. Episcopalian. Avocation: oil painting. Home and Office: 18 W Broad St Apt 2 Bethlehem PA 18018

WITTROCK, MERLIN CARL, educational psychologist; b. Twin Falls, Idaho, Jan. 3, 1931; s. Herman C. and Mary Ellen W.; m. Nancy McNulty, Apr. 3, 1953; children: Steven, Catherine, Rebecca. BS in Edn., Biology, U. Mo., Columbia, 1953, MEd in Ednl. Psychology, 1956; PhD in Ednl. Psychology, U. Ill., Urbana, 1960. Prof. grad. sch. edn. UCLA, 1960—, founder Ctr. Study Evaluation, chmn. divsn. ednl. psychology, chmn. faculty, exec. com.; univ. com. on outstanding teaching. Dir. math. and humanities program; co-founder Urban Tchr. Edn. Program; fellow Ctr. for Advanced Study in Behavioral Scis., 1967—68; vis. prof. U. Wis., U. Ill., Ind. U., Monash U., Australia; co-prin. investigator Calif. Reading Tchr's Insts.; chmn. com. on evaluation and assessment L.A. Unified Sch. Dist.; mem. nat. adv. panel for math. scis. NRC of NAS; chmn. nat. bd. Nat. Ctr. for Rsch. in Math. Scis. Edn.; chmn. charges com. UCLA; adv. bd. Kauffman Found.; bd. dirs. Western Edn. Lab. for Edn. Rsch., Far West Lab, 1989—2001. Author, editor: The Evaluation of Instruction, 1970, Changing Education, 1973, Learning and Instruction, 1977, The Human Brain, 1977, Danish transl., 1980, Spanish transl., 1982, The Brain and Psychology, 1980, Instructional Psychology: Education and Cognitive Processes of the Brain, Neuropsychological and Cognitive Processes of Reading, 1981, Handbook of Research on Teaching, 3d edit., 1986, The Future of Educational Psychology, 1989, Research in Learning and Teaching, 1990, Testing and Cognition, 1991, Generative Science Teaching, 1994, Problem-Solving Transfer, 1996, Taxonomy for Learning, Teaching and Assessing, 2001. Mentor Edn. Leadership Program. Capt. USAF, 1953-55. Recipient Thorndike award for outstanding psychol. rsch., 1987, Disting. Tchr. of Univ. award UCLA, 1990, Greenfield award for rsch. in learning UCLA Grad. Sch. Edn., 1988; Ford Found. grantee. Fellow: APA (pres. divsn. ednl. psychology 1984—85, assn. coun. 1988—91, award for Outstanding Svc. to Ednl. Psychology 1991, 1993, Disting. Svc. award for svc. to sci. adv. coun.), AAAS, Am. Psychol. Soc. (charter fellow); mem.: Am. Ednl. Rsch. Assn. (chmn. ann. conv., chmn. publs. 1980—83, assn. coun. 1986—89, bd. dirs. 1987—89, chmn. com. on ednl. TV, Outstanding Svc. award 1989, Outstanding Contbns. award 1986), Phi Delta Kappa. Office: UCLA 3339 Moore Hl Los Angeles CA 90095-1521

WITTSTEIN, EDWIN FRANK, stage and film production designer; b. Mt. Vernon, N.Y., Apr. 7, 1929; s. Nathan Harry and Miriam (Goldman) W. Student, Parsons Sch. Design, 1946-50; BS, NYU, 1950; postgrad., Cooper Union, 1950-52. Stage designer Dramatic Workshop prodn. The Inspector General, 1947; set designer Gertrude Stein's Yes Is for a Very Young Man; set and costume designer Ounga Opera, Phila., 1950, (opera) The Celebrated Jumping Frog of Calaveras County, Venice, Italy, 1953, The Transposed Heads, 1958, The Fantasticks, 1960 (still running); designer Broadway prodn. Kean, 1961; set and costume designer The Gondoliers, N.Y.C. Opera, 1963, The Knack (directed by Mike Nichols), 1964, The Marriage of Figaro, N.Y.C. Opera, 1965, The Amen Corner, 1965, Happy Birthday Wanda June, Enter Laughing, 1965, The Room, A Slight Ache, 1965, The Yearling, 1965, Serjeant Musgrave's Dance, 1966 (Obie award 1966), You Know I Can't Hear You When the Water's Running, 1967, set designer Merchant of Venice, Shakespeare Festival Conn., 1967, As You Like It, Richard II, Shakespeare Festival Conn., 1968, The Man in the Glass Booth, 1968, The Basement, The Tea Party, Celebration, 1969, (for Cin. Playhouse) The Miser, Volpone, The Good Woman of Setzuan, Angel Street, He Who Gets Slapped, 1968-70, The Country Wife, Shakespeare Theatre, Conn., 1973, Ulysses in Nightown, 1974 (Tony award nomination 1974, Maharam award 1974), The Torchbearers, 1978, The Aspern Papers, 1978, Love's Labors Lost, 1983, Berkshire Theatre Festival, 1988, Tusitala, 1988, Tete a Tete, 1989, The Hasty Heart, 1990, Trains, 1991, (sets, costumes 30th anniversary tour) The Fantasticks, 1990, Sarah, Plain and Tall, 1991 (Emmy nomination 1991), Colette Collage, 1991, March of the Falsettos, 1991, Falsettoland, 1991, (prodn. designer Hallmark Hall of Fame TV) An American Story, 1992, (prodn. designer Hallmark Hall of Fame TV) Skylark, 1993, (prodn. designer Hallmark Hall of Fame TV) A Place for Annie, 1993, (set designer off-Broadway) I Do! I Do!, 1996; designer TV shows Armstrong Circle Theatre, The Tonight Show with Steve Allen, NBC operas Cosi Fan Tutte, La Traviata, La Boheme, Boris Godounov, Cavalleria Rusticana, Blithe Spirit, The Diary of Anne Frank, Camino Real, The Royal Family, The Prince of Homburg; prodn. designer TV series The Adams Chronicles (Emmy nomination 1975); designer TV films A Memory of Two Mondays, 1971, For Ladies Only, 1982, Legs, 1982, Samson and Delilah, 1983, Heartsounds, 1984; designer TV spl. Echoes in the Darkness, 1987; designer films Bananas, 1971, Play It Again Sam, 1971, The Seven-Ups, 1972; art dir. films Smile, 1975, Fame, 1979; prodn. designer film Endless Love, 1981; set and costume designer (ballet) Coppelia, 1992; one-man show (painting) Hammond Museum, N. Salem, N.Y., 1999; drawer, writer Positano Sketch Book, 2000. Home: 339 E 87th St New York NY 10128-4801

WITTY, JOHN BARBER, health care executive; b. Vicksburg, Miss., Mar. 26, 1946; s. Neomah Wilks and Jennie (Barber) W.; m. Susan Deemer, June 26, 1976; children: Justin Michael, Adam David. BA, Miss. State U., 1968; MEd, U. Md., 1972, EdD, 1989. Cert. prin. regular edn. and spl. edn., curriculum coord. spl. edn., tch. spl. edn. K-12, Md. Tchr. Anne Arundel County Pub. Schs., Annapolis, Md., 1972-77, specialist in community affairs, 1977-78, sch. based adminstr., 1978-79, county based adminstr., 1979-87; dir. svcs. devel. Am. Internat. Health Rehab. Svcs., 1987-88, dir. tng. & devel., 1988-89, dir. cost containment svcs., 1989-90, v.p. svcs., 1990-91; chief oper. officer AIIA/Comp Care, Daytona Beach, Fla., 1991-94; pres. Med. Advantage, Orlando, 1994—. Bd. dirs. Anne Arundel County Sheltered Workshop, Glen Burnie, Md., 1987-89. Pres. Rolling Knolls Community Assn., Annapolis, 1980s, Gen.'s Hwy. Coun., Annapolis, 1980s; chmn. Anne Arundel County Stormwater Mgmt. Commn., 1984-85; mem. human rights com. Providence Ctr., 1984-85; pres. Oceantime Condominium Assn., Ocean City, Md., 1984-89, Huntington Community Assn., 1990-96. With USN, 1969-72. Recipient Jaycee of Month award, 1975, C. William Brownfield award Annapolis Md. Jaycees, 1975, Jaycee Award of Svc., 1976, Md. State Jaycee award, 1975, 77, Jaycee of Month, 1977, Harold Reece award, 1977. Mem. Rotary, Annapolis Jaycees (v.p., bd. dirs.), Phi Delta Kappa, Kappa Delta Pi, Phi Mu Alpha Sinfonia. Republican. Presbyterian. Avocations: golf, running, yard work, coin collecting, reading. Home: 2345 Westminster Ter Oviedo FL 32765-7554 Office: Med Advantage 3452 Lake Lynda Dr Ste 250 Orlando FL 32817-1445 E-mail: jwitty76@aol.com.

WITTY, ROBERT WILKES, insurance services company executive; b. Vicksburg, Miss., Apr. 20, 1941; s. N.W. and Jennie (Barber) W.; m. Sally Van Tilborg, Jan 26, 1964; children: Deborah, Theresa, Robin. BBA, U. Miss., 1964; LLB, LaSalle U., 1968; postgrad., Ga. State U., 1981. With Crawford & Co., 1964-85; adjuster Lima, Ohio, 1964-66, Findlay, 1966-68; sr. adjuster N.Y.C., 1969-72; supr. br. New Orleans, 1972-76; asst. field supr. home address Atlanta, 1976-78; asst. v.p., 1978-80; v.p., 1980-81; regional v.p., regional ops. mgr. Northeast region, Montvale, N.J., 1981-85; pres., COO Am. Internat. Adjustment Co. (subs. A.I.G.), 1985-90; pres., CEO Am. Internat. Health & Rehab. C. (subs. AIAC), 1986-90, also bd. dirs.; pres., CEO Gates McDonald & Co. (subs. Nationwide Ins. Group), Columbus, Ohio, 1991-93; exec. v.p. strategic devel. The Thomas Howell Group (Americas) Inc., 1994-95, divsn. pres. risk mgmt. svcs., 1995-96, also bd. dirs., exec. bd. mem., 1995; S.E. region v.p. GAB Robins, Atlanta, 1995-99; nat. acct. mgr. S.E. and S.E. region Prism, Inc., Crawford, 1999—. Bd. dirs. Am. Internat. Adjustment Co., Am. Internat. recoveries, Inc.; bd. trustees Kessler Rehab. Inst., 1989-90; v.p. Lindsey & Newsom Claims Mgmt., Inc., 1990, N.Am. Health & Rehab. Svcs., 1990. Recipient Outstanding Contbn. award East Orange City Council, 1987, Support award East Orange Womens Club, 1987. Mem. Atlanta Claims Assn., Profl. Ins. Agts. of N.Y., Profl. Inst. Agts. of Northeast, Loss Exec. Coun., Risk Ins. Mgmt. Soc., Inc., Grand Haven Golf Club. Presbyterian. Home: 79 Lagre St Grand Haven Palm Coast FL 32137 Office: 3728 Phillips Hwy Jacksonville FL 32207-9300 E-mail: robert-witty@prism-net.com.

WITTY, THOMAS EZEKIEL, III, psychologist, researcher; b. Greensboro, N.C., Oct. 11, 1955; s. Thomas Ezekiel Jr. and Peggy (Coggins) Witty; m. Ginger Lynell Kissee, June 28, 1997; children: Ezekiel Thomas, Zoe Anne, Zoe Anne. BA in English, U. N.C., Greensboro, 1980; MS, Va. Commonwealth U., 1989; PhD, U. Mo., 1995. Lic. psychologist Miss. Tchr. secondary English, debate and cross-country coach Henry County Pub. Schs., Collinsville, Va., 1981-87; fin. aid. counselor asst. Va. Commonwealth U., Richmond, 1987-89; substance abuse counselor Dist. 19 Alcoholism Svcs., Petersburg, Va., 1990; grad. rsch. asst. U. Mo., Columbia, 1990-94, grad. instr., 1992-94; postdoctoral fellow Rusk Rehab. Ctr., 1995-98; chief psychology Mo. Rehab. Ctr., Mt. Vernon, 1998-2001; psychologist North Miss. Med. Ctr., Tupelo, 2001—. Rsch. cons. Coun. on Rehab. Edn., Inc., Champaign, Ill., 1991; ad hoc reviewer Jour. Rehab. Psychology, 1995—98; internship selection com. U. Mo. Health Svcs. Consortium, Columbia, 1996—98. Contbr. articles to profl. jours. NIH postdoctoral fellow in rehab. rsch., 1995-98, Walter Scott Monroe rsch. fellow U. Mo., 1992-95; rsch. grantee U. Mo. Rsch. Bd., 1997. Mem.: Nat. Rehab. Counseling Assn., Am. Pain Soc., Miss. Psychol. Assn., APA (divsn. 17, 22, 38, 50, program rev. com. divsn. 22 1996—), Sierra Club, KC, Kappa Delta Pi. Democrat. Roman Catholic. Avocations: running, swimming, cycling, hiking, camping. Office: North Miss Med Ctr Dept Behavioral Health 830 S Gloster St Tupelo MS 38801 Fax: 662-377-7035. E-mail: twitty@nmhs.net.

WITWER, SAMUEL WEILER, JR. lawyer; b. Chgo., Aug. 5, 1941; s. Samuel Weiler and Ethyl Loraine (Wilkins) W.; m. Susan P. Stewart, Sept. 18, 1971; children: Samuel Stewart, Michael Douglas. AB with honors, Dickinson Coll., 1963; JD, U. Mich., 1966. Bar: Ill. 1967, U.S. Dist. Ct. (no. dist.) Ill. 1967, U.S. Ct. Appeals (7th cir.) 1972, U.S. Supreme Ct. 1973, U.S. Ct. Appeals (6th cir.) 1985, U.S. Dist. Ct. (ea. dist.) Mich., 1987. Assoc. Witwer, Moran, Burlage & Atkinson, Chgo., 1967-74; ptnr. Witwer, Poltrock & Giampietro, 1974— ; mem. Fed. Trial Bar Admissions Com. No. Dist. Ill., 1982-97. Governing mem. Chgo. Zool. Soc., 1986-90; trustee United Meth. Homes and Services, Chgo., 1974—, Dickinson Coll., Carlisle, Pa., 1976-97; mem. Cook County Home Rule Commn., Chgo., 1974-75; chmn. Agy. Appeals Com. Chgo., 1975-78; atty. Glenview Park Dist., 1982—; spl. asst. atty. gen. Auditor Gen. Ill., 1984-92. Mem. ABA, Meth. Bar Assn. (pres. 1972-73), Chgo. Bar Assn., Ill. Bar Assn., Law Club of Chgo., Sigma Chi, Phi Delta Phi. Republican. Methodist. Club: Union League. Home: 1330 Overlook Dr Glenview IL 60025-5166 Office: Witwer Poltrock & Giampietro 125 S Wacker Dr Chicago IL 60606-4402

WITYK, JOSEPH JOHN, radiologist; b. Krewecia, Ukraine, Oct. 21, 1931; BS, Ohio U., 1955; MD, Case Western Res. U., 1959. Diplomate Am. Bd. Radiology. Intern Pitts. Mercy Hosp., 1959-60; resident in surgery Cleve. Metro. Gen. Hosp., 1960-61, resident in radiology, 1961-64; radiologist Sinai Hosp., Balt., 1964-83; instr. Johns Hopkins Hosp. and Med. Sch., 1965-74, asst. prof. radiology, 1974-98; chief dept. radiology Homewood Hosp., 1983-91. Mem. Am. Coll. Radiology, Radiol. Soc. N.Am., Md. Radiol. Soc. Office: Oakwood Profl Bldg 7845 Oakwood Rd Glen Burnie MD 21061-4280

WITZ, GISELA, scientist, educator; b. Breslau, Federal Republic of Germany, Mar. 16, 1939; came to U.S., 1955. d. Gerhardt Witz and Hildegard (Sufeida) Minzak. BA, NYU, 1962, MS, 1965, PhD, 1969. Assoc. rsch. scientist NYU Med. Ctr., N.Y.C., 1970-73, rsch. scientist, 1973-77, asst. prof., 1977-80, Univ. of Medicine and Dentistry of N.J.-Rutgers Med. Sch., Piscataway, N.J., 1980-86; assoc. prof. U. Medicine and Dentistry N.J.-Robert Wood Johnson Med. Sch., 1986-93, prof., 1993-2000, prof. emeritus, 2001—. Dep. dir. Joint Grad. Program in Toxicology, Rutgers U./Univ. Medicine and Dentistry of N.J.-Robert Wood Johnson Med. Sch., 1988, assoc. dir. 1992-2000; cons. Nat. Rsch. Coun., Washington, 1982-83, 85-86. Recipient Dupont Teaching award, NYU, 1966, Univ. Scholar, Founders Day award, N.Y. U., 1969, Student Appreciation award Rutgers Assn. Toxicology Grad. Students, 1996; honoree 3d Ann. Women in Sci. Symposium, 2000. Fellow Oxygen Soc.; mem. Am. Assn. Cancer Rsch., Am. Chem. Soc., Soc. Toxicology, N.Y. Acad. Sci., Sigma Xi. Avocation: gardening. Office: U Medicine and Dentistry NJ Robert Wood Johnson Med Sch Piscataway NJ 08854 E-mail: witz@eohsi.rutgers.edu.

WITZIG, WARREN FRANK, nuclear engineer, educator; b. Detroit, Mar. 26, 1921; s. Arthur Judson and Mary (Bender) W.; m. Bernadette Sullivan, Mar. 31, 1942; children: Eric, Leah, Marc, Lisa Witzig Davidson. BEE, Rensselaer Poly. Inst., 1942; MS, U. Pitts., 1944, PhD, 1952. Registered profl. engr., Pa., Wash. Rsch. engr. Westinghouse Research, Pitts., 1942-48; mgr. reactor physics, engr. Bettis Atomic, 1948-60; co-founder, sr. v.p., dir. NUS Corp., Washington, 1960-67; head dept. nuclear engring. Pa. State U., 1967-87, emeritus, 1987—. Cons. nuclear engr. utilities industry; chmn. Pa. Gov.'s Com. on Atomic Energy Devel., 1970-80; mem. Saxton safety com., 1970-72; mem. waste com. Atomic Indsl. Forum, 1971-73; adv. com. Dept. Energy, 1980-82; mem. ops. rev. com. Tex. Utility; nuclear safety and compliance com., bd. dirs. GPU, 1983-92; mem. nuclear oversight com. PSE&G, 1983-91; mem. accrediting bd. Inst. Nuclear Power Ops., 1992-96; safety rev. bd. TVA, 1986-91; chmn. Westinghouse Nuclear Safety and Environ. Commn., 1988-93; chmn. safety audit bd. Centichem., 1989; safeguards com. Pa. State U., 1993—, interim dir. nuclear reactor, 1996-97; Designer S5W submarine reactor, 1956-60. Mem. bd. mgmt. YMCA, 1955-64. Fellow AAAS, Am. Nuclear Soc. (mem. exec. com. edn. div., past chmn. nat. com. on public info., chmn. nuclear engring. dept. head com. 1980); mem. Am. Phys. Soc., IEEE (past chmn. nuclear eng. and plasma div.), Sigma Xi, Eta Kappa Nu, Pi Kappa Alpha, Sigma Pi Sigma (Power Engring. Educator spl. citation) Presbyterian (elder). Achievements include design of S5W submarine reactor; criticality engineer on Nautilus maiden voyage; developed continuing and long distance education in nuclear engineering. Home: 1330 E Park Hills Ave State College PA 16803-3244 Office: Pa State U Breazeale Nuclear Reactor University Park PA 16802-1408 E-mail: wfw1@psu.edu.

WIVAGG, DANIEL EDWIN, biology educator, editor; b. Shrewsbury, Mass., Nov. 14, 1943; s. Edwin Nathaniel Wivagg and Hazel Viola Hokans; m. Ann Gray Havice, Sept. 6, 1969; children: Jonathan, Jennie, Peter, Eric. BA in Zoology, U. Mass., 1965; PhD in Botany, U. Tex., 1975. Secondary sci. tchr. North Reading (Mass.) H.S., 1966-69; asst. prof. Loyola U., Chgo., 1974-79; from lectr. to instr. to assoc. prof. Baylor U., Waco, Tex., 1979-95, prof., 1995—. Grant reviewer NSF, Arlington, Va., 1994, 99; dir. edn. reform Tapestry, The Inst. for Philosophy, Religion, and Life Scis., Inc., Waco, 1998-2000, chmn. bd. dirs., 2000—; cons. editor Saunders Coll. Pub., Phila., 1996-98; mem. Advanced Placement Biology Test Devel. Com., 2002—. Editor (assoc.): Am. Biology Tchr., Nat. Assn. Biology Tchrs., 1985—95; contbr.: Test Bank, 1993; editor (book) , 1996, Test Item File, 2002; contbr. articles to profl. jours.; editor: (other) Test Bank, 1999. Recipient Disting. Achievement award for editl. Ednl. Press Assn. of Am., 1986, Excellence in Print award for writing/editl. Washington Edn. Press Assn., 1986, 91; course improvement grantee NSF, 1993-95. Fellow Tex. Acad. Scis.; mem. Am. Inst. Biology Scis., Nat. Assn. Biology Tchrs. (publs. com. 1998-2001, mem. assessment task force 1997-2001, chair occasional publs. subcom. 1996-2001), Sci. Tchrs. Assn. Tex., Tex. Assn. Biology Tchrs. (pres.-elect 2003), Sigma Xi, Phi Kappa Phi. Avocations: timber frame construction, carpentry, shooting. Office: Baylor U 1311 S Fifth St PO Box 97388 Waco TX 76798-7388 Office Fax: 254-710-2969. E-mail: dan_wivagg@baylor.edu.

WIVEL, NELSON AUBURN, physician, medical researcher, educator; b. Denver, Sept. 4, 1935; s. Claude Burns and Aubrey (Angus) W.; m. Carol Henderson, June 16, 1963 (dec. 1999); children: Mark Auburn, Ashley Elizabeth. BS, Ea. N.Mex. U., 1957; MD, Stanford U., 1961. Diplomate Am. Bd. Pathology. Intern Cornell U., N.Y.C., 1961-62, asst. resident in medicine, 1962-63; asst. resident in pathology Stanford U., Calif., 1963-65; rsch. trainee in pathology Washington U., St. Louis, 1965-66; head ultrastructural studies sect. Nat. Cancer Inst., Bethesda, Md., 1966-70, head ultrastructural biology sect., 1970-86; med. officer for AIDS rsch. Gen. Clin. Rsch. Ctrs., NIH, 1986-89, dir. Office of Recombinant DNA Activities, 1989-96; dep. dir. Inst. Human Gene Therapy Sch. Medicine U. Pa., Phila., 1996—. Adj. prof. molecular and cellular engring., program chair ethics and pub. policy rsch. program U. Pa. Med. Ctr., Phila., 1996—; exec. dir. recombinant DNA adv. com. NIH. Assoc. editor Jour. Nat. Cancer Inst., 1968-70, Human Gene Therapy, 1993—, Jour. Biolaw and Bus., 1996—; contbr. more than 80 articles to profl. jours. including Sci., Nature, Jour. of Virology, Virology. Recipient Commendation medal USPHS, 1990. Mem. Am. Soc. Cell Biology, Am. Soc. Virology, Am. Soc. Gene Therapy. Achievements include research on murine retroviruses that can function as moveable genetic elements (transposons). Avocations: swimming, sailing. Office: U Pa Sch Medicine Inst Human Gene Therapy Maloney Bldg Rm M630.B 36th and Spruce Sts Philadelphia PA 19104-4283 E-mail: naw@mail.med.upenn.edu.

WIXOM, ROBERT LLEWELLYN, biochemistry educator; b. Phila., July 6, 1924; s. Clinton W. and Beatrice R. (Hunt) W.; m. Edith Ann Smith, Aug. 21, 1949 (dec. Feb. 1967); children: David G., Richard L.; m. Patricia McMillin, Aug. 2, 1986. BA, Earlham Coll., 1947; PhD, U. Ill., 1952. Instr. U. Ark. Sch. Medicine, Little Rock, 1952-54, asst. prof., 1954-60, assoc. prof., 1960-64, U. Mo., Columbia, 1964-72, prof., 1972-92, prof. emeritus, 1992—. Chmn. biol. scis. sector U. Mo., 1989-92, chair environ. affairs coun., 1991-94. Author: Environmental Challenges for Higher Education, 1996; co-editor, author: Chromatography--A Century of Discovery (1900-2000) The Bridge to the Sciences/Technology, 2001; contbr. articles to sci. jours. NIH rsch. fellow, 1970, recipient NIH Rsch. svc. award, 1978. Mem. AAAS, Am. Chem. Soc. (chmn. U. Mo. sect. 1984-85), Am. Soc. Biochemistry and Molecular Biology, Am. Inst. Nutrition, Protein Soc., Sigma Xi. Achievements include research in identification of essential amino acid requirements and metabolism in adult men, in biosynthesis of valine and isoleucine in microorganisms and plants, on the role of histidine in adult men, and in ferritin/hemosiderin/iron metabolism. Office: U Mo Sch Medicine Med Sci Bldg Dc008 00 Columbia MO 65212-0001

WIXOM, WILLIAM DAVID, art historian, museum administrator, educator; b. Phila., July 17, 1929; s. Clinton Wood and Beatrice Rachel (Hunt) W.; m. Nancy Coe, Aug. 8, 1959; 3 children. BA, Haverford (Pa.) Coll., 1951; MA, Inst. Fine Arts NYU, 1963. Lecturer The Barnes Foundation, Merion, Pa., 1951—52; asst. curator to curator medieval and renaissance decorative arts Cleve. Mus. Art, 1958-78, chief curator early western art, 1979; chmn. dept. medieval art and The Cloisters Met. Mus. Art, N.Y.C., 1979-98, curator emeritus. Lectr. Barnes Found., Merion, Pa., 1951—52; adj. assoc. prof. history of art Case Western Res. U., Cleve., 1967—78, adj. prof., 1978, N.Y.U., 1981—82; mem. adv. coun. Snite Mus. Art Notre Dame U., 1974—95; curatorial cons. for medieval art The Barnes Foundation, Merion, Pa., 2002—. Author: Treasures from Medieval France, 1967; Renaissance Bronzes from Ohio Collections, 1975; contbg. author The Royal Abbey of Saint Denis in the Time of Abbot suger, 1981, The Treasury of San Marco, 1985; Gothic and Renaissance Art in Nuremberg, 1986, Festschrift Gerhard Bott, 1987, Hommage a Hubert Landais, 1987, The Cloisters, Studies in Honor of the Fiftieth Anniversary, 1992, Festschrift Gerhard Schmidt, 1994, Enamels of Limoges 1100-1350, 1996, Studies in Honor of Kurt Weitzmann, 1995, The Dictionary of Art, 1996, The Glory of Byzantium, Art and Culture of the Middle Byzantine Era, AD 843-1261, 1997, Sculptures hors contexte, Louvre conférences et colloques, 1997, Mirror of the Medieval World, 1999, Romanesque Sculpture in American Collections, 1999, Tilman Riemenschneider, Master Sculptor of the Late Middle Ages, 1999, Picturing the Apocalypse: Illustrated Leaves from a Medieval Spanish Manuscript, 2002; contbr. articles to profl. jours. Bd. dirs. Internat. Ctr. Medieval Art, N.Y.C., 1971-82, pres., 1971-74. Belgium-Am. Ednl. Found. fellow, 1962; Nat. Endowment Arts grantee, 1973; fellow Pierpont Morgan Libr., 1979-2001; J. Paul Getty Mus. Guest Scholar, 1996. Fellow Soc. of Antiquaries of London; mem. Coll. Art Assn. (dir. 1979-83), Medieval Acad. Am., Internat. Ctr. Medieval Art. Mem. Soc. Of Friends. Office: Dept Medieval Art Met Mus Art New York NY 10028

WIXTROM, DONALD JOSEPH, translator; b. Republic, Mich., Oct. 14, 1928; s. Joseph Albert and Edith (Johnson) W.; m. Marilyn Jean Sjoquist, Oct. 14, 1961; children: Joe Alan, Lorna Jean, Aaron Matthew. Free lance translator, Republic, 1966—. Mem. Am. Translators Assn. Baptist. Home and Office: RR 1 Box 98 Republic MI 49879-9726

WIZARD, BRIAN, publisher, author; b. Newburyport, Mass., June 24, 1949; s. Russell and Ruth (Hidden) Willard. BA, Sonoma (Calif.) State U., 1976; D of Metaphysics, Universal Life Ch., 1997. Ordained to ministry Universal Life Ch., 1997. Pvt. practice as jeweler, sculptor and craftsman, Calif., 1974-79; Wallowa, Oreg., 1991—; prin. The Starquill Pub., Port Douglas, Queensland, Australia, 1981-86; owner Starquill Internat., Wallowa, Oreg. Author: (trilogy) The Will He Make it Saga (contender 1998 Pulitzer prize), Permission to Kill, 1985, Permission to Live, 1992, Back in the World, 1995; (novels) Shindara, 1990, Heaven on Earth, 1998, Coming of Age, 1990, Pollution IV, 1993, Nigerian 419 Scam "Game Over!", 2000; (short stories) Tropical Pair, 1986, Metempsychosis, 1988 (In Search of) The Silver Lining, 1994, The Moon Whistling By on a Cloud, 1994, (The Princess of the) Wildflowers, 1995, Mushroom Magic, 1996, Vietnam 1999! Make Friends Not War; contbr. to Smithsonian Inst.'s The Vietnam War Generation; contbr. to SpaceArc; prodr. (video documentary) Thunderhawks, 1987, Swift Action Newsteam, Tope Creek Lookout, 1995; songwriter, prodr. (cassette) Brian Wizard Sings for His Supper, 1989 (cert. of achievement Billboard 1993); songwriter, singer, prodr. (I Don't Want) Permission to Kill, 1989, Busker's Theme Song, Living in North Queensland, Circus Act, Hitch Hiking Man, Self-Portrait, The Love We Share Will Never End, 1994, Never Met a Girl Like You, Folk-Rock Opera: A Cover Story: After That Ugly Saloon Incident; contbr. to America's Finest Songwriter and Lyricists CD, 1997, (novels, video and music) Brian Wizard's 20th Century Anthology, 1998 (nominee Nobel Prize in Lit. 2000), (video) Vietnam '99, Make Friends Not War, 1999; contbr. to TV documentaries History of the Machine Gun, 2000, Vietnam, The Personal Experience, 2001. Renovator hist. landmark The Tope Creek Lookout (Skyship); mem. Nat. Hist. Lookout Register; sponsor Adopt A Hwy., 1995; min. Universal Life Ch.; amb. at large Africa Anti Fraud Alliance. With U.S. Army, 1967-70. Decorated Air medals (26), Aviator Flight Wings; recipient Cert. of Appreciation, Pres. Richard M. Nixon. Mem. Vietnam Helicopter Crewmember Assn., 145th Combat Aviation Bn. Assn. (Internet host), Vietnam Combat Vets. Assn., Vietnam Vets. Am., Vietnam Vets. Australia Assn. Office: PO Box 42 Wallowa OR 97885-0042 E-mail: bwizard@eoni.com.

WIZEN, SARABETH MARGOLIS, financial advisor; b. Ypsilanti, Mich., May 11, 1950; d. Isidor and Ada (Eglovitch) Margolis; m. Sidney K. Wizen, July 27, 1975. BA, Mich. State U., 1972; MA, Eastern Mich. U., 1974. Adminstr. Faulkner Dawkins & Sullivan, N.Y.C., 1976-77, Dean Witter Reynolds, N.Y.C., 1977-79; adminstrv. salesman Cowen & Co., 1979; v.p., dir. ops. Brookehill Equities, Inc., 1979-87; pres., bd. dirs. Brookehill Ptnrs., Inc., 1987-99; sr. fin. advisor First Union Securities, Westport, Conn., 2000—. Apptd. to NASD Bd. Arbitrators, 1996. Named to Willow Run H.S. Hall of Fame, 1998. Mem. Fin. Women's Assn. N.Y. (bd. dirs. 1989-95, 97-98, 2000—), Met. Mus. Art, Mich. State U. Alumni Assn., Eastern Mich. U. Alumni Assn., Alpha Epsilon Phi Alumni Assn. Office: First Union Securities One Penn Plaza New York NY 10119 E-mail: sarabethmw@aol.com.

WIZNIA, CAROLANN KAMENS, lawyer; b. Boston, Apr. 30, 1950; BA, Brandeis U., 1972; JD, Boston Coll., 1975. Bar: Conn. 1976. Pvt. practice, New Haven, 1976—. Mem. ABA, Conn. Bar Assn. Office: 850 Howard Ave New Haven CT 06519-1106

WLADIS, MARK NEIL, lawyer; b. Elizabeth, N.J., May 18, 1964; s. George L. and Roberta W. (Wolgin) W.; m. Diane F. Wladis, Nov. 18, 1990; children: Jacqueline P., Harrison S. BA, Muhlenberg Coll., 1986; JD, Syracuse U., 1989, LLM in Taxation, 1993. Bar: N.Y. 1990, Fla. 1995, U.S. Dist. Ct. (no. dist.) N.Y. 1991, U.S. Tax Ct. 1992. Tax assoc. Coopers & Lybrand, Syracuse, N.Y., 1989-90; assoc. Nottingham, Engel, Gordon & Kerr, 1991-92; ptnr. Melvin & Melvin, LLP, 1993-99, Devorsetz Stinziano Gilberti Heintz & Smith, P.C., Syracuse, 2000—01, Alderman Wladis PC, Syracuse, 2001—. Vice-chmn Trustee Onandaga C.C., 2001-; bd. dirs. Ctrl. N.Y. Lupus Soc., Syracuse, 1992-94, Jewish Fedn., Syracuse, 1996—. Mem. Lafayette Golf and Country Club (bd. dirs. 1994-95). E-mail. Office: Alderman Wladis PC 472 S Salina St Ste 444 Syracuse NY 13202 E-mail: mwladis@aldermanwladispc.com.

WLASCHIN, KEN, cultural organization administrator, writer; b. Bradish, Nebr., July 12, 1934; s. Bernard A. and Lucy M. (Stevens) W.; m. Maureen N. Kennedy Martin, Mar. 22, 1961; 1 child, Scott Martin. BA, Dartmouth Coll., 1956; MA, U. Coll., Dublin, Ireland, 1957; postgrad., U. Poitiers, France, 1960. Program dir. Nat. Film Theater, London, 1969-83, London Film Festival, 1970-83; artistic dir. L.A. Film Expn., 1984-86; dir. exhbn. Am. Film Inst., L.A., 1986-97, dir. preservation, 1998—. Theater critic Rome Daily Am. & Daily Sketch, Rome and London, 1962-67; art critic Art Voices Mag., Rome, 1962-68; film critic Films and Filming Mag., London, 1973-82; story editor London Weekend TV, 1968. Author: (TV play) Ticket to Trieste, 1961, (novel), The Italian Job, 1964, Rome A City, 1964, Guide to Cinema, 1970, Encyclopedia of Movie Stars, 1979, Faber Book of Movie Verse, 1994, Opera on Screen, 1997, Gian Carlo Menotti on Screen, 1999. With U.S. Army, 1958-61, ETO. Mem. Brit. Film Inst., Brit. Film Acad. Avocation: opera. Home: 2597 Dearborn Dr Los Angeles CA 90068-2239 Office: Am Film Inst 2021 N Western Ave Los Angeles CA 90027-1625 E-mail: kwlaschin@afionline.org.

WLEUGEL, JOHN PETER, manufacturing company executive; b. Hoyanger, Sogn, Norway, July 1, 1929; s. Johan and Helga (Faye) W.; m. Leonor Abaroa, Dec. 1959; children— Jan Andrew, Cecilia Maria. BA, U. Copenhagen, 1953; MBA, U. Toronto, 1957. With Belgium Machine Tool Assn., 1953-54, Massey-Ferguson Ltd., Toronto, 1954-71, treas., 1968-71, also dir. several subs.; sr. v.p. Bata Ltd., also bd. dirs.; dir., officer several subsidiaries (Bata Shoe Orgn.), Don Mills, Ont., Can., 1972-89; exec.-in-residence Schulich Sch. Bus., York U., North York, Can., 1990—. Bd. dirs. AMR Techs., Inc., Bloomen Networld Inc. Mem. Financial Execs. Inst., Univ. Club (Toronto). Home: 5 Campbell Crescent Toronto ON Canada M2P 1P1 Office: Schulich Sch Bus York U 4700 Keele St Toronto ON Canada M3J 1P3

WLUDYKA, PETER S. statistician, educator; b. Spartanburg, S.C., Mar. 16, 1949; s. Peter Wludyka and Margaret Reynolds; m. Catherine M. Beaver, May 7, 1994; 1 child Peter 1 child Deirdre Wludyka Seim. PhD, Clemson U., 1994. Assoc. prof. stats. U. North Fla.f, Jacksonville, 1994—. Dir. ctr. for rsch. and consulting in stats. U. North Fla., 1997—. Author: (novel) The Past is Another Country, 1988; contbr. articles to profl. jours. Recipient Best Applications Paper of Yr. award, Technometrics, 1997. Office: U North Fla Dept Stats St Johns Bluff Rd S Jacksonville FL 32210 Business E-Mail: pwludyka@unf.edu.

WNUK, WADE JOSEPH, manufacturing and service company executive; b. St. Louis, Sept. 2, 1944; s. Edward Joseph and Helen Evelyn (Millick) W.; m. Judith Kay Yohe, May 3, 1969; children: Russell Nicholas, Wade Gregory. BS in Math. magna cum laude, St. Louis U., 1966; MS in Engring. Sci., Calif. Inst. Tech., 19667; MBA, Harvard U., 1974. Govt. research analyst, Washington, 1967-69; planner FMC Corp., Chgo., 1974-75, mgr. bus. devel. petroleum equipment divsn. Houston, 1975-77, group planning mgr. petroleum equipment group, 1977-78; ops. mgr. FMC Petroleum Equipment, 1978-80; subsea mgr. FMC Wellhead Equipment div., 1980-81; dir. corp. devel. Marathon Mfg. Corp., 1981-82, v.p. corp. devel., 1982-84; exec. v.p. Marathon Power Tech., Houston and Waco, 1984-86; v.p., regional gen. mgr. TDW, Inc., Tulsa, 1986-90, sr. v.p. Tulsa and Singapore, 1990-94; pres. Norriseal, Houston, 1995-98, cons., 1999-2000, Echo Environ., N.Y.C.; pres. Wedco, 2001—. Served with U.S. Army, 1969-72. Mem. Internat. Bus. Club (past v.p.), St. Louis U. Alumni Assn., Calif. Inst. Tech. Assn., Harvard Alumni Assns., Harvard Club (Houston). Office: 53333 Westheimer Rd Houston TX 77056 E-mail: wwnul@icopolymers.com.

WOBBLETON, JUDY KAREN, artist, educator; b. Williamston, N.C., Aug. 31, 1947; d. Lloyd Thomas and Lillian Edith (Hudson) Letchworth; m. Albert Virgil Wobbleton Jr., Apr. 7, 1968; children: Olivia Elizabeth, Virgil Alan. Clk. Beaufort County Hosp., Washington, 1965-68; ins. supr. Mercy Hosp., Sacramento, 1968-72; adminstrv. asst. hosp. svcs. Fairbanks (Alaska) Meml. Hosp., 1972-75; basketry artist Williamston, 1983—. Instr. basketry N.C. Basketmakers, 1984-2000, co-founder, 1984; instr. Wayne C.C., Goldsboro, N.C., 1986-91. Contbg. artist: The Basket Book, 1988, Basketmaker's Baskets, 1990, Craft Works in The Home, 1990. Troop leader Girl Scouts U.S., Goldsboro, 1983-88, svc. unit mgr., 1987-91; active Roanoke Arts & Crafts Guild, 1991-98, v.p., 1991-97, pres., 1998-99; mem. Martin County Arts Coun., 2001—. Recipient 2d Pl. award Wilson Arts Coun., 1987, 3d Pl. award Martin County Arts Coun., 1992, 99. Mem. N.C. Basketmakers Assn. (hon., co-founder 1984, bd. dirs. 1984-94, membership chmn. 1984-87, pres. 1990-94, conv. rev. com. 1994-96, 96-2002, mem.-at-large 2000—), Goldweavers Basketry Guild (hon.). Avocations: reading, cooking, painting. Home and Office: Baskets By Judy 1325 Oakview St Williamston NC 27892-8664

WOBUS, REINHARD ARTHUR, geologist, educator; b. Norfolk, Va., Jan. 11, 1941; s. Reinhard Schaffer and Oral (Phares) W.; m. Sheridan Whitcher, Mar. 18, 1967; children: Erik Reinhard, Cameron Wright. BA, Washington U., St. Louis, 1962; MA, Harvard U., 1963; PhD, Stanford U., 1966. Asst. prof. geology Williams Coll., Williamstown, Mass., 1966-72, assoc. prof., 1972-78, prof., 1978-85, Edna McConnell Clark prof. geology, 1985—, dept. chmn., 1988-96. Geologist U.S. Geol. Survey, Denver, 1967-86; vis. prof. Colo. Coll., Colorado Springs, 1976, 82-83, Colo. State U., Ft. Collins, summers 1977-84; bd. dirs. Colo. Outdoor Edn. Ct., Florissant; co-founder Keck Twelve-Coll. Geol. Consortium, mem. gov. bd., 1986—. Contbr. maps and articles on Precambrian geology of So. Rocky Mountains to profl. jours. Danforth fellow, 1962, Woodrow Wilson fellow, 1962, NSF fellow, 1962-66. Fellow Geol. Soc. Am.; mem. Am. Geophys. Union, Nat. Assn. Geology Tchrs., Coun. on Undergrad. Rsch., Colo. Sci. Soc., Mineral Soc. Am., Phi Beta Kappa, Sigma Xi. Achievements include current work: Petrology and geochronology of Precambrian igneous and metamorphic rocks and mid-Tertiary volcanic rocks, so. Rocky Mountains. Subspecialties: Petrology, Geology. Home: 20 Grandview Dr Williamstown MA 01267-2528 Office: Williams Coll Dept Geoscis Williamstown MA 01267 E-mail: rwobus@williams.edu.

WOEBER, KENNETH ALOIS, physician; b. Feb. 2, 1935; MB, BChir, MD, U. Witwatersrand, Johannesburg, South Africa, 1957. Intern Johannesburg Hosp., 1958-59; resident Jackson Meml. Hosp., Miami, Fla., 1959-62; rsch. fellow Harvard Med. Sch., 1962-64, instr. medicine, 1965-68, asst. prof. medicine, 1968-70, assoc. prof. medicine, 1970-72, U. Calif., San Francisco, 1972-75, prof. clin. medicine, 1975—, vice-chmn. medicine, 1981-2000, chief clin. endocrinology, 2000—. Chmn. subsplty. bd. endocrinology and metabolism Am. Bd. Internal Medicine, 1985-87. Contbr. articles to profl. jours. Recipient Van Meter prize Am. Thyroid Assn. Fellow Royal Coll. Physicians of Edinburgh. Home: 6 Bartel Ct Belvedere Tiburon CA 94920-1656 Office: U Calif San Francisco at Mt Zion PO Box 1640 San Francisco CA 94143-1640 E-mail: woeber@itsa.ucsf.edu.

WOEHRLE, CONRAD A. photographer, poet; b. Seattle, Nov. 30, 1956; s. Karl Conrad and Vivian Olive (Williams) Woehrle; m. Laura Patricia Woehrle, Sept. 10, 1988; children: Colman Ariel, Austin Chase. BA, U. Wash., 1983. Freelance photographer, 1983—94. Author: books of poetry;exhibitions include Joseph Dee Mus. of Photography, San Francisco, 1988, Represented in permanent collections AP, UPI. Photographer Seattle Sister City Com., 1983—87. Named Poet Laureate, Internat. Libr. of Poetry, 2001. Mem.: Poets Soc. Am. Avocations: numismatics, woodcarving, collecting antique Japanese Netsuke. Home: PO Box 499 South Prairie WA 98385

WOEHRLE, JUDITH ANN, physical therapist, educator; b. St. Louis, Aug. 30, 1953; d. Rudy and Christine Yovandich; m. Mark A. Woehrle, Oct. 30, 1971; children: Erik A. BS, St. Louis Univ., St. Louis, MO, 1977—80; MHS, Wash. Univ., St. Louis, MO, 1980—85. Staff phys. therapist Profl. Phys. Therapy, St. Louis, 1980—82; asst. prof. St. Louis Univ., 1982—86; staff phys. therapist Midwest Orthop. Phys. Therapy, Inc., 1983—87; instr. Wash. Univ., 1986—2000; lead phys. therapist Christian Hosp. NE, 1995—2000; asst. prof. Maryville Univ., 2000—. Cons., phys. therapist Cons. Phys. Therapy Svcs., St. Louis, 1983—85; owner Phys. Therapy Care, St. Louis, 1997—2000. Vice chmn. Mo. Phys. Therapy Assn., Eastern District, Mo., 1996—2000, chmn. nominating comm. St. Louis, 1998—99; med. coord. St. Louis Olympic Festival, 1994. Recipient Outstanding Svc. in Edn., Mo. Phys. Therapy Assn., 2002. Office: Maryville University 13550 Conway Road Saint Louis MO 63141

WOEHRLEN, ARTHUR EDWARD, JR. dentist; b. Detroit, Dec. 9, 1947; s. Arthur Edward and Olga (Hewka) W.; m. Sara Elizabeth Heikoff, Aug. 13, 1972; 1 child, Tess Helena. DDS, U. Mich., 1973. Resident in gen. dentistry USAF, 1973-74; gen. practice dentistry Redwood Dental Group, Warren, Mich., 1976—. Instr. Sinai Hosp., Detroit, 1977—; chief of dentistry St. John's Hosp., Macomb Ctr., Mt. Clemens, Mich., 1982—; mem. dentistry staff Hutzel Hosp., Warren; reviewer Chubb Ins. Co. (malpractice claims), 1978-89; bd. mem. Mich. Acad. Gen. Dentistry (chmn. State of Mich. Continuing Dental Edn. Accreditation). Contbr. articles on dentistry to profl. jours. Served to capt. USAF, 1973-76. Fellow Internat. Coll. of Oral Implantologists; mem. ADA, Acad. Gen. Dentistry (Master), Mich. Dental Assn., Acad. Gen. Dentistry, Am. Acad. Oral Medicine, Fedn. Dentaire Internationale, Acad. Dentistry for the Handicapped, Am. Acad. Oral Implantologists, Internat. Coll. Oral Implantologists, Macomb Dist. Dental Soc.; panel mem. Am. Arbitration Assn. Republican. Home: 25460 Dundee Rd Royal Oak MI 48067-3018 Office: 13403 E 13 Mile Rd Warren MI 48088-3188

WOELFEL, JAMES WARREN, philosophy and humanities educator; b. Galveston, Tex., Aug. 16, 1937; s. Warren Charles and Mary Frances (Washinka) W.; m. Sarah Chappell Trulove, Nov. 24, 1982; children by previous marriages: Skye Caitlin, Allegra Eve, Sarah Judith; stepchildren: Ann Marie and Paul Trulove. BA, U. Okla., 1959; MDiv, Episcopal Div. Sch., Cambridge, Mass., 1962; MA, Yale U., 1964; PhD, U. St. Andrews, Scotland, 1967. Asst. prof. philosophy and religion U. Kans., Lawrence, 1966-70, asst. prof. philosophy, 1970-71, assoc. prof. philosophy and religion, 1971-75, prof. philosophy and religious studies, 1975-88, prof. philosophy, 1988—, acting chmn. dept. religious studies, 1983-84, dir. Humanities and Western civilization program, 1985—. Manuscript reader for various presses, jours. Author: Bonhoeffer's Theology, 1970, Borderland Christianity, 1973, Camus: A Theological Perspective (republished as Albert Camus on the Sacred and the Secular, 1987), 1975, Augustinian Humanism, 1979, The Agnostic Spirit as a Common Motif in Liberal Theology and Liberal Scepticism, 1990; editor, co-author: Patterns in Western Civilization, 1991, 3rd edit., 2002; ; editor: Portraits in Victorian Religious Thought, 1997; contbr. essays, revs. to profl. jours.; contbr. articles. Danforth grad. fellow Episcopal Div. Sch., Cambridge, Mass., 1959-62, U. St. Andrews, 1962-63, 65-66, Yale U., New Haven, 1963-65; Fulbright scholar U. St. Andrews, 1962-63, Pub. Scholar award Kans. Humanities Coun., 1997; grantee NEH, Exxon Found., Mellon Found., Menninger Found., Inst. for Ecumenical and Cultural Rsch. Mem. Am. Acad. Religion, Highlands Inst. for Am. Religious Thought, Assn. for Core Texts and Courses, Phi Beta Kappa. Democrat. Avocations: piano; walking. Home: 808 Alabama St Lawrence KS 66044-3942 Office: U Kans Humanities & Western Civilization Program Bailey Hall 1440 Jayhawk Blvd Rm 308 Lawrence KS 66045-7574

WOELFEL, JOSEPH DONALD, communications educator; b. Buffalo, June 3, 1940; s. Richard Joseph and Elizabeth Lillian (Graeber) W.; children: Charles, Joseph, Johanna, Evan, Alaina, Alec, Emary. BS in Sociology, Canisius Coll., 1962; MA in Sociology, U. Wis., 1963, PhD in Sociology, 1968. Asst. prof. sociology U. Ill., Urbana, 1968-72; assoc. prof. communications Mich. State U., East Lansing, 1972-78; prof. communications SUNY, Albany, N.Y., 1978-89, prof., chair communications Buffalo, 1989—. Pres. The Galileo Co., Amherst, N.Y., 1978—; dir. rsch. Terra Rsch. Computing Co., Birmingham, Mich., 1990—; cons. Agy. Internat. Devel., Albany Rsch. Svcs., Almeth Rsch., Am. Mktg. Assn., Arbitron, ASG, Blue Cross/Blue Shield Mich., others; bd. dirs. Multimedia Moguls, Lancaster, N.Y. Author: Communication and Science, 1992, 94, What's Wrong With This Picture?, 1995, Variational Principles of Communication, 1995, (with others) The Measurement of Communication Process: Galileo Theory and Method, 1980; editor Systemsletter, 1983-85; editor-in-chief RAH Press, 1995—; assoc. editor Human Communication Rsch., 1976, 79, Communication Quar., 1977-83, Informatologia Jugoslavia, 1985—; cons. editor Am. Sociol. Rev., Am. Jour. Sociology, Rural Sociology, Jour. Cross Cultural Rsch., Human Orgn., Human Communication Rsch., Communication Rsch.; contbr. chpts. in books and articles to profl. publs. Bd. dirs. WBFO, Buffalo, 1991-92. Sr. fellow East-West Communication Inst., Honolulu, 1977-83, Faculty fellow Rockefeller Inst. Govt., 1985—; Richard W.D. Nicholas Agrl. Sci. scholar U. Melbourne, 1986; recipient Pres.'s award for Excellence in Rsch., SUNY, 1983, Fulbright award Conf. Dubrovnik, 1983. Mem. AAAS, N.Am. Classification Soc., N.Y. Acad. Scis., Internat. Soc. Network Analysis, Neural Network Soc., Psychometric Soc., Soc. Scientific Study of Communication. Office: U Buffalo Dept Communication 337 Baldy Hall Buffalo NY 14261-0001

WOELFEL, SCOTT GERARD, Internet executive; b. St. Louis, Aug. 5, 1959; s. William Michael and Betty Lee (Smith) W.; m. Debra Ann Daugherty, Sept. 17, 1994. BJ, U. Mo., 1981. TV news photographer Sta. KTUL-TV, Tulsa, 1981; TV news prodr. Sta. WXEX-TV, Richmond, Va., 1981-83, Sta. WESH-TV, Orlando, Fla., 1983-85; prodr. Cable News Network (CNN), Atlanta, 1985-89, exec. prodr., 1989-94; editor-in-chief CNN Interactive, 1995-96, v.p., editor-in-chief, 1996-98, sr. v.p., editor-in-chief, 1998-2000, pres., editor-in-chief, 2000—. Bd. dirs. Atlanta Cmty. Food Bank; mem. adv. bd. FACSNET, L.A., 1996—. Avocations: computer, movies, golf. Home: 617 E Pelham Rd NE Atlanta GA 30324-5201 Office: CNN Interactive PO Box 105366 Atlanta GA 30348-5366

WOELFLEIN, KEVIN GERARD, banker; b. Haverhill, Mass., Feb. 9, 1933; s. John Henry and Helen Margaret (Hoar) W.; m. Ann Buckley, Sept. 9, 1957; children: Karl G., Luise A., Andrew B., Peter H. BS, MIT, 1954; MBA, U. Pa., 1958, postgrad., 1959-65. Venture analyst Atlas Chem. Industries, Wilmington, Del., 1959-66; economist Fed. Res. Bank Phila., 1966-67; asst. v.p. 1st Nat. Bank Chgo., 1967-70, v.p., 1970-72; v.p., gen. mgr. (Tokyo br.), 1972-75; pres., chief exec. officer, dir. UBAF Arab Am. Bank, N.Y.C., 1975-81; pres., chief operating officer, dir. Am. Security Bank, Washington, 1981-83; pres., dir. Mass. Co., Inc., Boston, 1983-86; pres. U.S. Capital Investments Co., Alexandria, Va., 1983—; chmn. bd. Conn. Bancorp, Inc., also bd. dirs.; chmn. bd. Norwalk (Conn.) Bank, 1990-92, also bd. dirs. Trustee Meridian Internat. Ctr., Washington, 1982—87, counselor, 1987—. Bd. dirs. Small Bus. High Tech. Inst., 1982-85; mem. exec. com. MIT Enterprise Forum, Washington, 1982-85; mem. MIT Corp. vis. com. Ctr. for Internat. Studies; mem. adv. council U.S.-Japan Study Ctr., Johns Hopkins U. Sch. Advanced Internat. Studies, 1982-85; trustee Convent of Sacred Heart, Greenwich, Conn., 1977-81; mem. U.S.-Saudi Arabian Joint Commn. on Econ. Cooperation, 1982-84. Served to lt. U.S. Army, 1954-56. Recipient Corp. Leadership award MIT, 1980; Knight of Malta, Fed. Assn., 1984. Mem. Columbia Country Club. E-mail: kevinwoelflein@aol.com.

WOERNER, ALFRED IRA, medical device manufacturer, educator; b. Jersey City, Sept. 21, 1935; s. Theodore and Miriam (Mann) W.; m. Margaret R. Martin, Nov. 27, 1959; children: John, Michael, Judith. DME, Stevens Inst., 1956; MS, Stevens, 1961; MBA, NYU, 1965; LLB, LaSalle U., 1963; PhD, Calif. State U., 1990. Gen. program mgr. Becton Dickenson & Co., Ruthuferd, N.J., 1959-63; group v.p., asst. to pres. Howmet Corp., N.Y.C., 1963-69; gen. mgr., v.p. Wide Range Industries, 1969-72; pres., owner New World Market Ltd., Westwood, N.J., 1972—, Fairfield Surg. Corp., Stanford, Conn., 1972—. Cons. Woerner Assocs., Westwood; prof. Fairleigh Dickinson U., Teaneck, N.J., 1969-96. Author: Program Management, 1988. Pres. Bd. Edn., Westwood, 1978-86; adv. Stevens Inst. Tech., Hoboken, N.J., 1972-80. Mem. AMA, ASME, Am. Acad. Cons., Am. Statistical Assn. Achievements include five patents in Medical Industry; development of new process in orthopedic surgery industry. Home: 7560 Bay Island Dr S South Pasadena FL 33707-4562 Office: Fairleigh Dickinson U 1000 River Rd Teaneck NJ 07666-1996 E-mail: mrwaiw@aol.com.

WOERNER, FRED FRANK, international relations educator; b. Phila., 1933; BS, U.S. Mil. Acad., 1955; MA in Latin Am. History, U. Ariz., 1965. Commd. 2d lt. U.S. Army, 1955, advanced through grades to gen., comdr. in chief U.S. So. Command, ret., 1989; prof. internat. rels. Boston U. Mem. Coun. Fgn. Rels. Disting. fellow U.S. Army War Coll. Office: Boston Univ Dept Internat Rels 152 Bay State Rd Boston MA 02215-1501 E-mail: woerner@bu.edu.

WOERNER, FREDERICK FRANK, international relations educator; b. Phila., Aug. 12, 1933; s. Frederick Frank and Mary Ann (McCabe) W.; m. Gennie Ehrhorn, Jan. 21, 1956; children: Frederick Frank III, Charles Anthony, Robert John, Michael Scott. BS, U.S. Mil. Acad., West Point, N.Y., 1955; MA, U. Ariz., 1965. Advanced through grades to U.S. Army, 1955-89, ret., 1989; prof. Boston U., 1990—. Chmn. Am. Battle Monuments Commn., Washington, 1994-2001. Mem. Assn. Grads. of Mil. Acad., Assn. U.S. Army, Coun. Fgn. Rels. Lutheran. Avocations: reading, jogging, fishing. Home: 4 Arbor Cir Natick MA 01760-2953 Office: Dept Internat Rels Boston U 152 Bay State Rd Boston MA 02215-1501

WOERNER, KLAUS D. manufacturing executive; b. Germany; arrived in Can., 1960; B.Indsl. Engring., Ryerson Poly. U. Process engr. truck divsn. Ford Motor Co.; founder, pres., CEO ATS Automation Tooling Systems, Inc., Cambridge, Canada, 1978—. Named Can.'s Entrepreneur of the Yr., Ernst & Young, 1997. Office: ATS Automation Tooling 250 Royal Oak Rd Cambridge ON Canada N3H 5M2*

WOERNER, ROBERT EUGENE, federal agency administrator, editor; b. Cadillac, Mich., Sept. 23, 1947; s. William Reginald and Ellen Hazel (Van Zoeren) W. BA in English summa cum laude, Grand Valley State U., 1969. Logistics coord. Colo. Outward Bound, 1979-80; writer, editor Bur. of Land Mgmt., U.S. Dept. Interior, Grand Junction, Colo., 1977-78, Elko, Nev., 1980-82, Craig, Colo., 1982-84, Denver, 1984—. Free-lance writer, Buena Vista, Colo., 1976-77; mem. computer tech. adv. bd. Warren Tech, Golden, Colo., 1994-97. Newsletter editor Urban Peak, Denver, 1989-95; author book rev.; contbr. articles to profl. jours. including Jour. of Forestry, Govt. Exec. Vol. Craig Hosp., Englewood, Colo., 1994. Capt. USAF, 1970-76. Honors scholar Grand Valley State U., 1966-69; recipient cert. Excellence in Accountability Reporting Assn. Govt. Accts. U.S. Dept of Interior, 2001. Mem. Colo. Friends of Tibet, Inst. Noetic Scis., The Nature Conservancy, So. Utah Wilderness Alliance. Avocations: hiking, astronomy, travel, reading, Reiki (master/tchr.). Office: Bur Land Mgmt PO Box 25047 Denver CO 80225-0047

WOERNER, ROBERT LESTER, landscape architect; b. Rochester, N.Y., Jan. 31, 1925; s. William John and Loretta Bertha (Hettel) W.; m. Mary Jane Warn, May 12, 1952; children: Jane Marie, Anne Louise. BS, SUNY Coll. Forestry, Syracuse, 1949. Cert. landscape architect, Wash., Idaho. Draftsman N.A., Rotunno Landscape Architects, Syracuse, 1947-49; landscape architect Park Dist., Plan Commn., Yakima, Wash., 1949-50; asst. supt. parks Spokane Park Dept., Spokane, 1950-56; dir. Denver Bot. Gardens, 1956-58; pvt. practice landscape architect Spokane, 1959-2000; chmn. bd. registration Landscape Architects State of Wash., 1976-78; pres. Council Landscape Archtl. Registration Bds., 1978-79. Mem. Zoning Bd. Adjustment, Spokane, 1983; mem. Urban Design Com., 1983; mem. Capitol Campus Design Adv. Com., 1982-94. Cpl. U.S. Army, 1943-45, ETO. Recipient Indsl. Landscaping Award Am. Assn. Nurserymen, Lincoln Bldg., Spokane, 1966; recipient Cert. of Merit Wash. Water Power, 1967, State Indsl. Landscaping award Wash State Nurserymen's Assn., Wash. Water Power, 1968 Fellow Am. Soc. Landscape Architects (pres. 1979-80, Disting. Svc. award 1976); mem. Kiwanis, Masons. Republican. Roman Catholic.

WOERTZ, PATRICIA A. petroleum industry executive; b. Mar. 1953; B in Acctg., Pa. State U. Acct. Ernst & Young, Pitts., 1974; with Gulf Oil Corp., 1977-81, Houston, 1981-85; with debt. reduction process, merger of Gulf and Chevron, 1985-87; fin. mgr. Chevron Info. Tech. Co., 1989-91, strategic planning mgr., 1991-93; pres. Chevron Can. Ltd., Vancouver, B.C., 1993-96, Chevron Internat. Oil Co., 1996-98; v.p. logistics and trading Chevron Products Co., Chevron Corp., 1996-98; pres. Chevron Products Co., 1998—2001; v.p. Chevron Corp., 1998—2001; exec. v.p. Chevron Texaco Corp., San Francisco, 2001—. Mem.: Calif. C. of C. (bd. dirs.), Am. Petroleum Inst. (bd. dirs.). Office: Chevron Corp 575 Market St San Francisco CA 94105

WOESSNER, FREDERICK T. composer, pianist; b. Teaneck, N.J., July 23, 1935; s. Fred and Bertha W.; m. Lise, Feb. 14, 1960 (div. 1973); children: Betty, Allison. Student, Peabody Conservatory of Music, Balt., 1960-61; MBA, NYU, 1968; MA, Calif. State U., Los Angeles, 1975; pvt. study with, David Diamond, Charles Haubiel, Albert Harris. Owner Al-Fre-Bett Music, Los Angeles, 1980—. Composer (concert music for orch.) Nursery Song, Variations on an Irish Air, Reflections for Strings, Fanfare for Winds, Concerto No. 1 and Concerto No. 2 for Piano Improvisations and Orch., String Quartet No. 1, Sonic studies for Piano I Elegy for Trumpet and Winds, Victorian Atmosphere Overture, (orch.) Fantasia in Ragtime, Mantra and Air for Piano and Strings, Far Far Away, Keepers of the Flame (lyrics K.L. Dunham), (music for films) Sky Bandits, Gunbus, Pale Horse, Pale Rider, The Curb Your Appetite Diet, Centerfold, Voices United, (title music for TV) Actors Forum, (for stage) From Berlin to Broadway, Oh Atlantis, Kurt, Lil Nell, Another Town, Victorian Atmospheres; composer and pianist, album-film/video, Vincent Moreaux, His Finest Hour In My Forest Cathedral, Songs from the Sea; rec. artist Sonic Arts and Repertoire Records; author: Free Improvisation, A Programmed Instruction Series. Pres. bd. dirs. Inst. for Recording and Multimedia Arts; mem. bd. govs.Music and the Arts Found. of Am., Inc.; dir. West Coast Musical Theatre Lab. Mem. ASCAP, NARAS Rec. Acad., Am. Soc. Music Arrangers and Composers (treas. 1978—), Composers and Arrangers Found. Am. (v.p., sec.-treas.). Democrat. Office: Al-Fre-Bett Music PO Box 45 Los Angeles CA 90078-0045

WOESSNER, JACOB FREDERICK, JR. biochemistry educator; b. Pitts., May 8, 1928; s. Jacob Frederick and Margaret Edith (Mueller) W.; m. Nina Mae Butler, June 13, 1953; children: Jeffrey Paul, Katharine Margaret. BA in Biology and Chemistry, Valparaiso U., 1950; PhD in Biochemistry, MIT, 1955; postgrad., U. Mich., 1956. Rsch. asst. MIT, Cambridge, 1953-55; investigator Howard Hughes Med. Inst., Miami, Fla., 1956-70; asst. prof. biochemistry U. Miami Sch. Medicine, 1956-70, assoc. prof., 1963-72, prof., 1972—, prof. medicine, 1980—. Author: Matrix Metalloproteinases and TIMPs, 2000; editor: Handbook of Proteolytic Enzymes, 1998; mem. editl. bd. Connective Tissue Rsch., Arthritis and Rheumatism, Biochem. Jour.; contbr. over 200 articles to sci. jours., chpts. in books. Recipient Internat. Geigy Rheumatism prize, 1981, prize Roussel-OsteoArthritis Rsch. Soc., 1994; rsch. grantee NIH, 1972-98. Fellow Gerontol. Soc.; mem. AAAS, Am. Chem. Soc., Am. Soc. Biol. Chemistry and Molecular Biology, Biochem. Soc., Soc. for Study Reprodn., Arthritis Found., Internat. Soc. for Matrix Biology, Sigma Xi (nat. lectr. 1995-97). Lutheran. Avocation: archaeology. Home: 7901 SW 54th Ct Miami FL 33143-5711 Office: U Miami Sch Medicine R-127 PO Box 16960 Miami FL 33101-6960

WOESSNER, WARREN DEXTER, lawyer; b. May 31, 1944; s. Warren Wendling and Flora Coffin (Dexter) W.; m. Iris Freeman, Jan. 6, 1990. BA, Cornell U., 1966; PhD in Chemistry, U. Wis., Madison, 1971, JD cum laude, 1981. Bar: Wis. 1981, N.Y. 1982, Minn. 1984, U.S. Patent Office 1981, U.S. Supreme Ct. 1999. Sr. rsch. scientist Miles Labs., Madison, Wis., 1972-78; assoc. Kenyon & Kenyon, N.Y.C., 1981-84, Merchant, Gould, Smith, Edell, Welter & Schmidt., Mpls., 1984-88, ptnr., 1989-93, Schwegman, Lundberg, Woessner & Kluth, Mpls., 1993—. Sr. editor Abraxas Press, Inc., 1981—, bd. dirs., 1981-84; contbr. to books, articles to profl. jours. Bd. dirs. Sta. WORT-FM, Madison, 1975-78; coun. Small Mag. Editors and Pubs., San Francisco, 1975-77, Coffee House Press, Mpls., 1988-99, Minn. Biotech. Trade Orgn., 1999—. Nat. Endowment for Arts Individual fellow creative writing, 1974; Wis. Arts. Bd. Individual fellow, 1975-76; Loft-McKnight fellow, 1985. Mem. ABA, Am. Intellectual Property Law Assn. (chair, chem. practice com. 1993-95), PTO Biotech. Customer Ptnrship., Am. Chem. Soc. E-mail: wwoessner@slwk.com.

WOESTENDIEK, JOHN, JR. (WILLIAM JOHN WOESTENDIEK), newspaper reporter; b. Winston-Salem, N.C., Sept. 5, 1953; s. William John Sr. and Josephine (Pugh) W.; 1 child, Joseph Yoon Tae. BJ, U. N.C., 1975. Reporter Ariz. Daily Star, Tucson, 1975-78; reporter, asst. city editor, city editor Lexington (Ky.) Herald-Leader, 1978-81; reporter Phila. Inquirer, 1981-90, nat. corr. West Coast bur. Calif., 1990-93, reporter, 1994-96, columnist, 1996-2000; enterprise editor Charlotte (N.C.) Observer, 2000-01; reporter Baltimore Sun, 2001—. Recipient Paul Tobenkin Meml. award Columbia U., 1984, Nat. Headliners award Press Club Atlantic City, 1987, Pulitzer Prize for Investigative Reporting Columbia U., 1987, Ernie Pyle award, 1994, Best Feature Story award Ky. Press. Assn., 1978, Best Investigative Story award Ky. Press Assn., 1979, Nat. Arc of Excellence Nat. Assn. Retarded Citizens, 1984, Best News Reporting First Place award AP Mng. Editors Pa., 1985, Sigma Delta Chi award for Feature Writing, 1994; John S. Knight fellow Stanford U., 1988-89.

WOFFORD, CINDY LYNN, lawyer; b. Athens, Tex., Feb. 3, 1952; d. William Avant and Nell (England) W.; m. Dan Henry Lee III, Dec. 1, 1993. BA, Stephen F. Austin U., 1974; JD, U. Tex., 1978; LLM in Tax., So. Meth. U., 1986. Bar: Tex. 1978, U.S. Dist. Ct. (ea. dist.) Tex. 1980, Md. 1989, D.C. 1989, U.S. Tax Ct. 1989. Assoc. Cox, Roady, Dawson/Sheinfeld, Maley & Kay, Houston, 1978-81, Superior Oil Co., Houston, 1981-83, Ray, Hemphill, Trotti, Finfrock, Dallas, 1983-84, Frank C. Hider, P.C., Dallas, 1984-86; chief counsel IRS, Washington, 1987-88; assoc. Linda J. Ravdin, PC, 1989-93; prin. Ravdin & Wofford PC, 1993—. Author: Divorce and Separation, Tax Management Portfolio, 1st edit., 2d edit.; panelist The Family Lawyers, Arlington County Cable TV, 1999; contbr. articles to profl. jours. Named one of 50 Best Divorce Lawyers, Washingtonian Mag., 2000. Mem. ABA (vice chair and chair elect domestic rels. com. tax sect.), State Bar Tex., State Bar Md., D.C. Bar Assn. Presbyterian. Office: Ravdin & Wofford PC 1700 K St NW Ste 650 Washington DC 20006-3812 E-mail: clwofford@ravdin-wofford.com.

WOFFORD, HARRIS, former senator, national service executive; b. N.Y.C., Apr. 9, 1926; s. Harris Llewellyn and Estelle (Gardner) W.; m. Emmy Lou Clare Lindgren, Aug. 14, 1948 (dec. Jan. 1996); children: Susanne, Daniel, David. BA, U. Chgo., 1948; study fellow, India, 1949, Israel, 1950; LLB, Yale U., 1954; LL.B., Howard U., 1954. Bar: D.C. 1954, U.S. Supreme Ct. 1958, Pa. 1978. Asst. to Chester Bowles, 1953-54; law assoc. Covington & Burling, Washington, 1954-58; legal asst. to Rev. Theodore Hesburgh, Commn. on Civil Rights, 1958-59; assoc. prof. Notre Dame Law Sch., 1959-60, on leave, 1961-66; asst. to Sen. Kennedy, 1960; spl. asst. to Pres. Kennedy, 1961-62; spl. rep. for Africa, dir. Ethiopian program U.S. Peace Corps, 1962-64; assoc. dir. Peace Corps, Washington, 1964-66; pres. Coll. at Old Westbury, SUNY, 1966-70, Bryn Mawr (Pa.) Coll., 1970-78; counsel firm Schnader, Harrison, Segal and Lewis, Phila., 1979-86; chmn. Pa. Dem. State Com., 1986; sec. labor and industry Commonwealth of Pa., 1987-91; U.S. senator from Pa., 1991-95; CEO Corp. Nat. Svc., Washington, 1995—2001; chmn. America's Promise: The Alliance for Youth, Alexandria, Va., 2001—. Vis. lectr. Howard Law Sch., 1956; chair America's Promise: the Alliance for Youth, 2002—. Author: It's Up to Us, 1946, (with Clare Wofford) India Afire, 1951, Of Kennedys and Kings, 1980; editor: Embers of the World, 1970; co-editor: Report of the U.S. Commission on Civil Rights, 1959. Mem. Coun. Fgn. Rels., 1968—; co-chmn. Com. for Study of Nat. Svc., 1977-80; mem. U.S. Adv. Com. on Nat. Growth Policy Processes, 1975-76; trustee The Am. Coll. , Bryn Mawr, 1975-83; mem. coun. U.S.-South Africa Leader Exch. Program, 1971-87; bd. dirs. Internat. League for Human Rights, 1979-87, pres., 1980-81; bd. dirs. Points of Light Found., Youth Svc. Am.; trustee Martin Luther King Ctr. for Nonviolent Social Change, 1983-87; governing coun. Wilderness Soc., 1983-87. With USAF, 1944-45. Mem. ABA, Nat. Commn. on Svc.-Learning. Roman Catholic. Home: 955 26th St NW Apt 501 Washington DC 20037-2040 Office: America's Promise 909 N Washington St Alexandria VA 22314 E-mail: harrisw@americaspromise.org.

WOFFORD, TERRY, artist; b. Leicester, Leicestershire, Eng., Apr. 5, 1943; d. Dan Gilbert and Marie Celeste Victoria Field; m. Robert L. Wofford. Nat. Diploma Design, Intermediate Degree, Birmingham (Eng.) U., 1964. Artist, NASA art program NASA, 1980—; developer and program mgr. Women's Channel Am. Online, Ariz., 1995—2000. Designer Alfred Shaheen of Hawaii, L.A., 1966—67; artist, designer, photographer, 1967—72; designer Jordan Sach Ltd., Scottsdale, Ariz., 1978—78; artist, Air Force Art Program USAF, 1980—; designer Barth & Dreyfuss of Calif., L.A. Artist, communicator Windstar Found., Snowmass, 1980—84. Recipient Looking at Earth award, Smithsonian Air & Space Mus., 1986, award of Distinction, Simuflight & Flying mag., 1993, award, Exptl. Aircraft Assn., Oshkosh, Several from this group. Fellow: Am. Soc. Aviation Artists (sec. 1985—86, chairperson ethics com. 1987—89). Personal E-mail: Terryflys2@aol.com.

WOGAMAN, GEORGE ELSWORTH, insurance executive, financial consultant; b. Mikado, Mich., May 29, 1937; s. Edgar R. and Leah Katherine (McGuire) W.; m. Sandra Lee Jensen, Apr. 10, 1965; children: Jennifer, Christopher. Grad. various ins. courses. CLU, registered rep.; cert. ChFc. With Blair Transit Co., Dun & Bradstreet, Chrysler Engring. Co., 1955-61; exec. chef Westward Ho!, 1961-68; owner, mgr. George Wogaman Ins. Agy., Grand Forks, N.D., 1969—. Mem. pres. coun. Farmers Ins. Group, 1988, 98, 99, 2000; alderman East Grand Forks (Minn.) City Coun., 1979—2000, v.p., 1982—2000. Corp. mem. United Hosp., Grand Forks, 1982—; mem. Nat. Rep. Congl. Com., Rep. Presdl. Task Force; mem. Red River Valley Estate Planning Coun.; mem. Wesley United Meth. Ch., Grand Forks. Recipient Pub. Svc. award East Grand Forks City Coun., 1979. Mem. Am. Soc. CLU's, North Valley Life Underwriters Assn. (Life Underwriter of Yr. 1988), Farmers Ins. Group Pres.'s Coun., Famers Financial Solutions, 2001-. Home: 1818 19 h St NW East Grand Forks MN 56721-1013 Office: 2612 Gateway Dr Grand Forks ND 58203-1406 E-mail: gwogaman@aol.com.

WOGAMAN, JOHN PHILIP, minister, educator; b. Toledo, Mar. 18, 1932; s. Donald Ford and Ella Louise (Kilbury) W.; m. Carolyn Jane Gattis, Aug. 4, 1956; children: Stephen Neil, Donald George, Paul Joseph, Jean Ann. BA, U. Pacific, 1954; STB, Boston U., 1957, PhD, 1960. Ordained to ministry United Meth. Ch., 1957. Pastor First Meth. Ch., Marlborough, Mass., 1956-58; staff asst. div. world missions United Meth. Ch., 1960-61; asst. prof., then assoc. prof. U. Pacific, 1961-66; prof. Christian social ethics Wesley Theol. Sem., Washington, 1966—, dean, 1972-83. Sr. pastor Foundry United Meth. Ch., Washington, 1992—2002; mem. com. religious and civil liberties Nat. Coun. Chs., 1966—; chairperson United Meth. Infant Formula Task Force, 1980-84, Muskie Com., 1982-91, World Meth. Coun., 1986-91, United Meth. Gen. Conf., 1988, 92, 96, 2000; pres. Interfaith Alliance, 1997-99; bd. dir. Interfaith Conf. of Greater Washington. Author: Methodism's Challenge in Race Relations, 1960, Protestant Faith and Religious Liberty, 1967; Guaranteed Annual Income: The Moral Issues, 1968, A Christian Method of Moral Judgement, 1976, Christians and the Great Economic Debate, 1977, Faith and Fragmentation, 1985, Economics and Ethics, 1986, Christian Perspectives on Politics, 1988, rev. edit., 2000, Christian Moral Judgement, 1989, Making Moral Decisions, 1990, Christian Ethics, 1993, To Serve the Present Age, 1995, Speaking the Truth in Love, 1999, From the Eye of the Storm: A Pastor to the President Speaks Out, 1999; editor: The Population Crisis and Moral Responsibility, 1973, Readings in Christian Ethics, 1996. Pres. Stockton (Calif.) Fair Housing Com., 1963-64, Suburban Md. Fair Housing, 1970; mem. Calif. Dem. Ctrl. Com., 1964-66. Lilly fellow, 1959-60; recipient rsch. award Assn. Theol. Schs., 1975. Mem.: Am. Theol. Soc., Soc. Christian Ethics (pres. 1976—77), Cosmos Club (Washington). Home: 4620 45th St NW Washington DC 20016-4479 E-mail: jpwogaman@aol.com.

WOGAN, ROBERT, broadcasting company executive; b. N.Y.C., Oct. 13, 1925; s. Robert and Johanna (Hilderbrandt) W.; m. Phyllis Jayn Volz, Nov. 21, 1965 (div. 1991); children— Robert, Stephen. Grad. pub. schs. Page NBC, 1943, asst. mgr. guest relations, 1945-46, night announcer, sec., 1946, asst. supr. announcing, 1946-47, NBC (prodn. div.), 1947-48, night adminstrv. asst., 1948-50, supr. network program operations, 1950-55, Eastern radio program and prodn. mgr., 1955-63, exec. producer "Monitor" program, 1963-65, v.p. radio network programs, 1965-73; exec. producer spl. programs NBC Radio Network, 1973-75, regional mgr. affiliate relations, 1975-81, regional dir. affiliate relations, 1981-89; regional mgr. Westwood One Cos., 1989—, Mut. Broadcasting System, 1989—, NBC Radio Network, 1989—, Talknet Programs, 1989—; exec. producer conv. entertainment, coordinator NBC/Mus. of Broadcasting to preserve history radio data. Exec. producer X Minus One radio program, 1974-75. Mem. Nat. council Boy Scouts Am., 1970— ; chmn. Radio com. United Hosp. Fund, 1972. Served with AUS, 1944-45. Recipient Radio-TV All-Am. of Year award for Experiment in Drama, 1963, Gabriel award for pub. service programming, 1967, Freedoms Found. award, 1972, Peabody awards for "Monitor", 1972, for "Project I Experiment", 1973. Mem. Broadcast Pioneers, Internat. Radio and TV Soc. Home: 360 W 22nd St New York NY 10011-2600 Office: 30 Rockefeller Plz New York NY 10112-0002 also: 1700 Broadway New York NY 10019-5905 also: 1775 S Jefferson Davis Hwy Arlington VA 22202

WOGAN, TERRI KAY, volunteer administrator; b. Honolulu, May 22, 1953; d. William Neil and Barbara Rose (Faus) Walton; m. W. Mark Wogan, Oct. 26, 1974; children: Lindsay Ann, Meghan Lynn, Jennifer Kay. BA in Elem. Edn., Libr. Endorsement, Ariz. State U., 1975. Libr., media specialist Paradise Valley Schs., Phoenix, 1976-80; vol. adminstr. State of Ariz. Dept. of Econ. Security, 1990—. Campaign worker Bill Walton, City Coun. Election, Scottsdale, Ariz., 1984-88. Named Clubwoman of Yr., Scottsdale Jr. Woman's Club, 1987, Outstanding Young Women of Am., 1988. Mem. Dirs. of Vols. in Agencies, GFWC Scottsdale Woman's Club (pres. 1989-90), Gen. Fedn. Woman's Clubs Jr. (2d v.p. 1992-94, 1st v.p. 1994—). Lutheran. Avocations: boating, water skiing, golf, reading. Home: 5401 E Marilyn Rd Scottsdale AZ 85254-2386

WOHL, ARMAND JEFFREY, cardiologist; b. Phila., Dec. 11, 1946; s. Herman Lewis and Selma (Paul) W.; m. Marylouise Katherine Giangrossi, Sept. 4, 1977; children: Michael Adam, Todd David. Student, Temple U., 1967; MD, Hahnemann U., 1971. Intern Bexar County Hosp., San Antonio, 1971-72; resident in internal medicine Parkland Hosp., Dallas, 1972-74; fellow in cardiology U. Tex. Southwestern Med. Ctr., 1974-76; chief of cardiology USAF Hosp. Elmendorf, Anchorage, 1976-78; chief cardiologist Riverside (Calif.) Med. Clin., 1978-79; cardiologist Grossmont Cardiology Med. Group, La Mesa, Calif., 1980-84; pvt. practice, 1985-2001; chief of cardiology Grossmont Hosp., 1988-90; assoc. clin. prof. Sch. Medicine. U. Calif., San Diego, 1990-2001; pvt. practice Kona, Hawaii, 2001—. Contbr. articles to profl. jours. Bd. dirs. Grossmont Healthcare Dist., 1995-98, San Diego County chpt. Am. Heart Assn., 1981-87, West Hawaii divsn., 2001--. Maj. USAF, 1976-78. Fellow Am. Coll. Cardiology (councilor Calif. chpt. 1991-99), ACP, Coun. on Clin. Cardiology. Avocations: tennis, travel. Office: 74-5620 Palani Rd #100 Kailua Kona HI 96740 *Personal philosophy: Work hard, respect others, enjoy life.*

WOHL, KENNETH ALLAN, lawyer; b. Denver, May 26, 1950; s. Milton and Leah (Liss) W. BA with honors, U. Calif., Berkeley, 1972; JD, U. Denver, 1975. Bar: Calif. 1975, U.S. Dist. Ct. (cen. dist.) Calif. 1975, Colo. 1976, U.S. Dist. Ct. Colo. 1976, U.S. Dist. Ct. (we. dist.) Tex. 1988. Trial atty. U.S. Equal Employment Opportunity Commn., Denver, 1976-79; regional counsel Mexican-Am. Legal Def. and Ednl. Fund, 1979-81; employment litigation cons., 1981-82; adminstrv. law judge State of Ariz., Tucson, 1982-83; sr. trial atty. U.S. Equal Employment Opportunity Commn., 1983-90; employment law counsel Continental Airlines, 1990-95; mgr. employment dispute resolution US West, 1995-97; asst. dir. EEO, U. Ariz., Tucson, 1997-98; pvt. practice Wheat Ridge, Colo., 1998-99; corp. counsel Colo. West Mental Health, 1999—. Cons. Rocky Mountain Assn. Indsl. Psychologists, Denver, 1977-79. Del. Colo. Dem. Conv., Denver, 1976. Mem. Calif. Bar Assn., Colo. Bar Assn. Avocations: hiking, short story writing. Home and Office: 350 Oak Run Rd Carbondale CO 81623-2811 E-mail: kwohl@cwrmhc.org.

WOHL, ROBERT, historian, educator; b. Butte, Mont., Feb. 13, 1936; s. Albert and Lani Wohl; m. Marisol Jacas-Santoll, Aug. 5, 1987; children: Robert, Alexnader. BA, UCLA, 1957; MA, Princeton U., 1959, PhD, 1963. Instr. U. So. Calif., L.A., 1961—64; asst. prof. UCLA, 1964—66, assoc. prof., 1966—69, prof., 1969—, chmn. history dept., 1970—73. Author: French Communism in the Making, 1966, The Generation of 1914, 1979 (Ames Book award, 1982), A Passion Far Wings, 1997. Fellow, Guggenheim, 1981—82, Getty, 1993—94, Nat. Air and Space Mus., 1994—95. Democrat. Roman Catholic. Avocation: tennis. Office: Dept History UCLA Los Angeles CA 90095-1473

WOHL, RONALD A. information technology executive; BS in Physics, MBA, Harvard U. Office: Oracle Corp 500 Oracle Pkwy Redwood City CA 94085*

WOHL, RONALD GENE, lawyer; b. N.Y.C., Dec. 10, 1934; s. Arthur and Bernice (Deutch) W.; m. Linda Susan Meltsner, May 2, 1965; children: Allison Brooke Wohl George, Arthur Evan, Amanda Kate. AB, Syracuse U., 1956, LLB, 1961; LLM, Bklyn. Law Sch., 1967. Bar: N.Y. 1962, U.S. Dist. Ct. (so. and ea. dists.) N.Y. 1963, U.S. Ct. Appeals (2d cir.) 1964, U.S. Supreme Ct. 1965, U.S. Dist. Ct. (no. dist.) N.Y. 1977, U. S. Dist. Ct. Conn. 1980, U.S. Tax Ct. 1986. Law clk. to judge Jacob Mishler U.S. Dist. Ct. (ea. dist.) N.Y., 1963-64; assoc. Edward Gettinger & Peter Gettinger, N.Y.C., 1962-63, 68-70; asst. U.S. atty. U.S. Dept. of Justice, 1964-68; ptnr. Squadron, Gartenberg, Ellenoff & Pleasant, 1970-71; pvt. practice, 1971-74; ptnr. Ferster, Bruckman, Wohl, Most & Rothman, LLP, 1974-96, sr. counsel, 1997-98, Goetz, Fitzpatrick, Most & Bruckman LLP, 1999—. Trustee Roslyn (N.Y.) Union Free Sch. Dist., 1981-93. Mem. N.Y. Bar Assn., N.Y. Dist. Attys. Assn., Assn. of Bar of City of N.Y., Nassau County Bar, Soc. of Med. Jurisprudence. Avocation: photography. Home: 70 The Intervale Roslyn NY 11576-1905 Office: Goetz Fitzpatrick Most & Bruckman LLP One Penn Plz New York NY 10119 E-mail: rwohl@goetzfitz.com.

WOHL, RONALD H. management consultant, writing and editorial expert; b. Washington, Sept. 3, 1942; s. Bernard Carl and Martha (Aberbach) W.; m. Myrna Zelda Chevelier, June 27, 1965; children: Jennifer Lynn, Amy Beth. Student, Fla. State U., 1960-62; BA in Anthropology, George Washington U., 1965; postgrad., George Washington U. Law Sch., 1965-67, Am. U., Washington, 1969-74. Cert. mgmt. cons. Asst. to regional credit mgr. Sears, Roebuck & Co., Bethesda, Md., 1966-67; supr. payroll & ins. Montgomery Coll., Rockville, 1967-71; supr. program info. & analysis Nat. Rural Elec. Coop. Assn., Washington, 1971-74; employee benefits comms. cons. Wyatt Co., 1974-77; pres. R.H. Wohl & Assocs./In Plain English, Gaithersburg, Md., 1977—. Columnist Gazette Newspapers, Gaithersburg, 1987, Montgomery Jour., Rockville, 1989-90; bd. dirs. Braille Tech., LLC, 1995, BookmarkSystems.com; prin. Future Solutions, 1997; mng. prin. Capital Human Resources Group, 1998; exec. dir. Libr. Connection Orgn., 2000. Co-author: The Employee Benefits Communication Tool Kit, 2000, Benefits Communication: A Guide, 2002, Benefit Communication Update, 2002; mem. editl. bd., author Employers Guide to Managed Health Care, 1994—, Civic Action Handbook, 1994—, In Plain English Guide to Preparing Summary Plan Descriptions, 1998, Enwisen Guidebook to the Electronic Summary Plan Description, 1998; co-author: Benefit Communication Edge, 1999. Precinct chair Montgomery County Dems., 1978—; Dem. candidate for Md. Ho. of Dels., Annapolis, 1986; chmn. Commn. on Humanities, Montgomery County Md., 1987—; dir. North Potomac (Md.) Citizens Assn., 1988-95; citizen mem. Comty. Policing Steering Com., Montgomery County, Md., 1992-96; tchr. Am. Jewish history and comparative religion; bd. dirs. Temple Beth Ami Congregation, Temple Beth Ami Brotherhood, Rockville, 1991-95, pres. 1990-92. Mem. Am. Assn. Home Based Bus. (nat. bd. dirs.), Inst. for Mgmt. Cons. (pres. Washington D.C. chpt. 1998-2000, nat. bd. dirs. and chair profl. devel. 2000). Home: 14501 Antigone Dr North Potomac MD 20878-2484 Office: R H Wohl & Assocs Inc In Plain English PO Box 3300 Gaithersburg MD 20885-3300 E-mail: rwohl@inplainenglish.com.

WOHLEBER, LYNNE FARR, archivist, librarian; b. Pitts., Mar. 16, 1939; d. Donald Elmer and Helen Rose (Lula) F.; m. David Louis Wohleber, Oct. 14, 1972 (div. Sept. 1989); 1 child, Jeffrey David. AB, Allegheny, 1961; MLS, U. Pitts., 1991. Comms. sec. Aluminum Co. of Am., Pitts., 1968-73; shop mgr. The Thread Shed, 1986-90; libr. Coun. Am. Embroiderer's Libr., Carnegie, Pa., 1985-93; archivist Episcopal Diocese of Pitts., 1989—; libr. com. Bower Hill Cmty. Ch., 1996—. Cons. Calvary Episcopal Ch. Archives, Pitts., 1992—93, Bapt. Home Libr., Mt. Lebanon, Pa., 1994, First United Meth. Ch. Archives, Pitts., 1995, Episcopal Diocese of Albany, 2000; archival cons. Christ Ch., New Brighton, 2001, Old St. Luke's, Scott Twp., 2002; bldg. archives workshop instr., 1995, 2000, 01, 02; presenter in field. Bd. deacons Bower Hill Cmty. Ch., rec. sec., 1996-99; mem. nominating com. Bower Hill Cmty. Ch., 1998-99; coord. presch. program Am. Lung Assn., Pitts., 1977-87; capt., ward chair Am. Cancer Soc., Pitts., 1978-84; mem. newsletter editor Mendelssohn Choir of Pitts., 1973-87; cub scout den leader Boy Scouts Am., Mt. Lebanon, Pa., 1983-84. Mem. Soc. Am. Archivists (planning com. 1999 Pitts. conf.), Mid-Atlantic Regional Archives Conf. (co-chair spl. events 1992, publs. com. 1996-2001, panelist 1999 spring conf.), Nat. Episcopal Historians and Archivists (Pitts. coord. for 1997 Episcopal Tri-History Conf., bd. dirs. 1996—, treas. 1999—), Hist. Soc. Episcopal Ch., Curators, Archivists and Record Profls. Western Pa. (co-chair Archives Week 1999 com.), Women's Episcopal History Project, Beta Phi Mu. Republican. Presbyterian and Episcopalian. Home: 110 Skylark Cir Pittsburgh PA 15234-1018 Office: Episcopal Diocese of Pitts 900 Oliver Bldg 535 Smithfield St Pittsburgh PA 15222-2403 E-mail: wohleber@pgh.anglican.org.

WOHLFORTH, ERIC EVANS, lawyer; b. N.Y.C., Apr. 17, 1932; s. Robert Martin and Mildred Campbell (Evans) W.; m. Caroline Penniman, Aug. 3, 1957; children: Eric Evans, Charles Penniman. AB, Princeton U., 1954; LLB, U. Va., 1957. Bar: N.Y. 1958, Alaska, 1967. Assoc. Hawkins, Delafield & Wood, N.Y.C., 1957-66; ptnr. McGrath & Wohlforth, Anchorage, 1966-70; commr. revenue State of Alaska, 1970-72; ptnr. McGrath, Wohlforth & Flint, 1972-74, Wohlforth & Flint, Anchorage, 1974-87, Wohlforth, Argetsinger, Johnson & Brecht, Anchorage, 1988-98, Wohlforth, Vassar, Johnson & Brecht, Anchorage, 1999—. Mem. Alaska Investment Adv. Com., 1973-80. Trustee Alaska Permanent Fund Corp., 1995—, vice-chair, 1995—97, 2001—, chmn., 1997—99; chancellor Episcopal Diocese of Alaska, 1972—. Mem. Alaska Bar Assn., Assn. of Bar of City of N.Y. Home: 7831 Ingram St Anchorage AK 99502-3965 Office: 900 W 5th Ave Ste 600 Anchorage AK 99501-2044

WOHLGEMUTH, WILLIAM K., JR. psychologist; b. Balt., July 25, 1963; s. William K., Sr. and Patricia D. W. BA, U. Louisville, 1985; MA, Loyola Coll. in Md., Balt., 1989; PhD, U. Miami, 1995. Lic. psychologist, N.C. Asst. clin. prof. Duke U. Med. Ctr., Durham, N.C., 1994—. Cons. Select Comfort Corp., Mpls., 1998-99; trainee Nat. Heart, Lung and Blood Inst., Miami, 1989-93; prin. investigator rsch. study Duke U. Med. Ctr., Durham, N.C. Consulting editor: Health Psychology, Psychosomatic Medicine, Jour. of Gerontology, 1995-99; monthly guest doctor: WRAL "Ask the Doctor", Raleigh, N.C., 1998—; contbg. author: Sleep Restriction Therapy, 1999, Handbook of Conceptualization and Treatment of Child Psychopathology. Recipient award of Acad. Merit U. Miami, 1995. Mem.: Soc. Behavioral Medicine, Am. Psychol. Assn., Am. Acad. Sleep Medicine. Office: Duke Univ Med Ctr Sleep Disorders Ctr 2908 Ctr Durham NC 27710-0001 E-mail: wkw@geri.duke.edu.

WOHLGENANT, RICHARD GLEN, lawyer, director; b. Porterville, Calif., Dec. 2, 1930; s. Carl Ferdinand and Sara Alice (Moore) W.; m. Teresa Joan Bristow, Dec. 27, 1959; children: Mark Thomas, Tracy Patrice, Timothy James. BA, U. Mont., Missoula, 1952; LL.B., Harvard U., Cambridge, Mass., 1957. Bar: Colo. 1957, U.S. Dist. Ct. Colo. 1957. Assoc. Holme Roberts & Owen LLP, Denver, 1957-62; ptnr./mem. Holme Roberts & Owen, 1962-99, of counsel, 2000—. Bd. dirs. Adopt-A-Sch., Denver, 1976-80, St. Joseph Found., Denver, 1990-93, Denver Com. Coun. Fgn. Rels., 1988-98, Japanese-Am. Soc. Colo., 1993-98, Rocky Mountain chpt. U.S. Mex. C. of C., 1993-00; bi-nat. bd. U.S./Mex. C. of C., 2000—; mem. Chamber of th Americas, 2001—; adv. bd. Human Med. Genetics Prgm., U. Colo. H.S.C., 2000—. Mem. ABA, Colo. Bar Assn., Denver Bar Assn., Am. Coll. Real Estate Lawyers, Univ. Club, Law Club, City Club. Republican. Roman Catholic. Home: 300 Ivy St Denver CO 80220-5855 Office: Holme Roberts & Owen LLP 1700 Lincoln St Denver CO 80203-4500

WOIKE, LYNNE ANN, computer scientist; b. Torrance, Calif., Oct. 20, 1960; d. Stephen J. and Virginia (Ursich) Shane; m. Thomas W. Woike, Feb. 13, 1988; 1 child, Karla. BSc in Computer Sci. cum laude, Calif. State U., Dominguez Hills, 1994. Computer cons. Unocal Oil Co., Wilmington, Calif., 1992-94; x-window/motif software developer Logicon Inc., San Pedro, 1994-95; reticle engr. TRW, Inc., Redondo Beach, 1982-88, sr. mem. tech. staff product data mgmt. database adminstr., 1995-98, chmn. product data mgmt. change control bd., 1995—98, sr. Unix/NT system adminstr., 1999; tech. lead, subscriber database DIRECTV, Inc., El Segundo, Calif., 1999—2002. Mem. IEEE, IEEE Computer Sci., Assn. for Computing Machinery (chmn. student chpt. 1993-94), Calif. State U. Sci. Soc. (computer sci. rep. 1993-95). Office: TRW One Space Park R5/B180 Redondo Beach CA 90578 E-mail: woike@pacbell.net.

WOJCICKI, ANDREW ADALBERT, chemist, educator; b. Warsaw, Poland, May 5, 1935; s. Franciszek Wojcicki and Janina (Kozlowa) Hoskins; m. Marba L. Hart, Dec. 21, 1968; children: Katherine, Christina. BS, Brown U., 1956; PhD, Northwestern U., 1960; postdoctoral fellow, U. Nottingham, Eng., 1960-61. Asst. prof. chemistry Ohio State U., Columbus, 1961-66, assoc. prof., 1966-69, prof., 1969-2000, prof. emeritus, 2001—, acting chmn., 1981-82, assoc. chmn., 1982-83, 84-86. Vis. prof. Case Western Res. U., 1967, U. Bologna, Italy, 1988, Nat. Sci. Council Chemistry Rsch. Promotion Ctr., Taiwan, 1994, U. Sydney, Australia, 1998; vis. researcher U. Coll. London, 1969; sr. U.S. scientist Alexander von Humboldt Found., Mulheim/Ruhr, Germany, 1975-76; vis. scholar U. Calif.-Berkeley, 1984; assoc. dean Coll. of Math. and Phys. Scis., Ohio State U., 1996-98. Contbr. articles to profl. jours. Guggenheim fellow U. Cambridge (Eng.), 1976; recipient Disting. Teaching award Ohio State U., 1968, Humboldt Sr. award Humboldt Found., 1975, 76. Mem. Am. Chem. Soc. (Columbus sect. award 1992), Royal Chem. Soc., Sigma Xi, Phi Lambda Upsilon. Home: 825 Greenridge Rd Columbus OH 43235-3411 Office: Ohio State U 100 W 18th Ave Columbus OH 43210-1106

WOJCIECHOWSKI, FRANK ANDREW, urologist; b. Nanticoke, Pa., Mar. 16, 1939; s. Andrew and Anna (Jaskowiak) W.; m. Dolores Zaziarski, July 20, 1963 (div. 1985); children: Christopher, Lisa Marie. BA with honors, Rutgers U., 1971; DO, Coll. Osteo. Medicine & Surg., Des Moines, 1975. Diplomate Am. Bd. Urology, Am. Osteo. Bd. Urol. Surgery; lic. physician, Pa., Ga., Ala. Intern Meml. Osteopathic Hosp., York, Pa., 1975-76; commd. capt. USAF, 1976—, advanced through grades to lt. col., 1988—; chief of flight medicine Andersen AFB, Guam; resident in urology Wilford Hall Med. Ctr., Lackland AFB, Tex., 1980-85; chief urology svc. 71st Tac Hosp., Homestead, Fla., 1985-88, Wiesbaden Regional Med. Ctr., Germany, 1988-91, Wright Patterson Med. Ctr., Dayton, Ohio, 1991-92; ret. USAF, 1992; urologist Clark-Holder Clinic, LaGrange, Ga., 1992—. Cons. in field. Decorated Nat. Def. medal, Air Force Meritorious Service medal. Mem. Am. Coll. Osteopathic Surgeons, Soc. of Air Force Clin. Surgeons, Soc. of Govt. Svc. Urologists, Assn. of Mil. Osteopathic Surgeons, Am. Osteopathic Assn., Am. Urology Assn. Roman Catholic. Avocations: lapidary, silversmithing, leathercraft, skiing.

WOJCIK, CASS, decorative supply company executive, former city official; b. Rochester, N.Y., Dec. 3, 1920; s. Emil M. and Casimira C. (Krawiecz) W.; student Lawrence Inst. Tech., 1941-43, Yale U., 1943-44, U.S. Sch. for European Personnel, Czechoslovakia, 1945; m. Lilliam Leocadia Lendzion, Sept. 25, 1948; 1 child, Robert Cass. Owner, Nat. Florists Supply Co., Detroit, 1948-88, Nat. Decorative, Detroit, 1950-89; co-owner Creation Ctr., Detroit, 1955-60, Wojcik Family Collection Collectables Mktg., 1995—; cons.-contractor hort.-bot. design auto show displays, TV prodrs., designers and decorators. Mem. Regional Planning and Evaluation Coun., 1969-75; city-wide mem. Detroit Bd. Edn., 1970-75; commr. Detroit Public Schs. Employees Retirement Commn., until 1975; mem. Area Occupl. Ednl. Commn., Ednl. Task Force; chmn., grand marshal Ann. Gen. Pulaski Day Parade, Detroit, 1970, 71; mem. Friends of Belle Isle; mem. Nat. Arboretum Adv. Coun., U.S. Dept. Agr., 1982-83; mem. pastoral coun. Archidiocese of Detroit, 1983-86, 88-92; v.p. rsch. Barna Coll., Ft. Lauderdale, Fla., 1989-94; vice chmn. 13th Congl. Dist. Rep. Party Mich., 1987-91; elected to 1988 electoral coll. With U.S. Army, 1944-46. Decorated Bronze Star; recipient citation Polish-Am. Congress, 1971, Art in Park 3d prize City of Oakland Park, Fla. Mem. S.E. Mich. Coun. Govts., Mich., Nat. sch. bd. assns., Big Cities Sch. Bd. Com., Nat. Coun. Great Cities Schs., Mcpl. Fin. Officers Assn. U.S., Nat. Coun. Tchr. Retirement, Ctrl. Citizens Com. Detroit, Internat. Platform Assn., Mich. Heritage Coun., Nat. Geog. Soc., Polish Century Club. Home: 1729 SW 14th Ct Fort Lauderdale FL 33312-4109

WOJCIK, EVA MARIA, physician, cytopathologist, educator; b. Gdansk, Poland, June 5, 1957; came to U.S., 1984; d. Tadeusz Wojcik and Maria Wojcik-Zimnicka; m. Michael Alan Brayne, Dec. 24, 1992; children: Adam, Mark. MD, Acad. Medicine, Gdansk, 1982. Diplomate Am. Bd. Anatomic Pathology, Clin. Pathology, Cytopathology; cert. phys. mgr. Chief resident dept. pathology Wayne State U. Med. Ctr., Detroit, 1990-91; faculty assoc. M.D. Anderson Cancer Ctr., Houston, 1992-93; asst. prof. Coll. Medicine and Med. Scis., Arabian Gulf U., Manama, Bahrain, 1993-95; pathologist UroCor Inc., Oklahoma City, 1995-97; asst. prof., dir. Quantitative Pathology Lab., Loyola U. Med. Ctr., Maywood, Ill., 1997—2000, cytopathologist, 2001—. Cons. cytopathology Salmaniya Med. Ctr., Manama, 1993-95; sect. head Image Analysis Lab., UroCor Inc., 1995-97; dir. Fine Needle Aspiration Svc.,

Loyola U. Med. Ctr., 1997—. Assoc. editor Jour. Histotechnology, 2000—; contbr. numerous articles to profl. jours. Mem. Internat. Acad. Cytopathology (evolving techs. com. 1996—), Am. Soc. Cytopathology (current concept and techs. com. 2000—, New Frontiers in Cytopathology award 1998), Southwest Oncology Group, Ill. Soc. Cytology (v.p. 1999—). Avocations: travel, books. Office: Loyola U Med Ctr 2160 S First Ave Maywood IL 60153 Fax: 708-327-2620. E-mail: ewojcik@lumc.edu.

WOJCIK, MARTIN HENRY, foundation development official; b. Chgo., May 10, 1948; s. Henry Martin and Mary Lorraine (Naughton) W. BS, Ill. Inst. Tech., 1970; M. in Humanities, Bonn U., W. Ger., 1975. Price adminstr. R.R. Donnelley & Sons., Chgo., 1970-72; dir. devel. Citizens for a Better Environment, Milw., 1976-79, pres. Chgo., 1979-85; dir. found. relations Northwestern U., Evanston, 1987-89; dir. corp. and found. rels. Mayo Found., Rochester, Minn., 1989—. Bd. dir. Citizens for Better Environ., Chgo., 1979—85, 1989—, chmn. bd. dir., 1990—91, 1999—2001; mem. policy adv. com. Ill. EPA, Springfield, Ill., 1980—82. Bd. dirs. Rochester Civic Theatre, 1991-97, pres. bd. dirs. 1994-95; mem. adv. panel Minn. State Arts Bd., 1995, 97, 99, 2001. Mem. AAAS, Ill. Inst. Tech. Alumni Assn. Roman Catholic. Home: 625 19th St NW Rochester MN 55901-4901 Office: Mayo Found Rochester MN 55905-0001 E-mail: wojcik.martin@mayo.edu.

WOJNAKOWSKI, MARY MELISSA, nurse anesthetist, researcher; b. Erie, Pa., Aug. 19, 1964; d. Thomas Jerome and Mary Patricia (Luedtke) W. BS in Nursing, U. Pitts., 1988, MS in Nursing, 1991, postgrad., 1994—, cert. registered nurse anesthetist, 1991. RN, Pa., W.Va. Staff registered nurse Children's Hosp. Pitts., 1988-91; staff nurse anesthetist Allegheny Gen. Hosp., Pitts., 1991-97, 99—, Weirton (W.Va.) Med. Ctr., 1997—. Pres. Pa. Assn. Nurse Anesthetists Ednl. Dist. V, Pitts., 1997-98, bd. dirs. 1993-98, trustee 1997-99. Recipient Pain Mgmt. Rsch. grant AANA Found. and Glaxo Wellcome, Park Ridge, Ill., 1997. Mem. Am. Assn. Nurse Anesthetists, U. Pitts. Alumni Assn., Sigma Theta Tau. Avocations: cooking, water sports, crafts. Office: Wierton Med Ctr 601 Colliers Way Weirton WV 26062-5014

WOJNILOWER, ALBERT MARTIN, economical consultant; b. Vienna, Austria, Feb. 3, 1930; came to U.S., 1939; s. Theodore and Lissy (Koppel) W.; m. Sue Freudenfels, Apr. 6, 1952; children: Daniel, Michael, Joel, Samuel. AB, A.M., Columbia U., 1951, PhD, 1960. Economist Fed. Res. Bank of N.Y., N.Y.C., 1951-62; assoc. economist First Nat. City Bank of N.Y.C., 1962-63; chief economist The First Boston Corp., 1964-86, sr. advisor, 1986-94; econ. cons. Craig Drill Capital, 1994—. Adj. prof. fin. NYU Grad. Sch. Bus. Adminstrn., N.Y.C., 1961-66 Author: The Quality of Business Loans, 1960; co-author: Financial Institutions and Markets, 1970, 2d edit., 1981. Recipient A.A. Green prize Columbia Coll., 1951 Mem. Am. Fin. Assn. (bd. dirs. 1979-81), Am. Econ. Assn., Phi Beta Kappa Democrat. Jewish. Office: Craig Drill Capital 767 5th Ave Ste 5000 New York NY 10153-5099 E-mail: awojnilower@cdccorp.com.

WOLAHAN, CARYLE GOLDSACK, nursing educator; b. Somerville, N.J., July 27, 1942; d. Wilbur Wood and Jane (Hadley) Goldsack; m. Thomas Warren Hussey, June 26, 1965 (dec. Oct. 1970); 1 child, Timothy Stephen; m. William Kevin Wolahan, Sept. 30, 1983 (dec. Jan. 2001). BS, Wagner Coll., 1964; MEd, Columbia U., 1973, EdD, 1979. Sch. nurse, tchr. Malverne (N.Y.) Pub. Schs., 1966-67, Dover-Wingdale Pub. Schs., Dover Plains, N.Y., 1967-68; head nurse Harlem Valley State Hosp., Wingdale, 1968-69; asst. prof., acting dir. div. nursing Trenton (N.J.) State Coll., 1973-77; assoc. prof., acting dir. Felician Coll., Lodi, N.J., 1979-80, dir. div. nursing, 1982-87; dir. nursing program Stern Coll., Yeshiva U., N.Y.C., 1980-82; assoc. dean Coll. Nursing SUNY Health Sci. Ctr., Bklyn., 1987-91, acting dean Coll. Nursing, 1991-92; dean sch. nursing Adelphi U., 1992-2000; prof. nursing Adelphi U. Sch. Nursing, 2000—. Contbr. articles to profl. jours., chpts. to books; editor Topics in Clin. Nursing, 1983. Trustee Cath. Med. Ctrs. Bklyn. and Queens, 1989-2000, chair continuous quality improvement com., 1998-2000; regional bd. St. Vincent's Cath. Med. Ctrs. Recipient NEAA award, Disting. Trustee award United Hosp. Fund, 2000; Named Woman of Achievement Alpha Omicron Pi; named to Nursing Hall of Fame Tchrs. Coll. Columbia U., 1999. Mem. ANA (del. 1978-87), N.J. State Nurses Assn. (coun. on edn. 1976-82, chmn. com. on ednl. preparation 1984-88), N.Y. State Nurses Assn. (chair pub. rels. com. 1990-92, spkrs. bur., recruitment com. Dist. 14, 1990, chair coun. on edn.), Nat. League for Nursing (accreditation com. 1985-90, site visitor 1984-98), Am. Acad. Nursing, Nursing Edn. Alumni Assn. Tchrs. Coll. (pres. 1990-94), Lake Hopatcong Yacht Club, Sigma Theta Tau. Episcopalian. Avocations: boating, reading, theater, hand crafts. Home: 13 Ford Rd Landing NJ 07850 E-mail: wolahan@adelphi.edu.

WOLAK, EDMUND L. engineering administrator; b. Calif. m. Hozumi Miyamchi, Apr. 26, 1992; 1 child, Anton. BS in Math. and Physics, U. Wash., 1983; PhD in Applied Physics, Stanford U., 1989. Rsch. asst. Stanford U., Palo Alto, Calif., 1983-89, rsch. assoc., 1989; product devel. engr. SDL, Inc., San Jose, 1991-94, engr., sect. mgr., 1995-97, sr. sect. mgr., 1997—. Vis. scientist Matsushita, Osaka, Japan, 1989-91. Co-patentee in field; contbr. articles to profl. publs. Mem. IEEE. Avocations: piano, travel, fitness, jogging. Office: JDS Uniphase Inc 80 Rose Orchard Way San Jose CA 95134-1356 E-mail: ewolak@sdli.com.

WOLANER, ROBIN PEGGY, internet and magazine publisher; b. Queens, N.Y., May 6, 1954; d. David H. and Harriet (Radlow) W.; m. Steven J. Castleman, 1992; children: Terry David, Bonnie Lee. BS in Indsl. and Labor Rels., Cornell U., 1975. Sr. editor Viva Mag., N.Y.C., 1975-76; editor Impact Mag., 1976-77; circulation mgr. Runner's World Mag., Mountain View, Calif., 1977-79; cons. Ladd Assocs., San Francisco, 1979-80; gen. mgr. Mother Jones Mag., 1980-81, pub., 1981-85; founder, pub. Parenting Mag., 1985-91, pres., 1991-92; v.p. Time Pub. Ventures, 1990-96; pres., CEO Sunset Pub. Corp., 1992-95; exec. v.p. CNET, 1997—. Jewish. Office: 150 Chestnut St San Francisco CA 94111 E-mail: robinw@cnet.com.

WOLANIN, BARBARA ANN BOESE, art curator, art historian; b. Dayton, Ohio, Dec. 12, 1943; d. William Carl and Elisabeth Cassell (Barnard) Boese; m. Thomas R. Wolanin, 1966 (div. 1980); children: Peter, Andrew; m. Phillip F. Brown, 2001. AB, Oberlin Coll., 1966, AM, 1969; MAT, Harvard U., 1967; PhD, U. Wis., 1981. Art tchr. Newton (Mass.) Pub. Schs., 1969-71; asst. prof. art history Trinity Coll., Washington, 1978-83, James Madison U., Harrisonburg, Va., 1983-85; curator U.S. Capitol, Architect of the Capitol, Washington, 1985—. Author: (exhbn. catalog) Arthur B. Carles, 1983, 2000, Constantino Brumidi, 1998; contbr. articles to profl. jours. Woodrow Wilson fellow, 1967, Kress fellow U. Wis., 1974, Smithsonian fellow, 1976; recipient Faculty Devel. award James Madison U., 1985. Mem. Women's Caucus for Art (pres. D.C. chpt. 1998-2001), Am. Assn. Mus., Coll. Art Assn., Am. Inst. for Conservation, Phi Beta Kappa (pres. Trinity Coll. 1982-83). E-mial. Home: 7807 Hamilton Spring Rd Bethesda MD 20817 Office: US Capitol Office Capitol Architect Washington DC 20515-0001 E-mail: bwolanin@aoc.gov.

WOLANIN, THOMAS RICHARD, educator, researcher; b. Detroit, Dec. 1, 1942; s. Chester Richard and Helen Theresa (Luszki) W.; m. Donna M. Christian; children: Peter, Andrew. BA magna cum laude, Oberlin Coll., 1965; MA, Harvard U., 1970, PhD, 1972. Staff dir. subcom. on labor-mgmt. rels. House Edn. and Labor Com., 1975-77, dep. staff dir. subcom. on select edn., 1977-78; exec. asst. to pres. NYU, 1981-82; analyst Senate Budget Com., 1982-83; staff dir. subcom. on investigations House P.O. and Civil Svc. Com., 1983-85, 87-91; staff dir. subcom. on postsecondary edn. House Edn. and Labor Com., 1978-81, 85-87;, 91-93; dep. ast. sec. legis. and congl. affairs U.S. Dept. Edn., Washington, 1993-96; sr. assoc. The Inst. for Higher Edn. Policy, 1996—. Instr. govt. Oberlin Coll., 1967-69; asst. prof. polit. sci. U. Wis., Madison, 1971-78; rsch. prof. edn. policy and polit. sci. George Washington U., Washington, 1997-00. Author: Presidential Advisory Commissions: Truman to Nixon, 1975; co-author: Congress and the Colleges: Higher Education in National Politics, 1976; contbr. articles to profl. jours. Voce chair bd. Am. Youth Policy Forum, vice chair adv. com. student fin. aid. Woodrow Wilson fellow, 1965-66, Harvard Grad. prize fellow, 1965-67, 69-71; guest scholar The Brookings Instn., 1970, Congl. fellow, 1971-72, Ford Found. travel and student grantee, 1972-73, 73-74, Spencer fellow Nat. Acad. Edn., 1975-81, acad. specialist grantee USIA, 1990. Mem. Am. Polit. Sci. Assn., Polish Am. Arts Assn. Washington, Congl. Fellowship Alumni Assn., Phi Beta Kappa. Democrat. Avocations: military history, Polish history, literature. Office: Inst Higher Edn Policy 1320 19th St NW Ste 400 Washington DC 20036-1635 E-mail: tom@ihep.com.

WOLBACH, ALBERT BOGH, JR. family practice physician; b. Allentown, Pa., Sept. 6, 1932; s. Albert Bogh and Gertrude Lillian (Mitchell) W.; m. Shirley Ann Mentzer, Dec. 21, 1957; children: Sheryl Ann, Wendy Sue, Ann Mentzer. AB, U. Pa., 1954; MD, Jefferson Med. Coll., 1958. Diplomate Am. Bd. Family Practice. Intern Lancaster (Pa.) Gen. Hosp., 1958-59; pvt. practice, Ephrata, Pa., 1961—; ret., 1997. Mem. med. staff Ephrata C.C., 1961—; pres. med. staff Ephrata Hosp., 1969-70, bd. dirs., 1971-86. Contbr. articles to med. jours. Dir. Ephrata Sch. Dist., 1971-83; mem. Ephrata Rep. Com., 1983—. Lt. comdr. USPHS, 1959-61. Mem. Train Collectors Assn. (life, treas. Keystone divsn. 1990—), Masons, Shriners, Nat. Honor Soc., Phi Beta Kappa, Alpha Epsilon Delta. Mem. Ch. of Brethren. Avocation: model railroading. Office: 923 W Main St Ephrata PA 17522-1329

WOLBERS, MARK EDWARD, music educator, musician, conductor; b. Kalamazoo; s. Harold John Sr. and Jennie W.; m. Miok Hong, May 12, 1995. MusB in Instrumental Music Edn., Mich. State U., 1981, MusM in Wind Instruments, 1985; DMA in Clarinet Performance, U. Mich., 1990. Cert. secondary tchg., Mich., 1981. Dir. bands Stockbridge (Mich.) Cmty. Schs., 1981-84; condr. Youth Band U. Mich., Ann Arbor, 1985-86; instr. music San Jose (Calif.) State U., 1989-92, San Jose City Coll., 1990-92; assoc. prof. music U. Alaska, Anchorage, 1992—. Head wind & percussion divsn., U. Alaska, 1992—, head Music Tchr. Edn., 1992—, condr. Univ. Wind Ensemble, 1992—; clarinet performer, Alaska Pro Musica, Anchorage, 1993—; condr. San Jose City Coll. Concert Band, 1990-92. Composer songs and instrumental works; contbr. articles to profl. jours. Grievance chair, United Academics, Anchorage, 2000—, treas. Faculty Assn., 1997—; mem. discipline rev. panel, Alaska State Coun. Arts, Anchorage, 1997-98. Mem. Music Educators Nat. Conf., Internat. Clarinet Soc., Chamber Music Am., Alaska Music Educators Assn. (region VIII rep. 1993—), Soc. Music Tchr. Edn. (Alaska state rep. 1993—), Mich. Sch. Band and Orch. Assn. (state com. chmn. Youth Arts Festival 1983-84, v.p. dist. VIII 1983-84), Phi Kappa Phi.. Office: U Alaska Music Dept 3211 Providence Dr Anchorage AK 99508 E-mail: afmew@uaa.alaska.edu.

WOLBRINK, JAMES FRANCIS, real estate investor; b. Charles City, Iowa, Sept. 8, 1942; s. Richard William and Anna (Bult) W.; m. Karen Ann Dunkerly, June 18, 1966. BS in Indsl. Engring., Iowa State U., 1966, postgrad., 1968-72. Cert. assn. exec. Tech. writer/editor Lawrence Radiation Lab., Livermore, Calif., 1966-67; editor, head engring. publs. Engring. Research Inst., Iowa State U., Ames, 1967-70; mng. dir., edn. and publs. Am. Inst. Indsl. Engrs., Norcross, Ga., 1971-83; commodities broker Clayton Brokerage, 1983-85; now pres. Wolbrink Properties, 1983—. Named Outstanding Young Alumnus Iowa State U., 1977. Mem. Sandy Springs Optimist Club (pres. 1989-90), Optimist Internat. (gov. Ga. dist. 1994-95), Delta Chi. Home and Office: 4520 Northside Dr NW Atlanta GA 30327-4548 E-mail: wolbrink@mindspring.com.

WOLCK, WOLFGANG HANS-JOACHIM, linguist, educator; b. Koenigsberg, Germany, Sept. 19, 1932; came to U.S., 1963; s. Walter Erich and Margarete (Brettschneider) W.; m. Carolyn Ann Burch, June 18, 1966. Student, Birkbeck Coll., London, 1956; Staatsexamen, Christian Albrecht U., Kiel, Germany, 1960; PhD, J.W. Goethe U., Frankfurt, Germany, 1963. Instr. German and Latin Liverpool (Eng.) Inst., 1957-58; instr. Albert Ludwig U., Freiburg, Germany, 1964-65; asst. prof. Ind. U., Bloomington, 1966-69; assoc. prof. linguistics SUNY-Buffalo, 1970-74, prof., 1975-97; disting. svc. prof. SUNY, Buffalo, 1997—; chmn. dept. SUNY-Buffalo, 1977-87, 89-91, dir. Latin Am. Studies program, 1972-76; research fellow Instituto de Estudios Peruanos, Lima, Peru, 1976-77; advisor Ministry of Edn., 1972, 82-83; rsch. prof. Belgian Nat. Sc. Found., 1991—. Cons. Fischer-Price Toys, Inc., East Aurora, N.Y., 1980— ; hon. prof. San Marcos Nat. U., Lima, 1972; mem. Fulbright Nat. Screening Com., 1993-96, E.C. Scientific Com. Linguistic Minorities, 1993-96, hon. mem. Rsch. Ctr. for Multilingualism, Brussels. Founding mem. Peru Earthquake Relief Com., Washington, 1972; field rep. United Way Campaign, Buffalo, 1977-81. Recipient Bronze medal Mazaryk U., Brno, Czech Republic, 1971; Fulbright grantee, 1963-64. Mem. Am. Dialect Soc., Linguistic Soc. Am., Societas Linguistica Europea, Linguistic Assn. Can. and U.S., Am. Assn. Applied Linguistics, Ctr. for Cognitive Sci., Centre for Multilingual Rsch., Sociedad Boliviana de Linguistica (hon.), Internat. Inst. Buffalo (bd. dirs. 1996—, pres. 1999—2001), Ellicottville Ski Club (bd. dirs. 1988-94). Home: 611 Skinnersville Rd Buffalo NY 14228-2503 Office: SUNY 609 Baldy Hall Buffalo NY 14260-1000 E-mail: wwolck@acsu.buffalo.edu.

WOLCOTT, HARRY F, anthropologist, educator; b. Oakland, Calif., Feb. 28, 1929; s. Leroy O and Alice S Wolcott. Bachelor Sci., U. Calif. Berkeley, Berkeley, California, 1947—51; Master Arts, San Francisco State, San Francisco, California, 1952—59; Phd, Stanford, Stanford, California, 1959—64. Prof. U. Oreg., Eugene, Oreg., 1964—2002. Author: (book) Kwakiutl Village and School , Writing Up Qualitative Research, 2nd Edition, Sneaky Kid and Its Aftermath. Sgt. U.S. Army, 1952—54, United States America. Recipient Fulbright, US Govt., 1985, 1991, Spindler, Coun. Anthropology Edn., 1989. Fellow: Soc. Applied Anthropology, Am. Anthrop. Assn.; mem.: Coun. Anthropology Edn. Constitution. Home: 85711 South Willamette Street Eugene OR 97405-9555 Office: Anthropology Department Eugene OR 97403

WOLCOTT, HUGH DIXON, obstetrics and gynecology educator; b. N.Y.C., Jan. 12, 1946; s. Charles Edmund and Joan Degrau (Loveland) W.; m. Jane Jarrell Smith; children: Allison, James. BS, U.S. Naval Acad., 1967; MSE, Princeton U., 1969; MD, Northwestern U., Chgo., 1979. Diplomate Am. Bd. Ob-Gyn, Am. Bd. Med. Examiners. Commd. ensign USN, 1967, advanced through grades to capt., 1990; aviator, Fighter Squadron 14 Naval Air Station, Oceana, Va., 1971-74; test pilot Naval Air Test Ctr., Patuxent River, Md., 1974-76; staff physician Naval Hosp., Portsmouth, Va., 1984, Jacksonville, Fla., 1984-86, dir. colposcopy and laser clins. Portsmouth, Va., 1986-89, dir. ob-gyn. residency program, 1989-91, acting chmn. dept. ob-gyn., 1990-91; ret., 1991; asst. prof. Med. Coll. Hampton Roads, Norfolk, Va., 1991—. Chmn. dept. ob-gyn. Sentara Hosps, Norfolk, 1996—2001; ob-gyn. splty. advisor Sentara Health Mgmt. Corp., 2000—; mem. Maternal Care Futurists Adv. Bd., Hill-Rom Corp., 1998—; pres.-elect, bd. mgrs. Mid-Atlantic Women's Care, LLC, 1999—. Contbr. articles profl. jours. Awarded 1st prize scientific paper by resident physician Am. Coll. Obstetricans and Gynecologists; recipient Guggenheim fellowship Princeton U., 1967-68; Trident scholar U.S. Naval Acad., 1966-67. Fellow Am. Coll. Ob.-Gyns. (chmn. Navy sect. armed forces dist. 1989-91), Assn. Profs. Ob.-Gyns. (assoc.); mem. Am. Assn. Gynecol. Laparoscopists. Episcopalian. Home: 835 Botetourt Gdns Norfolk VA 23507-1814 Office: Woman Care Ctrs 811 Med Tower 400 Gresham Dr Norfolk VA 23507-1901 E-mail: hdwolcott@aol.com.

WOLCOTT, JOHN WINTHROP, III, retired corporate executive; b. Balt., Dec. 3, 1924; s. John Winthrop, Jr. and Dorothy C. (Fraser) W.; m. Elizabeth Thelin Hooper, Apr. 24, 1948 (div. 1985); children: John Winthrop IV (dec.), Elizabeth T., Katherine C.; m. Karen E. Jones, Oct. 1, 1985; 1 child, Oliver Lund. B.Indsl. Engring., Gen. Motors Inst., 1951. Registered profl. engr., Ohio. With Gen. Motors Corp., 1946-53, Weatherhead Co., Cleve., 1957-60; v.p. H.K. Porter Co., Inc., Pitts., 1960-64; pres., dir., CEO Ametek, Inc., N.Y.C., 1964-66; v.p. Am. Machine & Foundry Co., 1966-77, group exec. process equipment group, 1967-70; exec. v.p. ops., dir. AMF, Inc., 1970-77; pres., chief exec. officer, dir. Transway Internat. Corp., N.Y.C., 1978-86, chmn. bd., 1982-86. Served with USCGR, 1943-46. Mem. Soc. Colonial Wars, Md. Club (Balt.) Episcopalian. Home: 210 Carrsbrook Dr Charlottesville VA 22901-1004 E-mail: wolcott@cstone.net.

WOLCOTT, NANCY BOOKOUT, music director; b. Rochester, N.Y., Sept. 20, 1932; d. Raymond and Esther Anna (Mohr) Bookout; m. Vernon Wolcott, July 6, 1956; children: Deborah Nan, David Miles. MusB, U. Rochester, 1954; Sacred Music Master, Union Theol. Sem., 1956. Music dir., organist St. Mark's Luth. Ch., Balt., 1957-58; soprano soloist Franklin St. Presbyn. Ch., 1959-62; youth choir dir. First United Meth. Ch., Bowling Green, Ohio, 1963-70; music dir. Ashland Ave. Bapt. Ch., Toledo, 1971-85, First Presbyn. Ch., Bowling Green, 1986—. Festival coord. Adult Choir Festival, Toledo, 1974, 85, Chorister's Guild Youth Choirs, Toledo, 1976, 84; staff tchr. creative arts Bowling Green State U., 1977-94; workshop leader Am. Guild Organists, Toledo, 1981, Choristers Guild, Toledo, 1981, 83, 85, 87. Editor (Renaissance Madrigal show) Music and Drama of Elizabethan England, 1969, (children's day pageant) An American Heritage, 1972. Mem. Am. Guild Organists (sec. 1983-84), N.W. Ohio Sigma Alpha Iota (pres. 1985-87, Sword of Honor Alumnae chpt. 1983). Democrat. Presbyterian. Avocations: reading, theater, traveling. Home: 1056 Fort Dr Bowling Green OH 43402-1205

WOLCZYK, JOSEPH MICHAEL, lawyer; b. Auburn, N.Y., June 16, 1955; s. Constantine J. and Mary E. (Burke) W.; 1 child, Sarah Marie. AA, Auburn (N.Y.) C.C., 1975; BA, SUNY, Buffalo, 1977; MA, U. Notre Dame, 1978; JD, Valparaiso U., 1982; AAS, Cayuga (N.Y.) C.C., 1987. Bar: N.Y. 1984, U.S. Dist. Ct. (no. dist.) N.Y. 1985, D.C. 1986, U.S. Ct. Appeals (fed. cir.) 1989, Maine 1990. Pvt. practice, Auburn, 1984-2000; commnr.'s hearing officer N.Y. State Dept. Corrections Office of Counsel, 2000—. Atty., engr. Integrated Concepts, Inc., Rochester, N.Y., 1989-90; v.p. legal ops. White Earth Environ., Auburn, 1988-90; owner Commonwealth Funding of Auburn, 1986-87. Author: Small Town Solo, 5 The Compleat Lawyer 4. Mem. exec. bd. Boy Scouts Am. #366, Auburn, 1991-95; incorporator, bd. dirs. Tomatofest of Ctrl. N.Y., Auburn, 1988; vice chmn. Auburn Zoning Bd. Appeals, 1986-88; bd. dirs. Legal Svcs. of Ctrl. N.Y., 1995-98. Named one of Outstanding Young Men of Am., 1988. Mem. ABA (sec. law student divsn. 1981, Silver Key award, D.C. Bar, Maine Bar Assn., Irish Lawyers Assn. N.Y., Cayuga Mus. of History (treas. 1991-94, pres. 1994-96), Rotary Club Auburn (pres. 1988-90, Group Study Exch. teams to Japan 1985, 96, Group Study Exch. dist. chmn. 1993-97, chmn. dist. 7150 found. com. 1996-99, chmn., dist. 7150 trainer 2002—), Auburn/Cayuga C.C. Alumni Assn. (bd. dirs. 1997—). Avocations: sailing, bicycling, hiking, skiing. Office: 164 State St Auburn NY 13021-1845

WOLD, JOHN SCHILLER, geologist, former congressman; b. East Orange, N.J., Aug. 31, 1916; s. Peter Irving and Mary (Helff) W.; m. Jane Adele Pearson, Sept. 28, 1946; children: Peter Irving, Priscilla Adele, John Pearson. AB, St. Andrews U., Scotland and Union Coll., Schenectady, 1938; MS, Cornell U., 1939; LLD (hon.), U. Wyo., 1991. Dir. Fedn. Rocky Mountain States, 1966-68; v.p. Rocky Mountain Oil and Gas Assn., 1967, 68; mem. Wyo. Ho. of Reps., 1957-59; Wyo. Republican candidate for U.S. Senate, 1964, 70; mem. 91st Congress at large from, Wyo.; chmn., CEO Wold Trona Co., Inc.; pres., chmn. Wold Talc Co.; ret. Wold Nuclear Co., Wold Mineral Exploration Co., Casper, Wyo.; founding pres. Wyo. Heritage Soc.; founder Central Wyo. Ski Corp. Chmn. Wyo. Natural Gas Pipeline Authority, 1987-91; chmn. bd. Nuclear Exploration and Devel. Corp., Mineral Engring. Co. Contbr. articles to profl. jours. Chmn. Wyo. Rep. Com., 1960-64, Western State Rep. Chmns. Assn., 1963-64; mem. exec. com. Rep. Nat. Com., 1962-64; chmn. Wyo. Rep. State Fin. Com.; Active Little League Baseball, Boy Scouts Am., United Fund, YMCA, Boys Clubs Am.; former pres. bd. trustees Casper Coll.; trustee Union Coll. Served to lt. USNR, World War II. Named Wyo. Man of Yr. AP-UPI, 1968; Wyo. Mineral Man of Yr., 1979, Wyo. Heritage award, 1992, Wyo. Oil/Gas and Mineral Man of 20th Century, Am. Heritage Ctr. of U. Wyo., 1999; named Benefactor of Yr., Nat. Coun. for Resource Devel., 1993. Mem. Wyo. Geol. Assn. (hon. life, pres. 1956), Am. Assn. Petroleum Geologists, Ind. Petroleum Assn. Am., AAAS, Wyo. Mining Assn., Sigma Xi, Alpha Delta Phi. Episcopalian (past vestryman, warden). Home: 1231 W 30th St Casper WY 82601-5372 Office: Mineral Resource Ctr 139 W 2nd St Casper WY 82601-2473 E-mail: WOPI@Trib.com.

WOLD, MARGARET BARTH, religion educator, author; b. Chgo., Mar. 6, 1919; d. Frank Philip and Esther Sophie (Pedersen) Barth; m. Erling Henry Wold, Oct. 4, 1942 (dec. Dec. 1999); children: John, Michael, Kristi Wold de Merlier, Stephen Ganzkow-Wold, Erling Jr. BA, Luther Coll., 1941; MA, Luther Sch. Theology, Chgo., 1950; DD (hon.), Luther Coll., 1986; LittD (hon.), Calif. Luth. U., 1973; DD (hon.), Wartburg Sem., 1985. Exec. bd. Am. Luth. Ch. Women, Mpls., 1966-73, exec. dir., 1973-74; dir. for ministry in changing communities So. Pacific dist., Am. Luth. Ch., 1977-84; assoc. prof. N.T. Calif. Luth. U., Thousand Oaks, 1985-89, coord. sr. mentor program, 1986-99. Organizer, dir. preschs., Calif. and N.D., 1960-72; cons. Pub. Welfare Bd., Bismarck, N.D., 1967-68; v.p. So. Calif. West Synod, Evang. Luth. Ch. in Am., 1987-90; keynote speaker Luth. World Fedn. Assembly, Budapest, Hungary, 1984; C.C. Hein Meml. lectr., 1985; study leader student conf. Sun-Moon Lake Edn. Ctr., U. Taiwan, 1977; spkr. in field. Author: The Shalom Woman, 1975, The Critical Moment, 1978, Women of Faith and Spirit, 1987, The Power of Ordinary Christians, 1988; also 5 books co-authored with Erling H. Wold. Bd. dirs. Grand Forks (N.D.) Unified Sch. Dist., 1968-70; bd. dirs. Pacific Luth. Theol. Sem., Berkeley, Calif., 1974-86, pres. bd. dirs., 1978-84, bd. dirs., Calif. Lutheran Homes, 1996-2000, mem. adv. bd., Ctr. for Spirituality and Ethics, Walnut Manor, Anaheim, 1999—. Recipient Martin Luther 450th Anniversary award Luth. Brotherhood, 1967, Disting. Svc. award Luther Coll., 1968, 125th Anniversary award Augustana Coll., S.D., 1968, Hon. Alumna award Pacific Luth. Theol. Sem., 2000. Mem. Am. Acad. Religion, Soc. for Bibl. Lit. Democrat. E-mail: marlingl@aol.com. *To live and survive with joy in today's kind of world demands the giving and receiving of hope and humor and hugs. As we bring these gifts into our daily contacts, they come back to enrich our individual lives and move out to increase the collective positive energies of the human spirit.*

WOLDEGABRIEL, GIDAY, research geologist; b. Mai Misham/Adwa, Tigray, Ethiopia, Sept. 3, 1955; arrived in U.S., 1982; s. Giday WoldeGabriel and Mislal Mesfin; m. Almaz Berhane Tesfamichael, Jan. 15, 1994. BS in Geology with honors, Addis Ababa (Ethiopia) U., 1978, MS in Geology, 1980; PhD in Geology, Case Western Res. U., 1987. Lectr. geology Addis Ababa U., 1980-82; dir.'s postdoctoral fellow Los Alamos (N.Mex.) Nat. Lab., 1987-90, cons., 1990-92, mem. tech. staff, 1992—. Mem.: Am. Geophys. Union. Avocations: running, camping, skiing, body building, swimming. Home: PO Box 4694 Los Alamos NM 87544-3638 Office: Los Alamos Nat Lab EES-6 1 Ms D462 Los Alamos NM 87545-0001 E-mail: wgiday@lanl.gov.

WOLDMAN, EVELYN JANDORF, computer information specialist, educator; b. Balt., Mar. 4, 1950; d. Bernard Joseph and Lottie (Kaufman) Jandorf; BA, Boston U., 1972, MEd, 1977; Cert. Advanced Grad. Study, Lesley Coll., 1986; m. James Arthur Woldman, Aug. 26, 1979; children: Robyn Nancy (dec.), Susan Ami, Rachel Lynne. Tchr., Holliston (Mass.) Pub. Schs., 1972-82; computer resource Miller Sch., 1982-83; computer coordinator K-12, Holliston Sch., 1983-85; part-time faculty Lesley Coll., 1983—; ptnr. Ednl. Techs.; software specialist Chpt. 1 Computer Ctr., 1989-95; software specialist Framingham State Coll., 1995-96; mem. Commonwealth Inservice Inst., Mass. Dept. Edn. Contbr. articles to profl. publs.; resource author: Computers and the Social Studies, 1988. Mem. ASCD, Mass. Coun. for Social Studies (newsletter editor), Nat. Council Social Studies, Internat. Council on Computers in Edn., Holliston Fedn. Tchrs., Pi Lambda Theta. Democrat. Jewish. Clubs: B'nai B'rith, Hadassah. Home and Office: 18 Cudworth Ln Sudbury MA 01776-1386

WOLDMAN, SHERMAN, pediatrician; b. Buffalo, Apr. 1, 1932; s. Joseph Harry and Sadie (Weinstein) W. m. Fern Marlene Weinstein, Dec. 28, 1952; children Deborah Janine Case, Scott Alan, Sabina Heide Muller. BS in Pharmacy Magna Cum Laude, U. Buffalo, 1953, MD with High Hons., 1957. Diplomate Am. Bd. Pediatrics. Intern Millard Fillmore Hosp., Buffalo, 1957-58; resident in pediats. Children's Hosp., 1958-60, active staff, 1961—; pvt. practice, 1961-66, Cheektowaga, N.Y., 1962—; mem. active staff Millard Fillmore Hosp., Buffalo, 1961—, chmn. dept. pediats., 1985-91. Adj. clin. asst. pediats., SUNY Sch. Medicine, Buffalo, 1962, clin. assoc. 1970, clin. asst. prof., 1973, clin. assoc. prof., 2001, preceptor Sch. Nursing, 1976-82; attending pediatrician Booth Meml. Hosp., Buffalo, 1969-72; sch. physician Williamsville (N.Y.) Ctrl. Schs., 1962-94, chmn. of physicians, 1970-94; courtesy staff St. Joseph Intercomty. Hosp., Cheektowaga, 1963-80, Kenmore (N.Y.) Mercy Hosp., 1963-70, 1974-82, Sisters of Charity Hosp., Buffalo, 1991—, Erie County Med. Ctr., Buffalo, 1979-83, Buffalo Gen. Hosp., 1987-95; provisional staff Mercy Hosp., Buffalo, 1982-83, courtesy staff, 2000—. Vol. Leukemia and Lymphoma Soc., 1975— , bd. trustees Western N.Y. and Finger Lakes chpt. 1975—, pres. 1977-79, v.p. 1979-81, mem. profl. edn. com. 1975—, mem. nat. bd. trustees 1978-87, vice chmn. patient aid com., 1980-87; mem. task force on sch. health Erie County (N.Y.) Health Dept; trustee Temple Beth David Ner-Israel, Buffalo, 1964-5. Recipient (with Mrs. Fern Woldman) recognition cert. Cheektowaga C. of C., 1982; Myron L.

Woldman Vol. of Yr. award Western N.Y. chpt. Leukemia Soc. Am., 1987, nat. chmn.'s citation 1999; Disting. Physician award MIllard Fillmore Health System, 1995. Fellow Am. Acad. Pediat. (PREP fellow 1979-85, 92-94, 94-96, 97-99); mem. Med. Soc. State of N.Y., Buffalo Pediatric Soc. (pres. 1969-70), Gibson Anat. Soc. (hon.), Med. Soc. County of Erie, N.Y. (chmn. pub. health com. 1978-79), Maimonides Med. Soc. (pres. Buffalo 1982-83), Alpha Omega Alpha, Rho Chi, Phi Lambda Kappa (alumni pres. 1965, v.p. alumni 1980-81) Avocations: gardening, computers. Office: 4427 Union Rd Cheektowaga NY 14225-2305

WOLDT, GERALD D. (JAY WOLDT), nurse anesthetist; b. Chippewa Falls, Wis., May 30, 1943; s. D.C. and Blanche A. (Patrie) W.; children: Michael B., Eve A. Diploma in Nursing, St. Mary's Sch. Nursing, Wausau, Wis., 1965; diploma, Tripler Army Sch. Anesthesia, Honolulu, 1970; BSN, Med. Coll. Ga., 1977; MSN, Oreg. Health Sci. U., 1980. Cert. RN Anesthetist. Staff nurse operating room Fitzsimons Army Hosp., Denver, 1966-67; commd. U.S. Army, 1966, advanced through grades to lt. col., 1981; staff anesthetist 93d Evacuation Hosp., Vietnam, 1970-71, 27th Surg. Hosp., Vietnam, 1971; clin. instr., staff anesthetist Madigan Army Hosp., Tacoma, 1971-72; staff anesthetist Munson Army Hosp., Leavenworth, Kans., 1972-76; chief anesthetist Dwight D. Eisenhower Hosp., Augusta, Ga., 1976-78, 2d Gen. Hosp., Landstuhl, Germany, 1980-83; nurse anesthesia cons. 7th MEDCOM, Germany, 1980-83; chief anesthetist, clin. instr. DeWitt Army Hosp., Ft. Belvoir, Va., 1983-97; staff anesthetist Potomac Hosp., Woodbridge, 1986-91, Mary Washington Hosp., Fredericksburg, 1991-93, dir. nurse anesthesia, 1993-95, Fredericksburg (Va.) Ambulatory Surgery Ctr., 1996-98; staff anesthetist, clin. instr. nurse anesthesia Regions Hosp., St. Paul, 1998—2000; staff anesthetist ambulatory surgery Mpls. Sports Medicine Ctr., 2000—. Co-facilitator death and dying seminars, 1980-83; lectr. in field. Mem. Am. Assn. Nurse Anesthetists, Sigma Theta Tau. Roman Catholic. Avocations: reading, racquetball, tennis, walking, painting. Home: 2830 Kenwood Isles Dr Minneapolis MN 55408-1977 E-mail: gdwoldt@mn.rr.com.

WOLDT, HAROLD FREDERICK, JR. newspaper publishing executive; b. Atlanta, July 4, 1947; s. Harold Frederick and Dorothy Rose (Lansdowne) W.; m. Lisa Diane Neves; children: Lauren Rae, Katherine Neves, Caroline Neves. BS in Journalism, So. Ill. U., 1969. Classified advt. rep. Chgo. Tribune, 1969-70, classified automobile staff mgr., 1970-72; nat. advt. sales rep. Chgo. Tribune newspapers, N.Y.C., 1972-74, city circulation mgr., 1974-77; nat. circulation mgr. Chgo. Tribune, 1977-80, circulation mgr., 1980-84; v.p., circulation dir. News & Sun Sentinel Co., Ft. Lauderdale, Fla., 1985; circulation mgr. Newsday, Inc., L.I., N.Y., 1985-86, circulation dir. Melville, 1986-88, v.p., circulation dir. Melville and L.I., 1988-94; sr. v.p. circulation Newsday, pres. Distbn. Systems. Am. subs. of Newsday, Inc., 1994-98; v.p. sales circulation mktg. The N.Y. Times, N.Y.C., 1998; dir. circulation Omaha World-Herald, 1999-2000; v.p. circulation San Jose (Calif.) Mercury News, 2001—. Speaker, participant Am. Press Inst.; bd. dirs. Abilities Health and Rehab. Svcs. (Nat. Ctr. for Disability Svcs.), Albertson, L.I., N.Y., 1992-94. Bd. dirs. Robert R. McCormick Boys Club, Chgo., 1980-81; chmn. United Way campaign, Chgo. Tribune, 1980, Omaha World-Herald United Way Campaign, 1999-2000, bd. dir. Children's Discovery Mus. Calif. Mem. Am. Pubs. Newspaper Assn. (circulation and readership com. 1988-93), Internat. Circulation Mgrs. Assn. (pres. 1991-92), Alpha Delta Sigma, Tau Kappa Epsilon. Office: San Jose Mercury News 750 Ridder Park Dr San Jose CA 95190 E-mail: hwoldt@sjmercury.com.

WOLENSKY, JOAN, occupational therapist, interfaith minister; b. Wilkes Barre, Pa., Mar. 4, 1954; d. Paul and Anna (Havrilla) W.; children: Maurisa Ann Fela, Jennifer Andrea Fela. BS, Coll. Misericordia, Dallas, Pa., 1985; DDiv (hon.), New Theol. Sem., N.Y.C., 1992. Cert. interfaith minister; cert. minister Order of Melchizedek, 1992; ordained minister Order of Holy Spirit, 1998; Reiki master, USUI and Karuna Sys.; cert. nat. and internat. spiritual response therapy counselor/tchr.; cert. master tchr. magnified healing. Founder, adminstr. N.E. Pa. Interfaith Ministries/Celestial Pathways Ctr., Harveys Lake, Pa., 1988; founder, dir., adminstr. Occupational Therapy Cons. Svcs., 1989; traveling occupational therapist. Dean, mem. adv. bd. Sage Inst., Shokan, N.Y.; mem. adv. bd. and quality assurance bd. At Home Health Care, Wilkes-Barre; mem., spkr. Am. Congress Rehab. Medicine, 1995. Contbr. articles to profl. jours. Recipient Supr.'s award City of Richmond Nursing Home, 1989; Mary K. Minglin scholar Am. Occupational Therapy Assn., 1984. Mem. Assn. for Interfaith Mins., Holistic Consortium of N.E. Pa., Inst. for Higher Healing/Wellness, Spiritual Response Assn., Universal Holistic Healers Assn. Avocations: martial arts, yoga, angels, guitar. Home: PO Box 197 Harveys Lake PA 18618-0197

WOLF, AIZIK LOFT, neurosurgeon; b. Bogota, Colombia, Jan. 17, 1956; came to U.S., 1963; s. Jose Wolf and Judy Grimberg Loft; m. Robyn Dinwoodie, Sept. 6, 1987; children: Jaelyn, Ariel. AB, U. Chgo., 1977; MD, Yale U., 1981. Diplomate Am. Bd. Neurol. Surgery. Asst. prof. neurosurgery, chief epilepsy surgery U. Md. Hosp., Balt., 1987-93, asst. prof. neurology, chief Gamma knife skull base surgery, 1990-93; dir. Miami Neurosci. Ctr. HealthSouth Doctor's Hosp., Coral Gables, Fla., 1993—. Office: HealthSouth Doctor's Hosp 5000 University Dr Coral Gables FL 33146-2094

WOLF, ALAN STEVEN, lawyer; b. Jersey City, Jan. 5, 1955; s. Lester Joel and Beatrice (Spiegel) W.; m. Donna Snow Wolf, Aug. 31, 1980; children: Lauren, Bradley. BA, Dartmouth Coll., 1977; JD, Southwestern U., L.A., 1980. Bar: Calif. 1980, U.S. Dist. Ct. (no., so., ea. and cen. dists.) Calif. 1980. With Alvarado, Rus & McClellen, Orange, Calif., 1981-84; ptnr. Cameron Dreyfuss & Wolf, 1984-89; pres. Gordon & Wolf, Newport Beach, Calif., 1989-91, Wolf & Pfeifer, Newport Beach, 1991-97, Wolf & Richards, Newport Beach, 1997—. Pres., founding dir. Laguna Beach (Calif.) Pop Warner Football, 1995-99, sec., 1996; chief Indian Princess Tribe, Laguna Beach, 1993; charter bd. dirs. Irvine Swim League, 1985. Mem. U.S. Foreclosure Network (bd. dirs. 1990-95, Com. Mem. of Yr. 1994), Calif. Mortgage Bankers Assn. (chmn. legal issues com. 1994-95), Dartmouth Club (pres. Orange County club 1991); fellow Am. Coll. Mortgage Attys. Avocations: computers, Internet. Office: The Wolf Firm 18 Corporate Plaza Dr Newport Beach CA 92660-7901

WOLF, ALFRED A. physicist, educator; b. Phila., July 21, 1925; s. Jacob Wolf, Anna Wolf; m. Enid G. Wolf, Nov. 24, 1957 (div. Dec. 1981); children: Marcus M., Laurence J. BSEE, Drexel U., 1948; MSEE, U. Pa., 1954, PhD, 1958; MD, U. Juarez, 1978. Engr.-in-charge Naval Air Devel., Johnsville, Pa., 1949—56; chief scientist Gen. Dynamics, Rochester, NY, 1957—60; dir. rsch. Litton Industries, Silver Spring, Md., 1960—63; disting. prof. elec. engring. Drexel U., Phila., 1963—65; tech. dir. RCA, Burlington, Mass., 1965—67; assoc. tech. dir. Naval Ship R&D Ctr., Annapolis, Md., 1967—78; pres. Prime Rsch. Found., 1978—. Asst. prof. elec. engring. U. Pa., Phila., 1949—59; sr. sci. advisor USN, 1971—76; adj. assoc. prof. U. Rochester, 1960—62; adj. prof. U. Md., Annapolis, 1967—69, George Washington U., Washington, 1969—99. Author: Biophysics of Wound Healing, 1989; contbr. Cpl. U.S. Army, 1943—46. Nominee Nobel Prize in Physics, 1972; named Notable Am. of Bicentennial Era, Am. Biog. Inst., 1976; recipient Honor citations (8), USN, 1972—83, Citation of Honor, Drexel U., 1961; grantee, NSF, 1956—59. Mem.: IEEE (life), Engring. in Medicine and Biology Soc. (chmn. Balt. sect. 1990—95), Sigma Xi. Democrat. Jewish. Achievements include patents for include 24 in field. Avocation: writing. Home: 562 Ferry Point Rd Annapolis MD 21403-1308 Office: Prime Rsch Found 562 Ferry Point Rd Annapolis MD 21403-1308

WOLF, ALFRED CLARENCE, retired economist; b. Nov. 5, 1911; s. Louis and Clara (Ost) Wolf; m. Agnes Strauss, June 30, 1945; children: Sally Kathryn, John Alexander, Steven Sidney, Andrew Michael David. AB, Harvard U., 1934, MPA, 1954; postgrad., Grad. Sch. Arts and Scis., 1935—37, Army Indsl. Coll., 1941. Rsch. supr., asst. rsch. economist, assoc. rsch. economist, divsn. rsch. Works Project Adminstrn., Washington, 1938—41; head Navy Indsl. Manpower Program USN, 1941—46; spl. asst. Vet. Emer. Housing Expediter Office of War Mobilization and Reconversion, 1946—47; mem. staff office of sec. of the interior U.S. Dept. Interior, 1947—49, dir., 1949—50, exec. asst. to the sec. for defense prodn. office of the sec. of interior, 1950—53; rsch. dir. Harvard-Pakistan Planning Bd. project Harvard U., 1953—55; asst. dir. overseas devel. program Ford Found., 1955—57, developed program in Africa, 1957—58, dir. program L.Am. and Caribbean, 1959—61; dir. social devel. divsn. Inter-Am. Devel. Bank, Washington, 1961—64, program advisor to pres., 1964—77, ret., 1977. Cons. Inter-Am. Devel. Bank, Devel. & Resources, Inc., Nat. Acad. Pub. Adminstrn., George Washington U., Carnegie Endowment for Internat. Peace, The Policies Sci. Ctr., Inc., Wilcox an dAssocs., others, 1977—. Comdr. USNR, 1938—68, ret. USNR, 1968. Decorated Legion of Merit; recipient Disting. Svc. awsard, Interior Dept., 1953; fellow Conservation fellow, Harvard U., 1953—54. Mem.: Cosmos Club (Washington), Harvard Club (N.Y.C.). Home: 1057 Rocky Run Rd Mc Lean VA 22102 Office: 2011 I St NW Ste 601 Washington DC 20006-1808

WOLF, ANDREW, food manufacturing company executive; b. Budapest, Hungary, May 20, 1927; came to U.S., 1947, naturalized, 1952; s. Alfred and Magda Farkas. Diploma, Baking Inst. Tech., Budapest, 1945; BSME, CCNY, 1962; postgrad., Ill. Inst. Tech., Chgo., 1962-64; MBA, U. Chgo., 1973. Pres., owner Mignon Pastry Shops, N.Y.C., 1948-54; cons. Hanscom Bakeries, new 1954-55; dir. new products Arnold Bakers, N.Y., Conn., 1955-60; dir. new products R & D Kitchens of Sara Lee, Deerfield, Ill., 1960-71, v.p. R & D, 1971-89, spl. asst. to pres., exec. cons., 1989—. Rep. Sara Lee Corp., Grocery Mfrs. Am. Tech. Com. for Food Protection, 1975—; spokesman Frozen Food Action Comm. Team, Inc., radio and TV, 1982—. Contbr. articles to profl. jours.; patentee bakery equipment and methods. Active White House Conf. on Food and Nutrition, 1959, Pres. Reagan's Task Force on Phys. Fitness and Nutrition, 1983. With U.S. Army, 1947-48, 51-52. Recipient Hon. Tex. Citizenship award State of Tex., 1969, Bishop award Tex. Dept. Mental Health, 1972. Mem. Am. Frozen Food Inst. (rsch. and tech. svcs. coun., quality maintenance task force coun.), Am. Bakers Assn. (liaison com. U.S. Dept. Agr.), Inst. Food Technologists, Am. Soc. Bakery Engrs., Sr. Rsch. Execs. Round Table, Tau Beta Pi, Pi Tau Sigma. Home: PO Box 91 Deerfield IL 60015-0091

WOLF, ARON S. health facility administrator, psychiatrist; b. Newark, Aug. 25, 1937; married; children: Jon, Lisa, Laurie. BA, Dartmouth Coll., 1959; MD, U. Md., 1963; cert. in med. mgmt., Tulane U., 1998, Master's in Med. Mgmt., 2000. Diplomate Am. Bd. Psychiatry and Neurology, Am. Bd. Forensic Psychiatry; cert. med. mgmt. Tulane U., 1999. Intern U. Md. Hosp., Balt., 1963-64; resident in psychiatry Psychiat. Inst. U. Md. Hosp., 1964-67, chief resident, 1966-67; pvt. practice specializing in adminstrv. medicine and psychiatry Anchorage, 1967—. Dir. Springfield Hosp. Alcholic Clinic, Balt., 1966-67; psychiat. cons. Levindale Hebrew Home and Infirmary, Balt., 1966-67, McLaughlin Youth Ctr., Anchorage, 1969-72; mem. staff Providence Hosp., chief psychiatry sect., 1977-81, 94; mem. staff Humana Hosp., Alaska, Kodiak Island Hosp., Palmer Valley Hosp., Valdez Cmty. Hosp., Bethel Cmty. Hosp., Cordova Alaska Hosp.; mem. staff Charter North Hosp., exec. com., 1984-86; staff psychiatrist Landon Psychiat. Clinic, 1970-71; ptnr. Langdon Clinic, Anchorage, 1971-97, clinic pres., 1981-95; clin. prof. U. N.Mex., 1991—; med. dir. Cordova Cmty. Mental Health Ctr., 1976-80, 84—, ptnr., dir. comprehensive substance dependence program Breakthrough, 1989; assoc. adminstr. Med. Affairs Providence Hosp., Anchorage, 1995-2000; rural adminstr. Providence Health Sys. Alaska, 2000--; cons. Alaska Native Med. Ctr., 1975-77, Woman's Resource Ctr., Anchorage, 1977-81; instr. dept. psychology U. Alaska, Anchorage, 1968-75; assoc. clin. prof. psychiatry U. Alaska, Fairbanks, 1974-85, clin. prof., 1985—; assoc. clin. prof. U. Wash., 1974-85, clin. prof., 1985—, clin. prof. psychiatry Sch. Medicine U. N.Mex.; participant weekly mental health TV talk show, Anchorage, 1970—; guest lectr. to various profl. and civic groups, 1967—. Contbr. articles to psychiatry to profl. jours. Vice pres. Greater Anchorage Area Borough Sch. Bd., 1971-72, pres. 1973-74; pres. Chugach Optional Sch. Parent Adv. Bd., 1976-77; mem. med. adv. com. Alaska Kidney Found., 1977-82; mem. Alaska Gov.'s Mental Health Adv. Bd., 1976-84, chmn., 1983; mem. Gov.'s Task Force on Criminally Committed Patients, 1980—; bd. dirs. Greater Anchorage Drug Mgmt. Group, 1972-73. With M.C., USAF, 1967-70. Recipient Wendell-Muncie award Md. Med. Soc. 1967. Fellow Am. Psychiat. Assn. (pres. Alaska dist. br. 1975, sec. Alaska br. 1984-85, del. assembly 1975-81, 86, 89-93, area III chmn. assembly procedures com. 1982—, nat. planning com. 1981, nat. membership com. 1981-86, 89—, chmn. confidentiality com., 1986—, recorder of assembly 1984-85, chmn. 1988, Alaska del., 1986—, chair nat. membership com. 1992—); mem. Am. Acad. Psychiatry and Law (mem. ethics com., 1987), Am. Soc. Law and Medicine, Soc. Air Force Psychiatrists, ACLU, AMA (chmn. mental health com. 1971-75, medicine and law com. 1980-81), Alaska Med. Assn., N.Y. Acad. Scis., Am. Assn. of Med. Adminstrn. Home: 8133 Sundi Dr Anchorage AK 99502-4198 Office: 4001 Dale St Anchorage AK 99508-5459 E-mail: aronwolf@aol.com., awolf@provak.org.

WOLF, ARTHUR HENRY, museum administrator; b. New Rockford, N.D., June 18, 1953; s. Louis Irwin and Vivian Joyce (Grinde) W.; m. Holly M. Chaffee, Oct. 18, 1984. BA in Anthropology, U. Nebr., 1975; MA, U. Ariz., 1977. Lab. asst., acting curator anthropology U. Nebr. State Mus., Lincoln, 1973-75; rsch. asst. Ariz. State Mus., Tucson, 1975-77; curator of collections Sch. Am. Rsch., Santa Fe, 1977-79; dir. Millcent Rogers Mus., Taos, 1979-87, Nev. State Mus. and Hist. Soc., Las Vegas, 1988-92, Mus. of Rockies, Bozeman, Mont., 1992-96; pres. High Desert Mus., Bend, Oreg., 1996—2000; pres. and CEO Mus. of No. Ariz., Flagstaff, 2000—. Speaker in field; cons. Pueblos of Zuni, Picuris, San Ildefonso and Taos. Contbr. articles and revs. to profl. jours. Trustee Kokopelli Archeol. Rsch. Fund, Bozeman, 1992-96; active Mont. Ambs. Recipient Young Alumnus award U. Nebr. Lincoln, 1990. Mem. Am. Assn. Mus. (bd. dirs. 1994—, vis. com. roster 1989—, vice chair 1996-97), Rotary, Assn. Sci. Mus. Dirs. Avocations: travel, reading, music. Office: Mus No Ariz 3101 N Fort Valley Rd Flagstaff AZ 86001*

WOLF, BARRY, genetics, pediatric educator; b. Chgo., June 19, 1947; s. Bert D. and Toby E. (Urkoff) W.; children: Michael Loren, Bryan Phillip. BS, U. Ill., 1969; MD, U. Ill. Coll. Medicine, 1974; PhD, U. Ill., 1974. Diplomate Am. Bd. Pediatrics, Med. and Biochem. Genetics. Intern, resident in pediatrics Childrens Meml. Hosp., Northwestern U., Chgo., 1974-76; fellow Yale U. Sch. Medicine, New Haven, 1976-78; prof. human genetics Med. Coll. Va., Richmond, 1978-2001, vice chair for rsch. dept. pediatrics, 1996-2000; dir. rsch. Conn. Children's Med. Ctr., 2001—. Assoc. chair, dir. rsch. dept. pediats. U. Conn. Sch. Medicine, 2001—. Author over 150 jour. articles and book chpts. dealing with inherited disorders of metabolism and biochem. genetics, specifically disorders of biotin metabolism. Recipient E. Mead Johnson award for pediatric rsch. Am. Acad. Pediatrics, 1988, Borden award in nutrition Am. Inst. Nutrition, 1987, Outstanding Scientist of Va. award Va. Sci. Mus., 1986, Ounce of Prevention award Action for Prevention of Va., 1985. Mem. Am. Soc. Clin. Investigation, Am. Pediat. Soc., Soc. Pediatric Rsch., Soc. for Inherited Metabolic Diseases, Am. Soc. Clin. Nutrition, Am. Inst. Nutrition, Soc. for the Study of Inborn Errors of Metabolism, Am. Soc. Human Genetics. Avocations: Japanese cloisonne. Office: Conn Childrens Med Ctr 282 Washington St Hartford CT 06106 E-mail: bwolf@ccmckids.org.

WOLF, BRUCE, lawyer; b. Phila., Dec. 16, 1955; s. Charles and Mary (Saionz) W. BA, Temple U., 1977; JD, Drake U., 1981. Bar: Pa. 1981, U.S. Dist. Ct. (ea dist.) Pa. 1981, U.S. Ct. Appeals (3d cir.) 1981. Assoc. LaCheen & Alva, Phila., 1981-88; pvt. practice, 1989—. Mem. Fed. Criminal Justice Act Panel, Phila., 1998—. Committeeman Phila. Dem. Party 63rd ward, 1994-2000. Mem. Phila. Bar Assn., Pa. Assn. Criminal Def. Lawyers. Democrat. Jewish. Office: 612 S 6th St 1st Fl Philadelphia PA 19147-2108 Fax: (215) 922-2194. E-mail: bwolf.esq@erols.com.

WOLF, CARL, lawyer; b. Phila., Dec. 3, 1950; s. Harry and Yetta (Boorstein) W. BA, Pa. State U., 1972; JD, U. San Diego, 1976. Bar: Calif. 1976, U.S. Dist. Ct. (no. dist.) Calif. 1976. VISTA and staff atty. San Francisco Neighborhood Legal Assistance Found., 1977-80; assoc. Allan Lerch & Assocs., San Francisco, 1981-83; ptnr. Hammill & Wolf, 1983-93; pvt. practice, 1993-95; ptnr. Callaway & Wolf, 1995—. Bd. dirs. Bay Area Lawyers for Individual Freedom, San Francisco, 1981-87, AIDS Legal Referral Panel, San Francisco, 1988-92, San Francisco Neighborhood Legal Assistance Found., 1992-95. Mem. State Bar Calif. (ethnic minority rels. com. 1984-87, Wiley Manuel award for pro bono svcs. 1991). Avocation: travel. Office: Callaway & Wolf 785 Market St Ste 1150 San Francisco CA 94103-2018

WOLF, CARL F.W. physician, biomedical engineer; b. New Hyde Park, N.Y., Feb. 4, 1933; s. Fritz J.C. and Bertha E. (Heidemann) W. BSChemE, MIT, 1953; MS in Chem. Engring. Practice, MIT, Cambridge, 1954; MD, Hahnemann Med. Coll., Phila., 1968. Diplomate Am. Bd. Pathology in Anatomic & Clin. Pathology. Intern in pathology N.Y. Hosp., N.Y.C., 1968-69, asst. pathologist II, 1969-71, provisional asst. pathologist, 1971-72, asst. dir. blood bank, 1971-76, asst. attending pathologist, 1972-79, assoc. attending pathologist, 1979-87, attending pathologist, 1987—, dir. Blood Bank & Transfusion Svc., 1976—; cons. in clin. pathology N.Y. Hosp.-Westchester Divsn., 1976-94; attending pathologist, dir. clin. lab. Burke Rehab. Ctr., White Plains, N.Y., 1974-96. Fellow in pathology Cornell U. Med. Coll., 1969-72, instr. in pathology, 1972-73, asst. prof. pathology, 1973-79, assoc. clin. prof. pathology, 1979-83, assoc. prof. clin. pathology, 1983-87, prof. clin. pathology, 1987—; vis. fellow dept. pathology Meml. Hosp. for Cancer and Allied Diseases, N.Y., 1970; USPHS trainee in exptl. pathology Cornell U. Med. Coll., 1969-71; rsch. assoc. N.Y. Blood Ctr., 1969-75; assoc. investigator Lindsley F. Kimball Rsch. Inst.-N.Y. Blood Ctr., 1975-83, 84-87. Contbr. numerous articles to profl. jours., chpts. to books; invited lectr. in field. Fellow Am. Soc. Clin. Pathologists, N.Y. Acad. Medicine; mem. AMA, AIChE, Am. Assn. Blood Banks, Coun. Hosp. Blood Bank Dirs. Greater N.Y. Region (bd. dirs., chmn.), Soc. for Study of Blood, Blood Banks Assn. N.Y. State, Am. Chem. Soc., Acad. Clin. Lab. Physicians and Scientists, Alpha Omega Alpha, Phi Lambda Upsilon, Tau Beta Pi. Home: 435 E 70th St Apt 21-j New York NY 10021-5347 Office: NY Presbyn Hosp Weill Cornell Ctr 525 E 68th St New York NY 10021-4870

WOLF, CHARLES, JR. economist, educator; b. N.Y.C., Aug. 1, 1924; s. Charles and Rosalie W.; m. Theresa van de Wint, Mar. 1, 1947; children: Charles Theodore, Timothy van de Wint. BS, Harvard U., 1943, M.P.A., 1948, PhD in Econs., 1949. Economist, fgn. service officer U.S. Dept. State, 1945-47, 49-53; mem. faculty Cornell U., 1953-54, U. Calif., Berkeley, 1954-55; sr. economist The Rand Corp., Santa Monica, Calif., 1955-67, head econs. dept., 1967-81; dean The Rand Grad. Sch., 1970-97, sr. econ. advisor, 1981—, corp. fellow in internat. econs., 1996—; sr. fellow Hoover Inst., 1988—. Bd. dirs. Capital Income Builder Fund, Capital World Growth Fund; lectr. econs. UCLA, 1960-72; mem. adv. bd. grad. ch. pub. policy Carnegie-Mellon U., 1992-2001; mem. adv. bd. ctr. internat. bus. and econ. rsch., UCLA Anderson Grad. Sch., 1996—. Author: The Costs and Benefits of the Soviet Empire, 1986, Markets or Governments: Choosing Between Imperfect Alternatives, 1989, 1993, Linking Economic Policy and Foreign Policy, 1991, Long-Term Economic and Military Trends: The United States and Asia, 1994-2015, 1995, The Economic Pivot in a Political Context, 1997; co-author: Economic Openness: Many Facets, Many Metrics, 1999, Asian Economic Trends and Their Security Implications, 2000; mem. bd. editors: Korean Jour. Def. Econs., 1995—, mem. editl. adv. bd.: Society, 1997—; contbr. articles to profl. jours.; co-author: (novels) European Military Prefects, Economic Constraints, and the Rapid Reaction Force, 2001. Mem. Assn. for Public Policy Analysis and Mgmt. (pres. 1980-81), Am. Econs. Assn., Econometric Soc., Coun. on Fgn. Rels., Internat. Inst. Strategic Studies London. Clubs: Cosmos (Washington); Riviera Tennis (Los Angeles); Harvard (N.Y.). Office: The Rand Corp 1700 Main St Santa Monica CA 90401-3208 Business E-Mail: wolf@rand.org.

WOLF, CHARLES BENNO, lawyer; b. Chgo., Apr. 16, 1950; s. Ludwig and Hilde (Mandelbaum) W.; m. Sarah Lloyd, Sept. 1, 1973; children: Walter Ludwig, Peter Barton. AB, Brown U., 1972; JD, U. Chgo., 1975. Bar: Ill. 1975, U.S. Dist. Ct. (no. dist.) Ill. 1975, U.S. Ct. Appeals (4th, 5th, 6th, 7th, 8th, 9th, 10th, and 11th cirs.) 1985, U.S. Supreme Ct. 1985. Ptnr. Vedder, Price, Kaufman & Kammholz, Chgo., 1975—, exec. com., 1999—. Co-author: ERISA Claims and Litigation, 10th edit., 1995; contbr. articles to profl. jours. Mem. ABA (co-chair labor sect. subcom. on multi-employer plans), Internat. Found. Employee Benefit Plans. Office: Vedder Price Kaufman & Kammholz 222 N La Salle St Ste 2600 Chicago IL 60601-1100 E-mail: cwolf@vedderprice.com.

WOLF, CHRISTINE STRELOW, piano teacher; b. Rochester, Minn., Jan. 27, 1964; d. Donald Eugene and Arlene Audrey Strelow; m. Michael Joseph Wolf, Nov. 02, 1991; children: Elizabeth and Gregory. MusB cum laude, St. Cloud State U., 1986; postgrad. piano performance, Hartt Sch. Music, 1987-89. Nat. cert. tchr. music. Ind. music tchr. Music Tchrs'. Nat. Assn., Rochester, St. Cloud, and Hartford, Minn., Conn., 1982-89, Apple Valley, Minn., 1992—; music link tchr. Nat. Assn. Music Tchrs., 1999—. Chmn. Nat. Guild Auditions, Apple Valley, 1999—; contest judge coord. Minn. Assn. Music Tchrs., 1991-98; accompanist Mayo H.S., Redeemer Lutheran Ch., Rochester, 1979-82, St. Cloud State U. choirs, vocal dept., 1982-86; dir. children's choir Emanuel Lutheran Ch., Hartford, 1988-89; music dir. Lutheran Ch. Our Savior, Rosemount, Minn., 1994—; min. of music All St. Eagen, 2002-. Composer, arranger contemporary Christian songs; TV and radio appearances including Live From Landmark, 1972-82, 86, 88-89. Performer various nursing homes, Dakota county; organizer student performances nursing homes, malls, Dakota County. Recipient Hiawathaland 1st place Rochester Keyboard Club, 1981, Duet Competition 1st place Dorian Music Festival Luther Coll., Decorah, Iowa, 1982; Ruth Gant Meml. scholar, St. Cloud State U., 1984-86. Mem.: Minn. Assn. Music Tchrs. (v.p. conv. 2002—), Minn. Music Tchrs. Assn. (judge 1991—, contest judge coord. 1992—, adjudication com. 2000—, convention com. 2001—, v.p. conventions 2002—, Young Artist of 1986), Am. Coll. Musicians (adjucator, chmn. 1991, judge 1999, Paderewski Gold medal, Piano diploma 1982), Music Tchrs. Nat. Assn., Nat. Fedn. Music Clubs. E-mail: wolfpiano@Prodigy.net.

WOLF, CHRISTOPHER ROBIN, technology executive; b. Richmond, Va., Apr. 29, 1954; s. Rene Arthur and Charlotte Elizabeth W.; m. Lise Holt Honoré; children: Eleonor Charlotte, Elyssa Harriet. BA summa cum laude, univ. honors, Ohio Wesleyan U., 1978; MBA, Yale U., 1983. Pres. Computer Data Designs Co., San Francisco, 1978-81; v.p. investment banking Kidder, Peabody & Co. Inc., N.Y.C., 1983-88; sr. v.p., ptnr. mergers and acquisitions Oppenheimer & Co., Inc., 1989-91; mng. ptnr. The Georgica Group, Inc., 1991-96; sr. v.p., group head investment banking Fahnestock & Co., Inc., 1996; exec. v.p., CFO Hyseq, Inc., Sunnyvale, Calif., 1996-99; pres., CEO Protogene Labs., Inc., Palo Alto, 1999—. Adj. prof. Columbia U. Grad. Sch. Bus. Trustee Arneson Inst., Delaware, Ohio; ptnr. Blue Hill Ptnrs., N.Y.C., 604 Ptnrs., San Francisco, Rock Creek Ptnrs., Boulder, Colo. Mem. Knickerbocker Club, River Club, St. Francis Yacht Club, Yale Club, Phi Beta Kappa. Episcopalian. Avocations: expedition trekking, tennis, collecting antiquities, sailing. Office: Protogene Labs Inc 303 Constitution Dr Menlo Park CA 94025-1110 E-mail: wolf@protogene.com.

WOLF, CYD BETH, lawyer, entrepreneur; b. N.Y.C., Oct. 6, 1957; d. Aaron Joseph and Sally (Marcus) Wolf; m. Germano Fabio Fabiani, Nov. 18, 1990; children: Alessandra Julia Fabiani, Francesca Isabella Fabiani. BA in Urban Studies with honors, U. Pa., 1977; JD, U. Balt., 1983. Bar: Md 1983, US Dist Ct Md 1983, US Ct Appeals (6th and 11th cir) 1986, US Ct Appeals (4th and 5th cir) 1989. Assoc. Weinberger, Weinstock, Sagner, Stevan & Harris, Balt., 1983-86, Semmes, Bowen & Semmes, Balt., 1986-90, Piper & Marbury, Balt., 1990-95; private practice, 1995-98, Owings Mills, Md., 1998—. Contbr. articles to profl jours. Mem leadership comt Univ Baltimore Educ Found, fundraiser, mentor. Mem.: ABA, Bar Asn Baltimore City (banking, bankruptcy and bus law sect), Bankruptcy Bar Asn (mem rules comt dist Md 1997—), Md State Bar Asn (banking and bus sect). Avocations: tennis, painting, drawing, fiction and non-fiction reading and writing. Home and Office: 5 Hillchase Ct Baltimore MD 21208-6306

WOLF, CYNTHIA TRIBELHORN, librarian, library educator; b. Denver, Dec. 12, 1945; adopted d. John Baltazar and Margaret (Kern) Tribelhorn; m. H.Y. Rassam, Mar. 21, 1969 (div. Jan. 1988); children: Najma Christine, Yousuf John; adopted children: Leonard Joseph Lucero, Lakota E. Rassam-Lucero, McKinley William Osborn, Kevin Trey, Jackson Andrew Lee; m. Walter Larry Peck, June 21, 1965 (div. Feb. 1967). BA, Colo. State U., 1970; MLS, U. Denver, 1985. Cert. permanent profl. librarian, N.Mex. Elem. tchr. Sacred Heart Sch., Farmington, N.Mex., 1973-78; asst. prof. libr. sci. edn. U. N.Mex., Albuquerque, 1985-91, dir. libr. sci. edn. divsn., 1989-91; pres. Info. Acquisitions, 1990-99; libr. dir. Southwestern Coll., Santa Fe, 1992-94; mem. youth resources Rio Grande Valley Libr. Sys., Albuquerque, 1994-95, adult reference svc., 1995-98; with Albuquerque Pub. Schs., 1998—; instr. U. N.Mex.,

1998-99. Fine arts resource person for gifted edn. Farmington Pub. Schs., 1979-83; speaker Unofficial Mentorships and Market Rsch., 1992-98. Mem. Farmington Planning and Zoning Commn., 1980-81; bd. dirs. Farmington Mus. Assn., 1983-84; pres. Farmington Symphony League, 1978. Mem. AAUW, N.Mex. Library Assn., LWV (bd. dirs. Farmington, 1972-74, 75, pres.). Avocations: mixed media graphics design, market research, creative approaches to personal journals, board game design.

WOLF, DALE EDWARD, state official; b. Kearney, Nebr., Sept. 6, 1924; BSc, U. Nebr., 1945; PhD in Agronomy and Weed Control, Rutgers U., 1949. With Dept. Agr., 1946; assoc. prof. agronomy Rutgers U., 1949; with E.I. duPont de Nemours & Co., Inc., from 1950, dir. agrichem. mktg., then gen. mgr. biochem. dept., 1972-79; v.p. biochems., also chmn. bd. subs. Endo Labs., Inc., Wilmington, Del., from 1979; group v.p. Agrl. Products, from 1983; dir. Del. Devel. Office, Dover, 1987-89; lt. gov. of Del., 1989-93; gov. State of Del., 1993; chmn. Daynel Internat. Inc., Wilmington, Del., 1996—; vice chmn. Emerald Bio Agrl. Corp. Vice chmn. WSFS Bank, 1998, Emerald Bioagr. Corp., 2002. Co-author: Principles of Weed Control, 1951. Bd. dirs. Del. chpt. ARC, 1975; gen. campaign chmn. United Way Del., 1978, also bd. dirs.; gen. campaign chmn. Girls Club Del., 1987; chmn. Del. Found. for Literacy, 1993-98. 1st lt. AUS, 1943-46. Decorated Bronze Star, Purple Heart. Mem. Nat. Agrl. Chem. Assn. (chmn. 1981-83), Pharm. Mfrs. Assn. (dir.), Masons, Sigma Xi, Alpha Zeta.

WOLF, DAVID, lawyer; b. Boston, July 11, 1927; s. Ezekiel and Ray (Cohen) W.; m. Maxine Laura Bunnin, June 29, 1963; children— Eric E., Douglas R., James A. BA, U. Mass., 1949; LLB, Harvard U., 1952; postgrad., Northeastern U., 1952-55. Bar: Mass. 1952, U.S. Patent Office 1952, U.S. Ct. Customs and Patent Appeals 1955, U.S. Supreme Ct. 1958, U.S. Ct. Appeals (fed. cir.) 1983. Ptnr. Wolf, Greenfield & Sacks, P.C., Boston, 1952—. Watercolor artist; exhibited various local shows; holder of 13 U.S. letters patents in various arts. Watercolor artist; exhibited various local shows. Bd. dirs. Newton Country Players, 1964-67, Killington East Homeowners Assn., pres. 1992-97; mem. Com. for Accuracy in Mid. East Reporting in Am., 1989—, bd. dirs., gen. counsel, 1993—. Recipient various awards for art. Mem. Am. Patent Law Assn. (lectr. trademark trial adv. programs 1986-89, 2000), Lic. Execs. Soc., U.S. Trademark Assn., Harvard Law Sch. Alumni Assn., Boston Patent Law Assn. (pres. 1976), New Eng.-Israel C. of C. (v.p., bd. dirs. 1984-98), Hadassah Men's Assn., B'nai B'rith, Free Sons Israel, Alpha Epsilon Pi. Office: Wolf Greenfield & Sacks PC Fed Res Plz 600 Atlantic Ave Boston MA 02210-2211 E-mail: dwolf@wolfgreenfield.com.

WOLF, DAVID BRIAN, social worker, writer, researcher, educator; b. Phila., Dec. 3, 1960; s. Julius and Nancy (Bank) W.; m. Miriam Yocheved Wolf, Dec. 26, 1987; children: Sita, Abhimanyu David. BS in Psychology, Penn State U., State College, Pa., 1983; MSW, Fla. State U., Tallahassee, 1997, PhD in Social Work, 1999. Crisis-intervention and short term counselor On Drugs, Inc., State College, Pa., 1981-83, dir. counselor tng., 1981-83; pres. Internat. Soc. for Krishna Consciousness, Tel-Aviv, Israel, 1987—; dir. arabic ednl. programs Internat. Soc. Krishna Consciousness, Rama, Israel, 1988-90; coll. campus dir. Fla. Vedic Coll., Zephyrhills, Fla., 1991-92; counselor State of Fla., Live Oak, 1994-95; dir. ctrl. office of child protection Internat. Soc. Krishna Consciousness, Alachua, Fla., 1998—; program mgr. Dept. Health State of Fla., Gainesville, 1995—, social worker svcs. program mgr., 1995—. Mem. bd. dirs. Multi-disciplinary Assessment Team, Starke, Fla., 1995—, Palatka, Fla., 1995—, Trenton, Fla., 1995—, Lake City, Fla., 1995—, Gainesville, Fla., 1995—, Svc. Assessment Team, Gainesville, Fla., 1995—, Family Svc. Planning Team, Trenton, Fla., 1995—, Gainesville, Fla., 1995—, Alachua Learning Ctr., 1999—; chmn. bd. dirs. Free U. Pa. State U, 1978-83, Vaisnava Acad. Day Sch., Alachua, Fla., 1996-98, Internat. Soc. Krishna Consciousness, Alachua. Fla., 1997—. Author: Krsna, Israel, and the Druze-An Interreligious Odyssey, 1994, Effects of the Hare Krsna Maha Mantra on Stress, Depression and the Three Gunas, 1999; editor: Fortunate Souls, 1996, North American Sankirtana Newsletter, 1991-92; contbr. articles to profl. jours. Recipient Fellowships Fla. State U., 1996-97, 1997-98. Mem. NASW, Phi Kappa Phi. Home: 17303 NW 112th Blvd Alachua FL 32615-4537 Office: Children's Med Svcs 1701 SW 16th Ave Gainesville FL 32608-1153 Fax: 904-418-0982. E-mail: dgovinda@aol.com.

WOLF, DAVID CARY, gastroenterologist, medical educator; b. Scarsdale, N.Y., June 11, 1959; married; two children. BA, Yale U., 1981; MD, Columbia U., 1985. Resident Presbyn. Hosp., N.Y.C., 1985-88; gastroenterology fellow Albert Einstein Coll. Medicine, Bronx, 1988-91; asst. prof. medicine U. Cin. Coll. Medicine, 1991-93, Mt. Sinai Sch. Medicine, N.Y.C., 1993-96; assoc. prof. medicine N.Y. Med. Coll., Valhalla, 1996—; med. dir. liver transplantation Westchester Med. Ctr., 1996—. Contbr. articles to profl. jours. Fellow ACP, Am. Coll. Gastroenterology. Avocation: race walking. Office: NY Medical Coll Munger Pavilion Rm 206 Valhalla NY 10595

WOLF, DONALD JOSEPH, industrial engineer, consultant; b. Waynesboro, Pa., Feb. 28, 1925; s. Joseph Herman and Olive Mae (Kepner) W.; m. Betty Irene Stull, May 26, 1950; children: Darrell Joseph, Robert Lee, David Wayne. BS in Wood Tech., N.C. State U., 1953; MS in Indsl. Engring., LaSalle U., 1995, PhD, 1996. Registered profl. engr., Calif., Md. Foreman, indsl. engr. York County Chair Co., Red Lion, Pa., 1953-57; supt. indsl. engr. Hoke Furniture Co., Thurmont, Md., 1957-60; plant mgr., indsl. engr. Statton Furniture Co., Hagerstown, 1960-70; internat. cons. Ross Assocs., Inc., Asheville, N.C., 1970-78; pres., prin. cons. Wood Arts, Inc., Frederick, Md., 1978—. Staff cons. Samuel Lawrence Furniture Co., Phoenix, 1990-98. Active Citizen Amb. program People to People Internat; forestry bd. vice chmn. Frederick County, Md.; cubmaster, scoutmaster Boy Scouts Am., Red Lion and Thurmont, 1957-60; v.p. Jr. C. of C., Red Lion, 1958-59; v.p. St. John's Luth. Ch., Thurmont, 1986-88, lay asst. min., 1988-93. Sgt. U.S. Army C.E., 1943-47, ETO. Mem. NSPE (life), Md. Soc. Profl. Engrs. (life), Calif. Soc. Profl. Engrs., Inst. Indsl. Engrs. (life, sr.), Order of the Engr., Md. Hist. Soc., Frederick County (Md.) Hist. Soc., Adams County (Pa.) Hist. Soc., York County (Pa.) Hist. Soc., Buckinghamshire (Eng.) Hist. Soc., Kitochtinny Hist. Soc., Libr. of Congress (assoc.), Nat. Trust, Smithsonian Resident Assoc., N.C. State Alumni Assn., Soc. of War of 1812, Elks, Am. Legion (life), VFW (life), SAR (past pres., v.p., newsletter editor, historian, Bronze medal, Cert. of Disting. Svc., War Svc. medal, Silver medal, Silver Disting. Svc. medal), Soc. of Wood Sci. and Tech., Forest Products Rsch. Soc. (divsn. chmn.), Nat. Congress of Patriotic Orgns. (founding fellow), Ho. of Gordon, Clan MacLean Internat. (life), Clan McLaine of Lochbuie, Xi Sigma Pi. Republican. Avocation: genealogy. Home and Office: Wood Arts Inc 6905 Balsam Ct Frederick MD 21703-7146

WOLF, E. DAN, veterinary ophthalmologist; b. Xenia, Ohio, July 28, 1943; s. Elmer Marcus and Wanda Jeanne (Hess) W.; m. Marja Elina Nieminen, Dec. 31, 1992; children: Adam Benjamin, Aida Elina. DVM, Ohio State U., 1968. Diplomate Am. Coll. Vet. Ophthalmologists. Rsch. assoc. U. Ill. Coll. Medicine, Chgo., 1973-79; asst. prof. Coll. Vet. Medicine U. Fla., Gainesville, 1979-84; med. cons. Animal Eye Clinic, Denver, 1984-86; asst. prof. Ohio State U., Columbus, 1986-92; med. cons. Animal Eye Clinic, Tampa, Fla., 1992—; pres., owner So. Eye. Clin. for Animals, Southwest, 1996—. Cons. Wil Rsch. Lab., Ashland, Ohio, 1988-92, Bushy Run Rsch. Lab., Export, Pa., 1986-92. Mem. AVMA, Fla. Vet. Med. Assn., Hillsborough County Vet. Med. Assn. (chmn.). Avocations: environmentalism, diversity tolerance, social equity, photography. Office: Animal Eye Clinic 8008 W Waters Ave Tampa FL 33615-1800

WOLF, EDITH MALETZ, retired educator; b. Warsaw, Nov. 12, 1922; came to U.S., 1923; d. Michael and Sonia Chai (Ingerov) Maletz; m. Jordan Melvin Wolf, July 7, 1946; 1 child, David Richard (dec.). BS, U. Wis., 1944, MS, 1968. Cert. tchr. Wis. Tchr. Milw. Pub. Schs., 1945-85, acting vice prin., 1980-81, ret., 1985. Author: The Magic Dreydle, 1962, The New Governess, 1970, (play) The Dream. Mem. Saturday Arts, Milw., 1970-80, Wis. Painters and Sculptors, Milw., 1944—. Scholarship Dudley Krafts Watson, 1944. Mem. AAUW, Hadassah (sec. 1980-81, pres. emeritus, donor chair, program chair), Nat. Mus. Women in the Arts, Florentine Opera Club (founding mem.), U. Wisc. Alumni Assn., Cousteau Soc. Avocations: reading, writing fiction, plays, painting, gardening.

WOLF, EDWARD LINCOLN, physics educator; b. Cocoa, Fla., Nov. 22, 1936; s. Norman Lincoln and Harriet (Burgess) W.; m. Carol Joyce Euwema, June 15, 1958; children: Douglas Wakefield, David Lincoln. BA, Swarthmore Coll., 1958; PhD, Cornell U., 1964. Postdoctoral fellow U. Ill. Dept. Physics, Urbana, 1964-66; research assoc. Eastman Kodak Co., Rochester, N.Y., 1967-75; prof. physics Iowa State U., Ames, 1975-85; head dept. physics, prof. Polytechnic U., Bklyn., 1986—, prof. physics, 1986—. Sr. vis. fellow Cavendish Lab. U. Cambridge, U.K., 1973-74; vis. prof. U. Pa., Phila., 1982; program dir. condensed matter physics NSF, 1996-98. Author: Principles of Electron Tunneling Spectroscopy, 1985; editor: Materials and Mechanisms of Superconductivity, 1985. Fellow Am. Phys. Soc.; mem. AAAS, Materials Rsch. Soc., Phi Beta Kappa, Sigma Xi. Presbyterian. Avocations: jogging, cycling, music. Office: Polytechnic U Dept Physics Six Metrotech Ctr Brooklyn NY 11201-3850 E-mail: ewolf@duke.poly.edu.

WOLF, FRANK, business educator, consulting executive; b. Dessau, Germany, Jan. 16, 1933; came to U.S., 1952; s. Erwin and Else Wolf; m. Sandra Lance; 1 child, Amelia. BS, Davis and Elkins Coll., 1960; MS, Poly. Inst. N.Y., 1965; D in Bus. Adminstrn., Nova U., Ft. Lauderdale, Fla., 1997. Dir. info. tech./MIS Am. Can. Corp., Greenwich, Conn., 1967-80; v.p. mktg. Marketronics, N.Y.C., 1980-81; pres. On Line Rsch., Greenwich, 1980-93, SB Software, Savannah, Ga., 1986—; adj. prof. bus. Nova Southeastern U., 1997—. Spkr. in field; arbitrator NASD, 2001—. Contbr. articles to profl. publs. Chmn. Inland Wetlands Agy., Town of Greenwich, 1975-86; non-govtl. orgn. rep. UN, N.Y., 1994-2000. White Ho. fellow Presdl. Interchange, Washington, 1972-73. Mem. Acad. Internat. Bus. Republican. Avocations: swimming, diving, flying glider. E-mail: wolff@nova.edu.

WOLF, FRANK R. congressman, lawyer; b. Phila., Jan. 30, 1939; m. Carolyn Stover; children: Frank, Virginia, Anne, Brenda, Rebecca. BA, Pa. State U., 1961; LL.B., Georgetown U., 1965. Bar: Va., D.C. Legis. asst. former Congressman Edward G. Biester, Jr., 1968-71; asst. to Sec. of Interior Rogers B. Morton, 1971-74; dep. asst. sec. for Congl. and Legis. Affairs, Dept. Interior, 1974-75; mem. U.S. Congress from 10th Va. dist., Washington, 1981—. Mem. appropriations com. Served with USAR, 1962—63. Republican. Presbyterian. Office: US Ho of Reps 241 Cannon Bldg Washington DC 20515-4610*

WOLF, FREDERICK GEORGE, environmental scientist, administrator; b. Paterson, N.J., Aug. 30, 1952; s. Frederick George and Doris (Miller) W. BS, U. S.C., 1974; postgrad., Clemson U., 1976-77; MS in Environ. Health, East Tenn. State U., 1978; MS in Sys. Mgmt., U. Denver, 1990; DBA in Mgmt., Nova Southeastern U., 2000. Phys. scientist U.S. Army Environ. Hygiene Agy., Edgewood, Md., 1974-75, S.C. Dept. Health and Environ. Control, Columbia, 1977-78; environ. scientist EPA, Atlanta, 1978-79, Boston, 1979—81, Seattle, 1981—86; mgr. hazardous waste sect. Parametrix Inc., Bellevue, 1986-88; regional mgr. environ. remediation Atofina Chems., Inc., Tacoma, 1988—. Lt. USNR, 1974-87. Recipient Spl. Svc. award EPA, 1982, Bronze medal, 1983. Mem. Acad. of Hazardous Materials Mgmt. (cert. hazardous materials mgr. master level), Soaring Soc. Am. (Bronze badge number 338), Sigma Xi, Epsilon Nu Eta, Sigma Beta Delta. Office: Atofina Chems Inc 2901 Taylor Way Tacoma WA 98421-4330

WOLF, G. VAN VELSOR, JR. lawyer; b. Balt., Feb. 19, 1944; s. G. Van Velsor and Alice Roberts (Kimberly) W.; m. Ann Holmes Kavanagh, May 19, 1984; children: George Van Velsor III, Timothy Kavanagh (dec.), Christopher Kavanagh, Elisabeth Huxley. BA, Yale U., 1966; JD, Vanderbilt U., 1973. Bar: N.Y. 1974, U.S. Dist. Ct. (so. dist.) N.Y. 1974, U.S. Ct. Appeals (2d cir.) 1974, Ariz. 1982, U.S. Dist. Ct. Ariz. 1982, U.S. Ct. Appeals (9th cir.) 1982. Agrl. advisor U.S. Peace Corps., Tanzania and Kenya, 1966-70; assoc. Milbank, Tweed, Hadley & McCloy, N.Y.C., 1973-75; vis. lectr. law Airlangga U., Surabaya, Indonesia, 1975-76; editor-in-chief Environ. Law Reporter, Washington, 1976-81; assoc. Lewis & Roca, Phoenix, 1981-84, ptnr., 1984-91, Snell & Wilmer, Phoenix, 1991—. Vis. lectr. law U. Ariz., 1990, Vanderbilt U., 1991, U. Md., 1994, Ariz. State U., 1995; cons. Nat. Trust Hist. Preservation, Washington, 1981. Editor: Toxic Substances Control, 1980; editor in chief Environ. Law Reporter 1976-81; contbr. articles to profl. jours. Bd. dirs. Ariz. divsn. Am. Cancer Soc., 1985—96, sec., 1990—92, vice-chmn., 1992—94, chmn., 1994—96, bd. dirs. S.W. divsn., 1996—, chmn., 1996—98, nat. bd. dirs., 1999—; bd. dirs. Herberger Theatre Ctr., 1998—, sec., 2001—; bd. dirs. Phoenix Little Theatre, 1983—90, chmn., 1986—88. Recipient St. George medal Am. Cancer Soc., 1998. Mem. ABA (vice-chmn. SONREEL commn. state and regional environ. coop. 1995-98, co-chmn. 1998-2000, vice-chmn. environ. audits task force 1998-99, vice-chmn. SONREEL ann. meeting planning com. 1998-99), Assn. of Bar of City of N.Y., Ariz. State Bar Assn. (coun. environ. & nat. res. law sect. 1988-93, chmn. 1991-92, CLE com. 1992-98, chmn. 1997-98), Maricopa County Bar Assn., Ariz. Acad., Union Club N.Y.C., Univ. Club Phoenix, Phoenix Country Club. Office: Snell & Wilmer 1 Arizona Ctr Phoenix AZ 85004-0001 E-mail: vwolf@swlaw.com.

WOLF, GARY HERBERT, architect; b. Lansing, Mich., July 15, 1950; s. Herbert C. and Margaret Wolf; m. Bonnie L. Grad, June 21, 1980; children: Alexander, Theodore. BA, Cornell U., 1972; M Archtl. History, U. Va., 1974; MArch, Princeton U., 1978. Assoc. Graham Gund Archs., Inc., Cambridge, Mass., 1983-87; prin. Adams & Wolf Archs., Inc., Belmont, 1987-91, Gary Wolf Archs., Inc., Boston, 1991—; dir. design Heliotrope, Providence, 1993-96. Mem. other archtl. firms, preservation orgns. and other instns. including constrn. mgmt. dept. Harvard U., Michael Graves Arch., Nat. Register Historic Places, 1974-83; vis. critic Harvard U. Grad. Sch. Design, Cambridge, Mass.; guest juror RISD, Providence, MIT, Cambridge. Prin. archtl. works include Leonard Street retail and office block, Belmont, Mass., 1988, Autumn Leaves House, Weston, Mass., 1988-94, Synectics Corp. Offices, Cambridge, 1987-88, 90-91, Mus. of Our Nat. Heritage Renovations, New Galleries, Conf. Ctr., Offices, Lexington, Mass., 1993-99, Brookline Music Sch., 1991-94, MIT Student House, 1999-2000; designer pvt. residences, Zephyr Hammock, Glass Curtain Lamp, other objects; contbr. articles to profl. jours. Recipient Thomas Jefferson Meml. Found. Scholarship U. Va., 1972-74, Merit award Internat. Conceptual Furniture Competition, Progressive Archiecture Mag., 1980,numerous nat. design awards including Gold Indsl. Design Excellence award Bus. Week/Indsl. Design Soc. Am., 1994, Best Products award Time Mag., 1994, Renovations of the Yr. award, 1996, Preservation award Victorian Soc.-New Eng., 1998. Mem. AIA, Am. Assn. Mus., Nat. Trust Hist. Preservation, Boston Soc. Archs. (past chmn. membership com., honor award citation 1997), Docomomo New Eng. (bd. dirs.). Office: Gary Wolf Archs 7 Marshall St Boston MA 02108-2404

WOLF, GARY WICKERT, lawyer; b. Slinger, Wis., Apr. 19, 1938; s. Leonard A. and Cleo C. (Wickert) W.; m. Jacqueline Weltzin, Dec. 17, 1960; children: Gary, Jonathan. BBA, U. Minn., 1960, JD cum laude, 1963. Bar: N.Y. 1964, U.S. Ct. Appeals (2d cir.) 1969, U.S. Dist. Ct. (so. dist.) N.Y. 1969, U.S. Supreme Ct. 1971. Assoc. Cahill, Gordon & Reindel, N.Y.C., 1963-70, ptnr., 1970—. Bd. dirs. N.J. Resources Corp., N.J. Natural Gas Co. Mem. N.Y. State Bar Assn. (com. on securities regulation), Anglers Club (N.Y.C.), Downtown Assn. (N.Y.C.), Mashomack Fish and Game Club. Home: 35 Fieldstone Dr Basking Ridge NJ 07920-1605 Office: Cahill Gordon & Reindel 80 Pine St Fl 17 New York NY 10005-1790

WOLF, GREGORY H. insurance company executive; b. Erie, Pa. married; 2 children. BS, Penn State U.; MS in Hosp. and Health Svcs. Adminstrn., Ctrl. Mich. U.; postgrad., Cornell U., U. Pa. V.p. mktg. and sales, then sr. v.p., exec. v.p., pres. Employers Health, Green Bay, Wis., 1988-95; sr. v.p. sales and mktg. Humana Inc., Louisville, 1995-96, COO, pres., 1996—97, CEO, pres., 1997—99; pres. Cigna Inc., Small Bus. Initiative, 2001—; mem. bd. of dir. Shopko Stores, Inc., Green Bay. Past bd. dirs. Boys and Girls Club of Green Bay, Cystic Fibrosis Found. Green Bay. Office: Cigna Corp 1 Liberty Place Philadelphia PA 19192-1550*

WOLF, HAROLD ARTHUR, finance educator, educator; b. Lind, Wash., Feb. 10, 1923; s. Edward and Olga (Limert) W.; March 23, 1961; children: Mark, Suellen. BA, U. Oreg., 1951; MA, U. Mich., 1952, PhD, 1958. Instr. Lehigh U., 1955-56; economist Prudential Life Ins. Co., Newark, 1957-58; asst. prof. fin., money, banking U. Colo., 1958-60, assoc. prof., 1961-64, prof., 1965-68; prof. fin. U. Tex., Austin, 1969—; pvt. practice consulting for fin. instns., 1960—. Author: Personal Finance, 1978, 8th edit., 1989, Managing Your Money, 1977, Personal Financial Planning, 8th edit., 1989, 3d custom edit., 2000. Served with U.S. Navy, 1941-47. Mem. Am. Economic Assn., Am. Fin. Assn., So. Fin. Assn. Home: 7004 Edgefield Dr Austin TX 78731-2926 Office: U Tex Dept Finance Austin TX 78712

WOLF, HAROLD HERBERT, pharmacy educator; b. Quincy, Mass., Dec. 19, 1934; s. John I. and Bertha F. (Sussman) W.; m. Joan Z. Silverman, Aug. 11, 1957; children: Gary Jerome, David Neal. BS, Mass. Coll. Pharmacy, 1956; PhD, U. Utah, 1961; LLD (hon.), U. Md., 1994. Asst. prof. pharmacology Coll. Pharmacy Ohio State U., 1961-64, assoc. prof., 1964-69, prof., 1969-76, Kimberly prof., 1975-76, chmn. div. pharmacology, 1973-76; dean Coll. of Pharmacy, U. Utah, Salt Lake City, 1976-89, prof. pharmacology, 1976—, dir. Anticonvulsant Drug Devel. Program, 1989—2002. Vis. prof. U. Sains Malaysia, 1973-74; mem. Nat. Joint Commn. on Prescription Drug Use, 1976-80; mem. NIH rev. com. Biomed. Rsch. Devel. Grant Program, 1978-79; external examiner U. Malaya, 1978, 92, 96, U. Sains Malaysia, 1980. Contbr. articles in field of central nervous system pharmacology and field of pharm. edn. Recipient Alumni Achievement award Mass. Coll. Pharmacy, 1978, Disting. Faculty award U. Utah, 1989, Rosenblatt prize, 1989, Disting. Alumnus award Coll. Pharmacy, U. Utah, 1991, Weaver prize, 2000. Fellow AAAS, Acad. Pharm. Scis.; mem. Am. Soc. Pharmacology and Exptl. Therapeutics, Am. Pharm. Assn. (task force on edn. 1982-84), Am. Assn. Colls. of Pharmacy (pres. 1977, Disting. Pharmacy Educator award 1988, scholar in residence 1989, chmn. commn. on implementing change in pharmacy edn. 1989-92, 95-96), Am. Soc. Hosp. Pharmacists (commn. on goals 1982-84), Am. Coun. on Pharm. Edn. (bd. dirs. 1985-88), Soc. Neurosci. Jewish. Home: 4467 Adonis Dr Salt Lake City UT 84124-3922 Office: Univ Utah Coll Pharmacy Salt Lake City UT 84112

WOLF, HARRY, retired dean and educator; b. Alameda, Calif., Dec. 26, 1922; s. Morris J. and Regina (Fischer) W.; m. Doris Zena Rackow, Feb. 15, 1947 (dec. Jan., 1999); children: Stephen F., Bernard N., Rebecca J. BA, U. Calif., Berkeley, 1947, MA, 1951. Salary and wage analyst Dept. of the Navy, San Francisco, 1947-57; chief salary adminstrn. U.S. Atomic Energy Commn., Washington, 1957-62, pers. dir. Berkeley, 1962-66, 72-77; dir. Exec. Seminar Ctr., U.S. Civil Svc. Commn., 1966-72; prof. Golden Gate U., San Francisco, 1965-87, dean pub. adminstrn., 1987-90; ret., 1990. Pers. cons. Exec. Mgmt. Svcs., Inc., Washington, 1977-82; chair county civil svc. revision bd. Contra Costa County, Calif., 1980. Contbr. articles to profl. jours. Bd. dirs. Shelter Inc. of Contra Costa County, 2001—; mem. sr. adv. coun. Congresswoman Ellen Tauscher; coord. Region VIII Fed. Emergency and Ednl. Assistance Program, 2001—; past pres. Temple Isaiah, Lafayette, Calif, 1973-74. Master sgt. U.S. Army, 1943-46. Recipient Bay Area Outstanding Contbr. award ASPA, 1983, Disting. Svc. award Golden Gate U., 1990. Mem. Nat. Assn. Ret. Fed. Employees (state pub. rels. chair 1995-98, dist. v.p. 1999-2000). Democrat. Jewish. Avocations: bridge, model trains. Home: 669 Montezuma Ct Walnut Creek CA 94598-2913 E-mail: harrynmi@aol.com.

WOLF, IRNA LYNN, psychologist; b. Dunottar, South Africa, Aug. 30, 1949; came to U.S., 1977; d. John and Tolsa W.; m. Raymond Frank Shamos, Feb. 22, 1976; children: Lorin Iver, Richard Lance, Ilan Hiram, Troy Joseph. MFA cum laude, U. Witwatersrand, 1976; MA, U. Rochester, 1983; PhD, Ariz. State U., 1991, postgrad., 1997. Lic. psychologist, Ariz., diplomate psychology; cert. sch. psychologist. Rsch., tchg. asst. Ariz. State U., Tempe, 1984-89; ind. rsch., 1989-97; pvt. practice Phoenix, 1997—. Lectr. in field; cons. Human Info. Processing, 1997—. Contbr. articles to profl. jours. Recipient Certificate of Appreciation Paradise Valley Police Dept., 1992. Mem. APA, Am. Psychol. Soc., Nat. Assn. Sch. Psychologists, We. Psychol. Assn., Ariz. Psychol. Assn., Phi Kappa Phi. Republican. Avocations: painting, drawing, hiking, swimming. Home: 4516 E Onyx Ave Phoenix AZ 85028-4200

WOLF, JAMES ANTHONY, insurance company executive; b. Washington, May 10, 1945; s. Arthur William and Marie Antoinette (Dalton) Wolf; m. Sheila Marie Regan, June 27, 1968; children: Jayne Ann, Elizabeth. BS in Fin. cum laude, Boston Coll., 1967. Mktg. rep. IBM, Newark, 1967-68, Boston, 1970-78, mktg. mgr. N.Y.C., 1978-81; 2nd v.p. Tchrs. Ins. & Annuity Assn., 1981-82, v.p., 1982-85, sr. v.p., 1985-98, exec. v.p., 1998-00; pres. Retirement Svcs., 2000—. Served to sgt. U.S. Army, 1968-70, Vietnam. Mem. Am. Mgmt. Assn. Republican. Roman Catholic. Home: 233 Ridge Common Fairfield CT 06430-7010 Office: Tchrs Ins & Annuity Assn Am 730 3rd Ave New York NY 10017-3206

WOLF, JOHN HOWELL, retired publisher; b. Narberth, Pa., Mar. 19, 1918; s. W. Dale and Ruth Coryell (Howell) W.; m. Jane Belmeur, May 18, 1946 (div. Dec. 16, 1969); children: John B., Wendy J.; m. Emily West Asbury, Dec. 21, 1969. Student, DePauw U., Greencastle, Ind., 1935-39, Xavier U., Cin., 1940-41. Pub. Cin. Suburban Newspapers, Inc., 1946-73; pres., pub. Cin. Suburban Newspapers, Inc./Clermont Newspapers, Inc., 1973-82. Chmn. Nat. Better Newspaper Contests, Washington, 1957-58; adv. bd. U.S. Suburban Press, Inc., Chgo., 1970-75. Dir. Suburban Press Found., Chgo., 1972; del. 5th UNESCO Conf., 1956; chmn. Police Media Adv. Com., Cin., 1968; chmn. small media com. United Appeal, Cin., 1965; mem. com. of mgmt. YMCA, Norwood, Ohio, 1947—; pres. Y Men's Club, Norwood, 1952, Carlisle (Ky.) Nicholas County Indsl. Authority, 1984-89, chmn., 1988-89. Maj. U.S. Army, 1942-46. Recipient Silver medal Advertisers Club, Cin., 1973. Mem. Soc. Profl. Journalists, Suburban Newspapers of Am. (pres. 1973, pres. suburban newspapers sect. 1968), Nat. Newspaper Assn. (dir. 1978-83, exec. com. 1980-83, fin. com. 1980-83, Outstanding Dir. 1980), Accredited Home Newspapers of Am. (dir. 1972), Norwood Club (pres. 1950), Masons. Presbyterian. Avocations: reading, travel. Home: 244 Azalea Ct Carlisle KY 40311-9053

WOLF, JOHN MICHAEL, adult education seminar consultant; b. Upper Darby, Pa., Aug. 21, 1946; s. Herbert Michael and Elizabeth (Collins) W.; m. Gloria Ann Pettinati, Feb. 1, 1969 (div. 1978); m. Diane Elaine Batterson, Sept. 10, 1983 (div. 1994); children: John Michael Jr., Jessica Diane. BS, Drexel U., 1969; MBA, Temple U., 1972; PhD, Walden U., 1990. Salesman Lit Bros., Upper Darby, 1961-63, Cousins Shoes, Upper Darby, 1963-69; purchasing agt. Philco-Ford Co., Phila., 1969-70; sales rep. Conn. Gen. Life Ins. Co., 1970-75, Provident Life & Accident Ins. Co., Cherry Hill, N.J., 1975-78; pres. Associated Cons., Haddonfield, 1978-96; sr. ptnr. Lifelong Learning Ptnrs., Bradenton, Fla., 1996—. Cons. Chrysler Corp., Detroit, 1987, Maccabbes Mut. Life Corp., Detroit, 1989, Security-Conn. Life, Hartford, 1989, U.S. Air Pitts., 1989, GE, Paris, 1991, Ashland Chem. Co., Columbus, 1992, Campbell Soup Co., 1993, N.J. Prins. Assn., 1994, F.T.D. Aetna Ins., Tex. Instruments, 1995, Starbucks Coffee Co., Fedex, SunAmerica, 1996, Met P&C, HBO, 1997, Time Warner Cable, 1998, AIG, 1999, Comcast Cable 2000, Great West Life, 2001, Danka, John Hancock, 2002. Chmn. U.S. Jaycees, Haddonfield, 1979; co-chmn. March of Dimes, Haddonfield, 1983. Mem. Am. Mgmt. Assn., Soc. for Accelerative Learning & Tchg., Internat. Alliance Learning Creative Edn. Found., Statue of Liberty Found., Tau Kappa Epsilon. Avocations: soccer, music, travel, skiing. Office: Lifelong Learning Ptnrs 4301 32nd St W Ste C14 Bradenton FL 34205-2796

WOLF, JOHN S. ambassador, federal agency administrator; b. Sept. 12, 1948; BA, Dartmouth Coll., 1970; postgrad., Princeton U., 1978-79. Fgn. svc. officer, 1970—; prin. dep. asst. sec. for int. orgn. affairs U.S. Dept. State, 1989—92; amb. to Malaysia Kuala Lumpur, 1992—95; coord. APEC, 1996; amb. APEC , 1997; spec. adv. to pres. & sec. state Caspian Basin Energy Diplomacy , 1999—2000; asst. sec. for non-proliferation U.S. Dept State , 2001—. Office: US Dept State Non-Proliferation Bureau 2201 C St NW Washington DC 20520*

WOLF, J(OHN) STEVEN, construction executive, land developer; b. Portsmouth, Ohio, Sept. 4, 1947; s. John Andrew and Betty Lee Wolf; m. Pamela Gahm, Mar. 11, 1995. BS in Civil Engring., Ohio U., 1975. Registered profl. engr., Ohio, Ind. Project engr. Columbus & So. Ohio Electric Co., 1974-75; staff project engr. Goodyear Atomic Corp., Piketon, Ohio, 1975-78; constrn. mgr. Am. Electric Power Svc. Corp., Lancaster, 1978-83; project mgr. F. and P. Mgrs., Inc., Columbus, 1983-85, Target Constrn. Co., Columbus, 1985-91; area mgr. Sherman R. Smoot Co., Indpls., 1991-93; dir. constrn. Pizzuti Devel., Inc., Columbus, 1993-2000; v.p. ops. Renier Constrn. Corp., 2000—01; land devel. projects dir. C.V. Perry & Co., Ohio, 2001—. Panel mem., speaker, seminars and classes in mgmt. and constrn. related areas. With U.S. Army, 1968-69, Vietnam. Decorated Army Commendation medal (2),

Combat Infantryman badge. Mem. NSPE, Ohio Soc. Profl. Engrs., Masons, Scottish Rite, Shriners. Methodist. Home: 13675 Bevelheimer Rd Westerville OH 43081-9651 Office: CV Perry & Co 370 S Fifth St Columbus OH 43215 E-mail: swolf@cvperry.com.

WOLF, JONATHON EDWARD, music educator; b. Denver, 1961; s. Walter Calvin and Marjorie Lydia Wolf. U. of Denver, MusB Edn., Denver, Colorado, 1984. Subsitute tchr. Kirkwood,parkway Sch. Dist., St.Louis, Mo., 1884—85; music tchr. (k_8) Cathedral sch., ST. louis, 1986—89; music tchr. (k-8) ST.gabriel sch., St.Louis, 1990—98; music tchr. Hillsboro sch. Dist, Hillsboro, 1999—2002. Music min. Apostolic Faith Ch., St. Louis, 1984—2001. Entertainer Local Nursing Home &Churches, St. Louis, 1989—2002; pvt. piano tchr. Local Nursing Homes&Churches, 1989—2002. Recipient 1St Pl. Nat. Talent Search, Gold City Gospel Qtet. Gadsen, Ala., 1989, Nat. Quartet Conv. Comp., Nat. Qtet. Conv. , Nashville, Tenn, 1989 to 2000, Nominated For Tchr. Of The Yr., Hillsboro Elementry Sch., Hillsboro,mo, 2002. Mem.: Mo. Music Edn. Assn. (assoc.; negotiation cntee's 1982—2002), Music Educators Nat. Conf. (assoc.; negotiation cmtee's 1982—2002), Mo. State Tchr. Assn. (assoc.; negotiation cmte, various comettes 1998—2002). Achievements include first to Recording My 1st Album Or Cd, Started In 6th Grade. Home: 4521 Frederickton Ct Saint Louis MO 63128 Personal E-mail: singsonggi@aol.com.

WOLF, JOSEPH ALBERT, mathematician, educator; b. Chgo., Oct. 18, 1936; s. Albert M. and Goldie (Wykoff) W. BS, U. Chgo., 1956, MS, 1957, PhD, 1959. Mem. Inst. for Advanced Study, Princeton, 1960-62, 65-66; asst. prof. U. Calif., Berkeley, 1962-64, assoc. prof., 1964-66, prof., 1966—94, Miller research prof., 1972-73, 83-84, prof. grad. sch., 1994—; prof. honorario Universidad Nacional de Cordoba, Argentina, 1989. Vis. prof. Rutgers U., 1969-70, Hebrew U., Jerusalem, 1974-76, Tel Aviv U., 1974-76, Harvard U., 1979-80, 86 Author: Spaces of Constant Curvature, 1967, 72, 74, 77, 84, Unitary Representations on Partially Holomorphic Cohomology Spaces, 1974, Unitary Representations of Maximal Parabolic Subgroups of the Classical Groups, 1976, Classification and Fourier Inversion for Parabolic Subgroups with Square Integrable Nilradical, 1979; co-editor, author: Harmonic Analysis and Representations of Semisimple Lie Groups, 1980, The Penrose Transform and Analytic Cohomology in Representation Theory, 1993, Geometry and Representation Theory of Real and P-Adic Grps., 1997, Global Differential Geometry: The Mathematical Legacy of Alfred Gray, 2000; editor Letters in Math. Physics, Jour. of Group Theory in Physics; contbr. articles to profl. jours. Alfred P. Sloan rsch. fellow, 1965-67, NSF fellow, 1959-62; recipient Médaille de l'Université de Liège, 1977, Humboldt prize, 1995. Mem. Am., Swiss Math. Socs. Office: U Calif Dept Math Berkeley CA 94720-3840 E-mail: jawolf@math.berkeley.edu.

WOLF, KARL EVERETT, aerospace and communications corporation executive; b. Hartford, Conn., Aug. 19, 1921; s. Carl Fred and Anna (Voss) W.; m. Lola Sue Stoner, Aug. 1, 1948; children: Paula R., Gloria J., Glenn K. BS, U.S. Mil. Acad., 1943; JD, U. Pa., 1953; SJD, George Washington U., 1963. Bar: D.C. 1953, Conn. 1953, U.S. Supreme Ct. 1960, Calif. 1971, Mich. 1975. Commd. 2d lt. U.S. Army, 1943, advanced through grades to lt. col., 1959, ret., 1963; assoc. counsel Philco. Corp., Phila., 1963-73; v.p., gen. counsel Ford Aerospace Corp., Detroit, 1973-88; ret., 1988. Mem. adv. bd. Bur. Nat. Affairs, Fed. Contract Reports, Washington, 1963-73 Author: State Taxation of Government Contractors, 1964. Decorated Silver Star, Bronze Star, Purple Heart; Croix de Guerre (Belgium) Mem. ABA, Calif. Bar Assn. Home: 1633 Castle Cove Cir Corona Del Mar CA 92625

WOLF, LARRY LOUIS, biology educator; b. Madison, Wis., Oct. 21, 1938; s. Mark Adam and Dorothy Alice (Test) W.; m. Janet Noelle Sorlien, Sept. 5, 1965; children: Alan Michael, Frederick Ian. BS, U. Mich., 1961; PhD, U. Calif., Berkeley, 1966. Prof. biology Syracuse (N.Y.) U., 1967—. Ecology adv. panel NSF, Washington, 1977-79. Co-author: General Ecology, 1973, 79; contbr. articles to profl. jours. Mem. gifted and talented adv. bd., Manlius, N.Y., 1981-85. Scientific grants NSF, 1968-88, 95-98. Fellow Am. Ornithologists Union, AAAS; mem. Ecol. Soc. Am. (editl. bd. 1984-87), Animal Behavior Soc., Internat. Soc. for Behavioral Ecology (coun. 1986-88, editor 1993-97), Phi Beta Kappa. Achievements include research on ecology and evolution of lek behavior in the long-tailed hermit hummingbird; species relationships in the Avian genus Aimophila. E-mail: llwold@mailbox.syr.edu.

WOLF, LAWRENCE, lawyer; b. L.A. BA, Calif. U., Northridge, 1972; JD, U. Calif., Santa Clara, 1975. Bar: Calif. 1975. Atty. City of Santa Monica, Calif., 1975-77, L.A. County Pub. Defender, 1977-79; pvt. practice law L.A., 1979—. Coord. law confs. Calif. Juvenile Cts., Inglewood, 1983. Mem. L.A. County Bar Assn., Juvenile Cts. Bar Assn. Office: 10390 Santa Monica Blvd Ste 300 Los Angeles CA 90025-5091 Fax: (310) 277-1500. E-mail: info@youareinnocent.com.

WOLF, LINDA S. advertising executive; Grad., Ohio Wesleyan U. Asst. account exec. Leo Burnett Group, Chgo., 1978; exec. v.p. new bus., dir. worldwide, group pres. N.Am. Leo Burnett Co., Inc., 1978-2000; CEO Leo Burnett USA, 2000—. Office: Leo Burnett Co Inc 35 W Wacker Dr Ste 3710 Chicago IL 60601-1648*

WOLF, MARCUS ALAN, lawyer; b. Mansfield, Ohio, July 6, 1946; s. Carl Merle and Eunice Virginia (Beekman) W.; m. Terrie L. Wolf, May 18, 2001; children: Stephanie Ariah, Marcus André. BA, Northeast La. U., 1969; JD, Ohio No. U., 1980. Bar: Ohio 1980, U.S. Dist. Ct. (no. dist.) Ohio 1980. Tchr. Clearfork Valley Schs., Butler, Ohio, 1969-70, Shelby City Schools, Shelby, 1972-77; prin. Marcus A. Wolf Co. L.P.A. (formerly Thompson & Wolf Co. L.P.A.), Mansfield, 1980—. Owner Marcus' Beauty Salon. Mem. exec. com. Richland County Dem. Com., 1986-93, 2000—, precinct committeeman, 1988, 90-93; chmn. adminstrv. bd. Main St. United Meth. Ch.; mem. dist. 7 Mansfield Power Squadron, 1985—. Mem. ABA, Ohio Bar Assn., Richland County Bar Assn., Masons, Elks. Methodist. Avocations: boating, fishing, skiing, hunting. Home: 457 Davis Rd Mansfield OH 44907-1121 Office: Marcus A. Wolf Co LPA 13 Park Ave W Mansfield OH 44902-1714 also: Marcus' Salon 310 Lexington Ave Mansfield OH 44907

WOLF, MARILYN, volunteer; b. Muncie, Ind., June 12, 1950; d. Richard D. and Jessie Clair; m. Dan Edward Wilson, June 13, 1970 (div. May 1982); children: Jorja Rae, Jacob Vincent; m. Burton Charles Weitzman, July 30, 1988. BS in Comms., U. Md., Rockville, 1999; AA, Montgomery Coll., Rockville, 1997. Office mgr., bookkeeper Dr. James L. Shoot, Indpls., 1982-85; budget asst. U.S. Mil. Acad., West Point, N.Y., 1985-87; mgmt. analyst FDA, Rockville, Md., 1987-95, consumer safety officer, 1995-99; freelance writer, 2000. Chief steward Nat. Treasury Employees' Union chpt. 282, 1999; GSA Interagy. Telecommuting Ctr. Pilot Project, 1993. Trustee Montgomery Coll., 1992; mem. Leadership Pasco, 2001, class pres., mem. comm. com., bd. dirs.; mem. agy. rels. com. United Way Pasco County, 2001-02. Mem. Women's Exec. Leadership Program, 1992, Federally Employed Women (Parklawn chpt. pres. 1991-92, regional bd. 1991-92, Parklawn exec. com. 1992-94), Pub. Health Svc. Women's Network (one of founding mem.), Am. Mensa Soc. (Met. Washington Mensa scholarship chair 1993-96, bus. mgr. 1998), Timber Greens Country Club (bd. dirs.), Phi Theta Kappa. Avocations: writing, reading. E-mail. Home: 9452 Conservation Dr New Port Richey FL 34655-6020

WOLF, MARTIN EUGENE, lawyer, educator; b. Balt., Sept. 9, 1958; s. Eugene Bernard and Mary Anna (O'Neil) W.; m. Nancy Ann Reinsfelder, May 9, 1980; children: Matthew Adam, Allison Maria, Emily Elizabeth. BA, Johns Hopkins U., 1980; JD, U. Md., 1991. Bar: Md. 1991, U.S. Dist. Ct. Md. 1992, U.S. Ct. Appeals (4th cir.) 1992, U.S. Ct. Appeals (2d cir.) 1993, U.S. Ct. Appeals (3d cir.) 1998, U.S. Ct. Appeals (11th cir.) 2000, U.S. Ct. Fed. Claims 2001. Mgmt. trainee Giant Foods, Inc., Landover, Md., 1980-82, dept. mgr., 1982-83, ops. analyst, 1983-86, fin. coord., 1986-89; law clk. Piper & Marbury, LLP, Balt., 1989-91, assoc., 1991-96; prin. Law Office of Martin E. Wolf, Abingdon, Md., 1996-99; ptnr. Quinn, Gordon & Wolf Chartered, Towson, 2000—. Dir. Giant Food Fed. Credit Union, Landover, 1984-89; pres. Stalagmite Properties, Ltd., Abingdon, Md., 1995-96; tchg. asst. U. Md. Sch. Law, Balt., 1992-94, adj. prof., 1996—. Pres. bd. dirs. Chesapeake Search & Rescue Dog Assn., Inc., 2000—. Mem. ABA, Md. State Bar Assn., Harford County Bar Assn., Harford County Bar Found. (Vol. Svc. award 1992, 94). Democrat. Roman Catholic. Avocations: Lacrosse, hockey. Home: 11 Mitchell Dr Abingdon MD 21009-1628 E-mail: mwolf@quinnlaw.com.

WOLF, MICHELE SUE, poet, writer, editor; b. Denville, N.J., June 21, 1954; d. Sheldon Wolf and Dorothy Joyce Yospe; m. Sanford Michael Herzon, Aug. 5, 2001. BS in Pub. Comm., Boston U., 1976; MS in Journalism, Columbia U., 1978. Publicist Boston Ballet, 1976—77; assoc. copy editor Charles Scribner's Sons, N.Y.C., 1979—81; copy editor Simon & Schuster, Inc., 1981—84; assoc. editor Harper's Bazaar, 1985—87; freelance writer and editor Chevy Chase, Md., 1987—. Author: (poetry books) The Keeper of Light, 1995 (winner Painted Bride Quar. poetry chapbook series, 1995), Conversations During Sleep, 1998 (Anhinga prize for poetry, 1997); contbr. poetry to jours., mags. Recipient Nat. Mag. award for personal svc., Am. Soc. Mag. Editors, 1993, Nat. Media award, Am. Speech-Lang.-Hearing Assn., 1994, Anna Davidson Rosenberg award for poems on the Jewish experience, Judah L. Magnes Mus., Berkeley, Calif., 1997; fellow residency, Va. Ctr. for the Creative Arts, 1987, residency fellow, 1988, Edward F. Albee Found., 1989, Corp. of Yaddo, Saratoga Springs, N.Y., 1990. Mem.: Poetry Soc. Am., Nat. Writers Union, Am. Soc. Journalists and Authors, PEN Am. Ctr. Home and Office: 4615 N Park Ave # 810 Chevy Chase MD 20815-4514 E-mail: michelewolf@juno.com.

WOLF, MILTON ALBERT, economist, former ambassador, investor; b. Cleve., May 29, 1924; s. Sam and Sylvia (Davis) W.; m. Roslyn C. Zehman, June 23, 1948 (dec.); children: Leslie Eric, Caryn Sue, Nancy Gail, Sherri Hope. BA in Chemistry and Biology, Ohio State U., 1948; BS in Civil Engring. summa cum laude, Case Inst. Tech., 1954; MA in Econs., Case Western Res. U., 1973, PhD in Econs., 1993, LHD (hon.), 1980; LLD (hon.), Cleve. State U., 1980; D in Diplomacy (hon.), Ohio State U., 1997. Pres. Zehman-Wolf Constrn. Co., Cleve., 1948-76; U.S. ambassador to Austria, 1977-80; disting. professorial lectr. in econs. Case Western Res. U., 1981-87; chmn. Milton A. Wolf Investors, 1980—. Bd. dirs. Town and Country Trust; U.S. del. UN conf. on Sci. and Tech. for Devel., 1979; U.S. del. dedication of UN Internat. Ctr., Vienna, 1979; host Salt II Summit, Vienna, 1979; trustee Cleve. Clinic; chmn. Fulbright Commn. for Austria, 1977-80. Trustee emeritus Ohio State U., 1986-96, chair, 1995-96; hon. trustee Case Western Res. U., Cleve. Orch.; chmn. Coun. Am. Ambs.; chmn. Am. Austrian Found.; chmn. Am. Jewish Joint Distbn. Com.; mem. econ. adv. task force Carter Presdl. Campaign, 1976; mem. Carter Inauguration Com.; nat. trustee United Israel Appeal, United Jewish Appeal, Coun. Jewish Fedns.; trustee United Way Svcs.; life trustee Park Synagogue, Cleve.; past pres., life trustee Jewish Cmty. Fedn., Cleve.; bd. dirs. Grad. Sch. Internat. Econs. and Fin., Brandeis U. With USAAF 1943-48. Recipient Austrian-Am. medal of honor, 1999, Austrian Cross of Honor for Sci. and Art 1st Class, 1997, Gt. Gold medal of honor with sash Republic of Austria, 1980, Gt. Gold medal of State Province of Salzburg, Republic of Austria, 1979, Eisenman award Jewish Cmty. Fedn. Cleve., 1990, Internat. Humanitarian award Raoul Wallenberg Com., 1995; Hooded A fellow Brandeis U. Mem. Am. Econ. Assn., Cleve. Engring. Soc., Cleve. Builders Assn., Coun. Fgn. Rels., Fgn. Policy Assn., Acad. Polit. Sci., Cleve. Com. World Affairs, UN Assn.- U.S. (bd. govs.), Tau Beta Pi. Home: 19200 S Park Blvd Shaker Heights OH 44122-1857 Office: 25700 Science Park Dr Beachwood OH 44122-7319

WOLF, MONICA THERESIA, small business owner, inventor; b. Germany, Apr. 26, 1943; came to U.S., 1953, naturalized, 1959; d. Otto and Hildegard Maria (Heim) Bellemann; children: Clinton, Danielle. BBA, U. Albuquerque, 1986. Developer Word Processing Ctr. Pub. Svc. of N.Mex., Albuquerque, 1971-74, word processing supr., 1974-78, budget coord., 1978-80, lead procedures analyst, 1980-88; owner Monika's Woodworks, 1988-91; founder Monidan Blue, 1992—; ind. dir. Royal Body Care, 1999—. Bd. dirs. Pub. Svc. Co. of N.Mex. Retirees; adv. bd., former student trainer APS Career Enrichment Ctr.; instr. firearm safety and pistol competition. Animal rights activist. Mem.: NAFE, Internat. Word Processing Assn. (founder N.Mex. chpt.), N.Mex. Inventors Club. Democrat. Home and Office: 305 Alamosa Rd NW Albuquerque NM 87107-5312

WOLF, MURIEL HEBERT, soprano, opera director, music educator; b. Boston, Nov. 15, 1925; d. Joseph Aurel and Gertrude May (Schellenger) Hebert; m. Anton Wolf, Feb. 5, 1949 (dec. Jan. 1989); m. Albert Paul Steger, Feb. 14, 1991. BMus in Voice with Distinction, New Eng. Conservatory of Music, 1949, MMus in Musical Rsch., 1950; Artist's Diploma with Highest Honors, Acad. of Music, Vienna, Austria, 1955; Postgrad. in Musicology, Brandeis U., 1956-57; Postgrad. in Opera, Ind. U., 1962-64. Instr. in music and theatre Verde Valley Sch., Sedona, Ariz., 1957-62; coord. of voice SUNY, Buffalo, 1979-84, prodr., dir. of opera, 1966-79, instr. of music, 1965-68, asst. prof. of music, 1968-71, assoc. prof. of music, 1971-84, prof. of music, 1984-93, prof. emeritus, 1993—. Guest lectr., dir. opera U. No. Ariz., Flagstaff, 1961—62; lectr., recitals Am. Psychiat. Assn., N.Y.C., Dallas, Montreal, 1979—88; co-chair Ctrl. Opera Svc. Nat. Conf. Met. Opera Auditions; founder Musictheater Advocates, Inc., Buffalo, 1974. Contbg. editor: Opera Quar., 1981—87; contbr. Founder, pres. The Anton and Muriel Wolf Found., Inc., 1999—. Grantee, N.Y. State Coun. of Arts, Buffalo, 1973, 1975, 1977, Cameron Baird Found., 1976, Polonia Cultural Inst., 1979; scholar Fulbright, Vienna and Salzburg, Austria, 1953—55. Mem.: Nat. Assn. Tchrs. Singing (conf. panelist, moderator and lectr.), Met. Opera Assn., Nat. Opera Assn. (conf. panelist, moderator and lectr., assoc. editor jour. 1962—82). Avocation: travel. E-mail: mhwolf@adelphia.net.

WOLF, NELSON MARC, cardiologist; b. Phila., Nov. 30, 1942; s. Max and Miriam (Wolensky) W.; m. Rochelle Barbara Hirshey, June 15, 1968; children: Michael Jason, Amy Jessica. Civ, U. Pa., 1964; MD, Temple U., 1968. Diplomate Am. Bd. Internal Medicine with subspecialty in cardiovascular disease, interventional subspecialty. Intern Temple U. Hosp., Phila., 1969; resident in medicine Georgetown U. Hosp., Washington, 1972-73, cardiology fellow, 1973-74, Temple U. Hosp., 1974-76; asst. prof. medicine dept. medicine, divsn. cardiology Med. Coll. Pa., Phila., 1976—, assoc. dir. CCU, mem. catheterization team, 1976—, dir. CCU, 1979—, assoc. prof. medicine, dir. Cardiac Catheterization Lab., 1980—, prof. medicine, 1984—. Cons. Sports Medicine Ctr., The Med. Coll. Pa. and West Park Hosp., Phila., 1985—, Scranton (Pa.) Temple Residency Program, 1993—; lectr. in field. Reviewer Annals of Internal Medicine, Archives of Internal Medicine; contbr. articles and abstracts to profl. jours. Lt. M.C., USNR, 1969-72. Fellow ACP, Am. Coll. Cardiology, Phila. Coll. Physicians, Undersea Med. Soc., Soc. Cardiac Angiography and Interventions, Clin. Coll. Cardiology; mem. Babcock Surg. Soc., Am. Heart Assn. (bd. govs. Southeastern Pa.), Phila. Acad. (founding mem. cardiology), Internat. Soc. for Cardiovascular Pharmacotherapy, Phila. Acad. Cardiology (v.p. 1991, pres.-elect 1992), Alpha Omega Alpha. Jewish. Avocations: biking, scuba diving. Home: 1320 Grenox Rd Wynnewood PA 19096-2403 Office: Med Coll Hosps Dept Medicine Divsn Cardiol 3300 Henry Ave Philadelphia PA 19129-1121

WOLF, PATRICK JOHN, political science educator; b. Washington, Mar. 10, 1965; s. Richard Delano and Sally Joan (Pollock) Watson; m. Kathleen Ann Beames, Dec. 31, 1994; children: Alexander Patrick, Brendan David. BA, U. St. Thomas, 1987; AM, Harvard U., 1993, PhD, 1995. Lobbyist Legis. Coalition for Hearing Impaired, St. Paul, 1985-87; program adminstr. Dept. Pub. Svc., 1987-88; teaching fellow Harvard U., Cambridge, Mass., 1990-92; asst. prof. polit. sci. Columbia U., N.Y.C., 1994-98; asst. prof. pub. policy Georgetown U., Washington, 1998—, faculty assoc. Harvard program on edn. policy and governance, 1999—. Guest scholar Brookings Instn., 2000 Book rev. editor Jour. Pub. Adminstrn. Rsch. & Theory; contbr. articles to profl. jours. Student chair grad. affairs com. Harvard U., 1992—93; mem. Nat. Commn. Choice in K-12 Edn., 2001—. Young Scholar grantee Minn. Elks, 1983, Minn. Nat. Hon. Soc. grantee, 1983, Mellon Dissertation grantee 1992-93, Harvard Univ., 1993, 94; Jacob Javits Grad. fellow Dept. Edn., Washington, 1988-92; recipient award for best article of 1997 Acad. Mgmt. Divsn. Pub. & Nonprofit Mgmt. Mem. Am. Polit. Sci. Assn. (exec. com. pub. adminstrn. sect. 1999—), Acad. Polit. Sci., Assn. Policy Analysis & Mgmt., Delta Epsilon Sigma Hon. Soc. (v.p. 1987). Roman Cath. Avocations: running, classical music. Office: GPPI Georgetown U 3600 N St NW Washington DC 20007-2670 E-mail: wolfp@georgetown.edu.

WOLF, PETER MICHAEL, investment manager, writer; b. New Orleans, Dec. 6, 1935; s. Morris and Ruth (New) W.; m. Alessandra Cantey, July 3, 1967; children: Phelan Godchaux, Alexis Ambler. BA, Yale U., 1957; MA, Tulane U., 1963; PhD, NYU, 1968. Ptnr. Wolf and Co., New Orleans, 1958-62; assoc. Wilbur Smith & Assocs., N.Y.C., 1968-70; faculty mem. NYU, 1966-67, Pratt Inst., N.Y.C., 1968-70; adj. prof. Cooper Union, 1971-87; chmn. bd. fellows, mem. faculty Inst. Arch. and Urban Studies, 1972-82; prin. Peter Wolf Assocs., 1970—. Participant, advisor Investment Policy com. Fiduciary Counsel Inc., 2000—; organizer of exhbns. Mus. Modern Art, N.Y.C., 1969; writer exhbns. Whitney Mus. Art, N.Y.C., 1970; contbr. exhbns. Mus. Modern Art, N.Y.C., 1973, Albany Inst Art, 1975; vis. scholar/artist Am. Acad. in Rome, 2001. Author: Hot Towns: The Future of the Fastest Growing Communities in America, 1999; Land in America: Its Value, Use and Control, 1981; On Streets, 1979; The Future of the City: New Directions in Urban Planning, 1974; The Evolving City, Urban Design Proposals by Ulrich Franzen and Paul Rudolph, 1974, Another Chance for Cities, 1970, Eugene Hénard and the Beginning of Urbanism in France 1900-1914, 1969. Trustee Guild Hall, East Hampton, N.Y., 1981-86, 99—, Van Allen Inst., 1995—, Godchaux Res. Plantation Fund, pres., 1994—; chmn. bd. trustees Van Allen Inst., N.Y., 1999-2000; adv. bd. Nat. Acad. Design, 1999—. NEA Fellow, 1979; Graham Found. Fellow, 1967-68, 94-95; Fulbright Fellow, 1965-66; Ford Found. grantee, 1971-74. Recipient Nat. Rsch. Ednl. Trust Fund, Charles P. Shattuck award 1983. Mem. Am. Inst. Cert. Planners, Contemporary Arts Coun. Museum of Modern Art, Inst. for Pvt. Investors. Avocation: tennis. Home: 325 W End Ave New York NY 10023-8135 Office: 36 W 44th St New York NY 10036-8102

WOLF, PETER OTTO, civil engineer, consultant; b. Vienna, Austria, May 9, 1918; s. Richard and Dora (Bondy) W.; m. Jennie Robinson, Aug. 12, 1944 (div. 1977); children: Ann Elizabeth, John Richard, Michael Stephen; m. Janet Elizabeth Robertson, Sept. 17, 1977. BSc in Engring., U. London, 1941; D in Engring. (hon.), Dresden (Germany) U. Tech., 1985. Chartered engr., U.K.; profl. hydrologist, U.S. Asst. Brundell & Farran, Doncaster, U.K., 1941-44; civilian asst. War Office, London, 1944-45; civil engr. Harold Marsh, King's Lynn, Eng., 1945; design engr., then chief designer James Williamson, Glasgow, Scotland, 1945-47; engr. for Mullardoch dam John Cochrane & Son Ltd., Cannich, 1947-49; lectr. in fluid mechanics and hydraulic engring. Imperial Coll., U. London, Eng., 1949-55, reader in hydrology, 1955-66; visiting prof. Stanford U., Palo Alto, Calif., 1959-60, Cornell U., N.Y., 1963, Nat. Univ. Mex., 1968; prof., head dept. civil engring. City Univ., London, 1966-82, cons., 1982-85; prof. emeritus, 1982—; dir. Pell Frischmann Cons. Engrs. Ltd., London, 1992—. Cons. in field, London, 1950—; chmn. U.K. Gov. Consultative com. Flood Protection Rsch. and Devel., 1983-85. Translator, editor: Engineering Fluid Mechanics, 1954; assoc. editor Water Internat., 1984-86; editl. bd. mem. Jour. Hydrology, 1959-79; contbr. articles to profl. jours. Mem. Natural Hazards Com., U.K., 1987-90, vice chmn., 1990-91, chmn., 1991-93; mem. exec. com. Hazards Forum, U.K., 1990-98, disting. mem. 1998—; mem. U.K. coordination com. Internat. Decade for Natural Disaster Reduction, 1992-98. Rsch. grantee Dept. Sci. and Indsl. Rsch., London, 1952, Natural Environment Rsch. Coun., Swindon, U.K., 1965, 66, IBM, London, 1965, 67. Fellow ASCE, Royal Acad. Engring., Instn. Civil Engrs. (vice chmn. Glasgow br. 1946-47, Telford Premium award 1953), Chartered Instn. Water and Environ. Mgmt. (rsch. com.), Royal Meteorol. Soc.; mem. Brit. Hydromech. Rsch. Assn. (hon.), Brit. Hydrological Soc. (hon., pres. 1987-89), Am. Geophys. Union, Internat. Commn. on Irrigation and Drainage, Internat. Assn. Hydraulic Rsch., Am. Inst. Hydrology (Ray K. Linsley award 1988), Athenaeum Club, Sigma Xi. Avocations: classical music, reading, walking, skiing. Home: 69 Shepherds Hill London N6 5RE England

WOLF, PHILIP ALAN, neurologist; b. N.Y.C., Mar. 19, 1936; m. Barbara Buck, Aug. 11, 1968; children: Alexander, Katherine. AB, NYU, 1956; MD, SUNY, Syracuse, 1960; cert. in preventive medicine, U. Pa., 1962. Diplomate Am. Bd. Psychiatry and Neurology, Nat. Bd. Med. Examiners. Intern Boston City Hosp., 1960-61; asst. resident Peter Bent Brigham Hosp., 1963-64; resident in neurology and neuropathology Mass. Gen. Hosp., 1964-67; fellow in neurology and neuropathology Harvard Med. Sch., Boston, 1964-67, instr. preventive medicine, 1967-69; assoc. rsch. prof. Boston U., 1979-83, adj. prof. pub. health, 1983-84, prof. pub. health, 1985—. Rsch. prof. medicine Boston U., 1983—, prof. neurology, 1978—; staff neurologist and chief cerebrovascular disease sect. VA Med. Ctr., Boston, 1969-97; sr. vis. neurologist Boston Med. Ctr., 1969—; mem. sci. adv. and coord. com. Am. Heart Assn., 1994-96, mem. stroke coun., exec. com., 1993-96, 83-87; mem. sci. issues com. Am. Acad. Neurology, Mpls., 1991-97; prin. investigator The Framingham (Mass.) Study, 1989—. Contbr. articles to profl. jours.; mem. editl. bd. Stroke, 1982—, Neuroepidemiology, 1988-93, dep. editor, 1990-93; mem. editl. bd. Am. Jour. Geriatric Cardiology, 1992, Jour. Cardiovascular Risk, 1993; ad hoc reviewer numerous profl. jours. Lt. USPHS, 1961-63. Recipient C. Miller Fisher M.D. award, Am. Heart Assn. (Boston), 2000, Jacob K. Javits Neurosci. award Nat. Adv. Neurol. Disorders and Stroke Coun., 1992, 1st Ann. Humana award for excellence in clin. stroke Am. Heart Assn., 1992. Fellow Coun. on Geriatric Cardiology, Am. Neurol. Assn., Am. Acad. Neurology, Am. Heart Assn. Coun. on Epidemiology, Am. Heart Assn. Stroke Coun., Am. Coll. Epidemiology, Am. Coll. Preventive Medicine; mem. AMA, Mass. Med. Soc., Internat. Soc. and Fedn. Cardiology Epidemiology and Prevention. Office: Boston U Sch Medicine 715 Albany St # B-608 Boston MA 02118-2526

WOLF, R. PETER, fundraising executive, harpsichordist; b. Washington, Dec. 5, 1942; s. Harry Edward and Virginia Anne (Simmons) W.; m. Rachel Irene Harrington Doggett, Sept. 2, 1994; m. Beniko Tsubaki, Apr. 15, 1977 (div. Oct. 1987). AB magna cum laude, Harvard U., 1965; MPhil, Yale U., 1969, PhD, 1977. Musician-in-residence N.C. State U., Raleigh, 1971-72; instr., asst. prof. SUNY, Stony Brook, 1972-78; asst. prof. U. Utah, Salt Lake City, Rutgers U., New Brunswick, N.J., 1980-85; editor, prodn. mgr. Broude Bros., Ltd., N.Y.C., 1985-89; dir. of devel. Hoboken (N.J.) Chamber Orchestra, 1989-90; devel. dir. Planned Parenthood/Essex County, Newark, 1991-93; dir. grants and spl. projects Nat. Coun. of Negro Women, Washington, 1994-96; devel. dir. Tudor Place Found., 1996-97, Family and Child Svcs. Washington, 1997—. Cons. Partnership in Philanthropy, Newark, 1993-94; concert adv. com. The Meadows Found., Franklin Twp., N.J., 1987-93; dir. Sanctuary Concert Series, Highland Park, N.J., 1990-94; harpsichordist numerous ensembles, 1971—; vis. asst. prof. U. Utah, Salt Lake City, 1978-80. Editor 14 musical edits., 1984—; contbr. articles to profl. jours. Recipient solo recitalist's grant Nat. Endowment for the Arts, 1983, grant-in-aid Am. Coun. Learned Socs., 1982; fellow Summer Humanities Inst. NEH, 1984, Fulbright Hays, Amsterdam, 1965-66. Mem. Nat. Soc. Fund-Raising Execs. (cert.), Am. Fedn. Musicians, Soc. Jean-Philippe Rameau, Am. Musicol. Soc. Democrat. Avocations: philately, computers, Cardigan Welsh corgies. Home: 7001 Barkwater Ct Bethesda MD 20817-4402

WOLF, ROBERT EDWARD, physician, educator; b. Houston, Jan. 20, 1942; s. John Eaton and Ruby Lucile (Bukowski) W.; m. Ann Elizabeth Killebrew, Dec. 23, 1967; 1 child, Robert Edward, Jr. BA, Baylor U., 1964; MA, U. Tex. Med. Br., 1968, MD, 1969, PhD, 1973. Diplomate Am. Bd. Internal Medicine. Intern in internal medicine U. Tex. Med. Br., Galveston, 1969-70, resident in internal medicine, 1970-71; fellowship in rheumatology U. Tex. Health Scis. Ctr., Dallas, 1973-75; rsch. assoc. VAMC, 1975-77; asst. prof. of medicine U. Tex. Health Scis. Ctr., 1975-77; assoc. prof. medicine La. State U. Health Scis. Ctr., Shreveport, 1977-89; prof. medicine La. State U. Med. Ctr., 1989—; staff physician VAMC, 1977—, dir. Arthritis Ctr., 1990—. Mem. faculty promotions com. La. State U. Med. Ctr., 1994-98, rsch. adv. coun., 1992—, adminstrv. coun., 1994—, utilization rev. com., 1983-95. Contbg. author: Selected Topics in Clinical Chemistry, 1972, Serum Protein Abnormalities, 1975; contbr. articles to profl. jours. Mem. undergrad. edn. com. Arthritis Found., Atlanta, 1979-82, pres., 1983-85, exec. com.; mem. Lupus Found., Shreveport. Lt. comdr. USPHS, 1971-73. Recipient Grand (Student) award Nat. Rsch. Forum, Galveston, 1968, 3rd (Resident) award, 1970, Multipurpose Arthritis Ctr. award NIH, Bethesda, md., 1977, Ctr. of Excellence-Arthritis award State of La., Baton Rouge, 1990—. Fellow Am. Coll. Rheumatology; mem. Am. Assn. Immunologists, Soc. for Leukocyte Biology, Internat. Soc. for Immunopharmacology, Clin. Immunology Soc. Office: La State U Health Scis Ctr PO Box 33932 1501 Kings Hwy Shreveport LA 71103-4228

WOLF, ROBERT IRWIN, psychoanalyst, art therapist, art therapy educator, sculptor, photographer; b. N.Y.C., Mar. 30, 1947; s. Arthur and Bernice (Rosenwasser) W.; children: Joshua Corey, Rebecca Melissa. B Indsl. Design, Pratt Inst., 1968, M Profl. Studies, 1973. Cert. Am. Bds. for Cert. and Accreditation in Psychoanalysis. Clin. dir. Henry Street Settlement Sch., N.Y.C., 1973-80; prof. art and art therapy Coll. of New Rochelle (N.Y.) Grad. Sch., 1980—. Pvt. practice psychoanalysis, art therapy and supervision, N.Y.C., 1974—; dir. Inst. for Expressive Analysis, N.Y.C., 1993-96; vis. prof. art Pratt Inst., Bklyn., 1976—; keynote speaker Delaware Valley Art Therapy Assn., 1979; guest lectr. Ill. Art Therapy Assn., 1980. Contbr. articles to profl. jours., chpt. to book; exhibited sculptures in numerous galleries throughout U.S. Recipient lst place sculpture award Ariel Gallery, N.Y.C., 1989. Mem. Nat. Psychol. Assn. for Psychoanalysis (sr.), Nat. Assn. for Advancement Psychoanalysis (cert.), Coun. Psychoanalytic Psychotherapists, Am. Art Therapy Assn. (registered, contbg. editor Art Therapy 1985—, workshop presenter 1970—), N.Y. Art Therapy Assn. (pres. 1975-76), Westchester Art Therapy Assn. (assoc.). Avocations: downhill skiing, jogging, snorkeling. Office: Coll New Rochelle Grad Art Programs New Rochelle NY 10801 also: 162 W 56th St Ste 502 New York NY 10019 E-mail: rwolf27102@aol.com.

WOLF, ROBERT B. lawyer; b. Phila., Aug. 18, 1914; s. Morris and Pauline (Binswanger) W.; children— Edwin David, Virginia. BA, Haverford Coll., 1936; LL.B., Harvard, 1939. Bar: Pa. 1939. Ptnr. Wolf, Block, Schorr & Solis-Cohen, 1940-43, 46-56, 57-85, of counsel, 1985—; gen. counsel FHA, Washington, 1956-57. Instr. humanities Haverford Coll., 1948-49, 71-72. Chmn. mayor's coordinated housing improvement program, Phila., 1951, Phila. Youth Svcs. Coordinating Com., 1978-84; past chmn. Pa. Com. Crime and Delinquency; mem. juvenile adv. com. Pa. Commn. on Crime and Delinquency, 1976-86; ct. master Phila. Youth Study Ctr., 1989-91; trustee Benjamin Franklin Found., Berlin, Germany, 1955-56 request Dept. State. Mem. Am., Pa., Phila. bar assns., Phi Beta Kappa. Home: 2101 Harts Ln Conshohocken PA 19428-2416 Office: Wolf Block Schorr & Solis-Cohen 1650 Arch St Fl 20 Philadelphia PA 19103-2029

WOLF, ROBERT CHARLES, writer, news correspondent; b. Storm Lake, Iowa, Feb. 27, 1955; s. Dennis Joseph and Loretta Carmel (Mackey) W. Animal caretaker, 1973-91; newspaper corr., 1993—. Author: Fossils of Iowa, 1983, Iowa's State Parks, 1991. Republican. Roman Catholic. Avocations: paleontology, photography, traveling in Iowa region. Home and Office: 3521 10th Ave N Fort Dodge IA 50501-2910

WOLF, ROBERT FARKAS, systems and avionics company executive, environmental planning consultant; b. N.Y.C., Feb. 19, 1932; s. Desidar Farkas and Christina (Hodosy) Wolf; m. Victoire M. Cullerot, Oct. 8, 1960. BS in Liberal Studies, SUNY, Albany, 1981; MBA in Econs., Rivier Coll., Nashua, N.H., 1987. Engring. designer Mpls. Honeywell Co., Manchester, N.H., 1956-63; design engr. Sanders Assocs., Nashua, 1963-79; systems analyst Kollsman Instruments Co., Merrimack, N.H., 1979-97; ret., 1997. Bd. dirs. Webster House Children's Home, Manchester, 1975-80; chmn. Mt Vernon (N.H.) Planning Bd., 1981—, N.H. Regional Planning Commn., Nashua, 1984—; mem. Solid Waste Mgmt. Bd. Mem. Nat. Assn. Regional Couns., N.H. Planners Assn. Republican. Home: 15 S Main St Mont Vernon NH 03057-1621 Office: Kollsman Co 220 Daniel Webster Hwy Merrimack NH 03054-4837

WOLF, ROBERT THOMAS, lawyer; b. N.Y.C., Apr. 14, 1936; s. Simon and Rose (Salzhauer) W.; divorced; l child, Lisa Eve. BS in Econs., U. Pa., 1955; LLB, Bklyn. Law Sch., 1963. Bar: N.Y. 1964. Asst. corp. counsel City of N.Y., 1970-80; ptnr. Weinberger & Wolf, Bronx, N.Y., 1980-83, Weinberger, Wolf, Rodrigues & Malach, Bronx, 1983-87, Weinberger, Wolf & Malach, Bronx, 1987-88, Wolf & Malach, Bronx, 1988-90; sole practice, 1990—. With U.S. Army, 1957-59. Mem. N.Y. State Bar Assn., Bronx County Bar Assn., Assn. Trial Lawyers Am., N.Y. State Trial Lawyers Assn. Avocations: sports, reading, swimming, Spanish literature and conversation.

WOLF, ROSALIE JOYCE, financial executive; b. Southampton, N.Y., May 8, 1941; d. Saul and Anne Wolf; m. Milton Stern, May 15, 1979; 1 child Dina G Pruzansky. AB, Wellesley Coll., 1961; MA in Math, Northwestern U., 1962. With Mobil Oil Corp., N.Y.C., 1962-77, asst. treas. internat., to 1977; v.p. venture capital group Donaldson, Lufkin, Jenrette, N.Y.C., 1977-79; asst. corp. contr. Internat. Paper Co., 1979—, treas., 1981-86; prin., chief fin. officer Aldrich, Eastman & Waltch Inc., Boston, 1986-89; mng. dir. pvt. equity Merchant Banking Group, Bankers Trust Co., N.Y.C., 1989-93; treas., chief investment officer The Rockefeller Found., 1994-2000; mng. dir. Laurel Mgmt. Co. LLC (now Offit Hall Capital Mgmt. LLC), 2001—. Dir, mem compensation cont Narragansett Capital Corp, 1983—86; dir Airborne, Inc; trustee TIAA, 1996—, N European Oil Royalty Trust, 2001—; dir Sanford C Bernstein Fund, 2000—. Scholar Durant, Wellesley Col, 1961. Mem.: Social Scis Research Coun (chmn fin comt), Women's Forum, Fin Women's Asn NY, Phi Beta Kappa. E-mail: rwolf@laurelmanagement.com.

WOLF, SHARON ANN, psychotherapist; b. Dallas, May 13, 1951; d. Frank Allan and Ursula (Mohnblatt) W.; 1 child, Allan. BA in Psychology, New Eng. Coll., 1973; MA in Counseling Psychology, Antioch Grad. Sch., 1976; PhD in Clin. Psychology, Union Grad. Sch., 1989. Cert. Mental Health Counselor, 1997. Behavioral spl. ednl. planner Philbrook Children's Learning Ctr., Concord, N.H., 1972; asst. to spl. edn. cons. N.H. Hosp., 1972-73; spl. edn. planner Rochester (N.H.) Child Devel. Ctr., 1973; counseling practicum Morrill Sch., Concord, N.H., 1973, Contoocook Valley Mental Health Ctr., Henniker, 1973-74, counseling psychology intern, 1974-76; lab. instr. New Eng. Coll., 1973; ednl. and guidance counselor asst. Hillsboro (N.H.)-Deering Sch. Dist., 1973-74; pediatric psychology intern parent-infant devel. program Ctrl. N.H. C.M.H. Ctr., Concord, 1986-87; assoc. psychologist Easter Seal Rehab. Ctr., Manchester, N.H., 1976-80, Ctrl. N.H. Community Mental Health Svcs., Concord, 1980-88; intern forensic psychology Concord Dist. Ct., 1987-88; pvt. practice Northfield, N.H., 1988—. Psychol. cons. children and youth program Twin Rivers Counseling Ctr., Franklin, N.H. 1980-83, therapist, 1984-86; therapist Ctrl. N.H. Comm. Mental Health Ctr., 1980-83, Parent-Infant Devel. Program, Concord, N.H., 1983-88. Fellow Am. Orthopsychiat. Assn.; mem. Am. Assn. Suicidology, Am. Assn. Counseling and Devel., New England Coun. on Crime and Delinquency, N.H. Assn. of the Deaf, N.H. Registry of Interpreters for the Deaf. Avocations: rug hooking, music, spending time with son. Office: PO Box 253 Tilton NH 03276-0253

WOLF, STEWART GEORGE, JR. physician, medical educator; b. Balt., Jan. 12, 1914; s. Stewart George and Angeline (Griffing) W.; m. Virginia Danforth, Aug. 1, 1942; children: Stewart George III, Angeline Griffing, Thomas Danforth. Student, Phillips Acad., 1927-31, Yale U., 1931-33; AB, Johns Hopkins U., 1934, MD, 1938; MD (hon.), U. Göteborg, Sweden, 1968. Intern N.Y. Hosp., 1938-39, resident medicine, 1939-42, NRC fellow, 1941-42; rsch. fellow Bellevue Hosp., 1939-42, clin. assoc. vis. neuropsychiatrist, 1946-52; rsch. head injury and motion sickness Harvard neurol. unit Boston City Hosp., 1942-43; asst., then assoc. prof. medicine Cornell U., 1946-52; prof., head dept. medicine U. Okla., 1952-67, Regents prof. medicine, psychiatry and behavioral scis., 1967—, prof. physiology, 1967-69; dir. Marine Biomed. Inst., U. Tex. Med. Br., Galveston, 1969-78, dir. emeritus, 1978—, prof. medicine univ., also prof. internal medicine and physiology med. br., 1970-77; prof. medicine Temple U., Phila., 1977—. V.p. med. affairs St. Luke's Hosp., Bethlehem, Pa., 1977-82; dir. Totts Gap Inst., Bangor, Pa., 1958—; supr. clin. activities Okla. Med. Rsch. Found., 1953-55, head psychosomatic and neuromuscular sect., 1952-67, head neuroscis. sect., 1967-69; adv. com. Space Medicine and Behavioral Scis., NASA, 1960-61; cons. internal medicine VA Hosp., Oklahoma City, 1952-69; cons. (European Office), Paris, Office Internat. Rsch., NIH, 1963-64; mem. edn. and supply panel Nat. Adv. Commn. on Health Manpower, 1966-67; mem. Nat. Adv. Heart Coun., 1961-65, U.S. Phamacopeia Scope Panel on Gastroenterology, Regent Nat. Libr. Medicine, 1965-69; chmn., 1968-69; mem. Nat. Adv. Environ. Health Scis. Coun., 1978-82; exec. v.p. Frontiers Sci. Found., 1967-69; mem. sci. adv. bd. Muscular Dystrophy Assns. Am., Inc., 1974-91, chmn., 1980-89; mem. gastrointestinal drug adv. com. FDA, 1974-77; bd. Internat. Cardiology Fedn.; mem. bd. visitors dept. biology Boston U., 1978-88; mem. vis. com. Ctr. for Social Rsch., Lehigh U., 1980-90; chmn. adv. com. Wood Inst. on History of Medicine, Coll. Physicians, Phila., 1980-90, mem. program com. Coll. Physicians, 1990-91; dir. Inst. for Advanced Studies in Immunology and Aging, 1988—. Author: Human Gastric Function, 1943, The Stomach, 1965, Social Environment and Health, 1981, others; adv. editor Internat. Dictionary Biology and Medicine, 1978—; editor in chief Integrative Physiol & Behavioral Sci.: The Official Jour. of Pavlovian Soc., 1990—. Pres. Okla. City Symphony Soc., 1956-61; mem. Okla. Sch. of Sci. and Math. Found., 1961—. Recipient Disting. Svc. Citation U. Okla., 1968, Dean's award for disting. med. svc., 1992; Horsley Gantt medal Pavlovian Soc., 1987, Hans Selye award Am. Inst. Stress, 1988, Rsch. award Carolinska Inst., Stockholm, 1994, Wilém Laufberger medal Acad. Scis. of Czech Republic, Citation for sci. and humanitarian achievement The J.E. Purkyně Bohemian Med. Assn. Fellow Am. Psychiat. Assn. (disting., trustee 1992—, Hofheimer prize for rsch. 1952); mem. AMA (coun. mental health 1960-64), Am. Soc. Clin. Investigation, Am. Clin. and Climatol. Assn. (pres. 1975-76), Assn. Am. Physicians, Am. Psychosomatic Soc. (pres. 1961-62), Am. Gastroent. Assn. (rsch. award 1943, pres. 1969-70), Am. Heart Assn. (chmn. com. profl. edn., com. internat. program, awards), Romanian Acad. Med. Sci. (hon.), Coll. Physicians Phila., Collegium Internat. Activitas Nervosae Superioris (exec. com. 1992—, pres. 1994), Philos. Soc. Tex., Sigma Xi, Alpha Omega Alpha, Omicron Delta Kappa. Clubs: Cosmos (Washington). Home: 1430 Totts Gap Rd Bangor PA 18013-5632 Office: Totts Med Rsch Labs Bangor PA 18013

WOLF, TRUDY J. FRAASE, music educator, librarian; b. Bismarck, N.D., Sept. 14, 1967; d. Rodger David and Sharleen Janet (Siewert) Fraase; m. Allen Nicholas Wolf; 1 child, Nicholas Sylvester. BS in Music Edn., Dickinson (N.D.) State U., 1990; MMus in Oboe Performance, U Ill., 1992, MS in Music Edn., 1996. Lic. tchr. music K-12, libr., N.D., music K-12, German 7-12, S.D. 6-8 band and choir dir. Rugby (N.D.) Pub. Sch., 1992-93; K-12 music instr. Lehr (N.D.) Pub. Sch., 1996-97; K-12 music instr., libr. Zeeland (N.D.) Pub. Sch., 1993—. Oboist Minot (N.D.) Symphony Orch., 1992-93, Mo. River Cmty. Band, 2000—; choral dir. ELCA Luth. Ch., Rugby, 1992-93; substitute English horn/oboe Bis-Man Symphony Orch., Bismarck, N.D., 1994—; clinician/judge, 1994—. Editor The Chorister, 1997-2001. Mem. Zeeland Econ. Devel. Com., 1997-98, v.p., 1998; dir. Cmty. Women's Chorus, Zeeland, 1997—; v.p. Zeeland Job Devel. Authority, 1998-2001. Mem. Music Educators Nat. Conf., Am. Choral Dirs. Assn. (state jour. editor 1997-2001), Nat. Band Assn., Mu Phi Epsilon (chpt. pres. 1988-90), Lions (chpt. pres. 1998-99). Avocations: gardening, reading, walking, crafts. Office: Zeeland Pub Sch PO Box 2 Zeeland ND 58581-0002

WOLF, WALTER ALAN, computer science educator, biochemist; b. N.Y.C., Mar. 9, 1942; s. Theodore B. and Tasia (Richman) W.; m. Doris Inez Buckley, June 13, 1962; children— Terri-Lynn, Patricia. B.A., Wesleyan U., 1962; M.A., Brandeis U., 1964, Ph.D. in Chemistry, 1967; M.S. in Computer Sci., Rochester Inst. Tech., 1985. Research assoc. MIT, Boston, 1967-70; asst. prof. Colgate U., Hamilton, N.Y., 1970-77; asst prof. Eisenhower Coll., Seneca Falls, N.Y., 1977-80, assoc. prof., 1980-84; asst. prof. computer sci. Rochester Inst. Tech., N.Y., 1984— . Author profl. papers, also articles. Feature editor Jour. Chem. Edn., 1972— . Grantee NSF, 1972, 74, 80— , Research Corp., 1972. Mem. Am. Chem. Soc. (dist. bd. dirs. 1984—), AAAS, Assn. Computing Machinery, Sigma Xi. Avocations: science fiction; community theatre. Home: 1229 Birdsey Rd Waterloo NY 13165-8458 Office: Rochester Inst Tech Dept Computer Sci Rochester NY 14623

WOLF, WAYNE HENDRIX, electrical engineering educator; b. Washington, Aug. 12, 1958; s. Jesse David and Carolyn Josephine (Cunningham) W.; m. Nancy Jane Porter, Aug. 12, 1989. BS with distinction, Stanford U., 1980, MS, 1981, PhD, 1984. Lectr. Stanford (Calif.) U., 1984; staff mem. AT&T Bell Labs., Murray Hill, N.J., 1984-89; asst. prof. elec. engring. Princeton (N.J.) U., 1989-95, assoc. prof., 1995-98, prof., 1998—. Program chair First Internat. Workshop Hardware-Software Co-Design, 1991, gen. chair, 1993; program chair Internat. Conf. on Computer Design, 1995. Author: Modern VLSI Design, 1994, Computers as Components, 2000; co-editor: High-Level VLSI Synthesis, 1991; contbg. author: Physical Design Automation of VLSI Systems, 1989. Fellow: IEEE (editor-in-chief Transactions on VLSI Sys. 1999—2000), Assn. Computing Machinery (editor-in-chief Transactions on Embedded Computing Sys. 2001—); mem.: ALM, Tau Beta Pi, Phi Beta Kappa. Avocations: bicycling, photography, films, flying. Office: Princeton U Dept Elec Engring Princeton NJ 08544-0001

WOLF, WERNER PAUL, physicist, educator; b. Vienna, Austria, Apr. 22, 1930; came to U.S., 1963, naturalized, 1977; s. Paul and Wilhelmina Wolf; m. Elizabeth Eliot, Sept. 23, 1954; children: Peter Paul, Mary-Anne Githa. BA, Oxford (Eng.) U., 1951, DPhil, MA, Oxford (Eng.) U., 1954; MA (hon.), Yale U., 1965. Rsch. fellow Harvard U., 1956-57; Fulbright travelling fellow, 1956-57; Imperial Chem. Industries rsch. fellow Oxford U., 1957-59, univ. demonstrator, lectr., 1959-62; lectr. New Coll., 1957-62; faculty Yale U., 1963—2001, prof. physics and applied sci., 1965-76, dir. grad. studies dept. engring. and applied sci., 1973-76, Becton prof., 1976-84, chmn. dept. engring. and applied sci., 1976-81, chmn. council engring., 1981-84, Raymond J. Wean prof. engring. and applied sci., prof. physics, 1984—2002, prof. emeritus, 2002—, dir. undergrad. studies dept. applied physics, 1987-94, dir. grad. studies coun. engring., 1989, chmn. dept. applied physics, 1990-97, chair commn. on econ. status of faculty, 1990-92, dir. ednl. affairs for engring., 1994-99. Cons. Dupont Exptl. Sta., Wilmington, Del., 1957, Hughes Aircraft, Culver City, Calif., 1957, GE Rsch. Lab., Schenectady, N.Y., 1960, Mullard Rsch. Labs., Salfords, England, 1961, IBM, Yorktown Heights, N.Y., 1962-66, Brookhaven Nat. Lab., 1966-80, GE R & D Ctr., Schenectady, 1966-93, U. Bridgeport, 1995-96, Nat. U. Singapore, 1994-96; vis. prof. Technische Hochschule, Munich, Germany, 1969; Sci. Research Council sr. vis. fellow Oxford U., 1980, 84; vis. fellow Corpus Christi Coll., 1984, 87; mem. program com. Conf. Magnetism and Magnetic Materials, 1963, 65, 86, chmn., 1968, mem. adv. com., 1964-65, 70-76, 85-88, chmn., 1972, steering com., 1970-71, conf. gen. chmn., 1971; mem. organizing, program coms. Internat. Congress on Magnetism, 1967, internat. program com., 1978-79, planning com., 1979-85; vis. physicist Brookhaven Nat. Lab., 1966, 68, vis. sr. physicist, 1970, research collaborator, 1972, 74, 75, 77, 80; mem. vis. com. dept. phys./sci. U. Del., 1980, 84, 86; mem. NATO Advanced Study Inst. Program Com., 1983, 85, internat. adv. bd. Yamada Conf. XXV on Magnetic Phase Transitions, 1990; mem. bd. visitors Fairfield U. Sch. Engring., 1996—. Editor: CASE Reports, 1988-90; contbr. papers on magnetic materials and low temperature physics. Named vis. guest fellow, Royal Soc. London, 1987; recipient sr. U.S. scientist award, Alexander von Humboldt Found, 1983, Sheffield Disting. Tchg. award, Yale U. Faculty Engring., 2000. Fellow IEEE (life), Am. Phys. Soc. (edn. com. 1977-80, program dir. Indsl. Grad. Intern Program 1978-79, chmn. fellowship com., Div. Condensed Matter Physics 1981-83); mem. Conn. Acad. Sci. and Engring., Yale Sci. and Engring. Assn. (Meritorious Svc. award 1985). Home: 37 Apple Tree Ln Woodbridge CT 06525-1258 Office: Yale U Dept Applied Physics PO Box 208284 New Haven CT 06520-8284 E-mail: werner.wolf@yale.edu.

WOLF, WILLIAM JOHN, lawyer; b. Grosse Pointe, Mich., 1963; s. John William and Marilyn Ann (Wazny) W.; m. Debra Rae Gibson. BA, Alma Coll., Alma, Mich., 1984; JD, Wake Forest U., Winston-Salem, N.C., 1987. Bar: N.C., Fed. Ct. Atty. Womble Carlyle Sandridge & Rice, Winston-Salem, 1987-90, Nye, Phears & Davis, Durham, 1990-92; ptnr., atty. Nye & Wolf, 1992-93; atty. Bugg & Wolf PA, 1993—. Pres. Durham Young Lawyers, 1995. Mem. N.C. Bar Assn., N.C. Assn. Constrn. (law sect. 1989—), Durham Cty. Bar Assn. Office: Bugg & Wolf 411 Andrews Rd Ste 160 Durham NC 27705-6507

WOLF, WILLIAM MARTIN, computer company executive, consultant; b. Watertown, N.Y., Aug. 29, 1928; s. John and Rose (Emrich) W.; m. Eileen Marie Jolly, Aug. 19, 1952 (div. 1974); children: Rose, Sylvia, William. BS, St. Lawrence U., 1950; MS, U. N.H., 1951; postgrad., U. Pa., 1951-52, MIT, 1952-55. Programmer digital computer lab. MIT, Cambridge, Mass., 1952-54; pres. Wolf R & D Corp., Boston, 1954-69, Wolf Computer Corp., Boston, 1969-76, Planning Systems Internat., Boston, 1976-81, Micro Computer Software Inc., Cambridge, 1981-88, Tech. Acquisition Corp., Boston, 1989-91, Planning Internat., Inc., Boston, 1989-94, Wolfsort Corp., Boston, 1989—; chmn. Wolf & McManus, Brookline, Mass., 1995—; dir., exec. dir. Tech. Capital Network MIT, 1992-94; founder Year 2000 Software Corp., Brookline, Mass., 1996—; co-founder, pres., CEO Eureka.Com, Inc., Rockport, 1999-2000, FocuSystems, Inc., Rockport, 2000—. Co-founder, pres. Assn. Ind. Software Cos., Washington, 1965-67, Design Sci. Inst., Phila., 1969-73, Nat. Coun. Profl. Svc. Firms, Washington, 1970-75; seminar leader MIT Sloan Sch., Cambridge, 1970; co-founder, bd. dirs. Harbor Nat. Bank, Boston. Author computer program; inventor management system, orbit calculator, sorting method; patent method for solving Yr. 2000 problem. Co-founder X-10 Orgn., Boston, 1962; trustee Addison Gilbert Hosp., Gloucester, Mass., 1963; v.p. Young Pres. Orgn., Boston, 1970; overseer Mus. Sci., Boston, 1989-97; mem. Computer Mus. Named Outstanding Young Man in Boston, Jaycees, 1962; recipient Speaker's award Data Processing Mgmt. Assn., 1966. Mem. World Bus. Coun., MIT Club (Alumni award 1991), Forty-Niners.

WOLFART, H.C. linguistics scholar, writer, editor; b. Lindau im Bodensee, Germany, 1943; Grad. (BA equivalent), Albert-Ludwigs-U., Freiburg im Breisgau, Fed. Republic Germany, 1964; MA, Cornell U., 1967, Yale U., 1966, M.Phil., 1967, PhD, 1969. Lectr. U. Alta., Edmonton, Can., 1967-68; asst. prof. U. Man., Winnipeg, 1969-72; assoc. prof. U. Manitoba, Can., 1972-77, prof., head anthropology dept. Can., 1977-78, prof., coord. linguistics program Can., 1978-87, prof., head linguistics dept. Can., 1987-93, Univ. Disting. prof., head linguistics dept. Can., 1993-96, Univ. Disting. prof., Killam rsch. fellow Can., 1996—. Author: Plains Cree: A Grammatical Study, 1973, (with F. Pardo) Computer-Assisted Linguistic Analysis, 1973, (with J.F. Carroll) Meet Cree: A Guide to the Cree Language, 2d edit., 1981, (with D.H. Pentland) Bibliography of Algonquian Linguistics, 1982, (with F. Ahenakew) The Student's Dictionary of Literary Plains Cree, 1998; editor: Essays in Algonquian Bibliography in Honour of V.M. Dechene, 1984; editor and translator: (told by L. Beardy) pisiskiwak kâ-pîkiskwêcik/Talking Animals, 1988, (told by Nêhiyaw/Glecia Bear, co-edited and co-translated with F. Ahenakew) wanisinwak iskwêsisak/Two Little Girls Lost in the Bush, 1991; editor: Linguistic Studies Presented to John L. Finlay, 1991, (told by Nêhiyaw/Glecia Bear and others, co-edited and co-translated with F. Ahenakew) kôhkominawak otâcimowiniwâwa/Our Grandmothers' Lives as Told in their Own Words, 1992, (co-edited and co-translated with F. Ahenakew) kinêhiyâwiwininaw nêhiyawêwin/The Cree Language is Our Identity: The LaRonge Lectures of Sarah Whitecalf, 1993; (told by Emma Minde, co-edited and co-translated with F. Ahenakew) kwayask ê-kî-pê-kiskinowâpahtihicik/Their Example Showed Me the Way: A Cree Woman's Life Shaped by Two Cultures, 1997, (co-edited and co-translated with F. Ahenakew) ana kâ-pimwêwêhahk okakêskihkêmowina/The Counselling Speeches of Jim Kâ-Nîpitêhtêw, 1998; (with F. Ahenakew) They Knew Both Sides of Medicine: Cree Tales of Curing and Cursing (told by Alice Ahenakew 2000); mem. editl. bd. Actes du Congrès des Algonquinistes, 1982-94, Revue canadienne de linguistique, 1983-86; assoc. editor (supplements) Algonquian and Iroquoian Linguistics, 1985-96, 99—; gen. editor Sociètè d'Edition de textes algonquiens, 1985—. Recipient Rh Inst. award in the humanities, 1980; fellow Studienstiftung des deutschen Volkes, 1966-67, Can. Coun./Social Scis. and Humanities Rsch. Coun., 1975-76, 82-83, 86-96. Fellow Philol. Soc., Algonquian Text Soc., Royal Soc. of Can.; mem. Assn. canadienne de linguistique, Societas Linguistica Europaea, Linguistic Assn. Gt. Britain, Linguistic Soc. Am., Soc. for the Study of Indigenous Langs. of the Ams., Soc. for Mesopotamian Studies, Rupert's Land Rsch. Ctr., British Assn. Can. Studies, Oxford Bibliog. Soc., Friends of the Bodleian, Henry Sweet Soc. Office: Linguistics Dept U Manitoba Winnipeg MB Canada R3T 2N2

WOLFBERG, MELVIN DONALD, optometrist, educational administrator, consultant; b. Altoona, Pa., June 24, 1926; s. Max Alex and Claire (Schiffman) Wolfberg; m. Audrey Iris Koch, Apr. 26, 1952; children: Debra Lynn, Michael Alex, Daniel Ben; m. Linda Diane Machesic, Dec. 4, 1979. OD, Pa. Coll. Optometry, Phila., 1951; D of Ocular Sci. (hon.), New England Coll. Optometry, 1989, Ill. Coll. Optometry, 1990; LHD (hon.), Pa. Coll. Optometry, 1998. Lic. optometrist, Pa. Pvt. practice and ptnr. optometric practice, Selinsgrove, Pa., 1951-79; pres. Pa. Coll. Optometry, Phila., 1979-89, chmn. bd., 1976-79; v.p. profl. rels. Bausch and Lomb, Rochester, N.Y., 1991-95; pres. In Vision Inst., Boston, 1991-95; ptnr./dir. Sylvan Learning Ctr., Vero Beach, Fla., 1996—. Cons. to sec. HEW, Washington, 1970-77; dir. Better Vision Inst., N.Y.C., 1960-80. Mem. Selinsgrove City Coun., 1961-62; pres. Selinsgrove Community Chest, 1957; chmn. Optometrists Rep. Nat. Com., 1972, 76; chmn. Nat. Inter-Profl. Health Coun., Washington, 1972-77; dir. Univ. City Sci. Ctr., Phila., 1980-87; adv. com. Coun. Higher Edn., Commonwealth Pa., 1980-89. Served with U.S. Army, 1944-46, ETO. Decorated Purple Heart, Bronze Star, Silver Star; named Man of Yr. Central Pa. Optometric Soc., 1964, Alumnus of Yr. Pa. Coll. Optometry, 1970; recipient Carel C. Koch Meml. medal, 1989. Fellow Am. Acad. Optometry (pres. 1985-86); mem. Pa. Assn. Colls. and Univs. (exec. com. 1982-89, sec.-treas. 1985-88, vice chmn. 1988-89), Pa. Optometric Assn. (pres. 1959-61, Optometrist of Yr.), Am. Optometric Assn. (pres. 1969-70, Disting. Svc. award 1994), Pa. Coll. Optometry Alumni Assn. (pres. 1957), Beta Sigma Kappa.

WOLF-CHASE, GRACE ANNAMARIE, astronomer, astrophysicist; b. N.Y.C., Dec. 12, 1957; d. Franz and Ruth Anna (Schnabel) Wolf; m. Dennis Arthur Chase, Apr. 25, 1994; children: Jaclyn Ruth Chase, Dennis Rolf Chase, Jason Arthur Chase. AB, Cornell U., 1981; PhD, U. Ariz., 1992. Undergrad. rsch./teaching asst. Cornell U., Ithaca, N.Y., 1980-81; grad. rsch./teaching asst. U. Ariz., Tucson, 1981-86; telescope operator Nat. Radio Astronomy Obs., Kitt Peak, 1986-90; instr. astronomy lab. U. Ariz., Tucson, 1990-91; lectr. astronomy U. Nev., Las Vegas, 1993; NRC postdoctoral fellow NASA/Ames Rsch. Ctr., Moffett Field, Calif., 1994-96; Pres.'s postdoctoral fellow U. Calif., Riverside, 1996-98; astronomer Adler Planetarium and Astronomy Mus., 1998—, project dir. Milky Way exhibit gallery; rsch. scientist U. Chgo., 1998—. Pub. lectr. Flandrau Sci. Ctr., U. Ariz., Tucson, 1990-92; lectr. astronomy camp Steward Obs., Tucson, 1991-92; presenter in field. Contbr. articles to sci. jours. and conf. procs. including Astron. Jour., Astrophys. Jour., Astrophys. Jour. Letters, Bull. Am. Aston. Soc., CO: 25 Years of Millimeter-wave Spectroscopy, The Far-Infrared and Submillimetre Universe, Science with the Atacama Large Millimeter Array, Proceedings of 3rd Three-Island Euroconf. on Clusters and Assns., From Darkness to Light: Origin and Early Evolution of Young Stellar Clusters, Infrared and Submillimeter Space Astronomy, Macmillan Space Sci. Reference; invited lectr. Templeton events. Mem. Am. Astron. Soc. Avocations: figure skating, science fiction, swimming, weightlifting, flying. Office: The Adler Planetarium/Astron Mus 1300 S Lake Shore Dr Chicago IL 60605-2403 E-mail: gwolfchase@adlernet.org.

WOLF-DEVINE, CELIA CURTIS, philosophy educator; b. Phila., Sept. 14, 1942; d. Robert Bunsen Wolf and Nancy Anne Brady; m. Philip Edwards Devine, June 28, 1986. BA, Smith Coll., 1964; MA, U. Wis., 1971, PhD in Philosophy, 1984. Instr. Tufts U., Medford, Mass., 1971-72, Simmons Coll., Boston, 1972-73, U. Mass., Boston, 1975, U. San Francisco, 1978-81; asst. prof. Coll. St. Benedict, St. Joseph, Minn., St. Cloud (Minn.) State U., 1986-87; assoc. prof., chair philosophy dept. Stonehill Coll., Easton, Mass., 1987—. Part-time instr. Chapman Coll., St. Marys, Moraga, Calif., Suffolk U., Boston State Coll., 1974-79; invited visitor NEH Summer Seminar on Early Modern Philosophy, Brown U., summer 1988; presenter in field. Author: Descartes on Seeing: Epistemology and Visual Perception, 1993, Diversity and Community in the Academy: Affirmative Action in Faculty Appointments, 1997, Sex and Gender: a Spectrum of Views, 2002 (co-edited with Philip Devine); (chpts. to books) The New Catholics, 1987, Affirmative Action and the University: A Philosophical Inquiry, 1993, The Affirmative Action Debate, 1995, Images of the Human, 1995, The Abortion Controversy, 1994, Social and Personal Ethics, 2d edit., 1997, The Family, Civil Society and the State, 1999, Descartes' Natural Philosophy, 2000, Liberalism at the Crossroads, 2d edit., 2002; contbr. articles to profl. jours. Sec. R.I. br. Nat. Assn. Scholars, 1996—. Grantee Carthage Found., 1995-96, Earhart Found., summer 1996. Mem. Am. Philos. Assn., Am. Cath. Philos. Assn., Soc. Christian Philosophers. Roman Catholic. Home: 41 Hilltop Ave Providence RI 02908-2810 Office: Stonehill Coll Philosophy Dept Washington St North Easton MA 02357-0001 E-mail: cwolfdevine@stonehill.edu.

WOLFE, AL, marketing and advertising consultant; b. Wyo., May 3, 1932; s. Clyde A. and Margaret V. (Joyce) W.; m. F. Carilouise, 1957 (div. 1994); m. Helen S., 1997; children: Kirk, Kelley, Alison. BA in Psychology, U. Wyo., 1958. Product mgr., merchandising mgr. Gen. Mills, Mpls., 1958-62; asst. mktg. dir., v.p., account supr. Compton Advt., Chgo. and N.Y.C., 1963-66; v.p., account supr., exec. v.p., gen. mgr. Wells Rich Greene, N.Y.C., 1967-76; exec. v.p., dir. N.W. Ayer ABH Internat., 1976-81; mng. dir., pres., bd. dirs. DDB Needham Worldwide, Chgo., 1981-87, pres. U.S. Div., 1987-88; pres. Al Wolfe Assocs., Inc., Mktg. and Advt. Cons., Sedona, Ariz., 1989—. Bd. dirs.

Clorox Co., Oakland, Calif. Bd. dirs. U. Wyo. Found., pres., 1993-94; past pres. bd. dirs. U. Wyo. Art Mus.; chmn. Sedona Med. Ctr. Found.; bd. dirs. Sedona Acad.; bd. dirs. Sedona Cultural Park. Recipient Disting. Alumnus award U. Wyo. 1981 Mem. Econ. Club (Chgo.), Sedona 30 Club. Home: 134 Back O Beyond Cir Sedona AZ 86336-6806 Office: Al Wolfe Assocs Inc PO Box 2367 Sedona AZ 86339-2367

WOLFE, ALAN, political science educator, writer; b. Phila., June 10, 1942; s. Leon L. and Jean (Birnbaum) W.; m. Jytte Klausen, Feb. 28, 1982; children: Rebekka, Jan, Andreas. BS, Temple U., 1963; PhD, U. Pa., 1967. Dean grad. faculty New Sch. Social Rsch., N.Y.C., 1990-93; univ. prof. Boston U., 1993-99; dir. ctr. for religion and am. pub. life Boston Coll., Chestnut Hill, Mass., 1999—. Summer seminar leader NEH, 1994-96; advisor State of the Union Address, President Clinton, Washington, 1995. Author: Whose Keeper?, 1989 (C. Wright Mills award 1989), America At Century's End, 1992, The Human Difference, 1993, Marginalized in the Middle, 1996, One Nation, After All, 1998, Moral Freedom, 2001; contbg. editor The Wilson Quar., 1993—, The New Republic, 1994—. Rsch. grantee Russell Sage Found., 1994—, Lilly Endowment, 1998. Office: Boston Coll 24 Quincy Rd Chestnut Hill MA 02467-3937 E-mail: wolfe@bc.edu.

WOLFE, ALLAN, physicist; b. Bklyn., Dec. 19, 1942; s. Isidore Irving and Florence (Rosenfeld) W.; m. Marta Elias Boneta, Dec. 30, 1967; 1 child, Daniel Duchaune. BS, Poly. Inst. Bklyn., 1964; MS, U. N.H., 1969, PhD, 1971. Physics chmn. Nasson Coll., Springvale, Maine, 1973-74; prof. physics N.Y.C. Tech. Coll., Bklyn., 1974—. Physicist, visitor AT&T Bell Labs.-Lucent Techs., Murray Hill, N.J., 1977-97; physics rschr. U. L'Aquila, Italy, 1989, Indian Inst. Sci., Bangalore, 1990, Japan Soc. for Promotion Sci., Tokyo, 1990. Contbr. articles to profl. jours. Avocations: chess, jogging, music, Masonry, Japanese, French and Hebrew langs. Office: NYC Tech Coll 300 Jay St Rm 812N Brooklyn NY 11201-1909 E-mail: awolfe@citytech.cuny.edu.

WOLFE, BARBARA L. economics educator, researcher; b. Phila., Feb. 15, 1943; d. Manfred and Edith (Heimann) Kingshoff; m. Stanley R. Wolfe, Mar. 20, 1965 (div. Mar. 1978); m. Robert H. Haveman, July 29, 1983; children: Jennifer Ann Wolfe, Ari Michael Wolfe. BA, Cornell U., Ithaca, N.Y., 1965; MA, U. Pa., 1971; PhD, U Pa., 1973. Asst. prof. Bryn Mawr (Pa.) Coll., 1973-76; rsch. assoc. Inst. Rsch. on Poverty, Madison, 1976-77, dir., 1994—2000; from asst. prof. to assoc. prof. U. Wis., 1977-88; prof., 1988—. Adj. prof. Australian Nat. U., 2002—; resident scholar NIAS, Wassenear, The Netherlands, 1984-85, 96-97; vis. scholar Russell Sage Found., N.Y., 1991-92. Co-author: Succeeding Generations, 1994; editor: (book) Role of Budgetary Policy in Demographic Transitions, 1994, contbr. articles to profl. jours. Active Commn. on Children with Disabilities, Washington 1994-95, Tech. Adv. Panel Social Security, Washington, 1994-95. Recipient Best Article of Yr. award Rev. Income and Wealth, 1992, Fulbright award Coun. Internat. Exch. of Scholars, 1984. Mem.: Assn. Pub. Policy Mgmt. (policy coun. 2001—, 2001—), Internat. Inst. Pub. Finance (bd. mgmt. 1994—2000, v.p. 2000—), Am. Econ. Assn. (bd. com. 1989—92, exec. bd. 1996—99). Office: U Wis Inst Rsch on Poverty 1180 Observatory Dr Madison WI 53706-1320 E-mail: wolfe@LaFollette.wisc.edu.

WOLFE, BRUCE MCLAREN, surgery educator; b. Oakland, Calif., May 22, 1942; s. Cameron Withgot and Jean (Brown) W.; children: John C., Michael B., Catherine B.; m. Marybeth Masters, Sept. 1, 1997. AB, Stanford U., 1963; MD, St. Louis U., 11967. Diplomate Am. Bd. Surgery. Intern, resident in surgery St. Louis U., 1967-73; rsch. fellow in surgery Harvard U. Med. Sch.-Peter Bent Brigham Hosp., Boston, 1975-77; asst. prof. surgery U. Calif.-Davis Sch. Medicine, Sacramento, 1977-81, assoc. prof., 1981-88, prof., 1988—, chief gastrointestinal surgery svcs., 1986—, dir. Surg. Rsch. Labs., 1982-89, clin. dir. pharm. home infusion svcs., 1990—. Mem. meit rev. bd. for surgery VA, 1986-90. Mem. editl. bd. Jour. Parenteral and Enteral Nutrition, 1978-96, Jour. Metabolism and Nutrition, 1995, Am. Jour. Clin. Nutrition, 1997—; contbr. over 75 articles and abstracts to med. jours., including Am. Jour. Surgery, Annals Surgery, Surg. Forum, Survery, Gynecology and Obstetrics, Lancet, Surgery, Annals Plastic Surgery, Practical Gastroenterology, Jour. Parenteral and Enteral Nutrition, Western Jour. Medicine, Surg. Clinics N.Am., Diagnostic Microbiol. and Infectious Diseases, Am. Jour. Clin. Nutrition, Am. Jour. Vet. Rsch., Jour. Lab. and Clin. Medicine, Nutrition in Clin. Practice, Metabolism, Toxicologic Pathology,, Nutrition in Clin. Practice, Jour. AMA, Life Scis., Surg. Endoscopy, World Jour. Surgery, Jour. Royal Coll. Surgeons Edinburgh, Fedn. Procs., also numerous chpts. to books. Physician Nat. Ski Patrol, Homewood, Calif., 1986—. Lt. comdr. USN, 1973-75. Rsch. grantee NIH, 1979-82, 1985-95, Abbott Labs., 1981, Mead Johnson Labs., 1982-84, 96-87, Nat. Inst. Gen. Med. Scis., 1993-98, Nat. Inst. Diabetes, Digestive and Kidney Diseases, 1990-94, Ethicon Endo-Surgery, 1992-94, Am. Women Surgeons, 1996-97. Mem. ACS, AMA, Am. Coll. Sports Medicine, Am. Inst. Nutrition, Am. Soc. for Cln. Nutrition (com. on subsplty. tng. 1988-91), Am. Soc. for Parenteral and Enteral Nutrition (bd. dirs. 1980-81, 87-96, pres. No. Calif. chpt. 1987-88, mem. exec. com. 1990-95, treas. 1990-92, v.p. 1992-93, pres.-elect 1993-94, pres. 1994-95), Am. Soc. Bariatric Surgery, Am. Surg. Assn., Soc. for Surgery Alimentary Tract, Soc. Am. Gastrointestinal Endoscopic Surgeons (ednl. resources com. 1994—, rsch. com. 1994—), Soc. Univ. Surgeons, Western Surg. Assn., Nat. Assn. Vascular Access Networks (bd. dirs. 1990-92), Nat. Found. for Iletis and Colitis, Pacific Coast Surg. Assn., Pancreas Club, Sacramental Surg. Soc., Sacramento-El Dorado Med. Soc., Sacramento Valley Gut Club, Sigma Xi. Avocations: skiing, bicycling. Office: U Calif-Davis Med Ctr 2221 Stockton Blvd 3d Fl Sacramento CA 95817-2214 Address: 131 Clunie Dr Sacramento CA 95864-6965 Fax: 916-734-3951. E-mail: bmwolfe@ucdavis.edu.

WOLFE, BURTON H. non-profit organization executive; b. Washington, Sept. 2, 1932; s. Simon and Gertrude (Hinkle) W.; m. Sandra Sue Smith, Jan. 22, 1962 (div. Nov. 1968); children: James Burton, Brendan Simon. BA, George Washington U., 1954. Reporter/editor Stars & Stripes, Darmstadt, Germany, 1955-56; reporter/feature writer Burlington (Vt.) Free Press, 1956-57, Internat. News Svc., San Francisco, 1957-58; editor/pub. The Californian, 1960-62; pub. rels. writer B'nai B'rith, Washington, 1963; pub. editor AFSCME, AFL-CIO, 1964-65; writer/editor Civic Edn. Svc., 1965-66; founder, dir. Homosapiens Ednl. and Legal Project, San Francisco, 1986—. Lectr. in field. Author: The Hippies, 1968, Hitler and the Nazis, 1970, The Devil and Dr. Noxin, 1973, Pileup on Death Row, 1973, The Devil's Avenger: A Biography of Anton Szandor Lavey, 1974 Sgt. U.S. Army, 1954-56. Recipient Newswriting award AP, 1956-57, Journalism award Cath. Press Assn., 1960, 70, Writing award Bar Assn. Calif., 1975. Mem. Am. Legion, Elks, Phi Beta Kappa. Avocations: working out, programming music tapes. Office: HELP PO Box 642836 San Francisco CA 94164-2836

WOLFE, CHRISTOPHER, political science educator; b. Boston, Mar. 11, 1949; s. Walter Brewster and Margaret Mary (Conway) W.; m. Anne, June 17, 1973; children: Julia, Jared, Rebecca, Thomas, Stephen, Trevor, Patrice, Elena, Marisa, Alex. BA, U. Notre Dame, 1971; PhD, Boston Coll., 1978. Instr. Assumption Coll., 1975-78; asst. prof. Marquette U., Milw., 1978-85, assoc. prof., 1985-92, prof., 1992—. Author: The Rise of Modern Judicial Review, 1986 (Benchmark Book of the Year 1998), Essays on Faith and Liberal Democracy, 1987, Judicial Activism Bulwark of Freedom or Precarious Security, 1991, How to Interpret the Constitution, 1996; editor: Liberalism at the Crossroads, 1994, The Family, Civil Society, and the State, 1998, Homosexuality and American Public Life, 1999, Natural Law and Public Reason, 2000, Same-Sex Matters, 2000. Earhart Found. Summer fellow Earhart Found., 1995, Nat. Endowment for the Humanities fellow, 1994, Presdl. grantee Randolph Found., 1994, Bradley Found. grante, 2000; named to Templeton Honor Roll, Templeton Found./Intercollegiate Studies Inst. Mem. Am. Pub. Philosophy Inst. (pres. 1989—), Am. Polit. Sci. Assn., The Federalist Soc., Fellowship of Cath. Scholars. Republican. Roman Catholic. Office: Marquette U., Poli. Sci. D. PO Box 1881 Milwaukee WI 53201-1881 E-mail: christopher.wolfe@marquette.edu.

WOLFE, CHRISTOPHER RANDALL, psychologist, researcher, educator; b. Ann Arbor, Mich., Mar. 10, 1959; s. Donald M. and Annette I (Grossman) W. BA in Philos. Analysis, Behavioral Scis., Denison U., 1981; MS in Psychology, U. Bridgeport, 1984; MS in Cognitive Psychology, U. Pitts., 1987, PhD in Cognitive Psychology, 1989. Prof. interdisciplinary studies Miami U., Oxford, Ohio, 1989—, assoc. dept. psychology, 1989—, dir. quantitative reasoning and instrnl. computing, 1989—; tech. editor, dir. assessment and DragonflyNet for project Dragonfly. Dir., creator websites; condr. workshops, presenter in field. Author: Learning and Teaching on the World Wide Web, 2001; contbr. articles and abstracts to profl. jours., chpts. to books; software developer Internet list owner; developer of world wide web; mem. exec. bd. Ctr. for Human Devel., Learning and Teaching. Grantee Miami U., 1990, 92, NSF, 1995, others; recipient awards for website, USA Today, 1997, Eisenhower Nat. Clearinghouse for Sci. and Math., 1997, Microsoft Internet Explorer Home Users website, 1998, Web This Week, 1999. Mem. Am. Psychol. Soc. (charter), Assn. for Integrative Studies, Psychonomic Soc. (assoc.), Soc. for Computers in Psychology (sect., treas.), Soc. for Judgment and Decision Making, Devel. and Tchg., Am. Assn. Advancement of Science Kinetic City Cyber Club (bd. mem.); Ctr. for Learning, Technology & Assessment U. Ariz. (affiliate). Home: 333 W Sycamore St Oxford OH 45056-1134 Office: Miami U Western Coll Program Oxford OH 45056 Fax: (513) 529-5849. E-mail: WolfeCR@MUOhio.edu.

WOLFE, DAVID LOUIS, lawyer; b. Kankakee, Ill., July 24, 1951; s. August Christian and Irma Marie (Nordmeyer) W.; m. Gail Lauret Fritz, Aug. 25, 1972; children: Laura Beth, Brian David, Kaitlin Ann. BS, U. Ill., 1973; JD, U. Mich., 1976. Bar: Ill. 1976, U.S. Dist. Ct. (no. dist.) Ill. 1976. Assoc., Gardner, Carton & Douglas, Chgo., 1976-82, ptnr., 1983—; lectr. estate planning Aid Assn. for Lutherans SMART Program, Chgo., 1980-84; lectr. Ill. Inst. Continuing Legal Edn., Chgo. Bar Assn., Lake Shore Nat. Bank, Ill. State Bar Assn. Contbr. articles to legal publs. Recipient Recognition award Ill. Inst. Continuing Legal Edn., 1981-84. Mem. ABA (sects. on taxation, corp. banking and bus. law 1981—, lectr.), NFL Players Assn. (cert. contract advisor 1983—), NCAA (cert. contract advisor), Chgo. Assn. Commerce and Industry (employee benefit subcom. 1983—), Ill. State Bar Assn. (employee benefits sect. council, 1986-95, recognition award 1983), Phi Kappa Phi, Beta Alpha Psi, Beta Gamma Sigma, Sigma Iota Lambda, Phi Eta Sigma. E-mail: dwolfe@gcd.com. Office: Gardner Carton & Douglas 321 N Clark St Ste 3300 Chicago IL 60610-4720

WOLFE, DEBORAH CANNON PARTRIDGE, government education consultant, educator, clergy; b. Cranford, N.J. d. David Wadsworth and Gertrude (Moody) Cannon; 1 son, H. Roy Partridge. BS, N.J. City Coll.; MA, EdD, Tchrs. Coll., Columbia U.; postgrad., Vassar Coll., U. Pa., Union Theol. Sem., Jewish Sem. Am.; hon. doctorates, Seton Hall U., 1963, Coll. New Rochelle, 1963, Morris Brown U., 1964, Glassboro/Rowan Coll., 1965, Bloomfield Coll., 1988, Monmouth Coll., 1988, William Paterson Coll., 1988; LLD (hon.), Kean Coll., 1981; LHD (hon.), Stockton State Coll., 1982; LLD (hon.), Jersey City State Coll., 1987, Centenary Coll., William Paterson Coll., 1989, Tuskegee U., 1989, Glassboro State Coll., 1985, Tuskegee U., 1989, St. Peter's Coll., 1989, Rider Coll., 1989, Georgian Court Coll., 1990; DSc (hon.), Stevens Inst. Tech., 1991; LLD (hon.), Rutgers U., 1992, Thomas Edison Coll., 1992; DSc, U. Med. and Dentistry N.J., 1989, CUNY, 2001; LHD (hon.) , Queens Coll., 2001. Former prin., tchr. pub. schs., Cranford, also Tuskegee, Ala.; faculty Tuskegee Inst., Grambling Coll., NYU, Fordham U., U. Mich., Tex. Coll., Columbia U.; supervision and adminstrn. curriculum devel., social studies U. Ill., summers; prof. edn., affirmative action officer Queens Coll.; prof. edn. and children's lit. Wayne State U.; edn. chief U.S. Ho. of Reps. Com. on Edn. and Labor, 1962—. Fulbright prof. Am. lit. NYU; U.S. rep. 1st World Conf. on Women in Politics; chair non-govtl. reps. to UN (NGO/DPI exec. com.), 1983—; editl. cons. Macmillan Pub. Co.; cons. Ency. Brit.; adv. bd. Ednl. Testing Svc.; mem. State Bd. Edn., 1964-94; chairperson N.J. Bd. Higher Edn., 1967-94; mem. nat. adv. panel on vocat. edn. HEW; mem. citizen's adv. com. to Bd. Edn., Cranford; mem. Citizen's Adv. Com. on Youth Fitness, Pres.'s Adv. Com. on Youth Fitness, White House Conf. Edn., 1955, White House Conf. Aging, 1960, White House Conf. Civil Rights, 1966, White House Conf. on Children, 1970, Adv. Coun. for Innovations in Edn.; v.p. Nat. Alliance for Safer Cities; cons. Vista Corps, OEO; vis. scholar Princeton Theol. Sem., 1989—; chairperson Human Rels. Coun., N.J., 1994—; vis. prof. U. Ill., U. N.C., Wayne State U.; theologian-in-residence Duke U.; mem. trustee bd. Sci. Svc.; mem. N.J. Commn. on Holocaust Edn., 1996. Contbr. articles to ednl. publs. Bd. dirs. Cranford Welfare Assn., Cmty. Ctr., 1st Bapt. Ch., Cranford Cmty. Ctr. Migratory Laborers, Hurlock, Md.; trustee Sci. Svc., Seton Hall U., bd. regents; mem. Pub. Broadcasting Authority, N.J. Commn. on Holocaust Edn., 1996—, Tuskegee U. Alumni, 1995; mem. N.J. Conv. of Progressive Baptists, 1995, v.p., 1996—; parliamentarian Progressive nat. Bapt. Conv.; sec. Kappa Delta Pi Ednl. Found.; mem. adv. com. Elizabeth and Arthur Schlesinger Libr., Radcliffe Coll., trustee Edn. Devel. Ctr., 1965—; assoc. min. 1st Bapt. Ch.; chair Human Rels. Commn., Monroe, 1995; v.p., then pres. N.J. Conv. Progressive Bapt., 1996—; parliamentarian Progressive Nat. Baptist Conv.; mem. exec. com. Nat. Coun. Agrl. Rsch., Ext. and Teaching, 1997—; mem. N.J. Holocaust Commn., 1996— Named to, NABSE Hall of Fame; recipient Woman of Yr. award, Delta Beta Zeta, Morgan State Coll., Medal of Honor, DAR, 1990, Disting. Svc. medal, Nat. Top Ladies of Distinction, 1991, Disting. Svc. award, Nat. Assn. State Bds. Edn., 1992, 1994, Disting. Svc. to Edn. award, N.J. Commn. on Status of Women, 1993, Svc. to Children award, N.J. Assn. Sch. Psychologists, 1993, Disting. Medal award, U. Medicine and Dentistry N.J., Union Coll., citation, N.J. State Coun. on Vacat. Edn., 1994, N.J. State Bd. Edn., 1994, Svc. award for 50 Yrs., Cranford Bd. Edn., 1995, Women Who Count award, Zonta Internat., 1996, Minister's Appreciation award, Progressive Nat. Bapt. Conv., 1996, Edn. award, Tuskegee U. Alumni, 1996, Women Who Make a Difference award, Zonta Internat., 1995, Dr. George Washington Carver award, Pa. Acad. Sci., 1998, Lifetime Svc. award, William Patterson U., 1999, Triumph award, N.J. Dept. State, 2001. Mem.: NAACP (Medal of Honor 1994), AAUP, AAUW (nat. edn. chmn.), NCCJ, NEA (life), ASCD (rev. coun.), AAAS (chmn. tchr. edn. com.), LWV, N.J. Conv. of Progressive Bapts. (1st woman elected pres. 1999), Alliance Black Clergywomen (pres.), Nat. Assn. State Univs. and Colls. and Land Grant Colls. (mem. exec. bd. 1996, mem. coun. on agr. ext. and tchg.), Ch. Women United (UN rep., mem. exec. com.), Internat. Platform Assn., Am. Coun. Edn. (mem. commn. fed. rels.), Nat. Soc. Study Edn., Internat. Assn. Childhood Edn., Am. Acad. Polit. and Social Sci., Comparative Edn. Soc., Internat. Reading Assn., Fellowship So. Churchmen, Am. Tchrs. Assn., N.Y. Tchrs. Assn., Nat. Assn. Black Educators (pres.), Nat. Assn. Negro Bus. and Profl. Women (chmn. spkrs. bur., Nat. Achievement award 1958), Nat. Panhellenic Coun. (dir.), Am. Coun. Human Rights (v.p.), Coun. Nat. Orgns. Children and Youth, N.J. Commn. Holocaust Edn., N.J. Holocaust Commn., N.J. Fedn. Colored Women's Clubs, UN Assn.-USA (mem. exec. com.). Home: 4102 Monroe Village Jamesburg NJ 08831 *I feel I am extremely fortunate to have been born into a family where love of God and love of knowledge have been major concerns. The knowledge we have sought has not been 'knowledge for knowledge's sake' but 'knowledge to improve society and the world'. I have always felt that 'God power' linked with 'Brain power' was the greatest force in the world and I knew that in order to achieve such strength one must work diligently and constantly. Because knowledge changes so rapidly this quest for wisdom must be eternal. Hence I hope I'm still learning and growing for education must be involved from 'the womb to the tomb'.*

WOLFE, EDWARD WILLIAM, II, music educator, composer; b. Albuquerque, Sept. 24, 1946; s. Edward William and Mary Ellen (Gabriele) W.; m. Nancy Jean Brown, Aug. 16, 1980. B in Music Edn., U. N.Mex., 1968, MA, 1973. Cert. tchr., N.Mex., Calif. Tchr Grant Jr. High Sch., Albuquerque, 1970-75, Manzano High Sch., Albuquerque, 1974-75, Hoover Mid. Sch., Albuquerque, 1975-77, San Dimas (Calif.) High Sch., 1977-85; instr. music Calif. Poly. State U., Pomona, Calif., 1984; tchr. Bonita High Sch., LaVerne, 1985-89, Lone Hill Mid. Sch. and Feeders, San Dimas, 1989—2001, San Dimas High Sch., 2001—. Tchr. Hummingbird Music Camp, Jemez, N.Mex., 1970-76; cons. BUSD, San Dimas, 1980—; presenter jazz edn. SCSBOA fall conf., 1995. Author: The Language of Music, 1974, rev. 1993; composer Quartet for Horns, 1967, Oboe Sonata, 1967, Trio for Flute, Violin and Horn, 1968, Caverna, 1972, Quintet for Brass, 1993, numerous compositions and jazz arrangements, 1972—. Mem. Task Force on Mid. Sch. Reform, 1990. Recipient award Juvenile Justice Commn. City of San Dimas, 1984, 93; named to BUSD Hall of Fame, 1991. Mem. Music Educators Nat. Conf. (adjudicator 1969-77, 80—, v.p. dist. 7 1972, pres. 1975-76), Calif. Music Educators Assn. (task force on mid. sch. reform 1990, Outstanding Music Edn. cert. 1991), Nat. Assn. Jazz Educators (adjudicator 1980—, treas. N.Mex. chpt. 1972), Calif. Tchrs. Assn., So. Calif. Sch. Band and Orch. Assn., Bonita United Teaching Assn., Phi Mu Alpha. Avocation: model railroader. Home: 817 S Dumaine Ave San Dimas CA 91773-3808 *Personal philosophy: America's children need and deserve the best we can provide in education. They have tried to do what we have demanded of them and by so doing have in many instances forfeited the very thing that is required for their emotional and physical growth. They have missed their childhood along with all its wonder and opportunities for healthy learning. As a muisc educator, I have dedicated my life to the pursuit of educational excellence for my students. To this end I Will continue to try to provide a loving atmosphere for their emotional growth, a challenging course of study for their intellectual stimulation and a promise of success for their all important self image. I'll endeavor to provide the best I can with the hope that after I'm gone, they will do the same.*

WOLFE, ELAINE CLAIRE DAUGHETEE, junior high school educator; b. Indpls., May 29, 1940; d. Arthur and Lois Eleanor (Grieger) D.; m. Steven Roger Allen, June 17, 1962 (dec. Oct. 1969); m. Howard Evans Wolfe, Jan. 30, 1971 (div. Dec. 1981); children: Leah Denise Wolfe-Garcia, Scott Arthur. BS in Biol. Scis., Purdue U., 1962; MA in Vertebrate Zoology, UCLA, 1964; EdS in Curriculum & Instrn./Sch. Admin., Ind. U., 1994, EdD in Sch. Admin./Curriculum & Instrn., 1997. Cert. tchr. Ind., Calif., Pa.; cert. prin., Ind.; cert. supt., Ind. Tchr. biology Canoga Park (Calif.) H.S., 1963-64; instr. biology Purdue U., West Lafayette, Ind., 1964-65; sci. instr. Tex. Christian U., Ft. Worth, 1965-66; sci. tchr. Ft. Worth Pub. Schs., 1966-67; tchr. biology Upper Merion H.S., King of Prussia, Pa., 1967-71, Fulton Jr. H.S., Indpls., 1982; tchr. sci. and chair sci. dept. Guion Creek Mid. Sch., 1982—. Free-lance artist, 1971—; evaluator N.Ctrl. Assn. visitation teams, 1986, 90; cons. in field. Contbr. articles and poetry to profl. jours.; exhibitor Ctr. for Creative Arts Gallery, Indpls., Rocky Mills Art Gallery, Indpls., Indpls. Art Mus. Mem. adv. bd. Pike Outdoor Classroom, Indpls., 1995—; mem. Project 2061 Benchmarks Sci. Com., State of Ind., 1995; piano accompanist Guion Creek Mid. Sch., 1982-90; mem. Guion Creek Mid. Sch. PTA, 1982—; active Am. Bapt. Women, 1981—. Named Tchr. of the Yr., Met. Sch. Dist. of Pike Twp., 1991; recipient Disting. Alumna award for excellence Purdue U. Sch. Sci., 1998, Golden Apple award, 1995; Mt. St. Helens Honors Workshop grantee Nat. Sci. Tchrs. Assn./NSF, 1988, Sigma Xi grantee, 1991, Take Pride in Am. awardee, 1992. Mem. Nat. Sci. Tchrs. Assn., Hoosier Assn. Sci. Tchrs., Nat. Mid. Sch. Assn., Ind. Mid. Sch. Edn. Assn., Purdue U. Alumni Assn., Purdue Assn. of Indpls., Nat. Wildlife and World Wildlife Assn., Nat. Geog. Soc., Nat. Parks Assn., Smithsonian Inst., Kappa Delta Pi, Phi Lambda Theta. Republican. Avocations: gardening, knitting, travel, photography, sewing. Home: 3541 Windham Lake Trace Indianapolis IN 46214-1400 Office: Guion Creek Middle Sch 4401 W 52d St Indianapolis IN 46254 Home Fax: 317-293-9180; Office Fax: 317-298-2794. E-mail: ewolfe@pike.k12.in.us.

WOLFE, ETHYLE RENEE (MRS. COLEMAN HAMILTON BENEDICT), college administrator; b. Burlington, Vt., Mar. 14, 1919; d. Max M. and Rose (Saiger) Wolfe; m. Coleman Hamilton Benedict, Dec. 4, 1954. BA, U. Vt., 1940, MA, 1942; postgrad., Bryn Mawr Coll., 1942—43; PhD, NYU, 1950; LHD (hon.) , CUNY, 1989; LittD (hon.) , Iona Coll., 1989. Tchg. fellow U. Vt., 1940—42; rsch. fellow Latin Bryn Mawr (Pa.) Coll., 1942—43; instr. classics Bklyn. Coll., 1947—49, instr. classical langs., 1949—54, asst. prof., 1954—59, assoc. prof., 1960—68, prof., 1968—, acting chmn. dept. classics and comparative lit., 1962—63, chmn. dept., 1967—72; dean Bklyn. Coll. Sch. Humanities, 1971—78; exec. officer Bklyn. Coll. Humanities Inst., 1980—89; provost and v.p. for acad. affairs Bklyn. Coll., 1982—88, provost emeritus, 1989. Exec. com., chmn. com. on undergrad. affairs, com. on univ.-wide programs CUNY; study group AAAS, 1987—89; dir. Nat. Core Visitors Programs, 1985—89, Fund for Improvement of Postsecondary Edn.-funded Ctr. for Core Studies, 1987—88; co-chair senate report Chancellor's Coll. Prep. Initiative, 1991; exec. com The Liberal Art of Sci.: Agenda for Action. Mem. editl. bd.: Classical World, 1965—71; co-editor: The Am. Classical Rev., 1971—76; contbr. articles to profl. jours. Named Ethyle R. Wolfe Inst. for the Humanities Bklyn. Coll. in her honor, 1989; named to Hall of Honor, U. Vt., 1991, Disting. U. Faculty Sen. Emeritus, CUNY, 1992; recipient Kirby Flower Smith award, 1939, Goethe prize, U. Vt., 1940, Alumni Achievement award, 1985, Presdl. medal, NEH, Charles Frankel prize, 1990; grantee, 1971, 1982—84. Mem.: Am. Soc. Papyrologists, Classical Assn. Atlantic States (exec. com.), Vergilian Soc. Am., Archeol. Inst. Am., Am. Philol. Assn., N.Y. Classical Club (past pres., exec. com.), Phi Beta Kappa (past pres. Rho chpt., pres. 1988—90, Spl. Citation of Honor on Sesquicentennial 1998). Home: 360 W 22nd St New York NY 10011-2600 Office: care Ethyle R Wolfe Inst Humanities Bklyn Coll Bedford Ave # H Brooklyn NY 11222

WOLFE, EVA AGNES, retired educator; b. Stockport, Iowa, Jan. 13, 1910; d. Marion J. and Hattie Florence (Webber) Munson; m. Donald Earl Wolfe, 1937; 1 child, Sharon Dawn. BA, Iowa Wesleyan U., 1951; student, U. Minn., 1928-89, State U. Iowa, 1928, 29, 30. Tchr. rural schs. Van Buren County, Stockport, 1929-30, grade sch. tchr. Keosauqua, Iowa, 1930-37, Pleasant Lawn Consol. Sch., Mt. Pleasant, 1946-50; tchr. home econs., English Danville (Iowa) Consol. High Sch., 1951-60; tchr. home econs. West Burlington (Iowa) Pub. Schs., 1961-74; ret., 1974. Mem. Am. Assn. Ret. Persons. Mem. DAR, AAUW, Henry County Ret. Tchrs. (pres. 1976-78), Daus of Nile, Order of Eastern Star, White Shrine, Alpha Xi Delta. Democrat. Methodist. Avocations: music, reading, sewing, dancing, exercise. Office: c/o Harold Munson 3199 Wheat Blvd Lockridge IA 52635-8054

WOLFE, GARY DONALD, library commissioner, state education official; b. Altoona, Pa., Mar. 19, 1941; s. Donald George and Norma Rosmond (Cooper) W.; m. Mary Susan Olex, Aug. 5, 1967; children: Mark Douglas, Michelle Marie. BS in Elem. Edn., St. Francis Coll., Loretto, Pa., 1970; MLS, U. Pitts., 1972. Libr. clk. Altoona Pub. Libr., 1959-61; acting children's libr. Coyle Free Libr., Chambersburg, Pa., 1961-63; asst. prof. librarianship St. Francis Coll., 1963-75; adminstr. Centre County Libr., Bellefonte, Pa., 1975-89; dir. libr. devel. State Libr. Pa., Harrisburg, 1989-95; dep. sec. edn., commr. for librs. State of Pa., 1995—. Editor: Automated Circulation: A Study, 1981. Sgt. USAR, 1963-69. Recipient Cert. of Merit, Pa. Library Assn., 1986, Disting. Svc. award Pa. Libr. Assn., 1997, Disting. Alumni award St. Francis Coll., 1997. Mem. ALA, Pa. Library Assn. (treas. 1983-85), Pa. Citizens for Better Libraries. Republican. Avocation: reading. Home: 2407 Wicklow Dr Harrisburg PA 17112-9620 Office: State Libr of Pa PO Box 1601 Harrisburg PA 17105-1601*

WOLFE, GARY JOHN, foundation administrator, wildlife biologist; b. Georgetown, Tex., Mar. 29, 1949; s. Ervin Wright and Faye Margaret (Houston) W.; m. Rita May Boulton, Aug. 30, 1980. BS in Biology, BA in Chemistry, U. N.Mex., 1971; MS in Wildlife Biology, Colo. State U., 1974, PhD in Wildlife Biology, 1985. Park ranger Nat. Park Svc., Mt. Rainier Nat. Park, Wash., 1968-71, Big Bend Nat. Park, Tex., 1972; wildlife biologist Vermejo Park Corp., Raton, N.Mex., 1974-81, v.p., gen. mgr., 1981-86; field dir. Rocky Mountain Elk Found., Ft. Collins, Colo., 1986-88, group mgr. field ops. Missoula, Mont., 1988-93, exec. v.p., COO, 1993-97, pres., CEO, 1998—2001; pres. Wildlife Conservation Cons., 2001—. Contbr. articles to prof. jours. Mem. exec. bd. Mont. coun. Boy Scouts Am. Recipient Disting. Svc. award Ducks Unlimited, 1983. Mem. Nat. Wildlife Fedn. (life), Nat. Eagle Scout Assn., The Wildlife Soc. (cert. wildlife biologist, wildlife administr. award N.W. sect. 1991), Trout Unlimited (life), N.Mex. Wildlife Fedn. (life, conservationist of yr. award 1978), Rocky Mountain Elk Found. (life, Sargent Wildlife Stewardship award 1999), Boone and Crockett Club (profl. mem.). Avocations: hunting, fishing, camping, rafting, personal fitness training.

WOLFE, GEORGE CROPPER, retired private school educator, artist, author; b. New Orleans, Sept. 6, 1933; s. Howard Edward and Amaryllis (Brannen) W.; m. Catherine Vasterling, June 2, 1955; children: David, Michael, Philip. BA in Fine Art, La. State U., 1956; MEd, U. New Orleans, 1972, MS in Urban Planning, 1975; postgrad., Tex. Tech U., Junction, 1986-93, Northwestern State U., La. Cert. tchr. art, social studies, La. Elem. tchr. Live Oak Manor Sch., Waggaman, La., 1962-65; tchr. art Isidore Newman Sch., New Orleans, 1965-96; adj. prof. art Northwestern State U., Natchitoches, La., 1997-99; co-owner design studio Wolf Patrol Prodns. Author: (video) Sculpture in Motion, 2000 (Silver Telly award 2001), 3-D Wizardry (also video), Papier Maché Plaster and Foam, 1995; author, pub.

video: Sculpture in Motion, 2000; sculpture projects include New Alexandria (La.) Mus. Art; contbr. articles to profl. jours.; solo exhbn. at Hanchley Gallery/Northwestern State U., 1999; installed two sculpture commns. "Echo Totem" and "Alex the Red" for Alexandria Mus. Art, 1998, "Hands Supporting Hands" for Wesley Found., 1999; outdoor sculpture "Pegasus Transformed" exhibited on Northwestern State U. campus, 1999; lifesize puppets for prodn. of Two by Two, Northwestern State U. Summer Theatre, 1999. Served with USCG, 1956-58. Recipient Telly award for How-to video 3D Wizardry, 1966, how-to video Sculpture in Motion, 2001. Mem. Nat. Art Edn. Assn. (La. Art Educator of Yr. 1990), La. Art Edn. Assn. (pres. 1978-79), Kappa Delta Pi, Phi Delta Kappa (v.p., Rsch. award 1996). Home: 342 Jefferson St Natchitoches LA 71457-4382

WOLFE, GERALDINE, administrator; b. Monticello, Ark., Mar. 29, 1944; d. John Wesley and Hazeline (Daniels) Fisher; 1 child, Arin. BA, Keuka Coll., 1965; MA, Mt. Holyoke Coll., 1967; MSEd, Elmira Coll., 1981; cert. ednl. adminstrn. SUNY-Brockport, 1985; PhD Cornell U., 1988. Tchr. biology and health Corning Sch. Dist., N.Y., 1967-90; asst. prof. SUNY, Plattsburgh, 1990-93; adminstr. Saranac Lake Ctrl. Sch. Dist., 1993-96; asst. supt. Schenectady City Sch. Dist., 1996-99; supt. Catskill (N.Y.) Ctrl. Sch. Dist., 1999—. Mem. Mid. States Evaluation Team, 1985; chmn. bd. trustees Friendship Bapt. Ch., Corning, 1984-90; bd. dirs. Hamilton Hill Arts Ctr., 1996-99, Oslo scholar U. Oslo, 1964, Coop. Ext., Common Ground of Catkill, Workforce Investment Act, Youth Coun., Grene County Collubirative Community Partnership for Youth; Mem. N.Y. State Profl. Health Educators Assn., Women in Ednl. Adminstrn., LWV, Sigma Xi, Sigma Lambda Sigma. Club: Cosmopolitan (officer 1979-81) (Elmira). Mem. allocations com. United Way, 1982-90; mem. edn. com. Planned Parenthood, 1984-90. Mem. NAACP, ASCD, Nat. Assn. Sec. Sch. Prins., Am. Assn. Sch. Adminstrs., Nat. Alliance Black Sch. Educators, N.Y.S. Assn. for Computers and Technologies in Edn., N.Y.S. Assn. Compensatory Educators, N.Y. State Coun. Sch. Supts., Cornell Edn. Soc., Jr. League of Elmira, Rotary Club of Catskill, Capital District Assn. of Women Adminstrs., Delta Kappa Gamma, Phi Delta Kappa. Avocations: tennis; cross countryskiing; travel; piano; reading. Home: 7 Forest Hills Dr Elmira NY 14905-1141 Office: Catskill Ctrl Sch Dist 343 W Main St Catskill NY 12414-1621

WOLFE, GREGORY BAKER, international relations educator; b. L.A., Jan. 27, 1922; s. Harry Norton and Laura May (Baker) W.; m. Mary Ann Nelson, June 15, 1946; children: Gregory Nelson, Laura Ann, Melissa Helene. AB, Reed Coll., 1943; MA, Fletcher Sch. Law and Diplomacy, 1947, PhD, 1961; Dr. honoris causa, U. Autonoma de Guadalajara, Mex., 1984; D.H.L., S.E. Coll. Osteo. Medicine, Miami, Fla., 1985; DHL, U. Tecnologica Equinoccial, Quito, Ecuador, 2000, U. Tecnologica de Santiago, Dominican Republic, 2001. With internat. div. Arthur D. Little, Inc., Cambridge, Mass., 1951-57; dir. Greater Boston Econ. Study Com., 1957-61; dir. Latin Am. program Com. Econ. Devel., 1961-64; dir. intelligence and rsch. for Am. republics State Dept., 1964-68; pres. Portland State U., 1968-74; dean Sch. Internat. Svc. Am. U., Washington, 1975-79; pres. Fla. Internat. U., Miami, 1979-86, prof. internat. rels., 1979—; vis. scholar Cambridge U., Eng., 1986-87; chmn. Ednl. Facility Authority, Dade County, Fla., 1998—. Fed. negotiator Joint Transp. Com. Washington 1962-66 Contbr. articles to profl. jours. Chmn. bd. trustees Internat. Fine Arts Coll., 1993—, U. de Palermo Found., Buenos Aires, 1998—; bd. dirs. Chopin Found. U.S., Inc., 1988-96, Concert Assn. Fla., Inc., 1988—; founding chmn. Brickell Ave. Lit. Soc., 1 988-96. Recipient Fla. Internat. Ctr. award, 1980, Leonard Abess award, 1984, Orden del Merito Civil, King of Spain, 1986, Fulbright lectr., Ecuador, 1989. E-mail: wolfeg@fiu.edu., andes79@hotmail.com.

WOLFE, J. MATTHEW, lawyer; b. Pitts., Mar. 29, 1956; s. James Michael and Mary Evangeline (Andrews) Wolfe; children: James M. Jr., Ross M. BA, U. Pa., 1978; JD, Villanova U., 1981. Bar: Pa. 1981, U.S. Dist. Ct. (ea. dist.) Pa. 1985, U.S. Ct. Appeals (3rd cir.) 1985, U.S. Supreme Ct., 1992, U.S. Dist. Ct. (we. dist.) Pa. 1997. Atty. Cmty. Legal Svcs., Phila., 1981-82; pvt. practice, 1981-82, 89-95, 97-99; asst. counsel Pa. Dept. of Transp., Phila, 1983-86; spl. prosecutor Pa., 1984-86; spl. asst. dist. atty. Berks County, Reading, 1984-86; dep. atty. gen. Commonwealth of Pa., Phila., 1986-89; spl. asst. dist. atty., 1991-92; chief counsel Pa. Dept. Law and Industry, 1995-97; atty. Law Offices of Alice Ballard, 1998—. Gen. counsel Univ. Bus. Machines, Inc., Upper Darby, Pa., 1989-95; instr. Pa. Bar Inst., Harrisburg, 1984; Pa. workers compensation rules com. Pa. Dept. Laor & Industry, 1995-97, Pa. Worker's Compensation Fraud task force, 1996-97. Assoc. editor The Docket newspaper, 1980-81; contbr. articles to The Univ. City Trumpet newspaper, 1981-95. Mem. Spruce Hill Cmty. Assn., Phila, 1980—, bd. dirs., 1982—96, 1999—; mem. sch. bd. task force on Scholastics and Sports Phila., 1986; mem. neighborhood adv. coun. 19th Police Dist., 1987—93; mem. Cedar Park Neighbors, 1986—; vice chmn. Woodland Dist. Phila.Coun. BSA, 1989—91; Ward leader 27th Ward Rep. Com., Phila., 1979—; chmn. Univ. City Rep.Com., 1990—96; eucharistic minister St. Francis de Sales Parish, 2000—; catechist Confraternity Christian Doctrine program, 1995—2002; lector St. Frances De Sales Parish, 1995—; bd. dirs. University City Town Watch, 1983—85. Mem. ABA, Pa. Bar Assn. (mem. com. legal ethics and profl. responsibility 1986-95), Phila. Bar Assn. (mem. com. labor and employment law, instr. 1995), West Phila. C. of C. (bd. dirs. 1989-95, gen. counsel 1993-95, 98—), Pi Sigma Alpha, Phi Delta Theta (editor Phi Oracle newsletter). Roman Catholic. Home: 4256 Regent Sq Philadelphia PA 19104-4439 Office: 1700 Lewis Tower 225 South 15th St Philadelphia PA 19102 E-mail: matthew@wolfe.org.

WOLFE, JAMES RONALD, lawyer; b. Pitts., Dec. 10, 1932; s. James Thaddeus and Helen Matilda (Corey) W.; m. Anne Lisbeth Dahle Eriksen, May 28, 1960 (dec. 1996); children: Ronald, Christopher, Geoffrey; m. Patricia D. Yoder, Oct. 30, 1999. BA summa cum laude, Duquesne U., 1954, DHL (hon.), 1997; LL.B. cum laude, NYU, 1959. Bar: N.Y. 1959. Assoc. Simpson Thacher & Bartlett, N.Y.C., 1959-69, ptnr., 1969-95, counsel, 1996-99. Co-editor: West's McKinney's Forms, Uniform Commercial Code, 1965. Served to 1st lt. U.S. Army, 1955-57. Mem. Assn. Bar City N.Y. Roman Catholic. Home: 500 SE 5th Ave Apt 601 Boca Raton FL 33432-5510 Office: Simpson Thacher & Bartlett 425 Lexington Ave New York NY 10017-3954

WOLFE, JANE, writer; b. Columbus, Ohio, Feb. 26, 1957; d. William Culver and Relna Fay (Kalfs) W.; m. Leon A. Harris, Jr., Sept. 27, 1996; 1 child, Lee Harris III. BA, Denison U., 1980. Soc. editor The Dallas Morning News, 1986-87; pub. The Gold Book of Dallas Soc., 1988-92. Author: The Murchisons: The Rise and Fall of a Texas Dynasty, 1989, Blood Rich: When Oil Billions, High Fashion and Royal Intimacies Are Not Enough, 1993; bus. reporter The N.Y. Times, 1999—. Home: 4300 Saint Johns Dr Dallas TX 75205-4335

WOLFE, JOAN LUEDDERS, non-profit organizations consultant; b. Detroit, May 2, 1929; d. William R. and Mary Lucinda (Deane) Luedders; m. Willard Wolfe, June 26, 1953; children: John Roberts, Peter Harper (dec.). BA in Econ., U. Mich., 1951; D.Public Service (hon.), Western Mich. U., 1973. Founder, chmn. West Mich. Environ. Action Coun., exec. dir., 1971-73; 1st woman mem. Mich. Natural Resources Commn., 1973-82, chair, 1977; bd. dirs. Dyer Ives Found., 1984-88, Mich. Wetlands Found., 1984-88, Mich. League Conservation Voters, 1999—. Author: Making Things Happen: The Guide for Members of Volunteer Organizations, 1981, updated 1991. Pres. Belmont Sch.-Community Club, Newcomers Club Grand Rapids, Grand Rapids Audubon Club, Mich. Pesticide Coun. Named Conservationist of Yr. Mich. United Conservation Club, 1971; inducted Mich. Women's Hall of Fame, 1996; recipient Women of Achievement and Courage award Mich. Women's Found., 1998, Environ. Quality award Mich. Soc. Internal Medicine, 1970, Conservation award Am. Motors Corp., 1973, others. Mem. Nat. Audubon Soc. (nat. bd. dirs. 1982-87).

WOLFE, JOHN THOMAS, quality assurance professional; b. Balt., June 8, 1953; s. Henry Raphael and Patricia Ann (Sweeney) W.; m. Denise Ann Duckworth, June 18, 1978 (dec. June 28, 2001) BS, Towson State Coll., 1975; repair tech., Lincoln Tech. Inst., 1976. Cert. quality engr., cert. mechanical inspector. Night mgr. Towson Park Svc. Ctr., Balt., 1969-76; mgr. Kelly Springfield Svc. Ctr., 1976-80; quality control inspector Nurad, Inc., 1980-89, product conformance system auditor, 1990, quality assurance engr., 1990—; quality assurance mgr. Nurad Tech. Inc., 1990—92, 1998—2001, dir. quality assurance, 1992-97, v.p. quality assurance, 1997-98, facility security officer, 1994—, occupl. safety and environ. officer, 1995-99. Mem. Am. Soc. Quality Control, Triple Nine Soc., I.S.P.E., Intertel, Mensa. Democrat. Roman Catholic. Avocations: archeology, history, science fiction, travel. Home: 825 Wedgewood Rd Baltimore MD 21229-1225 Office: Nurad Tech Inc 3110 Carlins Park Dr Baltimore MD 21215

WOLFE, LINDA, writer; b. N.Y.C., Nov. 15, 1932; d. Harry M. Friedman and Mina Romanoff Kaufman; m. Max Pollack; children: Jessica Wolfe Bernstein. MA, NYU, 1958. Editl. asst. Oxford U. Press, N.Y.C., 1955—60, Partisan Rev., N.Y.C., NY, 1958—60; writer, rschr. Time, Inc., 1960—71; contbg. editor N.Y. Mag., 1971—96; consulting editor Woman Mag. (Conde Nast), 1990—90. Author: (book) Love Me To Death: A Journalist's Memoir of the Hunt for her Friend's Killer, 1998, Double Life: The Shattering Affair Between New York's Chief Judge Sol Wachtler & Socialite Joy Silverman, 1994, Wasted: The Preppie Murder, 1989 (Notable Book of Yr., N.Y. Times, 1989), The Professor and the Prostitute and Other True Tales of Murder and Madness, 1986, Private Practices (a novel), 1981, The Cosmo Report: Women and Sex in the Nineteen-Eighties, 1981, Playing Around: Women and Adultery, 1975, The Cooking of the Caribbean Islands, 1970, The Literary Gourmet, 1962. Recipient Edgar Allan Poe award nominee, Mystery Writers of Am., 1989. Mem.: PEN (exec. bd. dirs. 1994—95), Nat. Book Critics Circle (v.p. 1997—2002). Avocations: 18th-century English dance, travel.

WOLFE, LISA ANN, financial consultant; b. New Kensington, Pa., Sept. 29, 1962; d. Otis Lawrence and Lois Ann (Smouse) Wolfe. BS, Ind. U. Pa., 1983; MBA, Duquesne U., 1992. Fin. mgmt. cons. Allegheny Energy, Greensburg, Pa., 1984-95, Allegheny Power Svc. Corp., N.Y.C., 1995—96, Pitts. Cultural Trust, Greensburg, Pa., 1996—. Mem. Zeta Tau Alpha (v.p. Ind. U. Pa. chpt. 1982-83). Republican. Avocations: crafts, skiing, golf, racquetball. Home: 420 Spring Run Dr Monroeville PA 15146-3385 Office: Allegheny Energy 800 Cabin Hill Dr Greensburg PA 15601-1689

WOLFE, MARY JOAN, physician; b. Pa., May 26, 1949; d. Dermot F. and Jean M. Wolfe; m. Thomas R. Roberts, June 9, 1979; children: Douglas Roberts-Wolfe, Rebecca Roberts-Wolfe. AB in Chemistry, Cornell U., 1971; MD, M.S. Hershey (Pa.) Med. Ctr., 1976. Diplomate Am. Bd. Internal Medicine, Am. Bd. Emergency Medicine. Intern Rochester (N.Y.) Gen. Hosp., 1976-77; resident in internal medicine Westchester County Med. Ctr., Valhalla, N.Y., 1977-79, attending physician emergency dept., 1979-83; practice medicine specializing in internal medicine Ossining, 1986—. Attending physician emergency room No. Westchester Hosp., Mt. Kisco, NY, 1986—89. Mem. ethics com. Phelps Meml. Hosp., 1994-97, mem. bylaws com., 1989-96, chmn., 1996—. Mem. N.Y. Soc. Internal Medicine, Am. Soc. Internal Medicine. Avocations: gardening, camping, swimming, computers, painting. Home: 6 Cecilia Ln Pleasantville NY 10570-1502 Office: 14 Church St Ossining NY 10562-4831 E-mail: robrtswolf@aol.com.

WOLFE, MAURICE RAYMOND, retired museum director, educator; b. Paris (Neuilly), France, Oct. 13, 1924; s. Guy Ellsworth and Genevieve (Plion) W.; m. Warwick Ellen Griffin, Nov. 4, 1955; 1 child, Shavaun. BA, U. Calif. in Sociology, Berkeley, 1948; MA in Sociology, U. Calif., Berkeley, 1952; postgrad. study, U. Paris Sorbonne, 1951; Cert. of Completion Sch. of Edn., U. Calif., Berkeley, 1954, postgrad., 1955. Rsch. asst. dept. of edn. U. Calif., Berkeley, 1949; tchr. of English and history Castlemont H.S., Oakland, Calif., 1954; lectr. in anthropology, philosophy, sociology and edn. U. Md. Overseas, 1956-59; lectr., instr. in philosopy and sociology U. Md., Munich, 1960-62; faculty mem. Merritt Coll., Oakland, Calif., 1962-88, chmn. dept. behavioral scis., 1967-87; dir. and founder Merritt Coll. Anthropology Mus., 1973-88; rsch. assoc. U. Calif. Lowie Mus. of Anthropology, 1985-89. Lectr. Pers. Mgmt. for Execs., U.S. Govt. Sponsored, Berkeley, Calif. 1966-67, San Francisco State U., 1967-68, Calif. State U., Hayward, Dept. Sociology, 1970-71; adj. instr. Monterey Peninsula Coll., 1990, 91, Hartnell Coll., Salinas, Calif., Chapman U., 1992-95, Golden Gate U., 1995-98; adj. prof. Golden Gate U., 1997—. Editor: (jour.) Socioloqus, 1952. Recipient French Govt fellowship, Sorbonne, Paris, 1956; named to list of Great Teachers of Calif., Calif. Assn. Comty. Colls., Santa Barbara, 1984. Home: 33751 E Carmel Valley Rd Carmel Valley CA 93924-9303 E-mail: azal@aol.com.

WOLFE, MELINDA BETH, human resources executive; b. Chgo., July 30, 1956; d. Seymour Louis and Muriel Sharlene (Hyman) W.; m. Kenneth D. Inadomi, Oct. 10, 1987; 1 child, Molly. BA magna cum laude, Wash. U., 1978; MCRP, Harvard U., 1981. Investment banker Merrill Lynch, N.Y., 1981-95, dir. diversity strategy, 1995-96; dir. global recruiting and tng. Credit Suisse First Boston, 1996-99; mng. dir. staffing and devel. Goldman Sachs, N.Y.C., 1999—2001, head office of global leadership and diversity, 2001—. Chair corp. cir. Nat. Coun. for Rsch. on Women, 1999—; mem. coun. of advocates Planned Parenthood, 1995—; mem. leadership cir. Women's Campaign Fund, 1996—97; mem. The Dalton Sch. Coun., 1999—, The Dalton Sch. Bd., 2000—; bd. dirs. Art Sweats Inc., 1995—. Mem. Fin. Womens Assn. Home: 607 W End Ave New York NY 10024-1606 Office: Goldman Sachs 85 Broad St New York NY 10004 E-mail: melinda.wolfe@gs.com.

WOLFE, MILDRED NUNGESTER, artist; b. Celina, Ohio, Aug. 23, 1912; d. Roy Clifford and Augusta Wilhelmina (Hoenie) Nungester; widowed; children: Karl Michael, Elizabeth Hoenie. AB, U. Monte Vallo, 1932; MA, Colo. Coll., 1944. Tchr. Decatur (Ala.) City Schs., 1933-42; tchr. art and art history Millsaps Coll., Jackson, Miss., 1960-70; artist Wolfe Fine Art Studio, 1945—. Artist 4 lithographs of So. scene, 1940s, lithographs displayed in Montgomery Mus. of Art, 1940, Libr. of Congress, London, Warsaw, Coventry, 1944; oil portrait of Eudora Welty, Nat. Portrait Gallery, Washington, 1989; represented in permanent collections at Miss. Mus. of Art, 1995, Huntsville Mus. of Art, 1996, Ga. Mus. of Art, 1996. Recipient 1st prize oil painting, Ala. Art League, Montgomery, 1935, 1st prize watercolor Miss. Art League, Jackson, 1949, award of merit, Grumbacher Internat., Lakeland, Fla., 1952, Visual Arts award Miss. Inst. of Arts and Letters, Jackson, 1989. Mem. Miss. Mus. of Art, Miss. Watercolor Soc. Office: Wolfe Fine Art Studio 4308 Old Canton Rd Jackson MS 39211-5920

WOLFE, RALPH STONER, microbiology educator; b. Windsor, Md., July 18, 1921; s. Marshall Richard and Jennie Naomi (Weybright) W.; m. Gretka Margaret Young, Sept. 9, 1950; children: Daniel Binns, Jon Marshall, Sylvia Suzanne. Mem. faculty U. Ill., Urbana, 1953—, prof. microbiology, 1961—. Cons. USPHS, Nat. Inst. Gen. Med. Scis. Contbr. microbial physiology rsch. papers to profl. jours. Guggenheim fellow, 1961, 75, USPHS spl. postdoctoral fellow, 1967; recipient Pasteur award Ill. Soc. for Microbiology, 1974, Selman A Waksman Award in Microbiology Nat. Acad. of Sciences, 1995, Applied Environ. Microbiology award Procter & Gamble, 1999. Mem. NAS (Selman Waksman award in microbiology 1995), Am. Acad. Arts and Scis., Am. Soc. Microbiology (Carski Disting. Teaching award 1971, Abbott Lifetime Achievement award 1996, hon. mem.), Am. Soc. Biol. Chemists. Office: U Ill Dept Microbiology B103 Chem & Life Scis Bldg 601 S Goodwin Ave Urbana IL 61801-3709

WOLFE, RICHARD PEEL, lawyer; b. Brookhaven, Miss., May 31, 1937; s. Hubert Heuck Wolfe and Nell Lyon Peel; m. Ann Perkins Terrell, Aug. 20, 1960; children: Susan Wolfe Huppman, Emily Wolfe Leigh. AB in History magna cum laude, Princeton U., 1959; JD, Harvard U., 1962; M in Civil Law, Tulane U., 1965. Bar: La. 1963, U.S. Dist. Ct. (ea. dist.) La. 1963, U.S. Ct. Appeals (5th cir.) 1963; cert. tax law specialist. Assoc. Monroe & Lemann, Attys., New Orleans, 1963-68, ptnr., 1968-96, Jones, Walker, Attys., New Orleans, 1997—. Mem. IRS-Tax Lawyers S.W. Regional Liaison Com., 1976-77; presenter in field. Mem. planning com. Tulane Corp. Law Inst., Tulane Law Sch., 1988-2000; bd. dirs. Met. Crime Commn. of New Orleans, 1997-2001, Bur. Govtl. Rsch., 1984-90; trustee La. Nature and Sci. Ctr., 1980-84; chmn. Gallier Ho. Mus. Coun., Tulane U., 1986-88, trustee, 1978-86; mem. com. to nominate alumni trustees Princeton U., 1979-81, chmn., 1981; mem. Audubon Pk. Commn., City of New Orleans, 1971-77; trustee Metairie Pk. Country Day Sch., 1973-77; mem. agy. rels. com. United Way of Greater New Orleans, 1973-75; bd. deacons St. Charles Ave. Presbyn. Ch., 1967-70, 72-75, chmn., 1970. Mem. ABA (corp. stockholder relationships com., sect. taxation 1967-77), La. State Bar Assn. (liaison com. with dist. dir. IRS 1974-80, chmn. sect. on taxation 1975-76, task force on legal practice designation and specialization 1981-83), New Orleans Bar Assn., Boston Club of New Orleans, La. Club, New Orleans Country Club, New Orleans Lawn Tennis Club, Harvard Club (N.Y.C.), Soc. of War of 1812, Phi Beta Kappa. Republican. Presbyterian. Home: 7916 Plum St New Orleans LA 70118 Office: Jones Walker 201 St Charles Ave Ste 5100 New Orleans LA 70170

WOLFE, ROBERT KENNETH, engineering educator; b. Chattanooga, Sept. 5, 1929; s. Robert Earl and Mae Bell (Hicks) W.; m. Mary Chacharonis, Oct. 31, 1959; children: Robert Kenneth Jr., Ann Marie. BSChemE, Ga. Inst. of Tech., 1952, PhD, 1956. Chem. engr. Mallinckrodt Chem. Works, St. Louis, 1955-60; mgr. systems engrng. IBM, Chgo., 1960-68; ops. rsch. mgr. Owens Ill., Toledo, 1968-73; prof. engrng. U. Toledo, 1973-96, prof. emeritus, 1997—. Chair sys. engrng PhD program U. Toledo, 1978-80. Contbr. articles to profl. jours. Mem. AIChE, Inst. Indsl. Engrs., Ops. Rsch. Soc. Am., Inst. Mgmt. Sci., Sigma Xi, Alpha Pi Mu (advisor 1987), Tau Beta Pi (Outstanding Undergrad. Prof. award 1995). Avocations: walking, swimming. Home: 4930 Spring Mill Ct Toledo OH 43615-1143 Office: U Toledo 2801 W Bancroft St Toledo OH 43606-3328

WOLFE, ROGER ALLEN, lawyer; b. Charleston, W.Va., Aug. 25, 1948; s. Jackson Clark and Imogene Ashley Wolfe; children: Matthew, Theresa, Katherine, Rebecca. BA in Psychology, W.Va. U., 1970, JD, 1973. Bar: W.Va. 1970, U.S. Ct. Appeals (4th cir.) 1975, U.S. Supreme Ct. 1979. Law clk. U.S. Dist. Ct., Charleston, 1973-74; mem. Jackson & Kelly, PLLC, 1974—. Mem. W.Va. State Bar (chair employment law com. 1993-2001), Order of the Coif. Avocations: music, gardening, reading, family activities, outdoor activities. Office: Jackson & Kelly PO Box 553 Charleston WV 25322-0553 E-mail: rwolfe@jacksonkelly.com.

WOLFE, SHEILA A. journalist; b. Chgo. d. Leonard M. and Rena (Karn) W. BA, Drake U. Reporter Chgo. Tribune, 1956-73, asst. city editor, 1973-75; day city editor Chgo. Tribune , 1975-79; city editor Chgo. Tribune, 1979-81, met. coordinator, 1981-83, adminstrv. asst. to mng. editor, 1983-2000. Pres. City News Bur. Chgo. 1986-88, 94-96. Recipient Beck award for outstanding profl. performance Chgo. Tribune, 1979; recipient Disting. Service award Drake U., 1982 Mem. Phi Beta Kappa. Home: 71 E Division St Chicago IL 60610-8307 E-mail: chicagoshe@aol.com.

WOLFE, STANLEY, composer, educator; b. N.Y.C., Feb. 7, 1924; s. Bert S. and Dorothy (Sanders) W.; m. Marguerite Wiberg, Aug. 10, 1960; children: Jeffrey, Madeleine. Student, Stetson U., 1946-47, Henry St. Music Sch., 1947-48; BS in Composition, Juilliard Sch. Music, 1952, MS in Composition, 1955. Faculty Juilliard Sch., N.Y.C., 1955—, dir. extension div., 1956-89; adj. prof. music Lincoln Ctr. campus Fordham U., 1969-73; lectr. N.Y. Philharmonic Pre-Concert Series, 1985—. Prin. compositions include King's Heart; dance score, 1956, Canticle for Strings, 1957, Lincoln Square Overture, 1958, Symphony Number 3, 1959, String Quartet, 1961, Symphony Number 4, 1965, Symphony Number 5 (Lincoln Center Commn.), 1970, Symphony Number 6, 1981; Violin Concerto, 1987. Served with AUS, 1943-46. Recipient award Am. Acad. and Inst. Arts and Letters, 1990; Guggenheim fellow in composition, 1957; Nat. Endowment for Arts grantee, 1969, 70, 77 Mem. ASCAP, Am. Music Center, Am. Symphony Orch. League (Alice Ditson award 1961), U.S. Chess Fedn. Home: 32 Ferndale Dr Hastings On Hudson NY 10706

WOLFE, SUZANNE L. artist, art educator; b. Chgo., Feb. 4, 1942; d. John Charles and Rosetta (Goselin) Wolfe; 1 child, Kalu Alexander Wolfe. BA in Anthropology, U. Mich., 1965, BFA, 1968, MFA, 1970. Prof. art U. Hawaii, Honolulu, 1971—. Dir., curator East-West Ceramics Collaboration, Honolulu, 1995, 98, Workshop, 1995, 98. Exhibited in solo shows at Contemporary Mus., Honolulu, 1988; group exhbns. at Bechtold Gallery, Amsterdam, 1992, Duchamp Gallery, Taipei, 1995, Dinnerworks, Louisville, 1993. Mem. Nat. Coun. Edn. in the Ceramic Arts. Office: U Hawaii Art Dept 2535 The Mall Honolulu HI 96822-2233

WOLFE, TOWNSEND DURANT, III, art museum director, curator; b. Hartsville, S.C., Aug. 15, 1935; m. Brooks Gibson Wolfe; children from previous marriage: Juliette Elizabeth, Mary Bryan, Townsend Durant, Zibilla Lee. BFA, Atlanta Art Inst., 1958; MFA, Cranbrook Acad. Art, 1959; postgrad, Harvard Inst. Arts Adminstrn., 1970; DFA (hon.), Memphis Coll. Art, 1996; PhD (hon.) , Montserrat Coll. Art, 2001, Ark. State U., 2002. Instr. Atlanta Art Assn., 1956-59, Memphis Acad. Art, 1959-64, Scarsdale Studio Workshop and Seamen Inst., N.Y.C., 1964-65; dir. Ford Found. Fund for Advancement of Edn. Wooster Community Art Ctr., Danbury, Conn., 1965-68; lectr. art U. Ark., Little Rock, 1969—; dir., chief curator The Ark. Arts Ctr., 1968—. Sec. Ark. Arts Ctr. Found., 1973—; pres. Ark. Consortium Arts, 1976-80; pres. Ark. Arts in Edn. Adv. Coun., 1977-79; bd. dirs. Mid-Am. Arts Alliance, 1982-89; mem. adv. bd. Ark. Artists Registry, 1986—, Ark. Repertory Theatre, 1976-84; reviewer Inst. Mus. Svcs., 1984-87, examiner mus. assessment program, 1985-87; overview panel Nat. Endowment for Arts, 1986-88, rev. panel utilization of mus. resources, 1986, grant rev. panel conservation and collection maintenance, 1987; curator 20th Century Am. Sculpture Exhbn., First Ladies' Garden, The White House, 1995, Powerful Expressions: Recent American Drawings Nat. Acad. Design, N.Y., 1996. One-man shows include Madison Gallery, N.Y.C., 1961, U. Miss., 1963, Soutwestern U., Memphis, 1964, Ark. State U., Jonesboro, 1964, 70; group shows include Ball State Tchrs. Coll., Muncie, Ind., 1959, 63,65, 67, Ann. New Eng. Exhbn., 1966-67, Wadsworth Atheneum, Hartford, Conn., 1967, Audubon Artists, N.Y.C., 1968; represented in permanent collections Ark. State U., Union Planters Nat. Bank, Memphis, Mint Mus. Art, Charlotte, N.C., East Tenn. State U., others; author: Trustee Handbook, 1978, Appraiser Handbook, 1979, Selections from the Permanent Collection of the Arkansas Arts Center Foundation catalogue, 1983, Twentieth Century American Drawings from the Arkansas Arts Center Foundation Collection, 1984, American Drawings, 1986, National Drawings Invitational, 1986, 87, 88, 91, 92, 93, 94, 96, National Objects Invitational, 1987, 88, 89, 91, National Crafts Invitational, 1987, Picasso: The Classical Years 1917-1925, 1987, Carroll Cloar Arkansas Collections, 1987, Revalations Drawing/America catalogue, 1988, The Face, 1988, 90, American Abstract Drawings, 1989, The Figure, 1990, Will Barnet Drawings: 1930-90, 1991, Silverpoint Etc., 1992, Edward Faiers Retrospective, 1994, exhbn. catalogue Memphis Coll. Art, Paul Zwietnig-Rotterdam, 1995, Hans Burkhardt Drawings: 1932-1989, 1996, Large Drawings and Objects, 1996, various catalog essays. Presdl. appt. Nat. Mus. Svcs. Bd., 1995, Elizabeth Found. for the Arts, 1995, Nat. Coun. on the Arts, 1995. Recipient 20 awards for painting, 1958-68, Winthrop Rockefeller Meml. award, 1973, James R. Short award Southeastern Mus. Conf., 1981, Individual Achievement award Ark. Mus. Assn., 1984, Ark. Art Edn. Advocacy award, 1985, Promethean award for excellence in the arts March of Dimes, 1986, Chevalier dans l'ordre des Arts et Lettres, 1988, Diamond award Ark. chpt. Pub. Rels. Soc. Am., 1996, Dr. Martin Luther King Jr. Cmty. Svc. award, 1996, Disting. Svc. award outside the profession Nat. Art Edn. Assn., 1997, Nat. Humanitarian award NCCJ, 1998, Edwin Hanlon Meml. award Individual Contbrn. to Arts Little Rock Arts & Humanities Promotion Commn., 1998, Creative Spirit award, Black Alumni Pratt Inst., N.Y.C., Bus. and Profl. Leader award, Rotary Club, 1999, Gov.'s Arts Awards Lifetime Achievement award, 2002; 75th Anniversary Paul Harris fellow Rotary Found., 1999. Mem. Assn. Art Mus. Dirs., Assn. Am. Museums (membership com. 1982-88, accreditation com., sr. examiner 1972—). Democrat. Episcopalian. Office: The Ark Arts Ctr MacArthur Park 9th and Commerce Little Rock AR 72202

WOLFE, TRACEY DIANNE, distributing company executive; b. Dallas, June 13, 1951; d. George F. Wolfe and Helen Ruth Cline Lemons; children: Bronson Alan, Travis Aaron. BS in Edn. and Social Sci., Tex. A&M U., Commerce, 1973, MS in Elem. Edn., 1976. Asst. to dir. student devel. East Tex. State U., 1973-74; corp. sec., v.p. Wolfe Distbg. Co. (beer distbrs.), Terrel, Tex., 1974-90, pres., 1990—. Mem. adv. bd. Tex. A&M U. Commerce Coll. Bus. and Tech., 1998—; mem. broadcast adv. bd. Tex. A&M U. Commerce Coll. Bus. and Tech., 1999—. Mem. chancellor's century coun. Tex. A&M U. , 1997—; panel mem. grievance com. State Bar Tex., 1994—2000; vol. CASA Rockwall County, 1996, bd. dirs., 1995—; active Rockwall Leadership Class, 1996—97, Leadership Tex., 2002, mem., 2002; bd. dir., exec. com., chmn. elect Tex. A&M U. Commerce Found.; bd. dir. Friends Terrell Libr., 1995—2001, Rockwall County Child Protective Svcs. Mem. Tex. A&M U.-Commerce Alumni Assn. (bd. dirs. 1992-96), Rotary,

Kappa Delta (nat. province pres. 1980-82). Republican. Methodist. Home: 3316 Lakeside Dr Rockwall TX 75087-5323 Office: 100 Metro Dr Terrell TX 75160-9104 E-mail: tdwolfe@flash.net .

WOLFE, VERDA NELL, pension consultant, financial planner; b. Sulphur Springs, Tex., Jan. 31, 1927; d. Marvin Alvin and Winnie Davis (Bass) Hamiter; m. James Braddy Wolfe, May 3, 1947; children: James Gordon, William Gregory, Charles Gary. Student, Baylor U., 1948-52, Tex. Tech U., 1974-76. CLU, CFP; cert. pension cons. Estate analyst Estate Fin. Planning Svc., Lubbock, Tex., 1973-76, Planning Cons., Lubbock, 1977-81; pres. DDRW Fin. Svcs., 1982-85, Pension Concepts and Administration, Lubbock, 1986—. Mem. Soc. Fin. Svcs. Profls. (chpt. pres. 1988-89), Inst. Cert. Fin. Planners, Am. Soc. Pension Actuaries and Cons. Avocations: music, oil painting, gardening. Home: 2125 57th St Lubbock TX 79412-2625 Office: Pension Concepts & Adminstn 2811A 74th St Lubbock TX 79423-1437 E-mail: vwolfe@door.net.

WOLFE, WILLIAM JEROME, librarian, English language educator; b. Chgo., Feb. 24, 1927; s. Fred Wiley and Helen Dorothea (Lovaas) W.; m. ViviAnn Lundin O'Connell, June 25, 1960 (div. 1962); 1 child, Lund. *Son Lund,U.S. Navy veteran and graduate of the University of Arizona, is a computer programmer. Father Fred Wolfe, World War I U.S. Army veteran, worked in the Railway Mail Service 1920-61 and practiced law in Chicago 1928-63. Grandparents Ludvig Lovaas (cabinetmaker) and Anna Anderson immigrated from Norway in 1888. Grandfather Alfred Wolfe, graduate of Tri-State Normal College, taught school in Kosciusko County, Indiana, 1897-1930. Great-grandfather James Knox Polk Wiley, served in the Union Army Ohio Regiment at the Battle of Shiloh. Great-great-great-grandfather Garret Wolfe served in the Pennsylvania militia during the American Revolution.* AB, U. Chgo., 1948; BA, Roosevelt U., Chgo., 1953; MEd, Chgo. State U., 1963; AA with high honors, Pima C.C., 1992; BA in Art magna cum laude, U. Ariz., 1994. Tchr. English John Marshall High Sch., Chgo., 1956-60; libr. Safford Jr. High Sch., Tucson, 1961-71, Santa Rita High Sch., Tucson, 1971-75, Tucson High Sch., 1975-87. Tutor Eastside Ctr., Literacy Vols. Tucson, 1988-2001, supr., 1993-2001. Co-founder Tucson Classic Guitar Soc., 1969-72; docent U. Ariz. Mus. Art, Tucson, 1989—; mem. adv. bd. U. Ariz. Sch. Music, 1995—; singer U. Ariz. Collegium Musicum, 1981-96, Lane Justus Chorale, 1996-2002; mem. U. Ariz. Scholarship Devel. Adv. Coun., 2000—. With U.S. Army, 1945-46, ETO. Recipient U. Ariz. Alumni Assn. Slonaker award, 2001. Mem. U. Ariz. Pres. Club, Assn. Literary Scholars and Critics, Tucson Guitar Soc. (treas. 2001—), Tucson Post Card Exch. Club, Phi Kappa Phi. Mem. Ch. of Christ Scientist. Avocations: poetry writing, drawing, singing, piano, classical guitar. Home: 8460 E Rosewood St Tucson AZ 85710-1702 E-mail: wjwolfe@earthlink.net. *Through every turn of events, a pleasing composition of life develops from love of family, wise counsel of teachers, inspiration of friends, and thankfulness to the Creator.*

WOLFEN, WERNER F. lawyer; b. Berlin, May 15, 1930; came to U.S., 1939; s. Martin and Ruth Eva (Hamburger) W.; m. Mary Glasier, July 1, 1956; children: Richard, James, Lawrence (dec.). BS, U. Calif., Berkeley, 1950, JD, 1953. Bar: Calif. 1953. Assoc. Irell & Manella, L.A., 1953-57, ptnr., 1957-98, sr. ptnr. emeritus, 1999—; pres. Capri Investment Co. LLC, 1999—. Bd. dirs. BroadCom Corp., Rokenbok Toy Co., Vixel Corp., Sequal Tech. Corp. Bd. govs. UCLA Found., 1992—, L.A. Goal, 1994—, pres., 1994-99 Mem. ABA. Democrat. Jewish. Office: Capri Investment Co LLC 1800 Avenue of the Stars Los Angeles CA 90067-4212 Business E-Mail: wwolfen@irell.com.

WOLFENDEN, RICHARD VANCE, biochemistry educator; b. Oxford, Eng., May 17, 1935; s. John Hulton and Josephine (Vance) W.; m. Anita Gaunitz, June 25, 1965; children: Peter, John. BA, MA, Exeter Coll., Oxford U., Eng., 1958; PhD, Rockefeller Inst., 1964. Asst. prof. chemistry Princeton U., N.J., 1964-70; assoc. prof. biochemistry U. N.C., Chapel Hill, 1970-73, prof. biochemistry, 1973-83, alumni disting. prof., 1983—. Vis. fellow Exeter Coll., Oxford, 1969; vis. prof. U. Montpellier, France, 1976; mem. molecular biology panel NSF, Washington, 1973-76; mem. bio-organic and natural products study sect. NIH, Washington, 1981-86. Mem. editl. bd. Bioorganic Chemistry, 1983—, Biomed. Chem. Letters, 1993—. Fellow AAAS, Am. Acad. Arts and Scis.; mem. NAS, Am. Chem. Soc. (chair biol. divsn. 2000-02), Am. Soc. Biol. Chemists. Democrat. Home: 1307 Mason Farm Rd Chapel Hill NC 27514-4609 Office: U North Carolina Dept Biochemistry Chapel Hill NC 27514

WOLFENSON, AZI U. electrical, mechanical and industrial engineer, consultant; b. Rumania, Aug. 1, 1933; arrived in Peru, 1937; s. Samuel G. and Polea S. (Ulanowski) Wolfenson; m. Rebeca Sterental, Jan. 10, 1983; 1 child Michael Ben ;children from previous marriage: Ida, Jeannette, Ruth, Moises, Alex. Mech., Elec. Engr., U. Nacional de Ingenieria, Peru, 1955; Indsl. Engr., U. Nacional de Ingenieria, 1967; MSc in Indsl. Engring., U. Mich., 1966; PhD in Engring. Mgmt., Pacific Western U., 1983; PhD in Engring. Energy, Century U., 1985; D in Philosophy of Engring. (hon.), World U. Roundtable, Ariz., 1987. Power engr. Peruvian Trading Co., 1956-57; gen. mgr. AMSA ingenieros S.A., 1957-60; prof. U. Nacional de Ingenieria, Peru, 1956-72, dean mech. and elec. engring., 1964-66, dean indsl. engring., 1967-72; dir. SWSA Automotive Parts, Peru, 1954-77; project mgr. Nat. Fin. Corp., Cofide, 1971-73; Peruvian dir. Corporacion Andina de Fomento, CAF, 1971-73; rep. in Peru CAF, 1973-74; pres. DESPRO cons. firm, 1973-76; exec. pres. Electroperu, 1976-80. Cons. engr., 1964—; dir. Tech. Transference Studies, 1971—72. *Among his numerous achievements Azi Wolfenson includes his outstanding executive presidency in Electroperu, while responsible of all the electricity in the country. During his presidency, Peru reached its most important electrical development. When he left Electroperu in 1980, after 5 years, he wrote a best seller book called "El Gran Desafio" (The Big Challenge). It includes not only the history of the electricity in Peru, but also the electrical planning for the next 25 years, and projects that are still in the process of planning and development. For his presidency he received recognition award and distinction from the President of Peru.* Author: (book) Work Communications, 1966, Programmed Learning, 1966, Production Planning and Control, 1968, Transfer of Technology, 1971, National Electrical Development, 1977, Energy and Development, 1979, El Gran Desafio, 1981, Hacia una politica economica alternativa, 1982, The Power of Communications: The Media, 1987; contbr. articles to newspapers and jours. Mem. Nat. Coun. Fgn. Investment and Tech. Transfer, 1972—73, Superior Coun. Electricity, 1964—66; metal mech. expert for andean group, 1970—71; promoter, co-founder, gen. mgr. La Republica Newspaper, Peru, 1981; pres. PROA Project promotion AG, Switzerland, 1982—; chmn. Inst. for the Devel. of the Ams., Inc., Fla., 1993—; co-founder El Popular, 1983, El Nacional, 1985, Todo Sport, 1993, El Chino, 1994, La Reforma, 1997, El Men, 1999, La Razon, 2001; pres. bd. dirs., newspapers; v.p. bd. dirs. Island Way Cmty. Assn., 1995—97; mem. exec. bd. dirs. Miami State Israel Bonds, 1997; mem. consultative coun. Instituto Pervano de Deportes, 1999; mem. consultive coun. Min. Econ. and Fin., 1973—74; councilman at the Concejo Provincial De Lima, 1969—75; pres. Peruvian Jewish Cmty., 1966—70, Peruvian Hebrew Sch., 1976—78. Named Exec., Gente Mag., 1979; recipient Disting. Svc. awards, Order Merit, Peru, 1980, Disting. award, City Coun. Huancayo, 1980, Trujillo, 1978, Huaral, 1979, piura, 1980, Disting. Contbn. award, City of Lima, 1970, 1971, Disting. Contbn. to Elec. Devel. in Peru, 1979, El Sol Radiante, City Hall of Magdalena, Peru, 1995, Recognition award, Israel Govt., 1967, Disting. Comision Integracion Electrica Regional medal, CIER, 1984. Fellow: Brit. Inst. Mgmt., Inst. Prodn. Engrs.; mem.: J.C.C. Fla., AAAS, AIIE (sr.), ASME, MTM Assn., FCL, Asociacion Periodistas Peru, Circulo Periodistas Peru, Swiss sect. PEN Club INternat., Swiss Soc. Writers, United Writers Assn., Assn. Energy Engrs., Am. Nuc. Soc. (vice chmn. 1988, 1990, chmn. Swiss sect. 1991—93, Significant Contbn. to Advancement of Nuc. Sci. award 1995), Inst. Adminstrv. Mgmt., Asociacion Peruana Avance Ciencia, Assn. Mgmt. Sci. (dir. 1968), Am. Inst. Mgmt. Sci., Am. Soc. Engring. Edn., Asociacion Electrotechnica del Peru, Inst. Peruano Ingenieros Mecanicos (pres. 1965—66, v.p. 1967, dir. 1969, 1970, 1976), Colegio Ingenieros Peru, Alumni Assn. Mich., Pacific Western and Century U., Hebraica Club, Club dr 2000. Home: 3781 NE 208th Ter Miami FL 33180-3835 E-mail: aziwolfenson@aol.com.

WOLFF, ALEXANDER NIKOLAUS, writer; b. Wilmington, Del., Feb. 3, 1957; s. Nikolaus Emanuel and Mary Whitney (Neave) W.; m. Vanessa James, June 20, 1998. BA in History cum laude, Princeton U., 1980. Reporter Sports Illustrated, N.Y.C., 1980-81, writer/reporter, 1981-82, staff writer, 1982-85, sr. writer, 1985—; commentator CNNSI.com, Atlanta, 1996—. Basketball commentator Atlanta Olympics, Brit. Broadcasting Corp., London, 1996; mentor-through-the-mail Young Writers Inst., West Hartford, Conn., 1991—; sports ethics fellow Inst. for Internat. Sport, Kingston, R.I., 1992; Ferris prof. journalism Princeton U., 2002. Author: 100 Years of Hoops, 1991, A March for Honor, 1997, Big Game, Small World, 2002; co-author: Raw Recruits, 1990, The In-Your-Face Basketball Book, 1980; mem. editl. com. Princeton Alumni Weekly, 1997-00. Mem. hons. com. Basketball Hall of Fame, Springfield, Mass., 1992-93. Recipient writing awards U.S. Basketball Writers Assn., Pro Basketball Writers Assn., Sports Journalism award Women's Sports Found., Best Sports Stories. Mem. U.S. Basketball Writers Assn. (pres. 1999-00, Hall of Fame), Pro Basketball Writers Assn., Nat. Sportscasters and Sportswriters Assn., Internat. Sports Press Assn. Office: Sports Illustrated 135 W 50th St New York NY 10020-1201

WOLFF, ANTONIO C. physician, educator, bio medical researcher; b. Rio de Janeiro, Brazil, Oct. 17, 1963; m. Jennifer Wolff. MD, Univ. Fed. Rio De Janeiro, Brazil, 1981-86. Asst. prof. med. Emory Univ., Atlanta, 1995-98; asst. prof. onc. Sidney Kimmel Comprehensive Cancer Ctr., Johns Hopkins Univ., Baltimore, Md., 1998—. Asst. prof. onc., THe Johns Hopkins Onc. Ctr., 1998—. Office: Bunting-Blausteon Cancer Rsch. Bldg Rm 189 1650 Orleans St Baltimore MD 21231-1000 E-mail: awolff@jhmi.edu.

WOLFF, BRIAN RICHARD, metal products executive; b. L.A., Dec. 11, 1955; s. Arthur Richard and Dorothy Virginia (Johnson) Wolff; children from previous marriage: Ashley Rachael, Taryn Nicole. BSBA, Calif. State U., Chico, 1980; postgrad., U. Phoenix, 1990—. Registered counseling practitioner Calif.; ordained min. Prog. Universal Life Ch., 1996; registered guidance practitioner Calif. Sales rep. Federated Metals Corp./ASARCO, Long Beach, Calif., 1980-82, dist. sales mgr., 1983-84; sales mgr. Copper Alloys Corp., Beverly Hills, 1982-83; dir. mktg. Federated-Fry Metals/Cookson, Long Beach, Industry and Paramount, 1984-87; regional sales mgr. Colonial Metals Co., L.A., 1987-91; nat. sales mgr. Calif. Metal X/Metal Briquetting Co., 1991-93; sales engr. Ervin Industries, Inc., Ann Arbor, Mich., 1993-95. Tech. sales mgr. GSP Metals & Chems. Co., 1987—91; cons. sales Calif. Metal Exch., L.A., 1987—91, Atlas Pacific, Inc., Bloomington, 1993—. Contbr. poetry to various publs. Mem. citizens adv. com. bus. Calif. Legislature., 1983; bd. dirs. How Hall, Inc., Huntington Beach, 1998—99; bd. trustees Newport Beach (Calif.) Alano Club, 2002—. Mem.: NRA, Soc. Die Cast Engrs., Am. Electroplaters Soc., Steel Structures Painting Coun., Calif. Cast Metals Assn., Am. Foundrymen Soc., Non Ferrous Founders Soc., Newport Beach Alamo Club (bd. dirs.). Republican. Presbyterian. Avocations: scuba diving, tennis, freshwater fishing, trap shooting, hunting.

WOLFF, CATHERINE ELIZABETH, opera company executive; b. Evanston, Ill., June 11, 1957; AB with honors, Vassar Coll., 1979; MA in Performing Arts Mgmt., Am. U., 1982. Adminstrv. asst. Opera Am., 1982-85; artistic adminstr. Pitts. Opera, 1985-94; exec. dir. Del. Symphony Orch., Wilmington, 1994-95; gen. dir. Syracuse (N.Y.) Opera Co., 1996—. Music panelist N.Y. State Coun. Arts, 2000—02. McGuire fellow Vassar Coll., 1979. Mem. Opera Am., Am. Symphony Orch. League, Phi Beta Kappa. Office: Syracuse Opera Co PO Box 1223 Syracuse NY 13201-1223

WOLFF, CHRISTOPH JOHANNES, music historian, educator; b. Solingen, Germany, May 24, 1940; came to U.S., 1970; s. Hans Walter and Annemarie (Halstenbach) W.; m. Barbara Mahrenholz, Aug. 28, 1964; children: Katharina, Dorothea, Stephanie. Ed., U. Berlin, 1960-63, U. Freiburg, Germany, 1963-65; Dr. Phil., U. Erlangen, Germany, 1966; MusD, New Eng. Conservatory, 1999; LHD, Valparaiso U., 2002. Lectr. U. Erlangen, 1966-69; asst. prof. U. Toronto, Ont., Can., 1968-70; assoc. prof. musicology Columbia U., 1970-73, prof., 1973-76; prof. musicology Harvard U., 1976—, William Powell Mason prof., 1985—2002, Adams Univ. prof., 2002—, dept. chmn., 1980-88, 90-91. Vis. prof. Princeton U., 1973, 75; hon. prof. U. Freiburg, Germany, 1990—; acting dir. Harvard U. Libr., 1991—92; dir. Bach Archive, Leipzig, Germany, 2001—; dean Grad. Sch. Arts and Scis., 1992—2000. Author: Der Stile Antico in der Musik J.S. Bachs, 1968, The String Quartets of Haydn, Mozart and Beethoven, 1980, Bach Compendium, 7 vols., 1986—89, Bach: Essays on His Life and Music, 1991, Mozart's Requiem, 1994, The World of Bach Cantatas, 1997, The New Bach Reader, 1998, Johann Sebastian Bach: The Learned Musician, 2000; contbr. articles to profl. jours.; editor: Bach-Jahrbuch, 1974—, critical edits. of music by Scheidt, Buxtehude, Bach, Mozart and Hindemith. Recipient Dent medal Royal Mus. Assn., London, 1978, Humboldt prize, 1996. Fellow: Am. Philos. Soc., Am. Acad. Arts and Scis.; mem.: Gesellschaft fuer Musikforschung, Saxon Acad. of Scis. (Leipzig), Am. Musicol. Soc., Internat. Musicol. Soc. Home: 182 Washington St Belmont MA 02478-3560 Office: Harvard U Dept Music Cambridge MA 02138-5723

WOLFF, CHRISTOPHER See KENDALL, CHRISTOPHER

WOLFF, DEBORAH H(OROWITZ), lawyer; b. Phila., Apr. 6, 1940; d. Samuel and Anne (Manstein) Horowitz; m. Morris H. Wolff, May 15, 1966 (div.); children: Michelle Lynn, Lesley Anne; m. Walter Allan Levy, June 7, 1987. BS, U. Pa., 1962, MS, 1966; postgrad., Sophia U., Tokyo, 1968; JD, Villanova U., 1979, LLM, 1988. Tchr. Overbrook H.S., Phila., 1962-68; homebound tchr. Lower Merior Twp., Mongomery County, 1968-71; asst. dean U. Pa., Phila., 1975-76; law clk. Stassen, Kostos and Mason, 1977-78; assoc. Spencer, Sherr, Moses and Zuckerman, Norristown, Pa., 1980-81; ptnr. Wolff Assocs., Phila., 1981—. Lectr. law and estate planning, Phila., 1980—. Founder Take a Brother Program; bd. dirs. Germantown Jewish Ctr.; h.s. sponsor World Affairs Club, Phila., 1962-68; mem. exec. com., sec. bd. Crime Prevention Assn., Phila., treas., bd. dirs., 1965—; v.p. bd. dirs. U. Pa. Alumnae Bd., Phila., 1965—, pres. bd. dirs., 1993—, v.p. organized classes, bd. crime prevention; chmn. urban conf. Boys Club Am., 1987, treas., 1999; active Hahnaman Brain Tumor Rsch. Bd.; v.p., bd. dirs. Crime Prevention; treas. Assn. of Alumnae Bd. Recipient 3d Ann. Cmty. Svc. award Phila. Mayor's Com. for Women, 1984; named Pa. Heroine of Month, Ladies Home Jour., 1984. Mem. Lions (pres. Germantown Club 1997—). Home and Office: 422 W Mermaid Ln Philadelphia PA 19118-4204 E-mail: debbyw@comcast.net.

WOLFF, DERISH MICHAEL, economist, company executive; b. Boston, May 14, 1935; s. Nathan and Ruth Mae (Derish) W.; m. Maureen Robinson; children: Jeffrey Scott, Hayley Beth Kissel. BA, U. Pa., 1957; MBA, Harvard U., 1959. Fin. analyst Sigmund Werner, Inc., Belleville, NJ, 1959-61; devel. economist Louis Berger, Inc., East Orange, 1961-65, chief economist, 1965-67, v.p., 1968-75, exec. v.p., 1976-82, pres., CEO, 1982—2002, chmn., 2002—. Dir. Louis Berger Internat., Bronkonsult, CHELBI, Ammann & Whitney, Va. Maintenance Svcs., Klohn-Crippen; guest lectr. UN, Fgn. Svc. Inst., Newark Inst. Tech., U. Nev., Harvard U., Rutgers U., U. Denver; mem. Bretton Woods Com., 1987—; lectr. on globalization MIT, 2001-; mem. industry adv. panel (IAP) Dept. of State, 2001—. Mem. editl. bd. Modern Engring. Tech, 1978-80, Nat. Devel.-Modern Govt., 1972-79, Constrn. Bus. Review, 1991—. Mem. adv. com. N.J. Inst. Tech.; class chmn. U. Pa. Ann. Giving, 1975-82, class pres., 1982-92, mem. adv. bd. Huntsman Program of Internat. Studies and Bus., U. Pa., 1997—; mem. U.S. Presdl. Trade Del. to Japan, 1986; mem. indsl. sector adv. com. Dept. of Commerce, 1988-92; mem. adv. com. U.S. Trade and Devel. Program, 1989-92. Mem. Am. Cons. Engrs. Coun. (chair internat. engring. com. 1983-85, vice chair 1986-93), Internat. Engring. and Constrn. Industries Coun. (del. 1986, 87, chmn. 1988-90), Bldg. Futures Coun. (vice chair 1994—), Ctr. for Strategic and Internat. Studies (steering group/GATT negotiations 1989), Phi Beta Kappa. Clubs: Harvard, Penn. Jewish. Office: Louis Berger Group 100 Halsted St East Orange NJ 07018-2699

WOLFF, DIANE PATRICIA, author, journalist, producer; b. N.Y.C., Oct. 12, 1945; d. Irving Mark and Catherine Halkett (Grossman); m. Wallace Gorell (div.). BS, Columbia U., 1968; postgrad., U. Calif., Berkeley, 1977-78, Stanford U., 1978-79; student, Interuniv. Ctr., Tokyo. Prodr. Sta. KRON-TV, San Francisco, 1983-87; prodr. ind. films, 1990-92; prodr. CD-ROM Exec. Prodrs., 1994-96; contbg. editor New Asia Pacific Review, Westport, Conn., 1996-98. Journalist Far Ea. Econ. Rev., Nat. Interest, N.Y. Times, San Francisco Chronicle, others. Author: Chinese Writing: An Introduction, 1975, Ghenghis Khan: A Memoir, 2001, Khubilai Khan: A Memoir, 2001, Gone with the Gator, 2001; project editor: A Sun-Herald Serial Novel. Nat. def. fgn. lang. fellow Columbia U., 1967; recipient Most Notable Book award Am. Libr. Assn., 1975. Mem. Author's Guild, Am. Soc. Journalists & Authors, Assn. For Asian Studies, Asia Soc. Avocations: sailing, swimming, fitness, cooking. Home: 1250 W Marion Ave Apt 143 Punta Gorda FL 33950-5388 E-mail: wuwolff@msn.com.

WOLFF, EDWARD, physician; b. N.Y.C., Apr. 15, 1941; s. Julius and Molly W.; m. Marilyn Alice Pels; children: Shanna, Loryn, Kimberly. BS, Muhlenberg Coll., 1962; MD, Georgetown U., 1966. Intern U. Ala. Hosp., Birmingham, 1966-67; resident N.Y. Med. Coll., N.Y.C., 1967-71; physician pvt. practice, Great Neck, N.Y., 1976—. Attending physician North Shore U. Hosp., Manhasset, NY, St. Francis Hosp. Heart Ctr., Roslyn, NY. Fellow Am. Coll. Physicians; mem. AMA, N.Y. State Med. Soc., NAssau County Med. Soc. Office: 560 Northern Blvd Ste 210 Great Neck NY 11021-3445

WOLFF, EDWARD ALVIN, electronics engineer; b. Chgo., Oct. 31, 1929; s. Samuel S. and Lillian P. W.; m. Anna Lee Tishk, June 19, 1951; children: David Steven, Elliot Marvin, Susan Toby. BSE.E., U. Ill., 1951; MS, 1953; PhD, U. Md., 1961. Electronic scientist Naval Research Lab., Washington, 1951-54; project engr. Md. Electronic Mfg. Corp., Litton Industries, College Park, Md., 1956-59, Electromagnetic Research Corp., College Park, 1959-61; engring. mgr. Aero Geo Astro-Keltec Industries/Aiken Industries, Alexandria, Va., 1961-67; v.p. Geotronics, Inc., Falls Church, 1967-71; supervisory electronics engr. NASA Goddard Space Flight Ctr., Greenbelt, Md., 1971—; system mgr. Network TDRS System, 1981-89, MRJ, Inc., Oakton, Va., 1989-98; cons. in field, 1998—. Instr. Tex. A&M U., 1962 Author: Spacecraft Technology, 1962, Antenna Analysis, 1966, 2d edit., 1988, Geoscience Instrumentation, 1974, Urban Alternatives, 1975, Microwave Engineering and Systems Applications, 1988. Mem. Md. Gov.'s Sci. Resources Adv. Bd., 1963-67; pres. U.S. Environment and Resources Council, 1972-75; treas. World Evironment and Resources Council, 1975-81. Served with U.S. Army, 1954-56. Fellow IEEE (dir. 1971-72), Washington Acad. Scis.; mem. AIAA, Nat. Soc. Profl. Engrs., Eta Kappa Nu, Sigma Tau, Phi Eta Sigma. Home: 16870 Island Cove Dr Apt 130 Jupiter FL 33477-2356 E-mail: ewolff@ieee.org. *Everything I have done has been with the help of others. In return, as I have acquired management responsibilities, a primary objective has been to help others achieve their goals.*

WOLFF, EDWARD NATHAN, economics educator; b. Long Branch, N.J., Apr. 10, 1946; s. Arthur Seymour and Ethel (Kalmenoff) W.; m. Jane Zandra Forman, Nov. 27, 1977; children: Spencer, Ashley. BA, Harvard U., 1968; PhD, Yale U., 1974. Rsch. assoc. Nat. Bur. Econ. Rsch., N.Y.C., 1974-77; asst. prof. NYU, 1974-79, assoc. prof., 1979-84, prof., 1984—; mng. editor Rev. of Income and Wealth, 1987—. Cons. UN, 1981-82, Com. Econ. Devel., N.Y.C., 1981-82, Inst. Rsch. Poverty, Madison, Wis., 1984-88, Inst. Social Rsch., Ann Arbor, Mich., 1982-85, Jerome Levy Econs. Inst., 1989-91, 95-96, Econ. Policy Inst., 1992-95, 20th Century Fund, 1992-93, Aspen Inst., 1993, World Bank, 1994-95. Author: Growth, Accumulation and Unproductive Activity, 1987, Top Heavy: A Study of Increasing Unequality of Wealth in America, 1995; editor: International Comparisons of Household Wealth Distribution, 1987, Research in Economic Inequality, Vol. 4, 1993; co-author: Productivity and American Leadership: The Long View, 1989, Competitiveness, Convergence, and International Specialization, 1993; co-editor: International Perspectives on Profitability and Accumulation, 1992, Poverty and Prosperity in the USA in the Late Twentieth Century, 1993, Convergence of Productivity, 1994; contbr. articles to profl. jours. Grantee NSF, 1984-90, Exxon Found., 1984-88, Fishman-Davidson Ctr. U. Pa., 1987-89, Sloan Found., 1990—, Mellon Found, 1991—. Mem. Am. Econ. Assn., Internat. Assn. Rsch. Income and Wealth (coun. 1987-94), Internat. Inst. Pub. Fin., Internat. Input-Output Assn. (coun. 1995—), European Soc. Population Economists. Avocations: tennis, skiing. Office: NYU Dept Econs 269 Mercer St Rm 700 New York NY 10003-6633

WOLFF, EDWIN RAY, retired construction engineer, consultant; b. Continental, Ohio, Mar. 24, 1933; s. Ray Simeon and Datha Ruth (Donaldson) W.; m. Elizabeth I. Sutterlin, Feb. 16, 1963; children: Sandra Jean, Donald Scott. BSME, U. Toledo, 1969. Registered profl. engr., Ohio. Mem. design staff City of Ft. Lauderdale, Fla., 1965-67; mem. design/spl. orders staff Devilbliss Co., Toledo, 1967-69; engineer, mem. R & D staff Toledo Scale, 1969-70; design/constrn. engr. Lucas County Engr., Toledo, 1970-98, ret., 1998. Cons. G.A.F., Inc., Oregon, Ohio, 1980—. Vol. Spl. Olympics, Lucas County, 1989—; trustee, bd. elders Fairgreen Ch., Toledo, 1975—; trustee Beneficial Union Pittsburg, 1986—; former bd. dirs. Lucas County ARC; bd. dirs. Cmty. Residential Svcs., Inc. With Combat Engrs. Corps, 1956-58. Mem. Phi Kappa Chi, Pi Kappa Alpha. Democrat. Presbyterian. Home: 4312 Grantley Rd Toledo OH 43613-3738

WOLFF, ELEANOR BLUNK, actress; b. Bklyn., July 10, 1931; d. Sol and Bessie (Schultz) Blunk; m. William Howard Wolff, June 19, 1955; children: Ellen Jill, Rebecca Louise. BA in Edn., Speech and Theatre, Bklyn. Coll., 1972, MS in Spl. Edn., 1975; postgrad., Adelphi U., 1980-81. Cert. tchr., N.Y. Fashion model Garment Ctr., N.Y.C., 1949-50; sec. to v.p. out-of-town/export sales Liebmann Breweries Inc., Bklyn., 1950-58; tchr. N.Y.C. Bd. Edn., 1971-76; sec. to dir. environ. programs, pub. affairs officers, speakers bur. project leader Power Authority State of N.Y., N.Y.C., 1976-85; tchr. Hewlett-Woodmere (N.Y.) Sch. Dist., 1986-89; instr. adult edn. County of Nassau, N.Y., 1986-97. Actress/model, N.Y.C., 1992—; mem. Love Creek Prodns. V.P. program devel. for youth ctr. Wavecrest Gardens Community Assn., Far Rockaway, N.Y., 1959-63; teen leader Far Rockaway Jewish Ctr. Youth Coun., 1965-68; pres. Parents Assn. P.S. 215Q, Far Rockaway, 1966-67; tutor N.Y. C. Bd. Edn. Sch. Vol. Program, Far Rockaway, 1969-71; chair civic affairs Dem. Club, Far Rockaway, 1961-63; committeewoman Dem. Ctrl. Com., Queens County, N.Y., 1963-64; v.p. membership, mem. constn. com. Nassau County Dem. Women's Caucus, 1988, 89; awards com. Bklyn. Coll., 1993-97, chair theatre arts affiliate, 1990-94, 2001-; mem. comm. adv. com. Hewlett-Woodmere Sch. Dist. 14, 1996-97; committeewoman Nassau County Dem. Party, 1998—; press/media steward vol. Goodwill Games, 1998. Named Mother of Yr. Congregation Shaaray Tefila, Far Rockaway, 1968; recipient Merit award Wavecrest Gardens Community Assn., 1960, Theater Arts Trophy for disting. svc. Bklyn. Coll. Alumni, 1992. Mem. AFTRA, SAG (awards nominating com. 2000-2001), Actors Equity Assn., Nassau Assn. Cmty. and Continuing Edn., Alumni Assn. Bklyn. Coll. (life). Avocations: painting, piano, gardening. Office: 1344 Broadway Ste 110 Hewlett NY 11557-1353

WOLFF, ELROY HARRIS, lawyer; b. N.Y.C., May 20, 1935; s. Samuel and Rose Marian (Katz) W.; children: Ethan, Anna Louise. AB, Columbia U., 1957, LL.B., 1963. Bar: N.Y. 1963, D.C. 1969. Assoc. Kaye, Scholer, Fierman, Hays & Handler, N.Y.C., 1963-65; atty.-adviser to commr. FTC, Washington, 1965-67; sr. trial atty. Dept. Transp., 1967-69; assoc. Leibman, Williams, Bennett, Baird & Minow, Washington, 1969-70, ptnr., 1970-72, Sidley & Austin, Washington, 1972-99; sr. counsel Sidley Austin Brown & Wood, 2000—. Mem. adv. com. on practice and procedure FTC, 1969-71; chmn. adv. com. on procedural reform CAB, 1975 Served to 1st lt. USAF, 1957-60. Mem. ABA (chmn. spring meeting program 1992-94, coun. 1995-98), Union Internationale des advocats (chmn. competition law com. 1994-98), Army and Navy Club. Office: Sidley Austin Brown & Wood 1501 K St NW Washington DC 20005 E-mail: ewolff@sidley.com.

WOLFF, FRANK PIERCE, JR. lawyer; b. St. Louis, Feb. 27, 1946; s. Frank P. and Beatrice (Stein) W.; m. Susan Scallet, May 11, 1984; children: Elizabeth McLane, Victoria Hancox. BA, Middlebury Coll., 1968; JD, U. Va., 1971. Bar: Mo. 1971, U.S. Ct. Appeals (5th cir.) 1974, U.S. Ct. Appeals (8th cir.) 1975, U.S. Supreme Ct. 1975. Ptnr. Lewis, Rice & Fingersh, St. Louis, 1971—90; ptnr., sect. leader, bus. and transactional counseling sect., mem. oper. group Bryan Cave LLP, 1997—. Bd. dirs. Misco Shawnee, Inc. Bd. dirs. Leadership St. Louis, 1985-88, Washington U. Child Guidance Clinic, St. Louis, 1976-79, Jewish Family and Children's Svc., St. Louis, 1981-83, John Burroughs Sch., 1995-2000, BJC Health Sys., Inc., 1998-2001, The Butterfly House, 2001—; gen. counsel Mo. Bot. Garden, St. Louis, 1981—, Mo. Hist. Soc., St. Louis, 1997—; trustee St. Louis Children's Hosp., 1995-2001, chairperson mission vision and values com., 1996-2001, mem. exec. com., 1997-99; co-chmn. Parks Task Force, 2004 Inc. . Capt. USAR, 1968-76. Mem. ABA, Mo. Bar Assn., Bar Assn. Met. St. Louis (chmn. corp. sect. 1984-85), Noonday Club,

Westwood County Club (chmn. fin. com. 1989-91, treas. 1989-91, v.p. 1991-93, pres. 1994-95, exec. com. 1989-95). Home: 17 Clerbrook Ln Saint Louis MO 63124-1202 Office: Bryan Cave 211 N Broadway Ste 3600 Saint Louis MO 63102-2733

WOLFF, GRACE SUSAN, pediatrician; b. Rome; BS, Le Moyne Coll., 1961; MD, Med. Coll. Wis., 1965. Diplomate Am. Bd. Pediatrics, Pediatric Cardiology. Intern St. Vincents Hosp., N.Y.C., 1965-66; pediat. resident Babies Hosp.-Columbia Presbyn., 1967-69; fellow in pediat. cardiology Childrens Hosp., Boston, 1969-71; pediatrician, pediatric cardiologist U. Miami (Fla.) -Jackson Meml. Hosp., 1977—; chief divsn. pediat. cardiology, 1995—; prof. U. Miami. Mem. Am. Acad. Pediats., Am. Bd. Pediats., NASPE, Am. Acad. Pediat., Am. Coll. Cardiology, Am. Heart Assn. Office: U Miami-Jackson Meml Hosp PO Box 016960-R76 Miami FL 33101

WOLFF, GREGORY STEVEN, insurance company executive; b. Manchester, Conn., Dec. 10, 1951; s. Thomas J. and M. Elizabeth (Grandburg) W.; m. Elizabeth Mae Heppenstall, June 3, 1971; children: Keith J., James T., Kyle M. BA in Edn., U. Conn., 1974. Cert. fin. planner. Insurance salesman Northwestern Mut. Life, Glastonbury, Conn., 1974-76, Wolff-Zackin & Assocs., Inc., Vernon, 1976—2001; chmn. bd. dirs., mng. mem. Wolff-Zackin Fin. LLC, 2001—. Lectr. in field; bd. dirs. Savs. Bank of Manchester, bd. dirs., exec. bd. Ea. Conn. Health Network, exec. bd. dirs. Greater Hartford Hosp. Club. Contbr. articles to profl. jours.; co-author: Financial Need Analysis I, cassette prog. Co-founder Manchester Soccer Camp, 1981. Mem. Nat. Assn. Life Underwriters, Conn. Assn. Life Underwriters, Hartford Assn. Life Underwriters (past pres.), Million Dollar Round Table, Ct. of Table. Methodist. Avocations: tennis, golf, coaching youth sports. Home: 126 Tamarac Dr Glastonbury CT 06033-1941 Office: Wolff-Zackin Fin LLC PO Box H Vernon Rockville CT 06066-1620

WOLFF, HENNING OTTO AUGUST, private public school administrator; b. Berlin, Jan. 9, 1928; s. Gunther E. W. and Andrea Elisabeth (Kühne) W.; m. Lieselotte K. C. Gerlach, Sept. 6, 1958; children: Cord-Michael, Dai-Aniela. Diploma in engring., Tech. U. Munich, Germany, 1954. Cert. in chem. engring. Co-owner Wolff & Co. KGaA, Walsrode, Germany, 1961-65; tech. mgr. Wolff Walsrode AG, 1965-77; mng. owner Henning Wolff GmbH & Co KG, 1989—; mgr. Otto-Kühne-Schule Godesberg GmbH, Bonn, 1980—; mng. ptnr. Paedagogium Godesberg GmbH, 1980—. Fellow Rotary Club; mem. Rotary Internat. (dist. gov. 1986-87). Avocation: golf. Office: Paedagogium Godesberg Otto-Kuhne-Platz 1 53173 Bonn Germany E-mail: hwolff.walsrode@t-online.de.

WOLFF, HERBERT ERIC, banker, former army officer; b. Cologne, Germany, May 24, 1925; s. Hugo and Juanna Anna (Van Dam) W.; m. Alice (Billy) Rafael, Nov. 13, 1946 (dec. July, 1987); children: Karen (dec. Jan., 1992), Herbert E., Allen R. BA, Rutgers U., 1953; BS, U. Md., 1957; MA, George Washington U., 1962; grad., U.S. Army War Coll., 1962, Harvard U., 1979. Commd. 2nd lt. U.S. Army, 1945, advanced through grades to maj. gen.; served in Fed. Republic of Germany, Greece, Iran, Republic of Korea, Australia, New Guinea, The Phillipines, Japan and Socialist Republic of Vietnam; dep. dir. ops. NSA Chief CSS, Ft. Meade, Md., 1973-75; dep. corps. comdr. V. Corps U.S. Army, Frankfurt, Germany, 1975-77, comdr. gen. U.S. Army Western Command Hawaii, 1977-81; with First Hawaiian Bank, Honolulu, 1981-2000, sr. v.p., corp. sec., to 2000; hon. consul gen. (Dató) U.S. Pacific region Govt. of Malaysia, 1985—. Author: The Man on Horseback, 1962, The Tenth Principle of War Public Support, 1964, The Military Instructor, 1968. Exec. bd. Aloha coun. Boy Scouts Am.; bd. dirs. USO, Girl Scouts of U.S., Hawaii; v.p. Hawaii Com. Fgn. Rels.; past pres. Pacific Asian Affairs Coun.; pres. Hawaii Army Mus. Soc. Decorated Bronze Star with V and 3 oak leaf clusters, Air medal (24) U.S. Army, Purple Heart, Gallantry Cross with 2 palms, Gallantry Cross with palm and silver star Nat. Order 5th class South Vietnam, Order Nat. Security Merit Choen-Su S. Korea, D.S.M. with oak leaf clusters (2), Silver Star with oak leaf cluster U.S. Army, Legion of Merit with 3 oak leaf clusters, D.F.C., Combat Infantry Badge with two stars, master parachutist, Army aviator; named Citizen of Yr. Fed. Exec. Bd., 1987. Mem. 1st Inf. Divsn. Assn., 1st Cav. Divsn. Assn., Plaza Club (pres., bd. dirs.), Honolulu Country Club, Waialae Country Club, Rotary, Phi Kappa Phi. Office: First Hawaiian Center 999 Bishop St Honolulu HI 96813-0001 E-mail: generalherbwolff@aol.com. *History is a gift we borrow and hope to pass on. Forget the past and be doomed to repeat it. Remember the past and accept the challenge to convince others.*

WOLFF, HUGH LIPMAN, urologist, educator; b. Apr. 24, 1931; m. Sylvia Musin; children: Stephanie, Timothy, Amy, Jane. BA, U. Iowa, 1952, MD, 1955. Diplomate Am. Bd. Urology. Intern King County Hosp., Seattle, 1955-56; resident in urology Univ. Hosps., Iowa City, 1958-62; pvt. practice San Antonio, 1962-94; v.p. med. affairs Santa Rosa Health Care, 1991-2000. Clin. prof. divsn. urology U. Tex. Health Sci. Ctr., San Antonio, 1971—; chmn. bd. Preferred Choice Health Plan, San Antonio, 1985-91. Capt. USAF, 1956-58. Home: 7510 Forrestglen Dr San Antonio TX 78209-2735 E-mail: hlwolff@swbell.net.

WOLFF, JAMES AUGUST, business educator; b. Lewiston, Idaho, Dec. 4, 1950; s. Ernest A. and Myrtle A. W.; m. Mia Louise Devereaux, Mar. 25, 1972; children: James Aaron, Jeremy Michael. BS in Agrl., U. Idaho, 1972; MBA, Wash. State U., 1990, PhD in Bus. Adminstrn., 1995. Asst. mgr., store mgr., seasonal purchasing coord. Drug Fair Northwest, 1972-87; grad. asst. Wash. State U., Pullman, 1988-94; asst. prof. Wichita (Kans.) State U., 1994-2000, assoc. prof., 2000—, assoc. dean grad. studies in bus., 2000—. Avocation: woodworking. Office: Wichita State U 1845 Fairmount St Wichita KS 67260-0001 E-mail: Jim.Wolff@wichita.edu.

WOLFF, JAMES AUGUST, finance educator, researcher; b. Lewiston, Idaho, Dec. 4, 1950; s. Ernest August Wolff, Myrtle Adair Wolff; m. Mia Louise Devereaux; children: J. Aaron, Jeremy. BS in Agr., U. Idaho, 1972; MBA, Wash. State U., 1990, PhD, 1995. Mgmt. Drug Fair Northwest, Great Falls, Mont., 1972—88; asst. prof. Wichita State U., Wichita, Kans., 1994—2000, assoc. prof., 2000—, assoc. dean grad. studies in Bus., 2000—. Contbr. articles. Mem.: Acad. Internat. Bus., Strategic Mgmt. Soc., Acad. Mgmt. Avocations: woodworking, gardening. Home: 218 Valley Stream Ct Derby KS 67037 Office: Wichita State Univ 1845 N Fairmount Wichita KS 67260-0048 Business E-Mail: Jim.Wolff@wichita.edu.

WOLFF, JEAN WALTON, writer, artist; b. San Rafael, Calif., Apr. 12, 1955; d. Warren and Alice Eleanor (Broadbent) W. BA with honors, U. Calif., Santa Cruz, 1978; MPH, U. Calif., Berkeley, 1987. Sr. account rep. Preferred Health Network, Emeryville, Calif., 1989-90; writer U. Calif., Berkeley, 1990-91, Aptos, Calif., 1987—. Editor: Long Baptisms, 1997; author: (play) Love Radio; contbr. articles to San Francisco Chroicle, San Jose Mercurty News-.contbr.; creator In Your Dreams greeting cards. Vol. Janus Recovery Ctr., Santa Cruz, 1979, Santa Cruz County Fair, 1991, In Celebration of Muse, Santa Cruz, 1998, 2001. Recipient Poetry award Santa Cruz County Fair, 1991, 93, 94; Regents fellow, 1986. Mem. Nat. Writers Union, Santa Cruz Art League. Avocations: painting, collages. Office: In Your Dreams Prodns PO Box 851 Capitola CA 95010

WOLFF, JESSE DAVID, lawyer; b. Mpls., Aug. 26, 1913; s. Maurice I. and Annalee (Weiskopf) W.; m. Elizabeth Hess, Nov. 22, 1939; children: Nancy Nicholas, Paula, Daniel Jesse. BA summa cum laude, Dartmouth Coll., 1935; JD, Harvard U., 1938. Bar: N.Y. 1938. Practiced in, N.Y.C., 1938—; assoc., then ptnr., to counsel Weil, Gotshal & Manges, 1938-88, 88—, sr. mng. ptnr., 1966-86. Past dir., dep. chmn. Sotheby Parke Bernet Group (Eng.); past mem. adv. bd. Sotheby's Inc. Hon. trustee Greatery N.Y. ARC; past mem. exec. com. Salvation Army, N.Y.C. Served with AUS, 1942-45. Mem. ABA, Judge Adv. Gen. Assn. Office: Weil Gotshal & Manges 767 5th Ave Fl Concl New York NY 10153-0119

WOLFF, JOEL HENRY, lawyer, human factors engineer; b. New Rochelle, N.Y., Oct. 29, 1966; s. Richard Eugene and Elise Leonora (Wolff) A.; m. Stacy J. Plotkin. BA, U. Nev. at Las Vegas, 1991; JD, Gonzaga U., 1995. Computer operator Sun Teleguide, Henderson, Nev., 1987-90; engring. aide Wojcik Engring., Las Vegas, 1989-90; computer cons. Ax Med. Interfaces, 1990-91; programmer Biosoft, 1991-92; computer cons., sys. analyst Wolff Legal Engines, 1995-99; mem. corp. legal dept. Graham and James LLP/Riddell-Williams P.S., Seattle, 1997-98; contractor for litigation dept. Preston, Gates and Ellis LLP, 1998; staff atty. U.S. immigration and Visa law Law Offices of Dan P. Danilov, 1999-2000; staff atty. immigration and Visa law Liebman-Mimbu, PLLC, 2000; atty., owner immigration law Law Offices of Joel H. Wolff, Kirkland, 2000—01; shareholder Bergstedt, Clegg & Wolff, P.S., Lynnwood, 2001—. Contract reviewer, document coder Perkins Coie LLP, Seattle, 1999; legal database designer and cons., King County Prosecuting Atty.'s Office, civil divsn., employment law sect., Seattle, 1998-99. Named Eagle Scout Boy Scouts Am., 1984. Mem. ASCE (sec. student chpt. 1986-87), ABA (law student divsn. 1992-95), Internat. Law Soc. of Gonazaga Univ., Nat. Eagle Scout Assn., Fed. Bar Assn., Wash. State Bar Assn., Wash. State Trial Lawyers Assn., Phi Alpha Delta, Sigma Nu. Achievements include rsch. on systems engring. with emphasis of man/machine interface; stats. analysis of social power structures and how they interface with sci. and tech.; specialist in immigration and Visa law as it applies to high tech. corps. Office: Bergstedt Clegg & Wolff PS 3500 188th St SW # 550 Lynnwood WA 98037-4762 Office Fax: 425-673-2908. E-mail: joel@bcwlaw.info.

WOLFF, KURT JAKOB, lawyer, director; b. Mannheim, Germany, Mar. 7, 1936; s. Ernest and Florence (Marx) W.; m. Sanda Lynn Dobrick, Dec. 28, 1958; children; Tracy Ellin, Brett Harris. AB, NYU, 1955; JD, U. Mich., 1958. Bar: N.Y. 1958, U.S. Supreme Ct. 1974, Hawaii 1985, Calif. 1988. Atty. pvt. practice, N.Y.C., 1958-2000; assoc. Hays, Sklar & HErzberg, 1958-60; sr. assoc. Nathan, Mannheimer, Asche, Winer & Friedman, 1960-65, Otterbourg, Steindler, Houston & Rosen, N.Y.C., 1965-68, sr. ptnr., 1968-70, dir., treas., 1970—, CEO, 1982-99, gen. counsel, 1999. Spl. master N.Y. Supreme Ct., 1977-85; vol. master U.S. Dist. Ct. (so. dist.) N.Y., 1978-82. Lectr., U. Mich. Law Sch.; mem. com. of visitors U. Mich. Law Sch., 1993—; spl. mediator Dept. Disciplinary Com. Appellate Divsn. First Judical Dept., 1991-99. Contbr. articles to profl. jours. Mem. ABA (chmn. ins. com. econs. sect. 1980-82, editor arbitratino newsletter, arbitration com. sect. litigation), N.Y. State Bar Assn. (lectr.), Am. Arbitration Assn. (arbitrator), N.Y.C. Bar Assn. (arbitration com. 197-83, state cts. of superior jurisdiction com. 1983-86, mem. com. legal edn. & admission to the bar 1991-94), Hawaii State Bar Assn., Calif. State Bar Assn., Gen. Arbitration Coun. Textile Industry N.Y.C., Fed. Bar Coun. Home: 4 Juniper Ct Armonk NY 10504-1356 also: 48-641 Torrito Ct Palm Desert CA 92260 also: John Hancock Bldg 175 E Delaware Pl Apt 6504 Chicago IL 60611-7731 Office: 230 Park Ave New York NY 10169-0005

WOLFF, L. THOMAS, medical director; b. Suffern, N.Y., 1942; MD, Albany Med. Coll., 1968. Dir. rural med. edn. program Upstate Med. U., Syracuse, NY; assoc. dir. N.Y. State Area Health Edn. Ctr. Co-investigator IDEATEL. Mem.: ABFP (elect bd. dirs. 1998, elect pres.). Office: Am Bd Family Practice 2228 Young Dr Lexington KY 40505-4294 Office Fax: 859-269-5626.*

WOLFF, MANFRED ERNST, medicinal chemist, pharmaceutical company executive; b. Berlin, Feb. 14, 1930; came to U.S., 1933; s. Adolph Abraham and Kate (Fraenkel) W.; m. Helen S. Scandalis, Aug. 1, 1953 (div. 1971); children: Stephen Andrew, David James, Edward Allen; m. Susan E. Hurbert, Jan. 19, 1973 (div. 1975); m. A. Gloria Johnson, Dec. 25, 1982. BS, U. Calif. at Berkeley, 1951, MS, 1953, PhD, 1955. Registered U.S. patent agt. Rsch. fellow U. Va., 1955-57; sr. medicinal chemist Smith, Kline & French Labs., Phila., 1957-60; mem. faculty U. Calif., San Francisco, 1960-82, prof. medicinal chemistry, 1965-82, chmn. dept. pharm. chemistry, 1970-82; dir. discovery rsch. Allergan Labs, Irvine, Calif., 1982-84; v.p. discovery rsch. Allergan Pharms., 1984-89; v.p. R & D Immunopharmaceutics Inc., San Diego, 1989-91, sr. v.p. R & D, 1991-95; pres. Intellepharm., Inc., Laguna Beach, Calif., 1997—. Adj. prof. medicinal chemistry U. So. Calif., 1982—; elected mem. U.S. Pharm. Conv. Com. of Revision, 1990—. Editor: Burger's Medicinal Chemistry and Drug Discovery, Vol. 1-5, 5th edit., 1995-97; asst. editor Jour. Medicinal Chemistry, 1968-71; mem. editl. bd. Medicinal Chemistry Rsch., 1991-95, PharmSci., 1999—; contbr. articles to profl. jours.; patentee in field. Fellow AAAS, Am Assn. Pharm. Scientists; mem. Am. Chem. Soc., Licensing Execs. Soc. Achievements include discovery of Alphagan and Lumigan medicines for glaucoma, Tazorac medicine for psoriasis, and Sitaxsentan medicine for congestive heart failure. E-mail: drwolff@aol.com.

WOLFF, MICHAEL A. state supreme court judge; Grad., Dartmouth Coll., 1967; JD, U. Minn., 1970. Lawyer Legal Svcs.; mem. faculty St. Louis U. Sch. Law, 1975-98; judge Mo. Supreme Ct., 1998—. Chief counsel to gov., 1993-94, spl. counsel, 1994-98. Co-author: Federal Jury Practice and Instructions. Chief counsel to Gov. St. Louis, 1993-94, spl. counsel, 1994-98. Office: Supreme Ct MO PO Box 150 Jefferson City MO 65102-0150*

WOLFF, OTTO, federal agency administrator; Grad., Pa. State U. Profl. staff mem. com. on house adminstrn. U.S. Ho. Reps.; dep. asst. sec. for adminstrn. Dept. Commerce, 1981—93, asst. sec., CFO for adminstrn., CFO, 2001—. Office: Dept Commerce Adminstrn CFO 14th and Constitution Ave NW Washington DC 20230*

WOLFF, PEGGY A. college administrator; b. Sidney, Nebr., Oct. 11, 1954; d. Paul T. Wolff and Ardene E. Clausen. BS, Coll. of Saint Mary, 1976; MBA, Butler U., 1986. Cert. health info. mgmt. Dir. med. record Immannel Med. Ctr., Omaha, 1976-82, Meth. Hosp., Indpls., 1982-86; sr. v.p. YPRO Corp., 1985—95; pres. Especially Yours, 1995—96; coding specialist United Med. Ctr., Cheyenne, Wyo., 1996-97; HIMS program dir. Western Nebr. C.C., Scottsbluff, Nebr., 1997—. Sr. cons. TRAID, Portland, Oreg., 1999—. Mem. Am. Health Info. Mgmt., Nebr. Health Info. Mgmt. (sec. 2000-2002). Democrat. Roman Catholic. Avocations: reading, crafts. Home: PO Box 516 Scottsbluff NE 69361 Office: Western Nebr CC 1601 E 27th Scottsbluff NE 69361 E-mail: pwolff@wncc.net.

WOLFF, PETER ADALBERT, physicist, educator; b. Oakland, Calif., Nov. 15, 1923; s. Adalbert and Ruth Margaret W.; m. Catherine C. Carroll, Sept. 11, 1948; children: Catherine Mia, Peter Whitney. AB in Physics, U. Calif., Berkeley, 1945, PhD in Physics, 1951. Rsch. scientist Lawrence Radiation Lab., 1951-52; staff scientist Bell Telephone Lab., Murray Hill, N.J., 1952-63, dept. head, dir. electronic rsch. lab., 1964-70; prof. physics U. Calif., San Diego, 1963-64; prof. physics, head solid state and atomic physics div., assoc. dir. Material Sci. Ctr. MIT, Cambridge, 1970-76, dir. rsch. lab. of electronics, 1976-81, prof. physics, 1976-89, prof. emeritus, 1994—, 1994—; dir. Francis Bitter Nat. Magnet Lab., 1981-87. Dir. Draper Lab. Contbr. articles to profl. jours. Served with C.E. U.S. Army, 1945-46. Fellow Nippon Electric Co. Rsch. Inst., Princeton, 1989-94. Mem. Am. Phys. Soc.

WOLFF, RICHARD CARL, financial planner, insurance agency and pension planning company executive; b. Boston, July 17, 1933; Student, Boston U., 1957-60. CLU. Pres. Richard C. Wolff Ins. Agy., Swampscott, Mass., 1960—, Fiscal Planning Corp., Swampscott, 1978—, Multi Pension Planning Co., Swampscott, 1979—. Mem. adv. bd. para-actuary program Bentley Coll., Waltham, Mass., 1979-90; past chmn. adv. bd. Elite Club of Western Life, St. Paul; lectr. on fringe benefits. Author: Measure of Success, 1987. Pres. Temple Israel, Swampscott, 1981-83, pres. Brotherhood, 1987-89. Recipient Legion of Honor, DeMolay, 1978, Man of Yr. award, Temple Israel, 1989. Mem. Top of Table (charter), Million Dollar Round Table (life), Mass. Assn. Accident/Health Underwriters (pres. 1965-66), Essex County Estate Planning Assn. (founder, pres. 1975-76), Boston Life Underwriters Assn. (founder, pres. North Shore br. 1979-80), Swampscott Bus. Council (pres. 1980), Lynn C. of C. (v.p. 1982-85, disting. svc. award 1984, community leader award 1985), Peabody C. of C. (bd. dirs. 1985-86, 96-97), Masons (master 1974), K.P., Rotary (Peabody award, Paul Harris fellow, pres. 1975-76), B'nai B'rith (pres. 1962-63, bd. dirs. 1991, Jewish family svc.), Kernwood Country Club (membership com., house com.). Avocations: golf, boating. Office: Fiscal Planning Corp PO Box 182 Swampscott MA 01907-0382

WOLFF, RICHARD JOSEPH, public relations executive, consultant, historian; b. Hackensack, N.J., Oct. 13, 1952; s. Richard Hamilton and Irene Marie (Ciruzzi) W. AB, Georgetown U., 1974; MA, Columbia U., 1976, PhD, 1979. Asst. dean, prof. St. John's U., Queens, N.Y., 1980-85; ptnr. pub. rels. Kekst & Co., Inc., N.Y.C., 1985-97; mng. dir. Eastern region and L.Am. Golin/Harris Internat., 1997—, worldwide mng. divsn. G/H Fin., 1997—. Mem. Columbia U. Seminar on Modern Italy, N.Y.C., 1983—; founding mem. St. John's U. Seminar on Vatican Studies, Queens, 1994—; mem. Legatus, 2000—. Author: Between Pope and Duce, 1990, Dorothy Day, 1994; contbr. articles to profl. jours.; editor Catholics, the State and the European Radical Right, 1987. Chmn., commr. North Hudson Sewerage Authority, Hudson County, N.J., 1988—; mem. adv. com. Congressman Robert Menendez, Jersey City, N.J., 1994—. Recipient Howard Marraro prize Am. Cath. Hist. Assn., 1982, Internat. fellow Columbia U., 1977. Mem. Phi Beta Kappa. Roman Catholic. Avocations: golf, reading, travel, politics. Office: Golin/Harris Internat Chrysler Bldg 405 Lexington Ave Rm 1602 New York NY 10174-1501

WOLFF, ROBERT PAUL, philosophy educator; b. N.Y.C., Dec. 27, 1933; s. Walter Harold and Charlotte (Ornstein) W.; m. Cynthia Griffin, June 9, 1962 (div. 1986); children: Patrick Gideon, Tobias Barrington; m. Susan Gould, Aug. 25, 1987. AB, Harvard U., 1953, MA in Philosophy, 1954, PhD, 1957. Instr. Harvard U., 1958-61; asst. prof. philosophy U. Chgo., 1961-63; vis. lectr. Wellesley Coll., 1963-64; assoc. prof. philosophy Columbia, 1964-69, prof., 1969-71; prof. philosophy U. Mass., Amherst, 1971-92, prof. Afro-Am. studies, 1992—; grad. program dir. doctoral program in Afro-Am. studies; devel. cons. U. QwaQwa, South Africa, 1998—. Author: Kant's Theory of Mental Activity, 1963, A Critique of Pure Tolerance, 1965, Political Man and Social Man, 1966, Kant: A Collection of Critical Essays, 1967, Poverty of Liberalism, 1968, The Ideal of the University, 1969, In Defense of Anarchism, 1970, 2d edit., 1998, Philosophy: A Modern Encounter, 1971, The Autonomy of Reason, 1973, About Philosophy, 1975, 8th edit., 2000. Exec. dir. Harvard-Radcliffe Alumni/ae Against Apartheid, 1988-90; pres., exec. dir. Univ. Scholarships for South African Students, 1990—; co-dir. inst. advanced study in humanities U. Mass., 1992-98, grad. program dir. Doctoral Program in Afro-Am. Studies, 1996—. Home: 107 Buffam Rd Amherst MA 01002-9723 E-mail: rwolff@afroam.umass.edu.

WOLFF, SHELDON, radiobiologist, educator; b. Peabody, Mass., Sept. 22, 1928; s. Henry Herman and Goldie (Lipchitz) W.; m. Frances Faye Farbstein, Oct. 23, 1954; children: Victor Charles, Roger Kenneth, Jessica Raye. BS magna cum laude, Tufts U., 1950; MA, Harvard U., 1951, PhD, 1953. Teaching fellow Harvard U., 1951-52; sr. research staff biology div. Oak Ridge Nat. Lab., 1953-66; prof. cytogenetics and radiology U. Calif., San Francisco, 1966-94; prof. emeritus, 1994—; dir. Lab. Radiobiology and Environ. Health U. Calif., San Francisco, 1983-95; vice chmn., chief rsch. Radiation Effects Rsch. Found., Hiroshima, Japan, 1996-2000. Vis. prof. radiation biology U. Tenn., 1962, lectr., 1953-65; cons. several fed. sci. agys.; mem. health and environ. rsch. adv. com. U.S. Dept. Energy, 1986—, chmn., 1987-95; co-chmn. Joint NIH/Dept. Energy Subcom. on Human Genome, 1989-94. Editor: Chromosoma, 1983-97 ; assoc. editor: Cancer Research, 1983-97; Editorial bd.: Radiation Research, 1968-72, Photochemistry and Photobiology, 1962-72, Radiation Botany, 1964-86, Mutation Research, 1964-97, Caryologia, 1967-96, Radiation Effects, 1969-81, Genetics, 1972-85; Contbr. articles to sci. jours. Recipient E.O. Lawrence meml. award U.S. AEC, 1973, 1st ann. Belle award, 1998. Mem. Genetics Soc. Am., Radiation Rsch. Soc. (counselor for biology 1968-72, Failla lectr. 1992, medal 1992), Am. Soc. Cell Biology, Environmental Mutagen Soc. (coun. 1972-75, pres. 1980-81, award 1982), Internat. Assn. Environ. Mutagen Socs. (treas. 1978-85), Sigma Xi. Democrat. Home: 41 Eugene St Mill Valley CA 94941-1717 Office: U Calif Dept Radiology San Francisco CA 94143-0001

WOLFF, SIDNEY CARNE, astronomer, observatory administrator; b. Sioux City, Iowa, June 6, 1941; d. George Albert and Ethel (Smith) Carne; m. Richard J. Wolff, Aug. 29, 1962 BA, Carleton Coll., 1962, DSc (hon.), 1985; PhD, U. Calif., Berkeley, 1966. Postgrad. research fellow Lick Obs, Santa Cruz, Calif., 1969; asst. astronomer U. Hawaii, Honolulu, 1967-71, assoc. astronomer, 1971-76; astronomer, assoc. dir. Inst. Astronomy, 1976-83, acting dir., 1983-84; dir. Kitt Peak Nat. Obs., Tucson, 1984-87, Nat. Optical Astronomy Observatories, 1987-2001; dir. Gemini Project Gemini 8-Meter Telescopes Project, 1992-94; astronomer, project scientist Large Synoptic Survey Telescope, 2001—. Pres. SOAR Inc., 1999—; project scientist Large Synoptic Survey Telescope. Author: The A-Type Stars--Problems and Perspectives, 1983, (with others) Exploration of the Universe, 1987, Realm of the Universe, 1988, Frontiers of Astronomy, 1990, Voyages Through the Universe, 1996, Voyages to the Planets, 1999, Voyages to the Stars and Galaxies, 1999; founding editor: Astronomy Edn. Rev., 2002; contbr. articles to profl. jours. Trustee Carleton Coll., 1989—. Rsch. fellow Lick Obs. Santa Cruz, Calif., 1967; recipient Nat. Meritorious Svc. award NSF, 1994. Fellow Royal Astronical Soc.; mem. Astron. Soc. Pacific (pres. 1984-86, bd. dirs. 1979-85), Am. Astron. Soc. (coun. 1983-86, pres.-elect 1991, pres. 1992-94). Office: Nat Optical Astronomy Obs PO Box 26732 950 N Cherry Ave Tucson AZ 85719-4933

WOLFF, TOBIAS (JONATHAN ANSELL WOLFF), writer; b. Birmingham, Ala., June 19, 1945; s. Arthur Saunders and Rosemary (Loftus) Wolff; m. Catherine Dolores Spohn, 1975; children: Michael, Patrick, Mary Elizabeth. BA, Oxford Univ., 1972, MA, 1975, Stanford Univ., 1978; LHD (hon.), Santa Clara Univ., 1996. Mem. faculty Stanford (Calif.) U., Goddard Coll., Plainfield, Vt., Ariz. State U., Tempe, Syracuse (N.Y.) U., Stanford (Calif.) U.; reporter Washington Post. Author: In the Garden of the North American Martyrs, 1981 (St. Lawrence award for fiction 1982), The Barracks Thief, 1984 (PEN/Faulkner award for fiction 1985), Back in the World, 1985, This Boy's Life: A Memoir, 1989 (L.A. Times Book prize 1989), In Pharaoh's Army: Memories of the Lost War, 1994 (Esquire-Volvo-Winterstone's award, Eng., 1994), The Night in Question, 1996; editor: Matters of Life and Death: New American Stories, 1983, The Stories of Anton Chekhov, 1987, Best American Short Stories, 1994, The Vintage Book of Contemporary American Stories, 1994. Recipient Wallace Stegner fellowship in creative writing, 1975-76; Nat. Endowment for the Arts fellowship in creative writing, 1978, 85; Mary Roberts Rinehart award, 1979; Ariz. Coun. on Arts and Humanities fellowship in creative writing, 1980, Guggenheim fellowship, 1982; Rea award, 1989; Whiting Writer's award, 1989, Lila-Wallace-Reader's Digest award, 1993, Lyndhurst Found. award, 1994, award of merit Am. Acad. Arts and Letters, 2001. Office: Stanford U Dept English Stanford CA 94305-2087

WOLFF, VIRGINIA EUWER, writer; b. Portland, Oreg., Aug. 25, 1937; d. Eugene Courtney and Florence Evelyn (Craven) Euwer; m. Art Wolff, July 19, 1959 (div. July 1976); children: Anthony Richard, Juliet Dianne. AB, Smith Coll., 1959; postgrad., Goddard Coll., Warren Wilson Coll., L.I. U., Portland State U., Lewis & Clark Coll. Cert. tchr., Oreg. Tchr. The Miquon Sch., Phila., 1968-72, The Fiedel Sch., Glen Cove, N.Y., 1972-75, Hood River Valley (Oreg.) H.S., 1976-86, Mt. Hood Acad., Govt. Camp, Oreg., 1986-98. 2d violinist Quartet con brio, Portland, 1989-94, Parnassius Quintet, Portland, 1996—. Author: Probably Still Nick Swansen, 1988, The Mozart Season, 1991, Make Lemonade, 1993, Bat 6, 1998, True Believer (Nat. Book award, Michael L. Printz honor, Pacific N.W. Booksellers Assn. award, Jane Addams Book award, 2002), 2001. Violinist Mid-Columbia Sinfonietta, Hood River, 1976—, Oreg. Sinfonietta, Portland, 1988—, Parnassius Chamber Ensemble, 2000-. Recipient Young Adult Book award Internat. Reading Assn., 1989, PEN U.S.A. Ctr. West, 1989, Best Young Adult Book of Yr. award Mich. Libr. Assn., 1993, Child Study Children's Book award Bank Street Coll., 1994, Oreg. Book award Oreg. Lit. Arts, 1994, 2001, Jane Addams Children's Book award Jane Addams Peace Assn. and the Women's Internat. League for Peace and Freedom, 1999, Nat. Book award, 2001, Printz Honor Book award, 2002; named to Carnegie medal Shortlist, ALA, 2002. Mem. Soc. Children's Book Writers/Illustrators (Golden Kite 1994, 2002), Chamber Music Soc. Oreg. Avocations: chamber music, swimming, hiking, playing violin, gardening. Office: Curtis Brown Ltd care Marilyn E Marlow 10 Astor Pl Fl 3 New York NY 10003-6982

WOLFF, WILLIAM F., III, investment banker; b. N.Y.C., Apr. 12, 1945; s. William F. Jr. and Nancy (Wimpfheimer) W.; m. Phyllis Fox, June 1, 1969; children: Kenneth, Laura, Jonathan, Gillian. BA, U. Mich., 1967; JD, Columbia U., 1970, MBA, 1971. Bar: N.Y. 1970. V.p. Salomon Bros., Inc., N.Y.C., 1971-78; prin. Morgan Stanley & Co., 1978-83; mng. dir. Lehman Brothers, 1983-2000, UBS Warburg, N.Y.C., 2000—02. Bd. dir. Ascent/Meredith Asset Mgmt. Trustee St. David's Sch., N.Y.C., 1985—; dir. City Harvest. Mem. Univ Club (N.Y.), Ocean Beach Club (Elberon, N.J.) (trustee 1985-89). Office: UBS Warburg 299 Park Ave New York NY 10171-0002 E-mail: rwolff3@yahoo.com.

WOLFF, WILLIAM I. surgeon, educator; b. N.Y.C., Oct. 24, 1916; s. Julius Louis and Matilda (Brick) W.; m. Lillian Myrick, June 30, 1952 (div. 1967); children: Richard, Deborah, David, Alan, Lisa, Mitchell, George, Rebecca, Barbara; m. Rita T. Smith, Feb. 15, 1972. BS, NYU, 1936; MD, U. Md., 1940. Diplomate Am. Bd. Surgery, Am. Bd. Thoracic Surgery. Intern Cornell U. divsn. Bellevue Hosp., 1940-42, resident specializing in chest surgery Columbia U. divsn., 1942-43; resident, chief Bronx Vets. Hosp., 1946-48; chief thoracic surgery Deshon Vets. Hosp., 1949; practice medicine specializing in surgery N.Y.C., 1950—; assoc. prof. surgery NYU, 1960—; dir. surgery Beth Israel Med. Ctr., 1962-76; prof. surgery Mt. Sinai Sch. Medicine, 1965—. 1st disting. lectr. soc. Am. Gastrointestinal Surgeons, 1987; vis. prof. or invited guest lectr. over 40 med. schs. univ. ctrs., over 150 tchg. hosps., numerous nat. and internat. cancer confs. in U.S., Eng., South Africa, Kenya, Israel, Mex., Can., USSR, France and P.R. Contbr. over 120 articles to med. jours., chpts. to books. Served to maj. M.C. AUS, 1943-46, ETO. Mem. ACS, Am. Coll. Gastroenterology (bd. govs.), Am. Assn. for Thoracic Surgery, Soc. Thoracic Surgeons (founding), Soc. for Surgery Alimentary Tract, Am. Coll. Chest Physicians, Am. Gastroenterologic Assn., Internat. Soc. Surgery, Internat. Cardiovasc. Surg. Soc., N.Y. Surg. Soc. (pres. 1980-81), N.Y. Acad. Medicine (chmn. sect. on surgery), Assn. Alumni Bellevue Hosp. (pres. 1982), Aspetuck Valley Country Club. Achievements include early contributor to subject of cardiac resuscitation by ccardiac message; originator of scientific procedure of colonoscopy and removal of colonic polyps. Avocations: gardening, ballet, tennis, theatre. Office: 44 Gramercy Park N New York NY 10010-6310

WOLFGANG, JERALD IRA, economic development educator; b. Niagara Falls, N.Y., Apr. 8, 1938; s. Louis and Rose (Jochnowitz) W.; m. Joan Barbara Winter, Aug. 18, 1968; l child, Lynn Jessica. BS in Edn., SUNY, Buffalo, 1962, MS in Adminstrn., 1966. Tchr. Niagara Falls Schs., 1962-68; asst. to Gov. Rockefeller Albany, N.Y., 1968-71; dep. commr. for State of N.Y. Dept. Motor Vehicles, 1971-75; with N.Y. State Senate, Buffalo, 1976; spl. asst. to minority leader N.Y. State Assembly Office of Minority Leader, 1977-83; dir. Western N.Y. Edn. Ctr. for Econ. Devel., 1983—. Bd. dirs., Southern Tier West Regional Planning and Devel.; adv. bd., State of N.Y. Small Bus. Assn., Western N.Y. Council for Edn. and Employment Equity, Western N.Y. Economic Devel. Corp., N.Y. State Economic. Devel. Corp., Western N.Y. Internat. Trade Council, Inc. Active Niagara County Am. Cancer Soc., Niagara Univ. Council, Mt. St. Mary's Hosp., Lewiston, Camp Nia-Y, Lewiston-Porter All Sports Scholarship Dinner; chmn. Niagara County Republican Com, 1978-86; sec. N.Y. Republican State Com, 1982-88; chmn. bd. dirs. A Festival of Lights, 1997—; sec. bd. dirs. St. Mary's Hosp., 1997-98; bd. vice chmn. St. Mary's Hosp. Found.; bd. dirs. United Way; apptd. mem. Work Investment Bd. Niagara County, 2000. Named Rep. of Year, 1977, Man of Year, Niagara Taxpayers League, Inc., 1987, Lewiston Kiwanian of Yr., 1999; recipient Top Hat award for Outstanding Svc. to Cmty., WHLD Radio and Niagara Frontier Svcs., 1978, Disting. Achievement award, SUNY Buffalo United U. Professions, Pres.'s award for outstanding club leadership, Lewiston Kiwanis, 1979, Pathfinder award, 1999, Leader of Year award, Leadership Niagara, 2001. Mem. Am. Vocational Assn., Assn. of Vocational Edn. Administrators of N.Y. State, Greater Buffalo C. of C., Help and Instruct Residents in Edn., Nat. Assn. of Small Bus. Internat. Trade Educators., N.Y. Assn. for Continuing Community Edn., N.Y. State Council on Vocational Edn., Niagara County Labor Mgmt. Council, Niagara Frontier Industry Edn. Council, Lewiston Kiwanis, Niagara Falls County Club. Republican. Jewish. Avocations: golf, racquetball. Home: 4267 Lower River Rd Youngstown NY 14174-9753 Office: NY Edn Ctr Econ Devel 355 Harlem Rd West Seneca NY 14224-1825

WOLFGANG, JOAN WINTER, insurance company executive; b. N.Y.C., May 19, 1944; d. Nathan and Miriam Winter; m. Jerald I. Wolfgang, Aug. 18, 1968; 1 child, Lynn Jessica. BS, SUNY, Buffalo, 1966, MS, 1970; student, Bryant and Stratton Coll, Buffalo. Lic. agt. and broker. Home econ. cons. Niagara Falls (N.Y.) Schs., 1966-68; tchr. home econs. Gaskill Jr. H.S., Niagara Falls, 1968-71; co-owner, operator Niagara Renal Ctr., 1993-98; owner Joan Wolfgang, Ins., Buffalo, 1980—. Trustee, vice chair Niagara County C.C., Sanborn, N.Y., 1982, 90; mem., chmn. Planning Bd., Town of Lewiston, N.Y., 1980—; chmn. N.Y. State Assn. C.C. TrusteesConf., 1994; mem. exec. com. Statewide Assn. Bds. C.C. Trustees. Recipient WJJL Top Hat of Week award, WHLD Good Neighbor award. Mem. Niagara Falls Area C. of C., Niagara Falls Coll. Club, State Univ. Coll. at Buffalo Alumni Assn., Profl. Ins. Agts. Assn., Niagara Falls Country Club. Republican. Avocations: golf, travel, cooking. Home: 4267 Lower River Rd Youngstown NY 14174-9753

WOLFGRAM, KENNETH CHARLES, agricultural engineer; b. Rochester, Minn., Dec. 6, 1944; s. Ellsworth Stanley and Helen Edith (Ranfranz) W.; m. Janet Caroline Waldron, Dec. 30, 1966; Derek Edwin, Sarah Caroline. BS in Agrl. Engring., U. Minn., 1966. Design engr. Allis Chalmers, Milw., 1965-69, project engr. Topeka, 1969-72, Omsteel Industries, Omaha, 1972-73; design engr. Caterpillar Inc., Aurora, Ill., 1973-75, sr. design engr., 1975-84, project engr., 1984-87, sr. project engr. Decatur, 1987-95, engring. supr. Joliet, 1995-98; tech. mgr. Claas Caterpillar Europe, Harsewinkel, Germany, 1998-2000, Caterpillar Agrl. Products, Dekalb, Ill., 2001—. Patentee in field. Mem. SAE (bd. dirs. 1995-98), Am. Soc. Agrl. Engring. E. Home: 417 Cambridge Ave Elburn IL 60119 Office: Caterpillar Agrl Products 12101 Barber Greene Rd Dekalb IL 60115 E-mail: ken.wolfgram@cat.com.

WOLFHARD, HANS GEORG, research scientist; b. Basel, Switzerland, Apr. 2, 1912; came to U.S., 1956, naturalized, 1961; s. Albert Georg and Helen (Buerck) W.; m. Adelheid Rohde, Jan. 18, 1940 (dec. 1995); children: George, John, Bernie; m. Clara Ralston, Jan. 4, 1997. Student, U. Berlin, 1934-35; Dr.Rer.Nat., U. Goettingen, 1938. Scientist Aero. Rsch. Sta., Brunswick, Germany, 1939-46; rsch. scientist Imperial Coll., London, Royal Aircraft Establishment, Eng., 1946-56, Bur. Mines, Pitts., 1956-59; head dept. physics reaction motors divsn. Thiokol Chem. corp., Denville, N.J., 1959-63; mem. sr. rsch. staff Inst. Def. Analyses, Alexandria, Va., 1963-96. Cons. Sverdrup Tech., AECD-Arnold AFB, Tenn., 1996—. Co-author: Flames, 4th edit., 1979, Chinese transl., 1990. Recipient 1st Gen. Goodpastor award for Excellence in Rsch., 1983. Fellow Am. Optical Soc., Mil. Sensor Symposium (First Jamieson award); mem. AIAA, Combustion Inst. Presbyterian. Home: 711 Bright Ave Fayetteville TN 37334-2255

WOLFINGER, AUDREY JANE, retired librarian; b. Mt. Penn, Pa., June 21, 1933; d. Harry Charles and Eva (Trace-Eckenroth) W. BS in Edn., Kutztown State Tchrs. Coll., 1955; tchrs. cert., Temple U., 19576; MS in Libr. Sci., Fla. State U., 1970. Mem. adminstrv. libr. staff Neshaminy Sch. Dist., Langhorne, Pa., 1955-84; libr., audio visual coord. Neshaminy Jr. High, 1955-76; libr. Neshaminy H.S., 1976-84; ret., 1984. Editor Wolfinger Family Newsletter, 1988—. Bd. dirs. Neshaminy Valley Music Theatre, Langhorne, 1964-65. Mem. Nat. Soc. DAR, Nat. Soc. Daus. of the Am. Colonists, Nat. Geneal. Soc., Geneal. Soc. Pa., Bucks County Geneal. Soc. (v.p. 1990-94, pres. 1994-98; resource ctr. dir. 1998, pres. protem 2001—), Kutztown U. Alumni Assn., Fla. State U. Alumni Assn. Avocations: piano Baroque music, reading British mysteries, researching family history. Home: 14 Brook Dr Furlong PA 18925-1037 Office: Bucks County Geneal Soc PO Box 1092 Doylestown PA 18901-0020 E-mail: a.j.wolfinger@rcn.com.

WOLFINGER, RAYMOND EDWIN, political science educator; b. San Francisco, June 29, 1931; s. Raymond Edwin and Hilda (Holm) W.; m. Barbara Kaye, Aug. 7, 1960; 1 son, Nicholas Holm. AB, U. Calif.-Berkeley, 1951; MA, U. Ill., 1955; PhD, Yale U., 1961. Asst. prof. polit. sci. Stanford (Calif.) U., Calif., 1961-66; assoc. prof. Stanford U., 1966-70, prof., 1970-71, U. Calif.-Berkeley, 1971—, Heller prof. polit. sci., 1995—. Dir. U. Calif. Data Archive and Tech. Assistance, 1980-92; chmn. bd. overseers Nat. Election Studies, Ann Arbor, Mich., 1982-86 Author: The Politics of Progress, 1974, (with others) Dynamics of American Politics, 1976, 80, (with Steven J. Rosenstone) Who Votes, 1980, (with others) The Myth of the Independent Voter, 1992; mem. editorial bd. Brit. Jour. Polit. Sci., 1980-84, Am. Polit. Sci. Rev., 1985-88. Bd. dirs. S.W. Voter Rsch. Inst., San Antonio, 1988-96, Consortium of Social Sci. Assns., 1987-93, pres. 1988-90. 1st lt. U.S. Army, 1951-53. Fellow Ctr. for Advanced Study in Behavioral Scis., 1960-61; Guggenheim fellow, 1965; Ford Found. faculty research fellow, 1970-71 Fellow Am. Acad. Arts and Scis. (chair Class III membership com. 1998-99); mem. Am. Polit. Sci. Assn. (sec. 1981-82), AAUP (council 1981-84), Western Polit. Sci. Assn. (v.p. 1988-89, pres. 1989-90). Democrat. Office: U Calif Dept Polit Sci Berkeley CA 94720-1950

WOLFLE, DAEL LEE, public affairs educator; b. Puyallup, Wash., Mar. 5, 1906; s. David H. and Elizabeth (Pauly) W.; m. Helen Morrill, Dec. 28, 1929 (dec. July 1988); children: Janet Helen (Mrs. Wilhelm G. Christophersen), Lee Morrill, John Morrill. BS, U. Wash., 1927, MS, 1928; postgrad., U. Chgo., summers 1929, 30; PhD, Ohio State U., 1931, D.Sc., 1957, Drexel U., 1956, Western Mich. U., 1960. Instr. psychology Ohio State U., 1929-32; prof. psychology U. Miss., 1932-36; examiner in biol. scis. U. Chgo., 1936-39, asst. prof. psychology, 1938-43, assoc. prof., 1943-45; on leave for war work with Signal Corps, 1941-43; with OSRD, 1944-45; exec. sec. Am. Psychol. Assn., 1946-50; dir. commn. on human resources and advanced tng. Assoc. Research Councils, 1950-54; exec. officer AAAS, 1954-70; editor Sci., 1955, pub., 1955-70; prof. pub. affairs U. Wash., Seattle, 1970-76, prof. emeritus, 1976—. Mem. sci. adv. bd. USAF, 1953-57; mem. def. sci. bd. Dept. Def., 1957-61; mem. adv. council on mental health NIMH, 1960-64; mem. nat. adv. health council USPHS, 1965-66; mem. commn. on human resources NRC, 1974-78; mem. adv. bd. Geophys. Inst., Fairbanks, Alaska., 1970-93, chmn. adv. bd., 1972-81 Author: Factor Analysis to 1940, 1941, Science and Public Policy 1959, The Uses of Talent, 1971, The Home of Science, 1972, Renewing a Scientific Society, 1989; editor: America's Resources of Specialized Talent, 1954. Trustee Russell Sage Found., 1961-78, Pacific Sci. Cent. Found., 1962-80, Biol. Scis. Curriculum Study, 1980-85; chmn. bd. J. McK. Cattell Fund, 1962-82. Named Alumnus Summa Laude Dignatus, U. Wash., 1979; named one of 100 Alumni of the Century, U. Wash., 1999. Mem. AAAS, (pres. Pacific divsn. 1991-92, exec. com. 1990—), AAUP, APA, Am. Acad. Arts and Scis. (exec. com. western sect. 1985-92), Sigma Xi. Office: U Wash Box 353055 Grad Sch Pub Affairs Seattle WA 98195-3055 Home: Apt 1900J 1208 Snyder Ln Blacksburg VA 24060-2141

WOLFMAN, BRUNETTA REID, education educator; b. Clarksdale, Miss., Sept. 4, 1931; d. Willie Orlando and Belle Victoria (Allen) Reid Griffin; m. Burton Wolfman, Oct. 4, 1952; children: Andrea, Jeffrey. BA, U. Calif., Berkeley, 1957, MA, 1968, PhD, 1971; DHL (hon.), Boston U., 1983; DP (hon.), Northeastern U., 1983; DL (hon.), Regis Coll., 1984, Stonehill Coll., 1985; DHL, Suffolk U., 1985; DET (hon.), Wentworth Inst., 1987; AA (hon.), Roxbury Community Coll., 1988. Asst. dean faculty Dartmouth Coll., Hanover, N.H., 1972-74; asst. v.p. acad. affairs U. Mass., Boston, 1974-76; acad. dean Wheelock Coll., 1976-78; cons. Arthur D. Little, Cambridge, Mass., 1978; dir. policy planning Dept. Edn., Boston, 1978-82; pres. Roxbury C.C., 1983-88, ACE sr. assoc., 1988-94, NAWE sr. assoc., 1994-98; assoc. v.p. acad. affairs George Washington U., Washington, 1989-92, prof. edn., 1992-96, prof. edn. emeritus, 1996—. Accreding commission on edn. on health svcs. administrn. (ACEHSA); ACE-MIVER cons.; pres. bd. dirs. Literacy Vols. of Capitol Region; mem. comm. com. bd., pub. rels. com. LVA, Inc.; bd. dirs. Am. Coun. Edn., Harvard Cmty. Health Plan. Author: Roles, 1983; contbr. articles to profl. jours. Mem. bd. overseers Wellesley Coll., 1981, Boston Symphony Orch.; trustee Mus. Fine Arts, Boston; mem. Coun. on Edn. for Pub. Health; chair Provincetown bd. Coun. on Aging, 1999—; trustee, sec. Provincetown Art Assn. and Mus.; bd. dirs. Boston-Fenway Program, 1977, Freedom House, Boston, 1983, Boston Pvt. Industry Coun., 1983; bd. dirs., co-chmn. NCCJ, Boston, 1983. Named Wolfman Courtyard in their honor, Evergreen Ctr., 2000; recipient Freedom award, NAACP No.Calif., 1971, Amelia Earhart award, Women's Edn. and Indsl. Union, Boston, 1983; scholar Nat. Assn. Women in Edn. Mem. AAUW, Am. Sociol. Assn., Assn. Black Women in Higher Edn., Greater Boston C. of C. (edn. com. 1982), Sierra Club, Mass. Audubon Soc., Cosmos Club (Washington), Provincetown Art Assn. (sec. bd. trustees, mus. sch. com.), Alpha Kappa Alpha (Humanitarian award 1984), Phi Delta Kappa. Home: 657 Commercial St Provincetown MA 02657-1759 E-mail: bruburt2@attbi.com.

WOLFMAN, EARL FRANK, JR. surgeon, educator; b. Buffalo, Sept. 14, 1926; s. Earl Frank and Alfreda (Peterson) W.; m. Lois Jeannette Walker, Dec. 28, 1946; children— Nancy Jeannette, David Earl, Carol Anne. BS cum laude, Harvard U., 1946; MD cum laude, U. Mich., 1950. Diplomate Am. Bd. Surgery. Intern U. Mich., Ann Arbor, 1950-51, asst. resident in surgery, 1951-52, resident in surgery, 1954-55, from jr. clin. instr. surgery to assoc. prof., 1955-66, asst. to dean, 1960-61, asst. dean, 1961-64; practice medicine specializing in surgery, 1957—, Sacramento, 1966—; prof. surgery Sch. Medicine, U. Calif., Davis, 1966—, chmn. dept. surgery, 1966-78, assoc. dean, 1966-76, mem. staff, chief surg. svcs. Med. Ctr., 1966-78, chmn. div. surg. scis., 1966-78. Contbr. articles to profl. jours. Served to lt. M.C. USNR, 1952-54. Fellow ACS; mem. AMA (del. 1987-99), Ctrl. Surg. Soc., Western Surg. Soc., Sacramento Surg. Soc., Pacific Coast Surg. Soc., Frederick A. Coller Surg. Soc., Soc. Surgery Alimentary Tract, Am. Assn. Endocrine Surgeons, Sacramento Med. Soc., Sierra Sacramento Valley Med. Soc., Calif. Med. Assn. (trustee 1991-2000), Am. Soc. Gen. Surgeons. Methodist. Home: 44770 N El Macero Dr El Macero CA 95618-1085 Office: U Calif Davis Sch Medicine Dept Surgery 2221 Stockton Blvd Fl 3 Sacramento CA 95817-2214 E-mail: efwolfman@ucdavis.edu.

WOLFMAN, IRA JOEL, editor, writer; b. Oct. 7, 1950; s. Aaron and Beatrice Ruth (Perlo) W.; m. Julia Diamant, June 24, 1979 (dec. 1982); m. Ronda Small, Dec. 20, 1991. BA cum laude, SUNY, Albany, 1971. News editor Washington Park Spirit, Albany, N.Y., 1971-73; sr. editor Smash mag., N.Y.C., 1975-76, Circus mag., N.Y.C., 1976-79; assoc. editor 3-2-1 Contact mag., 1979-80; editor Sesame St Parents' Newsletter, 1980-83; editor in chief Enter mag., 1983-85, Sesame St. mag., Parents Guide, 1990-94; v.p., editor-in-chief Adult Consumer mags. Children's Television Workshop, N.Y.C., 1994-97, v.p., editorial dir. mags. and sch. products, 1997-2000, group v.p. & publ., mags., Sesame Workshop, 2000-01; prin. IW Multiple Media Cons., 2001—. Newsletter editor Found. for Grandparenting, Mt. Kisco, N.Y., 1984-87; editor Am. Writer, 1988-89; freelance writer and editor, contbr. to Travel & Leisure, Architectural Record, Metropolis, N.Y. Daily News, Ms., Spy, 1985—. Author: Do People Grow on Family Trees? Genealogy for Kids and Other Beginners, 1991, My World and Globe, 1991, Climbing Your Family Tree: Online and Offline Genealogy, 2002. N.Y. State Legis. Corrs. scholar, 1970. Jewish.

WOLFMAN, NEIL T. physician; b. Bklyn., Dec. 29, 1943; s. Augustus and Lydia W.; m. Pamela Wolfman; children: Jessica, Benjamin, Austin. BA, NYU, 1964; MD, Albany Med. Coll., 1971. Resident, then fellow U. Pitts., 1975-78; asst. prof. Bowman Gray Sch. Medicine, Winston-Salem, N.C., 1978-85, assoc. prof., 1985-91, prof., 1991-99, prof. emeritus, 1999—, dir. ultrasound, 1978-99, chief body imaging sect., 1980-95, dir. radiographic anatomy NC, 1990—2000. Author: Basic Atlas Sectional Anatomy, 1998; editor: SCAR '94: Computer Applications to Assist Radiology, 1995; guest editor: Seminars in Roentegenology (jour.); contbr. chpts. to books, more than 50 articles to profl. jours. Bd. dirs. Temple Emanuel, Winston-Salem, 1983-88, 95—, co-chmn. Young Jewish Leadership, 1984-85, chmn. fundraising Temple Emanuel, 1992-94; bd. dirs. Russian Resettlement comm. Jewish Cmty. Coun., Winston-Salem, 1986. Lt. comdr. USN, 1975-77. Fellow Am. Coll. Radiology (alt. councilor/exec. com. N.C. chpt. 1992-98, councilor 1999—), Am. Inst. Ultrasound (chmn. continuing med. edn. com.); mem. AMA, Radiol. Soc. N.Am., Soc. Gastrointestinal Radiologists, Soc. Uroradiology. Office: Wake Forest U Sch Medicine Dept Radiology Medical Ctr Blvd Winston Salem NC 27157

WOLFMEYER, TESS C. special education educator; b. Oceanside, Calif., Mar. 31, 1953; d. Vernon G. and Janet N. Wolfmeyer. BA in Special Edn., U. Wis., Eau Claire, 1975; cert. in Biblical studies, Wheaton Coll., 1981; MS in Edn., U. Wis., Whitewater, 1993. Cert. tchr, Wis., cert. in early childhood exceptional ednl. needs. Tchr. Milw. Pub. Schs., 1975-80; spl. instr. Wheaton (Ill.) Coll., 1980-81; tchr. Curative Rehab. Ctr., Wauwatosa, Wis., 1981-85, 1993; assn. dir. Curative Rehab. Svcs., 1985—; sr. spl. edn. tchr. Curative Care Network. Mem. Coun. Exceptional Children. Avocations: reading, cross stitch, swimming, biking.

WOLFORD, NANCY LOU, medical and surgical nurse; b. Cumberland, Md., Feb. 22, 1956; d. Charles Leo and Shirley Lou (Weicht) Westfall; m. Harry Edward Wolford III, Aug. 20, 1977; 1 child, James. AA in Nursing, Allegany C.C., 1977. RN, Md.; cert. in med.-surg. nursing. Staff nurse in emergency dept. Frostburg (Md.) Community Hosp., 1978-88; staff nurse Staffbuilders of Pitts., 1985-86; staff nurse med. surg. unit Frostburg Hosp., Inc., 1988-95; staff nurse oncology/med.-surg. unit Meml. Hosp. and Med. Ctr., Cumberland, Md., 1995-97. Ind. beauty cons. Mary Kay Cosmetics, Inc., 1993—. Recipient Congl. scholarship Md. State Sen., 1974-77. Republican. Methodist. Avocations: art, music. Home: 412 Park St Frostburg MD 21532-1511 Office: Meml Hosp and Med Ctr Memorial Ave Cumberland MD 21502

WOLFORD, ROY, JR. publishing executive; b. Majestic, Ky., Sept. 6, 1946; s. Roy Sr. and Edith (Daugherty) W.; m. Judy Karen Wunder, June 19, 1969; children: Christopher Paul, Alexander Dean. Grad., Eastern Ky. U., 1967. Auditor Dispatch Printing Co., Columbus, Ohio, 1969-79; bus. mgr. Ohio Mag., Inc., 1979-89; gen. mgr. Ohio Mag. Inc., 1989—. Bd. dirs. Ohio Mag. and Consumer News Svc., 1996. With U.S. Army, 1967-69, Vietnam. Mem. Audit Bur. Circulations, City-Regional Mag. Assn., Internat. Regional Mag. Assn., Mag. Pub. Assn. Republican. Presbyterian. Avocations: boating, camping, computer hacking. Home: 1379 Birchwood Dr Columbus OH 43228-9790 Office: Ohio Mag Inc 62 E Broad St Ste 200 Columbus OH 43215-3522

WOLFOWITZ, PAUL DUNDES, federal official, former ambassador to Indonesia; b. N.Y.C., Dec. 22, 1943; s. Jacob and Lillian (Dundes) W.; m. Clare Selgin, Nov. 25, 1968; children: Sara Elizabeth, David Samuel, Rachel Dahlia. BA in Math. and Chemistry, Cornell U., 1965; MA, U. Chgo., 1967, PhD in Polit. Sci., 1972. Lectr., asst. prof. Yale U., 1970-73; with U.S. Arms Control and Disarmament Agy., 1973-77, spl. asst. to dir., 1974-75, dep. asst. dir., 1976; spl. asst. for SALT, 1976-77; with Dept. Def., Washington, 1977-80; dep. asst. sec. of def., regional programs, program analysis and evaluation Office of Sec. of Def., 1977-80; vis. assoc. prof. Sch. Advanced Internat. Studies, Johns Hopkins U., 1980-81; dir. policy planning staff U.S. Dept. State, 1981-82, asst. sec. of state for East Asian and Pacific affairs, 1982-86; U.S. amb. to Indonesia, 1986-89; undersec. def. for policy Office of Sec. of Def., Washington, 1989—. Recipient Presdl. Citizens medal. Office: Undersec Def for Policy Office of Sec Def The Pentagon Washington DC 20301-0001*

WOLFRAM, DAVID ANTHONY, computer scientist; b. Melbourne, Australia, Sept. 20, 1962; s. Hans Gerhard (dec.) and Bettine Rosalind (Kauffmann) W. BSc with honors, U. Melbourne, 1984, MSc, 1986; PhD, U. Cambridge (Eng.), 1990, U. Oxford (Eng.), 1991; Grad. Diploma Mgmt., U. New South Wales, 2000, U. Sydney, 2000. Chartered engr.; European engr., chartered info. sys. practitioner; chartered info. sys. engr. Rsch. asst. U. Oxford, 1990; jr. rsch. fellow Christ Ch., Oxford, 1990-94, BT fellow, 1994; lectr. in computer sci. Australian Nat. U., Canberra, 1995-2000, vis. fellow Rsch. Sch. Info. Scis. and Engring., 2000; with Microsoft Corp., USA, Redmond, Wash., 2000—02. Program chair Australasian Theory Symposium, 2000. Author (book) The Clausal Theory of Types, 1993; contbr. articles to profl. jours.; guest editor: Electronic Notes in Theoretical Computer Science, Vol. 31, 2000; guest editor spl. issue Theoretical computer Science, 2001. Fellow Cambridge Philos. Soc.; mem. Brit. Computer Soc., London Math. Soc., N.Y. Acad. Scis., Internat. Soc. for Philos. Enquiry (diplomate), Am. Australian Assn., Melbourne Cricket Club, Ordre du Tastevin (chevalier), Oxford and Cambridge Club (London). Avocations: photography, tennis, chess.

WOLFRAM, GARY LEE, economics educator, consultant; b. Redding, Calif., Nov. 1, 1950; s. Harold Walter and Hera Olga (Abbott) W.; m. Mary Bess Gompers; children: Elizabeth, Wyatt, Liam. BA in Econs., U. Calif., Santa Barbara, 1972; PhD in Econs., U. Calif., Berkeley, 1976. Asst. prof. Mt. Holyoke Coll., South Hadley, Mass., 1976-77; asst. prof. econs. U. Mich., Dearborn, 1979-83; sr. economist Mich. Senate Rep. Staff, Lansing, 1983-89; George Munson prof. Hillsdale (Mich.) Coll., 1989—; dep. state treas. State of Mich., Lansing, 1991-92; chief of staff U.S. Congressman Nick Smith, Washington, 1995-96. Vis. asst. prof. Wash. State U., Pullman, 1979-80; pres. Hillsdale Policy Group. Author: Towards a Free Society, 1993; contbr. articles to profl. publs. Mem. Mich. State Bd. Edn., Lansing, 1993—; chmn. Headline Blue Ribbon Commn., Lansing, 1993; mem. bd. scholars Mackinac Ctr., Midland, 1986—; mem. bd. advisors Adam Ferguson, Lorraine, Ohio, 1996—; mem. bd. adminstrn. Buckeye Inst., 1996—; bd. dirs. Mich. Enterprise Zone Authority, 1992-94, Mich. State Housing Devel. Authority, 1991-92, Mich. Strategic Fund. Recipient Lysander Spooner award Mackinac Ctr. for Pub. Policy, 1992. Republican. Roman Catholic. Avocation: running. Home: 3 Corona Cir Hillsdale MI 49242-5030 Office: Hillsdale Coll Dept Econs Hillsdale MI 49242

WOLFRAM, STEPHEN, physicist, computer company executive; b. London, Aug. 29, 1959; came to U.S., 1978; Degree, Eton Coll., 1976, Oxford U., 1978; PhD in Theoretical Physics, Calif. Inst. Tech., 1979. With Calif. Inst. Tech., Pasadena, 1979-82, Inst. for Advanced Study, Princeton, N.J., 1983-86; prof. physics, math, computer sci. U. Ill., Champaign, 1986-90; founder and dir. Ctr. Sysytems Rsch., 1986—87; pres., CEO Wolfram Rsch. Inc., Champaign, 1987—. Author: Theory and Applications of Cellular Automata, 1986, Mathematica: A System for Doing Mathematics by Computer, 1998, 2d edit., 1991, Mathematica Reference Guide, 1992, Mathematica: The Student Book, 1994, The Mathematica Book, 3rd edit., 1996, 4th edit., 1999, Cellular Automata and Complexity, 1994, A New Kind of Science, 2002; editor jour. Complex Systems, 1987— Fellow MacArthur Found., 1981; recipient World Leaders of Tomorrow, World Economic Forum, 1999. Office: Wolfram Rsch Inc 100 Trade Centre Dr Champaign IL 61820-7237 E-mail: s.wolfram@wolfram.com.

WOLFRAM, THOMAS, physicist, educator; b. St. Louis, July 27, 1936; s. Ferdinand I. and Audrey H. (Calvert) W.; m. Eleanor Elaine Burger, May 22, 1965; children: Michael, Gregory, Melanie, Susan, Steven. BA, U. Calif., Riverside, 1959, PhD in Physics, 1963; MA in Physics, UCLA, 1960. Dir. divsn. physics and chemistry; Engr. Atomics Internat., Canoga Park, Calif., 1960-63; mem. tech. staff N.Am. Aviation Corp. Sci. Ctr., Thousand Oaks, 1963-68; group leader in solid state physics Rockwell Internat. Sci. Ctr., 1968-72, dir. div. physics and chemistry, 1972-74; prof. physics, chmn. dept. physics and astronomy U. Mo., Columbia, 1974-83; dir. phys. tech. divsn. AMOCO Corp., 1983-87; v.p., gen. mgr. AMOCO Laser Co., 1987-95; bus. cons., 1995—. Cons. in field. Author: (novel) The Venture; (novel) The Dragon Tamers; editor: Inelastic Electron Tunneling Spectroscopy, 1978; contbr. rsch. articles to numerous publs. in field. Recipient Disting. Prof. award Argonne Univs. Assn., 1977 Fellow Am. Phys. Soc. Office: 2004 Somerset Ln Wheaton IL 60187-8128 *Crisis is the catalyst for constructive change.*

WOLFSCHMIDT, WILLI See FLINT, WILLIS WOLFSCHMIDT

WOLFSON, AARON HOWARD, radiation oncologist, educator; b. Nashville, May 13, 1955; s. Sorrell Louis and Jacqueline Adele (Falis) W.; m. Adrienne Sue Mates, Dec. 16, 1979; children: Alexis Ellyn, Andrew Lane. BA, U. Fla., 1978, MD, 1982. Diplomate Am. Bd. Radiology. Intern internal medicine Jackson Meml. Hosp., Miami, Fla., 1982-83; staff physician Pub. Health Svc., 1983-85; pvt. practice Palm Beach Gardens, Fla., 1985-86; resident in radiation oncology Med. Coll. Va., Richmond, 1986-89; instr. radiation oncology U. Miami Sch. Medicine, 1989-91, asst. prof., 1991-97, assoc. prof., 1997—. Co-dir. Gynecology Site dis. group, Sylvester Cancer Ctr., 2001—. Contbr. articles to profl. jours. Bd. dirs. Children's Home Soc., Ft. Lauderdale, Fla., 1993—, Temple Beth Israel, Sunrise, Fla., 1994—; mem. spkrs. bur. U. Miami, 1993—; vol. spkr. Broward County Schs., 1990—; exec. v.p. Temple Beth Israel, 1996-98, pres., 1998-99. Sylvester Cancer Ctr. grantee, 1992. Mem. Gynecologic Oncology Group, Radiation Therapy Oncology Group, Am. Soc. Therapeutic Radiology and Oncology. Jewish. Achievements include research on malignant tumors of the female genital tract. Avocations: bridge, tennis, reading science fiction. Office: Univ of Miami 1475 NW 12th Ave # D-31 Miami FL 33136-1002 E-mail: awolfson@med.miami.edu.

WOLFSON, ELLEN N. physician; b. Jamaica, N.Y., Feb. 13, 1947; BA, Skidmore Coll., 1968; MA, Columbia U., 1964; MD, NYU, 1981. Intern Greenwich (Conn.) Hosp., 1981-82, resident, 1982-84, attending physician, 1984—. Office: 4 Dearfield Dr Ste 2 Greenwich CT 06831-5333

WOLFSON, IRWIN M. insurance company executive; b. Bronx, N.Y., May 29, 1937; s. Herman M. and Kate (Greenstein) W.; m. Pauline S. Frechtel, Dec. 25, 1962; children: Fran M., Lisa G. BS in Econs., NYU, 1960. Owner/CEO Wolfson Agency, Yonkers, N.Y., 1973—. Instr., owner Successful Adult Fin. Seminars, Yonkers, 1990—. Mem. operating bd. Child Abuse Prevention Ctr., White Plains, N.Y. Sgt. U.S. Army, 1960-66. Recipient Achievement award Congressman Elliot Engel, 1992, proclamation From T. Zaleski (Mayor) City of Yonkers, 1992, letter of Recognition from M. Cuomo (Governor) N.Y. 1992; Irwin M. Wolfson Day proclaimed by A. O'Rourk (County Exec.) N.Y. 1992. Mem. Yonkers Exch. Club (pres. 1990-91, N.Y. dist. dir. 1991-95, 99–, N.Y. dist. pres. 1996-97). Home: 11 Jackson Ave Unit 4 Scarsdale NY 10583-3134 Office: Wolfson Agy 475 Tuckahoe Rd Yonkers NY 10710-5712

WOLFSON, LARRY MARSHALL, lawyer; b. Springfield, Ill., June 12, 1947; m. Cynthia Sherwood, 1972; children: Sharon Eve, Rachel Beth, Anna Faye, Blackie Perro, Natasha Molly. BSBA, Northwestern U., 1969; JD cum laude, U. Mich., 1974. Bar: Ill. 1974. Ptnr. Jenner & Block, Chgo., 1980—2002, Shaw, Gussis, Domanskis, Fishman & Wolfson, LLC , Chgo., 2002—. Mem. ABA, Ill. State Bar (lectr. Comml. Banking and Bankruptcy Law Edn. Series 1990), Chgo. Bar Assn., Chgo. Coun. Lawyers, Am. Bankruptcy Inst. Office: Shaw Gussis et al 1144 W Fulton St Market Chicago IL 60607 Fax: (312) 840-7362. E-mail: lwolfson@jenner.com.

WOLFSON, MARK ALAN, investor, business educator; b. Chgo., Sept. 25, 1952; s. Jack and Maribelle (Simen) W.; m. Sheila Rae Aronesti, Aug. 3, 1975; children: Laura Rachel, Charles Michael. BS in Acctg. and Fin., U. Ill., 1973, M Acctg. Sci., 1974; PhD in Acctg., U. Tex., 1977. Asst. prof. acctg. Stanford (Calif.) U., 1977-81, assoc. prof., 1981-85, prof., 1985-87, Joseph McDonald prof., 1987-92, assoc. dean, 1990-93; Dean Witter prof. acctg. and fin., 1992-96; prof. acctg. and fin., 1996-2000; mng. ptnr. Oak Hill Capital Mgmt., 1998—; ptnr. Oak Hill Venture Ptnrs., 1999—; prin. Oak Hill Platinum Ptnrs., 2001—. Ford Found. vis. assoc. prof. U. Chgo., 1981-82; Thomas Henry Carroll vis. prof. Harvard U., Boston, 1988-89; cons. Fin. Acctg. Stds. Bd., Norwalk, Conn., 1985, 89-92; rsch. assoc. Nat. Bur. Econ. Rsch., Cambridge, Mass., 1988—; steering com. Stanford Inst. Econ. Policy Rsch., 1990-2000, exec. com. 2001—; task force Fed. Home Loan Bank Bd., 1989; v.p. Keystone Inc., 1995—,; bd. dirs. Investment Tech. Group, Caribbean Restaurants, DaVinci I, eGain Comm., Fin. Engines, Inc., Oreck Corp., FEP Capital, 230 Park Investors; trustee Merlo Sch., 2001-. Contbr. numerous articles to profl. jours. Recipient Pomerance prize Chgo. Bd. Options Exch., 1981, Disting. Tchg. award Stanford U., 1990, Notable Contbn. to Lit. award AICPA-Am. Acctg. Assn., 1990, 92, Wildman award, 1991; named Disting. Accountancy Alumnus, U. Ill., 1989. Jewish. Office: Oak Hill Capital 2775 Sand Hill Rd Ste 220 Menlo Park CA 94025-7019

WOLFSON, MICHAEL GEORGE, lawyer; b. Chgo., Sept. 1, 1938; s. A. Lincoln M. Weingarten and Brina (Nelson) W.; m. Rita Sue Parsont, Sept. 11, 1966; children: Bethany Lynne, Sara Wynne, Deborah Kay. Student, MIT, 1956-58; BA, U. Chgo., 1961, JD, 1964, postdoctoral, 1964-65. Bar: Ill. 1964, N.Y. 1969. Assoc. Cravath, Swaine & Moore, N.Y.C., 1965-71, Brown, Wood, Fuller, Caldwell & Ivey, N.Y.C., 1971-73; ptnr. Sidley Austin Brown & Wood LLP, 1974—. Mediator, specializing in comml. and internat. disputes. Woodrow Wilson fellow, 1961; Ford Found. fellow in internat. trade and devel., 1965. Fellow Am. Bar Found. (life); mem. ABA. Avocations: reading, photography, fly fishing, bicycling. E-mail: mwolfson@sidley.com.

WOLFSON, ROBERT ALLEN, physician; b. N.Y.C., Nov. 11, 1952; s. Erwin and Marion (Asbell) W.; m. Donna Meluso, Dec. 9, 1983; children: Michele, Matthew. AB, NYU, Bronx, 1973; MD, SUNY Downstate, Bklyn., 1977. Diplomate Am. Bd. Internal Medicine. Intern, resident Kings County Hosp., Bklyn., 1977-80, chief resident, 1980-81; asst. prof. medicine Albert Einstein Coll. Medicine, Bronx, 1981-95; physician Mt. Kisco (N.Y.) Med. Group, 1995—. Office: Mt Kisco Med Group 90 S Bedford Rd Mount Kisco NY 10549-3412 E-mail: rwolfson@mkmg.com.

WOLFTHAL, MICHAEL EDWARD, director; b. N.Y.C. s. Paul Rubin and Phyllis Wolfthal; m. Diane Marie Lordi, Dec. 4, 1976; children: Jennifer, Debor, Jeffrey. BA, Monmouth Coll., 1973; MA, Seton Hall U., 1980. Tchr. social studies Bishop Ahr H.S., Edison, NJ, 1973—76, chmn. dept. social studies, 1976—81, athletic dir., 1981—. Sec. Greater Middles Conf., Middlesex County, NJ, 1981—. Named Athletic Dir. of Yr., Greater Middles Conf., 1996. Mem.: NJSDAA. Avocations: sports, reading, walking. Home: 1 Tingley Ln Edison NJ 08820 Fax: 732-494-2229.

WOLFZAHN, ANNABELLE FORSMITH, psychologist; b. N.Y.C., Jan. 23, 1932; d. Paul Phillip and Addie (Glassman) Forsmith; m. Herbert Eytan Wolfzahn, Feb. 4, 1956; children: Risa, Felice, Orna. BA, Hunter Coll., 1953; MA in Counseling Psychology, Manhattan Coll., 1971; PhD in Clin. and Community Psychology, Union Inst., 1979. Cert. sch. psychologist, sch. counselor, N.Y. Counselor for handicapped children Bklyn. Tuberculosis Assn., 1952; social worker Child Placement Svcs., N.Y.C., 1953-58; fellow in social and community psychiatry Albert Einstein Coll. Medicine, 1977-79; intern Bronx (N.Y.) Devel. Svcs., 1977-79; intern head trauma program Rusk Inst., NYU Med. Ctr., 1979; psychologist Creedmore Psychiat. Ctr., 1980-82, Harlem Valley Psychiat. Ctr., 1982-87; clin. coord. of group homes Green Chimneys Children's Svcs., 1987-88; with Ulpan Akiva and Assaf Harofeh Med. Ctr., Tel Aviv U., Israel, 1988-89; nursing home cons., psychotherapist Bklyn. Ctr. for Psychotherapy, 1989-91; pres., coord. Westchester chpt. Vols. for Israel, 1992—; freelance psychologist, counselor, 1994—; retired, 2001—. Mem. workshops in field; mem. staff Mother-Child Home Program of White Plains, N.Y., 1975-76; mem. curriculum com. Learning in Retirement Iona Coll. (LIRIC), 1994—; counselor with multiple sclerosis victims and their families. Exhibited in group shows at Wuchinich Gallery, Mt. Kisco Libr., 1998, Somers Gallery, Somers Libr., 1998, Greenberg Gallery, Greenberg Libr., 1998, Gallery at New Rochelle Libr., 1998, Woods Gallery, Burke Ctr., White Plains, N.Y., 1998, Levine Art Gallery, Putnam Arts coun., 1998, Mid-Rockland Arts Festival, 1998, The Bendheim Performing Arts Ctr., 1999, Reflection of Westchester Exhibit, 1999, Art on Main St., 1999, Open Studios, 2000, Westchester Arts Coun., 2000, Oresmond Art Exhibit, Oresmond Gallery, Larchmont, N.Y., 2002, others; contbr. articles to profl. jours. Vol. Vols. for Israel, 1988, 91-92, founder, pres., coord. Westchester Region chpt., 1993—; mem. archaeol. dig Bet Shaan, Israel; arts amb. White Plains Arts Coun., 2000—. Recipient Vol. award White Plains Hosp., 1974-76, John C. Klein Meml. Writing award Newspaper Inst. Am., 1965; Alvin Johnson scholar, 1953. Mem. APA, Westchester County Psychol. Assn., N.Y. Neuropsychology Assn., Am. Mental Health Affiliates of Israel, N.Y. Acad. Scis., Nat. Coun. Jewish Women, Am. Orthopsychiat. Assn. Avocations: oil painting, lap swimming, writing, travel, photography. Home and Office: 34 Springdale Rd Scarsdale NY 10583-7329

WOLGAMOTT, GARY DEAN, medical educator; b. Weatherford, Okla., July 23, 1940; s. Kenneth Blaine and Winona Irene Wolgamott; m. Sandra Jean Wolgamott, Apr. 26, 1962; children: Thad Dean, Dotti D'Lane Wolgamott-Forehand. BS in Biology and Chemistry, Northwestern Okla. State U., 1963; PhD in Microbiology, Okla. State U., 1968. Postdoctoral fellow U. Iowa Coll. Medicine, Iowa City, 1971, NASA, Houston, 1974-75; prof. Southwestern Okla. State U., Weatherford, 1968—, chmn. allied health scis., 1975—, assoc. dean Sch. Health Scis., 1994—. Mem. med. tech. rev. com. Nat. Accrediting Agy. of Clin. Lab. Scis., 1980-90. Editor/author Lambda Tau Newsletter, 1976—. Named Bernhard prof., Southwestern Okla. State U., 1996; named to Outstanding Professors Acad., 1999—2000. Fellow: Okla. Acad. Sci. (chmn.collegiate acad. 1968—80, pres. 1980); mem.: Am. Soc. Microbiology (edn1. coord. 1971—79), Kiwanis (bd. dirs., pres. 1990—91), Lambda Tau (nat. sec.-treas. 1976—), Beta Beta Beta (nat. pres. 2001—). Methodist. Avocations: bicycling, running, backpacking, guitar, skiing. Office: Southwestern Oklahoma State U 100 Campus Dr Weatherford OK 73096-3001 E-mail: wolgamg@host1.swosu.edu.

WOLGAST, ELIZABETH HANKINS, philosophy educator; b. Dunnellen, N.J., Feb. 27, 1929; d. Frank William and Evelyn Clara Hankins; m. Richard Wolgast, June 26, 1949; children: Stephen, Johanna. BA, Cornell U., 1950, MA, 1952; PhD, U. Wash., 1955. Vis. prof. U. Calif., Davis, 1966-67; prof. Calif. State U., Hayward, 1968-96. Vis. prof. Dartmouth Coll., Hanover, N.H., 1975-76, U.S. Mil. Acad., West Point, N.Y., 1987. Author: Paradoxes of Knowledge, 1977, Equality and the Rights of Women, 1980, Grammar of Justice, 1987, Ethics of an Artificial Person, 1992. Fellow AAUW, 1957, NEH, 1979, 91, Am. Coun. Learned Socs., 1975. Mem. Am. Philos. Assn. Mem. Soc. Of Friends. Avocation: painting. Home: 1536 Olympus Ave Berkeley CA 94708

WOLIN, DORIS DIAMOND, psychologist; b. N.Y.C., Oct. 18, 1929; d. Philip Charles and Hattie (Bentley) Diamond; m. Sidney Wolin; children: Laurie, James; m. Frank Norris, Sept. 20, 1986. Student, Wooster Coll., 1948-49; BA, NYU, 1951, MA, 1957; postgrad., Yeshiva U., 1958—; PhD, Heed U., 1988. Sch. psychologist Lawrence Sch. Systems, L.I., N.Y., 1959-60, New Hope Clinic, 1959-60, Jamaica Ctr. for Psychotherapy, 1960-61; instr. in psychology Bklyn. Coll., 1961-62; therapist Bklyn. Community Counseling Ctr., 1961-66; psychotherapist Testing and Advisement Ctr., NYU, 1951; pvt. practice clin. psychology N.Y.C., 1951—; theapist North Jersey Mental Health Assocs., Oakland, N.J., 1979-81; cons. Bd. of Edn., L.I., N.Y., 1987—; instr. L.I. U. Bklyn. Ctr., 1971—. Adj. prof. psychology L.I. U., 1971, Coll. New Rochelle, 1989; psychologist Save A Marriage, N.Y.C., 1977—; cons. Ctr. Psychotherapy and Counseling, Fairlawn, N.J., 1988-90, Astoria Blue Feather Presch. Intervention Program, 1989-90, Kingsbrook Jewish Med. Ctr., 1990-91, East River Child Devel. Ctr., 1991-92, Low Meml. Child Care Ctr., 1993-95. Mem. Rose Garden Bklyn., Botanic Garden, Hort. Soc. of N.Y.; mem. aux. Bklyn. Bot. Gardens. Mem. N.Y. Soc. of Clin. Psychologists, Am. Psychol. Assn., Am. Group Psychotherapy Assn., Bklyn. Psychol. Assn., N.Y. State Psychol. Assn., Soc. for the Sci. Study of Sex, Psychologists in Pvt. Practice. Avocations: gardening, landscaping, decorating, gourmet cooking. Home and Office: 90 8th Ave Brooklyn NY 11215-1553 E-mail: ddwolin@yahoo.com.

WOLIN, JAMES MICHAEL, budget analyst; b. Bklyn., Apr. 1, 1955; s. Sidney Harry and Doris (Diamond) W. BS in Bus. and Econs., Hofstra U., 1977, MBA in Fin., 1981. Analyst Aspen Systems, Inc., N.Y.C., 1979-80; prodn. coord. Hudson's Bay Co., 1980-85; systems coord. Morgan Guaranty Trust Co., 1985-86; info. mgr. Prudential-Bache Securities, 1986-88; unit head Office of Mgmt. and Budget, City of New York, 1988-98; dep. dir. Dept. Sanitation, 1998-2000; dir. ops. mgmt. and budget oral health programs and policy The Health and Hosp. Corp., N.Y.C., 2000—. Mem. jr. com. Nat. Ctr. Learning Disabilities. Mem. Am. Mgmt. Assn., Fin. Execs. Networking Group, Mensa (pres. greater N.Y. chpt.). Home: 240 Waverly Pl New York NY 10014-2213

WOLIN, MICHAEL STUART, physiology educator; b. Bklyn., Sept. 11, 1953; s. Emanuel and Anita (Klein) W.; m. Theresa Marie Burke, Oct. 25, 1987; children: Joshua Mark, Seth Adam, Sarah Rachel. BA in Chemistry, SUNY, Binghamton, 1975; MS, Yale U., 1977, MPhil, 1978, PhD, 1981. NIH Nat. Rsch. Svc. fellow Tulane U. Sch. Medicine, New Orleans, 1981-82, instr. pharmacology, 1982-83; asst. prof. physiology N.Y. Med. Coll., Valhalla, 1983-89, assoc. prof., 1989-95; prof., 1995—. Prin. investigator NIH, 1984—, mem. exptl. cardiovascular scis. study sect., 2001—. Editor (assoc.): Am. Jour. Physiology, 1993—98, Microcirculation, 1999—; mem. editl. bd.: Microcirculation Jour., 1994—, mem. editl. bd.: Free Radical Biology and Medicine, 1997—2002, mem. editl. bd.: Nitric Oxide Biology and Chemistry, 1997—, mem. editl. bd.: Am. Jour. Physiology, 1991—, mem. editl. bd.: Circulation Rsch., 1999—, mem. editl. bd.: Jour. Cardiovascular Pharmacology, 2001—. Trustee bd. edn. Elmsford Union Fre Sch. Dist., 2001—. Recipient Merit award NIH, 1996—, Mary E. Gerritsen award The Microcirculatory Soc., 2000; Biomed. rsch. scholar C.H. Revson Found., 1983-85. Mem.: AAAS, Oxygen Soc. Microcirculatory Soc. (chmn. devel. com. 1994—95), Nitric Oxide Soc., Am. Physiol. Soc., Am. Heart Assn. (mem. exec. com. 1992—94, mem. cardiovascular rsch. study com. 1992—95, co-chair lung and devel. rsch. study com. 1995—96, rsch. com. 1995—2000, com. on sci. sessions program 1996—99, chair sci. program com. cardiopulmonary and critical care coun. 1996—99, mem. exec. com. 1996—, chmn. lung, respiration and resuscitation rsch. study com. 1997—2000, vice chair cardiopulmonary critical care coun. 1999—2001, chmn. cardiopulmonary critical care coun. 2001—, sci. adv. and coord. com. 2001—, Established Investigator award 1989—94, Albert Hyman Rsch. award La. affiliate 1983), Am. Thoracic Soc. Jewish. Achievements include elucidation of novel mechanisms of regulating vascular tone, tissue respiration and guanylate cyclase by reactive oxygen and nitrogen species. Home: 40 Goodwin Ave White Plains NY 10607-1014 Office: NY Med Coll Dept Physiology Valhalla NY 10595 E-mail: mike_wolin@nymc.edu.

WOLIN, NEAL STEVEN, lawyer; b. Chgo., Dec. 9, 1961; s. Harry S and Doris (Wacker) Wolin. BA summa cum laude, Yale U., 1983; MSc, U. Oxford, Eng., 1985; JD, Yale U., 1988. Bar: Ill 1989, DC 1989, US Supreme Ct 1995. Adj. asst. prof. of law Bklyn. Law Sch., 1989; law clk. U.S. Judge Eugene H. Nickerson, Bklyn., 1988-89; assoc. Wilmer, Cutler & Pickering, Washington, 1989-90; spl. asst. to dirs. ctrl. intelligence Webster Gates & Woolsey, 1990-93; dep. legal adviser Nat. Sec. Coun. The White House, 1993-94; exec. asst. to the nat. sec. adviser The White House, 1994-95; dept. gen. counsel U.S. Dept. Treasury, 1995-99, gen. counsel, 1999-2001; exec. v.p., gen. counsel The Hartford Fin. Svcs. Group, Inc., Hartford, 2001—. Vis. fellow Brookings Inst., Washington, 2001; adj. lectr. in pub. policy JFK Sch. Govt., Harvard U., 2001. Bd. overseers Rand Inst. Civil Justice; mem. bd. regents U. Hartford; mem. Presdl. Adv. Commn.Holocaust Assets in U.S., 1999—2000, 2001—. Fellow Henry, Henry Trust, Oxford Univ, 1983—84, Coker Teaching, Yale Law Sch, 1987—88. Mem.: Coun on Foreign Relations, Phi Beta Kappa. Home: 14 West Hill Dr West Hartford CT 06119 Business E-Mail: nwolin@thehartford.com.

WOLINSKY, EMANUEL, physician, educator; b. N.Y.C., Sept. 23, 1917; s. Jacob and Bertha (Siegel) W.; m. Marjorie Claster, Nov. 15, 1946; children: Douglas, Peter. BA, Cornell U., 1938, MD, 1941. Diplomate Am. Bd. Med. Microbiology. Intern, resident medicine N.Y. Hosp., 1943-45; bacteriologist Trudeau Lab., Saranac Lake, N.Y., 1947-56; mem. faculty Case Western Res. U. Sch. Medicine, 1956-98, prof. medicine, 1968-88, prof. pathology, 1981-88, prof. emeritus, 1988-98, ret., 1998. Dir. microbiology Cleve. Met. Gen. Hosp., 1959-91, acting dir. dept. pathology, 1980-86, chief div. infectious diseases, 1961-83. Co-editor Textbook of Pulmonary Diseases, 5th edit., 1993; Asso. editor: Am. Rev. Respiratory Diseases, 1973-79; Contbr. articles to profl. jours., textbooks. Mem. Tb panel U.S.-Japan Co-op. Med. Sci. Program, 1969-75. Recipient Crystal Cross award Ohio Thoracic Soc., 1995, Louis Weinstein award Clin. Infectious Diseases, 1995, Maurice Saltzman award Mt. Sinai Healthcare Found., 1999; named to Med. Hall of Fame, Cleve. Mag., 1998. Mem. Am. Soc. Microbiology (Gardner Middlebrook award 1998), Am. Thoracic Soc. (Trudeau medal 1986), Infectious Diseases Soc. Am., Phi Beta Kappa, Alpha Omega Alpha. Home: 24761 S Woodland Rd Cleveland OH 44122-3327

WOLINSKY, IRA, nutritionist; b. N.Y.C., Mar. 30, 1938; s. Abraham and Rachel (Stupsky) W.; m. Mary Ann C. Leonard, Jan. 9, 1965; children: Daniella, David. BS, CCNY, 1960; MS, Kans. U., 1965, PhD, 1968. Lectr. Hebrew U., Jerusalem, 1968-74; assoc. prof. Pa. State U., University Park, 1974-79; prof. U. Houston, 1979—. Editor of books and series on nutrition sci., sports nutrition, nutrition methods, exercise physiology; contbr. rsch. articles to profl. jours. Office: U Houston Dept Human Devel Houston TX 77204-0001 E-mail: iwolinsky@uh.edu.

WOLINSKY, JERRY SAUL, neurology educator; b. Balt., Nov. 26, 1943; s. Morris and Anne Melinda (Smith) W.; m. Gerlind Stähler, Jan. 20, 1969; children: Anja Kerstin, Jean-Paul. BS in Biology, Ill. Inst. Tech., 1965; MD, U. Ill., Chgo., 1969. Diplomate Nat. Bd. Med. Examiners, Am. Bd. Psychiatry and Neurology. Instr. neurology U. Calif., San Francisco, 1973-75; rsch. assoc. neurology VA Hosp., 1975-78; asst. prof. neurology U. Calif., 1975-78; assoc. prof. neurology and immunology Johns Hopkins U., Balt., 1978-83; Bartels Family prof. neurology U. Tex., Houston, 1983—. Program dir. Multiple Sclerosis Update Series, Houston. Author book chpts.; mem. editorial bd. Annals of Neurology, 1980-87, Neuro Virology and Multiple Sclerosis, 1994—; assoc. editor Sci. Am. Medicine, 1995—; mem. editorial adv. bd. Critical Revs. in Clin. Neurobiology, 1983-88; ad hoc reviewer numerous jours.; contbr. over 200 articles to profl. jours. Comdr. USAR, 1970-77. Recipient David M. Oklon scholarship, 1968-69, Basil O'Connor Starter Rsch. grant Nat. Found. March of Dimes, 1975-78, NIH Rsch. Career Devel. award, 1979-83; rsch. grantee NIH, Nat. Multiple Sclerosis Soc., Clayton Found. for Rsch. Fellow Am. Acad. Neurology, AAAS; mem. Am. Neurol. Assn., Tex. Med. Assn., Am. Soc. Clin. Investigation, Tex. Neurol. Soc., Harris County Med. Soc. Home: 3311 Rice Blvd Houston TX 77005-2933 Office: Univ Tex 6431 Fannin St Ste 7 044 Houston TX 77030-1501

WOLINTZ, ARTHUR HARRY, physician, neuro-ophthalmologist; b. Bklyn., May 30, 1937; s. Louis and Celia (Ragofsky) W.; m. Carol Sue Bergstein, Nov. 28, 1963; children: Robyn Joy, Ellen Sharon. Student, NYU, 1955-58; MD summa cum laude, SUNY, Bklyn., 1962; postgrad., Columbia U., 1967-68. Diplomate Am. Bd. Psychiatry and Neurology, Am. Bd. Ophthalmology; licensee Nat. Bd. Med. Examiners, U. State of N.Y. Intern Maimonides Hosp., Bklyn., 1962-63, jr. resident in medicine, 1963-64; resident Nat. Inst. Neurol. Diseases and Blindness, Bethesda, Md., 1964-66; chief resident Mt. Sinai Hosp., N.Y.C., 1966-67; clin. asst. prof. neurology Downstate Med. Ctr. SUNY, Bklyn., 1968-69, resident in ophthalmology, 1969-71, from asst. prof. to prof., 1971—, prof. clin. ophthalmology and clin. neurology, 1977—, interim chief ophthalmology, 1983, acting regional chmn. dept. ophthalmology, 1984, prof. ophthalmology, 1987—, chmn. dept. ophthalmology, 1987-96; Disting. tchg. prof. to chair emeritus dept. ophthalmology SUNY-Health Sci. Ctr. Bklyn., 1995, 96—; asst. neurologist Presbyn. Hosp., N.Y.C., 1967-68; instr. neuropathology Coll. Physicians and Surgeons Columbia U., 1967-68; instr. neurology Mt. Sinai Sch. Medicine, 1967-68; assoc. dir. neurology Maimonides Med. Ctr., Bklyn., 1968-69; asst. neurologist Coney Island Hosp., 1968-69. Vis. neurologist Kings County Hosp. Ctr., Bklyn, 1968-69; chief div. ophthalmology and neuro-ophthalmology Kingsbrook Jewish Med. Ctr., Bklyn., 1971, sec. med. and dental staff 1976-77, v.p. 1978-79, pres. 1980-81, dir. ophthalmology 1981; attending physician State Univ. Hosp., Bklyn., 1971, Kings County Hosp. Ctr., Bklyn., 1971; cons. Luth. Med. Ctr., Beth Israel Med. Ctr., Brookdale Hosp. Med. Ctr., Bklyn., L.I. Coll. Hosp., Bklyn., Maimonides Med. Ctr., Cath. Med. Ctr. Bklyn. and Queens, Bklyn. VA Hosp. Author: Essentials of Clinical Neuro-Ophthalmology, 1976; contbr. chpts. to sci. textbooks and handbooks, articles to profl. jours. Pres. Flatbush Jewish Ctr., Bklyn. With USPHS 1964-66. Recipient J. Eugene Chalfin Meml. Lectr. award Alumni Assn. State Univ.-Kings County, 1981, Richard C. Troutman Master Tchr. award in Ophthalmology, Alumni Assn. SUNY Health Sci. Ctr., Bklyn., 1987, Tchr. of Yr. award dept. ophthalmology Interfaith Med. Ctr., 1988, Disting. Alumni Achievement award Alumni Assn., SUNY Health Sci. Ctr., Bklyn., 1997. Fellow ACP, ACS, Am. Acad. Ophthalmology and Otolaryngology, Am. Acad. Neurology; mem. AMA, AAAS, Med. Soc. County Kings, Med. Soc. State N.Y., Bklyn. Ophthal. Soc., N.Y. Acad. Medicine, Am. Acad. Neurology, Alumni Assn. SUNY (pres.-elect 1989, pres. 1990-91, Richard C. Troutman M.D. Master Tchr. award in ophthalmology 1987, Disting. Alumni Achievement award 1998), Oddfellows, Alpha Omega Alpha. Avocations: Torah reader, cantor. Home and Office: 100 Ocean Pky Brooklyn NY 11218-1755

WOLITARSKY, JAMES WILLIAM, securities industry executive; b. Tarrytown, N.Y., Feb. 19, 1946; s. Edward and Beulah (Kemmet) W.; m. Jean T. Nalle; children: James Jr., Matthew; stepchildren: Timothy, Joan. BA, Franklin and Marshall Coll., 1968; MBA, NYU, 1973. Auditor Hertz, Herson & Co., N.Y.C., 1970-73; comml. loan officer Phila. Nat. Bank, 1973-76; CFO, Almo Electronics Corp., Phila., 1976-80; dir. budget and control Paine Webber Inc., N.Y.C., 1981-82, dir. mktg. adminstrn., 1982-83, sr. v.p., dir. mut. funds and asset mgmt., 1983-84; sr. v.p., dir. product mgmt. Phila. Nat. Bank, 1984-86; exec. v.p., CFO, Moseley Holding Corp., N.Y.C., 1986-87; pres., CEO Moseley Securities Corp., 1987-88; exec. v.p. Gruntal Fin. Corp., 1988-91; CFO, Janney Montgomery Scott Inc., Phila., 1992-99, pres., 2000—, pres., CEO, 2001—, also bd. dirs. Bd. dirs. Independence Sq. Properties, Pa. Trust Co. Bd. dirs. Cliveden of Nat. Hist. Trust, Inc., World Affairs Coun. Phila., Securities Industry Assoc. Sgt. U.S. Army, 1968—70. Decorated Bronze Star, Vietnam Cross of Gallantry. Mem. Securities Industry Assn., Phila. Country Club. Episcopalian. Avocations: fishing, skiing, tennis, golf. Office: Janney Montgomery Scott Inc 1801 Market St Philadelphia PA 19103-1675 E-mail: jwolitarsky@jmsonline.com.

WOLITZER, STEVEN BARRY, investment banker; b. Bklyn., Mar. 14, 1953; s. Philip and Regina (Wurm) W.; m. Joyce Sue Lindower, Dec. 7, 1985; children: David Joel, Scott Richard, Rachel. BS, NYU, 1973; MBA, Harvard U., 1977. CPA, N.Y. Mng. dir. Lehman Bros. Inc., N.Y.C., 1977—, head global mergers and acquisitions, 1996—. Home: 1185 Park Ave Apt 6A New York NY 10128-1309 Office: Lehman Bros Inc 745 South Avenue New York NY 10019 E-mail: swolitze@lehman.com.

WOLK, MARTIN, physicist, electronics engineer; b. Long Branch, N.J., Jan. 13, 1930; s. Michael and Tillie (Barron) W.; 1 child, Brett Martin. BS, George Washington U., 1957, MS, 1968; PhD, U. N.Mex., 1973. Physicist Naval Ordnance Lab., White Oak, Md., 1957-59, Nat. Oceanic and Atmospheric Adminstrn., Suitland, 1959-66; solid state physicist Night Vision Lab., Fort Belvoir, Va., 1967-69; rsch. asst. U. N.Mex., Albuquerque, 1969-73; electronics engr. Washington Navy Yard, 1976-83, TRW, Inc., Redondo Beach, Calif., 1983-84; physicist Metrology Engring. Ctr., Pomona, 1984-85; electronics engr. Naval Aviation Depot North Island, San Diego, 1985—. Cons. Marine Corps Logistics Base, Barstow, Calif., 1985—, Naval Weapons Station, Fallbrook, Calif., 1987-89, Naval Weapons Support Ctr., Crane, Ind., 1989—. Contbr. articles to Jour. Quantitative Spectroscopy and Radiative Transfer, Monthly Weather Rev., Proceedings of SPIE, Procs. of EUROPTO. Cpl. 11th Airborne Div., 511 Parachute Infantry Reg., U.S. Army, 1946-49, Japan. Mem. IEEE, Soc. Photo-Optical Instrumentation Engring., European Optical Soc., Sigma Pi Sigma, Sigma Tau. Achievements include development of first Tiros meteorological satellites; research on electron-beam for micro-circuit device fabrication; development of electro-optical calibration systems for the TOW missile system optical and night vision sights for the Marine Corps; development of visible and infrared spectral radiometric system utilizing a Fourier Transform Interferometer spectrometer and dual conjugate Cassegrainian optical telescopes for primary standards calibration of thermal radiation sources for the Navy. Home: 740 Eastshore Ter Unit 91 Chula Vista CA 91913-2421

WOLKEN, JONATHAN, performing company executive; m. JoAnne Wolken; 4 children. Grad., Dartmouth Coll. Co-founder, artistic dir. Pilobolus Dance Theatre, Washington Depot, Conn., 1991, devel. dir., 1991—. Artist-in-residence USIS Arts Am. Program, Kuopio, Finland; tchr. Pilobolus Summer Workshop, Maine. Choreographer (Operas) Where the Wild Things Are, Glyndebourne Festival Opera, creator (television feature) Oneiric, Pilobolus/Danish TV. Office: Pilobolus Dance Theatre Bo 388 Washington Depot CT 06794*

WOLKOFF, EUGENE ARNOLD, lawyer; b. N.Y.C., June 9, 1932; s. Oscar and Jean (Zablow) W.; m. Judith Gail Edwards, Oct. 15, 1967; children—Mandy, Elana, Alexa, Justine. AB, Bklyn. Coll., 1953; LLB, St. John's U., 1961. Bar: N.Y. 1962, N.Mex. 1994. Practiced in, N.Y.C and Santa Fe; mem. Callahan & Wolkoff, N.Y.C., 1965—; gen. counsel BGK Group of Cos. Bd. dirs. Babylon Enterprises, Inc., Hist. Newspaper Archives, Inc., Beacon Concessions, Inc.; mem. nat. panel arbitrators Am. Arbitration Assn. Served to lt. col. USAFR, 1953-75. Mem. N.Y. State Bar Assn., N.Mex. Bar Assn., Pi Beta Gamma. Office: 2124 Broadway New York NY 10023-1722 also: 330 Garfield St Santa Fe NM 87501-2640 E-mail: gene@bgkgroup.com.

WOLKOV, HARVEY BRIAN, radiation oncologist, researcher; b. Cleve., Feb. 8, 1953; s. Sidney and Norma (Levin) W.; m. Lauren Cronin, Jan. 9, 1993; 1 child, Nicole. BSc, Purdue U., 1975, MSc, 1977; MD, Medical Coll. Ohio, 1979. Diplomate Am. Bd. Radiology. Intern U. Calif., San Francisco, 1979-80; res. Stanford Med. Ctr., Stanford, Calif., 1980-83; rsch. asst. Stanford (Calif.) U., 1982; from asst. clin. prof. to assoc. clin. prof. U. Calif., Davis, 1983-97, assoc. clin. prof., 1997—; medical dir. Mercy Hosps., Sacramento, 1987-90; med. dir. Sutter Cancer Ctr. Dept. Radiation Oncology, 1990—. Co-prin. investigator Pediat. Oncology Group, Chgo., 1989—; adv. bd. Nat. Graves Disease Found., Jacksonville, Fla., 1993—; dir. Sutter Gamma Knife Ctr., 1997—; bd. dirs. Sutter Hosps. Found., Sacramento. Author: (with others) Intraoperative Radiation, 1989, Frontiers in Radiation, 1991, Textbook Radiation Oncology, 1998, Internat. Jour. Bd. Biol. Physics; contbr. 30 articles to profl. jours. Fellow Am. Cancer Soc., 1978, 1983, Am. Coll. Radiology, 1997; recipient Travel award Am. Soc. Therapeutic Radiology Oncology, Reston, Va., 1987. Mem.: Sulter Inst. for Medical Rsch. (chair rsch. com.

1996—), Calif. Radiation Oncology Soc. (pres.-elect 1999, pres. 2000—01), Am. Soc. Therapeutic Radiology and Oncology (bd. dirs. 2000—, vice chair outcome rsch., fin. com., corp. rels., workforce, comm., coronary artery radiation therap coms.), Radiation Therapy Oncology Group (com. chair 1986—90, publication com. 1990—, mem. com. 1990—, lung and brain com. 1990—), No. Calif. Radiation Oncology Soc. (pres. 1999—2001), Coun. Affiliated Radiation Oncology Soc. (pres. 1999—2001), Assn. Residents Radiation Oncology (exec. com. 1997—2000), Am. Cancer Soc. (reviewer 1990—), Am. Coll. Radiology (chmn. standards accreditation com. 1997—, councilor at large 1999, alt. councilor 2000—, mem. expert panels). Jewish. Avocations: oil painting, sculpture, travel. Office: Sutter Cancer Ctr 2800 L St Ste 10 Sacramento CA 95816-5616 E-mail: hbwolkov@aol.com.

WOLKOW, ALAN EDWARD, chiropractic physician; b. Bklyn., Nov. 9, 1946; s. Benjamin and Leanora (Pliner) W.; m. Terri Lynn Blumenfeld, May 29, 1977; children: Jana, Darren, Michael. AA, CUNY, 1966; BSME, N.Y. Inst. Tech., 1969; postgrad. mech. engring., U. Conn., 1970-71, engr.-in-tng., 1976; DChiropractic cum laude, Life Coll., Marietta, Ga., 1983. Nat. bd. qualified chiropractic orthopedist; cert. CPR; lic. real estate salesman, Ga. Mech. engr. Pratt & Whitney Aircraft Co., East Hartford, Conn., 1969-72, Combustion Engring., Windsor, 1972-74, Ebasco Svcs., Norcross, Ga., 1974-77, Simons Eastern Co., Decatur, 1977-79, Austin Co., Atlanta, 1979-80; pvt. practice Wolkow Chiropractic Clinic PC, Duluth, Ga., 1984—. Injury prevention cons. Swift Atlanta, Suwanee, Ga., 1987-94. Area coord. Nat. Assn. for Seatbelt Safety,Duluth, 1984—; mem. spkr.'s bur. Ga. Safety Belt Coalition, Atlanta, 1985—, Arthritis Found. Ga., Atlanta, 1987—; asst. advisor B'nai B'rith Youth Orgn., Atlanta, 1978-93; vol./fundraiser March of Dimes, 1984—. Recipient Cornerstone award PMA, Inc., 1985, Comdr. award, 1986, Chancellor award, 1987; recognition award Found. for Advancement Chiropractic Edn., 1988. Mem. ASME, Am. Chiropractic Assn., Ga. Chiropractic Assn., Nat. Back Found., Am. Coll. Chiropractic Orthopedists, Coun. on Diagnostic Imaging, Parker Chiropractic Resource Found., Kiwanis. Democrat. Jewish. Avocations: clarinet, saxophone, tennis, racquetball. Home: 3754 Loveland Ter Atlanta GA 30341-1742 Office: 3675 Satellite Blvd Ste 840 Duluth GA 30096 E-mail: drawolkow@aol.com.

WOLKOWITZ, OWEN MARK, physician, psychiatrist, researcher; b. Washington, Oct. 3, 1952; s. Gabriel Wolkowitz and Mandzia Wolkowitz-Murik; m. Janet Anne Negley, Sept. 9, 1984. BA, NYU, 1974; MD, U. Md., 1979. Diplomate Am. Bd. Psychiatry and Neurology. Intern in psychiatry Stanford (Calif.) U. Med. Ctr., 1979-80, resident in psychiatry, 1980-82, chief resident in psychiatry, 1983; med. staff fellow NIMH, Bethesda, Md., 1983-86; attending psychiatrist, assoc. prof., rschr. U. Calif., San Francisco, 1986-87, staff psychiatrist, team leader Adult Inpatient Svcs., 1991-95; dir. Adult Psychopharmacology Clinic, 1995—; mem. dean's award com. U. Calif., 1986-93, mem. student rsch. fellowship com., 1986-87, mem. residency tng. objective com., 1986-87, prof. psychiatry, 1997—. Jour. reviewer Archives of Gen. Psychiatry, Biol. Psychiatry, Gen. Hosp. Psychiatry, Hosp. & Cmty. Psychiatry, Jour. Clin. Psychopharmacology, Jour. Nervous & Mental Disease, Jour. Neurosci., Jour. Psychiat. Rsch., Psychiatry Rsch., Psychosomatics, Schizophrenia Bull., Schizophrenia Rsch., Western Jour. Medicine; mem. behavioral scis. rev. bd. VA, 1988, 90, rsch. adv. group, 1993; mem. adv. bd. for clin. investigation Western Jour. Medicine, 1993; mem. steering com. Napa State Hosp., 1988-95. Contbr. more than 130 articles to profl. jours. Recipient Young Rschr. Neurosci. award Calif. Assn. for the Mentally Ill, 1989, Stanley award Nat. Assn. for the Mentally Ill, 1993, Young Investigator award Nat. Alliance for Rsch. on Schizo and Affective Disorder, 1989, established investigator award Nat. Alliance for Rsch. in Schizo and Affective Disorder, 1995; grantee S. Henderson Fund, 1988-90, Biomed. Rsch. Support, 1989-91, 93, AIDS Clin. Rsch. Ctr., 1990-91, NIMH, 1987-93, Scottish Rite Found., 1993-95, Stanley Found., 1993-95. Mem. AAAS, Am. Psychiat. Assn. (session chmn. ann. meeting 1993), Psychiat. Rsch. Soc., Soc. for Biol. Psychiatry, Am. Soc. Clin. Psychopharmacology, Internat. Soc. for Psycho-Neuro-Endocrinology (Carl P. Richter prize 1992), Collegium Internationale Neuropsychopharmacologicum, World Fedn. Socs. Biol. Psychiatry, West Coast Coll. Biol. PsychiatryNo. Calif. Psychiat. Soc., Psi Chi. Avocations: tennis, jogging, reading, biking. Office: U Calif/Dept Psychiatry Langley Porter Psychiat 401 Parnassus Ave # F984 San Francisco CA 94143-0984

WOLL, HARRY J. electrical engineer; b. Farmington, Minn., Aug. 25, 1920; s. Henry L. and Clara M. (Fredrickson) W.; m. Mary V. Cowan, Feb. 15, 1947; children: Daniel, Alice. BSE.E., N.D. State U., 1940; postgrad., Ill. Inst. Tech., 1940-41; PhD, U. Pa., 1953. With RCA Corp., 1941-85, chief engr. aerospace systems div. Mass., 1963-69, div. v.p. govt. engring. Moorestown, N.J., 1969-75; div. v.p., gen. mgr. RCA Automated Systems, Burlington, 1975-81; staff v.p., chief engr. RCA Electronic Products and Labs., Princeton, N.J., 1981-85. Patentee in field. Chmn. bd. trustees Moore Sch. Elec. Engring., U. Pa., 1976-90; trustee U. Pa., 1989-91. Recipient 50th Anniversary gold medal Moore Sch. Elec. Engring., U. Pa., 1973 Fellow AAAS, IEEE (past chmn. Phila. sect., past chmn. fellow com.), Aerospace Industries Tech. Council (past chmn.); mem. KC, Sigma Phi Delta, Phi Kappa Phi. Roman Catholic. Home: PO Box 679 Concord MA 01742-0679 E-mail: hjwoll@cs.com.

WOLLAN, CHRISTINE R. clinical social worker; b. Evanston, Ill., Feb. 21, 1954; m. Douglas Boleen, Oct. 11, 1980; children: Karl, Lauren. BA, Luther Coll., 1976; MSW, U. Minn., 1980. Bd. cert. diplomate clin. social work; lic. ind. clin. social worker. Clin. social worker Storefront/Youth Action, Edina, Minn., 1980-84, Cen. Minn. Mental Health Ctr., Buffalo, 1984-87, Storefront/Youth Action, Richfield, 1987-89; pvt. practice social worker Aspen Counseling Clinic, Plymouth, 1989—, Maple Grove (Minn.) Counseling Ctr., 1989-94, Prinsen Counseling Clinic, Maple Grove, 1991-94; sch. social worker Monticello Pub. Schs., 1994—. Cons. Project Charlie, Edina, 1986—; task force mem. Early Childhood Family Edn., Monticello, Minn., 1987-89. Bd. dirs. United Way. Recipient Scholarship award U. Minn. Hosps., 1978, Leadership in Ednl. Excellence award, 1999. Mem. Acad. Cert. Social Workers, NASW, Minn. Soc. for Clin. Social Work. Home: 9816 Kalenda Ave NE Monticello MN 55362-8675

WOLLAN, CURTIS NOEL, theater producer, theater director; b. Mpls., Nov. 10, 1951; s. Curtis Berdins and Lorraine Alice (Walser) Wollan; m. Jane Ellen Deter, May 17, 1980; children: Alexis Lorraine, Chet Curtis. BA in Speech and Theatre, Luther Coll., Decorah, Iowa, 1973; MFA in Directing, U. Iowa, 1976. Ptnr., artistic dir. Stage Two Prodns., Mpls., 1977-85; artistic dir. Chimera Theatre Co., St. Paul, 1985-87; ptnr., artistic dir. T.C.C. Prodns., Mpls., 1990-92; pres., prodr., dir. Troupe Am., Inc., 1987—. Guest dir. Circa 21 Prodns., Rock Island, Ill., 1983—, Big League Theatricals, N.Y.C., 1988—93, Ryman Auditorium, Nashville, 1999, Lucas Theatre for the Arts, Savannah, 2001, Theatre Under the Stars, Houston, 2001; past sec., bd. dirs. Midwest Citizens for Arts, Mpls., 1985—87; dir., asst. prodr. Sheehan Prodns. Medora Mus., Mpls., 1987—91; prodr., dir. Medora Musical, 1992—. (creator, dir. mus. concept revue): (plays) The Lovely Liebowitz Sisters, 1986—, Big River, 1988—89, Oil City Cymphony, 1989—90, Gifts of the Magi, 1990, Driving Miss Daisy, 1991—92, Steel Magnolias, 1992—93, On Golden Pond, 1994, A Christmas Carol, 1996—2002, The Odd Couple, 1997, Moon Over Buffalo, 1998—99, Lost Highway, 2000—01, The Sunshine Boys, 2001—, Same Time, Next Year, 2002; (co-author, dir. nat. tour): Mr. Pickwick's Christmas, 1987—92; prodr.(nat. tour): A Child's Christmas in Wales, 1988—89, Babes in Toyland, 1992—96, Tap Dance Kid, 1995, Mahalia, 1996, Miracle on 34th St., The Musical, 1997—98, Schoolhouse Rock Live!, 1997—2000, Here's Love, 1999; Hank and My Honky Tonk Heroes, 1999—; Forever Plaid, 1999—; actor: (films) Bix, 1990, The Childhood Friend, 1993. Recipient Best Prodn. award, Twin Cities Critics Cir., 1981, Best Direction award, 1981, Patriotism award, Am. Legion, 1995. Mem.: Southeastern Theatre Conf. Lutheran. Avocations: movies, restaurants, travel, history, horseback riding. Office: Troupe Am Inc 528 Hennepin Ave Ste 206 Minneapolis MN 55403-1810 E-mail: cwollan@mninter.net.

WOLLE, CHARLES ROBERT, federal judge; b. Sioux City, Iowa, Oct. 16, 1935; s. William Carl and Vivian (Down) W.; m. Kerstin Birgitta Wennerstrom, June 26, 1961; children: Karl Johan Knut, Erik Vernon, Thomas Dag, Aaron Charles. AB, Harvard U., 1959; JD, Iowa Law Sch., 1961. Bar: Iowa 1961. Assoc. Shull, Marshall & Marks, Sioux City, 1961-67, ptnr., 1968-80; judge Dist. Ct. Iowa, 1981-83; justice Iowa Supreme Ct., Sioux City and Des Moines, 1983-87; judge U.S. Dist. Ct. (so. dist.) Iowa, Des Moines, 1987-92, chief judge, 1992-99, sr. U.S. dist. judge, 2001—. Faculty Nat. Jud. Coll., Reno, 1983—. Editor Iowa Law Rev., 1960-61 Vice pres. bd. dirs. Sioux City Symphony, 1972-77; sec., bd. dirs. Morningside Coll., Sioux City, 1977-81 Fellow Am. Coll. Trial Lawyers; mem. ABA, Iowa Bar Assn., Sioux City C. of C. (bd. dirs. 1977-78) Avocations: sports, art, music, literature. Office e-mail: charles r. Office: Sr US Dist Judge US Courthouse Annex Ste 403 110 E Court Ave Des Moines IA 50309 E-mail: wolle@iasd.uscourts.gov.

WOLLE, WILLIAM DOWN, foreign service officer; b. Sioux City, Iowa, Mar. 11, 1928; s. William Carl and Vivian Lucille (Down) W.; m. Zanie L. Donahue, Feb. 7, 1992; children from previous marriage: Laila Jean, William Nicholas. BA, Morningside Coll., 1949; M.Internat. Affairs, Columbia U., 1951. Joined U.S. Fgn. Service, 1951; consular officer Baghdad, Iraq, 1951-52; econ. officer, 1952-53; consular officer Manchester, Eng., 1954-56; trainee Arab lang. and area Beirut, Lebanon, 1957-58; fgn. service officer gen. Aden, So. Yemen, 1958-59; econ. officer Jidda, Saudi Arabia, 1959-62; internat. relations officer, 1962-64; officer in charge Arab-Israeli affairs, 1965-67; detailed Nat. War Coll., 1967-68; counselor polit. affairs Kuwait City, Kuwait, 1968-70; econ. officer, dir. AID, Amman, Jordan, 1970-73; econ. officer Nairobi, 1973-74; ambassador to Oman, Muscat, 1974-78. Dir. Middle Eastern/South Asian Research Office, Dept. State, 1978-79; ambassador to United Arab Emirates, 1979-81; adviser internat. affairs Indsl. Coll. Armed Forces, 1982-84; chief sr. officer assignments, Washington, 1984-86. Served with AUS, 1946-47. Recipient Superior Service award Dept. State, 1974, Outstanding Civilian Service award Dept. Def., 1984. Home: PO Box 362 Occoquan VA 22125

WOLLENBERG, RICHARD PETER, paper manufacturing company executive; b. Juneau, Alaska, Aug. 1, 1915; s. Harry L. and Gertrude (Arnstein) W.; m. Leone Bonney, Dec. 22, 1940; children: Kenneth Roger, David Arthur, Keith Kermit, Richard Harry, Carol Lynne. BSME, U. Calif., Berkeley, 1936; MBA, Harvard U., 1938; grad., Army Indsl. Coll., 1941; D in Pub. Affairs (hon.), U. Puget Sound, 1977. Prodn. control Bethlehem Ship, Quincy, Mass., 1938-39; with Longview (Wash.) Fibre Co., 1939—, safety engr., asst. chief engr., chief engr., mgr. container operations, 1951-57, v.p., 1953-57, v.p. ops., 1957-60, exec. v.p., 1960-69, pres., 1969-78, pres., chief exec. officer, 1978-85, pres., chief exec. officer, chmn. bd., 1985—, also bd. dirs. Mem. Wash. State Council for Postsecondary Edn., 1969-79, chmn., 1970-73; mem. western adv. bd. Factory Mutual Ins Co. Trustee Reed Coll., Portland, 1962—, chmn. bd. 1982-90. Served to lt. col. USAAF, 1941-45. Recipient Alumni Achievement award Harvard U., 1994. Mem. NAM (bd. dirs. 1981-86), Pacific Coast Assn. Pulp and Paper Mfrs. (pres. 1981-92), Inst. Paper Sci. and Tech. (trustee), Wash. State Roundtable. Home: 1632 Kessler Blvd Longview WA 98632-3633 Office: Longview Fibre Co PO Box 606 Longview WA 98632-7391

WOLLER, JAMES ALAN, lawyer; b. Adrian, Mich., Dec. 27, 1946; s. Robert Arthur and Florence Emma (Jacob) W.; m. Jill Ann Samis, Aug. 18, 1968 (div. Aug. 1978); 1 child, Emily Erin; m. Elizabeth Julia Frey, May 22, 1982 (div. Apr. 1999); m. Carol Pierini, Oct. 29, 1999. BA, U. Mich., 1969; JD, Columbia U., 1974. Bar: N.J. 1974, U.S. Dist. Ct. N.J. 1974, U.S. Tax Ct. 1976, U.S. Supreme Ct. 1995. Assoc. McCarter & English, Newark, 1974-79; v.p. Pfaltz & Woller, PA, Summit, N.J., 1979-86, pres., 1987—. Editor Columbia U. Human Rights Law Rev., 1973-74. Mem.: ABA, Summit Bar Assn. (pres. 1987—88), Union County Bar Assn., NJ Bar Assn., Columbia Law Sch. Assn. NJ (trustee 1992—97, v.p. 1997—2001, pres. 2001—), Raritan Yacht Club (Perth Amboy, NJ) (fin. sec. 1988—89, treas. 1989—92, vice commodore 1993—94, commodore 1994—95), Downtown Club (trustee 1997—99, treas. 1999, v.p. 2000, pres. 2001). Republican. Methodist. Avocation: sailing. Home: The Gatehouse 249 Hanover St Annapolis MD 21401 Office: Pfaltz & Woller PA 382 Springfield Ave Ste 217 Summit NJ 07901-2780 E-mail: jimwoller@aol.com.

WOLLERSHEIM, JANET PUCCINELLI, psychology educator; b. Anaconda, Mont., July 24, 1936; d. Nello J. and Inez Marie (Ungaretti) Puccinelli; m. David E. Wollersheim, Aug. 1, 1959 (div. June 1972); children: Danette Marie, Tod Neil; m. Daniel J. Smith, July 17, 1976. AB, Gonzaga U., 1958; MA, St. Louis U., 1960; PhD, U. Ill., 1968. Lic. psychologist, Mont. Asst. prof. psychology, asst. dir. testing/counseling ctr. U. Mo., 1968-71; prof. psychology U. Mont., Missoula, 1971—, dir. chin. psychology, 1980-87; chair Mont. Bd. Psychologists, 1977-78; cons. Mont. State Prison, 1971-85, Trapper Creek Job Corps, 1973—; pvt. practice Missoula, 1971—. Author numerous rsch. articles. Bd. dirs. Crisis Ctr., Missoula, 1972-73; mem. profl. adv. bd. Head Start, Missoula, 1972-79. Recipient Disting. scholar award U. Mont., 1991. Fellow Am. Psychol. Assn. (bd. dirs. div. clin. psychology 1990-92); mem. Rocky Mountain Psychol. Assn. (pres. 1983-84), Nat. Coun. Univ. Dirs. Clin. Psychology (bd. dirs. 1982-88). Home and Office: 105 Greenwood Ln Missoula MT 59803-2401 E-mail: jpwoller2000@yahoo.com.

WOLLERT, GERALD DALE, retired food company executive, investor; b. LaPorte, Ind., Jan. 21, 1935; s. Delmar Everette and Esther Mae W.; m. Carol Jean Burchby, Jan. 26, 1957; children— Karen Lynn, Edwin Del. BS, Purdue U., 1957. With Gen. Foods Corp., 1959-89, dir. consumer affairs N.Y., 1973-74, mng. dir. Cottee Foods div. Sydney, Australia, 1974-76, gen. mgr. Mexico div. Mexico City, 1978-79, pres. Asia/Pacific ops. Honolulu, corp. v.p. worldwide coffee and internat. div., 1979-89; ret., 1989. Dir. Gen. Foods cos., Japan, Peoples Republic China, Korea, India, Taiwan, Singapore, Philippines. Webelos leader Boy Scouts Am., Mexico City, 1978-79; co. gen. chmn. United Fund campaign, Battle Creek, Mich., 1964-65, White Plains, N.Y., 1972-73. Served with U.S. Army, 1958. Mem. Asian-U.S. Bus. Coun., Oahu Country Club (Hawaii), Venice Golf and Country Club (Fla.), Beacon Hills and Beechwood (Ind.) Club.

WOLLETT, ELEANOR LEIGH, general education curriculum coordinator; b. Hudson, Mich. d. Lawrence and Eleanor H. (Zuchowski) Ball; m. James E. Wollett; children: Larry, Linda, Lisa. BA in English, Siena Heights Coll., 1971, MA in Edn., 1976; PhD in Curriculum, Tchg., Ednl. Policy, Mich. State U., 1996. Cert. tchr., Mich. Tchr., Addison, Mich., 1967-70, Hudson, 1971-99; lang. arts coord., 1992-97; adj. faculty Mich. State, East Lansing, 1992, 93, Siena Heights U., Adrian, Mich., 1996—. Cons., adv. bd. S.E. Mich. Writing Project, Adrian, 1981-94; tchr. cons. Red Cedar Writing Project, East Lansing, 1994—. Organist, choir dir. Our Saviour Luth., Hudson. Mem. ASCD, Nat. Writing Project (tchr. cons.), Lenawee Reading Coun. (pres. 1989-90), Nat. Coun. Tchrs. of English, Mich. Coun. Tchrs. of English, Internat. Reading Coun., Mich. Reading Coun., Nat. Sci. Tchrs. Assn., Nat. Coun. Tchrs. Maths. Lutheran. Avocations: reading, writing, walking, piano, line dancing. Home: 653 S Meridian Rd Hudson MI 49247-9334 Office: Lenawee Intermediate Sch Dist Edn Svc Ctr 4107 N Adrian Hwy Adrian MI 49221-9309

WOLLINS, DAVID HART, lawyer; b. N.Y.C., Nov. 1, 1952; s. Donald John Wollins and Constance Joy Graham; m. Leslie Bjerg Lilly, Apr. 1, 1989; children: Alexandra Bjerg Lilly W., David Hart Jr. BS in Fin. and Mktg., U. Pa., 1974; JD, New Eng. Sch. Law, 1978. Bar: N.Y. 1979, U.S. Dist. Ct. (ea. and so. dists.) N.Y. 1979, U.S. Dist. Ct. Colo. 1986, U.S. Dist. Ct. (ea. dist.) Calif. 1999 U.S. Ct. Appeals (10th cir.) 1986, U.S. Ct. Appeals (fed., D.C. and 2d cirs.) 1990, U.S. Ct. Appeals (9th cir.), 1992, U.S. Ct. Claims 1983, U.S. Supreme Ct. 1994. Pres. Nature's Way Recycling Co., Boston, 1974-75; summer assoc. Phillips, Nizer, Benjamin, Krim & Ballon, N.Y.C., 1976-78, assoc., 1978-86; of counsel Cortez and Friedman, P.C., Englewood, Colo., 1986-87; mem. firm, co-head litigation dept. Brenman, Raskin, Friedlob & Tenenbaum, P.C., Denver, 1987-91; shareholder, head litigation dept. McGe-ady Sisneros & Wollins, P.C., 1991-95; spl. counsel Jonathan J. Hellman & Assoc., P.C., Englewood, 1995-96; mng. ptnr. Wollins, Hellman & Green, Denver, 1996—2001, Wollins & Hellman, P.C., Denver, 2001—. Pro bono atty., City N.Y., 1978-86. Author short stories and numerous poems. Mem. N.Y. Bar Assn., Colo. Bar Assn., Colo. Trial Lawyers Assn., Denver Bar Assn. Home: 311 Bannock St # A/C Denver CO 80223-1174 Office: Wollins & Hellman PC 720 S Colorado Blvd Ste 620S Denver CO 80246-1943 Fax: 303-758-8111. E-mail: dhwollins@cs.com.

WOLLMAN, HARRY, health care and executive search consultant; b. Bklyn., Sept. 26, 1932; s. Jacob and Florence Roslyn (Hoffman) W.; m. Anne Carolyn Hamel, Feb. 16, 1957; children: Julie Ellen, Emily Jane, Diana Leigh. AB summa cum laude, Harvard Coll., 1954, MD, 1958. Diplomate Am. Bd. Anesthesiology. Intern U. Chgo. Clinics, 1958-59; resident U. Pa., 1959-63, assoc. in anesthesia, 1963-65, mem. faculty, 1965-87, prof. anesthesia, 1970-87, prof. pharmacology, 1971-87, Robert Dunning Dripps prof., chmn. dept. anesthesia, 1972-87; prin. investigator Anesthesia Rsch. Ctr., 1972-78; program dir. Anesthesia Rsch. Tng. Grant, 1972-87; sr. v.p., chief acad. officer, dean Sch. Medicine Hahnemann U., Phila., 1987-92, prof. anesthesiology, 1987-92, prof. pharmacology, 1987-92, univ. prof., 1992-96; prin. Alexander, Wollman and Stark, Health Care Cons. Exec. Search, Woodstock, Vt., 1996—. Mem. anesthesia drug panel, drug efficacy study, com. on anesthesia Nat. Acad. Scis.-NRC, 1970-71, com. on adverse reactions to anesthesia drugs, 1971-72; mem. pharm. and toxicology tng. grants com. NIH, 1966-68, anesthesia tng. grants com., 1971-73, surgery, anesthesia and trauma study sect., 1974-78; chmn. com. on studies involving human beings U. Pa., 1972-76, chmn. clin. practice exec. com., 1976-80 Assoc. editor for revs.: Anesthesiology, 1970-75; Contbr. and editor books. Hon. John Harvard scholar Harvard Coll., 1950-53, Harvard Coll. scholar, 1953-54, Detur award, 1951; NIH rsch. traineeship fellow, 1959-63, Pharm. Mfg. Assn. fellow, 1960-61. Mem. Pa. Soc. Anesthesiologists (pres. 1972-73), Am. Physiol. Soc., Assn. U. Anesthetists (exec. coun. 1971-74, chmn. scientific adv. bd. 1975-77), Soc. Acad. Anesthesia Chairmen (chmn. com. fin. resources 1973-77, pres. 1977-78), Am. Dental Soc., Anesthesiology (adv. bd. 1985-90), Assn. Am. Med. Coll., Phi Beta Kappa, Sigma Xi. Home: 13 Hathorn Hl Woodstock VT 05091-1238 Office: Alexander Wollman and Stark 13 Hathorn Hl Woodstock VT 05091-1238

WOLLMAN, JUNE ROSE, clothing executive; b. Bklyn., June 14, 1929; d. Louis and Ella (Klein) Nierenberg; m. Howard Louis Wollman, Sept. 29, 1922; children: Jodi Ann (dec.), Randi Sue. Interior designer June Rose Decors Ltd., Valley Stream, N.Y., 1951—; with Louella Realty, N.Y.C., 1956-85; designer Lou Nierenberg Corp., 1956-80; with Lou Nierenberg Internat., 1974-85, Lou Nierenberg Ltd., N.Y.C., 1985—, real estate pres., 1985—. Cons. fake furs, jackets, coats, N.Y.C., 1985—. Trustee Green Acres Civic Cos., Valley Stream, 1951—; bd. dirs. Mill Brov Civic Assn., 1990—; presenter Meml. Jodi Ann Wollman Scholarship Ann., South High Sch., Valley Stream, 1969—; life mem. Temple Emanu-El, Lynbrook, 1969—, asst. to chair Long Island (N.Y.) inter temple networking caring cmtys., 1989—, bd. dirs. sisterhood, 1990—; founding sponsor Mt. Sinai Med. Ctr., past v.p.; pres. Sam & Rose Klein Family Inc., 1975-85, CEO, 1985—; pres. Jodi Ann Wollman Glioblastomn Rsch. Fund, 1970-90. Recipient L.I.J.H. Med. Ctr. award Ladies Svc. Guild, New Hyde Park, N.Y., 1965-85, Mt. Sinai Med. Ctr. award, N.Y.C., 1969-89. Mem. Am. Jewish Congress (pres. South Shore chpt. 1957-63). Republican. Jewish. Avocations: reading, golf, tennis, swimming, travel. Home and Office: June Rose Decors Ltd 13 Cloverfield Rd Valley Stream NY 11581-2421

WOLLMAN, ROGER LELAND, federal judge; b. Frankfort, S.D., May 29, 1934; s. Edwin and Katherine Wollman; m. Diane Marie Schroeder, June 21, 1959; children: Steven James, John Mark, Thomas Roger. BA, Tabor Coll., Hillsboro, Kans., 1957; JD magna cum laude, U. S.D., 1962; LLM, Harvard U., 1964. Bar: S.D. 1964. Sole practice, Aberdeen, 1964—71; justice S.D. Supreme Ct., 1971—85, chief justice, 1978—82; judge U.S. Ct. Appeals (8th cir.), 1985—, chief judge, 1999—2002; states atty. Brown County, Aberdeen, 1967—71. Served with U.S. Army, 1957—59. Office: US Ct Appeals US Courthouse & Fed Bldg 400 S Phillips Ave Rm 315 Sioux Falls SD 57104-6851

WOLLMAN RUSOFF, JANE SUSAN, journalist, writer; b. N.Y.C., Oct. 15, 1942; d. Charles Saul and Fay Wollman; m. Garry B. Rusoff, Nov. 9, 1991. Student, Hunter Coll., 1963-65. Accredited film journalist Motion Picture Assn. Am. Publicity asst. Am. Internat. Pictures, N.Y.C., 1961-62, 63-64, L.A., 1962-63; writer, editor London Express Features, N.Y.C., 1964-69; editor home electronics Merchandising Mag., 1974-77, Chgo., 1977-79; freelance electronics writer N.Y.C., 1979-85; freelance entertainment writer, 1985-91; freelance entertainment and fin. writer L.A., 1991—; contbg. editor Rsch. Mag. and Investor Direct Mag., 1993—; stringer N.Y. Times, 1996—. Author: Computer Workplace: Ergonomic Design for Computing at Home, 1985; co-author: (with Steve Allen) How to Be Funny, 1987; contbr. articles to Washington Post, L.A. Times Syndicate, Good Housekeeping, USA Today. Mem. Soc. Profl. Journalists, Deadline Club. Avocations: ballet and drama study, tutoring learning-disabled children. Office: 920 N Kings Rd # 309 West Hollywood CA 90069

WOLLMER, RICHARD DIETRICH, statistics and operations research educator; b. L.A., July 27, 1938; s. Herman Dietrich and Alice Myrtle (Roberts) W. BA in Math., Pomona Coll., 1960; MA in Applied Math., Columbia U., 1962; MS in Engring. Sci., U. Calif., Berkeley, 1963, PhD Engring. Sci., 1965. Scientist Rand Corp., Santa Monica, Calif., 1965-70; prof. info. systems Calif. State U., Long Beach, 1970—, vis. prof. Northridge, 1981-82, dept. chair, 2000—. Cons. McDonnell Douglas, Long Beach, Calif., 1978-80, 82, 85-91, Logicon, San Pedro, Calif., 1979-81, Behavioral Tech. Labs., U. So. Calif., 1973-75; vis. assoc. prof. Stanford U., 1976; rsch. scientist Electric Power Rsch. Inst., Palo Alto, Calif., 1977; rsch. engr. Jet Propulsion Lab., Pasadena, Calif., 1971. Contbr. articles to profl. jours. Deacon Bel Air Presbyn. Ch., L.A., 1982-84, treas. 1983. Mem. So. Calif. Inst. Mgmt. Sci.-Ops. Rsch. Soc. (chmn. 1981, 89, vice chmn., 1980, 88, treas. 1979), Ops. Rsch. Soc. Am., Inst. Mgmt. Sci., Internat. Fedn. Ops. Rsch. Mgmt. Sci., Internat. Fedn. Ops. Rsch. and Mgmt. Sci., So. Calif. INFORMS (treas. 1999). Republican. Avocations: classical music, sports, reading, antique cars. Home: 6132 Fernwood Dr Huntington Beach CA 92648-5574 Office: Calif State U 1250 N Bellflower Blvd Long Beach CA 90840-0001

WOLLPERT, SANDRA COX, horse breeder; b. Phila., July 8, 1950; d. Robert Miller and Audrey Olive (Fullam) Cox; m. Worth Alan Wollpert, Sept. 29, 1973; children: Worth Douglas, Shaunna Lee. BA, BS, Pa. State U., 1971. Cert. secondary sch. tchr., Pa. Tchr. Cheltenham (Pa.) High Sch., 1972-73; officer Four Seasons Devel. Inc., Ohio, 1975-86; pres. SW Acquisitions and SW Realty Inc., Chardon, Blythswood Farm, Inc., Chardon. Bd. dirs. CW Holding Co., Wilmington, Del., Spruco Investment Co., Wilmington, Diamondtech Inc., Chardon; chmn. Arabian Race Com., Ohio, 1990-95. Author: Cerissa, 1976, Rebel's Honor, 1980, Winter Roses, 1983, Rapture's Fury, 1988; contbg. editor (pedigrees) Arabian, 1996—; contbr. articles to profl. jours. including Finish Line. Contbr. WWF, NRDC. Mem. Nat. Trust for Scotland, Arabian Jockey Club, Deep Springs Trout Club, Concord Country Club, Union League Phila., EARA, The Baronial Order of Magna Carta, Phi Kappa Phi (hon.). Avocations: horseback riding, fishing, horse racing, reading, traveling. Office: Blythswood Inc 401 South St Chardon OH 44024-2805

WOLMAN, ERIC, health care consultant; b. N.Y.C., Sept. 25, 1931; s. Leo and Cecil (Clark) W.; m. Sandra Rosman, July 27, 1963; children: Karin, Alastair. AB in Math., Harvard Coll., 1953; PhD in Applied Math., Harvard U., 1957. Mem. tech. staff AT&T Bell Labs., Murray Hill, Holmdel, N.J., 1957-66, dept. head traffic rsch. and network engring. Holmdel, 1966-77, dept. head ops. rsch. and computing syss. West Long Branch, N.J., 1977-82, dept. head human performance engring. Piscataway, Summit, 1983-87; v.p. cmty. programs and rsch. Mich. Cancer Found., Detroit, 1988-91; asst. leader cancer prevention and control program Prentis Comprehensive Cancer Ctr. Met. Detroit, 1990-94; mem. faculty grad. program in cancer biology Wayne State U. Sch. of Medicine, Detroit, 1992-96; vis. rsch. prof. dept. sys. engring and ops. rsch. George Mason U., Fairfax, Va., 1996—. Mem. evaluation panel for fire programs Nat. Bur. of Standards, Gaithersburg, Md., 1966-74, evaluation panel for nat. engring. lab., 1974-80, working group on info. tech. NSF, Arlington, Va., 1980-81. Contbr. articles to profl. jours. Trustee Rumson (N.J.) Country Day Sch., 1973-81, Sea Edn. Assn., Woods Hole, Mass., 1981—. Fellow AAAS; mem. APHA, Inst. Ops. Rsch. and The Mgmt. Scis. (coun. 1979-82), Seabright Beach Club, Harvard Club (N.Y.C.). Avocation: cruising. Home: 7806 Hidden Meadow Ter Potomac MD 20854-1792 E-mail: eric.wolman@erols.com.

WOLMAN, J. MARTIN, retired newspaper publisher; b. Elizabeth, N.J., Mar. 8, 1919; s. Joseph D. and Dora (Baum) W.; m. Anne Paley, Sept. 12, 1943; children: Natalie, Jonathan, Ruth Ellen, Lewis Joel. Student, U. Wis., 1937-42. With Wis. State Jour., Madison, 1936-84, pub., 1968-84; pres., gen. mgr. Madison Newspaper, Inc., 1969-84, ret., 1984, dir., 1969—, Lee Enterprises, Inc., 1971-74; treas. Lee Endowment Trusts, 1988—. Sec.-treas. Madison Improvement Corp., 1958-62 Treas. Wis. State Jour. Empty Stocking

Club, 1948, Children and Youth Services Inc., 1962— ; mem. Mayor Madison Adv. Com., 1965; bd. dirs. United Givers Fund, 1960-64, trustee, 1980— ; ex-officio Roy L. Matson Scholarship Fund, 1961, Central Madison Com., Madison Art Assn.; trustee Edgewood Coll., Madison, U. Wis. Hosp. and Clinic; chmn. Madison Area Arts Coalition, 1984-85; bd. dirs. Univ. Health Sci. Center, 1975; chmn. U.S. Savs. Bond Met. Wis., 1983; coordinator Barneveld Disaster Fund, Wis., 1985-86; mem. U. Wis. Found., 1968-95; bd. dirs., trustee Wisc. Clin. Cancer Ctr., 1986—; Dir. Wisc. Newspaper Found., 1986-88; v.p., treas. Lee Endowment Found., 1989—. Served with AUS, 1942-46. Named Advt. Man of Year Madison Advt. Club, 1969, Madison Man of Achievement, 1976, Man of Yr. Salvation Army, 1993; recipient Disting. Service award Wis. Newspaper Assn., 1982, Community Service award Inland Daily Press Assn., 1983, Ralph D. Casey Minn. award for Disting. Service in Journalism, 1987, First Ringling Bros. Silver Smile award, 1993, Outstanding Svc. for Youth award Wis. State Jour., 1995, Rounders Youth Lifetime award, 1997. Mem. Madison C. of C. (dir. 1966-70, 74-84), Inland Daily Press Assn. (dir. 1961-65), Wis. Daily Newspaper League (pres. 1961-65), Wis. Newspaper Assn. (dir. 1977-84) Clubs: B'nai B'rith. Office: 1901 Fish Hatchery Rd Madison WI 53713-1248

WOLMAN, M. GORDON, geography educator; b. Balt., Aug. 16, 1924; s. Abel and Anna (Gordon) W.; m. Elaine Mielke, June 20, 1951; children: Elsa Anne, Abel Gordon, Abby Lucille, Fredericka Jeannette. Student, Haverford Coll.; AB in Geology, Johns Hopkins U., 1949; MA in Geology, Harvard U., 1951, PhD, 1953. Geologist U.S. Geol. Survey, 1951-58, part-time, 1958—; assoc. prof. geography Johns Hopkins U., Balt., 1958-62; prof. Johns Hopkins, 1962—. Prof. Johns Hopkins U., 1962—, chmn. dept. geography and environ. engring., 1958—90, interim provost, 1987—90, prof. environ. health sci., 1998—; adv. com. geography U.S. Office Naval Rsch., Oak Ridge Nat. Lab.; exec. com. diysn. earth sci. NRC; internat. environ. programs com., environ. studies bd., com. water, com. mineral resources and environ., chmn. nat. commn. water quality policy NAS; chmn. NRC Com. Adv. U.S. Geol. Survey; chmn. NAS Commn. Geoscis., Environment and Resources, NRC Bd. Sustainability, 1995—2000; chmn. study land use and populationNRC Tri-Acad., China, India; environ. adv. com. Savannah River Tech. ctr.; chmn. U.S. Com. for IIASA. Author: Fluvial Processes in Geomorphology, 1964; editl. bd.: Science mag. Pres. bd. trustees Park Sch., Balt.; pres. bd. dirs. Sinai Hosp., Balt., Resources for Future, 1980-87; adv. com. Inst. Nuclear Power Ops., 1982-85; active Balt. City Charter Revision Commn., Cmty. Action Com., Balt. With USNR, 1943-46. Recipient Meritorious Contbn. award Assn. Am. Geographers, 1972, Disting. Career award Geomorphology, 1993, D.L. Linton award Brit. Geomorphological Rsch. Group, 1994, Rachel Carson award Chesapeake Appreciation Inc., Ian Campbell medal Am. Geol. Inst., 1997, Ned. med. Desert Rsch. Inst. Fellow Am. Acad. Arts and Scis.; mem. ASCE, NAS, NAE, Am. Geophys. Union (chmn. subcom. sedimentation, pres. hydrol. sect., Robert Horton medal 2000), Geol. Soc. Am. (v.p. 1983, pres. 1984, Penrose medal 1999), Am. Philos. Soc., Am. Geog. Soc. (councillor 1965-70, Cullum Geog. medal 1989), Washington Geol. Soc., Agrl. Hist. Soc., Md. Acad. Scis. (exec. com. 1970-75), Phi Beta Kappa, Sigma Xi. Home: 2104 W Rogers Ave Baltimore MD 21209-4553 Office: Johns Hopkins U Dept Geography/Environ Engr Baltimore MD 21218 E-mail: wolman@jhu.edu.

WOLMAN, MARTIN, lawyer; b. Albany, N.Y., Feb. 2, 1937; s. Benjamin S. and Sonya (Kogan) W.; children: Koren M. Wolman-Tardy, Barton T., William B., Brandon S. AB, Brown U., 1958; LLB, U. Calif., Berkeley, 1964. Bar: Calif., 1964, Conn., 1965. Atty. Conn. Bank & Trust Co., Hartford, 1964-67; assoc. Day, Berry & Howard, 1967-72, ptnr., 1972—. Mem. Conn. Law Revision Commn., 1985—. Trustee Russell-Sage Coll., Troy, N.Y., 1990-96, Wadsworth Atheneum, 1994—; trustee Kingswood-Oxford Sch., West Hartford, Conn., 1980-93, chmn., 1986-89; bd. dirs. Hartford Hosp., 1991—, Inst. of Living, 1994, Hartford Health Care Corp., 1996—; mem. bd. govs. Hill-Stead Mus., Farmington, Conn., 1990-94. Lt. (j.g.) USN, 1958-61. Fellow Am. Coll. Trust and Estate Counsel (chmn. Conn. chpt. 1981-86); mem. Conn. Bar Assn. (chmn. exec. com. probate sect. 1979-82). Office: Day Berry & Howard City Place I 25th Fl Hartford CT 06103-3499 Business E-Mail: mwolman@dbh.com.

WOLMAN, MOSHE, pathologist, educator; b. Warsaw, Oct. 19, 1914; s. Yehuda Leib and Leah (Cukier) W.; m. Brigitte Eva Koebbel, Jan. 25, 1939; children: Dan, Ruth, Naomi, Amnon. MD, U. Rome, 1938. Asst. to chief physician Hadassah Hosp., Jerusalem, 1940-59; asst. to assoc. prof. Hebrew U. Med. Sch., 1949-59; head pathology Tel Hashomer Hosp., Israel, 1959-79; prof. pathology Tel Aviv U. Med. Sch., Israel, 1964-85. Head pathology lab. Br. Army 27th Gen. Hosp., 1945-46; prof. histology & cell biology Tel Aviv Med. Sch., 1966-74. Author: Histochemistry of Lipids, 1964, Biological Peroxidation of Lipids, 1975, Demagoguery and Rhetoric, 1990, Lipid Pigments, 1993; contbr. articles to profl. jours.; demarcated and identified new metabolic disease Wolman disease, 1956-60. Capt. pathologist Brit. Army, 1941-46, Mid. East Forces. Recipient Pearse prize Royal Microscopical Soc., Eng., 1988, Pioneer award Internat. Fedn. Histochemical Socs., Washington, 1988. Fellow Leopoldina Acad. Sci. Jewish. Home: 15 Ido St 52233 Ramat Gan Israel Office: Tel Aviv U Med Sch Dept Pathology 69978 Tel Aviv Israel

WOLNEK, STEPHEN S. church administrator; Pres. United Synagogue of Conservative Judaism, N.Y.C. V.p. Jewish Nat. Fund. Office: United Synagogue of Conservative Judaism 155 5th Ave New York NY 10010-6802

WOLNITZEK, STEPHEN DALE, lawyer; b. Covington, Ky., Mar. 13, 1949; s. Frederick William Jr. and Mary Ruth (Meiners) W.; m. Katherine Anita Bishop, Dec. 15, 1972; children: Marcus Stephen, Justin Bishop. BA cum laude, U. Notre Dame, 1970; JD, U. Cin., 1974. Bar: Ky. 1975, U.S. Dist. Ct. (ea. dist.) Ky. 1976, U.S. Supreme Ct. 1978, U.S. Dist. ct. (we. dist.) Ky. 1981, U.S. Ct. Appeals (6th cir.) 1991. Dep. sheriff Kenton County, Covington, 1971-75; assoc. Taliaferro & Smith, 1975-80; ptnr. Taliaferro, Smith, Mann, Wolnitzek & Schachter, 1980-86; officer Smith, Wolnitzek, Schachter & Rowekamp P.S.C., 1986-96; pres. Wolnitzek, Rowekamp, Bender & Bonar, P.S.C., 1996-98, Wolnitzek, Rowekamp & Bonar, P.S.C., Covington, 1998—2002. Bd. dirs. Ky. Legal Svcs. Plan Inc., 1984-96; adj. prof. Samuel Chase Coll. Law, No. Ky. U., 1995-98; mem. Ky. Jud. Retirement and Removal Commn. (now Ky. Jud. Conduct Commn.), 1995—, chair, 1996—. Mem. exec. com. Kenton County Boys-Girls Club, 1981—, sec., 1995, v.p., 1996, pres., 1997; mem. exec. com. Ky. Law Enforcement Coun., Frankfort, 1984-93, vice chmn., 1991-93, chair cert. com., 1986-93; mem. City Coun., Ft. Wright, Ky., 1984-85, mem. Bd. Adjustment, 1986-97, vice chair, 1995-97; pres. No. Ky. Comty. Ctr., Covington, 1985-86; mem. bd. visitors Chase Coll. Law, no. Ky. U., 1995-97; bd. dirs. Kenton Housing Inc., 1986—, sec., 1991-93, v.p., 1993-95, pres., 1995-97; trustee No. Ky. Youth Leadership Found., 1992—, exec. com. bd. dirs., 1992—, pres., 1996-2001; gen. chair diocesean annual appeal Diocese of Covington, Ky., 2001. Recipient Roy Taylor award No. Ky. Legal Aid Soc., 1985, Disting. Lawyer award No. Ky. Bar Assn., 1998; named Vol. of Yr., Community Chest United Appeal, Cin., 1986. Master: Samuel P. Chase Am. Inns of Ct.; fellow: No. Ky. Bar Found. (charter life), Ky. Bar Found. (charter life, bd. dirs. 1989—94, 1995—2000), Am. Bar Found.; mem.: Fraternal Order Police (Ky. gen. counsel 1975—), U. Cin. Alumni Assn. (trustee, bd. dirs. 1999—), Def. Rsch. Inst., Ky. Def. Counsel. (bd. dirs. 1982—86), Nat. Coun. Sch. Bd. Attys., Ky. Coun. Sch. Bd. Attys. (bd. dirs. 1981—87), Assn. Def. Trial Attys., Ky. Bar Assn. (bd. govs. 1984—96, chmn. ann. conv. 1986, chmn. ho. of dels. 1986, v.p. 1992—93, pres. 1994—95), Notre Dame Club Cin. Democrat. Roman Catholic. Avocations: sports, reading. Home: 1836 Beacon Hl Covington KY 41011-3684 Office: PO Box 352 502 Greenup St Covington KY 41011-2522 E-mail: wolnitfam@fuse.net.

WOLOSHCHUK, CANDACE DIXON, secondary school educator, artist, consultant; b. Joliet, Ill., Jan. 11, 1947; d. Harold Russell and Beatrice Diane (Johnson) Dixon; m. Christopher Ralph Jose, Mar. 1, 1969 (div. Sept. 1982); children: Amy Russell, Jennifer Seavey; m. Thomas Woloshchuk, Dec. 23, 1988; stepchildren: Michael, Debbie, Paul, John. BA in Art, Salem Coll., 1969; postgrad., Merrimac Coll., 1969; MA in Art Edn., U. Hartford, 1977; Cert. Dir. Fine Arts, Fitchburg State Coll., 1994; student, CAGS Mus., 2000. Cert. tchr., Mass., Conn. Art dir. Fred D. Wish Sch., Hartford, Conn., 1969-71; art tchr. Timothy Edwards Jr. H.S., South Windsor, 1971-72; art coord. Hebron (Conn.) Elem. Sch., Gilead Hill Sch., 1974-78; art tchr. Longmeadow (Mass.) Pub. Schs., 1978-82, Agawan (Mass.) Pub. Schs., 1982-85; visual arts coord. Wilbraham (Mass.) Mid. Sch., 1985—. Coord. medieval festival Wilbraham Mid. Sch., 1986-87, coord. Oriental festival, 1987-88; pres., owner Scholarships Unltd., Monson, Mass., 1992-94; mem. tchr.-trainer program U. Hartford, 1974-78; enrichment, art tchr. Elms Coll., 1988-93; v.p. Pioneer Valley Decorative Painters, 1996-97. One-women show Garrett Gallery, 1981; group shows include Spencer Arts Ctr., 1993, Craft Adventure Expo '93, 1993 (2nd and 3rd pl. awards), Craft Expo '92, 1992 (2nd pl. award), Wilbraham Pub. Libr., 1992, 93, 94. Chairwomen, mem. Wilbraham Arts Lottery Coun., 1987-88; program chairwoman Pioneer Valley Decorative Painters of Mass., 1996—, v.p., 1997—. Recipient Outstanding Visual and Performing Arts Edn. award, Mass. Alliance for Arts Edn., 1988, gold award Am. Sch. Food Svc. Assn., 1987. Mem. ASCD, NAFE, Nat. Art Edn. Assn., Mass. Art Edn. Assn., Mass. Tchrs. Assn., Wilbraham Tchrs. Assn., Am. Craft Coun. Republican. Avocations: sailing, painting, equestrian riding. Office: Wilbraham Mid Sch 466 Stony Hill Rd Wilbraham MA 01095-1574 E-mail: cwoloshchuk@hwrsd.org.

WOLOSHEN, JEFFREY LAWRENCE, automobile executive, consultant, accountant; b. Highland Park, Mich., July 4, 1949; s. Michael and Virginia May (Rosenau) W.; m. Catherine Ann Nowakowski, June 24, 1972; children: Matthew, Veronica. BSBA with distinction, Wayne State U., 1971; MBA, Mich. State U., 1998. CPA, Mich., Ill., Cert. Mgmt. Acct. Auditor Plante & Moran, CPAs, Southfield, Mich., 1968-74; mgmt. acct. Caterpillar Tractor Co., Peoria, Ill., 1974-77; div. controller Household Mfg., Freeport, 1977-80, SPX Corp., Muskegon, Mich., 1980-85; fin. exec. Chrysler Corp., Auburn Hills, 1985-98; sr. fin. mgr. source planning Daimler Chrysler Corp., 1999—. Treas. United Way Fund, Aurora, Ill., 1976-77; century mem. Boy Scouts Am., Detroit, 1988—. Mem. AICPAs, Inst. Cert. Mgmt. Accts. Republican. Roman Catholic. Avocations: photography, watercolors.

WOLOSHIN, MURRAY I. investment company executive; b. N.Y.C. s. Leon and Rosilyn Woloshin. Student, U. Pa., 1978; BS cum laude, Boston U., 1980; postgrad., Columbia U., 1989. CFA. Rsch. analyst, asst. to chair Niederhoffer, Cross & Zeckhauser, N.Y.C., 1980-81; v.p., rsch. analyst and trader Niederhoffer, Cross & Zeckhauser; NCZ Commodities, 1981-83; rsch. analyst and trader Sci. Mgmt., Livingston, N.J., 1984; ptnr., cons. fin. svcs. and rsch. analyst Benchmark Fin. Counselors, Roseland, 1985-89, ptnr., cons. utilities, rsch. analyst and portfolio mgr. N.Y.C., 1989-95; pres. Furray Logic Ltd., 2000—. Cons., analyst Consol. Edison, N.Y.C.; contbr. Electric Power Rsch. Inst. project distributed generation; cons. trading sys. and models REFCO (Howard Olonoff), N.Y.C., 1992-95; grader CFA exam Assn. for Investment Mgmt. and Rsch., Charlottesville, Va., 1994-96; developer/cons. inventory, point of sale and mgmt. info. sys. McManus Tires, Hackensack, N.J., 1987-91, 96-99; cons. ops. rsch. related to customer svc., participant devel. advanced decision support sys. AT&T Bell Labs., 1996-98; cons. dept. global fixed income J.P. Morgan, 1998—; expert witness in field. Mem. N.Y. Soc. Security Analysts, Assn. Investment Mgmt. and Rsch., Am. Mensa. Achievements include co-developed patent pending structured language generator which translates unstructured languages like spread sheets into structured languages. Office: Benchmark Fin Counselors Ste 225 500 E 77th St New York NY 10162-0001

WOLOSONOVICH, STEPHEN, violinist; b. Linden, N.J., Nov. 7, 1934; s. Stephen and Mary Wolosonovich. Student, N.Y. Coll. of Music, 1949-51, Eastman Sch. of Music, 1951-54, Meadowmount Sch. of Music, 1954-55; BS, Juilliard Sch. Music, 1959. Violinist Rochester Philharm., 1952-54, Rudié Syfonietta, 1962-63, Montovani Orch., 1962; violin soloist Ballet Russ de Monte Carlo, 1962; violinist, prodr., dir. Music for Young Listeners, N.Y., N.J., 1962-75; violin solo recital, lectr., tchr. U. Beijing, 1986. Violin solo lectr. Lehigh U., 1980. Violin soloist Svc. Electric Cable T.V., Allentown, Pa., 1978, 79, 81, violin soloist, interview Channel T, Nutley, N.J., 1981-82; arranger (concerto) Butterfly Concerto, 1996, Polonaise, 1995; debut recital Carnegie Recital Hall, 1982.

WOLOTKIEWICZ, MARIAN M. business executive; b. Camden, N.J., Apr. 22, 1954; d. Edward J. and Rita J. Wolotkiewicz; m. Paul J. Sagan, Mar. 31, 1984 (div. Aug. 1, 1994). AB in Polit. Sci., Mount Holyoke Coll., 1976; JD, Suffolk U., 1979; MBA Clark U., 1995. Notary pub., Mass. Manuscript editor Little, Brown & Co., Boston, 1979-84; freelance editor, 1984-88; freelance writer Camp Dresser & McKee Inc., 1985-87; dir. pub. info. Regis Coll., Weston, Mass., 1988-90; assoc. dir. planned giving Clark U., Worcester, 1990-93; dir. gift planning & policy Mus. Fine Arts, Boston, 1993-94; pvt. practice cons., 1994-96; project mgr. Global Bus. Process Integration The Gillette Co., 1996-99; bus. cons., 1999—2001; adminstrv. dir. CMT Ind. Labs., Ltd., Ballston Spa, NY, 2001—; owner Photos4You.com , 1999—, AsktheDivas.com, 1999—. Various writing, editing and communications activities for Mass. Bar Assn., 1978-83, Womens Bar Assn., 1979-83; freelance editor for publishers including Little, Brown & Co., Artech Ho., Ballinger, Butterworth, 1984-88. Chmn. adv. com. Stow (Mass.) Cable TV, 1983-94; active fundraising Mass. Assn. Womens Lawyers charity auction, 1984, Mt. Holyoke Coll., 1986-96; pres. Boston Alumnae Club, Mt. Holyoke Coll., 1997-99. Mem. Phi Delta Phi.

WOLOWITZ, DAVID, lawyer; b. Washington, Apr. 3, 1946; s. William H. and Frances H. Wolowitz; m. Roxanne S. Tooker, Aug. 29, 1970. AB, Washington U., 1968; MA, Harvard U., 1971; JD, U. Mich., 1975. Bar: N.H. 1975, U.S. Dist. Ct. N.H. 1975, U.S. Dist. Ct. (1st cir.) 1981, Mass. 1985. Staff atty. N.H. Legal Assistance, Concord, 1975-76, mng. atty. Portsmouth, 1977-79, N.H. Pub. Defender, Exeter, 1979-83; ptnr. Sanders & McDermott, Hampton, N.H., 1983-91; ptnr., dir. McLane Law Firm, Portsmouth, 1991—. Guest faculty trial advocacy program Harvard Law Sch., 1983—. Jewish. Office: 10 Pleasant St Portsmouth NH 03801-3816 E-mail: david.wolowitz@mclane.com.

WOLPE, CLAIRE FOX, civic worker, psychotherapist; b. N.Y.C., June 24, 1909; d. David and Pauline (Hirsch) Fox; A.B., Mills Coll., 1930; M.A., U. So. Calif., 1936, M.S.W., 1965; Ph.D., Marquette U., 1970; postgrad. Smith Coll., summer 1931, Columbia U., summer 1963, U. Mexico City, summer 1964; m. Arthur S. Wolpe, Dec. 25, 1932 (dec. Mar. 1962); children— Ruth (Mrs. Roy Rose), Sheri (Mrs. Jerome Langer). Student advisor Jewish student orgn. UCLA, 1931-33; with Travelers Aid, Los Angeles, 1934; med. social work Los Angeles County Gen. Hosp., 1934-38; with USPHS, 1938; social worker Los Angeles County Health Dept., 1938-39; psychiat. social worker Gateways Psychiat. Hosp. and Mental Health Center, Los Angeles, 1962-63, 65-66, ret. 1996; exec. dir. Bay Cities Mental Health Center, Los Angeles, 1966-68; supr. Airport Marina Counseling Service; pvt. practice. Mem. Mayors Com. on Civil Def. 1950-52, Wilshire Coordinating Council, 1954-58; leader Girl Scouts U.S.A., 1954-58; mem. regional bd. NCCJ, 1951-55. Bd. dirs. So. Calif. Mental Health Assn., 1955-58, Los Angeles chpt. A.R.C., 1951-53, Community Relations Conf. So. Calif., 1950-60, Los Angeles Jewish Fedn. Council, 1952-58, B'nai B'rith Anti-Defamation League, 1973— , Hillel Assn., 1973— . Fellow Soc. Clin. Social Workers, Am. Assn. Orthopsychiatry; mem. Nat. Assn. Social Workers, Psychotherapy Assn. So. Calif. (dir. 1967— , pres.-elect 1984), Calif. Marriage, Family and Child Counseling Assn., Group Psychotherapy Assn. So. Calif. (tribute award 1989), Am. Group Psychotherapy Assn., Los Angeles Transactional Analysis Soc. (sec.-treas. 1966-68), Psi Chi. Jewish religion. Mem. B'nai B'rith Women. Home and Office: 234 S Orange Dr Los Angeles CA 90036-3011

WOLPE, PAUL ROOT, government administrator, science educator; b. Charleston, Sc, Feb. 26, 1957; s. Gerald Isaac Wolpe and Elaine Ring Wolpe; m. Valerie Hope Root, Sept. 2, 1984; children: Ariel Lilianne Root, Kendra Rachel Root. PhD, Yale U., New Haven, CT, 1979—86. Prof. of bioethics U. of Pa, Philadelphia, Pa., 1992—; chief of bioethics NASA (NASA), Washington, 2001—; dir. of rsch. Dept of Psychiatry, Jefferson Med. Coll., Philadelphia, Pa., 1988—92. Dir. Ethics and Psychiatry Program, U. of PA, Philadelphia, Pa., 2000—; sr. fellow Leonard Davis Inst. of Health Economics, U. of PA, Philadelphia, Pa., 1998—. Author: (textbook) Sexuality and Gender in Society, (book) In the Winter of Life. Mem.: Nat. Med. Com., Planned Parenthood of Am. Office: Center for Bioethics University of PA 3401 Market Street Ste 320 Philadelphia PA 19104 Office Fax: 215-573-3036. E-mail: wolpep@mail.med.upenn.edu.

WOLPER, ALLAN L. journalist, educator; b. N.Y.C. s. Sydelle Wolper; m. Joanna Wolper; children: Jill Miller, Richard, Kim Arminen. BS, NYU, 1965. Reporter Providence Jour., 1965-67; polit. writer AP, N.Y.C., 1967-69, N.Y. Post, N.Y.C., 1970-73; writer, producer WABC Eyewitness News, 1974-75; managing editor, columnist Soho Weekly News, 1974-82; host, writer, producer of Right to Know Suburban Cablevision and N.J. Network, Sta. WNYC-TV, N.Y.C., Newark and Avenel, N.J., 1982-89; host, producer series on media Right to Know Right to Know syndicated pub. radio series on the media, Newark, 1989-93; assoc. prof. journalism Rutgers U., 1978-92, prof. journalism, 1995—; commentator on media issues WBGO-FM, 1993—. Host, prodr., writer documentary The Marielitos, 1984, Hillside: Desegregation, 1985, Impact, 1988, TV spl. The First Amendment, 1989 (Brechner award 1995); columnist Sports Media, Washington Journalism Rev., 1980-82, media N.J. Reporter, Princeton, 1982-85; ethics columnist, contbg. editor Editor and Pub. mag., 1987—. Recipient best pub. affairs program award Internat. TV and Video Festival, 1985, Nat. Cable TV Assn., 1986, award for cable excellence, 1986, 3 Aces award Nat. Cable TV, 1985, 86, Lowell Mellett award Pa. State U., 1985, Alfred I. DuPont award Columbia U., 1985, award in broadcast journalism (1st cable prodr. to win) N.J. Press Assn., 1987, N.J. Bell Enterprise award for best radio documentary, 1992, Best Radio Commentary and Media Nat. Headliner award 1993, Hildy Johnson award North Jersey Press Club, 2000. Mem.: AAUP, Soc. Profl. Journalists (chmn. freedom of info. com. Deadline Club N.Y.C. br. 1980, Outstanding Broadcast Journalism award 1984, 1987, Disting. Svc. award 1989, spl. award N.J. chpt. media criticism 1991, radio documentary 1992, investigative report 1992, 1st pl. Pub. Svc. award Mag. N.J. chpt. 1994, Brechner 1st Amendment award 1996, Best Column, Deadline Club, N.Y. chpt. 2000, spl. award N.J. chpt., 1st pl. Bicentennial Broadcast Competition 1989). Office: 327 Central Park W New York NY 10025-7631 also: Rutgers U Journalism Dept Hill Hall Newark NJ 07102

WOLPER, BEATRICE EMENS, lawyer; b. New Haven, Nov. 28, 1945; BA, U. Cin., 1974; JD cum laude, No. Ky. U., 1978. Bar: Ohio 1979. Assoc., then ptnr. Emens, Kegler, Brown, Hill & Ritter, Columbus, Ohio, 1979-97; ptnr. Chester, Willcox & Saxbe, LLP, 1997—. Pres., founder Women's Bus. Bd., Columbus, 1984—; bd. mem., exec. com. Ctr. Sci. and Industry, Columbus, 1994—; bd. dirs. Attys. for Family Hold Enterprises, N.Y.C. Author: Family Business Basics, 2000. Participant NAFTA, Washington, 1993; del. White House Conf. on Small Bus., Washington, 1995. Named Entrepreneur of the Yr., YWCA, Columbus, 1993, Women of Achievement, Ernst & Young/Inc. Mag., Columbus, 1993. Mem. Internat. Women's Forum (pres. Ohio chpt. 1994—), Columbus Bar Assn. (chair securities commn. 1987-89), Capital Club (chair 1994-96), Columbus C. of C. (bd. mem. 1994—). Avocations: fly fishing, geology, hiking, reading. Home: 9592 Lake Of The Woods Dr Galena OH 43021-9622 Office: Chester Willcox & Saxbe LLP 17 S High St Ste 900 Columbus OH 43215-3442

WOLPER, DAVID LLOYD, motion picture and television executive; b. N.Y.C., Jan. 11, 1928; s. Irving S. and Anna (Fass) W.; m. Margaret Dawn Richard, May 11, 1958 (div.); children: Mark, Michael, Leslie; m. Gloria Diane Hill, July 11, 1974. Student, Drake U., 1946, U. So. Calif., 1948. V.p., treas. Flamingo Films, TV sales co., 1948-50, v.p. West Coast Ops., 1954-58; chmn., pres. Wolper Prodns., L.A., 1958—. Cons., exec. producer Warner Bros., Inc., 1976—. TV prodns. include Race for Space, Making of the President 1960, 64, Biography series, Story of... series, The Yanks are Coming, Berlin: Kaiser to Khrushchev, December 7: Day of Infamy, The American Woman in the 20th Century, Hollywood and The Stars, March of Time Specials, The Rise and Fall of the Third Reich, The Legend of Marilyn Monroe, Four Days in November, Krebiozen and Cancer, National Geographic, Undersea World of Jacques Cousteau, China: Roots of Madness, The Journey of Robert F. Kennedy, Say Goodbye, George Plimpton, Appointment With Destiny, American Heritage, Smithsonian, They've Killed President Lincoln, Sandburg's Lincoln, Primal Man, The First Woman President, Chico and the Man, Get Christie Love, Welcome Back, Kotter!, Collison Course, Roots, Victory at Entebbe, Roots: The Next Generations, Moviola, The Thorn Birds, North and South Books I, II, III, Napoleon and Josephine, Alex Haley's Queen, Men Of The Dragon, Unwed Father, The Morning After; feature films include The Hellstrom Chronicle, Devil's Brigade, The Bridge at Remagen, If It's Tuesday, This Must Be Belgium, Willy Wonka and The Chocolate Factory, Visions of Eight, This is Elvis, Murder in the First, Surviving Picasso, L.A. Confidential; live spl. events include Opening and Closing Ceremonies 1984 Olympic Games, Liberty Weekend July 3-6, 1986. Trustee L.A. County Mus. Art, Am. Film Inst., L.A. Thoracic and Cardiovascular Found., Boys and Girls Clubs Am., U.S. Golf Assn. Found.; bd. dirs. Amateur Athletic Assn. L.A., L.A. Heart Inst., Acad. TV Arts and Scis. Found., So. Calif. Com. for Olympic Games, U. Soc. Calif. Cinema/TV Dept.; bd. govs. Cedars Sinai Med. Ctr.; com. mem. U.S. Olympic Team Benefit; mem. adv. com. Nat. Ctr. Jewish Film. Recipient award for documentaries San Francisco Internat. Film Festival, 1960, 7 Golden Globe awards, 5 George Foster Peabody awards, Disting. Service award U.S. Jr. C. of C.; 40 Emmy awards, 145 Emmy nominations Acad. TV Arts and Scis.; Monte Carlo Internat. Film Festival award, 1964, Cannes Film Festival Grand Prix for TV Programs, 1964; Oscar award, 11 Oscar nominations, Jean Hersholt Humanitarian award Acad. Motion Picture and TV Scis., medal of Chevalier The French Nat. Legion of Honor, 1990; named to TV Hall of Fame, 1988. Mem. Nat. Acad. TV Arts and Scis., Acad. Motion Picture Arts and Scis., Producers Guild Am., Caucus for Producers, Writers and Dirs. Office: The David L Wolper Co Inc 617 N Rodeo Dr Beverly Hills CA 90210

WOLPERT, ETTA, artist, poet; b. Mpls., Dec. 6, 1930; d. Garrett and Gertrude G. (Gruenberg) W. BA, U. Minn., 1952, MA, 1954. Asst. to Allen Tate U. Minn., Mpls., 1952; tutor Harvard U. Bur. of Study Counsel, Cambridge, Mass., 1955-59; instr. English Emerson Coll., Boston, 1955-58; workshop leader in poetry Cambridge Ctr. for Adult Edn., 1956; asst. prof. English & Art No. Essex Community Coll., Haverhill, Mass., 1964-66; leader art history workshop Brandeis Study Group, Lexington, 1962; social worker Welfare Dept., Lowell, 1969-71; artist, poet freelance Lexington, 1975—. One-woman show includes Cary Meml. Libr., 1962; exhibited in shows at Habit Inst., 1991, Cambridge Art Assn., 1992, 4th Ann. Internat. Exhibit, 1989; author: (poems) Selections, 1973. Recipient Hon. Mention, World of Poetry, 1991, Hon. Mention in Poetry Contest, Harvard Summer Sch., 1965, Two First prizes New Eng. Poets Club, 1969. Mem. Ariel Gallery, Gallery of Art Investment, Cambridge Art Assn., New Eng. Poetry Club. Home: 4 Revere St Lexington MA 02420-4420

WOLPIN, MILES D. political science educator; b. Mt. Vernon, N.Y., Dec. 4, 1937; s. Arthur A. and Sylvia Wolpin; m. Natasha S. Shuaeva, Apr. 17, 1992. JD, Columbia U., 1962, MA, 1964, PhD, 1968. Instr. CUNY, N.Y.C., 1965-66; jr. faculty Marlboro (Vt.) Coll., 1968-70; asst. prof. St. Francis Xavier U., Antigonish, N.S., Can., 1970-72; vis. asst. prof. U. N.Mex., Albuquerque, 1972-73; assoc. prof. SUNY, Potsdam, 1973-84, prof., 1984—2000. Vis. rschr. Internat. Peace Rsch. Inst., Oslo, 1980—81, Oslo, 1989—90. Contbr. Town justice Town Ct., Hopkinton, NY, 1992—99. Mem.: Nat. Assn. Scholars. Avocation: Avocations: organic agriculture. Home: RR 3 Fletcher Rd 346 Potsdam NY 13676-9803 Office: Dept Politics State Univ Coll Potsdam NY 13676 Fax: 315-265-9421. E-mail: wolpin@northnet.org.

WOLRAICH, MARK LEE, pediatrician, educator; BA, SUNY, Binghamton, 1966; MD, SUNY, Syracuse, 1970. Diplomate Am. Bd. Pediatrics. Pediatric intern SUNY, Syracuse, 1970-71; pediatric resident U. Okla. Health Scis. Ctr., Oklahoma City, 1973-74; pediatric fellowship U. Oreg. Health Scis. Ctr., 1974-76; asst. prof. U. Iowa, 1976-81, assoc. prof., 1981-86, prof., 1986-90, Vanderbilt U., 1990-2001, dir. divsn. child devel., dir. child devel. ctr., 1990-99, dir. ctr. for chronic illnesses and disabilities in children, 1990-2000; investigator J.F. Kennedy Ctr. for Rsch. on Edn. and Human Devel., 1990-2001; Shaun Walters prof. pediatrics, dir. Child Study Ctr., Okla. U. Health Scis. Ctr., 2001—. Med. supr. U. Iowa Divsn. of Developmental Disabilities, 1980-90; vis. prof. Great Ormond St. Hosp. for Sick Children, London, 1983, U. Cape Town, Rondebosch Cape, South Africa, 1986, Columbus Children's Hosp., Ohio State U., Dept. Pediatrics, 1988; mem. Iowa State Foster Care Rev. Bd. Co-editor Advances in Developmental and Behavioral Pediatrics, 1981-92; cons. editor Am. Jour. on Mental Deficiency; editl. adv. bd. A Guide to Parent Counseling; editor The Classification of Child and Adolescent Mental Disorders in Primary Care-Diagnostic and Statistical

Manual for Mental Disorders in Primary Care Child and Adolescent Version, 1996; cons. reviewer Developmental Medicine and Child Neurology, Pediatrics, Nutrition and Behavior, Jour. Pediatrics, Jou. of Social and Personal Relationships, Applied Rsch. in Mental Retardation, Jour. of Clin. Psychology, Jour. Developmental and Behavioral Pediatrics, Clin. Pediatrics, others; contbr. numerous articles to profl. publs.* Recipient Disting. and Dedicated Svc. award Spina Bifida Assn. of Iowa, 1979, Lou Holloway award for rsch. Health Scis. Edn.; grantee NIMH, 1987-90, Nat. Inst. on Disability and Rehab. Rsch., 1987-89, 87-88, NIH, 1988-91, Iowa Dept. of Human Svcs., 1986-88, 88-89, U. Iowa, 1979, 80-87, United Cerebral Palsy Rsch. and Endl. Found., Inc., 1978-87, Iowa March of Dimes, 1980, Sugar Assn., Inc., 1983, Internat. Life Scis. Inst., 1988-91, W.T. Grant Found., 1989, NIMH, 1998—, MCH Lend grant, 1999—. Fellow Am. Acad. Pediatrics (com., grant 1992—, chair com. on psychosocial aspects of child and family health 1997-00, chair child & adolescent health action group), Am. Acad. Cerebral Palsy and Developmental Medicine; mem. Soc. for Developmental and Behavioral Pediatrics (pres. 1994-95, program dir. 1990-93), Soc. Pediatric Psychology Assn. (assoc., Lee Salk award for disting. svc.), Soc. for Pediatric Rsch. (sr.), Am. Acad. Physician and Patient (charter), Am. Pediatric Soc. Office: Okla U Health Scis Ctr 1100 NE 13th St Oklahoma City OK 73117

WOLSIFFER, PATRICIA RAE, retired insurance company executive; b. Indpls., Aug. 15, 1933; d. Charles L. and Dorothy M. (Smith) Bohlsen; m. Edward C. Wolsiffer, Oct. 5, 1956; children: John M., Anderson, Sherry L. Anderson Cooney, Edward J. Wolsiffer. Student, Ind. Central U., 1974-75. Various secretarial positions, 1964-71; with Blue Cross/Blue Shield Ind. (Associated Ins. Cos., Inc.), Indpls., 1971-88, supr. personnel, 1973-76, exec. asst. to pres., 1976-79, corp. sec., 1979-85, exec. asst. to chmn. bd., chief exec. officer, 1985-88; ret. Vol. Hancock Meml. Hosp. Guild. Mem.: Order Eastern Star, Daus. of Nile, Ladies Oriental Shrine. Republican. Presbyterian. Home: 5550 E 100 N Greenfield IN 46140-9445 Office: 120 Monument Cir Indianapolis IN 46204-4906

WOLSON, CRAIG ALAN, lawyer; b. Toledo, Feb. 20, 1949; s. Max A. and Elaine B. (Cohn) W.; m. Ellen Carol Schulgasser, Oct. 26, 1986; children: Lindsey, Michael and Geoffrey (triplets). BA, U. Mich., 1971, JD, 1974. Bar: N.Y. 1975, U.S. Dist. Ct. (so. and ea. dists.) N.Y. 1975, U.S. Ct. Appeals (2d cir.) 1975, U.S. Supreme Ct. 1978. Assoc. Shearman & Sterling, N.Y.C., 1974-81; v.p., asst. gen. counsel Thomson McKinnon Securities Inc., 1981-85; v.p., sec., gen. counsel J.D. Mattus Co., Inc., Greenwich, Conn., 1985-88; also bd. dirs. J.D. Mattus Co., Inc. and affiliated cos.; v.p., asst. gen. counsel Chem. Bank, N.Y.C., 1988-95; of counsel Williams & Harris, 1995-96; ptnr. Williams & Harris LLP, 1996-97; counsel Brown & Wood L.L.P., 1997-98, Mayer, Brown & Platt, N.Y.C., 1999-2001; spl. counsel Schulte Roth & Zabel LLP, 2001—. Dep. clk. Lucas County Courthouse, Toledo, 1968-69, 71-72. Articles and administrv. editor U. Mich. Law Rev., 1973-74. Mem. ABA, N.Y. State Bar Assn., Assn. of Bar of City of N.Y. (securities regulation com. 1994-97, corp. law com. 1997-2000, project fin. com. 2000—), Corp. Bar. Assn. of Westchester and Fairfield, Phi Beta Kappa, Phi Eta Sigma, Pi Sigma Alpha. Avocations: reading, playing piano, fine dining, theater. Home: 29 Punch Bowl Dr Westport CT 06880-2130 Office: Schulte Roth & Zabel LLP 919 Third Ave New York NY 10022

WOLSTEIN, ARTHUR, podiatrist; b. N.Y.C., Nov. 22, 1914; s. Hyman Wolstein and Rose Kornbluth; m. Diane Teichberg, May 29, 1947; children: Deborah, Lewis, Peter, Marianne. D in Podiatric Medicine, N.Y. Coll. Podiatric Medicine, 1937. Past chmn. Visions summer camp for the blind, 1997; chmn. bd. R.A.I.N., 1998—; treas. Bronx Rotary Club, 1997; vol. Chaplains Programs Bronx Vets. Med. Ctr. Staff sgt. U.S. Army, 1942—46. Mem.: DAV (elected comdr. Bronx chpt. #23 1999—2001), APHA, Am. Assn. Hosp. Podiatrists (past pres.), Bronx County Podiatry Soc. (pres. 1955), Am. Acad. Ambulatory Foot Surgery, Am. Podiatric Med. Assn. (del. 1955—65), Nat. Order Trenchor Rats, Disabled Am. Vets, B'nai B'rith, Bronx Hist. Soc., Bronx Coun. on Arts, AARP, Comdrs. Club. Jewish. Avocation: N.Y. Yankees fan. Home: 11 Morrison Dr New Rochelle NY 10804-1710

WOLSTON, JON, psychiatrist; b. Phila., Nov. 2, 1949; s. Edward Cristy and Maxine Louise (Askey) W.; m. Nancy Jean Laser, Aug. 18, 1978; children: Christopher, Ethan. AB cum laude, Dartmouth Coll., 1971, BMS, 1974; MD, Northwestern U., 1976. Diplomate Am. Bd. Psychiatry and Neurology, Nat. Bd. Med. Examiners; cert. cons. in hypnosis Am. Soc. Clin. Hypnosis. Resident in psychiatry Northwestern Med. Ctr., Chgo., 1976-79; fellow in psychiatry Dartmouth-Hitchcock Med. Ctr., Hanover, N.H., 1979-80; staff psychiatrist Providence Ctr. for Counseling and Psychiat. Svcs., 1980-83; mem. active staff Butler Hosp., Providence, 1980—2002, pres., 1991-93; psychiatrist pvt. practice, 1983—. Instr. clin. psychiatry dept. psychiatry Dartmouth Med. Sch., 1979-80; instr. psychiatry and human behavior Brown U. Med. Sch., 1981-82, clin. asst. prof. in psychiatry and human behavior, 1982-2002; part-time instr. dept. counselor edn. R.I. Coll., 1982-84; asst. physician dept. psychiatry R.I. Hosp., Providence, 1980-83; med. back-up alcohol and drug treatment svc. Butler Hosp., 1987-88; asst. inpatient unit chief Butler Hosp., 1988-91; mem. rev. bd. Inst. Behavioral Medicine, Providence, 1990-93; cons. psychiatrist Family Inst. R.I., 1983-84, Affiliates for Psychotherapy, 1993-95. Co-author: Psychosomatic Medicine and Liaison Psychiatry, 1985; contbr. articles to profl. jours.; presenter in field. Chair prof. adv. bd. R.I. chpt. Children and Adults with Attention Deficit Disorders, Providence, 1994-97; musicmeister Pack 88 Boy Scouts Am., Providence, 1994-98, asst. scoutmaster Troop 28, 1998-2002; mem. Interfaith Health Care Ministries Cmty. Adv. Bd., 2002. Recipient Disting. Tchr. award Brown U. Sch. Medicine, 2001. Mem. APA, New Eng. Soc. Clin. Hypnosis (pres. 1995-97), Am. Pain Soc., Am. Soc. Dowsers. Avocations: skiing, camping, canoeing, kayaking. Home: 6 Cooke St Providence RI 02906-2006 Office: 394 Angell St Providence RI 02906

WOLTER, ALLAN BERNARD, writer, educator; b. Peoria, Ill., Nov. 24, 1913; s. Bernard Gregory Wolter and Marianne Bernardette Strub. BA, Our Lady of Angels Sem., Cleveland, OH, 1937; MA, Cath. U. of Am., Washington, DC, 1942, PhD, 1947; LG, Franciscan Inst. St. Bonaventure U., Saint Bonaventure, NY, 1952; DSc (hon.) , Quincy U., Quincy, IL, 1967. Ordained Roman Catholic Priest Roman Cath. Ch., 1940. Asst. prof. chemistry Our Lady of Angels Franciscan Sem., Cleveland, Ohio, 1943—45, asst. prof. biology, 1943—45, asst. prof. philosophy, 1943—45; assoc. prof. philosophy Franciscan Inst., St. Bonaventure U., Saint Bonaventure, Nebr., 1946—52; prof., 1952—62; vis. prof. Cath. U. Am., 1952—63; rsch. assoc. Ctr. Medieval and Renaissance Studies, UCLA, 1978—97; vis. prof. franciscan theology Joseph Doino, 1997—; prof. emeritus philosophy The Cath. U. Am., 1984—84; vis. lectr. Princeton U., 1965—65; vis. prof. U. Mich., Mich., 1967—67, NYU, NY, 1969—69. Assoc. editor The New Scholasticism, 1949—51; editor Franciscan Studies, 1949—52, Franciscan Inst. Publications, 1946—62. Author books. V.p. Am. Cath. Philos. Assn., 1956—57, pres., 1957—58. Recipient Aquinas Medal, Am. Cath. Philos. Assn., 1998. Fellow: Nat. Endowment Humanities; mem.: Societas Internationalis Scotistica, Soc. for Medieval and Renaissance Studies, Am. Philos. Assn., Phi Beta Kappa. Office: Saint Bonaventure University Saint Bonaventure NY E-mail: awolter@sbu.edu.

WOLTER, JOHN AMADEUS, librarian, government official; b. St. Paul, July 25, 1925; s. Amadeus Frank and Marjorie (Wears) W.; m. Joan Patricia Venard, July 6, 1956; children: Mark, Thomas, Matthew, David. Student, Coll. of St. Thomas, 1950; BA, U. Minn., 1956, MA, 1965, PhD, 1975; postgrad., Georgetown U., 1957. Officer, seaman Isthmian Lines Inc., N.Y.C., 1943-50, 57-60; marine transp. officer Mil. Sea Transp. Ser., Washington, 1956-57; instr., map libr. U. Minn., 1961-64, asst. to dir. univ. librs., 1964-65, research fellow, 1965-66; asst. prof. Wis. State U., River Falls, 1966-68; asst. chief geography and map. div. Libr. of Congress, Washington, 1968-78, chief, 1978-91, acting dir. pub. svc. and collections MGMT I, 1989-90; cons. in geography, 1991-93. Mem. U.S. Bd. Geog. Names, 1969-83, vice chmn., 1980-81, chmn., 1981-83. Editor: Progress of Discovery: Johann Georg Kohl, 1993, Images of the World: The Atlas Through History, 1996, The Minto Collection: Essay and Bibliography, 1999; rev. editor cartography divsn. Surveying and Mapping, 1971-72; mem. editl. bd. Cartographica, 1971-80, Am. Cartographer, 1974-79, Terrae Incognitae, 1973-75, ACSM Bull., 1974-80, Surveying and Mapping, 1972-80; editl. advisor The Portolan, 1986—; contbg. editor Imago Mundi, 1979-91; contbr. articles to profl. jours. Served with U.S. Army, 1950-52. Libr. of Congress Disting. Svc. award, 1992, Smithsonian Inst. Cert. of award, 1986. Mem. Internat. Geog. Union (U.S. nat. com. 1972-80, 84-88), Internat. Cartographic Assn. (U.S. mem. commn. on history of cartography 1972-76, corr. 1976-92, Assn. Am. Geographers (editorial bd. Annals 1988-92), Spl. Librs. Assn. (sec.-treas. geog.and map div. 1965), Soc. History Discoveries (sec.-treas. 1972-75, coun. 1976-78, v.p. 1983-85, pres. 1985-87), Am. Congress Surveying and Mapping (chmn. publs. com. 1978-80, Presdl. citation 1985), N.Am. Soc. Oceanic History, N.Mex. Geog. Soc. (bd. dirs., governing bd.), Soc. for History of Discoveries, Washington Map Soc., Soc. Nautical Rsch., Ariz. Hist. Soc., U.S. Naval Hist. Found., Philip Lee Phillips Soc. (bd. dirs. ex officio), Theta Delta Chi. Home: 4555 S Mission Rd Apt 984 Tucson AZ 85746-2314 E-mail: johnamadeus@aol.com.

WOLTERING, MARGARET MAE, retired secondary school educational consultant; b. Trenton, Ohio, July 24, 1913; d. David Lindy and Nellie Stevenson; m. Elmer Charles Woltering, Apr. 9, 1938 (dec. Oct. 1994); 1 child Eugene Anthony. Student, Mercy Sch. Nursing, Hamilton, Ohio, 1931-34; BS, Miami U., 1962, MEd, 1968, postgrad., 1975. RN Ohio, cert. tchr., curriculum supr., Ohio Pub. Health. Pub. health nurse Ohio State Dept. Health, Butler County, 1936-49; supr. Swedish Hosp., Seattle, 1944-45; various h.s. teaching positions Cin., 1968-78; ednl. cons. Ohio, 1981-94. Cons., Ohio, 1981—96; ednl. cons. specializing in curriculum devel., 1980—91; book reviewer Friends of Libr., 1991—93; lectr. Sr. Citizens Ctr., 1992—98; instr. Bible Study, 2000—. Author: The National Library of Poetry Anthology, 2000—02, spelling book, numerous poems. Chmn. Hosp. Svc. for Children, Hamilton, 1981—85; chmn. vol. tutorial program Hamilton H.S., 1989—93, 1994—2000. Mem.: AAUW, Internat. Poetry Soc., Toastmasters. Democrat. Roman Catholic. Avocations: reading, theater , art collecting, China porcelain painting.

WOLTERS, RAYMOND, historian, educator; b. Kansas City, Mo., July 25, 1938; s. Raymond M. and Margaret G. (Reilly) W.; m. Mary McCullough, June 23, 1962; children— Jeffrey, Kevin, Thomas BA, Stanford U., 1960; MA, U. Calif.-Berkeley, 1962, PhD, 1967. Instr. dept. history U. Del., Newark, 1965-67, asst. prof., 1967-70, assoc. prof., 1970-75, prof., 1975-96, Thomas Muncy Keith prof., 1996—. Mem. editl. adv. bd. Acad. Am. Ency.; author: The New Negro on Campus, 1975, The Burden of Brown, 1984, Right Turn, 1996, Du Bois and His Rivals, 2002. Fellow NEH, 1971-72, Am. Coun. Learned Socs., 1978-79, Earhart Found., 1989-90; recipient Silver Gavel award ABA. Mem. Am. Hist. Assn., Orgn. Am. Historians, So. Hist. Assn. Home: 20 Bridlebrook Ln Newark DE 19711-2061 Office: U Del History Dept Newark DE 19716

WOLTZ, HOWARD OSLER, JR. steel and wire products company executive; b. Mt. Airy, N.C., Apr. 2, 1925; s. Howard Osler and Louise (Elliott) W.; m. Joan Elizabeth Moore, Dec. 29, 1949; children: Louise, Joan Woltz Robins, Howard O. III, Edwin Moore. LLB, U. Va., 1948. Bar: N.C., 1948. Ptnr. law firm, Mt. Airy, 1948-54; pres., founder Dixie Concrete Products, Inc., 1953-69; founder Dixie Exposaic, Inc., 1963; pres., chmn. bd. Insteel Industries (formerly Exposaic Industries, Inc.), 1969-89, chmn., CEO, 1989-91. Mem. N.C. Ho. of Reps., 1951-53; chmn. Mt. Airy-Surry County Airport Authority, 1987-93; former pres. Greater Mt. Airy United Fund. Mem. Nat. Concrete Masonry Assn. (pres. 1965), N.C. Concrete Masonry Assn. (pres. 1959), Wire Reinforcement Inst. (chmn. 1982), Am. Wire Producers Assn. (bd. dirs. 1987-91), N.C. State Bar Assn., Mt. Airy C. of C. (Citizen of Yr. 1991). Rotary (past pres. Mt. Airy). Republican. Home: 243 Old Green Hill Rd Mount Airy NC 27030-9240 Office: Insteel Industries Inc 1373 Boggs Dr Mount Airy NC 27030-2145 E-mail: howoltz@insteel.com.

WOLTZ, KENNETH ALLEN, consulting executive; b. Phila., Mar. 2, 1943; s. Herman and Florence (Varell) M.; m. Barbara Hand, June 18, 1966; children: Karyn, Diane, Kenneth. BS, U.S. Mil. Acad., 1966; MBA, Xavier U., 1971. Cert. mgmt. cons. Various mgmt. positions GE, Evansdale, Ohio and Bethesda, Md., 1968-73; mgr. systems Xerox Corp., Rochester, N.Y., 1973-75; dir. info. svcs. McGraw Edison, Des Plaines, Ill., 1975-77; mng. dir., mgmt. cons. KPMG, Chgo., 1977-80; mgmt. cons., CEO, Woltz & Assoc., Inc., Barrington, Ill., 1980—; mgmt. cons. Speaker at various Univs. With U.S. Army, 1966-68. Mem. Soc. Mgmt. Info. Systems, Inst. Mgmt. Cons., West Point Soc. (treas. 1975), Assn. Corp. Growth, Assn. Mgmt. Consulting Firms, Ind. Computer Cons. Assn. Home: 800 Ocean Dr Unit 1105 Juno Beach FL 33408-1724 Office: Woltz & Assocs Inc PO Box 158 West Dundee IL 60118-0189 also: Ste 203/284 4300 S US Hwy 1 Jupiter FL 33477-1198 E-mail: woltz@msn.com.

WOLVERTON, TERRY L(YNN), writer, consultant; b. Cocoa Beach, Fla., Aug. 23, 1954; d. Donald E. Wolverton and Ruth L. Miller Tackabery. PhB, Grand Valley State U., Allendale, Mich., 1977. Dir. The Woman's Bldg., L.A., 1977-89; mgmt. cons. Consult'Her, 1982—; creative writing instr. L.A. Gay and Lesbian Ctr., 1988-97; founder Writers at Work, L.A., 1997—. Bd. dirs. The Woman's Bldg., 1982-86, 96—; mem. adv. bd. L.A. Poetry Festival, 1990—, The Fringe Festival, L.A., 1987-88. Author: (novel) Bailey's Beads, 1996, (poetry collections) Black Slip, 1992, Mystery Bruise, 1999, (memoir) Insurgent Muse, 2002; editor (anthology series) His, 1995, 97, 99, Hers, 1995, 97, 99, (anthologies) Indivisible, 1991, Blood Whispers: L.A. Writers on AIDS, vol. 1, 1991, vol. 2, 1994, Circa 2000: Lesbian Fiction at the Millennium, 2000, Circa 2000: Gay Fiction at the Millennium, 2000. Mem. pub. policy com. Calif. Confedn. of the Arts, Sacramento, 1986-88. Recipient Lesbian Rights award So. Calif. Women for Understanding, 1986, Vesta award in lit. The Woman's Bldg., 1991, Movers and Shakers award for Women Writers, So. Calif. Libr. for Social Studies and Rsch., 1995, Lesbian and Bisexual Woman Active in Cmty. Empowerment award L.A. Gay and Lesbian Ctr., 1997, Harvey Milk award Christopher St. West Assn., 1997. Mem. PEN Ctr. USA West (bd. dirs.). Avocations: visual art, body building, gardening, yoga. E-mail: consulther@aol.com.

WOLVERTON, THOMAS FRANK, automotive company supervisor; b. Saginaw, Mich., Dec. 26, 1954; s. Francis Edward and Donna Muriel Wolverton; m. Holly Louise Muller, Dec. 20, 1978 (div. May 1980); 1 child, Brian Thomas; m. Trudy Reneé Surprenant, Oct. 26, 1985; 1 adopted child, Renee Lynn. Cert. Trident submarine test dir., Gen. Dynamics. With USN, 1974-83, missile technician Conn., 1974-80, lead instr., 1980-83; submarine test technician Gen. Dynamics, 1984, engrng. asst., 1985, program coord., 1986, test dir., 1987-94; skilled trades supr. Kelly Svcs./GM, Flint, Mich., 1995—. V.p. Electric Boat Mgmt. Assn., Groton, 1992-94; vol. Big Bros Am., Norwich, Conn., 1981-83. Mem. Am. Legion. Avocations: stamps, fishing, softball. Home: 9600 East Rd Burt MI 48417

WOLYNES, PETER GUY, chemistry researcher, educator; b. Chgo., Apr. 21, 1953; s. Peter and Evelyn Eleanor (Etter) W.; m. Jane Lee Fox, Nov. 26, 1976 (div. 1980); m. Kathleen Cull Bucher, Dec. 22, 1984; children: Margrethe Cull, Eve Cordelia, Julia Jean. AB with highest distinction, Ind. U., 1971; AM, Harvard U., 1972, PhD in Chem. Physics, 1976; DSc (hon.), Ind. U., 1988. Rsch. assoc. MIT, Cambridge, 1975-76; asst. prof., assoc. prof. Harvard U., 1976-80; vis. scientist Max Planck Inst. für Biophysikalische Chemie, Gottingen, Fed. Republic Germany, 1977; assoc. prof. chemistry U. Ill., Urbana, 1980-83, prof. chemistry, 1983-2000, prof. physics, 1985-2000, prof. physics and biophysics, 1989-2000, mem. Ctr. for Advanced Study, 1989-2000; William H. and Janet LyCan prof. chemistry Ctr. for Advanced Study U. Ill., 1993-96, Robert Eiszner prof., 1996-2000; prof. chemistry and biochemistry U. Calif., San Diego, 2000—, Francis H.C. Crick prof., 2001—. Vis. prof. Inst. for Molecular Sci., Okazaki, Japan, 1982, 87; vis. scientist Inst. for Theoretical Physics, Santa Barbara, Calif., 1987, Ecole normale Supérieure, Paris, 1992; Merski lectr. U. Nebr., 1986; Denkewalter lectr. Loyola U., 1986; Hinshelwood lectr. Oxford U., 1997; Harkins lectr. U. Chgo., 1997; FMC lectr. Princeton U., 1998; Matsen lectr. U. Tex., 2002. Contbr. numerous articles to profl. jours. Sloan fellow, 1981-83, J.S. Guggenheim fellow, 1986-87; Beckman assoc. Ctr. for Advanced Study, Urbana, 1984-85; Fogarty scholar NIH, 1994-98. Fellow AAAS, Am. Phys. Soc., Am. Acad. Arts and Scis.; mem. NAS, Am. Chem. Soc. (Pure Chemistry award 1986, Peter Debye award 2000), N.Y. Acad. Scis., Biophys. Soc., Phi Beta Kappa, Sigma Xi, Phi Lambda Upsilon (Fresenius award 1988), Sigma Pi Sigma, Alpha Chi Sigma. Home: 12737 Sandy Crest Ct San Diego CA 92130-2795 Office: U Calif San Diego Dept Chem and Biochemistry 9500 Gilman Dr La Jolla CA 92093-3617 E-mail: pwolynes@ucsd.edu.

WOLYNIES, EVELYN See GRADO-WOLYNIES, EVELYN

WOLZ, CARL E. astronaut; b. Cleve., Sept. 6, 1955; m. Pamela J. Glady; 2 children. BS in Physics, Kent State U., 1977; MS in Solid State Physics, John Carroll U., 1979. Commd. 2d lt. USAF, 1979, advanced through grades to col.; with Atomic Energy Detection Sys. 1155th Tech. Ops. Squadron, McClellan AFB, Calif., 1979—82; flight test engr. USAF Test Pilot Sch., Edwards AFB, 1983—84, F-16 Combined Test Force, Edwards AFB, 1984—87; flight test mgr. Detachment 3 Air Force Flight Test Ctr., 1987—90; astronaut NASA, Houston, 1990—; mission specialist STS-108 Endeavour, Internat. Space Sta., 2001. Decorated USAF Commendation medal, USAF Achievement medal with 1 oak leaf cluster; named to, Ohio Vets. Hall of Fame; recipient Disting. Alumnus award, Kent State U., 1997. Mem.: Kent State U. Alumni Assn., Am. Legion. Achievements include logged over 833 hours in space; mission specialist STS-51 Discovery (1993); Orbiter flight engr. STS-65 Columbia (1994); mission specialist STS-49 Atlantis (1996). Avocations: piano, vocal music, sports, lead singer MAX-Q (rock-n-roll band). Office: Astronaut Office/CB NASA Johnson Space Ctr Houston TX 77058*

WOMACK, DOUG C. labor union representative; b. Marshalltown, Iowa, Dec. 7, 1950; s. Robert J. and Mildred R. (Woods) W.; m. Paulette A. Junge, June 4, 1971. Grad. high sch., Garwin, Iowa. Steward local #893 UAW, Marshalltown, 1976-77, recording sec., 1977-82, chairperson consumer affairs dept., 1981-84, chairperson Lennox unit, 1982-86, v.p., 1983-85, pres., 1985-94. Mem. region 4 exec. bd. UAW, Chgo., 1985-94, mem. UAW internat. staff, 1994—, edn. dir. region 4, 2000—. Active Marshall County Dem. Com., 1984-93; co-chmn. Labor/Mgmt. Coun.; mem. City Econ. Devel. Commn., 1986-92; bd. dirs., local United Way, 1985-92; apptd. by gov. Iowa State Labor-Mgmt. Coop. Coun., 1990-93; participant Young Trade Union Leaders Exch. Program, Tokyo, 1988. Named to Top 25 Up and Coming Young State Leaders Des Moines Register, 1987. Avocations: motorcycling, politics. Office: Region 4 UAW 2700 S River Rd Ste 200 Des Plaines IL 60018-4105 E-mail: uawedguy@earthlink.net.

WOMACK, EDGAR ALLEN, JR. energy executive; b. Humboldt, Tenn., Oct. 29, 1942; s. Edgar Allen Sr. and Lucy Opal (George) W.; m. Linda Jane Cochran, Dec. 28, 1963; children: Connie Britton, Cynthia Womack. BS, MIT, 1963, MS, 1965, PhD, 1969. With U.S. Atomic Energy Commn., Washington, 1968-73, Babcock and Wilcox Co., 1975-85, v.p. sales and mktg., 1983-85; v.p. R&D, chief tech. officer McDermott Internat., 1985—; pres. BWX Techs., 1998—. Mem. bd. Naval Submarine League. Patentee in field. Served to lt. USNR, 1968-70. Hon. Woodrow Wilson Found. fellow. Fellow ASME (ind. adv. bd. 1988—, chmn. 1997), AAAS, Indsl. Research Inst. (bd. 1989-96, pres. 1994-95), Sigma Xi. Presbyterian. Avocations: photography, diving, golf. Home: 401 Saint Andrews Cir Lynchburg VA 24503-3750 Office: BWX Techs 2016 Mt Athos Rd Lynchburg VA 24504 E-mail: eawomack@mcdermott.com.

WOMACK, JAMES ERROL, college president; b. Eugene, Oreg., June 27, 1940; s. John Leon and Dorothy Laverne (Yarbrough) W.; m. Sharron Kay McCullough, June 8, 1963; children: Timothy, Stephen, Joseph, Marilee. BS, N.W. Christian Coll., 1963; M Teaching, Cen. Okla. State U., 1968; postgrad., Pacific Luth. U., 1958-60, U. Oreg., 1960-63, Phillips U., 1966-68, HHD (hon.), 1987. Cert. tchr., Okla., Calif.; cert. fund raising exec.; ordained to ministry Christian Ch. (Disciples of Christ, 1963. Youth min. Lowell (Oreg.) Christian Ch., 1962-63, First Christian Ch., The Dalles, Oreg., 1963-65; youth and edn. min. Putnam City Christian Ch., Oklahoma City, 1965-68; tchr. English and social studies, coach basketball Patterson (Calif.) High Sch., 1968-71; min. youth and edn. Maze Blvd. Christian Ch., Modesto, Calif., 1968-71; dir. devel. Nat. Benevolent Assn. (Colo. Christian Home), Denver, 1976-86; coord. campus activities, coach basketball N.W. Christian Coll., Eugene, 1971-73, dir. planned giving, 1973-76, pres., 1986—. Cons. Luth. Social Svcs. Colo., Denver, 1984-85, Dayton, Ohio, 1986-89, Florence Crittenton Home Svcs., Little Rock, 1985—; presenter in field. Mem. devel. coun. Woodhaven Learning Ctr.; mem. fin. com. and nurture commn. Cen. Rocky Mountain Region Christian Ch.; chmn. N.W. Oklahoma City Youth Week Activities; trustee N.W. Christian Coll.; active Denver Planned Giving Roundtable; regional bd. dirs. N.W. Regional Ch., Christian Ch. in Kans. Recipient Book Award for Acad. Excellence Christian Bd. of Pub. Mem. Nat. Soc. Fund Raising Execs., Nat. Benevolent Assn. (trustee best of caring fund), Oreg. Ind. Coll. Assn. (mem. exec. com.), Colo. Assn. Fund Raisers (past sec., bd. dirs.), Emerald Empire Fellowship of Christian Athletes (charter mem., sec., bd. dirs.), Ministerial Alliance (chmn. migrant ministries), Rotary (mem. program com. Eugene chpt. 1990), Optimists (bd. dirs. Highland Park chpt.), Civitan, Denver City Club. Avocations: fishing, reading, sports. Home: 1363 Windsor Ct Springfield OR 97477-8107 Office: NW Christian Coll 828 E 11th Ave Eugene OR 97401-3745*

WOMACK, MARY PAULINE, lawyer; b. Chattanooga, Dec. 3, 1942; d. Lucille (Thomas) W. BS, U. Chattanooga, 1964; JD, Woodrow Wilson Coll. Law, 1984. Bar: Ga. 1988, U.S. Dist. Ct. (no. dist.) Ga. 1988. Pvt. practice, Atlanta, 1988—. DeKalb County Dems., 66th dist., regional com. State of Ga. Mem. Ga. Bar Assn., Sigma Delta Kappa (past regional v.p.). Office: 100 Peachtree St NW Ste 1950 Atlanta GA 30303-1919 Home: 10170 Big Canoe Jasper GA 30143-5118

WOMACK, THOMAS HOUSTON, manufacturing company executive; b. Gallatin, Tenn., June 22, 1940; s. Thomas Houston and Jessie (Eckel) W.; Linda Walker Womack, July 20, 1963 (div. Dec. 1989); children: Britton Ryan, Kelley Elizabeth; m. Pamela Ann Reed, Apr. 20, 1991. BSME, Tenn. Tech. U., Cookeville, 1963. Project engr. U.S. Gypsum Co., Jacksonville, Fla., 1963-65; project mgr. Maxwell House Div. Gen. Foods Corp., 1965-68, mfg. mgr. Hoboken, N.J., 1968-71, div. ops. planning mgr., 1971-73; industry sales mgr. J.R. Schneider Co., Tiburon, Calif., 1973-79; pres., CEO Womack Internat., Inc., Mare Island, 1979—; chmn., CEO Ceramic Microlight Technologies, Inc., 1995—; pres., CEO WestAmerica Engring. and Mfg. Co., 1997—. Holder 5 U.S. patents. Mem. Soc. Tribologists and Lubrication Engrs., Am. Filtration Soc., Soc. Mfg. Engrs., Am. Soc. Chem. Engrs. Avocations: skiing, vintage exotic sports cars. Office: Womack Internat Inc PO Box 2175 Vallejo CA 94592-0175 Fax: 707-562-1010.

WOMACK, TOM D. lawyer; b. Forrest City, Ark., Oct. 28, 1946; s. Thomas Isaac and Ida Mae (Bannon) W.; m. Linda C. Cornish, Aug. 18, 1973; children: Thomas Andrew, John Derek. BS, Ark. State U., 1968; JD, U. Memphis, 1972. Bar: Ark. 1972, U.S. Dist. Ct. (ea. dist.) Ark. 1972, U.S. Ct. Appeals (8th cir.), U.S. Supreme Ct. 1977, U.S. Tax Ct. 1980. Assoc. Barrett, Wheatley, Smith & Deacon, Jonesboro, Ark., 1972-74, ptnr., 1975-93, Womack, Landis, Phelps, McNeil & McDaniel, Jonesboro, 1993—. Contbr. articles to law jours. Chpt. chmn. Craighead County Red Cross, Jonesboro, Ark., 1985; chmn., bd. dirs. Greater Jonesboro C. of C., 1987-88; bd. dirs. Ark. Cmty. Found., 1999—. Recipient Gavel award Ark. Bar Assn., 1984. Fellow Am. Coll. Trust and Estate Counsel; mem. Ark. Bd. Legal Specialization (tax law splst. 1986—). Baptist. Avocation: fishing. Office: Womack Landis Phelps McNeil & McDaniel 301 W Washington Ave Jonesboro AR 72401-2778 E-mail: twomack@wlpmm_firm.com.

WOMACK, WHITNEY AYN, English and American literature educator; b. Whiteman AFB, Mo., Aug. 30, 1970; d. Larry Francis Strait and Stephanie Burnette Chambers. AB in English magna cum laude, U. Mo., 1991, MA in English, 1993; PhD in English, Purdue U., 1999. Grad. instr. Purdue U., West Lafayette, 1993-98; asst. prof. English Miami U., Hamilton, Ohio, 1998—. Editl. asst.: DeGustibus: Festschrift for Alain Renoir, 1992; contbr. biog. articles to dictionaries and book collections on women writers. Mentor Alt. Cmty.-Based Schs., Lafayette, Ind., 1995-97. Pew Tchg. Leadership fellow Pew Found., 1995, Purdue Rsch. Found. fellow Purdue U., 1997. Mem. MLA, Nat. Coun. Tchrs. English, Brit. Women Writers, Gaskell Soc., Phi Beta Kappa, Phi Kappa Phi. Democrat. Avocations: reading, film, traveling. Home: 26 Twin Lakes Dr Fairfield OH 45014 Office: Miami U 1601 Peck Blvd Hamilton OH 45011 E-mail: womackwa@muohio.edu.

WOMBLE, WILLIAM FLETCHER, lawyer; b. Winston-Salem, N.C., Oct. 29, 1916; s. Bunyan Snipes and Edith (Willingham) Womble; m. Jane Payne Gilbert, Oct. 11, 1941; children: William Fletcher, Jr., Jane Womble Haver, Russell G., Ann Womble Strader. AB, Duke U., 1937, JD, 1939. Bar: N.C. 1939. Assoc. Womble Carlyle Sandridge & Rice P.L.L.C. and predecessors, Winston-Salem, 1939-47, mem., 1947—. Campaign chmn. Forsyth County Cmty. Chest, 1949; mem. N.C. Gen. Statutes Commn., 1953—55, N.C. Bd. Higher Edn., 1955—57, 1960—63, N.C. Adv. Budget Commn., 1957—58; life trustee, past chmn. High Point U.; trustee Winston-Salem State U., 1953—55; past trustee, past pres. Children's Home; bd. dirs. Triad United Meth. Home (now Arbor acres United Meth. Retirement Cmty.), 1976—87, treas., 1975—79, pres., 1979—85; hon. chair United Way, Forsyth County, 1998; mem. People-to-People Citizen Amb. Program, 1981, 1986, N.C. Ho. of Reps., 1953—58, chmn. com. higher edn., vice chmn. fin. com., 1957; chmn. adminstrv. bd. Centenary United Meth. Ch., 1961—63, chmn. bd. trustees, 1983—85; bd. dirs. Sr. Svcs., Inc., 1998—. Served to maj. USAAF, 1941—46. Named Trustee of the Yr., Gen. Bd. Global Mins. of United Meth. Ch., Health and Wlfare Minst. Dept., 1989. Fellow: Am. Bar Found. (life; state chmn. 1984—89, Fifty Yr. award 1995); mem.: ABA (ho. dels. 1978—87, bd. govs. 1982—85, exec. coun. Nat. Conf. Bar Pres. 1985—88, ethics com. 1985—91, resource devel. coun. 1986—92, chmn. jud. code subcom. 1988—91, chair affiliate outreach com. 1994—97, coun. mem. sr. lawyers divsn. 1995—97), Forsyth County Bar Assn. (pres. 1962), N.C. Supreme Ct. Hist. Soc., U.S. Supreme Ct. Hist. Soc., Am. Judicature Soc., N.C. State Bar (trustee interest on Lawyers Trust Accounts 1983—91, vice chmn. 1989—91, Chief Justice's Professionalism award 2001), N.C. Bar Assn. (pres. 1966—67, chmn. endowment founders campaign 1986—87, chair sr. lawyers divsn. 1994—95, Judge John J. Parker award 1984), Soc. Cin., Winston-Salem C. of C. (pres. 1960—61), Piedmont Club, Twin City Club, Old Town Club, Rotary (local pres. 1964). Democrat. Home: #441 1244 Arbor Rd Winston Salem NC 27104-1139 Office: Womble Carlyle Sandridge & Rice 1 W Fourth PO Drawer 84 Winston Salem NC 27102-0084 Fax: (336) 733-8369. E-mail: wwomble@wcsr.com.

WOMBWELL, JOHN FUTRELL, electrical contracting company executive; b. Lexington, Ky., Oct. 23, 1961; s. Joseph H. and Barbara F. Wombwell; m. Robin McCuistion, Sept. 19, 1987; children: Burkley Anne, John Stewart. BS in Econs., U. Ky., 1984; JD, U. Tex., 1987. Assoc. Andrews & Kurth LLP, Houston, 1987-94, ptnr., 1994-98; gen. counsel, sec., sr. v.p. Integrated Elec. Svcs., Inc., 1998-99, exec. v.p., 1999—. Office: Integrated Elec Svcs Inc 1800 West Loop S Ste 500 Houston TX 77027-3290 E-mail: john.wombwell@ielectric.com.

WOMELDORFF, PORTER JOHN, utilities executive; b. Milw., Feb. 26, 1933; s. Virgil Leslie and Leorra (Porter) W.; m. Marilyn Sapp, Jan. 7, 1966; children: John Porter, Michael Wayne. With Ill. Power Co., Decatur, 1954-95; beginning as elec. engr., successively results supr., instrumentation engr., supr. system planning, mgr. planning, 1954-79; v.p., 1979-93; global climate program exec., 1993-95; ret., 1995; pres. Womeldorff Assocs. Ltd., 1995—97. Mem. Ill. Coal Devel. Bd., 1982-95, chair. Chair adv. bd. U. Ill. Coll. Engring., 1986-89; former chair sci. com. Global Climate Coalition. Lay mem. Central Ill. Ann. Conf., United Methodist Ch., 1968—, lay leader, 1976-79, lay mem. North Central Jurisdictional Conf., 1972—, lay mem. Gen. Conf., 1976—; lay mem. Gen. Bd. Pubs., 1992—. Served to lt. C.E., AUS, 1955-57. Decorated Army Commendation Medal. Mem. Instrument Soc. Am. (v.p. 1971-73, Power Div. Achievement award 1983), IEEE, ASME, U. Ill. Elec. Engring. Alumni Assn. (pres., dir., Outstanding Alumni award 1994), Phi Kappa Phi, Tau Beta Pi, Sigma Tau, Eta Kappa Nu, Alpha Kappa Lambda. Home and Office: 735 Country Manor Dr Decatur IL 62521-2524 E-mail: pjwom@aol.com.

WOMER, CHARLES BERRY, retired hospital executive, management consultant; b. Cleve., Mar. 30, 1926; s. Porter Blake and Margaret (Berry) W.; m. Elizabeth Benson, Oct. 7, 1950; children: Richard B., Carol E., John C. MS in Hosp. Adminstrn., Columbia U., 1953; BS in Mech. Engring., Case Inst. Tech., 1949. Asst. dir. Univ. Hosps., Cleve., 1957-61, assoc. dir., 1961-65, pres., 1976-82; mgmt. cons., 1982-90; ret., 1990. Adminstr. Yale-New Haven Hosp., 1965-67, dir., 1968-76, pres., 1976; lectr. Yale U., 1965-78, 87-91; adj. asst. prof. Case Western Res. U., 1976-83; mem. Conn. Commn. on Hosps. and Health Care, 1973-76; bd. dirs. New Haven Savings Bank, 1969-76. Bd. govs. U. New Haven, 1972-76. Served with AUS, 1944-46. Fellow Am. Coll. Healthcare Execs. (life); mem. Am. Hosp. Assn. (chmn. coun. on mgmt. and planning 1977-79), Conn. Hosp. Assn. (trustee 1970-74, pres. 1972-73, Disting. Svc. award 1976), Assn. Am. Med. Colls. (exec. coun. 1974-77, 78-80, treas. 1975-76, chmn. 1979-80, adminstrv. bd. coun. tchg. hosps. 1972-77, chmn. 1975-76, Disting. Svc. Mem. 1982—). Home: 88 Notch Hill Rd Apt 382 North Branford CT 06471-1861

WON, DELMOND JACK HING, commissioner; b. Honolulu, Nov. 18, 1953; BS in Engring., U. Hawaii, 1975, MBA, 1977. Various positions, including dir. planning affairs Hawaiian Tug & Barge Corp. & Young Bros., Ltd., 1977-90; v.p. Hawaii Pacific Industries, Oahu, Hawaii, 1990-93; cons., 1993-94; commr. Fed. Maritime Commn., Washington, 1994—. Office: Fed Maritime Commn 800 N Capitol St NW Washington DC 20573-0001 E-mail: delmondw@fmc.gov.

WONDERS, WILLIAM CLARE, geography educator; b. Toronto, Apr. 22, 1924; s. George Clarence and Ann Mary (Bell) W.; m. Lillian Paradise Johnson, June 2, 1951; children: Karen Elizabeth, Jennifer Anne, Glen William. BA with honors, Victoria Coll., U. Toronto, 1946; MA, Syracuse U., 1948; PhD, U. Toronto, 1951; Fil. Dr. h.c., Uppsala U., 1981. Teaching asst. dept. geography Syracuse U., 1946-48; lectr. dept. geography U. Toronto, 1948-53; asst. prof. geography dept. polit. economy U. Alta., 1953-55, assoc. prof. geography, 1955-57, prof., head dept. geography, 1957-67, prof. dept. geography, 1967-87, Univ. prof., 1983—, prof. emeritus, 1987—. Vis. prof. geography U. B.C., 1954, U. Okla., 1965-66, St. Mary's U., 1977, U. Victoria, 1989, J.F. Kennedy Inst., Free U. Berlin, 1990; guest prof. Inst. Geography, Uppsala (Sweden) U., 1962-63; rsch. fellow in Geography U. Aberdeen, Scotland, 1970-71, 78; vis. fellow in Can. Studies, U. Edinburgh, Scotland, 1987. Author: Looking at Maps, 1960, The Sawdust Fusiliers, 1991, Norden and Canada-A Geographer's Perspective, 1992, Alaska Highway Explorer, 1994; (with T. Drinkwater et al) Atlas of Alberta, 1969, (with J.C. Muller et al) Junior Atlas of Alberta, 1979; contbr., editor: Canada's Changing North, 1971, The North, 1972, The Arctic Circle, 1976, Knowing the North, 1988, Geographica, 1999, Geographica's Pocket World Reference, 2000, Frontiersmen & Settlers, 2002; contbr. articles to jours. and encys., chpts. to books. Mem. Nat. Adv. Com. on Geog. Rsch., 1965-69; chmn. Boreal Inst. No. Studies (Can. Circumpolar Inst.), 1960-62; mem. Can. Permanent Com. on Geog. Names, 1981-94, Alta. Hist. Sites Bd., 1978-83, vice chmn., 1982-83; mem. policy bd. Can. Plains Rsch. Centre, U. Regina (Sask.), 1975-86; mem. adv. bd. Royal Tyrrell Mus. Paleontology, 1984-89; bd. dirs. The Muttart Found., 1986-93, 95-98, v.p., 1991-93, mem., 1991—. NSF sr. fgn. scientist fellow, 1965-66; Canada Council leave fellow, 1969-70, 77-78; Nuffield Found. fellow, 1970-71. Fellow Arctic Inst. N.Am., Royal Soc. Can., Royal Can. Geog. Soc. (Massey medalist 1998); mem. Can. Assn. Geographers (past pres.), Can. Assn. Scottish Studies (councillor 1974-77), Order of Can., Can. Forces Decoration, Scottish Soc. No. Studies, Champlain Soc. (councillor 1981-86), Sigma Xi, Gamma Theta Upsilon. E-mail: wwonders@home.com.

WONDOLOWSKI GERSTEIN, CHRISTINE RITA, academic librarian; b. Worcester, Mass., July 24, 1950; d. Anthony Stanislaus and Irene Zofia (Karolkiewicz) Wondolowski; m. Malvin Jay Gerstein, Mar. 9, 1992. BA, Emmanuel Coll., 1972; MusM, Ithaca Coll., 1979; MLS, SUNY, Geneseo, 1983. Cert. pub. libr. profl., N.Y. state; cert. tchr. music, Mass. Vocal music tchr. Southbridge (Mass.) Pub. Schs., 1973-76; lectr. in music Nazareth Coll., Rochester, N.Y., 1980-83; adult svcs. libr. Bklyn. Pub. Libr., 1983-85; corp. libr. Lazard Freres and Co., N.Y.C., 1985-86; evening libr. in charge York Coll./CUNY, Jamaica, NY, 1986-88; collection devel. libr., asst. prof. libr. svcs. Hofstra U., Hempstead, N.Y., 1988-94, assoc. prof., 1994—. Contbr. to ency., 1989; contbr. articles to profl. jours. Mem., soprano soloist Kingsborough Musical Soc., Bklyn., 1984-92, United Choral Soc., Hewlett, N.Y., 1990-91. Mem. AAUP (Hofstra U. chpt. 1988—, 2d v.p., 1997—, exec. com. 1997—, newsletter editl. bd. 1999—), Assn. Coll. Rsch. Librs. of N.Y., L.I. Libr. Resources Coun. (resource sharing com. 1989—, chair resource sharing com. 1995-97), Nassau County Libr. Assn. (acad. and spl. librs. divsn. 1990-96, exec. bd., continuing edn. divsn., chair program com. 1990-93, corr. sec. 1994-95), Am. Musical Instrument Soc. (bibliographer publ. prizes com. 1999—). Avocations: singing, travel. Office: 902D Axinn Libr Hofstra U Hempstead NY 11549-0123 E-mail: christine.gerstein@hofstra.edu.

WONG, ALFRED MUN KONG, lawyer; b. Honolulu, Sept. 12, 1930; s. Inn and Mew Kung (Choy) W.; m. Laureen Hong, Nov. 20, 1965; children— Peter Marn On, Julie Li Sharn. Student U. Hawaii, 1948-50; B.S., Marquette U., 1953; J.D., U. Calif., 1964. Bar: Hawaii 1964. With Thomas Lee, C.P.A., 1961-62, firm Scott and Balacco, San Francisco, 1962-64; contract atty. Honolulu Redevel. Agy., 1968-71; mng. dir. Takushi, Funaki Wong & Stone, Attys. at Law, Honolulu, 1964—; adj. prof. U. Hawaii Law Sch., 1980-82; mem. bd. bar examiners State of Hawaii, 1968-79; mem. Hawaii Jud. Selection Commn., 1979-85, chmn., 1983-85. Bd. dirs. Pacific coun. Girl Scouts U.S., 1973-78 (Outstanding Svc. award 1978, Cmty. Benefactor award 1992); pres. Niu Valley Community Assn., 1975, bd. dirs., 1974, 76, 77; mem. spl. review com. William S. Richardson Law Sch. U. Hawaii, 1995; dir. Maryknoll Schs., 1995—, v.p., 1999; mem. exec. Friends Hawaii Charities. Served to capt. C.E., U.S. Army, 1953-61. Recipient Chicago Tribune medal, 1952, 53, Soc. Am. Mil. Engrs. award, 1952, 53. Mem. ABA, Am. Law Inst., Hawaii Bar Assn. (dir., chmn. unauthorized practice of law com., nominating com., real property and fin. svcs. sect.), Hastings Coll. Law Alumni Assn. (bd. govs., 1978—, Disting. Service award 1987, nat. chair Hastings annual fund, 1993-94, mem. bd. trustees 1066 Found., 1992—, 2d v.p. 1995, Alumnus of the Yr. 1997), Am. Judicature Soc., Friends of U. Hawaii Law Sch. (bd. dirs. 1987-93, pres. 1991-93), Waialae Country Club (bd. dirs. 1991-93, pres. 1993), Honolulu Club (founding dir.), Beverly Hills Country Club. Office: Takushi Funaki Wong & Stone 733 Bishop St Honolulu HI 96813-4022

WONG, ANTONIO HAM, family physician; b. San Pedro Sula, Honduras, Oct. 7, 1960; came to U.S., 1973; s. Hui Chung and Maria (Wong) H.; m. Heidi Wong, Apr. 7, 1990; children: Lawrence, Catherine, Kristen, Keith. BS, U. Miami, Fla., 1984, MD, 1990. Chief resident dept. family medicine Jackson Meml. Hosp., Miami, 1992-93; med. dir. PCA-Century Med. Ctr., 1993-95; CEO, founder Caduceus Med. Inst., Pembroke Pines, Fla., 1995—. Mem. AMA, Am. Acad. Family Physicians, Am. Soc. Bariatric Physicians, Fla. Med. Assn., Broward County Med. Assn. Avocations: reading, gourmet cooking, swimming, painting, photography. Office: Doctors Plus Med Ctr 9877 Pines Blvd Pembroke Pines FL 33024-6164 also: 17901 NW 5th St Ste 101 Pembroke Pines FL 33029

WONG, BELLA TOY FUNND, lawyer; b. Boston, Feb. 5, 1961; d. Perry Wai Yee and Joan Hung (Lem) W.; m. Steven M. Brand, Sept. 18, 1993. BA, Harvard U., 1982, EdM, 1991; postgrad., Stanford U., 1982-84; JD, U. Calif., Davis, 1987. Bar: Calif. 1987, Mass., 1990; cert. gen. sci. and biology tchr., Mass. Assoc. LeBoeuf, Lamb, Leiby, MacRae, San Francisco, 1987-90; sci. instr. Lincoln Sudbury (Mass.) Regional H.S., 1991-98, head sci. dept., 1996-98; asst. supt. Wellesley (Mass.) Pub. Schs., 1998—. Mem. ABA, ASCD, Am. Assn. Sch. Personnel Officers, Calif. Bar Assn., Mass. Bar Assn., New Eng. Assn. Chemistry Tchrs., Mass. Assn. Sch. Supts., Mass. Assn. Sch. Personnel Officers. Office: Wellesley Pub Schs 40 Kingsbury St Wellesley MA 02481-4831

WONG, BERT YUAN SHU, internist, cardiologist; b. Shanghai, China, 1940; MD, Yale U., 1965. Diplomate in internal medicine and cardiovascular diseases Am. Bd. Internal Medicine. Intern Georgetown Hosp., Washington, 1965-66, resident in internal medicine, 1966-67; resident in cardiology VA Hosp., West Haven, Conn., 1969-70; resident in internal medicine Yale-New Haven Hosp., 1970-71, fellow in cardiology, 1971-73. Fellow ACP, Am. Coll. Cardiology, Am. Coll. Chest Physicians. Office: 215 Parkside Dr Colorado Springs CO 80910

WONG, CHING-PING, chemist, materials scientist, engineer, educator; b. Canton, China, Mar. 29, 1947; came to U.S., 1966; s. Kwok-Keung and Yun-Kwan W. BS in Chemistry, Purdue U., 1969; PhD in Organic/Inorganic Chemistry, Pa. State U., 1975. Postdoctoral scholar Stanford (Calif.) U., 1975-77; mem. rsch. staff AT&T Bell Labs., Princeton, N.J., 1977-82, sr. mem. tech. staff, 1982-87, disting. mem. tech. staff, 1987-92; AT&T Bell Labs. fellow, 1992-96; Regents prof. Sch. of Materials Sci. and Engring., Ga. Inst. Tech., Atlanta, 1996—; assembly, reliability and thermal mgmt. rsch. dir. NSF Packaging Rsch. Ctr. Program chmn. 39th Electronic Components Conf., 1989; gen. chmn. 41st Electronic Components and Tech. Conf., 1991; bd. govs. IEEE-Components, Hybrids and Mfg. Tech. Soc., 1987-89, tech. v.p., 1990-91, pres., 1992-93. Author, editor: Polymers for Electronic and Photonic Applications, 1993; contbr. articles to profl. jours. Recipient Outstanding Papers and Contbns. award IEEE-Components, Hybrids and Mfg. Tech. Soc., 1990, 91, 94, 96, 1998, Ga. Tech. Outstanding Faculty award, London, 1999, Award of Excellence U. Press, 2000. Fellow: Nat. Acad. Engring., IEEE (Outstanding Sustained Tech. Contbns. award 1995, Millenium medal 2000, EAB Exceptional Continuation Edn. award 2001, CPMT Outstanding Exceptional Tech.Contbn. award 2002). Achievements include over 40 U.S. and numerous internat. patents for integrated device passivation and encepsulation area; pioneer in application of gel polymers for device reliability without hermeticity, a new application on electronic device packaging. Office: Ga Inst Tech Sch Materials Sci & Engring 771 Ferst Dr Atlanta GA 30332-0001 Business E-Mail: cp.wong@mse.gatech.edu.

WONG, DAVID, pharmaceutical researcher; b. Canton, China, Oct. 15, 1962; came to the U.S., 1987; s. Ka-Yat and Yeuk-Bing (Lam) W.; m. Yong Kristine Chung, Aug. 29, 1992. BA, U. Tex., 1990, PhD, 1994. Diploma in psychiat. nursing, Hong Kong. Student nurse Hwai Chung Hosp., Hong Kong, 1984-87, psychiat. RN, 1987; co-supr. for undergrad. rsch. U. Tex., Austin, 1991-93, tchg. asst., 1990-94; postdoctoral rsch. CIBUS Pharm., Inc., Redwood City, Calif., 1994-95, scientist, 1995-96; sr. rsch. scientist Andrx Pharm. Inc., Ft. Lauderdale, Fla., 1996—. Cons. Shanghai Materia Medica Med. and Biotech. Inst., 1995—. Recipient Tex. Excellence in Tchg. award Student Coun. Coll. Pharmacy, Austin, 1991, Tex. Excellence in Tchg. award Ex-Student Assn. U. Tex., Austin, 1992, Pen Tchg. Leadership award Fourth Nat. Conf. on Tchg., Asst. Tng. and Employment, Chgo., 1993. Mem. Am. Assn. Pharm. Scientists, Am. Chem. Soc., Hong Kong Nurse's Assn. Office: Andrx Pharm Inc 4001 SW 47th Ave Ste 201 Fort Lauderdale FL 33314-4030 Home: 903 Coventry Cir Milpitas CA 95035-3534

WONG, DAVID T. biochemist, researcher; b. Hong Kong, Nov. 6, 1935; s. Chi-Keung and Pui-King Wong; m. Christina Lee, Dec. 28, 1963; children: Conrad, Melvin, Vincent. Student, Nat. Taiwan U., 1955-56; BS, Seattle Pacific U., 1961; MS, Oreg. State U., 1964; PhD, U. Oreg., 1966. Sr. biochemist Lilly Rsch. Labs., Indpls., 1968-72, rsch. biochemist, 1973-77, sr. rsch. scientist, 1978-89, rsch. advisor, 1990-97, Lilly rsch. fellow, 1997-99, cons., 2000—. Adj. prof. biochemistry and molecular biology Ind. U. Sch. Medicine, 1986—96, adj. prof. neurobiology, 1991. Mem. editl.bd.: Chinese Jour. Physiology, 1996—2000; contbr. articles to sci. jours. Named Alumnus of the Yr., Seattle Pacific U., 1998, Alumnus of Growing Vision, 1991; recipient Scientist of the Yr. Pres. award, Chinese Neurosci. Soc., 1991, Discoverers award, Pharm. Mfr. Assn., 1993, Lifetime Rsch. award, Mental Health Assn. Ind., 1996, World Difference award, Ind. Health Industry Forum, 1996, Pharm. Discover's award Prozac, Nat. Alliance Rsch. Schizophrenia and Depression, 1996, Outstanding Achievement in Neurosci. Rsch. award, Lilly Neuroscience Eli Lilly and Co., 2000, Cornerstone award, Am. Drugstore Mus. Indpls., 2000, Excellence award, Asian Am. Alliance, Inc., 2002, Pioneer Recognition award, Com. 100, 2002, Excellence award, U.S. Pan Asian Am. C. of C., 2002. Mem.: Soc. Chinese Bioscientists Am., Soc. Neurosci. (pres. Indpls. chpt. 1987, 1988), Am. Soc. Neurochemistry, Internat. Soc. Neurochemistry, Am. Soc. Pharmacology and Exptl. Therapeutics, Am. Coll. Neuropsychopharamcology, Indpls. Assn. Chinese Ams. (pres. 1987). Achievements include patents in field; research in on biochemistry and pharmacology of neurotransmission; discovery of and development of antidepressant drug, Prozac (Fluoxetine) and drug candidates including Atomoxetine, a selective inhibitor of norepinephrine uptake; daproxetine, a selective inhibitor of serotonin an dnorepinephrine; studies of potentially useful substances which enhance transmission of norepinephrine, dopamine, serotonin, acetycholine, and GABA-neurons; studies of natural products led to the discovery of caboxylic ionophores: Narasin and A204, which increase transport of cations across biomembranes. Home: 5812 E Fall Creek Parkway Nort Indianapolis IN 46226-1051 Fax: (317) 254-8688.

WONG, DAVID YUE, academic administrator, physics educator; b. Swatow, China, Apr. 16, 1934; came to U.S., 1953; s. Fan and Wen (Tsang) W.; m. Katherine Young, Sept. 3, 1960 (div. Mar. 1988); children: Amy, Eric; m. Elizabeth Lewis, Mar. 26, 1988 BA, Hardin Simmons U., 1954; PhD, U. Md., 1957. Theoretical physicist Lawrence Radiation Lab., U. Calif., Berkeley, 1958-59; asst. prof. physics U. Calif., San Diego, 1960-63, assoc. prof., 1963-67, prof., 1967—, chair dept. physics, 1977-80, provost Warren Coll., 1985-94. Alfred P. Sloan fellow, 1966-68 Mem. Am. Inst. Physics.

WONG, EDWINA A. LEE, real estate broker; b. Honolulu, Feb. 12, 1947; d. Edwin M.S. and Grace K. (Aipa) Lee; m. Michael Kam Hoong Wong, Feb. 15, 1970; children: Michelle L.M.Y., David M.K. Cet., Stapleton Real Estate Sch., Honolulu. Lic. real estate broker, Hawaii. Real estate broker Fin. Realty, Honolulu, 1976-80, Pacific Real Estate Investments, Honolulu, 1982-89; owner, mgr., broker Edwina A.L. Wong, 1989—. Sec. Bishop Estate, Honolulu, 1985-86; extra Walt Disney Inc., Honolulu, 1989. Alt. Hawaii Dem. Conv., 1988, 90; pres. bd. dirs. Makakilo (Hawaii) Gardens Assn., 1989; mem. planning com. Friends of Mike Wong for Hawaii Ho. of Reps., 1990. Mem. Nat. Assn. Realtors, Honolulu Bd. Realtors. Avocations: swimming, tennis, golf, volleyball, hula dancing. Home: 92-344 Hookili Pl Kapolei HI 96707-2802

WONG, ELAINE DANG, foundation executive; b. Canton, China, June 3, 1936 (parents Am. citizens); d. Robert G. and Fung Heong (Woo) Dang; A.A. (Rotary scholar), Coalinga Coll., 1956; B.S. (AAUW scholar, Grad. Resident scholar), U. Calif., Berkeley, 1958, teaching credential, 1959; m. Philip Wong, Nov. 8, 1959; children— Elizabeth, Russell, Roger, Edith, Valerie. Tchr. acctg. San Mateo (Calif.) High Sch., 1959-60; acct., 1960-75; substitute tchr. Richmond County Schs., Augusta, Ga., 1975-77; comptroller Central Savannah River Area, United Way, Augusta, 1977-82; asst. controller Hammermill Hardwoods div. Hammermill Paper Co., Augusta, 1982-84; controller SFN Communications of Augusta, Inc. (WJBF-TV), 1984-85; acct. Med. Coll. Ga. Found., Inc., 1986-88, Nat. Sci Ctr. Found., Inc., 1988-89; cons. small bus.; pvt. tutor acctg. Mem. adv. bd. Richmond County Bd. Edn., 1985-87; bd. dirs. Cen. Savannah River chpt. Girl Scouts US, 1986-92. Panel judge Jr. Achievement Treas. award, 1980, 81; treas. Chinese Lang. Sch., 1973-75, Merry Neighborhood Sch., 1974-75. Recipient Achievement award Bank of Am., 1954. Mem. Nat. Assn. Accts. (dir. 1978-85, treas. 1982-84), Chinese Assn. Republican. Presbyterian.

WONG, HENRY LI-NAN, bank executive, economist; b. Rangoon, Burma, Nov. 3, 1940; came to U.S., 1946; s. Chew King and Jenny (Yu) W.; m. Laurie Yap, Apr. 11, 1968; children: Rachael S.Y., Remle S.W. BS, Waynesburg Coll., 1965; MS, U. Hawaii, 1968, PhD, 1969. Economist Econ. Rsch. Svc., USDA, Washington, 1969-70, Hawaii Dept. Budget and Fin., Honolulu, 1970-73; dir. Hawaii film office Hawaii Dept. Planning and Econ. Devel., 1973-84; exec. v.p., chief adminstr. office of chmn. CB Bancshares Inc., 1984—. Vice chmn., dir. Hawaii Strategic Devel. Corp., Honolulu, 1991-95; mem. coun. of revenue State of Hawaii, 1995-98; v.p., bd. dirs. Friends of East West Ctr., Honolulu, 1983-84. Trustee, chmn. bd. Lanakila Rehab. Ctr.; mem. Salvation Army Adv. Coun. Honolulu; bd. dirs. WHKT Bnevolent Assn. NDEA fellow, 1965-69. Mem. Assn. Film Commrs. (pres. 1980), Am Econ. Assn., Am. Agrl. Econs. Assn., Hawaii Internat. Film Festival, Chinese C. of C., Hawaii Soc. Corp. Planners, Elks, Masons (trustee), Shriners, Alpha Kappa Psi, Theta Chi. Democrat. Presbyterian. Office: City Bank City Fin Tower 201 Merchant St Honolulu HI 96813-2928

WONG, IVAN GYNMUN, seismologist; b. Portland, Oreg., Feb. 23, 1948; s. Edward P. and Elizabeth K. (Lee) W.; m. Laly B. Flores, Oct. 22, 1988; children: Matthew W., Scott G. BS in Physics, Oreg. State U., 1970; BS in Geology, Portland (Oreg.) State U., 1972; MS in Geophysics, U. Utah, 1976. Phys. sci. technician/geologist U.S. Army Corps of Engrs., Portland, Oreg., 1967-72; seismol. field asst. U.S. Geol. Survey, Salt Lake City, 1974-75; rsch. asst. U. Utah, 1974-75, U. Calif., Berkeley, 1975-76; staff to sr. seismologist Woodward-Clyde Cons., Oakland, Calif., 1976-92; v.p., sr. seismologist, mgr. seismic hazard br. Woodward-Clyde Fed. Svcs., 1993-98; sr. seismologist, mgr. seismic hazards group URS Corp., Oakland, Calif., 1998—. Rsch. assoc. Ariz. Earthquake Info. Ctr., Northern Ariz. U., Flagstaff, 1986—; seismology instr. Calif. Acad. Scis., San Francisco, 1989—; cons. to several U.S. govt. agys. including Dept. Energy, U.S. Bur. Reclamation, FEMA, Govt. of Thailand; rev. and adv. panels, U.S. Geol. Survey, various locations, 1991—; invited spkr., guest lectr. various profl. orgns. including Asian Disaster Prevention Ctr., 1997. Author books; contbr. 2000 papers, maps and abstracts to profl. jours. Staff sgt. USMCR, 1970-79. Grantee Nat. Earthquake Hazards Reduction Program, U.S. Geol. Survey, 1986—. Mem. Am. Geophys. Union, Geol. Soc. Am., Seismol. Soc. Am., Earthquake Engring. Rsch. Inst., Internat. Assn. Earthquake Engring, Assn. Engring. Geologists. Office: URS Corp 500 12th St Ste 200 Oakland CA 94607-4010 E-mail: ivan_wong@urscorp.com.

WONG, JAMES BOK, economist, engineer, technologist; b. Canton, China, Dec. 9, 1922; came to U.S., 1938, naturalized, 1962; s. Gen Ham and Chen (Yee) W.; m. Wai Ping Lim, Aug. 3, 1946, (dec.)children: John, Jane Doris, Julia Ann. BS in Agr., U. Md., 1949, BS in Chem. Engring., 1950; MS, U. Ill., 1951, PhD, 1954. Rsch. asst. U. Ill., Champaign-Urbana, 1950-53; chem. engr. Standard Oil of Ind., Whiting, 1953-55; process design engr., rsch. engr. Shell Devel. Co., Emeryville, Calif., 1955-61; sr. planning engr., prin. planning engr. Chem. Plastics Group, Dart Industries, Inc. (formerly Rexall Drug & Chem. Co.), L.A., 1961-66, supr. planning and econs., 1966-67, mgr. long range planning and econs., 1967, chief economist, 1967-72, dir. econs. and ops. analysis, 1972-78, dir. internat. techs., 1978-81; pres. James B. Wong Assocs., 1981—. Chmn. bd. dirs. United Pacific Bank, 1988—; tech. cons. various corps. Author: Jade Eagle, 2000; contbr. articles to profl. jours. Bd. dirs., pres. Chinese Am. Citizens Alliance Found.; mem. Asian Am. Edn. Commn., 1971-81. Served with USAAF, 1943-46. Recipient Los Angeles Outstanding Vol. Service award, 1977. Mem. Am. Inst. Chem. Engrs., Am. Chem. Soc., VFW (vice comdr. 1959), Commodores (named to exec. order 1982), Sigma Xi, Tau Beta Pi, Phi Kappa Phi, Pi Mu Epsilon, Phi Lambda Upsilon, Phi Eta Sigma. Home: 2460 Venus Dr Los Angeles CA 90046-1646 *Personal philisophy: A man's reputation is his most prized possession.*

WONG, JAMES THOMAS, lawyer; b. N.Y.C., Sept. 15, 1955; s. Swee Chee and Dorothy Chuan-Ying (Yang) W.; m. Patricia Uyehara, Aug. 15, 1981; children: Thomas, Jordan, Cory, Sara. BA cum laude, U. Pa., 1976; JD, Case Western Res. U., 1979. Bar: Pa. 1979, U.S. Dist. Ct. (ea. dist.) Pa. 1979, Hi. 1982, U.S. Ct. Appeals (9th cir.) 1982. Dep. atty. gen., asst. gen. counsel Commonwealth of Pa., 1980-82; assoc. Law Offices Richard K. Quinn, Honolulu, 1982-85; assoc., ptnr. Libkuman, Ventura, Ayabe & Hughes, 1985-91; sr. trial atty., staff counsel AIG Ins. Cos., 1991-94, mng. atty., 1994-99; pvt. practice, 1999—. Bd. dir. Asian Am. Council Greater Phila., 1980-82, council of deacons Calvary by the Sea Luth. Ch., 1996-99. Mem. ABA, Pa. Bar Assn., Hi. Bar Assn., Am. Arbitration Assn. Lutheran. Home: 173 Kokololio Pl Honolulu HI 96821-2563 Office: 735 Bishop St Ste 200 Honolulu HI 96813

WONG, JEFFREY YUN CHUNG, radiation oncologist, medical researcher; b. Honolulu, Nov. 5, 1955; s. Tom Kam Yee and Rose Ah Moy (Chun) W.; m. Julia Kyoko Yoshikawa, Oct. 17, 1987; 1 child, Marisa Midori. BS in Biology, Stanford U., 1977; MD, Johns Hopkins U., 1981. Diplomate in radiation oncology Am. Bd. Radiology. Intern Harbor-UCLA Med. Ctr., Torrance, 1981-82; resident U. Calif., San Francisco, 1982-85; staff physician, chair radiation oncology and radiation rsch. City of Hope Med. Ctr., Duarte, 1985—. Contbr. articles to profl. jours. Am. Cancer Soc. clin. fellow, 1984. Mem. Am. Soc. Therapeutic Radiology and Oncology, Am. Soc. Clin. Oncology, Radiation Rsch. Soc., Phi Beta Kappa.

WONG, JOAQUIN, pediatric neurologist; b. Nov. 4, 1959; MD, U. Panama, 1984. Intern Social Security Hosp., Panama City, Panama, 1984-86, resident in pediatrics Panama, 1986-89, Albert Einstein Coll. Medicine./Montefiore

Med. Ctr., Bronx, N.Y., 1989-92, fellow in pediatric neurology, 1992-95; asst. prof. pediatric neurology La. State U. Med. Ctr., New Orleans, 1995—. Mem.: Am. Acad. Pediatrics, Child Neurology Soc. Office: 200 Henry Clay Ave New Orleans LA 70118-5720

WONG, JOHN WING-CHUNG, psychiatrist; b. Canton, China, Aug. 12, 1934; came to U.S., 1962; s. Min Sam and Yee Fern (Lau) W.; m. Lily Jent-Ju Chen, May 4, 1962; children: Diana, John Wing-Chung Jr., Gloria, Angela. MD, Queen's U., Kingston, Ont., Can., 1959. Diplomate Am. Bd. Psychiatry and Neurology. Resident physician in psychiatry Ohio State U. Hosp., Columbus, 1963-65; intern St. Michael's Hosp., Toronto, 1959-60; resident internal medicine univ. med. unit Queen Mary Hosp., Hong Kong, 1960-61; practice medicine specializing in psychiatry L.A., 1969-97; med. dir. inpatient unit Ventura County Health Care Agy., 1994-96, med. dir. behavioral health dept., 1996-2000; med. dir. Behavioral Medicine Ctr., San Gabriel Valley Med. Ctr., San Gabriel, Calif., 1991—; emeritus assoc. clin. prof. U. So. Calif. Sch. Medicine, 1998—. Dir. Pacific Clinic, Pasadena, Calif., 1987-90; med. dir. psychiat. consultation liaison svc. Hosp. of the Good Samaritan, L.A., 1989-90, Behavioral Medicine Ctr., Gabriel (Calif.) Valley Med. Ctr., 1991—; bd. dirs. Ea. Internat. Bank, Alhambra, Calif.; dir. day treatment program Resthaven Cmty. Mental Health Ctr., L.A., 1967-69; dir. area XXIV Profl. Standard Rev. Orgn., L.A., 1980-83; chmn. dept. psychiatry St. Vincent Hosp., 1978-79; dir. The Assocs.-Calif. Inst. Tech., Pasadena, 1990-91. Bd. dirs. San Marino (Calif.) Community Chest, 1986-88, pres., 1987-88; bd. dirs. San Gabriel Region United Way Inc., L.A., 1989-91, systemwide bd. dirs., 1990-91; mem. Los Angeles County Commn. on Aging, 1992-96. Mem. Am. Psychiat. Assn., So. Calif. Psychiat. Soc., Assocs. of Calif. Inst. Tech. Office: San Gabriel Valley Med Ctr Behavioral Medicine Ctr 438 W Las Tunas Dr San Gabriel CA 91776-1216 Home: 1005 Nightingale Pl Oxnard CA 93030-8507

WONG, KAINAM THOMAS, electrical engineer; b. Hong Kong, Nov. 24, 1960; s. Ying-Man and Wai-Ming (Pun) W. BS, UCLA, 1985; BSEE, U. Colo., 1987; MSEE, Mich. State U., 1990; PhD, Purdue U., 1996. Tchg. asst. Mich. State U., East Lansing, 1988-89; mfg. engr. Gen. Motors, Warren, Mich., 1990-91; rsch. asst. Purdue U., West Lafayette, Ind., 1994-96; sr. profl. staff Johns Hopkins U., Laurel, Md., 1996-98; asst. prof. Nanyang Tech U., Singapore, 1998, Chinese U. of Hong Kong, 1998—2001, U. Waterloo, Canada, 2001—. Asst. prof. Nanyang Tech. U., Singapore, 1998, Chinese U. Hong Kong, 1998-2001, U. Waterloo dept. elec. and computer engring., Canada. Mem.: IEEE (sr.). E-mail: ktwong@ieee.org.

WONG, KENNETH K. education educator; b. Hong Kong, May 11, 1955; s. H.C. Wong and C.K. Man; m. Michelle A. Chu, 1979; 1 child, Ellen E. BA with honors, U. Chgo., 1977, MA, 1980, PhD, 1983. Asst. prof. U. Oreg., Eugene, 1983-88; asst. prof. dept. edn. U. Chgo., 1988-93, assoc. prof., 1993—. Cons. Nat. Commn. for Employment Policy, 1990, U.S. Dept. Edn., 1988, Edn. Devel. Ctr. and NSF, 1994-96. Author: City Choices, 1990; co-author: When Federalism Works, 1986; editor: Politics of Policy Innovation, 1992, Rethinking School Reform in Chicago, 1996, Rethinking Policy for At-Risk Students, 1994; co-editor: Politics of Urban Education, 1992, Implementing School Reform, 1997; mem. editl. bd. Am. Ednl. Rsch. Jour., 1992-96, Ednl. Adminstrn. Quarterly, 1994—; series editor Advances in Ednl. Policy, 1995—. Mem. rsch. adv. com. Chgo. Urban League, 1988—; mem. human capital devel. com. United Way of Chgo., 1990—. Spencer fellow Nat. Acad. Edn., 1989-90; rsch. grantee Inst. Poverty Rsch., Madison, 1990-91, Benton Ctr., Chgo., 1990-93, Spencer Found., Chgo., 1992-93, Nat. Ctr. on Edn. in Inner Cities, 1993-95, Joyce Found., Chgo., 1993-95, U.S. Dept. Edn., 1994-95, 95-97, 97, NSF, 1996—, British Coun., 1997. Mem. Am. Ednl. Rsch. Assn., Am. Polit. Sci. Assn., Assn. for Policy Analysis and Mgmt., Midwest Polit. Sci. Assn. Avocation: hiking. Office: U Chgo Dept Edn 5835 S Kimbark Ave Chicago IL 60637-1635

WONG, KON MAX, electrical engineer educator; b. Macau, China, June 11, 1945; arrived in Can., 1976; s. Ho Ting and Sin Hung (Yung) Wong; m. Margaret Ellen Rumsey, Aug. 25, 1984; children: An Zhong Alexander, Hui Zhong Richard. BSc in Engring., U. London, 1969; DIC, Imperial Coll., London, 1972; PhD, U. London, 1974, DSc, 1995. Rsch. engr. Plessey Telecom Rsch., Taplow, 1969-76; assoc. prof. Tech. U. Nova Scotia, Halifax, Can., 1976-81; prof. McMaster U., Hamilton, Canada, 1981—, Mitel Prof. signal processing Canada, 1999—, chmn. Dept. Elec. Engring., 1985-86, 88-94; hon. prof. South East U., Nanjing, China, 1995—; vis. prof. Chinese U. Hong Kong, Hong Kong, 1997—. Cons. Defence Rsch. Establishments, Can., 1986—, Mitel Corp., Ottawa, Can., 1993—, Lockheed-Martin, Ottawa, 1993-94, Canadian Marconi, Ottawa, 1995-97, Spotwave wireless, 2000—; assoc. editor IEEE Transaction on Signal Processing, 1997-99. Contbr. articles to textbooks and to profl. jours. Fellow IEEE, Inst. Elec. Engrs., Inst. Physics, Royal Statistics Soc. Avocations: table tennis, swimming, squash, piano playing, painting. Office: Dept Elec & Computer Engring McMaster U Hamilton ON Canada

WONG, LEE-JUN CHANG, human geneticist; b. Taipei, Taiwan, Republic of China, Sept. 21, 1948; came to U.S., 1971; d. Yu-Shang and Tsui-Er Chiu Chang; m. Shan S. Wong, Feb. 16, 1973; children: Inyork H., I. Hansie. BS, Nat. Taiwan U., 1971; PhD, Ohio State U., 1975. Diplomate Am. Bd. Genetics; cert. clin. molecular genetics, clin. biochem. genetics. Asst. to assoc. prof. U. Mass., Lowell, 1978-92; trainee Baylor Coll. of Medicine, Houston, 1992-94; asoc. prof., lab. dir. U. So. Calif., L.A., 1995-97; assoc. prof. dept. oncology, pediats. & medicine, lab. dir. Georgetown U., Washington, 1997—. Office: Georgetown U Med Ctr 3800 Reservoir Rd NW # M4000 Washington DC 20007-2113 E-mail: wonglj@georgetown.edu.

WONG, LILIANE, architect, architecture educator; BA, Vassar Coll., 1981—81; MA, Harvard U., , 1985. Registered arch. Assoc. Perry Dean Rogers & Ptnrs., Boston, 1985—94; prin. Mahon Wong Assocs., Cambridge, 1994—; assoc. prof. RISD, Providence, 1998—. Furniture line. Named Bulfinch Arch Competition winner, Hist. Neighborhood Found., 1987; recipient Women in Arch. award, Boston Soc. of Archs., 1994. Mem.: AIA, Boston Soc. Archs.*

WONG, LINDA, lawyer; b. Hackensack, N.J., Nov. 15, 1953; d. Quing and Alice Wong; m. Richard Peres, June 14, 1980; children: Lindsay Peres, Jessica Peres. BA, Rutgers U., 1976, JD, 1982. Atty. Office Legis. Svcs., Divsn. Legal Svcs., Trenton, N.J., 1982-84, N.J. Dept. of the Pub. Adv., Divsn. Devel. Disabled, Trenton, 1984-90; asst. dir. divsn. civil rights N.J. Dept. Law and Pub. Safety, 1990-94; ptnr. Wong, Tsai & Fleming, Edison, N.J., 1994—. Adj. instr. Rutgers U., New Brunswick, N.J., 1994-95; mem. Supreme Ct. Com., N.J., 1994-96; presenter in field. Contbr. articles to profl. jours. Mem. ABA, N.J. State Bar Assn. (chairperson), N.J. Assn. Pacific Am. Lawyer Assn., Nat. Asian Pacific ABA, N.J. NOW. Web site: www.wongfleming.com. Office: Wong Fleming, PC P O Box 3663 821 Alexander Rd Ste 150 Princeton NJ 08543-3663

WONG, MICHAEL ANTHONY, financial analyst; b. Fresno, Calif., Apr. 27, 1967; s. Edsell Yew and Cynthia Marie (Fong) W. BA in Econs. summa cum laude, UCLA, 1988; MBA, Stanford U., 1996. Asst. bank examiner FDIC, San Francisco, 1988-90; small ent. devel. vol. U.S. Peace Corps, Guaranda, Ecuador, 1991-94; e-procurement fin. mgr., sr. fin. analyst, cons. Hewlett-Packard Co., 1999—. Fin. analyst spl. projects Hewlett-Packard Latin Am., 1996-98, founder Personal Success Cir. Mem. U.S. Tennis Assn., Palo Alto Tennis Club, Sierra Club, Omicron Delta Epsilon, Phi Beta Kappa. Avocations: tennis, mountain climbing, hiking. Home: 1093 Tanland Dr Apt 207 Palo Alto CA 94303-3755

WONG, NANCY L. dermatologist; b. Chung King, China, Aug. 23, 1943; came to U.S., 1947; d. YinPao Harry and Alice Wang; m. Robert Lipshutz; children: Seth, Alison, David. BS magna cum laude, Pa. State U., 1963; MS in Physics, Columbia U., 1965; MD, Jefferson Med. Coll., Phila., 1971. Diplomate Am. Bd. Dermatology. Intern Wilmington Med. Ctr., 1972; resident Jackson Meml. Hosp., Miami, Mount Sinai Med. Ctr., Miami, 1977; pvt. practice Palo Alto, Calif., 1987—. Woodrow Wilson fellow 1963-64, NSF fellow, 1963-64, AEC fellow, 1963-64. Fellow Am. Acad. Dermatology. Avocations: music, writing, painting. Office: 1101 Welch Rd Ste A2 Palo Alto CA 94304-1925

WONG, NGAI YING, educator; b. Hong Kong, Mar. 3, 1956; s. Hon Fan and Sau Ho (Kwok) W.; m. Fung Yee Ng., Dec. 18, 1983; children: Lok Ping, Lok Yin. BA, U. Hong Kong, 1977, MPhil, 1981, PhD, 1995; MA in Edn., Chinese U. Hong Kong, 1987. Tutor U. Hong Kong, 1977-80; tchr. Wong Tai Shan Meml. Coll, Hong Kong, 1980-85, sr. tchr., coord. extracurricular activities, 1985-89; lectr. Chinese U. Hong Kong, 1989-95, asst. prof., 1995—2001, prof., 2001—. Editor Math. Bull., 1980-89, EduMath, 2001—. Fellow Inst. Math. and Applications, Royal Statis Soc.; mem. Hong Kong Assn. for Sci. and Math. Edn. (math. com. 1981-89, convenor math. sec. 1981-83), Hong Kong Assn. Math. Edn. (pres. 1995-99). Buddhist. Avocations: Chinese martial art, seal carving. Office: Chinese U Faculty Edn Shatin Hong Kong E-mail: nywong@cuhk.edu.hk.

WONG, OTTO, epidemiologist; b. Canton, China, Nov. 14, 1947; came to U.S., 1967, naturalized, 1976; m. Betty Yeung, Feb. 14, 1970; children: Elaine, Jonathan. BS, U. Ariz., 1970; MS, Carnegie Mellon U., 1972, U. Pitts., 1973, ScD, 1975. Cert. epidemsiologist Am. Coll. Epidemiology, 1982. USPHS fellow U. Pitts., 1972-75; asst. prof. epidemiology Georgetown U. Med. Sch., 1975-78; mgr. epidemiology Equitable Environ. Health Inc., Rockville, Md., 1977-78; dir. epidemiology Tabershaw Occuopational Med. Assocs., 1978-80; dir. occupational rsch. Biometric Rsch. Inst., Washington, 1980-81; exec. v.p., chief epidemiologist ENSR Health Scis., Alameda, Calif., 1981-90; chief epidemiologist, pres. Applied Health Scis., San Mateo, 1991—. Adj. prof. epidemiology and biostats. Tulane U. Med. Ctr., New Orleans; vis. prof. epidemiology and occupl. health Nat. Def. Med. Ctr., Taipei, Taiwan, Shanghai Med. U.; adj. prof. dept. cmty. & family medicine Chinese U. Hong Kong; cons. WHO, Nat. Cancer Inst., Nat. Inst. Occupl. Safety and Health, Occupl. Safety and Health Adminstrn., Nat. Heart, Lung and Blood Inst., Internat. Agy. for Rsch. on Cancer, U.S. EPA, Ford Motors Co., Gen. Electric, Mobil, Chevron, Union Carbide, Fairfax (Va.) Hosp., Agy. for Toxic Substances and Disease Registry, U. Ariz. scholar, 1967-68. Assoc. editor Annals Epidemiology; contbr. articles to profl. jours. Fellow Am. Coll. Epidemiology, Human Biology Council; mem. Am. Pub. Health Assn., Biometric Soc., Soc. Epidemiologic Rsch., Phi Beta Kappa, Pi Mu Epsilon. Republican. Office: Applied Health Scis PO Box 2078 181 2nd Ave Ste 628 San Mateo CA 94401-3812

WONG, PATRICK SECK LAI, chemical engineer; b. Canton, China, 1936; came to U.S., 1957; m. Helen Wong, 1941; children: Julian, Francis, Alex. BSChemE, U. Mich., 1960; MS, MIT, 1962; PhD, Imperial Coll., London, 1967. Rsch. chemist W.R. Grace, Clifton, N.J., 1962-64; rsch. assoc. MIT, Cambridge, Mass., 1967-73; head transport process Alza Corp., Palo Alto, Calif., 1973-79, prin. scientist, 1981-85, dir. product rsch., 1985-87, sr. dir. rsch., 1987-91, exec. dir. R & D, 1991-94, v.p. rsch., 1994-97, v.p. oral product R&D, 1997—; v.p. R & D Collins Indls. Co., Hong Kong, 1979-81, Bio-Electro System, Palo Alto, 1988-91. Contbr. articles to Jour. Polymer Sci. (London), AIChemE Jour., Ency. Pharm. Tech. Recipient Founder's award ALZA Corp., 1996. Mem. Am. Chem. Soc., Am. Assn. Pharm. Scientists, Controlled Release Soc., Tau Beta Pi, Sigma Xi. Achievements include 170 patents for Controlled Drug Delivery. Office: Alza Corp 1900 Charleston Rd Mountain View CA 94043-1218 E-mail: Patrick.Wong@alza.com.

WONG, PHILLIP ALLEN, osteopathic physician; b. Oakland, Calif., Dec. 8, 1956; s. Timothy Him and Lillian (Lee) W.; m. Lisa Perreautt, Apr. 30, 1983; children: Ashley, Heather. BS in Microbiology and Chemistry, No. Ariz. U., 1979; DO, Kirksville Coll. Osteo. Med., 1983. Intern Kirksville Osteo. Health Ctr., 1983-84; staff family physician USAF, Kirtland AFB, N.Mex., 1984-87; CEO, pvt. practice Albuquerque, 1987—. Capt. USAF, 1984-87. Mem. Am. Acad. Osteopathy (bd. cert. in osteo. manipulative medicine), Am. Osteo. Assn., Am. Coll. Osteo. Family Physicians (bd. cert. family practice), N.Mex. Osteo. Med. Assn. (bd. mem.), Ariz. Acad. Osteopathy (bd. mem.), Cranial Acad. (bd. cert. in cranial in the osteo. field). Office: 10211 Montgomery Blvd NE Ste A Albuquerque NM 87111-3608

WONG, RAYMOND SHIU-LOONG, radiologist; b. Hong Kong, Jan. 25, 1942; came to U.S., 1958; s. Jason Y. and Nancy L. (Tamm) W.; m. Jo-Lien Hsieh; 1 child, Florence W. BS in Chemistry, UCLA, 1962; MD, U. Chgo., 1966. Diplomate Am. Bd. Radiology with subspecialty in nuclear radiology, Am. Bd. Pediats. Diagnostic radiologist Hollywood Presbyn. Med. Ctr., L.A., 1981-94, Huntington Meml. Hosp., Pasadena, Calif., 1994—. Contbr. articles to profl. jours. Mem. Am. Coll. Radiology, Soc. Nuclear Medicine, Calif. Radiol. Soc., L.A. Radiol. Soc., Radiol. Soc. N.Am. Office: Huntington Meml Hosp 100 W California Blvd Pasadena CA 91105-3097

WONG, RAYMOND Y. physician, educator; b. L.A., Nov. 20, 1954; s. Sam Tin and Bik See Wong; m. Lorna Ai, July 12, 1981; 1 child, Melanie. BS in Chemistry, Pacific Union Coll., Angwin, Calif., 1975; MD, Loma Linda U., 1979. Diplomate Am. Bd. Internal Medicine. Staff physician Loma Linda VA Hosp., 1983-84; attending physician Loma Linda U. Med. Ctr., 1984—; head divsn. gen. internal medicine and geriatrics Loma Linda U. Sch. Medicine, 1997—. Presenter workshops. Fellow ACP; mem. Soc. Gen. Internal Medicine (taskforce on clinician-educator 1995-98), Clerkship Dirs. Internal Medicine. Avocations: travel, chess. Office: Loma Linda U Sch Medicine Rm 1582 LLUMC Loma Linda CA 92354

WONG, RICHARD LEE, lawyer; b. Austin, Tex., May 5, 1964; s. Richard and Narcissus Faye (Lee) W. BA, Calif. State U., Hayward, 1987; JD, Georgetown U., 1990. Mem. Office of Presdl. Pers. The White House, Washington, 1989-90; with Sedgwick Detert Moran & Arnold, San Francisco, 1990-91; dist. office staff U.S. Senator John Seymour, 1991-92; atty.-advisor U.S. Dept. Transp., Washington, 1992—. Mem. Chinese Christian Ch. of Greater Washington. Recipient Nat. Performance Rev. Reinventing Govt. award, 1997, Govt. Tech. Mag. Leadership award, 1999, Pres.'s Coun. on Y2K Conversion award, 2001. Mem.: Asian Pacific-ABA, Conf. on Asian Pacific Am. Leadership., U.S. Naval Inst. Address: 1211 S Eads St Apt 601 Arlington VA 22202-2890

WONG, STEPHEN T.C. radiology, neurology, computer scientist, and bioengineer educator; b. Hong Kong, Sept. 8, 1959; came to U.S., 1985; s. Cheuk and Sam Kuk (Lam) W.; m. Sandie P.K. Ho, Jan. 26, 1960; children: Solomon, Gabriella. B of Engring., U. Western Australia, Perth, 1983; MSc in Computer Sci., Lehigh U., 1989, PhD in Computer Sci., 1991. Registered profl. engr., Pa. Mech. engr. Mass. Engring. Co., Manila, Philippines, 1977-78; rsch. assoc. Australian Nat. U., Canberra, 1982-83; elec. engr. Hewlett Packard Co., Singapore, 1984-85; tech. staff AT&T Bell Labs., Allentown, Pa., 1985-87; rsch. assoc. NSF Engring. Rsch. Ctr., Lehigh Valley, 1988-91; rschr. Japan MITI ICOT Lab., Tokyo, 1992-93; asst. prof. U. Calif., San Francisco, 1993—; sr. tech. staff Philips Rsch. Lab., Palo Alto, 1996-97; chief arch., dir., dir. engring. Philips Med. Sys., Best, The Netherlands, 1999-2000; v.p. info. tech. Charles Schwab & Co., 2000—01. Grant rev. com. NSF, Washington, 1995—, NIH, Bethesda, 1997—; tech. adv. com. Intenrat. Conf. Computer Assay Radiology, Berlin, 1996—. Editor: Medical Image Databases, 1997; mem. editl. bd. Jour. Computer Med. Imaging, 1997—; editor Digital Librs. in Medicine, 1998. Australian Nat. U. scholar, 1982, Gleddon Tour scholar, 1983; NSF fellow, 1987-91; Japan Sci. and Tech. grant, 1992-93. Mem. IEEE (chpt. chmn. 1984—), Am. Assn. Med. Physicists. Achievements include patent disclosures and product devel. in biometrics on the World Wide Web; digital trust center of medical imaging; broadcasting model of electronic medical record; personalization of electronic medical record; development of the first working prototype of optical time domain reflectometer and hospital-wide PACS in U.S. Academic Medical Centers, and product development of radiology information systems PACS, computerized patient record and Health-care systems and on-line global trading systems. Office: UC San Francisco Sch Medicine Dept Radiology 505 Parnassus Ave # 628 San Francisco CA 94122-2722 E-mail: swong@radiology.ucsf.edu.

WONG, SUN YET, engineering consultant; b. Honolulu, Dec. 6, 1932; s. Chip Tong and Shiu Inn (Chang) W.; m. Janet Siu Hung Lau; children: Cathleen, Bryan, Jonathan. BS in Civil Engring. with honors, U. Hawaii, 1954; MS in Civil Engring., Yale U., 1955. Engr. N.Am. Aviation, Downey, Calif., 1955-58; mem. tech. staff Ramo Woolridge Space Tech. Labs., Calif., 1958-64; exec. v.p., treas., tech. dir. Mechanics Rsch. Inc., El Redondo Beach, 1958-64; exec. v.p., treas., tech. dir. Mechanics Rsch. Inc., El Segundo, 1964-77; treas. System Devel. Corp., Santa Monica, 1977-79; chmn. bd., pres., treas. Applied Rsch. Inc., El Segundo, 1979-81; ind. cons. Rolling Hills Estates, Calif., 1981—. Cons. J.H. Wiggins Co., Redondo Beach, 1982—84, Intercon, Cerriots, Calif., 1982—84, Acurex, Mountain View, Calif., 1983, Applied Tech., Mountain View, Calif., 1983—85, Aston., Mountain View, 1983—85, Electromech. Sys. Inc., Anaheim, Calif., 1984, Measurement Analysis Corp., Torrance, Calif., 1984—96, MRJ, Fairfax, Va., 1984, Tompkins and Assocs., Torrance, 1984—, TRW, Redondo Beach, 1984, E Sys., Garland , 1986—93, Statis. Scis., Inc., Beverly Hills, Calif., 1986, Kodak Datatape, Pasadena, Calif., 1989, Odectics, Anaheim, 1990, Ampex, Redwood City, Calif., 1991, Swales & Assocs., Beltsville, Md., 1992—93, Hughes Space and Comms. Co., El Segundo, 1992, El Segundo, 94, El Segundo, 1996—2000, Lion Engring., Rancho Palos Verdes, Calif., 1994—. NASA Goddard, Greenbelt, Md., 1997, Boeing, El Segundo, 2000—, Raytheon, El Segundo, 2000—; dir. Lion Engring. Recipient Intelligence Cmty. Seal medallion, U.S. Govt., 2001, Nat. Reconnaisance Office Dir.'s award, 2001. Avocation: metal machining. Home and Office: 7 Club View Ln Rolling Hills Estates CA 90274 E-mail: sywong@GTE.net.

WONG, TAN FOON, electrical engineer, educator; b. Hong Kong, Hong Kong, Jan. 27, 1969; s. Kwan Wong and Siu Har Lee; m. Chak Lai Chan; children: Michael, Matthew. BS, Chinese U. Hong Kong, 1991; MSEE, Purdue U., 1992, PhD, 1997. Rsch. engr. Macquarie U., Sydney, NSW, Australia, 1993-95; postdoctoral rsch. assoc. Purdue U., West Lafayette, Ind., 1997-98; asst. prof. U Fla., Gainesville, 1998—. Contbr. articles to profl. jours. Recipient Ralph E. Powe Jr. Faculty Enhancement award, Oak Ridge Associated Univs., 2000. Mem. IEEE (editor Transactions on Vehicular Tech. 2001). Office: U Fla PO Box 116130 Gainesville FL 32611 Fax: 352-392-0044. E-mail: twong@ufl.edu.

WONG, THOMAS TANG YUM, engineering educator; b. Hong Kong, July 27, 1952; arrived in U.S., 1976; s. Kwai Sun and Yee Yuen (Fung) W.; m. Mini-i Lee, June 9, 1984; children: Clara Joyce, Lillian Denise. BSc in Engring., U. Hong Kong, 1975; MS, Northwestern U., Evanston, Ill., 1978, PhD, 1981. Product engr. Motorola Semiconductor, Inc., Hong Kong, 1975-76; teaching asst. Northwestern U., 1976-78, rsch. asst., 1978-80, postdoctoral fellow, 1980-81; asst. prof. Ill. Inst. Tech., Chgo., 1981-86, assoc. prof., 1986-96, prof., 1996—, dir. grad. program dept. elec. engring., 1987-95, chmn. dept. elec. and computer engring., 2001—; dir. rsch. and devel. Telecomm. Equipment Corp., 1994—; chief sci. authority Quintech Electronics & Comms., Inc., Indiana, Pa., 1997-99. Cons. to pvt. industry, 1981—; chmn. Chicagoland Microwave Symposium, 1988. Author: Fundamentals of Distributed Amplification, 1993; contbr. articles to profl. jours.; book reviewer tech. publs.:. Trustee Sch. Dist. 73.5, Ill., 1995—2001. GE fellow, 1983; rsch. grantee NASA, 1989-91, U.S. Dept. Energy, 1992—, pvt. industry, 1993—. Mem. IEEE (chmn. joint Chgo. chpt. Antenna Propagation and Microwave Theory Techniques Soc. 1987-88, mem. steering com. joint symposium Antennas Propagation Soc./Internat. Union of Radio Sci./Nuclear Electromagnetic Pulse 1992), AAUP, Am. Soc. Engring. Edn., Am. Phys. Soc., Tau Beta Pi, Eta Kappa Nu. Achievements include several patents in the areas of microwave electronics and communications. Office: Ill Inst Tech Dept Elec/Computer Engring Chicago IL 60616 E-mail: twong@ece.iit.edu.

WONG, TIMOTHY C. language professional/educator; b. Hong Kong, Jan. 24, 1941; came to U.S., 1951; s. Patrick J. and Rose (Poon) W.; m. Elizabeth Ann Steffens, Dec. 18, 1970; children: Sharon Elizabeth, Rachel Margaret, Laura Katherine. BA, St. Mary's Coll., Moraga, Calif., 1963; MA, U. Hawaii, 1968; PhD, Stanford U., 1975. Vol. U.S. Peace Corps, Thailand, 1963-65; asst. prof. Ariz. State U., Tempe, 1974-79, assoc. prof., 1979-85; resident dir. Coun. on Internat. Ednl. Exchange Peking (People's Rep. China) Univ., 1984-85; assoc. prof. Ohio State U., Columbus, 1985-95; prof. Ariz. State U., Tempe, 1995—, dir. Ctr. for Asian Studies, 1995—2002. Author: Wu Ching-tzu, 1978, Stories for Saturday: Twentieth-Century Chinese Popular Fiction, 2002. Mem. Chinese Lang. Tchrs. Assn., Assn. Asian Studies, Am. Oriental Soc. (dir.-at-large 1996-2000, v.p. western br. 2000-02, pres., 2002—). Democrat. Roman Catholic. Office: Ariz State U Dept Langs and Lits Tempe AZ 85287-0202 E-mail: timothy.wong@asu.edu.

WONG, WALLACE, medical supplies company executive, real estate investor; b. Honolulu, July 13, 1941; s. Jack Yung Hung and Theresa (Goo) W.; m. Amy Ju, June 17, 1963; children: Chris, Bradley, Jeffery. Student, UCLA, 1960-63. Chmn., pres. South Bay Coll., Hawthorne, Calif., 1965-86; chmn. Santa Barbara (Calif.) Bus. Coll., 1975—; gen. ptnr. W B Co., Redondo Beach, Calif., 1982—; CEO Cal Am. Med. Supplies, Rancho Santa Margarita, 1986-96, Cal Am. Exports, Inc., Rancho Santa Margarita, 1986-96, Pacific Am. Group, Rancho Santa Margarita, 1991-96; chmn., CEO Alpine, Inc., Calif., 1993-96; pres. Bayside Properties, 1993—, San Juan Capistrano, Calif., 1993—. Bd. dirs. Metrobank, L.A. FFF Enterprises; chmn. bd. 1st Ind. Fin. Group., San Juan Capistrano, 1994—; chmn. Affinity Fin. Corp., 1996—. Acting sec. of state State of Calif., Sacramento, 1982; founding mem. Opera Pacific, Orange County, Calif., 1985; mem. Hist. and Cultural Found., Orange County, 1986; v.p. Orange County Chinese Cultural Club, Orange County, 1985. Named for Spirit of Enterprise Resolution, Hist. & Cultural Found., Orange Country, 1987; recipient resolution City of Hawthorne, 1973. Mem. Westren Accred Schs. & Colls. (v.p. 1978-79), Magic Castle (life), Singapore Club. Avocations: travel, skiing. Office: Bayside Properties 31672 S Pacific Coast Hwy Ste A Laguna Beach CA 92651 E-mail: WWong1025@aol.com.

WONG, WALTER FOO, county official; b. San Francisco, Apr. 11, 1930; s. Harry Yee and Grace (Won) W. AA, Hartnell Coll., 1952; BS, U. Calif., Berkeley, 1955; MPH, U. Hawaii, 1968. Registered sanitarian, Calif. Sanitarian Stanislaus County Health Dept., Modesto, Calif., 1955-56, Monterey County Health Dept., Salinas, 1956-67, sr. sanitarian, 1968-69, supervising sanitarian, 1969-70, dir. environ. health, 1971—. Sec. Monterey County Solid Waste Mgmt. Com., 1976—, Monterey County Hazardous Waste Mgmt. Com., 1987—; coord. Monterey County Genetic Engring. Rev. Com., 1987—; mem. Monterey County Genetic Engring. Experiment Permit Rev. Panel, 1995; mem. Monterey County Hazardous Materials Response Task Force, 1988—; mem. tech. adv. com. Monterey Peninsula Water Mgmt. Dist., 1985—, Monterey Regional Water Pollution Control Agy., 1985—; chmn. task force Monterey Regional Wastewater Reclamation Study for Agr., EPA and State of Calif. Chmn. Salinas Bicentennial Internat. Day Celebration, 1974, Pollution Clean-up Com. of Fort Ord Task Force, 1992; mem. Calif. Bare Closure Environ. adv. com., 1993. Recipient Community Svc. award Monterey County Med. Soc., 1998. Mem. Calif. Conf. Dirs. Environ. Health (pres. 1982-83), Assn. Environ. Health Adminstrs. (pres. 1982-83), Salinas C. of C. (Mem. of Yr. award 1971), U. Calif. Berkeley Alumni Assn., U. Hawaii Alumni Assn. (Disting. Alumni award 1992), Monterey County Hist. Soc. (pres. 1995-96), Ethnic Cultural Coun. (chmn. 1995). Republican. Presbyterian. Avocations: sports, music, outdoor recreation. Home: 234 Cherry Dr Salinas CA 93901-2807 Office: Monterey County Health Dept 1270 Natividad Rd Rm 301 Salinas CA 93906-3198

WONG, WARREN JAMES, mathematics educator; b. Masterton, N.Z., Oct. 16, 1934; came to U.S. 1964; s. Ken and Jessie (Ng) W.; m. Nellie Gee, May 12, 1962; children: Carole Frances, Andrea. BSc, U. Otago, Dunedin, N.Z., 1955, MSc, 1956; PhD, Harvard U., 1959. Lectr. U. Otago, Dunedin, 1960-64, sr. lectr., 1964; assoc. prof. math. U. Notre Dame, Ind., 1964-68, prof., 1968—. Proceedings editorial bd. Am. Math. Soc., Providence, R.I., 1988-90; contbr. articles to profl. jours. Vestryman St. Michael and All Angels Episcopal Ch., South Bend, 1988-90. Mem. Am. Math. Soc., Math. Assn. Am., Australian Math. Soc. Episcopalian. Office: Dept Math Univ Notre Dame Notre Dame IN 46556-5641

WONG, WAYNE D. nutritionist; b. San Francisco, May 13, 1950; s. Chaney Noon and La Dean Maryan (Mah) W. m. Betty Lee, Oct. 16, 1977; children: Michael Gabriel, Elizabeth Catherine, Whitney Forbes, Ellesse Florence. BS in Dietetic Adminstrn., U. Calif., Berkeley, 1972; MS in Sch. Bus. Mgmt., Pepperdine U., 1976; student, Nikon Sch. Photography, San Francisco, 1969, Canyon Hills Bible Coll., Bakersfield, Calif., 1998. Cert. Food Svc. Dir., Calif. Community Coll. tchr.; Registered Dietitian, Sch. Bus. Official, Benefit specialist. Food svc. worker, lab. asst. U. Calif., Berkeley, 1968-69, 70-71; mgmt. intern Mich. State U., East Lansing, 1970; dietetic intern Milw. Pub. Schs., 1972-73; food svc. cons. Trader Vic's, San Francisco, 1973; dir. food svcs. Bakersfield (Calif.) City Sch. Dist., 1973—. Instr. Bakersfield Coll., 1978—; cons. Wong, R.D., Bakersfield, 1978—; registered Benefit Specialist Investors Retirement Mgmt., Carpinteria, Calif., 1988-99; mem. nat. child nutrition adv. coun. USDA, Washington, 1977-79; 1st v.p. Ptnrs. in Nutrition Coop., Lancaster, Calif., 1988-90; food svc. edn. task force Calif. Dept. Edn., Sacramento, 1979; project coord. nutrition edn. and tng. exemplary program adoption grant Bakersfield City Sch. Dist., 1982, webmaster food svcs. website; project dir. basic skills, basic foods course, curriculum and recipe devel. grant Calif. Dept. Edn., 1985, cons. tchg. course, 1985-88; mem. adv. coun. Calif. State U. Long Beach Child Nutrition Program Mgmt. Tng. Ctr., 1991; mem. Sch. Nutrition Adv. Coun., Bakersfield, 1990—; graphics and tech. writing cons. Cal-Pro-Net Ctr., Fresno City Coll., 1995—; program panelist Ptnrs. Nutrition Coop., Am. Sch. Food Svc. Assn., Ann. Nat. Conf., 1995; curriculum cons. Cal-Pro-Net Ctr., San Jose State U.; presenter Calif. Sch. Food Svc. Assn., 1999-2001, Bakersfield Coll., 1999; USDA field tester, trainer Food Safety Internet Course, 2000; Sch. Breakfast Survey field tester Nat. Food Svc. Mgmt. Inst.; website cons. Three Stranded Cord Ministries, 2001; mem. Kern Region Prayer Watch. Author: Food Service Equipment-How Long Should It Last?, 1985; co-author (videotape) Bettermade Plastics, 1991, Recycle: Save Earth's Resources Now; programmer Food Svc. Pers. Database, 1988, Dishmachine Labor and Energy Matrix, 1991; contbr. articles to profl. jours.; guest soloist classical guitar Highland High Orch., 1996, Glorious Christmas Prodn., 1997-98; classical guitarist Wong Family Trio, A Night to Honor Israel Prodn., 1996—; videographer Assembly of God, Canyon Hills; graphic artist Elizabeth in Recital; guest artist Barnes and Noble, 1999-00; mem. choir Bakersfield Centennial Spiritual Heritage Celebration, 1997. BBQ fund-raiser co-chmn. Citizens for Yes on Measure B, Bakersfield, 1989; legis. com. Child Nutrition Facilities Act 1975, Sacramento, 1973-76; expert witness State Senate Select Subcom. on Nutrition and Human Needs, Sacramento, 1973; asst. troop leader Boy Scouts Am., Troop 219, San Francisco, 1965-67; participant Chinese Family Life Study U. Calif., Berkeley; dir. polystyrene recycling project Bakersfield City Sch. Dist., 1990; team leader Healthy Kids, Healthy Calif. program Calif. Dept. Edn., 1985-87; sponsor Christian Broadcasting Network Satellite Comms. Ctr., 1978; world vision sponsor India Cmty. Devel. Program, 1974-92; guitarist Canyon Hills Assembly of God Ch. Orch., 1996—, choir mem., 2001; publicity coord. Bakersfield Youth Symphony, 1996-99; bd. dirs., MIS cons. Young Artists Internat., 1999; mem. nutrition adv. coun. Bakersfield Coll., 1999; mem. Men's Prison Ministry, 2001. Recipient Eastman Kodak Scholastic Photography award Hon. Mention All State, 1968, Leadership award Calif. State Dept. Edn., 1987, Outstanding Sch. Lunch Program award USDA, 1989, Outstanding Summer Food Svc. Program award, 1999; 1st pl. Calif. Sch. Food Svc. Assn. Country Cook-off, 1983, 84; Toto Wizard nominee Sabatasso Foods, 1985, Best Practice award USDA, 1992. Mem. Am. Dietetic Assn. (Young Dietitian of Yr. 1976), Am. Sch. Food Svc. Assn. (child nutrition mktg. bike ride 1991, Cycle Across Am. for Child Nutrition and Fitness 1993), Calif. Assn. Sch. Bus. Ofcls. (photographer 1985, food svc. R&D chmn. 1985-87, recognition 1987, food and nutrition R&D com. 1984), Calif. Sch. Food Svc. Assn. (edn. tng. chmn. 1975-76, wellness awareness bike ride 1990-91, child nutrition bike ride 1991, 1st pl. photo contest 1993, cover photographer assn. jour. Poppyseeds 1992), Sports and Cardiovasc. Nutritionists, Kern County Sch. Food Svc. Assn. (pres. 1987-90, Golden Poppy award 1990), Kern Wheelmen (v.p. 1992), MENSA, Pi Alpha Phi, Omicron Nu. Republican. Mem. Assemblies of God Ch. Avocations: long distance bicycling, tennis, photography, classical guitar, Bible study. Home: 4901 University Ave Bakersfield CA 93306-1773

WONG, WING-CHUN GODWIN, philosopher; b. Jan. 11, 1959; s. Shiu-Tong and Po-Hang (Yim) Wang; m. Lai-Wan Amy Wong. BA, U. Mich., 1983; MA, PhD, U. Ill., Urbana-Champaign, 1994. Tutor math. U. Mich., Ann Arbor, 1981-82; teaching asst. U. Ill., Urbana-Champaign, 1983-93; rsch. mem. Beckman Inst. Advanced Scis. and Tech., Urbana, 1989-93; asst. prof. Towson U., Balt., 1993-99, assoc. prof., from 1999. Author book chpts.; contbr. to internat. conf. procs.; contbr. articles to profl. jours. Grantee NEH, 1994, 95. Mem. AAAS, Am. Math. Assn., Am. Philos. Assn., N.Am. Kant Soc., Mich. Alumni Assn. Avocations: classical music, piano, mathmatics, physics, astronomy. Home: Baltimore, Md. Died June 2, 2001.

WONG, Y(ING) WOOD, real estate investment company executive, venture capital investment company executive; b. Hong Kong, Apr. 28, 1950; came to U.S., 1969; s. Loyee K.H. and Margaret M.C.L. Wong; m. Leslie K.P. Chan, Dec. 18, 1977; children: Joshua H., Jonathan H. AA in Biology, Menlo Coll., 1971, BS in Bus. Adminstrn., 1974; BA in Zoology, U. Calif., Berkeley, 1972; MBA, Northwestern U., 1976. Auditor Touche Ross & Co., CPAs, San Francisco, 1976-78; founder, mng. dir. Wong Properties, Palo Alto, Calif., 1976—; founder, venture capital ptnr. Wongfratris Investment Co., 1986—. Instr. Golden Gate U., 1977. Trustee Crystal Springs Uplands Sch., Hillsborough, Calif., 1993-98; advisor The Pui Ying Mid. Sch., Guangzhou, China, The Pui Ying Christian Svcs. Soc., Vancouver, Can.; bd. dirs. Peninsula Symphony, Los Altos, Calif., 2002--. Named Hon. Citizen of Taishan City, China; established Wood Wong Fgn. Students Exch. Grant, Menlo Coll., 1997—. Mem. Internat. Platform Assn., Commonwealth Club Calif., Beta Alpha Psi. Office: 51 Jordan Pl Palo Alto CA 94303-2903 E-mail: wood.wong@wongfratris.com.

WONG-DIAZ, FRANCISCO RAIMUNDO, lawyer, educator; b. Havana, Cuba, Oct. 29, 1944; came to U.S., 1961; s. Juan and Teresa (Diaz de Villegas) Wong; 1 child, Richard Alan. BA with honors, No. Mich. U., 1965; MA with highest honors, U. Detroit, 1967; PhD, MA, U. Mich., 1974; JD, U. Calif., Berkeley, 1976. Bar: Calif. 1980, U.S. Dist. Ct. (no. dist.) Calif. 1990, Fla. 1987. Prof. City Coll. San Francisco, 1975—, dept. chmn., 1978-85; rsch. atty. Marin Superior Ct., 1980-81; ct. arbitrator Marin Mcpl. Ct., 1985; atty. pvt. practice, Kentfield, Calif., 1980—. Adj. asst. prof. San Francisco State U., 1977; assoc. dean Miami-Dade Coll., 1986; dir. Cutcliffe Cons., Inc., Hawthorne, LaFamila Ctr., Inc., San Rafael, Calif., 1980-85, Small Bus. Inst., Kentfield, 1982-86; cons. ICC Internat., San Francisco, 1980-82; political commentator Univision KDTV, 1980—. Author: American Politics in a Changing World, 1999; bd. editors Indsl. Rels. Law Jour., 1975-76; mem. editl. bd. Calif. Lawyer, 1991-93. Lector St. Sebastian's Ch., 1984—, parish coun., 1995; bd. dirs. Am. Cancer Soc., 1999—. Vis. scholar U. Calif., Berkeley Sch. Bus., 1983-84, U.S. Dept. State scholar, Washington, 1976; Horace C. Rackham fellow U. Mich., 1970, summer fellow U. Calif. Berkeley, 1995, Nat. Security Law Ctr. U. Va., 1996; named Best New Vol. of Yr., Am. Cancer Soc., 2000, One of One Hundred Most Influential Hispanics in the Nation, Hispanic Bus. Mag., Oct. 2000. Mem. ABA, Am. Polit. Sci. assn., Latino Ednl. Assn. (treas. 1985), Cuban Am. Nat. Coun., World Affairs Coun. (sem. leader San Francisco 1980), U. Calif. San Francisco PC Advocates, Commonwealth Club. Roman Catholic.

WONG-MCDONALD, ANA, psychologist; b. Hong Kong, Hong Kong; BA in Mus., UCLA, 1987; MA in Psychology, Fuller Theol. Sem., Pasadena, Calif., 1997, MA in Theology, 1997, PhD in Clin. Psychology, 1999. Lic. psychologist, Calif. Owner, instr. Allegro Piano Instrn. Studio, L.A., 1985-99; choir dir. Golden West Christian Ch., 1982-89; v.p. Internat. Collection Corp., 1986-93; clin. psychologist L.A. County Dept. Mental Health, 1999—. Part time faculty Calif. State U., L.A., 1997-98, Azusa Pacific U., 2001; symposium chair Soc. Sci. Study of Religion, 1997; student award judge Christian Assn. Psychol. Studies, 1998. Reviewer: Jour. Psychology and Theology, 2001—. Ethnic minority scholar Calif. Psychol. Assn., 1993; Western Psychol. Assn. scholar, 1991. Mem. APA, Christian Assn. Psychol. Studies (paper award 1998), Phi Kappa Phi. Avocations: music, dance, pencil sketching, painting. Office: Hollywood Mental Health Ctr 1224 N Vine St Los Angeles CA 90038

WONHAM, WALTER MURRAY, electrical engineer, educator; b. Montreal, Que., Can., Nov. 1, 1934; m. Vera Anne Hale; children: Marjorie Jane, Cynthia Margaret. B of Engring., McGill U., Montreal, 1956; PhD, U. Cambridge, Eng., 1961. Asst. prof. elec. engring. Purdue U., Lafayette, Ind., 1961-62; rsch. scientist Rsch. Inst. for Advanced Studies, Balt., 1962-64; assoc. prof. Brown U., Providence, 1964-69; rsch. assoc. NASA, Cambridge, Mass., 1967-69, cons., 1969; prof. elec. engring. U. Toronto, Ont., Can., 1970—, J. Roy Cockburn prof., 1991-96, Cockburn chair, 1991, univ. prof., 1996—2000, univ. prof. emeritus, 2000—. Author: Linear Multivariable Control: A Geometric Approach, 1974, 3d edit., 1985 (Russian transl. 1980, Chinese transl. 1984); assoc. editor Soc. for Indsl. and Applied Math., Jour. on Control and Optimization, 1965-79, Sys. Control Letter, 1981-85. Recipient Brouwer medal Netherlands Math Soc., 1990; Athlone fellow, Gt. Britain, 1956-58; spl. scholar Nat. Rsch. Coun. Can., 1958-60; sr. postdoctoral resident rsch. assoc. NAS USA, 1967-69. Fellow IEEE (Control Sys. Sci. and Engring. award 1987), Royal Soc. Can. Office: U Toronto Dept Elec Engring 35 St George St Toronto ON Canada M5S 3G4

WONNACOTT, JAMES BRIAN, physician; b. Charlottetown, P.E.I., Can., Feb. 24, 1945; came to U.S., 1978, naturalized, 1984; s. Earl Lepage and Eunice Deborah (Eaton) W. Honors diploma, Prince of Wales Coll., 1964; BSc with honors in biology, Dalhousie U., 1966, MD, 1972. Diplomate Am. Bd. Family Practice, Coll. Family Physicians Can. Intern Victoria Gen. Hosp., Halifax, N.S., Can., 1971-72; gen. practice medicine Summerside, P.E.I., 1975-78; med. dir. alcoholism treatment unit Raleigh Hills Hosp., 1981-83; preceptor tchg. staff U. Tex. Med. Sch., Baylor Coll. Medicine, Houston, 1984-95; exec. med. dir. Oak Forest Med. Ctr., 1990-95, Vis. Nurse Assn., Hospice, Houston, 1991-95; pvt. practice family medicine rural Kans., 1996-2000; med. dir. Rural Health Clinic, Spearman, Tex., 2000—. Mem. med. adv. bd. Med. World News, 1983-90. Served as flight surgeon RCAF, 1967-75. Fellow Am. Acad. Family Physicians; mem. AMA. Methodist. Office: PO Box 8 Spearman TX 79081-0008

WONNACOTT, PAUL, economics educator; b. London, Can., Mar. 16, 1933; s. Gordon Elliott and Muriel Johnston Wonnacott; m. Donna Elizabeth Cochrane, July 2, 1960; children: David, Ann, Alan, Bruce. BA, U. Western Ont., 1955; MA, Princeton U., 1957, PhD, 1959. Instr., asst. prof. econs. Columbia U., N.Y.C., 1958-62; assoc. prof. then prof. econs. U. Md., College Pk., 1962-91, prof. emeritus, 1992. Mem. Pres.'s Coun. Econ. Advisers, 1991-93; Alan Holmes prof. econs. Middlebury Coll., 1994-2000; mem. rsch. staff Royal Commn. Banking and Fin., Toronto, 1962; sr. staff economist Coun. Econ. Advisers, Washington, 1968-70; assoc. dir. divsn. internat. fin. Fed. Res. Bd., Washington, 1974-75; vis. scholar Office Internat. Monetary Rsch., U.S. Treasury, 1980; econ. adviser to Under Sec. of State, 1990-91. Author: The Canadian Dollar, 1960, 2d rev. edit., 1965, (with R.J. Wonnacott) Free Trade between the United States and Canada: The Potential Economic Effects, 1967, (with H.G. Johnson and H. Shibata) Harmonization of National Economic Policies under Free Trade, 1968, Macroeconomics, 1974, 3d rev. edit., 1984, (with R.J. Wonnacott) Economics, 1979, 4th rev. edit. 1990, Spanish edit., 1981, 3d rev. edit., 1987, (with Y. and C. Crusius) Portuguese edit., 1982, 2d rev. edit., 1985, (with A. Blomquist) Can. edit., 1983, 4th rev. edit., 1994, Lithuanian edit., 1998, The United States and Canada: The Quest for Free Trade, 1987; contbr. numerous articles to profl. jours. Fellow Brooking Inst., 1957-58, Ford Found., 1963-64; vis. fellow Inst. Internat. Econs., 1986, 93-94 Mem. Am. Econ. Assn. Avocations: skiing, tennis. Home: 10100 Bevern Ln Potomac MD 20854-2130 E-mail: paulwon@wam.umd.edu.

WONNACOTT, RONALD JOHNSTON, economics educator; b. London, Can., Sept. 11, 1930; s. Gordon and Muriel (Johnston) W.; m. Eloise Howlett, Sept. 11, 1954; children: Douglas, Robert, Cathy Anne. BA, U. Western Ont., 1955; A.M., Harvard U., 1957, PhD, 1959. Mem. faculty U. Western Ont., London, 1958-96, prof. econs., 1964-96, chmn. dept., 1969-72, prof. emeritus, 1996—. Vis. assoc. prof. U. Minn., Mpls., 1961-62; cons. Resources for the Future, Econ. Council Can., Can.-Am. Com., Nat. Planning Assn., C.D. Howe Inst. *Mr. Wonnacott co-authored (with Paul Wonnacott) a 1967 Harvard Press Book on Canada-U.S. free trade, including numerous previously unrecognized effects. This triggered a debate in Canada that culminated in the 1989 Canada-U.S. FTA. This book also contributed theoretically by analyzing and estimating three factors which have since become broadly incorporated in trade theory: economies of scale and imperfect competition; transport costs and other geographical influences; and the benefits of removing partner's trade barriers, as well as your own. Since 1975, he developed the theory of hub-and-spoke trading systems. Before NAFTA, he urged Canadian participation to avoid becoming one of the spokes to a U.S. hub.* Author: Canadian-American Dependence: An Interindustry Analysis of Production and Prices, 1961, Canada's Trade Options, 1975, Selected New Developments in International Trade Theory, 1984, The Economics of Overlapping Free Trade Areas and the Mexican Challenge, 1991, (with G.L. Reuber) The Cost of Capital in Canada, 1961, (with Paul Wonnacott) Free Trade Between the U.S. and Canada, 1967, Economics, 1979, 4th edit., 1990, (with Thomas H. Wonnacott) Introductory Statistics, 1969, 5th edit., 1990, Econometrics, 1970, 2d edit., 1979, Regression, 1981 Fellow Royal Soc. Can.; mem. Am. Econ. Assn., Can. Econ. Assn. (pres. 1981), London Hunt Club, Sunningdale Golf Club (Eng.), Hon. Co. Edinburgh Golfers, Craigleith Ski Club. Home: 171 Wychwood Pk London ON Canada N6G 1S1 E-mail: Wonnacot@Julian.uwo.ca.

WONSER, MICHAEL DEAN, retired public affairs director, art history educator; b. Long Beach, Calif., Mar. 12, 1940; s. Franklin Henry and Dorothy Mae (Harris) W.; children: Therice Michele, Sherice Michele, Christopher Franklin; m. Mary L. Van Epps, Dec. 22, 1990. BS, U. Oreg., 1963, MFA, 1965; postgrad., U. Colo., 1976. Instr. Cen. Oreg. Coll., Bend, 1966-68; prof. Adams State Coll., Alamosa, Colo., 1969-91, dir. pub. affairs, 1982-90; adj. prof. art history Ctrl. Oreg. C.C., Bend. Pres. Colo. Faculty Com. Trustees, 1980-82. Mem. Chamber Edn. Com., Monte Vista, Colo., 1982-88; pres. Luth. Ch. Alamosa, 1980-85; bd. dirs. Creede Repertory Theatre, 1989-91; mem. Commerce Comm. and Resources Comm., 1995, Cmty. Improvement Commn., Sisters, Oreg., 1996-97. Mem. Higher Edn. Assn. of Rockies (pres. Colo. chpt. 1985-88), C. of C. Ambassador (treas. 1982), Alamosa, C. of C. Tourism Bd., Alamosa (chmn. 1987-89), Sisters C. of C. (pres. 1996-97, bd. dirs.), Rotary, Lambda Chi Alpha (Hall of Fame 1993). Republican. Avocations: golf, skiing. Home: 24 NW Shasta Pl Bend OR 97701-2633 E-mail: mmwonser@teleport.com.

WOO, ALEX, process engineer; arrived in U.S., 1990; BSChemE, Rensselaer Poly. Inst., 1996. Coop. engr. G.E. Silicones, Waterford, N.Y., 1995-96; process engr. Masonite Corp., Towanda, Pa., 1997—2001. Mem.: AIChE, Internat. Mgmt. Coun. (key rep. 1997—2001). Avocations: travel, outdoor activities. Home: 28R Village Grn Budd Lake NJ 07828 Office: Howmet Castings Dover NJ 07801

WOO, CHI-KEUNG, energy economist, consultant; b. Guangzhou, Guangdong, China, Oct. 22, 1955; came to the U.S., 1977; s. K.L. and L.H. (Fu) W.; m. Linda Ellen Burley, Apr. 3, 1982; 1 child, Alisha W.M. B in Comm., Concordia U., Montreal, Can., 1976; MA, Queens U., Kingston, Ont., 1977; PhD, U. Calif., Davis, 1982. Economist PG&E, San Francisco, 1982-84, 85-87, SMUD, Sacramento, 1984-85; sr. assoc. Analysis Group, San Francisco, 1985-87; assoc. prof. City U. Hong Kong, 1991-93; v.p. Energy & Environ. Econs., Inc., San Francisco, 1993—. Mem. adv. bd. Vocat. Tng. Coun., Hong Kong, 1991-93. Contbr. articles to profl. jours. including Energy Jour., Water Resources Rsch. Mem. Internat. Assn. Energy Economists (adv. bd. 1991-93, editl. bd. mem. 1991—), Am. Econs. Assn. Achievements include estimation of the costs of service interruption (electricity and water) that permits economic planning and pricing of reliability. Home: 1822 Humboldt Ave Davis CA 95616-3135 Office: Energy & Environ Econs 353 Sacramento St Ste 1700 San Francisco CA 94111-3655 E-mail: ck@ethree.com.

WOO, DAH-CHENG, hydraulic engineer; b. Shanghai, China, Dec. 18, 1921; came to U.S., 1947; s. Pei-Cho and Changtze (Chang) Woo. BS, Hangchow (China) Christ Coll., 1944; MA, U. Mich., 1948, PhD, 1956. Lic. profl. engr. Hydraulic engr. ALN&M Cons. Engrs., Ann Arbor, Mich., 1951-62; sr. hydraulic engr. Fed. Hwy. Adminstrn., Washington, 1962-96; cons. hydraulic engr., 1996—. Fellow ASCE (urban water resources rsch. coun. 1967-96); mem. Am. Geophys. Union,Internat. Water Resources Assn., Internat. Assn. Hydraulic Rsch., Internat. Assn. for Automation and Robotics in Construction. Achievements include contbns. to basic knowledge of sheet (or thin) flow over smooth to rough surfaces, in laminar and transition regions, without and with the raindrop impact effect. Home: 2300 Pimmit Dr Apt 712 Falls Church VA 22043-2820

WOO, JONATHAN C. G. chemist, management consultant; b. San Francisco, Oct. 22, 1968; s. Gar Lok and Julia Y. P. Woo. AB, U. Calif., Berkeley, 1990; MS, Northwestern U., 1992, PhD, 1994. Res. fellow Memorial Sloan Kettering Ctr., N.Y.C., 1994-97, Mitchell Madison Group, 1997-99, Bristol-Myers Squibb, 1999—. Contbr. articles to profl. jours. Fellow NIH, 1995. Mem. Am. Chem. Soc.

WOO, KAREN, physician; b. San Francisco, Sept. 3, 1960; d. Wayne and Jeannette Woo. BS, San Francisco State U., 1983; DO, Ohio U., 1987. Diplomate Am. Bd. Pediatrics, Am. Bd. Perinatal Neonatal Medicine. Intern O'bleness Hosp., Athens, Ohio, 1987-88; resident in pediats. Loma Linda (Calif.) U. Med. Ctr., 1988-91, fellow in neonatology, 1991-94; neonatologist Neonatology Med. Group, San Bernardino, Calif., 1994-95, Neonatal Svcs., Ventura, 1995-98, Kaiser Permanente Med. Group, Sacramento, 1998—. Fellow: Am. Coll. Osteopathic Pediatricians, Am. Acad. Pediat.; mem.: AMA, Am. Osteopathic Assn. Office: Kaiser Permanente Med Ctr 2025 Morse Ave Sacramento CA 95825-2115

WOO, PETER WING KEE, organic chemist; b. Canton, China, June 22, 1934; came to U.S., 1950; s. Yu Chang and Lim Tsing (Poon) W.; m. Katherine Liang, Aug. 27, 1966; children: Karen H.W., Lena H.A., Nelson H.Y. BS with great distinction, Stanford U., 1955; PhD, U. Ill., 1958. From assoc. chemist rsch. to sr. rsch. chemist Parke Davis & Co., Detroit, 1958-71; from rsch. scientist to sr. rsch. assoc. Parke Davis Pharm. Rsch. (divsn. Warner-Lambert Co.), Ann Arbor, Mich., 1971-2000; with Pfizer Global Rsch. & Devel., Ann Arbor Labs. Pfizer, Inc., 2000—. Co-inventor antileukemia drug (pentostatin); contbr. to devel. lipid-modifying drug (atorvastatin, lowering cholesterol) and anti-arrhythmia drug (pirmenol); patentee in field; reviewer in field; contbr. articles to profl. jours. Mem. AAAS, Am. Chem. Soc. (excellence in indsl. chem. rsch. award 1983, Huron Valley sect.), Internat. Isotope Soc., Sigma Xi, Phi Beta Kappa. Avocations: tennis, table tennis, swimming, soccer, piano. Office: Pfizer Global Rsch & Devel 2800 Plymouth Rd Ann Arbor MI 48105-2495 E-mail: peterwoo@mediaone.net.

WOO, S. B. (SHIEN-BIAU WOO), former lieutenant governor, physics educator; b. Shanghai, China, Aug. 13, 1937; came to U.S., 1955; s. C.K. and Kuo-Ying (Chang) W.; m. Katy K.N. Wu, July 20, 1963; children: Chih-I, Chih-Lan. BS in Physics and Math. summa cum laude, Georgetown Coll., Ky., 1956; MS in Physics, Washington U., St. Louis, 1962, PhD in Physics, 1964. Prof. physics U. Del., Newark, 1966—2002; lt. gov. State of Del., Dover, 1985-89. Pres. Del. State Senate; chmn. Bd. Pardons; cons. E.I. DuPont Co., Wilmington, Del., 1968, Del. State Coll., Dover, 1980—81; steering com. 80-20 initiative, 1998—; pres. 80-20 PAC, 2001—. Contbr. articles to profl. jours. Chmn. bd., chief exec. officer Chinese Am. Community Ctr., Hockessin, Del., 1982-83; sec. Asian-Am. caucus Democratic Nat. Conv., 1983-84; pres., co-chmn. Gov.'s Internat. Trade Council, 1985-89; chmn. Gov.'s task force on High Tech., 1985-89. Recipient Highest Achievement award Asian Am. High Tech. Conv., 1985; Army Rsch. grantee, 1972-87, NSF grantee, 1978-81; Inst. fellow Kennedy Sch., Harvard U. Mem. Am. Phys. Soc., AAAS, AAUP (exec. com. nat. council 1974-77), Orgn. Chinese Ams. (bd. dirs. 1977-79, nat. pres. 1990-91), Sigma Xi. Home: 5 Farm House Rd Newark DE 19711-7458 E-mail: sbw@udel.edu.

WOO, VERNON YING-TSAI, lawyer, real estate developer, judge; b. Honolulu, Aug. 7, 1942; s. William Shu-Bin and Hilda Woo; children: Christopher Shu-Bin, Lia Gay. BA, U. Hawaii, 1964, MA, 1966; JD, Harvard U., 1969. Pres. Woo Kessner Duca & Maki, Honolulu, 1972-87; pvt. practice law, 1987—. Judge per diem Honolulu Dist. Family Ct., 1978-84, 95—. Bd. dirs. Boys and Girls Club of Honolulu,. 1985-95, pres., 1990-92. Mem. ABA, Hawaii Bar Assn., Honolulu Bd. Realtors. Home: 1221 Victoria St Apt 2403 Honolulu HI 96814-1454 Office: Harbor Ct 55 Merchant St Ste 1900 Honolulu HI 96813

WOO, WALTER, computer systems consultant; b. San Antonio, May 12, 1948; s. Foon Foo and Man Yin (Wong) W.; m. Margaret Leong, Aug. 26, 1973; children: Ryan David, Ellery. BA, St. Mary's U., San Antonio, 1971; postgrad., U Houston, 1983. Spl. projects chemist Atlantic Richfield Chem., Channelview, Tex., 1977; programmer/analyst First City Svcs., Houston, 1978-80; systems analyst Aminoil USA, 1980-81; sr. systems analyst Occidental Petroleum Co., 1981-82; systems analyst Houston Export Crating Co., 1982-83; systems specialist (mgr.) Ford Aerospace and Comm., Houston, 1983-85; project mgr. Raytheon Corp., 1985-87; systems cons. Ciber Inc., 1987-89, Computer Horizons Corp., Houston, 1989-92; ind. cons. Innovative Tech. Info. Systems, 1992-97; regional MIS dir. Cushman & Wakefield, Inc., 1997-2000; sr. project mgr. Enron, 2000-01; mgr. project svcs. Tobin Internat., Ltd., 2001—. Adj. instr. Houston C.C. Vol. United Way. With Tex. Air N.G. Dow Chem. Co. acad. scholar, 1977. Mem. Data Processing Mgmt. Assn., Golden Key. Republican. Baptist. Avocations: travel, computers, reading, amateur tennis. Home: 2115 Gentryside Dr Houston TX 77077-3601 E-mail: kbtp1@aol.com.

WOOD, ALLEN JOHN, electrical engineer, consultant; b. Milw., Oct. 1, 1925; s. Alfred John and Kathleen Francis (Welch) W.; m. Barbara Ann Cook, Oct. 29, 1949; children: John Scott, Susan Beth Wood Richmond. BEE, Marquette U., 1949; MS in Elec. Engring., Ill. Inst. Tech., 1951; PhD, Rensselaer Poly. Inst., 1959. Registered profl. engr., N.Y. Engr. Allis Chalmers Mfg. Co., West Allis, Wis., 1949-50, GE, Lynn, Mass., 1951-52, Schenectady, N.Y., 1952-59, sr. engr., 1960-69; mem. tech. staff Hughes Aircraft Co., Culver City, Calif., 1959-60; cons., prin., dir. Power Techs., Inc., Schenectady, N.Y., 1969-91, treas., chief fin. officer, 1989-91, also bd. dirs., 1969-91; ind. cons., 1991—. Adj. prof. Rensselaer Poly. Inst., Troy, 1966-2000; cons. in field, 1992—. Author: Power System Reliability Calculations, 1973, Power Generation Operation and Control, 1984, 2d edit. 1996; contbr. numerous articles to profl. jours. With U.S. Army, 1942-46, ETO, PTO. Fellow IEEE (life); mem. AAAS. Republican. Mem. Reformed Ch. in Am. Avocations: amateur radio, photography. E-mial. E-mail: allenwood@hotmail.com.

WOOD, ANDRÉE ROBITAILLE, archaeologist, researcher; b. Chgo., Feb. 10, 1929; d. Andrew George and Alice Marie (Fortier) Robitaille; m. Richard Lawrence Wood, Jan. 14, 1956; children: Mary Wood Molo, Matthew William Wood, Melissa Irene Wood, Elizabeth Wood Wesel, John Andrew Wood. BA, No. Ill. Univ., DeKalb, 1977, MA, 1982. Freelance archaeologist, 1981-84; rsch. asst. Prehistoric Project Oriental Inst., Univ. Chgo., Ill., 1984—. Rsch., discovery, removal, analysis and identification of ancient blood residues on lithic material excavated at ten millenium old site, Çayönü in Ergani, Turkey. Contbr. articles to profl. jours. Avocations: writing poetry, boating, tennis, golf. Home: 356 Old Sutton Rd Barrington IL 60010-9113 also: 8735 Midnight Pass Rd Apt 604B Sarasota FL 34242-2892

WOOD, BENJAMIN CARROLL, JR. safety professional; b. Leonardtown, Md., June 16, 1956; s. Benjamin C. Sr. and Ethel M. (Cole) W.; m. Sheilaann P. Manibog; May 26, 1977; children: Dreamer K., Cinnamon K.; stepchildren: Reynaldo K. Yumul, Angelica K. Yumul. AGS, Chaminade U., Honolulu, 1984; BS in Fire Sci., U. Md., 1997; BA in environmental studies, U. Nev., Las Vegas. Cert. criminal justice instr., food svc./sanitation mgr., environ. health and safety law prof., Va.; notary pub., Va. Aviation ordnanceman USMC, 1974-90, non-nuclear safety officer Calif., 1990-94; ret., 1994; safety spec. Office of the Sheriff, Arlington, Va., 1995-98; safety coord. Monte Carlo Resort & Casino, Las Vegas, Nev., 1998-99, safety/loss prevention officer, 1999, Econ. Opportunity Bd., North Las Vegas, 1999-2000; loss prevention cons. Employers Ins. Co. Nev., Las Vegas, 2000—. Recipient Excellence in Pub. Svc. award, Arlington (Va.) County Govt., 1997, 98, Naval Commendation medal, Sec. Navy, Washington, 1982, Humanitarian Svc. medal CMA, Washington, 1984. Mem. Am. Soc. Investigative Specialists, Am. Soc. Safety Engrs., Soc. for Advancement of Safety and Health, Nat. Safety. Coun., Va. Safety Coun., Nev. Safety Coun., Am. Legion, Employers for Workers Compensation, Nat. Fire Protection Assn., Nev. Hotel/Lodging Assn., Nev. Restaurant Assn. Home: 7305 Hospitality Pl Las Vegas NV 89131-4588 Office: Employers Ins Co Nev 7180 Pollock Dr Las Vegas NV 89119-9003 E-mail: bwood@eicn.com.

WOOD, BERENICE HOWLAND, educator; b. Newport, R.I., Oct. 21, 1910; d. Horatio Gates and Margaret Lorraine (Doyle) W. AB, Vassar Coll., 1934; MA, Columbia U., 1936; postgrad., U. R.I., 1961-65. Clk. 1st Dist. Ct. R.I., Newport, 1942-50; home service dir. ARC, 1950-61; tchr. Cranston, R.I., 1961-62, Elmhurst Sch., Portsmouth, 1962-64, Newport, 1964-82. Sec. to mayor City of Newport, 1941. Pres. Coun. Social Agys., Newport, 1955-57; active Hist. Soc. Newport, Art Mus. Newport, Redwood Library, Newport, Preservation Soc. Newport. Mem. Point Assn. Newport. Roman Catholic. Avocations: maintaining and preserving antiquities, foreign travel. Home: 82 Mill St Newport RI 02840-3146

WOOD, BERNARD ANTHONY, anthropology educator; b. London, Apr. 17, 1945; came to U.S., 1997; s. Anthony Frederick and Joan Faith (Slocombe) W.; m. Hazel Pamela Francis, Aug. 21, 1965 (div. July 1980); children: Nicholas James, Penelope Clare; m. Alison Margretta Richards; 1 child, Hannah Elin. BSc, U. London, 1966, MD, 1969, PhD, 1975, DSc, 1996. S.A. Courtauld prof. anatomy U. London, 1982-85; Derby prof. anatomy U. Liverpool, Eng., 1985-97, dean Faculty of Medicine Eng., 1996-97; Henry R. Luce prof. human origins George Washington U., Washington, 1997—. Chair sci.-based archeology com. Natural Environment Rsch. Coun., U.K., 1989-96; mem. bioarcheology panel Wellcome Trust, U.K., 1994-2000. Author: Koobi Fora Research Project: Vol. 4, 1991; editor: Food Acquisition and Processing in Primates, 1984, Major Topics in Primate and Human Evolution, 1986. Avocations: running, woodchopping, Verdi. Home: 1705 Surrey Ln NW Washington DC 20007-2018 Office: George Washington U 2110 G St NW Washington DC 20052-0001 E-mail: bwood@gwu.edu.

WOOD, BERT CLARENCE, III, fire operations bureau administrator; b. Washington, Aug. 9, 1943; s. Bert Clarence and Ora Pearl (Allen) W.; m. Carol Elaine Deal, Aug. 14, 1971; children: Christina A., Gail Marie. A.A.S. in Fire Sci. Mgmt. with honors, No. Va. Community Coll., 1979; BS in Fire Sci. Mgmt. with honors, U. Md., 1983. Vice pres. systems devel. Nat. Data Ctrs., Silver Springs, Md., 1965-69; sta. comdr. Alexandria Fire Ops. Bur., Va., 1971—. Contbr. articles to profl. jours. Recipient Top Tech. Paper award Inst. Fire Engrs., Eng., 1984, Fireman of Yr. award Ins. Women, 1983. Mem. Internat. Fire Service Instrs. Club: Clans of Scotland (chief exec. officer 1984). Avocations: gardening, sailing.

WOOD, BONNIE BESS, library director; b. New Orleans, Jan. 28, 1945; d. Wiley Morgan, Jr. and Muriel Beatrice (Baudier) W.; m. John Wade Hoffpauir, Jan. 28, 1964 (div. 1972); 1 child, Bronwyn Bess; m. Frank Levy, Nov. 24, 1980. BA in Edn., U. Fla., 1971; MLS, La. State U., 1980. Libr. Keystone H.S., Keystone Heights, Fla., 1974-75, Covington (La.) H.S., 1975-87; field rep. Am. Fedn. Tchrs., Baton Rouge, 1987-89; libr. Philips Jr. Coll., New Orleans, 1989-91, Trinity Epis. Sch., New Orleans, 1991-93, Christ Episc. Sch., Covington, 1993-96; asst. prof. S.E. La. U., Hammond, 1996—2001; libr. dir. Rouquette Libr., St. Joseph Sem. Coll., St. Benedict, La., 2001—. Author: Introductory Research Skills, 1997; storyteller Stories-In-Motion, 1987—; reviewer websites: Electronic Resources REv., 1999—. Mem. control bd. St. Tammany Libr., Covington, 1981—83; mem. Northshore chpt. Crohn's and Colitis Found. Am., 1997—; mem. domestic violence coun. St. Tammany Parish, 1998—. Mem.: NOW (pres. St. Tammany chpt. 1999—2001, v.p. La. chpt., v.p. for comms. 1998—2001), La. Coalition Against Censorship, La. Libr. Assn., Am. Coll. and Rsch. Librs. Jewish. Avocation: genealogy.

WOOD, CAROLYN JANE, educational administration educator; b. Niles, Mich., Sept. 1, 1942; d. Jerome W. and Priscilla J. (Barbary) W. BA, Drake U., Des Moines, 1964; MA, U. Denver, 1968; PhD, Washington U., St. Louis, 1977. Cert. chr. social studies, 7-12, cert. adminstr. Social studies tchr. Howard Cmty. Schs., Niles, 1964-66; asst. residence hall dir. U. Denver, 1966-68; asst. dean of students Bowling Green (Ohio) State U., 1968-71; faculty Washington U., St. Louis, 1972-76; asst. prof. U. N.Mex., Albuquerque, 1977-81, assoc. prof., 1981-93, prof. ednl. adminstrn., 1993—. Part-time instr. Webster Coll., St. Louis, spring 1975, Maryville Coll., St. Louis, summer 1977; evaluator N.Mex. Fellows for the Advancement of Math. Edn., NSF, 1991-94; project dir. AWARE-NM (Assisting Women to Advance Through Resources and Encouragement), Albuquerque, 1987-92. Contbr. articles to profl. jours.; co-creator multimedia: Do Flowers Always Grow from Planted Seeds?, 1993, Does Systemic Change Teach Helplessness or Resourcefulness?, 1994, Are People Learning to be Helpless or Resourceful?, 1994. Sec. and mem. N.Mex. Corrections Commn., Santa Fe, 1983-85; chmn. bd. United Way of Greater Albuquerque, 1991. Recipient Rsch. award U. N.Mex. chpt. Phi Delta Kappa, 1979, Outstanding Tchr. of the Yr. for Grad. Instrn. award U. N.Mex., 1982, Gov.'s Award for Outstanding N.Mex. Women, 1991, Rsch. awrd Nat. Rural Edn. Assn., 2000. Mem. ASCD, Am. Ednl. Rsch. Assn., Phi Delta Kappa. E-mail. Home: 2521 Harold Pl NE Albuquerque NM 87106-2515 Office: Univ of N Mex Edn Office Bldg Albuquerque NM 87131-0001 E-mail: cwood@unm.edu.

WOOD, CHARLES EARL, obstetrician, gynecologist; b. Sterling, Colo., Oct. 4, 1930; s. Walter Earl and Dorothy Nancy (Long) W.; m. Patricia Taylor, Nov. 1, 1960; children: Lecia, Spencer, Christine. BA, Phillips U., 1959; MD, U. Colo., 1963. Diplomate Am. Bd. Obstetrics and Gynecology. Intern Denver Gen. Hosp., 1963-64, resident in ob-gyn, 1964-67, mem. staff, 1967-73; practice medicine specializing in ob-gyn Casper, Wyo., 1967-86; mem. staff Skaggs Cmty. Hosp., Branson, Mo., 1986—. Mem. staff Natrona County Meml. Hosp., Casper, 1967-84, chief of obstetrics, 1975, chmn. staff, 1981-83; mem. staff Converse County Hosp., Douglas, Wyo. 1967-85, Carbon County Hosp., Rawline, Wyo., 1968-75; mem. Wyo. Family Practice Residency program, 1978-83; clin. assoc. prof. family practice (ob-gyn) Univ. Hosp. of Wyo. Coll. Human Medicine, 1982-83. Mem. Natrona County Sch. Bd., 1974-80, vice chmn., 1976-77, chmn., 1978-79; pres. Casper YMCA, 1974-76, gen. chmn. fundraising campaign, 1976-77, mem. bldg. com. 1976-78; mem. Blue Envelope, 1970-84; pres., charter mem. Wyo. Right to Life, 1970-75; T-Bird booster Casper Coll., 1970-82; assoc. Sch. of the Ozarks, Pt. Lookout, Mo., 1985—. Served with USN, 1949-50, 52-53. Mem. Am. Coll. Obstetricians and Gynecologists, Am. Fertility Soc. (charter), Wyo. Med. Soc., Denver Med. Soc., Natrona County Med. Soc. (pres. 1979-80), Audubon Soc., Casper Air Modelers Assn. (charter, pres. 1969-76), Wyo. Handball Assn., Wyo. Arabian Horse Assn., Am. Hereford Assn., Irish Wolfhound Club Am., Wyo. Farm Bur., Elks. Home: 117 Woodside Ln Rogers AR 72756-0711

WOOD, C(HARLES) NORMAN, former association executive, military officer; b. Dallas, Mar. 7, 1938; s. Charles Camp Wood and Mary Louise (Wheatley) Ferguson; m. Jerre Louise Jones, June 10, 1961 (div. Sept. 1967); 1 child, Wende Louise; m. Elizabeth Burwell Dillard, June 27, 1969; 1 child, Elizabeth Burwell. BBA, U. Tex., 1960; MPA, Auburn U., 1974. Commd. 2d lt. USAF, 1960, advanced through grades to lt. gen., 1990; electronic warfare officer Strategic Air Command, Kans. and Okinawa, 1962-69; intelligence staff officer Hdqrs. Strategic Air Command, Offutt AFB, Nebr., 1969-72; chief def. analysis br. Hdqrs. Mil. Assistance Command, Saigon, Republic of Vietnam, 1972-73; air staff officer Hdqrs. USAF, Washington, 1974-76; exec. officer Office of Air Force History, 1976-77; student Nat. War Coll., 1978-79; dep. comdr. for ops. 544th Strategic Intelligence Wing, Offutt AFB, 1979, wing comdr., 1980; asst. dep. chief of staff intelligence Strategic Air Command, 1981-82; exec. dir. Pres.'s Fgn. Intelligence Adv. Bd. The White House, Washington, 1982-83; dep. dir. Nat. Strategic Target List, Joint Strategic Planning Staff, Offutt AFB, 1984; dep. asst. chief of staff intelligence USAF, Washington, 1985; dir. intelligence J-2 Hdqrs. U.S. European Command, Fed. Republic Germany, 1986-87; asst. chief of staff intelligence Air Force Hdqrs., Washington, 1988-90; dir. Intelligence Community Staff, 1990-92; sr. v.p., gen. mgr. BDM Fed., 1992-96; pres., CEO Armed Forces Comms. and Electronics Assn., Fairfax, Va., 1996—2001. Decorated D.S.M., Legion of Merit, Def. Superior Svc. medal. Mem. Nat. Mil. Intelligence Assn., Security Affairs Support Assn., Armed Forces Communications and Electronics Assn., Air Force Assn. Republican. Mem. Christian Sci. Ch. Home: 5440 Mt Corcoran Pl Burke VA 22015-2147 E-mail: woodcn@aol.com.

WOOD, CHARLES TUTTLE, history educator; b. St. Paul, Oct. 29, 1933; s. Harold Eaton and Margaret (Frisbie) W.; m. Susan Danielson, July 9, 1955; children: Lucy Eaton, Timothy Walker, Martha Augusta, Mary Frisbie. AB, Harvard, 1955, AM, 1957, PhD, 1962. Investment analyst, trader Harold E. Wood & Co., St. Paul, 1955-56; teaching fellow gen. edn. Harvard, 1959-61, instr. history, 1961-64; mem. faculty Dartmouth, 1964-96, prof. history, 1971-80, Daniel Webster prof. history, 1980-91, Daniel Webster prof. history and comparative lit., 1991-96, Daniel Webster prof. emeritus, 1996—, chmn. dept. history, 1976-79, chmn. dept. comparative lit., 1977. Vis. Keeney prof. of history Brown U., 1992-93; vis. prof. U. Coll. London, 1996. Author: The French Apanages and the Capetian Monarchy, 1223-1328, 1966, Philip the Fair and Boniface VIII, 2d edit., 1971, reprint 1976, Felipe el Hermoso y Bonifacio VIII: Mexico: UTEHA, 1968, The Age of Chivalry: Manners and Morals 1000-1450, 1970, The Quest for Eternity, reprint edit., 1983, Joan of Arc and Richard III, 1988, The Trial of Charles I, 1989, Fresh Verdicts on Joan of Arc, 1996; also articles. Chmn. Dresden Bd. Sch. Dirs., 1972-74. Guggenheim fellow, 1986-87; recipient Disting. Service award N.H. Sch. Bds. Assn., 1975; Am. Council Learned Socs. fellow, 1980-81; Am. Bar Found. fellow, 1981-82 Fellow Medieval Acad. Am. (treas. 1989-2001, fin. com. 1979-2001, council 1985-87); mem. Am. Hist. Assn. (chmn. nominating com. 1977, Adams prize com. 1976-78), Conf. Brit. Studies, Soc. for French Hist. Studies, N.H. Sch. Bds. Assn. (2d v.p. 1974-75), New Eng. Medieval Conf. (pres. 1978-79), Am. Soc. Legal History, Phi Beta Kappa (pres. Alpha of N.H. 1997-99). Clubs: St. Botolph (Boston). Home: 7 N Balch St Hanover NH 03755-1502 E-mail: charles.t.wood@dartmouth.edu.

WOOD, CHARLES W. financial services company executive; b. McAlester, Okla., Nov. 6, 1946; s. Edgar Scott and Jessie Doyle (Ray) W.; m. Maxie Rae Moss, July 3, 1975 (div. July 1988); 1 child, Whitney Rae. AA, Eastern Okla. State Coll., 1966; BS, Okla. State U., 1968. Regional planner Kiamichi Econ. Dist., Wilburton, Okla., 1969-73; state planner Okla. Crime Commn., Oklahoma City, 1973-75, dir. planning, 1975-80, dir., 1980-81; adminstr., mgmt. cons., logistics trainer Okla. Crime Victims Bd., 1981-89; registered rep. Waddell and Reed, Inc., Edmond, Okla., 1989-91, dist. mgr., mgmt. trainer, 1991—. Mgmt. cons. Author/editor/pub. Victims' Voice newsletter, 1985-91. Recipient Liberty Bell award Okla. Bar Assn., 1985. Mem. Nat. Assn. Victims Compensation (treas. 1983-87, v.p. 1987-89), Jaycees (charter pres. 1970-73), Rotary (treas. 1983-85). Democrat. Ch. of Christ. Avocations: golf, photography, astronomy, real estate. Office: Waddell and Reed Inc 508 W 15th St Edmond OK 73013-3615

WOOD, CHRISTOPHER L.J. real estate executive; b. London, Jan. 20, 1947; came to U.S., 1983; s. Sidney John and Lillian Ballantine (Pollock) W.; m. Pamela Wood, Dec. 14, 1978; 1 child, Alexander Wood. BSc, London U., 1969. Ptnr., dir. Debenham, Tewson & Chinnocks, London, 1972—96; COO America's Best, 1996—98; mng. dir. Peracon Inc.; prin. DTZ Debenham Thorpe Internat., 1996—. Mem. St. George's Soc. N.Y., Thames Rowing Club, Union League Club (Phila.). Office: DTZ PO Box 412 Pawling NY 12564

WOOD, CHRISTOPHER TODD, educator; b. Renton, Wash., June 25, 1970; s. James Herring and Linda P. W.; m. Angie Jeanette. BA, Gonzaga U., 1993; MS, Ea. Wash. U., 1996; PhD in Counseling, Oreg. State U., 2001. Home: 1325 S Marmot Dr Tucson AZ 85713 E-mail: woodc@u.arizona.edu.

WOOD, CLINTON WAYNE, middle school educator; b. Birmingham, Ala., Nov. 13, 1954; s. Clinton Mason and Dorothy Ann (Pullen) W. BA, U. Mobile, 1978. Cert. secondary edn. tchr., Ala. Tchr., coach Westminster Christian Sch., Gadsden, Ala., 1978-79, Simmons Mid. Sch., Hoover, 1979—. Author, editor: The Marble Valley Boys, 1986; co-author: Kiss Sweet Little Lillah For Me; contbr. articles to profl. jours. Named one of Outstanding Young Men of Am., 1985. Mem. Nat. Edn. Assn., Ala. Edn. Assn., Coaches Assn. (state and nat.), SAR, SCV. Baptist. Avocations: sports, camping, reading, hiking, traveling. Home: 3400 Treeline Ct Apt 604 Hoover AL 35216-5714 Office: Simmons Mid Sch 1575 Patton Chapel Rd Birmingham AL 35226-2257

WOOD, CONSTANCE RICE, psychiatric social worker; b. Marlboro, Mass., Feb. 1, 1922; d. John Edward and Helen Bullard (Ellis) Rice; AB, Syracuse U., 1943; MSW, Boston U., 1973; m. Robert K. Wood, Mar. 18, 1944; children: Robert K. Jr., Jeffrey Bullard, Durinda Rice. Clinician, psychiat. social worker Monadnock Family and Mental Health Service, Keene, N.H., 1972—; pvt. practice psychiat. social work, Keene, 1975—; owner Tavern Antiques, Keen, 1981—. Mem. adv. bd. Monadnock Area Women's Crisis Svc., 1980-82; founding mem. Keene Ctr. for Human Concerns, 1969, Women's Crisis Ctr., Keene, 1977-79; N.H. del. Nat. Democratic Conv., 1968, mem. exec. bd. N.H., Dem. Party, 1969-72, chmn. Cheshire County Dem. Party, 1972; pres. bd. trustees Keene Unitarian-Universalist Ch., 1969; recorder N.H. Women's Polit. Caucus, 1974. Mem. Nat. Assn. Social Workers, NOW, Nat. Women's Polit. Caucus, ACLU, LWV, Women's Internat. League for Peace and Freedom. Home: 63 Arch St Keene NH 03431-2232 Office: 331 Main St Keene NH 03431-4177

WOOD, CORINNE, state official; b. Barrington, Ill., May 28, 1954; m. Paul R. Wood; children: Ashley, Brandon, Courtney. BS, U. Ill.; JD, Loyola U. of Chgo. Pvt. practice; counsel Ill. Savs. and Residential Fin. Bd.; atty. Hopkins & Sutter, Chgo.; gen. counsel Ill. Commr. of Banks and trusts; state rep. 59th dist. 90th Ill. Gen. Assembly, Springfield; lt. gov. State of Ill., 1999—. Appointed spec. asst., Ill. Atty. Gen. Former co-capt. Shields Twp. Rep. Precinct; Lake Forest chmn. John E. Porter for Congress, 1994, 96; adv. mem. Coun. of Women Advisors to U.S. Congress; past 1st v.p., bd. dirs. Women's Rep. Club, past pres., bd. mem. 10th Congl. Dist. of Lake Forest/Lake Bluff chpt.; past pres. (fin. chmn.), mem. bd. govs. Lake County Rep. Fedn.; bd. dirs. Allendale Shelter Club, Allendale Assn.; adv. bd. A Safe Place; transition bd. dirs. Anne M. Kiley Ctr. for the Developmentally Disabled; mem. LWV of Lake Forest/Lake Bluff; mem. Lake Forest Open Lands Assn.; former Lake Forest chmn., sustaining mem. Jr. League of Chgo.; former new mems. chair, membership com., Sunday sch. tchr. First Presbyn. Ch. of Lake Forest; den leader Pack 43, Boy Scouts Am.; plan commr. City of Lake Forest, 1993-97, sr. housing commr., 1993-97, ad hoc com. on sr. housing bd. mem. Recipient City of Lake Forest Spl. Recognition of Pub. Svc.. award. Mem. ABA, Ill. Bar Assn., Lake County Bar Assn., Chgo. Bar Assn., House Financial Insts. Comm., Comm. on Aging, Edn. Appropriations Comm., Labor and Commerce Comm., appointed mem., Legislative Rsch. Bureau, bd. mem. Office: Office of Lt Governor 214 State House Springfield IL 62706-0001*

WOOD, CRAIG BRECKINRIDGE, paleobiologist, natural science educator; b. Washington, Jan. 27, 1943; s. William Ernest Wood and Christina Mae (DeBrito) Phillips; m. Sung He Lee, May 21, 1982; children: William, Violet, Virginia. AB in Geology, U. N.C., 1966; MS in Geology, U. Wyo., 1967; MA in Geology, Harvard U., 1980, PhD in Geology, 1992. Tchg. fellow geology, anthropology, biology depts. Harvard U., Cambridge, Mass., 1968-70, 73-74; rsch. assoc. geology dept. Princeton (N.J.) U., 1970-71; geologist Herbert & Assocs. Ltd., Virginia Beach, Va., 1972-73; instr. natural sci. Providence Coll., 1974-79, asst. prof. natural sci., spl. lectr. geology, 1979-92, assoc. prof. natural sci., 1993-2001, prof., 2001—, dir. natural sci. program, 1993-95; lectr. biology and geology Asian divsn. U. Md., Yokota AFB, Japan, 1981-82, Osan AFB, Korea, 1981-82. Harvard U. exch. scholar dept. paleontology U. Calif., Berkeley, 1988-89; rsch. assoc. in mammalogy Mus. Comparative Zoology, Harvard U., 1994—; expdn. mem. Rift Valley Rsch. Mission in Ethiopia, Addis Ababa, 1976, Blue Nile region, Ethiopia, 1993, 96, 97, 98; Mesozoic fieldwork in Gyeongsangdo, Korea, 1998-2000; fieldwork in Jilin Province, China, 2000-2002. Co-discoverer of "Bodo Man", 1976, first Ethiopian highland Mezozoic vertebrates, 1993, first Ethiopian dinosaurs, 1996, first Triassic vertebrates in Tigray Province, 1997-98, first Ethiopian Mesozoic mammal, 1999, first Mesozoic mammals in Jilin Province, China, 2000. Mem. AAAS, Soc. Vertebrate Paleontology, Paleontol. Soc., Soc. for Study of Mammalian Evolution, Tokalon Club, R.I. Carolina Club (treas. 1994-97), Sigma Xi, Phi Mu Alpha Sinfonia. Office: Providence Coll Biology Dept Providence RI 02918-0001 E-mail: cbwood@providence.edu.

WOOD, DANIEL BRIAN, educational consultant; b. Roseburg, Oreg., Mar. 5, 1960; s. Jack Livingston and E. June (Gamble) W. BS, U. Oreg., 1982, MS, 1985, PhD, 1989. Cert. folklore and ethnic studies. Fare policy analyst Lane Transit Dist., Eugene, Oreg., 1984-85; asst. to dean for internships Univ. Oreg., 1987-88; rsch. analyst Oreg. System Higher Edn., 1988; pvt. practice, ednl. rsch., 1988—. Co-designer, co-author statewide exam. and analysis of transfer student performance in Oreg. higher edn.; manuscript reviewer for refereed jours.; vis. asst. prof., rsch. assoc. U. Miss., 1992-93; active Statewide Task Force on Transfer Followup, 1987-88. Reviewer Internat. Jour. Intercultural Rels., 1995—; contbr. articles to profl. jours. Mem. Am. Soc. Pub. Adminstrn., Oreg. Sect. Pub. Adminstrn. Edn., Pi Lambda Theta (pres.), Phi Delta Kappa. Home and Office: 122 E Howard Ave Eugene OR 97404-2617 E-mail: drdbwood@webtv.net.

WOOD, DAVID LAURENCE, artist, art educator, consultant; b. Hollywood, Calif., Sept. 1, 1944; s. E. Laurence and Natalie Georgette (Sheckles) W.; m. Terry Lynn Ezell Wood, Aug. 11, 1973 (div. Aug. 1983); children: Caynan, Jennifer; m. Pamela Forster, July 14, 2000. BA in art history, U. Calif., 1968; MA in printmaking, Calif. State U., 1976. Fine art dept. chair John Burroughs H.S., Burbank, Calif., 1992-93, art instr., 1969-94, Santa Monica (Calif.) H.S., 1994—. Chmn. Partnership com. Visual Arts, Burbank, 1988-94; lectr. I.V.A.E. J. Paul Getty Ctr., Santa Monica, 1992-93. Pres. Fine Arts Fedn. Burbank, 1993—; bd. dirs. Task Force for the Cultural Arts, 1991-92, Glendale Regional Arts Coun., Glendale, Calif., 1988-92, Design Review Bd., Burbank, 1969-73. Recipient Bronze award Information Film Producers of Am., Hollywood, 1980; named Outstanding Art Tchr., Creative Art Ctrs., Burbank, 1989, 90, 91, 92, 93. Mem. Am. Soc. Appraisers. E-mial. Home: 3921 Davana Rd Sherman Oaks CA 91423-4633 E-mail: davidlwood@earthlink.net.

WOOD, DAVID LEE, entomologist, educator; b. Jan. 8, 1931; BS, SUNY, Syracuse, 1952; PhD, U. Calif., Berkeley, 1960. Lic. forester, Calif. Prof. entomology, emeritis dept. Environ. Sci. Policy, Mgmt. U. Calif., Berkeley, 1960—. Lectr., reviewer, cons. in field. Contbr. articles to profl. jours. Recipient Silver medal Swedish Coun. for Forestry and Agril. Rsch., 1983. Fellow Entomol. Soc. Can., We. Entomol. Soc. Am. (Founder's award 1986, Founder's award Western Forest Insect Work Conf. 1992); mem. AAAS, AIBS, Entomol. Soc. Am., Entomol. Soc. Can., Internat. Soc. Chem. Ecology (Silver medal 2001), Soc. Am. Foresters, Sigma Xi. Home: 26 Hardie Dr Moraga CA 94556-1134 Office: U Calif Divsn Insect Biology 201 Wellman Hall Berkeley CA 94720-3112 E-mail: bigwood@nature.berkeley.edu.

WOOD, DENNIS, communications executive; Mgr. Berkeley Walcoverings Inc.; chmn. bd. dirs., pres., CEO C-MAC Industries, Montreal, Canada. Bd. dirs. Gen. Trust Can., Maax Inc., Groupe Bocenor, Blue Mountain Coverings, Nat. Bank of Can. Bd. dirs. Orchestre Metropolitaine of Montreal. Office: C-MAC Industries 610 Sherbrook St W Ste 1610 Montreal QC Canada H3A 2R7

WOOD, DENNIS ALLEN, pathologist; b. Menominee, Mich., Mar. 5, 1951; m. Christine A. Wood, June 12, 1976. BA in Biochem., U. Wis., 1973, MD, 1977. Med. dir. lab. Sheboygan (Wis.) Meml. Med. Ctr., 1983—2000; ret., 2000; pathologist Logan Regional Hosp., Hyde Park, Utah, 2002—. Lt. comdr. USN, 1977—83. Fellow: Coll. Am. Pathologists. Home: 325N 575E Hyde Park UT 84318

WOOD, DIANE PAMELA, judge; b. Plainfield, N.J., July 4, 1950; d. Kenneth Reed and Lucille (Padmore) Wood; m. Dennis James Hutchinson, Sept. 2, 1978 (div. May 1998); children: Kathryn Hutchinson, David Hutchinson, Jane Hutchinson. BA, U. Tex., 1971, JD, 1975. Bar: Tex. 1975, D.C. 1978, Ill. 1993. Law clk. U.S. Ct. Appeals (5th cir.), 1975—76, U.S. Supreme Ct., 1976—77; atty.-advisor U.S. Dept. State, Washington, 1977—78; assoc. Covington & Burling, 1978—80; asst. prof. law Georgetown U. Law Ctr., 1980—81, U. Chgo., 1981—88, prof. law, 1988—95, assoc. dean, 1989—92, Harold J. and Marion F. Green prof. internat. legal studies, 1990—95, sr. lectr. law, 1995—; spl. cons. antitrust divsn. internat. guide U.S. Dept. Justice, 1986—87, dep. asst. atty. gen. antitrust divsn., 1993—95; judge U.S. Ct. Appeals (7th cir.), 1995—. Contbr. articles to profl. jours. Bd. dirs. Hyde Park-Kenwood Cmty. Health Ctr., 1983—85. Mem.: Internat. Acad. Comparative Law, Am. Law Inst., Am. Soc. Internat. Law, Phi Alpha Delta. Democrat.

WOOD, DIRK GREGORY, surgeon, physician, forensic consultant; b. Springfield, Ohio, Sept. 19, 1953; s. Carlos Paul and Evelyn Cecelia (Bird) W.. BA magna cum laude, Urbana (Ohio) U., 1973; postgrad., Ohio State U., 1973-75; MD, UAG Facultad de Medicina, Guadalajara, Mexico, 1980; mini pupilage, Inns of Court School of Law, London, 1990; JD, Capital Law Sch., Columbus, Ohio, 1991. Diplomate Am. Bd. Ob-Gyn, Am. Bd. Forensic Medicine. Intern Bronx (N.Y.) Lebanon Hosp., 1981-82; resident William Beaumont Hosp., Royal Oak, Mich., 1982-86; physician, surgeon Her Care, Inc., Springfield, 1986—. CEO Just What the Doctor Ordered, Springfield, 1992—; dir. of obstetrics Mercy Med. Ctr., Springfield, Ohio, 1999—; chief collaborative physician Nurse Midwives Ctr., 1999—. Coroner Clark County, Ohio, 1991-97; mem. Clark County Rep. Ctrl. Com., Clark County Dist. 14, 1992—. Named Ky. col., Ala. col. Fellow ACS, Am. Coll. Ob-Gyn., Internat. Coll. Surgeons, Am. Coll. Legal Medicine, Am. Coll. Forensic Examiners, Royal Soc. Medicine (London), Interam. Coll. Physicians and Surgeons; mem. SAR, Am. Soc. Law and Medicine, Phi Delta Epsilon (past chpt. pres.), Phi Alpha Delta. Republican. Avocations: scuba diving, bibliophilia, travel. Home: 202 Tuttle Rd Springfield OH 45503-5236 E-mail: club2042@core.com.

WOOD, DONALD CRAIG, retired marketing professional; b. Wilmington, Del., June 24, 1937; s. Thomas Henry and Madelyn (Brehm) W.; m. Elizabeth Haring, Apr. 28, 1962; children: Craig Standish, Allison Jean. BA, U. Del., 1959; MBA, Northwestern U., 1967. Sales engr. NVF Corp., Broadview, Ill., 1960-62, Synthane Corp., Morton Grove, 1962-68; account exec., mgr. sales Donnelley Mktg. subs. Dun and Bradstreet Corp., Oakbrook, 1968-76, from dir. to v.p. market devel. to v.p. mktg. Stamford, Conn., 1977-1980; from v.p., gen. mgr. to pres. Donnelley Mktg. Info. Svcs. subs. Dun and Bradstreet Corp., 1980-86; sr. v.p. Donnelley Mktg. Inc. subs. Dun and Bradstreet Corp., 1987-90; v.p., gen. mgr. info. svcs. Triad Systems Corp., Livermore, Calif., 1990-96; ret., 1996. Served to 1st lt. U.S. Army, 1959-60. Home: 6312 Providence CC Dr Charlotte NC 28277

WOOD, DONALD EURIAH, lawyer; b. Guymon, Okla., May 27, 1935; s. Theodore and Lula Elizabeth (Rider) W.; m. Lynda Sharon Harris, Sept. 30, 1960; children— Donald Craig, Tana Dawn, Kristen Lynn. BA, Panhandle A. and M. Coll., 1958; LL.B., Okla. U., 1964, JD, 1970. Bar: Okla. bar 1964. Asst. county atty., Texas County, 1964; county atty., 1965-67; dist. atty. Okla. 1st Jud. Dist., Guymon, 1967—. Mem. adv. com. Okla. Commn. Criminal and Traffic Enforcement Systems, 1972; mem. Gov.'s Commn. Community Affairs and Planning, 1972-75; mem. faculty Panhandle State Coll., 1974-92; mem. Okla. Dist. Atty. Tng. Council, 1976—; mem. Okla. Bur. Narcotics and Dangerous Drugs Commn., 1992-98. Served with inf. AUS, 1958-60. Named Okla. Prosecutor of Yr., Assn. Okla. Narcotic Enforcers, 1994-95. Mem. Okla. Bar Assn. (legal ethics com. 1971—), Texas County Bar Assn. (pres. 1966, 1970-71), Nat. Dist. Attys. Assn., Okla. Dist. Attys. Assn. (pres. 1972, exec. com. 1971—), Phi Alpha Delta. Clubs: Elk, Rotarian. Presbyterian. Home: 605 Hillcrest Dr Guymon OK 73942-3345 Office: 319 N Main St Guymon OK 73942-4843

WOOD, DONALD NEAL, educator in media, author; b. Chgo., Sept. 20, 1934; s. Claude Obern and Mary Elmina (Neal) W.; m. Marie Ann Vayo, June 9, 1956; children: Bridget Louise, Brian Hamilton. BA, Earlham Coll., 1956; MA, U. Mich., 1958, PhD, 1963. Cert. tchr. secondary schs., profl. adminstrs. cert. Elem. and secondary tchr. Economy (Ind.) Twp Schs, 1956-57; speech instr. Westminister Coll., New Wilmington, Pa., 1958-59; program coord. Nat. Ednl. TV and Radio Ctr., N.Y.C., 1959-60; area coord. Midwest Program on Airborne TV Instrn., Lafayette, Ind., 1960-63; asst. prof. speech, TV San Diego State U., 1963-65; dir. ednl. TV Hawaii Dept Edn., Honolulu, 1965-70; prof. radio-TV-film Calif. State U., Northridge, 1970-98; adj. lectr. Duke Inst. for Learning in Retirement, Durham, NC, 1999—2002. Author: (books) Educational Telecommunications, 1977, Designing the Effective Message, 1989, 96, Post-Intellectualism and the Decline of Democracy, 1996; (textbook) Mass Media and the Individual, 1983; co-author: (textbook) Television Production: Disciplines and Techniques, 1978, 2001. Bd. dirs. Monte Nido Valley Property Owners Assn., Calabasas, Calif., 1971-72, 73-74, 86-87; mem. Malibu (Calif.) Creek Docents, 1977-90, pres. 1977-78; sec. Pleasant Green Woods Cmty. Assn., 1999-2002. Recipient Broadcast Preceptor award San Francisco State U., 1978, Disting. Tchg. award Calif. State U. Northridge, 1995, Choice award Outstanding Acad. Book, 1997, Living History award Calabasas Hist. Soc., 1998; grantee Calif State U. Fund for Innovation, 1971. Mem. Broadcast Edn. Assn. Avocations: hiking, tennis, chess. E-mail: dnwood@nc.rr.com.

WOOD, DR. BENTON, retired editor, priest; b. Arlington, Mass., Aug. 14, 1927; s. Edward E. Wood, Jr. and Dorothy Benton Wood; m. Joan Spodnyak Wood, Sept. 4, 1954; children: John Benton. BS, Northwestern U., Evanston, IL, 1951; MS, State U. NY, Albany, NY, 1952; Religious Edn. Degree, Geneva Theol. Coll., Byfield, MA, 1974, Dr. (hon.) Humane Letters, 1979. Ordained Anglican Priest Diocese Albany, NY, 1957. Counsellor Camp Pasquaney, E. Hebron, NH, 1944—64; chaplain Northwood Sch., Lake Placid, NY, 1954—57, history dept. head, 1954—57; chaplain Trinity-Pawling Sch., Pawling, 1958—62; dir. of studies, summer sch. St. Andrew's Sch., Boca Raton, Fla., 1962—65; headmaster York Sch., Monterey, Calif., 1965—67; academic dean Trinity Prepatory Sch., Winter Park, Fla., 1967—74; rector Ch. Annunciation, Anna Maria Island, 1975—88. Dir. St. Alban's Stamp Mission, Parrish, Fla., 1974—2001; editor Northwestern U. Alumni newsletter, Sarasota, Fla., 1990—2001; chaplain Baker St. Irregulars, 1980—. Author: (reference) Philatelic & Numismatic Holmes. Chaplain Anna Maria Fire Dept., Anna Maria Island, Fla., 1978—88. Pvt. U.S. Army, 1945—46. Recipient Two Shilling award, Baker St. Irregulars, 1997. Fellow: Am. Geog. Soc. Avocations: philatelist, sherlockian. Home: 9840 Sucia Circle Parrish FL 34219 Personal E-mail: barscannusi@aol.com.

WOOD, EARL HOWARD, physiologist, educator; b. Mankato, Minn., Jan. 1, 1912; s. William Clark and Inez (Goff) W.; m. Ada C. Peterson, Dec. 20, 1936; children: Phoebe, Mark Goff, Guy Harland, Earl Andrew. BA, Macalester Coll., 1934, D.Sc., 1950; BS, U. Minn., 1939, MS, M.B., PhD, 1941, MD, 1942. Teaching fellow physiology U. Minn., 1936-39, instr., 1940; NRC fellow med. scis., dept. pharmacology U. Pa., 1941; instr. pharmacology Harvard Med. Sch., 1942; research asst. acceleration lab. Mayo Aero Med. Unit, 1943; asst. prof. physiology Mayo Found., U. Minn. Grad. Sch., 1944, prof. physiology and medicine, 1950—; staff mem. sect. physiology Mayo Clinic, 1947—; chmn. biophys. scis. unit Mayo Med. Sch.; career investigator Am. Heart Assn., 1961—. Sci. cons. air surgeon USAF Aero Med. Ctr., Heidelberg, Germany, 1946; vis. prof. U. Bern, 1965-66; vis. scientist dept. physiology Univ. Coll., London, 1972-73; rsch. cons. Canadian Air Force, DCIEM, Toronto, 1993-99. Contbr. articles to profl. jours., chpts. to books. Recipient Presdl. certificate of merit, Disting. Lectr. award Am. Coll. Chest Physicians, 1974, Sr. U.S. Scientist Humboldt award Kiel, Fed. Republic Germany, 1985, Phillips Meml. award ACP, 1983, Lucian award for research in cardiovascular diseases McGill U., 1985, Stewart Meml. lectr. Royal Aero. Soc., 1987, Outstanding Achievement award U. Minn., 1991. Fellow Aerospace Med. Assn. (Disting. Research award 1983); mem. Am. Physiol. Soc. (past chmn. circulation group, pres. 1980-81, Daggs award 1995), Am. Soc. Pharmacology and Exptl. Therapeutics, Am., Central socs. clin. investigation, Soc. Exptl. Biology and Medicine, Am. Heart Assn. (Research Achievement award 1973, past chmn. basic sci. sect.), AAAS, Nat. Acad. Medicine Mex., Nat. Acad. Arts and Scis. (Netherlands), Federated Am. Socs. Exptl. Biology (pres. 1981—), German Soc. for Heart and Circulation Rsch., Carl-Ludwig Ehrenmünze, Phi Beta Kappa, Sigma Xi, Alpha Omega Alpha (Outstanding Achievement award 1991). Achievements include research, numerous publs. on devel. instrumental techniques and procedures for study heart and circulation in health and disease; applications of these procedures to detection and quantitation of various types of acquired and congenital heart disease, study of effects and compensatory reaction of heart and circulation to various types of circulatory stress. Home: 211 2nd St NW Apt 1918 Rochester MN 55901-3101 E-mail: wood.earl@mayo.edu.

WOOD, EDWARD MANNING, fund raising counsel; b. Wabash, Ind., Apr. 21, 1948; s. Edward Emerson III and Gene Devere (Romig) W.; m. Deborah Smith, Aug. 15, 1970 (div. May 1982); children: Sarah Anne, Daniel Edward; m. Diana Lee Setree, Dec. 26, 1982; 1 child, Rebecca Romig. BA, Coll. of William and Mary, 1970; MDiv, Va. Theol. Sem., 1973. Cert. fund raising exec. Curate Galilee Ch., Virginia Beach, 1973-76; chaplain Trinity Episcopal Sch., Richmond, Va., 1976-79; asst. rector St. David's Ch., Venetia, Pa., 1979-81; v.p. Ketchum, Inc., Pitts., 1982-93; exec. dir. U. Pitts., 1993-95; prin. Wood Ptnrs., Fund-Raising Counsel, Allison Park, Pa., 1995—. Author: Setree Family History, 1986. Non-stipendiary priest Episcopal Diocese of Pitts., 1981—. Avocations: travel, philanthropy. Home and Office: Wood Ptnrs 2112 Coventry Dr Allison Park PA 15101-3356 E-mail: tedwood@pfnmail.net.

WOOD, EMILY CHURCHILL, educator, educational consultant; b. Summit, N.J., Apr. 11, 1925; d. Arthur Burdett and Ruth Vail (Pierson) Churchill; m. Philip Warren Wood, June 22, 1946; children: Martha, Arthur, Warren, Benjamin. BA, Smith Coll., 1946; MA in Teaching, Manhattanville Coll., 1971; postgrad., U. Tulsa, 1974-79, Langston U., 1990-92. Cert. tchr. social studies, learning disabilities, elem. edn., econs., Am. history, world history. Tchr. Miss Fines Sch., Princeton, N.J., 1946-47, Hallen Ctr. for Edn., Portchester, N.Y., 1973-74, Town and Country Sch., Tulsa, Okla., 1974-79, Tulsa Pub. Schs., 1979-97, Heritage Acad., Tulsa, 1998—; adj. instr. Tulsa C.C., Tulsa, 1998—. Ednl. cons. Tulsa, 1997—; leader colloquia Bill of Rights Arts and Humanities Coun., Tulsa, 1989; mem. literacy task force Tulsa 2000 Edn. Com., 1990-92; chmn. internat. student exch. Eisenhower Internat. Sch., Tulsa, 1992-97. Author: (with others) Visual Arts in China, 1988, Applauding Our Constitution, 1989, The Bill of Rights: Who Guarantees What, 1993; contbr. articles to profl. jours. Leader, founder Am. Field Svc., Tulsa, 1982—84; pres., v.p. Booker T. Washington H.S. PTA, 1985; campaign mgr. auditors race Dem. Party, 1988, 1992, 1994; bd. dirs. Smith Coll. Alumnae, Northampton, Mass., 1956—59, Sister Cities Internat., Tulsa, 1992—2001, nominations chair, 1999—2001; bd. dirs. Tulsa Global Alliance; trustee Okla. Found. for Excellence, 2000—. Named Tulsa Tchr. of Yr. Tulsa Classroom Tchrs. Assn., 1988, Nat. Elem. Tchr. of Yr., Nat. Bar Aux., 1992, Outstanding Elem. Social Studies Tchr., Nat. Coun. or Social Studies, 1999; recipient Elem. Medal of Excellence, Okla. Found. for Excellence, 1990, Valley Forge Tchrs. medal Freedoms Found., 1992, Paragon award Tulsa Commn. on Status of Women, 1996, Pinnacle award Mayor's Commn. on Status of Women, 1998, Liberty Bell award Tulsa Bar Assn., 1998, Global Vision award Tulsa Global Alliance, 2002. Mem. UN Assn. Ea. Okla. (pres. 2000—), Nat. Coun. Social Studies (religion program com. 1984—, bd. dirs. 1997—), DAR, Okla. Edn. Assn., Okla. Coun. Social Studies (pres. 1995, tchr. of yr. 1984), Okla. Bar Assn. (law related com. 1988—, tchr. of yr. 1990), Okla. Coun. Econ. Edn. (state and nat. awards 1981, 89, 92), Kent Place Alumnae Assn. (disting. alumna award 1992). Avocations: reading, swimming, travel, walking. Home: 3622 S Yorktown Pl Tulsa OK 74105-3452 E-mail: emily_wood46@hotmail.com.

WOOD, EMMA S. nurse practitioner; b. Lancaster County, Pa., June 20, 1945; d. Moses H. and Elizabeth M. (Shirk) Zimmerman; m. George Wood, Feb. 4, 1977 (dec. July 1989); 1 child, George William Jr. ADN, Edison C.C., 1979; BSN, U. South Fla., 1987, MSN, 1989. RN, Fla.; advanced RN practitioner; cert. psychiat. and mental health nurse, cert. profl. in health care quality, clin. specialist in psychiat. mental health. Agy. adminstr., home health nurse VNA of Desoto County, Arcadia, Fla., 1979-81; utilization rev. coord. G. Pierce Wood Meml. Hosp., 1981-85, RN specialist, 1985-89, sr. nurse supr., mgr., 1989-95, nurse educator, 1995—2000, advanced RN practitioner, 1990—. Mem. ANA, Fla. Nurses Assn., Nat. Assn. for Health Care Quality, Fla. Assn. for Health Care Quality, Am. Psychiat. Nurses Assn., NLN, Sigma Theta Tau. Home: 5847 SE Hwy 31 Arcadia FL 34266-1552 E-mail: goldwing@qtcom.net.

WOOD, FLOYD EDWARD, JR. pharmacist, consultant; b. Kirkwood, Mo., June 7, 1926; s. Floyd Edward and Gertrude Ethel Wood; m. Joye Carolyn Habertlier, July 24, 1952; children: Christine, Floyd III, Barbara, Keith, Kevin, Benjamin, Peter, Timothy. BS, St. Louis Coll. Pharmacy, 1952. Owner Wood Drug Co., Kirkwood, 1952-94; cons. Omnicare, Florissant, Mo., 1995—. Author: Policy and Procedure, 1978. With USN, 1944-45. Mem. Am. Soc. Cons. Pharmacists, Am. Pharm. Assn., Mo. Pharmacist Assn. Democrat. Methodist. Avocations: amateur radio, piano, gardening. Office: 10702 Manchester Rd Kirkwood MO 63122-1321

WOOD, FORREST E., JR. philosopher; b. Fairfield, Tex., Aug. 20, 1937; m. Evelyn Elaine Wood; children: Eric, Sharon Heinemann. PhD, Southwestern Bapt. Theol. Sem., Ft. Worth, Tex., 1964. Asst. prof. Tex. Wesleyan Coll., Ft. Worth, 1963—64, La. Coll., Pineville, 1964—66; prof. philosophy and religion U. So. Miss., Hattiesburg, 1966—. Author: (book) Whiteheadian Thought As A Basis for a Philosophy of Religion, 1986, The Delights and Dilemmas of Hunting, 1997. Mem.: Soc. for Philosophy of Religion (pres.), Am. Philos. Assn. Home: 2301 Eddy St Hattiesburg MS 39402 Office: U So Miss Hardy St Hattiesburg MS 39406 Personal E-mail: f.wood@usm.edu. E-mail: f.wood@usm.edu.

WOOD, FRANCES DIANE, medical secretary, artist; b. Caddo, Okla., Mar. 7, 1950; d. Clovis Lynn and Hilda Dee (Guthrie) Wood; m. Samuel Dante Wolfe, Aug. 20, 1990 (div. Mar. 1992). BA, Southeastern Okla. State U., 1972; postgrad., Grayson County Coll., 1984—87, Rose State Coll., 2001—02. Ins. clk. Sherman Cmty. Hosp., Tex., 1973-74; med. sec. Essin Clinic, Sherman, 1980-83; med. transcriptionist Texoma Med. Ctr., Denison, 1983-88, Wilson N. Jones Meml. Hosp., Sherman, 1989-95; CEO Designs by Diane, Caddo, Okla., 1995—. Conv. del. Blue Cross-Blue Shield Tex., Dallas, 1980-83; v.p. Jett Transcription, Denison, Tex., 1988. Exhibited paintings in cmty. art shows; Native Am. craft work in permanent collections Bryan County Nat. Bank, Caddo, Indian Terr. Mus., Caddo. Charter mem. Caddo Edn. Found., Okla., 1993-95; sponsor Save the Children, Philippines, 1995. Mem. Am. Soc. Prevention Cruelty to Animals, The Nature Conservancy, Physicians Com. for Responsible Medicine, Nat. Trust Historic Preservation, Okla. Sheriffs Assn. (hon.), Arts Coun. Co-op (life), Nat. Arbor Day Found., Sierra Club, Sacred Heart Auto League, People for the Ethical Treatment of Animals, So. Poverty Law Ctr. Supporters. Democrat. Avocations: pet care, interior decorating, astronomy, folk medicine, gardening.

WOOD, FRANK, actor; Grad. acting program, NYU; grad. theater program, Wesleyan U. Broadway debut in Side Man, (Tony award 1999); actor in shows including: Three Sisters, Tomorrowland, King of Rats, Dark Ride; many roles in Gil Kofman plays at Soho Rep, Adobe Theater and Dallas Theater Ctr.; has worked with Fifty Second Street Project; (TV appearances) Law and Order, Ed, The Sopranos, Third Watch; (films) Down To You, 2000, Small Time Crooks, 2000, Pollock, 2000, Thirteen Days, 2000, The Royal Tenenbaums, 2001. Recipient 1995 Drama-Logue award for best ensemble in Kofman's Entrevista 187, Padua Hills Playwrights Festival. Mem. East Coast Artists. Office: c/o SAG 1515 Broadway Fl 44 New York NY 10036-8901*

WOOD, GEORGE AMBOS, city manager; b. Savannah, Ga., Feb. 3, 1952; s. Herbert Lee and Louise (Ambos) W.; m. Pamela Sue Hinson, Dec. 9, 1979; 1 child, Andrew Hinson. BS in Polit. Sci., Ga. So. U., Statesboro, 1974; MPA, U. Kans., 1978. Adminstrv. asst. to city mgr. City of Salina, Kans., 1977-79; city adminstr. City of Lancaster, S.C., 1979-80; town mgr. Town of Kingstree, 1980-82; village mgr. Village of Pinehurst, N.C., 1982-88; city mgr. City of Kings Mountain, 1988-94, City of Cleveland, Tenn., 1994-2000, City of Statesboro, Ga., 2000—. Bd. dirs. United Way, Cleveland, 1994—; mem. Econ. Devel. Coun., Cleveland, 1994—. Recipient George C. Franklin award N.C. League of Municipalities, Raleigh, 1988, Excellence in Pub. Svd. award Am. Soc. Pub. Adminstrn., 2000. Mem. Tenn. City Mgmt. Assn. (award for excellence in mcpl. govt. 1997), Tenn. Mcpl. League (City Overall Improvement award 1995), Rotary (bd. dirs. Kings Mountain chpt. 1992-94), Local Govt. Stewardship award Tenn. Dept. Environment and Conservation, 1997, Disting. Budget Presentation award GFOA, 1999. Baptist. Avocations: golf, reading, travel. Office: City of Statesboro PO Box 348 50 E Main St Statesboro GA 30459

WOOD, GERALD DAVID, religious organization administrator; b. Narrows, Va., Oct. 16, 1947; s. Curtis Edmond and Myrtle Isabella (Jernigan) W.; m. Sandra Fay Harris, Aug. 24, 1968; children: Angela Dawn, Anthony David, Jonathan David, Beth Lynette. Student, Kjesaters, Vingaker, Sweden, 1966-67, Washington and Lee U., 1967-68, U. Va., 1968-69, Emmanuel Coll., 1973-81; MLitt, Oxford Grad. Sch., 2001; BREd, Maranatha Inst Christian Mins., 1994. Ordained to ministry Internat. Pentecostal Holiness Ch., 1968. Pastor Charlottesville (Va.) Pentecostal Holiness Ch., 1968-72, St. Paul Pentecostal Holiness Ch., Max Meadows, Va., 1972-82; sec.-treas. Va. Conf. Sunday Sch. Bd., Dublin, 1974-80; treas. Va. Conf. Christian Edn. Bd., 1980-86; pastor New Covenant Pentecostal Holiness Ch., Princeton, W.Va., 1982-86; dir. Christian edn. Appalachian Conf. Pentecostal Holiness Ch., Dublin, 1986-94; mem. Appalachian Conf. Bd., 1994; sr. pastor 1st Pentecostal Holiness Ch., Greenville, N.C., 1994-2000; pastor Shiloh Pentecostal Holiness Ch., Wilson, 2000—. Mem. gen. Christian edn. bd. Internat. Pentecostal Holiness Ch., 1987—91, 1993; mem. gen. bd. publs., 1993—2001; dir. radio ministry Wythe County Ministerial Assn., Wytheville, Va., 1978—80; pres. W.Va. Camp Meeting Assn., Princeton, 1982—84; bd. dirs. ATAM, Inc., Falcon, NC. Bd. dirs. Mountaineer Food Bank, Gassaway, W.Va., 1986, Marantha Inst., Dublin, 1986-94, treas., 1989-92, registrar, 1992-94, Greenville Cmty. Shelters, 1998-2000, chmn. ch. com., 1999-2000, v.p. 2000; pres. Dublin Elem. Sch. PTA, 1988-90, Pulaski County Advs. for Talented and Gifted, 1989-92, sec. New River Dist. PTA, 1990-92; chmn. bd. dirs., Ch. Ministries United, Greenville, N.C., 1996-97; mem. exec. com. Franklin Graham Crusade, Greenville, 1998. Mem. Pentecostal Fellowship N.Am. (v.p. Princeton chpt. 1982-83), Am. Assn. of Christian Counselors, Nat. Coun. on Family Rels. Republican. Avocation: amateur radio. Office: Shiloh Pentecostal Holiness Ch 5843 Shiloh Church Rd Wilson NC 27896 E-mail: GDWood1047@prodigy.net. *My father taught me: "Always be honest with God, with others and with yourself. Love others the way God loves you. Serve God with everything you are." I have chosen to live in this way.*

WOOD, GORDON STEWART, historian, educator; b. Concord, Mass., Nov. 27, 1933; s. Herbert G. and Marion (Friberg) W.; m. Louise Goss, Apr. 30, 1956; children: Christopher, Elizabeth, Amy. AB, Tufts U., 1955; AM, Harvard, 1959; PhD, Harvard U., 1964. Fellow Inst. Early Am. History and Culture, Williamsburg, Va., 1964-66; asst. prof. Harvard U., Cambridge, Mass., 1966-67; assoc. prof. U. Mich., Ann Arbor, 1967-69; prof. history Brown U., Providence, 1969—; Pitt prof. Cambridge U., 1982-83. Bd. trustees Tufts U.; Bancroft lectr. U.S. Naval Acad., 1986; Anson G. Phelps lectr. NYU, 1986; Charles Edmundson lectr. Baylor U., 1987; Samuel Paley lectr. Hebrew U., Jerusalem, 1987; presdl. lecture series on presidency, 1991. Author: The Creation of the American Republic, 1776-1787, 1969, The Rising Glory of America, 1760-1820, 1971; co-author: The Great Republic, 1977, The Radicalism of the American Revolution, 1992 (Pulitzer Prize for history 1993); co-editor: Imagined Histories: American Historians Interpret the Past, 1998, The American Revolution: A History, 2002. Mem. coun. Inst. Early Am. History and Culture, 1980-83; bd. trustees Colonial Williamsburg. With USAF, 1955-58. Recipient Bancroft prize Columbia U., 1970, Disting. Visitor award Australian-Am. Ednl. Found., 1976, Douglass Adair prize, 1984, Emerson prize Phi Beta Kappa, 1992, Kidger award New Eng. Tchrs. Assn., 2001; Sunderland fellow U. Mich. Law Sch., 1990, All Souls Coll. fellow, 1991, Fletcher Jones Found. Disting. fellow The Huntington, 1997-98; Woodrow Wilson Ctr. guest-scholar, 1993-94; named to Rhode Island Heritage Hall of Fame, 2000; Dr. of Letters, La Trobe Univ., Austrailia. Mem. Am. Hist. Assn. (John Dunning prize), Orgn. Am. Historians, Soc. Am. Historians, Nat. Hist. Soc. (chmn. bd. advisors), Soc. Historians of the Early Am. Republic (pres.), Am. Acad. Arts and Scis., Am. Philos. Soc. Office: Brown Univ Dept of History Box N Providence RI 02912-9040

WOOD, GREGORY BURTON , JR. brokerage house executive; b. Mpls., Apr. 1, 1943; s. Gregory Burton and Ramona Edith (Jackson) W.; m. Linda A. Payn, July 8, 1967 (div. 1984); children: Kelly L., G. Scott; m. Judith A. Clubb, Dec. 15, 1984; 1 child, Jennifer L. Student, Oreg. State U., 1962-66; grad., Securities Industry Inst., 1990. Sales rep. Itek Corp., Seattle, 1966-69; account exec. Shearson Hammill & Co., 1969-78, forest products commodities analyst, 1973-78; fin. advisor, forest products commodities analyst Prudential Securities, Inc., Bellevue, Wash., 1978-82, br. mgr., 1st v.p. Ft. Worth, 1982-95, dir. regional tng. Dallas, 1995-97; exec. dir. One Prudential, Phoenix, 1997-99; pres. Investment Mktg. Assocs., 1999; exec. v.p. George K. Baum & Co., Kansas City, Mo., 1999-2001; sr. v.p. Wells Fargo Pvt. Client Svcs., Salt Lake City, 2001—. Mem. Chgo. Mercantile Exchange, 1976-82. Contbr. articles to profl. jours. Past mem. bd. dirs. Ft. Worth Boys and Girls Club. Mem. Securities Industry Assn. (sales and mktg. com.), Rolls-Royce Owners Club, Classic Car Club Am. Republican. Avocations: collecting antique and classic automobiles. Office: Wells Fargo Bank 299 S Main St 7th Fl Salt Lake City UT 84111 E-mail: gwood@ix.netcom.com.

WOOD, HARLINGTON, JR. federal judge; b. Springfield, Ill., Apr. 17, 1920; s. Harlington and Marie (Green) W. AB, U. Ill., 1942, JD, 1948. Bar: Ill. 1948. Practiced in, Springfield, 1948-69; U.S. atty. So. Dist. Ill., 1958-61; mem. firm Wood & Wood, 1961-69; assoc. dep. atty. gen. for U.S. attys. U.S. dept. Justice, 1969-70; assoc. dep. atty. gen. Justice Dept., Washington, 1970-72, asst. atty. gen. civil div., 1972-73; U.S. dist. judge So. Dist. Ill., Springfield, 1973-76; judge U.S. Ct. Appeals (7th cir.), 1976—. Adj. prof. Sch. Law, U. Ill., Champaign, 1993; disting. vis. prof. St. Louis U. Law Sch., 1996—. Chmn. Adminstrv. Office Oversight Com., 1988-90; mem. Long Range Planning Com., 1991-96. Recipient Profl. Lifetime Achievement award, Inns of Ct., 2002. Office: US Ct Appeals PO Box 299 600 E Monroe St Springfield IL 62701-1626

WOOD, HEIDI, commissioner; BA with honors, Brown U., 1987. Analyst SG Cowen; fin. cons. Shearson Lehman Hutton, Wedbush Morgan; from v.p., sr. analyst to exec. dir. Morgan Stanley Dean Witter, 1999—; commr. aerospace investment Aerospace Commn., Arlington , Va. Mem.: N.Y. Aerospace Analyst Soc. (treas.). Office: Aerospace Commn Crystal Gateway One Ste 940 1235 Jefferson Davis Hwy Arlington VA 22202-3283*

WOOD, HELEN LUCILLE, civic volunteer; b. Cook, Nebr., July 22, 1912; d. Lewis and Lucy Ann (Ellam) Richards; m. Harry Harold Himes, June 1931 (div. 1940); m. Leroy Eugene Wood, Nov. 10, 1941; children: Edwin Kirk, Donald David (dec.). Sec. Pacific Gas & Electric Co., Oakdale, Calif., 1930-35; with clerical div. Real Estate & Ins., 1937-47; soc. editor Oakdale Leader, 1960-61; planning commn. mem. City of Oakdale, 1973-82, city council mem., 1982-86. Hon. Chmn. Stanislaus County Cerebral Palsy Telethon, Modesto, Calif., 1988; mem. Stanislaus County Solid Waste Com., Modesto, 1982-86; mem. Solid Waste Adv. Bd. State of Calif.; appointee planning commn. Stanislaus County, Calif., 1989—. Mem. Oakdale Women's Club, Oakdale C. of C. (dir. 1987-89), Oakdale Town Criers-Toastmasters. Republican. Methodist. Avocations: sewing, reading, writing, gardening, cooking. Home: 532 W F St Oakdale CA 95361-3733

WOOD, H(OWARD) JOHN, III, astrophysicist, astronomer; b. Balt., July 19, 1938; s. Howard John Jr. and Cara (Loss) W.; m. Austine Barton Read, June 10, 1961 (div. Jan. 1975); children: Cara Loss, Erika Barton; m. Maria Ilona Kovacs, May 22, 1977; 1 child, Andreas M. BA in Astronomy, Swarthmore Coll., 1960; MA, Ind. U., 1962, PhD, 1965. Lectr., asst. prof. then assoc. prof. U. Va., Charlottesville, 1964-70; staff astronomer European So. Obs., Santiago, Chile, 1970-75; Fulbright Rsch. fellow U. Vienna Obs., 1976-78; rsch. assoc. Ind. U., Bloomington, 1978-81; asst. to the dir. Cerro Tololo Inter-Am. Obs., La Serena, Chile, 1982-83; physicist, astronomer NASA/Goddard Space Flight Ctr., Greenbelt, Md., 1984—, mgr. instrument synthesis and analysis lab., 2000—. Optics lead engr. Mars Observer Laser Altimeter, 1989-90, Hubble Space Telescope, 1990—; adv. optics and outreach Next Generation Space Telescope, 1996—; advisor, participant Hubble Space Telescope Allen Comm., NASA, Danbury, Conn., 1990; co-chmn. Hubble Space Telescope Ind. Optical Rev. Panel, Columbia, Md., 1990-91; mem. panel The Townes/SAGE Panel-Jet Propulsion Lab., Pasadena, 1991-92. Co-author: Physics of Ap Stars, 1976; contbr. articles to profl. publs. Grantee NSF (10), 1965-82, Am. Astron. Soc., 1978. Mem. Internat. Astron. Union (Commn. 29 1962—), Optical Soc. Am. (chair optical tech. div. 1999-2001, co-chair ann. meeting 2002), Sigma Xi. Achievements include discovery of Balmer-Line variability of Ap stars; discovery of magnetic fields in southern Ap stars; alignment testing and delivery of the DIRBE photometric cryogenic telescope on the COBE spacecraft; alignment and optical prescription for Hubble Space Telescope while in orbit. Office: NASA/Goddard Space Flight Ctr Code # 551 Greenbelt MD 20771-0001 E-mail: jwood@mail.hst.nasa.gov.

WOOD, JACKIE DALE, physiologist, educator, researcher; b. Picher, Okla., Feb. 16, 1937; s. Aubrey T. Wood and Wilma J. (Coleman) Wood Patterson. BS, Kans. State U., 1964, MS, 1966; PhD, U. Ill., 1969. Asst. prof. physiology Williams Coll., Williamstown, Mass., 1969-71; asst. prof. U. Kans. Med. Ctr., Kansas City, 1971-74, assoc. prof., 1974-78, prof., 1978-79; prof., chmn. dept. physiology Sch. Medicine, U. Nev., Reno, 1979-85; chmn. dept. physiology coll. medicine Ohio State U., Columbus, 1985-97, prof. physiology and internal medicine, 1997—. Cons. NIH, Bethesda, Md., 1982—. Recipient Rsch. Career Devel. award NIH, 1974, Chancellor's award for teaching excellence U. Kans., 1975; named Hon. Citizen City of Atzugi Japan, 1987; Alexander von Humboldt fellow, W.Ger., 1976. Mem. AAAS, Am. Physiol. Soc. (assoc. editor 1984-96, rsch. award 1986), Soc. Neurosci., Am. Gastroent. Assn., Assn. Chmn. Depts. Physiology. Office: Ohio State U Dept Physiology 300 Hamilton Hall 1645 Neil Ave Columbus OH 43210-1218 E-mail: wood.13@osu.edu.

WOOD, JAMES ALLEN, retired lawyer; b. McMinnville, Tenn., Jan. 14, 1906; s. Ira and Emma (Calhoun) W.; m. Eva Beth Sellers, Dec. 28, 1941; 1 son, Eben Calhoun. AB, U. Tenn., 1929; LL.B., U. Tex., 1934. Bar: Tex. 1934. Tchr. Bolton H.S., Alexandria, La., 1929-32; since practiced in Corpus Christi, 1971-97; ret., 1998. State dist. judge, Corpus Christi, 1941-43; mem. rules adv. com. Supreme Ct. Tex., 1949-86. Author 7 vols. poetry; contbr. articles to profl. jours.; author: Life on a Warren County Farm (Tenn.) 1906-1923, 1996, Early Bench and Bar of Corpus Christi, 1996, Items: Serious of Not, 1997, Moody Shadows, 1962, Muted Echoes, 1970, For Exiles, 1973, Last Sunset, 1974, Blunt Arrows, 1979, Bottom Lines, 1987, Wandering Lines, 1993. Bd. dirs. Nueces River Authority, 1972-89, pres., 1981-84, life time hon. dir., 1989—. Lt. USNR, 1943-45. Fellow Am. Coll. Trial Lawyers; mem. ABA, Tex. Bar Assn., Nueces County Bar Assn. (pres. 1941) Home and Office: 458 Dolphin Pl Corpus Christi TX 78411-1514

WOOD, JAMES EDWARD, JR. religion educator, author; b. Portsmouth, Va., July 29, 1922; s. James E. and Elsie Elizabeth (Bryant) W.; m. Alma Leacy McKenzie, Aug. 12, 1943 (dec. Oct. 2000); 1 son, James Edward III BA, Carson-Newman Coll., 1943; BD, So. Bapt. Theol. Sem., 1947, ThM, 1948; MA, Columbia U., 1949; postgrad., U. Tenn., 1943-44; cert. in Chinese, Yale U., 1949-50; Japanese diploma, Naganuma Sch. Japanese Studies, Tokyo, 1950-51; PhD., So. Bapt. Theol. Sem., 1957; LLD, Seinan Gakuin U., Japan, 1983; LLD (hon.), Capitol U., 1996; DHC (hon.), Bucharest (Romania) U., 1998. Ordained to ministry So. Bapt. Ch., 1942. Pastor So. Bapt. chs., Tenn. and Ky., 1942-48; Bapt. missionary to Japan, 1950-55; prof. religion and lit. Seinan Gakuin U., Japan, 1951-55; assoc. prof. history of religions Baylor U., Waco, Tex., 1955-58, prof. hist. religions, dir. J. M. Dawson Inst. Ch. State Studies, 1958-73, 80-95, 1st dir. honors program, 1959-64, chmn. interdeptl. grad. degree program in ch.-state studies, 1962-73, 80-95; founder Ch. State Rsch. Ctr., 1968, founder, chmn. faculty-student Far Eastern exch. program, 1970-72, Simon and Ethel Bunn Disting. prof. ch.-state studies, 1980-99, Simon and Ethel Bunn Disting. prof. emeritus, 1999—. Exec. dir. Bapt. Joint Com. on Pub. Affairs, Washington, 1972-80; mem. ctrl. panel Bapt. World Alliance Commn. on Religious Liberty and Human Rights, 1965-75, 80-2000, Commn. on Freedom, Justice and Peace, 1976-80; chmn. Bapt. Com. on Bicentennial, 1973-76; mem. So. Bapt. Inter-Agy. Coun., 1972-80, vice chmn., 1975-76, sec. 1976-77; vis. prof. So. Bapt. Theol. Sem., 1974, N.Am. Bapt. Theol. Sem., Sioux Falls, S.D., 1974, 79, Okla. Bapt. U., Shawnee, 1977, vis. scholar, Christ Coll. Oxford U., 1983, Naval Coll. Chaplains, Providence, 1988—, others; vis. lectr. Ashland (Ohio) Theol. Sem., 1971; Vernon Richardson lectr. U. Bapt. Ch., Balt., 1975, Ea. Bapt. Theol. Sem., Phila., 1975, Duquesne U., 1976, Wake Forest U., 1978, U. Richmond, 1979; lectr. First World Congress on Religious Liberty, Amsterdam, 1977, Notre Dame Law Sch., 1980, 2d Congress, Rome, 1984, U. Faculty of Law, Warsaw, Poland, 1984, Chinese Inst. Religion, Beijing, 1986, Brigham Young U., 1986, 95, 97, Union Theol. Sem., Va., 1989, U. Kans. Law Sch., 1990, U. Tirana, Albania, 1992, U. Malta, 1994, Austin Coll., 1989, 95, U. Pitts. Law Sch., 1997, vis. prof. Bulgarian Baptist Theol. Sem., Sofia, 1998, Faculty of Canon Law, Cath. U., Leuven, Belgium, 1999, numerous others; chair Internat. Consultation on Relig. Rights and Ethnic Identity, Budapest, 1992; co-chair Internat. Conf. Religious Freedom, Moscow, 1993; mem. internat. adv. bd. World Report on Freedom Conscience Human Rights Ctr., U. Sussex, U.K.; co-chair consultation on Freedom of Conscience and Belief, Moscow, 1993; chair Internat. Consultation Religious Liberty and Social Peace, Malta, 1994; Carver-Barnes lectr. Southeastern Bapt. Theol. Sem., 1981; Asian Found. lectr. Seinan Gakuin U., Japan, 1983; ecumenical consultation on edn. Nat. Coun. Chs., 1974; numerous other com. coun. positions. Co-author: Church and State in Scripture, History and Constitutional Law, 1958; author: A History of American Literature: An Anthology, 1952, The Problem of Nationalism, 1969, Nationhood and the Kingdom, 1977, Secular Humanism and the Public Schools, 1986, Reflections on Church and State, 1995; (edited by Derek H. Davis) The Separation of Church and State Defended: Selected Writings of James E. Wood, Jr., 1995, Church-State Relations in the Modern World, 1999, and numerous others; editor: Markham Press Fund, Baylor U. Press, 1970-72; editor, contr.: Jewish-Christian Relations in Today's World, 1971, Baptists and the American Experience, 1976, Religion and Politics, 1983, Religion, the State, and Education, 1984, Religion and the State: Essays in Honor of Leo Pfeffer, 1985, Ecumenical Perspectives on Church and State, Protestant, Catholic and Jewish, 1988, Readings on Church and State, 1989, The First Freedom: Religion and the Bill of Rights, 1990, contr. coeditor: The Role of Religion in the Making of Public Policy, 1991, The Role of Government in Monitoring and Regulating Religion in Public Life, 1993, Problems and Conflicts Between Law and Morality in a Free Society, 1994, founding editor Jour. Ch. and State, 1959-73, 80-93, mem. editl. coun., 1973-80; mem. editl.

bd. Religion and Public Edn., Religious Freedom Reporter; area editor, contbr. Ency. So. Bapts., 1982, Church and State in Am. History, 1987; contbr. Changing Trends in Education, 1992, Law, Religion and Human Rights in Global Perspective, 1995, Dialogue of Democracy: An American Politics Reader, 1996, many others; contbr. over 300 articles to profl. jours. Speaker in field. Sponsor Ams. for Public Schs., 1963-68; bd. dirs. Waco (Tex.) Planned Parenthood, 1966-72, pres., 1971-72; sponsor Christians Concerned for Israel, 1968—, Tex. Conf. Chs. Consultation on Religion and Public Edn., 1971, Nat. Christian Leadership Conf. for Israel, 1978—; pres. Waco area ACLU, bd. dirs. Tex. unit, 1968-72; pres. Nat. Council Religion and Public Edn., 1979-83, exec. com., 1975-90, bd. dirs., 1972-90; chmn. exec. com. Council Washington Reps. on UN, 1977-80, mem. council exec. com., 1973-80; exec. com. Nat. Coalition on Public Edn. and Religious Liberty, 1973-95; mem. religious liberty com. Nat. Council Chs. U.S.A., 1972—, also mem. com. internat. concerns on human rights; Am. rep. Chs. Montreux Colloquium on Helsinki Final Act, 1977; v.p. Waco Conf. Christians and Jews, 1983-86, Internat. Acad. for Freedom of Religion and Belief, 1985-90, pres., 1990—, hon. pres., 2000—; mem. internat. adv. bd. World Report on Freedom of Conscience, Human Rights Ctr., U. Sussex, Eng.; trustee Internat. Devel. Conf., 1974-80; nat. coun. Am.-Israel Friendship League, 1977—; founder, chmn. Waco Human Rights Week, 1981-86; mem. ch. rels. com., U.S. Holocaust Meml. Coun., 1990-98; adv. com. on religious freedom abroad U.S. State Dept., 1998—. Recipient Disting. Alumnus award Carson-Newman Coll., 1974, Religious Liberty award Alliance for Preservation of Religious Liberty, 1980, Henrietta Szold award Tex. region Hadassah, 1981, Human Rights award Waco Conf. Christians and Jews, 1986, Cir. of Achievement award Baylor U. Mortar Bd., 1991, Religious Freedom Lifetime award Ams. United Ctrl. Tex., 1993, W.R. White Meritorious Svc. award, 1996, Human Rights Leadership award Freedom mag., 1998; hon. Tex. col., 1969. Mem. Am. Soc. Ch. History, Am. Acad. Religion, Am. Soc. Internat. Law, Am. Soc. Sci. Study of Religion, N. Am. Soc. Ecumenists, NCCJ (ad. com. on ch. state and taxation 1979-85), Supreme Court Hist. Soc., Soc. for Scholarly Publishing, Va. Hist. Soc., Phi Eta Sigma, Pi Kappa Delta, Alpha Psi Omega. Democrat. Home: 203 Barrington Ln Yorktown VA 23693-5622 E-mail: james_wood@baylor.edu.

WOOD, JAMES JERRY, lawyer; b. Rockford, Ala., Aug. 13, 1940; s. James Ronald and Ada Love Wood; m. Earline Luckie, Aug. 9, 1959; children: James Jerry, William Gregory, Diana Lynn. AB, Samford U., 1964, JD, 1969. Bar: Ala. 1969, U.S. Supreme Ct. 1976. Dir. legal affairs Med. Assn. State of Ala., Montgomery, 1969-70; asst. atty. gen. State of Ala., 1970-72; asst. U.S. atty. Middle Dist. Ala., 1972-76; pvt. practice, 1977-78; pres. Wood & Parnell, P.A., Montgomery, Ala., 1979-89; pvt. practice, 1990—. Gen. counsel Ala. Builders Self-Insurers Fund, Home Builders Assn. of Ala.; chmn. character and fitness com. Ala. State Bar, 1981-84, 86-89, chair task force on quality of life, 1990-92, chair task force on mem. svcs., 1994-96. Capt. USAR, 1974-79. Fellow Am. Bar Found. (Ala. state chair), Ala. Law Found.; mem. ABA (ho. of dels. 1990-98), FBA (pres. Montgomery chpt. 1974-75), Am. Nat. Inns of Ct., Am. Soc. Assn. Execs., Ala. Assn. Workers Compensation Group Self-Insured Funds (chmn.), Ala. Bar Assn., Montgomery Bar Assn., Ala. Def. Lawyers Assn., Ala. Law Inst., Ala. Coun. Assn. Execs. (pres. 2001), Def. Rsch. Inst., Rotary (pres. Montgomery Capital chpt. 1986-87, 96-97). Republican. Baptist. Office: PO Box 241206 Montgomery AL 36124-1206 E-mail: jjwood@mindspring.com.

WOOD, JAMES MICHAEL, lawyer; b. Oakland, Calif., Mar. 22, 1948; s. Donald James and Helen Winifred (Reimann) W.; children: Nathan, Sarah, Ruth, Alexandra; m. Cynthia Ahart Wood. BA, St. Mary's Coll., 1970; JD, U. San Francisco, 1973. Bar: Calif. 1973, U.S. Dist. Ct. (no., cen. and so. dists.) Calif. 1973. Rsch. atty. Alameda County Superior Ct., Oakland, 1973-76; ptnr. Crosby, Heafey, Roach & May, 1976—. Mem. adv. com. Food Drug Law Inst., 1999—; presenter profl. confs. Contbr. articles to profl. jours. Chair alumni-faculty devel. fund St. Mary's Coll. Alumni Bd. Dirs., 1990-94. Mem. ABA (litigation sect., health law litigation com., litigation products liability com.), ATLA (assoc.), State Bar Calif., Calif. Trial Lawyers Assn. (assoc.), No. Calif. Assn. Def. Counsel, Alameda County Bar Assn., Def. Rsch. Assn., Am. Acad. Hosp. Attys., Nat. Health Lawyers Assn., Drug Info. Assn., Food Drug Law Inst. Office: Crosby Heafey Roach & May 1999 Harrison St Ste 2200 Oakland CA 94612-3572 E-mail: jwood@chrm.com.

WOOD, JAMES MICHAEL, psychologist, researcher; b. Tucson, Aug. 13, 1951; s. Thomas A. and Joan Lenore (Kane) W.; m. Marie-Anne Salvio, Apr. 16, 1990 (div. Oct. 1991); m. M. Teresa Nezworski, June 14, 1997; stepchild, Maureen Mahoney. AB, Harvard Coll., 1973; MDiv, Yale U., 1979; PhD in Psychology, U. Ariz., 1990. Lic. psychologist, Ariz. Asst. prof. dept. psychology U. North Tex., Denton, 1990-91, U. Tex., El Paso, 1993—. Contbr. articles to profl. jours. Mem. Am. Profl. Soc. Abuse of Children, Internat. Soc. Preventon Child Abuse and Neglect, Am. Psychol. Soc. Office: U Tex El Paso Dept Psychology El Paso TX 79968-0001

WOOD, JAMES NOWELL, museum director and executive; b. Boston, Mar. 20, 1941; s. Charles H. and Helen N. (Nowell) W.; m. Emese Forizs, Dec. 30, 1966; children: Lenke Hancock, Rebecca Nowell. Diploma, Universita per Stranieri, Perugia, Italy, 1962; BA, Williams Coll., Williamstown, Mass., 1963; MA (Ford Mus. Tng. fellow), NYU, 1966. Asst. to dir. Met. Mus., N.Y.C., 1967-68, asst. curator dept. 20th century art, 1968-70; curator Albright-Knox Art Gallery, Buffalo, 1970-73, assoc. dir., 1973-75; dir. St. Louis Art Mus., 1975-80, Art Inst. Chgo., 1980—. Vis. com. visual arts U. Chgo., 1980-94; head com. Nat. Endowment Arts Mem. Intermuseum Conservation Assn. (past pres.), Assn. Art Mus. Dirs. Office: Art Inst Chgo 111 S Michigan Ave Chicago IL 60603-6492

WOOD, JEANNE CLARKE, charitable organization executive; b. Pitts., Dec. 21, 1916; d. Joseph Calvitt and Helen Caroline (Mattson) Clarke; m. Herman Eugene Wood, Jr., May 6, 1936 (dec.); children: Helen Hamilton (Mrs. John Harry Mortenson), Herman Eugene III. Student, Collegiate Sch. for Girls, Richmond, Va., 1932-33. Asst. to Dr. and Mrs. J. Calvitt Clarke, Christian Children's Fund, Inc., Richmond, 1938-64; founder Children, Inc., 1964, pres., internat. dir., 1964—. Author: (with Helen C. Clarke) In Appreciation: A Story in Pictures of the World-Wide Family of Christian Children's Fund, Inc. 1958, Children's Christmastime Around the World, 1962, Children's Games Around the World, 1962, Children-Hope of the World-Their Needs, 1965, Children-Hope of the World-Their Friends, 1966; Editor: CI News, 1964. Recipient citation Eastern Council Navajo Tribe, 1970, citations Mayor of Pusan (Korea), 1971, citations Mayor of Seoul, 1971, citations Gov. of Kanagawa Prefecture (Japan), 1972, commendation Pres. of U.S., 1972, citation Stephen Philibosian Found., 1975, citation Santa Ana (El Salvador) Dept. Edn., 1975, citation Nat. Sch. for Blind, Dominican Republic, 1982, citation Navajo Tribal Council of Navajo Nation, Window Rock, Ariz., 1982 Home and Office: Children Inc PO Box 5381 1000 Westover Rd Richmond VA 23220-6624 *While there are many things about which we can make no choice in this volatile world where change is constant and sometimes disastrous, it has seemed to me that one can make the choice between accepting things positively or negatively. I have chosen to accept them positively.*

WOOD, JEREMY SCOTT, architect, urban designer; b. Glen Ridge, N.J., Oct. 23, 1941; s. William Gamble and Alice-Marguerite (Scott) W.; m. Robin Benensohn-Rosefsky, June 14, 1970; children: Alexis, Jonas, Augusta. AB, Yale U., 1964, M in Architecture, 1970. Registered architect, Ma. Sr. assoc. TAC/The Architects Collaborative, Inc., Cambridge, Mass., 1970-94; sr. project mgr. Domenech Hicks & Krockmalnic, Inc., Boston, 1995-97; sr. project architect Elkus/Manfredi Architects, Ltd., 1997—. Instr. Boston Archtl. Ctr., 1970-76; head tutor Dept. of Art History and History of Modern Architecture Yale U., 1969-70, Emerson Coll. Performance & Production Ctr./Emerson Majestic Theatre Renovation, Boston MA, 2001—. Author: (sect. and chpt. in books) Adaptive Reuse: Issues and Case Studies in Building Preservation, 1988, Office Buildings, 1989, Exposed Structure in Building Design, 1993; prin. works include Emerson Coll. Prodn. and Performance Ctr., Boston, 2001—, Allen House Restoration & Condominiums, South End, Boston, 1998, Emerson Coll. Prodn. and Performing Ctr., Boston, 2001—, MBTA/AMTRAK North-South Rail Link Stations (Boston), MBTA Subway Station Modernization State St. and Govt. Ctr. Stations (Boston), Complejo Medico de las Americas, Guatemala City, Guatemala, Health Care Internat. Hosp. and Hotel, Clydebank, Glasgow, Scotland, Copley, Pa., Boston, The Westin Hotel at Copley Pl., Boston, Liberty Ctr. and Vista Internat. Hotel, Pitts., Wellington Bus. Ctr. Offices, Medford, Mass., Two Portland (Maine) Sq. Office Bldg., One Mifflin Pl., Cambridge, Groton (Mass.) Sch. Dormitories, Coll. Engring. and Applied Sci., Shuwaikh Campus, Kuwait U., Kuwait City, Kuwait, Hosp. U. Pa., Phila.; asst. editor Perspecta 11; corr. Architecture and Urbanism, 1976; contbr. articles to profl. jours. Recipient Award of Excellence, Assn. Sch. Bus. Ofcls., Coun. Ednl. Facilities Planners, AIA, 1976, Concrete Industry Bd. Spl. Recognition award The Westin Hotel, Boston, 1983, Prestressed Concrete Inst. award, 1983, Honor award Associated Gen. Contractors of Mass., 1985, Grand award Urban Land Inst., 1988, hon. mention New Eng. Healthcare Design Awards, 1994, 1997 Move Massachusetts 2000 design award for engring. and arch. of North South Rail Link Project. Mem. AIA, Boston Soc. Architects, Mass. State Assn. Architects, Am. Planning Assn., Soc. Archtl. Hists. (life, Nat. chpt.), Boston Inst. Contemporary Art, The Archtl. League N.Y. Home: 10 Pigeon Hill Rd Weston MA 02493-1620

WOOD, JOAN, retired chemist; b. Bklyn., May 19, 1934; d. Harry Christian Nintzel and Helen Pauline (Diviak) Levesen; m. Randall Leroy Field Sr., Nov. 15, 1952 (div. Feb. 1972); children: Randall Leroy Jr., Roland, Gary, Brian, Lorraine, Thomas; m. Bransford Wayne Almond, Dec. 9, 1986 (div. Apr. 1993); m. Roy Allen Wood, Sr., Oct. 9, 1999. Grad. high sch., Bklyn. Sec. Fulton Savs. Bank, Bklyn., 1952-53; mgr. reprodn. Air Pre-heater Corp., Wellsville, N.Y., 1958; chemistry technician fibers div. Allied Chem., Hopewell, Va., 1963-76; chemistry technician Va. Power Co.-North Anna Power Sta., Mineral, 1976-86, assoc. instr., 1987-92, sr. chemistry technician, 1992-94, sr. chemistry technician shift leader, 1992-94; ret., 1994; craft shop owner Stuffed Stuff and Other Stuff, Bumpass, Va., 1994-99. Recipient cert. of achievement Nat. Acad. for Nuclear Tng., 1988. Mem. Women of Moose (com. chmn. Moosehart Hopewell 1971). Roman Catholic.

WOOD, JOETTA KAY, special education educator; b. Kirksville, Mo., Sept. 30, 1951; d. Vernon John Wood and Hazel Ellen (Lake) Ammon. BS in Elem. Edn., N.W. Mo. State U., 1973; MS in Spl. Edn., S.W. Mo. State U., 1993. Cert. tchr., Mo. Kindergarten Livingston County Sch., Wheeling, Mo., 1973-75; 1st grade tchr. Mercer (Mo.) Sch., 1975-77, Maysville (Mo.) Sch., 1978-80; learning disabilities tchr. Lakeland Sch., Lowery City, Mo., 1980-81, Tri-County Sch., Jamesport, 1981-84, Plato (Mo.) Sch., 1984—. Adj. faculty Columbia Coll., 1995. Mem. Coun. for Exceptional Children, Mo. State Tchrs. Assn. Home: PO Box 8 Plato MO 65552-0008

WOOD, JOHN ARMSTEAD, planetary scientist, geological sciences educator; b. Roanoke, Va., July 28, 1932; s. John Armstead and Lillian Cary (Hall) W.; m. Elisabeth Mathilde Heuser, June 12, 1958 (div.); children: Crispin S., Georgia K.; m. Julie Marie Nason, Sept. 9, 1989. BS in Geology, Va. Polytech. Inst., 1954; PhD in Geology, Mass. Inst. Tech., 1958; post-doctoral study, U. Cambridge, Eng., 1959-60. Staff scientist Smithsonian Astrophys. Obs., Cambridge, Mass., 1959, 61-62, 65—; research asso. Enrico Fermi Inst. U. Chgo., 1962-65; prof. dept. geol. scis. Harvard, 1976-95; asso. dir. Harvard-Smithsonian Center for Astrophysics, 1981-98. Vice chmn. Lunar Sample Analysis Planning Team, 1971—72; mem. space studies bd. NRC, 1998—2001; chair Com. on Lunar and Planetary Exploration, 1999—2001. Author: Meteorites and the Origin of Planets, 1968, The Solar System, 1979, 2d edit., 2000. Recipient NASA medal for exceptional sci. achievement, 1973, J.L. Smith medal NAS, 1976, G.K. Gilbert award Geol. Soc. Am., 1992. Fellow AAAS, Am. Geophys. Union, Meteoritical Soc. (pres. 1971-72, Leonard medal 1980); mem. NAS, Am. Acad. Arts and Scis., Cosmos Club. Achievements include having asteroid no. 4736 named in his honor Johnwood. Home: 71 Langdon St Cambridge MA 02138-2501 Office: 60 Garden St Cambridge MA 02138-1516

WOOD, JOHN ARTHUR, nurse; b. Lincoln, Nebr., Mar. 30, 1964; s. Earl Wayne and Lorene Wilma (Kuhn) W.; m. Julie Kristin Gray, June 5, 1993; children: Amy, Will. BSN, U. Nebr., 1988. RN, Nebr. Nurse's asst. Tabitha Nursing Home, Lincoln, Nebr., 1986-88, staff nurse, 1988-89, Truman Med. Ctr. West, Kansas City, Mo., 1989-93, Via Christi-St. Francis, Wichita, Kans., 1993-96. Preceptor Med. ICU, Via Christi-St. Francis, Wichita, Truman Med. Ctr. CPR instr., ARC, Lincoln, 1982-86, mem. Red Cross Youth Leadership Camp Staff, Lincoln, 1978-84, first aid team instr., 1981-84, first aid instr., 1981-84. Recipient awards Adm. Nebr. State Navy, Lincoln, 2000, ARC, Lincoln, 1983. Mem. NRA (life). Republican. Avocations: sportsman, outdoorsman, reading, music.

WOOD, JOHN MARTIN, lawyer; b. Detroit, Mar. 29, 1944; s. John Francis and Margaret Kathleen (Lynch) W.; m. Judith Anne Messer; children: Timothy Peter, Meagan Anne. BA, Boston Coll., 1966; JD, Cath. U. Am., 1969. Bar: D.C. 1970, Va. 2001, U.S. Dist. Ct. D.C. 1970, Va., 2001, U.S. Ct. Appeals (D.C. cir., 3d cir., 4th cir.), U.S. Supreme Ct. 1973. Trial atty. tax divsn. Dept. Justice, Washington, 1969-73; assoc. Reed Smith LLP, 1973-80, ptnr., 1980—, mng. ptnr., 1989-95, dir. legal pers., 1995-98. Dir. adv. bd. Salvation Army, Va. and Met. Washington, Leadership Washington, 1993—. Mem. D.C. Bar, Econ. Club of Washington, Barristers Club (Washington), River Bend Golf and Country Club, The Currituck Club (N.C.), Phi Alpha Delta, Delta Sigma Pi. Home: 9490 Oak Falls Ct Great Falls VA 22066-4143 Office: Reed Smith LLP 3110 Fairview Park Dr Ste 1400 Falls Church VA 22042 E-mail: jwood@reedsmith.com.

WOOD, JOHN MICHAEL, writer; b. Seattle, June 7, 1975; s. James Michael and Maureen Theresa Wood. BA, U. Wash., 1999. Author: (screenplays) Footprints, 1998, (novels) The Savage Earth, 2000, The Further Room, 2001. Avocations: films, film criticism, traveling.

WOOD, JOHN THURSTON, cartographer, jazz musician; b. Chgo., Apr. 29, 1928; s. Clarence Leo and Hilda Bernice (Miller) W.; m. Erma Louise Vogt, July 3, 1957; children: John Thurston Jr., Holly Lynn, Joseph Miller II. BS, Iowa State U., 1952; postgrad., Ohio State U., 1962-64, Indsl. Coll. Armed Forces, Washington, 1974, Fed. Exec. Inst., Charlottesville, Va., 1985. Commd. 2d lt. USAF, 1952, advanced through grades to lt. col., 1968; combat airlift pilot 535th Troop Carrier Squadron, Vung Tau, Vietnam, 1966-67; comdr. USAF Operational Evaluation Detachment, Topeka, 1967-70; aerial and ground survey officer Def. Intelligence Agy., Washington (D.C.), Def. Mapping Agy., Washington (D.C.), Va., 1972-76; ret., 1976; chief user svcs. Nat. Cartographic Info. Ctr. U.S. Geol. Survey, Reston, 1976-83, dep. chief, 1983-85, chief, 1985-89, 1985-89; chief Earth Sci. Info. Office U. S. Geol. Survey, 1989-95. Tuba player Buck Creek Jazz Band, 1977—. Decorated Air medal with four oak leaf clusters. Mem. Masons, Shriners. Home: 4007 Terrace Dr Annandale VA 22003-1856

WOOD, JONATHAN STUART, economist, educator; b. New Orleans, Nov. 14, 1944; s. John Joseph and Linelle Marie (Waguespack) W.; m. Ann M., Apr. 7, 1973; children: Elizabeth, Christopher, Julie, Jonathan. Grad., NASA Summer Inst. in Space and Engring., 1965; BS in Mech. Engring., Tulane U., 1966; MS in Aerospace Engring., Princeton U., 1970; MBA in Econs., NYU, 1975, MPhil in Econs. and Fin., 1978, PhD in Econs. and Fin., 1980. Rschr. on bio-engring study of neck whiplashes Tulane Med. Sch. and Tulane Sch. Engring. (for US Dept Health, Edn. and Welfare), 1963; materials tester and lab. analyst Svc. Foundry, New Orleans, 1964; ops. rsch. & econ. analyst Grumman Aerospace Corp., Bethpage, N.Y., 1969-74; sr. investment analyst, cons. to common stock dept. Prudential Ins. Co., Newark, 1974-76; instr. fin. & acctg. Sch. Bus. U. Conn., Storrs, 1976-78; Liberty Fund Rsch. fellow Stanford U. Inst. Humane Studies Rsch. Seminar in Econs., Palo Alto, Calif., 1977; asst. prof. econs. & fin. Tulane U., New Orleans, 1978-84; assoc. prof. econs. & fin. Coll. Bus. Adminstrn. Loyola U., 1984—. Prof. econs. and fin. Pace U. Grad. Sch. Bus. Adminstrn., N.Y.C., 1975-76; vis. prof. fin. Grad. Sch. Bus. Adminstrn. NYU, 1980; vis. prof. fin. Grad. Sch. Bus. Tulane U., 1985, 91, lectr., 1990; presenter in field.; cons. economist; expert in bus. valuation; adj. prof. in econ. and fin. Pace U. Grad. Sch. Bus. Adminstrn., N.Y., 1975-76; appeared on WWL-TV discussing current econ. and fin. events focusing on La. econ. matters; rschr., lectr. in field; conducted interviews and seminars in field. Author: Chemical Kinetic Influences, 1968, Chemical Kinetic Influences in Liquid Propellant Rocket Combustion Instability, 1969, 70, Effectiveness Evaluation of Orbital Observatories (with Joseph R. Fragola), 1975, Heterogeneous Expectations and Security Price Distributions, 1978, Entrepreneurship and the Co-Ordination of Expectations in the Stock Market, 1980, 82, Some Refinements in the Austrian Trade-Cycle Theory, 1984, Capital Formation Problems in the United States and the Question of a Capital Shortage, 1984, Methodologies for Valuation of Closely-Held Companies (with Dr. Michael A. Dalton and Robert I. Glover), 1989, Valuation of Closely-Held Companies & Professional Practices by Experts (with Dr. Michael A. Dalton and Dr. Robert I. Glover), 1989, Real Value of Damage Caps for Medical Malpractice in Louisiana (with Michael A. Dalton), 1997; referee Quarterly Rev. Econs. and Bus., 1982, Rev. Austrian Econs., 1989; contbr. chpts., reviews to books. Chmn. fin. com., mem. exec. bd. Short-Fern St. Neighborhood Assn., 1984-85; lectro, Eucharistic min., mem. com. Univ. Parish St. Thomas More Tulane U.; dir. Operation New Start, Inc.; softball coach Carrollton Boosters; elected to u. senate, 1986—; U. Senate Parking Com., 1986-87; faculty acad. affairs budget com., 1986-89, 89-92; Blue Ribbon Task Force for libr.'s acad. future, 1986-87; u. senate designatee to Fin. Com. of bd. trustees, 1991-92, 92-93; advisor to Endowment Com. of Bd. Trustees, 1991-93. Recipient MBA Top Gun award as Outstanding Tchr., Loyola U., 1993. Mem. Am. Econ. Assn., Am. Fin. Assn., We. Econ. Assn., We. Fin. Assn., So. Econ. Assn., So. Fin. Assn., Ea. Fin. Assn., Southwestern Social Scis. Assn., Opers. Rsch. Soc. Am./Inst. Mgmt. Sci., Pontchartrain Astronomy Soc., Student Recruitment Team, Grad. Edn. Task Force, Entrepreneurship Task Force, Curriculum Com., Advising Com. (chmn. 1986-87), MBA Curriculum Task Force. Avocations: astronomy, music. Home: 500 Arlington Dr Metairie LA 70001-5516 Business E-Mail: jswood@loyno.edu. E-mail: jsjewood@aol.com.

WOOD, JOSEPH GEORGE, neurobiologist, educator; b. Victoria, Tex., Dec. 8, 1928; s. Harold Robert and Frances Josephine (Marcak) W.; 1 dau., Marian. BS, U. Houston, 1954, MS, 1958; PhD, U. Tex., Galveston, 1962. Teaching asst. biology, U. Houston, 1956-58; instr. anatomy U. Tex. Dental Br., Houston, 1961, Yale U., 1962-63; asst. prof. U. Ark. Med. Sch., Little Rock, 1963-66; assoc. prof. U. Tex., San Antonio, 1966-70, asst. dean acad. devel., 1967-69, prof. and chmn. dept. neurobiology and anatomy, 1970-84, prof. neurobiology and anatomy, 1984-88; prof., chmn. dept. anat. sci. U. Okla. Coll. Medicine, 1988-93; dir. Okla. Ctr. Neurosci., 1990-95. Guest prof. dept. pathobiology, cell biol. and neuroanatomy U. Minn., 1993-96; sr. lectr. molecular and cell biology U. Tex., Dallas, 1997—, asst. dean pre health professions, 1998—. Served with AUS, 1954-56. Recipient Basic Sci. Tchg. award U. Ark. Med. Ctr., 1963, U. Tex. Houston, 1972, 75, 86, Disting. Alumnus award U. Tex. Med. Br., 1976 Mem. Am. Assn. Anatomists (exec. com. 1974-78), Soc. Neurosci. (exec. com. Houston chpt. 1971-77, pres. 1973-77), Assn. Am. Med. Colls., Cajal Club, Histochem. Soc., Assn. Anatomy Chmn., Tex. Soc. Electron Microscopy (pres. 1970-71, exec. council 1971-79), Sigma Xi (research award 1962), Phi Kappa Phi, Alpha Omega Alpha. Office: U Tex at Dallas MS FN 32 PO Box 830688 Richardson TX 75083-0688 E-mail: woodj@utdallas.edu.

WOOD, JOSHUA WARREN, III, lawyer, foundation executive; b. Portsmouth, Va., Aug. 31, 1941; s. Joshua Warren and Mary Evelyn (Carter) W.; m. Marcia Neal Ramsey, Feb. 29, 1964; children: Lauren Elaine Yeh, Joshua Warren IV. AB, Princeton U., 1963; JD, U. Va., 1971. Bar: Va. 1971, N.J. 1976, U.S. Supreme Ct. 1977, N.Y. 1982. Comml. banking asst. Bankers Trust Co., N.Y.C., 1967-68; assoc. McGuire, Woods & Battle, Richmond, Va., 1971-75; v.p., gen. counsel, sec. The Robert Wood Johnson Found., Princeton, N.J., 1975—. Mem. AAA/ABA/AMA Commn. on Alternative Dispute Resolution in Health Care; master Marie L. Garbaldi Am. Inn Court for Alternative Dispute Resolution. Mem. editl. bd. Va. Law Rev., 1969-71. Capt. arty. U.S. Army, 1963-67. Decorated Army Commendation medal. Mem. ABA, Princeton Bar Assn., N.Y. Bar Assn., Va. Bar Assn., N.J. Bar Assn., Nat. Health Lawyers Assn., Am. Arbitration Assn. (bd. dirs., mem. panel of arbitrators, task force Mass torts & alternative dispute resolution), Order of Coif, Princeton Club. Office: College Rd PO Box 2316 Princeton NJ 08543-2316

WOOD, KATE, artist; b. Mesa, Az., Oct. 18, 1967; d. William W. and Andrea R. Wood. BA, U. Mass., 1992. Artist's model Art Assn. Martin Co., Stuart, Fla., 1992-98; fine artist Changes in Artitude, Ibor City, 1993-94, Unarmed Underground, 1994-96; portrait painter-freelance Fla., 1992—; senic artist Barn Theatre, Stuart, 1996-99, Shiloh Theatrical Prodns., Stuart, 1996—; art instr. Ctr. for Art and Soul, 1996-98. Free-lance muralist, Fla., 1993—; artistic dir. of murals Safari Signs, Stuart, Fla., 1999—; art instr. Alizarin Crimson Studio/Gallery, Stuart, 2000—.

WOOD, KENNETH ANDERSON, artist, designer, consultant; b. Cleve., May 11, 1913; s. George Robert and Leonore (Anderson) Wood; m. Ruth Eleanor Diehm, Sept. 14, 1937 (dec. May 1999). Student, Fenn Coll., Cleve., 1932-34, Cleve. Inst. Art, 1935-45. Artist Patterson Displays, Cleve., 1934-35; art dir. Bailey Meter Co., Wickliffe, 1936-71; owner Kenwood Designers and Assocs., Chesterland, 1971—; designer of stained glass windows, 1979—. Pres. Artist and Craftsman Assocs., Cleve., 1940—44, Geauga Artists Assn., Geauga County, Ohio, 1950—53. Exhibitions include nat., regional and local, 1939—97, Represented in permanent collections Butler Mus. Am., Youngstown, Ohio, Inlander Collection of Gt. Lakes Regional Patinaings, Cleve. Mus. Art, numerous pvt. collections; patents for product design. Mem.: Indsl. Desingers Soc. Am. (life). Republican. Seventh Day Adventist. Avocation: travel. Office: Kenwood Designers and Assocs 11950 Sperry Rd Chesterland OH 44026-2225

WOOD, KENNETH ARTHUR, retired newspaper editor, writer; b. Hastings, Sussex, Eng., Feb. 25, 1926; came to U.S., 1965; s. Arthur Charles and Ellen Mary (Cox) W.; m. Hilda Muriel Harloe, Sept. 13, 1952. Educated in Eng. Editor Stamp Collector newspaper Van Dahl Publs., Albany, Oreg., 1968-80, editor emeritus, 1980—. Author (ency.) This Is Philately, 1982, (atlas) Where in the World, 1983, Basic Philately, 1984, Post Dates, 1985, Modern World, 1987; author several hundred articles and columns published in the U.K. and U.S.A., 1960—. Served with Brit. Army WW II. Recipient Disting. Philatelist award Northwest Fedn. Stamp Clubs, 1974, Phoenix award Ariz. State Philatelic Hall of Fame, 1979, Disting. Philatelist award Am. Topical Assn., 1979. Fellow Royal Philatelic Soc. (London); mem. Am. Philatelic Soc. (Luff award 1987, Hall of Fame Writers Unit, 1984). Avocations: philately, aviation history, modern history, gardening. Office: 2430 Tudor Way SE Albany OR 97321-5661

WOOD, LARRY (MARY LAIRD), journalist, writer, university educator, public relations executive, environmental consultant; b. Sandpoint, Idaho; d. Edward Hayes and Alice (McNeel) Small; children: Mary, Marcia, Barry. BA summa cum laude, U. Wash., 1939, MA summa cum laude, with highest honors, 1940; postgrad., Stanford U., 1940-43, U. Calif., Berkeley, 1946-47, cert. in photography, 1971; postgrad. journalism, U. Wis., 1971-72, U. Minn., 1971-72, U. Ga., 1972-73; postgrad. in art, architecture and marine biology, U. Calif., Santa Cruz, 1974-76, Stanford Hopkins Marine Sta., 1977-80. Lifetime secondary and jr. coll. teaching cert., Wash., Calif. Feature writer and columnist Oakland Tribune and San Francisco Chronicle, Calif., 1939—; archtl. and environ. feature and travel writer and columnist San Jose (Calif.) Mercury News (Knight Ridder), 1972-90; teaching fellow Stanford U., 1940-43; dir. pub. rels. 2-counties, 56-park East Bay Regional Park Dist., No. Calif., 1948-68; pres. Larry Wood Pub. Rels., 1946—; pub. rels. dir. Calif. Children's Home Soc., 1947-58. Prof. (tenure) pub. rels., mag. writing, journalism, investigative reporting San Diego State U., 1974, 75; disting. vis. prof. journalism San Jose State U., 1976; assoc. prof. journalism Calif. State U., Hayward, 1978; prof. sci. and environ. journalism U. Calif. Berkeley Ext. grad. divsn., 1979—; press del. nat. convs. Am. Geophys. Union Internat. Conf., 1986—, AAAS, 1989—, Nat. Park Svc. VIP Press Tour, Yellowstone after the fire, 1989—, Nat. Assn. Sci. Writers, 1989—, George Washington U./Am. Assn. Neurol. Surgeons Sci. Writers Conf., 1990, Am. Inst. Biol. Scis. Conf., 1990, Nat. Conf. Sci. Writers, Am. Heart Assn., 1995, Internat. Cardiologists Symposium for Med./Sci. Writers, 1995, Annenberg Program Electronic Media Symposium, Washington, 1995; EPA del. to USSR and Ea. Europe; expert witness on edn., pub. rels., journalism and copyright; cons. sci. writers interne project Stanford U., 1989—; spl. media guest Sigma Xi, 1990—; mem. numerous spl. press corps; selected White House Spl. Media, 1993—; selected mem. Duke U. 14th Ann. Sci. Reporters Conf., 1995; internat. press guest Can. Consulate Gen. Dateline Can., 1995—, French Govt. Tourist Office, 1996—, Ministerio delle Risorse Agricole Alimentari e Forestali and Assocs. Conf., 1995; appeared in TV documentary Larry Wood Covers Visit of Queen Elizabeth II Contbr. over 5,500 articles on various topics for newspapers, nat. mags., nat. and internat. newspaper syndicates including L.A. Times-Mirror Syndicate, Knight-Ridder Syndicate, Washington Post, Phila. Inquirer, Chgo. Tribune, Miami Herald, Oakland Tribune, Seattle Times, San Francisco Chronicle, Parade, San Jose Mercury News (Nat. Headliner award), Christian Sci. Monitor, L.A. Times/Christian Sci. Monitor Worldwide News Syndicate, Washington Post, Phila. Inquirer, Hawaiian Airlines In Paradise and other in-flight mags., MonitoRadio, Donnelly Pubs., Sports Illus., Life, Mechanix Illus., Popular Mechanics, Parents (contbg. editor), House Beautiful, Am. Home (awards 1988, 89), Archl. Digest, Better Homes and Gardens, Sunset, Architectural Digest, National Geographic World, Travel & Leisure, Chevron USA/Odyssey (Calif. Pub.'s award 1984), Xerox Edn. Publs., Europe's Linguapress, PSA Mag., Off Duty, Oceans, Sea Frontiers, AAA Westways, AAA Via, Travelin', others. Significant works include home and garden columnist and editor, 5-part series Pacific Coast Ports, 5-part series Railroads of the West, series Immigration, Youth Gangs, Endangered Species, Calif. Lighthouse Chain, Lighthouses of the World, Pacific Coast Wetlands, Elkhorn Slough Nat. Estuarine Res., Ebey's Landing Nat. Hist. Island Res., Calif. Water Wars, BLM's Adopt a Horse Program, Mt. St. Helen's Eruption, Oreg's Covered Bridges, Loma Prieta Earthquake, Oakland Firestorm, Missing Children, Calif. Prison Reform, Columbia-Alaska's Receding Glacier, Calif. Underwater Parks, and many others; author: Wonderful U.S.A.: A State-by-State Guide to Its Natural Resources, 1989; co-author over 21 books including: McGraw-Hill English for Social Living, 1944, Fawcett Boating Books, 1956-66, Fodor's San Francisco, Fodor's California, 1982-89, Bell and Howell/Charles Merrill Focus on Life Science, Focus on Physical Science, Focus on Earth Science, 1983, 87, State of California's Golden State Travel Guide, 1998; contbr. Earth Science 1987; 8 works selected for use by Europe's Woltors-Nordoff-Longman English Language Texts, U.K., Netherlands, 1988; author: (with others) anthology West Winds, 1989; reviewer Charles Merrill texts, 1983-84; book reviewer Profl. Communicator, 1987—; selected writings in permanent collections Oakland Pub. Libr., U. Wash. Main Libr.; environ. works included in Dept. Edn. State of Md. textbook; contbr., author Journalism Quar.; author script PBS/AAA America series, 1992; contbg. editor: Parents, Fashion Showcase, Spokane Mag. Nat. chmn. travel writing contest for U.S. univ. journalism students Assn. for Edn. in Journalism and Mass Communication/Soc. Am. Travel Writers, 1979-83; judge writing contest for Nat. Assn. Real Estate Editors, 1982—; cons. S. Carolina Dept. Parks, Recreation and Tourism, 1999—; press del. 1st Internat. Symposium Volcanism and Aviation Safety, 1991, Coun. for Advancement of Sci. Writing, 1977—, Rockefeller Media Seminar Feeding the World-Protecting the Earth, 1992, Global Conf. on Mercury as Pollutant, 1992, Earth Summit Global Forum, Rio de Janeiro, 1992; invited Nat. Park Svc. Nat. Conf. Sci. Writers, 1985, Postmaster Gen.'s 1992 Stamps, 1991, Internat. Geophys. Union Conf., 1982—, The Conf. Bd., 1995—, Corp. Comm. Conf., Calif. Inst. Tech.'s Media and Sci. Seminar, 1995—, Medical Writers Delegation to Russia and Estonia, 1997, N.Y. Times Opinion Rsch. Co. Corp. Image Conf., 1999, EPA and Dept. Energy Tech. Conf., 1992, Am. Soc. Photogrammetry and Remote Sensing Internat. Conv. Mapping Global Change, 1992, U.S. Conf. on Oceans, 1998, N.Y. Mus. Modern Art Matisse Retrospective Press Rev. and all media previews, 1992—, celebration 150th anniversary Oreg. Trail, 1993, Nat. Coun. Advancement Sci. Writing, 1993-2002, Sigma Xi Nat. Conf., 1988-2002, Nat. Sci. Writers Confs., 1996-2002, PRSA Travel and Tourism Conf., 1993—, Internat. Conf. Environment, 1994, 95, Quality Life Europe, Prague, 1994, Calif. Sesquicentennial, 1996, 14th Ann. Sci. Writers Conf., 1996, Picasso Retrospective, 1996, many others; mem. Gov.'s Conf. Tourism N.C., 1993-2002, Calif., 1976—, Fla., 1987—, N.C. Govs. conf. on tourism and film, 2000-, U.C. Irvine Calif. Computer Sci. Symposium, 2000, Sea Grant's conf. on sci. in the news, 2000, N.Y. conf. bd. conf. on environ. journalism, 2000, on economics, 2001; press guest 14 U.S. states and 12 fgn. countries' Depts. Tourism, 1986—. Recipient numerous awards, honors, citations, speaking engagements, including induction into Broadway Hall of Fame, U. Wash., 1984, Broadway Disting. Alumnus award, 1995; citations for environ. writing Nat. Park Svc., U.S. Forest Svc., Bur. Land Mgmt., Oakland Mus. Assn., Oakland C. of C., Chevron USA, USN plaque and citation, best mag. articles citation Calif. Pubs. Assn., 1984, U.S. Treasury award, 1946; co-recipient award for best Sunday newspaper mag. Nat. Headliners, citation for archtl. features Oakland Mus., 1983; honoree for achievements in journalism Nat. Mortar Bd., 1988, 89; selected as one of 10 V.I.P. press for Yellowstone Nat. Park field trip on "Let Burn" rsch., 1989; named one of Calif.'s top 40 contemporary authors for writings on Calif. underwater parks, 1989, nat. honoree Social Issues Resources Series, 1987, Gov.'s Calif. Women of Achievement award, 1988, 89, 90; invited V.I.P. press, spl. press guest numerous events worldwide. Mem. AAAS, Am. Bd. Forensic Examiners, Calif. Acad. Scis., San Francisco Press Club, Nat. Press Club, Pub. Rels. Soc. Am. (charter mem. travel, tourism, environment and edn. divs.), Nat. Sch. Pub. Rels. Assn., Environ. Cons. N.Am., Am. Assn. Edn. in Journalism and Comm. (exec. bd. nat. mag. div. 1978, panel chmn. 1979, 80, author Journalism Quar. jour.), Women in Comm. (nat. bd. officer 1975-77, book reviewer Prof. Communicator), Soc. Profl. Journalists (nat. bd. for hist. sites 1980—), Nat. Press Photographers Assn. (hon. life, cons. Bay Area interne project 1989—, honoree 1995), Investigative Reporters and Editors (charter), Bay Area Advt. and Mktg. Assn., Nat. Assn. Sci. Writers, Calif. Writers Club (state bd., Berkeley bd. 1989—, honoree ann. conv. Asilomar, Calif. 1990), Am. Assn. Med. Writers, Internat. Assn. Bus. Communicators, Soc. Environ. Journalists (charter), Am. Film Inst., Am. Heritage Found. (citation 1986, 87, 88), Soc. Am. Travel Writers, Internat. Oceanographic Found., Oceanic Soc., Calif. Acad. Environ. News Writers, Seattle Advt. and Sales Club (former officer), Nature Conservancy, Smithsonian Audubon Soc., Nat. Wildlife Fedn., Nat. Parks and Conservation Assn., Calif. State Parks Found., Calif. Environ. Leadership Roundtable (trustee), Fine Arts Mus., San Francisco, Seattle Jr. Advt. Club (charter), U. Wash. Comm. Alumni (Sch. Comm. alumni, life, charter mem. ocean scis. alumni, Disting. Alumni 1987), U. Calif., Berkeley Alumni (life, v.p., scholarship chmn. 1975-81), Stanford Alumni (life), Mortar Board Alumnae Assn. (life, honoree 1988, 89), Am. Mgmt. Assn., Nat. Soc. Environ. Journalists (charter), Calif. Environ. Leadership Roundtable, Phi Beta Kappa (v.p., bd. dirs. Calif. Alumni Assn., statewide chmn. scholarship awards 1975-81), Purple and Gold Soc. (planning com., charter, 1995—), Pi Lambda Theta, Theta Sigma Phi. Home: Piedmont Pines 6161 Castle Dr Oakland CA 94611-2737 *A creed I follow is Ralph Waldo Emerson's statement: "Nothing great was ever achieved without enthusiasm.".*

WOOD, LARRY ALAN, packaging laboratory administrator, mechanical engineer; b. Batavia, N.Y., Sept. 27, 1951; s. Melvin George and Catherine Virginia Wood; m. M. Maureen Campbell, June 27, 1975; children: Catherine Maureen Wood Papierski, Suzanne Elizabeth. Grad. in Mech. Engring., Western Mich. U., 1974. Coop. Doehler-Jarvis Diecasting, Grand Rapids, Mich., 1969-74; tooling engr. St. Louis Diecasting, 1974-76; HVAC engr. Zurheide-Herrmann, St. Louis, 1976; tooling engr. McDonnell-Douglas, 1976-79, packaging engr., 1979-85, USAF, Wright-Patterson AFB, Ohio, 1985-89, packaging lab. supr., 1989—. Advisor engring. adv. bd., part-time mem. engring. faculty Sinclair C.C., Dayton, Ohio. Author: Wood Family Genealogy, 1999; editor: MIL-HANDBOOK-304, 1996. Advisor cmty. adv. com. Mad River Ohio Sch. Sys., 1989-91. Mem. ASTM, Nat Inst. Packaging Handling and Logistics Engrs. (pres. Dayton chpt. 1991-93, chmn. tech. svcs. 1993—, Cert. 1993), Nat. Def. Transp. Assn. (chair membership 1997—). Democrat. Unitarian Universalist. Avocations: wood working, clock repair, genealogy, antique car restoration. Office: Air Force Packaging Tech and Engring Facility 5215 Thurlow St Ste 5 Wright Pat OH 45433-5547 Fax: 937-656-1350. E-mail: lwood67976@aol.com., larry.wood@wpafb.af.mil.

WOOD, LESLIE ANN, retail administrator; b. Chgo., Apr. 9, 1957; d. Howard Arnold and Anita Eleanor (Andler) W. AA, Harper Coll., 1977; BS in Comm. Scis., Ill. State U., 1979; MBA, Olivet Nazarene U., 1998. Advt. asst. Harry Alter Co., Chgo., 1979-80; clk. typist Career Guild, Evanston, 1980-81; reporter Aparacor, 1981-82; sales mgmt. trainee Prudential Ins. Co. Am., Millburn, N.J., 1983-84; fin. cons. Summit Fin. Resources, Livingston, 1984; mgr. Chgo. area Renault Inc. div. AMC/Jeep/Renault, Elk Grove Village, Ill., 1985-87; customer relations specialist Chrysler Motors, Lisle, 1987-88; dist. svc. and parts mgr. Chrysler; dist. parts mgr. Subaru of Am., Addison, Ill., 1989-91, dist. fixed ops. mgr., 1992-95; univ. rep. Olivet Nazarene U., Schaumburg, 1996-97; mktg. cons. WZSR STAR 105.5, Crystal Lake, 1997-99; parts cons. Am. Isuzu Motors, Cerritos, Calif., 1999—2001; parts and svc. mgr. Hyundai Motor Am., Aurora, Ill., 2002—, dist. parts svc. mgr., 2002—. Mem. ch. choir, rainbows coord. Stephens Min. First Presbyn. Ch., Libertyville, Ill. Avocations: aerobics, circuit weight training, sewing, stained glass crafts. Home and Office: 230 Brett Cir Unit D Wauconda IL 60084-1587

WOOD, LIGA, small business owner, poet; b. Reichenberg, Czech Republic, Jan. 13, 1945; arrived in U.S., 1950; d. Herbert N. and Minna Sudmalis Briedis; m. Joseph Dakes Paparian (dec. Apr. 1987); 2 stepchildren. BA, SUNY, Oneonta, 1967. Tchr. Guilderland Ctrl. Sch. Dist., Guilderland, NY, 1967—2000; owner Woodhouse Pub. and Photography, Schenectady. Author: (book of free-verse poetry) Random Reflections in Free Verse, A Pocketful of Verse; author: (photographer) (book of humor) This is My Wife Princess Cecicly Rocketty Tyson. V.p. Zion Ch., Schenectady, 2000. Mem.: Therapy Dogs Internat. (assoc.), Delta Kappa Phi. Republican. Christian Ch. Avocations: oral interpretive reading, dog training, piano, writing, singing. Home and Office: 927 Northumberland Dr Schenectady NY 12309

WOOD, LINCOLN JACKSON, aerospace engineer; b. Lyons, N.Y., Sept. 30, 1947; s. William Hulbert and Sarah Brock (Strumsky) Wood. BS with distinction, Cornell U., 1968; MS in Aeronautics and Astronautics, Stanford U., 1969, PhD, 1972. Staff engr. Hughes Aircraft Co., El Segundo, Calif., 1974-77; mem. tech. staff Jet Propulsion Lab. Calif. Inst. Tech., Pasadena, 1977-81, tech. group supr. Jet Propulsion Lab., 1981-89, tech. mgr., 1989-91, dep. tech. section mgr., 1991-99, dep. leader Ctr. of Excellence for Deep Space Comm./Nav. Sys., 2000—. Bechtel instr. engring. Calif. Inst. Tech., Pasadena, 1972—74, lectr. in sys. engring., 1975—76, vis. asst. prof., 1976—78, vis. assoc. prof., 1978—84; cons. in field. Contbr. articles to profl. jours. Bd. dirs. Boys Republic, Chino Hills, Calif., 1991, 1997—. Fellow: AIAA (assoc.; tech. com .astrodynamics 1985—86, chmn. 1986—88, assoc. editor Jour. Guidance, Control and Dynamics 1983—89); mem.: AAAS, IEEE (sr.), Am. Astro. Soc. (sr.; space flight mechanics com. 1980—97, chmn. 1993—95, assoc. editor Jour. Astro. Scis. 1980—83, gen. chmn. AAS/AIAA Space Flight Mechanics Meeting 1993), Los Solteros (pres. 1991, 1997—), Sigma Xi. Office: Jet Propulsion Lab 4800 Oak Grove Drive Mail Stop 301-125L Pasadena CA 91109 E-mail: Lincoln.J.Wood@jpl.nasa.gov.

WOOD, LINDA MAY, librarian; b. Ft. Dodge, Iowa, Nov. 6, 1942; d. John Albert and Beth Ida (Riggs) Wiley; m. C. James Wood, Sept. 15, 1964 (div. Oct. 1984). BA, Portland State U., 1964; M in Librarianship, U. Wash., 1965. Reference libr. Multnomah county Libr., Portland, Oreg., 1965-67, br. libr., 1967-72, adminstrv. asst. to libr., 1972-73, asst. libr., asst. dir., 1973-77; asst. city libr. L.A. Pub. Libr., 1977-80; libr. dir. Riverside (Calif.) City and County Pub. Libr., 1980-91; county libr. Alameda County Libr., Fremont, Calif., 1991—. Adminstrv. coun. mem. Bay Area Libr. and Info. Svcs., Oakland, Calif., 1991—. Chair combined charities campaign County of Alameda, Oakland, Calif., 1992; bd. dirs. Inland AIDS project, Riverside, Calif., 1990-91; vol. United Way of Inland Valleys, Riverside, 1986-87, Bicentennial Competition on the Constitution, 36th Congl. Dist., Colton, Calif., 1988-90. Mem. ALA (CLA chpt. councilor 1992-95), Calif. Libr. Assn. (pres. 1985, exec. com., ALA chpt. councilor 1992-95), Calif. County Librs. Assn. (pres. 1984), League of Calif. Cities (cmty. svcs. policy com. 1985-90), OCLC Users Coun. (Pacific Network del. 1986-89). Democrat. Avocations: folk dancing, opera, reading. Office: Alameda County Libr 2450 Stevenson Blvd Fremont CA 94538-2326

WOOD, MARCIA J. human resources executive; b. Montego Bay, Jamaica; BA, NYU, 1995; MA, Columbia U., 1996. With Cunard Line, N.Y.C., 1984-85, sales rep., 1985-89, adminstrv. asst., 1989-91, asst. to sr. v.p. sales, 1991-96; human resources mgr. County Seat Stores, Inc., 1997—. Adj. prof. bus. mgmt., travel and tourism CUNY, N.Y., 1997—. Mem. Fundraising Com. for Econ. Redevel. of Jamaica; mem. adv. bd. bus. mgmt. dept. Borough of Manhattan C.C., 1992. Etta Kallman scholar, 1994. Mem. Phi Theta Kappa, Soc. Human Resource Mgmt., Soc. Industrial Organizational Psychology. Avocations: research, reading, fundraising. Home: 160 Belmont Ave Elmont NY 11003-2948

WOOD, MARCUS ANDREW, lawyer; b. Mobile, Ala., Jan. 18, 1947; s. George Franklin and Helen Eugenia (Fletcher) W.; m. Sandra Lee Pellonari, July 25, 1971; children: Edward Alan, Melinda Janel. BA cum laude, Vanderbilt U., 1969; JD, Yale U., 1974. Bar: Oreg. 1974, U.S. Dist. Ct. Oreg. 1974, U.S. Ct. Appeals (9th cir.) 1982. Assoc., then ptnr. Rives, Bonihadi & Smith, Portland, Oreg., 1974-78; ptnr. Stoel Rives LLP and predecessor firms, 1974—. Pres., bd. dirs. Indochinese Refugee Ctr., Portland, 1980, Pacific Ballet Theatre, Portland, 1986-87; bd. dirs. Outside In, Portland, 1989—. Lt. USNR, 1969-71. Mem. ABA, Phi Beta Kappa. Home: 9300 NW Finzer Ct Portland OR 97229-8035 Office: Stoel Rives 900 SW 5th Ave Ste 2300 Portland OR 97204-1229

WOOD, MARIAN STARR, publishing company executive; b. N.Y.C., Mar. 30, 1938; d. Edward James and Betty (Starr) Markow; m. Anthony Stuart Wood, Mar. 21, 1963 BA, Barnard Coll., 1959; postgrad., Columbia U., 1959-64. Teaching asst., lectr. Columbia U., N.Y.C., 1960-64; editor Praeger Pubs., 1965-71; sr. editor Henry Holt & Co., 1972-81, exec. editor, 1981-96; assoc. pub. Marian Wood Books, 1996-99; v.p. Marian Wood Books at G.P. Putnam's Sons, 1999—. Recipient Roger Klein Found. award career achievement, 2001.

WOOD, MARY ELLEN, nurse; b. Winchester, Mass., Dec. 12, 1957; d. Neil Terrence and Eleanor Claire (Kearns) Flathers; m. Bruce Benton, Aug. 8, 1987; children: Kelly Anne, Matthew Thomas. BS, U. N.H., 1979; MS, Boston U., 1985. RN, N.H., Bd. cert. advanced diabetes mgr. Staff nurse New Eng. Bapt. Hosp., Boston, 1979-82, The Children's Hosp., Boston, 1982-85; diabetes and rheumatology nurse coord. Dartmouth-Hitchcock Med. Ctr., Hanover, NH, 1985-89, diabetes clin. nurse specialist, 1989—, bd. cert. advanced diabetes mgr., 2002—. Mem. instnl. rev. bd. Dartmouth Med. Sch., Hanover, 1994-97; mem. N.H. Diabetes Adv. Group, Concord, N.H., 1996—. Author (chpt. in book) Mosby's Manual of Emergency Care, 1995; contbr. articles to profl. jours. Founder, chair Camp Dartmouth Hitchcock Adv. Coun. , Lebanon, 1991—97. Recipient Outstanding Alumni Recognition award, U. N.H., Dept. Nursing, 1995. Mem. Am. Diabetes Assn. (sec. N.H. affiliate 1987-89, Health Profl. of Yr. 1987), N.H. Assn Diabetes Educators (treas. 1989-91, pres. 1997-98, Diabetes Educator of Yr. 1999). Avocations: skiing, hiking, needlecrafts, gardening, travel. Office: Dartmouth-Hitchcock Med Ctr 1 Medical Center Dr Lebanon NH 03756-0002 E-mail: mary.e.wood@hitchcock.org.

WOOD, MAURICE, medical educator; b. Pelton, Eng., June 28, 1922; came to U.S., 1971; s. Joseph and Eugenie (Lumley) W.; m. Erica Joan Noble, May 1, 1948; children: Roger Lumley, Ashley Michael, Frances Jane. MB BS, U. Durham, Eng., 1945. Diplomate Am. Bd. Family Practice. Sr. ptnr. med. practice South Shields County, Durham, 1950-71; gen. practice teaching group U. Newcastle, Newcastle-on-Tyne, Eng., 1969-71; gen. clin. asst. dept. psychology-medicine South Shields Gen. Hosp., 1966-71; assoc. prof., dir. rsch. in family practice Med. Coll. Va.-Va. Commonwealth U., Richmond, 1971-73, prof., dir. rsch. in family practice, 1973-87, prof. emeritus, 1987—. Cons. advisor WHO, Geneva, 1979-90, chmn. working party to develop a classification for primary care, 1979-90; founding mem. exec. dir. N.Am. Primary Care Rsch. Group, Richmond, 1983-92, past pres., pres. emeritus, 1993—; chmn. com. on cmty. oriented primary care Insts. of Medicine, 1982-84. Assoc. editor Jour. Family Practice, 1976-83. Recipient award for meritorious svc. Va. Acad. Family Physicians, 1976; Maurice Wood award for career achievement in primary care rsch. founded in his honor, 1995. Fellow Royal Coll. Gen. Practitioners, Am. Acad. Family Physicians; mem. Inst. Medicine-Nat. Acad. Sci., Soc. Tchrs. Family Medicine (Curtis Hames Career Research award 1984), Inst. of Medicine, NAS, Ambulatory Sentinel Practice Network, Internat. Primary Care Network (treas., bd. dirs.), N.Am. Primary Care Rsch. Group (treas., bd. dirs., exec. dir., 1982-92). Lodges: Rotary. Episcopalian. Home and Office: RR 1 Box 672 Roseland VA 22967-9209 E-mail: wood150w@aol.com.

WOOD, MICHAEL B. CEO, president; Grad., McGill U. CEO, pres. Mayo Found. , 2002—; vice-chair bd. of gov. Mayo Regional Health Sys. , Rochester, Minn.; orthopedic surgeon Mayo Med. Sch., prof. of orthopedics; residency Mayo Grad. Sch. of Medicine; fellowship microvascular surgery, hand surgery U. Louisville. Pres. of bd. Malcolm Baldrige Nat. Quality Award Found., 2000; mem. Coalition Nonprofit Health Care. Mem.: Soc. of Med. Adminstrn., Minn. Med. Assn., Am. Med. Assn., Am. Soc. Reconstructive Microsurgery (pres. 1990—91). Office: Mayo Clinic Found 200 First St SW Rochester MN 55905*

WOOD, MICHAEL BRUCE, orthopaedic surgeon, researcher, educator; b. Glasgow, Mont., Oct. 7, 1943; s. Benjamin Joseph and LaVaun Adele (Gray) W.; m. Mary Elizabeth Magnotto, June 17, 1967; children: Michael S., Hadley M., Benjamin D., Luke E. BA in Chemistry, Franklin and Marshall Coll., 1965; MD CM, McGill U., 1969; MS in Orthopedic Surgery, U. Minn., 1974. Diplomate Am. Bd. Orthopedic Surgery, Sub-bd. Hand Surgery. Asst. prof. Med. Coll. Ohio, Toledo, 1977-79; from asst. prof. to prof. orthopedic surgery Mayo Med. Sch., Rochester, Minn., 1979—. Cons. orthopedic surgery Mayo Clinic, Rochester, 1979—. Author: Atlas of Microsurgery, 1990, Vascularized Bone, 1996; co-editor: Jour. of Microsurgery, 1986-92; dep. editor Jour. Bone and Joint Surgery, 1996, assoc. editor, 1989-94. Trustee Mayo Found., Rochester, 1995—, chair exec. com., 1998—, pres., CEO, 1999—; bd. govs. Mayo Clinic, 1993-98. Maj. U.S. Army, 1974-79, Germany. NIH grantee, 1987-97; Bunnell fellow, 1986-87. Fellow Am. Assn. Orthopedic Surgery, Am. Orthopedic Assn., Am. Soc. Surgery of Hand, Am. Soc. for Reconstructive Microsurgery, Internat. Soc. for Reconstructive Microsurgery, Orthopedic Rsch. Soc., Sigma Xi. Office: Mayo Clinic 200 1st St SW Rochester MN 55905-0002

WOOD, MICHAEL G. science educator, educator; b. St. George, Bermuda, May 26, 1959; s. Ernest M. and Janis G. Wood; m. Wood Laurie E., July 21, 1990; children: Abi W. Gengenbach, Eliabeth M. BS Biology, U. Tex., 1982, MS Biology, 1986. Author: (novels) Laboratory Text and Study Guide for Essentials of Anatomy and Physiology, 1997, Laboratory Textbook of Anatomy and Physiology, 2001. Pres. bd. dirs. Montessori Sch. Corpus Christi, Corpus Christi, Tex., 1999. Recipient Educator of Yr. award, Koch Industries, 1999. Avocations: guitar, camping.

WOOD, MICHAEL K. English educator, writer; b. Providence, Feb. 15, 1966; s. Irving and Esther Ann Wood. BA, U. R.I., 1988; MFA, Goddard Coll., 2000. Ramp tng. instr. Airport Terminal Svcs., Warwick, R.I., 1990—; instr. English C.C. R.I., 2000—; instr., acad. coord. Travler's Aid Soc., Providence, 2001. Editor (pub.): Hunted News, 1990—, Suburban Press, —; editor: (poems) The Moral ool, 1993—; author: I'm So Sick of What I Need, 1997—, (memoir) God Was Too Small, 2000—, (novels) The Hunted News, 2002. Roman Catholic. Avocations: music, writing. Home: 26 Blackstone Blvd #6 Providence RI 02906 Office: Subourbon Press PO Box 9101 Warwick RI 02889

WOOD, MYRA LINDEN FRANK, consultant; b. Richmond, Va., Oct. 26, 1950; d. J. C. and Myra Teresa (Lanzarone) Frank; m. Timothy Franklin Long (div. Jan. 1981); m. Robert Andrew Hudson (div. 1994); m. Frederick W. Wood, Sept. 25, 1999. BA, Erskine Coll., 1972; student, Inst. Fin. Edn., 1982-88. Chief activities therapist S.C. Dept. Corrections, Columbia, 1973-75, acting prin., 1975-77, coll. coord., 1977-78; owner, operator Carolina Coast Seafood, Aiken and Beaufort, S.C., 1978-80; from teller to savs. counselor Security Fed. Savs. & Loan, Aiken, 1981-83; customer svc. rep. Bankers 1st Savs. & Loans, Augusta, Ga., 1983-84, mgr. br. adminstrn., 1984-85; coord. automated teller machines, banking officer 1st Fed. Savs. Bank, Brunswick, 1985-88; ptnr., cons. electronic banking/software devel. RAH Systems, 1988-93; ptnr. specific application computer programming, software tng. Details & More, Greenville, S.C., 1989-90, ptnr. event planning, various mfg. positions and mktg./sales, 1989-91; cons. office and computer svcs. Mauldin, 1992-93. Lectr. S.C. Edn. Tchrs. Assn., Columbia, 1974, S.C. Assn. Social Workers , Columbia, 1975, Bus. and Profl. Women's Club, Columbia, 1978; small bus. owner, distbr. Nuskin product line, 1987—90; ind. mktg. rep. Network 2000/U.S. Spring, 1988—92; computer specialist Top Food Svcs. Carolina, Inc., Duncan, SC, 1989—90; admintrv./sales mgr. Cusom Catering, Duncan, 1990; cons. Contract Office/Computer Svcs., Greenville, 1992—; Shaklee ind. distbr., 1998—; dir., sec.-treas., CFO FMW Holdings, Inc., 2000—. Book rev. writer A Class Act, Greenville, 1996—; appeared with Aiken Cmty. Theatre, 1981. Bd. dirs. Quest Soc., Greenville, 1992-95; mem. hospice com. Am. Cancer Soc., Augusta, 1981; lectr. St. John's United Meth. Ch., 1981-82, A Class Act, 1998; registrar, treas. Sugar Creek Soccer Club, Greenville, 1996-97. Mem. A Creative Gathering Writers Group, Writer's Roundtable. Democrat. Avocations: writing, reading, travel, study/research exploring the internet. Home and Office: PO Box 333 Mauldin SC 29662-0333 E-mail: cobfrank@charter.net.

WOOD, NEIL RODERICK, real estate development company executive; b. Winnipeg, Man., Can., Aug. 22, 1931; s. Reginald and Pearl (Beake) W.; m. Jean Mitchell Hume, Aug. 10, 1957 (div.); children: Barbara, David, John, Brian. B.Com., U. Man., 1952; MBA, Harvard U., 1955. Asst. mgr. Ont. real estate investment office Gt. West Life Assurance Co., 1955-59; with Cadillac Fairview Corp. Ltd. (and predecessor), Willowdale, Ont., 1959-61, 63-81, exec. v.p., 1968-71, pres., 1971-81, vice chmn., 1980-81; pres. N.R. Wood Devel. Co. Ltd., 1982—; exec. v.p., dir. Campeau Corp., 1985-86; pres., CEO, dir. Markborough Properties Inc., 1986-95. Bd. dirs. Dorsay Devel. Corp.; past pres., trustee Internat. Coun. of Shopping Ctrs. Mem. Toronto Club, Rosedale Golf Club, Craigleith Ski Club, Beaumaris Club, Lost Tree Club, Loxahatchee Golf Club, Beacon Hall Club. Home and Office: RR # 3 Newmarket ON Canada L3Y 4W1

WOOD, NORMA J. nurse practitioner; b. R.I., Dec. 29, 1952; d. Marvin H. and Gertrude E. (Feather) Gentry; m. Charles Burrell Wood, Jr., Feb. 21, 1971; children: Holly Jean, John Russell. ADN magna cum laude, Coll. of the Albemarle, 1977; BSN magna cum laude, U. South Fla., 1985, MSN magna cum laude, 1987. Cert. in adult health ANA. Instr. nursing St. Petersburg (Fla.) Jr. Coll., 1987; nurse practitioner Humana Health Care Plans, St. Petersburg, 1987, Gateway Family Practice, St. Petersburg, 1988-90; instr. nursing U. Tampa, Fla., 1990-91; nurse practitioner VA Med. Facility, Bay Pines, 1990—. Adj. faculty So. Adventist U., 1996—. Contbr. articles to profl. jours. Grad. Coun. fellow Kellogg Found.

WOOD, OLIVER GILLAN, JR. economist, educator; b. Greer, S.C., Apr. 27, 1937; s. Oliver Gillan and Grace (McBrayer) W.; m. Jean Collier Wood; children: Brian Jay, Joseph Corey, Andrew Oliver. BBA, U. S.C., 1958, MA in Econs., 1963; PhD, U. Fla., 1965. Asst. prof. banking and fin. U. S.C., Columbia, 1965-68, assoc. prof. banking and fin., 1968-73, prof. banking and fin., 1973-94; disting. prof. emeritus, 1994—. Chmn. U. S.C. Press com. 1981-94. Author: Commercial Banking, 1978, (with others) Analysis of Bank Financial Statements, 1979, Introduction to Money and Banking, 1980, (with others) How to Borrow Money, 1981. Bd. dirs., founder Republic Nat. Bank, Columbia, 1975-87, Edisto Farm Credit ACA, 1990—; adv. bd. Lexington State Bank, 1990-94, BB&T Fin. Corp., 1994—. Mem. Am. Econs. Assn., Am. Fin. Assn., Fin. Mgmt. Assn., Beta Gamma Sigma (pres. 1972). Avocations: farming, golf. Home: 121 Running Fox Rd Columbia SC 29223-3020 Office: PO Box 24677 Columbia SC 29224-4677

WOOD, PATRICK HENRY, III, federal agency administrator; b. Tex. Grad., Tex. A&M U. With Baker & Botts, Washington; engr. Arco Indonesia; legal counsel to chmn. Tex. Railroad Commn.; staff mem. Fed. Energy Regulatory Commn., 1991—93; chmn. Pub. Utility Commn. Tex.; chmn. Fed. Energy Regulatory Commn. U.S. Dept. Energy, Washington, 2001—. Office: US Dept Energy 888 1st St NE Washington DC 20426-4205*

WOOD, PAUL NIGEL, film and television engineer; b. Suva, Fiji, Mar. 27, 1955; came to U.S., 1960; naturalized, 1996; s. John Leslie Stansfield and Dorothy Myrtle (Douglass) W.; m. Paulette Ramsay, Oct. 22, 1995. Student, Pasadena City Coll., 1973-75, Loyola Marymount U., Los Angeles, 1975-76. Mgr. videotape Superior Video Services, North Hollywood, Calif., 1975-76; senior engr. Bell and Howell video div., Newport Beach, 1976-80; chief engr. BDS Videoproduktion, Hamburg, Fed. Republic Germany, 1980-83; dir. engring. Howard A. Anderson Co., L.A., Calif., 1984-90, Sony Pictures Studios, Culver City, 1990—. Mem. Acad. TV Arts and Scis., Soc. Motion Picture and TV Engrs., Soc. TV Engrs. Office: Sony Pictures Post Prodn Svcs 10202 Washington Blvd Culver City CA 90232-3195

WOOD, PAUL WILLIAM, language educator, educator; b. Cin., Mar. 24, 1933; s. Walter John and Marie Sophie (Lott) W.; m. Mary Lou Donovan, Aug. 20, 1960; children: Paul Jr., Suzanne, Douglas, Rebecca. BA, Athenaeum of Ohio, Cin., 1954; MA, U. Cin., 1960; PhD, Northwestern U., 1970. Tchr. Forest Hills Sch. Dist., Cin., 1960-62; instr. Loyola U., Chgo., 1962-67; asst. prof. U. Akron, Ohio, 1967-71; prof. dept. modern lang. St. Bonaventure U., Olean, N.Y., 1971—. Participant Project Rendez-Vous, Ministry Affaires Etrangeres, Paris, 1985; mem. 2d Lang. Acquisition Coun., Buffalo, 1985-89; symposium leader Heidelberg (Germany) U., 1986; fgn. lang. program evaluator Commonwealth of Pa., Edinboro, 1987. Editor: Creating an Environment for Second Language Learning, 1987; contbr. to profl. publs. Pres. Friends of Libr., Olean, 1985-88; chmn. selection com. Big Thirty Acad. Scholarship, Olean, 1990; bd. dirs. Cattaraugus County Coun. on Alcoholism and Substance Abuse, Inc., 1993-2000. With U.S. Army, 1955-57, Korea. Named grand knight Olean Coun. 338, 1988-2000, faithfull navigator, 2000—. Mem. N.Y. State Assn. Fgn. Lang. Tchrs. (v.p. 1983-85, 93—, pres. 1985-86, Ferdinand D. Bartholo Disting. Leadership award 1985), Western N.Y. Fgn. Lang. Educators' Coun. (pres. 1978-80), Coll. Consortium Internat. Study (del. 1984-93), N.Y. State Coun. on Langs. (pres. 1986-88), Pi Delta Phi (v.p. 1991-97, pres. 1998—). Roman Catholic. Office: St Bonaventure U Box BQ Saint Bonaventure NY 14778 E-mail: pwood@sbu.edu.

WOOD, PRISCILLA LOUISE, property manager; b. Washington, Sept. 3, 1940; d. Thaddeus Francis and Leonise Ruth Aubry; m. Frank Tucker Wood, July 6, 1963; children: Elise Monette, Christopher Tucker. BS in Edn., Oswego State U., 1962; MS in Edn., Keane U., 1980. Jr. high sch. tchr., Plainfield, NJ, 1966—79; chmn. dept. English, 1968—79; program coord. Pakistan Am. Ctr., Karachi, 1981—83; asst. property mgr. Brooks, Torrey & Scott, Inc., Westport, Conn., 1985—, v.p. Norwalk, 1997—. Dfl. Roman Catholic. Avocation: writing. Office: Brooks Torrey & Scott Inc 542 Westport Ave 2d Fl Norwalk CT 06851 Office Fax: 203-840-4848.

WOOD, QUENTIN EUGENE, oil company executive; b. Mechanicsburg, Pa., Mar. 5, 1923; s. Lloyd Paul and Greta (Myers) W.; m. Louise Lowe, Apr. 14, 1958. BS, Pa. State U., 1948. Petroleum engr. Quaker State Oil Refining Corp., Parkersburg, W.Va., 1948-52, chief engr. Bradford, Pa., 1952-55, mgr. prodn., 1955-68, v.p. prodn. Pa., 1968-70, exec. v.p., 1970-73, pres., chief ops. officer, 1973-75, pres., chief exec. officer, 1975-82, chmn., chief executive officer, 1982-88, chmn. bd., 1988-90, dir., 1990-93. Bd. dirs. Pa. Mfrs. Ins. Co.; chmn. industry tech. adv. com. U.S. Bur. Mines, 1960-70, Penn Grade Tech. Adv. Com., 1955-69, Pa. Oil and Gas Conservation Commn., 1961-71. Trustee Pa. State U., 1976-94, pres., 1979-87. 1st lt. USAAF, 1943-46. Mem. Am. Inst. Metall. Engrs., Pa. Grade Crude Oil Assn. (dir.), Pa. Oil Producers Assn. (past pres., dir. Bradford dist.), Am. Petroleum Inst. (dir.), Nat. Petroleum Refiners Assn. (dir.). Home: 1402 Spinnakers Reach Dr Ponte Vedra Beach FL 32082

WOOD, R. STEWART, JR. retired bishop; b. Detroit, June 25, 1934; s. Raymond and Marjorie Wood; m. Kristin Lie Miller, June 25, 1955; children: Lisa, Raymond, Michael. AB, Dartmouth Coll., 1956; MDiv, Va. Theol. Seminary, 1969; MA in Counseling and Sociology, Ball State U., 1973; postgrad., Va. Seminary. Ordained to diaconate and priesthood Episc. Ch., 1959. Vicar Episc. Ch., Seymour and Bean Blossom, Ind.; assoc. rector Grace Ch., Muncie, rector, 1966-70; exec. dir. Episc. Community Svcs., Indpls., 1970-76; rector All Saint's Episc. Ch., Christ Ch., Glendale, Ohio, 1976—84, St. John's Ch., Memphis, 1984—88; elected Bishop Coadjutor Diocese Mich., Detroit, 1988-89, diocesan bishop, 1990-2000; ret., 2000. Dir. summer camps, conf. ctr.; dep. Gen. Conv. 1970, 73, 76, 82; exec. coun. Coalition for Ordination of Women, bd. dirs. Avocations: camping, golf, tennis, photography. Office: Box 968 255 Robert Frost Ln Quechee VT 05059-0968

WOOD, RICHARD COURTNEY, library director, educator; b. Spartanburg, S.C., Aug. 8, 1943; s. Herman Alva and Mildred Eloise (Porter) W.; m. Amy Louise Black, Aug. 16, 1974. BA, U. Tex., 1966; MLS, U. S.C., 1977. Head cataloging Wofford Coll. Libr., Spartanburg, 1969-78; hosp. libr. John Peter Smith Hosp., Ft. Worth, 1978-80; reference libr. Tex. Coll. Osteo. Medicine, 1980-82, assoc. dir. libr., 1982-91; dir. librs., assoc. prof. Sch. Medicine, chair HCOM dept. Tex. Tech U. Health Scis. Ctr., Lubbock, 1991—. Cons. Tarrant County Med. Libr. Assn., Fort Worth, 1978-82, 84, Med. Plaza Hosp., Fort Worth, 1979-82, Grand Prairie (Tex.) Community Hosp., 1980-81, Cook-Fort Worth Children's Hosp., 1988-91. Patron Kimball Art Mus. Fort Worth, 1987—; spokesman Neighborhood Assn., Fort Worth, 1989; vis. exec. United Way, Fort Worth, 1990. Recipient Dean's award Sch. Nursing, Tex. Tech U. Health Sci. Ctr., 1998. Mem. Dallas-Tarrant County Consortium (chmn. 1980-81), Metroplex Consortium Health Scis. (chmn. 1980-81), South Cen. Regional Group, Med. Libr. Assn. (chmn. osteo. librs. sect. 1986-87), South Cen. Acad. Med. Librs. (bd. dirs. 1991—, past chair), Nat. Network Librs. Medicine (bd. dirs. South Cen. region 1991-93), Deutsche Gesellschaft für Heereskunde, LIS Users Group (chair exec. bd.), Sigma Tau Delta. Republican. Presbyterian. Avocations: languages, travel, history, gardening, music. Home: 1805 Bangor Ave Lubbock TX 79416-5518 Office: Preston Smith Libr Health Scis 3601 4th St Lubbock TX 79430-0001 E-mail: hldir@ttacs.ttu.edu.

WOOD, RICHARD D. research scientist, educator; b. Boulder, Colo., June 3, 1955; s. Robert Dean and Maxine Louise W.; m. Enid Alison Vaag, Oct. 31, 1975. BS, Westminster Coll., 1977; PhD, U. Calif., Berkeley, 1981. Postdoctoral assoc. Yale U., New Haven, 1982-85; rsch. fellow Imperial Cancer Rsch. Fund, South Mimms Hertfordshire, England, 1985-92, sr. scientist England, 1992-95, prin. scientist England, 1995—2001; Richard Cyert prof. molecular and cellular oncology U. Pitts. Cancer Inst., 2001—. Trustee Marie Curie Cancer Care, London, 1999-2000; hon. prof. U. London, 1996-2001. Recipient Meyenburg prize for cancer rsch. German Cancer Ctr. 1998; named disting. alumnus Westminster Coll., 1999. Fellow Royal Soc.; mem. AAAS, European Molecular Biology Orgn. Avocations: playing bass, jazz music, cycling. Office: U Pitts Cancer Inst 5117 Centre Ave Pittsburgh PA 15232

WOOD, RICHARD HARVEY, JR. economics educator; b. Phila., Dec. 12, 1938; s. Richard Harvey and Frances (Manning) W.; m. Maria Graciela Jave, Aug. 17, 1968; 1 child, Maria Frances. B.A. in Geography, Antioch Coll., 1963; M.A. in Agrl. Econs., U. Wis., 1965, Ph.D. in Econs., 1972. Asst. prof. econs. U. Portland, Oreg., 1968-70; from asst. prof. to assoc. prof. econs. Stetson U., DeLand, Fla., 1970—; Fulbright lectr., Monterrey, Mex., 1978-79. Pres. bd. dirs. Sugar 'N Spice Day Care Ctr., DeLand, 1984-85, Wesley House, DeLand, 1984-85 . Land Tenure Ctr. fellow U. Wis., Madison, 1963-65. Mem. Am. Econ. Assn., Latin Am. Studies Assn. Democrat. Avocations: tennis; canoeing; hiking; running; camping. Home: 495 Oakridge Ave Deland FL 32724-2463 Office: Stetson U PO Box 8322 Deland FL 32720

WOOD, RICHARD ROBINSON, real estate executive; b. Salem, Mass., Nov. 8, 1922; s. Reginald and Irene Margaret (Robinson) W.; m. Pamela Vander Wiele, Mar. 8, 1951 (div. Apr. 1969); children: Christopher Robinson, Bryant Cornelius, Marcella Wood Mackenzie; m. Jane Philbin, Sept. 19, 1970. AB, Harvard Coll., 1944; postgrad., Mass. Inst. Tech., 1947-48. V.p. Hunneman & Co., Boston, 1959-72; trustee, sec. Mass. Real Estate Investment Trust, 1967-69; trustee Suffolk Franklin Savings Bank, 1967-74; pres., chmn. Continential Real Estate Equity, Boston, 1972-74; exec. v.p. ITEL Real Estate Corp., San Francisco, 1974-75; v.p. Baird & Warner, Chgo., 1976-80; pres., chmn. Renwood Properties, Inc., Peabody, Mass., 1981—. Founder Real Estate Securities 2d Syndication Inst., 1972, pres., 1976-78; v.p., dir. Common Goal Capitol Group, Balt., 1986—; gen. ptnr. Common Goal Mortgage Fund, Balt., 1986—; v.p., bd. dirs. St. Katherines Care Ctrs., 1990—; pres., chmn. ILCO Properties, Chgo., 1981-87; mem. Coun. for Rural Housing and Devel., 1988—; chmn. 19 Chauncy St. Trust, 1995—, Inst. for Responsible Housing Preservation, 1994-99. Mem. Mayor's Citizen Adv. Bd., Boston, 1965-67; pres. Boston Rep. city Com., 1965-67; committeeman, treas. Mass. Rep. State Com., Boston, 1964-72; mem. Coun. for Rural Housing and Devel., 1988—. With Med. Corps U.S. Army, 1943-44. Mem. Nat. Leased Housing Assn., Harvard Club Boston, Longwood Cricket Club, Harvard Club of N.Y., Badminton and Tennis Club, White Mountain Ski Runners. Avocations: tennis, skiing. Home: 19 Chauncy St Cambridge MA 02138-2549 Office: Renwood Properties Inc 875 Massachusetts Ave Cambridge MA 02139-3067 E-mail: renwoodprops@aol.com.

WOOD, ROBERT "BRYAN", music educator; b. Kingsport, Tenn., Apr. 8, 1976; s. Robert and Rita Wood. B in Music Edn., Ea. Tenn. State U., 2000. Lic. tchr. Tenn. Instr. area high schs., Tenn., 1996—2000; band dir. Vol. H.S., Church Hill, 2000—. Marching band instr. area high schs., 1996—99. Mem.: TMEA, MENC. Home: 2003 Timbers Edge Ct Kingsport TN 37660 Office: Volunteer High School Band PO Box 247 Church Hill TN 37642 Home Fax: 423-357-6694; Office Fax: 423-288-3223. Personal E-mail: bwood1@chartertn.net. Business E-Mail: bwood1@chartertn.net.

WOOD, ROBERT CHARLES, lawyer, real estate developer; b. Chgo., Apr. 8, 1956; s. Roy Edward and Mildred Lucille (Jones) W.; m. Jennifer Jo Briggs, Oct. 1984; children: Jacqueline Jones, Reagan Keith. BA in History, BBA in Real Estate, So. Meth. U., 1979, JD, 1982. Bar: Tex. 1983. Appraiser McClellan-Massey, Dallas, 1977-79; researcher, acquisitions officer Amstar Fin. Corp., 1979-80; prin. Robert Wood Cons., 1981-98; ptnr. Welch & Wood Attys. and Y2K Cons., 1998-2000; pvt. practice, 1995—; real estate investor and developer, 1998—. Cons. Plan Mktg. Cos., 1983-84; pvt. practice law, Dallas, 1983-84; gen. counsel Diversified Benefits, Inc., Dallas, 1984-86; nat. accts. mgr. Lomas & Nettleton Real Estate Group, Dallas, 1987-88; sr. pension cons., prin. Eppler, Guerin &Turner, 1988-93; chmn. adv. coun. on devel. Medisend, 1991; nat. consulting coord. fin. advisors coun., v.p. Callan Assocs., San Francisco, 1994-95; atty. at law, 1995—; exec. v.p., gen. counsel, Rushmore Investment Advisors, Plano, Tex., 2002-. Author: Electionomics: How the Money Managers View the Election, 1992, After the Congress Vote: How the Managers See Things Now, 1993, Y2K--The Year 2000 Issue: How Y2K Affects the Markets, 1998; mem. So. Meth. U. Law Rev., 1981-82; contbr. articles to profl. publs. Bd. dirs. Dallas unit Am. Cancer Soc., 1982-87, mem. spl. events com., 1986-87, mem. crusade com., 1987-88, mem. medisend adv. com., 1988-94, chmn. corp. devel. bd., 1989-95. Mem. Tex. Bar Assn., Phila. Bar Assn., Phi Gamma Delta. Avocations: skiing, tennis, bicycling. E-mail: rccwood@aol.com.

WOOD, ROBERT COLDWELL, political scientist; b. St. Louis, Sept. 16, 1923; s. Thomas Frank and Mary (Bradshaw) W.; m. Margaret Byers, Mar. 22, 1952; children— Frances, Margaret, Frank Randolph. AB, Princeton U., 1946; MA, Harvard U., 1947, MPA, 1948, PhD, 1950; LLD or DHL (hon.), St. Bonaventure Coll., U. Pitts., 1965, Bklyn. Poly. Inst., 1966, Princeton U., 1969, Rhode Island Coll., U. Mass., 1970, Worcester Poly. Inst., 1971, U. Maine, 1972, Hokkaido U., Japan, 1975, North Adams Coll., 1977, Boston U., 1978, Stonehill Coll., 1979. Assoc. dir. Fla. Legis. Reference Bur., Tallahassee, 1949-51; mgmt. orgn. expert U.S. Bur. Budget, Washington, 1951-54; lectr. govt. Harvard U., 1953-54, asst. prof., 1954-57; asst. prof. polit. sci. MIT, 1957-59, assoc. prof., 1959-62, prof., 1962-66, head dept., 1965-66, 69-70; undersec. HUD, Washington, 1966-68, sec., 1969; chmn. Mass. Bay Transp. Authority, Boston, 1969-70; dir. Harvard U.-MIT Joint Center for Urban Studies, Cambridge, 1969-70; pres. U. Mass., 1970-77; supt. Boston Public Schs., 1978-80; prof. U. Mass., Boston, 1981-83; Henry Luce prof. Dem. Instns. and the Social Order Wesleyan U., Middletown, Conn., 1983-93, John E. Andrus prof. govt., 1993; prof. emeritus U. Mass., Boston, 1994—. Sr. fellow McCormack Inst. Pub. Affairs, U. Mass., Boston, vis. prof. U. Mass., 1998—. Author: Suburbia, Its People and Their Politics, 1958, Metropolis Against Itself, 1959, 1400 Governments, The Political Economy of the New York Region, 1960, The Necessary Majority, Middle America and Urban Crisis, 1972, Whatever Possessed the President? Academic Experts and Presidential Policy, 1960-88, 1993; (with others) Schoolmen and Politics, 1962, Government and Politics of the U.S, 1965; author, editor: Eastward Ho: Options for Metropolitan Boston, 1997, Remedial Law: When Courts Become Administrators, 1990, Turnabout Time: New Choices for U/Mass, 1996. Trustee Coll. Bd., 1979-83, Kettering Found., 1971-76; mem. Commn. on Acad. Health Ctrs. and Economy New Eng.; bd. dirs. Lincoln Inst. Land Policy, 1976-80; chmn. Inst. for Resource Mgmt., 1982-84, 20th Century Task Force Fed. Ednl. Policy, 1983, Conn. Gov.'s Coalition on Adult Literacy, 1986-89; mem. Gov.'s Commn. on Quality and Integrated Edn., 1989-90. Served with inf. AUS, World War II, ETO. Decorated Bronze Star; recipient Hubert H. Humphrey award, 1985. Fellow Am. Acad. Arts and Scis., Am. Polit. Sci. Assn. (Career Achievment award 1989), Cosmos Club Washington, Phi Beta Kappa.

WOOD, ROBERT EMERSON, pediatrics educator; b. Jacksonville, Fla., Nov. 15, 1942; s. Waldo E. and Verda V. Wood. BS in Chemistry magna cum laude, Stetson U., 1963; PhD in Physiology, Vanderbilt U., 1968, MD, 1970. Bd. cert. pediatrics; bd. cert. pediatric pulmonology. Intern in pediatrics Duke U. Med. Ctr., Durham, 1970-71, resident in pediatrics, 1971-72; fellow pediatric pulmonology Case Western Res. U., Cleve., 1974-76, asst. prof. pediatrics, 1976-82, assoc. prof. pediatrics, 1982-83; assoc. prof. pediatrics, chief divsn. pediatric pulmonary medicine Dept. Pediatrics, U. N.C., Chapel Hill, 1983-88, prof. pediatrics, chief divsn. pediatric pulmonary medicine, 1988-94, dir. pediat. ICU, 1984-86, dir. Ctr. Pediat. Bronchology, 1994-99; prof. pediats. Children's Hosp. Med. Ctr., U. Cin., 1999—, chief, divsn. pulmonary medicine, 2001—. Mem. editorial bd.: Pediatric Pulmonology, 1992—, Jour. Bronchology, 1993—; contbr. chpts. to books and articles to profl. jours. Lt. comdr. USPHS, 1972-74. Named Grad. fellow Danforth Found., 1963-68, Med. Scientist fellow Life Ins. Med. Rsch. Found., 1965-70, Clin. Rsch. fellow Cystic Fibrosis Found., 1974-76. Mem. Am. Bronchesophagological Assn., Am. Assn. for Bronchology, Soc. for Pediatric Rsch., Am. Thoracic Soc., N.C. Pediatric Soc. Office: Children's Hosp Med Ctr Pediat Pulmonary Medicine 3333 Burnet Ave Cincinnati OH 45229-3026 Fax: 513-636-7734. E-mail: rewood@chmcc.org.

WOOD, ROBERT WARREN, lawyer; b. Des Moines, July 5, 1955; s. Merle Warren and Cecily Ann (Sherk) W.; m. Beatrice Wood, Aug. 4, 1979; 1 child, Bryce Mercedes. Student, U. Sheffield, Eng., 1975-76; AB, Humboldt State U., 1976; JD, U. Chgo., 1979. Bar: Ariz. 1979, Calif. 1980, Wyo. 2000, N.Y. 1989, D.C. 1993, Mont. 1998, U.S Tax Ct. 1980, Wyo.; Roll of Solicitors of Eng. and Wales, 1998. Assoc. Jennings, Strouss, Phoenix, 1979-80, McCutchen, Doyle, San Francisco, 1980-82, Broad, Khourie, San Francisco, 1982-85, Steefel, Levitt & Weiss, San Francisco, 1985-87, ptnr., 1987-91, Bancroft & McAlister, San Francisco, 1991-93; prin. Robert W. Wood, P.C., 1993—. Instr. in law U. Calif. San Francisco, 1981-82. *With over twenty years of domestic and international experience, Robert W. Wood is well known as a tax attorney specializing in taxation and mergers and acquisitions. The author of 28 tax books and over 1,000 articles, he represents entrepreneurs, U.S. and foreign investors, privately held companies and publicly traded entities. He regularly renders advice to companies and shareholders on the structuring and closing of taxable and tax-free acquisitions, and is routinely engaged by companies, law and accounting firms to provide specialized advice in this field. He also advises litigants and attorneys on the tax treatment of damage awards and settlement payments, an area in which he is a recognized U.S. authority.* Author: Taxation of Corporate Liquidations: A Complete Planning Guide, 1987, 2nd edit., 1994, The Executive's Complete Guide to Business Taxes, 1989, Corporate Taxation: Complete Planning and Practice Guide, 1989, S Corporations, 1990, The Ultimate Tax Planning Guide for Growing Companies, 1991, Taxation of Damage Awards and Settlement Payments, 1991, 2nd edit., 1998, Tax Strategies in Hiring, Retaining and Terminating Employees, 1991, The Home Office Tax Guide, 1991; co-author: (with others) California Closely Held Corporations: Tax Planning and Practice Guide, 1987, Legal Guide to Independent Contractor Status, 3d edit., 2000; editor: California Small Busines Guide, 4 vols., 1998, Home Office Money & Tax Guide, 1992, Tax Aspects of Settlements and Judgements, 1993, 2d edit., 1998, cumulative supplement, 2000; editor-in-chief The M & A Tax Report; editor: Limited Liability Companies: Formation, Operation and Conversion, 1994, 2d edit., 2001, Limited Liability Partnerships: Formation, Operation and Taxation, 1996; mem. editl. bd. Real Estate Tax Digest, The Practical Accountant, Jour. Real Estate Taxation. Fellow Am. Coll. Tax Counsel; mem. Calif. Bd. Legal Specialization (cert. specialist taxation), Can. Bar Assn., Bohemian Club, Law Coun. Australia. Republican. Office: 477 Pacific Ave # 300 San Francisco CA 94133-4614

WOOD, ROBIN, infectious diseases physician, researcher; b. Birmingham, England, Oct. 11, 1948; s. George and Joyce (Smith) W.; m. Nov. 10, 1979; children: Jonathan, Rebecca. BSc, London U., 1970; MB ChB, Oxford U., 1974; MD, U. Cape Town, 1990. Intern Radcliffe Infirmary, Oxford, England, 1974-76; gen. practitioner Lusaka, Zambia, 1979-85; resident U. Cape Town, South Africa, 1986-90; fellow in infectious diseases Stanford (Calif.) U., 1990-92; from head HIV clinic to head dept. medicine Somerset Hosp., Cape Town, 1993—. Assoc. prof. medicine U. Cape Town, 1999. Fellow South African Coll. Medicine, Royal Soc. Tropical Medicine; mem. AAAS, Infectious Diseases Soc. South Africa, N.Y. Acad. Sci. Avocations: sailing, squash, chess. Home: 2 Jewel Ct 5 Chepstow Rd Greenpoint Capetown 8001 South Africa Office: U Cape Town Dept Medicine 7925 Cape Town South Africa

WOOD, ROBIN D. food service executive, writer; b. Santa Monica, Calif., Dec. 14, 1973; d. Gene Raymond and Sherry Ann Wood; children: Alexander G., Haley H.

WOOD, SHELTON EUGENE, college educator, consultant, minister; b. Douglas, Ga., May 20, 1938; s. Shelton and Mae Lillie (Pheil) Wood; m. Edna Louise Wood, Aug. 25, 1961; children: Shelton John, Deirdre Louise. AA, St. John's U., 1958; BA, U. Nebr., 1959; MEd, Coll. William and Mary, 1971; PhD, Sussex U., 1973; EdD, Southeastern U., 1975; MBA, Ctrl. Mich. U., 1977; MA, U. Okla., 1980; D in Ministry, Wesleyan Bible Coll., 1999; Cert. in Internt. Rels., Fgn. Svc. Inst., 1971; Cert. in Mgmt., Indsl. Coll. Armed Forces, 1970. Area mgr. Marshall Fields Corp., Fla., 1957-58; transp. supr. Greyhound Corp., Jacksonville, 1959-62; officer U.S. Army, 1963, advanced through grades to infantry col., 1996; with Redstone Readiness Group, 1977-80; chief studies and analysis divsn. Korean Inst. for Def. Analysis, 1981-83; faculty St. John River C.C., 1984-90; nat. and internat. bus. and mgmt. cons., 1995—; sr. pastor Fellowship Wesleyan Ch., Spring Hill, Fla., 1998—. Mem. faculty Wesleyan Bible U., 1997—, dean Grad. Sch. Author: Strategic for Implementing A Family Life Ministry Center, 1997; contbr. over 120 articles and reports in field of mil. tng., edn., mgmt., pastoral studies, and practical theology. Active Boy Scouts Am., 1977—90; lay leader United Meth. Ch., Falls Church, Va., 1977—79, St. James United Meth. Ch., 1986—90; mem. dist. bd. ministerial devel. Fla. Dist. of Wesleyan Ch., 1999, chair evangelism and ch. growth com., 1999—. Decorated Bronze Star with 2 oak leaf clusters, Air medal with 3 oak leaf clusters, Purple Heart with 2 oak leaf clusters; Sussex Coll. fellow, 1969-70. Mem. NEA, Am. Soc. Trainers and Developers (pres. S.E. chpt. 1974-75), Am. Def. Preparedness Assn., Putnam County C. of C. (pres. 1990-91), Toastmasters Internat. (Disting. Toastmaster 1989), Kiwanis (pres. 1989-90), Phi Kappa Delta, Phi Delta Kappa. Address: 8485 Chatsworth St Spring Hill FL 34608

WOOD, STUART KEE, retired engineering manager; b. Dallas, Mar. 8, 1925; s. William Henry and Harriet (Kee) Wood; m. Loris V. Poock, May 17, 1951 (dec. June 1990); children: Linda S. Kuehl, Thomas N., Richard D.; m. Lois H. Morton, Nov. 25, 1994. BS in Aero. Engring., Tex. A&M U., 1949. Aircraft sheet metal worker USAF SAC, Kelly Field, San Antonio, 1942-45; structural design engr. B-52, 367-80, KC-135, 707 Airplanes Boeing, Seattle and Renton, Wash., 1949-55, thrust reverser design engr. 707 and 747 Airplanes Renton, 1955-66, supr. thrust reverser group 747 Airplane Everett, Wash., 1966-69; supr. rsch. basic engine noise 727 airplane FAA, NASA, 1969-74; supr. jetfoil propulsion Jetfoil Hydrofoil Boeing, Renton, 1974-75; supr. rsch. basic engine performance loss JT9D Pratt & Whitney, 1975-79; supr. propulsion systems 757 Airplane Boeing, Renton, 1979-90, supr., propulsion systems thrust reverser 737, 747, 757, 767 Kent, Wash., 1990-94, ret., 1994. Patentee in field. Recipient Ed Wells award AIAA, N.W. chpt., Bellevue, Wash., 1992. Republican. Presbyterian. Avocations: photography, computers, travel. Home: 3831 46th Ave SW Seattle WA 98116-3723 E-mail: stuwood@attbi.com.

WOOD, SUSANNE GRIFFITHS, environmental chemist, microbiologist; b. Buffalo, Dec. 28, 1933; d. John Arnold and Alice Fredericka (Wiede) Griffiths; m. Richard Bruce Wood, Aug. 8, 1970. BA in Biology, SUNY, Buffalo, 1954, MA in Biology, 1957; PhD in Plant Pathology, U. Ill., 1976. Asst. cancer rsch. scientist Roswell Park Meml. Inst., Buffalo, 1957-59, 64-66; clin. microbiologist Deaconess Hosp., 1959-64; teaching and rsch. asst. U. Ill., Urbana-Champaign, 1966-75, rsch. assoc., 1975-80; asst. profl. scientist Ill. Natural History Survey, Champaign, 1980-83, assoc. profl. scientist, 1983-92; lab. supv. Northern Ill. Water Corp., Ill., 1993-94; lab mgr. Integrated Analytical, Clinton, 1995-96; rsch. specialist dept. vet. bioscis. U. Ill., 1998—. Contbr. articles on microbial physiology and environ. chemistry to profl. jours. Assoc. chimesmaster U. Ill., 1971-94, chimesmaster, 1995—; carillonneur U. Luth. Ch., Champaign, 1968-2001; organist Philo (Ill.) Presbyn. Ch., 1987—; mem. libr. U. Ill. Russian Folk Orch., 1974-92. Mem. AAAS, Am. Chem. Soc., Soc. for Environ. Toxicology and Chemistry, Guild of Carillonneurs in N.Am., Am. Acad. Microbiology (reg. microbiologist). Home: PO Box 437 207 S Hayes St Philo IL 61864 E-mail: swood88888@aol.com.

WOOD, THOMAS E. lawyer; b. L.A., Apr. 20, 1939; s. Louis Earl and Youda (Hays) Wood; m. Sally Ann Wood, June 22, 1963; children: Julia W. DeVuono, Melissa W. Brewster. BA, Amherst Coll., 1961; LLB, U. Pa., 1966. Bar: Pa. 1966. Assoc. Drinker Biddle & Reath LLP, Phila., 1966-72, ptnr., 1972—, ptnr.-in-charge Berwyn office, 2001—. Chmn. Easttown Zoning Hearing Bd., Easttown Twp., Pa., 1976—. Mem. Phila. Club. Office: Drinker Biddle & Reath LLP 1000 Westlakes Dr Ste 300 Berwyn PA 19312-2409 E-mail: woodte@dbr.com.

WOOD, THOMAS WESLEY, humanities educator, editor; b. Hugo, Okla., Mar. 16, 1920; s. Thomas Wesley Wood Sr. and Alma Elora (Rogers) Daniel; m. L. Deloris Gray, May 31, 1968; m. Doreen Anderson, June, 1950 (div. 1966); children: John William, Thomas Wakefield. BA in History and Journalism, Tulsa U., 1951, MA in History, 1952; MS in Journalism, Northwestern U., 1953; PhD in European History, U. Okla., 1966. Reporter City News Bur. Chgo., 1952-54; prof. Tulsa (Okla.) U., 1954-73, So. Ill. U., Carbondale, 1973-76; vis. prof. Am. U., Cairo, Egypt, 1976-78, U. Ark., Little Rock, 1978-80; prof. Temple U., Phila., 1980-90, emeritus prof., 1990—. Reporter, corr. Tulsa World, 1954-84; editor, pub., founder Lost Generation Jour., Salem, Mo., 1973—. Author: Tulsa U. Editing Hankbook, 1956, 60, Tulsa U. Reporting Handbook, 1958, 60, 69, Outline History of American Journalism, 1961, Influence of the Paris Herald on the Lost Generation Writers, 1966; sub.-editor Egyptian Gazette, 1977-78. Recipient editing and writing award Mo. Press Women, 1985, writing award Pa. Press Club, 1983, writing award Ark. Press Women, 1979, 80, photography award Soc. Profl. Journalists, 1972. Mem. Overseas Press Club Am., Assn. Edn. Journalism and Mass Comm., Hemingway Soc., Soc. Scholar Editors, Coun. Editors Learned Journals, Pi Alpha Mu (nat. pres. 1956-60). Republican. Baptist. Avocation: fly fishing, traveling, interviewing expatriate 20's Americans. Home: RR 5 Box 134 Salem MO 65560-9008 Office: Lost Generation Jour RR 3 Box 387 Salem MO 65560-9315

WOOD, THOMAS WILLARD, health care industry executive; b. Logan, Utah, Jan. 21, 1939; s. Elmer Raymond and Leola (Pitkin) W.; m. Blanche Loila Dowdle, Sept. 11, 1959 (div.); children: Dianna Wood Perry, Jeffery Thomas (dec.); m. Charlene Taulbee, Oct. 5, 1974; children: Douglas Winston Remington, Angela Christine Douglas, Thomas Willard II, Michael Joseph, Matthew David. BA, Utah State U., 1962; MS, Cen. Mich. U., 1975; postgrad., Indsl. Coll. Armed Forces, 1975, Armed Forces Staff Coll., 1976. Commd. 2d lt. USAF, 1962, advanced through grades to col., 1983; chief protocol Hdqrs. Air Force Logistics Command, Wright-Patterson AFB, Ohio, 1972-75; chief spl. project div. Hdqrs. 21st Air Force, McGuire AFB, N.J., 1977-78; chief inquiries br. Office Legis. Liaison, The Pentagon, Washington, 1978-82; dep. dir. Directorate Competition Advocacy Ogden Air Logistics Ctr., Hill AFB, Utah, 1982-85; air attache U.S. Def. Attache Office, Am. Embassy, Wellington, New Zealand, 1985-88; chief protocol, dep. dir. pub. and govtl. affairs Hdqrs. U.S. Comdr.-in-Chief Pacific, Camp Smith, Hawaii, 1988-89; ret., 1989; adminstrv. asst. to v.p. mktg. Hawaii Med. Svc. Assn., Honolulu, 1989-91; sr. account exec. client rels. Baxter Internat. Inc., San Antonio, 1991-92; sr. account exec. prescription svc. divsn. Caremark, Inc., 1992-95; with corp. accts. prescription svc. divsn. Caremark Inc., 1996-97; sr. account exec. field ops. Caremark Pharm. Svcs., Medpartners Inc., 1997-99; sr. acct. mgr. field ops. CaremarkRx Inc., 1999-2000. Sr. nat. acct. mgr. SBC Comms., Inc., Caremark, Inc., San Antonio, 2000—; dean New Zealand Mil. Attache Corps, 1986-88. Elder LDS Ch., also ch. organist, pianist, tchr. Decorated DFC, Air medal with nine oak leaf clusters; Gallantry Cross with palm (Vietnam); named hon. Royal New Zealand Air Force Navigator, 1988. Mem. Disting. Flying Cross Soc. Republican. Avocations: jogging, swimming. Home: 1351 Grey Oak Dr San Antonio TX 78213-1602 Office: CaremarkRx Inc 7034 Alamo Downs Pkwy San Antonio TX 78238-4509

WOOD, TRACEY ANN, lawyer; b. Milw., June 21, 1967; d. Kenneth J. and Susan J. (Hayden) Wood; 1 child, Alexander Case Roller. BA, Marquette U., 1988; JD, U. Wis., 1992. Bar: Wis. 1993, U.S. Dist. Ct. (we. and ea. dists.) Wis. 1993, U.S. Ct. Appeals (7th cir.) 1993. Atty. Kalal & Assocs., Madison, 1993-96, Thomas, Kelly, Habermehl & Wood, S.C., Madison, 1996-98; ptnr. Van Wagner & Wood, S.C., 1998—. Mem. Nat. Assn. Criminal Def. Lawyers, Wis. Assn. Criminal Def. Lawyers, Dane County Criminal Def. Lawyers Assn. (pres. 1998). Avocations: bicycling, hiking, yoga. Office: Van Wagner & Wood SC 10 E Doty St Ste 701 Madison WI 53703 E-mail: traceyawood@yahoo.com.

WOOD, VIRGINIA ANN, educator; b. Petoskey, Mich., June 24, 1936; d. William Nelson and Mildred Alice (Cope) Reed; m. Frederick Lee Wood, Sept. 28, 1970 (dec. Apr. 1971); 1 child, Frederick Lee. BS, Ferris State U., 1957. Tchr. Reese (Mich.) Schs., 1957-59, Utica (Mich.) Schs., 1963-64, Richmond (Mich.) Cmty. Schs., 1959-63, 64—. Coach Sci. Olympiad, Richmond H.S., 1984—. Contbr. software revs. to Sci. Tchr. mag., 1987. Trustee Pub. Libr. Bd., 1980-98; mem. Richmond Cmty. Theatre, 1965-71; organist, choir dir. United Ch. of Christ. NSF grantee in chemistry and project physics, 1962-68. Mem. NEA, Nat. Sci. Tchrs. Assn., Mich. Edn. Assn., Mich. Sci. Tchrs. Assn. (sec., bd. dirs. 1961-70), Richmond Edn. Assn. (pres. 1966-67, sec. 1984-94), Alpha Delta Kappa (pres. 1968-70). Avocations: needlework, music. Home: 70109 Karen St Richmond MI 48062-1098 Office: Richmond High Sch 35320 Division Rd Richmond MI 48062-1392 E-mail: reedwood@klondyke.net.

WOOD, VIVIAN POATES, mezzo soprano, educator, writer; b. Washington, Aug. 19, 1923; d. Harold Poates and Mildred Georgette (Patterson) W. Studies with Walter Anderson, Antioch Coll., 1953-55; Denise Restout, Saint-Leu-La-Fôret, France and Lakeville, Conn., 1960-62, 64-70, Paul A. Pisk, 1968-71; Paul Ulanowsky, N.Y.C., 1958-68; Elemer Nagy, 1965-68, Vyautas Marijosius, 1967-68; MusB, Hartt Coll. Music, 1968; postgrad. (fellow), Yale U., 1968; MusM (fellow), Washington U., St. Louis, 1971, PhD (fellow), 1973. Debut in recital series Internat. Jeunesse Musicals Arts Festival, 1953; solo fellowship Boston Symphony Orch., Berkshire Music Ctr., Tanglewood, 1964, St. Louis Symphony Orch., 1969, Washington Orch., 1949, Bach Cantata Series Berkshire Chamber Orch., 1964, Yale Symphony Orch., 1968. Appearances in U.S. and European recitals, oratorios, operas, radio and TV, 1953-68; appeared as soloist in Internat. Harpsichord Festival, Westminister Choir Coll., Princeton, N.J., 1973; appeared as soloist in meml. concert, Landowska Ctr., Lakeville, 1969; prof. voice U. So. Miss., Hattiesburg, 1971-2000, ret. 2000; asst. dean Coll. Fine Arts, 1974-76, acting dean, 1976-77; guest prof. Hochschule für Musik, Munich, 1978-79; prof. Italian Internat. Studies Program, Rome, 1986; Miss. coord. Alliance for Arts Edn., Kennedy Ctr. Performing Arts, 1974—; mem. Miss. Gov.'s Adv. Panel for Gifted and Talented Children, 1974—; mem. 1st Miss. Gov.'s Conf. on the Arts, 1974—. Author: Polenc's Songs: An Analysis of Style, 1971. Recipient Young Am. Artists Concert award N.Y.C., 1955; Wanda Landowska fellow 1961-68. Mem. Miss. Music Tchrs. Assn., Nat. Assn. Tchrs. of Singing, Music Tchrs. Nat. Assn., Am. Musicology Soc., Golden Key, Mu Phi Epsilon, Delta Kappa Gamma, Tau Beta Kappa (hon.), Pi Kappa Lambda. Democrat. Episcopalian.

WOOD, WELLINGTON GIBSON, III, biochemistry educator; b. Balt., Dec. 29, 1945; s. Wellington Gibson Jr. and Elsie Bernice (Johnson) W.; m. Beverly Jean Beaver, Feb. 8, 1969; children: Wellington Gibson IV, Katherine Birmingham. BA, Tex. Tech U., 1971, PhD, 1976. Postdoctoral fellow Syracuse (N.Y.) U., 1976-77; staff scientist Bangor (Maine) Mental Health Inst., 1978-80; evaluation coord. VA Med. Ctr., St. Louis, 1980-89, assoc. dir. for edn. and evaluation Mpls., 1989—; asst. prof. St. Louis U. Sch. Medicine, 1982-87, assoc. prof., 1987-89; assoc. prof. dept. pharmacology U. Minn. Sch. Medicine, Mpls., 1990-96, prof. dept. pharmacology, 1996—. Mem. sci. editorial bd. Alcoholism and Drug Rsch. Comm. Ctr., Austin, Tex., 1990-96; mem. biochemistry, physiology and medicine study sect. NIH-Nat. Inst. Alcohol Abuse and Alcoholism, 1992-96, bd. sci. counselors, 1997—; bd. dirs. Minn. Inst. for Vets. Rsch. Assoc. editor Exptl. Aging Rsch., 1977-82; contbr. numerous articles to profl. jours. Nat. Inst. on Alcohol Abuse and Alcoholism postdoctoral fellow, 1976-77; grantee Nat. Inst. on Alcohol Abuse and Alcoholism, Nat. Inst. on Aging, Dept. Vets. Affairs, NATO Dept. Def. Mem. Am. Aging Assn. (bd. dirs. 1984-87), Rsch. Soc. on Alcoholism (chmn. membership com. 1988-91), Internat. Soc. for Biomed. Rsch. on Alcoholism, Am. Soc. for Neurochemistry, Internat. Soc. for Neurochemistry, Am. Soc. Biochemistry and Molecular Biology. Achievements include elucidating the role of cholesterol in brain neuronal structure and function, particularly with respect to the neuronal plasma membrane; this work has focused on mechanisms that are involved in the regulation of membrane cholesterol domains and how changes in cholesterol domains may contribute to neuronal dysfunction induced by alcoholism, aging, and Alzheimer's disease. Home: 16091 Huron Path Lakeville MN 55044-8874 Office: VA Med Ctr GRECC 11G Minneapolis MN 55417 E-mail: woodxoo2@tc.umn.edu.

WOOD, WENDY DEBORAH, filmmaker; b. N.Y.C., Oct. 4, 1940; d. John Meyer and Marion Emily (Peters) W.; m. William Dismore Chapple, Dec. 7, 1963; 1 child, Samuel Eliot. BA cum laude, Vassar Coll., 1962; MA, Stanford U., 1964. Tchg. asst. Stanford U., 1962-64; photographer, film editor Bristol (Eng.) U., 1964-66, asst. dir. Internat. Conf. Film Schs., 1966; rsch. asst. biology dept. U. Conn., Storrs, 1970-72; sr. media specialist Aetna Life & Casualty Co., Hartford, Conn., 1972-89; media writer, prodr., dir. U. Conn. Ctr. for Media and Tech., Storrs, 1989—. Pres. Chapple Films, Inc., 1972—. Films include: Yankee Craftsman, 1972, Alcoholism, Industry's Costly Hangover, 1974, Draggerman's Haul, 1975, Flight Without Wings, 1977, Auto Insurance Affordability, 1981 (2 awards), Where Rivers Run to the Sea, 1981 (award), Our Town is Burning Down, 1982 (6 awards), Wellness at the Worksite, 1984 (4 awards), Aenhance, 1989 (3 awards), Tiffany: Magician in Glass. Mem. jury N.Y. Internat. Video and Film Festival; bd. dirs. Windham Regional Arts Coun., 1987, 88, 89; mem. peer rev. com. Conn. Commn. Higher Edn., 1992-96. Recipient CINE Golden Eagle award Coun. on Internat. Non-Theatrical Events, 1972, 76, 84, 1st Place award Indls. Photography, 1974, cert. Outstanding Creativity U.S. TV Commls. Festival, 1974, EFLA award Am. Film Festival, 1974, 76, Dir's. Choice award Sinking Creek Film Festival, 1975, award Columbus Film Festival, 1975, award Excellence Life Ins. Advts. Assn., 1975, Silver Screen award U.S. Indsl. Film Festival, 1976, 81, 1st place award Conn. Film Festival, 1977, 1st prize Nat. Outdoor Travel Film Festival, 1978, 1st pl. Houston Film Festival, 1982, CINE Golden Eagle, 1982, 84, award Am. Film Festival, 1982, N.Y. Film Festival, 1982, 83, Silver CINDY award Assn. Visual Communicators, 1985, Conn. Film/Video Festival 1st pl. award, 1997, Gold award Conn. Film Festival, 1997, others. Mem. Info. Film Prodrs. Am. (nat. dir., pres. chpt. 1981-82, Cindy award 1971, 72, 81, 82, 85, 87), Internat. Quorum Motion Picture Prodrs., Audio Visual Communicators (pres. Conn. chpt. 1985, treas. 1988). Democrat. Mem. Soc. Of Friends. Home: 604 Phoenixville Rd Chaplin CT 06235-2211 E-mail: Chapple@uconnvm.uconn.edu., woodwendy@earthlink.com.

WOOD, WILLIAM JEROME, lawyer; b. Indpls., Feb. 14, 1928; s. Joseph Gilmore and Anne Cecillia (Morris) Wood; m. Joann Janet Jones, Jan. 23, 1954; children: Steven, Matthew, Kathleen, Michael, Joseph, James, Julie, David. Student, Butler U., 1945-46; AB with honors, Ind. U., 1950, JD with distinction, 1952. Bar: Ind. 1952. Mem. firm Wood, Tuohy, Gleason, Mercer & Herrin (and predecessor), Indpls., 1952—. Bd. dirs. Grain Dealers Mut. Ins. Co., Am. Income Life Ins. Co.; gen. counsel Ind. Cath. Conf.; city atty., Indpls., 1959—60; instr. Ind. U. Sch. Law, 1960—62. Author: (book) Indiana Pastor's Legal Handbook, 3d edit., 2001, Realtors' Indiana Legal Handbook, 2d edit., 1991. Mem. Ind. Corp. Survey Commn., 1963—, chmn., 1977—86; mem. Ind. Corp. Law Study Commn., 1985—87, Ind. Non Profit Corp. Law Study Commn., 1989—91; bd. dirs. Alcoholic Rehab. Ctr., Indpls., Indpls. Lawyers' Commn., Cmty. Svc. Coun. Indpls. With AUS, 1946—48. Recipient Brotherhood award, Ind. region NCCJ, 1973. Mem.: St. Thomas Moore Legal Soc. (pres. 1970), Indpls. Bar Found., Indpls. Bar Assn. (pres. 1972—73, coun. bd. mgrs. 1992—93), Ind. Bar Assn. (sec. 1977—78, award 1968), Audubon Soc., Indpls. Lit. Club (pres. 1973—74), Am. Legion. Democrat. Roman Catholic. Home: 3619 E 75th Pl Indianapolis IN 46240-3674 Office: Bank One Ctr Tower 111 Monument Cir Ste 3400 PO Box 44942 Indianapolis IN 46244-0942 E-mail: bwood@indylegal.com.

WOOD, WILLIAM MCBRAYER, lawyer; b. Greenville, S.C., Jan. 27, 1942; s. Oliver Gillan and Grace (McBrayer) W.; m. Nancy Cooper, 1973 (dec. 1993); children: Walter, Lewis; m. Jeanette Dobson Haney, June 25, 1994. BS in Acctg., U. S.C., 1964, JD cum laude, 1972; LLM in Estate Planning (scholar), U. Miami, 1980. Bar: S.C. 1972, Fla. 1979, D.C. 1973, U.S. Tax Ct. 1972, U.S. Ct. Claims 1972, U.S. Supreme Ct. 1977. Intern ct. of claims sect., tax divsn. U.S. Dept. Justice, 1971; law clk. to chief judge U.S. Ct. Claims, Washington, 1972-74; ptnr. firm Edwards Wood, Duggan & Reese, Greer and Greenville, 1974-78; asst. prof. law Cumberland Law Sch., Samford U., Birmingham, Ala., 1978-79; faculty Nat. Inst. Trial Advocacy: N.E. Regional Inst., 1979, 83-90, 95-97, Fla. Regional Inst., 1989; teaching team 5th intensive trial techniques course Hofstra U., 1983; assoc. then capital ptnr. firm Shutts & Bowen, Miami, 1980-85; sole practice, 1985—; also Rock Hill, S.C., 1994—; of counsel Griffin, Smith, Caldwell, Helder & Lee, Monroe, N.C., 2001—. Contbg. editor: The Lawyers PC; Fla. editor: Drafting Wills and Trust Agreements; substantive com. editor ABA: The Tax Lawyer, 1983—. Pres. Piedmont Heritage Found., Inc. 1975-78; del. State Rep. Conv., 1985, 87, 90; exec. committeeman Miami-Dade County Republicans, 1988-94, co-gen. counsel, 1990-91; apptd. Miami-Dade County Indsl. Devel. Authority, 1990-94; mem. vestry Episc. Ch., 1993-94. With USAF, 1965-69, Vietnam. Decorated Air Force Commendation medal; recipient Am. Jurisprudence award in real property and tax I, 1971; winner Grand prize So. Living Mag. travel photo contest, 1969. Mem. ABA (taxation sect., teaching law com., 1994—), Greer C. of C. (pres. 1977, Outstanding leadership award 1976), Greater Greenville C. of C. (dir. 1977), Order Wig and Robe, Estate Planning Council South Fla., Omicron Delta Kappa. Club: Bankers (bd. govs. 1989-94). Lodge: Masons, Rotary. Office: 5345 Wilgrove Mint Hill Rd Charlotte NC 28227-3467

WOOD, WILLIAM PRESTON, author, lawyer; b. Bronxville, N.Y., Apr. 23, 1951; s. Preston and Eleanor Catherine (Auby) W. BA, Middlebury Coll., 1973; JD, U. of the Pacific, 1976. Bar: Calif. 1976, U.S. Dist. Ct. (ea. dist.) Calif. 1976. Dep. dist. atty. Sacramento County District Atty., Sacramento, 1977-82; dir. publs. Calif. Dist. Attys. Assn., 1984-85; chief counsel Office Sec. State, 1999—; freelance writer, 1985—. Author: (novels) Rampage, 1985, Gangland, 1988, Fugitive City, 1990, Court of Honor, 1991, Stay of Execution, 1994, The Bone Garden, 1994, Quicksand, 1998, (motion picture) Rampage, 1992, Broken Trust, 1995; co-author (TV series) Kaz, 1978; contbr. articles to profl. jours. Pres. Citizens for a Better Sacramento, 1986. Mem. Writers Guild Am.-West. Republican. Episcopalian.

WOOD, WILLIS BOWNE, JR. retired utility holding company executive; b. Kansas City, Mo., Sept. 15, 1934; s. Willis Bowne Sr. and Mina (Henderson) W.; m. Dixie Gravel, Aug. 31, 1955; children: Bradley, William, Josh. BS in Petroleum Engring., U. Tulsa, 1957; grad. advanced mgmt. program, Harvard U., 1983; JD (hon.), Pepperdine U., 1996. With So. Calif. Gas Co., L.A., 1960-74, from v.p. to sr. v.p., 1975-80, exec. v.p., 1983-84; pres., CEO Pacific Lighting Gas Supply Co., 1981-83; from sr. v.p. to chmn., pres., CEO, Pacific Enterprises, 1984-93, chmn., CEO, 1993-98; ret., 1998. Bd. dirs. Washington Mut., Seattle, Automobile Club Soc. Calif.; trustee U. So. Calif. Trustee, past vice-chmn. Harvey Mudd Coll., Claremont, Calif., 1984—; trustee emeritus, past chmn. Calif. Med. Ctr. Found., L.A., 1983-2000; trustee, past pres. S.W. Mus., L.A.; trustee John and Dora Haynes Found., 1998—; past bd. dirs. L.A. World Affairs Coun.; past dir., past chmn. bus. coun. for Sustainable Energy Future, 1994—; past dir. Pacific Coun. for Internat. Affairs. Recipient Disting. Alumni U. Tulsa, 1995; inductee U. Tulsa Engring. Hall of Fame, 2001. Mem. Soc. Petroleum Energy Engrs., Pacific Energy Assn., Calif. State C. of C. (past bd. dirs.), Am. Automobile Assn. (vice-chmn. 2001), NAM (past bd. dirs.), Hacienda Golf CLub, Ctr. Club, Calif. Club. Republican.

WOOD, YVONNE MCMURRAY, retired nursing educator; b. Fulton County, Ind., July 23, 1931; d. Wesley Earl and Dortha (Bunn) McMurray; m. Bob C. Wood, Dec. 27, 1954; children: Teresa Wood Goble, Kevin. Diploma, Meth. Hosp. Sch. Nursing, 1955; BA, Indpls. U., 1955; MS in Nursing, Ind. U., Indpls., 1972; MS in Adult Edn., Ind. U., Bloomington, 1982. Instr. ARC, Dayton, Ohio, 1956-57; staff nurse Health and Hosp. Corp., Indpls., 1967-70; asst. prof. community health and psychiat. nursing Ind. U., 1967-70; instr. med. terminology No. N.Mex. Community Coll., Espanola, 1982-83; instr. McCurdy Practical Nurse Sch., 1979-82; staff nurse Mimbres Meml. Hosp., Deming, N.Mex., 1983-85, Pima County Health Dept., Tucson, 1985; day charge nurse intermediate care Presbyn. Village, Little Rock, 1986; sch. nurse McCurdy Schs., Espanola, 1989; instr. hospice program No. N.Mex. Community Coll., 1989-90. Night supr. Marion County Nursing Home and Rehab. Ctr., Indpls., 1965-66; vis. asst. prof. Coll. Nursing U. N.Mex., Albuquerque, 1979-81; staff nurse Home Health Svcs. Englewood (Fla.), 1986-87; instr. Edison Community Coll., Ft. Myers, Port Charlotte, Fla., 1988. Vol. cons. for establishment of family crisis ctr. in no. N.Mex., Rio Arriba County, 1991-92, local libr., 1996—, others, 1993-98; neighborhood vol.; libr. vol. Mem. Sigma Theta Tau. Home: 229 Caddy Rd Placida FL 33947-2223 E-mail: bwood76@home.com.

WOODALL, DAVID MONROE, research engineer, dean; b. Perryville, Ark., Aug. 2, 1945; m. Linda Carol Page, June 6, 1966; 1 child, Zachary Page. BA, Hendrix Coll., 1967; MS, Columbia U., 1968; PhD, Cornell U., 1976. Registered profl. engr., Idaho. Nuc. engr. Westinghouse Corp., Pitts., 1968-70; asst. prof. U. Rochester, N.Y., 1974-77, U. N.Mex., Albuquerque, 1977-79, assoc. prof., 1979-83, chair dept., 1980-83, prof., 1984-86; group physics mgr. Idaho Nat. Engring. Lab., Idaho Falls, 1986-92; assoc. dean, dir. rsch. U. Idaho, Moscow, 1992-99, acting dean, 1999; dean coll. sci., engring., math. U. Alaska, Fairbanks, 1999—; dir. Ctr. for Nanosensor Tech., 2001—. EAC commr. Accreditation Bd. Engring. Tech., 1990-95, bd. dirs., 1997-; cons. in field. Contbr. articles to profl. jours. Grantee NSF, DOE, AFOSR, Office Naval Rsch., DMEA, others. Mem. IEEE, Am. Nuc. Soc. (chpt. chair 1982-83), Am. Soc. Engring. Edn. (divsn. chair 1993, 95, bd. dirs. engring. rsch. coun.). Office: U Alaska Coll Sci Engring Math PO Box 755940 Fairbanks AK 99775-5940 E-mail: ffdmw1@uaf.edu.

WOODALL, SAMUEL ROY, JR. lawyer; b. July 8, 1936; s. Samuel Roy Woodall; m. Jane Marvin Brock, Aug. 5, 1958; children: Samuel Roy III, Lawrence B., Claiborne A., George G. BA, U. Ky., 1958, LLB, 1962; postgrad., Yale U., 1959. Bar: Ky. 1962. Atty. Ky. Dept. Ins., 1962-64, gen. counsel, 1965-66; commr. ins. Commonwealth Ky., 1966-68; assoc. firm Wyatt, Grafton and Sloss, Louisville, 1968-69, ptnr., 1969-72; pres. Western Pioneer Life Ins. Co. (and predecessors), Louisville, 1972-76; asst. to pres. Am. Life & Accident Ins. Co., 1976-80; pres. Nat. Assn. Life Cos., Washington, 1980-93; v.p. and chief counsel state rels. Am. Coun. Life Ins., 1993-98; with Morris, Manning & Martin (Atlanta-based firm), 1998—2001; ins. cons. Congl. Rsch. Svc., Libr. of Congres, 2001—. Guest instr. ins. law U. Louisville, 1968—69. Note editor: U. Ky. Law Rev., 1961—62. Pres. Citizen's Met. Planning coun., Louisville, 1970—71; chmn. City of Louisville Riverfront Commn., 1970—75, Ky. Heritage Commn., 1964—77; bd. dirs. Bingham Child Guidance Clinic, Louisville, 1969—76, Youth Performing Arts Coun., 1979—80. Named one of Ky.'s 3 Outstanding Young Men, Ky. Jr. C. of C., 1968; recipient Sullivan medallion, U. Ky., 1958; fellow Woodrow Wilson, Yale U., 1959. Mem.: ABA, Fedn. Ins. Counsel, D.C. Bar Assn., Ky. Bar Assn., Phi Beta Kappa, Phi Alpha Delta (pres. chpt. 1961—62). Home: 2851 29th St NW Washington DC 20008-4111 Office: CRS-Libr of Congress 101 Independence Ave SE Washington DC 20540-7000

WOODALL, SONJA DENISE, small business owner; b. Birmingham, Ala., Jan. 23, 1967; d. Clifford Merrill Woodall, Florence Edith Woodall. Diploma, Bauder Finishing Coll., Atlanta; AS, Jefferson State U.; student, U. Ala. Birmingham, Birmingham So. Coll. Clk. CMA Credit Union, Birmingham, 1992—95; owner Result Resume, 1995—. Author: (poetry): A Moment in Time, 2000 (Editors Choice award, 2000). Mem.: C. of C., Internat. Poetry Soc. (Editors Choice award 2000). Democrat. Avocations: literature, art, spirituality. Home: 1413 Wharton Ave Birmingham AL 35217

WOODALL, THOMAS A. state supreme court justice; b. Meridian, Miss., July 14, 1950; m. Debbie Bogan, 1972; children: Scott, Matthew, Claire. BA in History, Millsaps Coll., 1972; JD, U. Va., 1975. With Rives and Peterson, Birmingham, Ala., 1975—91; ptnr. Woodall and Maddox, 1991—96; circuit judge Jefferson County, 1996—2001; assoc. justice Ala. Supreme Ct., 2001—. Mem. Ala. Pattern Jury Instrn.-Civil Com., 1985—2001, vice chmn., 1992—2001. Republican. Methodist. Office: 300 Dexter Ave Montgomery AL 36104-3741*

WOODARD, ALVA ABE, business consultant; b. Roy, N.Mex., June 28, 1928; s. Joseph Benjamin and Emma Lurania (Watkins) W.; m. Esther Josepha Kaufmann, Apr. 5, 1947 (div. Sept. 1991); children: Nannette, Gregory, Loreen, Arne, Mark, Kevin, Steven, Curtis, Marlee, Julie, Michelle; m. Margaret Adele Evenson, Oct. 1, 1994. Student, Kinman Bus. U., 1948-49, Whitworth Coll., 1956, Wash. State U., 1953-54. Sec.-treas., dir. Green Top Dairy Farms, Inc., Clarkston, Wash., 1948-52; v.p., treas., sec., dir. ASC Industries, Inc. (subs. Gifford-Hill and Co.), Spokane, 1952-75; dir. Guenther Irrigation, Inc., Pasco, 1966-71; mng. dir. Irrigation Rental, Inc., 1968-75, Rain Chief Irrigation Co., Grand Island, Nebr., 1968-75; sec., dir. Keeling Supply Co., Little Rock, 1969-72; pres., dir. Renters, Inc., Salt Lake City, 1971-75, Woodard Western Corp., Spokane, 1976-86, Woodard Industries, Inc., Auburn, Wash., 1987-90; cons. Woodard Assocs., Spokane, 1985—. Pres., dir. TFI Industries, inc., Post Falls, Idaho, 1989-90; v.p., sec., treas., dir. Trans-Force, Inc., Post Falls, 1989-90, TFI Computer Scis., Inc., Post Falls, 1989-90. Newman Lake (Wash.) Rep. precinct committeeman, 1964-80; Spokane County del. Wash. Rep. Conv., 1968-80. Mem. Adminstrv. Mgmt. Soc. (bd. dirs. 1966-68), Optimists. Avocations: fishing, theater, golf, reading, dancing. Home and Office: 921 E 39th Ave Spokane WA 99203-3034

WOODARD, BETH STUCKEY, librarian, educator; b. Fairbury, Ill., Oct. 25, 1956; d. James Dale and Helenjean (Lauterbach) Stuckey; m. Billy Dean Woodard, July 14, 1979 (div. June 1993); children: Rebecca Lindsay, Sarah Lauren; m. Gregory Allen Wolfe, Oct. 21, 1995. BA, Ill. Wesleyan U., 1978; MS, U. Ill., 1979. Reference libr. U. S.C., Columbia, 1979-82; reference libr., asst. prof. libr. adminstrn. U. Ill., Urbana, 1983-85, cen. info. svcs. libr., 1985-99, 2001—, assoc. prof., 1990—, acting head of reference, 1993-94, 97, interim commerce librarian, 1999-2001. Cons. Oberlin (Ohio) Coll., 1996, Ea. Ill. U., 1999, So. Ill. U., Edwardsville, 1999. Contbr. book chpts. to Reference and Information Services, 1991, 95, 2001; editor: (spl. jour. issue) Ill. Librs., 1991. Chair fund raising com. Oakwood (Ill.) Twp. Pub. Libr., 1997-98; trustee Oakwood Twp. Pub. Libr., 2001—. Mem. ALA, Reference and User Svcs. Assn. (evaluation of reference and adult svcs. com. 1990-92, chair 1992-94, bd. dirs. 1994-2001, editor newsletter 1997-2001, Isadore Gilbert Mudge/ R.R. Bowker award 1998), Assn. Coll. and Rsch. Librs. (mem. continuing edn. com. 1988-90, chair 1990-92, chair guidelines for bibliographic instrn. programs 1994-96, sec. instrn. sect. 1992-93, chair comms. com. 1993-94, vice-chair instrn. sect. 2000-01, chair instrn. sect. 2001-2002, chair Dudley awards com.), Phi Kappa Phi, Beta Phi Mu, Alpha Lambda Delta. Office: U of Ill 1408 W Gregory Dr Urbana IL 61801-3607 E-mail: bswoodar@uiuc.edu.

WOODARD, CAROL JANE, educational consultant; b. Buffalo, Jan. 19, 1929; d. Harold August and Violet Maybelle (Landsittel) Young; m. Ralph Arthur Woodard, Aug. 19, 1950; children: Camaron Jane, Carsen Jane, Cooper Ralph. BA, Hartwick Coll., 1950; MA, Syracuse U., 1952; PhD, SUNY, Buffalo, 1972; LHD (hon.), Hartwick Coll., 1991; postgrad., Bank St. Coll., Harvard U. Cert. tchr., N.Y. State. Tchr., Orchard Park, N.Y., 1950-51, Danville, Ind., 1951-52, Akron, N.Y., 1952-54; dir. Garden Nursery Sch., Williamsville, 1955-65; tchr. Amherst (N.Y.) Coop. Nursery Sch., 1967-69; asst. prof. early childhood edn. SUNY, Buffalo, 1969-72, lab. demonstration tchr. and student teaching supr., 1969-76, assoc. prof., 1972-79, prof., 1979-88, prof. emeritus, 1988—; dir. Consultants in Early Childhood, 1988—. Cons. Lutheran Ch. Am., Villa Maria Coll., Buffalo Pub. Schs., Buffalo Mus. Sci., Headstart Tng. Programs, Erie Community Coll., N.Y. State Dept. Edn., numerous workshops.; cons. sch. systems, indsl. firms, pubs., civic orgns. in child devel.; vis. prof. The Netherlands and East China Univ., Shanghai, People's Republic of China; sci. trainer The Wright Group, 1995. Author 7 books for young children, 2 textbooks in field; co-author: Physical Science in Early Childhood, 1987; co-author nat. curriculum for ch. sch. for 3-yr.-olds; author: (booklet) You Can Help Your Baby Learn; author/coord. TAKE CARE child protection project, 1987; contbr. chpts. to books, articles to profl. jours. Trustee Hartwick Coll., Oneonta, N.Y., 1978-87; cons. EPIC Birth to Three Program, 1992; design cons. indoor playground Noah's Ark Jewish Ctr., Buffalo, 1992; Sites Project coord., cons. Let's Talk project Buffalo Pub. Schs., 1994—; student tchg. supr. SUNY, Fredonia, 1994—. Mem. Nat. Assn. Edn. Young Children, Early Childhood Edn. Council Western N.Y., Assn. Childhood Edn. Internat., Phi Delta Kappa, Pi Lambda Theta. Home: 1776 Sweet Rd East Aurora NY 14052-3028

WOODARD, CLARA VERONICA, nursing home official; b. Bayonne, N.J. d. William George and Lula (Langston) Yelverton; m. John Henry Woodard; children: John Michael, Stephen Jay. Grad., Bayonne Hosp. Sch. Nursing, 1951, Manhattan Sch. Radiology, 1953, NYU-Bellevue Med. Ctr., 1955, Valencia Community Coll., Orlando, Fla. RN, N.J., Fla. Head nurse Bayonne Hosp., 1949-50; office nurse Dr. D.G. Morris, Bayonne, 1951-52; pvt. duty nurse Christ Hosp and Bayonne Hosp., 1954-58; tchr. kindergarten, Nuremburg, Fed. Republic Germany, 1972-73; ICU-CCU nurse Holy Spirit Hosp., Camp Hill, Pa., 1973-74; head nurse Orlando Gen. Hosp., 1974-76, house supr., 1976-78; dir. nurses Winter Park (Fla.) Care Ctr., 1980-83; Medicare coord. Pinar Terrace Manor, Orlando, 1987-92, clin. instr., 1992—, house supr., nurse mgr. Alzheimer unit, 1993—. Instr. Valencia Coll., Orlando, Fla. Named Employee of Yr. and Employee of Month, Orlando Gen. Hosp., 1980, Employee of Month, Winter Park Care Ctr., 1983. Mem. NAFE, Nat. League Negro Women Democrat. Roman Catholic. Avocations: poetry, short stories, public speaking, theology. Home: 2931 De Brocy Way Winter Park FL 32792-4505 Office: Pinar Terrace Manor 7950 Lake Underhill Rd Orlando FL 32822-8229

WOODARD, DEANA SAFFORD, artist, travel consultant; b. Springfield, Mass., June 18, 1946; d. Dean Wilbur and Merle Watkins (Woodard) Safford; m. Richard Peter Bean, Oct. 17, 1968 (div. Oct. 1999); children: Duane Matthew (dec.) and David Andrew (twins), Dana Robert, Matthew Adams. Student, W.Va. Wesleyan Co., 1964-66. Cert. tax preparer. Co-owner McCarthy Gallery, Rockport, Mass., 1995, Gallery Six, Rocky Neck, 1996, Gallery 43, Rocky Neck Art Colony, Gloucester, 1997; travel cons. Magic World travel, Springfield, 1991-94, The Cruise and Vacation Store, East Longmeadow, 1994-97. Hist. and geneal. rschr.; vol. U.S. Peace Corps, Iran, 1968-69; distbr. Seamless Internat., Inc., 1996-97. Author: East and Me; A Personal Encounter With the Mid East, 1992; editor: Woodard Footprints, 2002; artist Sedona Art Mart, 2001-02. Mem. coun. Springfield Art League, 1992-95; host parent Internat. Exch. Students, 1986, 87, 89, 91; co-founder Verde Valley Single Campers, 2001. Recipient Watercolor awards Longmeadow Shops Art Exhibit, 1991, 94, Pastel awards, 1989, 93. Mem. N.Am. Marine Arts Soc. (award of excellence 1991), Acad. Artists Assn. (membership chmn. 1993-97, pres. 1997, Watson-Guptill award 1991), Nat. Mus. Women in the arts (charter), Am. Artist Profl. League, Rocky Neck Art Colony, Nat. Safety Assocs. (sales coord. 1995-2002, co-founder Verde Valley Single Campers 2001, Bronze medal 1995), Mingus Mountain Gem and Mineral Club. Avocations: biodynamic gardening, history, hiking, camping.

WOODARD, DOROTHY MARIE, insurance broker; b. Houston, Feb. 7, 1932; d. Gerald Edgar and Bessie Katherine (Crain) Floeck; student N.Mex. State U., 1950; m. Jack W. Woodard; June 19, 1950 (dec. May 1972); m. Norman W. Libby, July 19, 1982 (dec. Dec. 1991). Ptnr. Western Oil Co., Tucumcari, N.Mex., 1950—; owner, mgr. Woodard & Co., Las Cruces, N.Mex., 1959-67; agt., dist. mgr. United Nations Ins. Co., Denver, 1968-74; agt. Western Nat. Life Ins. Co., Amarillo, Tex., 1976—. Exec. dir. Tucumcari Indsl. Commn., 1979—; dir. Bravo Dome Study Com., 1979—; owner Libby Cattle Co., Libby Ranch Co.; regional bd. dirs. N.Mex., Eastern Plains Council Govts., 1979—. Mem. NAFE, Tucumcari C. of C., Mesa Country Club. Home: PO Box 823 Tucumcari NM 88401-0823 *Personal philosophy: A never ending search and quest for knowledge, through participation and understanding.*

WOODARD, H. TOM, entertainment company executive; b. Lebanon, Ind., May 5, 1948; s. Edgar Clifford and Edna Anne (Yaryan) W. AS in Music and Theater, Vincennes U., 1985; BA in Communication, Calif. State U., Sacramento, 1986, MA in Communication, 1988; postgrad. in comm., U. Nebr.,

1989; postgrad. in edn., U. Tenn., 1990. Actor TV series Timothy Churchmouse, Indpls., 1967-68; entertainer stage and TV L.A., 1969-71; tchr. dance Arthur Murray Sch. Dance, Fresno, Calif., 1973-75; tchr. dance, choreographer Dance Palace Studios, Tacoma, 1976-80; lectr. Purdue U., West Lafayette, Ind., 1987; producer, tchr. Aba-Daba Prodns., Lincoln, Nebr., 1988-90; lectr. U. Tenn., Knoxville, 1990-91, Pellissippi State Coll., Knoxville, 1991-96; pres. Pharaoh Records, 1993—. Promoter Saddle Talent Prodns., Knoxville, 1995-99; pub. trade mag. Country Note Connection, 1993-97, Steinwood Publishing, 1993—, Goliath Alliance Group, 1999—; personal mgr. Grand Trunk Talent Mgmt., 1999—. Author: To See the Sun Shine, 1997, George Fruits: Last Survivor of the American Revolution, 1999; producer dance videos Learning to Dance Vols. 1-12, 1989; exec. prodr. (CD series) Gold Rush Country, vol. 1-6, 1995-99, Alamo George: Last of the Original Frontiersmen. With USAF, 1966-67. Recipient Gold Double Honors Ballroom Dance award, 1979, First Place Forensic Speaking, West Coast Championship, 1980, Indie Record Lab of Yr. Country Music Assn. Am., 1995, Album of Yr., 1995, Trade Publ. of Yr., 1995. Mem. ASCAP, SAR, European Country Music Assn. (Tenn. rep. 1996-97), Broadcast Music Inc., Aircraft Owners and Pilots Assn. Democrat. Avocations: music, aviation, writing, computers, genealogy. Home and Office: Pharaoh Records 433 Gallaher View Rd Knoxville TN 37919-5350 E-mail: tsmith3@conc.tds.net.

WOODARD, NINA ELIZABETH, banker; b. L.A., Apr. 3, 1947; d. Alexander Rhodes and Harriette Jane (Powers) Matthews; divorced; children: Regina M., James. D. Grad., Pacific Coast Banking Sch., 1987; BS in Mgmt., Calif. Coast U., 1993; postgrad., Ctr. for Creative Leadership, 1994. Lifetime cert. sr. profl. in human resources. Dental asst. Donald R. Shire DDS, L.A., 1965-66; with Security Pacific Nat. Bank, Marina Del Rey, Calif., 1968-69, First Interstate Bank, Casper, Wyo., 1971—, adminstr. asst. pers., 1975-78, asst. v.p., asst. mgr. pers., 1978-82, v.p., dir. mktg. and pers., 1982-84, v.p., mgr. human resources, 1984-88; v.p., mgr. employee rels. First Interstate Bank Ltd., L.A., 1988-93; v.p., mgr. employee rels. Ams. region Standard Chartered Bank, 1993-95, sr. v.p. human resources, 1995-99, sr. v.p. advisor cultural integration and employee comm. Thailand, 1999-2000, sr. v.p. mgmt. cultural integration UAE, 2000—. Instr. mktg. Am. Inst. Banking, 1983, Casper Coll., 1982. Mem. Civil Svc. Commn., City of Casper, 1983-88; bd. dirs. YMCA, 1984-87, Downtown Devel. Assn.; pres. Downtown Casper Assn.; instr. St. Patrick's Parish Religious Edn., 1991-92, mem. parish coun., 1993-94; advisor to the parish coun. Parish of the Resurrection, Jersey City, 1999. Named Bus. Woman of Yr., Bus. and Profl. Women, 198, Young Career Woman, 1975. Mem. Nat. Assn. Bank Women, Bus. and Profl. Women (dist. dir.), Am. Soc. Pers. Adminstrn. (regional v.p., state coun. Wyo. 1987-88), Pers. and Indsl. Rels. Assn. (chmn. govt. affairs com. 1989-90, Fast Track award 1991, Pres.'s Achievement award 1993, conf. chmn. 1991, 92, dist. chair 1993, 2d v.p. 1994), Fin. Women Internat. (Wyo. state chair 1986, regional edn. and tng. chair 1987, dist. coord. L.A. 1993, L.A. group chair 1994, nat. bd. dirs.), Soc. Human Resource Mgmt. (area I v.p. 1996-99). Republican. Roman Catholic. Office: Standard Chartered Bank 2d Fl 23-25 MG Rd Fort Mumbai 400 100 Mumbai India

WOODARD, PAMELA KAREN, radiologist; b. Cambridge, Mass., July 24, 1964; d. Paul Esty and Marion (Boyajian) W.; m. Josh William McDonald, Apr. 28, 1993; 1 child, Gwyneth Anne McDonald. BA, Duke U., 1986, MD, 1990. Diplomate Am. Bd. Radiology. Med. intern U. N.C., Chapel Hill, 1990-91; resident in radiology Duke U. Med. Ctr., Durham, N.C., 1991-95; fellow in chest radiology Mallinckrodt Inst. Radiology, St. Louis, 1995-96, instr., 1996-97, asst. prof., 1997-2001; asst. prof., co-chief computed tomography, dir. cardiovascular MR program Yale U., Dept. Radiology, Yale-New Haven Hosp., New Haven. Contbr. articles to profl. jours. and chpts. to book. Recipient Michael Nathan award for cmty. svc., 1989-90, Arthritis Found. Med. Student Rsch. award, 1988-89, Ciba-Geigy award, 1990, Upjohn award for cmty. svc., 1990; Melvin M. Figley fellow, 1997, Siemens Med. Systems./Radiol. Soc. N.Am. fellow, 1996-98; Radiol. Soc. N.Am. Eastman Kodak scholar, 1999. Fellow: Am. Coll. Chest Physicians; mem.: AMA, N.Am. Soc. for Cardiac Imaging (bd. dirs.), Am. Coll. Radiology, Am. Heart Assn., Soc. Thoracic Radiology, Internat. Soc. Magnetic Resonance in Medicine, Radiol. Soc. N.Am., Am. Roentgen Ray Soc. Office: 333 Cedar St New Haven CT 06510-3206

WOODARD, PAUL ESTY, bibliotherapy librarian emeritus, nurse; b. Chico, Calif., Oct. 24, 1921; s. Herman Eugene and Cecile Ellen (Esty) W.; m. Marion Kathryn Boyajian, July 28, 1962; children: Pamela Karen, Geoffrey Esty. RN, Wichita-St. Joseph Hosp., 1950; BA, Friends U., 1952; PhD, Western U., 1955; cert. in libr. sci., Framingham State Coll., 1973. Dir. student health Friends U., Wichita, 1950-52; nurse Mt. Auburn Hosp., Cambridge, Mass., 1952-53; pvt. duty nurse Mass. Gen. Hosp., Boston, 1955-63; dir. insvc. edn. New Eng. Bapt. Hosp., 1963-69, dir. health scis. libr., 1970-95, notary pub., 1964—. Mem. phys. fitness coun. YMCA, Cambridge, 1961-63. Recipient Recognition awards ARC, 1955, 63, Svc. award Am. Friends Svc. Com., 1946, Med. Libr. Assn. award, 1995. Mem. Medieval Acad. of Am. (life), New Eng. Historic Geneal. Soc. (life), Nat. Geographic Soc. (life), Med. Libr. Assn., Alpha Kappa Tau. Avocations: numismatist, genealogist, mediaevalist. Home: 46 Hickory Cliff Rd Newton Upper Falls MA 02464-1209 Office: New Eng Bapt Hosp Paul E Woodard Health Scis Libr 125 Parker Hill Ave Ste 2 Boston MA 02120-2865

WOODARD, RICHARD CHARLES, college administrator; b. Utica, N.Y., Feb. 13, 1939; s. Albert Richard and Margaret Olwen (Williams) W.; m. Elizabeth Dorothy Vanderpool, Sept. 10, 1965; children: Lisa, Jennifer. BA, Utica Coll., 1961; MA, Syracuse U., 1966. With Peace Corps, Venezuela, 1962-64; high sch. tchr. N.Y. and Mich. pub. schs., 1966-71; teaching asst. Calif. State U., Chico, 1971-73; dir. rsch. United Way of Greater Rochester, N.Y., 1974-83; dir. prospect rsch. Hobart and William Smith Colls., Geneva, 1983-87, dir. devel. ops., 1989-96, dir. advancement svcs., computer ops., 1996—2002; assoc. dir. major gifts U. Rochester, 1987-88; dir. major gifts Utica (N.Y.) Coll., 1988-89. Mem.: APHA, Assn. Profl. Rsch. Am. (founder, bd. dirs. upstate N.Y. chpt. 1991—95, 1999—2002, pres. 2000—02). Presbyterian. Home: 1 Mountain Rd Rochester NY 14625-1816 E-mail: woodard.r@att.net.

WOODARD, WALLACE WILLIAM, III, quality advocate; b. Balt., May 25, 1950; s. Wallace William and Helen Cecelia (Berger) W.; m. Patricia Ann Dunphy, Dec. 31, 1976; children: Wallace William IV, Cassaundra Ann, Lauren Ashley. BS in Indsl. Engring., Georgia Tech., 1972; MS in Mgmt., Rensselaer Poly., 1977. Sr. quality control engr. Martin Marietta Aerospace, Orlando, Fla., 1972-75; nuclear quality assurance engr. NE Utilities, Hartford, Conn., 1975-78; prin. quality engr. Fla. Power and Light, Juno Beach, Fla., 1978—; nuclear energy adv. West Palm Beach, 1990. Speaker Pvt. Industry Council, West Palm Beach, Fla., 1986; coach Palm Beach Gardens Youth Athletics, 1983-86, YMCA, Palm Beach Gardens, 1984-85; exec. advisor Jr. Achievement, Miami, Fla., 1981; asst. scoutmaster Boy Scouts Am., 1989-95, Gulf Stream Coun. 1997-2000; bd. dirs. Homeowners, 1992-2000. Mem. Am. Soc. Quality Control (cert. quality engr., reliability engr. 1987, chmn. 1986-87, sec. mgmt. 1987-88, ISO 9000 lead assessor 1995—), Am. Inst. Indsl. Engrs., Am. Nuclear Soc., Sigma Phi Epsilon. Clubs: Toastmasters Internat. (treas. 1984-85). Roman Catholic. Avocations: water sports, skiing, tennis, travel. Home: 12774 S Normandy Way West Palm Beach FL 33410-1422 Office: Fla Power and Light 700 Universe Blvd North Palm Beach FL 33408-2657

WOODARD,JR. FREDRICK JAMES, music educator, musician; b. Kansas City, Mo., Mar. 2, 1961; s. Fredrick James Woodard,Sr and Sandra Josephine Woodard, Barbara Ann Woodard (Stepmother); m. Rochelle Mareace Breeden, May 4, 1996; children: Kahmal London, Fredrick Woodard,III, Deniece Woodard. MusB, Berklee Coll. of Music, Boston, 1983; MEd, U. of Mass., Boston, 2000. Cert. Tchr. Mass., 1990, Ednl Administr. Mass., 2000. Gen. music tchr. St Joseph and St. Patrick Schs., Roxbury, Mass., 1992—94; guitar tchr. and instrumental ensemble dir. Belmont Hill Sch., Belmont, 1992—94; guitar,electric bass and strings tchr. Roland Hayes Divsn. of Music, Roxbury, 1994—; pres./owner Ujam Records, 1996—; bandleader The Fred Woodard Trio, 1988—; freelance musician Various bands in the Boston area, Boston, 1983—. Musician (guitarist,producer,composer,arranger): (jazz compact disc) Arrival, 1999, (compact disc) 1715, 2001 (GBOS Image Award Jazz Artist of the Yr., 2002). Mem. Dudley St. Neighborhood Initiative, Roxbury, Mass., 2001—02. Mem.: Mass. Music Educators Assn., Internat. Assn. for Jazz Edn. Avocations: history, photography, travel. Office: Ujam Records PO Box 190586 Boston MA 02119 Personal E-mail: fwtrio@hotmail.com. E-mail: fwtrio@hotmail.com.

WOODBRIDGE, JOHN DUNNING, history and church history educator; b. Salisbury, N.C., May 24, 1941; s. Charles Jahleel and Ruth (Dunning) W.; m. Susan Jane Frerichs, June 28, 1970; children: Elisabeth Anne, Joshua, David. BA in History, Wheaton Coll., 1963; MA in History, Mich. State U., 1965; PhD de Troisième Cycle, U. Toulouse, France, 1969; MDiv, Trinity Evang. Div. Sch., Deerfield, Ill., 1971. Vis. prof. history U. Toulouse, 1968-69; asst. prof. history Trinity Coll., Deerfield, 1970-74; prof. ch. history Trinity Evang. Div. Sch., 1970—; vis. prof. history Northwestern U., Evanston, Ill., 1988-95. Vis. prof. religion Hautes Etudes, Sorbonne, U. Paris, 1996, 99. Author: Biblical Authority, 1982, Revolt in Pre-revolutionary France, 1995; editor: Great Leaders of the Christian Church, 1988; co-editor: Historische Kritik und biblischer kanon, 1988; sr. editor Christianity Today, 1997-99. NEH fellow, 1973-74, Herzog August Bibliothek fellow, 1982, ACLS fellow, Paris, 1976-77; NEH summer grant, Chgo., 1995. Mem. Am. Soc. Eighteenth Century Studies, Soc. French History. Mem. Evangelical Free Ch. Avocation: composing music.

WOODBRIDGE, JOHN MARSHALL, architect, urban planner; b. N.Y.C., Jan. 26, 1929; s. Frederick James and Catherine (Baldwin) W.; m. Sally Byrne, Aug. 14, 1954; children: Lawrence F., Pamela B., Diana B.; m. Carolyn Kizer, Apr. 8, 1975. BA magna cum laude, Amherst Coll., 1951; M.F.A. in Architecture, Princeton U., 1956. Designer John Funk, architect, San Francisco, 1957-58; designer, assoc. partner Skidmore, Owings & Merrill, 1959-73; staff dir. Pres.'s Adv. Council and Pres.'s Temporary Commn. on Pennsylvania Ave., Washington, 1963-65; exec. dir. Pennsylvania Ave. Devel. Corp., 1973-77. Lectr. architecture U. Calif., Berkeley; vis. prof. U. Oreg., Washington U., St. Louis. Co-author: Buildings of the Bay Area, 1960, A Guide to Architecture in San Francisco and Northern California, 1973, Architecture San Francisco, 1982, San Francisco Architecture, 1992. Recipient Fed. Design Achievement award Nat. Endowment for Arts, 1988; Fulbright scholar to France, 1951-52. Fellow AIA (emeritus); mem. Nat. Trust Historic Preservation, Soc. Archtl. Historians, Phi Beta Kappa. Democrat. Episcopalian. Home and Office: 19772 8th St E Sonoma CA 95476-3849

WOODBRIDGE, NORMA JEAN, registered nurse, writer; b. Flushing, N.Y., Apr. 21, 1931; d. Charles Jahleel Woodbridge and Ruth Eyman Dunning. BS in Nursing Edn., Temple U., 1958; RN, U. Pa., 1952; LittD, World Congress Poets, Cairo, 1990. RN, Fla. Sr. RN, forensic State of Fla. Dept. Corrections, 1992-95; staff RN Lee Convalescent Ctr., Ft. Myers, Fla., 1997-98; unit mgr. Tandem Health Care, N. Ft. Myers, 1998-99; nurse Cape Coral (Fla.) Gen. Staff Rehab., 1999—. Author-in-residence Highland Pk. (N.J.) Sch. Sys., 1988-90. Author: African Realities and Dreams, 1987, Resting Places, 1988, Meditations of a Modern Pilgrim, 1990; contbr. Christmas Blessings, 2002; composer (jazz album) Watercolor Dreams, 1982; playwright Switch: Switch, 1998; poetry reading on NPR, 2001. Yaddo fellow Yaddo Writing Colony, 1988. Mem. ASCAP, Nat. League Am. Pen Women (pres. Princeton br. 1982-85), N.J. Poetry Soc. (v.p. 1987-88). Avocations: travel, fishing, gourmet cooking, hiking, theatre. Home: 2606 Zoysia Ln Fort Myers FL 33917-2476

WOODBURY, DIXON JOHN, physiology educator, researcher; b. Seattle, Dec. 31, 1956; s. John Walter and Betty (Gunderson) W.; m. Susan Diana Harvey, Mar. 20, 1980; children: James Dixon, Thomas Walter, Emily Susan, Kara Leigh. BS in Physics and Chemistry magna cum laude, U. Utah, 1980; PhD in Physiology and Biophysics, U. Calif., Irvine, 1986. Postdoctoral fellow in biochemistry Brandeis U., Waltham, Mass., 1986-89; rsch. assoc. Howard Hughes Med. Inst., 1989-90; asst. prof. Wayne State U., Detroit, 1990-97, assoc. prof., 1997-2001, Brigham Young U., Provo, Utah, 2001—. Unit commr. Boy Scouts Am., 1984-86, 96-98; bishopric Ch. of Jesus Christ LDS, 1997-99. Fellow U. Calif., 1980, 81, 85, Muscular Dystrophy Assn., 1986-88. Mem. IEEE, Soc. for Neurosci., Biophys. Soc. Office: Brigham Young U 574 Widtsoe Bldg Provo UT 84602-5255

WOODBURY, NATHALIE FERRIS SAMPSON, anthropologist, editor; b. Humboldt, Ariz., Jan. 25, 1918; d. Frank Herbert Sampson and Nathalie Ferris; m. Richard Benjamin Woodbury, Sept. 18, 1948. AB, Barnard Coll., 1939; ABD, Columbia U., 1942. Instr. Bklyn. Coll., 1944-45; asst. prof. Eastern N.Mex. Coll., Portales, 1945-46; instr. anthropology U. Ariz., Tucson, 1946-47; lectr. anthropology Barnard Coll., N.Y.C., 1952-55, exec. officer anthropology, 1954-56, asst. dean studies, 1956-58. Co-author: History of Hawikuh, 1966; columnist Past Is Present, History of Anthropology, 1984-96; newsletter editor Am. Anthrop. Assn., 1965-74; assoc. editor Am. Anthropologist, 1973-75. Mem. Shutesbury (Mass.) Hist. Commn., 1995—. Recipient Disting. Svc. award Am. Anthrop. Assn., 1978, Disting. Svc. award Soc. Am. Archaeology, 1988, Presdl. Recognition award, 1990. Mem. Am. Anthrop. Assn. (sec. 1970-75, bd. dirs. 1975-78), Am. Ethnological Soc. (sec. 1960-66, treas. 1978-79), Soc. Am. Archaeology (treas. 1965-67), Nature Conservancy (hon., life). Avocations: wildlife, conservation, dogs.

WOODBURY, RICHARD BENJAMIN, anthropologist, educator; b. West Lafayette, Ind., May 16, 1917; s. Charles Goodrich and Marion (Benjamin) W.; m. Nathalie Ferris Sampson, Sept. 18, 1948. Student, Oberlin Coll., 1934-36; BS in Anthropology cum laude, Harvard U., 1939, MA, 1942, PhD, 1949; postgrad., Columbia U., 1939-40. Archeol. research, Ariz., 1938, 39, Fla., 1940, Guatemala, 1947-49, El Morro Nat. Monument, N.Mex., 1953-56, Tehuacan, Mex., 1964; archaeologist United Fruit Co. Zaculeu Project, Guatemala, 1947-50; assoc. prof. anthropology U. Ky., 1950-52, Columbia U., 1952-58; rsch. assoc. prof. anthropology interdisciplinary arid lands program U. Ariz., 1959-63; curator archeology and anthropology U.S. Nat. Mus., Smithsonian Instn., Washington, 1963-69, acting. head office anthropology, 1965-66, chmn. office anthropology, 1966-67; prof., chmn. dept. anthropology U. Mass., Amherst, 1969-73, prof., 1973-81, prof. emeritus, 1981—, acting assoc. provost, dean grad. sch., 1973-74. Mem. divsn. anthropology and psychology NRC, 1954-57; bd. dirs. Archaeol. Conservancy, 1979-84, Valley Health Plan, Amherst, 1981-84, Mus. of No. Ariz., 1983-90; liason rep. for Smithsonian Instn., Com. for Recovery of Archeol. Remains, 1965-69; assoc. seminar on ecol. systems and cultural evolution Columbia U., 1964-73; mem. exec. com. bd. dirs. Human Relations Area Files, Inc., New Haven, Conn., 1968-70; cons. Conn. Hist. Commn., 1970-72. Author (with A.S. Trik) The Ruins of Zaculeu, Guatemala, 2 vols., 1953, Prehistoric Stone Implements of Northeastern Arizona, 1954, Alfred V. Kidder, 1973, Sixty Years of Southwestern Archaeology, 1993; editor: (with I.A. Sanders) Societies Around the World (2 vols.), 1953, (with others) The Excavation of Hawikuh, 1966, Am. Antiquity, 1954-58, Abstracts of New World Archaeology; editor-in-chief: Am. Anthropologist, 1975-78; mem. editorial bd.: Am. Jour. Archeology, 1957-72. Mem. sch. com., Shutesbury, Mass., 1979-82; chmn. finance com. Friends of Amherst Stray Animals, 1983-85, trustee, 1991—. With USAF, 1942-45. Fellow Mus. No. Ariz., 1985. Fellow AAAS (coun. rep. Am. Anthrop. Assn. 1961-63, com. on desert and arid zones rsch. Southwest and Rocky Mountains divsn. 1958-64, vice-chair 1962-64, com. arid lands 1969-74, sec. 1970-72), Am. Anthrop. Assn. (exec. bd. 1963-66, A.V. Kidder award 1989), Archeol. Inst. Am. (exec. com. 1965-67); mem. Soc. Am. Archeology (treas. 1953-54, pres. 1958-59, chmn. fin. com. 1987-89, Fiftieth Anniversary award 1985, Disting. Svc. award 1988), Ariz. Archeol. and Hist. Soc., Nature Conservancy, Archeol. Conservancy (life). Office: U Mass Dept Anthropology Machmer Hall Amherst MA 01003

WOODBURY, ROBERT CHARLES, lawyer; b. Sheridan, N.Y., July 7, 1929; s. Wendell F. and Lillian S. (Towne) W.; m. Martha Bayard Page, Jan. 25, 1958. BEE, Rensselaer Poly. Inst., 1950; JD, Cornell U., 1953. Bar: N.Y. 1954, U.S. Dist. Ct. (so. dist.) N.Y. 1965, U.S. Dist. Ct. (we. dist.) N.Y. 1979, U.S. Ct. Appeals (4th cir.) 1964, U.S. Ct. Claims 1961, U.S. Ct. Mil. Appeals 1956, U.S. Patent Office 1961; lic. profl. engr., N.Y. Project engr. Army reactors program U.S. Atomic Energy Commn., 1957-60; assoc. Reid & Priest, N.Y.C., 1962-70; pvt. practice Dunkirk, N.Y., 1971—; ptnr. Aular & Woodbury, 1973-81, Morten & Woodbury, Dunkirk, 1982-88. Gen. counsel N.Y. State Temp. Commn. Environ. Impact Major Pub. Utility Facilities, 1970-71; del. N.Y. 8th Jud. Dist. Rep. Jud. Nominating Conv., 1985—; chmn. bd. dirs. Woodbury Farms, Ltd., 1965-98, Woodbury Vineyards, 1968-91. Assoc. trustee Buffalo Gen. Hosp. Found., 1994-96; trustees coun. Buffalo Gen. Healthcare Sys., 1996-98, steering com. 1996-98; mem. trustees coun. Kaleida Health Sys., Buffalo, 1998-2001, Kaleida Health Cmty. Coun., 2001—; founding pres. Chautauqua County Arts Coun., 1971; town atty. Town of Sheridan, 1972-75; dist. counsel city sch. dist. City of Dunkirk, 1973-82; co-founder No. Chautauqua Indsl. Roundtable, 1979; co-chmn. Chmn.'s Club, Chautauqua County Rep. Com. 1988-98; chmn., pres., dir., counsel Historic Harbor Renaissance, Inc., 1999—. Lt. USN, 1954-57. Fellow N.Y. Bar Found.; mem. N.Y. State Bar Assn. (chmn. com. atomic energy law 1967-69, chmn. com. pub. utility law 1969-71, mem. action unit 5 regulatory reform N.Y. 1980-83), Bar Assn. No. Chautauqua (pres. 1979), Cornell Law Assn., Rensselaer Alumni Assn., Dunkirk C. of C. (pres. 1979), Mid-Day Club Buffalo, Chautauqua Yacht Club. Republican. Presbyterian. Avocations: skiing, wine, sailing. Home: 3300 S Roberts Rd Fredonia NY 14063-9418 Office: PO Box 800 87 E 4th St Dunkirk NY 14048-2225 E-mail: bobhere@netsync.net.

WOODBURY, RODNEY DELWIN, music educator; b. Las Vegas, Nev., Jan. 20, 1976; s. Rodney Dennis and Patricia Woodbury; m. Cassia Marie Taylor, June 8, 1996; 1 child Maisy. MusB, U. Nev., Las Vegas, 1999. Cert. ID secondary edn.in music. Dir. of bands Century H.S., Pocatello, Idaho, 1999—. Mem.: Nat. Assn. of Music Edn., Phi Kappa Phi, Phi Mu Alpha. Avocation: worship music. Office: Century H S 7801 Diamondback Dr Pocatello ID 83204 E-mail: woodburo@d25.k12.id.us.

WOODBURY, SARA JEAN, poet; b. Eau Claire, Wis., Oct. 15, 1944; d. Thorwald Orstad W. and Jean McDermid; m. Lon E., Aug. 23, 1967 (div. July 1976); children: Ruth Ellen, Samuel Todd, Melanie. Student, U. Idaho, 1962—67; postgrad., U. Wash., 1972, Ea. Wash. U., 1980. Staff KXLY, Spokane, 1963-66; staff sec. Morgan & Morgan, Lewiston, Idaho, 1966, U.S. Ho. of Reps., Washington, 1967—69. Author: Edge of Night, 1999, Ways of Silence, 2000, A Field, A Mountain, 2001, also numerous poems; contbr. articles to profl. jours., 10 chpts. to books. Vol. Margaret Leonard Campaign, Spokane, 1982, Jack Gerraighty Campaign, Spokane, 1998; mem. Neighborhood Coun., Spokane. Named 1st Lady, Lake Hills Jaycees, Bellevue, Wash. Mem. Volume II, Spokane Open Poets Assn., Pen West USA. Avocations: music, walking, art galleries. Home: 1029 W 1st Ave Apt 514 Spokane WA 99201-4059

WOODBURY, STEPHEN ABBOTT, economics educator; b. Beverly, Mass., Oct. 25, 1952; s. Stephen E. and Barbara (Sandberg) W.; m. Susan Pozo, May 29, 1982 (div. June 1992); 1 child, Ricardo Pozo; m. Virginia Baldwin, Dec. 7, 1996. AB, Middlebury (Vt.) Coll., 1975; MS, U. Wis., 1977, PhD, 1981. Asst. prof. of econs. Pa. State U., University Park, 1979-82, Mich. State U., East Lansing, 1982-88, assoc. prof. econs., 1988-94; prof. econs., 1994—; sr. economist W.E. Upjohn Inst., Kalamazoo, 1984—. Dep. dir. Fed. Adv. Coun. on Unemployment Compensation, Washington, 1993-94, cons., 1994-96; cons. U. Hawaii/State of Hawaii, Honolulu, 1991-96, State of Mich. Task Force, Lansing, 1989-90, U.S. Dept. Labor, Washington, 1988, 96—, European Communities Commn., Brussels, 1987-88; vis. prof. U. Stirling, Scotland, 1992; vis. scholar Fed. Res. Bd., Washington, 1992. Author: Tax Treatment of Fringe Benefits, 1991; editor: Search Theory and Unemployment, 2002, Employee Benefits and Labor Markets in the U.S. and Canada, 2000, Reform of the Unemployment Insurance System, 1998, Long-Term Unemployment and Reemployment Policies, 2000; contbr. articles to profl. jours. Recipient Rsch. grants William H. Donner Found., 1991, U.S. Dept. Health and Human Svcs., 1985, 99, U.S. Dept. Labor, 1995, 98. Filene Rsch. Inst., 1996, Ctr. Credit Union Rsch., U. Wis., 1997, AMA, 2001. Mem. Am. Econ. Assn., Am. Statis. Assn., Assn. for Evolutionary Econs., Indsl. Rels. Rsch. Assn., Midwest Econs. Assn. (1st v.p. 1993-94, pres. 1998-99), Nat. Acad. Social Ins., Soc. Labor Economists, Nat. Tax Assn. Office: Dept Econs Marshall Hall Mich State U East Lansing MI 48824 also: WE Upjohn Inst 300 S Westnedge Ave Kalamazoo MI 49007-4630

WOODCOCK, CYNTHIA HARDIN, program development strategic planning; b. Jacksonville, Fla., Oct. 2, 1953; d. Jack Bealle and Doris Jane (Peebles) Hardin; m. Charles Edwin Woodcock III, June 21, 1975. BA summa cum laude, U. N.C., 1975; MBA in Fin., Columbia U., 1979. Asst. program officer The Robert Wood Johnson Foundation, Princeton, N.J., 1976-78; fin. analyst N.J. Dept. Health, Trenton, 1979-80; program officer The Commonwealth Fund, N.Y.C., 1980-85, sr. program officer, 1985-87, asst. v.p. program fin. and mgmt., 1987-90; mgmt. cons., 1990-95; dir. program devel. Internat. Life Scis. Inst., 1995-97; ptnr. Futures, Inc., Ellicott City, Md., 1997—. Bd. dirs. Piano Perspectives Sch. Music. Mem. Sigma Delta Pi, Phi Beta Kappa. Methodist. Avocations: dress design, piano, culinary arts. Office: Futures Inc 10154 Bracken Dr Ellicott City MD 21042-1673

WOODCOCK, DAVID GEOFFREY, architect, educator; b. Manchester, Eng., May 28, 1937; s. Herbert Edwin and Constance Mary (Bristol) W.; m. Kathleen Mary Bishop, Oct. 1, 1960 (dec. 1964); 1 child, Jonathan Alfred; m. Valerie Frances Gubbins, July 4, 1964; children: Frances Mary, Penelope Jane. BA with 1st class honors in Architecture, U. Manchester, 1960, D in Town Planning, 1966. Registered architect, Tex. Lectr. U. Manchester, 1961; asst. prof. Tex. A&M U., College Station, 1962-66, assoc. prof., 1970-76, prof., 1976—; sr. lectr. Kent. Inst. Art & Design, Canterbury, England, 1966-70. Pvt. practice, College Station, 1980—, Canterbury, 1966-70. Bd. dirs. Opera and Performing Arts Soc. Tex. A&M U., 1980-83, 88-91, pres., 1993-94, adv. bd. Hammons Sch. Architecture Drury Coll., Mo., 1990-93, Savannah (Ga.) Coll. Arts and Design/Architecture, 1987-93; active Episc. Diocese Tex. Archtl. Commn., 1987-95. Recipient Rsch. Excellence award Tex. Hist. Commn., 1991, Romieniec award for archtl. edn. Tex. Soc. Architecture, 1995, Truett Latimer Profl. award Preservation Tex., Inc., 1998. Fellow AIA; mem. Assn. for Preservation Tech. Internat. bd. dirs. 1990—, v.p. 1998-99, pres. 1999-2001), Nat. Coun. for Preservation Edn., Assn. Collegiate Schs. Architecture (regional dir. 1981-84, Disting. Prof. 1991). Avocations: drawing, creative and gifted education, choral singing. Office: Tex A&M U Dept Architecture College Station TX 77843-3137 E-mail: woodcock@archone.tamu.edu.

WOODCOCK, JANET, federal official; b. Washington, Aug. 29, 1948; d. John and Frances (Crocker) W.; m. Roger Henry Miller, Nov. 16, 1981; children: Kathleen Miller, Susanne Miller. BS cum laude, Bucknell U., 1970; MD, Northwestern U., Chgo., 1977. Diplomate Am. Bd. Internal Medicine. Intern Hershey Med. Ctr./Pa. State U., 1977-78, resident in internal medicine, 1978-80, chief resident in medicine, 1980-81; fellow in rheumatology U. Calif./VA Med. Ctr., San Francisco, 1982-84; instr. medicine divsn. rheumatology and immunology VA Med. Ctr., 1984-85; med. officer divsn. biol. investigational new drugs Ctr. for Biologics Evaluation and Rsch./FDA, Rockville, Md., 1986-87, group leader divsn. biol. investigational new drugs, 1987-88, dep. dir. divsn. biol. investigational new drugs, 1988, dir. divsn. biol. investigational new drugs, 1988-90; dir. Ctr. for Drug Evaluation and Rsch./FDA, 1994—; acting dep. dir. Ctr. for Biologics Evaluation and Rsch., FDA, 1990-92, dir. office of therapeutics rsch. and rev., 1992-94; dir. Ctr. for Drug Evaluation and Rsch., FDA, 1994—. Instr. medicine, asst. prof. divsn. gen. internal medicine Hershey Med. Ctr./Pa. State U., 1981; analytical chemist rsch. divsn. A.B. Dick Co., Niles, Ill., 1971-73. Nat. Merit scholar Bucknell U., 1966, Pa. State scholar, 1966; Rsch. fellow Am. Rheumatism Assn.; VA Investigator grantee, 1985. Mem. Alpha Omega Alpha, Alpha Lambda Delta. Office: Dept Health & Human Svc Center Drug Evaluation & Rsch 1451 Rockville Pike Rockville MD 20852-1420*

WOODCOCK, JOHN ALDEN, lawyer; b. Bangor, Maine, July 6, 1950; s. John Alden Woodcock and Joan (Carlin) Nestler; m. Beverly Ann Newcombe, July 14, 1973; children: John A., Patrick C., Christopher C. AB, Bowdoin Coll., 1972; MA, U. London, 1973; JD, U. Maine, 1976. Bar: Maine 1976, U.S. Dist. Ct. Maine 1976. Assoc. Stearns, Finnegan & Needham, Bangor, 1976-80; asst. dist. atty. Penobscot County, 1977-78; ptnr. Mitchell & Stearns, 1980-91, Weatherbee, Woodcock, Burlock & Woodcock, Bangor, 1991—. Mem. alumni coun. Bowdoin Coll., Brunswick, Maine, 1992—, pres., 1995-96, trustee, 1996—; bd. dirs. Ea. Maine Med. Ctr., Bangor, 1980—, chmn, 1996—, Ea. Maine Healthcare, Bangor, 1989—. Master Ballou Inn of Ct.; fellow Maine Bar Found.; mem. ABA, Maine State Bar Assn., Penobscot County Bar Assn. Home: 110 Main Rd N Hampden ME 04444-1404 Office: Weatherbee Woodcock Burlock & Woodcock 136 Broadway Bangor ME 04401-5206

WOODCOCK, JONATHAN HUGH, neurologist; b. Chelsea, Mass., Oct. 17, 1951; s. Hugh Wesson and Ann Harriet (Walker) W.; children: Rachel Ann, Mollie Christine, Sarah Margaret. BA, Houghton Coll., 1973; MD, SUNY, Buffalo, 1977. Diplomate Am. Bd. Internal Medicine, Am. Bd. Neurology and Psychiatry. Resident in internal medicine Case Western Res. Univ. Hosps., Cleve., 1977-79; resident in neurology Mass. Gen. Hosp., Boston, 1979-82; resident in psychiatry McLean Hosp., Belmont, Mass., 1982-84; asst. neurology Mass. Gen. Hosp., Boston, 1984-89; dir. neuropsychiatry unit McLean Hosp., Belmont, 1984-89; med. dir. NeuroBehavioral Inst. of Rockies, Boulder, Colo., 1989-90, Mediplex Rehab-Denver, Thornton, 1991-97, Greeley (Colo.) Ctr. for Independence, 1998—. Instr. psychiatry Harvard Med. Sch., Boston, 1984—89; clin. instr. neurologu U. Colo. Health Scis. Ctr., 1992—, asst. clin. prof., 1993, clin. assoc. prof., 2001—, asst. clin. prof. rehab. medicine, 1998—; pres. Colo. Health Injury Found., 1994—95; prof. adv. bd. Epilepsy Found. Colo., 1991—97. Co-author: Impulse Control Disorders, 1986, Behavioral Aspects of Huntington's Disease, 1990. Fellow rsch. fellow neurology, Mass. Gen. Hosp., 1981—84. Mem. Am. Acad. Neurology, Am. Neuropsychiat. Assn., Behavioral Neurology Soc., Am. Soc. Neurorehab. Avocations: skiing, snowboarding, hiking. E-makl. Office: 8515 Pearl St Ste 203 Denver CO 80229-4809 E-mail: woodcockmd@aol.com.

WOODCOCK, LES, editorial director; b. Amityville, N.Y., June 30, 1927; s. Horace Henry and Carol (Reimenschneider) W.; m. Mary Theresa Gill, Aug. 16, 1953 (div. Dec. 1992); children: Mark, Kathleen Lopes, Susan, Brian, Kevin, Maria Schiavello; m. Mary Peterson, Sept. 13, 1997. BS, Columbia U., 1954. Writer, editor Sports Illustrated, N.Y.C., 1954-68; corr. Time Inc. News Bur., Rome, 1968-69; mng. editor, v.p. Sportsworld Comm. Corp., N.Y.C., 1969-70; editor, v.p. Sports Guide, Inc., 1970-71; editor, pub., v.p. Turf & Sport Internat., Ltd., Balt., 1972-75; asst. editor, pub. Classic, N.Y.C., 1975-79; editor L.I. Life, Manhasset, N.Y., 1980-82; pres. Edit Aids, Douglaston and N.Y.C., 1983-88; editl. dir. Major League Mktg., Westport, Conn., 1985—. Contbr. articles to profl. jours. Pres. Plandome Civic Assn., 1967-68. With U.S. Army, 1946-47. Mem. Soc. of Silurians, Time-Life Alumni Soc. Democrat. Home and Office: 447 E 14th St Apt 3A New York NY 10009-2721 E-mail: cardwriter@aol.com.

WOODCOCK, RICHARD WESLEY, educational psychologist; b. Portland, Oreg., Jan. 29, 1928; s. Carol Wesley and Captola Winifred (Catterlin) W.; m. Annie Lee Plant, Aug. 16, 1951; children: Donna, Dianne, Judy, Wayne; m. Ana Felicia Muñoz-Sandoval, June 14, 1991. BS, U. Oreg., 1949, MEd, 1953, EdD, 1956. Diplomate of Am. Bd. of Profl. Psychol. Lt. USN, 1945-46, 50-51; elem. tchr. Arago Schs., Oreg., 1951-52; dir. spl. edn. Coos County Sch., Coquille, 1952-54, Corvallis (Oreg.) Pub. Schs., 1955-57; asst. prof. psychology Western Oreg. U., 1957-61; assoc. prof. spl. edn. U. No. Colo., Greeley, 1961-63; prof. spl. edn. Peabody Coll. Vanderbilt U., 1963-68; editor, dir. rsch. Am. Guidance Svc., 1968-72; dir. Measurement Learning Cons., Tenn., Oreg., 1972—; vis. scholar U. Ariz., 1985-88, U. So. Calif., L.A., 1988-91; rsch. prof. psychology U. Va., 1993-97. Cons. NCAA, 1989-94. Author: (battery tests) Mini-Battery of Achievement, 1994, Woodcock Language Proficiency Battery English and Spanish forms, 1991, 95, Woodcock-Muñoz Language Surveys, 1993, W-J Psycho-Edn. Battery, 1977, 89, 2001, Bateria Woodcock Psico-Educativa en Español, 1982, 96, Woodcock Reading Mastery Tests, 1973-87, Scales of Independent Behavior, 1984, 95, G-F-W Auditory Skills Battery, 1976, The Peabody Rebus Reading Program, 1967, The Colorado Braille Battery, 1966, Woodcock Diagnostic Reading Battery, 1997, Mather-Woodcock Group Writing Tests, 1997; contbr. numerous articles to profl. jours. Scholar vis. scholar, Vanderbilt U., 2002—. Fellow Am. Acad. Sch. Psychology.

WOODDELL, PHILO GLENN, fine arts educator, radio broadcaster and producer; b. Hutchinson, Kans., Sept. 3, 1941; s. Philo Davis and Jean Elise Wooddell. B of Music Edn., Southwestern Coll., Winfield, Kans., 1963; MM, Crane Sch. Music, Potsdam, N.Y., 1985; MA, NYU, 1989. Cert. in music and speech edn., N.Y. Tchr., chmn. fine arts/humanities dept. Jeffersonville (N.Y.)-Youngsville Ctrl. Sch. Dist. 1, 1965-97. Local host N.P.R.'s Morning Edit., WJFF-FM, prodr., host Sunday Brunch, Music of the Cinema, Music of the Stage, NPR spls., Nancy LaMott Remembrance and Kiowa Myths and Legends, Paul Winter and Friends, Rte. 66, Kans.: Am.'s Heartland; mem. programming and adv. bds. Radio Catskill, also pres. bd. trustees, 1991-92, v.p. bd. trustees, 1993; film music moderator Universal City, Calif., MOMA, N.Y.C., and Lowes Theatre, N.Y.C.; clinician on ednl. theatre N.Y. State Music Educators Assn., N.Y.C.; music and media clinician Western Heritage Mus., Glendale/Burbank, Calif.; mem. adv. com. Cities as Sch. Bldg. Leadership Team; media clinician Tisch Sch. of the Arts, N.Y.C., 1994; film music moderator UCLA, 1995; film music conf. presenter USC, L.A., 1996; lifetime career achievement m.c. honoring Steven Sondheim, NYU. Dir. profl. and semi-profl. prodns. for dinner, proscenium, exptl. and children's theatre; performed with Central City (Colo.) Opera Assn., Kansas City Starlight Theatre, Dallas Summer Musicals, N.P.R. Playhouse; shows at various Catskill resorts; vocalist with Phila. Orch., Saratoga Performing Arts Ctr., Saratoga Springs, N.Y., Prairie Fest Arts Festival, Walnut Valley Music Festival, Winfield, Kans.; voice over/narration experience; editor The Collegian; film music moderator Lowe's Theatre, N.Y.C., 1997; guest edn. contbr. Middletown N.Y.-Times-Herald Rev.; contbr. articles to profl. jours. Founder Sullivan County (N.Y.) Help Line; founder, bd. dirs. Sullivan County Festival of the Arts Program. Inductee Educator's Hall of Fame, Southwestern Coll. Mem. Am. Guild of Variety Artists, Music Educators Nat. Conf., Am. Choral Dirs. Assn., Am. Film Inst. (charter), Arts Alliance Assn., Arts in Edn. Assn., N.Y. State United Tchrs., Sullivan County Dramatic Workshop, N.Y. State Music Educators Assn., Film Music Soc., Lions Club Internat., Phi Mu Alpha Sinfonia. Home: PO Box 88 50 Durr Rd Jeffersonville NY 12748-5401 Office: Sta WJFF-Radio Catskill PO Box 797 Jeffersonville NY 12748-0797 E-mail: philo100@yahoo.com.

WOODELL, MARY ELIZABETH, social worker; b. High Point, N.C., Aug. 11, 1942; d. Zeno Clifton and Mary Elizabeth (Johnson) Tucker; m. Charles Harold Woodell, Aug. 22, 1964; children: Jennifer, Amy. BA, Wake Forest U., 1964; MSW, U. N.C., 1968. Cert. clin. social worker. Case aide Family Svc. Assn., Winston-Salem, N.C., 1964-65; sch. social worker Cen. Edn. and Rehab. Ctr., 1965-66; pediatric social worker N.C. Meml. Hosp., Chapel Hill, 1968-69; mental health counselor Oconee County Mental Health, Seneca, S.C., 1969—. Mem. NASW, Pilot Club, Phi Beta Kappa. Democrat. Episcopalian. Avocation: bird watching. Home: 1822 Sequoya Way Seneca SC 29672-8079 Office: 115 Carter Park Dr Seneca SC 29678-1152

WOODEN, JOHN ROBERT, former basketball coach; b. Martinsville, Ind., Oct. 14, 1910; s. Joshua Hugh and Roxie (Rothrock) W.; m. Nellie C. Riley, Aug. 8, 1932; children: Nancy Anne, James Hugh. BS, Purdue U., 1932; MS, Ind. State U., 1947. Athletic dir., basketball and baseball coach Ind. State Tchrs. Coll., 1946-48; head basketball coach UCLA, 1948-75. Lectr. to colls., coaches, business. Author: Practical Modern Basketball, 1966, They Call Me Coach, 1972; Contbr. articles to profl. jours. Served to lt. USNR, 1943-46. Named All-Am. basketball player Purdue U., 1930-32, Coll. Basketball Player of Yr., 1932, to All-Time All-Am. Team Helms Athletic Found., 1943, Nat. Basketball Hall of Fame, Springfield (Mass.) Coll., as player, 1960, as coach, 1970, Ind. State Baksetball Hall of Fame, 1962, Calif. Father of Yr., 1964, 75, Coach of Yr. U.S. Basketball Writers Assn., 1964, 67, 69, 70, 72, 73, Sportsman of Yr. Sports Illustrated, 1973, GTE Acad. All-Am., 1994; recipient Whitney Young award Urban League, 1973, 1st ann. Velvet Covered Brick award Layman's Leadership Inst., 1974, 1st ann. Dr. James Naismith Peachbasket award, 1974, medal of excellence Bellarmine Coll., 1985, Sportslike Pathfinder award to Hoosier with extraordinary svc. on behalf of Am. youth, 1993, GET All Am. Acad. Hall of Fame, 1994, 40 for the Age award Sports Illustrated, 1994, the 1st Frank G. Wells Disney award for role model to youth, 1995, Disting. Am. award Pres. Reagan, 1995, Svc. to Mankind award Lexington Theol. Sem., 1995, NCAA Theodore Roosevelt Sportsman award, 1995, Vince Lombardi award for excellence, 2000, Ind. Legend award, 2000; named Basketball Coach of the Century, 2000. *I have tried to live the philosophy of my personal definition of success which I formulated in the middle thirties shortly after I entered the teaching profession. Not being satisfied that success was merely the accumulation of material possessions or the attainment of a position of power or prestige, I chose to define success as "peace of mind which can be attained only through the self-satisfaction that comes from knowing you did your best to become the best that you are capable of becoming.".*

WOODFIELD, DENIS BUCHANAN, retired healthcare company executive; b. N.Y.C., Oct. 23, 1933; s. William Frederick and Margery Brunton (Hoyt) W.; m. Rosemary Humphries, Feb. 16, 1963; children: Katherine, Nicholas, Elizabeth. BA, Harvard U., 1954; PhD, Oxford U., 1962. Trainee Chase Manhattan Bank, N.Y.C., 1962-65; analyst Gen. Electric, 1965-68; banking dir. Pan Am. World Airways, 1968-74; dir. treasury svcs. Johnson & Johnson, New Brunswick, N.J., 1974-93; exec. dir. P.R. Industries and Svcs. Assn., Princeton, 1994-99; ret., 1999. Bd. dirs. Br. Schs. and Univs. Found. Author: Surreptitious Printing in England 1550-1640, 1973, English Armorial Bookbindings, 1958. Trustee Princeton Pub. Libr., 1978-92; bd. dirs. Friends of Princeton Univ. Libr., 1994—. Named hon. mem. Sr. Common Room, Lincoln Coll., Oxford U., 1978. Mem. Manorial Soc. Gt. Britain (U.S. chmn. 1981—), Grolier Club (N.Y.C.), Nassau Club (Princeton, N.J.). Clubs: Grolier (N.Y.C.), Nassau (Princeton, N.J.). Episcopalian. Avocations: geneaology, sailing, bibliographies. Home: 883 Lawrenceville Rd Princeton NJ 08540-4317

WOODFIN, MARTHA, interior designer; b. Georgetown, Tex., Mar. 26, 1939; d. John Edward and Lenora (Beckmann) Cloud, m. Ronald L. Woodfin, Jan. 28, 1962; children: Alfred John, Edward Claude. BS in Interior Design, U. Tex., 1961. Instr. interior design Seattle C.C., 1966-70, Corro Coso C.C., Ridgecrest, Calif., 1972-78; interior designer Wm. L. Davis and Sons Co., Seattle, 1965-71, Leishman-Taack Interiors, Albuquerque, 1986-91, Martha Woodfin Interiors, Sandia Park, N.Mex., 1991—. Mem. Am. Soc. Interior Designers (1st place residential design award 1993, various offices, bd. dirs.). Baptist. Office: Martha Woodfin Interiors PO Box 55 Sandia Park NM 87047-0055

WOODFORD, ANN MARGUERITE, social services administrator, social worker; b. Bklyn., Mar. 12, 1954; d. Nicholas Gonzaga and Lilly Marguerite (Nielson) W. BS cum laude, CUNY, Bklyn., 1976; MA, Fordham U., 1979, MSW, 1990. Cert. secondary edn. educator. Youth dir. tchr. Cath. Diocese Bklyn., 1976-88; therapist, social worker Angel Guardian Home, Bklyn., 1988-90; program coord. Talbot Perkins Childrens Svcs., N.Y.C., 1990-92; supr. Angel Guardian Home Intensive Med. Mgmt. Program, Bklyn., 1992-96; program coord., supr. Cardinal McCloskey Svcs., Therapeutic Foster Boarding Home, Bronx, N.Y., 1996-97; exec. dir. Amethyst House, S.I., 1997—. Resident vol. staff Providence House, Bklyn., 1981-96, Women Helping Women, Flushing, N.Y., 1984-85; cons. Providence House, Bklyn., 1981-97, Angel Guardian Home, Bklyn., 1996—. Mem. Sisters of Charity, Halifax, 1977—; bd. dirs. Advs. for Svcs. for the Blind Multihandicapped, 1994—, S.I. Com. on Alcoholism and Substance Abuse, 1997, co-chair, 1999—; leader Girl Scouts Am., 1994—. Named Outstanding Leader, Girl Scouts Am., Greater N.Y. Coun., 1996. Mem. NASW. Democrat. Roman Catholic. Avocations; gardening, cooking, camping, arts and crafts, singing. Office: Amethyst House Inc 75 Vanderbilt Ave Staten Island NY 10304-2604

WOODFORD, ARTHUR MACKINNON, library director, historian; b. Detroit, Nov. 23, 1940; s. Frank Bury and Mary-Kirk (MacKinnon) W.; children: Mark, Amy. Student, U. Wis., 1958-60; BA in History, Wayne State U., 1963; AM in LS, U. Mich., 1964. Libr. Detroit Pub. Libr., 1964-74; asst. dir. Grosse Pointe (Mich.) Pub. Libr., 1974-77; dir. St. Clair Shores (Mich.) Pub. Libr., 1977—. Author: All Our Yesterdays, 1969, Detroit and Its Banks, 1974, Detroit: American Urban Renaissance, 1979, Charting The Inland Seas, 1991, Tonnancour, 1994, vol. 2, 1996, This Is Detroit: 1701-2001, 2001. With USNR, 1958-64. Mem. Mich. Libr. Assn. (v.p. 1988-89), Gt. Lakes Maritime Inst., Prismatic Club Detroit (pres. 1982), Algonquin Club of Detroit and Windsor (treas. 1983-93). Methodist. Avocations: tennis, bridge, reading, model shipbuilding. Office: St Clair Shores Pub Libr 22500 Eleven Mile Rd Saint Clair Shores MI 48081-1399 Home: 3284 S Channel Dr Harsens Island MI 48028 E-mail: woodfora@libcoop.net.

WOODFORD, DIANNA LYNNE, communications executive; b. Sioux City, Iowa, Oct. 30, 1946; d. Donald Reed and Leah Elizabeth (Lathrum) W. BA, U. S.D., 1968; MA, U. Minn., 1970. Reporter Sioux City Jour., 1968-69; tape libr. Iowa Beef Processors, Dakota City, Nebr., 1971; communications dir. McCracken Concrete Pipe Machinery Co., Sioux City, 1971—. Com. chmn. Greater Sioux City Press Club, 1972-80. Contbr. articles to profl. jours; photographer cover photo Concrete Mag., 1985. Campaign coord. United Way of Siouxland, Sioux City, 1986-91; chmn. bd. dirs. Concrete Pipe Credit Union, Sioux City, 1979-82. Mem. Siouxland Postal Customer Coun., Phi Beta Kappa, Kappa Tau Alpha, Alpha Phi. Republican. Methodist. Avocations: photography, history, travel, diving, skiing. Home: 409 B St Sergeant Bluff IA 51054 Office: McCracken Concrete Pipe Machinery Co 111 S George St Sioux City IA 51103-4801

WOODHOUSE, GAY VANDERPOEL, former state attorney general, lawyer; b. Torrington, Wyo., Jan. 8, 1950; d. Wayne Gaylord and Sally (Rouse) Vanderpoel; m. Randy Woodhouse, Nov. 26, 1953; children: Dustin, Houston. BA with honors, U. Wyo., 1972, JD, 1977. Bar: Wyo. 1978, U.S. Dist. Ct. Wyo., U.S. Supreme Ct. Dir. student Legal Svcs., Laramie, Wyo., 1976—77; assoc. Donald Jones Law Offices, Torrington, 1977—78; asst. atty. gen. State of Wyo., Cheyenne, 1978—84, sr. asst. atty. gen., 1984—89, spl. U.S. atty., 1987—89, asst. U.S. atty., 1990—95, chief dept. atty. gen., 1995—98, atty. gen., 1998—2000. Chmn. Wyo. Tel. Consumer Panel, Casper, 1982—86; advisor Cheyenne Halfway House, 1984—93; chmn. Wyo. Silent Witness Initiative Zero Domestic Violence by 2010, 1997, Wyo. Domestic Violence Elimination Coun., 1999—2001; spl. projects cons. N.Am. Securities Adminstrs. Assn., 1987—89; Chmn. bd. Pathfinder, 1987; S.E. Wyo. Mental Health. Mem.: Laramie County Bar Assn. Republican. Avocations: inline speed skating, stained glass. Address: 211 W 19th St Ste 308 Cheyenne WY 82001 Office: 123 Capitol Bldg Cheyenne WY 82002-0001 Fax: 307-638-1975. E-mail: gwoodh@state.wy.us.*

WOODHOUSE, JOHN FREDERICK, food distribution company executive; b. Wilmington, Del., Nov. 30, 1930; s. John Crawford and Anna (Houth) W.; m. Marilyn Ruth Morrow, June 18, 1955; children: John Crawford II, Marjorie Ann Woodhouse Purdy. BA, Wesleyan U., 1953; DHL, 1997; MBA, Harvard U., 1955. Bus. devel. officer Can. Imperial Bank of Commerce, Toronto, Ont., 1955-59; various fin. positions Ford Motor Co., Dearborn, Mich., 1959-64, Cooper Industries, Inc., Mount Vernon, Ohio, 1964-67; treas. Houston, 1967-69, Crescent-Niagara Corp., Buffalo, 1968-69; exec. v.p., CFO Sysco Corp., Houston, 1969-71, pres., COO, 1972-83, pres., CEO, 1983-85, chmn., CEO, 1985-96, mem. exec. and fin. coms., 1996-98, chmn. bd. dirs., chmn. exec. com., 1998-2000, sr. chmn., 2000—01. Bd. dirs., men. exec. com. Shell Oil Co., 1991-2002; bd. dirs., mem. exec. com. Winrock Internat., 1993-2000; dir. Harvard Bus. Sch. Assocs., 1995-2001. Chmn. Mich. 16th dist. rep. Club, 1962-64; treas. Cooper Industries Found., 1967-69; trustee Wesleyan U., 1976-92, vice-chmn., 1986-92, chmn. comprehensive capital campaign, 1998—; ruling elder Presbyn.. Ch.; trustee, chmn. audit com., mem. exec. com. Mt. Holyoke Coll., South Hadley, Mass., 1996—; bd. dirs. Winrock Internat. Inst. for Agrl. Devel., 1993-2000, mem. fin. com., mem. exec. com., chmn. investment com.; bd. advisors The Retail Food Industry Ctr., U. Minn.; trustee The Am. Inst. Food Distbn., Elmwood Pk., N.J., 2001—, The Food Inst., 2001—. Recipient Herbert Hoover award for disting. svc. to food industry, 2000, Diplomate recognition Nat. Restaurant Assn., 2001. Mem. Nat. Am. Wholesale Grocers Assn. (bd. dirs. 1990—, vice chmn. 1992, chmn. 1994-96), Internat. Foodservice Distbrs. Assn. (Herbert Hoover award 2000), Houston Soc. Fin. Analysts, Fin. Execs. Inst., Harvard Bus. Sch. Club, Sigma Chi. Avocations: backpacking, canoeing, tennis. Office: Sysco Corp 1390 Enclave Pkwy Houston TX 77077-2099 E-mail: woodhouse.john.@corp.sysco.com.

WOODHOUSE, THOMAS EDWIN, lawyer; b. Cedar Rapids, IA, Apr. 30, 1940; s. Keith Wallace and Elinor Julia (Cherny) W.; m. Kiyoko Fujiie, May 29, 1965; children: Miya, Keith, Leighton. AB cum laude, Amherst Coll., 1962; JD, Harvard U., 1965. Bar: N.Y. 1966, U.S. Supreme Ct. 1969, Calif. 1975. Assoc. Chadbourne, Parke, Whiteside & Wolff, N.Y.C., 1965-68; atty./adviser AID, Washington, 1968-69; counsel Pvt. Investment Co. for Asia S.A., Tokyo, 1969-72; ptnr. Woodhouse Lee & Davis, Singapore, 1972-74; assoc. Graham & James, San Francisco, 1974-75; asst. gen. counsel Natomas Co., 1975-81; mem. Lasky, Haas, Cohler & Munter, 1982-90; trust adminstr. Ronald Family Trust A, 1989—, Gordon P. Getty Family Trust, 1994—; sole practice Berkeley, 1990—. Of counsel Wilson, Sonsini, Goodrich & Rosati, Palo Alto, Calif., 1992-95; instr. law faculty U. Singapore, 1972-74; CEO, Vallejo Investments, 1997—. chmn. Police Rev. Com. of Berkeley (Calif.), 1980-84; mem. Berkeley Police Res., 1986—; bd. dirs. Friends Assn. of Svcs. for Elderly, 1979-84; clk. fin. com. Am. Friends Svc. Com. of No. Calif., 1979-83; pres. Zyzzyva Inc., lit. quar., 1985-87. Trustee Freedom from Hunger, 1989-99, Coun. of Friends Bancroft Libr., 1997—, Dominican Sch. of Philosophy and Theology, 1998—. With U.S. Army, 1958. Fellow Am. Bar Found. (life); mem. Calif. Bar Assn., Assn. Internat. de Bibliophilie, Harvard Club, Univ. Club, Book Club Calif., Roxburghe Club, Travellers Club, Grolier Club, Faculty Club U. Calif.-Berkeley, Mira Vista Golf and Country Club. Republican. Roman Catholic. Home and Office: 1800 San Antonio Ave Berkeley CA 94707-1618 E-mail: tew@wodehus.com.

WOODHURST, ROBERT STANFORD, JR. architect; b. Abbeville, S.C., July 12, 1921; s. Robert Stanford and Eva (Ferguson) W.; m. Dorothy Ann Carwile, Aug. 4, 1945; 1 son: Robert Stanford III. BS in Architecture, Clemson U., 1942. Registered arch., S.C., Ga., NCARB. Designer Harold Woodward, Arch., Spartanburg, S.C., 1946-47; assoc. arch. F. Arthur Hazard, Arch., Augusta, Ga., 1947-54; ptnr. Woodhurst & O'Brien, Architects, 1954-83, Woodhurst Partnership, Augusta, 1983—. V.p. Southeastern Architects and Engrs., Inc., Augusta, 1964-83; lectr. history architecture N. Augusta Community Coll.; mem. nat. exam. com. Nat. Council Arch tl. Regis. Bds.; pres. Ga. State Bd. Archs. Chmn. Augusta-richmond County Planning Commn., 1966-68; trustee Hist. Augusta, Inc., active Mayor's Adv. Com., 1965-68; mem. Augusta Bldg. Code Bd. Appeals, 1955-58. Served to capt. U.S. Army, 1942-45. Decorated Air medal with 7 oak leaf clusters; Croix de Guerre avec palms (France); prisoner of war, Germany. Fellow AIA (Bronze medal 1942); mem. Ga. Assn. AIA (pres. 1977, Bronze medal 1977, Rothchild Silver Medal 1987), Soc. Archtl. Historians, Nat. Coun. Archtl. Registration Bds., Augusta Country Club, Pinnacle Club, Elks. Democrat. Baptist. Achievements include designed and built: 1st Bapt. Ch., Augusta, Univ. Hosp. Med Ctr., Augusta, Peabody Apts. and Irvin Towers, Augusta, W. Lake Country Club, Augusta, Med. Libr., Med. Coll. Ga., Libr. Voorhees Coll., Denmark, S.C., Ambulatory Care Ctr. Univ. Hosp. Augusta, Married Students Apts., Med. Coll. Ga., Covenant Presbyn. Ch., Augusta, Student Ctr. Voorhees Coll., Pres.' Home Voorhees Coll., others. Home: 810 Dogwood Ln Augusta GA 30909-2704 Office: Woodhurst Partnership 607 15th St Augusta GA 30901-2601 E-mail: twparch@aol.com.

WOODING, WILLIAM MINOR, medical statistics consultant; b. Waterbury, Conn., Aug. 24, 1917; s. George Lee and Ella Elizabeth (Asher) W.; m. Nina C. Peaslee, May 30, 1940; children: Barbara Lee Wooding Bose, Elizabeth Ann. B Chem. Engring. cum laude, Poly. Inst. Bklyn., 1953. Lab. asst. Am. Cyanamid Co., Stamford, Conn., 1941-44, chemist, 1945-50, rsch. chemist, 1950-56, rsch. adminstrv. svcs. coord., 1956-57; asst. chief chemist Revlon Rsch. Ctr., N.Y.C., 1957-60, assoc. rsch. dir., 1960-65, Carter-Wallace, Inc., Cranbury, N.J., 1965-67, dir. tech. svcs., 1967-75; dir. statis. svcs. Carter-Wallace, Inc. and Wallace Labs., 1975-82; cons. med. statis. and clin. trials BioStatistics, Swanton, Vt., 1982—. Instr. Stat-a-Natrix Inst., Edison, N.J., 1983-86. Author: Planning Pharmaceutical Clinical Trials, 1994. Home and Office: BioStatistics 298 Maquam Shore Rd Swanton VT 05488-9639

WOODKE, ROBERT ALLEN, lawyer; b. Schaller, Iowa, Dec. 23, 1950; s. Everett Albert and Helen Marie (Breihan) W.; m. Jan Melanie Lawrence, Aug. 15, 1987 (div. 1997). BS, Iowa State U., 1973; JD, Creighton U., 1977. Bar: Iowa 1977, Minn. 1978, U.S. Dist. Ct. (no. dist.) Iowa 1977, U.S. Dist. Ct.Minn. 1980. Law clk. Minn. 5th Dist. Ct., Marshall, 1977-78; assoc. Powell Law Office, Bemidji, Minn., 1978-82; pvt. practice, 1982—. Cons. Mgmt. Tng. Inst., Bemidji, 1987-88. Contbg. author: Flying Solo: A Survival Guide for Solo Lawyers, 1984, 2d edit., 1994, Going to Trial, 1989, 2d edit. 1999, Personal Injury Handbook, 1991. Bd. dirs. Bemidji chpt. Am. Red. Cross, 2001—. Recipient Ann. Legal Svc. award N.W. Minn. Legal Svcs., Moorehead, 1987. Mem. ABA (coun. mem. sect. gen. practice 1994-98; co-editor-in-chief Legal Tech. and Practice Guide 1996-98, mem. editl. bd.), Minn. Trial Lawyers Assn., Minn. Bar Assn. (chair sect. of gen. practice 1990-92, chair GP solo and small firm sect. 2000—), Beltrami County Bar Assn. (pres. 1988-89), 15th Dist. Bar Assn. (treas. 1986-87, pres. 1997-98), Downtown Bus. and Profl. Assn., Bemidji C. of C., Jaycees (v.p. 1986-87), Lions Club (2d v.p. Bemidji chpt. 1987-88, 1st v.p. 1988—, pres. 1989—). Republican. Lutheran. Office: Brouse Woodke & Meyer PLLP 312 America Ave NW Bemidji MN 56601-3121 E-mail: rawoodke@paulbunyan.net.

WOODLAND, IRWIN FRANCIS, lawyer; b. New York, Sept. 2, 1922; s. John James and Mary (Hynes) W.; m. Sally Duffy, Sept. 23, 1954; children: Connie, J. Patrick, Stephen, Joseph, William, David, Duffy. BA, Columbia U., 1948; JD, Ohio State U., 1959. Bar: Calif. 1960, Wash., 1991, U.S. Dist. Ct. (cen. dist.) Calif. 1960, U.S. Dist. Ct. (no. dist.) Calif. 1962, U.S. Dist. Ct. (so. dist.) Calif. From assoc. to ptnr. Gibson, Dunn & Crutcher, L.A., 1959-88. Bd. dirs. Sunlaw Energy Corp., Vernon, Calif. With USAF, 1942-45, ETO. Mem. ABA, Calif. Bar Assn., L.A. Bar Assn., Wash. State Bar Assn., Phi Delta Phi, Jonathan Club. Roman Catholic. Address: Gibson Dunn & Crutcher 333 S Grand Ave Ste 4400 Los Angeles CA 90071-1548

WOODLEY, DAVID TIMOTHY, dermatology educator; b. Aug. 11, 1948; s. Raoul Ramos-Mimosa and Marian (Schlueter) W.; m. Christina Paschall Prentice, May 4, 1974; children; David Thatcher, Thomas Colgate, Peter paschall. AB, Washington U., St. Louis, 1968; MD, U. Mo., 1973. Diplomate Am. Bd. Internal Medicine, Am. Bd. Dermatology, Nat. Bd. Internal Medicine. Intern Beth Israel Med. Ctr., Mt. Sinai Sch. Medicine, N.Y. Hosp., Cornell U. Sch. Medicine, N.Y.C., 1973-74; resident in internal medicine U. Nebr., Omaha, 1974-76; resident in dermatology U. N.C.., Chapel Hill, 1976-78; asst. prof. dermatology U. N.C., 1983-85, assoc. prof. dermatology, 1985-88; prof. medicine, co-chief divsn. dermatology Cornell U. Med. Ctr., N.Y.C., 1988-89; prof., vice chair dept. dermatology Stanford (Calif.) U., 1989-93; prof., chair dept. dermatology Northwestern U., Chgo., 1993-99; co-chief dermatology U. So. Calif. Sch. Medicine, L.A., 1999—. Research fellow U. Paris, 1978-80; expert NIH, Bethesda, Md., 1983-89; prof., assoc. chmn. dermatology Stanford U Sch. Medicine, 1989-93; chmn. dermatology Sch. Medicine Northwestern U., 1993-99; prof., chmn. dermatology U. So. Calif., 1999—; mem. study sect. NIH. Contbr. chpts. to books and articles in field to profl. jours. Mem. Potomac Albicore Fleet, Washington, 1982-83, Friends of the Art Sch., Chapel Hill, 1983—, Jungian Soc. Triangle Area, Chapel Hill, 1983—. Fellow Am. Acad. Dermatology; mem. ACS (assoc.), Dermatology Found., Am. Soc. for Clin. Rsch., Soc. Investigative Dermatology, Assn. Physician Poets, Am. Soc. for Clin. Investigation. Office: U So Calif Divsn Dermatology LAC & USC Med Ctr 8th Fl 1200 N State St Los Angeles CA 90033-1029 E-mail: dwoodley@hsc.usc.edu.

WOODLOCK, DOUGLAS PRESTON, judge; b. Hartford, Conn., Feb. 27, 1947; s. Preston and Kathryn (Ropp) W.; m. Patricia Mathilde Powers, Aug. 30, 1969; children: Pamela, Benjamin. BA, Yale U., 1969; JD, Georgetown U., 1975. Bar: Mass. 1975. Reporter Chgo. Sun-Times, 1969-73; staff mem. SEC, Washington, 1973-75; law clk. to Judge F.J. Murray U.S. Dist. Ct. Mass., Boston, 1975-76; assoc. Goodwin, Procter & Hoar, 1976-79, 83-84, ptnr., 1984-86; asst. U.S. atty., 1979-83; judge U.S. Dist. Ct., 1986—. Instr. Harvard U. Law Sch., 1980, 82; mem. U.S. Jud. Conf. Com. on Security Space and Facilities, 1987-95; chmn. New Boston Fed. Courthouse Bldg. Com., 1987-98. Articles editor Georgetown Law Jour., 1973-75; contbr. articles to profl. jours. Chmn. Commonwealth of Mass. Com. for Pub. Counsel Svcs., 1984-86, Town of Hamilton Bd. Appeals, 1978-79. Recipient Dir.'s award U.S. Dept. Justice, 1983, Thomas Jefferson award for Pub. Architecture, AIA, 1996. Mem. ABA, Mass. Bar Assn., Boston Bar Assn., Am. Law Inst., Am. Judicature Soc., Am. Bar Found., Fed. Judges Assn. (bd. dirs. 1996-01), Mass. Hist. Soc. Office: US Courthouse 1 Courthouse Way Ste 4110 Boston MA 02210-3006

WOODMAN, ARTHUR TULLIS, architect, consultant; b. Kans. City, Mo., Mar. 21, 1926; s. Clyde E. and Esther M. W.; m. Frances G., Sept. 15, 1946; children: Susan, Jo Ann, Scott, Sherry, Julie, Janet, Tom, Rebecca. Student in Engring., Washburn U., 1946; BS in Archl. Engring., U. Kans., 1948. Registered profl. architect, Kans. Mem. staff Overend & Boucher, Wichita,

Kans., 1948-49, Thomas & Harris, Wichita, 1950-52; assoc. arch. John M. Hickman and Arthur T. Woodman Archs. Associated, 1953-59; prin., owner Arthur T. Woodman Arch., 1959-62; sr. ptnr., architect Woodman Van Doren, 1962-82; prin., owner Woodman Archs., 1982—. Commr. for Kans., Okla., Ark. River Commn., 1990, 96, 2000—; cons. Wichita Art Mus., 1973-75, Wichita State U., 1970-83. Architect Hyperbolic Paraboloid Vickers Petroleum, 1957, First Nat. Bank, Wichita, 1965 (design award AIA 1967), Lincoln Park Cmty. Ctr., Wichita, 1975 (design award 1978). Mem. vestry St. Andrew's Episcopal Ch., Derby, Kans., 1964-94; environ. chair Water Resources, Wichita, 1975-95. With USN, 1944-46. Recipient Cert. of Appreciation Kans. Water Authority, Topeka, 1997; named to Hall of Fame Ark. River Hist. Soc., Tulsa, Okla., 1998. Mem. AIA, Ark. River Devel. Assn. (chmn.), Wichita C. of C. (environ. chair), Phi Delta Theta. Republican. Avocations: golf, tennis, classic cars.

WOODMAN, G. ROGER, management consultant; b. Point Pleasant, N.J., Feb. 25, 1953; s. George Emil and Emma (Stringham) W.; m. Jean Wilson; 1 child, Kevin Richard. AS, Ocean County Coll., 1981; student, Trenton (N.J.) State Coll., 1987. Sr. operator, night supr. Ocean County Nat. Bank, Point Pleasant, 1973-85; constrn. ofcl. N.J. Dept. Community Affairs, Trenton, 1985-87; pres., sr. cons. Cynosure Cons., Inc., Lakewood, N.J., 1987—. Environ. cons. Environ Health Inspections, Lakewood, 1988, N.J. Dept. Cmty. Affairs, Trenton, 1989-95, BNK, Restorations, Clifton, N.J., 1989—. Author: (with others) Uniform Construction Code, 1985. County committeeman Ocean County Reps., Lakewood, 1989-98; life mem. Bay Head Vo. Fire Co., 1971—; mem. Lakewood Rep. Club, 1989-98; mem. Fishermen's Meml. Fund, 1998—, chmn., 2001. Mem. Nat. Fire Protection Assn., N.J. Fireman's Assn., Am. Mgmt. Assn., Lakewood Soccer Club, Masons (Durand lodge master 1980, treas. 2000, sec. 2001—, jr. grand steward 2002-), Shriners. Avocations: gardening, hiking, travel, model trains, reading. Home: 1370 Red Oak Dr Lakewood NJ 08701-3923 Office: Cynosure Cons Inc 1370 Red Oak Dr Lakewood NJ 08701-3923

WOODMAN, GREY MUSGRAVE, psychiatrist; b. Birmingham, England, Jan. 26, 1922; came to U.S., 1959, naturalized 1963; s. Edward Musgrave and Ida (Cullen) W.; m. Irene Woodman; children: Sheila, Shonagh. BA, Oxford (Eng.) U., 1943, MA, BM, BChir, 1945; grad., Clinton Citizens Police Acad., 2001. Ship's surgeon Brit. Merchant Marines, 1946-48; intern Whipps Cross Hosp., London, 1949-50, med. registrar, 1951-53, Gen. Hosp., Newcastle-on-Tyne, England, 1953-54; gen. practice London, 1954-56; physician USAF Hosp., 1956-59; resident in psychiatry U. Okla. Med. Ctr., 1959-62; staff psychiatrist Western Mo. Mental Health Ctr., Kansas City, 1962-76; med. dir. Mental Health Ctr. Clinton County, Clinton, Iowa, 1976-87; pvt. practice, 1976—; founder, dir. Lincolnshire Clinic, The London Psychiat. Clinic, 1997—. Mem. staff Jane Lamb Health Ctr., Mercy Hosp., Comphealth; psychiat. cons. Mufon; mem. mental health specialist chpt. ARC. Mem. Prevent Child Abuse Coun. Recipient Internat. Order of Merit, 1999. Fellow Royal Soc. Medicine (London, life); mem. AMA (life), Am. Psychiat. Assn. (life), Am. Acad. Med. Hypoanalysts (clin.), Brit. Med. Assn., World Fedn. Mental Health, Iowa Med. Soc. (past chmn. hospice com.), Internat. Assn. Social Psychiatry, Clinton Co. Prevent Child Abuse Coun., Am. Red Cross (mental health specialist 1996—), Oxford Club (life). Republican. Episcopalian. Home: 515 N 13th St Clinton IA 52732-4816 Office: London Psychiat Clinic 212 Wilson Bldg 5th Ave Clinton IA 52732 E-mail: greyufo@sanasys.com.

WOODMAN, HAROLD DAVID, historian, educator; b. Chgo., Apr. 21, 1928; s. Joseph Benjamin and Helen Ruth (Sollo) W.; m. Leonora Becker; children— Allan James, David Edward. BA, Roosevelt U., 1957; MA, U. Chgo., 1959, PhD, 1964. Lectr. Roosevelt U., 1962-63; asst. prof. history U. Mo., Columbia, 1963-66, assoc. prof., 1966-69, prof., 1969-71, Purdue U., West Lafayette, Ind., 1971-97, Louis Martin Sears disting. prof., 1990-97, prof. emeritus, 1997—; chmn. Com. on Am. Studies, 1981-94. Author: Conflict and Consensus in American History, 1966, 9th rev. edit., 1996, Slavery and the Southern Economy, 1966, King Cotton and His Retainers, 1968, Legacy of the American Civil War, 1973, New South-New Law, 1995; mem. editorial bd. Jour. So. History, 1972-75, Wis. Hist. Soc., 1972-76, Bus. History Rev., 1971-77, Agrl. History, 1976-82, Am. Hist. Rev., 1981-84, Jour. Am. History, 1985-88. Served with U.S. Army, 1950-52. Recipient Otto Wirth award Roosevelt U., 1990; Woodrow Wilson Internat. Center for Scholars fellow, 1977; Social Sci. Rsch. Coun. faculty grantee, 1969-70; Nat. Humanities Ctr. Fellow, 1983-84 Mem. Am. Hist. Assn., Orgn. Am. Historians, Econ. History Assn., Agrl. History Soc. (pres. 1983-84), Everett E. Edwards award 1963), Soc. Am. Historians, Bus. History Conf. (pres. 1981-82), Ind. Assn. Historians (pres. 1983-84), So. Hist. Assn. (exec. coun. 1982-85, Ramsdell award 1965, pres. 1995-96). Home: 1100 N Grant St West Lafayette IN 47906-2460 Office: Purdue U Dept History West Lafayette IN 47907 E-mail: hwoodman@sla.purdue.edu.

WOODMAN, JEAN WILSON, educator, consultant; b. New Brunswick, N.J., June 3, 1949; d. Richard and Doris (Pappa) Wilson; m. G. Roger Woodman; 1 child, Kevin. BA in English, St. Mary-of-the-Woods Coll., Terre Haute, Ind., 1971; MA in Tchg. magna cum laude, Monmouth U., West Long Branch, N.J., 1981. Cert. tchr., N.J. Tchr., chmn. English dept. St. Peter Sch., Point Pleasant, N.J., 1973-77, 80-85, Holy Family Sch., Lakewood, 1985-89; tchr. ESL and supplemental instrn. Lakewood Prep. Sch., Howell, 1991-93; tchr. St. Gregory the Great Sch., Hamilton Square, 1993—. Ednl. cons. J.W. Woodman Assocs., Lakewood, 1982—; sr. v.p. Cynosure Cons., Inc., Lakewood, 1987—. Contbr. poems to profl. publs. Mem. ASCD, Nat. Cath. Ednl. Assn. Avocations: writing, swimming, theater, ice skating.

WOODMAN, LUCY RHODES, music educator; b. Tryon, N.C., Aug. 16, 1940; d. William Clarence and Ramona Edna (Brock) Rhodes; m. James W. Woodman; children: Claudia Catherine, James Jefferson, Andrew Brock. AA, Mars Hill Coll., 1960; MusB, U. N.C., Greensboro, 1962; MusM, U. Colo., 1965. Tchr. piano pvt. practice, Wheatland & Cheyenne, Wyo., 1965-78, 79—; instr. in pre-piano and adult piano Cheyenne Parks and Recreation Dept., 1999—. Adj. tchr. piano U. Wyo., Laramie, 1970-74, staff accompanist, 1973-74; instr. Laramie County C.C.; performer/clinician Wyo. Artist Roster, 1992-99; pianist Cheyenne A.M.E. Ch., 1998—; frequent adjudicator for piano students' events; workshop provider for piano tchrs.; authorized provider The Listening Program for enhanced learning. Author: The Musical Home; composer: piano pieces Wyoming Postcards, 1988, composer: piano pieces Prayer for Peace, 1990, composer: piano pieces Piano-Sonata, 1990, composer: also numerous songs, composer: 2 operettas and chamber works. Presenter Diversity!, chamber concerts. Recipient Hon. Mention in music composition, Wyo. Arts Coun. Performing Arts Fellowship Competition, 2001; fellow Wyo. Art Coun., 1990; grantee Individual Artist grantee, Wyo. Art Coun., 1995, Travel grantee, 1997. Mem. Wyo. Music Tchrs. Assn. (pres. Cheyenne chpt. 1970, 89), Nat. Guild Piano Tchrs. (faculty mem.), Am. Soc. Composers, Authors and Pubs., Music Tchrs. Nat. Assn., Cheyenne Music Tchrs. Assn. Avocations: art, gardening, decorating, walking, reading. Home and Office: 415 W 23rd St Cheyenne WY 82001-3518

WOODMAN, WALTER JAMES, lawyer; b. Talara, Peru, Jan. 21, 1941; s. Walter James and Nora Carmen (Wensjoe) W.; m. Ruth Meyer, Dec. 19, 1970; children: Justin Meyer, Jessica Hilary. BA, U. Miami, 1964; JD, So. Meth. U., 1967. Bar: Tex. 1967, La. 1980, U.S. Dist. Ct. (no. dist.) Tex. 1967, U.S. Ct. Appeals (5th cir.) 1981, U.S. Supreme Ct. 1971, U.S. Dist. Ct. (we. dist.) La. 1980, U.S. Dist. Ct. (ea. dist.) Tex. 1983, U.S. Dist. Ct. (mid. dist.) La. 1988, U.S. Dist. Ct. (ea. dist.) La. 1989. Pvt. practice, Dallas, 1967-72, Waxahachie, Tex., 1972-79, Shreveport, La., 1979—. Bd. dirs. N.W. La. Legal Svcs., Shreveport, 1993-96. Contbr. articles to profl. jours. Candidate Tex. Ho. of Reps., 1972; bd. dirs. Gov.'s Pan Am. Commn., Baton Rouge, 1993-96. Home: Nonesuch Farm 12250 Ellerbe Rd Shreveport LA 71115 Office: 9045 Ellerbe Rd Ste 103 Shreveport LA 71106-6799

WOODMANSEE, GLENN EDWARD, employee relations executive; b. Feb. 8, 1936; s. Glenn E. and Elaine (Turnquist) W.; m. Sharon E. Horne, Sept. 5, 1959; chidlren: Lynn Ann, Thomas Edward. Student, Coe Coll., 1954-55; BS, Ariz. State U., 1960. Assoc. group mem. Prudential Ins. Co., Seattle, 1960-64; regional mgr. Blue Cross, N.Y.C., 1964-72; mgr. employee benefits McDermott Inc./Babcock & Wilcox, New Orleans, 1972-82; dir. employee relations Tidewater Inc., 1982-95; v.p. S&E Enterprise Co., Carriere, Miss., 1995-96. Bd. dirs. CPC Hosp., New Orleans, 1988-94; pres. Manalapan Rep. Club, Englishtown, N.J., 1977; mem. Twp. Zoning Bd.; county committeeman N.J. Rep. Party, Englishtown, 1970-77. Served to cpl. U.S. Army, 1955-57. Recipient N.Y.C. Marathon medal N.Y.C. Track Club, 1987. Mem. SAR, Am. Soc. Pers. Assocs., Bus. Coalition Health (treas. 1986-88, pres. 1988-90), Tng. and Devel. Assn. Am., Risk Ins. Mgmt. Soc., Toastmasters, Masons (32 degree), Shriners, Tau Kappa Epsilon. Clubs: New Orleans Athletic, South Shore Yacht. Republican. Presbyterian. Avocations: running, swimming, golf, boating. Home: 104 Pine Burr Rd Carriere MS 39426-7704

WOOD PRINCE, WILLIAM NORMAN, investments and real estate professional; b. Tulsa, Oct. 25, 1942; s. William Henry and Eleanor (Edwards) W.P.; m. Jonna Rosamond Leanard, Nov.7, 1967 (div. 1983); children: Scott Clarkson, Patrick Bernard. BA, Vanderbilt U., 1964. Account exec. Needham Harper & Steers, Chgo., 1965-68; brand mgr. Armour-Dial, 1968-70; account supr. J. Walter Thompson, 1970-75; sr. v.p. D'Arcy, Masius, Wynn Williams, 1975-77; chmn. F.H. Prince & Co., 1977—. Bd. dirs. ACL Holdings Ltd.; advisor Arral Pacific Equity Trust, Hong Kong, 1987-93. Trustee Ill. Inst. Tech., Chgo., 1982-86, St. George's Sch., Newport, R.I., 1980-93, CETA/WTTW, Chgo., 1989-96; aux. bd. Art Inst. Chgo., 1974-92; bd. dirs. Hubbard St. Dance Chgo., 1990—, chmn., 1993-97. Mem. Racquet (gov. 1981-87), Chgo. Club, Old Elm, Racquet and Tennis Club, Shoreacres, Newport Country Club, Spouting Rock. Republican. Episcopalian. Avocations: tennis, windsurfing, traveling, oriental art. Office: 303 W Madison St Ste 1900 Chicago IL 60606 Office Fax: 312-419-9502.

WOODRESS, JAMES LESLIE, JR. English language educator; b. Webster Groves, Mo., July 7, 1916; s. James Leslie and Jessie (Smith) W.; m. Roberta Wilson, Sept. 28, 1940. AB, Amherst Coll., 1938; A.M., NYU, 1943; PhD, Duke U., 1950; LittD, U. Nebr., 1995. News editor Sta. KWK, St. Louis, 1939-40; rewriteman, editor UPI, N.Y.C., 1940-43; instr. English, Grinnell (Iowa) Coll., 1949-50; asst. prof. English, Butler U., Indpls., 1950-53, asso. prof., 1953-58; asso. prof. English, San Fernando Valley (Calif.) State Coll., 1958-61, prof., 1961-66, chmn. dept., 1959-63, dean letters and scis., 1963-65; prof. English, U. Calif.-Davis, 1966-87, chmn. dept., 1970-74; vis. prof. Sorbonne, Paris, 1974-75, 83. Author: Howells and Italy, 1952, Booth Tarkington: Gentleman from Indiana, 1955, A Yankee's Odyssey: The Life of Joel Barlow, 1958, Dissertations in American Literature, 1957, 62, 68, Willa Cather: Her Life and Art, 1970, 75, 81, American Fiction 1900-50, 1974, Willa Cather: A Literary Life, 1987; editor: Eight American Authors, 1971, American Literary Scholarship: An Annual, 1965-69, 75-77, 79, 81, 87, Critical Essays on Walt Whitman, 1983, Cather's The Troll Garden, 1983, (with Richard Morris) Voices from America's Past, anthology, 1961-62, 75. Served to lt. AUS, 1943-46. Ford Fund for Advancement Edn. fellow, 1952-53; Guggenheim fellow, 1957-58; Fulbright lectr. France, 1962-63; Fulbright lectr. Italy, 1965-66; recipient Hubbell medal, 1985 Mem. MLA (sec. Am. Lit. group 1962-63), AAUP, Phi Beta Kappa. Address: 892 Harrison Ave Claremont CA 91711-4128

WOODRING, DEWAYNE STANLEY, religion association executive; b. Gary, Ind., Nov. 10, 1931; s. J. Stanley and Vera Luella (Brown) W.; m. Donna Jean Wishart, June 15, 1957; children: Judith Lynn (Mrs. Richard Bigelow), Beth Ellen (Mrs. Thomas Carey). BS in Speech with distinction, Northwestern U., 1954, postgrad. studies in radio and TV broadcasting, 1954-57; MDiv, Garrett Theol. Sem., 1957; LHD, Mt. Union Coll., Alliance, Ohio, 1967; DD, Salem (W.Va.) Coll., 1970. Ordained to ministry, Meth. Ch., 1955. Assoc. youth dir. Gary YMCA, 1950-55; minister of edn. Griffith (Ind.) Meth. Ch., 1955-57; minister adminstrn. and program 1st Meth. Ch., Eugene, Oreg., 1957-59; dir. pub. relations Dakotas area Meth. Ch., 1959-60, dir. pub. relations Ohio area, 1960-64; adminstrv. exec. to bishop Ohio East area United Meth. Ch., Canton, 1964-77; asst. gen. sec. Gen. Council on Fin. and Adminstrn., United Meth. Ch., Evanston, Ill., 1977-79; assoc. gen. sec. Gen. Council on Fin. and Adminstrn., 1979-84; exec. dir., CEO Religious Conf. Mgmt. Assn., 1982—. Staff, dept. radio svcs. 2d assembly World Coun. Chs., Evanston, 1954; vice-chmn. commn. on entertainment and program North Ctrl. Jursidictional Conf., 1968-72, chmn., 1972-76; commn. on gen. conf. United Meth. Ch., 1972-93, bus. mgr., exec. dir., 1976-93, mem. divsn. interpretation, 1969-72; chmn. comm. commn. Ohio Coun. Chs., 1961-65; exec. com. Nat. Assn. United Meth. Found., 1968-72; del. World Meth. Conf., London, Eng., 1966, Dublin, Ireland, 1976, Honolulu, 1981, Nairobi, 1986, Singapore, 1991, Rio de Janeiro, Brazil, 1996, Brighton, Eng., 2001; exec. com. World Meth. Coun., 1986-2001; del. White House Conf. on Travel and Tourism, 1995, Ohio East Area United Meth. Found., 1967-78, v.p. 1967-76; chmn. bd. mgrs. United Meth. Bldg., Evanston, 1977-84; adv. bd. Nassau/Paradise Island, 1997-99, Red Lion Hotels and Inns, P.R. Conv. Ctr., GMG Solutions; lectr., cons. on fgn. travel. Creator: nationally distbd. radio series The Word and Music; producer, dir.: TV series Parables in Miniature, 1957-59. Adviser East Ohio Conf. Communications Commn., 1968-76; pres. Guild Assocs., 1971—; trustee, 1st v.p. Copeland Oaks Retirement Ctr., Sebring, Ohio, 1969-76; bd. dirs. First Internat. Summit on Edn., 1989. Recipient Cert. Meeting Profl. award, 1985, Cert. Expt. Mgr. award, 1988; named to Ky. Cols., 1989, Conv. Liaison Coun. Hall of Leaders honoree, 1994. Mem. Am. Soc. Assn. Execs., Ind. Soc. Assn. Execs. (Mtg. Planner of Yr. award 1990), Mtg. Profl. Internat., Conv. Industry Coun. (bd. dirs., past chmn.), Def. Orientation Conf. Assn. (chaplain), Ind. Conv. Visitors Assc. (bd. dirs., 1996-2000), Cert. Mtg. Profls. (bd. dirs. 1983-91), Internat. Assn. Exhbn. Mgmt., Found. for Internat. mtgs. (bd. dirs.), Marriott Cust. Leadership Forum (mem. cust. adv. bd.). Home: 7224 Chablis Ct Indianapolis IN 46278-1540 Office: 1 RCA Dome Ste 120 Indianapolis IN 46225-1023

WOODRING, MARGARET DALEY, architect, planner; b. N.Y.C., Mar. 29, 1933; d. Joseph Michael and Mary (Barron) Daley; m. Francis Woodring, Oct. 25, 1954 (div. 1962); m. Robert Bell, Dec. 20, 1971 (dec.); children: Ward, Gabrielle, Phaedra. Student, NYU, 1959-60; BArch, Columbia U., 1966; MArch, Princeton U., 1971. Registered architect; cert. planner. Architect, planner various firms, N.Y.C.; environ. design specialist Rutgers U., New Brunswick, N.J., 1966-68; programming cons. Davis & Brody, N.Y.C., 1968-71; planning cons. William H. Liskamm, San Francisco, 1971-74; mgr. planning Met. Transp. Commn., Oakland, Calif., 1974-81; dir. Internat. Program for Housing and Urban Devel. Ofcls. Ctr. for Environ. Design Rsch. U. Calif., Berkeley, 1981-89; prin. Woodring & Assocs., San Rafael, Calif., 1989—. Adj. lectr. dept. architecture U. Calif., Berkeley, 1974-84; founder New Horizons Savs. Assn., San Rafael, 1977-79; cons. U.S. Agy. for Internat. Devel., Washington, 1981-89; mem. jury Nat. Endowment Arts, others. Chair Bicentennial Com., San Rafael, 1976; bd. dirs. Displaced Homemakers Ctr., Oakland, 1981-84; pres. Environ Design Found., San Francisco, 1984-90. William Kinne Travel fellow Columbia U., 1965-66; Richard King Mellon fellow Princeton U., 1968-71. Mem. AIA (chair urban design com. San Francisco chpt. 1980-81), Am. Inst. Cert. Planners, Urban Land Inst., Soc. for Internat. Devel. (pres. San Francisco chpt. 1980-83), World Affairs Coun., Internat. World Congress on Land Policy. Avocations: hiking, gardening, reading, race walking. E-mail: mdwoodring@aol.com.

WOODROOF, ERIC AUBREY, engineer, consultant, researcher; b. L.A., Aug. 1, 1969; s. E. Aubrey and Nancy Pearl (Ward) W.; m. Andrea King, July 12, 1998. BS in Physics, U. Calif., Santa Barbara, 1992; MS in Environ. Sci., Okla. State U., 1995, PhD in Indsl. Engring. and Mgmt., 1998. Energy mgmt. cons. Okla. State U., Stillwater, 1994-98; project coord. Okla. Indsl. Assessment Ctr., 1994-98; indsl. account exec. Johnson Controls, Oklahoma City, 1998—. Cons. W.W. Hastings Indian Hosp., Talequah, Okla., 1995, Okla. State U., 1995, 96, Lawton Indian Hosp., 1995, Pawnee Indian Health Ctr., 1996, Anadarko Indian Hosp., 1996, GM, Flint, Mich., 1996; lectr. Soc. Environ. Scientists, 1994, USPHS, 1995, Sierra Club, 1996, Assn. Energy Engrs., Oklahoma City chpt., 1998, among others. Mem. editl. bd. Energy Engring., 1998—; contbr. articles to profl. jours. Recipient Presdl. fellow Engring., 1995-98, Mem. Assn. Energy Engring. (cert. energy mgr., cert. Environ. Inst., 1995-98. Mem. Assn. Energy Engring. (cert. energy mgr., cert. energy procurement profl., cert. lighting effeciency profl.), Internat. Facility Mgmt. Assn. (scholarship 1998), Illuminating Engring. Soc. N.Am., Phi Kappa Phi. Avocations: sailing, camping, hiking. Office: 2601 N Hemlock Ct Broken Arrow OK 74012-1106

WOODROW, KENNETH M. psychiatrist; b. Yonkers, N.Y., Mar. 20, 1942; s. Jack H. and Grace (Lewis) W.; m. Mary Mack, June 9, 1968 (div. 1985); 1 child, Laura; m. Patricia Robin Stokes, July 1, 1989. BA, Wesleyan U., 1964; postgrad., U. Calif., Davis, 1964; MD, U. Md., 1968. Diplomate Am. Bd. Psychiatry and Neurology. Intern Kaiser Found. Hosp., Oakland, Calif., 1968-69; resident psychiatry Stanford (Calif.) U. Med. Ctr., 1969-72; clin. assoc. NIMH Lab. Clin. Pschopharmacology, USPHS, 1972-74; pvt. practice psychiatry Menlo Park, Calif., 1977—; clin. assoc. prof. dept. psychiatry Stanford U. Sch. Medicine, 1975—; staff psychiatrist, chmn. pharmacy and therapeutics com. Stanford U. Hosp.; staff psychiatrist Sequoia Hosp., Redwood City, Calif. Examiner Am. Bd. Psychiatry and Neurology; rsch. assoc. NIH, Lab. Socioenviron. Studies, 1963-65; rsch. fellow U. Md. Psychiat. Inst., Balt., 1966; cons. Kaiser Permanente Med. Group, 1969; grant rev. cons. nSF, 1970; psychiat. emergency svc. and med. cons. Highland Alameda Hosp., 1970-72; clin. assoc. NIMH, 1972-74; exec. com. Com. for Concerned Psychiatrists, 1972-74; staff psychiatrist Palo Alto VA Hosp., 1974-76; psychiat. cons. Job Corps, San Jose, 1975-82; lectr. San Jose Hosp., 1976-83. Fellow Am. Psychiat. Assn. Fellow: Am. Psychat. Assn. Office: 1225 Crane St Ste 106 Menlo Park CA 94025-4253

WOODROW, RUTH, nurse; b. Indpls., Sept. 13, 1928; d. Herman C. and Irene M. (Ziliak) Fuchs; m. Roger Woodrow, July 22, 1955; children: Howard Charles, Arlene Marie. BA in Psychology cum laude, Marist Coll., Poughkeepsie, N.Y., 1976; MA in Edn., U. South Fla., 1983. RN, Ill. Med.-surg. nurse Jackson Meml. and Dade County Hosps., Miami, Fla.; oper. rm. nurse Dade County and Tampa Gen. Hosps.; emergency rm. nurse Suburban and Sibley Hosps., Washington area; pediatric nurse Phila. Gen. and Sarasota Meml. Hosps.; charge nurse, adolescents Sarasota Meml. Hosp., 1978-79; instr., coord. Sarasota County Vocat.-Tech. Ctr., 1979-90; instr. dept. edn. Doctors Hosp., Sarasota, 1990-91; dir. staff devel. Plymouth Harbor, Inc., 1991—. Author: Essentials of Pharmacology for Health Occupations, 1987, 3d edit., 1997. Mem. cmty. wellness com. Planned Approach to Cmty. Health, Sarasota, 1988-90; vol. Hospice of Sarasota, 1987; vol. nurse Cmty. Med. Clinic, Sarasota, 1992-93, Sr. Friendship Ctr. Med. Clinic, Sarasota, 1997—; mem. Ethics Com. of Plymouth Harbor, chmn., 1996—. Mem. Assn. for Profls. in Infection Control (sec. 1996, program chair 1997-98). Avocations: reading, hiking, bridge. Home: 6411 Woodbirch Pl Sarasota FL 34238-2509

WOODRUFF, BRADLEY ALLEN, epidemiologist; b. Jamestown, N.Y., May 24, 1953; s. Allen Gilbert and Caroline (Wilcox) Woodruff; life ptnr. Karen Lisa Cairns. BA, SUNY, Fredonia, 1975; MD, Upstate Med. Ctr., Syracuse, N.Y., 1980; MPH, Johns Hopkins U., 1986. Lic. Pa., 1983, N.Y., 1981, Md., 1985, diplomate Am. Bd. Pub. Health and Gen. Preventive Med. Intern in gen. surgery U. Cin. Med. Ctr., 1980—81; resident in gen. surgery Upstate Med. Ctr., Syracuse, NY, 1981—82; gen. physician Hôpital St. Jean de Dieu, Parakou, Benin, 1983; gen. physician P.C.E.A. Tumutumu Hosp., Karatina, Kenya, 1983; emergency physician Allegheny Valley Hosp., Natrona Heights, Pa., 1984—85; epidemic intelligence svc. officer CDC, Charleston, W.Va., 1987—89; resident in preventive med. CDC Enteric Disease Br., Atlanta, 1989—90; med. epidemiologist CDC Hepatitis Br., 1990—96, CDC Internat. Emergency and Refugee Health Br., Atlanta, 1996—. Author: (novels) Rapid Health Assessment Protocols for Emergencies, 1999; contbr. articles to profl. jours., chapters to books. Mem. tech. adv. com. Internat. Rescue Com., N.Y.C., 2000—. Recipient PHS citation, USPHS, 1989, Achievement medal, 1993, Secretary's award for Disting. Svc., Dept. of Health and Human Svcs., 2000, Outstanding Unit citation, USPHS, 1995, 1996, and 2001, Unit commendation, 1989 (2), 1992, 1993 (2), Group Spl. Recognition award, U.S. Dept. of Health and Human Svc., 1992, Group Honor award Internat. Health, 1997. Fellow: Am. Coll. of Preventive Med.; mem.: Am. Assn. Pub. Health, Phi Beta Kappa, Alpha Omega Alpha. Office: CDC 4770 Buford Hwy NE Atlanta GA 30341 Office Fax: 770-488-7829. Business E-Mail: BWoodruff@cdc.gov.

WOODRUFF, BRUCE EMERY, lawyer; b. Mason City, Iowa, June 23, 1930; s. Frederick Bruce and Grace (Emery) W.; m. Carolyn Clark, Aug. 18, 1956; children: David C., Douglas B., Lynn M., Daniel R. BS in Bus., U. Ill., 1952; JD, Washington U., St. Louis, 1959. Bar: Mo. 1959, D.C. Dist. Ct. (ea. dist.) Mo. 1959, U.S. Ct. Appeals (8th cir.) 1960, U.S. Supreme Ct. 1979. Assoc. Armstrong, Teasdale, Schlafly, Davis & Dicus, St. Louis, 1959-65; ptnr. Armstrong Teasdale, Schlafly & Davis (and predecessor firms), 1966-95; sr. counsel Armstrong Teasdale LLP, 1996—. Prin. counsel St. Louis C.C., 1962-89; bd. dirs. Cass Bank & Trust Co., Cass Info. Sys., Inc., Red Lion Beef Corp., Manor Grove Corp., Rainbow Village, Inc.; city atty., Kirkwood, Mo., 1986. Named Kirkwood Citizen of Yr., 1983. Mem. ABA (banking law com.), Mo. Bar Assn., Bar Assn. Met. St. Louis, Health Lawyers Assn. Clubs: Algonquin (Glendale, Mo.); Noonday (St. Louis (bd. dirs. 1988-91). Republican. Presbyterian. Avocations: golf, swimming, sailing, photography. Home: 9 Taylor Est Kirkwood MO 63122-2914 Office: Armstrong Teasdale LLP 1 Metropolitan Sq Ste 2600 Saint Louis MO 63102-2740

WOODRUFF, C(HARLES) ROY, professional association executive; b. Anniston, Ala., Sept. 27, 1938; m. Kay Carolyn Jernigan, June 26, 1962; children: Charles R. Jr., Earl David. BA, U. Ala., 1960; BD, So. Bapt. Theol. Sem., 1963, PhD in Psychology of Religion and Pastoral Care, 1966. Diplomate Am. Assn. Pastoral Counselors; lic. profl. counselor, Va. Asst. pastor Ft. Mitchell Bapt. Ch., South Ft. Mitchell, Ky., 1960-63; Protestant chaplain Silvercrest Hosp., New Albany, Ind., 1963-66; dir. dept. pastoral care and edn. Bryce State Hosp., Tuscaloosa, Ala., 1966-71; assoc. prof., chaplain supr. dept. patient counseling Med. Coll. Va., Richmond, 1971-76; assoc. prof., chmn. dept. psychology of religion and pastoral care Midwestern Bapt. Theol. Sem., Kansas City, Mo., 1976-78; exec. dir. Peninsula Pastoral Counseling Ctr., Newport News, Va., 1978-88, Am. Assn. Pastoral Counselors, Washington, 1988—. Lecturing fellow Interpreter's House, Lake Junaluska, N.C., 1966-78; pastoral counselor, clin. supr. Psychol. Clinic, U. Ala., Tuscaloosa, 1969-71; adj. staff mem. The Counseling Inst., Kansas City, 1976-78. *Credentials as minister and counselor, Dr. Woodruff's career in the field of pastoral care and counseling has included clinical practice, teaching and supervision, and management of the primary professional association for certified pastoral counselors. He has testified on two occasions before congressional committees regarding the role of pastoral counselors with federal mental health agencies, consumer organizations, and other professional associations. He has enabled his organization to secure grants from major pharmaceutical companies to implement training opportunities for clergy and has represented his field in Europe and Asia, as well s throughout America.* Author: Alcoholism and Christian Experience, 1968; (with others) Alcohol, In and Out of the Church, 1968, Work Adjustment: The Goal of Rehabilitation, 1973, Pastoral Theology and Ministry, Key Resources, 1983, The Dictionary of Pastoral Care and Counseling, 1990; also articles. Apptd. by Gov. of Va. to Bd. Profl. Counselors, Commonwealth of Va., 1987-95 (chmn. 1993-95); mem. Nat. Mental Health Leadership Forum, 1990-93; pres. Coalition on Ministry in Specialized Settings, 1996-2000. United Meth. Ch. Gen. Bd. Christian Social Concerns grantee, 1965; So. Bapt. Theol. Sem. teaching fellow, 1965-66. Fellow Coll. Chaplains of Am. Protestant Hosp. Assn.; mem. Assn. for Clin. Pastoral Edn. (cert. supr.), Assn. Couples for Marriage Enrichment (cert.). Home: 10827 Burr Oak Way Burke VA 22015-2416 Office: Am Assn Pastoral Counselors 9504A Lee Hwy Fairfax VA 22031-2303

WOODRUFF, ELLEN LOUISE, minister; b. Bertha, Minnesota, Jan. 30, 1942; d. Harold Ernest and Ruth Eleanor (Olson) Klebs; m. John S. Woodruff, July 31, 1969; children: Ruth Ellen, Jonathan C. BA, U. Minn., 1969; Assoc. in Ministry, Luther Sem., St. Paul, 2000. Recreation therapist St. Mary's Hosp., Mpls., 1969, Belgrade Nursing Home, 1971—73; dir. youth camp Elks Assn., Brainerd, 1976—95; student chaplain Regions Hosp., St. Paul, 1997—98, Good Samaritan Homes, Mpls. & St. Paul, 1998—99; conservator St. Paul, 2000—. Mem. program com. Mid-States Camping Assn., Chgo., 1992—94; leader/spkr. Ch. Retreats, 1985—. Author (editor): Klebs Family History, 2001, Awesome Angels, 2000. Mem. Shepherd of the Valley Luth. Ch. Recipient J.B. Fritzjerald award, Mpls. Park & Recreation, 1969; grantee, U. Minn., 1966—68. Mem.: Assn. Profl. Chaplains, Am. Camping Assn. (sec. newsletter 1983—95, bd. dirs. 1980—83, 1990—93, Sue Tinker award 1993). Home: 9391 Knighton Woodbury MN 55125-3721

WOODRUFF, FAY, paleoceanographer, geological researcher; b. Boston, Jan. 23, 1944; d. Lorande Mitchell and Anne (Fay) W.; m. Alexander Whitehill Clowes, May 20, 1972 (div. Oct. 1974); m. Robert G. Douglas, Jan. 27, 1980; children: Ellen, Katerina. RN, Mass. Gen. Hosp. Sch. Nursing, Boston, 1966;

BA, Boston U., 1971; MS, U. So. Calif., 1979. Rsch. assoc. U. So. Calif., L.A., 1978-81, rsch. faculty, 1981-96. Keynote spkr. 4th Internat. Symposium on Benthic Foraminifera, Sendai, Japan, 1990. Contbg. author: Geological Society of America Memoir, 1985; contbr. articles to profl. jours. Life mem. The Nature Conservancy, Washington, 1992; bd. dirs. Friends of Friendship Park, Inc., 1995-2001; co-founder, v.p. Resources Families Adopted Ea. European Children, Inc., L.A., 1996-2000. NSF grantee, 1986-94. Mem. Am. Geophys. Union, Geol. Soc. Am., Internat. Union Geol. Scis. (internat. commn. on stratigraphy, subcommn. on Neogene stratigraphy 1991-99), Soc. Woman Geographers (sec. So. Calif. chpt. 1990-96), Soc. Econ. Paleontologists and Mineralogists (sec., editor N.Am. Micropaleontology sect. 1988-90), Sigma Xi. Office: U So Calif Earth Scis Los Angeles CA 90089-0001

WOODRUFF, JANE, sales executive; b. Derby, Eng., July 20, 1945; d. George John Schwaegerman and Joyce (Robinson) Turnock; m. Charles Walter Woodruff, Aug. 1, 1964 (div. 1976); 1 child, Jon Bradley. BA, Purdue U., 1967, MS, 1968, MA, 1970. Tchr. Kansas City (Mo.) Schs., 1970-73; asst. dir. communicatons Skyline Corp., Elkart, Ind., 1974-77; market analyst Motor Wheel Corp. subs. Goodyear Tire and Rubber Co., Lansing, Mich., 1977-80, mgr. planning and research, 1980-82, mgr. car and light truck mktg., 1982-84; account exec. Motor Wheel Corp., Farmington Hills, 1984-96; acct. exec. Enkei Internat., Madison Heights, 1996-98, asst. dept. mgr., O.E.S., 1998—. Chmn. Motor Wheel Savs. Bond Drive, Lansing, 1980; fundraiser Capital Area United Way, Lansing, 1981; cons. bus. projects Jr. Achievement, Lansing, 1981-82. NDEA scholar U.S. Dept. Edn., 1967-68; teaching fellow Purdue U., 1968-70; recipient Cert. Achievement YWCA, Lansing, 1980. Mem. Indsl. Mktg. Group Am. Mktg. Assn. (treas.), Automotive Market Research Council, Soc. Automotive Engrs. Office: Enkei Internat 32400 Industrial Dr Madison Heights MI 48071-1527

WOODRUFF, JUDY CARLINE, broadcast journalist; b. Tulsa, Nov. 20, 1946; d. William Henry and Anna Lee (Payne) W.; m. Albert R. Hunt, Jr., Apr. 5, 1980; children: Jeffrey Woodruff, Benjamin Woodruff, Lauren Ann Lee. Student, Meredith Coll., 1964-66; BA, Duke U., 1968. News announcer, reporter Sta. WAGA-TV, Atlanta, 1970-75; news corr. NBC News, 1975-76, White House corr. Washington, 1977-83; anchor Frontline, PBS documentary series, 1983-90; corr. MacNeil-Lehrer News Hour, PBS, Washington, 1983-93; anchor, sr. corr. CNN, 1993—, prime anchor, sr. coord. Bd. advisors Henry Grady Sch. Journalism, U. Ga., 1979-82, Benton Fellowship in Broadcast Journalism, U. Chgo., 1984-90, Knight Fellowship in Journalism, Stanford U., 1985—; bd. visitors Wake Forest U., 1982-89; trustee Duke U., 1985—; founding bd. dirs. Internat. Women's Media Found. Author: This is Judy Woodruff at the White House, 1982. Active Commn. on Women's Health, The Commonwealth Fund. Recipient award Leadership Atlanta, Class of 1974, Atlanta chpt. Women in Comms., 1975, Edward Weintal award for excellence in fgn. policy reporting, 1987, Joan Shorenstein Barone award for series on def. issues, 1987, Helen Bernstein award for excellence in journalism N.Y. Pub. Libr., 1989, Pres.'s award Nat. Women's Hall of Fame, 1994, CableAce award for best newscaster, 1995, Allen H. Neuharth award for excellence in journalism, 1995. Mem. NATAS (Atlanta chpt. Emmy award 1975), White House Corrs. Assn. Office: Cable News Network 820 1st St NE Washington DC 20002-4243

WOODRUFF, KATHRYN ELAINE, English language educator; b. Ft. Stockton, Tex., Oct. 12, 1940; d. James Arthur and Catherine H. (Stevens) Borron; m. Thomas Charles Woodruff, May 18, 1969; children: Robert Borron, David Borron. BA, Our Lady of the Lake U., San Antonio, 1963; MFA, U. Alaska, 1969; PhD, U. Denver, 1987. Cert. tchr., Tex., Colo. English and journalism tchr. Owensboro (Ky.) Cath. High Sch., 1963-64, Grand Junction (Colo.) Dist. 12, 1964-66; English tchr. Monroe High Sch., Fairbanks, Alaska, 1966-67; teaching asst. U. Alaska, 1967-69, instr., 1969-70, U. Colo., Boulder, 1979, Denver, 1988-89, Regis Coll., Denver, 1987-89; asst. prof. Econs. Inst., Boulder, 1989-92; assoc. prof. English Colo. Christian U., Lakewood, 1993—. Tchr. Upward Bound, Fairbanks, 1968; instr. ethnic and women writers course U. Colo., Denver, 1988-93; mem. Assoc. Writing Programs; soprano Boulder Chorale, Cantabile Singers; mem. Women's Studies Delegation to South Africa, 1998; active in missionary work in Ecuador, 1998, European Singing Tour with Augustana Arts, 1998, 2000. Author: (poetry) Before the Burning, 1994; poetry readings in Colo., Tex. and Paris; poems publ. in Denver Quarterly, The Incliner, Southwestern Am. Lit. Friend Chautauqua Music Festival, Boulder, 1985—; dir. 12th Annual Arts Festival, Fairbanks, 1969; active Augustana Chamber Chorus, Augustana Classical Chorus. Recipient Poet's Choice award Internat. Soc. Poetry, 1997; named one of Outstanding Young Women Am., 1966; nominated for Poet Laureate of Colo., 1996; NEH grantee, 1996. Mem. AAUW, MLA, Am. Assn. Univ. Professors, Assoc. Writing Programs, Soc. Internat. Devel. UN Assn., Nat. Women's Hall of Fame, Acad. of Am. Poets, Internat. Women's Writing Guild. Democrat. Mem. Christian Ch. Avocations: singing, tennis, skiing, volleyball, travel. Office: Colo Christian U 180 S Garrison St Lakewood CO 80226-1053

WOODRUFF, MARK REED, magazine editor; b. Roanoke, Va., Jan. 3, 1957; s. James Moses and Elizabeth (Reed) W. BFA, Va. Commonwealth U., 1981; postgrad., San Francisco State U., 1983-84. Freelance writer, N.Y.C., 1984-88; features editor Taxi Mag., 1988-90; mng. editor Spin Mag., 1990-95; sr. editor Rolling Stone, 1995-97, asst. mng. editor, 1997-98; editor-in-chief Tennis mag., 1998—. Mem. Am. Soc. Mag. Editors. Democrat. Avocation: tennis. Home: 118 Glendale Rd Ossining NY 10562-1619 Office: Tennis Mag 810 7th Ave 4th Fl New York NY 10019-5818 E-mail: mwoodruff@tennis.com.

WOODRUFF, NEIL PARKER, agricultural engineer; b. Clyde, Kans., July 25, 1919; s. Charles Scott and Myra (Christian) W.; m. Dorothy Adele Russ, June 15, 1952; children: Timothy C., Thomas S. BS, Kans. State U., 1949, MS, 1953; postgrad., Iowa State U., 1959. Agrl. engr. Agrl. Research Service, Dept. Agr., Manhattan, Kans., 1949-63, research leader, 1963-75; cons. engr. Manhattan, 1975-77; civil engr. Kans. Dept. Transp., Topeka, 1977-79; prof., mem. grad. faculty Kans. State U., civil engr. facilities planning, 1979-84. Mem. sci. exchange team to, Soviet Union, 1974; with W/PT Cons., 1984—. Contbr. articles to tech. jours. and books. Fellow Am. Soc. Agrl. Engrs. (Hancor Soil Water Enginrg. award 1975); mem. Sigma Xi, Gamma Sigma Delta. Home and Office: 12906 W Blue Bonnet Dr Sun City West AZ 85375-2538

WOODRUFF, RANDALL LEE, lawyer; b. Anderson, Ind., July 31, 1954; s. Billy Max and Phyllis Joan (Helmick) W.; m. Lucetta Farnham, Aug. 15, 1976. BA, Ind. U., 1976, JD, 1985. Bar: Ind. 1985, U.S. Dist. Ct. (no. and so. dists.) Ind. 1985, U.S. Supreme Ct. 1989. Exec. dir Cmty. Justice Ctr., Anderson, 1979-85; assoc. Shearer, Schrock & Woodruff, 1985-87; pvt. practice, 1987-97, Woodruff Law Offices, P.C., 1997—. Bd. dirs. East Cen. Legal Svcs. Program, Anderson, 1986-89; trustee Chpt. 7 Bankruptcy Panel, So. Dist. Ind., 1991—. Bd. dirs. Offender Aid & Restoration of the U.S., 1988-93. Mem. Ind. Assn. Criminal Def. Lawyers, Ct. Appointed Spl. Advocates (bd. dirs. 1988), Madison County Bar Assn. (sec./treas. 1990, v.p. 1991, pres. 1992). Mem. Christian Ch. (Disciples Of Christ). Office: 109 E 9th St Anderson IN 46016-1509 E-mail: rlwtrustee@insightbb.com., rlwoodruff@insightbb.com.

WOODRUFF, THOMAS ELLIS, electronics consulting executive; b. Stockton, Calif., Feb. 8, 1921; s. Ennis Casselberry and Gracella (Scotford) W.; m. Doris Elaine Walters, Jan. 14, 1947 (div. Aug. 1962); children: Mary Ann Woodruff Mahaffy, Patricia Lee; m. Ruth Elizabeth Craik, Feb. 25, 1964; 1 child, Robert Peter; stepchildren: Gordon Lee Vickers, Barbara Ann Vickers, Mary Jean Vickers. AA, Stockton Jr. Coll., 1941; BSEE, U. Calif., Berkeley, 1943. Registered profl. engr., Calif. Engr. GE, Syracuse, N.Y., 1944-47; staff engr. Hughes Aircraft Co., Culver City, Calif., 1947-56; mgr. electronics design Sanders Assocs., Nashua, N.H., 1956-58, chief engr. preliminary design, 1958-60, mgr. spl. programs div., 1960-62, corp. dir. systems, 1962-65, v.p., gen. mgr. corp. systems group, 1965-73, v.p. antisubmarine weapons and communications, 1966-72, dir., 1968-70, sr. dir., 1970-76, v.p. gen. mgr. ocean systems group, 1972-76, v.p. sci. and tech., 1976-88, corp. cons., 1989—; v.p. Sanders Nuclear Corp., 1966-71. Mem. adv. com. Def. Intelligence Agy., Washington, 1978-83; joint adv. com. MIT Lincoln Lab., Bedford, Mass., 1988-89; cons. Superconductor Tech., Inc., Santa Barbara, Calif., 1988—, Oryx, Inc., Paramus, N.J., 1989—, Sanders/Lockheed, 1988-91, ret. 1992. Patentee, co-patentee 14 inventions in electronics for computers, control systems, video displays, submarine detection devices, others. Mem. IEEE (sr.). Republican. Avocations: skiing, photography, motorcycling, swimming. Home and Office: 8 Berkeley St Nashua NH 03064-2309

WOODRUFF, TRUMAN O(WEN), physicist, emeritus educator; b. Salt Lake City, May 26, 1925; s. Wilford Owen and Evelyn (Ballif) W.; m. Ambrosina Lydia Solaroli, Sept. 14, 1948 (dec. June 1991); m. Patricia O'Keefe Vincent, Sept. 23, 1995. AB, Harvard U., 1947; BA, Oxford (Eng.) U., 1950; PhD, Calif. Inst. Tech., 1955. Nat. scholar Harvard, 1942-44, 46-47, Sheldon traveling fellow, 1947-48; Rhodes scholar Oxford U., 1948-50; Dow Chem. Co. fellow, Howard Hughes fellow Calif. Inst. Tech., 1950-54; research asso. physics U. Ill., 1954-55; physicist Gen. Elec. Research Lab., 1955-62; prof. physics Mich. State U., 1962-85, prof. emeritus, 1985—, chmn. dept., 1972-75; sr. scientist research labs. Hughes Aircraft Co., Malibu, Calif., 1986-87; cons. in physics Los Angeles, 1987-91. Vis. prof. Scuola Normale Superiore, Pisa, Italy, 1982—. Contbr. articles to sci. jours. Served with USNR, 1944-46. Fulbright fellow U. Pisa, 1968-69 Fellow Am. Phys. Soc.; mem. Assn. Harvard Chemists, Phi Beta Kappa, Sigma Xi.

WOODRUFF, VIRGINIA, broadcast journalist, writer; b. Morrisville, Pa. d. Edwin Nichols and Louise (Meredith) W.; m. Raymond F. Beagle Jr. (div.); m. Albert Plaut II (div.); 1 child, Elise Meredith. Student, Rutgers U. News corr. Sta. WNEW-TV Metromedia, N.Y.C., 1967; nat., internat. critic-at-large Mut. Broadcasting System, 1968-75; lectr. Leigh Bur., 1969-71; byline columnist N.Y. Daily Mirror, N.Y.C., 1970-71; first Arts critic Teleprompter and Group W Cable TV, 1977-84; host/producer The First Nighter N.Y. Times primetime cable highlight program, 1977-84; pres., chief exec. officer Starpower, Inc., 1984-91; affiliate news corr. ABC Radio Network, N.Y.C., 1984-86; pres. Promarket People Inc., 1991-93; S.W. contbg. corr. Am. in the Morning, First Light, Mut. Broadcasting System, 1992; S.W. freelance corr. Voice of Am., USIA, 1992—. Perennial critic Off-Off Broadway Short Play Festival, N.Y.C., 1984—; was 1st Woman on 10 O'Clock News, WNEW-TV, 1967. Contbg. feature writer Vis a Vis mag., 1988-91. Mem. celebrity panel Arthritis Telethon, N.Y.C., 1976. Selected episodes of First Nighter program in archives N.Y. Pub. Libr., Billy Rose Theatre Collection, Rodgers and Hammerstein Collection, Performing Arts Rsch.Ctr. Mem. Drama Desk. Clubs: National Arts, Dutch Treat. Presbyterian.

WOODRUFF, WANDA LEA, elementary education educator; b. Woodward, Okla., May 2, 1937; d. Milton Casper and Ruth Arlene (Bradshaw) Shuck; m. William Jennings Woodruff, Aug. 18, 1962; children: Teresa Kaye, Bruce Alan, Neal Wayne. BS, Northwestern State U., 1959; MA in Edn., Olivet Nazarene U., 1973. Cert. K-8th grade tchr. Elem. tchr. Anthony (Kans.) Pub. Schs., 1959-60, transition class tchr., 1960-61, elem. tchr., 1961-62, Versailles (Ky.) Pub. Schs., 1962-63, Bradley (Ill.) Elem. Schs., 1968-93; presch. vol. Concern Ctr., Bartlesville, Okla., 1994—. Com. chmn. Bus. and Profl. Women, Anthony, 1959-62; sec. com. PTA, Anthony, 1959-63, Bradley (Ill.) PTA, 1968-93. Recipient grant for edn. First of Am. Bank, 1991-92, 92-93. Mem.: Nazarene World Mission Soc. (local pres. 1999—2002), Bartlesville Pilot Club Internat. (edn./patriotism chairperson 1994—95, dir. 1995—96, mem. Spl. Olympics Com. 1995—98, pres.-elect 1996—97, pres. 1997—98). Avocations: jogging, reading, baking, working with children and young people. Home: 2373 Mountain Dr Bartlesville OK 74003-6952

WOODRUFF, WILLIAM, economic history educator; b. Blackburn, Lancashire, Eng., Sept. 12, 1916; came to U.S., 1952, naturalized, 1972; s. William and Anne (Kenyon) W.; m. Kay Wright, Sept. 20, 1941 (dec. 1959); children: David, Roger; m. Helga Gaertner, Jyly 19, 1960; children: Kirsten, Mark, Peter, Andrew, Thomas. BA, Oxford U., 1940, MA, 1946; BSc, London U., 1949; D.Phil., Nottingham U., 1952; M.Com. (hon.), Melbourne U., Australia, 1957. Lectr. in econ. history Nottingham U., Eng., 1946-50; Houblon-Norman fellow Bank of Eng., London, 1950-51; prof. econs. U. Ill., 1953-56; prof. econ. history Melbourne U., 1956-64; mem. Inst. for Advanced Study, Princeton, N.J., 1964-65; grad. rsch. prof. econ. history U. Fla., Gainesville, 1966—. Author: The Rise of the British Rubber Industry, 1958, Impact of Western Man, 1966, 2d edit., 1982, Emergence of an International Economy, 1971, 6th edit., 1990, America's Impact on the World, 1975, The Struggle for World Power, 1980, 2d edit., 1982, Vessel of Sadness, 1969, 9th edit., 1992, Paradise Galore, 4th edit., 1990, A Concise History of the Modern World, 1991, Billy Boy, 1993, (with Lachlan McGregor) The Suez Canal and the Australian Economy, 1957, (with Helga Woodruff) Technology and the Changing Trade Patterns of the United States, 1968; co-author: The Victoria History of the Counties of England, A History of the County of Wiltshire, 1959, The Movement Toward Latin American Unity, 1969, Readings in Economic History and the History of Economic Theories, 1978. Recipient Sr. award Rockefeller Found., 1964, Japan Soc. for the Advancement of Sci., 1975; Fulbright scholar Harvard U., 1951-52. Home: 1710 NW 66th Ter Gainesville FL 32605-4132 Office: Dept Econs U Fla Gainesville FL 32611

WOODRUM, CLIFTON A., III, lawyer, state legislator; b. Washington, July 23, 1938; s. Clifton A. Jr. and Margaret (Lanier) W.; m. Emily Abbitt, Aug. 10, 1963; children: Robert, Meredith W. Snowden, Anne. AB, U. N.C., 1961; LLB, U. Va., 1964. Bar: Va. 1964, U.S. Dist. Ct. (we. dist.) Va. 1964, U.S. Ct. Appeals (4th cir.) 1968, U.S. Supreme Ct. 1970. Assoc. Dodson, Pence & Coulter, Roanoke, Va., 1964-68; ptnr. Dodson, Pence, Viar, Woodrum & Mackey, 1968-95; counsel Dodson, Pence & Viar, 1995-98; mem. Va. Ho. of Dels., 1980—. Chmn. 6th Dist. Dem. Com., Va., 1972-76; mem. State Water Commn., 1981-2000, State Crime Commn., 1982-2000, chmn., 1995-98; chmn. Med. Malpractice Study, Va., 1984-85, Freedom of Info. Study, 1998-2000; mem. Electric Utility Restructing Com., 1997—, Freedom of Info. Adv. Coun., 2000-2002, chair. Mem. ABA, Va. Bar Assn., Roanoke Bar Assn. Episcopalian. Home: 2641 Cornwallis Ave SE Roanoke VA 24014-3339 Office: Clifton A Woodrum PO Box 990 Roanoke VA 24005-0990

WOODRUM, PATRICIA ANN, librarian; b. Hutchinson, Kans., Oct. 11, 1941; d. Donald Jewell and Ruby Pauline (Shuman) Hoffman; m. Clayton Eugene Woodrum, Mar. 31, 1962; 1 child, Clayton Eugene, II. BA, Kans. State Coll., Pittsburg, 1963; MLS, U. Okla., 1966. Br. libr. Tulsa City-County Libr. System, 1964-65, head brs., 1965-66, head reference dept., 1966-67, chief extension, chief pub. svc., 1967-73, asst. dir., 1973-76, exec. dir., 1976-96; owner Paradigm Mgmt. Cons. Svcs., 1997—. Active Leadership Tulsa Alumni; mem. Ct. Apptd. Spl. Advocates Bd.; co-chmn. Bot. Garden/Edn. and Rsch. Ctr.; bd. dirs. Tulsa Garden Ctr., Oasis, Inc. Recipient Disting. Libr. award Okla. Libr. Assn., 1982, Leadership Tulsa Paragon award, 1987, Women in Comm. Newsmaker award, 1989, Outstanding Alumnus award U. Okla. Sch. Libr. Info. Studies, 1989, Headliner award Tulsa Press Club, 1996, Disting. Alumnus Coll. Arts and Scis., U. Okla., 2000; inducted into Tulsa City-County Libr. Hall of Fame, 1989, Okla. Womens Hall of Fame, 1993. Mem. ALA, Pub. Libr. Assn. (pres. 1993-94), Okla. Libr. Assn. (pres. 1978-79, Disting. Libr. award 1982, Meritorious Svc. award 1996), Tulsa Press Club. Democrat. Episcopalian. Avocations: swimming, gardening. E-mail: clayt59267@aol.com.

WOODRUM, ROBERT LEE, executive search consultant; b. Merkel, Tex., Mar. 3, 1945; s. Bill and Norma (Shea) W.; m. Linda Mary Larkin, July 20, 1968; children: Jennifer, Michael. BA, Calif. State U., Northridge, 1967; postgrad., U. Okla., 1974. Press sec. U.S. Senate, Washington, 1977-78; dir. pub. affairs U.S. Office Personnel Mgmt., 1979-80; pres. Corp. Communications, 1980-82; v.p. Norton Simon Inc., N.Y.C., 1982-83; spl. asst. to the commr. NFL, 1983-84; exec. dir. Ritz Paris Hemingway Award, 1984-87; pres. Ritz Paris Internat., 1984-86; sr. v.p. AmBase Corp., 1986-91; mng. dir. Korn/Ferry Internat., N.Y.C., 1991—; dir. DataBuilt, Inc., 2000—. Advisor USIA, Washington, 1980-93, ARC, 1983, White House Vets. Com., 1979-80. Trustee N.Y.C. Meals on Wheels, Inc. Lt. comdr. USN, 1968-77. Decorated Navy Achievement medal (2). Mem.: Ocean Reef Club, N.Y. Sky Club. Office: 6 Plumbridge Ln Hilton Head Island SC 29928-3360

WOODS, BARBARA A. SHELL, psychotherapist, mediator, career consultant; d. Oscar Ketron and Mamie Maruja (Perry) Shell; m. James Wesley Woods, May 7, 1966; children: Jonathan Scott, Eric Jason. BS in Bus. Mgmt., East Tenn. State U., 1961; MA in Counseling and Devel., George Mason U., 1983, postgrad., 1985-88. Cert. clin. mental health counselor, mediator, Va.; nat. cert. counselor, nat. cert. career counselor; lic. profl. counselor, lic. marriage and family counselor, Va. Office asst. vet. affairs East Tenn. State U., Johnson City, 1958-61; sec. purchasing dept. U. Tenn., Knoxville, 1961-62; social worker I and II Tenn. Welfare Dept., 1962-66; daycare coord. Econ. Opportunity of Atlanta, 1966-67; child welfare worker Forsyth County Dept. of Welfare, Winston Salem, N.C., 1967-68; dir., tchr. Woodland Pre-Sch., Alexandria, Va., 1975-78; pers. mgmt. Woodward & Lothrup, Tyson's Corner, 1983; career coord. Nat. Bd. for Cert. Counselors, Alexandria, 1984. Counselor, trainer The Women's Ctr. of Northern Va., Vienna, Va., 1985-90; counseling dir. The Women's Health Connection, Vienna, 1990-92; trainer, counselor City of Falls Ch. Youth At Risk Program, Falls Church, 1993-94; dir./owner Change & Growth Consulting, Springfield/Alexandria, Va., 1984—. Zoning chairperson West Springfield (Va.) Civic Assn., 1980-82; citizen mem. Fairfax County Citizens Planning Task Force, Springfield, 1979-82. Scholarship Am. Legion, 1957. Mem. ACA, No. Va. Chpt. clin. Counselors (chairperson 1990-92, Appreciation award 1992), Va. Clin. Counselor (regional rep. 1990-92), Nat. EAP Assn. (sec. 1989-90), Met. Area Career/Life Planning Network (founder, Appreciation award 1985), Va. Counselors Assn. Avocations: gardening, crafts, decorating, reading. Office: Change and Growth Cons 6220 Old Franconia Rd Alexandria VA 22310-2529

WOODS, BRYANT PRENTICE, National Park ranger; b. Kirbyville, Tex., Apr. 8, 1946; s. Hampton Oliphant and Maxine Armistead Woods. BA in Psychology, U. Colo., 1974; MS in Biology, Western State Coll. of Colo., 1983. Pk. ranger-interpretation Zion Nat. Pk., Springdale, Utah, 1986—89, Big Bend (Tex.) Nat. Pk., 1989—90, Acadia Nat. Pk., Bar Harbor, Maine, 1991—93, supervisory pk. ranger, 1993—. Songwriter: Just Can't Remember (recorded by Chairback Gap), 2000. Avocations: natural history, songwriting, bluegrass music. Home: 13 Des Iles AVe Bar Harbor ME 04609 Office: Acadia Nat Park Bar Harbor ME 04609 E-mail: acorvid@yahoo.com.

WOODS, CATHI L. human services administrator; b. Chattanooga, Oct. 4, 1961; d. Robert L. and Shirley Phillips Woods; 1 child, Joshua Barbour. Degree in exec. edn., Harvard U., 1999. Exec. dir. Hope Resource Ctr., Knoxville, 1996-97; CEO, pres. Daybreak, Boston, 1998—. Exec. dir. Women's Care Ctr., Dayton, Tenn., 1991-96; mem. Rhea County Health Coun., 1994-96; mem., bd. chair Adolescent Pregnancy Initiative Coun., 1994-96. Mem. NAFE. Avocations: reading, travel. Office: Daybreak Inc 3 Park St Boston MA 02108 E-mail: ceo@daybreakinc.org.

WOODS, CHRISTINE L. manufacturing company executive; b. Erie, Pa., Aug. 10, 1942; d. John Aaron and Frances Louise (Bauschard) Nelson; m. John William Andrews, Sept. 1, 1960 (div. 1971); children: Lynne Andrews Bargar, Denise; m. Robert W.H. Laughlin, Dec. 24, 1983 (dec. 1995); m. Joseph Woods, Oct. 16, 1999. Student, U. Md., 1963-64, Allegheny Coll., 1974-75. Cert. in prodn. and inventory mgmt. Master scheduling supr. Joy Mfg. Co., Franklin, Pa., 1977-82; materials mgr. Gerber Garment Tech., Tolland, Conn., 1984-86; chief master scheduler Thermos Co., Norwich, 1986-87; mfg. systems mgr. Rogers Corp., Manchester, 1987-88; mgr. prodn. planning Gerber Garment Tech., Tolland, 1988-90; materials mgr. KCR Tech., East Hartford, 1990-91; ops. mgr. Polyplastex Internat., Clearwater, Fla., 1992-95; mgr. logistics Tech Data Corp., 1995—. Vol. Erie Playhouse, 1970-72, Conn. Pub. Broadcasting, Hartford, 1985-86; cellist Allegheny Civic Symphony, Meadville, Pa., 1975-80, reader Recording for the Blind, Austin, Tex., 1982-83; former mem. managerial women's adv. bd. Behrend Coll. Mem. Am. Prodn. and Inventory Control Soc., Feather Sound Country Club. Republican. Presbyterian. Avocations: golf, bridge, rollerblading. E-mail: cris810@aol.com.

WOODS, CYNDY JONES, secondary educator, researcher; b. Phoenix, Oct. 26, 1954; d. Glenn Billy and Helen Marie (Harrison) Jones; m. Clifford R. Woods, Apr. 3, 1975; children: Sean, Kathleen, Connor. AA in English, St. John's Coll., 1974; BA in English, Ariz. State U., 1992, M in Secondary Edn., 1994. Cert. secondary and ESL tchr., c.c. instr., Ariz. Tchr. grades 6-8 John R. Davis Sch., Phoenix, 1993, Thomas J. Pappas Sch., Phoenix, 1994-98, Maya H.S., Phoenix, 1998—; adj. faculty English and lit. Glendale C.C., 1997-98; asst. prin. Maya H.S., Phoenix, 2000—. Adj. faculty English and lit. Rio Salado C.C., 1995—; treas. Martin Luther Sch. Bd., Phoenix, 1985-89; presenter in field; chair TIF tech. and specialist depts. Conn. U., 2000—. Contbr. poetry to anthologies Dance on the Horizons, 1993, The Sound of Poetry: Best Poems of 1995, Across the Universe, 1996; contbr. articles to profl. jours. Mem. St. Francis Xavier Sch. Bd., Phoenix, 1995; v.p. City/County Child Care Bd., Phoenix, 1988-92; youth group advisor Mt. Calvary Luth. Ch., Phoenix, 1988-96; mem. SRP Ednl. Adv. Coun., 1996-98; mem. Maricopa County Juvenile Cmty. Justice Com., 1997; Fulbright master tchr., 2001. Fulbright Tchr. scholar, 1998. Mem. Ariz. Edn. Assn., Brophy Coll. Prep. Mother's Guild, Xavier Coll. Prep. Mother's Guild. Democrat. Avocations: computers, homeless issues, at-risk issues, volleyball, writing. Home: PO Box 5115 Glendale AZ 85312-5115 E-mail: cyndywrites@yahoo.com.

WOODS, DAVID LYNDON, publishing and broadcast executive, former federal agency executive; b. San Jose, Calif. s. Donald Mason and Lynda Rosalia (Mueller) W.; m. Barbara Sue Vacin, June 9, 1956 (div. July 1987); children: Stephanie Lynn Woods Snide, Allison Elizabeth Woods Traba, Roberta Lee, Dana Royce Woods Bunce, Meredith Mason; m. Jeanne-Renee Jones, July 5, 1998. AB, San Jose State Coll., 1952; MA, Stanford U., 1955; postgrad., U. So. Calif., 1962-63; MBA, Rollins Coll., 1965, Oxford (U.K.) U., 1974; PhD, Ohio State U., 1976. Dir. univ. broadcasting Lehigh U., Bethlehem, Pa., 1953-54; project officer NARAD Briefing Reports Navy Chief of Naval Ops., 1956-59; mgr. presentations and advt. Bendix-Pacific divsn. Bendix Corp., North Hollywood, Calif., 1959-60; dir. pub. rels. and advt. Librascope divsn. GPI, Glendale, 1961-62; sr. writer-editor Martin-Marietta Corp., Orlando, Fla., 1963-65; head program support br. Navy Dept. Speech Bur., Washington, 1965-70; spl. asst. to chief naval material Naval Material Command, 1970-84; dir. Navy sci. and tech. info. Naval Material Command (later at Office Naval Rsch.), Arlington, Va., 1984-93; pres. DaleWood Enterprises, Inc., Middleway, W.Va., 1987—. Adj. prof. bus. and pub. adminstrn. George Washington U., 1975-86; instr. Stanford (Calif.) U., Lehigh U., Ohio State U., U. Md., U. Va., and other colls., 1953-88, 94-97, Marshall U., 1998—; bd. correction naval records Sec. of Navy, Washington, 1980-85; commentator, on-air musical host local radio, 1994-95, 96-97; ptnr. Cap'n Dave's Flotsam and Jetsam, 1996—. Author: A History of Tactical Communication Techniques, 1965, 82, The Development of Visual Signals on Land and Sea, 1976, (four histories): U.S. Naval and Marine Corps Bases (2 vols.), 1986; editor: Signaling and Communicating at Sea (2 vols.), 1984; author, editor numerous fed. publs.; editl. columnist newspaper, 1998—; contbr. over 300 articles and revs. to mags. and jours. Chmn. fin. Commn. on Aging, Alexandria, 1993; bd. dirs. Middleway Hist. Conservancy, 1994—, The Station at Shepherdstown, W.Va., 1998-2000; vice chmn. Coun. on Aging of Jefferson County, 1995—, Nat. Assn. for Uniformed Svcs., 1986-91; U.S. del. NATO Congress Internat. Res. Officers, 1984-91, U.S. v.p., 1988-89. Capt. USNR, 1949-87. Recipient Navy Superior Pub. Svc. medal, 1986. Mem. SAR, Nat. Def. Indsl. Assn. (life, author 1991-92), U.S. Naval Inst. (life, author 1966—), Naval Res. Assn. (life, dist. pres. 1974-75, 93-94, nat. pub. affairs officer 1966-72), Naval Enlisted Res. Assn. (life assoc., pub. 1987-93), Res. Officers Assn. (life, nat. pres. 1985-86, columnist 2000—01), Armed Forces Comm. and Electronics Assn. (life, author), Nat. Comm. Assn. (emeritus, chair mass comm. divsn. 1970-71), Sovereign Mil. Order of Temple of Jerusalem, Naval Order of the U.S. (life, recorder-gen. 1996-97), Army-Navy Club, Harper's Ferry/Bolivar Vets. Assn. Avocations: American musical comedy, acting and directing theatre, bluegrass and old-time banjo music, military signals, history of technology. E-mail: dwoods7807@aol.com.

WOODS, DENNIS CRAIG, school superintendent; b. Akron, Ohio, Nov. 29, 1946; m. Janice Mary Matvey, Apr. 21, 1971; children: Gregory, Jeffrey, Mark. BA, Brown U., 1968; MA, U. Akron, 1974; postgrad., Ohio State U., 1990-92. Job placement specialist Summit County Bd. Edn., Akron, 1971-72; tchr. English, athletic dir. South H.S., 1972-77; unit prin. Buchtel H.S., 1977-80; asst. prin. Firestone H.S., 1980-81, prin., 1987-90, Ellet H.S., Akron, 1981-87; grad. rsch. assoc. Policy Rsch. for Ohio Based Edn., Columbus, 1990-91; asst. dir. Sch. Study Coun. of Ohio, 1991-92; supt. Sandy Valley Local Schs., Magnolia, Ohio, 1992-96, Bay Village (Ohio) City Sch. Dist., 1996—. Instructional audit team Sch. Effectiveness Trainers, Columbus, 1992-96; presenter adminstr.'s acad. Middletown (Ohio) City Sch. Dist., 1994; presenter Ohio Acad. for Sch. Improvement, Columbus, 1993, Supts. Transition Project,

The Ohio State U., 2000—; site visitor Blue Ribbon Schs. Program, Washington, 1991; presenter in field. Founding mem. Sandy Valley TAP Group, Magnolia, 1993—96; advancement chair Troop 50, Boy Scouts Am., Akron, 1986—93; governance com. Ohio H.S. Athletic Assn., 2001—; trustee The Bay Village Ednl. Found., 1996—; mem. com. of practitioners Ohio Dept. Edn., 2002—; eucharistic min. St. Raphael Ch., 1994—; mem. cmty. bd. St. John West Shore Hosp., 1998—; mem. governing bd. Cuyahoga Spl. Edn. Svc. Ctr., 1999—; bd. dirs. Lake Erie Ednl. Computer Assn., 1999—, Mohican Inst., 2000—; mem. articulation and transfer adv. coun. Ohio Bd. Regents, 2001—. Lt. (j.g.) USNR, 1968—70. Recipient Outstanding Secondary Prin. award Akron Secondary Prins. Assn., 1985, 89, Pyramid award Nat. Sch. Pub. Rels. Assn., 1997, Exemplary Svc. award Sandy Valley Bd. Edn., 1996; E.E. Lewis fellow Ohio State U., 1991, Eikenberry scholar, 1990. Mem. ASCD, Horace Mann League (Amb. award 2000), Ohio Assn. Local Supts., Ohio Sch. Bds. Assn., Ohio Inst. Effective Sch. Leadership (first cohort 1995), Am. Assn. Sch. Adminstrs. (del. assembly 2000), Mid-Am. Assn. Sch. Supts., Ohio Assn. Local Sch. Supts., Greater Cleve. Sch. Supts. Assn., Buckeye Assn. Sch. Adminstrs. (exec. and pub. rels. com. 1995, legis. com. 1996-97, chmn. state dept. com. 1998-2000, pres.-elect 2000, pres. 2001, past pres. 2002, Exemplary Leadership award 2000), Sandy Valley C. of C., Bay Kiwanis Club, Touchdown Club, Phi Delta Kappa. Avocations: reading, physical fitness, ornithology. Office: Bay Village City Sch Dist 377 Dover Center Rd Bay Village OH 44140-2304 E-mail: dwoods@Leeca.org.

WOODS, DENNIS OLIVER, headmaster, market and political research analyst; b. Spirit Lake, Iowa, Mar. 11, 1947; s. Peter Ashton and Edna Elizabeth Woods; m. Jane Robertson; children: Miranda, Vijay, Catherine. BS in Agrl. Journalism, Iowa State U., 1970; MEd , Oreg. State U., 1973; postgrad., Multnomah Bible Coll., 1973—74, Computer Career Inst., 1974—75. Polit. rsch. asst., vol. several polit. and social action coms., Portland, 1976—79; market/polit. rsch. analyst Bardsley & Haslacher, 1980—84; market/statis. rsch. analyst Columbia Info. Sys., 1985—90; owner Target Market Strategies, Clackamas, 1991—2001; founder, headmaster ClassicalFree Virtual Acad., 2001—. Author: textbooks on hist., sociol. and religious influences leading to U.S. constnl. settlement. Vice chmn. Multnomah County Rep. Party, Portland, 1990—90; polit. rsch. cons. Target Market Strategies, Clackamas, 1990—2001; issues and strategy cons. Multnomah County Rep. Party, Portland, 1986—90; bd. mem. Oreg. Mktg. Assn., 1973—74. First lt. art. U.S. Army, 1971—72. Presbyterian. Avocation: woodworking. Office: ClassicalFree Virtual Acad PO Box 497 Clackamas OR 97015 Home Fax: 503-658-0385; Office Fax: 503-658-0385.

WOODS, DONALD DEWAYNE, advertising materials designer/manufacturer; b. Chattanooga, June 17, 1942; s. Wilburn William and Stella Elizabeth (Hooks) W.; m. Wanda Louise Hines, May 29, 1974 (div. Oct. 1989); m. Donna Maria Spanier, Feb. 21, 1992. GED (Gen. Ednl. Devel.), Tex. Camera/reprodn. mgr. Benco Plastics Inc., Knoxville, Tenn., 1964-69; sous chef Cherokee Country Club, 1967-69; auto/screen pressman Gibson Greeting Cards Inc., Cin., 1973-80; plant mgr. Am. Sign Co., Florence, Ky., 1984-86; gen. mgr., co-owner Trans-Acc Graphics, Cin., 1986; owner D & D Enterprises, 1986—. Cons. screen printing Levi Strauss, Cin., 1975-76, Journey Electronics Inc., Mason, Ohio, 1992; designer Screen Printed Products, 1986-89. Author: Screen Printing: Techniques for Point of Sale Merchandise, 1984; co-patentee utilization of night vision device in processing film. Cons., v.p. 7th Step Found., Cin., 1973-78; cons. Cin. Coalition for Homeless, 1992. With U.S. Army, 1960-64, Germany. Recipient Update award Printers Week/Cin. Enquirer, 1989. Mem. Profl. Photographers Assn., Advt. Specialties Assn. (imprinter 1986—), The Planetary Soc., Midwest Screen Printers Assn. (cons. 1978—), Civil War Soc. (participant drama reenactment 1974—). Republican. Mem. Ch. of God. Avocations: photography, boating, Civil War study, genealogy, biblical history. Home and Office: 3300 Gamble Ave Cincinnati OH 45211-5616

WOODS, EDYTHE B. psychology educator; b. Athens, Ga., Jan. 31, 1959; BS in Psychology, Duke U., 1981; MS in Psychology, Yale U., 1983, MPhil in Psychology, 1984, PhD in Psychology, 1986. Biology tchr. Westminster Schs., Atlanta, 1986-87; chemistry and math. tchr. Benjamin Sch., North Palm Beach, Fla., 1987-89; rsch. assoc. Wayne State U. Med. Sch., Detroit, 1989-91; asst. prof. psychology William Tyndale Coll., Farmington Hills, 1992-93, assoc. prof. psychology, 1993-98, chair divsn. arts and scis., 1993-94, v.p. acad. affairs, 1994-98; chair, assoc. prof. psychology Madonna U., Livonia, 1998—2002, prof., 2002—. Contbr. articles to profl. jours. Recipient Grad. fellowship NSF, 1982-84. Mem. APA, Am. Psychol. Soc., Soc. Tchg. Psychology, Phi Beta Kappa. Office: Madonna U 36600 Schoolcraft Livonia MI 48150 Fax: 734-432-5393. E-mail: ewoods@madonna.edu.

WOODS, FRANK J. health facility administrator; b. Kane, Pa., June 25, 1956; s. Lawrence Miller and Virginia Claire Woods; m. Kathleen Mary Smith, Nov. 28, 1981 (div. Aug. 3, 1998); children: Joshua, Danielle; m. Lora Sue Likins, Feb. 22, 2002; 1 child Thomas. BS in Liberal Arts, U. R.I., 1978. Cert. clin. lab. scientist R.I. Lab. technologist U. R.I. Health Svcs., Kingston, 1978—79; lab. mgr. Cranston (R.I.) Med. Lab., Inc., 1979—86; real estate broker Coldwell Banker, Warwick, RI, 1986—91; lab. mgr. Labcorp of Am., Inc., Cranston, 1991—2000, East Side Clin. Lab., Cranston, 2000—. Author: Love Stories, Poems and Letters, 2002. Vol. R.I. Watershed Watch U. R.I., Kingston, 2002. Roman Catholic. Avocations: bicycling, outdoor activities, cooking, body building. Home: 50 Glenwood Dr Warwick RI 02889

WOODS, GEORGE EDWARD, judge; b. 1923; m. Janice Smith. Student, Ohio No. U., 1941-43, 46, Tex. A&M Coll., 1943, Ill. Inst. Tech., 1943; JD, Detroit Coll. Law, 1949. Sole practice, Pontiac, Mich., 1949-51; asst. pros. atty. Oakland County, 1951-52; chief asst. U.S. atty. Ea. Dist. Mich., 1953-60, U.S. atty., 1960-61; assoc. Honigman, Miller, Schwartz and Cohn, Detroit, 1961-62; sole practice, 1962-81; judge U.S. Bankruptcy Ct., 1981-83, U.S. Dist. Ct. (ea. dist.) Mich., Detroit, 1983-93, sr. judge, 1993—. Served with AUS, 1943-46. Fellow Internat. Acad. Trial Lawyers, Am. Coll. Trial Lawyers; mem. Fed. Bar Assn., State Bar Mich. Office: US Dist Ct 277 US Courthouse 231 W Lafayette Blvd Detroit MI 48226-2700

WOODS, GERALD WAYNE, lawyer; b. Durham, N.C., Sept. 15, 1946; m. Deborah Jordan Bates, Apr. 30, 1983; children: Paul Ellis, Katherine Jordan. BS, U. N.C., 1968; JD, Emory U., 1973. Bar: Ga. 1973, U.S. Dist. Ct. (no. dist.) Ga. 1974, U.S. Supreme Ct. 1980, U.S. Dist. Ct. (so. dist.) Ga. 1987. With retail mgmt. Sears, Roebuck & Co., Atlanta, 1968-70; asst. to exec. sec. bd. regents U. Ga. System, 1973-76, asst. exec. sec., 1976-78; legal advisor to pres. Med. Coll. of Ga., Augusta, 1978-2000, v.p. for bus. ops., legal advisor to the pres., asst. prof. med. jurisprudence, 1990-2000; of counsel Kilpatrick Stockton LLP, 2001—. Mem. faculty Sr. Acctg. Officers Workshop Nat. Assn. of Coll. and Univ. Bus. Officers, Myrtle Beach, S.C., 1981; lectr. law seminars and med. confs., nationwide. Contbr. articles to profl. jours. Councilman City of Augusta, 1984-95; pres. YMCA of Augusta, Inc., 1987-88; bd. dirs. Leadership Augusta, 1982-85, 94-96, others; bd. dirs. Augusta Symphony, 1988-90, pres., 1990-91; trustee Augusta-Richmond County Pub. Libr., 1984-85; mem. Richmond County Dem. Exec. Com., 1983-86, Richmond County Bd. of Health, 1986-95, Augusta Symphony League, 1986—; bd. dirs. Augusta Youth Ctr., 1988-93, Southea. Nat. Scis. Acad., 1989—, Southeastern Natural Scis. Acad. Land Trust, Inc., 2001—; chmn. cultural action plan steering com. Greater Augusta Arts Coun., 1992, active, 1994-2001, pres., 1999; mem. air svc. task force Augusta C. of C., 1990-93; mem. Cmtys. in Sch. Inc. Bd., 1996-98, Southeastern Tech. Ctr. Bd., 1996-2000; trustee Historic Augusta, Inc., 1998—; active Ga.-Carolina coun. Boy Scouts Am., 1999—; co-chair exec. forum Leadership Augusta, 1994-96, 2002; asst. scoutmaster Boy Scouts Am., 1998—. Mem. State Bar Ga. (medico-legal liaison and mental health coms. 1979, vice chmn. coll. and univ. com., sch. and coll. law sect. 1986-88), Augusta Bar Assn., Ga. Soc. Hosp. Attys., Nat. Assn. Coll. and Univ. Attys. (exec. bd. 1983-86, co-vice chair fin. com. 2002--), Nat. Health Lawyers Assn./Am. Acad. Healthcare Attys., Kiwanis (treas. Ansley club 1977, bd. dirs. 1977-78), Nat. Assn. Coll. and Univ. Bus. Officers, Forrest Hills Assn. (pres. 1982-85, bd. dirs. 1985-94), Met. Augusta C. of C. (co-chair govt. affairs com.), U. N.C. Alumni Assn. (v.p. Augusta chpt. 1984-90), Pinnacle Club, Augusta Country Club, Rotary. Avocation: photography. Office: Kilpatrick & Stockton LLP 1400 First Union Bank Bldg Augusta GA 30903

WOODS, HARRIETT RUTH, retired political organization president; b. Cleve., June 2, 1927; d. Armin and Ruth (Wise) Friedman; m. James B. Woods, Jan. 2, 1953; children: Christopher, Peter, Andrew. Student, U. Chgo., 1945; BA, U. Mich., 1949; LLD (hon.), Webster U., 1988. Reporter Chgo. Herald-Am., 1948, St. Louis Globe-Democrat, 1949-51; prodr. Star, KPLR-TV, St. Louis, 1964-74; moderator, writer Sta. KETC-TC, 1962-64; council mem. University City, Mo., 1967-74; mem. Mo. Hwy. Commn., 1974, Mo. Transp. Commn., 1974-76, Mo. Senate, 1976-84; lt. gov. State of Mo., 1985-89; pres. Inst. for Policy Leadership, U. Mo., St. Louis, 1989-91, lectr., 1995—. Pres. Nat. Women's Polit. Caucus, 1991-95; dir. Federal Home Loan Mortgage Corp., 1995-98; fellow inst. politics J.F. Kennedy Sch. Govt., Harvard U., 1988; lectr. U. Mo., St. Louis, 1995—. Author: Stepping Up to Power: The Political Journey of American Women, 2000. Bd. dirs. LWV of Mo., 1963, Nat. League of Cities, 1972-74; Dem. nominee for U.S. Senate, 1982, 86. Jewish.

WOODS, HARRY ARTHUR, JR. lawyer; b. Hartford, Ark., Feb. 15, 1941; s. Harry Arthur and Viada (Young) W.; m. Carol Ann Meschter, Jan. 21, 1967; children: Harry Arthur III, Elizabeth Ann. BA in Econs., Okla. State U., 1963; JD, NYU, 1966. Bar: N.Y. 1966, Okla. 1970. Assoc. White & Case, N.Y.C., 1966—67, Crowe & Dunlevy, Oklahoma City, 1971—75, ptnr., 1976—. Councilman City of Edmond, 1975-79, mayor pro tem, 1977-79. Capt. JAGC U.S. Army, 1967-71. Mem. ABA, Am. Law Inst., Internat. Assn. Def. Counsel, Okla. Bar Assn. (bd. govs. 2001-03, profl. responsibility tribunal 1999-2004, Outstanding Svc. award 1982, Golden Gavel award 1998, Neil Bogan Professionalism award 1998), Ruth Bader Ginsburg Inn of Ct. (pres. 1998-2000), Okla. County Bar Assn. (bd. dirs. 2001-2003). Democrat. Methodist. Avocations: flying, jogging, bicycling, photography, rock climbing. Office: Crowe & Dunlevy 1800 Mid-America Tower 20 N Broadway Ave Ste 1800 Oklahoma City OK 73102-8273

WOODS, HOWARD JAMES, JR. civil engineer; b. Elizabeth, N.J., Oct. 11, 1955; s. Howard James and Catherine (Hurring) W.; m. Roseann Schmidt, Jan. 30, 1999. BCE cum laude, Villanova U., 1977, MCE, 1985. Registered profl. engr. N.Y., N.J., Pa., Md., N.Mex. Environ. engr. EPA, Phila., 1977-81; project engr. Johnson, Mirmiran & Thompson, Silver Spring, Md., 1981-83; dir. engring. ea. div. Am. Water Works Svc. Co., Haddon Heights, N.J., 1983-85, mgr. ops. ea. div., 1985-86, dir. planning, 1986-88, east regional mgr. ops., 1988-92; v.p. N.J. Am. Water Co., 1992-97, Am. Water Works Svc. Co., 1997-98; sr. v.p. Am. Water Svcs., Marlton, NJ, 1998-2000; pres. Howard J. Woods, Jr. & Assocs., LLC, 2000—. Apptd. by gov. to N.J. Water Supply Adv. Coun., 1991-97. Named one of Oustanding Young Men Am., Jaycees, 1984, Outstanding Civil Engring. Alumnus, Grad. Sch. Villanova U., 1986; recipient John J. Gallen award Villanova U. Coll. of Engring. Tech. Achievement award. Mem. ASCE, Nat. Water Well Assn., Am. Mgmt. Assn., Am. Water Works Assn., Amnesty Internat., Water Environ. Fedn., Villanova Club (So. N.J.), Tau Beta Pi. Democrat. Roman Catholic. Avocations: skiing, music, photography. Home: 138 Liberty Dr Newtown PA 18940-1111 Office: Howard J Woods Jr & Assocs LLC 138 Liberty Dr Newtown PA 18940-1111 E-mail: budwoods@earthlink.net.

WOODS, JOHN WILLIAM, electrical, computer and systems engineering educator, consultant; b. Washington, Dec. 5, 1943; s. John Gill and Margaret (McHugh) W.; m. Harriet Hemmerich, June 17, 1972; children: Anne, Christopher. BSEE, MIT, 1965, MSEE, 1967, PhD, 1970. Sr. rsch. engr. Lawrence Livermore (Calif.) Nat. Lab., 1973-76; asst. prof. Rensselaer Poly. Inst., Troy, N.Y., 1976-78, assoc. prof., 1978-84, prof., 1985—. Vis. prof. Delft Tech. U., The Netherlands, 1985, Heinrich-Hertz Inst., Berlin, 2000; program dir. NSF, Washington, 1987-88; assoc. dir. Ctr. for Image Processing Rsch., 1992—; cons. Kodak, Rochester, N.Y., 1985-86, Johns Hopkins Applied Physics Lab., Laurel, Md., 1987, Calian Comms. Ltd., 1990-91; co-founder Focus Interactive Tech., Inc., 1993; assoc. dir. NSF I/U Ctr. for Next Generation Video, 1998-01, dir. 2002—. Co-author: Probability and Random Processes fwith Appeals to Signal Processing, 2002, 3d edit., 1994; editor: Subband Image Coding, 1991; co-editor: Handbook of Visual Communications, 1995; mem. editl. bd. Graphical Models and Image Processing, 1989-93; contbg. author book chpts., articles to profl. jours. Mem. Com. Acad. Excellence, Clifton Park, N.Y., 1984. Capt. USAF, 1969-73. Grantee NSF, Army Rsch. Office, Advanced Rsch. Projects Agy., Ctr. Advanced TV Studies, 1978-01. Fellow IEEE (editl. bd. Trans. on Video Tech. 1990—, Third Millennium medal 2000); mem. IEEE Signal Processing Soc. (com. chmn. 1983-85, ednl. com. chmn. 1987-93, ad. com. mem. 1986-88, assoc. editor jour. 1979-82, co-chmn. tech. program com. 1st IEEE Internat. Conf. on Image Processing 1994, Best Paper awards 1977, 86, Meritorious Svc. award 1989, Tech. Achievement award 1993). Roman Catholic. Home: 43 Longview Dr Clifton Park NY 12065-2318 Office: Rensselaer Poly Inst ESCE Dept Troy NY 12180-3590

WOODS, JOHN BURTIS, protective services official; b. Houston, Apr. 6, 1961; s. Ezola Guidry; m. Cecelia Davis Woods, May 27, 1995 (div. May 8, 1998); children: John Elijah, Apryl Breanna. Assocaite Sci., Houston CC, Houston, Texas, 1985. Customer rels. Lincoln Hotel, Houston, 1987—88; geol. technician E.R.M. Inc., 1987—88; chem. technician Gulf States Analytical, Inc., 1988—90; dep. sheriff Harris County Sheriff Dept., 1990—93; police officer Houston Police Dept., 1993—. Midtown civic mem. Midtown Civic Club, Houston, 1988—2002. Democrat-Npl. Baptist. Avocation: billiards. Home Fax: 713-523-2310.

WOODS, JOHN ELMER, plastic surgeon; b. Battle Creek, Mich., July 5, 1929; m. Janet Ruth; children: Sheryl, Mark, Jeffrey, Jennifer, Judson. BA, Asbury Coll., 1949; MD, Western Res. U., 1955; PhD, U. Minn., 1966; DHL, Ashbury Coll., 1999. Intern Gorgas Hosp., Panama Canal Zone, 1955-56, resident in gen. surgery, 1956-57, Mayo Grad. Sch., Rochester, Minn., 1960-65, resident in plastic surgery, 1966-67, Brigham Hosp., Boston, 1968; fellow, transplant cons. Harvard Med. Sch., Cambridge, 1969; cons. in gen. and plastic surgery Mayo Clinic, Rochester, 1969-93, vice chmn. Dept. Surgery; asst. prof. Mayo Med. Sch., 1973-76, assoc. prof., 1976-80, prof. plastic surgery, 1980-93, Stuart W. Harrington prof. surgery. Vis. prof. Yale Sch. Medicine, New Haven, 1984, Harvard Sch. Medicine, Cambridge, 1984. Contbr. over 200 articles to profl. jours.; also 26 book chpts. and 1 film. Recipient Disting. Mayo Clinician award, 1991, Disting. Mayo Alumnus award, 1999. Mem. AMA (coun. on sci. affairs 1985-87), ACS (grad edn. com. 1985-87), Am. Bd. Med. Specialties, Am. Bd. Plastic Surgery (sec.-treas. 1985-88, chmn. 1988-89), Am. Soc. Plastic Surgeons Ednl. Fedn. (pres. 1984-85). Avocations: skiing, sailing, reading, the arts. Office: Mayo Clinic Plummer N-10 Rochester MN 55905-0001 E-mail: woods.john@mayo.edu.

WOODS, JOHN WILLIAM, retired lawyer; b. Ft. Worth, Dec. 10, 1912; s. John George and Eugenia (Smith) W.; m. Gertie Leona Parker, Apr. 15, 1954. BS, North Tex. State U., 1951, M.Ed., 1952; JD, St. Mary's U., San Antonio, 1967; postgrad., Fresno State Coll., 1952, West Tex. State U., 1959. Bar: Tex. bar 1966. Tchr., Corcoran, Calif., 1952-53, Pampa, Tex., 1953-63, Harlandale Sch. Dist., San Antonio, 1963-67; practicing atty. Amarillo, Tex., 1967-68; county atty. Sherman County, 1969-72; county judge, 1988, ret.; justice of peace, 1975-88; pvt. practice, Stratford, Tex., 1968-95; ret., 1995. Served to ensign USN, 1930-47, ETO. Mem. Tex. Bar Assn., Amarillo Bar Assn., Am. Legion, Masons, Shriners, Scottish Rite, York Rite. Democrat. Mem. Christian Ch. (Disciples Of Christ). Home: # 911 1300 S Jackson St Amarillo TX 79101-4146

WOODS, KATHY MARIE DELAPLAIN, humanities educator; b. San Francisco, Nov. 11, 1958; d. James Lisle Deplain, Jr. and Mary Kathyrn Hickman Deplain; m. Glen Allen Woods, May 30, 1981; children: Rachel Judy. BBA Mktg., U. of Oklahoma, Norman, OK, 1982, BA English, 1985, ME English Edn., 1994. Nat. Bd. Certified Teacher Okla., 2001. Educator West Mid H.S., Norman, Okla., 1985—97, Norman H.S. North, Norman, 1997—. Mem. Lang. Arts Adv. Bd., Norman, Okla., 1986—; sec. Oaklahoma Writing Project, Norman, Okla., 2001—, workshop presenter, Okla., 2001—. Contbr. text book; author: (poem) Writing Contest (2nd Pl., 1999). Elder & chair or nominating com. First Presbyn. Ch. of Moore, Moore, Okla., 1996—99, educator, 1993—99, newsletter author & pub., 1994—97. Recipient West Mid High Tchr. of The Yr., West Mid High Faculty, 1996, Norman Pub. Schools Tchr. of The Yr., Norman Pub. Schools, 1996. Mem.: Oaklahoma Coun. of Teachers of English, Norman Readers & Writers. Democrat-Npl. Presbyterian. Home: 912 Little River Road Norman OK 73071 Office: Norman High School North 1809 Stubbeman Norman OK 73069 Personal E-mail: mskwoods@webzone .net.

WOODS, LAWRENCE MILTON, airline company executive; b. Manderson, Wyo., Apr. 14, 1932; s. Ben Ray and Katherine (Youngman) W.; m. Joan Frances Van Patten, June 10, 1952; 1 dau., Laurie. B.Sc. with honors, U. Wyo., 1953; MA, N.Y. U., 1973, PhD, 1975; LL.D., Wagner Coll., 1973. Bar: Mont. 1957; C.P.A., Colo., Mont. Accountant firm Peat, Marwick, Mitchell & Co. (C.P.A.'s), Billings, Mont., 1953; supervisory auditor Army Audit Agy., Denver, 1954-56; accountant Mobil Producing Co., Billings, Mont., 1956-59; planning analyst Socony Mobil Oil Co., N.Y.C., 1959-63, planning mgr., 1963-65; v.p. North Am. div. Mobil Oil Corp., N.Y.C., 1966-67, gen. mgr. planning and econs., 1967-69, v.p., 1969-77, exec. v.p., 1977-85, also dir.; pres., chief exec. officer, dir. Centennial Airlines, Inc., 1985-87; pres., dir. Woshakie Travel Corp., 1988—, High Plains Pub. Co. Inc., 1988—. Bd. dirs. The Aid Assn. for Lutherans Mut. Funds. Author: Accounting for Capital, Construction and Maintenance Expenditures, 1967, The Wyoming Country Before Statehood, 1971, Sometimes the Books Froze, 1985, Moreton Frewen's Western Adventures, 1986, British Gentlemen in the Wild West, 1989; editor: Wyoming Biographies, 1991, Wyoming's Big Horn Basin, 1996, Agent R, 2000, John Clay, Jr., 2001; co-author: Takeover, 1980; editor: Wyoming Biographies, 1991; contbr.: Accountants' Encyclopedia, 1962. Bd. dirs. U. Wyo. Rsch. Corp. Served with U.S. Army, 1953—55. Mem. ABA, Mont. Bar Assn., Am. Inst. CPA's, Chgo. Club. Republican. Lutheran. Office: High Plains Pub Co PO Box 1860 Worland WY 82401-1860

WOODS, LEWIS CURRY, III, science educator, researcher; b. Harrodsburg, Ky., Oct. 20, 1953; s. Emeline Woods; m. Mary A. Newton, July 20, 1954; children: Anna, Luke. BS in Biology (Fisheries), Murray State U., 1975; MS in Zoology, Ohio State U., 1977; PhD in Zoology, N.C. State U., 1983. Fisheries biologist Ky. Dept. Fish and Game, Frankfort, 1973—75; fisheries supr. Ohio Divsn. Wildlife, Findlay, 1977—79; biologist, dir. Crane Aquaculture Facility, Balt. Gas & Electric, 1983—90; asst. prof. aquaculture dept. animal and avian scis. U. Md., College Park, 1998—. Assoc. editor N.Am. Jour. Aquaculture, Bethesda, 1988—90; dir. Striped Bass Grower's Assn., 1996; vis. scientist Woods Hole (Mass.) Oceanographic Inst., 1975; adj. assoc. prof. dept. pathology Sch. Medicine, U. Md., 1988—2001; adj. assoc. Horn Point Environ. Lab. U. Md., Cambridge, 1996—2001. Named Outstanding Young Man in Am., Jaycees, 1983, lead scientist aquaculture adv. del. to post-USSR Russia, Md. Dept. Agr., Office Aquaculture & Seafood, 1992; recipient Gamma Beta Phi Fellowship award, Gamma Beta Phi Honor Soc., 1971, Chesapeake Bay Conservation award, Izaak Walton League of Am., 1985, Urban Wildlife Conservation award, Nat. Inst. Urban Wildlife, 1986, Take Pride in Am. award, U.S. Dept. of the Interior, 1986; fellow Office, of Econ. and Coop. Devel., 1995. Mem.: USDA (adv. com. for nat. coord. for aquaculture new animal drug approvals, aquaculture adv. com. for nat. animal germplasm program, n.e. regional aquaculture ctr., industry and tech. adv. coms.), Fed. Joint Subcom. on Aquaculture (quality assurance in aquaculture workgroup), World Aquaculture Soc., U.S. Aquaculture Soc. (v.p. 2001—02, dir., v.p. 2001—02), Am. Fisheries Soc. (cert. fisheries scientist), Striped Bass Grower's Assn. (assoc.), Phi Kappa Phi.

WOODS, MICHAEL PATRICK, obstetrician, educator; b. Jackson, Mich., May 1, 1959; s. James Merrill and Marian Ruth (Allcorn) Woods; m. Anne Terese Giles, June 3, 1988; children: Rachel, Leah, Monica, Anna, Michaela. BA, Knox Coll., 1981; MD, Loyola U., Maywood, Ill., 1985. Diplomate Am. Bd. Ob-Gyn. Tchg. asst. histology U. Nebr. Med. Ctr., Omaha, 1981-82, resident, 1985-89, chief resident ob-gyn., 1988-89, clin. assoc. prof., 1989—; pvt. practice Council Bluffs, Iowa, 1989-95; med. dir. S.W. Iowa Maternal Care Clinic. Loyola U. Stritch Sch. Medicine admissions com., 1981-85; U. Nebr. Med. Sch. admissions com., 1985-86; Knox Coll. premed. advisor, 1982-85; adv. bd. Iowa Western C.C. med. asst. program; bd. dirs. S.W. Iowa Vis. Nursing Assn., 1989—. Contbr. articles to profl. jours. Recipient CIBA Pharm. Co. Cmty. Svc. award, 1986, Burroughs Welcome Co. Svc. to ACOG Jr. Fellows award, 1988, John McCain fellowship, 1995, Primary Health Care Policy fellow, 1998. Mem. AMA, ACOG, Ctrl. Assn. of Obs.-Gyn., Am. Soc. of Reproductive Medicine, Am. Assn. of Gynecologic Laproscopists, Nebr. Ob-Gyn. Soc., Alpha Sigma Nu. Avocations: volleyball, fishing, reading, coin collecting, refinishing antique furniture. Office: Bellevue Ob Gyn Assocs Ste 107 2206 Longo Dr Bellevue NE 68005-4247

WOODS, NANCY FUGATE, dean, women's health nurse; BS, Wis. State U., 1968; MSN, U. Wash., 1969; PhD, U. N.C., 1978. Staff nurse Sacred Heart Hosp., Wis., 1968, Univ. Hosp., 1969-70, St. Francis Cabrini Hosp., 1970; nurse clinician Yale-New Haven Hosp., 1970-71; instr. nursing Duke U., Durham, N.C., 1971-72, from instr. to assoc. prof., 1972-78; assoc. prof. physiology U. Wash., Seattle, 1978-82, prof. physiology, 1982-84, chairperson dept. parent and child nursing, 1984-90, prof. dept. parent and child nursing, 1990—, dean Sch. Nursing, 1998—; dir. Ctr. Women's Health Rsch., U. Wash., 1989—. Pres. scholar U. Calif., San Francisco, 1985-86. Contbr. articles to profl. jours. Fellow ANA, Am. Acad. Nursing, Inst. Medicare, N.A.S.; mem. AAUP, APHA, Am. Coll. Epidemiology, Soc. Menstrual Cycle Rsch. (v.p. 1981-82, pres. 1983-85), Soc. Advancement Women's Health Rsch. Office: U Wash Sch Nursing PO Box 357260 Seattle WA 98195-7260*

WOODS, PENDLETON, college director, author; b. Ft. Smith, Ark., Dec. 18, 1923; s. John Powell and Mabel (Hon) W.; m. Lois Robin Freeman, Apr. 3, 1948; children: Margaret, Paul Pendleton, Nancy Cox. BA in Journalism, U. Ark., 1948. Editor, asst. pub. mgr. Okla. Gas & Electric Co., Oklahoma City, 1948-69; dir. Living Legends of Okla., Okla. Christian U., 1969-82; project, promotion dir. Enterprise Square and Am. Citizenship Ctr., 1982-92, dir. Nat. Edn. Program and Am. Citizenship Ctr., 1992. Arbitrator BBB; leader youth seminars in field; state pub. affairs officer Employer Support Guard and Res. Author: You and Your Company Magazine, 1950, Church of Tomorrow, 1964, Myriad of Sports, 1971, This Was Oklahoma, 1979; recorded Sounds of Scouting, 1969, Born Grown, 1974 (Western Heritage award Nat. Cowboy Hall of Fame), One of a Kind, 1977, Countdown to Statehood, 1982, The Thunderbird Tradition, 1989, A Glimpse at Oklahoma, 1990; editor Libertas. Bd. dirs. Campfire Girls Coun., Okla. Jr. Symphony, past pres., Zoo Amphitheater of Oklahoma City, Will Rogers Centennial Commn., Greater Oklahoma City Tree Bank Found.; bd. dirs. Boy Scout Am. (life); bd. dirs., co-founder Ctrl. Park Neighborhood Assn.; dir. Okla. for Resource Preservation; chmn. State Directional Signage Task Force; vol. reader Okla. Libr. for the Blind; past pres. Okla. Assn. Epilepsy; past pres. Keep Okla. Beautiful, Oklahoma City Mental Health Clin.; pub. rels. chmn. Oklahoma County chpt. A.R.C.; past chmn. Western Heritage award Nat. Cowboy Hall of Fame; past pres., hon. lifetime dir. Variety Health Ctr.; dir. Am. Freedom Coun.; state pres. SAR; exec. dir. Oklahoma City Bicentennial Commn.; mem. Okla. Disabilities Coun.; charter dir. Okla. Vets. Med. Rsch. Found.; cons. Exec. Svc. Corps; mem. Coun. Pub. Affairs; vol. Oklahoma City VA Hosp. With AUS, WWII and Korean War; ret. col.; state historian Okla. N.G.; chmn. Oklahoma City Independence Day Parade; exec. com. Oklahoma City Centennial Commn.; Okla. pub. affairs officer Employer Support Guard and Res. Named Outstanding Young Man of Yr., Oklahoma City Jr. C. of C., 1953; recipient Silver Beaver award Boy Scouts Am., 1963, Wokan award Okla. City Coun. Camp Fire girls, 1968, Silver medal Advt. Fedn. Am., Disting. Cmty. Svc. award Neighborhood Devel. and Conservation Ctr., Gold and Silver Patrick Henry Patriotism medals Mil. Order of the World Wars, 2 Commendation awards Am. Assn. for State and Local History, 4 honor medals Freedoms Found., Jefferson Davis medal United Daus. of the Confederacy, Okla. Disting. Svc. medal (2), Outstanding Contbn. to Okla. Mus., Okla. Mus. Assn., 1987, Outstanding Contbn. to Okla. Tourism award Okla. Dept. Tourism, 1989, Cmty. Svc. award U. Ark. Alumni Assn., 1992, Citizenship and Patriot award SAR, 1992, 5 Who Care award KOCO-TV, 1993, Jefferson award Am. Inst. for Pub. Svc., 1993, Mayor's award in Beautification, 1994, George Washington award Youth Leadership Found., St. Augustine, Fla., 1993, Golden Rule award J.C. Penney Found., 1999, Lifetime Achievement award Keep Okla. Beautiful; inducted into Okla. Journalism Hall of Fame, 2001, Okla. Mil. Hall of Fame, 2002. Mem. DAV, Soc. Assoc. Indsl. Editors (past v.p.), Advt. Fedn. Am. (past dist. dir.), Ctrl. Okla. Bus. Communicators (past pres., hon. life mem.), Okla. Jr. C. of C. (hon. life, past internat. dir.), Okla. Distributive Edn. Clubs (hon. life), Oklahoma City Advt. Club (past pres. hon. life mem.),

Words of Jesus Found. (pres.), Okla. Zool. Soc., Okla. Geneal. Soc. (past pres.), Okla. County Sr. Nutrition Found. (sec., bd. dirs.), Nat. Eagle Scout Assn. (Okla. chmn.), U. Ark. Alumni Assn. (charter pres. Oklahoma City chpt.), Okla. Lung Assn. (pub. rels. com.), Am. Cancer Soc. (dir. Okla. County chpt.), Okla. Travel Industries Assn., Okla. Hist. Soc. (publ. editor), Okla. Heritage Assn. (publ. editor), Oklahoma City Beautiful (publ. editor), Okla. Safety Coun. (publ. editor), Oklahoma County Hist. Soc. (dir., past pres.), 45th Inf. Div. Assn. (past pres.), Korean War Vets Assn., Am. Legion, VFW, Mus. Unassigned Lands (chmn.), Mil. Order World Wars (regional comdr., Okla. City comdr., Okla. State comdr., nat. staff), Oklahoma City Hist. Preservation Commn., Oklahoma City Clean and Green Coalition, Sigma Delta Chi, Kappa Sigma (nat. commr. publs.), Lincoln Park Country (pres.), Am. Ex-Prisoners of War (state comdr.), Okla. Vets. Coun. (chmn.). Home: 541 NW 31st St Oklahoma City OK 73118-7334 E-mail: penwoods@cox.net.

WOODS, PHYLLIS MICHALIK, librarian; b. New Orleans, Sept. 12, 1937; d. Philip John and Thelma Alice (Carey) Michalik; 1 child, Tara Lynn Woods. BA, Southea. La. U., 1967. Cert. speech and English tchr., libr. sci., La. Tchr. speech, English and drama St. Charles Parish Pub. Schs., Luling, La., elem. tchr., secondary tchr. remedial reading, Chpt. I reading specialist, Wicat tchr. coord., elem. sch. libr.; media specialist Jefferson Parish Pub. Sch. System. Tchr. cons. St. Charles parish writing project La. State U. Writing Project. Author: Egbert, the Egret, Egbert's Picnic, Egbert Visits Sammy, Angel Without Wings, The Necklace and Egbert's Calf, The Hurricane, The Cleanup Day, The Rainbow, The Fair, The Tornado; songwriter; musical compositions include The Fruits of the Spirit, Father's Day Song, Mother's Day Song; contbr. articles and poems to River Parish Guide, St. Charles Herald. Sch. rep. United Fund, St. Charles Parish Reading Assn.; parish com. mem. Young Authors, Tchrs. Who Write; active 4-H leader; bd. trustees Michalik Scholarship Trust. Mem. ASCD, Internat. Platform Assn., Internat. Reading Assn., St. Charles Parish Reading Coun., Newspaper in Edn. (chmn., historian), La. Assn. Newspapers in Edn. (state com.).

WOODS, REGINALD FOSTER, management consulting executive; b. Charleston, W.Va., Sept. 25, 1939; s. Reginald Foster and Jean Lee (Hill) W.; m. Katharine Terry Norden, May 11, 1963; children: Eric Arthur, Elizabeth Terry, Tracy Lee. BME, Cornell U., 1961, MME, 1962, MBA, 1963. Mktg. specialist Gen. Electric Co., N.Y.C., 1963-64; dir. flight equipment and facilities planning Eastern Airlines, 1964-70; v.p. planning Butler Internat., Inc., Montvale, N.J., 1970, sr. v.p. fin., 1971-80, exec. v.p., 1980-86, pres., 1986-87; chmn. Mgmt. Resources Group, Inc., Saddle River, 1987-96; pres., ceo The Advantage Ptnrs., Chatham, 1992-94. Bd. dirs. Benedetto, Gartland & Co., Inc., N.Y.C., DCG Corp., Roseville, Calif., The Greenleaf Co., Cranford, N.J., pres. DCG Corp., 1994—. Mem. Ridgewood Country Club, Glenmore Country Club, Keswick Club, Keswick Hunt Club. Home and Office: Fox Ridge Farm PO Box 490 Keswick VA 22947-0490

WOODS, RICHARD DALE, lawyer; b. Kansas City, Mo., May 20, 1950; s. Willard Dale and Betty Sue (Duncan) W.; m. Cecelia Ann Thompson, Aug. 11, 1973 (div. July 1996); children: Duncan Warren, Shannon Cecelia; m. Mary Linna Lash, June 6, 1999. BA, U. Kans., 1972; JD, U. Mo., 1975. Bar: Mo. 1975, Kans. 2000, U.S. Dist. Ct. (we. dist.) Mo. 1975, U.S. Tax Ct. 1999. Assoc. Shook, Hardy & Bacon L.L.P., Kansas City, Mo., 1975-79, ptnr., 1980-2000; shareholder Kirkland & Woods, P.C., Overland Park, Kans., 2001—. Gen. chmn. Estate Planning Symposium, Kansas City, 1985-86; chair Northland Coalition, 1993. Chmn. fin. com. North Woods Ch., Kansas City, 1986-88, 93-96; mem. sch. bd. N. Kansas City Sch. Dist., 1990-97, treas., 1992-97; mem. North Kansas City Ednl. Found., 1998-2002, pres., 1999-2002; mem. planned giving com. Truman Med. Ctr., 1992—, chmn., 1992-98; mem. Clay County Tax Increment Fin. Commn., 1990-99; bd. dirs. Heart of Am. Family Svcs., 1998—, sec., 2000-2001. Fellow Am. Coll. Trust and Estate Counsel; mem. ABA, Mo. Bar Assn., Johnson County Bar Assn., Kansas City Met. Bar Assn., Lawyers Assn. Kans. City (sec., v.p., pres. young lawyers sect. 1981-84), Kans. City Estate Planning Soc. (bd. dirs. 1985-88, 93-95). Democrat. Office: Kirkland & Woods PC 6201 College Blvd Ste 250 Overland Park KS 66211 E-mail: rwoods@kcnet.com.

WOODS, ROBERT ARCHER, investment counsel; b. Princeton, Ind., Dec. 28, 1920; s. John Hall and Rose Erskine Heilman W.; m. Ruth Henrietta Diller, May 27, 1944; children— Robert Archer III, Barbara Diller (Mrs. Gregory Alan Klein), Katherine Heilman (Mrs. John E. Glennon), James Diller. AB, U. Rochester, 1942; MBA, Harvard, 1946. Account exec. Stein Roe & Farnham (investment counsel), Chgo., 1946-53, ptnr., 1954-90. Gov. Investment Co. Inst. Trustee U. Rochester; bd. dirs. Chgo. Juvenile Protective Assn., Chgo. Infant Welfare Soc., Chgo. Assn. Retarded Citizens. Served to lt. (s.g.) USNR, 1943-46. Mem. Am. Mgmt. Assn. (trustee 1973), Harvard Bus. Sch. Club Chgo. (pres. 1961), Phi Beta Kappa, Delta Upsilon. Clubs: Univ. Chgo, Chicago, Tower. Home: 470 Orchard Ln Winnetka IL 60093-4222 Office: 1 S Wacker Dr Chicago IL 60606-4614

WOODS, ROBERT EDWARD, lawyer; b. Albert Lea, Minn., Mar. 27, 1952; s. William Fabian and Maxine Elizabeth (Schmit) W.; m. Cynthia Anne Pratt, Dec. 26, 1975; children: Laura Marie Woods, Amy Elizabeth Woods. BA, U. Minn., 1974, JD, 1977; MBA, U. Pa., 1983. Bar: Minn. 1977, U.S. Dist. Ct. Minn. 1980, U.S. Ct. Appeals (8th cir.) 1980, Calif. 2000. Assoc. Moriarty & Janzen, Mpls., 1977-81, Berger & Montague, Phila., 1982-83, Briggs and Morgan, St. Paul and Mpls., 1983-84, ptnr., 1984-99; exec. v.p., gen. counsel InsWeb Corp., Redwood City, Calif., 1999-2000; gen. counsel BORN Info. Svcs., Inc., Mpls., 2000—. Adj. prof. William Mitchell Coll. Law, St. Paul, 1985; exec. com., bd. dirs. LEX MUNDI, Ltd., Houston, 1989-93, chmn. bd. 1991-92; bd. dirs. Midwest Asia Ctr., 1993-95, chmn. bd., 1994-95. Author (with others) Business Torts, 1989; sr. contbg. editor: Evidence in America: The Federal Rules in the States, 1987. Mem. ABA, Minn. State Bar Assn., State Bar of Calif., Hennepin County Bar Assn., Ramsey County Bar Assn. (chmn. corp., banking and bus. law sect. 1985-87), Assn. Trial Lawyers Am., Wharton Club of Minn., Phi Beta Kappa. Home: 28 N Deep Lake Rd North Oaks MN 55127-6506

WOODS, SANDRA KAY, real estate executive; b. Loveland, Colo., Oct. 11, 1944; d. Ivan H. and florence L. (Betz) Harris; m. Gary A. Woods, June 11, 1967; children: Stephanie Michelle, Michael Harris. BA, U. Colo., 1966, MA, 1967. Personnel mgmt. specialist CSC, Denver, 1967; asst. to regional dir. HEW, 1968-69; urban renewal rep. HUD, 1970-73, dir. program analysis, 1974-75, asst. regional dir. cmty. planning and devel., 1976-77, regional dir. fair housing, 1978-79; mgr. ea. facility project Adolph Coors Co., Golden, 1980, dir. real estate, 1981, v.p. chief environ. health and safety officer, 1982-96, v.p. strategic selling initiatives, 1996—2000; pres. Woods Properties LLP, 2000—. Mem. Exec. Exch., The White House, 1980. Bd. dirs. Golden Local Devel. Corp., 1981-82; fundraising dir. Coll. Arts and Scis., U. Colo., boulder, 1982-89, U. Colo.found.; mem. exec. bd. NCCJ, Denver, 1982-94; v.p. women in bus. Inc., Denver, 1982-83; mem. steering com. 1984 Yr. for All Denver Women, 1983-84; mem. 10th dist. Denver br. Fed. Res. Bd., 1990-96, chmn. bd., 1995-96; bd. dirs. Nat. Jewish Hosp., 1994—; chmn. Greater Denver Corp., 1991—. Named one of Outstanding Young Women Am., U.S. Jaycees, 1974, 78, Fifty Women to Watch, Businessweek, 1987, 92, Woman of Achievement YWCA, 1988. Mem. Indsl. Devel. Resources Coun. (bd. dirs. 1986-89), Am. Mgmt. Assn., Denver C. of C. (bd. dirs. 1988-96, Disting. Young Exec. award 1974, mem. Leadership Denver, 1976-77), Colo. Women's Forum, Nat. Assn. Office and Indsl. Park Developers (sec. 1988, treas. 1989), Committee of 200 (v.p. 1994-95), Phi Beta Kappa, Pi Alpha Alpha, PEO Club (Loveland). Republican. Presbyterian. E-mail: sandrawoods@qwest.net.

WOODS, SARAH KAREN, communications consultant; b. Wantage, U.K., Sept. 29, 1964; came to U.S., 1970; d. Robert Julian Preston and Andrea Jane Anderson; m. Christopher John Woods, Sept. 1, 1990; children: Henry, James. BA in Econs., U. of the South, 1986. Assoc. Security Pacific Hoare Govett Ltd., London and Hong Kong, 1986-89; officer syndications Westpac Fin. Asia Ltd., Hong Kong, 1989-90; asst. v.p. First Pacific Co. Ltd., 1990-94; exec. dir. Forrest Internat. Ltd., 1994-97; assoc. CS&A, N.Y.C., 1999—. Mem. Internat. Assn. of Bus. Communicators (pres. Hong Kong chpt. 1995, profl. devel. chair 1994, program chair 1993, Gold Quill award of Merit, 1998). Avocations: running, Vietnamese art. Home: 248 W 88th St Apt 17A New York NY 10024-2365 Office: CS&A 248 W 88th St Apt 17A New York NY 10024-2365

WOODS, SHARHONDA MICHELE, military officer; b. Jacksonville, N.C., Aug. 22, 1976; d. Richard Cecil and Linda Joyce Berry; m. David Lawrence Woods, Dec. 18, 1998. BA in Criminal Justice, U. Ala., 1998. Dir. Cmty. Svc. Ctr., U. Ala., Tuscaloosa, 1997—98; commd. USAF, 1998, advanced through grades to capt., 2000; chief, Logistics Plans 55th Logistics Support Squadron, Offutt AFB, Nebr., 1998—2000; installation deployment officer 42d Air Base Wing, Maxwell AFB, Ala., 2000—01; exec. officer 42d Logistics Group, 2001—. Facilitator Dorothy I. Height Leadership Inst., Washington, 1998—; trainer Faith Cmtys. Adv. Bd./Ala. Coalition Against Domestic Violence, Montgomery, Ala., 2001—. Vice chair Nat. Coun. Negro Women, Washington, 1999—; co-chair, mem. Black Youth Vote!, 2000—; judge Shell Oil Excellence in Tchg. Award, 2001; sec. Air Force Officer Mentor Action Program, 2001—. Mem.: Delta Sigma Theta, Inc. Avocations: reading, travel, volunteer work. Office: 12AF Logistics Plans 2915 S 12th Air Force Dr Davis Monthan AFB AZ 85707 Fax: 520-228-2077. E-mail: ladywoods23@yahoo.com.

WOODS, STEPHANIE ELISE, computer professional; b. Kansas City, Kans., July 26, 1962; d. Benoyd Myers and Lee Ann (Parks) Ellison; m. Reginald Elbert Woods; children: Erin Elise, Ryan Ellison. BA in Bus. Adminstrn., Wichita State U., 1984. Svcs. mgr. IBM, Houston, 1985—. Mem. NAFE, Alpha Kappa Alpha, Omicron Delta Kappa Alumni, Mortar Bd. Alumni. Democrat. Methodist. Avocations: sewing, needlework, puzzles, aerobics, weightlifting, singing. Office: IBM 2 Riverway Houston TX 77056-1939

WOODS, THOMAS STEPHEN, chemicals executive, researcher; b. Florence, Ala., Dec. 13, 1944; s. Clarence Augustus and Margaret Easter Woods; m. Susan Gesiene Schweers, Aug. 27, 1966; children: Kathryn Scott, Leslie Gesiene. PhD, U. of Ill., Champaign, Illinois, 1967—71; BS, Auburn U., Auburn, Alabama, 1963—67. Rsch. chemist Walter Reed Army Inst. of Rsch., Washington, 1972—74, DuPont Co., Wilmington, Del., 1974—84, mgr., licensing for the americas, 1985—87; directeur de la recherche et du developpement DuPont France, Paris, France (incl. Monaco), 1987—90; rsch. mgr., product delivery DuPont Co., Wilmington, Del., 1990—96; internat. tech. mgr. DuPont India, New Delhi, India, 1996—99; dir., intellectual assets mgmt. DuPont Co., Wilmington, Del., 2000—. Chmn., specifications expert group European Crop Protection Assn. and CropLife Internat., Brussels, 1999—. Author: (invited lecture) Industry Donation of Intellectual Property Rights to Universities, (encyclopedia chapter) Pesticide Formulations in Encyclopedia of Agrochemicals, (invited lecture) The Formulator's Toolbox - Product Forms for Modern Agriculture, (research paper in j. medicinal chemistry) Primaquine Analogs: Derivatives of 4-Amino-2-methoxyacridine, (chapter in adv. in heterocyclic chem.) Thioureas in the Synthesis of Heterocycles, (research paper in j. organic chemistry) 2-Amino-2-thiazoline. VIII., Cleavage of Sulfur-sulfur Bonds., 2-Amino-2- thiazoline. VII., (research paper in int. j. sulfur chem.) The Effect of Thiobenzoate Anion on Organic Thiosulfates, Use of Sodium Borohydride to Distinguish Organic Polysulfides from Disulfides, (research paper in tetrahedron) Equilibrium Studies: Substitutent Effects on Methoxypyridine-1-Methylpyridone Equilibria, (research paper in tetrahedron letters) Importance of Intermolecular Effects in Protomeric Equilibria, (research paper in inorganic chemistry) Substitution by Tridentate Groups in Platinum (II) Complexes, (ph.d. thesis, university of illinois) The Photochemistry of the 2,3-Piperazinediones and the 1,2,5,6-Tetrahydro-2-pyrazinones. Thermodynamic Studies of Equilibria of Some Methyltropic Nitrogen Heterocycles. Mem. Am. Sch. of Paris Bd. of Trustees, Paris, France (incl. Monaco), 1988—90. First lt. US Army, 1972—74, Walter Reed Army Medical Center. Decorated Army Commendation Medal for Sci. Rsch. US Army, Nat. Def. Svc. Medal; recipient Batchelor of Sci. with Honor, Auburn U., 1967; fellow NIH Predoctoral Fellowship, NIH, 1969-1971, NSF Undergraduate Rsch. Fellowship, NSF, 1966; scholar Geigy Scholarship, Geigy Chem. Co., 1965-66. Mem.: Am. Chem. Soc. (chmn., arrangements com. 1977—79), Phi Eta Sigma Academic Hon., Pi Mu Epsilon Math. Hon., Sigma Pi Sigma Physics Hon., Sigma Xi Rsch. Hon., Phi Lambda Upsilon Chemistry Hon. (pres. 1970—71), Theta Xi Frat. (life; pres. 1965—66). Methodist. Achievements include patents for Four US and international patents for novel crop protection products. Avocations: travel, gardening, piano. Home: 2 Top of the Oaks Chadds Ford PA 19317-9147 Office: E I du Pont de Nemours and Company Chestnut Run Plaza 708/182 Wilmington DE 19880-0708 Home Fax: 610-558-1218; Office Fax: 302-999-3409. Personal E-mail: thomas.s.woods@usa.dupont.com. E-mail: thomas.s.woods@usa.dupont.com.

WOODS, TOMIKA PATRICE, telecommunications area manager, author; b. Milwaukee, Wi, Oct. 27, 1970; d. Elsie Lee Woods and Hillard Bellamy; children: Brandice. Associates in Arts, Stratton College, Milwaukee, Wisconsin, 1989—91. Assistant manger Zales Jewelers, Milwaukee, Wis., 1988—89; circulation specialist Milwaukee Journal/Sentinel, 1989—89; sales consultant Rogers & Hollands Jewelers, Glendale, 1990—91; manager Afterthoughts, Milwaukee, 1991—92, Wohl Shoes, Milwaukee, 1992—94; intermodal biller C P Rail System, 1994—94; telecommunications area manager SBC/Ameritech, Waukesha, 1994—. Author: (book) Flip the Script, 2001, (movie screenplay) , 2000. Life skills mentor First Love Community Outreach Center, Milwaukee, Wi, 1995—2001, support group facilitator, 1995—2001. Non Denominational. Avocation: writing, traveling, singing & darts. Personal E-mail: TheJazzi1@aol.com.

WOODS, WALTER EARL, biomedical research and development executive; b. Phila., Sept. 26, 1944; s. Walter Earl and Janet I. (Ferguson) W.; m. Anna Maria Gianfreda, Dec. 4, 1975; children: Jeffrey, Elaine, Roberto, Carlo. BS in Biology, Del. Valley Coll. Sci. and Agr., 1966. Pilot plant operator Shell Chem., Woodbury, N.J., 1966-67; virologist, tissue culturist 1st U.S. Med. Lab., N.Y.C. and Ft. Meade, Md., 1967-69; virologist Merck, Sharpe & Dohme, West Point, Pa., 1969-70; quality control and assurance supr. Richardson-Merrell Inc., Swiftwater, 1970-74, cons., dir. influenza vaccine mfg. Naples, Italy, 1974-75, mgr. biol. prodn. Swiftwater, 1976-78, Connaught Labs., Inc., Swiftwater, 1978-81, dir. vaccine mfg., 1982-84, dir. mfg. resource planning, class A rating, 1984-88, dir. product devel. and mgmt., 1989-91; chmn. HIB and Pertussis bus. group, 1990-93; project co-dir. SAP software installation Connaught Labs., Inc., Swiftwater, 1997-98; exec. dir. project mgmt. Pasteur Mérieux Connaught, 1998—; project leader acellular combination vaccines, 1998—; project leader Lic. DAPTACEL in U.S., 2002—. Project dir. licensing Acellular Pertussis and Japanese Encepahlitis Vacines, 1992, HIB vaccine, 1993, licensed acP vaccine, Germany, 1994; bus. dir. for license of acellular pertussis vaccine, infant indications; mem. joint devel. com. Merck-Connaught Partnership; corp. sponsor for licensing of DTacP vaccine for infant use, 1996. Mem. visitors bd. East Stroudsburg U., bd. dirs. computer sci., 2000; bd. dirs. Northeastern Pa. Indsl. Resource Ctr., Wilkes-Barre, Pa., 1988—91. Recipient Banting-Best award, 1989. Mem. ASM, Pharm. Mfrs., Project Mgmt. Inst., Internat. Assn. Biol. Standardization. Avocations: soccer, music, gardening, reading. Home: 53 Deerfield Way Scotrun PA 18355-9637 Office: Aventis Pasteur Discovery Dr Swiftwater PA 18370-0187

WOODS, WALTER RALPH, retired agricultural scientist, administrator; b. Grant, Va., Dec. 2, 1931; s. John Wythe and Hazel Gladys (Hash) W.; m. Jacqulyn Rose Miller, Sept. 14, 1953; children: Neal Ralph, Diana Lyn. BS, Murray (Ky.) State U., 1954; MS, U. Ky., 1955; PhD, Okla. State U., 1957. Instr. animal sci. Okla. State U., 1956-57; asst. prof., then assoc. prof. Iowa State U., 1957-62; assoc. prof., then prof. U. Nebr., 1962-71; prof. animal sci., head dept. Purdue U., 1971-85; dean Kans. State U., Manhattan, 1985-92, dir. Agrl. Expt. Sta., 1985-92, dir. Coop. Ext. Svc., 1987-92; asst. adminstr. for regional rsch. CSRS USDA, Washington, 1993-94; acting dep. adminstr. USDA/CSREES, 1994-95. Author papers, articles in field. Bd. dirs. Ind. 4-H Found., 1979-81, Kans. 4-H Found., 1987-92; mem. leadership coun. Kans. Value Added Ctr., 1990-92; mem. exec. com. Kans. Rural Devel. Coun., 1990-93; chair Coun. Adminstrv. Head Agr., 1992, Great Plains Agr. Coun., 1990-92. Recipient Disting. Agrl. Alumni award Murray State U., 1969, Meritorious Service award Ind. Pork Producers Assn., 1975 Mem. Am. Soc. Animal Sci. (sec.-treas. Midwest sect. 1979-81, pres. Midwest sect. 1983-84). Mem. Christian Ch. (Disciples Of Christ). Home: 8318 Strathmore Ln Roanoke VA 24019-2236

WOODS, WARREN CHIP, civil engineer; b. Kansas City, Mo., Apr. 26, 1948; s. Russell McDonald and Sadie Maxine (Peatling) W.; m. Marie Annette Weyer, Aug. 22, 1970; children: Erica Grayce, Jenessa Marie. BSCE, U. Mo., Rolla, 1970, MSCE, 1972. Registered profl. engr., Kans.; registered land surveyor, Kans. Rd. supr. Marshall County, Marysville, Kans., 1972-76, county engr., 1976-80; project engr./project surveyor BG Cons., Inc., Manhattan, 1980-88; county engr. Lyon County, Emporia, 1988—. Mem. NSPE, Nat. Soc. Profl. Surveyors, Kans. Engring. Soc., Am. Congress on Surveying and Mapping, Kans. County Hwy. Assn. (sec.-treas. 1992, pres. 1994), Profl. Surveyors of the 6th P.M. (life), Kans. Soc. Land Surveyors (pres. 1991-93). Republican. Lutheran. Avocations: softball, hunting, fishing, Frisbee golf. Home: 1730 Thompson St Emporia KS 66801-6082 Office: Lyon County Hwy Dept 500 S Prairie St Emporia KS 66801-9478

WOODS, WILLIAM ELLIS, lawyer, pharmacist, association executive; b. Ballinger, Tex., Sept. 25, 1917; s. Cary Dysart and Gertrude Mae (Ellis) W.; m. Martha Brockman, May 28, 1954. BS, U. Tex. Sch. Pharmacy, 1938; JD, Sch. Law, 1953. Bar: Tex. bar 1954, U.S. Supreme Ct 1957. Dir. emergency med. service Tex. State Health Dept., 1942-43, USPHS, 1943-47; asst. dir. Nat. Pharm. Survey Office, 1947-48; with Eli Lilly & Co., 1948-51; first dir. U. Tex. Pharmacy Extension Service, Austin, 1953-54; pvt. practice law Corpus Christi, Tex., 1954-58; asst. to exec. v.p. Nat. Pharm. Council, N.Y.C., 1958-64, sec., 1964-65; Washington rep., assoc. gen. counsel Nat. Assn. Retail Druggists, 1965-76, exec. v.p., 1976-84, hon. past pres., 1984. Presenter testimony on health, pharmacy and small bus. before coms. of U.S. Congress and various fed. agys.; mem. Joint Commn. on Pharmacy Practitioners; chmn. Nat. Small Bus. Legis. Coun., 1981; pres. Nat. Drug Trade Conf., 1981; del. U.S. Pharmacopoeial Conv., 1975, 80. Contbr. articles to pharmacy publs. Recipient Achievement Medal award Alpha Zeta Omega, 1975, Lubin Profl. Pharmacy award U. Tenn., 1982; established Wm. E. Woods Endowed Presdl. Scholarship in Elder Law, U. Tex., 1994. Mem. ABA, Tex. Bar Assn., Law Sci. Acad., Phi Delta Phi, U. Tex. Chancellor's Coun., Nat. Assn. Execs., Capitol Hill Club, Can. Club (N.Y.C.). Methodist. Home: 8810 Walther Blvd Apt 1007 Baltimore MD 21234-5715

WOODS, WILLIE G. dean, English language and education educator; b. Yazoo City, Miss.; d. John Wesley and Jessie Willie Mae W. BA, Shaw U., Raleigh, N.C., 1965; MEd, Duke U., 1968; postgrad., Pa. State U., 1970, 80-82, Temple U., 1972, U. N.H., 1978, NYU, 1979, Indiana U. of Pa., 1986-88; PhD, Indiana U. of Pa., 1995. Tchr. schs. in N.C. and Md., 1965-69; mem. faculty Harrisburg (Pa.) Area Community Coll., 1969—99, assoc. prof. English and edn., 1976-82, prof., 1982-94, sr. prof., 1994—, supr. Writing Ctr., 1975-78, coord. Act 101/Basic Studies Program, 1978-83, dir. Acad. Founds. program 1983-87, asst. dean academ. affairs Acad. Found. and Basic Edn. Div., 1987-89, asst. dean acad. affairs, chmn. social sci., pub. svcs. and basic edn. div., 1989-94, dean social sci., pub. svcs. and basic edn. divsn., 1994-96, 1998—, chmn. dirs. coun., 1981-82, acting v.p. faculty and instrn., 1996—, acting vp fac. and instrn., 1996-98; tchr. Community Resources Inst., 1975-90, dean divsn. arts & sci., Chesapeake Coll., Md., 1999-; moderator workshops, cons. in field. Asst. editor Black Conf. Higher Edn. Jour., 1980. Sec., exec. com. People for Progress, 1971-73; bd. mgrs., exec. com. Camp Curtin br. YMCA, 1971-79; bd. dirs. Alternative Rehab. Communities, 1978—; bd. mgrs. Youth Urban Svcs., Harrisburg Area YMCA, 1981-92; bd. dirs. Dauphin Residences, Inc., 1981-88; mem. Harrisburg Mayor's Commn. Lit., 1995—, Pa. Gov.'s Interagy. Coun. Lit., 1997—. Kellogg fellow in expanding leadership diversity in cmty. coll. program, 1994-95; recipient cert. of merit for community svcs. City of Harrisburg, 1971, Youth Urban Svcs. Vol. of Yr. award, 1983, Black Student Union award Harrisburg Area Community Coll., 1984. Mem. Pa. Assn. Devel. Educators (chmn. conf. 1980, sec. 1981-82, v.p. 1986-87, pres. 1987-88), Pa. Black Conf. Higher Edn. (Outstanding Svc. award 1980, Central Region award 1982), Nat. Coun. Tchrs. English, Pa. Edn. Assn., Am. Assn. Community and Jr. Colls., Nat. Coun. on Black Am. (instl. rep. 1983—), AAUP, Alpha Kappa Alpha (Outstanding Svc. award 1983, 97, Basileus award 1984, Ida B. Wells Excellence in Media award 1994, Ivy Honor Roll of Clips award 1994), Alpha Kappa Mu, Phi Kappa Phi. Baptist. Home: PO Box 8 Preston MD 21655 Office: Chesapeake Coll 1000 College Dr PO Box 8 Wye Mills MD 21679

WOODS COGGINS, ALMA, artist; b. Canton, Pa., May 24, 1924; d. Fred and Essica Ortha (Manahan) Woods; m. Jack B. Coggins, Jan. 15, 1948. Grad. h.s., New Albany, Pa., 1941. Framer Exhibited in shows at Wyomissing Inst. Fine Arts, Reading Mus., Yellow Springs Art Show, Valley Forge Small Paintings Exhbn., Pa. State Delawre County Cmapus, MainlineArt Ctr. Ann. Exhbn., Chester County Art Assn. Shows, Small Paintings Nat. Exhbn./Ky. Highlands Mus., Pa. State U., Harrisburg, numerous others. Sec. zoning hearing bd. Zoning Commn., Pike Twp., 1965-99. Recipient awards for art. Mem. Berks Art Alliance, Chester County Art Assn., Pen and Brush. Avocation: gardening. Home: PO Box 57 Boyertown PA 19512-0057

WOODSIDE, ARCH G. marketing educator, researcher; b. Pittburgh, Pa., Jan. 9, 1943; s. Arch G Woodside, Sr. and Martah Elizabeth Woodside; children: Christine, Judy, Martha, Martha Jane. PhD, Penn State, 1965—68. Woldenberg prof. mktg. Tulane U., New Orleans, 1985—2000; prof. mktg. Boston Coll., Boston, 2000—02. Past pres. Soc. Consumer Psychology, Washington, Dc, 1978—79. Author advt. various rsch., mktg. mgmt. Capt. US Army, 1968—70, Ft. Belfouir. Fellow: APA, Soc. Mktg. Advances; mem.: Royal Soc. Can. Avocation: writing. Home: 135 Florence St Apt 11 Chestnut Hill MA 02467-1938 Office: Boston College 140 Commonwealth Ave Chestnut Hill MA 02467 Home Fax: 1-617-332-6677; Office Fax: 1-617-552-6677.

WOODSIDE, FRANK C., III, lawyer, educator, physician; b. Glen Ridge, N.J., Apr. 18, 1944; s. Frank C. and Dorothea (Poulin) W.; m. Julia K. Moses, Nov. 15, 1974; children: Patrick Michael, Christopher Ryan. BS, Ohio State U., 1966, JD, 1969; MD, U. Cin., 1973. Diplomate Am. Bd. Legal Medicine, Am. Bd. Forensic Medicine, Am. Bd. Profl. Liability Attys. Mem. Dinsmore & Shohl, Cin.; clin. prof. pediats.emeritus U. Cin., 1992—. Adj. prof. law U. Cin., 1973—. Editor: Drug Product Liability, 1985—. Fellow Am. Coll. Legal Medicine, Am. Coll. Forensic Examiners, Am. Soc. Hosp. Attys., Soc. Ohio Hosp. Attys.; mem. ABA, FBA, Ohio Bar Assn., Internat. Assn. Def. Counsel, Def. Rsch. Inst. (chmn. drug and med. svc. com. 1988-91), Cin. Bar Assn. Office: Dinsmore & Shohl 1900 Chemed Ctr 255 E 5th St Cincinnati OH 45202-4700 E-mail: woodside@dinslaw.com.

WOODSIDE, GEORGE ROBERT, computer software developer; b. Meadville, Pa., Oct. 29, 1949; s. William Clinton and Bernadette Lorena (Greene) W.; m. Diane Claire Hickenlooper, June 14, 1980 (div. 1996). Grad. h.s., Fairview, Pa. Programer GE Co., Erie, Pa., 1967-69; programmer-analyst Lovell Mfg. Co., 1969-70; mgr. data processing Eriez Mfg. Co., 1970-74; owner Woodside-Benson Assocs., Fairview, 1974-78; prin. mem. tech. staff Transaction Tech. Inc. (now Citicorp/TTI), Santa Monica, Calif., 1978-92; owner GRW Sys. and Programming, Sparks, Nev., 1993—. Contbr. articles to mags.; developer software to detect and eliminate computer viruses, software for laser cert., telecomm., spectography, and DSP applications. Mem. IEEE. Achievements include development of software for laser testing equipment; elevator control and performance analysis; numerous applications of spectrometers; oil analysis software; high precision equipment control and circuit testing; writer business and financial applications. Avocations: photography, woodworking. E-mail: grwsystems@charter.net.

WOOD-SMITH, DONALD, plastic surgeon; b. Sydney, Australia, June 30, 1931; s. William Frederick and Vera Mary; children: Christina Margaret, Donald William, Phillip Raynor. MB, BChir, Sydney U., 1954. Diplomate Am. Bd. Plastic Surgery. Sr. resident Lewisham Hosp., Sydney, 1954-56, Royal Marsden Hosp., 1957-58; resident plastic surgery NYU Hosp. Med. Ctr., 1960-64, asst., assoc. and attending surgeon, 1964-92; prof. plastic surgery Columbia Presbyn. Med. Ctr., 1991—. Vis. surgeon Bellevue Hosp., 1964-92, London Ind. Hosp., 1999—; chmn. plastic surgery Manhattan Eye Ear and Throat Hosp., 1975-77; assoc. prof. plastic surgery NYU, 1977-84, prof., 1984-92; surgeon, dir. plastic surgery Manhattan Eye Ear and Throat Hosp., 1977-84; cons. plastic surgeon N.Y. Eye and Ear Infirmary, chmn. dept. plastic and reconstructive surgery, 1984—. Author: Nursing Care of the Plastic Surgery Patient, 1967, Cosmetic Facial Surgery, 1973; contbr. articles to med. jours. Fellow ACS, Royal Coll. Surgeons of Edinburgh; mem. Am. Assn.

Plastic Surgeons, Am. Soc. Plastic Surgeons, Am. Soc. Maxillofacial Surgeons, N.Y. Acad. Medicine, Brit. Assn. Plastic Surgeons, N.Y. Athletic Club. Republican. Office: 830 Park Ave New York NY 10021-2757 also: 34 Hans Rd Knightsbridge London SW3 1RW England E-mail: dw830@aol.com.

WOODSON, ADRIANNE MARIE, secondary school educator; b. Chgo., Sept. 1, 1951; d. Theodore Roosevelt and Adah Mae Hull; m. Rudolph Woodson, June 26, 1976; children: Porsha M., Patrice A., Kellen E., Karley A. BS, Lincoln U., 1973; MS, Ind. U., South Bend, 1981. Lic. sch. adminstr. Spl. edn. tchr. Gary (Ind.) Cmty. Sch. Corp., 1973-76; spl. edn. multi-category tchr. South Bend (Ind.) Cmty. Schs., 1976-77; spl. edn. resource tchr. Sch. City of Hammond, Ind., 1977-86, facilitating tchr., 1986-97, homebound instr., 1997—, spl. edn. coord., 1998—. Student tchr. supr. Purdue U. Calumet, Hammond, summers 1993–; participant for standardizing nat. diagnostic test W.I.A.T., Westchester, Ind,. 1990; presenter at state conf. Coun. for Exceptional Children, Indpls., 1987, 99; spl. edn. dir.'s program Cohort 2000, Bloomington, Ind., 1999-2000. Pres. Jack and Jill Am., Inc.; children's program dir. Delaney United Meth. Ch. Mem. Lincoln U. Alumni Assn. (sec.-treas.), Sigma Gamma Rho (com. chairperson, Membership award 2000), Delta Kappa Gamma (v.p.). Democrat. Methodist. Avocations: travel, fashion, home and interior decorating, singing, playing the piano. Office: 5727 Sohl Ave Hammond IN 46320-2356 Fax: 219-933-2498. E-mail: amwoodson@m1.hammond.k12.in.us.

WOODSON, GAYLE ELLEN, otolaryngologist; b. Galveston, Tex., June 9, 1950; d. Clinton Eldon and Nancy Jean (Stephens) W.; m. Kevin Thomas Robbins; children: Nicholas, Gregory, Sarah. BA, Rice U., 1972; MD, Baylor Coll. Medicine, 1975. Diplomate Am. Bd. Otolaryngology (bd. dirs., residency rev. com. for otolaryngology). Fellow Baylor Coll. Medicine, Houston, 1976, Inst. Laryngology & Otology, London, 1981-82; asst. prof. Baylor Coll. Medicine, 1982-87; asst. attending Harris County Hosp. Dist., Houston, 1982-86; with courtesy staff Saint Luke's Episcopal Hosp., 1982-87; assoc. attending The Methodist Hosp., 1982-87; asst. prof. U. Calif. Med. Sch., San Diego, 1987-89; chief otolaryngology VA Med. Ctr., 1987-92; assoc. prof. U. Calif. Sch. Med., 1989-92; prof. otolaryngology U. Tenn., Memphis, 1993—. Mem. staff Bapt. Meml. Hosps., Meth. Hosps., Le Bonheur Children's Hosp.; numerous presentations and lectures in field. Contbr. numerous articles and abstracts to med. jours., also videotapes. Fellow ACS (bd. govs.), Royal Coll. Surgeons, Soc. Univ. Otolaryngologists (past pres.), Am. Soc. Head and Neck Surgery, Am. Laryngol. Assn. (coun.), Triological Soc.; mem. AMA, Am. Acad. Otolaryngology-Head and Neck Surgery (bd. dirs. 1993-96), Am. Med. Women's Assn. (past pres. Memphis br.), Soc. Head and Neck Oncologists Eng., Am. Physiol. Soc., Assn. Women Surgeons, Am. Soc. Head and Neck Surgeons. Office: U Fla PO Box 100264 Gainesville FL 32610-0264

WOODSON, HERBERT HORACE, retired electrical engineering educator; b. Stamford, Tex., Apr. 5, 1925; s. Herbert Viven and Floy (Tunnell) W.; m. Blanche Elizabeth Sears, Aug. 17, 1951; children: William Sears, Robert Sears, Bradford Sears. SB, SM, MIT, 1952, ScD in Elec. Engring., 1956. Registered profl. engr., Tex., Mass. Instr. elec. engring., also project leader magnetics divsn. Naval Ordnance Lab., 1952-54; faculty M.I.T., 1956-71, prof. elec. engring., 1965-71, Philip Sporn prof. energy processing, 1967-71; prof. elec. engring., chmn. dept. U. Tex., Austin, 1971-81, Alcoa Found. prof., 1972-75, Tex. Atomic Energy Research Found. prof. engring., 1980-82, Ernest H. Cockrell Centennial prof. engring., 1982-93, dir. Center for Energy Studies, 1973-88, assoc. dean devel. and planning Coll. Engring., 1986-87, acting dean, 1987-88, dean' chair for excellence in engring., 1988-96; ret. Staff engr. elec. engring. div. AEP Service Corp., N.Y.C., 1965-66; cons. in field. Author: (with others) Electromechanical Dynamics, parts I, II, III. With USNR, 1943-46. Recipient Fed. Engr. Yr. award Nat Soc. Profl. Engr., 1990. Fellow IEEE (life, pres. Power Engring. Soc. 1978-80); mem. AAAS, Am. Soc. Engring. Edn., Nat. Acad. Engring. Achievements include patents in field. Home: Apt 144 1034 Liberty Park Dr Austin TX 78746-6876 E-mail: hhwoodson@mail.utexas.edu.

WOODSON, LINDA TOWNLEY, English educator, writer; b. Clifton, Tex., Oct. 14, 1943; d. Richmond Alyet and Gena Lee (Wade) Townley; m. James Charles Woodson, Sept. 6, 1963 (div. Dec. 1982); 1 child, Rachel Woodson Garrett; m. Richard Patrick Smith, Mar. 24, 1983. BS in Edn., Tex. Christian U., Fort Worth, 1964, PhD, 1977. Cert. tchr., Tex., Calif. Elem. tchr. Fort Worth Ind. Dist., 1964-65, Austin (Tex.) Ind. Sch. Dist., 1965-67, Fairfield (Calif.)-Suisun Unified Sch., 1969-71; instr. English So. Meth. U., Dallas, 1977-79; asst. prof. English Tex. Tech. U., Lubbock, 1979-81; prof., chair dept. English U. Tex., San Antonio, 1981—. Author: A Handbook of Modern Rhetorical Terms, 1979, From Cases to Composition, 1982, The Writer's World, 1986; co-author: Writing in Three Dimensions, 1995; co-editor: Modes of Inquiry, 1998. Mem. Nat. Coun. Tchrs. English (commn. on composition 1980-82), Conf. Coll. Composition and Communication (nominating com. 1985, exec. coun. 1995-98), Cormac McCarthy Soc., South Ctrl. MLA. Avocations: reading philosophy, dogs, gardening. Home: 16519 Loma Lndg Helotes TX 78023-3438 Office: U Tex at San Antonio Dept English Classics & Philosophy San Antonio TX 78249 E-mail: lwoodson@utsa.edu.

WOODSON, STEPHEN WILLIAM, collection agency executive; b. Kansas City, Mo., May 31, 1950; s. William Albert and Patricia Marguerite (May) W. AA, Maple Woods C.C., 1977. Asst. mgr. Pub. Fin., San Pedro, Calif., 1973-74; asst. to v.p. MOAMCO, Mpls., 1974-75; collection cons. Blue Valley Fed. Savs. & Loan, 1975-86; pres. Met. Collection Svcs., Inc., North Kansas City, Mo., 1975-81, Regional Collection Svcs., 1981-84, Transam. Collection Svcs., Kansas City, Mo., 1986—. Collection agency executive; b. Kansas City, Mo., May 31, 1950; s. William Albert and Patricia Marguerite (May) W.; A.A., Maple Woods Community Coll., 1977. Asst. mgr. Pub. Fin., San Pedro, Calif., 1973-74; asst. to v.p. MOAMCO, Mpls., 1974-75; pres. Met. Collection Svcs., Inc., North Kansas City, Mo., 1975-81, Regional Collection Svcs., 1981-84; collection cons. Blue Valley Fed. Savs. & Loan, 1975-86; pres. Transam. Collection Svcs., 1986—; pres. Transam. Credit, 1988—, Trans-Am. Investigations Pvt. Detective Agy., 1996—. Active Big Bros. and Sisters, Kansas City, Mo., 1977—; counselor Mo. Dept. Probation and Parole; pres. Job Readiness, Inc., 1983-86; mem. citizens adv. bd. Kansas City Alliance Bus. Task Force. Served with USN, 1967-70. Recipient Whitehall Found. Scholastic award, 1968. Mem. Internat. Traders Assn., Am. Collectors Assn., Northland C. of C. Republican. Lutheran. Active Big Bros. and Sisters, Kansas City, Mo., 1977—; counselor Mo. Dept. Probation and Parole; pres. Job Readiness, Inc., 1983-86; citizens adv. bd. Kansas City Alliance Bus. Task Force. With USN, 1967-70. Recipient Whitehall Found. Scholastic award, 1968. Mem. Internat. Traders Assn., Am. Collectors Assn., Northland C. of C. Republican. Lutheran. Office: 1920 Swift Ave Ste 203 Kansas City MO 64116-3445 E-mail: swoodson@kc.rr.com.

WOODSON-GLENN, YOLANDA, social worker; b. L.A., July 29, 1958; d. Lewie B. and Clareece Woodson; children: James Glenn, Kimberly Glenn. MA in Counseling Psychology, Bowie State U.; postgrad. Social worker Dept. Children and Family Svcs., Baltimore, MD, 1994-95; victim advocate State's Atty's Office, Annapolis, 1995-96; social worker Children of the Village, Carson, CA, 1997-99, Dept. of Children and Family Svcs., Lakewood, 1999—. Counselor City of Refuge Ch., Compton, Calif., 2000—. Author: Suffering for Righteousness, 2001. Pentecostal. Avocations: cooking, crafts, museums, concerts. Home: 3908 Hathaway Ave # 964 Long Beach CA 90815 Office: 4060 Watson Plaza Dr Lakewood CA 90712

WOODSWORTH, ANNE, university administrator, librarian; b. Fredericia, Denmark, Feb. 10, 1941; came to U.S., 1983; d. Thorvald Ernst and Roma Yrsa (Jensen) Lindner; 1 child, Yrsa Anne. BFA, U. Man., Can., 1962; BLS, U. Toronto, Ont., Can., 1964, MLS, 1969; PhD, U. Pitts., 1987. Edn. libr. U. Man., 1964—65; reference libr. Winnipeg Pub. Libr., 1965—67; reference libr. sci. and medicine dept. U. Toronto, 1967—68; med. libr. Toronto We. Hosp., 1969—70; rsch. asst. to chief libr. U. Toronto, 1970—71, head reference dept., 1971—74; pers. dir. Toronto Pub. Libr., 1975—78; dir. librs. York U., Toronto, 1978—83; assoc. provost for librs. U. Pitts., 1983—88, assoc. prof., 1988—91; dean Palmer Sch. Libr. and Info. Sci., L.I. U., 1991—98; dean Sch. Edn. Dowling Coll., Oakdale, NY, 1999—2000; dean sch. info. and libr. sci. Pratt Inst., Bklyn., 2000—02, acting provost, 2002—. Pres. Anne Lindner Ltd., 1974-83; rsch. libraries adv. coun. OCLC, 1984-87. Author: The Alternative Press in Canada, 1972, Leadership and Research Libraries, 1988, Patterns and Options for Managing Information Technology on Campus, 1990, Library Cooperation and Networks, 1991, Managing the Economics of Leasing and Contracting Out Information Services, 1993, Reinvesting in the Information Job Family, 1993, The Future of Education for Librarianship: Looking Forward from the Past, 1994. Dir. Sr. Fellows Inst., 1995-98; trustee L.I. Librs. Resources Coun., 1993-96; bd. dirs. Population Rsch. Found., Toronto, 1980-83. Grantee Can. Coun., 1974, Ont. Arts Coun., 1974, Coun. on Libr. Resources, 1986, 88, 91, 93; UCLA sr. fellow, 1985. Mem. ALA (com. on accreditation 1990-94, councillor 1993-97), Can. Assn. Rsch. Librs. (pres. 1981-83), Assn. Rsch. Librs. (bd. dirs. 1981-84, v.p. 1984-85, pres. 1985-86), Assn. Coll. and Rsch. Librs. (chair K.G. Saur award com. 1991-93), Assn. for Libr. and Info. Sci. Edn. (chair honors and awards com. 1995, bd. dirs. 1998-99, v.p. 1998-99), Am. Soc. Higher Edn., Internet Soc., Am. Soc. Info. Sci. (convenor 1999-2000), Archons of Colophon.

WOODWARD, BEVERLY A. sociology researcher, writer; b. Cambridge, Mass., May 17, 1934; d. James Oscar Woodward, II and Beatrice Denke; m. Paul H. Monsky. BA, U. Calif. Berkeley, Berkeley, CA, 1955; MA, New Sch. U., New York, NY, 1961, PhD, 1972. Vis. fellow Ctr. Internat. Studies Princeton U., Princeton, NJ, 1973—73; coord. Internat. Seminars on Tng. for Nonviolent Action, 1975—87, Internat. Nonviolent Initiatives, Waltham, Mass., 1987—; rsch. assoc. philosophy & sociology Brandeis U., 1989—. Fellow fellow, U. Consortium World Order Studies, 1972-1973, Bunting Inst. Harvard U., 1987-1989. Mem.: ACLU, War Resisters League, Peace Studies Assn., Am. Soc. Law Medicine &Ethics, Boston Clavichord Soc. (bd. of directors 1995—2002), Boston Atheneum. Avocations: playing keyboards, baroque dance. Home: PO Box 515 Waltham MA 02454 Office: Brandeis University Ms 071 Waltham MA 02454

WOODWARD, CLARE KEATING, retired biochemist; b. Houston, Dec. 10, 1941; d. Carl R. Keating and Bernice J. McKinney; m. Val W. Woodward. Bachelor's degree, Smith Coll., Northampton, Mass., 1963. Prof. U. Minn., St. Paul, 1970—2000, prof. emeritus, 2000—. Assoc. editor: Biochemistry, 2000—02; contbr. Recipient numerous profl. awards, 1979—. Fellow: Biophys. Soc. (pres. 1997—98). Home: PO Box 333 899 Lakeview Dr Garden City UT 84028 Personal E-mail: clare@biosci.cbs.umn.edu. Business E-Mail: clare@biosci.cbs.umn.edu.

WOODWARD, CLIFFORD EDWARD, chemical engineer; b. Richmond, Va., Jan. 17, 1941; s. Clifford Rawlings and Myrtis (Wilson) W.; m. Katherine Roberts, June 1, 1967; children: Ted, Robert, Christopher, John. BSChemE, Va. Poly. Inst. and State U., 1962, MS in Nuclear Sci. and Engr., 1963; MSChemE, U. Houston, 1975. Registered profl. engr., Tex. Devel. engr. Olin Corp., 1963-65; supervising engr. Monsanto Co., 1965-72; lead engr. Brown & Root Inc., Houston, 1972-74; process mgr. Kvaerner Process Inc., 1974-77, 1979-81, process dir., 1983-88, process mgr., 1992—; prin. engr. Jacobs Engring. Group, Inc., 1977-79; process mgr. M.W. Kellogg, Amsterdam, N.C., 1981-83, sr. engr. mgr. Houston, 1988-89; process dept. mgr. BE&K, 1989-92. Pres. Process Resources, Houston, 1975-77. Mem. planning comm. City of Alvin, Tex., 1970-72; founder Cypress Creek Emergency Med. Svcs. Assn., 1975; pres. Klein (Tex.) Sch. Bd., 1979-90. Mem. AIChE, Engrs. Coun. of Houston (v.p., sec. 1991). Achievements include electrodeposition of polymers from latex solutions and surface kinetics and direct contact heat transfer. Home: 4114 Oxhill Rd Spring TX 77388-9705 Office: Kvaerner Process 7909 Parkwood Circle Dr Houston TX 77036-6565

WOODWARD, CLINTON BENJAMIN, JR. civil engineering educator; b. El Paso, Tex., Mar. 4, 1943; s. Clinton Benjamin and Iris Elizabeth (Zant) W.; m. Willie Ann Shollenbarger, June 14, 1969 (div. June 1976); m. Deon Bennett Speir, Nov. 22, 1979; 1 child, Clinton Benjamin III. BSET, N.Mex. State U., 1976; MS, Colo. State U., 1978; MSCE, N.Mex. State U., 1984, PhD, 1986. Registered profl. engr., N.Mex. From asst. mgr. to pres. Woodward Enterprises Co., Inc., Las Cruces, N.Mex., 1968-82; prof., program dir. structural engring. N.Mex. State U., 1987—. Contbr. articles to profl. jours. With USN, 1962-66., Mem. ASCE, Am. Soc. for Engring. Edn., Forest Products Soc., Soc. Wood Sci. and Tech., Tau Beta Phi, Chi Epsilon, Phi Kappa Phi, Sigma Xi. Avocations: camping, fly fishing.

WOODWARD, DANIEL HOLT, librarian, researcher; b. Ft. Worth, Oct. 17, 1931; s. Enos Paul and Jessie Grider (Butts) W.; m. Mary Jane Gerra, Aug. 27, 1954; children: Jeffrey, Peter. BA, U. Colo., 1951, MA, 1955; PhD, Yale, 1958; MSLS, Cath. U. Am., 1969. Mem. faculty Mary Washington Coll. of U. Va., 1957-72, prof. English, 1966-72, librarian, 1969-72, Huntington Library, Art Collections and Bot. Gardens, San Marino, Calif., 1972-90, sr. rsch. assoc., 1990-97; ind. scholar, 1997—. Editor: The Poems and Translations of Robert Fletcher, 1970, The Ellesmere Chaucer: A New Monochromatic Facsimile, 1997, Wallace Stevens, Vassar Viewed Veraciously, 1997; co-editor: New Ellesmere Chaucer Facsimile, Ellesmere Chaucer: Essays in Interpretation, 2 vols., 1995. Served with AUS, 1952-54. Mem. Bibliog. Soc. Am., Phi Beta Kappa, Beta Phi Mu. Home: 80 Runyon Mill Rd Hopewell NJ 08525 E-mail: danielwoodward@webtv.net.

WOODWARD, FREDERICK MILLER, publisher; b. Clarksville, Tenn., Apr. 15, 1943; s. Felix Grundy and Laura Henrietta (Miller) W.. m. Elizabeth Louise Smoak, Mar. 23, 1967; children: Laura Claire, Katherine Elizabeth BA cum laude, Vanderbilt U., 1965; postgrad., Tulane U., 1965-70. Manuscript editor U.S.C. Press, Columbia, 1970-73, mktg. dir., 1973-81; dir. U. Press of Kans., Lawrence, 1981—. Mem. adv. com. Kans. Ctr. for the Book, Topeka, 1987—; lectr. pub. U. Kans., Lawrence, Kans. State U., Manhattan, 1983—; book judge Western Heritage Ctr., Oklahoma City, 1988. Mem. Assn. Am. Univ. Presses (bd. dirs. 1988-91, pres. 1995-96, past pres. 1996-97), Kans. State Hist. Soc. (life), Phi Beta Kappa. Democrat. Avocations: racquetball, reading, music. Home: 2220 Vermont St Lawrence KS 66046-3066 Office: U Press Kans 2501 W 15th St Lawrence KS 66049-3905

WOODWARD, GRETA CHARMAINE, construction company executive, rental and investment property manager; b. Congress, Ohio, Oct. 28, 1930; d. Richard Thomas and Grace Lucetta (Palmer) Duffey; m. John Jay Woodward, Oct. 29, 1949; children: Kirk Jay, Brad Ewing, Clay William. Bookkeeper Kaufman's Texaco, Wooster, Ohio, 1948-49; office mgr. Holland Furnace Co., Wooster, 1948-49; acctg. clk. Columbus and So. Ohio Electric, 1949-50; interviewer, clk. State Ohio Bur. Employment Services, Columbus, 1950-51; clk. Def. Constrn. Supply Ctr. (U.S. Govt.) (formerly Columbus Gen. Depot), 1951-52; treas. Woodward Co., Inc., Reynoldsburg, Ohio, 1963—. Newspaper columnist Briarcliff News, 1960-63. Active Reynoldsburg PTA, 1960-67; Reynoldsburg United Meth. Ch.; mem. women's service bd. Grant Hosp. Avocations: bike riding, crocheting, writing poetry, stock market, water aerobics, line dancing, ballroom dancing. Office: Woodward Excavating Co Inc 7340 Tussing Rd Reynoldsburg OH 43068-4111

WOODWARD, HOLLY LOWELL, former educator, writer; b. Bronxville, N.Y., Dec. 13, 1957; d. John and Elizabeth (Prosser) R. BA, Wesleyan U., 1980; MFA, Columbia U., 1984; PhD, SUNY, Binghamton, 1998. With State Dept. Moscow Summit, 1988; tchr. Convent of Sacred Heart, N.Y.C., 1998; writer-in-residence St. Albans Washington Nat. Cathedral, 1990-91. Contbr. to newspapers and profl. publs. Yaddo fellow, 1994, 95, Geraldine Dodge fellow, 1995, 97, Ragdale fellow, 1996, 97, Edward Albee Found. fellow, 1998, Hawthorden Castle Fellow, Scotland, 1998, Vt. Studio fellow, 2001; Derassi fellow, 1998; writing fellow Bennington U., 1995; recipient 1st pl. New Letters Fiction prize, 1993, 2d pl. Literal Latte Fiction prize, 1997, 1st prize Story Mag, 1999, Robert Frost award, 2000; Atlantic Ctr. for Arts assoc. fellow, 2001, White fellow Costa Rica, 2002, Lediq Internat. Ho. fellow, 2002. Mem. MLA, AAUW, Nat. League Am. PEN Women. Episcopalian. Home: 76 Jackson St Apt 3 Hoboken NJ 07030-6057 E-mail: artictfox@aol.com.

WOODWARD, ISABEL AVILA, educational writer, foreign language educator; b. Key West, Fla., Mar. 14, 1906; d. Alfredo and Isabel (Lopez) Avila; m. Clyde B. Woodward, June 6, 1944 (dec.); children: Joy Avis Ball, Greer Isabel, Woodward Sucke. Student, Fla. State Coll. for Women, 1925, AB in Edn., 1938; cert. in tchg. Spanish, U. Miami, 1961; summer study, U. Fla., Eckerd Coll.; postgrad., St. Lawrence U., U. Miami. Tchr., Key West, 1927-42; remedial reading cons., 1941-42; reading tchr., asst. reading lab. and clinic St. Lawrence U., summer 1941; Spanish translator U.S. Office of Censorship, Miami Beach, 1943; tchr. Central Beach Elem. Sch., 1943-44, Silver Bluff Elem. Sch., 1943-50, Henry West Lab. Sch., Coral Gables, Fla., 1955-57, Dade Demonstration Sch., Miami, 1957-61. Author 125 sch. radio lessons for tchg. Spanish Workshop for Fla.; spkr. poetry and short story writing, 1977; guest lectr. on writing the short story Fla. Inst. Tech., Jensen Beach, 1981; guest lectr. Cicle Bay Yacht Club, Stuart, Fla., 1995. Freelance writer; contbr. to Listen Mag., Sunshine Mag., Lookout Mag., Christian Sci. Monitor, Miami Herald, Three/Four, Child Life, Wee Wisdom, Fla. Wildlife, Young World: sponsor Pcrt St. Lucie Jr. Woman's Club, 1983. Recipient Honoris Causa award Alpha Delta Kappa, 1972-74, award Contra Costa Times, Calif., 1985, 1st prize for short story in nat. Ark. writers conf. contest, 1992; named one of 5 Outstanding Fla. Tchrs. 1972-74. Mem. Nat. League Am. Pen Women (1st v.p. Greater Miami br. 1974-76, historian 1978—, librarian 1978—, awards for writing 1973, 74, 77, 1st and 3d pl. state writing awards for adult and juvenile fiction 1983, state 1st prize short story 1985), AAUW, Alpha Delta Kappa, Psi Psi Psi. Address: 1950 SW Palm City Rd Apt 6-301 Stuart FL 34994-4310

WOODWARD, JAMES HOYT, academic administrator, engineer; b. Sanford, Fla., Nov. 24, 1939; s. James Hoyt and Edith Pearl (Breeden) W.; m. Martha Ruth Hill, Oct. 13, 1956; children: Connie, Tracey, Wade. BS in Aero. Engring. with honors, Ga. Tech. Inst., 1962, MS in Aero. Engring., 1963, PhD in Engring. Mechanics, 1967; MBA, U. Ala.-Birmingham, 1973. Asst. prof. engring. mechanics USAF Acad., Colo., 1965-67, assoc. prof., 1967-68; asst. prof. engring. mechanics N.C. State U., 1968-69; assoc. prof. engring. U. Ala., Birmingham, 1969-70, assoc. prof., 1973-77, prof. civil engring., 1977-89, asst. v.p., 1973-78, dean engring., 1978-84, acad. v.p., 1984-89; chancellor U. N.C., Charlotte, 1989—. Dir. tech. devel. Rust Engring. Co., Birmingham, 1970-73; cons. in field. Contbr. articles to profl. jours. With USAF, 1965-68. Mem. ASCE, ASME, Am. Soc. Engring. Edn., Am. Mgmt. Assn., Sigma Xi. Methodist. Office: U NC Charlotte Office of Chancellor 9201 University City Blvd Charlotte NC 28223-0002

WOODWARD, JAMES KENNETH, retired pharmacologist; b. Anderson, Mo., Feb. 5, 1938; s. Audley J. and Doris Evelyn (Fields) W.; m. Kathleen Ruth Winget, June 25, 1960 (div. Nov. 1994); children: Audley J., Kimie Connette; m. Lisa Marie Stuart, Feb. 28, 1996. AB in Chemistry, S.W. Mo. State Coll., BS in Biology, 1960; postgrad., U. Kans. (USPHS fellow), 1960-62; PhD (USPHS fellow), U. Pa. Sch. Medicine, 1967. Pharmacologist Stine Lab., Newark, 1963-65, rsch. pharmacologist, 1967-71; sr. rsch. pharmacologist Merrell-Nat. Labs., Cin., 1972-73, sect. head, 1973-74, head dept. pharmacology, 1974-78; head dept. pre-clin. pharmacology Merrell Rsch. Ctr. Merrell Dow Pharms., Inc., 1978-83; assoc. dir. research adminstrn. Merrell Dow Rsch. Inst., 1983-88, dir. biol. devel., 1988-90, dir. int. reg. affairs, 1990-93; dir. clin. cand. prep. Marion Merrell Dow, 1993; ret., 1993; cons., 1993. Patentee in field. Pres. Golf Manor Recreation Commn., Cin., 1973-75. USPHS post-doctoral fellow U. Pa., 1967. Mem. AAAS, Phila. Physiol. Soc. Democrat. Baptist. Home: 972 Sheridan Dr Lancaster OH 43130-1923 E-mail: lisadocwoodward@aol.com.

WOODWARD, JOHN RUSSELL, motion picture production executive; b. San Diego, July 10, 1951; s. Melvin C. and Dora M. (Rorabaugh) W. BA in Visual Arts, U. Calif., San Diego, 1973; MA in Cinema Prodn., U. So. Calif., 1978. V.p. prodn. World Wide Motion Pictures Corp., 1982—. Asst. prodr. The Manitou, 1977; 1st asst. dir. Mortuary, 1981, They're Playing with Fire, 1983, Prime Risk, 1984, Winners Take All, 1986, Kidnapped, 1986, Slam Dance, 1986, Honor Betrayed, 1986, The Hidden, 1987, New Monkees, 1987, Bad Dreams, 1987, Night Angel, 1988, Disorganized Crime, 1988, UHF, 1988, The Horror Show, 1988, Fear, 1989, Tremors, 1989, Young Guns II, 1990, Shattered, 1990, Tales from the Crypt, 1990, Two-Fisted Tales, 1990, Buried Alive, 1990, Dream On, 1991, Strays, 1991, Universal Soldier, 1991, An Army of One, 1992, The Vanishing, 1992, Ghost in the Machine, 1992, The Shawshank Redemption, 1993, City Slickers II, 1993, Breach of Conduct, 1994, The Craft, 1995, Broken Arrow, 1995, The Rich Man's Wife, 1995, Gattaca, 1996, Liar, Liar, 1996, Wild Things, 1997, Dennis the Menace 2, 1997, The 13th Warrior, 1998, BASEketball, 1998, Swing Vote, 1999, LA Sheriff's Homicide, 1999, Mission to Mars, 1999, Road Hogs, 2000, The Further Adventures, 2000, From Hell, 2000, Two Against Time, 2000, Mark of Greatness, 2001, Paranormal Girl, 2002, American Family, 2002; location mgr. Star Chamber, 1982, To Be or Not to Be, 1983, Flashdance, 1983, Two of a Kind, 1983, Touch and Go, 1984, Explorers, 1984, Sweet Dreams, 1985, The Long Shot, 1985, The Running Men, 1985, A Different Affair, 1985, Walk Like a Man, 1986. Avocations: fishing, camping.

WOODWARD, JONATHAN MORGAN, mental health specialist; b. Vancouver, Wash., Dec. 18, 1955; s. Jessie Charles and Catherine (Agustus) W.; children: Shane, Joshua, Christopher, Miranda, Jacob. MBA, Oxford (Eng.) U., 1983; D in Naturopathy, LaSalle U., Mandeville, La., 1994. Lic. cert. counselor, Wash. CEO Rivercrest Health Care, Inc., Vancouver, Wash., 1986-94; owner, mgr. N.W. Counseling Ctr., 1994—. Keynote spkr. Drug Free Am., Washington; counselor Conf. on Excellence in Edn.; legis. chmn. Chem. Dep. Profl. Wash. Author: Instructions Not Included, 1999, 2001. Bd. dirs. Franklin House. Recipient Cert. Appreciation White House Conf. on Drug Free Am.; named Outstanding Vol. Dept. Social and Health Svcs. Mem. U.S. C. of C., Charles F. Menninger Soc., CDP Washington, NAADAC. Republican. Episcopalian. Address: 8000 NE Parkway Dr Ste 300 Vancouver WA 98662-6737 Office: Ste 300 8000 NE Parkway Dr Vancouver WA 98662-6737 E-mail: drjmw98@aol.com.

WOODWARD, KENNETH EMERSON, retired mechanical engineer; b. Washington, Oct. 30, 1927; s. George Washington and Mary Josephine (Compton) W.; m. Mary Margaret Eungard, Mar. 29, 1956; children: Stephen Mark, Kristi Lynn. BME, George Washington U., 1949, M Engring. Adminstrn., 1960; MS, U. Md., 1953; PhD, Am. U., 1973. Mech. engr. Naval Rsch. Lab., Washington, 1950-54; supr. med. engring. program, chief engring. support branch, chief reliability and assessment, value engring. program mgr. Harry Diamond Labs., 1955-74; sci. adviser U.S. Army Med. Bioengring. R & D Lab., Ft. Detrick, Md., 1974-75; mech. engr. Woolcott & Co., Washington, 1975-90; ret., 1990. Author: Solar Energy Applications for the Home, 1978; contbr. over 40 articles to profl. publs. With U.S. Army, 1946-47. Recipient Dept. of the Army Decoration for Exceptional Civilian Svc., Honors Achievement award Angiology Rsch. Found., Purdue Frederick Co., Engring. Alumni Achievement award George Washington U., Washington, 1987. Mem. ASME, Am. Soc. for Artificial Internal Organs. Republican. Baptist. Achievements include 12 U.S. and 2 foreign patents, development of artifical human heart. Home: 1701 Hunts End Ct Vienna VA 22182-1833

WOODWARD, LESTER RAY, lawyer; b. Lincoln, Nebr., May 24, 1932; s. Wendell Smith and Mary Elizabeth (Theobald) W.; m. Marianne Martinson, Dec. 27, 1958; children: Victoria L. Woodward Eisele, Richard T., David M., Andrew E. BSBA, U. Nebr., 1953; LLB, Harvard U., 1957; LLD (hon.), Bethany Coll., 1974. Bar: Colo., 1957. Assoc. Davis, Graham & Stubbs, Denver, 1957-59, 60-62, ptnr., 1962—. Teaching fellow Sch. Law Harvard U., 1959-60. Bd. dirs. Bethany Coll., Lindsborg, Kans., 1966-74, 87-95, chmn., 1989-92; bd. dirs. Pub. Edn. Coalition, Denver, 1985-92, chmn., 1988-89; mem. Colo. Commn. Higher Edn., Denver, 1977-86, chmn., 1979-81; mem. bd. edn. Denver Pub. Schs., 1999—. Mem. ABA, Colo. Bar Assn., Am. Law Inst. Republican. Lutheran. Home: 680 Bellaire St Denver CO 80220-4935 Office: Davis Graham & Stubbs 1150 17th St Ste 500 Denver CO 80202-5682

WOODWARD, NIEL W., III, astronaut; b. Chgo., July 26, 1962; s. Neil W. and Aileen S. Woodward; married. BS in Physics, MIT, 1984; MA in Physics, U. Tex., 1988; grad., Aviation Officer Candidate Sch., 1990; grad. with distinction, U.S. Naval Test Pilot Sch., 1996; M in Engring. Mgmt., George Washington U., 2000. Advanced through grades to lt. comdr. USN, commd. ensign, 1989, naval flight officer, 1990, assigned to Green Lizards of Attack Squadron 95; weaponeering officer, contingency cell officer Naval Strike Wafare Ctr., Fallon, Nev.; assigned to air vehicle/stores compatibility dept. Naval Strike Aircraft Test Squadron, Patuxent River, Md., 1996—98; astronaut, mission specialist candidate NASA, Johnson Space Ctr., Houston, 1998—. Recipient (2) Navy Commendation medals, (2) Navy Achievement medals. Achievements include research in use of optical spectroscopy to investigate neoclassical plasma rotation in fusion reactor; logged over 1500 flight hours in more than 25 different types of aircraft. Avocations: reading, running, computers, sailing, music. Office: Astronaut Office/CB NASA Johnson Space Ctr Houston TX 77058*

WOODWARD, RALPH LEE, JR. historian, educator; b. New London, Conn., Dec. 2, 1934; s. Ralph Lee and Beulah Mae (Suter) W.; m. Sue Dawn McGrady, Dec. 30, 1958; children: Mark Lee, Laura Lynn, Matthew McGrady; m. Janice Chatelain, Aug. 8, 1996. AB cum laude, Central Coll., Mo., 1955; MA, Tulane U., 1959, PhD, 1962. Asst. prof. history Wichita (Kans.) U., 1961-62, U. S.W. La., Lafayette, 1962-63; asst. prof. history U. N.C., Chapel Hill, 1963-67, asso. prof., 1967-70; prof. history Tulane U., New Orleans, 1970-99, head dept. history, 1973-75, chmn. dept. history, 1986-88; dir. Tulane Summer in C. Am., 1975-78; prof. in charge Tulane Jr. Year Abroad, Paris, 1975-76; Penrose prof. L.Am. studies Tex. Christian U., Ft. Worth, 1999—. Fulbright lectr. U. Chile, U. Catolica de Valparaiso, Chile, 1965-66, U. del Salvador, Universidad Nacional, Buenos Aires, 1968; vis. prof. U.S. Mil. Acad., West Point, N.Y., 1989; regional liaison officer Emergency Com. to Aid Latin Am. Scholars, 1974. Author: Class Privilege and Economic Development, 1966, Robinson Crusoe's Island, 1969, Positivism in Latin America, 1850-1900, 1971, Central America: A Nation Divided, 1976, 3d edit., 1999, Tribute to Don Bernardo de Galvez, 1979, Belize, 1980, Nicaragua, 1983, 2d edit., 1994, El Salvador, 1988, Guatemala, 1992, Rafael Carrera and the Emergence of the Republic of Guatemala, 1993 (Alfred B. Thomas Book award); editor: Central America: Historical Perspectives on the Contemporary Crises, 1988, Here and There in Mexico: The Travel Writings of Mary Ashley Townsend, 2001; assoc. editor: Revista del Pensamiento Centroamericano, 1975, Research Guide to Central America and the Caribbean, 1985, Encyclopedia of Latin American History and Culture, 1996; contbg. editor: Handbook of Latin American Studies, 1987-90; series editor: World Bibliographical Series, 1987—; contbr. articles to profl. jours. Capt. USMC, 1955-58. Recipient Alfred B. Thomas Book award Southeastern Coun. Latin Latin Am. Studies, 1994; Henry L. and Grace Doherty Found. fellow Tulane U., 1962; named La. Humanist of Yr. La. Endowment for Humanities, 1995. Mem. Am. Hist. Assn. (mem. Conf. L.Am. History, pres. 1989, mem. gen. com. 1974-76), Southeastern Conf. L.Am. Studies (program chmn. 1975, pres. 1975-76), L.Am. Studies Assn., Com. on Andean Studies (chmn. 1972-73), Geography and History Acad. Guatemala. Office: Tex Christian U PO Box 297260 Fort Worth TX 76129-0001 E-mail: r.woodward@tcu.edu.

WOODWARD, ROBERT SIMPSON, IV, economics educator; b. Easton, Pa., May 7, 1943; s. Robert Simpson and Esther Evans (Thomas) W.; m. Mary P. Hutton, Feb. 15, 1969; children: Christopher Thomas, Rebecca Marie. BA, Haverford Coll., 1965; PhD, Washington U., St. Louis, 1972. Econ. policy fellow HEW, Washington, 1975-76; asst. prof. U. Western Ont., London, Can., 1972-77; asst. prof. Sch. Medicine Washington U., St. Louis, 1978-86, assoc. prof., 1986-2001; McKerley prof. health econ. U. N.H., Durham, 2001—. Pres. Writing Assessment Software, Inc., 1987-91. Contbr. articles to profl. jours. Mem. adv. coun. Mo. Kidney Program, 1980-86, vice-chmn., 1983, chmn., 1984-85; coop. mem. Haverford Coll., 1968-90. NDEA fellow, 1968-71, Kellogg Nat. fellow, 1981-84. Mem. Am. Econs. Assn., Am. Statis. Assn. Home: 131 Wednesday Hill Rd Lee NH 03824-6546 Office: U NH Dept Health Mgmt and Policy Hewitt Hall Durham NH 03824-3563 E-mail: rsw@unh.edu.

WOODWARD, ROBERT UPSHUR, newspaper reporter, writer; b. Geneva, Mar. 26, 1943; s. Alfred E. and Jane (Upshur) W.; m. Elsa Walsh, Nov. 25, 1989; children: Tali, Diana. BA, Yale U., 1965. Reporter Montgomery County (Md.) Sentinel, 1970-71; reporter Washington Post, 1971-78, met. editor, 1979-81, asst. mng. editor, 1981—. Author: (with Carl Bernstein) All the President's Men, 1974, The Final Days, 1976, (with Scott Armstrong) The Brethren, 1979, Wired, 1984, Veil: The Secret Wars of the CIA, 1987, The Commanders, 1991, (with David S. Broder) The Man Who Would Be President, 1991, The Agenda: Inside the Clinton White House, 1994, The Choice, 1996, Shadow: Five Presidents and the Legacy of Watergate, 1999, Maestro, Greenspan's Fed and the American Boom, 2000. Served with USN, 1965-70. Office: Washington Post Co 1150 15th St NW Washington DC 20071-0002

WOODWARD, THEODORE ENGLAR, medical educator, internist; b. Westminster, Md., Mar. 22, 1914; s. Lewis Klair and Phoebe Helen (Neidig) W.; m. Celeste Constance Lauve, June 24, 1938; children: William E., R. Craig, Celeste L. Woodward Applefeld, Lewis O. (dec.). BS, Franklin and Marshall Coll., 1934, DSc (hon.), 1954; MD, U. Md., 1938; DSc (hon.), Western Md. Coll., 1950, Hahnemann U., 1993. Diplomate Am. Bd. Internal Medicine. Asst. prof. medicine U. Md. Sch. Medicine, Balt., 1946-48, assoc. prof., also dir. sect. infectious disease, 1948-54, prof., 1954-83, prof. emeritus, 1983—, chmn. dept., 1954-81; attending physician Balt. VA Med Ctr., 1949—. With Armed Forces Epidemiol. Bd., Washington, 1952-92, mem. commns., 1952-72, pres. bd., 1976-78, 80-92; mem. U.S./Japan Coop. Med. Sci. Program, Washington, 1965-95, emeritus, 1995—; disting. physician Cen. VA, Washington, 1981-87. Author: Chloramphemicol, 1958, 200 Years of Medicine in Baltimore, 1976, A History of the Department of Medicine, University of Maryland, 1807-1981, 1987, A History of Armed Forces Epidemiological Board, 1940-1990, 1990, Carroll County (Md.) Physicians of the 19th and Early 20th Centuries, 1990, The Armed Forces Epidemiological Board: The History of the Commissions, 1995, Make Room for Sentiment: A Physician's Story, 1998, Research on Infectious Diseases at the University of Maryland School of Medicine and Hospital. A Global Experience: 1807-2000, 2000; contbr. chpts. to textbooks. Life trustee Gilman Sch., Balt., 1955—. Lt. col. Medical Svc. Corp U.S. Army, 1941-46, ETO, PTO. Decorated Order of the Sacred Treasure Gold and Silver Star Govt. of Japan; recipient U.S.A. Typhus Commn. medal Dept. Def., 1945, also Exceptionally Disting. Svc. award, 1990, Outstanding Civilian Svc. medal with oak leaf cluster Dept. Army, 1981; recipient Louis Pasteur medal Inst. Pasteur, 1961, Student Coun. Faculty awardee of Yr., U. Md., 1966, 72, 74-78, 81-93, 85-89, 91, 93-96, 98, 2000, Disting. Svc. award AMA, 1995. Mem. ACP (master, gov. Md. regent 1969-70, James D. Bruce Meml. award 1970, Disting. Tchr. award 1992), Am. Clin. and Climatol. Assn. (pres. 1969-70), Infectious Disease Soc. Am. (pres. 1976-77, Finland award 1972, Bristol award, Kass award 1991), Inst. Medicine NAS, Elkridge Club (Towson, Md.), Mayo Fellows Assn. (hon.), Hamilton St. Club. Republican. Avocations: photography, gardening, raising wild fowl. Home: 1 Merrymount Rd Baltimore MD 21210-1908 Office: Balt VA Med Ctr 10 N Green St Baltimore MD 21210

WOODWARD, THOMAS MORGAN, actor; b. Ft. Worth, Sept. 16, 1925; s. Valin Ridge and Francis Louise (McKinley) W.; m. Enid Anne Loftis, Nov. 18, 1950; 1 child, Enid Anne. AA, Arlington State Coll., 1948; BBA, U. Tex., 1951. Motion picture and TV actor, 1955—; numerous TV appearances include Dallas; motion pictures include The Great Locomotive Chase, 1955, Slaughter on 10th Ave., 1957, The Gun Hawk, 1962, Cool Hand Luke, 1966, The Wild Country, 1973, Which Way Is Up, 1977, Speed Trap, 1978, Battle Beyond the Stars, 1980, Girls Just Want to Have Fun, 1985, Dark Before Dawn, 1987, Gunsmoke III, 1991. With USAAF, 1944-45; to capt. USAF, 1951-53. Recipient Golden Boot award Motion Picture and TV Fund, 1988, Golden Lariat award Nat. Western Film Festival, 1988, Lifetime Achievement award in the arts Arlington Tex. Arts Coun., 1994, Lifetime Achievement award for western film acting Wild West Film Festival, 1995, Internat. Star award 1997; named Disting. Alumnus of Arts U. Tex., 1969; inducted into the Walk of Western Stars William S. Hart Mus., L.A., 1990. Mem. Acad. Motion Picture Arts and Scis., SAR, Pi Kappa Alpha (Disting. Achievement award 1981, inducted into Order of West Range 1988). Office Fax: 323-969-1938.

WOODWARD, WILLIAM LEE, retired savings bank executive; b. Lexington, Ky., Jan. 12, 1926; s. Joel Henry and Ophelia Martha (Wallace) W.; m. Dorothy J. Dekle, Dec. 31, 1949; children: Pamela, William Lee, Martha. AB, U. Ky., 1950, MA, 1952. Tchr. Lafayette H.S., 1950-52; asst. prin. Ft. Benning (Ga.) Children's Schs., 1952-53; asst. mgr. Lexington Fed. Savs. & Loan Assn., 1953-54, exec. v.p., 1954-73, pres., 1973-96. Pres. Lexington Deaf Oral Sch., 1968; trustee Midway (Ky.) Coll., 1968-80; treas. Bluegrass Found., 1967-95; bd. dirs. Ky. Housing Corp., 1979-80. Served with USN, 1944-46. Mem. Ky. Savs. and Loan League (pres. 1969) Rotary. Mem. Christian Ch.

WOODWELL, GEORGE MASTERS, ecology research director, lecturer; b. Cambridge, Mass., Oct. 23, 1928; s. Philip McIntire and Virginia (Sellers) W.; m. Alice Katharine Rondthaler, June 23, 1955; children: Caroline Alice, Marjorie Virginia, Jane Katharine, John Christopher. AB, Dartmouth Coll., 1950; AM, Duke U., 1956, PhD, 1958; DSc (hon.), Williams Coll., 1977, Miami U., 1984, Carleton Coll., 1988, Muhlenberg Coll., 1990, Duke U., 1994, Dartmouth Coll., 1996. Mem. faculty U. Maine, 1957-61, assoc. prof. botany, 1960-61; vis. asst. ecologist, biology dept. Brookhaven Nat. Lab., Upton, N.Y., 1961-62, ecologist, 1965-67, sr. ecologist, 1967-75; founder, dir. Ecosystems Center, 1975-85; dep. and asst. dir. Marine Biol. Lab., Woods Hole, Mass., 1975-76; founder, pres. and dir. Woods Hole Research Ctr., 1985—. Founder, chmn. Conf. on Long Term Biol. Consequences of Nuclear War, 1982-83; bd. trustees Inst. Rsch. on Amazon Bason, Belem, Brazil, 1995—. Editor: Ecological Effects of Nuclear War, 1965, Diversity and Stability in Ecological Systems, 1969, (with E.V. Pecan) Carbon and the Biosphere, 1973, The Role of Terrestrial Vegetation in the Global Carbon Cycle: Measurement by Remote Sensing, 1984, The Earth in Transition: Patterns and Processes of Biotic Impoverishment, 1990, (with K. Ramakrishna) Forests for the Future, 1993, (with F.T. Mackenzie) Biotic Feedbacks in the Warming of the Earth, 1995. Founding trustee Environ. Def. Fund, 1967, Natural Resources Def. Coun., 1970, vice chmn., 1974—. World Resources Inst., 1982-96; bd. dirs. Conservation Found., 1975-77, Ctr. for Marine Conservation, 1990-98, World Wildlife Fund, 1970-84, chmn., 1980-84, Ruth Mott Fund, 1984-91, chmn., 1989-91; bd. trustees Inst. Environ. Rsch. in Amazon, 1996—; adv. com. TMI Pub. Health Fund, 1980-94. Recipient Joseph Priestley award Dickinson Coll., 1993, Hutchinson medal Garden Club of Am., 1993, Disting. Svc. award Am. Inst. Biol. Scis., 1982, Heinz Environ. prize, 1996. Fellow AAAS, Am. Acad. Arts and Scis.; mem. NAS, Brit. Ecol. Soc., Ecol. Soc. Am. (v.p. 1966-67, pres. 1977-78), Sea Edn. Assn. (bd. dirs. 1980-85), World Comm. on Forests and Sustainable Development, 1994-98, Sigma Xi. Achievements include rsch., pub. on structure and function of natural communities, biotic impoverishment, especially ecological effects of ionizing radiation, effects of persistent toxins, world carbon cycle and warming of the earth, sci. and internat. environ. affairs. Office: Woods Hole Research Ctr PO Box 296 Woods Hole MA 02543-0296

WOODWORTH, BETH ELAINE, business owner; b. Olean, N.Y., Feb. 22, 1951; d. Glenn Walter and Marjorie Elaine (Platt) Bernreuther; m. Donald James Woodworth; children: Mathew, Jennifer, Melissa. BA, SUNY, Albany, 1973; MS in Edn., St. Bonaventure U., 1977, MS in Edn., 1986; EdD, SUNY, Buffalo, 1996. Cert. elem. and secondary tchr., N.Y.; cert. sch. adminstr., N.Y. Tchr. English Scio (N.Y.) Ctrl. Sch., 1973-76; instructional support svcs. asst. Allegany County Bd. Coop. Ednl. Svcs., Belmont, N.Y., 1977-81; dir. Wellsville (N.Y.) Child Care Ctr., 1981; substitute tchr. various schs., N.Y., 1982; tchr. English Angelica (N.Y.) Ctrl. Sch., 1984-85; owner Woodworth Nurseries, Scio, 1982-89; sec., treas. Parallel Processing, Inc., Bergen, N.Y., 1982—; pres. Duotables, Inc., 1995—. Mem. rsch. team SUNY, Buffalo, 1988-90, Western N.Y. Ednl. Svc. Coun., Inc., Buffalo, 1989-90; presenter in field. Contbr. articles to profl. jours. Neighborhood chmn. Seven Lakes coun. Girl Scouts U.S., Phelps, N.Y., 1977-80, 84-85, leader, 1977-80, 84-85, bd. dirs. 1978-80, 81-84, educator family life., 1982-83, mem. troop com. Genesee Valley coun., Rochester, N.Y., 1987-90, leader, 1990-99; badge counselor Iroquois Trail coun. Boy Scouts Am., Lockport, N.Y., 1987-90; mem. coop. planning team Byron-Bergen (N.Y.) Ctrl. Sch., 1994-96. Presdl. fellow, 1987-90. Mem. ASCD, Am. Ednl. Rsch. Assn., Nat. Rural Edn. Assn., Rural Edn. Spl. Interest Group, Rsch. on Women Edn. Spl. Interest Group, Phi Delta Kappa, Pi Lambda Theta. Avocations: reading, writing. Home and Office: 5866 W Sweden Rd Bergen NY 14416-9516

WOODWORTH, STEPHEN DAVIS, investment banker; b. Stillwater, Okla., Nov. 4, 1945; s. Stanley Davis and Elizabeth (Webb) W.; m. Robin Woodworth; children: Lisa Alexander, Ashley Ives. BA, Claremont McKenna Coll., 1967; MBA, Calif. Lutheran U., 1975; grad. Mgmt. Policy Inst., U. So. Calif., 1981. Div. mgr. Security Pacific Bank, L.A., 1970-86; pres. Channel Island Equities, Oxnard, Calif., 1988—2002, Omni Lingual Svcs., Inc., Thousand Oaks, 2002—. Chmn. Cen. Coast MIT Enterprise Forum, Santa Barbara, Calif., 1992-94; moderator The White House Conf. on Small Bus., 1995; exec. com., dir. World Affairs Coun. of Ventura County, 1995-98; dir. Greater Oxnard Econ. Devel. Corp., 1996-99; vice chair Santa Barbara chpt. Am. Inst. Wine and Food, 1996-98; instr. fin. and banking Calif. Luth. U., 1978-79; active Calif. CPA Edn. Found., 1996; mem. adv. bd. Hanson Lab. Furniture Industries, Inc., Newbury Park, Calif., 1995-98, H.K. Canning, Inc., 1996-98, Blois Constrn., 1997—; co-founder Calif. Family Bus. Inst., 1996; dir. Ctrl. Coast Chpt. So. Calif. Software Coun., 1999-2001. Contbr. articles to profl. jours. Chmn. Alliance for the Arts, Thousand Oaks, Calif., 1988-95; chair bd. advisors Mary Health of the Sick Hosp., 2001—. Ret. Lt. Col. U.S. Army Res., 1970-96, Korea. Recipient Outstanding Alumnus Calif. Lutheran U., 1986. Mem. Res. Officers Assn. of the U.S., Ventura County Econ. Devel. Assn., Tower Club, Santa Barbara Vintners Assn., James Beard Found., Marine Meml. Club, Spanish Hills Country Club. Republican. Roman Catholic. Home: 661 Corte De Quintero Camarillo CA 93010-8340 Office: Network Omni 1329 E Thousand Oaks Blvd 2d Fl Thousand Oaks CA 91362-E-mail: swoodworth@networkomni.com.

WOODWORTH, THASIA GOODWIN, internist, nephrologist, immunologist; b. Niagara Falls, N.Y., May 28; d. William Jarrard and Alice (Becker) Goodwin; m. Warren Frederick Woodworth, Sept. 4, 1971; children: Mason Lefferts, Graeme Frederick, Garrett Jarrard, Avery Aislinn. BS, Rensselaer Poly. Inst., 1971; MD, Albany Med. Coll., 1971. Diplomate Am. Bd. Internal Medicine. Intern Albany (N.Y.) Med. Ctr., 1971-72; med. resident Cornell U./North Shore Univ. Hosp., Manhassett, 1972-74, renal fellow, 1975-76; nephrology fellow R.I. Hosp.-Brown U., Providence, 1982-86; med. dir. R.I. Renal Inst., Westerly, 1980-86; pvt. practice internal medicine/nephrology, 1976-86; rsch. physician Hoffman-LaRoche, Nutley, N.J., 1986-88; v.p. clin. regulatory affairs Seragen, Inc., Hopkinton, Mass., 1988-95; sr. assoc. dir. Pfizer Ctrl. Rsch., Groton, Conn., 1995—2001; dir., therapeutic area safety head Pfizer Global R&D, 2001—. Med. dir. Wood River Health Svc., Hope Valley, RI, 1976—80, R.I. Renal Inst., Hope Valley, 1981—86; chmn. NIH Osteoarthritis Biomarker Initiative, 1999—. Contbr. over 100 articles to profl. jours. Bd. dirs. Wood River Health Svc., 1980-92, Westerly-Pawcatuck YMCA, Westerly, 1978-84; chmn. Omeract Toxicity Task Force, 1992—. Haffenreffer fellow R.I. Hosp., 1984. Mem. Am. Coll. Rheumatology, Am. Soc. Nephrology, Am. Soc. Transplantation, Am. Coll. Clin. Pharmacology, Alpha Omega Alpha. Avocations: sailing, gardening, dressage. Home: 6 Wapan Rd Westerly RI 02891-5518 Office: Pfizer Global R&D New London CT 06320 E-mail: thasia_g_woodworth@groton.pfizer.com.

WOODY, CAROL CLAYMAN, data processing executive; b. Bristol, Va., May 20, 1949; d. George Neal and Ida Mae Clayman; m. Robert William Woody, Aug. 19, 1972. BS in Math., Coll. William and Mary, Williamsburg, Va., 1971; MBA with distinction, Wake Forest U., 1979. Programmer trainee GSA, 1971-72; systems engr. Citizens Fidelity Bank & Trust Co., Louisville, 1972-75; programmer/analyst-tng. coord. Blue Bell, Inc., Greensboro, N.C., 1975-79; supr. programming and tech. svcs. J.E. Baker Co., York, Pa., 1979-82; fin. design supr. bus. systems Lycoming divsn. AVCO, Stratford, Conn., 1982-83; project mgr. Yale U., New Haven, 1984-97; cons. ImageWork Technologies Corp., 1998-2001; co-owner Sign of the Sycamore, antiques; product developer Software Engring. Inst. Carnegie Mellon U., 2001—. Mem. Data Processing Standards Bd., 1977, CICS/VS Adv. Council, 1975; speaker Nat. Fuse Conf., 1989, Aion expert systems nat. conf., 1990, bus. sch. Coll. William & Mary, 1994. Author various manuals; contbr. articles to profl. jours. IBM Corp. fellow, 1978; Stephen Bufton Meml. Ednl. Found. grantee, 1978-79. Mem. Am. Bus. Woman's Assn. (chpt. v.p. 1978-79, Merit award 1978), NAFE (founder shoreline network 1993), Assn. for System Mgmt., Assn. for Image Info. Mgmt., Project Mgmt. Inst., Network Inc. of Conn. (treas. 1996-97), Delta Omicron (alumni pres. 1973-75, regional chmn. 1979-82). Republican. Presbyterian. Home: PO Box 1450 Guilford CT 06437-0550

WOODY, CLAUDIA LAVERGNE, computer company executive, consultant; b. Martinsville, Va., Jan. 30, 1955; d. N. Rees and LaVergne (Tuck) W. BA summa cum laude, Mary Baldwin Coll., 1977; MS, U. Tenn., 1979; MBA, U. Tex., 1989; cert., Project Mgmt. Inst.; JD, Ga. State U., 1999. Cert. project mgr. profl. Project Mgmt. Inst. Asst. basketball coach U. Tenn., Knoxville, 1977-79, asst. athletics dir., 1979-81, U. Tex., Austin, 1981-88, dir. external affairs, asst. dean Coll. Bus., 1988-91; dir. mktg. San Marcos Telephone Co. and San Marcos Telecorp, 1991-93; v.p. mktg. Century Telephone Enterprises, Dallas, 1993-95; program dir. tech. results sys. Atlanta Com. Olympic Games, 1995-96; dir. global application delivery IBM Global Svcs., 1996—. MacGregor Sporting Goods, Berlin, Wis., 1984-86, Apple Computer, Inc., 1987—; dir., tournament mgr. NCAA Nat. Championships, 1981-88; cons. in field. Mng. editor Texas: The Business School Mag. (Coun. Advancement and Support Edn. award 1990), 1987-91. Bd. dirs The Vol. Ctr., Austin, 1989-92, Greater Austin Sports Found., 1990-94; bd. dirs., v.p. The Artemis Found., Winter Park, Colo., 1990—; mem. adv. bd. Tex. Ctr. for Legal Ethics and Professionalism, 1994—, Legends of Golf, Austin, 1991-93, San Marcos Incubator, 1992-94, Bus. Sch. S.W. Tex. State U., 1991-94, Rotary Internat., 1994—; mem. Leadership Tex., 1993; bd. dirs. bd. visitors Mary Baldwin Coll., 1995—. Russell scholar Mary Baldwin Coll., Staunton, Va., 1977; Hilton A. Smith grad. fellow, 1979; recipient The Kozmetsky award U. Tex., Austin, 1989. Mem. Exec. Women Tex. Govt., Coun. Advancement and Support Edn., Coun. Coll. Women Athletics Adminstrs., NAFE, Nat. Soc. Fundraising Execs., Leadership Tex. Alumnae, Phi Beta Kappa, Omicron Delta Kappa, Psi Chi, Pi Lambda Theta, Kappa Delta Pi, Phi Kappa Phi, Beta Gamma Sigma. Democrat. Avocations: cycling, snow skiing, water skiing, softball. Home: 2996 Margaret Mitchell Dr NW Atlanta GA 30327-1708 E-mail: clwoody@us.ibm.com.

WOODY, CLYDE WOODROW, lawyer; b. Princeton, Tex., Oct. 3, 1920; s. James W. and Emma Mae (Heard) W.; m. Paula Fay Mullen, Aug. 23, 1969; children: Todd, Joe. BS, U. Houston, 1951, JD, 1951; postgrad. St. Mary's U., San Antonio, 1952, U. Colo., 1953. Bar: Tex. 1952, U.S. Ct. Appeals (5th cir.) 1956, U.S. Supreme Ct. 1958, U.S. Ct. Appeals (6th cir.) 1973, U.S. Ct. Appeals (11th cir.) 1981; cert. specialist in criminal law and family law Tex. Bd. Legal Specialization. Pvt. practice law Houston, 1952-66; ptnr., then sr. ptnr. Woody & Rosen, Houston, 1966-80; pvt. practice law, Houston, 1980—; city atty. Southside Pl., Houston, 1955-57; bd. dir. Unitedbank-Houston, Cen. Bank Holding Co., Miami, Fla.; lectr. Bd. dirs. Mossler Found., 1966-70; del. People to People Internat. Citizen Amb. Program, 1988, 91; sect. chmn. State Bar Tex., 1964-65; staff judge adv. N.Am. Air Def. Command, Ent ARB. Capt. U.S. Army, 1941-45, to capt. USAF, 1951-53; PTO, CBI. Mem. Am. Judicature Soc., Nat. Assn. Criminal Def. Lawyers, Tex. Trial Lawyers Assn., Assn. Trial Lawyers Am., ABA, Houston Bar Assn., Tex. Criminal Def. Lawyers Assn., Nat. Transp. Safety Bd. Bar Assn., Phi Delta Phi. Democrat. Methodist. Clubs: University, Texas, (Houston). Contbr. articles to legal jours. Home: 731 Brogden Rd Houston TX 77024-3003 Office: 731 Brogden Rd Houston TX 77024-3003

WOODY, JOHN FREDERICK, secondary education educator; b. Indpls., Apr. 27, 1941; s. Ralph Edwin and Crystal Oleta (Thomas) W.; m. Nancy Ann Henry, July 7, 1963; children: Michael, Laura. BS in Secondary Sch. Teaching, Butler U., 1963, MS in Edn., 1967, adminstrn. lic., 1979, postgrad., 1991—, UCLA, 1980-82, Ind. U., 1990, U. Amsterdam, The Netherlands, 1985, Mont. State U., 1993, Purdue U., 1994. Tchr. Pub. Sch. 90, Indpls., 1963-66, Broad Ripple High Sch., Indpls., 1966-89; tchr., head social studies dept. Arlington H.S., 1989—. Author: (resource kits for hist. events) Cram, Inc., 1976-81, (filmstrips) Lowe Sheldrew, 1976-81; contbr. articles to profl. jours. and sch. materials. Sponsor Rep. Nat. Com., 1982—; deacon Heritage Bapt. Ch., 1983—; mem. U.S. Congress German Bundestag Select Com. Ind., 1986-93. Fulbright scholar U.S. Info. Agy., 1985. Mem. ASCD, Nat. Coun. Social Studies, Ind. Coun. Social Studies, Arlington Acad. Com. Avocations: reading, writing, swimming, lifting weights. Home: 7362 Woodside Dr Indianapolis IN 46260-3137 Office: Arlington High Sch 4825 N Arlington Ave Indianapolis IN 46226-2499

WOODY, THOMAS CLIFTON, II, assistant district attorney; b. Portsmouth, Va., Mar. 31, 1962; s. Thomas Clifton Sr. and Jean (Whitehead) W.; m. Sherry Carpenter, Aug. 15, 1981; children: Thomas Clifton III, Seth Chandler, Spencer David. BA, Old Dominion U., 1984; JD, Mercer U., 1987. Bar: Ga. 1987, U.S. Dist. Ct. (mid. dist.) Ga. 1987, U.S. Ct. Appeals (11 cir.) 1987. Assoc. Adams & Hemingway, Macon, Ga., 1987-92; asst. dist. atty. Dist. Atty's. Office-Macon Judicial Cir., 1992—. Lectr. Ga. Coll., Milledgeville, 1992—. Pres. Bibb County Young Reps., Macon, 1986-90; mem. exec. coun. Bibb County Rep. Party, Macon, 1986-92; chmn. Peach County Rep. party. Mem. Ga. Bar Assn., Macon Bar Assn., Pros. Attys. Coun. Ga., The Federalist Soc. (exec. bd. Ctrl. Ga. Lawyers Divsn.). Republican. Baptist. Avocations: golf, reading, baseball, theological studies, coaching youth sports. Home: 153 Red Oak Rd Byron GA 31008-6311 Office: Macon Judicial Dist Office of Dist Atty 661 Mulberry St Macon GA 31201-2605

WOODYARD, DAVID OLIVER, religious studies educator, clergy member; b. Oak Park, Ill., Apr. 27, 1932; s. Wilfred Cole and Sara (Taylor) W.; m. Martha Joanne Adamson, June 18, 1955; children: Sara Jane, Kimberly Ann. BA, Denison U., 1954; MDiv, Union Theol. Seminary, 1958; DMin, Vanderbilt U., 1974. Dir. U. Christian Fellowship, Storrs, Conn., 1958; prof. religion Denison U., Granville, Ohio, 1960—, chair dept. religion, 1978—, Charles and Nancy Brickman Disting. Svc. chair, dept. religion, 2001—. Bd. dirs. Union Theol. Seminary, 1985-89, Am. Acad. Religion, 1979—. Author: Living Without God-Before God, To Be Human Now, The Opaqueness of God, Beyond Cynicism: The Practice of Hope, Strangers and Exiles: Living By Promises, Journey Towards Freedom: Economic Structures & Theological Perspectives, Risking Liberation: Middle Class Powerlessness and Social Heroism, Liberating Nature: Theology and Economics in a New Order. Pres. Hospice Svcs. of Licking County, Newark, Ohio, 1984-86, Planned Parenthood of East Ctrl. Ohio, 1982-84; adv. bd. Battered Women's Shelter, Newark, 1987-91; bd. dirs. Progressive Prisoner Movement, 1987-89 Home: PO Box 20 Granville OH 43023-0020

WOODYSHEK, J. DANIEL, lawyer; b. Englewood, N.J., May 27, 1948; s. Joseph John and Marjorie (Leahy) W.; m. Alice Ann Murphy (div.); children: David Daniel, Michael Patrick, Danielle. BS cum laude, Marywood Coll., Scranton, Pa., 1976; JD, Boston U., 1979. Bar: Mass. 1980, U.S. Dist. Ct. Mass. 1980. Assoc. Roche, Carens & DeGiacomo, Boston, 1980-83, Shocket, Dockser & Assocs., Boston, 1983-85; ptnr., head real estate dept. Shocket & Dockser, Natick, 1985—97; principal Goguen, McLaughlin, Richards & Mahoney, 2002—. Active local polit. campaigns. Mem. ABA (conveyance com. 1988—), Mass. Bar Assn. (real property sect.), Mass. Conveyancers Assn., Land Ct. Examiner, Pi Gamma Mu, Lambda Iota Tau, Delta Epsilon Sigma. Democrat. Roman Catholic. Avocations: racquetball, gardening, reading, fishing. Office: Goguen McLaughlin Richards & Mahoney 2 Pleasant St Natick MA 01760-0050 E-mail: dwoodyshek@gmrm1.com.

WOOG, DAN, journalist; b. Buffalo, Mar. 27, 1953; s. James Katten and Josephine Mildred (Holtsberg) W. BA, Brown U., 1975. Exec. editor Soccer America's Youth Soccer Letter, Oakland, Calif., 1987—; columnist "Woog's World", Westport News, 1987—. Author: School's Out: The Impact of Gay and Lesbian Issues on America's Schools, 1995, Jocks: True Stories of America's Gay Male Athletes, 1998, Friends and Family: True Stories of Gay America's Straight Allies , 1999, Gay Men, Straight Jobs, 2001. Co-founder Westport Soccer Assn., 1975, Staples High Sch. Gay/Straight Alliance, Westport, 1994; co-facilitator Outspoken, East Norwalk, Conn., 1993. Named Coach of Yr., Conn. Jr. Soccer Assn., 1981, Nat. Youth Coach of Yr., Nat. Soccer Coaches Assn. of Am., 1990; inductee Conn. Soccer Hall of Fame. Mem. Nat. Gay and Lesbian Journalists Assn., Gay, Lesbian and Straight Tchrs. Assn. Office: 301 Post Rd E Westport CT 06880-3624 E-mail: dwoog@optonline.net.

WOOG, JOHN J. eye plastic surgeon; b. Jamaica, N.Y., Feb. 28, 1958; BS, Pa. State Univ., 1978; MD, Thomas Jefferson Univ., 1980. Diplomate Am. Bd. Ophthalmology. Co-dir. Eye Plastics & Orbit Svc. Mass. Eye & Ear Infirmary, Boston, 1985-88; pvt. practice ophthalmology Sloane, Kraut, & Finkelstein, Brookline, Mass., 1985-89, Ophthalmic Cons. Boston, 1989—; dir. Eye Plastics & Orbit Svc. New England Medical Ctr., Boston, 1988-94, co-dir. Eye Plastics & Orbit Svc., 1994—; assoc. clinical prof. Tufts Univ. Sch. Medicine, 1994—; clinical instr. Harvard Medical Sch., 1989—. Bd. dirs. Ophthalmic Cons. Boston, 1989—, Boston Eye Surgery & Laser Ctr., 1992—. Sect. editor: Principles & Practices of Ophthalmology, Eye Trauma, 1994. Fellow Am. Acad. Ophthalmology (Honor award 1994, Sr. Achievement award 2002), Am. Soc. Ophthalmic Plastic & Reconstructive Surgery (Rsch. award 1985, 98). Office: Ophthalmic Cons Boston 50 Staniford St Fl 6 Boston MA 02114-2517

WOOGE, DANIEL LEE, music educator; b. Kansas City, Kans., Oct. 15, 1973; s. Norman Lee and Karen Louise W.; m. Darcie René Phillips, July 6, 1996. B in Music Edn., Baker U., Baldwin, Kans., 1997. 5-12 instrumental and vocal tchr. Usd 420, Osage City, Kans., 1997—. Mem. ednl. adv. coun. Baker U., Baldwin City, 1997—. Recipient Teacher's Who Make A Difference award, Channel 49 and Southwestern Bell, 1999. Home: 1430 E St Osage City KS 66523 Office: USD 420 515 Ellinwood Osage City KS 66523 Personal E-mail: danwooge@hotmail.com. E-mail: danwooge@yahoo.com.

WOOLAM, GERALD LYNN, surgeon; b. Lubbock, Tex., Apr. 16, 1937; s. Rawson Harp and Christine Leta (Rampy) W.; m. Nan Kelly, Feb. 28, 1959; children— Kelly Ann, Gerald Lynn, Gregory Alan. BA, Tex. Tech. U., 1958; MD, Baylor U., 1962. Diplomate Am. Bd. Surgery. Intern Parkland Meml. Hosp., Dallas, 1962-63; resident in gen. surgery Mayo Clinic and Mayo Grad. Sch. Medicine, U. Minn., Rochester, 1963-67, chief resident assoc. in surgery, 1967-68; surgeon Lubbock, 1968—; assoc. clin. prof. surgery Tex. Tech. U. Sch. Medicine, 1972-74, clin. prof., 1975—, prof., interim chmn. dept. surgery, 1980-81. Contbr. articles to profl. jours. Bd. dirs. Community Concert Assn. of Lubbock, 1968-71, 1st United Meth. Ch., Lubbock, 1970—, South Plains Health Systems, 1976-81; trustee West Tex. Found., 1971-74. With USNR. Recipient Outstanding Clin. Prof. award Tex. Tech. U., 1977. Fellow ACS; mem. AAAS, Priestley Soc. (dir. 1970-73, pres. 1981-82), Lubbock Surg. Soc. (pres. 1972), AMA, Lubbock-Crosby-Garza County Med. Soc. (treas., exec. com. 1971—, pres. 1986), Osler Soc., Am. Cancer Soc. (del. 1980-88, dir. 1988—, nat. pres. 1999-2000, pres. Lubbock unit 1972-73, pres. Tex. divsn. 1978-79), Am. Heart Assn. (pres. Lubbock County divsn. 1973-74), Tex. Surg. Soc., Soc. Surgery Alimentary Tract, Soc. for Surg. Oncology, Central Assn. Dentists and Physicians, So. Surg. Assn., Sigma Xi, Phi Chi, Alpha Omega Alpha, Phi Kappa Phi, Phi Eta Sigma, Alpha Epsilon Delta. Home: 4007 69th St Lubbock TX 79413-5945 Office: 3611 22d Pl Lubbock TX 79410 E-mail: gwoolam@lubbocksurgical.com.

WOOLARD, CONNIE WARD, artist, retired art gallery manager; b. Wilkes-Barre, Pa., Mar. 25, 1931; d. Harold Walton and Betty Bertha (Mandeville) Ward; m. Maurice Emmett Woolard, Oct. 25, 1952; children: Karin Elise Woolard Snoots. Student, U. Md., 1949-50, Abbott Art Sch., 1951-52. Comml. artist Rex Engraving Co., Silver Spring, Md., 1953-60, art dir., 1959-60; mgr. Town Ctr. Gallery, Rockville, 1978—90, Bethesda, 1990—99, ret., 1999. Freelance artist, fine artist, 1965—. One-woman shows include Town Ctr. Gallery, 1984, 1986, 1989, 1991, 1993, 1996, Art Contemporary, Bethesda, 1982, Sugar & Frichtl Gallery, 1993. Recipient Salmagundi Non-Member award Salmagundi Club, N.Y.C., 1983, Judges Choice award Nat. League Am. Penwomen, 1996, Juror's award Miniature Painters Sculptors and Gravors Washington, 1997, awards Cider Painters Am. Mem.: Potomac Valley Watercolorists, Balt. Watercolor Soc. (Mid Atlantic Regional award 1985), Miniature Painters, Sculptors & Engravers Soc. Washington, Nat. League Am. Penwomen (past sec., pres., named Women Yr. 1984), So. Watercolor Soc. (signature mem.), Phila. Watercolor Soc., Washington Watercolor Assn. (past pres.), Rockville Art League (past pres.), Salmagundi Club (Nat. Soc. Painters in Casein and Acrylic award, Maria Szerti Meml. award 2001). Avocations: gardening, reading, photography. Home: 3922 Havard St Silver Spring MD 20906-4311

WOOLARD, WILLIAM LEON, lawyer, electrical distributing company executive; b. Bath, N.C., Aug. 26, 1931; s. Archie Leon and Pearl Irene (Boyd) W.; m. Virginia Harris Stratton, June 17, 1961; children: William Leon Jr., Margaret Anne. AB, Duke U., 1953, LLB, JD, 1955. Bar: N.C. 1955, U.S. Dist. Ct. (we. and mid. dists.) N.C. 1960. Claims analyst Md. Casualty Co., Charlotte, N.C., 1955-56; dist. mgr. Chrysler Corp., 1956-60; ptnr. Jones, Hewson & Woolard, 1960-86, of counsel, 1986—; pres. Armature Winding Co., Inc., 1970—, also bd. dirs.; v.p. Power Products Mfg. Co., 1970—, also bd. dirs. Mem. adminstrv. bd. 1st United Meth. Ch., Charlotte, 1961-78, trustee, 1984-87; trustee Lawyers Ednl. Found., Charlotte, 1970-78, N.C. Sch. Sci. and Math., 1997—; bd. dirs. Christian Rehab. Ctr., Charlotte, 1972-73, N.C. Eye and Human Tissue Bank, Winston-Salem, 1978-79. Recipient Order of Civil Merit Moran award Republic of Korea, 1990, Disting. Svc. medal Republic of China, 1990, Medal of Friendship Pope John Paul II, 1990, Humanitarian Citizen of Merit medal Republic of China, 1990, Humanitarian medal France, 1990, Outstanding Svc. medal Mayor of Paris, 1990, Order of Long Leaf Pine, Gov. of N.C., 1990, numerous others; Angier B. Duke scholar Duke U., 1949-53; Carnegie Found. fellow Duke U., 1951-52, Melvin Jones fellow Lions Found., 1978. Mem. ABA, N.C. Bar Assn., N.C. State Bar Assn., 26th Jud. Dist. Bar Assn., Am. Judicature Soc., Lions (pres. Charlotte Ctrl. club 1972-73, pres., trustee ednl. found. 1973-87, dist. gov., chmn. coun. govs. internat. orgn. 1978-79, internat. bd. dirs. 1981-85, Ambassador of Goodwill award 1983, internat. 3rd v.p. 1986-87, 2nd v.p. 1987-88, 1st v.p. 1988-89, internat. pres. 1989-90, immediate past pres. 1990-91, chmn. bd. trustees 1990-91), Masons, Shriners, Phi Kappa Sigma, Delta Theta Phi. Avocations: collecting antique and rare books, opera, boating, fishing. Home: 638 Hempstead Pl Charlotte NC 28207-2320 Office: PO Box 32277 Charlotte NC 28232-2277

WOOLDREDGE, WILLIAM DUNBAR, health facility administrator; b. Salem, Mass., Oct. 27, 1937; s. John and Louise (Sigourney) W.; m. Johanna Marie; children: John, Rebecca Wistar. BA, Colby Coll., 1961; MBA, Harvard U., 1964. Staff assoc. Sun Oil Co., Phila., 1964-67; treas. Ins. Co. N.Am., 1967-72, B.F. Goodrich Co., Akron, Ohio, 1972-84, sr. v.p., 1978-79, exec. v.p., chief fin. officer, mem. mgmt. com., 1979-84; chief fin. officer, exec. v.p., dir. Belden & Blake Corp., North Canton, 1984-89; sr. v.p., chief fin. officer, dir. Belden & Blake Oil Prodn., Inc., 1984-89; prin. dir. Carleton Group, Cleve., 1989-92; CFO, COO, v.p. King's Med. Co., Hudson, Ohio, 1993—, also bd. dirs. Pres. Hudson Econ. Devel. Corp. Bd. dirs. Salvation Army, North Park Coll. and Seminary; trustee Children's Hosp. Med. Ctr., Akron. With U.S. Army, 1956-58. Mem. Fin. Execs. Inst. Clubs: Country of Hudson. Episcopalian. Home: 100 College St Hudson OH 44236-2925 Office: King's Med Co 1920 Georgetown Rd Hudson OH 44236-4060 E-mail: wdwooldred@aol.com.

WOOLDRIDGE, PATRICE MARIE, marketing professional, martial arts and meditation educator; b. Chgo., June 3, 1954; d. Charles E. and Marlys E. Reardon; m. Patrick Wooldridge, June 27, 1981. *Husband Patrick Wooldridge is Vice President of Wooldridge Associates, specializing in Technical Analysis and Competitive Intelligence, and sidelining as a computer consultant. From 1971-1991 he was a Paramedic, Chief Paramedic, and Instructor Trainer in First Aid and Emergency Medicine. Memberships include: Qualitative Research Consultants Association and Society of Competitive Intelligence Professionals. A past President of the Midwest Buddhist Council and former Co-Chair of the Chicago Catholic-Buddhist Conference, he holds Scouting's Distinguished Scoutmaster and Wood Badge Awards. He has studied various martial arts since he was 9 years old, and currently teaches T'ai Chi and the Arica method.* AS, Moraine Valley Coll., 1974; BA, Govs. State U., 1976, MA, 1977; MBA, Loyola U., Chgo., 1983. Community prof. Govs. State U., University Park, Ill., 1977-78; counselor, social worker Bloom Twp. High Sch., Chicago Heights, 1977-78; market analyst Dr. Scholl Footcare, Chgo., 1978-79; supr. consumer rsch. Unocal, Schaumburg, Ill., 1979-84; group rsch. dir. Tatham-Laird & Kudner, Chgo., 1984-87; v.p., assoc. dir. strategic planning & rsch. Bayer Bess Vanderwarker Advt., 1987-90; v.p. dir. qualitative svcs. Goldring/MIL Rsch., 1990-91; pres. Wooldridge Assocs., Inc., Chgo., 1991—. Instr. dancing, 1969-89; instr. T'ai Chi the Sch. of T'ai Chi Chuan, N.Y.C., 1986—; instr. Arica the Arica Inst., N.Y.C., 1978—. Performer The Anawim Players, Chgo., 1985-97; treas. Karma Thegsum Choling, Chgo., 1987-97; bd. dirs. Illustrated Theatre Co., Chgo., 1987, The Human Process, Chgo., 1992—, Tai Chi Found., Inc., 1994-97; adv. bd. N.W. Suburban Boy Scouts, Schaumburg, 1984; participant White House Conf. on Small Bus., 1996. Recipient Gold Medallion 2000 Ogilvy Awards. Mem. Am. Mktg. Assn., Qualitative Rsch. Cons. Assn., Union of Concerned Scientists, The Planetary Soc. Home and Office: 1717 W Rascher Ave Chicago IL 60640-1117

WOOLDRIDGE, THOMAS DEAN, nephrologist; b. Grenada, Miss., Feb. 25, 1946; s. Reuben Dean and Katherine (Shipp) W.; m. Luanne Lyle, Oct. 15, 1975; 1 child, Thomas Dean Jr. BS, BA, Millsaps Coll., Jackson, Miss., 1968; MD, U. Miss., 1972. Diplomate in internal medicine and nephrology Am. Bd. Internal Medicine. Intern U. Hosp., Jacksonville, Fla., 1972-73; resident, fellow U. Miss., 1973-77; med. dir. artificial kidney unit North Miss. Med. Ctr., Tupelo, 1977—; pvt. practice Nephrology & Hypertension Assocs., 1977—. Chmn. Network & Med. Rev. Bd., 1999—; mem. HCFA Forum, 1999—. Mem. ACP, AMA, Am. Soc. Nephrology, Miss. Nephrologic Soc. (pres. 1993-94), Miss. State Med. Assn. Methodist. Avocations: jogging, history, tennis. Home: 1848 Northwood Dr Tupelo MS 38804-1047 Office: Nephrology and Hypertension Assocs 1542 Medical Park Cir Tupelo MS 38801-6560

WOOLDRIDGE, WILLIAM CHARLES, lawyer; b. Miami, Fla., Feb. 24, 1943; s. Clarence Edward and Easter Marguerite (Souders) W.; m. Joyce L. Norton, June 15, 1968; children: William Charles, John Michael. BA, Harvard U., 1965; LLB, U. Va., 1969. Bar: Va. 1969. Atty. Norfolk and Western Ry. Co., 1973-82; with Norfolk So. Corp., 1982-2000, v.p. dept. law, 1996-2000. Pres. John Marshall Found., Richmond, Va., 1992-94; pres. Norfolk Hist. Soc., 1995-96; chair Friends of Chrysler Mus. Hist. Houses, 1997-99; bd. dirs. Sta. WHRO (FM and TV), 1997-2000, WHRO Found., Libr. of Va. Found. Capt. JAGC, U.S. Army, 1969-73. Mem. Va. Bar Assn. Republican.

WOOLEVER, NAOMI LOUISE, retired editor; b. Williamsport, Pa., Sept. 17, 1922; d. Samuel Bruce and Kathryn Elizabeth (Schmidt) W. BS, Pa. State U., 1944, MA, 1966, postgrad., 1974-76. Reporter, women's editor Gazette & Bulletin, Williamsport, 1944-53; women's editor Sun-Gazette, 1953-72, assoc. city editor, 1972-74; prof. journalism Williamsport Area Community Coll., 1974-76; nat. editor, mng. editor Grit Pub. Co., Williamsport, 1976-81, editor in chief, 1981-88. Career cons. high sch. and coll. journalism classes, Pa. Contbr. articles to profl. jours. Named Woman of Yr., Williamsport Univ. Women, 1967. Mem. Pa. Women's Press Assn. (pres. 1960-62, Pa. Newswoman of Yr. 1958), Nat. Fedn. Press Women (bd. dirs. 1960-62), Soroptimist Club (pres. Williamsport chpt. 1958-60), Univ. Women's Club (pres. 1961-63), Friends of James V. Brown Libr., Williamsport Country Club, Williamsport Woman's Club, Lycoming County Hist. Soc., Gen. John Burrow's Hist. Soc., Clio Club (pres. 1991-93), Pa. State Alumni Assn. (life mem.), Phi Kappa Phi, Kappa Tau Alpha, Zeta Tau Alpha. Republican. Mem. United Methodist Ch. Avocations: music, duplicate bridge, photography, sports. Home: 326 N Montour St Montoursville PA 17754-1832

WOOLEY, CHARLES FRANCIS, internist; b. Jersey City, 1929; MD, N.Y. Med. Coll., 1954. Diplomate Am. Bd. Internal Medicine, Am. Bd. Cardiovascular Disease. Intern U. Hosp., Columbus, Ohio, 1954-55, resident medicine, 1955, 58-60, fellow cardiovascular diseases, 1960-63; mem. staff Ohio State U. Hosps., 1961—; prof. medicine Ohio State U., 1972—. Fellow ACP, Am. Coll. Cardiology, Am. Heart Assn. Office: Ohio State U Heart & Lung Rsch Inst 473 W 12th Ave 2nd Fl Columbus OH 43210 E-mail: wooley_1@medctr.osu.edu.

WOOLEY, GERALDINE HAMILTON, writer, poet; b. Idlewild, Mich., Feb. 15, 1942; d. Charles Loren and Alice (Smith) Hamilton; m. David Wooley, June 11, 1961 (div. 1983); children: Vickie Wooley Houston, Monica Wooley Roberts, Deborah Wooley Williams. GED, Flint, Mich. Cosmetologist pvt. practice, Flint, Mich., 1967-70; tchr's. aide Flint Comty. Schs., 1969-71; nurse's aide Clara Barton Home, Flint, 1972; factory worker GM AC Plant, 1973-76; child care worker Beecher Cmty. Schs., 1987-89; poet, songwriter, 1994—. Songwriter Hilltop Records, Hollywood, Calif., 1996—. Author: (poems) Between The Raindrops, 1995 (Editor's Choice 1995), At Water's Edge, 1995 (Editor's Choice 1995), Tapestry, 1996 (Editor's Choice 1996), Memories of Tomorrow, 1996 (Editor's Choice 1996). Mem. PTA Flint Sch. Dist., 1969-70. Named to Internat. Poetry Hall of Fame, 1996. Mem. Internat. Soc. Of Poets, Nat. Writers Assn., Internat. Black Writers. Democrat. Avocations: camping, playing organ, exploring old houses, writing. Home: 2176 Flamingo Dr Mount Morris MI 48458-2610 E-mail: LadyKnight77@webtv.net.

WOOLF, KENNETH HOWARD, architect; b. N.Y.C., Aug. 19, 1938; s. Howard Walter and Elizabeth Ann (Levy) W.; m. Elizabeth Adair Rainwater, July 3, 1965; children: Robert Gregg, Susan Adair, Jennifer Adair. BArch, Cornell U., 1961. Staff arch. Look & Morrison, Archs., Pensacola, Fla., 1965-72; pvt. practice arch., 1972—. Instr. architecture Pensacola Jr. Coll., part-time 1967-76; chmn. Pensacola Archtl. Rev. Bd., 1970-81; mem. Gulf Breeze Planning Bd., 1976-78; chmn. Pensacola City Bd. Adjustment and Appeals, 1995—. Prin. works include Coca-Cola Bottling Co. Plant, Pensacola, 1974, 3 profl. office bldgs. towers, Pensacola, 1976, 84, 92, Bapt. Hosp. addition, 1977, The Village, Housing for Elderly, 1978, 81, 98, Azalea Trace Ret. Cmty. Complex, 1980, 99, Northview Cmty., 1981, Coca-Cola Bottling Plant, Beaumont, Tex., 1983, Episcopal Day Sch., Pensacola, 1993. With USN, 1961-65. Named Jaycee of Yr., 1970. Mem. AIA (sec. N.W. Fla. chpt. 1976-77, 77-78, pres. 1979-81, Comml. Design Hon. award 1975), Rotary. Episcopalian. Home: 15 N Sunset Blvd Gulf Breeze FL 32561-4051 Office: 100 W Gadsden St Pensacola FL 32501-3910 E-mail: khwarch@bellsouth.net.

WOOLF, NEVILLE JOHN, astronomer, educator; b. London, England, Sept. 15, 1932; s. Henry Robert and Lily Woolf; m. Patricia Lenore Martin, Sept. 26, 1972; children: David, Martin; m. Suzanne Hoff, Dec. 0, 1966 (dec. July 0, 1969). BSc, Manchester U., Manchester, England, 1956, PhD, 1959. Postdoctoral Lick Obs., Santa Cruz, Calif., 1959—61, Princeton U. Observation, Princeton, NJ, 1962—65; assoc. prof. astronomy Astronomy Dept. U. Tex., Austin, Tex., 1965—67; prof. astronomy U. Minn., Minneapolis, Minn., 1967—74; astronomy prof. Steward Obs. U. Ariz., Tucson, 1974—. Councilor Am. Astron. Soc., 1974—76. Cpl. Brit. Army, 1951—53. Fellow Fellow, Alfred P. Sloan Found., 1966. Achievements include discovery of Identification Of Silicate Dust Around Stars, In Interstellar Space And In Comets; development of Techniques For Observing Terrestrial Planets Around Other Stars. Avocations: contemplation, history of contemplation. Office: Steward Observatory University Arizona Tucson AZ 85721

WOOLF, WILLIAM BLAUVELT, retired association executive; b. New Rochelle, N.Y., Sept. 18, 1932; s. Douglas Gordon and Katharine Hulton (Blauvelt) W. AA, John Muir Jr. Coll., 1951; student, U. Calif. at Berkeley, 1951; BA, Pomona Coll., 1953; MA, Claremont (Calif.) Grad. Sch., 1955; PhD, U. Mich., 1960. Instr., asst. prof., assoc. prof. U. Wash., Seattle, 1959-68; assoc. sec., dir. adminstrn. AAUP, Washington, 1968-79; mng. editor Math. Revs., Am. Math. Soc., Ann Arbor, Mich., 1979-90, acting exec. editor, 1984-85; assoc. exec. dir. Am. Math. Soc., Providence, 1990-96. Bd. dirs. Nat. Child Rsch. Ctr., Washington, 1975-77; trustee Friends Sch., Detroit, 1985-90, treas., 1986-90; mem. Law and Justice Coun., Jefferson County, Wash., 1998—, chmn., 2001; mem. Wash. State U. Jefferson County Adv. Team, 1999—. Jefferson County Edn. Com., 1998—, chmn., 1999-2001. Fulbright Research fellow U. Helsinki, Finland, 1963-64 Fellow AAAS; mem. ACLU (life, treas. Washington 1966-68, bd. dirs. Washtenaw County and Mich. State 1989-90, bd. dirs. R.I. State 1993-95, treas. 1994-95), Am. Math. Soc., Math. Assn. Am. Mem. Soc. Of Friends. Home: PO Box 235 Port Townsend WA 98368-0235

WOOLFENDEN, JAMES MANNING, nuclear medicine physician, educator; b. L.A., Nov. 8, 1942; BA with distinction, Stanford U., 1964; MD, U. Wash., 1968. Diplomate Am. Bd. Nuclear Medicine (chmn. credentials com. 1993-94, vice chmn. exams. com. 1993-95, chmn. exam. com. 1995-96, sec. 1994-96, chmn. 1996-97), Nat. Bd. Med. Examiners. Med. intern L.A. County-U. So. Calif. Med. Ctr., 1968-69; med. resident West L.A. VA Med. Ctr., 1969-70; nuclear medicine resident L.A. County-U. So. Calif. Med. Ctr., 1972-74; from asst. prof. radiology to assoc. prof. radiology U. Ariz., Tucson, 1974-84, prof. radiology, 1984—. Mem. med. staff Univ. Med. Ctr., Tucson, 1974—; cons. VA Med. Ctr., 1974—; cons. med. staff Tucson Med. Ctr., 1975—. Carondelet St. Joseph's Hosp., 1974-98, St. Mary's Hosp., Tucson, 1976-90; mem. Nat. Cancer Inst. site visit team NIH, 1976, mem. NHLB Inst. site visit team NIH, 1976, mem. diagnostic radiology study sect., 1993-97, chmn., 1995-97; mem. med. liaison officer network EPA, 1983—; cons.-tchg. med. staff Kino Comty. Hosp., 1984-94; med. officer Clin. Ctr., NIH, Bethesda, 1984-85; mem. Ariz. Cancer Ctr., U. Ariz., 1988—, sr. clin. scientist Univ. Heart Ctr., 1990—; Ariz. bd. regents U. Ariz. Presdl. Search Com., 1990-91; chmn. Ariz. Atomic Energy Commn., 1979-80, Ariz. Radiation Regulatory Hearing Bd., 1981—; bd. dirs. Calif. Radioactive Materials Mgmt. Forum, 1989—, chmn.-elect, 1993-94, chmn., 1994-95, Western Forum Edn. in Safe Disposal of Low-Level Radioactive Waste, 1990—, vice chmn., 1991-92, chmn., 1992-94. Manuscript reviewer: Noninvasive Med. Imaging, 1983-84, Jour. Nuclear Medicine, 1985—, Investigative Radiology, 1989-94, Archives of Internal Medicine, 1990—; contbr. book chpts.: Diagnostic Nuclear Medicine, 2d edit., 1988, Adjuvant Therapy of Cancer, 1977, Fundamentals of Nuclear Medicine, 1988, others; contbr. articles and book revs. to profl. publs. Mem. Am. Heart Assn. Coun. on Cardiovasc. Radiology. Maj. U.S. Army, 1970-72, Vietnam. Fellow Am. Coll. Nuclear Physicians (long range planning com. 1981-83, govt. affairs com. 1984-94, exec. com. 1987-91, sec. 1989-91, parliamentarian 1991-95, treas. 1996-98, mem. publs. com. 1993—, chmn. publs. com. 1993-94, pres.-elect 1998-99, pres. 1999-2000, others); mem. AMA (diagnostic and therapeutic tech. assessment reference panel 1982-98), Am. Nuclear Soc., Soc. Nuclear Medicine (com. on audit 1992-99, trustee 1992-96, ho. dels. 1996—, fin. com. 1996-99, bd. dirs. 1997-99, bronze medal for sci. exhibit 1984, bd. dirs., sec.-treas. So. Calif. chpt. 1993-95, pres.-elect 1995-96, pres. 1996-99), Assn. Univ. Radiologists, Ariz. Med. Assn., European Assn. Nuc. Medicine, Pima County Med. Soc., Radiol. Soc. N.Am. Office: Ariz Health Scis Ctr Nuc Medicine 1501 N Campbell Ave Tucson AZ 85724-5068

WOOLFORD, DORNELL LARMONT, academic administrator; b. Easton, Md., Apr. 15, 1965; s. Calvin Henry and Shirley Eleanora (Simms) W. BA in Liberal Studies, Salisbury State U., 1988, MA in English, 1993. Coord. minority retention/outreach Chesapeake Coll., Wye Mills, Md., 1991-92, coord. transfer svcs., 1992-93; lectr. English U. Md. Ea. Shore, Princess Anne, 1993—; prospect rschr. Salisbury (Md.) State U., 1999; instr. devel. English Wor-Wic. C.C., Salisbury, 1999—. Mem. Md. Exec. Coun. for Ednl. Opportunities, 1992-96, Developmental Edn. Assn. Md., 1993-96; cons. Nat. Black Leadership Initiative on Cancer, Princess Anne, 1995-96. Bd. mem. Lower Shore chpt. ARC, Salisbury, 1997; bd. dirs. Bay Shore Svcs., 1997—, Nat. Kidney Found. Md. Mem. Rotary Club Salisbury (sec. 1997-98), Rotaract Club Salisbury (dir. 1993-96, Rotaractor of Yr. 1995), Salisbury State U. Alumni Assn. (bd. mem. 1995—). Episcopalian. Avocations: tennis, bowling, walking. Office: Wor-Wic Cmty Coll Dept English Salisbury MD 21804 E-mail: dornellw@hotmail.com.

WOOLHISER, DAVID ARTHUR, hydrologist; b. LaCrosse, Wis., Jan. 21, 1932; s. Algie Duncan and Blanche Lenore (Jasperson) W.; m. Kathryn Brown, Apr. 21, 1957; children: Carl David, Curt Fredric, Lisa Kathryn. BS in Agriculture, BSCE, U. Wis., Madison, 1955, PhD, 1962; MS, U. Ariz., 1959. Instr. U. Ariz., Tucson, 1955-58; hydraulic engr. Agrl. Rsch. Svc. USDA, Madison, Wis., 1959-61, Columbia, Mo., 1961-63; asst. prof. Cornell U., Ithaca, N.Y., 1963-67; rsch. hydraulic engr. Agrl. Rsch. Svc., Ft. Collins, Colo., 1967-81, Tucson, 1981-91, collaborator, 1991-92; faculty affiliate Colo. State U., 1994—. Vis. scientist Inst. Hydrology, Wallingford, Eng., 1977-78; vis. prof. Imperial Coll., London, 1977-78; faculty affiliate Colo. State U., 1967-84; adj. prof. U. Ariz., 1981-92; vis. prof. Va. Poly. Inst. and State U., 1992; sr. rsch. sci. Colo. State U., 1993-94, faculty affiliate, 1994—; vis. prof. U. Córdoba, Spain, 1993-94, 96. Contbr. articles to profl. jours. Recipient disting. svc. citation Coll. Engring. U. Wis., Madison, 1991, Feb. Lab. Consortium award for excellence in tech. transfer, 1998, Ray K. Linsky award Am. Inst. Hydrology, 2000. Fellow Am. Geophys. Union (Robert E. Horton award 1983); mem. NAE, ASCE (Hunter Rouse lectr. 1994, arid lands hydraulic engring. award 1988). Office: 1631 Barnwood Dr Fort Collins CO 80525-2069 E-mail: woolhiserd@aol.com.

WOOLLAM, JOHN ARTHUR, electrical engineering educator; b. Kalamazoo, Aug. 10, 1939; s. Arthur Edward and Mildred Edith (Hakes) W.; children: Catherine Jane, Susan June. BA in Physics, Kenyon Coll., 1961; MS in Physics, Mich. State U., 1963, PhD in Solid State Physics, 1967; MSEE, Case Western Res. U., 1978. Rsch. scientist NASA Lewis Rsch. Ctr., Cleve., 1967-80; prof. U. Nebr., Lincoln, 1979—, dir. Ctr. Microelectronic and Optical Materials Rsch., 1988—; pres. J.A. Woollam Co., Inc., 1987—. Editor Jour. Applied Physics Com., 1979-94. Grantee NASA, NSF, USAF, Advanced Rsch. Projects Agy. Fellow Am. Phys. Soc.; mem. Am. Vacuum Soc. (chmn. thin film divsn. 1989-91). Office: U Nebr Dept Elec Engring 209NWSEC Lincoln NE 68588-0511

WOOLLCOMBE, GRAHAM DOUGLAS, dean; b. Plymouth, Devon, Eng., Apr. 22, 1956; s. Richard Edward De Ambrosis and Phoebe (Morshead) W. MA, Cambridge U., 1982; MS in Creative Intelligence, Maharishi European Rsch. U., Seelisberg, Switzerland, 1982. Cert. Royal Inst. Brit. Archs.; cert. Maharishi Ayurveda cons. EEG asst. Maharishi European Rsch. U., Boppard-am-Rhein, Germany and Eng., 1982-85; rsch. and edn. cons. Ministry of Ayurveda, Sri Lanka, 1985; arch. Maharishi Nagar, Ghazhirbad Up, India, 1986; graphics designer Mentmore Video, Buckinghamshire, Eng., 1986-92; Ayurvedic cons. and bus. cons., The Hague, The Netherlands, 1993-94. Candidate Natural Law Party, Northampton, Eng., 1997. Anglican. Avocations: croquet, painting, computer graphics. Home and Office: 639 Whispering Hills Rd Boone NC 28607-5599

WOOLLEY, ALMA SCHELLE, nursing educator; b. N.Y.C., Oct. 3, 1931; d. Max Carl and Matilda Louise Schelle; m. Arthur E. Woolley Jr., Sept. 11, 1954; children: Mariel Therese, Mark Stephen, Peter James, Jane Frances. Student, CUNY, 1949-51; BSN, Cornell U., 1954; MSN, U. Pa., 1965, EdD, 1980. Instr. sch. nursing U. Pa., Phila., 1965-69; asst. prof. nursing Atlantic Community Coll., Mays Landing, N.J., 1969-74; coord. nursing program Stockton State Coll., Pomona, 1974-81; dir., Carolyn F. Rupert prof. nursing Sch. of Nursing, Ill. Wesleyan U., Bloomington, 1981-86; dean Sch. Nursing Georgetown U., Washington, 1986-92, prof., 1992-96, prof. emeritus, 1996—. Vis. prof. U. Md. and Uniformed Svcs. U. Health Scis., 1997—. Author: History of Georgetown University School of Nursing, 1903-2000, 2001; mem. editl. bd.: Nurse Educator; editor: Bull. of Am. Assn. for History of Nursing; contbr. articles to profl. jours. Recipient Dist. Alumni award Cornell U. Sch. Nursing, 1989. Mem. ANA, Am. Assn. Colls. of Nursing (bd. dirs. 1988-90), Nat. League for Nursing (bd. of rev.), Am. Assn. for History of Nursing, Cosmos Club, Sigma Theta Tau, Phi Delta Kappa. Episcopalian. Address: 13 Basswood Ct Catonsville MD 21228-5870 E-mail: awooll@aol.com.

WOOLLEY, AUDIE LEE, otolaryngologist; b. Cisco, Tex., June 28, 1962; MD, U. Tex., 1988. Diplomate Am. Bd. Otolaryngology. Intern Washington U., St. Louis, 1988-89, resident in otolaryngology-head and neck surgery, 1989-94; fellow pediat. otolaryngology St. Louis Children's Hosp., 1994-95; mem. staff John Cochran VA Hosp., St. Louis Children's Hosp., St. Louis, 1989-95, Barnes Hosp., Jewish Hosp., St. Louis, 1989-95, U. Ala. Sch. Medicine, Birmingham, 1995—, Children's Hosp. Ala., Birmingham, 1995—, med. dir. cochlear implant program; instr. otolaryngology, head-neck surgery Washington U., St. Louis, 1994—; clin. assoc. prof. otolaryngology, head-neck surgery Sch. Medicine U. Ala., Birmingham, 1995—. Mem. AMA, Am. Acad. Otolaryngology-Head and Neck Surgery, Soc. Ear, Nose, Throat, Advances in Children, Birmingham Ear, Nose and Throat Soc. Office: Children's Hosp Ala ACC320 1600 7th Ave S Birmingham AL 35233-1785

WOOLLEY, BRYAN (LOWELL BRYAN WOOLLEY), author, journalist; b. Gorman, Tex., Aug. 22, 1937; s. G.L. Jr. and Beatrice Voleta (Gibson) W.; m. Julianne Nelson, Aug. 31, 1958 (div. 1968); m. Margaret Ray Hilpert, July 13, 1968 (div. 1978); children: Bryan Edward, John Patrick; m. Isabel Catherine Rickert, Apr. 14, 1979. BA, U. Tex., El Paso, 1958; BDiv, Tex. Christian U., 1963; MTh, Harvard U., 1966. Reporter El Paso Times, 1955-58; tchr. Bel Air H.S., El Paso, 1958-59; bank teller Ft. Davis (Tex.) State Bank, 1959-60; corr. AP, Tulsa, 1967-68; city editor The Anniston (Ala.) Star, 1968-69; reporter, editl. writer The Courier-Jour., Louisville, 1969-76; sr. writer, columnist The Dallas Times Herald, 1976-89; sr. writer The Dallas Morning News, 1989—. Author: Some Sweet Day, 1974, We Be Here When the Morning Comes, 1975, Time and Place, 1977, November 22, 1981, Sam Bass, 1983 (Spur award 1984), The Time of My Life, 1984, Where Texas Meets the Sea, 1985, The Edge of the West, 1990, The Bride Wore Crimson, 1993, Generations, 1995, Mythic Texas, 1999. Named Bernard DeVoto fellow, Bread Loaf Writers Conf., 1975; named to Authors of the Pass: El Paso Writers Hall of Fame, 1989; recipient Tex. Headliner award, 1977, 1981, 1983, 1990, Lit. award in journalism, PEN West, 1993, U. Mo. Lifestyle Journalism award in arts and entertainment, 1995, Sweepstakes award, Tex. AP Mng. Editors Assn., 1999. Mem.: PEN West, Tex. Folklore Soc., West Tex. Hist. Assn., Tex. State Hist. Assn., Tex. Inst. Letters (pres. 1993—94, Stanley Walker Journalism award 1981, 1983, 1990, O. Henry award for mag. journalism 1991). Democrat. Home: 18040 Midway Rd Apt 215 Dallas TX 75287-6503 Office: Dallas Morning News 508 Young St Dallas TX 75202-4828 E-mail: lbwoolley@aol.com.

WOOLLEY, CATHERINE (JANE THAYER), writer; b. Chgo., Aug. 11, 1904; d. Edward Mott and Anna L. (Thayer) W. AB, UCLA, 1927. Advt. copywriter Am. Radiator Co., N.Y.C., 1927-31; freelance writer, 1931-33; copywriter, editor house organ Am. Radiator & Standard San. Corp., N.Y.C., 1933-40; desk editor Archtl. Record, 1940-42; prodn. editor SAE Jour., N.Y.C., 1942-43; pub. relations writer NAM, 1943-47. Condr. workshop on juvenile writing Truro Ctr. for Arts, 1977, 78, 92, Cape Cod Writers Conf., 1990, 91, 92; instr. writing for juveniles Cape Cod Writers Conf., 1965, 66, 92. Author: juvenile books (under name Catherine Woolley) I Like Trains, 1944, rev., 1965, Two Hundred Pennies, 1947, Ginnie and Geneva, 1948, paperback edit., 1988, David's Railroad, 1949, Schoolroom Zoo, 1950, Railroad Cowboy, 1951, Ginnie Joins In, 1951, David's Hundred Dollars, 1952, Lunch for Lennie, 1952 (pub. as L'Incontentabile Gigi in Italy), The Little Car That Wanted a Garage, 1952, The Animal Train and Other Stories, 1953, Holiday on Wheels, 1953, Ginnie and the New Girl, 1954, Ellie's Problem Dog, 1955, A Room for Cathy, 1956, Ginnie and the Mystery House, 1957, Miss Cathy Leonard, 1958, David's Campaign Buttons, 1959, Ginnie and the Mystery Doll, 1960, Cathy Leonard Calling, 1961, paperback edit., 1988, Look Alive, Libby!, 1962, Ginnie and Her Juniors, 1963, Cathy's Little Sister, 1964, paperback edit., 1988, Libby Looks for a Spy, 1965, The Shiny Red Rubber Boots, 1965, Ginnie and the Cooking Contest, 1966, paperback 1979, Ginnie and the Wedding Bells, 1967, Chris in Trouble, 1968, Ginnie and the Mystery Cat, 1969, Libby's Uninvited Guest, 1970, Cathy and the Beautiful People, 1971, Cathy Uncovers a Secret, 1972, Ginnie and the Mystery Light, 1973, Libby Shadows a Lady, 1974, Ginnie and Geneva Cookbook, 1975, adult book Writing for Children, 1990, paperback, 1990; (under name Jane Thayer) The Horse with the Easter Bonnet, 1953, The Popcorn Dragon, 1953, rev. edit. 1989, Korean edit., 1999, Where's Andy?, 1954, Mrs. Perrywinkle's Pets, 1955, Sandy and the Seventeen Balloons, 1955, The Chicken in the Tunnel, 1956, The Outside Cat, 1957, English edit., 1958, 83, Charley and the New Car, 1957, Funny Stories To Read Aloud, 1958, Andy Wouldn't Talk, 1958, The Puppy Who Wanted a Boy, 1958, rev., 1986, paperback edition, 1988, French translation Le Petit Chien Qui Voulait Un Garcon, 1991, Korean translation, 1998, The Second-Story Giraffe, 1959, Little Monkey, 1959, Andy and His Fine Friends, 1960, The Pussy Who Went To the Moon, 1960, English edit., 1961, A Little Dog Called Kitty, 1961, English edit., 1962, 75, The Blueberry Pie Elf, 1961, English edit., 1962, revised edit., 1994, Spanish edit., 1995, Andy's Square Blue Animal, 1962, Gus Was a Friendly Ghost, 1962, English edit., 1971, Japanese edit., 1982, A Drink for Little Red Diker, 1963, Andy and the Runaway Horse, 1963, A House for Mrs. Hopper; the Cat that Wanted to Go Home, 1963, Quiet on Account of Dinosaur, 1964, English edit., 1965, 74, paperback edit., 1988, Emerald Enjoyed the Moonlight, 1964, English edit., 1965, The Bunny in the Honeysuckle Patch, 1965, English edit., 1966, Part-Time Dog, 1965, English edit. 1966, The Light Hearted Wolf, 1966, What's a Ghost Going to Do?, 1966, English edit. 1972, Japanese edit., 1982, The Cat that Joined the Club, 1967, English edit. 1968, Rockets Don't Go To Chicago, Andy, 1967, A Contrary Little Quail, 1968, Little Mr. Greenthumb, 1968, English edit., 1969, Andy and Mr. Cunningham, 1969, Curious, Furious Chipmunk, 1969, I'm Not a Cat, Said Emerald, 1970, English edit. 1971, Gus Was A Christmas Ghost, 1970, English edit. 1973, Japanese edit., 1982, Mr. Turtle's Magic Glasses, 1971, Timothy And Madam Mouse, 1971, English edit., 1972, Gus And The Baby Ghost, 1972, English edit. 1973, Japanese edit., 1982, The Little House, 1972, Andy and the Wild Worm, 1973, Gus Was a Mexican Ghost, 1974, English edit. 1975, Japanese edit., 1982, I Don't Believe in Elves, 1975, The Mouse on the Fourteenth Floor, 1977, Gus Was a Gorgeous Ghost, 1978, English edit., 1979, Where Is Squirrel?, 1979, Try Your Hand, 1980, Applebaums Have a Robot, 1980, Clever Raccoon, 1981, Gus Was a Real Dumb Ghost, 1982, Gus Loved His Happy Home, 1989; contbr. stories to juvenile anthologies in U.S., Great Britain, France, Germany, and Holland, sch. readers, juvenile mags. Trustee Truro Pub. Libraries, 1974-84; Mem. Passaic (N.J.) Bd. Edn., 1953-56, Passaic Redevel. Agy., 1952-53; pres. Passaic LWV, 1949-52. Named mem. N.J. Literary Hall of Fame, 1987; recipient Phantom Friends Lifetime Achievement award, 1992; dedication of Catherine Woolley Children's Rm. in Truro Pub. Libr., 1999. Mem. Authors League Am., Friends of Truro Libr., Truro Hist. Soc., Amnesty Internat. U.S.A., Kenilworth Soc. Democrat. Home: PO Box 71 Truro MA 02666-0071

WOOLLEY, DONNA PEARL, timber and lumber company executive; b. Drain, Oreg., Jan. 3, 1926; d. Chester A. and Mona B. (Cheever) Rydell; m. Harold Woolley, Dec. 27, 1952 (dec. Sept. 1970); children: Daniel, Debra, Donald. Diploma, Drain High Sch. Sec. No. Life Ins. Co., Eugene, Oreg., 1943-44; sec., bookkeeper D & W Lumber Co., Sutherlin, 1944, Woolley Logging Co. & Earl Harris Lumber Co., Drain, 1944-70; pres. Woolley Logging Co., 1970—, Smith River Lumber Co., 1970—, Mt. Baldy Mill, 1970-81, Drain Plywood Co., 1970-81, Woolley Enterprises, Inc., Drain, 1973—, Eagle's View Mgmt. Co., Inc., Eugene, 1981—. Bd. dirs. Wildlife Safari, Winston, 1991, Oreg. Cmty. Found., Portland, 1990-99, chairperson, 1997-99; bd. trustees Linfield Coll., McMinnville, U. Oreg. Found., Eugene, Oreg. Trl. Coun., Boy Scouts Am., 1980—, Umpqua C.C. Fedn., 2001. Recipient Recipient Pioneer award, U. Oreg., 1982, Econ. and Social Devel. award, Soroptimist Club, 1991, First Citizen of Eugene award, 2000, Aubrey Watzek award, Lewis & Clark Coll., Howard Vollum award, 2001. Mem. Oreg. Women's Forum, Pacific Internat. Trapshooting Assn., Amateur Trapshooting Assn., Eugene C. of C. (bd. dirs. 1989-92), Arlington Club, Town Club (bd. dirs., pres.), Sunnydale Grange, Cottage Grove/Eugene Rod & Gun Club. Republican. Avocations: golf, travel. Office: Eagle's View Mgmt Co Inc 1399 Franklin Blvd Eugene OR 97403-1979

WOOLLEY, JOHN EDWARD, trade association executive; b. Jersey City, July 17, 1935; s. Ogden Price and Catherine Hildegard (Tanney) W.; m. Sandra Marina Turtzo, Oct. 23, 1984. BA, Rutgers U., 1957; MBA, U. Ala., 1970; grad., U.S. Naval War Coll., 1977. Commd. U.S. Army, 1957-82, advanced through grades to col., co. comdr. 1st Inf. Divsn. Vietnam, 1965-66; ops. staff officer, exec. officer Office of Dep. Chief of Staff, Ops., U.S. Army, Washington, 1967-69; ops. staff officer, White House briefer Orgn. of Joint Chiefs of Staff, 1970-73; bn. comdr. and chief of staff 1st Inf. div. U.S. Army, Germany, 1973-76; chief of ops. officer III US Corps, U.S. Army, Ft. Hood, Tex., 1977-78; comdr. 2nd Brigade, 2nd Armored div. U.S. Army, 1978-79; planner Office of Dep. Chief of Staff Ops., U.S. Army, Washington, 1979-82; v.p. and sr. v.p. United Coal Co., Bristol, Va., 1982-86; dir. Food Mktg. Inst., Washington, 1988-99, v.p. ops., 1999—. Contbr. articles to profl. jours. Bd. dirs. Jr. Achievement, Bristol, Va., 1984-86. Decorated Legion of Merit (3), Bronze Star medals (2), Army Commendation medal. Mem. Ret. Officers Assn., Am. Soc. Assn. Execs., Country Club of Bristol (bd. dirs. 1983-86), Army Navy Country Club, Tau Kappa Epsilon (chpt. pres. 1956-57). Republican. Roman Catholic. Avocation: golf. Home: 214 Skyline Dr Bristol TN 37620-4141 Office: Food Mktg Inst 655 15th St NW Ste 700 Washington DC 20005-5701 E-mail: jwoolley@fmi.org.

WOOLLEY, J(ONATHAN) MICHAEL, health economist, economic consultant; b. Norfolk, Va., Mar. 2, 1958; s. Herbert Thomas Woolley and Jane Kennedy (Dodson) Genet; m. Diana Elaine Gorrie, Aug. 1, 1987; children: Christian David, Thomas Michael, Jonathan James, David Alexander. BA in Econs., U. Calif., San Diego, 1981; MA in Econs., U. Calif., Santa Barbara, 1983, PhD in Econs., 1987. Economist Fed. Res. Bd., Washington, 1987-89; asst. prof. Sch. Pub. Adminstrn. U. So. Calif., L.A., 1989-93; health economist Amgen Inc., Thousand Oaks, Calif., 1993—. Econ. cons. Econ. Analysis Corp., L.A., 1990—. Co-author: (book) Handbook for Microeconomic Principles, 1983; bd. editors Internat. Jour. of Econs. of Bus., 1993—; contbr. articles to profl. jours. Regents fellow U. Calif., Santa Barbara, 1981-82, Earhart Found. fellow, 1985-86, Haynes Found. fellow, 1990-91. Mem. Internat. Health Econs. Assn., Am. Econ. Assn., Am. Fin. Assn., Western Econ. Assn., Health Econ. Rsch. Orgn. Home: 301 Regal Oak Ct Thousand Oaks CA 91320-4567 Office: Amgen Inc MS 27-4-8 One Amgen Center Dr Thousand Oaks CA 91320-1789

WOOLLEY, MARGARET ANNE (MARGOT WOOLLEY), architect; b. Bangor, Maine, Feb. 4, 1946; d. George Walter and Anne Geneva (Collins) W.; m. Gerard F. Vasisko, June 22, 1985. BA, Vassar Coll., 1969; MArch, Columbia U., 1974. Registered architect. N.Y. Urban designer Mayor's Office Lower Manhattan Devel., 1974-76, Mayor's Office Devel., N.Y.C., 1976-78; project mgr. Office Econ. Devel., 1978-81, dep. dir. design and engring., 1981-83; dep. dir. design. N.Y.C. Pub. Devel. Corp., 1983-85, asst. v.p. design, 1985—86; v.p. design N.Y.C. Econ. Devel. Corp., 1986—94; dep. program dir. corrections program unit N.Y.C. Dept. Design and Constrn., 1996-97, program dir. cts. and juvenile justice units, 1997—2002, asst. commissioner architecture and engring., 2001—. Mem. N.Y. State Licensing Bd. Architecture, 1994—; mem. archtl. registration exam. com. Nat. Coun. Archtl. Registration Bds., 1995—99, mem. practice analysis steering com., 1999—2001; chair archtl. registration exam. specifications task force, 2000—01; mem. archtl. registration exam. devel. task force, 2001—. Assoc. mem. bd. regents L.I. Coll. Hosp., Bklyn., 1982—93, mem. planning and devel. com., 1983—93, pres. assoc. bd. regents, 1988—89. William Kinne Fellows scholar, 1973. Mem. AIA (bd. dirs. N.Y.C. chpt. 1988-90, nat. pub. architects steering com. 1993-95) N.Y. State Assn. Architects (bd. dirs. 1990-92), Heights Casino Club, Vassar Club, Jr. League. Home: 135 Willow St Brooklyn NY 11201-2255

WOOLLEY, MARY ELIZABETH, research administrator; b. Chgo., Mar. 16, 1947; John Joseph and Ellen Louise (Bakke) McEnerney; m. John Stuart Woolley, Dec. 6, 1969 (div. 1985); children: George Newsom, Nora Ellen; m. Michael Howland Campbell, Jan. 1, 1989. BS, Stanford U., 1969; MA, San Francisco State U., 1972; postgrad., U. Calif., San Francisco and Berkeley, 1974-75. Assoc. dir. Inst. Epidemiology and Behavioral Medicine, San Francisco, 1979-81; adminstr. Med. Rsch. Inst. of San Francisco, 1981-82, v.p., adminstr., 1982-86, v.p., exec. dir., 1986-90; pres. Research! Am., Alexandria, Va., 1990—. Cons. in fin. and mgmt. NIH, Bethesda, Md., 1984—92; adj. faculty U. Calif. Sch. Pub. Health, Berkeley, 1983—92, mem. Dean's adv. coun., 1995—2002; founding mem. Whitehead Inst. Bd. Assocs., 1995—; bd. dirs. Lovelace Inst., Respiratory Rsch. Inst., vice chmn., 1999—; lectr. to profl. assns.; mem. bd. visitors Harvard U. Sch. Pub. Health, Cambridge, 2002—. Editor Jour. of Soc. Rsch. Adminstrs., 1986-89, mem. editl. rev. bd., 1989-95; mem. editl. bd. Jour. Women's Health, 1992—, Sci. Comm., 1994—; contbr. articles and editls. to profl. jours. Bd. dirs. Kensington (Calif.) Edn. Found., 1986-89, Enterprise for H.S. Students, 1990-92; mem. capital campaign com. Calif. Shakespeare Festival, 1989-91, v.p. Med. Rsch. Assns. Am., 1993-95; bd. advisors Friends of Cancer Rsch., 1996—; bd. dirs. Nat. Patient Safety Found., 1998-2000. Recipient Silver Touchstone award Am. Hosp. Assn., 1994, Disting. Svc. award Columbia Coll. Physicians and Surgeons, 1994, Advocacy award Fedn. Am. Socs. Exptl. Biology, 1998, Advocacy award Friends Nat. Inst. Nursing Rsch., 1999, Leadership award Coun. Scientific Soc. Pres.'s, 1999. Fellow AAAS; mem. Assn. Ind. Rsch. Insts. (pres.-elect 1987-89, pres. 1989-90), Inst. Medicine (elected), Soc. Rsch. Adminstrs. (bd. dirs. 1986-90, bd. advisors 1990-93, Hartford-Nicholson Svc. award 1990, Disting. Contbn. to Rsch. Adminstrn. award, 1993), Calif. Biomed. Rsch. Assn,. (bd. govs. 1986-90), Md. Gov.'s Commn. on Women's Health, 1993-96. Democrat. Office: Research! Am 908 King St Ste 400E Alexandria VA 22314-3067

WOOLLEY, ROGER SWIRE, lawyer; b. Chgo., Nov. 18, 1924; s/ Anthony Walter and Agnes Louise (MacMurray) W.; m. Patricia Ann Jundt, 1951 (dec. 1978); children: Elliott Payne, Merrit Ann. BA, Coll. William & Mary, 1947; student, Exeter Coll., London, 1947-48; LLB, Columbia U., 1951. Bar: Calif., U.S. Supreme Ct. Legal counsel Solar Aircraft, San Diego, 1952-54; prin. Law Offices of Roger S. Woolley, Rancho Santa Fe, Calif., 1954—. Active Automobile Club So. Calif., L.A., dir. 1974-98, chmn. 1988-90; active Am. Automobile Assn., Falls Church, Va., Orlando, Fla., dir., 1986-97, chmn., 1991-93; founding dir., sec. Bank La Jolla, 1962-68; founding dir., sec. Rancho Santa Fe Savs. & Loan, 1972-78; founding dir., sec. Torrey Pines Bank, 1979-84; dir. Scripps Meml. Hosp. Found., La Jolla, Calif. 1984—; trustee emeritus The Endowment Assn. of Coll. William & Mary, Williamsburg, Va.; chmn., mem. Calif. State Hwy. Commn., 1958-67. Mem. ABA, State Bar Calif., San Diego County Bar Assn., Rotary Club Rancho Santa Fe. Office: Law Offices of Roger S Woolley PO Box R 16903 Avenida de Acacias Rancho Santa Fe CA 92067

WOOLLEY, VICTORIA L. writer; b. Neptune, N.J., July 3, 1969; d. Frank K. Woolley and Marilyn P. Gordon. BA in Print Journalism, Northeastern U.; Spanish cert., U. Carabobo, Valencia, Venezuela; copywriting cert., Inst. Copywriting, Bagley, Eng., 2001—02. Tchr. ESL U. Carabobo, Valencia, 1993—94; mktg. asst. Sony Music Internat., N.Y.C., 1996—97; events coord., mktg. assoc. Am. Stock Exch., 1997—99; writer Victoria Woolley, Copywriting Svc., 2000—; ind. beauty cons. Mary Kay, 2001—. Mem.: Nat. Writers Union, Editl. Freelance Assn. Roman Catholic. Avocations: traveling, exercising. Home: Apt 6D 1482 York Ave New York NY 10021-8821

WOOLLING, KENNETH RAU, vascular internist; b. Indpls., Mar. 6, 1918; m. Catherine Margaret McColl, Mar. 20, 1948; 2 children. BA magna cum laude, Butler U., 1939; postgrad., Harvard U., 1939-40; MD, Ind. U., 1943; MS in Medicine, U. Minn., 1951. Diplomate Nat. Bd. Med. Examiners, Am. Bd. Internal Medicine, Am. Bd. Cardiovascular Disease. Intern Indpls. City Hosp. (now Wishard Meml.), Indpls., 1943-44; resident in internal medicine Marion County Gen. Hosp., 1947; fellow, first asst. internal medicine Mayo Found., Rochester, Minn., 1948-52; mem. med. staff, mem. tchg. staff postgrad. med. edn. Marion County Gen. Hosp. (name now Wishard Meml. Hosp.), Indpls., 1952—; founder, dir., peripheral vascular diseases clinic Indpls City & Marion County Gen. Hosp. (now Wishard Meml.), 1952-68; pvt. practice internal medicine and cardiovascular diseases Indpls, 1952—; founder, dir. peripheral vascular diseases clinic Meth. Hosp., Indpls., 1967-72, founder, dir. vascular lab., 1970-73, mem. med. staff, tchr. staff postgrad. med. edn., 1952—. Mem. med. staff St. Vincent Hosp., St. Francis Hosp. and Winona Meml. Hosp., Indpls., 1952—; charter mem. med. staff Cmty. Hosp., Indpls., 1952—; charter mem. med. adv. com. Butler U., Indpls, 1956—. Contbr. articles to profl. jours., 1950—. Capt. Med. Corps U.S. Army, 1944-46. Fellow ACP, Am. Coll. Chest Physicians, Coun. on Cardiology Am. Heart Assn., Am. Coll. Angiology (gov. state of Ind. 1979-80); mem. AMA (50 Yr. award 1993), SAR, Internat. Union Angiology, Am. Soc. Internal Medicine, Am. Diabetes Assn., Ind. State Med. Soc., Ind. Diabetes Assn., Am. Fedn. for Clin. Rsch., N.Y. Acad. Med. Scis., North Ctrl. Clin. Soc., Mayo Cardiovascular Soc., Ind. Hist. Soc., Res. Officers Assn., Indpls. Med. Soc., Am. Legion, Shriners, Masons (Scottish Rite and Mystic Tie Lodge, 50 yr. award 1989), Contemporary Club of Indpls., Indpls. Athletic Club, Highland Golf and Country Club, Phi Delta Theta (50 yr. award 1985), Phi Kappa Phi, Phi Chi. Presbyterian. Office: PO Box 80192 Indianapolis IN 46280-0192

WOOLSEY, DAVID ARTHUR, leasing company executive; b. Oakland, Calif., Nov. 27, 1941; BS, U. San Francisco, 1963; MBA, U. Calif., Berkeley, 1965. Mgr. lease and spl. projects fin. Kaiser Aluminum & Chem. Corp., Oakland, Calif., 1965-68; v.p. U.S. Leasing Internat., Inc., San Francisco, 1968-78; exec. v.p. GATX Capital Corp., 1978, 1982-88, also bd. dirs.; COO Orix U.S.A. Corp., 1988-98, also bd. dirs.; group pres. Capital Fin., Heller Fin., Inc., 1998—. Republican. Roman Catholic. Home: 308 Village View Ct Orinda CA 94563-2700 E-mail: dwoolsey@hellerfin.com.

WOOLSEY, JOHN MUNRO, JR. lawyer; b. N.Y.C., Apr. 22, 1916; s. John M. and Alice B. (Bacon) W.; m. Ledlie Laughlin, Dec. 27, 1948; children: John, Alice, Henry, Mary. BA, Yale U., 1938, LL.B., 1941. Bar: N.Y. 1941, Mass. 1947. Assoc. Debevoise, Stevenson, Plimpton & Page, N.Y.C., 1941-42; with Bd. Econ. Warfare, Washington, 1942; with firm Herrick & Smith and predecessor firms, Boston, 1946-86, ptnr., 1956-83, of counsel, 1984-86, Palmer & Dodge, 1986—. With Office of U.S. Chief of Counsel, Nürnberg Trials, Germany, 1945-46 Former pres. Trustees of Reservations, Shady Hill Sch. Served to lt. USNR, 1942-46. Decorated Order of White Lion (Czechoslovakia) Mem. Am. Antiquarian Soc., Am. Law Inst., Century Assn., Tavern Club. Office: Palmer & Dodge One Beacon St Boston MA 02108

WOOLSEY, LYNN, congresswoman; b. Seattle, Nov. 3, 1937; BS, U. San Francisco, 1981. Mem. U.S. Congress from 6th Calif. dist., 1993—; mem. edn. and workforce com., sci. com. Mem. Petaluma City Coun., 1984-92 Democrat. Office: US Ho Reps 2263 Rayburn Ho Office Bldg Washington DC 20515-0506*

WOOLSON, CHARLES E., JR. lawyer; b. Woodbury, N.J., June 6, 1953; s. Charles E. and Alice Woolson; 1 child, Jennifer E. BA, Temple U., 1975; JD, Widener U., 1977. Bar: N.J., Va., U.S. Dist. Ct. N.J., U.S. Ct. Appeals (3d cir.), U.S. Supreme Ct; cert. N.J. Supreme Ct. Asst. claims atty. Fidelity & Deposit, Richmond, Va., 1978-81; atty. Davidow & Davidow, Millville, NJ, 1981, Montano Summers Mullen Manuel & Owens, Cherry Hill, 1982—86, Law Offices of Roger Steedle, Absecon, 1986—2002; prin. Law Firm of Charles E. Woolson, Jr., L.L.C., Hammonton, 2002—. Mem. Atlantic County Rep. Com., 1996—. Mem. Trial Attys. of N.J. (trustee 1996—), N.J. Bar Assn. (spl. com. mcpl. ct. practice). Office: 104 Bellevue Ave PO Box 851 Hammonton NJ 08037 E-mail: woollaw@eticomm.net.

WOOLSTON-CATLIN, MARIAN, psychiatrist; b. Seattle, Jan. 20, 1931; d. Howard Brown and Katharine Nichols (Dally) Woolston; m. Randolph Catlin Jr., July 5, 1959; children: Laura Louise, Jennifer Woolston, Randolph III. BA cum laude, Vassar Coll., 1951; MD, Harvard U., 1955. Diplomate Nat. Bd. Med. Examiners. Intern in pediat. medicine Children's Hosp., Boston, 1956, asst. resident in pediat. medicine, 1956; resident in psychiatry Mass. Mental Health Ctr., 1957-59; fellow in child psychiatry Tavistock Clin., London, 1960; commonwealth fellow in child psychiatry Harvard U. at Gaebler Children's Unit, Waltham, Mass., 1975-78, clin. instr. psychiatry, 1978-79; pvt. practice Wellesley Hills, 1978-91, Medfield, 1991—. Clin. instr. psychiatry Harvard U. at Mass. Mental Health Ctr., Boston, 1957-59, 78-82, Tufts U. at Mass. Mental Health Ctr., 1957-59; mem. exec. bd. Parents' and Children's Svcs., Boston, 1983-86. Designer H.H. Hunnewell Meml. Garden for New England Flower Show Mass. Hort. Soc., 1975 (Ames Cup award). Mem. exec. bd. Ext. Divsn. New Eng. Conservatory Music., 1972-75; charter mem. reuse com. Medfield State Hosp., 1992—. Fellow Am. Acad. Child and Adolescent Psychiatry; mem. AMA, Am. Psychiat. Assn. (life mem.), Mass. Psychiat. Assn., Mass. Med. Soc., Boston Vassar Club (exec. bd. 1963-75), Hills Garden Club Wellesley (exec. bd. and design chief 1973-75). Episcopalian. Avocations: landscape design, sculpting. Home and Office: 314 North St Medfield MA 02052-1204

WOOLUMS, MARGARET CARMICHAEL, thoroughbred bloodline researcher; b. Charleston, W.Va., Aug. 8, 1935; d. H. St. G.T. Jr. and Margaret Lyle (MacCorkle) Carmichael; m. Dan Dudley Gravitt (div. 1956); 1 child Margaret Alexander Lyle; m. William Howard Woolums Jr. (dec. 1992); 1 child, Anna Hetzel Woolums Carney. BBA, U. Ky., 1960. Statistician Blood-Horse Mag., Lexington, Ky., 1954-66; adminstrv. asst., stats. bur. The Jockey Club, 1966-69; sec., treas. Pedigree Assocs., Inc., 1970-82, pres., 1982-96; v.p. info. Racing Corp. of Am., Inc. div. Ky. Horse Ctr., 1990-91; pres. Pedigree Prodns., Inc., Lexington, 1990—; breeder thoroughbred horses, 1988—. Adviser Internat. Cataloguing Stds., London, 1982—; editor, owner South Am. Thoroughbred Qtr. mag., 1990-92; divsn. dir. Ky. Racing Commn., 1992-93; prin. asst. Ky. Pub. Svc. Commn., 1993-95; coord. internat. info. Jockey Club Racing Svcs., Inc., 1995-2001. Editor Racing Update, Inc., 1993-95; contbr. articles to topical publs. Mem. Thoroughbred Club Am., Cen. Ky. Riding for Handicapped (bd. dirs. 1986-91), Va. Horse Ctr. (bd. dirs. 1985-91), Shoemaker Found. (host com. 1995-99). Democrat. Episcopalian. Office: Pedigree Prodns Inc 909911 N Broadway Lexington KY 40505 E-mail: arazi@mis.net.

WOOLWORTH, SUSAN VALK, primary school educator; b. Toledo, Apr. 24, 1954; d. Robert Earl and Alice (Melick) Valk; children: Alison Valk, Andrew Baker. BA, Pine Manor Jr. Coll., Chestnut Hill, Mass., 1974; BS, Boston U., 1976. Tchr. kindergarten Lancaster (Pa.) Country Day Sch., 1986—. Bd. dirs. Fulton Opera House; past bd. dirs. Planned Parenthood, Vis. Nurse Assn., Hands-On House. Mem. Jr. League (sustainer), Sigma Gamma. Republican. Episcopalian. Avocations: walking, gardening, tennis, decorating.

WOOSLEY, RAYMOND, pharmacology and medical educator; b. Ky., Oct. 2, 1942; m. Julianne Buchert. BS, Western Ky. U., 1964; PhD, U. Louisville, 1967; MD, U. Miami, 1973. Intern, resident Vanderbilt U. Hosp., Nashville, 1973-76; sr. pharmacologist, dir. rsch. Meyer (Glaxo) Labs., Ft. Lauderdale, Fla., 1968-71; instr. dept. medicine, pharmacology Vanderbilt U., Nashville, 1976-77, asst. prof., 1977-79, assoc. prof., 1979-84, assoc. dir. clin. rsch. ctr., 1981-88, prof., 1984-88; prof. pharmacology, medicine, chmn. dept. pharmacology Georgetown U. Sch. Medicine, Washington, 1988-2000; assoc. dean clin. rsch., 2001—; also chief divsn. clin. pharmacology Georgetown U. Sch. Medicine, Washington, 1988-94; dir. Inst. for Cardiovascular Scis., 1995-2000, Gen. Clin. Rsch. Ctr., Washington, 1999-2001; v.p. Ariz. Health Scis. Ctr., 2001—; dean Sch. Medicine U. Ariz., 2001—02. Bd. dirs. U.S. Pharmacopeia, 2000—; rschr. in field. Editor: Cardiovascular Pharmacology and Therapeutics, 1994; contbr. chpts. to books and articles to profl. jours. NIH Predoctoral fellow NIH, 1964-67, postdoctoral fellow U. Louisville, 1967-68, Vanderbilt U., 1976-77, Am. Coll. Clin. Pharmacology fellow, 1974; Ogden scholar Western Ky. U., 1960-64; recipient Career Devel. award in Clin. Pharmacology Pharm. Mfrs. Assn. Found., 1977-80. Fellow ACP, Am. Coll. Clin. Pharmacology; mem. Am. Heart Assn. (fellow coun. clin. cardiology 1985—), Am. Soc. Pharmacology and Exptl. Therapeutics (clin. pharmacology exec. com. 1981-92, Harry Gold award 2001), Am. Fedn. Clin. Rsch., Am. Soc. Clin. Pharmacology and Therapeutics (v.p. 1998-99, pres.1999, Rawls-Palmer award 1990), Am. Bd. Clin. Pharmacology, Assn. Med. Sch. Pharmacology (pres. 1996-98), Soc. for Women's Health Rsch. (bd. dirs. 1999—). Office: Ariz Health Sci Ctr 245018 AHSCCI 1501 N Campbell Ave # 2222 Tucson AZ 85724-5018 E-mail: WoosleyR@u.arizona.edu.

WOOSNAM, IAN HAROLD, professional golfer; b. St. Martins, Shropshire, U.K., Mar. 2, 1958; s. Harold and Joan Woosnam; m. Glendryth Mervyn Pugh, Nov. 12, 1983; children: Daniel Ian, Rebecca Louise, Ami Victoria. Ed., St. Martins Modern Sch. Profl. golfer, 1976—. Tournament winner News of the World under 23 match-play, 1979, Cacharel under 25 Championship, 1982, Swiss Open, 1982, Silk Cut Masters, 1983, Scandinavian Enterprise Open, 1984, Zambian Open, 1985, Lawrence Batley TPC, 1986, 555 Kenya Open, 1986, Hong Kong Open, 1987, Jersey Open, 1987, Cepsa Madrid Open, 1987, Bell's Scottish Open, 1987, 90, Lancome Trophy, 1987, 93, Suntory World Match-Play Championship, 1987, 90, World Cup (Wales) Team and Individual, 1987, Million Dollar Challenge, 1987, Welsh Pro Championship, 1988, Volvo PGA Championship, 1988, Panasonic European Open, 1988, Carrols Irish Open, 1988, 89, AmEx Med Open, 1990, Epson Grand Prix, 1990, Torras Monte Carlo Open, 1990, 91, Fujitsu Mediterranean Open, 1991, U.S. Masters, 1991, USF&G Classic, 1991, PGA Grand Slam of Golf, 1991, World Cup Individual, 1991, European Montecarlo Open, 1992, Murphy's English Open, 1993, Air France Cannes Open, 1994, Brit. Masters, 1994, Johnnie Walker Classic, 1996, Scottish Open, 1996, German Open, 1996, Heineken Classic, 1996, Volvo PGA Championship, 1997, Hyundai Motor Masters, 1997; ranked 1st Sony world rankings, 1991, Ryder Cup Team Mem., 1983, 85 (winners), 87 (winners), 89, 91, 93, 95 (winners), 97 (winners), Cisco World Match Play champaionship, 2001. Avocations: snooker, sports, water skiing.

WOOSNAM, RICHARD EDWARD, venture capitalist, lawyer; b. Anderson, Ind., June 27, 1942; s. Richard Wendelland and Ruth (Cleveland) W.; m. Diane Dalto, Jan. 12, 2002; children: Cynthia S., Elizabeth C. BS, Ind. U., 1964, JD, 1967, MBA, 1968. Bar: Ind. 1967, U.S. Dist. Ct. (so. dist.) Ind. 1967. Instr. bus. law Ind. U., Bloomington, 1966-68; assoc. Ferguson, Ferguson & Lloyd, 1967-68; dep. pros. Monroe County, 1967-68; tax acct. Price Waterhouse, Phila., 1968-69; v.p., treas. Innovest Group, Inc., 1969-82, chmn., pres., 1983—. Guest lectr. Wharton Sch. Bus., U. Pa., Ind. U., Bloomington, 1975—; bd. dirs. Capital Mgmt. Corp., N.Y. Achievement, L.L.C., Innovest Talent Svcs., Inc., Command Equity Group, LLC, Bridges Learning Sys., Inc., Ind. U. Found., World Affairs Coun. of Phila., Fairmount Park Conservancy, Phila. Hospitality, Inc., Ctr. for Entrepreneurship and Innovation; trustee Pa. Acad. Fine Arts. Bd. dirs. Walnut St. Theatre; mem. nat. adv. bd. Point Breeze Performing Arts Ctr. Mem. ABA, Ind. Bar Assn., Union League of Phila., Sunday Breakfast Club, The Pa Soc. Home: 1810 Spruce St Philadelphia PA 19103-6677 Office: 2000 Market St Ste 1400 Philadelphia PA 19103-3214

WOOSTER, MARTIN MORSE, author, editor; b. Washington, Nov. 30, 1957; s. Harold Abbott and Marcia Wooster. BA, Beloit (Wis.) Coll., 1980. Staff writer Network News, Washington, 1983; Washington editor Harper's Mag., 1983-87; assoc. editor Wilson Quarterly, 1987-88; contbg. editor Reason, 1988—2001, Washington editor, 1988-91; assoc. editor Am. Enterprise, 1994—2002. Vis. fellow Capital Rsch. Ctr., Washington, 1993—. Author: Angry Classrooms, Vacant Minds, 1994, The Great Philanthropists and the Problem of Donor Intent, 1994, rev., 1998, Should Foundations Live Forever: The Question of Perpetuity, 1998, Return to Charity, 2000, The

Foundation Builders, 2000; contbg. editor: Philanthropy, 2000—, Strategy & Business, 2000-02. Mem. Free Press Assn. (H.L. Mencken award 1988). Republican. Office: PO Box 8093 Silver Spring MD 20907-8093

WOOSTER, ROBERT, history educator; b. Beaumont, Tex., Aug. 27, 1956; s. Ralph Ancil and Edna Lee (Jones) W.; m. Catherine Cox, 1992. BA, Lamar U., 1977, MA, 1979; PhD, U. Tex., 1985. Scholar in residence Tex. State Hist. Assn., Liberty, 1985-86; asst. prof. Tex. A&M U., Corpus Christi, 1986-90, assoc. prof., 1990-95, prof., 1995—, chmn. dept. humanities, 1997—2002, Frantz prof. history, 2001—. Author: Soldiers, Sutlers and Settlers (Bates award 1987), U.S. Military and Indian Policy, 1988, History of Fort Davis, 1990, Nelson A. Miles and The Twilight of the Frontier Army, 1993, The Civil War 100, 1998, The Civil War Bookshelf, 2001; editl. adv. bd. Southwestern Hist. Quar., Austin, Tex., 1989—, Military History of the West, 1995—, Jour. of the West, 1996-2000. Dep. dir. U.S. Mil. Acad./ROTC fellowship U.S. Mil. Acad., West Point, N.Y., 1990. Mem. Tex. State Hist. Assn., Orgn. Am. Historians. Democrat. Home: 4600 Ocean Dr Apt 708 Corpus Christi TX 78412-2543 Office: Texas A&M Univ 6300 Ocean Dr Corpus Christi TX 78412-5599

WOOSTER, WARREN S(CRIVER), marine science educator; b. Westfield, Mass., Feb. 20, 1921; s. Harold Abbott and Violet (Scriver) W.; m. Clarissa Pickles, Sept. 13, 1948; children: Susan Wooster Allen, Daniel, Dana. Sc.B., Brown U., 1943; MS, Calif. Inst. Tech., 1947; PhD, UCLA, 1953. From research asst. to prof. Scripps Instn. Oceanography, U. Calif., 1948-73; dir. UNESCO Office Oceanography, 1961-63; dean Rosenstiel Sch. Marine Atmospheric Sci., U. Miami, 1973-76; prof. marine studies and fisheries U. Wash., Seattle, 1976-91, prof. emeritus, 1992, dir. Inst. Marine Studies, 1979-82. Contbr. to books, profl. jours. Served with USNR, 1943-46. Fellow Am. Geophys. Union, Am. Meterol. Soc.; mem. Sigma Xi. Office: U Wash Sch Marine Affairs 3707 Brooklyn Ave NE Seattle WA 98105-6715 E-mail: wooster@u.washington.edu.

WOOTAN, GERALD DON, osteopathic physician, educator; b. Oklahoma City, Nov. 19, 1944; s. Ralph George and Corrinne (Loafman) W. BA, Ctrl. State U., Edmond, Okla., 1970, BS, 1971, MEd, 1974; MB, U. Okla., Oklahoma City, 1978; DO, Okla. State U., 1985. Dir. mfg. engring. lab. GE, Oklahoma City, 1965-70; counseling psychologist VA Hosp., 1970-76; physician asst. Thomas (Okla.) Med. Clin., 1978-81; pvt. practice, Jenks, Okla., 1986—; intern Tulsa Regional Med. Ctr., 1985-86; assoc. prof. Okla. State U. Coll. Osteo. Medicine, 1986—, with Springer Clinic, 1995-98; owner Jenks (Okla.) Health Team LLC, 1998—. Chmn. gen. practice quality assurance Tulsa Regional Med. Ctr., 1989-91; v.p. New Horizons Counseling Ctr., Clinton, Okla., 1977-81; sr. aviation med. examiner FAA, Tulsa, 1991—; pres. S.W. Diagnostics, Inc., Tulsa, 1989-91, Okla. Edn. Found. Osteo. Medicine, Tulsa, 1988-89, 96, trustee Tulsa Long Term Care Authority; med. dir. Grace Living Ctr. Contbr. articles to profl. jours.; patentee for human restraint. Advancement chmn., chmn. Eagle bd. rev. Boy Scouts Am., Tulsa, 1987-88; trustee Tulsa Long Term Care Authority, 1988-91; trustee Tulsa Community Found. for Indigent Health Care, Inc., 1988-91. With USN, 1962-64. Named Clin. Preceptor of Yr., U. Okla., 1980, Outstanding Alumni award Okla. State U. Coll. Osteo. Medicine, 1990. Mem.: Am. Coll. Osteo. Family Physicians (cert. of added qualification in geriatrics 1982, bd. cert. 1993, pres. Okla. chpt. 1993—94, qualified hyperbaric oxygen therapy 2001, med. dir. Narconon Drug Treatment Ctr.), Okla. Acad. Gen. Practitioners (pres.), Am. Coll. Gen. Practitioners, Am. Acad. Physician Assts., Tulsa Dist. Osteo. Soc. (pres. 1991—92), Okla. Osteo. Assn. (legis. bur. 1986—2001, trustee 1998—2001, membership bur. 1998—2001, bur. on membership benefits 1998—2001), Am. Osteo. Assn., Okla. State U. Coll. Osteo. Medicine Alumni Assn. (pres. 1988—89). Avocations: scuba diving, aviation medicine. Home: 4320 E 100th St Tulsa OK 74137-5305 Address: 715 W Main St Ste S Jenks OK 74037-3553 Office: Ste S 715 W Main St Jenks OK 74037-3553

WOOTEN, AUSTIN FRANKLIN, lobbyist, educator, writer; b. Washington, May 14, 1951; s. Julius Jr. and Doris Issabelle (Abbott) W.; m. Diane Elizabeth Carelock, Dec. 26, 1981; 1 child, Austing Franklin Jr. BA, Howard U., Washington, 1973, MEd, 1980; MBA, Southeastern U., 2001. Cert. spl. edn. provisional tchr., D.C.; cert. tchr. secondary social studies, Va.; notary pub. Collection specialist Libr. of Congress, Washington, 1980-86; instrnl. svc. specialist D.C. Pub. Schs., 1986-91, inclusion specialist, 1997-98; assessment specialist Potomac Job Corps, 1992-95; residential advisor, tutor Grafton Sch./D.C. Tutors, Washington and Rockville, Md., 1995-97; spl. edn. tchr. Leary Sch., Oxon Hill, 1996-97; lobbyist Bonner and Assocs., Washington, 1999—; writer-editor Exec. Personnel Svcs., U.S. HUD, 2000—. Author; (poems) Precious Pieces (The Nameless People), 1995 (Mark Waxman Archives 1996); (novels) The Deprogrammer, 1983, Blind Luck, 1994; author, lyricist: What Shall We Do?, 1999; author instrnl. TV guides for first instrnl. fixed TV sys. D.C. Pub. Schs. Chief election judge P.G. County Bd. Elections, Oxon Hill, Md., 1991-95; fundraiser Dem. Nat. Com., Washington, summer 1996. Recipient cert. of appreciation U.S. Ho. of Reps. Page Sch., Washington, 1997, Editor's Choice award, 2000, award Internat. Libr. Poetry, Owings Mill, Md., 2000. Mem. Soc. Tng. and Devel., Soc. Tech. Comm., Washington Tchrs. Union, K.C. (2nd degree). Roman Catholic. Avocations: writing, poetry, chess, stamp collection, coin collecting.

WOOTEN, CECIL AARON, religious organization administrator; b. Laurel, Miss., June 3, 1924; s. Cecil A. and Alice (Cox) W.; m. Helen Moss, Apr. 4, 1947; children: Michael, Margaret, Martin, Marsha, Mark. BS in Mech. Engring, U. Ala., 1949. With CBI Industries, 1941—, bd. dirs., 1965-83; mng. dir. CBI Constructors Ltd., London, 1957-62; mgr. (Houston sales dist.), 1962-64; v.p., mgr. corp. services Oak Brook, Ill., 1968-69; sr. v.p.-gen. sales mgr., 1969-78; sr. v.p. comml. devel. Chgo. Bridge & Iron Co. (subs. CBI Industries), 1978-79; sr. v.p. corp. adminstrn. CBI Industries, Oak Brook, 1980-83; dir. devel. Christian Family Services, Gainesville, Fla., 1983-86, Denver Ch. of Christ, 1986-88, Boston Ch. of Christ, 1988-92; pres. Internat. Chs. of Christ, Inc., L.A., 1994-99; 2000chair Internat. Chs. Christ, 1999—2000. Bd. dirs. Oak Brook (Ill.) Bank. Former trustee Elmhurst (Ill.) Coll.; former bd. sponsors Good Samaritan Hosp., Downers Grove, Ill. Served to 1st lt. AUS, 1943-46. Mem. ASME, Nat. Soc. Profl. Engrs. Lodges: Rotary. Office: 3731 Wilshire Blvd Ste 800 Los Angeles CA 90010

WOOTEN, FRANK THOMAS, retired research facility executive; b. Fayetteville, N.C., Sept. 24, 1935; s. Frank Thomas and Katherine (McRae) Wooten; m. Linda Walker, July 14, 1962; children: Laurin Walker, Patrick Thomas, Ashley Tripp. BSEE, Duke U., 1957, PhD, 1964. Engr. Corning Glass Works, Raleigh, NC, 1964—66; from engr. to pres. Rsch. Triangle Inst., Research Triangle Park, 1966—89, pres., 1989—99, ret., 1999. Bd. dirs. N.C. Biotech. Ctr., Troxler Electronics Labs., N.C. Biosci. Investment Fund. Contbr. articles on semiconductors and biomedical engring. to profl. publs.; patentee semiconductors tech. Lt. (j.g.) USN, 1957—59. Recipient Disting. Engring. Alumnus award, Duke U., 1991; fellow, Shell, 1961. Mem.: IEEE, Nat. Inst. Stats. Scis. (corp. 1990—98), Ballistic Missile Def. Orgn. (tech. application rev. panel 1990—94), Assn. for Advancement Med. Instrumentation (chmn. com. on aerospace tech. 1971—77). Baptist.

WOOTEN, FREDERICK (OLIVER WOOTEN), applied science educator; b. Linwood, Pa., May 16, 1928; s. Frederick Alexander and Martha Emma (Guild) W.; m. Jane Watson MacPherson, Aug. 30, 1952; children: Donald, Bartley. BS in Chemistry, MIT, 1950; PhD in Chemistry, U. Del., 1955. Sr. scientist Lawrence Livermore (Calif.) Lab., 1957-72; prof. applied sci. U. Calif., Davis, 1972-99, prof. emeritus, 1999—. Vis. prof. physics Drexel U., Phila., 1964, Chalmers Tech. H.S., Goteborg, Sweden, 1967-68, Heriot-Watt U., Edinburgh, Scotland, 1979, Trinity Coll., Dublin, Ireland, 1986, Mich. State U., East Lansing, 1993, Boston U., 1996; vis. scholar in math. U. Mass., Amherst, 1991; staff physicist All-Am. Engring. Co., Wilmington, Del., 1955-57; chmn. applied sci. U. Calif., Davis, 1973-93, chmn. designated emphasis in computational sci., 1989-2000; cons. in field. Author: Optical Properties of Solids, 1972. Mem. AAAS, Am. Phys. Soc., N.Y. Acad. Scis., Sigma Xi. Home: 2328 Alameda Diablo Diablo CA 94528 Office: U Calif Dept Applied Sci Davis CA 95616 E-mail: wooten@netvista.net.

WOOTEN, HOLLIS DARWIN, engineer; b. South Pittsburg, Tenn., Sept. 29, 1939; s. Lawson Wade and Lila Mae (Hill) W.; m. Elserean Phelps, June 26, 1976. BS in Engring., U. Tenn., 1975. Advanced engr. Westinghouse, Richland, Wash., 1975-79, sr. engr. Oak Ridge, Tenn., 1979-84; sr. design engr. Los Alamos Tech. Assn., 1984-86; devel. assoc. Oak Ridge Gaseous Diffusion Plant, 1987-89; devel. staff mem. Oak Ridge Nat. Lab., 1989-92, devel. group leader, 1992—. Scoutmaster Boy Scouts Am., South Pittsburg, 1960; pres. McReynolds PTA, South Pittsburg, 1960; mem. South Pittsburg Aux. Police, 1967. Mem. ASHRAE, Tenn. Soc. Profl. Engrs., Order of Engr., K.C. (mem. coun.), Chattanooga Engrs. Club. Roman Catholic. Avocation: hunting. Office: Martin Marietta Energy Sys Oak Rigde Nat Lab K-25 Site PO Box 2003 Oak Ridge TN 37831-2003

WOOTEN, MICHAEL ERIC, United States Marine officer; b. San Diego, June 12, 1959; s. James Willis and Elease (Lewis) W. AA, DeKalb C.C., 1981; BA in Psychology, Chapman U., 1986; MA in Leadership and Orgnl. Mgmt., Norwich U., 1996; MS in Acquisition and Contract Mgmt., Naval Postgrad. Sch., 1997. Notary pub., Va.; U.S. contracting officer warrant; def. acquisition cert. Level III. Air traffic controller Hdqs. & Hdqs. Squadron, Tustin, Calif., 1983-86; commd. 2nd lt. USMC, 1987, advanced through grades to maj., 1997; officer student, 1987-88; asst. supply officer Second Maintenance Battalion, Camp LeJeune, N.C., 1988-89; supply officer Second Landing Support Battalion, 1989-90; protocol officer Marine Corps Logistics Base, Albany, Ga., 1990; asst. br. head Mgmt. Br. Integrated Logistics Support, 1990-91; aide-de-camp Marine Corps Logistics Base, 1991-92; logistics officer Hdqs. Battalion, 1992-93; supply officer First Light Anti Aircraft Missile Battalion, Yuma, Ariz., 1993—96; student Naval Postgrad. Sch., 1996-97; contracting officer Hdqs. USMC, Washington, 1998—2001, NATO Summit Staff, 1999—2001; dep. dir. Marine corps Regional Contracting Office, 2001—02; contracting officer, chief of contracting Coalition Forces Landing Component Command, 2002; comdg. officer Tenant Activities Co. Hdqrs. Btn., Marine Corps Base, Quantico, 2002. Nonresident dir. Navy Mut. Aid Assn., Arlington, Va., 1994; regional dir. NPS Taekwondo Assn. Schs., Va. Decorated Navy Commendation medal, Joint Svc. Commendation medal, Meritorious Svc. medal, Army Commendation medal, Mil. Outstanding vol. Svc. medal, Superior Svc. award Outstanding Marine Corps student, 1997. Mem. NAACP, Nat. Contract Mgmt. Assn., Marine Corps Assn., Mensa, Phi Beta Sigma. Episcopalian. Avocations: writing, tae kwon do (3d degree black belt). Office: Commanding Officer Tenant Activities Co Hdqrs and Svc Battalion 2006 Hawkins Ave Quantico VA 22134

WOOTON, WILLIAM ROBERT, state legislator, lawyer; b. Providence, Sept. 20, 1944; s. Robert O. and Beulah (Bennett) W.; m. Shirliebeth Wenzel, Aug. 25, 1968; children: William Robert Jr., Richard Bennett, Russell Owen. BBA, Marshall U., 1966; postgrad., Ohio U., 1966-67; JD, W.Va. U., 1971. Bar: U.S. Dist. Ct. (no. and so. dists.) W.Va. 1971, U.S. Ct. Appeals (4th cir.) 1972. Law clk. U.S. Cir. Judge John A. Field, Charleston, W.Va., 1971-72; asst. atty. gen. Atty. Gen. of W.Va., 1972-74; asst. prosecuting atty. Raleigh County Prosecuting Atty., Beckley, W.Va., 1974-76; ptnr. Wooton Law Firm, 1977—. Del. W.Va. Ho. of Dels., Charleston, 1977-86, 89-90; senator W.Va. Senate, Charleston, 1991—, chmn. jud. com. Col. W. Va. Army N.G., ret. Mem. Rotary. Democrat. Baptist. Office: PO Box 59 Beckley WV 25802-0059

WOOTTEN, JOHN ROBERT, investor; b. Feb. 5, 1929; s. Henry Hughes and Ella Gayle (Ditzler) W.; m. Mary Lou Schmausser, Mar. 15, 1952 (div.); children: Pamela Jean, Robert Hughes; m. Geraldine Ann Theisen, Aug. 14, 1982. BS, Colo. A&M U., 1953. Sec. S.W. Radio & Equipment Co., Oklahoma City, 1953-55; pres. Belcaro Homes, Inc., 1955-60, Bob Wootten Ford, Yukon, Okla., 1960-68, Bus. Data Sys., 1968-72; chmn., CEO 1st Nat. Bank, Moore, Okla., 1970-72; pres. Commn. Enterprises, Inc., Liberal, Kans., 1967-79, Trebor Leasing Co., 1965-87, Okla. Sch. Book Depository, Inc., Oklahoma City, 1976-80, S.W. Sch. Depository, Inc., Dallas, 1976-86; chmn., CEO Exch. Nat. Bank Del City, Okla., 1976-78; dir. S.W. Bancshares Corp., Oklahoma City. Pres. Okla. chpt. Am. Cancer Soc., 1966-67, Okla. chpt. Arthritis Found., 1973-76, Lyric Theater, Okla., 1976-77; chmn. bd. trustees Bone and Joint Hosp., 1976-81; bd. dirs. Okla. Theater Ctr., Dallas Theater Ctr.; trustee Oklahoma City U.; pres. Last Frontier coun. Boy Scouts Am., 1968-70; Rep. nominee for Lt. Gov. of Okla., 1966. Mem. Ind. Bankers Assn., Am. Bankers Assn., Tex. Bookmen's Assn., Okla. Bookmen's Assn., Tex. Assn. Sch. Adminstrs., Econ. Club Okla., Navy League, Rotary (pres. Oklahoma City 1963-64, dist. gov. 5520 1998-99). Home: 6760 Gato Rd El Paso TX 79932-3210 E-mail: woottens@aol.com.

WOOTTEN, PATRICIA EILEEN, director, educator; b. Washington, Jan. 3, 1968; d. Morgan Bayard and Katherine (Bourg) Wootten. BS History and Polit. Sci., U. Md., 1991. Cert. ESL tutor 1992, literacy tutor 1992. Author: (poetry) Keeping the Memories, 1997, My Mon Amie, 2000 (Poet of Merit award Internat. Soc. of Poets, 2001), Stitches, 2001 (Poet of Merit award Internat. Soc. of Poets, 2002), Defy the Impossible, 2001, Acknowledging Delores, 2001 (Poet of Merit award Internat. Soc. of Poets, 2000), (collection of poetry) Inspirations, 1989; editor (asst. editor): (newsletter) St. Mark's Family Newsletter of St. Mark's Cath. Ch., 1993—98; co-editor: MOSAIC Classified Staff Orgn. Internal Newsletter of Prince George's C.C., 1998—99. RCIA Sponsor St. Mark's Cath. Ch., Hyattsville, 1992—93; RCIC coord. and tchr. Acension Cath. Ch., Bowie, 2001—; mem. Folk Group Holy Redeemer Cath. Ch., College Park , 1994—97; chief election judge Prince George's County Bd. of Elections, Upper Marlboro, 1994—96; rep. Classified Staff Orgn. Prince George's C.C., Largo, 1995—; ESL & Literacy Tutor Literacy Coun. of Prince George's County, Landover, 1992—97; cheerleading coach St. Mark's Cath. Sch., Hyattsville, 1987—89. Mem.: Psi Beta. Roman Catholic. Avocations: swimming, gymnastics, travel, writing, photography. Office: Prince George's CC 301 Largo Rd Largo MD 20774-2199 Home Fax: 301-779-2763; Office Fax: 301-322-0850. Personal E-mail: triciawootten@hotmail.com. Business E-mail: woottepe@pg.cc.md.us.

WOOTTEN, THOMAS FRANKLIN, retired criminal justice administrator; b. Orlando, Fla., Jan. 13, 1931; s. John Franklin and Betty (Shadburn) W.; m. Ruth Marie Raiman, Sept. 26, 1953 (div. 1978); m. Heidi Herbold, Apr. 12, 1978. AB in Clin. Psychology, Ohio State U., 1953, postgrad., 1958-59, Nova U., 1977-82. Comdr. USN, 1949, active duty at sea and overseas, 1949-76, ret., 1976; mgmt. adminstr. Office Commonwealth Atty., Virginia Beach, Va., 1977-79; pres., CEO Inst. Applied Polygraph Sci., 1979-82; undersheriff Portsmouth (Va.) Sheriff's Office, 1982-93. Co-chair Va. Polygraph Adv. Bd., Va. Dept. Commerce, 1988-96. Decorated Legion of Merit (valor), Air Medal, Nat. Honor medal Republic of Vietnam. Mem. VFW (life), NRA (life), Am. Polygraph Assn. (various coms. 1976—, chair stds. and ethics 1985-86, co-chair accreditation com. 1991-92), Am. Assn. Police Polygraphists, Va. Polygraph Assn. (life, past pres.), South Eastern Bee Keeper's Assn., Trout Run Homeowners Assn., Pi Kappa Alpha, Psi Chi. Avocations: yachting, photography, marksmanship, genealogical research, bee keeping. Home: 2228 Windward Shore Dr Virginia Beach VA 23451-1728

WOOTTON, BROOKII E. investor relations professional; b. Uvalde, Tex., Mar. 4, 1965; d. Charles K. and Leona Agnus (Farley) W.; m. John J. Ferguson Jr. (div. 1999); 1 child, J. Grey Ferguson. BS, S.W. Tex. State U., 1988; MBA, U. Phoenix, 2000. Operator test floor Motorola, Austin, Tex., 1987-88; stockbroker's asst. Shearson Lehman Hutton, 1988-89; instr. office adminstrn. Devine (Tex.) Ind. Sch. Dist., 1989-91; asst. to chief exec. officer Turbeco, Inc., Houston, 1991-96, with investor rels., 1996-98, dir. investor rels., 1998—; mgr. investor rels. DSI Toys, Inc., 1999-2000; mgr. fin. comms. Hill & Knowlton, 2000—. Rep. for Turbeco, Inc. N.W. C. of C. Active community and charitable orgns.; sponsor cheerleading and twirling; judge, contest dir. Am. Twirling Festival. Mem. NEA, NAFE, AAUW, VOTAT, Bus. Profls. Am. Club (sponsor), Tex. Tchrs. Assn., Tex. Bus. Educators Assn., Devine Educators Assn. (v.p.), N.W. Houston C. of C. (rep.), Jr. League N.W. Harris County, Tex. Computer Edn. Assn., Golden Key Nat. Alumni Soc., Order of Omega, Phi Theta Kappa, Alpha Phi, Phi Upsilon Omicron. Office: Hill & Knowlton 808 Travis St Fl 21 Houston TX 77002-5706 E-mail: bwootton@hillandknowlton.com.

WOOTTON-GORGES, SANDRA LEE, radiologist; b. El Paso, Tex., Oct. 20, 1958; d. William Charles Jr. and Patricia Anne (Keates) Wootton; m. William Francis Gorges, May 27, 1995; 1 child, Melinda Anne Gorges. BS in Chemistry, San Jose State U., 1980; MD, U. Calif., 1985. Diplomate Am. Bd. Radiology. Intern in medicine Mt. Zion Hosp., San Francisco, 1985-86; resident in radiology U. Calif., San Diego, 1986-90; asst. prof. radiology U. Colo., Denver, 1992-99; asst. prof., dir. pediatric. radiology U. Calif., Davis, 1999—. Author (chpt. in book) Practical Pediatric Radiology, 1994. Mem. Radiol. Soc. N.Am., Am. Roentgen Ray Soc., Soc. Pediat. Radiology, Childrens Oncology Group, Am. Soc. Pediat. Neuroradiology. Avocations: photography, family, travel, bowling, pets. Office: Dept Radiology U Calif 4860 Y St Ste 3100 Sacramento CA 95817

WORACHEK, SUSAN, music educator; b. Bloomington, Ind., Feb. 18, 1952; m. James Allen Worachek, July, 1978; children: Jennifer Ann, Sarah Elizabeth. BS, Miami U., 1974; MEd, Xavier U., 1981. Cert. tchr., Ohio. Music educator Norwood (Ohio) Pub. Schs., 1974-85; gifted students educator P.A.G.E., Inc., Cin., 1992-94; coord. musical arts Cin. Hills Christian Acad., 1995—. Dist. chmn. cultural arts contest Valley Area Coun. PTA, Cin, 1990-93, advisor, 1990-91; chmn. bd. Christian edn. Messiah Luth. Ch., Cin., 1993—; mem. supt.'s adv. coun. Princeton Bd. Edn., Cin., 1993—; mem. bus. adv. com. Glendale Elem. Sch., Cin., 1993—, pres. No. Hills Piano Tchr's. Forum, 1991-93, Glendale PTA, 1993-95; judge Ohio Fedn. Music Clubs, Cin., 1986-94. Mem. Glendale Lyceum, Village Gardeners, Delta Omicron. Avocations: tennis, bridge, people, music. Office: Cin Hills Christian Acad 11300 Snider Rd Cincinnati OH 45249-2222

WORBOYS, ROGER DICK, retired communications executive; b. Syracuse, N.Y., Sept. 1, 1947; s. Carl Stape and Dorothy Elsa (Dick) W.; m. Mary Lee Tasker, Nov. 27, 1971; children: Thomas, Elizabeth. Bachelors degree, Alfred U., 1969; M in Bus., U. N.H., 1971. Asst. dir. residences U. N.H., Durham, 1971; mgr.- regional mgr. Continental Cablevision, Boston, 1974-86; v.p. ops. Simmons Comm., Stamford, Conn., 1986-88, Insight Comm., Glasgow, Scotland, N.Y.C., 1988-95, Bresnan Comms., White Plains, N.Y., 1996-98, sr. v.p., 1999-2000; ret., 2001. Sec. bd. Simmons Comm., Stamford, 1986-88. Chair Pub. Sch. Tech. Adv., Dover, N.H. Mem. Portsmouth N.H. C. of C. (pres.), Rotary Internat. (bd. dirs.). Roman Catholic. Avocations: recreational bike riding, hiking, climbing. Office: Bresnan Comms 709 Westchester Ave White Plains NY 10604-3103

WORBY, RACHAEL BETH, conductor; b. Nyack, N.Y., Apr. 21, 1949; d. Louis Lincoln and Diana (Zacharia) W.; m. David Obst, Sept. 7, 1986. BS in Music, Crane Sch. of Music, 1971; postgrad., Ind. U., 1971-72; ABD, Brandeis U., 1979. Music dir. N.H. Philharmonic, Manchester, 1979-82, New Eng. Conservatory Youth Orch., Boston, 1980-82; Exxon asst. conductor Spokane (Wash.) Symphony, 1982-84; asst. conductor L.A. Philharmonic, 1983-87; music dir. Carnegie Hall, N.Y.C., from 1984, Wheeling (W.Va.) Symphony, 1986—. Instr. New Eng. Conservatory of Music, Boston, 1979-82, MIT, Boston, 1980-82; lectr. N.Y. Philharmonic, N.Y.C., 1978-86. Rockefeller Found. grantee, 1981, Exxon/NEA grantee, 1982. Office: Wheeling Symphony Orch 1025 Main St Ste 811 Wheeling WV 26003-2724*

WORCESTER, CATHY PORTSCHE, violinist, teacher; b. Salt Lake City, Aug. 23, 1952; d. Vernon Willis and Gretchen Ann (Roeser) Portsche; m. Richard King Worcester, June 7, 1975; children: Benjamin, Elizabeth. MusB, Ariz. State U., 1976; MusM, Ind. U., 1981. Violinist Phoenix Symphony Orch., 1976-79; concertmaster Mesa (Ariz.) Symphony Orch., 1983-97, Sun Cities Symphony of the West Valley, Sun City, Ariz., 1996—; studio tchr. violin, viola and chamber music Mesa, 1983—. Bd. dirs. Mesa Symphony Orch., 1994-98; mem. Opus 2, violin and piano duo, 1998-. Mem. Am. Fedn. Musicians (local 586), Am. String Tchrs. Assn. Avocations: reading, racquetball, refinishing furniture. Home: 1108 W 6th St Mesa AZ 85201-4704

WORCESTER, DONALD EMMET, history educator, writer; b. Tempe, Ariz., Apr. 29, 1915; s. Thomas Emmet and Maud (Worcester) Makemson; m. Barbara Livingston Peck, July 5, 1941; children: Barbara Livingston and Elizabeth Stuart (twins), Harris Eugene. AB, Bard Coll., 1939; MA, U. Calif., 1940, PhD, 1947. Lectr. Calif. Coll. Agr., Davis, 1946, U. Calif., 1947; asst. prof. U. Fla., 1947-51, assoc. prof., 1951-55, head dept., 1955-59, prof. history, 1955-63; chmn. dept. history Tex. Christian U., 1963-72, Lorin A. Boswell prof. history, 1971-80, Ida and Cecil Green emeritus tutor, 1981-94. Vis. prof. U. Madrid, 1956-57; chmn. bd. Univ. Press Mgrs., 1961-63. Author: The Interior Provinces of New Spain, 1786, 1951, (with Wendell G. Schaeffer) The Growth and Culture of Latin America, 1956, 2d edit., 1971, Sea Power and Chilean Independence, 1962, Spanish edit., 1971, The Three Worlds of Latin America, 1963, (with Maurice Boyd) American Civilization, 1964, (with Robert and Kent Forster) Man and Civilization, 1965, Makers of Latin America, 1966, Brazil: From Colony to World Power, 1973; editor: Forked Tongues and Broken Treaties, 1975, Bolivar, 1977, The Apaches: Eagles of the Southwest, 1979, German edit., 1982, The Chisholm Trail: High Road of the Cattle Kingdom, 1981, Pioneer Trails West, 1985, The Spanish Mustang: From the Plains of Andalusia to the Prairies of Texas, 1986, The Texas Cowboy, 1986, The Texas Longhorn: Relic of the Past, Asset of the Future, 1987, (fiction) The War in the Nueces Strip, 1989, A Visit from father and other Tales of the Mojave, 1990, Brazos Scout, 1991, Man on Two Ponies, 1992, Gone to Texas, 1993, Western Horse Tales, 1994; also children's books; mng. editor: Hispanic Am. Hist. Rev, 1960-65; editor TCU Monographs in History and Culture, 1966-73; mem. editl. bd. The Am. West. Served to lt. comdr. USNR, 1941-45. Recipient Golden Spur award Western Writers Am., 1975, 80, 99; C.L. Sonnichsen Book award, 1985. Mem. Western Hist. Assn. (v.p. 1973-74, pres. 1974-75), Western Writers Am. (v.p. 1972-73, pres. 1973-74, Saddleman award 1988), N.Mex. Hist. Soc., Westerners Internat. (dir. 1975-80, pres. 1978, 79), Tex. Inst. Letters, Phi Beta Kappa, Phi Alpha Theta (pres. 1960-62). Home: 9321 Bear Creek Rd Aledo TX 76008-4004

WORCESTER, HOWARD LESTER, internist; b. Kansas City, Mo., Jan. 3, 1945; s. Howard Elmer and Alma Jane (Evans) W. div.; children: Tiffany, Chase. BS, U. Oregon, 1967, MD, 1971. Diplomate Am. Bd. Internal Medicine, Am. Bd. Forensic Pathology. Intern Harbor Gen. Hosp. UCLA, 1971-72; med. officer U.S. Army, West Germany, 1972-75; resident U. Calif., Irvine, 1975-77, chief med. resident, 1977-78; pvt. practice internal medicine Meml. Hosp., Long Beach, Calif., 1978—. Dir. utilization rev. Long Beach Meml. Hosp., 1983—, trustee, 1983—, also bd. dirs.; cons. Sultanate of Oman, Muscat, Oman, 1984—. Patron L.A. County Mus. Major U.S. Army, 1972-75. Recipient Merck scholarship U. Oreg. Med. Sch., 1969 Mem. Long Beach Meml. Hosp. Med. Group (pres. 1983—), Long Beach Meml. Med. Svc. Orgn. (pres. 1993-96), Phi Beta Kappa, Alpha Omega Alpha. Episcopalian. Avocations: cooking, wine collecting, travel, sports. Home: 11042 Skyline Dr Santa Ana CA 92705-2473 Office: Meml Med Group 2650 Elm Ave Ste 309 Long Beach CA 90806-1600

WORCESTER, PEGGY JEAN, medical/surgical nurse; b. Willard, Ohio, June 10, 1950; d. Cleon V. and Gertrude M. (Ayers) Smeltz; m. Kenneth H. Worcester, June 26, 1971; l child, Jennifer R. Diploma, Riverside White Cross Hosp., Columbus, Ohio, 1971; BSN, Ashland (Ohio) U., 1991; MSN, Med. Coll. Ohio, 2002. RN, Ohio; CNOR, CCRN. Head nurse intensive CCU, Fisher-Titus Med. Ctr., Norwalk, Ohio, 1973-74, relief supr., 1981-82, staff nurse operating room, 1985-91; staff nurse surg. ICU Med-Ctrl. Health Systems, Mansfield Hosp., 1992-98, staff nurse cardiovasc. ICU, 1998—. Mem. Assn. Operating Room Nurses (treas. 1986-88, pres. 1988-90).

WORD, RICHARD LAWRENCE, protective services official; b. San Francisco, Feb. 6, 1962; s. Robert Louis and Joyce Ann Word; m. Stacey Lynn Moore, Oct. 10, 1987; children: Noah Robert, Taylor Ann. BS, John F. Kennedy U., 1998; MPA, Golden Gate U., 2001; grad., Session 184, FBI Nat. Acad., 1996; grad., Session 24, FBI Nat. Exec. Inst., 2002. Police cadet San Francisco Sheriff's Dept., 1982—84; police officer Oakland (Calif.) Police Dept., 1984—89, sgt. of police, 1989—93, lt. of police, 1993—97, capt. of police, 1997—99, chief of police, 1999—. Adv. bd. Boys and Girls Clubs, Oakland, 2000—; bd. dirs. ARC, 2000—, Oakland Police Activities League, 1999—. Mem.: Police Execs. Rsch. Forum, Calif. Police Chiefs Assn. (bd. dirs. 1999—), Internat. Assn. Chiefs of Police. Avocations: reading, camping, weightlifting, fishing, watching football. Office: Oakland Police Dept 455 7th St Oakland CA 94607 Office Fax: 510-238-2251. E-mail: rword@oaklandnet.com.

WORD, TERRY MULLINS, lawyer; b. Corpus Christi, Tex., Dec. 30, 1943; s. Terrence Stuart and Leila Elba (Mullins) W.; m. ALice G. Hector, Jan. 27, 1971 (div. 1977); children: Morgan Anna, Zachary Hector; m. Mary Ann L. Rios Garcia, May 28, 1983; children: Jettie Laure, Terrence Rios; 1 stepson, John Jarrett Garcia. BA in Econs., Math., U. Tex., 1966, JD, 1973. Bar: Tex. 1973, N.Mex. 1973, U.S. Dist. Ct. N.Mex. 1973. Ptnr. Stribling, Anderson, Read & Word, Albuquerque, 1973-74; atty. N.Mex. Pub. Defender, 1974-76;

pvt. practice, 1976-77; assoc. Richard E. Ransom, P.A., 1977-83; pres. pvt. practice, 1983—. Workmen's compensation editor The N.Mex. Trial Lawyer, Albuquerque, 1982-84. Bd. dirs. Big Bros./Big Sisters Albuquerque, 1983—. Lt. USn, 1966-70, Vietnam. Fellow Am. Coll. Trial Lawyers; mem. ATLA (sustaining mem., bd. govs. 1991-94, N.Mex. Trial Lawyers Assn. (chmn. continuing legal edn. com. 1984-85, treas. 1984-85, bd. dirs. 1984—, pres. elect 1985-86, pres. 1986-87), Am. Bd. Trial Advocates (pres. N.Mex. chpt. 1996-97, N.Mex. Supreme Ct. Rules of Civil Procedures com., 1989-92). Democrat. Episcopalian. Home: 6401 Caballero Pkwy NW Albuquerque NM 87107-5635 Office: 500 Tijeras Ave NW Albuquerque NM 87102-3133 E-mail: twordpc@swcp.com.

WORDEN, ELIZABETH ANN, artist, author, comedy writer, singer, playwright; b. Karnes City, Tex., Nov. 8, 1954; d. Alan Walker and Mary Paralee (Long) W. BS in Comms., U. Tex., 1977. Disc jockey, newsperson KMMK Radio, McKinney, Tex., 1978, KPBC Radio, Irving, 1979-80, KDNT Radio, Denton, 1980-81, KJIM Radio, Ft. Worth, 1981-82, KPBC Radio, Irving, 1983, KRYS Radio, Corpus Christi, Tex., 1984; owner Worden Industries. Executed paintings for Am. Embassy, Bogota, Colombia; one-woman shows include Art Ctr., Corpus Christi, 1990; exhibited in group shows at Tex. A&M, Corpus Christi, 1986, 92, Galeria Chapparal, Corpus Christi, 1988, New Eng. Fine Art Inst., Boston, 1993, Am. Embassy, Bogota, Art Ctr. Corpus Christi, 2000; paintings in pvt. collections throughout the country. Mem. Art Ctr. Corpus Christi. Mem. Tex. Fine Arts Assn., Pastel and Colored Pencil Soc. Avocations: writing fiction and poetry, acting, photography, reading. Home and Office: Worden Enterprises 3842 Brookhill Dr Corpus Christi TX 78410-4404 E-mail: elizworden@aol.com.

WORDEN, KATHARINE COLE, sculptor; b. N.Y.C., May 4, 1925; d. Philip Gillette and Katharine (Pyle) Cole; m. Frederic G. Worden, Jan. 8, 1944; children: Fred, Dwight, Philip, Barbara, Katharine. Student, Potters Ch., Tucson, 1940-42, Sarah Lawrence Coll., 1942-44. Exhibited in group shows at Royce Galleries, Galerie Francoise Besnard, Paris, Cooling Gallery, London, Galerie Schumacher, Munich, Selected Artists Gallery, N.Y.C., Art Inst. Boston, Reid Gallery, Nashville, Weiner Gallery, N.Y.C., Boston Athanaeum, House of Humor and Satire, Gabrovo, Bulgaria, 1983, Newport Bay Club, 1984; pvt. collections Grand Palais, Paris, Dakar and Bathurst, Africa. Dir. Stride Rite Corp., 1980-85; occpl. therapist psychopathic ward L.A. County Gen. Hosp., 1953-57; Headstart vol., Watts, Calif., 1965-67; tchr. sculpture Watts Towers Art Ctr., 1967-69; participant White House Women Doers Luncheon meeting, 1968; dir. Cambridgeport Problem Ctr., Cambridge, Mass., 1969-71; mem. Jud. Nominating Commn., 1976-79; bd. overseers Boston Mus. Fine Arts, 1980-83; bd. govs. Newport Seamens Ch. Inst., 1989-91; tustee Comm. Rsch., Miami, Fla., 1960-69, chmn. bd., 1966-69; trustee Newport Art Mus., 1984-86, 92-94, Jamestown Cmty. Theatre, 1994-97, 99—, Newport Health Found., 1986-91, Hawthorne Sea Fund, 1990-93; bd. dirs. Boston Ctr. for Arts, 1976-80, Child and Family Svcs. of Newport County, 1983-97, 99—. Mem. Common Cause (Mass adv. bd. 1971-72, dir. 1974-75), Mass. Civil Liberties Union (exec. bd. 1973-74, dir. 1976-77). Home: 24 Fort Wetherill Rd Jamestown RI 02835-2908

WORDEN, MARNY, artist, musician; b. Williamsport, Pa., Sept. 23, 1926; d. Harold Ernest and Marion Francis (Tillinghast) W.; m. Richard Dean Blair, Sept. 9, 1949 (div. 1957); 1 child, Brian Eric; m. John Riley Olson, Dec. 19, 1957. BA, U. Toledo, 1946; MAT, Ind. U., 1968. English tchr. Tex. Sch. for Deaf, Austin, 1954-62, Ind. Sch. for Deaf, Indpls., 1962-65; French, Spanish tchr. Indpls. City Schs., 1965-70; curriculum projects dir. Ind. Sch. for the Deaf, Indpls., 1970-71, tchr. English, Latin, 1972-79. Symphony musician and pvt. tchr. flute, piccolo, 1942—; dir. Tillinghast Early Music Consort; adjudicator Ind. Sch. Music Competitions. Author: (textbooks) 1,2,3 Language Series, 1970, (adaptations for the deaf) Beowulf, 1973, Song of Roland, 1974. Recipient of craftsman's rating in lapidary work, silversmithing; stone sculptures. Mem. Internat. Porcelain Artists & Tchrs., Inc. Avocations: oil paintings, watercolors, porcelain painting, performing. Home: 178 Ladd Ridge Cir Kingston TN 37763-6964

WORDEN, ROBERT L. government agency administrator, researcher; b. Olean, N.Y., June 5, 1945; s. John L. and Leone E. (Borer) W.; m. Norma Jean Chue; children: Maia, Peter, Nathaniel. BA cum laude, St. Bonaventure U., 1967; MA, Georgetown U., 1969, PhD, 1972. Applicant screener, coder U.S. Peace Corps, Washington, 1967-68, statis. analyst, 1968-70; rsch. analyst Fed. Rsch. Divsn. Libr. of Congress, 1973-81, sr. rsch. analyst Fed. Rsch. Divsn., 1981-82, unit supr. Fed. Rsch. Divsn., 1982-85, sect. head Fed. Rsch. Divsn., 1985-98, acting chief Fed. Rsch. Divsn., 1997-98, chief Fed. Rsch. Divsn., 1998—, acting chief Asian divsn., 2002—. Co-author, editor: The Veterans Benefits Administration: An Organizational History, 1776-1994, 1995, India: A Country Study, 1996; co-author, co-editor: China and the Third World - Champion or Challenger?, 1986, China: A Country Study, 1988. Sec.-treas. Annapolis (Md.) Preservation Trust, Inc., 1987-95, pres., 1995-97, sec., 2000—; chmn. Bd. Elections Suprs., Annapolis, 1983-86. 1st lt. U.S. Army, 1971-73. Georgetown U. fellow, 1970-71. Mem. Libr. of Congress Profl. Assn., Libr. of Congress Asian Am. Assn., Assn. for Asian Am. Studies, Assn. for Asian Studies. Democrat. Roman Catholic. Avocations: genealogy, foreign travel, reading. Home: 30 Murray Ave Annapolis MD 21401-2843 Office: Libr of Congress Fed Rsch Divsn 101 Independence Ave SE Washington DC 20540-4840 Fax: (202) 707-3920. E-mail: rwor@loc.gov.

WORDEN, SUE JANINE, engineer, scientist; b. Dallas, Feb. 24, 1956; d. Ithiel Murray and Irene Elizabeth (Krepkovich) W.; m. Bapi Masroor Ahmad, May 1983 (div. Dec. 1984). BSME, U. Tex., 1978, MSEE, 1981, PhD in Elec. Engring., 1994. Engring. co-op Vought Corp., Grand Prairie, Tex., 1975-77; rsch. asst. U. Tex., Arlington, 1977; mech. engr. E.I. DuPont de Nemours, Wilmington, Del., 1978-79; tchg. asst. U. Tex., Austin, 1979-80; engr., scientist II Tracor Aerospace, 1980-86; rsch. engr., scientist asst. Applied Rsch. Labs., 1986-90; instr. Austin C.C., 1990-92; systems analyst U. Tex., Austin, 1992—99; engr. V BAE Systems, 1999—. Com. chair Expanding Your Horizons in Scis. and Math.; mentor Austin Ind. Sch. Dist. Mem. AAUW, IEEE, ACM, SIAM, Assn. for Women in Sci., Assn. of Women in Math., Soc. Women Engrs., Sigma Xi, Tau Beta Pi, Pi Tau Sigma. Avocations: astronomy, classical music, gardening, hiking/camping, sewing. Home: PO Box 4932 Austin TX 78765-4932 Office: BAE Systems MS 28-08 6500 Tracor Ln Austin TX 78725

WORDEN, WILLIAM PATRICK, deacon; b. Chgo., July 23, 1933; s. Shannon Gerard and Florence Marie (Chouinard) W.; m. Shirley Ann Poerio, Apr. 1, 1956; children: Mary Patricia Maloney, Judith Ann Laverdiere, Ellen Jean. BEE, Ill. Inst. Tech., 1955; MA in Pastoral Studies, Loyola U., Chgo., 1986; D Ministry, Grad. Theol. Found., Bristol, Ind., 1991. Deacon St. Peter and Paul Parish, Naperville, Ill., 1980-85, St. Thomas the Apostle Parish, Naperville, 1985—; chaplain DuPage County Jail, Wheaton, Ill., 1991-96; mem. reactor safety rev. com. Argonne Nat. Lab., Darien, 1989-97; dir. Diaconate for the Diocese of Joliet, 1997—. Del. Region VII Deaconal Orgn., 1981-84. Author: (with others) Decontamination and Decommissioning of Nuclear Facilities, 1980; contbr. articles to religious column in newspaper, jours. in field. Bd. dirs. Interfaith Counseling Svc., Naperville, 1980-85, Just of DuPage Jail Ministry, Wheaton, 1986-90. Office: St Thomas the Apostle Ch 1500 Brookdale Rd Naperville IL 60563-2129

WORDSMAN, ELIZABETH SCHMITT (BETSY WORDSMAN), senior manager print production; b. Milw., Mar. 1, 1955; d. Paul E. and Dorothy A. (Rehmer) Schmitt; m. Arthur Wordsman, Dec. 29, 1986. BFA, Boston U., 1981. Advt. mgr. Brills Inc., Milw., 1983-85; prodn. mgr. in tng. Allied Graphics Arts, N.Y.C., 1985-87; acct. supr. Bel-Aire Assoc., 1987-88; cons. Bloomingdale's, 1988-89; sales promotion prodn. dir. Lord & Taylor, 1989-95; sr. mgr. global print prodn. Avon Products, 1995—. Judge Gravure Assn. of Am. Golden Cylinder awards, 1998, 99; spkr. PIRA Internat. Catalog Conf., 1999. Judge Gold Ink Awards, 1998, 99. Recipient Gold Ink award Printing & Pub. Exec., 1992, 93, 96, 97, 98, Rose Achievement award Lord & Taylor, 1993, Avon Chmn.'s Achievement award, 1999. Mem. Direct Mktg. Assn., Gravure Assn. of Am.

WORELL, JUDITH P. psychologist, educator; b. N.Y.C. d. Moses and Dorothy Goldfarb; m. Leonard Worell, Aug. 11, 1947 (div.); children: Amy, Beth, Wendy; m. H.A. Smith, Mar. 23, 1985 BS magna cum laude, Queens Coll., 1950; MA, Ohio State U., 1952, PhD in Clin. Psychology, 1954; DHL (hon.), Colby-Sawyer Coll., 1993. Research assoc. Iowa Psychopathic Hosp., Iowa City, 1957-59; research assoc. Okla. State U., 1960-66; asst. prof. U. Ky., Lexington, 1969-71, assoc. prof., 1971-75, prof. ednl. and counseling psychology, 1976—, dir. counseling psychology tng. program, 1980-93, chairperson dept. ednl. and counseling psychology, 1993-97, prof. emerita, 1999—. Author: (with C.M. Nelson) Managing Instructional Problems, 1974; (with W.E. Stilwell) Psychology for Teachers and Students, 1981; Psychological Development in the Elementary Years, 1982; (with Fred Danner) The Adolescent as Decision-maker: Applications to Development and Education, 1989; (with Pam Remer) Feminist Perspectives in Therapy: An Empowerment Model for Women, 1992; (with N. Johnson) Shaping the Future of Feminist Psychology: Education, Research, and Practice, 1997, (with Norine Johnson & Michael Roberts) Beyond Appearance: A New Look at Adolescent Girls, 1999, Encyclopedia of Women and Gender: Sex Similarities and Differences and the Impact of Society on Gender, 2001, (with Pam Remer) Feminist Perspectives in Therapy: Empowering Diverse Women, 2002; assoc. editor Jour. Cons. and Clin. Psychology, 1976-79, mem. editl. bd., 1984-89; assoc. editor Psychol. Women Quar., 1984-89, editor, 1989-95; mem. editorial bd. Sex Roles, 1984—, Psychol. Assessment, 1991-97, Clin. Psychology Rev., 1991-97, Women and Therapy, 1992—; cons., reviewer 10 jours.; contbr. articles to profl. jours. Named U. Ky. Campus Woman of Yr., 1976, Outstanding Univ. Grad. prof., 1991, Disting. Ky. psychologist, 1990; USPHS fellow, 1953; NIMH rsch. grantee, 1962-69. Fellow APA (pres. Clin. Psychology of Women 1986-88, chmn. com. state assn. rels. 1982-83, fellow selection divsn. 35 com. 1983-84, policy and planning bd. 1989-92, publs. and comm. bd. 1992-99, chair 1996-98, chair jours. com., pres. divsn. psychology of women 1997-98, Disting. Leader for Women in Psychology 1990, coun. rep. 2000—), Ky. Psychol. Assn. (pres. 1981-82, rep. at large 1995-97), Southeastern Psychol. Assn. (exec. coun. mem.-at-large, pres.-elect 1993-94 pres. 1994-95), Am. Women in Psychology, Phi Beta Kappa. Home: 3892 Gloucester Dr Lexington KY 40510-9729 Office: U Ky Dept Ednl and Counseling Psychology 245 Dickey Hl Lexington KY 40506-0017 E-mail: jpwphd@aol.com.

WORENKLEIN, JACOB JOSHUA, lawyer; b. N.Y.C., Oct. 1, 1948; s. Abraham and Cela (Zyskind) W.; divorced; children: David, Daniel, Laura; m. Cindy Sternkler, Feb. 26, 1995. BA, Columbia U., 1969; MBA, JD, NYU, 1973. Bar: N.Y. 1974. From assoc. to ptnr. Milbank, Tweed, Hadley & McCloy, N.Y.C., 1973-93, chmn. firm planning com., 1988-90, exec. com., 1990-93, sr. advisor to exec. com., 1993-94; mng. dir., group head of global project fin. group Lehman Bros., 1993-96; mng. dir., head project fin, commodity fin., export fin. Soc. Gen., 1996-98, mng. dir., global head project and sector fin. Paris and N.Y.C., 1998—. Mem. investment banking mgmt. com. Lehman Bros., 1993-96; mem. adv. coun. Amoco Power Resources Corp., 1995—; adj. prof. fin. NYU Stern Sch. of Bus. Mem. editl. bd. Jour. Project Fin., 1996—; contbr. articles to profl. jours. Pres. Old Broadway Synagogue, N.Y.C., 1978—; trustee Fedn. Jewish Philanthropies, N.Y.C., 1984-86; bd. overseers United Jewish Appeal-Fedn. Jewish Philanthropies, 1987, chmn. lawyers divsn. major gifts, 1989-91, chmn. lawyers divsn., 1991-93, bd. dirs., 1991-97; trustee Jewish Cmty. Rels. Coun. N.Y., 1995-98, mem. coun. on fgn. rels., 1998—. Mem. Coun. on Fgn. Rels. Office: Soc Gen 1221 Avenue Of The Americas New York NY 10020-1001

WORGAFTIK, SUSAN CAROL, social worker; b. Bronx, N.Y., Feb. 13, 1946; d. Alex and Rose (Rosen) W. BA, U. Conn., 1968; MA, Columbia U., 1969; M in Social Svcs., Boston U., 1976. Cert. social worker, Mass. Coord. interagy. rels. Divsn. Alcoholism Commonwealth of Mass., Boston, 1976-77; mgr., planner contracts Federated Dorchester (Mass.) Neighborhood Houses, 1977-89; adminstr. Local 26 Trust Funds Greater Boston Hotel Employees, 1989-92; dir. cmty.-wide programs Federated Dorchester Neighborhood Houses, 1992—. Mem. delegation Lessons Without Borders, Jamaica, 1995. Bd. dirs. Bowdoin St.-Geneva Ave. Main Sts., Dorchester, com. chair, 1995—, treas.; mem. adv. bd. Safe Neighborhood Initiative, Dorchester, 1993—; mem. adv. com. CDC Cmty. Bus. Network, 1998—;; mem. loan rev. bd. Dorchester Bay Neighborhood Devel. Corp., 2002-; bd. dirs. Boston Greenspace Alliance, 2001-. Mem. NASW. Avocations: gardening, reading. Office: Federated Dorchester Neighborhood Houses 450 Washington St Dorchester MA 02124

WORK, BRUCE VAN SYOC, business consultant; b. Monmouth, Ill., Mar. 20, 1942; s. Robert M. and Evelyn (Rusken) W.; m. Janet Kay Brown, Nov. 12, 1966; children: Bruce, Terra. BA, Monmouth Coll., 1964; BS, U. Mo.-Rolla, 1966; postgrad., U. Chgo., 1978-79. Registered profl. engr., Ill. Various mgmt. positions Midcon Corp. (and subs.), 1966-79; pres. Indsl. Fuels Corp., Troy, Mich., 1979-85, Costain Coal Inc., Troy, 1985-89; pvt. practice small bus. cons., 1989-92; bus. cons. Wallis Oil Co., 1992-2000; small bus. cons., 2000—. Mem. various coms. Cuba United Meth. Ch. Mem. Detroit Athletic Club, Forest Lake Country Club, Blue Key. Office: 2280 Hwy DD Cuba MO 65453-9684 E-mail: jbwork@fidnet.com. *People are the key to our success. Treat each individual as you would like to be treated.*

WORK, CHARLES ROBERT, lawyer; b. Glendale, Calif., June 21, 1940; s. Raymond P. and Minna M. (Fricke) W.; m. Linda S. Smith, Oct. 4, 1965 (div.); children: Matthew Keehn, Mary Lucila Landis, Benjamin Reed; m. Veronica A. Haggart, Apr., 1985, 1 child, Andrew Haggart. BA, Wesleyan U., 1962; JD, U. Chgo., 1965; LLM, Georgetown U., 1966. Bar: D.C. 1965, Utah 1965. Asst. U.S. atty. D.C., 1966-73; dep. adminstr. law enforcement assistance adminstrn., U.S. Dept. Justice, 1973-75; ptnr. Peabody, Lambert & Meyers, Washington, 1975-82, McDermott, Will & Emery, Washington, 1982—. Recipient Rockefeller Pub. Service award 1978. Mem. D.C. Bar (pres. 1976-77). Office: McDermott Will & Emery 600 13th St NW Fl 12-8 Washington DC 20005-3005

WORK, GEORGE PAUL, musician; b. Lincoln, Nebr., June 20, 1957; s. George Arthur Work, Carol Puckett Work; m. Dawn Elizabeth Work MaKinne. cert. in performance, B in Music Performance, Eastman Sch. Music, 1979, M in Music Performance, 1981. Founder, dir. Iowa State Summer Chamber Music Workshop, Ames, Iowa, 1993—2000; prof. c.ello Iowa State U., 1981—. Cellist Ames Piano Quartet, Ames, 1981—; artist faculty mem. Luth. Music Program, Mpls., 1984—97, Bravo! Summer String Inst., Mpls., 1994; adj. prof. cello Drake U., Des Moines, 1997—98; artist faculty mem. Brevard (N.C.) Music Ctr., 1998—. Musician: (recording) Piano Quartets by Chausson and Saint-Saens, 1989, Dvorak: The Two Piano Quartets, 1990, Faure: The Two Piano Quartets, 1991, Piano Quartets by Strauss and Widor, 1993, Piano Quartets of Schumann and Brahms, 1994, Piano Quartets of Brahms, 1995, The Russian Piano Quartet, 2000, Dorian Sampler, Volume 2, 1989, Gemini, 2001, (chamber music performances) over 300 concerts throughout N.Am., also France, Austria, Taiwan, and Mex. Mem. Amnesty Internat., Ames, Iowa; case coord. Amnesty Internat, 1986—91. Grantee Grants for Ames Quartet concerts and workshops, Affiliated Arts Agencies of Upper Midwest, 1985—87, 1989—91, Grant for Ames Quartet concerts and workshops, Nat. Endowment for Arts, 1982—83. Mem.: Am. String Tchrs. Assn. (Studio Tchr. of Yr. award, Iowa 1991). Avocations: astronomy, travel. Office: Iowa State Univ Ames IA 50011 Business E-Mail: gwork@iastate.edu.

WORK, HENRY HARCUS, physician, educator; b. Buffalo, Nov. 11, 1911; s. Henry Harcus and Jeannette (Harcus) W.; m. Virginia Codington, Oct. 20, 1945 (dec. Nov. 1991); children: Henry Harcus III, David Codington, William Bruce, Stuart Runyon. AB, Hamilton Coll., Clinton, N.Y., 1933; MD, Harvard, 1937. Intern, resident Boston Children's Hosp., 1937-40, Emma P. Bradley Home Providence, 1940, Buffalo Children's Hosp., 1940-42, N.Y. Hosp., 1945-47; psychiat. services adviser, chief U.S. Children's Bur., Washington, 1948-49; assoc. prof. pediatrics U. Louisville, 1949-55; mem. faculty UCLA, 1955-72, prof. psychiatry and pub. health, 1966-72; chief profl. svcs. Am. Psychiat. Assn., Washington, 1972-83; clin. prof. George Washington U., Georgetown U., Uniformed Svcs. U. of Health Scis., U. Md., 1973—. Author: A Guide to Preventive Child Psychiatry, 1965, Minimal Brain Dysfunction: A Medical Challenge, 1967, Psychiatric Emergencies in Childhood, 1967, Crisis in Child Psychiatry, 1975, also articles. Served to capt. AUS, 1942-45. Recipient Simon Wile Award, Amer. Acad. of Child and Adolescent Psychiatry, 1994. Mem. So. Calif. Psychiat. Assn. (pres. 1966-67), Am. Orthopsychiat. Assn. (v.p. 1968-69), Am. Coll. Psychiatry (sec.-gen. 1979-93), Group for Advancement of Psychiatry (pres. 1982-85) Home: 4986 Sentinel Dr Apt 504 Bethesda MD 20816-3581

WORK, JANE MAGRUDER, retired professional society administrator; b. Owensboro, Ky., Mar. 30, 1927; d. Orion Noel and Willie May (Stallings) Magruder; m. William Work, Nov. 26, 1960; children: Paul MacGregor, Jeffrey William. BA, Furman U., 1947; MA, U. Wis., 1948; PhD, Ohio State U., 1959. Dir. radio U. South Miss., Hattisburg, 1948-51; pub. rels. assoc. Ohio Fuel Gas Co./Columbia Gas, Columbus, 1952-62; adj. prof. comm. Pace U., N.Y.C., 1963-75; dir. speechmodule ERIC, Washington, 1975-76; mgr. orgn. liaison, dir. legis. analysis Nat. Assn. Mfgs., 1977-84, asst. v.p. legis. analysis, 1984-87, v.p. legis. analysis, 1987-93, v.p. mem. comm., 1993-2001, ret., 2001. Adv. bd. public affairs NYU Grad. Bus. Sch., 1983-87; adv. bd. Proedn. Mag., 1984-87; cons. IBM, Xerox, 1963-77. Contbr. articles to profl. jours. Mem. transition team Consumer Product Safety Commn., Washington, 1979—80; chair No. Va. Pvt. Industry Coun., Fairfax County, 1979—85; co-chair Va. Gov.'s Employment & Tng. Task Force, Richmond, 1983; bd. dirs. Alzheimer's Assn. Nat. Capital Area, 2002—. Named to Acad. Women Achievers YWCA, 1987. Mem.: World Future Soc. (steering network 1993 Gen. Assembly), The Planning Forum (bd. dirs. Capital chpt. 1990—93), Speech Comm. Assn. (sect. chmn. 1980—82), Am. Soc. Assn. Execs. (rsch. adv. com. 1989—97), Nat. Assn. Industry-Edn. Coop. (bd. dirs. 1983—), Issue Mgmt. Assn. (bd. dirs. 1985—88), Future Homemakers of Am. (bd. dirs. 1985—88), Pi Kappa Delta (hon.), Alpha Psi Omega (hon.). Republican. Unitarian Universalist. Avocations: gardening, volunteering. Home: 6245 Cheryl Dr Falls Church VA 22044-1809

WORK, JANICE RENÉ, pediatric dentist; b. Porterville, Calif., Aug. 22, 1944; d. Weldon and Vivian May (Campbell) W. AA, Porterville Jr. Coll., 1964; BA, Brigham Young U., 1967, MFA, 1978; DDS, Georgetown U., 1984; pediatric cert., U. Nebr. Med. Ctr., 1991. Diplomate Am. Bd. Pediatric Dentistry. Dentist Dedicated Dental Svcs., Media, Pa., 1985, Lehigh Dental Assocs., Bethlehem, 1985-86, Grenfell Regional Health Svcs., Forteau, Labrador, Canada, 1986-88, Temporary Dental Help, Manhattan Beach, Calif., 1991, Dr. Randall G. Turner, Torrance, 1991, United Health Ctr. San Joaquim Valley, Inc., Huron, 1991; pediatric dentist Sacramento, 1992—. Chair Prevent Abuse and Neglect through Dental Awareness (PANDA) com., Sacramento; mem. bd. Sacramento Dist. Dental Found., 1993-98, Sacramento Dist. Midwinter Com., 1994-98, Sacramento Dist. Health Com., 1995-98. Fellow Acad. Gen. Dentistry, Acad. Dentistry Internat. Avocations: scuba diving, skiing, biking, camping. Home: PO Box 293690 Sacramento CA 95829-3690 Office: Dr Jan s Dentistry for Children 7260 E Southgate Dr Ste A Sacramento CA 95823-2609 E-mail: drjan3@juno.com.

WORK, MICHAEL JAY, lawyer; b. Maysville, Ky., Oct. 7, 1946; s. Clarence Lee and Marjorie (Lemon) W.; m. Christine Marion Dignan, Aug. 2, 1969; children: Thomas M., Meghan E., Kristen C. BA, Ohio State U., 1968, JD, 1971. Bar: N.H. 1972, U.S. Dist. Ct. N.H. 1972. Atty., examiner Pub. Utilities Commn. Ohio, Columbus, 1971; criminal justice planner N.H. Gov.'s Commn. on Crime and Delinquency, Concord, 1972-73; assoc. Law Offices of John C. Fairbanks, Newport, N.H., 1973-75; sole practice, 1975—. Mem. adv. bd. Lake Sunapee Bank, Newport, 1980—; mem. N.H. Supreme Ct. Profl. Conduct Commn., Concord, 1981-90. Dir. YMCA Camp Coniston, Inc., Croydon, N.H., 1981—. Named Outstanding Young Man Am., 1978. Mem. ABA, N.H. Bar Assn. (gov. 1982-84), Sullivan County Bar Assn. (pres. 1982), New London Bar Assn. (pres. 1983), Newport C. of C. (pres. 1980), Rotary (pres. Newport chpt. 1984-85). Democrat. Avocations: sports, coin collecting. Home: Burpee Ln PO Box 552 New London NH 03257-0552 Office: 7a Main St PO Box 627 Newport NH 03773-0627 E-mail: mjwork@earthlink.net.

WORK, WILLIAM, retired association executive; b. Ithaca, N.Y., Aug. 10, 1923; s. Paul and Helen Grace (Nicholas) W.; m. Jane Noel Magruder, Nov. 26, 1960; children— Paul Magregor, Jeffrey William. AB, Cornell U., 1946; MA, U. Wis., 1948, PhD, 1954; D Arts (hon.), Eastern Mich. U., 1986; LLD (hon)., Emerson Coll., 1987. Cert. assn. exec. Instr., assoc. dir theatre Purdue U., 1948-50; from instr. to prof., dir. theatre Eastern Mich. U., 1951-63; exec. sec. Speech Communication Assn., Annandale, Va., 1963-88, ret., 1988. Mem. faculty U. Wis., 1950-51, So. Ill. U., 1959; cons., reader, review panelist U.S. Office Edn., 1966-71; del. White House Conf. Children, 1970; pres. Alliance Assn. Advancement Edn., 1977, Coun. Communication Socs., 1974-77; past. mem. AAAS, AAUP, Internat. Communication Assn., Internat. Inst. Communications. Contbr. articles, revs. profl. jours. Mem. Mich. Cultural Commn., 1959-60; mem. Hastings-on-Hudson (N.Y.) Bd. Edn., 1972-75. Recipient Alex Drier award, 1962 Mem. Phi Kappa Phi. Democrat. Unitarian Universalist. Home: Falls Church, Va. *If, as George Santayana wisely noted, those who cannot remember the past are condemned to repeat it, then it must be equally true that those who fail to prepare for the future are condemned to endure it.* Died Sept. 4, 2001.

WORKMAN, GEORGE HENRY, engineering consultant; b. Muskegon, Mich., Sept. 18, 1939; s. Harvey Merton and Bettie Jane (Meyes) W.; m. Vicki Sue Hanish, June 17, 1967; children: Mark, Larry. AS, Muskegon C.C., 1960; BS in Engring., MS in Engring., U. Mich., 1966, PhD, 1969. Registered profl. engr., Ohio. Prin. engr. Battelle Meml. Inst., Columbus, Ohio, 1969-76; pres. Applied Mechanics Inc., Longboat Key, Fla., 1976—. Instr. dept. civil engring. Ohio State U., 1973, 82. Contbr. tech. papers to nat. and internat. confs. With USN, 1961-64. Mem. ASME, Am. Acad. Mechanics, Sigma Xi, Chi Epsilon, Phi Kappa Phi, Phi Thea Kappa. Congregationalist. Home and Office: 3431 Bayou Ct Longboat Key FL 34228-3028 E-mail: workman.ami@netsrq.com.

WORKMAN, JAMES E. retired school psychologist; b. Hillsboro, Ohio, Mar. 19, 1938; s. Russell Cochran and Stella Mae W.; m. Brenda Lee Staats, Oct. 8, 1960; children: Jennifer Nakayama, Loretta Workman. AB, Cin. Bible Sem., 1961; postgrad., Cin. Bible Grad. Sch., 1961-63; MEd, U. Cin., 1969; postgrad., 1969-72, Gestalt Inst. of Cleve., 1975. Cert. sch. psychologist Ohio; motorcycle riding instr. Motorcycle Safety Found. English tchr. Clermont Northeastern Local Schs., Owensville, Ohio, 1964-66; social worker Clermont County Human Svcs., Batavia, 1966-69; dir. Regional Spl. Edn. Ctr., Wilmington, 1969-71; intern Hamilton County Office Edn., 1971-72; psychologist Zanesville (Ohio) City Schs., 1972-97. Bd. dirs. SCI, Inc., Zanesville, 1975—, chairperson FY92, FY93; bd. dirs., v.p. Residential Resources, Inc., Zanesville, 1992—; bd. dirs. Southeastern Ohio Symphony, New Concord, Ohio, 1980—, Friends of the Libr., Zanesville, 1995—, pres., 2000. Mem. Ohio Sch. Psychologists assn., East Cen. Ohio Sch. Psychologists Assn. (pres. 1974). Avocations: flying, sailing, reading, writing, motorcycling. Home: 1450 Lectric Ln Zanesville OH 43701-6928

WORKMAN, JEROME JAMES, JR. chemist; b. Northfield, Minn., Aug. 6, 1952; s. Jerome James and Louise Mae (Sladek) W.; m. Rebecca Marie Zittel, Aug. 3, 1974; children: Cristina Louise, Stephannie Michelle, Daniel Jerome, Sara Marie, Michael Timothy. BA with honors, St. Mary's U., Winona, Minn., 1976, MA, 1980; PhD, Columbia Pacific U., San Rafael, Calif., 1984; postgrad., Columbia U., 1990-91, 99-00, MIT, Cambridge, Mass., 2001—. Prin. Workman & Assocs., Mankato, Minn., 1980-82; pres. Biochem. Cons., 1982-84; sr. chemist Technicon Instruments, Tarrytown, N.Y., 1984-87; supervising scientist Bran & Luebbe/Technicon, 1987; sr. scientist Hitachi Instruments, Danbury, Conn., 1987-89; mgr. tech. support NIR Systems/Perstorp Analytical, Silver Spring, Md., 1989-90, mgr. mktg., 1990-92, dir. mktg., 1992-93; assoc. advisor Inst. Textile Tech., Charlottesville, Va., 1992—; prin. scientist Perkin Elmer Corp., Norwalk, Conn., 1993-96; sr. rsch. fellow Kimberly-Clark Corp., Analytical and Measurement Tech., Neenah, Wis., 1996—. Instr. Fedn. Analytical Chemistry and Spectroscopy Socs.; external examiner U. Guelph, Ont., Can., 1993-94, chair rep. indsl. adv. bd. Ctr. for Process Analytical Chemistry 1993—; apptd. mem. subcom. on process analytical techs. U.S. FDA, 2002, vis. prof., 2002. Author: Handbook of Organic Compounds: NIR, IR, Raman, and UV-Vis Spectra Featuring Polymers and surfactants, 3 vols., 2000; co-author: Statistics in Spectroscopy, 1991, (series) Chemometrics in Spectroscopy, UV-Vis Spectroscopy, 1993, Introduction to Near Infrared Spectroscopy, 2002; editor: The Process Pages for NIRnews, Internat. Com. for Near Infrared Spectroscopy, 1993-98, Spectroscopy Letters, 1999—; co-editor: Applied Spectroscopy: A Compact Reference for Practitioners, 1998; contbg. editor Spectroscopy Mag.; editl. adv. bd. for Spectroscopy, 1995—; assoc. editor Applied Spectroscopy Reviews, 1995—, Lab. Robotics and Automation, 1995-98, Wiley-Interscı. Series in Lab. Automation, 1993; process editor: Jour. of Near Infrared Spectroscopy, 1995; contbr. articles to profl. jours. Recipient Heart of Gold award Minn. affiliate Am. Heart Assn., 1984; Am. Heart Assn. H.N. and H.B. Shapira scholar, 1971, 72; NSF grantee, 1977, 78. Fellow: ASTM (exec. com., chair main com. on molecular spectroscopy, 2 awards of appreciation for contbns. 2000, Eastern Analytical Symposium award 2002, award of merit 2002), Am. Inst. Chemists, Royal Soc. Chemistry U.K. (chartered chemist); mem.: Coblentz Soc. (bd. mgrs. 2002—), Joint Com. Atomic and Molecular Phys. Data (chmn. UV-VIS, exec. coun.), Coun. Near-Infrared Spectroscopy (pres.), Soc. for Applied Spectroscopy, Am. Chem. Soc. (instr. course on Practical Near-IR Analysis), Nat. Honor Soc., Sigma Xi, Delta Epsilon Sigma. Achievements include research in molecular spectroscopy, statistics and chemometrics; development and applications of spectroscopic methods and sensors to consumer products and processes. Office: Argose Inc 230 Second Ave Waltham MA 02451 E-mail: jworkman@argose.com.

WORKMAN, JOHN MITCHELL, chemist; b. Uniontown, Pa., Oct. 25, 1949; s. Hugh Lawrence and Mary Louise (Mitchell) W.; m. Gayle Sue Zappin, Nov. 20, 1987. BA in Psychology, Miami U., Oxford, Ohio, 1971; MS in Edn., Kans. State U., 1976; MS in Chemistry, U. Cin., 1985, PhD in Chemistry, 1987; MBA in Fin., Wright State U., Dayton, Ohio, 1995. Teaching and rsch. asst. dept. chemistry Wright State U., Dayton, Ohio, 1977-81; grad. teaching asst. U. Cin., 1982-83, grad. rsch. asst., 1983-86; sr. scientist Chemsys Inc., Fairborn, Ohio, 1986-89, dir. elemental analysis, 1989—; lab. dir., 1994—. Contbr. articles to jours. Analytical Chemistry, Applied Spectroscopy. With U.S. Army, 1972-75. Mem.: Am. Phys. Soc., Am. Chem. Soc., Sigma Iota Epsilon, Sigma Pi Sigma, Sigma Xi. Episcopalian. Office: Chemsys Inc PO Box 427 Fairborn OH 45324-0427 E-mail: gopackard@aol.com.

WORKMAN, KAYLEEN MARIE, special education and adult education educator; b. Paola, Kans., Aug. 25, 1947; d. Ralph I. and Pearl Marie (Shults) Platz; m. John Edward Workman, Aug. 10, 1980; children: Andrew Ray, Craig Michael. BS in Edn., Emporia State U., 1969, MS in Edn., 1983. Tchr. English/speech Lincoln (Kans.) High Sch., 1969-70, substitute tchr., 1970-71, Hudson (Wis.) Sch. Dist., 1971-72; tchrs. aide learning disabilities Park Forest South (Ill) Jr. High Sch., 1977-78; learning disabilities/English instr. George York Sch., Osawatomie, Kans., 1978-97; adult edn. instr. Adult Edn. Ctr., Osawatomie State Hosp., 1997-2000; spl. edn. tchr. Ottawa (Kans.) H.S., 2000—. Supr. Loose Ends Clown Troop, 1988-91; presenter in field. Author of poems. Com. mem., sec. Cub Scouts, Osawatomie, 1987-88, com. mem. Boy Scouts Am., 1988-91, sec., 1990-91; forensics judge Osawatomie H.S. Forensics Team, 1991-92; hunter's safety instr. Osawatomie Sportsman's Club, 1982-86; mem. Osawatomie Cmty. Band, 1990-92. Mem. Osawatomie-NEA (v.p. 1982-83, 93-94, pres. 1983-84, 94-95, sec. 1986), Kans.-NEA (Sunflower uniserv adminstrv. bd. 1985, Sunflower uniserv coord. coun.), Learning Disabilities Assn., Delta Kappa Gamma. Avocations: hunting, fishing, collecting Santa Clauses, writing poetry, shopping.

WORKMAN, NORMAN ALLAN, accountant, graphic arts consultant; b. Boston, Apr. 20, 1918; s. William Horace and Estelle Emily (Hanlon) W.; m. Harriet Patricia Banfield, Aug. 1, 1946; children: Stephen, Mark, Brian, Patricia. Student, Coll. William and Mary, 1938-39; BS in Econs. magna cum laude, Bowdoin Coll., 1941. CPA, Oreg. Staff acct. Lybrand Ross Bros. & Montgomery, Boston, 1941-43, Whitfield Stratford & Co., Portland, Oreg., 1946-51; ptnr. Workman, Shephard & Co., CPAs, 1951-60; sole practitioner, 1961-96. Newsletter columnist Good Impressions, 1993-98. Chmn. bd. Sylvan Sch., Portland, 1956-57; pres. Doernbecher Children's Hosp. Found., Portland, 1963-85, Bowdoin Club Oreg., Portland, 1963—; trustee Oreg. Episcopal Schs., Portland, 1974-76. Lt. (j.g.) Supply Corps, USNR, 1944-46. Mem. AICPA, Inst. Mgmt. Accts. (pres. Portland chpt. 1954-55), Oreg. Soc. CPA's, Pacific Printing and Imaging Assn., Arlington Club, Multnomah Athletic Club, Phi Beta Kappa. Avocations: bird hunting, fishing, horticulture. Home: 4381 SW Fairview Blvd Portland OR 97221-2709 Office: 1750 SW Skyline Blvd Portland OR 97221-2533

WORKMAN, ROBERT PETER, artist, cartoonist; b. Chgo., Jan. 27, 1961; s. Tom Okko and Virginia (Martin) W. Doctorate d'Etat, Diplome 3d Cycle, Sch. of Louvre, Paris, 1997; prof. habilite, France, 1997; DEA, French U. Lumiere, Lyon; Doctorate in Hieroglyphics, Nat. Inst. Lang./Civilizations, Egypt, 1997; PhD, Roosevelt U., Belgium; postgrad., Sch. of Art Inst. Chgo.; Ecole Doctorale des Sciences, U. Blaise-Pascal/U. D'Auvergue, 1998. Freelance artist, Chgo.; artist Villager Newspaper, 1991—; instr. St. Xavier Coll., 1985; cartoonist Bridge View News, Oak Lawn, Ill., 1983-89, Village View Pubs., Oak Lawn, 1989; artist Villager News, 1991; creator acrylic sculpture ArtStyle. TV art dir. Media-In-Action, Oak Lawn; lectr. Oxford U., Eng., U. Ariz., 1996; substitute tchr. Morgan Park Acad., Chgo.; artist-in-residence Chgo. Pub. Libr.; featured voice Am. Radio, 1992; maitre de confs., Paris; creator acrylic sculpture art style. Author: (cartoon strip) Cypher, 1983-89; Sesqui Squirrel Coloring Book, 1982, Sesqui Squirrel History of Chicago, 1983, Book of Thoth, The Great Pyramid A Book in Stone, 1998, Easter Island and Egypt,(artists' books) Sesqui Squirrel History of the Constitution, Sesqui Squirrel Presents How Columbus Discovered America, The Sesqui-Squirrel Chicago Millennium Book, 1999; author: (novel) Angels of Doom, Book of THOTH, The Great Pyramid a Book in Stone, 1998, Easter Island and Egypt; artworks and books in collections of over 120 mus. and librs. and pvt. collections, including Mus. du Louvre, Paris, France, Lincoln Collection, Ill., Smithsonian, Art Inst. Chgo., Daley Br. Libr., Chgo., Ill. Exec. Mansion Mus., Musee du Louvre, Paris, Lincoln Collection State of Ill., Sesquicentennial Archives Chgo. Pub. Libr. (awards and honors), Vatican Libr., Rome, Bodleian Libr. Oxford (Eng.) U., Mt. Greenwood br. Pub. Libr. Chgo., Ill. Collection, Libr. Nat. Mus. Am. Art, Nat. Portrait Gallery, Carter Presdl. Libr., Reagan Presdl. Libr., Expo. U.S. Pavilion Lisbon, Portugal, 1998; exhibited Am. Pavilion, Expo 92, Seville, Spain, Royal Acad. Arts, 1995, Am. Pavilion, Expo 98, Lisbon, Portugal, inaugural exhbn. of the New Millennium/Chgo. Pub. Libr., 2000; featured on Sta. WBBM-TV, Chgo., 1998; contbr. poetry to books: Journey to Infinity, America at the Millennium, Treasured Poems of America; creator of Planetnet Concept; inventor Tri-CAR; inventor millenium star explorer spacecraft, Tri-CAR. Mem. nat. adv. bd. Am. Security Coun., Boston, Va.; founder Kennedy Pk. Libr., Chgo. Featured in Artist's mag., 1990; recipient Resolution City Coun. Chgo., 1992. Mem. Am. Watercolor Soc., Gen. Med. Coun. (Eng.), No. Ill. Newspaper Assn., Art Inst. Chgo. (freelancer 1991), Artists' Resource Trust Ft. Wayne Mus. Art, Ridge Art Assn., VFW, S.W. Archdiocesan Singles, Friends Oxford U., Alumni Sch. Art Inst. Chgo., KC, Mensa. Roman Catholic. Home and Office: 2509 W 111th St Apt 2E Chicago IL 60655-1325

WORKMAN, WILLARD ALLYN, association executive; b. Milford, Del., Oct. 30, 1946; s. Willard Harold and Louise Elizabeth Workman; 1 child, Amanda. BA in Polit. Sci., L.I. U., 1969. Spl. negotiator internat. trade controls Dept. State, Washington, 1987-88; v.p., gen. mgr. internat. U.S. C. of C., 1988-2001, sr. v.p. Internat. Affairs, 2001—. V.p. Ctr. Internat. Pvt. Enterprise, Washington, 1992; trustee U.S. Coun. for Internat. Bus., N.Y.C., 1993-2001. With USN, 1969-73. Mem. Univ. Club. E-mail: wworkman@uschamber.com.

WORLEY, DAVID, lawyer; b. Stuttgart, Germany, Sept. 30, 1958; AB, Harvard U., 1980; JD, U. Va., 1985. Atty. Arnall, Golden & Gregory, Atlanta, 1985-87; pvt. practice Jonesboro, 1987-90; atty. Glave, Glave, Fincher and Breakfield, 1991-94, Jacobs and Slowsky, Atlanta, 1994—; chmn. Dem. Party, 1998—2001. Chmn. Ga. State Dem. Party, 1998—; chmn. bd. trustees Clayton County Libr. Bd., 1993—. Mem. Assn. of State Dem. Chairs. Office: Jacobs and Slowsky 100 Peachtree St NW Ste 1950 Atlanta GA 30303-1919 also: 1100 Spring St NW Ste 710 Atlanta GA 30309-2829*

WORLEY, JANE LUDWIG, lawyer; b. Reading, Pa., Sept. 4, 1917; d. Walter Schearer and Marion Grace (Johns) L.; m. Floyd Edwin Worley, Oct. 30, 1946 (dec. Jan. 1982); children: Laetitia Anne, Thomas Allen, Christopher Ludwig. AB, Bryn Mawr Coll., 1938; JD, Temple U., 1942. Bar: Pa. 1943, U.S. Dist. Ct. (ea. dist.) Pa. 1980, U.S. Supreme Ct. 1968. Assoc. Richardson Moss & Richardson, Reading, 1943-48; pvt. practice Wernersville, Pa., 1948—. V.p., bd. dirs. Worley Lumber Co. Inc., Wernersville, 1955—. Sec. Friends of Reading Mus., 1986-91; sec. Berks County chpt. ARC, 1986-87, v.p., 1987-91. Mem. ABA, Pa. Bar Assn., Berks County Bar Assn., DAR, Jr. League Reading. Republican. Mem. United Ch. of Christ. Avocations: antique and art collecting, travel. Office: 6210 Penn Ave Wernersville PA 19565

WORLEY, LLOYD DOUGLAS, English language educator; b. Lafayette, La., Sept. 11, 1946; s. Albert Stiles and Doris (Christy) W.; m. Maydean Ann Mouton, Apr. 4, 1966; children: Erin Shawn, Albert Stiles II. BA, U. SW La., 1968, MA, 1972; PhD, So. Ill. U., 1979. Ordained priest, Liberal Cath. Ch. 1982. Tchr. Lafayette H.S., 1969-74; vis. asst. prof. dept. English So. Ill. U., Carbondale, 1979-80; asst. prof. dept. English Pa. State U., DuBois, 1980-87; assoc. prof., assoc. dir. composition dept. English U. No. Colo., Greeley, 1987-88, prof. dept. English, 1988—. Acting dir. Writing Component Ctr. Basic Skills, So. Ill. U., 1980. Editor: Ruthven Literary Bull., 1988-92; contbr. book chpts., articles. Rector Parish of St. Albertus Magnus, sec-treas. Am. Province; provost Am. Clerical Synod Chpt.; Sovereign Grand Master, Order of Holy Sepulchre, 1982—. Decorated Knight Bachelor, 1996, Hereditary Knight of San Luigi, 1996, Knight Cmdr. Order of Merit St. Angilbert, 1993, Prelate Comdr. Order of Noble Companions of Swan, 1993, Grand Chamberlain, 1995, Knight Order of Guadalupe, 1995, Knight Comdr. Justice Sovereign Order St. John, Knight Grand Cross of Bear of Alabona, 1995, Knight Grand Cross Order St. Stanislaus, 1998, Knight Comp. Crown of Alabona, 1998, Knight Grand Cross Order St. John, 1998, Knight Grand Cross Order Sts. Constantine the Great and Helen, Grand Cross with Collar of Order of Noble Companion of Swan, 2000; created hereditary Baron, Royal and Serene House of Alabona-Ostrogojsk et de Garama, HRSH Prince William I, created Count Palatine of Maxalla, 1996, created Hereditary Duke of Maxalla, 2000. Fellow Philalethes Soc.; mem. ASCD, Internat. Assn. for Fantastic in Arts (divsn. head Am. Lit. 1987-93), Lord Ruthven Assembly (pres. 1988-94, founding pres. emeritus 1994), Conf. Coll. Composition and Comm., Nat. Coun. Tchrs. English, Am. Conf. Irish Studies, Sigma Tau Delta (bd. dirs. 1990-96, high plains regent various states 1992-96, 10-Yr. Outstanding Advisor award 1997), Masons (century lodge #190), Order of DeMolay (chevalier, cross of honor, legion of honor), Knights Holy Sepulchre (Sov. Grand Master), Rose Croix Martinist Order (pres. premier nat. coun.). Democrat. Office: 3620 W 10th B-150 Greeley CO 80634-9655 Fax: 419-793-6884.

WORLEY, MARGARET ANN, apparel designer, writer; b. Presque Isle, Maine, Sept. 6, 1935; d. Charles Lawrence and Charlotte Lavinia (Baker) Trombley; m. Francis Wybe Kortecamp, July 31, 1957; children: Shari Ann Kortecamp, Stanny Rae Kortecamp; m. Garland Thornton Worley, Oct. 1, 1972 (div.); children: Doell Marie. Lic. Cosmetology Hartford Regional Tech, cert. Fashion Design Bishop Sch. of Design. Designer / seamstress self-employed, Loma Linda, Calif., 2002—02, Hollywood; designer, seamstress, hairstylist & colorist Miss Am. Pageant, Dallas, Houston. Mem. Adv. Bd., Redlands Yucaipa ROP, Adv. Bd., Colton Sch. Dist., Colton, Calif. Author: (book) It's Not Good That Man or Woman Should Be Alone. Amb. chairperson Loma Linda Chamber, Loma Linda, Calif., 2000—02, amb., 1990—2002; mem. Joseph Princ, Inc., 1999—2002. Recipient Amb. of the Yr., Loma Linda Chamber, 1995 & 2000, Mem. of the Yr., 1998. Non-Denominational. Achievements include design of Wheelchair Bag. Avocations: writing, reading, discussion groups. Home: 1411 Anderson St Loma Linda CA 92354

WORLEY, ROBERT WILLIAM, JR. retired lawyer; b. Anderson, Ind., June 13, 1935; s. Robert William and Dorothy Mayhew (Hayler) W.; m. Diana Lynn Matthews, Aug. 22, 1959; children: Nathanael, Hope Hillegas. BS in Chem. Engring., Lehigh U., 1956; LLB, Harvard U., 1960. Bar: Conn. 1960, U.S. Supreme Ct. 1966, Fla. 1977. Assoc. then ptnr. Cummings & Lockwood, Stamford, Conn., 1960-91; gen. counsel Consol. Asset Recover Corp. sub. Chase Manhattan Corp., Bridgeport, 1991-94; v.p., asst. gen. counsel The Chase Manhattan Bank, N.Y.C., 1994-2001; ret., 2001. Mem. trustees com. on bequests and trusts Lehigh U., 1979—; mem. Conn. Legis. Task Force on Probate Court Sys., 1991-93; chmn. Greenwich Arts Coun., 1981-82; v.p., bd. dirs. Greenwich Choral Soc., 1962-77, 80, mem., 1960-95; bd. dirs. Greenwich Ctr. for Chamber Music, 1981-85, Greenwich Symphony, 1986-89; commr. Greenwich Housing Authority, 1972-77; past mem. Rep. Town Com. Greenwich; mem. bldg. com. for sr. ctr. Greenwich Bd. Selectman, 1980-81. Capt. JAGC, AUS, 1965. Mem. Conn. Bar Assn. (exec. com. probate sect. 1980), Harvard Club Boston. Christian Scientist. Home: PO Box 1055 Marion MA 02738-0019

WORLEY, WILL J, engineering consultant; b. Gibson City, Ill., Aug. 2, 1919; s. William Carlton and Anna (Osborn) W.; m. Carolyn Juergensmeyer, Aug. 22, 1954; children: James Logan, Thomas Richard, Fred Burton. BSME, U. Ill., 1943, MS in Theoretical and Applied Mechanics, 1945, PhD in Engring., 1952. Registered profl. engr., Ill. Instr. Theoretical and Applied Mechanics U. Ill., Urbana, 1943—49, asst. prof., 1949-57, assoc. prof., 1957-60, prof., 1960-89, prof. emeritus, 1989—. Cons., instr. acoustics lab. IBM, Endicott, N.Y., summer 1960, mech. analyst, instr., San Jose, Calif., summer 1961; cons. acoustics lab., Poughkeepsie, N.Y., summer 1963; cons. on accident reconstrn., indsl. accidents, fires and explosions to comml. and ins. cos. and lawyers; organizer session on sports medicine Acoustical Soc. Am. Contbr. articles to profl. jours.; patentee in field. Mem. ASME (life, past chmn. com. applied mechanics div. and machine design div., editor shock and vibration symposium 1962), Sigma Xi, Pi Tau Sigma, Pi Mu Epsilon. Home: 2106 Zuppke Urbana IL 61801-6706

WORMACK, KAREN ELISE, small business owner, poet; b. Newark, Sept. 6, 1962; d. John Wesley Wormack Jr. and Gloria Marlena (Erwin) Wormack-Davis. BA in English/Comms., Kean Coll., 1985; MPA, Marywood U., Scranton, Pa., 2000. Cert. hypnotherapist. Customer svc. agt. Piedmont Airlines, Newark, 1986-87; investment rep. First Investor's Corp., Piscataway, N.J., 1987-90; sales assoc. Weichert Realtors, Morristown, 1991-93; real estate salesperson Shawnee Resort, Shawnee-on-Delaware, Pa., 1995-96; owner The Pocono Love Basket, 1995—; clin. hypnotherapist The Hypnosis Inst. N.Y., 1998; quality assurance coord. Cmty. Access Unltd., Human Svc. Agy. for Devel. Disabled, Elizabeth, N.J., 1999-2000; team leader Home Based Waiver Program Servicing Children and Adults with devel. disability; team leader Home Based Waiver Program Step-By-Step, Inc., 2000—; therapeutic staff support Colonial Intermediate Unit 20, Easton, Pa., 2001, Youth Advocate Program, 2001—; owner The Fancy Cone, The Fancey Cone, 2002—. Sec./counselor Hugh O'Brian Youth Found., North Brunswick, N.J., 1988-89. Author: A Voice Crying in the Wilderness, 1990, The Adventures of Prissy and Missy, 1993, Enchanted Seraphim!, 1999, Emmanuel's Accolades!, 2000; contbg. author: Great Poems of the Western World, 1990, On Terrorism, 1990, Spirit of the Age, 1996, Sound of Poetry, 1996. Mem. Hergott Fund. Found. Com. Recipient Outstanding Poet award World of Poetry, Sacramento, 1990, Clearance C. and Elizabeth Walton Medal of Honor for Excellence in Pub. Adminstrn., Marywood U., 2000. Mem. The Assn. for the Severely Handicapped, Nat. Bd. Realtors, Pi Alpha Alpha, Alpha Epsilon Lambda. Mem. Christian Ch. Avocations: poetry, song writing, modeling, philanthropy, exploring caves. Home: 503 Thomas St Stroudsburg PA 18360-2104 E-mail: kewormack@aol.com.

WÖRMAN, ANDERS LARS EDVARD, civil engineering educator; b. Stockholm, Mar. 19, 1961; s. Lars-Erik and Charlotte (Thunberg) W.; m. Ulrike Elisabeth Melin, Oct. 7, 1989; children: Johannes, Oscar, Jacob. MSc in Civil Engring., Royal Inst. Tech., Stockholm, 1985, PhD in Hydraulic Engring., 1991. Asst. prof. engring. Royal Inst. Tech., Stockholm, 1988—91; rsch. engr. Swedish State Power Co., Sweden, 1991—93; assoc. prof. engring. Uppsala (Sweden) U., 1992—2002; assoc. prof. biometry and informatics Swedish U. Agrl. Scis., Uppsala, 2002—. Coord. aquatic and environ. engring. programs, Uppsala U., 1993-2000; dir. of studies, 1993-2001; assoc. prof. engring. Royal Inst. of Tech., Stockholm, 2001-2002. Contbr. articles to profl. jours. Recipient Thernwall prize Royal Acad. Engring. Sci., Sweden, 1992. Mem. Internat. Assn. Hydraulic Rsch., N.Y. Acad. Sci., Am. Geophys. Union. Avocation: climbing. Office: Swedish U Agrl Scis PO Box 7013 SE 75007 Uppsala Sweden E-mail: anders.worman@bi.slu.se., worman@aom.kth.se.

WORMAN, HOWARD JAY, internist, educator; b. Paterson, N.J., May 21, 1959; s. Louis and Dora (Rubin) W. BA, Cornell U., 1981; MD, U. Chgo., 1985. Diplomate Am. Bd. Internal Medicine. Intern N.Y. Hosp., N.Y.C., 1985-86, resident, 1986-87; guest investigator Rockefeller U., 1987-90; asst. prof. Mt. Sinai Sch. Medicine, 1990-94; asst. attending physician Mt. Sinai Hosp., 1990-94; asst. prof. Columbia U. Coll. Physicians and Surgeons, 1995-98, assoc. prof., 1998—; asst. attending physician N.Y. Presbyn. Hosp., Columbia-Presbyn. Ctr., 1995-98, assoc. attending physician, 1998—; dir. divsn. digestive and liver diseases Presbyn. Hosp., 1999—. Mem. med. adv. com. Muscular Dystrophy Assn., 2000—. Mem. editl. bd. Hepatology, Frontiers in Biosci., World Jour. Gastroenterology; contbr. articles to profl. jours. Recipient Physician-Scientist award NIH, 1987-92; Charles E. Culpeper scholar in Med. Scis., 1994-95, Irma T. Hirschl scholar, 1997—. Mem. AAAS, ACP, Am. Chem. Soc., Am. Fedn. Med. Rsch. (Trainee award in clin. rsch. 1989, Henry Christian award 1990), Am. Soc. Cell Biology, Am. Assn. Study of Liver Diseases, Am. Gastroent. Assn., Am. Soc. Clin. Investigation, N.Y. Acad. Scis. (vice chmn. biol. scis. sect. 1992-93, chmn. 1993-94), Hon. Order Ky. Cols., Phi Beta Kappa. Democrat. Jewish. Avocations: music, reading. Office: Columbia U Coll Physicians-Surgeons 630 W 168th St New York NY 10032-3795 E-mail: hjwl4@columbia.edu.

WORMAN, JAMES VINCENT, music educator; b. Raritan, N.J., Oct. 3, 1960; s. George Robinson and Katherine Yawger Worman; m. Amy Virginia Worman, July 1, 1989; 1 child, Jared Thomas. B in Mus. Edn., Shenandoah Conservatory, 1983; MusM, Va. Commonwealth U., 1987; PHD, U. Wis., 1997. Band dir. South Carroll H.S., Sykesville, Md., 1983-84, Laurel Park H.S., Martinsville, Va., 1984-85; isntr. saxophone U. Richmond, 1985-86; band dir. Orange County H.S., Orange, 1987-93; adj. prof. music Edgewood Coll., Madison, Wis., 1996-97; asst. prof. Trinity U., San Antonio, 1997—. Score reader for prodn. Wis. Pub. TV, Madison, 1996; mus. cons. San Antonio Sch. Dist., 1998-2000; chief adjudicator Ctrl. Ark. Marching Championship, Little Rock, 1998—. Editor (mus. composition) Beau Ideal, 1998; arranger (mus. composition) Old American Country Set, 1999. Recipient Excellence in Mus. Direction award Alamo City Theatre Arts Coun., San Antonio, 2000. Mem. Nat. Band Assn., Soc. Am. Music (com. chair 1999-01), Coll. Band Dirs. Nat. Assn., Internat. Jazz Educators Assn., Tex. Music Educators Assn. (region coll. chair 1998—). Avocations: U.S. history, American culture, baseball, travel. Home: 15747 Wood Sorrel San Antonio TX 78247 Office: Trinity Univ Dept Music 715 Stadium Dr San Antonio TX 78212 E-mail: jworman@trinity.edu.

WORMAN, LINDA KAY, nursing administrator; b. Buffalo, Sept. 28, 1959; d. Robert Kindig and Winifred (Hostetter) W. BSN, Emory U., 1980; MPH, U. N.C., 1986. RN; cert. lactation cons.; cert. advanced nursing adminstr.; cert. inpatient obstet. nurse. Staff nurse SICU U. Hosp., Cleve., 1980-81; staff nurse labor and delivery Med. Ctr., Columbus, Ga., 1981; dep. prin. tutor Macha (Africa) Mission Hosp., 1981-85; staff nurse neurosci. ICU Duke U. Hosp., Durham, N.C., 1985-86; nurse mgr. maternal-child Woodland (Calif.) Meml. Hosp., 1986-88; nurse mgr. obstetrics Pa. State U. Hosp., Hershey, 1988-94; v.p. nursing svcs. Jersey Shore (Pa.) Hosp., 1994-96; dir. maternal-child health Newton (N.J.) Meml. Hosp., 1996-98, with maternal-child health, rehab. and behavioral svcs., 1998—. Rape and domestic violence crisis vol. Harrisburg YWCA, 1992—94; bd. dirs. N.W. N.J. Maternal Child Health Network, 1996—2000. Mem. Pa. Perinatal Assn. (bd. dirs. 1989-94). Home: 4 Peregrine Point Newton NJ 07860-1468 Office: Newton Meml Hosp 175 High St Newton NJ 07860-1099

WORMAN, SYLVIA EASLER, artist; b. Evansville, Ind., Sept. 5, 1935; d. Earl and Ruth (Alley) Easler; m. James M. Worman, Jan. 29, 1955; 1 child, Kathy Sue. Student, U. Evansville, 1959-61, U. So. Ind., 1980-83. Watercolor tchr. U. So. Ind., Evansville, 1990-95. Tchr. watercolor workshops for Ky. and Ind. watercolor groups; demonstrator Ind. and Ky. Watercolor Socs., others. Mem. Am. Watercolor Soc. (assoc.), Ky. Watercolor Soc. (signature, Purchase and Merit awards 1981-85), Ind. World Orgn. China Painters (pres. 1981-82), Watercolor West (exhibiting), Brown County Art Guild (artist), Hoosier Salon (artist, Purchase and Merit awards 1981-87), Watercolor Soc. Ind. (signature artist, purchase and merit awards). Avocations: watercolor, acrylic, collage, printmaking, photography. Home: 890 Sycamore Lake Dr Evansville IN 47712-3628

WORMER, THOMAS ANDREW, surgeon; b. Buffalo, Dec. 3, 1956; s. Donald Andrew and Elinor Ann (Bliss) W.; m. Melissa Jane Ertell, Apr. 11, 1988; children: Matthew Thomas, Margaret Elizabeth, Samuel James, Sarah Jane. BS, Allegheny Coll., 1979; MD, Albany Med. Coll., 1984. Diplomate Am. Bd. Surgery. Intern Millard Fillmore Hosp., Buffalo, 1984-85, resident in gen. surgery, 1985-89; attending surgeon F.F. Thompson Hosp., Canandaigua, N.Y., 1989-95, chief surgery, 1994-99. Fellow ACS; mem. Canandaigua Med. Soc. (pres. 1994), N.Y. State Med. Soc. Presbyterian. Office: Canandaigua Medical Group 335 Parrish St Canandaigua NY 14424-1794 E-mail: tandw@aol.com.

WORMSER, GARY PAUL, epidemiologist, researcher; b. Wilmington, Del., Jan. 17, 1947; MD, Johns Hopkins U., Baltimore, MD, 1972; BA, U. of Pa, Philadelphia, PA, 1968. Chief of infectious diseases NY Med. Coll., Valhalla, NY, 1981—, vice chair dept. of medicine, 1998—. Contbr. articles to profl. jours. Recipient Dean's Rsch. Award, NY Med. Coll., 1999. Fellow: IDSA; mem.: ASM. Achievements include research in early descriptions of AIDS; HGE in New York; Borrelia Lonestare Infection. Office: New York Medical College Munger 2nd floor Valhalla NY 10595 Office Fax: 914-493-7289.

WORNER, THERESA MARIE, internist, educator; b. Breckenridge, Minn., Feb. 19, 1948; d. William Daniel and Elizabeth (Stelten) W.; m. Martin Herbst, Mar. 24, 1979. AB, St. Theresa Coll., 1970; MD, U. Minn., 1974. Diplomate Am. Bd. Internal Medicine. Rotating intern Kings County Hosp., Bklyn., 1974-75, resident medicine, 1975-77; fellow VA Med. Ctr., Bronx, N.Y., 1977-78, chief med. sect. Alcoholism treatment program, 1978-87; asst. prof. medicine Mt. Sinai Sch. Medicine, N.Y.C., 1984-87; mem. faculty Postgrad. Ctr., 1985-90; physician in charge alcoholism svcs. L.I. Coll. Hosp., Bkyn., 1987-92; assoc. prof. clin. medicine SUNY, Health Sci. Ctr., 1988—; dir. rsch. 32BJ Health Fund, 1992-99; clin. assoc. prof. Pub. Health Cornell U. Med. Coll., 1996—; pres. Menachem Publ., Bethlehem, N.H., 1999—. Pres./founder Alcohol. Info, 1995-97; advisor Patient Care Mag., 1984—; cons. REA, 1996—. Referee Hepatology, 1986, Jour. Study Alcohol, 1984—, Substance Abuse, 1992—, Alcoholism: Clinical and Exptl. Rsch., 1992—, Drug and Alcohol Dependence, 1993—, Drug Therapy, 1994—, Addiction, 1996—; contbr. numerous articles to profl. jours. Active Bronx Bot. Garden, Mus. Modern Art, Met. Mus. Art, Mus. Natural History, Bklyn. Mus. Art, Turtle Bay Civic Assn., Bklyn. Lyric Opera, Empire State Opera, Amato Opera. Grantee Child Welfare Adminstrn., 1991, 92, 93; recipient Physicians Recognition award AMA, 1984, 89, 91, 96, Cert. of Merit Govt. Employees Ins. Co., 1986, PACT Intern Site award, 1991, 92. Fellow ACP, N.Y. Acad. Medicine; mem. AAAS, Am. Med. Soc. on Alcoholism and Other Drug Dependence, Am. Soc. Internal Medicine, Am. Assn. for Study Liver Diseases (Travel award 1978), N.Y. Acad. Scis., Rsch. Soc. on Alcoholism, Internat. Soc. Biologic Rsch. in Alcoholism. Office: 322 E 50th St New York NY 10022-7902

WORONOFF, ISRAEL, former psychology educator; b. Bklyn., Dec. 30, 1926; s. Samuel and Lena (Silberman) W.; m. Fay Goldberg, Feb. 11, 1950; 1 child, Gary. AB in Psychology, U. Mich., 1949, MA in Sociology, 1952, PhD in Edn., 1954. Lic. psychologist, Mich. Instr. Flint (Mich.) Jr. Coll., 1953-54; asst. prof. St. Cloud (Minn.) State Coll., 1954-56, Ea. Mich. U., Ypsilanti, 1956-59, assoc. prof., 1959-62, prof., 1962-92. Cons. psychologist Midwest Mental Health Clinic, Dearborn, Mich., 1978-83, Orchard Hills Psychiat. Ctr., Novi, Mich., 1983—; mem. Bd. Jewish Fedn. Washtenaw County, 1997—; co-chair Bd. Jewish Family Svc. of Ann Arbor, 1997. Author: Educator's Guide to Stress Management, 1986. Mem. bd. Jewish Family Svc. of Ann Arbor, 1996—, Jewish Fedn., Ann Arbor, 1997—; mem. cmty. rels. com. Jewish Cmty. Assn., Ann Arbor, Mich., 1990-92; v.p. edn. Beth Israel Congregation, Ann Arbor, 1985-87; mem. adv. bd. Mich. Anti-Defamation League of B'nai B'rith, 1958—. Mem. APA, Mich. Psychol. Assn., Am. Ednl. Rsch. Assn. Democrat. Home: 2519 Londonderry Rd Ann Arbor MI 48104-4017 E-mail: ted_woronoff@online.emich.edu.

WORRALL, JOHN DENNIS, economics educator, consultant, writer; b. Wildwood, N.J., July 29, 1942; s. John and Adele Veronica (McKenna) W.; m. Suzanne Elizabeth Hopkins; children: Heather, John; m. Janet Priscilla Moran; 1 child, Kevin. BA, Rutgers U., 1969, MA, 1972, PhD, 1976. Asst. dir. Rutgers Bur. Econ. Rsch., New Brunswick, N.J., 1974-77; dir. rsch. Nat. Ctr. for Employment Handicapped-Human Resources Ctr., L.I., N.Y., 1977-78; v.p., dir. econ. rsch. NCCI, N.Y.C., 1979-83; prof. econs. Rutgers U., Camden, N.J., 1983—, asst. dir. Bur. Econ. Rsch. New Brunswick, 1983—. Advisor Courier Post newspaper, Camden, 1994-97; John R. Commons lectr. U. Wis. Bus. Sch.,

Madison, 1991. Co-author: An Evaluation of Policy Related Rehabilitation Research, 1975; co-editor: Placement in Rehabilitation, 1979, Benefit Issues in Workers' Compensation, 1985; editor: Safety and the Workforce, 1983; assoc. editor Jour. Ins.: Math. and Econs., 1990—, Jour. Risk and Ins., 1992—. Del. White House Conf. on Handicapped, Washington, 1977; pres. South Jersey Irish Am. Unity Conf., Fedn. Irish Am. Socs., Phila., 1996-98; bd. dirs. St. Patrick's Day Observance Com., Phila., 1996-98, Phila. Immigration Resource Ctr., 1999-2001. Sgt. U.S. Army, 1960-66. Named Outstanding Faculty Mem. Rutgers U. Alumni Assn., 1991; honoree Gaelic Ball, Ladies Ancient Order Hibernians, Phila., 1998. Fellow Risk Theory Soc. (sec. 1990, pres. 1991); mem. Nat. Acad. Social Ins., Am. Econs. Assn., Am. Risk and Ins. Assn. (Robert I. Mehr award 2001), Commodore John Barry Soc. (pres. 1996-98). Roman Catholic. Avocations: golf, fishing. Office: Rutgers U Armitage Hall Camden NJ 08102 Fax: 609-354-3274. E-mail: jworrall@crab.rutgers.edu.

WORRALL, JUDITH RAE, health and welfare plan consultant; BA, Simpson Coll., Indianola, Iowa, 1984. Fin. planner IDS/Am. Express, West Des Moines, Iowa, 1987-89; client mgr. Haake Cos., Kansas City, Mo., 1993-95; asst. v.p. Aon Cons. Group, 1995—2000; sr. cons. Gallagher Benefit Svcs., 2000—. Bd. dirs. Arthritis Found., Kansas City, 2000—. Named Woman of Yr., Leukemia Soc. Am., 1997. Mem.: Greater Kansas City Health Underwriters Assn. (pres. 2001—02). Office: Gallagher Benefit Svcs Ste 800 2345 Grand Blvd Kansas City MO 64108

WORRELL, ANNE EVERETTE ROWELL, newspaper publisher; b. Surry, Va., Mar. 7, 1920; d. Charles Gray and Ethel (Roache) Rowell; m. Thomas Eugene Worrell, Sept. 12, 1941; 1 child Thomas Eugene. Student, Va. Intermont Coll., 1939, LittD (hon.), 1991; student, U. Richmond, 1965. Founding stockholder Worrell Newspapers Inc., 1949, v.p., dir., 1969-73; v.p., sec. Worrell Investment Co., Charlottesville, Va.; pres. The Genan Co. (formerly Bristol Newspapers). Pres. Bristol Jr. League, 1959; bd. dirs. The Corp. for Thomas Jefferson's Poplar Forest Found., Va. Hist. Soc., Va. Intermont Coll., Antiquities; active Bayly Mus., Monticello Cabinet. Named Outstanding Alumna, Va. Intermont Coll., 1981. Mem.: DAR (Shadwell chpt.), Nat. Trust for Hist. Preservation, Greencroft Club, Farmington Country Club, Contemporary Club. Episcopalian. Home: Seven Sunset Circle Farmington Charlottesville VA 22901 Office: Pantops PO Box 5386 Charlottesville VA 22905-5386

WORRELL, BILLY FRANK, health facility administrator; b. Columbia, Ala., Oct. 12, 1939; s. Beachum Worrell and Madeline (Scott) Wells; children: Jon, Kevin, Heather; m. Lorna Faye Jones, Nov. 26, 1991. A in Bus., Thomas Coll., Thomasville, Ga., 1978; BS magna cum laude, Albany State Coll., 1990, MBA, 1991; MS, LaSalle U., 1995, PhD, 1996. Registered respiratory therapist, respiratory care profl., arterial blood gas technician, neo-natal advanced life support technician. Electrician USN, 1957-60, Newport News (Va.) Shipbldg., 1960-63; mfg. mgr. Lockheed Aircraft, Marietta, Ga., 1963-70, Champion Homes, Thomasville, 1970-74; salesman Cadillac dealership, 1974-76; estimator Knight-Dodson Constrn. Co., 1976-78; adminstr. Ga. Army Nat. Guard, 1978-84; ret., 1984; allied health mgr. Phoebe Putney Meml. Hosp., Albany, 1988-93; dir. cardiopulmonary dept. Mitchell County Hosp., Camilla, Ga., 1994-95; dir. cardiopulmonary contract svcs. Sumter County Hosp., Americus, 1995—. Columnist newspaper column Lee County Ledger, 1990; actor film and plays. Vol. Salvation Army, Thomasville, 1978-83, Sr. Citizens Group, Thomasville, 1980-83, Kidney Found., Thomasville, 1980-85. Mem. Nat. Bd. Respiratory Care, Ga. Respiratory Care, Toastmasters. Republican. Avocations: guitar, singing, reading, photography, restoring old cars. Home: 1142 Philema Rd Leesburg GA 31763-3237 Office: Sumter County Hospital Americus GA 31709

WORRELL, CYNTHIA CELESTE, school nurse; b. Des Moines, Feb. 13, 1948; d. Ralph E. and Mary (Nading) W.; children: Steven F. Durand II, Sonya R. Bellson. BSN, Ariz. State U., 1977, MS, 1983; postgrad. in law, Newport U.; PhD cand. in Health Svcs., Walden U., 2002. RN, Ariz. Adminstrv. nurse mgr. Humana Hosp.; charge nurse med./surg. floor Humana Hosp. Desert Valley, Phoenix; staff nurse Staff Builders; sch. nurse Creighton Sch. Dist., 1978-81, Scottsdale Sch. Dist., 1986—. Instr. nursing dept. U. Phoenix, 1990—; mem. comprehensive sch. health essential skills adv. com. Ariz. Dept. Edn. Allstate Found. scholar. Mem.: AAUW, NEA, Space Nursing Soc., Scottsdale Edn. Assn. (exec. bd.), Ariz. Edn. Assn., Soc. Integrative Medicine, Am. Holistic Nurses Assn. (cert.). E-mail: cynandra@aol.com.

WORRELL, ERNST, energy and environmental analyst, researcher; b. Goor, Netherlands, Feb. 22, 1964; s. Cornelis Wijnandus and Marijke (Schets) W.; m. Antoinette Françoise Van Der Haagen, Dec. 5, 1997. MSc in Chemistry, Utrecht (The Netherlands) U., 1989, PhD in Chemistry, 1994. Asst. tchr. Utrecht U., 1986-89, sci. rschr., 1988-94, sr. scientist, 1995-98; scientist Princeton (N.J.) U., 1994-95; staff scientist Lawrence Berkeley (Calif) Nat. Lab., 1998—. Vis. prof. U. Sao Paulo, 1996; mem. roster of experts African Energy Policy Rsch. Network, 1996—; chmn. Summer sStudy on Energy Efficiency in Industry, 2001. Author: Potentials for Improved Use of Industrial Energy and Materials, 1994; assoc. editor Energy, the Internat. Jour., 1995—, Ency. of Energy; editor-in-chief Resources, Cons. and Recycling, 1998—; contbr. chpts. to books, articles to profl. jours. Office: Lawrence Berkeley Nat Lab MS 90-4000 1 Cyclotron Rd Berkeley CA 94720-0001 E-mail: eworrell@lbl.gov.

WORRELL, MARY THORA, loan officer; b. Montreal, Quebec, Can., July 8, 1932; came to U.S., 1974; d. Samuel R. and Rose E. Lewis; m. Henry G. Worrell, July 18, 1953 (div. Aug. 1974); children: Deborah, Geoffrey, John. BA, Sir George Williams U., Montreal, 1957. Lic. real estate agt., Mass. Rschr. Pvt. Stock, Palo Alto, Calif., 1979-90; loan officer Gt. We. Bank, Dublin, 1990-91, San Francisco Fed. Savs. Bank, 1991-92; residential loan specialist Eureka Bank, Foster City, Calif., 1992-93; residential loan officer First Interstate Bank, Oakland, 1993-94; loan officer First Nationwide Bank, Walnut Creek, 1994-95, Chase Manhattan Mortgage, San Francisco, 1995-96; sr. loan officer Pacific Bay Bank, San Pablo, Calif., 1996-97, Wausau Mortgage Corp., Pleasanton, 1997—. Speaker, mem. panel nat. prayer breakfast Ho. Commons, Ottawa, Can., 1972; speaker Wharton Sch. Human Resources, Phila., 1976; group leader Nat. Sci. Found. and George Washington U., 1976-77; mem. prison visitation com. Antioch Missionary Bapt. Ch., Oakland, Calif., 1992-98. Recipient Outstanding Svc. Conf. Speaker Pub. Rels. Student Soc. Am., 1976. Avocations: American Jurisprudence, prison fellowship, eagle watching, golf, ballroom dancing. E-mail: mthora@yahoo.com.

WORRELL, MASON DEWEY, b. Princeton, W.Va., July 12, 1941; s. Rufus Dewey and Margaret Helen Worrell; m. Shirley Jean White, Oct. 18, 1969; 2 children. BS in Music Edn., Concord Coll., Athens, W.Va., 1964; MA in Guidance, Radford U., 1973. Instrumental music tchr. Boone County Bd. Edn., Madison, W.Va., 1964; vocal and gen. music tchr. 7-9 Baltimore County Schs., Balt., 1964—65; gen. music and choral tchr. 1-12 Tazewell (Va.) County Schs., 1965—71; gen. music and choral tchr., presch.-6 Mercer County Schs., Princeton, W.Va., 1971—. Elem. music chmn. Mercer County Schs., 1986—. Mem.: W.Va. Music Educators Assn., Music Educators Nat. Conf., W.Va. Edn. Assn., NEA. Office: Mercer County Schs 1403 Honaker Ave Princeton WV 24740

WORRELL, PETER, professional hockey player; b. Pierrefonds, Que., Can., Aug. 18, 1977; Left wing Fla. Panthers, Sunrise, 1997—. Office: Fla Panthers Nat Car Rental Ctr 2555 Panther Pkwy Sunrise FL 33323*

WORRELL, RICHARD VERNON, orthopedic surgeon, college dean, dean; b. Bklyn., June 4, 1931; s. John Elmer and Elaine (Callender) Worrell; m. Audrey Frances Martiny, June 14, 1958; children: Philip Vernon, Amy Elizabeth. BA, NYU, 1952; MD, Meharry Med. Coll., 1958. Diplomate Am. Bd. Orthop. Surgery, Nat. Bd. Med. Examiners. Intern Meharry Med. Coll., Nashville, 1958—59; resident in gen. surgery Mercy-Douglass Hosp., Phila., 1960—61; resident in orthop. surgery State U. N.Y. Buffalo Sch. Medicine Affiliated Hosps., 1961—64; resident in orthop. pathology Temple U. Med. Ctr. , Phila., 1966—67; pvt. practice orthop. surgery, 1967—68; asst. prof. acting head divsn. orthop. surgery U. Conn. Sch. Medicine, 1968—70; attending orthop. surgeon E.J. Meyer Meml. Hosp., Buffalo, Millard Fillmore Hosp., Buffalo, VA Hosp., Buffalo, Buffalo State Hosp.; clin. instr. orthop. surgery SUNY, Buffalo, 1970—74; chief orthop. surgery VA Hosp., Newington, Conn., 1974—80; asst. prof. surgery (orthop.) U. Conn. Sch. Medicine, 1974—77, assoc. prof., 1977—83, asst. dean student affairs, 1980—83; prof. clin. surgery SUNY Downstate Med. Ctr., Bklyn., 1983—86; dir. orthop. surgery Brookdale Hosp. Med. Ctr., 1983—86; prof. orthop. U. N.Mex. Sch. Medicine, 1986—97, prof., vice chmn. dept. orthop., 1997—99, prof. emeritus, 1999—; dir. orthop. oncology U. N.Mex. Health Scis. Ctr., 1987—99; mem. med. staff U. N.Mex. Cancer Ctr., 1987—99; chief orthop. surgery VA Med. Ctr., Albuquerque, 1987—97. Cons. in orthop. surgery Newington (Conn.) Children's Hosp., 1968—70; mem. sickle cell disease adv. com. NIH, 1982—86. Bd. dirs. Big Bros. Greater Hartford. Served to capt. M.C. USAR, 1962—69. Fellow: ACS, Royal Soc. Medicine, London, Am. Acad. Orthop. Surgeons; mem.: AMA, N.Mex. Soc. Clin. Oncology, Internat. Soc. Orthop. Surgery and Traumatology, Orthop. Rsch. Soc., Internat. Fedn. Surg. Colls. (assoc.), Am. Soc. Clin. Oncology, Am. Soc. Clin. Pathologists, Am. Orthop. Assn., Alpha Omega Alpha.

WORSHAM, BERTRAND RAY, psychiatrist; b. Atkins, Ark., Feb. 14, 1926; s. Lewis Henry and Emma Lavada (Burris) W.; m. Margaret Ann Dickson, June 4, 1947 (div. 1960); children: Eric Dickson, Vicki Gayle; m. Lynne Ellen Reynolds, Aug. 27, 1976; children: Mary Ellen Clarice, Richard Andrew (dec.). BA, U. Ark., 1951; MD, U. Ark., Little Rock, 1955. Intern Hillcrest Med. Ctr., Tulsa, 1955-56; resident in psychiatry Menninger Sch. Psychiatry, Topeka, 1956-59; pvt. practice, 1959-78; clin. instr. U. Okla. Sch. Medicine, 1965-78; coord. drug and alcohol treatment unit Washington D.C. VA Med. Ctr., 1978-84; med. dir. Norman divsn. Okla. State Vets. Ctr., 1984-89; psychiat. cons. Comty. Counselling Ctr., Oklahoma City, 1989—. Cons. Oklahoma City Vets. Hosp., 1959-72, State Dept. Pub. Health, 1960-65, helping to establish cmty. mental health ctrs. throughout Okla.; dir. Cmty. Mental Health Ctr., Shawnee, Okla., 1965-72; mem. staff Coyne Campbell Hosp., 1960-78, Bapt. Med. Ctr., 1960-78, Mercy Health Ctr., 1960-78, Deaconess Hosp., 1963-78, Dr.'s Gen. Hosp., 1963-78, Presbyn. Hosp., 1962-78, U. Health Sci. Ctr., 1962-78, Children's Meml. Hosp., 1968-78, Oklahoma City VA Hosp., 1960-78, Washington D.C. Va. Hosp., 1978-84, Okla. Vets. Ctr., Norman, 1984-89. Mem. Civil Disaster Com., Oklahoma City, 1966, USN League, Okla., 1972—. With USAF, 1944-46; capt. USNR, 1957-86, ret. Fellow Menninger Found., Charles F. Menninger Found.; mem. AMA, Am. Psychiat. Assn. (Okla. dist. br. 1959-78, 84—), Assn. Mil. Surgeons of U.S., Ret. Officers Assn., World Fedn. for Mental Health, Internat. Platform Assn., Washington Psychiat. Assn., No. Va. Mental Health Assn., Masons (32 degree), VFW, Phi Beta Pi (Beta Theta chpt.). Republican. Episcopalian. Avocations: golf, church activities. Home: 9915 N Kelley Ave Oklahoma City OK 73131-2022 Office: 9915 N Kelley Ave Oklahoma City OK 73131-2022 *Man's ability to do goal-directed work is mans greatest asset. And as results add together we more nearly approach an infinitely profound civilization.*

WORSHAM, CHRISTINE BEHRENS, healthcare administrator; b. Portsmouth, Ohio, June 29, 1958; d. Carl William Behrens and Karin Rita (Roeder) Behrens-Ellis; m. Willia Scott Worsham, Oct. 7, 2000. AS in Sci., Brunswick Coll., 1979, AS in Nursing, 1981; BA in Econs., George Mason U., 1987; M in Healthcare Adminstrn., Xavier U., 1989. CCRN. Staff nurse Bath County Community Hosp., Hot Springs, Va., 1981-82; critical care nurse U. Va. Med. Ctr., Charlottesville, 1982-85; med. paralegal Donahue, Ehrmantraut, Montedonico, Washington, 1986; adminstrv. intern U. Va. Med. Ctr., Charlottesville, 1987; adminstrv. resident Alleghany Regional Hosp., Lowmoor, Va., 1989-95; exec.v.p. Odin Co., 1995—. Bd. dirs. Odin Co.; v.p. comms. Odin Sys. Internat. Mem. aux. Safe Harbor, St. Simons, Ga., 1991; active Med. Assistance Program, Brunswick, 1990, Rep. Women's Orgn., St. Simons, 1990; mem. found. bd. S.E. Ga. Regional Med. Ctr. Mem. AACCN, Am. Hosp. Assn., Am. Coll. Healthcare Execs., Golden Isles Investment Club St. Simons (pres. 1994), Omicron Delta Epsilon Theta. Presbyterian. Home: 1335 Hilltop Rd Charlottesville VA 22903

WORSLEY, GREGORY JOHN, creative director; b. Fall River, Mass., May 23, 1954; s. Leonard Joseph and Beatrice (Machado) W.; m. Kathleen Page Griffin, May 1, 1981; children: Kimberly Page, Benjamin Leonard. AA, Community Coll. of Balt., 1976. Art dir. The Reeves Agy., Balt., 1979-83, Hottman Edwards Advt., Balt., 1983-85, Farrar Network, White Marsh, Md., 1985-87; sr. art dir. Mktg. and Design, Inc., Columbia, 1988-89; creative dir. The Blum Group, Balt., 1989—. Designer: Hall of Fame Plaques for Balt. Orioles baseball team, 500 Home Run Club logo Am. Baseball League. Home: 150 Marburth Ave Baltimore MD 21286-1144 Office: The Blum Group 17 Warren Rd Baltimore MD 21208-5334

WORSLEY, JAMES RANDOLPH, JR. lawyer; b. Rocky Mount, N.C., July 28, 1924; s. James Randolph and Helen Marie (Killian) W.; m. Cornelia Cheston, Feb. 11, 1956; children: Cornelia Worsley Newell, Julia Worsley Neilson, Charlotte Cheston Worsley. BS, E. Carolina U., 1944; postgrad., Harvard U., 1944-45, LLB, 1949. Bar: N.C. 1949, D.C. 1949. Assoc. Klagsbrunn, Hanes & Irwin, Washington, 1949-54; ptnr. Ober, Kaler, Grimes & Shriver (and predecessor firm), 1955-94, coun., 1995—. Chmn. Md. Potomac Water Authority, 1969-71, Montgomery County (Md.) Charter Revision Commn., 1967; mem. pastoral coun. Archdiocese of Washington, 1975-78; bd. dirs. Madeira Sch., McLean, Va., 1975-81. Fellow Am. Bar Found.; mem. Chevy Chase Club, Met. Club, Knights of Malta. Democrat. Roman Catholic. Avocations: sailing, tennis. Home: 11 Quincy St Chevy Chase MD 20815-4226 Office: Ober Kaler Grimes & Shriver 1401 H St NW Ste 500 Washington DC 20005-2175

WORTH, DOUGLAS GREY, poet, songwriter, saxophonist; b. Mar. 14, 1940; s. Charles Brooke and Merida Grey; m. Karen Weisskopf (div.); children: Colin, Daniel; m. Patricia Hourihan, Feb. 14, 1998. BA, Swarthmore (Pa.) Coll., 1962; MA, Columbia U., 1964. English tchr. N.Y.C. Pvt. Schs., 1965-69, Newton (Mass.) Pub. Schs., 1970-90. Author: (poetry books) Of Earth, 1974, Invisibilities, 1977, Triptych, 1979, From Dream, From Circumstance, 1984, Once Around Bullough's Pond, 1987, Some Sense of Transcendence, 1999; contbr. poetry to anthologies, including New American Poetry, The Logic of Poetry, A Year in Poetry. Organizer Poets for Nuclear Disarmament, 1980s. Recipient 1st prize Internat. Poetry Awards, 1981; Artists Found. fellow in poetry, 1979; poetry grantee Mass. Arts Lottery Coun., 1983. Address: 31 Maple Ave # 1 Cambridge MA 02139-1115

WORTH, GARY JAMES, communications executive; b. Berkeley Township, N.J., Dec. 13, 1940; s. Melvin Raymond and Viola Vista (Landis) W. Student, Trenton State Coll., 1964, Palm Beach Jr. Coll., 1958-59. Dir. sta. relations MBS, Inc., N.Y.C., 1972, v.p. sta. relations, 1972, exec. v.p., 1972-79, mem. exec. com., 1978-79; v.p. Mut. Reports, Inc., Washington, 1972-79, dir., 1972-79; v.p., dir. WCFL, Inc., Chgo., 1979, Mut. Radio N.Y., Inc., N.Y.C., 1979; pres., dir. Robert Wold Co. Inc. and subs. Wold Communications, Inc., L.A., 1980-85; pres., chief exec. officer, dir. WesternWorld Inc. and subs. WesternWorld TV, 1986-93, The Video Tape Co., North Hollywood, Calif., 1987-93; sec. dir. WesternWorld Video Inc., L.A., 1986-87; CEO Starcom Television Svcs., Inc., 1993—96; chmn., CEO Starcom Entertainment, Inc., 1993—; CEO Starcom Mgmt. Svcs. Inc., 1993—, New Age Conversions, Inc., 1996—. Producer, dir.: USAF movie Assignment McGuire. Served to capt. USAF, 1960-66, Vietnam. Decorated Air Force Commendation medal, Armed Forces Expeditionary medal.; recipient Chief Herbert H. Almers Meml. award Bergen County (N.J.) Police Acad., 1972 Mem. Nat. Assn. Broadcasters, Nat. Assn. TV Program Execs., Nat. Informercial Mktg. Assn. Methodist. E-mail: star2874@msn.com.

WORTH, GEORGE JOHN, English literature educator; b. Vienna, Austria, June 11, 1929; came to U.S., 1940, naturalized, 1945; s. Adolph and Theresa (Schmerzler) W.; m. Carol Laverne Dinsdale, Mar. 17, 1951; children: Theresa Jean (Wilkinson), Paul Dinsdale. AB, U. Chgo., 1948, MA, 1951; PhD, U. Ill., 1954. Instr. English U. Ill., Urbana, 1954-55; faculty U. Kans., Lawrence, 1955—, assoc. prof., 1962-65, prof. English lit., 1965-95; prof. emeritus English, 1995—; asst. chmn. dept. U. Kans., Lawrence, 1961-62, assoc. chmn., 1962-63, acting chmn., 1963-64, chmn., 1964-79. Author: James Hannay: His Life and Work, 1964, William Harrison Ainsworth, 1972, Dickensian Melodrama, 1978, Thomas Hughes, 1984, Great Expectations: An Annotated Bibliography, 1986; editor: (with Harold Orel) Six Studies in Nineteenth Century English Literature and Thought, 1962, The Nineteenth Century Writer and His Audience, 1969, (with Edwin Eigner) Victorian Criticism of the Novel, 1985. Mem. AAUP, MLA, Dickens Fellowship, Dickens Soc., Midwest Victorian Studies Assn., Rsch. Soc. for Victorian Periodicals. Office: U Kans Dept English Wescoe Hall Lawrence KS 66045-7590 E-mail: GJWorth@aol.com.

WORTH, JAMES GALLAGHER, engineer, chemist; b. Phila., Sept. 20, 1922; s. Wilmon W. and Elsie (Gallagher) W.; m. Esther Alberta Cring, Sept. 11, 1943 (dec. 1981); children: Nancy Jeanne, Constance Anne, James Gallagher, Jr.; m. Barbara Marie Demarest, Mar. 22, 1985. AS, Rochester Inst. Tech., 1949; BS, U. Miami, 1951; postgrad., U. So. Calif., 1961—. Registered profl. engr., Calif., Fla. Chem. technician Internat. Paper Co., 1942-43, Eastmand Kodak Co., 1946-49; pres., founder, engr.-chemist Applied Rsch. Labs. Fla., Inc., Hialeah, 1949-84; chmn. bd., 1956-84; pres., chmn. bd. Ra-Chem Lab., Inc., Hialeah, 1964-66, Worth Engring., Inc., Hialeah, 1984—2001. Maj. USAAF, 1943-46; with USAFR, 1946-82. Fellow Am. Inst. Chemists; mem. Am. Chem. Soc., Am. Soc. Testing Materials, Am. soc. Metals, Nat. Soc. Profl. Engrs., Fla. Engring. Soc., Nat. Fire Protection Assn., Masons. Democrat. Methodist. Home: 751 Oriole Ave Miami FL 33166-3811 E-mail: justgworth@aol.com.

WORTH, LYNN HARRIS, writer; b. Flushing, N.Y., Sept. 21, 1934; d. Andrew Lamar Harris and Jean Hofmann; m. Chauncey Merrill Smith, Jr., June 20, 1992. AA, Vt. Coll., 1954; degree in Interior Design, NY Sch. Interior Design, 1971. Editl. asst. Time Mag., N.Y.C., 1954—56; pub. rels. asst. Silver Hill Found., New Canaan, Conn., 1958—61. Ptnr. Chameleon Interiors, Westport, Conn., 1972—84. Editor and pub.: Va. Gamebird Jour., editor, pub.: Magyar Vizsla News; contbr. articles to mags. Publicity dir. Westport Young Woman's League, 1967—68; publicity/pub. rels. Girl Scouts Am., Dist. 2, Fairfield County, 1967—69, LWV, Westport, polit. campaign for Gov. Tom Meskill, Westport. Mem.: Magyar Vizsla Soc. (founding mem.), numerous regional dog clubs, Vizsla Club of Am. (Am. Kennel Club del., v.p., sec. 1980—2002). Home: PO Box 1755 Clarksville VA 23927 Personal E-mail: Lynhar@aol.com.

WORTH, MARY PAGE, mayor; b. Balt., Jan. 23, 1924; d. Christian Allen and Margaret Pennington (Holbein) Schwarzwaelder; m. William James Worth, Nov. 4, 1947 (dec. May 1986); children: Margaret Page, William Allen, John David III. Student, Ladycliff Coll., Highland Falls, N.Y., 1941-42, Abbott Sch. Art, Washington, 1942-44; grad., Packer Coll. Inst., Brooklyn. Selectman Town of Searsport, Maine, 1973-75; mayor City of Belfast, 1986-2000. Recreation chmn. Town of Searsport, 1970-72. Del. Rep. State Conv., Maine, 1970-94; pres. Searsport Reps., 1974-76; active ARC Overseas Assn., 1976—; pres. Searsport C. of C., 1976-79; mem. exec. bd. Waldo County Com. for Social Action, Belfast, 1986—; mem. Abnacki coun. Girl Scouts U.S.; tutor Literacy Vols. Am.; recreation specialist ARC, Camp Haugen, Japan, 1946-47; bd. dirs. RSVP-Waldo County, Heat Start Waldo County; vol. tchr. Sch. for Blind, Cholon, Republic Vietnam, 1959-61, Am. Sch. at Saigon, Republic Vietnam, 1959-61; club dir. USAF Spl. Svcs., Ft. Meyer, Va., 1962-63, U.S. Army Spl. Svcs., Ft. Belvoir, Va., 1963-64; mem. Congresswoman Olympia Snow's Mpcl. Adv. Bd.; town chair Rep. Party; mem. adv. Belfast History Project. Mem. Gibson Island Club, 1938-73, mem. DAR (officer Maine 1986—), Internat. Platform Assn., Ret. Officers Assn. (life), 11th Airborne Assn./511th Parachute Infantry Regiment Korea War Vets. Assn., Waldo County Humane Soc. (pres. 1990—), Waldo County Law Enforcement (v.p. 1990—), VFW Aux., Am. Legion Aux., Belfast Garden Club (parliamentarian 1984—), Rotary (bd. govs. com. Maine St. '90), ARC Overseas Assoc.. Avocations: Great Dane breeding, antiques. Home: 5 Seaside Dr Belfast ME 04915-6039 Office: City of Belfast Mayor's Office 71 Church St Belfast ME 04915-6208

WORTH, MELVIN H. surgeon, educator; b. Norwich, Conn., July 14, 1930; s. Melvin H. and Stella E. (Cline) W.; m. Alice Tenzer, May 17, 1953; children: Nancy, David. AB, Clark U., 1950; MD, NYU, 1954. Diplomate Am. Bd. Surgery. Intern Bellevue Hosp., N.Y.C., 1954-55, resident, 1957-61, dir. trauma svc., 1966-79; dir. surgery S.I. U. Hosp., 1979-96; assoc. prof. NYU, 1968-69; prof. clin. surgery SUNY, Bklyn., 1979—, Uniformed Svc. U. Health Sci. Ctr., 1996—. Chmn. trauma designation com. N.Y.C. Emergency Med. Svc., 1990; mem. Office of Profl. Med. Conduct of N.Y. State, 1983-98. Vice chmn. N.Y. State Health Rev. and Planning Coun., 1988-94, chair, 1995. Capt. USMC, 1955-57. Scholar-in-residence Inst. Medicine, 1996—. Fellow ACS, Am. Coll. Gastroenterology; mem. Internat. Soc. Surgery, Soc. Am. Gastrointestinal Endoscopic Surgeons, Am. Assn. for Surgery of Trauma, Assn. Acad. Surgery, Soc. Critical Care Medicine, Assn. Surg. Edn., N.Y. Surg. Soc. (pres. 1989), Alpha Omega Alpha. Home: 4914 Jamestown Rd Bethesda MD 20816-1756

WORTHAM, JAMES CALVIN, retired mathematics educator; b. Oconee County, Ga., Sept. 12, 1928; s. James Notley and Effie (Cross) W.; m. Mary Helena Shelley, Dec. 23, 1953; children: Sharon Elaine, Marilyn Kay, Deborah Louise, James Donald. BA, U. Akron, 1957; MA (NSF Scholar), Ohio State U., 1969. Tchr. jr. H.S. Akron Pub. Schs., 1956-62, tchr. sr. H.S., 1962-66; math. curriculum specialist Akron (Ohio) Pub. Schs., 1966-90; instr. math. U. Akron, 1966-90; ret., 1990. Served with USAF, 1951-55. Mem. NEA, Ohio Edn. Assn., Math. Assn. Am., Nat., Ohio couns. tchrs. of Math., Nat. Coun. Suprs. of Math., Greater Akron Math. Educators Soc. (pres. 1984-86), Pi Mu Epsilon. Republican. Mem. Ch. of Nazarene. Home: 229 Sand Run Rd Akron OH 44313-5364

WORTHAM, JAMES MASON, gas supply company official; b. Ft. Worth, Nov. 21, 1954; s. John Lilburn and Mary Elizabeth (Mason) W.; m. Rhonda Dee Richards, Aug. 16, 1980 (div. 1995); children: James Mason Jr., William Charles. Student, USAF Acad., 1973-75; BBA in Stats., U. Tex., Austin, 1977; MBA in Fin., U. Houston, 1989. Teller Capital Nat. Bank, Austin, 1976-77; abstractor First Title Co., Houston, 1977-78, escrow officer, 1978-80; div. order analyst Mitchell Energy Corp., The Woodlands, Tex., 1980-81, landman I, 1981-83, landman II, 1983-89, sr. landman, 1989-97, sr. gas supply & bus. devel. rep., 1997—. Pres. Genesis Class St. Luke's Meth., Houston, 1983. Recipient Young Texan award, Ft. Worth Optimist Club, 1973, award, Woodlands YMCA Marathon Competition, 1985, Multiple Sclerosis 150 Mile Bike Ride, 1995—97, 2002, Houston-Tennaco Marathon, 1996, Houston Meth. Hosp. Marathon, 1997—2000, Cinco Ranch Triathelon, 1999—2000, Sugarland Triathelon, 1999, Compaq Houston Marathon, 2001—02, John Newcombe Tennis Ranch, 2001. Mem.: Houston Assn. Petroleum Landmen (2d pl. tennis 1983, 1989), Natural Gas and Elec. Power Soc. North Tex. (1st pl. tennis 1998, 2d pl. tennis 1999, 2001), Tex. Alliance of Energy Prodrs., Gas Processors Assn. Houston, Gas Processors Assn. North Tex., Nat. Energy Svcs. Assn./Houston Energy Assn. (1st pl. tennis 1998, 2001), Woodlands Coun. Realtors Benefit, Houston Jr. League Charity Ball, The Woodlands Lions Club (lion tamer 1990—91, 1st v.p. 1992—93, pres. 1993—94). Republican. Methodist. Avocations: tennis, bridge, running, biking, swimming. Home: 10600 Six Pines Rd Apt 131 The Woodlands TX 77380-1469 Office: Devon Energy Corp 2001 Timberlock Pl The Woodlands TX 77380- E-mail: jim.wortham@dvn.com.

WORTHAM, THOMAS RICHARD, English language educator; b. Liberal, Kans., Dec. 5, 1943; s. Tom and Ruth (Cavanaugh) W. AB, Marquette U., 1965; PhD, Ind. U., 1970. From asst. prof. to assoc. prof. UCLA, 1970-82, prof., 1982—, vice-chmn. and dir. undergrad. studies, 1993-97, chmn. dept., 1997—. Vis. prof. Am. lit. U. Warsaw, Poland, 1976-77; sr. rsch. fellow Am. Coun. of Learned Socs., 1983-84. Editor: James Russell Lowell's The Biglow Papers: A Critical Edition, 1977, Letters of W. D. Howells, vol. 4, 1892-1901, 1983, The Early Prose Writings of William Dean Howells, 1853-1861, 1990, William Dean Howells' My Mark Twain, 1996, Mark Twain's Chapters From My Autobiography, 1999; asst. editor Nineteenth-Century Fiction, 1971-75, mem. adv. bd., 1976-83, co-editor, 1983-86; co-editor Nineteenth-Century Literature, 1986-95, editor, 1995—; mem. editl. bd. The Collected Works of Ralph Waldo Emerson, 1996—, Am. Documentary Heritage Libr., 1999—. Regent's faculty fellow in the humanities U. Calif., 1971; travel grantee Nat. Endowment for the Humanities, 1985-86, 88-89; grants-in-aid of rsch. Am. Philos. Soc., 1976, 81. Mem. MLA Am. (Norman Foerster prize com. of Am. Lit. sect. 1973, chmn. Pacific coast region, com. on manuscript holdings of Am. Lit. sect. 1972-78, mem. Hubbell prize com. of Am. Lit. sect. 1989-91), Am. Studies Assn., Ralph Waldo Emerson Soc. (bd. dirs. 1992-95), Assn. for

Document Editing, Internat. Assn. Univ. Profs. English, Soc. Textual Scholarship. Episcopalian. Avocations: breeding and training Arabian horses. Office: U Calif Dept English 405 Hilgard Ave Los Angeles CA 90095-1530 E-mail: wortham@humnet.ucla.edu.

WORTHEN, JOHN EDWARD, retired academic administrator; b. Carbondale, Ill., July 15, 1933; s. Dewey and Annis Burr (Williams) W.; m. Sandra Damewood, Feb. 27, 1960; children: Samantha Jane, Bradley Edward. BS in Psychology (Univ. Acad. scholar), Northwestern U., 1954; MA in Student Pers. Adminstrn., Columbia U., 1955; EdD in Adminstrn. in Higher Edn. (Coll. Entrance Exam. Bd. fellow), Harvard U., 1964; PhD (hon.), Yeungnam U., Daegu, Korea, 1986; DL (hon.), Ball State U., 2001. Dean of men Am. U., 1959-61; dir. counseling and testing and asst. prof. edn., 1963-66; asst. to provost and asst. prof., 1966-68; acting provost and v.p. acad. affairs, 1968; assoc. provost for instrn., 1969; v.p. student affairs, 1970-75; v.p. student affairs and adminstrn., 1976-79; pres. Ind. U. of Pa., 1979-84, Ball State U., Muncie, Ind., 1984-2000; ret., 2000. Cons. to universities and public schs. Bd. dirs. Ball State U. Found., Muncie-Delaware County Cmty. Found. Mem. Bus. Modernization and Tech. Corp., Am. Assn. State Colls. and Univs. (chair, bd. dirs. 1999), First Merchants Corp., Crossmann Cmtys., Inc., Rotary Internat., Phi Delta Kappa, Kappa Delta Pi. E-mail: johneworthen@aol.com.

WORTHEN, WILLIAM JAMES, architect; b. Syracuse, N.Y., Apr. 30, 1971; s. William Sidney and Anna Marie Worthen. BS in Bldg. Sci., Rensselaer Poly. Inst., Troy, N.Y., 1995. Registered architect, D.C. Archtl. designer The Kearns Group, Troy, 1992-95; architect Bernard Johnson Young, Bethesda, Md., 1995-96, Blackburn Architects, Washington, 1996-97; project architect Hellmuth, Obata & Kassabaum, Washington, San Francisco, 1997—. Vol. coord. Clinton 98 Re-election Campaign, Washington, 1998; mem. Human Rights Campaign. Mem AIA, Lambda Chi Alpha. Avocation: marathon running. Office: Hellmuth Obata & Kassabaum 71 Stevenson St Ste 2200 San Francisco CA 94105-2979

WORTHEY, CAROL, composer; b. Worcester, Mass., Mar. 1, 1943; d. Bernard Krieger and Edith Lilian (Cramer) Symonds; m. Eugene Worthey III, June 1969 (div. 1980); 1 child, Megan; m. Raymond Edward Korns, Sept. 21, 1980. BA in Music Composition, Columbia U., 1965; grad., Dick Grove Sch. Music., L.A., 1979; grad. filmscoring prog., UCLA, 1978; music studies with Darius Milhaud, Walter Piston, Elliot Carter, Vincent Persichetti, Grant Beglarian, Karl Korte, Otto Luening, Eddy Lawrence Manson, Dick Grove; studied, RISD, 1948-54, Columbia U., 1965. Sr. composer, arranger Celebrity Ctr. Internat. Choir, Hollywood, Calif., 1985—. Composition lectr. Calif. Luth. U., UCLA, U. So. Calif., Borders Books; judge piano and composer competitions Armenian Allied Arts Assn., 2001; judge vocal and art competitions Armenian Allied Arts Assn., 2002. Composer, arranger The Hollywood Chorale; composer ballets Athena, 1963, The Barren, 1965, piano works performed in France, Italy, Germany, Canada, U.S., Eng. by Mario Feninger, 1992, Pastorale, performed in Mex., 1994, Neighborhood of the Heart, 1994, (choir) Unquenchable Light, 1993, (film score) The Special Visitor, 1992; compositions performed at Aspen Music Festival, 1963, Carnegie Hall, 1954, Dorothy Chandler Pavilion, 1986-89; appeared as singer-songwriter L.A. Songwriter's Showcase, 1977; arranger Merv Griffin Show, 1981, The Night Before Christmas, L.A. Children's Theater, 1988-91, Capistrano Valley Symphony, 1994, Very Old Merry Old Christmas, Dorothy Chandler Pavilion, 1994, Judge, 1994; (CD) David Arkenstone Return of the Guardian, 1996, Celtic Book of Days, 1998; composer, lyricist, librettist full-length musical The Envelope Please, 1988; conductor, composer J'allume un cierge à la Liberté, 2000, Human Rights Concert, Paris, 2000; music dir. Writers of the Future award ceremony Authors Svcs., L.A., 2002; author: Treasury of Holiday Magic, 1992, (poems) The Lonely Wanderer Comes Home, 1994; art work exhibited RISD, 1952, Folk and Art Mus., L.A., 1975, 1st Internat. Art Exhibit Celebrity Ctr. Pavilion, 1992, Music Ctr., L.A., 2001; cable tv show: Neighborhood of the Heart, 1995, 96. Vol. performer various childcare ctrs., old folks homes, etc.; judge Composer's Competition Inner City Cultural Ctr., 1995—97. Recipient Silver Poet award World of Poetry, 1987, 2nd place winner, 1st BarComposers and Songwriters Competition for "Fanfare for Joy & Wedding March", 1990, Golden Poet award World of Poetry, 1992. Mem.: Songwriters and Composers Assn., Film Music Network, Nat. Acad. Songwriters, Broadcast Music Inc., Nat. Assn. Composers, USA, Film Adv. Bd., Toastmasters Internat. (Advanced Toastmaster Silver 2001), Mu Phi Epsilon. Jewish. Avocations: gourmet cooking, films, macrame, creative writing, calligraphy. E-mail: carol@worthgold.com.

WORTHING, CAROL MARIE, minister; b. Duluth, Minn., Dec. 27, 1934; d. Truman James and Helga Maria (Bolander) W.; children: Gregory Alan Beatty, Graydon Ernest Beatty. BS, U. Minn., 1965; MDiv, Northwestern Theol. Seminary, 1982; DMin, Grad. Theol. Found., Notre Dame, Ind., 1988; MBA in Ch. Mgmt., Grad. Theol. Found., Donaldson, Ind., 1993; cert., Austin Presbyn. Theol. Sem., 2001; PhD, Grad. Theol. Found., 2002. Secondary educator Ind. (Minn.) Sch. Dist., 1965-78; teaching fellow U. Minn., 1968-70; contract counselor Luth. Social Svc., Duluth, 1976-78; media cons. Luth. Media Svcs., St. Paul, 1978-80; asst. pastor Messiah Luth. Ch., Fargo, N.D., 1982-83, vice pastor, 1983-84; assoc. editor Luth. Ch. Am. Ptnrs., Phila., 1982-84; editorial assoc. Luth. Ptnrs. Evang. Luth. Ch. Am., Phila. and Mpls., 1984—; parish pastor Resurrection Luth. Ch., Pierre, S.D., 1984-89; assoc. pastor Bethlehem Luth. Ch., Cedar Falls, Iowa, 1989-90; exec. dir. Ill. Conf. Chs., Springfield, 1990-96, Tex. Conf. of Chs., 1996—. Mem. pub. rels. and interpretation com. Red River Valley Synod, Fargo, 1984-86, mem. ch. devel., Pierre, 1986-87; mem. mgmt. com. office comm. Luth. Ch. in Am., N.Y.C., Phila., 1984-88; mem. mission ptnrs. S.D. Synod, 1988, chmn. assembly resolutions com., 1988; mem. pre-assembly planning com., ecumenics com., chmn. resolutions com. N.E. Iowa Synod, 1989-90; mem. ch. and society com., 1990-96; ecumenical com., 1995-96; Luth. Ecumenical Rep. Network, 1995—; mem. Cen. and So. Ill. Synod, 1996; mem. S.W. Tex. Synod, 1996—, mem. ecumenical com., 1998-2001; nat. edn. cons. Am. Film Inst., Washington, 1967-70; chaplain state legis. bodies, Pierre, 1984-89; mem. exec. bd. Luth. Ecumenical Rep. Network for Region 4, Evang. Luth. Ch. in Am., 2002—. Author: Cinematics and English, 1967, Peer Counseling, 1977, Tischrede Lexegete, 1986, 88, 90, Way of the Cross, Way of Justice Walk, 1987, Introducing Collaboration as a Leadership Stance and Style in an Established Statewide Conference of Churches, 1993, The Anointing of Jesus--A Christological Necessity, 2001. Co-facilitator Parents of Retarded Children, 1985; bd. dirs. Countryside Hospice, 1985; cons. to adminstrv. bd. Mo. Shores Women's Ctr., 1986. Named John Macquarrie fellow, Grad. Theol. Found., 2002. Mem. NAFE, Nat. Assn. Ecumenical Staff (chair of site selection com. 1991-92, chair of scholarship com. 1993-94, mem. profl. devel. com. 1993-94, chair program planning com. 1996, bd. dirs. 1995-96), Pierre-Ft. Pierre Ministerium (v.p. 1986-87, pres. 1987-88). Democrat. Avocations: writing prose and poetry, concerts, theater, art, photography. Home: Ste 2B4 40 N I H 35 Austin TX 78701-4339 Office: Tex Confs Chs Ste 125 1033 La Posada Dr Austin TX 78752-3830 E-mail: cworthing@txconfchurches.org. *Ecumenism is, I believe, about full coherence between our ecclesiology and our ethics. The Spirit of God calls the church to come together for a compassionate purpose: to respond to all who suffer, so that the world might be transformed into God's own vision of peace, justice, and love.*

WORTHINGTON, CAROLE YARD LYNCH, lawyer; b. Knoxville, Tenn., Aug. 29, 1951; d. Charles R. and Alma (Allred) Yard; m. Robert F. Worthington Jr., Sept. 14, 1996; 1 child, Allison Kathleen. BA, U. Tenn., 1972, JD, 1977. Bar: Tenn. 1977, Ga. 1982. Assoc. Thomas, Leitner, Mann, Warner & Owens, Chattanooga, 1977-78, Thomas, Mann & Gossett, Chattanooga, 1978-81, ptnr., v.p., 1981-86; prin. Grant, Konvalinka & Harrison, P.C., 1987-96, Carole Lynch Worthington, Atty. at Law, Knoxville, 1996—. Sec. Nat. Transp. Rsch. Ctr., Inc.; mem. U. Tenn. Alliance of Women Philanthropists. Author: Estate Planning Tennessee Practice, 1992; asst. editor Tenn. Law Rev., 1976-77. Vice chmn. allocations United Way of Chattanooga, 1985, pilot campaign, 1986; active Jr. League of Chattanooga, 1981-92; mem. alumnae adv. coun. U. Tenn. Coll. Law, 1983-92, dean's cir., 1989—; bd. dirs. Mental Health Assn. Chattanooga Inc., 1986-92, 1st v.p., 1988-89, sec., 1989-92; trustee St. Nicholas Sch., 1992-95, East Tenn. Opera Guild, 2001—. Recipient Alumni Leadership award U. Tenn. Coll. Law, 1988, 92. Fellow Am. Bar Found., Tenn. Bar Found., Chattanooga Bar Found.; mem. ABA (assembly del. 1991-97, 98-2001), com. on legal aid and indigent defendants 1994-95, select com. of house 1994-96, standing com. on charter and by laws 1999-2000, standing com. on credentials and admissions 1999-2000, standing com. on credentials and admissions 1999-2000, com. on client rels. 2000-2002), Chattanooga Bar Assn. (bd. govs. 1982-89, sec.-treas. 1985-86, pres. 1987-88), Knoxville Bar Assn. (chair pro bono com. 2002), Tenn. Bar Assn. (vice chair comml. law, banking and bankruptcy 1988-90, unified bar study com. 1990-91, chair bar leadership conf. 1990, editl. bd. Tenn. Bar Jour. 1991-94, Tenn. Bar Assn. long range planning com. 1992-95, 97-99, bd. govs. 1994-96, chair long range planning com. 1995-96, future of bar com. 1998-2001), Ga. Bar Assn., Nat. Conf. Lawyers and Realtors (ABA del. 1990-92), Nat. Conf. Bar Pres.'s (exec. coun. 1989-92, treas. 1992-93, sec. 1993-94, pres.-elect 1994-95, pres. 1995-96), Tenn. Bd. Profl. Responsibility, Phi Alpha Delta, East Tenn. Opera Guild Bd., 2001-02. Home: First Tennessee Plaza Ste 1950 800 S Gay St Knoxville TN 37929 E-mail: carole@clw-law.com.

WORTHINGTON, DANIEL GLEN, lawyer, educator; b. Rexbury, Idaho, Aug. 15, 1957; BA magna cum laude, Brigham Young U., 1982, MEd, 1986, EdD, JD cum laude, Brigham Young U., 1989. Bar: Utah 1990. Asst. to assoc. dean students Brigham Young U., 1986-88, cons., 1987-89, mgr. planned giving, tech. cons., 1989-90, adj. prof. law and edn., 1989—; asst. dean students Coll. Eastern Utah, 1985-86; assoc. dean, exec. dir. devel. Porterville Coll. Found., 1990-91; prin. Worthington & Assocs., Provo, Utah, 1991-93; mng. atty., ptnr. Walstad & Babcock; assoc. dean U. S.D. Sch. Law, 1994-95, exec. v.p. found., 1995—. Assoc. v.p. gen. counsel U. Ctrl. Fla. Found., Orlando, adj. faculty Masters of Tax Program; sr. cons. Fla. Hosp. and the U. S.D. Bus. Sch., 1997—2001; cons. Citigroup Trust Svcs., 1997—2001; sr. cons. Fla. Hosp., 1997—99, v.p. gen. counsel, 1999—. Editor-in-chief jour. Edn. & Law Perspectives, 1986-88, co-chair, exec. adv. bd., dir., 1988-91; contbr. articles to profl. jours. Exec. v.p. S.D. Planned Giving Coun., 1994—; nat. assembly del. Nat. Com. on Planned, 1994—; pres. Greater Orlando Planned Giving Round Table, 1999—; v.p., gen. counsel Fla. Hosp. Found., 1999—. With USAFR, 1982-88. Mem. Supreme Ct. Hist. Soc., Federalist Soc., Nat. Soc. Fund Raising Execs., Phi Kappa Phi. Address: 7853 Horse Ferry Rd Orlando FL 32835 E-mail: dan_worthington@mail.fhmis.net.

WORTHINGTON, GEORGE RHODES, retired naval officer; b. Louisville, July 11, 1937; s. William Bowman and Elizabeth (Frost) W.; m. Sydna Anne Alexander, Mar. 28, 1981 (div. Oct. 1990); children: Rhodes Ballard, Graham Rankins, Greer Anne. BS, U.S. Naval Acad., 1961; postgrad., USMC, Quantico, Va., 1975-76, Nat. War Coll., 1978-79. Commd. ensign USN, 1961, advanced through grades to rear adm., 1989, communications officer USS Halsey Powell, 1961-63, flag lt., aide comdr. cruiser-destroyer Flotilla Seven, 1963-65, exec. officer Underwater Demolition Team Eleven Coronado, Calif., 1965-68, ops. officer USS Strong Charleston, S.C., 1969-71, exec. officer Naval Spl. Warfare Group Saigon, Vietnam, 1971-72, comdg. officer SEAL Team One Coronado, 1972-74, naval attache Def. Attache Office Phnom Penh, Cambodia, 1974-75, comdg. officer Undersea Warfare Group One Coronado, 1976-78, program sponsor Office of Chief of Naval Ops, Washington, 1979-85; comdr. Naval Spl. Warfare Group One, Coronado, 1985-87; chief of staff Spl. Ops. Command Europe USN, Stuttgart, Fed. Republic Germany, 1987-88; dep. asst. sec. of def. (spl. ops.) Def. Dept., Washington, 1988-89; comdr. Naval Spl. Warfare Command, Coronado, 1989-92; mktg. agent, cons. PIDEAC Inc., 1992-96. Naval adv. IFG Ltd.; with Burdeshaw Assoc., Inc.; former v.p. govt. rels. WarRoom Rsch., Inc.; bd. dirs. ZODIAC N.Am., WESCAM-Sonoma, Inc., Spl. Ops. Warrior Found. Decorated D.S.M., Legion of Merit (2), Def. Superior Svc. medal, Meritorious Svc. medal. Mem. Res. Officers Assn. (past chpt. pres.), U.S. Parachute Assn., Underwater Demolition Team-Seal Assn. (life), Mayflower Soc. D.C. (life) , Naval Acad. Alumni Assn., Naval Inst., Navy League San Diego, Nat. Def. Indsl. Assn. (life), Army-Navy Club, Army-Navy Country Club. Republican. Episcopalian. Avocations: masters swimming, skiing, sport parachuting. Address: 1118 Pacifica Ave Chula Vista CA 91913-1550 Fax: 619-216-1712. E-mail: grw7@cox.net.

WORTHINGTON, MELVIN LEROY, minister, writer; b. Greenville, N.C., June 17, 1937; s. Wilbur Leroy and Alma Lee (Braxton) W.; m. Anne Katherine Wilson, Sept. 12, 1959; children: Daniel Edward, Lydia Anne. Diploma, Imperial Detective Acad., Cin., 1965; B.Bibl.Edn., Columbia Bible Coll., S.C., 1959; B.Th., Luther Rice Sem., Jacksonville, Fla., 1967, B.Div., 1969, M.Th., 1970, D.Th., 1974; M.Ed., Ga. State U.-Atlanta, 1979; EdD, Vanderbilt U., 1998. Ordained to ministry, Central Conf. Free Will Baptists, 1957. Pastor Union Chapel Free Will Bapt. Ch., Chocowinity, N.C., 1959-62, Palmetto Free Will Bapt. Ch., Vanceboro, 1959-62, First Free Will Bapt. Ch., Darlington, S.C., 1962-66, Wesconnett Free Will Bapt. Ch., Jacksonville, Fla., 1967, First Free Will Bapt. Ch., Amory, Miss., 1967-72, Albany, Ga., 1972-79; exec. sec. Nat. Assn. Free Will Bapt., Inc., Antioch, 1979—2002, chmn. Sunday Sch. bd., 1975-77, asst. moderator, 1977-79, chmn. grad. study com., 1976-77, exec. sec. emeritus, 2002—. Clk. S.C. State Assn. Free Will Bapt., Florence, 1966-67; asst. moderator Ga. State Assn. Free Will Bapt., Moultrie, 1973-74, moderator, 1975-79; pres. Ga. Bible Inst., Albany, 1978 Editor in chief: Contact mag., 1979—2002, author editorial, 1980—2002; contbr. articles to profl. jours. Adv. bd. Nat. Fedn. Decency, 1985; nat. bd. dirs. Christian Leaders for Responsible TV, 1986 Mem. Evang. Press Assn., Religious Conf. Mgmt. Assn. (dir. 1983, v.p. 1986, pres. 1989-92), Nashville C. of C., Future Farmers Am. (N.C. Farmer degree 1955, Am. Farmer degree 1957). Democrat. Office: Nat Assn Free Will Bapt Inc 5233 Mount View Rd Antioch TN 37013-2306 E-mail: mlw@nafwb.org. *The basic principle which has guided, governed and guarded my life has been a burning desire to find, follow and finish the will of God.*

WORTHINGTON, SAMUEL ANDREW, social welfare administrator; b. Boston, Sept. 3, 1958; s. Courtenay Pope Jr. and Helen Shauneen (McFetridge) W.; m. Renée JoAnne Vizzard, Sept. 1, 1984; children: Rachel, James, Lindsay. BA, U. Vt., 1979; MA with honors, Monterey Inst. Internat., Monterey, Calif., 1984. Project coord./mgr. tng. programs Delphi Internat. Group, Washington, 1986-88, dir. programs, 1988-93, exec. dir., 1990-92; mng. dir. program Childreach, U.S. mem. of PLAN Internat., Warwick, R.I., 1993-94, dep. nat. exec. dir., 1994, nat. exec. dir., CEO, 1994—. Bd. dirs., exec. com. InterAction, Washington, 1994-2002; chair gender awareness program PLAN Internat., Woking, U.K., 1995-2001. Editor: (acad. jour.) Monterey Rev., 1983-84. Mem. Nat. Adv. Com. on Diversification Nat. Coun. for Internat. Visitors, Washington, 1990-93; cmty. fellow Internat. Leadership Devel. Inst., 1991; v.p., bd. dirs. Westminster Unitarian Ch., 1998-2001; bd. dirs. R.I. World Affairs Coun., 1999—; treas., bd. dirs. Global R.I., 2000—; chair Commn. on the Advancement of Women, InterAction, 2000—; program policy coun. Hope for African Children Intiative, 2001—; chair nat. exec. dir. team Plan Internat., 2002—, global exec. mgmt. team, 2002—. Fulbright scholar Inst. Internat. Studies, Geneva, 1985; recipient Claiborne Pell Internat. Leadership award Internat. Exch. Assn., 1991; feature on PBS TV series The Visionaries, 1996-97. Unitarian Universalist. Avocations: travel, reading, skiing, hiking, sailing. Office: Childreach US mem of PLAN Internat 155 Plan Way Warwick RI 02886-1099 E-mail: worthins@childreach.org.

WORTHINGTON, WARD CURTIS, JR. university dean, anatomy educator; b. Savannah, Ga., Aug. 8, 1925; s. Ward Curtis I and Pearl Mabel (Farris) W.; m. Floride Calhoun McDermid, June 21, 1947; children: Ward Curtis III, Amy Lynne Worthington Hauslohner. BS, The Citadel, 1952; MD, Med. U. S.C., 1952. Intern Boston City Hosp., 1952-53; instr. anatomy John Hopkins, 1953-56; asst. prof. anatomy U. Ill., 1956-57; asst. prof., assoc. prof. Med. U. S.C., Charleston, 1957-66; prof. anatomy Med. U. S.C., Charleston, 1966-91; prof. emeritus, 1991—. prof. history med. scis. U. S.C., Charleston, 1987—, asst. dean curriculum, 1966-69, chmn. dept. anatomy, 1969-77, acting v.p. acad. affairs, 1975-77, v.p. acad. affairs, 1977-82, assoc. dean acad. affairs, 1982—, dir. Waring Hist. Library, 1982—. Contbr. articles to profl. jours. Bd. dirs. Charleston Symphony Orch. Assn., 1980-84, 2d v.p., 1982. Served with USNR, 1944-46. Research grantee The Commonwealth Fund, 1957-61, NIH, 1962-73; NIH spl. fellow, 1964-65. Mem. Waring Library Soc., S.C. Acad. Sci., S.C. Med. Assn., Charleston County Med. Soc., Endocrine Soc., Am. Physiol. Soc., Am. Assn. Anatomists, Sigma Xi, Alpha Omega Alpha. Episcopalian. Lodge: Rotary (bd. dirs. 1982-83). Home: 17 Morton Ave Charleston SC 29407-7231 Office: 171 Ashley Ave Charleston SC 29425-0001

WORTHINGTON, WILLIAM ALBERT, III, lawyer; b. June 26, 1950; s. William Albert Jr. and Patricia Lou (Reynolds) W.; m. Melanie Ann McDonald, Oct. 30, 1993; children: Elizabeth Clark, Emily Robin, Katherine Anne, William Jackson. BS, U. Utah, 1972; JD, Washington and Lee U., 1976. Bar: Tex. 1976, U.S. Dist. Ct. (so. dist.) Tex. 1977, U.S. Ct. Appeals (5th cir.) 1977, U.S. Ct. Appeals (11th cir.) 1981, U.S. Supreme Ct. 1981, U.S. Dist. Ct. (we. dist.) Tex. 1982, U.S. Dist. Ct. (ea. dist.) Tex. 1986, U.S. Dist. Ct. (no. dist.) Tex. 1993. Assoc. Sewell & Riggs, Houston, 1976-82, ptnr., 1982-89, shareholder, 1990-94; ptnr. Strasburger & Price, LLP, 1994—. Exec. editor Washington and Lee Law Rev., 1976; contbr. articles to law jours. Active Houston YMCA, Amnesty Internat. U.S.A., ARC; del. state bar of Tex. to Rep. Cuba, 2001. Mem. Am. Law Inst., Tex. Assn. Def. Counsel, Def. Rsch. Inst., Product Liability Adv. Coun., Houston Bar Found., Tex. Bd. Legal Specialization (cert. civil trial lawyer, personal injury trial lawyer), U.S. Cycling Fedn., Sierra Club. Office: Strasburger & Price LLP 1301 Mckinney St Ste 3200 Houston TX 77010-3033 E-mail: bill.worthington@strasburger.com.

WORTHINGTON-WHITE, DIANA ALICE, research scientist; b. Cleve., Jan. 7, 1956; d. Cyril Frank and Jerroldyn Faye (Paul) Worthington-White. BS, U. Cin., 1977, MEd, 1978. Rsch. technician U. Hosp. Cleve., 1979-81; asst. instr. U. Fla., Gainesville, 1981-90, assoc. instr., 1990-95; applied rsch. lead specialist U. S.C., Columbia, 1996—. Editor: Bone Marrow Purging & Processing, 1990, Advances in Bone Marrow Purging & Processing, 1992, Advances in Bone Marrow Purging & Processing, 1994; contbr. articles to profl. jours. Treas. Alachua County CROP Walk, Gainesville, 1988-95; vol. Ronald McDonald House, Gainesville, 1984-95; fin. sec., 1st Luth. Ch., Gainesville, 1984-86, youth dir., 1986-89. Recipient NIH rsch. grant, 1992. Mem. AAAS, Internat. Soc. for Hematotherapy & Graft Engrng. (founding mem., sec. 1992—), Am. Med. Writers Assn. Avocations: semi-profl. classical flutist, phys. fitness, sports, choral music. Office: Univ SC Divsn Transplantation CCTR 7 Medical Park Columbia SC 29203 Home: 1040 Carlyle Lk Decatur GA 30033-4632

WORTHLEY, HAROLD FIELD, minister, educator; b. Brewer, Maine, Nov. 3, 1928; s. Herbert Morrison and Aline May (Field) W.; m. Barbara Louise Bent, June 25, 1955; children: Susan Louise Field, Laura May, David Bruce. AB, Boston U., 1950, MA, 1951; STB, Harvard Div. Sch., 1954, STM, 1956, ThD, 1970. Ordained to ministry United Ch. of Christ, 1954. Min. Congl. chs., Maine, N.H. and Mass., 1952-62; assoc. prof. religion, chaplain Wheaton Coll., Norton, Mass., 1963-77; exec. sec., archivist Congl. Christian Hist. Soc., Boston, 1971—; exec. dir. Am. Congl. Assn., 1999—; libr. Congl. Libr., Boston, 1977—. Editor Bull. of Congl. Library, 1976— , Hist. Intelligencer, 1980-86. Author: Inventory of the Records of the Particular Churches of Massachusetts, 1620-1805, 1970; contbr. articles to profl. jours. Mem. Hist. Coun. United Ch. of Christ. Fellow Pilgrim Soc., Congl. Christian Hist. Soc. Home: 14 Mansfield Ave Norton MA 02766-2212 Office: The Congregational Libr 14 Beacon St Ste 206 Boston MA 02108-3782

WORTHY, K(ENNETH) MARTIN, retired lawyer; b. Dawson, Ga., Sept. 24, 1920; s. Kenneth Spencer and Jeffrie Pruett (Martin) W.; m. Eleanor Vreeland Blewett, Feb. 15, 1947 (dec. July 1981); children: Jeffrie Martin, William Blewett; m. Katherine Teasley Jackson, June 17, 1983. Student, The Citadel, 1937-39; BPh, Emory U., 1941, JD with honors, 1947; MBA cum laude, Harvard U., 1943. Bar: Ga. 1947, D.C. 1948. Assoc. Foley & Lardner (formerly Hopkins & Sutter and Hamel & Park), Washington, 1948-51, ptnr., 1952-69, 72-90, sr. counsel, 1991—; asst. gen. counsel Treasury Dept., 1969-72; chief counsel IRS, 1969-72. Dir. Beneficial Corp., 1977-96, emeritus, 1996-98; mem. Nat. Coun. Organized Crime, 1970-72; cons. Justice Dept., 1972-74. Author: (with John M. Appleman) Basic Estate Planning, 1957; contbr. articles to profl. jours. Del. Montgomery County Civic Fedn., 1951—61, D.C. Area Health and Welfare Coun., 1960—61; mem. coun. Emory U. Law Sch., 1976—, chmn., 1993—95; trustee Chelsea Sch., 1981—2001, trustee emeritus, 2001—; trustee St. John's Coll., Annapolis, Md., Santa Fe, 1987—93, 1995—2001, Sherman Found., Newport Beach, Calif., 1991—, Associated Marine Inst. Found., 1999—2001, Ga. Wilderness Insts., 1997—, St. Simons Island Libr. Found., 2000—, chmn., 2001—; fellow Aspen Inst., 1982—92; chmn. dept. fin. Episcopal Diocese, Washington, 1969—70. Capt. U.S. Army, 1943—46, capt. U.S. Army, 1951—52. Recipient Army Commendation Ribbon, 1945, Treasury Exceptional Svc. award and medal, 1972, IRS Commrs. award, 1972, Disting. Alumnus award Emory U., 1992. Fellow Am. Bar Found., Am. Coll. Tax Counsel (bd. regents 1980-88, chmn. 1985-87), Atlantic Coun. (counselor 1989-99); mem. ABA (coun. taxation sect. 1965-69, 72-75, chmn. 1973-74, del. Nat. Conf. Lawyers and CPAs 1981-87, ho. of dels. 1983-89, chmn. audit com. 1985-90), Fed. Bar Assn. (nat. coun. 1969-72, 77-79), Ga. Bar Assn., D.C. Bar, Am. Law Inst., Nat. Tax Assn., Am. Tax Policy Inst. (trustee 1989-98), Rotary, Chevy Chase Club, Met. Club, Sea Island Club, Harvard Club N.Y.C., Phi Delta Theta, Phi Delta Phi, Omicron Delta Kappa. Home: PO Box 30264 189 W Gascoigne Sea Island GA 31561 Office: Foley & Lardner 3000 K St NW Ste 500 Washington DC 20007-5143 E-mail: kworthy@foleylaw.com., kmartinworthy@aol.com.

WORTHY, PATRICIA MORRIS, law educator, lawyer; b. Fort Benning, Ga., May 28, 1944; d. Walter and Ruby Mae (Lovett) Morris. AA, Queensborough Community Coll., 1964; BA, Bklyn. Coll., 1966; JD, Howard U., 1969. Bar: D.C. 1971. Trial atty. NLRB, Washington, 1969-71; dep. gen. counsel ACTION, 1971-74; assoc. Dolphin, Branton, Stafford & Webber, 1974-77; dep. asst. sec. for regulatory functions HUD, 1977-80; adj. prof. Howard U. Sch. Law, 1979-92; chmn. D.C. Pub. Service Commn., 1980-91, Washington Met. Area Transit Commn., 1980-91; chief of staff Office of Mayor Sharon Pratt Kelly, Washington, 1991-92; prof. law Howard U., 1992—; dean acad. affairs Howard U. Law Sch., 2001—. Bd. dirs. Yankee Energy System, Inc.; chmn. D.C. Jud. Nomination Commn. Bd. dirs. Nat. Black Child Devel. Inst., 1975-80, Anacostia Econ. Devel. Corp., 1970-74; chmn. Occupl. Safety and Health Bd., Washington, 1979-80; trustee WETA-TV Channel 26, 1984-94. Mem. ABA, Nat. Conf. Black Lawyers, Nat. Conf. Bar Examiners (multistate profl. responsibility com. 1986-89), World Peace Through Law (chairperson young lawyers sect. 1973-75). Office: Howard U Sch Law Van Ness & Connecticut Ave NW Washington DC 20001

WORTLEY, GEORGE CORNELIUS, government affairs consultant, investor; b. Syracuse, N.Y., Dec. 8, 1926; s. George C. and Arlene (Hirsh) W.; m. Barbara Jane Hennessy, May 13, 1950; children: George C. IV, Ann Wortley Lavin, Elizabeth Wortley Ring. BS, Syracuse U., 1948. Newspaper pub., pres. Manlius Pub. Corp., Fayetteville, N.Y., 1950-92; pres. Nat. Editorial Found., 1968-73; mem. 97th-100th Congresses from 27th N.Y. Dist., 1981-89, mem. Banking, Fin. and Urban Affairs com., mem. Select Com. on Aging, Select Com. on Children, Youth and Family; pvt. bus. cons., investor Washington, 1989—; prin. Dierman, Wortley, Zola & Assocs., 1995—. Pres. Am. Newspapers Reps., 1966—68. Pres. Hiawatha coun. Boy Scouts Am., 1972-75; mem. Nat. Commn. on Hist. Publs. and Records, 1977-80, Fayetteville Sr. Citizen Housing Commn., 1977-80; mem. allocations com. United Way of Ctrl. N.Y., 1979-81; mem. pub. rels. com. St. Camillus Health Care Ctr., 1971-78; mem. fed. legis. com. Am. Lung Assn., 1974-77; bd. dirs. Crouse-Irving Meml. Hosp. Found., 1975-87, pres. 1979-81; bd. dirs. Am. Heart Assn., Upstate N.Y., 1960-80, chmn. pub. rels. com., 1970-74, chmn. legis. com. 1977, mem. fund raising adv. com., 1974-79; trustee Cazenovia Coll., 1981-94; bd. dirs. Onondaga Hist. Assn., 1980-90; dir. Global Leadership Inst., 1987-2001. Served with MMR, USNR, WWII. Recipient Silver Beaver award Boy Scouts Am., 1973, Silver Antelope award, 1981 Mem. Nat. Newspaper Assn. (legis. com. 1976-80), Greater Syracuse C. of C. (dir. 1979-81), Upstate Coun. Indsl. Editors, LeMoyne Coll. Pres.'s Assocs., Syracuse U. Alumni Assn. (nat. treas. 1973-77), Former Mems. of U.S. Congress Assn., Navy League of U.S., Cosmos Club, Georgetown Club, Coral Ridge Yacht Club, Lions, KC, Kappa Sigma (pres. 1957-59). Republican. Roman Catholic. Office: 1776 K St NW Ste 400 Washington DC 20006-2326

WORTMAN, RICHARD S. historian, educator; b. N.Y.C., Mar. 24, 1938; s. Joseph R. and Ruth (Nacht) W.; m. Marlene Stein, June 14, 1960; 1 child, Leonie. BA, Cornell U., 1958; MA, U. Chgo., 1960, PhD, 1964. Instr. history U. Chgo., 1963-64, asst. prof., 1964-69, asso. prof., 1969-76, prof., 1976-77; prof. history Princeton U., 1977-88, dir. Russian studies, 1982-88; prof. history Columbia U., 1988—; Bryce prof. history, 2001—. Trustee Nat. Council for Soviet and Eastern European Research, 1983-89; sr. fellow Harriman Inst., 1985-86 Author: The Crisis of Russian Populism, 1967, The

Development of a Russian Legal Consciousness, 1976, (with Leopold Haimson and Ziva Gallili) The Making of Three Russian Revolutionaries: Voices from the Menshevik Past, 1987, Scenarios of Power: Myth and Ceremony in Russian Monarchy, vol. I, 1995, vol. II (George L. Mosse prize Am. Hist. Assn.), 2000. Social Sci. Rsch. Coun. grantee, 1975-76; Guggenheim fellow, 1981-82 Mem. Am. Assn. Advancement Slavic Studies (pres. Mid-Atlantic Slavic Conf. 1982-83), AAUP, Am. Hist. Assn. Home: 410 Riverside Dr Apt 91 New York NY 10025-7924 E-mail: rsw3@columbia.edu.

WORTMAN, WILLIAM ALLEN, librarian; b. Council Bluffs, Iowa, Sept. 19, 1940; s. Allen and Jean (McCullough) W.; m. Susan Howlett, Aug. 26, 1966; children: Emily, Alice. BA, Wesleyan U., 1962; MA, U. Nebr., 1965; PhD, Case Western Res. U., 1972; MLS, Columbia U., 1975. Humanities libr. Miami U., Oxford, Ohio, 1975—. Founder, dir. Native Am. Women Playwrights Archive, Oxford, 1996—. Author: Collection Management, 1989, Guide to Serial Bibliographies, 2d edit., 1995, Literature in English: A Guide for Librarians, 2000. Mem. ALA, MLA, Soc. for History of Authorship, Reading and Pub. Democrat. Avocations: hiking, playing tuba in community band. E-mail: wortmawa@muohio.edu.

WORTMAN, WILLIAM JEROME, JR. obstetrician-gynecologist; b. Morganton, N.C., Aug. 2, 1934; s. William Jerome and Roberta May (Royster) W.; m. Carolyn Mabel Cane, Mar. 28, 1957 (div. 1974); children— Laura Wortman Solitario, Richard Ashley; m. 2d, Mary Ellen Moore, Jan. 18, 1975 (div.); m. Andrea Denise Edwards, May 20, 1995. A.B., Duke U., 1956; M.D., Wake Forest Coll., 1964. Diplomate Am. Bd. Ob-Gyn. Intern, U.S. Naval Hosp., Charleston, S.C., 1964-65; resident Virginia Mason Med. Center, Seattle, 1965-66, Kings County Hosp., Bklyn., 1966-69; practice medicine specializing in ob-gyn, Charlotte, N.C., 1969—; mem. staff Presbyn. Hosp., Mercy Hosp.; instr. ob-gyn SUNY-Downstate Med. Center, 1968-69; prin. Tryon Distbg., also bd. dirs.; cons. in field. Served to lt. USN, 1957-64; bd. dirs. Opera Carolina; to lt. comdr. M.C., USN, 1964-67. Mem. So. Med. Assn., Am. Coll. Obstetricians and Gynecologists, Am. Fertility Soc., Am. Assn. for Colposcopy and Colpomicroscopy, Am. Assn. Gynecol. Laparoscopists, Am. Assn. Sex Educators, Counsellors and Therapists, Am. Physicians Poetry Assn. (treas.), Royal Soc. Medicine Great Britain, Les Chevaliers du Tastevin. Clubs: Peninsula Club, Chaine Des Rotisseurs Peninsula Yacht Club. Contbr. numerous articles to profl. jours. Home: PO Box 1250 Cornelius NC 28031-1250 Address: PO Box 1250 Cornelius NC 28031-1250

WOSK, JULIE, humanities educator; m. Averill M. Williams. BA, Washington U., St. Louis, 1966; MAT, Harvard U., 1967; PhD, U. Wis., 1974. Prof. SUNY Maritime Coll., Bronx, 1975—. Author: Breaking Frame, 1992, Women and the Machine, 2001; contbr. articles to profl. jours. Grantee Alfred P. Sloan Found., N.Y.C., 2000. Mem. Soc. for History of Tech., Internat. Soc. for History of Tech. Office: SUNY Maritime Coll Dept Humanities 6 Pennyfield Ave Ft Schuyler Bronx NY 10465

WOSK, MIRIAM, artist; b. Vancouver, B.C., Can., Aug. 17, 1947; d. Morris J. and Dena W.; 1 child, Adam. Student, U. B.C., Can., 1966; AAS, Fashion Inst. Tech., N.Y.C., 1969; postgrad., Sch. Visual Arts, New Sch. Social Rsch., N.Y.C., 1969-74. Freelance illustrator 1st cover of Ms. mag., 30th ann. cover Ms. mag., Mademoiselle, N.Y. Times, Esquire, Vogue, N.Y. Mag., Viva, McCalls, Saturday Rev., Sesame St., New West, Psychology Today, 1969—79; curator group show The Inner Lives of Women: Psyche, Spirit and Soul Spring St. Gallery, L.A., 1996. One woman shows include Transam. Ctr., L.A., 1983, West Beach, L.A., 1988, Wilshire Pacific Bldg., L.A., 1991, 2001, Robert Berman Gallery, Santa Monica, Calif., 1991, 2001, Drago, Santa Monica, 1992, Jazz, Pacific Design Ctr., West Hollywood, Calif., 1995, Robert Berman Gallery, Santa Monica, Calif., 2001; exhibited in group shows at Harkness House Gallery, N.Y.C., 1979-80, Dist. 1199 Cultural Ctr. Inc., N.Y., 1981, Smithsonian Inst., Washington, 1981, Transam. Pyramid, San Francisco, 1983, Barnsdall Art Gallery, L.A., 1983, Functional Art Gallery, L.A., 1985, One Market Plaza, San Francisco, 1986, Laforet Mus., Tokyo, 1986, Art et Industrie Gallery, N.Y.C., 1986, Otis Parsons Sch. Design, L.A 1987, B1 Gallery, Santa Monica, 1987, Katharina Rich Perlow Gallery, N.Y.C., 1988, Sam Francis Studio, Santa Monica, 1988, Gallery Functional Art, Santa Monica, 1989, 91, Santa Monica Mus. Art, 1990, 99, 2000, Getty Mus., Malibu, Calif., 1990, James Corcoran Gallery, Santa Monica, 1990, Joan Robey Gallery, Denver, 1992, Cultural Ctr., Eureka, Calif., Calif. State U., Long Beach, 1992, Pacific Design Ctr., L.A., 1992, U. Art Mus., Long Beach, 1992, L.A. County Mus. Art, 1992, 96, Helander Gallery, Palm Beach, Fla., 1993, Spring Street Gallery, L.A., 1994, 96, Anderson Ranch Art Ctr., Aspen, Colo., 1995, Park Ave. Armory, N.Y.C., 1997, 98, 2000, Adam Baumgold Gallery, N.Y.C., 1997, Pub. Corp. Arts, Long Beach Arts, 1998, Boritzer Gray Hamano, Santa Monica, 1999, Santa Monica Fine Arts Studio, 1999, Jan Baum Gallery, L.A., 2000; pub. in nat. and internat. mags., books and newspapers including The Golden Age of Magazine Illustration: The Sixties and Seventies. New Feminist Criticism-Art-Identity Action, Los Angeles Times, Washington Post, Casa Vogue, L'Express Paris and Idea Internat. (Japan). Recipient Merit award Art Dirs. Club N.Y., cert. of merit Soc. Illustrators, cert. excellence Am. Inst. Graphic Artists; named guest editor Maedmoiselle Mag. Studio: 436 Adelaide Dr Santa Monica CA 90402

WOSKOW, CATHERINE ROSE, artist; b. Ukiah, Calif., Jan. 21, 1958; d. Donald Thomas and Mary Jane W. Student, Bradford Liberal Arts Coll., 1976-77, Sonoma State U., 1978-79, Koningkijke Acad. Kunsten Vormgeving, The Netherlands, 1980-81. One-woman shows include Eleonore Austerer Gallery, San Francisco, 1996, 98, 2001, Kimzey Miller Gallery, Seattle, 1998, Davis & Cline Gallery, Ashland, Calif., 2002; group exhbns. include Gallery Marckant, Langelo, The Netherlands, 1992, San Francisco Mus. Modern Art Rental Gallery, 1992, William Zimmer Gallery, Mendocino, Calif., 1992—, Solomon Dubnick Gallery, Sacramento, 1994, 2002, Eleonore Austerer Gallery, San Francisco, 1996—, Tercera Gallery, Palo Alto, Calif., 1996-2002, Kimzey Miller Gallery, Seattle, 1997-2001, Gwenda Jay Addington, Chgo., 1998-2001, Davis & Cline Gallery, Ashland, Calif., 1998-2002, Austerer Crider Gallery, 2001-02. Grantee Rotary Internat., The Netherlands, 1980-81. Avocations: whitewater kayaking, gardening, dancing.

WOSNITZER, MOREY, urologist; b. Passaic, N.J., Sept. 4, 1944; s. Morris and Ethel (Saltzman) W.; m. Nancy Joell Coplin, Sept. 18, 1978; children: Matthew, Brian. BS, Rutgers U., 1951, MS, 1952; MD, Columbia U., 1956. Diplomate Am. Bd. Urology, Am. Bd. Sexology. Intern in surgery Mt. Sinai Med. Ctr., N.Y.C., 1956-57, asst. resident in surgery, 1957-58; asst. resident in urology Columbia Presbyn. Med. Ctr., 1958-59, Mass. Gen. Hosp., Boston, 1959-60; resident in urology Peter Bent Brigham Hosp., 1962-63; pvt. practice Springfield, N.J., 1964—. Assoc. in Clin. Urology Columbia U., N.Y.C., 1975—; clin. instr. in Urology Cornell U., N.Y.C., 1989—. Lt. Comdr. USN, 1960-62. Fellow ACS, Internat. Coll. Surgeons, Soc. Urology and Engring., Am. Assn. Clin. Sexologists. Avocations: gardening, computer, reading, music, horticulture. Office: 420 Morris Ave Springfield NJ 07081-1149

WOSTREL, NANCY JO, painter, illustrator; b. San Diego, Feb. 21; d. George Jerome Wostrel and Imogene Marie Nelson. BFA, Famous Artists Schs., 1972. Staff artist Marikle & Kelly Advertising, San Diego, 1960-61; illustrator, 1961-62, 66-67; art dir., illustrator J. Jessop & Sons, 1962-66; v.p., art dir. Concept Advt. Inc., 1967-68; advt. mgr. Streicher & Seaman Inc., 1968-70; painter, illustrator, 1970—. Bd. dirs. publicity Watercolor West, Riverside, Calif., 1980-82. Represented in over 12 solo, invitational exhbns. Recipient First award for watercolor S.D. Art Inst., 1975, Lloyd award for watercolor SDWS Nat. Exhbn., 1980, 2nd prize watercolor So. Calif. Expo, 1979. Mem. Am. Watercolor Soc. (signature mem.), Watercolor West (signature mem., bd. dirs. 1980-82). Avocations: writing, Collies, gardening, collecting blue and white porcelain. Studio: 2505 Montclair St San Diego CA 92104-5348

WOTT, JOHN ARTHUR, arboretum and botanical garden executive, horticulture educator; b. Fremont, Ohio, Apr. 10, 1939; s. Arthur Otto Louis and Esther Wilhelmina (Werth) W.; children: Christopher, Timothy, Holly. BS, Ohio State U., 1961; MS, Cornell U., 1966, PhD, 1968. Mem. staff Ohio State Coop. Extension Svc., Bowling Green, 1961-64; rsch. asst. Cornell U., Ithaca, N.Y., 1964-68; prof. Purdue U., West Lafayette, Ind., 1968-81; prof. Ctr. Urban Horticulture U. Wash., Seattle, 1981—; assoc. dir. Ctr. Urban Horticulture U. Wash., 1990-93; dir. arboreta Washington Park Arboretum, 1993—. Writer columns for Nursery Mgmt. Profession, Balls and Burlap, Am. Nurseryman, The Arboretum Found.; contbr. articles to profl. jours. and papers including Nursery Mgr. Profl., Balls and Burlap, Arboreteum Found. Bull., Am. Nurseryman. Mem. Am. Soc. Hort. Sci. (com. chmn. 1967-82), Am. Assn. Bot. Gardens and Arboreta, Internat. Plant Propagators Soc. (internat. pres. 1984, internat. sec.-treas. 1985—). Avocations: music, antiques. Office: Internat Plant 2300 Arboretum Dr E Seattle WA 98112-2300 Personal E-mail: jwott10623@aol.com. Business E-Mail: jwott@u.washington.edu.

WOUK, HERMAN, writer; b. N.Y.C., May 27, 1915; s. Abraham Isaac and Esther (Levine) W.; m. Betty Sarah Brown, Dec. 9, 1945; children: Abraham Isaac (dec.), Nathaniel, Joseph. AB with gen. honors, Columbia U., 1934; LHD (hon.), Yeshiva U., 1954; LLD (hon.), Clark U., 1960; LittD (hon.), Am. Internat. Coll., 1979; PhD (hon.), Bar-Ilan U., 1990, Hebrew U., 1997; DLitt (hon), George Washington U., 2001, Trinity Coll., 1998. Writer radio programs for various comedians, N.Y.C., 1935; asst. writer weekly radio scripts comedian Fred Allen, 1936-41. Presdl. cons. to U.S. Treasury, 1941; vis. prof. English Yeshiva U., 1952-57; scholar-in-residence Aspen Inst. Humanistic Studies, 1973-74 Author: (novels) Aurora Dawn, 1947, The City Boy, 1948, Slattery's Hurricane, 1949, The Caine Mutiny, 1951 (Pulitzer Prize award for fiction, 1952), Marjorie Morningstar, 1955, Youngblood Hawke, 1962, Don't Stop the Carnival, 1965, The Winds of War, 1971, War and Remembrance, 1978, Inside, Outside, 1985 (Washingtonian Book award, 1986), The Hope, 1993, The Glory, 1994, (dramas) The Traitor, 1949, The Caine Mutiny Court-Martial, 1953, (comedy) Nature's Way, 1957, (non-fiction) This is My God, 1959, The Will to Live On, 2000, (screenplays for TV serials) The Winds of War, 1983, War and Remembrance, 1986. Trustee Coll. of V.I., 1961-69; bd. dirs. Washington Nat. Symphony, 1969-71, Kennedy Ctr. Prodns., 1974-75. Exec. officer U.S.S. Southard USNR, 1942-46, PTO. Recipient Richard H. Fox prize, 1934, Columbia U. medal for Excellence, 1952, Alexander Hamilton medal, 1980, U. Calif.-Berkeley medal, 1984, Golden Plate award Am. Acad. Achievement, 1986, USN Meml. Found. 'Lone Sailor' award, 1987, Yad Vashem KaZetnik award, 1990, Bar Ilan U. Guardian of Zion award, 1998, USCD medal U. Calif.-San Diego, 1998. Mem. Naval Res. Assn., Dramatists Guild, Authors Guild, Internat. Platform Assn. (Ralph Waldo Emerson award 1981), PEN Clubs: Bohemian (San Francisco); Cosmos, Metropolitan (Washington); Century Assn. (N.Y.C.). Jewish. Office: care BSW Literary Agy 3255 N St NW Washington DC 20007-2845

WOUNG-CHAPMAN, MARGUERITE NATALIE, lawyer; b. Kingston, Jamaica, Aug. 11, 1965; came to U.S., 1978; d. Maurice Lascelles and Lois (Ogle) W.; m. Kevin Troy Bingham May 27, 1990 (div. Apr. 1998); 1 child, Jordan Nile Bingham; m. Stanley G. Chapman III, May 28, 1999. BSLI, Georgetown U., 1986, JD, 1989. Bar: D.C., 1989, U.S. Dist. Ct. D.C., 1991. Assoc. Arter & Hadden, Washington, 1989-91; sr. atty. Tenneco Energy, Houston, 1991-95, counsel, 1995-97; atty. ARCO Pipeline Co., 1995; sr. counsel El Paso Corp., 1997-99, assoc. gen. counsel, 2000—; gen. counsel Tenn. Gas Pipeline Co., 2000—, ANR Pipeline Co., 2000—. Contbg. author: Banks and Thrifts - Government Enforcement and Receivership, 1991. Mem.: D.C. Bar Assn., Energy Bar Assn. Office: El Paso Corp 9 E Greenway Plz Ste 740 Houston TX 77046-0908 E-mail: Marguerite.Woung-Chapman@ElPaso.com.

WOYCZYNSKI, WOJBOR ANDRZEJ, mathematician, educator; b. Czestochowa, Poland, Oct. 24, 1943; came to U.S., 1970; s. Eugeniusz and Otylia Sabina (Borkiewicz) W.; m. Elizabeth W. Holbrook; children: Lauren Pike, Gregory Holbrook, Martin Wojbor. MSEE, Wroclaw (Poland) Poly., 1966; PhD in Math., Wroclaw U., 1968. Asst. prof. Inst. Math. Wroclaw U., 1968-72, assoc. prof., 1972-77; prof. dept. math. Cleve. State U., 1977-82; prof., chmn. dept. math. and stats. Case Western Res. U., Cleve., 1982-91, dir. Ctr. for Stochastic and Chaotic Processes in Sci. and Tech., 1989-2001, chmn. dept. stats, 2001—. Rsch. fellow Inst. Math. Polish Acad. Scis., Warsaw, 1969-76; postdoctoral fellow Carnegie-Mellon U., Pitts., 1970-72; vis. assoc. prof. Northwestern U., Evanston, Ill., 1976-77; vis. prof. Aarhus (Denmark) U., 1972, U. Paris, 1973, U. Wis., Madison, 1976, U. S.C., 1979, U. N.C., Chapel Hill, 1983-84, Gottingen (Germany) U., 1985, 91, 96, U. NSW, Sydney, Australia, 1988, Nagoya (Japan) U., 1992, 93, 94, U. Minn., Mpls., 1994, Tokyo U., 1997, Princeton U., 1998. Dep. editor in chief: Annals of the Polish Math. Soc., 1973-77; assoc. editor Chemometrics Jour., 1987-94, Probability and Math. Stats., 1988—, Annals of Applied Probability, 1989-96, Stochastic Processes and Their Applications, 1993-99; co-editor: Martingale Theory and Harmonic Analysis in Banach Spaces, 1982, Probability Theory and Harmonic Analysis, 1986, Nonlinear Waves and Weak Turbulence, 1993, Nonlinear Stochastic PDE's: Hydrodynamic Limit and Burgers' Turbulence, 1995, In a Reporter's Eye: The Life of Stefan Banach, 1996, Stochastic Models in Geosystems, 1997; author: (monograph) Martingales and Geometry in Banach Spaces I, 1975, part II, 1978, Burgers-KPZ Turbulence: Göttingen Lectures, 1998; co-author: Random Series and Stochastic Integrals: Single and Multiple, 1992, Distributions in the Physical and Engineering Sciences, vol. 1: Distributional and Fractal Calculus, Integral Transforms and Wavelets, 1997, Introductory Statistics and Random Phenomena. Uncertainty, Complexity and Chaotic Behavior in Engineering and Science, 1998. Rsch. grantee NSF, 1970, 71, 76, 77, 81, 87—, Office of Naval Rsch., 1985-96. Fellow Inst. Math. Stats.; mem. Am. Math. Soc., Am. Statis. Assn., Polish Math. Soc. (Gt. prize 1972), Polish Inst. Arts and Scis., Racquet Club East. Roman Catholic. Avocations: tennis, music, skiing, sailing, rare books collecting. Home: 3296 Grenway Rd Cleveland OH 44122-3412 Office: Case Western Res U Dept Statistics Cleveland OH 44106 E-mail: waw@po.cwru.edu.

WOYSKI, MARGARET SKILLMAN, retired geology educator; b. West Chester, Pa., July 26, 1921; d. Willis Rowland and Clara Louise (Howson) Skillman; m. Mark M. Woyski, June 19, 1948; children: Nancy Elizabeth, William Bruno, Ronald David, Wendelin Jane. BA in Chemistry, Wellesley (Mass.) Coll., 1943; MS in Geology, U. Minn., 1945, PhD in Geology, 1946. Geologist Mo. Geol. Survey and Water Resources, Rolla, 1946-48; instr. U. Wis., Madison, 1948-52; lectr. Calif. State U., Long Beach, 1963-67, lectr. to prof. Fullerton, 1966-91, assoc. dean Sch. Natural Sci. and Math., 1981-91, emeritus prof., 1991—. Contbr. articles to profl. jours.; author lab. manuals; editor guidebooks. Fellow Geol. Soc. Am. (program chmn. 1982); mem. South Coast Geol. Soc. (hon. pres. 1974), Mineral Soc. Am. Home: 880 Morningside Dr Apt M-320 Fullerton CA 92835-3577

WOYT, JAMES CHARLES (JIM WOYT), actor; b. Passaic, N.J., Feb. 2, 1950; s. Francis John and Esther Mary Wojdyla. Actor, 1986—. Appeared in (films) Something in Common, 1987, Homeboy, 1987, Throwback, 1987, Toxic Avenger II, 1988, Harry Met Sally, 1988, True Convictions, 1989, The Kill Off, 1989, Gremlins II, 1989, Long Time Companions, 1989, Cadillac Man, 1989, Bonfire of the Vanities, 1989, Rocky V, 1990, Beni Hana Story, 1990, Soapdish, 1990, Godfather III, 1990, Fisher King, 1990, Three Men & a Little Lady, 1990, Other People's Money, 1990, Return to Kansas City, 1991, Sublet, 1991, Breakfast at Tiffany's, 1991, Lucky Stiff, 1991, In Search of Bobby Fisher, 1992, Last Action Hero, 1993, The Quiz Show, 1993, Special Unit 2, 1999, The Pretender, 1996, America's Most Wanted, 1996, Melrose Place, 1996, Volcano, 1996, Seinfeld, 1996, Dr. Bean, 1996, Bulworth, 1996, Mr. and Mrs. Smith, 1996, Family Matters, 1996, Buffy the Vampire Slayer, 1997, The Last Don, 1997, Recoil, 1997, Soldier, 1998, Third Rock From the Sun, 1998, Man on the Moon, 1998, E.R., 1998, Seven Days, 1998, Lords of Mafia, 1999, Special Unit 2, 1999, Mighty wind, 2002; (TV) Third Rock from the Sun, 1998, Any Day Now, 1998, ER, 1998, Seven Days, 1998, L.A. Confidential (pilot), 2000, Jack & Jill, 2000, That 70s Show, 2000, West Wing, 2000, The Miracle, 2000, Popular, 2000, Collateral Damage, 2001, Crossroads, 2001, Fighting Fitzjerolds, 2001, Strong Medicine, 2001, Big Time, 2001, Like mike, 2002, Scribs, 2002, Push Nevada, 2002, American Dreams, 2002, Daredevil, 2002, Judging Amy, 2002, Intolerable Cruelty, 2002; (comml.) Nick At Night, 1988, Diesel Jeans, 1996, Pepsi Cola, 2002; (stage) Our Town, 1988; comml. includes Kirin Beer, 1988, Miller High Life, 1991, Nestea, 1996; (video) Spoof Bruce Springsteen Concert, 1991; (indsl. film) N.Y. Life, 1992; (theme park) Universal Studio's Halloween Horror Nights I, 1997, II, 1998. Democrat. Roman Catholic. Avocations: photography, body building. Home: 15515 S Crenshaw Blvd Apt 118 Gardena CA 90249 Office: c/o Starting Point Agy 1827 12th Ave Los Angeles CA 90019

WOZNIAK, DEBRA GAIL, lawyer; b. Rockford, Ill., Oct. 3, 1954; d. Richard Michael and Evalyn Louise Wozniak. BA, U. Nebr., 1976, JD, 1979. Bar: Nebr. 1980, Iowa 1980, Ill. 1982. CPCU. Asst. legal counsel Iowa Ho. of Reps., Des Moines, 1980-81; mng. atty. Rapp & Gilliam, 1981; from asst. counsel to counsel and asst. dir. Alliance of Am. Insurers, Schaumburg, Ill., 1981-87; from asst. counsel to counsel StateFarm Ins. Cos., Bloomington, 1987—. Bd. dirs. Mo. Property and Casualty Ins., Guaranty Fund, NCIGF. Mem. Nebr. Bar Assn., Iowa Bar Assn. Avocation: antiques. Office: State Farm Ins Cos One State Farm Plz Bloomington IL 61710

WOZNIAK, JOYCE MARIE, sales executive; b. Detroit, Aug. 3, 1955; d. Edmund Frank and Bernice (Liske) W. BA, Mich. State U., 1976; MA, Nat. U., San Diego, 1988; postgrad., U.S. Internat. U., 1989-90. Probation officer San Diego County Probation, 1979-81; prodn. engr. Tuesday Prodns., Inc., San Diego, 1981-85; nat. sales mgr. Advance Rec. Products, 1986-88; acct. exec. Joyce Enterprises, 1986-95; sales exec. Audio-Video Supply Inc., 1988-98; account exec. M.C.S.I. (formerly Consol. Media Sys., Inc.), 2000—02; sys. integration specialist TV Magic, Inc., 2002—. Producer (video) Loving Yourself, 1987, southwest cable access program, 1986-95; registered marriage, family and child counselor-intern, Calif., 1989. Active Zool. Soc. San Diego. Mem.: Internat. TV Assn. (treas. San Diego chpt. 1990—91), NAFE, NATAS, Calif. Assn. Marriage and Family Therapists, Art Glass Assn. So. Calif., Nat. Assn. Broadcasters. Office: 4887 Ronson Ct Ste D San Diego CA 92111 E-mail: joycew@tvmagic.tv.

WOZNIAK, RICHARD ANTHONY, computer engineer; b. Buffalo, Aug. 24, 1959; s. Richard Anthony and Julia Marie (Cefaratti) W. BA, U. Buffalo, 1981, MS, 1983. Software engr. Sierra Rsch., Buffalo, 1983-85; sr. analyst Marine Midland Bank, 1985-91, project mgr., 1991-93, tech. specialist, 1993—. Pres. South Cheektowaga Baseball Assn., Cheektowaga, N.Y., 1984—. Recipient award Cheektowaga C. of C., 1992. Home: 33 Grand Prix Dr Cheektowaga NY 14227-3613 Office: HSBC 241 Main St Fl 5 Buffalo NY 14203-2703

WOZNIAK, RICHARD MICHAEL, SR. retired city and regional planner; b. rural Fullerton, Nebr., Nov. 28, 1928; s. Theo Charles and Monica (Lesiak) W.; m. Evalyn Louise Pickett, Sept. 9, 1951; children: Debra, Karen, Richard Michael, Steve. BS, Iowa State U., 1954. Cert. landscape architect. Landscape architect Rockford (Ill.) Nurseries, 1954-55; landscape architect, city planner Harland Bartholomew & Assocs., St. Louis, 1955-58; sr. planner Springfield/Sangamon County Regional Planning Commn., Springfield, Ill., 1958-60; city planner City of Omaha, 1960-64; owner, cons. Richard M. Wozniak & Assocs., Fremont, Nebr., 1964-74; exec. v.p. Mits Kawamoto & Aassocs., Omaha, 1974-76; owner, planning cons., racher Richard M. Wozniak & Assocs., Long Pine, Nebr., 1976-84; dir. planning and community devel. City of Norfolk (Nebr.)/Madison County, 1984-97; ret., 1997. Cons. to more than 45 cities and counties in Ill., Mich. and Nebr., 1955-84; v.p., pres. Nebr. State Bd. Landscape Architects, Lincoln, 1967-84; treas. Nat. Coun. Landscape Architecture Bds., 1976. Author numerous studies and reports, comprehensive plans; designer land planning for parks and subdivs. Bd. mem. Madison County Bd. Adjustment, Nebr. With U.S. Army, 1946—49, with USAF, 1954—68. Recipient numerous awards. Mem. Am. Planning Assn. (charter), Am. Inst. Cert. Planners (charter), Nebr. Assn. County Ofcls. (v.p., pres. 1985-91), Am. Legion, Nebr. Planning and Zoning Assn. Avocations: woodworking, fishing, sculpturing. Home: 208 Skyline Dr Madison NE 68748-6231

WOZNIAK, ROBERT, physician; b. Nowa Deba, Tarnobrzeg, Poland, Mar. 29, 1964; came to U.S., 1989; s. Wladyslaw and Wanda Wozniak; m. Silvia Regina Miranda. MD, Med. Acad., Cracow, Poland, 1989. Diplomate in internal medicine and in endocrinology diabetes and metabolism Am. Bd. Internal Medicine, cert. in hyperbaris medicine. Rsch. coord. Mt. Sinai Med. Ctr., N.Y.C., 1992-94; intern St. Luke's-Roosevelt Hosp. Ctr., 1994-95, resident, 1995-97; clin. fellow endocrinology Albert Einstein Coll. Medicine, Montefiore Med. Ctr., 1997-99; pvt. practice Rock Hill and Lancaster, S.C., 1999—. Contbr. articles to profl. jours. Recipient merit award and scholarships Med. Acad., Cracow, 1984-88. Mem.: ACP-ASIM, AMA, Endocrine Soc. Roman Catholic. Avocations: computing, tourism. Office: Lancaster Endocrinology 834 W Meeting St Ste B Lancaster SC 29720-6220 E-mail: woznis01@pol.net.

WOZNIAK, STEPHEN GARY, high technology company executive; b. San Jose, Calif., Aug. 11, 1950; Co-chmn. Axlon, Inc., Sunnyvale, Calif., 1986—. Recipient Nat. Medal Tech., 1985, Grace Murray Hopper award, Assn. Computing Machinery, 1979. Invented Apple computer.*

WOZNICKI, JOHN RAYMOND, literature educator; b. Bristol, Pa., Nov. 1, 1967; s. Stanley Raymond and Maria (Brooks) W.; m. Jill Elizabeth Overlien, May 12, 1990 (div. Aug. 12, 1996); m. Leslie Tamara Kendig, June 18, 1999. BA, Worcester State Coll., 1992; MA, Coll. N.J., 1994; PhD, Lehigh U., 1998. Instr. Lehigh U., Bethlehem, Pa., 1994-98, Middlesex County Coll., Edison, N.J., 1995-96, Pa. State U., Hazleton, 1996-97, Allentown Coll., Center Valley, Pa., 1997-98, Bloomsburg (Pa.) U., 1997-98; asst. prof. Fairmont (W.Va.) State Coll., 1998-2001, C.C. Phila., 2001—. Author: Ideological Content and Political Significance of 20th Century Amercian Poetry; contbr. to Robert Frost Ency., Am. Lang. Poetry, Moria Poetry Jour. Mem. AAUP, MLA. Democrat. Avocations: running, personal computing, sports, writing poetry, cooking. Office: Georgian Ct Coll 900 Lakewood Ave Lakewood NJ 08701 Home: 24 Jean St Lambertville NJ 08530-2210 E-mail: woznickij@cgeorgian.edu.

WRAASE, DENNIS RICHARD, utilities company executive, accountant; b. Washington, Mar. 15, 1944; s. Richard Harold and Esther Morelle (Cowan) W.; m. Cecilia Anne Kirby, Dec. 30, 1987; children: Richard Reid, Elisabeth Kirby. BS, U. Md., 1966; MS, George Washington U., 1975. CPA, Md. Acct. Exxon Corp., Balt., 1966-70, fin. analyst Houston, 1970-74; mgr. fin. systems Potomac Electric Power Co., Washington, 1974-78, asst. comptr., 1978-81, dir. computer and gen. svcs., 1981-83, comptr., 1983-92, v.p., 1986-89, sr. v.p., 1989—, CFO, 1996—; dir. Potomac Capital Investment, 1998—, exec. v.p., 1999, pres., COO, 2000—. Pepco Holding Inc., 2002. Pres. Olney Jaycees, Md., 1978; bd. dirs., v.p. Nat. Capital area Boy Scouts Am., Washington, 1987-2002, Better Bus. Bur., Washington Bd. Trade, Federal City Coun., 2001—; bd. dirs. Washington Performing Arts Soc., 2002–. With USAR, 1967-73. Mem. Am. Inst. CPAs, Fin. Execs. Inst. Democrat. Lutheran. Office: Potomac Electric Power Co 701 NInth St NW Ste 1000 Washington DC 20068

WRAGA, WILLIAM GERARD, educator; b. Teaneck, N.J., Mar. 21, 1957; s. William Francis and Maryjane M. (Conlon) W.; m. Amy Jeanne Schneider, June 26, 1982; children: William Frederic, Ian Thomas. AB, Rutgers Coll., 1979; MAT, U. Chgo., 1980; EdD, Rutgers U., 1991. Tchr. Hillsborough H.S., Belle Mead, N.J., 1980-81, Green Brook (N.J.) H.S., 1981-84, Mendham (N.J.) H.S., 1984-86; dept. supr. Freehold (N.J.) Twp. H.S., 1986-87; dist. supr. K-12 Bernards Twp. Pub. Schs., Basking Ridge, N.J., 1987-94; adj. asst. prof. Rider U., Lawrenceville, 1994; asst. prof. dept. edn. leadership U. Ga., Athens, 1995-99, assoc. prof., 1999—, interim head dept. ednl. adminstrn. and policy, 2002—. Chmn. civics com. N.J. State Dept. Edn., 1988-90, mem. social studies core course proficiencies panel, 1989-91; bd. dirs. N.J. Coun. for Social Studies, 1988-90, chmn. publ. com., 1988-89; mem. exec. bd. N.J. ASCD, 1992-93; mem. adv. com. N.J. Vietnam Vets. Meml. Ednl. Ctr., 1993-94; presenter in field. Author: Democracy's High Sch., 1994; contbg. author: Readings in Middle Sch. Curriculum, 1993, Curriculum Issues and the New Century, 1995, Handbook on Teaching Social Issues, 1996; exec. editor Focus on Edn. Jour., N.J. ASCD, 1993 edit.; co-editor Rsch. Rev. for Sch. Leaders, 1996, 98, 00; guest co-editor Social Edn., 1990; contbr. articles and book revs. to profl. jours. Grad. Merit scholar Rutgers U., 1984-85, 85-86; recipient Excellence in Dissertation award Rutgers Grad. Sch. Edn. Alumni Assn., 1992. Fellow John Dewey Soc. (bd. dirs. 2000—); mem. Am. Ednl. Rsch. Assn., Profs. of Curriculum (Factotum 1998-99), Soc. Study Curriculum History (pres. 2001—), Phi Delta Kappa, Pi Lambda Theta, Kappa Delta Pi. Office: U Ga Coll Edn Dept Ednl Adminstrn and Policy 850 College Station Rd Athens GA 30605-4808 E-mail: wwraga@coe.uga.edu.

WRAY, BETTY BEASLEY, allergist, immunologist, pediatrician; b. Ga., 1935; MD, Med Coll. Ga., 1960. Diplomate Am. Bd. Allergy and Immunology, Am. Bd. Clin. Lab. Immunology. Intern Talmadge Meml. Hosp., Augusta, Ga., 1960-61, resident in pediatrics, 1962, 64-65, fellow in pediatric allergy, 1966-68; staff mem. U. Hosp., 1974—, Med. Coll. Ga., Augusta, 1979—, prof. pediat. medicine, interim dean Sch. Medicine, v.p. clin. activities, 2000—02, prof. emeritus, 2002—. Mem. Am. Acad. Allergy and Immunology, Am. Acad. Pediatrics, Am. Coll. Allergy and Immunology, So. Med. Assn. Office: Med Coll of Georgia BG 1009 Augusta GA 30912 E-mail: bettyw@mail.mcg.edu.

WRAY, CECIL, JR. lawyer; b. Memphis, Nov. 19, 1934; s. Thomas Cecil and Margaret (Malone) W.; m. Gilda Gates, Sept. 11, 1964; children: Christopher A., Kathleen Wray Baughman. Student, U. Va., 1952-53; BA magna cum laude, Vanderbilt U., 1956; LLB, Yale U., 1959. Bar: Tenn. 1959, N.Y. 1961, U.S. Supreme Ct. 1964. Registered counseil juridique, France, 1978-82. Law clk. to justice Tom C. Clark U.S. Supreme Ct., Washington, 1959-60; assoc. Debevoise & Plimpton, N.Y.C., 1960-67, ptnr., 1968-96, of counsel, 1997-99, resident ptnr. Paris, 1976-79. Adj. prof. N.Y. Law Sch., 1997—. Co-author: Innovative Corporate Financing Techniques, 1986. Pres. Search & Care, Inc., N.Y.C., 1981-87, Episcopal Charities, N.Y.; vestryman St. James' Ch., N.Y.C., 1982-87, warden, 1988-94; trustee Fondation des Etats-Unis, Paris, 1976-79, Ch. Pension Fund; bd. dirs. East Side Comty. Ctr., Inc.; bd. fgn. parishes Episcopal Ch., 1995—; bd. dirs. Hudson Highlands Land Trust; commr. Adirondack Park Agy.; bd. dirs. Ch. Life Ins. Co. Fellow Am. Coll. Investment Counsel (trustee 1981-86, pres. 1983-84); mem. ABA, Am. Law Inst., Assn. Bar City N.Y., Coun. Fgn. Rels., Ausable Club (St. Huberts, N.Y.), Union Club, Century Club, Order of Coif, Phi Beta Kappa. Episcopalian. Home: 47 E 88th St New York NY 10128-1152 Office: Debevoise & Plimpton 919 3rd Ave New York NY 10022-3902

WRAY, CHARLES HERMAN, JR. nursing educator, mental health nurse; b. Leaksville, N.C., Feb. 1, 1950; s. Charles Herman Sr. and Ruby (Cruise) W.; m. Patricia Ann Hall; 1 child, Anne Marie. BSN, U. N.C., 1979; MSN, U. Va., 1985. RN, N.C. Asst. head nurse Children's Psychiat. Unit-Duke U., Durham, N.C., 1985-87; asst. to v.p., dir. nursing Duke Med. Ctr., 1987-90; course coord. mental health Piedmont C.C., Roxboro, N.C., 1990—. Recipient NIMH traineeship, 1984. Mem. ANA, MENSA, Reed Organ Soc. Episcopalian. Avocation: music. Office: Piedmont CC PO Box 1197 Roxboro NC 27573-1197

WRAY, GERALDINE SMITHERMAN (JERRY WRAY), artist; b. Shreveport, La., Dec. 15, 1925; d. David Ewart and Mary Virginia (Hoss) Smitherman; m. George Downing Wray, June 24, 1947; children: Mary Virginia Hill, Deanie Galloway, George D. Wray III, Nancy Armistead. BFA with honors, Newcomb Art Sch., Tulane U., 1946. Tchr. children's art. One woman shows include Don Batman Gallery, Kansas City, Mo., 1982, Gallery II, Baton Rouge, 1985, McNeese Coll., Lake Charles, La., 1987, Dragonfly Gallery, Shreveport, La., 1987, Barnwell Garden and Art Ctr., Shreveport, 1988, 95, Southdown Mus., Houma, La., 1989, La. State U., Shreveport, 1991, WTN Radio Station, Shreveport, 1993, The Cambridge Club, Shreveport, 1993, Centenary Coll., 1993, Northwestern State U., Natchitoches, La., 1995, Goddard Mus., Ardmore, Okla., 1996, Art Buyers Caravan, Atlanta, 1996, Lockhaven (Pa.) U., 1996, Billingsley Gallery, Pensacola, Fla., 1996, Casa D'Arte, Shreveport, La., 1996, N.E. State U., Monroe, La., 1997, Art Expo, N.Y.C., 1997, Palmer Gallery, Hot Springs Ark., 1998, Tower Art Gallery, Shreveport, La., 1999; Group shows include Watercolor USA Springfield., Mo., 1988, Waddell's Gallery, Shreveport, 1988, 91, Water Works Gallery, Dallas, 1990, Southwestern Watercolor Show, 1991 (D'Arches award, Creative Artist award 1997), Masur Mus. Exhibition (honorable mention 91, 92), , Bossier Art Ctr., Bossier City, La., 1992, Irving Art Assn. (honorable mention), 1992, Leon Loard Gallery, Montgomery, Ala., 1993, Ward-Nasse Gallery, N.Y.C., 1993, 97, Soc. Experimental Artists Internat. (1st. place, honorable mention), 1993, Palmer Gallery, Hot Springs, Ark., 1994, Nat. Watercolor Soc. Ann., 1994-96, 98, Art Expo, N.Y.C., 1996, Casa D'Arte, Shreveport, 1996, Art Buyers Caravan, Atlanta, 1996, Off The Wall Gallery, Savannah, Ga., 1997, Art Effects Gallery, Merian, Pa., Boulevard Art Gallery, Macon, Ga., 1997, Visual Inspirations, Newton, N.J., 1997, Mossey Brake Gallery, Tex., 1997, Barnwell Ctr. (with children & grandchildren), Shreveport LA, 1998, Manhattan Arts Mag. Showcase Award, Nat. Assn. Women Artist Traveling Show; permanent collections include NAWA, Zimmerli Mus., Rutgers Univ., N.J.-Meir Mus., Lynchburg, Va., Goddard Mus. Ardmore, Okla., Bibl. Arts Ctr., Dallas, La. State Capitol Bldg., Lockhaven Univ. Penn., LSUS Med. Ctr., Shreveport, LA. Art chmn. Jr. League, Shreveport, 1955-60; bd. dirs. Holiday-in-Dixie Cotillion, Shreveport, 1974-76. Inducted into Visual Artists Hall of Fame, Shreveport, La., 1998. Mem. Nat. Assn. Women Artists, Nat. Watercolor Soc. (signature mem. 1994, 96), Southwestern Watercolor Soc. (signature mem. 1991), La. Watercolor Soc. (signature mem. 1990), La. Artists Inc. (elected mem.), Internat. Soc. Exptl. Artists (signature mem.), Western Fedn. Soc. Artists (signature mem.). Episcopalian. Avocation: tennis. Home: 573 Spring Lake Dr Shreveport LA 71106-4603 E-mail: jwray@softdisk.com.

WRAY, JOHN LAWRENCE, engineer; b. Maryville, Mo., June 17, 1935; s. Lawrence Paul and Roberta Inez Wray; m. Jane Eloise Wray, Aug. 18, 2001; m. Sally Blair Wray, Dec. 28, 1958 (div. Jan. 11, 2001); children: Mary Anne Deauville, Nancy Cook Rummel, Carolyn Gerdes Wheeler. MBA, Santa Clara U., Santa Clara, CA, 1964—66; MSME, Stanford U., Stanford, CA, 1957—58; BSME, U. of Mo., Columbia, MO, 1953—57. Professional Engineering Registration, Ca, NY, Or, WA, TX. Sr. cons. Mollerus Engrng. Corp., Los Gatos, Calif., 1990—98; pres. Renewable Resources, Inc., Palo Alto, 1985—89; v.p. engrng. services Quadrex Corp., Campbell, 1978—84; engrng. mgr. GE, San Jose, 1962—78; staff engr. Kans. City Power and Light, Kansas City, Mo., 1956. Educator West Valley Coll., Saratoga, Calif., 1984—88, Nat. U., San Jose, Calif., 1984; pres. Systrol, Inc., Saratoga, Calif., 1984—87. Sponsoring manager (analysis methods plan) Nuclear Reactor Operating Safety Analysis; author: (air force publication) Effects of Nuclear Weapons in Eyes (Commendation Medal, 1962); editor: (book) Effects of Nuclear Weapons, Glasstone. Precinct worker Polit. Com., Saratoga, Calif., 1964; pres., dir., chmn., tennis com. Brookside Swim and Racquet Club, 1964—2000. Capt. USAF, 1957—62, Washington, DC. Mem.: ASME (nuc. power divsn. 1957—2002), Leavenworth, WA and Maryville, MO Masons (warden 1957—2002), Leavenworth Lions Svc. Club (sec. 2000—02). Methodist. Avocations: classic car renovation, radio controlled model airplanes, radio controlled model airplanes, stamp collection. Home: 9722 Dye Road Leavenworth WA 98826 Home Fax: 509-548-7551. Personal E-mail: jlwray5@msn.com.

WRAY, ROBERT, lawyer; s. George and Ann (Moriarty) W.; m. Lila Keogh (dec.); children: Jennifer, Edward, Hillary. BS, Loyola U., 1957; JD, U. Mich., 1960. Bar: D.C., Ill. 1960. Assoc. Hopkins & Sutter, Chgo., 1964-69; gen. counsel Agy. for Internat. Devel., 1969-71; sr. counsel TRW, Inc., 1972-73, Export-Import Bank of the U.S., 1974-79; prin. Robert Wray Assocs., 1979-86; internat. ptnr. Pierson, Ball & Dowd, 1986-87; prin. Robert Wray Assocs., 1988—; spec. counsel Graham & James, 1988-97; ptnr. Holland & Knight, Washington, 1997—. Recipient medal of superior honor Dept. of State. Mem.: ABA, Internat. Bar Assn., Am. Soc. Internat. Law, Fed. Bar Assn., Chevy Chase Club, Annapolis Yacht Club, Talbot Country Club, Met. Club, Bretton Woods Com. Office: 2099 Pennsylvania Ave NW Washington DC 20006-6800

WRAY, THOMAS JEFFERSON, lawyer; b. Nashville, July 17, 1949; s. William Esker and Imogene (Cushman) W.; m. Susan Elizabeth Wells, Aug. 19, 1972; children: William Clark, Caroline Kell. BA, Emory U., 1971; JD, U. Va., 1974. Bar: Tex. 1974, U.S. Dist. Ct. (so., no. and ea. dists.) Tex. 1976, U.S. Ct. Appeals (5th and 11th cirs.) 1976, U.S. Supreme Ct. 1987. Assoc. Fulbright & Jaworski, L.L.P., Houston, 1974-82; ptnr. Fulbright & Jaworski, 1982—. Mem. ABA, Coll. Labor and Employment Lawyers, Houston Bar Assn., Houston Mgmt. Lawyers Forum (chmn. 1981-82), Briar Club, Phi Beta Kappa. Republican. Episcopalian. Home: 3662 Ella Lee Ln Houston TX 77027-4105 Office: Fulbright & Jaworski 1301 Mckinney St Ste 5100 Houston TX 77010-3095 E-mail: tjwray@fulbright.com.

WREFORD, DAVID MATHEWS, magazine editor; b. Perth, Australia, Dec. 17, 1943; emigrated to Can., 1966; s. Peter Mathews and Mary Lichfield (Edquist) W.; m. Donna Diane Campbell, Sept. 28, 1970; children— Elizabeth Mary, Catherine Anne. B.Sc. in Agr. with honours, U. Western Australia, 1966. Field editor Southam Bus. Publns. Ltd., Winnipeg, Man., Can., 1967-73; field editor Country Guide, Public Press Ltd., Milton, Ont., 1973-75; editor Country Guide, United Grain Growers Ltd., Winnipeg, 1975—. Mem. Man. Inst. Agrologists, Agrl. Inst. Can., Canadian Fedn. Farm Writers and Broadcasters. Mem. Ch. Of Eng. Home: 294 Elm St Winnipeg MB Canada R3M 3P3 Office: United Grain Growers Ltd PO Box 6600 Winnipeg MB Canada R3C 3A7 also: Toronto-Dominion Centre 25th Fl 201 Portage Ave Winnipeg MB Canada R3C 3A7 E-mail: dwreford@fbc.agricoreunited.com.

WREGE, CHARLES DECK, management educator; b. Newark, Mar. 11, 1924; s. Carl and Louise (Deck) W.; m. Beulah Marion Cippel, May 28, 1950. BA, Upsala Coll., 1952; MA, New Sch. for Social Rsch., 1955; MBA, NYU, 1956, PhD, 1961. Owner, operator Yearound Display Co., N.Y.C., 1946-50; indsl. engr. Weston Elec. Instruments, Newark, 1952-56; instr. in mgmt. Sch. Commerce NYU, 1956-61; asst. prof. mgmt. Univ. Coll. Rutgers U., New Brunswick, N.J., 1961-80, assoc. prof. mgmt. Sch. Adminstrv. Scis., 1980-85, assoc. prof. mgmt. Sch. Bus., 1985-91, prof. emeritus, 1992; adj. prof. Cornell U., Ithaca, N.Y., 1991—. Vis. prof. Cornell U., 1980, vis. rschr., 1981; adv. TV series on history of technology Uden Assocs., London, 1993; adv. tv docudrama on F.W. Taylor, Quest Prodns., 1998; guest speaker Canal History and tech. Symposium Hugh Moore Hist. Park and Mus., Lafayette, Coll., 1992, 93, 94, 95, 96, 98, 99; reviewer Entrepreneurship Theory and Practice, 1996—; contbr. spcl. rsch. forum Acad. of Mgmt., 1999; commentator TV docudrama "Stopwatch", Sloan Found., 1999; advisor TV docudrama proposal on This Working Life, Australian Broadcasting Corp., 1999. Author: Spring Lake: An Early History, 1976, Facts and Fallacies of Hawthorne: Historical Analysis of the Hawthorne Illumination Texts and Their Influence on the Hawthorne Studies, 1986, Trolley Treasures, vol. 1, 1987, vol. 2, 1991, Frederick W. Taylor, Father of Scientific Management: Myth and Reality, 1991; contbg. author: The History of Science in the United States: An Encyclopedia, 2001; commentator (film) A Question of Management, 1986, (video tape series) Methods of Management History, 1995; reviewer Acad. of Mgmt. Rev., 1994—, Entrepreneurship Theory and Practice, 1996—; mem. editl. bd. Pub. Adminstrn. and Mgmt.: An Interactive Jour., 1996—. Internat. Jour. of Organizational Theory and Behavior, 1997—, Jour. Decision, 2001-; advisor tv docudrama This Working Life Australian Broadcasting Corp. documentary series, 1999. Active Spring Lake (N.J.) Bicentennial Com., 1975-76; hist. advisor Kheel Labor Mgmt. Documentation Ctr., Cornell U., Ithaca, N.Y., 1980—, vis. researcher, 1980-81; advisor bus. history archives, Kettering U., Flint, Mich., 1989—; active, cons. archivist Friends of N.J. R.R. and Transp. Mus., Inc., 1992—. With USAAF, 1943-46. Recipient Disting. Paper award So. Mgmt. Assn., 1985, Midwest Case Writers Assn., 1986, Outstanding Paper award Literati Club MCB Univ. Press, Eng., 1998. Mem. Acad. Mgmt. (historian 1979—, editor history divsn. newsletter 1979-86, chmn. history divsn. 1985, chmn. centennial com. 1979-85, feature editor acad. news 1988—, editorial bd. Jour. Mgmt. History 1994—), Am. Inst. Hist. Tech. (v.p. 1987—), Ctr. for Canal History and Tech. Avocations: railway history. Home: 23 Worthington Ave Spring Lake NJ 07762-1659

WREN, HAROLD GWYN, arbitrator, lawyer, legal educator; b. Big Stone Gap, Va., May 19, 1921; s. James H. and Jessie M. (Reeve) W.; m. Beryl E. Bird, Nov. 20, 1948; children: James H., II, Geoffrey G. AB, Columbia U., 1942, LL.B., 1948; J.S.D., Yale U., 1957. Bar: N.Y. 1948, Okla. 1956, Tex. 1959, Ky. 1983. Assoc. firm Willkie Farr & Gallagher, N.Y.C., 1948-49; assoc. prof. law U. Miss., Oxford, 1949-54; prof. law U. Okla., Norman, 1954-57, So. Meth. U., Dallas, 1957-65, Boston Coll., 1965-69; dean, prof. law Lewis and Clark Law Sch., Portland, Oreg., 1969-72, U. Richmond, Va., 1972-76; prof. law U. Louisville, 1976-91, dean, 1976-81; arbitrator Am. Arbitration Assn., 1958—, Fed. Mediation and Conciliation Service, 1958—, Nat. Arbitration Forum, 1995—, NASD Regulation, Inc., 2002—; of counsel James R. Voyles, Atty. at Law, Louisville, 2001—. Bd. dirs. Health Care Excel, Inc.; rep. Area III Citizen Adv. Ctr., 2002—. Author: Creative Estate Planning, 1970, Problems in Corporate Changes, 1958, Problems in Texas Estates, 1961, (with Gabinet and Carrad) Tax Aspects of Marital Dissolution, 1987, 2d edit., 1997, (with Glascock) The Of Counsel Agreement, 1991, 2d edit., 1998. Served to capt. USNR, 1942-80. Fulbright scholar, 1953-54 Fellow Am. Coll. Trust and Estate Counsel, Am. Coll. Tax Counsel, Am. Bar Found. (life); mem. ABA, Louisville Bar Assn., Conversation Club, Order of Coif, Phi Beta Kappa, Phi Kappa Phi. Democrat. Episcopalian. Home: 5944 Ashwood Bluff Dr Louisville KY 40207-1269 Office: 200 S 5th St Ste 400 S Louisville KY 40202-3236 E-mail: HWrenbirdwren@aol.com.

WREN, JOHN D. advertising executive; Pres., CEO Omnicom Group, Inc., N.Y.C. Office: Omnicom Group Inc 437 Madison Ave Fl 9 New York NY 10022-7001*

WREN, ROBERT JAMES, aerospace engineering manager; b. Moline, Ill., May 12, 1935; m. Jordis Wren; children: James, Patrick, Kiley. BSCE, U. Tex., 1956; MSCE, So. Meth. U., 1962; doctoral candidate, U. Houston. Registered profl. engr. Tex. Engrng. aide Ctrl. Power and Light Co., Corpus Christi, 1954; sta. clk. City of Austin (Tex.) Power Plant, 1954-55; assoc. engr., hydraulic engr. U.S. Bur. of Reclamation, Austin, 1955-57; structural test engr. Gen. Dynamics, Ft. Worth, 1957-62; sr. structural dynamics engr., mgr. vibration and acoustic test facility NASA-Manned Spacecraft Ctr., Houston, 1962-63, 63-66, head exptl. dynamics sect., 1965-70; mgr. Apollo Spacecraft 2TV-1 CSM Test Program, 1966-68, Apollo Lunar Module-2 Drop Test Program, 1968-70; mgr. structural design space sta., space base, lunar base, mars mission NASA-Manned Spacecraft Ctr., Houston, 1970-73; mgr. structural design and devel., space shuttle carrier aircraft-747 NASA Johnson Space Ctr., 1973-74, mgr. structural divsn. space shuttle payload systems, 1974-84; mgr. engrng. directorate for space shuttle payload safety NASA-Johnson Space Ctr., 1984-94, mem. space shuttle payload safety rev. panel, 1984-2000, alternate chmn. space shuttle payload safety review panel, 1990-2000, mgr. engrng. dir. vehicle and payload flight sys. safety, 1994-2000. Mem. NASA Internat. Space Sta. Flight sys. safety panel, 1994-2000; dir. safety and mission assurance Internat. Space Sta. Program Office, United Space Alliance Hdqs., Houston, 2000—. Pres. Friendswood Little League Baseball, 1980-83; bd. dirs. Bay Area YMCA, Houston, 1982—, chmn., 1983-84. Recipient Sustained Superior Performance award NASA, Personal Letter of Commendation, George Low NASA Apollo Program, Outstanding Svc. award NASA, Group Achievement awards NASA; Paul Harris fellow Rotary. Mem. Space Ctr. Rotary (dir., treas., sec., v.p. 1979-85, pres. 1985-86, Rotary dist. 5890/govt. rep. 1986-87, area coord. 1987-89, zone leader 1988-89, gov.'s aide 1989-90, chmn. dist. assembly 1989-90, 93-94, fin. com. 1989-91, Rotary Nat. award for Space Achievement Found./co-founder, bd. dirs. 1984—), Rotary World Health Found. Plastic Surgery for Children (co-founder, bd. dirs. 1985—), Rotary Space Meml. Found. (co-founder, bd. dirs. 1986—, co-founder, bd. dirs. Space Ctr. Rotary Endowment Found., 1987—). Methodist. Avocations: snow and water skiing, running, scuba diving, tennis, sailing. Home: PO Box 1466 Friendswood TX 77549-1466 Office: United Space Alliance Hdqrs 1150 Gemini Houston TX 77058 E-mail: robert.j.wren@usahq.unitedspacealliance.com.

WREN, STEPHEN COREY, mathematician, inventor; b. St. Louis, Sept. 4, 1956; s. Donald W and Jo V (Mask) Wren; 1 child Corey. BA in Math./Computer Sci. , Washington U., St. Louis, 1979. Actuary William Mercer, St. Louis, 1980-83; pres. CIM, 1983—2000; managing mem Variant USA, St. Louis, 2000—. Instr St Louis Univ, 1986—87, Webster Univ, 1985—86. Achievements include invention of computerized marketing networks. E-mail: stevewr@synerty.net.

WREN, THOMAS EDWARD, philosopher, educator; b. Kansas City, Mo., July 16, 1938; s. Alfred Augustus and Mary Wren; m. Carol Ann Thompson, Sept. 9, 1969; children: Kathleen Marie, Michael Thomas. BA, St. Mary's Coll., Winona, Minn., 1959, MEd, 1965; MA in English, DePaul U., 1962; MA in Philosophy, Loyola U., Chgo., 1965; PhD, Northwestern U., 1969. Lectr. Lewis U., Lockport, Ill., 1965, Northwestern U., Chgo., 1966; prof. Loyola U., 1967—, Loyola U. Rome (Italy) Ctr., 1968—69, 1996—97. Vis. prof. Calif. State U., Fullerton, 1987—88. Office: Loyola U Chgo Philosophy Dept 6525 N Sheridan Rd Chicago IL 60626

WRENN, WALTER BRUCE, marketing educator, consultant; b. Mobile, Ala., Nov. 9, 1950; s. Walter P. and Winona A. (Jeffrey) W.; m. Jan F. Carmichael, June 12, 1971. BS, Auburn U., 1973; M of Mgmt., Northwestern U., 1974, PhD, 1989. Market analyst The UpJohn Co., Kalamazoo, 1974-78; asst. prof. mktg. Andrews U., Berrien Springs, 1978-89; assoc. prof. Ind. U., South Bend, 1995—. Cons. The UpJohn Co., Kalamazoo, 1982, N.Am. Div. SDA, Washington, 1983, Worthington (Ohio) Foods, 1985—, Adventist Health System, Austin, Tex., 1986, Leco, 1991, Bio-Met, 1991, Maple Leaf Farms, 1998. Author: (instr. manuals) Principles of Marketing, 1983, 86, Marketing Management, 1984, 88, 91, 94; co-author: Marketing for Congregations, 1994, The Marketing Research Guide, 1997, Marketing Planning Guide, 1997; contbr. articles to profl. jours. Dir. University Press, Berrien Springs, 1986-89, Sta. WAUS, Berrien Springs, 1987—. Named Outstanding Young Man of Am. Jr. C. of C., 1980; univ. scholar Northwestern U., 1980-83. Mem. Am. Mktg. Assn. (Outstanding Mktg. Student 1973), Acad. Mktg. Sci., Phi Kappa Phi, Alpha Mu Alpha, Omicron Delta Epsilon, Delta Sigma Pi, Delta Mu Delta. Seventh Day Adventist. Avocations: racketball. Home: 5027 E Bluffview Dr Berrien Springs MI 49103-1435 Office: Ind Univ 1700 Mishawaka Ave South Bend IN 46615-1400

WRESCH, ROBERT RICHARD, ophthalmologist, medical educator; b. Portland, Oreg., July 19, 1943; s. Richard Charles and Faith M. (Griffith) W.; m. Eunice Elnora Jewell, Feb. 14, 1971; children: Keith, Alysia. BA in Chemistry, Walla Walla Coll., College Place, Wash., 1965; MD, Loma Linda (Calif.) U., 1969. Diplomate Am. Bd. Ophthalmology. Intern Kettering (Ohio) Meml. Hosp., 1969-70, resident in gen. surgery, 1970-71; gen. physician and surgeon Blantyre Adventist Clinic, Malawi, 1971-73; gen. physician and surgeon, instr. to health assts. Malamulo Hosp., Makwasa, Malawi, 1973-74; family practice physician Riverside Gen. Hosp. and Loma Linda U. Health Svc., Loma Linda, Calif., 1974-76; resident in ophthalmology Loma Linda U., 1976-79; chief ophthalmology, instr. ophthalmology residents Pettis Meml. VA Hosp., Loma Linda, 1979-80; head dept. ophthalmology, instr. nursing, instr. residents Maluti Adventist Hosp., Mapoteng, Lesotho, 1980-89; ophthalmologist Guam Seventh-Day Adventist Clinic, Tamuning, 1990—. Instr. dept. ophthalmology Loma Linda U., 1979-80, clin. instr. ophthalmology, 1980-90, asst. clin. prof. ophthalmology, 1990—. Contbr. papers to Ophthalmic Soc. of South Africa, 1988, 89. Named 1 of 4 Honored Alumni, Alumni Assn. Sch. Medicine Loma Linda U., 1992. Fellow Am. Acad. Ophthalmology. Adventist. Avocations: computer software development, bible education, scuba diving, kayaking. Office: Guam SDA Clinic 388 Ypao Rd Tamuning GU 96913-3701 E-mail: wresch@kuentos.guam.net.

WRIGHT, AMOS JASPER, III, medical librarian; b. Mar. 3, 1952; m. Dianne Vargo; children: Amos Jasper IV, Rebecca Caitlin. BA in English, Auburn U., 1973; MLS, U. Ala., 1982. Libr. asst. microforms and documents dept. Draughon Libr. Auburn U., 1973-81; grad. asst. Health Scis. Libr. U. Ala., Tuscaloosa, 1981-82; cataloger, head tech. svcs. Tuscaloosa Pub. Libr., 1982-83; clin. libr. dept. anesthesiology U. Ala., Birmingham, 1983—. Sec. Libr. Ops. Com. Draughon Libr. Auburn U., 1975-76; mem. student adv. com. U. Ala. Grad. Sch. Libr. Svc., 1981-82; mem. Ala. planning com. Second White House Conf. on Librs. and Info. Svcs., 1989, joint conf. planning com. Ala. Libr. Forum, 1989-90, planning com. and conf. agenda subcom. Ala Govs. Conf. on Librs. and Info. Svcs.; cons. Wood Libr.-Mus. of Anesthesiology, 1987, Shelby Med. Ctr. Libr., 1987-88; reviewer Spl. Study Section H., Div. Rsch. Grants, NIH, 1989. Author: (poetry books) Frozen Fruit, 1978, Right Now I Feel Like Robert Johnson, 1981, Criminal Activity in the Deep South, 1700-1939: An Annotated Bibliography, 1989; co-editor: Incipit: History of the Health Scis. News, 1988-89; assoc. editor: Bulletin of Anesthesia History, 1998—; contbr.: (Gregory VL editor) A Dynamic Tradition: A History of Alabama Academic Libraries, 1991; columnist: Anesthesia History Assn. Newsletter, 1985—, Synapse 1989; contbr. articles to Anesthesia and Analgesia, Health Care Ala., Anesthesiology, Ala. Jour. Med. Sci., Middle East Jour. Anesthesiology, Int. Surg.; also over 400 poems in anthologies, jours. and popular mags, over 50 articles and reviews on jazz and rock music in newspapers. Mem. Pelham Pub. Libr. Bd., 1988-2001. Recipient NEH Youthgrant, 1981, Wood Libr.-Mus. fellowship, 1988. Mem. Assn. Librs. in the History of Health Scis., Am. Assn. for History of Medicine (local arrangements com. 1988-89), Med. Libr. Assn. (oral hist. com. 1988-90), Ala. Libr. Assn. (bibliog. com. 1984-86, pubs. com. 1990-92, membership com. 1991-92), Anesthesia Hist. Assn. (v.p. 1999-2000, pres. 2000-02), Ala. Hist. Assn., Birmingham Hist. Soc., Shelby County Hist. Soc., Ala. Health Librs. Assn. (v.p. 1988, pres. 1989). Home: 119 Pintail Dr Pelham AL 35124-2121 Office: Dept Anesthesiology U Ala Sch Medicine 619 19th St S Birmingham AL 35294 E-mail: ajwright@uab.edu.

WRIGHT, ANDREW, English literature educator; b. Columbus, Ohio, June 28, 1923; s. Francis Joseph and Katharine (Timberman) W.; m. Virginia Rosemary Banks, June 27, 1952; children: Matthew Leslie Francis, Emma Stanbery. AB, Harvard U., 1947; MA, Ohio State U., 1948, PhD, 1951. Prof. English lit. U. Calif., San Diego, 1963—, chmn. dept. lit., 1971-74; dir. U. Calif. Study Center, U.K. and Ireland, 1980-82. Vis. prof. U. Queensland, Australia, 1984, Colegio de la Frontera Norte, San Antonio del Mar, Baja, Calif., 1991-92. Author: Jane Austen's Novels: A Study In Structure, 1953, Joyce Cary: A Preface to His Novels, 1958, Henry Fielding: Mask and Feast, 1965, Blake's Job: A Commentary, 1972, Anthony Trollope: Dream and Art, 1983; Fictional Discourse and Historical Space, 1987; contbg. author numerous books, articles to profl. jours., numerous short stories to lit. mags.; editorial bd. Nineteenth Century Fiction, 1964-86. Bd. dirs. Calif. Coun. Humanities, 1983-87. Guggenheim fellow, 1960, 70; Fulbright Sr. Research fellow, 1960-61 Fellow Royal Soc. Lit.; mem. MLA, Jane Austen Soc., Athenaeum (London), Trollope Soc., Santayana Soc., Phi Beta Kappa. Home: 7227 Olivetas Ave La Jolla CA 92037-5335 Office: U Calif San Diego Dept Lit La Jolla CA 92093-0410 E-mail: ahwright@ucsd.edu.

WRIGHT, ANTONY POPE, research chemist; b. Charlottesville, Va., Apr. 28, 1943; s. David McCord and Caroline J. (Jones) W.; m. Judith A. Brown, Apr. 26, 1975; children: Christopher W., David M., Simon K., Amy E. BSc, McGill U., Montreal, Que., Can., 1963; PhD, U. Wis., 1973. Chemist Stauffer Wacker Silicones, Adrian, Mich., 1967-70; scientist Dow Corning Corp., Midland, 1973-99; assoc. tech. dir. Strem Chems., Inc., Newburyport, Mass., 1999—. Vis. fellow U. Durham, Eng., 1989-90; vis. scientist MIT, 1999-2000. Contbr. chpt. to book. Lt. (j.g.) USNR, 1963-67. Fellow Royal Soc. Chemistry; mem. Am. Chem. Soc. Achievements include patents in fields of catalysis, organofluorine and organosilane/silicone products and synthesis; understanding the synthetic chemistry of elemental silicon; co-discovery of the Wright West Rearrangement in Organosilicon Chemistry, the telomerization of diiodochlordtrifluorethylene in organofluorine chemistry. Home: 151 Crane Neck St West Newbury MA 01985-2316 Office: Strem Chems Inc 7 Mullikan Way Newburyport MA 01950-4098

WRIGHT, BERNICE MARTHA, librarian; b. Bartlett, Tex., July 23, 1948; d. Rudolph Frank and Martha Hattie Anna (Foerster) Persky; m. Michael David Wright, June 17, 1972. BA, Tex. Woman's U., 1970, MLS, 1971. Asst. acquisitions libr. Baylor U., Waco, Tex., 1971-76; acquisitions libr. Stephen F. Austin State U., Nacogdoches, 1976-91, reference libr., 1992—. Treas. Tex. Dem. Women, Austin, 1997, exec. bd., 1996, historian, 1998-2000; pres., Nacogdoches County Dem. Women, 1995-96. Mem. Tex. Libr. Assn. (publs. com. 1980-81, scholarship com. 1985), Nacogdoches Bus. and Profl. Women (com. chmn. 1996), Univ. Women's Club (nominating com.), Univ. Profl. Women (pres. 1995). Home: 2024 Cedar Crest Dr Nacogdoches TX 75964-9049 Office: Univ Libr Nacogdoches TX 75962-0001

WRIGHT, BETH SEGAL, art historian, educator; b. N.Y.C., July 23, 1949; d. Ben and Ella (Litvack) Segal; m. Woodring Erik J. Wright, Sept. 5, 1971; children: Benjamin, Joshua. AB cum laude, Brandeis U., 1970; MA, U. Calif., Berkeley, 1972, PhD, 1978. Instr. Mountain View Coll., Dallas, 1978-82; lectr. U. Tex., 1980-81, Tex. Christian U., Ft. Worth, 1981; asst. prof. U. Tex., Arlington, 1984-88, assoc. prof., 1988-98, prof., 1998—. Adj. and vis. asst. prof. art history U. Tex., Arlington, 1981-84. Author: Painting and History During the French Restoration. Abandoned by the Past, 1997; author, editor: The Cambridge Companion to Delacroix, 2001; contbr. articles to Art Bull., Arts Mag., Word & Image, Oxford Art Jour., Nouvelles de l'Estampe, Clio, others. Kress Found. hon. traveling fellow, 1975-76; NEH Travel to Collections grantee, Paris, 1987, 93; U. Tex. Arlington Rsch. Enhancement grantee, Paris, 1990, 93, 99, Coll. Art Assoc. Meiss grant, 1996; recipient Dallas Mus. Art Vasari award Painting and History, 1998. Mem. Soc. Histoire Art Français (contbr. articles to bull.), Am. Soc. for 18th-Century Studies, Coll. Art Assn., Midwest Art History Soc. (bd. dirs. 1990-93).

WRIGHT, BETTY REN, children's book writer; b. Wakefield, Mich., June 15, 1927; d. William and Revena Evelyn (Trezise) W.; m. George Albert Frederiksen, Oct. 9, 1976. BA, Milw.-Downer Coll., 1949. With Western Pub. Co., Inc., 1949-78, mng. editor Racine Editl., 1967-78. Author numerous juv. and jr. novels, including The Doll House Murders, 1983, Christina's Ghost, 1985, The Summer of Mrs. MacGregor, 1986, A Ghost in the Window, 1987, The Pike River Phantom, 1988, Rosie and the Dance of the Dinosaurs, 1989, The Ghost of Ernie P., 1990, A Ghost in the House, 1991, The Scariest Night, 1991, The Ghosts of Mercy Manor, The Ghost of Popcorn Hill, 1993, The Ghost Witch, 1993, A Ghost Comes Calling, 1994, Out of the Dark, 1995, Haunted Summer, 1996, Too Many Secrets, 1997, The Ghost in Room 11, 1998, A Ghost in the Family, 1998, The Moonlight Man, 2000, The Wish Master, 2000; also numerous picture and ednl. books including Pet Detectives, 1999; contbr. fiction to mags. Recipient Alumni Svc. award Lawrence U., 1973, Lynde and Harry Bradley Maj. Achievement award, 1997, numerous awards for books including Mo. Mark Twain award, 1986, 96, Tex. Bluebonnet award, 1986, 88, Young Readers award Pacific N.W. Libr. Assn., 1986, Reviewer's Choice Booklist, Ala. Young Readers award, 1987, Ga. Children's Choice award, 1988, Ind. Young Hoosier Book award, 1989, 96, Children's Choice Book/Internat. Reading Assn.—CBC, 1984, S.C. Children's Choice award, 1995, Okla. Sequoyah Children's Choice award, 1988, 95, award Fla. Sunshine State, 2001. Mem. AAUW, Allied Authors, Coun. for Wis. Authors (juv. book award 1985, 96), Phi Beta Kappa. Avocations: reading, travel. Home and Office: 6223 Hilltop Dr Racine WI 53406-3479

WRIGHT, BLANDIN JAMES, lawyer; b. Detroit, Nov. 29, 1947; s. Robert Thomas and Jane Ellen (Blandin) Wright; m. Gina Almente; children: Steven Blandin, Martha Kay, Oliver Steffan. BA, U. Mich., 1969; JD, Dickinson Law Sch., 1972; LLM in Taxation, NYU, 1973; MS in Taxation with honors, Am. U., 1992. Bar: Pa. 1973, Fla. 1976, U.S. Tax Ct. 1977, D.C. 1979, U.S. Supreme Ct. 1979, Va. 1984, N.Y. 1991; CPA, Tex., 1978, Va., 1985. Atty. Office Internat. Ops. Nat. Office IRS, Washington, 1973-76; tax dir. Intairdril Ltd., London, 1976-78; tax atty. Allied Chem. Corp., Houston, 1978-79; v.p., gen. counsel Assoc. Oiltools, Inc., London, 1979-82; v.p. taxes, gen. counsel J. Lauritzen (USA), Inc., Charlottesville, Va., 1982-85; sole practice, 1985-88; ptnr. Richmond & Fishburne, 1988-90, of counsel, 1990-91; tax counsel Mobil Oil Corp., N.Y.C., 1990, Fairfax, Va., 1990-95; vice chmn., gen. counsel Cruise Holdings, Ltd., Miami, 1996-97; pres. Maritime Capital Group, Inc., 1998—; chmn. Internat. Hospitality, Inc., 1999—. Officer Pamaco Partnership Mgmt. Corp., Va., 1986-91, CRW Energy Corp., 1986-90, Transp. & Tourism Internat., Inc., 1986—, Hotsprings Assocs., Inc., 1989-91, MDM Hotels, Inc., 1992-95, Internat. Shipping & Resorts, Inc., 1992—, United Holdings Ltd., 1993-96, Cruise and Resorts Internat., Inc., 1994—; bd. dirs. Blandin J. Wright, P.C., Internat. Hospitality, Inc., CRS Holdings, Inc. Contbr. articles to profl. jours. Coach Charlottesville Youth Soccer, Baseball and Basketball, 1984-89; coach London Youth Baseball, 1982. Mem. ABA, AICPA, Am. Arbitration Assn. (arbitrator 1985—), Tex. Soc. CPAs, Va. Soc. CPAs, Fairfax County Bar Assn., Farmington Country Club, Deering Bay Yacht and Country Club, Mensa, Beta Gamma Sigma. Roman Catholic. Office: 4770 Biscayne Blvd Ph G Miami FL 33137-3251 E-mail: blandin@earthlink.net.

WRIGHT, BURTON, retired sociologist; b. Detroit, Jan. 31, 1917; s. Burton and Hazel Marie (Thomas) W.; m. Marie Fidelis Gallivan, Jan. 26, 1942; children: Burton III, Catherine Margaret (dec.). AA, C.Z. Coll., 1944; BA, U. Wash., 1947, MA, 1949; PhD, Fla. State U., 1972. Enlisted USN, 1937, commd. and advanced through grades to comdr., 1957; dir. Naval Res. Recruiting, 1960-64; ret., 1964; mem. faculty U. Wash., 1947-49, George Washington U., Washington, 1954-60, Rollins Coll., Winter Park, Fla., 1966-69; prof. dept. sociology U. Ctrl. Fla., Orlando, 1972-82, prof. emeritus, 1982-89; ret., 1989; prof. sociology Troy State U., 1991—. Cons. Ford Found., 1951, Dept. Air Force, 1955, U.S. Army Chem. Corps, 1956; mem. faculty Northwestern U., summers 1956-59; vis. prof. sociology Troy State U., Dothon; dir. Am. Sociol. Assn. Nat. Honors Program, 1981-89; vis. prof. Troy State U., Dothan. Author: (with J.P. Weiss and C.M. Unkovic) Perspective: An Introduction to Sociology, 1975, (with V. Fox) Criminal Justice and the Social Sciences, 1978, (with J.P. Weiss) Social Problems, 1980. Decorated Navy Commendation medal. Fellow Am. Anthrop. Assn.; mem. AAUP, Am. Sociol. Assn. (membership com. 1983-86), Soc. Psychol. Study Social Problems, Am. Acad. Arts and Scis., Soc. Study Social Problems, So. Sociol. Soc., North Ctrl. Sociol. Soc., Univ. Club (Winter Park). Roman Catholic. Home: 502 Dunleith Blvd Dothan AL 36303-2936

WRIGHT, C. T. ENUS, former academic administrator; b. Social Circle, Ga., Oct. 4, 1942; s. George and Carrie Mae (Enus) W.; m. Mary Stephens, Aug. 9, 1974. BS, Fort Valley State U. (Ga.), Ga., 1964; MA, Atlanta U., 1967; PhD, Boston U., 1977; LHD, Mary Holmes Coll., 2000. Tchr. Ga. Pub. Schs., Social Circle, 1965-67; mem. faculty Morris Brown Coll., Atlanta, 1967-73, divsn. chmn., 1973-77; program dir., asst. provost Eastern Wash. U., Cheney, 1977-81; v.p. acad. affairs Talladega Coll. (Ala.), 1981-82; pres. Cheyney U. Pa., Cheyney, 1982-85; v.p. and provost Fla. Meml. Coll., 1985-89; pres. Internat. Found. and Coord. African-African Am. Summit, 1989-2001; pres., CEO IFESH, 2001—. Cons. and lectr. in field; bd. dirs. IFESH, England, Leow Sullivan Trust, So. Africa, Peoples Investment Fund for Africa. Author: (booklet) The History of Black Historical Mythology, 1980; contbr. articles to profl. jours. Commnr., Wash. Pub. Broadcasting, Olympia, 1980-84; exec. com. Boy Scouts Am., Phila., 1982—; Goodwill Amb. State of Ga., 1997—. Human Rels. scholar, 1969, Nat. Tchg. fellow Boston U., 1971. Mem. Am. Assn. Colls. and Univs. (coms. 1982—), Am. Hist. Assn. (coms. 1970—), Assn. Study Afro-Am. Life & History (coms. 1965—), Nat. Assn. Equal Opportunity in Higher Edn. (coms. 1982—), NEA (coms. 1965—). Am. Baptist. Clubs: Lions (Cheyney, Wash. (v.p. 1979-81)), Tuscan, Fountain Hills Times, Atlanta Constitution. Address: 17420 E Dull Knife Dr Fountain Hills AZ 85268 E-mail: wrightjack@aol.com.

WRIGHT, CAMERON HARROLD GREENE, electrical engineer; b. Quincy, Mass., Jan. 21, 1956; s. Frederick Herman Greene and Dorothy Louise (Harrold) W.; m. Robin Michele Rawlings, May 14, 1988. BSEE summa cum laude, La. Tech. U., 1983; MSEE, Purdue U., 1988; PhD, U. Tex., 1996. Registered profl. engr., Calif. Commd. 2d lt. USAF, 1983, advanced through grades to lt. col., 1999; avionics design engr. USAF Avionics Lab., Wright-Patterson AFB, Ohio, 1983-86; divsn. chief space test range space divsn. USAF, L.A. AFB, 1988-90, dir. advanced satellite systems, 1990-91; instr. elec. engring. USAF Acad., Colorado Springs, 1991-93, asst. prof., 1996-98, assoc. prof., 1998—2001, prof., 2001—, dep. dept. head, 2000—. Mem. exec. com. Nat. Aerospace and Electronics Conf., Dayton, Ohio, 1983-86; bd. dirs. Rocky Mountain Bioengring. Symposium. Contbr. chpts. to book, articles to profl. jours.; reviewer profl. jours.; co-author, editor: An Introduction to Electrical Engineering, 1994. Coord. tech. career motivation Dayton Sch. Dist., 1983-86; speaker engring. careers Colorado Springs Sch. Dists., 1991-93, 98—; vol. computer/network cons. Project Transitions Hospice, Austin, Tex., 1995-96. Mem. IEEE (sr., founder and chmn. Pikes Peak Region Signal Processing Soc. 1997-99, chmn. Pikes Peak sect. 1999-2001), Air Force Assn. (life, dir. L.A. Young Astronaut program 1988-91, Officer of Yr. 1991), Am. Soc. for Engring. Edn., Rocky Mt. Bioengring. Soc. (bd. dirs. 1997—). Achievements include development of unique process to detect incoming missile warheads for Strategic Defense Initiative, robotic laser system for eye surgery. Office: Dept Elec Engring 2354 Fairchild Dr Ste 2f6 U S A F Academy CO 80840

WRIGHT, CAROLE DEAN, reading specialist; b. Mt. Clemens, Mich., Aug. 18, 1943; d. Edward Lawrence and Alice Agnes Hundt; m. David John Wright, Dec. 20, 1964 (div. Sept. 1984); 1 child, Amy Elizabeth. BA, Mich. State U., 1964, MA, 1967. Reading specialist Holt (Mich.) Pub. Schs., 1965-70, Ypsilanti (Mich.) Pub. Schs., 1970-71, Aurora (Colo.) Pub. Schs., 1972—; pres. Aurora Edn. Assn., 1978-80, Colo. Edn. Assn., Denver, 1982. Mem. adv. com. Nat. Assessment of Ednl. Progress, Denver, 1975; chair unit accreditation bd. Nat. Coun. Accreditation of Tchr. Edn., Washington, 1990-99; trustee Pub. Employees Retirement Assn. Colo., 1993X. Contbg. author to Idea's for Children's Literature, 1976. Mem. Colo. Comm. on Tchr. Edn. and Accreditation, Denver, 1976-82; vice chair Gov.'s Chpt. 2 Adv. Com., Denver, 1987-93. Named Outstanding Educator, Fed. Programs Adminstr. Coun. U.S. Dept. Edn., 1991. Mem. NEA (bd. dirs. 1984-87), Internat. Reading Assn., Colo. Edn. Assn. (v.p. 1980-81, 83-84, pres. 1982, award 1999), Phi Delta Kappa (Leadership award 1998). Home: 2268 Clermont St Denver CO 80207-3740

WRIGHT, CAROLE YVONNE, chiropractor; b. July 12, 1932; d. Paul Burt and Mary Leoan (Staley) Fickes; 1 child, Morgan Michelle. D. Chiropractic, Palmer Coll., Davenport, Iowa, 1976. Instr. Palmer Coll., Davenport, Iowa, 1975-76; dir., owner Wright Chiropractic Clinic, Rocklin, Calif., 1978-88, Woodland, 1980-81; co-owner Ft. Sutter Chiropractic Clinic, Sacramento, 1985-89; owner Wright Chiropractic Health Ctr., 1989-93, Capitol Chiropractic, Sacramento, 1993-95. Cons. in field; lectr., speaker on radio and TV programs, at seminars. Contbr. articles to profl. jours. Co-chmn. Harold Michaels for Congress campaign, Alameda, Calif., 1972; dist. dir. 14th Congle. Dist., 1983-95. Mem. Internat. Chiropractic Assn. Calif. (bd. dir. 1978-83), Rocklin C. of C. (bd. dirs. 1979-81). Republican. Avocations: reading, travel. Home: 425 Cirby Way Ste 70 Roseville CA 95678-4244

WRIGHT, CHARLES LEE, information systems consultant; b. Dalton, Ga., Dec. 18, 1949; s. Charlie William and Catherine Christine (Quarles) W.; children: Charles Lee, Christina, Leana. AA in Bus., Dalton Jr. Coll., 1971; BS in Bus., U. Tenn., Chattanooga, 1977; student, IBM classes. Trainee Ludlow Carpets, Dalton, 1971, EDP supr., 1971-73, EDP mgr., 1973-77; ops. mgr. Walter Carpet Mills, Industry, Calif., 1977-80; ptnr., cons. TCT Systems, San Dimas, 1978-92; ptnr., CEO Williams, Wright and Assocs., Upland, 1978-92; v.p. ops. Roland Corp., U.S., 1993—. Served as sgt. U.S. Army, 1969-71; Vietnam, Cambodia. Decorated Bronze Star, Army Commendation medal with oak leaf and oak leaf cluster, Air medal. Mem. Data Processing Mgmt. Assn., Am. Mgmt. Assn., Small Systems User Group, COMMON. Home and Office: 11635 Firestone Blvd # 112 Norwalk CA 90650 E-mail: cwright@rolandus.com., chuckmanchu@yahoo.com. *Personal philosophy: Efficient work and dedication to detail is the key to success.*

WRIGHT, CHARLES PENZEL, JR. English language educator; b. Pickwick Dam, Tenn., Aug. 25, 1935; s. Charles Penzel and Mary Castleman (Winter) W.; m. Holly McIntire, Apr. 6, 1969; 1 child, Luke Savin Herrick. BA, Davidson (N.C.) Coll., 1957; M.F.A., U. Iowa, 1963; postgrad., U. Rome, 1963-64. Mem. faculty U. Calif., Irvine, 1966-83, prof. English, 1976-83; mem. faculty U. Va., Charlottesville, 1983—. Fulbright vis. prof. N.Am. lit. U. Padua, Italy, 1968-69; disting. vis. prof. U. Degli Studi, Florence, Italy, 1992. Author: The Dream Animal, 1968, The Grave of the Right Hand, 1970, The Venice Notebook, 1971, Hard Freight, 1973, Bloodlines, 1975, Colophons, 1977, China Trace, 1977, Wright: A Profile, 1979, The Southern Cross, 1981, Country Music: Selected Early Poems, 1982, The Other Side of the River, 1984, Zone Journals, 1988, Halflife, 1988, Xionia, 1990, The World of the 10,000 Things, 1990, Chickamauga, 1995, Quarter Notes, 1995, Black Zodiac, 1997, Appalachia, 1998, Negative Blue, 2000, A Short History of the Shadow, 2002; trans.: The Storm and Other Poems (Eugenio Montale), 1978, Orphic Songs (Dino Campana), 1984. Served with AUS, 1957-61. Recipient Pen Translation Prize, 1979, Nat. Book award for poetry, 1983, citation in poetry Brandeis U. Creative Arts Awards, 1987, Merit medal Am. Acad. and Inst. Arts and Letters, 1992, Ruth Lilly Poetry prize, 1993, Lenore Marshall Poetry prize, 1996, L.A. Times Book prize, 1997, Nat. Book Critics Circle award 1997, Pulitzer Prize, 1998, Ambassador Book award, 1998; Fulbright scholar, 1963-65; Guggenheim fellow, 1976, Ingram Merrill fellow, 1980, 93. Mem. Fellowship of So. Writers, Am. Acad. Arts and Letters, Am. Acad. Arts and Sci., Acad. Am. Poets (chancellor). Home: 940 Locust Ave Charlottesville VA 22901-4030 Office: English Dept Univ Va Charlottesville VA 22901

WRIGHT, CHATT GRANDISON, academic administrator; b. San Mateo, Calif., Sept. 17, 1941; s. Virgil Tandy and Louise (Jeschien) W.; children from previous marriage: Stephen Brook, Jon David, Shelley Adams; m. Janice Teply, Nov. 28, 1993. Student, U. Calif., Berkeley, 1960-62; BA in Polit. Sci., U. Calif., Davis, 1964; MA in Econs., U. Hawaii, 1968. Instr. econs. U. Hawaii, Honolulu, 1968-70; mgr. corp. planning Telecheck Internat., Inc., 1969—70; economist State of Hawaii, 1970—71; adminstr. manpower City & County of Honolulu, 1971-72; bus. adminstr., dean. Hawaii Pacific U., Honolulu, 1972-74, v.p., 1974-76, pres., 1976—. Mem. City and County of Honolulu Manpower Area Planning Comm., 1976-82; mem. Mayor's Salary Commn. City of County of Honolulu, 1977-80; mem. Honolulu City Ethics Commn., 1978-84; mem. City and County of Honolulu Labor Market Adv. Coun., 1982-84; bd. dirs. Hawaii Econ. Devel. Corp., 1980-84; trustee Queen's Med. Ctr., Honolulu, 1986-92, Honolulu Armed Svcs. YMCA, 1984-86, Hawaii Maritime Ctr., 1990-92; chmn. bd. trustees Hist. Hawaii Found., 1995-96, trustee, 1990-96; mem. adv. bd. Cancer Rsch. Ctr. Hawaii, 1987; trustee St. Andrew's Priory Sch., 1994-98; bd. dirs. Hawaii Visitors Bur., 1995-97, Hawaii Coun. on Econ. Edn., 1998—; bd. dirs. Downtown Improvement Assn., 1988-96, Outrigger Duke Kahanamoku Found., 1996-98, Hawaii Opera Theatre, 1997-99; trustee Oceanic Inst., 1998—; mem. Hawaii Execs. Coun., 1996—, chmn. 2002; bd. govs. Hawaii Med. Libr., 1989-92; mem. adv. bd. Aloha coun. Boy Scouts Am., 1991-2002; trustee Molokai Gen. Hosp., 1991-92; mem. Pacific Asian Affairs Coun., 1998-2001; steering com. Asian Devel. Bank, 2000—. With USN, 1968-70. Recipient Pioneer award Pioneer Fed. Savs. Bank, 1982, Stephen J. Jackstadt award, 1998; named Sales Person of Yr., Sales and Mktg. Execs. of Honolulu, 1998; Paul Harris fellow Rotary, 1986. Mem. Am. Assn. Higher Edn., Assn. Governing Bds. Univs. and Colls., Japan-Am. Soc. Honolulu, Soc. Sci. Assn., Nat. Assn. Intercollegiate Athletics (vice chair NAIA coun. of pres. 1994, mem. 1985-98), Hawaii Joint Coun. Econ. Edn. (bd. dirs. 1982-88), Western Coll. Assn. (exec. com. 1989-92), Hawaii Assn. Ind. Colls. and Univs. (chmn. 1986), Outrigger Canoe Club, Pacific Club (Honolulu), Plaza Club (bd. govs. 1992-97), Waialae Country Club. Republican. Episcopalian. Avocations: hunting, fishing, reading, travel. Office: Hawaii Pacific U Office of Pres 1166 Fort Street Mall Honolulu HI 96813-2708 E-mail: president@hpu.edu.*

WRIGHT, CLARK PHILLIPS, computer systems specialist; b. Orange, Tex., Aug. 30, 1942; s. Madison Brown and Mary Elizabeth (Phillips) W.; m. Stacy Charlotte Klutz, June 5, 1965 (div. Oct. 1979); m. Cora Lou Alexandria Schelling, Oct. 31, 1979; 1 child, Isaac Schelling. BA, U. Tex., 1965. Computer programmer Lockheed Electronics Co., Houston, 1965-67; prin. analyst Control Data Corp., St. Paul, 1967-76; computer scientist DBA Systems, Inc., Lanham, Md., 1976-79; engring. specialist Ford Aerospace Corp., Houston, 1979-90, Loral Aerospace Corp., 1990-97, Lockheed Martin Space Mission, 1997—. Precinct chmn. Rep. Party of Tex., 1982-86. Mem. IEEE, Math. Assn. Am., Assn. Computing Machinery, SAR (chartered, sec., treas.), Sons Republic Tex., Info. Sys. Security Assn., Masons, Rotary. Avocations: travel, photography. Home: 5000 Park Ave Dickinson TX 77539-7013 Office: Lockheed Martin Space Ops PO Box 58487 Houston TX 77258-8487 E-mail: cpwright@ghg.net., ClarkP.Wright@csoconline.com.

WRIGHT, CLIFFORD SIDNEY, accounting educator; b. New Orleans, Mar. 7, 1943; s. Samuel H.P. and Winifred (Vonderhaar) W.; m. Jane Eniz Truch, Aug. 2, 1969; children: Mark, Christopher, Erin. BA, BS, U. New Orleans, 1967; MBA, Loyola U., 1970; JD, Northwestern Calif. Sch. Law, 1990. CPA, La. Mgr. FNBC, New Orleans, 1967-70; prof. bus. Xavier U., 1970—. Pvt. practice, Metairie, La., 1970—. Deacon Archdiocese of New Orleans, 1987—; bd. dirs. Hospice, Metairie, 1996, St. Vincent de Paul Soc., Metairie, 1996. Mem. AICPA, La. Soc. CPAs, Am. Acctg. Assn., Nat. Acctg. Assn., Nat. Soc. Pub. Accts., Assn. Govt. Accts. Democrat. Roman Catholic. Avocations: running, music, travel. Home: 3716 Fran St Metairie LA 70001-2730 Office: Xavier U La 7325 Palmetto St New Orleans LA 70125-1056

WRIGHT, CONNIE SUE, special education educator; b. Nampa, Idaho, Aug. 26, 1943; d. Ruel Andrew and Renabel Carol (Graham) Farwell; m. Roger R. Wright, July 5, 1968; 1 child, Jodi C. BA, N.W. Nazarene Coll., 1967; MA in Spl. Edn., Boise State U., 1990. Cert. elem. tchr. grades kindergarten through 8th, cert. spl. edn. tchr. grades kindergarten through 12th, Idaho. Tchr. 3rd and 4th grades Vallivue Sch. Dist. 139, Caldwell, Idaho, 1967-69; tchr. 2nd grade Nampa Sch. Dist. 131, 1969-70; tchr. 3rd grade Caldwell Sch. Dist. 132, 1970-73; tchr. spl. edn. grades kindergarten through 3rd Hubbard Elem. Sch., Kuna (Idaho) Joint Sch. Dist. 3, 1985-92; tchr. adolescents CPC Intermountain Hosp. of Boise, 1992-93; tchr. spl. edn. Pioneer Elem. Sch., Meridian, Idaho, 1993—, Spalding Elem. Sch., Meridian, 1997—. Mem. Internat. Edn. Conf. Between Russia and U.S., 1994. Libr. Horizon's Reading Coun., 1990-91. Named Tchr. Yr. Pioneer Elem. Sch., 1994-95; recipient Cert. of Recognition, Devel. D.C. Mem. Coun. for Exceptional Children, Coun. for Learning Disabilities, Coun. Learning Disabilities, Assn. Curriculum & Supr., Delta Kappa Gamma Soc. Internat. (Omicron chpt.). Avocations: reading, doll making, computers.

WRIGHT, CREIGHTON BOLTER, cardiovascular surgeon, educator; b. Washington, Jan. 29, 1939; s. Benjamin Washington and Catherine Adele (Bolter) W.; m. Carolyn Eleanor Craver, Jan. 29, 1966; children: Creighton Bolter, Benson, Kathryn, Elizabeth. BA, Duke U., 1961, MD, 1965; MBA, Xavier U., Cin., 1995. Diplomate Am. Bd. Surgery, Am. Bd. Thoracic Surgery, Am. Bd. Gen. Vascular Surgery. Intern Duke U., Durham, N.C., 1965-66; resident in surgery U. Va., Charlottesville, 1966-71; asst. prof., then assoc. prof. George Washington U., Washington, 1974-76; assoc. prof., then prof. surgery U. Iowa, Iowa City, 1976-81; prof. clin. surgery U. Cin., 1982-89, Uniformed Svcs. U., 1982—; dir. dept. surgery Jewish Hosp., Cin., 1989—; med. dir. cardiovascular svcs. Health Alliance Cin., 1999—. Editor: Vascular Grafting, 1983, (with others) Venous Trauma, 1983; contbr. articles to med. jours., chpts. to books. Col. USAR, 1966-93. Decorated Bronze Star; recipient Kindred Resident Tchr. award, 1967, Golden Apple Tchg. award, 1975, Kaplan award Am. Heart Assn., 1999, Tchg. award Jewish Hosp., 2001. Mem. Assn. Acad. Surgery (pres. 1980), Soc. Univ. Surgeons, Soc. Vascular Surgery, Am. Assn. Thoracic Surgery, Soc. Thoracic Surgery, Ctrl. Surg. Assn., Internat. Soc. Cardiovasc. Surgery, Am. Heart Assn. S.W. Ohio (v.p. 1998—, pres. 2000), Muller Surg. Soc. (pres. 1985-87), So. Thoracic Surg. Assn., Midwestern Vascular Surg. Soc., Cin. Surg. Soc. (pres. 1996), Greater Cin. Vascular Soc. (pres. 1997-98), Comml. Club, Alpha Omega Alpha, Sigma Chi (Significant Sig award 1993). Home: 312 E 2d St Covington KY 41011-1704 Office: Cardiovascular & Thoracic Surgeons 2123 Auburn Ave Cincinnati OH 45219-2906 E-mail: wrightcr@healthall.com.

WRIGHT, DANIEL, wine specialist, consultant; b. Hull, Yorkshire, Eng., June 24, 1931; came to U.S., 1971; s. Edwin Vincent and Agnes Mary W.; m. Agnes Macdonald Doull, July 9, 1955 (div. 1977); children: Oliver Hamish, Alistair Louis, Edwina Moira, William Joseph, Jeffrey Peter. Diploma in hotel and catering ops.-mgmt., Westminster Tech. Coll., London, 1952. Trainee, asst. mgr. wine dept. Fortes & Co., Hoteliers, London, 1952-57; tech. mgr. Asher Storey & Co., wine shippers, 1958; wine mgr. St. James Bonded Warehouses, 1958-64; gen. mgr. wine and spirits dept. Hunt Edmonds Brewery, Banbury, Oxford, Eng., 1964-68; wine and spirit contr. Vaux Brewery, Sunderland, Durham, Eng., 1968-71; corp. wine dir. Ga. Crown Distbg. Co., Atlanta, 1978-89; wine specialist, cons. Jax Beer & Wine (formerly Greens Beer & Wine Stores), 1990-97. Mem. adv. bd. Atlanta Wine Festival, 1981—, judge wine competitions, 1981—. Bd. dirs. Park North Homeowners Assn., Atlanta, 1986-88; chief judge Atlanta Wine Festival, 1991. With Brit. Army, 1949-51. Fellow Brit. Bottlers Inst.; mem. Chaine des Rotisseurs (chevalier Atlanta 1977—), Companions of Beaujolais. Avocations: mycology, tennis, walking, studying languages, running. Home: 6709 Park Ave NE Atlanta GA 30342-2366

WRIGHT, DANIEL A. lawyer; b. Washington, Sept. 30, 1946; s. William L. and Mary J. Wright; m. Deborah J. Wright, Sept. 5, 1981. BA, U. Calif., Davis, 1968; JD, Golden Gate U., 1978; Cert. in Pub. Adminstrn., U. Ala., 1969. Bar: Wash., U.S. Dist. Ct. (we. dist.) Wash. Claims officer Dept. Social and Health Svcs., Olympia, Wash., 1979—85; staff atty. Dept. of Licensing, 1985—95; sole practitioner Tumwater, Wash., 1986—96; atty. William B. Pope & Assocs., Olympia, 1996—2001, McConnell, Meyer & Assocs., LLP, Olympia, 2001—. Adjudicator VA, San Francisco, 1979; law examiner Wash. State Bar Assn., Seattle, 1998. Asst. scoutmaster Boy Scouts Am., 1990—2001. Capt. U.S. Army, 1969-71, Vietnam. Regional Tng. Program in Pub. Adminstrn. fellow, 1968-69. Mem.: Wash. State Bar Assn. (fee dispute arbitration com. 1988—90, com. on professionalism 1998—2000, law office mgmt. assistance program com.), Clan Gregor (elections com., fundraising chmn. Pacific N.W. chpt. 1995—, fundraising chmn. 2000—). Avocations: woodworking, auto racing, astronomy, photography. Office: McConnell, Meyer & Assocs 2112 Black Lake Blvd SE Olympia WA 98512 E-mail: dwright@lewiscountylaw.com.

WRIGHT, DAVID ALAN, music educator; s. James Kenneth Wright and Mary Agnes Haney; m. Shari Deane Holmes, Aug. 31, 1981; children: Meagan, Patrick, Ryan; m. Kathleen Kee Marks, Aug. 17, 1968 (div. Feb. 1, 1979); children: Kristin Ann, Shelly Renea. Bachelor Music, W.Va. U., Morgantown, West Virginia, 1965—69. Band dir. Marion County Schools, Monongah, W.Va., 1969—73; band/choral dir. Salem Junion H.S., Salem, 1973—81; music tchr. Logan County Schools, Logan, 1981—90; band dir. Catawba County Schools, Hickory, NC, 1990—93; salesman Far East Motors, 1993—96; closing agt. Piedmont Housing, Lincolnton, 1996—2000; music tchr. Iredell-Statesville Schools, Statesville, 2000—. Choir/music dir. Various Churches, Various Cities, 1981—2002. Mem.: Profl. Educators NC, Music Educators, masons. Home: 1837 Smyrna Lane Catawba NC 28609-8964 Office: West Iredell Middle School 303 Watermelon Road Statesville NC 28625

WRIGHT, DAVID BURTON, retired newspaper publishing company executive; b. Fowler, Ind., Aug. 29, 1933; s. Claude Matthew and Rose Ellen (Lavelle) W.; m. Geraldine F. Gray, May 9, 1964; children— David Andrew, Anne Kathleen AB, Wabash Coll., 1955. C.P.A., Ind. Audit staff George S. Olive & Co. C.P.A.s, Indpls., 1958-63, mgmt. cons., 1963-65; controller Herff Jones Co., 1965-69, corp. controller, asst. sec., 1970-71; asst. bus. mgr. Indpls. Newspapers Inc., 1971-77, asst. sec., treas., 1975-93, bus. mgr., 1977-93, v.p., 1982-93; asst. sec., treas. Central Newspapers Inc., Indpls., 1975-79, sec., treas., 1979-89; asst. sec., treas. Muncie Newspapers Inc., Ind., 1975-93. Mem. St. Francis Hosp. Adv. Bd., Indpls., 1983-99. Sec. St. Francis Hosp. Adv. Bd., 1986-87, v.p., 1987-91, pres., 1991-93. Served with U.S. Army, 1956-58. Mem. Ind. Assn. CPAs, Indpls. Econ. Club, KC. Roman Catholic. Home: 6713 Forrest Commons Blvd Indianapolis IN 46227-2396

WRIGHT, DAVID JONATHAN, finance educator; b. Joliet, Ill., July 6, 1951; s. Thomas and Miriam (Mosiman) W.; m. Kristin Joyce Holmberg, May 31, 1980; three children. BS, U. Ill., 1973, MBA, 1975, PhD, 1979. Asst. prof. fin. Ind. U., Bloomington, 1979-84, U. Notre Dame, Ind., 1985-92; prof. fin. U. Wis. Parkside, Kenosha, 1992—. Prof. fin., advisor Ryan Labs, Inc., N.Y.C., 1988-97; fin. com. Kenosha Area Bus. Alliance, 1993—, chair, 2000—, awards selection com., 1996-97; adv. to bus. editor Racine (Wis.) Jour. Times, 1997. Bd. appeals Village of North Bay, Wis., 1993-97. Mem. Fin. Mgmt. Assn. Internat. (European program com. 1997), Fin. Mgmt. Assn., Acad. Fin. Svcs., Ea. Fin. Assn., Midwest Fin. Assn. (awards selection com. 1992), U. Ill. Alumni Assn. Office: U Wis Parkside Sch Bus & Technology Kenosha WI 53141 E-mail: wright@uwp.edu.

WRIGHT, DAVID L. food and beverage company executive; b. Wenatchee, Wash., Mar. 12, 1949; s. Franklin Sven and Mary Elizabeth (Collins) W.; m. Karen Sue Rice, Mar. 28, 1981; children: Kara, Erin, Jonathan, Anna Catherine. BA, U. Calif., Davis, 1971. Chief of rsch. dept. of benefit payments State of Calif., Sacramento, 1972-75; profl. staff mem. com. on agr. U.S. Ho. Reps., Washington, 1975-77; adminstrv. asst. Rep. William C. Wampler, 1977-81; spl. asst. for legis. affairs to Pres. The White House, 1981-84; dir. govt. affairs Pepsico Inc., Purchase, N.Y., 1984-87; v.p., govt. affairs Pepsico, Inc., 1987—. Mem. exec. com. U.S. Coun. for Internat. Bus., 1997—. Capt. USAR, 1971-79. Mem Capitol Hill Club. Republican. Office: Pepsico Inc 700 Anderson Hill Rd Purchase NY 10577-1444

WRIGHT, DEIL SPENCER, political science educator; b. Three Rivers, Mich., June 18, 1930; s. William Henry and Gertrude Louise (Buck) W.; m. Patricia Mae Jaffke, Aug. 22, 1953; children: David C., Mark W., Matthew D., Lois L. BA, U. Mich., 1952, M in Pub. Adminstrn., 1954, PhD, 1957. Asst. prof. polit. sci. Wayne State U., Detroit, 1956-59; from asst. to assoc. prof. U. Iowa, Iowa City, 1959-67; assoc. prof. U. Calif., Berkeley, 1965-66; prof. U. N.C., Chapel Hill, 1967-83, alumni disting. prof., 1983—; Carl Hatch vis. prof. U. N.Mex., Albuquerque, 1987. Lectr. USIA, Washington, various dates; cons. Office Mgmt. and Budget, Washington, 1979-80. Author: Understanding Intergovernmental Relations, 3d edit., 1988; editor: Federalism and Intergovernmental Relations, 1984, Globalization and Decentralization, 1996; contbr. over 100 articles to various polit. sci. and pub. adminstrn. jours. Mem. dir's.

adv. com. NIH, Bethesda, Md., 1970-74, N.C. Coun. on State Goals and Policies, Raleigh, 1973-77, N.C. State Internship Coun., Raleigh, 1985-93. Internat. Inst. Mgmt. research fellow, Berlin, 1977. Fellow Nat. Acad. Pub. Adminstrn.; mem. AAAS, Am. Polit. Sci. Assn., Am. Soc. Pub. Adminstrn. (Waldo Lifetime Career Achievement award), Midwest Polit. Sci. Assn., Policy Studies Orgn., So. Polit. Sci. Assn. (pres. 1981-82). Lodges: Rotary (bd. dirs. Chapel Hill club 1981, 84, 90, v.p. 2000-01, pres. 2001-02). Republican. Methodist. Home: 204 Velma Rd Chapel Hill NC 27514-7641 Office: U North Carolina Dept Polit Sci CB 3265 Chapel Hill NC 27599-3265

WRIGHT, DIXIE LEE, educational consultant; b. Winslow, Ind. d. Edward Franklin and Ann Berenece Corne; m. Lendon L. Wright; children: Kevin, LeeAnn, Michael. BS in Edn., Ind. U.; postgrad., U. No. Colo. Self employed workshop developer for schs. and agys.; career coord. postsecondary sch. Colo.; ind. contractor Colo. State Rehab. and other govtl. and ind. agys. working with spl. needs persons. Cons., assessor state non-profit agys., Colo.; presenter in field. Author: Know How is the Key, 1997, Job Survival: How to Adjust and Keep Your Job, 2000, Stuff You Need to Know to Teach Job Retention, 2000. Bd. dirs. Littleton C. of C. Mem.: AARP (state coord. works program), Bus. Profl. Women (adv. bd., pres.). Avocations: art, drawing, public speaking. Address: PO Box 632 Bailey CO 80421-0632

WRIGHT, DONALD FRANKLIN, retired newspaper executive; b. St. Paul, July 10, 1934; s. Floyd Franklin and Helen Marie (Hansen) W.; m. Sharon Kathleen Fisher, Dec. 30, 1960; children: John, Dana, Kara, Patrick. BME, U. Minn., 1957, MBA, 1958. With Mpls. Star & Tribune Co., 1958-77, research planning dir., then ops. dir., 1971-75, exec. editor, 1975-77; exec. v.p., gen. mgr. Newsday, Inc., L.I., 1977-78, pres., chief operating officer, 1978-81, L.A. Times, 1981-87; sr. v.p. Times Mirror Co., L.A., 1988—98; pres., CEO L.A. Times; exec. v.p. Times Mirror Co., L.A., 1998-99; ret., 1999. Former vice chmn. bd. trustees Claremont Grad. Sch. and Univ. Ctr.; chmn. L.A. Area coun. Boy Scouts Am., 1988, pres. western region, 1998-2000, mem. nat. exec. bd., 1998--; dir. emeritus Assocs. Calif. Inst. Tech.; chmn. bd. dirs. U. Minn. Found.; past bd. dirs. United Way Long Island, Calif. Mem. Am. Newspaper Pubs. Assn. (past chmn. telecom. com. and prodn. mgmt. com.), Newspapers Pubs. Assn., U. Minn. Alumni Assn., Mpls. Club. Presbyterian.

WRIGHT, DONALD GENE, accountant; b. Grand Junction, Tenn., June 7, 1950; s. Ernest Young and Frances Irene (Reeder) W.; children: Richard Benjamin, Jacqueline; m. Helen "Vicki" Elizabeth Holt Wright, Oct. 1, 1988; step children: Veronica Reynolds Garcia, Mindy Reynolds Barrett. A Engring. (equivalent), U. Tenn., Martin, 1970; BBA in Acctg., Lambeth U., 1995. Cost acctg. clk. Harman Automotive, Inc., Bolivar, Tenn., 1975-79, sr. acct., 1979-85, budget & spl. projects mgr., 1985-92, acctg., estimating mgr., 1992-95; contr. Hutchinson Sealing Sys., Inc., Wytheville, Va., 1995-2000, Hutchinson Rubber Mixing Tech. Ctr., Wytheville, 1995-99, Dura Automotive Sys., Pikeville, Tenn., 2000—. Bd. dirs. West Tenn. Chpt. NAA, Jackson, Tenn., 1987-95. Editor: VP Communications Monthly Newsletter, 1991, Director of Newsletter Monthly Newsletter, 1989. Mem. Nat. Assn. Accts. (pres. West Tenn. chpt.), Gideon's Internat. Methodist. Avocations: martial arts, home improvement, travel. Home: 235 South 10th St Wytheville VA 24382 Office: Dura Automotive Sys Inc 132 Ferro Rd Pikeville TN 37367 also: Rubbu Mixing Tech Ctr 455 Industry Rd Wytheville VA 24382-3491

WRIGHT, DONNA MARIE, real estate company executive; b. Wenatchee, Wash., Feb. 17, 1940; d. Donald O. and Marie A. (Ritter) Doud; m. Gary Donald Wright, June 26, 1962; children: Donald, Pamela, Penny, Gregory, Theodore. Student, Shoreline Community Coll., Everett Community Coll., 1976-78. With traffic dept. Cedargreen Frozen Foods, Wenatchee, 1959-62; owner Colwell Banker-Gary Wright Realty, Inc., Marysville, Wash., 1974—. Mem. adv. com. Marysville-Pilchuck H.S., 1982—; edn. chmn. Fedn. Dem. Women, 1973—76, region dir., 1977—79; pres. Cascade Dem. Women, Snohomish County, Wash., 1976—80. Recipient Paul Harris award, Rotary, 2000. Mem. Nat. Assn. Realtors (sub-com. 1982-83, dir. 1995-98), Wash. Assn. Realtors (c om. chmn. 1984—, bd. dirs. 1994, Realtor Achievement award 1995), Women's Council of Realtors (state sec. 1988, v.p. 1989, nat. del. 1988, 89, nat. nominating commn. 1988), Snohomish County Bd. Realtors (sec., treas. 1979-82, v.p. 1988, pr es. elect 1989, pres. 1990, bd. dirs., Outstanding Service award 1983, Community Service award 1985, Realtor of Yr. 1988). Mem. Ch. Assemblies of God. Club: Bus. and Profl. Women (Marysville) (pres. 1981-82); adv. bd. Everett C.C. Women's Programs, 1999—. Lodge: Soroptimists (local pres. 1985-86). Avocations: community involvement, traveling. Home: 5533 Parkside Dr Marysville WA 98270-4138 Office: Coldwell Banker Gary Wright REalty Inc 9323 State Ave Marysville WA 98270-2203

WRIGHT, DOUGLAS TYNDALL, business executive, university executive emeritus; b. Toronto, Ont., Can., Oct. 4, 1927; s. George C. and Etta (Tyndall) W. BASc. with honors in Civil Engring, U. Toronto, 1949; MS in Structural Engring, U. Ill., 1952; PhD in Engring, U. Cambridge, 1954; D.Eng. (hon.), Carleton U., 1967; LLD (hon.), Brock U., 1967, Concordia U., 1982; DSc (hon.), Meml. U. Nfld., 1969; DHL (hon.), Northeastern U., 1985, U. Waterloo, 1995; DUniv (hon.), Strathclyde U., Glasgow, 1989; D de L'Université, Compiegne U., France, 1991; D Univ. (hon.), Université de Sherbrooke, 1992; DSc, McMaster U., 1993, Queen's U., 1993; LLD (hon.), U. Waterloo, 1995. Lectr. dept. civil engring. Queen's U., 1954-55, asst. prof., 1955-58, assoc. prof., 1958; prof. civil engring. U. Waterloo, 1958-67, chmn. dept. civil engring., 1958-63, dean engring., 1959-66; chmn. Ont. Com. on Univ. Affairs Govt. of Ont., 1967-72, Ont. Commn. Post-Secondary Edn., Toronto, 1969-72, dep. provincial sec. for social devel., 1972-79; dep. minister culture and recreation, 1979-80; pres. U. Waterloo, Ont., Ont., 1981-93, prof. engring., 1981—, pres. emeritus, 1995—. Vis. prof. U. Autónoma Mex., 1964, 66, U. Sherbrooke, 1966—67; cons. engr. Netherlands and Mexican Pavillions Expo, 1967, Olympic Sports Palace, Mexico City, 1968, Ont. Place Dome and Forum, 1971; tech. advisor Toronto Skydome, 1984—92, Com Dev Ltd., bd. dirs.; tech. advisor Geometrica Inc., Meloche, Monnex, Inc., Goeken Groiup Corp., RIM Ltd., Pinetree Cap. Corp., Security Nat. Ins. Co., Waterloo Regional Children's Mus., Glenmount Theoret. Physics; mem. Premier's Coun. on Sic. and Tech., Ont., 1985—91; Can. rep. Coun. Internat. Inst. Applied Sys. Analysis, Laxenburg, Austria, 1986—97; prime min.'s personal rep. to Coun. Misn. of Edn., 1990—91. Contbr. articles to profl. jours. Bd. dirs. African Students Found., Toronto, 1961-66, Ont. Curriculum Inst., 1964-67, Ont. R&D Challenge Fund, 1998—; bd. govs. Stratford Shakespearian Festival, 1984-86, mem. senate, 1987. Decorated officer Order of Can., chevalier Ordre National du Mérite (France); recipient Gold medal Ont. Profl. Engrs., 1990, Can. Engrs. Gold Medal award Can. Coun. Profl. Engrs., 1992, Sir. John Kennedy Medal award Engring. Inst. Can., 1995, Can. Entrepreneur of Yr. award, 1997; Athlone fellow, 1952-54. Fellow ASCE, Can. Acad. Engring., Engring. Inst. Can. (del. Engrs. Coun. Profl. Devel., N.Y.C. 1961-70); mem. Assn. Profl. Engrs. Province Ont., Internat. Assn. Bridge and Structural Engring., Internat. Assn. Shell Structures, Royal Can. Yacht Club, Univ. Club (Toronto). Office: U Waterloo Waterloo ON Canada N2L 3G1 E-mail: dtwright@uwaterloo.ca.

WRIGHT, DOUGLASS BROWNELL, retired judge, lawyer; b. Hartford, Conn., May 30, 1912; s. Arthur Brownell and Sylvia (Stephens) W.; m. Jane Hamersley, Sept. 24, 1938 (dec. Feb. 1997); children: Jane C., Douglass B., Hamersley S., Elizabeth B., Arthur W.; m. Ann Hallowell Ferguson, Nov. 7, 1998. AB, Yale U., 1933; LL.B., Hartford Coll. Law, 1937. Bar: Conn. 1937. Legal dept. Aetna Life Ins. Co., 1937-39; partner Davis, Lee, Howard & Wright, Hartford, 1939—; lectr. law U. Conn., 1946—; asst. state's atty. State of Conn., 1952-59; judge Conn. Circuit Court, 1959-65, Conn. Superior Ct., 1965—98; ret., 1998. Leader orch. Judge Wright and the Four Wrongs Author: Connecticut Law of Torts, 1956, Connecticut Legal Forms, 5 vols., 1958, Connecticut Jury Instructions, 3 vols., 1960, 76. Sec., dir. Captioned Films for the Deaf, Inc.; bd. dirs., pres. Am. Sch. for Deaf, 1942— ; trustee Hartt Mus. Found., 1949— , Good Will Boys Club Hartford, 1950— ; regent U. Hartford; bd. dirs. Vis. Nurse Assn., Newington Home for Crippled Children, Hartford Times Farm, Loomis Sch.; incorporator Conn. Inst. for Blind. Served as lt. USNR, 1942-45. Mem. Phi Beta Kappa, Psi Upsilon. Clubs: University (Hartford), Hartford Golf (Hartford), Hartford Tennis (Hartford), 20th Century (Hartford); Coral Beach and Tennis (Bermuda); Hillsboro (Pompano Beach, Fla.). Congregationalist. Home: 20 Loeffler Rd Apt T519 Bloomfield CT 06002-2273 Office: 95 Washington St Hartford CT 06106-4431

WRIGHT, ETHEL, secondary education educator; b. Apr. 5, 1947; m. James A. Wright, Sept. 26, 1969; children: Cassandra, Hannibal, Omari. BS in English, Alcorn State U., Lorman, Miss., 1970; MS in Edn., Butler U., Indpls., 1975. Tchr. Simmons H.S., Arcola, Miss., 1970-71; tchr. English Indpls. Pub. Schs., 1971—. Mem. textbook adoption com. Indpls. Pub. Schs., 1979, liaison for Tchrs. Ctr., mem. film preview com. Clk., Dem. Com., Indpls. Recipient ABCD award Indpls. Pub. Schs., 1985, 92; Gregg and Reed scholar Indpls. Pub. Schs. Mem. NEA, Indpls. Edn. Assn. Avocations: reading, gardening, sewing, growing houseplants, travel.

WRIGHT, EUGENE ALLEN, federal judge; b. Seattle, Feb. 23, 1913; s. Elias Allen and Mary (Bailey) W.; m. Esther Ruth Ladley, Mar. 19, 1938; children: Gerald Allen, Meredith Ann Wright Morton. AB, U. Wash., 1935, JD, 1937; LLD, U. Puget Sound, 1984. Bar: Wash. 1937. Assoc. Wright & Wright, Seattle, 1937-54; judge Superior Ct. King County, 1954-66; v.p., sr. trust officer Pacific Nat. Bank Seattle, 1966-69; judge U.S. Ct. Appeals (9th cir.), Seattle, 1969—. Acting municipal judge, Seattle, 1948-52; mem. faculty Nat. Jud. Coll., 1964-72; lectr. Sch. Communications, U. Wash., 1965-66, U. Wash. Law Sch., 1952-74; lectr. appellate judges' seminars, 1973-76, Nat. Law Clks. Inst., La. State U., 1973; chmn. Wash. State Com. on Law and Justice, 1968-69; mem. com. on appellate rules Jud. Conf., 1978-85, mem. com. on courtroom photography, 1983-85, com. jud. ethics, 1984-92, com. Bicentennial of Constn., 1985-87. Author: (with others) The State Trial Judges Book, 1966; also articles; editor: Trial Judges Jour., 1963-66; contbr. articles to profl. jours. Chmn. bd. visitors U. Puget Sound Sch. Law, 1979-84; mem. bd. visitors U. Wash. Sch. Law, 1996; bd. dirs. Met. YMCA, Seattle, 1955-72; lay reader Episc Ch. Served to lt. col. USAR, 1941-46, col. Res., ret. Decorated Bronze Star, Combat Inf. badge; recipient Army Commendation medal, Disting. Service award U.S. Jr. C. of C., 1948, Disting. Service medal Am. Legion. Fellow Am. Bar Found.; mem. ABA (coun. div. jud. adminstrn. 1971-76), FBA (Disting. Jud. Svc. award 1984), Wash. Bar Assn. (award of merit 1983), Seattle-King County Bar Assn. (Spl. Disting. Svc. award 1984. William L. Dwyer Outstanding Jurist award 2001), Order of Coif, Wash. Athletic Club, Rainier Club, Masons (33 degree), Shriners, Delta Upsilon (Disting. Alumni Achievement award 1989), Phi Delta Phi. Office: US Ct Appeals 9th Cir 902 US Courthouse 1010 5th Ave Seattle WA 98104-1195

WRIGHT, FAYE See DAYA MATA, SRI

WRIGHT, FRANCES JANE, educational psychologist; b. L.A., Dec. 22, 1943; d. step-father John David and Evelyn Jane (Dale) Brinegar. BA, Long Beach State U., 1965; MA, Brigham Young U., 1968, EdD, 1980; postgrad., U. Nev., 1970, U. Utah, 1972-73; postdoctoral, Utah State U., 1985-86. Cert. secondary tchr., adminstr., Utah. Asst. dir. Teenpost Project, San Pedro, Calif., 1966; caseworker Los Angeles County, 1966-67; self-care inservice dir. Utah State Tng. Sch., American Fork, Utah, 1968, vocat. project designer, 1968; tchr. mentally handicapped Santa Ana Unified Schs., Calif., 1968-69; state specialist intellectually handicapped State Office Edn., Salt Lake City, 1969-70; vocat. counselor Manpower, 1970-71; tchr. severely handicapped Davis County Schs., Farmington, Utah, 1971-73, diagnostician, 1973-74, resource elem. tchr., 1974-78; instr. Brigham Young U., Salt Lake City, 1976-83; resource tchr. jr. high Davis County Schs., Farmington, 1978-90; ednl. cons. Murray, Utah, 1973-90; chief ednl. diagnostician Ctr. for Evaluation of Learning and Devel., Layton, 1989-90. Clin. dir. assessment and observation program Idaho Youth Ranch, 1990-95, clin. dir. intake program, 1992-94, supr. family preservation svc./aftercare teams, 1993-95, co-ranch treatment dir. and placement officer, 1995; cons. juvenile correctional dist. 5, 1996-2000; cons., counselor address issues with youth and families, 2001—; clin. cons. Magic Hot Springs Youth Camp, 1996-97; program dir. Liberty Care Svcs., 2001—; mem. cmty. accountability bd. McNeil Assn., 1996—, Dist. 5 Juvenile Justice Coun., 1997—, parent project facilitator, 1998—; trainer Detour prison prevention programfor adolescents, 1997-2000; cons. Northstar Family Preservation, 1997—; acting chmn . Dist. 5 Juvenile Justice Coun., 1998-99, chmn. 1999-2001; mem. Idaho Juvenile Justice Commn., 1999-2001; adv. bd. So. Central Learning Ctr., 1999-2001; mem. oversight bd., evaluator Status Offender prog. 1997-2000; program dir. Liberty Care Svc.; lectr. in field; pvt. cons./counselor lic. in juvenile justice, youth, edn. and other related concerns. Named Profl. of Yr. Utah Assn. for Children with Learning Disabilities, 1985. Mem. Assn. Children/Adults with Learning Disabilities (del. 1979-85, 87, nat. nominating com., 1985-86, nat. bd. dirs. 1988-91), Utah Assn. Children/Adults with Learning Disabilities (exec. bd. 1978-84, profl. adv. bd. 1985-90, coord. LDA orgn. Idaho 1991—), Coun. Exceptional Children (div. learning disabilities, ednl. diagnostics, behavioral disorders), Coun. Learning Disabilities, ASCD (regional adv.), Windstar Found., Nat. Wildlife Found., World Wildlife Fedn., Best Friends Animal Sanctuary, Cousteau Soc., Nat. Assn. Sch. Adminstrs., Job's Daughters. Democrat. Mem. Lds Ch. Avocations: geneaology research, horseback riding, sketching, crafts, reading. Home: 2176 Julie Ln Twin Falls ID 83301-8361 Office: Youth Ctr Juvenile Corrections 2469 Wright Ave Twin Falls ID 83301-7972 *Personal philosophy: I dream of the day when man will value man and his surrounding world for their intrinsic value instead of what they can or could do for a specific person.*

WRIGHT, FRANK, artist, educator; b. Washington, Oct. 10, 1932; s. John Franklin and Margaret (Young) W.; m. Mary Eleanor Dow, May 31, 1957; 1 child, Suzanne Elizabeth. BA, Am. U., 1954; MA in Art History, U. Ill., 1960. Instr. Am. U., Washington, 1958-59; Paul J. Sachs fellow Nat. Gallery of Art, 1959-60, Harvard U., Cambridge, Mass., 1960-61; instr. Corcoran Sch. Art, Washington, 1966-70; asst. prof. to prof. fine arts George Wash. U., 1970—. Exhbns. include Corcoran Gallery of Art, Washington, 1981, Kennedy Galleries, N.Y, 1981, Md. Hall, Annapolis, 1998, Strathmore Hall, Bethesda, Md., 1998. Mem. Hist. Soc. D.C. Fellow Leopold Schepp Found., 1956, Print Coun. Am., 1959. Mem. Nat. Soc. Arts and Letters (advisor 1992—), Cosmos Club (art com. 1993), Omicron Delta Kappa (Alpha Cir.). Avocations: collecting Washingtoniana material, lecturer on Washington, D.C. Home: 3520 Bradley Ln Chevy Chase MD 20815-3260 E-mail: fwright@gwu.edu.

WRIGHT, FRANK GARDNER, retired newspaper editor; b. Moline, Ill., Mar. 21, 1931; s. Paul E. and Goldie (Hicks) W.; m. Barbara Lee Griffiths, Mar. 28, 1953; children: Stephen, Jeffrey, Natalie, Gregory, Sarah. BA, Augustana Coll., Rock Island, Ill., 1953; postgrad., U. Minn., 1953-54. Suburban reporter Mpls. Star, 1954-55; with Mpls. Tribune, 1955-82, N.D. corr., 1955-56, Mpls. City Hall reporter, 1956-58, asst. city editor, 1958-63, Minn. polit. reporter, 1963-68, Washington corr., 1968-72, Washington bur. chief, 1972-77, mng. editor, 1977-82; mng. editor/news Mpls. Star and Tribune, 1982-84, assoc. editor, 1984-98; ret., 1998. Juror for Pulitzer Awards, 1983-84 Chmn. Golden Valley Human Rights Commn., 1965-67; mem. exec. com. Nobel Peace Prize Forum, 2000; mem. faculty Augsburg Coll., 3d Age, U. St. Thomas, Ctr. for Sr. Citizens Edn., 2000; bd. dirs. Luth. Social Services, Washington. Recipient several Page 1 awards Twin Cities Newspaper Guild, 1950's, 60's, Worth Bingham prize Worth Bingham Meml. Fund, 1971; runnerup Raymond Clapper award for Washington correspondence, 1971; Outstanding Achievement award Augustana Alumni Assn., 1977; citation for excellence in internat. reporting Overseas Press Club, 1985; Minn. SPJ/SDX 1st Place Page One award for in-depth reporting, 1988, MWAP award Human Interest Reporting, 1995. Mem. Am. Newspaper Guild (chmn. Mpls. unit 1961-67, editorial v.p. Twin Cities 1963-67), Minn. AP Editors Assn. (pres. 1981), Phi Beta Kappa Home: 4912 Aldrich Ave S Minneapolis MN 55409-2353 E-mail: fgwright@aol.com.

WRIGHT, FRANZ PAUL, poet, writer, translator; b. Vienna, Austria, 1953; Translator, author of introduction Rainer Maria Rilke, The Unknown Rilke, 1990; translator modern and contemporary French and German poets; author: (poems) Tapping the White Cane of Solitude, 1976, The Earth Without You, 1980, Eight Poems, 1981, The One Whose Eyes Open When You Close Your Eyes, 1982, No Siege Is Absolute, 1983, Going North in Winter, 1986, Entry in an Unknown Hand, 1989, Midnight Postscript, 1990, And Still the Hand Will Sleep in Its Glass Ship, 1990, Rorschach Test, 1995, The Night World and the Word Night, 1993, Knell, 1998, ILL LIT: Selected and New Poems, 1998, The Beforelife, 2001; represented in anthologies; contbr. articles to profl. publs. Recipient Witter Bynner Prize for Poetry, 1995, PEN/Voelcker award, 1996; NEA fellow, 1985, 92, Guggenheim fellow, 1989, Whiting fellow, 1991. E-mail: franzwright@earthlink.net.

WRIGHT, FRED W., JR. writer; b. Nashville, Apr. 21, 1940; s. Frederick William Sr. and Mary (Boring) W.; m. Rosemary Spenser Warren, June 12, 1965 (div. 1973). BA, Eckerd Coll., 1964; MA, U. South Fla., 1971. Writer, critic Times Pub. Co., St. Petersburg, Fla., 1964-75; freelance writer, editor, 1975—. Author, editor: The Radiance Technique on the Job, 1993; author: City Smart: Tampa/St. Petersburg, 1997. Mem. Soc. Am. Travel Writers, Mensa. Democrat. Avocation: duplicate bridge. Home and Office: PO Box 86158 Saint Petersburg FL 33738-6158

WRIGHT, FREDERICK HERMAN GREENE, II, computer systems engineer; b. Quincy, Mass., Feb. 23, 1952; s. Frederick Herman Greene and Dorothy Louise (Harrold) W. Student, MIT, 1968-69. Test and measurement technician The Foxboro (Mass.) Co., 1968; hardware and software designer MIT Project MAC, Cambridge, Mass., 1969, Info. Internat., Brookline, 1969, Stanford Artificial Intelligence Lab, Palo Alto, Calif., 1971-73, Systems Concepts, San Francisco, 1970, 73-74, 1976-90; hardware and software designer, then pres. Resource One, 1974-76; pvt. cons. San Rafael, Calif., 1991—. Computer cons. Langley-Porter Neuropsychiatric Inst., San Francisco, 1976. Membership chmn. Pacific Soaring Coun., San Francisco, 1983-85, bd. dirs., 1984-85; active Mayflower Cmty. Chorus, 1993—. Recipient Gold Soaring Badge Fed. Aeronautique Internat., 1983. Mem. Soaring Soc. Am., Aircraft Owners and Pilots Assn., Nat. Space Soc., Bay Area Soaring Assn. Avocations: soaring, flying, singing. Home and Office: 251 C St San Rafael CA 94901-4916

WRIGHT, GARY KENNEDY, educational administrator; b. Hillsboro, Ohio, July 12, 1936; s. Homer Donald and Mary Elizabeth (Kennedy) W.; m. Chris Lee Wright, Oct. 13, 1984; children: Cris, Nikki, Jeff, Kevin, Katy. BS in Edn., Wittenberg U., 1962, MEd, 1966; PhD, Ohio U., 1977. Tchr. Mills Lawn Sch., Yellow Springs, Ohio, 1958-63; mid. sch. prin. Bryan Sch., 1963-65; elem. prin. McLane Sch., West Bend, Wis., 1965-68; dir. curriculum and instrn. West Bend Sch. Dist., 1968-70; rsch. asst. Ohio U., Athens, 1970-72; area dir. Madison (Wis.) Met. Sch., 1972-78; assoc. supt. Montgomery County Schs., Rockville, Md., 1978-80; supt. Lindberg Sch. Dist., St. Louis, 1980-90; program dir. Danforth Found., 1990-92; exec. dir. Coop. Sch. Dists., 1992—. Author: (monograph) Reinventing Leadership, 1991; co-author: (book chpt.) St. Louis Currents, 1986, (monograph) A New Platform for Preparing Administrators, 1991. Bd. dirs. South St. Louis County YMCA, 1991—; mem. long range planning com. United Way, St. Louis, 1994—; chmn. program com. Met. YMCA, St. Louis, 1992—. Named Citizen of Yr., Crestwood-Sunset Hills C. of C., 1985. Mem. Am. Assn. Sch. Adminstrs., Mo. Assn. Sch. Adminstrs. (25 Yr. Svc. award 1990), Suburban Sch. Supts., Phi Delta Kappa. Office: Coop Sch Dists 1460 Craig Rd Saint Louis MO 63146-4842

WRIGHT, GEORGE CULLEN, electronics company executive; b. Anderson, S.C., June 28, 1923; s. Benjamin Norman and Essie Floride (Cole) W.; m. Kathleen Ashe, Oct. 19, 1947; children: Carol Ann (Mrs. John C. Marquardt), George Cullen, Florenda Jean, William Norman. BS, Clemson U., 1948. Asst. supt. Duke Power Co., 1949-56; city mgr. Gaffney, S.C., 1956-60; v.p. mktg. Hubbard & Co., Chgo., 1960-65; dir. Methode Electronics, Inc., Rolling Meadows, Ill., 1956—; v.p., dir. Anchor Coupling Co., Inc., Libertyville, 1973-76. Pres., dir. Exec. Extension & Ventures, Inc., Barrington, Ill., 1976-78, White Marlin Marine, Inc., Anderson, S.C., 1976-86, Piedmont Corp., 1986-2001. Patentee in field. Pres. Barrington East Ass., 1968-70. Served with AUS, 1942-45. Mem. AIEE Electron Industry Assn., Am. Mgmt. Assn. Lodges: Rotary, Sertoma (pres. 1963-65). Home: 224 Jolly Rd Townville SC 29689-3540

WRIGHT, GLADYS STONE, music educator, composer, writer; b. Wasco, Oreg., Mar. 8, 1925; d. Murvel Stuart and Daisy Violet (Warren) Stone; m. Alfred George Wright, June 28, 1953. BS, U. Oreg., 1948, MS, 1953. Dir. bands Elmira (Oreg.) U-4 High Sch., 1948-53, Otterbein (Ind.) High Sch., 1954-61, Klondike High Sch., West Lafayette, Ind., 1962-70, Harrison High Sch., West Lafayette, 1970-84. Organizer, condr. Musical Friendship Tours, Cen. Am., 1967-79; v.p., condr. U.S. Collegiate Wind Band, 1975—; bd. dirs. John Philip Sousa Found. 1984—; chmn. Sudler Cup, 1986—, Sudler Flag, 1982; pres. Internat. Music Tours, 1984—, Key to the City, Taxco, Mex., 1975. Editor: Woman Conductor, 1986—; composer: marches Big Bowl and Trumpets and Tabards, 1987; contbg. editor: Informusica (Spain). Bd. dirs. N. Am. Wildlife Park, Battleground, Ind. 1985. Recipient Medal of the order John Philip Sousa Found., 1988, Star of Order, 1991, Internat. Contbrn. to Music award Phi Beta Mu, 2000; 1st woman guest conductor U.S. Navy Band, Washington D.C., 1961, Goldman Band, N.Y.C., 1958, Kneller Hall Band, London, 1975, Tri-State Music Festival Massed Orch., Band, Choir, 1985; elected to Women Bd. Dirs. Hall of Fame of Disting. Women Conductor, 1994; inductee Hall of Fame Disting. Condrs., Nat. Band Assn., 1999. Mem. Am. Bandmasters Assn. (bd. dirs. 1993, 1st woman mem.), Women Band Dirs. Nat. Assn. (founding pres. 1967, sec. 1985, recipient Silver Baton 1974, Golden Rose 1990, Hall of Fame 1995), Am. Sch. Band Dirs. Assn., Nat. Band Assn. (Citation excellence 1970), Tippecoanoe Arts Fedn. (bd. dirs. 1986-90), Tippecanoe Fife and Drum Corps. (bd. dirs. 1984), Daughters of Am. Revolution, Col. Dames-Pre Quitanen Chpt., New England Women, Tau Beta Sigma (Outstanding Svc. to Music award 1970), Phi Beta Mu (1st hon. women mem. 1972), North Am. Wildlife Park (bd dirs, 1990—). Avocations: historic preservation, environ. activities.

WRIGHT, GORDON BROOKS, musician, conductor, educator; b. Bklyn., Dec. 31, 1934; s. Harry Wesley and Helen Philomena (Brooks) W.; m. Inga-Lisa Myrin Wright, June 13, 1958 (div. 1979); children: Karin-Ellen Sturla, Charles-Eric, Daniel Brooks. MusB, Coll. Wooster, 1957; MA, U. Wis., 1961; postgrad., Salzburg Mozarteum, 1972, Loma Linda U., 1979; studied with, René Leibowitz, Carl Melles, Wilfred Pelletier, Herbert Blomstedt, Hans Swarowsky. Founder, music dir. Wis. Chamber Orch., 1960-69; music dir. Fairbanks (Alaska) Symphony Orch., 1969-89; prof. music Univ. Alaska, Fairbanks, 1969-89, prof. emeritus, 1989—; founder, music dir. Arctic Chamber Orch., 1970-89; exec. dir. The Reznicek Soc., Indian, Alaska, 1982—. Guest condr. Philharmonia Hungarica, Philomusica London, Norwegian Radio Orch., Orch. St. Luke's, Anchorage Symphony Orch., Musashino Orch., Tokyo, Tohoku Orch., Sendai, Japan; composer: Suite of Netherlands Dances, 1965, Six Alaskan Tone Poems, 1974, Symphony in Ursa Major, 1979 (Legis. award 1979), 1984 Overture, Scott Joplin Suite, 1987, Toccata Festiva, 1992; columnist Alaska Advocate. Founder, bd. dirs. No. Alaska Environ. Ctr., Fairbanks, 1971-78. Served as pvt. AUS, 1957-59. Mem.: Am. Fedn. Musicians, Arturo Toscanini Soc., Condr.'s Guild, Am. Symphony Orch. League, Royal Musical Assn., Am. Musicol. Soc., Ctr. for Alaskan Coastal Studies (bd. dirs. 1982—), Alaska Conservation Soc. (editor Rev. 1971—78), Audubon Soc., Wilderness Soc., Friends of Earth-Alaska (bd. dirs. 1978—), Sierra Club (chmn. Fairbanks Group 1969—71). Avocations: hiking, kayaking, collecting books, photography. Home: HC 52 Box 8899 Indian AK 99540-9604 E-mail: turnagain@earthlink.net.

WRIGHT, GWENDOLYN, art center director, writer, educator; b. Chgo., May 14, 1946; d. William Kemp and Mary Ruth (Brown) W.; m. Paul Rabinow, Nov. 18, 1980 (div. 1982); m. Thomas Bender, Jan. 14, 1984; children: David, Sophia. BA, NYU, 1969; MArch, U. Calif., Berkeley, 1974, PhD, 1980. Assoc. prof. Columbia U., N.Y.C., 1983-87, prof., 1988—; dir. Buell Ctr. for Study Am. Architecture, 1988-92. Cons. Fulbright Scholars, Coun. Internat. Exch. Scholars, Washington, 1988-91, ArchNet, 1999—, Nat. Bldg. Mus., Washington, 2001—. Author: Building the Dream: A Social History of Housing in America, 1980, Moralism and the Model Home, 1981, The History of History in American Schools of Architecture, 1990, The Politics of Design in French Colonial Urbanism, 1991; writer N.Y. Times, 1999. Fellow Ford Found., 1979-80; Stanford Inst. for Humanities, 1982-83, Mich. Inst. for Humanities, 1991, Getty Ctr. for History of Art and the Humanities, 1992—. Fellow Soc. Am. Historians, N.Y. Inst. for Humanities; mem. Soc. Archtl. Historians, Coll. Art Assn., Am. Hist. Assn., Orgn. Am. Historians. Democrat. Home: 54 Washington Mews New York NY 10003-6608 Office: Columbia U Avery Hall New York NY 10027

WRIGHT, HARRISON MORRIS, historian, educator; b. Phila., Oct. 6, 1928; s. Sydney L. and Catharine W. (Morris) W.; m. Josephine Stearns Cole, July 20, 1957; children— Rebecca H., J. Rodman, Thomas F., Daniel H., James L. BA, Harvard, 1950, MA, 1953, PhD, 1957. Teaching fellow Harvard,

1955-57; mem. faculty Swarthmore Coll., 1957—, prof. history, 1968-87, Isaac H. Clothier prof. history and internat. relations, 1987-93, chmn. dept., 1968-79, provost, 1979-84, Clothier prof. and provost emeritus, 1993—, acting pres., 1982. Author: New Zealand, 1769-1840: Early Years of Western Contact, 1959, The Burden of the Present: Liberal-Radical Controversy over Southern African History, 1977; Editor: The New Imperialism— Analysis of Late Nineteenth-Century Expansion, 1961, 2d edit., 1976, Sir James Rose Innes: Selected Correspondence (1884-1902), 1972. Fulbright scholar New Zealand, 1950-51; Ford Found. fgn. areas fellow Eng. and Ghana, 1961-62; grantee Am. Philos. Soc., S. Africa, 1966-67; grantee Old Dominion Fund, S. Africa, 1971 Mem.: Hist. Soc. Pa. (coun. 1984—91, coun. emeritus 1992—, v.p. 1986—88, chmn. 1989—91), African Studies Assn., Jamestown (R.I.) Harbor Commn., Internat. Sailing Inst. (bd. dirs. 1998—), Humanities Forum R.I. (bd. dirs. 1995—2000), R.I. Hist. Soc. (bd. dirs. 1998—), Newport Hist. Soc. (bd. dirs. 1973—88), Am. Hist. Assn., Phi Beta Kappa. Home: PO Box 209 Jamestown RI 02835-0209

WRIGHT, HARRY HERCULES, psychiatrist; b. Charleston, S.C., Jan. 4, 1948; s. Harry Vernon and Agnes Lucile (Simmons) W. BS, U. S.C., 1970; MD, MBA, U. Pa., 1976. Resident in psychiatry Wm. S. Hall Psychiat. Inst., Columbia, S.C., 1977-79; adminstrv. fellow in psychiatry NIMH, Rockville, Md., 1979; fellow in child psychiatry William S. Hall Psychiat. Inst., 1979-81, teaching child psychiatrist, 1981—; instr. dept. neuropsychiatry and behavioral sci. U. S.C. Sch. Medicine, 1981-82, asst. prof., 1982-86, assoc. prof., 1986-90, prof., 1990—. Contbr. articles to profl. jours. Bd. dirs. Carolina Children's Home, 1992—, Zero to Three, 1997—; bd. trustees, First Steps to Sch. Readiness, 2000—; mem. landmarks commn. City of Columbia, 1986-98. Falk fellow, 1977-79; Laughlin fellow, 1979; recipient Freed award Hall Psychiat. Inst., 1978, Outstanding Service award Sickle Cell Found. Mem. AAAS, Am. Acad. Child Psychiatry, World Psychiat. Assn., World Assn. Infant Mental Health, Am. Soc. Adolescent Psychiatry, Am. Pub. Health Assn., Am. Psychiat. Assn., So. Med. Assn., Riverbank Zool. Soc., Autism Soc. Am., Acad. Orgnl. and Occupl. Psychiatry, Soc. Study Psychiatry and Culture, Omicron Delta Kappa, Sigma Xi. Methodist. Home: PO Box 12474 Columbia SC 29211-2474 Office: 3555 Harden Street Ext Ste 104 Columbia SC 29203-6894

WRIGHT, HASTINGS KEMPER, surgeon, educator; b. Boston, Aug. 28, 1928; s. Donald M. and Lucia (Durand) W.; m. Nancy E. Howell, June 19, 1954; children: Mark, Kenneth, Barbara, Donald. AB, Harvard U., 1950, MD, 1954, MA, 1973. Diplomate: Am. Bd. Surgery. Intern Univ. Hosps. Cleve., 1954, resident, 1957-61; asst. prof. surgery Western Res. U., Cleve., 1961-66; assoc. prof. surgery Med. Sch. Yale U., New Haven, 1967-72, prof. Med. Sch., 1972-95; prof. surgery emeritus, 1995—; chief gen. surgery Yale-New Haven Hosp., 1968-79, asst. chief surgery, 1979-95. Author: Complications of GI Surgery, 1972; asst. chief editor Archives of Surgery, Chgo., 1977-89. Capt. U.S. Army, 1955-57. Fellow ACS, Am. Surg. Assn.; mem. Soc. Univ. Surgeons (program dir. 1972), Am. Gastroent. Assn., Soc. Surgery Gastrointestinal Tract Clubs: Mory's Assoc. (New Haven); Yale (N.Y.C.). Republican. Episcopalian. Home: 35 Wood Rd Branford CT 06405-4935 Office: Yale U Med Sch Dept Surgery 333 Cedar St New Haven CT 06510-3289

WRIGHT, HELEN PATTON, professional society administrator; b. Washington, Jan. 15, 1919; d. Raymond Stanton and Virginia (Mitchell) Patton; m. James Skelly Wright, Feb. 1, 1945 (dec. 1988); 1 son, James Skelly; m. John H. Pickering, Feb. 3, 1990. Student, Sweet Briar Coll., 1936-38; grad., Washington Sch. Secretaries, 1939, Am. U., 1989. Tchr. Washington Sch. Secs., N.Y.C., 1939-40; sec. The White House, 1941-43, Am. Embassy, London, 1943-45; asst. to exec. dir. Senate Atomic Energy Com., 1946-47. Bd. dirs. Constitution Project, 2001—. Author: My Journey Recollections of the First Seventy Years, 1995. V.p., mem. budget and admissions com. United Fund New Orleans, 1960-62; chmn. met. divsn., campaign; v.p. Dept. Pub. Welfare, Orleans Parish and City New Orleans, 1960-62, Milne Asylum for Destitute Orphan Boys, New Orleans, 1958-62; mem. bd. New Orleans Social Welfare Planning Coun., 1954-62, New Orleans Cancer Soc., 1958-60; v.p. Juvenile Ct. Adv. Com. New Orleans, 1961; successively sec., v.p., pres. Parents' Assn. Metairie Park Country Day Sch., 1956-59; v.p. La. Assn. Mental Health, 1960-62; del. dir. to Nat. Assn. Mental Health, 1960-62; bd. mem. Washington Health and Welfare Coun., 1962-64, Hillcrest Children's Ctr., Washington, 1963-69, D.C. Mental Health Assn., 1962-72, 73-76; bd. dirs. Hospice Care of D.C., 1981-88, 90-96, pres., 1986-88; mem. adv. bd. civil commitment project Nat. Ctr. for State Cts., 1981; bd. dirs. Nat. Assn. Mental Health, 1960-66, 67-74, sec., 1968-70, pres.-elect, 1970-71, pres., 1972-73, cons. on assn. film, 1972; mem. commn. on mentally disabled ABA, 1973-80, commn. on legal problems of elderly, 1997; mem. adv. bd. Alzheimer's Assn. Greater Washington chpt., 1996, bd. dirs. Constn. Project; chmn. altar guild Christ Ch. Cathedral, New Orleans, 1960, Little Sanctuary of St. Albans Sch., Washington, 1965; pres. Altar Guild, St. Alban's Ch., 1976, 77; chmn. Washington com. Nat. Cathedral Assn., 1976-79, trustee, 1976-90, sec., 1977, v.p., 1980-83, trustee emeritae, 1997; bd. dirs. Nat. Ctr. Voluntary Action; mem. task panel Mental Health Problems, Scope and Boundaries, Pres.'s Commn. Mental Health, 1977; mem. tech. rev. com. Md. Psychiat. Rsch. Ctr., 1979-81. Mem. ABA (commn. on legal problems of the elderly 1997-99). Address: Apt 1007 8100 Connecticut Ave Chevy Chase MD 20815

WRIGHT, HELEN KENNEDY, retired professional association administrator, publisher, editor, librarian; b. Indpls., Sept. 23, 1927; d. William Henry and Ida Louise (Crosby) Kennedy; m. Samuel A. Wright, Sept. 5, 1970 (dec. 1998); 1 child, Carl F. Prince II (dec.). BA, Butler U., 1945, MS, 1950, Columbia U., 1952. Reference libr. N.Y. Pub. Libr., N.Y.C., 1952-53, Bklyn. Pub. Libr., 1953-54; reference libr., cataloger U. Utah, 1954-57; libr. Chgo. Pub. Libr.; asst. dir. pub. svcs. ALA, Chgo., 1958-62, editor Reference Books Bull., 1962—85, asst. dir. for new product planning, pub. svcs., 1985-89, dir. office for libr. outreach svcs., 1987—88, mng. editor yearbook, 1988-89. Contbr. to Ency. of Careers, Ency. of Libr. and Info. Sci., New Book of Knowledge Ency., Bull. of Bibliography, New Golden Book Ency. Recipient Louis Shores/Oryx award, 1991. Mem. Phi Kappa Phi, Kappa Delta Pi, Sigma Gamma Rho. Roman Catholic. Home: 1138 W 111th St Chicago IL 60643-4508

WRIGHT, HUGH ELLIOTT, JR. association executive, writer; b. Athens, Ala., Nov. 20, 1937; s. Hugh Elliott and Martha Angeline (Shannon) W. AB, Birmingham-So. Coll., 1959; M.Div., Vanderbilt U., 1962, D.Ministry, 1967; postgrad., Harvard U., 1963. Ordained to ministry Methodist Ch., 1963; pastor Baxter (Tenn.) Meth. Ch., 1963-64; assoc. pastor Waverly Pl. Ch., Nashville, 1965-66; field sec. Tenn. Heart Assn., 1964-65; editorial asst. Motive mag., 1965-67; Protestant-Orthodox editor Religious News Service, N.Y.C., 1967-75; research fellow Auburn Theol. Sem., 1976; editor project on mediating structures and public policy Am. Enterprise Inst., 1979-80; coordinator project on ch., state and taxation NAt. Conf. of Christians and Jews, N.Y.C., 1980-83; v.p. for program NCCJ, 1983-88, sr. v.p., dep. to pres., 1988-91; program cons., 1992—. Cons. Hartford Sem. Found., 1972, United Meth. Bd. Global Ministries, 1975-78, 92—. United Meth. Communications, 1979-81, Nat. Congress for Cmty. Econ. Devel., 1996—; bd. dirs. Internat. Coun. Christians and Jews, DePaul Coll. Law Ctr. on Ch. State Rels., Nat. Coun. Chs. Com. on Religious Liberty, Nat. Coun. Religious and Pub. Edn. Host: Challenge to Faith, Sta. WOR, 1973-77; author: (with R. Lecky) Can These Bones Live, 1969, The Big Little School, 1971, (with R. Lynn) Go Free, 1973, Challenge to Mission, 1973, (with Juanita Wright) Viewers Guide to Six American Families, 1977, (with Howard Butt) At the Edge of Hope, 1978, (with Douglas McGaw) A Tale of Two Congregations, 1980, Holy Company: Christian Heroes and Heroines, 1980, RNS Reporting...Sixty Years of Religious News Service, 1993; editor: (with Robert Lecky) Black Manifesto: Religion, Racism and Reparations, 1969. Recipient award Birmingham Council Indsl. Editors, 1959, Founders medal Vanderbilt U., 1962, Shepherd prize Vanderbilt, 1962, Religious Heritage of Am. award in journalism, 1972, Asso. Ch. Press Feature Article award, 1980 Mem. Authors League and Guild, Am. Acad. Religion, Phi Beta Kappa, Sigma Delta Chi, Alpha Tau Omega, Alpha Psi Omega, Eta Sigma Phi. Democrat. Home: 1346 Midland Ave Bronxville NY 10708-6840 Office: 475 Riverside Dr New York NY 10115-0122 E-mail: ewright@gbgm.umc.org.

WRIGHT, ISAAC WILSON, JR. quality assurance professional; b. Nashville, Oct. 22, 1948; s. Isaac Wilson and Julia Frances (Nixon) W.; m. Giovanna Finn, Nov. 12, 1988. BS in Elec. Engring., U. Tenn., 1970, MBA in Indsl. Mgmt., 1973. Staff asst. to prodn. mgr. disposal med. devices Baxter-Travenol Labs., Cleveland, Miss., 1974-75; quality engr. Stephens-Adamson, Inc., divsn. Allis-Chalmers Corp., Clarksdale, 1976-81, supr. quality assurance, 1981-84; mgr. quality assurance and safety Fontaine Fifth Wheel Co., Birmingham, Ala., 1985-90, dir. quality assurance, 1990-95; sr. quality assurance engr. Harley-Davidson Motor Co., Milw., 1996—. Book reviewer Quality Progress. Mem. Am. Soc. Quality (sr., cert. quality engr., quality auditor, quality mgr., organizer, sect. chair Birmingham sect. 1986-88, organizer Montgomery sub-sect. 1992-93, dir. at large Birmingham sect. 1990-91, Milw. sec. bd. dirs. 1998—, Testimonial award 1994), Singles South Civitan (newsletter editor 1986-87, dist. award 1987), Cleveland Evening Lions (pres. 1981-82, dist. publicity and info. chmn., newsletter editor 1980-81, dist. award 1981), 40 Plus of Southwestern Wis. (bd. dirs. 1998-2000), Exchange Club (bd. dirs. 1975), U. Tenn. Alumni Assn. and Century Club, Beta Theta Pi. Methodist. Office: 11800 W Capitol Dr Wauwatosa WI 53222-1005 E-mail: wwright@execpc.com., wilson.wright@harley-davidson.com.

WRIGHT, JAMES EDWARD, college president, history educator; b. Madison, Wis., Aug. 16, 1939; s. Donald J. and Myrtle (Hendricks) W.; m. Joan Bussan, Sept. 3, 1962 (div.); children: James J., Ann Marie, Michael J.; m. Susan DeBevoise, Aug. 18, 1984. BS, Wis. State U., 1964; MS, U. Wis., 1966, PhD, 1969; MA (hon.), Dartmouth Coll., 1980. From asst. prof. to assoc. prof. history Dartmouth Coll., Hanover, N.H., 1969-80, prof. history, 1980—, assoc. dean faculty, 1981-85, dean faculty, 1989-97, acting pres., 1995, provost, 1997-98, pres., 1998—. Sr. historian U. Mid Am., Lincoln, Nebr., 1976-77; humanist-in-residence Colo. Humanities Coun., Georgetown, 1975. Author: Galena Lead District, 1966, Politics of Populism, 1974, Progressive Yankees, 1987; author, co-editor: Great Plains Experience, 1978. Trustee Kimball Union Acad., Meriden, N.H., 1990-94; dir. Sherman Fairchild Found., Greenwich, Conn., 1991—. NCAA Divsn. I, 2001--; chair Hanover Dem. Town Com., 1970-74. Cpl. USMC, 1957-60. Fellow Danforth, 1964—69, Guggenheim, 1973—74, Charles Warren, Harvard U., 1980—81, Am. Acad. Arts and Scis., 2001—. Mem. Orgn. Am. Historians (chair film, media com. 1983-85), The Century Assn., Western History Assn. (chair Caughey prize 1986-87), Phi Beta Kappa. Home: 1 Tuck Dr Hanover NH 03755-3575 Office: Dartmouth College Office of the President 207 Parkhurst Hall Hanover NH 03755 E-mail: james.wright@dartmouth.edu.*

WRIGHT, JAMES C. lawyer; b. Topeka, Apr. 1, 1938; s. Forest E. and Naomi (Sheafor) W.; m. Judith E. Baker, Sept. 2, 1961 (div. June 1982); children: Lori Batchman, Jeb, Ashley Friend; m. Patricia A. Slider, Apr. 28, 1984; stepsons: Andy, Charlie. BA, Kans. U., 1960; LLB, Washburn U., 1963. Bar: Kans. 1963, U.S. Dist. Ct. Kans. 1963, U.S. Ct. Appeals (10th cir.) 1970. Assoc. Shaw, Hergenreter & Quarnstrom, Topeka, 1963-69; ptnr. Shaw, Hergenreter, Quarnstrom & Wright, 1969-81; atty. pvt. practice, 1981-86; ptnr. Wright & Shafer, 1986-99; pvt. practice, 1999—. Bd. dirs., pres. Crittenton Home, Topeka, 1979; bd. dirs. Vol. Ctr., Topeka, 1974-80. Mem.: Topeka Bar Assn. (bd. dirs. 1991—95), Kans. Golf Assn. (bd. dirs. 1996—98), Shawnee Country Club (v.p., bd. dirs. 1974—80), Topeka Country Club (bd. dirs. 1993—97, pres. 1996), Topeka Lawyers Club. Avocations: golf, travel. Office: Wright Law Office 700 SW Jackson St Topeka KS 66603-3731 Office Fax: 785-234-8997. E-mail: wright.jc@worldnet.att.net.

WRIGHT, JAMES CORWIN, international management consultant; b. Watertown, S.D., 1959; s. Patrick and Delores Wright; m. Susan Kathleen Mohr, Nov. 7, 1981 (div. Oct. 1983); m. Lynda Renelle Prettyman, Jan. 4, 1986. HHD (hon.), D in Internat. Mgmt. (hon.), , 1993. With delivery dept. San Juan (P.R.) Star Newspaper, 1972-74; asst. diving instr. Caribbean Sch. of Aquatics, San Juan, 1973-74; freelance musician various locations, 1975-81; detail draftsman AiResearch Mfg. Co. of Ariz., Phoenix, 1977-79; project designer McMartin Industries, Inc., Omaha, 1980-82; chief exec. officer Aztron Corp., Council Bluffs, Iowa, 1982-86; pres. Aztron Prodns., Fountain Hills, Ariz., 1986-88; chief exec. officer Jalyn Entertainment Group, Scottsdale, 1988—; pub. Roadrunner Mag., Phoenix, 1988-89; v.p. Zent & Assocs., 1989-93. Cons. Tripp and Assocs., Inc., Blair, Nebr., 1982-85, Control Data Corp., Omaha, 1984, Fast Lane Mag., Omaha, 1984-87, Salt River Project, Ariz., 1986-87, MEMCON, Nebr., 1984, Tricon, Ltd., Iowa, 1982-84, Doane Western Co. Inc., Nebr., 1984; gen. mgr. Tight Fit Enterprises, Council Bluffs, 1983-85; trustee Jalyn Internat. Trust, 1991-94, Bus. Intercontinental Trust, 1991-94, West African Devel. Trust, 1991-93; writer syndicated column, 1984-89. Author: Newsletters: A Report, 1985, Developing Presentation Skills; editor: (jour.) The Wintight Letter, 1985; contbr. articles to profl. jours. Active Nat. Congl. Com., 1985-86, Rep. Nat. Com., 1985; chmn. G.P.V. Community Assistance Team, Inc., 1990-92. Recipient Cert. of Merit Pres. Ronald Reagan, 1984, Cert. of Merit Presdl. Task Force, 1986, Cert. of Appreciation Nat. Congl. Com., 1985-86, World Decoration Excellence award, 1990, Disting. Leadership award, 1991, Medal of Honor, 1993; named Cert. Internat. Financier Internat. Soc. of Financiers, 1987, 89; Decorated titled knight Paupers Commilitones Christi Templique Solomonis, cpt. Légion de L'Aigle de Mer Baron. Mem. Internat. Traders, Internat. Parliment for Safety and Peace, Internat. Platform Assn., Inst. des Affaires Internat. (assoc.), Maison Internat. des Intellectuels-Academie Midi (sec., pres.), Am. Mgmt. Assn., Nat. Assn. of Underwater Instrs., Liberia-Am. C. of C. (trustee 1991-93). Avocations: sailing, scuba diving. Office: Jalyn Internat Trust PO Box 5065 Scottsdale AZ 85261-5065

WRIGHT, JAMES DAVID, sociology educator, writer; b. Logansport, Ind., Nov. 6, 1947; s. James Farrell and Helen Loretta (Moon) W.; m. Christine Ellen Stewart, July 25, 1987; children: Matthew James, Derek William. BA, Purdue U., 1969; MS, U. Wis., 1970, PhD, 1973. Cert. specialist social policy and evaluation rsch. Asst. prof. sociology U. Mass., Amherst, 1973-76, assoc. prof., 1976-79, prof., 1979-88; Favrot prof. human rels. Tulane U., New Orleans, 1988-2001; prof. sociology U. Ctrl. Fla., Orlando, 2001—. Author/co-author: The Dissent of the Governed, 1976, Under the Gun, 1983, The State of the Masses, 1986, Homelessness and Health, 1987 (commendation Nat. Press Club 1988), Address Unknown: Homeless in America, 1989, The Greatest of Evils: Urban Poverty and the Urban Underclass, 1993, Beside the Golden Door, 1998, Fixin' to Git, 2002others; editor: (book series) Social Institutions and Social Change, 1984—, (jour.) Social Sci. Rsch. Jour., 1978—; contbr. numerous articles, essays, book chpts. to profl. publs. Mem. Am. Sociol. Assn. Democrat. Avocations: cooking, gardening, travel. Office Fax: 407-823-6738. E-mail: jwright@mail.ucf.edu.

WRIGHT, JAMES EDWARD, judge; b. Arlington, Tex., Jan. 15, 1921; s. James Robert and Clairette (Smith) W.; m. Eberta Adelaide Slataper, June 25, 1946; 1 child, Patricia Diane Wright Rogers. JD, U. Tex., 1949. Bar: Tex. 1949. Practice in, Ft. Worth, 1949-69; city atty. Arlington, 1951-61; judge 141st Dist. Ct., Ft. Worth, 1970-88, sr. dist. judge, 1988—. Served with USAAF, World War II. Paul Harris fellow, 1981; named Disting. Alumnus U. Tex.-Arlington, 1982; named to Mil. Sci. Dept. Hall of Honor, U. Tex.-Arlington, 1985 Fellow Tex. Bar Found. (life); mem. ABA, Ft. Worth-Tarrant County Bar Assn. (pres. 1958-59), Tex. Bar Assn., Sons of the Rep. of Tex., Rotary (pres. Downtown Ft. Worth club 1966-67), Masons (32 degree), Shrinersm Moslah Temple Patrol (life, pres. 1962-63), Royal Order Jesters (life), Phi Alpha Delta. Methodist. Home: 717 Briarwood Blvd Arlington TX 76013-1502 E-mail: bewright2@earthlink.net.

WRIGHT, JAMES EDWARD, secondary school educator; s. James Edward Wright and Artela Thomas Sapp. BS in Music Edn., Fla. A&M U., 1999. Cert. tchr. Fla., 2001. Tchr., dir. bands Blanche Ely H.S., Pompano Beach, Fla., 1999—; min., tchr. Bible Teacher's Internat., Ft. Lauderdale, 2000—. Mem.: Phi Mu Alpha Sinfonia. Office: Blanche Ely High Sch 1201 NE 6th Ave Pompano Beach FL 33060

WRIGHT, JAMES SYLVESTER, state agency administrator, writer; b. Dorsey, Md., Oct. 30, 1948; s. James Sylvester Wright, Estelle Wright Thomas, Barbara Jean Wright (Stepmother), Francis Thomas (Stepfather); m. Jacqueline Brogdon Brogdon; children: Alan. AA, Anne Arundel C.C., 1975. Unit mgr. Md. Dept. Pub. Safety, Balt., 1972—. Author: American Apartheid, 1997. Corp. U.S. Army, 1968—74, Camp Lejune. Mem.: Black Writers Guild Of Md. (Events Coord. 1999—2001), Masons. Baptist. Avocation: sports. Home: P.O. Box 26664 Baltimore MD 21207 Home Fax: 410 265 9505. Personal E-mail: jswltd@hotmail.com.

WRIGHT, JANE COOKE, physician, educator, consultant; b. N.Y.C., Nov. 30, 1919; d. Louis T. and Corinne (Cooke) W.; m. David D. Jones. AB, Smith Coll., 1942; MD with honors, N.Y. Med. Coll., 1945; D in Med. Scis., Women's Med. Coll. Pa., 1965; ScD, Denison U., 1971. Intern Bellevue Hosp., N.Y.C., 1945-46, resident, 1946, mem. staff, 1955-67; resident Harlem Hosp., 1947, chief resident, 1948; clin. Cancer Rsch. Found., Harlem Hosp., 1949-52; dir., 1952-55; mem. staff Harlem Hosp., 1949-55; practice medicine specializing in clin. cancer chemotherapy N.Y.C.; mem. faculty dept. surgery Med. Ctr., N.Y. U., 1955-67, adj. assoc. prof., 1961-67, also dir. cancer chemotherapy services research, 1955-67; prof. surgery N.Y. Med. Coll., N.Y.C., 1967-87, prof. surgery emeritus, 1987—, assoc. dean, 1967-75; mem. staff Manhattan VA Hosp., 1955-67, Midtown, Met., Bird S. Color, Flower-Fifth Ave. Hosps., all N.Y.C., 1967-79, Westchester County Med. Center, Valhalla, N.Y., 1971-87, Lincoln Hosp., Bronx, 1979-87. Cons. Health Ins. Plan of Greater N.Y., 1962-94; cons. Blvd. Hosp., 1963—, St. Luke's Hosp., Newburgh, N.Y., 1964—; pelvic malignancy rev. com. N.Y. Gynecol. Soc., 1965-66, St. Vincent's Hosp., N.Y.C., 1966—, Dept. Health, Edn. and Welfare, 1968-70, Wyckoff Heights Hosp., N.Y.C., 1969—, NIH, 1971—, others; adv. bd. Skin Cancer Found. Contbr. articles to profl. jours. Mem. Manhattan coun. State Commn. Human Rights, 1949—, Pres.'s Commn. Heart Disease, Cancer and Stroke, 1964-65, Nat. Adv. Cancer Coun. NIH, 1966-70, N.Y. State Women's Coun., 1970-72; bd. dirs. Medico-CARE, Health Svcs. Improvement Fund Inc.; trustee Smith Coll., Northampton, Mass., 1970-80. Recipient numerous awards, including; Mademoiselle mag. award, 1952; Lady Year award Harriet Beecher Stowe Jr. High Sch., 1958; Spirit Achievement award Albert Einstein Sch. Medicine, 1965; certificate Honor award George Gershwin Jr. High Sch., 1967; Myrtle Wreath award Hadassah, 1967; Smith medal Smith Coll., 1968; Outstanding Am. Women award Am. Mothers Com. Inc., 1970; Golden Plate award Am. Acad. Achievement, 1971; Exceptional Black Scientists Poster Ciba Geigy, 1980 Fellow N.Y. Acad. Medicine; mem. Nat. Med. Assn. (edit. bd. jours.), Manhattan Ctrl. Med. Soc., N.Y. County Med. Soc. (nominating com.), AMA, AAAS, Am. Assn. Cancer Rsch. (dir. Rsch. Salute 1971-74), N.Y. Acad. Scis., N.Y. Cancer Soc., Internat. Med. and Rsch. Found. (v.p.), Am. Cancer Soc. (dir. div.), N.Y. Cancer Soc. (pres. 1970-71), Am. Soc. Clin. Oncology (sec. treas. 1964-67), Contin Soc., Sigma Xi, Lambda Kappa Mu, Alpha Omega Alpha. Clubs: The 400 (N.Y. Med. Coll.). Address: 7002 Kennedy Blvd East Apt 9C Guttenberg NJ 07093

WRIGHT, JANE M. small business owner, educator; b. Chicago, Ill., May 15, 1963; d. James Weatherspoon and Elizabeth Hillard; m. Donald Wright, Apr. 24, 1999. AAA, Truman Coll., Chicago, IL, 1988; BAS, Chgo. State U., Chicago, IL, 1991—95. Educator Cath. Charities, Chicago, Ill., 1988—93, Ounce of Prevention Fund, Chicago, 1994—99, Chgo. City Coll., Chicago, 1999—. Author: (book) A New Name for Jane. Entertainer African Am. Stuied Assn., Chicago, Ill., 2001. Avocations: bowling, swimming, acting. Home: 8352 South Ellis Apartment 103 Chicago IL 60619

WRIGHT, JEFFREY CYPHERS, publisher, editor; b. Wilmington, Del., Dec. 29, 1951; s. John Collins and Margaret Ann (Cyphers) W.; children: Seth Damon, Jarrett Colin. BA, W.Va. U., 1975; MFA, Bklyn. Coll., 1985. Officer mgr. Theatre Arts Books, N.Y.C., 1976-78; poet, tchr. Comprehensive Employment Tng. Act, 1980-82, Tchrs. and Writers, N.Y.C., 1983-87; tchr. Bklyn. Coll., 1983-87; pub., editor Cover Mag., N.Y.C., 1986—. Editor (poetry anthology) 30-Turning Thirty, 1986; author of poetry; works featured in N.Y. Times, ARTnews, Art and Auction Archive. Bd. mem. Poetry Project, St. Marks Ch., N.Y.C., 1980-83, Rutgers U. Gallery, New Brunswick, 1995—. Ind. Press Support grantee Coordinating Coun. of Lit. Mags., N.Y.C., 1981. Mem. Poets and Writers, Inc. Democrat. Unitarian Universalist. Office: Cover Mag 632 E 14th St Apt 18 New York NY 10009-3379 E-mail: covermag@yahoo.com.

WRIGHT, JESSE HARTZELL, psychiatrist, educator; b. Altoona, Pa., Sept. 21, 1943; s. Jesse H. and Marion (Stone) W.; m. Susanne Judy Wright, July 9, 1967; children: Andrew, Laura. BS, Juniata Coll., 1965; MD, Jefferson Med. Coll., 1969; PhD, U. Louisville, 1976. Diplomate Am. Bd. Psychiatry and Neurology, Am. Bd. Med. Examiners; lic. psychiatrist, Ky. Asst. prof. U. Louisville, 1975-79, assoc. prof., 1979-87, prof., 1987—; clin. dir. Norton Psychiat. Clinic, Louisville, 1975-83, med. dir., 1983—; chief adult psychiatry U. Louisville, 2000—; resident in psychiatry U. Mich., Ann Arbor, 1970-73. Author first multimedia computer program for psychotherapy, chpts. to books; contbr. articles to profl. jours; author: (self help book for depression) Getting Your Life Back. Fellow APA; mem. Ky. Psychiat. Assn. (sec. 1979-80, v.p. 1980-81, pres. 1982-83), Acad. Cognitive Therapy (founding pres.). Avocations: gardening, running, theater, skiing. Home: 15 Indian Hills Trl Louisville KY 40207-1532 Office: Norton Psychiat Clinic 200 E Chestnut St Louisville KY 40202-1822

WRIGHT, JO ANNE, Episcopal priest; b. Wichita, Kans., May 31, 1935; d. Everett Joseph and Agnes Josephine (Ketcham) Steinheimer; m. John Cook Wright, June 25, 1955 (div. June 1976); children: Elizabeth, Jennifer, Melanie, Kennedy Weston. AB, Oberlin Coll., 1955; MDiv, Ch. Divinity Sch. of Pacific, Berkeley, Calif., 1987. Ordained deacon Episcopal Ch., 1987, ordained priest, 1987. Pre-sch. tchr. Children's Hour Headstart, Lawrence, Kans., 1977-79; reference libr. Lawrence (Kans.) Pub. Libr., 1979-84; rector St. Luke's Episcopal Ch., Wamego, Kans., 1987-98, St. John's Episcopal Ch., Vinita, Okla., 1999—; mem. diocesan coun. Diocese of Okla., 2000—01, dean NE region, 2001—. Youth officer Diocese of Kans., Topeka, 1987-92, rural missioner, 1992-98, mem. standing com., mem. diocesan coun., 1997-98; pres. Vinita Minsterial Alliance, 2001. Writer monthly column Plenteous Harvest, 1987-92. Chair Wamego Coun. Chs., 1998, CROP walk organizer, 1988, 92, 95; tour leader Ednl. Opportunities, Israel, 1998. Roanridge grantee Episcopal Ch. U.S.A., 1995. Mem. Phi Beta Kappa. Democrat. Avocations: reading, travel. Home: 221 S Bell St Vinita OK 74301-3408 Office: St John's Episcopal Ch 522 W Canadian Ave Vinita OK 74301-3612 E-mail: jowright@junct.com.

WRIGHT, JOHN, classics educator; b. N.Y.C., Mar. 9, 1941; s. Henry and Dorothy (Chaya) W.; m. Ellen Faber, June 16, 1962; children: Jennifer, Emily. BA, Swarthmore Coll., 1962; MA, Ind. U., 1964, PhD, 1971. Instr. classics U. Rochester, 1968-72, asst. prof., 1972-75; assoc. prof. Northwestern U., Evanston, Ill., 1975-77, prof., 1977-83, John Evans prof. Latin lang. and lit., 1983-2001, chmn. dept., 1978-97, 00-01, prof. emeritus in svc., 2002—. Author: The Play of Antichrist, 1967, Dancing in Chains: The Stylistic Unity of the Comoedia Palliata, 1974, The Life of Cola de Rienzo, 1975, Essays on the Iliad: Selected Modern Criticism, 1978, Plautus: Curculio, Introduction and Notes, 1981, rev. edit., 1993, Ralph Stanley and the Clinch Mountain Boys: A Discography, 1983, The Five-String Banjo Stanley Style, 1984, rev. edit. (Clyde Pharr) Homeric Greek: A Book for Beginners, 1985, It's the Hardest Music in the World to Play: The Ralph Stanley Story in His Own Words, 1987, Traveling the High Way Home: Ralph Stanley and the World of Traditional Bluegrass Music, 1993; albums Everything She Asks For, 1993, Traveling the High Way Home, 1995, Promises, 1996, Ellen and John Wright 1, Ellen and John Wright 2, 1998; columnist: Banjo Newsletter; contbr. articles to profl. jours. Fellow Am. Acad. Rome, 1966-68; Nat. Endowment Humanities Younger humanist fellow, 1973-74; named to Honorable Order of Ky. Colonels; recipient songwriting prize Santa Fe Bluegrass and Old Time Music Festival, 1996. Mem. Am. Acad. in Rome Soc. of Fellows, Am. Philol. Assn., Ill. Classical Conf., Petronian Soc., Met. Opera Guild, Chgo. Area Bluegrass Assn., Minn. Bluegrass and Old-Time Music Assn., Internat. Bluegrass Music Assn. (Print Media Personality of Yr. 1994), BMI, Nat. Acad. Recording Arts and Scis. Clubs: Ralph Stanley Fan. Home: 1137 Noyes St Evanston IL 60201-2633 Office: Northwestern U Dept Classics Evanston IL 60208-2200 E-mail: jhwright@northwestern.edu.

WRIGHT, JOHN CHARLES, air force intelligence officer; b. Alexander City, Ala., Oct. 11, 1958; s. Bill Acton and Betty Lou (Tidwell) W.; m. Andrea Lyn Clark, July 20, 1982; children: Jennifer Diane, William Clark, Julianne Sabrina, John Charles Jr. BS in Mil. History, USAF Acad., 1982; MBA, Embry Riddle Aero. U., 1992. Student pilot 14th Flying Tng. Wing, Columbus AFB, Miss., 1982-83; chief of intelligence 4477th Test and Evaluation Squadron, Nellis AFB, Nev., 1984-86; chief operational intelligence Air

Forces Iceland, Keflavick Navl Air Sta., 1986-87; chief command briefing team Hdqs. Tactical Air Command, Langley AFB, Va., 1987-90; chief joint intelligence assignments Air Force Mil. Pers. Ctr., Randolph AFB, Tex., 1990-93; chief of intelligence 3d Composite Wing, Elmendorf AFB, Alaska, 1993-95; chief issues and analysis Hdqs. USAF, Pentagon, 1995-96, chief air force briefing team, 1996-98; chief advanced sys. U.S. Strategic Command SAC, Offutt AFB, Nebr., 1998-99, chief intelligence sys. divsn., 1999—. Author, editor: Low Altitude Threat to Tactical Air Forces, 1988, Intelligence Officer Force Plan, 1993, Deployment Requirements for Combined Wings, 1995. Scout master Boy Scouts Am., San Antonio, 1991-93, Anchorage, 1994-95, Springfield, Va., 1995-98, asst. commr., Bellevue, Nebr., 2002-. Lt. col. USAF. Mem. USAF Acad. Assn. of Grads., Autism Soc. of Am., Ret. Officers Assn. Mem. Lds Ch. Avocations: distance running, camping. Home: 2605 Ellsworth Ave Bellevue NE 68123-1776 E-mail: wrightx6@cox.net.

WRIGHT, JOHN COLLINS, retired chemistry educator; b. Oak Hill, W. Va., Aug. 5, 1927; s. John C. and Irene (Collins) W.; m. Margaret Ann Cyphers, Sept. 11, 1949; children: Jeffrey Cyphers, John Timothy, Curtis Scott, Keith Alexander. BS, W.Va. Wesleyan Coll., 1948, LLD, 1974; PhD, U. Ill., 1951; DSc (hon.), U. Ala., 1979, W.Va. Inst. Tech., 1979. Research chemist Hercules, Inc., 1951-57; mem. faculty W.Va. Wesleyan Coll., 1957-64; asst. program dir. NSF, 1964-65; dean Coll. Arts and Scis., No. Ariz. U., 1966-70, W.Va. U., Morgantown, 1970-74; vice chancellor W.Va. Bd. Regents, Charleston, 1974-78; pres. U. Ala., Huntsville, 1978-88, prof. chemistry, 1988-95, prof. emeritus, 1995—; interim pres. W.Va. Coll. Grad. Studies, Institute, 1975-76. Hon. research asso. Univ. Coll., London, Eng., 1962-63; cons. NSF, 1965— , Army Sci. Bd., U.S. Army, 1979-82. Served with USNR, 1945-46. Mich. fellow Center Study Higher Edn., U. Mich., 1965-66 Mem. AAAS, NSTA. Office: 4724 Panorama Dr SE Huntsville AL 35801-1215

WRIGHT, JOHN F. state supreme court justice; BS, U. Nebr., 1967, JD, 1970. Atty. Wright & Simmons, 1970-84, Wright, Sorensen & Brower, 1984-91; mem., coord. Commn. on Post Secondary Edn., 1991-92; judge Nebr. Ct. Appeals, 1992-94; assoc. justice Nebr. Supreme Ct., 1994—. Chmn. bd. dirs. Panhandle Legal Svcs., 1970 Mem. Scottsbluff Bd. Edn., 1980-87, pres., 1984, 86. Served with U.S. Army, 1970, Nebr. N.G., 1970-76. Recipient Friend of Edn. award Scottsbluff Edn. Assn., 1992. Office: Nebr Supreme Ct 2207 State Capitol PO Box 98910 Lincoln NE 68509-8910*

WRIGHT, JOHN RICKEN, chemist, educator; b. Batesville, Ark., Jan. 3, 1939; s. John Adam and Alice Lanelle Wright; m. Barbara Ruth Martin, Feb. 1, 1964; children: Karen Elizabeth Frings. BS, Ark. State U., Jonesboro, AR, 1960; MS, U. Miss., Oxford, MS, 1967, PhD, 1971, MS, 1967, PhD, 1971. Chemistry educator Wynne H.S., Wynne, Ark., 1960—61; commd. officer USAF, 1961—65; chemistry educator Southeastern Okla. State U., Durant, Okla., 1973—; postdoctoral rschr. U. Miss., Oxford, Miss., 1966—67, Wash. U., Saint Louis, Mo., 1967—68, Fla. State U., Fla., 2002—02. Consulting grant reviewer Nat. Institutes Health, Bethesda, Md., 1978—. Contbr. articles to profl. jours. Pres. Durant Texoma Kiwanis, Durant, Okla., 1978. Capt. USAF, 1961—65. Recipient Burlington-Northern Faculty Achievement Award, Burlington-Northern, 1988; grantee Amendment Grant Two, USAF/AF0SR, 1997, grant, NIH/NIGMS, 1996-2000, Rsch. Program Grant, NIH/RISE/SCORE, 2000-2004, Instrument grant, NIH, 1987, Continuing instl. support, NIH/MBRS, 1988-1991, USAF minigrant, USAF, 1989, Contract award, 1989, Rsch. Grant, USAF/AF0SR, 1989-1990, Grant Ext., 1991, Chemiluminescent dosimetry and structural investigations grant, 1992-1993, Polymer Characterization grant, 1993-1998. R-Consevative. Baptist. Achievements include patents for Patent 3,699,024. Avocations: private pilot, amateur astronomy, cross country hiking. Office: Southeastern Oklahoma State University 1405 North 4th Street Durant OK 74701 Office Fax: 580-745-7494. E-mail: jwright@sosu.edu.

WRIGHT, JOHN ROBERT, pathologist, educator; b. Winnipeg, Man., Can., Aug. 18, 1935; came to U.S., 1961, naturalized, 1968; s. Ross Grant and Anna Marie (Crispin) W.; m. Deanna Pauline Johnson, June 25, 1960; children—Carolyn Deanna, David John. MD with honors, U. Man., 1959. Diplomate: Am. Bd. Pathology. Intern Winnipeg Gen. Hosp., 1959-60, resident, 1960-61, Balt. City Hosp., 1961-63, Buffalo Gen. Hosp., 1963-64; teaching fellow in medicine U. Man., 1960-61; instr. in pathology, Buswell fellow SUNY-Buffalo, 1965-67, prof. pathology, chmn. dept. pathology, 1974-96, interim dean medicine, v.p. clin. affairs, 1997-98, dean medicine, 1998—2001; asst. chief pathology Balt. City Hosps. and; asst. prof. Johns Hopkins U., 1967-74; cons. Roswell Park Meml. Inst., 1975—, bd. visitors, 1981-97, interim dir., 1985-86, chmn. bd. visitors, 1987-97. Recipient Louis A. and Ruth Siegel Disting. Teaching award SUNY-Buffalo, 1977, 78, 88, Deans award SUNY, 1987. Fellow Assn. Pathology Chairs (sr., pres. 1994-96); mem. AMA, AAAS, Coll. Am. Pathologists, Am. Soc. Investigative Pathologists, Am. Soc. Clin. Pathologists, U.S. and Can. Acad. Pathology, Am. Heart Assn., Alpha Omega Alpha. Achievements include research in amyloidosis and aging. Home: 46 Wynngate Ln Williamsville NY 14221-1840 Office: 204 Farber Hall SUNY Buffalo NY 14214 E-mail: jrwright@buffalo.edu.

WRIGHT, JOSEPH ROBERT, JR. corporate executive; b. Tulsa, Sept. 24, 1938; s. Joe Robert and Ann Helen (Cech) W. BS, Colo. Sch. Mines, 1961; M.I.A., Yale U., 1964. Vice pres. Booz, Allen & Hamilton, 1965-71; dep. dir. Bur. Census, Dept. Commerce, 1971-72; dep. adminstr. Social and Econ. Statis. Adminstrn., 1972-73, acting asst. sec. econ. affairs, 1973; asst. sec. adminstr. Dept. Agr., 1973-76; pres. Citicorp Retail Inc. and Retail Consumer Services Inc., N.Y.C.; v.p. Citicorp, Inc., 1976-81; dep. sec. Dept. Commerce, Washington, 1981-82; dep. dir. Office Mgmt. and Budget, 1982-88; chmn. Pres.'s Council on Integrity and Efficiency, 1982-89; chmn. Pres.'s Coun on Mgmt. Improvement, 1984-89; dir. Office Mgmt. and Budget, 1988-89; exec. v.p., vice chmn. W.R. Grace & Co., N.Y.C., 1989-94; chmn., CEO and Dir. AmTec, Inc., New York, 1994—. Chmn. Grace Environ., Inc., 1989-94, Amtec, Inc., 1995-2000, GRC, Internat., 1997-2000; co-chmn. Baker & Taylor, 1996—; vice-chmn. Jefferson Consulting, 1998—, Tennemark Worldwide, 2000—; bd. dirs. Pan Am. Sat, Inc., AT&T Govt. Mkts., Titan Corp., Real Med, Inc., Fusion Tech., Inc., Terremark Worldwide, Baker & Taylor, Verso Tech., Bion Enviorn. Tech., Travelers, 1990-99, Harcourt Brace Janovich, 1990-92, GRC Internat., 1994-99; fed. co-chmn. Coastal Plains Regional Commn., 1981-82, Four Corners Regional Commn., 1981-82, New Eng. Regional Commn., 1981-82, Old West Regional Commn., 1981-82, Pacific N.W. Regional Commn., 1981-82, S.W. Border Regional Commn., 1981-82. Mem. Pres. Export Coun., 1989-93, adv. bd. Coun. for Excellence in Govt., 1988-96; trustee Hampton U., 1990-98. 1st lt. AUS, 1963-65. Recipient Pres.'s Citizens award and medal, 1989; named Govt. Exec. of Yr., Govt. Computer News Mag., 1988, medal disting. achievement Colo. Sch. Mines, 1985. Mem. Young Pres. Orgn. (coun. on fgn. rels.), Nat. Acad. Pub. Adminstrn. (com. for responsible fed. budget), Colo. Sch. Mines Alumni Assn., Chief Execs. Orgn., World Bus. coun., Reagan Alumni Assn., Hampton Hills Golf Club (N.Y.), Banyon Country Club (Fla.), Sky Club (N.Y.C.), N.Y. Econ. Club (N.Y.C.). Office: Terremark 36th Fl 405 Lexington Ave New York NY 10174 Address: 10 Gracie Sq # 7G New York NY 10028-8031

WRIGHT, JUDITH MARGARET, law librarian, educator, dean; b. Jackson, Tenn., Aug. 16, 1944; d. Joseph Clarence and Mary Catherine (Key) Wright; m. Mark A. Johnson, Apr. 17, 1976; children— Paul, Michael BS, U. Memphis, 1966; MA, U. Chgo., 1971; JD, DePaul U., 1980. Bar: Ill. 1980. Librarian Oceanway Sch., Jacksonville, Fla., 1966-67; program dir. ARC, South Vietnam, 1967-68; documents and reference librarian D'Angelo Law Library, U. Chgo., 1970-74, reference librarian, 1974-77, dir., lectr. in law, 1980-99, assoc. dean for libr. and info. svcs., lectr. in law, 1999—. Mem. adv. bd. Legal Reference Svcs. Quar., 1981—. Mem. ABA, Am. Assn. Law Libraries, Chgo. Assn. Law Libraries. Democrat. Methodist. Office: U Chgo Law Sch D'Angelo Law Libr 1121 E 60th St Chicago IL 60637-2745 Fax: 773-702-2889. E-mail: jm-wright@uchicago.edu.

WRIGHT, JUDITH RAE, retired accountant; b. Paoli, Ind., Feb. 16, 1929; d. Samuel Earl and Bernice Louise (Lomax) Hudelson; m. James Edward Walters, July 11, 1947 (div. June 1971); children: Jamie Jo, Jennifer Rae; m. George Ralph Wright, Feb. 20, 1972 (dec. Apr. 1977). Student, Northwood Inst., West Baden, Ind., 1968-69, Ind. U.-Purdue U., Indpls., 1972-77. Acct. Ind. Hwy. Commn., Indpls., 1969-75, Ind. Dept. Correction, Indpls., 1972-76, Ind. Dept. Pub. Welfare, Indpls., 1976-78, Ind. Office Social Svcs., Indpls., 1978-79; acct. supr. Ind. Dept. Pub. Welfare, 1979-92, ret., 1992. Mem. First Christian Ch. Recipient Gov.'s Spl. Achievement award, 1992. Mem. Assn. Govt. Accts., Am. Legion Aux., Order of Eastern Star, Kappa Kappa Kappa. Republican.

WRIGHT, KATIE HARPER, educational administrator, journalist; b. Crawfordsville, Ark., Oct. 5, 1923; d. James Hale and Connie Mary (Locke) Harper; m. Marvin Wright, Mar. 21, 1952; 1 child, Virginia K. Jordan. BA, U. Ill., 1944, MEd, 1959; EdD, St. Louis U., 1979. Elem. and spl. edn. tchr. East St. Louis (Ill.) Pub. Schs., 1944-65, dir. Dist. 189 Instrnl. Materials Program, 1965-71, dir. spl. edn. Dists. 188, 189, 1971-77, asst. supt. programs, 1977-79; interim supt. East St. Louis Sch. Dist. 189, 1993-94. Adj. faculty Harris/Stowe State Coll., 1980; mem. staff St. Louis U., 1989—; interim supt. Dist. 189 Schs., 1994—; mem. Pres.'s Commn. on Excellence in Spl. Edn. Author: Delta Sigma Theta/East St. Louis Chapter History, 1992; contbr. articles to profl. jours.; feature writer St. Louis Argus Newspaper, 1979—. Mem. Ill. Commn. on Children, 1973-85, East St. Louis Bd. Election Comms., East St. Louis Fin. Adv. Authority, 1999—; pres. bd. dirs. St. Clair County Mental Health Ctr., 1970-72, 87—; bd. dirs. River Bluff coun. Girl Scouts USA, 1979—, nat. bd. dirs., 1981-84; bd. dirs. Jackie Joyner-Kersee Youth Ctr. Found., 1991—, United Way, 1979—, Urban League, 1979—, Provident Counseling Ctr., 1995-98; pres. bd. trustees East St. Louis Pub. Libr., 1972-77; pres., bd. dirs. St. Clair County Mental Health Ctrs., 1987; mem. adv. bd. Magna Bank; charter mem. Coalition of 100 Black Women; mem. coord. coun. ethnic affairs Synod of Mid-Am., Presbyn. Ch. U.S.A.; mem. Ill. Dept. Corrections Sch. Bd., 1995—; charter mem. Metro East Links Group, Gateway chpt. The Links, Inc.; mem. Ill. Minority/Female Bus. Coun., 1991—; mem. Pres.'s Commn. on Excellence in Spl. Edn., 2001--. Recipient of more than 150 awards including Lamp of Learning award East St. Louis Jr. Wednesday Club, 1965, Outstanding Working Woman award Downtown St. Louis, Inc., 1967, Ill. State citation for ednl. document Love is Not Enough, 1974, Delta Sigma Theta citation for document Good Works, 1979, Girl Scout Thanks badge, 1982, award Nat. Coun. Negro Women, 1983, Cmty. Svc. award Met. East Bar Assn., 1983, Journalist award Sigma Gamma Rho, Spelman Coll. Alumni award, 1990, A World of Difference award, 1990, 92, Edn. award St. Louis, YWCA, 1991, SIU-E-Kimmel award, 1991, St. Clair County Mental Health award, 1992, Gateway East Met. Ministry Dr. M.L. King award, 1993, Nat. Coun. Negro Women Black Leader of Yr., 1995, Disting. Alumni award U. Ill., 1996, Pioneer award Mosque 28B, 2000, Tri Del Globe award, 2001; named Woman of Achievement, St. Louis Globe Democrat, 1974, Outstanding Adminstr. So. region III Office Edn., 1975, Woman of Yr. in Edn. St. Clair County YWCA, 1987, Nat. Top Lady of Yr., 1988, Disting. Alumnus U. Ill., 1996, Vashon H.S. Hall of Fame, 1989, Citizen Amb., South Africa, 1996, Sr. Illinoisan Hall of Fame, 1997, award United Way, 2000, Urban League Merit award, 2002, Ill. State Bd. of Edn. award, 2002. Mem. Am. Librs. Trustees Assn. (regional v.p. 1978-79, 92, nat. sec. 1979-80), Ill. Commn. on Children, Mensa, Coun. for Exceptional Children, Top Ladies of Distinction (pres. 1987-91, nat. editor 1991—, Journalism award 1992, Media award 1992), Delta Sigma Theta (chpt. pres. 1960-62, Letters award 2000), Kappa Delta Pi (pres. So. Ill. U. chpt. 1973-74), Phi Delta Kappa (Svc. Key award 1984, chpt. pres. 1984-85), Iota Phi Lambda, Phi Lambda Theta (chpt. pres. 1985-87), East St. Louis Women's Club (pres. 1973-75). Republican. Home: 733 N 40th St East Saint Louis IL 62205-2138

WRIGHT, KENNETH BROOKS, lawyer; b. Whittier, Calif., June 5, 1934; s. Albert Harold and Marian (Schwey) W.; m. Sandra Beryl Smith, June 20, 1959; children: Margo Teresa, Daniel Brooks, John Waugh. BA cum laude, Pomona Coll., 1956; JD, Stanford U., 1960. Bar: Calif. 1961, U.S. Supreme Ct. 1979. Assoc., then ptnr. Lawler, Felix & Hall, 1961-77; ptnr. Morgan, Lewis & Bockius, Los Angeles, 1978-99, counsel, 1999—. Teaching team leader Nat. Inst. Trial Advocacy, 1978-80; mem. governing com. Calif. Continuing Edn. of Bar, 1973-77, chmn., 1975-76; nat. panel arbitrators Am. Arbitration Assn., 1970—; lectr. ABA Sect. Litigation Nat. Inst., 1979-86; bd. dirs. L.A. Internat. Comml. Arbitration Ctr. Chmn. bd. editors: Am. Bar Jour, 1977-81. Pres. Pomona Coll. Alumni Assn., 1970-71; pres. parent tchr. coun. Campbell Hall Sch., 1973-74, bd. dirs., 1976—, vice chmn., 1994—; counsel Vol. League San Fernando Valley, 1979-81; chmn. sect. adminstrn. of justice Town Hall of Calif., 1970-71; sr. warden Episcopal Ch., 1973-74. Served with U.S. Army, 1956-57. Mem. ABA (dir. programs litigation sect. 1977-81, mem. con. 1982-88, mem. standing com on comm. 1978-88, chmn. 1987-88, chmn. sect. book pub. com. 1986-89, pres. fellows young lawyers 1985-86, bd. dirs. 1980-89), Internat. Bar Assn., Assn. Bus. Trial Lawyers (chair com. alt. dispute resolution 1991-93, bd. dirs. 1993-96), Am. Law Inst., Am. Bar Found., State Bar Calif. (mem. gov. com. continuing edn. of the bar 1972-77, chmn. 1975-76), Conf. Barristers (exec. com. 1966-69, 1st v.p. 1969), L.A. County Bar Assn. (com. on judiciary 1981-83, chmn. continuing legal edn. adv. com. 1989-91, vice-chmn. continuing legal edn. com. 1991-93, bd. dirs. L.A. Lawyers 1989-94), L.A. County Bar Found. (bd. dirs., trustee 1993-99, mem. exec. com. internat. sect. 1996-99), U.S. Supreme Ct. Hist. Soc., Jonathan Club, Chancery Club, Phi Beta Kappa. Republican. Avocations: skiing, tennis. Home: 3610 Longridge Ave Sherman Oaks CA 91423-4918 Office: Morgan Lewis & Bockius 300 S Grand Ave Los Angeles CA 90071-3109

WRIGHT, KIRBY MICHAEL, writer, editor; b. Honolulu, Sept. 1, 1955; s. Harold Stanley and June Gertrude (McCormack) W.; m. Darcy Laureen Mobraaten, Dec. 28, 1991. BA, U. Calif., San Diego, 1983; MFA, San Francisco State U., 1994. Pub. rels. dir. Winners Circle Resorts, Carlsbad, Calif., 1987-90; instr. Palo Alto (Calif.) Adult Sch., 1994-95; writer GT Prodn. Co., Palo Alto, 1995-96, editor, 1997—. Author: The Rainbow Warrior, 1998; (screenplay) Gordon & Al, 1996; (dramatic monologue) Blue Mesa Review, 1994 (1st pl. award Browning Soc. 1993, 94); (play) Houdini, 1999, (novel) Ulua Lines, 2000. Rschr. Ctr. for Auto Safety, Washington, 1980; advisor SAT Success, Palo Alto, 1998. Recipient Poetry prize Ann Fields Trust, San Francisco, 1993, 1st pl. Poets award Acad. Am. Poets, San Francisco, 1993. Fellow Arts Coun. Santa Clara County, Arts Coun. Silicon Valley. Democrat. Roman Catholic. Avocations: boxing, surfing, gourmet cooking. Office: GT Prodn Co 3259 Alma St Palo Alto CA 94306-2925 Home: 740 McGavran Terrace Vista CA 92083 E-mail: kirby33@earthlink.net.

WRIGHT, LINDA ELLEN, nursing educator; b. Elmira, N.Y., Mar. 4, 1943; d. Marcus Alton and Helen Marie (Eaton) Wright. Diploma, Arnot-Ogden Meml. Hosp., 1964; BSN, Alfred U., 1987; MS, Syracuse U., 1990. Staff med.-surg. nurse Arnot-Ogden Meml. Hosp., Elmira, 1964-67, charge nurse, 1967-72, charge nurse NICU, 1972-76, asst. ob.-gyn. coord., 1976-78, asst. instr. Sch. Nursing, 1978-87, instr., 1987—, asst. dir. Sch. Nursing, dir. faculty and student affairs. Exch. nurse Rainbow Babies and Children's Hosp., Univ. Hosp., Cleve., 1971; vis. nurse Med. Coll. Va., Richmond. Supporter, vol. Children's Miracle Network. Mem.: AAUW, NOW, Am. Cancer Soc. (edn. com.), Oncology Nursing Soc. (cons.), N.Y. State Nurses Assn., Assn. Women's Health, Obstetrics and Neonatal Nurses, World Wildlife Fund, Nat. Parks and Conservation Assn., Ctr. Marine Conservation, Nature Conservancy, Wilderness Soc., Colonial Dames XVII Century, Sigma Theta Tau. Presbyterian. Home: 915 Lincoln St Elmira NY 14901-1806 Office: Arnot Ogden Med Ctr Grove St Elmira NY 14905 E-mail: lwright@aomc.org.

WRIGHT, LINDA JEAN, manufacturing company executive; b. Chgo., Dec. 14, 1949; d. Eugene F. and Rosemary Margaret (Kiley) Kemph; m. Kelly W. Wright, Jr., Feb. 1979 (div. 1984); m. Samuel Neuwirth Klewans, Aug. 28, 1986 (div. 1991). Student, Loretto Heights Coll., 1967-69, U. Ill., 1970-71. Asst. to v.p. Busey 1st Nat. Bank, Urbana, Ill., 1969-72; spa mgr., supr. sales tng. Venus and Apollo Health Club, San Antonio, 1973-76; owner Plant Shop, 1976-77; with Enterprise Bank, Falls Church, Va., 1977-84, comml. lending officer, 1978-84, sr. v.p., 1979-84, corp. sec. of bd. dirs., 1980-84; pes., CEO Fairfax Savs. Bank, 1984-87, Bankstar, N.A. (formerly Bank 2000 of Reston, N.A.), 1988-90; v.p. Ryan-McGinn Inc., Arlington, Va., 1991-95, Bethlehem Corp., 1995—. Bd. dirs. INOVA Inst. Rsch. and Edn., 1990-94. Apptd. pub. ofcl., chmn. Va. Small Bus. Fin. Authority, Richmond, 1984-88; trustee Inova Health System, 1992-95; mem. exec. com. Fairfax-Falls Church United Way, United Way Capital Area, Washington, 1984-85; mem. Fairfax County Spl. Task Force, 1986; bd. dirs. Fairfax Com. of 100, 1993095; mem., bd. dirs. Hospice No. Va., Arlington, 1985-86, chmn. No. Va. Local Devel. Corp., 1986; mem. ops. bd. Fairfax Hosp., 1987-94; pres. No. Va. Transp. Alliance, 1987-92; bd. dirs. Va. Found. for Rsch. and Econ. Edn., 1989-91, No. Va. coun. Am. Heart Assn., 1989-94. Mem. Fairfax County C. of C. (dir., v.p., pres. 1987-88), Nat. Assn. Bank Women (chmn. No. Va. group 1980-81), Fairfax Hunt Club, Tower Club (bd. govs. 1989-95). Roman Catholic. Avocations: aviation, fox hunting.

WRIGHT, MAE A. engineering, communications and nuclear waste management specialist; b. Northampton, Mass., Nov. 14, 1956; d. Lawrence Shepard and Caroline Mary (La Rose) W. BSME, Worcester Poly. Inst., 1980. Assoc. engr. nuclear safety Westinghouse Electric Corp., Monroeville, Pa., 1978-80, engr. nuclear safety, 1980, shift tech. advisor Salem nuclear plant, 1980-81, engr. info. program, 1981-84, sr. engr. info. program, 1984, mgr. info. program, 1984-86, mgr. bus. rels., 1987-88; mgr. community rels. West Valley (N.Y.) Demonstration Project, 1988-90, mgr. community rels. and total quality, 1990-91, mgr. ops. support, 1991-97, mgr. waste mgmt., 1997-2000; owner The Wright Group Strategic Comm. Specialists, 2000—. Spkr. Campus Am., 1979-81; pres. bd. dirs. Energy Source Edn. Coun., Washington, 1988-90; mgmt. com. Electric Info. Coun., N.D. Mem. Project Mgmt. Inst. (cert.). E-mail: wrightgroup@hotmail.com..

WRIGHT, MALCOLM STURTEVANT, nuclear facility manager, retired career officer; b. Orange, N.J., Sept. 2, 1941; s. Malcolm Everett and Margaret Sommer (Kohler) W.; m. Barbara Jean Larsen, June 5, 1963 (div. Aug., 1988); children: Tracy Ann, Karen Elizabeth; m. Lya Hanfri Baughman, Nov. 5, 1988; children: Zachary Seth, Sara Ann. BS in Engring., U.S. Naval Acad., 1963; MA in Polit. Sci., Villanova U., 1974. Commd. ensign USN, 1963, advanced through grades to capt., 1983, retired, 1993; dir. tactical tng. dept. US Naval Submarine Sch., Groton, Conn., 1982-84; commanding officer USS Alabama, Silverdale, Wash., 1984-87; planner polit.-mil. strategy Staff of Chmn. Joint Chiefs of Staff, Pentagon, Washington, 1987-90; comdr. Submarine Squadron Seventeen, Silverdale, Wash., 1990-92; chief of staff to comdr. Naval Base Seattle, 1992-93; mgr. waste and decontamination plant Westinghouse Hanford Co., Richland, Wash., 1993-96; mgr. 324/327 facility stabilization project Babcock and Wilcox Hanford Co., 1996-99; dir. 324 bldg. deactiviation project Fluor Hanford Co., 1999—. Tech. advisor Disney Studios, Burbank, Calif., 1994-95. Vol. ARC, East Orange, N.J., 1957-59. Decorated Legion of Merit, USN, 1982, 86, 92, 93, Meritorious Svc. medal 1984, Defense Superior Svc. medal, 1990. Mem. U.S. Naval Inst., U.S. Naval Submarine League, U.S. Naval Acad. Alumni Assn. Republican. Presbyterian. Avocations: military history, civil war, Scottish culture, golf. Home: 3512 W 30th Ave Kennewick WA 99337-2500 Office: Flour Hanford Inc PO Box 1000 Richland WA 99352-1000

WRIGHT, MARGARET TAYLOR, marketing consultant, publisher; b. Wilmington, N.C., Nov. 8, 1949; d. Thomas Henry and Margaret (Taylor) W. BA, U. N.C., 1972; MBA, Wake Forest U., 1978. Child advocacy specialist Child Advocacy Council Dept. Human Resources, Raleigh, N.C., 1973-74; region dir. N.C. Office for Children Dept. Human Resources, Winston-Salem, 1974-76; product mgr. food div. Am. Home Products, N.Y.C., 1978-80; account exec. Ted Bates Advt., 1981; product mgr. C.F. Mueller div. McKesson, Inc., Jersey City, 1981-83; mgr. new products Popsicle div. Sara Lee Corp., Englewood, N.J., 1983-86; pres. Wright Mktg. Blueprint, Old Chatham, N.Y., 1987—; chmn. Equatorial Group, Ltd., 1994—; pub. Grey Play Round Table Mag. on African Grey Parrots, 1994—. Pub. web pages www.Africangreys.com and www.Africanature.com Author: African Grey Parrots, A Complete Owner's Manual, 2001; co-author: (pamphlets) Children--Helping Them Grow, 1973; pub.: Grey Play Round Table mag., 1994—. Youth coord. Jim Holshouser Gubernatorial Campaign, New Hanover County, N.C., 1972; mem. Jr. League, N.Y. and N.C., 1972-84. Episcopalian. Avocations: tennis, sailing, golf, traveling. Office: Wright Mktg Blueprint PO Box 190 Old Chatham NY 12136-0190 E-mail: maggie@africangreys.com.

WRIGHT, MARIE ANNE, management information systems educator; b. Albany, N.Y., Oct. 21, 1953; d. Arthur Irving and Ethel (Knickerbocker) W. BS, U. Mass., Boston, 1981; MBA, Clarkson U., 1984; PhD, U. Mass., Amherst, 1989. Grad. asst. Clarkson U., Potsdam, N.Y., 1982; sys. analyst St. Lawrence U., Canton, 1983-84; instr. Bentley Coll., Waltham, Mass., 1984-85; tchg. asst. U. Mass., 1985, rsch. asst., 1986; computer cons. Amherst (Mass.) Police Dept., 1986-88; asst. prof. Elms Coll., Chicopee, Mass., 1986-89; assoc. prof. Western Conn. State U., Danbury, Conn., 1990—2002, prof., 2002—. Cons. Ctr. for Human Devel., Springfield, Mass., 1986-87, Early Childhood Ctr., 1986-87. Contbr. articles to profl. jours. and mags. Recipient MIS award U. Mass., 1981. Mem. AAUW, IEEE, Assn. Computing Machinery, Internat. Computer Security Assn., Info. Sys. Security Assn,. Computer Security Inst., Beta Gamma Sigma. Democrat. Avocations: cross-country skiing, swimming, reading. Office: Western Conn State U MIS Dept Danbury CT 06810

WRIGHT, MARIE BEULAH BATTEY, retired advertising executive; b. Cordell, Okla., Jan. 12, 1917; d. John William and Mary (Yoder) Battey; m. Joseph Barney Gifford, Sept. 3, 1948 (dec. 1960); m. Harold Arthur Wright, May 18, 1979. BFA, U. Okla., 1937; posTgrad., Oklahoma City Symphony, 1939—40; postgrad., Baylor U., 1943-44. Host 15-minute daily piano show U. Okla. Radio Sta., 1935; supt. music Woodward (Okla.) Pub. Schs., 1937-38; sales and promotion mgr. KOME, Tulsa, 1940-43; instr. Sch. Radio Baylor U., Waco, Tex., 1943-45; asst. program mgr. KWKH, Shreveport, La., 1945-47; salesman KTBS Radio, Shveveport, 1947-55; comml. mgr. KTBS-TV, 1955-57, KEEL Radio, Shveveport, 1957-62, v.p., gen. mgr., 1963-75; v.p. Lin Broadcasting, Shreveport, 1963-75; gen. mgr. KEEL/AM and KMBO/FM, 1968-80; v.p. Multimedia Broadcasting, 1975-80. Freelance mus. in arrangements Okla. City radio stas., 1938-39; editl. writer radio stas.; author: The Killing of the Presidency, 1974 (RTNDA Best Editl. 1973). Mem. publicity com. United Fund, 1955-62, exec. com. Shreveport Symphony, 1976-82, Strand Theatre of Shreveport Corp., 1977-94; bd. dirs. Downtown Devel. Corp., 1975-81; La. rep. So. Growth Policies Bd., 1985-96; mem. La. State Arts Coun., 1992-96; bd dirs. Caddo-Bossier Cmty. Action, 1969-71; mem. housing com. Caddo Parish, Shreveport, 1969; mem. City Charter Com., Shreveport, 1970; bd. dirs. Amb. Club, Shreveport, 1971-74; bd. dirs. David Raines Assn., Shreveport, 1969; mem. Com. of 500 March of Dimes, Shreveport, 1969; exec. asst. Shreveport Summer Theatre, 1950-60. Named Broadcaster of Yr., La. Assn. Broadcasters, Shreveport, 1970, Women Who Have Made a Diffence, YWCA, Shreveport, 1988; recipient Humanitarian award Shreveport Negro C. of C., 1969, Humanitarian award for outstanding contbn. to the arts, 1995. Mem. Shreveport C. of C. (bd. dirs. 1968-71, 1st woman mem.). Democrat. Avocations: theatre, symphony, reading, politics. Home: 701 Livingston Ave Shreveport LA 71107-3914

WRIGHT, MARSHALL, retired manufacturing executive, former diplomat; b. El Dorado, Ark., July 14, 1926; s. John Harvey and Helen Vaughan (Williams) W.; m. Mable Olean Johnson, Sept. 12, 1950 (dec. June 1989); children: William Marshall, Jefferson Vaughan; m. Lind Groseclose Vaughan, Mar. 31, 1990. Student, U. Ark., 1946-48, Cornell U., 1957-58; BS in Fgn. Service, Georgetown U., 1951. Joined U.S. Fgn. Service, 1953; vice consul Egypt, 1953-55; adminstrv. officer Can., 1955-56; econ. officer Burma, 1958-60; polit. officer Thailand, 1966-67; spokesman for State Dept., 1964-66; country dir. for Philippines, 1969; sr. mem. NSC, 1967-68, dir. long range planning, 1970-72; asst. sec. state for congl. relations, 1972-74; sr. fellow Nat. War Coll., 1969-70; v.p. govt. affairs Eaton Corp., 1974-76, v.p. pub. affairs, 1976-80, v.p. corp. affairs, 1980-91. Chmn. Cleve. ARC; trustee Cleve. Orch., Cleve. Inst. Music; chmn. Cleve. Com. Fgn. Rels.; vice chmn. Govtl. Rsch. Inst.; mem. Conf. Bd. Pub. Affairs Rsch. Coun., MAPI, Pub. Affairs Coun.; bd. dirs. Cleveland Town Hall, Bus. Industry Polit. action Com. With USMC, 1944-46. Recipient Meritorious Service award State Dept., 1966, Distinguished Service award, 1972 Mem. Am. Fgn. Svc. Assn., Met. Club, Dacor, Mayfield Country, Union, Moss Creek Golf Club, Berkeley Hall Golf Club. Home: 304 Corning Dr Cleveland OH 44108-1014 also: Moss Creek Plantation 80 Toppin Dr Hilton Head Island SC 29926-1025

WRIGHT, MARY E. (MARY E. GUEN), clinical psychologist; b. Rochester, Minn., Jan. 3, 1951; d. Robert George and Rosemarie Celine (Nowicki) Tompkins; m. Scotty Kane Wright, Mar. 17, 1977 (div. May 1984); children: Drew Robert, Rosemary Elizabeth. BA, U. South Ala., 1985; MA, U. Mo., 1989, PhD, 1993. Lic. psychologist, Calif., Ark. Family therapist Boone County Juvenile Ct. Svcs., Columbia, Mo., 1986—87; psychology extern, adolescent dept. Charter Hosp. of Columbia, 1987; psychology clk. Psychology Clinic, 1987—88, Mid-Mo. Mental Health Ctr., Columbia, 1988—89, Biggs Forensic Ctr./Fulton (Mo.) State Hosp. Sex Offender Program, 1989—90; psychology intern Atascadero (Calif) State Hosp., 1990—91; psychologist, program coord., team leader Fulton State Forensic Hosp. Sex Offender Program, 1991—93; primary therapist coord. Boone County Juvenile Sex Offender Project, Columbia, 1992—93; staff psychologist Atascadero State Hosp., 1993—96; staff adolescent psychologist team leader Wyo. State Hosp., Evanston, 1996—97, forensic psychologist, forensic examiner, 1996—98, core faculty psychologist, 1998—99; clin. psychologist, dir. psychol. svcs. Cornerstone Med. Group, Van Buren, Ark., 1999—2000; pvt. practice Ft. Smith, 1999—. Author publs.; presenter in field. Mem. Crawford County Child Sexual Abuse Task Force, 1999—. Recipient awrds and grants. Mem. APA, Nat. Alliance for Mentally Ill, Ark. Psychol. Assn., Children and Adults with Attention Deficit. Democrat. Roman Catholic. Avocations: horticulture, books, historic preservation, human rights, outdoors. Home: 623 N 5th St Fort Smith AR 72901-1439 E-mail: cheekypin@hotmail.com.

WRIGHT, MARY JAMES, senior education consultant; b. Charlottesville, Va., Aug. 20, 1946; d. Harry Beech and Virginia Allen (Root) James; m. Paul Sims Wright, July 26, 1969; children: Christopher Brennan, Keith Allen. BA summa cum laude, Mary Washington Coll., 1968; MA, Northwestern U., 1969. Instr. drama and speech Mary Washington Coll., Fredericksburg, Va., 1969-71, Charles County Community Coll., La Plata, Md., 1973-79; arts and media coord. Charles County Arts Coun., 1973-82, Gen. Smallwood Mid. Sch., Indian Head, Md., 1980-82, No. Va. Community Coll., Annandale, 1982-84; computer-based learning specialist USDA Grad. Sch., Washington, 1984-85, U.S. Army Engr. Sch., Ft. Belvoir, Va., 1985-87, Battelle Meml. Inst., Columbus, Ohio, 1987-88; videodisc designer Kendrick & Co., Washington, 1988-90; instrnl. design mgr. The Discovery Channel, Bethesda, Md., 1990-93; instnl. design mgr., writer Edunetics Corp., Arlington, Va., 1994-97. Project mgr., instl. designer Toby Levine Comms., Inc., 1990-97; mng. editor Time-Life Edn., Alexandria, Va., 1997-99, sr. edn. cons. ThinkNet, 1999—. Author, dir.: Story-Theatre for Children, 1979; contbr. articles to profl. jours.; pub. children's books, videos, videodiscs, CD-ROMS, Web sites, multimedia kits and classroom guides for Time Life, PBS, Discovery Channel, Nat. Geographic Soc., Edunetics/Steck Vaughn. Pres. Am. Christian Television System of No. Va., Action for Women, Charles County AAUW; sign lang. interpreter Deaf Ministry; ministry vol. Sports and Rec Plus. Nat. Danforth fellow 1969; recipient Achievement award Dept. of Army, 1986, Kendrick & Co., 1989; recipient Outstanding Arts Programming award Md. Dept. Parks and Recreation, 1980, Silver and Bronze Cindy awards (Cinema in Industry and Edn.), 1992, Red Ribbon Am. Film & Video Assn. Festival, Special Gold Jury award Houston Internat. Film Festival, 1992, Gold award Nebr. Interactive Media, 1993, award for Excellence, Time Life, Inc., 1999. Mem. Internat. Interactive Courseware Soc. (Mark of Excellence award 1992), Assn. for Devel. Computer-Based Instrn. Systems (coord. spl. interest groups D.C. chpt. 1989-90), Mortar Bd., Alpha Psi Omega, Alpha Phi Sigma. Home and Office: 4302 Rolling Stone Way Alexandria VA 22306-1225 E-mail: wrightl1mj@aol.com.

WRIGHT, MARY POWERS, counselor; b. N.C. AAS with honors, Ctrl. Carolina C.C., Sanford, N.C., 1992; BAS, Campbell U., Buies Creek, N.C., 1994; MA, Campbell U., 1999. Dep. clk. of ct. Adminstrv. Office of the Cts., Raleigh, N.C., 1978-83; computer lab. asst., news reporter Campbell U., 1992-94, asst. to curriculum materials coord., 1994-95; tutorial coord. Ctrl. Carolina C.C., 1995-96; data entry staff N.C. Dept. Environ. Health, Raleigh, 1997; counseling intern North Harnett Elem. Sch., Angier, N.C., 1997-98. Interviewer, counselor Employment Security Commn., 1998-2000; admissions counselor Campbell U., 2000—. Mem. Cape Fear Friends of the Fine Arts, Buies Creek, 1996—. Mem. Omicron Delta Kappa, Delta Kappa Pi. Democrat. Baptist. Avocations: reading, singing, horseback riding, photography, computers. Home: PO Box 234 Buies Creek NC 27506-0234

WRIGHT, MARY ROSE, parks and recreation director; b. Hartford, Conn., Jan. 12, 1949; d. J. William and Eileen J. (Walsh) Bigoness; m. Roy C. Gunter III, June 24, 1972 (div. Feb. 1988); m. Kenneth Ross Wright, Dec. 1, 1988. BA, Marquette U., 1970; MS, U. Mo., 1972. Prgram analyst State Calif. Dept. Health, Sacramento, 1972-76; tng. ctr. dir. State Calif. Dept. Parks and Recreation, Pacific Grove, 1976-81, visitor svcs. mgr. Monterey, 1981-83, Monterey dist. supr., 1983-92, dep. dir., 1992-93; Monterey dist. supt. Calif. Dept. Parks and Recreation, 1993-99, chief dep. dir., 1999—. Hist. preservation commr. City of Monterey, 1984-92. Bd. dirs. Big Sur Health Ctr., 1993—; bd. govs. Santa Lucia Conservancy, 1995-99. Office: Calif Dept Parks and Recreation Chief Dep Dir 1416 9th St Rm 1405 Sacramento CA 95814-5511

WRIGHT, MATTIE PEARL, civic worker; b. St. Petersburg, Sept. 22, 1938; d. Willie and Mattie Watkins; m. Ernest Rayfield Wright, July 26, 1958; children: Patricia, Vincent, Kimberly. Student, St. Petersburg Jr. Coll., 1986, Lakewood C.C., St. Petersburg, 1993, U. South Fla., 1995. Tchr. pvt. sch., 1986-90. Owner, mgr. 17 house rental properties. Contbr. poems to anthologies. Coord. Crime Watch, South St. Petersburg, 1984—; pres. Neighborhood Assn., South St. Petersburg, 1985—; vol. Pinellas County Sch. Sys., Exch. Ctr. for Prevention Child Abuse, North St. Pe6ersburg, 1995—. Republican. Baptist. Home: 3634 2nd Ave S Saint Petersburg FL 33711-1312

WRIGHT, MAX, information processing executive, consultant, youth leadership corporate training executive; b. Windsor, England, June 14, 1954; came to the U.S., 1989; s. Harold Edwin and Sheila Doreen (Young) W.; 2 children: Robyn, Devan Lucien. Electronics tech. Electricity Supply Commn., Germiston, South Africa, 1972-74, R. Muller, Johannesburg, South Africa, 1974-75; svc. mgr., sr. technician OKTV, George, South Africa, 1975-77; field engr. Burroughs Machines, Johannesburg, 1978-79; systems analyst Sidha Assocs. (Pty.) Ltd., 1980-84, mng. dir., 1984-88; v.p. Arisoft, Inc., Fairfield, Iowa, 1989-97, pres., 1997—, DogMatch, Inc. Pres. DogMatch, Inc., 2000—. Contbr. articles to profl. jours. Tchr. Transcendental meditation, 1979—; treas. South African Assn. Age of Enlightenment, 1980-87; founder, pres. Life Force, Inc., 1994—. Winner 2001 ComputerWorld/Smithsonian Honors Program Laureate. Mem. T'ai Chi Assn. South Africa, Fairfield T'ai Chi Assn. (founding instr. and dir. 1992—). Avocations: Transcendental meditation, T'ai Chi Ch'uan, peaceful warrior training. E-mail: arisoft@compuserve.com.

WRIGHT, MICHELLE MARIA, English language educator; b. Oct. 31, 1968; BA, Oberlin Coll., 1992; MA, U. Mich., 1995, PhD, 1997. McCandless prof. English, Carnegie Mellon U., Pitts., 1997-2000. Thomas E. Critchett vis. asst. prof. English, Macalester Coll., 2000-01; mem. editl. bd. Collegiate Press, San Diego, 1998—; asst. prof. English, Macalester Coll., 2001—. Book rev. editor: Callaloo Journal Postcolonial Studies, 1999—. Apnelist Metro. Regional Arts Council, Minn. Recipient Mellon fellow Social Scis. and Rsch. Coun., 1991-97, Rackham Merit fellow, 1992-96, Rackham Predoctoral fellow, 1996-97. Mem. Phi Kappa Phi. Office: Macalester Coll 200 Old Main/1600 Grand Ave Saint Paul MN 55105 E-mail: mmwright@andrew.cmu.edu.

WRIGHT, MINTURN TATUM, III, lawyer; b. Phila., Aug. 7, 1925; s. Minturn T. and Anna (Moss) W.; m. Nonya R. Stevens, May 11, 1957; children: Minturn T., Richard S., Robert M., Marianne F. BA, Yale U., 1949; LLB, U. Pa., 1952. Bar: Pa. 1953, U.S. Ct. Appeals (3d cir.) 1953, U.S. Supreme Ct. 1962. Law clk. U.S. Ct. Appeals (3d cir.), 1952-53; assoc. Dechert, Price & Rhoads, Phila., 1953-61, ptnr., 1961-95, chmn., 1982-84. Bd. dirs. Cotiga Devel. Co.; vis. prof. U. Pa. Law Sch., 1965—69, 1993—97. Contbr. articles to profl. jours. Trustee Acad. Natural Scis. Phila., 1958—, chmn., 1976-81; trustee Hawk Mountain Sanctuary Assn., chmn. bd. dirs., 1992-97; trustee Rare Ctr., Pa. chpt. The Nature Conservancy, Exec. Svc. Corps.; trustee Marshall-Reynolds Found. Served with U.S. Army, 1943-46. Mem. ABA, Pa. Bar Assn., Phila. Bar Assn., Nat. Coal Lawyers Assn., Eastern Mineral Law Assn. (trustee), Phila. Club, Milldam Club. Episcopalian. Office: Dechert Price & Rhoads 4000 Bell Atlantic Tower 1717 Arch St Ste 4000 Philadelphia PA 19103-2793

WRIGHT, MURIEL DEASON See WELLS, KITTY

WRIGHT, NANCY HOWELL, interior designer; b. Sept. 6, 1932; d. David Austin and Catherine Howell; m. Hastings Kemper Wright, June 19, 1954; children: Mark, Barbara; children: Kenneth, Donald. BFA, Ohio Wesleyan U.; student, Parsons Sch. Design, 1977. Interior decorator Country Manor of Branford (Conn.), 1971-75; design mgr., 1976-97; pres., owner Nancy Wright Interiors, 1997—. Sec. Branford Art League, 1977; chmn. Harrison House Hist. House, Branford, Conn., 1983-84; mem. Rep Town Com., Branford, 1990-92; recording sec. Branford Garden Club, 1991—. Mem. Am. Soc. Interior Designers (award for best Conn. retail store design, 1980, Conn. Coalition), Branford Garden Club (rec. sec. 1990-94, membership chmn. 1995, v.p. 1997-99, pres. 1999-2000), Delta Phi Delta. Republican. Episcopalian. Home and Office: 35 Wood Rd Branford CT 06405-4935

WRIGHT, NANCY MEANS, author, educator; b. Glen Ridge, N.J. d. Robert Thomas and Jessie Washington (Thomson) Means; m. Spencer V. Wright (div. June 1990); children: Gary, Lesley, Donald, Catharine; m. Dennis J. Hannan, Aug. 30, 1992. AB, Vassar Coll.; MA, Middlebury Coll., 1965. Head French dept. Proctor Acad., Andover, N.H., 1960-70; owner, mgr. Cornwall (Vt.) Crafts, 1971-86; scholar Vt. Coun. on Humanities, Hyde Park, Vt., 1985—, Vt. Ctr. for the Book, Chester, 1985-92. Adj. prof. Burlington (Vt.) Coll., 1986-90, C.C. of Vt., Middlebury, 1984-90; adj. lectr. Marist Coll., Poughkeepsie, N.Y., 1990-98; mem. faculty in fiction Writer's Digest Sch., Cin., 1991-2001, N.E. Young Writers Conf., 1986-90, 97—. Author: The Losing, 1973, Down the Strings, 1982, Make Your Own Change, 1985, Vermonters at Their Craft, 1988, Mad Season, 1996, Harvest of Bones, 1998, Poison Apples, 2000, Stolen Honey, 2002, Fire and Ice, 2002, (poems) Split Nipple, 1992, Walking up into the Volcano, 2000. Scholar Bread Loaf Writer's Conf., Vt., 1959. Mem.: Author's Guild, Soc. Children's Book Writers (grantee 1988), League Vt. Writers (pres. 1976—80), Unitarian-Universalist Assn. Democrat. Avocations: theater, singing, travel, gardening, cross-country skiing. E-mail: nancyden@shoreham.net.

WRIGHT, NANNIE BELL, retired secondary school educator; b. Laing, W.Va., May 7, 1934; d. Samuel Thomas and Edna (Irving) W. BS in Edn. magna cum laude, W.Va. State Coll., 1956; MA, U. Chgo., 1960; postgrad., NYU, 1966, L.I. U., 1990. Tchr. social studies, math., and English Wiley H. Bates Jr. H.S., Annapolis, Md., 1956-63; English tchr. Copiague (N.Y.) Jr. H.S., 1963—95. Resource tchr. Copiague Jr. High Sch., 1970-75. Chmn. edn. com. AAUW, Annapolis, 1960; pres. women' s aux. Crownsville Hosp., 1960—61. Mem.: NAACP (v.p.Long Island br. 1992—), Nat. Coun. English Tchrs., Inst.Gen. Semantics, Noetic Scis., U. Chgo. Alumni Assn., Copiague Retired Tchrs. Assn., Delta Sigma Theta (v.p. Annapolis alumnae chpt. 1961), Pi Lambda Theta, Alpha Kappa Mu. Republican. Roman Catholic. Avocations: reading, traveling, energy healing, writing poetry, attending plays and concerts. Home: 27 Wellington Pl Amityville NY 11701-3030 E-mail: nanbwlucky@aol.com.

WRIGHT, NORMAN ALBERT, JR. middle school educator; b. Suffern, N.Y., July 21, 1948; s. Norman A. and Eleanor (Schultz) W.; 1 child, Kami Renee. BA, Pace U., Pleasantville, N.Y., 1970; MA, William Paterson Coll., Wayne, N.J., 1974. Tchr. 6th grade Nanuet (N.Y.) Pub. Schs., 1970-77; tchr. 5th grade Alpine (N.J.) Pub. Schs., 1977-78; tchr. 6th grade Englewood Cliffs (N.J.) Pub. Schs., 1978-79; tchr. 5th grade Woodcliff Lake (N.J.) Pub. Schs., 1979-80, tchr. middle sch. math., 1980-82, tchr. middle sch. sci., 1982—. Mem. profl. devel. com. Woodcliff Lake Pub. Schs., 1988-90, co-chair, 1990-2000, mem. supts. curriculum coord. com., 1988-2000, dist. and regional sci. articulation team, 1988—, chmn. dist. sci. team, 1994-2000, mid. sch. program devel. com., 1990—; clin. faculty Montclair State U., 1998—. Judge Seiko Challenge Nat. Sci. Competition, Our Lady of Mercy Sch. Sci. Fair; mem. Woodcliff Lake PTA. Mem. NEA, ASCD, NSTA, Nat. Mid. Level Sci. Tchrs. Assn., Nat. Coun. Tchrs. Math., Nat. Coun. Tchrs. English, Am. Mus. Natural History, Nat. Geog. Soc., N.J. Edn. Assn., N.J. Sci. Tchrs. Assn. (conf. presenter) N.J. Marine Edn. Assn., N.J. Earth Sci. Tchrs. Assn., North Jersey Weather Observers, Am. Chem. Soc. (tchr. affiliate), N.J. Assn. Environ. Edn., N.J. Assn. Mid. Level Educators, Hudson Valley Orienteering, U.S. Orienteering Fedn., Woodcliff Lake Edn. Assn., N.Y. Zool. Soc., Internat. Soc. Tech. in Edn., Internat. Reading Assn., Astron. Soc. Pacific, Activities Integrating Math. and Sci. Edn. Found., N.Y. State Middle Sch. Assn., The Planetary Soc., N.Y. Acad. Scis. Avocations: walking, rowing, bicycling, photography, reading. Office: Woodcliff Sch 134 Woodcliff Ave Westwood NJ 07677-8296

WRIGHT, OLGA, artist, aesthetician; b. Mangum, Okla., Feb. 6, 1932; m. George Wayne Polly, Jr., Aug. 21, 1956. Student, N.Y. Art Students League, 1959; BS, Arts and Industries U., Kingsville, Tex., 1962. Owner Olga Wright Aesthetics, Corpus Christi, Tex., 1937—. One-woman shows include Centennial Mus., 1978. Recipient Best of Show award Dimension Show, 1977, Best Oil of Show award, 1977, 79, All Membership Show of Art Ctrs. Artfest '96. Mem. Art Ctr. Corpus Christi, Art Assn., Art Guild, Pastel Soc., South Tex. Art League, Water Color Soc. South Tex. Avocations: photography, philately, writing, botany, jewelry making. Home: 4238 Estate Dr Corpus Christi TX 78412-2429 Office: Olga Wright Aesthetics 4238 Estate Dr Corpus Christi TX 78412-2429

WRIGHT, PAMELA JEAN, administrator; b. Flint, Mich., Mar. 7, 1947; d. Richard Dardine and Mary Louise Smith; m. Arnold Freeman Wright, Dec. 11, 1972; 1 child, Jason Freeman. AA in Edn., Harford C.C., 1969; BA in Edn., Augusta Coll., 1972; MEd of Guidance Counseling, U. S.C., 1975. Employment counselor Fla. State Employment Svcs., Miami, 1975-79, area counseling supr., 1979-80; cons. Tradcom Internat., 1986-87; dir. student employment and career svcs. and One Stop Ctr. Miami-Dade C.C., 1981—. Bd. dirs. Dade Employ the Handicapped Com., 1978-80. Mem. Fla. Assn. C.C. (pres., v.p., membership chair, region V dep. dir.), Coral Gables C. of C., South Dade C. of C., Fla. Coll. Placement Assn. (bd. dirs. 1994-97). Roman Catholic. Avocations: sailing, camping, skiing, reading. Office: Miami-Dade Cmty Coll 11011 SW 104th St Rm 3105 Miami FL 33176-3393 E-mail: pwright@mdcc.edu.

WRIGHT, PETER MELDRIM, lawyer; b. Charlottesville, Va., Apr. 10, 1946; s. David McCord and Caroline Wallace (Jones) W.; m. Astrid Gabriella Mercedes Sandberg, June 4, 1972; children: David Habersham, Christian Langdon. AB, U. Ga., 1967, JD, 1972. Bar: Ga. 1972, U.S. Dist. Ct. (no. dist.) Ga. 1972. Assoc. Jones, Bird & Howell, Atlanta, 1972-77, ptnr., 1977-82, Alston & Bird, Atlanta, 1982-2001; gen. counsel Resource Healthcare of Am., Inc., 2001—. Author: A Survey of State Blue Sky Laws Applicable to Tax Exempt Bonds, 1987, Long Term Care Facilities, Chapter 7 of Health Care Corporate Law—Facilities and Transactions, 1996. Sec. Atlanta coun. Soc. Colonial Wars in Ga., 1975-88, dep. gov., 1989-91; mem. Soc. Cin. Ga., Savannah, historian, 1996—, v.p., 1998—. Mem. Ga. Bar Assn., Nat. Assn. Bond Lawyers (chmn. blue sky laws and legal investment law coms. 1982-85, bd. dirs. 1985-86), Ga. Hist. Soc. (bd. curators 1993-2000, sec. 1994-98; v.p. Atlanta chpt. 1998-2000), Oglethorpe Club (Savannah, Ga.), St. Andrew's Soc. Savannah. Home: 3502 Woodhaven Rd NW Atlanta GA 30305-1011 Office: One Breckhead Plaza Ste 900 3060 Peachtree Rd NW Atlanta GA 30305

WRIGHT, RANDOLPH EARLE, retired petroleum company executive; b. Brownsville, Tex., Dec. 22, 1920; s. William Randolph and Nelle Mae (Earle) W.; m. Elaine Marie Harris, May 9, 1943; 1 son, Randolph Earle. BS, U. Tex., 1942. With Texaco Inc., 1946-82, mgr. gas div., 1968-70, gen. mgr. producing dept., 1970-71, v.p. gas dept., 1971-82, v.p., sr. officer, 1972-80; past pres., dir. Sabine Pipe Line Co.; v.p., asst. to pres. Texaco U.S.A., 1980-82, ret., 1982; past v.p. Texaco Mineral Co. Past chmn. engring. found. adv. council U. Tex., Austin. Past mem. exec. bd. Sam Houston Area coun. Boy Scouts Am.; past bd. dirs., past pres. Jr. Achievement S.E. Tex.; past bd. dirs. Houston Symphony Soc., Tex. Research League, Houston C. of C.; past trustee U. St. Thomas, S.W. Rsch. Inst. Served with USNR, World War II.

WRIGHT, RICHARD KIRK, physicist, materials researcher, consultant; b. Portland, Oreg., May 24, 1945; s. Roscoe Kirk and Esther Agnes (Hobbs) W.; m. Judie Kay Patterson, June 9, 1969; children: Kimberlee, Jamie, Ashlee, Lindsay. BS, Ariz. State U., 1975; DSc, Eurotech. Rsch. U., Palo Alto, Calif., 1989. Engr. Motorola Semicondr., Phoenix, 1973-77, Tektronix Inc., Beaverton, Oreg., 1977-83; sr. engr. Amdahl Corp., Sunnyvale, Calif., 1983-90; mfg. engr. TAQ Comms., Santa Clara, 1990-93; cons. Loral Fairchild, Milpitas, 1993-94; sr. mem. tech. staff Infineon Techs. Corp. (formerly Siemens Microelectronics), San Jose, 1994—2001; ret., 2001; cons., 2001—. Cons. Ultra Fine Assembly Co., Fremont, 1990-2001. Author articles and procs. Served with U.S. Army, 1966-68, Germany. Mem. Am. Phys. Soc. Achievements include research in thermal fatigue in semiconductor packaging; room temperature re-crystallization of tin; Brownian motion of tin whiskers; also patents applied for in micro electronic assembly. Avocations: fishing, hunting, flying. Home: 2702 E River Rd Livingston MT 59047 E-mail: richard@wrights-stuff.com.

WRIGHT, RICHARD LEE, engineer; b. Wichita, Kans., Dec. 4, 1949; s. Junior Lee and Mary Jane (Pray) W.; m. Randi L. Fell, Sept. 12, 1969 (div. 1971); 1 child, Mark Erin; m. Beverly Ann Moore, Mar. 2, 1973; children: Richelle LeAnn, Rita Linn. Diploma, Fairview High Sch., Boulder, Colo., 1968. Drafting engr. Beech Aircraft, Boulder, 1968-69, with aircraft assembly dept., 1973-74, design engr., 1974, with Level I & II Q.C. dept., 1975-77; with Level III Q.C. dept. Wichita Brass & Aluminum Foundry, 1977-82; Level III NDT engr. Ind. Gear Works Systems Inc., Indpls., 1982—. Active Am. Legion, Oaklandon, Ind., 1986—. Served as sgt. U.S. Army, 1969-71. Mem. Am. Soc. Non-Destructive Testing, Am. Soc. Quality Control, U.S. Chess Fedn., Freelance Photographers Assn. Republican. Baptist. Avocations: photography, camping, archery. Office: IGW Systems Inc PO Box 895 Carmel IN 46082-0895

WRIGHT, RICHARD NEWPORT, III, retired civil engineer; b. Syracuse, N.Y., May 17, 1932; s. Richard Newport and Carolyn (Baker) Wright; m. Teresa Rios, Aug. 23, 1959; children: John Stannard, Carolyn Maria, Elizabeth Rebecca, Edward Newport. BCE, Syracuse U., 1953, MCE (Parcel fellow), 1955; PhD, U. Ill., 1962. Jr. engr. Pa. R.R., Phila., 1953-55; instr. civil engring. U. Ill., Urbana, 1957-62, asst. prof., 1962-65, assoc. prof., 1965-70, prof., 1970-74, adj. prof., 1974-79. Chief structures sect. Bldg. Rsch. divsn. U.S. Bur. Stds., Washington, 1971—72; dep. dir. tech. Ctr. Bldg. Tech., 1972—73, dir., 1974—91; pres. Internat. Coun. Bldg. Rsch., Studies and Documentation, 1983—86; dir. Bldg. and Fire Rsch. Lab., 1991—99; chmn. Bd. Infrastructure and Constructed Environ., 1999—2002. Contbr. articles to profl. jours. Pres. Montgomery Village Found., 1989—90, 2001—, bd. dirs., 1985—. With AUS, 1955—57. Named Fed. Engr. of the Yr., Nat. Soc. Profl. Engrs.; recipient Henry L. Michel award Industry Advancement Rsch., Civil Engring. Rsch. Found., 1999. Mem.: AAAS, ASCE (hon.; mem. tech. activities com. 2000—). Home: 20081 Doolittle St Montgomery Village MD 20886-1354 Office: Dept of Commerce Nat Inst Standards & Tech Bldg And Fire Research Labs Gaithersburg MD 20899-0001 E-mail: dickwrig@erols.com.

WRIGHT, RICHARD OSCAR, III, pathologist, educator, clinical ethicist; b. La Junta, Colo., Aug. 9, 1944; s. Richard O. Jr. and Frances R. (Curtiss) W.; m. Bernale Trout, May 31, 1969; children: Lauren Diane, Richard O. IV. BS in Biology, Midwestern State U., 1966; MS in Biology, U. Houston, 1968; DO, U. Health Sci., 1972; MA in Bioethics, Midwestern U., 2001. Cert. anatomic pathology and lab. medicine Am. Osteo. Bd. Pathology. Sr. attending pathologist Normandy Met. Hosps., St. Louis, 1977-81, Phoenix (Ariz.) Gen. Hosps., 1981-97, dir. med. edn., 1989-92, 96—; clin. asst. prof. pathology Coll. Osteo. Medicine, Western U., Pomona, Calif., 1985—; dir. labs., chmn. dept. John C. Lincoln Hosp., Deer Valley, 1997—, dir. med. edn., dir. labs. Ariz., 1997—; v.p. Osteo. Postdoctoral Tng. Inst., Kirksville, Mo., 1998—. Clin. instr. pathology Ohio U. Coll. Osteo. Medicine, Athens, 1976—77; clin. prof. pathology Kirksville Coll. Osteo. Medicine, 1985—; vis. lectr. pathology New Eng. Coll. Osteo. Medicine, Biddeford, Maine, 1989—92; clin. asst. prof. pathology Midwestern U. Ariz. Coll. Osteo. Medicine, 1997—; cons. pathologist Phoenix Indian Med. Ctr., 1992—94; adv. bd. Inter Soc. Coun. Pathology, Chgo., 1992—; sec. med. staff John C. Lincoln Hosp.-Deer Valley, 1997—99, v.p. med. staff, 2000—; dir. John C. Lincoln Health Network Bd., 2001—. Active Ariz. Rep. Party, Phoenix, Rep. Nat. Coun., Washington; precinctman Dist. 18 Maricopa County, Ariz., 1996-98, Madison Heights Precinct, 1996-98; dir. John C. Lincoln Healthcare Network, 2001—; chmn. bd. trustees Phoenix (Ariz.) Gen. Hosp., 1994-95; ex-officio, trustee, 1995-97; dir. John C. Lincoln Health Network Guild, 1997—; dir., v.p. found. adv. coun. Lincoln Health Found.-Phoenix Gen. Hosp. Osteo. Endowment Fund. Recipient Mead-Johnson award Nat. Osteo. Assn., 1975. Fellow Am. Osteo. Coll. Pathologists (disting., pres. 1989-90, bd. govs. 1984-91), Coll. Pathologists, Coll. Am. Pathologists, Am. Soc. Clin. Pathologists; mem. Ariz. Osteo. Med. Assn. (del. dist. 2 ho. of dels. 1998), Ariz. Soc. Pathologists, Century Club Alumni Assn., AAAS, Alpha Phi Omega, Rho Sigma Chi, Psi Sigma Alpha. Presbyterian. Office: Anatomic Pathology Assoc 19829 N 27th Ave Phoenix AZ 85027-4001 E-mail: rwrigh@jcl.com.

WRIGHT, RICHARD W. lawyer, law educator; b. St. Louis, Nov. 10, 1946; s. Frederick Sylvester and Marguerite Elizabeth (Payne) W.; m. Diane Elizabeth Ponti, June 15, 1968; children: Jessica Lara, Jennifer Erin, Kelsey Sera. BS with honors, Calif. Inst. Tech., 1968; JD summa cum laude, Loyola U., L.A., 1973; LLM, Harvard U., 1976. Bar: Calif. 1973. Atty.-advisor Solicitor's Office U.S. Dept. Interior, Washington, 1974-75; mem. profl. staff Office of Tech. Assessment, U.S. Congress, 1975-77; from asst. prof. to assoc. prof. law Benjamin N. Cardozo Sch. Law, Yeshiva U., N.Y.C., 1977-85; assoc. prof. law Chgo.-Kent Coll. Law, Ill. Inst. Tech., 1985-89, prof. law, 1990—; Leroy Jeffers Centennial vis. prof. law U. Tex., Austin, 1989-90. Vis. fellow Brasenose Coll., vis. lectr. Faculty of Law, U. Oxford, Eng., 1995; adviser Restatement of the Law Third of Torts on Apportionment, 1993-99; Sir George Turner lectr. and vis. fellow U. Melbourne, Australia, 1997; vis. lectr. U. Canterbury, New Zealand, 1997. Contbr. essays to books. Recipient Monrad G. Paulsen award Yeshiva U. Faculty of Law, 1985; Norman and Edna Freehling scholar Chgo.-Kent Coll. Law, 1992-95. Mem. ABA (tort and ins. practice sect. task forces and adv. groups), Calif. Bar Assn., Am. Law Inst., Assn. Am. Law Schs. (exec. com. torts sect. 1992-98, chair 1997), Am. Soc. for Polit. and Legal Philosophy, Internat. Assn. Art, Intelligence and Law. Office: Chgo-Kent Coll Law 565 W Adams St Chicago IL 60661-3613

WRIGHT, ROBERT, broadcasting executive; b. Rockville Center, N.Y., Apr. 23, 1943; m. Suzanne Werner, Aug. 26, 1967; children: Kate, Christopher, Maggie. AB in History, Coll. Holy Cross, 1965; LL.B., U. Va., 1968. Bar: N.Y. 1968, Va. 1968, Mass. 1970, N.J. 1971. With Gen. Electric Co., 1969-70, 73-80, gen. mgr. plastics sales dept., 1978-80; law sec. to chief judge U.S. Dist. Ct., N.J., 1970-73; pres. Cox Cable Communications, Atlanta, 1980-83; exec. v.p. Cox Communications, 1980-83; v.p., gen. mgr. housewares, audio and cable TV ops. GE, 1983-84; pres., chief exec. officer GE Fin. Svcs. Inc., 1984-86, NBC, N.Y.C., 1986—. Office: GE 3135 Easton Tpke Fairfield CT 06431-0001

WRIGHT, ROBERT ERIC, economist; b. Rochester, NY, Jan. 1, 1969; s. Robert Gene and Elizabeth Gayle Wright; m. Deborah Anne Vasta; children: Madison, Alexander. PhD, SUNY, Buffalo, 1991—97. Asst. prof. Intellectual Heritage Program Temple Univ., Phila., 1998—99; lect. Dept. of Econ., U. Va., Charlottesville, Va., 1999—. Cons. Winthrop Group, Cambridge, 2001—; content expert Jones Internat., Englewood, Colo., 2001—; founding faculty cons. MAPS Program, Thomas Edison State Coll., Trenton, NJ, 1998—. Author: (book) Hamilton Unbound: Finance and the Creation of the American Republic, 2002, The Wealth of Nations Rediscovered: Integration and Expansion in American Financial Markets, 1780-1850, 2002, Origins of Commercial Banking in America, 1750-1800, 2001; editor: History of Corporate Finance: Development of Anglo-American Securities Markets, Laws, and Financial Practices and Theories, 2002; contbr. jour. article, articles (Best Article in Early U.S. Economic History, 1999). Conf. coord. Assn. for Core Texts and Courses, Phila., 1998—99. Grantee Rsch. grantee, Harvard Bus. Sch., 2001, Am. Antiquarian Soc., 1999, SUNY Buffalo, 1994, NSF, 1998. Libertarian. Deism. Business E-Mail: rewright@virginia.edu.

WRIGHT, ROBERT JOSEPH, lawyer; b. Rome, Dec. 13, 1949; s. Arthur Arley and Maude T. (Lacey) W.; m. Donna Ruth Bishop, Feb. 18, 1972; children: Cynthia Ashley, Laura Christine. BA cum laude, Ga. State U., 1979; JD cum laude, U. Ga., 1983. Bar: GA. 1983, U.S. Dist. Ct. (no. dist.) Ga. 1983, U.S. Dist. Ct. (mid. dist.) Ga. 1985. Assoc. Craig & Gainer, Covington, Ga., 1983-84, Heard, Leverett & Adams, Elberton, 1984-86; gen. counsel Group Underwriters, Inc., 1987—. Editorial staff Ga. Jour. Internat. and Comparative Law, 1981-82 Mem. State Bar Ga. (sec. legal econs. sect. 1987-88, chmn. legal econs. sect. 1988-90), Order of the Coif, Masons, Phi Alpha Delta. Baptist. Home: 1030 E Canyon Creek Ct Watkinsville GA 30677-1500

WRIGHT, ROBERT PAYTON, lawyer; b. Beaumont, Tex., Feb. 15, 1951; s. Vernon Gerald and Huberta Read (Nunn) W.; m. Sallie Chesnutt Smith, July 16, 1977; children: Payton Cullen, Elizabeth Risher. AB, Princeton U., 1972;

JD, Columbia U., 1975. Bar: Tex. 1975. Ptnr. Baker Botts L.L.P., Houston, 1975—. Author: The Texas Homebuyer's Manual, 1986. Mem. Am. Coll. Real Estate Lawyers (bd. govs. 2002—), State Bar Tex. (chmn. coun. real estate, probate, trust law sect. 1994-95), Houston Bar Assn. (chmn. real estate sect. 1989-90), Tex. Coll. Real Estate Lawyers, Houston Real Estate Lawyers Coun., Houston Club. Episcopalian.

WRIGHT, ROBERT ROSS, III, law educator; b. Ft. Worth, Nov. 20, 1931; m. Susan Webber; children: Robert Ross IV, John, David, Robin. BA cum laude, U. Ark., 1953, JD, 1956; MA (grad. fellow), Duke U., 1954; SJD (law fellow), U. Wis., 1967. Bar: Ark. 1956, U.S. Supreme Ct. 1968, Okla. 1970. Instr. polit. sci. U. Ark., 1955-56; mem. firm Forrest City, Ark., 1956-58; ptnr. Norton, Norton & Wright, 1959; asst. gen. counsel, asst. sec. Crossett Co., Ark.; atty. Crossett div. Ga.-Pacific Corp., 1960-63; asst. sec. Pub. Utilities Co., Crossett, Triangle Bag Co., Covington, Ky., 1960-62; faculty U. Ark. Law Sch., 1963-70; asst. prof., dir. continuing legal edn. and research, then asst. dean U. Ark., Little Rock, 1965-66, prof. law, 1967-70; prof. U. Okla., 1970-77; dean U. Okla. Coll. Law; dir. U. Okla. Law Center, 1970-76; vis. prof. U. Ark., Little Rock, 1976-77; Donaghey Disting. prof. U. Ark, 1977-99, Donaghey disting. prof. emeritus, 1999—. Vis. disting. prof. U. Cin., 1983; vis. prof. law U. Iowa, 1969-70; vis. prof. U. Ark., Little Rock, 1976-77; Ark. commr. Nat. Conf. Commrs. Uniform State Laws, 1967-70; past chmn. Com. Uniform Eminent Domain Code; past mem. Com. Uniform Probate Code, Ark. Gov.'s Ins. Study Commn.; chmn. Gov. Commn. on Uniform Probate Code; chmn. task force joint devel. Hwy. Research Bd.; vice chmn. Okla. Jud. Council, 1970-72, chmn., 1972-75; chmn. Okla. Center Criminal Justice, 1971-76 Author: Arkansas Eminent Domain Digest, 1964, Arkansas Probate Practice System, 1965, The Law of Airspace, 1968, Emerging Concepts in the Law of Airspace, 1969, Cases and Materials on Land Use, 3d edit., 1982, supplement, 1987, 5th edit., 1997, Uniform Probate Code Practice Manual, 1972, Model Airspace Code, 1973, Land Use in a Nutshell, 1978, 4th edit., 2000, The Arkansas Form Book, 1979, 2d edit., 1988, Zoning Law in Arkansas: A Comparative Analysis, 1980, Old Seeds in the New Land: A History and Reminiscences of the Bar of Arkansas, 2001; contbr. articles to profl. jours. Mem. Little Rock Planning Commn., 1978-82, chmn., 1982. Named Ark. Man of Year Kappa Sigma, 1958. Fellow: Am. Coll. Trust and Estate Counsel (acad.), Am. Law Inst.; mem.: ABA (past chmn., exec. coun. gen. practice, solo and small firm sect., former chmn. new pubs. editl. bd., sect. officers conf., ho. of dels. 1994—2000, standing com. fed. jud. improvements 1998—), Pulaski County Bar Assn., Ark. Bar Assn. (life; exec. coun. 1985—88, ho. of dels., chmn. eminent domain code com., past mem. com. new bar ctr., past chmn. preceptorship com., exec. com. young laywers sect.), Okla. Bar Assn. (past vice-chmn. legal internship com., former vice-chmn. gen. practice sect.), U. Ark. Alumni Assn., U. Wis. Alumni Assn., Duke U. Alumni Assn., Omicron Delta Kappa, Phi Alpha Delta, Phi Beta Kappa, Order of Coif. Episcopalian. Home: 249 Pleasant Valley Dr Little Rock AR 72212-3170 Office: U Ark Law Sch 1201 McMath St Little Rock AR 72202-5142

WRIGHT, ROBERT THOMAS, JR. lawyer; b. Detroit, Oct. 4, 1946; s. Robert Thomas and Jane Ellen (Blandin) W.; m. Diana Feltman, June 8, 1994; children: Sarah Allison, Jonathan Brian. BA in History and Polit. Sci., U. N.C., 1968; JD, Columbia U., 1974. Bar: Fla. 1974. Assoc. Paul & Thomson, Miami, Fla., 1974-77, Mershon, Sawyer, Johnston, Dunwoody & Cole, Miami, 1977-81, ptnr., 1981-95, Shutts & Bowen, Miami, 1995-98, Verner, Liipfert, Bernhard, McPherson & Hand, Miami, 1998—2001; founding ptnr. Coffey & Wright, L.L.P., 2002—. 1st lt. U.S. Army, 1968-71. Mem. ABA, Fla. Bar, Dade County Bar Assn. Avocations: golf, rugby, African cichlids. Home: 11095 SW 84th Ct Miami FL 33156-4311 Office: Coffey & Wright LLP Penthouse 2-B 2665 S Bayshore Dr Miami FL 33133 E-mail: RTWJr1@aol.com., rtwright@coffeylaw.org.

WRIGHT, RODNEY H. architect; b. Valparaiso, Ind., June 2, 1931; s. George and Lena May (Cahoon) W.; m. Sydney Sullivan Goelitz, Feb. 16, 1966; children by previous marriage: Weston, Julie-An; stepchildren: Louise Goelitz, Ann Marie Goelitz, Thomas Goelitz. Grad. high sch. With various archtl. firms, 1953-60; pvt. practice architecture, 1960—; architect Hawkweed Group Ltd., Chgo., 1978-85; sole propr. Rodney Wright, Architect; lectr Northwestern U., 1971. Keynote speaker First Solar Symposium, Sao Paulo, Brasil, 1976; presenter 1987 European Conf. on Architecture, Munich, 1st/2d conf. How Successful Directors Manage, 1986-93; speaker for various child care mtgs. and workshops. Author: Hawkweed, 1975, Passive Solar House Book, 1980, Urban Brickyard, Saving Energy Serving Children, 1993. Bd. dirs. Lake County Urban League, 1961-69, chmn., 1961-65; bd. dirs. Uptown Devel. Ctr., Chgo., 1969-73. With U.S. Army, 1950-53 Design fellow Nat. Endowment for Arts, 1975; recipient award U. Wis./Early Childhood Edn. Conf. Fellow AIA (chpt. dir. 1971, co-chmn. task force 1 1969-72, mem. nat. com. community devel. ctrs. 1970-72). Achievements include pioneering in design of passive solar and superinsulated bldgs. Research design of child care environments, including use of color, equipment, natural nonpolluting materials. Address: 2722 Woodrum Ridge Rd Liberty KY 42539-7772

WRIGHT, SARAH ELIZABETH, writer, poet; b. Wetipquin, Md., Dec. 9, 1928; d. Willis Charles and Mary Amelia (Moore) Wright; m. Joseph Gilbert Kaye, June 17, 1960; children: Michael, Shelley. Student, Howard U., 1945—49, Pa. State Tchrs. Coll., 1950—52, New Sch. Social Rsch., L.I. U.; BS, SUNY, Albany. MacDowell Colony fellow MacDowell Colony, Peterborough, NH, 1973; writer-in-residence Finkelstein Meml. Libr., Spring Valley, NY, 1978, 1979, 1980. Pres. Pen & Brush, Inc., N.Y.C., 1992—93, cons., prodr. Black History Month celebration and commemoration; cons. for creative artists pub. svc. program N.Y. State Coun. on the Arts. Co-author (with L. Smith): Give Me A Child, 1955; author: (novels) This Child's Gonna Live, 1969, A. Philip Randolph, 1990 (N.Y. Pub. Libr. award, 1990). Recipient Disting. Writer award, Middle Atlantic Writers Assn., 1988, The Sarah E. Wright Best Grad. Paper award, Salisburg State U., 1997, Outstanding Contbn. to Am. Lit. award, Zora Neale Hurston Assn., U. Md. Ea. Shore, Princess Anne, Md., 1999. Mem.: Pen Am. Ctr. (events com.), Authors Guild, Inc. (coun. mem. 1980—90), Harlem Writers Guild, Inc. (v.p., pres. 1958—65, award enduring commitment 1998), Nat. Assn. for Poetry Therapy (cert. poetry therapist). Home: 780 West End Ave New York NY 10025

WRIGHT, SCOTT OLIN, federal judge; b. Haigler, Nebr., Jan. 15, 1923; s. Jesse H. and Martha I. Wright; m. Shirley Frances Young, Aug. 25, 1972. Student, Central Coll., Fayette, Mo., 1940-42; LLB, U. Mo., Columbia, 1950. Bar: Mo. 1950. City atty., Columbia, 1951-53; pros. atty. Boone County, Mo., 1954-58; practice of law Columbia, 1958-79; U.S. dist. judge Western Dist. Mo., Kansas City, from 1979. Pres. Young Democrats Boone County, 1950, United Fund Columbia, 1965. Served with USN, 1942-43; as aviator USMC, 1943-46. Decorated Air medal. Mem. ABA, Am. Trial Lawyers Assn., Mo. Bar Assn., Mo. Trial Lawyers Assn., Boone County Bar Assn. Clubs: Rockhill Tennis, Woodside Racquet. Lodges: Rotary (pres. Columbia 1965). Unitarian Universalist. Office: Charles E Whitaker Courthouse 400 E 9th St Ste 8662 Kansas City MO 64106-2684

WRIGHT, STEPHEN NATHAN, religious organization administrator; b. Springfield, Ill., Oct. 18, 1956; s. William Nathan and Judith Elaine Wright; m. Rebecca Lynne Wright, July 9, 1976; children: Daniel, Jonathan, Mary, Benjamin. BA in Bus. Adminstrn., Grand Rapids Bapt. Coll., 1991, MDiv, 1995; postgrad., Grand Rapids Bapt. Sem., 1995—. Ordained min. Bapt. Ch., 1995. Various mgmt. positions The ServiceMaster Co., Downers Grove, Ill., 1977—89; pastor Pleasantview Family Ch., Dowling, Mich., 1992-97; v.p. Kent Cmty. Hosp., Grand Rapids, 1997-99; pres. David's House Ministries, Wyoming, 1999—. Adj. faculty Cornerstone U., Grand Rapids, 1995—. Grad. Leadership Grand Rapids, 2001. Mem. Hastings Area Ministerial Assn. (sec.-treas., 1996-97, pres. 2000-2001), Alliance Christian Providers Individuals with Disabilities (chair 2000—), Downtown Grand Rapids Rotary Club. Mem. Hastings Area Ministerial Assn. (sec.-treas. 1996-97, pres. 2000—). Achievements include Boston Marathon finisher. Office: David's House Ministries 2375 Banner Dr SW Wyoming MI 49509-1929 E-mail: snwdhm@aol.com.

WRIGHT, STEVEN RANDALL, minister; b. Griffin, Ga., Aug. 9, 1947; s. Garnett A. and Ellis (Boyt) W.; m. Patricia Anne Wright, Jan. 21, 1967; children: Christopher, Kevin. BA, Cen. Wesleyan Coll., 1969; postgrad., No. Bapt. Theol. Sem., 1976-78. Ordained to ministry Wesleyan Ch., 1969. Min. youth and music 1st Wesleyan Ch., Westminster, S.C., 1965-66, Pickens View Wesleyan Ch., Pickens, 1966-67; pastor Wesley Chapel, Greensboro, Ga., 1967-70; sr. pastor 1st Wesleyan Ch., Savannah, 1970-73, Farnham St. Wesleyan Ch., Galesburg, Ill., 1973-76, Wesleyan Community Ch., Oak Lawn, 1976—. Dist. pres. Wesleyan Youth, Ga., 1969-71; treas. So. area Wesleyan Youth, 1970-73; mem. bd. ministerial standing, Ga. and Ill., 1970-88; sec., mem. adminstrn. bd. Ga. dist. Wesleyan Ch., Inc., 1969-73, adminstrn. bd. Ill. dist., 1976-80, 88; chmn. Ill. dist. bd. Evangelism and Ch. Growth, 1988—, sec., 1988—; chmn. bds. mission and evangelism Bd. Christian Edn., Ga. dist., 1970-72. Contbr. articles to profl. jours. Pres. local Young Reps., S.C., 1968; founder New Life, 1974—, Men Alive Prayer Breakfast, 1976—, Orland Park Community Ch., 1980, HOPES, 1977—. Mem. Nat. Assn. Evangls., So. Mins. Alliance, Kiwanis (various spiritual aims coms. Oak Lawn club 1977-84, Outstanding Achievement award 1979) Home: 10340 S Kolin Ave Oak Lawn IL 60453-4808 Office: Wesleyan Community Ch 8844 Austin Ave Oak Lawn IL 60453-1130 *The real sanctuary for ministry is our life, not a structure made from mortar, wood and glass. Worshipping and serving our living Lord daily causes effective ministry.*

WRIGHT, SUSAN WEBBER, judge; b. Texarkana, Ark., Aug. 22, 1948; d. Thomas Edward and Betty Jane (Gary) Webber; m. Robert Ross Wright, III, May 21, 1983; 1 child, Robin Elizabeth. BA, Randolph-Macon Woman's Coll., 1970; MPA, U. Ark., 1972, JD with high honors, 1975. Bar: Ark. 1975. Law clk. U.S. Ct. Appeals 8th Cir., 1975-76; asst. prof. law U. Ark., Little Rock, 1976-78, assoc. prof., 1978-83, prof., 1983-90, asst. dean, 1976-78; dist. judge U.S. Dist. Ct. (ea. dist.) Ark., 1990—, chief judge, 1998—. Vis. assoc. prof. Ohio State U., Columbus, 1981, La. State U., Baton Rouge, 1982-83; mem. adv. com. U.S. Ct. Appeals 8th Circuit, St. Louis, 1983-88. Author: (with R. Wright) Land Use in a Nutshell, 1978, 2d edit., 1985; editor-in-chief Ark. Law Rev., 1975; contbr. articles to profl. jours. Mem. Am. Judicature Soc., Ark. Bar Assn., Pulaski County Bar Assn., Am. Law Inst., Ark. Assn. Women Lawyers (v.p. 1977-78), Ark. Women's Forum. Episcopalian. Office: US District Court 600 W Capitol Ave Ste 520 Little Rock AR 72201-3329

WRIGHT, SYLVIA HOEHNS, computer systems specialist; b. Richmond, Va., July 8, 1946; d. John Richard and Elsie (Compton) Hoehns; m. Garland Malcolm Wright, Mar. 13, 1965; children: Garland, Donald, Bonnie, Mark, Karen. BS in Mgmt. of Info. Sys., Va. Commonwealth U., 1980. Bus. application analyst Va. Power Co., Richmond, 1981-95; project mgr. First Health Svcs., 1996—2001. Freelance writer, lectr., Richmond, 1981—. Editor newsletter Massey Cancer Ctr. of Va., 1995-98; contbr. column to mag. Va. Women, 1993-95. Bd. dirs., lobbyist for hist. preservation Laurel Hist. Dist., Richmond, 1986—; lobbyist cmty. planning Henrico Citizens Com., Richmond, 1981—. Mem. Richmond Profl. Women's Network, Nat. Assn. Am. Pen Women (treas. 1984-98, nat. membership chair 1988-2001), Va. Master Gardeners. Avocations: arts, gardening, hist. preservation, genealogy, photography. Home: 9363 Hoehns Rd Glen Allen VA 23060-3237

WRIGHT, THEODORE OTIS, forensic engineer; b. Gillette, Wyo., Jan. 17, 1921; s. James Otis and Gladys Mary (Marquiss) W.; m. Phyllis Mae Reeves, June 21, 1942 (div. 1968); children: Mary Suzanne, Theodore Otis Jr., Barbara Joan; m. Edith Marjorie Jewett, May 22, 1968; children: Marjorie Jane, Elizabeth Carter. BSEE, U. Ill., 1951, MS in Engring., 1952; postgrad., Air Command and Staff Coll., 1956-57, UCLA, 1958. Registered profl. engr. Wash. 2d lt. U.S. Air Force, 1942-65, advanced through grades to lt. col., 1957, ret., 1965; dep. for engring. Titan SPO, USAF Sys. Command, L.A., 1957-65; rsch. engr. The Boeing Co., Seattle, 1965-81; pres. The Pretzelwich, Inc., 1981—2002; cons., forensic engr. in pvt. practice Bellevue, 1988—. Adj. prof. U. Wash., Greenriver Jr. Coll., both 1967-68. Contbr. articles to nat. and internat. profl. jours. Decorated Purple Heart, Air medal. Fellow NSPE (life; v.p. western region 1985-87); mem. ASTM (com. E-43 metric practice 1988—), Nat. Coun. Weights and Measures, Wash. Soc. Profl. Engrs. (state pres. 1981-82, Disting. Svc. award 1980, Engr. of Yr. 1996, Columbia award 1996), U.S. Metric Assn. (life, cert. advanced metrication speciallist), Am. Nat. Metric Coun. (bd. dirs. 1978-94), Air Force Assn. (charter life, state pres. 1974-76, 90-91, Jimmy Doolittle fellow 1975), Order of Daedalians (life), Eta Kappa Nu, Pi Mu Epsilon, Tau Beta Pi. Democrat. Presbyterian. Avocations: flying, photography, classical music, archaeology. Home: 141 140th Pl NE Bellevue WA 98007-6939 E-mail: wto@Qwest.net.

WRIGHT, THEODORE PAUL, JR. political science educator; b. Pt. Washington, N.Y., Apr. 12, 1926; s. Theodore Paul and Margaret (McCarl) W.; m. Susan Jane Standfast, Feb. 18, 1967; children: Henry Sewall, Margaret Standfast, Catherine Berrian (Mrs. Matthew H. Smith). BA magna cum laude, Swarthmore Coll., 1949; MA, Yale U., 1951, PhD, 1957. Instr. govt. Bates Coll., Lewiston, Maine, 1955-57; asst. prof., 1957-64; assoc. prof., 1964-65; assoc. prof. polit. sci. Grad. Sch. Public Affairs, SUNY, Albany, 1965-71, prof., 1971-95; prof. emeritus SUNY, 1995—. Author: American Support of Free Elections Abroad, 1964; contbr. chpts. to books, articles to profl. jours. Trustee Am. Inst. Pakistan Studies, 1973-82; bd. dirs. Am. Coun. Study of Islamic Studies, 1998—, European Conf. on Modern South Asian Studies, 1974--. Served with USNR, 1944-46. Carnegie intern Indian civilization U. Chgo., 1961-62; Fulbright rsch. prof. India, 1963-64; Am. Inst. Indian Studies rsch. fellow India, 1969-70; Am. Coun. Learned Socs. grantee on South Asia in London, 1974-75; Am. Inst. Pakistan Studies/Fulbright rsch. fellow, Pakistan, 1983-84, Fulbright lectr., 1990-91. Mem. South Asian Muslim Studies Assn. (pres. 1988-2000), Assn. Asian Studies (chmn. N.Y. Conf. on Asian Studies 1988-89), Dutch Settlers Soc. of Albany (pres. 1988-90, 98-2001), The New Netherland Project (bd. dirs. 2000-), Adirondack Mountain Club, Phi Beta Kappa (chpt. pres. 1992-93), Phi Delta Theta. Republican. Unitarian Universalist. Home: 27 Vandenburg Ln Latham NY 12210 E-mail: wright15@juno.com.

WRIGHT, THEODORE ROBERT FAIRBANK, biologist, educator; b. Kodaikanal, Tamil Nadu, India, Apr. 10, 1928; s. Horace Kepler and Adelaide Caskey (Fairbank) Wright; m. Eileen Marie Yongen, Jan. 6, 1951 (dec. Jan. 2002). AB in Biology, Princeton U., 1949; MA in Biology, Wesleyan U., 1954; PhD in Zoology, Yale U., 1959. Asst. professor biology Johns Hopkins U., Balt., 1959-65; assoc. prof. biology U. Va., Charlottesville, 1965-75, prof. biology, 1975-95; prof. emeritus, 1995—. Vis. scientist Max Planck Inst. for Biology, Tubingen, 1975-76, Devel. Biology Ctr., U. Calif., Irvine, 1982. Editor: The Genetics and Biology of Drosophila, vol. 2a-c, 1978, vol. 2d, 1980, Genetic Regulatory Hierarchies in Development, 1990; co-editor: Advances in Genetics, 1988-92. With U.S. Army, 1950-52. NIH postdoctoral fellow Max Planck Inst. for Biology, Tubingen, Fed. Republic Germany, 1958-59; NSF grantee, 1967-72, 90-93; NIH grantee, 1972-93; Am. Cancer Soc. grantee, 1988-90. Fellow AAAS; mem. AAUP, Genetics Soc. Am., Soc. for Devel. Biology, Va. Acad. Sci., Sigma Xi. Office: U Va Dept Biology Gilmer Hall Charlottesville VA 22903-2477

WRIGHT, THOMAS PARKER, application developer; b. Springfield, Mo., July 3, 1924; s. James Lewis and Vesta Marie (Parker) Wright; m. Elizabeth Jane Smith; children from previous marriage: Jeffrey, Kathleen, Thomas, Ramona, Karen. BA in Math., Henderson State U., 1948; MA in Math., La. State U., 1962. Math., sci. tchr. Hondo (N.Mex.) Union H.S., 1950-53; prin. Westridge (Ark.) H.S., 1954-55; math. tchr. Santa Ana (Calif.) Unified Sch. Dist., 1955-63; math., computer instr. Santa Ana Coll., 1963-71; adminstrv. dean Rancho Santiago CC., 1971-79; art gallery mgr. Lahaina (Hawaii) Galleries, Inc., 1979-80; pres. Maui Fine Arts, Inc., Kihei, 1981—; computer sci. instr. Maui C.C., Kahului, 1983-94. Software cons. Babock Electronics, Costa Mesa, Calif., 1964—66; sys. programmer Santa Ana Coll., 1966—71, Maui C.C., 1983—94, multi-media and internet software developer, 1989; dir. Maui Ednl. Tech. R&D Ctr. Internet Website, 1995—. Author computer programs;one-man shows include Maui C.C., 1989, exhibited in group shows at Art Maui, 1984, 1986, 1989. Pres. Santa Ana Tchrs. Assn., 1960, Santa Ana Coll. Faculty Assn., 1965. 1st lt. USMCR, 1944—46, 1st lt. USMCR, 1950—52. Mem.: NEA, U. Hawaii Profl. Assembly. Republican. Presbyterian. Avocations: water color and acrylic painting, computer art, ocean fishing, photography. Home: 811 S Kihei Rd Apt 3L Kihei HI 96753-9086 Office: Maui CC 310 Kaahumanu Ave Kahului HI 96732 Business E-Mail: wrightt@hawaii.edu.

WRIGHT, TIM EUGENE, packaging development executive; b. Weed, N.Mex., Oct. 13, 1943; s. Clyde Everett and Juanita Delores (Barrett) W.; m. Nancy Ann Ausenbaugh, Oct. 2, 1965 (div. 1975); 1 child, Ramsey Jordan. Diploma, Dayton Art Inst., 1967; MFA, U. Idaho, 1969. Designer Lawson Mfg. Co., Troy, Idaho, 1968-70, Boise Cascade, Burley, 1970-72, project coord. Golden, Colo., 1972-76; product devel. mgr., designer Greybeard Audio, Vancouver, Wash., 1996—. Patentee folding carton, spacer for rolls, collapsible pallet. Recipient silver award for packaging, 1978, design and engrng. showcase award Innovations '99. Mem. Western Pckg. Assn. (bd. dirs., past pres. Columbia chpt.), Soc. Plastics Engrs. Office: Matrix Applications Co PO Box 3668 Pasco WA 99302-3668

WRIGHT, VERNON HUGH CARROLL, bank executive; b. Bronxville, N.Y., Sept. 24, 1942; s. Dudley Hugh and Helen Margurite (Carroll) W. m. Lucy Hiss Babb, June 7, 1966; children: Dudley Hugh II, Katherine Babb. BS in acctg., U. Balt., 1969. Sr. v.p. Maryland Nat. Bank, Balt., 1969-90, 91, MNC Fin., Balt., 1990-91; vice chmn., chief corporate fin. officer MBNA Am. Bank, N.A., Wilmington, Del., 1991—. Bd. dirs. MBNA Am. Bank, Wilmington, Del. Exec. v.p., chief corp. fin. officer MBNA Corp. With USN, 1962-66. Avocations: farming, teaching. Office: MBNA Am Bank 1100 N King St Wilmington DE 19884-2821 Business E-Mail: vernon.wright@mbna.com.

WRIGHT, WADELL, engineer; b. Greenville, S.C., Aug. 29, 1944; s. Thomas C. and Marie (Tate) W.; m. Ines Rosario Teran, Sept. 1, 1977; children: Andre Tyrone, Anthony Wadell, Fionna Michelle, Aljonn Jerome. Diploma, Control Data Inst., Burlington, Mass., 1970. With RCA, Marlboro, Mass., 1971, Honeywell Info. Systems, Waltham, 1971-74, Bendix Field Engring. Corp., Columbia, Md., 1975-79, Ford Aerospace & Communications Corp., Palo Alto, Calif., 1979-80, Kentron Internat., Pasadena, 1980-82, Rockwell Internat., Anaheim, 1983-84; sr. computer engr. Al-Johi Internat., Dhahran, Saudi Arabia, 1984-85; sr. test engr. Gen. Dynamics, San Diego, 1985-87, sr. standards lab. engr. Rancho Cucamonga, Calif., 1987-88; owner, mgr. WRIGHT Vending Svc., Colton, 1988—; CEO Wright's Adolescent Devel. Ctr. Inc., San Bernardino, 1990—; owner Cyber-Bus. Network Internet, 2001—. Performed work related duties Ascension Island, Atlantic Ocean, Quito, Ecuador, S.Am., Kauai, Hawaii, Seychelles Island, Indian Ocean, Dharan, Saudi Arabia. Author: Its Up to You in America, 1987-88; inventor in field. Vice chmn. Utility Commn. City of Colton, 1997—. With U.S. Army, 1962-65. Home: 1397 N Topsail Ave Colton CA 92324-6211 Office: Wright's Adolescent Dev Ctr PO Box 1107 Colton CA 92324-0818 E-mail: wcyberbusiness@aol.com.

WRIGHT, WALTER EDWARD, county official, retired army officer; b. Farmville, Va., Dec. 2, 1950; s. Grady Hartwell and Evelyn Pearl (Andrews) W.; m. Barbara Lindsay, May 28, 1983; children: Laura Christine Shafer, Jessica Evelyn. BA, Va. Mil. Inst., 1973; M Pub. Svc., Western Ky. U., 1977; AAS, Columbia (Mo.) Coll., 1986; MEd, Tex. Tech U., 1992; disaster mgmt cert., U. Wis., 1998. Cert. disaster mgmt., cert. emer. mgr. Commd. 2d lt. U.S. Army, 1973, advanced through grades to lt. col., 1993; ops. officer U.S. Army Civil Affairs, Lubbock, Tex., 1991-93, Pensacola, Fla., 1993-95; ret., 1995; dir. emergency mgmt. Linn County Emergency Agy., Cedar Rapids, Iowa, 1995—. Emergency mgmt. cons. ARC and City of Lubbock, Tex., 1991—93, Escambia County, Pensacola, Fla., 1993—95; instr. Nat. Mass Fatality Inst. Kirkwood C.C., Cedar Rapids, Iowa. Contbr. articles to profl. jours. Chmn. Linn County Local Emergency Planning Com., 1995—; mem. Linn County Hazardous Material Task Force, 1995—; mem. E911 Commn., Linn County, 1995—; mem. strategic planning com. Linn-Mar Sch. Dist., Marion, Iowa, 1996-2000. Recipient svc. award ARC, Lubbock, 1993, cert. of appreciation IES Utilities/Iowa Emergency Mgmt. Divsn., Cedar Rapids, 1996. Achievement award Iowa State Assn. of Counties, Exemplary Performance award Federal Emergency Mgmt. Agy., Achievement award Nat. Assn. Counties. Mem. Internat. Assn. of Emergency Mgrs., Nat. Emergency Mgmt. Assn., Am. Soc. Profl. Emergency Planners, Iowa Emergency Mgmt. Assn. Office: Linn County Emergency Mgmt Agy 50 2d Ave Bridge Cedar Rapids IA 52401 E-mail: linnena@hmbest.net.

WRIGHT, WAYNE KENNETH, federal agency statistician; b. Chelsea, Mass., Jan. 26, 1944; s. Wayne K. and Louise Annette (Olson) W.; m. Sharon Kay Brown, Aug. 30, 1964 (div. 1974); 1 child, Trent Edward; m. Linda Susan Berkel, Mar. 15, 1975 (div. 1979); 1 child, Stacey Danielle; m. Bonnie Sue Oberhelman, Apr. 3, 1982; 1 child, Forrest Kenneth. BS in Sociology, U. Iowa, 1971; postgrad., U. North Iowa, 1971-72; cert. in marketing, Atlanta U., 1988. Survey asst. Shive-Hall-Hattery Engring., Cedar Rapids, Iowa, 1962-66; chem. lab technician Wilson Packing Plant, 1966-71; grad. rsch. asst. U. No. Iowa, Cedar Falls, 1971-72, grad. teaching asst., 1972-73; demographic and economic statistical asst. U.S. Bur. of Census, Charlotte, NC, 1973—; survey statistician U.S. Bur. Census, Kansas City, Kans., 1973-74, info. specialist, 1974-83, Charlotte, NC, 1983—2002; data specialist U.S. Bur. of Census, N.C., 1991—. Named Ky. Col., 1987; named Hon. Citizen, City of Beloit (Wis.), 1974. Fellow Alpha Kappa Delta. Lutheran. Avocations: tennis, boating, fishing, camping, hiking. Home: 1417 Morrocroft Trl Gastonia NC 28054-6499 Office: US Bur Census 901 Center Park Dr Ste 106 Charlotte NC 28217-2935 E-mail: w.kenneth.wright@census.gov., wrghtgmp@aol.com.

WRIGHT, WILEY REED, JR. lawyer, retired judge, mediator; b. Seattle, Jan. 31, 1932; s. Wiley Reed and Gertrude Ellen (Datson) W.; m. Sally Harrison Clarke, 1955 (div. 1963); children: Wiley III, Margaret, Andrew; m. Roberta Hostinsky, Oct. 18, 1963; children: Cathryn, Amy, Susan. BS in Commerce, Washington and Lee U., 1954, LLB, 1956. Bar: Va. 1956, U.S. Dist. Ct. (ea. dist.) Va. 1956, U.S. Ct. Appeals (4th cir.) 1956, U.S. Supreme Ct. 1993. Law clk. to hon. judge U.S. Dist. Ct., Alexandria, Va., 1958-59; ptnr. Clarke, Richard, Moncure & Whitehead, 1959-68; judge corp. and cir. cts., 1968-79; chief judge cir. ct., 1979-84; ptnr. Hazel & Thomas P.C., 1984-96; mediator McCammon Mediation Group Ltd., Richmond, Va., 1996—. Mem. at large Va. State Bar Coun., 1984-90; mem. Jud. Coun. Va., 1982-84, vice chmn. jud. conf. Va., 1980-82. Assoc. editor: Virginia Circuit Judges Benchbook, 1987. Legal counsel to Alexandria C. of C., 1984-88. 1st lt. U.S. Army, 1956-58. Fellow: Va. Law Found., Am. Bar Found.; mem.: Boyd-Graves Conf., Va. Bar Assn., Omicron Delta Kappa, Phi Delta Phi. Avocations: boating, fishing. Home: PO Box 358 Lively VA 22507-0358 Office: McCammon Mediation Group Ltd Nations Bank Ctr 700 1111 E Main St Richmond VA 23219-3531

WRIGHT, WILLIAM BIGELOW, retired financial executive; b. Rutland, Vt., Dec. 21, 1924; s. Earl Smith and Christine (Bigelow) W.; m. Polly Pardee, Aug. 27, 1949; children: Christine, Henry, John, Lucy. Graduated, Phillips Exeter Acad., 1943; AB, Princeton U., 1950. With Chubb & Son, N.Y.C., 1950-53; various positions Am. Internat. Group, N.Y.C., Havana, Tokyo, Seoul, Hong Kong, 1953-57; asst. to the pres. Johnson & Higgins, Caracas, Venezuela, 1957-63; pres. Marble Bank, Rutland, 1968-83; chmn. bd. Marble Bank, Marble Fin. Corp., 1983-94; mem. adv. bd. Marble divsn. Albank, 1994-98; ret., 1998. V.p. Windham Found., Grafton, Vt.; sch. commr. City of Rutland, 1966-75; chmn. Vt. Blue Cross and Blue Shield, 1980-83; pres. Northeast chpt. 10th Mountain Divsn. Assn., 1993-95; trustee Green Mountain Coll., Poultney, Vt., 1973-98; pres. Princeton Alumni Assn. of Vt., 1989-99; trustee Calvin Coolidge Meml. Found., Plymouth, Vt., 1992—. With U.S. Army, 1943-46; ETO. Mem. Ivy Club (Princeton, N.J.), Princeton Club N.Y.C., Alumni Coun. Princeton U. (exec. com. 1992-95, v.p., exec. com. Class of '47 1992—). Republican. Congregationalist. Avocations: skiing, golfing, sailing, traveling. Home: 15 Cream Hill Rd-Mendon Rutland VT 05701-9673

WRIGHT, WILLIAM COOK, archivist, historian, researcher; b. Jersey City, July 11, 1939; s. Harry Cook and Edna Marguerite Tompkins) W. BA, Gettysburg Coll., 1961; MA, U. Del., 1965, PhD, 1971. Tchr. Salem (N.J.) High Sch., 1961-65; adj. instr. U. Del., Newark, 1968-70; assoc. dir. N.J. Hist. Commn., Trenton, 1970-76; head Bur. Archives and History N.J. State Libr., 1976-83; dir. Div. Archives and Records Mgmt., N.J. State Dept., 1983-85; chief Bur. Records Mgmt., 1985-89, ret., 1989. Coord. state hist. records adv. bd. Nat. Hist. Publs. and Records Commn. 1976-87; mem. adv. com. for papers of William Livingston; sec. N.J. State Records Com., 1976-85, chmn., 1985; mem. adv. bd. dirs. N.J. Archives Series, 1971-86; mem. region 2 adv. coun. Nat. Archives and Records Svc., 1976-77; mem. adv. com. N.J.

Newspaper Project, 1983-85, state rev. com. for hist. sites, 1976-79; mem. implementation and planning com. N.J. Supreme Ct., 1982 Author monograph: The Secession Movement in the Middle Atlantic States, 1972; compiler Directory of N.J. Newspapers, 1765-1970; contbr. articles and book revs to profl. jours. Mem. Lawrence Twp. Cultural and Heritage Adv. Com., 1989-92, chmn., 1991. Recipient Award of Recognition N.J. Hist. Commn., 1992. Mem. Acad. Cert. Achivists (cert.), N.J. Hist. Soc. Home: 10 Windsor Ct Sewell NJ 08080-2815 E-mail: wcwright@comcast.net.

WRIGHT, WILLIAM EDWARD, historian, educator; b. Fairfield, Ala., Nov. 5, 1926; s. Cecil Augustus Wright and Leila Myrtle Greer; m. Norma Louise Lacy, Sept. 2, 1950; children: Mariellen Wiemann, Amber. BS in Bus., U. Colo., 1951, MA in History, 1953, PhD, 1957. Instr. to prof. history U. Minn., Mpls., 1957—93, dir. immigration history rsch. ctr., 1965—66, assoc. dean office internat. programs, 1969—70, assoc. v.p. internat. programs, 1970—76, founding dir. ctr. Austrian studies, 1977—88. Author: (book) Serf, Seigneur, Sovereign, 1966 (Phi Alpha Theta award for Best Book in History, 1966); editor (editor and contbg. author): Austria, 1938-1988. Anschluss and Fifty Years, 1995; editor: Austria in the Age of the French Revolution, 1789-1815, 1990, Austria Since 1945, 1982, (jour.) Austrian History Yearbook, 1982—89. Founding dir. Am. Alpbach Found., Washington, 1984—88; chmn. Dem.-Farmer-Labor Party Legis. Task Force, Mpls., 1966—67; campaign mgr. Donald Fraser Reelection Campaign, 1968—68; candidate Minn. state senate Dem.-Farmer-Labor Party, 1966—66. Staff sgt. U.S. Army, 1945—47, ETO. Recipient Oesterreichisches Ehrenkreuz fuer Wissenschaft und Kunst, erste Klasse, Republic of Austria, 1994, Das Grosse Goldene Ehrenzeichen fuer Verdienste um die Republik Oesterreich, 1989, McKnight Found. Humanities award for European history, McKnight Found., 1961; fellow Fulbright Rsch. fellow, Austro-American Ednl. Commn., 1962-1963, Fulbright fellow to Austria, 1954-1955. Mem.: Czechoslovak History Conf., German Studies Assn., Am. Hist. Assn. Dfl. Avocations: photography, travel, music, auto mechanics. Home: 18200 Honeysuckle Ln Wayzata MN 55391-3618 Office: U Minn 267 Nineteenth Ave S Minneapolis MN 55455 Personal E-mail: wrigh001@umn.edu.

WRIGHT, WILLIAM EVAN, physician; b. N.Y.C., Aug. 1, 1946; s. Samuel and Frances Elnora (Perpente) W.; m. Diana Claire Dryer, Aug. 15, 1970; children: Jason William, Elizabeth Garland, Edwin Samuel. BA in Music, U. Rochester, 1968; MD, U. Pa., 1972; MSPH, U. Utah, 1979; MS in Physiology, Harvard U., 1980. Diplomate Am. Bd Internal Medicine, Am. Bd. Preventive Medicine, Occupl. Medicine, Am. Bd. Ind. Med. Examiners; ACOEM cert. med. rev. officer; cert. FAA med. examiner. Intern LDS Hosp., Salt Lake City, 1972-73, resident, 1973-75, U. Utah Med. Ctr., Salt Lake City, 1978-79, Harvard Sch. Pub. Health, Boston, 1979-80; asst. prof. U. So. Calif., L.A., 1980-86; med. dir. U.S. DEA, Arlington, Va., 1986-96; program mgr., site med. dir. DynCorp, Reston, 1991-96; med. dir. Md. Office, CORE, Inc., Irvine, Calif., 1996—. Cons. in field. Contbr. articles to profl. jours. Maj. M.C., U.S. Army, 1975-77. Fellow ACP, Am. Coll. Occupl. and Environ. Medicine, mem. Alpha Omega Alpha. Avocation: performing music. Home: 6801 Wemberly Way Mc Lean VA 22101-1532

WRIGHT, WILLIAM EVERARD, JR. lawyer; b. New Orleans, Dec. 4, 1949; s. William E. and Claire (Carter) W.; m. Alice Marquez, May 26, 1972; children: Matthew, Caroline. BA, Tulane U., 1971, JD, 1974. Bar: La. 1974. Assoc. Little, Schwartz & Dussom, New Orleans, 1974-76; ptnr. Baldwin & Haspel, 1976-91, Deutsch, Kerrigan & Stiles, New Orleans, 1991—. Mem. La. Bd. Examiners, 1981-84. Mem. ABA (chmn. profl., officers' and dirs. liability law com. 1997-98, constrn. forum), Associated Builders and Contractors (bd. dirs.), La. Bar Assn. (bd. dels. 1985—), New Orleans Bar Assn. (exec. com. 1980-86, officer 1983-86), New Orleans C. of C. Home: 700 Eleonore St New Orleans LA 70115-3249 Office: Deutsch Kerrigan & Stiles 755 Magazine St Ste 100 New Orleans LA 70130-3672 E-mail: wwright@dkslaw.com.

WRIGHT, WILLIAM WYNN, chemist; b. Balt., Aug. 13, 1923; s. Andrew Wynn and Margaret Mary (Peters) W.; m. Mary Theresa Mead, Feb. 10, 1945; children: Ann Wynn, Jane Frances, Stephen William, Kathleen Theresa, Drew Edward. BS magna cum laude, Loyola Coll., Balt., 1944; MS, Georgetown U., 1946, PhD, 1948. Rsch. fellow Georgetown U. Grad. Sch., Washington, 1944; chemist Nat. Bur. Standards, 1945, FDA, Washington, 1945-79; sr. scientist U.S. Pharmacopeia, Rockville, Md., 1979—. Cons., advisor WHO, Geneva, 1960-2000. Recipient Superior Svc. award U.S. Dept. Health, Edn. and Welfare, Washington, 1964, USPHS, Washington, 1979. Fellow AAAS (life), Assn. Ofcl. Analytical Chemists (pres. 1967); mem. Am. Chem. Soc., N.Y. Acad. Sci. (life), Sigma Xi. Roman Catholic. Achievements include development of numerous chemical analytical methods for antibiotics and pharmaceuticals; studies into absorption and excretion of antibiotics; standardization of antibiotic susceptibility discs and of their use in clinical laboratories.

WRIGHT CARRIER, J. T. business owner; b. McKenzie, Tenn., July 31, 1952; d. Gilbert M. and Mildred B. Wright; m. William W. Carrier III, July 28, 1973; 1 child, Morgan Bailey. BA in Psychology cum laude, Memphis State U., 1974, MA in Ednl. Counseling, Pers. Svcs., 1976, PhD, 1992. Sales rep. API Inc., Memphis, 1980—; casting dir. Theatrics Etc., 1980—. Profl. model; casting dir., crew svcs. staff for nat. feature and advt. accts. including Warner Bros., Disney, Phillips 66, Exxon, KC Masterpiece BBQ Sauce, Northwest Airlines; scriptwriter for corp. videos, Fed. Express, Memphis Bus. Jour. Pub. Crisis Intervention Studies for Memphis Police Dept.; crew svcs. for U.S. Def. Dept. tng. videos. Co-founder Memphis and Shelby County Film, Tape and Music Commn. Named Miss Memphis, 1972, Top Casting Co. Adweek Mag., 1986. Mem. Nat. Career Devel. Assn. Avocations: environmentalism, ballet, modern dance, theatre. Office: Theatrics Etc PO Box 11862 Memphis TN 38111-0862

WRIGHTON, MARK STEPHEN, chemistry educator; b. Jacksonville, Fla., June 11, 1949; s. Robert D. and Doris (Cutler) Wrighton; children: James Joseph, Rebecca Ann. BS, Fla. State U., 1969; PhD, Calif. Inst. Tech., 1972; DSc (hon.) , U. West Fla., 1983. From asst. prof. chemistry to provost MIT, Cambridge, 1972—90, provost, 1990—95; prof., chancellor Washington U., St. Louis, 1995—. Bd. dirs. A.G. Edwards, Inc., Cabot Corp., Ionics, Inc., Helix Tech. Corp., Optical Imaging Sys., Inc., Danforth Plant Sci. Ctr., Nidus Ctr. for Sci. Enterprise, Barnes Jewish Hosp., BJC HealthCare; mem. Nat. Sci. Bd.; bd. dirs. Nat. Assn. of Independent Colleges and Univs. Author: Organometallic Photochemistry, 1979. Trustee St. Louis Art Mus., Mo. Bot. Garden, St. Louis Symphony, St. Louis Sci. Ctr., Mary Inst. Country Day Sch.; bd. dirs. United Way Greater St. Louis, Chem. Heritage Found. Recipient Herbert Newby McCoy award, Calif. Inst. Tech., 1972, Disting. Alumni award, 1992, E.O. Lawrence award, Dept. Energy, 1983, Halpern award in photochemistry, N.Y. Acad. Scis., 1983, Fresenius award, Phi Lambda Upsilon, 1984, Dreyfus tchr.-scholar, 1975—80; fellow, Alfred P. Sloan, 1974—76, MacArthur fellow, 1983—88. Fellow: AAAS; mem.: Electrochem. Soc., Am. Chem. Soc. (award in pure chemistry 1981, award in inorganic chemistry 1988), Am. Philos. Soc., Am. Acad. Arts and Scis. Office: Washington Univ Office of Chancellor One Brookings Dr # 1192 Saint Louis MO 63130-4899

WRIGHTSON, KEITH EDWIN, historian; b. Croxdale, Eng., Mar. 22, 1948; s. Robert and Evelyn (Atkinson) W.; m. Eva Mikusovä, Aug. 19, 1972; children: Nicholas Mikus, Eliska Anne. BA, U. Cambridge, 1970, MA, PhD, U. Cambridge, 1974. Rsch. fellow Fitzwilliam Coll., Cambridge, 1972-75; univ. lectr. U. St. Andrews, U.K., 1975-84; Can. commonwealth fellow U. Toronto, 1983-84; univ. lectr. U. Cambridge, Eng., 1984-93, reader in English social history Eng., 1993-98, prof. social history Eng., 1998-99; prof. history Yale U., New Haven, 1999—. Fellow Jesus Coll., Cambridge, 1984-99, dir. studies in history, 1990-98; vis. prof. U. Alta., 1988, U. Toronto, 1992. Author: English Society 1580-1680, 1982, Earthly Necessities, Economic Lives in early modern Britain, 2000; co-editor: The World We Have Gained, 1986; co-author: (with D. Levine) Poverty and Piety in an English Village, 1979, The Making of an Industrial Society, 1991; contbr. articles to profl. jours. Fellow, British Acad., Royal Hist. Soc.; mem. Social History Soc., Econ. History Soc. Avocations: modern jazz, contemporary literature. Office: Yale U Dept History PO Box 208324 New Haven CT 06520-8324 E-mail: keith.wrightson@yale.edu.

WRIGLESWORTH, VICKI LEE, nurse; b. Clearfield, Pa., Oct. 18, 1959; d. James Lee and Janet Hazel (Livergood) Price; m. Dennis Lee Wriglesworth, July 1, 1978; children: Eric, Shane. LPN, Clearfield County Votech Sch., 1978. Practical nurse DuBois (Pa.) Hosp., 1979-80, Tri County Oral Facial Surgeons, Clearfield, 1980—, Drs. Craig and Doerfler Office, Clearfield, 1997—. Office: Tri-County Oral Facial Surgeons 807 Turnpike Ave Clearfield PA 16830-1238

WRIGLEY, VIRGINIA MARIE, accountant; b. Highland, Ill., Nov. 27, 1938; d. James Lemen and Clara Marie (Shea) Oatman; m. Clarence L. Wrigley, Nov. 16, 1957 (div. Mar. 1980); children: Margot Ann Wrigley Crowell, Michael Sean, Mitchell, Dean. Cert. in tax preparation, H&R Block, 1982; cert. in acctg. I, Belleville Area Coll., 1984, cert. in acctg. II, 1985. Tax preparer H&R Block, Collinsville, Ill., 1972-76, supr. office Fairview Heights, 1976-78, regional coordinator St. Louis, 1978-79, asst. dist. mgr. Belleville, 1978-79, dist. mgr. Warson Woods, Mo., 1979-83; co-owner A1 Bookkeeping & Income Tax Service, Collinsville, 1983-87; owner Accredited Acctg. & Tax Service, 1987—. Fellow Nat. Accts. Assn. Ill., Accreditation Coun. Accountancy & Enrolled Agts., Nat. Assn. Tax practitioners, Cert. Tax Accts., Nat. Soc. Pub. Accts., Coll. Bus. and Profl. Women, Collinsville C. of C., Masons (sec. 1972-73), Women-of-the-Moose. Republican. Roman Catholic. Home: 1279 Vandalia St Collinsville IL 62234-4060 Office: Accredited Acctg & Tax Svc 1279 Vandalia St Collinsville IL 62234-4060

WRINKLE, JOHN NEWTON, lawyer; b. Chattanooga, July 31, 1929; s. John Stuart and Anne (Ownbey) W.; m. Louise Rucker Agee, Feb. 1, 1958; children: Anne Blair, Margaret Rucker. BA, Vanderbilt U., 1951; LLB, Yale U., 1955. Bar: Ala. 1955, U.S. Dist. Ct. (no. dist.) Ala. 1956, U.S. Ct. Appeals (5th cir.) 1958, U.S. Ct. Appeals (11th cir.) 1981, U.S. Tax Ct. 1957. Assoc. White, Bradley, Arant, All & Rose, Birmingham, Ala., 1955-63; ptnr. Bradley Arant Rose & White LLP, 1963-92, counsel, 1993—. Coord. pre-law students Birmingham So. Coll., 1989—. Trustee Birmingham Symphony Assn., 1970-79, 80-83, Episcopal Found. Jefferson County, 1994-2000; mem. bd. advisors St. Andrew's Sewanee Sch., 1985—. With USAF, 1951-52. Disting. fellow Birmingham-Southern Coll., 1995—. Fellow Am. Coll. Trust and Estate Counsel; mem. ABA, So. Employee Benefits Conf. (steering com. 1970-73), Birmingham Bar Assn., Assn. of Bar of City of N.Y., Birmingham Com. Fgn. Rels., Redstone Club, Mountain Brook Club, Summit Club, Knickerbocker Club (N.Y.C.), Yale Club (N.Y.C.), Phi Beta Kappa, Phi Alpha Delta. Episcopalian. Home: 2 Beechwood Rd Birmingham AL 35213-3914 Office: Bradley Arant Rose & White LLP 1819 5 Ave N Birmingham AL 35203 E-mail: jnwrinkle@bradleyarant.com.

WRISTON, KATHRYN DINEEN, lawyer, business executive; b. Syracuse, N.Y. d. Robert Emmet and Carolyn (Bareham) Dineen; m. Walter B. Wriston, Mar. 14, 1968; 1 stepchild. Student, U. Geneva, 1958-59; BA cum laude, Smith Coll., 1960; LLB, U. Mich., 1963. Bar: N.Y.1964, U.S. Ct. Appeals (2d cir.) 1964, U.S. Supreme Ct. 1968. Assoc. Shearman & Sterling, N.Y.C., 1963-68. Bd. dirs. Goodyear Tire and Rubber Co., 2002—, audit. com., corp. responsibility com., 2002—; bd. dirs. Northwestern Mut. Life Ins. Co., mem. ins. products and mktg. com., 1986-89, audit com., 1989—, chmn. audit com., 2001—, investment and fin. policy com., 1989-95; dir. Santa Fe Snyder Corp., 1990-2000, mem. audit com. 1990-93, 95-2000, nominating com., 1990-99, compensation com., 1998-99, conceptual framework task force Indep. Standards Bd., 1998—, dir. 1990-2000; trustee Fin. Acctg. Found., 1992-97, selection com., 1992-97, audit com., 1992-96, chair, 1993-96, chair devel. com., 1996-97, fin. com., 1994-97. exec. com., 1996-97; task force on timely fin. reporting guidanace Fin. Acctg. Stds. Bd., 1982-83, mem. bd. agenda adv. com., 1981-85, process and structure com., 1981-85, chair, 1983-85, adv. coun., 1981-85; exec. com. CPR Inst. for Dispute Resolution, 1994-99; dir. The Stanley Works, 1996—, mem. pub. policy, 1996—, mem. fin. and pension coms., 1996-97, 2002—, chair audit com., 1997-2002, exec. com., 1997—. Vis. com. U. Mich. Law Sch., 1973—; trustee Fordham U., Bronx, N.Y., 1971-81, vice-chair bd. trustees, 1980-81, student affairs com., 1971-77, chair, 1974-77, faculty affairs com., com. on law sch., 1978-81, grievance com., 1971-81; ea. region selection panel Pres. Commn. on White House Fellowships, 1981-83, chair, 1982-83; bus. com. Nat. Ctr. for State Cts., 1982-88; bd. overseers Rand Inst. for Civil Justice, 1985-93; trustee John A. Hartford Found., 1991—, pres., 2002—, grant com., 1991—, vice-chair, 1992—, chair evaluation com., 1998—, audit com., 1992—, chair, 1993—, sec., 1996-02; mem. Gov. Wilson's N.Y. Little Hoover Commn., 1974. Mem. ABA, Nat. Assn. Accts., Practicing Law Inst. (exec. 1976—, programs and publs. com., chair 1979—, membership com. 1976-79, chair 1977-79, nominating com. 1978, 81-85, v.p., 1985—, mem. bar rev. courses 1978-79, fin. com. 1989—, mem. Am. Law Inst./ABA subcom. on Am. law network 1989-91), Fin. Women's Assn. N.Y., N.Y. County Lawyers Assn. (legal aid com. 1972-76), N.Y. State Bar Assn., Assn. of Bar of City of N.Y.

WRISTON, WALTER BIGELOW, retired banker; b. Middletown, Conn., Aug. 3, 1919; s. Henry M. and Ruth (Bigelow) W.; m. Barbara Brengle, Oct. 24, 1942 (dec.); 1 dau., Catherine B.; m. Kathryn Ann Dineen, Mar. 14, 1968. BA with distinction, Wesleyan U., Middletown, Conn., 1941; LL.D., Wesleyan U., 1984; postgrad., Ecole Francaise Middlebury, Vt., 1941, Am. Inst. Banking, 1946; MA, Fletcher Sch. Internat. Law and Diplomacy, 1942; LLD, Lawrence Coll., 1962, Tufts U., 1963, Brown U., 1969, Columbia U., 1972, Morehouse Coll., 1985; D.C.S., Pace U., 1974; DCS, St. John's U., 1974; DHL, Lafayette Coll., 1975; LLD, Fordham U., 1977, Hamilton Coll., 1996; DCS, NYU, 1977. Officer spl. div. Dept. State, Washington, 1941-42; jr. insp. comptrollers div. Citibank (N.A.), 1946-50, asst. cashier, 1950-52, asst. v.p., 1952-54, v.p., 1954-58; sr. v.p., 1958-60; exec. v.p., 1960-67; pres., 1967-70; chmn., 1970-1984; also dir. Bd. dirs. ICOS Corp., Cygnus, Inc., Vion Pharms., Inc.; trustee Rand Corp., 1973-83; mem. Nat. Commn. on Productivity, 1970-74, Nat. Commn. for Indsl. Peace, 1973-74; chmn. Pres.' Econ. Policy Adv. Bd., 1982-89. Author: Risk and Other Four-Letter Words, 1986, The Twilight of Sovereignty, 1992. Trustee, pres. N.Y.Presbyn.Hosp.; trustee Manhattan Inst. for Policy Rsch. Inc. Served with AUS, 1942-46. Mem. Bus. Coun., Links Club, Univ. Club, River Club, Sky Club, Palm Beach Bath and Tennis Club, Ocean Club Fla. Office: 425 Park Ave Fl 3 New York NY 10022-3506

WROBEL, JERZY MICHAL, physicist, educator; b. Wroclaw, Poland, May 7, 1954; s. Edmund and Jadwiga Wrobel; m. Theresa Ligus, Oct. 4, 1980. PhD, Wroclaw U. Tech., 1984. Rsch. assoc. Nat. Rsch. Coun. Can., Ottawa, Ont., 1987-89; vis. scientist MIT, Cambridge, 1989; asst. prof. physics U. Mo., Kansas City, 1989-95, assoc. prof., 1995—. Mem. Am. Phys. Soc., Am. Assn. Physics Tchrs., Materials Rsch. Soc., Soc. Photo-Optical Instrumentation Engrs., Sigma Xi. Office: U Mo Dept Physics 5100 Rockhill Rd Kansas City MO 64110-2499 E-mail: wrobelj@umkc.edu.

WROBEL, LANCE J. orthopedic surgeon; b. Chgo., July 14, 1944; s. John Joseph and Virginia Gertrude Wrobel; m. Susan L. Wrobel, Oct. 12, 1968; children: Scott, Kristin, Craig. MD, Loyola U., Maywood, Ill., 1969. Diplomate Am. Bd. Orthopedic Surgery. Intern Cook County Hosp., Chgo., 1969-70; resident U.S. Naval Hosp., San Diego, 1970-74; comdr.-elect overseas surg. team USN, 1970-77; assoc. South County Orthopedic Specialists, Laguna Hills, Calif., 1978—. Team physician orthopedic cons. Santa Margarita Cath. H.S., Rancho Santa Margarita, Calif., 1987—. Mem. ACS, Am. Acad. Orthopaedic Surgeons, Am. Assn. Hip and Knee Surgeons, Arthroscopy Assn. N.Am., Calif. Orthopaedic Assn. Roman Catholic. Avocation: golf. Office: South County Orthopaedic Specialists 24331 El Toro Rd 2nd Flr Laguna Hills CA 92653

WROBLE, ARTHUR GERARD, judge; b. Taylor, Pa., Jan. 21, 1948; s. Arthur S. and Sophia P. Wroble; m. Mary Ellen Sheehan, Nov. 19, 1977; children: Sophia Ann, Sarah Jean, Stacey Margaret. BSBA with honors, U. fla., 1970, MBA, 1971, JD, 1973. Bar: Fla. 1973, U.S. Ct. Appeals (5th cir.) 1974, U.S. Ct. Appeals (11th cir.) 1981, U.S. Dist. Ct. (so. dist.) Fla. 1974, U.S. Dist. Ct. (mid. dist.) 1982, U.S. Dist. Ct. (no. dist.) Fla. 1986, U.S. Army Ct. Mil. Rev. 1989, U.S. Ct. Mil. Appeals 1990, U.S. Supreme Ct. 1976. Ptnr. Burns, Middleton, Farrell & Faust (now Steel, Hector, Davis, West), Palm Beach, Fla., 1973-82, Wolf, Block, Schorr & Solis, Cohen, Phila. & West Palm Beach, 1982-87, Scott, Royce, Harris & Bryan, P.A., Palm Beach, 1987-89, Grantham and Wroble, P.A., Lake Worth, 1989-92; prin. Arthur G. Wroble, P.A., West Palm Beach, 1992-2000; cir. judge 15th Jud. Ct. Fla., Palm Beach, 2000—. Mem. 15th Jud. Cir. Ct. Nominating Commn., 1979-83; mem. U. Fla. Law Ctr. Council, 1981-84, U.S. Magistrate Merit Selection Panel, so. dist. Fla., 1987; mem. adv. bd. alternative sentencing program Palm Beach County Pub. Defender's Office; adj. instr. bus. law Coll. of Boca Raton (now Lynn U.), 1988; mem. U.S. Military Acad. Screening com., 16th Dist., Fla., 2001-. Contbr. to profl. jours. Bd. dirs. Palm Glades Girl Scout Coun., 1996—. Served to lt. col. JAG, USAR. Named Eagle Scout, Boy Scouts Am., 1962. Mem. ABA, Fla. Bar (bd. govs. young lawyers sect. 1979-83, bd. govs. 1985-89), Palm Beach County Bar Assn. (pres. young lawyers sect. 1978-79, bd. dirs. 1979-81, sec.-treas. 1981-83, pres. 1984-85), Fla. Bar Found. (bd. dirs. 1990-93), Fla. Assn. Women Lawyers, Fla. Coun. Bar Assn. Pres. (bd. dirs. 1986-92), Guild Cath. Lawyers Diocese Palm Beach, Inc. (pres. 1980-81, bd. dirs. 1981—, Monsignor Jeremiah P. O'Mahoney Outstanding Lawyer award 1993), Legal Aid Soc. Palm Beach County, Inc. (bd. dirs. 1981-2000), Univ. Fla. Alumni Assn., Palm Beach County Club (pres. 1983-84), Kiwanis (pres. 1980-81, pres. West Palm Beach found. 1989-2000, dir. 1991—, Citizen of Yr. 1994, George F. Hixon fellowship 1999), KC (grand knight 1978-79), Am. Inns of Ct LIV (West Palm Beach chpt. pres. 1999-2000, bd. dirs. 1995-2000). Roman Catholic. Office: Palm Beach County Cthse 205 N Dixie Hwy West Palm Beach FL 33401-4522

WROBLE, LISA ANN, writer, educator; b. Dearborn, Mich., June 17, 1963; d. Robert Frank and Ruth Marie (Schiller) W. Diploma, Inst. Children's Lit., 1983; BA cum laude, Ea. Mich. U., Ypsilanti, 1985. Cert. ESL tchr., ltd. profl. class B, Libr. Mich. Asst. editor cmty. rels. Vets. Adminstrn., Ann Arbor, Mich., 1983-85; prodn. coord. Cmty. Crier Newspaper/COMMA Graphics, Plymouth, 1985-86; proofreader Valassis Inserts, Livonia, 1986-89; tech. writer Nat. TechTeam, Dearborn, 1989-90; freelance writer Plymouth, 1990—. Publicist Garden City (Mich.) Osteo. Hosp., 1990-91; creative writing instr. Cmty. Edn. Plymouth (Mich.)-Canton Schs., 1992-93, 97—; instr. Inst. of Children's Lit., 2000—. Author: (12 book series) Kids Throughout History, 1997, 98, The Oceans, 1998, How Things Work, Childcraft, vol. 9, 2000, The New Deal in American History, 2002; contbg. editor Metroparent, 1991-93; contbg. tech. writer Cleaner Times, 1992-95, Facilities Planning News, 1993-96, FM Data Monthly, 1997-2000, Mich. Learning, 1998—, Wonder Years, Partnership for Learning, 2000—; book rev. editor Parenting Today's Teens, 1998-2001; columnist Christian Libr. Jour., 1999—; book reviewer BookPage Promotions, 1997—, The ALAN Rev., 1993—, Christian Libr. Jour., 1997—, The Wonder Years, 2001—; software reviewer Compute Publs., 1989-92, Falsoft Inc., 1991-94; contbr. articles, essays and sects. to reference books, multi-media CD ROMs and textbooks; contbg. writer Eye on the Web, 1998, Bridges CX, 1999-2000, Career Explorer, 1999-2000, Teach-Michigan Found., 1998-2000, Partnership for Learning, 2000—. Tutor Cmty. Literacy Coun., Plymouth, 1989-93; vol. spkr. in schs. Recipient Reading Tutor award Cmty. Literacy Coun., 1991-93. Mem. Soc. Childrens Book Writers and Illustrators (adv. com. Mich. chpt. 1993-94, 98—, workshop facilitator 1990, 97—, mentorship coord. 2000—), Internat. Reading Assn., Nat. Writers Assn. (vol. critiquer 1989-93), Childrens Lit. Assn., Mich. Reading Assn., Womens Nat. Book Assn., Text and Acad. Authors Assn., Peninsula Writers, Livonia Writers Group. Republican. Roman Catholic. Avocations: swimming, photography, crafting, cross country skiing, cooking. Home: 2614 Fountain View Cir #102 Naples FL 34109-1705 E-mail: lisawtoo@yahoo.com.

WROBLESKI, JEANNE PAULINE, lawyer; b. Phila., Feb. 14, 1942; d. Edward Joseph and Pauline (Popelak) W.; m. Robert J. Klein, Dec. 3, 1979. BA, Immaculata Coll., 1964; MA, U. Pa., 1966; JD, Temple U., 1975. Bar: Pa. 1975. Pvt. practice law, Phila., 1975—; pres., shareholder Jeanne Wrobleski & Assocs., LLC, 1999—. Lectr. on bus. law Wharton Sch., Phila. Mem. Commn. on Women and the Legal Profession, 1986-89; v.p. Center City Residents' Assn.; Eisenhower Citizen Amb. del. to Soviet Union; judge Pro Tem Phila. Ct. Common Pleas; bd. dir. Charlotte Cushman Found. Bd. dirs., mem. exec. com. Temple Law Alumni; del. Moscow Conf. on Law and Econ. Coop., 1990; del. to jud. conf. 3d Cir. U.S. Ct. Appeals, 1991; mediator U.S. Dist. Ct. (ea. dist.) Pa., 1996; bd. trustees Phila. Prisons, Charlotte Cushman Found.; Bd. dirs. South St. Dance Co., Women in Transition; bd. dirs., vice chair The Wilma Theater. Rhea Liebman scholar, 1974. Mem.: ABA, AAUW, Jagiellonian Law Soc., Am. Judicature Soc., Phila. Bar Assn. (chmn. women's rights com. 1986, com. on jud. selection and retention 1986—87, chmn. appellate cts. com. 1992, bus. cts. task force, com. on bus. litigation), Pa. Bar Assn., Phila. Art Alliance, Nat. Mus. Women in the Arts, Pa. Acad. Fine Arts, Penn Club, Lawyers Club, Founders Club, The Cosmopolitan Club, Lambda Iota Tau, Alpha Psi Omega. Democrat. Office: Jeanne Wrobleski & Assocs LLC 1845 Walnut St Fl 24 Philadelphia PA 19103-4708 E-mail: jwrobleski@wwdlaw.com.

WROBLEWSKI, MARY STEVENSON, women's health nurse; Diploma, Mercy Hosp. Sch. Nursing; BS, Coll. of St. Francis, Joliet, Ill.; MS in Nursing, Aurora U. RN, Ill. Mgr. perinatal svcs. Ctrl. Dupage Hosp., Winfield, Ill. Alexian scholar, 1988. Mem.: AWHONN, Am. Hosp. Assn. (governing coun. for women and children).

WROBLEY, RALPH GENE, lawyer; b. Denver, Sept. 19, 1935; s. Matthew B. and Hedvig (Lyon) W.; m. Madeline C. Kearney, June 13, 1959; children: Kirk Lyon, Eric Lyon, Ann Lyon. BA, Yale U., 1957; JD, U. Chgo., 1962. Bar: Mo. 1962. With Bell Tel. Co., Phila., 1957-59; asoc. Stinson, Mag & Fizzell, Kansas City, Mo., 1962-65, mem., 1965-88; ptnr. Bryan, Cave, McPheeters & McRoberts, 1988-92; ptnr., exec. com. Blackwell, Sanders, Peper, Martin LLP, 1992-2000. Bd. dirs. Human Resources Corp., 1971; mem. Civic Coun. Kansas City, 1986-2001; chmn. Pub. Housing Authority of Kansas City, 1971-74; vice chmn. Mayor's Adv. Commn. on Housing, Kansas City, 1971-74; bd. govs. Citizens Assn., 1965—. vice chmn., 1971-75, chmn., 1978-79; bd. dirs. Coun. on Edn., 1975-81, v.p., 1977-79; bd. dirs., pres. Sam E. and Mary F. Roberts Found., 1974-96; trustee Clearinghouse for Mid Continent Founds., 1977-96, chmn. 1987-89; bd. dirs. Bus. Innovation Ctr., 1984-91, vice-chmn. 1987-91, adv. bd. dirs., 1993-99, Midwest Regional Adv. Bd. Inst. Internat. Edn., 1989-93, Internat. Trade Assn., 1989-92, v.p., 1990; vice chmn., bd. dirs. Mid-Am. Coalition on Healthcare, 1991—. Mem. Mo. Bar Assn., Yale Club (pres. 1969-71, outstanding mem. award 1967). Republican. Presbyn. (elder) Home: 1015 W 67th Ter Kansas City MO 64113-1942 Office: 2300 Main St Kansas City MO 64108-2416 E-mail: rwrobley@blackwellsanders.com.

WROBLOWA, HALINA STEFANIA, electrochemist; b. Gdansk, Poland, July 5, 1925; came to U.S., 1958, naturalized, 1970; 1 child: Krystyna Wrobel-Knight, grandson Christopher E. Knight. MSc, U. Lodz, Poland, 1949; PhD, Warsaw Inst. Tech., 1958. Chmn. dept. prep. studies U. Lodz, 1950-53; adj. Inst. for Phys., Chemistry Acad. Scis., Warsaw, Poland, 1958-60; dept. dir. electrochemistry lab. energy inst. U. Pa., Phila., 1960-67; dir. electrochemistry lab., 1968-75; prin. research scientist Ford Motor Co., Dearborn, Mich., 1976-91; pvt. practice cons., 1991. Chmn. Gordon Rsch. Conf. on Electrochemistry, 1983. Contbr. chpts. to books, articles to profl. jours., patent lit. Served with Polish Undeground Army, 1943-45, decorated Mil. Silver Cross of Merit with Swords. Mem. Electrochem. Soc., Internat. Electrochem. Soc., Mensa, Sigma Xi. E-mail: hzuk@voicenet.com.

WRONG, DENNIS HUME, sociologist, educator; b. Toronto, Nov. 22, 1923; s. Humphrey Hume and Mary Joyce (Hutton) W.; m. Elaine L. Gale, Nov. 24, 1949 (div. Oct. 1965); 1 child, Terence Hume; m. Jacqueline Conrath, Mar. 26, 1966. BA, U. Toronto, 1945; PhD, Columbia U., 1956. Tchr. Princeton U., 1949-50, Rutgers U., 1950-51, U. Toronto, 1954-56, Brown U., 1956-61; mem. grad. faculty New Sch. Social Research, 1961-63; prof. sociology, chmn. dept. Univ. Coll., NYU, 1963-65; prof. sociology NYU, 1966-94, prof. emeritus, 1994—; retired. Vis. prof. U. Nev., 1965-66; vis. fellow Oxford (Eng.) U., 1978, European U. Inst., 1996-97; Simon vis. prof. U. Manchester, Eng., 1978. Author: American and Canadian Viewpoints, 1955, Population, 1956, 59, Population and Society, 1961, 67, 77, Skeptical Sociology, 1976, Power: Its Forms, Bases and Uses, 1979, 88, 95, Class Fertility Trends in Western Nations, 1980, The Problem of Order: What Unites and Divides Society, 1994, 95, The Modern Condition: Essays at Century's End, 1998, The Oversocialized Conception of Man (reissue of Skeptical Sociology), 1999; editor: Social Research, 1961-64, (with Harry L. Gracey) Readings in Introductory Sociology, 1967, 72, 77, Contemporary Sociology: A Journal of Reviews, 1972-74, Max Weber, 1970; mem. editl. bd. Dissent, 1966—; contbg. editor Partisan Rev., 1981-87, Guggenheim fellow, 1984-85, Woodrow

Wilson Internat. Ctr. for Scholars fellow, 1991-92. Mem.: Soc. for Adavncement of Socio-Econs., Eastern Sociol. Soc., Am. Sociol. Assn. Home: 144 Drakes Corner Rd Princeton NJ 08540-7519 E-mail: dhwrong@voicenet.com.

WRONSKI, STANLEY PAUL, education educator; b. Mpls., Apr. 8, 1919; s. John and Katherine (Kotvis) W.; m. Geraldine Breslin, May 27, 1943; children: Linda A., Mary Jo Tewinkel, Sandra J., John S., Paul S. BS in Edn., U. Minn., 1942, MA, 1947, PhD, 1950. Counselor Bur. Vet. Affairs U. Minn., Mpls., 1946-47, instr. Coll. Edn., 1948-49; tchr. Marshall High Sch., 1947-48; asst. prof. Ctrl. Wash. Coll., Ellensburg, 1950-51; from asst. to assoc. prof. Boston U., 1951-57; from assoc. prof. to prof. Mich. State U., East Lansing, 1957-84, prof. emeritus, 1984—. Advisor Ministry of Edn., Bangkok, Thailand, 1964-66; pres. New Eng. Assn. Social Studies Tchrs., Boston, 1955-56, Mich. Coun. for Social Studies, 1960-61, Nat. Coun. for Social Studies, 1974. Co-author: Teaching Social Studies in High School, 1958, 73, Modern Economics, 1964, School and Society, 1964, Social Studies and Social Sciences, 1986; creator "The Sustainable Planet" interactive display at Impression 5 Mus., Lansing, Mich., 2000. Active U.S. Nat. Commn. for UNESCO, Washington, 1974-76, mil. adv. coun. Ctr. for Def. Info., Washington, 1988—; pres. Greater Lansing UN Assn., 1986-88, 99-2000, chair Mich. UN at Fifty Planning Com., 1995. Comdr. USN, 1942-64. Recipient Internat. Educator award Pacific Rim Consortium, 1992, Glen Taggart award Mich. State U., 1995; named Outstanding Social Studies Educator, Social Studies Tchr. Jour., 1981. Mem. NEA (life), Nat. Peace Found. (charter), Univ. Club (charter). Avocations: golf, reading, volunteer work. Home: 4520 Chippewa Dr Okemos MI 48864-2008 Office: Mich State U Coll Edn Erickson Hall East Lansing MI 48824 E-mail: wronskis@msu.edu.

WROSCH, CARSTEN, psychologist; b. Berlin, Oct. 19, 1965; s. Wolfgang Wrosch and Helga (Seils) Mueller. MA, Free U. of Berlin, 1994, PhD, 1997. Predoctoral fellow Max-Planck Inst. for Human Devel., Berlin, 1994-97, postdoctoral fellow, 1997-99; vis. scientist U. Pitts., 1998, Carnegie Mellon U., Pitts., 1999-2001, Concordia U., Montreal, Que., Can., 2001—. Mem. Am. Psychol. Assn. Office: Concordia U Dept Psychology Montreal QC Canada H4B 1R6

WROTH, JAMES MELVIN, data processing executive, retired military officer; b. Lincoln, Nebr., Feb. 2, 1929; s. Charles M. and Reba (Sharp) Wroth; m. Donna Mae Benson, June 4, 1951 (dec.); children: Mark, David S., Mary E. Bannon; m. Molly B. Mullan, June 15, 1975; stepchildren: Edward H. Mullan(dec.) , Philip C. Mullan. BS, U. Nebr., 1951; MBA, Syracuse U., 1963; postgrad., F.A. Sch., 1957, Command and Gen. Staff Coll., 1962, Armed Forces Staff Coll., 1967, Army War Coll., 1968, Harvard U., 1972. Commd. 2d lt. U.S. Army, 1951, advanced through grades to brig. gen., 1973, 40th inf. divsn. Republic of Korea, 1952-53; instr. A.A.A. Sch., Ft. Bliss, Tex., 1954-56; with 3d Inf. Div., Ft. Benning, Ga., 1957-61; with Office Chief of Staff U.S. Army, 1963-66; comdg. officer 1st Bn. 31st Arty., Republic of Korea, 1967; exec. asst. to asst. sec. Army U.S. Army, 1968-70; exec. officer I Field Force Vietnam Arty., 1970; comdg. officer 52d Arty. Group, Vietnam, 1971; with Office Dep. Chief Staff for Personnel, Dept. Army, 1972-75; comdg. gen. VII Corps Arty. and Augsburg Germany Mil. Community, 1975-77; comdr. 2d ROTC region, Ft. Knox, Ky., 1977-79; ret., 1979; v.p., dir. mgmt. scis. ops. Gen. Research Corp., McLean, Va., 1979-82; group v.p Info. Systems & Network Corp., Bethesda, Md., 1982-93; chmn., pres. J-Tech, Inc., White Stone, Va., 1993—. Trustee Washington Adventist Hosp. Found., 1989—93. Decorated D.S.M., Legion of Merit, Bronze Star, Air Medal with V device, Army Commendation medal, Vietnamese Gallantry Cross with palm; recipient F. A. Assn. award, 1950, John J. Pershing award, 1951, 40 and 8 award, 1951. Mem.: U.S. Coast Guard Aux. (flotilla comdr.), Ret. Officers Assn. (past chpt. pres.), Nat Soc. Pershing Rifles (past nat. comdr.), Indian Creek Yacht and Country Club (dir. 2000—03), Indian Creek Yachting Assn. (commodore), Beta Gamma Sigma, Alpha Kappa Psi. Home: 286 Breezy Pt White Stone VA 22578-2400

WROTH, L(AWRENCE) KINVIN, lawyer, educator; b. Providence, July 9, 1932; s. Lawrence Counselman and Barbara (Pease) W.; m. Susan Collins, May 2, 1958 (div. 1972); children: Ann K., Caroline D., Eliza H.; m. Deborah Bethell, Aug. 10, 1972; 1 dau., Katharine L.; stepchildren— John H., David H., Elizabeth T. and Sarah B. Zobel. BA, Yale U., 1954; LLB, Harvard U., 1960. Bar: Mass. 1960, Maine 1974. Teaching fellow, asst. prof. law Dickinson Sch. Law, 1960-62; rsch. assoc. Harvard U., 1962-64; assoc. prof. law U. Maine Sch. Law, Portland, 1964-66, prof., 1966-96; assoc. dean Sch. Law U. Maine, 1977-78, acting dean, 1978-80, dean, 1980-90; dean, prof. Vt. Law Sch., 1996—. Rsch. fellow Charles Warren Center Studies in Am. History, Harvard U., 1968-74; cons. civil and probate procedure, profl. and jud. responsibility, and ct.-bar rels. Maine Supreme Jud. Ct., 1967-96; cons. civil, probate, family ct. and criminal procedure and evidence Vt. Supreme Ct., 1969—. Author (with R.H. Field and V.L. McKusick) Maine Civil Practice, 2d edit., 1970; editor-in-chief: Province in Rebellion, 1975; editor: (with H.B. Zobel) Legal papers of John Adams, 1965; reporter: Vermont Rules of Civil Procedure, 1971, Vermont Rules of Criminal Procedure, 1974, Maine Rules of Probate Procedure, 1980, (with J. Dooley) Vermont Rules of Evidence, 1982, Maine Code of Judicial Conduct, 1993, Vermont Code of Judicial Conduct, 1994. Pres. Greater Portland Landmarks, Inc., 1966-69, adv. trustee, 1969-85; adv. coun. Nat. Trust Hist. Preservation, 1967-70; bd. dirs. Maine Bar Found., 1983-89, sec., 1983-86, v.p., 1987, pres., 1988, fellow, 1991; bd. dirs. Pine Tree legal Assistance Inc., 1985-96; mem. bd. dirs. Nat. Assn. IOLTA Programs, Inc., 1988-90; bd. dirs. Portland Symphony Orch., 1990-98, v.p. for ops. and resources, 1991-95, pres., 1995-96; mem. Maine Commn. on Legal Needs, 1989-90, Commn. to Study Future of Maine's Cts., 1991-93; Commn. on Future of Vt.'s Judiciary, 1998-99; mem. Vt. Bus. Roundtable, 1998—. Recipient Littleton-Griswold prize Am. Hist. Assn., 1966, Howard H. Dana award Maine Bar Found., 1991, Justice Louis Scolnik award Maine Civil Liberties Union, 1992, Herbert Harley award Am. Judicature Soc., 1994. Fellow Am. Bar Found.; mem. ABA, Maine Bar Assn. (Disting. Svc. award 1990), Am. Law Inst., Vermont Bar Assn., Colonial Soc. Mass., Mass. Hist. Soc. Office: Vt Law Sch PO Box 96 South Royalton VT 05068-0096 E-mail: kworth@vermontlaw.edu.

WRUBEL, SUSAN MAZANEK, physician assistant; b. Garden Grove, Calif., Nov. 23, 1959; d. John Otto and Doris Anna Mazanek; m. David Aaron Wrubel, Sept. 1, 1996. AA in Human Svcs., Golden West Coll., 1980, AA in Nursing, 1981; physician asst. cert., Stanford U., 1988. RN, Calif.; FNP; cert. physician asst. RN Long Beach (Calif.) Meml., 1981-85, St. Francis Hosp., Santa Barbara, Calif., 1986; physician asst. Camino Med. Group, Sunnyvale, 1988-98, Saad Shakir MD, Inc., Los Altos, 1997—, Jeff McClanahan MD, Los Gatos, 1999. Mem. Am. Acad. Physician Assts., Calif. Acad. Physician Assts., Bay Area Non Docs (pres. 1997—). Lutheran. Avocations: playing tennis, scuba diving, jet skiing. E-mail: susanmwrubel@yahoo.com.

WRUBLE, BERNHARDT KARP, lawyer; b. Wilkes-Barre, Pa., Mar. 21, 1942; s. Maurice and Ruth Yvonne (Karp) W.; m. Judith Marilyn Eyges, Nov. 16, 1968 (div. 1987); children: Justine, Vanessa, Alexis; m. Jill Diamond, Nov. 24, 1990; children: Mattia, Austin. BA in Polit. Sci., Williams Coll., Williamstown, Mass., 1963; LLB, U. Pa., 1966; postgrad., NYU, 1972-74, Harvard U., 1978. Bar: U.S. Dist. Ct. (so. dist.) N.Y. 1969, U.S. Dist. Ct. (ea. dist.) N.Y. 1972, U.S. Ct. Appeals (2d cir.) 1972, U.S. Supreme Ct. 1972, U.S. Ct. Appeals (7th cir.) 1974, U.S. Ct. Appeals (D.C. and 4th cirs.) 1984, U.S. Ct. Appeals (5th cir.) 1985, U.S. Ct. Appeals (11th cir.) 1986. Law clk. to presiding judge U.S. Ct. Appeals (3d cir.), 1966-67; assoc. Simpson, Thacher & Bartlet, N.Y.C., 1968-73; ptnr. Simpson, Thatcher & Bartlett, 1974-77; prin. dep. gen. counsel U.S. Dept. Army, Washington, 1977-79; dir. Office Govt. Ethics, 1979; exec. asst. to sec. and dep. sec. U.S. Dept. Energy, 1979-81; dir. Pres.'s Interagy. Coal Export Task Force, 1980-81; ptnr. Verner, Liipfert, Bernhard, McPherson and Hand, 1981-99; sr. v.p. legal affairs Northwest Airlines, St. Paul, 1999—2001. Bd. dirs. Epilepsy Found. Am., 1983, chmn., 1991. Mem. ABA, D.C. Bar Assn., N.Y. State Bar Assn., Williams Coll. Alumni Assn. (pres. Washington chpt. 1986-91), Williams Coll. Soc. Alumni Assn. (exec. com. 1988-91). Democrat. E-mail: bkwruble@yahoo.com.

WRUBLE, BRIAN FREDERICK, private investor; b. Kalamazoo, Apr. 18, 1943; s. Milton and Rose Muriel (Nathanson) W.; m. Susan Roberta Shifrin, June 23, 1968 (div. Oct. 1984); children: Amy Carolyn, Jordan Todd; m. Kathleen Wilson Bratton, Apr. 20, 1985; 1 child, Henrietta Zane Bratton. BEE, Cornell U., 1965, MEE, 1966; MBA with distinction, NYU, 1976. Field engr. Sperry Corp., Lake Success, N.Y., 1966-69; v.p. Alliance One Instl. Services, Inc., N.Y.C., 1970-76, H. C. Wainwright and Co., Inc., N.Y.C., 1976-77, Wainwright Securities, Inc., N.Y.C., 1977; v.p., co-mgr. fundamental equities research Smith Barney, Harris Upham & Co., 1977-79; exec. v.p. chief fin. ops. Equitable Life Assurance Soc. U.S., 1979-92; chmn., pres., chief exec. officer Equitable Capital Mgmt. Corp., 1985-92; chief investment officer Equitable Life Assurance Soc. U.S., 1991-92; pres. chief oper. officer, dir. Delaware Mgmt. Holdings, Inc., 1992-95; pres., CEO The Delaware Group, 1992-95; pres., chief oper. officer Delaware Mgmt. Co., 1992-95; chmn. Delaware Distributors, Inc., 1992-95; chmn., chief exec. officer Delaware Svc. Co., Inc., 1992—95; gen. ptnr. Odyssey Ptnrs., L.P., N.Y.C., 1995—; mng. prin. Odyssey Investment Ptnrs., L.L.C., 1997-98, spl. ltd. ptnr., 1999—. Chmn., pres. Equitable Realty Assets Corp., Atlanta, 1983—92; v.p., dir. TELMARI, Inc., N.Y.C., 1982—83, Equitable Variable Life Ins. Co., 1987—92; chmn. Equico Capital Corp., N.Y.C., 1984—92; CEO Equitable Gen. of Okla., Oklahoma City, 1985—86; trustee Equitable Retirement Plans, N.Y.C., 1980—86, Oppenheimer Quest Funds, 2001—; pres. Hudson River Trust, 1991—92, Equitable Funds, 1991—92. Vice-chmn. Boys Choir of Harlem, N.Y.C., 1984—92; vice chmn. Corp. Ptnrs. Phila. Art Mus., 1993—95; bd. govs. Jerome Levy Econ. Inst., 1990—2001; bd. dirs. Harlem Youth Devel. Found., 1989—92, Corp. Ptnrs. Phila. Art Mus., 1992—95, The Jackson Lab., Inc., 1990—, Inst. for Advanced Study, 1992—. Recipient Heroes award Boys Choir Harlem, 1990, Founders award, 1993. Mem.: IEEE, Phila. C. of C. (bd. dirs. 1992—95, mem. exec. com. 1993—95), Inst. CFAs (CFA, bd. trustees 1992—98, vice chmn. 1993—94, chmn. 1994—95, bd. trustees rsch. found. 1994—95, 2000—02, assoc. editor CFA Digest 1983—), N.Y. Soc. Security Analysts, Assn. Investment Mgmt. and Rsch. (gov. 1992—98). Republican. Jewish. Avocations: running, skiing, sailing, amateur radio.

WRUCK, ERICH-OSKAR, retired foreign language educator, adminstrator; b. Gross-Kroessin/Pomerania, Germany, Oct. 29, 1928; came to U.S., 1952, naturalized, 1954; s. Erich Albert and Erna (Kroening) W.; m. Esther Emmy Schmidt, Oct. 3, 1953; children: Eric Gordon, Karin Esther, Krista Elisabeth. BA magna cum laude, Rutgers U., 1959; MA, 1961, PhD, 1969. Asst. instr. Rutgers U., New Brunswick, N.J., 1959-62; asst. prof. Davidson (N.C.) Coll., 1962-69, assoc. prof., 1969-73, prof., chmn. dept. German, 1983-87; established exch. program Marburg (Germany) U., 1963; with U. Würzburg, Germany, 1985; dir. Davidson abroad program Marburg, 1966-67, 71-72; jr. yr. abroad program Würzburg, 1986-87, 89-92; ret., 1994. Cons. faculty U.S. Army Command and Gen. Staff Coll., 1974-85. 1st lt. U.S. Army, 1953-57, to col. USAR, 1988. Recipient Julius Maximilians medal U. Wuerzburg, 1987; named to Arty. OCS Hall of Fame, 1996; Henry Rutgers scholar. Mem. Goethe Assn., Freies Deutsches Hochstift, Schiller Assn., Goethe Soc. of N. Am. (charter), Soc. German Am. Studies. Lutheran. Avocations: painting, photography, soaring, skiing, running.

WRUCK, MICHELLE MINGINO, pediatric nurse practitioner; b. Mastic, N.Y., Dec. 14, 1957; d. Michael A. and Vivian Mingino; m. Ernest R. Wruck, Oct. 14, 1979; children: Kristanya, Alexander, Natalia. RN, Beth Israel Hosp., 1978; BS, St. Joseph's Coll., 1989; MS, SUNY, Stony Brook, 1993. Staff nurse pediatrics/pediatric ICU SUNY, Stony Brook, 1980-86, clin. coord. outpatient transfusion clinic, 1988-90; dir. nursing Infants and Children's Health Svcs., Middle Island, N.Y., 1990-93; PNP, Suffolk County Dept. Health, Hauppauge, 1993-94, SUNY, Stony Brook, 1994—2000; pediat. pvt. practice Hampton Cmty. Health Care, Water Mill, NY, 2000—. Lectr. in field , 1980—. Mem.: Nurse Practitioners Assn. L.I., N.Y. State Nurses Assn. (bd. dirs. dist. # 19 1990—93), Nurse Practitioners Assn. N.Y. State, Sigma Theta Tau. Home: 8 Drew Dr Eastport NY 11941-1335

WRUCKE-NELSON, ANN C. elementary education educator; b. Mankato, Minn., Nov. 5, 1939; d. G.F. and Dorothy (Thomas) Wrucke; children: Chris, Dor-Ella. BS, Mankato State U., 1961; MLA, So. Meth. U., 1974; postgrad., U. Minn., 1963, Tex. Woman's U., EdD in Early Childhood Edn., 1992. Cert. elem., kindergarten, ESL, history tchr., Tex. Tchr. Rochester (Minn.) Pub. Schs., Christ the King Sch., Dallas; dir., tchr. Norway Christian Presch.; Every Student Learns Lang. program kindergarten tchr. Dallas Ind. Sch. Dist., 1971—. Tchr. summer session Tex. Woman's U., 1991; presenter in field. Producer video: A Year of Language Learning, 1990. Sunday sch. tchr. Holy Trinity Ch. Recipient Tchr. of Yr. award, 1989, Tex. TESOL scholarship, 1994; Bill Martin Literacy Conf. scholar; named ESL Tchr. of Yr., 1991. Mem. Internat. Reading Assn., Assn. for Childhood Edn. Internat., So. Assn. on Children Under Six, TESOL, Kindergarten Tchrs. Tex., Tex. TESOL, Dallas Assn. for Edn. of Young Child, Phi Delta Kappa. Office: 201 N Adams Ave Dallas TX 75208-4624

WU, ALBERT W. medical educator; b. N.Y.C., July 27, 1957; s. Ray J. and Christina (Chan) W. BA, Cornell U., 1980, MD, 1984; MPH, U. Calif. Berkeley, 1990. Resident in medicine Mt. Sinai Hosp., N.Y.C., 1984-86, U. Calif. San Diego, 1986-87, clin. instr., 1987-88; Robert Wood Johnson scholar U. Calif. San Francisco, 1988-90; asst. prof. Johns Hopkins U., Balt., 1990-96, assoc. prof., 1996—. Pres. Internat. Soc. for Quality of Life Rsch., 2003—. Office: Johns Hopkins U 624 N Broadway Baltimore MD 21205-1900 E-mail: awu@jhsph.edu.

WU, ANDY TING, research scientist; b. Fuzhou, Fujian, China, Jan. 18, 1963; m. Ge Song; children: Wilton, Daniel. PhD, The Norwegian Inst. Tech., Trondheim, Norway, 1992. Rschr. The Norwegian Inst. Tech., Trondheim, Norway, 1992—93; rsch. fellow to chief rschr. Superconductivity Rsch. Lab., ISTEC, Tokyo, 1993—98; rschr. U. Alberta, Edmonton, Canada, 1998—2001; staff scientist Thomas Jefferson Nat. Accelerator Facility (Jefferson Lab.), Newport News, Va., 2001—. MS student co-advisor Tokyo U., 1995—97; rsch. U. Alberta, Edmonton, Alberta, Canada, 1998—2001; rsch. fellow to chief rschr. Superconductivity Rsch. Lab., ISTEC, Tokyo, 1993—98; rschr. The Norwegian Inst. Tech., Trondheim, Norway, 1992—93; Summer PhD student advisor Denmark U. Tech., Tokyo, 1996, Seoul U., Tokyo, 1995.

WU, CARL CHERNG-MIIN, ceramic engineer; b. Taiwan, Republic of China, July 10, 1938; s. Sung-Pai and Yueh-Oh (Lin) W.; m. Lisa Cheng, Aug. 1, 1970; 1 child, Priscilla Pei-i. BS, Nat. Taiwan U., 1962; ScM, Brown U., 1967, PhD, 1970. Postdoctoral fellow U. Md., College Park, 1970-73, vis. asst. prof., 1973-77; ceramic engr. Naval Rsch. Lab., Washington, 1977-86, supv. ceramic engr., 1986—. Contbr. papers to profl. publs. Pres. Washington China Post, 1987-88; pres. Chines Cmty. Benevolent Alliance, 1994-97. Mem. Am. Ceramic Soc., Nat. Inst. Ceramic Engrs., Assn. Chinese Schs. (pres. 1984-85), Chinese-Am. Profl. Assn. (pres. 1984-85), Chinese-Am. Soc. (v.p. 1988-94, exec. dir. 1994—), Chinese Consol. Benevolent Assn. (chmn. 1993). Home: 9605 Newbridge Dr Potomac MD 20854-4435 Office: Naval Rsch Lab Code # 6354 Washington DC 20375-0001 E-mail: lisacar/wu@aol.com.

WU, CHAI WAH, research scientist; b. Hong Kong, China; BA in Computer Engrng., BA in Cognitive Sci., Lehigh U., 1990; MSEE, MA in Math., PhD in Elec. Engrng., U. Calif., Berkeley, 1995. Rschr. U. Calif., Berkeley, 1996; fellow IBM, Yorktown Heights, NY, 1996—97, rsch. staff mem., 1997—. Author: (book) Synchronization in coupled chaotic circuits and systems, 2002; contbr. invention. Fellow: IEEE (assoc. editor 1997—99, Fellow 2001); mem.: Am. Math. Soc. Office: IBM T J Watson Rsch Ctr PO Box 218 Yorktown Heights NY 10598

WU, DAVID, congressman; b. Taiwan, Apr. 8, 1955; came to U.S., 1961; m. Michelle Wu; children: Matthew, Sarah. BS, Stanford U., 1977; student, Harvard Med. Sch.; JD, Yale U., 1982. Ptnr. Cohen & Wu, 1988-98; mem. edn. and workforce com., sci. com. 106th Congress from 1st Oreg. dist., 1999—. Mem. Congl. Asian Pacific Caucus (vice chair), New Democrat Coalition also: 620 NW Main Ste 606 Portland OR 97205 Office: 1023 Longworth House Office Building Washington DC 20515*

WU, DONGDONG, software engineer; b. Zhengzhou, Henan, China, Aug. 18, 1959; came to U.S., 1992; d. Xuemin Wu and Qi Wang; m. Gregory Lafrance, Dec. 2, 2000; children: Phillip Tao, Arthur Lafrance. BS in Physics, Zhengzhou U., 1982; MS in Optics, Shanxi U., Taiyuan, China, 1987; MS in Physics, Miss. State U., 1996. Tchg. asst. Henan U. Agr., Zhengzhou, 1982-84; asst. prof. S.W. Jiaotong U., Chengdu, China, 1987-92; cons. Gates Rubber Co., Denver, 1997; info. tech. engr. Broadbase Info. Sys., Inc., Menlo Park, Calif., 1997—2000; software engr. Kana Software, Inc., 2000—. Rsch. asst. Shanxi U., Taiyuan, 1984-87, Miss. State U., 1994-96. Contbr. articles to Applied Optics, Acta Optica Sinica. Recipient 2nd award Sci. Tech., Govt. Shanxi, 1991. Mem. China Soc. Computer Sci., Chengdu Soc. Laser, Sigma Xi (assoc.). Achievements include first to experimentally observe self-defocusing optical bistability and establish theoretical model to explain experimental results, demonstrate laser phtofragmentation-laser induced fluorescence can be used to detect and measure TNT concentration in soil. Home: 11060 Firethorne Dr Cupertino CA 95014

WU, DONGPING (DON WU), optical and electrical engineer; b. Shi-jia-zhuang, Hebei, China, Apr. 21, 1960; came to U.S., 1992; s. Hongquan and Shujian Wu; m. Helen Hongwei Zhu, July 30, 1988; children: Yue, Eric Z., Alicia Tianshu. BS, Harbin Inst. Elec. Tech., Heilongjiang, China, 1982; MS, Beijing U. Posts & Telecomms., 1987, U. Cin., 1996. Nat. profl. tng. in integrated optics, China. Sr. engr. Ma'anshan 2d H.S., Anhui, China, 1977—78; mfg. engr. Shanghai Electric. Cable Rsch. Inst., 1982—84; asst. prof. S.E. U., Nanjing, China, 1987—92; engr. Nanometrics, Inc., Sunnyvale, Calif., 1996—98; sr. engr. JDS Uniphase Corp., San Jose, 1998—. Vice-sec. gen. Jiangsu Inst. Electronics, Nanjing, 1989-91; dept. sec. for rsch. and acad. affairs S.E. U., Nanjing, 1989-91. Contbr. articles to Beijing U. of Posts and Telecomms. jour., Procs. of IEEE-EMC Symposium, others. Recipient 2d prize sci. and tech. progress China Ministry Machinery Industry, 1986. Mem. IEEE Electromagnetic Compatibility Soc., Electron Devices Soc., China Inst. Electronics, Jiangsu Inst. Electronics. Achievements include E-M theory of anisotropic optical fibers; unified formula for E-M effects of power lines on telecommunication lines; processing and characterization of PCD and DLC semiconductor materials; anisotropic ellipsometry and reflectometry; optical characterization of copolymers; semiconductor lasers with waveguide-cavity combined structure; R&D and product development and manufacturing of gas lasers (argon and He-Ne); precision cleaning chemistry and precious metal brazing; correction to Marcatili's model of channel waveguides. Avocations: American history, reading, classical music, Chinese classical literature, language learning. Office: JDS Uniphase-Comml Lasers 90 Rose Orchard Way San Jose CA 95134-1623 E-mail: wudg@hotmail.com.

WU, ESTHER UN-WAH, managment consultant; b. Pasadena, Calif., Feb. 24, 1960; d. Wilson and Louise W. BS in Pub. Adminstrn., U. So. Calif., 1982; MS in Pub. Health, UCLA, 1984. Supr. corp. disability plans Security Pacific Corp., L.A., 1983-84; rsch. assoc. Robert Wood Johnson Found./U. Lowell, Mass., 1984; sr. employee benefits rep. McDonnell Douglas Corp., Long Beach, Calif., 1984-89, adminstr., 1989-91; fin. benefits adminstr. Carter Hawley Hale, 1992-93; sr. cons. B. Castle Smith & Co., Pasadena, 1994—. Com. mem. data collection Employers Health Care Coalition Los Angeles, 1984-91; mem. Orange County Health Care Coalition, 1984-91. Contbr. chpt. to book in field. Mem. Am. Soc. Pub. Adminstrn., Am. Pub. Health Assn., U. Soc. Calif. Pub. Adminstrn. Support Group. Democrat. Episcopalian. Avocation: tennis. Home: 1716 Grand Oaks Ave Altadena CA 91001-3612 E-mail: estherwu@bcastlesmith.com.

WU, FRANK H. law educator, journalist; b. Cleve., Aug. 20, 1967; s. Hai and Grace (Ma) W. BA, Johns Hopkins U., 1988; JD, U. Mich., 1991. Bar: Calif. 1992, D.C. 1995. Assoc. Morrison & Foerster, San Francisco, 1992-94; fellow Stanford U. Law Sch., Palo Alto, 1994-95; assoc. prof. Howard U. Law Sch., Washington, 1995—; clinic dir., 2000—. Scholar-in-residence Deep Springs Coll., 2001. Author: Yellow: Race in America Beyond Black and White, 2001; co-author: Beyond Self Interest, 1996, Race, Rights and Reparation: Law and the Japanese American Internment, 2001; contbg. author: The Affirmative Action Debate, 1996, Illegal Immigration Viewpoints, 1996. Bd. trustees Gallaudet U., 2000—; chmn. hearing com. D.C. Bar Bd. Profl. Responsibility, 2000—, D.C. Human Rights Commn., 2001—. Mem. Asian Pacific ABA (dir. ednl. fund 1995-98). Home: 4423 35th St NW Washington DC 20008-4203 Office: Howard U Law Sch 2900 Van Ness St NW Washington DC 20008-1100

WU, GUOFA FELIX, manufacturing executive; b. Nanchang, Jiangxi, China, Oct. 19, 1945; s. Luxing Wu and Guande Xiong; m. Juan Liu; children: Libby; m. Youming Zhong (div. Nov. 15, 1985); children: Zhehui. M in Engring., Tsinghua U., Beijing, China, 1984; M in Sci., U. Toledo, Ohio, 1993; Ph. D., Harrington, Eng., 1995. Pres. Global Internet Corp., Boston, 1999—. Tech. specialist Nat. Transp. Systems Ctr. of U.S. Dept. Transp., Cambridge, Mass. Fellow: North Am. Soc.Experts and Entrepreneurs (pres. 2001—02). Home: 36 Parsons St Boston MA 02135

WU, HARRY PAO-TUNG, retired librarian; b. Jinan, Shandong, China, May 1, 1932; came to U.S., 1960; s. James Ching-Mei and Elizabeth Hsiao (Lu) W.; m. Irene I-Len Sun, June 23, 1961; children: Eva Pei-Chen, Walter Pei-Liang. BA, Nat. Taiwan U., Taipei, 1959; student, Ohio State U., 1962; MLS, Kent State U., 1966. Archive and libr. asst. Taiwan Handicraft Promotion Ctr., Taipei, 1959-60; student asst. Kent State U. Libr., 1960-61; reference libr. Massillon (Ohio) Pub. Libr., 1964-65, acting asst. dir., 1965, asst. dir., head adult svcs., 1966; dir. Flesh Pub. Libr., Piqua, Ohio, 1966-68, St. Clair County Libr. Sys., Pt. Huron, Mich., 1968-96; founder, dir. Blue Water Libr. Fedn., 1974-96; ret., 1996. Pres. Mich. Library Film Circuit, Lansing, 1977-79; mem. St. Clair County Literacy Project Com., 1986-96; bd. dirs. Blue Water Reading Coun., 1987-88, Mich. Waterways council Girl Scouts U.S.A., Port Huron, 1985-86; bd. dirs. United Way St. Clair County, Mich., 1990-91; bd. trustees Libr. Mich., 1992-95. Cmty. mem. editl. bd. Times Herald, 1998-99. Mem. ALA, Mich. Libr. Assn. (chmn. libr. sys. roundtable 1974-75), Am. Mgmt. Assn., Assn. Ednl. Comms. and Tech., Detroit Suburban Librs. Roundtable, Chinese-Am. Librs. Assn., Pt. Huron Internat. Club (pres. 1988), Rotary (dir. 1972-74, 88-90, Paul Harris fellow 1988). Home: 1518 Holland Ave Port Huron MI 48060-1511

WU, HSIU KWANG, economist, educator; b. Hankow, China, Dec. 14, 1935; came to U.S., 1952, naturalized, 1963; s. Kao Cheng and Edith (Huang) W.; m. Kathleen Gibbs Johnson, Aug. 17, 1968. Grad., Lawrenceville Sch., 1954; AB, Princeton U., 1958; MBA, U. Pa., 1960, PhD, 1963. Prof., group coordinator fin., econs. and internat. bus. Boston U., 1968-72; prof., chmn. fin., econs. and legal studies faculty U. Ala., 1972-81, Lee Bidgood prof. fin. and econs., 1978-97, Ala. Banker Edn. Found. Banking Chair prof., 1973-78, prof. emeritus fin., 1997—; econ. adviser Office of Comptroller of Currency, U.S. Treasury, 1966-69, 75-80; dir. Ala. Fed., 1984-88, SECOR Bank FSB, 1988-93, chmn. bd., 1992-93. Cons. instl. investor study SEC, 1969-70; mem. com. examiners undergrad. program for counseling and evaluation test in bus. Ednl. Testing Service, 1971, 77 Co-editor: Elements of Investments, 2d rev. edit, 1972; Contbr. articles to law and econ. jours. Sloan Faculty fellow Sloan Sch. Mgmt., Mass. Inst. Tech., 1965-66 Mem. Am. Fin. Assn., Fin. Mgmt. Assn. Home: 3201 Old Barn Ct Ponte Vedra Beach FL 32082-3713

WU, JAMES CHEN-YUAN, aerospace engineering educator; b. Nanking, China, Oct. 5, 1931; came to U.S., 1953, naturalized, 1963; s. Chien Lieh and Cheng-Ling Wu; m. Mei-Ying Chang, Sept. 7, 1957; children— Alberta Yee-Hwa, Norbert Mao-Hwa. Student, Nat. Taiwan (Formosa) U., 1949-52; BS, Gonzaga U., 1954; postgrad., Columbia U., 1954; MS (univ. fellow), U. Ill., 1955, PhD, 1957. Engr. Wah Chang Corp., N.Y.C., 1954; researcher Mass. Inst. Tech. at Cambridge, 1957; asst. prof. Gonzaga U., Spokane, Wash., 1957-59; research specialist Douglas Aircraft Co., 1959-65, group leader, 1960-61, supr., 1961-62, br. chief, 1963-65; prof. aerospace engrng. Ga. Inst. Tech., 1965-96; pres. Applied Aero, LLC, 1996—. Cons. N.Am. Aviation Co., Geophys. Tech. Corp., European Atomic Energy Commn., Ispra, Italy, European Atomic Energy Commn. (research center), U.S. Army Research Office, Durham, S.C. Contbr. articles to profl. jours. Chmn. bd. dirs. Chinese-Am. Inst. Recipient profl. achievement award Douglas Aricraft Co., 1963, Outstanding Tchrs. award Gonzaga U., 1959; Assn. fellow Am. Inst. Aeros. and Astronautics Mem. Am. Soc. Engrng. Sci. (founding), Soc. Indsl. and Applied Math. (vice-chmn. Pacific N.W. 1958-59), Am. Astron. Soc. (sr.), Am. Phys. Soc., Nat. Assn. Chinese Ams. (pres. Atlanta chpt.), Sigma Xi, Tau Beta Pi, Sigma Alpha Nu. Office: Sch Aerospace Engring Georgia Inst Tech 48365 Avalon Heights Ter Fremont CA 94539-8005

WU, JIE, molecular biologist, educator; b. Xiamen, China, Aug. 10, 1959; BS, Xiamen (China) U., 1982; PhD, U. Kans., 1988. Asst. prof. dept. med. microbiology and immunology U. South Fla., Tampa, 1991-2001, assoc. prof., 2001—, assoc. prof. interdisciplinary oncology program, 2001—; asst. prof.

H. Lee Moffitt Cancer Ctr., 1995-2001, assoc. prof., 2001—. Editor Frontiers in Bioscience, 2001—; contbr. articles to profl. jours. Postdoctoral fellowship Juvenile Diabetes Found. Internat., 1992-94; recipient Jr. Faculty Rsch. award Am. Cancer Soc., 1996-99, Young Investigator award Am. Diabetes Assn., 1993. Mem. AAAS, Am. Assn. for Cancer Rsch., Soc. of Chinese Bioscientist in Am. Office: Molecular Oncology Program H Lee Moffitt Cancer Ctr 12902 Magnolia Dr Tampa FL 33612 E-mail: wu@moffitt.usf.edu.

WU, JUNJIE, agricultural economics educator; b. Luyi, Henan, China, Sept. 1, 1963; married. PhD in Agrl. Econs., U. Conn., 1992. Assoc. prof. Oreg. State U., Corvallis, 1987—. Contbr. articles to profl. jours. Mem.: Am. Agrl. Econs. Assn. Office: Oreg State U Ballard 200A Corvallis OR 97331 Office Fax: 541-737-1441. Business E-Mail: junjie.wu@orst..edu.

WU, KENNETH KUN-YU, physician, scientist; b. Kaohsiung, Taiwan, Taiwan, July 6, 1941; came to U.S., 1967; m. Lung-Chin Wu, Mar. 29, 1969; children: Stanley, David. MD, Nat. Taiwan U., 1966; MS, Yale U., 1968; PhD, The Univ. London, 1997. Diplomate in internal medicine and hematology Am. Bd. Internal Medicine, 1973. Assoc. in medicine U. Iowa, Iowa City, 1973-74, asst. prof. medicine, 1974-76; assoc. prof. medicine, dir. coagulation and thrombosis unit Rush Med. Coll., Chgo., 1976-81, prof. medicine, dir. coagulation and thrombosis unit, 1981-83; prof. medicine, dir. divsn. hematology and oncology U. Tex. Med. Sch., Houston, 1983—, prof. pathology and lab. medicine, 1984—, dir. Gen. Clin. Rsch. Ctr., 1985-91, dir. Vacular Biology Rsch. Ctr., 1988—, vice chmn. dept. medicine, 1990—; adj. prof. Biomed. Rsch. Lab. Rice U., 1984—; vis. prof. The William Harvey Rsch. Inst. St. Bartholomew's Hosp. Med. Coll., London, 1991-92; Royl M. and Phyllis Gough Huffington prof. in gerontology U. Tex. Health Sci. Ctr. Mem. hematology study sect. NIH, Bethesda, Md.; mem. rev. com. Nat. Heart Lung and Blood Inst., Nat. Neurologic and Stroke Inst. Contbr. over 300 articles to profl. jours. Mem. Assn. Am. Physicians, Am Soc. Clin. Investigation, Academia Sinica (Taiwan). Office: U Tex Health Sci Ctr 6431 Fannin St Houston TX 77030-1501 E-mail: Kenneth.K.Wu@uth.tmc.edu.

WU, LAWRENCE MG HLA MYIN, physician; b. Rangoon, Burma, May 12, 1937; arrived in U.S., 1964; s. John and Maria (Wong) W.; m. Margaret Perez, June 1968. MBBS, U. Rangoon, Burma, 1961. Internship Knickerbocker Hosp., N.Y.C., residency, chief residency; house phys. (fell.) St. Mary's Hosp., Bklyn.; surgeon Harrison Cmty. Hosp., Cadiz, Ohio, Harris Walker Clin., S. Williamsoms, Ky.; priv. prac. Boenger Clin., Edgerton, Ohio. Med. dir., Boenger Clin., Edgerton, Ohio, 1991—; bd. govs., Community Meml. Hosp., Hicksville, Ohio, 1996—. Mem. C. of C., Edgerton, Ohio. Fellow Am. Coll. Emergency Medicine (life, charter); mem. AMA, Am. Coll. Gen. Practice (life, charter), Ohio St. Med. Assn., Williams Co. Med. Assn., Am. Coll. Internal Phys., Midwest Burma Med. Assn. Republican. Roman Catholic. Home: 3804 Lake Rd Edgerton OH 43517-9536 Office: 104 N West St Edgerton OH 43517-9697

WU, LI-PEI, banker; b. Changhwa, Taiwan, Sept. 9, 1934; came to U.S., 1968; m. Jenny S. Lai, Mar. 24, 1963; children: George T., Eugene Y. BA, Nat. Taiwan U., 1957; MBA, Kans. State U., Ft. Hays, 1969; Comml. Banking Exec. Program, Columbia U., 1974. Staff acct., asst. controller, asst. v.p., v.p. Nat. Bank Alaska, Anchorage, 1969-73, v.p. controller, 1973-76, sr. v.p. chief fin. officer, 1976-78; chmn. exec. com. Alaska Nat. Bank of the North, 1978-79, chief adminstrv. officer, 1979-80, pres., 1980-81; pres., chief exec. officer Gen. Bank & GBC Bancorp, Los Angeles, 1982-84, chmn., pres, chief exec. officer, 1984-98, chmn., CEO, 1998-2000, chmn., 2001—. Sr. adv. to pres. of Taiwan, 2000—; dir. Pacific Coast Banking Sch., 1995—99; bd. advisors Asia Soc., 1998—; mem. Pacific Coun. on Internat. Policy, 1999; chmn. United Taiwanese Found. of So. Calif., 1998—2001; founder and chmn. Formosa Found., 2001—; benefactor Pacific Coun. Internat. Policy, 2000—01. Founder, pres. Taiwanese Am. Polit. Action Com., 1992-93; pres. Taiwanese United Fund, 1990-92; founder, 1st pres. Nat. Taiwanese Am. Citizens League, 1989-91; mem. White House Pacific Rim Econ. Conf., 1995. Recipient Alumni Achievement award Fort Hays U., 1995, Entrepreneur of Yr. award Greater L.A. Ernst & Young, 1998. Office: Gen Bank 800 W 6th St Los Angeles CA 90017-2704 E-mail: lpw@generalbank.com.

WU, MARGARET ANNE, computer scientist, educator; b. Chgo., Apr. 11, 1935; d. Aloys Joseph and Beatrice Rose (Kubal) Schlosser; m. Shih-Yen Wu, June 24, 1967; children: Jennifer, Gregory. BS in Math., Ill. Inst. Tech., 1956; MS in Math., Northwestern U., 1958; PhD in Computer Sci., U. Iowa, 1980. Rsch. computer scientist IIT Rsch. Inst., Chgo., 1958—67; rsch. assoc. U. Iowa, 1967—71, vis. asst. prof. mgmt. info. sys., 1979—93. Author: Computers and Programming: An Introduction, 1973, Introduction to Computer Data Processing, 1975, 2d edit., 1979, Introduction to Computer Data Processing with Basic, 1980; author: (with Shih-Yen Wu) Systems Analysis and Design, 1994. Mem.: Assn. Computing Machinery, Ariz. Sr. Acad.

WU, MICHAEL MING-KUN, software engineer; b. Taoyuan, Republic of China, Dec. 20, 1958; came to U.S., 1961; s. Pei-Rin and Susan Suh-Jin (Lin) W.; m. Cheryl Ann Patton, July 9, 1994. AB in Biochemistry, Harvard Coll., 1979; PhD in Bioengring., U. Pa., 1990. Asst. staff mem. Lincoln Lab., MIT, Lexington, 1979-82; rsch. fellow Inst. Brain Rsch., U. Tokyo, 1984-86; sr. software engr. Lab. Techs. Corp., Wilmington, Mass., 1990-94; prodn.-line mgr. Axon Instruments, Inc., Foster City, Calif., 1994—. Monbusho scholar (Japanese Ministry Sci., Edn. and Culture), Tokyo, 1984-86. Mem. IEEE, Assn. for Computing Machinery, Soc. Gen. Physiologists, Biophys. Soc. Home: 1911 Fort Myer Dr Ste 1100 Arlington VA 22209-1603 Office: Axon Instruemnts Inc 3280 Whipple Rd Union City CA 94587-1217

WU, MING-LU, management consultant; b. Nanyang, Henan, China, Mar. 3, 1963; s. Chang-Hai Wu and Xiang-Lan Zheng; m. Jin-Hong Guo, Apr. 4, 1987 (wid. Oct. 1993); 1 child, Di; m. Chung Shing, Feb. 12, 1996. B Engring, Jilin U. Tech., Changchun, China, 1983; MS, Chinese Acad. Scis., Beijing, 1986, PhD, 1994. Asst. prof. Nat. Rsch. Ctr. for Sci. and Tech. for Devel., Beijing, 1986-91, assoc. prof., 1994-95; rsch. fellow City U. of Hong Kong, 1995—. Invited rschr. China's Enterprises Evaluation Ctr., Beijing, 1987-88; rsch. asst. Beijing Info. and Control Inst., Beijing, 1984-85. Co-author: (books) China's Economic Development and Some Related Factors' Analysis, 1991, International Competitiveness, 1992 (3rd prize for technology progress, China's State S&T Commn. 1994). Avocations: Chinese poetry and prose composition, games. Office: City U Hong Kong Dept Mgmt Scis 83 Tat chee Ave Kowloon Hong Kong China Personal E-mail: ng0312@hongkong.com. Business E-Mail: msminglu@cityu.edu.hk.

WU, QIAO, nuclear engineer, educator, nuclear engineer, researcher; b. Yibin, Sichuan Province, China, July 4, 1960; s. Ronghui Liu; m. Jianping Xu, Aug. 15, 1987. PhD, Purdue U., 1995. Sr. rschr. Purdue U., West Lafayette, Ind., 1995—98; asst. prof. Oreg. State U., Corvallis, 1998—2001. Contbr. articles to profl. jours. Mem.: Am. Nuc. Soc. (Best Paper award Thermal Hydraulics Divsn. 1997). Office: Oreg State U 130 Radiation Ctr Corvallis OR 97331 Office Fax: 541-737-0480. Business E-Mail: qiao@engr.orst.edu.

WU, RONGLING, geneticist, researcher; b. Rugao, Jiangsu, China, Jan. 27, 1964; s. Youpeng Wu and Xiuying Zhang; m. Helen Rong Chen, Mar. 12, 1989; 1 child, Louie. BS, Nanjing (China) Forestry U., 1984, MS, 1987; PhD, U. Wash., 1995. Asst. prof. Nanjing Forestry U., 1987-90; postdoctoral rsch. assoc. U. Wash., Seattle, 1995-96, N.C. State U., Raleigh, 1996-98, rsch. assoc., 1998-2000; asst. prof. dept. stats. U. Fla., Gainesville. Advisor Chinese Acad. Forestry, Beijing, 1997—, Nanjing Forestry U., 1997—, Beijing Forestry U., 2001—. Contbr. articles to profl. jours. Recipient Rsch. Excellence prize, State Economy Commn. and State Sci. and Tech., China, 1990, 2d Sci. and Ext. prize, Ministry of Forestry, China, 1991, 3d Sci. Invention prize, State Sci. and Tech. Commn., China, 1994, award, USDA, 2001, Outstanding Young Investigator award, Nat. Natural Sci. Found., China, 2001. Avocations: running, swimming, camping, movies. Home: 11929 NW 10th Rd Gainesville FL 32606

WU, RU-SHAN, geophysicist; b. XingYang, Henan, China, Dec. 9, 1938; came to U.S., 1990; s. Yue Ren Wu and Song Zhen Zhang; children: Xili, Hui-han. BSc in Physics, North-Western Univ., Sian, China, 1962; PhD in Geophysics, MIT, 1984. Rsch. asst. Inst. Geophysical Prospecting, Min. Geology, Peking, China, 1962-65, rsch. scientist, 1966-77, sr. rsch. scientist, 1977-78; asst. rsch. physicist Univ. Calif., Santa Cruz, 1986, assoc. rsch. geophysicist, 1987-88, 90-95; rsch. geophysicist Inst. Geophys. and Planet Phys., Univ. Calif., 1995—; dir. modeling and imaging lab. Inst. Tectonics, Univ. Calif., 1997—; assoc. rsch. geophysicist Inst. Geophysics, Chinese Acad. Scis., Beijing, 1988-89, rsch. geophysicist, 1989-90. Vis. sci. MIT, Cambridge, 1978-80, postdoc. assoc., 1984-85; vis. sci. Nat. Rsch. Ctr. Disaster Prevention, Tsukuba, Japan, 1988-89; vis. prof. Fed. Univ. Bahia, Salvador, Brazil, 1990-91; Karlsruhe (Germany) Univ., 1992. Guest editor Jour. Pure Applied Geophysics, 1987-88; mem. editl. bd. Acta Geophysica Sinica; contbr. over 100 articles to profl. publs. Recipient Cert. of Merit, Nat. Conf. Sci. Tech. China, 1977. Fellow Chinese Geophys. Assn.; mem. Am. Geophy. Union, Soc. Exploration Geophys., Seismol. Soc. Am., Internat. Assn. Seismology Physics Earth Interior (mem. com. heterogeneity, chair subcom. heterogeneity, com. wave propagation). Avocations: music, arts, poetry, languages. Office: Inst Geophys and Phys/Earth Scis Univ Calif Santa Cruz 1156 High St Santa Cruz CA 95064-1077

WU, SARAH ZHENG, investment banker; b. Shanghai, China, Dec. 2, 1963; came to U.S., 1987; d. Chunzhuo Wu and Zhifen Chen; m. Sagun Raj Tuladhar, Jan. 28, 1995. Student, Tongji U., Shanghai, 1979-82; BA in Town and County Planning, Manchester (Eng.) U., 1987; MS in Urban and Regional Planning, Columbia U., 1989. Rsch. asst. Manchester U. Sch. Town and Country Planning, 1987-89, Columbia U. Grad. Sch. Arch., Planning & Hist. Preservation, N.Y.C., 1987-89; urban and transp. planner Parsons Brinckerhoff, 1989-92, sr. environ. planner Honolulu, 1992-95; fin. analyst, privatization and project fin. Parson Brinckerhoof Infrastructure Devel. Co., N.Y.C., 1995-97; portfolio mgr. Global Project Fin. Credit Suisse First Boston, 1997—. Editor Jour. Chinese Student Assn. Manchester U., 1987; rsch. asst.: Parks and Gardens of Cheshire Park and Plains, U.K., 1987, The Global City: New York, London and Tokyo, 1991. Recipient William Kennie fellowship Columbia U., N.Y.C., 1988. Mem. Internat. Chinese Transp. Profls. Assn. (treas., bd. dirs.), Am. Planning Assn. (Robert C. Weinberg award for acad. excellence in urban planning 1989), Chinese Am. Assn. Engrs. Avocations: Asian art, Chinese antique furniture and porcelain, stamp collecting, travel, opera. Home: 800 Palisade Ave Fort Lee NJ 07024-4193 Office: Credit Suisse First Boston Global Project Fin 11 Madison Ave New York NY 10010-3698

WU, SHI-QI (SAMUEL WU), medical geneticist; b. Anhuei, China, Oct. 14, 1945; s. Wu Qi-Qiang and Xu Yi-Fang. MD, Shanghai First Med. Coll., China, 1971. Diplomate Am. Bd. Med. Genetics. Internist Xian 52 Hosp., China, 1972-73, res. gen. surgery China, 1973-78; res. hematololgy Zhongshang Hosp., Shanghai, China, 1979-84; fellowship clin. cytogenetics U. Wis., 1985-88; fellowship cytogenetics U. British Columbia, Vancouver, Canada, 1988-90; co-dir. cytogenetics. rsch. lab Comp. Cancer Ctr. U. Wisc., Madison, Wis., 1993-98; cons. cytogenetics Wis. State Lab Hygiene, 1993-98; assoc. scientist human oncol. U. Wis. Med. Sch., 1990-92, sr. scientist human oncology, 1992-98; assoc. prof. dept pediat. U. So. Calif., 1998—; dir. cytogenetics lab Children's Hosp., L.A., 1998—; program dir. Am. Bd. Med. Genetics program in CHLA, Chiildren's Hosp., U. So. Calif. Med. Sch., 1999—. Mem. ACMG, Am. Assn. Cancer Rsch., Am. Soc. Med. Gene. Office: Children's Hosp Cytogenetics Lab Mailstop 11 4650 W Sunset Blvd Los Angeles CA 90027-6062 E-mail: SWU@chla.usc.edu.

WU, SUSAN YING CHU LIN (YING-CHU LIN), engineering company executive, engineer; b. Beijing, June 23, 1932; came to U.S., 1957; d. Chi-yu and K.C. (Kung) Lin; m. Jain-Ming Wu, June 13, 1959; children: Ernest H., Albert H., Karen H. BSME, Nat. Taiwan U., 1955; MS in Aero. Engring., Ohio State U., 1959; PhD in Aeros., Calif. Inst. Tech., 1963. Sr. engr. Elecro-Optical Systems, Inc., Pasadena, Calif., 1963-65; asst. prof. aero. engring. U. Tenn. Space Inst., Tullahoma, 1965-67, assoc. prof., 1967-73, prof., 1973-88; adminstr. Energy Conversion R&D Programs, 1981-88; pres., chief exec. officer ERC, Inc., Huntsville, Ala., 1987-2000, chmn., 2000—. Presdl. appointee adv. bd. Nat. Air and Space Mus., Smithsonian Inst., 1993-2000. Contbr. over 90 articles to profl. jours. Mem. Better Sch. Task Force, Tullahoma, 1985-86; founding mem. Tullahoma Edn. Found. for Excellence; trustee Rochester Inst. Tech., 1992-94; mem. adv. com. NASA Aeronautics and Space Transp. Tech., 1994-2000. Recipient Chancellor's Rsch. award U. Tenn., 1978, Outstanding Educator of Am. award, 1973, 75; Amelia Earhart fellow, 1958, 59, 62, Plasmadynamics and Lasers award AIAA, 1994, Faraday Meml. medal Internat. Liaison Group for MHD Pow Generation, 1999. Fellow ASME, AIAA (assoc.); mem. Soc. Women Engrs. (hon., life; achievement award 1985), Sigma Xi. Office: ERC Inc 555 Sparkman Dr NW Ste 1622 Huntsville AL 35816-3431 E-mail: swu@erc-incorporated.com.

WU, TAI TE, biological sciences and engineering educator; b. Shanghai, China, Aug. 2, 1935; m. Anna Fang, Apr. 16, 1966; 1 son, Richard. MB, BS, U. Hong Kong, 1956; BS in Mech. Engring. U. Ill., Urbana, 1958; SM in Applied Physics, Harvard U., 1959, PhD in Engring. (Gordon McKay fellow), 1961. Rsch. fellow in structural mechanics Harvard U., 1961-63; rsch. fellow in biol. chemistry Harvard U. (Med. Sch.), 1964, rsch. assoc., 1965-66; rsch. scientist Hydronautics, Inc., Rockville, Md., 1962; asst. prof. engring. Brown U., Providence, 1963-65; asst. prof. biomath. Grad. Sch. Med. Scis., Cornell U. Med. Coll., N.Y.C., 1967-68, assoc. prof., 1968-70; assoc. prof. physics and engring. scis. Northwestern U., Evanston, Ill., 1970-73, prof., 1973-74, prof. biochemistry and molecular biology and engring. scis., 1973-85, acting chmn. dept. engring. scis., 1974, prof. biochem., molecular biology, cell biology and biomed. engring., engring. scis., applied math., 1985-94, prof. biochemistry, molecular biology, cell biology, biomed. engring., 1994—. Author (with E.A. Kabat and others): Variable Regions of Immunoglobulin Chains, 1976, Sequences of Immunoglobulin Chains, 1979, Sequences of Proteins of Immunological Importance, 1983, Sequences of Proteins of Immunological Interest, 1987, 5th edit., 1991; editor: New Methodologies in Studies of Protein Configuration, 1985, Analytical Molecular Biology, 2001; contbr. Recipient progress award Chinese Engrs. and Scientists Assn. So. Calif., Los Angeles, 1971; C.T. Loo Scholar, 1959-60; NIH Research Career Devel. awardee, 1974-79 Mem. Am. Soc. Biochem. and Molecular Biology, Biophys. Soc., Sigma Xi, Tau Beta Pi, Pi Mu Epsilon. Office: Northwestern U Dept Biochem Molecular and Cell Biology Evanston IL 60208-0001 E-mail: tt@immuno.bme.nwu.edu.

WU, THOMAS XINZHANG, engineering educator, researcher; b. Urumqi, Xinjiang, China, Nov. 21, 1968; came to U.S., 1995; m. Nadine Xiufang Guo, June 15, 1992; 1 child, Lucy. BS in Engring., U. Sci. and Tech., Hefei, Anhui, China, 1988, MS in Engring., 1991, U. Pa., 1997, PhD, 1999. Asst. U. Sci. and Tech., Hefei, 1991-93, lectr., 1993-95; asst. prof. Sch. Elec. Engring./Computer Sci. U. Cen. Fla., Orlando, 2000. Presenter in field. Contbr. articles to profl. jours. Head evangelism of the core group of mandarin svc. Chinese Christian Ch. and Ctr., Phila., 1998, worship leader mandarin svc., 1997—. Rsch. fellow U. Pa., 1995-99; recipient Pres. award Chinese Acad. Scis., 1991, Excellent Papers award China Microwave Soc., 1993, Young Scientist Found. award U. Sci. and Tech., 1994-95. Mem. IEEE (reviewer 1996—), Optical Soc. Am. (reviewer 1999—). Achievements include research in RF ICS, packaging, chaotic electromagnetics, electromagnetic metamaterials, China C-band satellite beam forming network design using rectangular coaxial waveguide technology; invention of omnidirectional leaky wave antenna. Avocations: Bible reading, music, travel, sports, friends. Office: U Central Fla EE Program Sch Elec Engring Orlando FL 32817 Fax: 407-823-5835. E-mail: tomwu@mail.ucf.edu.

WU, TIEN HSING, civil engineering educator, consulting engineer; b. Shanghai, China, Mar. 2, 1923; came to U.S., 1947, naturalized, 1957; s. Chong-Yung and Ying Mei (Pih) Woo; m. Peihsing Lin, Aug. 14, 1952; children: Mei, Anne. B.S., St. John's U., Shanghai, 1947; M.S., U. Ill., 1948, Ph.D., 1951. Registered profl. engr., Ohio, Mich. Civil engr. DeLeuw Cather & Co., Chgo., 1951-52, Ill. Div. Hwys., Springfield, 1952-53; from asst. prof. to prof. Mich. State U., East Lansing, 1953-65; prof. civil engring. Ohio State U., Columbus, 1965—; vis. prof. Norwegian Geotech. Inst., Oslo, 1959, 70, 76, Nat. U. Mex., Mexico City, 1964, Royal Inst. Tech., Stockholm, 1980; UN cons. Punjab Agrl. U., Ludhiana, India, 1981. Author: Soil Mechanics, 2d, rev. edit., 1976; Soil Dynamics, 1970; also papers, numerous articles. Recipient Antarctica Svc. medal, 1967, Lichtenstein award Ohio State U., 1973, research award Ohio State U., 1984. Fellow ASCE (State of the Art award 1990); mem. Transp. Rsch. Bd., Sigma Xi. Home: 160 Brookside Oval Columbus OH 43085-3638

WU, TSE CHENG, research chemist; b. Hong Kong, Aug. 21, 1923; came to U.S., 1947, naturalized, 1962; s. Shau Chuan and Shui (Chan) W.; m. Janet Ling, June 14, 1963; children: Alan, Anna, Bernard. BS, Yenching U., 1946; MS, U. Ill., 1948; PhD, Iowa State U., 1952. Prodn. chemist Yungli Industries, Tangku, China, 1946-47; rsch. assoc. Iowa State U., Ames, 1952-53; rsch. chemist duPont Co., Waynesboro, Va., 1953-60, GE, Waterford, N.Y., 1960-71; sr. rsch. chemist Abcor, Inc., Wilmington, Mass., 1971-77; rsch. assoc. Allied-Signal, Inc., Morristown, N.J., 1977-88; cons., 1989—. Contbr. articles to profl. jours; patentee in polymer chemistry and organosilicon chemistry. Mem. Troy Arts Guild, 1968-71, Morris County Art Assn., 1981, Rossmoor Art Assn., 1999. Recipient Gold medallion award for inventions GE, 1967; Allied Corp. patent award, 1983; Eastman Kodak Rsch. fellow, 1951-52. Mem. Am. Chem. Soc., Sigma Xi, Phi Kappa Phi, Phi Lambda Upsilon, Alpha Chi Sigma. Home: 601 Red Wing Ct Walnut Creek CA 94595-3927

WU, TSONG-HO, operations researcher; b. Pingtung, Taipei, Nov. 29, 1952; came to U.S., 1980; s. Ching-Chiang and Li-Shiang (Huang) W.; m. Shu-Jen S. Shei, Dec. 28, 1979; children: Arthur, Mae, Sandy. BA in Math., Nat. Taiwan U., Taipei, Taiwan, 1976; MS in Ops. Rsch., SUNY, Stony Brook, 1981, PhD in Ops. Rsch., 1983. Sr. network architect Sprint Data, Lenexa, Kans., 1983-86; mem. tech. staff Bellcore, Red Bank, N.J., 1986-94, dir., 1995-99; tech. cons. AT&T Labs., Middletown, 1999-2000; pres., CEO, Transtech Networks, Inc., 2000—. Guest mem. tech. rev. bd. Ministry Transp. and Comm., Taipei, 1993-94, 96. Author: Fiber Network Service Survivability, 1992, ATM Transport and Network Integrity, 1997; editor IEEE Jour., Jan. 1994; patentee passive protected SONET ring architecture. Recipient N.J. Inventors of Yr. award N.J. Inventors Hall of Fame, 1997. Fellow IEEE (Disting. Lectr. award 1998—). Avocations: writing, music, table tennis, travel. E-mail: twu@transtechnetworks.com.

WU, TUNG, curator, art historian, art educator, artist; b. Fuzhou, Fukien, China, Dec. 10, 1940; came to U.S., 1965; s. Chin-Wen and Jingrong (Chen) W.; m. Ying Chin, July 16, 1974. BA, Normal U., Taipei, Taiwan, 1962; postgrad., U. Mich., 1967-70, Harvard U., 1979—. Rsch. asst. Nat. Palace Mus., Taichung, Taiwan, 1962-65; with photography archive U. Mich., 1966-68; rsch. asst. Cleve. Mus. Art, 1968; Ford Found. curatorial intern Nelson-Atkins Mus. Art, Kansas City, Mo., 1969; rsch. fellow Mus. Fine Arts, Boston, 1971-79, asst. curator, 1980-84, assoc. curator, 1985-86, curator Asian art, 1986-92, Matsutaro Shoriki curator Asian art, 1992—, head dept. art of Asia, Oceania and Africa, 1999—. Teaching asst. U. Kans., Lawrence, 1969, Harvard U., 1978; vis. lectr. Harvard U., Cambridge, Mass., 1975, Emmanuel Coll., Boston, 1992, Simmons Coll., Boston, 1993; advisor Chinese Inst. Am., N.Y.C., 1985—, Chinese Cultural Found., San Francisco, 1985-87, Nat. Mus. History, Taipei, 1984—; cons. Project Emperor-One, Boston, 1983-86; panelist mus. program NEA, 1995; panelist Korea Found. Workshop on Korean painting, Seoul, South Korea, 2000. Mem. Nat. Com. on U.S.-China Rels., Washington, 1985—; mem. Nat. Devel. Seminar Taipei, 1989, 92, Nat. Edn. Reform, Taipei, 1994; advisor dept. Asian trade art Peabody Mus., Salem. Mass., 191—; trustee W.A. Compton Found. Oriental Arts. Grantee Freer Found. U. Mich., 1968, Ford Found., Kansas City, 1969, Smithsonian Instn., Washington, 1978; recipient Outstanding Alumnus award Taiwan Normal U., 1997. Mem. Taoist Soc. Japan, Soc. Chinese Kunqu Opera, Soc. Chinese Calligraphy. Office: Mus Fine Arts Asiatic Dept 465 Huntington Ave Boston MA 02115-5597

WU, WAYNE WEN-YAU, artist; b. Tachia, Taiwan, Republic of China, Oct. 5, 1935; s. K.C. Kau and Chin-Fong (Chen) W.; m. Amy Hsueh, Dec. 25, 1961; children: Ingrid, Judy, David. BA in Fine Arts, Taiwan Normal U., 1959. Supr. art edn. ctr. Taichung (Taiwan) Libr., 1970-74; instr. fine arts dept. Taiwan Normal U., Taipei, 1973-74; instr. paintings Hunter Mus. of Art, Chatanooga, Tenn., 1980-92; artist, painting instr. Wayne Wu's Art Studio, Atlanta, 1994-2000, San Jose, Calif., 2000, Salinas, 2000—. Represented in 23 solo shows including Taiwan Mus. of Art, 1995, Hunter Mus. of Am. Art, 1980, 98, Taipei Internat. Art Fair, 2001, and over 100 group shows. Mem. Am. Watercolor Soc. Home: 815 Cactus Ct Salinas CA 93905-4606

WU, YING, economics educator, researcher; b. Beijing, Sept. 22, 1955; s. Dazhi and Chengying (Mao) W.; m. Hong Yao, Jan. 20, 1987; children: Danke, Danlei. BA in Econs., Peking (China) U., 1984, MA in Econs., 1987; PhD in Econs., U. Oreg., 1992. Instr. Peking U., 1986-87; grad. tchg. fellow U. Oreg., 1987-92; asst. prof. U. Portland, 1992-93; instr. Lane C.C., 1993-94; lectr. Nanyang Technol. U., Singapore, 1994-98; asst. prof. Salisbury U., 1998—2002, assoc. prof., 2002—. Guest prof. Peking U., 1995; guest commentator Asia Bus. News, Singapore, 1996-97, Brit. Broadcasting Corp., 1997. Author: An Analysis of Credit and Equilibrium Credit Rationing, 1994; jour. referee Journ. Macroecons., 1996; contbr. articles to profl. jours. Libr. svc. coord. Nanyang Techol. U., 1997-98. Recipient 20th Century Achievement award Internat. Biog. Ctr., U.K., 1998, 2000 Millennium medal, Am. Biog. Inst., 1999. Mem. Am. Econ. Assn., Western Econ. Assn., Pi Gamma Mu. Avocations: table tennis, jogging, swimming, hiking, movies. Office: Salisbury U Franklin P Perdue Sch Bus 1101 Camden Ave Salisbury MD 21801-6860 E-mail: yxwu@salisbury.edu.

WU, YUNG C. retired chemist; b. Canton, China, Oct. 3, 1923; BS, Sun Yat-Sen U., Guangzhou, China, 1947; MS, U. Houston, 1952; PhD, U. Chgo., 1957. Rsch. chemist Portland Cement Assn., Skokie, Ill., 1958—62, IBM, Yorktown Heights, NY, 1963—66, Oak Ridge (Tenn.) Nat. Lab., 1966—67, Nat. Inst. Stds. and Tech., Gaithersburg, Md., 1967—95. Inventor in field. Office: Nat Inst Stds & Tech 100 Bureau Dr Gaithersburg MD 20899

WU, YUNYING, engineer, researcher; b. Beijing, Jan. 26, 1968; came to U.S., 1990; d. Cang-Pu Wu and Huiqi Gao; m. Shiawpyng Yang, May 6, 1995. BS in Engring. Mechanics, Peking U., 1990; M Sys. Sci. and Math., Washington U., 1992, DSc in Engring., 1996. Rsch. and tchg. asst. Washington U., St. Louis, 1990-95; sr. engr. Computer Scis. Co., Fairview Height, Ill., 1996—. Contbr. articles to profl. jours. Scholar Washington U., St. Louis, 1990-95. Mem. IEEE. Avocations: music, painting, reading, chatting. Office: Computer Scis Corp 8 Executive Dr Ste 300 Fairview Heights IL 62208-1352

WUBAH, DANIEL ASUA, microbiologist, educator, dean; b. Accra, Ghana, Nov. 6, 1960; came to U.S., 1984; s. Daniel Asua and Elizabeth Bruba (Appoe) W.; m. Judith A. Dadson, Dec. 17, 1993; children: Vera Brubak, Araba. BSc with honors, BEd, U. Cape Coast, Ghana, 1984; MS, U. Akron, 1988; PhD, U. Ga., 1990. Cert. in hazardous waste site ops. and emergency response health and safety. Postdoctoral fellow U.S. EPA Rsch. Lab., Athens, Ga., 1991-92; asst. prof. dept. microbiology Towson (Md.) U., 1992-97, assoc. prof., 1997-2000, dept. chair, 1998-2000; assoc. dean Coll. Sci. and Math. James Madison U., 2000—, prof., 2002—. Councillor Coun. Undergrad. Rsch. Assoc. editor: Mycologia; contbr. articles to profl. publs. Sr. warden Sherwood Episcopal Ch., Cockeysville, Md., 1998-2000; bd. govs. Nat. Aquarium Balt. Recipient Paul Acquarone award U. Akron, 1985, Palfrey award U. Ga., 1989; Faculty Rsch. grantee Towson State U., 1992, 94, 97; grantee NSF, 1993, 98—, USDA, 1994, Univ. Sys. Md., 1998-2000, NIH Bridges, 1998—, NSF Undergrad. Mentoring in Environ. Biology, 2000—. Mem. AAAS, Mycological Soc. of Am., Am. Soc. Microbiology, Med. Mycological Soc. of Am., Internat. Soc. for Human and Animal Mycology, CUR (councilor biology divsn.), Sigma Xi (pres. Towson chpt. 1996-97), Coun. on Undergrad. Rsch. (listserver adminstr.), Project Kaleidoscope F21. Episcopalian. Achievements include first description of the resting stage of anaerobic zoosporic fungi from rumen; first isolation of rumen zoosporic fungi from nature; description of a novel morphological development in rumen fungus; demonstration that hitherto fungi belonging to different species were the same. Home: 415 Confederacy Dr Penn Laird VA 22846-9625 Office: James Madison U Office Dean Coll Sci And Math Harrisonburg VA 22807-0001 E-mail: wubahda@jmu.edu.

WUBBELS, GENE GERALD, chemistry educator; b. Preston, Minn., Sept. 21, 1942; s. Victor and Genevieve M. (Sikkink) W.; m. Joyce Ruth Honebrink, Aug. 26, 1967; children: Kristen, Benjamin, John. BS, Hamline U., 1964; PhD, Northwestern U., 1968. Asst. prof. Grinnell Coll., Iowa, 1968-73; assoc. prof., 1973-79; prof. chemistry, 1979-92; Dack prof., 1986-92; provost, dean of coll., prof. chemistry Washington Coll., Chestertown, Md., 1992-95; sr. vice chancellor acad. affairs, 1995-97; prof. chemistry U. Nebr., Kearney, 1995—. Editor: Survey of Progress in Chemistry, vol. 10, 1983. Program dir. NSF, Washington, 1990-92; moderator United Ch. of Christ Congl., Grinnell,

1980-82, 83-84. Grantee NSF, 1971-95; recipient Sci. Faculty Prof. Devel. award NSF, 1981-82, Catalyst award for excellence in tchg. Chem. Mfrs. Assn., 1989. Fellow Iowa Acad. Sci.; mem. ACS (rsch. grantee 1970-86, mem. editl. adv. bd. Accounts Chme. Rsch. 1977-83, adv. bd. Petroleum Rsch. Fund 1986-89, pres. Chem. Coun. Undergrad. Rsch. 1986-87). Republican. Avocation: music. Office: U Nebr Kearney 905 W 25th St Kearney NE 68849-0002 E-mail: wubbelsg@unk.edu.

WUCHERER, RUTH MARIE, business owner; b. Milw. d. Frank Edward and Helen Antoinette Wucherer. BA in Journalism, U. Wis., Milw.; MA in Journalism, Marquette U. Owner Ruth's Writing and Speaking Svc., Milw., 1987—. Spkr. in field. Author: Write To Sell, 1988, 2 other books; contbr. articles, travel articles, book revs. to profl. publs. Mem. Internat. Women's Writing Guild, Wis. Regional Writers Assn. Avocations: watching and attending baseball games, travel, guitar. Home: 3370A S 12th St Milwaukee WI 53215-5006 E-mail: ruthw@uwm.edu.

WUCHTER, RICHARD B. retired research scientist, real estate agent; b. Wadsworth, Ohio, July 21, 1937; s. Harold I. and Ruth M. Wuchter; m. Fay H. Gauger, Mar. 17, 1972. BS in Chemistry magna cum laude, Case Western Res. U., 1959; PhD in Organic Chemistry, Cornell U., 1963. Tchg. asst. Cornell U., Ithaca, NY, 1961—63; sr. scientist Rohm & Haas Co., Spring House, Pa., 1963—99, cons., 2000—01; ret., 2001; real estate agt. Weichert Realtors, Ft. Washington, Pa., 2001—. Fellow, Cornell U., 1959—60. Mem.: Pa. Bd. Realtors (Rookie of Yr. 2000), Phi Beta Kappa. Achievements include patents for phosphorus catalysts, specialty monomers, chelating resins, reactive polymers, modifiers for PVC plastics, recycle processes using toxic chemicals. Avocations: skiing, gardening, reading, jogging. Home: 1521 Old Welsh Rd Huntingdon Valley PA 19006 Office: Weichert Realtors 535 Pennsylvania Fort Washington PA 19034 Home Fax: 215-646-2245. Business E-Mail: rwuchter@weichert.com.

WU-CHU, STELLA CHWENYEA, nutritionist, consultant; b. Kaohsiung, Taiwan, Sept. 22, 1952; came to U.S., 1976; d. Jin-Shoui and Sue-Tuan (Ling) Wu; children: Christine, Whitney. BS, Fu-Jen Cath. U., Taiwan, 1974; MA, San Francisco State U., 1979. Registered dietitian. Intership U. Calif., Berkeley, 1978; food svc. supr. Calif. Surgery Hosp., Oakland, 1979—80; nutritionist, cons. Solano Napa Agy. on Aging, Vallejo, 1980—; nutrition cons. Marin County Div. of Aging, San Rafael, 1981—; nutritionist San Francisco Commn. on Aging, 1990—; nutrition cons. Contra Costa Office on Aging, 1995—. Mem. adv. bd. Staying Health project Am. Soc. on Aging, 1999—2000; nutritional advisor Veggie Life Mag., Walnut Creek, Calif., 1993, Salt Free Cooking Made Easy. Chief editor quar. publ. Taiwanese Assn. publ., 1991-94. Cmty. liaison East Bay Taiwanese Assn., Walnut Creek, 1992-93; v.p. No. Calif. Formosan Fedn., 1993; dist. supportive com. chair United Meth. Women, 1995-97, Bayview dist. social actions mission coord., 1997-98; adv. bd. Overseas Chinese Inst. on Aging, 2000—, Am. Soc. Aging, 2000. Mem. Am. Dietetic Assn., Am. Pub. Health Assn., Jacob Inst. of Women's Health, Nat. Assn. Nutrition and Aging Svcs., Formosan Assn. for Pub. Affairs, Am. Assn. of Meals on Wheels. Avocations: reading, concerts, dancing, creative writing (in Chinese). Home: 70 Seabreeze Dr Richmond CA 94804-7410 Office: San Francisco Commn Aging 25 Van Ness Ave Ste 650 San Francisco CA 94102-6057 E-mail: stellawc@aol.com.

WUDL, FRED, chemistry educator; b. Cochabamba, Bolivia, Jan. 8, 1941; came to U.S., 1958; s. Robert and Bertha (Schorr) W.; m. Linda Raimondo, Sept. 2, 1967. BS, UCLA, 1964, PhD, 1967. Postdoctoral rsch. fellow Harvard U., 1967-68; asst. prof. dept. chemistry SUNY, Buffalo, 1968-72; mem. tech. staff AT&T Bell Labs., Murray Hill, N.J., 1972-82; prof. chemistry and materials U. Calif., Santa Barbara, 1982-97; Courtaulds prof. UCLA, 1997—. Recipient arthur C. Cope scholar award Am. Chem. Soc., 1993, Award for Chemistry of Materials, 1996, Natta medal Italian Chem. Soc., 1994, Wheland medal U. Chgo., 1994. Fellow AAAS. Office: UCLA Dept Chemistry Los Angeles CA 90095-1569 E-mail: wudl@chem.ucla.edu.

WUEBKER, COLLEEN MARIE, librarian; b. LaCrosse, Wis., June 22, 1943; d. Harris M. and Mary Frances (Collins) Gruber; m. William Joseph Wuebker, Aug. 14, 1965; children: Jon Paul, Timothy William, Maree Jean. BA, Mount Mercy Coll., 1965; MS, Mankato State U., 1975. Cert. permanent profl. media specialist, tchr., Iowa. Secondary tchr. Luverne Community Sch., Minn., 1965-66; tchr. St. Mary's Sch., Larchwood, Iowa, 1966; secondary tchr. SEMCO Community Sch., Gilman, 1966-67; substitute tchr. West Bend (Iowa) Community Schs., 1968-74, sch. media specialist, 1975—, Mallard Community Schs. (Iowa), 1974-75. Mem. selection com. Lakeland Area Edn. Agy., Cylinder, Iowa, 1977—; mem. Gov.'s Sch. Efficiency Task Force, West Bend, 1987; mem. sch. evaluation team Dept. Pub. Instrn., Des Moines, 1986. Mem. Sts. Peter and Paul Parish Coun., West Bend, 1987—, liturgy and music coord., song leader, 1987—; speaker Marriage Encounter Movement, Sioux City Diocese, 1985—, Pre-Cana Workshops, Emmetsburg, 1985—; chmn. Parish Liturgy Com., West Bend, 1987—. Mem. NEA, Iowa Edn. Assn., Iowa Ednl. Media Assn., Cath. Daus. Am. (past v.p. West Bend). Roman Catholic. Avocations: genealogy, music. Home: Box 426 11 1st Ave NE West Bend IA 50597-5010 Office: West Bend Community Sch 300 3rd Ave SW West Bend IA 50597-8573

WUENSCH, BERNHARDT JOHN, ceramic engineering educator; b. Paterson, N.J., Sept. 17, 1933; s. Bernhardt and Ruth Hannah (Slack) W.; m. Mary Jane Harriman, June 4, 1960; children: Stefan Raymond, Katrina Ruth. SB in Physics, MIT, 1955, SM in Physics, 1957, PhD in Crystallography, 1963. Rsch. fellow U. Bern, Switzerland, 1963-64; asst. prof. ceramics MIT, Cambridge, 1964-69, assoc. prof. ceramics, 1969-74, prof., 1974—, TDK chair materials sci. and engring., 1985-90, dir. Ctr. Materials Sci. and Engring., 1988-93, acting dept. head dept. materials sci. and engring., 1980. Vis. prof. Crystallographic Inst., U. Saarland, Fed. Republic Germany, 1973; physicist Max Planck Institut für Festkorperforschung, Stuttgart, Fed. Republic Germany, 1981; mem. U.S. nat. com. for crystallography NRC, NAS, 1980-82, 89-94; mem. N.E. regional com. for selection of Marshall Scholars, 1970-73, chmn., 1974-80. Co-editor: Modulated Structures, 1979, Neutron Scattering in Materials Science, 1995; adv. editor: Physics and Chemistry of Minerals, 1976—85; assoc. editor Can. Mineralogist, 1978—80; editor: Zeitschrift fuer Kristallographie, 1981—88, Jour. Ceramic Processing Rsch., 2000—. Ford Found. postdoctoral fellow, 1964-66. Fellow Am. Ceramic Soc. (Outstanding Educator award 1987), Mineral. Soc. Am.; mem. AAAS, Am. Crystallographic Assn., Mineral. Assn. Can., Materials Rsch. Soc. Episcopalian. Home: 190 Southfield Rd Concord MA 01742-3432 Office: MIT 77 Massachusetts Ave Rm 13-4037 Cambridge MA 02139-4307 E-mail: wuensch@mit.edu.

WUENSCHE, VERNON EDGAR, construction company executive; b. Elgin, Tex., Nov. 25, 1945; s. Harry Edwin Jacob and Emma Martha (Dube) W. BBA, U. Tex., 1967, MBA, 1968. CPA, Tex. Audit asst. Arthur Andersen & Co., Houston, 1968-70; tax cons. Peat Marwick Mitchell & Co., 1970; cost acct. Bemis Bros. Bag Co., 1970-71; asst. controller Prodn. Systems Internat., Inc., 1971-72; controller Am. Housing Guild, Inc., 1972-73, Wood Bros. Homes, Inc., Houston, Dallas, 1973-74, Oklahoma City, 1975; pres., founder, custom home builder Woodmark Homes, Inc., Houston, Dallas, Austin, Tex., 1975—; founder, kitchen and bath renovator Woodmark Kitchen & Bath, Inc., 1994—. Election judge Harris County, Houston, 1978, Rep. state del., Tex., 1978, 80, 94, 96, 98; elder Meml. Luth. Ch., Houston, 1982—; finisher marathon, Galveston, Tex., 1970, 71; founder Texans for Efficiency in Govt., 1991, Bus. Consensus, 1999; dir. Houston Entrepreneurs Forum. With USAR, 1968-74. Recipient Builder of Tex. Design award Tex. Arch. Mag., 1994. Mem. Alley Theater Guild, Tex. Wendish Heritage Soc., U. Tex. Ex-Students Assn., Rice Design Alliance, Mus. of Fine Arts, Arts Symposium of Houston, Phi Kappa Phi, Beta Gamma Sigma. Avocation: distance running. Home: 14211 Swiss Hill Dr Houston TX 77077-1029

WUENSCHEL, PETER CYRIL, educational association administrator, social worker; b. Pitts., Feb. 3, 1959; s. Cyril Alloysious and Mary Jo (Dunn) Wuenschel; m. Debbie Bodine; children: Diedra, Jeremiah, Matthew, Erica. B in Sociology, U.Tulsa, 1981; MSW, U. Houston, 1996, postgrad., 1997—2002. Lic. master social worker. Dir. youth and music St. Thomas More, Tulsa, 1981—86; social worker State of Okla., 1986—91; dir. cmty. life St. Cyril of Alexandria, Houston, 1991—96; exec. dir. Bridgeport Communities in Schs., 1996—2002. Field instr. U. Houston, 1996—2002; adv. com. U. Houston Clear Lake, Houston, 2000—02. Mem. steering com. United Way Cmty. Resources, Houston, 1998—2000; vice-chair Assn. Vol. Adminstrs. - Bay Area Satelite, 1998—2000. Mem.: NASW, Space Center Rotary, Phi Kappa Phi. Democrat. Roman Catholic. Avocation: musician. Office: Bridgeport Communities In Schs PO Box 580096 Houston TX 77258 Home Fax: 281-486-0405; Office Fax: 281-486-0405. Personal E-mail: Peterw@ghg.net. Business E-Mail: Peterw@ghg.net.

WUEST, LARRY CARL, tax examiner; b. Blue Ash, Ohio, Oct. 14, 1940; s. Carl William and Billie Asalee (Lanham) W. AA in Acctg., Long Beach City Coll., 1961; BS in Acctg., Miami U., Oxford, Ohio, 1969; MBA, Xavier U., 1977. Acct. Ohio River Co., Cin., 1969-79; computer programmer Bertke Electric, 1979-81, Great Am. Ins., Cin., 1982, Belcan Svcs., Cin., 1983-84, PDR Svcs., Cin., 1985; retail shop owner Raven's Records, Harrison, Ohio, 1986-87; tax examiner IRS, Covington, Ky., 1988—. Mem. Mensa, World Affairs Coun. of Greater Cin. Avocations: travel, music collecting, art, computer programming. Home: 217 S Vine St Harrison OH 45030-1354

WUHL, CHARLES MICHAEL, psychiatrist; b. N.Y.C., Sept. 24, 1943; s. Isadore and Sali (Ackner) W.; m. Gail; children— Elise, Amy. M.D., U. Bologna, 1973. Diplomate Am. Bd. Psychiatry and Neurology. Intern, N.Y. Med. Coll., 1975-76, resident in psychiatry, 1976-77; fellow in child psychiatry Columbia Presbyn. Med. Center, 1977-78; practice medicine specializing in psychiatry and child psychiatry, Englewood, N.J., 1978— ; attending staff, mem. faculty N.Y. Med. Coll.; psychiatrist NYU, also asst. clin. prof. psychiatry NYU Sch. Medicine. Contbr. to Psychosocial Aspects of Pediatric Care, 1978, World Book Ency., 1980—. Mem. Am. Psychiat Assn., AMA, Am. Acad. Child Psychiatry. Office: 163 Engle St Englewood NJ 07631-2530

WUKOVITS, JOHN FRANCIS, secondary school educator; b. Akron, Ohio, Nov. 3, 1944; s. Thomas William and Grace Annette Wukovits; children: Amy Dickerman, Julie, Karen. BA in History, U. Notre Dame, 1967; M in Am. History, Mich. State U., 1968. Cert. secondary tchr. Mich. Tchr. St. Timothy Sch., Trenton, Mich., 1968—71, Trenton Pub. Schools, 1971—73, St. Joseph Sch., Trenton, 1981—91, Trenton Pub. Schools, 1991—. Author: (book) Devotion to Duty: A Biography of Admiral Clifton A. F. Sprague, 1995, Barry Sanders, 1995; contbg. author: book Men of War: Great Naval Leaders of World War II, 1992, contbg. author: book Reference Guide to United States Military History, 1995, contbg. author: book Quarterdeck & Bridge: Two Centuries of American Naval Leaders, 1997, : book The Great Admirals: Command at Sea, 1587-1945, 1997; author: Jesse James, 1997, The Gunslingers, 1997, Vince Lombardi, 1997, Wyatt Earp, 1997, Annie Oakley, 1997, The Black Cowboys, 1997, Butch Cassidy, 1997; : book Scientists & Inventors, 1998; author: John Stockton, 1998, Jack Nicklaus, 1998, Tim Allen, 1998, The Composite Guide to Auto Racing, 1998, The Composite Guide to Soccer, 1998, Anne Frank, 1998, Martin Luther King, Jr., 1998, Stephen King, 1999, Jim Carrey, 1999, Life of an American Soldier in Europe, 2000, Life As A POW, 2000, Colin Powell, 2000, The 1910s, 2000, The 1920s, 2000, George Bush, 2000 (NY Pub. Library's "Books for the Teen Age List", 2001), Bill Gates, 2000, The Encyclopedia of World Sports, 2001, The Persian Gulf War: Leaders and Generals, 2001, History of Sports: Hockey, 2001, The Spanish-American War, 2001, Strategic Battles of World War I, 2001, World War I Flying Aces, 2002, The Encyclopedia of The Winter Olympics, 2002, Michael J. Fox, 2002; contbg. author: book Book of Days, 1988, 1988, contbg. author: book Best Little Stories from World War II, 1989, contbg. author: book Best of the Wild West, 1996. Mem.: Orgn. Am. Historians, The Golf Writers Assn. Am., Soc. for Mil. History. Roman Catholic. Avocations: golf, reading. Home: 1235 Harbour # 22 Trenton MI 48183 Office: Trenton Pub Schs 4000 Marian Dr Trenton MI 48183 Home Fax: 734-676-1073. Personal E-mail: johnwukovits@comcast.net.

WULBERT, DANIEL ELIOT, mathematician, educator; b. Chgo., Dec. 17, 1941; s. Morris and Anna (Greenberg) W.; children: Kera, Noah. BA, Knox Coll., 1963; MA, U. Tex., Austin, 1964, PhD, 1966. Research assoc. U. Lund (Sweden), 1966-67; asst. prof. U. Wash., Seattle, 1967-73; prof. U. Calif.-San Diego, La Jolla, 1973—. Vis. prof. Northwestern U., Evanston, Ill., 1977. Contbr. articles in field. Office: U Calif San Diego Dept Math # 0112 La Jolla CA 92093 E-mail: dwulbert@ucsd.edu.

WULF, JANIE SCOTT MCILWAINE, gifted and talented education educator; b. Smithfield, Va., Mar. 30, 1934; d. Porter O'Brien and Claire (Bennett) Scott; m. Harro Biner Wulf, Sept. 22, 1962; children: Susan, Thomas, Katherine, Jane. BS, Longwood Coll., Farmville, Va., 1955; MEd in Guidance, George Mason U., Fairfax, Va., 1975; postgrad., U. Va. Cert. home econs., upper elem. tchr., guidance counselor, g/t cert., Va. Tchr. kindergarten Faith Luth. Day Sch., Arlington, Va.; tchr. home econs. Annandale H.S., Fairfax; tchr. sci. Chesterfield County Pub. Schs., Chester; tchr. English gifted and talented edn. Fairfax County Pub. Schs., Fairfax, also mid. sch. team leader, 1990-91; team leader, supervising tchr. Fairfax County Frost Sch., 1990-98; ret., 2000. Mem. Am. Fedn. Tchrs. English, Nat. Geneal. Soc., Va. Mid. Sch. Assn., Va. Assn. Tchrs., VA. Hist. Soc., Va. Geneal. Soc., Fairfax County Fedn. of Tchrs.,

WULF, MELVIN LAWRENCE, lawyer; b. N.Y.C., Nov. 1, 1927; s. Jacob and Vivian (Hurwitz) W.; m. Deirdre Howard, Dec. 18, 1962; children: Laura Melissa, Jane Miranda. BS, Columbia U., 1952, LL.B., 1955. Bar: N.Y. 1957. Asst. legal dir. ACLU, 1958-62, legal dir., 1962-77; Distinguished vis. prof. Hofstra Law Sch., 1975, spl. prof. law, 1976-77; mem. firm Clark Wulf & Levine, 1978-83, Beldock, Levine & Hoffman, 1983—. Author articles. Served to lt. (j.g.) USNR, 1955-57. Ford Found. fellow, 1967 Home: 340 Riverside Dr New York NY 10025-3423 Office: 99 Park Ave New York NY 10016-1601 E-mail: mwulf@blhny.com.

WULF, NORMAN, federal official; b. ; married; two children. BA, Iowa Wesleyan Coll.; JD, U. Iowa; LLM, U. Miami. Office dir. State Dept.; dep. gen. counsel ACDA; acting asst. dir. for Nonproliferation/Regional Arms Control U.S. Arms Control and Disarmament Agy., Washington, 1985—. Leader efforts to strengthen the internat. inspections regime underpinning the Nuclear Non-Proliferation Treaty in sixty countries, Internat. Atomic Energy Agy., Vienna; active North Korean issues. Office: Office Pub Affairs Us Arms Control Disarm Agy Washington DC 20451-0001*

WULF, SHARON ANN, management consultant; b. New Bedford, Mass., Aug. 23, 1954; d. Daniel Thomas and Norma Dorothy (McCabe) Vieira; m. Stanley A. Wulf, 1983. BS in Acctg. cum laude, Providence Coll., 1976; MBA, Northeastern U., 1977; PhD, Columbia Pacific U., 1984. Staff acct., intern Laventhol & Horwath, Providence, 1977; jr. fin. analyst Polaroid Corp., Waltham, Mass., 1977-78, fion. analyst Freetown, 1978-79, Cambridge, 1979-81; sr. fin. cons., mktg. strategic planner Digital Equipment Corp., Stow, 1981-82, Maynard, 1982-83, mgr. fin. devel. program, 1983-84, strategic fin. cons. engring. divsn., 1984-86, group mgr. planning & strategic ops. Hudson, 1986-87, group mgr. strategic bus. planning, 1987-89; mktg. planning mgr. Diigital Equipment Corp., Marlboro, 1989-90, new ventures bus. devel. mgr., 1990-92; pres. Enterprise Sytems, Framingham, 1993—; sr. instr. Cambridge Coll., 1997—, prof., 1998—. Lectr. fin. acctg. Southeastern Mass. U., 1979—81; adj. prof. acctg., mgmt. & fin., knowledge mgmt. strategies Northeastern U., Boston, 1980—; instr. Nat. Tech. U ., 1991—; instr., vis. prof. mgmt. Framingham State Coll., 1999—; exec. com. enterprise forum MIT, 1987—92; prin. Work Sys. Assocs., Inc., Marlborough, Mass., 1992—93; bd. advisors Spaceball Tech., Inc., Lowell, Mass., Terasys., Inc.; sr. faculty advisor healthcare master's degree program Mass. Gen. Hosp., 2000—02; cons. in field. Author: Building Performance Values, 1996, Customer Service Action Plans, 1997, LEadership in Action: The Way It Is Cersus The Way It Should Be, 1997. Chair pub. support and fund raising ARC, New Bedford, 1974-84; bd. dirs. Vets. Outreach Ctr., Metrowest, Framingham, 1989-93; v.p. MIT Leadership Found., Cambridge, 1991-93; mem. exec. com. MIT Enterprise Forum, also co-chair stant up clinics, 1986-92. Mem. Black Alumni of MIT (bd. advisors 1989-92), Univ. Coll. Faculty Soc., Phi Sigma Tau. Home: 902 Salem End Rd Framingham MA 01702-5532 Office: Enterprise Systems 1257 Worcester Rd Ste 301 Framingham MA 01701-5217 Fax: 508-626-9038. E-mail: sharonw@enters.com.

WULF, STANLEY ARTHUR, engineering executive; b. Adrian, Minn., Aug. 14, 1943; s. Arthur Harry and Dena (Huisenga) W.; m. Sharon A. Vieira Wulf, Oct. 1, 1983. BSME, Mass. Inst. Tech., Cambridge, 1965; PhD, Northwestern, Evanston, Ill., 1970. Rsch. engr. Argonne (Ill.) Labs., 1971-73; dir. Materials Testing Lab. Brewer Engring. Labs., Marion, Mass., 1973-81; v.p. AMPS Ltd., 1981-92; OEM sales mgr. HBM, Inc., Marlborough, Mass., 1982-90; mktg. dir. NMB Tech., Chatsworth, Calif., 1990-93; pres. Enterprise Sys., 1993—. Dir. Psi Delta Corp., Boston, Marine Biotech Inc., Beverly, Mass. Mem. Internat. Soc. Weighing and Measurements, Soc. for Experimental Mechanics, Soc. of Automotive Engrs. Home: 902 Salem End Rd Framingham MA 01702-5532 Office: Enterprise Systems 1257 Worcester Rd Ste 301 Framingham MA 01701-5217 E-mail: sawulf@alum.mit.edu.

WULF, WILLIAM ALLAN, computer information scientist, educator, federal agency administrator; b. Chgo., Dec. 8, 1939; s. Otto H. and Helen W. (Westermeier) Wulf; m. Anita K. Jones, July 1, 1977; children: Karin, Ellen. BS, U. Ill., 1961, MSEE, 1963; PhD in Computer Sci., U. Va., 1968. Prof. computer sci. Carnegie-Mellon Univ., Pitts., 1968—81; chmn., CEO Tartan Labs., 1981—87; AT&T prof. computer sci. U. Va., Charlottesville, 1988—; asst. dir. Nat. Sci. Found., Washington, 1988—90; pres. Nat. Acad. of Engring., 1996—. Bd. dirs. Charles Strak Draper Labs., Cambridge, Mass., Nat. Action Coun. Minorities Engring., Inst. Women and Tech. Biblioteque; cons. various computer mfrs., Alexandria, Egypt. Author: Fundamental Structures of Computer Science, 1981. Bd. dirs. Pitts. High Tech. Coun., 1982—88; trustee Charles Babbage Inst., Bibliotheca Alexandrina. Fellow: AAAS, IEEE, Assn. Women in Sci., Assn. Computing Machinery; mem.: Am. Acad. Arts and Scis., Nat. Acad. Engring. Avocations: woodworking, photography. Office: Nat Acad Engring 2101 Constitution Ave NW Washington DC 20418-0007

WULFERS, MONIKA, artist; came to U.S., 1963; d. Hans Hinrich and Eva Wulfers; children: Christopher, Jennifer BA, North Ctrl. Coll., Naperville, Ill., 1968; MFA, Sch. Art Inst. Chgo., 1973. Bd. dirs. Artists, Residents Chgo., 1973-74, dir. Ednl. Found., 1974-75; rsch. assoc. Argonne (Ill.) Nat. Lab., 1975-82, visual artist in residence, 1980-82; dir., owner Washington Island (Wis.) Gallery & Gardens, 1988—; patient advocate nuclear medicine, 1992—. Vis. prof. Barat Coll. DePaul U., 2000—02, dir. Reicher Gallery, 2000—02. Exhibited in group shows at Mus. Moderner Kunst/Mus., Vienna, Austria, 1985, Art Inst. Chgo., 1985, Wilhelm-Hack Mus., Germany, 1992. Chair wastewater com. Town of Washington, Washington Island, 1989-91; sole proprietor Cmty. Mgmt. Specialists, Washington Island, 1991—. Recipient travel award Peterson Found., Sturgeon Bay, Wis., 1993, Exhbn. award Peninsula Art Found., Door County, Wis., 1994, operational grant Wis. Med. Physics Found., Madison, 1997-98. Mem. Proton Therapy Coop. Group. Avocations: tennis, skiing, sailing, garden design. Home: 1650 Green Bay Pl Lake Bluff IL 60044 E-mail: mwulfers@barat.edu.

WULFF, ROBERT JOSEPH, lawyer; b. St. Louis, Aug. 27, 1961; BSEE, U. Mo., Columbia, 1983; JD cum laude, St. Louis U., 1986. Bar: Mo. 1986, U.S. Dist. Ct. (ea. dist.) Mo. 1986, U.S. Ct. Appeals (8th cir.) 1986, Ill. 1987, U.S. Supreme Ct. 1990. Shareholder Amelung, Wulff & Willenbrock, P.C., St. Louis, 1986—. Mem. Mo. Orgn. Def. Lawyers, Bar Assn. Met. St. Louis, Phi Alpha Delta. Office: Amelung Wulff & Willenbrock PC 515 Olive St Ste 17 Saint Louis MO 63101-1849 E-mail: rjw@awwstl.com.

WULFF, ROGER LAVERN, museum administrator; b. Olean, N.Y., Nov. 16, 1940; s. LaVern Theodore and Marjorie (Perkins) Wulff; m. Geraldine Schepker Wulff, July 3, 1971. AA, Montgomery Jr. Coll., Rockville, Md., 1968; BA, U. Md., 1970; postgrad., Pa. State U., 1971-73, The George Washington U., 1975-79. Cultural instn. value methodology specialist. Pres., chmn. bd. dirs. Mus. Svcs. Internat., Washington, 1980—. Founder Mus. Svcs. Internat., 1980—; speaker at various mus. confs.; mem. panel experts Tourism Sector Devel. Project, The Hashemite Kingdom of Jordan. Contbr. articles to profl. jours. Chmn. Internat. Com. on Mus. Security, 1986-92, editor, 1986—. With U.S. Army, 1959-62. Recipient Excellence in Leadership Svcs. award, Smithsonian Inst., Washington, 1989, Cert. Appreciation, African Am. Mus. Assn., Washington, 1988 Mem. U.S. Com. of the Internat. Coun. of Mus., Internat. Com. for Mus. Security, Internat. Coun. of Mus. (former chmn. internat. com. on mus. security), Internat. Com. on Exhbn. Exch., U.S./Internat. Coun. on Monuments and Sites (steering com.), Internat. Cultural Assistance Network, Am. Assn. Mus., Nat. Assn. Mus. Exhbn., Com. on Mil. Mus. in Am., Mus. Assn. Security Com., Com. on Mus. Evaluation and Rsch., Washington Mus. Collaborative. Avocation: gardening. Home: c/o General Delivery San Ignacio Post Office Cayo Belize E-mail: museplan@bll.net.

WULFF, VIRGINIA MCMILLAN, association executive; b. Glendale, Calif., May 27, 1958; d. Reginald Joseph and Virginia Ellen (Cavett) McMillan; m. Robert Reid Wulff, June 20, 1981; children: Kellyn Melissa, Katharine Cooper, Kyle Reid. BA in English with honors, Stanford U., 1980. Prodn. mgr. Addison Wesley/Benjamin Cummings Pub., Menlo Park, Calif., 1980-82; ways and means chair Oak Elem. PTA, Los Altos, 1988-89, pres., 1990-91, Los Altos/Mountain View PTA Coun., Los Altos, 1992-93; v.p. comms. Sixth Dist. PTA, San Jose, Calif., 1995-99, editor The Bell, 1995-99. Sec., mem. exec. bd. Peninsula Youth Theatre, Mountain View, Calif., 1994—; pres. San Juan Sensations Team, Los Altos, 1995—. Editor: The Bell, 1995-98. Oak chair Measure A Com., Los Altos, 1993, 95, 97; mem. parcel taxes bond measure coms. Los Altos Elem.; mem. Mountain View/Los Altos H.S. Dist. Bond Com., 1996, 97; lead parent rep. Castilleja Sch., 1998—; legislation chair Blach PTA, 1999—, Sixth Dist. PTA, San Jose, CA, 1995-98. Mem. AAUW. Home: 136 Waverly Pl Mountain View CA 94040-4573

WULFHORST, DIETER, music educator, musician; b. Essen, Germany, May 29, 1961; s. Traugott Wulfhorst, Ursula Wulfhorst; m. Susan J. Doering. D in Musical Arts, U. Md., 1996—96. Asst. prof. music Ind. U. of Pa., Indiana, 1996—2000, Calif. State U., Fresno, 2001—. Cellist Santa Fe Pro Musica, 1991—. Mem.: ASTA. Home: POBox 2580 Clovis CA 93613-2580 Office: Calif State Univ Fresno 2380 E Keats Ave Fresno CA 93740-8024 Office Fax: 559-278-6800. Personal E-mail: dwulfhorst@csufresno.edu. Business E-Mail: dwulfhorst@csufresno.edu.

WULKE, JOY, artist; b. San Bernardino, Calif., May 23, 1948; d. Harold and Minnie-Lou (Sisson) W.; m. David Connell, Sept. 11, 1983; 1 child, Gioia Montana. BA in Architecture, Wash. State U., 1970; M Environ. Design, Yale U., 1974. Owner, mgr. Old Mole Art Coop., Pullman, Wash., 1970-71; owner, designer, artist Fiberworks, 1972-76, Joy Wulke Studio Art & Design, Stony Creek, Conn., 1976—. Seminar instr. Yale U. New Haven, 1974; product designer Dansk, Armonk, N.Y., 1975-79, GEAR & Schumacher, N.Y.C., 1978-80; assoc. prof. Mont. State U., Bozeman, 1981-83; mem. adj. faculty RISD, Providence, 1983-85; mem. guest faculty Glastgow (Scotland) Sch. Art, 1988; founding dir. Projects for New Millennium, Stony Creek, 1993—; environ. and space cons. Tchr. Ctr., Inc., New Haven, 1973-98; mem. adv. coun. Wash. State U. Sch. Architecture, Pullman, 1995—; cons. on pub. art Conn. Commn. on Arts, Hartford, 1980—. Group exhbns. include Wadsworth Athenaeum Gallery of the Senses, Hartford, Conn., 1981, NYU, 1992, Lyman Allyn Museum, New London, Conn., 1992, San Bernardino County Museum, 1993, Delaware Ctr. for Contemporary Art, Wilmington, 1995, Urban Glass, Bklyn., 1996, Rockville (Md.) Arts Place, 1999, Discovery Museum, Bridgeport, 2000; commd. works include La. World's Fair, New Orleans, 1984, Lincoln Ctr. Film forum, N.Y.C., 1991, Middlesex Hosp., Middletown, conn., 1994, Mont. State U., Missoula, 1996, Cermack Plaza, Chgo., 1998, So. Conn. State U., New haven, 2000. Bd. dirs. David Bermant Found., Santa Barbara, Calif., 1989-98; mem. cultural planning coun. Greater N.H. Arts Coun., New Haven, 1997—. Grantee Conn. Commn. on Arts, 1986—, Comm. Found. Greater New Haven, 1996, New Eng. Found. for Arts, 1994. Avocations: travel, photography, installations in abandoned buildings using light and reflection. Home: 26 Prospect Hill Rd Branford CT 06405-5711

WULKER, LAURENCE JOSEPH, portfolio manager, educator, financial planner; b. Cin., Apr. 6, 1945; s. Joseph Laurence and Dorothea Clare (Link) W. BS, Xavier U., Cin., 1967, MA, 1971; cert. fin. planner, Coll. Fin. Planner, 1985. Instr. Lloyd High Sch., Erlanger, Ky., 1967-68, Elder High Sch., Cin., 1968-73, Peoples High Sch., Cin., 1973-74, Regina High Sch., Cin. Tech. U., Cin., 1974-75; stockbroker Harrison-Bache, 1976-78; portfolio mgr., fin. planner, v.p. investments Paine Webber, 1978—, formed Wulker Group, 1997; instr. U. Cin., 1981-98, Nat. Inst. Fin., South Plainfield, N.J., 1986-88; systems operator, Fin. Planning Forum Tristate Online, Cin., 1991—. Speaker at numerous seminars 1984—; systems operator Investor Forum, Compuserve, 1985-86. Author column Japanese-Am. League Newsletter, 1985-96; contbr.

articles to Cin. Enquirer, Cin. Post, Cin. Bus. Courier. Bd. dirs., v.p., pres. No. Ky. Symphony, 1993-99; treas. Friends of Findlay Market, Findlay Market Assn., 1999—; bd. dirs. Riverwinds Condo Assn. Fulbright scholar Dept. Health, Edn. and Welfare, 1972; named one of best 200 Stockbrokers, Country-Money mag., 1987. Mem. Stock and Bond Club, Fulbright Soc., Order Ky. Cols. Roman Catholic. Avocations: computers, tennis, golf, volleyball, reading. Home: Riverwinds Condos 558 Davenport Ave No 11 Cincinnati OH 45204-1362 Fax: 513-369-4020. E-mail: laurence.wulker@ubspainewebber.com., lwulker@juno.com.

WUNDER, CHARLES C(OOPER), physiology and biophysics educator, gravitational biologist; b. Pitts., Oct. 2, 1928; s. Edgar Douglas and Annabel (Cooper) W.; m. Marcia Lynn Barnes, Apr. 4, 1962; children: E(dgar) Douglas, David Barnes, Donald Charles. AB in Biology, Washington and Jefferson Coll., 1949; MS in Biophysics, U. Pitts., 1952, PhD in Biophysics, 1954. Assoc. U. Iowa, Iowa City, 1954-56, asst. prof. physiology and biophysics, 1956-63, assoc. prof. physiology and biophysics, 1963-71, prof. physiology and biophysics, 1971-98, prof. emeritus, 1998—. Cons. for biol. simulation of weightlessness U.S. Air Force, 1964; vis. scientist Mayo Found., Rochester, Minn., 1966-67. Author: Life into Space: An Introduction to Space Biology, 1966; also chpts., numerous articles, abstracts Recipient Research Career Devel. award NIH, 1961-66; AEC predoctoral fellow U. Pitts., 1951-53; NIH spl. fellow, 1966-67; grantee NIH, NASA Mem. Am. Physiol. Soc., The Biophys. Soc. (charter), Aerospace Med. Assn., Iowa Acad. Sci. (chmn. physiology sect. 1971-72, 83-84, 96-97), Am. Soc. Biomechanics (founding), Aerospace Physiologist Soc., Iowa Physiol. Soc. (pres. 1996-97), Am. Soc. for Gravitational and Space Biology (Founders award 2000). Presbyterian. Achievements include the establishment of chronic centrifugation as an approach for investigating gravity's role as a biological determinant. Home: 702 W Park Rd Iowa City IA 52246-2425 Office: U Iowa BSB Iowa City IA 52242 E-mail: charles-wunder@uiowa.edu.

WUNDER, HAROLDENE FOWLER, accounting educator; b. Greenville, S.C., Nov. 16, 1944; d. Harold Eugene Fowler and Sarah Ann (Chaffin) Crooks. BS, U. Md., 1971; M Acctg., U. S.C., 1975, PhD, 1978. Vis. asst. prof. U. S.C., Columbia, 1977-78; asst. prof. U. Pa., Phila., 1978-81; vis. asst. prof. U. N.C., Chapel Hill, 1981-82; asst. prof. U. Mass., Boston, 1982-86; vis. assoc. prof. Suffolk U., 1986-87; assoc. prof. U. Toledo, 1987-93; prof. acctg. Calif. State U., Sacramento, 1993—. Contbr. articles to profl. and academic jours. George Olson fellow, 1975. Mem.: AICPA, Nat. Tax Assn., Am. Taxation Assn., Am. Acctg. Assn., Calif. Soc. CPAs, Beta Gamma Sigma. Avocation: reading. Office: Calif State U Sch Bus Adminstrn Sacramento CA 95819-6088 E-mail: wunderh@csus.edu.

WUNDERLICH, ALFRED LEON, artist, art educator; b. Salem, Oreg., June 26, 1939; s. Joseph Anthony and Anna Margaret (Meyer) W.; children: Annelise, Jonathan Resor. Cert., Cooper Union, 1961; B.F.A., Yale U., 1962, M.F.A., 1968. Dir. visual studies program Hopkins Ctr., Dartmouth Coll., Hanover, N.H., 1965-66; asst. prof. art Hopkins Ctr., Darmouth Coll., 1966-74; assoc. prof. R.I. Sch. of Design, Providence, 1983-94; prof. R.I. Sch. of Design, 1994—. Adj. lectr. Hunter Coll. CUNY, 1973, adj. prof., vis. artist Pahlavi U., Shiraz Iran, 1978, vis. artist U. Edinburgh, Scotland, Edinburgh Internat. Arts Festival, 1973, Kansas City Art Inst., Art Inst. Chgo., Ohio State U., 1986, Carnegie Mellon U., 1987, Moscow State U., 1991, Ariz. State U., 1995; fine arts advisor Inst. for Internat. Edn.; mem. U.S. Art in Space team, met with Soviet Artists Union team, Moscow, 1990; owner, artistic dir. GAS-523 project to fly aboard NASA Space Shuttle; executor first bacteria based living paintings, Rich Biology Labs. M.I.T., 2001. Solo shows Dartmouth Coll., 1969, Kyoto, Japan, 1969, Pahlavi U., 1978, Kwanghow Mus., Canton, China, 1979, Chang-tu Mus., Szechwan, China, 1978, MIT, 1981, Swarthmore Coll., 1985, Knoerdler Gallery, N.Y.C., 1995, 97, Alfonz Ver Gallery, San Francisco, 1997, 98; group exhbns. Harvard U. 1995, MIT 1996, also numerous other group exhbns.; represented in permanent collections Mus. Modern Art, N.Y.C., Art Inst. Chgo., Yale U. Art Gallery, Nat. Gallery Scotland, 1st Nat. Bank Boston, Dartmouth Coll., Smithsonian-Cooper Hewitt Mus., Stanford U. Art Mus., also others. Recipient Bocour Color award, 1960; Yale ALumni fellow, 1962-63; Yaddo fellow, 1973; Dartmouth Faculty fellow, 1968; Fulbright grantee to India, 1963-64; Dartmouth Coll. research grantee, 1970-72; SUNY research grantee, 1983 Home: 3326 22d St San Francisco CA 94110 Office: RISD 2 College St Providence RI 02903-2784 E-mail: awunderl@risd.edu.

WUNDERLICH, BERNHARD, physical chemistry educator; b. Brandenburg, Germany, May 28, 1931; came to U.S., 1954, naturalized, 1960; s. Richard O. and Johanne (Wohlgefahrt) W.; m. Adelheid Felix, Dec. 28, 1953; children: Caryn Cornelia, Brent Bernhard. Student, Humboldt U., Berlin, Germany, 1949-53, Goethe U., Frankfurt, Germany, 1953-54, Hastings Coll., 1954-55; PhD, Northwestern U., 1957. Instr. chemistry Northwestern U., Evanston, Ill., 1957-58, Cornell U., Ithaca, N.Y., 1958-60, asst. prof., 1960-63; assoc. prof. phys. chemistry Rensselaer Poly. Inst., Troy, 1963-65, prof. phys. chemistry, 1965-88, prof. emeritus, 1988—; prof. chemistry U. Tenn., Knoxville, 1988-2001, prof. emeritus, 2001—; Disting. scientist div. chemistry Oak Ridge Nat. Lab., 1988-2001. Cons. E.I. duPont de Nemours Co., 1963-88; dir. Lab. for Advanced Thermal Analysis; rsch. in solid state of linear high polymers and thermal analysis, 1980-2001. Author: Macromolecular Physics, Vol. 1, 1973, Vol. 2, 1976, Vol. 3, 1980, Thermal Analysis, 1990; author computer and audio courses on Crystals of Linear Macromolecules, and Thermal Analysis of Materials; contbr. over 500 articles to profl. jours.; mem. editl. bd. Chemistry, 1965-68, Makromolekulare Chemie, 1966-96, Jour. Thermal Analysis and Calorimetry, 1963-2001; mem. adv. bd. Jour. Polymer Sci., 1963-2001, Macromolecules, 1984-88, Polymers for Advanced Tech., Macromolecular Sci., 1988-2001, Phys. and Thermochim. Acta, 1996-2001. Recipient Humboldt award, 1987-88, award for applied chem. thermodynamics Swiss Soc. for Thermal Analysis and Calorimetry, 1993, TA Instruments award Internat. Conf. Thermal Analysis and Calorimetry, 1996. Fellow Am. Phys. Soc., N.Am., Thermal Analysis Soc. (Mettler award in thermal analysis 1971); mem. Am. Chem. Soc. Home: 200 Baltusrol Dr Knoxville TN 37922-3707

WUNDERLICH, GENE LEE, economist; b. Bottineau, N.D., Sept. 29, 1928; s. Arnold Arthur and Evelyn (Olson) W.; m. Gooloo Sahiar, Mar. 19, 1957; children: Karl, Roshna. BS, U. N.D., 1949; MS, Iowa State U., 1951, PhD, 1955. Economist USDA, Washington, 1955-95. Advisor Bulgarian Ministry Agr., 1992, Armenian Ministry Agr., 1993, Ukrainian Ministry Agr., 1993; cons. World Bank, Moldova, 1994, USAID, Ukraine, 1996, Va. Poly. Inst. and State U., Albania, 1996-97. Editor Jour. Agrl. Econs. Rsch., 1987-92; author: Land Ownership and Taxation in American Agriculture, 1993, Agricultural Landownership in Transitional Economies, 1995; contbr. chpts. to books and numerous articles to profl. jours. Recipient Superior Svc. award USDA, 1976, 93, award Econ. Rsch. Svc., 1992, 93; Fulbright scholar Bombay U., 1953-54, 62-63; fellow Yale U. Law Sch., 1966-67. Mem. Am. Econ. Assn., Am. Agrl. Econs. Assn., Internat. Assn. Agrl. Econs. Home: 4704 Randolph Ct Annandale VA 22003-6216

WUNDERLICH, HOWARD JEFFREY, lawyer; b. Bklyn., Feb. 18, 1961; BS, Rensselaer Poly. Inst., 1983; JD, Nova U., 1986. Bar: Fla. 1986, N.Y. 1987, N.J. 1987, U.S. Dist Ct. (no. and we. dists.) N.Y. 1987, U.S. Dist. Ct. N.J. 1987, U.S. Dist. Ct. (so. and ea. dists.) N.Y. 1988, U.S. Ct. Internat. Trade 1991, U.S. Tax Ct. 1987, U.S. Ct. Mil. Appeals 1987, U.S. Ct. Appeals (fed. cir.) 1987, U.S. Ct. Appeals (11th cir.) 1988, U.S. Ct. Appeals (6th cir.) 1991, U.S. Supreme Ct. 1991. Pvt. practice, Lake Grove, N.Y., 1987—. Of counsel Richard J. McCord, P.C., 1991-95, Goldman, Horowitz & Cherno, 1992-95. Mem.: VFW, ABA, Nat. Assn. Consumer Bankruptcy Attys., Am. Bankruptcy Inst., Res. Officers Assn., Armed Forces Communications and Electronics Assn., Soc. Am. Mil. Engrs., Suffolk County Bar Assn., Bar Assn. Nassau County, Fed. Bar Assn., Assn. Trial Lawyers Am. E-mail: hjwesq@hotmail.com.

WUNDERMAN, JAN DARCOURT, artist; b. Winnipeg, Man., Can., Jan. 22, 1921; d. Rene Paul and Georgette Marie (Guionet) Darcourt; m. Frank Joseph Malina, 1938 (div. 1945); m. Lester Wunderman (div. 1967); children: Marc, Geroge, Karen Renee. BFA, Otis Art Inst., L.A., 1942. One man shows include Easthampton Guild Hall, L.I., 1977, Denise Bibro Fine Art Gallery, N.Y.C., 1996-98, 2002, Roko Gallery, 1963, 66, 68, 71, 73, 76; represented in numerous permanent pub., corp. and pvt. collections including Zimmerli Mus., NYU Loeb Collection, Norfolk Mus., Alfred Kouri Collection, Skidmore Coll. Print Collection, Nat. Assn. of Women Artists, Rutgers U., 1994, Albright Knox Mus., 1998-99, Daimler Chrysler Coll., Germany, 2002. Recipient Ohashi award Pan Pacific Exhbn., Tokyo and Osaka, 1962, Emily Lowe award 1965, J.J. Akston Found. prize, 1965, Canaday Meml. prize, 1979, Marian De Solo Mendes prize, 1981, Charles Horman Meml. prize, 1983, Amelia Peabody award Nat. Assn. Women, 1991, Grumbacher Gold medal of honor, 1992, Doris Kreindler award 1992. Mem. Nat. Assn. Women Artists (medal of honor 1966, Marcia Brady Tucker award 1965, E. Holzinger prize 1966, Jane C. Stanley prize 1977, Marge Greenblatt award 1990, Amelia Peabody award 1991, Solveig Stomsoe Palmer prize 1997), Am. Soc. Contemporary Artists (corr. sec. 1977-78, Bocour award 1980, Elizabeth Erlanger Meml. award 1990, Kreindler award 1992), Contemporary Artists Guild (rep. by Denise Bibro Fine Art N.Y.C.). Avocations: history, travel. Studio: 41 Union Sq W Rm 516 New York NY 10003-3208 Fax: 212-677-0246.

WUNNICKE, BROOKE, lawyer; b. Dallas, May 9, 1918; d. Rudolph von Falkenstein and Lulu Lenore Brooke; m. James M. Wunnicke, Apr. 11, 1940; (dec. 1977); 1 child, Diane B. BA, Stanford U., 1939; JD, U. Colo., 1945. Bar: Wyo. 1946, Colo. 1969, U.S. Dist. Ct. Wyo. 1947, U.S. Dist. Ct. Colo. 1970, U.S. Supreme Ct. 1958, U.S. Ct. Appeals (10th cir.) 1958. Pvt. practice law, 1946-56; ptnr. Williams & Wunnicke, Cheyenne, Wyo., 1956-69; of counsel Calkins, Kramer, Grimshaw & Harring, Denver, 1969-73; chief appellate dep. atty. Dist. Atty's Office, 1973-86; of counsel Hall & Evans L.L.C., 1986—. Adj. prof. law U. Denver Coll. of Law, 1978-97; lectr. Internat. Practicum Inst. Denver, 1978—. Author: Ethics Compliance for Business Lawyers, 1987; co-author: Standby Letters of Credit, 1989, Corporate Financial Risk Management, 1992, Legal Opinion Letters Formbook, 1994, (Supplement 2002), UCP 500 and Standby Letters of Credit-Special Report, 1994, Standby and Commercial Letters of Credit, 1996, 3d edit., 2000, Supplement, 2002; contbr. articles to profl. jours. Pres. Laramie County Bar Assn., Cheyenne, Wy., 1967-68; Dir. Cheyenne C. of C., Cheyenne, Wy., 1965-68. Recipient awards for Outstanding Svc., Colo. Dist. Attys. Coun., 1979, 82, 86, Disting. Alumni award U. Colo. Sch. of Law, 1986, 93, Lathrop Trailblazer award Colo. Women's Bar Assn., 1992, William Lee Knous award U. Colo., 1997, Eleanor P. Williams award disting. svc. to legal profession, 1997, Potter Lifetime Profl. Svc. award, 1999, Def. Rsch. Inst. Ann. Nat. award, 1999; named first Frank H. Ricketson Jr. Adj. Prof., U. Denver Coll. Law, 1997. Fellow Colo. Bar Found. (hon.); mem. ABA, Wyo. State Bar, Denver Bar Assn. (hon. life; trustee 1977-80), Colo. Bar Assn. (hon., life, Award of Merit 1999), Am. Arbitration Assn. (nat. panel, regional panel), William E. Doyle Inn of Ct. (hon.), Order of Coif, Phi Beta Kappa. Republican. Avocations: reading, writing, teaching, lecturing. Office: Hall & Evans L L C 1200 17th St Ste 1700 Denver CO 80202-5817

WUNSCH, ANNA CATHERINE MARY O'BRIEN HORTON, artist, consultant; b. Jersey City, Jan. 22, 1921; d. James Joseph and Clara Josephine (Doyle) O'B.; m. Lester William Horton, Mar. 10, 1942 (div. Apr. 17, 1947); children: William Horton, Marianne Horton; m. Alfred Joseph D. Wunsch, July 10, 1948 (dec. Dec. 1989); children: Rosmarie, Irene, Alfred, Kathleen Wunsch. Student, Western Electric AT&T Spec. Mech. Drawing Sch., 1936, St. Paul of the Cross, Jersey City, N.J., 1936, Art Instruction Co., N.Y.C., 1946; GED, Martin Luther King Coll., Jersey City, 1986; child care degree (hon.), Jersey City State Coll., 1989. Emergency cert. ARC, 1965. Comml. artist, engr.'s quality control, design cons. We. Electric Co., Inc./AT&T, Kearney, N.J., 1938-48; timesetter Union City (N.J.) br. Arrow Mfg. Co., 1950; jig artist, box designer Spiedel Watch Bands Co.; art instr. (summer), asst. tchr. head start St. Bridget Sch., 1969; leader, tchr. Mont Gardens Housing, 1970; asst. tchr./Foster Grandparent Act J.C. Med. Cen. Hosp./Cath. Charities, Newark, 1985, 86; asst. tchr. YHMA JC, Sch. Spl. Child Arts and Crafts/Cath. Charities, 1985, 86. Prodn. timer (vol.), engr. advisor, cons. bench hand AT&T, Bell Sys., Kearny, South Kearny, Jersey City, West Side, Bayonne, Marion plants, 1938-48. Permanent collections include Jersey City (N.J.) Mus., Jersey City Main Libr., numerous pvt. collections; featured in N.J. Artist, N.Y. State Artist. Den mother Cub Scouts Boys Scouts Am., 1960-69; group mother, leader Girl Scouts USA, 1959; pres. PTO, 1964; soprano J.C. Dollies, 1965-75. Recipient Congl. Medal Honor for vol. work during WWII, Pres. Johnson, 1969, Head Start award, 1969—; subject of personal interview, TV. Democrat. Roman Catholic. Avocations: beadwork, knitting, crochet, paper flowers, cooking. Home: Middle Rd Sr Village 96 Golden Ln Bldg 10 Hazlet NJ 07730-2516

WUNSCH, JARED, mathematician; b. Boston, Aug. 1, 1971; s. Carl I. and Marjory M. Wunsch. AB, Princeton U., 1993; PhD, Harvard U., 1998. NSF postdoctoral fellow, instr. Columbia U., N.Y., NY, 1998—2000; asst. prof. SUNY , Stony Brook, 2000—.

WUNSCH, KATHRYN SUTHERLAND, retired lawyer; b. Tipton, Mo., Jan. 30, 1935; d. Lewis Benjamin and Norene Marie (Wolf) Sutherland; m. Charles Martin Wunsch, Dec. 22, 1956 (div. May 1988); children: Debra Kay, Laura Ellen. AB, Ind. U., 1958, JD summa cum laude, 1977; postgrad., Stanford (Calif.) U., 1977. Bar: Calif. 1977, U.S. Dist. Ct. (no. dist.) Calif. 1977. Founder Wunsch and George, San Francisco, 1989-93, Kathryn Wunsch and Assoc. Counsel, San Francisco, 1993-99; ret., 1999. Articles editor Ind. U. Law Rev., 1975-76. Mem. Phi Beta Kappa (v.p. no. calif. 1995-97), Psi Chi. Republican. Avocations: collecting fine art and antiques, theater, opera, gardening, hiking.

WUNSTELL, ERIK JAMES, non-profit organization administrator, communications consultant; b. Fresno, Calif., Dec. 24, 1951; s. John Wunstell and Rose Soldorian. Grad. comml. law, Dept. U.S. Treas., 1976; grad., N.Am. Sch. Acctg., 1978. Owner Camden Comm., Fresno, Calif., 1974—; founder, dir. Earth Ecology Found., 1980—. Author: Corporate Strategies in Ecological Capitalization, 2000, Environmental Investments in the New Millennium, 2001, Eco-Logical Eco-Nomics, 2002. Office: Earth Ecology Found A16-303 6120 W Tropicana Ave Las Vegas NV 89103-4694 E-mail: erikwunstell@aol.com.

WUORINEN, CHARLES PETER, composer; b. N.Y.C., June 9, 1938; s. John Henry and Alfhild (Kalijarvi) W. BA, Columbia U., 1961, MA, 1963; DMus (hon.), Jersey City State Coll., 1971. Lectr. Columbia U., 1964-65, instr., 1965-69, asst. prof., 1969-71, co-dir. Group Contemporary Music, 1962—; prof. music Rutgers U., 1984—. Vis. lectr. Princeton U., 1967-68, New England Conservatory, 1968-71, Yale U., 1983; adj. lectr. U. South Fla., 1971-72; faculty Manhattan Sch. Music, 1972-79, U. So. Calif., 1981; artistic dir., chmn. Am. Composers Orch., 1973-87; composer-in-residence Ojai Festival, 1975, Santa Fe Chamber Music Festival, 1993, 2001, Tanglewood Music Festival, 2001; San Francisco Symphony, 1984-89; condr. Cleve. Orch., 1976, Finnish Radio Orch., 1979, Helsinki Philharm., 1979; disting. prof. Rutgers U., 1984—; vis. prof. SUNY, Buffalo, 1989-94, NYU, 1990 Author: Simple Composition; mem. editorial bd. Perspectives of New Music; bd. mem. Composers Recs. Inc., 1962-89; composer numerous works including Music for Orchestra, 1956, Be Mery All That Be Present, mixed chorus, 1957, Concert for Four Trombones, 1960, Madrigale Spirituale, 1960, Turetzky Pieces, 1960, Evolutio: organ, 1961, Evolution Transcripta for chamber orch., 1961, Tiento Sobre Cabezon, 1961, Concert for Double Bass Alone, 1961, Trio No. 1 for flute, cello and piano, 1961, Invention for percussion quintet, 1962, Octet, 1962, Duuiensela for cello and piano, 1962, Bearbeitungen über das Glogauer Liederbuch, 1962, The Prayer of Jonah, 1962, 2d Flute Trio: Piece for Stefan Wolpe, 1962, Chamber Concerto for cello and 10 players, 1963, Piano Variations, 1963, Flute Variations, 1963, Composition for violin and 10 instruments, 1964, Chamber Concerto for flute and 10 players, 1964, Orchestral and Electronic Exchanges, 1965, Composition for oboe and piano, 1965, Chamber Concerto for oboe and 10 players, 1965, Super Salutem for male voices and instruments, 1964, Piano Concerto, 1966, The Bells for carillon, 1966 (revised 1997), Bicinium, 2 oboes, 1966, Janissary Music for 1 percussionist, 1966, Harpsichord Divisions, 1966, Making Ends Meet for piano four-hands, 1966, John Bull: Salve Regina Versus Septem, 1966, Duo for violin and piano, 1967, The Politics of Harmony: A Masque, 1967, String Trio, 1968, Flute Variations II, 1968, Time's Encomium (electronic), 1969, Adapting to the Times for cello and piano, 1969, The Long and the Short for violin, 1969, Contrafactum for orch., 1969, Nature's Concord trumpet and piano, 1969, Piano Sonata, 1969, Ringing Changes for percussion, 1970, A Song, 1970, Tuba Concerto, 1970, A Message to Denmark Hill, 1970, Cello Variations, 1970, String Quartet, 1971, Canzona for 12 instruments, 1971, Grand Bamboula for string orch., 1971, Amplified Violin Concerto, 1972, Harp Variations, 1972, Bassoon Variations, 1972, Violin Variations, 1972, On Alligators for 8 instruments, 1972, Speculum Speculi for 6 players, 1972, Third Trio for flute, cello and piano, 1973, 12 Short Pieces for piano, 1973, Grand Union for cello and drums, 1973, Arabia Felix for 6 Instruments, 1973, Second Piano Concerto, 1974, Fantasia for violin and piano, 1974, Reliquary for Igor Stravinsky for orch., 1975, The W. of Babylon (opera), 1975, TASHI, 1975, Hyperion for 12 instruments, 1975, Cello Variations 2, 1975, 2d Piano Sonata, 1976, Percussion Symphony, 1976, The Winds, 1977, Fast Fantasy for cello and piano, 1977, Archangel for trombone and string quartet, 1977, Six Pieces for violin and piano, 1977, Six Songs for two voices, Wind Quintet, Self Similar Waltz for piano, Ancestors for chamber ensemble, 1978, Two-Part Symphony, 1978, Archaeopteryx for bass trombone and chamber ensemble, 1978, The Magic Art, A Masque for chamber orch, 1979, Fortune for 4 instruments, 1979, 2d String Quartet, 1979, The Celestial Sphere for chorus and orch., 1979, Psalm 39 for baritone and guitar, 1979, Percussion Duo, 1979, Joan's for 5 instruments, 1979, Blue Bamboula for piano, 1980, Capriccio for piano, 1981, Horn Trio, 1981, Short Suite for orch., 1981, Trio for bass instruments, 1981, New York Notes for 6 players, 1982, Mass, 1982, Divertimento for alto sax and piano, 1982, Divertimento for string quartet, 1982, Spinoff for violin, double bass and congas, 1983, Trio for violin, cello and piano, 1983, Third Piano Concerto, 1983, Rhapsody for violin and orch., 1984, Concertino, 1984, Crossfire for orch., 1984, Movers and Shakers for orch., 1984, Bamboula Squared for orch. and computer-generated sound, 1984, Natural Fantasy for organ, 1985, Horn Trio Continued, 1985, Trombone Trio, 1985, Prelude to Kullervo for tuba and orch., 1985, Double Solo for Horn Trio, 1985, Fanfare for the Houston Symphony, 1986, The Golden Dance for orch., 1986, Third Piano Sonata, 1986, Third String Quartet, 1987, Galliard for chamber orch., 1987, Bamboula Beach for orch., 1987, FIVE: Concerto for amplified cello and orch., 1987, Sonata for violin and piano, 1988, Bagatelle for piano, 1988, Ave Christe for piano, 1988, Another Happy Birthday for orch., 1988, Machault Mon Chou for orch., 1988, String Sextet, 1989, Twang for soprano and piano, 1989, A Solis Ortu for chorus, 1989, Genesis for chorus and orch., 1989, Astra for orch., 1990, Delight of the Muses for orch., 1991, Missa Brevis, 1991, A Winter's Tale for Soprano and Six Instruments, 1992, Microsymphony, 1992, Missa Renovata for Chorus and Orch., 1992, Saxophone Quartet, 1992, Concerto for Saxophone Quartet and Orch., 1993, The Mission of Virgil for orch., 1993, Percussion Quartet, 1994, Piano Quintet, 1994, Christes Crosse, 1994, Lightenings VIII, 1994, Guitar Variations, 1994, Sonata for Guitar and Piano, 1995, The Great Procession, 1995, Katz Fugue for piano, 1995, Windfall for band, 1994, Schoenberg Op. 31 Variations, (remade for two pianos, 1996), The River of Light (for string orch. and percussion, 1996), Epithalamium (for two instruments, 1997), Symphony Seven, 1997, Fenton Songs, 1997, Cello Variations III, 1997, Lepton trio for celeste, piano and harp, 1998, An Orbicle of Jasp for cello and piano, 1999, Brass Quintet, 2000, Fourth String Quartet, 2000,Cyclops for chamber orchestra, 2000, Haroun and the Sea of Stories (opera), 1997-2001, Stanzas Before Time (tenor and harp), 2001, Buttons and Bows (cello and accordion), 2001. Recipient Philharmonic Young Composers award, 1954; Bennington Composers Conf. scholar, 1956-60; Bearns prize, 1958-59, 61; MacDowell Colony fellow, 1958; Alice M. Ditson fellow, 1959; Arthur Rose teaching fellow, 1960; Broadcast Music-Student Composers award, 1959, 61, 62, 63; Lili Boulanger Meml. award, 1963; Festival fellow Santa Fe Opera, 1962; Festival fellow World's Fair Music and Sound, 1962; commd. by Koussevitzky Found., 1964, Berkshire Music Center, 1963, Fromm Found., 1963-71, Ford Found., 1962, Orch. of Am., 1958, Columbia U., 1956, Washington and Lee U., 1964, Fine Arts Quartet, 1969, Naumberg Found., 1971, U. South Fla., 1972, Nat. Opera Inst., 1973, Light Fantastic Players, 1973, N.Y. State Council on the Arts, 1974, N.Y. Philharm., 1974, Balt. Chamber Music Soc., 1974, Buffalo Philharm., 1974, Ojai Festival, 1974, Contemporary Chamber Ensemble, 1974, TASHI, 1974, Beethoven Festival, Bonn, 1978, Albany Symphony, 1981, San Francisco Symphony, 1984, 86, 88, 89, Cleve. Orch., 1984, Balt. Symphony, 1984, Houston Symphony, 1986, N.Y.C. Ballet, 1987, 90, Libr. of Congress, 1988, New World Symphony, 1987, Chamber Music Soc. Lincoln Ctr., 1989, 92, Am./ Soviet Youth Orch., 1990, Phila. Orch., 1992, Beethorenhalle Orch., Bonn Mönchengladbach and Ludwig Forum, Germany; grantee Nat. Inst. Arts and Letters, 1967, Nat. Endowment Arts, 1974, 76; Guggenheim fellow, 1968, 72; Ingraham Merrill fellow, 1972, Rockefeller Found. fellow, 1979, 80, 81, John D. and Catherine T. MacArthur fellow, 1986-91; recipient Pulitzer prize, 1970, Brandeis U. creative arts award, 1970, Creative Artists Pub. Svc. award, 1976; Arts and Letters award Finlandia Found., 1976, Koussevitzky Internat. Rec. award, 1970, 72. Mem. AAAS, AAAL, Am. Soc. Univ. Composers, Am. Composers Alliance (former bd. dirs.), Am. Music Ctr. (bd. dirs.), Internat. Soc. Contemporary Music (bd. dirs.), Am. Acad. Arts and Scis., Phi Beta Kappa. Office: care Howard Stokar Mgmt 870 W End Ave New York NY 10025-4918

WURBS, RALPH ALLEN, civil engineering educator, consultant; b. Bryan, Tex., Aug. 17, 1949; s. Herman Carl and Edna Maxine Wurbs; m. Kerry Wesson, Aug. 21, 1971; children: Sarah Elizabeth, Amy Rebecca, Jeremy David. BS in Civil Engring., Tex. A&M U., 1971; MS in Civil Engring., U. Tex., Arlington, 1974; PhD in Civil Engring., Colo. State U., 1978. Registered profl. engr., Tex. Surveyor, constrn. inspector Tex. Dept. Transpl., 1969-70; civil engr. U.S. Army Corps Engrs., Ft. Worth, 1971-80; faculty mem. civil engring. dept. Tex. A&M U., College Station, 1980—, prof., divsn. head environ. and water resources divsn. Vis. rsch. engr. Waterways Experiment Sta., Environ. Lab., Mil. Hydrology Program, USACE, Vicksburg, Miss., 1983-85; vis. rsch. engr. and scholar Hydrologic Engring. Ctr., USACE, Davis, Calif., 1989, 90, 94, 95; vis. scholar Inst. Water Resources, USACE, Alexandria, Va., 1992-93; cons. UN Devel. Program, Nat. Inst. Hydrology, India, Roorkee, 1996; vis. prof. Cath. U. Leuven, Belgium, 1998; spkr. in field. Author: Water Management Models, 1994, Modeling and Analysis of Reservoir System Operations, 1996; contbr. chpts. to books and articles to profl. jours. Corps of Engrs. Water Resources Planning fellow, 1976-77. Mem. ASCE (Hawley award for best paper Tex. sect. 1996), Internat. Water Resources Assn., Am. Soc. for Engring. Edn., Assn. Environ. Engring. and Sci. Profs., Univs. Coun. on Water Resources (Tex. A&M U. rep.), Chi Epsilon, Tau Beta Pi, Phi Kappa Phi. Home: 1804 Lawyer Pl College Station TX 77840-4837 Office: Civil Engring Dept Tex A&m Univ College Station TX 77843-0001 E-mail: r-wurbs@tamu.edu.

WURDEMAN, LEW EDWARD, photographer; b. Colorado Springs, Colo., Oct. 31, 1949; s. Robert Martin and Shirley Gladys (Reetz) W. Student, U. Tex., 1967-69, U. Minn., 1969-72. Adminstr. Control Data Corp., Bloomington, Minn., 1969-81; product splst., 1981-83; sys. mgr., 1983-84; cons., 1984-89; mgr. The Roach Orgn., Inc., Mpls., 1989-90; computer cons. Wurdeman Enterprises, Inc., Farmington, Minn., 1991-93; sr. cons. Norstan Consulting, Minnetonka, 1993-2001; photographer Vividere Glamour Photography, 1996—. Glamour photographer. Commr. Parks and Recreation Dept., City of Farmington, Minn., 2001—. Mem. Internat. Freelance Photographers Orgn., Internat. Glamour Photographers Assn., Photog. Soc. Am. Profl. Photographers Am., German Shepherd Dog Club Mpls., German Shepherd Dog Club Am. Republican. Lutheran. Avocations: dog breeding and training, computers, photography. Office: Vividere Photography PO Box 332 Farmington MN 55024-0332

WURLITZER, FRED PABST, surgeon; b. San Francisco, Dec. 26, 1937; s. Raimund Billings and Pauline (Pabst) W.; m. Lee Jones Wurlitzer (div. Jan. 1991); children: Ricky, Arnisha, Susan, Elena; m. Ann Marie Allan, June 2, 1992; children: Melanie, Heather, Gregory. BA, Stanford U., 1960; MD, U. Cin., 1965; MBA, Golden Gate U., 1985. Diplomate Am. Bd. Gen. Surgery. Intern, resident Highland-Almeda County Hosp., 1965-67; resident in surgery UCLA Sch. Medicine/VA Hosp., 1967-60; fellow in surg. oncology U. Tex./M.D. Anderson Hosp., Houston, 1970-71; instr. surgery U. So. Calif., Los Angeles, 1971-73; physician Pasadena (Calif.) Tumor Inst., 1971-73, San Mateo (Calif.) Med. Clinic, 1973-77; pvt. practice, Burlingame, Calif., 1977-84; vol. surgeon various hosps., 1989-93; pres. Wurlitzer Properties, Burlingame, 1976—. Contbr. articles to profl. jours. Comdr. USPHS, 1992—. Recipient Acknowledgement of Outstanding Svc. award Am. Cancer Soc.,

1974, Disting. Svc. award Health Vols. Overseas, 1994. Fellow ACS; mem. AMA, Soc. Head and Neck Surgeons, Southwestern Surg. Congress, So. Med. Assn. Unitarian Universalist. Avocations: skiing, tennis. Home: 8129 Regents Ct University Park FL 34201-2234

WURMAN, RICHARD SAUL, architect; b. Phila., Mar. 26, 1935; s. Morris Louis and Fannie (Pelson) W.; m. Gloria Nagy; children: Joshua, Reven, Vanessa, Anthony. BArch (T.P. Chandler fellow), MArch with highest honors, U. Pa.; DFA (hon.), U. of the Arts, 1994; LHD (hon.), Art Ctr College of Design, 1995. Mem. faculty N.C. State U., Raleigh, 1962-64, 77, Washington U., St. Louis, 1965, Princeton U., 1965-67, Cambridge (Eng.) U., 1967-68, N.Y.C. program Cornell U., 1968-70, CCNY, 1968-70, UCLA, 1976, U. So. Calif., 1976; prof. architecture, dean Sch. Environ. Design, Calif. State Poly. U., Pomona; chmn. dept. Otis/Parsons, Los Angeles; with Archtl. Office Louis I. Kahn, London, 1960-62; chmn. dept. environ. design Otis Parsons Calif. Founding dir. Group Environ. Edn., 1968; bd. dirs. Internat. Design Conf., Aspen, Colo., 1970-2002, chmn., 1972; co-chmn. 1st Fed. Design Assembly, 1973; trustee Center Bldg. Edn. Programs, 1976—; dep. dir. Phila. Office Housing and Community Devel., 1977; bd. dirs., chmn., creative dir. TED Confs.-Tech. Entertainment Design Conf., 1984—, Kobe, Japan, 1992, Monterey, Calif., 1994—, Med. Comm. Conf., Charlestown, S.C., 1995; pres. Access Press Ltd., The Understanding Bus., 1981-91; designer exhbns., cons. in field; vis. scholar MIT, 1993—, RISD, 1995—; found. bd. eBook. Author 80 books including The Notebooks and Drawings of Louis I. Kahn, The Nature of Recreation, Urban Atlas, Man Made Philadelphia, Aspen Visible, Our Man Made Environment; also author 27 vols. ACCESS travel and info. guidebook series; editor: What Will Be Has Alway Been: The Words of Louis I. Kahn, Information Anxiety 2, Follow the Yellow Brick Road, The Wall Street Journal Guide to Understanding Money and Markets, Fortune Guide to Understanding Personal finance, 1992, USAtlas, 1990, N, The Newport Guide, 1995, Information Architects, 1996, C, Understanding USA, 1996, The Charleston Guide, 1997, Wills, Trusts and Estate Planning, 2001, Diagnostic Tests for Men, 2001, Diagnostic Tests for Women, 2001, Heart Disease and Cardiovascular Health, 2001, Drugs Prescription, non-prescription and Herbal, 2001, Can I Afford to Retire?, 2001, Information Anxiety, 2001, Understanding Children, 2002; DE contbr. articles to profl. jours.; retrospective exhbn. AXIS Design Gallery, Tokyo, 1991. Recipient Thornton Oakley medal, 1954, Arthur Spayd Brookes Gold medal, 1958, Kevin Lynch award MIT, 1991, Stars of Design award and Chrysler award for innovation in design Pacific Design Ctr., 1996, Chrysler award for Innovation in Design, 1996; Graham fellow, 1966, 76; T.P. Chandler fellow, 1968; fellow Guggenheim Found., 1969; fellow Rockefeller Bros. Fund, 1972; fellow Nat. Endowment Arts, 1970, 73, 74, 76, 79-80; fellow World Econ. Forum, Davos, Switzerland, 1994—; grantee Fels Found., 1970; grantee Ednl. Facilities Lab., 1972, 74; grantee Rohm & Haas Co., 1976 Fellow AIA (medal 1958); mem. Am. Inst. Graphic Artists (v.p., bd. dirs. 1985), Alliance Graphique Internat. Address: The Orchard 180 Narragansett Ave Newport RI 02840-6929

WURMFELD, SANFORD, artist, educator; b. N.Y.C., Dec. 6, 1942; s. Charles Jacob and Esther (Witzling) W.; m. Rella Stuart-Hunt, Dec. 11, 1971; children: Jeremy Philip, Treva. BA in Art with honors, Dartmouth Coll., 1964; ind. study, Rome, 1964-65. Lectr. Hunter Coll., N.Y.C., 1967-72, asst. prof., 1972-77, assoc. prof., 1977-80, chmn. dept. art, 1978—, prof. art, 1980—, Caroff prof., 2000—. Vis. artist lectr. Calif. State Coll., Hayward, Cooper Union, NY, Bar Coll., Arondale-on-Hudson, NY, Drexel U., Phila., 1970, SUNY, Fredonia, 1971, Livingston Coll., New Brunswick, NJ, 1973, Whitney Mus., 1982, Met. Mus. Art, 1987, 87, Princeton U., 1990, The Slade Sch. U. Coll., London, 1991, Chelsea Coll. Art, London, 1991, Whitney Mus., 1992, Hochschule der Kurst, Berlin, 1995, Simon Fraser U., Vancouver, 1996, U. Victoria, B.C., 1996, Acad. Minerva, The Netherlands, Glasgow Sch. of Art, Scotland, 1997, external examiner, 1999—2002. One-man shows include Karl Ernst Osthaus Mus., Hagen, Germany, 2000, Susan Caldwell Gallery, Inc., N.Y., 1978, Bard Coll. Invitational Exhibit, 1977, Susan Caldwell Gallery, 1976-77, Galarie Denise Rene, 1974, Rockefeller Meml. Gallery, Fredonia, N.Y., 1971, Tibor de Nagy Gallery, 1968, Bryant Park, N.Y., Fischbach Gallery, 1969; group shows include Mus. Modern Art, N.Y., 1968, Grank Palais, Paris, 1968, Kunsthaus, Zurich, 1968, Tate Gallery, London, 1968, Ft. Worth Art Ctr., 1969, Galerie de Gestlo, Kunstfair, Basel Switzerland, 1970, 72, Columbia Film Festival, 1973, Galerie Denise Rene, 1974, Hopkins Ctr. Galleries, 1974, Lehigh U., 1976, Susan Caldwell Gallery, 1977-79, Toni Birckhard Gallery, Cin., 1980, Carnegie Internat., 1983, Shanghai Exhbn. Hall Shanghai, China, 1986, Long Beach Mus. of Art, Calif., 1989, William Paterson Coll. of N.J., 1990, Hallwells Contemporary Arts Ctr., Buffalo, 1991, Louis Stern Fine Arts, L.A., 1995, Andre Zarre Gallery, N.Y., 1996, Karl Ost Haus-Mus., Hagen, Germany, others; represented in permanent collections at Met. Mus. Art, N.Y., Guggenheim Mus., N.Y., SUNY, Fredonia, Cen. Trust Co., Cin., Am. Telephone and Telegraph, N.Y., Baxter Travenol Labs., Deerfield, Ill., Gen. Electric Corp., Fairfield, Conn., Sprengler Mus., Hanover, Fed. Republic of Germany, City of Hannover, Fed. Republic of Germany, Shreve, Lamb & Harmon Corp., N.Y., Silkscreeners Guild, W. Ger., Warner Nat. Corp., Cin., U. N.C., William Hayes Ackland Meml. Art Ctr., Chapel Hill, Karl Ernst Osthaus Mus., others; contbr. articles to profl. jours. Recipient Ames award Dartmouth Coll., 1964; fellow Guggenheim Found., 1974, Nat. Endowments for the Arts Individual Artist's, 1987-88; CUNY faculty rsch. grantee. Home: 18 Warren St New York NY 10007-1066 Office: Hunter Coll Dept Art 695 Park Ave New York NY 10021-5024 E-mail: sanford.wurmfeld@hunter.cuny.edu.

WURMSDOBLER, PETER, engineer; b. Schaerding, Austria, Aug. 14, 1968; s. Alois and Marianne Wurmsdobler; m. Claude Ducker. MME, Vienna U. Tech., Austria, 1986—92, PhD in Control Engring., 1993—97. Tchg. and rsch. asst. Inst. for Machine and Process Automation, Vienna, Austria, 1992—97; post-doctoral rsch. and devel. engr. Centre de Transfert des Microtechniques, Besancon, France, 1998—2001; open control lab. dir. Control.com, Westborough, Mass., 2001—. Dir. Real Time Linux Found., Boise, 2000—. Dir.: (Organization) Real Time Linux Workshop, 1999. Gefreiter Army Data Processing Unit, 1997—98, Vienna. Personal E-mail: peter@wurmsdobler.org.

WÜRSIG, BERND GERHARD, marine biology educator; b. Barsinghausen, Hanover, Fed. Republic of Germany, Nov. 9, 1948; s. Gerhard Paul and Charlotte Annemarie (Yorkowski) W.; m. Melany Anne Carballeira, Nov. 19, 1969; children: Kim, Paul. BS, Ohio State U., 1971; PhD, SUNY, Stony Brook, 1978. Postdoctoral researcher U. Calif., Santa Cruz, 1978-81; prof. Moss Landing (Calif.) Marine Labs., 1981-89; dir. Marine Mammal Lab. Tex. A&M U., Galveston, 1989—. Govt. cons. Minerals Mgmt. Service, Washington, 1980—. Contbr. articles to profl. jours.; contbr. seven-part miniseries to TV on lives of dolphins, dolphin problems induced by humans, also Discovery Channel show on Life of B. Würsig; co-author: The Hawaiian Spinner Dolphin, 1994, Whales, Dolphins and Porpoises, 1995; sr. advisor IMAX film Dolphins, 2000; sr. author: The Marine Mammals of the Gulf of Mexico, 2000. Recipient Chmn.s award for Rsch. and Exploration Nat. Geographic Soc., 1998, Alban-Heiser award for excellence in Tex. conservation rsch. Zool. Soc. Houston, 1991, Student Body award for most effective tchr. Tex. A&M U., 1994-95; Fulbright Found. scholar, 2001—. Mem. Marine Mammal Soc. (pres. 1991-93), N.Y. Acad. Scis., Soc. Cryptozoology, Am. Behavior Soc., Am. Mus. Natural History, Soc. Archimedes. Clubs: Explorers (N.Y.C.) (fellow of research). Avocations: photography, diving, airplane piloting, skiing, hiking. Home: 2402 Creekridge Pearland TX 77581- Office: Tex A&M U Marine Mammal Rsch Program 4700 Avenue U Ste 303 Galveston TX 77551-6900

WURSTER, CHARLES FREDERICK, environmental scientist, educator; b. Phila., Aug. 1, 1930; s. Charles Frederick and Helen B. Wurster; m. Eva M. Tank-Nielsen, Aug. 26, 1970; children: Steven Hadley, Nina F., Erick Frederick. SB, Haverford Coll., 1952; MS, U. Del., 1954; PhD, Stanford U., 1957. Teaching asst. U. Del., 1952-54; research asst. Stanford U., 1954-57; Fulbright fellow Innsbruck, Austria, 1957-58; research chemist Monsanto Research Corp., 1959-62; research assoc. biol. scis. Dartmouth Coll., 1962-65; asst. prof. biol. scis. SUNY, Stony Brook, 1965-70; assoc. prof. environ. scis. Marine Scis. Rsch. Ctr., 1970-94, prof. emeritus, 1994—. Vis. prof. Macquarie U., Sydney, Australia, 1988; founding trustee, sec., mem. exec. com. Environ. Def. Fund, Inc., 1967—; mem. adminstr.'s pesticide policy adv. com. EPA, 1975—78. Contbr. articles to profl. publs. Fellow: AAAS; mem.: Nat. Pks. and Conservation Assn. (trustee 1970—79), Defenders of Wildlife (dir. 1975—84, 1987—96). Achievements include research in on DDT, PCBs, other chlorinated hydrocarbon effects on phytoplankton, birds; relationship between environmental sciences and public policy; instrumental in banning several insecticides, including DDT, Dieldrin and Aldrin. Office: SUNY Marine Scis Research Ctr Stony Brook NY 11794-5000 E-mail: CFWurster@Yahoo.com.

WURSTER, DALE ERIC, pharmacy educator; b. Madison, Wis., Jan. 19, 1951; s. Dale Erwin and June M. (Peterson) W.; m. Pamela Ann Marvin, May 31, 1975; children: Elizabeth Ann, Kristin Gail, Dale Edward. BS in Chemistry, U. Wis., 1974; PhD in Phys. Pharmacy, Purdue U., 1979. Asst. prof. Sch. Pharmacy U. N.C., Chapel Hill, NC, 1979—82; asst. to assoc. prof. Coll. Pharmacy U. Iowa, Iowa City, 1982—95, prof. Coll. Pharmacy, 1996—, divsn. head pharmaceutics, 2000—01, assoc. dean Grad. Coll., 2002—. Cons. Nat. Assn. Bds. of Pharmacy, Park Ridge, Ill., 1982—; apptd. to U.S. Pharmacopeial Conv. Com. of Revision, 1995—; cons. in field. Contbr. articles to profl. jours. Fed. and indsl. grantee. Fellow Am. Assn. Pharm. Scientists; mem. Am. Chem. Soc., Am. Assn. Colls. Pharmacy, Materials Rsch. Soc., Sigma Xi. Achievements include research in tablet coatings for controlled release, surface phenomena, solution and differential scanning calorimetry, chemical kinetics; dissolution kinetics and testing, physics of tablet compression, analytical applications of Fourier transform infrared spectroscopy. Home: 3808 County Down Ln NE North Liberty IA 52317-9388 Office: U Iowa Coll Pharmacy S215 Iowa City IA 52242 E-mail: dale-e-wurster@uiowa.edu.

WURSTER, DALE ERWIN, pharmacy educator, university dean emeritus; b. Sparta, Wis., Apr. 10, 1918; s. Edward Emil and Emma Sophia (Steingraeber) W.; m. June Margaret Peterson, June 16, 1944; children: Dale Eric, Susan Gay. BS, U. Wis., 1942, PhD, 1947. U. Wis. Sch. Pharmacy, Madison, 1958-71, mem. faculty, 1947-71; prof., dean N.D. State U. Coll. Pharmacy, 1971-72; prof. U. Iowa Coll. Pharmacy, Iowa City, 1972—, dean, 1972-84, dean emeritus, 1984—. George B. Kaufman Meml. lectr. Ohio State U., 1968; Hancher Finkbine Medallion prof. U. Iowa, 1984; Joseph V. Swintosky disting. lectr. U. Ky., 2000; cons. in field; phys. sci. adminstr. USN, 1960-63; sci. advisor U. Wis. Alumni Rsch. Found., 1968-72; mem. revision com. U.S. Pharmacopoeia, 1961-70; mem. pharmacy rev. com. USPHS, 1966-72; mem. tech. adv. com. contraceptive R&D program Ea. Va. Med. Sch., 1987-2002, rsch., U. Wis. Contbr. articles to profl. jours., chpts. to books; patentee in field. With USNR, 1944-46. Recipient Superior Achievement citation Navy Dept., 1964, merit citation U. Wis., 1976, Disting. Alumni award U. Wis. Sch. Pharmacy, 1984. Fellow Am. Assn. Pharm. Scientists (founder, sponsor Dale E. Wurster rsch. award 1990—, Disting. Pharm. Scientist award 1991); mem. Am. Assn. Colls. Pharmacy (exec. com. 1964-66, chmn. conf. tchrs. 1960-61, vis. scientist 1963-70, Disting. Educator award 1983), Acad. Pharm. Scis. (exec. com. 1967-70, chmn. basic pharmaceutics sect. 1965-67, pres. 1975, Indsl. Pharm. Tech. award 1980), Am. Pharm. Assn. (chmn. sci. sect. 1964-65, rsch. achievement award 1965, Wis. Disting. Svc. award 1971), Iowa Pharmacists Assn. (Robert G. Gibbs award 1983), Wis. Acad. Scis., Arts and Letters, Soc. Investigative Dermatology, Rumanian Soc. Med. Sci. (hon.), Am. Found. Pharm. Edn. (bd. grants 1987-92), Sigma Xi, Kappa Psi (past officer), Rho Chi, Phi Lambda Upsilon, Phi Sigma. Home: 16 Brickwood Cir NE Iowa City IA 52240-9129

WURTELE, CHRISTOPHER ANGUS, paint and coatings company executive; b. Mpls., Aug. 25, 1934; Valentine and Charlotte (Lindley) W.; m. Heather Campbell (div. Feb. 1977); children: Christopher, Andrew, Heidi; m. Margaret Von Blon, Aug. 21, 1977. BA, Yale U., 1956; MBA, Stanford U., 1961. V.p. Minn. Paints, Inc. (merged with Valspar Corp. 1970), Mpls., 1962-65, exec. v.p., 1965, pres., CEO, 1973-96, chmn., 1973-98. Dir. Bemis Co., IDS Mutual Fund Group. Bd. dirs. Bush Found., Walker Art Ctr. With USN, 1956-59. Mem. Mpls. Club. Episcopalian. Home: 2970 Gale Rd Wayzata MN 55391 Office: 4900 IDS Ctr 80 S 8th St Minneapolis MN 55402

WURTELE, MORTON GAITHER, meteorologist, educator; b. Harrodsburg, Ky., July 25, 1919; s. Edward Conrad and Emily Russell (Gaither) W.; m. Zivia Syrkin, Dec. 31, 1942; children— Eve Syrkin, Jonathan Syrkin. S.B., Harvard, 1940; MA, UCLA, 1944, PhD, 1953. Asst. prof. meteorology Mass. Inst. Tech., Cambridge, 1953-58; asso. prof. meteorology U. Calif. at Los Angeles, 1958-64, prof., 1964—, chmn. dept., 1971-76. Vis. prof. U. Buenos Aires, 1962, U. Jerusalem, 1965; vis. scholar U. Calif.-Berkeley, 2000—. Prin. contbr.: Glossary of Meteorology; co-editor: Progress in Desert Research; contbr. articles to profl. jours. Trustee Univ. Corp. for Atmospheric Rsch.; pres., dir. Sage Resources, Inc. With USNR, 1940-41. Fulbright grantee, 1949-50, 65; NATO sr. fellow, 1961-62 Fellow Am. Meteorol. Soc.; mem. Am. Profs. for Peace in Middle East (nat. exec. 1974—), Royal Meteorol. Soc., Am. Geophys. Union, Phi Beta Kappa, Sigma Xi. Clubs: Harvard So. Calif. Home: 1317 Shattuck Ave Berkeley CA 94709-1414 Office: Hilgard Hall U Calif Berkeley CA 94720 E-mail: wurtele@home.com.

WURTH, PATSY ANN, geographic information systems specialist; b. Paducah, Ky., Dec. 5, 1947; d. James Edward and Olean Barbara (Sietz) W.; m. Jerry Leon Scarbrough, Aug. 7, 1965 (div. 1985); children: Tracy Ann, Ashli Michele, Scott Jeremy; m. Robert W. Luther, Feb. 25, 1995 (div. 1998). BS magna cum laude, Murray (Ky.) State U., 1988, MS, 1991. Cert. EMT. Instr. Ky. Cabinet for Human Resources, Frankfort, 1983-93, Vocat. Edn. Region I, Paducah, Ky., 1983-91, Murray State U., 1983-91, Calloway County Red Cross, Murray, 1985-89; exec. dir. Marshall County Red Cross, Benton, Ky., 1985-88; profl. intern Johnson Controls, Cadiz, 1986; grad. asst. Murray State U., 1988-91; fellow U.S. Dept. Energy/Oak Ridge (Tenn.) Nat. Lab., 1989-90; rsch. fellow U.S. Army Corps Engrs. Constrn. Engring. Rsch. Lab., Champaign, Ill., 1991-92, acting team leader spatial techs. support team, 1992-93; GIS facility mgr. environ. scis. divsn. Oak Ridge (Tenn.) Nat. Lab., 1993-95; mgr. GIS svcs. Solutions to Environ. Problems, Inc., Oak Ridge, 1995-96, Aegis Svcs. Corp., Clinton, Tenn., 1996-97; GIS program coord. Roane State C.C., Oak Ridge, 1996—; GIS program mgr. Sci. Applications Internat. Corp., Tenn., 1998—2001. Exec. dir. Marshall County Red Cross, Benton, Ky., 1985-88; first aid attendant Ohio River Steel, Calvert City, Ky., 1985-86. Troop leader Kentuckiana Girl Scouts, Benton, 1973-84, fund drive chair, 1973-84. Mem. LWV, Am. Soc. Safety Engrs., Ky. EMT Instrs. Assn. (instr.), Western Ky. EMT Assn., Am. Soc. Photogrametry and Remote Sensing (Western Great Lake region sec.-treas. 1992), Nat. Safety Coun. (cmty. health and emergency svcs. com.), Assn. Women in Sci., Women in Tech. and Sci. (chmn. 1997-98), Tenn. Geog. Info. Coun. (bd. dirs. 1997-2000), S.E. Regional ESRI Users Group (chair 1995), Nat. Assn. Environ. Profls., Oak Ridge Area ESRI Users Group (chmn. 1996-2000), Epsilon Pi Tau, Alpha Chi. Democrat. Roman Catholic. Home: 330 Melton Hill Dr Clinton TN 37716-7106 Office: Roane State CC 701 Briarcliff Ave Oak Ridge TN 37830

WURTH, SUSAN WINSETT, health facility case manager; b. McKenzie, Tenn., Dec. 17, 1953; d. James Edward and Betty Arnold (Winsett) Paris; m. Michael Wurth, Sept. 21, 1974; children: Jonathan MIchael, Brandi Michelle. AS, Paducah (Ky.) C.C., 1974; BSN, Murray State U., 1998, MSN, 2001. RN, cert. clin. nurse specialist. Staff nurse, team leader Cmty. Hosp., Mayfield, Ky., 1974-76, Western Bapt. Hosp., Paducah, 1976-87, day charge nurse orthop. and urology unit, 1987-96, case mgr. orthop. and neurology units, 1996-99, case mgr. ortho and urology, 1999—. Spkr. in field; edn. com., policy and procedure com. Educator for Free Prostate Cancer Screening Yearly. Developer patient care pathways for total knee, total hip and radical prostatectomy, 1994, 95; developer protocol for total hip and total knee patients for orthop. group, 1998. Mem. Nat. Assn. Clin. Nurse Specialists, Sigma Theta Tau. Home: 7305 Wurth Rd Paducah KY 42001-9227 E-mail: swurth@bhsi.com.

WURTMAN, RICHARD JAY, physician, educator, inventor; b. Phila., Mar. 9, 1938; s. Samuel Richard and Hilda (Schreiber) W.; m. Judith Joy Hirschhorn, Nov. 15, 1959; children: Rachael Elisabeth, David Franklin. AB, U. Pa., 1956; MD, Harvard U., 1960. Intern Mass. Gen. Hosp., 1960-61, resident, 1961-62, fellow medicine, 1965-66, clin. assoc. in medicine, 1985—; research assoc., med. research officer NIMH, 1962-67; mem. faculty MIT, Cambridge, 1967—, prof. endocrinology and metabolism, 1970-80, prof. neuroendocrine regulation, 1980-94, Cecil H. Green disting. prof., 1994—; dir. Clin. Rsch. Ctr., MIT, 1985—; prof. neuroscience MIT, 1984-94. Lectr. medicine Harvard Med. Sch., 1969—; prof. Harvard-MIT Divsn. Health Scis. and Tech., 1978—; Smithies lectr. Oxford U., 2002; sci. dir. Ctr. for Brain Scis. and Metabolism Charitable Trust, 1981—; invited prof. U. Geneva, 1981; Sterling vis. prof. Boston U., 1981; vis. fellow Balliol Coll., Oxford U., 1997; mem. small grants study sect. NIMH, 1967-69, preclin. psychopharmacology study sect., 1971-75; behavioral biology adv. panel NASA, 1969-72; coun. basic sci. Am. Heart Assn., 1969-74; rsch. adv. bd. Parkinson's Disease Found., 1972-80, Am. Parkinson's Disease Assn., 1978—; com. phototherapy in newborns NRC-Nat. Acad. Scis., 1972-74, com. nutrition, brain devel. and behavior, 1976, mem. space applications bd., 1976-82; mem. task force on drug devel. Muscular Dystrophy Assn., 1980-87; chmn. life scis. adv. com. NASA, 1979-82; chmn. adv. bd. Alzheimer's Disease Assn., 1981-84; assoc. neuroscis. rsch. program MIT, 1974-82; chmn. life scis. adv. bd. USAF, 1985—; Bennett lectr. Am. Neurol. Assn., 1974; Flexner lectr. U. Pa., 1975; founder, chmn. sci. adv. bd. Interneuron Pharms., Inc., 1989-99; co-founder Wurtco, 1999, Back Bay Sci., 1999. Author: Catecholamines, 1966; (with others) The Pineal, 1968; editor: (with Judith Wurtman) Nutrition and the Brain, Vols. I and II, 1977, Vols. III, IV, V., 1979, Vol. VI, 1983, Vol. VII, 1986, Vol. VIII, 1990, also numerous other articles and books; mem. editl. bd. Endocrinology, 1967-73, Jour. Pharmacology and Exptl. Therapeutics, 1968-75, Jour. Neural Transmission, 1969-88, Neuroendocrinology, 1969-72, Metabolism, 1970-80, Circulation Research, 1972-77, Jour. Neurochemistry, 1973-82, Life Scis., 1973-81, Brain Rsch., 1977—. Mem. bd. overseers Boston Symphony Orch., 1997—; bd. dirs. Combined Jewish Philanthropies, Boston, 1997—; bd. dirs. Fenwy Cmty. Health Ctr., Boston, 1998—, Provincetown Art Assn. and Mus., 2000—. Recipient Alvarenga prize and lectureship Phila. Coll. Physicians, 1970, CIBA-Geigy Drew award in Biomed. Rsch., 1982, Roger Williams award in Preventive Nutrition, 1987, Roger J. Williams award in Preventive Medicine, 1989, NIMH Merit award, 1989—, Internat. Prize for Modern Nutrition, 1989, Hall of Fame Disting. Alumni award Ctrl. H.S. Phila., 1992; Disting. lectr. Purdue U., 1984; Rufus Cole lectr., Rockefeller U., 1985; Pfizer lectr. NYU Med. Sch., 1985; Grass Fedn. lectr. U. Ga., 1985, Alan Rothballer Meml. lectr., N.Y. Med. Coll., Valhalla, N.Y., 1989, Gretchen Kerr Green lectr in the neuroscis., 1989; Wellcome Vis. Prof. Washington State U., Pullman, 1989; Julius Axelrod Disting. lectr. in neurosci., CUNY, 1990, Sigma Tau Found. lectr. on aging, Rome, 1990, Disting. lectr. in neurosci. La. State U., 1991, McEwen lectr. Queen's U., Ont., 1991; Plenary lectr. 3d Internat. Symposium on Microdialysis, 1993; Hans Lindner Meml. lectr. Weizmann Inst., 1993, Waldo E. Nelson Meml. lectr. St. Christopher's Hosp., Phila., 1997, Sidney Kibrick M.D. lectr. Boston U. Med. Sch., 1998. Mem. Am. Soc. Clin. Investigation, Endocrine Soc. (Ernst Oppenheim award 1972), Am. Physiol. Soc., Am. Soc. Biol. Chemists, Am. Soc. Pharmacology and Exptl. Therapeutics (John Jacob Abel award 1968), Am. Soc. Neurochemistry, Soc. Neuroscis., Am. Soc. Clin. Nutrition, Am. Inst. Nutrition (Osborne & Mendel award 1982). Clubs: Harvard (Boston). Achievements include some 40 U.S. patents on new treatments for diseases and conditions; invention of melatonin for promoting sleep, of dexfenfluramine for treating obesity, of citicoline for treating stroke and of Prozac (Sarafem) for the treatment of premenstrual syndrome. Home: 300 Boylston St Boston MA 02116-3923 Office: Mass Inst Tech 45 Carleton St # E25-604 Cambridge MA 02142-1323 E-mail: dick@mit.edu.

WURTZ, MARGARET JOHNSTON, artist, calligrapher; b. Yonkers, N.Y., Feb. 19, 1930; d. James and Leontine (Orbanes) Johnston; m. Elmer S. Wurtz, May 5, 1951; children: Marguerite, Raymond, Eileen, James, Jeanette. BA, Molloy U., 1973; MA/L.S., SUNY, Stonybrook, 1985. Art tchr. St. Joseph, Babylon, N.Y., 1963-80; freelance artist and calligrapher, 1980—; propr. Marline Designer Shirts, Bolton Landing, NY, 1986-90. Student workshops Soc. of Scribes, N.Y.C., 1984-2000; active artist/exhibitor Wet Paints, Sayville, N.Y., 1994-2000. Artist fabric collage, 1985, pastel painting, 1998-2002. Vol. L.I. Maritime Mus., 1998-2002, St. Lawrence Soup Kitchen, Sayville, N.Y., 1998-2002, St. Patrick Soup Kitchen, Bay Shore, N.Y., 1995-2002. Mem. Sumpwams Garden Club (various awards). Roman Catholic. Avocations: gardening, piano, golf, bicycling. Home: 15 Poplar St Sayville NY 11782-3116

WURTZ, ROBERT HENRY, neuroscientist; b. St. Louis, Mar. 28, 1936; s. Robert Henry and Alice Edith (Popplwell) W.; m. Sally Smith, Dec. 20, 1958 (div.); children: William, Erica; m. Emily Otis, Apr. 23, 1983. AB, Oberlin Coll., 1958; PhD, U. Mich., 1962. Rsch. assoc. Com. for Nuclear Info., St. Louis, 1962-63; fellow Sch. Medicine, Washington U., 1962-65; rsch. psychologist NIH, Bethesda, Md., 1965-66, physiologist, 1966-78, chief lab. sensorimotor rsch., 1978—. Vis. scientist Cambridge U., Eng., 1975-76. Editor: Neurobiology of Saccadic Eye Movement, 1989. Recipient Karl Spencer Lashley award Am. Philos. Soc., 1995. Fellow AAAS; mem. APA (Disting. Sci. Contbn. award 1997), NAS, Inst. of Medicine, Am. Acad. Arts and Scis., Soc. Neurosci. (pres. 1991), Am. Physiol. Soc., Assn. for Rsch. in Vision and Opthalmology, Soc. Exptl. Psychologists. Office: NIH Nat Eye Inst Bldg 49 Rm 2A50 Bethesda MD 20892-4435

WURTZEL, ALAN LEON, retail company executive; b. Mount Vernon, N.Y., Sept. 23, 1933; s. Samuel S. and Ruth (Mann) W.; m. Irene C. Rosenberg, Oct. 9, 1988; children from previous marriage: Judith Halle, Daniel Henry, Sharon Lee. AB, Oberlin Coll., 1955; postgrad., London Sch. Econ., 1955-56; LLB cum laude, Yale, 1959. Bar: Conn. 1959, D.C. 1960, Va. 1968. Law clk. Chief Judge David L. Bazelon, U.S. Ct. Appeals, D.C., 1959-60; assoc. Fried, Frank, Harris, Shriver & Kampelman, Washington, 1960-65; legisl. asst. to Senator Joseph Tydings, 1965-66; with Cir. City Stores, Inc. (formerly Wards Co., Inc.), Richmond, 1966-2001, v.p., 1968-70, pres., 1970-83, chief exec. officer, 1973-86, chmn., 1983-94, vice chmn., 1994-2001; chmn. emeritus, 2002—. Pres. NATM Buying Corp., 1978-86; pres. Operation Independence, 1987-88; bd. dirs. Office Depot, Inc., Boca Raton, Fla., 1989-96, Dollar Tree Stores, Norfolk, Va., Nat. Alliance of Bus., Washington, 1992-1999, SchoolNet, Bethesda, MD, Metametrics, Inc., Durham, NC, Storetrax, Inc., Bethesda, MD; mem. Nat. Skills Stds. Bd. Bd. visitors Va. Commonwealth Ednl. U., 1985-92; trustee Oberlin Coll., 1989-96; dir. Washington Ednl. Television Assn., 1989-95; pres. Jewish Community Fedn., Richmond, 1983-85. Mem. Va. State Bd. Edn., 1992-1996, Gov.'s Econ. Adv. Coun. 1990-1991. Office: 2134 R St NW Washington DC 20008-1907 E-mail: alwurtzel@aol.com.

WURZBACH, LINDA, educational consultant; b. San Antonio, Jan. 21, 1954; d. Delmar Earl Wurzbach, Dorothy Lang Wurzbach; m. Mark Allison Tatom. BS, U. Tex., 1975, MEd, 1978. Lic. tchr. Tex. Tchr. Austin Indep. Sch. Dist., Austin, Tex., 1976—81; project mgr. Tex. Sch. for the Blind and Visually Impaired, 1981—82, tchr., 1982—89; project dir. The Psychol. Corp., San Antonio, 1989—90; planner Tex. Edn. Agy., Austin, 1990—96; sr. project assoc. Coun. Chief State Sch. Officers, Washington, 1996—98; pres. Resources for Learning, Austin, 1998—. Cons. Tex. Edn. Agy., Austin, 1998—, Region 20 Edn. Svc. Ctr., San Antonio, 1998—, State Bd. Educator Cert., Austin, 1998—, Calif. Comm. Tchr. Credentialing, Sacramento, 1998—2000, Alain Locke Charter Acad., Chgo., 1998—99, Ill. State Bd. Edn., Springfield, Ill., 1998—99, Ky. Profl. Standards Bd., Frankfort, 1999—2000, Region 13 Edn. Svc. Ctr., Austin, 2000—, Chgo. Children's Choir, 2000—00, Parks and Recreation Dept., Austin, 2001—, Charles A. Dana Ctr., U. Tex., Austin, 2001, Inner-City Tchg. Corps, Chgo. Editor: TxBESS Activity Profile, 2001, Fine Arts Curriculum Frameworks, 2000; author: Works in Progress, 1997, Portfolio Assessment for Beginning Teachers , 1999, Performance Assessment System, 2000; prodr.: (video) If You Love It, Teach It., 2000, Express Yourself, 2001; contbr. articles. Mem.: Nat. Coun. Measurement in Edn., Am. Ednl. Rsch. Assn., Nat. Staff Devel. Coun., Assn. Supervision and Curriculum Develop. Home: 4504 Moose Dr Austin TX 78749 Office: Resources for Learning 3530 Bee Caves Rd Ste 211 Austin TX 78746 Office Fax: 512-327-8577. Business E-Mail: lindaw@resourcesforlearning.net.

WURZBERGER, BEZALEL, psychiatrist; b. Medias, Romania, June 28, 1945; came to U.S., 1967; s. Joshua and Isabella Wurzberger; m. Gladys Schmidt, Mar. 19, 1971; children: Tamar, David. BA, Columbia U., 1972; MD, Nat. U., Tegucigalpa, Honduras, 1982. Diplomate, Am. Bd. Psychiatry and Neurology. Intern North Gen. Hosp., N.Y.C., 1982-83; resident in psychiatry Creedmoor Psychiat. Ctr., Queens Village, N.Y., 1983-86; clin. psychiat. fellow N.Y. Med. Coll., Valhala, 1986-87; staff psychiatrist Glens Falls (N.Y.) Hosp., 1987-92, chmn. dept. psychiatry, 1993-98. Med. dir., Samaritan Counseling Ctr., Keene, N.Y., 1987—; psychiat. cons., Uihlein Mercy Ctr., Lake Placid, N.Y., 1988—, Psychol. Assocs., Queensbury, N.Y., 1998—; forensic psychiatry cons. Fed. Bur. Prisons, 1999—, N.Y. State Office of

Mental Health. V.p. Jewish Community Tegucigalpa, 1978-80; bd. dirs. Congregation Shaarey Tefily, Glens Falls, 1989—, v.p., 1993-96, pres., 1996-97. Sgt. Israeli Air Force, 1964-67. Mem. AMA, Am. Psychiat. Assn., Soc. Liaison Psychiatry, Acad. Psychosomatic Medicine, Honduran Coll. Physicians. Office: PO Box 794 Glens Falls NY 12801-0794 E-mail: bwurzberger@yahoo.com.

WURZEL, LEONARD, retired candy manufacturing company executive; b. Phila., Feb. 4, 1918; s. Maurice L. and Dora (Goldberg) W.; m. Elaine Cohen, Aug. 18, 1949; children— Mark L., Lawrence J. BS, Washington and Jefferson Coll., 1939; MBA, Harvard, 1941. With Loft Candy Corp., Long Island City, N.Y., 1946-64, v.p., 1949-56, exec. v.p., 1956-57, pres., 1957-64, dir., 1949-64; chmn., dir. Calico Cottage Candies, Inc., 1964-94; ret., 1994; mayor Village of Sands Point, N.Y., 1989—. Capt. U.S. Army, 1941—46. Decorated Bronze Star. Mem. Assn. Mfrs. Confectionery and Chocolate (bd. dirs., past pres., chmn.), Candy Chocolate and Confectionery Inst. (bd. dirs., treas.), Retail Confectioners Internat. (bd. dirs., past pres.) Home: 25 Woodland Dr Sands Point NY 11050-1136 Office: 26 Tibbits Ln Sands Point NY 11050-1135

WUSSLER, ROBERT JOSEPH, broadcasting executive, media consultant; b. Newark, Sept. 8, 1936; s. William and Anna (MacDonald) W.; children: Robert Joseph, Rosemary, Sally, Stefanie, Christopher, Jeanne. BA in Communication Arts, Seton Hall U., 1957, LLD (hon.), 1976, Emerson Coll., 1976. With CBS News, N.Y.C., 1957-72; v.p., gen. mgr. Sta. WBBM-TV, Chgo., 1972-74; v.p. CBS Sports, N.Y.C., 1974-76, pres., 1977-78, Sta. CBS-TV, N.Y.C., 1976-77, Pyramid Enterprises Ltd., N.Y.C., 1978-80; exec. v.p. Turner Broadcasting System Inc., Atlanta, 1980-87, sr. exec. v.p., from 1987, bd. dirs.; pres. Atlanta Sports Teams, Inc., 1981-87; pres., chief exec. officer COMSAT Video Enterprises, Inc., Washington, 1989-92; pres. Wussler Group, 1992—. Chmn. bd. dirs. Nat. Acad. TV Arts and Scis., 1986-90; bd. dirs. Atlanta Hawks Ltd., Atlanta Braves Nat. League Baseball Club, Inc.; co-owner Denver Nuggets, NBA, 1989-92. Bd. regents Seton Hall U., 1978-84; trustee Marymount Manhattan Coll., 1977-81. Recipient Emmy awards, numerous other nat. and internat. news and sports awards. Mem. Dirs. Guild Am., Internat. Radio and TV Soc., Ariz. Heart Inst., Cable Advt. Bur., Nat. Cable TV Assn. (satellite network com.), European Broadcasting Union. Roman Catholic.

WÜTHRICH, KURT, molecular biologist, biophysical chemist, educator; b. Oct. 4, 1938; MS in Chemistry, Physics and Maths., U. Bern, Switzerland, 1962; Eidenössisches Turn-und Sportlehrerdiplom, PhD in Chemistry, U. Basel, Switzerland, 1964; D Chem (hon.), U. Siena, Italy, 1997; PhD (hon.), U. Zürich, Switzerland, 1997, Ecole Poly. Lausanne, 2001. Postdoctoral tng. U. Basel, U. Calif., Berkeley, Bell Telephone Labs., Murray Hill, N.J., 1964-69; prof. biophysics Swiss Fed. Inst. Tech., Zürich, 1972—, chmn. dept. biology, 1995-2000. Mem. coun. Internat. Union Pure and Applied Biophysics, 1975-78, 87-90, sec. gen., 1978-84, v.p., 1984-87; mem. gen. com. Internat. Coun. Sci. Unions, 1980-86, standing com. on free circulation of scientists, 1982-90. Editor Jour. Biomolecular NMR, Quar. Rev. Biophysics, Macromolecular Structures; contbr. articles to profl. jours. Recipient Friedrich Miescher prize Schweizerische Biochemische Gesellschaft, 1974, shield of faculty of medicine Tokyo U., 1983, P. Bruylants medal Cath. U. Louvain, 1986, Stein and Moore award Protein Soc., U.S., 1990, Louisa Gross Horwitz prize Columbia U., 1991, Gilbert N. Lewis medal U. Calif., Berkeley, 1991, Marcel Benoist prize Swiss Confederation, 1992, Disting. Svc. award Miami Winter Symposia, 1993, Prix Louis Jeantet de Médecine, Geneva, 1993, Kaj Linderstrøm-Lang prize Kaj Linderstrøm-Lang Found., Copenhagen, 1996, Eminent Scientist of RIKEN (Tokyo), 1997, Kyoto prize in Advanced Tech., 1998, Guenther Laukien prize Exptl. Nuclear Magnetic Resonance Conf., 1999, Otto Warburg medal Soc. for Biochemistry and Molecular Biology, Germany, 1999; Fgn. fellow Indian Nat. Sci. Acad.; hon. fellow NAS India. Fellow: AAAS; mem.: Schweizerische Akademie der Technischen Wissenschaften, Academia Europea, European Molecular Biology Orgn., Deutsche Akad. der Naturforscher Leopoldina, Nat. Magnetic Resonance Soc. India (hon.), Japanese Biochem. Soc. (hon.), Am. Acad. Arts and Scis (hon.), Acad. Scis., Inst. France (assoc.), U.S. Nat. Acad (assoc.). Office: Inst Molecular Biology & Biophysics ETH Hönggerberg 8093 Zurich Switzerland

WUTHRICH, PAUL, electrical engineer, researcher, consultant; b. Ziefen, Switzerland, Feb. 25, 1931; came to U.S., 1956; s. Emil and Hulda (Degen) W.; m. Irmgard Ann Garbe, Dec. 3. 1960; children: Christine, Marc. BSEE, U. New Haven, 1970; MSEE, U. Conn., 1973. Prin. engr., mgr. R & D Timex Corp., Waterbury, Conn., 1956-88, staff scientist, 1988-96; cons., 1996—. Mem. Opitcal Soc. Am., Instrument Soc. Am., Phys. Soc. Am. Achievements include 45 patents on watch movement and instrumentation from electric to solid state watches; develop. of first 3D nimslo camera; rsch. on first infusion pump device for med. implant. Home and Office: 760 Hamilton Ave Watertown CT 06795-2311

WYAND, MARTIN JUDD, economics educator, retired military officer; b. Greenwich, Conn., May 28, 1931; s. Charles Samuel and Marian (Winter) W.; m. Margaret Alison Knox, May 26, 1974. BA in Social Sci., Pa. State U., 1953, MA in Econs., 1954; JD in Law, U. Denver, 1969; PhD Econs., U. Ill., 1964. Graduate teaching asst. Pa. State U., Univ. Park., 1953-54; grad. teaching asst. U. Ill., Urbana, 1960-64; from asst. prof. to prof. U. Denver, 1964-82; adj. prof. econs. Metro State Coll., Denver, 1982-84. Adj. prof. Coll. Bus. Adminstrn., U. Colo. Denver, 1984-90; lectr. Coll. Bus. Adminstrn., Pa. State U., 1990—; instr. Armed Forces Intelligence Tng. Ctr., 1974-76. Contbr. articles to profl. jours. Adminstrv. bd. dirs. Washington Park Meth. Ch., Denver, 1977-85. Served to col. USAFR, 1953-83, ret. 1991. Grantee Shell Oil Co., 1966, U. Denver, 1976. Mem. Am. Econ. Assn., Am. Collegiate Sch. Bus., Rocky Mountain Social Sci. Assn., Res. Officers Assn. (pres. Geddes chpt. 1978-82, ret.), Ret. Officers Assn., Air Force Assn., Alpha Kappa Psi, Pi Gamma Mu, Alpha Phi Omega. Avocations: reading, chess, classical music, swimming. Home: 1066 Crabapple Dr State College PA 16801-4252 Office: Pa State U 427 Beam Bldg University Park PA 16802

WYANT, CAROL SHUMAKER, not for profit management consultant; b. Alameda, Calif., May 26, 1939; d. Paul Russell and Helen Carolyn (Overstreet) Shumaker; m. Clyde William Wyant, Jr., Sept. 4, 1960 (div. Apr. 1984); children: John Russell, James William. BA, Stanford U., 1961; MA, Tulsa U., 1980. Fin. feasibility analyst Williams Realty Corp., Tulsa and San Antonio, 1980, real estate developer, 1981-84, leasing and bldg. mgr., 1984-85, cmty. affairs, 1985-87; exec. dir. Landmarks Preservation Coun. Ill., Chgo., 1987-94; dir. statewide partnerships Nat. Trust for Hist. Preservation, Washington, 1995-99; founder, pres. Pathfinder Cons., Chgo., 1999—. Vice chmn. Sales Tax Overview Com., Tulsa, 1983; v.p. Univ. Roundtable, San Antonio, 1982. V.p. Jr. League Tulsa, 1976; chmn. Citizens Coalition for Cmty. Devel., Tulsa, 1980; chmn. com. Downtown Owners Assn., San Antonio, 1982; advisor Isle La Motte Reef Preservation Trust. Named one of Outstanding Young Women of Am., 1968. Mem.: AIA (Chgo. br. hon.), The Chgo. Network, Mensa, Lambda Alpha Internat. Avocations: hiking, bicycling, singing, jogging, travel. Home: 161 W Harrison St Unit 407 Chicago IL 60605-1019 Office: Pathfinder Cons 302 N Wabash Ave Ste 1800 Chicago IL 60601 E-mail: carolwyant@mindspring.com.

WYANT, CLYDE W., JR. manufacturing company executive; b. Ada, Okla., Sept. 20, 1938; s. Clyde W. and Geneva Pauline (George) W.; m. Anne L. Edgerton, Nov. 23, 1984; children: Lynn, John, James, Markham, Carolyn BA in History, Stanford U., 1960; MBA, Harvard U., 1965. Asst. to pres. Helmerich & Payne, Inc., Tulsa, 1965-68, fin. v.p., 1968-85; exec. v.p., chief fin. officer Purolator Products Co. (formerly Facet Enterprises, Inc.), 1985-90; exec. v.p., CFO, treas. Lennox Internat., Inc., 1990-2001. Dir. Am. Nursery Products, Tahlequah, Okla., Hawkins Energy Co., Tulsa. Vice pres., trustee Holland Hall Sch., Tulsa, 1978-86; trustee Hillcrest Med. Ctr., Tulsa; vice chmn. admissions com. Tulsa Area United Way, 1979-86, chmn. allocations com., 1987, pres.-elect 1989, pres., 1990; fin. com. chmn. Community Network for Public Edn., Tulsa, 1983-85, Okla. Prof. Affairs Tribunal, 1989—; pres., treas., dir. Jr. Achievement of Greater Tulsa, 1978-86; community advisor Jr. League of Tulsa, 1979-82. Served to lt. U.S. Army, 1960-62 Recipient Bronze Leadership award Jr. Achievement, 1983 Mem. Fin. Execs. Inst. (pres. 1979-80), Am. Petroleum Inst., Mid-Continent Harvard Bus. Sch. Assn. (pres. 1980-82) Clubs: Tulsa Tennis (pres. 1985). Avocations: tennis; fishing; cooking. Office: Lennox Internat Inc PO Box 799900 Dallas TX 75379-9900 also: Two Warren Pl E 61st St Ste 1100 Tulsa OK 74136-0523 Home: 2140 Lake Park Blvd Richardson TX 75080-2252

WYANT, JAMES CLAIR, engineering company executive, educator; b. Morenci, Mich., July 31, 1943; s. Clair William and Idah May (Burroughs) W.; m. Louise Doherty, Nov. 20, 1971; 1 child, Clair Frederick. BS, Case Western Reserve, 1965; MS, U. Rochester, 1967, PhD, 1968. Engr. Itek Corp., Lexington, Mass., 1968-74; instr. Lowell (Mass.) Tech. Inst., 1969-74; prof. U. Ariz., Tucson, 1974—; pres. WYKO Corp., 1984-97; dir. optical sci. ctr. U. Ariz., 1999—. Chmn. Gordon Conf. on Holography Plymouth (N.H.) State Coll., 1984; vis. prof. U. Rochester, N.Y., 1983. Editor: Applied Optics and Optical Engineering, vols. VII-X, 1979-80, 83, 87. Recipient of Joseph Fraunhofer-Robert M. Burley Prize, 1992, Optical Soc. Am. Mem. Optical Soc. Am. (bd. dirs. 1979-81, Joseph Fraunhofer award 1992), Soc. Photo-Optical Instrumentation Engring. (pres. 1986). Home: 1881 N King St Tucson AZ 85749-9367 Office: U Ariz Optical Scis Ctr Tucson AZ 85721-0001 E-mail: jcwyant@optics.arizona.edu.

WYARD, VICKI SHAW, investment and insurance company executive; b. L.A., Oct. 29, 1945; d. Clinton Gilbert and Lois (Griswold) Shaw; m. Gary Edwin Wyard, July 1, 1966; children: Brett, Lori, Lisa. Student, Carleton Coll., 1963-65; BS, U. Minn., 1967. Cert. fin. planner. Systems analyst Univac Fed. Systems Div., Mpls., 1967-69, Internat. Timesharing Corp., Chaska, Minn., 1973-76; dir. Minnetonka Bd. of Edn., Excelsior, 1978-81, vice chairperson, 1981-84; fin. planner IDS Fin. Svcs., Mpls., 1986-89, trainer of planners, 1988-89; fin. planner, rep. Fin. Network Investment Corp., Torrance, Calif., 1989-91, Multi-Fin. Securities Corp., Mpls., 1991—. Bd. dirs. Westerlund Products Corp., Homescape Systems; seminar presenter in field. Contbr. articles to profl. jours. Trustee Washburn Child Guidance Ctr., Mpls., 1986-98; bd. dirs. Perspectives, Inc., St. Louis Park, Minn., 1988-2002, pres. bd., 1989-96; chmn. stewardship campaign Wayzata Cmty. Ch., 1996-98, mem. pers. com., 1999-2002. Mem. Internat. Assn. Fin. Planners, Fin. Profls. Assn. (bd. dir., v.p. legis. and regulatory task force Mpls. chpt. 1990-92). Avocations: snow skiing, writing, reading, music, golf. Home and Office: 3630 Northome Rd Wayzata MN 55391-3021

WYATT, BILL, airport executive; b. Astoria, Oreg. Student, Willamette U., U. Oreg. Mem. Oreg. Legislature, 1975; dir. employee benefits and govt. rels. Oreg. State Employees Assn.; dir. intergovtl. affairs City of Portland; exec. dir. Assn. for Portland Progress; pres. Oreg. Bus. Coun.; chief of staff Gov. of Oreg., Salem, 1995—2001; airport exec. PDX, Portland, Oreg., 2001—. Bd.dirs. Crabbe-Huson family mut. funds. Past chmn. bd. Urban League of Portland; bd. dirs. Oreg. Pub. Broadcasting. Mem. City Club of Portland (past bd. govs.). Office: PDX 7000 NE Airport Way Portland OR 97218 Mailing: U.S Headquarters Port of Portland P.O. Box 3529 Portland OR 97208*

WYATT, BRETT MICHAEL, secondary school educator; b. Toledo, Dec. 31, 1958; s. Warren Dale and Jacqueline Elizabeth (Angelides) W.; 1 child, Adrian. BA in Geography, Calif. State U., San Bernardino, 1981; MA in Geography, U. Calif., Davis, 1985. Elem. tchr. Sacramento City Unified Sch. Dist., 1987-89, tech. resource tchr., 1989-91; ednl. cons. IBM, Sacramento, 1989-92; asst. editor Computers in the Schs., Reno, 1991-93; media specialist L.A. Unified Sch. Dist., 1998—. Author: Jewish Settlement in Sacramento, A Pictorial History, 1987; prodr.: (video) Sacramento Educational Cable Consortium, 1991, 92; contbg. poet: Nevada High Desert Rev., 1997, 98; contbr. articles to profl. jours. Advisor Tech. Preparation Com., Sacramento, 1991; founding dir. Nev. Schs. Network, Reno, 1992; advisor WCSD Internet Task Force, Reno, 1994—; archivist Temple B'hai Israel, Sacramento, 1986-87; computer technician vol. Ptnrs. in Edn., Sparks, Nev., 1994—. Named Vol. of the Yr., Ptnrs. in Edn., Sparks, 1995; recipient award for outstanding ednl. video Sacramento Ednl. Cable Consortium, 1991, 92. Democrat. Home: 2614 S Harcourt Ave Los Angeles CA 90016-2827

WYATT, CHARLES H. cardiovascular surgeon; b. Aug. 22, 1960; BA, Wesleyan U., Middletown, Conn., 1982; MD, Baylor Coll. Medicine, 1986. Intern Baylor Coll. Medicine, Houston, 1986-87, resident in gen. surgery, 1987-91; fellowship cardiothoracic surgery U. Miami Affiliated Hosps., Fla., 1991-93; clin. asst. prof. surger U. Miami, 1993-95; attending cardiovasc. surgeon St. Clair Cardiovasc. Surgeons, Inc., 1995-98; attending cardiovascular surgeon Cardiovascular Inst. of the South, Lafayette, La., 1998—. Fellow ACS, Am. Coll. Cardiology, Am. Coll. Chest Physicians, Soc. Thoracic Surgeons. Home: 429 Farmington Dr Lafayette LA 70503-8412 Office: Cardiovascular Inst of the South 4212 W Congress St Ste 2100 Lafayette LA 70506-6768 E-mail: chwmd@prodigy.net.

WYATT, EDITH ELIZABETH, elementary education educator; b. San Diego, Aug. 13, 1914; d. Jesse Wellington and Elizabeth (Fultz) Carne; m. Lee Ora Wyatt, Mar. 30, 1947 (dec. Jan. 1966); children: Glenn Stanley (dec.), David Allen. BA, San Diego State Coll., 1936. Elem. tchr. Nat. Sch. Dist., National City, Calif., 1938-76. Sec. San Diego County Parks Soc., 1986-96, sec.-treas., 1998—; librarian Congl. Ch. Women's Fellowship, Chula Vista, Calif., 1980—; active Boy Scouts Am, 1959—. Recipient Who award San Diego County Tchrs. Assn., 1968, Silver Fawn award Boy Scouts Am. Mem. AAUW (sec. 1978-80, pub. rels. 1985—), Calif. Ret. Tchrs. Assn. (scholarship com. 1985-90, 92-95, treas. South Shores divsn. # 60 1996—), Starlite Hiking Club (sec.-treas. 1979—). Avocation: hiking. Home: 165 E Millan St Chula Vista CA 91910-6255

WYATT, EDWARD AVERY, V, city manager; b. Petersburg, Va., Nov. 1, 1941; s. Edward Avery and Martha Vaughan (Seabury) W.; m. Regina Helen Stec, Aug. 23, 1969; children: Edward Avery VI, Stephen Alexander, Kent Seabury. AS in Bus., Bluefield Coll.; BS in Bus., Pub. Adminstrn., Va. Poly. Inst. and State U., 1964; M.Commerce, U. Richmond, 1969; MA in Polit. Sci., Appalachian State U., 1977. Chief gen. svc. City of Petersburg, Va., 1966-67, asst. to city mgr., 1967-70; city mgr. City of Washington, N.C., 1970-73, City of Morganton, 1973-78, City of Greenville, 1978-82, City of Fairfax, Va., 1982-91, City of Wilson, N.C., 1991—. Adj. lectr. George E. Mason U. Bus. Sch., 1985-86; bd. dirs. Electricities of N.C., sec. 2000; commr. N.C. Ea. Mcpl. Power Agy. Contbr. numerous articles to profl. jours. and newsletters. Chmn. N.C. Code Ofcls. Qualification Bd., 1980-82; mem. adv. bd. Wilson Salvation Army, 1992—; mem. adv. com. Wilson Boys and Girls Club. Served with USNG and USAR, 1964-70. Paul Harris fellow Rotary Internat.; Dennis Duffey Meml. award Fairfax Police Youth Club. Mem. ASPA (ea. N.C. chpt.), Internat. City Mgmt. Assn. (endowment com. 1985-2000, chair 1991-92, coun. mgr. plan task force 1993-94), Va. Local Govt. Mgmt. Assn. (pres. 1989-90), N.C. City/County Mgmt. Assn. (pres.), Soc. Cincinnati in Va., Descendants of Francis Epes of Va. (pres.), Wilson Rotary (dir.). Home: 1307 Waverly Rd NW Wilson NC 27896-1483 Office: City of Wilson PO Box 10 Wilson NC 27894-0010

WYATT, ELNORIA, real estate broker; b. Fountain Run, Ky., July 22, 1927; d. George Harrison Simmons and Mamie Elizabeth (Shockley) Oaks; m. Lexie Lee Wyatt, Jan. 23, 1943; children: Ronald E., Donald Lee. Student in real estate, Bemis Lawrence Coll., Louisville, Ky., 1976, Western Ky. U., 1984-85. Cert. real estate appraiser, 1991. Skill worker Glasgow (Ky.) Mfg. Co., 1947-77; sec., treas. Wyatt Enterprises, Inc., Glasgow, 1980-85; real estate broker Wyatt Realty & Auction Services, 1978—; apprentice auctioneer, 1985—. Exec. com. Barren County Polit. Orgn., Glasgow, 1980-84; mem. county exec. bd. Dem. Women's Club, 1978—; exec. officer Ky. Citizens for Quality Long Term Care, 1990—. Mem. Ladies Garmentworkers Union (pres. 1958-72), Glasgow-Barren County Bd. Realtors (treas. 1984, sec. 1985, pres. 1987), Ky. Realtors' 200 Club. Mem. Ch. of Christ. Office: Glasgow-Barren County Bd Realtors Glasgow KY 42141

WYATT, GERARD ROBERT, biology educator, researcher; b. Palo Alto, Calif., Sept. 3, 1925; came to Can., 1935; s. Horace Graham and Mary Aimee (Strickland) W.; m. Sarah Silver Morton, Dec. 19, 1951 (dec. Mar. 1981); children— Eve Morton, Graham Strickland, Diana Silver; m. Mary Evelyn Rogers, Mar. 16, 1985 BA, U. B.C., Can., 1945; postgrad., U. Calif.-Berkeley, 1946-47; PhD, Cambridge U., 1950. Research scientist Can. Dept. Agr., Sault Ste. Marie, Ont., 1950-54; asst. prof. biochemistry Yale U., New Haven, 1954-60, assoc. prof., prof. biology, 1960-73; prof. biology Queen's U., Kingston, Ont., 1973-94, prof. emeritus, 1994—; sci. dir. Insect Biotech Can., 1990-93. Contbr. articles to profl. jours. Guggenheim fellow, 1956; Killam Research fellow, 1985 Fellow Royal Soc. Can.; mem. Am. Soc. Biol. Chemistry, Am. Entomol. Soc. Avocation: natural history. Home: 114 Earl St Kingston ON Canada K7L 2H1 Office: Queen's Univ Dept Biology Kingston ON Canada K7L 3N6 E-mail: wyattg@biology.queensu.ca.

WYATT, JAMES FRANK, JR. lawyer; b. Talladega, Ala., Dec. 1, 1922; s. James Frank and Nannie Lee (Heaslett) W.; m. Rosemary Barbara Slone, Dec. 21, 1951; children: Martha Lee, James Frank III. BS, Auburn U., 1943; JD, Georgetown U., 1949, postgrad., 1950. Bar: D.C. 1949, Ala. 1950, Ill. 1953, U.S. Supreme Ct 1953. Atty. Office Chief Counsel, IRS, 1949-51; tax counsel Universal Oil Products Co., Des Plaines, Ill., 1951-63, asst. treas., 1963-66, v.p. fin., treas., 1966-75; treas. CF Industries, Inc., Long Grove, Ill., 1976-78, v.p. fin., treas., 1978-82; assoc. Tenney & Bentley, 1983-85, Arnstein, Gluck, Lehr, Barron & Milligan, 1985-88; pvt. practice, 1989—. Dir. 1st Nat. Bank, Des Plaines. Village trustee, Barrington, Ill., 1963-75; bd. dirs. Buehler YMCA, Barrington Twp. Republican Orgn., 1963— ; pres. Barrington Area Rep. Workshops, 1962-63. Served to capt., Judge Adv. Gen. Corps AUS, 1944-47. Mem. Tax Execs. Inst. (v.p. 1965-66, chpt. pres. 1961-62), Fed., Am., Chgo. bar assns., Barrington Home Owners Assn. (pres. 1960-61), Newcomen Soc., Assn. U.S. Army, Scabbard and Blade, Phi Delta Phi, Sigma Chi. Clubs: Barrington Hills Country; Economics, University (Chgo.). Episcopalian. Home: 625 Concord Pl Barrington IL 60010-4508 Office: 200 Applebee St Barrington IL 60010-3063

WYATT, JAMES LUTHER, drapery hardware company executive; b. Williamsburg, Ky., May 13, 1924; s. Jesse Luther and Grace Edwina (Little) W.; m. Barbara Christman, Aug. 28, 1946; children— Linda Lou, William Charles Christman (dec.). BS, U. Ky., 1947, MS, 1948; Sc.D., Mass. Inst. Tech., 1952. Registered profl. engr., Ohio, Pa. Devel. engr. titanium div. Nat. Lead Co., Sayreville, N.J., 1948-50; tech. mgr., head, dept. metall. engring., mgr. new products Horizons, Inc., Cleve., 1953-57; cons., asso. Booz, Allen & Hamilton, N.Y.C., 1957-61; v.p. program devel. Armour Research Found., Chgo., 1961-63; v.p. new product devel. Joy Mfg. Co., Pitts., 1963-67; v.p. corp. devel. Nat. Gypsum Co., Buffalo, 1967-69, Max Factor & Co., Hollywood, Calif., 1969-71; pres. Wyatt & Co., 1971—, Jimbabs, Inc., 1983—, Ambassador Industries, Inc., Los Angeles, 1988—. U.S. del. 1st World Metall. Congress. Contbr. tech., mgmt. papers to profl. lit.; patentee in field. Mem. Pompano Beach Power Squadron, adminstr. officer, 1991, exec. officer, 1992, comdr., 1993; chmn. bd. trustees Meth. Ch., 1992, mem. fin. com., 1993, mem. adminstrv. bd.; chmn. bd. trustees 1st United Meth. Ch., Boca Raton; bd. dirs., v.p. Golden Harbour Homeowners Assn., 1997—. Lt. col. USAAF, 1942-46. Elected to U. Ky. Hall of Distinction, 2001. Mem. AIME, Am. Soc. Metals, Econ. Club (Chgo.), Execs. Club (Chgo.), Univ. Club (N.Y.C.), Calif. Yacht Club, Pompano Beach Power Squadron (comdr.), Sigma Phi Epsilon, Alpha Chi Sigma. Clubs: Econs. (Chgo.), Execs. (Chgo.); Univ. (N.Y.C.); Calif. Yacht. Home: 510 Golden Harbour Dr Boca Raton FL 33432-2942 Office: 510 Golden Harbour Dr Boca Raton FL 33432-2942 E-mail: jim_wyatt@juno.com.

WYATT, JOE BILLY, academic administrator; b. Tyler, Tex., July 21, 1935; s. Joe and Fay (Pinkerton) Wyatt; m. Faye Hocutt, July 21, 1956; children: Joseph, Sandra Faye. BA, U. Tex., 1956; MA, Tex. Christian U., 1960. Systems engr. Gen. Dynamics Corp., 1956—65; mgr. Digital Computer Lab., 1961—65; dir. computer ctr., assoc. prof. computer sci. U. Houston, 1965—72; dir. Office Info. Tech. Harvard U., 1972—76, sr. lectr. computer sci., 1972—82, v.p. adminstrn., 1976—82; chancellor Vanderbilt U., Nashville, 1982—2000, chancellor emeritus, 2000. Faculty Harvard U. Kennedy Sch., 1976—82; bd. dirs., chmn. com. on math/sci. Am. Coun. of Edn.; bd. dirs. El Paso Energy, Inc., Ingram Mills., Inc., Advanced Networking and Sys. Corp. Author (with others): Financial Planning Models for Colleges and Universities, 1979; editor-in-chief: Jour. Applied Mgmt. Sys., 1983; contbr. articles to profl. jours.; patentee in field. Trustee EDUCOM, Princeton, NJ, 1973—81, Harvard U. Press, 1976—83, pres., 1975—76, chmn. bd., 1976—79; trustee Leadership Nashville, 1983—93; active Coun. Competitiveness; bd. dirs. Nashville Inst. Arts, 1982—83, Ingram Industries, 1990—96; chmn. adv. com. IST, NSF, 1978—85; vice-chmn. bd. Mass. Tech. Devel. Corp., Boston, 1977—83; alumni bd. dirs. Harvard Bus. Sch., 1982—92. Named Outstanding Tennessean, Gov. of Tenn., 1986; recipient award for exemplary leadership, CAUSE, 1982, Nat. Tree of Life award, Jewish Nat. Fund, 1988; fellow, Gallaudet Coll., 1981—83. Fellow: AAAS; mem.: IEEE, Bus. Higher Edn. Forum (exec. com. 1990—93), So. U. Rsch. Assn., Inc. (chmn. coun. pres. 1988—89), U. Rsch. Assn. (bd. trustees 1988—, chmn. 1997—), Assn. Computing Machinery (pres. Dallas and Ft. Worth chpt. 1963—65), Am. Coun. Edn. (chmn. adv. com. on tech. edn. 1980—81, bd. dirs. 1990—92), Nat. Assn. Ind. Colls. and Univs. (policy bd. 1980—82), Hosp. Corp. Am. (bd. dirs. 1984—89), Assn. Am. Univs. (chmn. exec. com. 1990—91), Govt. Univ. Industry Rsch. Roundtable (chmn. 1998—), Nashville C. of C. (bd. dirs. 1983—86, pres. 1996—97), Experimental Aircraft Assn. (pres. adv. com., found. bd. 1997—), Aircraft Owners and Pilots Assn., Harvard Club, Beta Gamma Sigma, Sigma Xi, Phi Beta Kappa (hon.). Methodist. Office: Vanderbilt U 2525 West End Ave Nashville TN 37203 E-mail: joe.b.wyatt@vanderbilt.edu.

WYATT, JOSEPH LUCIAN, JR. lawyer, writer; b. Chgo., Feb. 21, 1924; s. Joseph Lucian and Cecile Gertrude (Zadico) W.; m. Marjorie Kathryn Simmons, Apr. 9, 1954; children: Daniel, Linn, Jonathan. AB in English Lit. with honors, Northwestern U., 1947; LLB, Harvard U., 1949. Bar: Calif. 1950, U.S. Dist. Ct. (cen. dist.) Calif. 1950, U.S. Ct. Appeals (9th cir.) 1950, U.S. Tax Ct., U.S. Supreme Ct. 1965. Assoc. firm Brady, Nossaman & Walker, Los Angeles, 1950-58, ptnr. L.A., 1958-61; pvt. practice, 1961-71; sr. mem. Cooper, Wyatt, Tepper & Plant, P.C., 1971-79; of counsel Beardsley, Hufstedler & Kemble, 1979-81; ptnr. Hufstedler & Kaus, 1981-95; sr. of counsel Morrison & Foerster, 1995—. Mem. faculty Pacific Coast Banking Sch., Seattle, 1963-92, Southwestern Grad. Sch. Banking, 1988-89; adviser Am. Law Inst., 1988—, Restatement, Trusts 3d, 1988—. Author: Trust Administration and Taxation, 4 vols., 1964—; editor: Trusts and Estates, 1962-74. Lectr. continuing legal edn. programs, Calif. and Tex.; trustee Pacific Oaks Coll. and Children's Sch., 1969-97; counsel, parliamentarian Calif. Democratic party and presdl. conv. dels., 1971—; mem. Calif. State Personnel Bd., 1961-71, v.p., 1963-65, pres., 1965-67; bd trustees Calif. Pub. Employees Retirement System, 1963-71. Served with USAAF, 1943-45. Fellow Am. Coll. of Trust and Estate Counsel; mem. ABA, Internat. Acad. Estate and Trust Law (treas. 1990-96), Am. Law Inst., Calif. State Bar Assn. (del. state conf. 1956, 62-67), L.A. Bar Assn. (trustee 1956). Democrat. Christian Scientist. Avocations: poetry, fishing. Home: 1119 Armada Dr Pasadena CA 91103-2805 E-mail: jwyatt@mofo.com., jwyatt3@earthlink.net.

WYATT, LENORE, civic worker; b. N.Y.C., June 12, 1929; d. Benedict S. Rosenfeld and Ora (Copel) Kanner; m. Bernard D. Copeland, May 17, 1953 (dec. March 1968); children: Harry (dec.), Robert (dec.); m. C. Wyatt Unger, Mar. 26, 1969 (dec. Feb. 1992); 1 child, Amy Unger; m. F. Lowry Wyatt, Sept. 12, 1992 (dec. Nov. 1996). Student, Mills Coll., 1946-48; BA, Stanford U., 1950, MA, 1952; postgrad., NYU, 1952-53. Instr. Stanford U., Palo Alto, Calif., 1952, Hunter Coll., N.Y.C., 1952-53, Calif. State U., Sacramento, 1956-60, U. Calif., Davis, 1965-69; property mgr. Unger, Demas & Markakis, Sacramento, 1974-83. Former actress and model; fin. com. Charles Wright Acad.; fin. mgr. several trusts. Pres. Sacramento Opera Assn., 1972—73; treas. Sacramento Children's Home, 1990—92, v.p., 1992—; former mem. bd. dirs. Sutter Hosp. Aux., Sutter Hosp. Med. Rsch. Found., Sacramento Symphony League, Temple B'nai Israel Sisterhood, Sacramento chpt. Hadassah, Sacramento Children's Home Guild; formerly active Sacramento Opera Assn., Crocker Soc. of Crocker Art Gallery, Sacramento Symphony Assn., Sacramento Reportory Theater Assn.; founding mem. Tacoma Cmtys. Art Sch.; past mem. bd. dirs. Charles Wright Acad.; mem. Temple Beth El of Tacoma; past mem., bd. dirs. Tacoma Art Mus. Mem.: Stanford U. Alumni Assn. (past bd. dirs. Sacramento), Sacramento Pioneer Assn., Am. Contract Bridge League, Del Paso Country Club (past capt. women's golf group, Sacramento), Thunderbird Country Club, Tacoma Club, Wash. Athletic Club, Maui Country Club, Tacoma Country and Golf Club, Sutter Club. Republican. Jewish. Avocations: golf, duplicate bridge. also: 1 Bryn Mawr Dr Rancho Mirage CA 92270

WYATT, MARCIA JEAN, fine arts educator, administrative assistant; b. Petersburg, Va., Nov. 2, 1959; d. Andrew Ezekiel and Lillian (Bonner) Wyatt; m. Nicholas Charles Cooper-Lewter, Nov. 29, 1986 (div. 1998). BS in Elem. Edn., Va. State U., Ettrick, 1984; MEd in Spl. Edn., 1993; Degree in Adminstrv. Ednl. Leadership, St. Mary's U., Mpls., 2000. Lic. minister, 1987; ordained to clergy, 1990. Tchr. Marion (Ind.) Community Schs., 1985-86, Inglewood (Calif.) Unified Schs., 1986-87; office mgr. C.R.A.V.E. Christ Counseling, Tustin, Calif., 1986—; asst. minister New Garden of Gethsemane B.C., L.A., 1987-90; assoc. minister New Hope Bapt. Ch., St. Paul, 1990—; assoc. pastor New Garden of Gethsemane B.C., L.A., 1990—; assoc. minister New Hope Bapt. Ch., 1990—, pulpit coord., 2002; pres. C.R.A.V.E. Christ Singers, L.A., 1987-90; adminstr. asst. Eldorado Bank, Orange, Calif., 1988-90; tchr. fine arts Broadway Cmty. Sch., Mpls., 1996—, Mpls. Sch. Dist., 1990—; assessment coord. Broadway Cmty. Sch., Mpls., 1999—; with Wyatt Consulting, Shoreview, 1986—; 4th grade tchr. Hall Cmty. Sch., Mpls. Founder, dir. Diversity in Motion program for A.A. students, 1992—; stage dir. Babu's Magic with dancer Chuck Davis, 1994; cons. Everyday Learning Corp., 1996—; assessment coord., curriculum writer Mpls. Pub. Schs., 1999—. Nominated to Pres.'s Commn. White House Fellowships, 1993; mem. C.R.A.V.E. Christ Ministries (Relax in Christ, Affirm with Christ, Visualize Christ, Experience Christ); pulpit coord. New Hope Bapt. Ch. Imagination grantee Star Tribune, 1994, 95-96, Fulbright grantee, Namibia, 1996, African studies grantee U. Wis., 1995-96, FASSE grantee U. Minn., 1996. Mem. NAFE, Alpha Kappa Alpha. Avocations: reading, music, fish breeding. E-mail: mwyatt@mpls.k12.mn.us.

WYATT, MICHAEL KENDALL, lawyer; b. Charleston, W.Va., Jan. 13, 1945; s. Noble Kendall Wyatt and Virginia Louisa Litton; m. Karen E. Anthony, June 21, 1969 (div. Aug. 1, 1993); children: Lauren Kendall Wyatt Simmons, Julia Litton. AB, Princeton U., 1967; BA, Oxford U., 1969, MA, 1973; JD, Harvard U., 1972. Bar: D.C. 1973, Md. 1998. Ptnr. Hamel & Park, Washington, 1980—89; assoc. dep. sec. lab. U.S. Dept. Labor, 1989—91; gen. counsel U.S. Small Bus. Adminstrn., 1991—93; ptnr. Proskauer, Rose, N.Y.C., 1993—95, Washington, 1993—95, Semmes, Bowen & Semmes, Washington, 1995—99, Hogan & Hartson, Washington, 1999—. Dir. Washington Internat. Coll., 1975—76; adj. prof. Cornell U., Ithaca, NY, 1992—96. Prin. editor: Small Business Compliance Advisor, 1994; editor: Harvard Internat. Law Jour., 1971—72; contbr. articles to profl. jours. Dir. Woodside Lake Corp., McLean, Va., 1985—87; v.p. Princeton (N.J.) Class of 1967, 1997—. Fellow Woodrow Wilson fellowship, 1967; grantee, Keasbey Scholarship Found., 1967, McConnell Found., 1967. Mem.: Washington Soc. for Close Harmony Singing, Met. Club D.C., Ivy Club, Phi Beta Kappa. Republican. Episcopalian. Avocations: singing, tennis, squash, antique autos, drawing. Home: 1155 Daleview Dr Mc Lean VA 22102 Office: Hogan & Hartson LLP 555 13th St NW Washington DC 20004

WYATT, PHILIP RICHARD, geneticist, physician, researcher; b. St. Louis, Oct. 22, 1951; s. John Poyner and Isabel (Gillespie) W.; m. Sharon Lorraine Parker, June 23, 1978; children: Geoffrey, Kathryn. BS, U. Man., 1972; PhD, U. Man., Winnipeg, Man., Can., 1976; MD, U. Ky., 1980. Lic. Med. Coun. Can. Chief genetics dept. North York Gen. Hosp., Toronto, 1983—, chair instnl. rev. bd. Advisor Ministry Health, Toronto, 1984-90; mem. Mins. Adv. Com. on Genetics, Ont., 2000; chmn. Maternal Serum Screening Com., Ont., 2000. Recipient Karger prize Karger Pub., Switzerland, 1976. Fellow Human Biology Coun.; mem. Am. Soc. Human Genetics, Ont. Med. Assn. (sect. chmn. genetics 1995-98, rev. bd. 1998—). Office: Genetics North York 4001 Leslie St North York ON Canada M2K 1E1 E-mail: pwyatt@nygh.on.ca.

WYATT, RICHARD JED, psychiatrist, educator; b. L.A., June 5, 1939; children: Elizabeth, Christopher, Justin. BA, Johns Hopkins U., 1961, MD, 1964; MD (hon.), Ctrl. U. Venezuela, 1977. Intern in pediat. Western Res. U. Hosp., Cleve., 1964-65; resident in psychiatry Mass. Mental Health Ctr., Boston, 1965-67; with NIMH, 1967—, asst. dir. intramural rsch., 1977-87, chief neuropsychiatry br., chief Neurosci. Ctr., 1972—; clin. prof. psychiatry Stanford U. Med. Sch., 1973-74, Duke U. Med. Sch., 1975—, Uniformed Svcs. Sch. Medicine, 1980—, Columbia U., 1987—; practice medicine specializing in psychiatry Washington, 1968—. Cons. Psychiatry Shelter Program for the Homeless, Columbia U., 1987—; mem. sci. adv. bd. Nat. Alliance for Rsch. Schizophrenia and Depression, 1991. Mem. editl. bd. Advances in Neurosci., 1989, Harvard Rev. Psychiatry, 1992; assoc. prodr. PBS spls. To Paint the Stars, Moods in Music. Recipient A.E. Bennett award, Soc. Biol. Psychiatry, 1971, Psychopharm. award, APA, 1971, Superior Achievement award, USPHS, 1980, dean award, Am. Coll. Psychiatrists, McAlpin Rsch. Achievement award, Nat. Mental Health Assn., 1986, Media award for To Paint the Star, 1991, Arthur P. Noyes award, Commonwealth of Pa., 1986, Arieti award, Am. Acad. Psychoanalysts, 1989, Robert L. Robinson award for Moods in Music, 1990, Mental Health Bell Media award for Moods in Music, Mental Health Assn. Atlanta, 1991, Lieber Ctr. for Schizophrenia Rsch. award, Columbia U., 2001, Outstanding Achievement award, Nat. Assn. VA Psychiatrists, 2001. Fellow Am. Psychiat. Assn., Am. Coll. Neuropsychopharmacology (Efron award 1983); mem. AMA, Washington Psychiat. Assn. Office: MSC 2610 Ste 106B 5415 W Cedar Ln Bethesda MD 20892

WYATT, ROBERT LEE, IV, lawyer; b. Las Cruces, N.Mex., Mar. 9, 1964; s. Robert Lee III and Louise Carole (Bard) W.; m. Vicki Harris Wyatt. BS, Southeastern Okla. State U., 1986; JD, U. Okla., 1989. Bar: Okla. 1989, U.S. Dist. Ct. (we. dist.) Okla. 1990, U.S. Ct. Appeals (10th cir.) 1990, U.S. Dist. Ct. (no. dist.) Okla. 1991, U.S. Ct. Appeals (8th cir.) 1991, U.S. Supreme Ct. 1993. Intern Okla. State Bur. Investigation, Oklahoma City, 1988-89, guest lectr., 1989; dep. spl. counsel Gov. of Okla., 1995; atty. Jones & Wyatt, Enid, Okla., 1989-2000. Mem. criminal justice panel atty. We. Dist. Okla. Contbr. Counsel to Fire Civil Svc. Commn. City of Enid, 1998-2000. Mem. ABA (mem. criminal and litigation sects.), Okla. Bar Assn. (mem. ins., mem. criminal law com.), Oklahoma County Bar Assn., Okla. Criminal Def. Lawyers Assn., Nat. Inst. for Trial Advocacy, Nat. Assn. Criminal Defense Lawyers, Luther Bohanon Am. Inn of Ct. (barrister), Phi Delta Phi, Alpha Chi. Democrat. Baptist. Home: 408 Timberdale Dr Edmond OK 73034 Office: Wyatt Law Office 228 Robert S Kerr Ave Ste 750 Oklahoma City OK 73102-3420 E-mail: bobwyatt@wyattlaw.com.

WYATT, ROBERT SAUNDERS, executive search consultant; b. Kingston, Pa., June 7, 1947; s. Robert Harry and Mary Elizabeth W.; m. Brenda Jean Weir, June 17, 1972; children: Matthew Weir, Scott Andrew. BS in Psychology, Denison U., 1969; MBA in Bus., Golden Gate U., 1975, PhD in Bus., 1983. Dir. tng. The Emporium, San Francisco, 1972-77; mgr. exec. compensation Carter Hawley Hale Stores Corp. Office, L.A., 1977-79; sr. v.p. human resources Broadway Southwest, Mesa, Ariz., 1979-90; exec. v.p. human resources Broadway Stores, L.A., 1990-92; v.p. human resources Bombay Co., Ft. Worth, 1992-93; exec. dir. Dallas Helstrom Turner & Assocs., Dallas, 1993-95; prin., owner, founder R.S. Wyatt Assocs., Inc., Colleyville, 1995-2000; prin. Korn/Ferry Internat., Dallas, 2000—01; mng. ptnr. Dallas office The Ansley Cons. Group, Irvine, 2001—. Author: Who is Minding the Store, A Demographic and Attitudinal Profile of Retail Sales Clerks, 1983. V.p. Hills of Monticello Homeowner Assn., Southlake, Tex., 1993-97; bd. dirs. Challenge Soccer Club, Southlake, 1998—; Stephen min./leader Meth. Ch., 2000--. Capt. USAF, 1969-72. Mem. Mensa. Avocations: distance running, golf, tennis.

WYATT, ROSE MARIE, clinical social worker; b. San Angelo, Tex., Feb. 16, 1937; d. James Odis and Annie LaVernia (Lott) W. BA, Fisk U., 1957; MS, U. So. Calif., 1963; MA, MSW, U. Chgo., 1972; postgrad., Ill. Inst. Tech., 1976—. Tchr. Chgo. Bd. Edn., 1959-63, clin. social worker, 1979—; adult program dir. Chgo. YWCA, 1963-64; youth counselor Chgo. Commn. on Youth Welfare, 1964-66; supervising social worker for Head Start, Chgo. Com. on Urban Opportunity, 1966; social worker Chgo. Commn. on Youth Welfare, 1966-68, Jewish Vocat. Svc., 1968; social worker sch. cmty. rels. Detroit Pub. Schs., 1968-70; social worker Rosman-Wyatt and Assocs., Chgo., 1980—, pres., 1981—; instr. dept. corrections Chgo. State U., 1972—. Adj. instr. Chgo. State U. Mem. adv. bd., chmn. program com. Calumet area United Chritities, 1974-80; vol. Assn. Cmty. Agts., 1968-70, Southside Sr. Citizens Coalition, Chgo., 1963-66, Roseland Health Planning Com., 1974-76, Teen Pregnancy Caucus, 1978-82; mem. social work adv. coun. Chgo. Bd. Edn., 1976. Recipient Outstanding Employee award for med.-social work svcs. Maternal dn Child Health Scis. divsn. HEW, 1971; Ford Found. scholar Fisk U., 1953-57, U. Chgo. scholar, 1970-72, United Charities scholar, 1970-72. Mem. NASW, NEA, Acad. Cert. Social Workers, Ill. Cert Social Workers, Chgo. Psychol. Club. Ill. Acad. Criminology, Ill. Assn. Sch. Social Workers, Am. Assn. Mental Deviciency, Qualified Mental Retardation Profls., Fisk U. Alumni Assn., Am. Bridge Assn., Alpha Kappa Alpha.

WYATT, SUSAN MELINDA CLOUGH, career counselor, writer; b. Ft. Worth, Feb. 6, 1943; d. Forrest Weldon and Mildred (Wyatt) Clough; m. David W. McClintock, Dec. 29, 1968 (div. Mar. 1987); children: Lesley Karen, Nathan Crane; m. Richard H. Williams, Apr. 24, 1999. BA in Polit. Sci., Whittier Coll., 1965; MA in Lit., Sci., and Arts, U. Mich., 1966; MAT in Secondary Edn., Antioch-Putney Grad. Sch. Edn., 1968; PhD in Human Resource Devel. and Counseling, Columbia Pacific U., 1992. Nat. cert. counselor; lic. profl. clin. counselor, N.Mex. Rsch. asst. U. Mich., Ann Arbor, 1969-70; fgn. svc. sec., rschr. U.S. Dept. State, Sanaa, Yemen, Washington, 1966-68, 70-72; English tchr. U. Jordan, Amman, 1972-74; cons. Washington, 1974-78; personnel officer U.S. Dept. State, 1978-82; pvt. practice Rome, 1982-84; dir. career svcs. The Women's Ctr., Raleigh, N.C., 1985-86; dir. edn. Hospice of N.C., 1986; placement counselor N.C. State U., 1987-92; group therapist Duke Alcoholism and Addictions Program, 1992-93. Pvt. practice, Raleigh, Albuquerque, 1985-98; career mgmt. cons. Right Mgmt. Consultants, 1991—. Recipient Nathaniel Hill rsch. award Am. Soc. Tng. Devel., 1990; Woodrow Wilson vis. fellow, 1978-82. Mem. Southwest Writers Assn.

WYATT, WILSON WATKINS, JR. communications and public affairs executive; b. Louisville, Dec. 3, 1943; s. Wilson Watkins Sr. and Anne (Duncan) W.; m. Jane Clay, Aug. 15, 1964 (dec. 1975); children: Carol, Wilson III, Sarah Wyatt; m. Kathleen Valonis, June 14, 1998. Student, U. of the South, 1961-65. Reporter The Courier-Jour., Louisville, 1965-67; pub. rels. account exec. Doe-Anderson Advt., 1967-68; account exec. Zimmer-McClaskey-Lewis (McCann-Ericksn Advtsg.), 1968-70; ptnr. Bennett & Wyatt Pub. Rels., 1970-71; state rep., vice chair appropriations and revenue com. Ky. Gen. Assembly, Frankfort, 1969-71; exec. dir. Louisville Cen. Area Inc., 1971-77; dir. corp. affairs and communications Brown & Williamson Tobacco Corp., Louisville, 1977-82; v.p. pub. policy BATUS Inc., Washington, 1982-86, v.p. corp. affairs Louisville, 1986-90; sr. v.p. corp. affairs PNC Fin. Corp., Pitts., 1990-92; sr. v.p. corp. comm. and govt. rels. The Travelers Cos., Hartford, 1992-94; exec. dir., CEO Am. Acad. of Actuaries, Washington, 1995-98; CEO Wyatt Comm. Cons., 1998—. Lead U.S. def. pub. rels. activities against hostile takeover for B.A.T. Industries, U.K., 1989-90; chmn. Travelers Found., 1991-94, Travelers Good Govt. Com., 1992-94. Mem. youth adv. com. Atlantic Inst., 1967-68; del. North Atlantic Treaty Assn. Young Leaders Conf., 1967; chmn. Leadership Effort for All Dems., Ky., 1967-68; regional campaign coord. for Robert F. Kennedy, Ky.-Ind., 1968; mem. Pres.'s Forum, Washington, 1988-91; trustee Conn. Policy Econ. Commn., 1992-95; mem. exec. com. Hartford Downtown Coun., 1992-94; mem. adv. bd. Dem. Leadership Coun., Washington; mem. Am. Savings Edn. Campaign U.S. Dept. Labor, 1996. Named one of Outstanding Young Men in Am., Ky. Jaycees, 1973. Mem. The Pres.'s Forum, Pub. Affairs Rsch. Coun. (conf. bd. 1986-95), Forum I, Assn. Chief Execs. Coun., Pub. Affairs Coun. (bd. dirs. 1982—, exec. com. 1982-86), Speakers Club (Washington), Greater Hartford C. of C. (exec. com. 1992-94), Hartford Stage (bd. dirs. 1993-95), Louisville Country Club, Congl. Country Club (Bethesda, Md.), University Club (Washington), Louisville Country Club. Avocations: boating, photography, writing. Home and Office: PO Box 298 7291 Bozman-Neavitt Rd Bozman MD 21612 E-mail: wwwtwo@aol.com.

WYATT-BROWN, ANNE MARBURY, linguistics educator; b. Balt., Apr. 8, 1939; d. William Luke and Natalie Jewett Narbury; m. Bertram Wyatt-Brown, June 30, 1962; children; Laura (dec.), Natalie. AB, Radcliffe Coll., 1961; MAT, Johns Hopkins U., 1962; PhD, Case Western Res. U., 1972. Instr. Cleve. Inst. Art, 1974-77, assoc. prof., 1978-83; asst. in linguistics U. Fla., Gainesville, 1989-92, asst. prof. linguistics, 1992-96, assoc. prof. linguistics, 1996—. Assoc. vis. prof. Am. studies U. Richmond. Author: Barbara Pym: A Critical Biography, 1992; editor Age Studies, Univ. Press Va., 1993—; mem. editl. bd. Jour. Aging Studies, 1989—. Mem. Gerontol. Soc. Am. (chmn. humanities and arts com.). Democrat. Episcopalian. Avocation: singing. Home: 3201 NW 18th Ave Gainesville FL 32605-3705 Office: U Fla Linguistics Program PO Box 115454 Gainesville FL 32611-5454

WYATT-BROWN, BERTRAM, historian, educator; b. Harrisburg, Pa., Mar. 19, 1932; s. Hunter and Laura Hibbler (Little) Wyatt-Brown; m. Anne Jewett Marbury, June 30, 1962; children: Laura(dec.) , Natalie. BA, U. of South, 1953, LLD (hon.), 1985; BA with honours, King's Coll., Cambridge (Eng.) U., 1957, MA, 1961; PhD, Johns Hopkins U., 1963. Faculty Colo. State U., Ft. Collins, 1962-64, U. Colo., Boulder, 1964-66, Case Western Res. U., Cleve., 1966-83, prof. history, 1974-83; Richard J. Milbauer prof. history U. Fla., Gainesville, 1983—; Fleming lectr. La. State U., Baton Rouge, 1995; Douglas Southall Freeman prof. U. Richmond, 2002—. Vis. prof. U. Wis.-Madison, 1969—70. Author: The Shaping of Southern Culture: Honor, Grace, and War, 2001, Lewis Tappan and the Evangelical War Against Slavery, 2d edit., 1971, Lewis Tappan and the Evangelical War Against Slavery, 3d edit., 1997, Southern Honor: Ethics and Behavior in the Old South, 1982, Southern Honor: Ethics and Behavior in the Old South, paperback edit., 1983, Yankee Saints and Southern Sinners, 1985, Yankee Saints and Southern Sinners, paperback edit., 1990, Honor and Violence in the Old South, 1986, The House of Percy: Honor, Melancholy and Imagination in a Southern Family, 1994, 1996, The Literary Percys: Family History, Gender, and the Southern Imagination, 1994; editor: The American People in the Antebellum South, 1973, Southern Biography Series, 1995—; contbr. ; author: The Shaping of Southern Culture: Honor, Grace and War, 2001. Lt. USNR, 1953—55. Finalist Am. Book award and Pulitzer prize for History, 1983; named assoc., Woodrow Wilson Internat. Ctr. Scholars, 1975; recipient History prize, Ohio Acad. History, 1983, Clio award, ABC, 1989, Jefferson Davis Meml. prize for History, 1983, Commonwealth Fund Lectr., Univ. Coll., London, 1985, Lamar lectr., Mercer U., 1993, Webb lectr., U. Tex., Arlington, 1994, Franklin-Littleton lectr., Auburn U., 1998, Henry Luce Found., Nat. Humanities Ctr., Research Triangle Park, N.C., 1998—99, Joanna Cowden lectr., Calif. State U., Chico, 2001; fellow, Guggenheim, 1974—75, Davis Ctr. Princeton U., 1977—78, NEH, 1985—86, NEH, Nat. Humanities Ctr., 1989—90, 1998—98; grantee, Am. Philos. Soc., 1968—69, 1972—73, summer, NEH, 1975. Mem.: Soc. for History Early Am. Republic (pres. 1994—95), So. Hist. Assn. (exec. coun. 1994—, v.p. 1999—2000, pres. 2000—01, Ramsdell award 1971), Soc. Am. Historians, Orgns. Am. Historians (exec. coun. 1990—93), St. George Tucker Soc. (pres. 1998—2000), Phi Alpha Theta (History prize 1983), Phi Beta Kappa. Episcopalian. Home: 3201 NW 18th Ave Gainesville FL 32605-3705

WYCHE, CYRIL THOMAS, lawyer; b. Greenville, S.C., Jan. 28, 1926; C. Granville and Mary (Wheeler) W.; m. Harriet Smith, June 19, 1948; children: Sara McCall, Bradford Wheeler, Mary Frances. BE, Yale U., 1946; LLB, U. Va., 1949; LLD (hon.), Clemson U., 1997, Furman U., 1997; HLD (hon.), Wafford Coll. Bar: S.C. 1948, U.S. Dist. Ct. S.C. 1950, U.S. Ct. Appeals (4th cir.) 1952, U.S. Ct. Claims 1964, U.S. Supreme Ct. 1970. Ptnr. Wyche, Burgess, Freeman & Parham, P.A., Greenville, S.C., 1948—. Pres., bd. dirs. YMCA, Greenville, 1960; pres. Greenville Little Theatre, 1965, Arts Festival Assn., Greenville, 1970, Greenville Community Corp., 1976—; bd. dirs. Greater Greenville C. of C., 1980. Served with USN, 1943-46. Named Environmentalist of Yr., State of S.C., 1979; recipient Conservation award Gulf Oil Corp., 1983, Alexander Calder award, 1996, Garden Clubs Am., 1999, Oak Leaf award The Nature Conservancy, 1996, Order of the Palmetto award S.C. Gov., 1996. Mem. ABA, S.C. Bar Assn., Greenville County Bar Assn., Am. Judicature Soc. Presbyterian. Avocations: skiing, scuba diving, piano, tennis, white water canoeing. Office: Wyche Burgess Freeman & Parham 44 E Camperdown Way PO Box 728 Greenville SC 29602-0728 E-mail: twyche@wyche.com.

WYCHE, MADISON BAKER, III, lawyer; b. Albany, Ga., Aug. 11, 1947; s. Madison Baker Jr. and Merle (McKemie) W.; m. Marguerite Jernigan Ramage, Aug. 7, 1971; children: Madison Baker IV, James Ramage. BA, Vanderbilt U., 1969, JD, 1972. Bar: Ga. 1972, U.S. Dist. Ct. (mid. dist.) Ga. 1972, U.S. Ct. Appeals (5th cir.) 1973, S.C. 1976, U.S. Dist. Ct. S.C. 1977, U.S. Ct. Appeals (4th cir.) 1977, U.S. Supreme Ct. 1980, U.S. Ct. Appeals (11th cir.) 1981, U.S. Dist. Ct. (no. dist.) Ga. 1995. Assoc. Perry, Walters, Lippitt & Custer, Albany, 1972-76, Thompson, Ogletree & Deakins, Greenville, S.C., 1976-77, Ogletree, Deakins, Smoak & Stewart, Greenville, 1977-80; ptnr. Ogletree, Deakins, Nash, Smoak & Stewart P.C., 1980—. Bd. dirs. Happy Ho., Inc., Albany. Co-editor Labor and Employment Law for South Carolina Lawyers, 1999. Co-incorporator, sec. State of Tenn. Intercollegiate State Legislature, Nashville, 1967-69; state sec.-treas. Coll. Young Dems., Nashville, 1968; mem. employer and employee rels. com. N.C. Citizens for Bus. and Industry, Raleigh, 1984—; mem. United Way Greenville; mem. Christ Episcopal Ch., Greenville, vestry, 1981-85; mem. bd. visitors Clemson U., 1998-2001; bd. dirs. Blue Ridge Coun., Boy Scouts Am., 1999-2000. Capt. U.S. Army, 1969-77. Recipient Eagle Scouts award Boy Scouts Am., 1961. Mem. ABA, S.C. Bar Assn. (unauthorized practice of law com. 1977-95, chmn. 1982-92, ho. of dels. 1991-98, nominating com. 1992-95, CLE divsn., chmn., 1997-98, exec. com. 1995-99, chmn. seminars subcom. 1995-97), Ga. Bar Assn., Atlanta Bar Assn., Indsl. Rels. Rsch. Assn., S.C. Def. Trial Lawyers Assn., St. Andrews Soc. Upper S.C. (bd. dirs. 1979-81, v.p. 1986-87, pres. 1988-90, scholarship chmn. 1998—), Palmetto Soc. (bd. dirs. 1992—), Vanderbilt U. Alumni Assn. (pres. S.C. chpt. 1990-95, bd. dirs. 1994—), The Poinsett Club (v.p., bd. dirs.) (Greenville, S.C.), Rotary (bd. dirs. 1982-84, Paul Harris fellow 1986), Commerce Club of Greenville (bd. dirs. 1990—), Phi Delta Phi. Office: Ogletree Deakins Nash Smoak & Stewart PO Box 2757 Greenville SC 29602-2757

WYCHE, RUTH SKYLER, rehabilitation contractor, researcher; b. Houston, Aug. 10, 1955; d. Malcolm Joseph and Dorothy Earlene (King) LeGrande; 1 child: Patricia Ann. BS, Sam Houston State U., 1977, lic. min., 1996; cert., Inst. Child Lit., 1988; postgrad., San Jacinto Coll., 1993, Sam Houston State U., 1996-2000. Cert.elem. tchr., Tex., 1977. Med. records Green Acres Convalescent Home, Huntsville, Tex., 1979-80, 81-82; tchr. Magnolia (Tex.) High Sch., 1980-81; sec. Harris Engring., Huntsville, 1982-83; artist M&M Design, 1983-84; fin. sec. First United Meth. Ch., 1984-87, nursery sch. coord., 1986-87; contractor Tex. Rehabilation Commn., 1986-87, Pasadena, Tex., 1990-92; counselor Houston Substance Abuse Clinic, Pasadena and Houston, 1992-93, Lake Charles Substance Abuse Clinic, 1992-93; adminstr. Johnson Glass & Mirror, Pasadena, 1993-96; contractor Tex. Rehab. Commn., 1996-97. Author poetry, 1985. Ballot counter Voting Polling places, Huntsville, 1977, 78, 79. Recipient Lady Kentiggerma Soc. Creative Anachronism, 1986, Sable Comet, 1986. Mem. NAFE, Tex. Acad. Sci., Phi Beta Chi. Republican. Avocations: biology, mathematics, writing, crochet, driving.

WYCHE, SAMUEL D(AVID), sportscaster; b. Atlanta, Jan. 5, 1945; m. Jane Wyche; children— Zak, Kerry BA, Furman U., 1966; M, U. S.C., 1969. Profl. football player Continental Football League, Wheeling Ironmen, 1966; profl. football player Cin. Bengals, 1968-70, Washington Redskins, 1971-73, Detroit Lions, 1974-75, St. Louis Cardinals, 1976, Buffalo Bills, 1976; owner sporting goods store, Greenville, S.C., 1974-92; asst. coach San Francisco 49ers, 1979-82; head coach Ind. U., Bloomington, 1983, Cin. Bengals, 1984-91, Tampa Bay (Fla.) Buccaneers, 1992-95; sports analyst NBC Sports, 1996-97, former co-host NFL on NBC Pre-Game Show, 1998—; sports analyst NFL on CBS, N.Y.C., 1999—. Named Coach of Yr. NFL, 1988. Office: 1909 Whisperwood Way Daytona Beach FL 32128-6677

WYCHECK, FRANK, football player; b. Phila., Oct. 14, 1971; m. Cherryn, Feb. 18, 1995; children: Deanna, Madison. Student, U. Md. Full back Washington Redskins, 1993-95, Houston Oilers, 1995—; tight end Tennessee Titans, Nashville. Active weekly radio call-in show. Named to Pro Bowl, 1998; named Dr.Z's All-Pro, 1998, USA Today's All-Joe Team, 1998. Office: Tenn Titans 460 Great Circle Rd Nashville TN 37228*

WYCKOFF, E. LISK, JR. lawyer; b. Middletown, N.J., Jan. 29, 1934; m. Elizabeth Ann Kuphal; children: Jenny Adele, Edward Lisk III, Elizabeth Hannah Longstreet. BA, Duke U., 1955; JD, U. Mich., 1960. Bar: N.Y. 1961, U.S. Dist. Ct. (so. and ea. dists.) N.Y. 1962, U.S. Ct. Appeals (2d cir. 1963), U.S. Tax Ct. 1974. Ptnr. Trubin Sillcocks, 1975—79, Kelley Drye & Warren, 1979—93, Kramer, Levin, N.Y.C., NY, 1993—2001. Lectr. Practising Law Inst., 1970—, Kelley, Drye & Warren, 1979-93, various profl. and bus. orgns. in U.S. and abroad; spl. counsel N.Y. Bankers Assn., 1974-98; counsel N.Y. State Senate Com. Housing and Urban Renewal, 1969-71, N.Y. State Senate Com. Judiciary, 1963-64, Com. Affairs of the City of N.Y., 1962; mem. N.Y.C. Mayor's Taxi Study Commn., 1967 Directing editor, commentator West's McKinney's Forms on Estates and Trusts, 1974—; commentator McKinney's Not-For-Profit Corp. law, 1995—; contbr. articles to profl. jours. Trustee N.Y. Gen. and Biog. Soc., 1993—, Inner-City Scholarship Fund., Inc., 1993—; chmn., bd. dirs. 1652 Wyckoff House and Assn., Inc., 1982—; trustee The Bard Ctr. Bard Coll., 1994—, Goodspeed Opera Co., 1996—, Florence Griswold Mus., 1997—, Wildlife Conservation Soc., 1993—; elector Wadsworth Atheneum; trustee, pres. Homeland Found., 1988—; mem. Concilium Socalium to Vatican Mus., 1991—; dir., treas. NY Geneal. and Biographic Soc., 2002—. Named papal hon. Knight Commdr. with star, Order of St. Gregory the Great, 1998. Fellow: Am. Bar Found., Am. Coll. Trust and Estate Counsel; mem.: ABA, St. Nicholas Soc., Holland Soc., Assn. of Bar of City of N.Y., N.Y. State Bar Assn., Internat. Bar Assn., Internat. Fiscal Assn., N.Y. Yacht Club, Essex Yacht Club (Conn.), Mashomack Fish and Game Preserve Club (Pine Plains, N.Y.), Racquet and Tennis Club (N.Y.C.), Knickerbocker Club. Avocations: tennis, sailing. Office: 20th Fl 505 Park Ave New York NY 10022 E-mail: eliskwyckoff@aol.com.

WYCOFF, CHARLES COLEMAN, writer, retired anesthesiologist; b. Glazier, Tex., Sept. 2, 1918; s. James Garfield and Ada Sharpe (Braden) W.; m. Gene Marie Henry, May 16, 1942 (dec.); children: Michelle, Geoffrey, Brian, Roger, Daniel, Norman, Irene, Teresa. AB, U. Calif., Berkeley, 1941; MD, U. Calif., San Francisco, 1943; postgrad., U. London, 1954-55. Diplomate Am. Bd. Anesthesiology. Intern San Francisco County Hosp., 1943-44; resident in anesthesiology U. Calif. Hosp., San Francisco, 1944-45; tng. in anesthesiology Walter Reed Genl. Hosp., 1945; founder The Wycoff Group of Anesthesiology, San Francisco, 1947-53; chief of anesthesia St. Joseph's Hosp., 1947-52, organizer residency tng. program in anesthesiology, 1950, San Francisco County Hosp., 1954, chief anesthesia, 1953-54; tchr. practice anesthesiology Presbyn. Med. Ctr., N.Y.C., 1955-63; asst. prof. anesthesiology Columbia U., 1955-63; clin. practice anesthesiology St. Francis Meml. Hosp., San Francisco, 1963-84. Producer, dir. films on regional anesthesia; contbr. articles to sci. jours. Scoutmaster Boy Scouts Am., San Francisco, 1953-55. Capt. M.C., U.S. Army, 1945-47. Mem. Alumni Faculty Assn. Sch. Medicine U. Calif.-San Francisco (councilor-at-large 1979-80). Democrat. Avocations: research in origins of human behavior, freelance writing, Sierra hiking, gardening. Home: 1400 Carpentier St unit 133 San Leandro CA 94577-3655 E-mail: ccwycoff@pacbell.net.

WYCOFF, WILLIAM MORTIMER, lawyer; b. Pitts., Jan. 1, 1941; s. William Clyde and Margaret (Shaffer) W.; m. Deborah Seyl, Jan. 25, 1963; children: Ann Richardson, Pieter Claesen. AB, Cornell U., 1963; JD, Northwestern U., 1966. Bar: Pa. 1967, U.S. Ct. Appeals (3d cir.) 1967), U.S. Dist. Ct. (we. dist.) Pa. 1967. Assoc., now ptnr. Thorp Reed and Armstrong, Pitts., 1966—. Pres. Children's Home Pitts., 1976-78, 86-88, now bd. dirs.; pres. Pressley Ridge Schs., Pitts., 1988-90, now bd. dirs.: pres. Pressley Ridge Found.; pres., bd. dirs. Pitts. Dance Coun., 1991-94; trustee Pitts. Cultural Trust, 1991-94. Fellow Internat. Acad. Trial Lawyers, Am. Coll. Trial Lawyers; mem. Acad. Trial Lawyers Allegheny County. Avocations: photography, skiing, biking, hiking, golf. Office: Thorp Reed & Armstrong LLP One Oxford Ctr 14th Fl 301 Grant St Pittsburgh PA 15219 E-mail: wwycoff@thorpreed.com.

WYDEN, RON, senator; b. Wichita, Kans., May 3, 1949; s. Peter and Edith W.; m. Laurie Oseran, Sept. 5, 1978; 1 child, Adam David Student, U. Santa Barbara, 1967-69; AB with distinction, Stanford U., 1971; JD, U. Oreg., 1974. Campaign aide Senator Wayne Morse, 1972, 74; co-founder, co-dir. Oreg. Gray Panthers, 1974-80; dir. Oreg. Legal Services for Elderly, 1977-79; instr. gerontology U. Oreg., 1976, U. Portland, 1980, Portland State U., 1979; mem. 97th-104th Congresses from 3d Oreg. dist., Washington, 1981-96; senator from Oreg. U.S. Senate, 1996—, mem. aging com., mem. budget com., mem. commerce sci. and transp. com., mem. energy and natural resources com., mem. environ. and pub. works com. Recipient Service to Oreg. Consumers award Oreg. Consumers League, 1978, Citizen of Yr. award Oreg. Assn. Social Workers, 1979, Significant Service award Multnomah County Area

Agy. on Aging, 1980; named Young Man of Yr. Oreg. Jr. C. of C., 1980 Mem. Am. Bar Assn., Iowa Bar Assn. Democrat. Jewish. Office: US Senate 516 Hart Senate Office Bldg Washington DC 20510-0001*

WYDEVEN, JOSEPH JUDE, university dean, educator; b. Appleton, Wis., Aug. 31, 1940; s. Joseph Henry and Anna Wydeven; m. Alice Camille Laoang, May 7, 1983; children: Rachel, John Eric. PhD, Purdue U., 1979. Prof. English, humanities Bellevue (Nebr.) U., 1979—, dean Coll. Arts and Scis., 1995—. Author: Wright Morris Revisited, 1998. Vol. Joslyn Art Mus., Omaha, 2000—. Staff sgt. USAF, 1966-70. Recipient Tchg. and Campus Leadership award Sears Roebuck Found., 1990. Mem. Western Lit. Assn. Avocations: writing, photography, travel. Home: 807 Waterford Cir Papillion NE 68046 Office: Bellevue Univ 1000 Galvin Rd S Bellevue NE 68005 Fax: 402-293-2023. E-mail: aliceandjoe@cox.net., jjw@bellevue.edu.

WYDICK, JUDITH BRANDLI JAMES, volunteer; b. Eldon, Mo., Aug. 14, 1937; d. William Bruce and Helen James; m. Richard Crews Wydick, Aug. 26, 1961; children: William Bruce, Derrick Cameron. Student, U. Colo., 1955-57; BS in Edn., U. Mo., 1959, MA in Eng., 1960. Cert. secondary tchr., Mo., Calif. Tchr. English Oakland (Calif.) Tech. H.S., 1960-61, Awalt H.S., Mountain View, Calif., 1961-62. Author: Preparing for College, 1982-89, Mad Capers, 1993-94. Organizer Univ. Farm Circle, Davis, Calif., 1972-77, 83, pres. 1976-77; pres., organizer Lawyers Wives Yolo County, Davis, 1973-75; pres., bd. dirs. Pence Art Gallery, Davis, 1979-81; pres., chair adv. coun. Jr. H.S. PTA, Davis, 1980-82; co-chair fundraising Yolo County Mental Health Assn., Davis, 1981; organizer Davis. H.S. Madrigal Choir, 1983-85, pres. PTA, 1984-85; full-time organizer Internat. House-Davis, 1981—, pres., 1985-87, 89-91, 97-2001, bd. dirs., 1984-94, 1997-2001; mem. Calif. State Bd. Food and Agr., 1992-94. Recipient Madrigal Parent award Davis H.S., 1985, PTA Honorary Svc. award, 1985; named Citizen of Yr., City of Davis, 1986. Episcopalian. Home: 2620 Corona Dr Davis CA 95616-0112

WYDICK, RICHARD CREWS, lawyer, educator; b. Pueblo, Colo., Nov. 1, 1937; s. Charles Richard and Alice Wydick; m. Judith Brandli James, 1961; children: William Bruce, Derrick Cameron. BA, Williams Coll., 1959; LL.B., Stanford U., 1962. Bar: Calif. bar 1962. Asso. firm Brobeck, Phleger & Harrison, San Francisco, 1966-71; mem. faculty U. Calif. Law Sch., Davis, 1971—, prof. law, 1975—, dean, 1978-80. Author: Plain English for Lawyers, 4th edit., 1998. Served to capt. USAR, 1962-66. Office: Sch Law U Calif Davis CA 95616

WYDLER, HANS ULRICH, lawyer, banker, accountant; b. Hamburg, Germany, Nov. 11, 1923; came to U.S., 1927, naturalized, 1932; s. John Joseph and Grethe Adolfine (Heitmann) W.; m. Susan Gail Hart, Sept. 1, 1965; children: Hans Laurence, Steven Courtney. BS, Ohio State U., 1944, BME with honors, 1947; BIE with honors, 1949; MS, MIT, 1948; LLB, Harvard U., 1951. Bar: Mass. 1951; registered profl. engr. Mass. Atty., systems engr., trustee Louis J. Hunter Assocs., Boston, 1951-57; asst. v.p. Chem. Bank, N.Y.C., 1958-64; v.p. Mfrs. Nat. Bank Detroit, 1964-65; sr. v.p. Security Nat. Bank, Huntington, N.Y., 1973-74; internat. and tax atty., acct. Hans U. Wydler, N.Y.C., 1966—; dir. Volume Mdse., Inc., Buning Internat. Inc., 1977-84. With USN, 1944-46. Mem. Acad. Polit. Sci. (life), ABA, N.Y. County Lawyers Assn., ASME. Home and Office: 945 5th Ave New York NY 10021-2655

WYDRA, FRANK THOMAS, healthcare executive; b. Republic, Pa., May 11, 1939; s. Frank T. and Anne M. (Kois) W.; m. Karen Branch, June 24, 1961; children: Denise Lee, Sheryl Lynn, Frank Thomas III. BS in Mgmt., U. Ill., 1961. V.p. Allied Supermarkets, Inc., Detroit, 1967-75; sr. v.p. HGH Health System, 1975-85; pres. Radius Health Care Sysytems, Inc., 1983-85; cons. Birmingham, Mich., 1985-88; exec. v.p. The Chi Group, Ann Arbor, 1988-91; mng. ptnr., CEO, owner IRI, Mgmt. Cons., Detroit, 1991—. Lectr. various profl. groups; bd. dirs. Mich. Health Systems Inc., Saber-Salisbury Assocs. Inc., Midwestern Health Ctr., MultiCare Med. Inc., RHS Inc. Author: Learner Controlled Instruction, 1980, (with others) Hospital Survival Guide, 1984, The Cure, 1992; creator 2 mgmt. games Performulations, 1978, The Dynamics of Power and Authority, 1981; contbr. articles to profl. jours. Personnel program advisor Mich. State U. Sch. Labor Relations, 1979-83; chmn. new programs Wayne County Community Coll., Detroit, 1979-80; bd. dirs. Detroit Metro Youth Found., 1980-83, State Mich. Health Occupations Council, Lansing, 1982-85. Capt. U.S. Army, 1961-63. Recipient numerous awards ASTD, Nat. Soc. Performance and Instrn., Mich. SOc. Instructional Tech., Supermarket Inst. Mem. Am. Hosp. Assn., Planning Soc. of Am. Hosp. Assn., Hosp. Personnel Adminstrs. Assn. (pres. 1981-82, numerous awards), Am. Mgmt. Assn., Am. Soc. Hosp. Pers.Adminstrs. (bd. dirs. 1981-83), Mich. Soc. Instrnl. Tech. (life, pres. 1973-74), Mich. Hosp. Assn., Employers Assn. Detroit (bd. dirs. 1982-85), Detroit Athletic Club. Avocations: writing, sailing. Home: 7960 Perry Lake Clarkston MI 48348

WYER, JAMES INGERSOLL, lawyer; b. Denver, June 9, 1923; s. William and Katherine (Rolfe) W.; m. Joan Best Connelly, Aug. 13, 1960; children: Joan Connelly Tatnall, Peter Ford, June Wyer Nugent. BA, Yale U., 1945, LL.B., 1949. Bar: N.Y. 1950, N.J. 1987. Assoc. Dewey, Ballantine, Bushby, Palmer & Wood, N.Y.C., 1949-56, Am. Cyanamid Co., Wayne, N.J., 1956, v.p., gen. counsel, 1973-86; of counsel St. John & Wayne, Newark, 1987—. Bd. dirs. TherMold, Inc., William Penn Life Ins. Co. N.Y. Bd. dirs. Nat. Legal Ctr. for the Pub. Interest. Served with USNR, 1943-46. Mem. Assn. Gen. Counsel (1st v.p. 1982-84, pres. 1985-86), ABA, Assn. of Bar of City of N.Y., Atlantic Legal Found. (chmn. 1986-97). Clubs: Jupiter Island (Hobe Sound, Fla.); Seabright (N.J.) Beach, Seabright Lawn, Tennis and Cricket (Rumson, N.J.); Coral Beach and Tennis (Bermuda), Hobe Sound (Fla.) Yacht, Rumson (N.J.) Country. Republican. Office: St John & Wayne 2 Penn Plz E Ste 1 Newark NJ 07105-2249

WYGAN, DOROTHY CAMILLA, foundation administrator; b. N.Y.C., Apr. 10, 1932; d. Paul and Dorothy Eliza (Grout) Reznikoff; m. Anton Kazimierz Wygan, Nov. 7, 1960 (div. 1974); 1 child, Paul A. BS, Am. U., 1953; MS in Edn., Coll. of New Rochelle, 1973; EdD, Columbia U., 1961. Copywriter J. Walter Thompson, N.Y.C., 1953-58, London, 1958-63; copy chief London Press Exchange, 1963-68; dir. New Rochelle (N.Y.) Day Nursery, 1970-73; devel. learning specialist Wappingers Ctrl. Sch. Dist., Wappingers Falls, N.Y., 1973-76; dir. learning resources ctr. Culinary Inst. Am., Hyde Park, 1976-82; dir. fund devel. Dutchess C.C., Poughkeepsie, 1982-87; v.p. fund devel. Rockland C.C., Suffern, 1987-90; exec. dir. Sarah Wells Girl Scout Coun., Middletown, NY, 1990—97; adj. lectr. Dutchess C.C., 1998—. Contbr. articles to profl. jours.; author of TV commls. Den mother Boy Scouts Am., Chelsea, N.Y., 1973-76; v.p. Wappingers Conservation Assn., 1973-82; pres. Leewood Arms Homeowner's Assn., 1977-87; trustee Vassar Temple, 1985-97, treas., 1988-90, 94-97; vol. cook Dutchess Outreach Soup Kitchen, 1985-97; bd. dirs. YWCA in Dutchess County, Poughkeepsie, N.Y., 2000—, pub. addairs com., Planned Parenthood of the Mid-Hudson Valley, 1998—; mem. County Exec. Affirmative Action Task Force Group, Suffern County, N.Y., 1987-90, N.Y. State Gov.'s Environ. Coun., 1988-91, N.Y. State Gov.'s Adv. Coun. on Women's Issues, 1989-90, County Exec. AIDS Prevention Task Force, Orange County, N.Y., 1994-97; bd. dirs., Stony Kill Environ. Edn. Ctr. Mem. Northfield Mt. Hermon Alumni Assn., Older Womens League (leader Hudson Valley chpt. 1999-2001), Mid-Hudson Women's Network. Home: 160 Academy St # 1K Poughkeepsie NY 12601-4504

WYGANT, FOSTER LAURANCE, art educator, educator; b. Dayton, Ohio, Oct. 30, 1920; s. Harold F. and M. Esther (Weber) W.; m. Rae E. Hoyt, 1 child, Nancy Laura Profl. diploma, Juilliard Sch. Music, 1942; BA, Columbia U., 1949, MA, 1956, Ed.D., 1959; postgrad., Am. Art Sch., Art Students League, 1951-53. Clarinetist Dallas Symphony and free-lance clarinetist, N.Y.C., 1945-47; publicity, fund-raising positions, and free-lance artist, 1952-56; tchr. art, pub. schs., 1956-59; asst. prof. Montclair State Coll., N.J., 1959-63, assoc. prof., 1963-68; prof. art edn. U. Cin., 1968-87, chmn. dept., 1968-84, dir. Sch. Art Edn. and Art History, 1984-86, emeritus prof., 1987—. Vis. sr. lectr. Leeds Coll. Art, Eng., 1966; regional chmn. Scholastic Awards Program, 1968-84; chmn. Action for Arts in Ohio Schs., 1974-75 Author: Art in American Schools in the Nineteenth Century, 1983, School Art in American Culture 1820-1970, 1993, School Art in American Culture Supplement: 1900-1915, 1997; editor, prin. author: Standards for Art Teacher Preparation Programs, 1979, Principles, Purposes and Standards for School Art Programs, 1982; contbr. numerous articles to profl. jours. Served with U.S. Army, 1941-45 N.Y. State and Juilliard Sch. Music scholar, 1939-41; Kellogg Found. fellow Columbia U., 1955-56 Mem. Nat. Art Assn. (nat. dir. higher edn. divsn. 1975-79, Recognition award 1980, Disting. Svc. award 1982, Disting. fellow 1995), Ohio Art Edn. Assn. (pres. 1972-74, Disting. fellow 2000), Seminar for Rsch. in Art Edn., Coun. for Policy Studies in Art Edn., Am. Fedn. Musicians. Home: 3562 Interwood Ave Cincinnati OH 45220-1824 E-mail: wygantfl@ucmail.uc.com.

WYGANT, PATRICIA BRYANS, artist; b. Marion, Ohio, Nov. 10, 1926; d. Ralph Armond and Frances Annetta (Kilbury) Bryans. BFA, Syracuse U., 1950. Resident Millay Colony for Arts, Austerlitz, N.Y., 1979. Exhibited in 62 nat. juried exhbns. including Watercolor USA, Nat. Watercolor Soc., Watercolor Workshop Greek Islands Sifnos Amorgos, Paros, 1988; paintings publ. in A Gallery of Marine Art, 1988, 98, The Best of Watercolor, 1995. Recipient Winsor Newton award Rochester Art Club, 1994. Mem. Am. Artists Profl. League, Ga. Watercolor Soc. (signature mem.), Niagara Frontier Watercolor Soc. (signature mem.). Avocation: traveling. Office: Anderson Alley Artists 250 N Goodman St Rochester NY 14607

WYGANT, RICHARD W. music educator; b. Waldwick, N.J., Sept. 17, 1966; s. Edward G. and Cherie L. Wygant; m. L. Monique Weber, Dec. 4, 1993; children: Michael, Lauren, Ryan. BS in Music Edn., William Paterson U., 1988. Cert. tchr. N.J., Pa. Band dir. Denville Twp. Pub. Schs., NJ, 1988—89, Parsippany H.S., 1989—94, Stroudsburg Jr. H.S., Pa., 1994—. Brass instr. Crossmen Drum & Bugle Corps, West Chester, 1989—93; brass arranger Jersey Surf Drum & Bugle Corps, Berlin, 1995—, Juliana Drum & Bugle Corps, Middelburg, Netherlands, 2001—. Named Outstanding Educator, Parsippany/Troy Hills Rotary, 1993; recipient Outstanding Svc. Citation, U.S Ho. of Reps., 1993, Cert. of Merit, N.J. Senate and Gen. Assembly, 1993. Mem.: NEA, Music Educators Nat. Conf., Pa. Music Educators Assn., Internat. Trumpet Guild. Home: 340 Keller Dr Stroudsburg PA 18360 Office: Stroudsburg Jr HS 1198 Chipperfield Dr Stroudsburg PA 18360 Home Fax: 570-421-0897. Personal E-mail: doublc@ptd.net. Business E-Mail: rwygant@stroudsburg.k12.pa.us.

WYGANT, WILLIS EDWARD, JR. retired minister; b. Mansfield, Ohio, Sept. 3, 1921; s. Willis Edward Wygant Sr. and Ruth May Wooden Wygant; m. Lina Stearns; children: Willis Edward III, Scott Devinney. AB, Denison U., 1943; MDiv, Pacific Sch. of Religion, Berkeley, 1955; ThM, San Francisco Theol. Sem., 1968; PhD, Calif. Inst. Integral Studies, 1976. Lic. vocat. nurse; cert. profl. hosp. chaplain, profl. mental health chaplain, marriage, family and child counselor. Chaplain Fed. Bur. Prisons, San Francisco, 1955—56; chaplain in the juvenile hall San Mateo County Parole Authority, 1957—65; chaplain Chope Gen. Hosp., 1961—81. Supr. clin. pastoral edn. students Assn. for Clin. Pastoral Edn., San Mateo, 1965—69. Author: Of One Blood, 2000. With USN, 1944—52. Mem.: AARP, Assn. of Profl. Chaplains. Mem. United Ch. Of Christ. Avocation: sailing. Home: 45-090 Namoku St Apt 801 Kaneohe HI 96744

WYKLE, MAY L. dean, educator, researcher; BSN, Case Western Res. U. , 1956, MSN Psychiat. Nursing, PhD Edn., Case Western Res. U. Dean, Cellar prof. gerontological nursing Frances Payne Bolton Sch. Nursing, Ohio, 1988—; dean, dir. u. ctr. aging and health Case Western Res. U. Established ednl. programs, Europe, Africa, Asia; vis. prof. U. Mich., U. Tex.-Houston, U. Zimbabwe-Africa; del., served on planning com. White Ho. Conf. on Aging , 1993. Contbr. articles, chapters to books; author: Decision Making in Long-Term Care, Practicing Rehabilitation with Geriatric Clients, Stress and Health Among the Elderly , Family Caregiving Across the Lifespan, Service Minority Elders in the 21st Century (AJN Book of Yr. award, 2000). Dir. Robert Wood Johnson Tchg. Nursing Home Project; project dir. several tng. grants; cons. nursing homes, psychiat. hosps.; mem. bd. dirs. numerous cmty. orgns., nursing homes, profl. assns. Named first Pope Eminent scholar, Rosalynn Carter Inst. Human Devel. Southwestern State U. , Americus, Ga., Outstanding Rschr. in State of Ohio, Ohio Rsch. Coun. on Aging, Ohio Network Edn. Cons. in field of Aging, 1992; recipient Humanitarian award, Outstanding Contbns. to Nursing Profession, 1999, Acad. award, NIMH Geriatric Mental Health, Merit award, Cleve. Coun. Black Nurses, Gerontological Doris Schwartz Nursing Rsch. award, Gerontological Soc. Am., Belle Sherwin award, Cleve. Vis. Nurse Assn., Leadership award excellence in geriatric care, Midwest Alliance in Nursing, Disting. nurse-scholar lectr. award, Nat. Coun. Nursing Rsch., Nursing Educator award, New Cleve. Woman mag. . Fellow: Gerontological Soc. Am., Am. Acad. Nursing; mem.: NIA, NIMH, NINR, Vets Adminstrn. (geriatric/gerontology adv. com.), Sigma Theta Tau Internat. (pres.-elect 1999). Office: 10900 Euclid Ave Cleveland OH 44106*

WYKOFF, BEVERLY YOUNG, social worker; b. Barberton, Ohio, Oct. 8, 1942; d. William Bishop and Carol Myrna (Bell) Young; m. Thomas William Wykoff, July 21, 1960 (div. Sept. 1986); children: Pieter, Cynthia, Caroline. MSSA, Mandel Sch. Social Scis., 1973; MS in Urban Studies, Cleve. State U., 1979; MA in Theater, Kent State U., 1987. Lic. ind. social worker. Social worker City of Cleve., 1973-97, case rev. facilitator, resource developer, 1995—; social worker Cuyahoga County, Ohio, 1988—; family devel. specialist SAFY, Las Vegas, 2000—. Mem. alumni bd. Mandel Sch. Social Scis., 1986-90; active polit. campaigner, Ohio. Democrat. Episcopalian. Avocations: tennis, dance, theater, politics.

WYLAN, BARBARA, artist; b. Providence, 1933; divorced; children: Andrea, Brock. BFA, R.I. Sch. of Design, Providence, 1955; studied with Donald Stoltenberg, Claude Croney, Murray Wentworth, Ruth Wynn, Charles Movalli, Dong Kingman. Tchr. watercolor workshops; juror various exhbns. 27 one-person shows; exhibited in over 100 group shows including Watercolor USA (Springfield award 1982), Nat. Soc. Painters in Casein and Acrylic 38th Ann., Nat. Arts club, N.Y.C. (Dr. David Soloway award 1991); represented in permenant collections, pvt., corp. and instnl. collectors including Mobile (Ala.) Mus. Art, Cahoon Mus. Am. Art, Cotuit, Mass.; represented by The Spectrum of Am. Artists and Craftsmen, Brewster, Hyannis, Nantucket, Mass., Newport, R.I., Palm Beach Gardens, Fla., North Conway, N.H., Woods Hole (Mass.) Art Gallery. Mem. Nat. Soc. Painters in Casein and Acrylic, Watercolor USA Honor Soc., New Eng. Watercolor Soc., Copley Soc. Boston, and Twenty-one in Truro.

WYLE, FREDERICK S. lawyer; b. Berlin, Germany, May 9, 1928; came to U.S., 1939, naturalized, 1944; s. Norbert and Malwina (Mauer) W.; m. Katinka Franz, June 29, 1969; children: Susan Kim, Christopher Anthony, Katherine Anne. BA magna cum laude, Harvard U., 1951, LL.B., 1954. Bar: Mass. 1954, Calif. 1955, N.Y. 1958. Teaching fellow Harvard Law Sch., 1954-55; law clk. U.S. Dist. Ct., No. Dist. Calif., 1955-57; assoc. firm Paul, Weiss, Rifkind, Wharton & Garrison, N.Y.C., 1957-58; pvt. practice San Francisco, 1958-62; spl. asst. def. rep. U.S. del. to NATO, Paris, 1962-63; mem. Policy Planning Council, Dept. State, Washington, 1963-65; dep. asst. sec. def. for European and NATO affairs Dept. Def., 1966-69; v.p. devel., gen. counsel Schroders, Inc., N.Y.C., 1969-71, atty., cons., 1971-72; chief exec. officer Saturday Rev. Industries, Inc., San Francisco, 1972-76; individual practice law, 1976—. Internat. counsel to Fed. States Micronesia, 1974-82; cons. Rand Corp., Dept. of Def., Nuclear Regulatory Commn.; trustee in bankruptcy, receiver various corps since 1974. Contbr. to: Ency. Brit, 1972, also articles in profl. publs., newspapers. Trustee for U.S. Interest Bicycle Club Casino, 1996-99. Served with AUS, 1946-47. Mem. Internat. Inst. Strategic Studies, Phi Beta Kappa. Office: 3 Embarcadero Ctr Fl 7 San Francisco CA 94111-4065

WYLIE, JAMES MALCOLM, educator; b. N.Y.C., Mar. 16, 1938; s. James M. and Nancy Beatrice (Worthy) W. BS, Boston U., 1960. Columnist Mexico City Times, 1964; assoc. prof. The Cooper Union Coll., N.Y.C., 1986—. Author: The Lost Rebellion, 1971, The Homestead Grays, 1977, The Sign of Dawn, 1981; participant Spoleto Festival U.S.A., 2001. Office: 51 Astor Pl New York NY 10003-7132

WYLIE, LAURIE JEAN, health education center administrator, nurse; b. Seattle, Mar. 13, 1951; d. Alexander James and Edna O. (Pulis) Wylie II; m. John W. Iverson, Sept. 21, 1974 (div.); children: Sara Jean, John Berger. BS in Nursing, U. Wash., 1975, postgrad., 1977; MA in Nursing, Columbia U., 1990. Cert. sch. nurse practitioner, community health nurse, nursing adminstr. Nurse practioner Child Devel. and Mental Retardation Ctr., Seattle, 1975-76; EPSDT nurse coord. State of Wash., 1976; sch. nurse Snohomish (Wash.) Sch. Dist., 1976-80; interim sch. nurse Lake Stevens (Wash.) Sch. Dist., 1980-81; cons. nurse Group Health Coop., Redmond, Wash., 1980-91; maternal infant nurse cons. Vis. Nurse Assn. Snohomish, 1986-88; nursing practice and govt. rels. coord. King County Nurses Assn., Seattle, 1987-90; exec. dir. Western Wash. Area Health Edn. Ctr., 1990—. Mem.: Nat. AHEC (pres.-elect, treas.), Wash. Rural Health Assn. (past pres., past sec.), Wash. State Nurses Assn. (PAC trustee, dist. pres.), ANA (senatorial coord., congl. dist. coord., com. of examiners for sch. nurse practitioner cert.). Office: 2033 6th Ave Ste 310 Seattle WA 98121-2566 E-mail: lauriewwahec@qwest.net.

WYLIE, MARY ANN, critical care nurse; b. Huron, S.D., Oct. 5, 1954; d. Paul P. and Ruth Esther (Glanzer) H.; m. Charles Owen Wylie, Nov. 18, 1983; children: Paul C., Jacob Ryan. LPN, Mitchell Area Vocat. Tech.Sch., 1974; diploma in nursing, Dakota Wesleyan U., 1978. RN, Tex.; CCRN; cert. med. surg. Staff LPN Meml. Hosp., Watertown, S.D., 1974-77; staff nurse, charge nurse Community Meml. Hosp., Redfield, 1978-80; staff nurse, charge nurse, critical care nurse Huron Regional Med. Ctr., 1980-83, Greater Bakersfield (Calif.) Meml. Hosp., 1983-89, VA Med. Ctr., Big Spring, Tex., 1990—. Mem. AACN. Avocations: outdoor activities, reading, travel, family time. Home: Box 3118 2204 S Main St Big Spring TX 79720-5537

WYLIE, PAMELA JANE, writer, producer, consultant, small business owner; BA in English, U. So. Calif., 1967, MFA in Profl. Writing, 1983, postgrad., 1979-83. Sys. programmer IBM, Poughkeepsie, N.Y., 1967-68; cons. CS/SD, Fountain Valley, Calif., 1968-69, Price Waterhouse, L.A., 1969-72; ind. cons., 1973-77; pres. PJW Enterprises, Inc., Fullerton, Calif., 1977—; dir. info. sys. NorthWest Quadrant, Newport Beach, 1985-86; sr. cons. Richard J. Yost & Assocs., San Gabriel, 1986-87; pres. Thorn Tree Prodns., L.A., 1998-99. Bd. dirs. Valdy Corp., L.A. Author: Power Your Way Through Y2K, 1999, (play) Doctor Franklin and Madam President, 1998, (internet) Harambee! Year 2000 Action Pack, 1998, (play) Heather on the Battlefield, 2001.

WYLIE, PAUL RICHTER, JR. lawyer; b. Dec. 25, 1936; s. Paul Richter and Alice (Dredge) W.; m. Arlene Marie Klem, Mar. 6, 1982; children: Lynne Catherine, John Michael, Thomas Robert. BSChemE, Mont. State U., 1959; JD, Am. U., 1965. Bar: Utah 1978, Calif. 1970, U.S. Supreme Ct. 1971, Mont. 1990. Patent examiner U.S. Patent and Trademark Office, Washington, 1962-64; asst. gen. patent counsel Dart Industries Inc., L.A., 1967-81; pvt. practice, 1981-86, Pacific Palisades, Calif., 1986-90, Bozeman, Mont., 1990—. Mem. ABA, AIChE, Am. Intellectual Property Law Assn., L.a. Intellectual Property Law Assn., Am. Chem. Soc., Licensing Execs. Soc., Tech. Transfer Soc. Home: 106 Silverwood Dr Bozeman MT 59715-9255 Office: 1805 W Dickerson St Ste 3 Bozeman MT 59715-4131

WYLIE, RICHARD THORNTON, aerospace engineer; b. Long Beach, Calif., July 11, 1956; s. Howard Hance and Marcella Dart (Metcalf) W. BS, Calif. State Poly. U., Pomona, 1978; MS, U. Calif., Berkeley, 1979. Registered profl. engr., Calif. Engr. Aerocraft Heat Treating, Paramount, Calif., 1991-94, TRW, Inc., Redondo Beach, 1980-91, 94—. Vol. tutor TRW Bootstrap, 1981-2001. Mem. Mensa (scholarship chmn. Harbor area 1995—, editor Harbor area newsletter 1996-99). Avocation: Graphoanalysis. Home: 1005 Kornblum Ave Torrance CA 90503-5113

WYLLIE, ELAINE, physician; b. Evanston, Ill., Aug. 26, 1953; MD, Ind. U., Indpls., 1978. Fellow in pediats. Ind. U./Case Western Res. U., 1981; fellow in child neurology Cleve. Clinic, 1984, fellow in epilepsy and clin. neurophysiology, 1985, profl. staff, 1985—, head sect. pediatric epilepsy. Office: The Cleve Clinic Found Dept Neurology 9500 Euclid Ave Cleveland OH 44195-0001

WYLLIE, F(RANCES) ROSEMARY (ROMY WYLLIE), interior designer, educator; b. Hull, England, Nov. 6, 1932; came to U.S., 1961; d. Robert Bertram and Frances Mary (Woodhouse) Blair; m. Peter John Wyllie, June 9, 1956; children: Andrew James, Elizabeth Jean (dec.), Lisa Margaret, John David. MA, U. St. Andrews, Scotland, 1955; diploma in design, Harrington Inst. Interior Design, Chgo., 1974. Cert. interior designer. Sec. Pa. State U., State College, 1956-59; mng. editor Jour. Geology U. Chgo. Press, 1967-72; designer Space Design Group, Chgo., 1974-77; pres. Intekton, Pasadena, Calif., 1977—. Substitute instr. Harrington Inst. Interior Design, Chgo., 1974-77, instr., 1977-83. Author: Caltech's Architectural Heritage: From Spanish Tile to Modern Stone, 2000. Mem. Internat. Interior Design Assn. (profl., cert.), Caltech Archtl. Tour Svc. (co-founder, bd. dirs. 1985—), Alumni Assn. Calif. Inst. of Tech. (hon. mem.). Clubs: Caltech Women's (pres. 1985-86). Avocations: tennis, hiking, art, photography, travel. Home: 2150 Kinclair Dr Pasadena CA 91107-1020 Office: Intekton 2150 Kinclair Dr Pasadena CA 91107-1020 E-mail: romy@caltech.edu.

WYLLIE, STANLEY CLARKE, retired librarian; b. Clearwater, Fla., Nov. 19, 1935; s. Stanley Clarke and Euginia Lee (Tison) W.; m. Martha Ann Thomason, June 14, 1963; children: Stanley Clarke Jr., Susan Lynne De-Herder, Patricia Anne. BS in History and Social Scis., Fla. So. Coll., 1958; MS in Libr. Sci., Fla. State U., 1963. Tchr. civics and English Lakeland (Fla.) Jr. H.S., 1960-61; libr. I Tampa (Fla.) Pub. Libr., 1962; dir. Chestatee Reg. Libr. Sys., Gainesville, Ga., 1963-64; ind. and sci. ref. libr. Dayton and Montgomery County Pub. Libr., Dayton, Ohio, 1964-66, collection libr., 1967-73, social scis. and genealogy ref. libr., 1973-90; ret. Editor Mad River Currents newsletter, 1996-97, Bits, 1964-66. Corr. sec. Montgomery County Geneal. Soc., 1990-91, rec. sec., 1997-98; pres. Dayton and Montgomery County Pub. Libr. Staff Assn.; pres. Men's Rep. Club, Lakeland, 1960-61; mem. tV cable commn. City of Riverside, Ohio, 1997-98; presiding judge Riverside, Montgomery County Bd. Elections, 1992—. Recipient Edward M. Selby award Ohio Chpt. of Rsch., 1991-92, Alumnus Disting. svc. award Fla. So. Coll., 1991; Knight York Cross of Honor, Ohio Priory #18, KYCH, 1983; named Ky. Col. Mem.: AARP (dist. coord. 1997—99), Mensa, Pub. Employee Retirees Inc. (chpt. pres. 1998, dist. 3 rep. 1999—), United Ancient Order of Druids (noble arch Franklin Grove #2), SAR (pres. Richard Montgomery chpt. 1990—91, Silver Good Citizenship medal 1997), Fla. Geneal. Soc., Fla. State Geneal. Soc., Pres.'s Club of Dayton (pres. 2000—01), Far Hills High Twelve Club, Odd Fellows (Noble Grand Steuben Rebekah Lodge 1997, chief patriarch Mad River Encampment # 16 1998—99, Noble grand 1998—2001, grand lodge rep. 1998—2000, Noble Grand Steuben Rebekah Lodge 2000, pres. S.W. Boosters Assn. 2001—, pres. S.W. Promotional Assn. 2001—, Grand Encampment Ohio 2002—, capt. occidental Canton patriarchs militant 2001—), Grand Stenteros, El Aliman Sanctorum, Ancient Mystic Order of Samaritans, Toastmasters (area 3 gov. 1995, v.p. edn. 1997), Audubon Soc., Order of DeMolay (adv. bd. 3d dist. 1996—, Cross of Honor, Legion of Honor), Order Rainbow for Girls (Grand Cross of Color), Dayton High Twelve (pres. 1994), Lions (pres. 1996—97, zone chmn. 1996—98, Pres. Excellence award 1997), Orange Order (Detroit), Improved Order of Redmen (Sr. Sagamore Lone Eagle Lodge), Elks (lecturing knight Dayton Lodge), KP (chancellor comdr. Red Star Lodge 2000—01, Grand Lodge rep. 2002—), Shriners, Masons. Anglican Catholic. Avocations: reading, stamp collecting. Home: 4960 Franlou Ave Dayton OH 45432-3120

WYMAN, DAVID SWORD, historian, educator; b. Weymouth, Mass., Mar. 6, 1929; s. Hollis Judson and Ruth (Sword) W.; m. Mildred Louise Smith, Sept. 13, 1950; children: James Nayler, Teresa Carol. AB, Boston U., 1951; EdM, Plymouth State Coll., 1961; AM, Harvard U., 1962, PhD, 1966; DHL (hon.), Hebrew Union Coll. Jewish Inst. Religion, 1986, Yeshiva U., 1988. Various positions, 1951-57; tchr. pub. schs. Tilton, N.H., 1957-60; tchr. pub. high sch. Penacook, 1960-61; prof. history U. Mass., Amherst, 1966-91, Josiah DuBois prof. history, 1986-91, Josiah DuBois prof. emeritus, 1991—, chmn. Judaic Studies Program, 1977-78, 82-84. Acad. advisor Simon Wiesenthal Ctr., L.A., 1983—; nat. coun. Nat. Christian Leadership Conf. for Israel, 1986, numerous radio and TV appearances; historian advisor to films. Author: Paper Walls: America and the Refugee Crisis, 1938-4l, 1968, The Abandonment of the Jews: America and the Holocaust, 1941-45, 1984 (Anisfield-Wolf award 1984, Stuart Bernath award 1984, Theodore Saloutos book award 1984, Present Tense Lit. award 1984, Boston Hadassah Myrtle Wreath award 1985, Nat. Jewish Book award 1985), new edit., 1998; editor: America and the Holocaust, 13 vols. documents, 1989-90, The World Reacts to the Holocaust, 1996; contbr. articles to profl. jours., chpts. to books. Recipient Chancellor's medal, U. Mass., 1986, Achievement award Isaac M. Wise Temple, Cin. 1986, Humanitarian award Bklyn. Holocaust Meml. Com., 1986, Herbert Katzki award Am. Jewish Joint

Distbn. Com., 1999; elected to Boston U. Collegium Disting. Alumni, 1986; Woodrow Wilson fellow, 1961-62, 65-66; grantee Social Sci. Rsch. Coun., 1969-70, Am. Coun. Learned Socs., 1969-70, Charles Warren Ctr. at Harvard U., 1969-70. Mem. Soc. for Am. Baseball Rsch., N.H. Hist. Soc., Friends Hist. Assn., Phi Beta Kappa. Avocations: baseball, greyhounds as pets, local N.H. history. Home: 61 Columbia Dr Amherst MA 01002-3105

WYMAN, JAMES THOMAS, petroleum company executive; b. Mpls., Apr. 9, 1920; s. James Claire and Martha (McChesney) W.; m. Elizabeth Winston, May 6, 1950; children: Elizabeth Wyman Wilcox, James Claire, Steven McChesney. Grad., Blake Prep. Sch., Mpls., 1938; BA, Yale U., 1942. With Mpls. Star and Tribune, 1946-50; advt. mgr. Super Valu Stores, Inc., Eden Prairie, Minn., 1951-54, store devel. mgr., 1955-56, gen. sales mgr., 1956-57, sales v.p., 1957-60, dir., 1959-87, exec. v.p., 1961-64, pres., chief exec. officer, 1965-70, chmn. exec. com., 1970-76, ret., 1976. Bd. dirs. Marshall & Winston, Inc. Served to lt. (s.g.) USNR, World War II. Mem.: Minneapolis; Woodhill Country (Wayzata). Home: 2855 Woolsey Ln Wayzata MN 55391-2752 Office: 1105 Foshay Tower Minneapolis MN 55402

WYMAN, JAMES VERNON, newspaper executive; b. Brockton, Mass., Nov. 17, 1923; s. George Dewey and Christine Laverne (Skinner) W.; m. Viola Marie Bousquet, June 24, 1950; children: J. Vernon, Douglas Phillip, Carolyn Anne. Student, Northeastern U., Boston, 1946-48; BS in Journalism, Boston U., 1951. From staff to dep. exec. editor Providence Jour.-Bull., 1951-88, v.p., exec. editor, 1989-95, ret., 1995. Served with AUS, 1942-46, PTO. Recipient Yankee Quill award, 1989, Disting. Alumni award Boston U. Coll. of Comm. Alumni Bd., 1996; named to R.I. Journalism Hall of Fame, 1999. Mem. New Eng. AP News Execs. Assn. (past pres.), AP Mng. Editors Assn., New Eng. Soc. Newspaper Editors, Acad. New Eng. Journalists (past dir.), New Eng. Newspaper Assn., Sigma Delta Chi (past pres. New Eng. chpt.). Roman Catholic. Home: 44 Starflower Ct Wakefield RI 02879-5475 E-mail: vijimwyman@aol.com.

WYMAN, RALPH MARK, corporate executive; b. Usti, Czechoslovakia, Feb. 7, 1926; came to U.S., 1941, naturalized, 1946; s. Hans and Stella (Parnas) W.; m. Lotte Ann Novak, Oct. 25, 1947; 1 dau., Leslie Andrea Wyman Cooper. Student, Upper Can. Coll., 1942, Bucknell U., 1942-43; BS in Bus. Adminstrn., NYU, 1945; postgrad., Columbia U., 1945-46. Asst. mgr. export dept. Liebermann Waelchi & Co., Inc., N.Y.C., 1946-47; trainee White Weld Co. (investment brokers), 1947-48; v.p. H.O. Canfield Co., 1948-65, vice chmn. bd., 1965-79, dir., 1953-79, Pantasote Inc., 1960-89, vice chmn. bd., 1967-89; mng. partner United Eagle Mgmt. Co., Eagle Mgmt. Co., 1960-95; pres. Veritas Co., 1960—; dir., chmn. Eagle Capital Internat. LLC, 1985—; dir., vice chmn. Affiliate Artists, Inc., 1971-88. Pres. Panwy Found.; bd. dirs. United Way of Greenwich, 1980-86; bd. dirs. Kids in Crisis, Greenwich, 1993-2001, sec., 1995; trustee Princeton Theol. Sem., 1976-2001, vice chmn., 1997-2001, trustee emeritus, 2001—; trustee Ctr. Theol. Inquiry, 1997—, Greenwich Acad., 1963-71, chmn. 1968-90. Mem. Greenwich Country Club, Lambda Chi Alpha. Presbyterian (elder, trustee Synod of N.E. 1974-76). Home: 34 Baldwin Farms N Greenwich CT 06831-3307 Office: # 9 Greenwich Office Park Greenwich CT 06831-5246 E-mail: rwyman@eaglecapllc.com.

WYMAN, RICHARD THOMAS, information services consultant; b. Wilmington, Del., June 4, 1951; s. William Harper and Marian Kathryn (Bode) W. . Pa. State U., 1969-71, Def. Language Inst., 1974-75, Control Data Inst., Dallas, 1979. Enlisted U.S. Army, 1971, served to staff sgt., 1979; data ctr. mgr. thrift svcs. divsn. ADP Inc., Dallas, 1979-80; support mgr. Electronic Data Sys., Inc., 1980-85, info. modeling analyst, 1985-90; pres. Strategic InfoSource, Plano, Tex., 1991-93; sr. cons. The SABRE Group, Ft. Worth, 1993-97; assoc. Perot Sys. Corp., Richardson, Tex., 1997-98; info. architect The Technical Resource Connection, Inc., Tampa, Fla., 1998—. Rep. 101st Airborne Divsn. Nat. Conf. Skill Maintenance, Ft. Meade, Md., 1977. Author: (spl. course) U.S. Army Intelligence, 1978-79. Co-chmn. sub-com. City Bond Referendum Com., Plano, 1990; mem. City of Plano Historic Landmark Com., 1993-97, vice chmn. 1996, chmn. 1996-97. Recipient Army Commendation medal, 1978, 79, Vol. Svc. award, Office of Mayor, Plano, 1990. Home: 717 Kipling Dr Plano TX 75023-6818 Office: Technical Resource Connection Inc 12320 Race Track Rd Tampa FL 33626-3115 E-mail: rwyman@trcinc.com.

WYMAN, RICHARD VAUGHN, engineering educator, exploration company executive; b. Painesville, Ohio, Feb. 22, 1927; s. Vaughn Ely and Melinda (Ward) W.; m. Anne Fenton, Dec. 27, 1947; 1 son, William Fenton. BS, Case Western Res. U., 1948; MS, U. Mich., 1949; PhD, U. Ariz., 1974. Registered profl. engr., Nev., Ariz.; registered geologist, Ariz., Calif.; lic. water right surveyor, Nev. Geologist N.J. Zinc Co., 1949, 52-53, Cerro de Pasco Corp., 1950-52; chief geologist Western Gold & Uranium, Inc., St. George, Utah, 1953-55, gen. supt., 1955-57, v.p., 1957-59; pres. Intermountain Exploration Co., Boulder City, Nev., 1959-93; tunnel supt. Reynolds Electric & Engring. Co., 1961-63, mining engr., 1965-67; asst. mgr. ops. Reynolds Electric and & Engring. Co., 1967-69; constrn. supt. engr. Sunshine Mining Co., 1963-65; lectr. U. Nev., Las Vegas, 1969-73, assoc. prof., 1973-80, dept. chmn., 1976-80, prof., 1980-92, prof. emeritus, 1992—, chmn. dept. civil and mech. engring., 1984-90, chmn. dept. civil and environ. engring., 1990-91. Mineral rep. Ariz. Strip Adv. Bd., 1976-80, U.S.B.L.M.; mem. peer rev. com. Nuclear Waste Site, Dept. Energy, Las Vegas, 1978-82; pres. Ariz. Juno Resources, Boulder City, 1980-87, v.p., 1990-97; pres. Wyman Engring. Cons., 1987—; cons. Corp. Andina de Fomento, Caracas, Venezuela, 1977-78; v.p. Comstock Gold, Inc., 1984-93; program evaluator Accreditation Bd. for Engring. and Tech., 1995-2001. Contbr. articles to profl. jours. Sec. Washington County Republican Party, Utah, 1958-60; del. Utah Rep. Conv., 1958-60; scoutmaster Boy Scouts Am., 1959-69; mem. citizens adv. com., tech. adv. com. Clark County Regional Flood Control Dist., 1998—. Served with USN, 1944-46. Recipient Order of Engr. award, 2000. Fellow ASCE (life; edn. divsn. 1990, local rep. nat. conv. Las Vegas), Soc. Econ. Geologists (life); mem. AIME/SME (life, chmn. So. Nev. sect. 1971-72, dir. 1968—, sec.-treas. 1974-92, chmn. Pacific S.W. Minerals Conf. 1972, gen. chmn. nat. conv. 1980, Disting. Mem. award 1989, Legion of Honor 1999), Assn. Engring. Geologists (dir. S.W. sect. 1989-91), Am. Inst. Minerals Appraisers, Am. Water Works Assn., Nev. Mining Assn. (assoc.), Assn. Ground Water Scientists and Engrs., Arctic Inst. N.Am. (life), Am. Soc. Engring. Edn., Soc. for History of Discoveries, Am. Philatelic Soc., SAR, Am. Legion, Kiwanis, Sigma Xi (pres. Las Vegas sect. 1986-91), Phi Kappa Phi (pres. U. Nev. Las Vegas chpt. 100 1982-83), Sigma Gamma Epsilon, Tau Beta Pi (hon.). Congregationalist. Home: 610 Bryant Ct Boulder City NV 89005-3017 Office: Wyman Engring PO Box 60473 Boulder City NV 89006-0473

WYMAN, SAMUEL H. international business consultant; b. Ft. Sill, Okla., Feb. 4, 1939; s. Leslie Haynes and Josephine Ann (Firor) W.; m. Laura Pilar Garzon, Aug. 19, 1961; 1 child, Lyndsey. BS, Georgetown U., 1961; MA, Columbia U., 1963. Sr. intelligence svc. CIA, Washington, 1965-94; sr. v.p. Jefferson Waterman Internat., 1994—. Recipient Meritorious Honor award Dept. State, 1976. Episcopalian. Avocations: philately, physical fitness, scuba, gardening, computers. Office: Jefferson Waterman Internat 1350 New York Ave NW Washington DC 20005-4709

WYMER, ROBERT ERNEST, metals company executive; b. Marlinton, W.Va., Feb. 9, 1947; s. Elmer and Blanche Margaret (Harper) W.; m. Holly Elizabeth Cline, Dec. 28, 1968; children: Robert Ernest Jr., Jill Allison. AS, W.Va. Inst. Tech., 1968, BS, 1986. Dir. recreation area W.Va. Dept. Natural Resources, Charleston, 1965-67; insp. hwy. constrn. W.Va. Dept. Hys., Elkins, 1968; supr. shift prodn. Union Carbide Corp., Alloy, W.Va., 1969-73, indsl. engr., 1973-74, mgr. mobile equipment dept., 1974-79; asst. plant mgr., supt. mines and calcite Acme Limestone Co., Ft. Springs, 1979-81; supr. maintenance Elkem Metals Co. LP, Alloy, 1981-83, master mechanic, 1984-87, mgr. maintenance project, 1987-88, mgr. maintenance and engring., 1988—. Coach Montgomery (W.Va.) Little Rockets Midget Football, 1976-77; pres. Pratt Vol. Fire Dept., Inc., 1977—; scout leader Boy Scouts Am., Handley, W.Va., 1978. Mem. ASTM, Soc. for Maintenance and Reliability Profls. (charter), KC. Republican. Roman Catholic. Avocations: rappelling, spelunking, woodworking. Office: Elkem Metals Co LP PO Box 613 Alloy WV 25002-0613

WYNAR, BOHDAN STEPHEN, librarian, writer, editor; b. Lviv, Ukraine, Sept. 7, 1926; came to U.S., 1950, naturalized, 1957; s. John I. and Euphrosina (Doryk) W.; m. Olha Yarema, Nov. 23, 1992; children: Taras, Michael, Roxolana, Yarynka. Diplom-Volkswirt Econs., U. Munich, Germany, 1949, PhD, 1950; MA, U. Denver, 1958. Methods analyst, statistician Tramco Corp., Cleve., 1951-53; freelance journalist Social Econs., 1954-56; adminstrv. asst. U. Denver Librs., 1958-59, head tech. svcs. div., 1959-62; assoc. prof. Sch. Librarianship, U. Denver, 1962-66; dir. div. libr. edn. State U. Coll., Geneseo, N.Y., 1966-67, dean Sch. Libr. Sci., prof., 1967-69; pres. Libraries Unlimited Inc., 1969—. Author: Soviet Light Industry, 1956, Economic Colonialism, 1958, Ukrainian Industry, 1964, Introduction to Bibliography and Reference Work, 4th edit, 1967, Introduction to Cataloging and Classification, 8th edit, 1992, Major Writings on Soviet Economy, 1966, Library Acquisitions, 2d edit, 1971, Research Methods in Library Science, 1971, Economic Thought in Kievan Rus', 1974; co-author: Comprehensive Bibliography of Cataloging and Classification, 2 vols., 1973, Ukraine: A Bibliographic Guide to English Language Publications, 1990, Independent Ukraine: A Bibliographic Guide to English Language Publications, 1989-99, 2000, Wynar's Introduction to Cataloging and Classification, 2000; editor Ukrainian Quar., 1953-58, Preliminary Checklist of Colorado Bibliography, 1963, Studies in Librarianship, 1963-66, Research Studies in Library Science, 1970— , Best Reference Books, 3d edit., 1985, 4th edit., 1992, Colorado Bibliography, 1980; gen. editor: American Reference Books Ann., 1969-2001; editor: ARBA Guide to Subject Encyclopedias and Dictionaries, 1985, ARBA Guide To Biographical Dictionaries, Reference Books in Paperback, An Annotated Guide, 2d edit., 1976, 3rd edit., 1991, Dictionary of Am. Library Biography, 1978, Ukraine-A Bibliographic Guide to English-Language Publications, 1990, 99, International Writings of Bohdan S. Wynar 1949-1992, 1993, Independent Ukraine, Bibliographic Guide, 2000, Recommended Reference Books for Medium-Sized and Small Libraries, 1981-2001; co-editor, contbr. Ency. Ukraine, 1955—; editor Library Sci. Ann., 1984-90, 98, Libr. Info. Sci. Annual 1984-90, 98—. Bd. dirs., mem. exec. bd. ZAREVO, Inc. Mem. ALA (pres. Ukrainian Congress com. br., Denver 1976), Colo. Library Assn., N.Y. Library Assn., Am. Assn. Advancement Slavic Studies (pres. Ukrainian Research Found. 1976-90), AAUP, Ukranian Hist. Assn. (exec. bd.), Sevčenko Societe Scientifique (Paris), Ukrainian Acad. Arts and Scis. (N.Y.C.).

WYNDRUM, RALPH WILLIAM, JR. communications executive consultant; b. N.Y.C., Apr. 20, 1937; s. Ralph W. and Virginia M. (Woolley) W.; m. Meta Schmidt, Apr. 23, 1960; children: Dorothy, Jeanne, Ralph, Joan. BS, Columbia U., 1959, MS in Elec. Engring., 1960, MS in Bus. Adminstrn., 1978; Sc.D., NYU, 1963. Mem. tech. staff Bell Labs., Murray Hill, N.J., 1963-65, supr. exploratory circuit design, 1965-69, head loop transmission tech. dept. N.J., 1969-79, head advanced loop transmission systems dept. Whippany, 1979-87, head internat. loop systems dept., 1987, dir. systems analysis ctr., 1987-90, dir. quality process ctr., 1990-92, dir. quality, engring., software and techs., 1993-94; v.p. AT&T World Svcs., 1994—, dir. process engr. ctr., 1995-96; tech. v.p. AT&T Labs., 1996-99, v.p. program mgmt., 1999-2000, exec. cons., 2000—; staff exec. SmartOrg, Inc., Menlo Park, Calif., 2001—; CEO, Wyndrum Assocs., 2000—. Adj. prof. N.J. Inst. Tech., 1965; adj. prof. Stevens Inst. Tech., 1980-88, mem. industry adv. bd., 2000—. Contbr. articles to profl. jours.; patentee in field. Fellow: IEEE (bd. dirs. 1988—90, 2000—01, v.p. publs. 1990—91, Pres.'s Leadership award 1991); mem.: IEEE-USA (v.p. tech. policy 2002—), IEEE Components, Packaging and Mfg. Tech. Soc., IEEE Comm. Soc. (chmn. conf. bd. 1981—87), Sigma Xi, Beta Gamma Sigma, Eta Kappa Nu. Republican. Roman Catholic. Home: 35 Cooney Ter Fair Haven NJ 07704-3001 Office: 35 Cooney Ter Fair Haven NJ 07704-3001 E-mail: rww@monmouth.com., r.wyndrum@ieee.org., rww@wyndrum.com.

WYNER, JUSTIN L. laminating company executive; b. Boston, Aug. 6, 1925; s. Rudolph H. and Sara G. Wyner; m. Genevieve Gloria Geller, July 3, 1955; children: George Michael, Daniel Mark, James Henry. BS cum laude, Tufts Coll., 1946; MBA, Harvard U., 1948. Chmn. bd. Shawmut Mills div. R.H. Wyner Assocs., West Bridgewater, Mass. Trustee Beth Israel Hosp., Boston, 1966-96, mem. fin. com., 1972-80; trustee Temple Israel, Boston, 1964—, pres., 1979-82, chmn. bd. mgrs., 1983-94; trustee Am. Jewish Hist. Soc., 1987—, pres., 1992-98; trustee Hebrew Coll., 1967—, chmn. cultural affairs com., 1977-78, trustee Temple Kehillath Israel, 1967—; trustee Combined Jewish Philanthropies, Boston, 1966-96, bd. mgrs., 1989—; trustee Roxbury Latin Sch., 1985-89; moderator Town of Brookline, Mass., 1970-82, 91-94, chmn. fin. com., 1961-64; nat. chmn. Reps. for Eugene McCarthy, 1968; chmn. Brookline United Fund, 1960; pres. Jewish Community Rels. Coun., 1971-73, mem. adminstrv. com., 1967—; dir. Brookline Taxpayer's Assn., 1956-61, Brookline Cmty. Coun., 1957-61; gov. Hebrew Union Coll.-Jewish Inst. Religion, 1987-92; del. to Mass. Rep. Conv., 1998; bd. dirs. Mass. div. Am. Cancer Soc., 1987-97; pres. Hebrew Free Loan Soc. Boston, 1972-88; active various other civic and religious orgns.; exec. com. bd. overseers Beth Israel Deaconess Hosp., 1996-98; dir. Ctr. for Jewish History, 1996—; justice of the peace, 1976—; trustee Martha's Vineyard Hosp., 1999—. Mem. Nat. Assn. for Textile Tech. (nat. bd. govs. 1970-73), Nat. Knitwear Mfrs. Assn. (past dir., bd. dirs., present hon. life dir.), Harvard Club Boston, Belmont Country Club. Avocations: sailing, amateur radio, golf. Home: 20 Rowes Wharf Boston MA 02110-3325 Office: Shawmut Mills 208 Manley St West Bridgewater MA 02379-1086 E-mail: jlwyner@shawmut-mills.com.

WYNER, YEHUDI, composer, pianist, conductor, educator; b. Calgary, Alta., Can., June 1, 1929; s. Lazar and Sarah Naomi (Shumiatcher) Weiner; m. Nancy Joan Braverman, Sept. 16, 1951 (div. 1967); children: Isaiah, Adam, Cassia; m. Susan M. Davenny, June 15, 1967. Diploma, Juilliard Sch. Music, 1946; AB, Yale U., 1950, B.Mus., 1951, M.Mus., 1953; MA, Harvard U., 1952. Vis. assoc. prof. Hofstra Coll., 1959; lectr. Queens Coll., N.Y.C., 1959-60; instr. Hebrew Union Coll., 1957-59; music dir. Westchester Reform Temple, 1959-68; asst. prof. theory Yale U., 1963-69, assoc. prof. theory, 1969-77, chmn. composition dept., 1969-73; prof. music SUNY, Purchase, 1978-89, dean music, 1978-82. Faculty Tanglewood Music Ctr. (formerly Berkshire Music Ctr.), 1975-97; vis. prof. composition Cornell U., 1987, Ziskind vis. prof. composition Brandeis U., 1987-88, Walter Naumburg prof. composition, dir. contemporary ensemble, 1989—; vis. prof. Harvard U., 1991-93, 96-98; Mary Duke Biddle Disting. composer Duke U., 1995. Mus. dir., New Haven Opera Soc., 1968-77, Turnau Opera Assn., 1961-64; mem., Bach Aria group, 1968—; composer-condr., Tanglewood, 1961; composer-in-residence, Santa Fe Chamber Music Festival, 1982, Am. Acad. in Rome, spring 1991; composer: Easy Suite for Piano, 1949, Songs, 1950-97, Two Chorale Preludes for Organ, 1951, Partita for piano, 1952, Dance Variations for wind octet, 1953, rev., 1959, Psalm 143, chorus, 1952, Sonata for piano, 1954, Concert Duo for violin and piano, 1955-57, Dedication Anthem, 1957, Serenade for Seven Instruments, 1958, Passover Offering, 1959, Three Informal Pieces for violin and piano, 1961, Friday Evening Service for Cantor, Chorus, Organ, 1963 (orchestrated 1992), (incidental music for play) The Old Glory, 1964, Torah Service with Instruments, 1966, Da Camera for piano and orch., 1967, Cadenza for clarinet and harpsichord, 1969, De Novo for cello and small ensemble, 1971, Liturgical Fragments for the High Holidays, 1971, Three Short Fantasies for piano, 1963-71, Canto Cantabile for soprano and concert band, 1972, (music for play) The Mirror, 1972-73, Memorial Music for soprano and 3 flutes, 1971-73, Intermedio for soprano and string orchestra, 1974, Wedding Music, 1976, Dances of Atonement for violin and piano, 1976, Fragments from Antiquity: 5 songs for soprano and symphony orch., 1978, Romances for Piano Quartet, 1980, All the Rage for flute and piano, 1980, Processionals and Marches, 1979, 80, Tanz and Maissele for clarinet, violin, cello, piano, 1981, On This Most Voluptuous Night for soprano and 7 instruments, 1982, Passage for 7 instruments, 1983, Wind Quintet, 1984, String Quartet, 1985, Composition for viola and piano, 1987, Toward the Center for piano, 1988, Sweet Consort for flute and piano, 1988, Leonardo Vincitore for 2 sopranos, string bass and piano, 1988, O To Be a Dragon, four songs for women's chorus and piano, 1989, Trapunto Junction for brass trio and percussion, 1991, Changing Time for small ensemble, 1991, New Fantasies for piano, 1991, Amadeus' Billiard for small ensemble, 1991, Il Cane Minore for 2 clarinets and bassoon, 1992, Wedding Dances: From the Notebook of Suzanne de Venné, 1993, Post Fantasies for piano, 1993, Prologue and Narrative for cello and orch., 1994, Song Cycle for soprano, baritone and piano: Restaurants, Wines-Bistros, Shrines, 1994, More Fantasies for piano, 1994, Lyric Harmony for orch., 1995, Praise Ye the Lord for soprano and ensemble, 1996, Brandeis Sunday for string quartet, 1996, A Mad Tea Party for soprano, 2 baritones, flute, violin, cello and piano, 1996, Epilogue for orch., 1996, Horntrio, 1997, Madrigal for string quartet, 1999, The Second Madrigal: Voices of Women for soprano and eleven players, 1999, Quartet for oboe and string trio, 1999. Recipient Inst. Arts and Letters grant, 1961, Brandeis Creative Arts award, 1963, Elise Stoeger prize Lincoln Ctr. Chamber Music Soc., 1998; commns. from Yale U., 1958, Mich. U., 1959, Fromm Found., 1960, Koussevitzsky Found. at Library Congress, 1960, 91, Ford Found., 1971, Yale Band, Yale Repertory Theater, Cantilena Chamber Players, Aeolian Chamber Players, Santa Fe Chamber Music Festival, Collage of Boston, N.Y. Woodwind Quintet, Frank Taplin project, NEA Consortium, Boston Symphony Chamber Players, Atlantic Sinfonietta, Carnegie Hall Am. Composers Orch., RNCM Manchester Internat. Cello Festival; Rome Prize fellow, 1953-56; Alfred E. Hertz fellow U. Calif., 1953-54, Guggenheim fellow, 1960, 76-77, Rockefeller Found. fellow Bellagio, 1998; NEA grantee, 1976. Mem. Am. Composers Alliance, Am. Music Center, Am. Acad. Arts and Letters (elected). Office: Music Dept Brandeis U Waltham MA 02454

WYNESS, STEVEN CHARLES, illustrator; b. Carmel, N.Y., Sept. 25, 1967; s. Tom and Marion J. (Sewell) W.; m. Lorraine E. Disanza, June 20, 1992; children: Erin Skylar, Logan Scott. AAS, Dutchess C.C., Poughkeepsie, N.Y., 1987; BA, We. Conn. State U., 1990. Mgr. photography, illustrator Cannondale Corp., Georgetown, Conn., 1987-92; illustrator, designer Steven C. Wyness Designs, Middletown, N.Y., 1991-98; print prodn. specialist Seiko Corp., Mahwah, N.J., 1995-96; art dir. The Orton Group, Salt Lake City, 1998-99, HGM Med. Lasers, Salt Lake City, 1999—2002. Sculptor, painter Aesthetic Concerns Inc., Middletown, N.Y., 1997. Executed woodstock mural Peace Now, 1994; designed Seiko trademark Windward, 1995, Freedom, 1988; photographer nat. and internat. photos for pubs. including Forbes, VeloVert, L.L. Bean. Home: 6329 S Fairwind Dr West Jordan UT 84084-6211 E-mail: sclwyness@earthlink.net.

WYNGAARDEN, JAMES BARNES, physician; b. East Grand Rapids, Mich., Oct. 19, 1924; s. Martin Jacob and Johanna (Kempers) W.; m. Ethel Vredevoogd, June 20, 1946 (div. 1977); children: Patricia Wyngaarden Fitzpatrick, Joanna Wyngaarden Gandy, Martha Wyngaarden Krauss, Lisa Wyngaarden, James Barnes Jr. Student, Calvin Coll., 1942-43, Western Mich. U., 1943-44; MD, U. Mich., 1948; DSc (hon.), U. Mich. and Med. Coll. of Ohio, 1984, U. Ill., 1985, George Washington U., 1986; PhD (hon.), Tel Aviv U., 1987; DSc. (hon.), U. S.C., West Mich. U., 1989. Diplomate: Am. Bd. Internal Medicine. Intern Mass. Gen. Hosp., Boston, 1948-49, resident, 1949-51; vis. investigator Pub. Health Rsch. Inst., N.Y.C., 1952-53; investigator NIH, USPHS, Bethesda, Md., 1953-56; asso. prof. medicine and biochemistry Duke U. Med. Sch., 1956-61, prof., 1961-65; vis. scientist Inst. Biologie-Physiochemique, Paris, 1963-64; prof., chmn. U. Pa. Med. Sch., 1965-67; physician-in-chief Med. Svc. Hosp. U. PA., Phila., 1965-67; Frederic M. Hanes prof., chmn. dept. medicine Duke U. Sch. of Medicine, Durham, N.C., 1967-82; physician-in-chief Med. Svc. Duke U. Hosp., 1967-82; chief of staff Duke U. Hosp., 1981-82; dir. NIH, Bethesda, MD, 1982-89; assoc. dir. life scis. Office of Sci. and Tech. Policy, Exec. Office of Pres., The White House, 1989-90; dir. Human Genome Orgn., 1990-91; fgn. sec. NAS, 1990-94; prof. medicine, assoc. vice chancellor for health affairs Duke U., Durham, N.C., 1990-94, ret., 1994; mem. staff VA, Durham County Hosps.; sr. assoc. dean internat. med. programs U. Pa., Phila., 1995-97. Cons. Office Sci. and Tech. Exec. Office of Pres., 1966-72; Mem. Pres.'s Sci. Adv. Com., 1972-73; mem. Pres.'s Com. for Nat. Medal of Sci., 1977-80; mem. adv. com. biology and medicine AEC, 1966-68; mem. bd. sci. counselors NIH, 1971-74; mem. adv. bd. Howard Hughes Med. Inst., 1969-82; mem. adv. council Life Ins. Med. Research Fund, 1967-70; adv. bd. Sci. Yr., 1977-81; vice chmn. Com. on Study Nat. Needs for Biomed. and Behavioral Research Personnel, NRC, 1977-81; bd. dirs. Hybridon Corp., Human Genome Scis., Genaera Pharm., Van Andel Rsch. Inst.; prin. Washington Adv. Group, 1995-2002. Author: (with W.N. Kelley) Gout and Hyperuricemia, 1976; mem. editorial bd. Jour. Biol. Chemistry, 1971-74, Arthritis and Rheumatism, 1959-66, Jour. Clin. Investigation, 1962-66, Ann. Internal Medicine, 1964-74, Medicine, 1963-90; editor: (with J.B. Stanbury, D.S. Fredrickson) The Metabolic Basis of Inherited Disease, 1960, 66, 72, 78, 83, (with O. Sperling and A. DeVries) Purine Metabolism in Man, 1974, (with L.H. Smith, Jr.) Cecil Textbook of Medicine, 16th edit., 1982, 19th edit., 1992. Bd. dirs. Royal Soc. Medicine Found., 1971-76, The Robert Wood Johnson Found. Clin. Scholar Program, 1973-78. Ensign USNR, 1943-46; sr. surgeon USPHS, 1951-56, rear adm. USPHS, 1982-90. Recipient Borden Undergrad. Research award, U. Mich., 1948, N.C. Gov.'s award for sci., 1974, Disting. Alumnus award We. Mich. U., 1984, Robert Williams award Assn. Profs. Medicine, 1985, Dalton scholar in medicine, Mass. Gen. Hosp., 1950, Richard Schweiker Excellence in Govt. award, 1985, Fedn. of Am. Socs. of Exptl. Biology Pub. Svc. award, 1989, Humanitarian award Nat. Orgn. for Rare Diseases, 1990; Royal Coll. Physicians fellow, 1984. Mem. Am. Rheumatism Assn., Am. Fedn. Clin. Research, So. Soc. Clin. Investigation (pres. 1974, founder's medal 1978), ACP (John Phillips Meml. award 1980), Am. Soc. Clin. Investigation, AAAS, Am. Soc. Biol. Chemists, Assn. Am. Physicians (councillor 1973-77, pres. 1978, Kober medal 1991), Endocrine Soc., Nat. Acad. Scis., Royal Acad. Scis. Sweden, Am. Acad. Arts and Sci., Inst. Medicine, Sigma Xi. Clubs: Interurban Clinical (Balt.). Democrat. Presbyterian. Avocations: tennis, skiing, painting. Office: The Washington Advisory Group 1275 K Street NW, Suite 1025 Washington DC 20005

WYN-JONES, ALUN (WILLIAM WYN-JONES), software developer, mathematician; b. Tremadoc, Gwynedd, Great Britain, Aug. 15, 1946; came to U.S., 1976; s. Goronwy Wyn and Mai Jones; m. Jocelyn Ripley, July 29, 1977; 1 stepchild, Electra Truman. BSc with honors, U. Manchester, U.K., 1968; MSc, Univ. Coll. London, 1970. Rsch. engr. Marconi-Elliott Computer Labs., Borehamwood, U.K., 1970-71; asst. tutor math. Poly. North London, 1971-72; programmer CRC Info. Sys., Ltd., London, 1972-76; mgr. devel. Warner Computer (now Warner Ins.), N.Y.C., 1976-80; pres., owner, developer Wallsoft Sys., Inc., 1982-92, Integrity Sys. Corp., N.Y.C., 1980-94. Software cons. investment banking divsn. Goldman, Sachs & Co., N.Y.C., 1994-2000, FirstRain, Inc., N.Y.C., 2000—; invited spkr. at profl. confs. Author, co-author computer software. Recipient Byte Award Distinction Byte Editors and Columnists, 1988, Readers Choice award Data Based Advisor Readers, 1990, 91. Mem. AAAS, Am. Math. Soc., Math. Assn. Am. Achievements include development of template programming in automatic code generation. Home: 609 Columbus Ave Apt 14D New York NY 10024-1436 E-mail: awynjones@firstrain.com.

WYNN, ALBERT RUSSELL, congressman; b. Phila., Sept. 10, 1951; m. Jessie Jackson, Jan. 14, 1994 (sep.); 1 child, Gabrielle. BS, U. Pitts., 1973; student, Howard U.; JD, Georgetown U., 1977. Intern African Regional Affairs, U.S. State Dept., 1972-73; exec. dir. consumer protection divsn. Prince George's County, 1977-81; mem. Md. Ho. of Dels., 1983-86; lawyer Albert R. Wynn & Assocs., 1982-86; mem. Md. State Senate from Dist. 25, 1987-92, U.S. Congress from 4th Md. Dist., Washington, 1993—; dep. Dem. whip; mem. commerce com. Mem. banking & fin. svcs com., internat. rels. com., Patuxent Inst. reform task force, 1988-92, joint com. econ. devel. strategy, 1989-92; del. Dem. Nat. Conv. 1984, 88,96; pres. Metro. Washington coun. consumer agencies. Mem. NAACP legal assistance program, coalition on black affairs, voter registration, edn. coalition, gov.'s task force drunk & drugged driving; 1st vice chmn. legis. black caucus; chmn. Prince George's County black elected officials alliance. Mem. J. Franklin Bourne Bar Assn., Kappa Alpha Psi (past pres.). Democrat. Baptist. Office: US Ho of Reps 434 Cannon House Ofc Bldg Washington DC 20515-0001*

WYNN, BETTY JEAN, columnist; b. Sanford, Fla., Aug. 30, 1948; d. James Henry Wearen and Katie Faniel; children: Cheri, Sean, Ruth, Tasha. GED, Seminole C.C., Sanford, Fla., 1979. Cert. tng. (Better Writing) Sear's Nat. Tng., Chgo., 1987, tutor workshop Laubach Literacy Action, Miami, 1994. Freelance writer, Fla., 1990—; guest columnist Sanford Herald, 1996—98. Mem.: Ea. Star (Martin Luther King chpt.). Avocation: reading. Home: 185 Mt Hope Ave # 514 Rochester NY 14620

WYNN, JOHN CHARLES, clergyman, retired religion educator; b. Akron, Ohio, Apr. 11, 1920; s. John Francis and Martha Esther (Griffith) W.; m. Rachel Linnell, Aug. 27, 1943; children: Mark Edward, Martha Lois Borland, Maryan Kay Ainsworth. BA, Coll. Wooster, 1941; BD, Yale U., 1944; MA, Columbia U., 1963, EdD, 1964; DD, Davis and Elkins Coll., 1958. Ordained to ministry Presbyn. Ch. (U.S.A.), 1944. Student asst. pastor Trinity Luth. Ch., New Haven, 1943-44; assoc. minister First Presbyn. Ch., Evanston, Ill.,

1944-47; pastor El Dorado, Kans., 1947-50; dir. family edn. and research United Presbyn. Bd. Christian Edn., Phila., 1950-59; prof. Colgate Rochester/Bexley Hall/Crozer Theol. Sem., 1959-85, prof. emeritus, 1985—; pvt. practice family therapy; adj. prof. U. Rochester, San Francisco Theol. Sem., St. Bernard's Sem., Wesley Theol. Sem., Hartford Theol. Found.; postdoctoral fellow Cornell U., 1973-74, St. John's U., 1980; lectr. Sch. Continuing Edn. Johns Hopkins U. Mem. summer faculty Union Theol. Sem., N.Y.C., San Francisco Theol. Sem.; del. study conf. World Coun. Chs., 1953, 57, 64, 65, 67, 75, 80; lectr. 5 univs., Republic of South Africa, 1968; chmn. com. on sexuality in human cmty. U.P. Ch.; vol. mem. chaplaincy staff Charlestown Care Ctr., Balt. Author: How Christian Parents Face Family Problems, 1955, Pastoral Ministry to Families, 1957, Families in the Church, A Protestant Survey, 1961, Christian Education for Liberation and Other Upsetting Ideas, 1977, Family Therapy in Pastoral Ministry, 1982 (rev. and expanded as Family Therapy in Pastoral Ministry: Counseling for the Nineties, 1991), The Family Therapist, 1987; Editor: Sermons on Marriage and Family Life, 1956, Sex, Family and Society in Theological Focus, 1966, Sexual Ethics and Christian Responsibility, 1970; Contbr. articles to mags. and religious jours. Bd. dirs. Presbyn. Life, Planned Parenthood League Rochester and Monroe County, Family Service Rochester, Samaritan Pastoral Counseling Ctr. Fellow Am. Assn. Marriage and Family Therapy (approved supr.); mem. Religious Edn. Assn., Nat. Coun. Chs. of Christ in U.S.A. (chmn. com. family life 1957-60), Nat. Coun. Family Rels., Family Svc. Assn. Am., Rochester Coun. Chs. (dir.) Address: 717 Maiden Choice Ln Apt 523 Catonsville MD 21228-6173 E-mail: RLWynn@erols.com.

WYNN, JOHN THOMAS, retired college president, farming executive, economic consultant, oil and gas producer; b. Corsicana, Tex., May 4, 1938; s. Sam Grady and Marjorie (Reese) W.; m. Sally Ruth Adams, Mar. 19, 1958 (div. 1975); children: Martha Maria, Catherine Clarissa, Lorraine Lemae; m. Myra Louise Alexander, Oct. 30, 1976; 1 child, John Thomas. AA, Wharton County Jr. Coll., 1960; BBA in Gen. Bus., Agrl. and Mech. Coll. Tex., 1962; MBA, Tex. A&M U., 1965; PhD in Higher Edn. Mgmt., U. So. Miss., 1973. Asst. registrar, then. instr. Tex. A&M U., College Station, 1962-67; exec. dean Delgado Community Coll., New Orleans, 1967-74, program dir., 1977-78; asst. exec. sec. So. Assn. Colls and Schs., Atlanta, 1974-77; pres. emeritus Williamsburg Tech. Coll., Kingstree, S.C., 1978-94; pres., CEO econ. cons. M&W Farm & Ranch, Egypt, Tex., 1994—. Cons. AID, Dominican Republic, 1966; bd. govs. Coastal Edn. Consortium, Conway, S.C., 1982-90; mem. exec. com. pres.'s coun. S.C. Tech. Edn. Coll., Columbia, 1985-86. Vestryman St. Thomas Episc. Ch., College Station, 1962-67, St. George Episc. Ch., New Orleans, 1969-72; vestryman St. Thomas' Episc. Ch., Wharton, Tex., 1998-2001, sr. warden, 1999-2000; Rep. precinct 2 chmn., Wharton County, Tex., 1998-2000. Served as sgt. USAR, 1955-62. Recipient Order of the Palmetto S.C. Gen. Assembly, 1994; named Hon. Order of Ky. Cols.; col. Aide-de-Camp, La., col. Aide-de-Camp, N.Mex. Mem. Future Farmers Assn. (hon.), S.C. Tech. Edn. Assn. (bd. dirs. 1985-88), Kingstree C. of C. (bd. dirs. 1981-84), Kiwanis, Masons (32 degree), Shriners (hon.), Phi Delta Kappa, Kappa Delta Pi. Avocations: chess, camping, music composition, reading. Home and Office: PO Box 307 Egypt TX 77436 Fax: 979-677-3672. E-mail: egypt@intertex.net.

WYNN, KARLA WRAY, artist, agricultural products company executive; b. Idaho Falls, Idaho, Oct. 1, 1943; d. Wiliam and Elma (McCowin) Lott; m. Russell D. Wynn, June 7, 1963 (div. 1996); children: Joseph, Jeffrey, Andrea. Student, Coll. of Holy Names, 1962-63, Providence Coll. Nursing, 1962-63; BFA, Idaho State U., 1989; postgrad., Alfred U., 1993. Co-owner R.D. Wynn Farms, American Falls, Idaho, 1963-96, office mgr., 1975-84; co-owner Redi-Gro Fertilizer Co., 1970-96, office mgr., 1980-84; pres. Lakeside Farms, Inc. (name now Redi-Gro Fertilizer Inc.), 1975—96; artist, 1990—. Owner Blue Heron, Pocatello, Idaho, 1991-96. Watercolors, oil paintings and ceramic clay sculptures exhibited at various art shows and galleries. Buddhist.

WYNN, STANFORD ALAN, lawyer; b. Milw., May 9, 1950; s. Sherburn and Marjory (Tarrant) W. BBA, U. Wis., Milw., 1972; JD, Case Western Res. U., 1975; LLM in Taxation, U. Miami, 1976. Bar: Wis. 1975, Fla. 1976. Assoc. Walsh and Simon, Milw., 1976-78; atty., asst. dir. advanced mktg. Northwestern Mut. Life Ins. Co., 1978—. Author: The Insurance Counselor-Split Dollar Life Insurance, 1991; cons. editor: The Insurance Counselor-The Irrevocable Life Insurance Trust, 1995. Bd. dirs. Waukesha Estate Planning Coun., 1985-86. Office: Northwestern Mut Life Ins Co 720 E Wisconsin Ave Milwaukee WI 53202-4703

WYNN, THOMAS JOSEPH, judge, educator; b. Chgo., Aug. 30, 1918; s. Phillip H. and Delia B (Madden) W.; m. Bernadette L. Lavelle, Apr. 17, 1948; children: Thomas Joseph, John P. AB, DePaul U., 1941, JD, 1942. Bar: Ill. 1942. Spl. investigator Phoenix & Murphy, Chgo., 1942; pvt. practice law, 1946-59; ptnr. Wynn & Ryan, 1959-79; assoc. judge Cir. Ct. Cook County, Ill., 1979-83, judge chancery div. mechanic's lien sect., 1983-96, retired, 1996. Lectr. bus. law Latin Am. Inst., Chgo., 1946-47; mem. faculty Coll. Commerce, DePaul U., Chgo., 1947-98, assoc. dean Evening div., 1957-73, prof., 1972-79, part-time faculty, 1979-83, adj. prof. bus. law, 1983-98; asst. atty. gen. Ill., 1957-58; bd. dirs., gen. counsel Suburbanite Bowl, Inc., 1958-79; gen. legal counsel Chgo. Consortium Colls. and Univs., GM Tool Corp.; pres., bd. dirs. Metroplex Leasing and Financing, Inc. Candidate for alderman Chgo. City Coun., 1951; candidate for judge Mcpl. Ct. Chgo., 1956; exec. sec., bd. dirs. Ill. Good Govt. Inst., 1958-79; mem. adv. bd. to dean Coll Law DePaul U., 1992—. Ensign-lt. (S.G.) USNR, 1942-46. Mem. Ill. Bar Assn., Chgo. Bar Assn. (mem. arbitration and alternative dispute resolution com., civil practice coms., mem. internat. law com., mem. judiciary com., mem. cir. ct. com.), Ill. Judges Assn. (com. mandatory arbitration alt. dispute resolution, com. pubs.), Assn. Univ. Evening Colls. (past chmn.), Am. Bus. Law Assn. (pres. 1972-73), Am. Real Estate and Urban Econs. Assn., Chgo. Area Evening Deans and Dirs. Assn., U.S. Adult Edn. Assn., Ill. Adult Edn. Assn., Am. Right-of-Way Assn. (advisor chmn., nat. ednl. com., 1963-64), St. Vincent DePaul Soc., DePaul Law Alumni Assn. (past pres.), Smithsonian Inst., Pres.'s Club, (DePaul U. 1986—), Blue Key, Gamma Eta Gamma, Beta Gamma Sigma, Delta Mu Delta. Home: 27592 W Cuba Rd Barrington IL 60010-2770

WYNNE, BRIAN JAMES, former association executive, consultant; b. N.Y.C., Dec. 2, 1950; s. Bernard and Dolores (Doyle) W. Student, Institute des Sciences Politiques, Paris, 1970-71; BA, Coll. Holy Cross, 1972; MA, U. So. Calif., 1974. Staff Exec. Cons., Inc., McLean, Va., 1974-76; prin., 1976-78; exec. dir. Indsl. Designers Soc. Am., Washington, 1978-88. Cons. to various non-profit orgns.; dir. Worldesign 85, founder Worldesign Found. Mem. Am. Soc. Assn. Execs., Indsl. Designers Soc. Am. (hon.), Phi Sigma Iota. Home: 5200 N Ocean Blvd Apt 1004 Lauderdale By The Sea FL 33308-3019

WYNNE, JAMES, research scientist; B Physics, M Physics, PhD Physics, Harvard U. Mgr. Laser Physics and Chemistry Group IBM T.J. Watson Rsch. Ctr.; rsch. scientist IBM Watson Rsch. Ctr. , 1971—. Contbr. articles, scientific papers. Achievements include patents in field. Office: Watson Rsch Ctr 1101 Kithawan Rd Ste 134 Yorktown Heights NY 10598*

WYNNE, JAMES WARREN, physician; b. Passaic, NJ; s. Warren John and Irene Agnes W.; m. Patricia Gillen Wynne, June 29, 1968, children: Kathleen, Maureen, Amy, Megan, John. BS, St. Peter's Coll., Jersey City, NJ, 1961-65; MD, Cornell Univ. Med. Coll., New York, NY, 1965-69. Bd. Cert. Int. Med., Pulm. Med., Crit. Care. Med. Int. Univ. Fla. Coll. of Med., Gainesville, FL, 1969-70, res., 1970-72, fell. in pulm. med., 1972-74, chief med. res., 1974-75, asst. prof. of med., 1975-78, assoc. prof. med., 1978-82, clin./assoc. prof. med., 1982—, priv. prac./pulm. med., 1982—. Bd. dirs. Shands Healthcare; bd. mem., bd. dirs. Alachua Gen. Hosp., Gainesville, Fla., 1989—96, chief of staff, 1989. Mem. Fla. Med. Assn., 1975—, Am. Thoracic Soc., 1975—, Fla. Thoracic Soc. (pres.), 1981-83. Roman Catholic. Office: 4741 NW 8th Ave Ste C Gainesville FL 32605

WYNNE, LOUIS, psychologist; b. Leeds, Yorkshire, Eng., Mar. 29, 1938; came to U.S., 1951; s. Philip and Rachel (McLinsky) W.; m. Rochelle L. Harris, Nov. 26, 1959 (div. Aug. 1968); children: Mark R., Ronald J., Roberta E.; stepchildren: Heather L. Edison, Cheryl A. Edison, James A. Edison; m. Sema Wynne, Dec. 28, 1968. BS, Mass. State Tchrs. Coll., 1959, MEd, 1961; PhD, Ohio State U., 1967. Cert. clin. psychologist, N.Mex. Chief Combat Intelligence br. 494th Bombardment Wing Strategic Air Command, Sheppard AFB, Tex., 1963-65, dep. dir. Comparative Psychology divsn. Holloman AFB, N.Mex., 1969-73; assoc. prof. psychiatry and psychology U. N.Mex., 1973-81; clin. dir. N.Mex. State Hosp., Las Vegas, 1983-85; pvt. practice psychology Albuquerque, 1988—. Cons. Blue Cross/Blue Shield of N.Mex., 1992—, Albuquerque Job Corps Ctr., 1996—. Author: Deliver Us From Evil, 2002; co-author: Warm Logic: The Art of the Intuitive Lifestyle, 1990; editl. bd. mem. Jour. Analysis of Verbal Behavior; contbr. articles to profl. jours. Mem. Internat. Ctr. for Study of Psychiatry and Psychology (adv. coun.), Assn. For Behavior Analysis. Avocations: trap shooting, skeet shooting, cross country skiing, films of the 40s, soccer. Office: 1420 Carlisle NE Albuquerque NM 87110 E-mail: landswy@aol.com.

WYNNE, LYMAN CARROLL, psychiatrist; b. Lake Benton, Minn., Sept. 17, 1923; s. Nels Wind and Ella C. (Pultz) W.; m. Adele Rogerson, Dec. 22, 1947; children: Christine, Randall, Sara, Barry, Jonathan. War certificate, Harvard, 1943, MD, 1947, PhD in Social Psychology, 1958; MD (hon.), Oulu U., Finland, 1989. Med. intern Peter Bent Brigham Hosp., Boston, 1947-48; grad. fellow social relations dept. Harvard, 1948-49; resident neurology Queen Square Hosp., London, Eng., 1950; resident psychiatry Mass. Gen. Hosp., Boston, St. Elizabeth's Hosp., Washington, also NIMH, 1951-54; psychoanalytic tng. Washington Psychoanalytic Inst., 1954-60, teaching analyst, 1965-72. Cons., investigator WHO, 1965— ; staff NIMH, 1954-57, chief sect. family studies, 1957-61, chief adult psychiatry br., 1961-72; mem. faculty Washington Sch. Psychiatry, 1956-72; prof. U. Rochester Sch. Medicine and Dentistry, 1971-98, chmn. dept. psychiatry, 1971-77, dir. div. family programs, 1971-83; psychiatrist-in-chief Strong Meml. Hosp., Rochester, N.Y., 1971-77, prof. emeritus psychiatry, 1998—; vis. lectr. Am. U., Beirut, Lebanon, 1963-64 Bd. dirs. Family Process, 1969-97; mem. editl. adv. bd. Jour. Nervous and Mental Diseases; sr. editor: The Nature of Schizophrenia, 1978; editor: The State of the Art in Family Therapy Research; co-editor: Psychosocial Intervention in Schizophrenia, 1983, Children at Risk for Schizophrenia, 1984, The Language of Family Therapy, 1985; sr. editor Systems Consultation, 1986 Chmn. AAMFT Rsch. & Edn. Found., 1992-94. Med. dir. USPHS, 1961-72; mem. NRC, 1969-72. Recipient Commendation medal USPHS, 1965; Hofheimer prize Am. Psychiat. Assn., 1966; Frieda Fromm-Reichmann award Am. Acad. Psychoanalysis, 1966; Meritorious Service medal USPHS, 1966; Stanley Dean award Am. Coll. Psychiatrists, 1976; McAlpin Research Achievement award, 1977, Disting. Achievement in Family Therapy Research, Am. Family Therapy Assn., 1981; Disting. Research Achievement award Assn. Marriage and Family Therapy, 1982, Disting. Profl. Contbn. award Am. Assn. for Marriage and Family Therapy, 1985, Disting. Contbn. to Family Therapy award Am. Family Therapy Assn., 1989. Fellow: Am. Acad. Psychoanalysis, Am. Psychiat. Assn. (life); mem.: Soc. for Rsch. in Psychopathology, Nat. Coun. for Family Relations, Assn. for Clin. Psychosocial Rsch. (coun. 1984—91), Am. Psychoanalytic Assn., Am. Assn. for Marriage and Family therapy (bd. dirs. 1992—94), Am. Family Therapy Acad. (pres. 1986—87), Am. Coll. Psychoanalysts, Western N.Y. Psychoanalytic Soc. (pres. 1986—87), Psychiat. Rsch. Soc. Home: 17 Tobey Brk Pittsford NY 14534-1819 Office: Strong Meml Hosp Rochester NY 14642-8409 E-mail: lcwynne@rochester.rr.com.

WYNNE, MARION EVERETT, lawyer; b. Mobile, Ala., Sept. 17, 1942; s. Marion Everett and Maria (Lyon) W.; m. Susan J., Sept. 6, 1970; children: Jessica C., Elizabeth M. BA, Occidental Coll., 1964; JD, U. So. Calif., 1967. Bar: Calif. 68, Ala. 76. Pub. defender LA. County, L.A., 1968-70; sole practice, 1971-75, Fairhope, Ala., 1976-88; mcpl. judge City of Fairhope, 1981-88; city atty., 1988—; ptnr. Wilkins, Bailkester, Biles & Wynne, Fairhope, 1988—. Vol. Ala. State Bar; tchr. Ala. Jud. Coll., 1992. Vice chmn. Thomas Hosp., Fairhope, 1996—; sr. warden St. James Episcopal ch., Fairhope, 1994; lay rector Cursillo, Fairhope, 1996. Mem. Calif. Bar Assn., Ala. Bar Assn., Ala. Trial Lawyer Assn. (bd. govs. 1995—), Baldwin County Bar Assn. (past pres. 1976—), Rotary (past pres.). Episcopalian. Avocations: guitar, yard work. Home: 711 Greenwood Ave Fairhope AL 36532 Office: Wilkins Bankester Biles & Wynne PA PO Box 1367 Fairhope AL 36533 E-mail: twynne@wbbwlaw.com.

WYNNE, TERRY LYNNE, career counselor, trainer, writer; b. Ridgeland, S.C., Mar. 28, 1951; d. Herbert Ray and Carolyne (Taylor) W. BA, Ga. State U., 1972, MEd, 1974, EdS, 1977. Lic. profl. counselor, Ga.; nat. cert. counselor; nat. cert. career counselor; master career counselor; master career devel. profl.; cert. practitioner Myers-Briggs Type Indicator. Asst. Ernest L. Robinson, PhD, Atlanta, 1976-77; various SunTrust Bank, 1971-75, 77-84; trainer, spkr., writer, 1980-90; product info. specialist Unisys Corp., 1984-87; career counselor Emory U., 1987-96, 97—, Charter Behavioral Health Sys., Atlanta, 1995-97; owner, sole propr. Profl. Edge, Tucker, Ga., 1990—. Ice skating instr. Omni Internat. Ice Skating, 1980-82; career counselor, tng. cons. grad. sch. USDA, Atlanta, 1996—. Freelance writer, 1980—. Recipient 3d pl. Maupintour Travel Photography Contest, 1991, Sullivan award Furman U., 1969; Ednl. Opportunity grantee Furman U., 1968. Mem. ACA, MENSA, Nat. Career Devel. Assn., Llc. Profl. Counselors Ga. Assn., Ga. Career Devel. Assn. Avocations: ballroom dance, writing, ice skating, travel, photography.

WYNNE-EDWARDS, HUGH ROBERT, geologist, educator, entrepreneur; b. Montreal, Que., Can., Jan. 19, 1934; s. Vero Copner and Jeannie Campbell (Morris) W.-E.; married; children from previous marriages: Robin Alexander, Katherine Elizabeth, Renée Elizabeth Lortie, Krista Smyth, Jeannie Elizabeth, Alexander Vernon. B.Sc. with 1st class honors, U. Aberdeen, Scotland, 1955; MA, Queen's U., 1957, PhD, 1959; D.Sc. (hon.), Meml. U., 1975. Registered profl. engr. B.C., 1995—. With Geol. Survey Can., 1958-59; lectr. Queen's U., Kingston, Ont., 1968-72, asst. prof., then assoc. prof., 1961-68, prof., head dept. geol. scis., 1968-72; prof., then Cominco prof., head dept. geol. scis. U. B.C., Vancouver, 1972-77; asst. sec. univ. br. Ministry of State for Sci. and Tech., Ottawa, 1977-79; sci. dir. Alcan Internat. Ltd., Montreal, 1979-80, v.p. R&D, chief sci. officer, 1980-89; CEO Moli Energy Ltd., Vancouver, 1989-90; pres. Terracy Inc., 1989—; sci. advisor Teck Corp., 1989-91; pres., CEO B.C. Rsch. Inc., 1993-97, exec. chmn., pres., 1997-2000. Chmn. Silvagen Inc., 1996-99; advisor Directorate Mining and Geology, Uttar Pradesh, India, 1964, Grenville project Que. Dept. Natural Resources, 1968-72; vis. prof. U. Aberdeen, 1965-66, U. Witwatersrand, Johannesburg, South Africa, 1972; UN cons., India, 1974, SCITEC, 1977-78; mem. sci. adv. com. CBC, 1980-84; mem. Sci. Coun. Can., 1983-89, Nat. Adv. Bd. on Sci. and Tech., 1987-90 indsl. liaison com. UN Ctr. for Sci. and Tech. in Devel., 1982-84; vice chmn. tech. adv. group Bus. Coun. for Sustainable Devel., Geneva, 1991; mem. Nat. Biotech. Adv. Coun., 1995-98; chmn. Neurosci. Can. Partnership, 1999—; pres. Silvagen Holdings Inc., 1999-2000; bd. dirs. Atomic Energy Can. Ltd., CST Coldswitch Techs., Inc., Welichem Biotech Inc. Bd. dirs. Royal Victoria Hosp., Montreal, 1984-89. Decorated officer Order of Can., 1991; recipient Spendiarov prize 24th Internat. Geol. Congress, Montreal, 1972. Fellow Can. Acad. Engring., Royal Soc. Can.; mem. Can. Rsch. Mgmt. Assn. (vice chmn. 1982-84, chmn. 1984-85, assn. medal 1987), Univ. Club (Montreal). Mem. United Ch. Canada. Avocations: tennis, skiing, carpentry. Office: Terracy Inc 2030 27th St West Vancouver BC Canada V7V 4L4 E-mail: hughwynn@terracy.com.

WYRSCH, JAMES ROBERT, lawyer, educator, author; b. Springfield, Mo., Feb. 23, 1942; s. Louis Joseph and Jane Elizabeth (Welsh) W.; m. B. Darlene Wyrsch, Oct. 18, 1975; children: Scott, Keith, Mark, Brian, Marcia. BA, U. Notre Dame, 1963; JD, Georgetown U., 1966; LLM, U. Mo., Kansas City, 1972. Bar: Mo. 1966, U.S. Ct. Appeals (8th cir.) 1971, U.S. Ct. Appeals (10th cir.) 1974, U.S. Ct. Appeals (5th cir.) 1974, U.S. Ct. Appeals (6th cir.) 1982, U.S. Ct. Appeals (11th cir.) 1984, U.S. Ct. Appeals (7th cir.) 1986, U.S. Ct. Appeals (4th cir.) 1990, U.S. Ct. Appeals (9th cir.) 1998, U.S. Ct. Mil. Appeals 1978, U.S. Tax Ct. 1983, U.S. Dist. Ct. Ohio 1965, U.S. Supreme Ct. 1972. Assoc. Wyrsch, Hobbs & Mirakian P.C., Kansas City, 1970-71; of counsel, 1972-77; ptnr., 1978—; pres., shareholder, 1988—; adj. prof. U. Mo., 1981—. Mem. com. instrns. Mo. Supreme Ct. 1983—; mem. adv. coun. legal assts. program U. Mo. at Kansas City , 1985-88; mem. cir. ct. adv. com. Jackson County, Mo., 1998—; mem. jud. selection com. U.S. Magistrate we. dist., Mo., 1985; mem. fed. practice subcom. we. dist. U.S. Dist. Ct., Mo., 1985-88; mem. subcom. to draft model criminal instrns.for dist. cts. of 8th cir., 1986—; bd. dirs. Kansas City Bar Found. Co-author: Missouri Criminal Trial Practice, 1994; contbr. articles to profl. jours. Capt. U.S. Army, 1966—69. Recipient Joint Svcs. Commendation medal U.S. Army, 1969, U. Mo. Kansas City Svc. award Law Found., 1991-92, Lawyer of Yr. award Mo. Lawyers Weekly, 2001, Dean of Trial Bar award Kansas City Met. Bar Assn., 2002. Fellow: Mo. Bar Found. (vice-chmn. crmiinal law com. 1978—79), Am. Coll. Trial Lawyers, Am. Bar Found. (life); mem.: ATLA, ABA, Am. Coll. Barristers (sr. counsel), Mo. Assn. Criminal Def. Attys. (dir. 1978, sec. 1982, dir. 1983), Nat. Assn. Criminal Def. Attys., Am. Bd. Trial Advs. (adv.), Kansas City Bar Assn. (chmn. anti-trust com. 1981, chmn. bus. tort, anti-trust, franchise com. 1998), Mo. Bar Assn., Am. Arbitration Assn. (panel arbitrators 1976—2000), Country Club of Blue Springs, Kansas City Club, Phi Delta Phi. Democrat. Roman Catholic. Home: 1501 NE Sunny Creek Ln Blue Springs MO 64014-2044 Office: Wyrsch Hobbs & Mirakian PC 1101 Walnut St Fl 13 Kansas City MO 64106-2134

WYRTKI, KLAUS, oceanography educator; b. Tarnowitz, Germany, Feb. 7, 1925; came to U.S., 1961; s. Wilhelm and Margarete (Pacharzina) W.; m. Helga Kocher, June 6, 1954 (div. 1970); children: Undine, Oliver; m. Erika Maassen. PhD magna cum laude, U. Kiel, Germany, 1950. With German Hydrographic Inst., Hamburg, 1950-51; German Rsch. Coun. postdoctoral rsch. fellow U. Kiel, 1951-54; head Inst. Marine Rsch., Djakarta, Indonesia, 1954-57; sr. rsch. officer, then prin. rsch. officer div. fisheries and oceanography Commonwealth Sci. and Indsl. Rsch. Orgn., Sydney, Australia, 1958-61; assoc. rsch. oceanographer, then rsch. oceanographer Scripps Instn. Oceanography, U. Calif., 1961-64; prof. oceanography U. Hawaii, Honolulu, 1964—, prof. emeritus, 1993. Chmn. North Pacific Expt., 1974-80, com. on climate changes and ocean Internat. Assn. Phys. Scis. of the Oceans; mem. Spl. Com. on Ocean Rsch. Working Group on Prediction of El Nino, Sci. Working Group on Topography Expt., panel on climate and global change NOAA. Author: El Nino—The Dynamic Response of the Equatorial Pacific Ocean to Atmospheric Forcing, 1975; editor: Oceanographic Atlas of the International Indian Ocean Expedition, 1971; mem. editl. bd. Jour. Phys. Oceanography, 1971-79. Recipient Excellence in Rsch. award U. Hawaii, 1980, Rosenstiel award U. Miami, 1981. Fellow Am. Geophys. Union (Maurice Ewing medal 1989), Am. Meteorol. Soc. (Harald Ulrick Sverdrup Gold medal 1991), Deutsche Meteorologische Gesellschaft (Albert Defant medal 1992). E-mail: wyrtki@aloha.net.

WYRWICH, KATHLEEN W. health research educator; b. Houston, Apr. 2, 1958; m. John J. Wyrwich, June 27, 1981; children: Thomas, Matthew, Luke, Mary. BS in Stats., So. Ill. U., 1979, MS in Math., 1981; PhD in Health Svcs. Rsch., St. Louis U., 1999. Cert. secondary math. edn., Mo. Chmn. dept. math. Gibault H.S., Waterloo, Ill., 1981-82; instr. math. Harris-Stowes State Coll., St. Louis, 1994-95, St. Louis U., 1995-96; asst. prof. math. St. Louis Coll. Pharmacy, 1995-96; rsch. asst. Washington U., St. Louis, 1996-97; sr. rsch. asst. St. Louis U., 1997-99, asst. prof. health svcs. rsch., 1999—, asst. prof. rsch. methodology, 2001—. Contbr. articles to profl. jours. Pres. Sch. Bd. St. Pius V, St. Louis, 1992-93, chmn. fin. com., 1995-96. Mem. Assn. for Health Svcs. Rsch., Greater St. Louis Lead Poisoning Prevention Coun. (pres., treas. 1985—), Delta Omega (hon.). Avocations: home renovation, skating, sewing. Office: Saint Louis U 221 N Grand Ave Saint Louis MO 63103- E-mail: wyrwichk@slu.edu.

WYSE, LOIS, advertising executive, author; b. Cleve. d. Roy B. Wohlgemuth and Rose (Schwartz) Weisman; m. Marc Wyse (div. 1980); m. Lee Guber (dec. 1988). Pres. Wyse Advt. Inc., 1951—. Contbg. editor Good Housekeeping, 1983-98. Author: 60 books; syndicated columnist: Wyse Words. Trustee Beth Israel Med. Ctr. Ctr. for Communications, N.Y.C. Mem. Woman's Forum, PEN, Author's Guild, League of Profl. Theater Women. Office: 3 E 71st St New York NY 10021 E-mail: loisw@thirdage.com.

WYSE, WILLIAM WALKER, lawyer, real estate executive; b. Spokane, Wash., July 20, 1919; s. James and Hattie (Walker) W.; m. Janet E. Oswalt, Jan. 30, 1944; children: Wendy L., Scott C., Duncan E. AB, U. Wash., 1941; JD, Harvard U., 1948. Bar: Oreg. 1948. Pvt. practice, Portland; ptnr. Stoel, Rives, Boley, Jones & Gray, 1953-88; pres. Wyse Investment Svcs., 1988—. Past dir. Treasureland Savs. and Loan Assn.; past trustee, sec. Pacific Realty Trust; past trustee Holladay Park Plaza; dir. Costa Pacifica Co., 1999-2000. Chmn. ctrl. budget com. United Fund, 1958—60; 1st v.p. United Good Neighbors; chmn. bd. dirs. Portland Sch. Bd., 1959—66; pres. Tri-County Cmty. Coun., 1970—71; bd. dirs., sec. Oreg. Parks Found.; bd. dirs. Cmty. Child Guidance Clinic, 1956—57, pres., 1956—57; bd. dirs. Oreg. Symphony Soc., 1965—74, 1993—99, pres., 1968; bd. dirs. Loaves and Fishes Ctrs., Inc., 1997—. Mem. ABA, Oreg. Bar Assn., Multnomah County Bar Assn., Am. Coll. Real Estate Lawyers, Univ. Club, Arlington Club, Portland City Club (past gov.), Wauna Lake Club, Delta Upsilon. Republican. Presbyterian. Home: 3332 SW Fairmount Ln Portland OR 97201-1446 Office: 200 SW Market St Ste 345 Portland OR 97201-5753 Personal E-mail: jwwyse@aol.com. E-mail: wwyse@nyseinvestment.com.

WYSHAK, LILLIAN WORTHING, lawyer; b. N.Y.C., July 19, 1928; d. Emil Michael and Stefanie (Dvorak) Worthing; m. Robert H. Wyshak, 1961 (div. 1986); children: Robin, Susan, Jeanne, Patricia. BS in Acctg., UCLA, 1948, MA in Anthropology, 1971; JD, U. So. Calif., L.A., 1956. Bar: Calif. 1956, U.S. Dist. Ct. (ctrl. dist.) Calif. 1956, U.S. Ct. Appeals (9th cir.) 1967, U.S. Supreme Ct. 1967; cert. specialist in taxation law Calif. Bd. Legal Specialization; lic. real estate broker, Calif. Assoc. Boyle, Bissell & Atwill, Pasadena, Calif., 1956-57, Parker, Milliken, Kohlmeier, L.A., 1957-58; asst. U.S. atty. Tax Div., Office of U.S. Atty., 1958-62; ptnr. Wyshak & Wyshak, Beverly Hills, Calif., 1963-86; pvt. practice, 1986—. Former referee State Bar Ct., L.A.; arbitrator La. County Bar Dispute Resolution Svcs. Contbr. articles to profl. jours. Trustee U. Redlands, 1972-81. Mem. ABA (civil and criminal tax penalties com. tax sect.), Assn. Tax Counsel, Beta Gamma Sigma, Phi Alpha Delta. Presbyterian. E-mail: lillin@pacbell.net.

WYSK, RICHARD A. engineering educator, researcher; b. Holyoke, Mass., Sept. 22, 1948; s. Stanley and Sophia Dorothy (Mazurowski) W.; m. Caryl Lynne Ray, Jan. 18, 1969; children: Richard Patrick, Rebecca Jeanne, Robyn Caryl. BS in Indsl. Engring. & Ops. Rsch., U. Mass., 1972, MS in Indsl. Engring. & Ops. Rsch., 1973; PhD in Indsl. Engring., Purdue U., 1977. Prodn. control mgr. Gen. Electric, Erie, Pa., 1973-75; rsch. analyst Caterpillar Tractor, Inc., Peoria, Ill., 1975-76; assoc. prof. Va. Polytechnic Inst., Blacksburg, 1977-83; prof. Pa. State U., State College, 1983-90, William Lionhard chair in engring., 1995—; dir. Inst. Mfg. Systems, College Station, 1990-94; Royce Wisenbaker chair Tex. A&M U., 1990-94; William Lionhard chair in engring. William Leonhard chair in engring., State College, 1995—. Co-author: A Study Guide for the P.E. in I.E., 1982, An Intro to Automated Proc. Plan., 1985, Modern Manufacturing Process Engineering, 1989, Computer-aided Manufacturing, 1991 (Book-of-the-Yr. award Inst. Indsl. Engrs. 1992, E. Eugene Merchant Mfg. Textbook award Soc. Mfg. Engrs. 1992). Pks. commr. Montgomery County Pks. & Recreation, Blacksburg, 1982-83; adv. mem. Inst. Systems Rsch. U. Md., 1991-95. With U.S. Army, 1969-71, Vietnam. Decorated Army Commendation medal with 2 oak leaf clusters. Fellow Inst. Indsl. Engrs. (chpt. pres. 1990—, Region III Award of Excellence 1982, D. Baker award 1993), Soc. Mfg. Engrs. (sr., Outstanding Young Mfg. Engr. 1981), Engring. Accreditation Commn. (commr. 1990-92), Sigma Xi. Avocations: racquetball, basketball. Office: Pa State U 310 Leonard Bldg University Park PA 16802

WYSS, DAVID ALEN, financial service executive; b. Ft. Wayne, Ind., Nov. 14, 1944; s. Alen G. and Anne W. (Winicker) W.; m. Grace H. Hawes, June 11, 1966; children: Sarah J., Alen D. BS, MIT, 1966; PhD, Harvard U., 1971. Economist Fed. Res., Washington, 1970-74, sr. economist, 1975-77; advisor Bank Eng., London, 1974-75; sr. staff economist Council Econ. Advisers, Washington, 1977-79; v.p. DRI Ltd., London, 1979-83; rsch. dir. DRI/McGraw Hill, Lexington, Mass., 1983-97; chief economist Std. & Poor's/DRI, 1997-99, Std. & Poor's, N.Y.C., 2000—. Contbr. numerous articles to profl. jours. Mem. Am. Econ. Assn., Am. Statis. Assn., Nat. Assn. Bus. Economists. Office: Std & Poors 55 Water St Ste Conc12 New York NY 10041-0003 E-mail: david_wyss@standardandpoors.com.

WYSS, JOHN BENEDICT, lawyer; b. Evanston, Ill., Nov. 23, 1947; s. Walther Erwin and Caroline Nettie (Benedict) W.; m. Joanne P. Comstock, Oct. 22, 1994; children: John Christian, Kirsten Dunlop. BS in Physics summa cum laude, Stanford U., 1969; JD, Yale U., 1972. Bar: Calif. 1972, D.C. 1974, U.S. Supreme Ct. 1976. Trial atty. antitrust div. U.S. Dept. Justice, Washington, 1972-74; assoc. Kirkland & Ellis, 1974-78, ptnr., 1978-83, Wiley, Rein & Fielding, Washington, 1983—. Mem. ABA, Phi Beta Kappa. Office: Wiley Rein & Fielding 1776 K St NW Washington DC 20006-2304 E-mail: jwyss@wrf.com.

WYSZYNSKI, RICHARD CHESTER, musician, writer, conductor, educator; b. Chgo., Feb. 15, 1933; s. Ignatius John and Victoria (Gerlich) W. MusB, B of Music Edn., Northwestern U., 1955; cert. in music criticism, U. So. Calif., 1967; studies with Marcel Moyse, Brattleboro, Vt., 1961-65. Instr. flute DeLaSalle Inst., Chgo., 1952-56; chmn. music dept. Adult Edn. Ctrs., 1957-60; prin. flutist N.C. Symphony Orch., Chapel Hill, 1960, Shreveport (La.) Symphony Orch., 1960-61, Camelot Nat. Touring Co., N.Y.C., 1964; asst. condr., flutist Man of La Mancha Nat. Touring Co., 1967-70; dir., solo flutist Cardinal Woodwind Quintet, Chgo., 1970—; condr. Cardinal Chamber Orch., 1972—; prin. flutist Jesus Christ Superstar Nat. Tour, N.Y.C., 1977; instr. Monnacep-Oakton Community Coll., Des Plaines, Ill., 1977—; co-prin. flutist Chgo. Symphonic Wind Ensemble, 1978—. Instr. music Exptl. Coll. U. So. Calif., Los Angeles, 1972, Cen. YMCA Community Coll., Chgo., 1976, Norris Ctr., Northwestern U., Evanston, Ill., 1979-81, Loyola Continuing Edn., Chgo., 1980-84; condr. Lincolnwood (Ill.) Community Mus. Theatre, 1976, Stuart Ctr., De Paul U., Chgo., 1978-80; lectr. music Newberry Library, Chgo., 1979, Chgo. Office Fine Arts, 1985-86; dir. Singleforum, Chgo., 1986—. Editor, pub. Interplay mag., 1951-54; music critic Old Town Voice, 1962-65; scriptwriter documentary films for Atwood Films, 1964-65 (N.Y. Film Festival, Cine award); producer, announcer Sta. WHPK-FM, 1973-76; featured in 1995 Reading series, by Chgo. Writers in the Emerging Artists Project, A. Montgomery Ward Found., Chgo. Dept. Cultural Affairs and Ill. Arts Coun.; dir. demonstration Cardinal Chamber Ensemble. Rockefeller Found. fellow, 1965-67, Chgo. Office Fine Arts grantee, 1985-86. Mem. Am. Fedn. Musicians. Clubs: Classical Music Rap Sessions for Singles (dir. 1984—) (Chgo.). Roman Catholic. Avocations: tennis, discussions. Home and Office: 851 N Leavitt St Chicago IL 60622-7116

WYZAN, MICHAEL LOUIS, economist, researcher; b. Albany, N.Y., Feb. 3, 1955; s. Henry S. and Marjorie Hope (Burger) W.; m. Kie Min Tang, July 30, 1985; 1 child, Rebecca Ling. AB, Miami U., Oxford, Ohio, 1975; PhD, U. N.C., 1979. Assoc. prof. econs. Ill. State U., Normal, 1982-91; vis. staff economist planning and econ. analysis staff U.S. Dept. State, Washington, 1990-91; advisor to Bulgarian Fin. Ministry U.S. Treas. Dept., Sofia, Bulgaria, 1994-95; sr. economist Open Media Rsch. Inst., Prague, 1995-97; assoc. prof. Stockholm Sch. Econs., 1993—; rsch. scholar Internat. Inst. for Applied Sys. Analysis, Laxenburg, Austria, 1997-2000; econ. advisor USAID, Yerevan, Armenia, 2000—. Editor: The Political Economy of Ethnic Discrimination and Affirmative Action: A Comparative Perspective, 1990, First Steps Toward Economic Independence: New States of the Post-Communist World, 1995; co-editor: Economic Change in the Balkan States: Albania, Bulgaria, Romania and Yugoslavia, 1991, The Mixed Blessing of Financial Inflows: Transition Countries in Comparative Perspective, 1999. Jewish. Avocations: travel, fiction, horseback riding. Office: 7020 Yerevan Pl Dulles VA 20189-7020 E-mail: wyzan@arminco.com., mwyzan@usaid.gov.

WYZNER, EUGENIUSZ, diplomat; b. Chelmno, Poland, Oct. 31, 1931; s. Henryk and Janina (Czaplicka) W.; m. Elzbieta Laudanska, June 27, 1961; 1 child, Jaroslaw. Student, U. Warsaw, Poland, 1952; LLM, U. Warsaw, 1954; postgrad., Hague (The Netherlands) Acad. of Internat. Law, 1958. With Ministry Fgn. Affairs, Poland, 1952-54; sec. of the neutral supervisory com. Korea, 1954-55; mem. staff Ministry Fgn. Affairs, Warsaw, 1956-61; ambassador to Geneva, 1973-78; dir. dept. internat. orgns. Ministry Fgn. Affairs, Warsaw, 1978-81; chmn. UN Disarmament Commn., 1982; undersec. gen. conf. services and spl. assignments UN, N.Y.C., 1982-92, undersec. gen. pub. info., 1992-94; dep. min. for fgn. affairs Republic of Poland, Warsaw, 1994-95, 1st dep. min. for fgn. affairs, sec. of state Poland, 1996-97; permanent rep. amb. to UN N.Y.C., 1998-99; vice-chmn. Internat. Civil Svc. Commn., 1999—. Vice-chmn. preparatory com. Internat. Conf. on Human Rights, chmn. com. on periodic reports on human rights, 1965-68; chmn. sub-com. of UN Com. on Peaceful Uses of Outer Space, 1967-82; pres. Rev. Conf. of Parties to Treaty on Prohibition of Nuclear Weapons, 1977; mem. Polish del. of UN Gen. Assembly, UN Programme Planing and Budgeting Bd., 1984-93; chmn. UN Publs. Bd., 1982-93; chmn. com. for 2000 review conf. of the parties to the treaty on the non-proliferation of nuclear weapons, 1998-99. Decorated Cross of Polonia Restituta Polish Council of State, 1969, 77, Golden Cross of Merit, 1964, Comdr.'s Cross with a star Order of Polonia Restituta, 1996, Comdr. of the Legion d'Honneur, Pres. of France and Grand Comdr.'s Cross of the Order of the Phoenix, Pres. of Greece, 1996. Mem. Internat. Inst. Outer Space Law (bd. dirs. 1974—, Citation 1977), Internat. Peace Acad. (bd. dirs. 1983-91), Internat. Congress Inst. (bd. dirs. 1987-90), Internat. Congress Acad. (mem. senate 1990-95). Office: Internat Civil Svc Commn Rm 1050 2 United Nations Plz New York NY 10017-4403 E-mail: wyzner@un.org.

XAGAS, STEVEN GEORGE JAMES, executive search firm executive, consultant, researcher; b. St. Charles, Ill., May 9, 1951; s. Gus and Carolyn Ann (Schneider) X.; m. Yvonne Schafer, Oct. 19, 1985; 1 child, Jacob Steven. BS in Psychology, Guilford Coll., 1973; postgrad., George Williams Coll., 1975. Cert. pers. cons. Homebound detention supr., sr. counselor 16th Judicial Ct. Dist., Geneva, 1974-77; project coord., psychotherapist Tri City Family Project and Kane County Sch. Office, 1977-80; exec. recruiter Search Dynamics, Chgo., 1980-82, CPS, Inc., Westchester, 1982-83; founder, pres. Xagas & Assocs., Geneva, 1983—. Career columnist, Chronicle Newspaper, St.Charles, Il., 1987-91, Am. Soc. Quality-Chgo. Newsletter, 1987-90; condr. job search seminars., employment cons., met. area Chgo., 1980—; spkr. in field. Columnist Y2K Line, Kane County Chronicle, 1999-2000; moderator, exec. prodr. video Face The People: Roundtable 2000, 1999-2000. Fundraiser Cancer Soc., Kane County, Ill., 1975—, Heart Assn., Kane County, 1982—; moderator city govt. and utilities reps. Year 2000 Panel Forum, Kane County, 1998; chmn. St. Mark's Year 2000 Task Force, Kane County, 1999-2000; cmty. vol. numerous social and human svc. orgns., Kane County, 1974—. Recipient Community Svc. Recognition, Tri City Family Project, Geneva, 1980, Honorable Mention award, Nat. Communicator Awards, 2001, Svc. recognition award Am. Soc. Quality, 1986, Exemplary status Law Enforcement Assistance Adminstrn., 1980. Mem. Am. Soc. Quality (sr.), Ill. Mgmt. and Exec. Search Consortium (charter mem.). Lutheran. Avocations: martial arts (black belt), bridge, lumberjacking, teaching adult self-defense, model ship building. Office: Xagas & Assocs 1127 Fargo Blvd Ste 1 Geneva IL 60134-2949 Fax: (630) 232-7154.

XANTHOPOULOS, PHILIP, SR. brokerage house executive; b. Pottstown, Pa., Sept. 20, 1944; s. Sopho and Beatrice Ann (Rudwolis) X.; m. Diane Mae Johnson, June 17, 1966 (div. 1976); children: Philip, Sherri Lynn; m. Iris Elana Bowden, Dec. 31, 1977. Student, Valley Forge Mil. Acad.; BA, Pa. State U., 1966. CFP. Owner several businesses, Pottstown, 1967-79; account exec. Merrill Lynch Pierce Fenner & Smith, Ft. Walton Beach, Fla., 1979-83; 1st v.p., portfolio mgr. Prudential Securities, Inc., 1983-97, v.p. tng. ctr. instr., mgmt. tng. assoc., 1997-98, v.p., br. mgr. Venice, Fla., 1999-2000, v.p., instr. Sr. Tng. Inst. N.Y.C., 2001—. Past. pres. Okaloosa Symphony Orch.; bd. dirs. Panhandle Animal Welfare Soc., Speech and Hearing Clinic. Mem. Internat. Assn. for Fin. Planning, Ft. Walton Bech Hosts Coun., Ft. Walton Beach C. of C., Ft. Walton Yacht Club, Millionaires Club, Krewe of Bowlegs, Masons, Sertoma (past pres.), Rotary (past pres.). Avocations: golf, stereo and electronics, collecting records, 50s music. Office: Prudential Securities Inc 2000 PGA Blvd Ste 2104 North Palm Beach FL 33408 E-mail: philip_xanthopoulos@prusec.com., philipx@earthlink.net.

XENAKIS, STEPHEN NICHOLAS, psychiatrist, army officer; b. Washington, July 5, 1948; s. Stanley Steve and Mary Alexandria (Poulos) X.; m. Mary Elizabeth Boddie, Jan. 19, 1974 (dec.); children: Nicholas John, Lea Elizabeth. AB, Princeton U., 1970; MD, U. Md., Balt., 1974; postgrad., Balt.-D.C. Psychoanalytic Inst., 1972-75, Armed Forces Staff Coll., 1984-85, U.S. Army War Coll., 1989-90. Diplomate Am. Bd. Psychiatry and Neurology. Commd. U.S. Army, 1972, advanced through grades to brig. gen., 1994; resident U. Md., Balt., 1974; intern Letterman Army Med. Ctr., Presidio of San Francisco, 1974-75, resident in psychiatry, 1975-78; fellow in child and adolescent psychiatry Letterman Army Med. Ctr., U. Calif., San Francisco, 1978-80; chief dept. psychiatry Darnell Army Cmty. Hosp., Ft. Hood, Tex., 1980-82; divsn. surgeon 1st Cav. Divsn., 1982-84; chief child, adolescent, family psychiatry Eisenhower Army Med. Ctr., Ft. Gordon, Ga., 1985-86, dep. comdr. clin. svcs., dir. med. edn., 1986-89; comdr. Blanchfield Army Cmty. Hosp., 1990-93; project mgr. AMEDD Vanguard, Fairfax, Va., 1993, TRICARE S.E., Augusta, Ga., 1994-95; cmdg. gen. Southeast Regional Command Eisenhower Army Med. Ctr., Ft. Gordon, 1995-97, asst. surgeon gen., 1997-98. Pres., CEO XenaLex, 1998—; clin. prof. Uniformed Svcs. of Health Scis., Bethesda, Md., 1985—, Med. Coll. of Ga., Augusta, 1985—; lectr., author Porter Lecture, 1989. Contbr. articles to profl. jours. Bd. dirs. Univ. Health Found., 1998. Fellow Am. Acad. and Adolescent Psychiatry, Am. Psychiat. Assn., Am. Coll. Physician Execs., Assn. Mil. Surgeon U.S. Greek Orthodox. Office: Xana Lex 730 Somerset Way Augusta GA 30909 E-mail: sxenakis@alltel.net.

XENOPHONTOS, CHRISTOS A. university educator; b. Nicosia, Cyprus, Dec. 25, 1967; s. Andreas Xenophontos, Maro Xenophontos; m. Cally Alevrofas; children: Roman, Lucas. PhD in Applied Math., U. Math., 1996. Vis. asst. prof. Ohio State U., Lima, 1996—97; asst. prof. Clarkson U., Potsdam, NY, 1997—2001. Office: Loyola Coll Math Scis 4501 N Charles St Baltimore MD 21117-2699 Office Fax: 410-617-2803. Business E-Mail: cxenophontos@loyola.edu.

XEPAPAS, ANARGYROS, architect; b. Sparta, Greece, Apr. 10, 1932; came to U.S., 1951. s. Nicholaos and Penelope N. X.; m. Aliki A. B in Architecture, Catholic U. Am., 1956, M in Architecture, 1957, PhD in Architecture, 1958. lic. Nat. Coun. Architects. Architect Murphy and Locraft, Washington, U.S. Dept. Edn. and Welfare, Washington, U.S. Dept. Defense, Washington, Vets. Adminstrn., Washington. Bd. trustees Riddle Aeronautical U., Daytona Beach, Fla., 1984, Bethune Cookman, U., Daytona Beach, 1983; bd. commn. Halifax Hosp., 1983; delegate (Fla.) Nat. Democratic Convention, San Francisco, 1984. Recipient Architect of Yr., Catholic U. Am., 1977, Key to the City award, Daytona Beach, Fla., 1977, St. Paul's award, Greek Orthodox Ch., 1992, Superior Performance award U.S. Govt., 1961. Mem. Am. Hellenic Progressive Assn. (Aristotelian award 1996, Ahepan of Yr. 1999), Nat. Democratic Com. Greek Orthodox. Avocations: design, soccer. Home: 2612 N Halifax Ave Daytona Beach FL 32118-3244

XI, HONGKANG, medical sciences researcher; b. Shanghai, China, Apr. 14, 1967; s. Xin Xi and Qindi Nee; m. Lei Wang, Dec. 26, 1999. BS, Fudan U., Shanghai, 1989; PhD, U. South Fla., 2001. Rsch. asst. Shanghai Textile Hosp., 1989-92; rsch. assoc. Shanghai Inst. Immunology, Shanghai 2d Med. U., 1992-96; grad. rsch. asst. U. South Fla. Coll. Medicine, Tampa, 1996-2001; postdoctoral fellow Emory U. Sch. Medicine, Atlanta, 2001—. Contbr. articles to profl. jours. Mem. AAAS, AAI. Office: Emory U Sch Medicine Dept Pathology and Lab Med 1639 Pierce Dr WMB 7206 Atlanta GA 30322

XI, NING, engineering educator, researcher; came to U.S., 1985; s. Fulin Xi and Guanling Wen; m. Li Liu. MS, Northeastern U., Boston, 1987, Washington U., St. Louis, 1990, DSc, 1993. Postdoctoral rschr. Washington U., St. Louis, 1993-94, asst. prof., 1994-97; assoc. prof. Mich. State U., E. Lansing, 1997—. Editor: IEEE Transactions on Robotics and Automation, 1998. Recipient Career award NSF, 1997. Mem. IEEE (Acad. Career award 1999), ASME. Avocations: sports, fishing, travel. Office: Mich State U 2120 Engineering Bldg East Lansing MI 68824 E-mail: xin@egr.msu.edu.

XIA, JIDING, chemical engineering educator; b. Jiangyin, Jiangsu, China, Mar. 23, 1921; s. Baogen Xia; m. Ming Yu, Oct. 1, 1958; children: Wei, Men. BS, Zhejiang U., Hangzhou, China, 1945, MS, 1948. Assoc. prof. Haijiang U., Fujian, China, 1949-50, Nanjing (China) Normal U., 1953-54; dir. teaching and rsch. divsn. Southeast U. (China), 1954-58; assoc. prof. and dir. teaching/rsch. divsn. Wuxi (China) U. Light Industry, 1958-85; prof. chem. engring. Wuxi U. of Light Industry, 1985-92; rsch. chemist U. Wis., Madison, 1995-96. Vis. prof. Wayne State U., Detroit, 1993-95; mem. expert group synthetic detergents and fatty acids, Ministry of Light Industry China, 1979-86; vis. prof. The VI Univ. of Paris, 1986; , evaluation com. acad. degree Authorized U., 1980-84, Jiangsu Light Industry Sr. Engrs., 1982-92; project evaluator China Nat. Natural Sci. Found. Surface Chemistry, 1985—; cons. Chemithon Co., Seattle, 1990-93, Aging Toilet Soap Factory, China, 1991—, Tianjin Rsch. Inst. Interface and Colloid Scis., 1993, Stepan Co., Chgo., 1994, Proctor & Gamble Co., Cin., 1994-95, Vista Chem. Co., Houston, 1994—;mem. adv. com. Internat. Symposium on Surfactants in Solution, 1993. Author: Synthetic Detergents, 1976, Chemistry and Technology of Surfactants and Detergents, 1997; author and editor: Protein-Based Surfactants, 2001; editor: Composite Soaps, 1987; translator: Comprehensive Refining of Sunflower Seed Oil, 1956, Chemistry of Oil and Fats, 1958, Manufacture of Detergents, 1986; mem. editl. bd. Jour. Surfactant Industry, 1982-90, Jour. Petro-Finechemicals, 1982, Chinese Ency. LIght Industry, 1987-91; contbr. more than 120 articles to acad. jours. Recipient award Ministry of Petroleum Industry for EOR Project, 1992, Outstanding Contbn. to Chinese Higher Edn. award State Coun., 1992, Ministry of Light Industry for rsch. on composite soaps, 1983, Remarkable Achievement in Sci. and Tech. Invention and Innovation, UN, 1994; Excellent Advanced Sci. Rsch. fellow Wuxi, 1990, 93. Mem. China Assn. Surfactants and Detergent Industry (hon. dir. 1992, standing dir. 1983-92), Jiangsu Soc. of Daily Chem. Industry (chmn. 1978-85), Am. Chem. Soc. Home: Wuxi U Light Industry Box 66 Wuxi Jiangsu 214036 China Fax: 248-577-1453. E-mail: xiajiding@aol.com.

XIA, LULIN, former securities dealer; b. Shanghai, China, Nov. 16, 1973; s. Taichun Xia and Huazhen Wang. BA summa cum laude, Mount Holyoke Coll., 1997. Rsch. fellow Rockefeller U., N.Y.C., 1996; fin. analyst Credit Suisse 1st Boston, 1997-99; investment profl. Forstmann Little & Co., 1999—. Recipient Achievement award Chemistry Rubber Co., 1994, Abby Howe Turner Found. award, 1996; Sarah Williston scholar Mount Holyoke Coll., 1995, 96, 97. Mem. Sigma Xi, Phi Beta Kappa. Avocations: travel, photography, cooking. Office: Forstmann Little and Co 767 Fifth Ave New York NY 10153 Fax: 212-759-9059. E-mail: lxia@forstmannlittle.com.

XIA, RENJIE, civil engineer, researcher; b. Shanghai, China, Dec. 25, 1943; came to U.S., 1986; s. Yalun and Xizhu (Mao) X.; m. Aifang He, Aug. 25, 1988; children: Tao, Fangzhou. BS, U. Agrl. Engring., Beijing, 1968; ME, East China Tech. U. Water Resources, Nanjing, 1982; PhD, U. Ill., 1991. Registered profl. engr., Ill. Engr. East China Tech. U. Water Resources, 1979-86; rsch. asst. U. Ill., Urbana-Champaign, 1986-87, Ill. State Water Survey, Champaign, 1987-91, assoc. profl. scientist, 1991-96, profl. scientist, 1996—. Contbr. articles to profl. jours. Mem. ASCE, Internat. Assn. for Hydraulic Rsch. Achievements include contribution to the discovery of significance of momentum and pressure coefficients on using Saint-Venant equations to solve unsteady flow problems; contribution to the detection of distribution of turbulent velocity fluctuations and relation between mean and maximum velocities in natural rivers. Avocations: playing piano, watching movies, travel. Office: Ill State Water Survey 2204 Griffith Dr Champaign IL 61820-7495

XIAO, GUISHAN, research scientist; b. Shaoyang, China, Aug. 20, 1963; came to U.S., 1995; s. XiangLi Xiao and Jingfeng Zhou; m. Hongyu Chen, Feb. 21, 1967. Master's degree, Beijing Agrl. U., 1992; PhD, Chinese Acad. Scis., Beijing, 1995. Instr. asst. Hunan Agrl. U., China, 1980-84; fellow Hunan U., Changsha, 1986-87, Peking U., Beijing, 1987-88; rsch. asst. Beijing Agrl. U., 1989-92, Chinese Acad. Scis., Beijing, 1992-95; postdoctoral fellow U. Tex. Health Sci. Ctr., Houston, 1995-97. Postdoctoral assoc. fellow Baylor Coll. Medicine, Houston, 1997—. Recipient III Grade prize Advancement of Sci. and Tech. China, 1987. Mem. AAAS, Am. Soc. for Biochemistry and Molecular Biology, Chinese Soc. for Biochemistry and Molecular Biology, Chinese Soc. for Biophysics and Structural Biology. Buddhist. Achievements include patent for separation techniques of PC factor in algae; biological and pathophysiological functions of Tyrosine free radical in catalysis of prostaglandin synthesse from human cells; findings of P152 factor participates the reaction of graft compatibility. Home: # 2 3100 Sawtelle Blvd Apt 204 Los Angeles CA 90066-1479

XIAO, YING, medical physicist, researcher, educator; b. Wuhan, China; d. Weiping Xiao and Shuping Shen; m. Zhibao Fu, Jan. 12, 1990; children: Michelle, Howard. BS, Qinghua U., Beijing, 1989; MS, Temple U., 1992, PhD, 1996. Diplomate Am. Bd. Radiology. Tchg. asst. Temple U., Phila., 1990-92, rsch. asst., 1992-96; postdoctoral fellow U. Pa., 1996-98; asst. prof. Thomas Jefferson U., 1998—. Contbr. articles to profl. jours. Mem. IEEE Computer Soc., Am. Phys. Soc., Am. Assn. Physicists Medicine, Del. Chpt. Am. Assn. Physicists in Medicine. Office: Thomas Jefferson U 111 S 11th St Philadelphia PA 19107 Fax: 215-955-5331. E-mail: ying.xiao@mail.tju.edu.

XIE, JINGPING, microbiologist, pediatrician; b. Anshan, Liaoning, China, Dec. 26, 1961; came to U.S., 1998; d. Baokui Xie and Guizhen Yu; m. Qiang Liu, Aug. 26, 1986; 1 child, Jingxiao Liu. MD, China Med. U., Shenyang, Liaoning, 1984; MS, Peking Union Med. Coll., Beijing, 1989. Med. diplomate. Postdoct. fellow Capital Inst. Pediats., Beijing, 1984-86, rsch. assoc., 1989-91, asst. researcher, 1991-97, assoc. researcher, 1997—. Vis. scholar U. Ala., Birmingham, 1998-99, U. Mich., Ann Arbor, 1999-2000. Contbr. articles to profl. jours. Established Scientist travel grantee 9th Internat. Congress Internat. Orgn. Mycoplasmology, 1992, chapter grantee Beijing Municipality, 1996; recipient Achievements in Sci. and Tech. Beijing Municipality, 1987. Mem. Am. Soc. Microbiology, Chinese Microbiology Soc., Infectious Diseases Soc. Am. Avocations: singing, swimming, running. Home: 5913 Lafayette Ln Ann Arbor MI 48103 Office: U Mich 109 S Observatory St Ann Arbor MI 48109

XIE, RUI-HUA, physicist, researcher; b. Ganxian, Jiangxi, China, Sept. 21, 1969; arrived in Can., 1997; s. Xiangan Xie and Yuying Yang; m. Qin Rao, Dec. 28, 1995; 1 child, Jianing. BS, Wuhan U., 1991, M of Engring., 1993; PhD, Nanjing U., 1996. Rsch. asst. Wuhan (China) U., 1991-93, Nanjing (China) U., 1993-96; rschr. CCAST, Beijing, 1996-97, U. Toronto, Ont., Can., 1997-98; Alexander von Humboldt fellow Max-Planck Inst. Ströngsforschung, Göttingen, Germany, 1998-2000; tchg., rsch. asst. Queen's U., Ont., 2000—. Contbr. articles to profl. jours. Avocation: philately. Home: 11-203 17 Van Order Dr Kingston ON Canada K7M 1B5 Office: Queen's U Dept Chemistry Kingston ON Canada K7L 3N6 E-mail: xie@chem.queensu.ca.

XIE, SHANG-PING, environmental studies educator; b. Quzhou, Zhejiang, China, Aug. 8, 1963; s. Chang-Tu Wang, Aug. 17, 1988; children: Weijiang Cordelia. BSc, Shangdong Coll., 1984; MSc, Tohoku U., 1988, DSc, 1991. Program scientist Princeton (N.J.) U., 1991-93; rsch. assoc. U. Washington, Seattle, 1993-94; assoc. prof. Hokkaido U., Sapporo, Japan, 1994-99, Univ. Hawaii, 1999—. Session convenor Am. Geophys. Union, Washington, 1996; spkr. in field; vis. fellow Nat. Sci. Found. of China, 1996. Editor Jour. Meteorol. Soc. Japan; contbr. articles to profl. jours. Reciepient Young Investigator award Ministry of Edn., Culture and Sci. of Japan. Mem. Am. Geophys. Union, Oceanographical Soc. of Japan, Meteorol. Soc. Japan (Yamamoto-Shyono medal 1996, Soc. medal 2002). Avocations: travel, swimming, reading. Office: Intl Pacif Rsch Ctr SOEST U Hawaii 2525 Correa Rd Honolulu HI 96822 E-mail: xie@soest.hawaii.edu.

XIE, YU, adult education educator; b. Zhenjiang, Jiangsu, China, Oct. 12, 1959; s. Liangyao Xie and Huazhen Zhao; m. Yijun Helen Gu, Dec. 1985; children: Raissa, Kevin. BA in Metallurgical Engring., Shanghai U. of Tech., China, 1982; MA in History of Sci., MS in Sociology, U. Wis., Madison, 1984, PhD in Sociology, 1989. From asst. to assoc. prof. U. Mich., Ann Arbor, 1989-96, John Stephenson Perrin prof. sociology, 1996—. Mem. adv. panel sociology program NSF, 1995-97; bd. dirs. Bd. Overseers of Gen. Social Survey. Dep. editor Am. Sociol. Review, 1996—; mem. editl. bd. Sociol. Methods and Rsch., 1989—, Am. Jour. Sociology, 1994-96, Sociol. Methodology, 1994-97; presenter in field; contbr. articles to profl. jours. Spencer fellow Nat. Acad. Edn., 1991-92; recipient Young Investigator award NSF, 1992-97, Faculty Scholar award William T. Grant Found., 1994-99. Mem. Am. Stat. Assn., Am. Sociol. Assn., Sociol. Rsch. Assn. (elected mem.), Population Assn. of Am. Office: U Mich Population Studies Ctr 426 Thompson St Ann Arbor MI 48104-2321 Fax: 734-998-7415. E-mail: yuxie@umich.edu.

XIE, YULONG, geostatistician, researcher; b. Wugang, Hunan Province, China, Jan. 21, 1964; s. Qi Wen Xie and Jin E. Zhang; m. Xiao Li Zhang, 1986; children: Xiao Hai, Xi. BS, Xiangtan U., China, 1983; MS, Hunan U., Changsha, China, 1988, PhD, 1993. Asst. prof. Xiangtan U., 1983—85, 1988—91; vis. scientist U. Valencia, Spain, 1993—95; postdoctoral rsch. assoc. Idaho State U., Pocatello, 1995—96, Clarkson U., Potsdam, NY, 1996—98, U. Alta., Edmonton, Canada, 1998—2000, Pacific N.W. Nat. Lab., Richland, Wash., 2000—02, sr. rsch. scientist, 2002—. Co-author: (book chpt.) Rule Induction Algorithm for Application to Geological and Petrophysical Data, 2002; contbr. articles to profl. jours. Recipient Tier-one reward for Promotion of Sci. and Tech., State Edn. Commn. China, 1994, Tier-two reward for Promotion of Sci. and Tech., Ministry Machinery Industry China, 1994; fellow Visiting Scientist, Spanish Ministry Edn. and Sci., 1994; scholar, DuPont Inc., 1992. Mem.: AAAS, Am. Geophysical Union, Am. Chem. Soc., Soc. Petroleum Engrs., Internat. Assn. Hydrological Scis., Internat. Assn. Math. Geology. Home: 1930 George Washington Way #208 Richland WA 99352 Office: Pacific NW Nat Lab PO Box 999 MS K6 81 Richland WA 99352 Office Fax: 509-376-5368. Business E-Mail: YuLong.Xie@pnl.gov.

XIONG, FUQIN, electrical engineering educator; b. Neijiang, China, Apr. 21, 1946; s. Yicheng Xiong and Beiying Huang; m. Jialan Min, Oct. 1, 1971; childrren: Yan Xiong, Wei Xiong. BSc, Tsinghua U., Beijing, 1970, MSc, 1982; PhD, U. Man., Winnipeg, Can., 1989. Tchr. Tsinghua U., 1970-82, lectr., 1982-85; from asst. to assoc. prof. elec. engring. Cleve. State U., 1990—2002, prof. elec. engring., 2002—. Vis. prof. Tsinghua U., 1997; fellow City U. Hong Kong, 1997; chmn. grad. program, dept. elec. and computer engring. Cleve. State U. Author: Digital Modulation Techniques, 2000; contbg. author: Wiley Encyclopedia of Telecommunications, 2002; contbr. articles to profl. jours.; reviewer IEEE Trans. on Comm., Inst. Elec. Engring. Procs. on Comm., Great Britain and No. Ireland. Rsch. fellow Natural Sci. and Engring. Rsch. Coun. Can., 1990; Rsch. grantee NASA, 1991-94, 2001-02. Mem. IEEE (sr.). Office: Cleveland State U Euclid at E 24th Cleveland OH 44115 E-mail: fxiong@csuohio.edu.

XIONG, TOUSU SAYDANGNMVANG, minister; b. Hmong Long Chieng, Laos, June 23, 1966; arrived in U.S., 1976; s. Nhialue Saydang and May (Vang) X.; m. Zoua Pahoua Moua, Sept. 14, 1993; children: Chivkeeb Genesis Toupa, Naamonunas Ruth, Nujsimloob Hebrews. BA in Bibl. Studies, Simpson Coll., San Francisco, 1989; MA in Theology, Mennonite Brethren Bibl. Sem., Fresno, Calif., 1991; AS in Computerized Acctg., Phillips Jr. Coll., Fresno, Calif., 1993. Ordained to ministry Christian and Missionary Alliance, 1991. Assoc. min. Hmong San Raphael (Calif.) Bapt. Ch., 1986-88; youth min. Hmong Alliance Ch. of Santa Barbara, Goleta, Calif., 1984-85, Hmong Alliance Ch. of Fresno, 1989—. Scoutmaster Boy Scouts Am., 1984—85, Eagle Scout, 1983. Home: PO Box 12068 Brooksville FL 34603-2068 Office: Hmong Alliance Ch Fresno 8234 E Belmont Ave Fresno CA 93727-9725 E-mail: xteagle76@wmconnect.com. *In my life as I have experienced both the world of the Hmong Animistic Religion in the East and the Christian faith from the West, I have come to realize that Jesus Christ is superior, for Jesus is the way, the truth and the life pointing us towards the Supreme and Creator Being.*

XIONG, YONGLIANG, geochemist; b. Guiyang , Guizhou Province, China, Aug. 7, 1960; parent Weici Xiong, Jinghua Li; m. Jie Tang; children: Yoni. PhD, U. Idaho, 1999. Rsch. assoc. Rutgers U., Piscataway, NJ, 2000—02; rsch. scientist Sandia Nat. Labs., Carlsbad, N.Mex., 2002—. Contbr. articles to profl. jours. Grantee, Geol. Soc. Am., 1997. Mem.: Am. Geophys. Union. Home: 1300 N Pate St J186 Carlsbad NM 88220 Office: Sandia Nat Labs 4100 National Parks Hwy Carlsbad NM 88220 Personal E-mail: yongliangxiong@netscape.net. Business E-Mail: yxiong@sandia.gov.

XU, BIN, research scientist; b. Xin Chang, ZheJiang, China, May 14, 1964; s. PeiTing Xu and Xia Lu; m. YueCai Meng, Oct. 12, 1994; 1 child, Meng Yuan. BS, East China Normal U., Shanghai, 1984, MS, 1987; D Econs., Fudan U., Shanghai, 1998. Cert. tchr., Shanghai. Traine rsch. fellow Shanghai U. Fin. and Econs., 1987-89, East China U. Sci. and Tech., Shanghai, 1989-90, asst. rsch. fellow, 1990-98, assoc. rsch. fellow, 1998—. Recipient Excellent Paper award Constrn. Dept. HeNan Provincial Govt., 1990. Mem. Chinese Assn. Sci. Poets, Shanghai Acad. Soc. Ecol. Economy, Shanghai Acad. Soc. Urban Economy. Avocations: reading newspapers, television, walking, library. Home: Apt 302 Bldg 2 Ln 135 Guonian Rd Shanghai 200433 China Office: East China U Sci and Tech 130 Meilong Rd Shanghai 200237 China E-mail: drxubin@163.net.

XU, CHEN-WEI, data processing executive; b. Nanjing, Jiangsu, China, Nov. 6, 1956; s. Danian Xu and Nonghua Qiu; m. Hongqi Duan; children: Shengjun, Peter. PhD, U. Toronto, Ont., Can., 1995. Mgr. statis. modeling Bank of Montreal, Toronto, 1997—2000; mgr. database and analysis GM, Detroit, 2000—. Contbr. rsch. papers to profl. jours. Pres. PhD Student Assn., Faculty of Mgmt., U. Toronto, Canada, 1994—95. Recipient Reviewership for Math. Rev., Am. Math. Soc., 1990—96. Home Fax: 519-967-0059. Personal E-mail: chenweixu@aol.com.

XU, CHUNHUI, systems engineer, educator; b. Daye, China, Mar. 15, 1964; m. Ping Ding, 1990; children: Zhouyuan, Kaylin. B in Engring., Huazhong U. Sci. & Technology, 1984, M in Engring., 1987, PhD, 1990; D in Engring., Tokyo Inst. Technology, 1995. Asst. prof. Hiroshima Inst. Tech., Japan, 1995-99, assoc. prof. Japan, 1999—2000; rsch. fellow Harvard U., 2001—. Mem.: IEEE, Int Fedn Automatic Control, Japan Soc Mgmt Info, Opers Research Soc Japan. Office: Harvard U DEAS 33 Oxford St MD 317 Cambridge MA 02138 E-mail: xchunhi@yahoo.com.

XU, HAO, electrical engineer; b. Wuhan, China, Feb. 28, 1971; s. Shizheng Xu and Daolan Zhang; m. Lin Jiang. Grad., Moscow Power Engring. Inst. and Tech. U.; PhD, Va. Tech. U., 2000. Rsch. asst. Mobile and Portable Radio Rsch. Group, Blacksburg, Va., 1996—2000; mem. tech. staff Bell-labs, Holmdel, NJ, 2000—. Contbr. articles to profl. jours.; editor: IEEE Transactoins on Wireless Comm. Mem.: IEEE (mem. tech. com. ICC conf., Comm. Soc. Steve O. Rice award 1999), Internat. Conf. Comms., Sigma Xi, Eta Kappa Nu. Office: Bell-labs/Lucent Techs 791 Holmdel-Keyport Rd R-111 Holmdel NJ 07733 Office Fax: 732-888-7074. Business E-Mail: haoxu@lucent.com.

XU, KANG, research electrochemist; b. Chengdu, Sichuan, China, July 3, 1964; s. Guang qing Xu and Qi lin Zhang; m. Ying Zhang; children: Alice, Michael. PhD, Ariz. State U., 1996. Cert. electrochemistry and polymer chemistry. Rsch. chemist Chengdu Inst. Organic Chemistry, Acad. Scis., Chengdu, China, 1988—92; postdoctoral Ariz. State U., Tempe, Ariz., 1996—97; assoc. NRC NAS, Washington, 1997—2000; rsch. contractor Am. Soc. Engring., 2000—02. Active mem. Electrochemical Soc., Pennington, NJ, 1995—2002. Mem.: Electrochemical Soc. Achievements include patents in field. Home: 10521 Polk Square Ct North Potomac MD 20878 Office: Army Rsch Lab 2800 Powder Mill Road Adelphi MD 20878 Home Fax: 301-279-5952; Office Fax: 301-394-0273. Personal E-mail: kang_xu@hotmail.com. Business E-Mail: kangxu@mail.com.

XU, LI, science educator; b. Changsha, China, Sept. 30, 1963; came to U.S., 1992; s. Xitang Wang and Qiuhua Xu; m. Liping Yu; 1 child, Matt Alex. MB, Hengyang (China) Med. Coll., 1985; M in Medicine, Capital U. Med. Scis., Beijing, 1988; PhD, U. Fla., 1999. Resident in otolaryngology Beijing Tong Ren Hosp., 1988-91; rsch. asst. Beijing Inst. Otorhinolaryngology, 1988-91; rsch. fellow U. Basel, Switzerland, 1991-92; postdoctoral fellow U. Mich., Ann Arbor, Mich., 1999—2001; asst. prof. Ohio U., Athens, 2001—. Rsch. fellow Swiss Nat. Rsch. Found., 1991, fellow NIH, Bethesda, Md., 2000. Mem. Assn. for Rsch. in Otolaryngology, Collegium Oto-rhino-laryngologicum Amicitiae Sacrum. Office: Ohio U Sch Hearing Speech & Lang Scis Athens OH 45701 E-mail: xul@ohio.edu.

XU, PING, chemist; b. Shanghai, China, Apr. 29, 1957; came to U.S., 1985; s. Yuan Xu and Changfu Zhu; m. Shuhong Wang, Feb. 17, 1987; children: Helen W., Olivia W. BS, East China U. Chem. Tech., Shanghai, 1982, MS, 1984, U. Cin., 1987, PhD, 1991. Asst. prof. East China U. Chem. Tech., 1984-85; Paul J. Flory meml. fellow U. Cin., 1990-92; sr. rsch. chemist Quantum Chem. Corp., Cin., 1991-94; polymer scientist W.L. Gore & Assocs., Inc., Elkton, Md., 1994—. Vis. scientist Oak Ridge (Tenn.) Nat. Lab., 1998—; vis. scientist Nat. Inst. Stds. and Tech., Gaithersburg, Md., 1999—. Contbr. numerous articles to sci. jours. Mem. AAAS, Am. Chem. Soc., Material Rsch. Soc. Achievements include research in engineering, rubber elasticity, polymer morphology and polymer physics. Home: 22 Piersons Rdg Hockessin DE 19707-9291 Office: WL Gore & Assocs Inc 2401 Singerly Rd Elkton MD 21921-2733 E-mail: pxu@aol.com.

XU, XIAO-BANG, engineering educator; b. Huize, Yunnan, China, Feb. 15, 1945; came to U.S., 1981; s. Bailing Xiong and Lan Xu; m. Yi Hong Wu, Sept. 30, 1973; 1 child, Jack J. Xiong. BSe, Tsinghua U., Beijing, China, 1968; PhD, U. Miss., 1985. Lectr. U. Houston, 1985; vis. instr. Clemson (S.C.) U., 1985, vis. asst. prof., 1986-88, asst. prof., 1988-94, assoc. prof., 1994—. Contbr. articles to profl. jours. Rsch. grant Elec. Power Rsch. Inst., 1992, NSF, 1996, Duke Power Co., 1992, 99, S.C. Elec. and Gas Co., 1992. Mem. IEEE, Electromagnetics Acad., Profl. Soc. of Antennas and Prop., Prof. Soc. of Microwave T&T, Phi Kappa Phi. Avocations: music, tennis, gardening, walking, reading. Office: ECE Dept Clemson U Clemson SC 29634-0001

XU, XIAOCHUN, biologist, researcher; b. Qianshan, Anhui, China, Aug. 13, 1958; came to U.S., 1992; s. Daren Xu and Shuping Wang; m. Gouqing Ge, July 1, 1983; 1 child, Jany. MD, Anhui Med. Coll., Hefei, 1982, MS, 1985; PhD, U. Göttingen, Germany, 1991. Rsch. asst. Anhui Med. U., 1985-86, asst. prof., 1987-88; rsch. assoc. U. Göttingen, 1988-91; postdoctoral fellow U. Tex., M.D. Anderson Cancer Ctr., Houston, 1992-95, asst. prof., 1995—. Author: (books) Meth. Mol. Biol. Retinoids, 1998, Handbook Exp. Pharm. Retinoids, 1999; contbr. rsch. papers to profl. jours. Grantee NIH, Nat. Cancer Inst., 1998. Mem. AAAS, Am. Assn. for Cancer Rsch., Am. Assn. for Preventive Oncology, M.D. Anderson Assn. Avocations: jogging, travel, movies, playing chess. Office: U Tex M D Anderson Cancer Ctr 1515 Holcombe Blvd Houston TX 77030-4009 E-mail: xxu@mdanderson.org.

XU, XIAOQING ELEANOR, finance educator; d. Dingwu Xu and Liqing Chen; m. Jiong Liu. BA in Econs., Zhongshan (Sun Yat-Sen) U., Guangzhou, China, 1992; MBA, Ind. State U., 1994; PhD in Fin., Syracuse U., 1998. Asst. prof. fin. St. Louis (Mo.) U., John Cook Sch. Bus., 1998—2002; assoc. prof. fin. Seton Hall U. Stillman Sch. Bus., South Oarange, NJ, 2002—. Mem.: Am. Fin. Assn., Fin. Mgmt. Assn. (program com. 2002). Office: Seton Hall Univ 400 S Orange Ave South Orange NJ 07079

XU, YING, computational biologist; b. Changchun, Jilin, People's Republic of China, Dec. 21, 1960; came to U.S., 1985; s. Ruran and Wengin (Pang) X.; m. Cindy Chenxin Zeng, Aug. 1, 1988; 1 child, Tony DongYi. BS in Computer Sci., Jilin U., Changchun, 1982, MS in Computer Sci., 1985; PhD in Computer Sci., U. Colo., 1991. Rsch. assoc. Oak Ridge (Tenn.) Nat. Lab., 1993-95; staff scientist Oak Ridge Nat. Lab., 1995-97, group leader, 1997—. Vis. asst. prof. Colo. Sch. Mines, Golden, 1991-93. Guest editor Jour. Combinational Optimization; contbr. more than 40 articles to profl. jours. including Jour. Computer and Sys. Scis., Jour. Computational Biology. Mem. AAAS, N.Y. Acad. Scis. Avocations: reading, popular science books, photography, Chinese chess. Office: Oak Ridge Nat Lab MS 6480 1060 Commerce Park Dr Oak Ridge TN 37830-8043

XU, YING-PEI, artist; b. Ningbo, Zheijiang, China, Jan. 31, 1941; came to U.S., 1992; s. Tong-Da and Yu-Mei(Ding) X.; m. Man-Li Bao, Jan. 1968; 1 child, Bing-Li; m. Jun Bi, Feb. 4, 1974; 1 child, Jing. BA, China Acad. Art, 1965, MA, 1980. Editor Fedn. Jiangxi Province, Nan Chang, China, 1965-68; artist Mus. Jiangxi Province, 1968-78; prof. China Acad. Art, Hangzhou, 1980-92; freelance artist Two World Arts Inc., N.Y.C., 1993-94; artist Julia Gray Ltd., 1994—. Exch. scholar Acad. Bildenden Kust, Hamburg, Germany, 1992. Author: Canadian Eskimos Art (translated), 1987, The World of Print, 1988; lectr. Hammand Mus., North Salem, N.Y., 1997; exhibited in group shows at Salmagundi Club, N.Y., 1997, Hecksher Mus. Art, L.I., N.Y., 1997, Internat. Graphic Art Exhbn., Stockholm, 1997, Oriental and Western Arts Auction, L.A., 1995, N.Y. State Mus., 1998, Cmty. Arts Assn., 1999; one man shows include Interchurch Ctr., N.Y., 1996, Gallery of Amerasia Bank, N.Y., 1994. Mem. Am. Artists Profl. League, All-China Artist Assn., All-China Printmaking Artist Assn. Avocation: dancing. Home: 18524 Dunlop Ave Saint Albans NY 11412-1514

XU, YONGZHI STEVE, mathematician; b. Guangzhou, Guangdong, China, Apr. 19, 1954; s. Xing Xu and Dayou Lu; m. Weiqun Feng Feng; children: Fei, Katie. PhD, U. Del., Newark, N.J., 1990. Asst. prof. Georgetown U., Washington, 1992—95; prof. math. U. Tenn., Chattanooga, 1995—. Editor: (book) Complex Analysis and Computer Algebra, 1999. Fellow China Bridge Internat. fellow, China Bridge Internat., 1996—2000. Office: U Tenn Dept Math Chattanooga TN 37403 Office Fax: 423-755-4586. Business E-Mail: yxu@cecasun.utc.edu.

XU, ZHENGYUAN, engineering educator; b. Taixing, China; s. Penghua Xu and Sanying Ji; m. Yan Deng, Oct. 1, 1992. PhD, Stevens Inst. Tech., 1999. Engr. Tsinghua UInisplendour Group Corp., Beijing, China, 1991-96; asst. prof. U. Calif., Riverside. Mem.: IEEE (sr.). Office: U Calif Dept EE 900 University Ave Riverside CA 92521 Fax: 909-787-2425. E-mail: dxu@ee.ucr.edu.

XU, ZHONG LING, mathematician, educator; b. Beijing, Mar. 6, 1937; came to U.S., 1984, naturalized; s. Chang L. and Ying (Yu) X.; m. Ling Wang, June 23, 1963; children: Nan, Rong. MS, U. Mass., 1987, PhD, 1990. Asst. prof. Acad. Scis. China, Beijing, 1978-84; assoc. prof. U. Tex. Pan Am., Brownsville, 1990-92, U. Tex., Brownsville, 1992-99, prof., 1999—. Mem. AIAA, IEEE Soc. Control and Decision, Am. Math. Soc., Soc. Indsl. and Applied Maths. Achievements include research in Hoo control for attitude of spacecraft, control of flexible smart structures and robotic control by fuzz logic. Avocations: oil painting, water color, calligraphy. Office: U Tex 80 Fort Brown St Brownsville TX 78520-4956 E-mail: zhong@utbl.utb.edu.

XU, ZONG-RONG, chemist, educator; b. Xiamen, Fujian, China, Oct. 14, 1958; arrived in Can., 1998; s. Huo-Cheng and Jin-Lian (Huang) X.; m. Yan-Ling Gao, July 30, 1978; 1 child: Xianbin. BSc, Sichuan U., Chengdu, China, 1977, MSc, 1986, PhD, 1989, U. Coimbra, Portugal, 2000. Engr. Xiamen 3d Pharm. Factory, 1977-83; lectr. Sichuan U., 1986-89, assoc. prof., 1987—. Vis. scholar Inst. for Molecular Scis., Okazaki, Japan, 1990-92; academician Acad. Sci. Rsch., Chengdu, 1995—; postdoctoral asst. U. Ottawa, Can., 2001-02 Contbr. articles to profl. jours. Recipient Excellent Scholar prize Province Edn. Com., Sichuan, 1991, Sci. and Tech. prize Nat. Edn. Com., China, 1992. Mem. AAAS, Chinese Soc. Chemistry, Chinese Soc., Physics. Avocations: poetry, painting, writing. Home: 3404 Crompton Cres Mississauga ON Canada Office: #179 180 Mississauga Valley Blvd Mississauga ON Canada L5A 3M2

XUAN, JIE, environmental science educator; b. Beijing, Jan. 4, 1946; came to U.S., 2000. s. Huaiyuan X. and Yihui Bai; m. Wengui Duo, Dec. 4, 1973 (div. Aug. 1993); children: Mingyu, Mingyue; m. Zhenhua Dai, Mar. 10, 1994. Diploma, Peking U., Beijing, 1970, MS, 1981, PhD, 1988. Tchr. H.S. no. 9, Boading, China, 1970-78; instr. Beijing Meteorology Inst., 1981-85; assoc. prof. Peking U., 1988-2001; rsch. assoc. U. Colo., Boulder, 2001—. Divsn. dir. China State Key Lab. Environ. Simulation, 1991-95; dir. Lab Environ. Wind Tunnel Peking U., 1990-95. Author: Physical Modeling of Atmospheric Diffusion, 2000; contbr. articles to profl. jours. Mem. Chinese Soc. Wind Engring. (sec. 1994—). Buddhist. Avocations: reading, music, fast walking. Office: U Colo Boulder Program Atmos & Ocean Scis Boulder CO 80309 E-mail: xuan@spot.colorado.edu.

XUE, JUE, solution architect, management science educator, consultant; b. Suzhou, Jiangsu, China; m. Xiaonong Liu; children: Lester, Gilbert. MSc, Acad. Sinica, China; MS, PhD, Carnegie Mellon U. Asst. prof. Clark U., Worcester, Mass., 1991—96; from asst. to assoc. prof. mgmt. sci. City U. Hong Kong, Kowloon, 1996—2000; solution arch. SWG, IBM, 2001—. Cons. SCS, IGS, IBM, 1998-2001. Contbg. author: Ency. of Combinatorial Optimization, Handbook of Optimization; contbr. articles to sci. jours., including SIAM, Networks, Algorithmica, Info. Processing Letters. Mem. INFORMS. Fax: (240) 358-2347.

XUE, YONGKANG, science educator; m. Su Q. Liu, Jan. 10, 1973; children: Fransis, Cathleen. PhD, U. Utah, 1987. Rsch. scientist Ctr. for Ocean-Land-Atmosphre Studies , Bletsville, Md., 1993—97, U. Md., College Park, 1997—99; assoc. prof. UCLA, 1999—. Mem.: Am. Assn. Geography, Am. Geophys. Union, Am. Meteorol. Soc. Office: UCLA 1255 Bunche Hall Los Angeles CA 90094-1524 Office Fax: 310-206-5976. Personal E-mail: yxue@geog.ucla.edu. Business E-Mail: yxue@geog.ucla.edu.

YABLON, JAY RUSSELL, lawyer; b. N.Y.C., Jan. 15, 1954; s. Bernard and Muriel D. Yablon; m. Deborah Ann Happ, Aug. 7, 1977; children: Joshua, Paula. BSEE in Computer Sci., BS in Polit. Sci., MIT, 1976; JD, SUNY, Buffalo, 1979. Bar: U.S. Patent and Trademark Office 1982, N.Y. 1983. Productivity engr. GE, Schenectady, N.Y., 1980-82; sr. sys. engr. Data Gen. Corp., Albany, 1982-86; chief counsel N.Y. State Legis. Commn. on Scis. and Tech., 1986-92; exec. dir. N.Y. State Gov.'s Telecom. Exch., 1992-95; founding ptnr. Law Office of Jay R. Yablon, Niskayuna, 1995—. U.S. exch. program rep., German Acad. Exch. Svcs., 1992. Committeeperson Niskayuna Dem. Com., 1996-98. Mem. N.Y. State Bar Assn., Schenectady County Bar Assn., Ea. N.Y. Intellectual Property Law Assn., Eta Kappa Nu, Tau Beta Phi, Sigma Psi. Home: 910 Northumberland Dr Schenectady NY 12309-2814 Office: Law Office of Jay R Yablon 910 Northumberland Dr Schenectady NY 12309-2814 E-mail: jay_r_yablon@msn.com.

YABLON, JEFFERY LEE, lawyer; b. Chgo., June 28, 1948; s. Robert R. and Faye I. (Goldberg) Y.; m. Jean C. LaPrade, Apr. 17, 1983. BA with honors, U. Wis., 1970; JD, Stanford U., 1973. Bar: Calif. 1974, D.C. 1975. Law clk. to Judge Cynthia Holcomb Hall, U.S. Tax Ct., Washington, 1973-75; Fulbright scholar U. Florence, Italy, 1975-76; assoc. Covington & Burling, Washington, 1976-80, Lee, Toomey & Kent, Washington, 1980-82, Shaw Pittman, Washington, 1982-84, ptnr., 1984—. Mem. bd. advisors Taxation of Exempts Jour., 1998—. Contbr. articles to legal jours.; editl. adv. bd. Moment Mag., 2000—. Mem. ABA, State Bar Calif., D.C. Bar. Jewish. Office: Shaw Pittman 2300 N St NW Washington DC 20037-1172

YABLON, LEONARD HAROLD, publishing company executive; b. N.Y.C., June 3, 1929; s. Philip A. and Sarah (Herman) Y.; m. Carolyn Sydney Torgan (dec. Aug. 1995); children: Scott Richard, Bonnie Michelle; m. Pamela Gallin; children: Laura, Abigail, Hilary, Peter. BS, L.I. U., 1950; MBA, CCNY, 1969. CPA, N.Y. Acct., 1950-63; dir. Forbes Inc., N.Y.C., 1963—; chmn. Forbes Family Holdings Inc.; pres. Sangre de Cristo Ranches, Fiji Forbes; v.p. Forbes Investors Adv. Inst.; pres. Forbes Trinchera, Forbes Europe. Sec.-treas. Forbes Found.; bd. dirs. Yablon Found., Mack Goldner Found.; vice chmn., bd. dirs. 21i.NET; mem. bd. advisors Ctr. for Study of UN Sys. and Global Legal Order. Home: 2 Fargo Ln Irvington NY 10533-1202 Office: 60 5th Ave New York NY 10011-8802

YACAVONE, DAVID WILLIAM, military officer, consultant, researcher; b. Newark, Feb. 5, 1945; s. William Michael and Rose Marie (Cerrato) Y.; m. Nancy Weissman; children: Nancy Christine, Rebecca Noel, Jason David, Briana Lynn. BA in Non-Western History, Seton Hall U., 1966, MA in Chinese History, 1968; DO, Chgo. Coll. Osteo. Medicine, 1974; MPH, Harvard U., 1986. Diplomate Am. Bd. Gen. and Preventive Medicine, Am. Bd. Aerospace Medicine. Rotating intern Chgo. Osteo. Med. Ctr., 1975; asst. prof. community medicine Mich. State U., East Lansing, 1975-76; bn. surgeon USN, Lansing, Mich., 1975-77; flight surgeon U.S. Naval Aerospace Med. Inst., Pensacola, Fla., 1977, USN, Jacksonville, 1977-79, sr. med. officer USS Saratoga, 1979; resident aerospace medicine U.S. Naval Aerospace Med. Inst., Pensacola, Fla., 1986-88; capt. med. corps USN USN, USS Dwight D. Eisenhower, 1988-90, 93-96; head aeromed. div. Naval Safety Ctr., Norfolk, Va., 1990-93; capt. med. corps USN USS Harry S. Truman, 1996-98, USS Nimitz, 1998—2001; comdr. carrier Airborne Early Warning Wing, 2001—. Staff mem. Lansing (Mich.) Gen. Hosp., 1975-76, Jackson (Much.) Gen. Hosp., 1976-77, Jacksonville (Fla.) Gen. Hosp., 1977-81, Daytona Beach (Fla.) Gen. Hosp., 1979-81, Naval Hosp., Corpus Christi, Tex., 1982-85, dir. mil. medicine, 1982-84; adj. instr. W.Va. Coll. Osteo. Medicine, 1977-79; tng. instr. Flight Instr.'s Tng., 1982-85, flight surgeon's sch. Naval Aerospace Med. Inst., 1986-88, 90-93, aircraft accident investigation technique, Armed Forces Inst. Pathology, 1990—; presenter in field. Author: (with others) Aviation, Space and Environmental Medicine, 1987, edit., 1992; editor: Aeromedical News, 1990-93. ACLS instr. Tex. Heart Assn., 1983-85. Recipient Steinbaum Meml. award, Kirksville Coll. Osteo. Medicine, 1971. Fellow Aerospace Med. Assn.; mem Soc. U.S. Naval Flight Surgeons (past officer), Assn. Mil. Surgeons of U.S., numerous coms.

YACK, PATRICK ASHLEY, editor; b. Little Rock, Oct. 25, 1951; s. Leo Patrick and Sarah Ann (Dew) Y.; children: Alexander Ryan, Kendall Elizabeth. BFA, So. Meth. U., 1974. Staff asst. U.S. Rep. Alan Steelman, Washington, 1975-76; press aide U.S. Senator Charles Percy, Chgo., 1977-78; reporter Fla. Times-Union, Jacksonville, 1979-80, regional reporter Atlanta, 1981-82; reporter The Denver Post, 1983-85, Washington bur. chief, 1985-87; nat. editor Atlanta Constitution, 1987-89; mng. editor The Register-Guard, Eugene, Oreg., 1989-94; editor News & Record, Greensboro, N.C., 1994-98, Fla. Times-Union, Jacksonville, 1998—. Sec. The dePaul Sch., Fresh Ministries; mem. univ. coun. Jacksonville U. Mem. Am. Soc. Newspaper Editors (past membership com. chair), Fla. Soc. Newspaper Editors (bd. dirs., pres.), Jacksonville World Affairs Coun. E-mail: payack@jacksonville.com.

YACKEL, JAMES WILLIAM, mathematician, academic administrator; b. Sanborn, Minn., Mar. 6, 1936; s. Ewald W. and Marie E. (Heydlauff) Y.; m. Erna Beth Seecamp, Aug. 20, 1960; children: Jonathan, Juliet, Carolyn. BA, U. Minn., 1958, MA, 1960, PhD, 1964. Rsch. instr. dept. math. Dartmouth Coll., Hanover, N.H., 1964-66; asst. prof. dept. stats. Purdue U., West Lafayette, Ind., 1966-69, from assoc. prof. to prof., 1969-76, assoc. dean sci., 1976-87; vice chancellor acad. affairs Purdue U. Calumet, Hammond, 1987-90, chancellor, 1990-2001, chancellor emeritus, 2001—. Rsch. mathematician Inst. Def. Analysis, Washington, 1969. Author: Applicable Finite Mathematics, 1974; editor Statistical Decision Theory, 1971; contbr. articles to profl. jours. Fellow AAAS; mem. Am. Math. Soc., Math. Assn. Am., Inst. Math. Stats. Achievements include research on Ramsey's theorem and finite graphs. E-mail: yackelj@calumet.Purdue.edu.

YACKLE, ALBERT REUSTLE, retired aeronautical engineer; b. Willow Grove, Pa., May 13, 1922; s. Albert J. and Marion D. (Reustle) Y.; m. Ruth E. Everett, Sept. 18, 1948; children: Linda McCann, Tom, Brad. BS in Mech. Engring. Aeronautical Option, Pa. State U., 1943. Registered profl engr., Calif. Structures engr. Ea. Aircraft, 1944, Kellett Aircraft Corp., 1946-48, chief structures engr., 1950-60; structures engr. Chase Aircraft, 1948-50; advanced design and program mgr. Lockheed Aircraft Corp., 1960-91; ret., 1991. Cons. Huntington Med. Rsch. Inst., Pasadena, Calif., 1991-96. Contbr. tech. papers to profl. jours. Lt. (j.g.) USN, 1944-46. Recipient Lockheed Spl. Achievement awards, 1976, 77, 79, 87; inducted into H.S. Hall of Fame, 1996. Fellow (assoc.) AIAA; mem. Am. Helicopter Soc. Achievements include 2 patents in rigid rotor helicopters. Home: 5105 Quakertown Ave Woodland Hills CA 91364-3538

YACKLEY, LUKE EUGENE, nursing educator; b. Elmhurst, Ill., Apr. 20, 1950; s. Lawrence E. and Patricia Anne (Neumann) Y.; m. Teresa D. Thompson, Apr. 27, 1973; children: Gregory Scott, Julia Ann, Timothy Kevin, Kathleen Mary. BA in Sociology, Quincy (Ill.) U., 1972; AA in Nursing, Kankakee (Ill.) C.C., 1977; BSN, U. Md., 1991, MS, 1994. RN, Md. Mental health specialist Dept. Mental Health, Manteno, Ill., 1974-78; staff nurse acute psychiatry Vets. Adminstrn., Perry Point, Md., 1978-82, head nurse addictions, 1982-00; edn. specialist EES/VA, 2000—. Scoutmaster Boy Scouts Am., Charlestown, Md., 1993-97, scouter 1985—; Lector, Eucharistic min. Good Shepherd Parish, Perryville, Md., 1987—; dist. venturing tng. coord.; adviser for explorer post Boy Scouts Am., Perry Point, 1993-00; h.s. sports ofcl. NEMOA, Harford County, Md., 1982—. Recipient Outstanding Performance award VA Med. Ctr., 1987, 95, Team Building award, 1992, Supr. of Yr. award VA Md. Health Care Sys., 1998, Nurse of Yr. VA Md. Health Care Sys., 2000. Mem. Elk Neck Trail Assn. (bd. dirs.). Roman Catholic. Avocations: scouting, officiating, camping, backpacking. Home: 1616 Carpenters Point Rd Perryville MD 21903-2009 Office: Employee Edn Office Bldg 82/11E VA Med Ctr Perry Point MD 21902 E-mail: luke.yackley@lrn.va.gov.

YACKTMAN, DONALD ARTHUR, financial executive, investment counselor; b. Chgo., Sept. 12, 1941; s. Victor and Matilda (Chamberlain) Y.; m. Carolyn I. Zuppann, June 15, 1965; children: Donald, Stephen, Jennifer, Melissa, Brian, Robert, Michael. BS, U. Utah, 1965; MBA, Harvard U., 1967. Chartered investment counselor. Trainee Continental Bank, Chgo., 1967-68; assoc. Stein Roe & Farnham, 1968-74, ptnr., 1974-82; pres. Selected Am. Shares; sr. v.p. Prescott Asset Mgmt., 1982-92; pres. Yacktman Asset Mgmt. Co., The Yacktman Funds, 1992—. Past pres. N.W. Suburban coun. Boy Scouts Am. Mem. Investment Analysis Soc. Chgo. Office: Yacktman Asset Mgmt Co 1110 Lake Cook Rd Ste 385 Buffalo Grove IL 60089

YACOB, YOSEF, lawyer, economist; b. Dire Dawa, Harar, Ethiopia, Nov. 12, 1947; s. Yacob and Egziaraya (Osman) Zanios; m. Betsy Ann Boynton; children: Sarah Ann, Matthew Yosef, Ezra Yosef, Jarred Yosef, Rachel Helen. BA, Linfield Coll., 1971; JD, Lewis and Clark U., 1974; LLM in Internt. Law, U. San Diego, 1999. Bar: Oreg. 1975, U.S. Dist. Ct. Oreg. 1979, U.S. Ct. Appeals (9th cir.) 1980. Rschr. criminal justice State of Oreg., Salem, 1974, sr. administrv. analyst, 1974-76; adjudications specialist, legal counsel, law enforcement coun. Office of the Gov. State of Oregon, 1976-78; chief administrv. law judge State of Oregon, Milwaukie, 1978-83, dir. hearings, appeals, 1982-84; mng. atty. Hyatt Legal Services, Clakamas, Oreg., 1984-86; pres., sr. ptnr. Yacob & Assocs. P.C., Clackamas, 1986-93; dir. gen. for legal affairs, gen. counsel Ministry of Fgn. Affairs, Govt. of Ethiopia, 1993—94; pres. N.W. Fin. Svcs., Wilsonville, Oreg., 1999—2002; fellow Grad. Law Program York U., Toronto, 1999—2002, dir. for internat. cooperation Ctr. for Refugee Studies, 2002—. Co-author: Evaluation of Multnomah County District Attorney's High Impact Project, 1978. Avocations: alpine skiing, nordic skiing, water skiing, reading. Office: Yacob & Assocs PC Northwest Legal Svcs 6885 SW Montgomery Way Wilsonville OR 97070-6739

YACOUB, IGNATIUS I. university dean; b. Dwar Taha, Syria, Jan. 5, 1937; came to U.S. 1978; s. Immanuel and Martha (Kharma) Y.; m. Mary Haddad, Sept. 14, 1961; children— Hilda, Lena, Emile. AB, Middle East Coll., Beirut, Lebanon, 1960; MA, Pacific Union Coll., Angwin, Calif., 1964; PhD, Claremont Grad. Sch., Calif., 1976. Dean studies Middle East Coll., Beirut, 1967-73, 75-78; dir. dept. edn. Afro-Mideast div. Seventh-Day Adventist Ch., 1970-73, dir. dept. pub. affairs, 1975-78; prof., chmn. dept. bus. econs. Southwestern Union Coll., Keene, Tex., 1978-80; prof., chmn. dept. bus. and econs. Loma Linda U., Riverside, Calif., 1980-86, founding dean Sch. of Bus. and Mgmt., 1986-90; prof. mgmt., 1995—; founding dean Sch. Bus. and Mgmt., La Sierra U., Riverside, Calif., 1990—95; prof. adminstrn. and mgmt. Loma Linda U., Loma Linda, 1995—. Bd. dirs. Riverside Nat. Bank; bd. advisors City Nat. Bank, 1997—. Mem. Exec. 2000 Coun. Riverside Cmty. Hosp. Found., 1991-95. Recipient Gov.'s Appreciation award, Lions Club, Lions Club award, Beirut, cert. Appreciation Exec. 2000 Coun., 1994, 95, Cert. of Appreciation Claremont Grad. Sch. Alumni Coun., 1996, Mentemereles Univ. Mex., 1992, 94. Mem. Am. Mgmt. Assn., Acad. Mgmt., Soc. for Advancement Mgmt., Greater Riverside C. of C. (Svc. award 1995), Corona C. of C. Seventh-day Adventist Home: 2722 Litchfield Dr Riverside CA 92503-6213

YACOWITZ, HAROLD, biochemist, nutritionist; b. N.Y.C., Feb. 17, 1922; s. Louis and Clara (Kurtzberg) Y.; m. Ann Ruth Barnett, Dec. 31, 1941; children: Caryn R., Richard S., Suzanne Yacowitz Dragan. BS, M in Nutritional Sci., Cornell U., 1948, PhD, 1950. Rsch. biochemist Parke-Davis Inc., Detroit, 1950-51; assoc. prof. Ohio State U., Columbus, 1951-55; head nutrition rsch. dept. Squibb Inst. for Med. Rsch., New Brunswick, N.J., 1955-59; dir. rsch. Nopco Chem. Co. Inc., Harrison, 1959-61, Amburgo Co. Inc., Phila., 1961-80; rsch. assoc. Fairleigh Dickinson U., Madison, N.J., 1961-80; pres., dir. rsch. Dr. H. Yacowitz & Co., Piscataway, 1961—, Animal Identification & Marking Systems Inc., Piscataway, 1982-97. Pres. Peninsula Investment & Devel. Inc., Cambridge, Md., 1961—; pres., bd. dirs. rsch. Drug Delivery Devices Inc., Piscataway, 1991—. Contbr. articles to profl. jours.; patentee in field. Leader Boy Scouts Am., Ithaca, N.Y., 1946-50, Piscataway, 1955-59. With U.S. Army, 1943-46, ETO, PTO. Grange League Fedn. fellow Cornell U., 1947-48, Robert Gould rsch. fellow, Cornell U., 1949-50, Coun. on Arteriosclerosis fellow Am. Heart Assn., 1970. Fellow N.Y. Acad. Scis. (chmn. sect. biology and medicine 1972-76); mem. Am. Chem. Soc., Am. Inst. Nutrition, Am. Assn. Lab. Animal Scientists, Exptl. Investors Club (New Brunswick, pres. 1955-59). Jewish. Avocations: gardening, sailing, fishing, swimming. Office: Drug Delivery Devices Inc 221 2nd Ave Piscataway NJ 08854-3519 E-mail: halyacowitz@webtv.net.

YADALAM, KASHINATH GANGADHARA, psychiatrist; b. Bangalore, India, Dec. 17, 1954; came to U.S., 1980; s. Gangadhara N. and Ramarathna G. (Daglur) Y.; m. Jyothi Kashinath, Feb. 26, 1981; children: Akhila, Adithya. MD, Kasturba Med. Coll., Manipal, India, 1977. Diplomate Am. Bd. Psychiatry and Neurology. Resident in psychiatry U. Nebr., Omaha, 1980-83; clin. fellow psychopharmacology Med. Coll. Pa., Phila., 1983-84, instr., 1984-85, asst. prof., 1985-89, dir. neuropsychiatry clinic, 1987-91, assoc. prof., 1989-91; med. dir. Diagnostic and Consultation Ctr. Med. Coll. of Pa.; assoc. dir. The Neuropsychiat. Clinic of La., Lake Charles, 1991-96, med. dir., 1996—. Med. dir. Schizophrenia Diagnostic and Consultation Ctr., 1990. Author: (with others) Drug Induced Dysfunction in Psychiatry, 1992; contbr. articles to profl. jours. Grantee, NIMH, 1987; recipient Young Investigator award, Internat. Congress Schizophrenia Rsch., Balt., 1987, Young Scientist award Winter Workshop on Schizophrenia, Badgastein, Austria, 1990. Fellow Am. Psychiat. Assn.; mem. Am. Coll. Clin. Pharmacology, Nat. Alliance of the Mentally Ill. Hindu. Avocations: table tennis, chess, squash, fitness. Office: 2829 4th Ave Ste 150 Lake Charles LA 70601-7897

YADAV, SUNIL, mechanical engineer; came to U.S., 1991; BS, Indian Inst. Tech., Kanpur, India, 1991; MS, Johns Hopkins U., 1994, PhD, 1996. Postdoctoral rsch. scholar Calif. Inst. Tech., Pasadena, 1996-98; engr. II Fermi Nat. Accelerator Lab., Batavia, Ill., 1998—. Contbr. papers to profl. jours. Mem. AAAS, ASME, Am. Acad. Mechanics, Sigma Xi.

YADAV, SURYA B. information scientist, educator, information scientist, consultant; b. Jaunpur, Uttar Pradesh, India, July 11, 1951; s. Sabhajeet Yadav, Dulari Devi; m. Sheela Singh; children: Barakha, Naveen, Menaka. M in Tech., Indian Inst. Tech., Kanpur, India, 1974; PhD, Ga. State U., 1981; diploma in German Lang., 1971. Sys. analyst Indian Inst. Mgmt., Ahmedabad, India, 1974—76; asst. prof. Tex. Tech. U., Lubbock, 1981—86, assoc. prof., 1986—92, prof., 1992—94, dept. head, prof., 1994—. Contbr. articles to profl. jours. Scholar, Government of India, 1965—72. Mem.: Assn. for Computing Machinery, IEEE Computer Soc. (assoc.), Phi Beta Delta, Upsilon Pi Epsilon. Office: Texas Tech U Dept ISQS Rawls Coll Bus Lubbock TX 79409 Personal E-mail: Surya.Yadav@ttu.edu.

YADEKA, THEOPHILUS ADENIYI, hospital administrator; b. Ibadan, Nigeria, Apr. 16, 1939; came to U.S., 1971; s. Joshua A. and Alice (Opawole) Y.; m. Julianah M., Aug. 23, 1965; children: Olatunde, Mofoluke, Ayoola, Mobolaji, Adedoja. Diploma, S.D.A. Nursing Sch., 1965, SUNY, 1972; BS in Healthcare Adminstrn., St. Francis Coll., 1976; MS in Healthcare & Hosp. Adminstrn., L.I. U., 1977. Lic. pvt. sch. tchr. clin. instr. Charge and staff nurse Met. City Hosp., N.Y.C., 1971—74, Barnabas Hosps., N.Y.C., 1974—77; prin. hosp. adminstr. Ministry of Health/State Hosp. Mgmt. Bd., Ibadan, Nigeria, 1978-85; asst. chief hosp. adminstr. State Hosps. Mgmt. Bd., Nigeria, 1985-89; asst. DON Lincoln Hosp., Bronx, NY, 1977—78, N.Y., 1989-90, Bronx Lebanon Hosp. Ctr., 1990—95; clin. instr., healthcare cons., 1999—. Mem. Am. Coll. Hosp. Adminstrs., Am. Coll. Nursing Home Adminstrs., Inst. Health Svc. Adminstrs. Nigeria. Home: Bronx GPO 496 Bronx NY 10451 Office: Bronx Lebanon Hosp Ctr Bronx NY 10457

YADRICK, ROBERT MARTIN, occupational analyst; b. Kansas City, Mo., Oct. 24, 1949; s. John George and Joanne Jean Yadrick; m. Patricia Eileen Koelzer, May 30, 1986; children: Lauren Nicole, John Nicholas. BA, Rockhurst Coll., 1971; MA, U. Mo., 1973, PhD, 1975. Cert. profl. ergonomist Bd. Certification in Profl. Ergonomics, Inc. Asst. prof. psychology Columbia (Mo.) Coll., 1975-78; rsch. assoc. U. Mo., Columbia, 1978-79; sr. rsch. assoc. Ctrl.-N.E. Colo. Health Sys. Agy., Inc., Denver, 1979-82; sr. human factors engr. McDonnell Douglas Corp., St. Louis, 1982-90; rsch. scientist Metrica, Inc., San Antonio, 1991; pers. rsch. psychologist USAF Rsch. Lab., Brooks AFB, 1991-99; occupl. analyst USAF, Randolph AFB, 1999—, quality assurance mgr., 2001—. Adj. lectr. U. Tex. San Antonio, Our Lady of the Lake U., St. Mary's U.; editor newsletter Insight, Human Factors and Ergonomics Soc., Santa Monica, Calif., 1994-96, reviewer visual performance tech. group, 1995-97; reviewer jour. Behavior Rsch. Methods, Instruments and Computers, 1996. Contbr. articles to profl. jours. Mentor, tutor Judson Sch. Dist., San Antonio, 1999—. Recipient Lab. Dir.'s award Armstrong Lab., 1996. Mem. Soc. for Indsl. and Orgnl. Psychology, Sigma Xi. Avoations: flying, hiking, water sports. E-mail: robert.yadrick@randolph.af.mil.

YAEGER, THERESE FRANCIS, management professional; b. Chgo., 1955; d. Walter W. and Eileen O'Brien Bronson; m. Paul Alan Yaeger, 1975; children: Colleen Rose, Elizabeth Marie, Anne Thirise, Julia Eileen. BA in Lit. and Comm. magna cum laude, Benedictine U., 1995, MS in Mgmt. and Orgnl. Behavior, 1996, PhD in Orgn. Devel., 2001. Gen. mgr. Bestway Carpeting Inc., Naperville, Ill., 1976—; assoc. dir. PhD dept. Orgn. Devel. Benedictine U., Lisle, 1995—. Mem. presenter Midwest Acad. Mgmt., 1996—, Orgn. Devel. Network, 1995—, Acad. Mgmt., 1996—, APA, Divsn. 13, 2001; adj. faculty Mgmt. & Orgnl. Behavior Benedictine U., 1996—; exec. bd. Midwest Acad. Mgmt. Author: (with others) Appreciative Inquiry: Rethinking Human Organization Toward a Positive Theory of Change, 1999, Appreciative Inquiry: An Emerging Direction for Organization Development, 2001; editor (mag.) DuPage Arts Life, 1995, 96; asst. editor (newsletter) rsch. O.D. Inst. OD Jour., 1996—; columnist Chgo. ASTD's Tng. Today, 1997—. Mem. ASTD., Chgo. Orgn. Devel. Inst. Chpt., Soc. Profl. Journalists. Roman Catholic.

YAFFA, JACK BER, healthcare administrator, educator, surgeon; b. Camden, N.J., Apr. 28, 1941; s. Harry and Rose (Plotkin) Y.; m. Phyllis A. Pollack, June 21, 1964; children: Andrew, Samuel, Jodi, Gregory. BA, U. Richmond, 1963; MD, Med. Coll. of Va., 1968. Cert. Am. Bd. Surgery; cert. Fla. Bd. Med. Examiners, Va. Bd. Med. Examiners. Surg. intern U. Miami (Fla.) Med. Ctr., 1968-69, surg. resident, 1969-73, chief resident in surgery, 1972-73; pvt. practice in gen.-vascular surgery Miami, 1973-95; assoc. chief of staff ambulatory care Miami VA Med. Ctr., 1995—; asst. prof. clin. surgery U. Miami Med. Sch., 1995—2001, asst. prof. clin. medicine, 1998—; med. dir. Baptist Hosp. Miami, 2001—. Chief med. officer Oakland Park Outpatient Clinic, Dept. VA Med. Ctr.; asst. chief of surgery Bapt. Hosp. Miami, 1978-79, chief of surgery, 1980-81, 91-93, chief of cardiac surgery, 1982-84, chief of trauma surgery, 1983, chmn. peripheral vascular lab., 1982-83, chief of staff, 1984-88, adminstrv. dir. critical care, 1988-92; active staff South Miami Hosp.; mem. governing bd. emergency med. svcs. tng. U. Miami Sch. Medicine, 1989-95. Fellow ACS (gov.-at-large 1990, bd. govs. 1991-96, instr. advanced trauma life support 1981-93, mem. state com. trauma 1985-93, sec.-treas. Miami chpt. 1983-85, pres. Miami chpt. 1985-87, councilor Miami chpt. 1990-92); mem. AMA, Fla. Med. Assn. (com. on emergency med. svcs., com. on hosp. med. staffs), Fla. Surg. Soc. (bd. dirs. 1990—), South Fla. Noninvasive Vascular Soc., Miami Surg. Soc., Jackson Surg. Soc., Dade County Med. Assn., Soc. Laparendoscopic Surgeons, Southeastern Surg. Congress, So. Med. Congress (assoc. councilor 1989), Surg. Hist. Soc. Jewish. Avocations: boating, fishing. Office: Miami VA Med Ctr 1201 NW 16th St Miami FL 33125-1624

YAFFE, BARBARA MARLENE, journalist; b. Montreal, Que., Can., Mar. 4, 1953; d. Allan and Anne (Freedman) Y.; m. Wilson E. Russell, Aug. 30, 1985. Student, McGill U., 1970-73; BA, U. Toronto, 1974; B in Journalism, Carleton U., 1974. Reporter Montreal Gazette, 1975-76, Toronto Globe and Mail, 1976-79, reporter, columnist N.S., 1979-81; TV bur. chief CBC-TV, St. Johns, Nfld., 1981-84, Edmonton, Alta., 1983; reporter Toronto Globe and Mail, St. John's, 1984-86; editor Sunday Express, 1987-88, Vancouver Sun, 1988-93, columnist, 1993—. Recipient Gov. Gen.'s award Roland Michener Found., 1977. Jewish. Office: c/o Vancouver Sun 200 Granville St Vancouver BC Canada V6C 3N3 E-mail: byaffe@pacpress.southam.ca.

YAFFE, JAMES, writer; b. Chgo., Mar. 31, 1927; s. Samuel and Florence (Scheinman) Y.; m. Elaine Gordon, Mar. 1, 1964; children: Deborah Ann, Rebecca Elizabeth, Gideon Daniel. Grad., Fieldston Sch., 1944; BA summa cum laude, Yale U., 1948. Prof. Colo. Coll., Colo. Springs, 1968—2002, prof. emeritus, 2002—. Author: Poor Cousin Evelyn, 1951, The Good-for-Nothing, 1953, What's the Big Hurry?, 1954, Nothing But the Night, 1959, Mister Margolies, 1962, Nobody Does You Any Favors, 1966, The American Jews, 1968, The Voyage of the Franz Joseph, 1970, So Sue Me!, 1972, Saul and Morris, Worlds Apart, 1982, A Nice Murder for Mom, 1988, Mom Meets Her Maker, 1990, Mom Doth Murder Sleep, 1991, Mom Among the Liars, 1992, My Mother the Detective, 1997; play The Deadly Game, 1960, (with Jerome Weidman) Ivory Tower, 1967, Cliffhanger, 1985; also TV plays, stories, essays, revs. Served with USNR, 1945-46. Recipient Nat. Arts Found award, 1968 Mem. P.E.N., Authors League, Writers Guild of Am., Dramatists Guild, A.A.U.P., Mystery Writers of Am., Phi Beta Kappa. Clubs: Elizabethan (Yale). Jewish. Avocations: music, bridge, movies. Home: 12 W 72 St New York NY 10023

YAFFE, STUART ALLEN, physician; b. Springfield, Ill., July 6, 1927; m. Natalie, 1952; children: Scott, Kim Yaffe Schoenburg. BS cum laude, U. Alaska, 1951; MD, St. Louis U., 1956. Diplomate Am. Bd. Family Practice. Intern St. Louis CIty Hosp., 1956-57, resident, 1957-58; physician pvt. practice, 1958—; clin. assoc. prof. So. Ill. U. Sch. Medicine., Springfield, 1971—; ptnr. Springfield Clinic, 1989—. With U.S. Army, 1945-47. Mem. AMA, Am. Acad. Family Physicians, Ill. Acad. Family Physicians, Ill. State Med. Soc., Sangamon County Med. Soc. Office: 1100 Centre West Dr Springfield IL 62704-2100

YAFFE, SUMNER JASON, pediatrician, educator; b. Boston, May 9, 1923; s. Henry H. and Ida E. (Fisher) Yaffe; m. Anita Yaffe (div. 2001); children: Steven, Kris, Jason, Noah, Ian, Zachary. AB, Harvard U., 1945, MA, 1950; MD, U. Vt., 1954. Diplomate Am. Bd. Pediatrics. Intern Children's Hosp., Boston, 1954-55, resident, 1955-56; resident in pediatrics St. Mary's Hosp., London, 1956-57; instr. pediatrics Stanford U., Palo Alto, Calif., 1959-60, asst. prof., 1960-63; assoc. prof. pediatrics SUNY-Buffalo, 1963-66, prof., 1966-75, adj. prof. biochem. pharmacology, 1968-75, acting chmn. dept. pediatrics, 1974-75; prof. pediatrics and pharmacology U. Pa., Phila., 1975-81; clin. prof. pediat. Johns Hopkins Hosp., 1996—2001; vis. prof. pediat. UCLA Sch. Medicine, 2001—. Vis. prof. pharmacology Karolinska Inst. , Stockholm, 1969—70; dir. Pediat. Renal Clinic, Stanford Med. Ctr., 1960—63; dir. newborn nursery svc. Palo Alto-Stanford Hosp., 1960—63, program dir. Clin. Rsch. Ctr. for Premature Infants, 1962—63; dir. Clin. Rsch. Ctr. for Children Children's Hosp., Buffalo, 1963—70, dir. Poison Control Ctr., 1967—75, dir. divsn. clin. pharmacology, Phila., 1975—81; dir. Ctr. for Rsch. for Mothers and Children Nat. Inst. Child Health and Human Devel., NIH, 1981—2001, program cons., 1963—71, mem. tng. grant com., 1963—65, mem. reproductive biology com., 1965—67; mem. adv. panel on maternal and child health WHO, Geneva, 1970—; liaison rep. drug rsch. bd. NRC, 1971—75, com. on drug dependence, 1972—75, mem. com. on problems of drug safety, 1972—75; mem. adv. panel in pediat. U.S. Pharmacopeia, 1970—, mem. adv. panel in toxicology, 1974—75; cons. Am. Found. for Maternal and Child Health, Inc., 1973—; pres. Maternal and Child Health Rsch. Found., Children's Hosp., 1974—75; Wall Meml. lectr. Children's Hosp., Washington, 1968—; Dr. W.E. Upjohn lectr. Can. Med. Assn., 1974; Louisville pediat. lectr. Sch. Medicine U. Louisville, 1974; William N. Creasy vis. prof. clin. pharmacology SUNY, 1976; advisor Internat. Childbirth Assn. Greater Phila., 1979—83; guest lectr. pediat. Georgetown U. Hosp., Washington, 1988—2001; lectr. in pediat. Johns Hopkins Sch. Medicine, Balt., 1988—2001; mem. Roundtable on Drug Devel., Inst. of Medicine. Author: (book) Clinics in Perinatology, 1974, Drug Assessment: Criteria and Methods, 1979, Pediatric Pharmacology, 1980, Pediatric Pharmacology, 2d edit., 1992; author: (with R. Galinsky) Clinical Therapeutics, 1978; editor (with R. H. Schwartz): Drug and Chemical Risks to the Fetus and Newborn, 1980; editor: (with G. G. Briggs, T. w. Bodendorfer, R. K. Freeman) Drugs in Pregnancy and Lactatin, A Reference Guide to Fetal and Neonatal Risk, 1983, Drugs in Pregnancy and Lactatin, A Reference Guide to Fetal and Neonatal Risk, 2d, edit., 1986, Drugs in Pregnancy and Lactatin, A Reference Guide to Fetal and Neonatal Risk, 4th edit., 1994, Drugs in Pregnancy and Lactatin, A Reference Guide to Fetal and Neonatal Risk, 5th edit., 1998; editor: (with J. V. Aranda) Pediatric Phyarmacology, 2d edit., 1993; mem. editl. bd.: Pediatric Alert, 1977—, mem. editl. bd.: Pharmacology, 1977—, mem. editl. bd.: Devel. Pharmacology and Therapeutics, 1979—95, mem. editl. adv. bd.: Drug Therapy, 1979—, cons. editor: Clin. Pharacokinetics, 1977; co-editor: Developmental Pharmacology, 1979—94; contbr. articles to profl. jours. With U.S. Army, 1943—44. Recipient Lederle Med. Faculty award, Lederle Found., 1962; scholar Fulbright, 1956—57. Fellow: Acad. Pharm. Scis.; mem.: AAUP, AMA (com. on drugs 1963—68), Soc. Maternal Fetal Medicine, Soc. Pediat. Rsch., Perinatal Rsch. Soc., Fedn. Am. Socs. Exptl. Biology, Am. Soc. Pharmacology and Exptl. Therapeutics, Am. Soc. Clin. Pharmacology and Therapeutics (chmn. sect. pediatric pharmacology 1977—83), Am. Pub. Health Assn., Am. Pharmaceutics Assn., Am. Pediat. Soc., Am. Fedn. for Clin. Rsch., Am. Coll. Clin. Pharmacology and Chemotherapy, Am. Acad. Pediat. (chmn. com. drugs 1967—76), Alpha Omega Alpha, Sigma Xi. Home: 416 Comstock Ave Los Angeles CA 90024 Office: 10833 Le Conte Ave Los Angeles CA 90095-3075 Fax: 310-267-0154. E-mail: sjyla@aol.com.

YAGAN, NEDA, physician, medical educator; b. Ankara, Turkey, Mar. 25, 1965; came to U.S., 1966; d. Rauf and Handan Yagan. BA, Case Western Res. U., 1987, MD, 1991. Intern Lenox Hill Hosp., N.Y.C., 1991—92; resident in diagnostic radiology Mallinkrodt Inst. Radiology/Washington U. Med. Ctr., St. Louis, 1992—96; fellow in abdominal imaging U. Pitts. Med. Ctr., 1996—97; asst. prof. radiology N.Y. Presbyn. Hosp.-N.Y. Weill Cornell Med. Ctr., N.Y.C., 1997—. Contbr. articles to profl. jours. Mem. Am. Assn. U. Radiologists, Am. Assn. Women Radiologists, Am. Roentgen Ray Soc., Radiol. Soc. N.Am., N.Y. Roentgen Soc., Turkish Am. Med. Assn. (sec. 2000—). Avocations: reading, drawing, painting. Office: NY Weill Cornell Med Ctr Dept Radiology 525 E 68th St New York NY 10021 E-mail: ney2001@med.cornell.edu.

YAGER, JOSEPH ARTHUR, JR. economist; b. Owensville, Ind., Apr. 14, 1916; s. Joseph Arthur and Edna (Pratt) Y.; m. Virginia Estella Beroset, Sept. 2, 1938; children: Thomas, Martha. AB, U. Mich., 1937, JD, 1939, MA, 1940; grad., Nat. War Coll., 1955. Economist OPA, 1942-44; economist State Dept., 1946-47, chief China research br., 1949-50, chief div. research for Far East, 1952-57; attaché U.S. consulate gen., Canton, China, 1947-48, consul Hong Kong, 1950-51; econ. counselor Taipei, 1957-59; dep. chief of mission, 1959-61; dir. Office Chinese Affairs, 1961, Office East Asian Affairs, 1961-63; 1963-66, vice chmn., 1966-68; dep. dir. mem. Policy Planning Council, 1963-66, vice chmn., 1966-68; dep. dir. internat. and social studies div. Inst. Def. Analyses, 1968-72; sr. fellow Brookings Instn., 1972-83, guest scholar, 1983-86; resident cons. Sci. Applications Internat. Corp., 1986-89, sr. fellow, 1989-96; cons., 1996—. Author: Transforming Agriculture in Taiwan, 1988, Prospects for Nuclear Weapons Proliferation in a Changing Europe, 1992; co-author: Energy and U.S. Foreign Policy, 1974, New Means of Financing International Needs, 1978, Military Equation in Northeast Asia, 1979, Nonproliferation and U.S. Foreign Policy, 1980, International Cooperation in Nuclear Energy, 1981, Energy Balance in Northeast Asia, 1984, Energy Policy Experience of Asia Countries, 1987. Served in AUS, 1944-45. Mem. Phi Delta Phi, Delta Tau Delta. Home: 10450 Lottsford Rd #5109 Bowie MD 20721

YAGER, THOMAS C. judge; b. L.A., Feb. 16, 1918; s. Thomas C. and May M. (McGowan) Yager; m. Antonia M. Gussenhoven, Nov. 2, 2000. AB in pol. sci., UCLA, 1939, gen. secondary lifetime tchg. credential, 1940; JD, USC, 1948; LLD, Western State U., Calif., 1972. Reader UCLA Philosophy Dept., 1940; atty., 1949-57; legal advisor Gov. Calif., 1957, 58; superior ct. sr. judge Calif., 1959-78; founder Cmty. Betterment Svc., L.A. Author: numerous legal and religious books; contbr. articles to profl. jours. Founder Judge Thomas C. Yager Found., L.A., Cmty. Betterment Svc., L.A. Maj. U.S. Army, 1942—46. Office: The Cmty Betterment Svc 108 N Gower St Los Angeles CA 90004-3828 E-mail: pvtsecty@aol.com.

YAGER, VINCENT COOK, bank executive; b. Chgo., June 15, 1928; s. James Vincent and Juanita (Cook) Yager; m. Susan Marie Gallagher, Sept. 28, 1957; children: Susan Marie, Sheila Ann. BA, Grinnell Coll., 1951. Asst. cashier Chgo. Nat. Bank, 1954-60, Harris Trust & Savs. Bank, Chgo., 1960-63; v.p. comml. loan dept. Madison Bank & Trust, 1963-68; v.p. fin. Cor-Plex Internat. Corp., 1968-70; pres., CEO, dir. First Nat. Bank Blue Island, 1970-89; pres., CEO Great Lakes Fin. Resources, Inc., Matteson, 1982-96, also bd. dirs. With U.S. Army, 1951—53, ETO. Mem.: Econ. Club Chgo., Bankers Club Chgo., Robert Morris Assocs. (pres. chpt. 1981—82), Midlothian Country Club, Rotary. Home: 1032 S Rand Rd Villa Park IL 60181-3145 Office: Great Lakes Bank Blue Island 13057 S Western Ave Blue Island IL 60406-2418

YAGI, FUMIO, mathematician, systems engineer; b. Seattle, July 14, 1917; s. Saihichiro and Kima (Okabe) Y.; m. Shizuko Nakagawa, June 24, 1954. BS, U. Wash., 1938, MS, 1941; PhD, MIT, 1943. Asst. prof. U. Washington, Seattle, 1946-53; app. math. Ballistic Rsch. Lab, Aberdeen Proving Ground, Md., 1953-56; rsch. specialist Jet Prop. Lab, Pasadena, Calif., 1956-63; systems engr., group head Grumman, Bethpage, N.Y., 1963-77; retired, 1977. With U.S. Army, 1944-46, Japan. MIT scholar, 1941-42; Inst. for Advanced Study fellow, 1943, U. Washington fellow, 1940-41. Home: 2914 Sahalee Dr E Sammamish WA 98074-6353

YAGIZ, OKTAY BORA, management consultant; b. Hozat, Turkey, Aug. 2, 1942; s. Cemal Huseyin and Munevver (Istemi) Y.; m. Esin Remziye Akcakoyunlu, Sept. 14, 1996; 1 child, Bora. Student, Am. U. Beirut, 1961-63; BS, Middle East Tech. U., Ankara, 1968; postgrad. in internat. relations, Ankara U. Econ. planner State Planning Orgn., Ankara, 1969-72; gen. mgr. Viking Pulp and Paper Inc., Izmir, Turkey, 1973-82; mng. ptnr. Obey Mgmt. Cons. Inc., Istanbul, 1984—; mng. dir. Point Mgmt. Cons., Inc., 1993—; gen. mgr. DynaChange Mgmt. Cons. Inc., McLean, Va., 1995—. Exec. dir., cons. Dedeman Group of Cos., Istanbul, 1993—; exec. dir. Std. Profil Inc., Istanbul, 1989—, Fox Printing Industries, Istanbul, 1995—, also 37 other cos.; led more than 90 corp. restructuring, instnl. devel. and change mgmt. projects. Mem. Econ. and Social Studies Found., Istanbul, 1992-95; mem. Taksim Round Table, Istanbul, 1991—. 2d lt. Turkish Army, 1972-73. Rockefeller scholar, 1961-63. Mem. Turkish Mgmt. Cons. Assn. (charter mem.; pres. 1994-96, chmn. emeritus 1996), Am. Mgmt. Assn., Talas/Tarsus Alumni Assn., Middle East Tech. U. Alumni Assn. Avocations: travel, horseback riding, chess, literature, essays in management. also: OBEY Mgmt Cons Selcuklar Sok 51-3 Levent 80630 Istanbul Turkey E-mail: dynachange@msn.com.

YAGLE, ANDREW EMIL, engineering educator; b. Ann Arbor, Mich., Sept. 17, 1956; s. Raymond Arthur and Anne Joan Yagle. BSEE, U. Mich., 1978; PhD, MS in Engring., MIT, 1985. Exxon tchg. fellow MIT, Cambridge, Mass., 1982—85; prof. elec. engring. U. Mich., Ann Arbor, 1985—. Contbr. numerous tech. papers to profl. jours. Recipient Presdl. Young Investigator award, NSF, 1988—93, Young Investigator award, Office of Naval Rsch., 1990—93. Mem.: IEEE (mem.-at-large, bd. govs. Signal Processing Soc. 1998—2000). Office: U Mich 1301 Beal Av. Ann Arbor MI 48109-2122 Office Fax: 734-763-1503. Business E-Mail: aey@eecs.umich.edu.

YAGODA, BEN JAMES, author, English educator; b. N.Y.C., Feb. 22, 1954; s. Louis and Harriet (Lewis) Y.; m. Gigi Simeone, May 17, 1987; children: Elizabeth Gloria Simeone Yagoda, Maria Louise Simeone Yagoda. BA, Yale U., 1976; MA, U. Pa., 1991. Asst. editor The New Leader, N.Y.C., 1976-78; asst. editor, exec. editor N.J. Monthly, Princeton, 1980-82; articles editor Philadelphia Mag., 1982-85; movie critic Phila. Daily News., 1986-88; asst. prof. English U. Del., Newark, 1992-96, assoc. prof., 1996-2001, prof., 2001—. Author: Will Rogers: A Biography, 1993, About Town: The New Yorker and the World it Made, 2000; co-editor: The Art of Fact: A Historical Anthology of Literary Journalism, 1997; contributing editor: Philadelphia Mag., 1985—, Edging West Mag., 1994-99; contbr. more than 100 articles to mags. and reviews. Mem. AAUP, Nat. Book Critics Circle, Authors Guild. Home: 618 Parrish Rd Swarthmore PA 19081-1005 Office: U Del English Dept Memorial Hall Newark DE 19716-2595 E-mail: byagoda@udel.edu.

YAHALOM, JOACHIM, radiologist, educator, oncologist, researcher; b. Tel Aviv, Dec. 21, 1949; came to U.S., 1985; s. Lipa and Lea Yahalom; m. Rina Yahalom-Feller, Feb. 15, 1974 (div. Nov. 1984); children: Shira, Roni, Tali, Orlee. MD, Hebrew U., Jerusalem, 1976. Diplomate Am. Bd. Radiation Oncology. Lectr. Hebrew U., 1982-86; asst. attending physician Meml. Sloan-Kettering, N.Y.C., 1985-92, assoc. attending physician, 1992-97, attending physician, 1997—; asst. prof. Cornell U., 1987-93, assoc. prof., 1993-98, prof., 1998—. Tenured mem. Meml. Sloan-Kettering Cancer Ctr., N.Y.C., 1997—, co-leader Lymphoma Disease Mgmt. Team, 1998. Contbr. articles to profl. jours.; mem. editl. bd. Leukemia & Lymphoma, 1991—. Served with Israel Def. Forces, 1980-85. Recipient clin. rsch. prize Astro/Varian, 1990; named one of Best Drs. in Am., Woodward/White, 1994-95, Castle Connoly, 1996-2002. Mem. Am. Assn. Cancer Rsch., Am. Soc. Clin. Oncology, Am. Soc. Therapeutic Radiology and Oncology, Am. Soc. Hematology, Am. Coll. Radiology, Am. Radium Soc. Office: Meml Sloan Kettering Cancer Ctr 1275 York Ave New York NY 10021 E-mail: yahalomj@mskcc.org.

YAHYA, MUHAMMAD JAVAID, financial consultant, economist; b. Lahore, Panjab, Pakistan, Mar. 21, 1945; came to U.S., 1971; s. Mohammed Raza Shamsi and Syeda Zamina Khatoon; m. Ansa S. Yahya, June 19, 1971; children: Sofia, Sadia, Daniel. MS in Chem. Tech., U. Panjab, Lahore, 1967, MA in Econs., 1970; MBA, Pace U., 1978; advanced studies in banking, Am. Inst. of Banking, 1979; diploma in bank mktg., U. Colo., 1980. Sr. officer Muslim Comml. Bank, Lahore, 1967-71; asst. mgr. Habib Bank Ltd., n.Y.C., 1971-73; asst. treas. Bankers Trust Co., N.Y.C., 1973-79, asst. v.p., 1979-82, v.p., 1982-91; asst. v.p. Merrill Lynch, East Brunswick, N.J., 1991—. Advisor DHL Internat. Ltd., N.Y.C., 1983-85. Gen. sec. Am. Muslim Assn., N.J., 1995-97. Republican. Moslem. Avocations: stamps, coins, poetry, traveling, economics. Home: 857 Inman Ave Edison NJ 08820-1236 Office: Merrill Lynch 197 Route 18 Ste 301 East Brunswick NJ 08816-1400

YAITES, LILLIANN, minister; b. Kansas City, Kans., Mar. 30, 1951; d. Irvin and Gladys Lovie Cushon; m. James Roy Yaites; children: James Brewer, Reginald Brewer, James, Natosha. AA in Bus. Adminstrn., Kansas City Cmty. Jr. Coll., 1971; BSBA, Emporia State U., 1973. Mgr. info. tech. Sabre Inc., Ft. Worth, 1984—2000, GetThere Inc., Dallas, 2000—01; min., treas. Campus Dr. United Meth. Ch., Fort Worth, 2002—. Counselor Campus Dr. United Meth. Ch., Ft. Worth, 2000—. Author: (book) I'm Saved, Now What?, 2001 (Book of the Month for Oct. Black Book Worm, 2001). Mem.: Christian Writers Fellowship Internat. Avocations: singing, writing. Office: Yaites Ministries PO Box 163674 Fort Worth TX 76161-3674 Office Fax: 817-306-1843. Business E-Mail: yaites@yaitesmin.org.

YAKATAN, GERALD JOSEPH, pharmaceutical consultant; b. Phila., May 20, 1942; s. Nathan and Bella (Resnick) Y.; m. Una Gittleman, Dec. 20, 1964; children: Nicole Blayne, Brook Noel. BS, Temple U., 1963, MS, 1965; PhD, U. Fla., 1971. Asst. prof. U. Tex., Austin, 1971-76, assoc. prof., 1976-80; dir. pharmacokinetics and drug metabolism Warner Lambert Co., Ann Arbor, Mich., 1980-83, v.p. product devel. Morris Plains, N.J., 1983-87; exec. v.p. R & D, Immunetech Pharm., San Diego, 1987-90; pres., chief exec. officer Tanabe Rsch. Labs., USA, Inc., 1990-95; pres., CEO, CSO IriSys R&D, 1996—. Contbr. articles to profl. jours. NIH fellow, 1965-69, NSF fellow, 1964. Fellow Am. Coll. Clin. Pharmacology (hon. regent), Am. Assn. Pharm. Sci., Acad. Pharm. Sci.; mem. Drug Info. Assn., U.S. Profl. Tennis Registry, Fla. Blue Key. Democrat. Jewish. Avocations: tennis, reading, travel. Address: IriSys R&D 11760 Sorrento Valley Rd Ste E San Diego CA 92121-1018 Office: Avanir Pharmaceuticals 11388 Sorrento Valley Rd., Ste. 200 San Diego CA 92121

YAKE, DANIEL GLEN, civil engineer; b. Spokane, Wash., Oct. 2, 1952; s. Glen Alvin and Irene Olsen Y.; m. Laura Bracciotti, Aug. 21, 1993; children: David Randall, Jonathan Bracciotti. BS, U. Idaho, 1976, MS, 1985. Registered profl. engr., Calif., Idaho, Wash.; cert. geologist, profl. ski instr., sr. level ski patroller. Commd. 2nd lt. U.S. Army, 1976, advanced through grades to maj., 1991, airborne and ranger qualified Ga., 1982, protocol officer Berlin, 1984-86, co. comdr. 649th Engr. Battalion Schwetzingen, Germany, 1986-88, constrn. mgr. engring. Heidelberg, Germany, 1988-90, aide-de-camp Germany, 1991-93, exec. officer 864th Engr. Battalion Ft. Lewis, Wash., 1993-94, army res. advisor Oakland, Calif., 1995-96, ret., 1996; facilities planner W. County Sch. Dist., Richmond, Calif., 1997-98; sr. project engr. Cal Engring. and Geology, Walnut Creek, 1998-99; dir. growth svcs. City of Coeur d'Alene (Idaho), 1999—. Contbr. articles to profl. jours. Precinct committeeman Rep. Party, Spokane, 1980-82. Mem. ASCE (program chmn. 1980-82, Daniel W. Meade winner 1981), Wash. Soc. Profl. Engrs. (treas. 1981-82, Young Engr. of Yr. 1982), Soc. Mil. Engrs. (sec. 1984-86), Rotary Internat. (mem. internat. outreach com. 1981-85). Avocation: skiing. Home: 3103 E Fernan Hill Rd Coeur D Alene ID 83814-7564 Office: City Coer d'Alene Stormwater Coord 710 E Mullan Ave Coeur D Alene ID 83814-3958 E-mail: yake@adelphin.net.

YAKE, WILLIAM ELLSWORTH, environmental scientist, poet; b. Spokane, Wash., Mar. 9, 1947; s. William Albert and Barbara (Ellsworth) Y. BS in Zoology, Wash. State U., Pullman, 1969, MS in Environ. Sci., 1972, MS in Environ. Engring., 1977. Investigator Spokane County Air Pollution Control Authority, Spokane, 1973-77; head ambient and compliance monitoring sect. Wash. State Dept. Ecology, Olympia, 1977-87, head toxics investigation sect., 1987-93, sr. scientist, 1993—2002; poet, freelance writer, cons., 2002—. Mem. Puget Sound Rsch. Coun., 1986-89; mem. Lake Roosevelt Sci. Adv. Bd., 1992-95. Author: Confluence, 1995, Faces of Birds, 1998; sponsor, designer Wash. State Pesticide Monitoring Program, 1990; prin. author Washington State Dioxin Source Assessment, 1998; author, sponsor Dioxin in Washington State Soils, 1999, sponsor, designer Wash. State Toxics Monitorine Program, 2001. Bd. dirs., treas. Olympia Poetry Network, 1993—, Olympia Zen Ctr., 1995-96. Mem. Wash. Poets Assn., Phi Beta Kappa. Avocations: poetry, photography, nonfiction writing. Home and Office: 4032 Green Cove St NW Olympia WA 98502-3520 E-mail: yake@thurston.com.

YAKICH, DAVID ELI, international sales executive; b. Denver, May 31, 1957; s. Eli and Josephine (Goodnough) Y. Jr.; m. Carrie Elizabeth. BS, Colo. State U., 1979; postgrad., U. Minn., 1980-82; BA, U. Colo., 1984. Geophys. tech. Amoco Prodn. Corp., Denver, 1980-81; cons. geophycist Lear Petroleum, 1982-84; computer svc. mgr. Daniel Geophys., 1984-87; nat. sales mgr. Graphics Info. Inc., 1987-89; area mgr. Far East Auto-trol Tech., 1989-91; v.p. sales and support GeoGraphix Inc., 1991; dir. internat. sales Visual Numerics Inc., 1992-93; Japan distbn. bus. mgr. Xilinx, Inc., Boulder, Colo., 1994—. Computer cons. Daniel Geophysical, Denver, 1983. Mem. Soc. Exploration Geophysics, Denver C. of C. Republican. Roman Catholic. Avocations: skiing, softball, tennis, golf, fishing. *Personal philosphy: Success is founded in your attitude. Remain positive and you can succeed.*

YAKLICH, RICHARD E. music educator; b. Pueblo, Colo., Mar. 9, 1964; s. Edward Eldon Yaklich, Virginia Rose Ursick. BA, U. So. Colo., 1989; MMus, Colo. State U., 1992; D of Musical Arts, U. S.C., 1996. Cert. Music tchg. cert. K-12 Fla., 1997. Dir. music U. So. Colo. Chamber Orch., Pueblo, 1985—89, Kingsport Youth Orch., Kingsport, Tenn., 1992—94, South Miami Sch. Arts, Miami, Fla., 1997—2001; asst. prof. Music Fla. Meml. Coll., 2001—. Asst. condr. Kingsport Symphony, 1992—94; dir. music Jubilate Chamber Orch., Miami, 2001—; prin. guest condr. Alahambra Orch., Miami, 1997—2001. Author: Orchestra Conductors Handbook, 2001; composer: numerous works for orch., chamber orch. Recipient Arts and Humanities award, State of Colo., 1991. Mem.: Condrs. Guild, Music Educators Nat. Conf., Am. Symphony Orch. League. Office: Fla Meml Coll Humanities 15800 NW 42d Ave Miami FL 33054

YAKOBOVITCH, MICHAEL, aviation executive; b. Kalish, Poland, Nov. 24, 1937; arrived in Israel, 1949; s. Morris and Fella (Gottlieb) Y.; m. Mania Goldberg, Sept. 22, 1959; children: Amir, Shirly. Degree in advanced bus. mgmt., U. Jerusalem, 1989. Line mechanic El Al Airlines, Israel, 1957-59, crew chief Israel, 1959-65, foreman Israel, 1965-80, dep. dir. line maintenance Israel, 1980-86, mgr. airline svcs. Israel, 1986-90, dir. maintenance divsn. Israel, 1994-99; dep. gen. mgr., North and Ctrl. Am./maintenance El Al Israel Airlines, N.Y.C., 1999—. Sgt. Israel Air Force, 1954-57. Home: Ben Sira 16 62916 Tel Aviv Israel

YAKOWICZ, VINCENT X, lawyer, consultant; b. New Castle, Pa., July 29, 1932; s. Vincent William and Anna (Kahocka) Y.; m. Marlene Brown, Apr. 2, 1977; children: Meredythe, Megan, Michelle. BA in Polit. Sci., Pa. State U., 1953; JD, U. Pa., 1956; postgrad., U. Va., 1968-69. Bar: Pa. 1957, U.S. Dist. Ct. (mid. dist.) Pa. 1962, U.S. Supreme Ct. 1970, U.S. Ct. Appeals (3d cir.) 1983. Asst. atty. gen. Pa. Dept. Revenue, Harrisburg, 1958-59, bur. dir., 1959-62; dep. atty. gen. State of Pa., Harrisburg, 1962-71, dep. sec. of revenue, 1971-74, sec. of revenue, 1974-75, solicitor gen., 1975-78; chief dep. counsel, chief of litigation Pa. Dept. Treasury, Harrisburg, 1979-87; pvt. practice law, 1987—. Chief of litigation, Pa. Dept. Ins., 1979; chief tax litigation, Pa. Dept. Justice, 1979; adv. com. Decedent Estate Laws of Joint State Govt. Com.; legal counselor to Pa. Constl. Conv. on Revisions; author, lectr. tax seminars, U. Pa., Pa. Bar Inst. Mem. ABA, Pa. Bar Assn., Lawrence County Bar Assn., Nat. Tax Assn., Nat. Assn. Tax Adminstrs., Fed. Bench-Bar Exec. Com., Nat. Assn. Atty. Gens. (antitrust subcom.), Gov.'s Tax Reform Com., Multi-state Taxation Commn. (chmn. subcom.). Home and Office: 227 Oak Knoll Rd New Cumberland PA 17070-2836

YAKSICH, JOHN JOSEPH, music educator; b. Warren, Ohio, Aug. 15, 1969; s. John Howard and Cynthia Kay Yaksich; m. Belinda Maria Colon, July 16, 1994; children: Andrew, Elizabeth. MusB, Youngstown State U., 1992; MusM, Kent State U., 1997. Cert. tchr. Ohio. Band dir., music tchr. Canfield (Ohio) Local Schs., 1992—96, Weathersfield Local Schs., Mineral Ridge, 1996—. Freelance musician, pvt. music tchr. Precinct committeeperson Trumbull County Rep. Ctrl. Com., Niles, Ohio, 1988—92; dir. music First Christian Ch. Girard, 1990—. Mem.: NEA, Am. Fedn. Musicians, Western Star Masons (worshipful master 2000—01). Mem. Christian Ch. (Disciples Of Christ). Avocations: reading, music, gaming. Home: 1545 W Park Ave Niles OH 44446 Office: Mineral Ridge HS 1334 Seaborn St Mineral Ridge OH 44440 Personal E-mail: john.yaksich@neomin.org.

YALAMANCHILI, KISHORE KUMAR, quantitative analyst; b. Juvvanapudi, Ap, India, Nov. 14, 1960; came to U.S., 1985; s. Sankara Rao and Jhansi Laxmi (Gullapalli) Y.; m. Padmaja Vejalla, June 8, 1991. B.E., Andhra U., Waltair, India, 1983; M. Tech., Indian Inst. Tech., Kanpur, 1985; PhD, Clemson U., 1990; MBA, U. Chgo., 1997. Mem. tech. staff Universal Analytics, Torrance, Calif., 1990-94; engr., scientist McDonnell Douglas, Long Beach, 1994-96; rsch. asst. Chgo. Bd. Trade, 1996-97; with State St. Rsch. and Mgmt., Boston, 1997—. Adj. asst. prof. Bentley Coll., Waltham, Mass., 1998—. Contbr. articles to profl. jours. Mem. Internat. Assn. Fin. Engrs., Bond Analysts Soc. Boston. Avocations: reading, jogging, stamp collecting. Office: State St Rsch and Mgmt 1 Financial Ctr Boston MA 02111-2621

YALCINTAS, M. GÜVEN, medical physicist; b. Milas, Turkey, Apr. 11, 1946; came to U.S., 1968; s. Kazim and Samiye Yalcintas; 1 child, Banu. BS in Physics, Ankara U., 1967; MS in Health Physics, U. Rochester, 1971, PhD in Med. Physics, 1974. Dir. EGE Med. Sch., Izmir, Turkey, 1975-76, EMI Med., Chgo., 1976-77; group leader Oak Ridge (Tenn.) Nat. Lab., 1977-88; dir. tech. transfer Lockheed Martin, Oak Ridge, 1988-93, dir. tech. transfer of environ. techs., 1993-96; pres. Applied Profls., 1996-97; v.p. mktg. and govt. rels. Nat. Inst. for Environ. Renewal, Mayfield, Pa., 1997-98; dir. tech. transfer Okla. State U., 1999-2001; v.p., dir. tech. transfer SUNY, Albany, 2001—. Adj. prof. radiation biology Tenn. Tech U.; adj. prof. environ. scis. Tusculcum Coll., adv. bd. environ. sci. program. Contbr. articles to profl. jours. Lt. Turkish Army, 1975-76. Mem. Am. Nuc. Soc. (chmn. 1986—, newsletter editor), East Tenn. Health Physics Assn., Health Phys. Soc. Avocations: soccer, chess, writing, boating, skiing. Home: 3 Mallard Rexford NY 12148 Office: PO Box 9 Albany NY 12201-0009

YALDEN, MAXWELL FREEMAN, Canadian diplomat; b. Toronto, Ont., Can., Apr. 12, 1930; s. Frederick and Marie (Smith) Y.; m. Janice Shaw, Jan. 28, 1952; children: Robert, Cicely (dec.). BA, Victoria Coll., U. Toronto, 1952; MA, U. Mich., 1954, PhD, 1956; D.U. (hon.), U. Ottawa, 1982; LLD (hon.), Carleton U., 1998. With Can. Dept. External Affairs, 1956-69, asst. undersec. state, 1969-73, dep. minister communications, 1973-77, commr. ofcl. langs., 1977-84; Can. amb. to Belgium and Luxembourg, 1984-87; chief Can. Human Rights Comms., Ottawa, 1987-96; elected UN Human Rights Com., 1996—. Office: 52 Crichton St Ottawa ON Canada K1M 1V7

YALE, JOHN PAUL, computer systems developer; b. Uhrichsville, Ohio, Sept. 4, 1945; s. Vernon Elna and Joan (Papworth) Y.; m. Mary Anne Hinkley, Feb. 9, 1966; children: John Vernon, Eric Kendall. AAS, Orange County C.C., 1968; BS, Ohio U., 1971. Dir. Pub. Broadcasting, Athens, Ohio, 1969-71; freelance prodr./dir. GGT, Niantic, Conn., 1971-79; dir. media svcs. L & M Hosps., New London, 1979-96; dir. sys. devel. C&E group MPTN, Ledyard, 1996—. Mem. Internat. TV Assn., Internat. Teleconf. Assn., Assn. fo Multimedia Internat., Internat. Internet Assn., Internat. Platform Assn. Home: 38 Sea Spray Ave Niantic CT 06357-3336 Office: 110 Pequot Trail PO Box 3180 Mashantucket CT 06339-3180 E-mail: john@jpyale.com., jyale@mptn.org.

YALE, SEYMOUR HERSHEL, dental radiologist, educator, university dean, gerontologist; b. Chgo., Nov. 27, 1920; s. Henry and Dorothy (Kulwin) Y.; m. Muriel Jane Cohen, Nov. 6, 1943; children: Russell Steven, Patricia Ruth. BS, U. Ill., 1944, D.D.S., 1945, postgrad., 1947-48, Spertus Inst. Jewish Studies, 1995—. Pvt. practice of dentistry, 1945-54, 56—; asst. clin. dentistry U. Ill., 1948-49, instr. clin. dentistry, 1949-53, asst. prof. clin. dentistry, 1953-54, assoc. prof. radiology Coll. Dentistry, 1956, prof., head dept. Coll. Dentistry, 1957-65, adminstrv. asst. to dean Coll. Dentistry, 1961-63, asst. dean Coll. Dentistry, 1963-64, acting dean Coll. Dentistry, 1964-65, dean, 1965-87, dean emeritus, 1987—, also mem. grad. faculty dept. radiology Coll. Medicine, prof. dentistry and health resources mgmt. Sch. Pub. Health, 1987—. Sr. dental dir. Dental Care Plus Mgmt. Corp., Chgo.; pres., dir. dental edn. Dental Care Plus Mgmt. Ednl. Svcs., Ltd.; health care facilities planner; dir. tng. Dental Technicians Sch., U.S. Naval Tng. Ctr., Bainbridge, md., 1954-56; mem. subcom. 16 Nat. Com. on Radiation Protection; mem. Radiation Protection Adv. Bd., State of Ill., 1971, City of Chgo. Health Sys. Agy.; founder Ctr. for Rsch. in Periodontal Disease and Oral Molecular Biology, 1977; organizer, chmn. Nat. Conf. on Hepatitis-B in Dentistry, 1982; organizer, dir. Univ. Taskforce Primary Health Care Project, U. Ill., Chgo.; chmn. U. Ill.-U. Stockholm-U. Gothenberg Conf. on Geriatrics, 1985; dir. planning AMVETS/UIC Tchg. Nursing Home Project, 1987-91; co-sponsor 1st Egyptian Dental Congress, 1984; adj. prof. Ctr. for Exercise Sci. and Cardiovasc. Rsch., Northeastern Ill. U., Chgo., 1991, Northwestern U. Sch. Dentistry Divsn. Behavioural Scis., Evanston, Ill., 1996—. Editor-in-chief Dental Care Plus Mgmt. Digest, 1995—. Bd. dirs., co-benefactor (with wife) World Heritage Mus., U. Ill., Urbana, 1985; mem. Hillel Bd., U. Ill.-Chgo.; life mem. (with wife) Bronze Circle of Coll. Liberal Arts, U. Ill., Urbana; mem. (with wife) Pres.' Council, U. Ill. Recipient centennial research award Chgo. Dental Soc., 1959; Distinguished Alumnus award U. Ill., 1973; Harry Sicher Meml. Lecture award Am. Coll. Stomologic Surgeons, 1983 Fellow Acad. Gen. Dentistry (hon.), Am. Coll. Dentists; mem. Ill. Dental Soc. (mem. com. on radiology), Chgo. Dental Soc., Internat. Assn. Dental Rsch., Am. Acad. Oral Roentgenology, Am. Dental Assn., Odontographic Soc. Chgo. (Award of Merit 1982), Council Dental Deans State Ill. (chmn.), N.Y. Acad. Scis., Gerontol. Soc. Am., Pierre Fauchard Acad. (Man of Yr. award Ill. sect. 1988), Am. Pub. Health Assn., Gerontol. Soc. Am., Omicron Kappa Upsilon, Sigma Xi, Alpha Omega (hon.) Achievements include established (with wife) collection of Coins of Ottoman Empire and Related Mohammedan States and supplemental antique map collection at World Heritage Mus., U of Ill.; established Muriel C. Yale Collection, antique maps of Holy Land collection at Spertus Inst. Jewish Studies. Home: 155 N Harbor Dr Chicago IL 60601-7364 Office: 30 N Michigan Ave Chicago IL 60602-3402 E-mail: ddssy@uic.edu.

YALE-LOEHR, STEPHEN WILLIAM, lawyer, editor; b. Newport News, Va., June 10, 1954; s. Raymond Charles and Joan Mary (Briggs) Loehr; m. Amy Janet Yale, July 16, 1977; children: Elizabeth, Jonathan, Alexander. BA, Cornell U., 1977, JD cum laude, 1981. Bar: D.C. 1981, U.S. Dist. Ct. D.C. 1982, U.S. Ct. Appeals (D.C. cir.) 1983, U.S. Supreme Ct. 1990, N.Y. 1993. Co-founder, editor Imagework mag., 1977; law clk. to chief judge U.S. Dist. Ct. (no. dist.) N.Y., Syracuse, 1981-82; assoc. Sutherland, Asbill & Brennan, Washington, 1982-86; co-editor Interpreter Releases, 1986-94; exec. editor Immigration Briefings, 1988-94; of counsel True, Walsh & Miller, Ithaca, N.Y., 1990—. Adj. prof. Georgetown U. Law Sch., 1988-90, Cornell Law Sch., 1991—; cons. Ford Found., 1997-99. Author: (with others) Understanding the 1986 Immigration Law, 1987, Understanding the Immigration Act of 1990, 1991, Immigration Law and Procedure, 1994— (20 vols.), Carnegie Endowment For Internat. Peace, 1994-96, Balancing Interests: Rethinking U.S. Selection of Skilled Immigrants, 1996; immigration law columnist N.Y. Law Jour., 1997—; contbr. articles to profl. jours. Mem.: ABA (immigration coord. com. 1998—2001), Am. Immigration Lawyers Assn. (chmn. investors com., bus. immigration com., Elmer Fried award for excellence in tchg. 2001), D.C. Bar Assn., N.Y. Bar Assn., Amnesty Internat., Phi Beta Kappa. Democrat. Avocations: photography, hockey. Home: 301 Highgate Rd Ithaca NY 14850-1437 Office: True Walsh & Miller 202 E State St Ithaca NY 14850-5551 E-mail: syl@twmlaw.com.

YALEN, GARY N. insurance company executive; b. N.Y.C., May 17, 1942; s. Sidney Leo and Mildred (Epstein) Y.; m. Rena Lynn Gear, Nov. 3, 1968; children— Robert, Lesley BEE, Rensselaer Poly. Inst., 1964; MBA, U. Mich., 1965. Chartered fin. analyst. Mktg. engr. N.Y. Telephone Co., N.Y.C., 1965-69; security analyst Merrill Lynch, 1969-74, Irving Trust Co., N.Y.C., 1974-80, research dir., 1980-83, sr. v.p., chief investment officer, 1983-87, exec. v.p., 1987-89, Bank of N.Y., 1989-90; chief investment officer, exec. v.p. Fortis Asset Mgmt. (formerly Amev), 1990-95; pres., chief investment officer Fortis Advisers, 1995-2001, Fortis Asset Mgmt., 2001—. Served with U.S. Army, 1966-68, Vietnam Mem. N.Y. Soc. Security Analysts, Beta Gamma Sigma Avocations: chess, golf. Home: 175 Nancy Ln Wyckoff NJ 07481-2522 Office: Fortis Advisers One Chase Manhattan Plz New York NY 10005

YALEN, SANDRA ELLEN, marriage and family therapist; b. Bklyn., Oct. 2, 1945; d. Herman Hy and Dorothy (Rackoff) Goldstein; m. William Leslie Yalen, Sept. 5, 1965; children: Renee Yalen Hulsey, Allen, Wendy. AAS in Social Svcs., Pima C.C., Tucson, 1992; BA in Psychology, U. Ariz., 1994, MS in Gerontology, 1996; M Counseling Marriage and Family Therapy, U. Phoenix, Tucson, 2001. Sr. coord. Armory Park Apts., Tucson, 1996-98; sub-acute social svc. worker La Canada Care Ctr., 1998—99; dir. social svcs. Desert Gardens Clin. Care Ctr., 1999-2000; holocaust survivors case mgr., cmty. resource specialist Jewish Family and Children's Svc., 2000—01; pvt. practice, 2001—. Co-pres. Elena group Hadassah, Tucson, 1998-2000, also past pres. and fin. sec., co-chmn. Al Galgamim group, 1998-2001, program vice chmn. Tucson chpt., also former pres., v.p., treas., corr. sec., rec. sec., life mem.; past Brownie troop leader, cookie chmn. Girl Scouts U.S.; team mother soccer team, Tucson. Recipient Ima award Tucson chpt. Hadassah, 1999. Mem. ACA, Assn. for Deaath Edn. and Counseling, Am. Assn. Marriage and Family Therapists, Ariz. Mental Health Counselors Assn. Jewish. Avocations: weightlifting, bicycling, walking. E-mail: seysbily@aol.com.

YALMAN, ANN, judge, lawyer; b. Boston, June 9, 1948; d. Richard George and Joan (Osterman) Y. BA, Antioch Coll., 1970; JD, NYU, 1973. Trial atty. Fla. Rural Legal Svcs., Immokalee, Fla., 1973-74; staff atty. EEO, Atlanta, 1974-76; pvt. practice Santa Fe, 1976—; probate judge Santa Fe County, 1999—. Part time U.S. magistrate, N. Mex., 1988-96. Commr. Met. Water Bd., Santa Fe, 1986-88. Mem. N.Mex. Bar Assn. (commr. Santa Fe chpt. 1983-86). Home: 441 Calle La Paz Santa Fe NM 87505-2821 Office: 304 Catron St Santa Fe NM 87501-1806

YALOW, ROSALYN SUSSMAN, biophysicist; b. N.Y.C., N.Y., July 19, 1921; d. Simon and Clara (Zipper) Sussman; m. Aaron Yalow, June 6, 1943; children: Benjamin, Elanna. AB, Hunter Coll., 1941; MS, U. Ill., Urbana, 1942, PhD, 1945; DSc (hon.) , U. Ill., Chgo., 1974, Phila. Coll. Pharmacy and Sci., 1976, N.Y. Med. Coll., 1976, Med. Coll. Wis., Milw., 1977, Yeshiva U., 1977, Southampton (N.Y.) Coll., 1978, Bucknell U., 1978, Princeton U., 1978, Jersey City State Coll., 1979, Med. Coll. Pa., 1979, Manhattan Coll., 1979, U. Vt., 1980, U. Hartford, 1980, Rutgers U., 1980, Rensselaer Poly. Inst., 1980, Colgate U., 1981, U. So. Calif., 1981, Clarkson Coll., 1982, U. Miami, 1983, Washington U., St. Louis, 1983, Adelphi U., 1983, U. Alta. (Can.), 1983, SUNY, 1984, Tel Aviv U., 1985, Claremont (Calif.) U., 1986, Mills Coll., Oakland, Calif., 1986, Cedar Crest Coll., Allentown, Pa., 1988, Drew U., Madison, N.J., 1988, Lehigh U., 1988; LHD (hon.) , Hunter Coll., 1978; DSc (hon.) , San Francisco State U., 1989, Technion-Israel Inst. Tech., Haifa, 1989, Med. Coll. Ohio Toledo, 1991; LHD (hon.) , Sacred Heart U., Conn., 1978, St. Michael's Coll., Winooski Park, Vt., 1979, Johns Hopkins U., 1979, Coll. St. Rose, 1988, Spertus Coll. Judaica, Chgo., 1988; DHC (hon.) , U. Rosario, Argentina, 1980, U. Ghent, Belgium, 1984; D. Humanities and Letters (hon.) , Columbia U., 1984; DSc (hon.) , Fairleigh Dickinson U., 1992, Conn. Coll., 1992, Smith Coll., Northampton, Mass., 1994, Union Coll., Schenectady, 1994. Diplomate Am. Bd. Scis. Lectr., asst. prof. physics Hunter Coll., 1946-50; physicist, asst. chief radioisotope service VA Hosp., Bronx, N.Y., 1950-70, chief nuclear medicine, 1970-80, acting chief radioisotope service, 1968-70, sr. med. investigator emeritus; research prof. Mt. Sinai Sch. Medicine, CUNY, 1968-74, Disting. Service prof., 1974-79, Solomon A. Berson Disting. prof.-at-large, 1986—; Disting. prof.-at-large Albert Einstein Coll. Medicine, Yeshiva U., 1979-85, prof. emeritus, 1986—; chmn. dept. clin. scis. Montefiore Med. Ctr., Bronx, 1980-85. Cons. Lenox Hill Hosp. , N.Y.C., 1956—62, WHO, Bombay, 1978; sec. U.S. Nat. Com. on Med. Physics, 1963—67; mem. nat. com. Radiation Protection, subcom. 13, 1957, Pres.'s Study Group on Careers for Women, 1966—72; sr. med. investigator VA, 1972—92, sr. med. investigator emeritus, 1992—. Co-editor: Hormone and Metabolic Research, 1973—79; editl. adv. coun. Acta Diabetologica Latina, 1975—77, Ency. Universalis, 1978—, editl. bd. Mt. Sinai Jour. Medicine, 1976—79, Diabetes, 1976, Endocrinology, 1967—72, contbr. numerous articles to profl. jours. Bd. dirs. N.Y. Diabetes Assn., 1974. Recipient VA William S. Middleton Med. Rsch. award, 1960, Eli Lilly award, Am. Diabetes Assn., 1961, Van Slyke award, N.Y. met. sect. Am. Assn. Clin. Chemists, 1968, award, ACP, 1971, Dickson prize, U. Pitts., 1971, Howard Taylor Ricketts award, U. Chgo., 1971, Gairdner Found. Internat. award, 1971, Commemorative medallion, Am. Diabetes Assn., 1972, Bernstein award, Med. Soc. State N.Y., 1974, Boehringer-Mannheim Corp. award, Am. Assn. Clin. Chemists, 1975, Sci. achievement award, AMA, 1975, Exceptional Svc. award, VA, 1975, A. Cressy Morrison award, N.Y. Acad. Scis., 1975, sustaining membership award, Assn. Mil. Surgeons, 1975, Disting. Achievement award, Modern Medicine, 1976, Albert Lasker Basic Med. Rsch. award, 1976, La Madonnina Internat. prize, Milan, 1977, Golden Plate award, Am. Acad. Achievement, 1977, Nobel prize for Physiology/Medicine, 1977, citation of esteem, St. John's U., 1979, G. von Hevesy medal, 1978, Rosalyn S. Yalow R&D award established, Am. Diabetes Assn., 1978, Banting medal, 1978, Torch of Learning award, Am. Friends Hebrew U., 1978, Virchow Gold medal, Virchow-Pirquet Med. Soc., 1978, Gratum Genus Humanum Gold medal, World Fedn. Nuc. Medicine or Biology, 1978, Jacobi medallion, Assoc. Alumni Mt. Sinai Sch. Medicine, 1978, Jubilee medal, Coll. of New Rochelle, 1978, VA Exceptional Svc. award, 1978, Fed. Woman's award, 1961, Harvey lectr., 1966, Am. Gastroenterol. Assn. Meml. lectr., 1972, Joslin lectr., New Eng. Diabetes Assn., 1972, 1st Hagedorn Meml. lectr., Acta Endocrinologica Congress, 1973, Franklin I. Harris Meml. lectr., 1973, Sarasota Med. award for achievement and excellence, 1979, Gold medal, Phi Lambda Kappa, 1980, Achievement in Life award, Ency. Britannica, 1980, Theobald Smith award, 1982, Pres.'s Cabinet award, U. Detroit, 1982, John and Samuel Bard award in medicine and sci., Bard Coll., 1982, Disting. Rsch. award, Dallas Assn. Retarded Citizens, 1982, Nat. medal of Sci., 1988, Abram L. Sachar Silver medallion, Brandeis U., 1989, Disting. Scientist of Yr. award, ARCS, N.Y.C., 1989, Golden Scroll award, The Jewish Advocate, Boston, 1989, spl. award, Clin. Ligand Assay Soc., Washington, 1988, numerous others. Fellow: Clin. Soc. N.Y. Diabetes Assn., Am. Coll. Radiology (assoc. in physics), N.Y. Acad. Scis. (chmn. biophysics divsn. 1964—65); mem.: NAS, Am. Physiol. Soc., Endocrine Soc. (pres. 1978, Kocn award 1972), Soc. Nuc. Medicine, Soc. Nuc. Medicine (hon.), Am. Gastroenterol. Assn. (hon.), Am. Coll. Nuc. Physicians (hon.), Harvey soc. (hon.), Med. Assn. Argentina (hon.), Diabetes Soc. Argentina (hon.), The N.Y. Acad. Medicine (hon.), N.Y. Roentgen Soc. (hon.), Biophys. Soc., Am. Assn. Physicists in Medicine, Radiation Rsch. Soc., Am. Phys. Soc., Am. Acad. Arts and Scis., Tau Beta Pi, Sigma Delta Epsilon, Pi Mu Epsilon, Sigma Pi Sigma, Sigma Xi, Phi Beta Kappa. Office: Vet Affairs Med Ctr 130 W Kingsbridge Rd Bronx NY 10468-3904

YAM, AILEEN LYNETTE, programmer; m. Keith L. Yam, June 26, 1990. MA, So. Ill. U., Carbondale, 1979. Statis. cons. Mich. State U. Computer Lab., 1985-87; rsch. exec. Young & Rubicam, Detroit, 1987-88; sci. programmer Carter-Wallace, Inc., Cranbury, N.J., 1988-90; tech. dir. statis. programming, SAS programming cons. Covance Inc., Princeton, 1990-98; lead programmer PharmaNet Inc., 1998—2002; pres. Clin. Info. Analysis, Inc., 2002—. Invited spkr. various orgns. Contbr. articles to profl. jours. Recipient Best Paper award SAS Inst., Inc., Cary, N.C., 1990, 1st pl. award in tng. materials, 1996, Best Paper award PharmaSUG, 1997. Avocations: piano, traveling. Home: 40 Linden Ln Plainsboro NJ 08536-2521 Office: PharmaNet Inc 504 Carnegie Ctr Princeton NJ 08540-6242

YAMADA, KENNETH MANAO, cell biologist; b. Mpls., Sept. 18, 1944; s. Paul Manao and Masaye (Uriu) Y.; m. Susan Jane Sleeper, July 1, 1973. BA in Biol. Scis., Stanford U., 1966, PhD in Biol. Scis., 1971, MD, 1972. Intern Mary's Help Hosp./Seton Med. Ctr., Daly City, Calif., 1972-73; commd. lt. USPHS, 1974, advanced through grades to capt., 1982—; sect. chief Nat. Cancer Inst., Bethesda, Md., 1980-90; lab. chief Nat. Inst. Dental and Craniofacial Rsch., NIH, 1990-96, br. chief, 1996—. Mem. NIH Cell Biology Study Sect., 1979-83; mem. external adv. com. Howard U. Cancer Rsch. Ctr., 1979-88; co-chmn. Gordon Conf. on Fibronectin, 1982; Stadtler lectr. U. Tex. Sys. Cancer Ctr., M.D. Anderson Hosp., 1988; Swerling lectr. Dana-Farber Cancer Inst., Harvard Med. Sch., 1988. Editor Jour. Cell Physiology, 1989—, Jour. Cell Biology, 1999—; contbr. more than 300 articles to profl. jours. Postdoctoral fellow U. Oreg., Dept. Biology, Eugene, 1973-74; recipient Eli Luke and Jacob David Rsch. award, 1972. Fellow AAAS; mem. Am. Soc. Cell Biology (coun. mem. 1992-95), Am. Soc. Biochemistry and Molecular Biology, Internat. Soc. Matrix Biology (coun. mem. 1994—), Southeastern Cancer Rsch. Assn. (bd. dirs. 1980-83), Soc. Devel. Biology, Phi Beta Kappa (Undergrad. Rsch. award), Sigma Xi. Office: Nat Inst of Dental and Craniofacial Rsch Rm 421 30 Convent Dr Bldg 30 Bethesda MD 20892-4370 E-mail: kenneth.yamada@nih.gov.

YAMADA, TAKESHI, artist, language and cultural consultant, educator, writer; b. Osaka, Japan, June 25, 1960; s. Yoshihiko and Yoshie Yamada. Student, Yamamoto Fine Art Acad., Osaka, 1970-73, Atorie Ribera Sch. Art, 1977, Nakanoshima (Japan) Coll. Art, 1978-80, Osaka Art U., 1980-83; ed., Calif. Coll. Arts and Crafts, Oakland, 1983; BFA, Md. Inst. Coll. Art, 1985; MFA, U. Mich., 1987, Wealth U., Seattle, 2002. Owner, pres. Yamada Art Ctr., Bklyn., 1983—; sr. translator Chgo. Japanese Am. News, 1997-99; sr. interpreter Unipac Tours, Inc., Chgo., 1997-2000, Hope Svc., Chgo., 1997-2000, Global Mgmt. Svcs., Inc., Chgo., 1997—2000, C.P. Lang. Inst., Bklyn., 2000—. Instr. Yamada Art Ctr., 1983—, Wicker Pk. Sch. Art, Chgo., 1995-96, Ill. Inst Tech., Chgo., 1993, Ann Arbor (Mich.) Art Assn., 1987-88, Jyuku Pvt. H.S., Osaka, 1978-83; instr., counselor Camp Northwestern, Lake Geneva, Wis., 1993, French Woods Summer Camp, N.Y., 1988, Shirahama Summer Marine Camp, Wakayama, Japan, 1982; lectr. Mont. State U., Billings, 1995, Mt. Vernon (Ohio) Nazarene Coll., 1995, Marwen Found., Chgo., 1993, Lauren Rogers Mus. Art, Laurel, Miss., 1993, La. State Mus., New Orleans, 1990, Ann Arbor Elem. Sch., 1987, Ea. Oreg. U., La Grande, 1998, Chemeketa C.C. Salem Oreg., 1999, Salem State Coll., 1999, Nagoya (Japan) U. Arts, 1988, Osaka (Japan) Coll. Arts, U. Minn., Mpls., 2000, Internat. Mus. Surg. Sci., 2001. One-man shows include Posselt-Baker Gallery, New Orleans, 1985, 87, Neville-Sargent Gallery, Chgo., 1988, 91, 92, 94, La. State Mus., New Orleans, 1990, Chgo. Cultural Ctr., 1991, Gallerie Charlotte Daneel, Amsterdam, The Netherlands, 1992, Lauren Rogers Mus. Art, Laurel, Miss., 1993, Mt. Vernon Nazaren Coll., 1995, Peltz Gallery, Milw., 1995, Mont. State U., Billings, 1995, Pauline Art Ctr., Chgo., 1994, 95, 98, Yamada Art Ctr., Chgo., 1995, 96, 97, 98, David Adler Cultural Ctr., Libertyville, Ill., 1996, Artemisia Gallery, Chgo., 1996, Holiday Inn, Elmhurst, Ill., 1997, Brownsboro Gallery, Louisville, Ky., 1998, Shinsen Art Gallery, Chgo., 1998, Ea. Oreg. U., La Grande, 1998, Salem State Coll., Salem, Mass., 1999, Belloc Lowdnes Fine Art, 1999, Japan Information Ctr., 1999, Hyde Park Art Ctr., 1999, Collins Fine Art, Chgo., 2000, Internat. Museum of Surg. Sci., 2001; exhibited in over 213 group shows, most recently at Chgo. Belloc Lowndes Fine Art, 1999, Japan Info. Ctr., 1999, Hyde Park Art Ctr., 1999, Belloc Lowndes Fine Art, Chgo., 1999, Japan Info. Ctr., 1999, Hyde Park Art Ctr., Chgo., 1999, Barrister's Gallery, New Orleans, 2000, Bloomsburg U., Pa., 2000, Athenaeum Mus., 2001, James Thompson Ctr., 2000, Drake Hotel, 2000, Red Bud Gallery, Houston, 2000, Barrister's Gallery, 2000, Bloomsburg U., 2000, Chemeketa C.C., Salem, Oreg., 1999, Pfister Hotel, Milw., 1996, 97, 98, 99, 2000, 2001, Peltz Gallery, 1995, 96, 97, 98, 99, 2000, 2001, Neville-Sargent Gallery, 1996, 97, 98, 99, 2000, 2001, Nadaismo Gallery, Chgo., 1996, Brownsboro Gallery, Louisville, 1996, 97, Bixler Gallery, Stroudsburg, Pa., 1996, Shinsen Gallery, 1999, 2000, James Thompson Ctr., 2000, Drake Hotel, Milw., 2000, Red Bud Galler Kentler Internat. Drawing Space, Bklyn., 2001, BWAC, 2001, Augen Gallery, Portland, Oreg., 2001, Chgo. Athenaeum Mus., Schaumburg, Ill., 2001, Peltz Gallery, Milw., 2001, Shinsen Art Gallery, Chgo., 2001; represented in permanent collections, including Chgo. Athenaeum Mus., Internat. Mus. Surg. Sci., Six Flags 'Power Plant' Amusement Pk., Balt., Holister Inc., Libertyville, H & H Graphics, Chgo., Dann Bros. Ins. Co., Chgo., Ann Arbor (Mich.) Observer Co., SGI-USA Detroit Cmty. Ctr., SGI-USA Chgo. Culture Ctr., Northwestern Mil.

and Naval Acad., Lake Geneva, Wis., Ohio State U., Newark, Mont. State U., Billings, Kishwaukee Coll., Malta, Ill., U. Mich. Mus. Art, New Orleans Mus. Art, La. State Mus., Salem State Coll., Salem, Mass., Ea. Oreg. U., La Grande, Mt. Vernon Nazaren Coll., Mt. Vernon, Ohio, U. Mich. Sch. Art, Ann Arbor, Chemeketa C.C., Salem, Oreg., Internat. Mus. Surg. Sci., Chgo.; other pvt. and corp.; commd. works include murals, photographs, illustrations for various publs.; author, artist (20 books): Comments on the New York Street Scene Paintings, 1987, New York: The City and Its People, 1987, Chicago: Citizen Kings, 1988, Divine Comedy: New Orleans Mardi Gras, 1990, Chicago Chronicle: From the Great Fire to the Great Flood, 1992, Grand Illusions: Chicago: 1893-1994, 1994, Iron Phoenix: Chicago Architecture, 1994, Eternity: Amsterdam Nightscapes, 1994, New Orleans: Street Scenes 1993, 1994, Dukes and Saints: New Orleans Jazz 1990-92, 1994, Louisville, 1998, Urban Portraits, 1998, Visual Anthropology, 1998, Miniatures, 1999, Milwaukee: Phantom City, 1999, Graphic Works 1996-99, 2000, City of Night: New Orleans, 2000, Takeshi Yamada's Chicago, 2000, Visual Anthropology, 2000, Medical Journal of the Artist, 2001; contbr. over 134 major articles and reviews in Japan and U.S. in various newspapers, mags., and books; over 258 visual art performances gen. pub. include James Thompson Ctr., 2000, Collias Fine Art, Chgo., 2000, Yamada Art Ctr., Chgo., 2000, Bklyn. Mus. Art, 2001, Kentler Internat. Drawing Space, 2001, Internat. Mus. Surg. Sci., Chgo., 2001, Chgo. Athenaeum Mus., 2001, Excalibur, Chgo., Bklyn. Borough Hall, N.Y., 2002, Evonne Davis Gallery, N.Y., Ridge St. Gallery, N.Y., 2002, Holland Tunnel Gallery, N.Y., 2002, BWAC, N.Y., 2002, Kentler Internat. Drawing Space, N.Y., 2002. Recipient Key to City, Mayor of City of New Orleans, 1990, Key to City of Gary, Ind., 1998, numerous art competition and exhbn. awards; fellow Artist's fellowship, N.Y., 2001; grantee Holbein Acryla grantee, Holebin Arts Inc., Tokyo, 1989; scholar, U. Mich. Sch. Art, 1985—87. Avocations: carnivorous plants, breeding tropical giant insects, travel, cooking, composition and performance of classical music. Home and Office: Yamada Art Center 1405 Neptune Ave Brooklyn NY 11224 E-mail: takeshiyamada@hotmail.com.

YAMADA, TETSUJI, health economist, educator; M of Internat. Affairs, Columbia U., 1978; MPhil, CUNY, 1983, PhD in Econs., 1987. Instr. CUNY, NYC, 1982—86; postdoc. fellow Grad. Ctr., CUNY, N.Y.C., 1987; asst. prof. dept. econs. Rutgers U., Camden, NJ, 1987—91; assoc. prof. Ritsumeikan U., Kyoto, 1991-92; rsch. fellow NBER, 1987-90, rsch. assoc., 1991-94; health economist Internat. Leadership Ctr. Longevity and Society, 1993-94; rsch. assoc. Ctr. Pacific Basin Fed. Res. Bank, San Francisco, 1990—; assoc. prof. Rutgers U., 1992—, chair dept. econs., 1996-99; exec. bd. China East Inst. Soc. Ins., China, 1998—. Rep. Japan Econ. Fedn., Ditchley, Oxford, England, 1994; vis. rsch. scholar Inst. Policy and Planning Scis., Tsukuba U., Japan, 1997—2002; temp. advisor WHO, 1999; faculty assoc. The Walter Rand Inst., 1999—; ctr. assoc. The Ctr. for Children and Childhood Studies, 2000—; cons. Japan Found., 2001; reviewer and referee profl. jours., books and rsch. grants. Contbr. articles to profl. jours. Fellow postdoctoral fellow, Grad. Ctr. CUNY, 1987; grantee Ministry of Edn., Japan, 1991, Iryo Kagaku Kenkyu Jo, Japan, 1991-92, 96-97, Pfizer Health Rsch. Found., 1992-93, 21st Century Cultural Rsch. Found., Japan, 1993, Ministry of Health and Welfare, Japan, 1993-94, Nomura Found., Japan, 1995-96, Iryo Keizai Kenkyu Kiko, Japan, 1997-98, Rutgers U. ORSP, 1992-, Ctr. for Children and Childhood Studies, 2000-2001 . Mem. Am. Econ. Assn., So. Econs. Assn., Western Econ. Assn., Internat. Health Econ. Assn., Japan Econ. Sem., Omicron Delta Epsilon (award). Home: 300 East 40th St #4M New York NY 10016 Office: Dept Econs-CCAS Rutgers Univ State Univ NJ Camden NJ 08102 Fax: 212-297-0192. E-mail: ytetsuji@aol.com., tyamada@crab.rutgers.edu.

YAMADA, TOSHIKATSU AUGUSTINE, academic administrator, mechanical engineer; b. Nagoya, Aichi, Japan, Jan. 23, 1923; s. Etsujiro and Yuki (Takeuchi) Y.; m. Chizuko Shirota, Nov. 22, 1956; children: Takahisa, Chieko. B in Engring., Nagoya (Japan) U., 1948, D in Engring., 1977. Asst. Nagoya (Japan) U., 1963-66; asst. prof. Toyota Coll. Tech., Japan, 1966-70, prof. Japan, 1970-87; pres. Aichi Coll. Tech., Gamagori, Japan, 1987—. Author: Milling With Plain Milling Cutters, 1977, Under The Beautiful Purple-Blue Flag, 1987. Mem. ASME, Japan Soc. Mech. Engrs., Gamagori (Japan) Internat. Assn. (dir. 1992—, v.p. 1994—). Avocations: classical music, tea ceremonies, bird watching, Judo. Home: 3-8-10 Wakamuzu Chikusa Nagoya 464 Japan Office: Aichi Coll Tech 50-2 Manori Nishihasama Aichi Gamagori 443 Japan

YAMAGUCHI, KRISTI TSUYA, ice skater; b. Hayward, Calif., July 12, 1971; d. Jim and Carole (Doi) Y. Gold medalist, Figure Skating Albertville Olympic Games, 1992; U.S. Skating champion, 1992; World Skating champion, 1991, 1992; World Junior champion, 1988; world profl. figure skating champion, 1994. Recipient Women First award YWCA, 1993, Inducted World Figure Skating Hall of Fame, 1999. Avocations: tennis, rollerblading, reading, and dancing.*

YAMAGUCHI, TADANORI, electrical engineer; b. Jan. 17, 1949; BSEE, Miyakonojyo Inst. Tech., Miyazaki, Japan, 1969. Rsch. and devel. engr. Sony Corp., Atsugi, Japan, 1969-76; fellow, project mgr. Tektronix, Inc., Beaverton, Oreg., 1977-94; fellow, exec. dir. Maxim Integrated Products, 1994—. Home: 12757 NW Hartford St Portland OR 97229-3769

YAMAGUCHI, YUKIO, chemistry research scientist; b. Hiroshima, Japan, Feb. 22, 1941; came to U.S., 1970; s. Tameo and Miyuki (Kodama) Y.; m. Masako Iwamura, Aug. 3, 1994. BE, Kyushu U., Fukuoka, Japan, 1964, ME, 1966; PhD, U. Tex., Austin, 1978. Research assoc. Kyushu U., Fukuoka, 1966-70; postdoctoral fellow U. Tex., Austin, 1979-80, U. Calif. and Lawrence Berkeley Lab., Berkeley, 1980-82, chemistry rsch. scientist, 1982-87, U. Ga., Athens, 1987—. Author: (with Y. Osamura, J.D. Goddard and H.F. Schaefer) A New Dimension to Quantum Chemistry: Analytic Derivative Methods in Ab Initio Molecular Electronic Structure Theory; contbr. articles to profl. jours. Mem. Am. Chem. Soc., Chem. Soc. of Japan. Avocations: reading, travel, swimming. Office: U Ga Ctr Computational Quantum Chem Athens GA 30602

YAMAGUCHI, YURIKO FUJITA, artist; b. Japan, Jan. 25, 1948; came to the U.S., 1971; d. Alexander and Michi (Hirose) Fujita; m. Hiroyuki Yamaguchi, Mar. 25, 1975; children: Seiji, Mariko. BA, U. Calif., Berkeley, 1975; MFA, U. Md., 1979. Instr. U. Md., College Park, 1982-83; adj. faculty Corcoran Sch. Art, Washington, 1988-97. Vis. artist Md. Inst. Art, Balt., 1991, 95, Mass. Coll. Art, Boston, 1994. Exhibited in group shows at Hirshhorn Mus., 1984, L.A. County Mus., 1987, Penine Hart Gallery, N.Y., 1989, 1994, Koplin Gallery, L.A., 1991, 1994, 1996, 1999, 2002, Gallery Emon, Japan, 1997, 2000, Numark Gallery, 1999, Hand Workshop Art Ctr., 2000, Howard Scott Gallery, N.Y.C., 2001, Del. Ctr. for Contemporary Arts, 2001, Suyama Space, Seattle, 2002, commd. wall mural, Represented in permanent collections Hirshhorn Mus., Nat. Mus. Women in Arts, Nat. Mus. Am. Art, Smith Coll. Art Mus., exhibited in group shows at Sheehan Gallery, Whitman Coll., Washington, 2002. Va. Mus. Fine Arts fellow, 1988, 85, 2001; Mid-Atlantic Found. fellow, 1995; Va. Commn. Arts grantee, 1994, 2000, Salzburg Kunstlerhaus Residency grantee, 1993. E-mail: yuriko414@aol.com. Home: 1517 Snughill Ct Vienna VA 22182-1724

YAMAKAWA, ALLAN HITOSHI, academic administrator; b. San Francisco, Oct. 18, 1938; s. Victor Tadashi and Alice Tsugie (Sato) Y.; m. Nancy Ann Habel, Apr.17, 1977 (div. Mar 1987); children: Bryan Allan, David Scott. BS, Roosevelt U., 1962, MEd, 1970. Tech. svcs. dir. audio visual libr. Roosevelt U., Chgo., 1958-60; dean, exec. dir. Ency. Britannica Schs., Inc., 1960-67; curriculum svcs. dir. Field Enterprises Newspaper Div., 1967-70; edn. svcs. dir. Chgo. Tribune Co., 1970-76; tng. svcs. dir. Dialogue Systems Inc., N.Y.C., 1976-79; orgn. devel. dir. U. Ill., Chgo., 1979-99. Cons., trainer Can. Daily Newspaper Pub. Assn., Toronto, 1973-84, Am. Newspaper Pub. Found., Reston, Va., 1972-80, Gifted Students Found. Dallas, 1974-75; cons. Cedars Sinai Med. Ctr., Beverly Hills, Calif., 1983-98, W. K. Kellogg Found., 1987-2000; faculty Internat. Ctr. for Health Leadership Devel., 1996-2000. Author: Handbooks of Teaching Methods, 1974, Communicate, 1975, Catalysts For Change, 1976, Evaluation of Senior Administrators, 1994; patentee experiential learning method. Instr. ARC, Chgo., 1954-85; bd. dirs. Edison Regional Gifted Ctr. Sch., Chgo., pres., 1989-93; dist. program chmn. Boy Scouts Am., 1985—. Recipient Founders award Boy Scouts Am., 1997. Mem. ASTD, ASCD, Soc. Programmed and Automated Learning, Toastmasters (pres. 1974-76), Order of Arrow. Avocations: photography, computer programming, electronics, pyrotechnics, film production. Office: 1524 W Pratt Blvd Unit G Chicago IL 60626-4297 E-mail: ahy26@hotmail.com.

YAMAMOTO, IRWIN TORAKI, editor, publisher investment newsletter; b. Wailuku, Maui, Hawaii, Apr. 5, 1955; s. Torao and Yukie (Urata) Y. B in Bus. Adminstrn., Mktg., Chaminade U., 1977. Pres., editor, publisher The Yamamoto Forecast, Kahului, Hawaii, 1977—. Author: (book) Profit Making in the Stock Market, 1983; columnist The Hawaii Herald, 1978—. Named Top Market Timer, Top Gold Timer, Top Bond Timer, and to Timer Digest Honor Roll by Timer Digest, also honored by Select Info. Exchange and Rating the Stock Selectors. Avocations: exercise, music, reading, philosophy. Home and Office: PO Box 573 Kahului HI 96733-7073

YAMAMOTO, JOE, psychiatrist, educator; b. Los Angeles, Apr. 18, 1924; s. Zenzaburo and Tomie (Yamada) Y.; m. Maria Fujitomi, Sept. 5, 1947; children: Eric Robert, Andrew Jolyon. Student, Los Angeles City Coll., 1941-42, Hamline U., 1943-45; BS, U. Minn., 1946, M.B., 1948, MD, 1949. Asst. prof. dept. psychiatry, neurology, behavioral sci. U. Okla. Med. Center, 1955-58, asst. prof., 1958-60; assoc. prof. dept. psychiatry U. So. Calif. Sch. Medicine, Los Angeles, 1961-69, prof., 1969-77, co-dir. grad. edn. psychiatry, 1963-70; prof. UCLA, 1977-94, emeritus prof., 1994—; dir. Psychiat. Outpatient Clinic, Los Angeles County-U. So. Calif. Med. Center, 1958-77; dir. adult ambulatory care services UCLA Neuropsychiat. Inst., 1977-88, chief Lab. for Cross Cultural Studies. Contbr. articles in field to profl. jours. Served to capt., M.C. U.S. Army, 1953-55. Fellow Am. Psychiat. Assn. (life), Pacific Rim Coll. Psychiatrists, Am. Acad. Psychoanalysis (trustee, mem. exec. com., pres. 1978-79), Am. Coll. Psychiatrists, Am. Orthopsychiat. Assn. (pres.-elect 1993-94, pres. 1994-95, past pres.), Am. Assn. for Social Psychiatry (trustee 1981-84, v.p. 1984-86); mem. So. Calif. Psychoanalytic Inst. and Soc. (pres. 1972-73), Soc. for Study of Culture and Psychiatry, Group for Advancement Psychiatry (bd. dirs. 1992-94), Kappa Phi, Alpha Omega Alpha. Office: UCLA Neuro psychiat Inst 760 Westwood Plz Los Angeles CA 90095-8353 *Learning about the diverse peoples of America, I have been fascinated with how we can be Asian, Hispanic, Black, European, and Native American and still identify with our national values. We value our freedom, individual rights and our ability to be someone different but equal. In mental health also there is a need for recognition of cultural differences and the need of treatment response to the individual.*

YAMAMOTO, KAORU, retired psychology and education educator; b. Tokyo, Mar. 28, 1932; arrived in U.S., 1959; s. Saburo and Hideko (Watanabe) Y.; m. Etsuko Hamazaki, Apr. 6, 1959 (div. 1986); m. Carol-Lynne Moore, Oct. 4, 1986; children: Keita Carey Moore, Kiyomi Lynne Moore. BS in Engring., U. Tokyo, 1953; MA, U. Minn., 1960, PhD, 1962. Engr. Toppan Printing Co., Tokyo, 1953; engr., rsch. chemist Japan Oxygen Co., 1954-57, 58-59; asst. prof. Kent (Ohio) State U., 1962-65; from asst. to assoc. prof. U. Iowa, Iowa City, 1965-68; prof. Pa. State U., University Park, 1968-72, Ariz. State U., Tempe, 1972-87, U. Colo., Denver, 1987-99, prof. emeritus, 1999—. Vis. prof. U. Minn., Mpls., 1974, Simon Fraser U., Burnaby, B.C., Can., 1984, U.Victoria, B.C., 1986, U. Wash., Seattle, 1987, Zhejiang Normal U., Jinhua, China, 1991; Fulbright lectr. U. Iceland, 1985. Author: The Child and His Image, 1972, Their World, Our World, 1993; author, editor 7 books, including Children and Stress, 2001; co-author: Beyond Words, 1988; editor Am. Ednl. Rsch. Jour., 1972-75, Ednl. Forum, 1984-92; contbr. chpts. to books and articles to profl. jours. Recipient Disting. Tchr. award Ariz. State U., 1980; Landsdowne scholar U. Victoria, 1985, Ctr. scholar Ctr. for Rsch. on Ethics and Values Azusa Pacific U., 1998-2000. Fellow: APA; mem.: Motus Humanus. Avocations: winter sports, travel, classical music, reading. Office: 13651 W 54th Ave Arvada CO 80002

YAMAMOTO, KEITH ROBERT, molecular biologist, educator; b. Des Moines, Feb. 4, 1946; BS, Iowa State U., 1968; PhD, Princeton U., 1973. Asst. prof. biochemistry U. Calif., San Francisco, 1976-79, assoc. prof., 1979-83, prof. biochemistry, 1983—, dir. biochemistry and molecular biology program, 1988—2001, prof., chmn. cellular and molecular pharmacology, 1994—; vice dean for rsch. UCSF Sch. Medicine, 2002—. Co-author: Gene Wars: Military Control Over the New Genetic Technologies, 1988; co-editor: Transcriptional Regulation, 1992; assoc. editor: Jour. Molecular Biology, 1988—2001; editor: Molecular Biology of the Cell, 1991—2001; editor-in-chief: , 2002—. Testifier hearings on biol. warfare com. on govtl. affairs U.S. Senate, Washington, 1989. Recipient Gregory Pincus medal Worchester Found. for Exptl. Biology, 1990; Dreyfus tchr.-scholar, 1982-86. Fellow: Am. Acad. Arts and Scis.; mem.: NAS. Office: U Calif San Francisco Dept Cellular Molecular Phm 513 Parnassus Ave San Francisco CA 94143-0450

YAMANE, STANLEY JOEL, optometrist, consultant; b. Lihue, Kauai, Hawaii, Mar. 13, 1943; s. Tooru and Yukiko (Miura) Y.; m. Joyce Mitsuko Tamura; children— Stanley Tooru Aiichi, Karen Margaret BS in Optometry, O.D., Pacific U., 1966. Diplomate Am. Acad. Optometry. Practice optometry, Waipahu, Hawaii, 1967-73; ptnr. with Dr. Dennis M. Kuwabara, 1973-81; ptnr. Drs. Kuwabara & Yamane, Optometrists, Inc., Waipahu, 1981-91, with br. office Honolulu; with DBA Eye Care Assocs. of Hawaii, 1989-91; dir. profl. affairs Vistakon, Inc., 1991-92; v.p. profl. affairs Vistakon Inc., 1992—, chair global profl. affairs coun., 1996-99. Lectr., cons. in field; sec.-treas. Hawaii Bd. Examiners in Optometry, 1975-76, v.p., 1976-78, pres., 1978-80; mem. adj. faculty Coll. Optometry, Pacific U., 1977-91, Pa. Coll. Optometry, 1981-91, So. Coll. Optometry, 1982-91, U. Mo., St. Louis, 1990-91; bd. dirs. Hawaii Vision Svc. Plan, 1984-91. Cons. editor Optometric Mgmt. Jour., 1981-91, Contact Lens Forum Jour., 1987-91, editor, 1991; contbr. articles to profl. jours. Bd. mgrs. Leeward Oahu Br. YMCA, 1967-70, Hi-Y advisor, 1967-71, mem. Century Club, 1967-91, bd. mgrs. West Oahu Br., 1971-78, gen. chmn. sustaining membership, 1976; 2d v.p. August Ahrens Elem. Sch. PTA, 1969; mem. Leeward Mental Health Adv. Council, 1975-76, Friends of Waipahu Cultural Garden Park Found., 1976—, Aloha council Boy Scouts Am., 1976-91; mem. bus. adv. council Waipahu High Sch., 1976-81, Parent-Tchr.-Community Adv. Council, 1978-80; bd. dirs. Central/Leeward unit Am. Cancer Soc., 1977-80, pub. edn. dir., 1978-79, v.p., 1979-80, founder, chmn. Celebrity Auction, 1980, dir. Oahu Baseline Survey, 1978; bd. dirs. Barbers Point council Navy League Am., 1981-85; profl. bd. advisors U. Houston Inst. for Contact Lens Research. Recipient Merit award Nat. Eye Research Found., 1974, Disting. Service award, 1976, Founder's award Pacific U., 1996, Heart of Am. Contact Lens Soc. Vision Svc. award, 1998. Fellow Am. Acad. Optometry (cornea and contact lens diplomate, vice chair cornea and contact lens sect. 1992-94, chair cornea and contact lens sect. 1994-96, immediate past chair, 1997-99, sec., 1990-92, vice chair ethics com. 1991-92, corp. support for Jour. com. 1981, chair diplomate awards com. 1988-90), AAAS, Am. Optometric Assn. (ann. congress del. 1978, pub. health com. 19738, optometric paraoptometric personnel com. 1978-79, contact lens project team 1979-80, task force on R&D 1984-87, contact lens sect. coun. 1988-92, sec., 1989-90, vice chair 1990-91, chair elect 1991-92, numerous coms.), Leeward Oahu Jaycees (Disting. Service award 1969, Top Outstanding Young Man award 1975), Hawaii State Jaycees, Am. Optometric Found. (bd. dirs. 1981-91 , chmn. task force clin. research 1981-83, nominations com. 1982, treas. 1985-86, sec., 1987-88, pres.-elect, 1988-89, pres. 1989-90), Am. Pub. Health Assn., Better Vision Inst., Coll. Optometrists in Vision Devel., Hawaii Optometric Assn. (corr. sec. 1968-70, state newsletter editor 1968-70, rec. sec. 1971, 2d v.p. 1972, pres. 1974-75; Man of Yr. 1975, Optometrist of Yr. 1979), Internat. Optometric & Optical League, Internat. Soc. Contact Lens Rsch., Brit. Contact Lens Assn., Japan Contact Lens Acad., Nat. Assn. of the Professions, Nat. Eye Research Found. (fellow Internat. Orthokeratology sect.; editorial bd. Contacto Jour. 1979, contact lens cert. com. 1981-85), Nat. Fedn. Ind. Bus., Optometric Cons. in Contact Lens Optometric Extension Program Found. (chmn. study group 1969-70, state dir. 1971-73), Optometric Hist. Soc., Optometric Polit. Action Coms., Soc. Contact Lens Specialists, Hawaii Assn. Children with Learning Disabilities, Hawaii Assn. Intellectually Gifted Children (pub. relations chmn. 1st Ann. State Conf. 1975, legis. lobbyist 1975-76), Waipahu Bus. Assn. (bd. dirs. 1974-78, chmn. pub. relations 1974-75, legis. lobbyist 1974-75, pres. 1974-75), Nat. Acad. Practice in Optometry (mem.-at-large on exec. com., disting. practitioner in optometry) Democrat. Baptist. Home: 8609 Autumn Green Dr Jacksonville FL 32256-9560 Office: Vistakon Inc Vp Profl Affairs 7596 Centurion Pkwy Jacksonville FL 32256-0517

YAMANI, MOHAMAD HILAL, cardiologist; b. Beirut, Lebanon, Sept. 22, 1956; came to the U.S., 1991; m. Zahra Adel Jishi, Mar. 14, 1998. MD, Am. U. Beirut, 1981. Bd. cert. internal medicine and cardiovasc. disease. Faculty cardiology Cleve. Clinic Found., 1999—. Mem. Internat. Soc. for Heart and Lung Transplantation, Am. Soc. Transplantation, Am. Heart Assn., Am. Coll. Cardiology, Heart Failure Soc. Am. Office: Cleve Clinic Cardiology F25 9500 Euclid Ave # F25 Cleveland OH 44195-0001 E-mail: yamanim@ccf.org.

YAMASHITA, AYAKO, research scientist; b. Japan; d. Fumio and Mitsuko Yamashita. Postdoctoral Assoc. Chemistry, Harvard Med. Sch., Boston, Massachusetts, 1974—76, Cornell U., Ithaca, New York, 1973—74; PhD Pharm. Sci., Kyushu U., Fukuoka, Japan, 1973, BS Chemistry, 1968. Sr. rsch. scientist Am. Home Products Co., Pearl River, NY, 1994—2002, Am. Cyanamid Co., Pearl River, 1991—94, DuPont Co., Wilmington, Del., 1989—91, Upjohn Co., Kalamazoo, 1980—89; rsch. staff, dept. of chemistry Princeton U., Princeton, NJ, 1978—80; rsch. staff dept. of chemistry Cornell U., Ithaca, NY, 1976—78. Peer rev. ad hoc cons. Nat. Inst. of Health, Bethesda, Md., 1997—, peer rev. cons., Md., 1993—97. Mem.: Am. Chem. Soc. Home: 52 Dwight Place #F Englewood NJ 07631 Office: Wyeth Company American Home Products Middletown Road Pearl River NY 10965 Office Fax: 845-602-5561. E-mail: yamasha@wyeth.com.

YAMATO, KEI C. international business consultant; b. Honokaa, Hawaii, Sept. 21, 1921; s. Kango and Shizuka (Tanaka) Y.; children: Karen, Marla, Kei Tracy. BA, U. Hawaii, 1946; LLD, Yale, 1950; DD, World Christianship Ministries, 1994. Ordained to ministry Ind. Universal Ch. of God, 1994. Pres. Internat. Bus. Mgmt. Co., 1950; founder Pacific-Asia Bus. Council, 1950; pres. Orchids of Hawaii Internat., Inc., 1951, Polynesian Products, Inc., Holiday Promotions Internat., Inc., 1952, Orchawaii Internat. Travel Corp., 1962, Pacific Area Landscaping, Inc., 1970—, Hawaii Hort. Enterprises, Inc., 1970—, Agrisystems, Inc., 1971-95; minister Ind. Universal Ch. God, Honolulu, 1995—. V.p., dir. Sperry & Hutchison Travel Awards, Inc., 1964, Copley Internat. Corp., 1967; all N.Y.C.; pres. Internat. Cons. Co., 1968, Asia-Pacific Corp., 1968; chmn. Asia Internat. Group of Cos., Asia Internat. Cons.; mng. dir. Internat. Cons. Assocs., 1993; universal cons. svcs. God's Universal Ch. and Ministries. Bd. dirs. Internat. Execs. Assn., World Trade Club N.Y.C., Sales Execs. Club N.Y.C.; mem. Regional Export Expansion Council, U.S. Dept. Commerce; organizer Asia Pacific Inst.; pres. Saudi Arabia Pacific Asia Bus. Council, Arab Asian Assocs. Served to 1st lt. AUS, World War II, ETO. Decorated Silver Star, Purple Heart with 2 oak leaf clusters. Mem. Advt. Club N.Y.C., Nat. Indsl. Conf. Bd., Profl. Mgmt. Cons. Assn. Am., Sales Promotion Execs. Assn., Chgo. Execs. Club, Sales and Marketing Execs. Internat., N.Y. Hort. Soc., Asia Soc., Japan Soc., Am. Mgmt. Assn. (lectr.), 442d Regimental Combat Team Assn., Landscape Contractors Assn. Hawaii, Gen. Contractors Assn. Hawaii, Friends East-West Center, East-West Philosophers Conf., Hawaii Assn. Nurserymen, Hawaii Bot. Soc., Honolulu Execs. Assn., U. Hawaii Alumni Assn., Navy League, Nat. Fedn. Ind. Bus., Am. Assn. Nurserymen, Pacific Area Travel Assn., Assn. U.S. Army, Hawaii Visitors Bur., Hawaii C. of C., U.S. Arab C. of C., Saudi Arabia Bus. Council. Clubs: Rotary, Bankers. Home: PO Box 22564 Honolulu HI 96823-2564

YAMAUCHI, EDWIN MASAO, history educator; b. Hilo, Hawaii, Feb. 1, 1937; s. Shokyo Yamauchi and Haruko (Owan) Yamauchi Higa; m. Kimie Honda, Aug. 31, 1962; children: Brian, Gail. Student, U. Hawaii, 1957-58; BA, Shelton Coll., 1960; MA, Brandeis U., 1962, PhD, 1964. Instr. Greek lang. Shelton Coll., Ringwood, N.J., 1960-61; grad. asst. Brandeis U., Waltham, Mass., 1962-63; asst. prof. Rutgers U., New Brunswick, N.J., 1964-69; assoc. prof. Miami U., Oxford, Ohio, 1969-73, prof. dept. history, 1973—, dir. grad. studies, 1978-82. Author: Pre-Christian Gnosticism, 1973, World of the First Christians, 1981, Foes from the North Frontier, 1982, Persia and the Bible, 1990, 7 other books, 1966-99; sr. editor Christianity Today, 1992-94; editor: Africa and Africans in Antiquity, 2001; co-author 2 books, co-editor 2 books. Fellow NEH, 1968, Inst. for Holy Land Studies, Jerusalem, 1968, Inst. for Advanced Christian Studies, 1974-75; grantee Am. Philos. Soc., 1970. Fellow Am. Sci. Affiliation (pres. 1983), Inst. Bibl. Rsch. (chair 1984-86, pres. 1987-89); mem. Conf. on Faith and History (pres. 1974-76), Near East Archaeol. Soc. (v.p. 1978-79), Archaeol. Inst. Am. (chpt. pres. 1973-74), Evang. Theol. Soc. (chair ea. sect. 1965-66). Office: Miami Univ Dept History Oxford OH 45056 E-mail: yamauce@muohio.edu.

YAMAYEE, ZIA AHMAD, engineering educator, dean; b. Herat, Afghanistan, Feb. 2, 1948; came to U.S., 1974; s. Sayed and Merjan Ahmad. BSEE, Kabul (Afghanistan) U., 1972; MSEE, Purdue U., 1976, PhD, 1978. Registered profl. engr., Calif., Wash. Mem. faculty of engring. Kabul U., 1978; engr. Systems Control, Inc., Palo Alto, Calif., 1979-81; sr. engr. Pacific N.W. Utilities, Portland, Oreg., 1981-83; assoc. prof. elec. engring. Clarkson U., Potsdam, N.Y., 1983-85; assoc. prof. Gonzaga U., Spokane, 1985-87, dean Sch. Engring., 1988-96; prof., chair elec. engring. dept. U. New Orleans, 1987-88. Part-time rsch. engr. La. Power and Light Co., New Orleans, 1987-88; sr. cons. Engring. and Cons. Svcs., Spokane, 1989-96. Contbr. articles, reports to profl. jours. Bd. dirs. Wash. State Math., Engring. Sci. Achievement, Seattle, 1989-96; mem. Spokane Intercollegiate Rsch. and Tech. Inst. Adv. Coun., 1990-96. NSF grantee. Mem. Am. Soc. Engring. Edn., IEEE (sr.). Office: University of Portland 5000 N Willamette Blvd Portland OR 97203-5798 E-mail: yamayee@up.edu.

YAMAZAKI, MAKOTO, economics educator; b. Tokyo, Dec. 19, 1948; s. Motoi and Mutsuko (Yamamoto) Y.; m. Abigail Elizabeth Burford, Aug. 4, 1984. BA in Law, Keio U., Japan, 1971; BA in Econs. and Polit. Sci., Wittenberg U., 1972-74; MA in Internat. Rels., The Fletcher Sch. of Law and Diplomacy, 1976; PhD in Econs., Duke U., 1984. Instr. Wittenberg U., Springfield, Ohio, 1972-74, asst. to program dir., 1973-75; vis. lectr. Tufts U., Medford, Mass., 1976, teaching asst. 1977-79; teaching asst. Duke U., Durham, N.C., 1982; asst. prof. W.Va. State Coll., Institute, 1984-85; vis. asst. prof. Wittenberg U., Springfield, Ohio, 1985-87; asst. prof. Aguinas Coll., Grand Rapids, Mich., 1987—; prin. Grand Rapids Japanese Sch., 1990-91; pres. Global Trade Cons., Grand Rapids, 1990-91; chmn. M&M Hilmont Internat., Inc., 1991—; faculty advisor Internat. Honor Soc. in Econs., 1988—; exec. com. U.S./Japan Grassroots Seminar, 1993—. Advisor Assn. Internat. des Etudients en Scis. Economiques Commerciales in French acronym, Grand Rapids, 1990. Wittenberg U. scholar, 1972; Grad. scholar Duke U., 1980; recipient rsch. grants Wittenberg U., 1986, Aquinas Coll., 1988. Mem. Am. Econ. Assn., Omicron Delta Epsilon. Congregationalist. Avocations: tennis, running, swimming, cooking, gardening. Home: 1131 Fernridge Ave SE Grand Rapids MI 49546-3818 Office: Aguinas Coll Econs Dept Grand Rapids MI 49506

YAMAZAKI, SHINJI, research scientist; b. Fuji, Shizuoka, Japan, Dec. 10, 1962; came to U.S., 1998; s. Mitsuru and Mie (Takeuchi) Y.; m. Yoshiko Nakaizumi, Aug. 5, 1993; 1 child, Yumi. BS in Pharmacy, Tokyo Coll. Pharmacy, 1985, MS in Molecular Pharmacology, 1987; PhD in Molecular Pharmacology, Tokyo U. Pharmacy & Life Sci., 1999. Scientist drug metabolism rsch. Upjohn Pharm., Ltd., Takasaki, Japan, 1987-88, scientist drug metabolism and analytical chemistry rsch. Tsukuba, Japan, 1988-96, Pharmacia & Upjohn Ltd., Tsukuba, 1996-98; rsch. scientist pharmacokinetics and bioanalytical rsch. Pharmacia & Upjohn Inc., Kalamazoo, 1998—2001, sr. rsch. scientist global drug metabolism, 2001—. Contbr. articles to profl. jours. Avocations: golf, soccer, wildlife. Office: Pharmacia 301 Henrietta St Kalamazoo MI 49007-4940 E-mail: shinji.yamazaki@pharmacia.com.

YAMBRUSIC, EDWARD SLAVKO, lawyer, consultant; b. Conway, Pa., Mar. 9, 1933; s. Michael Misko and Slavica Sylvia (Yambrusic) Y.; m. Natalie Visniak, 1990. BA, Duquesne U., 1957; postgrad., Georgetown U. Law Ctr., 1959-61; JD, U. Balt., 1966; cert., The Hague (Netherlands) Acad. Internat. Law, 1967, 69; diploma, Ctr. Study and Rsch. Internat. Law and Internat. Rels., 1970; PhD in Pub. Internat. Law, Cath. U. Am., 1984. Bar: Md. 1969, U.S. Ct. Customs and Patent Appeals 1972, U.S. Supreme Ct. 1972, U.S. Ct. Internat. Trade 1988. Copyright examiner U.S. Copyright Office, Libr. of Congress, Washington, 1969-80; atty. adviser Office Register of Copyrights, 1969-98; pvt. practice internat. and immigration law, 1969—. Legal counsel Nat. Ethnic Studies Assembly, 1976—, Soc. Fed. Linguists, 1980; pres. AMCRO Internat. Consulting, Inc., 1995—. Author: Treat Interpretation: Theory and Reality, 1987, The Trade-Based Approaches to the Protection of Intellectual Property, 1990; contbr. articles to ofcl. newsletter Nat. Confedn.

Am. Ethnic Groups, also legal jours. Pres. Nat. Confedn. Am. Ethnic Groups, Washington; nat. chmn. Croatian-Am. Bicentennial Com. nat. chmn. Nat. Pilgrimage of Croatian-Ams. to Nat. Shrine of Immaculate Conception, Washington; v.p. Croatian Acad. Am. Served to capt. U.S. Army, 1957-59. Duquesne U. Tamburitzans scholar, 1953-57; Hague Acad. Internat. Law fellow, 1970. Mem. ABA, Md. Bar Assn., Internat. Law Assn., Internat. Fiscal Assn., Am. Soc. Internat. Law, Croatian Cath. Union Am., Croatian Frat. Union Am. Republican. Roman Catholic. Certificate issued by the Librarian of Congress in recognition of 40 years of distinguished service to the people of the United States of America, 1957-98. Home and Office: 4720 Massachusetts Ave NW Washington DC 20016-2346

YAMIN, ALICIA ELY, lawyer; b. N.Y.C., Oct. 25, 1965; d. Jerome Sanford and Ida Elizabeth Rubin; m. Michael Jeremy Yamin, Oct. 5, 1991; children: Nicolas Ely, Samuel Ely. AB, Harvard Coll., 1987; JD, Harvard U., 1991; MPH, Harvard Sch. Pub. Health, Boston, 1996. Bar: N.Y., D.C. Founding mem. Dept. Human Rights, Archdiocese of Mexico City, 1991-93; assoc. Cleary, Gottlieb, Steen & Hamilton, N.Y.C., 1993-95; staff atty. law and policy project, asst. prof. Columbia U., 1996—. Bd. dirs. Physicians for Human Rights, Boston, 1996-2001; mem. com. Com. on Scientific Freedom/AAAS, Washington, 1999-2002; com. mem. Internat. Human Rights Com./Assn. of the Bar of the City of N.Y., 1998-99. Contbr. articles to profl. jours. Recipient Francois-Xavier-Bagnoud Essay award Francois-Xachen Bagnood Ctr., Boston, 1991, fellowship Echoing Green Found., N.Y., 1991. Office: Law and Policy Project/CSPH 60 Haven Ave Apt B2 New York NY 10032-2605 E-mail: aey3@columbia.edu.

YAMIN, DIANNE ELIZABETH, judge; b. Danbury, Conn., June 4, 1961; d. Raymond Joseph and Linda May (Bucko) Goetz; m. Robert Joseph Yamin, Sept. 3, 1988; children: Samantha Blythe, Rebecca Anne. AB, Lehigh U., 1983; JD, Mercer U., 1986. Bar: Conn. 1986, U.S. Dist. Ct. Conn. 1989. Lawyer Gerald Hecht & Assocs., Danbury, 1986-92; judge State Conn., 1991—. Atty. Yamin & Yamin, Danbury, 1992—; chmn. ethics com. Conn. Probate Assembly, 1994—; mem. Conn. Coun. on Adoptions, 1992—, Conn. Probate Assembly, 1991—. Bd. dirs. Big Bros./Big Sisters, Danbury, 1987-94, Conn Brass Soc., Inc., 1991—, Lions Club Danbury, 1993-94, Friends of Tarrywile Park, Inc., Danbury, 1993-99, Danbury Music Ctr., 1996—, Hispanic Ctr. Greater Danbury, 1999—; pres. coun. women Lehigh Univ., 2000—. Recipient outstanding young citizen award Conn. Jaycees, 1994, pro bono award Conn. Legal Svcs., 1993; named as one of 21 Young Lawyers Leading Us into the 21st Century, ABA Mag., 1995. Mem. ABA, Conn. Bar Assn., Conn. Health Lawyers Assn., Danbury Bar Assn, Omicron Delta Kappa. Republican. Roman Catholic. Avocations: ballet, volunteerism, travel, outdoor activities. Home: 66 Barnum Rd Danbury CT 06811-2938 Office: 155 Deer Hill Ave Danbury CT 06810-7726

YAMIN, JOSEPH FRANCIS, lawyer, counselor; b. Detroit, Mar. 12, 1956; s. Raymond Samuel and Sadie Ann (John) Y. 1975; BA, U. Mich., 1978; J.D., London Sch. Econs., 1981; JD, Detroit Coll. Law, 1982. Bar: U.S. Ct. Appeals (6th cir.) 1982, U.S. Dist. Ct. (ea. dist.) Mich. 1982. Atty. Alan R. Miller, P.C., Birmingham, Mich., 1981-93; ptnr. Beier Howlett PC, Bloomfield Hills, Mich., 1993—; bd. dir. Am. Wash Systems, Birmingham, 1979—; instr. Detroit Coll. Law Rev., 1984-86; mediator Wayne County, Oakland County. Recipient Am. Jurisprudence Book award Am. Jurisprudence Soc., 1981. Mem. ABA, Oakland County Bar Assn., Oakland County Mediation, Wayne County Mediator Litigation Panel, State of Mich. Bar Assn., Law Rev., Chi Phi, Oakland County Real Property Sect. Roman Catholic. Office: Beier Howlett PC 200 E Long Lake Rd Ste 110 Bloomfield Hills MI 48304-2328

YAMIN, MICHAEL GEOFFREY, lawyer; b. N.Y.C., Nov. 10, 1931; s. Michael and Ethel Yamin; m. Martina Schaap, Apr. 16, 1961; children: Michael Jeremy, Katrina. AB magna cum laude, Harvard U., 1953, LLB, 1958. Bar: N.Y. 1959, U.S. Dist. Ct. (so. and ea. dists.) N.Y., U.S. Ct. Appeals (2d cir.) 1966, U.S. Supreme Ct. 1967. Assoc. Weil, Gotshal & Manges, N.Y.C., 1958-65; sr. ptnr. Colton, Hartnick, Yamin & Sheresky, 1966-93, Kaufmann, Feiner, Yamin, Gildin & Robbins, LLP, N.Y.C., 1993—. Trustee Gov.'s Com. Scholastic Achievement, 1976—; mem. Manhattan Cmty. Bd. 6, 1974—88, chmn., 1986—88; mem. Manhattan Borough Bd., 1986—88. Mem. ABA, N.Y. State Bar Assn., Assn. Bar City N.Y., Fed. Bar Coun., Am Fgn. Law Assn. (Am. br.), Internat. Law Assn., Societe de Legislation Comparee, Internat. Bar Assn., Harvard Faculty Club (Cambridge, Mass.), Harvard Club of N.Y.C. (trustee N.Y. Found. 1981—, pres. 1999—, sub-chmn. schs. and scholarships com. 1972-93, bd. mgrs. 1985-88, 93-98, chair house com. 1992-95, v.p. 1995-98, chair comms. com. 1997-99, chair membership svcs. com. 1999-2000), Harvard Alumni Assn. (bd. dirs. 1995-98). Office: 777 3rd Ave New York NY 10017-1401

YAMIN-GARONE, MARY SULTANY, writer, graphic designer; b. Troy, N.Y., Oct. 24, 1957; d. George John and Edna Mary Yamin; m. Gene Garone, Jan. 11, 1994. AAS in Liberal Arts, Hudson Valley C.C., Troy, N.Y., 1977; BA in English and Journalism, SUNY, Albany, 1979. Writer, editor N.Y. State Dept. State, Office Fire Prevention & Control, Albany, 1981-95; owner, operator The Y's One Writing and Editing Svc., Niskayuna, N.Y., 1996—. Contbr. articles to profl. jours. Vol. Cuomo for Gov., Albany, 1986, 90, 94, Victory '88 Dukakis for Pres., Albany, 1988. Avocations: boxing, reading. Home and Office: The Ys One 3550 Consaul Rd Niskayuna NY 12304 E-mail: myaminga@nycap.rr.com., the_ysonewrite@hotmail.com.

YAMMARINO, FRANCIS JOSEPH, management educator, consultant; b. Buffalo, Dec. 25, 1954; s. Peter Anthony and Helen Ann (Giangrisostomi) Y.; m. Cathy Ann Apa, July 4, 1982; children: Kayla M., Anthony J. BS, SUNY-Buffalo, 1976, MBA, 1979, PhD, 1983. Services coordinator Buffalo Savs. Bank, 1972-76; research assoc., instr. SUNY-Buffalo, 1977-79, research fellow, 1979-81, project dir., 1980-81; asst. prof. mgmt. U. Ky., Lexington, 1982-85, SUNY-Binghamton, 1985-90, assoc. prof., 1990— ; mgmt. cons. Fortune 500 cos., several orgs. and agys. Author: (with F. Dansereau and J.A. Alutto) Theory Testing in Organizational Behavior: The Varient Approach, 1984, 1 other; sr. editor Leadership Quarterly; contbr. articles to profl. jours. Recipient Corning Glass Rsch. and Innovation award, numerous others. Fellow Am. Psychol. Soc., Ctr. for Leadership Studies SUNY-Binghamton (rsch. grantee); mem. Am. Psychol. Assn., Soc. Indsl. and Organizational Psychology, Soc. for Human Resources Mgmt., N.Y. Acad. Scis., Acad. Mgmt., Internat. Assn. Applied Psychology, Beta Gamma Sigma. Democrat. Office: SUNY-Binghamton Sch Mgmt PO Box 6000 Binghamton NY 13902-6000

YAMMINE, RIAD NASSIF, retired oil company executive; b. Hammana, Lebanon, Apr. 12, 1934; came to U.S., 1952, naturalized, 1963; s. Nassib Nassif and Emilie (Daou) Y.; m. Beverly Ann Hosack, Sept. 14, 1954; children: Kathleen Yammine Gross, Cynthia Yammine Rotman, Michael. BS in Petroleum Engring., Pa. State U., 1956; postgrad. advanced mgmt. program, Harvard U., 1977. Registered profl. engr., Ohio. Engr. Trans-Arabian Pipe Line Co., Saudia Arabia, 1956-61; with Marathon Pipe Line Co., 1961-75, mgr. we. divsn. Wyo., 1971-74, mgr. Ea. divsn. Martinsville, Ill., 1974-75; mktg. ops. divsn. mgr. Marathon Oil Co., 1975-83, pres., 1983-84; v.p. supply and transp. Marathon Petroleum Co., 1984-88, dir., 1984-90; pres. EMRO Mktg. Co., 1988-98; exec. v.p. Marathon Ashland Petroleum, 1998-99; ret. Bd. dirs. Marathon Oil Co.; chmn. bd. Findlay Devel. LLC. Patentee in field. Past trustee Wright State U. Found., Fisk U; bd. dirs. Findlay C. of C., bd. mgrs. Findlay Devel. LLC. Mem. ASME, Am. Petroleum Inst. (bd. dir.), Springfield and Clark C. of C. (bd. dirs.), Findlay C. of C. (bd. dirs.), Findlay Country Club. Republican. Home: 200 Penbrooke Dr Findlay OH 45840-8301

YAMORI, NOBUYOSHI, economist; b. Nagahama, Shiga, Japan, Aug. 13, 1963; s. Yoshitsugu and Etsuko (Sumida) Y.; m. Mieko Araki. BA in Econs., Shiga U., 1986; MA in Econs., Kobe U., 1988; PhD, Nagoya U., 1996. Rsch. assoc. Himeji Dokkyo U., Japan, 1989-91, asst. prof. Japan, 1991-94, assoc. prof. Japan, 1994-95; asst. prof. Nagoya U., Japan, 1995, assoc. prof. Japan, 1996—. Vis. scholar Columbia U., N.Y.C., 1990-91, 98, 2000, Fed. Res. Bank of San Francisco, 1999. Author: An Economic Analysis of Japanese Life Insurance Companies, 1995; contbr. articles to profl. jours. Grantee Ministry of Edn., 1995-2001; scholarship Rotary Internat. Found., 1990. Mem. Am. Econ. Assn. Avocation: tea ceremony. Office: Nagoya U Sch of Econs Furo-cho Chikusa-ku Nagoya 464-8601 Japan E-mail: yamori@soec.nagoya-u.ac.jp.

YAMPOLSKY, PHYLLIS, artist; b. Phila. d. Louis Jacob Yampolsky and Bassia Yampolsky Green; m. Peter Forakis, June 12, 1959 (div. 1964); children: Gia, Jozeph Peter. Student, Phila. Mus. Sch. Arts, 1950-52, Inst. Allende, San Miguel de Allende, Mex., 1954-55, Ecole Beaux Arts, Fontainbleau, France, 1956, Hans Hofmann Atelier, N.Y.C., 1956-58. Founder, dir., tchr. Workshop Yampolsky, N.Y.C., 1956-66; art instr. 92d St. YMHA, 1958-60; founder, dir. Hall of Issues, 1960-61; 1st artist-in-residence, 1966-67; creator, dir. Portrait of Ten Towns N.Y. State Coun. Arts, 1967-70; founder, officer Northeast Windham Coun. Arts, Vt., 1978-79; instr. Vt. Acad., Saxton's River, 1979-81, Vt. C.C., Springfield, 1979-81; co-founder, instr. New Vt. Sch. Arts, 1981; founder, pres. Ind. Friends McCarren Pk., Inc., N.Y.C., 1988—. Creator, dir., prodr. Hoving Happenings, 1966, 67; cons. Model Cities, Columbus, Ohio, 1968, Province Ont. Coun. Arts, 1968-70, Phila. Bicentennial Commn., Smithsonian Inst. Bicentennial Travelling Festival Kit; cons., panelist, performance artists Arcosanti, Ariz., 1977-78, 80, 81; facilitator NEA, 1970-75; cons., organizer, program dir. Habitat II CBO Host Com., N.Y.C., 1995-96; spl. events dir. Youth Pavilion, World's Fair, San Antonio, 1968; writer, dir. art curriculum Marylerose Acad., Albany, 1969, Bennett Coll., 1970; presenter Habitat II, UN conf., Istanbul, Turkey, 1996. One-woman shows include Phila. Art Alliance, 1953, Judson Gallery, N.Y.C., 1960, 62, Walker Gallery, N.Y.C., 1974, Kulicke Gallery, N.Y.C., 1975, Graham Gallery, N.Y.C., 1977, O.K. Harris and Susan Caldwell Galleries, N.Y.C., 1978, Stryke Gallery, N.Y.C., Windam Coll., Vt., 1978, Marlboro Coll., Vt., 1981, A Place Apart, N.Y.C., 1984, City Bank Gallery, Bklyn., 1986, Loft Lawyers, N.Y.C., 1987, 479 Gallery, N.Y.C., 1996, Stephan Gang, 1999, The Cave, 2000; exhibited in group shows at Park Place Gallery, N.Y.C., Brata Gallery, Cornell U., Dallas Mus. Fine Arts, Mus. Erotic Art, San Francisco, Mus. Erotic Art, Stockholm, Whitney Mus., Weisner Gallery, N.Y.C., City Without Walls Gallery, Newark, Green Gallery, N.Y.C., Leo Castelli Gallery, N.Y.C., Allan Stone Gallery, N.Y.C., Franklin Furnace, N.Y.C., Dorsky Gallery, N.Y.C., Bklyn. Terminal Show, N.Y.C., Food Stamp Gallery, N.Y.C., ABC No Rio, N.Y.C., Blue Mountain Gallery, N.Y.C., Boriqua Coll., N.Y.C., Phila. Mus. Art, Holland-Goldowsky, Chgo., Peter David, Mpls., Mc Nay Inst., San Antonio, Tex., Stephen Gang Gallery, N.Y.C., The Cave, Bklyn., Bklyn. Brewery; represented in permenant collections Am. Town Hall Wall Sys. used in Robert Kennedy Presdl. Primary, 1968, Clinton Presdl. Campaign and Inaugural Festivities, 1993, 97, UN Women's Conf., Beijing, 1995, UN 50th Celebration, N.Y.C., 1995, V.P. Gore's Reinvention Revolution Conf., Washington, 1996-97, March Against Cancer, Washington, 1998, W.A.F.E. Festival/Conf. on the Environment, Bklyn., 1998, The Hague (The Netherlands) Appeal Peace Conf., 1999, Main St. Millennium, Washington, Dallas Mus. Fine Arts, Mus. Erotic Art, Pres. Clinton Libr.; contbr. articles to profl. jours. Recipient Cue Mag., 1967, Betsy Barlow Rogers award Ind. Friends McCarren Pk., 1995; Ecole Beaux Arts scholar, Hans Hofmann Atelier scholar; grantee Ind. Friends McCarren Pk., J.M. Kaplan Fund, Andy Warhol Found., N.Y. Found., Vincent Astor Found., Citizen's Com. N.Y.C. Inc., 1990—. Fax: 718-383-5785. E-mail: ifmp@earthlink.net.

YAMPOLSKY, VICTOR, conductor; b. Frunze, Kirgizskaj, SSR, Oct. 10, 1942; s. Vladimir and Fanny (Zaslavsky) Y. Student, Moscow Conservatory, 1961-66, Leningrad Conservatory, 1968-72. Violinist Moscow Radio Orch., 1965; violinist, asst. condr. Moscow Philharm. Orch., 1965-72; violinist Boston Symphony Orch., 1973-77; music dir. Atlantic Symphony Orch., Halifax, N.S., Can., 1977-83; condr. Tanglewood Inst., Boston U., 1977-84; prof. music Boston U., 1979-84; assoc. prof. music Northwestern U., 1984—, Carol R. and Arthur L. Rice Jr. prof. in music performance, 1993—; music dir. Peninsula Festival, Fish Creek, Wis., 1986—; hon. dir. Scotia Festival of Music, Halifax; music dir. Omaha (Nebr.) Symphony Orch., 1995—. Office: Omaha Symphony Orch 1605 Howard St Omaha NE 68102-2797*

YAN, AIMIN, educator; b. Siping, China, Sept. 6, 1956; came to U.S., 1987; s. Mingrun Y. and Shuwen Liu; m. Huimin Lu, Apr. 21, 1985; children: Linda, Esther. B of Engring., U. Shanghai, China, 1982, MBA, 1984; PhD in Bus. Adminstrn., Pa. State U., 1993. Machine operator, supr. Tractor Components Co., Lishu, China, 1974-77; lectr., asst. dean U. Shanghai, China, 1984-88; instr., rsch. assoc. Pa. State U., University Park, 1990-93; asst. prof. Boston U., 1993-99, assoc. prof., 1999—, dir. internat. mgmt. program, 2000—. Rsch. dir. Human Resources Policy inst., Boston, 1997—; cons. in field. Author: International Joint Ventures, 2001; contbr. articles to profl. jours. Mem. Acad. Mgmt., Acad. Internat. Bus. Home: 37 Heritage Rd Acton MA 01720-5302 Office: Boston U 595 Commonwealth Ave Boston MA 02215-1704

YAN, LAIBIN, chemist, researcher; b. Xian Tao, Hubei Province, China, Sept. 26, 1962; arrived in U.S., 1992; s. Jin-Ting Yan and You-Zhi Yu; m. Xiaoxia Zhang, Apr. 4, 1988; children: Ellen (Xu), Jeffrey. BS in Agrl. Chemsitry & Soils, Huazhong Agrl. U., 1982; MSc in Soil Chemistry, Beijing Agrl. U., 1985; PhD, Purdue U., 1996. Lectr. Beijing Agrl. U., Beijing, 1985—92; rsch. assoc. U. of Ill., Urbana, Ill., 1996—98, US Nat. Rsch. Council/US EPA, Athens, Ga., 1998—2000; sr. staff scientist GE Betz, Trevose, Pa., 2000—. Contbr. chapters to books, articles to profl. jours. Fellow, The Gt. Brain-China SBFSS Fellowship Found., 1988—89; grantee, US Nat. Rsch. Council-US EPA, 1998—2000, U.S. Dept. of Agr., 1998—2000; scholar George D. Scarseth scholarship, Purdue U., 1994. Mem.: ACS, Soil Sci. Soc. of Am., Clay Mineral Soc., Am. Geophys. Union, Sigma Xi, Gamma Sigma Delta. Office: GE Betz PO Box 3002 4636 Somerton Rd Trevose PA 19053-6783 Office Fax: 215-633-4101.

YAN, PEI-YANG, electrical engineer; b. Tianjin, People's Republic of China, July 18, 1957; came to U.S., 1981; d. Zhi-Da and De-Qiu (Yu) Y.; m. Xiao-Chun Mu, June 2, 1984; children: Wendy Mu, Kevin Mu. MS in Physics, Wayne State U., 1983; PhD in Elec. Engring., Pa State U., 1988. Sr. staff engr. Intel Corp., Santa Clara, Calif., 1988—. Cotnbr. articles to profl. jours. including, Phys. Rev., IEEE Jour. Quantum Electronics, Jour. Optical Soc. Am., Optical Engring., and Jour. Photopolymer Sci. and Tech. Mem. Internat. Soc. Optical Engring., Optical Soc. Am. Achievements include theoretical and experimental demonstration of optical transverse bistability in transmission through nonlinear nematic liquid crystal film; development of excimer laser lithography process for 0.5, 0.35, 0.25, and 0.18 micron integrated circuit patterning technology, extreme ultraviolet lithography mask fabrication processes for 0.05 micron integrated circuit patterning technology. Office: Intel Corp PO Box 58119 Santa Clara CA 95052-8119

YAN, XIAO-HAI, science center director, educator; b. Shanghai, China, May 23, 1952; arrived in U.S., 1985; s. De Lian and Su jin (Wu) Y.; m. Yi-Hong Wang, Jan. 20, 1980; children: Jian-Ming, Lisa Christine. BS, Tongchi U., 1977; MS equivalent, Academia Sinica, 1981; PhD, SUNY, Stony Brook, 1989; postgrad., U. Calif., San Diego, 1990. Remote sensing physicist Inst. Tech. Physics, Acad. Sinica, 1977-85; teaching asst. Marine Scis. Rsch. Ctr. SUNY, Stony Brook, 1985-87, rsch. asst. Marine Scis. Rsch. Ctr., 1987-89; post doctoral rsch. scientist Scripps Inst. Oceanography U. Calif., San Diego, 1989-90; asst. prof. Coll. Marine Studies U. Del., Newark, 1990-93, assoc. dir. Ctr. Remote Sensing, 1990—, assoc. prof. Coll. Marine Studies, 1993-95, prof., 1995—. Contbr. articles to profl. jours. Recipient Rsch. award Rockefeller Inst., 1987, Grad. Student Rsch. award NASA, 1989, Internat. Travel award NSF, 1991, Global Change Rsch. award Nat. Oceanic and Atmospheric Adminstrn., 1993, U.S. Presdl. Faculty Fellow award, NSF, 1994. Mem. IEEE, Am. Geophys. Union, Am. Meteorol. Soc., Soc. Space Sci., Oceanography Soc. Avocations: swimming, reading, music, dancing, basketball. Office: U Del Coll Marine Studies Ctr Remote Sensing Newark DE 19716 E-mail: xiaohai@udel.edu.

YAN, YU, optical and laser engineer; b. Jiang Ling, Hubei, China, June 12, 1965; came to U.S., 1995; s. Jifa and Xuer (Xiong) Y. BS, Changchun Inst. Optics/Mechs., Jiling, China, 1987; MS, Shanghai Inst. Optics/Mechs., 1994. Optical and laser engr. Shanghai Inst. Optics and Fine Mechanics, Academia Sinica, 1987-94; rsch. assoc. Howard U., Washington, 1995, U. Ariz., Tucson, 1996; rsch. scientist Innovative Lasers Corp., 1997—; sr. engring. semiconductor Laser Internat. Corp., Binghamton, 1998; opto-mech. engr. IMRA Am. Inc., Ann Arbor, 1999—. Mem. SPIE, Optical Soc. Am. Achievements include patent in field. Home: 1044 Woodridge Ave Ann Arbor MI 48105-9748

YAN, ZHIXIN, engineer; b. Shanghai, China, Jan. 11, 1941; came to U.S., 1996; s. Mao-de Yan and Zhu-ying Wu; m. Man-ping Zhou, Oct. 1, 1966; children: Jiong, Bing. BSc, Shanghai U. Sci. & Tech., 1963; M of Applied Sci., Simon Fraser U., Burnaby, B.C., Can., 1992. Instr. Shanghai U. Sci. and Tech., 1963-80, prof., 1982-88; vis. scholar Carnegie Mellon U., Pitts., 1980-81, U. Md., College Park, 1981-82; rsch. assoc. Simon Fraser U., Burnaby, 1989-96; staff engr. Conexant Sys. Inc. (formerly Rockwell Semiconductor Sys. Inc.), Newport Beach, Calif., 1996—. Mem. IEEE-Electron Device Soc., IEEE-Electrochem. Soc., IEEE-Microwave Theory and Tech. Soc. Achievements include patent for modulation circuit. Avocations: travel, movie, sports. Office: Conexant Sys Inc 4311 Jamboree Rd Newport Beach CA 92660-3007

YANAGAWA, TSUTOMU, technology transfer company engineer; b. Osaka, Japan, Nov. 29, 1956; s. Hazime and Hiroko (Konishi) Y.; m. Masami Kawabata, Oct. 16, 1983 children: Sakiko, Fumitoshi. B Engring., U. Osaka Prefecture, Sakai, Japan, 1980, M Engring., 1982; D Engring., Osaka U., Suita, Japan, 1993. Rschr. Nippon Telegraph and Telephone Pub. Corp., Musashino, Japan, 1982-85; rsch. scientist NTT Basic Rsch. Labs., 1985-89, sr. rsch. scientist, 1989-91; sr. rsch. engr. NTT Opto-Electronics Labs., Atsugi-shi, Japan, 1991-97; mgr. NTT Affiliated Bus. Hdqrs., Tokyo, 1997-99; sr. rsch. engr. NTT Photonics Labs., Atsugi-shi, 1999-2000; mgr. NTT Advanced Tech. Corp., Japan, 2000—. Author: Sensor Dictionary, 1991; patentee semiconductor laser equipment, waveguide, optical equipment; contbr. articles to profl. jours. Mem. Japanese Soc. Applied Physics, Phys. Soc. Japan, Internat. Soc. Life Info. Sci. Avocations: art, flower arrangement, tea ceremony. Home: Ishida 861-1-8-401 Isehara Kanagawa 259-1116 Japan Office: NTT Advanced Tech Corp 3-1 Morinosato Atsugi-shi Kanagawa 243-0124 Japan E-mail: yanagawa@atsugi.ntt-at.co.jp.

YANAGISAWA, EIJI, otolargyngologist, educator; b. Yokohama, Japan, May 12, 1930; came to U.S., 1955; s. Jiro and Sue Yanagisawa; m. June Yanagisawa, Sept. 16, 1960; children: Ken, Kay, Amy Ray. MD, Nihon U., Tokyo, 1955. Intern Hosp. of St. Raphael, New Haven, 1962, U.S. Tokyo Army Hosp., 1955—56; resident in otolaryngology Yale-New Haven Hosp., 1956—59; instr. otolaryngology Yale U. Sch. Medicine, New Haven, 1959-61, 63-64, clin. instr., 1964-67, asst. clin. prof., 1967-72, assoc. clin. prof., 1972-83, clin. prof., 1983—; pvt. practice, 1964—. Author (with G. Gardner): The Surgical Atlas of Otology and Neuro-Otology, 1983; author: Color Atlas of Diagnostic Endoscopy in Otorhinolaryngology, 1997, Atlas of Rhinoscopy--Endoscopic Sinonasal Anatomy and Pathology, 2000; author: (with D.A. Christmas and J.P. Mirante) Powered Instrumentation in Otolaryngology and Head and Neck Surgery, 2001; contbg. authoer 246 chpts. and jour. articles, assoc. editor Ear, Nose & Throat Jour., 1999—, monthly contbr. Rhinoscopic Clinic sect. Ear, Nose and Throat Jour., 1993—. Mem.: AMA, ACS (coord. Clin. Congress, Otolaryngol. Movie Session 1999—2000), Am. Rhinologic Soc., New Eng. Otolaryngol. Soc. (pres. 1992), Triological Soc. (v.p., chmn. ea. sect. 1990), Am. Otol. Soc., Am. Broncho-Esophagological Assn. (pres. 1994), Am. Laryngol. Assn., Am. Acad. Otolaryngology-Head and Neck Surgery (co-chmn. interactive multimedia faculty 1998—2000, chmn. continuing edn. through TV subcom. 1988—98). Avocations: photography, videography, digital imaging. Office: So New Eng ENT and Facial Plastic Surg Group 98 York St New Haven CT 06511

YANAI, MICHIO, aerospace scientist; b. Jan. 16, 1934; came to U.S., 1970; s. Kin (Watanabe) Y.; m. Yoko Miyazaki, Apr. 25, 1965; children: Takashi, Satoshi. BS, U. Tokyo, 1956, MS, 1958, DSc, 1961. Rsch. meteorologist Meteorol. Rsch. Inst. Japan Meteorol. Agy., Tokyo, 1961-65; asst. prof. U. Tokyo, 1965-70; from assoc. prof. to prof. UCLA, 1969-99, prof. emeritus, 1999—. Fellow Am. Meteorol. Soc. (awards com. 1992, assoc. editor Jour. Atmos. Scis. 1988-90, Jule Charney award 1986); mem. Am. Geophys. Union, Royal Meteorol. Soc., Meteorol. Soc. Japan (Soc. award 1962, Fujiwara award 1993). Achievements include discovery of a large-scale wave in the equatorial stratosphere called the Yanai wave; formulated a method of diagnosing mass flux in cumulus ensemble called Q1-Q2 diagnosis; revealed the role of the Tibetan Plateua in the onset of the Asian summer monsoon. Office: UCLA Dept Atmos Scis 405 Hilgard Ave Los Angeles CA 90095-1565 E-mail: myanai@ucla.edu.

YANCEY, ASA GREENWOOD , SR. physician; b. Atlanta, Aug. 19, 1916; s. Arthur H. and Daisy L. (Sherard) Y.; m. Carolyn E. Dunbar, Dec. 28, 1944; children: Arthur H. II, Carolyn L., Caren L., Asa Greenwood Jr. BS, Morehouse Coll., 1937, ScD (hon.), 1991; MD, U. Mich., 1941; ScD (hon.), Howard U., 1991. Diplomate Am. Bd. Surgery. Intern City Hosp., Cleve., 1941-42; resident Freedmen's Hosp., Washington, 1942-45, U.S. Marine Hosp., Boston, 1945; instr. surgery Meharry Med. Coll., 1946-48; chief surgery VA Hosp., Tuskegee, Ala., 1948-58; chief surgery of Hughes Spalding Pavilion, 1958-72; pvt. practice specializing in surgery Atlanta, 1958-86; med. dir. Grady Meml. Hosp., 1972-89; mem. staff Hughes Spalding Hosp., St. Joseph Hosp., Emory U. Hosp., up to 1986-88; asst. prof. surgery Emory U., 1958-72, assoc. prof., 1972-75, prof. surgery, 1975-86, prof. emeritus, 1986—, assoc. dean Emory U. Sch. Medicine, 1972-89; clin. prof. surgery Morehouse Sch. Medicine, 1985—. *While in Tuskegee, Dr. Asa Yancey began clinical research work at the Tuskegee Veterinary School of Medicine. As a result of this animal research on dogs, Dr. Yancey published a paper in the Journal of National Medical Association in September 1952, page 356, entitled "A Modification of the Swenson Technique for Congenital Megacolon." This paper was published ten years before Soave published the identical work in 1962. The operation today bears Soave's name. Soave did a fine work of performing this procedure on a sufficient number of patients to well-establish it as a clinically acceptable operative technique.* Contbr. articles to profl. jours. Mem. Atlanta Bd. Edn., 1967-77, Fulton-De Kalb Hosp. Authority, trustee Body for Grady Meml. Hosp., 1989-93. 1st lt. M.C., AUS, 1942. Fellow ACS, Am. Surg. Assn.; mem. Nat. Med. Assn. (1st v.p. 1988-89, trustee 1960-66, editorial bd. jour. 1964-80), Inst. Medicine of NAS, So. Surg. Assn. Baptist. Home and Office: 2845 Engle Rd NW Atlanta GA 30318-7216

YANCEY, CAROLYN DUNBAR, educational policy maker; b. Detroit, Feb. 10, 1921; d. Henry Steward and Annie Louise (Dye) Dunbar; m. Asa Greenwood Yancey Sr., Dec. 28, 1944; children: Arthur H. II, Carolyn L., Caren L., Asa Greenwood, Jr. BA, Wayne State U., 1941. Cert. tchr., Mich. Mem. Bd. Edn. Atlanta Pub. Schs., 1982-97, v.p. Bd. Edn., 1993. Mem. bd. regents Univ. Sys. of Ga., 1985-92; trustee Spelman Coll., Atlanta, 1972-2001; bd. dirs. Women's C. of C. of Atlanta, 1972-74. Pres. PTA, Frank L. Stanton Sch., Atlanta, 1960; active in voter registration Atlanta Voters League, 1963. Recipient Daniel James Gen. Edn. award Tuskegee Airmen, Inc., 1993, Achievement award Atlanta Med. Assn., 1982, Leadership award NAACP, 1981. Mem. Links Inc. (pres. 1968), Delta Sigma Theta. Congregationalist. Avocations: sewing, homemaking. Home: 2845 Engle Rd NW Atlanta GA 30318-7216

YANCEY, GEORGE, science educator; b. Mose Lake, Wash., Sept. 8, 1962; s. Rose Taylor; m. Sherelyn Whittum. BA, West Tex. State U., 1985; Doctorate, U. Tex., 1994. Asst. prof. U. Wis., Whitewater, 1996—99, U. North Tex., Denton, 1999—. Cons. Reconcilation Consulting, Ft. Worth, 1996—2002. Author: (book) Beyond Black and White, 1996. Recipient Multiracial Congregations and Their People, Lilly Endowment, 1999—2001. Mem.: Antioch Global Network, Mavin Found., Christian Comty. Devel. Assn., Soc. for Sci. Study of Religion, So. Sociol. Soc., Southwestern Social Sci. Assn. Office: U North Texas PO Box 311157 Denton TX 76203 Home Fax: 940-369-7035; Office Fax: 940-369-7035. Personal E-mail: yancey@scs.cmm.unt.edu. Business E-Mail: yancey@scs.cmm.unt.edu.

YANCEY, JAMES D. bank executive; AS, Columbus State U., 1964; grad. Sch. of Banking, La. State U.; grad. Stonier Sch. of Banking, Rutgers U.; D (hon.) , Columbus State U., 1997. Various positions Columbus Bank and Trust Co., Synovus Finl. Corp., 1959—83, pres., 1983—90, vice chmn. bd., 1992; pres. Synovus, 1990, vice chmn. bd., 1992, pres., COO Ga., 1997—. Bd. dirs. Synovus Finl. Corp., Columbus Bank & Trust Co., TSYS, Shoney's Inc. Former mem. Bus. Coun. Ga.; former campaign chmn. United Way; former pres. Met. Boys Club; former dir. YMCA; former vice chmn. Southern Open; former pres. Historic Columbus Found.; former bd. trustee Brookstone Sch.; former chmn. bd. trustees Columbus State U. Recipient Thomas Y. Whitley Dist. Alumnus award, Columbus State U. Alumni Assn., 1987. Mem.: Ga. C. of C. (former bd. dirs.). Office: Synovus Finl Corp PO Box 120 Columbus GA 31902 Office Fax: 706-641-6555.

YANCEY, KATHERINE BEAN, writer, editor; b. Urbana, Ill., May 1, 1950; d. Charles Palmer and Elizabeth (Harriman) B.; m. Matthew Lee Yancey, Oct. 23, 1976 (div. Dec. 1989). BA, Middlebury Coll., 1971; MA in Journalism, U. Mo., 1974. Writer United Press Internat., Nashville, 1975-76; writer, editor 13-30 Corp., Knoxville, Tenn., 1977-81; cover story editor USA Today, Arlington, Va., 1982-86, dep. mng. editor Life sect., 1986-99, travel writer, 1999—. E-mail: kyancey@usatoday.com.

YANCEY, RICHARD CHARLES, investment banker; b. Spokane, Wash., May 28, 1926; s. George R. and M. Ruth (Yenney) Y.; m. Mary Anne Shaffer, Feb. 5, 1956; children: Leslie, Jennifer, Richard C. Jr. BA in Econs., Whitman Coll., Walla Walla, Wash., 1949; MBA with distinction, Harvard U., 1952. Assoc. Dillon, Read & Co. Inc., N.Y.C, 1952-63; v.p. Dillon, Read & Co., Inc., N.Y.C., 1963-75, mng. dir., 1975-89, dir., 1990; sr. adv., 1992; ret. Dillon, Read & Co., Inc., N.Y.C., 1992. Trustee, lead trustee W.M. Group of Funds, Seattle, Ad Media Ptnrs., Inc., N.Y.C., Czech and Slovak Am. Enterprise Fund, Westport, Conn.; former mem. partnership bd. Whittle Comms. L.P., Knoxville, Tenn. Former bd. overseers Whitman Coll.; former trustee, former pres. Plymouth Ch. of Pilgrims, Bklyn.; former trustee N.Y. Infirmary-Beekman Downtown Hosp. Served with USNR, 1944-46, PTO. Mem. N.Y. Soc. Security Analysts, Assn. for Investment Mgmt. and Rsch., Harvard Club, Met. Club, N.Y.C., Pilgrims of the U.S. Republican. Home: 42 Monroe Pl Brooklyn NY 11201-2603 Office: Ad Media Ptnrs Inc 19th Fl 444 Madison Ave Fl 19 New York NY 10022-6903 E-mail: ryancey@admediapartners.com.

YANCIK, JOSEPH JOHN, government official; b. Mt. Olive, Ill., Dec. 1, 1930; s. Joseph John and Anna (Gubach) Y.; m. Rosemary Panich, Feb. 19, 1955; children— Geri Anne, Ellen Marie. BS, U. Ill., 1954; MS in Mining Engring., Mo. Sch. Mines, 1956; PhD, U. Mo., Rolla, 1960. Mining research engr. St. Joe Lead Co., Bonne Terre, Mo., 1955-58; mgr. research and devel. Monsanto Co., St. Louis, 1960-70; asst. dir. mining U.S. Bur. Mines, Washington, 1970-77; v.p. research Nat. Coal Assn., 1977-82; pres. Bituminous Coal Research, Inc., 1980-82; dir. Coal Export Office U.S. Dept. Commerce, 1982-84; dir. Office of Energy Internat. Trade Adminstrn., 1984-95; pvt. practice Mc Lean, 1995—. Cons. energy in internat. trade and investment; dir. energy affairs U.S.-Russia Bus. Coun., Washington, 1996—2002. Contbr. articles to profl. jours. Served with C.E. U.S. Army, 1950-52. Recipient Alumni Achievement award U. Mo.-Rolla, 1975, Silver Medal award U.S. Dept. Commerce, 1986, Gold Medal award Dept. Commerce, 1992. Mem. Cosmos Club (Washington). Roman Catholic. Home and Office: 1703 James Payne Cir Mc Lean VA 22101-4223

YANCURA, ANN JOYCE, library director; b. Ft. Smith, Ark., Oct. 1, 1943; d. John Michael and Elizabeth Ann (Grcevic) Traub; m. Nicholas Daniel Yancura, Dec. 26, 1966; children: Daniel, Elizabeth. BA, U. Akron, 1965; MLS, Kent (Ohio) State U., 1982. Tchr. Akron Pub. Schs., 1966-70; mgr. SCM Corp., Strongsville, Ohio, 1982-85; exec. dir. Nola Regional Libr., Youngstown, 1985-90, McKinley Meml. Libr., Niles, 1990-98. Bd. dirs. Info. Access, Foster City, Calif., 1993-97; mem. Niles Hist. Soc., 1990—, Leadership Mahoning Valley, 1996-97. Named Outstanding Grad., Kent State U./Crawford Bindery, 1982, Boss of the Yr., Am. Bus. Women, 1992, Outstanding Cmty. Leader, Youngstown Vidicator, 1993; recipient Recognition award Friends of Libr., Niles, 1992. Mem. ALA (mem. coms.), Ohio Libr. Assn. (bd. dirs., mem. coun.), Ohio Mus. Assn., Pub. Libr. Assn. (mem. coms.), Niles C. of C. (bd. dirs. 1991-94), Niles Rotary (bd. dirs. 1990-95, Outstanding Svc. award 1992, 93, 94), Beta Phi Mu. Republican. Roman Catholic. Avocations: reading, travel, gardening. Home: 2180 Brittany Oaks Trl NE Warren OH 44484-3900 Office: McKinley Meml Libr 40 N Main St Niles OH 44446-5049

YANCY, WILLIAM SAMUEL, pediatrician; b. Pittsboro, Miss., Aug. 17, 1939; s. Lester Truman and Maxyne (Lindsey) Y.; m. Susan Elizabeth Guest, June 19, 1965; children: Amy Lynn Yancy, William Samuel Jr., James Michael. BA, Duke U., 1961, MD, 1965. Diplomate Am. Bd. Pediat. Resident in pediatrics Duke U. Med. Ctr., Durham, N.C., 1965-66, 67-68; resident in pediatrics, then fellow in adolescent medicine U. Rochester (N.Y.) Med. Ctr., 1966-67, 70-71; pediatrician Durham Pediatrics, 1971—. Dir. adolescent medicine tng. program Duke U. Med. Ctr., 1971-99, dir. behavioral pediat. tng. program, 1978-90, assoc. clin. prof. psychiatry, 1982-2000, clin. prof. pediatrics, 1984—; dir. pediat. tng. program Durham Regional Hosp., 1977-80, med. coun., 1980-86, chmn. dept. pediatrics, 1980-86, chmn. nursery com., 1986-96; pediatrician Duke U. Affiliated Physicians, 1995—; bd. mem. Am. Bd. Pediatrics, 1992-2000; chmn. Coalition for Healthy N.C. Youth, 1991-95; editl. bd. Jour. Devel. and Behavioral Pediatrics, 1984—. Bd. dirs. Child Advocacy Commn. Durham, 1973-76, 79-85, pres. 1973-74; bd. dirs. Durham Cmty. Guidance Clinic, 1974-76; N.C. State Coordinating Coun., Raleigh, 1994-95; vestry St. Stephen's Episcopal Ch., Durham, 1985-87, 95-98. Lt. cmdr. U.S. Navy, 1968-70. Fellow Am. Acad. Pediatrics (com. on adolescence), Soc. Adolescent Medicine (exec. sec.-treas. 1978-83, pres. 1985-86, chmn. fin. com. 1989-93); mem. AMA, Internat. Assn. Adolescent Health, Soc. Devel. & Behavioral Pediatrics (pres. 1984-85), N.C. Pediat. Soc. (chmn. com. on adolescents 1989-96), Beta Omega Sigma, Omicron Delta Kappa. Avocations: stamp collecting, writing, golf. Home: 59 Kimberly Dr Durham NC 27707-5418 Office: Durham Pediatrics 2609 N Duke St Ste 1000 Durham NC 27704-3048 E-mail: yancy002@mc.duke.edu.

YANDA, TIMOTHY GEORGE, cable television engineer; b. Cleve., Sept. 4, 1961; s. George Charles and Anna Marie (Voigt) Y.; m. April Ann Stankivicz, June 28, 1986; 1 child, Chelsea Ann. BA in Comms., Cleve. State U., 1987. Field engr. Cox Comms., Cleve., 1981-82, constrn. coord., 1982-84, systems security supr., 1984-85, constrn. supr., 1985-87, plant maintenance supr., 1987-89, project supr., 1990, project mgr., 1991-94, plant mgr., 1995-96; dir. engring., Primestar mgr. Cox Comms. Inc., 1996-98, dir. tech. ops, 1998—, interim v.p. field ops. no. Va., 2001. Corp. engring. material-evaluation com. Cox Comms., Inc., Atlanta, 1995—, mem. engring. adv. bd., dir. network ops. and engring., 2002—; trustee cable TV, Ohio Utlity Protection Svc., Youngstown, Ohio, 1985-87. Mem. Lakewood Hist. Soc., 1995-97; mem. Properties Chmn. Rejoice! Luth. Ch., Hudson, Ohio, 1999—. Mem. Soc. of Cable Telecom Engring., Lorain Yacht Club (commodore 1996-97), Sigma Phi Epsilon (pres. 1987-88, Best Brother 1986). Republican. Lutheran. Avocations: sailing, model boat building, old home restoration. Home: 7446 N Marblehead Rd Hudson OH 44236-4641 Office: Cox Communications-Cleve Area 12221 Plaza Dr Parma OH 44130-1059

YANDELL, CATHY MARLEEN, foreign language educator; b. Anadarko, Okla., Dec. 27, 1949; d. Lloyd O. and Maurine (Dunn) Y.; m. Mark S. McNeil, Sept. 7, 1974; children: Elizabeth Yandell McNeil, Laura Yandell McNeil. Diplôme d'études, Inst. des Professeurs de Français à l'Etranger, Sorbonne, Paris, 1970; BA, U. N.Mex., 1971; MA, U. Calif., Berkeley, 1973, PhD, 1977. Teaching asst. U. Calif., Berkeley, 1971-75, acting instr., 1976-77; asst. prof. Carleton Coll., Northfield, Minn., 1977-83, assoc. prof., 1983-89, prof. French, 1989—. Chair commn. on the status of women Carleton Coll., Northfield, 1983-85, ednl. policy com., 1985-86, 96-97, romance langs. and lits., 1990-94, chair faculty affairs com., 2000—, pres. of faculty, 1991-94, Bryn-Jones disting. tchg. prof. humanities, 1996-99, mentor to jr. faculty, 1996—, W.I. and Hulda F. Daniell prof. French lit. lang. and culture, 1999—; dir. Paris French Studies Program, 1998. Author: Carpe Corpus: Time and Gender in Early Modern France, 2000; co-author: Vagabondages: Initiation à la litt. d'expression française, 1996; contbr. to Art & Argumentation: The Sixteenth Century Dialogue, 1993, French Texts/American Contexts: French Women Writers, 1994, Montaigne: A Collection of Essays, Vol. 4, Language and Meaning, 1995, Reflexivity in Women Writers of the Ancien Régime, 1998; editor: Pontus de Tyard's Solitaire Second, ou prose de la musique, 1980; contbr. articles to profl. jours. Active exec. com., then mem. Amnesty Internat., Northfield, 1980—. Regents' Travelling fellow U. Calif. at Berkeley, 1975-76; Faculty Devel. grantee Carleton Coll., 1988, 91; NEH Rsch. fellow., 1994-95. Mem. MLA (del. 1989-92, exec. com. French 16th century lit., 2001—, 16th century studies coun. 2001—). Democrat. Home: 514 5th St E Northfield MN 55057-2220 Office: Carleton College 1 N College St Northfield MN 55057-4044 E-mail: cyandell@carleton.edu.

YANDERS, ARMON FREDERICK, biological sciences educator, research administrator; b. Lincoln, Nebr., Apr. 12, 1928; s. Fred W. and Beatrice (Pate) Y.; m. Evelyn Louise Gatz, Aug. 1, 1948; children: Mark Frederick, Kent Michael. AB, Nebr. State Coll., Peru, 1948; MS, U. Nebr., 1950, PhD, 1953. Rsch. asso. Oak Ridge Nat. Lab. and Northwestern U., 1953-54; biophysicist U.S. Naval Radiol. Def. Lab., San Francisco, 1955-58; asso. geneticist Argonne (Ill.) Nat. Lab., 1958-59; with dept. zoology Mich. State U., 1959-69; prof., asst. dean Mich. State U. (Coll. Natural Sci.), 1963-69; prof. biol. scis. U. Mo., Columbia, 1969—, dean Coll. Arts and Scis., 1969-82, rsch. prof., dir. Environ. Trace Substances Rsch. Ctr., 1983-93, dir. Alzheimer's Disease and Related Disorders Program, 1994—; research prof., dir. Environ. Trace Substances Research Ctr. and Sinclair Comparative Medicine Rsch. Farm, 1984-94; prof. emeritus, 1994—. Trustee Argonne Univs. Assn., 1965-77, v.p., 1969-73, pres., 1973, 76-77, chmn. bd., 1973-75; bd. dirs. Coun. Colls. Arts and Scis., 1981-82; mem. adv. com. environ. hazards VA, Washington, 1985-2002, chmn. sci. coun., 1988-2000, chmn. of com., 1990-2002. Contbr. articles to profl. jours. Trustee Peru State Coll., 1992-2001. Served from ensign to lt. USNR, 1954-58. Recipient Disting. Svc. award Peru State Coll., 1989. Fellow AAAS; mem. AAUP (Robert W. Martin acad. freedom award 1971), Environ. Mutagen Soc., Genetics Soc. Am., Radiation Rsch. Soc., Soc. Environ. Toxicology and Chemistry. Home: 1204 Castle Bay Pl Columbia MO 65203-6257 Office: U of Mo 521 Clark Hall Columbia MO 65211-4420 E-mail: YandersA@umsystem.edu.

YANDLE, STEPHEN THOMAS, dean; b. Oakland, Calif., Mar. 7, 1947; s. Clyde Thomas and Jane Walker (Hess) Y.; m. Martha Anne Welch, June 26, 1971. BA, U. Va., 1969, JD, 1972. Bar: Va. 1972. Asst. dir. admissions U. Va. Law Sch., Charlottesville, 1972-76; from asst. to assoc. dean Northwestern U. Sch. Law, Chgo., 1976-85; assoc. dean Yale U. Law Sch., New Haven, 1985—2000; exec. dir. Housing Authority of New Haven, 2002—. Bd. dirs. The Access Group; lectr. in law Yale Law Sch., 2002—. Commr. New Haven Housing Authority, 1998—; trustee Nat. Assoc. for Law Placement Found. for Rsch. and Edn., 2000—. Capt. U.S. Army, 1972. Mem. Law Sch. Admission Coun. (programs, edn. and prelaw com. 1978-84), Assn. Am. Law Schs. (chmn. legal edn. and admissions sect. 1979, nominations com. 1987, chmn. adminstrn. of law schs. sect. 1991), Nat. Assn. for Law Placement (pres. 1984-85, co-chmn. Joint Nat. Assn. com. on placement 1986-88), New Haven Legal Assistance Assn. (bd. dirs., treas. 1992-98). Office: Yale Law Sch PO Box 208215 New Haven CT 06520-8215 E-mail: stephen.yandle@yale.edu.

YANDLE, SYLVESTER ELWOOD, II, sales executive, inventor; b. Lafayette, La., Sept. 14, 1932; s. Arthur Ray and Marie (Delhomme) Y.; m. Gretchen Ehrensing, June 28, 1957; children: Gretchen Marie, Sylvester E. III, Gladys Anne, Henry Arthur. Student, Southwestern La. Inst. Well logger Core Labs., Lafayette, La., 1954-56; salesman Security Rock Bits, 1956-61, Orbit Valve, New Orleans, 1961-62, So. Engine & Pump, New Orleans, 1962-66; owner, pres. Indsl. Pump Sales, Inc., Belle Chasse, La., 1967—, Commodore Boat Stores, Belle Chasse, 1978—, Hydro Damp Inc., Belle Chasse, 1992—. Inventor: Air bag for airlines (patent 1991), Hydro Damp (patent 1989), Indicators Studs for Railroads (patent pending), 2 others pending. Active mem. Aurora Civic Assn., La. Sgt. 1st class, M.C., USAR, 1948-59. Mem. New Orleans C.C., Airplane Owners & Pilots Assn. Republican. Roman Catholic. Avocations: duck carving, knife making, painting, inventing, flying. Home: 5883 Rhodes Ave New Orleans LA 70131-3925 Office: Indsl Pump Sales Inc 2814 Engineers Rd Belle Chasse LA 70037-3153

YANEV, GEORGE P, mathematician, educator; b. Pomorie, Bulgaria, May 27, 1961; s. Petar G and Christina Y Yanev; m. Reneta P Getova, June 16, 1991; 1 child Petar. MS in Math., U.Sofia, Bulgaria, 1986—86; PhD in Math., U. Sofia, Bulgaria, 1991; PhD in Stats., U.South Fla., Tampa, 2001—01. Rsch. fellow Inst. of Math., Bulgarian Acad. of Sciences, Sofia, Bulgaria, 1991—97; vis. rsch. scholar U. South Fla., Tampa, Fla., 1996—97, vis. asst. prof. St. Petersburg, 2000—01; asst. prof. U. South Fla., 2001—. Advance NATO fellowship Mid. East Tech. U., Ankara, Turkey, 1995—96; grad. studies U. of Ioannina, Greece, 1996. Contbr. articles to profl. jours., chpt. to book. Soldier Bulgarian army, 1979—81. Recipient Bulgarian Nat. Award for Young Mathematicians, Second Prize, Union of Bulgarian Mathematicians, 1988, Ann. Award, First Prize, Inst. of Math., Nat. Found. for Sci. Investigation of Bulgaria, 1995, Student Paper Presentation, First Prize, Ann. Meeting of the Fla. Chpt. of Am. Statis. Assn., 2000. Mem.: Internat. Indian Statis. Assn., Am. Statis. Assn., Soc. for Indsl. and Applied Math., Am. Math. Soc., Inst. of Math. Stats. Greek Orthodox. Office: Univ South Florida 140 Seventh Ave S DAV258 Saint Petersburg FL 33701

YANEY, GEORGE, history educator; b. Teaneck, N.J., Oct. 30, 1930; s. Arthur J. and Frances (Levings) Y.; m. Ann Hinrichs, June 7, 1952; children: Brian, Dale, Carolyn, Tara. B in Mgmt. Engring., Rensselaer Poly. Inst., 1952; MA in History, U. Colo., 1956; PhD, Princeton U., 1961. Instr. Coll. Wooster, Ohio, 1957-58; prof. history U. Md., College Park, 1960-92, prof. emeritus, 1992—. Author: Systematization of Russian Government, 1973, Urge to Mobilize, 1982, World of the Manager, 1994. Served to capt. USMC, 1952-54. Rsch. fellow Harvard U., 1969-70, fellow Slavic Rsch. Ctr., U. Hokkaido, Japan, 1990-91; Fulbright grantee, 1975, 77, 85, Internat. Rsch. Exchanges Bd. grantee 1965, 75, 77, 85, 89. Home: 7303 Baylor Ave College Park MD 20740-3001 Office: Univ of Maryland Dept Of History College Park MD 20742-0001 E-mail: geoyaney@aol.com.

YANG, CHEN NING, physicist; b. Hefei, Anhwei, China, Sept. 22, 1922; , naturalized, 1964; s. Ke Chuan and Meng Hwa Lo; m. Chih Li Tu Yang, Aug. 26, 1950; children: Franklin, Gilbert, Eulee. BS, Nat. S.W. Assoc. U., China, 1942; PhD, U. Chgo., 1948; DSc (hon.) , Princeton U., 1958, Bklyn. Poly. Inst., 1965, U. Wroclaw, Poland, 1974, Gustavus Adolphus Coll., 1975, U. Md., 1979, U. Durham, Eng., 1979, Fudan U., 1984, Swiss Fed. Inst. Tech., Switzerland, 1987, Moscow State U., 1992, Drexel U., 1995, Tsinghua U., Taiwan, 1996, Chinese U., Hong Kong, 1997, U. Michigan, 1998, SUNY, 1999. Instr. U. Chgo., 1948—49; mem. Inst. Advanced Study, Princeton, NJ, 1949—55, prof., 1955—66; Albert Einstein prof. SUNY, Stony Brook, 1966—99, prof. emeritus, 1999—, dir. Inst. Theoretical Physics, 1966—99, dir. emeritus C.N.Yang Inst. Theoretical Physics; disting. prof.-at-large Chinese U., Hong Kong, 1986—. Trustee Rockefeller U., 1970—76, Salk Inst., 1978—89, Ben Gurion U., 1980—. Recipient Nobel prize for Physics, 1957, Rumford prize, 1980, Nat. medal of Sci., 1986, Benjamin Franklin medal, 1993, Bower prize, 1994, Onsager prize, 1999, King Faisal Internat. prize, 2001. Mem.: NAS, AAAS (bd. dirs. 1975—79), Pontifical Acad. Scis., Am. Philos. Soc., Korean Acad. Sci. & Tech., Russian Acad. Scis., Russian Acad. Scis., Polish Acad. Scis., Royal Spanish Soc. Scis., Venezuelan Acad. Scis., Brazilian Acad. Scis., Academia Sinica, Chinese Acad. Scis., Royal Soc. London (fgn. mem.), Am. Phys. Soc., Sigma Xi. Office: SUNY Inst Theoretical Physics Stony Brook NY 11794-0001

YANG, DARCHUN BILLY, research scientist, consultant; b. Taipei, Taiwan, July 17, 1945; came to U.S., 1971; s. Wan-chi and Chao-Di (Lee) Y.; m. Lifang Chen, May 29, 1971; children: James Elmer, Charlene Alice. BS, Tamkang U., Taiwan, 1969; MS, Furman U., 1973; PhD, U. Ga., 1977. Rsch. asst. U. Ga., Athens, 1973-77, rsch. assoc., 1978-80; staff chemist Exxon Rsch. & Engring. Co., Baytown, Tex., 1980-87; staff cons. Stanley Corp. Rsch. Lab., New Britain, Conn., 1987-89; sr. scientist Loctite Corp., Rocky Hill, 1989-97; sr. rsch. assoc. Avery Rsch. Ctr., Pasadena, Calif., 1997-2000; dir. rsch. and devel. Waterfall Comp., Santa Cruz, 2001—. Contbr. over 50 articles to books, profl. jours.; patentee in field. Pres. Taiwanese Assn., West Hartford, Conn., 1990, Houston, Tex., 1983. 2d. lt. Taiwan Army, 1969-70. Mem. Am. Chem. Soc., Adhesion Soc., Soc. Applied Spectroscopy. Democrat. Achievements include expert in adhesive and coating technology and surface modification. Avocations: golfing, fishing, skiing, swimming, bicycling. Bus. Home: 2226 Calle Escarlata San Dimas CA 91773-5102 Office: Waterfall Co 399 Encinol St Santa Cruz CA 95060-2132 E-mail: byang@waterfallco.com., darchun@aol.com.

YANG, DAVID CHIE-HWA, business administration educator; b. Taiwan, Republic of China, Nov. 7, 1954; came to U.S., 1977; s. Wen-Shen and Chin-Huei (Lee) Y. BA, Nat. Taiwan U., Taipei, 1977; MBA, U. Calif., Berkeley, 1979; PhD, Columbia U., 1985. Prof., sch. accountancy U. Hawaii, Honolulu, 1985—. Rsch. assoc. Acctg. Rsch. Ctr. Grad. Sch. Bus. Columbia U., N.Y.C., 1981-84; vis. prof. Beijing (People's Republic of China) Inst. Chem. Engring. Mgmt., 1988-89; cons. to China Nat. Chem. Constrn. Corp., 1990, 91, CIEC CPAs, Shanghai Acad. Social Scis. CPAs, China; past tchr. Peking U., Nat. Taiwan U. Author: Modern Western Financial Management, 1992, The Association Between SFAS 33 Information and Bond Ratings, 1985, Accounting and Auditing in China, 1998, China's Economic Powerhouse, 2002; co-author: FASB Statement 33 Data Bank Users Manual, 1985, FASB Statement 36 Data Bank Users Manual, 1985. Recipient Title VI Grant U.S. Dept. Edn., 1987, curriculum devel. grant Coopers S. Lybrand Found, N.Y.C., 1987, ednl. improvement fund award U. Hawaii, 1987. Mem. Inst. Mgmt. Accts., Am. Acctg. Assn., Inst. of Internal Auditors, EDP Auditors Assn., Assn. Chinese Scholars in Hawaii (pres. 2000-01), Chinese Acctg. Profs. Assn. N.Am. (pres. 1997-98), Assn. for Chinese Mgmt. Educators (v.p. 1999-2000), Inst. Mgmt. Accts., Beta Gamma Sigma, Beta Alpha Psi (Outstanding Prof. 1989, 91, 92, 96, 97, Dennis Ching 1st Interstate Bank Meml. Teaching award 1993). Office: U Hawaii Coll Bus Adminstrn 2404 Maile Way Honolulu HI 96822-2223

YANG, DAVID XIAO DONG, electrical engineer, entrepreneur; b. Shanghai, China, Aug. 12, 1969; came to U.S. 1985; s. Rong Yang and Xiang-He "Lily" Shi. BSEE, BS in Physics, Stanford U., 1992, MSEE, 1993, PhD in Elec. Engring., 1999. V.p., tech. PiXIM, Inc., Mountain View, Calif., 1998—. Cons. MSI Semiconductor, San Jose, Calif., 1995, Lightspeed Semiconductor Corp., Mountain View, Calif., 1997. Fellow Intel Found., 1998-99, Hewlett Packard, 1996-98. Mem. IEEE, SPIE, Tau Beta Pi (winner mathemat. modeling contest 1991). Achievments include 10 patents; inventions. Avocations: reading, board games, hiking. Office: PiXIM Inc 883 N Shoreline Blvd Mountain View CA 94043

YANG, FAN, electrical engineering research scientist; b. Wuhan, Hubei Province, China, 1975; s. Zhixi Yang, Weidong Zhou; m. Jianxia Xue. Ph. D, UCLA, Los Angeles, 1999—2002; MS, Tsinghua University, Beijing, 1997—99, BS, 1992—97, MS, 1997—99, BS, 1992—97. Research scientist UCLA electrical engineering, Los Angeles, CA, 2002—02; Graduate student researcher UCLA electrical engineering Dept., 1999—2002; research assistant State key laboratory of microwave and digital communication, Beijing, China, 1995—99; teaching assistant Tsinghua University, China, 1996—99; Research assistant State key laboratory of Microwave and Digital Communication, China, 1994—99. Publicity officer IEEE AP society, Los Angeles Chapter, Los Angeles, CA, 2002—02; Session chair 2001 IEEE AP-s International Symposium Committee, Boston, 2001—01; reviewer IEEE Transactions on Antenna and Propagation, Piscataway, NJ, 2001—01. Author: (jounal articles) IEEE Transactions on antenna and propagations, 2001 (Honorable mention of IEEE APS student paper competition, 2000), (journal papers) microwave and optical technology letters, 2001, electronic letters, 2001, microwave and wireless components letters, 2002, (papers and presentations) in various international symosium from 1997 to present. Vice president Chinese student and scholar association at UCLA, Los Angeles, CA, 2001—02. Mem.: IEEE. Office: UCLA Electrical Engineering Dept. 420 Westwood Plaza Los Angeles CA 90095 Office Fax: (310)206-8495. Personal E-mail: ygfn@ee.ucla.edu. Business E-Mail: ygfn@ee.ucla.edu.

YANG, GUANGBIN, engineer; b. Jiexie, China, Aug. 22, 1964; s. Xitan and Meirong Y.; m. Ling Jin, Nov. 19, 1991; children: Benjamin, Laurence. BS, Hangzhou Inst. Elec. Engring., China, 1986, M of Engring., 1989; MS, Wayne State U., 1998, DPhil, 2000. Engr., team leader China Elec. Product Reliability & Environ. Testing, Guangzhou, China, 1989-95; rsch. asst. Wayne State U., Detroit, 1995-96; rschr. Ford Motor Co., Dearborn, Mich., 1996-98; reliability engr. Yazaki N.Am., Inc., Canton, 1998-2000, Ford Motor Co., Dearborn, 2000—. Mem. tech. com. Fault-Tolerance Computation Soc., Beijing, 1994-95; cons. in field. Contbr. articles to profl. jours. Mem. IEEE (sr.), Am. Soc. Quality (sr.), N.Y. Acad. Sci. Avocations: poetry, classical music. Office: Ford Motor Co Powertrain Reliability MD 25 21500 Oakwood Blvd Dearborn MI 48121 E-mail: gyang@peoplepc.com.

YANG, GUOBIN, sociologist, sinologist; b. Zibo, Shandong, China, Oct. 18, 1963; came to U.S., 1994; m. Lan Lin, 1987; 1 child, Yufeng. MA, U. N.C., 1996; PhD, Beijing Fgn. Studies U., 1993, NYU, 2000. Adj. instr. NYU, N.Y.C., 1998-99; asst. prof. U. Hawaii, Honolulu, 2000—. Hon. vis. fellow dept. English and related lit. U. York, Gt. Britain, 1995; vis. scholar U. Calif., Berkeley, 2001; faculty fellow Social Sci. Rsch. Coun., 2001. Editor: A Companion to Masterpieces in World Poetry, 1990; editor (jour.) Wen Yuan: Studies in Lang., Lit. and Culture, 1991; contbr. articles to profl. jours. Recipient Travel award Dept. Fgn. Affairs and Trade, Australia, 1990, Henry Luce Found. fellowship U. N.C., 1994-96, Sino-Brit. fellowship Brit. Acad., 1995. Mem. Am. Sociol. Assn. (asst. editor Sociol. Theory 1997-2000), Assn. Asian Studies. Office: Univ Hawaii Manoa 2424 Maile Way SSB Rm 247 Honolulu HI 96822

YANG, HENRY (HONG) S. metallurgist, materials engineer; b. Tai Xin, Jiang Su, China, Oct. 27, 1964; came to U.S., 1989; s. Xiao-Wen and Yan-Hua (Li) Y.; m. Xiao-Ping (Susan) Su, May 1, 1992; children: Jenny Su, Rachel Su. BS, Harbin (China) Inst. Tech., 1984; MPhil, U. Birmingham, Eng., 1987, PhD, 1989. Postdoctoral rsch. fellow U. Calif., Davis, 1989-92, staff rsch. assoc., 1992-93; staff rsch. metallurgist Kaiser Aluminum & Chem. Corp., Pleasanton, Calif., 1994-98; sr. metall. Kaiser Aluminum Engineered Products, L.A., 1999—. Instr. Laney Coll., Oakland, Calif., 1994-95. Contbr. articles to internat. sci. jours. Recipient Emsley award Inst. Materials, London, 1988, Pfeil medal and prize Inst. of Materials, London, 1993, Buehler Tch. Paper Merit award Internat. Metallographic Soc., 1997. Mem. The Minerals, Metals and Materials Soc., Materials Rsch. Soc. Christian. Achievements include contributions to the understanding of superplasticity in aluminum alloys, titanium alloys, and intermetallics; study of physical and mechanical metallurgy problems of aluminum alloys. Avocations: inventions, table tennis, tennis. Office: Kaiser Aluminum Engrd Products 6250 Bandini Blvd Los Angeles CA 90040-3168

YANG, HENRY T. university chancellor, educator; b. Chungking, China, Nov. 29, 1940; s. Chen Pei and Wei Gen Yang; m. Dilling Tsui, Sept. 2, 1966; children: Maria, Martha. BSCE, Nat. Taiwan U., 1962; MSCE, W.Va. U., 1965; PhD, Cornell U., 1968; D honoris causa, Purdue U., 1996. Structural engr. Gilbert Assocs., Reading, Pa., 1968-69; asst. prof. Sch. Aeros. and Astronautics, Purdue U., West Lafayette, Ind., 1969-72, assoc. prof., 1972-76, prof., 1976-94, Neil A. Armstrong Disting. prof., 1988-94, sch. head, 1979-84; dean engring. Purdue U., 1984-94; chancellor U. Calif., Santa Barbara, 1994—. Mem. sci. adv. bd. USAF, 1985-89; mem. aero. adv. com. NASA, 1985-89; mem. engring. adv. com. NSF, 1988-91; mem. mechanics bd. visitors ONR, 1990-93; mem. def. mfg. bd. DOD, 1988-89, def. sci. bd., 1989-91; mem. acad. adv. bd. Nat. Acad. Engring., 1991-94; mem. tech. adv. com. Pratt & Whitney, 1993-95; bd. dirs. Allied Signal, 1996-99; mem. Naval Rsch. Adv. Com., 1996-98. Recipient 12 Best Tchg. awards Purdue U., 1971-94, Outstanding Aerospace Engr. award Purdue U., 1999. Fellow AIAA, Am. Soc. Engring. Edn. (Centennial medal 1993, Benjamin Garver Lamme award 1998); mem. NAE, Academia Sinica. Office: U Calif Chancellors Office Santa Barbara CA 93106

YANG, HSIN-MING, immunologist; b. Taipei, Taiwan, Dec. 2, 1952; came to U.S., 1980; s. Sze Piao and Yun-Huan (Chang) Y.; m. Yeasing Yeh, June 28, 1980; children: Elaine, Albert. BS, Nat. Taiwan U., 1976, MS, 1983; PhD, U. Wash., 1985. Rsch. assoc. Tri-Svc. Gen. Hosp., Taipei, 1979-80; fellow Scripps Clinic and Rsch. Found., La Jolla, Calif., 1986-88, sr. rsch. assoc., 1988-90; asst. prof. U. Nebr. Med. Ctr., Omaha, 1990-91; sr. rsch. scientist Pacific Biotech, Inc., San Diego, 1991-95; mgr. Scantibodies Lab., Inc., Santee, Calif., 1995-99, dir., 1999-2000; staff scientist Wyntek Diagnostics, Inc., San Diego, 2000—, Genzyme Diagnostics, 01—. Lectr. Yun-Pei Coll. Med. Tech., Shinchiu, Taiwan, 1979-80. Contbr. articles to profl. jours., chpt. to book; inventor in field; patentee on analyte detection device including a hydrophobic barrier for improved fluid flow. Joseph Drown Found. fellow, 1986, Nat. Cancer Ctr. fellow, 1987-88. Mem. Am. Assn. for Cancer Rsch., Am. Assn. Clin. Chemistry, N.Y. Acad. Scis. Avocations: tennis, swimming, table tennis. Office: Scantibodies Lab Inc 9336 Abraham Way Santee CA 92071-2861

YANG, HUIXING, chemistry researcher; b. Huian, Fujian, China, Oct. 10, 1936; came to the U.S., 1990; s. Jingfang Yang and Wuhan Zheng; m. Enhui Lu, Dec. 25, 1969; children: Hao, Han. BS, Peking U., Beijing, 1960; PhD, U. Del., 1981, U. Tex., 1990. Tchg. asst. Beijing U., 1960-78, lectr., 1978-81, 82-85, assoc. prof., 1985-90; rsch. fellow U. Tex., Austin, 1990-93, rsch. assoc., 1993-98, rsch. scientist, 1998—. Postdoctoral fellow U. Del., Newark,

1981-82. Mem. editl. com. Acta Chimica Sinica, 1983-93, Chinese Jour. Chemistry, 1989-93; contbr. articles to profl. jours. Achievements include research in experimental and theoretical chemical kinetic studies in high temperature; investigation of the catalyst and surface science using the kinetic networks method for estimation of catalytic activity. Home: 304 N Kings Canyon Dr Cedar Park TX 78613-2346 Office: Univ Tex Austin TX 78712 E-mail: h.yang@mail.utexas.edu.

YANG, IN CHE, hydrologist, researcher; b. Hsinchu, Taiwan, Feb. 7, 1934; s. Ho Mu Yang and Tsin Huang; m. Lih Huey Sheu, Oct. 9, 1966; 1 child Bayard 1 child George 1 child Norman. BSc in Chem. Engring., Nat. Taiwan U., Taipei, 1956; MSc in Nuc. Chemistry, Carleton U., Ottawa, Can., 1965; PhD in Nuc. Chemistry, U. Wash., 1971. Sect. chief US Geol. Survey, Lakewood, Colo., 1980—84, project chief, 1985—. Rsch. asst. prof. U. Wash., Seattle, 1974—78; mem. water-data acquisition Nat. Handbook of Recommended Methods, 1980—98; joint task group on part 700, radioactivity Std. Methods, 1978—. Author: (textbook) Science at Work: in Earth Science , 1993. Mem.: Am. Water Work Assn. Home: 11899 W 74th Way Arvada CO 80005 Office: US Geological Survey Denver Federal Center MS 421 Lakewood CO 80225 Office Fax: 303-236-5047. Personal E-mail: icyang78@hotmail.com. E-mail: ayang@usgs.gov.

YANG, JIASHI, engineering educator; B in Engring., Tsinghua U., B in Engring., M in Engring., Tsinghua U., Beijing, 1986; MS, Syracuse U., 1988; MA, PhD, Princeton U., 1993. Rsch. assoc. U. Mo., Rolla, 1993—94; rsch. fellow Rensselaer Poly. Inst., Troy, NY, 1994—95; sr. engr. Motorola, Inc., Schaumburg, Ill., 1995—97; prof. U. Nebr., Lincoln , Nebr., 1997—. Contbr. articles to profl. jours. Mem.: IEEE. Achievements include patents in field. Office: Dept Engring Mechanics U Nebr Lincoln NE 68588-0526 Office Fax: 402-472-8292. Business E-Mail: jyang1@unl.edu.

YANG, JOHN ERIC, journalist; b. Chillicothe, Ohio, Feb. 10, 1958; s. Yih-Chang and Cynthia Norma (Poon) Y. BA cum laude, Wesleyan U., 1980. Staff writer The Boston Globe, 1980-81; corr. Time Mag., Boston, Atlanta, Washington, 1981-86; staff reporter Wall St. Jour., Washington, 1986-90; staff writer The Washington Post, 1990—. Recipient Cert. Merit ABA, 1985, Page One award Newspaper Guild N.Y., 1986. Mem. Asian-Am. Journalists Assn. (2d Pl. 1989), Am. Polit. Sci. Assn. Office: The Washington Post 1150 15th St NW Washington DC 20071-0002

YANG, JUNPING, physician; b. Luokou, People's Republic of China, Aug. 12, 1962; came to U.S., 1987; s. Shuyi and Guoxiong Y.; m. Karen Shuk Ha Yu, June 10, 1993; children: Sonia Huimin, Monica Jiamin. MBBS, Wuhan Med. Coll., Hubei, 1983; MS in Pharmacology, Tongji Med. U., Wuhan, Hubei, 1986; PhD, Harvard U., 1993. Diplomate Am. Bd. Internal Medicine; cert. endocrinology, diabetes, metabolism. Med. intern U. Okla., 1993-94, med. resident, 1994-95; clin. investigator Washington U. Sch. Medicine, St. Louis, 1995—99; asst. prof. medicine U. Ill., Chgo., 1999—2000; dir. endocrinology Heartland Health, St. Joseph, Mo., 2000—. Author: Endocrinology, 1992, Molecular Endocrinology, 1993. Recipient Outstanding Presentation award Okla. Soc. Internal Medicine, Okla. Chpt. Am.Coll. Physicians, 1994. Mem. ACP, The Endocrine Soc. Office: 5301 Faraon St Ste 140 Saint Joseph MO 64506

YANG, KEWU, chemist; b. Xian, Shanxi, China, Dec. 25, 1956; s. Yongfa Yang and Shuqin Wu; m. Fang Dong, July 22, 1982; 1 child, Yang Yang. BSc, Northwestern Normal U., Lanzhou, China, 1982; MSc, Lanzhou U., 1991; PhD, Chem. Physics Inst., Chinese Acad. of Scis., 1994. Nat. postdoctoral fellow Fudan U., Shanghai, 1994-96, prof. chemistry, 1996-98; rsch. chemist Miami U., Oxford, Ohio, 1998—. Contbr. 50 articles to profl. jours. Ind. rsch. grantee China Postdoctoral Sci. Found., 1994-96, Shanghai City Postdoctoral Sci. Found., 1995-97. Mem. AAAS, Am. Chem. Soc., Sigma Xi. Home: 616 Brill Dr Oxford OH 45056 Office: Dept of Chemistry Miami Univ High St Oxford OH 45056 E-mail: yangk1@muohio.edu.

YANG, KEY PAIK, librarian, archivist; b. Naju, Chollo Namdo, Korea, Jan. 8, 1919; s. Yunmuk and Yunhui Yang; m. Hazel K. Yang; children: Won Kyung, A Kyung, Mal Kyung. BA Polit. Sci., Monmouth Coll., Monmouth, IL, 1949; MSLS, Libr. Sci., Cath. U. of Am., Washington, DC, 1960; Doctorate of Philosophy (hon.) , Dongguk U., Seoul, Korea, 1975. Shoki Choen Kinyu Kumiai, Seoul, Korea, 1939, Chosen Kinsoku Butshi Eidan, Seoul, Korea, 1939—43; chief of d Property Custodian Office, Korea, 1943—45; head of sect. Pub. Works Divsn., Korea, 1945—47, Pub. Info., Seoul, Korea, 1947—49; cataloger Libr. of Congress, Washington, 1949—50. Panel mem. Bd. of US Civil Svc. Examiners, 1955—55; chmn. Subcommittee on East Asian Libraries, 1980—80. Co-author: (book) The School of Yi Confucianism; author: Phsiology of Korean Culture, Art and Civilization, Introduction to Koreanology; contbr. articles to profl. jours. Recipient Fulbright Lectr., Korean U., Seoul, 1983, Meritorious Award, The Libr. of Congress, 1984; fellow Sr. Fellowship in Korea, State Dept., Korea, 1965; grantee Harvard U. Grant, Korean Ecology, 1960. Mem.: Assn. of Asian Studies. Democrat-Npl. Home: 5104 Marlyn Drive Bethesda MD 20816

YANG, LIQIU, physicist; b. China, 1965; m. Zenia Yang, 1990; children: Joyce, Justina, Julia. PhD in Physics, Kans. State U., 1991. Lectr. physics Kans. State U., Manhattan, 1991; postdoctoral fellow in chemistry Ames Lab., U.S. Dept. Energy, Iowa, 1991-93; postdoctoral fellow in computational biology U. Houston, 1993-96, instr. chemistry, 1996; asst. scientist III Ames Lab., 1997-98; pres. The Yang Acad., Inc., Rockville, Md., 2001—. Contbr. articles to profl. jours. Bd. dirs. Suzuki Assn. of Greater Washington Area, 1999-2001; chmn. bd. Mei-Hwa Chinese Sch., Silver Spring, Md., 2000-02. Office: The Yang Academy PO Box 1073 Rockville MD 20849

YANG, NING-SUN, biotechnology researcher; b. Beijing, June 21, 1947; came to U.S., 1970; s. Shei-Mei Yang and Shieu-Yien Wu; m. Vina W.H. Yang, Aug. 15, 1970; children: Kayva, Shaun. BA, Nat. Taiwan U., Taipei, 1969; PhD, Mich. State U., 1970; postgrad., Roche Inst. Molecular Biology, 1974-76. Rsch. scientist, lab chief dept. biology Mich. Cancer Found., Detroit, 1976-82; sr. scientist fellow, dir. Agracetus Inc., Madison, Wis., 1982-89; clin. assoc. prof. Wis. Med. Sch., 1993-96; prin. investigator U. Wis. Comprehensive Cancer Ctr., U. Wis. Med. Sch., 1990—; prof. biotech. Nat. Taiwan U., 1998—. Adj. and cons. prof. Fudan U., Shanghai, United Med. Coll., Beijing, 1990—; dir., disting. rsch. fellow Inst. BioAgrl. Scis., Academia Sinica, Taipei, 1998—; mem. fgn. adv. com. human gene therapy program Chinese Acad. Scis., Beijing, 1993—; mem. adv. bd. various U.S. and Taiwan biotech. cos.; lectr. in field. Editor: Particle Bombardment Technology for Gene Transfer, 1994; contbr. over 75 articles to profl. jours.; patentee in field of gene transfer on therapy utility. 2d lt. Taiwan Army, 1969-70. Mem. AAAS, Am. Soc. Gene Therapy (mem. program subcom. non-viral gene delivery 1999—), N.Y. Acad. Scis. Avocations: gardening, cooking, classical music, museums.

YANG, RUIKANG, research scientist; b. Nei Monggol, China, July 9, 1963; s. Bingnan and Jiacheng (Hong) Y.; m. Li Song, Feb. 1989; 1 child, Betty. BSEE, U. Elec. Sci. and Tech., China, 1983, MSEE, 1986; D of Technology, Tampere U. of Tech., 1996. Asst. lectr. U. Elec. Sci. and Tech. of China, 1986-88, lectr., 1988-91; rsch. fellow Tampere U. of Tech., 1991-93; sr. rsch. engr. Nokia Rsch. Ctr., Tampere, 1994-96; mem. tech. staff Bell Labs Lucent Tech., Murray Hill, N.J., 1996—. Contbr. articles to profl. jours. including IEEE Trans. Signal Processing, IEEE Trans. Cirs. and Systems, IEEE Signal Processing Letters, Signal Processing; reviewer IEEE Trans. on Signal Processing, IEEE Trans. on Image Processing. Mem. IEEE, Internat. Soc. Optical Image, European Speech Comm. Assn., N.Y. Acad. Sci. Avocations: reading, sports. Home: 3 O Keefe Rd Bridgewater NJ 08807-5694

YANG, SHENG-PING, economist, educator; b. Taipei, Taiwan, June 19, 1966; s. Wan-Sheng Yang and Sue-Jen Chen; m. Bee Ling Ong; children: Natalie. PhD, U. Nebr., 1998. Adj. instr. Houston C.C., 1998—99; asst. prof. econs. Chadron (Nebr.) State Coll., 1999—2000; lead prof. bus. LeTourneau U., Houston, 1999—; asst. prof. econs. and fin. Wayland Bapt. U., Plainview, 2000—. Contbr. articles to profl. jours. Mem.: So. Econs. Assn. Home: #405 13131 Fallsview Ln Houston TX 77077 Office: Wayland Bapt Univ #330 1900 W 7th St Plainview TX 79042 Office Fax: 806-291-1957.

YANG, SHU-CHIN, economist, consultant; b. Tieling, Liaoning, China, Nov. 20, 1917; came to U.S., 1946; s. Pei-chang and Shu-Fong (Wang) Y.; m. Nancy Shu-Teh Cheng, Dec. 23, 1947 (dec. Sept. 1985); 1 child, Catherine Tsai; m. Flora Kai-wah Quek, July 27, 1991. BA, Nat. Cheng-Chi U., Nanking, China, 1939; MA, Nankai Inst. Econs., Chung-King, China, 1943; PhD, U. Wis., Madison, 1954. Economist for joint head office of 4 nat. banks, Chung-King, 1939-41; economist Cen. Planning Bd., 1943-46; econ. affairs officer, br. chief UN Econ. Commn. for Asia and the Far East, Bangkok, 1950-63; sr. economist The World Bank, Washington, 1963-82; econ. mission chief, mem. The World Bank Mission for Korea, Taiwan, Egypt, India, etc., various locations, 1968-80; coord., mgr. UN Devel. Program/The World Bank, Washington, Beijing, Shanghai, 1983-86; dir. Inst. Internat. Econs., Nankai U., Tianjin, China, 1987-97; pres., cons. Svcs. for Econs. and Trade, Chevy Chase, Md. Econ. advisor Nat. Econ. Coun. of The Philippine Govt., Manila, 1956; adv. prof. Fu-dan U., Shanghai, 1987—; cons. World Bank, Shanghai, 1987-91; hon. prof. Shanghai, Dongbei and Cen. Fin. and Econs. univs., Shanghai, Dalian, and Beijing, 1987—. Author: (books) A Multiple Exchange Rate System, 1957, Theories and Strategies of Economic Development, 2d edit., 1989, China: Economic Reform, Development and Stability, 2000; author, editor: (book) Manufactured Exports of East Asia, 1994. Mem. Am. Econ. Assn., Chinese Econ. Assn. in N.Am. Died Apr. 4, 2001.

YANG, SONG-YU, research biochemist; b. Wu-Xi, Jiangsu, China, Oct. 27, 1938; came to U.S., 1981; s. Rong-Geng Zhong and Su-Fei Yang; m. Xue-Ying He, Jan. 1965; children: Ying-Zi, Yu-Xiao. MD, Beijing U. Med. Ctr., 1960; MS, CCNY, 1983; PhD, CUNY, 1984. Diplomate Beijing U. Med. Ctr. Instr. Peking Med. Coll./Beijing U. Med. Ctr., 1960-75; asst. prof. Shanghai Inst. Biochem. and Cell Biology, Acad. Sinica, 1975-80; tchg. asst. CCNY, 1981-84; rsch. assoc. Rsch. Found. of CUNY, 1984-88; rsch. scientist NYS OMRDD, 1988—; head med. biochem. lab. Inst. for Basic Rsch. in Devel. Disabilities, 1994—. Contbr. chpts. to books and numerous articles to profl. jours. Investigator Am. Heart Assn., N.Y.C., 1991-94. Recipient L.J. Curtman prize CCNY, 1984, Wall Street Fellowship award, 1991, NIH Rsch. award, 1994, Alzheimer's Assn. Rsch. award, 1999. Mem. AAAS, Am. Chemistry Soc., Am. Soc. Biochemistry and Molecular Biology, N.Y. Acad. Scis., Sigma Xi. Research contribution to the fatty acid beta-oxidation and the sex steroid hormone metabolism; enzymes and related genes. Office: NYS Inst Basic Rsch in Devel Disabilities Dept of Pharmacology 1050 Forest Hill Rd Staten Island NY 10314-6356 E-mail: yang_songyu@yahoo.com.

YANG, SUE, artist; b. Taipei, Taiwan, Aug. 26, 1955; d. Quei-Tzeng Yang and Jeng Yuan Liu; children: Olivia Hsin, Ronald Hsin. BA, Nat. Taiwan U., 1977; MA, Ohio State U., 1979; diploma, Sch. of Mus. of Fine Arts, Boston, 2001. Art educator Chinese Culture Ctr., Boston, 1994—98, Mus. of Fine Arts, Boston, 1996—, gallery instr. of western and Asian arts, 1995-99, gallery instr. assoc., 1999—. Lectr., demonstrator Bennington Coll., Vt., 1998, Middlebury Coll., Vt., 1997, 99; demonstrator Harvard U., Boston, 1997. Author: Masterpieces by the Chinese-American Artist, 1999; works featured Always Bright: Paintings by Chinese American Artists 1970-1999, 1999; four solo exhbns.; numerous group exhbns. Painting juror Newton's Festival of Arts/mayor's office, 1997. Recipient award of excellence Forte Cup 20th Century Asian-Pacific Art Competition, Washington, D.C., 1999, 2nd prize Newton Art Assn., 1998. Mem. Chinese Calligraphy Assn. (v.p. 1993-95). Budhist. Avocations: travel, gardening, reading, vis. museums and galleries. Office: Mus of Fine Arts 465 Huntington Ave Boston MA 02115-5523

YANG, TAO, information science educator, researcher; b. Wuhan, Hubei, China, Jan. 1, 1970; arrived in U.S., 1995; s. Linbao Yang and Hengqing Zou; m. Chunmei Yang. BS, Tongji U., Shanghai, 1990, ME, 1993. Tchr. Shanghai U., 1993—95; rschr. U. Calif., Berkeley, 1995—2001; chief scientist Yangs Sci. Rsch. Inst., Tucson, 2002—. Author: Impulsive Control Theory, 2001, Cellular Image Processing, 2001, Advances in Computational Verb Systems, 2001, Impulsive Systems and Control:Theory and Applications, 2001, Cellular Neural Networks and Image Processing: The Science of Cellular Local Rules, 2002, Chaotic Communication Systems, 2002, Handbook of CNN Image Processing: All You Need to Know about Cellular Neural Networks, 2002, Computational Verb Theory: From Engineering, Dynamic Systems to physical Linguistics, 2002; editor: Internat. Jour. Computational Cognition; contbr. articles to profl. jours. Achievements include invention of chaotic digital code-division multiple access communication systems; research in theory of computational verb systems which provide quantitative tools for research of verbs and machine understanding of verbs. Office: Yangs Sci Rsch Inst Dept EECS 741 E 1st St Tucson AZ 85719-4830 E-mail: taoyang@yangsky.com.

YANG, WEN-CHING, chemical engineer; b. Taipei, Taiwan, Nov. 11, 1939; came to U.S., 1964; s. Ting-Lien and Ho (Lee) Y.; m. Rae Tien, Aug. 24, 1968; children: Evonne R., Peter T. BSChemE, Nat. Taiwan U., Taipei, 1962; MSChemE, U. Calif., Berkeley, 1965; PhD in Chem. Engring., Carnegie Mellon U., 1968. Sr. engr. rsch. and devel. ctr. Westinghouse Electric Co., Pitts., 1968-76, fellow engr., 1976-93, adv. engr. sci. and tech. ctr., 1993-98, Siemens Westinghouse Power Corp., Pitts., 1998—. Instr. U. Pitts., 1980, 83; chmn. rsch. rev. panel Office Fossil Energy, Dept. Energy, Washington, 1990; hon. guest prof. Tsinghua U., Beijing, 1996—; co-chair 10th Internat. Conf. on Fluidization, Beijing, 2001. Author: (with others) Encyclopedia of Fluid Mechanics, 1986, 92; editor spl. vol. Powder Tech. jour., 1987, 98; editor: Fluidization, Solids Handling, and Processing, 1999; contbr. over 100 papers to sci. jours. Lt. Army Tank Corp., 1962-63. Fellow AIChE (programming chair and sec. group 3, editor 9 symposium series vols. 1987-88, 92-93, sec. particle tech. forum 1993—, Fluidized Processes Recognition award 1993, George Westinghouse Signature award of excellence 1995. Fluidization Lectureship award 2000); mem. Am. Chem. Soc., Chinese Am. Chem. Soc. (pres. Pitts. chpt. 1994), Orgn. Chinese Am. Achievements include patents in field; development of widely-used correlations and design equations in pneumatic transport and fluidization areas. Avocations: Chinese calligraphy, painting, tennis, gardening. Home: 2376 Mt Vernon Ave Export PA 15632-9028 Office: Siemens Westinghouse Power Corp Sci & Tech Ctr 1310 Beulah Rd Pittsburgh PA 15235-5068

YANG, XIANBIN, chemist, researcher; BSc in Chemistry, Beijing Med. U., 1988, MSc in Pharm. Chemistry, 1995; PhD in Bioorganic Chemistry, Polish Acad. Scis., 1998. Lab. asst. Beijing Med. U., 1988-89, rsch. asst., 1989-94, rsch. assoc. Nat. Rsch. Labs. Natural and Biomimetic Drugs, 1994-95; rsch. asst. Polish Acad. Scis., Lodz, 1995-98; postdoctoral fellow Sealy Ctr. for Structural Biology U. Tex. Med. Br., Galveston, 1998—. Tchr., advisor Univ. of Traditional Chinese Medicine, 1992-95; mgr. NMR lab., Beijing Med. U., 1991-95, tchr. 1988-94. Contbr. articles to profl. jours.; patentee in field. Postdoctoral fellow Dept. Def., Def. Advanced Rsch., 1998—; scholar Polish State Com. for Sci. Rsch., 1995-98. Mem. Am. Soc. for Biochemistry and Molecular Biology, Biophys. Soc., Sigma Xi. Office: U Tex Med Br Sealy Ctr for Structural Biology Dept Human Biol Chem & Genet Galveston TX 77555-0001

YANG, XIANG YANG, engineer, entrepreneur; b. Beijing, May 15, 1961; came to U.S., 1989; s. Jingqi and Shuying (Liu) Y.; m. Meiyuan Wen, Jan. 9, 1986; 1 child, Yifei. BSEE, Tsinghua U., 1983, MSEE, 1986; PhD in Elec. Engring., Pa. State U., 1991. Sr. scientist Quantex Corp., Rockville, Md., 1991-95; asst. prof. U. New Orleans, 1995-96; programmer, analyst Freddie Mac, McLean, Va., 1996-97; sr. design engr. GE Info. Svcs., Rockville, Md., 1997-98; co-founder, v.p., COO CompuSensor Tech. Corp., Gaithersburg, 1998—. Prin. investigator R&D projects Dept. of Def., Quantex Corp., and U. New Orleans, 1991-96. Author: Introduction to Optical Engineering, 1997; contbr. chpts. to books, more than 40 articles to profl. jours.; guest editor of tech. jours. Mem. IEEE (sr.). Achievements include patents in field. Office: CST Corp 352C Christopher Ave Gaithersburg MD 20879-3660

YANG, XIANGZHONG, research scientist, administrator, educator; b. Weixian, Hebei, China, July 31, 1959; came to U.S., 1983; s. Wukui Yang and Fengrong Zhang; m. Xiuchun Tian, Jan. 5, 1986; 1 child, Andrew Chun. BS in Animal Sci. with honors, Beijing Agrl. U., 1982; diploma, Nanjing (China) Agrl. U., 1982; MS in Reproductive Physiology, Cornell U., 1986, PhD in Reproductive Physiology, 1990. Rsch. asst. Cornell U., Ithaca, N.Y., 1983-89, lab. program coord., 1987-90, postdoctoral fellow, 1990-91, sr. rsch. assoc., Facility, Biotech Ctr./Animal Sci., U. Conn., Storrs, 1996-2000, prof., 2000—; dir. Embryo Engring. Program, 1992-96; assoc. prof., head Transgenic Animal dir. Ctr. Regenerative Biology U. Conn. Adj. prof. Beijing Agrl. U., 1992—; adj. prof. Cornell U., 1996—; hon. prof. Chinese Acad. Agrl. Scis., Beijing, 1991—, Beijing Agrl. U., 1992—, Xinjiang (China) Acad. Animal Scis., 1993—; dir. China-Cornell Fellowship Programs, Ithaca, 1992-96; dir. China Bridges Internat., Storrs, 1996—; chmn. local arrangement com. Reprodn. in Farm Animals Symposium, Ithaca, 1992; mem. internat. program com. Ann. M.C. Chang Meml. Conf., 1992; cons. sci. dir. Baylor Ctr. Reproductive Health, Dallas, 1993-94; cons. Gencyme Transgenics, Inc., Framingham, Mass., 1993—, PPL Therapeutics, Blacksburg, Va. Author: Biotechnology of Preimplantational Embryos, 1993; editor-in-chief Agr. Scis. Overseas, 1990-94; contbr. numerous articles to sci. jours., abstracts, tech. papers to conf. procs. Grantee CU Biotech, 1993—, EAIC Inc., 1993-96, USDA, 1991-94, 92-95, 96-98, 2001--, Rockefeller Found., 1991-95, 92-95, Rockefeller Found., 1991-95, 92-97, 97—, Lingnan Found., 1995-97, 97-99, Vet Sch., 1993-94, 94-96, NIH, 2001--, Transpharm. Inc., 1994—, Baylor U., 1994-96, Genzyme Transgenic Corp., 1996—, Conn. Innovations Inc., Biotech. R & D Corp.; fellow China State Edn. Commn., 1983-85, Cornell U. Grad. Sch., 1985. Mem. Internat. Embryo Transfer Soc. (edn. com. mem. 1992-94), Soc. Study of Reproduction (com. chair 1991-93), The N.Y. State Acad. of Scis., Chinese Agrl. Assn. Students and Scholars (founder, pres. 1988-89, conf. chair 1989), Am. Fertility Soc., Chinese Soc. and Tech. Assn., Sigma Xi. E-mail: jyang@canr.uconn.edu.

YANG, XIAOPING, engineering researcher; b. Sichuan, People's Republic of China, 1966; BS with honors., S.W. Jiaotong U., Sichuan, People's Republic of China, 1986; MS, Dalian U. Tech., People's Republic of China, 1989; PhD, Purdue U., 2001. Engr. Cummins, Inc., 2001—. Contbr. chpts. to books and rsch. articles to profl. jours. Dean's fellow U. Mo., 1995, Andrew's fellow Purdue U., 1996. Mem. Am. Soc. Mech. Engrs., Tau Beta Pi Nat. Honor. Soc.

YANG, XINJIAN (SAM YANG), environmental engineer; b. Changde, Peoples Republic of China, Nov. 15, 1954; came to the U.S., 1988; m. Shui Bing, Feb. 4, 1982; 1 child, Yanfei. BS, Xiangtan U., 1981; MS in Engring., U. Cin., 1991. Asst. lectr. Xiangtan (Peoples Republic of China) U., 1982-86, lectr., 1986-87; rsch. scholar U. Cambridge, England, 1987-88; rsch. asst. U. Cin., 1988-91; sr. engr. process and devel. Noell Inc., Long Beach, Calif., 1991-96; sr. project engr. Mitsubishi Heavy Industries Am. Inc., 1997-2000; with Alstom Power Inc., Knoxville, Tenn., 2000-2001; Sr. Engring. Supvr. Advanced Envirnmental Controls, Newport Beach, CA, 2001—. Contbr. articles to profl. jours. Hon. rsch. fellow Salford U., 1987-88, Chinese Ednl. Commn. fellow, 1985. Mem. Air and Waste Mgmt. Assn., So. Calif. EPA. Achievements include discovery of temperature programmed reaction for determination of activation energy, ammonia regeneration for a combined NH3/CaO FGD process, urea/ammonia catalytic conversion process, engineering design for 20 multi-million dollar projects, six patent applications including high level oxygen air conditioning. Home: 12001 Cherry St Los Alamitos CA 90720-4171 Office: Advanced Environmental Controls Ste 102 4019 Westerly Pl Newport Beach CA 92660 E-mail: samyang2000@yahoo.com., sam.yang@advancedenvironmentalcontrols.com.

YANG, YANG, science educator; b. Kaohsiung, Taiwan, Nov. 7, 1958; came to U.S., 1985; s. Shun-Wen and Huang-Yin Yang; m. Danmei Lee, May 30, 1987; 1 child, Jonathan Lee Yang. BS in Physics, Nat. Cheng Kung U., 1982; MS in Physics, U. Mass., 1988, PhD in Physics, 1992. Rsch. asst. U. Mass., Lowell, 1989-91; rsch. assoc. U. Calif., Riverside, 1991-92; rsch. scientist UNIAX Corp., Santa Barbara, Calif., 1992-96; prof. UCLA, 1997—. Contbr. articles to profl. jours. Mem. Am. Phys. Soc., Material Rsch. Soc. Office: UCLA Dept Materials Sci Engring Los Angeles CA 90095-0001

YANG, YIQI, textile chemist, educator, consultant; b. Shanghai, Aug. 28, 1956; came to U.S., 1986; s. Fuji and Shaohua (Sha) Y. M.Engring., China Textile U., 1984; PhD, Purdue U., 1991. Technician Shanghai No. 2 Yarn Mill, 1973-77; instr. Shanghai Textile Inst., 1980-82, China Textile U., Shanghai, 1984-86; asst. prof. U. Ill., Urbana, 1991-94; prof. and sr. rsch. engr. Inst. Textile Tech., Charlottesville, Va., 1994-95, prof. and sr. rsch. assoc., 1997—; sr. rsch. specialist Monsanto Co., Pensacola, Fla., 1996-97. Cons. in field. Contbr. articles to profl. jours., chpts. to books.; patentee in field. Recipient numerous rsch. grants. Mem. Am. assn. Textile Chemists and Colorists. Achievements include research on salt effect in dyeing; non-formaldahyde durable press finishing for silk; carpet nylon fiber recycle; wet-on-wet dyeing; one-step polyester/cellulosics dyeing with disperse/reactive dyes; continuous fabric stationary phases for liquid chromatography. Avocations: calligraphy, poems, singing, fishing, basketball. Office: Inst of Textile Tech 2551 Ivy Rd Charlottesville VA 22903-4614 Home: 3206 Watercress Ln Lincoln NE 68504-4626 E-mail: uiqiy@itt.edu.

YANG, YONGGAO, computer scientist, researcher; b. Chongren, Jiangxi, China, June 9, 1965; s. Shaozhen Yang and Luo Honghua; m. Qing Yan; 1 child Yanming. Master's degree, S.W. Jiaotong U., Chengdu, Sichuan, China, 1987; PhD, S.W. Jiaotong U., Chengdu, Sichuan, China, 1997, George Mason U., 2002. Cert. assoc. prof. Asst. prof. dept. computer sci. S.W. Jiaotong U., Chengdu, 1989—93, assoc. prof. dept. computer sci., 1994—97; tchg./rsch. assoc. George Mason U., Fairfax, Va., 1998—; asst. prof. Prairie View (Tex.) A&M U., 2002. Assoc. dean Sch. Computer and Comm. Engring. S.W. Jiaotong U., Chengdu, 1994—98. Author: (book) Local Area Networks: Principle and Application, 1994 (Second grade awards of Sci. and Tech. Progress, 1993), Computer Communication Interfaces Technology, 1995 (Second grade awards of Sci. and Tech. Progress, 1996). Mem.: Chinese Computer Soc. Home: #7D 11109 Cavalier CT Fairfax VA 22030 Personal E-mail: yyang2@gmu.edu. Business E-Mail: yyang2@gmu.edu.

YANG, YUANYUAN, computer science and electrical engineer, educator; came to the U.S., 1987; d. Li and Lijin (Liu) Y.; m. Jianchao Wang, Dec. 29, 1984; children: Xi Wang, Christina Wang. BS in Computer Sci. and Engring., Tsinghua U., Beijing, China, 1982, MS in Computer Sci. and Engring., 1984; MS Engring. in Computer Sci., Johns Hopkins U., 1989, PhD in Computer Sci., 1992. Rsch./teaching asst. Parallel Processing Lab. Tsinghua U. Dept. Computer Sci. and Engring., Beijing, 1982-87; teaching asst. dept. computer sci. Johns Hopkins U., Balt., 1987-89, rsch. asst. dept. computer sci., 1989-92; faculty mem. dept. computer sci. and elec. engring. U. Vt., Burlington, 1992—99; assoc. prof. dept. elec. and computer engring. grad. program State U. of N.Y., Stony Brook, 1999—. Editor: IEEE Trans. parallel and distributed sys., program chair, 6th Internat. COnf. on COmputer Sci. and Informatics, program vice, 2002, Internat. Conf. of Parallel Processing, program vice chair, 10th Internat. Conf. on High Performance Computing; Contbr. articles to profl. jours.; patentee in field. Mem.: IEEE Comm. Soc., IEEE Computer Soc., ACM, IEEE (sr.). Office: SUNY STony Brook Dept ECE 215 Light Eng Bldg Stony Brook NY 11794

YANGA, ISMAEL DURAN, surgeon; b. Bocaue, The Philippines, Feb. 5, 1932; s. Ismael Eusebio Yanga Sr. and Sofia Rodriguez Duran; m. Ruth Morter, Dec. 17, 1971; children: Michele Marie, I. David III. AA, U. Santo Thomas, Manila, 1951, MD, 1956. Diplomate Am. Bd. Surgery, Am. Bd. Disability Analysts. Rotating intern Mercy Hosp., Buffalo, 1963; surg. resident meml. Hosp., Albany, 1964, Hurley Med. Ctr., Flint, Mich., 1965-69, fellow in surgery, 1969-70; practice medicine specializing in surgery Howell. Chief med. staff McPherson Hosp., Howell, Mich., 1994, 95; pres. Dr. Yanga's Hosp., Inc., Bocaue Bulacan, Philippines, 2000, bd. dirs. Pres. mission bd. Christ for the Philippines. Fellow ACS, Am.Soc. Laser Medicine and Surgery (diplomate), Internat. Coll. Surgeons; mem AMA, Mich. State Med. Soc., Livingston County Med. Soc. (pres. 1979), Am. Bd. Disability Analysts, Livingston Physicians Group (pres. 1991-94), chmn. bd. dirs. 1994—), Livingston Physicians Orgn., Am. Coll. Managed Care Medicine (diplomate), Am. Coll. Med. Quality, Howell C. of C. Baptist. Office: 1315 Byron Rd Howell MI 48843-1008 E-mail: Iyanga@Ismi.net.

YANKAUER, ALFRED, physician, educator; b. N.Y.C., Oct. 12, 1913; s. Alfred Sr. and Teresa (Loewy) Y.; m. Marian Wynn, May 22, 1948; children: Kenneth and Douglas (twins). BA, Dartmouth Coll., 1934; MD, Harvard U., 1938; MPH, Columbia U., 1947. Diplomate Am. Bd. Pediatrics, Am. Bd. Preventive Medicine and Pub. Health. Health officer N.Y.C. Dept. Health, 1947-50; asst. commr. of health Rochester (N.Y.) Health Bur., 1950-52; dir. maternal and child health bur. N.Y. State Dept. Health, Albany, 1952-61; WHO prof. child health Madras (India) Med. Sch., 1957-59; regional maternal and child health advisor Pan-Am. Health Orgn./WHO, Washington, 1961-66; sr. rsch. assoc. Sch. of Pub. Health Harvard U., Boston, 1966-73; prof. family and cmty. medicine and pediatrics Med. Sch. U. Mass., Worcester, 1973—. Asst. prof. health Cornell U. Med. Coll., N.Y.C., 1948-50; med. dir. pediatric nurse practitioner program Mass. Gen.Hosp./Northeastern U. Coll. of Nursing, Boston, 1972-79. Editor Am. Jour. Pub. Health, 1975-90; contbr. over 200 articles to profl. jours. Mem. health adv. com. Pub. Affairs Assn., N.Y.C., 1980-88; bd. dirs. Am. Social Health Commn., Research Triangle Park, N.C., 1984-90, chmn. rsch. adv. com., 1990—. Maj., M.C., U.S. Army, 1941-45, ETO. Fellow AAAS, Am. Acad. Pediatrics (Job Lewis Smith award 1979); mem. APHA (Excellence award 1990), Mass. Pub. Health Assn. (Lemuel Shattuck award 1987). Democrat. Office: U Mass Med Ctr 55 Lake Ave N Worcester MA 01655-0002 E-mail: alfred.yankauer@umassmed.edu.

YANKWICH, PETER EWALD, chemistry educator; b. L.A., Oct. 20, 1923; s. Leon Rene and Helen (Werner) Y.; m. Elizabeth Pope Ingram, July 14, 1945; children: Alexandra Stone Yankwich, Leon Rene II, Richard Ingram. BS, U. Calif., Berkeley, 1943, PhD, 1945. Mem. sci. staff Radiation Lab., U. Calif., Berkeley, 1944-48; faculty U. Calif., 1947-48; mem. faculty U. Ill., Urbana, 1948-88, prof. chemistry, 1957-88; head div. phys. chemistry U. Ill., Urbana, 1962-67, v.p. acad. affairs, 1977-82. Mem. Adv. Coun. on Coll. Chemistry, 1961-68; NSF Sr. Postdoctoral fellow, 1960-61, exec. officer Directorate for Sci. and Engring. Edn., 1985-90, Directorate for Edn. and Human Resources, 1990-92, sr. staff assoc., 1992-99. Mem. Urbana Bd. Edn., 1958-73. Fellow AAAS, Am. Phys. Soc.; mem. Am. Chem. Soc. (chmn. phys. chemistry div. 1971-72, chem. edn. planning and coordinating com. 1974-77, chmn. edn. commn. 1977-81, bd. dirs. 1982-91), Phi Beta Kappa, Sigma Xi. Home: 2665 Tallant Rd Apt W305 Santa Barbara CA 93105-4889

YANNAS, IOANNIS VASSILIOS, polymer science and engineering educator; b. Athens, Apr. 14, 1935; s. Vassilios Pavlos and Thalia (Sarafoglou) Y.; m. Stamatia Frondistou (div. Oct. 1984); children: Tania, Alexis. AB, Harvard U., 1957; SM, MIT, 1959; MS, Princeton U., 1965, PhD, 1966. Asst. prof. mech. engring. MIT, Cambridge, 1966-68, duPont asst. prof., 1968-69, assoc. prof., 1969-78, prof. polymer sci. and engring. dept. mech. engring., 1978—, prof., dept. materials sci. and engring., 1983—; prof. Harvard-MIT Div. Health Scis. and Tech., 1978—. Vis. prof. Royal Inst. Tech., Stockholm, 1974. Author: Tissue and Organ Regeneration in Adults, 2001; mem. editorial bd. Jour. Biomed. Materials Rsch., 1986—, Jour. Materials Sci. Materials Medicine, 1990—, Tissue Engineering, 1994—; contbr. over 100 tech. articles. to profl. jours.; 15 patents in field. Recipient awards for design of first successful artificial skin for treatment of massively burned patients and for identification of regeneration templates for dermis and peripheral nerves, including Founders award Soc. for Biomaterials, 1982, Clemson award Soc. for Biomaterials, 1992, Fred O. Conley award Soc. Plastics Engrs., 1982, award in medicine and genetics Sci. Digest/Cutty Sark, 1982, Doolittle award Am. Chem. Soc., 1988; fellow Pub. Health Svc., Princeton U., 1963, Shriners Burns Inst., Mass. Gen. Hosp., Boston, 1980-81. Fellow Am. Inst. Chemists, Am. Inst. Med. and Biol. Engrs. (founding mem.), Biomaterials Sci. and Engring.; mem. Inst. Medicine of Nat. Acad. Scis. Office: MIT Bldg 3-332 77 Mass Ave Cambridge MA 02139-4307

YANNELLA, DONALD, educator; b. N.Y.C., May 12, 1934; s. Donald Joseph and Johanna (Meehan) Y.; m. Kathleen Malone, May 23, 1959; children: Susan Y. Harrigan, Katherine Y. Jennings, Donald III, Christopher, Clare. BS, Fordham U., 1956, MA, 1963, PhD, 1971. Teaching asst. dept. English Auburn U., 1956-57; prof. dept. English U. So. Miss., 1981-83, Rowan U. (formerly Glassboro State Coll.), 1964-81, 83-91, prof. emeritus, 1991—; prof. dept. English Barat Coll., 1991-94, disting prof. Am. lit., 1995—2000. Dir. grad. studies English Rowan U., 1973-81, co-dir. Am. studies program, 1974-81; chair dept. English U. So. Miss., 1981-83; v.p. acad. affairs, dean coll. Barat Coll., 1991-94; cons. in field. Author: American Prose to 1820, 1979, Ralph Waldo Emerson, 1982, The Perfect Prodigy: Melville on the Birth of Malcolm, 1986, Herman Melville's Malcolm Letter: "Man's Final Lore", 1992, New Essays on Billy Budd, 2002; contbr. articles to profl. jours. With U.S. Army, 1957-58. Recipient Merit awards Rowan U., 1979-80, 85-86; NEH fellow, 1978-79. Mem. AAUP (chpt. pres. 1968-69, mem. cons. group Coll. and Univ. Govt. 1969, v.p. N.J. State Conf. 1969-71, founding editor N.J. Conf. newsletter 1969-71, nat. spl. com. non-tenured faculty 1971-72, chair 1973-79), Modern Lang. Assn. (Am. lit. sect., sec.-treas. 1982-85, exec. com. 1982-86, 88, adv. coun. 1986-88, nominating com. 1987-89, chair 1989, award 1988), Melville Soc. (program chair 1972-73, acting sec.-treas. 1973-74, acting editor 1973-74, sec.-treas. 1975-89, editor 1976-89, pres. 1990), Nat. Project Ctr. Film & Humanities (adv. com. 1974-75). Home: 219 Hilliard Blvd Manahawkin NJ 08050-3230 E-mail: yannellakd@aol.com.

YANNI, JOHN MICHAEL, pharmacologist; b. St. Mary's, Pa., Nov. 3, 1952; s. John Paul and Regina (Emmert) Y.; m. Nancy Jane Reedy, Sept. 22, 1979; children: Susan Elizabeth, Jennifer Ruth, Steven Reedy. BS, Allegheny Coll., 1974; MS, Va. Commonwealth U., 1979, PhD, 1982. Biologist A.H. Robins Co., Richmond, Va., 1980-82, sr. rsch. biologist, 1982-86, rsch. assoc., 1986-88; group leader Eastman Kodak Co., Rochester, N.Y., 1988-90; asst. dir. Alcon Labs., Inc., Ft. Worth, 1990-92, dir., 1992-93, sr. dir., 1993-2000, v.p. pharm rsch. R & D, 2001—. Contbr. articles to profl. jours.; patentee in field. Alden scholar Allegheny Coll., 1974. Mem. Am. Soc. Pharmacology and Exptl. Therapeutics, N.Y. Acad. Sci., Assn. for Rsch. in Vision and Ophthalmology, Soc. for Leukocyte Biology. Achievements include patents in area of allergy; described thromboxane A2's muco-secretory effect; identified antiallergic potential of Arylalkly-heterocyclic amines; discovered drugs Patanol and Emadine for treatment of ocular allergy; described secretory response of human conjunctival and choroidal mast cells. Office: Alcon Labs Inc 6201 South Fwy Fort Worth TX 76134-2099

YANNITELL, DANIEL WILLIAM, engineer, educator; b. Johnson City, N.Y., Sept. 26, 1941; s. Wilford A. and Marione E. (Ralston) Y.; m. Cyryl Ann Pogon, July 4, 1970; children: Anthony P., Gina M. BS in Naval Architecture/Marine Engring., Webb Inst., 1962; PHD in Theoretical and Applied Mechanics, Cornell U., 1967. Mem. faculty engring. La. State U., Baton Rouge, 1967—. Office: La State U Mech Engring Dept Baton Rouge LA 70803-0001

YANNUZZI, ELAINE VICTORIA, food and home products executive; b. Summit, N.J. d. Emil and Alice (Vance) Y. BA, Seton Hall U., 1968. Pres. Expression Unltd., Warren, N.J., 1971-89; pvt. practice cons. pub. industry and bus. Bedminster, 1989—. Presenter seminar N.Y. Food and Wine Show, Splty. Food Show; lectr. NYU, Rutgers U.; moderator Am. Women's Econ. Devel., N.Y.C., 1985-87; spkr. Women Bus. Owners N.J., Princeton, 1986. Author: Gift Wrapping Food, 1985; editorial advisor Fancy Food mag., 1985—; editorial cons. Family Circle Gt. Ideas mag., 1987-89. Named Entrepreneur of Yr. N.J. Living mag., 1983, Woman of Yr. NYU, 1986. Mem. Roundtable for Women (bd. dirs. 1986-89, Pacesetter award 1985), Nat. Assn. for Splty. Food Trade (steering com. 1986). Home and Office: 612 Timberbrooke Dr Bedminster NJ 07921-2106

YANNUZZI, GIUSEPPE ALBERTO, elementary education educator, writer; b. Florida, Cuba, Jan. 19, 1939; came to U.S., 1965; s. Miguel and Juana A. Yannuzzi; m. Gilda C. Yannuzzi, Aug. 3, 1968; children: Carlos, Jorge, Nancy. B of Letters, Inst. Camagüey, Cuba, 1958; BA, Mercy Coll., 1971; MA, Montclair U., 1973. Instr. Spanish Coll. New Rochelle, N.Y., 1976-77, Mercy Coll., Dobbs Ferry, 1979-80, State Coll. at New Paltz, 1982-85; tchr. ESL, elem. edn. Pub. Schs. of the Tarrytowns, 1971—. Author: (hist. novels) Un cuarto de siglo de republica, 1991, La Habana Virtual, 1998; contbr. articles and essays to profl. jours. Recipient Juan J. Remos award Cruzada Educativa Cubana, 1983, Fellowship award N.Y. State Congress Parents and Tchrs., 1974, Diplome de Medaille d'Argent, 2001. Mem. Cuban Nat. Assn. Journalists in Exile (v.p. 1994-99, Silver medal 1989), Pen Club Internat., Circulo de Cultura Panamericano (dir. cultural affairs 1983—), Forum Civico Cubano (pres. 1989—), Société Academique Arts-Scis.-Lettres. Republican. Roman Catholic. Avocation: photography.

YANOFF, ARTHUR SAMUEL, artist, art therapist; b. Boston, May 9, 1939; s. Jack and Sheila (Molensky) Y.; m. Carol Marie Meider (div.); 1 child, Lenya Alexis; m. Joan Elizabeth Zito, Jan. 10, 1977 (div.); 1 child, Almaisa Marishka. Student, Mus. Sch. of Fine Arts, Boston, 1958-61; studied with Jason Berger, Brookline, Mass., 1962-65. Instr. children's summer art program Temple Beth Jacob, Concord, N.H., 1969; art design cons. Lillabulero Press, Northwood Narrows, 1967-74; art therapist for emotionally disturbed children N.H. Hosp., Concord, 1970-71, designer therapeutic program for children with learning disabilities, 1970-71; art instr. adult edn. program Coe-Brown Acad., Northwood, N.H., 1972; instr. Manchester Inst. Art, Concord, 1973-74, art therapist, 1975—. Instr. landscape painting, Berkshire C.C., Great Barrington, Mass., 1997—; instr. Interlaken Sch. Art, Stockbridge, Mass., 1998—. Author: The Paste-Up Autobiography: A Visual Memoir; An Approach to Psychotherapy and Remedial Teaching, 1973; del. to N.H. Bicentennial Com., 1974-75; one-man shows include Brooks Sch., N. Andover, Mass., 1966, B.E.L. Gallery, Westport, Conn., 1972, Boston Ctr. for Arts, 1974, Addison Gallery Am. Art, Andover, Mass., 1974, New Hampton Sch., N.H., 1976, Ithaca House Gallery, N.Y., 1976, Mus. Fine Arts, Boston, 1983, Babson Coll., Wellesley, Mass., 1983, Currier Gallery Art, Manchester, N.H., 1985, Concordia Coll., Bronxville, N.Y., 1986, Symposium '88 Le Centre D'Art, Baie-St-Paul, Quebec, Prix, Rene Richard, Lingo Fine Arts Gallery, West Stockbridge, Mass., 1999; group shows include Sarah Y. Rentschler Gallery, Hudson, N.Y., 2000; exhibited in painting series including The Teaching of Isaac Luria, New Eng. Coll. Gallery, Henniker, N.H., 1995, Yeshiva U. Mus., N.Y.C., 1996-97, Koussevitzky Arts Festival, Berkshire C.C., Pittsfield, 1997, The Ea. Sprit in Contemporary Art, Coun. for Creative Projects, Warehouse Gallery, Lee, Mass., 1997, Gallery Talk: Renoir's Portraits and Landscapes, Sterling and Francine Clark Art Inst. (with Berkshire C.C.), Williamstown, Mass., 2000; represented in permanent collections Congregation Ahavath Chesed, Jacksonville, Fla., Mus. Fine Arts, Boston, Santa Fe, Addison Gallery Am. Art, Andover, New Hampton Sch., N.H. Commn. on Arts, Concord, N.H. Savs. Bank, Concord, Lee (Mass.) Bank, Hampshire Coll., Amherst, Mass., Yeshiva U. Mus., Babson Coll., MFA/Hines Indsl. Found., Cambridge, Mass., Rose Art Mus., Brandeis U., Waltham, Mass., Currier Gallery Art, Manchester, Le Centre D'Art, Baie-St-Paul, Quebec, Chabad House Lubavitch of N.H., Manchester, Detroit Inst. Arts, Mus. Art, Ft. Lauderdale, Fla., Concordia Coll. Gallery, Bronxville, Temple Beth Shalom, Santa Fe; exhibited in numerous shows in Mass., Va., N.H., Maine, Sante Fe, L.A. Meml. Found. Jewish Culture fellow, N.Y.C., 1989-90; recipient grant Max and Anna Levinson Found. and Ctr. for Jewish Culture and Creativity, 1996-98. Mem. Boston Painters and Sculptors, Am. Art Therapy Assn., N.H. Art Assn., Livestock Guard Dog Assn. Hampshire Coll., Am. Southdown Breeders Assn., N.H. Sheep and Wool Growers Assn., Greater Boston Kerry Blue Terrier Club (chmn. sheep guarding project), Am. Working Terrier Assn. (field trial judge). Jewish. Avocations: study and evaluate terriers and other dogs for predator control and livestock protection. Home: 624 S Egremont Rd Great Barrington MA 01230-1930 Address: Deborah Davis Fine Arts Inc 345 Warren St Hudson NY 12534-

YANOFF, MYRON, ophthalmologist; b. Phila., Dec. 21, 1936; s. Jacob and Lillian S. (Fishman) Y.; m. Karin Michelle Lindblad, Aug. 8, 1980; 1 dau., Alexis A.; children by previous marriage: Steven L., David A., Joanne M. AB, U. Pa., 1957, MD, 1961. Prof. ophthalmology and pathology U. Pa. Med. Sch., Phila.; William F. Norris and George E. de Schweinitz prof. ophthalmology, chmn. dept., dir. Scheie Eye Inst., 1977-86; chmn., prof. ophthalmology MCP/Hahnemann U., Phila., 1988—. 1st exchange vis. prof. U. Vienna, 1992. Author: Ocular Pathology, Textbook of Ophthalmology; contbr. articles to profl. jours. Served to maj. M.C. USAR. Recipient Humboldt award, 1988. Mem. Am. Ophthalmic Soc., Verhoeff Soc., Am. Acad. Ophthalmology (Sr. Honor award 1995). Office: Hahnemann U Hosp Dept Ophthalmology Broad & Race Sts Philadelphia PA 19102

YANOFSKY, CHARLES, biology educator; b. N.Y.C., Apr. 17, 1925; s. Frank and Jennie (Kopatz) Y.; m. Carol Cohen, June 19, 1949, (dec. Dec. 1990); children: Stephen David, Robert Howard, Martin Fred; m. Edna Crawford, Jan. 4, 1992. BS, CCNY, 1948; MS, Yale U., 1950, PhD, 1951, DSc (hon.), 1981, U. Chgo., 1980. Rsch. asst. Yale U., 1951-54; asst. prof. microbiology Western Res. U. Med. Sch., 1954-57; mem. faculty Stanford U., 1958—, prof. biology, 1961—, Herzstein prof. biology, 1966—. Career investigator Am. Heart Assn., 1969-95. Served with AUS, 1944-46. Recipient Lederle Med. Faculty award, 1957, Eli Lilly award bacteriology, 1959, U.S. Steel Co. award molecular biology, 1964, Howard Taylor Ricketts award U. Chgo., 1966, Albert and Mary Lasker award, 1971, Townsend Harris medal Coll. City N.Y., 1973, Louisa Gross Horwitz prize in biology and biochemistry Columbia U., 1976, V.D. Mattia award Roche Inst., 1982, medal Genetics Soc. Am., 1983, Internat. award Gairdner Found., 1985, named Passano Laureate, Passano Found., 1992; recipient William C. Rose award in biochemistry and molecular biology, 1997, Abbott Lifetime Achievement award Am. Soc. Microbiology, 1998. Mem. NAS (Selman A. Waksman award in microbiology 1972), Am. Acad. Arts and Scis., Genetics Soc. Am. (pres. 1969, Thomas Hunt Morgan medal 1990), Am. Soc. Biol. Chemists (pres. 1984), Royal Soc. (fgn. mem.), Japanese Biochem. Soc. (hon.) Home: 725 Mayfield Ave Stanford CA 94305-1016 Office: Stanford U Dept Of Biological Sci Stanford CA 94305

YANOV, ALEXANDER L. social sciences educator, educator; b. Odessa, Ukraine, Apr. 18, 1930; arrived in U.S., 1974; m. Lidia N. Nechaeva, Apr. 2, 1956; 1 child Marina A. MA History, U. Moscow, 1953; PhD, Inst. Nat. Econ., Moscow, 1970. Vis. lectr. U. Tex., Austin, 1975; asst. prof. U. Calif., Berkeley, 1976—83; assoc. prof. U. Mich., Ann Arbor, 1983—86; prof. polit. sci. and history CUNY, N.Y.C., 1986—90. Cons. Pres. of Russia, Moscow, 1990—92, European Commn., Moscow, 2001—. Author: (novels) The Russian New Right, 1977, The Origins of Autocracy, 1981, Russia vs. Russia, 1999; contbr. articles to profl. jours. Grantee grant, Nat. Endowment for the Humanities, 1979, Nat. Coun. for Soviet and EE Rsch., 1980, The Harry Frank Guggenheim Found., 1981. E-mail: ayanov@estart.com.

YANOWITZ, EDWARD STANLEY, allergist, educator; b. N.Y.C., July 4, 1950; s. Robert Donald and Betty (Lewis) Y.; m. Jean Wendy Temeck, Oct. 25, 1986. BA, Yale U., 1972; MD, Autonomous U. Guadalajara, 1978; student 5th pathway program, Booth Meml. Med. Ctr., 1978-79. Diplomate Am. Bd. Pediat., Am. Bd. Allergy and Immunology. Intern in pediat. The Roosevelt Hosp., N.Y.C., 1979-80; resident in pediat. St. Luke's-Roosevelt Hosp. Ctr., 1980-82; fellow in allergy and immunology N.Y. Hosp./Cornell Med. Ctr., 1982-84; allergy assoc. Allergy Care Assocs., 1984-87; asst. prof. medicine George Washington U. Med. Ctr., Washington, 1987-97, clin. asst. prof., 1997—; allergy assoc. Asthma and Allergy Care Am. of Md., P.C., 1997-2000, pres., 2000—, assoc., 2000—. Vis. clin. fellow Columbia U., 1979-82; clin. fellow divsn. allergy and immunology dept. pediat., Cornell U., 1982-84, instr. pediat., 1984-87; asst. attending physician The New York Hosp., 1984-87; cons. staff dept. pediat. St. Luke's Hosp., Newburgh, N.Y., 1984-87. Co-author: Handbook of Pulmonary Drug Therapy, 1994. Fellow Am. Acad. Pediat., Am. Acad. Allergy and Immunology; mem. AMA, Joint Coun. Allergy and Immunology, N.Y. Med. Soc. (mem. com. fgn. med. grads. 1982, mem. membership com. 1986), N.Y. Allergy Soc., Med. Soc. State of N.Y., Alumni Assn. Autonomous U. Guadalajara, Am. Profl. Practice Assn. Office: Allergy and Asthma Care of Md PC 8508 Cedar St Silver Spring MD 20910-4322 E-mail: eyanowitz@juno.com.

YANTS, SVETLANA VLADIMIROVNA, librarian, lecturer; b. Pavlovsk, Voronezh, Russia, Oct. 14, 1933; d. Vladimir Mikhailovich and Anastasiya Lavrent'evna (Gubanova) Bukovshina; m. Villi Yakovlevich Yants, Nov. 17, 1956; children: Vladimir, Andrei. diploma of higher edn., excellence diploma, Voronezh State U., 1956. Librarianship diplomate Moscow Inst. Culture. Jr. mem. tchg. staff dept. of hydrology of land Voronezh State U., 1956-59; jr. libr. Voronezh State U. Sci. Libr., 1959-61, reference libr., 1961-64, head circulation dept., 1964-68, dir., 1968—. Author: The State & Prospects for Development of the Catalog System in the Libraries of Institutions of Higher Education, 1983; editor Catalogs of Russian and Fgn. Periodicals, 1969—. Chairperson Com. for Aesthetic Edn. of Young People Voronezh State U., 1973-83. Recipient Labour Prowess medal Supreme Soviet of USSR, Moscow, 1976, Honoured Culture Worker award Pres. of Russian Fedn., 1994. Mem. Regional Coun. Libr. Dirs. Edn. Insts. (chairperson), State Com. for Higher Edn. of Russian Fedn. (libr. and info commn. 1969—). Avocations: theatre, handicrafts, gardening. Office: Sci Libr Pr Revolyutsii 24 Voronezh 394000 Russia E-mail: yants@lib.vsu.ru.

YAO, BIN, mechanical engineering educator; b. Shaanxi, China, Dec. 23, 1968; came to U.S., 1992; s. Weikuan Yao and Qingrong Liu; m. Ying Xie, July 14, 1999. PhD, U. Calif., Berkeley, 1996. Postdoctoral rschr. mech. engring. dept. U. Calif., Berkeley, 1996; asst. prof. Sch. Mech. Engring. Purdue U., West Lafayette, Ind., 1996—. Summer faculty sabbatical leave Advanced Hydraulics Group, Joliet (Ill.) plant, Caterpillar Inc., 1997. Contbr. numerous tech. articles to profl. publs. (NSF Career award 1998). Regents fellow U. Calif., 1992. Mem. IEEE, ASME. Avocations: sports, travel, art, music. Office: Purdue U Sch Mech Engring West Lafayette IN 47907 Office Fax: 765-494-0539. E-mail: byao@ieee.org.

YAO, DAVID DA-WEI, engineering educator; b. Shanghai, China, July 14, 1950; came to U.S., 1983, naturalized, 1990; s. William Kang-Fu and Nancy Yun-Lan (Lu) Y.; m. Helen Zhi-Heng Chen, Jan. 31, 1979; children: Henry, John. MASc, U. Toronto, Ont., Can., 1981, PhD, 1983. Assoc. prof. systems engring. Harvard U., Cambridge, Mass., 1986-88; asst. prof. indsl. engring. and ops. rsch. Columbia U., N.Y.C., 1983-86, prof., 1988—, Thomas Alva Edison prof., 1992—. Acad. visitor AT&T Bell Labs., Holmdel, N.J., 1989, T.J. Watson Rsch. Ctr., IBM, Yorktown, N.Y., 1990—. Co-author: Monotone Structure in Discrete-Event Systems, 1994, Fundamentals of Queueing Networks, 2001; editor: Stochastic Modeling and Analysis of Manufacturing Systems, 1994; contbr. more than 150 articles to sci. jours. including Maths. Ops. Rsch., Jour. of Assn. Computing Machinery, Advances in Applied Probability, 1983—. Recipient Presdl. Young Investigator award NSF, Washington, 1987-92, Guggenheim fellow John Simon Guggenheim Meml. Found., N.Y.C., 1991-92. Fellow IEEE; mem. Soc. Indsl. and Applied Math., Ops. Rsch. Soc. Am. (George Nicholson prize 1983, Franz Edelman award 1999). Achievements include development of theory of algebraic structures in discrete-event systems, theory of stochastic convexity and its applications in queuing networks, stochastic network models for manufacturing systems and supply chains, methodologies in the optimization and control of stochastic discrete-event systems. Home: 1261 Underhill Ave Yorktown Heights NY 10598-5718 Office: Columbia U EOR 302 Mudd Bldg New York NY 10027-6699 E-mail: yao@ieor.columbia.edu.

YAO, GANG, biomedical engineer, researcher; b. Nanjing, China; s. Meng Yao and Yiqing Ding; m. Zhixuan Li, Nov. 11, 1969; 1 child, Rujie. PhD, Tex. A&M U., 2000. Scientist China Inst. Atomic Energy, Beijing, 1992-96; rsch. asst. Tex. A&M U., College Station, 1998-2000. Contbr. articles to profl. jours. Recipient 1st place young Conf. Laser Tech., 1993.

YAO, HILDA MARIA HSIANG, banker, strategic planner; b. Honolulu, Sept. 11, 1956; d. Hsin-Nung and Dorothy Wen (Wu) Y. BA cum laude, U. Pacific, 1975; MA, U. Wis., 1976. Ops. analyst Visa Internat., San Mateo, Calif., 1977-80; sr. product mgr. Bank of Am., San Francisco, 1980-81, asst. v.p., strategic planner Calif. electronic banking div., 1981-84, v.p., div. strategic planner U.S. wholesale svcs. world banking div., 1984-85, v.p., head dealer corp. svcs., 1985-89, v.p., dir. retail banking adminstrn., 1989-90, v.p., CFO internat. pvt. banking divsn., 1990-92, v.p., dir., deputy mgr. internat. investment svcs., 1992-93, v.p., head fiduciary policy, 1993-95, sr. v.p., dir. pvt. banking, trust and investment mgmt., 1995-97, sr. v.p., dep. mng. dir. internat. pvt. banking, 1997—. Bd. regents U. Pacific, Stockton, Calif., 1984-85, 91—; treas. pres.'s jr. adv. coun. Bank of Am., 1982-83; active exec. com. Campaign for Wis., 1991—; bd. dirs. U. Wis. Found., 1995—; bd. visitors Coll. of Letters and Sci. U. Wis., Madison, 1995—; mem. adv. bd. program in medicine and philosophy Calif. Pacific Med. Ctr., San Francisco, 1993—; mem. Pacific Coun. on Internat. Policy, 1996—; mem. China study group Pacific Coun. on Internat. Policy and Rand Corp., 1996—; hon. advisor China Soc. for People's Friendship Studies, 1992—. U. Wis. fellow, 1975-76, alumni fellow U. Pacific, 1983, Outstanding Young Alumna award U. Pacific, 1989. Mem. Nat. Vehicle Leasing Assn. (treas. 1988-89), World Affairs Counc., Calif. Acad. Scis., Commonwealth Club Calif., Bank Am. Club, Bankers Club San Francisco, World Trade Club, Univ. Club, The Mus. Soc., Calif. Legion of Honor, Bascom Hill Soc. U. Wis., President's Circle U. Pacific, Nat. Soc. Hist. Preservation, 1841 Club-Punahou Sch., Odyssey Club. Avocations: Shakespeare, opera, languages, swimming, golf. Home: Gramercy Towers 1177 California St San Francisco CA 94108-2212 Office: Bank of Am 50 California St Ste 233 San Francisco CA 94111-4624

YAO, JAMES TSU-PING, retired civil engineer; b. Shanghai, China, July 7, 1933; came to U.S. 1953; s. C.C. and Mae Jane (Wang) Y.; m. Anna Lee, June 14, 1958; children: Tina Lee, Timothy H.J., Shana Lynn. BSCE, U. Ill., 1957, MSCE, 1958, PhD, 1961. Lic. profl. engr. Tex., N.Mex. Postdoctoral preceptor Columbia U., N.Y.C., 1964-65; asst. prof. civil engring. U. N.Mex., Albuquerque, 1961-64, assoc. prof., 1965-69, prof., 1969-71, Purdue U., W. Lafayette, Ind., 1971-88, asst. head sch. civil engring., 1983-88, asst. dean grad. sch., 1984-87; prof. Tex. A&M U., College Station, 1988—2002, head dept. civil engring., 1988-93, Carolyn S. and Tommie E. Lohman prof. engring. edn., 1996—2002. Editor Jour. Structural Engring., 1990-92. Recipient Max Planck Rsch. award Alexander Von Humboldt Found., 1990, Civil Engring. Disting. Alumnus award, U. Ill., Urbana, 1991, Centennial medallion Am. Soc. Engring. Edn., 1993. Fellow Am. Soc. Engring. Edn.; mem. Am. Soc. Civil Engrs. (hon., State-of-the-Art of Civil Engring. award 1973, 83, Alfred M. Freudenthal medal 1990, Richard R. Torrens award 1992, Pres.'s medal 1995, Norman medal 1999, Jour. Profl. Issues Best Paper award 2000). Avocations: volleyball, paperfolding. Office: Tex A&M Univ Dept Civil Engring 3136 TAMU College Station TX 77843-3136 E-mail: jtpyao@tamu.edu.

YAO, JIANHUA, research chemist; b. Suzhou, People's Republic of China, Feb. 26, 1962; d. Dawu Yao and Xiuzhen Lu; m. Youlu Yu, Mar. 21, 1987. BSc, Nanjing (China) U., 1982, MSc, 1985; PhD, Concordia U., Montreal, Can., 1992. Mem. tchg. and rsch. staff Nanjing U., 1985-87; postdoctoral fellow Concordia U., 1992-93; rsch. assoc. Nat. Rsch. Coun. Can., Ottawa, 1993-95; rsch. chemist Phillips Petroleum Co., Bartlesville, Okla., 1995—. Contbr. over 25 articles to profl. jours.; patentee in field. Mem. ACS. Home: 1532 Whitney Ln Bartlesville OK 74006-6037 Office: Phillips Petroleum Co 332 Pl Rsch Ctr Bartlesville OK 74004-0001

YAO, JOHN SEN, physician; b. Honolulu, Aug. 28, 1954; s. Hsin-Hung and Dorothy W. Yao; m. Pauline A. Mysliwiec, Oct. 16, 1993. MPH, Columbia U., 1978, MD, 1983; MBA, UCLA, 1998; MPA, Harvard U., 1999. Diplomate Am. Bd. Internal Medicine, Nat. Bd. Med. Examiners. Resident in internal medicine U. Calif.-San Francisco Med. Ctr., 1983-86, asst. clin. prof., 1988-94; chief med. officer USPHS, Calif., 1990-98; med. dir. Cigna Healthcare, inc., 1997-98; fellow in policy studies Harvard U., Cambridge, Mass., 1998—. Mem. exec. com. State of Calif. TB Control, 1994—; mem. steering com. Breast and Cervical Cancer Prevention, Stte of Calif., 1991-94; med. advisor State of Calif. Medicaid Reform com., 1994-95. Contbr. articles to profl. jours. Med. advisor Gov.'s Coun. on Exercise and Health, Calif., 19945; mem. Calif. HIV-AIDS Commn., 1990-93. Fellow ACP. Avocations: golf, tennis, skiing, classical music, opera. Office: 14531 Benjamin Franklin Sta Washington DC 20044-4531 E-mail: jyaomd@aol.com.

YAO, SHANG J. retired research scientist; b. Canton, Quangdong, China, June 6, 1934; s. Wan-Nien Yao and Kong Liyao; m. Hui-Ying Sun Yao, Feb. 14, 1936; children: Gene J. Diploma Chem. Engring., Nat. Taipei U. of Tech., Taipei, Taiwan, 1955; MA, U. of Oreg., Eugene, Oregon, 1961; PhD, U. of Minn., Minneapolis, Minnesota, 1966. Robert a. welch found. fellow Tex. A&M U., College Station, Tex., 1966—67; postdoctoral fellow Northwestern U., Evanston, Ill., 1967—68; asst. prof. Wilbur Wright Coll., Chicago, 1968—69; instr. U. of Chgo., 1969—71; asst. prof. U. of Pitts. Sch. of Medicine, Pittsburgh, Pa., 1971—79, rsch. assoc. prof., 1979—87, rsch. prof., 1987—99. Vis. prof. chemistry Peking U., Beijing, 1985; vis. prof. chemestry Nanjing U. and Hudan U., Nanjing and Shanhai, China, 1988; disting. lectr. and lingnam prof. of chemestry Sundjatsen U., Canton, China, 1988. Mem. of divsn. of rsch. grants NIH, Bethesda, Md., 1987—99. Grantee Prin. Investigator, John A. Hartgord Found., 1977-1980, NIH, 1979-1989, 1996, Survivors Diabetes Found., 1989-1991. Mem.: Sigma XI, Phi Lambda Upsilon. Achievements include patents for Awarded six U.S. patents; research in Principal author of Biomedical Services and Sensors. Home: 1695 Hastings Mill Road Pittsburgh PA 15241

YAO, TITO GO, pediatrician; b. Manila, May 30, 1943; came to U.S., 1970, naturalized, 1984; s. Vincente and Sin Keng (Go) Y.; m. Lilia Ytem, July 3, 1976; children: Robert, James, Richard. MD, Far Ea. U., Manila, 1969. Diplomate Am. Bd. Pediatrics, Am. Bd. Quality Assurance. Intern Evang. Deaconess Hosp., Milw., 1970-71; resident in pediatrics T.C. Thompson Children's Hosp., Chattanooga, 1971-72, Meth. Hosp., Bklyn., 1972-73; fellow St. Christopher Hosp. Children, Phila., 1973-74, Cook County Children's Hosp., Chgo., 1974-75; dir. GSK Med. Ctr., 1976—. Chmn. dept. pediat. St. Anne's Hosp., Chgo., 1986-88, Loretto Hosp., Chgo., 1988—; dir. RJ Med. Center, Chgo., 1980—; mem. staff Norwegian Am. Hosp., St. Anthony's Hosp., St. Mary of Nazareth Hosp. Fellow Am. Acad. Pediatrics (life), Am. Coll. Utilization Rev. Physicians; mem. AMA (life, Physician Recognition award 1973—), Assn. Philippine Physicians Practicing in Am., Ill. Med. Assn., Am. Assn. Individual Investors, Chgo. Med. Soc., Chgo. Pediatric Soc. Office: 5351 W North Ave Chicago IL 60639-4350 also: 5140 W Chicago Ave Chicago IL 60651-2903 E-mail: titogyao@aol.com.

YAO, XIAOTIAN STEVE, electrical engineer, optical scientist; b. Hongzhou, Zhejiang, China, July 29, 1960; came to U.S., 1985; s. Dunli and Xianrong Yao; m. Yuanyuan Fang; 1 child, Leon. BS in Physics, Hebei U., China, 1982; MS in Applied Physics, N.W. Telecom. Engring. Inst., China, 1984; MSEE, U. So. Calif., 1989, PhD in Elec. Engring., 1992. Researcher N. China Electro-Optic Rsch. Inst., Beijing, 1982-84; optical engr. ADC Fiber Optics, Westboro, Mass., 1985-87; rsch. asst. U. So. Calif., L.A., 1987-90; mem. tech. staff Jet Propulsion Lab., Pasadena, Calif., 1990-96, sr. mem. tech. staff, 1996—2000; pres., CEO Gen. Photonics Corp., 2000—. Mem. adv. bd. Nat. Network Electro-Optic Mfg. Tech., Vandergrift, Pa., 1996—; mem. tech. com. Optical Fiber Comm. Conf., Washington, 1997-00. Contbr. more than 20 articles to profl. jours.; patentee in field. Recipient 18 NASA Tech Innovations award; rsch. grantee NASA, 1992-, USAF, 1996—. Mem. IEEE, Optical Soc. Am. Achievements include invention of opto-electronic oscillator, brillouin microwave oscillator, dual microwave and optical wave oscillator, brillouin selective sideband amplification technique, index-switched variable optical delay device, Polarite polarization controller, polarization independent electro-optic modulator. Office: Jet Propulsion Lab 4800 Oak Grove Dr Pasadena CA 91109-8001

YAO, XINGDONG, analytical chemist; b. Yangzhou, Jiangsu, China, Oct. 18, 1965; s. Wenwei Yao and Yuzhen Liu(Stepmother); m. Yuanmei Nie. Ph.D, Wuhan (China) University, 1990. Lectr. in Chemistry Shantou (China) U., 1990—91; dir. analysis ctr. associate prof. Shantou U., China, 1992—98; rsch. scientist S.C. State U., Orangeburg, SC, 1998—. Author: (rsch. paper) Studies on the Tolerance of Polysaccharides of Different Plants for Ultraviolet Radiation, 1996 (Ann. Excellent Rsch. Paper: Chinese Biochem.and Med.Assn., 1997), Speciation of Mercury in Natural Water by Reversed- Phase HPLC, 1992 (Ann.Excellent Rsch.Paper: Shantou Chem.and Chem.Enging. Soc., 1992). Mem.: Am. Chem. Soc. Personal E-mail: xdyao@oburg.net.

YAO, Y. LAWRENCE, engineering educator; b. Shanghai, China, May 25, 1953; came to U.S., 1982; s. Da-Jun Yao and Mei Fen Xu; m. Nancy Yao, June 24, 1984; children: David, Phillip. BE, Shanghai Jiao Tong U., China, 1982; MS, U. Wis., 1984, PhD, 1988. Grad. asst. U. Wis., Madison, 1983-87; lectr. U. NSW, Sydney, Australia, 1989-91, sr. lectr. Australia, 1991-94; assoc. prof. Columbia U., N.Y.C., 1994—. Cons. Unisearch & CAMIA, Australia, 1989-94, Med. Devices Mfrs., N.Y. and N.J., 1994—. Assoc. editor Jour. High Temperature Materials Processes, 1998—; contbr. tech. papers to profl. jours. and conf. procs. Rsch. grantee NSF, 1995—, Australian Rsch. Coun., 1990-95, collaborative rsch. grantee Commonwealth Sci. and Indsl. Rsch. Orgn., Australia, 1990-92. Mem. ASME (assoc. editor Jour. Mfg., Sci. and Engring. 2000—), Soc. Mfg. Engrs. (sr. mem., assoc. editor Jour. Mfg. Processes 1999—), N.Am. Mfg. Rsch. Inst., Am. Soc. Engring. Edn., Laser Inst. Am. (bd. dirs. 2000—). Avocations: traveling, movies, skiing, popular music. Office: Columbia U Dept Mech Engring 220 Mudd Bldg New York NY 10027 E-mail: yly1@columbia.edu.

YAP, KENG C. engineer; b. Kuala Lumpur, Selangor, Malaysia, Feb. 21, 1970; s. Yean Sieng Yap and Lan Ang Tiew; m. Lauren L. Sum; 1 child Shannon. BS in Engring., Meml. U.Newfoundland, St. John's, NF, Can., 1995; MS in Engring., U.Houston, Tex., 1997; DS in Engring., U. Houston, Tex., 2000. Rsrch. asst. U. Houston, Tex., 1995—2000; project engr. ACTA, Inc., Torrance, Calif., 2000—. Recipient Gerald E. Smith award, Am. Soc. Nondestructive Testing, 1998. Home: 29641 S. Western Ave. #107 Palos Verdes Estates CA 90275 Office: ACTA, Inc. 2790 Skypark Dr Ste 310 Torrance CA 90505 Personal E-mail: kyap@eudoramail.com. Business E-Mail: kyap@actainc.com.

YAPIJAKIS, CONSTANTINE, environmental engineering educator, consultant; b. Drama, Macedonia, Greece, July 18, 1948; arrived in U.S., 1971; s. Nikos and Stella (Voyagi) Yapijakis; m. Lily Huang, July 10, 1993; 1 child Nicole Isako. MS in Civil Engring., Nat. Tech. U., Athens, Greece, 1971; MS in Environ. Engring., NYU, 1973; PhD in Environ. Engring., Polytechnic U., N.Y.C., 1981. Registered profl. engr., N.Y., civil engr., Tech. Chamber of Greece. Jr. engr. Dr. Panaghiotakis' Cons. Group, Athens, 1969-71; intern engr. Dutch Pub. Wks. Dept., Amsterdam, 1970; environ. lab. asst. NYU, N.Y.C., 1971-73; environ. engr. City Planning Dept., 1972, John J. Kassner & Co., N.Y.C., 1973, Hazen and Sawyer, P.C., N.Y.C., 1973-78; adj. prof. CCNY/Polytechnic U., 1977—; assoc. prof. Pratt Inst., N.Y.C., 1980-86; prof. environ. engring., environ. rsch. lab dir. The Cooper Union, 1986—. Founding ptnr. Hellenic EnvironTech, Inc., Athens, Greece, 1991—; cons., presenter in field. Co-author: (book) Scale-up of Treatment Processes, 1983, Industrial Wastes Treatment Handbook, 1993, Hazardous Waste Site Remediation Mgmt., 1999, Water Quality-Reflection of Land Use, 1999, Environmental Engineering and Pollution Control, 2001, Handbook of Industrial Hazardous Wastes Treatment, 2002; contbr. articles to profl. jours. Recipient Earth Day award and medallion, City Club N.Y., 1995, Intern Egnr. award, Inst. Internat. Edn., 1972; grantee, NSF, 1988, 1992; scholar Intern. Engr., Internat. Assn. Students Tech. Edn., 1970, Sr. scholar, Fulbright Program, Greece, 1993—94, Fulbright Program, Aegean Initiative, 2002. Mem.: Environ. Law Inst., N.Y. Water Environment Assn. (Met. chpt. bd. dirs. 1992—94, 2001—03, chmn. edn. com., Svc. award 1995, Membership award 1996—99), N.Y. Acad. Scis. (judge h.s. sci. projects ann. competition 1994—), Internat. Assn. Water Quality, Am. Water Wks. Assn., Water Environment Fedn. (VIP Cir. 1994, Recruiters Recognition Club 1996). Achievements include development and design of preozonation - D.E. filtration process for New York City's water supply; development of new design for rotating biological contractors for application to industrial and hazardous wastes; research that established extensive lead contamination in surface soil of parks and playgrounds in New York City; research in perc pollution prevention study for 2000 drycleaners in N.Y.C; fast-rate bioremediation for protection of groundwater; enhanced solar evaporation for treatment of hazardous wastes; research in pollution prevention in the construction industry and brownfields development in N.Y.C. metro area. Avocations: travel, photography, reading, movies. Office: The Cooper Union 51 Astor Pl New York NY 10003-7185

YAPLE, HENRY MACK, library director; b. Vicksburg, Mich., May 30, 1940; s. Henry J. and Pauline B. (Spencer) Y.; m. Marilyn Lou Bales, Dec. 31, 1971; children: Sean H., Kendra S. BA in English with hons., Kalamazoo Coll., 1963; MA, U. Idaho, 1966; postgrad., U. d'Aix-Marseille, France, 1965-66, U. Toronto, 1966-69; MLS, W. Mich. U., 1972. Order libr. Mich. State U., E. Lansing, 1972-74, humanities bibliographer, 1974-78; acquisitions libr. U. Wyo., Laramie, 1978-87; libr. dir. Whitman Coll., Walla Walla, Wash., 1987—. Mem. Wyo. Coun. for the Humanities, 1982-86. U. Toronto scholar, 1966-69; Rotary fellow, 1965, 66; U. Wyo. rsch. grantee, 1982, 86. Mem. ALA, Wyo. Libr. Assn. (pres. 1984-85), Nat. Ski Patrol System (sr. patroller 1978-95, nat. #6946 1988), Wash. Libr. Assn., Northwest Assn. of Pvt. Colls. and U. Librs. (pres. 1987-88, 94-95), Beta Phi Mu. Avocations: book collecting, skiing, kayaking. Home: 1889 Fern St Walla Walla WA 99362-9393 Office: Whitman Coll Penrose Libr 345 Boyer Ave Walla Walla WA 99362-2067 E-mail: yaple@whitman.edu.

YARAR, BAKI, mining and metallurgical engineering educator; b. Adana, Turkey, Feb. 28, 1941; came to U.S., 1980; s. Salih and Sidika Yarar; m. Ruth G. Yarar; children: Deniz, Defne. BSc in Chemistry, Mid. East Tech. U., Ankara, Turkey, 1965, MSc in Chemistry, 1966; PhD in Surface Chemistry, U. London, 1969; DIC in Mineral Tech., Imperial Coll. London, 1969. Instr. Mid. East Tech. U., 1970-71, asst. prof., 1971-76, assoc. prof., 1976-79; vis. prof. U. B.C., Vancouver, Can., 1979-80; assoc. prof. Colo. Sch. of Mines, Golden, 1980-86, prof., 1986—. Pvt. practice cons. in mineral processing, worldwide, 1980—. Author chpts. to books, over 120 papers; editor books; mem. editl. bd. 4 jours. Lt. Turkish Army, 1970-71. Holder numerous awards and certificates of recognition. Mem. Soc. Mining Engrs. (chmn. fundamental com. 1989), Am. Chem. Soc., Materials Rsch. Soc., Sigma Xi (life, pres. CSM chpt.). Achievements include pioneering work in selective flocculation; invention of the gamma floation process; patent for superconductivity meter device. Home: 13260 Braun Rd Golden CO 80401-1643 Office: Colo Sch Mines Dept Mining Engring Golden CO 80401

YARBER, ROBERT EARL, writer, retired educator; b. East St. Louis, Ill., Sept. 28, 1929; s. Earl Yarber and Dorothy Anastasia Dwyer; m. Mary Roberta Winzerling, Nov. 27, 1952; children: Robert D., Charles C., Mary L. BA, McKendree Coll., 1951; MA, St. Louis U., 1953; postgrad., Exeter Coll. Oxford U., 1969. Prof. Mesa Coll., San Diego, 1963-89. Author: Writing for College, 1995, Reviewing Basic Grammar, 1996; contbr. articles to textbooks, revs., articles to profl. jours. Democrat. Roman Catholic. Home: 4125 Rochester Rd San Diego CA 92116-2123

YARBOROUGH, CLINTON JOSEPH, lawyer; b. Ft. Leavenworth, Kans., Dec. 28, 1969; s. William Glenn and Betsy Yarborough; m. Patsy Lee, Aug. 16, 1997; child, CJ. BS, Coll. Charleston, 1991; JD, U. S.C., 1993. Bar: S.C. 1994, Ga. 1995, U.S. Dist. Ct. (so. dist.) S.C. 1995, U.S. Supreme Ct. 2000. Title abstractor Woodward, Leventis, Unger, Daves, Herndon & Cothran, Columbia, S.C., 1992-94; forclosure atty. Ronald C. Scott, P.A., 1994-95; asst. pub. defender Defender Corp. Aiken County, Aiken, S.C., 1995-98; asst. dist. atty. Toombs Judicial Cir., Thomson, Ga., 1998-99; assoc. Jackson R. Massey & Assocs., P.C., Augusta, 1999-2000, Rogers, Townsend & Thomas, P.C., Columbia, S.C., 2000—adr. Mem. ABA, Sigma Chi, Rotary Internat. Roman Catholic. Avocations: archaeology, reading, anthropology, forestry. Office: PO Box 100200 Columbia SC 29202-3200 E-mail: yarborough@rtt-law.com, soca@cutthroats.com.

YARBOROUGH, WILLIAM GLENN, JR. military officer, forest farmer, defense and international business executive; b. June 21, 1940; s. William Glenn and Bessie (Rainsford) Y.; m. Betsy Gibson, Jan. 24, 1969; children: Bill, Clinton, Frank, Elizabeth. BS, U. S.C., 1961, MBA, 1969; postgrad., Command and Gen. Staff Coll., 1970, Naval War Coll., 1979, U. Va., 1983. Commd. to U.S. Army, advanced through grades to col., 1980, co. and troop comdr., squadron staff officer Vietnam and Europe, 1961-71, strategist, 1971-73; chief of assignments Office Pers. Mgmt. Mil. Pers. Ctr., 1973-76; comdr. 1st Squadron 1st Cavalry, Europe, 1976-78; chief of staff, spl. asst. to chief of staff 1st Armored Divsn., Europe, 1978; br. chief Office of Chief of Staff, Washington, 1979-80; exec. to dep. comdg. gen. Material Devel. and Readiness Command, 1980-81; mil. dep. for asst. sec. for rsch., devel. and acquisition, 1981-85; army mktg. dir. Grumman Corp., Bethpage, N.Y., 1990-93; pres., CEO Am. Conv. Corp., Vienna, 1993—2001; prin. WG4 & Assocs., 2001—. Bd. dirs. Carleton Techs., Access Rsch. Corp., Am. Conversion Corp. Trustee Patton Mus.; bd. dirs. So Others Might Eat (Some), Easter Seals. Decorated Silver Star, Bronze Star medal with 4 oak leaf clusters and V device, Purple Heart. Mem. VFW, SAR, Assn. U.S. Army (George Washington chpt., v.p. membership), Am. Legion, Armed Forces Comms. and Electronics Assn., U.S. Army Armor Assn., Nat. Def. Indsl. Assn. (bd. dirs. N.Y. chpt.), N.G. Assn., Res. Officers Assn., Army-Navy Club, Army Navy Country Club, Belle-Meade Country Club, Tower Club. Home: Box 115 Thomson GA 30824 Office: Box 828 Mc Lean VA 22101 E-mail: wgyarc@aol.com.

YARBOROUGH, WILLIAM PELHAM, writer, lecturer, retired army officer, consultant; b. Seattle, May 12, 1912; s. Leroy W. and Addessia (Hooker) Y.; m. Norma Mae Tuttle, Dec. 26, 1936 (dec.); children: Norma Kay (dec.), William Lee, Patricia Mae. BS, U.S. Mil. Acad., 1936; grad., Command and Gen. Staff Coll., 1944, Brit. Staff Coll., 1950, Army War Coll., 1953. Commd. 2nd lt. U.S. Army, 1936, advanced through grades to lt. gen., 1968, ret., 1971, various assignments U.S., Philippines and ETO, 1936-42; exec. officer Paratroop Task Force, North Africa, 1942; comdr. 2d Bn., 504th Par. Inf. Regt., 82d Airborne Div., Sicily invasion, 1943, 509th Parachute Inf., Italy and France, 1943-44; comdg. officer 473 Inf., Italy, 1945; provost marshal 15th Army Group, ETO, 1945, Vienna Area Command and U.S. Forces, Austria, 1945-47; mem. staff, faculty U.S. Army Info. Sch., 1948-49; operations officer, gen. staff Joint Mil. Assistance Adv. Group, London, Eng., 1951-52; mem. faculty Army War Coll., 1953-56, 57; dep. chief Mil. Assistance and Adv. Group, Cambodia, 1956-57; comdg. officer 66th CIC Group, Stuttgart, Germany, 1958-60, 66th M.I. Group, Stuttgart, 1960; comdg. gen. U.S.A. Spl. Warfare Ctr.; also comdt. U.S. Army Spl. Warfare Sch., Ft. Bragg, 1961-65; sr. mem. UN Command Mil. Armistice Comm., Korea, 1965; asst. dep. chief staff DCSOPS for spl. operations Dept. Army, Washington; chmn. U.S. delegation Inter-Am. Def. Bd., Joint Brazil U.S. Def. Commn., Joint Mexican-U.S. Def. Commn.; Army mem. U.S. sect. permanent Joint Bd. on Def., Can.-U.S. Def. Commn., Washington, 1965; asst. chief of staff intelligence Dept. Army Washington, 1966-68; comdg. gen. I Corps Group, Korea, 1968-69; chief staff, also dep. comdr.-in-chief U.S. Army, Pacific, Hawaii, 1969-71. Contbr. Internat. Mil. and Def. Ency., 1993, MacMillan Ency. of the Am. Mil., 1994; William P. Yarborough collection papers and artifacts donated to Mugar Meml. Librs., Boston U. Decorated Disting. Svc. medal with three oak leaf clusters, Silver Star, Legion of Merit with three oak leaf clusters, Bronze Star, Joint Svc. Commendation medal with oak leaf clusters, Croix de Guerre with Palm (France), Cross for Valor and Diploma (Italy), Order of Merit Second Class (Korea), Order of Ulchi (Korea). Fellow Co. Mil. Historians; mem. Kiwanis Club. Home: 160 Hillside Rd Southern Pines NC 28387-6727

YARBRO, ALAN DAVID, lawyer; b. Huntington, W.Va., Sept. 16, 1941; s. John David and Bernice (Bulette) Y.; m. Lee Merryman Myers, July 1961; children: Wendy, Jennifer, Caroline. AB magna cum laude, Harvard U., 1962, LLB cum laude, 1966. Bar: Md. 1966, U.S. Ct. Appeals (4th cir.) 1966, U.S. Dist. Ct. Md. 1966. Assoc. Venable Baetjer & Howard, Balt., 1966-72, ptnr., 1973-96, of counsel, 2002—; gen. counsel Mercantile Bankshares Corp., 1996—2002, corp. sec., 2002. Pres. W.S. Baer Corp., 1990-99. Trustee Children's Hosp., Balt., 1986-99, Children's Hosp. at Sinai Found., 1999—, Sinai Hosp. of Balt., 1999—; bd. dirs. The Park Heights St. Acad., Balt., 1986-89. Fellow Am. Bar Found., Md. Bar Found.; mem. ABA, Md. Bar Assn., Bar Assn. of Balt. (chmn. ethics com. 1988-89).

YARBROUGH, ALLYSON DEBRA, electrical engineer; b. Peterborough, England, Feb. 14, 1958; d. Freddy Dekhoma and Rosalind Mavis Y.; m. John Russell Scarpulla, May 8, 1990. BSEE, N.Mex. State U., 1979; MSEE, Cornell U., 1985, PhD in Elec. Engring., 1988. Rsch. asst. Nat. Atmospheric and Ionospheric Ctr., Arecibo, P.R., 1979; microwave applications engr. Hewlett-Packard Co., Santa Rosa, Calif., 1979-82; assoc. prof. Calif. State U., L.A., 1988-89; tech. staff Aerospace Corp., El Segundo, Calif., 1989-93, sect. mgr., 1993-99, dept. dir., 1999—. Mem. IEEE, Microwave Theory and Techniques Soc., Alpha Kappa Alpha, Eta Kappa Nu. Democrat. Roman Catholic. Avocations: woodworking, sewing, collecting vintage radios. Home: 26821 Grays Lake Rd Palos Verdes Estates CA 90275

YARBROUGH, EDWARD MEACHAM, lawyer; b. Nashville, Dec. 17, 1943; s. Gurley McTyeire and Miriam (Mefford) Y. BA, Rhodes Coll., 1967; JD, Vanderbilt U., 1973. Bar: Tenn. 1973. Asst. dist. atty. Davidson County, Nashville, 1973-76; ptnr. Hollins, Wagster & Yarbrough, 1976—. Chmn. com. Crime Commn., Nashville, 1981-82; mem. task force House Judiciary Com., Nashville, 1984; chmn. Crimestoppers Inc., Nashville, 1983—; trustee United Way, Nashville, 1983—, Belmont U., 1993—, Cumberland Sci. Mus., 1996—; bd. dirs. Big Bros. Inc., Nashville, 1983-85; mem. nat. devel. bd. Lipscomb U., 2000—; vice chmn. deacons Forest Hills Bapt. Ch. Served to 1st lt. U.S. Army, 1969-71, Vietnam. Decorated Bronze Star; named Best Criminal Def. Atty., Bus. Nashville mag., 1999. Fellow Nat. Speleological Soc. (bd. dirs. 1960—); mem. ABA (bd. dirs. 1985), Tenn. Bar Assn., Nashville Bar Assn. (pres. 1983), Tenn. Criminal Def. Lawyers, Nashville Kiwanis (pres. 1992), Am. Legion, Richland Country Club, City Club (Nashville). Democrat. Baptist. Avocations: cave exploration, photography, skiing, golf, running. Home: 5230 Granny White Pike Nashville TN 37220-1715 Office: Hollins Wagster & Yarbrough 424 Church St Ste 2210 Nashville TN 37219-2303

YARBROUGH, ISABEL MILES, dentist, educator; b. Columbus, Ga., May 24, 1956; d. Wiley and Lillie Miles; m. David E. Yarbrough; children: Davida Elizabeth, David Earl Jr. BS in Zoology, Ala. A&M U., 1978; DDS, Loyola U., 1982. Instr. endodontics Howard U. Sch. Dentistry, Washington, 1989-91; asst. prof. biology Ala. A&M U., Normal, 1991-94; dentist Drs. David and Isabel Yarbrough, Huntsville, Ala., 1993—. Mem. NAACP, Huntsville, 1996. Capt. U.S. Army, 1986-89. Mem. North Ala. Med. Assn., Huntsville-Madison Dental Soc., Delta Sigma Theta, Psi Omega. Avocations: reading, swimming, jogging. Home: 204 Cheswick Dr Madison AL 35757-8720 Office: 4530 Bonnell Dr NW Ste A Huntsville AL 35816-2002

YARBROUGH, KATHRYN DAVIS, public health nurse; b. Montrose, Colo., Aug. 31, 1947; d. L.O. and V. Jean (Dunn) Davis; m. James H. Yarbrough, Aug. 8, 1970; children: James, Jason. Diploma, Good Samaritan Hosp. Sch. Nursing, Phoenix, 1971; BSN, Kennesaw State Coll., 1996. RN, Ga.; cert. NAACOG. Supr. Cherokee County Health Dept., Canton, Ga., 1976-97. Den mother Boy Scouts Am., Canton, 1986-87; bd. dirs. Cancer soc., Canton, 1987—, Cherokee County Violence Ctr., 1990, First Steps Bd., 1993-97, Cherokee County Advocacy Ctr., 1994-97; HIV cons. ARC, Canton, 1988—, disaster vol., Cherokee County, 1993-99; co-chair Early Intervention Coun., Canton, 1991-93; mem. Leadership Cherokee, 1994, Interagy Coun., 1994; mem. Blue Ridge Jud. Cir. Domestic Violence Task Force, 1994. Mem. ANA, Ga. Nurses Assn., Svc. League Cherokee County (hon.). Methodist. E-mail: Kyarbro216@aol.com.

YARBROUGH, MARTHA CORNELIA, music educator; b. Waycross, Ga., Feb. 8, 1940; d. Henry Elliott and Jessie (Sirmans) Y. BME, Stetson U., 1962; MME, Fla. State U., 1968, PhD, 1973. Choral dir. Ware County High Sch., Waycross, 1962-64; asst. choral dir. Fla. State U., 1970-72; cons. in music Muscogee County Sch. Dist., Columbus, Ga., 1972-73; cons. in tchr. edn. Psycho-Edno. Cons., Inc., Tallahassee, 1972-73; asst. prof. music edn., dir. choruses and oratorio socs. Syracuse U., 1973-76, assoc. prof. music edn., 1976-83, prof., 1983-86, acting asst. dean Coll. Visual and Performing Arts, 1980-82, acting dir. Sch. Music, 1980-82, chmn. music edn., 1982-86; prof. music La. State U., Baton Rouge, 1986—, coordinator music, edn., 1986—, Haymon prof. of music, 1995—. Artist in residence Sch. Music U. Ala., Tuscaloosa, 1989-90, 98; chair exec. com. Music Edn. Rsch. Coun., 1992-94. Co-author: Competency-Based Music Education, 1980; mem. editl. com.: Jour. Rsch. in Music Edn., editor-in-chief: , 2000—; contbr. chapters to books, articles to profl. jours. Mem. Music Educators Nat. Conf. (sr. rschr. award 1996), La. State Music Assn., Am. Ednl. Rsch. Assn., Soc. Rsch. Music Edn. (mem. exec. com. 1988-90, program chair 1990-92,c hair 1992-94), AAUP, Coll. Music Soc., Pi Kappa Lambda, Phi Beta, Kappa Delta Pi. Office: Sch Music La State U Baton Rouge LA 70803-2504

YARBROUGH, TERRY PINCKNEY, physician; b. Columbia, S.C., Apr. 2, 1940; s. Dabney Randolph and Frances Horton (Colcock) Y.; m. Alexandra Mayo, Aug. 28, 1965; children: Alexandra, Laurens. MD, Med. Coll. of Va., 1965. Intern U. of Tex. Med. Br., Galveston, 1965-66; resident in internal medicine Med. Coll. Va., Richmond, 1968-71; pvt. practice Internal Medicine of Portsmouth Ltd., 1971—. Capt. USAR, 1966-68. Mem. ACP, Am. Coll. of Cardiology, Coun. Clin. Cardiology, Am. Heart Assn., Am. Soc. of Internal Medicine, Med. Soc. of Va. Episcopalian. Office: Internal Medicine of Portsmouth Ltd 3300 High St Portsmouth VA 23707-3321

YARBROUGH, WYNN W. secondary school educator; b. Fairfax, Va., Aug. 26, 1969; s. Thomas Gibson and Patricia Cullum Yarbrough; m. Karen Hancock, Oct. 18, 2000. BA, Mary Washington Coll., 1991; MA, Va. Commonwealth U., 1995; postgrad., Goddard Coll. Tchr. James Wood H.S., Winchester, Va., 1997—2000, Park View H.S., Sterling, 2000—01, Clark County H.S., Berryville, 2001—. Adj. prof. NVCC, Sterling, 1999—2001, LFCC, Middletown, Va. Interview editor: Pedestal Mag. Fellow, Shenandoah Arts Coun., Winchester, 2001, 2002. Home: 981 Briggs Rd Berryville VA 22611

YARCHOAN, ROBERT, clinical immunologist, researcher; b. N.Y.C., July 21, 1950; s. Zachary and Anne Mae (Veneroso) Y.; m. Giovana Tosato; children: Mark, John. BA magna cum laude, Amherst Coll., 1971; MD, U. Pa., 1975. Diplomate Am. Bd. Internal Medicine, Am. Bd. Allergy and Immunology. Resident in medicine U. Minn. Hosps., Mpls., 1975-78; clin. assoc. metabolism br. Nat. Cancer Inst., Bethesda, Md., 1978-80, investigator metabolism br., 1980-83, investigator clin. oncology program, 1983-87, sr. investigator clin. oncology program, 1988-91, chief retroviral diseases sect. medicine br., 1991-96, chief HIV and AIDS malignancy br., 1996—. Co-author: (chpt.) Cecil Textbook of Medicine, 1992, 95, 99; assoc. editor Jour. Immunology, 1985-89, AIDS Rsch. and Human Retroviruses, 1986—, AIDS, 1990-00, Jour. AIDS, 2000—, Jour. Human Virology, 2002—; sect. editor Thymus, 1992-97; contbr. articles to sci. jours.; patentee in field. Capt. USPHS, 1978—. Recipient Commendation medal USPHS, 1991, Asst. Sec. Health award U.S. govt. Dept. Health & Human Svcs., 1989, Inventors award U.S. Dept. Commerce, 1986, 87, Fed. Tech. Transfer Act award, 1999, 2000, 01, Outstanding Svc. medal USPHS, 2002. Fellow AAAS; mem. Am. Soc. Hematology, Am. Assn. Immunologists, Clin. Immunology Soc., Am. Soc. for Clin. Investigation, Internat. AIDS Soc. Achievements include co-inventor of therapies for AIDS and AIDS malignancies including ddI (didanosine) and ddC (zalcitabine) and IL-12 for Karposi's sarcoma; co-developer of therapies for AIDS and AIDS malignancies including AZT (zidovudine) for AIDS and paclitaxel for Kaposi's sarcoma; research in interactions between HIV and the immune system; AIDS-related tumors.

YARDE, RICHARD FOSTER, art educator; b. Boston, Oct. 29, 1939; s. Edgar St. Clair and Enid (Foster) Y.; m. Susan Donovan, July 8, 1967; children: Marcus, Owen. BFA in Painting cum laude, Boston U., 1962, MFA, 1964; DFA (hon., Mass. Coll. Arts, Boston, 1998. Asst. prof. art Boston U., 1965-71; assoc. prof. art Wellesley Coll., 1971-76; vis. assoc. prof. Amherst Coll., 1976-77, Mt. Holyoke Coll., 1980-81; vis. artist Mass. Coll. Art, 1977-80; prof. art U. Mass., Boston, 1981-90, Amherst, 1990—. Visual arts panelist Mass. Coun. Art and Humanities, 1976-78; bd. overseers Inst. Contemporary Art, Boston, 1991—. Exhibited in one-man shows Studio Mus. in Harlem, San Diego Mus.; Balt. Mus., Smith Coll. Mus. Art, Northampton, Mass., 1997, Mass. Coll. Art, 1996-99; exhibited in group shows Newport (R.I.) Art Mus., NAD, NYC, Mass., Smitsonian Inst., Washington, 1999, New Mus. Contemporary Art, N.Y.C., 1999, Mus. Fine Arts, Boston, 1999. Recipient Alumni award for disting. contbn. to arts Boston U., 1987, Chancellor's award for disting. scholarship U. Mass., Boston, 1984, Acad. award in art Am. Acad. Arts and Letters, 1995, Disting. Tchg. award U. Mass. Amherst, 1997. Works on Paper award New Eng. Found. for the Arts, Boston, 1998; Nat. Endowment for Arts fellow, 1976, Samuel F. Conti faculty fellow U. Mass., 2000, When the Spirit Moves Group Exhib., Spelman Coll. Mus., 2000, award Charles Wright Mus., 2000, Commonwealth Award, Artist Category, Mass. Cultural Council, 2001, William P. and Gertrude Schweitzer Prize National Academy of Design, NY, other awards. Office: U Mass Amherst care Arts Dept Fine Arts CtrBox 32150 Amherst MA 01003

YARDLEY, JONATHAN, journalist, columnist; b. Pitts., Oct. 27, 1939; s. William Woolsey and Helen (Gregory) Y.; m. Rosemary Roberts, June 14, 1961 (div. 1975); children: James Barrett, William W. II.; m. Susan L. Hartt, Mar. 23, 1975 (div. 1998); m. Marie Arana, Mar. 21, 1999. AB, U. N.C., Chapel Hill, 1961; DHL (hon.), George Washington U., 1987. Writer N.Y. Times, 1961-64; editorial writer, book editor Greensboro (N.C.) Daily News, 1964-74; book editor Miami (Fla.) Herald, 1974-78, Washington Star, 1978-81; book critic, columnist Washington Post, 1981—. Author: Ring: A Biography of Ring Lardner, 1977, Our Kind of People: The Story of an American Family, 1989, Out of Step: Notes from a Purple Decade, 1991, States of Mind: A Personal Journey Through the Mid-Atlantic, 1993, Misfit: The Strange Life of Frederick Exley, 1997, Monday Morning Quarterback, 1998; editor: My Life as Author and Editor (H.L. Mencken), 1993, Selected Stories (Ring Lardner), 1997. Recipient Pulitzer prize for criticism, 1981, Disting. Alumnus award U. N.C., 1989; Nieman fellow in journalism Harvard U., 1968-69. Home: 100 5th St NE Washington DC 20002-5936 Office: Washington Post 1150 15th St NW Washington DC 20071-0001 E-mail: yardley@twp.com.

YARED, LINDA S. mechanical engineer; b. East Grand Rapids, Mich., July 31, 1952; d. Forest S. and Penny (Bassler) Y. BS in Mech. Engring., U. Md., 1987. Sr. tech. rep. Xerox Corp., Rosslyn, Va., 1979-84; sr. engr. Mack Trucks, Allentown, Pa., 1987-90, Allied Signal Braking Systems, South Bend, Ind., 1990-95; project engr. Tri/Mark Corp., New Hampton, Iowa, 1995-99, Up and Running Inc, Granger, Ind., 1999—. Patentee in field. Mem. ASME, NOW (treas. 1994), Soc. Automotive Engrs. (sec. 1988-90), Soc. Women Engrs. Avocation: dog obedience training. Office: Up and Running Inc 227 E Cleveland Rd Ste 6 Granger IN 46530-7098

YAREMCHUK, MICHAEL JOHN, plastic surgeon; b. Detroit, Feb. 8, 1950; 1 child, Kaitlin. BA magna cum laude, Yale Coll., 1972; MD, Columbia Coll. Physicians and Surgeons, 1976. Diplomate Am. Bd. Surgery, Am. Bd. Plastic Surgery. Intern in surgery Harvard surg. svc. Deaconess Hosp., 1976-77, jr. and sr. asst. resident, 1977-79, sr. resident, 1980-81, chief resident gen. surgery, 1981-82; resident in plastic surgery Johns Hopkins Hosp., Balt., 1982-84; instr. divsn. plastic surgery sch. medicine Johns Hopkins U., 1984-85, asst. prof., 1985-87, asst. prof. orthopaedic surgery, 1985-87; asst. clin. prof. plastic surgery med. sch. U. Md., 1985-87; asst. clin. dir. plastic and maxillofacial surgery Md. Inst. Emergency Med. Systems Svcs., 1985-87; asst. surgery Mass. Gen. Hosp., Boston, 1987-89, asst. surgeon, 1989-92, assoc. vis. surgeon, 1993—, chief craniofacial surgery, 1994—; asst. prof. surgery Harvard Med. Sch., 1987-93, assoc. prof., 1993—, clinical prof., 2000. Clin. fellow surgery Harvard Med. Sch., 1977-82; rsch. and clin. fellow microsurgery Mass. Gen. Hosp. and Shriners Burn Inst., Boston, 1979-80; fellow dept. surgery divsn. plastic surgery sch. medicine Johns Hopkins U., 1982-84; mem. active staff Johns Hopkins Hosp., 1984-87, Children's Hosp. and Ctr. Reconstructive Surgery, 1984-87, Francis Scott Key Med. Ctr., 1985-87, VA Hosp., 1985-87; mem. courtesy staff U. Md. Hosp., 1985-87; mem. oper. rm. com. Johns Hopkins Hosp., 1985-87, mem. tissue com., 1985-87; attending surgeon plastic surgery Md. Inst. Emergency Med. Svcs. Systems, 1985-87; fellow craniofacial surgery U. Pa., Children's Hosp. Phila., 1987-88; co-organizer Craniofacial and Maxillofacial Surgery Combined Plastic and Oral Surgery Conf., 1988—; mem. consulting staff Shriners Burns Inst., Boston, 1988—; Kazanjian fellow craniofacial surgery Mass. Gen. Hosp., 1987-88, mem. oper. rm. com., 1990—, mem. adv. com. physician referral svc., 1991—; mem. planning group com. Breast Health Ctr., 1991—; mem. ad hoc com. AIDS GEC, 1991—; mem. Surg. Day Care Unit/GATA Sub-Com., 1991—; mem. Harvard resource-based relative value scale study sch. pub. health Harvard U., 1991; guest examiner qualifying exam Am. Bd. Plastic Surgery, 1992, 93; lectr., rschr. in field. Author: (with others) Microsurgery in Orthopedic Practice, 1989, Blunt Multiple Trauma: Comprehensive Pathophysiology and Care, 1990, Principles and Practices of Ophthalmology: Clinical Practice, Vol. 5, 1993, others; editor: (with R.J. Brumback and A.B. Burgess) Lower Extremity Salvage and Reconstruction: Orthopedic and Plastic Surgical Movement, 1989, (with J.S. Gruss, P.N. Manson) Rigid Fixation of the Craniomaxillofacial Skelton, 1992; contbr. articles to profl. jours. Recipient 1st prize in essay contest Harvard Med. Alumni Assn., 1982, Kappa Delta Ward award Am. Acad. Orthopaedic Surgeons, 1990; Royal Coll. Surgeons traveling fellow, 1996. Mem. ACS (Mass. chpt.), AMA (rep. alt. del. young physicians sect. 1988-90), Am. Soc. Plastic and Reconstructive Surgeons (mem. sci. program sub-com. 1993 meeting 1993—), AO/ASIF (mem. maxillofacial edl. com. 1987—, mem. scholarship com. 1990), Am. Soc. Maxillofacial Surgeons (mem. young maxillofacial surgeons com. 1989—, mem. rsch. com. 1990—, mem. local arrangement com. ann. meeting 1990, local chmn. basic course 1993), Am. Assn. Surgery Trauma, Am. Soc. Craniofacial Surgery, Am. Assn. Plastic Surgeons, Mass. Soc. Plastic and Reconstructive Surgeons, Mass. Med. Soc., Northeastern Soc. Plastic and Reconstructive Surgeons (mem. by-laws com. 1989-90, chmn. local arrangements 1992 meeting 1990, program chmn. 1994 meeting 1992, mem. nominating com. 1992—, Outstanding Sci. Presentation by Resident award 2d ann. meeting 1985), New Eng. Soc. Plastic and Reconstructive Surgeons (mem. nominating com. 1991), Boston Surg. Soc., Pan Am. Soc. Trauma, Ea. Assn. Surgery Trauma, Assn. Acad. Surgery, Plastic Surgery Rsch. Coun., Orthopaedic Rsch. Soc., Plastic Surgery Ednl. Found. (chmn. craniofacial-maxillofacial subcom. 1989-91, chmn. plastic surgery in-svc. exam. 1991, mem. mktg. com. 1991), Assn. Acad. Chmn. Plastic Surgery (assoc.), Internat. Soc. Craniofacial Surgery (assoc.), Mass. Gen. Hosp. Hand Club. Address: 15 Smith Farm Trl Lynnfield MA 01940-1019 E-mail: myaremchuk@partners.org.

YARGER, JAMES GREGORY, chemical company executive; b. Waverly, Iowa, Sept. 15, 1951; s. Glen Virgil and Lillian Maxine Yarger; m. Jeannie Rae Van Vickle; children: Benjamin, Jason. BA, U. Iowa, 1974; PhD, Brandeis U., 1981. Fellow Harvard U., Cambridge, Mass., 1981-83; sr. rsch. scientist Miles Inc., Elkhart, Ind., 1983-87; staff scientist Amoco Tech. Co., Naperville, Ill., 1987-92, sr. rsch. scientist and regulatory affairs officer, 1993-94; mgr. regulatory affairs, quality control and quality sys., 1994-95; dir. quality control-regulatory affairs Cambridge Chem., Inc., Germantown, Wis., 1996; pres., founder Cedaburg Labs., Inc., Grafton, 1997—, Cedaburg Pharms., LLC, 2000—. Contbr. chpts. to books, articles to profl. jours. including Biol. Chemistry, Molecular and Cellular Biology, Devels. in Indsl. Microbiology, Jour. Cell Sci., Poultry Sci. Participant Gov.'s Voluntary Action Program, Ind., 1987; pres. Hunters Woods Homeowners Assn., St. Charles, Ill., 1991, Charlemagne Homeowners Assn., St. Charles, 1992; dep. registrar Kane County, Ill., 1993-96; bd. dirs. Cedarburg Cultural Ctr., Wis., 1998, pres., bd. dirs., 2001-. Am. Cancer Soc. fellow, 1981-83. Achievements include founding Cedarburg Pharmaceuticals; patents for Lycopene biosynthesis in genetically engineered hosts and for Beta-Carotene biosynthesis in genetically engineered hosts and zeaxanthin biosynthesis in genetically engineered hosts. Home: W71n391 Cedar Pointe Ave Cedarburg WI 53012-2243 Office: 870 Badger Cir Grafton WI 53024-9436

YARGER, SAM JACOB, dean, educator; b. Pontiac, Mich., Oct. 8, 1937; s. Ralph And Eva L. (Little) Y.; m. Gwen Polk (div. 1982); 1 child, Mark Alan; m. Sally K. Mertens. BS in Elem. Edn., Eastern Mich. U., 1959; MA in Sch. Psychology, U. Mich., 1962; PhD in Ednl. Psychology, Wayne State U., 1968. Asst. prof. Oakland (Mich.) Community Coll., 1967-68, U. Toldeo, 1968-71; assoc. prof. Syracuse (N.Y.) U., 1971-77, prof., 1977-84, assoc. dean, 1980-84; dean, prof. U. Wis., Milw., 1984-92, U. Miami, Fla., 1992—. Rschr. Assessment Pre-Vocat. Skills Mentally Retarded Youth, 1964-65, Tchr. Attitude Change in REls. to Program Input, 1968, Leader Behavior in a Task Oriented Setting in Relation to Group Activity, 1968, Attitudes Inner-City Residents Toward Ednl. Programs and Tchrs., 1970, Dimensions Tchr. Ctr. Movement in Am. Edn., 1972-75, Dimensions Field Derived Content in Tchr. Edn. Programs, 1973-75, Nat. Study Inservice Edn., 1976-77, Nat. Study Preservice Edn., 1976-77, Nat. Study Preservice Edn., 1976-77, Nat. Study Federally-Funded Tchr. Ctr., 1979-82, Nat. Study Tchr. Edn., 1985-94; developer, dir. tchr. edn. programs, various U.S. locations; mem., chmn. various univs. coms.; cons., spkr. in field. Author: Improving Teacher Education, 1978, Documenting Success - A Guidebook for Teacher Centers, 1979, Inservice Teacher Education, 1980; author monographs; contbr. articles to profl. jours., chpts. to books. Mem. Am. Ednl. Rsch. Assn. (assoc. editor 1983-85, chair elect Orgn. Instl. Affiliates 1994-95), Am. Assn. Colls. for Tchr. Edn. (bd. dirs. 1984-87, exec. com. 1985-87). Office: U Miami Sch Edn PO Box 248065 Coral Gables FL 33124-8065 E-mail: syarger@miami.edu.

YARINGTON, CHARLES THOMAS, JR. surgeon, administrator; b. Sayre, Pa., Apr. 26, 1934; s. C.T. and Florence (Hutchinson) Yarington; m. Barbara Taylor Johnson, Sept. 28, 1963; children: Leslie Anne, Jennifer Lynne, Barbara Jane. AB, Princeton, 1956; MD, Hahnemann Med. Coll., 1960; grad., Army Command and Gen. Staff Coll., 1969, Air War Coll., 1973, Indsl. Coll. Armed Forces, 1974. Intern Rochester (N.Y.) Gen. Hosp., 1960-61; resident Dartmouth Hosp., 1961-62, U. Rochester Strong Meml. Hosp., 1962-65; instr. otolaryngology U. Rochester Sch. Medicine, 1962-65; asst. prof. surgery W.Va. U. Sch. Medicine, 1967-68; assoc. prof., chmn. dept. otorhinolarygology U. Nebr. Med. Center, 1968-69, prof., chmn. dept. otorhinolarygology, 1969-74; clin. prof. otolaryngology U. Wash., Seattle, 1974—; clin. prof. surgery Uniformed Services U. Health Scis., Bethesda, 1985—; chief otolaryngology Virginia Mason Med. Ctr., Seattle, 1978-88, 92-95, chief dept. surgery, 1988-91; surgeon Mason Clinic, 1974-97. Cons. Surg. Gen. USAF, Hunter Group Med. Mgmt. Cons., 1996-98, Seattle Multispecialty Panel, 1998—; pres. Virginia Mason Rsch. Ctr., Seattle, 1983-85; trustee Mason Clinic, 1988-91; adv. coun. Nat. Inst. Neurol. Diseases, Communicative Diseases, Stroke of NIH, Bethesda, Md., 1986-90; bd. dirs. Virginia Mason Hosp., Virginia Mason Med. Ctr., bd. govs., 1989-98. Author books and articles in field.; Mem. editorial bd. Aviation, Space, Environ. Med. Jour., Otol. Clinics of N. Am., Mil. Medicine, Otolaryngology-Head and Neck Surgery Trustee Seattle Opera Assn., 1983-89. Maj., M.C. AUS, 1965-67; brig. gen. USAF Res., to 1986. Decorated D.S.M., Legion of Merit; named Commdr. Venerable Order St. John (Gt. Britain), Companion with Star, Order Orthodox Hospit, Republic of Cypress; recipient Sir Henry Wellcome medal, 1984, Knight Grand Cross, Mil. and Hospitaller Order of St. Lazarus. Fellow ACS, Royal Soc. Medicine, Am. Acad. Otolaryngology (Barraquer Meml. award 1968, mem. standing com., bd. govs. 1982-88, Honor award 1974); mem. AMA, Am. Broncho-Esophagological Assn. (council, treas. 1982-86, pres. 1987-88), Am. Laryngol. Assn., Pacific Coast Soc. Ophthalmology and Otolaryngology (coun., pres. 1987-88), Soc. Med. Cons. to Armed Forces, Am. Soc. Head and Neck Surgery, N.W. Acad. Head and Neck Surgery (pres. 1984-86), Am. Soc. Otology, Rhinology and Laryngology (v.p. 1992-93, coun. 1997-2000), Res. Officers Assn. (past pres. Seattle chpt., nat. officer), Pan-Pacific Surg. Assn., Soc. Colonial Wars, Sons of Revolution (pres. Wash. 1985-87, Internat. Power Boat Assn. (comdr. 1999-2000), Seattle Yacht Club (trustee 2001—), Princeton Quadrangle Club, Broadmoor Golf Club, RAF Club (London), Sigma Xi.

YARINGTON, DAVID JON, retired educator; b. Auburn, N.Y., Sept. 13, 1936; s. Charles T. and Florence Yarington; m. Maybelle Yarington, Nov. 10, 1982; children: John, Susan. BA, Duke U., 1960; MEd, Cornell U., 1961; DEd, U. Pa., 1966. Cert. fundraising exec. Prof. Ohio U., Athens, 1964-66, U. Mass., Amherst, 1967-71; prof., head dept. Aquinas Coll., Grand Rapids, Mich., 1972-76; v.p. acad. affairs Lake Superior State U., Sault, 1976-78; dir. devel. Ea. Conn. State U., Willimantic, 1979-89, U. Maine, Orono, 1990-94; devel. officer Yale U., New Haven, 1995-97; ret., 1997. Rsch. fellow U. Pa., Phila., 1962-65. Author: Surviving In College, 1976, The Great American Reading Machine, 1977; contbr. articles to profl. jours. V.p. Rotary Internat., Willimantic, 1988, Bangor, 1994. With U.S. Army, 1956-58. U.S. Office Edn. fellow, 1966-67; rsch. grantee U.S. Office Edn. Mem. Peninsular Club. Methodist. Avocation: collecting rare books. Home: 0-1710 W Leonard Rd Grand Rapids MI 49544

YARIV, AMNON, electrical engineering educator, scientist; b. Tel Aviv, Israel, Apr. 13, 1930; arrived in U.S., 1951, naturalized, 1964; s. Shraga and Henya (Davidson) Y.; m. Frances Pokras, Apr. 10, 1972; children: Elizabeth, Dana, Gabriela. BS, U. Calif., Berkeley, 1954, MS, 1956, PhD, 1958. Mem. tech. staff Bell Telephone Labs., 1959-63; dir. laser research Watkins-Johnson Co., 1963-64; mem. faculty Calif. Inst. Tech., 1964—, Martin Summerfield prof. applied physics, 1966—. Co-founder, bd. mem. Arroyo Optics, Inc. Author: Quantum Electronics, 1967, 75, 85, Introduction to Optical Electronics, 1971, 77, 89, Theory and Applications of Quantum Mechanics, Propagation of Light in Crystals. Served with Israeli Army, 1948-50. Recipient Pender award U. Pa., Harvey prize Technion, Israel, 1992. Fellow IEEE (Quantum Electronics award 1980), Am. Optical Soc. (Ives medal 1986, Esther Beller medal 1998), Am. Acad. Arts and Scis.; mem. NAS, NAE, Am. Phys. Soc. Office: 1201 E California Blvd Pasadena CA 91125-0001

YARKONY, GARY MICHAEL, physician, researcher; b. N.Y.C., May 22, 1953; m. Kirsten Kohlmeyer; children: Judith, Rachel, Seth, Lauren. BA in Biology, SUNY, Buffalo, 1974; MD, SUNY, Syracuse, 1978; Master in Mgmt., Northwestern U., 1994. Intern, then resident in physical medicine, rehab. Northwestern U., Chgo., 1978—81, chief resident dept. rehab. medicine, 1980; asst. dir. head trauma program Rehab. Inc. Chgo., 1981—84, attending staff, 1981—94; chief of rehab. svcs. . U. Chgo. Hosps. Rehab. Ctr., 1994—2000; clin. prof. sect. orthopaedic surgery and rehab. medicine U. Chgo. Med. Ctr., 1995—2000, clin. prof. dept. surgery and neurology, 1995—2000; clin. prof. dept. rehab. medicine Chgo. Med. Sch., 2000—. Attending physician Northwestern Meml. Hosp., Chgo., 1984-94, Provera St. Joseph's Hosp., Elgin, Ill., 2000—; assoc. prof. dept. rehab. medicine Northwestern U. Med. Sch., 1985-94; adj. prof. Pritzker Inst. for Med. Engring., Ill. Inst. Tech., 1991-97; dir. rehab. Midwest Regional Spinal Cord Injury Care Sys., Chgo., 1984-94; dir. rsch. Schwab Rehab. Hosp., 1997-2000. Contbr. articles to profl. jours. and chpts. to book. Fellow Am. Acad. Physical Medicine and Rehab.; mem. Assn. Academic Physiatrists, Am. Spinal Injury Assn., Internat. Med. Soc. Paraplegia, Internal Rehab. Medicine Assn., Phi Beta Kappa, Phi Eta Sigma. Office: Rehab Medicine Specialists 87 N Airlite St Ste G16 Elgin IL 60123-4990

YARMOLA, ELENA GEORGIYEVNA, research scientist; b. Simpheropol, Ukraine, Feb. 11, 1958; came to the U.S., 1998; d. Georgiy Aleksandrovich and Galina Alekseevna Savchenko; m. Valeriy Vladimirovich Yarmola, Jan. 31, 1981; children: Tatiana Valeryevna, Andrew Valeryevich. MS in Biophysics, Moscow Inst. Physics & Tech., 1980, PhD in Biophysics, 1986. Rsch. scientist Engelhardt Inst. Molecular Biology, Moscow, 1985—2001; contractor rsch. in biophysics NIH, Bethesda, Md., 1994-98; postdoctoral assoc. U. Fla., 1998—. Sci. editor Molekuliathia Biologiia, Moscow, 1998; contbr. articles to profl. jours. Mem. Biophys. Soc. Avocation: kayaking. Office: VA Med Ctr Rsch Svc 151 1601 SW Archer Rd Gainesville FL 32608-1197 E-mail: yarmola@hotmail.com.

YARNALL, D. ROBERT, JR. entrepreneur, investor; b. Phila., Feb. 11, 1925; s. D. Robert and Elizabeth (Biddle) Y.; m. Rie Gabrielsen, June 24, 1954 (dec. Oct. 1980); children: Joan, Sara, Kristina; m. Anne Gates, July 3, 1982; stepchildren— Sarah, Michael, Amy Gates B.M.E., Cornell U., 1948. Mech. engr. Westinghouse Electric Co., Phila., 1947; dir. relief mission to Poland Am. Friends Service Com., 1948-49; with Yarnall Waring Co. (name changed to Yarway Corp. 1965), Phila., 1949-86, v.p., 1957-62, pres., chief exec. officer, 1962-78, chmn. bd., 1968-86. Founder, chmn. bd. Envirite Corp., Plymouth Meeting, Pa., 1975—; dir. James G. Biddle Co., Plymouth Meeting, Pa., 1957-78, chmn. bd., 1976-78; dir. Fed. Res. Bank of Phila., 1965-72, dep. chmn., 1971-72; dir. S.K.F. Industries, King of Prussia, Pa., Quaker Chem. Co., Phila., Meritor Fin. Group (PSFS), Keystone Internat. Inc., Houston; Cons. UN Indsl. Devel. Orgn. mission to, Indonesia, 1968; exec.-in-residence on faculty Centre d'Etudes Industrielles, Geneva, Switzerland, 1971-72; Bd. dirs. World Affairs Council, Pa., 1957-61, 64-68, 74— , chmn. bd., 1978-80 Trustee Internat. House, Phila., chmn., 1972-76; trustee U. Pa., 1981—, Phila Art Mus., 1978—, Greater Phila. Partnership, 1975—; trustee St. John's Coll., Annapolis, Md., 1975-86, vice chmn., 1978-82; bd. dirs. Pa. Environ. Council, 1976— , WHYY, Phila., Greater Phila. First Corp., 1984-86, Chestnut Hill Hosp., 1986—. Served with Am. Field Service with Brit. Army, World War II. Mem. ASME, Chief Execs. Orgn. Clubs: Philadelphia, Union League, Divotee Golf (Phila.). Home: 6706 Springbank St Philadelphia PA 19119-3713 Office: Envirite Corp Plymouth Meeting PA 19462

YARNELL, MICHAEL ALLAN, lawyer; b. Chgo., Sept. 10, 1944; s. Howard Winfred and Mary Elizabeth (Card) Y.; m. Karen Alice Hockenyos, June 12, 1971 (div. Mar. 1994); children: Sarah Munro, Jacob Rainey; m. Kristina Louise Renshaw, July 17, 1996. BS, Ariz. State U., 1967; JD with honors, U. Ill., 1971. Bar: Ariz. 1971. Ptnr. Streich, Lang, Weeks & Cardon, Phoenix, 1971-91, also bd. dirs.; mem. Myers, Barnes & Jenkins, 1991; judge Maricopa County Superior Ct., 1991—; adj. prof. Az. State U. Law Sch., 2002—. Author: Ins and Outs of Foreclosure, 1981, 11th edit., 2000; projects editor Law Rev. U. Ill. Law Forum, 1970; contbr. articles to profl. jours. Chairperson Phoenix Children's Theatre, 1987; vol. Habitat for Humanity, Adopt-a-Home sponsor; chmn. Legal Cmty. Builds, 1999. 1st lt. U.S. Army, 1971-72, Korea. Fellow Ariz. Bar Found.; mem. ABA, Am. Judicature Assn., Maricopa Bar Assn., State Bar Ariz. (Outstanding Contbn. to Continuing Legal Edn. award 1988, Com. on Profl. Conduct award 2000), Order of Coif, Lorna Lockwood Inn of Ct. (co-pres. 2000-2001), Phi Kappa Phi, Ariz. Yacht Club (vice comdr. 2000, comdr. 2001-02, staff comdr. 2002—). Republican. Avocations: computers, small boat sailing, white water rafting. Office: Maricopa County Superior Ct 101 W Jefferson St Phoenix AZ 85003-2206 E-mail: michael@yarnell.net.

YARNO, WENDY, pharmaceutical executive; BA, Portland State U., 1982; MBA, Temple U., 1988. Profl. rep. U.S. Human Health, 1983—85, mktg. analyst, 1985—87, product mgr. pediatric vaccines, 1988, assoc. dir. econ. affaris, 1989, sr. dir. mktg. planning, 1990—91, nat. account exec., 1991, sr. dir. managed health care affairs, 1992, project leader for U.S. Health Care Reform, 1992—93; v.p. ctrl. region Merck-Medco, 1994; v.p. hypertension and heart failure therapeutic bus. group U.S. Human Health, 1994—97; v.p. Ortho McNeil Pharm., Johnson & Johnson, 1997—98; v.p. worldwide human health Merck & Co., Inc., Whitehouse Station, NJ, 1999, v.p. human resources, 1999, sr. v.p. human resources, 2000—. Named Hon. Chairperson for Dinner of Hope, Somerset Hills Handicapped Riding Ctr. Office: Merck and Co Inc One Merck Dr Whitehouse Station NJ 08889-0100*

YAROS, CONSTANCE GREENBERG, painter, sculptor; b. Phila., Aug. 03; d. Harry William and Dorothy (Hofberg) Greenberg; m. Irvin Yaros, June 17, 1950 (dec. Nov. 6, 1983); children: Michael J. Yaros, Aimee Y. Silverman, Nancy S. Yaros. Student, Temple U., Tyler Sch. of Art, 1957-60, Blai Studio, 1976-81, Pa. Acad. Fine Arts, 1978-79, 87, Schuler Sch. of Art, 1990. One-woman shows include Tyler Alumni Gallery, 1992; exhibited in group shows icluding Woodmere Art Mus., Phila., 1995, Am. Artists Profl. League, N.Y., 1993, Oil Painters Am., 1994, Art at the Armory, Phila., 1990-92, Artists Equity Assn. Triennial, 1984, 88, 91, Allied Artists of Am., 1988, Catherine Loriliard Wolfe Art Club, 1988, Salmagundi Art Club, 1988, Tyler Alumni Gallery-Diamond Club, Temple U., 1988-92, Phila. Sketch Club, 1987, Old York Rd. Art Guild, 1975; public collections at Temple U., Jefferson Park Hosp., Bd. City Trusts, Fed. Dist. Ct. House, Bd. City Trusts; numerous pvt. collections. Mem. Portrait Soc. Am., Am. Technion Assn., Greenpeace, Phila. Mus. Art, Allied Artists Am., Am. Soc. Portrait Artists, Am. Artist Profl. League, Pa. Acad. Fine Arts, Oil Painters Am., Artists Equity Assn., Woodmere Art Mus., Phila. Art Alliance, Archives of Women's Mus. of Art, Alumni Pa. Acad. Fine Arts, Alumni Tyler Sch. Art. Avocations: music, ballet, fitness, photography, animal protection. Home and Office: 2401 Pennsylvania Ave Ste 4a5 Philadelphia PA 19130-3002

YARRIGLE, CHARLENE SANDRA SHUEY, realtor, investment counselor; b. Redlands, Calif., July 25, 1940; d. Troy Frank and Anna (Miskew) Shuey; m. Robert Charles Yarrigle, Oct. 16, 1965 (div. July 1985); children: Stephanie Ann, Steven Charles. AA, San Bernardino (Calif.) Coll., 1965; student, Ariz. State U., 1965-66; BS, Northern Mich. U., 1976, postgrad., 1976-77. Clk. Bungalow Grocery, Redlands, 1957-59; operator Pacific Tel. Co., San Bernardino, 1958-61; svc. rep. So. Calif. Gas, 1961-66; tchr. bus. Gwinn (Mich.) H.S., 1976-78; realtor, investment counselor Remax Fair Oaks, Fair Oaks, Calif., 1978—; broker, 1990—. Tchr. Project 100,000, Sheppard AFB, Wichita Falls, Tex., 1966-70. Mem. steering com., adv. bd. Sacramento (Calif.) Bd. Realtors, 1981—; vol. Easter Seal Soc., Humane Soc., Coventry House; adv. for mentally ill; tchr. Family-to-Family classes for Nat. Alliance for the Mentally Ill, 1999—. Mem. NAFE, Nat. Alliance for Mentally Ill (advocate), Calif. Alliance for Mentally Ill (advocate), Nat. Alliance Female Execs., Nat. Assn. Realtors (lic.), Calif. Assn. Realtors (Outstanding life mem., Master's Club 1981-2002). Republican. Avocations: financial planning for seniors, physical fitness, stock market, gardening. Office: Remax Gold Internat 5252 Sunrise Blvd Ste 6 Fair Oaks CA 95628-3535 E-mail: charrigle@aol.com.

YARRINGTON, GEORGE A. retired public relations executive, advertising executive, writer; b. Springfield, Mass., Oct. 20, 1906; s. George Timberlake and Jennie Elizabeth Yarrington; m. Katherine Peter Yarrington, Apr. 15, 1944. BA, Comml. Sci., Northeastern Univ., Boston, MA, 1930—34. Free-lance writer Self Employed, Belleville, Ill., 1972—2002; pub. rels. dir. Builders Assn., Boston, 1968—72; exec. dir. Quincy Taxpayers Assn., Quincy, 1953—68; instr. Burdette Coll., Boston, 1946—53; electronics instr. USAF, Scott Field, 1942—46; radio advt. writer CBS Sta. WMAS, Inc., Springfield, 1940—42; owner-mgr. Yarrington's Ser. Sta., Melrose, 1930—40; dept. store buyer Forbes & Wallace, Inc., Springfield, MA, 1925-1930. Pub. speaking instr. Dale Carnegie Inst., New York, NY, 1946—48; chmn. Old Colony Area Transp. Comm., Boston, 1958—60. Author: (book) Tales of the 20th Century. Campaign mgr. Ronald Reagan for Pres., North Conway, NH, 1972; admin. asst. to gov. foster furcolo Mass., 1958—60. Sargeant USAF, 1942—46, Scott Field, IL. Home: 726 Community Drive Apt 75 Belleville IL 62223

YARRISH, ROBERT L. internist; b. N.Y.C., Mar. 16, 1948; s. Herbert M. and Ruth (Rothenberg) Yarrish; m. Lynda A. Mack, Aug. 3, 1986. AB, Harvard U., 1970; MD, U. Pa., 1974. Diplomate Am. Bd. Internal Medicine, Am. Bd. Infectious Diseases. Intern Hunterdon Med. Ctr., Flemington, N.J., 1974-75; resident Phila. Gen. Hosp., 1975-76, Pa. Hosp., Phila., 1976-78; fellow U. Rochester, N.Y., 1978-80; attending physician U. Ky. Med. Ctr., Lexington, 1982-83, Westchester Med. Ctr., Valhalla, N.Y., 1983-86, Changhua (Taiwan) Christian Hosp., 1986-87; assoc. dir. clin. rsch. Lederle Labs., Pearl River, N.Y., 1987-89; program dir. infectious diseases St. Vincent's Med. Ctr., N.Y.C., 1989-96, Beth Israel Med. Ctr., N.Y.C., 1996-99; med. dir. Peter Krueger Clinic, Beth Israel Med. Ctr., 1999—2000; attending physician Sound Shore Med. Ctr., New Rochelle, NY, 2001—. Mem.: N.Y. Soc. Tropical Medicine, N.Y. Soc. Infectious Diseases, Infectious Diseases Soc. Am., Am. Soc. Microbiology. Office: 16 Guion Pl New Rochelle NY 10801-5503 E-mail: rlylam@erols.com.

YARROW, ANDREW LOUIS, writer, journalist, educator, international relations consultant; b. Washington, June 11, 1957; s. Leon Jay and Marian Jeannette (Radke) Y.; 1 child, Richard. BA, UCLA, 1979; MA, Princeton U., 1981; MPA, Harvard U., 1994. Reporter N.Y. Times, N.Y.C., 1981-92; prof. Am. U., Washington, 1994-97; spl. asst. to sec. labor U.S. Dept. Labor, 1995-99; speechwriter Export-Import Bank, 1999—. Internat. rels. cons. World Bank, Washington, 1994-95, UNICEF, 1999—; cons. U.S. Dept. Edn., 2000—. Author: Latecomers: Children of Parents Over 35, 1991; contbr. articles to profl. jours. and popular mags. Inst. for Internat. Edn. fellow, Eng., 1979; recipient Visitors Program award European Union, Brussels, 1993; Rsch. grant Govt. France, 1992-93. Mem. Phi Beta Kappa. Democrat. Avocations: photography, creative writing. Home: 4122 Jenifer St NW Washington DC 20015-1952 Office: Export-Import Bank Washington DC 20571

YARROW, CAROL WELLS, fund raiser; b. Lock Haven, Pa., Oct. 7, 1943; d. Alfred Gates and Edna Bertha (Tressler) Williams; m. Roy E. Wells, Jr., July 17, 1961 (div. 1972); children: Gregory Wells, Gina Wells Moore, Gate E. Wells; m. Harry C. Yarrow, Apr. 26, 1978 (div. 1998). Student, Cabrini Coll. Cert. Feng Shui Practitioner 2001. Devel. coord. Camphill Soltane, Glenmore, Pa., 1993-95; state fin. devel. specialist nat. hdqs. ARC Graphic Stds., 1995-97, regional devel. officer, 1997-99, chief pub. support officer Hyattsville, Md., 1999—. Pres., founder Garden Guild Malvern (Pa.) Preparatory Sch., 1986-90. Co-author: American Bed and Breakfast Cookbook, 1985; weekly columnist Bounty of the Brandywine, 1987, 88. Mem.: Prince George's Pub. Rels. Assn., Assn. Fundraising Profls. Home: 102 Roosevelt Ct Annapolis MD 21403 Office: ARC 6206 Belcrest Rd Hyattsville MD 20782 E-mail: yarrowc@usa.redcross.org., yarrowannapolis@fengshuitthebay.com.

YARVIS, JEFFREY SCOTT, military officer, social worker; b. Morristown, N.J., Oct. 9, 1965; s. Stephen Harlen Yarvis and Arlene Haskin; m. Laura Suzanne Gabrielle Yarvis, Aug. 31, 1997; children: Jacob, Olivia. BA, Ind. U., 1988; MEd, Cambridge Coll., 1992; MSW, Boston Coll., 1994. Clin. social work diplomate ABECSW, 1997, psychotherapy diplomate DAPA, 1997, domestic violence counseling CDV-III ABFE, 1997, cert. sch. social work N.J., 1994, LMSW-ACP Tex., 1996, ACSW NASW, 1996. With U.S. Army; occupl. social worker 85th Med. Detachment, Fort Hood, Tex., 1994—97; chief social work and family advocacy Dewitt Army Cmty. Hosp., Fort Belvoir, Va., 1997—99; instr. U.S. Army Med. Dept. Ctr. & Sch., Fort Sam Houston, Tex., 1999—. Tank platoon leader 1/63 Armor Bn., Fort Irwin, 1989—91; prevention team leader 47th Field Hosp., Port-au-Prince, Haiti, 1994—95, 85th Med. Detachment, Eagle Base, Bosnia-Herzegovina, 1997. Contbr. articles to profl. jours. Critical incident stress debriefing Bell-Coryell County Chpt. of ICISF, Killeen, 1994—97. Decorated 26 military decorations and badges; recipient Mental Health Profl. Yr. award, Internat. Critical Incidence Stress Found., Tex., 1997, Social Policy Grad. assistantship, Boston Coll. Grad. Sch. of Social Work, 1993—94. Mem.: Am. Soc. of Clin. Hypnosis, Assn. of Mil. Surgeons of the U.S., 5th U.S. Cavalry Assn., Nat. Guild of Hypnotists, Soc. for Social Work and Rsch., Assn. of U.S. Army, Nat. Assn. of Social Workers, Am. Legion. Democrat. Jewish. Avocations: running, boating. Home: 235 Terrell Dr Athens GA 30606 Office: U Ga Tucker Hall Sch Social work Athens GA 30602 Home Fax: 706-542-6644; Office Fax: 706-542-6644. Personal E-mail: yarvis831@aol.com. Business E-Mail: armymsw@arches.uga.edu.

YARWOOD, DEAN LESLEY, political science educator; b. Decorah, Iowa, Mar. 17, 1935; s. Harold Nicholas and Elsie Mabel (Roney) Y.; m. Elaine Delores Bender, Sept. 2, 1956; children: Lucinda, Kent, Keith, Douglas, Dennis. BA, Iowa U., 1957; MA, Cornell U., 1961; PhD, U. Ill., 1966. Tchr. social studies, acting jr. high prin. Mid-Prairie Community Sch., Wellman, Iowa, 1957-59; asst. prof. Coe Coll., Cedar Rapids, 1963-66, U. Ky., Lexington, 1966-67, U. Mo., Columbia, 1967-70, assoc. prof., 1970-78, prof., 1978—, dir. grad. studies dept. polit. sci., 1970-72, 88, 94-97, chmn. dept. polit. sci., 1988-91, 98-99, Frederick A. Middlebush prof. polit. sci., 1992-95, prof., 1978-2000, prof. emeritus, 2000—. Editor: The National Administrative System: Selected Readings, 1971, Public Administration, Politics, and the People: Selected Readings for Managers, Employees and Citizens, 1987; author, co-author numerous articles in polit. sci. jours. Recipient Bradish Meml. scholarship, 1953-57, Iowa Merit scholarship, 1956-57, Woodrow Wilson fellowship, 1959-60, James Garner fellowship, 1961-62, Woodrow Wilson Dissertation fellowship, 1962-63. Mem. Am. Soc. Pub. Adminstrn. (chmn. sect. on pub. adminstrn. edn. 1986-87, publs. com. 1986-89, com. on orgnl. rev. and evaln. 1995-97, Ctrl. Mo. chpt. coun. 1979-80, pres. 1980-81, ex-officio mem. coun. 1981-83), Am. Polit. Sci. Assn., Mo. Polit. Sci. Assn. (v.p. 1990-91, pres. 1991-92), Mo. Inst. for Pub. Adminstrn. (coun. 1976-77, v.p. 1977-78, pres. 1978-79, Pub. Adminstr. of Yr. 1998), Phi Beta Kappa. Office: U Mo Dept Polit Sci 206 Professional Building Columbia MO 65211-6040

YARYAN, RUBY BELL, psychologist; b. Toledo, Apr. 28, 1938; d. John Sturges and Susan (Bell) Y.; m. John Frederick Buenz, Jr., Dec. 15, 1962 (div. 1968). AB, Stanford U., 1960; PhD, U. London, 1968. Lic. clin. psychologist; diplomate Am. Bd. Psychology, Am. Acad. Experts in Traumatic Stess. Rsch. dir., univ. radio and TV, U. Calif., San Francisco, 1968-70; dir. delinquency coun. U.S. Dept. Justice, Washington, 1970-73; evaluation dir. Office Criminal Justice Planning, Sacramento, 1973-76; CAO project mgr. San Diego County, 1977-92; dir. devel. svcs. Childhelp USA, Woodland Hills, Calif., 1992-94; rsch. coord. Neuropsychiat. Inst. and Hosp., UCLA, 1986-87; exec. dir. Centinela Child Guidance Clinic, Inglewood, Calif., 1987-89; clin. dir. Nat. Found. Emotionally Handicapped, North Hills, 1990-93; pvt. practice, Beverly Hills, 1973—; supr. psychologist Los Angeles County Dept. Mental Health, 1998—. Psychologist Sr. Psychology Svcs., North L.A. County, 1994-98; cons. White House Conf. Children, Washington, 1970; mem. Nat. Adv. Com. Criminal Justice Standards and Goals, Washington, 1973; clin. affiliation UCLA Med. Ctr. Contbr. articles to profl. jours.; chpts. to books and monographs in field. Chair Human Svcs. Commn., City of West Hollywood, Calif., 1986; first vice-chair United Way/Western Region, L.A., 1988; mem. planning-allocations-rsch. coun. United Way, San Diego, 1980-82. Grantee numerous fed., state and local govt. orgns. Mem. Am. Psychol. Assn., Western Psychol. Assn., Calif. Psychol. Assn., Am. Orthopsychiat. Assn., Am. Profl. Soc. on Abuse of Children, Phi Beta Kappa. Episcopalian. Avocations: painting, music, theatre, writing, reading. Office: 337 S Beverly Dr Ste 107 Beverly Hills CA 90212-4307

YASHER, MICHAEL, retired accountant; b. United, Pa., Aug. 17, 1928; s. Michael and Mary (Sasik) Y.; m. Margaret Jean Wallace, June 23, 1956 (dec. July 12, 1987); 1 child, Michael. BS, Penn State U., 1956; diploma, Air Command & Staff Coll., 1972, Nat. Defense U., 1977; MA, Ctrl. Mich. U., 1983. CPA, D.C.; cert. profl. contract mgr., D.C. Enlisted USAF, 1948; commd. 1st lt. U.S. GAO, Washington, 1956, advanced through grades to col., 1982; ret. USAF, 1988; mem. appropriations com. U.S. House of Reps., 1978-79; acct. to the comptroller U.S. Air Materials Command, 1979-83; acct., cons. E. K. Williams Co., Silver Spring, Md., 1985-98. Contbr. numerous papers and articles to profl. publs. Treas. Boy Scouts Am., Rockville, Md., 1970; bd. dirs. Sr. Softball Assn., Montgomery County, 1993—94, Montgomery County Sr. Sports Assn., 1999—2001; pres. Leisure World (Md.) Billiards Club, 1994—96, treas., 1997, 1999; commr., organizer Sr. Softball League, Montgomery County, 1994; participant Nat. St. Olympics, San Antonio, 1995, Tucson, 1997, Orlando, 1999, Baton Rouge, 2001; std. bearer, Montgomery County rep. Md. Sr. Olympics, 1997—; news corr. Billiards Club-Leisure World, 2000—. Decorated with 14 mil. decorations; recipient Bronze medal for softball Md. Sr. Olympics, 1992, 1993, 96, 97, 98, Gold medal, 1994, 98, 99, volleyball, 1999, Bronze medal for volleyball, 1993, 1995, 96, 97, billiards, 1998, 2000, Silver medal for Softball, 1995, 2000, 2001, volleyball, 1998, 2000, Gold medal for Billiards, 2000, Meritorious Svc. award, U.S-.G.A.O., 1975, Data Systems Design Ctr. Outstanding Officer Mobilization Augmentee, 1978. Mem. AICPA, Nat. Capital Area Bowling Assn., Res. Officers Assn., Disabled Am. Vets. Comdrs. Club, Leisure World Billiards Club, Nat. Sr. Games Assn. (charter mem.), Am. Legion, VFW. Democrat. Roman Catholic. Avocations: coin collecting, sports. Home: 15107 Interlachen Dr Apt 318 Silver Spring MD 20906-5629

YASHIN, ALEXEI, hockey player; b. Sverdlovsk, Russia, Nov. 5, 1973; Profl. hockey player Ottawa Senators, 1992—2001, NY Islanders, 2001—. Hockey player CIS jr. team, 1992 World Jr. Championships, Russia jr. team, 1993, Russia team World Championships, 1994, 96, NHL All-Star Game, 1994. Office: New York Islanders Nassau Veterans Memorial Coliseum Hempstead NY 11553*

YASHON, DAVID, neurosurgeon, educator; b. Chgo., May 13, 1935; s. Samuel and Dorothy (Cutler) Y.; children— Jaclyn, Lisa, Steven. BS in Medicine, U. Ill., 1958, MD, 1960. Diplomate Am. Bd. Neurol. Surgery. Intern U. Ill., 1961, resident, 1961-64, asst. in neuroanatomy, 1960; clin. instr. neurosurgery U. Chgo., 1965-66; asst. prof. neurosurgery Case Western Res U., Cleve., 1966-69; assoc. prof. neurosurgery Ohio State U., Columbus, 1969-74, prof., 1974-89, prof. emeritus, 1989—; mem. staff St. Ann's Hosp., Children's Hosp., Grant Med. Ctr., Ohio State U. East Med. Ctr. Cons. Med. Research and Devel. Command, U.S. Army; mem. Neurology B Study Sect NIH. Author: Spinal Injury; contbr. articles to med. jours. Served as capt. U.S. Army, 1960-68. Fellow Royal Coll. Surgeons Can. (cert.), A.C.S.; mem. AMA, Am. Physiol. Soc., Congress Neurol. Surgeons, Am. Assn. Anatomists, Canadian, Ohio neurosurg. socs., Am. Assn. Neurol. Surgeons, Research Soc. Neurol. Surgeons, Acad. Medicine Columbus and Franklin County, Soc. for Neurosci., Soc. Univ. Surgeons, Am. Acad. Neurology, Assn. for Acad. Surgery, Am. Acad. Neurol. Surgery, Am. Assn. for Surgery of Trauma, Central Surg. Soc., Ohio Med. Soc., Columbus Surg. Soc., Sigma Xi, Alpha Omega Alpha. Address: 500 Columbia Pl Bexley OH 43209-1677

YASNOFF, WILLIAM ALAN, computer scientist, health facility administrator; b. Chgo., Apr. 7, 1953; s. Meyer Yasnoff and Doris Norwell; m. Joanene Lois Feldman. BS, Northwestern U., 1974, MD, 1975, PhD in Computer Sci., 1980. Asst. prof., med. computer sci. dept. U. of Tex. Health Sci. Ctr., Dallas, 1980—83; asst. prof. and dir., cardiology image processing Med. Coll. of Ohio, Toledo, 1983—85; v.p. rsch. Cell Analysis Sys., Inc., Lombard, Ill., 1985—86; pres., founder Morphometrix, Inc., Western Springs, 1986—87; med. dir. AMA/Net AMA, Chgo., 1987—90; assoc. dir., health network svcs. Oreg. Health Scis. U., Portland, 1990—93; dir. immunization registry and DOLPHIN network Oreg. Health Divsn., 1994—97; assoc. dir. for sci., pub. health practice program office Ctrs. for Disease Control and Prevention, Atlanta, 1997—. Assoc. editor Jour. of Biomed. Informatics, San Diego, 2000—; adj. prof. biostatistics Emory U., Atlanta, 2002—; cons. Compuserve, Inc., Columbus, OHIO, 1995, Ea. Va. Med. Sch., Norfolk, VA., 1995, Abbott Labs., Inc., San Jose, 1993—94, Columbine Venure Ptnrs., Englewood, 1989—91. Author: (book) Public Health Informatics and Information Systems, 2002; contbr. articles to profl. jours. Grief recovery counselor NE Bapt. Ch., Atlanta, 2000. Fellow: Am. Coll. of Med. Informatics; mem.: APHA, Assn. for Computing Machinery, IEEE Computer Soc., Am. Med. Informatics Assn. (sci. program chair spring meeting 2001). Avocation: tennis. Office: Ctrs for Disease Control and Prevention Mail Stop K-36 4770 Buford Hwy Atlanta GA 30341 Office Fax: 770-488-2574. Business E-Mail: wyasnoff@cdc.gov.

YASNYI, ALLAN DAVID, communications company executive; b. New Orleans, June 22, 1942; s. Ben Z. and Bertha R. (Michalove) Y.; m. Susan K. Manders; children: Benjamin Charles, Evelyn Judith, Brian Mallut. BBA, Tulane U., 1964. Free-lance exec. producer, producer, writer, actor, designer TV, motion picture and theatre, 1961-73; producer, performer the Second City; dir. fin. & adminstrn. Quinn Martin Prodns., Hollywood, Calif., 1973-76, v.p. fin., 1976-77, exec. v.p. fin. & corp. planning, 1977; vice chmn., CEO QM Prodns., Beverly Hills, 1977-78, chmn. bd., CEO, 1978-80; pres., CEO The Synapse Comm. Group, Inc., 1981—, ASI Entertainment, 1998-99. Exec. dir., adj. prof. U. So. Calif. Entertainment Tech. Ctr., 1994-99, exec. dir. emeritus, 1999—; participant IC IS Forum, 1990-95; exec. prodr. first live broadcast combining Intelsat, Intersputnik, The Voice of Am., and The Moscow World Radio Svc., 1990; resource guest Aspen Inst. Exec. Seminars, 1990; chmn. bd. dirs. Found. of Global Broadcasting, Washington, 1987-93; nat. adv. bd. DeSantis Ctr. Fla. Atlantic U., 1998-. Trustee Hollywood Arts Coun., 1980-83; exec. v.p., trustee Hollywood Hist. Trust, 1981-91; bd. dirs. Internat. Ctr. Intergative Studies, N.Y.C., 1988-92; bd. dirs. Asthma and Allergy Found. Am., 1981-85. With U.S. Army, 1964-66, Viet Nam. Named Tulane U. Hall of Fame. Mem. Acad. TV Arts and Scis., Inst. Noetic Scis., Hollywood Radio and TV Soc., Hollywood C. of C. (dir., vice chmn. 1978-93), Screen Actors Guild, Assn. Transpersonal Psychology (keynote spkr. 1988). Office: 4132 Fulton Ave Sherman Oaks CA 91423-4340

YASSIN, ROBERT ALAN, museum administrator, curator; b. Malden, Mass., May 22, 1941; s. Harold Benjamin and Florence Gertrude (Hoffman) Y.; m. Marilyn Kramer, June 9, 1963; children: Fredric Giles, Aaron David. BA (Rufus Choate scholar), Dartmouth Coll., 1962; postgrad., Boston U., 1962-63; MA, U. Mich., 1965, postgrad. (Samuel H. Kress Found. fellow), 1968-70, PhD candidate, 1970; postgrad (Ford Found. fellow), Yale U., 1966-68. Asst. to dir. Mus. Art U. Mich., 1965-66, asst. dir., 1970-72, asso. dir., 1972-73, acting dir., 1973, instr. dept. history of art, 1970-73; co-dir. Joint Program in Mus. Tng., 1970-73; chief curator Indpls. Mus. Art, 1973-75, 87-89, acting dir., 1975, dir., 1975-89; exec. dir. Tucson Mus. Art, 1990—2001, Palos Verdes Art Ctr., Calif., 2002—. Adj. prof. Herron Sch. Art Ind. U./Purdue U., 1975-89. Contbr. to mus. publications. Mem.: Western Mus. Assn., Nat. Trust Historic Preservation, Coll. Art Assn. Am., Am. Assn. Mus. (bd. dirs. Internat. Coun. Mus. 1986—89). Jewish. Office: Palos Verdes Art Ctr 5509 W Crestridge Rd Hermosa Beach CA 90254 Home: 7321 Marina Pacifica Dr N Long Beach CA 90803-3808 E-mail: rayassin@aol.com.

YASUDA, HIROTSUGU KOGE, chemical engineering professor; b. Kyoto, Japan, Mar. 24, 1930; s. Mitsuo and Kei (Niwa) Y.; m. Gerda Lisbeth Schmidtke, Apr. 6, 1968; children: Ken Eric, Werner Akira, Lisbeth Kay. BSChemE, Kyoto U., 1953; MS in Polymer Chemistry, SUNY, Syracuse, 1959, PhD in Polymer and Phys. Chemistry, 1961. Rsch. assoc. Ophthalmic Plastic Lab., Mass. Eye & Ear Infirmary, Boston, 1962-63; head biomaterial sect. eye rsch. Cedar-Sinai Med. Ctr., L.A., 1963-65; vis. scientist Royal Inst. Tech., Stockholm, 1965-66; sr. chemist Rsch. Triangle Inst., Rsch. Triangle Pk., N.C., 1966-72, mgr. Polymer Rsch. Lab., 1972-78; prof. chem. engring. U. Mo., Rolla, 1978-88, dir. Thin Films Inst., 1974-88, prof. chem. engring. Columbia, 1988—, chmn. dept., 1988-90, James C. Dowell rsch. prof., 1989—, dir. Ctr. for Surface and Plasma Techs., 1989—. Author: Plasma Polymerization, 1985. Home: 1004 Lake Point Ln Columbia MO 65203-2900 Office: Ctr For Surface Sci & Plasma Columbia MO 65211-0001 E-mail: yasudah@missouri.edu.

YASWEN, GORDON, artist, writer; b. N.Y.C., May 25, 1937; children: Montbor, Cheratra. Student, U. Vt., 1955—57; B.Design, U. Mich., 1959. Cert. instr. Calif. C.C. Instr. art, auto tech., auto biography San Francisco C.C., 1977—84, Coll. of Alameda, 1987—92, Santa Rosa Jr. Coll., 1979—. Proprietor Yascom Endeavors, Sebastopol, Calif., 1970—. Author: Life-Lists, 1997, Beyond the Bubble, 2000, Car Savvy, 2000, numerous poems. With USAFR, 1954—62. Avocations: camping, dancing, singing, hiking, acting. Home: 740 First St Sebastopol CA 95472

YATES, ALBERT CARL, academic administrator, chemistry educator; b. Memphis, Sept. 29, 1941; s. John Frank and Sadie L. (Shell) Y.; m. Ann Young; children: Steven, Stephanie, Aerin Alessandra, Sara Elizabeth. BS, Memphis State U., 1965; PhD, Ind. U., 1968. Research assoc. U. So. Calif., Los Angeles, 1968-69; prof. chemistry Ind. U., Bloomington, 1969-74; v.p. research, grad. dean U. Cin., 1974-81; exec. v.p., provost, prof. chemistry Washington State U., Pullman, 1981-90; pres. Colo. State U., Fort Collins, 1990—; chancellor Colo. State U. System, 1990—. Mem. grad. record exam. bd. Princeton (N.J.) U., 1977-81; undergrad. assessment program coun. Ednl. Testing Svc., 1977-81, NRC, 1975-82, Office Edn., HEW, 1978-80; mem. exec. coun. acad. affairs Nat. Assn. State Univs. and Land Grant Colls., 1983-87, Am. Coun. on Edn., 1983-87, nat adv. coun. gen. med. scis. NIH, 1987-90. Contbr. research articles to Jour. Chem. Physics; research articles to Phys. Rev.; research articles to Jour. Physics, Phys. Rev. Letters, Chem. Physics Letters. Served with USN, 1959-62. Recipient univ., state and nat. honors and awards Mem. AAAS, Am. Phys. Soc., Am. Chem. Soc., Sigma Xi, Phi Lambda Upsilon. Home: 1744 Hillside Dr Fort Collins CO 80524-1965 Office: Colo State U 102 Administration Bldg Fort Collins CO 80523-0100 E-mail: ayates@lamar.colostate.edu.*

YATES, ALLISON A. scientific organization administrator; BS, MS, Univ. of Calif.; PhD, Univ. of Calif. at Berkley, 1974. Dean Univ. of Southern Miss., 1988—97; dir. food and nutrition bd. Inst. of Medicine, the Nat. Acads., 1994-1996, 1998—. Office: Inst Medicine, the Nat Acads 2101 Constitution Ave NW Washington DC 20418*

YATES, CHARLES RICHARDSON, former arts center executive; b. Atlanta, Sept. 9, 1913; s. Presley Daniel and Julia (Richardson) Y.; m. Dorothy Malone, May 20, 1944; children: Dorothy Y. Kirkley, Charles R., Sarah F., J. Comer. BS with honors, Ga. Inst. Tech., 1935; DLitt (hon.), Emory U., 1999. With 1st Nat. Bank Atlanta, 1935-47, asst. v.p., 1940-47; with Joshua L. Baily & Co., Inc., Atlanta, 1947-60, v.p., 1956-60; v.p. finance Atlantic Coast Line R.R. Co. and L. & N. R.R. Co., 1960-67; v.p. Seaboard Coast Line R.R. Co., 1967-71, v.p. finance, 1971-73, L. & N. R.R. Co., 1967-73; pres. Atlanta Arts Alliance, 1973-83. Dir. Technology Park/Atlanta. Trustee Ga. Tech. Found., Woodruff Arts Ctr. Served with AUS, 1941-42; lt. USNR, 1942-46. Mem. Ga. C. of C. (dir., pres. 1965-67), East Lake Golf Club (pres. 1995—), Augusta Nat. Club (sec.), Atlanta Athletic Club, Peachtree Golf Club, Capital City Club, Royal and Ancient Golf Club. Episcopalian.

YATES, DAN CHARLES, insurance company official; b. Spring Valley, Ill., Oct. 14, 1952; s. Earl John Jr. and Charlotte Elaine (Sandberg) Y.; m. Margaret Mary McBride, Mar. 1, 1980; 1 child, Keith. B Bus. in Fin., Western Ill. U., 1977. CPCU. Claims adjuster G.A.B. Bus. Svcs., Kansas City, Mo., 1978-80; claims mgr. Dodson Group, 1980—. Mem. conf. com. Property Loss Rsch. Bur., Schaumburg, Ill., 1994-96, vice chair, 1994-95, chair, 1995-96; chair legal subcom. of the western regional adv. com. of property Loss Rsch. Bur., 1996; adv. coun. midwest region Nat. Assn. Ind. Ins. Adjusters, 1986-89, 97-2000, mem. Credit Com. for Bee Dee Co. Credit Union, 1992-97, pres., chair 1994-97, also bd. dirs., 1997—, chmn., 1998—. Vol. Jr. Achievement. With U.S. Army, 1972-74. Mem. Am. Inst. for CPCU, Kansas City Property Claims Assn. (pres. 1992). Avocations: bowling, basketball, blood donor. Office: Dodson Group 9201 State Line Rd Kansas City MO 64114-3234 E-mail: dyates@dodsongroup.com.

YATES, DAVID JOHN C. chemist, researcher; b. Stoke-on-Trent, Staffordshire, Eng., Feb. 13, 1927; came to U.S., 1958; s. Eric John and Beatrice Victoria (Street) Y.; m. Natalie Chmelnitsky, June 22, 1983 BS with honors, U. Birmingham, U.K., 1949; PhD, U. Cambridge, Eng., 1955, Sc.D., 1968. Rsch. physicist Kodak Labs., Wealdstone, London, 1949-50; rsch. chemist Brit. Ceramic Rsch. Assn., Stoke-on-Trent, 1950-51; rsch. assoc. dept. colloid sci. U. Cambridge, 1951-58; lectr. Sch. Mines and dept. chemistry Columbia U., N.Y.C., 1958-60; sr. rsch. fellow Nat. Phys. Lab., Teddington, U.K., 1960-61; rsch. assoc. corp. labs. Exxon Rsch. and Engring., Annandale, N.J., 1961-86; rsch. prof. dept. of chem. engring. Lafayette Coll., Easton, Pa., 1986-87; rsch. prof. dept. materials sci. Rutgers U., Piscataway, N.J., 1987-88; cons. San Diego, 1988—. Contbr. over 70 articles to profl. jours., chpts. to books; 13 U.S. patents, numerous fgn. patents. Fellow Inst. of Physics (U.K.), Royal Soc. Chemistry (U.K.), N.Y. Catalysis Club (chmn. 1966-67). Clubs: N.Y. Catalysis (chmn. 1965-66). Avocations: photography, bicycling, gliding, travel, sports cars.

YATES, DERRICK K. music educator, director; s. Alfredo V. Yates and Audrey A. Vawters. BS in Music Edn., Ala. A&M U., 1997, MEd, MusM, Ala. A&M U., 2002. Cert. Tchr. Ala., 1997. Band dir. Oakwood Acad., Huntsville, Ala., 1995—97, Huntsville City Schools Chapman Mid. Sch., Huntsville, 1997—2001; prof., asst. dir. of bands Ala. A&M U., Normal, 2001—. From adj. asst. dir. bands. to asst. dir. Ala. A&M U., 1997—2001, asst. dir. of bands, Ala., 2001—. Musician: Mid-West Music Festival, 2001 (1st Pl. trophy, 2001), Heritage Music Festival, 1999. Counselor Heritage Home for Children, Huntsville, Ala., 1995—2002; organizer Voter Registration, 2000—02. Mem.: Music Educator Nat. Conf., Internat. Trumpet Guild, Prince Hall Lodge of Master Masons, Phi Mu Alpha (adv. 1999—2002), Alpha Phi Alpha (edn. officer 2001—02). Baptist. Avocations: swimming, travel, exercising, movies. Office: Alabama A&M University PO Box 1925 Normal AL 35762 Home Fax: 256-851-5974; Office Fax: 256-851-5974. Personal E-mail: dyates@aaum.edu. E-mail: dyates@aamu.edu.

YATES, DIANE GREINER, librarian; b. Lancaster, Pa., Nov. 16, 1939; d. Arthur Kreider and Catharine Mae (Hersh) Greiner; m. Robert James Yates, Aug. 13, 1960; children: Robert, Andrew, Karen. BA, Grove City Coll., 1961; MLS, U. Pitts., 1972. Cert. med. libr., Pa. Hotel rep. Glenn Fawcett, Inc., San Francisco, 1961-63; bookmobile libr. Carnegie Libr., Pitts., 1963; reference libr. North Hills Libr., Glenshaw, Pa., 1969-81, libr. dir., 1981—. Bd. dirs. ElNetwork. Contbr. articles to mags., book revs. to local newspapers and Voice of Youth Advocates. Bd. dirs. Zoar Home, Allegheny County Libr. Assn. Mem. ALA, AAUW, Pa. Libr. Assn. (chmn. various coms. and task forces, chair pub. libr. divsn.), Victorian Soc. In Am., Music Box Soc., Magic Lantern Soc. Republican. Office: North Hills Libr 1822 Mount Royal Blvd Glenshaw PA 15116-2195

YATES, DONALD ALFRED, retired literature educator; b. Ayer, Mass., Apr. 11, 1930; s. Alfred Craig Yates and Bessie Mae Cambridge; m. Mary Dodd, June 24, 1951 (div. Mar. 1961); children: Brian Donald, Juliet Marie; m. Lynn P. Taylor, Mar. 31, 1962 (div. May 1975); 1 child, John Allan; m. Joanne Margaret Mueller, Mar. 21, 1977. AB in Spanish, U. Mich., 1951, MA in Spanish, 1954, PhD in Spanish, 1961. Tchg. fellow U. Mich., Ann Arbor, 1953-57; instr. Mich. State U., East Lansing, 1957-61, asst. prof. Spanish-Am. lit., 1961-64, assoc. prof., 1964-67, prof., 1967-83, prof. emeritus, 1983—. Pres. Internat. Inst. Latin-Am. Lit., Pitts., 1971-73. Author: Jorge Luis Borges: Life, Work & Criticism, 1985; editor, translator: Latin Blood: Best Crime Stories of Latin America, 1972; co-editor, translator: Labyrinths: Selected Writings of Jorge Luis Borges, 1962; co-editor: (textbook) Imaginación y Fantasía, 1960, 6th edit., 1999. With U.S. Army, 1951-53. Translation grantee NEA, 2000-01. Mem. MLA, Mystery Writers of Am., Baker St. Irregulars (The Greek Interpreter 1972), Sherlock Holmes Soc. London. Democrat. Home: 555 Canon Park Dr Saint Helena CA 94574-9726 E-mail: shsirene@earthlink.net.

YATES, ELLA GAINES, library consultant; b. Atlanta, June 14, 1927; d. Fred Douglas and Laura (Moore) Gaines; m. Joseph L. Sydnor (dec.); l child, Jerri Gaines Sydnor Lee; m. Clayton R. Yates (dec.). AB, Spelman Coll., Atlanta, 1949; MS in L.S, Atlanta U., 1951; JD, Atlanta Law Sch., 1979. 1954Asst. br. librarian Bklyn. Pub. Library, 1951; head children's dept. Orange (N.J.) Pub. Library, 1956—59; br. librarian East Orange (N.J.) Pub. Library, 1960—69; med. librarian Orange Meml. Hosp., 1967—69; asst. dir. Montclair (N.J.) Pub. Library, 1970—72, Atlanta-Fulton Pub. Library, 1972—76, dir., 1976—81; dir. learning resource ctr. Seattle Opportunities Industrialization Ctr., 1982—84; asst. dir. adminstrn. Friendship Force, Atlanta, 1984—86; state librarian Commonwealth of Va., 1986—90; library cons. Price Waterhouse, 1991; adv. bd. Library of Congress Center for the Book, 1977—85; interim dir. Atlanta-Fulton Pub. Libr., 1998—99; cons., dir. Woodruff Libr., Atlanta, 2000—02. Cons. in field; vis. lectr. U. Wash., Seattle, 1981-83; mem. Va. Records Adv. Bd., 1986-90; mem. Nagara Exec. Bd., 1987-91. Contbr. to profl. jours. Vice chmn. N.J. Women's Coun. on Human Rels., 1957-59; chmn. Friends Fulton County Jail, 1973-81; bd. dirs. United Cerebral Palsy Greater Atlanta, Inc., 1979-81 Coalition Against Censorship, Washington, 1981-84, YMCA Met. Atlanta, 1979-81, Exec. Women's Network, 1979-82, Freedom To Read Found., 1979-85, Va. Black History Mus., Richmond, 1990-91; sec., exec. dir. Va. Libr. Found. Bd., 1986-90. Recipient meritorious svc. award Atlanta U., 1977, Phoenix award City of Atlanta, 1980, Serwa award Nat. Coalition 100 Black Women, 1989, Black Caucus award, 1989, disting. svc. award Clark-Atlanta U., 1991, ednl. support svc. award Tuskegee Airmen, 1993, Alumnae Achievement award Spelman Coll., 1998, Annie McPheters award Atlanta-Fulton Pub. Libr., 1998, Disting. Alumnae award Clark Atlanta U., 2001; named profl. woman of yr. NAACP N.J., 1972, outstanding chum of yr., 1976; named outstanding alumni Spelman Coll., 1977, named to alumni hall of fame, 1995. Mem. ALA (exec. bd. 1977-83, commn. freedom of access to info.), NAACP, Southeastern Libr. Assn., Nat. Assn. Govt. Archives and Records Adminstrn. (exec. bd. 1987-91), Delta Sigma Theta (Pinnacle leadership award 2001). Baptist. Home and Office: 1171 Oriole Dr SW Atlanta GA 30311-2424

YATES, GARY L. marriage and family therapist; b. Washington, Aug. 16, 1944; s. Lewis Edward and Norma Jean (Andruss) Y.; m. Cynthia Ann Pagay, Aug. 16, 1974; children: David, Jonathan, Daniel, Matthew, Nathan. BA, Am. U., 1967; MA, U. No. Colo., 1978. Tchr. St. Anthony's, Kailua, Hawaii, 1970-74, Acad. of Pacific, Honolulu, 1974-79; adminstr. Dept. Pub. Health, San Bernardino, Calif., 1979-81, Charles Drew Sch. of Medicine, L.A., 1981-82; assoc. dir. Divsn. of Adolescent Medicine/Children's Hosp., 1982-92; sr. program officer Calif. Wellness Found., Woodland Hills, Calif., 1992-93, program dir., 1993-94, pres., CEO, 1995—. Asst. clin. prof. U. So. Calif., 1988—; bd. dirs. Calif. Wellness Found., Grantmaker in Health, Hispanics in Philanthropy, So. Calif. Assn. Philanthropy, Coun. Found. Contbr. articles to profl. jours.; contbg. author: Multi Agency System of Care, 1990. Mem. L.A. Roundtable for Children, 1988-92, United Way Task Force on AIDS, L.A., 1988-92, San Bernardino Comm. Coun., 1980-82; chmn. Hawaii Sch. Counseling Assn., Honolulu, 1978-79. S(sgt.) U.S. Army, 1968-70. Recipient NACO Achievement award Nat. Assn. U.S. Counties, 1980, 3rd Century award Hollywood Coord. Coun., 1989, Gov.'s Victim's Svc. award Gov. of Calif., 1990, Commendation award Calif. State Senate, 1992, Hispanic Health Leadership award, 1999, L.A. Free Clinic Lenny Somberg award, 1998. Mem. Am. Assn. Humanistic Psychologists, Soc. for Adolescent Medicine, Calif. Assn. Marriage and Family Therapists, Am. Pub. Health Assn. Democrat. Methodist. Avocations: reading, walking. Office: Calif Wellness Found 6320 Canoga Ave Ste 1700 Woodland Hills CA 91367-2565

YATES, JAMES ARTHUR, plastic surgeon; b. Butler, Pa., June 5, 1935; s. Adolph Walter and Laura Marie (De Foggie) Y.; m. Debra Lynne Stringer, June 19, 1983; 1 child, Jamie Dale Yates Reynolds. BA, Cornell U., 1956; MD, U. Md., Balt., 1960. Diplomate Am. Bd. Plastic Surgery, Nat. Bd. Med. Examiners, Am. Bd. Surgery; lic. physician, Pa., Ohio, R.I. Intern Cleve. Clinic Hosp., 1960-61, resident in gen. surgery, 1961-62, U. Pitts. Med. Ctr., 1963-65; resident in plastic surgery R.I. Hosp., 1966-67, chief resident, 1967-68; pvt. practice Plastic Surg. Ctr. Ltd., Camp Hill, Pa., 1968—; med. dir. Grandview Surgery Ctr., Mechanicsburg and Camp Hill. Tchg. fellow gen. surgery U. Pitts. Med. Ctr., 1963-65, instr. gen. surgery, 1965-66; clin. instr. plastic surgery Milton S. Hershey (Pa.) Med. Ctr., 1968—; staff maxillofacial and plastic surgery dept. Harrisburg (Pa.) Hosp., 1968—; chief plastic and aesthetic surgery dept. Holy Spirit Hosp., Camp Hill, 1968—; staff Polyclinic Med. Ctr., Harrisburg, 1968—, Seidle Meml. Hosp., Mechanicsburg, Pa., Cmty. Gen. Osteo. Hosp., Harrisburg, Mechanicsburg Rehab. Hosp., Carlisle (Pa.) Hosp.; med. dir. Grandview Surgery and Laser Ctr., Camp Hill; cons. Harrisburg State Hosp.; physician surveyor Am. Assn. Ambulatory Health Care; physician trainer plastic surgery residency program Am. Coll. Osteo. Surgery; bd. dirs. Am. Assn. Ambulatory Surgery Facilities. Contbr. articles to profl. jours.; adv. bd. Town and Country Mag. Police commr. West Shore Regional Police Dept.; pres. Boro Coun. Lemoyne Boro; mem. credentialling com. Keystone Health Plan; mem. task force on ambulatory surgery Pa. Dept. Health;mem. coun. Lemoyne (Pa.) Borough Coun., pres.; credentialing officer Freedom Health Care HMO. Fellow ACS; mem. AMA, Pa. Med. Soc., Am. Burn Assn., Am. Soc. Plastic and Reconstructive Surgeons, Am. Burn Victim Found., Am. Soc. Aesthetic Plastic Surgery, Vail Cosmetic Surgery Soc., Pa. Plastic Surgery Soc., Am. Soc. Automobile Medicine, Northeastern Soc. Plastic Surgeons, Royal Soc. Medicine, Lipolysis Soc. N.Am., Internat. Soc. Clin. Plastic Surgeons, South Ctrl. Pa. Regional Med. Dirs., Am. Coll. Physician Execs. Republican. Roman Catholic. Avocation: biking, skiing, model airplaning, Ferrari sports cars. Home: 833 Kiehl Dr Lemoyne PA 17043-1201 Office: Plastic Surgery Ctr Ltd 205 Grandview Ave Camp Hill PA 17011-1708 E-mail: jay5plas@msn.com.

YATES, JAMES NEWTON, English educator; b. Booneville, Ark., Aug. 13, 1961; s. Kenneth James and Margaret Juanita (Skinner) Y.; m. Margaret Colleen McKelvey, Dec. 29, 1990; 1 child, Brendan Daniel. BA, Ouachita Bapt. U., 1983; MA, Ark. State U., 1985; PhD, Okla. State U., 1995. Instr. English Rich Mountain C.C., Mena, Ark., 1985-88; tchg. assoc. Okla. State U., Stillwater, 1988-90; instr. English Northwestern Okla. State U., Alva, 1990-95, asst. prof. English, 1995-2000, assoc. prof. English, 2000—, chair, 2002—. Sponsor Student Govt. Assn., N.W. Okla. State U., 1995—, pres. faculty senate. Mem. MLA, S.W. Tex. Popular Culture Assn., Nat. Coun. Tchrs. English, Melville Soc., Rotary, Phi Delta Kappa. Democrat. Episcopalian. Avocations: writing fiction, reading, drawing, guitar, singing. Home: 711 7th St Alva OK 73717-2721 E-mail: jnyates@nwosu.edu.

YATES, JEFFREY A. municipal official; b. Nashville, Oct. 28, 1974; s. Sandy J. Yates; m. Jennifer E. Buschhorn, July 19, 1997. MPA, Regent U., 2001. Secondary edn. tchr. lic. Social sci. tchr. Shiloh Hills Christian Sch., Kennesaw, Ga., 1997—99; grad. assisstant Regent U., Virginia Beach, Va., 1999—2001; mgmt. and budget analyst City of Virginia Beach, 2001—. Libertarian. Avocations: kite surfing, surfing. Office: City of Virginia Beach Bldg 1 2401 Courthouse Dr Virginia Beach VA 23456 Business E-Mail: jayates@vbgov.com.

YATES, JOHN MELVIN, retired ambassador; b. Superior, Mont., Nov. 25, 1939; s. Leon Glen and Violet May (McPheeters) Y.; m. Peggy Maureen Simpson, Mar. 26, 1961 (dec. Apr. 1986); children: Catherine Diener, John Simpson, Maureen Cole, Paul Marion, Leon Gregory; m. Mary Barbara Carlin, Jan. 30, 1988. AB, Stanford U., 1961; MA, Fletcher Sch. Law and Diplomacy, 1962, MAL.D., 1963, PhD, 1972. Fgn. service officer U.S. Dept. State, Washington, 1964—, Algiers, Algeria, 1964-66, Blantyre, Malawi, 1967-68, Bamako, Mali, 1969-71, New Delhi, 1973-75, Ankara, Turkey, 1975-77, Libreville, Gabon, 1977-80, Washington, 1971-73, 80-82; amb. to Republic of Cape Verde, Am. Embassy, 1983-86, counselor for polit. affairs, 1986-89, dep. chief of mission Lagos, Nigeria, 1989-91, Kinshasa, Zaire, 1991-93, chief of mission Zaire, 1993-95, amb. to Republic of Benin, Cotonou, 1995-98, amb. to Republic of Cameroon and Republic Equatorial Guinea, Yaounde, 1998—2001. Recipient Presdl. award for sustained superior accomplishment in conduct of fgn. policy. Mem. Am. Fgn. Service Assn. Address: 3143 Tennyson St NW Washington DC 20015 E-mail: johnmyates@hotmail.com.

YATES, JOHN ROBERT, JR. engineer, educator; b. Boston, Feb. 9, 1930; s. John Robert and Rosemary Natalie (Logue) Y.; m. Virginia Dianne Finocchio, July 3, 1954 (dec. Feb. 1988); children: Deborah A., John Robert, Thomas F., Catherine I.; m. Barbara Marandola, Dec. 28, 1990. AB, Northeastern U., 1954. Commd. 2d lt. USMC, 1954, advanced through grades to lt. col., 1970; action officer, constrn. team, joint logistics rev. bd. Office Sec. Def., 1969-70; engr. III Marine Amphibious Force, Fleet Marine Force, Okinawa, 1970-71; comdg. officer, marine barracks U.S. Naval Base, Boston, 1971-74, ret., 1974. Dir. engring. Soldiers' Home, Chelsea, Mass., 1974-85; energy conservation coord. Exec. Office of Human Svcs., Commonwealth of Mass.; faculty Energy Mgmt. in Healthcare Instns., HEW, 1977. Mem. exec. bd. USO Coun. New Eng., 1971-84, pres., 1988-94; trustee Charlestown YMCA, 1974—, pres. 1988-94, vice chmn., 1977-79, chmn., 1980-82. Decorated Joint Svc. Commendation medal, Navy Commendation medal, Army Commendation medal. Mem. Soc. Am. Mil. Engrs. (dir. Boston post), Am., New Eng. hosp. engrs. socs., Navy League U.S. (v.p. Mass. Bay coun.), Am. Legion, VFW, Bostonian Soc., Wardroom Club (Boston), Army-Navy Club (Washington). Roman Catholic. Home and Office: 39 Chapman Rd Boxford MA 01921-2330

YATES, JOHN THOMAS, JR. chemistry educator, research director; b. Winchester, Va., Aug. 3, 1935; s. John Thomas and Kathryn (Barnett) Y.; m. Kerin Joyce Narbut, Oct. 18, 1958; children: Geoffrey, Nathan. BS, Juniata Coll., 1956; PhD, MIT, 1960. Asst. prof. chemistry Antioch Coll., Yellow Springs, Ohio, 1960-63; NRC fellow, research chemist Nat. Bur. Standards, Washington, 1963-82; R.K. Mellon prof. chemistry U. Pitts., 1982—, dir. Surface Sci. Ctr., 1982—. Co-dir. materials rsch. ctr. U. Pitts., 1994, R.K. Mellon prof. chemistry and physics, 1994—. Author: Experimental Innovations in Surface Science, 1997; co-author: The Surface Scientist's Guide to Organometallic Chemistry, 1987; co-editor: Vibrational Spectroscopy of Molecules on Surfaces, 1987, Chemical Perspectives of Microelectronic Materials, Vol. 131; assoc. editor: Studies in Surface Science and Catalysis, 1986; series editor: Methods of Surface Characterization, 1987; bd. editors Ann. Rev. Phys. Chemistry, 1983-85, Jour. Phys. Chemistry, 1983-88, Jour. Chem. Physics, 1984-87, Jour. Catalysis, 1987-91, Chem. Revs., Langmuir, Surface Sci., Applications of Surface Sci., Accounts Chem. Rsch.; assoc. editor Langmuir, 1991-98; contbr. revs. and articles to profl. jours.; inventor desorption spectrometer, 1981. Sherman Fairchild Disting. scholar Calif. Inst. Tech., 1977-78; recipient Silver medal Dept. Commerce-Nat. Bur. Stds., 1973, Stratton award, 1981, Gold medal Dept. Commerce Nat. Bur. Stds., 1981, Pres.'s Disting. Rsch. award U. Pitts., 1989, Proctor & Gamble award, 1989, Alexander von Humboldt Sr. Rsch. award, 1994, Linnett lectr. Cambridge U., 2000, named Among 100 Most Highly Cited Chemists in World 1984-Present; fellow Sidney Sussex Coll., 2000. Fellow Am. Phys. Soc. (bd. dirs. divsn. chem. physics 1991—, chmn. divsn. chem. physics 1989), Am. Vacuum Soc. (chmn. surface sci. divsn. 1973, 92, trustee 1975, bd. dirs. 1982-85, M.W. Welch award 1994, fellow 1994); mem. NAS, Am. Chem. Soc. (chmn. divsn. colloid and surface chemistry, Langmuir lectr. 1979, Kendall award in colloid of surface chemistry 1986, Morley prize Cleve. chpt. 1990, Peter Debye lectr. Cornell U. 1993, Pitts. award 1998, A.W. Adamson award 1999), Pitts.-Cleve. Catalysis Soc. (award 1996, G.N. Lewis award 2002). Office: U Pitts Surface Sci Ctr Dept Chemistry Pittsburgh PA 15260

YATES, KEITH LAMAR, retired insurance company executive; b. Bozeman, Mont., Oct. 29, 1927; s. Thomas Bryan and Altha (Norris) Y.; m. Dolores Hensel, Aug. 30, 1948; children: Thomas A., Molly Yates McIntosh, Richard A., Nancy Yates Sands, Penny Dannielle Yates, Pamela Yates Beeler. BA, Eastern Wash. U., 1953. Salesman Ancient Order United Workmen, Spokane, Wash., 1952-53, sales mgr., 1953-56, corp. sec., 1956-73, Neighbors of Woodcraft, Portland, Oreg., 1973-89, pres., 1989-92; ret., 1992. Author: Life of Willie Willey, 1966, The Fogarty Years, 1972, History of The Woodcraft Home, 1975, An Enduring Heritage, 1992; tuba player Beaverton Cmty. Band, 1987—, One More Time Around Again Marching Band, 1987—, Rose City Banjoliers, 1993—. Pres. Wash. State Christian Mens Fellowship, Seattle, 1965-67; pres. Met. Area Assn. Christian Chs., 1981-83; mem. regional bd. Christian Chs. Oreg., 1990-94. Command sgt.-maj., ret., 1987; served with USN, USAF, USANG, 1946-87. Mem. Wash. State Frat. Cong., (cert. Commendation 1969, sec. 1957-68, pres., mem. exec. bd., chmn. conv. program advt. com. 1960-73), Oreg. State Frat. Cong. (Outstanding Frat. 1975-76, Spl. Appreciation award 1984, Frat. Family of Yr. 1986, 98, sec. 1975-87, pres., mem. exec. bd. 1974—), Nat. Fraternal Congress Am. (conv. arrangement com. 1964, 90, publicity com. 1964, 65, 68, 90, credentials com. 1970, 77, 78, pres. press & pub. rels. sec. 1971-72, pub. rels. com. 1971-73, chmn. 1972, co-chmn. press and pub. rels. frat. seminar 1972, frat. monitor com. 1974-75, mem. com. 1975-76, family life com. 1978-80, constitution com. 1980, pres. state frat. congs. sec. 1981-82, historian 1987—), Washington County's Disting. Patriot, Portland Ins. Acctg. and Statis. Soc. Assn. Records Mgrs. and Adminstrs. (Oreg. chpt.), Portland C. of C., Wash. Ins. Coun., Wash. Claims Assn., Seattle Underwriting Assn. Home: 29860 SW Buckhaven Rd Hillsboro OR 97123-8821 E-mail: kayndee@email.msn.com.

YATES, LEIGHTON DELEVAN, JR. lawyer; b. Atlanta, Sept. 4, 1946; s. Leighton Delevan and Stella Louise (Hill) Y.; m. Phyllis Jeanne Hummer, Dec. 22, 1968; children: Leighton Delevan III, Laurence Jeanne. BA, Hampden-Sydney Coll., Va., 1968; JD with high honors, U. Fla., 1973. Bar: Fla. 1974, U.S. Dist. Ct. (middle dist.) Fla. 1975. Assoc. Maguire, Voorhis & Wells, P.A., Orlando, Fla., 1974-77, shareholder, 1978-98, dept. chmn., 1985-90; ptnr. Holland & Knight LLP, 1998—. Bd. dirs. Hubbard Constrn. Co., Winter Park, Fla., 1985—, Blythe Constrn., Inc., Charlotte, NC, 1999—; adminstrv. dir. SunTrust Bank, Orlando, Fla., 1990—. Exec. editor U. Fla. Law Rev., 1973. Mem. Fla. Bd. Bar Examiners, 1992-97, vice chmn., 1995-96, chmn. 1996-97, 2002—; chmn. Ctrl. Fla. Blood Bank, 1995—, vice chmn., 1980-95; chmn. 2002—; chmn. Ctrl. Fla. Blood Bank, 1995—, vice chmn., 1980-95; chmn. Fla. Bar Assn., Orange County Bar Assn., Univ. Club of Orlando, Country Club of Orlando, Order of the Coif, Omicron Delta Kappa, Phi Kappa Phi. Republican. Presbyterian. Avocations: scuba diving, cycling, music, reading. Home: 3218 S Osceola Ave Orlando FL 32806-6251 Office: Holland & Knight LLP 200 S Orange Ave Ste 2600 Orlando FL 32801-3453 Personal E-mail: lyates@cfl.rr.com. Business E-Mail: lyates@hklaw.com.

YATES, LINDA SNOW, financial services marketing executive, real estate; b. St. Louis, July 20, 1938; d. Robert Anthony Jerrue and June Alberta (Crowder) Armstrong; m. Charles Russell Snow, Nov. 26, 1958 (div. 1979); children: Cathryn Louise, Christopher Armstrong, Heather Highstone, Sean Webster; m. Alan Porter Yates, July 22, 1983. BBA, Auburn U., 1973, MEd, 1975, EdD, 1998. Cert. profl. sec. Div. head placement div. Solutions Group, Atlanta, 1981-83; employment coord. Fulton Fed. Savs., 1983-84; owner, recruiter Data One, Inc., 1984-85; ops. mgr. Talent Tree Temporaries, 1985-87; legal asst., sec. Rice & Keene, 1987-90; legal word processing asst. Kilpatrick & Cody, 1990-94; pres., owner Power Comm., Cashiers, N.C., 1994-98; regional coord. S.E. region, regional mktg. rep. WorldConnect Comms., Tulsa; dir. mktg. electronic collection divsn. Am. Fin. and Credit Svcs., Inc.; area v.p., loan agent Enterprise Lenders, LLC; bd. dirs., corp. sec. The Hilltop Assocs. Inc., 1999—; real estate sales Apex Realty, Inc. Adj. instr. DeKalb Coll., Atlanta, 1980-84, Mercer U., Atlanta, 1981-82; instr. bus. So. Union State Jr. Coll., Valley, Ala., 1974-75; legal sec. Swift, Currie, McGhee & Hiers, Atlanta, 1979-80, Samford, Torbert, Denson & Horsley, Opelika, Ala., 1969-71; dir. acad. planning, chmn. edn. divsn., mem. part-time faculty in ednl. adminstrn. CEU Grad. Coll., Nuevo Leon, Mex. Columnist Neon News Flash, 1995. Mem. Paralegal Assn. Beaufort County (charter mem., sec. 1993-94), Women Bus. Owners, Nat. Assn. Pers. Cons., Internat. Soc. Poets (Disting. mem., Internat. Poet of Merit 1996, Internat. Poetry Hall of Fame 1996), Cashiers Writers Group, Phi Delta Kappa, Alpha Xi Delta. Republican. Episcopalian. Avocations: golf, writing, international travel. Office: 1 Wade Hampton Dr Beaufort SC 29902-1912

YATES, MARYPAUL, textile company executive; d. Paul and Peggy Adelle (Bryan) Y.; m. Benjamin H. Weisgal, June 5, 1983; children: Bryan Asher Weisgal, Leah Yates Weisgal. Student, U. Ga., 1973-75; BFA magna cum laude, Syracuse U., 1977; AAS, Fashion Inst. Tech., N.Y.C., 1979. Designer, studio mgr. Jeffrey Aronoff Inc., N.Y.C., 1978-81; stylist Gerli & Co., 1982-83; dir. design Maharam, Hauppauge, N.Y., 1983-87; prin. Yates Weisgal Inc., N.Y.C., 1987—, Maverick Group, N.Y.C., 1994—. Adj. instr. CUNY-Hunter Coll., 1978-82, Fashion Inst. Tech. SUNY, N.Y.C., 1985, Parsons Sch. Design, N.Y.C., 1988-93; guest speaker various groups, lectr., condr. workshops in field, 1980—. Author: Textiles, A Handbook for Designers, 1986, revised, 1995, Fabrics, A Guide for Interior Designers and Architects, 2001; group exhibits include The Galleries, Fashion Inst. Tech., 1984, R.I. Sch. Design, 1985. Mem. Textile Mus., Washington; mem. industry adv. coun. Fashion Inst. Tech., 1984—; bd. dirs. CityArts, 1998-2000. Designer products awarded Coty award Fashion Critics Circle, 1980, Roscoe award Resource Coun., 1982, Product award Inst. Bus. Designers, 1986; grantee Ford Found., 1976. Mem. ASTM, Assn. for Contract Textiles (industry standards com. 1986-88, edn. com. 2000—, sustainability com. 2001—), Color Assn. U.S. (interior forecasting com. 1988—), Color Mktg. Group (color projections com. 1983—), Textile Study Group N.Y., Am. Craft Coun., Surface Design Assn. Office: 185 E 85th St Apt 20F New York NY 10028-2149 E-mail: mpy@maverickgroup.net.

YATES, MICHAEL FRANCIS, management consultant; b. N.Y.C., Feb. 9, 1946; s. John Berchmans and Jane Ann (Gretz) Y.; m. Christine Mary Dallos, Jan. 14, 1967; children: Erik Michael, Alison. BA, U. Buffalo, 1968. Mgmt. trainee, dept. mgr. Sears, Roebuck & Co., Buffalo, 1968-69; cons. Rothman & D'Alessandro, Inc., N.Y.C., 1969-71; sr. cons. Martin & Segal & Co., Inc., 1971-75, A.S. Hansen, Inc., N.Y.C., 1975-78; exec. v.p. A.M. D'Alessandro & Co., Inc., North Haledon, N.J., 1978-81; mng. dir. Alexander & Alexander Cons. Group, Inc., Lyndhurst, 1981-97; pres. Michael F. Yates & Co., Inc., Hampton, 1997—. Bd dirs. Am. Intercon, Inc. Host of Your Human Resources Resource, WALE AM, 2001—. Pres. Lincoln Sch. PTA, 1975-77, Bethlehem Twp. Rep. Club, mem. Hunterdon County com.; chmn. Bethlehem Twp. Econ. and Indsl. Devel. Bd., 1980-83; active Rep. Nat. Com. Mem. Am. Mgmt. Assn., Am. Compensation Assn., Soc. Human Resource Mgmt., Adminstrv. Mgmt. Soc., Aircraft Owners and Pilots Assn. Home: 519 Lannon Ln Glen Gardner NJ 08826-3817 Office: 2 Manor Dr Hampton NJ 08827-5409

YATES, NORRIS WILLIAM, JR. lawyer; b. Alamo Heights, Tex., July 6, 1926; s. Norris William and Maggie Barkley (Curry) Y.; m. Mary Hutchings Spencer, Dec. 30, 1947 (div. Aug. 1949); 1 child, William Spencer; m. Jimmie Carolyn Cook, Sept. 17, 1955; children: Victoria Carolyn Marullo (dec.), Rebecca Elizabeth Yates Bird. BA in Econs., Tex. A&M U., 1950; JD, U. Tex., 1957. Bar: U.S. Ct. of Military Appeals, 1963, U.S. Supreme Ct., 1964, Tex., 1957. Asst. to mgr. rates and tariffs Slick Airways, Inc., San Antonio, 1950; assoc. Beckmann, Stanard, Wood, Barrow & Vance, 1957-60; pvt. practice, 1960-67, 83—; asst. criminal dist. atty., chief civil sect. Bexar County Dist. Atty.'s Office, 1967-82. Mcpl. ct. judge City of San Antonio, 1966-67. Editor The Subpoena, 1958-59. Exec. com. Bexar County Dem. Party, San Antonio. Cpl. U.S. Army, Airborne Infantry, 1944-46, ETO; 1st lt. USAF, 1951-55, B-29 Bomber Pilot, Korea, JAG lt. col. USAFR, ret. 1978. Decorated Bronze Star medal, combat infantry badge, glider badge, pilot's wings, three battle stars; Eagle Scout. Mem. Daedalians, USAF Pilot Class 52-George Assn. (recording sec.), 307th Bomb Group/Wing Inc. (past pres.), Toastmasters (past pres., Disting. Dist. Gov. 1969-70, Disting. Toastmaster 1984, Presdl. citation 1992), Masons (past master, 32 degree), San Antonio A&M Club (dir.), San Antonio Ret. Officers Assn. (sec.), Neighborhood Assn. (dir.), Ft. Sam Houston Officers Club (mem. coun.). Democrat. Presbyterian. Avocations: travel, photography. Home: 2118 Kenilworth Blvd San Antonio TX 78209-2329

YATES, PATRICIA ENGLAND, human resources company executive; b. Sparta, Tenn., Sept. 18, 1958; d. Edsel and Gladys Mary (Garland) England; m. Dennis Eugene Yates, Nov. 30, 1990. BS in Home Econs., Tenn. Tech. U., 1982. Purchasing sec. Porelon, Inc., Cookeville, Tenn., 1982-87; buyer purchasing dept. Tenn. Tech. U., 1987-88; dir. pers. J & S Constrn. Co., Inc., 1988-93; placement coord. Holland Employment, 1993-95; svc. specialist Hamilton-Ryker Co., Shelbyville, Tenn., 1995-97; human resource mgr. Monterey Mills, Inc., Cowan, 1998-1999; agt. Randstad N.Am., Lewisburg, 2000—01. Dir. projects Nat. and Internat. Issues Rsch., Sparta, Tenn., 1982—. Mem. Internat. Assn. Adminstrv. Profls. (chpt. v.p. 2001, chpt. pres. 1998), Bus. and Profl. Women's Orgn. (treas. 1990, 2d v.p. 1992), Internat. Platform Assn., Marshall County C. of C., Kiwanis (chpt. pres. 2001). Avocations: reading, theater, drama, landscaping.

YATES, ROBERT, professional sports team executive; b. Apr. 19, 1943; m. Carolyn Yates; children: Doug, Amy. Team owner, founder Robert Yates Racing, Mooresville, NC, 1988—; air gauge dept. mgr. Holman-Moody Racing, Charlotte, 1968—71; overseer engine devel. Jr. Johnson, 1971; chief engine builder DiGard Racing, 1976—86; team mgr. Rainer/Lundy, 1986—88. Office: Robert Yates Racing 292 Rolling Hill Rd Mooresville NC 28117-6843

YATES, ROBERT DOYLE, anatomy educator; b. Birmingham, Ala., Feb. 28, 1931; s. James William Jr. and Mildred (Doyle) Y.; m. Jane Congleton, 1955; children: Robert Lee, Pamela C. BS, U. Ala., 1954, MS, 1956, PhD, 1959; Dr honoris causa (hon.) , Romania. Postdoctoral fellow U. Ala., Birmingham, 1959-60; with U. Tex., Galveston, 1961-72; prof. anatomy Tulane U. Med. Sch., New Orleans, 1972—, chmn. dept. structural and cellular biology, 1972—. Vis. investigator Harvard U. Med. Sch., Boston, 1962-63, Yale U. Med. Sch., New Haven, 1965-67. Mem. editl. bd. Am. Jour. Anatomy, Anat. Record; contbr. articles to profl. jours. and chpts. to books. Vestryman Trinity Episc. Ch., Galveston, 1965-68; vestryman, jr. warden Trinity Episc. Ch., New Orleans, 1985-89, sr. warden, 1989-92. With U.S. Army, 1960-61. Recipient numerous awrds NIH, 1965-72, Rsch. Career Devel. award, Golden Apple Tchg. award AMA Student Assn., 1971. Fellow: Royal Soc. Medicine (life); mem.: Pan Am. Assn. Anatomy (pres. 1999—2002), Am. Soc. Cell Biology, Pan Am. Congress of Anatomy (pres. 2000), Assn. Anatomy Cell Biology and Neurobiology Chairpersons (sec.-treas. 1976—98), Internat. Fedn. Assn. Anatomists (treas. 1989—99), Am. Assn. Anatomists (chmn. nominating com. 1980, sec.-treas. 1988—96, pres. 1999—2001), Costa Rican Assn. Anatomists (hon.), Anat. Soc. South Africa (hon.), Anat. Soc. West Africa (hon.), Romanian Soc. Anatomy (hon.), Italian Soc. Anatomy (hon.). Republican. Avocations: tennis, stained glass, beveled glass, hunting. Office: Tulane U Sch of Medicine 1430 Tulane Ave New Orleans LA 70112-2699

YATES, ROBIN CORRIENE, freelance writer; b. Detroit, Jan. 28, 1953; d. Roy C. and Mary L. Y. AA, Ind. U., 1982, BA in Liberal Arts, 1983. List rschr. Indpls. Bus. Jour., 1983-85; donor prospect rsch. organizer Butler U., Indpls., 1985-86; freelance writer, 1986—. Mem. Ind. Tchrs. of Writing, Soc. Profl. Journalists, Writer's Ctr. of Ind. Avocations: antiquing, oil painting, needlepoint. Home: 8120 Glenwillow Ln # U103 Indianapolis IN 46278-2257 E-mail: robinyat@prodigy.net.

YATES, RONALD EUGENE, newspaper editor, journalist, educator; b. Kansas City, Mo., Feb. 19, 1941; s. Guy Raymond and Willadene (Peterson) Y.; m. Ingeborg Zoelss, May 7, 1966; children: Jennifer Christina, Nicole Brigitte. BS (Gannett Newspapers scholar 1968-69, Angelo C. Scott Meml. scholar 1969), U. Kans., 1969. Reporter Kansas City (Kans.) Star, 1968; editor Univ. Daily Kansan, 1969; reporter, asst. city editor, fgn. corr. Chgo. Tribune, Chgo. and Tokyo, 1969-76, Asia and Latin Am. corr., 1976-82, met. editor, 1983—, nat. editor, 1984—, chief Asia corr., 1985—, sr. writer, 1992—; prof., chmn. dept. journalism U. Ill., Champaign, 1997—. Lectr. Calif. State U., Fullerton. Contbr. articles to mags. Served with U.S. Army Intelligence, 1962-66. Recipient award for excellence in staff leadership William Allen White Sch. Journalism, 1968, Edward Scott Beck award for best fgn. reporting, 1975, 87, 89, Inter-Am. Press Assn. award for reporting on Latin Am., 1979, Peter Lisagor award for bus. and fin. reporting, 1993; named Outstanding Sr. U. Kans., 1969 Mem. Fgn. Corrs. Club of Japan (v.p. 1989—), Los Angeles Press, Sigma Delta Chi. Lutheran. Office: U Ill 810 S Wright St Champaign IL 61820

YATES, STEVEN BRADLEY, publisher; b. Springfield, Mo., June 17, 1968; s. Carl Eugene and Joy Lynn (Evertz) Y.; m. Tamara Sue Gebhart, Nov. 16, 1991. BA in English Lit., Southwest Mo. State U., 1990; MFA in Writing, U. Ark., 1994. Sportswriter Springfield News Leader, 1984-90; grad. asst. dept. English U. Ark., Fayetteville, 1990-94, asst. to dir. of composition, 1991-94; constrn. inspector, surveyor State of Ark. Dept. Hwys. and Transp., Springdale, summers 1991-94; asst. mktg. mgr. U. Ark. Press, Fayetteville, 1994-98, U. Press of Miss., Jackson, 1998—. Contbr. articles, novel excerpts and short stories to mags. and revs. Sec. planning commn. City of Elkins, Ark., 1996-98. Fellow Miss. Arts Commn./NEA, 2000, Ark. Arts Coun., 1999, Lily Peter Found., 1990-91; scholar Mildred Henderson Ewing Found., 1989-90, Southeast Outdoor Press Assn., 1993-94; recipient Nat. Fiction Contest prize Analecta, 1992. Mem. Am. Assn. Univ. Presses (mktg. com. 2001—). Office: U Press of Miss 3825 Ridgewood Cir Jackson MS 39211

YATES, WILLIAM JOHN, business owner, counselor; b. Wurtzburg, Fed. Republic of Germany, Mar. 15, 1959; came to U.S., 1959; s. Jack John and Georgia Ann (McFeron) Y.; m. Jacqueline Renee Wheeler, July 20, 1982 (div. July 1987). Grad., high sch., Wharton, Tex., 1977; PhD Counseling, PhD Theocentric Psy., 1995. Ordained minister, Calif. Autobody shop mgr. Don Elliot Chevrolet, Wharton, 1978-79; autobody mechanic/painter Cochran Motor Co., 1979-80; truck driver The Orlgmud Co., Needville, Tex., 1980-81; dewatering plant operator Valero Energy Corp., Boling, 1981-83; auto parts counterperson Dependable Motor Parts, Wharton, 1983-84; automotive restoration specialist Bud's Quality Shop, 1984-85; power plant mechanic, asst. operator, asst. boiler fireman Imperial Sugar Co., Sugarland, Tex., 1985-87; autobody repairman, painter Gary's Body Shop, Texarkana, 1987-88; autobody repairman Helfman Ford, Houston, 1988-89, Jack Roach Ford, Houston, 1989; automotive sales rep. Mac Haik Ford, 1990, Luke Johnson Ford, Houston, 1991; bus. owner Yates and Assocs., Wharton, 1991—. Mem. Hazelden Grass Roots Polit. Network, Tex., 1994; cmty. liaison counselor Area Counties Coun. on Alcoholism and Drug Abuse, Wharton, 1993-95. With USAF and Tex. Air N.G., 1977-83; sys. integrator Info. Technology Tech. VAR/VAD. Mem. N.G. Assn. Tex., Nat. Assn. of the Self-Employed Bus. Owner. Republican. Avocations: automobile drag racing, volleyball, snowskiing, listening to music, motorcycle roadracing. Office: Apt 204 6803 N Navarro St Victoria TX 77904-1535

YATES, WILLIAM TENNYSON, II, educational consultant, management consultant; b. Tuskeegee, Ala., Mar. 26, 1944; s. William Tennyson Yates, Sr. and Dorothea Jordan Yates; m. Sue Wilson, Aug. 4, 1984. BS, Temple U., 1968; MS, Troy State U., 1975; PhD, St. Louis U., 1987. Commd. lt. USAF, 1969, advanced through grades to lt. col., ret., 1989; program dir., grant writer Woodrow Wilson Nat. Fellowship Found., Princeton, NJ, 1990—92; asst. v.p. Temple U., Phila., 1993—96; founding exec. dir. Moore Multi-Cultural Ctr., Cocoa, Fla., 1996—99; mgmt. cons. Phoenix Orgn., Indialantic , 1999—2001; regional v.p. Hire Golden, Inc., Valley Forge, Pa., 2001—. Mem. Civilian/Mil. Affairs Com., Melbourne, Fla., 1997—2002; v.p. Hosts of Brevard, Inc., Melbourne, 1999, pres., 2000—. Decorated Def. Meritorious Svc. medal, Air Force Meritorious Svc. medals, Air Force Commendetion Medal. Republican. Avocations: music, martial arts, computers, writing, photography.

YATES-CARTER, LYNNE, lawyer; b. Oakland, Calif., June 1, 1950; d. Charles and Bernice (Rose) Yates; m. William Matthew Carter, July 9, 1972; 1 child, Alexander. BA in English, U. Santa Clara, 1972, JD, 1976. Bar: Calif. 1976, U.S. Dist. Ct. (no. dist.) Calif. Pvt. practice, San Jose, 1976—. Judge pro tempore family law dept. Santa Clara County Superior Ct., 1979—, spl. master, 1988—, arbitrator in family matters, 1988—; adj. prof. family law Santa Clara U., 1989-90, 92; lectr. in field. Contbr. articles to profl. jours.; cons./contbr.: California Family Law Service, 1986. Active various polit. and civic orgns. Recipient Resolution of Commendation Santa Clara County Bd. Suprs., 1986. Mem. ABA, Santa Clara County Bar Assn. (conf. of dels. 1984—, sec. 1986, program com. chmn. 1991, Justice Bryl R. Salsman award for community svc. 1986, Cert. of Appreciation 1983, 86, family law exec. com.), Am. Acad. Matrimonial Lawyers (past pres. No. Calif. chpt.), Calif. State Bar Assn. (former chair family law sect.), Calif. Women Lawyers. Democrat. Avocations: cooking, reading, gardening. Office: 111 W Saint John St Ste 300 San Jose CA 95113-1104

YATSENKO, NIKOLAI AFANASYEVICH, physics researcher, educator; b. Russia, Jan. 1, 1948; came to the U.S., 1996; s. Afanasii and Vera (Bogacheva) Y.; m. Lyudmila Yegorovna Fedyanina, May 6, 1972; 1 child, Marina. MS in Physics, Moscow Inst. Physics & Tech., 1973, PhD in Physics and Math., 1978; DSc in Physics and Math., Russian Acad. Scis., Moscow, 1992. Rschr. Zhukovsky Mil. Air Force Acad., Moscow, 1973-75; rschr., sr. rschr. Inst. for Problems in Mechanics, Russian Acad. Scis., 1978-95, head rschr., 1995—. Assoc. prof. physics Russian Inst. Textile and Light Industry, Moscow, 1980-93, full prof. physics, 1993-2000; project scientist Optical Engring., Inc., Santa Rosa, Calif., 1996-98, Macken Instruments, Inc., Santa Rosa, Calif., 1998—; referee Soviet Union State Com. for Inventions and Discoveries, Moscow, 1986-91; mem. sci. coun. Inst. for Problems in Mechanics, Moscow, 1992—; mem. spl. PhD coun. Moscow Inst. Physics and Tech., 1995—. Co-author: Thermal Plasma Diagnostics, 1994, Radio-Frequency Capacitive Discharges, 1995, Gas Lasers-Recent Developments and Future Prospects, 1996; mem. editl. bd. Jour. Edn. Experiment in U., 1997—; referee Jour. Physics D: Applied Physics, 1998—, Measurement Sci. and Tech., 2000—; contbr. articles to jours. on plasma physics and gas lasers. Decorated Medal of Hon. 850th Ann. Moscow, 1997; recipient 6 awards Inst. Problems in Mechanics, Russian Acad. Scis., 1984-90, Outstanding Achievement medal Internat. Biog. Ctr., Cambridge, Eng., 1999, 20th Century Achievement award Am. Biog. Inst., 1999; grantee Ministry of Edn., Moscow, 1992, 94, 95, 97, Internat. Sci. Found., Russia, 1993, 94, Joint Russian and Internat. Sci. Found., 1995. Fellow Internat. Biog. Assn., Am. Biog. Inst. (life), Inst. Physics (London); mem. IEEE (sr.), AAAS, Am. Phys. Soc., European Phys. Soc., Am. Vacuum Soc., Am. Assn. Physics Tchrs., Nat. Geog. Soc., Sigma Xi. Achievements include experimental discoveries relating to radio-frequency capacitive discharges at moderate pressures; invention and demonstration of a slab CO_2 laser; 10 patents including laser apparatus utilizing a magnetically enhanced electrical discharge with transverse AC stabilization; Russian patent for gas-flow CO_2 laser. Avocations: books, travel. Office: Macken Instruments Inc 3186 Coffey Ln Santa Rosa CA 95403-2555 E-mail: nyatsenko@ieee.org.

YATVIN, JOANNE INA, education educator; b. Newark, Apr. 17, 1931; d. John and Mary Edna (Cohen) Goldberg; m. Milton Brian Yatvin, June 8, 1952; children: Alan, Bruce, Lillian, Richard. Ba, Douglass Coll., 1952; MA, Rutgers U., 1962; PhD, U. Wis., 1974. Cert. sch. adminstr. Tchr. Hamburg (N.J.) Pub. Schs., 1952-53, New Brunswick (N.J.) Pub. Schs., 1953-55, Mayaguez (P.R.) Schs., 1958-59, Milltown (N.J.) Pub. Schs., 1959-62, East Brunswick (N.J.) Pub. Schs., 1962-63; tchr., prin. Madison (Wis.) Met. Sch. Dist., 1963-88; supt. Cottrell Sch. Dist., Boring, Oreg., 1988-97, prin., 1997-2000; mem. faculty Portland State U., 2000—. Adv. bd. mem. Big Books Mag., 1990-91; cons. various sch. dists.; apptd. to nat. reading panel Nat. Inst. of Child Health and Devel., 1998-2000. Author: Learning Language Through Communication, 1986, (monograph) A Whole Language Program for a Whole School, 1991, (monograph) Beginning a School Literacy Improvement Project: Some Words of Advice, Kdg Teachers Guide, Pegasus Reading Program, Kendall Hunt, 2000; contbr. chpts. in books and articles to profl. jours. Named Elem. Prin. of Yr., Wis. Dept. Edn., 1985, Wis. State Reading Assn., 1985; recipient Excellence in Print award, Washington Edpress, 1987, Disting. Elem. Edn. Alumni award, U. Wis., 1988, Kenneth S. Goodman In Def. of Good Tchg. award, Dept. Lang. and Learning, U. Ariz. Mem.: ASCD, Oreg. Coun. Tchrs. English, Oreg. Reading Assn., Nat. Coun. Tchrs. English (chair com. on ctrs. excellence 1986—89, mem. commn. on curriculum 1999—2002), Internat. Reading Assn., Phi Delta Kappa. Home: 5226 SW Northwood Ave Portland OR 97201-2832 Office: Grad Sch Edn Portland State U PO Box 751 Portland OR 97207-0751

YAU, EDWARD TINTAI, toxicologist, pharmacologist; b. Canton, China, Dec. 29, 1944; came to U.S., 1967; s. Wing S. and Fong K. (Wong) Y.; m. Assumpta Koo, July 3, 1979; 1 child, Jonathan C. BS in Biology, Bapt. Coll., Hong Kong, 1967; PhD in Pharmacology, U. Miss., 1974. Diplomate Am. Bd. Toxicology. Postdoctoral fellow, then asst. prof. Purdue U., West Lafayette, Ind., 1974-77; toxicology supr. Wyeth Labs., Great Valley, Pa., 1977-79; sr. toxicologist CIBA-GEIGY Corp., Summit, N.J., 1979-82, mgr., 1982-86, asst. dir., 1986-88, dir., 1988-92, exec. dir., 1993-96; exec. dir. of toxicology and pathology Novartis Pharm. U.S., 1997-98; dir. toxicology Roberts Pharm. Corp., Eatontown, N.J., 1998-99, Forest Labs., N.Y.C., 1999-2000, Vertex Pharm. Inc., Cambridge, Mass., 2000—. Adj. prof. U. Miss., Oxford, 1989-92, 95—. Contbr. articles to sci. pubis. Recipient NSF award, 1970. Mem. Am. Chem. Soc., Am. Coll. Toxicology, Soc. Toxicology, Teratology Soc., Sigma Xi. Republican. Baptist. Home: 67 Grant Ave Clifton NJ 07011-3522

YAU, KEVIN KAM-CHING, astronomer; b. Hong Kong, July 11, 1959; came to U.S., 1992; s. Ching-Fat and Ping-Kiu (Leung) Y.; m. Florence Wai-Chung Liu, Aug. 22, 1987; children: Stephanie, Cherrymay. BS in Physics, U. Liverpool, Eng., 1982; MS in Astrophysics, U. Durham, Eng., 1984, PhD in Astronomy, 1988. Sr. rsch. asst. U. Durham, 1987-92; postdoctoral fellow Jet Propulsion Lab., Pasadena, Calif., 1992-94, mem. tech. staff, 1994—. Co-author: Halley's Comet in History, 1985; contbr. articles to profl. jours. Rsch. scholar U. Durham, 1984-87; awardee Victor Nadarov Fund, Royal Astron. Soc., 1983. Fellow Royal Astron. Soc.; mem. Internat. Astron. Union, Am. Astron. Soc. Achievements include expert status on the long-term motion of cometary orbits; successfully determining the past orbit of comet Halley and Swift-Tuttle and identified their returns from hist. records back to 200 B.C.; co-discoverer of the 164 BC return of Halley's comet from Babylonian clay tablets; world authority on the application of early astronomical observations to solve contemporary problems in astronomy. Office: Jet Propulsion Lab MS 230-101 4800 Oak Grove Dr Pasadena CA 91109-8001

YAU, STEPHEN SIK-SANG, computer science and engineering educator, computer scientist, researcher; b. Wusei, Kiangsu, China, Aug. 6, 1935; came to U.S., 1958, naturalized, 1968; s. Pen-Chi and Wen-Chum (Shum) Y.; m. Vickie Liu, June 14, 1964; children: Andrew, Philip. BS in Elec. Engring, Nat. Taiwan U., China, 1958; MS in Elec. Engring, U. Ill., Urbana, 1959, PhD, 1961. Asst. prof. elec. engring. Northwestern U., Evanston, Ill., 1961-64, assoc. prof., 1964-68, prof., 1968-88, prof. computer scis., 1970-88, Walter P. Murphy prof. Elec. Engring. and Computer Sci., 1986-88, also chmn. dept. computer scis., 1972-77, chmn. dept. elec. engring. and computer sci., 1977-88; prof. computer and info. sci., chmn. dept. U. Fla., Gainesville, 1988-94; prof. computer sci. and engr. Ariz. State U., 1994—, chmn. dept. computer sci. and engring., 1994—2001. Conf. chmn. IEEE Computer Conf., Chgo., 1967; gen. chmn. Nat. Computer Conf., Chgo., 1974, First Internat. Computer Software and Applications Conf., Chgo., 1977; Trustee Na. Electronics Conf., Inc., 1965-68; chmn. organizing com. 11th World Computer Congress, Internat. Fedn. Info. Processing, San Francisco, 1989; gen. co-chmn. Internat. Symposium on Autonomous Decentralized Systems, Japan, 1993, gen. chmn., Phoenix, 1995; conf. co-chair 24 Annual Internat. Computer Software and Applications Conf., Taipei, 2000. Editor-in-chief Computer mag., 1981-84; assoc. editor Jour. Info. Scis., 1983-99; editor IEEE Trans. on Software Engring., 1988-91; contbr. numerous articles on software engring., distributed and parallel processing systems, computer sci., elec. engring. and related fields to profl. publs.; patentee in field. Recipient Louis E. Levy medal Franklin Inst., 1963, Golden Plate award Am. Acad. of Achievement, 1964, The Silver Core award Internat. Fedn. Info. Processing, 1989, Spl. award, 1989. Fellow IEEE (mem. governing bd. Computer Soc. 1967-76, pres. 1974-75, dir. Inst. 1976-77, chmn. awards com., 1996-97; Richard E. Merwin award Computer Soc. 1981, Centennial medal 1984, Extraordinary Achievement 1985, Outstanding Contbn. award Computer Sci. Soc. 1985), AAAS, Franklin Inst.; mem. Assn. for Computing Machinery, Am. Fedn. Info.-Processing Socs. (mem. exec. com. 1974-76, 79-82, dir. 1972-82, chmn. awards com. 1979-82, v.p. 1982-84, pres. 1984-86; chmn. Nat. Computer Conf. Bd. 1982-83), Am. Soc. Engring. Edn., Sigma Xi, Tau Beta Pi, Eta Kappa Nu, Pi Mu Epsilon. Office: Ariz State U PO Box 875406 Tempe AZ 85287-5406

YAVARKOVSKY, JEROME HAROLD, library director; b. N.Y.C., May 12, 1940; B Mech. Engring., Rensselaer Poly. Inst., 1960; MS in Mgmt., MIT, 1962; M Libr. Sci., Columbia U., 1971. Lic. pub. libr. Adminstrv. specialist Bell Labs., Murray Hill, N.J., 1963-64; systems analyst J.C. Penney Co., N.Y.C., 1965-67; tech. cons. Auerbach Assocs., 1967-68; head programming Columbia U., 1969-71, chief systems, 1971-72, asst. univ. libr., 1972-83; dean librs. Adelphi U., Garden City, N.Y., 1983-85; dir. N.Y. State Libr., Albany, 1985-95; univ. libr. Boston Coll., Chestnut Hill, 1995—. Office: Thomas P O'Neill Libr Boston Coll Chestnut Hill MA 02467

YAVITZ, BORIS, business educator, corporate director; b. Tbilisi, USSR, June 4, 1923; came to U.S., 1946, naturalized, 1950; s. Simon and Miriam (Mindlin) Y.; m. Irene Bernhard, July 17, 1949; children— Jessica Ann, Judith, Emily. MA, Cambridge (Eng.) U., 1943; MS, Columbia U., 1948, PhD, 1964. Economic cons. Jewish Agy. for Palestine, N.Y.C., 1948-49; mgmt. cons. Werner Mgmt. Cons., Larchmont, N.Y., 1949-54; owner, mgr. Simbar Devel. Corp., N.Y.C., 1954-61; faculty Columbia U., 1964-94, prof. mgmt., 1964-94; dean Columbia U. (Grad. Sch. Bus.), 1975-82, Paul Garrett prof. pub. policy and bus. responsibility, 1982-94; dep. chmn., dir. Fed. Res. Bank N.Y., 1976-82; dean emeritus, Paul Garrett prof. emeritus Columbia U., 1994—; prin. Lear, Yavitz & Assocs. L.L.C., 1995—. Bd. dirs. J.C. Penney Co. Inc., Barnes Group Inc., Israel Discount Bank of N.Y., Crane Co., Ruder-Finn Inc., Medusa Corp.; trustee Am. Assembly, N.Y.C., 1975-82; vice chmn. The Inst. for the Future, 1984—; bd. govs. Media and Soc. Seminars, 1983-84; mem. nat. adv. coun. W. Averill Harriman Inst. Advanced Study of Soviet Union, 1983—; chmn. Nat. Assn. Corp. Dirs. Blue Ribbon Commn. on Corp. Governance. Author books; contbr. articles in field to profl. jours. Served to lt. British Royal Navy, 1943-46. Mem. ASME, Inst. Mgmt. Sci. Home and Office: Old Canoe Place Rd Hampton Bays NY 11946

YAVORSKY, JAMES ANTHONY, chemist, educator; b. Beaver Falls, Pa., Feb. 29, 1956; s. Paul John and Gene (Studdard) Yavorsky; m. Loretta Bryson, June 24, 1978; children: Cristin, James, Kaitlyn. BS in Chemistry, Wake Forest U., 1978; PhD in Chemistry, Clemson U., 1984. Devel. assoc. ICI Polyurethanes, West Deptford, NJ, 1984-99, Huntsman Polyurethanes, West Deptford, 1999—2001; adj. prof. Rowan U., 2002—; cons., 2002—. Hazmat annex dir. East Greenwich Twp. Emergency Mgmt., Clarksboro, NJ, 1990—. Bd. dirs. Selective Svc. Sys., Gloucester County, NJ; pres. Casa Dance Studio Parents Assn., Woodbury Heights, 1994—. Mem.: Am. Chem. Soc. Achievements include patents in field. E-mail: jayavorsky@yahoo.com.

YAVRU-SAKUK, BEDROS, dental educator; b. Istanbul, Turkey, Feb. 25, 1951; came to U.S., 1975; s. Arsavir and Adrine Rita Y-S.; m. Seta Azaduhi Sahinoglu, July 28, 1974; children: Alex, Nadine. Chirurgien dentiste de France, Paris U. Dentistry, 1975; DDS, NYU, 1977, postgrad. cert. prosthodontics, 1993, 96. Pvt. practice, Rego Park, Queens, N.Y., 1977—; clin. instr. divsn. restorative prosthodontic sci. NYU Coll. Dentistry, N.Y.C., 1988-91, group practice coord. restorative prosthodontic sci., 1991, clin. asst. prof. restorative and prosthodontic sci., 1993-98, clin. asst. prof. divsn. comprehensive care adminstrn., 1994—, clin. assoc. prof. divsn. comprehensive care adminstrn., 1997—. Chmn. bd. trustees Constantinople Armenian Relief Soc., N.Y.C., 1992; bd. dirs., dental adv. com. Karagheusian Comm. Co., N.Y.C., 1992; ch. del. St. Thomas Armenian Ch., Tenafly, N.J., 1993. Mem. ADA, Internat. Dental Fedn., Internat. Acad. Periodontology, Assn. of Dental Surgeons of France Avocations: tennis, fishing, biking, swimming. Office: Ste 1G 92-29 Queens Blvd Rego Park NY 11374

YAZAMI, RACHID, research scientist, consultant, editor; b. Fez, Morocco, Apr. 16, 1953; arrived in France, 1972; s. Abdelkader and Fatima (Attar) Y.; m. Michèle Dauriat, Oct. 3, 1992; 1 child, Jehane. Engring. Diploma in Electrochemistry, Technol. U. Grenoble, France, 1978, PhD in Electrochemistry, 1985. Assoc. rsch. dir. CNRS, Grenoble, 1985—, rsch. dir., 1998—; cons., 1992—. Invited scientist Kyoto U. and Shinshu U., Japan, 1988-90; sabbatical Calif. Inst. Tech., Jet Propulsion Lab., Pasadena, Calif., 2000—; mem. internat. adv. bd. Internat. Meetings on Lithium Batteries. Editor ITE-Battery Letters; inventor of carbon-lithium for lithium-ion batteries. Recipient Rsch. award, Hawaii Battery Conf., 2002. Mem. Electrochem. Soc. (v.p.), Internat. Battery Assn. (chmn. European office IBA-ITE, Rsch. award 1999), French Group Carbon Studies. Avocations: sports, tennis, skiing, soccer. Office: Caltech Mail Code 138-78 1200 E California Blvd Pasadena CA 91125 E-mail: ryazami@aol.com.

YBARRA, KATHRYN WATROUS, systems engineer; b. Middletown, Conn., Aug. 7, 1943; d. Claude Philip Jr. and C. Lyle ((Crook)) Watrous; m. Norman L. Adams (div.); children: Cynthia Anne Leonard, Suzette Mae Gross, Daniel Joseph Adams; m. Raul M. Ybarra, Dec. 11, 1976 (dec. June 16, 2001); stepchildren: Esther Ingram, Yolanda , Lisa. BA in Computer Sci., U. Tex., 1985. Scientific programmer Tracor, Inc., Austin, 1978-86; tech. staff engr. Honeywell, Inc. Comml. Avionics, Phoenix, 1986-2000; staff engr. L-3 Comm., Inc., 2000-01, ACSS, LLC, Phoenix, 2001—. Mem. Friends of Phoenix Libr., v.p. Juniper chpt., 1996-97, pres., 1998-99. Mem. RTCA (spl. com. # 147, Traffic Alert and Collision Avoidance Sys. II, chair requirements working group 1991—, leadership citation 1995, spl. com. 186, co-chair working group 4 1997-99, chair enhancement subgroup 1997-98, Cert. Achievement 1998), Nat. Soc. of DAR (registrar Camelback chpt. 1998-2002). Achievements include 5 patents for algorithms related to aircraft tracking systems for collision avoidance. Home: 17681 W Spencer Dr Surprise AZ 85374-3039

YBARROLA, STEVEN JAMES, anthropology educator, researcher; b. Stockton, CA, Feb. 6, 1955; s. James Martin Ybarrola, Leona Fern Ybarrola; m. Lorie Vivian Fletcher; children: Micah, Brianna. PhD, A.M., Brown University, Providence, RI, 1985—95; BA, Bethel College, St. Paul, MN, BA, 1983—85. Associate Professor Central College, Pella, IA, 1997—2002, Assistant Professor, 1994—96, Frank and Grace Moore Chair in Anthropology, 2001—02. Consultant Intel, Portland, OR, 1999—2000. Mem.: National Association for Ethnic Studies, Central States Anthropological Society, Society for the Anthropology of Europe, American Anthropological Association. Christian. Home: 1514 Edgewood Dr. Pella IA 50219 Office: Central College 812 University Pella IA 50219 Office Fax: (515) 628 5316. Personal E-mail: ybarrolas@central.edu. Business E-Mail: ybarrolas@central.edu.

YE, BIQING, biomedical engineer, researcher; b. Wenzhou, Zhejiang, China, Dec. 16, 1938; came to the U.S., 1987; d. Jing Ye and Suxin Li; m. Wenda Shen, Aug. 3, 1962 (div. Nov. 1995); children: Jiong, Han, Lu. BS, Peking U., Beijing, 1960, MS, 1962. Asst. Inst. Electronics, Chinese Acad. Sci., Beijing, 1962-64; asst. prof. Shanghai Inst. Optics & Fine Mechanics, Chinese Acad. Sci., 1964-85, assoc. prof., 1985-89; rsch. fellow Coll. Medicine, U. Fla., Gainesville, 1987-89, asst., 1989-90; assoc. scientist N.E. Deaconess Hosp., Harvard Med. Sch., Boston, 1990-94; scientist R&D Instrumentation Lab., Lexington, Mass., 1994—. Co-author: Pulse and CW Lasers, 1977, Lasers in Cardiovascular Medicine and Surgery, 1990; contbr. over 40 articles to profl. jours. Recipient Outstanding Achievement award in sci. and tech. Shanghai City Govt., 1982; grantee A. Ward Ford Meml. Inst., 1990-94. Mem. Am. Assn. for Clin. Chemistry, Optical Soc. China, Laser Soc. Shanghai. Achievements include patents for optical fiber coupler and power supply for laser flashlamp; applications of laser to medical areas; improvements of related laser devices; optical and spectroscopic studies in animal models. Office: Instrumentation Lab 526 Route 303 Orangeburg NY 10962-1309

YE, CANG, electrical engineer; b. Fuan City, China; came to U.S., 2001. s. Rongze Ye and Lanying Miao; m. Hong Kang, June 7, 1968; 1 child, Zixin. B in Engring., U. Sci. & Tech. China, Hefei, 1988, M in Engring., 1991; PhD, U. Hong Kong, 1999. Sr. rsch. engr. Lab. Intelligent Transp. Sys. Rsch. U. Hong Kong, 1998-99; rsch. fellow Nanyang Tech. U., Singapore, Singapore, 1999-2001, U. Mich., Ann Arbor, 2001—. Mem. IEEE. Office: Atl Bldg 1101 Beal Ave Ann Arbor MI 48109-2106

YE, NAN, engineer; b. Linan, Zhejiang, China, Dec. 23, 1959; d. Zhongjie Ye and Zhiying Ruan; m. Guiqiao Li, Mar. 12, 1984; 1 child, Brett Yichen. MS, Zhejiang U., Hangzhou, China, 1987; PhD, U. Md., 1994. Staff engr. DMC Corp., Houston, Aspen Tech., Houston, 1994-97, GSE Systems, Inc., Columbia, Md., 1997—2001, project leader, 1998—2001; prin. software engr. Avantium Tech., Inc., 2001—. Contbr. articles to profl. jours. Mem. The Instrumentation Systems and Automation Soc. Office: Avantium Tech Inc 10500 Little Patuxent Pkwy Ste 400 Columbia MD 21044 E-mail: nan.ye@avantium.com.

YE, XIU, mathematician, educator; b. Wuhan, China, May 17, 1957; s. Zizao and Guolin (Ye) Z.; m. Yijun Ding, Mar. 14, 1957; 1 child, Don. MS in Math., U. Pitts., 1987, MSME, 1991, PhD in Math., 1990. Lectr. U. Pitts., 1989-90, postdoctoral fellow, 1991; asst. prof. U. Ark., Little Rock, 1991-96, assoc. prof., 1996-99, prof., 1999—. Contbr. articles to profl. jours. Mem. Am. Math. Soc., Soc. of Indsl. Applied Math. Office: Dept Math U Ark 2801 S University Ave Little Rock AR 72204-1000

YE, YIMING, computer scientist, researcher; b. Xian, Shaanxi, China, Feb. 14, 1963; came to the U.S., 1997; s. Jizhong Ye and Chu Ying Wang. BS, Huazhong U. Sci. & Tech., Wuhan, China, 1985; MS, Chinese Acad. Sci., Beijing, 1988; PhD, U. Toronto, Ont., Can., 1997. Rschr. Chinese Acad. Sci., Beijing, 1988-91; postdoctoral rsch. fellow U. Toronto, 1996-97; rsch. staff mem. IBM T.J. Watson Rsch. Ctr., Yorktown Heights, N.Y., 1997—. Assoc. editor Electronic Commerce Rsch. Jour., 1999—; contbr. chpt. to book. Open fellow U. Toronto, 1991-93, rsch. fellow Ctr. for Advanced Studies IBM C Achievements include provided a way of calculating length, area and volume of a geometric entity without analytical expression; provided a method for knowledge re-organization in machine translations; provided an object search algorithm; provided a people tracking algorithm. Avocation: travel. Office: IBM TJ Watson Rsch Ctr PO Box 704 Yorktown Heights NY 10598-0704 E-mail: yiming@watson.ibm.com.

YEADON, TAMMY PAMELA, information specialist; b. Bayonne, N.J., Feb. 3, 1967; d. Tom and Betty Yeadon. BS in Polymer and Plastics Engring., U. Detroit, 1989; MLS, Rutgers U., 1994. Engr. Whirlpool Corp., Benton Harbor, Mich., 1988, Ford Motor Co., Detroit, 1989-90, MedTech Group, South Plainfield, N.J., 1991; quality assurance analyst Block Drug, Jersey City, 1992-93; info. mgr. John Brown, Bridgewater, 1994-97; tech. knowledge specialist A.T. Kearney, N.Y.C., 1998-99; sys. mgr. Berkshire Capital Corp., 2000—. Computer cons. Tyrell the Collection, Linden, N.J., 1991—; libr. cons. The Penn of N.Y., 1998-99. Tutor Literacy Vols. of Am., Elizabeth, N.J., 1993; vol. Gay Men's Health Crisis, N.Y.C., 1993. Mem. ALA, Am. Soc. of Info. Scis., Spl. Libr. Assn.

YEAGER, ANSON ANDERS, writer, former columnist and newspaper editor; b. Salt Lake City, June 5, 1919; s. Charles Franklin and Elise Marie (Thingelstad) Yeager; m. Ada May Bidwell, Sept. 10, 1944; children: Karen Ann, Anson Anders, Harry H., Terry Douglas, Ellen Elise. *When Capt. Yeager returned in 1952 he told Ada May he never wanted to move again. Couple completed 50 years in Sioux Falls home Oct. 1, 2002. Karen Ann was born in Alaska in 1952. Grandson Mark, son of Army doctor Terry, was born in Fairbanks, Alaska. Grandson Andy was born just before his father Maj. Anson Yeager Jr. (also a doctor) served briefly in Persian Gulf call-up. Son, Harry, is an electrical engineer in Santa Clara. Daughter, Ellen Hartman, is a physician's assistant in Denver. Other grandchildren are Seanna and Craig Yeager, Harry's children; Alexandra and Austin Hartman, and Chris Yeager, Andy's brother.* BS, S.D. State U., Brookings, 1947; LLD (hon.), Dakota State Coll., Madison, S.D., 1972; DPub.Svc. (hon.), S.D. State U., Brookings, 1991. Printer's devil, linotype operator Faith Ind. and Gazette (S.D.), 1935-38; printer S.D. State U., 1940-41; staff writer Argus Leader, Sioux Falls, S.D., 1947-55, Sunday editor, 1955-60, exec. editor, 1961-77, assoc. editor, 1978-84, editor editl. page, 1961-84, columnist, 1984-98, author travel articles and commentary. Lectr. dept. journalism U. S.D., 1953—55. *Anson Yeager made extensive use of Gregg shorthand throughout his career. His notes produced verbatim quotes in interviews and meetings. He acquired shorthand at Faith, S.D., High School. He also photographed news subjects and scenery. He used retirement to retrace career and military trips and to view historic World War II sites. A Japan and China tour presented a Yokohama and Tokyo area with no trace of the fire bombings of World War II. Extensive motor-home trips in Alaska, Canada, the lower 48 United States, and Mexico produced many columns. So did travel to the United Kingdom, Western Europe, the former Soviet Union, Hawaii, and the Caribbean.* Contbr. to World Book Ency., 1966—84; author: Anson Yeager's Stories, 2000. Bd. dirs. Sioux Falls Area C. of C., 1964—70, Sioux Falls Devel. Found., 1967, Boys Club of Sioux Falls, 1966—68, S.D. State U. Found., 1987—99, chmn., 1988—89; bd. dirs. Sioux Coun., Boy Scouts Am., Sioux Falls, 1967—72, v.p., 1970—72. Lt. col. U.S. Army, 1942—46, lt. col. U.S. Army, 1950—52, ret. S.D. Army N.G., 1947—64. Decorated Army Commendation medal; named Newsman of Yr., 1978; named to S.D. Newspaper Hall of Fame, 1994, S.D. Hall of Fame, 1998; recipient S.D. Sigma Delta Chi award, 1956, Editl. Excellence award, William Allen White Found., 1976, Disting. Alumni award, S.D. State U., 1980, Friend of Augustana Coll. award, 1980, Ralph D. Casey Minn. award for disting. svc. in journalism, U. Minn., 1981, Eminent Svc. award, East River Elec. Power Coop., 1984, Mass. Comms. award, S.D. State U., 1984, Les Helgeland Cmty. Svc. award, S.D. AP Mng. Editors, 1985, Disting. Svc. award, S.D. Press Assn., 1988, A.H. Pankow award, 1995, Jerome J. Lohr award, S.D. State U. Found., Western Am. award, Ctr. for Western Studies, Augustana Coll., 2000.

YEAGER, ARTHUR LEONARD, health company executive; b. Newark, Oct. 31, 1929; s. Samuel W. and Rose (Glassman) Y.; m. Lorayne P. Shuart, Nov. 25, 1980. DMD, Tufts U., 1954; MMH, Drew U., 2000. Pvt. practice dentistry, Westwood, N.J., 1957-94; DMO, N.J. state dir. Prudential Ins. Co., Parsippany, 1985-94; v.p. profl. rels. Direct Dental Network Blue Cross and Blue Shield of N.J., Newark, 1994-98; pres. AmeriDent of N.J., Lawrenceville, 1998—. Examiner N.E. Reg. Bd. Dental Examiners, chief examiner, mem. steering com.; dental adv. panel Blue Cross Blue Shield Assn.; dental plan orgn. bd. N.J. Dept. Ins.; mem. "supertooth" com. Delta dental Plan of N.J. Mem. Bergen County Adv. Pub. Health Coun.; v.p. Physicians for Automotive Safety, chmn. sch. bus safety), Nat. Coalition for Sch. Bus Safety (nat. coord.), mem. steering com. on sch. bus safety N.J. State Bd. Edn.; mem. N.Y. State Sch. Bus Std. Adv. Com.; mem. safety-pupil transp. task force N.J. Divsn. Hwy. Safety. Recipient Safety award N.J. Congress of Parents and Tchrs., 1981, Cert. of Appreciation, U.S. Dept. Transp., 1983, Gov.'s Hwy. Safety award, 1986, Johnson & Johnson/Safe Kids, N.J. honoree of the yr., 1993, Safety Leader award Advocates for Hwy. and Auto Safety, 1994. Mem. ADA (commn. on dental accreditation, coun. on dental edn.), N.J. Dental Assn. (coun. on legis., chmn. polit. action com., Pres.'s Svc. award 1991), Bergen County Dental Soc. (trustee), N.J. State Bd. Dentistry (pres., anesthesia com. chmn.), Am. Assn. Dental Examiners, Nat. Child Passenger Safety Assn. Home: 33 Park Gate Dr Edison NJ 08820-4029 Office: AmeriDent of NJ Princess Rd Office Pk 4 Princess Rd Lawrenceville NJ 08648 E-mail: healthnetgroup@aol.com.

YEAGER, CATHERINE ANNE, research psychologist; b. Hammond, Ind., Nov. 30, 1958; d. Andrew A. and Catherine T. (Janowski) Mudroncik; m. Robert Phillips Yeager, Sept. 8, 1985; children: Christopher, Caroline, Madeline, Ian. BA, Ind. U., 1980; MA, NYU, 1983; postgrad., Fielding Inst., 1998—. Systems engr. Bell Labs., Piscataway, N.J., 1980-83; project mgr. Bell Comm. Rsch., 1984-87; rsch. scientist NYU Sch. Medicine, N.Y.C., 1987—, asst. dir. Dissociative Disorders Clinic, 1992-98. Editor: Juveinle Violence, Child and Adolescent Psychiatric Clinics of North America, 2000; contbr. artitlce to sci. jours. Vol. therapist Union County Rape Crisis Ctr., Westfield, N.J., 1989—. Mem. APA, Nat. Acad. Neuropsychology, Phi Beta Kappa. Achievements include research in biopsychosocial correlates of violence, dissociative disorders, intergenerational transmission of violent behavior. Avocations: sailboat racing, skiing. Home: 145 Harrison Ave Westfield NJ 07090-2432 Office: NYU Sch Medicine 550 1st Ave New York NY 10016-6402 E-mail: catherine.yeager@med.nyu.edu.

YEAGER, CHARLES WILLIAM, lawyer, newspaper publisher; b. Frederick, Md., Sept. 18, 1921; s. Ralph A. and Ina Jane (Nuckles) Y.; m. Charlotte L. Matthews, Nov. 26, 1958; children: Gretchen A. Murphy, Kristin A. Bridge, Charles W. Yeager Jr., Matthew R. Yeager. BA, W.Va. U., 1943; LLB, U. Va., 1948. Bar: W.Va. 1948, Fla. 1969, U.S. Supreme Ct. 1968. Ptnr. Steptoe & Johnson, Charleston, W.Va., 1948-93; of counsel Rose and Atkinson, 1993—. Pub., editor The Nicholas CHronicle. Maj. U.S. Army, 1942-46. Democrat. Office: Nicholas Chronicle PO Box 503 Summersville WV 26651-0503

YEAGER, GEORGE MICHAEL, investment counsel executive; b. Pelham Manor, N.Y., Sept. 5, 1934; s. Harold Caldwell and Marybelle Alden (Glos) Y.; m. Barbara Gow, July 7, 1962; children: Scott Alden, Kathryn Gow. AB, Dartmouth Coll., 1956, MBA, 1957. Adminstrv. asst. Fed. Res. Bank N.Y., 1957-59; v.p. Yeager & Anderson, Inc., N.Y.C., 1959-60; pres. Yeager, Wood & Marshall, Inc., 1960—. Author: Investing Your Nest Egg: A Sensible Approach to Building a Profitable Portfolio in the New Golden Age of Capitalism, 2002. Mem. Assn. Investment Mgmt. & Rsch., Investment Counsel Assn. Am. (gov.), N.Y. Soc. Security Analysts, Univ. Club, Econ. Club of N.Y., U.S. Global Leaders Growth Fund (pres. 1995—), Internat. Soc. Financial Analysts, Mill Reef Club, Siwanoy Country Club. Home: 2 Elm Rock Rd Bronxville NY 10708-4904 Office: 630 5th Ave Ste 2900 New York NY 10111-0100

YEAGER, KURT ERIC, research institute official; b. Cleve., Sept. 11, 1939; s. Joseph Ellsworth and Karolyn Kristine (Pedersen) Y.; m. Rosalie Ann McMillan, Feb. 5, 1960; children: Geoffrey, Phillip; m. Regina Ursula Querfurt, May 12, 1970; 1 dau., Victoria. BA in Chemistry, Kenyon Coll., 1961; postgrad., Ohio State U., 1961-62; MS in Physics, U. Calif., Davis, 1964. Tchg. asst. Ohio State U., 1961-62; officer, program mgr. Air Force Tech. Applications Ctr., Alexandria, Va., 1962-68; assoc. dept. dir. Mitre Corp., McLean, 1968-72; dir. energy rsch. and devel. planning EPA, Washington, 1972-74; dir. fossil power plants dept. Electric Power Rsch. Inst., Palo Alto, Calif., 1974-79, dir. coal combustion systems, 1979-83, v.p. coal combustion systems, 1983-88, v.p. generation and storage, 1988-96, pres., CEO, 1996—. Mem. commerce tech. adv. bd., Oak Ridge fossil energy adv. bd. Nat. Acad. Engring.; mem. exec. bd. Nat. Coal Council. Contbr. articles to profl. jours. Pres. No. Va. Youth Football Assn., 1973-74. Capt. USAF, 1962-68. Decorated Air Force Commendation medals (2); recipient Outstanding Svc. award EPA, 1974. Mem. ASME (Rsch. Policy Bd.), AAAS, Am. Chem. Soc., Palo Alto C. of C. Republican. Episcopalian. E-mail: KYeager@EPRI.com.

YEAGER, LOUISE BARBARA LEHR, secondary education educator; b. New Haven, Feb. 24, 1943; d. Michael Adolf and Rosa (Gabold) Lehr; m. Charles Edward Yeager, Sept. 13, 1967; 1 child, William. BS in Math. and Physics, Cen. Conn. State U., 1965, postgrad., 1974. Tchr. math. West Haven (Conn.) High Sch., 1965—67, 1971—2002. Mem. Nat. Coun. Tchrs. Math., Assoc. Tchrs. Math. in Conn. Lutheran. Avocation: golf. Home: 30 Cedar Ln Northford CT 06472-1608 Office: West Haven H S Circle St West Haven CT 06516

YEAGER, MARK LEONARD, lawyer; b. Chgo., Apr. 7, 1950; BA, U. Mich., 1972; JD, Northwestern U., 1975. Bar: Ill. 1975, Fla. 1985. Ptnr. McDermott, Will & Emery, Chgo., 1975—. Mem. ABA.

YEAGER, MYRON DEAN, English language educator, business writing consultant; b. Evansville, Ind., Oct. 27, 1950; s. Robert Paul and Sarah Mazol (Hunt) Y. BA, Grace Coll., 1972; MA, Purdue U., 1974, PhD, 1980. Cert. tchr., Calif. Prof. Grace Coll., Winona Lake, Ind., 1976-84, Chapman U., Orange, Calif., 1984—. Cons. numerous firms, 1980—; faculty chmn. Chapman U., Orange, 1991-92, dept. chmn., 1990-93, dean sch. comm. arts, 2001—; dept. chmn. Grace Coll., Winona Lake, 1981-84. Author: (chpt.) Business Writing, 1989; co-author: The Hutton Story, 1998; co-editor The Chesterfield Papers Project, 1998, Procedings of the West Coast Conf. on Corp. Commn., 1994; contbr. articles to profl. jours. and mags. Recipient UCLA Clark postdoctoral fellowship, 1982, David Ross fellowship Purdue U., 1980, Valerie Scudder award for outstanding tchg., 1992. Mem. ACLU, AAUP, Am. Soc. Eighteenth-Century Studies, Johnson Soc. Western Region, Assn. Bus. Communication, Phi Beta Delta, Sigma Tau Delta. Office: Chapman Univ One University Dr Orange CA 92866-1099 E-mail: yeager@chapman.edu.

YEAGER, PETER CLEARY, sociologist, educator; b. Terre Haute, Ind., Nov. 29, 1949; s. Ralph Oscar and Dorothy (Cleary) Y.; m. Kathy Ellen Kram, Aug. 9, 1981; 1 child, Jason Kram Yeager. BA in Journalism, U. Minn., 1971; MS in Sociology, U. Wis., 1976, PhD in Sociology, 1981. Writer, photographer Sun Newspapers, Mpls., 1971-72; from lectr. to asst. prof. sociology Yale U., New Haven, 1979-82; from asst. to assoc. prof. sociology Boston U., 1982—. Rsch. fellow ethics and the professions program Harvard U., Cambridge, Mass., 1989-90. Co-author: Illegal Corporate Behavior, 1979, Corporate Crime, 1980 (named one of Choice's outstanding acad. books 1981); author: The Limits of Law, 1991. Bd. assessors 1st Parish in Framingham, Mass., 1992-94. Managerial Ethics Rsch. grantee Amsterdam Found., 1989-92, Human Resources Policy Inst. Boston U., 1986-87, 93-94. Mem. Am. Sociol. Assn., Am. Soc. Criminology, Law and Soc. Assn., Soc. for Study of Social Problems, Phi Beta Kappa, Kappa Tau Alpha. Avocations: hiking, reading, creative writing, tennis, travel. Office: Dept Sociology Boston U 96-100 Cummington St Boston MA 02215

YEAGER, ROBERT JULIUS, priest, financial consultant; b. Toledo, Apr. 20, 1938; s. Edmund Nicholas and Geraldine Mary (Small) Y. BA in Edn., Athaenaeum of Ohio, Cin., 1960, MA in Philosophy, 1962; MEd, U. Toledo, 1969, D of Ednl. Adminstrn., 1974. Ordained priest Cath. Ch., 1962. Prin. Delphos (Ohio) St. John H.S., 1965-67, Sandusky (Ohio) St. Mary's H.S., 1967-72; local supt. Tiffin (Ohio) Calvert H.S., 1972-80; exec. dir. Nat. Cath. Edn. Assn., Washington, 1980-82, v.p. devel., 1982-87; exec. dir. The Metanoia Group, Winona, Minn., 1987-91; prin. Cardinal Stritch H.S., Oregon, Ohio, 1991-97; exec. dir. Diocesan Fiscal Mgmt. Conf., Waterville, 1993—. Vis. lectr. U. Dayton, Ohio, 1965-80; adj. prof. St. Mary's U., Winona, 1987-91; bd. dirs. Lourdes Coll., Sylvania, Ohio, 1997-2000. Author: Understanding and Implementing Development, 1984; co-author: The Catholic High School-A National Portrait, 1981, Catholic High Schools: Their Impact on Low Income Students, 1983. Mem. Elks. Roman Catholic. Office: Diocesan Fiscal Mgmt Conf PO Box 199 Waterville OH 43566-0199 E-mail: 104227.110@compuserve.com.

YEAGER, THOMAS NELSON, lawyer, radio personality; b. Laurel, Md., Jan. 18, 1964; s. Thomas Merle and Olivia Lee (Scaggs) Y.; m. Jeanne Michelle MacLeod, June 14, 1997. BA, U. Md., 1986; JD, U. Md., Balt., 1990; grad., Nat. Coll. Dist. Attys., Houston, 1994. Bar: Md. 1990. Law clk. Kent County Circuit Ct., Chestertown, Md., 1990-91; asst. state's atty. Kent County, 1991-96, dep. state's atty., 1996-99; sole practitioner, 1995—. Radio personality WNAV Radio, Annapolis, Md., 1986-95, WCEI Radio, Easton, Md., 1995—; mem. Gov.'s Exec. Adv. Coun., Balt., 1991-94; ex-officio bd. mem. Crime Solvers of the Upper Eastern Shore, Chestertown, 1996—. Mem. Old Chestertown Neighborhood Assn., 1995—. Mem.: Nat. Eagle Scout Assn., 2d Cir. Bar Assn., Kent County Bar Assn., Md. State Bar Assn., Chestertown Optimist Club (past pres.), K.C. (past dep. Grand Knight). Republican. Roman Catholic. Avocations: skiing, rowing, boating. Office: 100 C Memorial Plz Chestertown MD 21620-1514 E-mail: tnyesq@dmv.com.

YEAGER, TWYNETTE, antiques and gift shop owner, retired educator; b. Atmore, Ala., Feb. 18, 1924; d. Q.E. and Bettie (Webb) Wells; m. William B. Watson Sr. (div. 1960); children: William B. Jr., Byron W., Karen Watson Thomas; m. Thomas B. Yeager, Jr., 1972 (dec.). BA, Samford U., 1958; MA, U. Ala., Tuscaloosa, 1962, EdD, 1972. Edn. dir. First Bapt. Ch., Atmore, 1954-56; counselor Parrish H.S., Selma, Ala., 1958-60; dean of students Judson Coll., Marion, 1965-70; prof. edn., 1970-89; owner Twink's Antiques and Gifts, Marion, Ala., 1995—. Mem. Area Agy. on Aging, Silver Haired Legislator, Marion City Coun., 1992—2002, Siloam Bapt. Ch.; mem. steering com., bd. dirs. Perry County Project, Cooperative Bapt. Fellowship; bd. dirs., vice chair Marion Acad. , 1992—2002; bd. dirs. Ala. Bapt. Hist. Commn., 1995—2002. Named Outstanding Alumnus Coll. Bus., Samford U., 1972. Mem.: Nat. Fellowship Bapt. Educators, Ala. Hist. Soc., Perry County Assn. Elected Ofcls. (treas.), Delta Kappa Gamma (past pres., legis. chmn. 2002). Republican. Avocations: music, reading, antiques. Home: 207 E Lafayette St Marion IL 36756

YEAGLEY, JOAN HOWERTON, writer; b. Denver, Jan. 25, 1930; d. Harold Emery Howerton and Jeannette Louise Boule; m. Harold Arthur Yeagley, Apr. 14, 1951; children: Jan, Donn, Jeff, Jeanne. BSc in Edn., Kans. State U., 1984. Cons. N.E. Kans. Libr. Sys.; tchr. creative writing Mo. Southern State Coll., Joplin, Crowder Coll.; workshop leader in field. Author: Four Bookmark Poets, The Studs of McDonald County, 1987; contbr. articles and stories to mags. Great books cord. Kans. City Pub. Libr./Great Books Found., Chgo. Recipient Kans. City Star award, Kans. City Star, 1965—67, Gold Quill award, Crowder Coll., 1988, Sager Creek Arts Ctr. award, John Brown U., 1995—96. Home: Rt 1 Box 1306 Stella MO 64867 E-mail: jhyeagley@lero.com.

YEAGLEY, KATHLEEN LUX, community health educator, nurse; b. Columbus, Ohio, Nov. 17, 1953; d. Donald Gregory and Harriet Hope (Harmer) L. BS, Ohio State U., 1975; MS, U. Hawaii, 1988; PhD, Ohio State U., 1992. Cert. health edn. specialist. Asst. charge nurse Doctor's North Hosp., Columbus, 1975-76; team leader Ohio State U. Hosp., 1976-77; flight nurse USAF, 1977-84; EMT instr. City Colls. Chgo., 1981-82; nursing and health svcs. chair ARC, Rhein Main, Fed. Republic Germany, 1984-85; parent educator, clinic coord. Kapiolani Hosp., Honolulu, 1985-86; family planning nurse student and health svcs. U. Hawaii, 1986-87, rsch. asst., 1988; grad. teaching assoc. Ohio State U., Columbus, 1988-92, lectr., 1992-93, asst. prof., 1993-96; tng. and rsch. coord. Next Era Med., 1997-98; asst. prof. Ohio State U., 1999—; perinatal program mgr. Columbus Health Dept., 2000—. Mem. APHA, AAHPERD, Res. Officer's Assn., Ohio Assn. Health, Phys. Edn., Recreation and Dance (exec. dir. 1993—), Sigma Theta Tau, Eta Sigma Gamma, Phi Kappa Phi. Republican. Roman Catholic. Office: Columbus Dept of Health 1204 W Broad St Columbus OH 43222 E-mail: klux@cmhhealth.org.

YEAMANS, GEORGE THOMAS, librarian, educator; b. Richmond, Va., Nov. 7, 1929; s. James Norman and Dolphine Sophia (Manhart) Y.; m. Mary Ann Seng, Feb. 1, 1958; children: Debra, Susan, Julia. AB, U. Va., 1950; MLS, U. Ky., 1955; EdD, Ind. U., 1965. Asst. audio-visual dir. Ind. State U., Terre Haute, 1957-58; asst. film librarian Ball State U., Muncie, Ind., 1958-61, film librarian, 1961-69, assoc. prof. libr. sci., 1969-72, prof., 1972-95; prof. emeritus, 1995—; cons. Pendleton (Ind.) Sch. Corp., 1962, 67, Captioned Films for the Deaf Workshop, Muncie, Ind., 1963, 64, 65, Decatur (Ind.) Sch. System, 1978; adjudicator Ind. Media Fair, 1979-93, David Letterman Scholarship Program, 1993. Author: Projectionists' Programmed Primer, 1969, rev. edit., 1982; Mounting and Preserving Pictorial Materials, 1976; Tape Recording, 1978; Transparency Making, 1977; Photographic Principles, 1981; Computer Literacy— A Programmed Primer, 1985; Building Effective Creative Project Teams, 1996, revised edit., 2000; Designing Dynamic Media Presentations, 1996, revised edit., 2000; songwriter Branson Bound, 1996; contbr. articles to profl. jours. Campaign worker Wilson for Mayor, Muncie, Ind., 1979. Served with USMC, 1950-52. Recipient Citations of Achievement, Internat. Biog. Assn., Cambridge, Eng., 1973, Am. Biog. Assn., 1976, Mayor James P. Carey award for achievement for disting. contbns. to Ball State U. and City of Muncie, 1988; Video Information Systems grantee Ball State U., 1993. Mem. NEA (del. assembly dept. audiovisual instrn. 1967), ALA, Am. Assn. Sch. Librs., Audio-Visual Instrn. Dirs. Ind. (exec. bd. 1962-68, pres. 1966-67), Ind. Assn. Ednl. Communications and Tech. (dist. dir. 1972-75), Assn. Ind. Media Educators (chmn. auditing com. 1979-81), Autism Soc. Am., Assn. Ednl. Comm. & Tech., Ind. Libr. Fedn., Ind. Corp. and Network Libr. Assn., Ind. Acad. Libr. Assn., Ind. Pub. Libr. Assn., Thomas Jefferson Soc. Alumni U. Va., Phi Delta Kappa. Republican. Unitarian. Home: 4507 W Burton Dr Muncie IN 47304-3575

YEASIN, MOHAMMED, electrical engineer, educator; b. Bhola, Bangladesh, Mar. 24, 1966; s. Abdus Sattar and Julekha Begum; m. Rehana Yasmeen; children: Maisa Munawara, Mohammed Hyder. BSEE, Bangladesh Inst. of Tech., 1989; MS in Computer Engring., Bangladesh U. of Engring. & Tech., 1994; PhD, Indian Inst. of Tech., 1998. Lectr. Bangladesh Inst. of Tech., Chittagong, Bangladesh, 1990—98; rsch. fellow Electro-Technical Lab., Tsukuba, Japan, 1998—99; vis. asst. prof. U. of West Fla., Pensacola, Fla., 1999—2000; asst. prof. Pa. State U., State Coll., Pa., 2000—. Cons. Advanced Interface Technologies, Inc., State Coll., 2000—. Contbr. chapters to books. Recipient Gold medal, Bangladesh Inst. of Tech., Khulna, 1989. Mem.: IEEE, Inst. of Engr. Bangladesh, BIT Chittagong Tchr. Club (life; gen. sec. 1993—94). Home: 801 C W Aaron Dr 3 State College PA 16803 Office: Pennsylvania State University 220 Pond Lab CSE University Park PA 16803 Home Fax: 814-865-3176. Personal E-mail: yeasin@cse.psu.edu.

YEATMAN, HARRY CLAY, biologist, educator; b. Ashwood, Tenn., June 22, 1916; s. Trezevant Player and Mary (Wharton) Y.; m. Jean Hansford Anderson, Nov. 24, 1949; children— Henry Clay, Jean Hansford. AB, U. N.C., Chapel Hill, 1939, MA, 1942, PhD, 1953; student, Cornell U., summer 1937. Asst. prof. biology U. of South, Sewanee, Tenn., 1950-54, asso. prof., 1954-60, prof., 1960—, Kenan prof., 1980—, chmn. dept., 1972-76, elderhostel tchr., 1987-88. Vis. prof. marine biology Va. Inst. Marine Sci., Gloucester Point, summer 1967; cons. Smithsonian Instn., Sci. Applications, Inc., La Jolla, Calif., Ctrs. for Disease Control, Atlanta, WHO, Ecol. Analysts, Inc., Balt., Duke Power Co., Charlotte, N.C. Contbr. articles to profl. jours. Served with AUS, 1942-46. Gen. Edn. Bd. fellow, 1941-42; Brown Found. fellow, 1984 Fellow AAAS; mem. Soc. Systematic Biology (charter), Soc. Limnology and Oceanography (charter), Soc. Ichthyology and Herpetology, Tenn. Acad. Sci., Am. Micros. Soc., Am. Ornithologists Union, Tenn. Ornithol. Soc., Tenn. Archeol. Soc., Nat. Speleological Soc., Blue Key, Phi Beta Kappa, Sigma Xi, Omicron Delta Kappa, Sigma Nu. Republican. Episcopalian. Home: PO Box 356 Jumpoff Rd Sewanee TN 37375 Office: Woods Lab Sewanee TN 37383-1000

YEATON, CECELIA E(MMA), human services administrator; b. Suffern, N.Y., Sept. 7, 1939; d. Cornelius and Marguerite Augusta (von Lueck) Schoolcraft; m. M. Bruce Yeaton, June 30, 1961; 1 child, Cecily Marguerite (dec.). BA, U. Maine, 1961. Diplomate Am. Coll. Health Care Execs. Adminstr. asst. Roger Williams Hosp., Providence, 1974-75; office mgr. radiology Hillcrest Hosp., Pittsfield, Mass., 1975-79, dir. quality assurance/risk mgmt., 1980-88; asst. adminstr. Univ. Hosp., Bklyn., 1988—2001; cons. Risk Mgmt./Performance Improvement, 2001—. Cons. Dalton (Mass.) Nursing Home, Inc., 1985-87; asst. libr. dir. Mary C. Wheeler Sch., Providence. Active Ind. Women's Forum. Mem. Mass. Soc. Hosp. Risk Mgmt. (bd. dirs. 1984-88, pres. 1986-87), Am. Soc. Healthcare Risk Mgmt. (edn. com. 1985-86), Greater N.Y. Hosp. Assn. (regional adv. group 1993-97), Am. Coll. Healthcare Execs., Met. Healthcare Adminstrs. Assn., Am. Soc. Quality. Republican. Episcopalian. Avocations: writing, cooking, watercolors, computers. E-mail: cyeaton@cox.net.

YEATS, ROBERT SHEPPARD, geologist, educator; b. Miami, Fla., Mar. 30, 1931; s. Robert Sheppard and Carolyn Elizabeth (Rountree) Y.; m. Lillian Eugenia Bowie, Dec. 30, 1952 (dec. Apr. 1991); children: Robert Bowie, David Claude, Stephen Paul, Kenneth James, Sara Elizabeth; m. Angela M. Hayes, Jan. 7, 1993. BA, U. Fla., 1952; MS, U. Wash., 1956, PhD, 1958. Registered geologist, Oreg., Calif. Geologist, petroleum exploration and prodn. Shell Oil Co., Ventura and Los Angeles, Calif., 1958-67; Shell Devel. Co., Houston, 1967; assoc. prof. geology Ohio U., Athens, 1967-70, prof., 1970-77; prof. geology Oreg. State U., Corvallis, 1977-97, prof. oceanography, 1991-97, prof. emeritus, 1997—, chmn. dept., 1977-85; geologist U.S. Geol. Survey, 1968, 69, 75; Glomar Challenger scientist, 1971; co-chief scientist, 1973-74, 78; mem. Oreg. Bd. Geologist Examiners, 1981-83; chmn. Working Group 1 Internat. Lithosphere Program, 1987-90; mem. geophysics study com. NRC, 1987-94; chmn. task force group on paleoseismology Internat. Lithosphere Program, 1990-98; chmn. subcom. on Himalayan active faults Internat. Geol. Correlation Program, Project 206, 1984-92. Researcher on Cenozoic tectonics of So. Calif., Oreg., New Zealand and Himalaya; active faults of Calif. Transverse Ranges, deep-sea drilling in Ea. Pacific; vis. scientist N.Z. Geol. Survey, 1983-84, 99, Geol. Survey of Japan, 1992, Inst. de Phys. du Globe de Paris, 1993; sr. cons. Earth Conss. Internat., 1997—. Author: The Geology of Earthquakes, 1997, Living with Earthquakes in the Pacific Northwest, 1998, Living with Earthquakes in California-A Survivor's Guide, 2001. Mem. Ojai (Calif.) City Planning Commn., 1961-62, Ojai City Council, 1962-65. 1st lt. U.S. Army, 1952-54. Named Richard H. Jahns Disting. Lectr. in Engring. Geology, 1995; Ohio U. rsch. fellow, 1973-74; grantee NSF, U.S. Geol. Survey. Fellow AAAS, Geol. Soc. Am. (chmn. structural geology and tectonics divsn. 1984-85, Cordilleran sect. 1988-89, assoc. editor bull. 1987-89); mem. Am. Assn. Petroleum Geologists (Outstanding Educator award Pacific sect. 1991, Michel T. Halbouty human needs award 1998), Am. Geophys. Union, Seismol. Soc. Am., Oreg. Acad. Sci. Home: 1654 NW Crest Pl Corvallis OR 97330-1812 Office: Oreg State U Dept Geoscis Corvallis OR 97331-5506

YEATTS, DOROTHY ELIZABETH FREEMAN, nurse, retired county official, educator; b. Richmond, Va., Jan. 19, 1925; d. Robert Franklin and Elizabeth Bell (Wiggins) Freeman; m. Roy Earl Yeatts, Nov. 27, 1948; children: Martha Jane Yeatts Couch, Robert Patrick. Diploma in nursing, Stuart Circle Hosp., Richmond, Va., 1947; BS in Nursing, Coll. William and Mary, 1947; cert. pub. health nursing supr., U. N.C., 1974. RN, Va., N.C. Vis. nurse Instructive Vis. Nurses Assn., Richmond, 1947-49; maternity nurse N.C. Bapt. Hosp., Winston-Salem, 1969-71; pub. health nurse I, Forsyth County Health Dept., 1971-72, pub. health nurse coord., 1972-74, pub. health nurse supr., 1974-78. Sunday sch. tchr. Tuckahoe Presbyn. Ch., Richmond, 1954-57, Trinity Presbyn Ch., Winston-Salem, 1960-84; pres. Buckingham Park Garden Club, Richmond, 1956-58, Women of Trinity Presbyn. Ch., 1963-64; elder Trinity Presbyn. Ch., 1978-81, circle bible moderator, 1984-97; bd. dirs. Forsyth Cancer Soc., Winston-Salem, 1980-86; instr. ARC, Winston-Salem, 1978-97, vol., 1993-97. Republican. Avocations: arts and crafts, fishing, stamp collecting, woodcarving, sewing. Home: 310 Coventry Park Ln Winston Salem NC 27104-3676 E-mail: dfyeatts@triad.rr.com.

YEATTS, ROBERT PATRICK, ophthalmologist; b. Richmond, Va., Sept. 10, 1952; s. Roy Earl and Dorothy Elizabeth (Freeman) Y.; m. Virginia Elizabeth Kimball, Aug. 4, 1974; children: John Patrick, Thomas Patrick, Patrick Kimball. BS, Hampden-Sydney (Va.) Coll., 1974; MD, Wake Forest U., 1978. Lic. N.C., Minn., Mass., S.C. Resident in internal medicine N.C. Baptist Hosp./Bowman Gray Sch. of Medicine, Winston-Salem, N.C., 1978-79; resident in ophthalmology Mayo Clinic and Mayo Grad. Sch. Medicine, Rochester, Minn., 1979-82; fellow ophthalmic plastic reconstructive surgery Mass. Eye and Ear Infirmary and Harvard U., Boston, 1982-83; instr. ophthalmology Mayo Clinic, Rochester, 1983-84, asst. prof. ophthalmology Boston, 1984; asst. clin. prof. ophthalmology Duke U., Durham, N.C., 1985-87; asst. prof. ophthalmology and otolaryngology Sch. Medicine Wake Forest U., Winston-Salem, 1987-93, assoc. prof. ophthalmology and otolaryngology, 1993—. Med. advisor CIGNA-Medicare, Greensboro, N.C., 1995-96; cons. product devel. Leibinger, 1996; spkr. in field. Contbr. , chapters to books. Supt. ch. sch. Home Moravian Ch., Winston-Salem, N.C., 1994-95. Mayo scholar Mayo Clinic, 1982-83; recipient award Heed Found., 1982, Physician Recognition award AMA, 1998. Fellow Am. Acad. Ophthalmology; mem. Am. Soc. Ophthalmic Plastic and Reconstructive Surgery, Internat. Soc. Orbital Disorders (bd. dirs. 1995—), N.C. Med. Soc. (del.), N.C. Soc. Eye Physicians and Surgeons (pres. 1997-98), Forsyth, Stokes, Davie County Med. Soc. (treas. 1996, sec. 1997, pres.-elect 1998, pres. 1999), Phi Beta Kappa, Chi Beta Chi. Republican. Mem. Moravian Ch. Avocation: sailboat racing. Home: 125 Windham Farm Ln Lewisville NC 27023 Office: Wake Forest U Sch of Medicine Medical Center Blvd Winston Salem NC 27157-0001 E-mail: pyeatts@wfubmc.edu.

YEAZEL, KEITH ARTHUR, lawyer; b. Fayetteville, N.C., Feb. 14, 1956; s. Russell E. and Barbara E. (Weaver) Y.; m. Deborah M. MacDonald, Aug. 30, 1986. BA, Ohio State U., 1983; JD, Capital U., 1989. Bar: Ohio 1989, U.S. Dist. Ct. (so. dist.) Ohio 1989, U.S. Ct. Appeals (6th cir.) 1990, U.S. Supreme Ct. 1992. Law clk. to judge George C. Smith U.S. Dist. Ct., Columbus, Ohio, 1988-89; prin. Keith A. Yeazel, Atty. at Law, 1989—. Mem. ABA, Ohio Bar Assn., Columbus Bar Assn., Nat. Assn. Criminal Def. Lawyers, Ohio Assn. Criminal Def. Lawyers, Order of Curia. Republican. Lutheran. Office: 65 S 5th St Columbus OH 43215-4307

YEE, ALBERT HOY, writer, retired psychologist, educator; b. Santa Barbara, Calif., June 14, 1929; children: Lisa Diane, Hoyt Brian, Cynthia Rae. BA, U. Calif., Berkeley, 1952; MA, San Francisco State U., 1959; Ed.D., Stanford U., 1965. Post-doctoral research fellow U. Oreg., Eugene, 1966-67; assoc. prof. edn. U. Wis., Madison, 1967-70, prof., 1970-73; prof. ednl. psychology, dean grad. studies and research Calif. State U., Long Beach, 1973-79, originating founder Grad. Ctr., 1974; prof. edn. U. Mont., 1979-83, dean Sch. Edn., 1979-82; sr. lectr. psychology Chinese U. of Hong Kong, 1985-89; dean, prof. psychology Am. Coll., Singapore; sr. lectr. psychology Nat. U., Singapore, 1989-90; dir. program U. Md., Hongkong, 1990; disting. vis. prof. ednl. psychology spl. adviser coll. grad. studies and internat. programs Marist Coll., 1990-92; prof. ednl. psychology Fla. Internat. U., Miami, 1992-94, rsch. scholar, 1994-95. Chmn. 1st Fed. Adv. Com. for Asian and Pacific Island Ams., Bur. Census, 1976-81. Author: Man, Society and the World, 1968; co-author: Comprehensive Spelling Instruction: Theory, Research and Application, 1971; editor: Social Interaction in Educational Settings, 1971, Perspectives on Management Systems Approaches to Education: A Symposium, 1973, Search for Meaning, 1984, A Study on Possible Future Developments for Hong Kong: Strategic Planning and Innovations, 1985, A People Misruled: Hong Kong and the Chinese Stepping-Stone Syndrome, 1989, 2d edit., 1992; editor: East Asian Higher Education: Traditions and Transformations, 1994, Whither Hong Kong: China's Shadow or Visionary Gleam?, 1999. With AUS, 1952-55, Korea, Japan. Recipient Civic Commendation Madison, 1973; sr. Fulbright lectr. Tokyo and Tamagawa Univs., Japan; also 1st Fulbright scholar to People's Republic China, 1972. Fellow AAAS, Nat. Conf. Research in English, Am. Psychol. Assn. , Am. Psychol. Soc.; mem. Calif. Coll. and Univ. Faculty Assn. (founder 1961), Chinese Hist. Soc. Am. and Orgn. of Chinese Americans (Bicentennial speaker), Asian-Am. Psychol. Assn. (pres. 1979-82, jour. editor 1981-82), Western Mont. Stanford Alumni Club (founding pres. 1997—). Home: 3822 Lincoln Rd Missoula MT 59802-3039 E-mail: alyee@montana.com.

YEE, ALFRED ALPHONSE, structural engineer, consultant; b. Honolulu, Aug. 5, 1925; s. Yun Sau and Kam Ngo (Lum) Y.; m. Janice Ching (div.); children: Lailan, Mark, Eric, Malcolm, Ian; m. Elizabeth Wong, June 24, 1975; children: Suling, Trevor, I'Ling. BSCE, Rose Hulman Inst. Tech., 1948, Dr. of Engring. (hon.), 1976; MEng in Structures, Yale U., 1949. Registered profl. engr., Hawaii, Calif., Guam, Tex., Minn., No. Marianas Islands. With civil engring. dept. Dept. Pub. Works, Terr. of Hawaii, Honolulu, 1949-51; structural engr. 14th Naval Dist., Pearl Harbor, Hawaii, 1951-54; pvt. practice structural engring. cons. Honolulu, 1954-55; structural engring. cons. Park & Yee Ltd., Honolulu, 1955-60; pres. Alfred A. Yee & Assocs. Inc., 1960-82; v.p., tech. adminstr. Alfred. A. Yee div. Leo A. Daly, 1982-89; pres. Applied Tech. Corp., 1984—. Patentee in concrete tech., land and sea structures; contbr. articles to profl. jours. Served with U.S. Army, 1946-47. Named Engr. of Yr., Hawaii Soc. Profl. Engrs., 1969, one of Men Who Made Marks in 1970, Honolulu, 1970. Mem. ASCE (hon.), NSPE, CASE, ACEC, NAE, Am. Concrete Inst. (hon.), Post-Tensioning Inst., Precast-Prestressed Concrete Inst. (PCI medal of honor award 1997), Prestressed Concrete Inst. (State of Art award 1991), Structural Engrs. Assn. Hawaii, Yale Sci. and Engring. Assn. (Martin P. Korn award 1965, Robert J. Lyman award 1984), Singapore Concrete Inst. Avocations: golfing, swimming. Office: 1441 Kapiolani Blvd Ste 810 Honolulu HI 96814-4457 E-mail: atc@lava.net.

YEE, DAVID, chemist, technology analyst; b. Albany, N.Y., Sept. 26, 1948; s. Fook On and King Sau (Seto) Y.; m. Vivien Chee-Nan Yeo, May 11, 1974; children: Daniel Ming-dao, Peter Ming-de. BS (cum laude), Rensselaer Polytech. Inst., 1970; MS, Cornell U., 1973, PhD, 1978. Fellow Max Planck Inst. for Exptl. Medicine, Göttingen, Germany, 1978—80; rsch. assoc. Harvard U., 1980—85; rsch. dir. Advance Biofactures Corp., Lynbrook, NY, 1985—99; sr. technology analyst Adis Internat., Langhorne, Pa., 2000—. Contbr. articles to profl. jours. including Analytical Chemistry, Jour. of Molecular Evolution, Biochemistry, Hoppe-Seyler's Zeitschrift für Physiologische Chemie, FEBS Letters, European Jour. Biochemistry; patentee in field. Mem. Am. Chem. Soc., Am. Sci. Affiliation, N.Y. Acad. Scis. Office: 820 Town Center Dr Langhorne PA 19047 E-mail: David.Yee@US.Adis.com.

YEE, H.C. engineer; b. Hangchow, China, July 15, 1959; s. K.C. Yee and P.C. (Cai) Y.; m. Bolina Long, Feb. 6, 1992; children: Philina, Derek. MD, Cheking Med. Coll. Sch., 1981; MS in Bioengring., U. Wash., 1987, PhD in Bioengring., 1991. Engr. IHE, Inc., Seattle, 1988-93; v.p. Ameritek, Inc., 1993—. Patentee in field. Mem. Am. Clin. Tech. Assn. Home: 7338 23rd Ave NE Seattle WA 98115-5806 Office: 7338 23rd Ave NE Seattle WA 98115-5806 E-mail: hcyee@ameritek.org.

YEE, KAREN KALUN, research scientist; b. Hong Kong, China, Feb. 8, 1968; d. Kwok Wai and Jean Yee. BS, U. Calif., Davis, 1990; MS, Va. Commonwealth U., 1993, PhD, 1997. Postdoc. fellow Monell Chem. Senses Ctr., Phila., 1997—2000, rsch. assoc., 2000—. Contbr. articles to profl. jours. Recipient Interdisciplinary Tng. Chem. Senses, NIH, 1997—2000, Graduate Tchg. assistantship, Med. Coll. of Va., Va. Commonwealth U., 1994—97; fellow Tuition fellowship, 1994—97, Commonwealth of Va. fellowship, 1993; grantee Small Rsch. grant, NIH, 2000—. Mem.: Soc. for Neurosci., Assn. Chemoreception Senses. Democrat. Avocations: biking, drawing. Office: Monell Chem Senses Ctr 3500 Market St Philadelphia PA 19104-3308 Office Fax: 215-898-2084.

YEE, KEITH PHILIP, accountant, finance company executive; b. Luton, Eng., Apr. 26, 1958; came to the U.S., 1985; m. Ginny Sung, Feb. 9, 1985; children: Ashley, Brittany. BA in Acctg. with honors, Exeter (Eng.) U., 1979. CPA, Calif. Audit sr. Ernst & Whinney, London, 1979-83, investigation supr. Hong Kong, 1983-85, audit mgr. Memphis, 1985-86; audit sr. mgr. Ernst & Young, San Francisco, 1986-91, internat. resident, 1991-93, audit sr. mgr., 1993-95, Price Waterhouse, San Jose, Calif., 1995-97, Adaptec, Milpitas, 1997-98, Synnex Info. Tech., Fremont, 1998-2000, Tripath Tech., Inc., Santa Clara, 2000—. Vice chmn. adv. coun. for svcs. to srs. Salvation Army, San Francisco, 1989. Grad. leadership San Francisco program San Francisco C. of C., 1990. Fellow Inst. Chartered Accts. in Eng. and Wales; mem. AICPA, Asian Am. CPAs (mem. adv. bd. 1994-95), Calif. Soc. CPAs, Inst. for Internat. Edn. (student programs com. 1990-95), San Francisco C. of C. (internat. bus. devel. com. 1993-95), Asian Am. Mfrs. Assn., Churchill Club. Avocations: internat. travel, music, sports. Office: Tripath Tech Inc 3900 Freedom Cir Santa Clara CA 95054-1204 E-mail: keith@tripath.com.

YEE, KUO CHIANG, neuroscientist, neurologist; b. Shanghai, Jan. 18, 1935; came to U.S., 1981; s. Hun and Wang J. Yee; m. Pei Ching Cai, Oct. 1, 1954; children: Hsiao Chiang, Hsiao Pei. MD, Zuzhen Med. Sch., Cheking, China, 1954; MS, U. Wash., 1983; PhD, U. B.C., Vancouver, Can., 1992. Prof. U. B.C., Vancouver, 1992-93; dir. Neurosci. Med. Ctr., Seattle, 1981—; pres. AmeriTek, Inc., 1993—. Author: Biological Effects and Dosimetry of Nonionizing Radiation, 1982; contbr. numerous articles to profl. jours. Achievements include development of advanced rapid in-vitro immunodiagnostic and clinical chemical reagent systems diagnostic test kits. Home: 7338 23rd Ave NE Seattle WA 98115-5806 Office: 7338 23rd Ave NE Seattle WA 98115-5806 E-mail: kcyee@ameritek.org.

YEE, LESLIE MITCHELL, physician executive, educator; b. Cin., Dec. 10, 1954; s. Harry W.K. and Lily Yee; m. Kim-Oanh Nguyen, June 4, 1986; 1 child, April. BS, Edgecliff Coll., 1975; MD, U. Cin., 1979; MPH, Harvard U., 1986. Diplomate Am. Bd. Preventive Medicine. Commd. 2d lt. USAF, 1975, advanced through grades to maj., 1985; chief environ. medicine Kadena Air Base, Japan, 1980-82; chief aerospace medicine Soesterberg Air Base, The Netherlands, 1982-85; chief flight medicine evaluation function USAF Sch. Aerospace Medicine, San Antonio, 1987-89; chief physician Whiting (Ind.) Refinery, Amoco Oil Co., 1989-90; sr. mgr. occupl. and environ. epidemiology Procter & Gamble Co., Cin., 1990-93, assoc. med. dir., 1993-94, corp. med. dir., 1994—. Vol. asst prof. U. Cin., 1991-96, vol. assoc. prof., 1996—; bd. dirs. Medichem. (USA rep.). Reviewer Am. Jour. Tropical Medicine and Hygiene, 1998—; contbr. articles to profl. jours. Recipient Sikorsky Helicopter Rescue award Sikorsky Aircraft Corp., Japan, 1982. Fellow Am. Coll. Preventive Medicine; mem. Am. Coll. Physician Execs., Internat. Commn. Occupl. Health, Am. Coll. Occupl. and Environ. Medicine (chmn. coun. sci. affairs 1996-99). Office: Procter and Gamble Co 2 Procter And Gamble Plz Cincinnati OH 45202-3315 E-mail: lesyee@email.com.

YEE, RAYMOND, healthcare executive; b. N.Y.C., N.Y., Apr. 30, 1960; s. Jimmy and Yuen-Hing Yee. BA in Biology, Columbia Coll., 1982; MPH in Health Adminstrn., Columbia U., 1985; MBA in Fin., NYU, 1989. Asst. credit mgr. Xerox Corp., N.Y.C., 1982-84; fin. systems analyst Montefiore Med. Ctr., Bronx, N.Y., 1984-85; mgmt. cons. Deloitte & Touche, N.Y.C., 1985-87; sr. cons. Ernst & Young, 1989-91; sr. project mgr. Columbia-Presbyn. Med. Ctr., 1992-96; mgr. health mgmt. fin. Schering Labs., Kenilworth, N.J., 1996-98; asst. dir. data analysis and reporting Contract Mgmt. Orgn., Yonkers, NY, 1999—2001; dir. faculty practice fin. Columbia U., N.Y.C., 2002—. Recipient citation of Merit, B'nai Brith, Bronx, N.Y., 1978, Westinghouse Sci. Talent Search, 1978. Mem. APHA, Am. Coll. Healthcare Execs. Office: Columbia University 630 W 168th St BB-2-239 New York NY 10032 E-mail: raymond_yee@yahoo.com.

YEE, ROBERT DONALD, ophthalmologist; b. Beijing, Feb. 21, 1945; came to U.S., 1947, naturalized, 1947; s. James and Marian Y.M. (Li) Y.; m. Linda Margaret Neil, June 28, 1968; children: Jillian Neil, Allison Betram. AB, Harvard U., 1966; MD, 1970. Diplomate Am. Bd. Ophthalmology. Fullbright scholar, 1966; intern U. Rochester, N.Y., 1970-71; resident in ophthalmology Jules Stein Eye Inst. UCLA, 1971-74; fellow in neuro-ophthalmology Nat. Eye Inst., Bethesda, Md., 1974-76; chief ophthalmology Harbor-UCLA Med. Ctr., Torrance, Calif., 1976-78; asst. prof. ophthalmology Sch. Medicine UCLA, 1976-78, assoc. prof., 1978-82, prof., 1982-87; prof., dept. chmn. ophthalmology Ind. U. Sch. Medicine, Indpls., 1987—. Mem. residency rev. com. for ophthalmology Accrediation Coun. for Grad. Med. Edn., 1995—, vice-chmn. 1998—. Mem. editorial bd. Investigative Ophthalmology and Visual Sci., 1982— , von Graefe's Archives of Ophthalmology, 1983-89; Feldman endowed chair ophthalmology UCLA, 1984-87. Author numerous med. research papers. Lt. comdr. USPHS, 1974—76. Grantee, NIH, 1976—84; scholar Dolly Green Rsch. scholar, 1984—86. Fellow: ACS, Am. Acad. Ophthalmology; mem.: AMA, Accreditation Cou. for Grad. Med. Edn. (residency rev. com., chair 2000—02), Indpls. Ophthal. Soc., Ind. Med. Soc., Chinese Am. Ophthal. Soc. (pres. 1996—98), Ind. Acad. Ophthalmology, Am. Ophthal Soc., Assn. Rsch. in Vision and Ophthalmology (chmn. eye movement sect. 1981, 1987, trustee 1996—2001, v.p. 2000—01), Phi Beta Kappa, Alpha Omega Alpha. Office: Ind U Med Ctr 702 Rotary Cir Indianapolis IN 46202-5133 E-mail: ryee@inpui.edu.

YEE, STEVE, artist; b. Sacramento, Jan. 22, 1953; s. J. Bok Yee. Art dir. Photo Design Studios, Sacramento, 1974-76, Griswold Advt., Sacramento, 1976-79, Hubbard Advt., Sacramento, 1979-82, Corcoran Co., Sacramento, 1982-84; artist State of Calif., 1984-88. Tchr. Argonaunt Ctr., Sacramento, 1976; program advisor info. tech. and multimedia, U. Calif., Davis; mem. Calif. State Personnel Task Force for Graphic Artists. Author: The World Alters as We Walk in it, 1976, Art in the Third Century, 1976. Active Religious Community for Peace, Sacramento, Am. Soc. for Aesthetics, N.Y.C. Named Selected Artist Palais Des Congres, Paris, 1975, Centro De Arte y Commicacion, Buenos Aires, 1979, Bradford Mus., Yorkshire, Eng., 1982, U. Man., Winnipeg, 1984; recipient Nat. Sch. Pub. Rels. Assn. award for web site design, 1997, Am.'s Disting. Achievement award for electronic media, 1998, Nat. Sch. Pub. Rels. Assn. award for electronic media, 1998, CalSPRA award for web site design, 1998, 99. Democrat. Baptist. Home: PO Box 188499 Sacramento CA 95818-8499

YEGGE, ROBERT BERNARD, law educator, dean; b. Denver, June 17, 1934; s. Ronald Van Kirk and Fairy (Hill) Y. AB magna cum laude, Princeton U., 1956; MA in Sociology, U. Denver, 1958, JD, 1959. Bar: Colo. 1959, D.C. 1978. Ptnr. Yegge, Hall and Evans, Denver, 1959-78; with Harding Shultz & Downs successor to Nelson and Harding, 1979—; prof. U. Denver Coll. Law, 1965—, dean, 1965-77, 97-98, dean emeritus, 1977—; asst. to pres. Denver Post, 1971-75; v.p., exec. dir. Nat. Ctr. Preventive Law, 1986-91. Author: Colorado Negotiable Instruments Law, 1960, Some Goals; Some Tasks, 1965, The American Lawyer: 1976, 1966, New Careers in Law, 1969, The Law Graduate, 1972, Tomorrow's Lawyer: A Shortage and Challenge, 1974, Declaration of Independence for Legal Education, 1976. Mng. trustee Denver Ctr. for Performing Arts, 1972-75; chmn. Colo. Coun. Arts and Humanities, 1968-80, chmn. emeritus, 1980—; mem. scholar selection com. Henry Luce Found., 1975—; Active nat. and local A.R.C., chmn. Denver region, 1985-88; trustee Denver Symphony Soc., Inst. of Ct. Mgmt., Denver Dumb Friends League, 1992—, chmn. 2000—, Met. Denver Legal Aid Soc., 1994-99, Colo. Legal Svcs., 2000—, Colo. Acad.; chmn. Colo. Prevention Ctr., 2000—; trustee, vice chmn. Nat. Assembly State Arts Agys.; vice chmn. Mexican-Am. Legal Edn. and Def. Fund, 1970-76. Recipient Disting. Svc. award Denver Jr. C. of C., 1965; Harrison Tweed award Am. Assn. Continuing Edn. Adminstrs., 1985, Alumni Faculty award U. Denver, 1993. Mem. ABA (chmn. lawyers conf. 1987-88, chmn. accreditation commn. for legal asst. programs 1980-90, standing com. legal assts. 1987-92, 98-2001, standing com. delivery legal svcs. 1992-95, 2001—, com. on Gavel award 1995-98, del. to jud. adminstrn. coun. 1989-95, Robert B. Yegge award 1996), Law and Soc. Assn. (life, pres. 1965-70), Colo. Bar Assn. (bd. govs. 1965-77, 97-98), Denver Bar Assn., D.C. Bar Assn., Am. Law Inst., Am. Judicature Soc. (bd. dirs. 1968-72, 75-85, Herbert Harley award 1985), Am. Acad. Polit. and Social Sci., Am. Sociol. Soc., Assn. Am. Law Schs., Order St. Ives, Phi Beta Kappa, Beta Theta Pi, Phi Delta Phi, Alpha Kappa Keta, Omicron Delta Kappa. Home: 3472 S Race St Englewood CO 80110-3138 Office: U Denver Coll Law 1900 Olive St Denver CO 80220-1857

YEGULALP, TUNCEL M. mining engineer, educator; b. Konya, Turkey, Nov. 5, 1937; came to U.S., 1963; s. Faik Suleyman and Selma Safiye (Karatay) Y.; m. Sevinc Guneri, July 5, 1963; children: Ali, Serdar. BS, Tech. U., Istanbul, 1961; DEngring. Sci., Columbia U., 1968. Mining engr. M.T.A., Ankara, Turkey, 1961-63, chief feasibility studies group Turkey, 1971; rsch. engr. Mobil Rsch., Paulsboro, N.J., 1967-69; chief sys. cons. Sisag Ltd., Ankara, 1971-72; asst. prof. Columbia U., N.Y.C., 1972-75; assoc. prof. Henry Krumb Sch. Mines, 1975-85, prof., 1985—. Dir. N.Y. Mining and Mineral Resources Inst. Rsch., 1987—; elected permanent mem. U.S. del. World Mining Congress, 1993. Author articles in field. Served to 2d lt. C.E. Turkish Army, 1969-71. Internat. AEC fellow, Vienna, 1963; Krumb fellow, Columbia U., 1964, Campbell fellow, 1965. Mem. AIME, Internat. Higher Edn. Acad. Scis., Turkish Studies Assn., Inst. for Ops. Rsch. and the Mgmt. Scis., Sigma Chi. Moslem. Office: Columbia U 924 SWM New York NY 10027 E-mail: yegulalp@columbia.edu.

YEH, HSIAO YEN C. artist, art educator; b. Chung-Qing, China, Mar. 4, 1942; arrived in U.S., 1963; d. Chien-Chung Chen and Gin-Ger Fan; m. Raymond W.H. Yeh, Sept. 16, 1967; children: Bryant P.Y., Clement C.Y., Emily S.Y. BA, U. Oreg., 1967; MEd, U. Minn., 1969. Owner, artist Art Inc., Oklahoma City, Honolulu, 1984—. Art instr. Firehouse Art Sta., Norman, Okla., Ctrl. State U., Edmond, Okla., 1989-91; art specialist U. Hawaii, Honolulu, 1993-95. Mem. AAUW (bd. mem.), Assn. Chinese U. Women (bd. mem. 1997-99), Nat. Assn. Art Educators. Home: 1821 Kumakani Pl Honolulu HI 96821-1327

YEH, HSU-CHONG, radiology educator; b. Taipei, Taiwan, Mar. 30, 1937; came to U.S., 1973; s. Ping-Hui and Ah-Chu (Chuang) Y.; m. Cha-Pying Yeh, Sept. 26, 1964; children: David, Benjamin. MD, Nat. Taiwan U., Taipei, 1962. Diplomate Am. Bd. Radiology. Rotating intern U. Alberta Hosp., Edmonton, Can., 1964-65; resident in diagnostic radiology Montreal (Can.) Gen. Hosp., McGill U., 1969-72, fellow in diagnostic ultrasound, 1972-73; mem. active med. staff Soldier's Meml. Hosp., Campbellton, N.B., Can., 1967-69; assoc. Mt. Sinai Sch. Medicine, N.Y.C., 1973-75, asst. prof. radiology, 1976-78, assoc. prof., 1979-86, prof., 1986—. Cons. radiology VA Hosp., Bronx, N.Y., 1977-87. Author: Radiology of the Adrenals, 1982; contbg. author: Progress in Liver Disease, 1979, Frontiers in Liver Disease, 1981, Ultrasound Annual, 1982, 85, Ultrasound in Urology, 1984, Ultrasonography of the Urinary Tract, 1991, Surgical Management of Urologic Disease, 1991; contbr. articles to med. jours. 2d lt. Armored Corps, Taiwan Army, 1962-63. Fellow Soc. Radiologists in Ultrasound, Royal Coll. Physicians and Surgeons Can.; mem. Am. Inst. Ultrasound in Medicine (sr.), Radiol. Soc. N.Am. (sci. exhibit award 1988-2000), Computerized Radiology Soc., Am. Roentgen Ray Soc. (sci. exhibit award 1988), N.Y. Roentgen Ray Soc. Avocations: fine art painting, sculpture, jogging, movies. Office: Mt Sinai Med Ctr One Gustave L Levy Pl New York NY 10029-6574

YEH, JAMES KUEN-JANN, nutritionist; b. Kuen-Ming, Yuen Nang, China, June 27, 1942; came to U.S., 1967; s. Jin Gee-shan Yeh and Shing (Lan) Tsao; m. Jenny Ming, Feb. 1, 1969; children: Berhan S., Bervan Y. BS, Nat. Taiwan U., 1965; MS, U. Wis., 1968, PhD, 1974. Rsch. asst. U. Wis., Madison, 1969-74; rsch. assoc. Brookhaven Nat. Lab., Upton, N.Y., 1974-76; rsch. biochemist Nassau County Med. Ctr., East Meadow, 1976-78; dir. metabolism lab. Winthrop-Univ. Hosp., Mineola, 1978—; asst. prof. SUNY, Stony Brook, 1980-87, assoc. prof., 1988-97, prof., 1998—. Adj. prof. L.I. U., Brookville, N.Y., 1980-83; nutrition cons. Life Health Ctr., West Babylon, N.Y., 1986-88; dir. metabolism lab. Winthrop-Univ. Hosp., Mineola, 1978—. Contbr. articles to profl. jours. Grantee NIH, 1975, Retirement Rsch. Found., 1986. Fellow: Am. Coll. Nutrition; mem.: Internat. Chinese Hard Tissue Soc., Am. Coll. Sports Medicine, Internat. Conf. on Calcium Regulating Hormones, Am. Soc. of Bone Mineral Rsch. Home: 10 Wisteria Pl Syosset NY 11791-2824 Office: Winthrop-Univ Hosp 259 1st St Mineola NY 11501-3987 E-mail: JYEH@Winthrop.org.

YEH, JIEH REN, engineer; b. Taipei, Taiwan, Feb. 25, 1956; s. Cheng and Ying Y.; m. Bih Jing Lin; children: Jeffrey, Brendan. PhD, Rensselaer Polytech. Inst., 1985. R&D engr. Alcoa Inc., Pitts., 1985—. Contbr. articles to profl. jours. Mem. ASME. Office: Alcoa Inc 100 Technical Dr Alcoa Center PA 15069 E-mail: jerry.yeh@alcoa.com.

YEH, JUNG-HUA, senior mechanical engineer; b. Taipei, Taiwan, Nov. 03; parents Min-An and Hsiu-Ming Y.; m. Shu-Ting Tsai, Nov. 7, 1987; 4 children. BA, Nat. Taipei Inst. Technology, 1984; MS, U. Mo., 1993, PhD, 1997. Mech. engr. Lotun Technic Co., Taipei, 1986-87, Logitech, Inc., Taipei, 1987-88, YFY Paper Mfg. Co., Taipei, 1988-90, Pro-Tech. Engrs. & Constructors Co., Taipei, 1990-91; sr. mech. engr. prediction maintenance team Inteplast Group, Ltd., Lolita, Tex., 1997—. Worked on equipment failure detection and performance by using advanced vibration techniques. Contbr. articles to profl. jours. including Jour. Machine Tools and Manufacture, 1999, ASME 14th Reliability, Stress Analysis, Jour. Mfg. Processes, 2000; contbr. to confs. including Mechanisms Session of the 21st ASME Design Automation Conf., 1995, ASME 14th Reliability, Stress Analysis, and Failure Prevention Conf., 2000. Christian Fellowship chmn., deacon; chmn. Comfort Chinese Ch. Coun. Recipient Disting. Leadership award in field of System Failure Detection and Prevention. Mem. AAAS, Soc. Automotive Engrs., ASME, Sigma Xi. Discovered dominant frequency shift when a bolted connection is slightly loosened. Virtual spring element to model contact conditions. Expertise includes detection of machine and structure assemblies with bolt looseness, failure diagnosis for civil and mechanical structures, multi-body contact condition modeling, fixture clamping condition modeling and monitoring, mechanical drive and transmission component design, hybris control of seismic structures. Avocations: reading, research, jogging, hiking. E-mail: jyehtx@yahoo.com.

YEH, KUO HSING, bank executive; b. Taipei, Taiwan, Republic of China, Feb. 1, 1932; m. Hsiu-Mei Yeh Tsang. BA, Nat. Taiwan U., 1954. Exec. v.p. Hwa Nan Comml. Bank, Ltd., Taiwan, 1955-81; pres. Banking Inst. Republic China, 1981-88; CEO Fin. Info. System Group Ministery Fin., Taiwan, 1984-88; pres. Chang Hwa Comml. Bank Ltd., Taiwan, 1988-94; chmn. Taipeibank, Taipei, 1994-97, Taiwan First Investment & Trust Co Ltd, Taipei, 1998, Cathay United Bank Co Ltd., Tapei, Taiwan, 1998—. Author: Theory and Practice of Lending Management, 1980; editor: Practice of Bank's Consumer Loan, 1983. Recipient Disting. Fin. Staffer award Ministry Fin., Taipei, 1974. Mem. Banker's Assn. Taiwan (chmn. 1988-92), Banker's Assn. Taipei (chmn. 1992-97), Taiwan U. Alumni Assn. (mng. dir. Taipei chpt. 1994), Taiwan U. Alumni Club, Taipei Yuen-Shan Club. Home: 3 Fl No 432 Chi Lin Rd Taipei 104 Taiwan Office: Cathay United Bank Co Ltd 218 Sec 2 Tun Hwa S Rd Taipei 104 Taiwan

YEH, LUN-SHU RAY, electrochemist; b. Taoyuan, Taiwan, Oct. 2, 1946; came to U.S., 1970; s. Ming-Ching and Lan-Kwei Yeh; m. Ming Mavis Lu; children: Leon Allen, Rick Norman. BS in Engring., Cheng-Kung U., Tainan, Taiwan, 1969; MS, U. Ky., 1972; PhD, U. Tex., 1976. Postdoctoral fellow Rice U., Houston, 1977; rsch. chemist Allied Chem. Corp., Morristown, N.J., 1978-83; sr. rsch. chemist Allied Signal Inc., 1983-87; scientist Philips Electronic Instruments Co., Mahwah, N.J., 1988-92, sr. scientist, 1993-97, Edax Internat. Co. subs. Philips Electronics Instruments Co., Mahwah, 1993-97, Edax Inc., Mahwah, 1998—. Contbr. numerous articles to profl. publs. Inventor award Allied Signal Inc., 1987. Mem. IEEE, Electrochem. Soc., Phi Kappa Phi, Phi Lambda Upsilon. Achievements include 5 patents in areas of bipolar batteries, solid state x-ray detectors, cryostat designs. Office: Edax Inc 85 Mckee Dr Mahwah NJ 07430-2121 E-mail: ray.yeh@ametek.com.

YEH, MING-NENG, obstetrician, gynecologist; b. Taiwan, Oct. 13, 1938; came to U.S., 1966; s. Chao-Chieh and Pu-Tseng (Song) Y.; m. Lisa Lie-Yu Lin, Oct. 18, 1965; children: Angela, Rubina, Noreen, Janet. MD, Nat. Taiwan U., Taipei, 1964. Diplomate Am. Bd. Ob-Gyn. Intern Johnston-Willis Hosp., 1966-67; resident Bklyn.-Cumberland Hosp., 1967-68, St. Luke's Hosp. Ctr., N.Y.C., 1968-71; fellow fetal medicine Columbia-Presbyn. Med. Ctr., 1971-73, attending obstetrician, 1987—; clin. prof. Columbia U., 1987—. Fellow N.Y. Acad. Medicine, N.Y. Acad. Sci.; mem. Am. Fertility Soc., Am. Inst. Ultrasound Medicine, Am. Coll. Ob-Gyn., N.Y. Obstet. Soc., N.Y. Gyn. Soc. Office: Columbia-Presbyn Med Ctr 161 Fort Washington Ave New York NY 10032-3713

YEH, PAUL PAO, electrical and electronics engineer, educator; b. Sung Yang, Chekiang, China, Mar. 25, 1927; came to U.S., 1956, naturalized, 1963; s. Tsung Shan and Shu Huan (Mao) Y.; m. Beverley Pamela Eng, May 15, 1953; children: Judith Elaine, Paul Edmond, Richard Alvin, Ronald Timothy. Student, Nat. Cen. U., Nanking, China, 1946-49; BSEE, U. Toronto (Ont., Can.), 1951; MSEE, U. Pa., 1960, PhD, 1966. Registered profl. engr., Ont. Design engr. Can. Gen. Electric Co., Toronto, 1951-56; asst. prof. SUNY, Binghamton, 1956-57; sr. engr. H.K. Porter, ITE & Kuhlman, Phila. and Detroit, 1957-61; assoc. prof. N.J. Inst. Tech., Newark, 1961-66; supr. rsch. and devel. N.Am. Rockwell, Anaheim, Calif., 1966-70; sr. R&D engr. Lockheed Calif. Co., Burbank, 1970-72, 78-89; mem. tech. staff The Aerospace Corp., El Segundo, 1972-78; sr. R&D engr. Lockheed Advanced Devel. Co., Burbank, 1978-89; chief scientist Advanced Systems Rsch., Pasadena, Calif., 1989—. With Consol. Edison Co., N.Y.C., 1963-64, Pub. Svc. Elec. and Gas Co. N.J., 1965-66, Zhejiang Sci. and Tech. Exch. Ctr. with Fgn. Countries, 1995—; sr. lectr. State U. Calif., Long Beach, 1967-73; cons. prof. Chung Shan Inst. Sci. and Tech., 1989-92; vis. prof. Tsinghua U., 1993—, South China U. Sci. and Tech., 1997—; vis. chair prof. S.E. U., 1994—, Zhejiang U., 1994—; cons. prof. Northwestern Poly. U., 1993—, Shanghai U., 1994—; hon. prof. Beijing U. Aeronautics and Astronautics, 1993—, Zhejiang U. Sci. and Tech., 1994—; chair, prof. Nanjing U. Aeronautics & Astronautics, 1999—, Wuyi U., 1999—; rschr. power sys. design and control, 1951-66; investigator R&D Stealth tech. electronic warfare, avionics, IR/EO Tech, nuclear hardening, anti-submarine warfare. Recipient Achievement award for anti-submarine warfare/magnetic anomaly detection sys. Lockheed Corp. Mem. IEEE (sr., life), Nat. Mgmt. Assn. (life), Nat. Def. Indsl. Assn., Assn. O ld Crows, Chinese Am. Engring./Sci. Assn. So. Calif. (pres. 1969-71), Nat. Ctrl. U. Alumni Assn. (pres. 1977), Beijing Assn. for Sci. and Tech. Exchs. with Fgn . Countries, (hon. dir.), Assn. Profl. Engrs. of Ont., N.Y. Acad. Scis., Air Force Assn., Zhejiang Assn. for Sci. and Tech. Exchs. with Fgn. Countries (advisor), Armed Forces Comms. and Electronics Assn., U.S. Naval Inst., Assn. U.S. Army. Republican. Presbyterian. Achievements include patent for Non-Capacitive Transmission Cable. Home: 78278 Quail Run Palm Desert CA 92211 Office: Advanced Systems Rsch Inc 33 S Catalina Ave Ste 202 Pasadena CA 91106-2426 E-mail: Drpaulpyeh@ieee.org.

YEH, RAYMOND WEI-HWA, architect, educator; b. Shanghai, China, Feb. 25, 1942; came to U.S., 1958, naturalized, 1976; s. Herbert Hwan-Ching and Joyce Bo-Ding (Kwan) Y.; m. Hsiao-Yen Chen, Sept. 16, 1967; children—Bryant Po Yung, Clement Chung-Yung, Emily Su-Yung. BA, U. Oreg., 1965, B.Arch., 1967; M.Arch., U. Minn., 1969. Cert. Nat. Coun. Archtl. Registration Bds.; registered architect, Tex., Okla., Calif., Hawaii. Draftsman, designer various archtl. firms, 1965-68; design architect Ellerbe Architects, St. Paul, 1968-70; v.p., dir. design Sorey, Hill, Binnicker, Oklahoma City, 1973-74; prin. architect Raymond W.H. Yeh & Assos., Norman, Okla., 1974-80; asst. prof. to prof. U. Okla., 1970-79; head dept. architecture, prof. Calif. Poly. State U., San Luis Obispo, 1979-83; dean Coll. Architecture U. Okla., Norman, 1983-92; prin. architect W.H. Raymond Yeh, 1983-93; dean sch. architecture U. Hawaii at Manoa, Honolulu, 1993—. Profl. adviser Neighborhood Conservation and Devel. Center, Oklahoma City, 1977 79 Works include: St. Thomas More U. Parish and Student Center, Norman, Summit Ridge Center Retirement Community, Harrah, Okla., (recipient Nat. Design award Guild Religious Architecture 1978). Nat. Endowment for Arts fellow, 1978-79 Fellow AIA (dir., pres. Okla. chpt. 1986, design awards, nat. com. chmn. 1989); mem. Calif. Coun. Archtl. Edn. (dir., pres. 1982-83), Okla. Found. for Architecture (founding chair bd. 1989-90), Asian Soc. Okla. (award of Excellence 1992), Asia Pacific Ctr. for Arch. (founding bd. dirs. 1996). Presbyterian. Office: U Hawaii Manoa Sch Architecture Honolulu HI 96822

YEH, YING CHIN, electrical engineer; b. Tainan, Taiwan, June 1, 1945; came to U.S., 1978; s. Tso Hsueh and Ai Lien (Yen) Y.; m. Su Chin Lee, Oct. 24, 1972; children: Karen Y.C., Cindy S.C. BSEE, Nat. Cheng Kung U., 1967; MSEE, Nat. Taiwan U., 1970; PhDEE, U. Ottawa, Can., 1973. Indsl. postdoctoral fellow RCA Ltd. R&D Lab., Montreal, Can., 1973-76; sr. engr. Canadair Ltd., 1976-78; sr. mem. tech. staff Otis Elevator Co. R&D Ctr., Farmington, Conn., 1978-81; assoc. tech. fellow The Boeing Co., Comml. Airplane Group, Seattle, 1981—. Mem. Internat. Fedn. for Info. Processing Working Group on Dependable Computing and Fault Tolerance. V.p. Taiwanese Am. Citizen League, Seattle, 1993-95. Mem. IEEE, Taiwanese Assn. for Greater Seattle (bd. dirs. 1998—). Achievements include development in 7J7 Control System Performance Study for synchronous PFC and Autonomous ARINC 629 operation; development 777 flight controls ARINC 629 Bus Requirement; design and validation testing of 777 PFC (primary flight computer) redundancy management. Office: Boeing Comml Airplane Group PO Box 3707 Seattle WA 98124-2207 E-mail: ying.c.yeh@boeing.com.

YEHL, RICK J. secondary school educator; b. Olean, N.Y., July 9, 1969; s. Ronald John and Patricia Anne Yehl; m. Sarah J. Yehl. BS in Phys. Edn., SUNY, Brockport, 1992; postgrad. driver's edn., SUNY, Buffalo, 1998; MS, U. New Eng., 2000. Alternative edn. phys. edn. and health Salamanca (N.Y.) City Schs., 1992—94; adaptive phys. edn. tchr. Corning (N.Y.) Sch. Dist., 1996—98; driver's edn. tchr. Greenwood (N.Y.) Ctrl. Sch., 1995—, Campbell (N.Y.) Savona Sch., 1995—, head softball coach, 1995—. Asst. football coach Alfred (N.Y.) State Coll., 1998—. Mem.: NEA. Avocations: coaching, weight lifting, camping, bicycling, golf. Home: 8455 Ct Rt 125 Campbell NY 14821 Office: 17 Mountainview Rd E Bath NY 14810

YELDANDI, VEERAINDER ANTIAH, engineer, consultant; b. Hyderabad, India, Jan. 31, 1929; came to U.S., 1979; s. Antiah Venkatswamy and Rangamma (Chippa) Y.; m. Suvarna Nagiah Bet, Mar. 15, 1952; children: Vinod, Vivek, Vijay, Vandana. BSCE, Osmania Univ., Hyderabad, India, 1951; MS, Univ. Roorkee, Roorkee, India, 1957. Registered profl. engr., Ill., Wis. Jr. engr. Hyderabad Pub. Works, Hyderabad, 1952-57; lectr. civil engr. Univ. Roorkee, 1957-59; project engr. Bhilai (India) Steel Plant, 1959-79; structure cons. Sargent & Lundy, Chgo., 1980-85, Westinghouse Engring., Chgo., 1986; estimating engr. Chgo. Dept. of Transp., 1987-91; civil engr. Dept. of Water, Chgo., 1991—. Pres. Rotary Club, Bhilai, 1969-70, v.p. Telugu Assn. Chgo., 1986-87. Fellow Am. Soc. Civil Engrs. (life); mem. Am. Water Works Assn. Achievements include preparation of technical report for water supply facilities for Bhilai Steel Plant complex expansion and township, design of the facilities and participated in construction of the project design of water mains project for the City of Chicago Dept. Water. Home: 4170 N Marine Dr Apt 18K Chicago IL 60613-2340 Office: City of Chgo Dept Water CWP 1000 E Ohio St Chicago IL 60611-3416

YELENICK, MARY THERESE, lawyer; b. Denver, May 17, 1954; d. John Andrew and Maesel Joyce (Reed) Y. B.A. magna cum laude, Colo. Coll., 1976; J.D. cum laude, Georgetown U., 1979. Bar: D.C. 1979, U.S. Dist. Ct. D.C. 1980, U.S. Ct. Appeals (D.C. cir.) 1981, N.Y. 1982, U.S. Dist. Ct. (so. and ea. dists.) N.Y. 1982, U.S. Supreme Ct. 1992, U.S. Ct. Appeals (5th cir.) 1995. Law clk. to presiding justices Superior Ct. D.C., 1979-81; ptnr. Chadbourne & Parke, LLP, N.Y.C., 1981—. Editor Jour. of Law and Policy Internat. Bus., 1978-79. Mem. Phi Beta Kappa. Democrat. Roman Catholic. Home: 310 E 46th St New York NY 10017-3002 Office: Chadbourne & Parke LLP 30 Rockefeller Plz Fl 31 New York NY 10112-0129

YELICH, LYNNE, member of parliament; b. Mar. 24, 1953; m. Matt Yelich; 2 children. Grad., Kenaston HS, 1971. Farmer, Kenaston; mem. House of Commons, Ottawa, Canada, ofcl. opposition dep. critic for citizenship and immigration. Office: House of Commons Rm 686 Confederation Bldg Ottawa ON K1A 0A6 Canada Address: Unit #71 Market Mall 2325 Preston Ave Saskatoon SK S7J 2G2 Canada Office Fax: 613-995-0126., 306-975-6492. E-mail: yelic.l@parl.gc.ca.

YELIN, ROBERT BRUCE, musician, recording artist, composer, lyricist; b. Yonkers, N.Y., Sept. 25, 1944; s. Paul and Libby (Watinsky) Y.; m. Harriet Ann Hunter, Mar. 22, 1980. Student, NYU, 1962-65. Jazz guitarist, performer, educator, N.Y., 1962-80, Colo., 1981-85; pres. Arbee Why Music Publs., Colo., Conn., 1981-87; prof. jazz guitar studies U. Colo., Denver, 1982; pres. Chord Master Records, Colo., Conn., 1983-88; jazz performer, educator Conn., 1985-88. Pvt. guitar tchr., 1962-88. Jazz guitarist (solo guitar albums) Night Rain, 1981 (Reviewer's Choice 1982), Talents of the Heart, 1990, Robert Yelin Plays the Music of Jobim & Brazil, 1999; (jazz trio album) Song for My Wife, 1983; performer N.Y. Jazz Guitar Festival, 1976, Breckenridge (Colo.) Jazz Festival, 1982, Winter Park (Colo.) Jazz Festival, 1983; (CD recordings), Bossa, Ballads and Blues Vols. 1-5, 1997, Welcome to my World, 1999, Enchanted, The Beauty of the 14-String Guitar, 1999; jazz clubs, concerts nationwide, 1962—; author: (with others) The Tal Farlow Jazz Guitar Method Book, 1973-74; contbg. editor Guitar Player mag., 1968-82, Frets mag. 1978-80; Wes Montgomery's Book, 1984-85(newsletter) The Jazz Guitar Soc. We. Australia, 1989—; contbg. cons. , article writer Just Jazz Guitar, 1994—; arranger also; co-prodr. (videos) Legends of Jazz Guitar, vols. 1-3, 1995-96; commd. 1st 14-string archtop guitar. Donates audio and video tape recordings to music schs., colls., univs. and guitar socs. all over the world. Mem. Broadcast Musician, Inc. Clubs: Jazz Guitar Record Library and Club (pres. 1981—). Home and Office: 17709 Fieldbrook Cir N Boca Raton FL 33496-1534

YELISEEV, ALEXEI ARKADIEVICH, biochemist, researcher; b. Moscow, Nov. 3, 1959; s. Arkadii Aleksandrovich and Tatiana Georgievna (Sokolova) E.; m. Elena Dmitrievna Polonnikova, Aug. 20, 1985; children: Ekaterina, Tatiana. MS in Chemistry, Moscow State U., 1981; PhD in Biochemistry, Russian Acad. Scis., 1987. From trainee rschr. to sr. rschr. A.N. Bakh Inst. Biochemistry, Russian Acad. Scis., Moscow, 1981-92, sr. rschr., 1992—. Vis. rsch. scientist U. Tex., Houston, 1993-99; sr. rsch. scientist Roche Vitamins, Inc., 1999-2001; sr. scientist Kosan Bioscis., Inc., 2001—. Author: (chpt.) Biosynthesis of Corrinoids, 1993, Control of Photosystem Formation in Rhodobacter sphaeroides, 1998; contbr. articles to profl. jours. Rsch. fellow Alexander von Humboldt Stiftung, 1989-92, Internat. Union Biochemistry, 1992, Royal Soc. London, 1993; grantee Internat. Sci. Found., 1994-95. Mem. AAAS, Am. Soc. Microbiology, Russian Biochem. Soc. (lectureship 1987). Avocations: travelling, music, books. Office: Kosan Bioscis Inc 3832 Bay Center Pl Hayward CA 94545 E-mail: alexeieliseev@aol.com., yeliseev@kosan.com.

YELLEN, JOHN EDWARD, archaeologist; b. N.Y.C., Nov. 1, 1942; s. Julius and Ruth (Blumenthal) Y.; m. Alison Spence Brooks, Dec. 21, 1971; children: Elizabeth Spence, Alexander Brooks. BA, Hobart Coll., 1964; MA, Harvard U., 1966, PhD, 1974. Predoctoral fellow Smithsonian Inst., Washington, 1971-72, postdoctoral fellow, 1972-73, rsch. assoc., 1973-77; program dir. NSF, 1977-92, archaeology program dir., 1993—. Author: Archaeological Approaches to the Present, 1977; co-editor: Experimental Archeology, 1977. Pres. Sousa Neighborhood Assn., Washington, 1991. Grantee Nat. Geog. Soc., 1973, NSF, 1975-77. Fellow Explorers Club (chair exploration com. 1996—); mem. Internat. Union Pre and Proto-Historic Scis. (exec. com. 1991—), Paleoanthropology Soc. (founder). Achievements include research in ethnographic and archaeological research in Botswana; archaeological research in Zaire, Ethiopia and Kenya. Home: 810 E St SE Washington DC 20003-2842 E-mail: jyellen@nsf.gov.

YELLIN, VICTOR FELL, composer, music educator; b. Boston, Dec. 14, 1924; s. Mendl and Sarah (Fell) Y.; m. Isabel Joseph, May 26, 1948; 1 son, Garo. AB cum laude, Harvard U., 1949, A.M., 1952, PhD, 1957. Teaching fellow Harvard U., Cambridge, Mass., 1952-56; asst. prof. NYU, N.Y.C., 1956-58, assoc. prof., 1961-64, prof., 1964—; asst. prof. Williams ., Williamstown, Mass., 1958-60; assoc. prof. Ohio State ., Columbus, 1960-61; coordinator N.Y. Metro-Fulbright-Hayes Vis. Scholars, 1978-82. Mem. editorial adv. bd. Am. Music. Composer: (opera) Abaylar, 1974 (song cycle) Dark of the Moon, 1986; conductor: Mrs. H.H.A. Beach's Grand Mass in E-flat, N.Y.C., 1982; author: Chadwick, Yankee Composer, 1990, Bye Bye Blues Variations for Violin and Piano, Tully Hall, N.Y.C., 1992, for Cello and Piano, Merkin Hall, N.Y.C., 2002, The Omnibus Idea, 1998; contbr. articles in Early Melodrama in Am., The Aethiop, Orchestral Restoration, Am. Music, A Celebration Am. Music, Jour. Musicology. Served with U.S. Army, 1943-46, ETO. Recipient grant Nat. Endowment Humanities, 1978 Mem. Am. Musicol. Soc., Sonneck Soc. Home: 52 Washington Mews New York NY 10003-6608 Office: NYU 100 Washington Sq E New York NY 10003-6688

YELLIS, KENNETH, museum administrator; Rsch. historian Office of Small Exhibits, Nat. Portrait Gallery, curator edn.; dir. pub. programs Plimoth Plantation; dir. First Lights Mus. Consultants; asst. dir. pub. programs Peabody Mus. Natural History, Yale U. Office: Peabody Mus Natural History Yale Univ 170 Whitney Ave New Haven CT 06520-8118*

YELNICK, MARC M(AURICE), lawyer; b. N.Y.C., Jan. 30, 1947; s. Louis and Jeanne (Friedman) Y.; m. Linda Sherwin, Dec. 20, 1973; children: Sandy, Shauna. BA, Bklyn. Coll., 1967; postgrad., NYU, 1967-70; JD, St. John's U., 1976. Bar: N.Y. 1977, U.S. Dist. Ct. (ea. and so. dists.) N.Y. 1977, U.S. Dist. Ct. (no. dist.) Calif. 1985. Assoc. Billet, Billet & Avirom, N.Y.C., 1977-79, Whitman & Ransom, N.Y.C., 1979-84; sole practice San Mateo, Calif., 1984—. Mem. ABA, Am. Immigration Lawyers Assn. (no. Calif. chpt.). Office: 520 S El Camino Real Ste 320 San Mateo CA 94402-1716 Fax: 650-341-4640. E-mail: MarcYelnick@Bigfoot.com.

YEN, DAVID CHI-CHUNG, management information systems educator; b. Tai-Chung, Taiwan, Republic of China, Nov. 15, 1953; s. I-King and Chi-Ann (Ro) Y.; m. Wendy Wen-Yawn Ding, July 4, 1981; children: Keeley Ju, Caspar Lung, Christopher Jai. MBA in Gen. Bus., Cen. State U., Edmond, Okla., 1981, BS in Computer Sci., 1982; MS in Computer Sci., PhD in Mgmt. Info. Systems, U. Nebr., 1985. Asst. prof. Miami U., Oxford, Ohio, 1985-89, assoc. prof., 1989-93, prof., 1994—, MIS advisor computer study com., 1986-90; asst. chmn., 1993-95; chmn. Miami U., Oxford, Ohio, 1995—; sr. faculty teaching excellence, 1994. Chmn., mem. computer policy com. Miami U., 1991-94, computer adv. group, 1993-94, com. evaluation adminstrs., 1993, conf. and session chair, seminar dir., Smucker prof. internship, mem. exec. com., 1995—, program chair; mem. Hong Kong Coun. for Acad. Accreditation, 2000—. Author two textbooks; editor Proceedings; contbr. articles to profl. jours. External assesser Can. Rsch. and Grants Coun., Hong Kong Rsch. and Grants Coun. Served to 2d lt., Rep. China Navy. Alumni teaching scholar Miami U., 1987-88; named Prof. of Yr. Delta Sigma Pi, 1993; grantee GE, Cleve. Found., Smucker, Microsoft. Mem. IEEE, Am. Chinese Mgmt. Educators Assn. (pres.-elect 1995, pres. 1996, program com. 1997—, MIS track chair 1998—), Soc. Info. Mgmt., Internat. Chinese Info. Sys. Assn., Internat. Bus. Sch. Computer User Assn., Internat. Sch. Bus. Computer User Group (chair conf., proceedings editor 1988), Assn. Computing Machinery, Ohio Mgmt. Info. System Assn., Decision Sci. Inst., Soc. Data Educators. Office: Miami U 309 Upham Hall Oxford OH 45056

YEN, DUEN HSI, corporate executive, physicist; b. Nyack, N.Y., Apr. 24, 1949; s. Ernest Chu and Louise (Loo) Y.; m. Linda Leiko Takai, June 22, 1989. BS in Physics, Rensselaer Polytech. Inst., 1971; MA in Biophysics, Johns Hopkins U., 1974; MSEE, U. Vt., 1978. Mem. tech. staff Bell Telephone Labs., Holmdel, N.J., 1978-83; pres. Multipath Systems, Inc., Honolulu, 1984—; exec. dir. Malama Learning Facility, 1999—. Violinist Oahu Civic Orch. Inventor noise detector, electronic travel aids for blind; contbr. articles to profl. jours. Small Bus. Innovation Rsch. grantee, NSF grantee 1984, Nat. Eye Inst. grantee 1988, 89, 91. Mem. Acoustical Soc. Am., Audio Engring. Soc., Sigma Pi Sigma. Avocations: binaural recording, stereo photography, violin.

YEN, FRANCES T. professional society administrator; b. Taipei, Taiwan, June 20, 1977; arrived in U.S., 1983; BS, SUNY, Binghamton, 1999; MPA, NYU, 2002. With Cmty. Svc. Soc., N.Y.C., Assn. to Benefit Children, N.Y.C., J.P. Morgan and Chase, N.Y.C. Avocations: theater , ice skating. Home: 15905 Laburnum Ave Flushing NY 11358-3618

YEN, GILI, economics researcher; b. Taipei, Taiwan, Mar. 8, 1953; s. Tzeng-song and Yueh-yun Yen; m. Eva Chung-Chiung; 1 child, Bernard Chih-hsun. BA. Nat. Taiwan U., Taipei, 1975, MA, 1978; PhD, Wash. U., 1983. Assoc. rsch. fellow Chung-Hua Instn. for Econ. Rsch., Taipei, 1983-86; assoc. prof. Inst. Indsl. Econs. Nat. Ctrl. U., Chung-li, 1985-87, prof., then dir., 1987-89, prof., founding dir. Inst. Fin. Mgmt., 1989-92; sr. rsch. fellow, divsn. dir. Taiwan Inst. Econ. Rsch., Taipei, 1992-93; sr. rsch. fellow Taiwan Rsch. Inst., 1994—; 1st v.p. China Devel. Bank (formerly China Devel. Corp.), 1994-97; dir., supr. China Steel Corp., Kaohsiung, 1990-97; dean Sch. Mgmt. Chaoyang U. of Tech., 1998—2001; prof. Dept. Bus. Adminstrn., 2001—. Advisor Exec. Yuan (the Adminstrv. Br. of the Ctrl. Govt.), Taipei, 1983-84, 89-90, Everfortune Bus. Group, 1999-2000, sen. advisor, 2001-; adj. prof. Nat. Taiwan U., Taipei, 1987-93. Author: (collection of acad. papers) Empirical Studies on Business Finance and Government Policy in Taiwan, 1996; editor: New Directions in Regional Trade Liberalization and Investment Cooperations, APEC, 1994, Proceedings Annual Acad. Nat. Conf. Mgmt.-related Topics, 2000—; mem. editl. bd. Advances Pacific Basin Bus., Econs., Fin., 1995; : Review of Pacific Basin Fin. Markets and Policies, 1998—; contbr. articles to profl. jours. including Jour. Econs. and Bus., Am. Jour. Econs. and Sociology, Rev. Quantitative Fin. and Acctg., Managerial and Decision Econs., Advances in Fin. Planning and Forecasting, and others. Recipient numerous rsch. awards Nat. Sci. Coun. Mem. Chinese Econ. Assn. (gov. 1991-94), Chinese Fin. Assn. (sec.-gen., exec. dir. 1992-96), Internat. Soc. for Instnl. Econs. (country rep. 1997). Avocations: reading, listening to music, playing table tennis, traveling, playing mahjong. Home: 6F No 233 Song-Der St Taipai 110 Taiwan E-mail: hjlee@mail.cyut.edu.tw.

YEN, HENRY CHIN-YUAN, computer systems programmer, software engineer, consulting company executive; b. Mpls., Apr. 18, 1958; s. James and Elizabeth Y.; m. Michele Calen, Oct. 8, 1988; children: Andrew, Matthew. Sr. systems programmer Grumman Data Systems Corp., Bethpage, N.Y., 1978-83; mgr. Data Ctr. On-Line Software Internat., Inc., Ft. Lee, N.J., 1983-85, lead systems programmer, 1985-88; v.p. The Galamery Co., Inc., Del., 1988—, Aegis Info. Systems, Inc., 1989—. Bd. dirs. Personal Computer Systems Corp. Bd. trustees Syosset Pub. Libr., NY, 2002. Mem. IEEE, Assn. Computing Machinery, Network and Sys. Profls. Assn., Mensa (v.p. greater N.Y. chpt. 2002-), Intertel. Avocations: bicycling, profl. musician. Home: PO Box 1 Hicksville NY 11802-0001 Office: Aegis Info Systems Inc PO Box 730 Hicksville NY 11802-0730 E-mail: henry@AegisInfoSys.com.

YEN, MICHAEL C. physician; b. Shanghai, China, Dec. 24, 1942; Came to U.S., 1965. s. Leo and Ching Ying (Lee) Y.; m. Peggy K. Yen, Aug. 20, 1977; 1 child, Elizabeth. MD, Sch. Shanghai, 1965. Diplomate Am. Bd. Internal Medicine, Am. Bd. Nephrology; cert. clin. hypertension specialist. Assoc. head of nephrology Md. Gen. Hosp., Balt., 1976-80, chmn. dept. medicine, 1980-93. Fellow ACP. Office: 821 N Eutaw St Baltimore MD 21201-4648 E-mail: mcy2@juno.com.

YEN, SAMUEL S(HOW)-C(HIH), obstetrics and gynecology educator, reproductive endocrinologist; b. Beijing, Feb. 22, 1927; s. K.Y. and E.K. Yen; children: Carol Amanda, Douglas Amelia, Margaret Rae. BS, Cheeloo U., China, 1949; MD, U. Hong Kong, 1954, DSc, 1980. Diplomate Am. Bd. Ob-Gyn, Am. Bd. Reproductive Endocrinology. Intern Queen Mary Hosp., Hong Kong, 1954—55; resident Johns Hopkins U., Balt., 1956—60; assoc. prof. reproductive biology Case Western Res. U., Cleve., 1967—70; prof. ob-gyn U. Calif., San Diego, 1972—83, chmn. dept. reproductive medicine, 1972—83, prof. reproductive medicine, 1983—; dir. reproductive endocrinology U. Calif. Med. Ctr., 1983—98, W.R. Persons chair, 1987. Assoc. dir. obstetrics Univ. Hosp., Cleve., 1968—70; DeGroof lectr., 1987; Van Campenhaut lectr. Can. Fertility and Andrology Soc., 1995; bd. examiners Am. Bd. Ob-Gyn., 1973—78, Am. Bd. Reproductive Endocrinology, 1976—82. Editor: Reproductive Endocrinology Physiology, Pathophysiology and Clinical Management, 1978, 1999. Named to Soc. of Scholars, Johns Hopkins U., 1992; recipient Axel Munthe Found. award, 1982, Simpson medal, U. Edinburgh, Scotland, 1996; fellow, Oglebay, 1968—69. Fellow: Royal Coll. Ob-Gyn. (ad eundem, London); mem.: Am. Fertility Soc., Endocrine Soc. (Rorer Clin. Investigator award 1992, Disting. Scientist award 1992), Soc. Gynecol. Investigation (pres. 1981, Disting. Scientist award 1992), Assn. Am. Physicians, NAS Inst. Medicine. Office: U Calif San Diego Reproductive Medicine # 0633 La Jolla CA 92093

YEN, TEH FU, civil and environmental engineering educator; b. Kun-Ming, China, Jan. 9, 1927; came to U.S., 1949; s. Kwang Pu and Ren (Liu) Y.; m. Shiao-Ping Siao, May 30, 1959 BS, Cen. China U., 1947; MS, W.Va. U., 1953; PhD, Va. Poly. Inst. and State U., 1956; hon. doctoral degree, Pepperdine U., 1982, Internat. U. Dubna, Russia, 1996, All Russian Petroleum Exploration Inst., St. Petersburg, Russia, 1999. Sr. research chemist Good Yr. Tire & Rubber Co., Akron, 1955-59; fellow Mellon Inst., Pitts., 1959-65; sr. fellow Carnegie-Mellon U., 1965-68; assoc. prof. Calif. State U., Los Angeles, 1968-69, U. So. Calif., 1969-80, prof. civil engring. and environ. engring., 1980—. Hon. prof. Shanghai U. Sci. and Tech., 1986, U. Petroleum, Beijing, 1987, Daqing Petroleum Inst., 1992; cons. Universal Oil Products, 1968-76, Chevron Oil Field Rsch. Co., 1968-75, Finnigan Corp., 1976-77, GE, 1977-80, United Techs., 1978-79, TRW Inc., 1982-83, Exxon, 1981-82, DuPont, 1985-88, Min. Petroleum, Beijing, 1982—, Biogas Rsch. Inst.-UN, Chengdu, 1991. Author numerous tech. books; contbr. articles to profl. jours. Recipient Disting. Svc. award Tau Beta Pi, 1974, Imperial Crown Gold medal, Iran, 1976, Achievement award Chinese Engring. and Sci. Assocs. So. Calif., 1977, award Phi Kappa Phi, 1982, Outstanding Contbn. honor Pi Epsilon Tau, 1984, Svc. award Republic of Honduras, 1989, award in Petroleum Chem. Am. Chem. Soc., 1994, Kapitsa Gold medal Russian Fedn., 1995. Fellow Royal Chem. Soc., Inst. Petroleum, Am. Inst. Chemists; mem. Am. Chem. Soc. (bd. dirs. 1993, councillor, founder and chmn. geochemistry divsn. 1979-81, Chinese Acad. Scis. (standing com.), Acad. Scis. Russian Fedn. (academician, fgn. mem.). Home: 2378 Morslay Rd Altadena CA 91001-2716 Office: U So Calif 3620 S Vermont Ave Rm 224A Los Angeles CA 90089-2531 E-mail: tfyen@usc.edu.

YEN, T.S. BENEDICT, pathologist, educator; b. Taipei, Taiwan, Oct. 15, 1953; came to U.S., 1965; s. Yen-Chen and Er-Ying Yen; m. Maria He Yen, Mar. 26, 1983; children: Cecilia, Brian. BS, Stanford U., 1973; MD, PhD, Duke U., 1982. Diplomate Am. Bd. Pathology. Asst. prof. U. Calif., San Francisco, 1985-91, assoc. prof. pathology, 1991-97, prof., 1997—, vice chmn. dept., 1996—. Contbr. more than 90 articles to profl. jours. Recipient SCBA-Cathay award Soc. Chinese Bioscientists Am., 1990. Office: Pathology 113B 4150 Clement St San Francisco CA 94121-1545 Fax: 415-750-2038. E-mail: yen@itsa.ucsf.edu.

YEN, WEN LIANG, retired aerospace engineer; b. Taipei, Taiwan, Dec. 13, 1937; came to U.S., 1963; s. Ping Ting and Mei Yen; m. Fina H. Kuo, Mar. 9, 1966; 1 child, AnnFrances. BS, Nat. Taiwan U., 1960; MS, Nat. Tsinghua U., Taiwan, 1962; PhD, Purdue U., 1969. Asst. prof. Ind. U.-Purdue U., Indpls., 1968-73, assoc. prof., 1973-80; mem. sci. staff Deutsches Elektronen-Synchrotron, Hamburg, Germany, 1978-80; programmer/analyst Computer Scis. Corp., Greenbelt, Md., 1980-82; sys. specialist Lockheed Engring. and Mgmt. Svcs. Co., Inc., 1982-87; sr. analyst Honeywell Tech. Solutions Inc., 1987—2002. Contbr. articles to profl. jours. Recipient Group Achievement award NASA, 1993. Achievements include development of spacecraft battery model which predicts whether the battery of a spacecraft will support proposed loads.

YEN, WEN-HSIUNG, language and music professional, educator; b. Tainan, Taiwan, June 26, 1934; came to U.S., 1969; m. Yuan-yuan Yen, Jan. 6, 1961; children: Tin-ju, Tin-jen, Tin-Tao. BA, Nat. Taiwan Normal U., 1960; MA, UCLA, 1971; PhD in Music, World U., 1988; Candidate Philosophy in Ethnomusicology, UCLA, 1995; cultural doctorate philosophy of music, The World Univ., 1988. Instr. Nat. Taichung Tchr. Coll., 1961-62; prof. Chinese Culture U., Taipei, 1964-69; lectr. West L.A. C.C., 1978-82; founder Chinese Culture Sch. L.A., 1976—. Grad. tchg. asst. U. Md., 1982-83; instr. L.A. City Coll., 1983—, Calif. State U. L.A., 1984—, Pasadena City Coll., 1989—; prof. Chinese Santa Monica (Calif.) Coll., 1986—, Calif. State U. Northridge, 1986—; founder Wen Yen Piano Studio, 1972—; founder, dir. Chinese Mus. Orch. So. Calif., 1974—; founder, pres. Chinese- Amer. Musicians Assn. of So. Calif., 1990—; co-chair Conf. Students of Chinese Lang. and Culture. Musical compositions include: Collection of Works by Mr. Yen, 1969; recordings: Art Songs and Chinese Folk Songs, 1982; author: Taiwan Folk Songs, 1967, vol. 2, 1969, A Dictionary of Chinese Music and Musicians, 1967, A Collection of Wen-hsiung Yen's Songs, 1968, vol. 2, 1987, vol. 3, 2000, Achievement and Methodology for Comparative Musicology, 1968; transl. Chinese Musical Culture and Folk Songs, 1989, Silk and Bamboo Expresses Emotion and Meaning, 2000, Ethnomnsicology Series (a collection of chinese mus. papers) in english, 2002; composer of 100 songs and instrumental music; exhibitor traditional Chinese musical instruments and publs. Chinese Culture Ctr., 1995, 96, Arcadia Pub. Libr., 1999; organizer concerts and conductor; contbr. to profl. jours.; presenter Triwanese Opera for the Chinese, Found. for Chinese Mus. Rsch. at Univ. of Sheffield, Eng.,2002 Bd. dirs. So. Calif. Coun. Chinese Sch., 1998—; bd. dirs. Chinese Studies Ctr., Calif. State U., L.A., 1990—. Mem. Chinese-Am. Musicians Assn. So. Calif. (pres.), Chinese Choral Soc. So. Calif. (music dir.), Chinese Performing Arts Assn. of Am. (CPAAA) (bd. dirs), Chinese Writers Assn. So. Calif. (v.p. 2000), Soc. Ethnomusicology, Coll. Music Soc., Internat. Coun. Traditional Music, Soc. Asian Music, Alumni Assn. Chinese Culture U. in USA, Taiwan Benevolent Assn. Am. (bd. dirs.), Taiwan Benevolent Assn. Calif. (bd. dirs., v.p. 1986, pres. 1987-89), Chinese Am. PTA So. Calif. (supr. 1985—), So. Calif. Coun. Chinese Schs. (chmn. exec. com., v.p. 2000—). Avocations: walking, table tennis, Tai Chi Chuan. Office: Chinese Culture Sch 615 Las Tunas Dr Ste B Arcadia CA 91007-8469 E-mail: wenhyen2000@yahoo.com.

YEN, WILLIAM MAO-SHUNG, physicist, consultant; b. Nanking, Kiangsu, China, Apr. 5, 1935; came to U.S., 1952; s. Wanli and Jane Hsanlin (King) Y.; m. Delane Robinson, Aug. 16, 1968 (div. May 1974); m. Laurel Frances Curtis, Aug. 18, 1978; 1 child, Jane Luhsan Bess. BS, U. Redlands, 1956; PhD, Washington U., 1962. Rsch. assoc. Stanford (Calif.) U., 1962-65; asst. prof. U. Wis., Madison, 1965-68, assoc. prof., 1968-72, prof., 1972-90, ret., 1990; Graham Perdue prof. U. Ga., Athens, 1986—. Cons. Lawrence Livermore (Calif.) Nat. Labs., 1975-84, Argonne (Ill.) Nat. Labs., 1976-82, Rosemount Corp., Eden Prairie, Minn., 1988-95, Chromonix LLD, Beverly Hills, Mich., 1995-1999. Editor: Laser Spectroscopy of Solids I, 1981, II, 1988, Dynamical Processes in Disordered Solids, 1989, Phospor Handbook, 1998; contbr. more than 230 articles to scholarly and profl. jours. Washington U. fellow, 1960, J.S. Guggenheim Found. fellow, 1979, Fulbright Sr. fellow, 1995; recipient Sr. U.S. Scientist award A.V. Humboldt Found., 1985, 90; named hon. prof. U. St. Antonio de Abad, Cusco, Peru, 1983, hon. prof. Inst. Physics, Acad. Sinica, 1995. Fellow AAAS, Am. Physical Soc., Optical Soc. Am., Electro Chem. Soc.; mem. Materials Rsch. Soc., Ceramics Soc. Am., Sigma Xi. Achievements include pioneering establishment of laser spectroscopy as a tool to study optical properties of solids. Home: 180 River Oak Way Athens GA 30605-2677 Office: U Ga Dept Physics and Astronomy Athens GA 30602-3451 E-mail: willyen@charter.net.

YENCHKO, SUZANNE, government relations executive; b. Hazleton, Pa., Aug. 5, 1946; d. Joseph and Anna (Mital) Y.; m. Edward Jules Weintraub, Aug. 2, 1975 (div. Sept. 1993); stepchildren: Jessica Anne Lawrence, Morris Harry Weintraub. BA in English Lit., Susquehanna U., 1968; MBA, Mt. St. Mary's Coll., 1981. Legis. liaison Pa. Dept. Commerce, Harrisburg, 1969-71; asst. exec. dir. Pa. Assn. for Retarded Children, 1971-73; exec. dir. Pa. Joint Coun. on the Criminal Justice Sys., 1973-76; dir. Adams County Office for Aging, Gettysburg, Pa., 1976-83; dir. house consumer affairs com. Pa. Ho. of Reps., Harrisburg, 1983-85; dir. environ. resources Pa. Chamber Bus. and Industry, 1985-95; dir. state govt. rels. AMP Inc., 1995-99; regional pub. affairs mgr. Internat. Paper, Camp Hill, 1999—. Mem. steering com. White House Conf. on Aging, Harrisburg, 1980-81; com. mem. Capitol Region Econ. Devel. Com., Harrisburg, 1990-97, bd. dirs., 2001-. Bd. mem. Ctrl. Pa. Youth Ballet, Carlisle, 1994-2000, Theatre Harrisburg, 1995-2001, Whitaker Ctr. for Sci. and Arts, 2001-; chair Pa. Commn. for Women, Harrisburg, 1995-2001; chair literary house tour West Shore Pub. Libr., Camp Hill, Pa., 1998; grad. Leadership Pa., 1991, Pub. Affairs Inst., 1995; bd. dirs. Ctrl. Pa. Tech. Coun., chair govt. affairs com.; environ. com. chair Pa. Bus. Roundtable. Named to 50 Best Women in Bus. in Pa., 1999. Mem. Women in Pa. Govt. Rels. (com. chair 1985—), Susquehanna U. Alumni Bd. (com. chair 1996—), Harrisburg Young Profls., N.C. Citizens for Bus. and Industry (com. 1996-99), Soc. Women Environ. Profls. Republican. Lutheran. Avocations: photography, historic preservation, gardening, skiing, architecture. Home: 13 Cumberland Rd Lemoyne PA 17043-1616 E-mail: synech@aol.com.

YENIKA-AGBAW, VIVIAN S. English studies educator, researcher; b. Tiko, Cameroon, Africa, May 21, 1959; came to U.S., 1991; d. Mathias Bayena and Teresa Joy Yenika; m. Steven Ekema Agbaw, June 30, 1984; children: Stephen Y., Michael L., Joy E. BA, U. Yaounde, Cameroon, 1983; MA, U. Conn., 1986; PhD, Pa. State U., 1996. Grad. asst. Pa. State U., University Park, 1993-96; asst. prof. Clarion (Pa.) U., 1997-98; assoc. prof. Bloomsburg (Pa.) U., 1998—; literacy cons., 2000—. Lit. cons. Bloomsburg U., 2000—; ad hoc reviewer Jour. Adolescent and Adult Literacy, 1997—. Contbg. author: Running for the Lives, 2000; contbr. articles to profl. jours. including Lang. Arts, Internat. Rev. Edn.; mem. editl. bd. Lang. Arts-Nat. Coun. Tchrs. English, 1998-2001. Program co-chair Columbia-Montour Women's Conf., Bloomsburg, 2000; chair acad. program com. 2002 Children's Lit. Assn. Conf. Grantee Bloomsburg U., 1998—. Mem. MLA, Internat. Reading Assn., Nat. Coun. Tchrs. English, Children's Lit. Assn., Comparative Internat. Edn. Soc. Home: 365 Hillside Dr Bloomsburg PA 17815 E-mail: vyenika@chusky.bloomu.edu.

YENKIN, BERNARD KALMAN, coatings and resins company executive; b. Columbus, Ohio, Dec. 2, 1930; s. Abe I. and Eleanore G. Yenkin; m. Miriam Schottenstein, Mar. 31, 1957; children: Leslie Mara, Jonathan, Allison Katsev, Amy. BA, Yale U., 1952; MBA, Harvard U., 1954. V.p. Yenkin-Majestic Paint Corp., Columbus, 1968-77, pres., 1977-85, chmn. bd., 1985—. Pres. Columbus Jewish Fedn., 1980-82, Pro Musica Chamber Orch., Columbus, 1983-85, Columbus Torah Acad., 1977-79; bd. v.p. Jewish Ednl. Svc. N.Am., N.Y.C., 1991-95. Recipient Mayor's award for Vol. Svc. City of Columbus, 1984, Young Leadership award Columbus Jewish Fedn., 1965. Mem. Yale Club of Cen. Ohio (pres. 1979-81), Yale Club of N.Y., Athletic Club (Columbus). Office: Yenkin-Majestic Industries 1920 Leonard Ave Columbus OH 43219-2514

YEO, KIM ENG, artist; b. Singapore, Apr. 24, 1947; came to U.S., 1978; d. Cheng Chye and Seok Kim (Chew) Lee; m. Bock Cheng Yeo; children: Beng Lin, Beng Jene. Student, Nanyang Acad. Fine Arts, Singapore, 1963; BSc with honors, U. Singapore, 1968. Watercolor demonstrator Flushing Art League, N.Y.C., 1980-84; art instr. Poppenhusen Inst., 1984; substitute art tchr. UN Internat. Sch., 1984-85; freelance paper product designer, 1981-87; textile designer J. Brown Designs, N.Y.C., 1987-91; tchg. artist Flushing (N.Y.) Town Hall, 1995-2001; artist-in-residence Pub. Sch. 214, 165, Francis Lewis H.S., Flushing, 1997-2001. Art cons. Corp. Art Directions, N.Y.C., Art Reps., L.A.; visual arts panelist, Flushing Coun., 1985-87, Queen's Coun., 1998-99, 2001. One person shows at Alliance Francais, 1975-77, Bhirasri Inst. Modern Art, Bangkok, Thailand, 1975-77, Flushing Coun. on Arts, 1995, 2000; exhibited Mallette Gallery, L.I., N.Y., 1998, 99, Artfolio Gallery, Singapore, 2000; exhibited in group shows at Womanart Gallery, N.Y.C., 1979-80, Nat. Art League, Douglastown, N.Y., 1979-86, Flushing Coun. on Arts, 1984-88, Postcrypt Art Gallery, N.Y.C., 1997, Singapore Watercolor Soc., 1997-99; represented in corp. and pvt. collections; artist greeting cards UNICEF, 1997-98; featured on QPATV Artists Series, 1993, QPTV Queens Jour., 2000. Benefit show UN Devel. Fund for Women Singapore, 1999. Mem. Flushing Art League (bd. dirs., treas. 1979-85, award 1986), Flushing Coun. on Arts, Nat. Art League. Buddhist. Avocations: gardening, bookmaking. Home: 16202 77th Ave Flushing NY 11366-1022 Fax: (718) 591-8483. E-mail: artist@kimengyeo.com.

YEO, RON, architect; b. Los Angeles, June 17, 1933; s. Clayton Erik and Rose G. (Westman) Y.; m. Birgitta S. Bergkvist, Sept. 29, 1962; children: Erik Elov, Katarina Kristina. B.Arch., U. So. Calif., 1959. Draftsman Montierth & Strickland (Architects), Long Beach, Calif., 1958-61; designer Gosta Edberg S.A.R. Arkitekt, Stockholm, 1962; partner Strickland & Yeo, Architects, Garden Grove, Calif., 1962-63; pres. Ron Yeo, Architect, Inc., Corona del Mar, 1963—. Cons., lectr. in field. Archtl. works include Garden Grove Civic and Community Center, 1966, Hall Sculpture Studio, 1966, Garden Grove Cultural Center, 1978, Gem Theater, 1979, Festival Amphitheatre, 1983, Los Coyotes Paleontol. Interpretive Ctr., 1986, Calif. State U. Fullerton Alumni House, 1997, O'Neill Regional Pk. Nature Ctr., 1998, Upper Newport Bay Interpretive Ctr., 2000, Stough Canyon Nature Ctr., 2000. Mem. Orange County Planning Commn., 1972-73, 1975-76; chmn. Housing and Community Devel. Task Force, 1978, Orange County Fire Protection Planning Task Force, City of Newport Beach City Arts Commn., 1970-72; pres. Orange County Arts Alliance, 1980-81; gen. plan advisory com. Newport Beach, 2002; dir. Orange Coast Watch, 2002. Fellow AIA; mem. Constrn. Specifications Inst. Democrat. Office: Ron Yeo FAIA Architect Inc 500 Jasmine Ave Corona Del Mar CA 92625-2308

YEOM, CHOONG KYUN, chemical engineer, researcher; b. Ookcheon, Republic of Korea, Mar. 26, 1958; s. Chul Hoon and Duk Soon (Kim) Y.; m. Mi Kyong Jeon, Nov. 4, 1984; children: Joomin, Jooyoung. BA in Chem. Engring., Hanyang U., Seoul, 1982; M in Chem. Engring., Korea Advanced Inst Sci & Tech, Taejon, Republic of Korea, 1984; D Chem. Engring., U. Waterloo, Waterloo, Can., 1991. Rschr. SK Chem., Inc., Seoul, 1984-88; rsch. asst., tchg. asst. U. Waterloo, 1989-91; postdoctoral fellow U. Alta., Edmonton, Can., 1991-92, McMaster U., Hamilton, Can., 1992-94; prin. rschr. Korea Rsch. Inst. Chem. Tech., Taejon, 1994—2001; sr. rschr. Petro Sep Inc., Oakville, 2001—. Adj. exec. B.S. Chem., Inc., Taejon, 1999—2001. Rschr. in field. Recipient Republic of Korea scholarship, 1982-83, Faculty of Engring. scholarship, U. Waterloo, 1989-91, Ont. Grad. scholarship, 1990-91, Best Student Papers award, Bakish Materials Corp., Englewood, N.J., 1989. Mem. AAAS, N.Am. Membrane Soc. Home: 1376 Bramble Wood Green Oakville ON Canada Office: Petro Sep Inc 2270 Speers Rd Oakville ON Canada L6L 2X8 E-mail: ckyeom@petrosepmembrane.com.

YEOMANS, DONALD KEITH, astronomer; b. Rochester, N.Y., May 3, 1942; s. George E. and Jessie Y.; m. Laurie Robyn Ernst, June 20, 1970; children: Sarah, Keith. BA, Middlebury (Vt.) Coll., 1964; MS, U. Md., 1967, PhD, 1970. Supr. Computer Scis. Corp., Silver Spring, Md., 1973-76; sr. rsch. astronomer Jet Propulsion Lab., Pasadena, Calif., 1976-92, supr., 1993—. Discipline specialist Internat. Halley Watch, 1982-89; sci. investigator NASA Comet Mission, 1987-91, Near-Earth Asteroid Rendezvous Mission, 1994-2001, Multi-Comet Flyby Mission, 1997—, Comet Impact Mission, 1999—; project scientist for asteroid sample return mission, 1998—. Author: Comet Halley: Once in a Lifetime, 1985, The Distant Planets, 1989, Comets: A Chronological History of Observation, Science, Myth, and Folklore, 1991. Recipient Space Achievement award AIAA, 1985, Exceptional Svc. medal NASA, 1986, Achievement award Middlebury Coll. Alumni, 1987; named NASA/JPL Sr. Rsch. Scientist, 1993. Mem. Internat. Astron. Union, Am.

Astron. Soc. Democrat. Presbyterian. Avocations: tennis, history of astronomy. Office: Jet Propulsion Lab #301-150 4800 Oak Grove Dr Pasadena CA 91109-8001 E-mail: donald.k.yeomans@jpl.nasa.gov.

YEOMANS, DONALD RALPH, Canadian government official, consultant; b. Toronto, Ont., Can., Mar. 25, 1925; s. Ralph and Louise (Weismiller) Y.; m. Catherine Simpson Williams, May 13, 1950; children: Patricia Ann, Nancy Louise, Jane Elizabeth. BASc, U. Toronto, 1947. Registered profl. engr., Ont.; cert. mgmt. acct. Mem. Bur. of Govt. Orgns., Ottawa, Ont., 1962-64; dep. sec. Treasury Bd., 1964-69; asst. dep. minister Dept. Supply and Services, 1969-75; assoc. exec. dir. Anti-Inflation Bd., 1975-76; asst. dep. minister Dept. Nat. Health-Welfare, 1976-77; commr. Correctional Services of Can., 1977-85; chmn. Tariff Bd., 1985-89; spl. advisor Can. Jud. Centre, 1989-92; mem. bd. govs. Carleton U., 1980-93, chmn., 1989-91. Spl. advisor Royal Com. Govt. Orgns., 1961, Royal Com. Fin. Accountability, 1977; assoc. Cons. and Audit Can., 1992-97; exec. counsellor Pub. Svc. Commn., 1990-95; cons. to govt. and industry, 1990-97, bd. dirs. Corrections Corp. Can.; mem. bd. govs. Can. Comprehensive Audit Found., 1989-94; mem. ind. adv. com. Auditor Gen. Can., 1989-95; chmn. Coun. Adminstrv. Tribunals, 1986; chmn. Coun. Chairs Ont. Univs., 1991-93; mem. Expert Com. on AIDS in Prisons, 1992-94; chmn. awards com. Am. Correctional Assn., 1992-97; bd. dirs. Corrections Corp. Can., Baker Group Internat., Inc. Recipient Centennial medal Govt. Can., 1967, Jubilee medal Govt. Can., 1977, E.R. Cass award Am. Corr. Assn., 1991, Corr. Svc. of Can. Exemplary Svc. medal, 2000, Founder's award Carleton U., 2000; Australian Commonwealth fellow, 1985. Fellow: Soc. Mgmt. Accts. Can. (pres. 1977); mem.: Fed. Superannuates Nat. Assn. (pres. Ottawa br. 1998—2000, bd. dirs.), Inst. Pub. Adminstrn. Can. (pres. 1974), Assn. State Correctional Adminstrs. (pres. 1983), Ottawa Heart Inst. Alumni Assn. (v.p.), Five Lakes (pres. 1975); Canadian (Ottawa, pres. 1978), Canadian Club (Ottawa, pres. 1978), Five Lakes Club (pres. 1975). Home and Office: 205-211 Second Ave Ottawa ON Canada K1S 2H8 Fax: 613-231-4557. E-mail: kdyeom@cyberus.ca.

YEOMANS, GORDON ALLAN, retired educator; b. Cherry Valley, Ohio, Sept. 30, 1921; s. Ralph Carey Yeomans and Margaret Warner; m. Marjorie Jo Roberts, Feb. 27, 1949; 1 child, Lynne Leigh Yeomans Craver. BA, U. S.W. La., 1951; MA, La. State U., 1952, PhD, 1966. Instr. U. Miss., Oxford, 1952; assoc. prof. Samford U., Birmingham, Ala., 1952-66, U. S.W. La., Lafayette, 1966-67; prof., dept. head Miss. U. for Women, Columbus, 1967-68; prof. U. Tenn., Knoxville, 1968-87, prof. emeritus, 1987. Cons. Andersen Electric Corp., Leeds, Ala., 1958, John Williamson Co., Birmingham, 1960-61, Birmingham (Ala.) Trust Bank, 1962, Union Carbide Corp., Oak Ridge, Tenn., 1969-81, Magnavox Corp., Asheville, N.C., 1975. Author: A Handbook for Speakers, 1969; contbr. author: The Heart of the Valley, 1976, Pamphlets and The American Revolution, 1976; contbr. articles to profl. jours. Program chmn. Knoxville Religious Bicentennial, 1976; adv. coun. Knoxville Alcohol and Drug Rehab. Ctr.; mem. 1st United Meth. Ch., Knoxville, religious drama dir.. With USAAF, 1940-45. Tchr. grantee Danforth Found., 1956-57, summer 1963, Rsch. grantee U. Tenn., 1974, 75; named Speech Tchr. of Yr., State of Tenn., 1984. Mem. Speech Communication Assn., So. Speech Communication Assn., East Tenn. Hist. Soc., Knoxville Civil War Roundtable. Democrat. Avocations: antiquarian book dealer and collector. Home: 805 Noragate Rd Knoxville TN 37919-7016

YEOMANS, SHEILA ALLEN, music educator, musician; b. Chico, Calif., Sept. 20, 1944; d. Hiram Mayhew and Mardelle Ladoris Allen; m. David John Yeomans, June 14, 1975; 1 child, Sheryl Anne. MusB in Voice Performance, Oberlin Conservatory, 1966; MusM in Voice, Eastman Sch. Music, 1967, D in Musical Arts Voice and Music Lit., 1974, performers cert. From instr. to assoc. prof. voice SUNY, Fredonia, N.Y., 1969-80; owner pvt. studio Pullman, Wash., 1980-85; assoc. prof. voice Tex. Christian U., Ft. Worth, 1985—. Vis. prof. voice and opera Wash. State U., Pullman, 1983-84; vocal soloist various orchs. and univ. artist series, 1974—; operatic roles with Eugene Opera, Buffalo Opera, Balt. Opera, 1972-84. Author: (book chpt.) Diction for Singers, 1992; contbr. articles to profl. jours. Fulbright grantee Staatliche Hochschule für Musik, Stuttgart, Germany, 1968-69, NEH Summer Seminar grantee for univ. profs., Dartmouth Coll., 1989, Tex. Christian U. rsch. grantee, 1995, 96; summer fellow Boston Symphony Orch., Tanglewood, 1976. Office: Tex Christian U Sch Music PO Box 297500 Fort Worth TX 76129-0001 E-mail: s.allen@tcu.edu.

YEOSOCK, JOHN JOHN, army officer; b. Wilkes-Barre, Pa., Mar. 18, 1937; s. John A. and Elizabeth B. Yeosock; m. Betta Lynn Hoffner, July 20, 1960; children— John John, Elizabeth John BS in Indsl. Engring., Pa. State U., 1959; MS in Ops. Rsch., U.S. Naval Postgrad. Sch., Monterey, Calif., 1969; postgrad., Nat. War Coll., 1976. Commd. officer U.S. Army, 1959, advanced through grades to lt. gen.; brigade comdr. 194th Armored Brigade, Ft Knox, Ky., 1978-80; chief of staff 1st Cavalry div. U.S. Army, Ft. Hood, Tex., 1980-81, asst. div. comdr., 1983-84; project mgr. Saudi N.G., Riyadh, Saudi Arabia, 1981-83; dep. chief of staff ops. Forces Command., Atlanta, 1984-86; comdr. 1st Cavalry Div., Ft. Hood, 1986-88; asst. dep. chief of staff for ops. The Pentagon, Washington, 1988-89; comdr. 3d Army and dep. comdg. gen. Forces Command, Ft. McPherson, Ga., 1989—&; comdr. U.S., U.K., French Army Forces, Kuwaiti Theater Ops., Desert Storm, Saudi Arabia, 1990-91; internat. cons., 1993—. Decorated D.S.M. (3), Legion of Merit (2), Bronze Star (2), French Legion of Honor, King Faisal award Class II, King Abdul Aziz medal Class II (Saudi Arabia), Combat Infantryman badge; recipient Nat. Vets. award, 1994, AUSA Inspiration award Atlanta, 1992; named Outstanding Engring. Alumnus, Pa. State U., 1990, Disting. Alumni, 1992, Disting. Alumnus, Valley Forge Mil. Acad., 1994; named to Pi Kappa Phi Hall of Fame. Mem. Wilkes-Barre C. of C. (hon., Achievement award 1991). Home: 223 Newport Dr Peachtree City GA 30269-4277

YEOSOCK, MICHAEL MICHAEL, funeral director, civil engineer; b. Wilkes-Barre, Pa., July 28, 1962; s. Michael J. and Patricia A. (Sauerwein) Y.; m. Mary Jacqueline Clemente; children: Adriana Grace, Christopher Michael. Student, Pa. State U., 1980-82; BS, W.Va. U., 1984; diploma in mortuary sci., New Eng. Inst., 1985; MS in Environ. Engring., U. New Haven, 1993. Cert. engr.-in-tng.; lic. profl. engr., Pa., Conn., N.Y. Project mgr. M.J. Pasonick, Jr., Inc., Wilkes-Barre, 1986-89; asst. civil engr. in tng. City of Norwalk (Conn.) Dept. of Pub. Works, 1989—, sr. engr., 1994—; supr. Jan Fabian Funeral Chapel, Hanover, Pa., 1990-91. Mem. AIME, ASCE, Soc. Mining Engrs., Can. Mining and Metallurgy, N.Y. Acad. Scis., Am. Rock Mechanics Assn., Internat. Soc. Rock Mechanics, Geospatial Info. and Tech. Assn. Republican. Russian Orthodox. Avocations: flying, white-water rafting. Home: 40 S Main St Wilkes Barre PA 18705-1915 Office: City of Norwalk 125 East Ave Norwalk CT 06851-5702 E-mail: myeosock@aol.com.

YERGIN, DANIEL HOWARD, writer, consultant; b. Los Angeles, Feb. 6, 1947; s. Irving H. and Naomi Y.; m. Angela Stent, Aug. 10, 1975; children: Alexander George, Rebecca Isabella. BA, Yale U., Eng., 1968; MA with first class honors, Cambridge U., Eng., 1970, PhD, 1974; PhD (hon.), U. Mo., 1980, U. Houston, 1994. Contbg. editor New York mag., 1968-70; research fellow Harvard U., Cambridge, Mass., 1974-76, lectr. bus. sch., 1976-79, lectr. Kennedy Sch. Govt., 1979-83, research assoc., 1983-90; chmn. Cambridge Energy Research Assoc., 1982-98, also chmn., sec. energy task force on strategic energy R&D, 1998—. Mem. policy adv. com. Program on U.S.-Japan Rels., Harvard U.; mem. bd. energy experts Dallas Morning News; mem. internat. panel advisors Asia-Pacific Petroleum Conf.; fellow World Econ. Forum, Davos. Author: Shattered Peace: The Origins of the Cold War and the National Security State, 1977, rev. edit., 1990, The Prize: Epic Quest for Oil, Money and Power, 1991 (Pulitzer Prize for non-fiction 1992, Eccle prize 1992); co-author: Cold War, 1977, Energy Future, 1979, Global Insecurity, 1982, Future of Oil Prices: Perils of Prophecy, 1984, Russia 2010: And What It Means for the World, 1993, the Commanding Heights, 1998; contbg. editor Atlantic Monthly, 1977-83. Mem. adv. bd. Solar Energy Rsch. Inst., Golden, Colo., 1979-81; sec. Energy Adv. Bd. Fellow Univ. Consortium for World Order Studies, 1974-75, Rockefeller Found., 1975-79, German Marshall Fund, 1980-81, Harvard U., Ctr. for Bus. and Govt., 1997—; Marshall scholar Cambridge U., 1974; recipient U.S. Energy award, 1997. Mem. PEN, Coun. on Fgn. Rels. (com. on studies), Nat. Petroleum Coun., Internat. Assn. for Energy Econs., Am. Hist. Assn., Am. Polit. Assn., Royal Inst. Internat. Affairs, Assn. Marshall Scholars (bd. dirs. 1988-91), U.S. Energy Assn. (bd. dirs.), Nat. Petroleum Coun., Yale Club (N.Y.C.), Harvard Club (N.Y.C.). Office: Cambridge Energy Rsch Assocs 20 University Rd Ste 7 Cambridge MA 02138-5756

YERION, MICHAEL ROSS, civil engineer; b. Jacksonville, Ill., Oct. 18, 1955; s. Billie Ross and Lucia Theresa (Schlegel); m. Charlene Helen Hochard, May 2, 1981; children: Gretchen, Erich. BSCE, So. Ill. U., 1979; MS in Engring. Mgmt., U. Mo., 1994. Registered profl. engr., Ill., Mo. Test engr. Panhandle Eastern Pipeline Co., Kansas City, Mo., 1979-80, pipeline engr. Springfield, Ill., 1981-83; civil engr. City of St. Peters, Mo., 1983-89, engring. supr., 1989-91, dir. engr., 1991-94, constrn. mgr., 1994—. Chmn. Local Emergency Planning, St. Charles County, Mo., 1991-94. Dir. O'Fallon Community Band, 1991; bd. dirs. Assumptions Grade Sch., 1997—, pres., 1998-99. Mem. ASCE, Nat. Soc. Profl. Engrs., Am. Pub. Works Assn., Am. Soc. Engr. Mgrs., Knights of Columbus (treas. 1997-2000, dep. grand knight 2000-02, grand knight 2002—). Roman Catholic.

YERKES, ADELINE MEISMER, public health administrator; b. Aurora, Nebr., Mar. 25, 1943; d. Dennis LaVerne and Phyllis (Zehr) Meismer; m. Michael King Yerkes, Apr. 11, 1964; 1 child, David. BSN, U. Nebr., 1964; MPH, U. Okla., 1980. School nurse Omaha Pub. Schs., 1964-69; nursing supr. Tulsa City-County Health Dept., 1969-71; dist. nursing supr., cons. Omaha-Douglas County Vis. Nurses Assn., 1971-74; dist. nursing supr. Okla. State Dept. Health, Lawton, 1975-78, eldercare and home care cons. Oklahoma City, 1978-80, dir. chronic disease, home care and elder care, 1980-87, chief chronic disease, 1987—. Adj. prof. Coll. Nursing Okla. U., Oklahoma City, 1983—, Coll. Pub. Health, 1985—; cons. case mgr. commn. child and youth Vis. Nurse Assn., Oklahoma City, 1983-86, home care Hospice Ctrl. Okla., Oklahoma City, 1984-87. Aging enabler Presbyn. Ch., Okla., 1990. Named Outstanding Chpt. Women Bus. and Profl. Women, 1981. Mem. ANA, Nat. League for Nursing (com. chair), Okla. League for Nursing, Am. Diabetes Assn. (Okla. chpt., pres. 1983-86, Outstanding Health Profl. 1986, com. chair legis., patient edn. ann meeting), Assn. State and Territorial Chronic Disease (bd. dirs. program, treas., 1988-92, pres. 1995, treas. 1997-99, bd. dirs., Outstanding Ledership award with CDC 1992), Sigma Theta Tau. Republican. Avocations: reading, gardening, traveling. Office: Okla State Health Dept 1000 NE 10th St Oklahoma City OK 73117-1207 E-mail: adeliney@health.state.ok.us.

YERKES, DAVID NORTON, architect; b. Cambridge, Mass., Nov. 5, 1911; s. Robert Mearns and Ada (Watterson) Y.; m. Catharine Noyes, Oct. 7, 1939 (dec. 1969); 1 dau., Catharine; m. Sarah Hitchcock Satterlee, July 9, 1972. BA, Harvard U., 1933; M.F.A., Yale U., 1935. Draftsman, designer, Chgo. and Washington, 1937-39, Deigert & Yerkes and Assos., Washington, 1945-69, David N. Yerkes & Assos., Washington, 1970-80, Yerkes, Pappas and Parker, 1980-83. Mem. panel archtl. advisers Nat. Commn. Fine Arts, 1961-63, 79-82; vice chmn. Presdl. Inaugural Parade Com., 1965 Prin. works include Voice of America Studios, Washington, 1958, Nat. Arboretum Hdqrs. Bldg. Am. Embassy, Somalia, also Madeira Sch. Auditoriu, 1969; 4 stas. Washington subway sys., 1971-81, hdqrs., Nat. Trust Historic Preservation, Washington, 1977, suite, Time, Inc., Washington, 1980, also various schs., labs; paintings exhibited in New Eng. and Washington. Served to capt. AUS, 1943-45. Firm recipient numerous regional and nat. awards; recipient Kemper award AIA, 1972 Fellow AIA (bd. dirs. 1965-68, v.p. 1968-69, chmn. nat. honor awards jury 1966, chmn. Reynolds Meml. award jury 1969, pres. found. 1974-76) Home: 3050 Military Rd NW #449 Washington DC 20015

YERKES, JAY ALAN, financial planner; b. Vallejo, Calif., June 7, 1971; s. Robert Alfred and Ruth Eileen Yerkes; m. Wendy E. Nichols, Nov. 6, 1999. BA in Classical Civilization, UCLA, 1993; MBA, U. Judaism, L.A., 1995. Owner Yerkes Enterprises, Tarzana, Calif., 1994-96; dist. mgr. Ind. Capital Mgmt., Calabasas, 1996-98; real estate broker Vacaville, 1996—; notary pub., 1996—; br. office mgr. SunAmerica Securities, 1998—. Named Most Valuable Skier UCLA Waterski Team, 1993. Mem. Vacaville C. of C. (chief amb. 2001—). Avocations: snowskiing, waterskiing, windsurfing. Office: SunAmerica Securities 137 Nighthawk Ct Vacaville CA 95688-1035 E-mail: jyerkes@pacbell.net.

YERKES, SUSAN GAMBLE, newspaper columnist; b. Evanston, Ill., Sept. 5, 1959; d. Charles Tyson and Darthea (Campbell) Higgins. BA in Liberal Arts (hon.), U. Austin, 1974; MA in Mass Comms., Wichita State U., 1976. Pub. affairs dir. anchor KAKE-TV, Wichita, Kans., 1977-81; freelance writer pub. rels. YS Comms. Global, 1981-84; metro columnist San Antonio Light, 1986-93; lifestyle columnist S.A. Express News, San Antonio, 1993—. Radio TV host WOAI-AM, San Antonio, 1993—; nat. assn. broadcast editls., Boston, 1978-81. Recipient 1st Place Column Writing Nat. Press Women, 1988, Tex. AP Mng. Editors, 1995, 97, Vivian Castelberry award Assn. for Women in Journalism, 1997. Mem. Internat. Women's Forum, Women in Comm., Pub. Rel. Soc. Am., Rotary, Phi Beta Kappa. Episcopalian. Avocations: horseback riding, travel, reading, friends, the Internet. E-mail: syerkesexpress-news.net. Home: 68 Granburg Cir San Antonio TX 78218-3011

YERKESON, DOUGLAS ALAN, lawyer; b. Cin., Aug. 12, 1967; s. Richard Douglas and Sally Em (Gatch) Y.; m. Michelle Ann Brueggeman, Sept. 11, 1993. BSME, U. Cin., 1990, JD, 1993. Bar: Ohio 1994, U.S. Patent & Trademark Office 1996, U.S. Dist. Ct. (so. dist.) Ohio 1998, U.S. Ct. Appeals (fed. cir.) 1998. Engr. KDI Precision Prod., Inc., Cin., 1990-92; intern U. Cin. Intellectual Property Office, 1992-93; reference atty. Lexis-Nexis, Dayton, Ohio, 1994-96; assoc. Biebel & French, LPA, 1996-2001, Bose McKinney & Evans, LLP, Indianapolis, 2001—. Recipient Jacob D. Cox scholarship U. Cin., 1990-93. Mem. ABA, ASME, Ohio State Bar Assn., Ind. State Bar Assn., Indpls. Bar Assn., Am. Intellectual Property Law Assn., Am. Railway Engring. Assn. (pres. U. Cin. chpt. 1990-92, student writing competition award 1992, 93), Intellectual Property Law Soc. (v.p. U. Cin. chpt. 1992-93), Cin. Railroad Club (trustee, v.p. 1995-01), U. Cin. Col. Eng. Alumni Assn. (bd. trustees), Ind. Trans. Mus. Home: 12267 Top Rock Ct Fishers IN 46038 Office: Bose Mckinney & Evans LLP 2700 1st Ind Plz 135 N Pennsylvania St Indianapolis IN 46204-2400 E-mail: dyerkeson@boselaw.com., yerkeson@fworldnet.att.net.

YERMAN, FREDRIC WARREN, lawyer; b. N.Y.C., Jan. 8, 1943; s. Nat W. and Tina (Barotz) Y.; m. Ann R. Rochlin, May 31, 1965; children: Emily, Deborah. BA, CUNY, 1963; LLB, Columbia U., 1966. Bar: N.Y. 1967. Assoc. Kaye, Scholer, Fierman, Hays & Handler, N.Y.C., 1966-74, ptnr., 1974—, chmn. exec. com., 1990-92. Bd. dirs. Lawyer's Com. for Civil Rights under Law, N.Y. Bd. dirs. United Way Tri-State, N.Y., Legal Aid Soc., N.Y.C.; chmn. Jewish Bd. Family and Children Svcs., N.Y.C., 1994—. Fellow Am. Coll. Trial Lawyers. Home: 31 Sheridan Rd Scarsdale NY 10583-1523 Office: Kaye Scholer Fierman Hays & Handler 425 Park Ave New York NY 10022-3506

YERUSHALMI, YOSEF HAYIM, historian, educator; b. N.Y.C., May 20, 1932; s. Leon and Eva (Kaplan) Y.; m. Ophra Pearly, Jan. 4, 1959; 1 child, Ariel. BA, Yeshiva U., 1953; M in Hebrew Lit., Jewish Theol. Sem. Am., 1957, DHL (hon.), 1987; MA, Columbia, 1961, PhD, 1966; MA (hon.), Harvard, 1970; LHD (hon.), Hebrew Union Coll., 1996; PhD (hon.), U. Haifa, Israel, 1997, Ludwig Maximilians U., Munich, 1997. Instr. Jewish history Rutgers U., New Brunswick, N.J., 1963-66; asst. prof. Hebrew and Jewish History Harvard U., 1966-70, prof., 1970-78, Jacob E. Safra prof. Jewish history and Sephardic civilization, 1978-80, chmn. dept. near eastern langs. and civilizations, 1978-80, Salo Wittmayer Baron Prof. of Jewish History, Culture, Soc.; dir. Ctr. for Israel and Jewish Studies Columbia U., N.Y.C., 1980—. Author: From Spanish Court to Italian Ghetto: Isaac Cardoso, A Study in Seventeenth-Century Marranism and Jewish Apologetics, 1971, Haggadah and History, 1975, The Lisbon Massacre of 1506, 1976, Zakhor: Jewish History and Jewish Memory, 1982, Freud's Moses: Judaism Terminable and Interminable, 1991, A Field in Anatot: Essays on Jewish History (in German), 1993, Servants of Kings and Not Servants of Servants: Some Aspects of the Political History of the Jews (in German), 1995, Sefardica: Essays on the History of the Jews, Marranos and New Christians of Hispano-Portuguese Origin (in French), 1998; author (in Hebrew): Spinoza on the Survival of the Jews, 1983; contbr. articles to profl. publs. on Spanish and Portuguese Jewry and history of psychoanalysis; chmn. publs. com. Jewish Publ. Soc., 1972-84; pres. Leo Baeck Inst., 1986-91. Bd. dirs. Conf. Jewish Social Studies, Psycho analytic Research and Devel. Fund, Editorial Bd., History and Memory. Recipient Newman medal CUNY, 1975, Nat. Jewish Book award, 1983, 92,Ansley award Columbia U. Press, 1968, medal of achievement in history Nat. Found. for Jewish Culture,1995; Kent fellow, 1963, travel fellow Nat. Found. for Jewish Culture, 1964, fellow NEH, 1976-77, Rockefeller fellow in humanities, 1983-84, Guggenheim fellow, 1989-90; Carl Friedrich von Siemens Stiftung fellow (Munich), 1996-97. Fellow Am. Acad. Jewish Research, Am. Acad. Arts and Scis., Academia Portuguesa da História Lisbon (hon.) Home: 450 Riverside Dr New York NY 10027-6801 Office: Columbia U 511 Fayerweather Hall 1180 Amsterdam Ave New York NY 10027-7039

YESAIR, DAVID WAYNE, biochemist; b. Newbury, Mass., Sept. 9, 1932; s. Wayne and Roma Jackson (Arlin) Y.; m. Ruth Elizabeth Avery, June 6, 1954; children: Karen, Catherine, Peter. BS in Chemistry, U. Mass., 1954; PhD in Biochemistry, Cornell U., 1958. NSF postdoctoral fellow Nat. Inst. for Rsch., Shinfield, England, 1961-62; sr. scientist biochemistry group Arthur D. Little, Inc., Cambridge, Mass., 1962-66, head biochemistry/biomed. and pharmacology group, 1966-71, 72-77, mgr. biomolecular scis. sect., 1977-82, v.p., 1978-84; pres. BioMolecular Products, Inc., 1984—; founder, pres. Lym-Med Nutritional Products LLC, 2000, Lym-Drug Products, LLC, 2000. NIH sabbatical fellow L'Inst. de Chemie des Substances Naturelle, CNRS, Gif-Sur-Yvette, France, 1971-72; drug metabolism chmn. Gordon Rsch. Conf., 1983; mem. biotech. adv. bd. U. Conn., 1986-94; guest lectr. toxicology curriculum MIT, 1972-82. Contbr. numerous articles to profl. jours. and chpts. to books; holder more than 50 worldwide patents. Active Newbury Hist. Soc., Newburyport Maritime Mus., Sons and Daus. First Settlers of Newbury, pres., 1975, 76; active Newburyport Choral Soc.; class agt., Mass. capital fund chairperson Gov. Dummer Acad. Fellow Leukemia Soc. Am., NSF, NIH. Fellow Am. Inst. Chemists; mem. N.Y. Acad. Scis., Internat. Lecithin and Phospholipid Soc., AAAS, Am. Chem. Soc., Mass. Inst. Chemists, Am. Assn. for Cancer Rsch., Am. Soc. Toxicology, Am. Soc. Pharmacology Exptl. Therapeutics, Internat. Soc. for Studying Xenobiotics, Sigma Xi. Avocations: woodworking, antique furniture restoration, creative landscape gardening, choral singing, swimming. Office: BioMolecular Products Inc PO Box 929 Byfield MA 01922-0929

YESAWICH, PETER CHARLES, advertising executive; b. Ithaca, N.Y., Oct. 28, 1950; s. Paul Joseph Jr. and Elizabeth (Larkin) Y.; m. Paris Pyne; children: Peter Charles, Paul Christopher, Logan Baker. BS, Cornell U., 1972, MS, 1974, PhD, 1976; AMP, Yale U., 1994. Dir. rsch. Robinsons, Inc., Orlando, Fla., 1976-78, v.p., 1978-81, exec. v.p., 1981-83; pres., CEO Yesawich, Pepperdine & Brown, 1983—. Vis. assoc. prof. Cornell U., Ithaca, 1977—, U. Ctrl. Fla., Orlando, 1988—; chmn. Pope Tourism Inst., Orlando, 1988-90. Contbr. articles to profl. jours. Recipient World Travel award Am. Assn. Travel Editors, 1985, Silver Medal award Am. Assn. Advt. Agys., 1992, Adrian award Hospitality Sales and Mktg. Assn. Internat., 1993; named Author of Yr. Cornell Quar., 1986. Mem. Cornell Hotel Soc., Am. Hotel & Motel Assn., Caribbean Hotel Assn., Hotel Sales Mktg. Assn., Am. Mktg. Assn. Avocations: jogging, writing. Office: Yesawich Pepperdine & Brown 423 S Keller Rd # 100 Orlando FL 32810-6102

YESILADA, BIROL ALI, political science educator; b. Nicosia, Cyprus, Aug. 12, 1956; came to U.S., 1971; s. Ali and Sermin (Mustafa) Y.; m. Susan Diana Lesea, Aug. 20, 1980; children: Sermin, Selin. AB, U. Calif., Berkeley, 1977; MA, San Francisco State U., 1979; PhD, U. Mich., 1984. Vis. asst. prof. U. Mo., Columbia, 1984-85, asst. prof., 1985-91; vis. asst. prof. Middle East Tech. U., Ankara, Turkey, 1987-88; vis. rsch. specialist State Planning Orgn., Turkey, 1987-88; assoc. prof. U. Mo., Columbia, 1991-98, chair dept. polit. sci., 1994-98; pres. Oceania Corp., 1992-98; prof. Portland (Oreg.) State U., 1998—, endowed chair Turkish polit. economy and trade, 1998—; exec. dir. Northwest Am. Turkish Rsch. Inst., 1999—; ptnr. BCM Internat., LLC, 2000—. Cons. State Planning Orgn., Ankara, 1987-88, Libr. of Congress, Washington, 1988-92, Coun. on Fgn. Rels., N.Y.C., 1990-91, U.S. State Dept. Fgn. Svc. Inst., 1995-99, Nat. Intelligence Coun., Washington, 1996-97, 99—, U.S. Inst. Peace, 1996, U.S. State Dept., 1995—; chair internat. studies adv. com. U. Mo., Columbia, 1992-94; adv. coun. Inst. Turkish Studies Georgetown U., 2000; adv. bd. Istanbul Strategic Rsch. Ctr. Bahcesehir U., 2000—. Author, co-editor: Agrarian Reform in Reverse: The Food Crisis in the Third World, 1987, The Political and Socioeconomic Transformation of Turkey, 1993; co-author: The Emerging European Union, 1996, 2001; editor Comparative Polit. Parties and Party ELites, 1999; mem. editl. bd. Cyprus Rev. Jour., 1987-98, New Perspectives on Turkey, 1987-95; contbr. articles to profl. jours. Bd. dirs. U. Mo. Peace Studies, Columbia, 1988-92; adv. bd. Constl. Studies Found. Mo., 1996-98. Rsch. fellow Am. Coun. Learned Socs. and Social Sci. Rsch. Coun., 1987, Fulbright-Hays, 1982, Turkish Econ. and Social Studies Found. of Eczacibasi Holding, 1995, William T. Kemper fellow for tchng. excellence U. Mo. and Commerce Bank, 1996; recipient Purple Chalk Tchg. Excellence award U. Mo., Columbia Arts and Scis. Coll., 1991; rsch. bd. grantee U. Mo., 1996. Mem. Am. Polit. Sci. Assn., Internat. Studies Assn., European Union Studies Assn., Middle East Studies Assn., Rotary (Tigard, Oreg.), Golden Key Honor Soc. Moslem. Avocations: jogging, swimming, camping, stamp collecting, ballroom dancing. Home: 12556 SW 114th Ter Tigard OR 97223-4061 E-mail: yesilada@pdx.edu.

YESLOW, ROSEMARIE, real estate professional; b. Detroit; d. Karl E. and Madeline E. (Paret) Norberg; widowed; children: Bradford (dec.), Tod, Eric (dec.), Mark. Student, U. Miami, 1947-49; AA in Journalism, Broward Jr. Coll., 1972; student, Fla. Atlantic U., 1973-75. Grad. Real Estate Inst., 1995. Ins. agt. Wittenstein Ins. Agy., Hollywood, Fla., 1965-75; owner, operator The Karl Motel/Apartments, Hallandale, 1980-95; realtor/assoc. The Keyes Co., Hollywood, 1990-93; realtor, assoc. Ebby Halliday Real Estate, Dallas, 1993—. Real estate investor, Hollywood, 1960—. Contbr. articles to profl. jours. Edn. v.p. Nat. Coun. Jewish Women, Hollywood, 1960-66; unit and dept. chmn. LWV, Ft. Lauderdale, Fla., 1960-72; edn. chmn. Dem. Exec. Com., Broward County, Fla., 1976-78; mem. planning and zoning bd. City of Hallandale, 1988-92. Mem. Nat. Assn. Realtors, Tex. Real Estate Assn., Greater Dallas Assn. Realtors, Hallandale Adult Cmty. Ctr. (adv. com., Cert. of Appreciation 1989), Hallandale Citizens United, Hallandale C. of C. (bd. dirs. 1987-92, Small Bus. Person of Yr. award 1990), Sierra Club. Democrat. Jewish. Avocations: camping, reading, hiking, swimming. Home: 4247 Throckmorton St Dallas TX 75219-2206 Office: Ebby Halliday Real Estate 8333 Douglas Ave Ste 100 Dallas TX 75225-5892 E-mail: ryeslow@aol.com.

YESNER, RAYMOND, pathologist, consultant; b. Columbus, Ga., Apr. 18, 1914; s. Benjamin Nabrisky and Anna (Tolbert) Y.; m. Bernice Lieberman, Feb. 16, 1947; children: David, Donna, Steven. AB, Harvard U., 1935; MD, Tufts U., 1941; MA (hon.), Yale U., 1969; DHL (hon.), Quinnipiac, 1992. Chief lab. svc. VA Hosp., Newington, Conn., 1947-53, VA Med. Ctr., West Haven, 1953-74, chief pathologist, 1974-77, dir. electron microscope lab., 1974-80, dir. pathology, 1977-87, chief of staff, 1968-74; dir. autopsy svc. Yale Med. Ctr., New Haven, 1987-96. Prof. pathology Yale Med. Ctr., 1972-84, prof. emeritus, 1984—, sr. rsch. scientist, 1984—, assoc. dean, 1972-84, Raymond Yesner chair in pathology, 1998. Author: (chpt.) Pulmonary Diseases and Disorders, 1988, Clinics in Chest Medicine, 1982; editor: Histological Typing of Lung Tumours, 1981, Atlas of Lung Cancer, 1998. Pres. Am. Cancer Soc. Conn. div., Wallingford, 1986-88, chmn. Pub. Issues, 1988-91; chmn. Lung Cancer com. WHO, Geneva, 1977-81. Capt. U.S. Army, 1944-47. Recipient Heath Meml. award, U. Tex., 1984, St. George medal, Am. Cancer Soc., 1989. Founding mem. Internat. Assn. for Study of Lung Cancer (pathology com. 1983-91); mem. Arthur P. Stout Surgical Pathology Soc., Radiation Therapy Oncology Group (pathology com. 1985-91), Sigma Xi. Home: 16 Sunbrook Rd Woodbridge CT 06525-1833

YETMAN, LEITH ELEANOR, academic administrator; b. Kellits, Clarendon, Jamaica, West Indies; came to U.S., 1967; d. 2nd child of 12 children of Percival Augustus and Grace Elizabeth (Anderson) Y.; m. Noel W. Miller, Apr. 8, 1961 (div. 1977); children: Donovan, Jo-Ann, Kirk, Lori-Anne; adopted children: LaFara, Samantha, Brandon Ryan. Attended, Bethlehem Teachers Coll., St. Elizabeth, Jamaica, 1960; BSC, Baruch Coll., 1976; MA, Columbia U., 1978. Cert. tchr., N.Y.; accredited Grace Inst. Bus. Tech., 1998. Legal sec. various law firms, N.Y.C., 1969-76; instr. Taylor Bus. Inst., 1977-79; founder, pres., dir. N.Y. Inst. Bus. Tech., 1981—. Founder Grace Inst. Bus. Tech., Bklyn., 1996. Recipient Outstanding Achievement award Baruch Coll. Alumni

Assn., 1989; Leith E. Yetman Day proclaimed June 1, 1994 by Manhattan Borough Pres. Mem. Better Bus. Bur. N.Y.C. Office: NY Inst Bus Tech 248 W 35th St New York NY 10001 E-mail: NY1EB02@aol.com.

YETMAR, SCOTT ANDREW, accountant, educator; b. Riverside, Calif., July 22, 1963; s. Donald Thomas and Adele Mae (Allen) Y.; m. Janice Katherine Merkey, June 22, 1985; children: Joshua Donald, Melissa Marie, Zachary Andrew. BA in Acctg., U. No. Iowa, 1985; MBA, Drake U., 1991; PhD in Acctg., Okla. State U., 1995. CPA Iowa. Sr. auditor KPMG Peat Marwick, Des Moines, 1985-88; contr. R and R Investors, West Des Moines, 1988-90; fin. planning mgr. Farm Bur. Ins., 1990-91; grad. asst. Okla. State U., Stillwater, 1991-95; asst. prof. acctg. U. So. Colo., Pueblo, 1995-96, Drake U., Des Moines, 1996—; expert witness taxation, acctg. Wiggens & Anderson, West Des Moines, 1998—99; expert witness acctg. and auditing Dickinson Law Firm, 2001. Expert witness on taxation Parrish, Kruidenier, Moss, Dunn law firm, Des Moines, 1996—97; reviewer MicroMash-CPA, Englewood, Colo., 1997—, Prentice Hall, Upper Saddle River, NJ, 1997—; instr. Becker/Conviser CPA Rev., Chgo., 1996—; ethics tng. cons. GuideOne Ins. Co., 1998—; cons. Pub. Defender's Office, Iowa Divsn., 2001—; Delta Sigma Pi's faculty advisor Drake U., 1997—2001, assessment com., Kemper Scholar selection com., Nat. Alumni Scholars selection com.; presenter in field. Author, reviewer acctg. textbook supplements; contbr. articles to profl. jours.; columnist for newsletters in field. Bd. dirs. Jr. Achievement, Pueblo, 1995-96, project bus. instr., Des Moines, 1989-91; bd. dirs. Cmty. Compacts for Student Success, Pueblo, 1995-96; parent vol. Westwood Elem. Sch., Ankeny, Iowa, 1996—; lector, commentator, eucharistic min. St. Theresa Ch., 1985-91; lector St. Francis Ch., 1991-95; fin. com., lector St. Paul the Apostle Ch., Pueblo West, 1995-96; fin. com., lector, commentator Our Lady's Immaculate Heart Ch., Ankeny, 1996—; coach West Des Moines Little League, 1986-88, Ankeny Little League, 1998, Ankeny Leisure Svcs. Basketball, 1997-; bd. dirs. Ankeny YMCA, 2000-01. Named Prof. of Yr., Drake U. Internat. Students Orgn., 1998; grantee Drake U., 1997, Kelley Ins. Ctr., 1997, Kaufmann Entrepreneur, 2000—01. Fellow: Life Mgmt. Inst.; mem.: AICPA (responsibilities in tax practice com. 1997—2000, mem.'s life ins. and disability com. 2001—, grantee tax divsn. 1994), Inst. Mgmt. Accts. (cert. fin. mgr., cert. managerial acct.), Am. Acctg. Assn. (computer resources com. 1997—2000, midyear planning com. 2000—01), Iowa Soc. CPAs (career awareness com. 1997—), Am. Taxation Assn. (ad hoc reviewer jour. 1999—, midyear com. 2000—01), KC. Republican. Roman Catholic. Avocations: golf, tennis, coaching, collecting sports cards, racquetball. Office: Drake U Aliber Hall 2507 University Ave Des Moines IA 50311-4505 Personal E-mail: fiveyetmars@mchsi.com. Business E-Mail: scott.yetmar@drake.edu.

YETT, FOWLER REDFORD, mathematics educator; b. Oct. 18, 1919; s. James William, Sr. and Rebecca Jane (Stribling) Y.; m. Mary Sue Lytle, June 17, 1945 (div. 1977); children: Jane Marie, Rebecca Yett Root, Mary Wester Yett. BS in Chem. Engring. (Univ. scholar), U. Tex., Austin, 1943, MA in Math., 1952; PhD, Iowa State U., 1955. Rsch. chemist, rsch. chm. engr. Manhattan Project, U. Chgo., 1943-44, Richland, Wash., 1944-45, Dow Chem. Co., Freeport, Tex., 1945; owner, mgr. Camera Supplies of Houston, 1946-49; tchg. fellow math. U. Tex., Austin, 1949-52, asst. prof., 1956-65; instr. math. Iowa State U., Ames, 1952-55; asst. prof. math. Long Beach (Calif.) State Coll., 1955-56; prof. math. U. So. Ala., Mobile, 1965-89, chmn. dept., 1965-68. Sr. rsch. engr. N.Am. Aviation, Inc., Downey, Calif., summers 1956-57, 59; faculty rsch. assoc. Boeing Co., Seattle, summer 1958; pres. Dr. Fowler Redford Yett & Daus., Inc., Solar, Inc.; gen. mgr. Dr. Fowler Redford Yett's World Acad. of Faith, Health, Langs., and Scis. Active all Lyndon Baines Johnson election campaigns, 1937-68; Sunday sch. tchr., Meth. Ch., 1970-71. Mem. Am. Math. Soc., Tau Beta Pi, Omega Chi Epsilon, Phi Lambda Upsilon, Phi Eta Sigma, Pi Mu Epsilon. Methodist. Home: 660 Merritt Dr Mobile AL 36609-6026

YETT, SALLY PUGH, elementary education educator, art specialist; b. St. Louis, Feb. 15, 1935; d. John D. and Esther Ruth P.; m. Donald Edward Yett, June 19, 1964; children: Stephen Edward, John Harold. BFA, Washington U., St. Louis, 1956; tchg. credential, Calif. State U., L.A., 1989. Cert. gen. clear multiple subject and art supplementary, Calif. Dept. Edn. Recreation therapist ARC, San Antonio, 1956-58; dir. recreation therapy dept. Jewish Hosp., St. Louis, 1958-64; tchr. art-gifted class Juan Cabrillo Elem., Malibu, Calif., 1975-78; educator pre-kindergarten Malibu Meth. Pre-Sch., 1979-81; educator grades 9-12 Santa Monica (Calif.) Sch. Dist., 1981-89; educator grades 1-6 art L.A. Unified Sch. Dist.-Visual and Performing Arts Magnet, 1990—; resource tchr., art edn. advisor Calif. State U., L.A., 2001—. Participant UCLA Tchrs. and Scholars Symposium, 1999—2002; cons. edn. dept. Calif. State U., L.A. Exhibitions include Malibu Art Festival, 1976 (3rd place award), Malibu Art Assn. Show, 1984 (3rd place award), Roberts Art Gallery, 1989, CAEA State Conv.-Calif. State Bakersfield Exhibit, 2001, Calif. State U., Bakersfield, 2001; contbr. articles to profl. jours. PTA pres. Juan Cabrillo Elem., Malibu, 1976-78, Malibu Park Jr. H.S., 1981-82; pres. Santa Monica Jr. Programs, 1979-81; 2nd, 3rd and 4th v.p. Santa Monica/Malibu PTA Coun., 1982-85; pres. Malibu Art Assn., 1982-83. Honoree Bravo award L.A. Music Ctr. Mem.: Internat. Studies Overseas Program, Pacific Asia Mus., Metro. Mus. Art, East West Players Orgn., Craft and Folk Mus., Calif. Alliance for Arts Edn., Ams. for the Arts, Shakespeare Festival/L.A., Smithsonian Inst., Huntington Mus., Gene Autrey Mus., Nat. Mus. Women, Mus. Natural History, Mus. Contemporary Art, S.W. Mus., L.A. County Art Mus., UCLA Fowler Mus. Cultural History, Calif. Art Edn. Assn., Calif. Coun. for Social Studies, Soc. for Calligraphy (bd. dirs., pub. rels. 1987—91), Tchrs. and Writers Collaborative, Nat. Art Edn. Assn., Mus. L.Am. Art, People to People Internat. (Indigenous Art del. to New Zealand, Australia 1998), UCLA Book Club. Avocations: travel, reading, painting, calligraphy, hiking. Home: 2042 Hanscom Dr South Pasadena CA 91030-4012

YETTER, R. PAUL, lawyer; b. Milw., Aug. 5, 1958; s. Richard and Lobelia (Gutierrez) Y.; m. Patricia D. Yetter, May 6, 1983; children: Chris, Mark, Michael, Joseph, Thomas, Andrew, Daniel. BA, U. Tex., El Paso, 1980; JD, Columbia U., 1983. Bar: Tex. 1983, U.S. Dist. Ct. (so., ea., no. and we. dists.) Tex., U.S. Ct. Appeals (5th cir.); bd. cert. in civil trial law and personal injury trial law Tex. Bd. Legal Specialization. Law clk. to Hon. John R. Brown U.S. Ct. Appeals (5th cir.), Houston, 1983-84; assoc. Baker & Botts, L.L.P., 1984-89, ptnr., 1990-97; name ptnr. Yetter & Warden, L.L.P., 1997—. Chair state judiciary rels. com. State Bar, 1995-96; mem. Funding Parity Task Force, 1995-97; mem. ex officio Jud. Selection Task Force, 1995-97; chair Alliance for Jud. Funding, Inc., 1996—; mem. ex officio contbns. com. Tex. Ctr. for the Judiciary, mem. com. on admissions, So. Dist., Tex., 2000—. Contbr. articles to profl. jours. Recipient Presdl. citation State Bar Tex., 1996; Southwestern Legal Found. rsch. fellow. Fellow Tex. Bar Foun., Houston Bar Found. Office: Yetter & Warden LLP 909 Fannin Ste 3600 Houston TX 77010-

YETTER, RICHARD, lawyer; b. Phila., Mar. 14, 1929; s. Frederick Jacob and Marie (Kircher) Y.; m. Lobelia Gutierrez, Feb. 4, 1955; children: Bruce, Tina Marie, Richard Paul, Erich David. BS, Pa. State U., 1951; JD, Marquette U., 1960. Bar: Wis. 1960, U.S. Dist. Ct. (ea. dist.) Wis. 1960, Tex. 1961, U.S. Dist. Ct. (we. dist.) Tex. 1971, U.S. Ct. Appeals (5th cir.) 1972. Adjuster Md. Casualty Co., El Paso, Tex., 1960-62; pres. Richard Yetter & Assocs. Inc., 1970-90; sole practitioner, 1962-70, 90—. Assoc. judge Mcpl. Ct., El Paso, 1967-71; adj. prof. law Webster U., St. Louis. Pres. Pleasantview Home for Sr. Citizens, Inc., 1968-76; state committeeman Tex. Rep. Com., El Paso, 1968-70; chmn. adv. bd. SBA, Lubbock, Tex., Salvation Army, El Paso; life mem. El Paso County Civil Svc. Commn., 1992-96. Served with USAF, 1951-60. Recipient William Booth award Salvation Army, 1997. Mem. Wis. State Bar, Tex. State Bar, El Paso Bar Assn., El Paso Trial Lawyers Assn. (past bd. dirs.), El Paso Probate Bar Assn. (past bd. dirs.), Optimist (life, pres. El Paso), Mil. Order World Wars (life). Methodist. Avocation: walking. Office: 6070 Gateway Blvd E Ste 501 El Paso TX 79905-2031

YETTO, JOHN HENRY, company executive; b. N.Y.C., Apr. 25, 1928; s. Michael and Josephine Yetto; m. Nancy A. Cagliostro, June 9, 1957; children: Sheryl, Kay, Michelle. BSChemE, CCNY, 1950; postgrad., Bklyn. Poly., 1951, Rutgers U., 1952. Devel. engr. Materials Lab., N.Y. Naval Shipyard, Bklyn., 1951-52; process engr. Bakelite Co., Div. UCC, Bound Brook, N.J., 1953-57; asst. plant engr. Revlon, Inc., Passaic, 1957-59; dept. mgr. Aerojet, Inc., Sacramento, 1959-71; pres. Systemedics, 1971-85, Proserv, Inc., Sacramento, 1975—. Chmn. YMCA Bd. of Mgrs., San Juan, Sacramento, Calif., 1964; pres. Fairway Pines Homeowners Assn., 1989-99, Sunrise Knolls Townhouse Owners' Assn., 1995. 1st lt. USAF, 1952-53. Mem. Fair Oaks C. of C. (pres. 1984), Rotary (pres. Fair Oaks 1982). Avocations: computers, tennis. E-mail: johnyetto@aol.com.

YEUNG, EDWARD SZESHING, chemist; b. Hong Kong, Feb. 17, 1948; arrived in U.S., 1965; s. King Mai Luk and Yu Long Yeung; m. Anna Kunkwok Seto, Sept. 18, 1971; children: Rebecca Tze-Mai, Amanda Tze-Wen AB magna cum laude, Cornell U., 1968; PhD, U. Calif., Berkeley, 1972. Instr. chemistry Iowa State U., Ames, 1972-74, asst prof., 1974-77, assoc. prof, 1977-81, prof. chemistry, 1981-89, disting. prof., 1989—. Contbr. articles to profl. jours. Alfred P. Sloan fellow, 1974-76; recipient Am. Chem Soc. award in Analytical Chemistry, 1994. Fellow AAAS; mem. Soc. Applied Spectrosci. (Lester Strock award 1990), Am. Chem. Soc. (award in chem. instrumentation 1987, award in analytical chemistry 1994, award in chromatography 2002). Home: 1005 Jarrett Cir Ames IA 50014-3937 Office: Iowa State U Gilman Hall Ames IA 50011

YEUNG, SAI-KEE, mathematician, educator; b. Nanan, Fujian, China, Aug. 27, 1963; arrived in U.S., 1985; s. Han-Chong and Why-Suen Yeung; m. Victoria C. Leong, Aug. 10, 1991; 1 child Joshua. PhD, Columbia U., 1989. Moore instr. MIT, Cambridge, Mass., 1989—91; visitor Inst. Advanced Study, Princeton, NJ, 1991—92; prof. Purdue U., West Lafayette, Ind., 1992—. Fellow, Sloan Found., 1994—96.

YEVI, GILBERT YAOVI, petroleum engineer; b. Cotonou, Benin, Feb. 4, 1965; came to U.S., 1992; s. Frederick A. and Cecile Amouzouvi (Fande) Y. BS in Drilling and Prodn., U. Mining & Geology, Sofia, Bulgaria, 1991; MS in Petroleum Engring., Miss. State U., 1994, PhD in Computational Engring., 1996; MBA in Fin., Tulane U., 2000. Asst. prodn. engr. Bulgarian Geol. Prospecting Co., Pleven, 1990, asst. well testing engr., 1991; rsch. asst. in Petroleum Engring. Miss. State U., Starkville, 1992-93; rsch. asst. NSF Ctr. for Computational Field Simulation, 1994-96; reservoir engr. Shell Offshore Inc., New Orleans, 1996-99; sr. reservoir engr. Shell Internat. E&P Inc., Houston, 2000—, Shell Nigeria, Lagos, Nigeria, 2002—. Contbr. articles to profl. jours.; patentee in field. Mem. Soc. Petroleum Engrs., Nat. Petroleum Engring. Honor Soc. Avocations: fishing, tennis, badminton, table tennis, travel. Office: 200 N Dairy Ashford St Houston TX 77079-1101 E-mail: gyaovi@yahoo.com.

YEVICK, GEORGE JOHANNUS, scientist; b. Berwick, Pa., May 8, 1922; s. John and Theresa Yevick; m. Miriam Amalia Lipschutz-Yevick, May 15, 1945; 1 child, David Owen. BS, Mass. Inst. Tech., Cambridge, 1942; PhD, Mass. Inst. Tech., 1947. Prof. physics Stevens Inst. Tech., Hoboken, N.J., 1947-92. Lectr. Lucent Corp., 1997-2001; founder, prin. investigator Personal Comms., Stanford, Conn., 1979-87. Contbr. articles to sci. jours.; patentee in field. Primary candidate of congress Dem. Party, Bergen County, N.J., 1964. Rsch. grantee U.S. Govt. Achievements include discovery of (with Jerome K. Percus) P.Y. equation, fundamental to the theory of liquids. Avocations: sculpture, painting, mosaic work. Home: 22 Pelham St Princeton NJ 08540-5315 Office: Stevens Inst Tech Hoboken NJ 07030

YGLESIAS, HELEN BASSINE, author, educator; b. N.Y.C., Mar. 29, 1915; d. Solomon and Kate (Goldstein) Bassine; m. Bernard Cole, 1938 (div. 1950); children: Tamar Cole, Lewis Cole; m. Jose Yglesias, Aug. 19, 1950 (div. 1992); 1 child, Rafael. Student pub. schs.; LHD (hon.), U. Maine, 1996. Literary editor Nation Mag., 1965-70; adj. assoc. prof. writing Columbia Sch. Arts, N.Y.C., 1973—. Vis. prof. creative writing Writers Workshop, U. Iowa, Iowa City, 1980. Author: (novels) How She Died (Houghton Mifflin award), 1972, Family Feeling, 1976, Sweetsir, 1981, The Saviors, 1987, The Girls, 1999, (non-fiction) Starting: Early, Anew, Over and Late, 1978, Isabel Bishop, 1989. Home: Apt 1303 1261 5th Ave New York NY 10029-3866

YGLESIAS, RAFAEL JOSE, novelist; b. N.Y.C., May 12, 1954; s. Jose and Helen (Bassine) Y.; m. Margaret Joskow, Oct. 15, 1977; children: Matthew, Nicholas. Author: Dr. Neruda's Cure for Evil, 1996, The Murderer Next Door, 1990, Only Children, 1988; screenwriter, author (film) Fearless, 1993; screenwriter (films) Death and the Maiden, 1995, Les Miserables, 1998, From Hell, 2001. Mem. The Author's Guild, Writer's Guild of Am., Acad. Motion Picture Arts and Scis.

YGUADO, ALEX ROCCO, economics educator; b. Lackawanna, N.Y., Jan. 17, 1939; s. Manuel and Rose (Barrillio) Y.; m. Patricia Ann Rieker; children: Gary Alexander, Melissa Rose, Charissa Ann. BA, San Fernando State Coll., Northridge, 1968; MA, Calif. State U., Northridge, 1970; MS, U. So. Calif., 1972. Contractor, L.A., 1962-69; instr. Calif. Poly. State U., San Luis Obispo, 1969-70, U. So. Calif., L.A., 1970-74; prof. econs. L.A. Mission Coll., San Fernando, Calif., 1975—, acad. senate pres., 1992-93, cluster chair profl. studies, 1993-2001, dean acad. affairs, 2001—. Cons. Community Service Orgn., Los Angeles, 1969-71. Author: Principles of Economics, 1978; contbr. chpts. in books. Served with U.S. Army, 1957-60. Recipient: Blue Ribbon landscape design City of Albuquerque, 1962, Cert. Appreciation Los Angeles Mission Coll., 1978; Fulbright scholar, 1986-87. Mem. Calif. Small Bus. Assn. Clubs: Newman (Los Angeles), Sierra Retreat (Malibu, sponsor). Democrat. Roman Catholic. Avocations: gardening, skiing, photography. Home: 25323 Oak Ridge Dr Santa Clarita CA 91350-3300 Office: LA Mission Coll 13356 Eldridge Ave Sylmar CA 91342-3200 E-mail: yguadoar@laccd.cc.ca.us.

YI, XIAOXIONG, political scientist, educator; b. Beijing, China, July 8, 1953; s. Lirong Yi, Xin Yu. BA, Beijing Normal U., 1982; MA, Pa. State U., 1985; PhD, Am. U., Washington, 1993. Instr. Dickinson Col., Carlisle, Pa., 1988—89; dir. internat. programs Marietta Coll., Ohio, 1999—2001, assoc. prof. polit. sci., 1989—. Guest prof. U. Internat. Relations, Beijing, China, 2000—; vis. prof. Fgn. Affairs Coll., Beijing, China, 1996—97. Contbr. articles. Named Outstanding Prof. of the Yr., Marietta Coll., 1995; fellow John Fletcher Hurst fellow, Am. U., 1985—88, Mershon Ctr. Rsch. fellow, Ohio State U., 1994—96; grantee Travel grantee, Korea Inst. for Def. Analysis, 1997. Mem.: Internat. Studies Assn., Assn. fir Asian Studies, Am. Polit. Sci. Assn. Home: 110 Cornerstone Dr Marietta OH 45750 Office: Marietta College Thomas Hall 215 5th St Marietta OH 45750 Office Fax: 740-376-7501. Business E-Mail: yix@marietta.edu.

YIELDING, K. LEMONE, physician; b. Auburn, Ala., Mar. 25, 1931; s. Riley Lafayette and Bertie (Dees) Y.; m. Lerena Wade Hauge, Dec. 7, 1973; children: K. Lemone, Michael Lafon, Teresa Louise, Riley Lafayette, Katrina Elizabeth, Elaine Louise Blodgett, Laura Carlen Blodgett. BS, Ala. Poly. Inst., 1949; MS, U. Ala., 1952, MD, 1954. Intern U. Ala. Med. Center, 1954-55; clin. assoc. Nat. Inst. Arthritis and Metabolic Diseases, NIH, 1955-57, sr. investigator, 1958-64; resident med. service USPHS Hosp., Balt., 1957-58; physician in practice of oncology and emergency medicine, 1995—. Adj. asst. prof. medicine Georgetown U. Med. Sch., 1958-64; cons. USPHS, 1964-68, 75—; prof. biochemistry, assoc. prof. medicine, chief lab. molecular biology U. Ala. Med. Ctr., Birmingham, 1964-80; prof., chmn. dept. anatomy, prof. medicine U. So. Ala. Coll. Medicine, Mobile, 1980-87; dean grad. sch. U. Tex. Med. Br., Galveston, 1987-95, dean emeritus, 1995—; cons. Am. Heart Assn., Arthritis Found., NIH, NASA. Contbr. to profl. jours., books. Served with USPHS, 1955-64. Grantee USPHS, Am. Cancer Soc., Nat. Found.-March of Dimes, U.S. Army, Am. Inst. Cancer Research. Mem. Am. Soc. Biol. Chemistry, Am. Assn. Cancer Research, Am. Assn. Photobiology, Assn. Research Vision and Ophthalmology, Soc. Exptl. Biology and Medicine, Am. Soc. Pharm. and Exptl. Therapeutics, Am. Assn. Pathologists, So. Soc. Clin. Investigation, Am. Assn. Anatomy, Soc. Toxicology, Sigma Xi. E-mail: yielding@hiwaay.net.

YIGIT, NUYAN, journalist; b. Istanbul, Turkey, Oct. 25, 1927; s. Ibrahim Sureyya and Ayse (Mediha) Y.; m. Fatos, July 2, 1958; children: Ipek, Ibrahim Sureyya. BA in Arts and Philosophy, Robert Coll., 1948; postgrad., Istanbul U., 1951, Columbia U., 1961. Cub reporter, editor Cumhuriyet newspaper, Istanbul, 1948-60; asst. bur. chief Time and Life, 1957-59; dep. gen. mgr. Hurriyet News Agy., 1963; Istanbul corr. Reuters, 1965-70; London bur. chief Hurriyet newspaper, London, 1970-83; gen. mgr. Gunaydin Newspaper Group, Istanbul, 1983-90. Freelance journalist, Istanbul, 1996—. Author travelog, 1995, short stories, 1996. Candidate for Turkish Parliament, Dem. Party, Istanbul, 1991. 1st lt. Turkish Cavalry, 1952-54. Moslem. Avocations: sports writing and commenting, rowing, reading. Home: 437 Golden Isles Dr Hallandale FL 33009

YIH, YUEHWERN, engineering educator; b. Keelung, Taiwan, Dec. 16, 1962; came to the U.S., 1984; p. Ren-Ku Yih and Guey-Ron Cheng. BS, Nat. Tsing Hua U., Hsin-Chung, Taiwan, 1984; PhD, U. Wis., 1988. Project asst. U. Wis., Madison, 1985, tchg. asst., 1985-88; asst. prof. Purdue U., West Lafayette, Ind., 1989-94, assoc. prof., 1994—. Vis. rschr. Nat. Inst. Stds. and Tech., Gaithersburg, Md., summer 1992-95; rsch. asst. U. Wis., Madison, summer 1985-88; cons. Heritage Environ. Svcs., Indpls., 1993-94. Editor: Manufacturing Cells - A System Engineering View, 1995; contbr. articles to profl. jours. Recipient Young Investigator award NSF, 1993, Dell K. Allen Outstanding Young Mfg. Engr. award Soc. Mfg.. Engrs., 1998; GE Faculty fellow GE Found., 1992, NEC Faculty fellow NEC Corp., 1993. Mem. Inst. Indsl. Engrs. (pres. Ctrl. Ind. chpt. 1993-94, dir. Ctrl. Ind. chpt. 1994-95, dept. editor 1994—), Coll. on Artificial Intelligence-Inst. for Ops. Rsch. and Mgmt. Sci. (v.p. 1996-99), Artificial Intelligence Com. Ind. Corp. for Sci. and Tech. Office: Purdue Univ 1287 Grissom Hall West Lafayette IN 47907-1287 Fax: 765-494-1299. E-mail: yih@purdue.edu.

YII, HUNG SIONG, computer engineer; b. Sibu Sarawak, Malaysia, May 25, 1965; came to U.S., 1986; s. Hee C. and Su C. (Lau) Y. BS in Computer Sci. Engring., U. Tex., Arlington, 1989; MSEE, St. Mary U., San Antonio, 1993. Rsch. engr. U. Tex., Arlington, 1989; computer engr. Flight Safety Internat., San Antonio, 1989-93; software engr. Spectrum Cellular Inc., Dallas, 1994-95, DSc Comms., Plano, Tex., 1995—. Co-chmn., instr. Alamo PC, San Antonio. Mem. Assn. for Computing Machinery. Home: 1608 Hearthstone Dr Plano TX 75023-7411 Office: DSc Comms MS # 121 1000 Coit Rd Plano TX 75075-5802

YIM, SOLOMON CHIK-SING, civil engineering educator, consultant; b. Hong Kong, Sept. 11, 1952; came to U.S., 1972; s. Fuk-Ching and San-Chan (Leung) Y.; m. Lenore S. Hata, Aug. 27, 1983; children: Rachel L., Joshua A. BSCE, Rice U., 1976; MSCE, U. Calif., Berkeley, 1977, MA in Math., 1981, PhD in Civil Engring., 1983. Registered profl. engr., Oreg. Rsch. asst. U. Calif., 1976-83, vis. lectr., 1983-84, vis. assoc. prof., 1993-94; sr. rsch. engr. Exxon Prodn. Rsch. Co., Houston, 1984-87; asst. prof. civil engring. Oreg. State U., Corvallis, 1987-91, assoc. prof., 1991-97, prof., 1997—, asst. dept. head, 1998-2000, dir. Transp. Rsch. Inst., 1999—. Cons. engr., 1977—; mem. ship structures com. NRC, 1990-96; mem. grad. fellowship com. in sci. and engring. Dept. Def., 1989-99; sr. vis. scientist Norwegian Coun. for Sci. and Indsl. Rsch., Trondheim, 1994. Fellow Office Naval Rsch., 1988-91; sr. faculty rsch. fellow USN, 1993. Mem. ASCE (publ. com. 1993-96, editl. bd. 1996—), ASME (assoc. editor 2000—), Soc. Naval Architecture and Marine Engrs., Internation Soc. Offshore and Polar Engrs. (charter, conf. tech. program com. 1992-98). Achievements include research in nonlinear stochastic dynamics and reliability of ocean and structural systems, in nonlinear response of structures to earthquakes. Office: Oreg State U 202 Apperson Hall Corvallis OR 97331-8522 E-mail: solomon.yim@orst.edu.

YIN, BEATRICE WEI-TZE, medical researcher; b. Taipei, Taiwan, Mar. 9, 1959; came to U.S., 1970; d. Chuan Keun and Ming Hsien (Huang) Y. BS, CUNY, Flushing, 1982, MS, 1988. Rsch. asst. Meml. Sloan-Kettering Cancer Ctr., N.Y.C., 1982—. Inventor Monoclonal antibodies to human gastrointestinal cancers, 1992. Avocations: readings, travel, gardening. Office: Meml Sloan Kettering Cancer Ctr 1275 York Ave New York NY 10021-6094

YIN, FANG-FANG, medical physicist, educator; b. Ningbo, Zhejiang, China, Sept. 14, 1958; came to U.S., 1985; s. Shisheng Yin and Xiaoxian Ma; m. Li Sun, Feb. 14, 1986; children: Moli Yin, Lucy Yin. BS, Zhejiang U., 1982; MS, Bowling Green (Ohio) State U., 1987; PhD, U. Chgo., 1992. Cert. medical physicist Am. Bd. Radiology. Lectr. Industry U. of East China, Shanghai, 1982-85; grad. asst. Bowling Green State U., 1985-87; rsch. asst. U. Chgo., 1987-88, researcher, 1989-91; asst./med. physicist U. Rochester, N.Y., 1992-93, sr. instr./med. physicist, 1994—, asst. prof./med. physicist, 1994—. Chief Oncologic Imaging Rsch. Lab., Rochester, 1994—; divsn. head med. physics Henry Ford Health System, Dept. Radiation Oncology, Detroit, 1998—. Contbr. articles to profl. jours.; patentee for automated method and system for the detection and classification of abnormal lesions and parenchymal distortions in med. images. Recipient Overman Summer fellowship Bowling Green State U., 1986; rsch. grantee Am. Cancer Soc., 1994, The Whitaker Found., 1995-98. Mem. Am. Assn. Physicists in Medicine. Avocations: tennis, ping pong. Office: Henry Ford Health Sys Dept Radiation Oncology 2799 W Grand Blvd Detroit MI 48202-2608

YIN, HENRY CHIH-PENG, educator; b. Nanjing, China, May 12, 1933; came to U.S., 1964; s. Fu-Hai and Yu-Min (Hsu) Y.; m. Terry Tsi-Chieh Liao, July 3, 1971; children: Connie Kang, Shonna Hsiang, Liang. BA, Taiwan Normal U., Taipei, 1959; MA, Columbia U., 1965, EdD, 1973. Asst. registrar Bronx C.C., 1967-68; fin. aid counselor Pratt Inst., N.Y.C., 1969-70; tchr. Chinese Seward Park H.S., 1970-95. Author: Letters to Three Places, 1984, New York Notes, 1988, Teachers and Friends, 1996, My Student Life in England and America, 1999, C.T. Hsia's Friends and Literature, 2001. Dr. Sun Yat-Sen's scholar, Chung-San Scholar Com., Taipei, 1961. Mem. Overseas Chinese Writers Assn. (founder, cons. 1980—), United Fed. Tchrs. Democrat. Avocations: swimming, theater, travel, reading, writing. Home: 50-40 201st St Bayside NY 11364

YIN, KENNETH JOSEPH, language educator; b. Lakewood, N.J., Aug. 5, 1967; s. John En Shen and Pauline (Li) Y. AB with distinction in Russian and Soviet Studies, Cornell U., 1989; MS in Linguistics, Georgetown U., 1992. Grad. fellow Georgetown U., Washington, 1990-93; coord. internat. bus. tng. programs World Trade Inst., N.Y.C., 1993; instr., registrar English Lang. Sch. N.Y. Assn. for New Ams., 1993-95; adj. lectr. ESL Touro Coll., 1995, Mercy Coll., Dobbs Ferry, N.Y., 1995; vis. instr. English and humanities Pratt Inst., Bklyn., 1996-98, asst. prof. English and humanities, 1998-99, adj. asst. prof. English and humanities, 1999—. Adj. lectr. ESL Fiorello H. LaGuardia C.C. CUNY, L.I. City, 1998—, classical, Middle Eastern and Asian langs. and cultures Queens Coll. CUNY, Flushing, 1999, Coll. ESL, 1999; contract interpreter, translator Appearance Assistance Program, Vera Inst. Justice, U.S. Immigration and Naturalization Svc., N.Y.C., 1999; instr. Sch. Chinese Studies China Inst. Am., N.Y.C., 1999—; tchg. fellow N.Y.C. Bd. Edn., 2000; adj. assoc. in Chinese, Fiorello H. LaGuardia C.C., CUNY, Long Island City, 2001--. Contbr. MLA Internat. Bibliography, 1995. Mem. local com. Cornell Alumni Admissions Ambassador Network, 1996—, Georgetown Career Network, 1993—, Cornell Career Networking Svc., 2000—, ESL Coun., CUNY, 2001—. Scholar N.Y. State Regents, 1985-89, Georgetown U., 1993-94, Thomas J. Watson Meml. scholar IBM, 1985-89. Mem. Golden Key Internat. Honour Soc. Avocation: ice skating. Office: Fiorello H LaGuardia CC CUNY 21-10 Thomson Ave Long Island City NY 11101-3071 Fax: 718-482-6032. E-mail: kennethy@lagcc.cuny.edu.

YIN, KEWEN KAREN, chemical engineer, educator; b. Beijing, June 21, 1946; Came to U.S., 1985; d. Yixin Yin and Wanzhen Zhu. MSChemE, Beijing Inst. Chem. Tech., 1982; MA in Math., U. Md., 1990, PhD in Chem. Engring., 1991. Engr. Lanzhou (China) Chem. Industry Co., 1969-78; rsch. asst. Beijing Inst. Chem. Tech., 1978-82; engr. Chem. Industry Design Corp., Beijing, 1983-84; lectr. Wuhan Inst. Material Sci., 1984-85; grad. asst. U. Md., College Park, 1986—91, asst. prof. chem. engring., 1991—96; assoc. prof. U. Minn., Duluth, 1996—98, Mpls.-St. Paul, 1998—. Mem. program com. The 1997 Am. Control Conf., Albuquerque, 1997. Contbr. numerous articles to profl. jours. Rsch. grantee NSF, 1994, Minn. Sea Grant, 1996, 98, Minn. Dept. Natural Resources, 1999. Mem. AIChE (vice-chair internat. meeting program 1997), Am. Stats. Soc. Avocation: classical music. Office: U Minn Dept Wood and Paper Sci 2004 Folwell Ave Saint Paul MN 55108-6128

YINDRA, MINA ANNELIESE, nursing administrator; b. Washington, June 9, 1961; d. Charles and Nettie Lou (Price) Wissler; m. Joseph John Yindra, Sept. 21, 1998; children: Donald Michael, Robert Charles. AAS in Nursing summa cum laude, No. Va. C.C., Annandale, 1992; BSN summa cum laude, SUNY, Albany, 1994; MSN summa cum laude, George Mason U., 1996. With Fairfax County Police Dept., 1978-87; security adminstr. TropWorld Casino, 1988-89; musician, 1989-92; orthopedic, neurol., surg. and pediat. nurse Mt. Vernon Hosp., Alexandria, Va., 1992-93, charge nurse acute joint replacement unit, 1994, dir. geriatric unit, asst. DON, 1994-95; nursing dir. subsacute unit HCR Corp., Adelphi, Md., 1995-96; nursing supr. Beebe Med. Ctr., Lewes, Del., 1996; pediat. ICU specialist Vis. Nurses Assn., Dover, 1997-2000; psychiat. nurse/unit supr. Meadows Physiat. Ctr., Centre Hall, Pa., 2000—;

police officer Dewey Beach, Del., 1999; stabilization unit supr. Meadows Psychiat. Ctr., Centre Hall, Pa. Counselor P.W. Women's Aid, Woodbridge, Va., 1978-81, diabetic edn. coord., 1994—. Profl. musician, 1983-92. Active People for Ethical Treatment Animals, 1996—, Human Rights Campaign, 1989—. Mem. ANA, Fraternal Order of Police, Mensa, Phi Theta Kappa, Phi Beta Kappa. Avocations: civic activism, animal rights, reading.

YING, JACKIE, chemical engineer, educator; Prof. MIT, Cambridge, 1992—. Mem. editl. bd. Advances in Chem. Engring., Jour. Metastable and Nanostructured Materials, Nanoparticle Sci. and Tech., Jour. of Electroceramics, Jour. of Porous Materials, Applied Catalysis A, Acta Metallurgica, Scripta Metallurgica. David and Lucile Packard fellow, 1995; recipient Exxon Solid-State Chemistry Fellowship award Am. Chem. Soc., 1997, Camille Dreyfus Tchr.-Scholar award, 1996, Colburn award Am. Inst. Chem. Engrs., 2000. E-mail: jyying@mit.edu.

YINGLING, JACOB MATTHIAS, independent investor; b. Aspers, Pa., Sept. 30, 1930; s. Jacob Charles and Emma Bell (Grimes) Y.; m. Genevieve Jean Koontz, Apr. 5, 1951; children: Stephen Jacob, Randall Matthew. BA, Gettysburg Coll., 1952. Del. from Carroll County Md. Ho. of Dels., Annapolis, 1963-72; asst. sec. Md. Dept. Econ. and Cmty. Devel., 1972-77. Former chmn. bd. dirs. TBT Investmens, Inc., Wilmington, Del.; bd. dirs. Monocacy Bancshares Inc., Taneytown, Md., Westminster Devel. Corp. Author: A Man from the Palatinate, An Autobiography. Pres. Westminster (Md.) Town Ctr. Corp.; former pres. Md. Sch. for Deaf, Frederick; trustee St. Joseph's Hosp., Towson, Md., 1980-88; pres. Carroll Haven, Westminster, 1987-91. Mem. Nat. Soc. SAR, Md. Soc. SAR (bd. mgrs., v.p. Carroll chpt.), Sons of Union Vets. of Civil War, Spkrs. Soc., Masons, Knights Templar, Boumi Temple, Zempo Temple, Elks, Moose, Alpha Tau Omega, Kappa Phi Kappa. Home: 24 Kalten Rd Westminster MD 21158-3036 E-mail: jgsr@cct.infi.net.

YINGLING, JOHN A. military officer; b. Alexandria, Va. Grad., Wake Forest U., 1975. Commd. U.S. Army, 1975, advanced through grades to brig. gen.; firing platoon comdr. Weapons Support Detachment, 3d Bn., 81st Field Artillery; from battery exec. officer to comdr. A Battery, 3d Bn., 6th Field Artillery U.S. Army, comdr. C Battery, 1st Bn., 76th Field Artillery Germany, bn. ops. officer Germany; field artillery assignment officer Mil. Pers. Ctr., 1984—86; 1st corps officer ps. mgr., fire support officer 1st Brigade, 9th Inf. Divsn., Ft. Lewis, 1987—91; staff officer Joint Staff, Nat. Mil. Command Systems, Pentagon, 1991—93; comdr. 7th Bn., 8th Field Artillery, Red Dragons, 25th Inf. Divsn., 1993—95, 3d Inf. Divsn. Artillery, 1996—98; dir. Fire Support and Combined Ops. Dept., Ft. Sill, 1998—99; asst. divsn. comdr. 2d Inf. Divsn., 1999; chief of staff USAR Command, Ft. McPherson, Ga. Decorated Legion of Merit with one oak leaf cluster, Meritorious Svc. medal with 4 oak leaf clusters, Joint Commendation medal, Army Commendation medal with 2 oak leaf clusters, many others. Office: Army Reserve Command Fort Mcpherson GA 30330-1069*

YINGLING, ROBERT GRANVILLE, JR. accountant; b. Lakewood, Ohio, Nov. 8, 1940; s. Robert Granville and Natalie (Phillips) Y.; m. Linda Kay Patterson, Mar. 30, 1968; 1 child, Michael Philip. AB in Polit. Sci., U. Mo., 1963; postgrad., U. Ariz., 1966-67, Portland State U., 1971-73. CPA, Oreg.; cert. govt. fin. mgr. Mgmt. trainee Mich. Nat. Bank, Flint, 1963-65; comml. note teller First Nat. Bank Ariz., Tucson, 1965-67; spl. asst. Travelers Ins. Cos., Phoenix, then Portland, Oreg., 1967-70; chief acct. Am. Guaranty Life Ins. Co., Portland, 1970-73; supr. Peat, Marwick, Mitchell & Co., 1973-79; ptnr. Dietrich, Bye, Griffin & Youel, 1979-84; prin. Isler, Collins & McAdams, 1984-85; owner, acct. R.G. Yingling Jr., CPA, 1985—. Adj. asst. prof., U. Portland, 1988. Treas. Portland Amateur Hockey Assn., 1977-78; mem. exec. bd. Columbia Pacific coun. Boy Scouts Am., 1985—, asst. treas., 1986-87, treas. 1988-91, dist. chmn. Mt. View, 1991; bd. dirs. Artist Repertory Theatre, Inc., 1992-96, St. Andrew Legal Clinic, Inc., 1992—, treas.; dir., treas. Mt. Hood Repertory Theatre, 1997—. Recipient Silver Beaver award, Boy Scouts Am., 1986. Mem. AICPA, Oreg. Soc. CPAs, Inst. Mgmt. Accts. (nat. dir. 1985-87), Assn. Govt. Accts. (nat. v.p. 1983), Nat. Conf. CPA Practitioners, Rotary. E-mail: bob@yinglingcpa.com., bob@yingling.com.

YINGST, BAMBI, transportation executive; b. Mpls., Mar. 6, 1958; d. Ronald and Nancy Pieri; m. Robert A. Yingst; children: Erin, Aileen, Jeremy. Student, Andrews U., 1987—88. Owner, operator Travel Reservation Ctr., Berrien Springs, Mich., 1982; supr. U.S. Airways, 1983—89, mgr., 1999—. Project dir. Am. Cancer Soc., Niles, Mich., 1981. Office: US Airways Washington Nat Airport Washington DC 20001 : 12901 Alton Sq #103 Herndon VA 20170 Fax: 703-872-2530. E-mail: bambi_yingst@usairways.com.

YINH, VICTOR MARIUS, electrical engineer; b. Panama, Dec. 19, 1946; came to U.S., 1988; s. Juan and Elena (Wong) Y.; m. Luz Aura Clop, Mar. 5, 1977; children: Victor, Daniel, Marius. BSEE, BSME, U. Panama, 1970, BS in Indsl. Engring., 1975. Cert. code enforcement and adminstrn. profl.; cert. bldg. ofcl. Elec. designer Amado's Engring., Inc., Panama, 1977-79; gen. mgr., project engr. Yinh & Assocs., 1979-88; mech. engr. AJT & Assocs., Inc., Cape Canaveral, Fla., 1989-90; substa. project engr. Fla. Power & Light Co., Juno Beach, 1990-93; plans examiner & inspector Town of Jupiter, Fla., 1994-2000, chief plans examiner, 2000—. Mem. Bldg. Ofcls. Assn. Fla. Mem. NSPE, IEEE, Fla. Assn. Plumbing, Gas, Mech. Inspectors (2d v.p. 1997), Bldg. Offcls. Assn. of Fla. Home: 5592 Eagle Lake Dr Palm Beach Gardens FL 33418-1550 Office: Town of Jupiter Bldg Divsn 210 Military Trl Jupiter FL 33458-5786

YIP, CHI YAN TOBY, social worker, journalist, researcher; b. Hong Kong, Oct. 13, 1966; s. Kam Hon and Chiu Yung Y.; m. Betty L.F. Wong, Mar. 2, 1997. BSW, Hong Kong Bapt. U., 1989; MPhil in Comm., Chinese U. Hong Kong, 1993; postgrad., Simon Fraser U., Can., 1997—. Registered social worker Hong Kong, B.C., Can. Asst. social work officer St. Christopher's Home, Hong Kong, 1994; rsch. asst. City U. Hong Kong, 1994-95; asst. social work officer Against Child Abuse, Hong Kong, 1995-97; reporter, announcer Fairchild Radio Sta. 1470 AM&FM 96.1, Can., 1997-98; child care worker The Ministry for Children and Families, 1998—2000. Vis. lectr. Swire Sch. Design, Hong Kong Polytechnic, 1994; dir. Adventure Ship, Hong Kong, 1993—97, Hong Kong, 2000—. Author (with others): Hong Kong Popular Culture Studies, 1993, Popular Culture: Its impact on Young People in Guangdong , 1996; freelance writer: Sing Tao Daily, freelance writer: The Hong Kong Econ. Times, 1995; editor: The History of Adventure-Ship, 20th Anniversary, 1997; co-author: (procs.) Theory and Practice-The Service Model of Adventure Ship and Its Buddies Program, Procs. of Symposium on Children's Agenda for Hong Kong in the 21st Century, 2000. Mem. Centre for Child Devel., Hong Kong Bapt. U., 1996—97, Newbern Meml. Chinese Alliance Ch., Canada; vol. newsletter editor Culture Regeneration Rsch. Soc., Canada, 1997—98; intake vol. Family and Youth Counseling, United Chinese Cmty. Enrichment Svcs. Soc. (SUCCESS), Canada, 1997—99. Named Champion Chinese Calligraphy competition Coll. & Univ. sect., 1998; recipient Team award of Merit Chinese Lit. Competition Hong Kong Urban Coun., 1993, Team award 2d runners up, Lyrics to Hymn Tune Competition, Herald Monthly, Vancouver, Can., 1999, 1st runner up, Creative Writing Competition, Chinese sect. UBC Student Newspaper, 1999; fellow Sch. Comm. Grad. fellow, Simon Fraser U. Canada, 1998, 1999, Dr. Cheng Yu Teng and Dr. Lee Shau Kee Student fellow, Chinese U. Hong Kong, 1992, Faculty of Applied Scis. Dean's Fund PhD grad. fellow, Simon Fraser U., Can., 1999, 2000; scholar Hong Kong TV Broadcasts Ltd. scholar, Chinese U. Hong Kong, 1991, Lion Dr. Francis K. Pan scholar, 1991. Mem.: Newbern Meml. Chinese Alliance Ch., Can. Assn. Media Edn., Nat. Geog. Soc., Can. Soc. Info., Hong Kong Social Work Assn., Assn. for Exptl. Edn., Chinese Comm. Assn., Hong Kong Profl. Counseling Assn. (sr.). Avocation: swimming. Office: 6673 Clarendon St Vancouver BC Canada V5S 2K2 E-mail: cyyip@sfu.ca.

YIRA, MARKUS CLARENCE, lawyer; b. St. Croix Falls, Wis., Feb. 6, 1971; s. Robert Gordon and Ruth Elizabeth Yira; m. Dawn Susanne Nelson, June 19, 1993; children: Jordan M., Kaitlin E., Alison M., Brandon M. BA magna cum laude, Hamline U., 1993; JD, William Mitchell Coll. Law, St. Paul, 1996. Bar: Minn. 1996, Wis. 2002, U.S. Dist. Ct. Minn. 1996, U.S. Ct. Appeals (8th cir.) 1997, U.S. Supreme Ct. 1999. Rsch. asst. William Mitchell Coll. Law, 1993-95; assoc. Eckman, Strandness & Egan, P.A., Wayzata, Minn., 1996-99, Lommen, Nelson, Cole & Stageberg, P.A., Mpls., 1999—. Mem. ATLA, Minn. Bar Assn., Minn. Trial Lawyers Assn., Hennepin County Bar Assn., Phi Beta Kappa. Office: Lommen Nelson Cole & Stageberg PA 1800 IDS Ctr 80 S 8th St Minneapolis MN 55402-2100 E-mail: markus@lommen.com.

YITTS, ROSE MARIE, nursery school executive; b. Bridgeport, Conn., Apr. 29, 1942; m. Richard Francis Yitts, Dec. 28, 1963; children: Anthony Michael, Jennifer Lisa, Heather Michelle. BS, So. Conn. State Coll., 1963; MS, So. Conn. State U., 1983. Tchr. Trumbull (Conn.) Bd. Edn., 1963-69; substitute tchr. Seymour (Conn.) and Oxford (Conn.) Bd. Edn., 1970-79; tchr. aide spl. edn. Oxford (Conn.) Bd. Edn., 1979-82; dir., founding ptnr., pres. and treas. Strawberry Tyme Nursery Sch. and Day Care Ctr. Ltd., Seymour, 1983—. Corr. sec. student senate So. Conn. State Coll., 1963; den leader, con. chmn. Boy Scouts Am., Seymour, 1973-77; troop leader Girl Scouts U.S., Seymour, 1978-80; chair fundraisers, coach George J. Hummel Little League, Seymour, 1982-86, 1st woman pres., 1987-88, player agt., 1990; tchr., spl. edn. curriculum developer Ch. of Good Shepherd, mem. parish coun., 1984-86; elected mem., corr. sec. Seymour Libr., bd. dirs., 1983-89; elected mem. Republican Town Com., 1996, mem. exec. bd., 2000, GOP 5 State, 1998—2002; elected mem. Seymour Bd. Edn., 1999—. Recipient award of merit, honorable mention, Golden Poet award, World of Poetry, 1987, Editor's Choice award, Nat. Libr. Poetry, 1994, 1995, Joseph Gido award, Seymour Rep. Town. Com., 2001—. Mem. Oxford Bus. Assn. (membership com. 1993-95), Seymour Hist. Soc. Republican. E-mail: michmax2@aol.com.

YIU, FANG, structural engineer, researcher; b. Shanghai, Apr. 21, 1972; d. Boxian Yiu and Jingfang Hua. BS, Shanghai Inst. Ry. Tech., 1993; MS, Tongji U., Shanghai, 1995; PhD, Cornell U., 2002. Cost evaluation cert., cert. fundamental engr. Structural engr. Shanghai Posts & Telecoms. Design Inst., 1993-95; rsch. asst. dept. civil and environ. engring. Cornell U., Ithaca, NY, 1998—2002; sr. staff tech. profl. Mustang Engring., L.P., 2002—. Asst. engring. mgr. Shanghai Designing INst. Telecomms., Shanghai, 1993—95; peer advisor dept. civil and environ. engring. Cornell U., Ithaca, 1999—2000, engring. grad. student assn. rep., 2000—02. Referee: for profl. jours. Mem. civil engring. del. People to People Amb., Spokane, Wash., 2000—; treas. Chinese Students and Scholars Assn., Ithaca, 1998—99. Mem.: ASCE, Soc. Woman Engrs., Earthquake Engring. Rsch. Inst. (treas. 2000—). Home: Rm 3 717 E Buffalo St Ithaca NY 14850 Office: Cornell U Dept Civil/Environ Engring 220 Hollister Hall Ithaca NY 14853 E-mail: fy16@cornell.edu.

YLAGAN, LOURDES ROSAL, cytopathologist; b. Cebu, The Philippines, Mar. 23, 1968; d. Mariano Magtoto and Salustiana Rosal Ylagan. BA, Queens Coll., Flushing, N.Y., 1988; MD, Ohio State U., 1993. Diplomate Am Bd Pathology, Am Bd Cytopathology. Resident in pathology NYU, N.Y.C., 1994-98; gynecol. pathology fellow Albert Einstein Coll. Medicine, Bronx, 1998-99; cytopathology fellow Washington U., St. Louis, 1999-2000, instr. pathology and immunology, 2000—. Contbr. articles to profl jours. Roman Catholic. Avocation: ballroomd dancing (Argentine Tango). Office: Box 8118 660 S Euclid Ave Saint Louis MO 63110-1010 E-mail: lylagan@path.wustu.edu.

YLVISAKER, JAMES WILLIAM, insurance executive; b. Mpls., Feb. 26, 1938; s. Johannas Wilhelm and Lucille Elizabeth (Torgeson) Y.; m. Judith Diane Stevens, May 19, 1943 (div. Aug. 1980). BA, Luther Coll., 1960. Assoc. actuary North Am. Life & Casualty, Mpls., 1961-76; actuary IDS Life Ins. Co., 1976-80; exec. v.p., chief operating officer Cologne Life Reinsurance Co., Stamford, Conn., 1980-89; pres., chief exec. officer IdeaLife Ins. Co., 1989-90, also bd. dirs.; pres., COO, Horizons LLC, Hartford, Conn., 1997-99, U.S. Living Benefits, LLC, Hartford, 1999—. Bd. dirs. Reassurance Corp. of Del., Stamford, Stamford Life Ins. Co., 1983-90, cons. actuary, 1991—. Dist. chmn. United Way of Mpls., 1966; regional coord. Carlson for Mayor Campaign, Mpls., 1968; state chmn. Head for Gov. Campaign, Mpls., 1970; mem. bd. regents Luther Coll., Decorah, Iowa, 1990. Fellow Soc. Actuaries; mem. Am. Acad. Actuaries, Internat. Actuarial Assn. Avocations: reading, music, golf, travel. Home and Office: 40 Prides Crossing 312 Elm St New Canaan CT 06840-5305 E-mail: jimuslb@optonline.net.

YLVISAKER, JOHN RICHARD, real estate developer, consultant; b. Decorah, Iowa, May 2, 1919; s. Sigurd Christian and Norma Marie (Norem) Y.; m. Tekla Valborg Strom, Dec. 31, 1951; children: Jon Erik, Jeffrey Alan, Nancy Jo, Susan Marie. AA, Bethany Luth. Coll., Mankato, Minn., 1938; BA, Concordia Sem., St. Louis, 1942; BS, U. Minn., 1945, MD, 1949. Diplomate Am. Bd. Surgery. Pvt. practice, Pontiac, Mich., 1956-69; med. dir. St. Joseph Mercy Hosp., 1969-80; pres., gen. ptnr. Ylvisaker Cos., Bloomfield Hills, 1967-. Adj. prof. health sci. Oakland U., Rochester, Mich., 1977—97. Capt. USAF, 1951-53. Fellow ACS; mem. AMA, Mich. State Med. Soc. (treas. 1967-79, pres. 1980-81), Oakland County Med. Soc., Village Club. Republican. Avocations: flying, sailing, gardening. Home: Ylvisaker Investment Co 9860 Pine Knob Rd Clarkston MI 48348-2144 E-mail: jry19@aol.com.

YNDA, MARY LOU, artist, educator; b. Los Angeles, Apr. 4, 1936; d. Ernest Pastor Ynda and Mary Estella (Ruiz) Zapotocky, m. Gary Lynn Coleman, Sept. 1, 1956 (div. Feb. 1983); children: Debra Lynn, Lisa Annette, David Gary; m. Miles Ciletti, May 25, 1991. Student, Immaculate Heart Coll., Los Angeles, 1973-79; AA in Fine Arts, Los Angeles City Coll., 1976; BA, Calif. State U., L.A., 1993. Instr. Fashion Inst. Design, L.A., 1980-81; tchr. art to disabled First St. Gallery, Claremont, Calif., 1991-94; tchr. art Tierra Del Sol Found., Sunland, 1995-96. Exhibited in group shows at Double Rocking G Gallery, L.A., 1983, Improv Theater West, West Hollywood, Calif., 1983, Exposition Gallery Calif. State U., L.A., 1983, L.A. Art Core Gallery, 1985, Poly. Tech. Sch., Pasadena, Calif., 1986, Bad Eye Gallery, L.A., 1987, Art in the Hall VI West Hollywood City Hall, 1989, Echo Park Gallery, L.A., 1991, Art N Barbee Gallery, 1992, A Celebration of City Life, 1993, DADA Show-Downtown Lives, L.A., 1994, 96, Spirit Exhbn. for Women's Caucus for Art, Santa Ana, Calif., 1995; designer Spoken Word CD Long Days and Monster Nights, 1994; contbg. author poetry Spoken Word Voices of the Angels, 1982; book rev. Yesterday and Tomorrow: California Women Artists, 1989. Archetypes and Contemporary Images in The Hispanic World. The City of Lancaster Mus./Art Gallery, Lancaster Calif. Mem. Women's Caucus for Art. Democrat. Avocations: mask making, fetish art, study of animal behavior.

YNGVE, VICTOR H. linguist, researcher; b. Niagara Falls, N.Y., July 5, 1920; s. Victor and Miriam (Huse) Y.; m. Jean Huber, Sept. 6, 1943; children: Marna, David, Alan. BS in Physics, Antioch Coll., Yellow Springs, Ohio, 1943; MS in Physics, U. Chgo., 1950, PhD in Physics, 1953. Staff mem., rsch. assoc. MIT, Cambridge, Mass., 1953-65; prof. linguistics U. Chgo., 1965-90, prof. emeritus, 1990—. Co-founder, editor Mechanical Translation and Computational Linguistics, 1954-70; cons. Standardization of Am. Std. Code for Info. Interchange (ASCII); founder, editor, pub. Comms. of the Workshop for Sci. Linguistics, 1990—. Author: Computer Programming with Comit II, 1972, Linguistics as a Science, 1986, From Grammar to Science, 1996. Mem. Linguistic Soc. Am., Soc. Linguistica Europaea, Linguistic Assn. of Can. and the U.S. (v.p. 1984-85, pres. 1985-86), Assn. for Computational Linguistics (co-founder, 1st pres. 1962-63).

YNTEMA, MARY KATHERINE, retired mathematics educator; b. Urbana, Ill., Jan. 20, 1928; d. Leonard Francis and M. Jean (Busey) Y. BA in Math., Swarthmore Coll., 1950; MA in Math., U. Ill., 1961, PhD in Math., 1965. Tchr., secondary math. Am. Coll. for Girls, Istanbul, Turkey, 1950-54, Columbus (Ohio) Sch. for Girls, 1954-57; computer programmer MIT Lincoln Lab., Lexington, Mass., 1957-58; tchr., secondary math Roundup (Mont.) High Sch., 1959-60; asst. prof. math U. Ill., Chgo., 1965-67; asst. prof. computer sci. Pa. State U., University Park, 1967-71; assoc. prof. to prof. math. Sangamon State U., Springfield, Ill., 1971-91; ret., 1991. Avocation: enjoyment of nature.

YOCAM, DELBERT WAYNE, retired software products company executive; b. Long Beach, Calif., Dec. 24, 1943; s. Royal Delbert and Mary Rose (Gross) Y.; m. Janet McVeigh, June 13, 1965; children— Eric Wayne, Christian Jeremy, Elizabeth Janelle. BA in Bus. Adminstrn., Calif. State U.-Fullerton, 1966; MBA, Calif. State U., Long Beach, 1971. Mktg.-supply changeover coordinator Automotive Assembly div. Ford Motor Co., Dearborn, Mich., 1966-72; prodn. control mgr. Control Data Corp., Hawthorne, Calif., 1972-74; prodn. and material control mgr. Bourns Inc., Riverside, 1974-76; corp. material mgr. Computer Automation Inc., Irvine, 1976-78; prodn. planning mgr. central staff Cannon Electric div. ITT, World hdqrs., Santa Ana, 1978-79; exec. v.p., COO Apple Computer, Inc., Cupertino, 1979-91; pres., COO, dir. Textronix Inc., Wilsonville, Oreg., 1992-95; chmn., CEO Borland Internat., Inc./Inprise Corp., Scotts Valley, Calif., 1996-2000, ret., 2000. Mem. faculty Cypress Coll., Calif., 1972-79; bd. dirs. Adobe Sys Inc., San Jose, Calif., Rogue Wave Software, Inc., Boulder, Colo., Softricity, Inc., Boston ; vice chmn. Tech. Ctr. Innovation, San Jose, Calif., 1989-90. Mem. Am. Electronics Assn. (nat. bd. dirs. 1988-89), Control Data Corp. Mgmt. Assn. (co-founder 1974), L.A. County Heart Assn. (active 1966). E-mail: yocam@aol.com.

YOCHELSON, ELLIS L(EON), paleontologist; b. Washington, Nov. 14, 1928; s. Morris Wolf and Fannie (Botkin) Y.; m. Sally Witt, June 10, 1950; children: Jeffrey, Abby, Charles. BS, U. Kans., 1949, MS, 1950; PhD, Columbia U., 1955. Paleontologist U.S. Geol. Survey, 1952-85, scientist emeritus, 1991; biostratigrapher, specializing in Paleozoic gastropods and minor classes of extinct mollusks; lectr. night sch. George Washington U., 1962-65; rsch. assoc. dept. paleobiology Smithsonian Instn., Washington, 1965—; lectr. Univ. Coll., U. Md., 1966-74; rsch. assoc. Smithsonian Instn., 1967—; lectr. U. Del., 1981; vis. prof. U. Md., 1986-87; organizer N.Am. Paleontol. Conv., 1969, editor proc., 1970-71. Co-editor: Essays in Paleontology and Stratigraphy, 1967; editor: Scientific Ideas of G.K. Gilbert, 1980; editorial bd. Nat. Geog. Rsch. and Exploration; contbr. numerous articles to profl. jours. Author: Charles Doolittle Walcott, Paleontologist, 1998, Smithsonian Institution Secretary Charles Doolittle Walcott, 2001. Fellow AAAS (chmn. sect. E 1971); mem. Soc. Systematic Zoology (sec. 1961-66, councilor 1973), Internat. Paleontol. Assn. (treas. 1972-76), Paleontol. Soc. (pres. 1976), History of Earth Sciences Soc. (sec.-treas. 1982-85, sec. 1986-87, pres. 1989), N.Am. Paleontol. Conv. (hon. life; sec.), Smithsonian Instn. (150th Anniversary com.), Sigma Xi. Office: Smithsonian Instn E-305A Mus Natural History Washington DC 20560-0121 E-mail: yochelson.ellis@nmnh.si.edu.

YOCHEM, BARBARA JUNE (RUNYAN), sales executive, lecturer; b. Knox, Ind., Aug. 22, 1945; d. Harley Albert and Rosie (King) Runyan; m. Donald A. Yochem (div. 1979); 1 child, Morgan Lee; m. Don Heard, Dec. 12, 1987 (div. 1998). Grad. high school, Knox, Ind., 1963. Sales rep. Hunter Woodworks, Carson, Calif., 1979-84, sales mgr., 1984-87; sales rep. Comml. Lumber and Pallet, Industry, 1987-92; mgr. Desert Shadows Apts., Herperia, 1998—, Hesperia, 1998; real estate agt. Marina Properties, Victorville, Spring Valley Lake, 2000—01, Coldwell Banker Home Real Estate , 2001—. Owner By By Prodns., Glendora, Calif., 1976—. Author: Barbara Yochem's Inner Shooting; contbr. articles to profl. jours. Head coach NRA Jr. Olympic Shooting Camp, 1989-94. Recipient U.S. Bronze medal U.S. Olympic Com., 1976, World Bronze medal U.S. Olympic Com., 1980; inductee Calif. Trapshooting Hall of Fame, 1998. Avocation: reading. Address: 9936 SVL Box Victorville CA 92392-5144 E-mail: BYochem@hotmail.com.

YOCKIM, JAMES CRAIG, state senator; b. Williston, N.D., Feb. 13, 1953; s. Daniel and Doris (Erickson) Y.; children: Jenna, Ericka. BSW, Pacific Luth. U., 1975; MSW, San Diego State U., 1979. Caseworker Dyslin Boys Ranch, Tacoma, 1975-77, head caseworker, program dir., 1979-80; landman Fayette Oil & Gas, Williston, 1980-82; owner Hy-Plains Energy, 1982-87; city fin. commr. City of Williston, 1984-88, 98—, 1998—2002; therapist Williston, 1983; senator N.D. State Senate, 1986-98; owner James C. Yockim Resources, Williston, 1987—. Dir. Bethel Luth. Found., 1993—; del. N.D. Dem. Conv., 1984, 86, 88, 90, 92, 94, 96, 98, 2000. 02; dist. chmn. Dem. Party, Williston, 1988; caucus chmn. Dem. Caucus N.D. State Senate; mem. N.D. Legis. Coun., 1997-98. Recipient Ruth Meiers award N.D. Mental Health Assn., 1989, Legislator of Yr. award N.D. Children's Caucus, 1989; named Outstanding Young North Dakotan N.D. Jaycees, 1988. Mem. NASW. Avocations: racquetball, golf. Home: 1123 2nd Ave E Williston ND 58801-4302 Office: 417 1st Ave E PO Box 2344 Williston ND 58802-2344

YOCUM, HARRISON GERALD, horticulturist, botanist, educator, researcher; b. Bethlehem, Pa., Apr. 2, 1923; s. Harrison and Bertha May (Meckes) Y. BS, Pa. State U., 1955; MS, Rutgers U., 1961. Horticulture instr. U. Tenn., Martin, 1957-59; biology tchr., libr. asst. high schs., El Paso, Tex., 1959-60; rsch. asst. geochronology lab. U. Ariz., Tucson, 1960-67, rsch. asst. environ. rsch. lab., 1969-76; landscaping supt. Tucson Airport Authority, 1976-82; instr. Pima C.C., Tucson, 1976—. Contbr. articles to profl. jours. Founder Tucson Bot. Gardens, 1964. Recipient 1st Unique Gardener award Gardeners Am. Mem. Am. Hort. Soc., Nat. Trust Historic Preservation, Ariz. Preservation Found., Men's Garden Club Tucson (pres. 1991), Tucson Cactus & Succulent Soc. (pres. 1991, 92), Internat. Palm Soc. (charter), El Paso Cactus and Rock Club, Tucson Gem and Mineral Soc., Old Pueblo Lapidary Club, Deming Mineral Soc., Nat. Geog. Soc., Ariz.-Sonora Desert Mus., Huachuca Vigilantes, Penn State Alumni Assn. (life), Pa. Club Tucson, Fraternal Order Police Assocs., N.Am. Hunting Club (life), Boyce-Thompson Arboretum, Shriners, Masons, Scottish Rite (life). Lutheran. Home: 1628 N Jefferson Ave Tucson AZ 85712-4204

YOCUM, TONIA SHEETS, physician assistant; b. Charleston, W.Va., May 29, 1971; d. Alden Mason and Linda Jane (Hartley) Sheets; m. Chalmer Clee Yocum II, Dec. 29, 1995. BS in Sports Medicine, Alderson-Broaddus Coll., 1996, BS in Med. Sci., 1992-96. Cert. physician asst. Surg. physician asst. Mt. Vernon Hosp., Alexandria, Va., 1996-98, Othopacdic Surgery and Sports Medicine Specialist of Hampton Rds., Newport News, 2002—. Fellow Am. Acad. Physician Assts., Va. Acad. Physician Assts. Home: 112 Panther Paw Path Williamsburg VA 23185 Mailing: Apt 210 594 Hollins Ct Newport News VA 23608 E-mail: cyocum2@hotmail.com

YODAIKEN, RALPH E. pathologist, occupational medicine physician; b. Johannesburg, South Africa, 1928; BS, U. Witwatersrand, Republic of South Africa, 1956; MPH, Johns Hopkins U., 1976. Diplomate Am. Bd. Pathology, Am. Bd. Forensic Medicine. Intern Coronation Hosp., Johannesburg, 1956-57; resident U. Witwatersrand Med. Ctr., 1957-58, Johannesburg Gen. Hosp., 1958; assoc. pathologist Buffalo Gen. Hosp., 1965-67; mem. staff Cin. Gen. Hosp., 1968-71; rsch. assoc. Johns Hopkins U. Sch. Hygiene and Pub. Health, Balt., 1976—; sr. staff mem. Nat. Inst. Occupational Safety and Health, Washington, 1977—, chmn. sr. adv. staff, 1983; dir. office occupational medicine Occupational Safety and Health Adminstrn., U.S. Dept. Labor, 1983-91, sr. med. advisor Bethesda, 1991-98; clin. prof. preventive medicine U. Health Scis., Washington, 1983—. Lectr. U. Witwatersrand, 1958-63; asst. prof. pathology, SUNY Buffalo, 1963-67; assoc. prof. pathology U. Cin., 1968-71; prof. pathology, assoc. prof. medicine Emory U., Atlanta, 1971-75; adj. clin. prof. George Washington U., 1975—; sr. assoc. Johns Hopkins Sch. Hygiene and Pub. Health; clin. prof. preventive medicine uniformed svcs. U. Health Scis. Served to lt. Israeli Army, 1948-50. Fellow Coll. Am. Pathologists, Am. Coll. Occupl. and Environ. Health, Am. Coll. Forensic Medicine.

YODER, ANNA A. elementary school educator; b. Beach City, Ohio, Sept. 5, 1934; d. Abram J. and Barbara D. (Miller) Y. BS, Ea. Mennonite Coll., 1966; MEd, Frostburg State Coll., 1974. Cert. elem. tchr., Ohio, recreational leader. Tchr. Garrett County Schs., Oakland, Md., 1966-70, prin. elem. sch., 1970-74; tchr. E. Holmes Local Schs., Berlin, 1974-98, ret., 1998. Chairperson edn. com. German Culture Mus., Berlin, Ohio, 1987-90; cons. bilingual edn. E. Holmes Local Schs., Berlin, Ohio, 1982-98, ret., 1998. Supporting mem. German Culture Mus., Berlin, Ohio, 1983—; mem. Killbuck (Ohio) Valley mus., 1988—, Holmes County Hist. Soc., Millersburg, Ohio, 1989—; life mem. Mennonite Info. Ctr., Berlin, Ohio, 1985—; sustaining mem. The Wilderness Ctr., Wilmot, Ohio, 1974—. Jennings scholar Martha Holden Jennings Found., 1983-84; Silver Poet award World of Poetry, 1986. Mem. AAUW (v.p. Holmes County chpt. 1994), Creative Arts Soc. (sec.-treas. 1987-89), Delta Kappa Gamma (sec. Beta Iota chpt. 1987-90, pres. 1990-92, pres. 1998-2000). Mennonite. Avocations: nature studies-birds and flowers, handcrafts. Home: 5229 State Route 39 Millersburg OH 44654-8408

YODER, ANNA MARY, reading educator; b. Iowa County, Iowa, Nov. 14, 1933; d. Kores M. and Sadie Rebecca (King) Y. BS in Elem. Edn., Ea. Mennonite U., 1959; MA in Linguistics, Hartford Sem. Found., 1968; MA in Curriculum and Instruction, U. Tenn., 1975; postgrad., U. Iowa, 1975-81. Tchr. Am. Sch., Tegulcigalpa, Honduras, 1969-70, Escuela Internat. Sch., San Pedro Sula, Honduras, 1970-75; tchr. bilingual Muscatine (Iowa) Cmty. Schs., 1977-78, tchr., supr. title I, 1978-79; tchr. Escuela Internat. Sch., 1979-80; tchr. home room Muscatine Cmty. Schs., 1980-87, reading tchr., 1987-99. Nat. dir.

adult educators Alfalit Spanish wun of Lit, Honduras, 1963-69. Author/editor: Pre-Cartilla de Alfalit, 1968. Mem. Sisters Cities, Muscatine, 1994, bd. dirs., 1995-99; vol. Mid Prairie Sch. Dist., Wellman, Iowa. Mem. NEA, Internat. Reading Assn., Reading Recovery Coun. N.Am. (tchr. 1995-2000). Avocations: gardening, cats, reading, volunteering.

YODER, BRUCE ALAN, chemist; b. Seward, Nebr., Apr. 29, 1962; s. Elwood John and Elda Raye (Stutzman) Y. BS in Chemistry, Wayne State Coll., 1983. Lab. technician Wayne (Nebr.) State Coll., 1982-83, Harris Labs., Lincoln, Nebr., 1984, chemist, 1984; scientist Dorsey Labs., 1984-86, scientist A, 1986-88; product stability analyst Sandoz Pharms., 1988-89, Sandoz Rsch. Inst., Lincoln, 1989-91; mgr. lab. computer ops. Sandoz Pharms., 1991-97; pres., CEO Data Mgmt. Svcs., Inc., 1997—. Active Lancaster County Young Reps., Lincoln, 1988—, co-chmn., 1990-91, pres., 1991-93; mem. Nebr. Fedn. Young Reps., 1988—, exec. com., 1990—, chmn., 1998-99; exec. com. Lancaster County Rep. Party, 1990-97; mem. Def. Adv. Com. Lancaster County, 1992-00; active Lincoln Mayor's Cmty. Cabinet, 1992-93, Lincoln City Charter Revision Commn., 1994—, co-chmn., 1998-2000, chmn., 2000—, v.p., 1999-2000, pres., 2000—; trustee Wayne State Coll. Found., 1991—; advisor Jr. Achievement, 1993-97; bd. dirs. Lincoln Meadows Assn., 1998-99. Recipient Dwight M. Frost, MD award for overcoming a phys. disability Immanuel Rehab. Ctr., 1993, Verdi Smith award for outstanding voluntary contbns. to Lancaster County Rep. Party, 1995-96, First Dist. Outstanding Vol. award Nebr. Reps., 1996-97, Daniel D. Fahrnbruch Leadership award 2000. Mem. Internat. Soc. for Pharm. Engrs., Am. Inst. Chemists, Am. Chem. Soc., Lincoln Ind. Bus. Assn., Jaycees, Elephant Club. Mennonite. Achievements include design of a sample holder for solid dosage forms when using a hunter color instrument, design of a new computer system for Sandoz Pharmaceuticals laboratory computer operations, design of a new computer system for Novartis Consumer Health, Inc. Home: 2240 Winding Way Lincoln NE 68506-2846 Office: Novartis Consumer Health Inc 10401 Hwy 6 Lincoln NE 68517-9626

YODER, CAROL YVONNE, psychologist, educator; b. Kingsville, Tex., Sept. 21, 1954; d. Richard Norman Yoder and Lila Jean Nichols Yoder Jasserand. BA, Pan Am. U., 1976; PhD, Tex. Tech. U., 1983. Post doctoral fellow Tex. Rsch. Inst., Houston, 1983—85; asst. prof. Ind. State U., Terre Haute, 1985—90, assoc. prof., 1990—2001, interim chairperson, 2001—02; prof., chairperson Trinity U., San Antonio, 2002—. Contbr. articles to profl. jours. Mem.: APA, Midwestern Psychol. Assn., Sigma Xi (pres. Wabash Valley chpt. 2001—02). Office: Ind State U Dept Psychology 7th & Cherry Terre Haute IN 47809

YODER, EDGAR PAUL, education educator; b. Millersburg, Ohio, June 20, 1946; s. Albert Daniel Yoder and Ella Marie (Bontrager) Erb; m. Deborah Jean Barnhart, June 12, 1971; children: Scott, Susan. BSA, Ohio State U., 1968, MS, 1972, PhD, 1976. Cert. tchr., counselor, prin., Ohio, Va. Tchr. agr. and sci. Conotton Valley Schs., Bowerston, Ohio, 1968-69, East Holmes Schs., Berlin, 1969-72; curriculum specialist Ohio State U., Columbus, 1972-74, project dir., 1974-76; asst. prin. Montgomery County Schs., Blacksburg, Va., 1976-77; asst. prof. Va. Poly. Inst. and State U., 1977-78, Pa. State U., University Park, 1978-84, assoc. prof. tchr. edn., 1984-94, prof., 1994—, interim dept. head, 1995-98. Cons. Poland Ministry Edn., Warsaw, 1994, Swaziland Ministry Agr., Mbane, 1985, 87, U. Peredenyia, Kandy, Sri Lanka, 1984. Author text: Ag Supplies and Services, 1974; (with others) Undergraduate Education in Agriculture, 1989, also chpt. to book. Chmn. community svc. Sertoma Internat., Columbus, 1975; asst. dir. Va. HSA Assn., Blacksburg, 1978; sect. chmn. Am. Heart Assn., State College, Va., 1981; pres. Ferguson Twp. PTO, State College, 1983-84; bd. dirs. RAFT Drug Rehab. Ctr., Radford, 1976-78, Nat. Future Farmers Am., Alexandria, Va., 1981-83. Recipient hon. degree, Nat. Future Farmers Am., 1983. Mem. Nat. Assn. Coll. Tchrs. Agr. (pres., teacher fellow 1987, Regional Outstanding Teaching award 1992), Am. Assn. Agr. Educators (legis. chmn. 1985), Am. Assn. Ednl. Rsch., Am. Vocat. Edn. Rsch. Assn., Assn. Internat. Agr. and Extension Edn., Phi Delta Kappa, Gamma Sigma Delta (Teaching award of Merit 1987). Avocations: collecting sports memorabilia, restoring antiques, classic cars. Office: Penn State U Rm 323 Ag Adminstrn Coll University Park PA 16802

YODER, EDWIN MILTON, JR. columnist, educator, editor, writer; b. Greensboro, N.C., July 18, 1934; s. Edwin M. and Mytrice M. (Logue) Y.; m. Mary Jane Warwick, Nov. 1, 1958; children: Anne Daphne, Edwin Warwick. BA, U. N.C., 1956; BA, MA (Rhodes scholar), Oxford (Eng.) U., 1958; D.H.L. (hon.), Grinnell Coll., 1980, Elon Coll., 1986; DLitt (hon.), U. N.C., 1993, Richmond Coll., London. Editorial writer Charlotte (N.C.) News, 1958-61; editorial writer Greensboro Daily News, 1961-64, assoc. editor, 1965-75; asst. prof. history U. N.C., Greensboro, 1964-65; editorial page editor Washington Star, 1975-81; syndicated columnist Washington Post Writers Group, 1982-97; prof. journalism and humanities Washington and Lee U., 1992—2002, prof. emeritus, 2002—. Hon. fellow Jesus Coll., Oxford, Eng., 1998—. Author: Night of the Old South Ball, 1984, The Unmaking of a Whig, 1990, Joe Alsop's Cold War, 1995, The Historical Present, 1997; contbr. articles to periodicals. Trustee Inst. for Early Am. History and Culture, Nat. Humanities Ctr., 1991-97. Recipient awards editorial writing N.C. Press Assn., 1958, 61, 66, Walker Stone award Scripps-Howard Found., 1978, Pulitzer prize editorial writing, 1979; Disting. Alumnus award U. N.C., Chapel Hill, 1980 Mem. Nat. Conf. Editorial Writers, Am. Soc. Newspaper Editors. Democrat. Episcopalian. Home: 4001 Harris Pl Alexandria VA 22304-1720 E-mail: yoderem@aol.com.

YODER, HATTEN SCHUYLER, JR. petrologist; b. Cleve., Mar. 20, 1921; s. Hatten Schuyler and Elizabeth Katherine (Knieling) Y.; m. Elizabeth Marie Bruffey, Aug. 1, 1959 (dec.); children: Hatten Schuyler III (dec.), Karen Marianne Yoder Wallace. AA, U. Chgo., 1940, SB, 1941; postgrad., U. Minn., 1941; PhD, Mass. Inst. Tech., 1948; PhD (hon.), U. Paris VI, 1981; DEngring. (hon.), Colo. Sch. of Mines, 1995. Petrologist Geophys. Lab., Carnegie Instn., Washington, 1948-71, dir., 1971-86, dir. emeritus, 1986—; cons. Los Alamos (N.Mex.) Nat. Lab., 1972—, chmn. external adv. com. earth & environ. scis. divsn., 1991-97. Author: Generation of Basaltic Magma, 1976, Planned Invasion of Japan, 1945, The Siberian Weather Advantage, 1997; editor: The Evolution of the Igneous Rocks: Fiftieth Anniversary Perspectives, 1979; co-editor: Geochemical Transport and Kinetics, 1974; co-editor Jour. of Petrology, 1959-69; assoc. editor Am. Jour. Sci, 1972-90; mem. editl. bd. Earth Scis. History, 1993—; contbr. articles to profl. jours. Trustee The Cutler Trust, 1992—; bd. advisors Coll. of Democracy of the Nat. Grad. U., founders com. 1985, exec. com./sec.-treas. 1995—. Lt. comdr. USNR, 1942-58. Naval Expedition to Siberia, 1945-46. Recipient Bicentennial medal Columbia U., 1954, A.G. Werner medal German Mineral Soc., 1972, Cert. of Recognition for Svc. in Cold War 1945-1991, U.S. Dept. Def., Profl. Achievement award U. Chgo. Club Washington, 2000; named to Disting. Alumni Hall of Fame, Lakewood (Ohio) H.S., 1990; mineral yoderite named in his honor, Yoder Symposium named in his honor, 2001. Fellow Geol. Soc. Am. (coun. 1966-68, A.L. Day medal 1962, History Geology award 1998), Geol. Soc. London (hon. Wollaston medal 1979), Geol. Soc. South Africa (du Toit lectr. 1987), World Innovation Found. (hon.), Am. Acad. Arts and Scis., Mineral. Soc. Am. (coun. 1962-64, 69-73, pres. 1971-72, MSA award 1954, Roebling medal 1992), Am. Geophys. Union (pres. volcanology, geochemistry and petrology sect. 1962-64); mem. NAS (chmn. geology sect. 1973-76, A.L. Day prize and lectr. 1972), Mineral Soc. London (hon., Hallimond lectr. 1979), Geol. Soc. Finland, Russian Mineral Soc. (hon.), Geochem. Soc. (organizer, founding mem., coun. 1956-58, spl. publ. 1 named in his honor 1987), Am. Chem. Soc., Mineral Assn. Can., Washington Acad. Sci., Geol. Soc. Washington, Chem. Soc. Washington, French Soc. Mineralogy and Crystallography (hon.), Am. Philos. Soc. (coun. 1983-85, 94—), Pub. Mems. Assn. of Fgn. Svc. (bd. dirs. 1993-96, 97—, v.p. 1994, 98-2000, treas. 2000—), History of Earth Scis. Soc. (pres. 1995-96), History of Sci. Soc. (Forum lectr. 1998), SAR, Sigma Xi, Phi Delta Theta (Golden Legion award). Home: 6709 Melody Ln Bethesda MD 20817-3152 Office: Geophys Lab 5251 Broad Branch Rd NW Washington DC 20015-1305 E-mail: yoder@gl.ciw.edu.

YODER, JOHN CLIFFORD, producer, consultant; b. Orrville, Ohio, Jan. 30, 1927; s. Ray Aquila Yoder and Dorothy Mildred (Hostetler) Yoder Hake; m. Alice Vigger Andersen, Mar. 2, 1963 (div. Nov. 1992); children: Gorm Clifford, Mark Edward. BA in Philosophy and Polit. Sci., Ohio Wesleyan U., 1951. Prodn. supr. Sta. WFMJ-TV, Youngstown, Ohio, 1954-62; producer Sta. NBC-TV, Chgo., 1964-72; ind. producer cons. Evanston, Ill., 1972—. Producer radio program Conversations From Wingspread, 1972-90 (George Foster Peabody Broadcasting award 1974, Ohio State award 1978, Freedoms Found. Honor medal 1978); appeared in film The Untouchables, 1994, TV program Missing Persons, 1993. Pub. rels. and pub. info. com. Chgo. Heart Assn. (Meritorious Svc. award 1978); electronic media advisor The White House, Washington, 1972; bd. dirs. Youngstown (Ohio) Symphony Soc., 1959-63, Youngstown Playhouse, 1952-63, Bensenville (Ill.) Home Soc. 1985-89. With USAF, 1945-47 PTO. Recipient Disting. Svc. award Inst. Medicine of Chgo. 1971. Mem. Am. Fedn. Television & Radio Artists, , Nat. Acad. TV Arts and Scis., Screen Actors Guild, Midwest Pioneer Broadcasters, Soc. Profl. Journalists, Mus. Broadcast Comms., Masons, Am. Legion, Chgo. Headline Club. Avocations: tennis, golfing, sailing, fishing, reading. Home: 720 Noyes St Apt D 2 Evanston IL 60201-2848

YODER, JONAS, music educator; b. Corvallis, Oreg., Nov. 7, 1979; s. Stanley Vernon and Paula Jo (Miller) Yoder. BA, Goshen Coll., 2001. Orchestral asst. Goshen (Ind.) Mid. Sch., 1998—2001; violin, cello and orchestra tchr. Denison Montessori Sch., Denver, 2001—. Vol. violin tchr. pub. schs. Mem.: Music Educators Nat. Conf., Am. String Tchrs. Assn., Suzuki Assn. Am. Mennonite. Office: Denison Montessori 1821 S Yates St Denver CO 80219

YODER, MARIANNE ELOISE, software developer, consultant; b. Phoenix; d. William Amber and Maryanne King; m. William Ernest Yoder, Dec. 26, 1977. BSN, U. San Francisco, 1972; MS, U. Ariz., 1982, PhD, 1989. RN, Ariz. Nurse U.S. Navy, 1971-80, 91; grad. teaching asst. U. Ariz., Tucson, 1980-82, faculty, 1982-85, grad. rsch. assoc., 1985-90; faculty, dir. coll. health profl. Computer Learning Ctr. No. Ariz. U., Flagstaff, Ariz., 1990-92; software developer, 1992-96, Carson City, Nev., 1996—. Chair Ariz. state commn. nursing rsch., 1992-96; chair of PILOT group, Assn. Devel. of Computer-Based Instructional Systems, Columbus, Ohio, 1990-92. Author: Software Integration Plan Introduction to Nursing Diagnosis, 1992, 2nd edit., 1993, contbg. author: Computer Applications in Nursing Education and Practice, 1993; contbr. articles to profl. jours. Vol. Flagstaff Pub. Libr., 1993-96. Recipient Pioneer in Nursing Edn. Informatics award Nurse Educator's Microworld & Fuld, 1994, Meritorious Tchg. Asst. award U. Ariz. Found., 1987. Mem. NLN (exec. bd. 1993-97), N.Y. Acad. of Scis., WEB Soc., Sigma Xi, Sigma Theta Tau (treas. 1970-71), Pi Lambda Theta. Avocations: quilting, skiing, puzzle-making. Home and Office: 631 Roundup Rd Carson City NV 89701-7615

YODER, MARY JANE WARWICK, psychotherapist; b. Corryton, Tenn., Nov. 20, 1933; d. Harry Alonzo and Mary Luzelle (Furches) Warwick; m. Edwin Milton Yoder, Jr., Nov. 1, 1958; children: Anne Daphne, Edwin Warwick. BA, U. N.C., Chapel Hill, 1956; MFA, U. N.C., Greensboro, 1969; MSW, Va. Commonwealth U., 1987; cert. individual psychotherapy, Smith Coll., 1991. Lic. ind. clin. social worker, D.C.; lic. clin. social worker, Va. Editorial asst. Harper & Bros., N.Y.C., 1956-57; flight attendant Pan Am. Airlines, 1957-59; adj. faculty mem. in ballet Guilford Coll., Greensboro, 1961-64; ballet tchr., adminstr. Jane Yoder Sch. of Ballet, 1964-75; homilitics listener Va. Theol. Sem., Alexandria, 1978-80; social worker, dance therapist Woodbine Nursing Ctr., 1983-87; staff psychotherapist D.C. Inst. Mental Health, 1987-92; pvt. practice Capitol Hill Ctr. Individual and Family Therapy, 1992—. Ballet and book critic Greensboro Daily News, 1961-75. Dancer, choreographer Greensboro Civic Ballet, 1961-75. Mem. Nat. Assn. Social Workers, Greater Washington Soc. for Clin. Social Work, Inc., Washington Sch. Psychiatry, Washington Soc. for Jungian Psychology, Jungian Venture, Army-Navy Country Club, Phi Beta Kappa. Episcopalian. Avocations: ballet, modern dance, horseback riding, swimming, reading. Office: Capitol Hill Ctr Individual and Family Therapy 530 7th St SE Washington DC 20003-2768

YODER, MYRON EUGENE, secondary school educator; b. Reading, Pa., Oct. 28, 1953; s. Robert W. and Carmen D. (Keinard) Y.; m. Debra Kuper, Dec. 27, 1975; children: Joshua B., Rebecca A. BE cum laude, Kutztown U., 1976; Masters Equavalency, Pa. Dept. Edn., 1979; MEd cum laude, Kutztown U., 1981. Cert. secondary social studies tchr., Pa. With maintenance ride repair Dorney Pk, Allentown, Pa., 1968-72; postal asst. Lehigh County U.S. P.O. SCF180, 1972-73; insp. Fairtex Mills, 1973-74; correctional officer Lehigh County Prison, 1974-76, emergency prison counselor, 1979-84; mgr., supr. Hosp. Cen. Svcs., Allentown, 1976; curriculum coord. Allentown Sch. Dist., 1986—. Adj. prof. edn. Cedar Crest Coll., 2000—; tchr. trainer Ctr. for Civic Edn., Bicentennial Commn., Calabasas, Calif., 1987—, Temple U. LEAP, 1987-2000; sch. coord. Boy Scouts Am. Awareness Post, Allentown, 1989-2000; scholar Pa. Humanities Coun., Phila., 1991; Pa. Congl. Dist. 15 coord. for We the People Citizen and Constn. Program, 1992—; apptd. commr. Pa. Profl. Standards and Practices Commn.; mem. social studies student standards devel. team Pa. Dept. Edn., 1996; mem. assessment and student standard exercise devel. team Social Studies State Collaborative, 1996. Photographer (Kinisa Local award 1980, 83); computer programmer Class Dues Record Keeper, 1987-88 (1st dist., 2nd regional runner-up computer learning award), Study Hall Record Keeper, 1988 (1st dist., 2nd regional award); contbr. articles to profl. publs. Chmn. Borough of Emmaus Operation Homecoming, 1991; discussion leader Pa. Humanities Coun., Emmaus, 1992, Allentown, 96; 1991; com. mem. Allentown Columbus Quincentenary, 1991, Allentown Black History Month Com., 1990-91; coord. We the People program Pa. Congl. Dist. 15; bd. dirs. Jr. Achievement of Lehigh Valley, 1993, Korea/Vietnam Meml. Nat. Ednl. Ctr., 1993. Recipient Applied Econs. Tchr. Yr. award Jr. Achievement of Lehigh Valley, 1990, 93, Jr. Achievement Applied Econs. Tchr. of Yr. for Pa. award, 1991, Pa. DAR Am. History Tchr. of Yr. award, 1993, Nat. Soc. DAR Am. History medal, 1993, cooperating Tchr. award Kutztown U., 1994, SAR Silver Good Citizenship medal, 1994, Letter of Commendation Pa. Sec. Edn., 1999; selected by Jr. Achievement to travel to Soviet Union to train Soviet tchrs. in using Jr. Achievment applied econs., 1991; finalist Pa. Tchr. of Yr., 1995. Mem. NEA, Nat. Coun. Social Studies, Pa. Coun. Social Studies (Outstanding Secondary Social Studies Tchr. 1992), Pa. State Edn. Assn. (internat. rels. com. region chmn. 1987, vice chmn. state com., 1996-97, tchr. trainer student assessment tng. cadre), Lehigh Valley Coun. Social Studies, Lehigh U. Coll. Edn. Alumni Coun. (Outstanding Tchr. award 1992), Allentown Edn. Assn. (v.p. 1991-96), Kiwanis. Republican. Lutheran. Avocation: photography. E-mail: yoderm@allentownsd.org., mey11@aol.com.

YODER, PATRICIA DOHERTY, public relations executive; b. Pitts., Oct. 30, 1939; d. John Addison and Camella Grace (Conti) Doherty; children: Shari Lynn, Wendy Ann; m. James Ronald Wolfe, Oct. 30, 1999. BA, Duquesne U., 1961. Press sec. U.S. Ho. of Reps., 1965-69; dir. Office of Pub. Info., City of Ft. Wayne, 1973-76; asst. mgr. pub. and corp. comm. Mellon Bank N.A., Pitts., 1977-79; v.p. pub. affairs Am. Waterways Operators Inc., Washington, 1980-83, sr. v.p., gen. mgr., 1983-86, exec. v.p., dir. banking, 1989-91; exec. v.p., dir. internat. banking Hill and Knowlton Inc., Pitts.; sr. v.p. corp. and pub. affairs PNC Fin. Svcs. Group, 1987-89; v.p., mgr. corp. pub. rels. and advt. GE Capital Svcs. Corp., Stamford, Conn., 1991-95; corp. v.p. pub. affairs and comm. GTE Corp., 1995-96; sr. v.p. corp. comm. Avis Group Holdings, Garden City, N.Y., 1996-99; prin. PDY Assocs., 1999—. Trustee Shadyside Hosp., Pressley Ridge Sch., Pitts., Ellis Sch.; bd. dirs. Children's Mus., Civic Light Opera, Pitts. Ballet Theatre, Jr. League of City of N.Y. Recipient Outstanding Woman Bus. and Industry, 1988, Disting. Alumni award Duquesne U., 1996. Mem. Pitts. Field Club, Duquesne Club, Indian Harbor Yacht Club. Roman Catholic. Home and Office: 500 SE 5th Ave Apt 601 Boca Raton FL 33432-5510 also: 535 E 86th St Apt 16E New York NY 10028-7533 E-mail: pdyoder@att.net.

YODER, RANDALL D. music educator; b. Lancaster, Pa., Jan. 21, 1949; s. David J. and Mary Lou Yoder; m. Leslee Ann Brenneman, Jan. 24, 1992; stepchildren: Dustin M. Kemper, Jelee Elizabeth Kemper. BS in Music Edn., Susquehanna U., 1971; MusM in Choral Conducting, Westminster Choir Coll., 1978. Tchr., choral dir. Northeastern Sch. Dist., Manchester, Pa., 1971—88, York (Pa.) City Schs., 1997—. Dir. The York County Honors Choir, 1998—2002; choral dir. Pa. Ambs. of Music, European Concert Tour, 2001, Sound of Am. Honor Choir, European Concert Tour, 2002. Composer: (original music for documentary) Historic Pennsylvania, 1996 (Emmy award, 1997), Hershey Park Memories, 1998, (CD) Christmas Rose, 2000. Mem.: Music Educators Nat. Conf., Am. Choral Dirs. Assn. Avocation: travel.

YODER, RONNIE A. judge; b. Knoxville, Tenn., July 10, 1937; s. Raymond Abraham and Veryl Hope (Hostetler) Y.; m. Shirley Mae Grimes, June 28, 1961; children: Susan Elizabeth Torres, Mary Amanda Anderson, Elizabeth Anne Lee, John Anthony Gerhard. BA in Polit. Sci. with honors, U. Va., 1958, JD, 1961. Bar: Va. 1961, N.Y. 1963, D.C. 1965, U.S. Dist. Ct. D.C. 1965, U.S. Dist. Ct. (so. dist.) N.Y. 1969, U.S. Ct. Claims 1964, U.S. Supreme Ct. 1968. Assoc. Mudge Rose Guthrie & Alexander, N.Y.C. and Washington, 1962-70; of counsel Zuckert Scoutt & Rasenberger, Washington, 1970-72, ptnr., 1972-75; adminstrv. law judge U.S. Dept. Labor, 1976, CAB, Washington, 1976-84, U.S. Dept. Transp., Washington, 1985-98, acting chief adminstrv. law judge, 1999-2001, chief adminstv. law judge, 2001—. Adminstrv. law judge Nat. Transp. Safety Bd., 1979-80, Maritime Adminstrn., 1983, 86-88, FDIC, 1982-83, SBA, 1983, FAA, 1985—, Fed. Hwy. Adminstrn., 1985—, Fed. R.R. Adminstrn., 1993-95, Rsch. and Spl. Programs Adminstrn., 1991—, Surface Transp. Bd., 1996-97; mem. Adminstrv. Conf. of U.S., 1994-95. Mem. editorial bd. U. Va. Law Rev., 1959-61; contbr. articles to profl. jours. Sec., co-counsel Capital Headstart, 1966-68; narrator Lincoln Commn., 1985, 86; mem. permanent jud. commn. Nat. Capital Presbytery, 1985-91. Rockefeller fellow, 1961. Fellow Am. Bar Found.; mem. ABA (jud. divsn. coun. 1994-95, exec. com. nat. conf. adminstrv. law judges 1980-83, 85-89, 90-96, 97-2001, sec. 1991-92, parliamentarian 1991-92, 96-2001, vice chmn. 1992-93, chmn.-elect 1993-94, chmn. 1994-95, mem. Nat. Ctr. for State Cts. working group on asbestos litig. 1982-84, reporter Model Code Jud. Conduct for Fed. Adminstrv. Law Judges 1989, adminstrv. law sect., sect. of sect. officers chmn. task force on participation in profl. assns. by govt. employees 1991-92, vice chmn. social security com. sr. lawyers sect. 1996-2000, govt. employees sect., pub. contract law sect., litigation sect., judges adv. com. on ethics and profl. responsibility 2001—), ATLA, FBA (judiciary divsn. leadership coun. 1999—, bd. dirs. D.C. chpt. 1999—), Am. Judicature Soc., Fed. Adminstrv. Law Judges Conf. (exec. com. 1976-81, 85, 87, 99—), Nat. Assn. Adminstrv. Law Judges, Va. Bar Assn. (bd. govs. adminstrv. law sect. 1981-87), D.C. Bar Assn., Am. Guild Musical Artists, Prettyman Levanthal Am. Inn of Ct., SAR, Phi Beta Kappa, Phi Eta Sigma. Home: 1400 Summit Ave Alexandria VA 22302-2735 Office: Dept Transp Rm 5411 400 7th St SW Washington DC 20590-0001 E-mail: ronnie.yoder@ost.dot.gov., honron@aol.com.

YODER-WISE, PATRICIA SNYDER, educator; b. Wadsworth, Ohio, July 2, 1941; d. Belford Grant and Leona Cora (Mohler) Snyder; m. Robert Thomas Wise, Feb. 17, 1973; children: Doreen Ellen, Deborah Ann. BSN, Ohio State U., 1963; MSN, Wayne State U., 1968; EdD, Tex. Tech. U., 1984. RN, Tex. Interim dir. nursing ctr. Tex. Tech. U. Health Sci. Ctr. Sch. Nursing, Lubbock, 1988-89, interim assoc. dean practice program, 1989-90, interim dean, prof., 1991-93, dean and prof., 1993-2000, prof., 2000—; clin. prof. U. Tex. Health Sci. Ctr., San Antonio, 1993—2000. Mem. rev. panel Nursing Outlook, 1993—; mem. adv. com. GlaxoWellcome, 1996-2000; v.p. Am. Nurses Credentialing Ctr., 2000-02. Author (editor): Leading and Managing in Nursing, 1994 (Book of Yr. award, 1996), 2002; : peer reviewer Jour. Profl. Nursing, 1984—93, : mem. editl. bd. Jour. Continuing Edn. in Nursing, 1978—; editor, 1988—. Participant Leadership Tex.-Found. for Women's Resources, 1997-98; mem. Leadership Tex., 1998-99, Leadership Am., 1999-2000. Recipient of Woman of Excellence in Medicine, YWCA, Lubbock, 1996. Fellow: Am. Acad. Nursing (chair Inst. for Nursing Leadership 1999—2002); mem.: ANA (del. 1995—2000, chair constituent assembly 1998—2000, sec. 2000—02, 1st v.p. 2002—), Tex. Nurses Assn. (pres. 1995—99). Office: Texas Tech Univ HSC Sch Nursing 7309 93rd St Lubbock TX 79424-4939

YODOWITZ, EDWARD JAY, lawyer; b. N.Y.C., 1943; BS, Long Island U., 1965; JD, U. Balt., 1969. Bar: N.Y. 1972. With Skadden, Arps, Slate, Meagher & Flom, L.L.P., N.Y.C., 1969—, now sr. ptnr. Chmn. securities litigation seminar Practicing Law Inst., 1984-95; bd. trustees L.I. U., 1990-99. Mem.: ABA. Home: 105 Ocean Ave Lawrence NY 11559-2006 Office: Skadden Arps Slate Meagher & Flom LLP Four Times Sq New York NY 10036-6522 Business E-Mail: eyodowit@skadden.com.

YOERGER, ROGER RAYMOND, agricultural engineer, educator; b. LeMars, Iowa, Feb. 17, 1929; s. Raymond Herman and Crystal Victoria (Ward) Y.; m. Barbara M. Ellison, Feb. 14, 1953; 1 child, Karen Lynne; m. Laura M. Summitt, Dec. 23, 1971; stepchildren: Daniel L. Summitt, Linda Summitt Canull, Anita Summitt Smith. BS, Iowa State U., 1949, MS, 1951, PhD, 1957. Registered prof. engr., Ill. Instr., asst. prof. agrl. engring. Iowa State U., 1949-56; assoc. prof. Pa. State U., 1956-58; prof. U. Ill., Urbana, 1959-85, head agrl. engring. dept., 1978-85, prof. emeritus, 1985—. Contbr. articles to profl. jours. Patentee in field. Mem. Ill. Noise Task Force, 1974-80. Fellow Am. Soc. Agrl. Engrs. (Massey-Ferguson medal 1989); mem. Am. Soc. Engring. Edn., Phi Kappa Phi (dir. fellowships, dir. 1971-83, pres.-elect 1983-86, pres. 1986-89), Rotary. Roman Catholic. Home: 107 W Holmes St Urbana IL 61801-6614 Office: 1304 W Pennsylvania Ave Urbana IL 61801-4713 E-mail: ryoerger@uiuc.edu.

YOFFIE, DAVID B. educator; b. Worcester, Mass. s. William A. and Judy S. Yoffie; m. Terry Svagr, Oct. 21, 1979; children: Ariel Rachel, Elana Lauren. BA, Brandeis U., 1976; MA, Stanford U., 1978, PhD, 1981; MA (hon.), Harvard U., 1990. Lectr. Stanford (Calif.) U., 1980-81; prof. bus. strategy Bus. Sch. Harvard U., Boston, 1981—. Vis. scholar Stanford U., 1995-96; bd. dirs. Intel Corp., Santa Clara, Calif., Nat. Bur. Econ. Rsch., Cambridge, Mass., E-Ink Corp., Cambridge, Englishtown.com, Cambridge, 1992-97. Mem. Coun. on Fgn. Rels., N.Y., 1983—; mem. internat. competition policy adv. com. U.S. Dept. Justice, Washington, 1997-2000. Mem. Am. Polit. Sci. Assn., Phi Beta Kappa. Avocations: biking, squash, skiing, photography, computers. Office: Harvard Bus Sch Soldiers Fld Boston MA 02163-1317

YOGESWARAN, PARARAJASINGAM, physician; b. Jaffna, Sri Lanka, Dec. 6, 1963; s. Pararajasingam and Ahilandeswary Vallipurum; m. Anitha Yogeswaran, June 9, 1990; children: Vidhushei, Shaiesh. MD, Southampton (Eng.) Med. Sch., 1994. House officer in medicine and surgery Southampton (Eng.) Gen. Hosp., Southampton, England, 1994—94; sr. house officer in emergency medicine Bromley Hosp., Kent, England, 1996; sr. house officer medicine and gerontology Hillingdon Hosp., Uxbridge, England, 1996—96; registrar internal medicine Queen Elizabeth Hosp. II, Welwyngarden City, 1996—98; registrar radiology St. Mary's Hosp., Paddington, London, 1998—2000; resident internal medicine Coney Island Hosp., Bklyn., 2000—. Mem.: Royal Coll. Physicians (London). Home: 2610 Olean Pkwy #2B Brooklyn NY 11235 Office: Coney Island Hosp 2601 Ocean Pkwy Brooklyn NY 11235*

YOGEV, RAM, pediatrician, educator; b. Rehovot, Israel, Oct. 27, 1942; came to U.S., 1975; s. Samuel and Jenny (Proper) Y.; m. Sara Frankel; children: Eldad, Shelly, Tomer. MD, Hebrew U., 1970. Diplomate Am. Bd. Pediatrics. Pediatric resident Hadassah Hosp., Israel, 1972-75, fellow pediatric infectious disease Israel, 1975-77; asst. prof., assoc. prof., prof. Northwestern U., Chgo., 1977—. Dir. pediatric and maternal HIV infection Children's Meml. Hosp., Chgo., 1987—. Recipient Exceptional Merit award Ill. Dept. Pub. Health, 1996, Jonas Salk award March of Dimes, 1999, Pub. Svc. award Chgo. Med. Soc., 2002. Mem. Am. Acad. Pediatrics. Office: Children's Meml Hosp 2300 N Childrens Plz Chicago IL 60614-3394 E-mail: r-yogev@northwestern.edu.

YOGEV, SARA, psychologist; b. Tel Aviv, May 23, 1946; came to U.S., 1975; d. Israel and Cila (Fink) Frankel; m. Ram Yogev, Oct. 2, 1967; children: Eldad, Shelly, Tomer. BA, Hebrew U., 1965-69, MA, 1970-73; PhD, Northwestern U., Evanston, Ill., 1976-79. Cert. clin. psychologist, Ill. Clin. experience dist. sch. psychologist Office Edn. and Culture, Jerusalem, Israel, 1968-71; intern. Beer Yaakov Psychiatric Hosp., Israel, 1971-72; asst. dir. Dept. Psychology, Hebrew U., Jerusalem, Israel, 1972-73; psychotherapist Mental Health Ctr., Hebrew U., Israel; clin. psychologist Inst. Psychoanalysis, Israel, 1973-75; psychotherapist, supr. Youth and Family Services, Ill., 1977-80; pvt. practice psychology Skokie and Chicago, 1981—. Academic experience instr. counseling psychology, 1977-79, asst. prof., Northwestern U., 1979-82, research psychologist at the rank asst. prof., 1983-86, visiting scholar, Ctr. Urban Affairs and Policy Research, 1987. Author: For Better or Worse But Not for Lunch: Making Your Marriage Work in Retirement, 2001;

contbr. articles to profl. jours. and books. Mem. American Assn. for Marriage and Family Therapy, American Psyhological Assn., Nat. Register Health Service. Jewish. Office: # 32 5225 Old Orchard Rd Skokie IL 60077-1027

YOGMAN, MICHAEL WILLIAM, pediatrician; b. Jersey City, Mar. 1, 1947; s. Harvey J. and Estelle (Rapport) Y.; m. Elizabeth Kasen Ascher, June 9, 1985; children: Madeline, Alexandra. BA, Williams Coll., 1968; MD, Yale U., 1972; MS, Harvard U., 1978. Diplomate Am. Bd. Pediats. Assoc. chief divsn. child devel. Children's Hosp., Boston, 1980-84; dir. infant and health devel. program Harvard U. Med. Sch., 1984-88, asst. prof. pediats., 1982-92, Tufts U. Med. Sch., Boston, 1993-98; pvt. practice Cambridge, 1989—; asst. clin. prof. pediats. Harvard U. Med. Sch., Boston, 2001—. Mem. statewide adv. com. Mass. Office for Children, Boston, 1983-85; mem. adv. bd. Yearbook of Health and Medicine 1980-98. Editor: Insupport of Families, 1986, Followup of the High Risk Infant, 1987; editor series Theory and Research in Behavioral Pediatrics, 1982-88; creator film Father-Infant Interaction, 1976; editl. bd. Child Devel., 1982-87. Trustee Children's Mus. Boston, 2000—. Rsch. grantee Nat. Found. March of Dimes, 1981-86. Fellow Am. Acad. Pediats.; mem. Soc. Pediat. Rsch., Soc. Rsch. in Child Devel., Ambulatory Pediat. Assn., Internat. Conf. on Infant, Soc. Devel. Behavior Pediats. Avocations: sailing, tennis, skiing. Home: 14 Wyman Rd Cambridge MA 02138-2218 Office: 575 Mount Auburn St Ste 202 Cambridge MA 02138-4627 E-mail: myogman@massmed.org.

YOHALEM, HARRY MORTON, lawyer; b. Phila., Jan. 21, 1943; s. Morton Eugene and Florence (Mishnun) Y.; m. Martha Caroline Remy, June 9, 1967; children: Seth, Mark. BA with honors, U. Wis., 1965; JD cum laude, M in Internat. Affairs., Columbia U., 1969. Bar: N.Y. 1969, D.C. 1981, Calif. 1992, U.S. Supreme Ct. 1985. Assoc. Shearman & Sterling, N.Y.C., 1969-71; asst. counsel to gov. State of N.Y., Albany, 1971-73, counsel office planning svcs., 1973-75; asst. gen. counsel FEA, Washington, 1975-77; mem. staff White House Energy Policy and Planning Office, 1977; dep. gen. counsel for legal svcs. Dept. Energy, 1978-80, dep. under sec., 1980-81; ptnr. Rogers & Wells, 1981-91; gen. counsel Calif. Inst. Tech., Pasadena, 1991—. Editor comments Columbia Jour. Transnat. Law, 1967-68, rsch. editor, 1968-69. Prin. Coun. for Excellence in Govt., Washington, 1990—; pres. Opera Bel Canto, Washington, 1984-87; mem. Lawyers Com. for Arts, Washington, 1981-88; bd. visitors dept. English U. Wis., 1999—. Harlan Fiske Stone scholar Columbia U., 1967, 69. Mem. ABA, Calif. Bar Assn., D.C. Bar Assn. Athenaeum, Phi Kappa Phi, Columbia Club N.Y. Home: 702 E California Blvd Pasadena CA 91106 Office: Calif Inst Tech JPL 180-305 4800 Oak Grove Dr Pasadena CA 91109-8001 E-mail: harry.yohalem@caltech.edu.

YOHANNES, DANIEL W. banker; b. Addis Ababa, Ethiopia, Sept. 22, 1952; m. Saron Yohannes; children: Tsedeye Daniel, Michael yohannes, Rebecca yohannes. BS in Econs., Claremont Coll., 1976; MBA, Pepperdine U., 1980. From trainee to exec. v.p. Bank of America (formerly Security Pacific), 1977-92; pres. US Bancorp (formerly Colo. Nat. Bank), Denver, 1992-96, CEO, 1996-99, vice chmn., 1999—. Bd. dirs. Nat. Jewish Med. and Rsch. Ctr., Denver, 1995—, Smithsonian Instn., Washington, 1997—; co-chmn. host com. G-8 Summit, Denver, 1997. Avocations: travel, reading. Office: US Bancorp 950 17th St Denver CO 80202

YOHAY, STEVEN JACOB, healthcare company executive, consultant; b. N.Y.C., N.Y., Nov. 28, 1950; s. Nathan and Natalie (Modlinger) Y.; children: Charlotte, Paige. BS in Psychology, SUNY-Empire State Coll., Saratoga Springs, N.Y., 1977. Cert. addiction specialist, alcoholism and substance abuse counselor. Staff counselor-trainee AREBA Casriel Inst., N.Y.C., 1971-72, asst. resident dir., 1972-73, resident dir., 1973-75, exec. dir., 1975-82, pres., chief exec. officer, 1982—. Cons. Long Lane Sch., Middletown Conn., Brookside Acad., Mt. Freedom, N.J., The Key, Ghent, Belgium, New Ctr. for Psychotherapies, Boston, Psychiat. Engring. Standards Assn. Contbr. articles to profl. jours. Bd. dirs. N.Y. Regional Therapeutic Communities of Am. Recipient Community Svc. award Bronx Borough Pres.'s Officer, 1966; Regents scholar N.Y. State Bd. Regents, 1966. Fellow Am. Soc. New Identity Process; mem. Am. Coll. of Addiction Treatment Adminstrs., Am. Coll. Healthcare Adminstrs., Nat. Assn. Alcoholism and Drug Abuse Counselors, Alcohol and Drug Problems Assn. N.Am., Nat. Assn. Addiction Treatment Providers, N.Y. State Assn. Practicing Psychotherapists. Jewish. Avocations: motorboating, sailing, tennis, scuba diving, mountain biking. Home: 78 Hawser Dr Oak Beach NY 11702 Office: AREBA Casriel Inc 500 W 57th St New York NY 10019-2902

YOHE, GARY WYNN, economics educator; b. Abington, Pa., May 10, 1948; s. Jack Wensel and Dorothy June (Hall) Y.; m. Linda Rosemary Citrano, Sept. 21, 1974; children: Marielle Elizabeth, Courtney Jeanne. BA, U. Pa., 1970; MA, SUNY, Stonybrook, 1971; M. Philosophy, Yale U., 1974, PhD, 1975. Asst. prof. SUNY, Albany, 1975-77; assoc. prof. Wesleyan U., Middletown, Conn., 1977-82, prof., 1982—; dir. John E Andrus Ctr. for Pub. Affairs, 1992-94, 95-96; dir. sponsored rsch., 1994-99; chair dept. econs., 1996-98; vis. prof., fellow Yale U., New Haven, 1983, 85, 88, John E. Andrews chair econs., 2001—. Rsch. cons. NAS, Washington, 1982-83, EPA, U.S. Dept. Energy, Washington, 1985—; project leader program on climate change Sigma Xi, Research Triangle Park, N.C., 1988-92; mem. adv. panel for Office Tech. Assessment of Systems at Risk from Climate Change, 1992-00; mem. rev. panel on global change NSF, 1992-96; mem. standing adv. com., exec. com. human dimension of global change program, 1993-96. Auhor: (with Edwin Mansfield) Microeconomics; chpts. lead author: 3d Assessment Report of the Intergovernmental Panel on Climate Change; contbr. numerous articles on issues of global change to profl. jours. Pres. 1st Congl. Ch., Portland, Conn., 1989-92; chmn. Gov.'s Commn. on Conn.'s Future, Hartford, 1985-88. Mem. Am. Econ. Assn., Assn. Environ. and Resource Economists, Conn. Acad. Sci. and Engring., Sigma Xi. Avocations: golf, gardening. Home: 84 High St Portland CT 06480-1229 Office: Wesleyan U Dept Econs Middletown CT 06459 E-mail: gyohe@wesleyan.edu.

YOHN, DAVID STEWART, virologist, science administrator; b. Shelby, Ohio, June 7, 1929; s. Joseph Van and Agnes (Tryon) Y.; m. Olivetta Kathleen McCoy, June 11, 1950; children: Linda Jean, Kathleen Ann, Joseph John, David McCoy, Kristine Renee (dec.). BS, Otterbein Coll., 1951; MS, Ohio State U., 1953, PhD, 1957; M.P.H., U. Pitts., 1960. Research fellow, scholar in microbiology Ohio State U., Columbus, 1952-56, prof. virology Coll. Veterinary Medicine, 1969-95, prof. emeritus, 1995—, dir. Comprehensive Cancer Ctr., 1973-88, dep. dir. Comprehensive Cancer Ctr., 1988-94, dir. emeritus Comprehensive Cancer Ctr., 1994—. Research assoc., asst. prof. microbiology U. Pitts., 1956-62; assoc. cancer research scientist Roswell Park Meml. Inst., Buffalo, 1962-69; mem. nat. med. and sci. adv. com. Leukemia Soc. Am., 1970-91, trustee, 1971-91; pres. Ohio Cancer Research Assocs., 1982— ; mem. cancer research centers rev. com. Nat. Cancer Inst., 1972-77 Pres. bd. deacons North Presbyn. Ch., Williamsburg, N.Y., 1967-68. Recipient Pub. Service award Lions, 1968 Mem. Am. Assn. Cancer Rsch., Am. Soc. Microbiology, Am. Assn. Immunologists, Internat. Assn. Comparative Rsch. on Leukemia and Related Diseases (sec.-gen. 1974-95), Ohio Valley-Lake Erie Assn. Cancer Ctrs. (sec. 1978-95), Sertoma (pres. 1992-93, chmn. bd. dirs. 1993-94, Dist. Sertoman of Yr. award 1987). Home: 974 Willow Bluff Dr Columbus OH 43235-5047 Office: Ohio State U Comprehensive Cancer Ctr 300 W 10th Ave Ste 1132 Columbus OH 43210-1240 E-mail: yohn.1@osu.edu.

YOHN, SHARON A. manufacturing executive; b. Altoona, Pa., Mar. 1, 1952; AS in Retail cum laude, Harcum Jr. Coll. (Pa.), 1972; BSBA, Villanova U., 1976. V.p. legal dept. Items Internat., Inc., Altoona, Pa., 1987-95, v.p., 1995—. Active ch. choir and choral soc. Republican. Methodist. Avocations: needlework, sewing, music, performing arts, travel. Office: Items Internat Inc 1540 E Pleasant Valley Blvd Altoona PA 16602-7224

YOHN, WILLIAM H(ENDRICKS), JR. federal judge; b. Pottstown, Pa., Nov. 20, 1935; s. William H. and Dorothy C. (Cornelius) Y.; m. Jean Louise Kochel, mar. 16, 1963; children: William H. III, Bradley G., Elizabeth J. AB, Princeton U., 1957; JD, Yale U., 1960. Bar: Pa. 1961, U.S. Dist. Ct. D.C. 1961. Ptnr. Wells Campbell Reynier & Yohn, Pottstown, 1961-71; mem., chmn. coms. Pa. House of Reps., Harrisburg, 1968-80; ptnr. Binder Yohn & Kalis, Pottstown, 1971-81; judge Montgomery County Ct. of Common Pleas, Norristown, Pa., 1981-91, U.S. Dist. Ct., ea. dist., 1991—. Asst. D.A., Montgomery County D.A. Office, 1962-65; instr. Am. Inst. of Banking, 1963-66; bd. dirs. Fed. Jud. Ctr., 1999—. Bd. dirs. Greater Pottstown Drug Abuse Prevention Program, 1970-76, Pottstown Meml. Med. Ctr., 1974-95, chmn., 1984-95; mem. exec. com. Yale LAw Sch. Alumni Assn., 1998—. Cpl. USMCR, 1960-66. Mem. Pa. Bar Assn., Montgomery Bar Assn. (bd. dirs. 1967-70). Republican. Office: US Dist Ct 14613 US Courthouse 601 Market St Philadelphia PA 19106-1713

YOKE, CARL BERNARD, English language educator, critic; b. Clarksburg, W.Va., Mar. 23, 1937; s. John Bernard and Doris Elma (Groghan) Y.; m. Beverly Jean Crow, Oct. 26, 1962 (div. 1968); 1 child, Christopher Carl; m. Sherry Elizabeth Gray, Oct. 6, 1973; children: Alexander Adam Gray (dec.), Andrea Elizabeth. BS, Kent State U., 1959, MA, 1961; postgrad., U. Wis., 1961-62, Case Western Res. U., 1962-68. Instr. English, Kent (Ohio) State U., 1962-68, asst. prof., 1968-74, assoc. prof., 1974—, dir. Euclid Acad. Ctr., 1965-66, various mid. level acad. positions, 1966-80, asst. to v.p. regional campuses, 1980-87. Author: (criticism) Readers Guide-Zelazny, 1979; author, co-editor: Death and the Serpent, 1985; author, editor: Phoenix from the Ashes, 1988; assoc. editor Extrapolation, 1978-86; contbr. over 100 articles, book revs. and radio shows to profl. publs. Ohio Wesleyan U. scholar, 1955; U. Wis. fellow, 1961. Mem. Internat. Assn. for Fantastic in Arts (v.p. 1985-89, bd. dirs. 1985-98, exec. editor, founder, pub. Jour. Fantastic Arts, 1987-98, mem. editl. bd. 1998—). Avocations: tennis, swimming, bicycling. Office: Kent State U Trumbull 4313 Mahoning Ave NW Warren OH 44483-1930 also: 4544 Bunker Ln Stow OH 44224-5158 E-mail: yokec@trumbull.kent.edu.

YOKEN, MEL B(ARTON), French language educator, writer; b. Fall River, Mass., June 25, 1939; s. Albert Benjamin and Sylvia Sarah (White) Y.; m. Cynthia Stein, June 20, 1976; children: Andrew Brett, David Ryan, Jonathan Barry. BA, U. Mass., 1960; MAT, Brown U., 1961, PhD, 1972. Instr. French U. Mass., Dartmouth, 1966-72, asst. prof., 1976-81, prof., 1981-2001, chancellor prof., 2001—. Dir. French summer study program French Inst., 1981-88; vis. prof. Wheaton Coll., 1987, U. of Montreal, 1981-88; translator New Bedford Superior Ct., New Bedford, Mass., 1985—, Fall River Superior Ct., Fall River, Mass., 1985—; reader, cons. AP Exams in French, 1997—; mem. nominating com. Nobel Prize for lit., 1972—, Acad. Am. Poets, 1999—. Author: Claude Tillier, 1976, Speech is Plurality, 1978, Claude Tillier (1801-44): Fame and Fortune in His Novelistic Work, 1978, Entretiens Quebecois I, 1986, Entretiens Quebecois II, 1989, Letters of Robert Molloy, 1989, Festschrift in Honor of Stowell Goding, 1993, Entretiens Quebecois III, 1999; contbr. articles to profl. jours. Pres. Friends of Fall River Pub. Libr., 1972-80, pres., bd. dirs., 1972-80; pres. New Bedford Pub. Libr., 1980-82; pres., dir. Am. Field Svc., 1980—; v.p. Friends of U. Mass. Libr., 1998—, pres., 1999—; dir. Boivin Ctr., 1999—. Decorated Officier dans l'Ordre des Palmes académiques, 2001—; recipient Disting. Svc. award City Fall River, 1974, 80, Excellence in Tchg. French award, 1984, 85, Gov.'s citation, 1986, Nat. Disting. Leadership award, 1990, Dist. Svc. award Mass. Foreign Lang. Assn., 1992, Medaille de Vermeil du Rayonnement de la Langue Française, L'Academie Française, 1993, Outstanding Cmty. Svc. award, 1997, Disting. Alumni award, Durfee H.S., 1998, Golden Apple award Fall River Herald News, 1998; Govt. of Que. grantee, 1981-85, 87-89, Can. Embassy grantee, 1986, 87, Southeastern Mass. U. grantee, 1985, 89, 90; Mel Yoken Day proclaimed by Mayor of New Bedford, 1990. Mem. MLA (life), Am. Assn. Tchrs. French (life), Am. Coun. Tchrs. Fgn. Langs., Middlebury Amicale (life), N.E. MLA (coord. 1987-91), New Eng. Fgn. Lang. Assn., Mass. Fgn. Lang. Assn. (bd. dirs. 1985-90, disting. svc. award 1992), N.Y. State Assn. Fgn. Lang. Tchrs., Internat. Platform Assn., Francophone Assn. (v.p. 1990—), Assn. Literary Scholars and Critics, Fall River C. of C., Brown U. Alumni Assn. (rep.), Richelieu Internat., Universal Manuscript Soc. (v.p. 1993-95). Avocations: traveling, languages, baseball, postcards, meteorology. Home: 261 Carroll St New Bedford MA 02740-1412 Office: U Mass Dartmouth Lang Dept Old Westport Rd North Dartmouth MA 02747-2512 E-mail: myoken@umassd.edu.

YOKIMISHYN, STEPHEN, state agency professional; b. Scranton, Pa., Dec. 12, 1954; s. Stephen and Xenia Yokimishyn; 1 child, Tracy. BS, U. Scranton, 1976. Cir. riding mgr. Econ. Devel. Coun. of Northeastern Pa., 1977-79; payroll clk. Avoca Borough, 1980—; various positions Luzerne County C.C., 1980-90; regional dir. Pa. Dept. Cmty. and Econ. Devel. Govs. Action Team, Wilkes-Barre, Pa., 1990—. Councilman Duryea (Pa.) Borough, 1987-95, coun. pres., 1992-94; adv. coun. Leadership Wilkes-Barre, 1998-2000, Blue Cross of Northeastern Pa., 1994—; coun. of dels. Econ. Devel. Coun. of Northeastern Pa., 1990—; bd. dirs. Child Devel. Coun. Northeastern Pa. Melvin Jones fellowship Internat. Assn. of Lions Clubs, 1994. Mem. Duryea Lions Club, Bishop's Adv. Commn., Duryea Ambulance Assn. (dir. 1997—), Duryea Baseball Assn. (dir. 1997—), Nat. Assn. of Cmty. Leadership. Avocations: sports, travel. Office: Govs Action Team 600 Baltimore Dr Wilkes Barre PA 18702-7901 Home: 130B Elmcrest Dr Dallas PA 18612-9168 E-mail: syokimishy@state.pa.us.

YOKLEY, RICHARD CLARENCE, protective services official; b. San Diego, Dec. 29, 1942; s. Clarence Ralph and Dorothy Junese (Sackman) Y.; m. Jean Elizabeth Liddle, July 25, 1964; children: Richard Clarence II, Karin Denise. Student, San Diego City Coll., 1967; AS, Miramar Coll., 1975; student, London Fire Brig. Tng. Acad., 1994, Fire Svc. Coll., Eng., 1994. Cert. fire officer, fire instr., Calif. Disc jockey Sta. KSDS-FM, San Diego, 1966-67; bldg. engr. Consolidated Systems, Inc., 1968-72; with Bonita-Sunnyside Fire Dept., Calif., 1972-99, fire marshal, 1981-91, ops. chief, 1991-93, maintenance officer, 1993-99. Med. technician Hartson Ambulance, San Diego, 1978-80, Bay Gen. Hosp. (now Scripps Hosp.), Chula Vista, Calif., 1980-83, EMT-D Sea World of San Diego, 1997—; chmn. South Bay Emergency Med. Svc., 1988; mem. firefighter adv. coun. to San Diego Burn Inst., 1989, 1999, mem. Coun. of Courage, 1991-99; mem. Emergency Med. Care Com. for San Diego County, 2001--. Contbr. articles to jours., newspapers and mags. Asst. curator Firehouse Mus., San Diego, 1972-89, docent, 1990-93; scoutmaster troop 874 Boy Scouts Am., Bonita, Calif., 1978-79. With USAF, 1962-66. Recipient Heroism and Community Svc. award Firehouse Mag., N.Y.C., 1987, Star News Salutes award Chula Vista Star News, 1987, Golden Svc. award San Diego County Credit Union, 1988, SeaWorld San Diego Excellence award, 2000. Mem. Internat. Assn. Firefighters (pres. local chpt. 1981-82), Calif. State Firefighters Assn. (dep. dir. so. divsn. 1994-97), Calif. Fire Mechanics, San Diego County Fire Prevention Officers (v.p. 1984, pres. 1985), Bonita Bus. and Profl. Assn. (bd. dirs. 1991-93, Historian award 1987, Pioneer award 1997), Fire Mark Cir. of the Ams. (dir. 1994-2000), Smokey Bear Collectors Assn. (co-founder, dir. 1995-97, advisor 1998-2000), South Bay Commn., Bonita Hist. Mus. (co-founder 1986, adv. bd. 1997, v.p. 1998, 99), Sport Chalet Dive Club (v.p. 1991). Republican. Methodist. Avocations: scuba diving, visit fire departments of foreign countries, collect fire memorabilia, snow skiing. Office: Seaworld San Diego Med Svcs & Life Safety 500 Sea World Dr San Diego CA 92109-7904

YOKUBAITIS, ROGER T. lawyer; b. Wharton, Tex., Jan. 9, 1945; Student, St. Louis U.; BA, JD, U. Houston, 1969. Bar: Tex. 1969. Formerly ptnr. Carmody & Yokubaitis, L.L.P., Houston, 1995—2000; mem. Roger T. Yokubaitis, P.L.L.C., 2000—. Mem. ABA, Houston Bar Assn., State Bar of Tex., Houston Bankruptcy Bar Assn., Am. Bankruptcy Inst. Office: Roger T Yokubaitis PLLC 1177 W Loop S Ste 1650 Houston TX 77027-9086 E-mail: Yokubaitis@msn.com.

YOLDAS, BULENT ERTHER, ceramics engineer, educator; b. Isaparta, Turkey, Feb. 19, 1938; arrived in U.S., 1958, permanent resident; s. Mustafa and Hatice Yoldas; m. Lubomyra Anne Ivanycky; children: Erol, Kim. BS in Ceramic Engring, Ohio State U., Columbus, 1963; MS, Ohio State U., 1964, PhD, 1966. Sr. engr. Owens Ill. Tech. Ctr., Toledo, 1966—74; fellow scientist Westinghouse Rsch. Ctr., Pitts., 1974—84, PPG Industries R&D Ctr., Pitts., 1984—96; adj. prof. Carnegie Mellon U., 1996—99. Mem. editl. bd. Jour. of Sol-gel Sci. of Tech., 2000—. Contbr. articles to profl. jours. Named one of top 100 Internat. Innovators, Tech. Mag. (pemier issue), 1981. Fellow: Am. Ceramic Soc.; mem.: AAAS, Materials Rsch. Soc. Achievements include invention of A radical glass forming method, 1980; image transfer technology, 1999; research in in ceramic and glass formation by chemical polymerization-so-called sol-gel technology; patents in field of 75. Avocations: gardening, hiking, music, poetry. Home: 1605 Jamestown Pl Pittsburgh PA 15235 Home Fax: 412-731-2382. E-mail: yoldas.pgh@worldnet.att.net.

YOLEN, JANE, author; b. N.Y.C., Feb. 11, 1939; d. Will Hyatt and Isabelle (Berlin) Y.; m. David Wilber Stemple, Sept. 2, 1962; children: Heidi Elisabet, Adam Douglas, Jason Frederic. BA, Smith Coll., 1960; M.Ed., U. Mass., 1978; LL.D. (hon.), Coll. of Our Lady of the Elms, 1980. Asst. editor This Week mag., 1960; mem. staff Saturday Rev., 1960; asst. editor Gold Medal Books, 1961, Rutledge Press, 1961-63; asst. juvenile editor A.A. Knopf, Inc., 1963-65; free-lance writer, 1965—; lectr. dept. edn. Smith Coll., 1979-84; editor Jane Yolen books, imprint Harcourt Brace Jovanovich, 1988-97. Tchr. writers confs. Centrum, Cape Cod Writers Conf., Soc. Children's Book Writers, U. Mass.; mem. Mass. Council on Arts, 1974 Author: Welcome to the River of Grass, 2001, The Fish Prince and Other Merman Stories, 2001, Odysseus in the Serpent's Maze, 2001, Dear Mother/Dear Daughter, 2001, Pirates in Petticoats, 1963, The Witch Who Wasn't, 1964, The Emperor and the Kite, 1968, Writing Books for Children, 1973, The Girl Who Cried Flowers, 1974, The Hundredth Dove, 1978, The Dream Weaver, 1979, Commander Toad in Space, 1980, The Gift of Sarah Barker, 1981, Touch Magic, 1981, Dragon's Blood, 1982, Tales of Wonder, 1983, Heart's Blood, 1984, Cards of Grief, 1984, Dragonfield, 1985, Merlin's Booke, 1986, The Lullabye Songbook, 1986, Ring of Earth, 1986, Favorite Folktales From Around the World, 1986, Piggins, 1987, Owl Moon, 1987, Three Bears, 1987, A Sending of Dragons, 1987, The Devil's Arithmetic, 1988, Sister Light/Sister Dark, 1988, White Jenna, 1989, Dove Isabeau, 1989, Baby Bear's Bedtime Book, 1990, Tam Lin, 1990, Bird Watch, 1990, Sky Dogs, 1990, Wizard's Hall, 1991, All those Secrets of the World, 1991, Wings, 1991, Hark! A Christmas Sampler, 1991, Encounter, 1992, Briar Rose, 1992, Letting Swift River Go, 1992, What Rhymes with Moon, 1993, Welcome to the Greenhouse, 1993, Honkers, 1993, Here There Be Dragons, 1993, Grandad Bill's Song, 1994, Good Griselle, 1994, The Girl in the Golden Bower, 1994, Old Dame Counterpane, 1994, Old Macdonald's Songbook, 1994, Here There Be Unicorns, 1994, Beneath the Ghost Moon, 1994, The Wild Hunt, 1995, Ballad of the Pirate Queens, 1995, And Twelve Chinese Acrobats, 1995, Water Music, 1995, Among Angels, 1995, Here They Be Witches, 1995, O. Jerusalem, 1996, Welcome to the Sea of Sand, 1996, Passager, 1996, Hobby, 1996, Sacred Places, 1996, Here There Be Angels, 1996, Milk and Honey, 1996, Meet The Monsters, 1996, Once Upon Ice, 1997, Merlin, 1997, Child of Faerie, 1997, Twelve Impossible Things Before Breakfast, 1997, Miz Berlin Walks, 1997, Nocturne, 1997, Armageddon Summer, 1998, House/House, 1998, Prince of Egypt, 1998, Raising Yoder's Barn, 1998, The Wizard's Map, 1999, The Pictish Child, 1999, The Fairies' Ring, 1999, Moonball, 1999, Gray Heroes: Elder Tales From Around the World, 1999, How Does a Dinosaur Say Goodnight, 2000, Off We Go, 2000, Queen's Own Fool, 2000, Not One Damsel in Distress, 2000, Mirror/Mirror, 2000, Color Me a Rhyme, 2000. Mass. del. Democratic Nat. Conv., 1972; town coordinator Robert Drinan's campaign, 1970; chmn. bd. trustees Hatfield (Mass.) Library, 1978-83. Mem. Soc. Children's Book Writers (bd. dirs. 1974—), Children's Lit. Assn. (bd. dirs. 1977-79), Sci. Fiction Writers Am. (pres. 1986-88), Nat. Assn. for Preservation and Perpetuation of Storytelling, Authors Guild, Bay State Writers Guild, Western New Eng. Storytellers Guild (founder), Mystery Writers Am., Horror Writers Am., Authors Guild. Democrat. Jewish/Quaker. Home: PO Box 27 Hatfield MA 01038-0027

YOLLICK, BERNARD LAWRENCE, otolaryngologic surgeon; b. Toronto, Mar. 24, 1922; came to U.S., 1949; s. Samuel and Beatrice (Roth) Y.; m. Liny L. Pajgin, 1947; children: Ingrid, Eric Lyf. Sr. Matriculation, Harbord Collegiate Inst., Toronto, 1939; MD, U. Toronto, 1945. Diplomate Am. Bd. Surgery, Am. Bd. Otolaryngology. Intern Sunnybrook Hosp., Toronto, 1945-46; resident D.C. Gen. Hosp., Washington, 1950, St. Louis County Hosp., Clayton, Mo., 1952-53; Am. Cancer Soc. fellow M.D. Anderson Cancer Hosp., Houston, 1953-54; resident in pathology Cook County Hosp., Chgo., 1949; surgeon Houston, 1953-59; fellowship in otolaryngology VA Hosp., Dallas, 1960-63; asst. prof. anatomy Baylor Med. Sch., Houston, 1953-59; assoc. prof. anatomy U. Tex. Dental Sch., 1953-59, Baylor Coll. Dentistry, Dallas, 1987-90; mem. staff Children's Med. Ctr., 1990—; mem. staff, chief dept. otolaryngology St. Paul Med. Ctr., 1990-98. Cons. Tex. Workers Compensation Ins. Fund, 1996—, Dept. Defense, Dallas, 1997—; mem. otolaryngology staff Vets. Adminstrn. Hosp., Dallas, 1990—. Contbr. articles to profl. jours. Served to capt. Royal Can. Army Med. Corps, 1942-45. Recipient fellowship Am. Cancer Soc., 1953. Fellow Am. Coll. Surgeons; mem. Tex. Otolaryn. Assn. (pres. 1979).

YOLTON, JOHN WILLIAM, philosopher, educator; b. Birmingham, Ala., Nov. 10, 1921; s. Robert Elgene and Ella Maude (Holmes) Y.; m. Jean Sebastian, Sept. 5, 1945; children: Karin Frances Yolton Griffith, Pamela Holmes Yolton Smith. BA with honors, U. Cin., 1945, MA, 1946; postgrad., U. Calif., Berkeley, 1946-50; DPhil (Fulbright fellow), Balliol Coll., Oxford, Eng., 1952; LL.D. (hon.), York U., 1974; D.Litt. (hon.), McMaster U., 1976. Vis. lectr. philosophy Johns Hopkins U., 1952-53; asst. prof. Princeton U., 1953-57; assoc. prof. Kenyon Coll., 1957-61; prof. U. Md., 1961-63; prof. philosophy York U., Toronto, 1963-78, chmn. dept., 1963-73, acting dean grad. studies, 1967-68, acting pres., 1973-74; prof. philosophy Rutgers U., New Brunswick, N.J., 1978—, dean Rutgers Coll., 1978-85, John Locke prof. history of philosophy, 1989-92, prof. emeritus philosophy, 1992—. Cons. Bertrand Russell Archives, McMaster U., 1973-86. Author: John Locke and the Way of Ideas, 1956, Metaphysical Analysis, 1967, Locke and the Compass of Human Understanding, 1970, Thinking Matter, 1983, Perceptual Acquaintance from Descartes to Reid, 1984, Locke and French Materialism, 1991, Perception and Reality, 1996, Realism and Appearances, 2000, other books; gen. editor Clarendon Edit. of Works of John Locke, Oxford U. Press, 1984-92, Blackwell's Companion to the Enlightenment, 1992, Locke Dictionary (Blackwell), 1993, Library of the History of Ideas, 5 books in field; mem. editl. bd. jours. in field; editor (with Jean S. Yolton) Some Thoughts Concerning Education, by Locke, 1989; v.p., bd. dirs. Jour. of the History of Ideas, 1991-98; contbr. articles to profl. jours. Mem. N.J. Com. for Humanities, 1978-85, treas., 1980-85. Am. Coun. Learned Socs. fellow, 1960-61; Can. Coun. fellow, 1968-69. Mem.: Hume Soc., Am. Soc. for 18th Century Studies, Can. Philos. Assn., Mind Assn., Am. Philos. Assn. Fax: 732-545-7134.

YONDA, ALFRED WILLIAM, mathematician; b. Cambridge, Mass., Aug. 10, 1919; s. Walter and Theophelia (Naruscewicz) Y.; m. Mary Jane McManus, Dec. 19, 1949 (dec.); children: Nancy, Kathryn, Elizabeth, John; m. Peggy A. Terrel, June 22, 1975. BS, U. Ala., 1952, MA in Math., 1954. Registered profl. engr. Mathematician rocket rsch. Redstone Arsenal, Huntsville, Ala., 1953, U.S. Army Ballistic Rsch. Labs., Aberdeen, Md., 1954-56; instr. math. U. Ala., Tuscaloosa, 1954, Temple U., Phila., 1956-57; assoc. scientist, rsch. & devel. divsn. Avco Corp., Wilmington, Mass., 1957-59; sr. mem. tech. staff RCA, Camden, N.J., 1959-66; mgr. computer analysis and programming dept. Raytheon Co. Space and Info. Systems Divsn., Sudbury, Mass., 1966-70, mgr. software systems lab., 1969-70, prin. engr. missiles systems divsn., 1970-73; mgr. sys. analysis & programming GTE Govt. Systems Corp., 1973-77, mgr. software engring. Atlantic ops., 1977-82, sr. mem. tech. staff Command Control & Comm. Sector, 1983-91; software systems engr. Yonda Software Systems Cons., 1991—. Contbr. articles to profl. jours. Pres. Milford Area Assn. Retarded Children, 1970-74, vice chmn. fin. com. Town of Medway, 1973; bd. dirs. Blackstone Valley Mental Health and Retardation Area, 1970-76; trustee Medway Librs., 1973-82, chmn., 1974-81. With USAAF, 1943-46. Hon. fellow Advanced Level Telecomm. Tng. Ctr., Ghaziabad, India, 1981. Mem. AAAS, IEEE, Math. Assn. Am., N.Y. Acad. Scis., Sigma Xi, Phi Eta Sigma, Pi Mu Epsilon (pres. Ala. chpt. 1953-54), Sigma Pi Sigma. Office: 1622 Worcester Rd Apt 225B Framingham MA 01702-4415 E-mail: awyonda@aol.com.

YONG, RAYMOND NEN-YIU, civil engineering educator; b. Singapore, Apr. 10, 1929; naturalized, 1966; s. Ngim Djin and Lucy (Loh) Y.; m. Florence Lechensky, July 8, 1961; children— Raymond T.M., Christopher T.K. BA in Math. and Physics, Washington and Jefferson Coll., 1950; BS, MIT, 1952; MS, Purdue U., 1954; MEngring., McGill U., Montreal, Que., Can., 1958, PhD, 1960. Mem. faculty McGill U., 1959-95, prof. civil engring., 1965-72, William Scott prof. civil engring. and applied mechanics, 1972-95; dir. Geotech Rsch. Ctr., 1973-95; assoc. mem. Ctr. for Medicine, Ethics and Law McGill U., 1991-95. Adj. prof. civil engring. U. Fla., Gainesville, 1984—; adj. rsch. prof. civil engring. Carleton U., Ottawa, 1990; disting. rsch. prof. U. Wales, Cardiff, 1995—; sr. sci. dir. Geoenviron. Engring. Rsch. Ctr., Cardiff Sch. Engring., U. Wales,1995. Author: Soil Properties and Behavior, 1975

(Japanese edit. 1977), Introduction to Soil Behavior, 1966 (Japanese edit. 1974), Vehicle Traction Mechanics, 1985, Principles of Contaminant Transport in Soils, 1992 (Japanese edit. 1995), Geoenvironmental Engineering: Contaminated Soils, Pollutant Fate and Mitigation, 2000. Decorated chevalier Ordre National du Que., 1985; recipient Killam prize Can. Coun., 1985, ASTM Charles B. Dudley award, 1988, Can. Environ. Achievement award, Lifetime Achievement Environment Can., 1991. Fellow Royal Soc. Can., Engrng. Inst. Can., Can. Soc. for Civil Engrng.; mem. ASCE, ASTM (Charles B. Dudley award 1988), Inst. Civil Engrs., Soc. Rheology, Clay Minerals Soc., Internat. Soc. Terrain-Vehicle Systems (pres. 1993—), Can. Geotech. Soc. (R.F. Legget award 1993). E-mail: RNYong@islandnet.com.

YONKER, RICHARD AARON, rheumatologist; b. Phila., Aug. 8, 1952; BA, George Washington U., 1974; DO, Coll. Osteopathic Medicine, 1978. Diplomate Am. Bd. Internal Medicine, Am. Bd. Rheumatology. Rheumatologist Sarasota (Fla.) Arthritis Ctr., 1984—. Fellow Am. Coll. Rheumatology; mem. Am. Osteopathic Assn., Fla. Osteopathic Med. Assn., Fla. Rheumatology Soc. Office: Sarasota Arthritis Ctr 3500 S Tamiami Trl Sarasota FL 34239-6026

YONKMAN, FREDRICK ALBERS, lawyer, management consultant; b. Holland, Mich., Aug. 22, 1930; s. Fredrick Francis and Janet Dorothy (Albers) Y.; m. Kathleen VerMeulen, June 9, 1953 (div. Sept. 22, 1980); children: Sara, Margriet, Nina.; m. Barbara Anne Sullivan, Aug. 22, 1981 (div. Mar. 31, 1994); 1 child, Fredrick Ryan; m. Jewel Marie Humphrey, July 4, 1998. BA, Hope Coll., Holland, 1952; JD, U. Chgo., 1957. Bar: N.Y. 1958, Mass. 1968, D.C. 1984. With Winthrop, Stimson, Putnam & Roberts, N.Y.C., 1957-64; sec., gen. counsel Reuben H. Donnelley Corp., 1964-66, Dun & Bradstreet, Inc., N.Y.C., 1966-68; ptnr. Sullivan & Worcester, Boston, 1968-72; gen. counsel Am. Express Co., N.Y.C., 1972-78, exec. v.p., 1975-80; pres. Buck Cons., N.Y.C., 1980-81; mgmt. cons., psychoanalyst, 1981—; counsel Peabody, Lambert & Myers, Washington, 1983-84. Chmn. Outward Bound, Inc., Garrison, N.Y., 1980-81; mem. bd. and chmn. audit com. Kennecott Corp., 1978-81; adj. prof. law Georgetown U., 1976-78; chmn. Georgetown Internat. Law Inst., 1980-81; vis. com. U. Chgo. Law Sch., 1980-82; mem. exec. com. Warner-Amex, 1978-80; bd. dirs. Sageworks Inc., Raleigh, N.C. Bd. dirs. Washington Campus Program, 1976-81; bd. dirs. Young Audiences, 1978-83. With CIC, U.S.Army, 1952-54. Recipient Silver Anniversary award Nat. Coll. Athletic Assn., 1977 Mem. ABA, N.Y. State Bar Assn., Rsch. Soc. for Process Oriented Psychology (Zurich) (diplomate). Methodist. Home: 925 Rock Rimmon Rd Stamford CT 06903-1213 E-mail: fyonkman@optonline.net.

YONKOSKY, REENA ANN, emergency physician; b. Ironwood, Mich., 1947; MD, Mich. State U., 1974. Intern U. N.Mex. Affiliate Hosps., Albuquerque, 1975-76, resident surgery, 1976-77, USPHS Hosp., San Francisco, 1978-81; emergency physician Hyperbaric Physicians Ga., Marietta, Ga.; affiliated physician St. Joseph's Hosp. Atlanta. Fellow Am. Coll. Emergency Physicians; mem. Am. Med. Women's Assn., So. Med. Assn., Undersea and Hyperbaric Med. Soc. Home: 6410 Concord Rd Cumming GA 30040-8501 Office: Hyperbaric Physicians Ga Ste 200 55 Whitcher St Marietta GA 30060

YONTZ, KENNETH FREDRIC, medical and chemical company executive; b. Sandusky, Ohio, July 21, 1944; s. Kenneth Willard and Dorothy (Kromer) Y.; m. Jean Ann Marshall, July 21, 1962 (div. Aug. 1982); children: Terri, Christine, Michael, Jennifer; m. Karen Glojek, July 7, 1984 (wid. Dec. 1994); m. Karen Mc Diarmid, Jan. 10, 1997. BSBA, Bowling Green State U., 1971; MBA, Eastern Mich. U., 1979. Fin. planning mgr. Ford Motor Co., Rawsonville, Mich., 1970-74; fin. mgr. Chemetron Corp., Chgo., 1974-76, pres. fire systems div., 1976-80; pres. electronics div. Allen Bradley Co., Milw., 1980-83, group. pres. electronics, 1983-85, exec. v.p., 1985-86; chmn. bd. Apogent Techs., 1986—, Sybron Dental Specialities, Milw., 1986—. Bd. dirs. Viasystems, St. Louis, Rockwell Int., Milw. Bd. dirs. Boys and Girls Club; founder Karen Yontz Womens Cardiac Awareness Ctr.. Mem. Bluemound Country Club, Milw. Athletic Club, Muirfield Village Golf Club, Vintage Club (Indian Wells, Calif.), Tradition Golf Club (La Quinta, Calif.) Roman Catholic. Office: Sybron Corp 411 E Wisconsin Ave Ste 2400 Milwaukee WI 53202-4412 *Positive results are seldom achieved from negative thoughts.*

YONTZ, TIMOTHY GENE, music educator; b. Elkhart, Ind., June 8, 1961; s. Clifford Eugene and Beverly Jean Yontz; m. Brenna Lynn Ruble, June 9, 1984; children: Brent, Bess. MusB Edn., Ind. U., 1984; MusM, Butler U., 1990; PhD, U. Nebr., 2001. Dir. of bands New Albany (Ind.) H.S., 1984—86, New Palestine (Ind.) H.S., 1986—92, Marinette (Wis.) H.S., 1992—97; asst. prof. of music/assoc. dir. of univ. bands U. Nebr., Omaha, 1997—. Music dir. Nebr. Wind Symphony, Omaha, 1998—. Mem.: Nebr. State Bandmasters Assn., Nebr. Music Educators Assn., Nat. Band Assn., Music Educators Nat. Conf., Coll. Music Soc., Coll. Band Directors Nat. Assn., Christian Instrumentalists and Directors Assn., Assn. of Concert Bands, Phi Beta Mu, Kappa Kappa Psi. R-Consevative. Christian. Office: U Nebr Omaha Strauss Performing Arts Center 222 Omaha NE 68182 E-mail: tyontz@mail.unomaha.edu.

YOO, BONG, mechanical and structural engineer, researcher; b. Pusan, South Korea, Aug. 29, 1953; s. Chi-Bong and Sung-Up (Song) Y.; m. Young-Min Kim, Sept. 17, 1954; children: Shin, Ji-Yun. BS, Seoul Nat. U., 1977, MS, 1981, U. Calif., San Diego, 1986; PhD, KAIST, South Korea, 2002. Designer Korea Heavy Machinery Co., Seoul, 1977-79; rschr. Korea Atomic Energy Rsch. Inst., Taejon, 1980—83, sr. rschr., 1983—92, head sect., prin. rschr., 1992—2002; mech. engr. Argonne Nat. Lab., Chgo., 2002—. Vis. scientist Argonne Nat. Lab., Chgo., 2001—. Contbr. articles; patentee (invention) in field. Pvt. South Korean mil., 1977-78. Mem. ASME, Earthquake Engrng. Rsch. Inst., Korean Soc. Mech. Engrs. (life), Korean Nuclear Soc. (life), Earthquake Engrng. Soc. Korea (life). Presbyterian. Avocations: tennis, soccer, baseball, go-game. Home: 7413 Brookdale Dr Apt 204 Darien IL 60561 Office: Argonne Nat Lab 9700 S Cass Ave Argonne IL 60439 E-mail: byoo@ra.anl.gov.

YOO, BOONGHEE, marketing professional, researcher; b. Kanghwa Island, Kyonggido, Korea, Nov. 22, 1961; s. Joonsoo and Yunhee Namgoong Yoo; m. Sungnan Ahn; children: Kiwoong, Heeyoung. PhD in Bus. Adminstrn., Ga. State U., 1996. Assoc. prof. mktg. St. Cloud (Minn.) State U., 1998—2002, Hofstra U., Hempstead, NY, 2002—. Asst. mktg. mgr. Cheil Comms., Inc., Seoul, 1986—91. Cpl. 67th Divsn. Korean Army, 1983—85. Mem.: Am. Mktg. Assn. (Best Paper award in the 2001 Summer AMA Conf. 2001). Office: Hofstra U Mktg Dept Rm 222 Weller Hall Hempstead NY 11549 Home: 15 Amby Ave Plainview NY 11803 Office Fax: 516-463-4834. Business E-Mail: mktbzy@hofstra.edu. E-mail: boongheeyoo@yahoo.com.

YOO, CHAI HONG, civil engineering educator; b. Seoul, Korea, Sept. 16, 1939; came to U.S., 1967, naturalized, 1976; s. Chong Ryul Yoo and Kwi Rhe Lim; m. Chum Sook Lee, June 19, 1970; children— Anna, Laura. B.S., Seoul Nat. U., 1962; M.S., U. Md., 1969, Ph.D., 1971. Registered profl. engr., Va., Ala. Structural engr. Pacific Architects and Engrs., Inc., Saigon, Vietnam, 1966-67, McGaughy, Marshall and McMillan Assoc., Norfolk, Va., 1971-72; faculty research assoc. dept. civil engring. U. Md., College Park, 1972-73, vis. asst. prof., 1973-74; asst. prof. civil engring. Marquette U., Milw., 1975-80, assoc. prof., 1980-81; assoc. prof. Auburn U. (Ala.), 1981-86; prof., 1986—. cons. in field. Served to 1st lt. Korean Airforce, 1962-66. NSF grantee, 1979-80, 83-86. Mem. ASCE, Am. Soc. for Engring. Edn., Structural Stability Research Council, Sigma Xi, Chi Epsilon, Tau Beta Pi. Contbr. numerous articles to profl. jours. Home: 2041 Janabrooke Ln Auburn AL 36830-6997

YOO, CHOON WANG, financial consultant; b. Seoul, Korea, July 11, 1960; came to U.S., 1986; s. Seung Ahn and Song Hee (Kim) Y.; m. Yeong Mee Kwon, May 26, 1990; 1 child, Sean. BA in Econs., Korea U., 1986; MBA in Acctg., CUNY, 1989; MBA in Fin., C.W. Post Coll., 1991. Acctg. mgr. Kenney Transport, Inc., N.Y.C., 1986-89, controller, 1989-92; fin. cons. Equitable Fin. Co., 1992-94; dist. mgr. Equitable/Equico Security Co., Paramus, N.J., 1994-95; pres. Hexagon Internat. Group Co., Ft. Lee, 1995—. Cons. Korean-Am. One-Hour Photo Assn., Massapequa, N.Y., 1993—, Korean Producers Assn., Bronx, 1995—, Pa. Merchant Group, Radnor, 1995—, 1st Security Co., Ltd., Seoul, Korea, 1995—, Hangil Merchant Bank, Seoul, 1996. Pres. Korean Am. 1.5 Generation Assn., 1994—. Young Poong Found. scholar, Seoul, 1984-86. Mem. Internat. Assn. Fin. Planning, Nat. Assn. Securities Dealers, Nat. Assn. Life Underwriters, Assn. Investment Mgmt. and Rsch. Presbyterian. Avocations: skiing, golf, tennis, art collecting. Office: Hexagon Internat Group Co 2175 Lemoine Ave Ste 400 Fort Lee NJ 07024-6033 Address: 576 Valley Rd # 173 Wayne NJ 07470-3526

YOO, CHRISTOPHER S. law educator; b. East Lansing, Mich., Oct. 12, 1964; s. Man Hyong and Sung Ja Yoo; m. Kris K. Shibuya, July 9, 1996; children: Marshall W., Brendan J. AB, Harvard U., 1986; MBA, UCLA, 1991; JD, Northwestern U., Chgo., 1995. Bar: D.C., Ill. Tchr. high sch. Seoul Internat. Sch., 1986-87; legis. asst. to Senator Carl Levin, U.S. Senate, Washington, 1987-89; asst. brand mgr. Procter & Gamble, Cin., 1991-92; law clk. to Judge A. Raymond Randolph, U.S. Ct. Appeals for D.C. Circuit, Washington, 1995-96; law clk. to Justice Anthony M. Kennedy, Supreme Ct. U.S, 1997-98; assoc. Hogan & Hartson L.L.P., 1996—97, 1998—99; asst. prof. law Vanderbilt U. Law Sch., Nashville, 1999—. Office: Vanderbilt U Law Sch 131 21st Ave S Nashville TN 37203-1181 Fax: 615-322-6631. E-mail: christopher.yoo@law.vanderbilt.edu.

YOO, JI SUNG, economics educator; b. Buyeo, Korea, July 22, 1945; s. Hong Yeol Yoo and Young Soon Lee; m. Wol Jie Lee, Aug. 10, 1974. BA in Polit. Sci., Yonsei U., Seoul, Korea, 1968, MA in Pub. Adminstrn., 1972; BA in Econs., Am. U., Washington, 1975; MA, PhD in Econs., Cath. U. Am., Washington, 1980. Instr. No. Va. C.C., Alexandria, 1978-80; researcher IBRD, Washington, 1979; prof. econs. Hanyang U., Seoul, 1980—, dean planning, coordination, 1988-92, dean Coll. Bus. and Econs., 1999-2001. Dir. Hanyang Econ. Rsch. Inst., 1996-99. Author: Statistics, 1983, Introduction to Econometrics, 1985, International Finance, 1987, Understanding IMF and IBRD, 1988, Introduction to Economics, 1997, Money and Banking, 1998; editor-in-chief Jour. Econ. Rsch., 1966—. Lt. with Korean armed forces, 1968-70. Mem. Korean Econ. Assn. (bd. dirs. 1985-90), Korean Internat. Econ. Assn. (bd. dirs. 1985-90), Korean Econometric Soc. (bd. dirs. 1985—), Asia Pacific Econ. Assn. (pres. 1997-99). Avocation: mountain climbing. Office: Hanyang U Dept Econs 17 Haengdand-dong Seongdong-gu Seoul Republic of Korea

YOO, MAN HYONG, materials scientist; b. Seoul, Republic of Korea, June 27, 1935; arrived in U.S., 1956; s. Hae Chang Yoo and Chang Kyu Lee; m. Sung Ja Choo, Sept. 10, 1960; children: Phillip Seung-Ho, Terry Seung-Won, Christopher Seung-Gil. BS, Mich. State U., 1960, MS, 1962, PhD, 1965. Rsch. assoc. Mich. State U., E. Lansing, 1966—67; mem. rsch. staff Oak Ridge (Tenn.) Nat. Lab., 1967—79, sr. rsch. staff, 1979—86, task leader, 1979—84, disting. scientist, 1986—. Guest scientist Nuc. Rsch. Ctr., Julich, Germany, 1984—85; vis. prof. Tohoku U., Sendai, Japan, 1988—89; guest scientist Max Planck Inst., Dusseldorf, Germany, 1994; vis. prof. Tech. U., Hamburg, Germany, 1995. Contbr. articles to profl. jours.; , editor conf. proceedings. Recipient Metallography award, Japan Inst. Metals, 1990, Outstanding Sci. award, U.S. Dept. Energy, 1991, Sr. U.S. Scientist award, Alexander von Humboldt, Germany, 1995, H. Mathewson award, TMS, 2002. Fellow: Am. Soc. Metals Internat., Minerals, Metals and Materials Soc.; mem.: Sigma Xi. Avocations: music appreciation, golf, squash, reading, calligraphy. Home: 966 W Outer Dr Oak Ridge TN 37830 Office: Oak Ridge Nat Lab PO Box 2008 Oak Ridge TN 37831-6115

YOOD, HAROLD STANLEY, retired internist; b. Plainfield, N.J., Feb. 23, 1920; s. Raphael and Netta (Newcorn) Y.; m. Helen H. Hull, Nov. 8, 1941; children: Pamela, Patricia Yood Herskovitz, Paula Yood Peterson, Andrew H. BA, U. Va., 1940, MD, 1943. Intern Syracuse (N.Y.) U. Med. Ctr., 1943; pvt. practice Plainfield, N.J., 1946-91; med. dir. Cen. Jersey Individual Physicians Assn., 1987-2000; ret. Staff dept. medicine Muhlenberg Hosp., 1946—, pres. staff, 1980-86, cons., 1991-95, emeritus, 1995—. Contbr. articles to Jour. Med. Soc. N.J., Communication for Ciba, others. Pres. vol. med. staff Raritan Valley Hosp., Greenbrook, N.J., 1969; bd. govs. Muhlenberg Regional Med. Ctr., 1980-86, exec. com.; trustee, v.p. United Way Plainfield/Fanwood, 1975-81; bd. dirs. United Way Union County, 1978-81; pres. Jewish Community Ctr., Plainfield, 1970-71; v.p. Jewish Fedn. Cen. N.J., 1971-73, Cen. N.J. Jewish Home for Aged, 1973-80. Capt. M.C. AUS, 1944-45, ETO. Decorated Purple Heart, Combat Med. badge, Combat Glider badge. Fellow Am. Coll. Gastroenterology (sr.), Am. Coll. Angiology (ret.), Internat. Coll. Angiology (ret.); mem. AMA, Med. Soc. N.J. (governing coun. hosp. med. staff sect. 1983-92, chmn. 1988-90; trustee 1989-90), Union County Med. Soc., Lions (life). *Enjoyment in my profession, pleasure in relationship with patients, a belief in the necessity for civic and community volunteer involvement, a commitment to support causes that aid the unfortunate and do no harm to individuals.*

YOOD, ROBERT A. rheumatologist; b. Ithaca, N.Y., Jan. 18, 1949; s. Bertram and Shirley (Saffran) Y.; m. Joan D. Schlachter, Aug. 3, 1975; children: Sara, David, Benjamin. BA, Yale U., 1970; MD, U. Oreg., Portland, 1974. Rheumatologist Fallon Clinic, Worcester, Mass., 1979—, treas., 1988-96, acting med. dir., 1995-96, bd. dirs., 1984-98, 2002—; chair divsn. rheumatic diseases and musculoskeletal medicine St. Vincent Hosp. Assoc. prof. medicine U. Mass. Med. Sch. Contbr. articles to profl. jours. Fellow ACP, Am. Coll. Rheumatology (fin. com.); mem. New Eng. Rheumatism Soc. (former pres.), Am. Med. Group Assn., Arthritis Found. (former med. adv. bd. Mass. chpt.). Office: Fallon Clinic 425 N Lake Ave Worcester MA 01605

YOOK, CHONG CHUL, engineering educator; b. Kyngbuk, Sunsan, Korea, Jan. 1, 1926; s. Jae Kyun Yook and Choi (Shoon) Ie; m. Sook Kae Chang, Aug. 15, 1949; children: Myung-Hi, Oak-Soo, Sun-Hi. BS in Engrng., Seoul (Republic of Korea) Nat. U., 1950; postgrad., Oak Ridge Inst., Argonne Internat. Inst., 1961, U. Ill., 1962; PhD in Nuclear Engrng., Hanyang U., Seoul, 1967. Prof. Chung-Nam Nat. U., Taejon, Republic of Korea, 1957-64, dean Engrng. Coll. Republic of Korea, 1962-64; prof. Hanyang U., 1964-91, prof. emeritus, 1991—. Mem. tech. adv. bd. Ministry of Sci. and Tech., Seoul, 1988-90; advisor inspection, testing and examination cons. ITEC Svc. Co., Ltd., Seoul, 1991—. Author: Radiation Safety Handling, 1982, East and West, 1991 (Panel award 1991); patent for applied measuring device of engine ring wear. Mem. energy and resources adv. com. Rep. of Korean Govt., Seoul, 1981-83. Mem. Korean Assn. for Radiation Protection (pres. Seoul chpt. 1977-79), Internat. Radiation Protection Assn. (rep. Netherlands chpt. 1977-1977-79), Internat. Radiation Protection Assn. (rep. Netherlands chpt. 1977-80, adv. com. Fed. Republic of Germany 1978-81), Korean Atomic Energy Rsch. Inst. (standing com. Taejon chpt. 1989-90), Korean Radioisotapes Assn. (audit treas. Seoul chpt. 1985-91). Mem. Christian Ch. Avocations: reading, mountain climbing, swimming.

YOOL, GEORGE RICHARD, consultant; b. Orange, Calif., Apr. 16, 1969; s. George Malcolm and Norma Susan Cravey; m. Megan Tiffaney Jacksen, June 6, 1991 (div. Nov. 1997); children: Thor Alexander, Logan Anthony, Ashley Rene; m. Liliana Matilde Cuzzocrea, Mar. 13, 2000. BS in Criminal Justice, No. Ariz. U., Flagstaff, 1993, MEd in Ednl. Leadership, 1995. Cons. dir. Cons. Unltd., Apache Junction, Ariz., 1988—; co-founder Barbarian Corp., 1996. Author: The Blue Rose/Silence, 1986 (1st pl. art contest 1986), Silent Dreams, 1992, The Writer's Cookbook, 1992, An Introduction to Zen Thought, 1993, rünLi Ching (Classic of Ethic), 1994, LiJie Ching (Classic of Knowledge), 1997, Metamorphosis of the Flying Rose, 1997, Unified Field Theory, 1998, Survey of Information Systems Technologies, 1999, Introduction to Web Design, 2000, Practical Algorithms and Logic, 2000, Chan Ching, 2002, The PuMa Tse, 2002; co-author: Handbook for Humanizing Higher Education, 1995; creator, author: (discovery) Problem Solving Using Paradology, 1995, Integrated Theory of Learning and Development, 1995; author, discoverer: (book, presentation, discovery) Mensonnomy: A New Unified Cosmology, 1994; inventor: Virtual Keyboard, 1995; contbr. articles to profl. jours. Recipient grad. scholarship No. Ariz. U., Flagstaff, 1995. Mem. Ariz. Grad. Student Assn. (del. 1995), Students and Tchrs. Instrnl. Needs Group (pres. 1995—), Grad. Student Assn. No. Ariz. U. (pres. 1995). Avocations: reading, research, writing, math, physics, guest lecturing. com. E-mail: god@barbaria.

YOON, E. YUL, retired career officer; b. Pyungyang, Korea, Feb. 10, 1927; s. Jung Soon and Jung Duk (Lee) Y.; m. Sun Sam Lee Yoon, Nov. 29, 1931; children: Kyung Ran, Kyung Im, Kwang Ho. Grad., Mil. Acad. Seoul, 1948; BS in Politics and Fgn. Policy, Dangook U., Seoul, Korea, 1955; grad., U.S. Air U., Montgomery, Ala., 1957. Squadron comdr. The 12th Fighter SQ F-51, Korea, 1952-53; armed force attache Korean Embassy, Paris, 1959-61; wing comdr. The 1st Combat Wing, The 10th Fighter Wing, Seoul, 1961-63; pres. Korean Air Force Coll., 1963-64; supt. Korean Air Acad., 1964-66; command-ing gen. Combat Air Command, Korea, 1968-70; minister plenipotentiary Korean Embassy, France, Mexico, 1966-68; vice minister for def. devel. Ministry of Def., Seoul, 1970-73; pres., CEO Korea Tacoma Shipbuilding Indsl. Co., Korea, 1973-76, Buyeon Co., Ltd., Seoul, 1976-86; cons. United Tech./Martin Marieta, 1976-85. Mem. Korean Heavy Industrialization Com., Seoul, 1970-73. Recipient Eulchi and two Gold Stars, Chungmoo Meritorious Svc. medals, Korea, 1952, 53, Korean Disting. Svc. medal, 1955; decorated U.S. Disting. Flying Cross, U.S. Air medal, Repub. of China Disting. Svc. medal. Mem. The Disting. Flying Cross Soc. (life), Ministry of Nat. Def. of Korea (rsch. assoc.). Avocations: photography, art collecting, golf. E-mail: yulyoon@hotmail.com.

YOON, JAY MYOUNG, oncologist, hematologist, internist; b. Korea, Sept. 30, 1946; married. BA Coll. Liberal Arts & Sci. summa cum laude, Seoul Nat. U., 1967, MD summa cum laude, 1971. Diplomate Am. Bd. Internal Medicine, 1978, Am. Bd. Oncology, 1979, Am. Bd. Hematology, 1980. Intern in medicine Bklyn. Hosp. Ctr.-Cornell U., N.Y.C., 1974-75; resident in medicine Bronx-Lebanon Hosp.-Albert Einstein Coll. Medicine, 1975-76; fellow in hematol. oncology Baystate Med. Ctr.-Tufts U. Sch. Medicine, Springfield, Mass., 1976-78; fellow in oncology Roswell Park Cancer Inst.-SUNY, Buffalo, 1978-79, rsch. clinician in oncology dept. surg. develop. oncology, 1979-80; rsch. instr. medicine SUNY, 1978—80; attending physician, med. oncologist St. Francis Hosp. and Health Ctr., Clarian Health Ptnrs., Beech Grove and Indpls., 1980-98; rsch. instr. medicine SUNY, 1978—80; prof. medicine Ulsan U. Med. Sch., 1997—98; CEO, pres. Yoon Clinic, P.C., Edmonds, Wash., 1999—; mem. med. staff Stevens Meml. Hosp., 1999—, Northwest Hosp., Seattle, 1999—, Swedish Med. Ctr., Seattle, 2000. Contbr. articles to profl. jours. Mem. AAAS, AMA, ADA, AACR, Am. Assn. Blood Banks, Am. Soc. Clin. Oncology, Am. Soc. Hematology, N.Y. Acad. Sci. Home: 11901 59th Ave W Mukilteo WA 98275-5569 Office: Yoon Clinic PC Edmonds Med and Profl Ctr 7631 212th St SW Ste 106 B Edmonds WA 98026-7565 Fax: 425-697-6222. E-mail: dryoomnd@msn.com.

YOON, JI-WON, virology, immunology and diabetes educator, research administrator; b. Kang-Jin, Chonnam, Korea, Mar. 28, 1939; came to U.S., 1965; s. Baek-In and Duck-Soon (Lee) Y.; m. Chungja Rhim, Aug. 17, 1968; children: John W., James W. MS, U. Conn., 1971, PhD, 1973. Sr. investigator NIH, Bethesda, Md., 1978-84; prof., chief div. virology U. Calgary, Alta., Can., 1984—, assoc. dir. Diabetes Rsch. Ctr. Canada, 1985—90, dir. Canada, 1990—99, Julia McFarlane prof. Canada, 1990—99, dir. Lab. Viral and Immunopathogenesis of Diabetes Canada, 1999—, Can. rsch. chair diabetes Canada, 2001—. Mem. editl. bd. Diabetologia, 1977, Ann. Rev. Advances Present Rsch. Animal Diabetes, 1990—, Diabetes Rsch. Clin. Practice, 1989—, Jour. Biomed. Rsch., 1992—, Jour. Exptl. Molecular Medicine, 1996—; mem. editl. adv. bd. Jour. Diabetologia, 1996—99; vis. prof. Diabetes Endocrinology Rsch. Ctr., Yale U., New Haven, 1997—. Contbr. articles to New England Jour. Medicine, Jour. Virology, Sci., Nature, The Lancet, Jour. Diabetes, Jour. Immunology, Jour. Biochemistry, Jour. Exptl. Medicine. Rsch. fellow Sloan Kettering Cancer Inst., 1973-74, Staff fellow, Sr. Staff fellow NIH, 1974-76, 76-78; recipient NIH Dir. award, 1984, Heritage Med. Scientist award, Alberta Heritage Found. Med. Rsch., 1984, Lectrship. award, 3d Asian Symposium Childhood Diabetes, 1989, 8th Annual Meeting Childhood Diabetes, Osaka, Japan, 1990, 9th Korean/Can. Heritage award, 1989, 1st Compatriot award Fedn. Korean-Can. Assn., 1996. Mem. Am. Soc. Immunologists, Am. Diabetes Assn., Am. Soc. Microbiology, N.Y. Acad. Sci., Soc. Virology, Internat. Diabetes Fedn. Baptist. Achievements include first isolation of diabetogenic virus from patients with recent onset of IDDM; first demonstration of prevention of virus-induced diabetes by vaccination with nondiabetogenic virus in animals; discovery that autoimmune IDDM can be prevented by depletion of macrophages in autoimmune diabetic NOD mice, certain viral glycoproteins (rubella virus E2 glycoprotein) can induce organ-specific autoimmune disease; research on molecular identification of diabetogenic viral gene in animal models, discovery of a nontoxic organic compound with no side effects that completely prevents type I diabetes in NOD mice, discovery that bacterial superantigens such as staphylococcal enterotozins (SEC1, SEC3) can prevent autoimmune type I diabetes by activation of CD4+ suppressor T cells in NOD mice; research on the role of cloned T-Cells in the pathogenesis of autoimmune Type I Diabetes at cellular and molecular level, molecular role TGFB in prevention of Autoimmune IDDM, molecular role of macrophages in pathogenesis of virus-induced diabetes. Home: 206 Edgeview Dr NW Calgary AB Canada T3A 4X5 Office: Julia McFarlane Diabetes Rsch Ctr 3330 Hospital Dr NW Calgary AB Canada T2N 4N1

YOON, YONG JOON, economist, educator; b. Dongrae, Korea, Apr. 10, 1945; s. In-Bok Yoon and Duck-Yung Sohn; m. Miryung Min Yoon, Mar. 25, 1983; 1 child, Benjamin. BS, Seoul Nat. U., 1967; PhD in Math., U. Fla., 1977; PhD, Northwestern U., 1986. Asst. prof. Tenn. Technol. U., Cookeville, 1976-77, U. Mo., columbia, 1985-89; economist Pub. Svc. Commn., Washington, 1990-96; sr. rsch. scholar George Mason U., Fairfax, Va., 1997—. Vis. assoc. prof. Va. Poly. Inst., Blacksburg, 2000—; vis. lectr. Yokohama (Japan) City U., 2001. Editor (with James Buchanan) The Return to Increasing Returns, 1994; contbr. articles to profl. jours. Mem. Am. Econ. Assn., Korean-Am. Econ. Assn., Pub. Choice Soc. Avocation: river watching, salpuri dance. Home: 7592 Vogels Way Springfield VA 22153 Office: George Mason U Buchanan House 1E6 Fairfax VA 22030

YORDAN, EDGARDO LUIS, gynecologist; b. Ponce, P.R., June 6, 1946; BA, Columbia U., 1968; MD, U. Md. Sch. Medicine, 1972. Diplomate Am. Bd. Obstetrics & Gynecology. Intern U. Chgo. Hosps. and Clinics, 1972-73; resident in ob/gyn Columbia U.-Presbyn. Med. Ctr., N.Y.C., 1973-77, Meml. Sloan-Kettering Cancer Ctr., N.Y.C., 1976; fellow U. So. Calif.-L.A. County Med. Ctr., 1977-79, Rush-Presbyn.- St. Luke's Med. Ctr., Chgo., 1980-95. Assoc. prof. ob/gyn Rush Med. Coll., Chgo., 1980—, Luth. Gen. Hosp., Chgo., 1987—. Mem. Soc. Gynecol. Oncology, Western Assn. Gynecol. Oncology, Ctrl. Assn. OB-GYN, Am. Coll. Surgeons, Soc. Gynecol. Laparascopy, Chgo. Gynecol. Soc., Ctrl. Travel Club. Office: Advocate Med Group Lutheran Gen Hosp 1700 Luther Ln Park Ridge IL 60068-1270 E-mail: edgardo.yordan@advocatemedical.com.

YORK, ALEXANDRA, writer, lecturer; m. Barrett Randell. BA in Comm. Arts, Teaching Degree in Speech Edn., Mich. State U. Cert. speech, English, French educator, Mich. Writer, profr., reporter bi-weekly feature Sta. WPIX-TV, N.Y.C., 1968; host two interview/talk shows on contemporary art scene ABC Radio Network, 1968; free-lance writer, 1968—; prin. actress radio and TV commls., including nat. Clairol TV spokesperson, 1970-82; pres. Promethena Artist Rep. Co., 1989—; editor Art Ideas mag., 1994-2000; editor, pub. Silver Rose Press, 2000—. Founding pres. Am. Renaissance for 21st Century, 1992—; lectr. in field. Author three books on self-help 1973, 77, 81, From the Fountainhead to the Future and Other Essays on Art and Excellence, 2000; editor, pub. Imprint of Art, Silver Rose Press, 2000-; series editor: Silver Rose Anthology--Award-Winning Short Stories, 2001; prodr. and curator major art exhibits Romantic Realism: Visions of Values, 1992, The Legacy Lives: The World at its Most Beautiful and Man and Woman at Their Best, 1996, 97; contbr. articles to newspapers and mags. including Reader's Digest, Vogue, USA Today, Vital Speeches; featured guest TV shows including The Today Show, To Tell the Truth, Larry King Live, ABC's Eyewitness News. Recipient Whiting Meml. award for outstanding svc. to cultural world from the Internat. Soc. for Philos. Enquiry, 1997. Mem. Authors Guild, Nat. Arts Club (literary com. 1993—), Rolls-Royce Owners' Club (v.p. comm., editor 1991-94, McFarlane award 1992), Classic Car Club Am., Urasenke Internat. Tea Ceremony Soc. Avocations: travel, sports, cars, food/wines, ceremonial Japanese tea, opera. Office: FDR Sta PO Box 8379 New York NY 10150-1919 Fax: (212) 759-1922.

YORK, CANDACE A. marketing professional, writer; b. Lubbock, Tex., Mar. 7, 1954; d. Billy John and Francis Ann York; m. James R. Callahan, Feb. 17, 1947. BFA in Art History, U. Tex., 1976. Archival asst. S.W. collection Tex. Tech. U., Lubbock, 1976—77; claims analyst Met. Life, Austin, 1977—78; mktg. software engr., info. devel. IBM Corp., 1978—. Author numerous poems. Vol. Ctrl. Tex. Food Bank, Austin, 2000—01. Laguna Gloria Art Mus., Austin, 1996—98. Named Internat. Poet of Merit, Internat. Libr. Poetry, 2001; recipient Excellence award, Soc. Tech. Comm., 1980, Honorable Mention award, Iliad Press, 2001, 1st pl. poetry in motion competition, 2001. Mem.: Assn. Interactive Media, Pub. Rels. Soc. Am. (programs com. Austin chpt. 2002), Acad. Am. Poets. Avocations: poetry, photography, guitar, painting, tai chi. Home: 8210 Bent Tree Rd #213 Austin TX 78759 Home Fax: 512-418-2919. E-mail: canyork@aol.com.

YORK, CAROLYN PLEASANTS STEARNS, English educator; b. High Point, N.C., Aug. 23, 1949; d. Frank Ellis and Jessie May (Pleasants) Stearns; m. Guy Aaron York, July 11, 1970; children: Adam Landon, Emily Pleasants, Jonathan Aaron. BA, U. N.C., Greensboro, 1971; MEd, U. N.C., Chapel Hill, 1985. Project Head Start asst. Forsyth County Schs., Winston-Salem, N.C., 1968; publicity dir. House in the Horseshoe Outdoor Drama, Southern Pines, 1975-76; chpt. I reading tchr. Lee County Schs., Sanford, 1977-86, English instr., 1987—. Reading instr. Ctrl. Carolina C.C., Sanford, 1985; reading chmn. So. Assn., Sanford, 1978; workshop dir., conf. spkr. N.C. Assn. Compensatory Educators, Raleigh, 1983. Author: (poetry) Pleasantries, 1996, Weaver of Destiny, 1999; contbr. poems and stories to books; editor newsletter Creations, 1976; appeared on Friday Noon Poets Assn. Pub. TV Program, 1997; photographer Lee High Rev. lit. mag., 1998-99; advisor Internat. Thespian Soc., 2002. Founding mem. Lee County Arts Coun., Sanford, 1975; sec. Footlight Players, Lee County Recreation Dept., 2002; Sunday Sch. tchr., Bible sch. tchr. First Presbyn. Ch., Sanford, 1982, 86-89; bd. dirs. Child Devel. Ctr., Sanford, 1980-82; mem. adv. coun. Cmty. Playhouse of the Temple Theater, 1997-99; Builders Club sponsor Kiwanis Club of Lee County, Sanford, 1978-80. Recipient local and state prize N.C. Reading Assn., 1995, 1st prize Fields of Earth Poetry Symposium, 1996, 1st place Am. Scholastic Press Assn., 2000. Mem. N.C. Poetry Soc. (bd. dirs., 3d v.p. 1997-2002, workshop dir. 1993, 2d prize 1993, 1st prize 1999), San-Lee Writers (pres. 1993—, co-founder), Tri County English Alliance (coord., English Fair rep. 1995-2001), Lee County Reading Assn. (young authors' chmn. 1996-97; advisor lit. mag. Lee High Rev. 1998-99), Guild Am. Papercutters. Avocations: snorkeling, playing the dulcimer, weaving, collecting antique valentines, cutting schrenschnitte. Home: 315 N Steele St Sanford NC 27330-3956 E-mail: Yorkshome@wave-net.net.

YORK, COURTNEY CARTER, retired engineering executive, genealogist; b. Roland, Okla., Jan. 26, 1929; s. Jacob A. York and Rosa Pauline Bias; m. Gerlene Joy Gibson, Jan. 8, 1931 (dec.); children: Barbara Ann, Darlene Rosa; m. Roberta Louise Gale, Mar. 8, 1936. AA in Electronics, West Valley Coll., 1968. Signal dept. crew So. Pacific R.R., Calif., 1953-63; foreman, engr. Ampex Corp., Redwood City, 1963-73; engr. Vesatel-Printers, Sunnyvale, 1974-76; engrng. corp mgr. Racal-Vadic, 1986; ret., 1986. Author 30 books on genealogy. Home: 2035 Smokey Dr Los Banos CA 93635-5107

YORK, DONALD GILBERT, astronomy educator, researcher; b. Shelbyville, Ill., Oct. 28, 1944; s. Maurice Alfred and Virginia Maxine (Huntwork) Y.; m. Anna Sue Hinds, June 12, 1966; children: Sean, Maurice, Chandler, Jeremy. BS, MIT, 1966; PhD, U. Chgo., 1971. Rsch. asst. Princeton (N.J.) U., 1970-71, rsch. assoc., 1971-73, rsch. astronomer, 1973-78, sr. rsch. astronomer, 1978-82; assoc. prof. U. Chgo., 1982-86, prof., 1986-92, Horace B. Horton prof. astronomy and astrophysics, 1992—. Dir. Apache Point Obs., Astrophys. Rsch. Consortium, Seattle, 1984-98, Sloan Digital Sky Survey, 1990-97. Contbr. articles to profl. jours. Recipient Pub. Svc. award NASA, 1976; grantee NASA, 1978—, NSF, 1984—. Mem. Internat. Astron. Union, Am. Astron. Soc. (publs. bd. 1980-83). Democrat. Avocations: squash, white water canoeing, science history, religion history, swimming. Office: 5640 S Ellis Ave Chicago IL 60637-1433 E-mail: don@oddjob.uchicago.edu.

YORK, E. TRAVIS, academic administrator, former university chancellor, consultant; b. Mentone, Ala., July 4, 1922; s. E.T. and Leila (Hixon) Y.; m. Vermelle Cardwell, Dec. 26, 1946; children: Lisa Carol, Travis Loften. BS, Auburn U., 1942, MS, 1946, DSc (hon.), 1982; PhD, Cornell U., 1949; postgrad., George Washington U., 1957-59; D.Sc. (hon.), U. Fla., 1984, Ohio State U., 1996. Rsch. fellow Cornell U., Ithaca, 1946-49; Assoc. prof. N.C. State Coll., 1949-52, prof., 1952-56, head dept. agronomy, 1953-56; Eastern dir. Am. Potash Inst., 1956-59; dir. Ala. Extension Service, Auburn U., 1959-61; adminstr. Fed. Extension Service, U.S. Dept. Agr., 1961-63; provost for agr. U. Fla., 1963-67, v.p. agrl. affairs, 1967-73, exec. v.p., interim pres., 1973-74, Disting. Svc. prof., 1988-96. Chancellor State U. System of Fla., 1975-80, chancellor emeritus, 1980— Mem. Am. Food for Peace Coun., 1961-62, Freedom from Hunger Com., 1961-62, Pres.'s Panel Vocat. Edn., 1961-62; chmn. coun. grad. edn. in agrl. scis. So. Regional Edn. Bd., 1964-66, mem., 1975-80, exec. com., 1978-80, mem. pres. coun., Pres.' Sci. Adv. Coun. Task Force on World Food Problems, 1966-67; mem. senate, exec. com. Nat. Assn. State Univs. and Land Grant Colls., 1967-70; mem. Edn. Commn. of States, 1975-79, steering com., 1977-79, treas., exec. com., 1978-79; bd. dirs. Nat. 4-H Svc. Com., 1963-75, AV Med. Corp., Sante Fe, 1987-96; trustee, bd. dirs Hlth Improvement Inc mem., 1996-98, mem. exec. com. Nat. 4-H Found., 1968-73; mem.-at-large nat. coun. Boy Scouts Am., 1962-75; dir., pres. Alpha Gamma Rho Edn. Found., 1965-72; bd. dirs. Nat. Ctr. for Voluntary Action, 1970-74; mem. bd. for Internat. Food and Agrl. Devel., 1980-86, chmn., 1983-86; trustee Escuela Agrícola Panamericana, 1980-88, Found. for Agronomic Rsch., 1980-92; tech. adv. com., cons. Group for Internat. Agrl. Rsch., 1983-89; trustee Agronomic Sci. Found., 1989-92; chmn. bd. Internat. Fertilizing Devel. Ctr., 1999-. Officer AUS, 1943-45. Recipient B.B. Comer award excellence natural sci. Auburn U., 1942; disting. svc. award Fla. Vet. Med. Assn., 1966; Nat. 4-H Alumni award, 1967; George Washington honor medal award Freedoms Found., 1967; nat. ptnr. in 4-H award, 1970; disting. faculty award U. Fla., Fla. Blue Key, 1972; E.T. York, Jr. disting. svc. award U. Fla., 1973; honors medal U. Fla. Acad. Scis., 1974; E.T. York svc. award Fla. Bd. Regents, 1983, disting. svc. award Am. Farm Bur., 1991, svc. above self award, Rotary Internat., 1994, Medal of Honor, DAR, 1998; named to Fla. Agrl. Hall of Fame, 1990, Ala. Agrl. Hall of Honor, 1995, Internat. Adult and Continuing Edn. Hall of Fame, 1996; designated as Great Floridian, Fla. History Mus., 1997. Fellow AAAS, Am. Soc. Agronomy, Soil Sci. Soc. Am., AM. Crop Sci. Soc.; mem. Am. Soc. Hort. Sci. (hon.), Assn. So. Agrl. Scientists (pres. 1968), Blue Key, Rotary (dist. gov. 1981-82), Sigma Xi, Phi Kappa Phi, Alpha Zeta, Gamma Sigma Delta (internat. disting. svc. award 1973), Omicron Delta Kappa, Phi Delta Kappa, Epsilon Sigma Phi, Alpha Gamma Rho (named to Hall of Fame 1982). Methodist. Address: 4020 SW 78th St Gainesville FL 32608-3608

YORK, ELINOR JANICE, retired psychiatric social worker, consultant; b. St. Joseph, Mo., Mar. 10, 1939; d. Clarence Green and Ruth Anita (Lee) Mabin; m. Phil A. York, Aug. 19, 1961; children: Kimberly Ann, Brian A. BA, Mt. St. Scholastica Coll., Atchison, Kans., 1960; MSW, U. Nebr., 1965. Lic. psychiat. social worker, Colo. Social worker Family and Children's Svc., Lincoln, Nebr., 1965-67; psychiat. social worker Ft. Logan Mental Hosp., Denver, 1974-75; social worker Jefferson County Schs., Golden, Colo., 1978-98. Social work cons. Gen. Douglas MacArthur Boys Ranch, Colo., 1980-82; parent educator Foothills Ch., Littleton, Colo., 1991-92. Mem. NASW (lic.), Christian Educators Assn., Jefferson County Ecucators Assn. (assoc. rep. 1985—, polit. action com. 1991-92). Mem. Littleton Foursquare Gospel Ch. Avocations: reading, music, travel, writing poetry. Home: 8096 S Vance Ct Littleton CO 80128-5635

YORK, ELIZABETH JANE, innkeeper; b. Camden, N.J., July 27, 1934; d. Charles Evans and Christine (Taggart) York; m. Anthony Neil Gaeta, Apr. 2, 1960 (div. Jan. 1986); children: Gregory Gaeta, Anthony Gaeta, Anne Gaeta; m. Robert Newbergh, July 26, 1996 (dec. Mar. 2001). BA, Wheaton (Ill.) Coll., Ill., 1957; postgrad., U. N.C., 1957-58. Owner Designing Woman, Minot, Mass., 1976-81; broker Vin Doyle Real Estate, Scituate, 1978-81; owner, innkeeper The Four Chimneys, Nantucket Island, 1981-90; gen. mgr. The Roberts House Group, 1992-95; writer, 1995—; pres. North Eastham, Mass., 1998—. Consult in field; advisor INN-Partners, 1992—. Group dir Scituate Newcomer's Club, 1976—81; vol Hosp Thrift Shop, Nantucket, 1982—, Second Shop, Nantucket, 1982—; mem Nantucket Conserv Found. Mem.: Hospice, Nantucket Lodging Asn, Nantucket Hist Soc, Cape Cod CofC, Nantucket CofC, Antheneum. Democrat. Avocations: sailing, antiques, books, travel. Home and Office: 94 Hopkins Ln Orleans MA 02653-3463

YORK, GARY ALAN, lawyer; b. Glendale, Calif., Aug. 29, 1943; m. Lois York, 1987; 1 child, Jonathan Alan. BA, Pomona Coll., 1965; LLB, Stanford U., 1968. Bar: Calif. 1969. Ptnr. Dewey Ballantine, L.A., 1985-95, Buchalter, Nemer, Fields & Younger, L.A., 1995-98, Le Boeuf, Lamb, Greene & MacRae, L.A., 1998—2002. Instr. law sch. UCLA, 1968-69. Bd. editors Stanford Law review, 1966-68. Mem. ABA (chmn. real estate fin. com., real property probate and trust sect. 1987-89, chmn. usury com. 1992-93), L.A. County Bar Assn. (chmn. real estate fin. sect. 1993-96, exec. com. 1995—), State Bar of Calif., Am. Coll. Real Estate Lawyers, Am. Coll. Mortgage Attys. Office: Baker & Hostetler LLP 333 S Grand Ave Ste 1800 Los Angeles CA 90071 E-mail: GYork@Bakerlaw.com.

YORK, HERBERT FRANK, physics educator, government official; b. Rochester, N.Y., Nov. 24, 1921; s. Herbert Frank and Nellie Elizabeth (Lang) Y.; m. Sybil Dunford, Sept. 28, 1947; children: David Winters, Rachel, Cynthia. AB, U. Rochester, 1942, MS, 1943; PhD, U. Calif., Berkeley, 1949; DSc (hon.), Case Inst. Tech., 1960; LL.D., U. San Diego, 1964, Claremont Grad. Sch., 1974. Physicist Radiation Lab., U. Calif., Berkeley, 1943-58, assoc. dir., 1954-58; asst. prof. physics dept. U. Calif., 1951-54, assoc. prof., 1954-59, prof., 1959-61; dir. Lawrence Radiation Lab., Livermore, 1952-58; chief scientist Advanced Rsch. Project Agy., U.S. Dept. Def., 1958; dir. advanced rsch. projects divsn. Inst. for Def. Analyses, 1958; dir. def. rsch. and engrng. Office Sec. Def., 1958-61; chancellor U. Calif.-San Diego, 1961-64, 70-72, prof. physics, 1964—, chmn. dept. physics, 1968-69, dean grad. studies, 1969-70, dir. program on sci., tech. and pub. affairs, 1972-88; dir. Inst. Global Conflict and Cooperation, 1983-88, dir. emeritus, 1988—. Amb. Comprehensive Test Ban Negotiations, 1979-81; trustee Aerospace Corp., Inglewood, Calif., 1961-87; mem. Pres.'s Sci. Adv. Com., 1957-58, 64-68, vice chmn., 1965-67; trustee Inst. def. Analysis, 1963-96; gen. adv. com. ACDA, 1962-69; mem. Def. Sci. Bd., 1977-81; spl. rep. of sec. def. at space arms control talks, 1978-79; mem. coun. nat. labs. Pres. U. Calif., 1991—; mem. task force future nat. labs. Sec. Emergy, 1994-95; cons. Stockholm Internat. Peach Rsch. Inst.; rschr. in application atomic energy to nat. def. problems of arms control and disarmament, elem. particles. Author: Race to Oblivion, 1970, Arms Control, 1973, The Advisors, 1976, Making Weapons, Talking Peace, 1987, Does Strategic Defense Breed Offense?, 1987, (with S. Lakoff) A Shield in the Sky, 1989, Arms and the Physicist, 1994; also numerous articles on arms or disarmament; bd. dirs. Bull. Atomic Scientists. Trustee Bishop's Sch., La Jolla, Calif., 1963-65. Recipient E.O. Lawrence award AEC, 1962, Vannevan Bush award, 2000, Clark Kerr award, 2000, Enrico Fermi award, 2000; Guggenheim fellow, 1972. Fellow AAAS, Am. Phys. Soc. (forum on physics and soc. award 1976, Leo Szilard award 1994), Am. Acad. Arts and Sci.; mem. Fedn. Am. Scientists (chmn. 1970-71, exec. com. 1969-76, 95-2000, pub. svc. award 1992), Pugwash Movement 1969—, Phi Beta Kappa, Sigma Xi. Home: 6110 Camino De La Costa La Jolla CA 92037-6520 Office: U Calif San Diego Mail Code 0518 La Jolla CA 92093 E-mail: hyork@ucsd.edu.

YORK, JAMES MARTIN, judge; b. Abilene, Tex., Feb. 22, 1939; s. James Orville and Hazel Mae (Martin) Y.; m. Sandra L. Zunker, June 5, 1959 (div. 1967); children: Debra Lynn, James Martin Jr.; m. Nora Darlene Buechman, Nov. 3, 1972; 1 child, Victoria Lee. Student, Baylor U., 1957-60, LLB, 1962. Bar: Tex. 1962; bd. cert. in family law and civil trial law, Tex. Pvt. practice, Houston, 1965-94. Sect. editor Baylor Law Rev., 1962. State Rep. primary candidate Rep. Party, Houston, 1970; del.-at-large Rep. State Conv., Houston, 1971; Rep. primary cand. for judge 310th Dist. Ct., 1994; coach Westbury Nat. Little League, Houston, 1967, Voss West Little League, Houston, 1969, 70; apptd. assoc. judge 246th Dist. Ct., 1995, Rep. nominee state dist. judge, 246th Dist. Ct. gen. election, 2002. Named Boss of Yr. Houston Assn. Legal Secs., 1973. Mem. Inwood Forest Golf Club, Houston Bar Assn., State Bar of Tex., Baylor Alumni Assn., Baylor Lettermen's Assn. Baptist. Avocations: golf, swimming, reading. Office: 246th Dist Ct 7th Fl Family Law Ctr 1115 Congress St Houston TX 77002-1927

YORK, JAMES ORISON, real estate executive; b. Brush, Colo., June 27, 1927; s. M. Orison and Marie L. (Kibble) Y.; m. Janice Marie Sjoberg, Aug. 1, 1959; children: Douglas James, Robert Orison. Student, U. Calif. at Berkeley, 1945-46; BA cum laude, U. Wash., 1949. Tchg. fellow U. Wash., Seattle, 1950-52; econ. rsch. analyst Larry Smith & Co. (real estate), Seattle and N.Y.C., 1953-60, ptnr. Seattle, 1960-66, pres. San Francisco, 1966-71; pres., chief exec. officer R.H. Macy Properties, N.Y.C., also sr. v.p. planning and devel., dir. R.H. Macy & Co., Inc., 1971-88; chmn. James York Assocs. (real estate and venture capital), 1988—. Dir. emeritus UBP Properties, Inc.; chmn., N.Y.C. retail div. Am. Cancer Soc. Contbg. author: Shopping Towns-USA, 1960. Trustee ICSC Ednl. and Rsch. Found. With USNR, 1945-47. Recipient Disting. Alumnus award U. Wash., 1989. Fellow Phi Beta Kappa; mem. Am. Soc. Real Estate Counselors, Urban Land Inst., Internat. Real Estate Fedn., Internat. Council Shopping Centers, Lambda Alpha. Clubs: Olympic (San Francisco); American Yacht (Rye, N.Y.); Corinthian Yacht (Seattle); Union League (N.Y.C.); Knights of Malta, Order St. John, Washington Athletic (Seattle), Royal Victoria (B.C.) Yacht. Episcopalian. Home and Office: 4 Riverstone Laguna Niguel CA 92677-5309 also: Sunrise Country Club 6 Malaga Dr Rancho Mirage CA 92270-3820 E-mail: jysail@aol.com.

YORK, JAMES WESLEY, JR. theoretical physicist, educator; b. Raleigh, N.C., July 3, 1939; s. James Wesley and Mary Smedes (Poyner) York; m. Betty Louise Mattern, Aug. 19, 1961 (div. Apr. 2002); children: Virginia York Setzer, Guilford Mattern. BS with high honors in Physics, N.C. State U., Raleigh, 1962, PhD in Physics, 1966. Asst. prof. N.C. State U., Raleigh, 1965-68; rsch. assoc. Princeton (N.J.) U., 1968-69, lectr., 1969-70, asst. prof., 1970-73; assoc. prof. U. N.C., Chapel Hill, 1973-77, prof. dept. physics, 1977-89, Agnew H. Bahnson, Jr. disting. prof. physics, 1989—2001, dir. Inst. Field Physics, 1984-90; vis. asst. prof. U. Md., College Park, 1972; prof. associe U. Paris, 1976; vis. scientist Harvard U., Cambridge, 1977; vis. prof. U. Tex., Austin, 1979, 87; prof. physics Cornell U., 2002—. Spkr. Internat. Symposium on Methods of Differential Geometry in Physics and Mechanics, Warsaw, 1976; Alfred Schild Meml. lectr. U. Tex., 1979; del. Seventh Internat. Congress on Math. Physics, Boulder, Colo., 1983, Tex. Symposium on Relativistic Astrophysics, Jerusalem, 1984, Marcel Grossman Meeting, Rome, 1985, Jerusalem, 97, NATO Advanced Study Inst., Lees Houches, France, 1982, Huelva, Spain, 92, Paris, 92, Banff, Canada, 92, other internat. and nat. meetings; co-organizer sci. meetings including Neutron stars and pulsars, Princeton, 1969; Spacetime dynamics Aspen Ctr. for Theoretical Physics, 1981, Classical Problems in Gravitation, 1990, Cosmic Censorship, 1992; coord. lectr. Inst. Theoretical Physics, U. Calif., Santa Barbara, 2000—; mem. com. of visitors physics divsn NSF, 1991; plenary lectr. Fifth Can. Conf. on Gen. Relativity and Astrophysics, Waterloo, 1993, Directions in Gen. Relativity, College Park, Md., 1993, Pacific Coast Gravity Mtg., Salt Lake City, 1996, 2d Samos meeting, Greece, 1998; hon. physics chmn. Cornelius Lanczos Internat. Centenary, Raleigh, NC, 1993; vis. prof. dept. physics N.C. State U., 1998—99, Inter-Instl. Disting. prof. physics, 2001—02. Mem. editl. bd. Jour. Math. Physics, 1989-92; contbr. chpts. to books, articles to sci. jours. Decorated Companion of St. Patrick, 1960; recipient 3d prize Gravity Rsch. Found. Essay award, 1975; Ford Found. fellow, 1962-65, NSF postdoctoral fellow, 1969-70; Battelle Found. grantee, 1967, Nat. Rsch. Com. France grantee, 1976, NSF grantee, 1974—, travel grantee, 1971, 76, 83, 84; U.S.A.-Israel Binat. Sci. Found. grantee, 1987-90, 90-93, Kenan Found. grantee, 1990, W.N. Reynolds Found. grantee, 1998; recipient Disting. Alumnus award, 1997. Fellow Am. Phys. Soc.; mem. AAAS, Internat. Soc. Gen. Relativity and Gravitation, Sigma Xi, Phi Kappa Phi, Tau Beta Pi, Sigma Pi Sigma, Pi Mu Epsilon, Phi Eta Sigma. Episcopalian. Avocations: literature, music, sports. Office: Cornell U 604 Space Scis Dept Physics Ithaca NY 14853 Business E-Mail: york@astro.cornell.edu.

YORK, JANET BREWSTER, nurse, family and sex therapist, sculptor; b. N.Y.C., Mar. 5, 1941; d. Edward Cox and Janet Stone Brewster; m. Albert Thompson York, Mar. 31, 1962 (dec.); children: Clifton Gaston, Torrance Brewster, 1 adopted child, Justin Brigham. AA with honors, Briarcliff Coll., 1961; RN with highest honors, U. Iowa, 1965; BA summa cum laude, Marymount Manhattan Coll., 1975; MA with honors, NYU, 1978. Nurse Manhattan Eye, Ear and Throat Hosp., N.Y.C., 1966-74; nurse, counselor Washington Free Clinic, 1969-71; family therapist Ackerman Family Inst., N.Y.C., 1976-80; sex therapist N.Y. Med. Coll., Flower Fifth Ave. Hosp., 1976-80; pvt. practice pvt. practice, 1978—. Supervisory staff grad. edn. program in human sexuality N.Y.U. Med. Ctr., 1982-89, sculptor, 1988—, operator Piccadil Kennel, breeder Cavalier King Charles Spaniels and Chinese Cresteds; bd. dirs. Animal Med. Ctr. Represented in permanent collection The Dog Mus. of Am., St. Louis; author: Corneel the Cavalier, Corneel at the Plaza; contbr. articles to profl. jours; author: (videotape) Death as a Part of Life. Named Vita fellow Internat. Coun. Sex Edn. and Parenthood, Am. U., 1981; recipient Evelyn Monte Sculpture award, 1988, 94, Ellsworth Howell Art Sculpture award Pen & Brush Club, 1991, 93, 96, 99, 2000, 02, Dog Fanciers Club, 1999. Mem. Nat. Assn. Women Artists, Am. Medallic Soc., Nantucket Art Assn., Walker Art Ctr., Nat. Sculpture Soc., Am. Kennel Club (art adv. com.), Nat. Mus. Women in Arts, Lawrence Beach Club, Rockaway Hunting Club, Millbrook Club, Progressive Dog Club, L.I. Kennel Club. Home: 155 E 72nd St New York NY 10021-4371 E-mail: Piccadiljy@aol.com.

YORK, KAREN KAY, accountant, farmer; b. Cedar Falls, Iowa, Jan. 30, 1950; d. Richard Arthur and Betty Lenore Wittren; m. Edward Louis York, June 28, 1969; 1 child, David Christian. AAS, McHenry C.C., Crystal Lake, Ill., 1978. Layout artist Black Dot Publ. Co., Crystal Lake, 1972-74; sch. bus. driver Sch. Dists. 47, 155, 1975-83; gen. acct., office mgr. Yornell Tool & Mold, 1976-87; staff acct. Scot Forge Co., Spring Grove, Ill., 1987—. Advisor and ednl. dir. Scot Forge Employee Ownership Coun., 1981—; spkr. in field. Contbr. articles to co. newsletter. Trustee Employee Ownership Found., 1998-99. Named Employee Owner of Yr. Employee Stock Ownership Assn., 1998, Ill. Employee Owner of Yr. Ill. Employee Ownership Assn., 1998. Mem. Nat. Employee Ownership (at-large bd. govs. 1992—). Avocations: raising and training horses, SCUBA diving, gardening, motorcycling. Office: Scot Forge Co 8001 Winn Rd # 8 Spring Grove IL 60081-9687

YORK, MICHAEL (MICHAEL YORK-JOHNSON), actor; b. Fulmer, Eng., Mar. 27, 1942; s. Joseph Gwynne and Florence Edith (Chown) Johnson; m. Patricia McCallum, Mar. 27, 1968. BA with honors in English, Univ. Coll., Oxford U. (Eng.), 1964; DFA (hon.), U. S.C. Created Chevalier de l'ordre Nat. des Arts Et Letter (France) 1995, Created Officer of the Order of the British Empire (OBE),1996. Profl. debut with Dundee Repertory Theatre, Scotland, 1964; mem. Nat. Theatre Co., London, 1965-66; TV film or miniseries appearances include: Much Ado About Nothing, The Forsyte Saga, Rebel in the Grave, True Patriot, Jesus of Nazareth, 1977, A Man Called Intrepid, 1979, The Phantom of the Opera, 1983, The Master of Ballantrae, 1984, Space, 1985, The Far Country, 1985, Are You My Mother, 1986, Ponce de Leon, 1987, Till We Meet Again, 1989, The Road to Avonlea, 1991, Gardens of the World, 1993; The Four Minute Mile, The Lady and the Highway Man, 1988, The Heat of the Day, 1988, The Hunt for Stolen War Treasure, 1989, The Night of the Fox, 1990, The Magic Paintbrush, 1993, David Copperfield's Christmas, 1994, Teklab, 1994, Fall From Grace, 1994, Not of This Earth, 1995, Duel of Hearts, September, 1995, A Young Connecticut Yankee in King Arthur's Court, 1995, A Knight in Camelot, (TV series) Knots Landing, 1987, SeaQuest, 1995, The Naked Truth, 1995, Babylon 5, 1995, The Ring, 1996, Un Coup De Baguette Magique, True Women, 1997, Sliders, 1997, The Magnificat, 1997, the Long way home, 1997, A Christmas Carol, 1997, The Search for Nazi Gold, 1998, The Ripper 1998, Dead Man's Gun, 1998, Perfect Little Angels, 1998, The Haunting of Hell House, 2000, The Lot, 2000; stage appearances include: Any Just Cause, 1967, Hamlet, 1970, Broadway prodns. of Outcry, 1973, Ring Round the Moon, 1975, Bent, 1980, Cyrano de Bergerac, 1981, Whisper in the Mind, 1990, The Crucible, 1991, Someone Who'll Watch Over Me, 1993, Nora, 1993, Ira Gershwin at 100, 1996; appeared in motion pictures including: The Taming of the Shrew, 1966, Accident, 1966, Red and Blue, 1967, Smashing Time, 1967, Romeo and Juliet, 1967, The Strange Affair, 1967, The Guru, 1968, Alfred the Great, 1968, Justine, 1969, Something for Everyone, 1969, Zeppelin, 1970, La Poudre D'Escampette, 1971, Cabaret, 1971, England Made Me, 1971, Lost Horizon, 1972, The Three Musketeers, 1973, Murder on the Orient Express, 1974, Great Expectations, 1974, Conduct Unbecoming, 1974, The Four Musketeers, 1975, Logan's Run, 1976, Seven Nights in Japan, The Last Remake of Beau Geste, 1977, The Island of Dr. Moreau, 1977, Fedora, 1977, The Riddle of the Sands, 1978, Final Assignment, 1980, The White Lions, Success is the Best Revenge, Perfect Little Angels, 1998, , 1984, Dawn, 1985, Vengeance, 1986, The Secret of the Sahara, 1987, Imbalances, 1987, Lethal Obsession, 1987, Midnight Cop, 1988, The Return of the Musketeers, 1989, The Long Shadow, 1991, Eline Vere, 1991, Wide Sargasso Sea, 1991, Rochade, 1991, Discretion Assured, Shadow of a Kiss, 1993, Gospa, 1994, Goodbye America, Austin Powers, Dark Planet, The Treat, 1997, Wrongfully Accused, 1998, One Hell of a Guy, 1998, Lovers and Liars, 1998, The Ghostly Rental, 1999, Austin Powers: The Spy Who Shagged Me, 1999, The Omega Code, 1999, Borstal Boy, 2000, Megiddo, 2001; radio performances The Dark Tower, 1977, (recipient Peabody award), A Matter of Honor, 1986, Babbitt, 1987, The Crucible, 1988, Are You Now, UTZ, 1989, McTeague, 1992, Make and Break, 1993; recs. include: Mere Christianity, 1982, Anna Karenina, 1985, Don Quixote, 1986, The King Must Die, 1988, British Rock: The First Wave, UTZ, 1989, The Modigliani Scandal, 1989, The Mummy, 1989, Candide, 1989, The Vampire Lestat, 1989, The Berlin Stories, 1990, The Remains of the Day, 1990, City of Joy, 1991, Beyond Love, 1991, Memories, Dreams, Reflections, 1991, A Poet's Bible, 1992, Einstein's Dreams, 1993, Accidentally on Purpose, 1993, The English Patient, 1993, Fortune's Favorite, 1993, The Three Musketeers, 1993, Paradise Lost, 1993, The Book of Psalms, 1994, The Book of Virtues, 1994, The Magic Paw-Paw, 1994; contbr. (books) The Courage of Conviction, 1985, Voices of Survival, 1987; author: Accidentally on Purpose, 1992; co-author: A Shakespearean Actor Prepares, 2000; (recordings) The Rubaiyat of Omar Khayyam, 1995, Aesop's Fables, 1995, The Poetry of Edgar Allen Poe, 1995, The Hunting of the Snark, Caesar's Women, 1996, Treasure Island, 1996, (Grammy Nomination) The Wind in the Willows, 1996, Rose, 1996, Daily Word, 1997, Les Miserables, 1998, Caesar, 1998, Brave New World, 1998, Titanic Hearings, 1998, The Fencing Master, 1999 (Audie award), Rikki Tikki Tavi, 1999, King Rat, 1999, Going Home: Jesus and Buddha, 2000, The Lion, The Witch and The Wardrobe, 2000. Chmn. Calif. Youth Theatre. Avocations: travel, music, art. Office: Paul Kohner Agy 9300 Wilshire Blvd Ste 555 Beverly Hills CA 90212

YORK, MICHAEL CHAREST, librarian; b. Newton, Mass., Jan. 2, 1947; s. Richard Francis and Frances Winship (Thibaut) Y.; m. Carol Roberts, June 26, 1982; 1 child, Michael Bradley. BA, U. N.H., 1971; MS, La. State U., 1972; MBA, Plymouth State Coll., 1990. Ref. libr. Ithaca (N.Y.) Coll., 1973-77; asst. dir. libr. Castleton (Vt.) State Coll., 1977-81; libr. dir. Merrimack Valley Coll., Manchester, N.H., 1981-85, U. N.H., Manchester, 1985-91, univ. libr. Durham, 1991-95; libr. dir. Colby-Sawyer Coll., New London, N.H., 1996-98; dir. The Libr. and Archives of N.H. Polit. Tradition, Concord, 1998-99; libr. N.H. State Libr., 1999—. Mem. ALA, New Eng. Libr. Assn. (pres. 1988-89), N.H. Libr. Assn. (pres. 1999—), N.H. State Libr. Adv. Coun. Avocations: sailing, skiing, woodworking. Home: 15 Catamount Rd Goffstown NH 03045-2700 Office: NH State Libr 20 Park St Concord NH 03301-6316 Fax: 603-271-2082. E-mail: myork@finch.nhsl.lib.nh.us.

YORK, RICHARD TRAVIS, art dealer; b. Nashville, Oct. 22, 1950; s. James Samuel and Jeane (Townes) Y. BA, Vanderbilt U., 1972. Dir. Am. art Hammer Galleries, N.Y.C., 1974-76; in charge Am. dept. M. Knoedler & Co., 1976-77; assoc. Hirschl & Adler Galleries, 1977-81; dir., owner Richard York Gallery, 1981—. Mem. adv. bd. Nat. Acad. Design, N.Y.C. Author: (exhbn. catalogs) American Folk Art, 1977, The Eye of Steiglitz, 1978 (Arlis award), Buildings Architecture in American Modernism, 1980, Ellen Day Hale, 1981 (Arlis award), The Natural Image: Plant Forms in American Modernism, 1982, An American Gallery, 1986, vols. I & II, 1987, III & IV, 1988, V, 1989, VI, 1990, VII, 1992, VIII, 1997, Charles G. Shaw: Abstractions of the Thirties, 1987, Will Henry Stevens: A Modernist's Response to Nature, 1987, Joseph Stella: The Tropics, 1988, Joseph Goldyne: Twenty Years of Work, 1992, American Paintings from the Collection of James H. Ricau, 1993, Modernism at the Salons of America, 1922-1936, 1995, California: One-hundred Forty Years of Art Produced in the State, 1996, Passion and Reverence—Joseph Stella and Nature, 1998, John Marin: The 291 Years, 1998, John Marin, The Painted Frame, 2000, Lockwood de Forest: Plein-Air Oil Sketches, 2001, Movement: Marin, 2001, Paintings by Walter Beck, 2002, John Graham's Renaissance and Revolution, 2002, No Record So True: The Wildflower Photographs of Edwin Hale Lincoln (1848-1938), 2002. Mem. art adv. com. Colby Coll., 1990-94; mem. art adv. panel IRS, 1991-97; mem. steering com. Direct Effect for AIDS Rsch., Rockefeller U., 1997—; mem. am. fellows Whitney Mus. Am. Art, N.Y.C.; mem. dirs. cir. Nat. Gallery Art, Washington, 2002—. Mem.: William Cullen Bryant Fellows, Pa. Acad. Art (adv. com. 1998—), Art Dealers Assn. Am. (bd. dirs. 1992—95, v.p. 1997—2000, art show com. 1997—2001, chmn.

membership com. 1998—2001), Nat. Arts Club, Met. Mus. of Art N.Y.C., Lotos Club (art com. 2000—), Ky. Cols. Office: Richard York Gallery 21 E 65th St New York NY 10021-6524 Business E-Mail: richard@ryorkgal.com.

YORK, STAR LIANA, sculptor; b. Washington, Apr. 14, 1952; d. Robert Erastus and Adele York Northam; m. Rodney James Barker. Student, Prince Georges C.C.; BFA, U. Md.; postgrad., Balt. Inst. Art. Tchr., artist in residence CETA Program, Md., 1974-76. Subject of book and mags. articles; exhibited in group shows at Prince Georges Com Coll., 1970-72, U. of Md., 1972-74, Balt. Inst. Art, 1975, Artist in Residence at Prince Georges Com Coll, CETA, Medicine Man Gallery: Leading The West, 1997, Southwest Art Mag. traveling exhibit of all mag. cover artist, 1998; one person show at Gilcrease Mus., Tulsa, Okla., 1998; group mus. shows at Tuscon Fine Art, 1991, 92, 93, 94, Beninington Fie Art, Vermont, 1997, Wildlite Fine Art, Jackson, Wyo., 1997, Albuquerque Fine Art, N.M., 1992; AWA group shows at Total Arts Gallery, Taos, N.M., 1999, Trailside Gallery, Scottsdale, Ariz., 1998; one and two person shows at Zaplin Lampert, Sante Fe, N.M. 1994, 95, 98, 99, Dewey Gallery, Sante Fe, 1992, 93, Meyer Gallery, Scottsdale, Ariz., 1992, 93, Mountain Trails Gallery, Jackson, Wyo., 1997, Shriver Gallery, Taos, N.M., 1983, 84, 85, 86, 87, 88, 89, 90, 91, 92, 93, 94, 95, 96, 97, 98, 99, Pendragon Gallery, Annapolis, Md., 1980, 81, 82, 83, Squashblossom Gallery, Aspen, Colo., 1984, 85, 86, 87, 88, Coggswell Gallery, Vail, Colo., 1986, 87, 88, Dakota Gallery, Boca Raton, Fla., 1985, 86, 87, 88, 89, 90, Ton Atim Gallery, Durango, Colo., 1992, 94, 96, 98, Silverado Skies Gallery, Miami, 1989, 1990, Christi Lee Gallery, Basalt, Colo., 1997, Hawthorn Gallery, Branson, Mo., 1990. Recipient first place Lance Internat. award Nat. Sculpture Soc., N.Y.C., 1978-80, first place sculpture Catherine Lorillard Soc., N.Y.C. Mem. Am. Women Artists Assn. (chairperson 1996—), Am. Polocrosse Assn., Am. Quarter Horse Assn. Avocation: polocrosse. Home: 533 Onate Pl Santa Fe NM 87501-3676 Office: Am Women Artists 533 Onate Pl Santa Fe NM 87501-3676

YORK, THEODORE ROBERT, retired consulting company executive; b. Mitchel Field, N.Y., May 4, 1926; s. Theodore and Helen (Zierak) Y.; m. Clara Kiefer, Jan. 3, 1952; children: Theodore R. II, Sharon L., Scott K., Krista A. Miller. BS, U.S. Mil. Acad., 1950; MBA, George Washington U., 1964; MPA, Nat. U., 1984. Commd. 2d lt. USAF, 1950, advanced through grades to col., 1970, ret., 1974; pres. T. R. York Cons., Fairfax, Va., 1974-79, T. R. Cons., San Diego, 1979-85; dir. Software Productivity Consortium, Herndon, Va., 1985-90; pres. ULTRAPLECS Intelligent Bldgs., Sandy, Utah, 1991—2002, ret., 2002. Mem. Loudoun County Rep. Com., Leesburg, Va., 1990-91. Decorated DFC, Air medal (5), Meritorius Svc. medal, Joint Svcs. Commendation medal, Air Force Commendation medal (5). Mem. Internat. Facilities Mgmt. Assn., Intelligent Bldgs. Inst. (advisor), Instituto Mexicana Del Edificios Intelegente (hon.), Office Planners and Users Group, Shriners, Masons. Avocations: computers, electronics. Office: ULTRAPLECS Intelligent Bldg 12189 Bluff View Dr Sandy UT 84092-5922 E-mail: tedusma50@hotmail.com. *Success is measured in terms of help from others. I believe in building a team to manage any project. Always use the word "we" and forget the word "I" when addressing a successful project and loyalty will follow.*

YORK, TINA, painter; b. Germany, Feb. 9, 1951; Student, Sch. Mus. Fine Arts, Boston, 1967-71; studied with, George Dergalis, Wayland, Mass., 1967-75; BA cum laude, Brandeis U., 1978; postgrad., N.Y. Med. Coll., 1980-83. Contbr. of works to numerous publications, 1987-99, 2000. Solo Show: L.A. Mus. of Arts, 2002, solo exhbns. include Gallery of Contemporary Art, Provincetown, Mass., 1969, Springfield (Mass.) Art Assn., 1971, Copley Soc., Boston, 1972, 73, Boston U., 1974, Mendler Gallery, Rockport, Mass., 1974, Cambridge (Mass.) Art Assn., 1975, Ames Gallery, N.Y.C., 1976, Gallery Seven, Boston, 1977, Brandeis U., Waltham, Mass., 1978, Rue Oker Gallery of Art, Sturbridge, Mass., 1979, Art Collectors Gallery, N.Y.C., 1981, 153 Gallery, Inc., N.Y.C., 1982, Creative Concepts, L.A., 1984, Alpha Contemporary Exhibits, L.A., 1985, Darraby Gallery, L.A., 1986, 8th St. Gallery, L.A., 1986, Koplin Gallery, L.A., 1987, Galerie Beverly Hills, Calif., 1988, Convention Ctr., Rome, 1988, Merck, Sharpe & Dohme, Rahway, N.J., 1988, Erlgangen Kultur Borse, Germany, 1989, Arwell Gallery, Laguna, Calif., 1989, Deutsch-Amerikanisches Inst., Regensburg, Germany, 1990, Art in Pub. Bldgs., Nuremberg, Germany, 1990, Art Expo, N.Y.C., 1990, Amerikahaus, Nuremberg, 1990, Art 5, Nuremberg, 1990, Dresdner Bank, Nuremberg, 1990, Amer. Hosp. Assn., Wash. DC, 1990, South. Med. Assn., Nashville, 1990, 94, 95, Studio Gallery, North Hollywood, Calif., 1991, 92, Galerie Lehman, Germany, Galerie Sud, Studio la Citta, Italy, Studio gall., Calif., 1991 La Foire Internat d'Art Contemporain, Paris, 1992, 94, Med. Heritage Gall., Waco, Tex., 1991, Herbstmesse, Frankfurt, Germany, 1992, 93, Kunstforum Internat., Aachen, Germany, 1993, Kunstlerhaus, Germany, 1993, Ambiente, Frankfurt, 1993, 94, 95, 96, 97, 98, 2000, ART/LA, Los Angeles, Calif., 1993, 94, 95, Internatl. Art Fair, Czech, 1993, 94, 95, 96, 97, 98, 99, 2000, Art Fair, Seattle, 1993, 94, Art Expo, Chicago, 1993, 94, Frankfurter Buchmesse, Frankfurt, Germany, 1993, Art Expo, New York, 1993, 94, 95, 96, Chicago Trade Show, Chicago, 1993, 95, 97, Toronto Trade Show, Toronto, 1993, Art Cologne, Cologne, Germany, 1993, 94, 96, Centre d'Art Contemporain, Switzerland, Dresdner Bank, Germany, Galerie Littmann, Switzerland, Galerie Fischer, 1994 Art Asia, Hong Kong, 1994, 95, 96, Art Expo, Calif., 1994, 96, PPFA Toronto Trade Show, 1994, 95, Limited Edit. Expo, New Orleans, 1994, 95, Frankfurt Book Fair, Frankfurt, Germany, 1994, 97, 98, 2000, Internat. Spring Fair, Birmingham, Eng., 1994, 95, Art Miami, Miami Fla., 1994, 95, Exposition of Art, Sydney, Australia, 1993, Art Taipei, Taipei, Taiwan, 1993, 94, 95, Art Santa Fe, Santa Fe, New Mex., 1993, 94, 95, NASA Ames Rsch. Ctr., Moffett Field, Calif., 1994, NASA Johnson Space Ctr., Houston, 1995, Galerie Rudelko, Germany, Scheffler Galerie, Germany, 1995, Studio Gall., Ariz., 1996, Jahns House, Germany, 1996, Internatl. Contemporary Art Fair, Madrid, Spain, 1995, West Valley Mus. Art, Pheonix, 1998; represented in permanent collections, St. Joseph Galleries, Las Vegas, Nev., Rio Decar, Mus. of Art, Las Vegas, Downey (Calif.) Mus. Art, Mus. Fine Arts, Salt Lake City, Mcpl. Art Mus., Osaka, Japan, Regional Mus. Art, Bautzen, Germany, Carter Ctr., Atlanta, Kennedy Space Ctr., Fla., New Zealand Space Adminstrn., Auckland, New Zealand, NASA (Natl. Aeronautics and Space Admin.), Internatl. Peace Acad., NY, US Information Agency, BBC (Brit. Broadcasting Co.), Lagan Jute, Ltd., India, Natl. Inst of Hlth., Maryland, Universitet Kliment Orchridski, Bulgaria, Hiatt Internatl., Bev. Hills, Calif., Paris, Gall. Dmovrosek, Yugoslavia, Colombia Univ., NY, Natl. Cancer Inst., Maryland, Kulturamt der Stadt Nurnberg, Germany, Planetary Soc., Calif., Mayo Clin., Ariz.; represented on Artrain USA a show that travels through the entire U.S. for 5 yrs. Hon. mention: mixed media painting, Waltham Art League, Waltham, MA, 1969; first prize: painting, Arts Fest., Scituate, MA, 1969; hon. mention: works on paper, Springfield Art Assn., Springfield, MA, 1970; first prize: painting, Internatl. Show, Fall River, MA, 1971; third prize, mixed media painting, De Cordova Mus., Lincoln, MA, 1972; second prize, painting, Amer. Artists in Paris, Paris, 1975; first prize, mixed media painting, Inst. of Contemporary Art, 1979; gold medal, Painting, Spring Arts Fest., Los Angeles, CA, 1985; first prize, mixed media painting, One Fifty Three Gall., Inc., 1987. Studio: Tina York Studio 7750 Abalone Bay St Las Vegas NV 89139

YORK, VERMELLE CARDWELL, real estate broker and developer; b. Evergreen, Ala., Jan. 30, 1925; d. Frederick Lofton and Emmie Mildred (Pitts) Cardwell; m. E. Travis York, Jr., Dec. 26, 1946; children: Lisa, Travis. BS, Auburn U., 1946. Pres. Tralisa Corp., Gainesville, Fla., 1966-87, sec., treas., 1988-94, Caret Corp., Gainesville, 1979-86, pres., 1987—. Mem. devel. com. Harn Mus., Gainesville, Fla., 1990-96, Hospice House, Gainesville, 1992-96; co-chair March of Dimes, Gainesville, 1995, Red Ribbon Campaign, 1989, 90; bd. dirs. Keep Alachua County Beautiful. Recipient President's Medallion, U. Fla., 1980; named Woman of Distinction Santa Fe C. C., 1988. Mem. Gainesville Builders Assn. (bd. dirs. 1997—), The Heritage Club (mem. amb. com. 1991-96), P.E.O. (pres. 1989-90), Surfside N. Club, (dir. 1988-91), Gainesville Women's Forum (membership chair 1994-96), Altrusa, Rotary, DAR, Phi Kappa Phi. Avocations: genealogy. Office: Caret Corp 4020 SW 78th St Gainesville FL 32608-3608

YORK, WALTER ALLEN, cinematographer; b. Knoxville, Tenn., Aug. 7, 1938; s. James Claude and Mary Louise (Sherrill) Y.; m. Victoria Ann Mix, June 1967 (div.); 1 child, Shannon Michelle; m. Bettye June Kiser, Dec. 27, 1986 (div. Nov. 2000). AA, Hiwassee Coll., 1959; BFA, Art Ctr. Coll. of Design, Pasadena, Calif., 1982; cert. level II film, TV and new media, UCLA, 1998. Freelance cinematographer, L.A., 1971—. V.p. Internet Broadcasting Network, sr. v.p., 2000, pres., CEO, 2001; instr. film prodn. 1 Watkins Coll. Art and Design, 2001-02. Mentor Pasadena City Schs., 1994—; judge Nat. CableAce Awards, 1993-96; feature film judge Nashville Ind. Film Festival, 2000. With USAF, 1960-61. Mem. Internat. Alliance Theatrical and Stage Employees (locals 600 and 728), Am. Soc. Lighting Designers, Soc. Operating Cameramen (assoc.), Siggraph, UCLA Alumni Assn. (life), Sigma Phi Epsilon (life).

YORKE, HAROLD W. astrophysicist; b. Riverside, Calif., Aug. 24, 1948; s. Harold W. and Wilda Mercedes (Bender) Y.; m. Ruth Barbara Rossbach, Nov. 7, 1969; children: Colleen Olivia, Vanessa Alexandra. BS, UCLA, 1970; Dipl. phys., U. Goettingen, Germany, 1972, Dr. rer. nat., 1974, Dr. habil., 1979. Rsch. asst. Calif. Inst. Tech., Pasadena, 1970-71; fellow, Fulbright scholar U. Goettingen, 1971-73, sci. asst., 1973-75; staff scientist Max Planck Inst. for Astrophysics, Munich, 1975-78; tenured scientist U. Goettingen, 1978-88; prof. Wuerzburg (Germany) U., 1988-98; sr. rsch. scientist Jet Propulsion Lab., Calif. Inst. Tech., Pasadena, 1998—, JPL lead scientist for astrophysics, 2000—; project scientist Herschel Space Obs., 2001—. Co-author: Radiation in Moving Gaseous Media, 1988; contbr. articles to Astronomy & Astrophysics, Astrophysical Jour. Regents' scholar U. Calif., 1966, Fulbright scholar, 1971, Fulbright fellow, 1972, NSF fellow Calif. Inst. Tech., 1970. Mem. Internat. Astron. Union, Am. Astron. Soc., Astronomische Gesellschaft, Phi Beta Kappa. Office: Jet Propulsion Lab MS 169-506 4800 Oak Grove Dr Pasadena CA 91109-8099 E-mail: Harold.Yorke@jpl.nasa.gov.

YORKE, JAMES ALAN, chaos mathematician; b. Plainfield, N.J., Aug. 3, 1941; married; three children. AB in Math., Columbia U., 1963; PhD in Math., U. Md., 1966. Cmem. faculty U. Md., College Park, 1963—, prof., 1973—, dir. Inst. for Phys. Sci. and Tech. 1College Park, 0985—2001. Guggenheim fellow, 1980—81. Mem.: AAAS, Soc. Indsl. and Applied Math., Math. Assn. Am., Am. Phys. Soc., Am. Math. Soc. Office: U Md Inst For Phys Sci And Tech College Park MD 20742-2431

YORSZ, STANLEY, lawyer; b. Norwich, Conn., June 5, 1953; s. Stanley and Helen (Chimilewski) Y.; m. Margaret A. McLean, June 14, 1986. BA, Colgate U., 1975; JD, Dickinson U., 1978. Bar: Pa. 1978, U.S. Dist. Ct. (we. dist.) Pa. 1978, U.S. Ct. Appeals (3d cir.) 1980, U.S. Supreme Ct. 1980. Law clk. to judge Pa. Superior Ct., Pitts., 1978-80; assoc. Buchanan Ingersoll P.C., 1980-86, ptnr., 1986—. Editor comments Dickinson Law Rev., 1978. Mem. ABA, Allegheny County Bar Assn., Pa. Bar Assn., Rivers Club. Roman Catholic. Avocations: tennis, squash, golf. Office: Buchanan Ingersoll PC 1 Oxford Ct Pittsburgh PA 15219-1407 E-mail: yorszs@bipc.com.

YORUK, EYUP SELAHATTIN, small business owner; b. Istanbul, Turkey, Feb. 20, 1928; s. Mustafa and Serife (Hamzabeyoglu) Y.; m. Emine Aysan Belen, May 3, 1962; children: Suleyman, Mustafa, Muzaffer, Kadir. Acct. Vittol Co., Istanbul, 1946-49; exec. Ismail Akgun Printing Co., 1950-58; exec. ptnr. Nur Printing Co., 1958-63; owner, exec. Yoruk Printing Co., 1963—. Expert Min. Justice, Istanbul, 1963—. Editor: History of Turkish Pharmacy, 1968, Hitler's Death, 1969, Love and Truth, 1968, Galata Tower, 1969, others. 2d lt. Turkish army, 1949-50. Mem. Istanbul C. of C., Istanbul Erkek Lisesi Alumni Orgn. Avocations: antiques, coins, stamps. Home: Etiler Camlik Mevkii 16/5 80630 Istanbul Turkey Office: Yörük Matbaasi Bağimisiz Sk 7 4 Levent Istanbul Turkey

YOSELOFF, JULIEN DAVID, publishing company executive; b. N.Y.C., June 25, 1941; s. Thomas and Sara (Rothfuss) Y.; m. Darlene Starr Carbone, Aug. 6, 1967; children— Michael Ian, Anthony Alexander. BA, U. Pa., 1962; student, London Sch. Econs., 1962-63; MA, Rutgers U., 1994. With A.S. Barnes and Co., Inc., Cranbury, N.J., 1963-80; dir. Associated Univ. Presses, Inc., 1966—; pres. Rosemont Pub. and Printing Corp., 1985—. Served with AUS, 1964. Mem. Phi Beta Kappa Assocs., Phi Beta Kappa, Pi Sigma Alpha. Avocations: amateur radio, photography, biking. Office: 2010 Eastpark Blvd Cranbury NJ 08512-3518

YOSELOFF, THOMAS, publisher; b. Sioux City, Iowa, Sept. 8, 1913; s. Morris and Sarah (Rabinowitz) Y.; m. Sara Rothfuss, Apr. 30, 1938; children: Julien David, Mark Laurence; m. Lauretta Sellitti, Apr. 23, 1964; 1 dau., Tamar Rachel. AB, U. Iowa, 1934; Litt.D. (hon.), Bucknell U., 1982; L.H.D. (hon.), Fairleigh Dickinson U., 1982. Chmn. Rosemont Pub. & Printing Corp., 1969—, Associated Univ. Presses, 1969—, Golden Cockerel Press, London, 1969—. Author: A Fellow of Infinite Jest, 1946, (with Lillian Stuckey) Merry Adventures of Till Eulenspiegel, 1944, Further Adventures of Till Eulenspiegel, pub. 1957, The Time of My Life, 1979; Editor: Seven Poets in Search of an Answer, 1944, Voyage to America, 1961, Comic Almanac, 1963, The Man from the Mercury, 1986. Pres. Center for War/Peace Studies, 1977-91. Recipient award of merit Bucknell U., 1975, award of merit U. Del., 1987. Mem. Phi Beta Kappa, Sigma Delta Chi, Delta Sigma Rho. Home: Unit 413 2325 Windmill Pkwy Apt 413 Henderson NV 89074-5436 Office: 440 Forsgate Dr Cranbury NJ 08512-3518

YOSHIDA, AKIRA, biochemist; b. Okayama, Japan, May 10, 1924; came to U.S., 1961; s. Isao and Etsu (Kagawa) Y.; m. Michiko Suzuki, Nov. 10, 1954; 1 child, Emmy. MSc, U. Tokyo, 1947, DSc, 1954. Assoc. prof. U. Tokyo, 1952-60; sr. rsch. fellow U. pa., Phila., 1960-63; rsch. scientist NIH, Bethesda, Md., 1963-65; rsch. prof. U. Wash., Seattle, 1965-72; dir. dept. biochem. genetics City of Home Med. Ctr., Duarte, Calif., 1972—98, emeritus prof., 1998—. Contbr. more than 300 articles to profl. jours. Scholar Rockefeller Found., 1955-56; recipient Merit award jfapanese Soc. Human Genetics, 1980, Achievement award City of Hope, 1981, Merit Grant award NIH, 1988. Mem. AAAS, Am. Soc. Biol. chemists, Am. Soc. Human Genetics (assoc. editor), Am. Soc. Hematology, N.Y. Acad. Scis. Home: 2140 Pinecrest Dr Altadena CA 91001-2121 Office: City of Hope Beckman Inst 1450 Duarte Rd Duarte CA 91010-3011 Home Fax: 626-791-7065. E-mail: ma3024@earthlink.net.

YOSHIDA, HIROYUKI, mathematician, educator, computer scientist, educator, medical science educator; b. Yokote, Akita, Japan, Mar. 16, 1961; s. Tadashi Yoshida; m. Shinobu Muto. PhD , U. of Tokyo, 1989. Asst. prof. Tokyo Inst. of Polytechnics, Atsugi, Japan, 1989—93; from vis. rsch. assoc. to asst. prof. The U. of Chgo., Chgo., 1993—97, asst. prof., 1997—. Author: Windows Magic, 1992, The Best Guide to NeXT Computers, 1992; editor: Introduction to the BASIC Programming Language, 1992, Essential LAN Terminology 100, 1993, The Best Guide to the World Wide Web, 1996, Essential Network Terminology 100, 1997, The Internet Dictionary, 1997; contbr. chapters to books, articles to profl. jours. Recipient Cum Laude award Edn. Exhibit, Radiol. Soc. of N.Am., 2000; grantee, Whitaker Found., 1995, Lewis Block Fund grant, The U. of Chgo., 1999, Am. Cancer Soc., 2000, NIH, 2000, Cancer Rsch. Found. of Am., 2001, Nat. Cancer Inst., 2002, Dept. Def., 2002. Mem.: IEEE, Inst. Electronics, Info. and Comm. Engrs., Info. Processing Soc. Japan, Internat. Soc.Optical Engring., Am. Assn. Physicists Medicine. Home: 5140 S Greenwood Ave 2 Chicago IL 60615 Office: U of Chicago Dept Radiology 5841 S Maryland Ave MC2026 Chicago IL 60637 Office Fax: 773-702-0371. Business E-Mail: yoshida@uchicago.edu.

YOSHIDA, LISA M.T. accountant; b. L.A., Aug. 25, 1969; d. Ralph Masaru and Lenette Dorothy Toma; 1 child, Logan Jacintho. BBA in Acctg., U. Hawaii, 1991, M Acctg., 1995. CPA, Hawaii. Mgr. KPMG Peat Marwick LLP, Honolulu, 1992-96, 97-98, Richard C. Drayson, CPA, Inc., Wailuku, Hawaii, 1998-99; asst. contr. Sheraton Maui, Lahaina, 1996-97; ptnr. Toma & Drayson, CPA's, LLP, Wailuku, 1999—. Mem.: AICPA, Hawaii Assn. Pub. Accts., Hawaii Soc. CPAs, Rotary (bull. editor Wailuku 1999, treas. 2000—01). Avocation: travel. Office: Toma & Drayson CPA's LLP 2241 W Vineyard St Wailuku HI 96793-1621

YOSHIDA, TAKASHI, historian, researcher; b. Maebashi, Gunma, Japan, Oct. 28, 1963; BA in Pvt. Law, Aoyama Gakuin U., 1988; BA in Polit. Sci., U. Ill., 1989; M in Internat. Affairs, Columbia U., 1992, MA in History, 1996, MPhil, 1998, PhD in History, 2001; advanced cert., CU East Asian Inst., 1997. Rsch. asst. Columbia U., N.Y.C., 1995-98, jr. fellow in Japan Studies, East Asian Inst., 2000-01; lectr. modern Japanese history Yale U., New Haven, 2001—02; asst. prof. modern Japanese history Western Mich. U., 2002—. Vis. scholar Hitosubashi U., 1998-99; adj. prof. Marymount Manhattan U., N.Y., 1995-98, Pace U., N.Y., 1998; lectr. modern Japanese history Yale U., 2001—. Contbr. articles to profl. jours.; author: The Nanjing Massacre in Japan in The Nanjing Massacre in History and Historiography, 2000. Fulbright-Hays DDRA fellow, 1998-99; Toyota Found. Rsch. grantee, 1999-2000. Mem. Am. Hist. Assn., Assn. for Asian Studies, Ctr. for Rsch. and Documentation of Japan's War Responsibility. Home: 81 Hubinger St 3d fl New Haven CT 06511 E-mail: ty44A@Columbia.edu.

YOSHIKAWA, CARY YUJI, physicist, software engineer; b. Honolulu, Mar. 16, 1963; s. Sueo and Mary Sumiko (Iwahara) Y.; m. Colleen (Choy), Feb. 13, 1993; 1 child, Emily Kiana. BSEE, U. Hawaii, 1987, MS in Physics, 1990, PhD in Physics, 1996. Rsch. asst. U. Hawaii, Honolulu, 1990-96; tech. staff mem. Lucent Technologies (Bell Labs.), Naperville, Ill., 1996—. Contbr. articles to Phys. Rev. Letters, Phys. Rev. D, Nuclear Instruments & Methods, Phys. Letters B. Achievements include devel. of transverse energy top quark mass analysis yielding smallest systematic error in the world at time of PhD completion; prin. devel. of optimization technique leading to top quark discovery by Dzero collaboration. Home: 1024 Asbury Dr Aurora IL 60504-9024 Office: Lucent Technologies 2000 N Naperville Rd Naperville IL 60563-1443

YOSHIKI-KOVINICK, MARIAN TSUGIE, author; b. L.A., Feb. 17, 1941; d. Eddie Junichi and Teruko Ruth (Kawamoto) Yoshiki; m. Philip Peter Kovinick, June 17, 1973. BA, U. So. Calif., 1963; MA, Azusa Pacific U., 1980. Tchr. Pasadena (Calif.) Unified Sch. Dist., 1964-66, Centinela Valley Union H.S. Dist., Lawndale, Calif., 1966-83; freelance writer, rschr. L.A., 1983—; archivist Archives of Am. Art Smithsonian Instn., 1996—. Rsch. supr. NEH project Calif. Asian Am. Artists Biog. Survey, 1999—, Huntington Libr. Reader, The Getty Rsch. Inst. Extended Reader. Rschr., cons. for various exhbns., including The Woman Artist in the American West, 1976, California Light, 1990, rschr. for books Elsie Palmer Payne, 1990, Guy Rose, American Impressionist, 1995, American Scene Painting, 1991, In Living Color: The Art of Hideo Date, 2001; co-author: An Encyclopedia of Women Artists of the American West, 1998, Publications in Southern California Art, vol. 6, 1999; contbg. author Grove's Ency. of American Art Before 1914, 1999, Southwest Art, 1998. Recipient Western Heritage award, 1999. Mem. Huntington Corral of Westerners, Art Librs. Soc. Democrat. Avocations: calligraphy, crocheting, needlepoint, gardening, photography. Home and Office: 4735 Don Ricardo Dr Los Angeles CA 90008-2812

YOSHIMURA, VALERIE NAO, educator, cultural organization administrator; b. Aug. 13, 1968; BA in French and Sociology, U. Calif., Santa Barbara, 1990; MA in French Lit., U. Mich., 1994, PhD in French Lit., 2000. Pres. Japanese Am. Citizens League, Detroit, 1994-98. E-mail: VYoshimura@beld.net.

YOSHIOKA, MARIANNE RUTH MIDORI, social worker, educator; b. Oakville, Ont., Can., Oct. 15, 1960; d. John Michio and Josie Teresa Yoshioka; m. Ernst Oliver VanBergeijk, June 1, 2002; children: Charlie Turner, Kees VanBergeijk, Sam Turner. BA, U. Western Ont., 1982; MSW, U. Mich., 1986; PhD, Fla. State U., 1995. Social worker U. Mich., Ann Arbor, 1987—90; therapist Fla. State U. Marriage and Family Clinic, Tallahassee, 1991—92; chair, exec. bd. dirs. Asians and Pacific Islanders Coalition on HIV/AIDS, N.Y.C.; assoc. prof. Columbia U. Sch. Social Work, 1995—. Cons. Sarah Burke Ho., Sanctuary for Families Domestic Violence Agy., N.Y.C., 1996—98, The N.Y. Asian Women's Ctr., N.Y.C., 1998—, The Asian Task Force Against Domestic Violence, Boston, 1998—, Devel. Svc. Group, Office of Minority Health, Washington, 1998, Chinatown Svc. Ctr., L.A., 1998—2001. Contbr. articles to profl. jours.; mem. editl. bd.: Rsch. on Social Work Practice, 1997—2000, mem. editl. bd.: Jour. Immigrant and Refugee Svcs., 2000—, mem. editl. bd.: Social Work jour., 2001—. Recipient Dissertation award, 8th Nat. Symposium on Doctoral Rsch. in Social Work, 1995; fellow Mental Health Leadership, Okura Found., 1998; grantee, NIDDK, 1996—2000, NIMH, 1997—99, Lois and Samuel Silberman Fund, 1998—99, Ctr. for Study of Social Work Practice, 2001—02. Mem.: NASW, Coun. on Social Work Edn. (Minority Rsch. Dissertation grantee 1993, 1995, grantee 1996—98). Office: Columbia U Sch Social Work 622 W 113th St New York NY 10025-4600

YOSHIUCHI, ELLEN HAVEN, childbirth educator; b. Newark, Apr. 15, 1949; d. Michael Joseph and Adeline V. (Lindblom) Haven; m. Takeshi Yoshiuchi, Dec. 1, 1973; children: Teri Takumi, Niki Noboru. BA summa cum laude, CUNY, 1980; M Profl. Studies in Human Rels., N.Y. Inst. Tech., 1991. Cert. bereavement svcs. counselor. Pvt. practice childbirth edn., 1983-89; program asst. parent/family edn. St. Luke's/Roosevelt Hosp. Ctr., N.Y.C., 1989-93, mem. faculty parent/family edn. program, 1990—; mem. faculty Family Ctr. at Riverdale Neighborhood House, Bronx, N.Y., 1991-96; faculty mem. The Greater N.Y. March of Dimes, N.Y.C., 1996—; mgr. patient svcs. N.Y.C. chpt. The Leukemia & Lymphoma Soc., 1998—. Mem. perinatal bereavement com. St. Luke's/Roosevelt Hosp. Ctr., N.Y.C., 1989-95. Editor ASPO/N.Y.C. News, 1983-86; contbr. articles to profl. jours. Bd. trustees Pan Asian Repertory Theatre, N.Y.C., 1996-2001. Fellow: Am. Coll. Childbirth Educators; mem.: ACA, Lamaze Internat. (cert. tchr., pres. N.Y.C. chpt. 1987—91, nominating com. 1991—93, dir. ednl. program 1991—93), Assn. for Specialists in Group Work, N.Y. State Perinatal Assn. Office: 475 Park Ave S New York NY 10016-6901

YOSHIZUMI, DONALD TETSURO, dentist; b. Honolulu, Feb. 18, 1930; s. Richard Kiyoshi and Hatsue (Tanouye) Y.; BS, U. Hawaii, 1952; DDS, U. Mo., 1960, grad. cert. prosthodontics, 1962, MS, 1963; m. Barbara Fujiko Iwashita, June 25, 1955 (dec. Feb. 1998); children: Beth Ann E., Cara Leigh S., Erin Yuri. Clin. instr. U. Mo. Sch. Dentistry, Kansas City, 1960-63; pvt. practice, Santa Clara, Calif., 1963-70, San Jose, Calif., 1970—. With USAF, 1952-56. Mem. Am. Dental Assn., Calif. Dental Assn., Santa Clara County Dental Soc., Omicron Kappa Upsilon, Delta Sigma Delta. Contbr. articles to profl. jours. Home: 5054 Parkfield Ave San Jose CA 95129-3225 Office: 2011 Forest Ave San Jose CA 95128-4813

YOSHIZUMI, TERRY TAKATOSHI, medical physicist; b. Osaka, Japan, July 2, 1949; came to U.S., 1975; s. Akira and Fumie Yoshizumi; m. Rebecca P. Peterson; 1 child, Alexander J. BS, Ehime U., Japan, 1973; MS, UCLA, 1975, U. Cin., 1977, PhD, 1980. Rsch. fellow Sloan-Kettering Inst., N.Y.C., 1980-81; chief radiation safety officer Bklyn. Hosp., 1981-82; instr. U. Cin., 1982-83; asst. prof. W.Va. U., Morgantown, 1983-87; physicist Howard U. Hosp., Washington, 1987-90; radiation safety officer Va. Conn. Health Care Sys., 1990—; assoc. rsch. scientist Yale U. Sch. Medicine, New Haven, 1991-96, lectr., 1996-97; asst. prof. radiology, dir. radiation safety Duke U., Durham, N.C., 1997—, radiation safety officer. Author: (with others) Physics of Nuc. Medicine, 1984; contbr. articles to profl. jours. including Physics Medicine and Biology, Jour. of Nuc. Medicine, Nuc. Med. Biology, Health Physics, Radiology, KSO Mag., Radiology, Operational Health Physics. Sloan-Kettering Ins./Cornell Grad. Sch. Med. Scis. postdoctoral fellow, 1980-81, Soc. Nuc. Medicine student rsch. fellow, 1980; U. Cin. scholar, 1975-80. Mem. Am. Coll. Radiology, Health Physics Soc., Am. Assn. of Physicists in Medicine. Office: Duke U Med Ctr PO Box 3155 Durham NC 27710-0001

YOSKIN, JON WILLIAM, II, insurance company executive; b. Phila., Oct. 16, 1939; s. Lewis William and Louise (Houck) Y.; m. Dorothea James, Sept. 25, 1961 (div. Mar. 1992); children: Nicholas, Dorothea, Maurice P.; m. Elizabeth Anne Groves, Sept 26, 1992. Pvt. practice, Phila., 1959-74; sr. v.p. Mid. Atlantic Gen. Investment Co., 1974-80; exec. v.p. Transatlantic Life Assurance Co., 1980-85, Meritor Life Ins. Co., Phila., 1985-88; owner, CEO Tri-Arc Fin. Svcs., 1988—; chmn., CEO Magellan Ins. Co. Ltd., Bermuda, Tri-Arc Fin. Svcs. Ltd., Life Re (Holdings), Ltd. Bd. dirs. Concerto Soloist, Phila., 1990-92, Nat. Media Corp., 1994-98, Phila. Commn. to End. Homelessness, 1995—; mem. Spl. Olympics Adv. Com. Mem. Nat. Assn. Life Underwriters, Coun. Ins. Agts. and Brokers (bd. dirs.), Profl. Assn. Ins. Agts., Sons of Am. Revolution, Mil. Order Loyal Legion of U.S. Republican. Episcopalian. Avocation: big game hunting. Home: 1606 Pine St Philadelphia PA 19103-6711 Office: Tri-Arc Fin Svcs PO Box 6745 983 Old Eagle School Rd Ste 616 Wayne PA 19087-1711 E-mail: jyoskin@triarcfs.com.

YOSSIF, GEORGE, psychiatrist; b. Bucharest, Romania, Nov. 18, 1939; arrived in U.S., 1975; s. Yuan and Eugenia (Paun) Yossif; m. Valentina Blanaru, Dec. 20, 1967 (div. 1978); 1 child Anamaria Verona ; m. Michaela Alexandru, Oct. 18, 1996; 1 child Stefan Oliver Felix. MD, Faculty of

Medicine, Bucharest, 1962; PhD in Neurophysiology cum laude, Scuola Normale Superiore, Pisa, Italy, 1971. Cert. specialist Endocrinology, Romania; diplomate Am. Bd. Psychiatry and Neurology. Intern in pharmacology Faculty of Medicine of Bucharest, 1962-63, intern in endocrinology, 1963-65; researcher div. neuroendocrinology Inst. Endocrinology, Bucharest, 1965-69; fellow in neurophysiology Scuola Normale Superiore and Istituto di Fisiologia, Pisa, Italy, 1969-71; postdoctoral fellow physiology Laval U. Faculty of Medicine, Quebec City, Can., 1971-73, asst. prof. neurophysiology Can., 1973-74; resident in neurology Ottawa Gen. Hosp., Ont., Can., 1974; research fellow Lipid Research Clinic of St. Michael's Hosp. U. Toronto, Can., 1974-75; rotating intern Cooper Med. Ctr., Camden, N.J., 1975-76; resident in psychiatry Johns Hopkins Hosp., Balt., 1976-79; instr. psychiatry, dir. Liaison-Cons. Service Dept. Psychiatry Howard U., Washington, 1979-80; staff psychiatrist, chief Intermed. Treatment Unit Bryce State Hosp., Tuscaloosa, Ala., 1980-82; med. dir. Stress Ctr. Lloyd Nolnd Hosp., Fairfield, 1982-83; practice medicine specializing in psychiatry Birmingham, 1982-92, Georgetown, Del., 1992-95; spl. in psychiatry, functional medicine, chelation therapy Millsboro, 1994-97. Adj. clin. asst. prof. Coll. Community Health Scis. U. Ala., Tuscaloosa, 1980-82. Contbr. articles to profl. jours. and popular press. Med. Research Council grantee, Laval U., 1973. Russian Orthodox. Office: PO Box 23667 Baltimore MD 21203-5667 Fax: 410-243-8708.

YOST, BERNICE, detective agency owner; b. Houston; d. Kenneth Wayne and Georgia (Sampson) Cox; m. Matthew Yost. Student, L.A. Trade Tech, 1968-70, Compton Coll., 1974-76, Ariz. State U., 1983-85. Staff acct. Moultrie, Liggens, Terrel CPA's, L.A., 1969-71; spl. agt. IRS, 1972-79, supervisory spl. agt. Phoenix, 1979-91, Washington, 1991-93; owner, operator Yost Detective Agy., Silver Spring, Md., 1995-2000, Culver City, Calif., 1998—2001, Beverly Hills, 2001—. Recipient Albert Gallatin award for merit, 1993. Mem. Nat. Orgn. of Black Law Enforcement Execs. Democrat. Baptist. Avocations: tennis, jogging, sewing. E-mail: berniceyost@aol.com.

YOST, ELLEN G. (ELLEN YOST LAFILI), lawyer; b. Buffalo, May 30, 1945; d. Irwin Arthur and Sylvia Rosen Ginsberg; m. Louis Lafili; children: Elizabeth Anne, Peter Andrew, Benjamin Lewis Yost. AB, Mt. Holyoke Coll., 1966; JD, SUNY, Buffalo, 1983. Bar: N.Y., U.S. Dist. Ct. (we. dist.) N.Y. 1984. Assoc. Jaeckle, Fleischmann & Mugel, Buffalo, 1983-89, Saperston & Day, P.C., Buffalo, 1989—; ptnr. Griffith & Yost, 1991-2000, Fragomen, Del Rey, Bernsen & Loewy, P.C., Buffalo, 2000—. Pres. Buffalo Coun. on World Affairs, 1987-89; bd. dirs. Buffalo World Trade Assn., 1988-90, Legal Svcs. for Elderly, Disabled, Disadvantaged, 1984—. Mem. ABA (co-chair Can. law com. of internat. law and practice sect. 1990-94, vice chair immigration and nationality law com. 1994-95, co-chair 1995-2000, co-chair task force N.Am. Free Trade Agreement 1991-94, immigration coord. com. 1996-2000, coun. internat. law and practice sect. 1998—), Can. Bar Assn., Internat. Bar Assn., N.Y. State Bar Assn. (chmn. U.S. Can. law com. 1987-89, mem. exec. com. internat. law and practice sect. 1987-89, sec. commn. in internat. trade and transactions 1984-87), Am. Immigration Lawyers' Assn. Jewish. Avocations: travel, skiing, sailing. Office: Fragomen Del Rey Bernsen Et Al 50 Fountain Plz Ste 1320 Buffalo NY 14202-2212 also: Vossendreef 6 1180 Brussels Belgium

YOST, EMERY JOSEPH, music industry producer, educator; b. Chgo., May 1, 1964; s. Thomas Joseph and Jean Ann (Kawa) Yost. BA in Music, Columbia Coll., 1988; postgrad., DePaul U., 1997—. Cert. tchr. Ill. Music instr. Chgo. Pk. Dist., Chgo., 1989—; music tchr. Immaculate Heart of Mary Sch., 1994—95; internat. recording and performance artist Smash/Polygram Records, 1995—97; CEO Spl. Music by Spl. People Inc., 1998—; cons. music programming Little City, Palatine, 1999—2000; pres., dir. House of Song, Chgo., 2000—; prodr. House of Records Records/Media Products, 2001—. Finalist Osterman awards, 1996, 1998; named Stan Greanias scholar, Spl. Childrens Charities, 1997, Anne Burke scholar, 1998. Mem.: Music Educators Nat. Conf., Nat. Acad. Recording Arts and Scis. Democrat. Home: 6015 W Ardmore Chicago IL 60646 Office: Chgo Pk Dist 3420 N Long Chicago IL

YOST, GERALD B. lawyer; b. Harvey, Ill., Dec. 21, 1954; s. Richard Dennis and Marilyn Patricia (Moore) Y.; m. Kay Lynn Benton, Apr. 16, 1977; children: Matthew Brian, Benjamin Gerald, Andrew Richard. BA in Journalism, Drake U., 1973-76; student, Purdue U., 1975; JD, Hamline U., 1980. Bar: Minn. 1980, U.S. Dist. Ct. Minn. 1980, Wis. 1987. Assoc. Bergman, Street & Ulmen, Mpls., 1980-84; ptnr. Wasserman and Baill, 1984-90, Yost, Stephenson & Sanford, Mpls., 1990-95, Yost & Baill LLP, Mpls., 1996—. Editor: Student Osteo. Med. Assn. Publ. mag., 1976; mem. Law Review Hamline U., 1978-80. Active YMCA, St. Paul. Recipient Am. Jurisprudence award, Lawyers Coop. Pub. Co., St. Paul, 1979. Mem. ABA, Minn. State Bar Assn., Wis. Bar Assn., Phi Alpha Delta, Sigma Delta Chi. Avocations: tennis, racquetball, boating and water skiing, jogging. Home: 422 Mt Curve Blvd Saint Paul MN 55105 Office: Yost & Baill LLP 2350 One Fin Plz 120 S 6th St Minneapolis MN 55402-1803 E-mail: gyost@yostbaill.com.

YOST, KELLY LOU, pianist; b. Boise, Idaho, Aug. 10, 1940; d. Roy Daniel and Helen Roberta (Kingsbury) Frizzelle; m. Nicholas Peter Bond, Dec. 27, 1961 (div. 1973); 1 child, Brook Bernard; m. Samuel Joseph Yost, June 16, 1984. MusB, U. Idaho, 1962; postgrad., U. So. Calif., 1965-69. Pvt. tchr. classical piano, Twin Falls, Idaho, 1962-88; rec. artist, owner ind. record label Channel Prodns., 1986—. Soloist U. Idaho Symphony Orch., Moscow, 1962; pianist, keyboardist Magic Valley Symphony Orch., Twin Falls, 1985, 86; touring guest piano soloist Vandaleer Concert Choir, Moscow, 1961. Recorded record albums: Piano Reflection (excerpts included in Simple Abundance by Sarah Ban Breathnach), 1987, recorded record albums: (selection synchronized with Japanese film Gaia Symphony #4 , 2001, recorded record albums: Quiet Colors, 1991, recorded record albums: Roses and Solitude, 1996, recorded record albums: Still...Still...Still, 1998, recorded record albums: Brand New Feel (in Japan), 2002. Mem. NARAS, Assn. Ind. Music, Music Tchrs. Nat. Assn., Idaho Music Tchrs. Assn. (sec. 1981-82), Magic Valley Cmty. Concert Assn. (bd. dirs. 1964-87), Phi Beta Kappa, Kappa Kappa Gamma (Alumnae Achievement award 1996). Avocations: snow skiing, hiking, philosophy. Office: Channel Prodns PO Box 454 Twin Falls ID 83303-0454

YOST, LARRY D. automotive company executive; Mgr. prodn. and inventory control Rockwell Internat., from 1971, pres. heavy vehicles sys. divsn., 1994-97; pres., CEO, Meritor Automotive Inc. (merger with Arvin Co.), Troy, Mich., 1997—, chmn., 1998—. Office: Arvin Meritor Inc. 2135 W Maple Rd Troy MI 48084-7121*

YOST, LYLE EDGAR, retired farm equipment manufacturing company executive; b. Hesston, Kans., Mar. 5, 1913; s. Joseph and Alma (Hensley) Y.; m. Erma Martin, July 31, 1938; children: Byron, Winston, Susan, Cameron. BS B.A, Goshen Coll., 1937; postgrad., U. Ind., 1940. With St. Joseph Valley Bank, Elkhart, Ind., 1938-41; tchr. Wakarusa (Ind.) High Sch., 1942-45; founder Hesston Corp., Kans., 1947, pres., 1949-83, now chmn. bd.; ret., 1991. Bd. dirs., past pres. Farm and Indsl. Equipment Inst.; mem. Gov.'s Com. for Ptnrs. for Progress Kans.-Paraguay; chmn. com. establishing creamery in Uruguay, 1967; mem. State Dept. cultural del. to USSR, 1967; past chmn. pres.'s adv coun. Hesston Coll. (Kans.); chmn. Prince of Peace Chapel, Aspen, Colo. Named Farmarketing Man of Year Nat. Agrl. Advt. and Marketing Assn., 1969, Kansan of Achievement in Bus., 1972, Kansan of Year, 1974, One of the Most Significant Contbrs. to Mechanization of Agrl. and Constrn. Equipment Mfrs. Inst., 1993. Mem. Alpha Kappa Psi (hon.). Home: 123 Kingsway Hesston KS 67062-9271

YOST, NANCY RUNYON, artist, designer, art educator; b. Eaton, Ohio, July 16, 1933; d. Stanley Everett and Treva (Geeting) Runyon; m. Kenneth John Yost, Aug. 17, 1952 (div. Dec. 1962); 1 child, Debra Colleen Yost Mayne. BS in Art Edn., Miami U., Oxford, Ohio, 1966, MEd in Art, 1970. Cert. profl. permanent tchr., Ohio. Sec. N.Am. Aircraft, Columbus, Ohio, 1957, Miami U., Oxford, 1957-61, textile instr., 1978, Living Arts Ctr., Dayton, Ohio, 1972-73; coord. art, music and phys. edn. Stewart Jr. High Sch., Oxford, 1981-86; art instr. Talawanda Sch. System, 1965-90, dist. coord., 1986-90; owner, creator Allegro Adornments Bus., 1988—. Postgrad. Sem. Charles Jeffrey, Cleve., Inst. Art, Miami U., 1973, David Van Dommelen Penn State at U. Tenn., 1975, Bill Helwig, N.Y., 1975, Nik Krevitsky, N.Y., 1976, Tom Shafer, Columbus, Ohio, 1982; mem. curriculum coun. Talawanda Sch. Dist., 1982—; rep. Amway Corp., 1980-81, World Book Co., Chgo., 1986-88; lectr. Miami U., 1986; invited workshop speaker, presenter Nat. Art Edn. Assn. Conv., Phoenix, 1992. One-woman shows include Creative Fibers Studio, Buffalo, 1974, exhibited in group shows at Dayton Art Inst., Invitational Fiber Artists Am., Ball State U., 1974, Christkindl Markt, Canton Art Inst., 1994 (hon. mention), Art All Over, Oxford, Ohio, 2002. Supr. Community Artworks, 1986; mem. adv. bd. Miami U. Summer Theatre, 1991-93; mem. spl. events planning com. Miami U. Art Mus., 1993—. Recipient Winner Most Creative Costume Ohio Mart, 1992, 93, First Pl. awards Community Photo Contest, 3d Pl. and Hon. Mention award Oxford Audubon Photo Show, 1994, 1st Pl. 3D Design, Greater Hamilton Art Exhibit at Fitton Ctr, 1995, Cash award ribbon and Purchase award Wyo. Art Show, 1996, Cash award ribbon Minnetrista Arts Fair, 1996, Best in Show Preble Co. Arts Assn. Juried Show, 1997, First Pl. Sculpture, 1997, 2d Pl Ribbon cash award Christ Kindl Markt, Canton Art Inst., 1999, 1st Pl. 3D Design award, Greater Hamilton Art Exhibit, 2000. Mem. Southwestern Art Edn. Assn., Ohio Art Edn. Assn., Ohio Edn. Assn., Talawanda Edn. Assn., Ohio Designer Craftsmen, Ohio Arts and Crafts Guild, Oxford Arts Club, Kappa Delta Pi. Avocations: commissioned artwork, sculpture, wearable art, fabric, metal collages, limited edition prints, painted wood furniture. Home: 6674 Fairfield Rd Oxford OH 45056-8813

YOST, PAUL ALEXANDER, JR. foundation executive, retired coast guard officer; b. Phila., Jan. 3, 1929; s. Paul Alexander Sr. and Jeanne Moore (Bailey) Y.; m. Jan Worth, June 2, 1951; children: Linda L., Paul Alexander III, David J., Lisa L., Christopher J. BS, USCG Acad., 1951; MS, U. Conn., 1959; MA, George Washington U., 1964; grad., Naval War Coll., 1964. Commd. ensign USCG, 1951, advanced through grades to adm., 1986, comdr. 8th dist., 1978-81, chief staff hdqrs. Washington, 1981-84, comdr. 3d dist., maritime Atlantic def. zone, and Atlantic area N.Y.C., 1984-86, commandant Washington, 1986-90, ret., 1990; pres. James Madison Found., 1990—. Decorated D.S.M. with gold star, Silver Star, Legion of Merit combat "V" with gold star, Meritorious Service Medal. Office: James Madison Meml Fellowship Found 2000 K St NW Washington DC 20006-1809

YOST, PAULA LYNN, accountant; b. Nashville, June 4, 1967; d. Glenn C. Gill and Paulette (Hendrixson) McDonald; m. Joseph Paul Yost, Apr. 18, 1992; 1 child, Justin Tyler. BS, Tenn. Tech. U., 1989, MBA, 1991. CPA Tenn. Tech. U. Sr. auditor Kraft CPAs, Nashville, 1995—; with Plodzik & Sanderson, Concord, N.H., 2000—.

YOST, R. DAVID, healthcare manufacturing company administrator; b. 1947; married. BS, USAF Acad., 1969; MBA, UCLA, 1970. From v.p. to pres. Kauffman-Lattimer Co., Columbus, Ohio, 1969-74; from group v.p. to group pres. cen. region Alco Health Systems Corp., Malvern, Pa., 1989-97; pres., CEO, chmn. AmeriSource Health Corp., 1997—2001; pres., CEO Amerisource Bergen Corp. (formerly Amerisource Health Corp.), 2001—. Capt. USAF, 1969-74. Office: AmeriSource Bergen Corp 1300 Morris Dr, Ste 100 Wayne PA 19087-5594*

YOST, RICHARD ALAN, chemistry educator; b. Martins Ferry, Ohio, Mar. 31, 1953; s. Donald Errold and Jessie Lee (Hoover) Y.; m. Katherine Sarah Fitzgerald, June 16, 1979; children: Sarah Elizabeth, Michael Patrick, Matthew Jefferson. BS in Chemistry, U. Ariz., 1974; PhD in Analytical Chemistry, Mich. State U., 1979. Asst. prof. chemistry U. Fla., Gainesville, 1979-83, assoc. prof., 1983-89, prof., 1989—, head divsn. analytical chemistry, 1994—2000, assoc. dean rsch., 2000—01. Cons. Lawrence Livermore Nat. Lab., Finnigan MAT Corp., Bristol-Myers Squibb; mem. sci. adv. and rev. bd. Lawrence Livermore Nat. Lab., 1994—. Mem. editl. bd. Jour. Am. Soc. Mass Spectrometry, 1990-97, Internat. Jour. Mass Spectrometry, 1996—; patentee in field. Dist. commr. Boy Scouts Am., 1981-84. Fellow NSF, 1975-79, Am. Chem. Soc. Analytical Divsn., 1977-78. Mem. Am. Chem. Soc., Am. Soc. Mass Spectrometry (sec. 1997-99, Disting. Contbn. award 1993), Phi Beta Kappa, Phi Kappa Phi. Office: U Fla Dept Chemistry Gainesville FL 32611 E-mail: ryost@chem.ufl.edu.

YOST, WILLIAM ALBERT, psychology educator, hearing researcher; b. Dallas, Sept. 21, 1944; s. William Jacque and Gladys (Funk) Y.; m. Lee Prater, June 15, 1969; children: Kelley Ann, Alyson Leigh BA, Colo. Coll., 1966, DSc (hon.), 1997; PhD, Ind. U., 1970. Assoc. prof. psychology U. Fla., Gainesville, 1971-77; dir. sensory physiology and perception program NSF, Washington, 1982-83; prof. psychology Loyola U., Chgo., 1977-89, dir. Parmly Hearing Inst., 1977—, prof. hearing scis., 1990—, dir. interdisciplinary neurosci. minor, 1997—. Adj. prof. psychology and otolaryngology Loyola U., Chgo., 1990—, acting v.p. rsch., 1999—2001, assoc. v.p. rsch., dean Grad. Sch., 2001—; individual expert bio-acoustics Am. Nat. Stds. Inst., 1983—; mem. study sect. Nat. Inst. Deafness and Other Communication Disorders, 1990—94; mem. hearing bioacoustics and biomechanics com. NRC, 1992—. Author: Fundamentals of Hearing, 1977, 4th edit., 2000; editor (with others) New Directions in Hearing Science, 1985, Directional Hearing, 1987, Auditory Processing of Complex Sounds, 1987, Classification of Complex Sounds, 1989, Psychoacoustics, 1993; assoc. editor Auditory Neurosci., 1994-97; ad hoc reviewer NSF, Air Force Office Sci. Rsch., Office Naval Rsch., 1981—; contbr. chpts. to books, articles to profl. jours. Pres. Evanston Tennis Assn., Ill., 1984, 90. Grantee NSF, 1974—, NIH, 1975—, AFOSR, 1983—, ONR, 1989-90. Fellow AAAS, Am. Phys. Soc., Acoustical Soc. Am. (assoc. editor jour. 1984-91, chair tech. com. 1990-94, exec. com. 1999—, v.p. 2002--), Am. Speech-Lang.-Hearing Assn.; mem. NAS (exec. com. on hearing bioacoustics, biomechanics 1981-87, chmn. 1993-97), Assn. Rsch. in Otolaryngology (sec.-treas. 1984-87, pres.-elect 1987-88, pres. 1988-89), Acoustics Soc. Am. (chair com. psychol. and physiol. acoustics 1990-94, mem. exec. coun. 1999—), Nat. Inst. Deafness and Other Comm. Disorders (task force, rev. panel 1990-94, chmn. 1994), Am. Auditory Soc. (exec. bd. 1993-98). *I am fortunate that I am in an occupation that is so much fun. Teaching and research are very enjoyable. Most days for me are fun.*

YOSTE, CHARLES TODD, lawyer; b. Vicksburg, Miss., Nov. 11, 1948; s. Harry M. and Charlene (Todd) Y. BS, Miss. State U., 1971; JD, U. Miss., 1976. Bar: Miss. 1976, U.S. Dist. Ct. Miss. 1976, U.S. Ct. Appeals, 1982, U.S. Supreme Ct. 2002. Sole practice, Starkville, Miss., 1976—; city atty., 1979-85; pros. atty., 1977-79; city judge, 1981-82. Candidate for Congress 2d dist., Miss., 1980. Served to capt. U.S. Army, 1971-73. Recipient Outstanding Young Man award Starkville Jaycees, 1980. Mem. ABA, Miss. Bar Assn., Am. Trial Lawyers Assn., Miss. Trial Lawyers Assn. (bd. govs. 1988-94), Starkville C. of C. (pres. 1982), Am. Legion, Rotary, Am. Coll. Barristers, Internat. Acad. Litigators. Republican. Roman Catholic. Home: 902 Montgomery St Starkville MS 39759 Office: PO Box 80288 Starkville MS 39759-0488 E-mail: cyoste@netdoor.com.

YOU, ALETA, education educator; b. Honolulu, Apr. 13, 1947; d. Richard W. and Eleanor (Chun) You; children: Aaron, Erika Mastny BS in Secondary Edn., Bradley U., 1970; MA in Speech Communication, U. Hawaii, 1971; PhD in Philosophy of Edn., Ariz. State U., 1975. Assoc. prof. student tchg., dir. Incarnate Word Coll., San Antonio, 1978-82; adj. assoc. prof. edn. The Coll. of N.J., Ewing, 1983-85; asst. dir. Princeton (N.J.) U., 1985-86; project dir. Rutgers U., New Brunswick, N.J., 1986-89, dir. program devel., 1989-94, sr. equity specialist, 1994—. Co-author: Science Teams Teachers Manual, 1992, (handbook) Linking Schools & Community Services, 1989; contbr. chpt. to book; project dir. (tchg. techniques video) Science Teams, 1994 (Bronze Apple award); contbr. articles to profl. jours.; editor Eisenhower Nat. Math. & Sci. Edn. newsletter, Rutgers U., 1991-94. Fellow Philosophy of Edn. Soc.; mem. AAUW, Nat. Alliance Bus., Nat. Assn. Ptnrs. in Edn., N.J. Assn. Ptnrs. in Edn. (exec. dir., New Brunswick, 1991-99). Avocations: reading, Biblical research, travel, dancing. Office: NJ Statewide Systemic Initiative Rutgers U 640 Bartholomew Rd Piscataway NJ 08854-8003

YOUD, T. LESLIE, civil engineer; b. Spanish Fork, Utah, Apr. 2, 1938; s. Thomas Leslie and Mary (Evans) Y.; m. Denice Porter, June 26, 1962; children: Verlin, Lance, Melinda, Thomas, Emily. BS, Brigham Young U., 1964; PhD, Iowa State U., 1967. Rsch. civil engr. U.S. Geological Survey, Menlo Park, Calif., 1967-84; prof. Brigham Young U., Provo, Utah, 1984--. Recipient Maeser Rsch. award Brigham Young U., 1991, Utah Engring. Educator of Yr., 1995, ASCE H. Bolton Seed medal, 2002.. Mem. ASCE, Internat. Soc. for Soil Mechanics and Fnd. Engring., Earthquake Engring. Rsch. Inst. Mem. Lds Ch. Achievements include development of techniques for mapping earthquake induced liquefaction hazard and techniques for estimating earthquake induced laterial spread displacements; inventor system for coupling accelerometers into bore hole casings. Home: 1132 E 1010 N Orem UT 84097-4306 Office: Brigham Young U Dept Civil Engring Provo UT 84602

YOUDELMAN, ROBERT ARTHUR, financial executive, lawyer; b. L.I., N.Y., Mar. 28, 1942; s. Jack and Marjorie Vivian (Baer) Y.; m. Karen Leita Schneier, July 30, 1966; children: Mara, Sondra. BBA in Acctg., Case Western Res. U., 1963; LLB, NYU, 1966, LLM in Taxation, 1975. Bar: N.Y. 1969, U.S. Tax Ct. Vol. U.S. Peace Corps, Salvador, Brasil, 1966-68; mgr. Arthur Andersen & Co., N.Y.C., 1969-77; v.p., dir. taxation The Allen Group Inc., Melville, N.Y., 1977-89, exec. v.p., CFO NY, 1989—. Mem. N.Y. State Hazardous Waste Task Force, Albany, 1985-87; pres. Residents for a More Beautiful Port Washington, N.Y., 1981-92. Recipient Individual Environ. Quality award for Region 2 EPA, 1992; named Citizen of Yr., Port Washington Rotary Club, 1989. Mem. ABA. Avocations: camping, hiking, environmental education and awareness. Office: Allen Telecom Inc 25101 Chagrin Blvd Beachwood OH 44122-5643

YOUKER, ROBERT BLISS, economist; b. Cuba, N.Y., Feb. 10, 1934; s. Bliss Jacob and Marion (Ostrander) Y.; m. Susan Lindsay, Aug. 25, 1962. BA in History, Colgate U., 1955; MBA, Harvard U. Internat. Econs., Fin. with distinction, 1961; postgrad studies in behavioral scis., George Washington U., 1975-82. Project dir. Checchi and Co., Washington, 1961-65; dep. dir. divsn. private and internat. orgns. Peace Corps, 1965-66; bus. devel. and rsch. staff Xerox Corp., Rochester, N.Y., 1966, systems analyst, info. systems, 1967; pres. Planalog Mgmt. Systems, Phila., 1968-74; lectr. Econ. Devel. Inst. World Bank, Washington, 1975-83; mgmt. specialist World Bank, 1983-87; cons. and trainer Mgmt. Planning and Control Systems, Bethesda, Md., 1988—. Adj. prof. George Washington U., 1988-91, adv. bd. 1988; dir. Project Mgmt. Inst., 1968-70, Internat. Project Mgmt. Assn., Europe, 1976-84; advisor PMC Washington chpt., 1995-2000; lectr. UCLA, 1974-83, U. Wis., Madison, 1975-82, 88-92, U. Bradford, Eng., 1979, 86, 88, Arthur D. Little Project Mgmt., 1986, 90, Acad. Ednl. Devel., 1989-2000. Tech. author: (CD ROM) Managing the Implementation of Development Projects. Lt. U.S. Navy, 1956-59. Mem. Congregational Ch. Avocations: white water canoeing, gardening. Home: 5825 Rockmere Dr Bethesda MD 20816-2443 E-mail: bobyouker@worldnet.att.net.

YOULA, SANDRA LYNN, land use planner, consultant; b. Bklyn., Nov. 23, 1956; d. Dante Ciriaco Youla and Patsy Lee Peters; m. Charles David Toy, Mar. 10, 1984; 1 child, Alana May Youla Toy. AB, Wellesley Coll., 1978; MCP, U. Pa., 1983. Rsch. asst. Dallas Dept. Urban Design, 1977; planning asst. Harvard U. Planning Office, Cambridge, Mass., 1978-80; cons. Cemrel/Ednl. Cons., 1980-81; planning asst. Dela. Valley Regional Planning Auth., Phila., 1982-83; rsch. officer/planning Hong Kong Housing Dept., 1986-88; sr. town planner Townland Cons. Ltd., Hong Kong, 1989-90; zoning analyst Md. Nat. Capital Park & Planning Commn., Silver Spring, 1997—. Lectr. U. Pa. Dynamics Orgn., Phila., 1993, 94, 95; conf. organizer Am. Planning Assn., N.Y.C., 1994. Coord. soup kitchen Ch. Epiphany, N.Y.C., 1992-94; lay coord. water ministry St. Columba's, Washington, 1994-97; vol. Cmty. Coun. Homeless, Washington, 1995. Mem. Am. Inst. Cert. Planners (cert.), Hong Kong Inst. Planners (cert.), Am. Planning Assn., Washington Wellesley Club (pres. Hong Kong club 1985-88). Democrat. Episcopalian. Avocations: church outreach programs. Office: Montgomery County Dept Park & Planning 8787 Georgia Ave Silver Spring MD 20910-3760 E-mail: sandra.youla@mncppc-mc.org.

YOUMAN, ROGER JACOB, editor, writer; b. N.Y.C., Feb. 25, 1932; s. Robert Harold and Ida (Kellner) Y.; m. Lillian Frank, June 22, 1958; children: Nancy, Laura, Joshua, Andrew. BA, Swarthmore Coll., 1953. Desk asst. CBS News, N.Y.C., 1953; program editor TV Guide, 1956, regional editor Memphis, 1956-57, Houston, 1957, asst. programming editor N.Y.C., 1957-60, assoc. editor Radnor, Pa., 1960-65, asst. mng. editor, 1965-72, mng. editor, 1972-76, exec. editor, 1976-79, 80-81, co-editor, 1981-90, editor, 1990-93, Panorama, 1979-80; editl. dir. TV Guide On Screen, 1993-96; freelance writer, editorial cons., 1996—. Del. U.S.-Soviet Bilateral Info. Talks, 1988, 90. Author: How Sweet It Was, The Television Years, Tuscan Notes; contbr. articles to various publs. Served with AUS, 1954-55. Home: 752 Mancill Rd Wayne PA 19087-2043

YOUMANS, JOYCE M. curator, researcher; d. Jasper D. and Karen S. Youmans. BA, U. Mo., Kansas City, 1995; MA in Art History, U. Kans., 2002. Rsch. asst. The Nelson-Atkins Mus. of Art, Kansas City, Mo., 1994—99, curatorial asst., 1999—2002, asst. curator African art, 2002—. Lectr. U. Kans., Lawrence, 2002—; rschr., Shawnee Mission, Kans., 1995—. Contbr. articles to profl. jours. Office: The Nelson-Atkins Mus of Art 4525 Oak St Kansas City MO 64111-1873

YOUMANS, JULIAN RAY, neurosurgeon, educator; b. Baxley, Ga., Jan. 2, 1928; s. John Edward and Jennie Lou (Milton) Y.; children— Reed Nesbit, John Edward, Julian Milton. BS, Emory U., 1949, MD, 1952; MS, U. Mich., 1955, PhD, 1957. Diplomate: Am. Bd. Neurol. Surgery. Intern U. Mich. Hosp., Ann Arbor, 1952-53, resident in neurol. surgery, 1953-55, 56-58; fellow in neurology U. London, 1955-56; asst. prof. neurosurgery U. Miss., 1959-62, assoc. prof., 1962-63, Med. U. S.C., 1963-65, prof., 1965-67, chief div. neurosurgery, 1963-67; prof. U. Calif., Davis, 1967-91; prof. emeritus, 1991—; chmn. dept. neurosurgery U. Calif., 1967-82. Cons. USAF, U.S. VA, NRC. Editor: Neurological Surgery, 1973; contbr. articles to profl. jours. No. vice chmn. Republican State Central Com. of Calif., 1979-81. Served with U.S. Navy, 1944-46. Mem. ACS (bd. govs. 1972-78), Congress of Neurol. Surgeons (exec. com. 1967-70), Am. Acad. Neurology, Am. Assn. Neurol. Surgeons, Am. Assn. Surgery of Trauma, Pan-Pacific Surg. Assn., Western Neurosurg. Soc., Neurosurg. Soc. Am., Soc. Neurol. Surgeons, Soc. Univ. Neurosurgeons, N. Pacific Soc. Neurology and Psychiatry, Royal Soc. Medicine, Am. Trauma Soc., U.S. C. of C., Bohemian Club, Sutter Club, Capital Club of Sacramento, Rotary. Republican. Episcopalian.

YOUMANS, WILLIAM BARTON, physiologist; b. Cin., Feb. 3, 1910; s. Charles Trimble and Lucy May (Gardiner) Y.; m. Cynthia McCreary Holbrook, Nov. 24, 1932; children: William Barton, Carol Anne, Charles Gilbert. Student, Vanderbilt U., 1928—29; BS, Western Ky. State Coll., Bowling Green, 1932; MS, Western Ky. State Coll., 1933; PhD, U. Wis., 1938; MD, U. Oreg., 1944. Intern Henry Ford Hosp., Detroit, 1944-45; instr. biology Western Ky. U., Bowling Green, 1932-35; rsch. asst. physiology U. Wis., Madison, 1935-36, instr. physiology, 1936-38; instr. physiology to assoc. prof. physiology U. Oreg. Med. Sch., Portland, 1938-42, prof. physiology, 1942-46, head physiology dept., 1946-52; prof. and chmn. dept. physiology U. Wis., Madison, 1952-71, prof. physiology, 1971-76, prof. emeritus, 1976—. Mem. physiology study sect. USPHS, 1952-56, mem. tng. grant and fellowship rev. panels, 1956-60, 60-64. Author: Nervous and Neurohumoral Regulation of Intestinal Motility, 1949, Hemodynamics in Failure of the Circulation, 1951, Basic Medical Physiology, 1952, Fundamentals of Human Physiology, 1957, others; contbr. articles to profl. jours. including the Pharos. Recipient Meritorious Achievement award, U. Oreg. Med. Sch. Alumni Assn., 1967, Emeritus Faculty award, U. Wis. Med. Alumni Assn., 1985. Fellow AAAS; mem. Am. Physiol. Soc., Am. Soc. Pharmacology and Exptl. Therapeutics, Am. Heart Assn., Alpha Omega Alpha, Phi Sigma, Gamma Alpha. Avocations: tenor banjo, gardening, camping. Home: 3212 S Old Ridge Rd Columbia MO 65203-9513

YOUNAN, JOSEPH, bishop; b. Hassakeh, Syria, Nov. 15, 1944; came to U.S., 1986; Student, Our Lady Deliverance Sem., Sharfet, Lebanon, Pontifical Coll. Propagation, Rome. Ordained priest Roman Cath. Ch., 1971. Served Syrian Caths. in U.S.; bishop Our Lady of Deliverance, Union City, N.J., 1996—. Office: Chancery Office Our Lady of Deliverance 502 Palisade Ave Union City NJ 07087-5213

YOUNESSI, HOUMAN, computer scientist, consultant; b. Tehran, May 28, 1963; s. Parviz and Farah Younessi; m. Sheyda Delavari; 1 child Zhubin Daniel. PhD, Swinburne U. Tech., Melbourne, Australia, 1988. Mng. dir. Australian Bus. Cons. PL, Melbourne, 1987—96; sr. lectr. Swinburne U. Tech., Australia, 1992—99; prof. Rensselaer at Hartford, Conn., 1999—. Victorian dir. COTAR, Melbourne, 1998—99; mem. internat. adv. com. SQM, Southampton, 1995—; mem. The OPEN Consortium, Sydney, NSW, Australia, 1996—. Author: (book) The OPEN Process Specification, 1997, The OPEN Toolbox of Techniques, 1998, Object-oriented Defect Mangement of Software, 2002, (book chpt.) Handbook of Object Technology, 1998; contbr. Mem.: IEEE. Avocations: tennis, skiing. Home: 34 Doria Ln South Windsor CT 06074 Office: Rensselaer at Hartford 275 Windsor St Hartford CT 06120

YOUNG, ALICE, lawyer; b. Washington, Apr. 7, 1950; d. John and Elizabeth (Jen) Y.; m. Thomas L. Shortall, Sept. 22, 1984; children: Amanda, Stephen. AB magna cum laude, Yale U., 1971; JD, Harvard U., 1974. Bar: N.Y. 1975. Assoc. Coudert Bros., N.Y.C., 1974-81; mng. ptnr. Graham & James, 1981-87; ptnr. Milbank, Tweed, Hadley & McCloy, 1987-93; ptnr., chair Asia Pacific Practice (U.S.) Kaye, Scholer LLP, 1994—. Bd. dirs. Mizuho Trust & Banking Co. Contbr. articles to profl. jours. Bus. com. Nat. Com. on U.S.-China Rels., 1993—, U.S.-China Bus. Coun., 1993—, Com. of 100, 1993—, vice-chmn., 1999—; bd. overseers visitation com. to Law Sch. Harvard U., 1994—99, chair subcom. on grad. program, 1996; trustee Lingnan Found., N.Y.C., 1984—91, Pan-Asian Repertory Theatre, N.Y.C., 1987—90, Aspen (Colo.) Inst., 1988—, Am. Assembly, 2000—; bus. com. Met. Mus. Art, N.Y.C., 1989—94; active Pres.'s Forum, 2000—, Coun. on Fgn. Rels., 1977—. Named one of Top 100 Minority Leaders, 1998, one of 40 Under 40 Crain's Bus., N.Y.C., 1989; Bates fellow Yale U., 1970, NDFL fellow Harvard U., 1967-68; recipient Star award N.Y. Women's Agenda, 1992. Mem. ABA, N.Y. State Bar Assn. (fgn. investment com.), Assn. Bar City N.Y. (spl. com. on rels. with Japanese bar, Union Internat. des Avocats), Nat. Asian Pacific Am. Bar Assn., Asian Am. Bar Assn. N.Y., Coun. on Fgn. Rels., Chmn.'s Fourm, Harvard Law Sch. Assn. N.Y.C. (trustee 1990-94), Japan Soc. (sec. 1989-97), Asia Soc. (pres.'s coun. 1984—). Office: Kaye Scholer LLP 425 Park Ave New York NY 10022-3506 E-mail: ayoung@kayescholer.com.

YOUNG, (ARTHUR) ALLEN, writer; b. Washington, July 4, 1918; s. Arthur N. and Nellie May Y.; m. Barbara Jean Young; children: Sarah Abigail, David Allen, Andrew Nichols, Elizabeth Corlett. Student, Occidental Coll., L.A., 1937-40, U. Chgo., 1940-41, 1946. Music columnist The Denver Post, 1948-57; arts editor Cervi's Jour., Denver, 1959-63; exec. dir. Young Audiences, Inc., 1963-70; asst. editor Rocky Mountain Med. Jour. (Colo. State Med. Soc.), 1972-80. Author: (book) Opera in Central City, 1993. Pres. Allied Arts, Inc., Denver, 1973-90; sec. Friends of Chamber Music, Denver, 1970-73, 1989-2002. T/5 U.S. Army Air Force, 1941-45. Democrat. Episcopalian. Avocations: piano, reading, writing. Home: 460 S Marion Pkwy Apt 451B Denver CO 80209-2507 E-mail: AYoung1425@aol.com.

YOUNG, ANDERSON BRIGGS, recreation educator, administrator; b. Rochester, N.Y., Dec. 2, 1949; s. Lawrence E. and Annette (Briggs) Y.; m. Mary Susan Quinby, July 28, 1990; children: Elaine Kathleen, Allison Olivia. BA, Ohio Wesleyan U., 1971; MDiv, Union Theol. Sem., N.Y.C., 1975; PhD, Ohio State U., 1981. Living learning programs coord. Capital Univ., Columbus, Ohio, 1976-79; teaching assoc. Ohio State Univ., 1979-81; asst. prof. SUNY Coll., Cortland, N.Y., 1981-84, assoc. prof., 1984-88, prof., 1988—, recreation and leisure studies dept. chair, 1985-98. Bd. chair Coalition for Edn. in Outdoors, Cortland, 1987—; trustee Ohio WesleyanUniv., Delaware, 1971-74, 83-86; mem. Curriculum Adv. Bd., Tompkins-Cortland Community Coll., Dryden, N.Y., 1986-98; Reynold Carlson Disting. lectr. Ind. U., 1999. Contbr. over 40 articles to profl. publs.; assoc. editor Schole Jour., 1989-93; presenter over 50 profl. meetings, 1981—. Dir. Ohio Wesleyan Univ. Alumni, 1975-81. Mem. Nat. Coun. on Outdoor Edn. (chair 1987-88, Julian Smith award 1992), Soc. of Park and Recreation Educators (bd. dirs. 1993-96), Nat. Recreation and Park Assn., Am. Assn. for Leisure and Recreation (com. chair 1989-91), N.Y. Outdoor Edn. Assn. (N.Y. leadership award), Nat. Parks and Conservation Assn., Phi Kappa Phi (chpt. treas. 1983-85), Phi Delta Kappa. Democrat. Avocations: wilderness, woodworking, basketball, folk music. Home: 561 Lime Hollow Rd Cortland NY 13045-9346 Office: SUNY Park Center Cortland NY 13045 E-mail: younga@cortland.edu.

YOUNG, ANDREW BRODBECK, lawyer; b. Phila., Feb. 8, 1907; s. Edward E. and Estelle (Brodbeck) Y.; m. Olive C. Sherley, Apr. 22, 1933; children: Andrew Oliver (dec.), Sherley. AB, Princeton U., 1928; LL.B., Harvard U., 1931. Bar: Pa. 1931. Ptnr. Stradley, Ronon, Stevens & Young, Phila., 1935-95, assoc., 1995—. Bd. dirs. Welex Inc., Holmes Investment Co., Phila.; lectr. finance U. Pa., 1939-66; lectr. various tax insts., 1953-81; mem. Mayor's Com. Exec. and Elective Salaries Phila. City Govt., 1959, Mayor's Com. Port Promotion Phila., 1959-63; mem. adv. coun. Phila. Cmty. Renewal Program, 1964-66; chmn., dir. Phila. Indsl. Devel. Corp., 1963-68, pres., 1963-70, chmn., 1970-86; mem. Mayor's Tax Study Commn., 1960, mem. Commr. Internal Revenue's Adv. Group, 1965; voting trustee Phila. Belt Line Ry. Co. Trustee Lovett Found.; mem. coun. pres.'s advisers LaSalle Coll., 1969-74. With Surgeon Gen.'s Office, AUS, 1942-45. Fellow Am. Bar Found.; mem. ABA (mem. ho. of dels. 1966-70, mem. council tax sect. 1958-70, chmn. sect. 1963-65), Pa. Bar Assn., Am. Law Inst. (tax adv. group, corps.-stockholders project 1957-59), Am. Coll. Tax Counsel, Am. Law Inst. (estate and gift tax project 1964-67), Phila. C. of C. (pres. 1958-60, chmn. bd. 1960-62, dir.), Am. Arbitration Assn. (nat. panel arbitrators), Phi Beta Kappa. Clubs: Philadelphia, Sunday Breakfast, Sunnybook Golf, Anglers, Wilderness. Republican. Episcopalian. Home: 613 Foulkeways Gwynedd PA 19436-1024 Office: Stradley Ronon 2600 One Commerce Sq 2005 Market St Philadelphia PA 19103-7042 E-mail: ayoung@stradley.com.

YOUNG, ANDREW JACKSON, civil rights leader, clergyman, former mayor, former ambassador, former congressman; b. New Orleans, Mar. 12, 1932; s. Andrew J. and Daisy (Fuller) Y.; m. Jean Childs, June 7, 1954; children— Andrea, Lisa Dru, Paula Jean, Andrew J. III. Student, Dillard U., 1947-48; BS, Howard U., 1951; B.D., Hartford Theol. Sem., 1955; D.D. (hon.), Wesleyan U., 1970, United Theol. Sem. Twin Cities, 1970; LL.D. (hon.), Wilberforce U., 1971, Clark Coll., 1973, Yale U., 1973, Swarthmore Coll., Atlanta U., others; numerous other hon. degrees. Ordained to ministry Congl. Ch., 1955; pastor Thomasville, Ga., 1955-57; assoc. dir. dept. youth work Nat. Council Chs., 1957-61; mem. staff So. Christian Leadership Conf., 1961-70, adminstr. citizen edn. program, 1961-64, exec. dir., 1964-70, exec. v.p., 1967-70; bd. dirs., mem. 93d-95th Congresses from 5th Ga. Dist.; mem. Rules com.; U.S. ambassador to UN, 1977-79; mayor of Atlanta, 1982-89; co-chmn. Atlanta Com. for the Olympic Games, 1996. Chmn. Atlanta Community Relations Commn., 1970-72; chmn. bd. Delta Ministry of Miss.; bd. dirs. Martin Luther King, Jr. Center for Social Change, Robert F. Kennedy Meml. Found., Field Found., So. Christian Leadership Conf. Recipient Pax-Christi award St. John's U., 1970; Springarn medal.; Medal of Freedom, 1980, French Legion of Honor medal, 1982; co-recipient, Martin Luther King, Jr., Award for Public Svc. (Ebony mag.), 1990. Mem. Ams. Dem. Action.

YOUNG, ARTHUR PRICE, librarian, educator; b. Boston, July 29, 1940; s. Arthur Price and Marion (Freeman) Y.; m. Patricia Dorothy Foss, June 26, 1965; children: John Marshall, Christopher Price. BA, Tufts U., 1962; MA in Tchg., U. Mass., 1964; MSLS, Syracuse U., 1969; PhD, U. Ill., 1976. Head reader svcs., social sci. bibliographer SUNY-Cortland, 1969-72; rsch. assoc. U. Ill. Libr. Rsch. Ctr., Urbana, 1972-75; asst. dean pub. svcs., assoc. prof. U. Ala., Tuscaloosa, 1976-81; dean librs., prof. U. R.I., Kingston, 1981-89; dir. Thomas Cooper Libr., U. S.C., Columbia, 1989-93; sr. fellow UCLA, 1991; dean librs., mem. adj. faculty dept. history No. Ill. U., DeKalb, 1993—. Mem. adj. faculty Syracuse (N.Y.) U., 1970-71, Dominican U., River Forest, Ill., 1994-96; pres. Consortium R.I. Acad. and Rsch. Librs., 1983-85; mem. bd. govs. Univ. Press New England, 1987-89; mem. exec. bd. Ill. Libr. Computer Sys. Orgn., 1995-99; chair Coun. Dirs. State Univ. Librs., 1994-95, 2001—; sr. fellow UCLA, 1991; pres. Ill. Libr. Assn., 2002. Author: Books for Sammies: American Library Association and World War I, 1981, American Library History: A Bibliography of Dissertations and Theses, 1988, Higher Education in American Life, 1636-1986: A Bibliography of Dissertations and Theses, 1988, Cities and Towns in American History: A Bibliography of Doctoral Dissertations, 1989, Academic Libraries: Research Perspectives, 1990, Religion and the American Experience, 1620-1900: A Bibliography of Doctoral Dissertations, 1992, Religion and the American Experience, the Twentieth Century: A Bibliography of Doctoral Dissertations, 1994; editl. bd. various jours. Chair Coun. of Dirs. Ill. State Univ. Librs., 1994-95, 2001-02. Served to capt. USAF, 1964-68. Recipient Berner Nash award U. Ill., 1976. Mem. ALA (chmn. editl. bd., chair Libr. Rsch. Seminar I, 1996), Assn. Coll. and Rsch. Librs. (publs. in librarianship 1982-88, chmn. Jesse H. Shera Endowment Fund com. 1991-94), Ill. Libr. Assn., S.C. Libr. Assn. (chmn. libr. adminstrn. sect. 1991-92), Assn. Rsch. Librs. (scholarly commn. com. 1991-93), Orgn. Am. Historians, Am. Hist. Assn., Horatio Alger Soc. (pres. 1999-2000), Caxton Club (Chgo.), Phi Kappa Phi, Beta Phi Mu, Phi Delta Kappa. Episcopalian. Home: 912 Borden Ave Sycamore IL 60178-3200

YOUNG, BARBARA, psychiatrist, psychoanalyst, psychiatry educator, photographer; b. Chgo., Oct. 27, 1920; d. William Harvey and Blanche (DeBra) Y. AB, Knox Coll., 1942; MD, Johns Hopkins U., 1945; grad., Balt. Psychoanalytic Inst., 1955. Intern Univ. Hosps., Iowa City, 1945-46, asst. resident in neurology, 1945-47; asst. resident in psychiatry Phipps Clinic, Johns Hopkins U. Hosp., Balt., 1947-49; staff psychiatrist Perry Point (Md.) VA Hosp., 1949-51; practice medicine specializing in psychiatry/psychoanalysis Balt., 1951—; instr. Johns Hopkins U., 1953-69, asst. prof. psychiatry, 1969—, prof. emeritus, 1997—; freelance photographer, 1958—. Lectr. dept. psychiatry Johns Hopkins U.; lectr. Lucy Daniels Found., Carey, N.C., dept. humanities Yale U. Med. Sch., Boston Inst. for Psycho-therapy, local psychiat. and social orgns. Works represented in Mus. Modern Art, N.Y.C., Balt. Mus. Art, Santa Barbara (Calif.) Mus. Art, Eastman House, Rochester, N.Y., Yale U. Gallery of Art; photographer: The Plop-A-Lop Tree, 1995. Mem. Am. Psychoanlytic Assn., Am. Psychiat. Assn., Balt.-Washington Soc. for Psychoanalysis. Democrat. Address: 5307 Herring Run Dr Baltimore MD 21214-1937

YOUNG, BARNEY THORNTON, lawyer; b. Chillicothe, Tex., Aug. 10, 1934; s. Bayne and Helen Irene (Thornton) Y.; m. Sarah Elizabeth Taylor, Aug. 31, 1957; children: Jay Thornton, Sarah Elizabeth, Serena Taylor. BA, Yale U., 1955; LLB, U. Tex., 1958. Bar: Tex. 1958. Assoc. Thompson, Knight, Wright & Simmons, Dallas, 1958-65; ptnr. Rain, Harrell, Emery, Young & Doke, 1965-87; mem. firm Locke Purnell Rain Harrell (A Profl. Corp.), 1987-98; of counsel Locke, Liddell & Sapp LLP, 1999—. Mem. adv. coun. Dallas Cmty. Chest Trust Fund, Inc., 1964-66; bd. dirs. Mental Health Assn. Dallas County, Inc., 1969-72, Trammell Crow Family Found., 1984-87; trustee Hockaday Sch., Dallas, 1971-77, 90—, chmn., 1994-96, Dallas Zool. Soc., 1986-92, Lamplighter Sch., Dallas, 1976-99, chmn., 1983-86, St. Mark's Sch., Dallas, 1970—, pres., 1976-78, The Found. for Callier Ctr. and Comm. Disorders, 1970—, pres., 1976-78, The Found. for Human Nutrition, 1988—, Shelter Ministries of 1988-99, Friends of Ctr. for Human Nutrition, 1988—, Shelter Ministries of Dallas Found., 1993—, Dallas Hist. Soc., 1993-2001; bd. dirs. Susan G. Komen Breast Cancer Found., 2000—, Nat. Assn. Ind. Schs., 2000—; mem. Yale Devel. Bd., 1984-91, 1998—. Fellow Tex. Bar Found., Dallas Bar Found.; mem. ABA, Tex. Bar Assn., Dallas Bar Assn., Am. Judicature Soc., Order of Coif, Phi Beta Kappa, Pi Sigma Alpha, Phi Gamma Delta, Phi Delta Phi, Dallas Country Club., Petroleum Club (Dallas), Yale Club (Dallas, N.Y.C.). Home: 6901 Turtle Creek Blvd Dallas TX 75205-1251 Office: Locke Liddell & Sapp LLP 2200 Ross Ave Ste 2200 Dallas TX 75201-6776

YOUNG, BETTE ANN, writer; b. Columbus, Ohio, Jan. 9, 1937; d. Richard Jack Abel and Gussie Ruth Dean Seiden; m. robert David Roth Mar. 17, 1957 (div. Dec. 1980); children: Deborah Anne Fay, Diane Hope Helbig, Robert David Roth Jr.; m. Sheldon Mike Young, Nov. 11, 1988. BA in Sociology, Oakland U., 1971; MA in Am. Culture, U. Mich., 1974, postgrad., 1977. Dir. libr. Jewish Cmty. Ctr., Detroit, 1980-82; edn. dir. Jewish Parents' Inst., 1980-82; lectr. Adult Coll. Jewish Studies, Columbus, Ohio, 1985-87; adminstrv. sec. Nat. Coun. Jewish Women, 1985-90; cons., membership dir., grant writer Columbus Jewish Hist. Soc., 1987-90, oral historian, 1990—. Author: Congregation Shaarey Zedek, 1981, The History of the Association of Jewish Community Organization Personnel, 1969-87, 1987, The Columbus Jewish Foundation, 1994, Emma Lazarus in Her World, 1995; book critic Jewish News, 1980-82, Ohio Jewish Chronicle, 1991—, Columbus Dispatch, 1992—. Cmty. cons. Anti-Defamation League, Detroit, 1982-83. Democrat. Home: 4776 Smoketalk Ln Westerville OH 43081-7838

YOUNG, BRUCE KENNETH, film director; b. Reno, Dec. 1, 1960; s. Kenneth Evans and Mae Wittenmyer Y.; m. Jennifer Law, Aug. 7, 1993. BA, Washington and Lee U., 1982. Dir. (documentary film) Stolen Years, 1999 (Capital Region emmy, 1999). Mem. Nat. Press Club, White House News Photographers' Assn. Office: Evans-McCan Group PO Box 763 Lexington VA 24450 E-mail: bruce@evans-mccan.org.

YOUNG, BRYAN ALAN, musician, educator; b. Brockton, Mass., Feb. 19, 1964; s. Douglas Alan and Judith Ann Young; m. Beth Anne Vasil, June 24, 1990; children: Jeremy, Benjamin. MusB in Classical Performance, Boston Conservatory Music, 1986; MusB in Edn., Berklee Coll. Music, 1988; MusM, U. Conn., 1996. Orff cert. K-3 coord. Ward After-Sch., Newton, Mass., 1989—93; music educator Hastings Mid. Sch., Fairhaven, 1993—. Freelance musician, pvt. instr., Boston, 1982—; dir. music Acushnet Classic Ensemble, Fairhaven, 1998—. Mem.: Music Educator Nat. Conf. Episcopalian. Avocations: painting, woodworking, gardening, cooking. Home: PO Box 1102 Lakeville MA 02347 Office: Hastings Mid Sch 30 School St Fairhaven MA 02719 Personal E-mail: bayoung@massed.net.

YOUNG, BRYANT LLEWELLYN, lawyer, business executive; b. Rockford, Ill., Mar. 9, 1948; s. Llewellyn Anker and Florence Ruth Y. AB, Cornell U., 1970; JD, Stanford U., 1974. Bar: Calif. 1974, Nev. 1975, D.C. 1979. Law clk. U.S. Dist. Ct. (no. dist.) Calif., San Francisco, 1974-75; assoc. Dinkelspiel, Pelavin, Steefel & Levitt, 1975-77; White House fellow, spl. asst. to sec. HUD, Washington, 1977-78, spl. asst. to sec., 1978-79, acting dep. exec. asst. for ops. Office of Sec., 1979; from dep. gen. mgr. to acting gen. mgr. New Cmty. Devel. Corp., 1979-80; mgmt. cons. AVCO Corp., 1980; spl. asst. to chmn. bd., CEO U.S. Synthetic Fuels Corp., Washington, 1980-81, project dir., 1981; pres. Trident Mgmt. Corp., San Francisco, 1981-87; of counsel Pelavin, Norberg, Harlick & Beck, 1981-82, ptnr., 1982-87; mng. ptnr. bus. section Carroll, Burdick & McDonough, 1987-90; founding ptnr. Young, Vogl & Harlick, 1990-93, Young, Vogl, Harlick, Wilson & Simpson, LLP, San Francisco, 1993-99; pres. Young Enterprises, Inc., 1995—; mgr. SRY Industries LLC, 1997—, KML Hospitality Industries LLC, 1997—; ptnr. Young Vogl LLP, 1999—2001; prin. Law Offices of Bryant L. Young, 2002—. Dir. The Whitman Inst. Pub. affairs com. San Francisco Aid Retarded Citizens, Inc., 1977; U.S. co-chmn. New Towns Working Group, U.S.-USSR Agreement on Cooperation in Field of Housing and Other Constrn., 1979-80; treas., bd. dirs. White House Fellows Found., 1980-84; prin. Coun. Excellence in Govt., Washington, 1986-94; adv. com. Nat. Multi-Housing Coun., 1987-92; mem. Ross Sch. Found., 1994-97, sec., 1995-97; bd. dirs. Marin AIDS Project, 1996-97, sec., 1997; trustee Ross Sch., 1997-2001. Mem. ABA (real property, trust and probate law sects. 1975-96), White House Fellows Assn. (chmn. ann. meeting 1979, del. China 1980), Marin County Sch. Bds. Assn., Am. Field Svc. Returnees Assn., Can.-Am. C. of C. No. Calif. (v.p., bd. dirs. 1992), Chile-Calif. Found. (exec. com., bd. dirs. 1993-96). Office: 425 California St Ste 2550 San Francisco CA 94104-2212 E-mail: bly@ebzlaw.net.

YOUNG, C. CLIFTON, state supreme court justice; b. Nov. 7, 1922, Lovelock, Nev.; m. Jane Young. BA, U. Nev., 1943; LLB, Harvard U., 1949. Bar: Nev. 1949, U.S. Dist. Ct. Nev. 1950, U.S. Supreme Ct. 1955. Justice Nev. Supreme Ct., Carson City, 1985—, chief justice, 1989-90. Office: Nev Supreme Ct 201 S Carson St Carson City NV 89701-4702*

YOUNG, C. W. (BILL YOUNG), congressman; b. Harmarville, Pa., Dec. 16, 1930; m. Beverly Young; children: Robert, Billy, Patrick. Mem. Fla. State Senate, 1961—71, minority leader, 1967—71; chmn. ho. appropriations/intelligence coms. 92nd-107th Congresses from 10th dist. Fla., 1971—; mem. Fla. Constn. Revision Commn., 1965-67; chmn. So. Hwy. Policy Com., 1966-68; mem. Electoral Coll., 1968. Appropriations com., chmn. subcom. Def., Labor, HHS and Edn. Fla. Legislature. With Nat. Guard USAR, 1948—57. Named Most Valuable Senator, Capitol Press Corps, 1969. Methodist. Office: US Ho Reps 2407 Rayburn Ho Office Bldg Washington DC 20515-0910 E-mail: bill.young@mail.house.gov.*

YOUNG, CHARLES EDWARD, university chancellor emeritus; b. San Bernardino, Calif., Dec. 30, 1931; s. Clayton Charles and Eula May (Walters) Young. AA, San Bernardino Coll., 1954; AB, U. Calif., Riverside, 1955; MA, UCLA, 1957, PhD, 1960; DHL (hon.), U. Judaism, L.A., 1969; DHL (hon.), Occidental Coll., L.A., 1997. Congl. fellow, Washington, 1958—59; adminstrv. analyst Office of the Pres., U. Calif., Berkeley, 1959—60; asst. prof. polit. sci. U. Calif., Davis, 1960, UCLA, 1960—66, assoc. prof., 1966—69, prof., 1969—97, asst. to chancellor, 1960—62, asst. chancellor, 1962—63, vice chancellor, adminstrn., 1963—68, chancellor, 1968—97; interim pres. U. Fla., Gainesville, 1999—. Bd. dirs. Intel Corp., Acad. TV Arts and Sci. Found., L.A. Met. Project; cons. Peace Corps., 1961—62, Ford Found. on Latin Am. Activities, 1964—66. Mem. Nat. Com. on U.S.-China Rels.; adminstrv. bd. Internat. Assn. Univs; mem. Knight Found. Commn. on Intercollegiate Athletics, Calif. Coun. on Sci. and Tech., Town Hall of Calif., Carnegie Comm. Task Force on Sci. and Tech. and the States, Pacific Coun. on Internat. Policy, NCAA Pres.'s Commn., Coun. for Govt.-Univ.-Industry Rsch. Roundtable and the Nat. Rsch. Coun. Adv. Bd.-Issues in Sci. and Tech.; chancellor's assocs. UCLA; coun. trustees L.A. Ednl. Alliance for Restructuring Now; past chair. Assn. Am. Univs., Nat. Assn. State Univs. and Land-Grant Colls.; past co-chair Calif. Campus Compact; trustee UCLA Found.; bd. dirs. Found. Internat. Exchange Sci. and Cultural Info. by Telecom., L.A. Internat. Visitors Coun., Greater L.A. Energy Coalition, L.A. World Affairs Coun. With USAF, 1951—52. Named Young Man of Year, Westwood Jr. C. of C., 1962; recipient Inter-Am. U. Cooperaton award, Inter-Am. Orgn. Higher Edn., Neil H. Jacoby Internat. award, UCLA Student Ctr., 1987, Edward A. Dickson Alumnus of Yr. award, UCLA Alumni Assn., 1994, Disting. Svc. award, U. Calif. Riverside Alumni Assn., 1996, Treasure of L.A. award, L.A. Ctrl. City Assn., 1996, Albert Schweitzer Leadership award, Hugh O'Brien Youth Found., 1996; fellow, UCLA Coll. Letters and Sci., 1996. Fellow: AAAS. Office: U Fla 226 Tigert Hall PO Box 113150 Gainesville FL 32611-3150

YOUNG, CHARLES RANDALL, software and marketing professional; b. Phila., Dec. 18, 1950; s. Charles Calvin and Henrietta Emma (Sorber) Y.; m. Mary Frances Hoey, June 8, 1973. BS with honors in Math., Drexel U., 1973; MS in Computer and Info. Sci., Ohio State U., 1975. Programmer coop Princeton (N.J.) Time Sharing Svcs., 1969-71; grad. tchg. asst. Ohio State U., Columbus, 1973-75; compiler programmer Burroughs, Paoli, Pa., 1975-76; simulation programmer Sperry, Blue Bell, 1976-78, computer security lead programmer, designer, 1978-84, operating sys. group mgr., 1984-89; disk program devel. mgr. Unisys, 1989-91, compiler and posix program mgr., 1991-93, open/oltp program mktg. mgr., 1993-94, superserver, internet and security bus. product, mktg. dir., 1995—. Contbr. articles to profl. jours. Mem. IEEE, Assn. Shareware Profls. Reformed Episcopal. Avocations: swimming, opera, church bass soloist, tennis. Home: 412 Norristown Rd Ambler PA 19002-2737 Office: Unisys PO Box 500 Blue Bell PA 19424-0001

YOUNG, C(ORNELIUS) B(RYANT), JR. electronics engineer; b. Sardis, Miss., Sept. 2, 1926; s. Cornelius Bryant Sr. and Ethel (Dorr) Y.; m. Marguerite Esther Grosso, May 27, 1950; children: Mark Joseph, Roy Neil, Annette Georgette, Neil Bryant. BEE, Ga. Inst. Tech., 1948; MEE, Bklyn. Poly. Inst., 1954; MS in Computer Sci., Stevens Inst. Tech., 1981. From jr. engr. to dir. applications engring. Western Union, N.Y.C., Upper Saddle River, N.J., 1948-84; sr. engring. specialist ITT Fed. Electric Corp., Paramus, 1985-89; mgr. commns. and comptrs. The BARC Group, Totawa, 1990-92; cons. C Squared Systems Engring., Ramsey, 1990—. Contbr. articles to profl. jours.; inventor microwave lens. Pres. Ramsey (N.J.) Ambulance Corps., 1987-89, 90-91, 96; chmn. Ramapo Valley ARC, Ramsey, 1987-88; chmn. troop 31, Boy Scouts of Am., Ramsey, 1968-76; vol. emergency room Valley Hosp., Ridgewood, N.J., 1980-94; mem. Ramsey Bd. Health, 1987—, Soc. of Valley Hosp., 1990—; vol. FISH Network, N.W. Bergen County, 1970-95. Lt. (j.g.) USNR, 1944-46, with res. 46-64, ret., 1964. Recipient Citizen of Yr. award Troop 31 Boy Scouts of Am., 1987. Mem. IEEE (life, sr.), Cons. Networks of N.Y. and N.J., Sigma Xi (assoc.). Republican. Baptist. Avocation: emergency medical services. Home: 68 Deer Trl Ramsey NJ 07446-2110

YOUNG, CRAIG C. sports medicine physician, educator; b. Inglewood, Calif., Aug. 1962; BS in Biol. Scis.,-U. Calif., Irvine, 1984; MD, U. Calif., San Diego, 1988. Diplomate Am. Bd. Sports Medicine, Am. Bd. Family Practice. Resident in family medicine UCLA, 1988-91; fellow in sports medicine Cleve. Clinic Found., 1991-92; asst. prof. Med. Coll. of Wis., Milw., 1992-98, med. dir. sports medicine, 1992—, assoc. prof., 1998—. Team physician Milw. Mustangs, 1993-2001, Milw. Brewers, 1994—, U.S. Nat. Snowboard Team, Salt Lake City, 1996—; co. physician Milw. Ballet, 1992—. Contbr. articles to profl. jours.; assoc. editor Sports Medicine Alert, 1995—; mem. editl. bd., reviewer Your Patient and Fitness, 1999-2001. Recipient Resident Tchr. award Soc. of Tchrs. of Family Medicine, 1991. Fellow Am. Coll. Sports Medicine, Am. Acad. Family Physicians; mem. Am. Med. Soc. for Sports Medicine, Major League Baseball Team Physicians Assn., Wilderness Med. Soc. Office: Med Coll of Wis 9200 W Wisconsin Ave Milwaukee WI 53226-3522

YOUNG, DALE LEE, banker; b. Palmyra, Nebr., Mar. 13, 1928; s. Mike P. and Grace (Clutter) Y.; m. Norma Marie Shalla, June 18, 1950; children—Shalla Ann, Philip Mike. BBA, U. Nebr., 1950. With FirsTier Bank N.A. (formerly First Nat. Bank & Trust Co.), Lincoln, Nebr., 1950-91, cashier, 1966-91, v.p., 1966-76, exec. v.p., 1976-92; sec. ISCO, Inc., 1991—, also bd. dirs. Bd. dirs. Woodmen Accident and Life Co.; sec., bd. dirs. Leasing Corp. Treas. Lincoln City Library Found.; Treas., mem. exec. com. Nebr. Republican Com., 1968— ; bd. dirs., v.p. Lincoln Symphony; bd. dirs. Lincoln Community Services, ARC, Lincoln Found.; trustee Bryan Meml. Hosp., 1976-80; mem. Lincoln City Coun., 1991-98, elected mayor, 1998. Served with AUS, 1946-48, 50-51. Mem. Nebr. Art Assn., Omaha-Lincoln Soc. Fin. Analysts, Lincoln C. of C. (pres.), Theta Xi. Clubs: Nebraska, Lincoln Country, Univ. Presbyterian. Home: 3911 Firethorn Ct Lincoln NE 68520-1466 Office: PO Box 81008 Lincoln NE 68501-1008

YOUNG, DARLENE ANN, small business owner; b. Pasadena, Calif., Nov. 02; d. James Burdick and Alice (Fussell) Slemons; m. F. Thomas Meehan, (div.); children: Tamara Meehan D'Ornellas, Michael Thomas; m. John R. Young, July 10, 1970. BS in Econs., U. Calif., Davis. Owner, mgr. Royal Coach Village and Royal Coach Trails, Houston, 1978—. Past pres. Glendale (Calif.) Philharm., Child Help, Performing Arts Coun. Orange County. Mem. Rsch. Assn. U. Calif.-Irvine Coll. Medicine (hon.). Republican. Presbyterian. Office: Royal Coach Village 700 W Greens Rd Houston TX 77067-4435 also: Royal Coach Trails 14003 W Hardy Rd Houston TX 77060-5329

YOUNG, DAVID BENNION, artist; b. Provo, Utah, Sept. 22, 1932; s. Karl Egbert and Elma Bennion Y.; m. Annette Deaton, June 5, 1956 (div. 1972); children: David Karl, Karen Ruth, Charri Young Sutherlin, Stanton Edwin; m. Mary Ann Futa, Feb. 27, 1994. BA in Art Edn., San Jose State U., 1959, MA in Art Landscape Painting, 1963; MFA in Painting, U. Ariz., 1978. Tchr. art Mt. Whitney H.S., Visalia, Calif., 1959-62, Saratoga (Calif.) H.S., 1963-64; lectr. art San Jose State U., 1964-65; tchr. art Mesa State Coll., Grand Junction, Colo., 1967-68, Douglas (Ariz.) H.S., 1971-75; assoc. prof. art Ctrl. Wyo. Coll., Riverton, 1980-89; retired, 1989. One-man shows include Brigham Young U., Provo, 1966, 78, 80, 88, 92, Visual Art Assn., Jackson Hole Wyo., 1992, Western Colo. Ctr. for the Arts, 1988, Ctrl. Wyo. Coll. , 1981, 82, 84, 90, 99. With inf. U.S. Army, 1952-54, Korea. Avocations: fishing, hunting, reading, exercising, photography. Home: 1578 17 Rd Loma CO 81524-9783

YOUNG, DAVID BRADLEY, lawyer; b. Delaware, Ohio, Aug. 1, 1970; BA, Ohio State U., 1993; JD, Willamette U., 1997; LLM, U. San Diego, 1998. Bar: Oreg. 1997, Calif. 1998. Staff counsel SANYO N.Am. Corp., San Diego, 1998—. Evans scholar Western Golf Assn., 1988. Avocations: golf, skiing, basketball. Office: SANYO N Am Corp 2055 Sanyo Ave San Diego CA 92154-6229

YOUNG, DAVID MICHAEL, biochemistry and molecular biology educator, physician; b. Bluffton, Ind., Oct. 11, 1935; s. Eli and Ruth (Comer) Y.; m. Diane Tangeman, Dec. 28, 1957 (div. 1971); children: Peter Michael, Amy Katherine; m. Lucia Virginia Patat, Sept. 2, 1972; children: David Michael II, Allison Amelia. BS, Duke U., 1957, MD, 1959. Diplomate: Nat. Bd. Med. Examiners. Intern pediatrics dept. Duke U. Med. Ctr., Durham, N.C., 1958-60; staff scientist Lab Cellular Physiology and Metabolism Nat. Heart Inst., NIH, 1960-62; vis. scientist McCollum-Pratt Inst., Johns Hopkins U., Balt., 1962-63, asst. prof. biology, 1963-64; asst. prof. Harvard U. Med. Sch., Boston, 1965-72, assoc. prof. Biol. chemistry, 1972-79, tutor biochem. scis., 1966-76, mem. grad. program for advanced study in immunology, 1971-76, assoc. chmn. div. med. scis., chmn. program for cell biology, 1972-76; head Lab Phys. Biochemistry Mass. Gen. Hosp., 1965-79; prof. biochemistry U. Fla. Coll. Medicine, Gainesville, 1979—, prof. medicine, 1979-86, chmn. dept. biochemistry and molecular biology, 1979-81, prof. molecular biology, 1981-86, prof. pediatrics, 1986—. Mem. cell physiology study sect. NIH, Bethesda, Md., 1978-82, sect. chmn., 1980; acad. assoc. Nichols Inst., San Juan Capistrano, Calif., 1976—; vis. prof. biology Johns Hopkins U., 1994, 95.

Editor-in-chief: Jour. Molecular and Cellular Biochemistry, 1983— ; patentee nerve growth factor, nerve growth factor antibody. Served to sr. surgeon USPHS, 1959-63. USPHS spl. fellow, 1962; recipient career devel. award USPHS, 1967-72; NIHresearch grantee, 1964— ; grantee John A. Hartford Found., 1968-73 Fellow AAAS; mem. Am. Soc. Biol. Chemists, Am. Chem. Soc., Biophys. Soc., Am. Soc. for Clin. Investigation, Am. Heart Assn. (research allocations com. 1976-79), Am. Soc. for Cell Biology, Alpha Omega Alpha Home: HC 33 Box 213 A Seal Cove ME 04674

YOUNG, DAVID NELSON, media and communications consultant; b. Baton Rouge, Nov. 12, 1953; s. Nelson Joseph and Agnes (LeBlanc) Young; m. Michéle Marie-Therese Bedél, May 7, 1979; children: Jason, Jessica. Student, La. State U., 1972, U. S.W. La., 1975. News editor Gonzales (La.) Weekly, 1976-77. Organizer Soviet/Am. Culinary Exch., 1989, Soviet/Am. High Sch. Basketball Excha., 1990; cons. in field. Host, Ascension Jour. TV Show. Bd. dirs. Ascension Cancer/Leukemia Soc., Gonzales, 1978—; organizer Societ/Am. High Sch. Basketball Exch.; nat. conmmitteeman La. Dem. Ctrl. Com., 1996-2000. Recipient Best-in-Depth Reporting award La. Newspaper Assn., 1984, Appreciation award USIA, 1988, Sovincentr Medal Honor, Moscow World Trade Ctr., 1988. Mem. East Ascension Genealogical Soc. (pres. 1980-81), East Ascension Sportsman League. Roman Catholic. Avocations: reading, computing, cooking. Office: DN Young & Assocs Inc 203 W Ascension St Gonzales LA 70737-2803

YOUNG, DAVID SAMUEL, minister; b. Mechanicsburg, Pa., Nov. 3, 1944; s. Grace Wolf Young; m. Joan Elizabeth Reznar, Nov. 26, 1966; children: Jonathan, Andrew. BS magna cum laude, Elizabethtown (Pa.) Coll., 1966; MDiv cum laude, Bethany Theol. Sem., Oak Brook, Ill., 1970, DMin, 1976. Ordained to ministry Ch. of the Brethren, 1970. Pastor Bush Creek Ch. of Brethren, Monrovia, Md., 1970-78, Everett (Pa.) Ch. of Brethren, 1978-80, Goshen (Ind.) City Ch. of Brethren, 1980-82, Mingo Ch. of the Brethren, Royersford, Pa., 1983-86; hospice pastor Crozer Chester Med. Ctr., Upland, 1987-95; interim assoc. pastor Elizabethtown Ch. of Brethren, 1996-97; interim pastor Mohler Ch. of Brethren, 1997-99, Hatfield Ch. of the Brethren, 1999—. Adj. prof. spiritual formation and ch. renewal Ea. Bapt. Theol. Sem., Phila., 1986—; bd. dirs. Bethany Theol. Sem., Oak Brook, 1978-83; chmn. nurture Mid-Atlantic Dist., Md., 1977-78; dean Ctr. for Bibl. Studies, Frederick, Md., 1977-78, co-chair Spiritual Renewal Team of Atlantic NE Dist.; congregation transformation specialist Am. Bapt. Ch., 2000—; bd. dirs. Light House Vocat. Svcs. Editor: Study War No More, 1981; author: James: Practical Faith and Active Love, 1992, A New Heart and A New Spirit, A Plan for Renewing Your Church, 1994, Servant Leadership for Church Renewal, Shepherds by the Living Springs, 1999; contbr. chapters to books, articles to profl. jours. Chair Regional Renovaire Conf. in 2000; bd. dirs. Lighthouse Vocat. Svcs. NSF fellow, 1966, 66, 67. Mem. Ministers Assn., Alban Inst., Greenleaf Ctr. for Servant Leadership. Home: 464 Ridge Ave Ephrata PA 17522-2559 E-mail: davidyoung@churchrenewalservant.org. *Awakened to God's living presence, the life of faith is one of gratitude, strength, and obedience. In an era of spiritual renewal, our life of continual prayer is joyously turned into faithful action.*

YOUNG, DAVID WILLIAM, management educator; b. L.A., Feb. 8, 1942; s. William Albert and Hilda Mary (Cook) Y.; m. Ernestine M.L. Van Schaik, Oct. 4, 1968 (div. 1975); m. Francesca Michela Larson, Jan. 28, 1984; children: Christian William, Anthony Edwin. BA, Occidental Coll., 1963; MA, UCLA, 1966; D in Bus. Adminstrn., Harvard U., 1977. Systems engr. IBM, Glendale, Calif., 1963-64; asst. to pres. Lundberg Survey, Inc., Hollywood, 1964-66; program economist U.S. AID, El Salvador, 1966-69; cons. Thomas Goldsmith & Assoc., Cambridge, Mass., 1969-71; mng. dir. Commonwealth Mgmt. Sys., 1971—; assoc. prof. mgmt. Harvard U. Sch. Pub. Health, Boston, 1976-85, adj. faculty mem., 1985—; prof. mgmt. Boston U. Sch. Mgmt., 1985—, chmn. dept. acctg., 1986-91, dir. acctg. MBA program, 1989-93, dir. inst. acctg. rsch. and edn., 1989-93, dir. health care mgmt. program, 1991-94; prin. The Crimson Group, Cambridge, 1994—. Vis. prof. mgmt. control Instituto de Estudios Superiores de la Empresa, Barcelona, Spain, 1984. Author: The Managerial Process in Human Service Agencies, 1979, Financial Control in Health Care, 1984, The Hospital Power Equilibrium, 1985, Management Control in Nonprofit Organizations, 1984, 88, 94, 99, 2002,Introduction to Financial and Management Accounting: A User Perspective, 1994, Primer on Financial Accounting, 1998, Primer on Management Accounting, 1999, Managing Integrated Delivery Systems: A Framework for Action, 1999; contbr. articles to profl. jours. Trustee Roxbury Comprehensive Cmty. Health Ctr., 1983-86, Art Inst., Boston, 1990-96, Mass. Eye and Ear Infirmary, Boston, 1990-92, Symmes Hosp., Arlington, 1993-94, The Atrium Sch., 1995-97, Youville Hosp., 1997-2000, Coolidge Corner Theatre Found., 2000—, Spaulding Rehab. Hosp., 2001—; commr., chair Mass. Hosp. Payment Sys., 1992-95. Milton Fund fellow Harvard Med. Sch., 1984. Mem. Am. Acctg. Assn. Democrat. Office: Boston U Sch Mgmt 595 Commonwealth Ave Boston MA 02215-1704 E-mail: dwy204@cs.com.

YOUNG, DAVID YEW WING, urologist; b. Honolulu, May 23, 1940; s. Jim Ting and Rose G.L. (Ne) Y.; m. Marie Louise Benito, June 3, 1995; children: Michelle, Glenn. BA, U. Hawaii, 1962; MD, Tulane U., 1966. Diplomate Am. Bd. Urology. Intern Harbor Gen. Hosp., 1966-67, resident in gen. surgery Calif., 1967-68; resident in urology U. Oreg. Health Scis., 1970-74; urologist Portland (Oreg.) Clinic, 1974-78; clin. instr. OHSU, Portland, 1974-94; pvt. practice urology, 1978—. Mem. AMA, Western Sect. of Am. Urology Assn., , Am. Urol. Assn., Oreg. Med. Assn., Oreg. Urol. Assn., N.W. Urol. Assn., Washington County Med. Assn. Avocations: gardening, fishing, golf, woodworking. Office: Westside Urology Assocs 421 SE 6th St Hillsboro OR 97123

YOUNG, DEBORAH (DEBORAH AYLING YANOWITZ), social worker, librarian; b. Syracuse, N.Y., June 27, 1950; d. David and Jean (AyLing) Y. Student, Pa. State U., Wilkes-Barre and Altoona; postgrad., Pa. State U., Wilkes-Barre, 1988; BA magna cum laude, Wilmington Coll., 1972; MSW, Western Mich. U., 1979; postgrad., Elmira Coll, 1983-84; MLS, U. Pitts., 1994. Cert. social worker, Mich., Pa., N.Y.; cert. pub. libr., N.Y., Va.; cert. homemaker-home health aide Found. Hospice and Homecare. Homeworker Kalamazoo Pub. Schs., 1974-76; group leader, project coord. Kalamazoo Parks-Recreation Dept.-Youth Conservation Corps, 1977, 78; dir. summer camp Huntington Family Ctrs., Inc., Syracuse, 1980-82; agy. dir. Schuyler Head Start-Day Care, Inc., Watkins Glen, Montour Falls, N.Y., 1982-87; pvt. practice child and elder care, N.Y., Mich., Pa, 1988-90; social worker, discharge planner VA Med. Ctr., Altoona, Pa., 1990-91; libr. worker U. Pitts. Sch. Libr. and Info. Scis., 1993-94; vocat. worker Laurelton (Pa.) Ctr., 1994-95; children-young adult svcs. coord., reference libr. Petersburg (Va.) Pub. Libr., 1996-97; libr. dir. Berwick (Pa.) Pub. Libr., 1997-98, Hollidaysburg (Pa.) Free Pub. Libr., 1999—2002. Mem., past camp staffer Cir. Pines Ctr., Delton, Mich., 1967—; vol. ARC, N.Y., Mich., Pa., 1965—; mem, rotating chmn. Watkins Glen Human Svcs. Com., 1982-87; reference and children's vol. Helper Altoona Area Pub. Libr., 1992-96; mem. choir Blessed Sacrament Cathedral, Altoona, 1991—; caregiver Babysitter Heaven Referral Svc., Altoona, 1995-96; mem. Blair County Health and Welfare Coun., Altoona, 1990-95, ARC; help-line tel worker Contact, Altoona, 1992; bd. dirs. Mental Health Assn. Human Svcs. Coalition, Columbia and Montour counties, Pa., 1997, 98; affiliation Religious Soc. Friends. Scholar Wilmington Coll., 1968-72, Office Vocat. Rehab., Pa. Dept. Labor and Industry, 1993-94; grad. fellow Western Mich. U., 1976. Mem. NASW, ALA, Green Key Honor Soc. Democrat. Roman Catholic. Avocations: swimming, travel, cooking, reading, writing.

YOUNG, DEIDRA JANE, educational researcher; b. Ottawa, Ont., Can., Nov. 19, 1955; came to Australia, 1970; d. Douglas Pedar and Elizabeth Alice (Allison) Holmberg; 1 child Lauren. BS, U. Western Australia, Perth, 1977; diploma of edn., Murdoch U., Perth, 1988; M in Applied Sci., Curtin U., Perth, 1988, PhD, 1991. Postdoctoral rsch. fellow Curtin U. Tech., 1991-94, Australian rsch. fellow, 1995-2000; sec. Western Austrlian Inst. Ednl. Rsch., Perth, 1998-2000; dir. Academe Consultancies, Karrinyup, Australia, 2000—. Sec. Western Australian Inst. Ednl. Rsch., Perth, 1998—. Author: How to Use HLM2, 1993, A Comparison of Student Performance in Metropolitan, Rural and Remote Western Australian Government Schools, 1994; contbr. numerous articles to profl. jours. and conf. procs., chpt. to book; conf. presenter in field; assoc. editor Education in Rural Australia. Recipient Brce Chopin Meml. award Internat. Assn. Ednl. Achievement, 1994. Mem. Am. Ednl. Rsch. Assn. (divsns. D and H, various spl. interest groups), Internat. Congress Sch. Effectiveness and Improvement, Nat. Assn. Rsch. in Sci. Tching., Australian Assn. Rsch. in Edn., Western Australian Inst. Ednl. Rsch. (exec. mem.), Australian Rural Edn. Rsch. Assn. (exec. mem.). Avocations: quilting, cross-stitching, crafts, swimming, walking. Home: 18 George St Stirling WA 6021 Australia Office: Academe Cons PO Box 21 Karrinyup WA 6921 Australia E-mail: deidrayoung@bigpond.com.

YOUNG, DIANE CAROLINE, pharmaceutical executive; b. Balt., Apr. 11, 1956; d. John Edwin and Violet Koski Young; m. Robert John Mich, Sept. 28, 1985; children: Shannon Mich, Ryan Mich. AB magna cum laude, Harvard U., 1977, MD, 1981. Diplomate Am. Bd. Internal Medicine, Am. Bd. Med. Oncology. Resident in internal medicine Johns Hopkins Hosp., Balt., 1981-83, Vanderbilt U. Hosp., Nashville, 1983-84; fellow in med. oncology Dana Farber Cancer Inst., Boston, 1984-87; instr. oncology Meml. Hosp., N.Y.C., 1987-88; asst. dir. R & D Hoffman-LaRoche, Nutley, N.J., 1988-90; dir. R & D Sandoz Pharms., East Hanover, 1990-92; from sr. dir. to v.p. global devel. Johnson & Johnson, Raritan, 1993—. Contbr. articles to profl. jours. Fellow Cancer Rsch. Inst., Cambridge, Mass., 1987; recipient TWIN award YWCA, Raritan, 1996. Mem. AMA, Am. Soc. Hematology, Am. Soc. Clin. Oncology, Soc. Biologic Therapy, Am. Assn. Pharm. Physicians, Phi Beta Kappa. Avocations: swimming, tennis, golf, piano. Home: 76 Prospect Hill Ave Summit NJ 07901

YOUNG, DONALD ALAN, physician; b. Oakland, Calif., Feb. 8, 1939; s. Leo Alan and Pearl Anita (Walker) Y.; children: Jennifer, Karen BA, U. Calif., Berkeley, 1960, MD, 1964. Diplomate Am. Bd. Internal Medicine. Intern, then resident in internal medicine U. Calif. Hosp., San Francisco, 1964-66; resident in internal medicine Parkland Hosp., Dallas, 1966-67; fellow chest diseases U. Calif. Hosp., San Francisco, 1967-68; mem. staff Palo Alto (Calif.) Med. Clinic, 1970-75; med. dir. Am. Lung Assn., 1975-77; scholar adminstrv. scholars program VA, Washington, 1977-80. Dep. dir. policy Bur. Program Policy Health Care Financing Adminstrn. HHS, Washington, 1980—84; exec. dir. Prospective Payment Assessment Commn., Washington, 1984—97; sr. v.p. Am. Assn. Health Plans, 1997—99; COO, med. dir., pres. Health Ins. Assocs. Am., 1999—; clin. instr. U. Calif. Med. Sch., San Francisco, 1968—70, Stanford U. Med. Sch., 1970—75. Bd. visitors Ind. U. Served with M.C. AUS, 1968-70. Decorated Commendation medal.; Recipient Borden award, 1964 Home: 6109 Trotter Ridge Ct Columbia MD 21044-4919 Office: Ste 500 1201 F St NW Washington DC 20004

YOUNG, DONALD ALLEN, writer, consultant; b. Columbus, Ohio, June 11, 1931; s. Clyde Allen and Helen Edith (Johnston) Y.; m. Rosemary Buchholz, Feb. 26, 1955 (div. Nov. 1976); children: Kent Allen, Kelly Ann; m. Marjorie Claire Shapiro, Aug. 20, 1977; stepchildren: Jo Alene, Andrea Lynn, Beth Ellen. Student, Ohio State U., 1949-51, Columbia Coll., 1952, North Cen. Coll., Naperville, Ill., 1956, Coll. DuPage, 1978. Editor various newspapers, mags., Detroit, Chgo., Columbus, 1946-63, 1973-74, 1978-79; v.p. Frydenlund Assocs., Chgo., 1963; pub. relations mgr. info. systems divsn. Gen. Electric Co., Phoenix, 1963-70; publs. dir. Data Processing Mgmt. Assn., Park Ridge, Ill., 1970-72; pub. relations mgr. Addressograph-Multigraph Corp., Arlington Heights, 1975-76; acct. exec. John Ripley & Assocs., Glenview, 1977-78; editorial dir. Radiology/Nuclear Medicine mag., Des Plaines, 1979-81; pres. Young Byrum Inc., Hinsdale, 1982-83; writer, consultant Tucson, 1983—. Cons. in field; sports reporter, Copley newspapers, 1975-83; mem. adv. council Oakton C.C., 1970-75. Author: Principles of Automatic Data Processing, 1965, Data Processing, 1967, Rate Yourself as a Manager, 1985, Nobody Gets Rich Working for Somebody Else, 1987, 2d edit., 1993, Rate Your Executive Potential, 1988, If They Can...You Can, 1989, The Entrepreneurial Family, 1990, How to Export, 1990, Women in Balance, 1991, Sleep Disorders: America's Hidden Nightmare, 1992, Small Business Troubleshooter, 1994, Crime Wave: America Needs a New Get-Tough Policy, 1996, Popcorn Publications, 1996, Adventure Guide to Southern California, 1997, Romantic Weekends: America's Southwest, 1998, Adventure Guide to the Pacific Northwest, 1998, Momentum: How to Get It-How to Keep It, 1999, Don't Get Mad-Get Rich, 1999, Walking Places in Washington DC, 2000. Arbitrator Better Bus. Bur., Tucson, 1987-92; docent Ariz. Sonora Desert Mus., 1988-92, Tucson/Pima Arts Coun., 1993-94. With USAF, 1952-56. Recipient Jesse Neal award Assn. of Bus. Pub., 1959, 61, Silver Anvil award Pub. Rels. Soc. of Am., 1976. Mem. Publicity Club of Chgo. (pres. 1978-79). Soc. Southwestern Authors (pres. 1992), Glen Ellyn (Ill.) Jaycees (bd. dirs., SPOKE award 1959, Outstanding Jaycee 1960), Young Reps. Club (v.p. 1960). Avocations: photography, travel, hiking, fishing. Home: 4866 N Territory Loop Tucson AZ 85750-5948 E-mail: dyoung1030@aol.com.

YOUNG, DONALD CLIFFORD, chemist, consultant; children: Mark Jefferson, Martha Diane Thompson, Rachel Jane Rhea, Steven John. PhD, U. Of Calif., Riverside CA, 1963—66. Sr. staff cons. Unocal, Brea, Calif., 1953—95; v.p. and chief tech. officer Enteck Corp., 1995—97. Pres. Donald C. Young & Associates, Fullerton, Calif., 1997—. Recipient Svc. Through Chemistry, Am. Chem. Soc., 1983, Presidents Prestigious Engring. Award, Orange County Engeering Coun., 2000. Fellow: Inst. For the Advancement Of Engring.; mem.: Am. Chenical Soc. Achievements include patents for Over 300 Patents in the chemical field. Avocation: faa certified flight instructor. Office: Donald C Young & Associates 245 Altura Drive Fullerton CA 92835-1301 Office Fax: 714-525-2228. E-mail: don1young@aol.com.

YOUNG, DONALD E. congressman; b. Meridian, Calif., June 9, 1933; m. Lula Fredson; children— Joni, Dawn. AA, Yuba Jr. Coll., 1952; BA , Chico (Calif.) State Coll., 1958. Former educator, river boat capt.; mem. Fort Yukon City Council, 6 years, mayor, 4 years; mem. Alaska Ho. of Reps., 1966-70, Alaska Senate, 1970-73, U.S. Congress from Alaska, 1973—; now ranking mem. transp. & infrastructure com., chmn. resources com., steering com. With U.S. Army, 1955-57. Republican. Episcopalian. Office: US Ho Reps 2111 Rayburn House Ofc Bldg Washington DC 20515*

YOUNG, DONALD FREDRICK, engineering educator; b. Joplin, Mo., Apr. 27, 1928; s. Oral Solomon and Blanche (Trent) Y.; m. Gertrude Ann Cooper, Apr. 15, 1950; children: Michael, Pamela, Susan, Christopher, David. BS, Iowa State U., 1951, MS, 1952, PhD, 1956. Research engr. AEC Ames Lab., 1952-55; asst. prof. Iowa State U., Ames, 1955-58, assoc. prof., 1958-61, prof. engring. sci. and mechanics, 1961-74, Anson Marston Disting. prof. engring., 1974-99, Anson Marston Disting. prof. emeritus, 1999—. Author: Introduction to Applied Mechanics, 1972, (with others) Essentials of Mechanics, 1974, (with others) Fundamentals of Fluid Mechanics, 1990, 4th edit., 2002, (with others) A Brief Introduction to Fluid Mechanics, 1997, 2d edit., 2001; contbr. articles to profl. jours. Recipient Outstanding Tchr. award Standard Oil, 1971, Faculty citation Iowa State Alumni Assn., 1972, Spl. Recognition award Iowa State U. Rsch. Found., 1988, David R. Boylan Eminent award for rsch., 1995. Fellow ASME (chmn. bioengring. div. 1973-74); mem. Am. Heart Assn., Am. Soc. Engring. Edn., Pi Tau Sigma, Pi Mu Epsilon, Phi Kappa Phi, Sigma Xi Home: 2042 Prairie Vw E Ames IA 50010-4558 Office: Iowa State U 2271 Howe Hall Ames IA 50010

YOUNG, DONALD ROY, pharmacist; b. Belfast, Pa., Oct. 7, 1935; s. Roy Clifford and Gladys Nicholas (Ealer) Y.; m. Joyce Anne Waldridge; children: Donald, Lynda, David. BS in Pharmacy, U. Md., Balt., 1957. Pharmacist Brookside Rhodes Drugs Co., Newark, 1956-57; pharmacist, mgr. Newark Rhodes Drugs Co., 1957-64; pharmacist, owner, mgr. Hudson's Pharmacy, St. Michaels, Md., 1964—. Bd. dirs., officer St. Michaels Bank; treas. Calvert Drug Co. Balt., 1970-76. Pres. St. Michaels Improvement Corp., 1966—. Mem. Nat. Assn. Retail Druggists, Ea. Shore Pharm. Assn. (pres. 1967-68, 82-86), Talbot County C. of C. (Outstanding Small Bus. Man of Yr. award 1989), St. Michaels Bus. Assn. (pres.), U. Md. Sch. Pharmacy Alumni Assn. (life), Isaac Walton League, Miles River Yacht Club, Rotary (pres. St. Michaels 1970, Most Outstanding Mem. award 1988, Paul Harris fellow award 1995), Elks, Masons (32 degree, master 1969-70, apptd. jr. grand deacon of Grand Line 1989-90). Republican. Methodist. Avocations: golf, boating, fishing, travel, hiking. Home: PO Box 130 118 Tricefields Rd Saint Michaels MD 21663 Office: Hudsons Pharmacy PO Box 130 Saint Michaels MD 21663-0130

YOUNG, DONALD STIRLING, clinical pathology educator; b. Belfast, N. Ireland, Dec. 17, 1933; s. John Stirling and Ruth Muir (Whipple) Y.; m. Silja Meret; children: Gordon, Robert, Peter. MB, ChB, U. Aberdeen, Scotland, 1957; PhD in Chem. Pathology, U. London, 1962. Terminable lectr. materia medica U. Aberdeen, 1958-59; fellow Postgrad. Med. Sch., U. London, 1959-62, registrar, 1962-64; vis. scientist NIH, Bethesda, Md., 1965-66, chief clin. chemistry service, 1966-77; head clin. chemistry sect. Mayo Clinic, Rochester, Minn., 1977-84; prof. pathology and lab. medicine U. Pa., 1984—; dir. William Pepper Lab. Hosp. of U. Pa., 1984—; dir. R. Philip Custer Lab., Presbyn. Med. Ctr., 1997—. Past bd. dirs. Nat. Com. Clin. Lab. Standards. Co-editor: Drug Interference and Drug Metabolism in Clinical Chemistry, 1976, Clinician and Chemist, 1979, Chemical Diagnosis of Disease, 1979, Drug Measurement and Drug Effects in Laboratory Health Science, 1980, Interpretation of Clinical Laboratory Tests, 1985, Effects of Drugs on Clinical Laboratory Tests, 1999, Effects of Preanalytical Variables on Clinical Laboratory Tests, 1996. Recipient Dir.'s award NIH, 1977, Gerard B. Lambert award, 1974-75, MDS Health Group award Can. Soc. Clin. Chemists, 1978; Roman lectr. Australian Assn. Clin. Biochemists, 1979; Jendrassik award Hungarian Soc. Clin. Pathologists, 1985, ATB award Italian Soc. Clin. Biochemistry, 1987. Mem. Am. Assn. Clin. Chemistry (J.H. Roe award Capital sect. 1973, Bernard Gerulat award N.J. sect. 1977, Ames award 1977, Van Slyke award N.Y. met. sect. 1985, J.G. Reinhold award Phila. sect. 1993, past pres.), Internat. Fedn. Clin. Chemists (past pres.), Acad. Clin. Lab. Physicians and Scientists (past exec. com.), Assn. Clin. Biochemists (Ciba-Corning lectr. 1985). Achievements include research in clinical chemistry, optimized use of the clinical laboratory. Home: 1116 Remington Rd Wynnewood PA 19096-4045 Office: Hosp U Pa 3400 Spruce St Philadelphia PA 19104-4206 E-mail: donaldyo@mail.med.upenn.edu.

YOUNG, DOUGLAS REA, lawyer; b. L.A., July 21, 1948; s. James Douglas and Dorothy Belle (Rea) Y.; m. Terry Forrest, Jan. 19, 1974; 1 child, Megann Forrest. BA cum laude, Yale U., 1971; JD, U. Calif., Berkeley, 1976. Bar: Calif., 1976, U.S. Dist. Ct. (no. dist.) Calif. 1976, U.S. Ct. Appeals (6th and 9th cirs.) 1977, U.S. Dist. Ct. (ctrl. dist.) Calif. 1979, U.S. Dist. Ct. Hawaii, U.S. Dist. Ct. (so. dist.) Calif., U.S. Supreme Ct. 1982; cert. specialist in appellate law. Law clk. U.S. Dist. Ct. (no. dist.) Calif., San Francisco, 1976-77; assoc. Farella, Braun & Martel LLP, 1977-82, ptnr., 1983—. Spl. master U.S. Dist. Ct. (no. dist.) Calif., 1977-78, 88, 96, 2000; mem. Criminal Justice Act Def. Panel no. dist. Calif.; mem. faculty Calif. Continuing Edn. of Bar, Berkeley, 1982—, Nat. Inst. Trial Advocacy, Berkeley, 1984—, Practicing Law Inst., 1988—; adj. prof. Hastings Coll. Advocacy, 1985—; vis. lectr. law Boalt Hall/U. Calif., Berkeley, 1986; judge pro tem San Francisco Mcpl. Ct., 1984—, San Francisco Superior Ct., 1990—. Author: (with Purver and Davis) California Trial Handbook, ed edit., (with Hon. Richard Byrne, Purver and Davis), 3d edit., (with Purver, Davis and Kerper) The Trial Lawyers Book, (with Hon. Eugene Lynch, Taylor, Purver and Davis) California Negotiation and Settlement Handbook; contbr. articles to profl. jours. Bd. dirs. Berkeley Law Found., 1977-78, chmn., 1978-79; bd. dirs. San Francisco Legal Aid Soc., pres., 1993—; bd. dirs. Pub. Interest Clearinghouse, San Francisco, chmn., 1987—, treas., 1988—; chmn. Attys. Task Force for Children, Legal Svcs. for Children, 1987—; mem. State Bar Appellate Law Adv. Commn., 1994—. Recipient award of appreciation Berkeley Law Found., 1983. Fellow Am. Coll. Trial Lawyers, Am. Acad. Appellate Lawyers; mem. ABA (Pro Bono Pub. award 1992), San Francisco Bar Assn. (founding chmn. litigation sect. 1988-89, award of appreciation 1989, bd. dirs. 1990-91, pres. 2001), Calif. Acad. Appellate Lawyers, McFetridge Am. Inn of Ct. (master), Lawyers Club San Francisco. Democrat. Office: Farella Braun & Martel 235 Montgomery St Ste 3000 San Francisco CA 94104-2902

YOUNG, EDWIN HAROLD, chemical and metallurgical engineering educator; b. Detroit, Nov. 4, 1918; s. William George and Alice Pearl (Hicks) Y.; m. Ida Signe Soma, June 25, 1944; children: David Harold, Barbara Ellen. BS in Chem. Engring, U. Detroit, 1942; MS in Chem. Engring, U. Mich., 1949, MS in Metall. Engring, 1952. Chem. engr. Wright Air Devel. Center, Dayton, Ohio, 1942-43; instr. U. Mich., Ann Arbor, 1946-52, asst. prof., 1952-56, assoc. prof., 1956-59, prof. chem. and metall. engring., 1959-89, prof. emeritus chem. and metall. engring., 1989—. Mem. Mich. Bd. Registration for Profl. Engrs., 1963-78, chmn., 1969-70, 72-73, 75-76; mem. Mich. Bd. Registration for Architects, 1963-78 Author: (with L.E. Brownell) Process Equipment Design, 1959; contbr. articles to profl. jours. Dist. commr. Boy Scouts Am., 1961-64; mem. Wolverine coun., 1965-68. With USNR, 1943-46, to capt. Res. ret., 1978. Fellow ASME, ASHRAE, AIChE (Donald Q Kern award 1979), Am. Inst. Chemists, Engring. Soc. Detroit; mem. Am. Chem. Soc., Am. Soc. Engring. Edn., Nat. Soc. Profl. Engrs. (pres. 1968-69, award 1977), Mich. Soc. Profl. Engrs. (pres. 1962-63, Engr. of Year award 1976), Mich. Assn. of Professions (pres. 1966, Distinguished award 1970), Nat. Council Engring. Examiners, Naval Res. Assn., Res. Officers Assn., Sigma Xi, Tau Beta Pi, Phi Kappa Phi, Phi Lambda Upsilon, Alpha Chi Sigma. Republican. Baptist. Home: 609 Dartmoor Rd Ann Arbor MI 48103-4513 E-mail: ehyoung@engin.umich.edu.

YOUNG, ELIZABETH BELL, consultant; b. Franklinton, N.C., July 2, 1929; d. Joseph H. and Eulalia V. (Miller) B.; m. Charles A. Young, Nov. 27, 1964. BA, N.C. Cen. U., 1948, MA, 1950; PhD, Ohio State U., 1959. Cert. speech pathologist; cert. audiologist. Chairperson dept. English Barber Scotia Coll., Concord, N.C., 1949-52; dir. speech area, prof. Talladega (Ala.) Coll., 1954-56; dir. speech clinic, prof. Va. State U., Petersburg, 1956-57; prof. Fla. A&M U., Tallahassee, 1959; chmn. dept. English Fayetteville (N.C.) State U., 1959-63; speech pathologist, rsch. assoc. Howard U. Sch. Dentistry, Washington, 1963-64; prof., chairperson dept. English U. Md.-East Shore, Princess Anne, Md., 1965-66; prof., supr. Speech Clinic Cath. U. Am., Washington, 1966-79; congl. staff aide U.S. Ho. of Reps., 1981-82, 88-90; prof. speech U. D.C., 1983-84; cons. nat. and local orgns., 1985-88, 90—. Lectr. over 250 speeches, seminars and workshops; speechwriter, cons. Nat. Assn. Equal Opportunity in Higher Edn., Washington, 1990. Contbr. articles to profl. jours. Fundraiser, pub. rels. polit. candidates, 1963-90; bd. dirs. United Negro Coll. Fund, 1970-80, D.C. Gen. Hosp. Handicapped Intervention Program, 1970-91. Recipient Citations and Certs. of Achievement community and nat. orgns., 1959-90. Fellow Am. Speech-Lang.-Hearing Assn.; mem. Pub. Mems. Assn. (bd. mem. 1980-91, 97—), Ohio State U. Alumni Assn., N.C. Cen. U. Alumni Assn. Democrat. Baptist. Avocations: reading, collecting sculpture of foreign countries, travel, writing, public speaking.

YOUNG, ESTELLE IRENE, dermatologist, educator; b. N.Y.C., Nov. 2, 1945; d. Sidney D. and Blanche (Krosney) Young. BA magna cum laude, Mt. Holyoke Coll., 1967; MD, Downstate Med. Ctr., 1971. Intern Lenox Hill Hosp., N.Y.C., 1971-72, resident in medicine, 1972-73; resident in dermatology N.Y. U. Hosp., 1973—74; resident in dermatology Columbia Presbyn. Hosp., N.Y.C., 1974-75; resident in dermatology Boston U. Hosp., 1975-76; asst. dermatologist Harvard U. Health Svcs., Cambridge, Mass., 1975-76; assoc. staff mem. dermatology Boston U. Med. Ctr., 1976-77; practice medicine specializing in dermatology Petersburg, Va., 1976-97; mem. staff Poplar Springs Hosp., 1976—, Southside Regional Med. Ctr. (formerly Petersburg Gen. Hosp.), 1976—, Ctrl. State Hosp., 1976—. Clin. instr. dept. dermatology Med. Coll. Va., 1976—, asst. clinic prof., 1988-94, assoc. clin. prof., 1994—; sec. med. staff Petersburg Gen. Hosp., 1982. Contbr. articles to profl. jours. Fellow Am. Acad. Dermatology; mem. Va. Med. Soc., Va. Dermatology Soc., Tidewater Dermatology Soc. (pres. 1982-83), Physicians for Social Responsibility Soc., Tidewater Physicians for Social Responsibility (pres. 1990), Internat. Physicians for Prevention of Nuclear War, Southside Va. Med. Soc., Sigma Xi. Home and Office: PO Box 20182 New York NY 10021-0063 Fax: (212) 249-5948. E-mail: eiy112@aol.com.

YOUNG, EVELINE, social worker; b. Tucson, July 30, 1950; d. A. Hor and Lii Yee (Lum) Y.; m. Ka-Sing Lau, June 14, 1974; children: Helen, Elaine. BS, Pa. State U., 1972; MA, U. Chgo., 1974. Cert. social worker, Pa.; cert. tchr., Pa. Tng. specialist Chgo. City Colls., 1972-73; program liaison, social worker Pressley Ridge Sch., Pitts., 1975-76; program counselor, instr. Kans. State U., Manhattan, 1976-77; social worker I Mayview State Hosp., Bridgeville, Pa., 1977-78, 80-81, program dir., residential svc. supr., 1981—2001; inspector western region Pa. Personal Care Home, Pitts., 2001—. Tchr., tutorial specialist Pa. State U., University Park, 1972; counselor Dept. Pks. and Recreation, Phila., 1971. Sec. exec. com. Falk Sch. PTA, Pitts., 1989—90; mem. com. Orgn. of Chinese Ams.-Vietnamese Boat People Com., 1978—80; mem. fundraising com. Nat. Assn. Chinese Ams., 1977; bd. dirs. YWCA, 2000—, asst. sec., 2000, sec., 2001—02, nominating com., 2001. Named one of Outstanding Young Woman of Am., 1986. Mem. NASW, Nat. Coun. Tchrs.

Math., Soc. Am. Mil. Engrs. Democrat. Avocations: international travel, camping, hiking, swimming, cooking. Home: 5888 Marlboro Ave Pittsburgh PA 15217 Office: 750 Kossman Bldg 400 Stanwix St Pittsburgh PA 15222-1311 Fax: 412-565-5633.

YOUNG, EVERETT J. management consultant, agricultural economist; b. Webberville, Mich., Mar. 14, 1913; s. J.P. and Ullie Josephine (Sigourney) Y.; m. Irene Elizabeth Olick, June 18, 1949. BS in Agrl. Econs., Mich. State U., 1939, MBA, 1960. Field rep. Mich. Fam Bur., Lansing, Mich., 1940-45; asst. exec. sec. Mich. Assn. Farmer Coops., Lansing., 1945-55; fin., mktg. advisor U.S. State Dept., Thailand, 1955-57; mktg. specialist Mich. Dept. Agrl., Lansing, 1957-58; mgr. Dairy Assn. Retail Inds., Detroit, 1961-63; ast. dir. Agrl. Coop. Devel. Internat., Washington, 1968-70; appraiser County of Eaton, Charlotte, Mich., 1974-83; farm mgr. 2 farms pvt. practice, 1972-96. Cons. E. Jay Young Mktg., Detroit, 1962-68, Experience, Inc., Mnpls., 1969-71, Africa, Asia Internat. Devel. Svcs., Washington, 1971-73; chief of party Internat. Coop. Devel. Assn., Uruguay, 1969-70. Author: Agricultural Cooperative, 1952; (USDA Aid Pub.) Food Mktg. in Developing Countries, 1970. Bd. dirs. Episc. Westrn Diocese Mich., Kalamzaoo, 1978-82; exec. com. Eaton County Rep. Club, Charlotte, 1983. Recipient Bishop's cross Episc. Ch., Kalamazoo, 1978. Mem. Internat. Assn. Agrl. Economists, Am. Fgn. Svc. Assn., Internat. Platform Assn., Circumnavigators Club (life), Shriners, Patriarch Mich. State U., Knights Templar, Lansing Farmers Club. Republican. Methodist. Avocations: travel, organ, French lang. Home: 1797 Packard Hwy Charlotte MI 48813-9717

YOUNG, FRANK EDWARD, former federal agency administrator, religious organization administrator; b. Mineola, N.Y., Sept. 1, 1931; s. Frank E. and Erma F. Y.; m. Leanne Hutchinson, Oct. 20, 1956; children: Lorrie, Debora, Peggy, Frank, Jonathan. MD, SUNY, 1956; PhD, Case Western Res. U., 1962; DSc (hon.), Roberts Wesleyan Coll., 1983, Houghton Coll., 1984, SUNY, 1986, L.I. U., 1986, Western Bapt. Coll., 1988. Asst. prof. pathology Western Res. U., Cleve., 1962-65; assoc. mem. microbiology Scripps Clinic & Rsch. Found., LaJolla, Calif., 1965-68; assoc. prof. biology U. Calif., San Diego, 1967-70; mem. microbiology & exptl. pathology Scripps Clinic & Rsch. Found., LaJolla, 1968-70; prof. microbiology and chmn. dept., prof. pathology and radiation biology and biophysics U. Rochester, N.Y., 1970-79, dir. Med. Ctr., 1979-81, dean Sch. Medicine and Dentistry, 1979-84, v.p. for health affairs, 1981-84; commr. FDA, Rockville, Md., 1984-89, dep. asst. sec. for health sci. and environ., 1989-93; dir. office emergency preparedness, 1993-96; pastor adult ministries 4th Presbyn. Ch., Bethesda, Md., 1996—; exec. dir. Reformed Theol. Sem. Met. Washington, 1996-99; v.p. Reformed Theol. Sem., Md., 1999—. U.S. rep. WHO exec. bd., Geneva, 1985-88; bd. dirs. High Tech., Rochester, N.Y., 1983-84. Contbr. numerous articles on cloning, gene mapping, gene shuttle vectors, 1970-84; initiator Fed. Regulations rules to increase access to exptl. drugs to desperately ill, 1987-88. Lectr. Christian orgns., 1970—; mem. United Way, Rochester, N.Y., 1982-84, N.Y. State Statutory Adv. Com. on DNA, Albany, N.Y., 1978. Recipient sec.'s spl. citation Dept. Health and Human Svcs., 1989, Surgeon Gen.'s Exemplary Svc. medal, 1988, Disting. Svc. medal Pub. Health Svc., 1986, Edward Mott award, 1985, Surgeon Gen.'s Medallion, 1992. Mem. Inst. Medicine of NAS, AAAS, Am. Acad. Microbiology (bd. govs.). Avocations: fishing, boating, yard work. Office: Congregational Care 5500 River Rd Bethesda MD 20816-3342 E-mail: fyoung@4thpres.org.

YOUNG, FREDERIC HISGIN, information systems executive, data processing consultant; b. Boston, Sept. 7, 1936; s. Ralph Randel Jr. and Wilhelmina Amalia (Imberger) Y.; m. Carol Joan Costello, Sept. 7, 1963 (div. Dec. 1971); children: Tracy Jean, Jodi Ann; m. Kathleen Paula Thorne, Dec. 1, 1984. BBA, U. Mass., 1961; JD, Suffolk U., 1966. Mgr. systems and programs Matrix Corp., Burlington, Mass., 1968-69; sr. cons. Programming Dimensions, Inc., 1969-70; bus. mgr. JTB Rehab. Ctr., North Reding, Mass., 1970-75; regional bus. mgr. Mass. Dept. Mental Health, Waltham, 1975-78, dir. personnel mgmt. Boston, 1978-81; prin. cons. Lafayette Assocs., Chelsea, Mass., 1980-81; asst. regional dir. Corp. for Applied Systems, Indpls., 1982-84; v.p. cons. svcs. HAS, Inc., Carmel, Ind., 1984-88; v.p. info. sytems Ind. Fed. Credit Union, Anderson, 1988-95; sys. cons. AIC, Inc., Indpls., 1995-96; sr. cons. Whittman-Hart, Inc., 1996-98; pres. FHY Assoc., Inc., Rio Rancho, N.Mex., 1999-2000; sr. cons. MarchFIRST, Spencer, Ind., 2000-01; divsn. mgr. PACE, 2001—. With USN, 1954-56. Republican. Avocation: woodworking. Home: 1840 Carmichael Ln Spencer IN 47460 E-mail: f-young4@ccrtc.com.

YOUNG, GARY EUGENE, editor, poet; b. Santa Monica, Calif., Sept. 8, 1951; s. Claude Eugene Young and Jeanne Ewing; m. Margaret Orenstein, Apr. 19, 1986; children: Jake Gordon, Cooper Gene. BA, U. Calif. Santa Cruz, 1973; MFA, U. Calif. Irvine, 1975. Editor Greenhouse Rev. Press, Santa Cruz, 1973—. Author: Hands, 1979, The Dream of a Moral Life, 1990, Days, 1997, Braver Deeds, 1999, No Other Life, 2002. Recipient Pushcart prize in poetry, 1992, Poetry prize Peregrine Smith Books, 1999; fellow Nat. Endowment Arts, 1981, NEH, 1986. Mem. Acad. Am. Poets, Poetry Soc. Am., Fresno Poetry Assn., Jackalope Soc. Home and Office: 3965 Bonny Doon Rd Santa Cruz CA 95060-9706

YOUNG, GENEVIEVE LEMAN, publishing executive, editor; b. Geneva, Sept. 25, 1930; came to U.S., 1945, naturalized, 1968; d. Clarence Kuangson and Juliana Helen (Yen) Y.; m. Cedric Sun, 1955 (div. 1972); m. Gordon Parks, Aug. 26, 1973 (div. 1979). BA (Wellesley Coll. scholar), Wellesley Coll., 1952. Asst. editor Harper & Row (pubs.), N.Y.C., 1960-62, editor, 1962-64, asst. mng. editor, 1964-66, mng. editor, 1966-70; exec. editor J.B. Lippincott Co., N.Y.C., 1970-77, v.p., 1972-77; sr. editor Little, Brown & Co., N.Y.C., 1977-85; editor-in-chief Lit. Guild Am., 1985-88; v.p., editorial dir. Bantam Books, 1988-92. Alumna trustee Phillips Acad., Andover, Mass., 1975-78, class agt., 1979-85; mem. Wellesley Bus. Leadership Coun., 1989-98; mem. Youth Counseling League, 1986-98, pres., 1989-96, mem. com. of 100, 1991-93; mem. Literacy Ptnrs., Inc., N.Y.C., 1992-2001, sec., 1996-2001; mem. Andover Devel. Bd., 1993-98; trustee Jewish Bd. Family and Children's Svcs., 1996-98. Recipient Alumna Achievement award Wellesley Coll., 1982, Matrix award, 1988. Mem. Assn. Am. Pubs. (exec. coun. gen. pub. div. 1975-78, 85-87, freedom to read com. 1972-75), Women's Media Group (pres. 1981-82, 2d v.p. 1994-95), Century Assn. Home: 30 Park Ave New York NY 10016-3801

YOUNG, GEORGE CRESSLER, federal judge; b. Cin., Aug. 4, 1916; s. George Philip and Gladys (Cressler) Y.; m. Iris June Hart, Oct. 6, 1951; children: George Cressler, Barbara Ann. AB, U. Fla., 1938, LLB, 1940; postgrad., Harvard Law Sch., 1947. Bar: Fla. 1940. Practice in, Winter Haven, 1940-41; asso. firm Smathers, Thompson, Maxwell & Dyer, Miami, 1947; adminstrv., legislative asst. to Senator Smathers of Fla., 1948-52; asst. U.S. atty. Jacksonville, 1952; partner firm Knight, Kincaid, Young & Harris, 1953-61; U.S. dist. judge No., Middle and So. dists. Fla., 1961-73; chief judge Middle Dist., 1973-81, sr. judge, 1981—. Mem. com. on adminstrn. fed. magistrates system Jud. Conf. U.S., 1973-80 Bd. dirs. Jacksonville United Cerebral Palsy Assn., 1953-60. Served to lt. (s.g.) USNR, 1942-46. Mem. Rollins Coll. Alumni Assn. (pres. 1968-69), ABA (spl. com. for adminstrn. criminal justice), Fla. Bar Assn. (gov. 1960-61), Jacksonville Bar Assn. (past pres.), Order of Coif, Fla. Blue Key, Phi Beta Kappa, Phi Kappa Phi, Phi Delta Phi, Sigma Alpha Epsilon. Home: 2424 Shrewsbury Rd Orlando FL 32803-1334 Office: US Dist Ct 635 US Courthouse 80 N Hughey Ave Orlando FL 32801-2278

YOUNG, GEORGE HAYWOOD, III, investment banker; b. Washington, Feb. 10, 1959; s. George H. Jr. and Jeanne Marie (Collins) Y.; m. Adina Chouequet, Oct. 12, 1996; children: Nathalie Haywood, George Haywood IV. BA in Internat. Rels. with honors, Brown U., 1982; MPhil in Internat. Rels., Magdalene Coll., U. Cambridge, Eng., 1983; M in Pub. and Pvt. Mgmt., Yale U., 1987. Assoc. cons. Bain & Co., Boston, 1983-85; assoc. CS First Boston, N.Y.C., 1987-90, v.p., 1990-91, dir., 1992-94; White House fellow U.S. Dept. Treasury, Washington, 1991-92; sr. v.p. Lehman Bros., N.Y.C., 1994-96, mng. dir., 1996—, mng. dir., co-head of global comms. group, 2000—. Spkr. in field. Application reader White House Fellows Commn., N.Y.C., 1993—; mem. alumni coun. exec. com. Phillips Acad., Andover, Mass., 1994—98, vis. mem. fin. and investment com. bd. trustees, 1998—; mem. regional selection panel White House Fellows Commn., N.Y.C., 2002—; vol. Ch. of the Holy Trinity, 1990—97. Mem. Coun. Fgn. Rels., Assn. U.S. Army, Harrow Sch. Assn., Oxford and Cambridge U. Club, Yale Golf Club, Metedeconk Nat. Golf Club. Roman Catholic. Home: 138 W 17th St Apt 8 New York NY 10011-5412 Office: Lehman Bros 745 7th Ave New York NY 10019-0001 E-mail: gyoung@lehman.com.

YOUNG, GEORGE R. educator; b. Eldorado, Ill., May 7, 1958; s. George R. Young, Wilma L. Young; m. Sherry L. Vega, June 30, 1997. AS, Shawnee C.C., Ullin, IL, 1978; BS, So. Ill. U., Carbondale, IL, 1980, M in Accountancy, 1989; PhD, U. Tex., Arlington, 1996. CPA Ill. Staff acct. Weldon Birch, Acct., Eldorado, 1981—83; pvt. practice, 1983—89; ptnr. Tate & Young, CPAs, 1989—92; instr. Ind. State U., Terre Haute, Ind., 1989—93; asst. prof. Fla. Atlantic U., Ft. Lauderdale, 1996—. Contbr. articles to profl. jours. Bd. mem., treas Rotary Internat., Eldorado, 1985—88; founding mem., first treas. Friends of Eldorado Meml. Libr., 1985—86; bd. mem., treas. Eldorado Teen Town, 1986—91; pres. Eldorado C. of C., 1986—88; bd. mem. Saline County Indsl. Devel. Com., 1986—87. Mem.: AICPA, Am. Acctg. Assn., Ill. CPA Soc., Assn. Cert. Fraud Examiners (assoc.), Beta Gamma Sigma, Phi Kappa Phi, Beta Alpha Psi.

YOUNG, GLENNA ASCHE, elementary education educator; b. Lodi, Ohio, Apr. 14, 1955; d. Virgil Eugene and B. Lucille (Johnson) Asche; m. William Young, Aug. 6, 1983. BS, Ohio State U., 1977, cert. learning-behavioral disorders, 1981; MS, Ashland Coll., Columbus Ohio, 1988. Cert. K-12 phys. edn. tchr., Ohio. Kindergarten and elem. phys. edn. tchr. West Jefferson (Ohio) Local Schs., 1979-82; high sch. tchr. severe behavioral handicapped Madison County Schs., London, 1982-86; elem. tchr. learning disabled SW Licking Local Schs., Etna, 1986-88, tchr. elem. phys. edn., 1988—. Treas. Etna Sch. PTO, 1989-91. Recipient Golden Apple award Ashland Oil Co. Mem. West Jefferson Edn. Assn. (Disting. Svc. award, President's award), SW Licking Local Edn. Assn. (bldg. rep. 1989-92, sec. 2002—). Home: 9550 Haaf Farm Dr Pickerington OH 43147-8401 E-mail: gyoung@laca.org.

YOUNG, GWYNNE A. lawyer; b. Durham, N.C., 1950; AB, Duke U., 1971; JD, U. Fla., 1974. Bar: Fla. 1974. Asst. state atty. 13th Judicial Cir., Fla.; mem. Carlton, Fields, Ward, Emmanuel, Smith & Cutler P.A., Tampa. Instr. U. Fla. Coll. Law, 1974. Exec. editor U. Fla. Law Review, 1973-74. Pres. Jr. League Tampa, Inc., 1985-86; bd. dirs. Assn. Jr. Leagues, Inc., 1987-89, Duke U. Nat. Alumni Assn., 1993—, pres., 1999-2000; trustee Duke U., 1999—. Fellow Am. Bar Found.; mem. ABA., Office: Carlton Fields Ward Emmanuel Smith & Cutler PA 1 Harbour Pl 777 S Harbour Island Blvd Tampa FL 33602-5729

YOUNG, HENRY E. tissue engineering medical educator; b. Dayton, Ohio, Dec. 5, 1951; s. Henry O. and Lucille M. Y.; m. Valerie E. Achorn, May 16, 1976; 1 child, Katherine. BS in Biology, Ohio State U., 1974; MS in Zoology, U. Ark., 1977; PhD, Tex. Tech. U., 1983. Instr.biochemistry Rush-Presbyn.-St. Luke's Med. Ctr., Chgo., 1987-88; asst. prof. anatomy Mercer U. Sch. Medicine, Macon, Ga., 1988-95, asst. prof. surgery, 1988-94, assoc. prof. anatomy, pediatrics, 1995—. Inventor in field. NIH Postdoctoral fellow biochemistry Case Western Res. U., Cleve., 1983-85, Muscular Dystrophy Assn. postdoctoral fellow, 1985-87; recipient Hooding award Excellence in Teaching and Rsch. Mercer U. Med. Sch., 1993, 94, Gender Equity award Am. Med. Women's Assn., 1997. Mem.: Am. Soc. Cell Biology, Stem Cells and Regen Medicine, Tissue Culture Soc., Am. Assn. Anatomists. Avocations: reading, lapidary, stain glass, singing. Office: Mercer U Sch Medicine 1550 College St Macon GA 31207-1500

YOUNG, HOBART PEYTON, economist, mathematician, educator; b. Evanston, Ill., Mar. 9, 1945; s. Hobart Paul and Louise (Buchwalter) Y.; m. Fernanda Toueg, Mar. 27, 1982; children: Hobart Patrick, Benjamin Morris Chandler. BA, Harvard Coll., 1966; PhD, U. Mich., 1970. Econ. Nat. Water Commn., Arlington, Va., 1971; from asst. to assoc. prof. CUNY, 1971-75; rsch. scholar, dep. chmn. systems and decision sci. Internat. Inst. for Applied Systems Analysis, Laxenburg, Austria, 1975-81; prof. pub. policy U. Md., College Park, 1981-94; prof. econ. Johns Hopkins Univ., 1994—; sr. fellow in econ. The Brookings Inst., 1998—. Adv. panel John D. and Catherine T. MacArthur Found., 1997-99; external faculty Santa Fe Inst., 2001—. Author: Fair Representation, 1982, Equity, 1994, Individual Strategy and Social Structure, 1998; editor: Cost Allocation, 1985, Fair Allocation, 1985, Negotiation Analysis, 1991, Social Dynamics, 2001; assoc. editor: Games and Economic Behavior, 1989—, Social Choice and Welfare, 1990-97. NSF grantee, 1975-86, 90-91, 96—, Office Naval Rsch. grantee, 1986-89, Russell Sage Found. grantee, 1989-91; Erskine fellow in Econs., 1990; recipient Lester R. Ford award Math. Assn. Am., 1976. Fellow Econometric Soc.; mem. Am. Polit. Sci. Assn., Ops. Rsch. Soc. Am., Cosmos Club, European Econ. Assn. Episcopalian. Avocation: choral singing, canoeing. Office: Johns Hopkins Univ Dept Econ Baltimore MD 21218 also: The Brookings Instn 1775 Massachusetts Ave NW Washington DC 20036-2103 E-mail: pyoung@jhu.edu.

YOUNG, HOWARD THOMAS, foreign language educator; b. Cumberland, Md., Mar. 24, 1926; s. Samuel Phillip and Sarah Emmaline (Frederick) Y.; m. Carol Osborne, Oct. 5, 1949 (div. 1966); children: Laurie Margaret, Jennifer Anne; m. Edra Lee Airheart, May 23, 1981; 1 child, Timothy Howard BS summa cum laude, Columbia U., 1950, MA, 1952, PhD, 1954. Lectr. Columbia U., N.Y.C., 1950-54; asst. prof. Romance langs. Pomona Coll., Claremont, Calif., 1954-60, assoc. prof., 1960-66, Smith prof. Romance langs., 1966-98, prof. emeritus, 1998—. Vis. prof. Middlebury Program in Spain, Madrid, 1986-87, U. Zaragoza, 1967-68, Columbia U., summer 2000; chief reader Spanish AP Ednl. Testing Service, Princeton, 1975-78, chmn. Spanish lang. devel. commn., 1976-79; mem. fgn. lang. adv. commn. Coll. Bd., N.Y.C., 1980-83; mem. West Coast selection commn. Mellon Fellowships for Humanities, Princeton, 1984-86, European selection com., 1987, 90; trans. cons. Smithsonian. Author: The Victorious Expression, 1964, Juan Ramón Jiménez, 1967, The Line in the Margin, 1980; editor: T.S. Eliot and Hispanic Modernity, 1995; contbr. London Times Higher Edn. Supplement; contbr. numerous articles and book revs. to profl. jours. Dir. NEH summer seminar for Sch. tchrs., 1993. Served with USNR, 1944-46, ETO Fellow Del Amo Found., 1960-61, NEH, 1975, 89-90; Fulbright fellow; 1967-68; Rockefeller Study Ctr. scholar, 1976 Mem. MLA, Assn. Tchrs. Spanish and Portuguese, Am. Comparative Lit. Assn., Acad. Am. Poets, Assn. Lit. Scholars and Critics. Home: 447 W Redlands Ave Claremont CA 91711-1638 Office: Pomona Coll Romance Lang Dept 550 Harvard Ave Claremont CA 91711-6380 E-mail: htyoung@pomona.edu.

YOUNG, HUBERT HOWELL, JR. lawyer, real estate investor and developer; b. Franklin, Va., May 30, 1945; s. Hubert Howell and Elizabeth Ann (Davidson) Y.; m. Christine P. Brooks, Dec. 31, 1964; 1 son, Hubert Howell, III. BA, Washington Lee U., 1967, LLB, magna cum laude, 1969. Bar: Va. 1969, U.S. Supreme Ct. 1972, Tex. 1974, U.S. Dist. Ct. Tex. 1974, U.S. Dist. Ct. (ea. dist.) Va. 1980. Assoc., Johnson, Bromberg, Leeds and Riggs, Dallas, 1973-75; gen. counsel Trammel Crow Co., Dallas, 1975-79; sole practice, Suffolk, Va., 1979— ; gen. counsel Young Properties, Suffolk, 1979— ; dir. Young Properties Devel. Corp., Trammel Crow Investment Corp., Suffolk Broadcasting Corp. Pres. Suffolk (Va.) Found. Trust, 1982-83; vice chmn. Suffolk Coalition for Sr. Citizen Housing, Inc., 1982-83; mem. Suffolk Substance and Abuse and Youth Council, 1982-84; chmn. Suffolk Rep. Party, 1982-85; commr. Med. Coll. Hampton Roads, 1990-96; dir. Va. Symphony, 1991-94. Served as lt. JAG, USN, 1969-73. Designated col. Confederate Army The Lee-Jackson Meml. Inc., 1981. Mem. ABA, Suffolk Bar Assn. (pres. 1994), Property Owners and Mgrs. Assn. (pres. 1995-96). Club: Cedar Point, Town Point, Sports, Ducks Unlimited (Suffolk). Fax: 757-539-5130. E-mail: yprop@msn.com. Office: Young Properties 444 N Main St Suffolk VA 23434-4425

YOUNG, HUGH DAVID, physics educator, writer, organist; b. Ames, Iowa, Nov. 3, 1930; s. Hugh Surber and Nellie Sibella (Peters) Y.; m. Alice Carroll, June 25, 1960; children: Gretchen Carroll, Rebecca Susan BS in Physics, Carnegie-Mellon U., 1952, MS in Physics, 1953, PhD in Physics, 1959, BFA in Music, 1972. From instr. to assoc. prof. physics Carnegie-Mellon U., Pitts., 1956-77, prof., 1977—; head dept. natural scis. Margaret Morrison Carnegie Coll., Carnegie-Mellon U., 1962-67, acad. coordinator, lectr. modern engring. mgrs. program, 1966-82. Vis. assoc. prof. physics U. Calif., Berkeley, 1967-68, vis. prof. physics, 1974; asst. organist St. Paul's Cathedral, Pitts., 1978-82 Author: Statistical Treatment of Experimental Data, 1962, Fundamentals of Mechanics and Heat, 2d edit., 1974, Fundamentals of Optics and Modern Physics, 2d edit., 1976; (with Sears and Zemansky) College Physics, 7th edit., 1990, University Physics, 9th edit., 1996. Bd. dirs. Renaissance and Baroque Soc., 1980-86. Recipient Ryan Tchg. award Carnegie Inst. Tech., 1965, Doherty award for excellence in edn. Carnegie Mellon U., 1997. Mem. Am. Assn. Physics Tchrs., Am. Phys. Soc., Am. Guild Organists (assoc.) Democrat. Avocations: organ, rock climbing. Home: 5746 Aylesboro Ave Pittsburgh PA 15217-1412 Office: Carnegie-Mellon Univ Dept Physics Pittsburgh PA 15213 E-mail: hdy@andrew.cmu.edu.

YOUNG, INA WEINSTEIN, association administrator; b. New Haven, Aug. 28, 1939; d. Nathan and Sarah (Brown) Weinstein; m. Morton H. Halperin, June 19, 1960 (div.); children: David Halperin, Mark Halperin, Gary Halperin; m. Joseph Leslie Young, Mar. 19, 1988; step-children: Michal Fandel, Avigayl Young. AB, Barnard Coll., 1961; MEd, Am. U., 1975. Tchr. Little Sch., North Reading, Mass., 1961-62, cons., 1963-75; career counselor Am. U., Washington, 1976-79; exec. dir. Jewish War Vets. Aux., 1979-85; adminstr. The Brookings Instn., 1985-87; dir. career svcs. Am. U. Law Sch., 1987-93; exec. adminstr. Population Assn. Am., 1993-95; program mgr. U.S. C. of C., 1995-98; mgr. continuing edn. Am. Indsl. Hygiene Assn., Fairfax, Va., 1999-2000; cons. AARP Found., Bethesda, Md., 2000—. Mem. Greater Washington Soc. Assn. Execs., Barnard Club. Democrat. Jewish. Avocations: arts, theatre, film, lit., travel. Home: 4846 Montgomery Ln Bethesda MD 20814-5302 Office: AARP Foundation 4846 Montgomery Ln Bethesda MD 20814-5302 E-mail: inajoe@earthlink.net.

YOUNG, IVEN S. physician; b. Bklyn., May 31, 1934; AB, U. Pa., 1955; MD, NYU, 1959. Chief endocrinology St. Vincent Hosp. 7 Med. Ctr., N.Y.C., 1966—; asst. clin. prof. medicine NYU, 1968—; assoc. clin. prof. medicine N.Y. Med. Coll., Valhalla, 1968—. Fellow Am. Coll. Physicians; mem. Am. Assn. Clin. Endocrinologists, Am. Diabetes Assn., Endocrine Soc., Phi Beta Kappa, Alpha Omega Alpha. Office: 130 W 12th St New York NY 10011-8271

YOUNG, J. LOWELL, soil chemist, biologist; b. Perry, Utah, Dec. 13, 1925; s. I.A. and Elzada (Nelson) Y.; m. Ruth Ann Jones, Sept. 15, 1950; children: Gordon, LoAnn, Colene, Kathryn. BS, Brigham Young U., 1953; PhD, Ohio State U., 1956. Rsch. asst. Ohio Agrl. Expt. Sta., Columbus, 1953-56, postdoctoral fellow, 1956-57; chemist Agrl. Research Service USDA, Corvallis, Oreg., 1957-64, rsch. chemist, 1964-78; asst. prof. Oreg. State U., 1957-63, assoc. prof., 1963-78, prof. soil sci., 1978-90, Courtesy prof. soil sci., 1990—; rsch. chemist Horticultural Crops Rsch. Unit USDA, 1978-88; collaborator Horticultural Crops Rsch. Unit U.S. Dept. Agrl., 1988-91. Contbr. articles to profl. jours. Served with USAAF, 1944-46. Mem. AAAS, Internat. Soil Sci. Soc., Internat. Humic Substances Soc., Soil Sci. Soc. of Am. (officer 1972-75, assoc. editor jour. 1975-80), Am. Soc. Agronomy (officer western 1966-72), Western Soc. Soil Sci. (officer 1966-71), Inst. for Alternative Agrl. Office: Oreg State U Crops & Soil Sci Dept Corvallis OR 97331

YOUNG, J. WARREN, magazine publisher; Pub. Boys' Life Mag., Irving, Tex. Office: Boys' Life PO Box 152079 Irving TX 75015-2079

YOUNG, JACK ALLISON, financial executive; b. Aurora, Ill., Dec. 31, 1931; s. Neal A. and Gladys Young; m. Virginia Dawson, Jan. 24, 1959; children: Amy D., Andrew A. BS in Journalism, U. Ill., 1954. CLU; chartered fin. cons.; registered security rep. Advt. writer Caterpillar Tractor Co., 1956-58; inst. agent Equitable Life Assurance Soc., St. Geneva, Ill., 1958—, ins. broker, 1972—; pres. Jack A. Young and Assocs., 1978—, Creative Brokerage, Inc., 1982-95. Past pres., gen. securities prin. Chartered Planning, Ltd., 1984-2000; past trustee Equitable CLU Assn.; past chmn. Equitable Nat. Agents Forum. Bd. dirs. Tri-City Famiy Services, 1975-83, pres., 1979-81; trustee Delnor-Community Health System, 1985-97, chmn., 1988-91; bd. dirs. St. Charles Ctr. Phys. Rehab., 1991-97; chmn., pres. Delnor-Cmty. Health Care Found., 1986-88; dir. Kane County Bar Found., Inc., 1997-2000. Lt. (j.g.) USN, 1956. Named to Equitable Hall of Fame, 1978. Mem. Million Dollar Round Table (life), Am. Soc. C.L.U.s, Am. Coll. C.L.U. Golden Key Soc., Fox Valley Estate Planning Council, Internat. Assn. for Fin. Planning, Inc., Aurora Assn. Life Underwriters (past pres., nat. committeeman), Nat. Assn. Securities Dealers (registered prin.), Geneva Golf Club (pres. 1994). Home: 18 Campbell St Geneva IL 60134-2732 also: 2706 Laurel Dr Vero Beach FL 32960-5063 Office: 28 N Bennett St Geneva IL 60134-2207 E-mail: jayassoc@aol.com., yjackayoung@aol.com.

YOUNG, JACK PHILLIP, chemist; b. Huntington, Ind., Oct. 28, 1929; s. Jacob P. and Marie Young; m. Jean Elizabeth Kennedy, June 18, 1955; children: James, Mark, David, Timothy, Karen. BS, Ball State U., 1950; PhD, Ind. U., 1955. Chemist Kraus Lab., Huntington, Ind., 1950, Huntington Lab., 1952-53, Oak Ridge (Tenn.) Nat. Lab., 1955-82, sr. staff, 1982—. Co-editor: Radiation and Public Perception, 1995; contbr. more than 180 articles to profl. jours. Patentee in field. Bd. dirs., pres. Children's Mus., Oak Ridge, 1983-89; bd. dirs. Oak Ridge Civic Music Assn., 1993—. Recipient award Indsl. Rsch., 1983. Fellow AAAS; mem. Am. Chem. Soc. (local pres. 1993), Sigma Xi. Roman Catholic. Achievements include development of methods to detect and identify single atoms and demonstration of the chemical consequences of radioactive transmutation and characterization of nuclear isomers. Office: Oak Ridge Nat Lab PO Box 2008 Oak Ridge TN 37831-2008 E-mail: youngjp@ornl.gov.

YOUNG, JACK W. elementary school educator; b. Salem, Ohio, Aug. 8, 1948; s. Jack Wayne Young, Geraldine Young; m. Elizabeth K. Young; children: Lindsay Killeen, Chad Justin. BS in Elem. Edn., Kent State U., 1973. Tchr. East Liverpool City Schs., East Liverpool, Ohio, 1972—73, Streetsboro City Schs., Streetsboro, 1973—. Scholar Jennings scholar, Jennings Scholar Bd., 1978. Avocation: Avocations: coaching soccer, gardening, motorcycling. Home: 550 E Riddle Ave Ravenna OH 44266

YOUNG, JACQUELINE EURN HAI, former state legislator, consultant; b. Honolulu, May 20, 1934; d. Paul Bai and Martha (Cho) Y.; m. Harry Valentine Daniels, Dec. 25, 1954 (div. 1978); children: Paula, Harry, Nani, Laura; m. Daniel Anderson, Sept. 25, 1978 (div. 1984); m. Everett Kleinjans, Sept. 4, 1988 (div. 1998). BS in Speech Pathology, Audiology, U. Hawaii, 1969; MS in Edn., Spl. Edn., Old Dominion U., 1972; advanced cert., Loyola Coll., 1977; PhD in Communication, Women's Studies, Union Inst., 1989. Dir. dept. speech and hearing Md. Sch. for the Blind, Balt., 1975-77; dir. deaf-blind project Easter Seal Soc. Oahu, Hawaii, 1977-78; project dir. equal ednl. opportunity programs Hawaii State Dept. Edn., Honolulu, 1978-85, state ednl. specialist, 1978-90; state rep. dist. 20 Hawaii State Legislature, 1990-92, state rep. dist. 51, 1992-94; vice-speaker Hawaii Ho. of Reps. Apptd. to U.S. Dept. Def. Adv. Commn. on Women in the Svc.; cons. spl. edn. U.S. Dept. Edn., dept. edn. Guam, Am. Samoa, Ponape, Palau, Marshall Islands, 1977-85; cons. to orgns. on issues relating to workplace diversity; adj. prof. commn., anthopology, mgmt. Hawaii Pacific U.; dir. mktg. Am. Cancer Soc. Hawaii Pacific, 1985—, dir. mktg., 1999—. TV writer, host, producer, 1992—. 1st v.p. Nat. Women's Polit. Caucus, 1988-90; chair Hawaii Women's Polit. Caucus, 1987-89; bd. dirs. YWCA Oahu, Kalihi Palama Immigrant Svc. Ctr., Hawaii Dem. Movement, Family Peace Ctr.; appointee Honolulu County Com. on the Status of Women, 1986-87; mem. Adv. Coun. on Family Violence: campaign dir. Protect Our Constn., 1998; trustee St. Louis Sch., 1997-99. Recipient Outstanding Woman Leader award YWCA of Oahu, 1994, Pres.'s award Union Inst., 1993, Fellow of the Pacific award Hawaii-Pacific U., 1993, Headliner award Honolulu chpt. Women in Commn., 1993, Korean Am. Alliance Washington Spl. Recognition award, 1998, Hawaii Women Lawyers Disting. Svc. award, 1999, Disting. Equity Adv. award Hawaii chpt. Nat. Coalition for Sex Equity in Edn., 1998, NEA Mary Hatwood Futrell for advancing women's rights award, 1999, Friend of Social Work award Hawaii chpt. NASW, 1998, Allan Saunders award Hawaii chpt. ACLU, 1999; named one of Extraordinary Women Hawaii, Found. Hawaii Women's History, 2001. Home: 212 Luika Pl Kailua HI 96734-3237

YOUNG, JAMES HARVEY, historian, educator; b. Bklyn., Sept. 8, 1915; s. W. Harvey and Blanche (DeBra) Y.; m. Myrna Goode, Aug. 25, 1940 (dec. Oct. 2000); children: Harvey Galen, James Walter. BA, Knox Coll., 1937, D.H.L., 1971; MA, U. Ill., 1938, PhD, 1941; D.Sc., Rush U., 1976. Mem. faculty Emory U., 1941-84, prof. history, 1958-80, Charles Howard Candler prof. Am. social history, 1980-84, prof. emeritus, 1984—, chmn. dept., 1958-66. Vis. assoc. prof. Columbia U., 1949-50; mem. nat. adv. food and drug council FDA, 1964-67; mem. Consumers Task Force, White House Conf. on Food, Nutrition and Health, 1969; mem. history life scis. study sect. NIH, 1970-73, 79-80, 91-93, chmn., 1992-93; vis. lectr. Am. Assn. Colls. Pharmacy Vis. Lectrs. Program, 1970-73; cons.-panelist NEH, 1970-83; cons. in history Centers for Disease Control; advisor Am. Coun. Sci. and Health; Logan Clendening lectr. U. Kans. Med. Ctr., 1973; Samuel X. Radbill lectr. Phila. Coll. Physicians, 1978; Beaumont lectr. Yale U., 1980; vis. hist. scholar Nat. Library Medicine, 1986; Harold J. Lawn lectr. U. Minn., 1990; David L. Cowen lectr. Rutgers U., 1990; James Campbell lectr. Rush U., 1992; Waring lectr. Med. U. S.C., 1993; Charles Jackson lectr. U. Tenn., 2001. Author: The Toadstool Millionaires, 1961, The Medical Messiahs, 1967, expanded edit., 1992, American Self-Dosage Medicines, An Historical Perspective, 1974, Pure Food: Securing the Federal Food and Drugs Act of 1906, 1989, American Health Quackery: Collected Essays, 1992; editor: (with W.A. Beardslee and T.J.J. Altizer) Truth, Myth and Symbol, 1962, (with T.L. Savitt) Disease and Distinctiveness in the American South, 1988. Served with AUS, 1943-45. Recipient Arts and Scis. award of distinction Emory U., 1999; FDA rsch. appointee, 1977-85; Carnegie rsch. grantee, 1947, USPHS grantee, 1960-65, Nat. Libr. Medicine grantee, 1990-94; Faculty fellow Fund Advancement Edn., 1954-55, Social Sci. Rsch. Coun. fellow, 1960-61, Guggenheim fellow, 1966-67. Mem. Am. Hist. Assn., So. Hist. Assn. (pres. 1982), Orgn. Am. Historians, Soc. Am. Historians, Am. Assn. History of Medicine (coun., Fielding H. Garrison lectr. 1979, William H. Welch medal 1982, Continuing Lifetime Achievement award 1992), Am. Inst. History of Pharmacy (coun., hon. pres. 1993-95, Edward Kremers award 1962), Phi Beta Kappa, Sigma Xi, Phi Kappa Phi, Omicron Delta Kappa, Phi Alpha Theta. Congregationalist. Home: 272 Heaton Park Dr Decatur GA 30030-1027 E-mail: jyoun02@emory.edu.

YOUNG, JAMES E. business executive, engineer; b. Celina, Ohio, Sept. 1, 1941; s. Thomas D. and Margaret E. (Flora) Y.; m. Patricia C. Teare, June 13, 1964; children: Kathleen M., Peter C. BSME, Rose-Hulman Inst. Tech., 1963; MBA, Ind. U., 1965; EdS, Ind. State U., 1998. V.p. Citicorp, N.Y.C., 1965-73; pres. James E. Young & Assoc., Inc., Indpls., 1974-91, The Young Group, Naples, Fla., 1991—. Vis. prof. guest lectr. Purdue U., Lafayette, Ind., 1986—; adv. bd. Purdue-Anderson, Inc., 1985—, Rsch. Inst. for Devel. of Interactive Learning Sys., Terre Haute, Ind., 1986—; pres. Remote Equipment Corp., Indpls., 1988-90; pres. Forum for Internat. Profl. Svcs., Inc., 1988-91, bd. dirs.; chmn. bd. WKJM, Inc., 1989-90; chmn. World Competitiveness Conf., 1990—; pres. G & G Angola, Inc., 1991-98, Ramco of Ind., 1992-98, Jaymer, Inc., 1996—. Author: Industrial Communications Networks, 1987, Load Rating Analysis For Steel Manhole Covers, 1995; Load Rating Analysis for Composite Manhole Covers, 1996, What Makes Steel Manhole Covers Unsafe?, 1999; Smart Choices for Composite Manhole Covers, 2000; patentee in field. Co-founder, chmn. bd. Ind. Amateur Baseball Assn., Inc., 1982—; mktg. chmn. Ind. Major League Baseball Commn., Indpls., 1982-86. Mem. ASME, Soc. Mfg. Engrs., Bus. Modernization and Tech. Corp. (chmn. telecom. 1984—), Rotary, Beta Gamma Sigma. Avocations: reading, boating, golf. Office: Young Group 1875 Verona Ct Naples FL 34109-7120 E-mail: jimyoung41@aol.com.

YOUNG, JAMES EARL, ceramics educator, educational administrator; b. Chgo., Dec. 20, 1922; s. James Alexander and Ellen (Chedister) Y.; children: Hugh Parker, Katherine Sue. BS, U. Ill., 1948; PhD, State U. N.Y. Coll. Ceramics Alfred U., 1962. Ceramic engr. Republic Steel Co., Chgo., 1948-52; ceramic engr. Armour Research Found., 1952-55; research supr. Structural Clay Research Found., Geneva, 1955-57; research fellow State U. N.Y. Coll. Ceramics at Alfred U., 1957-61, asst. prof., 1961-63, assoc. prof., 1963-67, prof., chmn. dept., 1967-70; dean Coll. Arts and Scis., Rutgers U., Camden, N.J., 1970-73; provost Rutgers U., Newark, 1973-82; exec. dir. Commn. on State Colls. of N.J., 1982-84; prof. Rutgers U., 1984-93, prof. emeritus, 1993—. Contbr. articles to tech. jours. Served with AUS, 1943-46. Am. Council Edn. fellow acad. adminstrn., 1966-67 Mem. Am. Ceramic Soc. Home: 130 Kingsberry Dr Somerset NJ 08873-4309

YOUNG, JAMES EDWARD, lawyer; b. Painesville, Ohio, Apr. 20, 1946; s. James M. and Isabel P. (Rogers) Y. BBA, Ohio U., 1968; JD, Ohio State U., 1972. Bar: Ohio 1972. Law clk. to chief judge U.S. Ct. Appeals, Nashville, 1972-73; chief counsel City of Cleve., 1980-81, law dir., 1981-82; assoc. Jones, Day, Reavis & Pogue, Cleve., 1973-79, ptnr., 1983—. Office: Jones Day Reavis & Pogue 901 Lakeside Ave E Cleveland OH 44114-1190 E-mail: jameseyoung@jonesday.com.

YOUNG, JAMES JULIUS, university administrator, retired army officer; b. Fort Ringgold, Tex., Nov. 28, 1926; s. John Cooper and Violet Thelma (Ohl) Y.; m. June Agnes Hillstead, Dec. 17, 1948; children: Robert Michael, Steven Andrew, Patrick James, Mary Frances. BS, U. Md., 1960; M.H.A., Baylor U., 1962; PhD in Hosp. and Health Adminstrn, U. Iowa, 1969. Commd. 2d lt. U.S. Army, 1947, advanced through grades to brig. gen., 1977; comdr., med. ops. officer, dir. tng. field med. units in European Command, 1949-53; comdr. Mil. Med. Leadership Sch., 1953-54; med. advisor (Nationalist Army of China), 1955-57; asst. adminstr. Fitzsimons Army Med. Center, 1957-60; med. plans and ops. officer (US Forces), Korea, 1962-63; sr. field med. instr., chief field med. service Med. Field Service Sch., 1963-66; dir. health care orgn. and mgmt. analysis Office of Surgeon Gen., 1969-71; dir. med. plans and ops. directorate Office of the Surgeon, Military Assistance Command, Vietnam, 1971-72; exec. officer, chief adminstrv. services Silas Hays Army Hosp., 1973-74; military health analyst, military health care study OMB, Exec. Office of Pres., 1974-76; dep. dir. resources mgmt. and cons. for health care adminstrn. Office of Surgeon Gen., 1976-77; chief med. svcs. corps U.S. Army, 1977-81; dir. resources mgmt. Office of Surgeon Gen., 1977-81; ret., 1981; instr. U. Iowa, 1967-69; asst. prof., preceptor Baylor U., 1973-74; vice chancellor for health affairs W.Va. Bd. Regents, Charleston, 1982-87; dean sch. of allied health scis. U. Tex. Health Sci. Ctr., San Antonio, 1987-90, interim dean Sch. Medicine, 1988-89, dean Sch. Medicine, 1989—, dean emeritus, 2000—. Cons. to Min. of Health, Republic of Vietnam, 1971-72, 1989-2000; adj. prof. Baylor U., 1977-81, George Washington U., 1975-76, W.Va. U., 1986; prof. U. Tex. health Sci. Ctr., San Antonio, 1989-2000. Contbr. articles to profl. jours. Decorated D.S.M., Legion of Merit, Meritorious Service medal and; others; recipient Walter Reed medallion for service, 1981; Army Med. Dept. medallion for contribution to health service, 1981, Order of Mil. Med. Merit, 1981, U T Health Scis. Ctr. Hon. medallion Fountains of Progress, 2000; recipient in Humanism in medicine award Health Care Foun. N.J., 2000. Mem. APHA, Coun. Deans, Assn. of Am. Med. Colls., Bexar Cty. Med. Soc., Tex. Med. Assn., Assn. Mil. Surgeons (chmn. med. svc. sect. 1978), Assn. U.S. Army, Interagy. Inst. Fed. Health Execs., Phi Kappa Tau. Roman Catholic. Home: 1610 Anchor Dr San Antonio TX 78213-1943 E-mail: jyoung51@rr.com.

YOUNG, JAMES MORNINGSTAR, physician, naval officer; b. Massillon, Ohio, Oct. 28, 1929; s. Ralph Louis and Pauline Louise (Morningstar) Y.; m. Bettylu Jones, July 3, 1952; children: Anne Christine, Mark Andrew, Patricia Jane, Elizabeth Lynne, Judith Pamela, Claudia Dianne; m. Mariette M. Aubuchon, Oct. 11, 1970; children: Gretchen Camille, Jason Paul. AB, Duke U., 1951, MD, 1955. Diplomate Am. Bd. Internal Medicine. Intern Bethesda Naval Hosp., 1955-56, asst. dir. tissue bank, 1956-58, resident, 1958-61; commd. lt. (j.g.) USN, 1955, advanced through grades to lt. comdr., 1961, promoted to temporary rank capt., 1963; White House physician to Presidents Kennedy and Johnson, Washington, 1963-66. Asst. chief medicine and dir. of interns, Oakland (Calif.) Naval Hosp., 1966-69; chief medicine Naval Hosp. Boston, Chelsea, Mass., 1969-74; med. officer Naval Air Sta., South Weymouth, Mass., 1974-75; assoc. clin. prof. medicine Boston U. Sch. Medicine, 1969-75; v.p. med. affairs Mass. Blue Shield/Blue Cross, 1975-87; lectr. Harvard Sch. Pub. Health, 1987-90; sr. advisor Beijing Coll. Traditional Chinese Medicine, 1987-88; med. advisor U.S.-China People's Friendship Assn., Washington, 1988-90; cons. USPHS, Office Asst. Sec. for Health, Nat. Ctr. for Health Svcs., Rsch. and Health Care Tech. Assessment, HHS, 1985-90; v.p. for med. affairs Greenery Rehab. Group, Inc., 1988-90; assoc. med. dir. New. Eng. Rehab. Hosp., 1992-95, chief medicine, 1992-95. Contbr. articles to med. publs. Decorated knight comdr. with star Equestrian Order of the Holy Sepulchre of Jerusalem; named Disting. Citizen of Washington H.S., Massillon, Ohio, 1993. Fellow ACP, AMA, Alpha Omega Alpha, Omicron Delta Kappa, Beta Omega Sigma, Sigma Alpha Epsilon. Home: 77 Harvey Mill Rd Lee NH 03824-6302 E-mail: jmyoung9@hotmail.com.

YOUNG, JAMES OLIVER, dentist, communication company executive; b. Parris Island, S.S., Apr. 19, 1945; s. William Oliver and Ruth Cherokee (Risner) Y.; m. Virginia Evelyn Koontz; children: Amy Robyn, Jenny Elizabeth, Thomas William. BS, Southeast State U., Okla., 1967; DDS, Baylor U., 1972. Ordained deacon Episc. Ch., 2001. Tchr. pub. schs., 1967-68; practice dentistry Ardmore, Okla., 1972-93; v.p. Cherokee Telephone Co., Calera, Okla., 1963-94, pres. Okla., 1994—. V.p. Cherokee Cellular, Inc., 1989—; pres. Comm. Equipment Co., Calera, 1984—, Ardmore Soup Kitchen, Inc., 1999—; bd. dirs. Good Shepherd Med. Clinic. Trustee Ardmore Devel. Authority, 1980-85. Bd. dirs. Ardmore Cmty. Concerts Assn., 1980-90, Salvation Army, 1990-91; scoutmaster Boy Scouts Am., pres. Arbuckle Area Coun., 1994-95; Okla. state adv. bd. Easter Seal Soc. Named one of Outstanding Young Men Am., 1981. Fellow Acad. Gen. Dentistry, Acad. Dentistry Internat.; mem. ADA, Okla. Dental Assn., Ind. Dentists Southern Okla. (pres. 1986), Okla. C. of C. (bd. dirs. 1984-85), Masons. Republican. Episcopalian. Avocations: skiing, sailing. Home: 2207 Ridgeway St Ardmore OK 73401-3405 Office: PO Box 445 Calera OK 74730-0445

YOUNG, JAY ALFRED, chemical safety and health consultant, writer, editor; b. Huntington, Ind., Sept. 8, 1920; s. Jacob Phillip and Marie (Skully) Y.; m. Anne Elizabeth Neff, June 29, 1942 (dec. June 1962); children: John, Paul, Cecelia, Michael, Joseph, Andrea, Therese, Gregory, Thomas, Lucy, Margaret, Antonia; m. Mary Ann Owens, Aug. 15, 1962; children: James, Laurence; 4 stepchildren. BS, Ind. U., 1939; AM, Oberlin Coll., 1940; PhD, U. Notre Dame, 1950. Chief chemist Asbestos Mfg. Co., Huntington, Ind., 1941-42; ordnance engr. U.S. War Dept., Washington, 1942-44; from instr. to prof. chemistry King's Coll., Wilkes-Barre, Pa., 1949-69; vis. prof. Carleton U., Ottawa, Ont., Can., 1969-70, Fla. State U., Tallahassee, 1975-77; Hudson prof. Auburn (Ala.) U., 1970-75; mgr. tech. publs. Chem. Mfrs. Assn., Washington, 1977-80; chem. safety and health cons. Silver Spring, Md., 1980—. Pro bono cons. OSHA, EPA, Consumer Product Safety Commn., Washington, 1980—; invited lectr. chem. edn. and chem. health and safety U.S., Can., Mex., Brazil, Argentina, Chile, Great Britain, Norway, France, Italy, India, Indonesia, Australia, New Zealand, Japan, 1963—. Author: Practice in Thinking, 1958, Elements of General Chemistry, 1960, Chemical Concepts, 1963, Selected Principles of Chemistry, 1963, Arithmetic for Students of Science, 1968, Instructor's Guide for Chemistry, a Cultural Approach, 1971, Study Guide for General Chemistry, 1974, Fire!, 1977, Actions and Reactions, 1978, Chemistry, A Human Concern, 1978, Kitchen Chemistry, 1980, Electron Microscopy Safety Handbook, 1985; co-author: Study Guide for Continental Classroom Chemistry, NBC/TV, vols. I and II, 1959, 60, Keys to Chemistry, 1973, Chemistry Preparation Laboratory, 1973, Keys to Oxidation-Reduction, 1974, Things that Last, 1977, Principles of Laboratory Safety (with videotape), 1980, OSHA Hazard Communication Regulations, 1984, Chemical Safety Manual for Small Businesses, 1st edit., 1989, 2d edit., 1992, Developing a Chemical Hygiene Plan, 1990; editor: Guidelines and Recommendations for the Preparation and Continuing Education of Secondary School Teachers of Chemistry, 1977, Improving Safety in the Chemical Laboratory: A Practical Guide, 1st edit., 1989, 2d edit., 1992 (also contbr.), Safety in Academic Chemistry Laboratories, 7th edit., 2002, Chemical Safety for Teachers and Their Supervisors, Grades 7-12, 2001; co-editor: Heath Chemistry Laboratory Experiments, 1987, Handbook of Chemical Health and Safety, 2001 (also contbr.); contbr. and cons. numerous books; contbr. Encyclopedia Britannica, and over 100 articles to profl. jours. Tech. resource person to media and expert witness regarding chem. hazards, precautions, transp. incidents involving chems.; mem. NSF Coll. Chemistry Commn., 1962-68. Lt. USNR, 1944-46. Recipient Disting. Chemistry Alumnus award U. Notre Dame, 1968, Excellence in Chemistry Teaching award Mfg. Chemists Assn., 1970. Fellow AAAS; mem. Am. Chem. Soc. (councilor 1963-87, policy com. 1970-81, sec. divsn. chem. edn. 1969-78, chmn. divsn. chem. health and safety 1979-80, mem. chem. safety com. 1982—, Chem. Health and Safety award 1991). Roman Catholic. Avocations: wood and metalworking, gardening. Home and Office: 12916 Allerton Ln Silver Spring MD 20904-3105

YOUNG, JAY MAITLAND, healthcare communications consultant; b. Louisville, Nov. 26, 1944; s. Clyde Dudley and Olive May (Tyas) Y. BA in Chemistry and Math magna cum laude, Vanderbilt U., 1966; MS in Biochemistry, Yale U., 1967, MPhil in Phys. Chemistry, 1968, PhD in Chemistry, 1971. Asst. prof. chemistry Bryn Mawr (Pa.) Coll., 1970-76; rsch. biochemist Abbott Labs., Ill., 1977-78, project mgr. physiolog. diagnostics, 1978-80, project mgr. cancer product devel., 1980-82, internat. clin. specialist sci. affairs, 1982-85, clin. project mgr. physiol. diag. quality and sci. support, 1986-90, staff quality assurance and sci. support, 1990-93, fertility, pregnancy, thyroid mgr., quality and sci. support, 1993-95, fertility, pregnancy, thyroid, cancer mgr., product quality assurance, 1995-97, staff noninfectious disease diagnostics sci. affairs, 1997—2001; cons. and med. writer pharm. and diagnostic areas, 2002—. Cons. Inst. for Cancer Rsch., Fox Chase, Phila., 1974, vis. scientist, 1975-76; honors examiner Swarthmore Coll., 1973, 74; mem. vis. evaluation com., 1975; presenter to med. groups on cancer markers, viral hepatitis and epidemiology of AIDS, 1982-84. Contbr. articles to profl. jours.; patentee in med. field. Vol. Episcopal Ch. Outreach Commn. Named to Hon. Order Ky. Cols.; predoctoral fellow NSF, Yale U., 1966-70; postdoctoral fellow, NIH, U. Oxford, 1971-72; grantee NSF, NATO Travel grant, U. Salford, Eng., 1974, Amer. Med. Writer's Assn. Care (Multi-disciplinary), 1999. Mem. Am. Med. Writers Assn.

YOUNG, JENNIFER LAW, photojournalist, documentary producer; b. Houston, Aug. 31, 1964; d. Louis Lester and Emma Louise (Barron) Law; m. Bruce Kenneth Young. BA in Philosophy, Journalism, Baylor U., 1987. Photojournalist UPI, Denver, 1987-89, staff photojournalist, editor Washington, 1989-90; photojournalist, editor Agence France Presse, 1990-96; prodr. The Evans-McCan Group, 1995—. Mem. Soc. Profl. Journalists, Women in Film, White House News Photographers Assn., Washington Film and Video Coun. Republican.

YOUNG, JERRY WESLEY, retired animal nutrition educator; b. Mulberry, Tenn., Aug. 19, 1934; s. Rufus William and Annie Jewell (Sweeney) Y.; m. Charlotte Sullenger, July 8, 1959; children: David, Jeretha. BS, Berry Coll., 1957; MS, N.C. State U., 1959, PhD, 1963. Asst. prof. Iowa State U., Ames, 1965-70, assoc. prof., 1970-74, prof. in animal sci., 1974-2000. Contbr. articles to profl. jours. Recipient Dist. Achievement award Berry Coll., 1998; postdoctoral fellow NIH, 1963-65. Fellow Am. Dairy Sci. Assn. (Outstanding Dairy Nutrition Rsch. 1987); mem. Am. Soc. Nutritional Scis., Am. Soc. Animal Sci., Am. Chem. Soc., Sigma Xi, Phi Kappa Phi, Gamma Sigma Delta. Baptist. E-mail: youngtn@comcast.net.

YOUNG, JESS RAY, retired internist; b. Fairfield, Ill., Feb. 4, 1928; s. Edgar S. and Clara B. (Musgrave) Y.; m. Gloria Wynn, July 10, 1953; children—James C., Patricia A. BS, Franciscan U., 1951; MD, St. Louis U., 1955. Intern Highland Alameda County Hosp., Oakland, Calif., 1955-56; resident in internal medicine Cleve. Clinic Hosp., 1956-59, mem. staff dept. vascular medicine, 1959-97, chmn. dept., 1976-97; ret., 1998. Co-author: Leg Ulcer, 1975, Peripheral Vascular Diseases, 1991, 1996; contbr. articles to profl. jours., chpts. to books. Served with AUS, 1946-47. Mem. AMA, Am. Heart Assn. (stroke council), Am. Coll. Cardiology, Internat. Cardiovascular Soc., ACP, Am. Fedn. Clic. Research, Ohio Soc. Internal Medicine, Soc. for Vascular Medicine and Rsch., Inter-Urban Club. Methodist. Home: 1503 Burlington Rd Cleveland OH 44118-1216 E-mail: jesyoung@aol.com.

YOUNG, JESS WOLLETT, lawyer; b. San Antonio, Sept. 16, 1926; s. James L. and Zetta (Alonso) Y.; m. Mary Alma Keeter, Apr. 17, 1954 (dec. Dec. 1996); children— Zetta, Imogen. BA, Trinity U., San Antonio, 1957; LLB, St. Mary's U., 1958. Bar: Tex. 1957, U.S. Dist. Ct. (we. dist.) Tex. 1960, U.S. Dist. Ct. (so. dist.) Tex. 1961, U.S. Tax Ct. 1970, U.S. Ct. Appeals (5th cir.) 1981, U.S. Supreme Ct. 1981. Ptnr. Thompson, Thompson, Young & Jones, San Antonio, 1958-63, Moursund, Ball & Young, San Antonio, 1965-73; v.p., dir. Moursund, Ball & Young, Inc., San Antonio, 1973-78; pres., dir. Young & Richards, Inc., San Antonio, 1978-81, Young, Murray & Richards, Inc., San Antonio, 1981-82, Young & Murray, Inc., 1983-87, sole practice, 1987-91, 94—; staff atty., sheriff Bexar County, Tex.; county judge, Bexar County (Tex.), 1964; city atty. City of Olmos Park (Tex.), 1965-70, City of Poteet (Tex.), 1975-76; spl. county judge, Bexar County, 1967. Mem. Tex. State Dem. Exec. Com., 1970-72, Tex. State Rep. Exec. Com., 1984-92, Rep. Precinct committeeman, 1984-92; Dem. precinct committeeman, San Antonio, 1964-76. Served with USNR, 1944-46. Mem. ABA, Tex. Assn. Def. Counsel, Tex. Assn. Bank Counsel, San Antonio Bar Assn., Delta Theta Phi. Episcopalian. Clubs: San Antonio Petroleum, San Antonio Gun (dir. 1958-63, 80-82). Home: 1221 Wiltshire Ave San Antonio TX 78209-6056 Office: 40 NE Loop 410 Ste 210 San Antonio TX 78216-5826

YOUNG, JOAN CRAWFORD, advertising executive; b. Hobbs, N.Mex., July 30, 1931; d. William Bill and Ora Maydelle (Boone) Crawford; m. Herchelle B. Young, Nov. 23, 1971 (div.). BA, Hardin Simmons U., 1952; postgrad., Tex. Tech. U., 1953-54. Reporter Lubbock (Tex.) Avalanche-Jour., 1952-54; promotion dir. Sta. KCBD-TV, Lubbock, 1954-62; account exec. Ward Hicks Advt., Albuquerque, 1962-70; v.p. Mellekas & Assocs. Advt., 1970-78; pres. J. Young Advt., 1978—; dir. advt. So. Therapy, Austin, Tex., 1999—. Author: (with Louise Allen and Audre Lipscomb) Radio and TV Continuity Writing, 1962. Bd. dirs. N.Mex. Symphony Orch., 1970-73, United Way of Greater Albuquerque, 1985-89; bd. trustees N.Mex. Children's Found., 1994-96. Recipient Silver medal N.Mex. Advt. Fedn., 1977. Mem. N.Mex. Advt. Fedn. (bd. dirs. 1975-76), Am. Advt. Fedn., Greater Albuquerque C. of C. (bd. dirs. 1984), Albuquerque Petroleum Club (membership chmn. 1992-93, bd. dirs. 1993—, sec. 1994-95, v.p. 1995-97, pres. 1997-99). Republican. Office: 6009 Belfast Dr Austin TX 78723-1832

YOUNG, JOHN HARDIN, lawyer, corporate executive; b. Washington, Apr. 25, 1948; s. John D. and Laura Virginia (Gwathmey) Y.; m. Mary Frances (Farley) Crosby. JD, U. Va., 1973; BCL, Oxford U., Eng., 1976. Bar: Va. 1973, D.C. 1974, U.S. Dist. Ct. (Va.) 1974, U.S. Dist. Ct. D.C. 1974, Internat. Trade Ct. 1974, U.S. Ct. Fed. Claims 1974, (U.S. Ct. Appeals (4th, 5th, Fed.and D.C. cirs.)), Pa. 1976, U.S. Supreme Ct. 1977, U. S. Dist. Ct. (Md.) 1989, cert.: Va. Supreme Ct. (mediator 1998-2001). Pvt. practice , 1973—80, 1983—88; ptnr. Porter Wright Morris & Arthur, Washington, 1988-92, of counsel, 1992-99, Sandler, Reiff & Young, PC, 2001—. Mem. adv. bd. Antitrust Bull.; mem. U.S. Sec. State's adv. com. Pvt. internat. Law, 1987-95; chmn. Va. Retirement Sys. Rev. Bd., 1990-94; asst. atty. gen. Commonwealth of Va., 1976-78; moderator Alexandria Forum, 1993-98, Fedn. Forum/TV Channel 10, 1989-91; gen. counsel various profit and not-for-profit tech. cos. Contbr. articles to profl. jours. and books on litigation, evidence, technology contracting and election law., Spl. counsel Dem. Nat. Com., 1998—99, chair lawyers coun., 1998—; gen. counsel adminstr. Exec. Office of Pres., Washington, 2000; gen. counsel Dem. Fla. Lead Recount Coun. Fellow: ABA (chmn. trade regulation and competition com. 1983—86, chmn. dispute resolution com. 1984—96, chmn. adminstrv. law sect. 1999—2000); mem.: Temple Bar Found. (founding mem., bd. dirs.), Am. Inns of Ct., Comml. Bar Assn. U.K. (overseas mem.), George Mason Am. Inn of Ct. (master 1990—, pres. 2002—), Am. Law Inst., Phi Alpha Theta (history honors), Hon. Soc. Mid Temple U.K. Episcopalian. E-mail: young@sandlerreiff.com.

YOUNG, JOHN ALAN, electronics company executive; b. Nampa, Idaho, Apr. 24, 1932; s. Lloyd Arthur and Karen Eliza (Miller) Y.; m. Rosemary Murray, Aug. 1, 1954; children: Gregory, Peter, Diana. BSEE, Oreg. State U., 1953; MBA, Stanford U., 1958. Various mktg. and fin. positions Hewlett Packard Co. Inc., Palo Alto, Calif., 1958-63, gen. mgr. microwave divsn., 1963-68, v.p. electronic products group, 1968-74, exec. v.p., 1974-77, COO, 1977-78, pres., 1977-92, CEO, 1978-92; ret., 1992. Bd. dirs. ChevronTexaco Corp., Agere Sys., Affymetrix, Inc., Ciphergen, Lucent Technologies, Perlegen, Fluidigm. Chmn. ann. fund Stanford U., 1966-73, nat. chmn. corp. gifts, 1973-77, mem. adv. coun. Grad. Sch. Bus., 1967-73, 75-80, Univ. trustee, 1977-87; bd. dirs. Mid-Peninsula Urban Coalition, 1971-80, co-chmn., 1983-85; chmn. Pres.'s Commn. on Indsl. Competitiveness, 1983-85, Nat. Jr. Achievement, 1983-84; pres. Found. for Malcolm Baldrige Nat. Quality Award; mem. Adv. Com. on Trade Policy and Negotiations, 1988-92. With USAF, 1954-56. Mem. Nat. Acad. Engring., Coun. on Competitiveness (founder, founding chair computer systems policy project 1986), Bus. Coun. (co-chair pres. com. of adcisors on sci. & tech. 1993-2001).

YOUNG, JOHN BYRON, retired lawyer; b. Bakersfield, Calif., Aug. 10, 1913; s. Lewis James and Gertrude Lorraine (Clark) Y.; m. Helen Beryl Stone, Dec. 26, 1937; children: Sally Jean, Patricia Helen, Lucia Robin. BA, UCLA, 1934; LLB, U. Calif., Berkeley, 1937; student, U. Chgo., 1943. Pvt. practice law Hargreaves & Young, later Young Wooldridge, Bakersfield, 1937-40; dep. county counsel County of Kern, 1940-42; dep. rationing atty. U.S. OPA, Bakersfield and Fresno, Calif., 1942; ptnr. firm Young Wooldridge and predecessors, Bakersfield, 1946-78, assoc. law firm, 1978-91. Bd. dirs., legal counsel Kern County Water Assn., Bakersfield, 1953-76. Mem., chmn. Kern County Com. Sch. Dist. Orgn., Bakersfield, 1950s and 60s; mem. Estate Planning Coun. of Bakersfield, 1960-76, pres., 1965-66. Capt. JAGC, U.S. Army, 1943-46. Mem. Kern County Bar Assn. (prs. 1948, Bench and Bar award 1978). Home: 13387 Barbados Way Del Mar CA 92014-3501 Office: Young Wooldridge 1800 30th St Fl 4 Bakersfield CA 93301-5298

YOUNG, JOHN EDWARD, lawyer; b. Tulsa, July 11, 1935; s. Russell Edward and Frances Lucille (Wetmore) Y.; m. Mary Moore Nason, Dec. 27, 1966; children: Cynthia Nason, Abigail Brackett. BS with honors, Calif. Inst. Tech., 1956; LLB magna cum laude, Harvard U., 1959. Bar: N.Y. 1961, U.S. Dist. Ct. (so. dist.) N.Y. 1973. Assoc. Cravath, Swaine & Moore, N.Y.C., 1960-67, ptnr., 1968-95, resident ptnr. Paris, 1971-73, London, 1990-95, sr. counsel, 1996—. Editor Harvard Law Rev., 1958-59. Trustee Internat. Sculpture Ctr., 1997—, vice chmn., 2000-02; trustee Royal Oak Found., 1997—, chmn., 1999-2002; gov. Am. Crafts Mus., 1997-2000. Sheldon Traveling fellow Harvard U., 1959-60. Mem. Assn. of Bar of City of N.Y., Century Assn., Harvard Club of N.Y.C., N.Y. Yacht Club, City Univ. Club London. Democrat. Episcopal. Home: 1088 Park Ave New York NY 10128-1132 Office: 380 Madison Ave 7th Fl New York NY 10017-2513 E-mail: jeyoung@attglobal.net.

YOUNG, JOHN WATTS, astronaut; b. San Francisco, Sept. 24, 1930; s. William H. Y.; m. Susy Feldman; children by previous marriage: Sandra, John. BS in Aero. Engring, Ga. Inst. Tech., 1952; LLD (hon.), Western State U., 1969; D Applied Sci. (hon.), Fla. Technol. U., 1970; DSc (hon.), U. S.C., 1981, Brown U., 1983; DEng. (hon.) , Glasgow U., 2001. Joined USN, 1952, advanced through grades to capt.; test pilot, program mgr. F4 weapons systems projects, 1959-62; then maintenance officer Fighter Squadron 143, Naval Air Sta., Miramar, Calif.; chief astronaut office Flight Ops. Directorate, 1974-87; spl. asst. dir. JSC for engring. ops., safety, 1987-96; assoc. dir. (tech.) JSC, 1996—. Decorated DFC (3), D.S.M. (2); recipient NASA Disting. Svc. medal (3), NASA Exceptional Svc. medal (2), NASA Engring. Achievement medal, 1988, NASA Outstanding Leadership medal, 1992, NASA Outstanding Achievement medal, 1994, AIAA Goddard Astronautics award, 2000, Congl. Space medal of honor, 1981; named Disting. Young Alumni Svc. award Ga. Tech. Acad. Disting. Engrs., 1994; named to Nat. Aviation Hall of Fame, 1988. Fellow Am. Astronautical Soc. (Flight Achievement award 1972, 81, 83, Space Flight award 1993), Soc. Exptl. Test Pilots (Iven Kincheloe award 1972, 81), AIAA (Haley Astronautics award 1973, 82, 84, NASA Disting. Exec. 1998, Rotary Space Trophy 2000); mem. Sigma Chi. Achievements include being an astronaut NASA, made 1st two-man 3 orbit flight, Gemini 3, Mar. 1965, Gemini 10 3 day flight, 1966, Apollo 10 8-day flight lunar landing dress rehearsal, 1969, Apollo 16 11 day lunar landing and surface exploration, 1972; comdr. 54 hour, 36 orbit 1st flight of Space Shuttle, 1981, and 10-day orbital flight 1st flight Space Lab, 1983; dir. space shuttle br., astronaut office, 1973-75. Office: NASA Johnson Space Ctr Houston TX 77058

YOUNG, JON NATHAN, archeologist; b. Hibbing, Minn., May 30, 1938; s. Robert Nathan Young and Mary Elizabeth (Barrows) Roy; m. Karen Sue Johnson, June 5, 1961 (div. May 1980); children: Shawn Nathan, Kevin Leigh; m. Tucker Heitman, June 18, 1988 (div. Apr. 1996). BA magna cum laude, U. Ariz., 1960, PhD, 1967; MA, U. Ky., 1962. Archeologist Nat. Park Svc. Southwest Archeol. Ctr., Globe and Tucson, Ariz., 1967-75; exec., camp dir. YMCA of Metro. Tucson, 1976-77; asst. dir. Kit Carson Meml. Found., Taos, N.Mex., 1978; co-dir. Las Palomas de Taos, 1979; archeologist Nat. Forest Svc., Carson Nat. Forest, Taos, 1980-99, Taos Ski Valley, 2000—. Exec. order cons. U.S. Sec. Interior, 1973-75. Author: The Salado Culture in Southwestern Prehistory, 1967; co-author: Excavation of Mound 7, 1981, First-Day Road Log in Tectonic Development of the Southern Sangre de Cristo Mountains, 1990, The Gila Pueblo Salado, 1997. Advisor Boy Scouts Am.; active YMCA

White Rag Soc.; mem. Kit Carson Hist. Mus. Grantee NEH, 1978; Ariz. Wilson Found., NSF, Ky. Rsch. Found. fellow, 1960-62; Baird Found., Bausch and Lomb, Elks; recipient cert. merit USDA, 1987, 89. Fellow AAAS, Am. Anthrop. Assn., Explorers Club, Royal Anthrop. Inst.; mem. Current Anthropology (assoc.), Ariz. Archaeol. and Hist. Soc., Ariz. Hist. Soc., Ctr. Anthropol. Studies, Coun. on Am.'s Mil. Past, Friends of Taos Pub. Libr., Friends of Taos Land Trust, Kit Carson Hist. Mus., New Mex. Heritage Preservation Alliance, Soc. Hist. Archaeology, Soc. Am. Archaeology, Harwood Found., Millicent Rogers Mus., Taos Archaeol. Soc., San Juan County Mus. Assn., Taos County Hist. Soc. (bd. dirs.), Sigma Xi, Phi Beta Kappa, Alpha Kappa Delta, Phi Kappa Phi, Delta Chi. Home: HCR 74 Box 24826 El Prado NM 87529-9549

YOUNG, JUDITH ANNE, animal conservationist; b. L.A., Feb. 11, 1953; d. John Mahlstedt Young and Cynthia Sheilds Tunniccliff. Grad. h.s., L.A. CEO Otter Conservation Ctr., Statesboro, Ga., 1983—. Copyright U.S. Govt., 1995. Avocations: animal keeping, water gardens, agriculture. E-mail: judy@g-net.net.

YOUNG, JULIA ANNE, librarian, elementary education educator; b. El Campo, Tex., July 25, 1958; d. Harold Lane and Marcella Jeanne (Payne) Y. BA in English and French, Sam Houston State U., Huntsville, Tex., 1979; MBA, Sam Houston State U., 1982; M in Libr. and Info. Sci., U. Tex., 1986. Cert. tchr. secondary bus., elem. and secondary English 1-12, talented and gifted K-12, PK-12 learning resource ctrs., K-8 elem. gen., Tex. Cataloguer Sam Houston State U., 1976-85; mem. acquisitions and serials staff Tex. State Libr., Austin, 1985-86; cataloguer PCL Grad. Libr. U. Tex., 1985-86; libr., tchr. Dallas Ind. Sch. Dist., 1986—. Vol. voter registration, Huntsville, 1982—83; mem. Common Cause, Dallas, 1976; leader Girl Scouts U.S., Huntsville , 1976, Dallas, 1987—88; sec. PTA, 1998—2000; mem. fin. com. adminstrv. bd. Highland Park United Meth. Ch., 1995—97; mem. ch. choir and handbell choir Oak Lawn United Meth. Ch., 2001—02. Grantee Jr. League, Dallas, 1994, 96. Mem. Dallas Emmaus Cmty., Dallas Assn. Sch. Librs. Democrat. Avocations: swimming, reading, walking, needlework, writing. Home: PO Box 190403 Dallas TX 75219-0403

YOUNG, KENNETH EVANS, educational consultant; b. Toronto, Ont., Can., Mar. 21, 1922; s. John Osborne Wallace and Gwendolyn May (Evans) Y.; m. Mae Catherine Wittenmyer, July 1, 1945; 1 child, Bruce Kenneth. AB, San Francisco State Coll., 1943; MA, Stanford U., 1947, PhD, 1953; LLD (hon.), U. Nev., 1972. Instr. journalism and speech San Francisco State Coll., 1946-48; instr. journalism and English Calif. State Poly. Coll., San Luis Obispo, 1949-50; from asst. prof. to acting dean Coll. Arts and Scis. Kellogg-Voorhis Campus, Pomona, 1951-57; dean faculty U. Alaska, College, 1957-59; fellow in coll. adminstrn. U. Mich., Ann Arbor, 1959-60; exec. v.p. U. Nev., Reno, 1960-64; pres. SUNY, Cortland, 1964-68; v.p., dir. Washington office Am. Coll. Testing Program, 1968-75; pres. Council on Postsecondary Accreditation, Washington, 1975-80; exec. dir. Nat. Univ. Continuing Edn. Assn., 1980-84; dir. Inst. for Learning in Retirement, Am. U., 1984-89. Sr. assoc., cons. Diane U. Eisenberg Assocs., Washington, 1984-95; chmn. Evans-McCan Group, 1996—. Prin. editor: Understanding Accreditation, 1983; contbr. articles to profl. jours. Sgt. U.S. Army, 1943-45. Republican. Home: 5 Stratford Ln Lexington VA 24450-1778

YOUNG, KEVIN C. executive of industrial company; b. Toronto, Ontario, Can., Sept. 21, 1966; s. Robert and Joyce Young; m. Kerstin A. Lack; children: Madeleine. BA with honors, U. Western Ont., 1989; MBA, U. Pa., 1993. V.p. mktg. and bus. devel. Indalex Aluminum Solutions, Toronto, 1997—99, v.p. sales and mktg. Vancouver, Canada, 1999—2001, pres. L.A., 2001—. Office: Indalex Aluminum Solutions 18111 E Railroad St La Puente CA 91748 Office Fax: 624-581-1451. E-mail: kevin.young.wg93@wharton.upenn.edu.

YOUNG, KIM ANN, health facility administrator; b. Akron, Ohio, Mar. 8, 1956; Harold Oscar and Shirley Mae (Witwer) Knight; m. John William Young, Oct. 2, 1982; children: Steven, Paul. Diploma in nursing with honors, Akron Gen. Med. Ctr. Sch. Nurs, 1977; BSN cum laude, U. Akron, 1984, MSN, 1992. RN, Ohio; cert. nursing adminstr. Staff nurse pediatric med-surg. Children's Hosp. Med. Ctr. Akron, 1977-83, charge nurse in pediatric med./surg., 1983-85, staff nurse pediatric ICU, 1985-88; head nurse in pediatric ICU Children's Hosp. Med. Ctr. of Akron, Ohio, 1988-93, head nurse in pediatric post anesthesia care unit, 1993-96; nurse mgr. post anesthesia care unit, presurg. unit (adult) Akron (Ohio) Gen. Med. Ctr., 1996—; dir.nursing, surgery adminstrn., anesthesia and surg. svcs. regional burn unit and pain ctr. Children's Hosp. Med. Ctr. of Akron, 2000—. Instr. advanced cardiac life support, pediatric advanced life support. Mem. Am. Soc. of Post Anesthesia Nurses, Ohio Orgn. Nurse Execs., Sigma Theta Tau, (Delta Omega chpt.).

YOUNG, LARRY JOE, insurance agent; b. Chanute, Kans., July 19, 1958; s. Larry Louis and Judith Ann (Leslie) Y.; m. Vickie Lea Everhart; children: Tyler Jay, Joseph Michael, Katherine LeAnn, Hayleigh Imogene, Larry Joe Jr. Student, Kans. City (Kans.) Community Coll., 1976-78; BGS in Meterology, Kans. U., 1980. Reg. rep., FDIC; security lic. mutual funds. Sales rep. Met. Life, Overland Park, Kans., 1981-86; deposit broker Union Cen. Life, 1986—; pres. Young & Assocs., Shawnee, Kans., 1988-95; Young & Assocs. Inc. (now incorporated), 1995—; owner/broker 1st Nat. CD Exch., 1996—; multiple line gen. agent Am. Nat. Ins. Co., mgr., 1998—. Coach Shawnee (Kans.) Soccer Club, 1986. Fellow, Life Underwriting Tng. Coun. Mem. Nat. Assn. Securities Dealers, Profl. Ind. Ins. Agts. Kans. Avocations: flying, pole vaulting.

YOUNG, LAURA, dance educator, choreographer; b. Boston, Aug. 5, 1947; d. James Vincent and Adelaide Janet Young; m. Anthony Charles Catanzaro, Sept. 26, 1970 (div. Nov. 1981); m. Christopher Edward Mehl, Aug. 23, 1987. Grad. high sch., Cohasset, Mass. Dancer Met. Opera Ballet, N.Y.C., 1971-73, Boston Ballet Co., 1963-65, prin. dancer, 1965-71, 73-89, ballet mistress, 1989-91. Guest tchr. Dance Tchrs. Club Boston, 1978—82, Dance Masters Assn., 1979, 90, 92, 93, Walnut Hill Sch., Natick, Mass., 1984—87, Natick, 1990—91, Granite State Ballet, 1993, Portland Ballet, Maine, Nat. Dance Theatre Bermuda, 1993, Worcester Performing Arts Sch., Mass., 1994, Alwin Sch. Dance Summer Intensive, Albuquerque, 1994—95, Ashland Youth Ballet, Ky., 1995, N.E. Regional Festival, 1996, Okla. Summer Arts Inst., 2000, Pitts. Ballet Theater Summer Program, 2000; asst. dir. Boston Ballet II, 1984—86, tchr., dir., 1986—96, dir. summer dance program, 1986—94; dir. DanceLab, 2001—; 1st hon. mem. Dance Masters Assn., Chpt. 5, 1992; mem. faculty Boston Conservatory, 1990—94; prin. Boston Ballet Sch., 1993—. Choreographer (ballets) Occasional Waltzes, 1984, Albinoni Suite, 1986, Champ Dances, 1987, A Place of Sound and Mind, 1988, Deadlock, 1989, Rumpelstiltskin, 1989. Recipient Leadership award Greater Boston C. of C., 1987; named Disting. Bostonian, Boston's 350th Jubilee Com., 1980. Mem. Am. Guild Mus. Artists, Dance Masters Am. (hon.). Office: Boston Ballet Co 19 Clarendon St Boston MA 02116-6100

YOUNG, LAURA WEN-YU, lawyer; b. San Francisco, Aug. 3, 1962; d. Timothy Shou-peng and Diane Yang. JD, U. Calif., Berkeley, 1987, AB in History, 1984. Bar: Calif. 1988. Assoc. Wang & Wang LLP, San Francisco, 1988-97, ptnr., 1997—, mng. ptnr., 2000—. Mem. adv. bd. Internat. Lawyers Newsletter, Portland, Oreg., 2000—, Boalt Hall Alumni Assn., Berkeley, 1995-2000. Contbr. articles to profl. jours. Dir. Wang Family Found., San Francisco, 1994—, Soc. for Song-Yuan Studies, Berkeley, 2000—, Berkeley War Crimes Study Ctr., 2000—. Mem. Internat. Trademark Assn. (chair Chinese subcom. 1999-2002), State Bar Calif., Taipei Univ. Club. Office: Law Offices Wang & Wang 8th Fl 180 Montgomery St San Francisco CA 94104

YOUNG, LAUREN SUE JONES, education educator; b. San Diego, July 21, 1947; d. Warren Calvin and Lola Esther Jones; 1 child, Forest McRay Young. AB, Occidental Coll., 1969; MS, San Diego State U., 1971; EdM, Harvard U., 1979, EdD, 1984. Adminstrv. asst. Child Devel. Research Unit, Nairobi, Kenya, 1969-70; asst. prof. San Diego State U., 1974-78, assoc. dir. tchr. corps., 1971-78; co-chmn. and mem. Harvard Ednl. Review, Cambridge, Mass., 1979-81; research assoc. The Huron Inst., 1980-82, Atari Cambridge Research Lab., Cambridge, 1982-84; policy analyst N.Y. State Dept. Social Services, Albany, 1984-85, spl. asst. to commr., 1985-87; assoc. prof. Mich. State U., East Lansing, 1987-2001; dir., sr. program officer The Spencer Found., Chgo., 1998—. Cons. Am. Insts. for Rsch., Cambridge, 1980, Tchr. Corps, Boston area, 1978-80, instr., Pago Pago, Am. Samoa, 1979; rsch. assoc. A Study of H.S.'s, Cambridge, 1980-82; disting. visitor John D. and Catherine T. MacArthur Found., 1995-96. Co-editor: Too Little, Too Late, 1988; mem. editorial bd. Evaluation Rev. Jour., L.A., 1984-88, Jour. Negro Edn. Team mem. Operation Crossroads Africa, Morogoro, Tanzania, 1968; mem. program adv. bd. Spencer Found., 1992. Recipient Danforth Found. fellow, St. Louis, 1978-84, tchr. scholar award, M.S.U., 1993. Mem. Am. Ednl. Research Assn. Office: The Spender Found 875 N Michigan Ave Ste 3930 Chicago IL 60611-1803

YOUNG, LAWRENCE, electrical engineering educator; b. Hull, Eng., July 5, 1925; arrived in Can., 1955; naturalized, 1972; s. Herbert and Dora Y.; m. Margaret Elisabeth Jane, Jan. 5, 1951. BA, Cambridge (Eng.) U., 1946, PhD, 1950, ScD, 1963. Asst. lectr. Imperial Coll., London, 1952-55; mem. research staff B.C. Research Council, 1955-63; assoc. prof. U. B.C., Vancouver, 1963-65, prof. dept. elec. engring., 1965-90, prof. emeritus, 1990—. Author: Anodic Oxide Films, 1961; contbr. articles to profl. jours. Recipient Callinan award Dielectrics div. Electrochemical Soc., 1983, Can. Electrochem. Gold medal, 1990. Fellow IEEE, Royal Soc. Can., Electrochem. Soc. Office: U BC Dept Elec Engring Vancouver BC Canada V6T 1W5 E-mail: youngl@interchange.ubc.ca.

YOUNG, LEO, electrical engineer; b. Vienna, Austria, Aug. 18, 1926; came to U.S., 1953, naturalized, 1958; s. Samuel and Marie Y.; m. Fay Merskey, Jan. 4, 1953 (dec. May 1981); children— Philip Michael, Sarah Anne, Joseph David; m. Ruth Breslow, Jan. 2, 1983 (dec. Nov. 1996); m. Jo-Ellen Turner, July 9, 1999. BA, Cambridge U., 1946, MA, 1950; MS, Johns Hopkins U., 1956, D.Engring. (Westinghouse-B.G. Lamme grad. scholar), 1959, D.H.L. (hon.), 1989. Lab. mgr. Decca Radar, Ltd., Surbiton, Eng., 1951-53; adv. engr. Westinghouse Electric Corp., Balt., 1953-60; staff scientist, program mgr. Stanford Research Inst., Menlo Park, Calif., 1960-73; staff cons., asso. supt. Naval Research Lab., Washington, 1973-81; dir. research Office of Undersec. for Def. Research and Engring., Dept. Def., 1981-94; cons. to dir. def. rsch. and engring. Dept. Def., 1994—. Bd. dirs. Filtronic-Comtek (U.K.); mem. NSF delegation to Japan, 1995, 99; chair NSF Rev. Panel on Critical Techs., 1997. Author: Microwave Filters, 1964, Systems of Units in Electricity and Magnetism, 1969, Advances in Microwaves, Vols. 1-8, 1966-74, Everything You Should Know About Pensions Plans, 1976; also articles; patentee in field. Recipient Woodrow Wilson award for Disting. Govt. Svc., 2001. Fellow: IEEE (pres. 1980, pres. Microwave Soc. 1969, hon. life mem. Microwave Soc., Microwave prize 1963, Microwave Career award 1988, Disting. Contbns. to Engring. Professionalism IEEE-USA 1993, Pinnacle award 1995), AAAS; mem.: NAE, Electromagnetics Acad., Royal Acad. Engring. U.K. (fgn. fellow), Sigma Xi. E-mail: youngturner@earthlink.net. *It has been my goal to serve the public and my belief that engineering and science improve the quality of life. I have enjoyed doing engineering research and am fortunate in receiving recognition.*

YOUNG, LESTER REX, engineering and construction company executive; b. Marion, Ind., Aug. 26, 1946; s. Harold Leroy and Willow Marie (May) Y.; m. Bonnie Darline Denison, Sept. 5, 1965; children: Tamara Lynn, Kelby Gene, Kadee Lynn. BSEE, Kans. State U., 1969; MBA, Wichita State U., 1979. Reg. engr. Colo., Kans., Ohio, Mont., Utah, La. Plant engr. Beech Aircraft Corp., Wichita, Kans., 1973-75, asst. to v.p. mfg., 1975-77; sr. project mgr. Smith & Boucher, Inc., Overland Park, Kans., 1977-80; dir. engring. R.M. Henning, Inc., New Philadelphia, Ohio, 1980-82; mgr. indsl. engring. Williams Internat., Ogden, Utah, 1982-84; mgr. plant engring. Sundstrand Corp., Denver, 1984-86; pres. ECS Engrs. Inc., Arvada, Colo., 1986-90; dir. bus. devel. Morrison Knudsen Corp., Denver, 1990-96; v.p. western region R&R Internat., Inc., 1996-99; v.p. ops. Aguirre Engrs., Inc., 1999-2000; ind. cons. strategic mktg., 2000—. Cons. Compliance Recycling Industries, Denver, 1984-87. Author: (reference manuals) Selection of Reverse Osmosis for Boiler Applications, 1987, Applications for Enzyme Activated Carbon, 1989, Integrated Refinery Waste Management, 1992. Capt. U.S. Army, 1969-73, Europe. Republican. Nazarene. Avocation: winter sports. E-mail: lyoung@ecsassociates.com.

YOUNG, LINDA DIANE, speech pathology/audiology services professional; b. Mt. Vernon, Ill., Sept. 4, 1949; d. Ramona Reed and John W. Davis (Deceased); children: Brian Young. BS in Elem. Edn., Murray State U., 1971, MS in Comm. Disorders, 1977. Cert. early childhood edn., elem. edn., H.S. edn., early intervention specialist, lic. speech/lang. pathologist. Second grade tchr. Pinellas County Pub. Schs., St. Petersburg, Fla., 1971—74; speech/lang. pathologist Orange County Pub. Schs., Orlando , 1978—80; parent educator Valencia C.C., 1978—80; sales rep. Kleinhenn Fund Raising Co., Anderson , Ind., 1983—86; speech/lang. pathologist Ea. Ill. Area Spl. Edn., Mattoon , 1986—87, Trico Cmty. Unit Sch. Dist., Campbell Hill , 1988—89, Cmty. Unit Sch. Dist. #186, Murphysboro, 1989—, Sullivan Cmty. Unit Sch. Dist., Sullivan. Game creator, author The Bee Safe or Bee Sorry Game , 1985; author: The Bee Safe or Bee Sorry Game, revised, 1999, (book and activities for children) The Adventures of Buzzie and Stinger, 2000. Mem. Govs. Coun. for the State of Ill. for the Dept. Children and Family Svcs., Springfield , 2002—. Recipient Benefactor award, The Amy Schulz Child Advocacy Ctr., Mt. Vernon, Cert. Appreciation, The Amy Schulz Child Advocacy Ctr., 1999, 2000, 2001. Mem.: So. Ill. Speech/Lang./Hearing Orgn., Philanthropic Ednl. Orgn. (asst. chairperson scholar awards 1999). Home: 1500 West Tripoli St Carbondale IL 62901 Office: Murphysboro CUSD #186 - Carruthers Elem 80 Candy Ln Murphysboro IL 62966

YOUNG, LORETTA ANN, auditor; b. Reading, Pa., Dec. 2, 1962; d. Milton and Delois Jean (Ridley) Y. BS, Towson U., 1985. CPA, cert. fin. svcs. auditor, internal auditor. Auditor Irving Burton Assocs., Inc., Washington, 1984-88; tax technician Gen. Bus. Svcs., Germantown, Md., 1989; auditor Montgomery County Govt., Rockville, 1989-90; dir. membership devel. Nat. Forum for Black Pub. Adminstrs., Washington, 1990-91; sr. acct.-analyst Cox & Assocs. CPAs, P.C., Hyattsville, Md., 1992; mgr. ops. LKA Computer Cons., Inc., 1992-94; supervisory auditor Office Specialists, Inc., Washington, 1994-97; sr. auditor Amtrak, 1997-2000; mgr. Deloitte & Touche, 2000—. Mem. AICPA, Inst. Internal Auditors, Md. Assn. CPAs., Assn. Govt. Accts. Home: PO Box 479 Germantown MD 20875-0479 Office: 1750 Tysons Blvd Mc Lean VA 22102-4219 E-mail: lyoung@deloitte.com.

YOUNG, LUCY H.Y. physician, retina surgeon; b. Taipei, Taiwan, Dec. 8, 1957; came to U.S., 1974; d. TsenMen Young and PeiLan Liu; m. Henning A. Gaissert, Aug. 12, 1989; children: Anna Gaissert, Philipp Gaissert, Henry Gaissert. BS in Biology, U. Wis., 1977, MD, 1981; PhD, Harvard U., 1984. Diplomate Am. Bd. Ophthalmology. Intern Framingham (Mass.) Union Hosp., 1984-85; resident in ophthalmology Mass. Eye and Ear Infirmary, Boston, 1985-88, retina fellow, 1988-90; instr. in ophthalmology Mass. Eye and Ear Infirmary/Harvard U., 1990-92, asst. prof. ophthalmology, 1992-97, assoc. prof., 1998—. Contbr. articles to profl. jours. Grantee Mass. Lions Eye Rsch. Fund, NIH, Cancer Rsch. Inst. Fellow ACS; mem. Am. Acad. Ophthalmology, Assn. for Rsch. in Vision and Ophthalmology, New Eng. Ophthal. Soc., Retina Soc., Macula Soc., Mass. Soc. Eye Physicians and Surgeons, Soc. for Neurosci. Office: Mass Eye and Ear Infirmary 243 Charles St Boston MA 02114-3096

YOUNG, MARGARET ALETHA MCMULLEN (MRS. HERBERT WILSON YOUNG), social worker; b. Vossburg, Miss., June 13, 1916; d. Grady Garland and Virgie Aletha (Moore) McMullen; m. Herbert Wilson Young, Aug. 19, 1959. BA cum laude, Columbia Bible Coll., 1949; grad., Massey Bus. Coll., 1958; MSW, Fla. State U., 1965; postgrad., Jacksonville U., 1961-62; MA in Old Testament, Tulane U., 1967, Columbia Internat. U., 1992. Dir. Christian edn. Eau Claire Presbyn. Ch., Columbia, S.C., 1946-51; prin. Bible Sch., Columbia, 1950-51; caseworker Fla. Children's Commn., 1951-52; Jackson County Welfare, 1952-54; tchr. Massey Bus. Coll., Jacksonville, Fla., 1954-57, office mgr., 1957-59; tchr. Massey Bus. Coll., Jacksonville, Fla., 1954-57, office mgr., 1957-59; social worker, unit supr. Fla. divsn. Family Svcs., St. Petersburg, 1960-66, dist. casework supr., 1966-71; social worker, project supr., program supr. Project Playpen, Inc., 1971-81, pres. bd., 1982-83, cons., 1986-89; pvt. practice family counselor, 1982—. Mem. coun. Child Devel. Ctr., 1983-89; mem. transitional housing com. Religious Cmty. Svcs., 1984-90. Mem. Acad. Cert. Social Workers, Nat. Assn. Social Workers (pres. Tampa Bay chpt. 1973-74), Fla. Assn. for Health and Social Svcs. (pres. chpt. 1971), Nature Conservancy, Rotary Ann (pres. 1970-71), Eta Beta Rho. Democrat. Presbyterian. Home: Presbyterian Home 201 W 9th North St Unit 13 Summerville SC 29483-6712

YOUNG, MARGARET BUCKNER, civic worker, author; b. Campbellsville, Ky.; d. Frank W. and Eva (Carter) Buckner; m. Whitney M. Young, Jr., Jan. 2, 1944 (dec. Mar. 1971); children: Marcia Elaine, Lauren Lee. BA, Ky. State Coll., 1942, MA, U. Minn., 1946. Instr. Ky. State Coll., 1942-44; instr. edn. and psychology Spelman Coll., Atlanta, 1957-60; dir. emeritus N.Y. Life Ins. Co.; alt. del. UN Gen. Assembly, 1973. Mem. pub. policy com. Advt. Coun. Trustee emerita Lincoln Ctr. for Performing Arts; chmn. Whitney M. Young, Jr. Meml. Found., 1971-92; trustee Met. Mus. Art, 1976-90; bd. govs. UN Assn., 1975-82; bd. visitors U.S. Mil. Acad., 1978-80; dir. Philip Morris Cos., 1972-91. Author: The First Book of American Negroes, 1966, The Picture Life of Martin Luther King, Jr., 1968, The Picture Life of Ralph J. Bunche, 1968, Black American Leaders-Watts, 1969, The Picture Life of Thurgood Marshall, 1970, pub. affairs pamphlet.

YOUNG, MARGARET CHONG, elementary education educator; b. Honolulu, May 8, 1924; d. Henry Hon Chin and Daisy Kyau (Tong) Chong; m. Alfred Y.K. Young, Feb. 21, 1948; children: Robert S.W., Richard S.K., Linda S.K. EdB, 5th yr. cert., U. Hawaii, 1945. Cert. tchr., Hawaii. Tchr. Waipahu (Hawaii) Elem. Sch., Manoa Housing Sch., Hawaii Dept. Edn., Honolulu, Pauoa Elem. Sch., Honolulu. Author: And They Also Came, History of Chinese Christian Association, Hawaii's People From China; contbr. numerous articles to profl. jours. Ch. sch. tchr., supt. United Ch. Christ-Judd St. Grantee San Francisco State Coll. Mem. NEA, Hawaii State Tchrs. Assn., Hawaii Congress of Parents and Tchrs. (hon. life mem.), Kappa Kappa Iota (Disting. Educator award 1986-87), Delta Kappa Gamma (internat.).

YOUNG, MARGARET LUBASH, librarian, information consultant, editor; b. Bridgeport, Conn., Aug. 17, 1926; d. George and Mary (Feltovic) Labash; m. Harold Chester Young, June 7, 1958 (div. July 1991); children: Jeffery Avery, Amy Margaret. BA, Cornell U., 1948; AMLS, U. Mich., 1959. Mktg. grader Harvard Bus. Sch., Boston, 1949-52; ops. rsch. sales asst. Arthur D. Little, Inc., 1953-57; reference libr. U. Mich., Dearborn, 1959-62; editor Gale Rsch., Detroit, 1964-74, Mpls., 1977-88; libr. Salzburg (Austria) Seminar, 1981-83; editor, info. cons. self employed, Hopkins, Minn., 1989—. Tax libr. cons. KPMG Peat Marwick, LLP, Mpls., 1991—; indexer Small Bus. Innovation Rsch., Minn. Project Innovation, Mpls., 1990-97. Co-editor: Directory of Special Libraries and Information Centers, edits. 3-6, 1974-81, Life Sciences Organizations and Agencies Directory, 1988; editor: Scientific and Technical Organizations and Agencies Directory, 1985, 2d edit., 1987. Host family Am. Field Svcs., 1979-80, 80-81; mem. steering com. Twin Cities Internat. Citizens Award, 1996-99. Mem. Spl. Librs. Assn. (internat. rels. chair Minn. chpt. 1994—, Fannie Simon award Pub. divsn. 1989), Am. Soc. Indexers, Beta Phi Mu. Democrat. Episcopalian. Avocations: gardening, classical music, dancing, yoga. Home: 313 Farmdale Rd W Hopkins MN 55343-7111

YOUNG, MARJORIE ANN, librarian; b. Ann Arbor, Mich., Jan. 30, 1945; d. Robert and Laura Kirstine (Larsen) Y. BA in French, Mich. State U., 1968; AMLS, U. Mich., 1969; MA in French Lang. and Lit., NYU, 1976. Asst. catalog libr. SUNY, New Paltz, 1969-73, asst. ref. libr., 1974-77, sr. asst. catalog libr., 1978-81, assoc. catalog libr., 1982-2000, catalog libr., 2000—. Sch. bd. libr. Adventist Sch., Poughkeepsie, N.Y., 1987—. Mem. Assn. Coll. and Rsch. Librs., SUNY Librs. Assn., Phi Beta Kappa. Avocations: singing, travel, languages, cooking, classical music. Home: PO Box 341 New Paltz NY 12561-0341 E-mail: youngm@newpaltz.edu.

YOUNG, MARVIN OSCAR, lawyer; b. Union, Mo., Apr. 4, 1929; s. Otto Christopher and Irene Adelheide (Barlage) Y.; m. Sue Carol Mathews, Aug. 23, 1952; children: Victoria Leigh, Kendall Marvin. AB, Westminster Coll., 1951; JD, U. Mich., 1954; LLD, Westminster Coll., 1989. Bar: Mo. 1954. Practice law firm Thompson, Mitchell, Thompson Douglas, St. Louis, 1954-55, 57-58; atty. Mo. Farmers Assn., Columbia, 1958-67; exec. v.p. First Mo. Corp., 1965-68; v.p. ops. MFA-Central Coop., 1967-68; v.p., gen. counsel, sec. Peabody Coal Co., St. Louis, 1968-82; gen. counsel Peabody Holding Co., Inc., 1983-85; also dir., sec. subs. and affiliates Peabody Coal Co.; ptnr. Gallop, Johnson & Neuman, St. Louis, 1986—, chmn. corp. dept., 1988-90, chmn. energy dept., 1990—. City atty. Warson Woods, Mo., 1990—; speaker at legal insts. Assoc. editor Mich. Law Rev., 1953-54; contbr. articles to profl. jours. Pres. Warson Woods PTA, 1974-75; trustee Met. Sewer Dist. St. Louis, 1974-80, chmn. 1978-80; mem. Mo. Energy Coun., 1973-77, Mo. Environ. Improvement and Energy Resources Athority, 1983-87, vice chmn. 1986-87; trustee Eastern Mineral Law Found., 1983-98; pres. Alumni Assn. Westminster Coll., Fulton, Mo., 1978-80, trustee coll., 1977—, mem. exec. com., 1978—, chmn. 1986-90, chmn. investment com., 1998-; chmn. Churchill Meml. and Libr., Fulton, 1992-2000; mem. chancellor's coun. adv. bd. U. Mo., St. Louis, 1992—; mem. lawyers adv. coun. Gt. Plains Legal Found., Kansas City, Mo., 1976-84; mem. Rep. Com. Boone County, Mo., 1962-68, chmn. legis. dist. com., 1962-64, 66-68; alt. del. Rep. Nat. Conv., 1968; pres. Clayton Twp. Rep. Club, 1973-77; sr. warden Episcopal Ch., 1988-89. Served to capt. USAF, 1955-57. Recipient alumni award of merit, 1972; named Coal Lawyer of Yr., Nat. Coal Assn., 1994; Churchill fellow, 1990. Mem. ABA, Mo. Bar Assn., Bar Assn. Met. St. Louis, Barristers Soc., Round Table Club of St. Louis, John Marshall Rep. Lawyers Club (pres. 1977), Mo. Athletic Club, Sjamrock Club of St. Louis County, Rotary (bd. dirs. St. Louis club 1993-95), Masons, Order of Coif, Shriners. Home: 555 Flanders Dr Saint Louis MO 63122-1617 Office: Gallop Johnson & Neuman LC 101 S Hanley Rd Ste 1600 Saint Louis MO 63105-3489 E-mail: moyoung@gjn.com.

YOUNG, MARY ELIZABETH, history educator; b. Utica, N.Y., Dec. 16, 1929; d. Clarence Whitford and Mary Tippit Y. BA, Oberlin Coll., 1950; PhD (Robert Shalkenbach Found. grantee, Ezra Cornell fellow), Cornell U., 1955. Instr. dept. history Ohio State U., Columbus, 1955-58, asst. prof., 1958-63, assoc. prof., 1963-69, prof., 1969-73; prof. history U. Rochester, N.Y., 1973—, prof. emeritus, 2000—. Cons. in field. Author: Redskins, Ruffleshirts, and Rednecks: Indian Allotments in Alabama and Mississippi, 1830-1860, 1961; co-editor, contbr.: The Frontier in American Development: Essays in Honor of Paul Wallace Gates, 1969. Recipient Pelzer award Miss. Valley Hist. Assn., 1955, Award Am. Studies Assn., 1982, Ray A. Billington award, 1982; Social Sci. Research Council grantee, 1968-69 Mem. Am. Hist. Assn., Orgn. Am. Historians, Soc. for Historians of the Early Am. Republic, Am. Antiquarian Soc. Home: 2230 Clover St Rochester NY 14618-4124 Office: U Rochester Dept History Rochester NY 14627 E-mail: yngm@mail.rochester.edu.

YOUNG, MARY FRANCES BRACCIO, educational consultant; b. Johnson City, N.Y., July 21, 1947; d. Louis and Helen (Petrini) Braccio; married Nov. 27, 1971. BA in History, SUNY, Geneseo, 1969; MS in Student Personnel Svcs. Guidance, SUNY, Albany, 1970. Cert. tchr., N.Y., Mass.; cert. guidance tchr., N.Y., Mass., N.J. Social studies tchr. Clarksburg (Mass.) Elem. Sch., 1972-73; guidance counselor Mt. Greylock Regional H.S., Williamstown, Mass., 1973-77, Hillsborough (N.J.) Middle Sch., 1977-78, Readington (N.J.) Twp. Schs., 1978-88; prin. Hoppock Middle Sch., Asbury, N.J., 1988-89, Readington Middle Sch., 1989-92; dir. edn. projects The Hostetter Group, Harrisburg, Pa., 1992—. V.p. InteResource Corp., York, Pa., 1978-79. Mem. Union Twp. Sch. Bd., Hampton, N.J., 1980-81; mem., v.p. Union Twp. Hist. Soc., 1983-87; bd. dirs. ARC, Flemington, N.J., 1989-92; scholar com. Bldg. 33 Found., 1995-2000; deacon Presbyn. Ch. Mem. ASCD, Nat. Mid. Sch. Assn. Avocations: gardening, reading, cooking, foreign travel. Home: 222 Heatherstone Way Lancaster PA 17601-4975

YOUNG, MELVIN ASHER, accountant, researcher; b. St. Louis, June 8, 1930; s. Leon Joel and Mary (Sorkin) Y.; m. Sonia Lee Winer Young, Feb. 24, 1957; 1 daughter, Melanie Anne. BS, U.S. Military Acad., West Point, N.Y., 1952. CPA, 1963. Indsl. engr., 1956-57; staff, ptnr. Winer, Levine & Young, 1957-97, Chattanooga; pvt. practice, 1998—. Author: (nonfiction) Where They Lie, 1991, Last Order of the Lost Cause, 1996; contbr. articles to profl. jours. Maj. U.S. Army, Korea, 1952-56, USAR. Mem. AICPA, Tenn. Soc. CPAs, Chattanooga Chpt. TSCPA (pres. 1973-74). Home: 1025 River Hills Cir Chattanooga TN 37415-5611 Office: PO Box 4509 Chattanooga TN 37405-0509 Fax: 423-266-0303.

YOUNG, MERWIN CRAWFORD, political science educator; b. Phila., Nov. 7, 1931; s. Ralph Aubrey and Louise (Merwin) Y.; m. Rebecca Conrad, Aug. 17, 1957; children: Eva Colcord, Louise Conrad, Estelle Merwin, Emily Harriet. BA, U. Mich., 1953; postgrad., Inst. Hist. Rsch. U. London, 1955-56,

Inst d'Etudes Politiques, U. Paris, 1956-57; PhD, Harvard U., 1964; DSc (hon.), Fla. Internat. U., 1998. Asst. prof. polit. sci. U. Wis., Madison, 1963-66, assoc. prof., 1966-69, prof., 1969—2001, emeritus, 2001—, Rupert Emerson prof., 1983; H. Edwin Young prof., 1994; chmn. African Studies Program U. Wis., Madison, 1964-68, chmn. dept. polit. sci., 1969-72, 84-87, assoc. dean Grad. Sch., 1968-71, acting dean Coll. Letters and Sci., 1992-93. Vis. prof. Makerere U. Coll., Kampala, Uganda, 1965-66; dean Faculty of Social Sci. Nat. U., Lubumbashi, Zaire, 1973-75; Fulbright prof. U. Dakar, Senegal, 1987-88. Author: Politics in the Congo, 1965, The Politics of Cultural Pluralism, 1976 (Herskovits prize 1977, Ralph Bunche prize 1979), Ideology and Development in Africa, 1982, The African Colonial State in Comparative Perspective, 1994 (Gregory Luebbert prize 1995); co-author: Cooperatives and Development, 1981, The Rise and Decline of the Zairian State, 1985; editor: The Rising Tide of Cultural Pluralism: The Nation-State at Bay?, 1993, Ethnic Diversity and Public Policy, 1998, The Accommodation of Cultural Diversity, 1999; co-editor: Dilemmas of Democracy in Nigeria, 1995, Beyond State Crisis? Postcolonial Africa and Post-Soviet Eurasia in Comparative Perspective, 2002. Served to 1st lt. U.S. Army, 1953-55. Social Sci. Rsch. fellow, 1967-68, Ford Faculty fellow, 1967-68, Guggenheim Found. fellow, 1972-73; vis. fellow Inst. for Advanced Study, Princeton, 1980-81; fellow Woodrow Wilson Internat. Ctr. for Scholars, 1983-84. Mem. AAAS, Am. Acad. Arts and Scis., Am. Polit. Sci. Assn., African Studies Assn. (pres. 1982-83, Disting. Africanist award 1991), Coun. Fgn. Rels. Home: 639 Crandall St Madison WI 53711-1836 Office: U Wis Dept Polit Sci North Hall 1050 Bascom Mall Madison WI 53706-1389 E-mail: young@polsci.wise.edu.

YOUNG, MICHAEL ANTHONY, lawyer; b. Lima, Ohio, Sept. 3, 1960; s. William John and Bettye Jean (Day) Y. BS magna cum laude, U. Cen. Fla., 1981; JD with honors, Fla. State U., 1984. Bar: Ga. 1984, Fla. 1985. Assoc. Kilpatrick & Cody, Atlanta, 1984-86, Stokes, Lazarus & Carmichael, Atlanta, 1986-89; pvt. practice, 1989—. Jud. intern U.S. Dist. Ct. (no. dist.) Fla., 1984; weekend atty. Atlanta Legal Aid Soc., 1985-86. Rsch. editor Fla. State U. Law Rev., 1982-84; contbr. articles to legal jours. Dir., pres. ChildKind Found. Mem. ABA, Assn. Trial Lawyers of Am., Fla. Bar Assn., Ga. Bar Assn., Atlanta Bar Assn. Avocations: scuba diving, golf, weightlifting. Home: 5275 S Trimble Rd NE Atlanta GA 30342-2174 Office: 17 Executive Park Dr NE Ste 440 Atlanta GA 30329-2222

YOUNG, MICHAEL CHUNG-EN, allergist, immunologist, pediatrician; b. Chgo., July 10, 1953; s. Koon C. and Siu Fun (Hui) Y.; m. Karen Lee Young, Apr. 7, 1979; 1 child, Liane. AB cum laude, Harvard Coll., 1975; MD, Yale U., 1979. Diplomate Am. Bd. Allergy and Immunology, Am. Bd. Pediatrics, Nat. Bd. Med. Examiners. Resident pediat. Children's Hosp., Boston, 1979—82, fellow in allergy and immunology, 1982—84, asst. in medicine (immunology), attending physician, 1984—; asst. clin. prof. pediat. Harvard Med. Sch., 2002—. Clin. instr. pediatrics Harvard Med. Sch., Boston, 1984—; mem. active staff South Shore Hosp., South Weymouth, Mass., 1985—. Author: Peanut Allergy Answer Book, Fair Winds Press, 2001; Contbr. articles to profl. jours. Named physician honoree, Asthma and Allergy Found. Am., 2001; recipient Nat. Rsch. Svc. award, NIH, 1982—84. Fellow Am. Coll. Allergy and Immunology (Parke Davis Allergy Fellows award 1983), Am. Acad. Allergy and Immunology, Am. Coll. Chest Physicians, Am. Acad. Pediatrics; mem. New Eng. Soc. Allergy, Mass. Allergy Soc. (pres. 1992-94), Mass. Med. Soc. Office: South Shore Allergy & Asthma Specialists 851 Main St South Weymouth MA 02190-1612

YOUNG, MICHAEL EDWARD, optometrist; b. Denver, Oct. 3, 1956; BS, Colo. State U., 1979; OD, Pacific U., 1983; M in Human Rels, U. Okla., 2000. Commd. USAF, 1980, advanced through grades to lt. col., 1997; comdr. optometry flight 30th Aerospace Medicine Squadron, Vandenberg AFB, Calif., 1994-97, dep. comdr., 1997-98, RAF, Lakenheath, Eng., 1998-2000; comdr. 314 Aeromed. Dental Squadron, Little Rock AFB, 2000—. Biomed. scis. corps advisor 30th Med. Group, Vandenberg AFB, 1994-98, 48th Med. Group, 1998-2000. Fellow Am. Acad. Optometry; mem. Am. Optometric Assn., Optometric Extension Program, Phi Beta Kappa. Home: 101 Arizona Ave Jacksonville AR 72076

YOUNG, MICHAEL KENT, dean, lawyer, educator; b. Sacramento, Nov. 4, 1949; s. Vance Lynn and Ethelyn M. (Sowards) Young; m. Suzan Kay Stewart, June 1, 1972; children: Stewart, Kathryn, Andrew. BA summa cum laude, Brigham Young U., 1973; JD magna cum laude, Harvard U., 1976. Bar: Calif. 1976, N.Y. 1985. Law clk. to Justice Benjamin Kaplan, Supreme Jud. Ct. Mass., Boston, 1976-77; assoc. prof., prof., Fuyo prof. Japanese law Columbia U., N.Y.C., 1978-98; dir. Ctr. Japanese Legal Studies Ctr. for Korean Legal Studies, 1985-98; dir. Program Internat. Human Rights and Religious Liberties Columbia U., 1995-98; dep. legal advisor U.S. Dept. State, Washington, 1989-91, dep. under sec. for econ. affairs, 1991-93, amb. for trade and environ. affairs, 1992-93; law clk. to Justice William H. Rehnquist U.S. Supreme Ct., 1977-78; dean, Lobingier prof. comparative law and jurisprudence George Washington U. Sch. of Law, 1998—. Chair U.S. Commn. on Internat. Religious Freedom, 2001—02; vis. scholar law faculty U. Tokyo, 1978—80, 1983; vis. prof. Waseda U., 1989; chmn. bd. advisors Japan Soc.; counsel select subcom. on arms transfers to Bosnia U.S. Ho. of Reps., 1996; mem. steering com. Law Profs. for Dole, 1996; mem. com. on internat. jud. rels. U.S. Jud. Conf., 1999—; mem. Brown v. Bd. Edn. 50th Anniversary Commemoration Com.; chair NAFTA labor agreement adv. com. Dept. of Labor, 2002—. Author: Fundamentals of U.S. Trade Law, 2001, Japanese Law in Context, 2001. Bd. visitors USAF Acad., 2002—03. Fellow, POSCO Rsch. Inst., 1995—98, Japan Found., 1979—80, Fulbright, 1983—84. Fellow: Am. Bar Found.; mem.: Coun. Fgn. Rels. Mem. Lds Ch. Avocations: Avocations: skiing, scuba diving, photography. Fax: 202-994-5157. E-mail: myoung@law.gwv.edu.

YOUNG, MICHAEL WARREN, geneticist, educator; b. Miami, Fla., Mar. 28, 1949; s. Lloyd George and Mildred (Tillery) Y.; m. Laurel Ann Eckhardt, Dec. 27, 1978; children: Natalie, Arissa. BA, U. Tex., 1971, PhD, 1975. NIH postdoctoral fellow Stanford (Calif.) U. Med. Sch., 1975-77; asst. prof. genetics The Rockefeller U., N.Y.C., 1978-83, assoc. prof., 1984-88, prof., 1988—, dir. Levy/White Ctr. Mind, Brain and Behavioral Studies, 2002—; head Rockefeller unit NSF Sci. and Tech. Ctr. Biol. Timing, 1991—. Investigator Howard Hughes Med. Inst., N.Y.C., 1987-96; adv. panel on genetic biology NSF, Washington, 1983-87; spl. advisor Am. Cancer Soc., N.Y.C., 1985—; spl. reviewer genetics study sect. NIH, Bethesda, Md., 1990—, cell biology study sect., 1993-97. Contbr. articles to profl. jours. Meyer Found. fellow, N.Y.C., 1978-83. Fellow N.Y. Soc. Fellows; mem. AAAS, Genetics Soc. Am., Am. Soc. Microbiologists, N.Y. Acad. Scis., Harvey Soc. Achievements include research on transposable DNA elements, molecular genetics of nerve and muscle development, biological clocks, molecular control of circadian rhythms. Home: 51 Greenwoods Rd Old Tappan NJ 07675-7018 Office: The Rockefeller Univ 1230 York Ave New York NY 10021-6399

YOUNG, MILTON EARL, retired petroleum company executive; b. San Angelo, Tex., Dec. 3, 1929; s. Edward Earl and Annie Mae (North) Y.; m. Clara Louise Sens, June 1, 1957; children— Vanessa, Bradley. AA, San Angelo Coll., 1950; BS in Petroleum Engring, U. Tex., 1953. Various positions Continental Oil Co., 1953-73; v.p. for prodn., drilling, engring. Tesoro Petroleum Corp., San Antonio, 1973-74, sr. v.p., 1974-85, group v.p. exploration and prodn., 1985-86, retired, 1986. Served with USNR, 1948-49. Mem. Soc. Petroleum Engrs. Republican. Lutheran. Home: 1932 Frazar Rd Sealy TX 77474-8439

YOUNG, MORRIS, electrical engineering consultant; b. Alexandria, Egypt, Aug. 28, 1937; came to U.S., 1949; s. Nessim and Anna Yahia; m. Susan Slater, Dec. 22, 1962; children: Bruce Leonard, Amy Ellen. Assoc., chief elec. engr. I.M. Robbins P.C., 1973-94; with Nassau Tech. Svcs., Wantagh, N.Y., 1995—. Trustee bd. edn. Wantagh Schs., dist. liaison to B.O.C.E.S., chmn. subcom. citizen's adv. com. for capital improvement project, budget adv. com., guest lectr. in indsl. arts dept.; appointee Nassau County Exec. Francis Purcell's Task Force; officer L.I. Planning Coun.; coach, mgr., Am. league pres. Wantagh Little League; chmn. cub pack 185 Boy Scouts Am.; v.p. Wantagh/Seaford Homeowners Assn.; mem. L.I. R.R. Commuter's Coun.; vol. Friends in Svc. to Humanity; bd. dirs. Temple Beth Emeth, Hewlett; mem. Christmas in April/Rebldg. in Am. Mem. Nat. Soc. Archtl. Engrs., Am. Legion, Jewish War Vets. U.S., Masons (mastermason), Scottish Rite (32nd degree), Shriner (pub. rels. dir. and chaplain Kismet Shrine). Republican. Home: 3452 Beltagh Ave Wantagh NY 11793-2552 Office: Lehr Assocs 130 W 30th St New York NY 10001-4092

YOUNG, MORRIS NATHAN, ophthalmologist, writer; b. Lawrence, Mass., July 20, 1909; s. Charles Michael and Ida (Davis) Y.; children: Cheryl Lesley Deknatel, Charles Chesley. BS, MIT, 1930; MA, Harvard U., 1931; MD, Columbia U., 1935; PhD, U. San Marino, 1998. Diplomate Am. Bd. Ophthalmology. Intern Queens (N.Y.) Gen. Hosp., 1935-37; resident in ophthalmology Harlem Eye and Ear Hosp., N.Y.C., 1938-40; pvt. practice in ophthalmology, 1945—. Med. advisor N.Y.C. Dir. Selective Svs. Sys., N.Y.C. Dept. Health; asst. ophthalmologist NYU Univ. Hosp., 1947-61; cons. Beth Israel Hosp., 1972-93, hon., 1994, St. Vincent's Hosp. and Med. Ctr., N.Y.C., 1978—; dir. emeritus ophthalmology N.Y. Downtown Hosp.; v.p. Life Music, Inc.; pres. Denton & Haskins Corp. Author: Presto Prestige, 1929, Hobby Magic, 1950, Houdini on Magic, 1953, Bibliography of Memory, 1961, Houdini's Fabulous Magic, 1961, How to Develop an Exceptional Memory, 1962, How to Read Faster and Remember More, 1965, A Complete Guide to Science Fair Competition, 1972, Radio Music Live, 1999, Original Magicol and Indices, Vols. 1-3, 1998 ; editor MAGICOL mag., 1949-52; contbr. articles to profl. jours. Bd. dirs. Houdini Hist. Ctr., Houdini Mus., Las Vegas; mem. exec. bd. Houdini Picture Corp.; hon. cons. Libr. Congress. Col. USAR, 1930-69, ret. Mem. AMA, ASCAP, Am. Assn. Ophthalmology, Am. Acad. Ophthalmology (life), N.Y. State Med. Soc., Pan Am. Med. Assn., Queens Gen. Hosp. Alumni Assn., Res. Officers Assn., Ret. Officers Assn., Soc. of Mil. Ophthalmologists, Glaucoma Found. (adv. bd.), Chinatown Lions Club (hon.), Lawrence United Lodge, Nat. Sojourners (pres. Manhattan chpt., trustee Knickerbocker chpt.), Heroes of '76, Soc. Am. Magicians (hon.), Internat. Brotherhood Magicians, Magic Collectors Assn. (founding), N.Eng. Magic Collectors Assn. (hon.), Mil. Order of World Wars (surgeon 1997—), Order of Lafayette (surgeon gen. 1998—), Magic Cir. (Inner Magic Cir.), Harvard Magic Club (hon.), Soc. of Osiris (hon. mem.). Office: 2 Fifth Ave Apt 16M New York NY 10011

YOUNG, NANCY MELINDA, otolaryngologist; b. N.Y.C., 1956; m. Mitchell L. Marinello; children: Samantha, Michelle Lindsey. BA, Wesleyan U., 1978; MD, NYU, 1982. Resident in gen. surgery Montefiore Hosp., Bronx, N.Y., 1982-84; resident in otolarnygology-head and neck surgery Northwestern Meml. Hosp., Chgo., 1984-87; fellow in neurotology Chgo. Otology Group-Hinsdale Hosp., 1987-88; head sect. neurotology and otology Children's Meml. Hosp., Chgo., 1988—. Asst. prof. Northwestern Dental Sch., 1988-90; asst. prof. Northwestern U., 1990-2002, assoc. prof., 2002; mem. med. adv. bd. Advanced Bionics Corp., Sylmar, Calif., 1997—, Cochlear Corp., Englewood, Colo.. Bd. dirs. Chgo. Hearing Soc., 1992-97, Anixter Ctr., 1997—. Fellow Am. Acad. Otolaryngology-Head & Neck Surgery; mem. ACS, AMA, Am. Neurol. Soc., Chgo. Med. Soc., Ill. Med. Soc. Office: Dept Otolaryngology 2300 Children Plz # 25 Chicago IL 60614-3318 E-mail: nyoung@northwesternuniversity.edu.

YOUNG, NICHOLAS, physician; b. Pui, Romania, Dec. 6, 1914; s. Melchior and Ella (Abraham) Y.; m. Anne Diaz, May 28, 1943 (dec. Feb. 1966); m. Marianne P. Low-Beer, May 20, 1967. MD, U. Basel Med. Faculty, Switzerland, 1937. Cert. Am. Bd. Neurology Psych. in Psychiatry. Intern, resident & sr. psychiatrist Manhattan State Hosp., Ward's Island, N.Y., 1943-47; sr. supervising psychiatrist King's Cty. Psychiatric Hosp., N.Y., 1947-48; lectr. N.Y. Psychoanalytic Inst., 1952-56, 56—. tng. and supervising analyst, 1971-75, chmn. ednl. com., 1975-77, chmn. faculty. Fellow Am. Psychiat. Assn. (life); mem. Am. Psychoanalytic Assn., Internat. Psychoanalytic Assn., N.Y. Psychoanalytic Soc. & Inst., N.Y. City & State Med. Soc. Office: 45 E 89th St Apt 26B New York NY 10128-1230

YOUNG, NORMAN GREGORY, law educator; b. L.A., Oct. 16, 1949; s. Andrew Spurgeon Nash and Hazel Marionette Y.; m. Shahla Rahman, Nov. 26, 1993; children: Christopher, Braedon. BA, Calif. State U., 1970; JD, Loyola Law Sch., 1973; pub. cert., Stanford U., 1982; cert., USAR JAG Sch., Charlottesville, Va., 1986; LLM in internat. law, U. San Diego, 1997; cert. The Hague Acad. of Internat. Law, 1998, cert. The Hague Acad. of Pub. Internat. Law, 1999. Bar: Calif. 1973, US Supreme Ct. 1987. Atty. SEC, L.A., 1973-76; trustee-in-bankruptcy U.S. Bankruptcy Ct., 1976-83; pvt. atty. Edwards & Young, 1976-91; prof. Calif. Poly. U., Pomona, 1976—; commr. Calif. Bldg. Stds. Commn., Sacramento, 1985-89. Vis. fellow U. Cambridge, 2000, 2001; vis. lectr. Econs. Coll., Ho Chi Minh City, Vietnam, 1997, Hanoi Nat. U., Vietnam, 1999, Wuhan Law Sch., China, 2000; adv. exec. com. internat. practice sect. State Bar Calif., 2001—. Mem. ABA, Am. Soc. Internat. Law, Golden Key. Office: Calif State Poly U 3801 W Temple Pomona CA 91768 E-mail: ngy@csupomona.edu.

YOUNG, OLIVIA KNOWLES, retired librarian; b. Benton, Ark., Sept. 3, 1922; d. Wesley Taylor and Med Belle (Crawford) Knowles; m. Calvin B. Young, Oct. 6, 1951; 1 child, Brigham Taylor. BA, Tenn. Tech. U., 1942, BS in Libr. Sci., 1946. Head periodicals and documents dept. Peabody Coll. Library, Nashville, 1946-49; area libr. U.S. Army, Austria, 1949-51; libr. Cairo Pub. Libr., Ga., 1955-57, Caney Fork Regional Libr., Sparta, Tenn., 1957-58; chief libr. Ft. Stewart (Ga.) U.S. Army, 1959-63; dir. Watauga Regional Libr., Johnson City, Tenn., 1963-70; dir. devel. and extension Tenn. State Libr. and Archives, Nashville, 1971-82, state libr. and archivist, 1982-85; ret., 1985. Mem. Tenn. Library Assn. (treas. 1970, Honor award 1985), Southeastern Library Assn., ALA, Boone Tree Library Assn. (pres. 1968), Altrusa Club (sec. 1967). Methodist. Home: 1825 N Atlantic Ave Apt 108 Daytona Beach FL 32118

YOUNG, PAMELA RUTH, social worker, consultant, therapist; b. Providence, Oct. 29, 1945; d. Morris P. and Esther (Frank) Y.; m. Murray Low, June 15, 1986. BA, Simmons Coll., 1967; MSW, Hunter Coll., 1969; cert., Ackerman Inst., 1978, Family Inst. of Westchester, 1980. Cert. social worker, N.Y.; diplomate Am. Bd. Examiners in Clin. Social Work; lic. marriage and family therapist, Conn. Social worker Met. Hosp., N.Y.C., 1969, Community Svc. Soc., N.Y.C., 1969-71; sr. social worker Hillside Hosp., L.I. Jewish-Hillside Med. Ctr., Glen Oaks, N.Y., 1971-87, cons. rsch. dept. psychiatry, 1987-88; dir. clin. svcs. Family Inst. of Westchester, White Plains, 1990-98; pvt. practice, 1980—. Mem. faculty Family Inst. Westchester, 1980—99, Adelphi U., 1980—87. Contbg. author: Reweaving the Family Tapestry, 1991. Mem.: NASW, Am. Family Therapy Acad., Am. Assn. Marriage and Family Therapists (approved clin. supr.), Acad. Cert. Social Work (diplomate). Jewish. Home and Office: 15 Springdale Rd Scarsdale NY 10583-7320 E-mail: PamL1@aol.com.

YOUNG, PATRICIA JANEAN, speech pathology/audiology services professional; b. San Dieto, Nov. 30, 1953; d. Bernarr E. and Janean Romig Young. AA, Palomar C.C., San Marcos, Calif., 1976; BA, Calif. State U., Chico, 1978; MA, Calif. State U., Long Beach, 1981. Cert. clin. competence Am. Speech-Lang.-Hearing Assn., speech pathologist Calif., tchr. Calif. Mgmt. trainee Robinson's Dept. Store, L.A., 1976—78; speech and hearing screening coord. Riverview Hearing, Speech, Lang. Ctrs., Long Beach, 1978—81, speech pathologist, 1981—84; speech pathologist, dir. Speech Pathology Svcs., Carlsbad and Temecula, 1984—; speech pathologist, augmentative comm. coord. Lake Elsinore (Calif.) Unified Sch. Dist., 1998—. Prodr. TV shoes on comm. disorders Long Beach Cable TV, 1983; coord. pub. svc. announcement and interviewee for Disabilities Awareness Week ABC TV, San Diego, 1986, San Diego, 88. Contbr. poetry to lit. publs.; author: (game) Match This!, 1995. Named to Outstanding Young Women Am. Mem.: Calif. Speech-Lang-Hearing Assn. (region rep., Outstanding Achievement award 1987), Am. Speech-Lang-Hearing Assn., Zeta Tau Alpha. Avocations: writing, theater, decorating. Home: 31935 Calle Espinoza Temecula CA 92592 Office: Lake Elsinore Unified Sch Dist 545 Chaney St Lake Elsinore CA 92530

YOUNG, PATRICIA JEAN HEDRICK, mental health nurse, educator; b. Fairmont, W.Va., June 2, 1952; d. Raymond and Mary Jean (Sapp) Hedrick; m. David Martin Young, Apr. 7, 1973; children: William Glen, Georgia Lynn. ADN, W.Va. No. C.C., Wheeling, 1977; AB in Edn., West Liberty State Coll., 1973, BSN, 1980; MS in Nursing, W.Va. U., 1987, EdD in Curriculum and Instrn., 1997. Cert. in psychiat./mental health nursing. Staff nurse Ohio Valley Med. Ctr., Wheeling, W.Va., 1977-89; instr. Washington (Pa.) Sch. Nursing, 1989—. Co-facilitator Nurse Educators Network. Mem. ch. coun., lay leader West Liberty Federated Ch. Mem.: NOW, AAUW, TriState Psychiat. Nurses Assn. (co-pres.), W.Va. Nurses Assn., Nat. League Nurses, Sigma Theta Tau. Home: PO Box 218 West Liberty WV 26074-0218 E-mail: DrPJHYoung@aol.com.

YOUNG, PATRICK, writer, editor; b. Ladysmith, Wis., Oct. 19, 1937; s. Rodney and Janice (Wolf) Y.; m. Leah Ruth Figelman, Oct. 8, 1966; 1 child, Justine Young Gottshall. BA, U. Colo., 1960. Reporter UPI, Washington, 1961-62; journalist USN, 1963-64; staff writer Nat. Observer, Silver Spring, Md., 1965-77; free-lance writer Laurel, 1977-79; mem. sr. staff Pres.'s Commn. on the Accident at Three Mile Island, Washington, 1979; chief sci. and med. writer Newhouse News Svc., 1980-88; editor Sci. News, 1988-95; ind. writer, editor, cons., 1995—. Sci. writer in residence U. Wis., 1986. Author: Asthma and Allergies, 1980, Drugs and Pregnancy, 1987, Schizophrenia, 1988; co-author: Keeping Young Athletes Healthy, 1991. With USN, 1963-64. Recipient Howard W. Blakeslee award Am. Heart Assn., 1971, Sci. Writing award in physics and astronomy Am. Inst. Physics, 1974, James T. Grady award Am. Chem. Soc., 1977. Mem. Nat. Assn. Sci. Writers, Nat. Press Club, Am. Assn. Adv. Sci. E-mail: young@nasw.org.

YOUNG, PAUL RAY, medical board executive, physician; b. Fairfield, Nebr., June 27, 1932; s. Earl Edward and Louisa May (Saunders) Young; m. Irene Marie Gray (div. 1971); children: Michael, Susan, Jean, James; m. Faye Elizabeth Hall, Oct. 28, 1972. BA, U. Nebr., Lincoln, 1953; MD, U. Nebr., Omaha, 1958. Diplomate Am. Bd. Family Practice. Intern Rsch. Hosp., Kansas City, Mo., 1958—59, dir. continuing med. edn., 1967—71; pvt. practice Raytown, 1961—67; assoc. prof. family practice U. Mo. Coll. Medicine, Columbia, 1971—75; chmn. dept. U. Nebr. Coll. Medicine, 1975—80, U. Tex. Med. Br., Galveston, 1980—88; dep. dir. Am. Bd. Family Practice, Lexington, Ky., 1988—90, exec. dir., 1990—97, sr. exec., 1998—. Chmn. RRC for Family Practice, Chgo., 1979—87. Founding editor: Family Practice Recert, 1979, founding editor: Jour. Am. Bd. Family Practice, 1987. Pres. Nicholas J. Piscano Meml. Found., 1990—97. Capt. M.C. USAF, 1959—61. Fellow: Am. Acad. Family Physicians; mem.: Soc. Tchrs. Family Practice (bd. dirs. 1970—72), Alpha Omega Alpha. Office: Am Bd Family Practice Inc 2228 Young Dr Lexington KY 40505-4219 E-mail: pyoung@abfp.org.

YOUNG, PAUL ANDREW, anatomist; b. St. Louis, Oct. 3, 1926; s. Nicholas A. and Olive A. (Langford) Y.; m. Catherine Ann Hofmeister, May 14, 1949; children— Paul, Robert, David, Ann, Carol, Richard, James, Steven, Kevin, Michael. BS, St. Louis U., 1947, MS, 1953; PhD, U. Buffalo, 1957. Asst. in anatomy U. Buffalo, 1953, instr. anatomy, 1957; asst. prof. anatomy St. Louis U., 1957, asso. prof., 1966, prof., 1972—, chmn. dept., 1973—. Author: (with B.D. Bhagat and D.E. Biggerstaff) Fundamentals of Visceral Innervation, 1977, (with P.H. Young) Basic Clinical Neuroanatomy, 1996, also computer assisted neurological anatomy tutorials; contbr. articles to profl. publs. Recipient Golden Apple award, Student AMA, 1974, 2000, Tchg. award, Acad. Sci. St. Louis, 1993, Emerson Excellence in Tchg. award, 2001. Mem. Am. Assn. Anatomists, Am. Assn. Clin. Anatomists, Soc. Neurosci., Sigma Xi, Alpha Omega Alpha. Office: St Louis U Dept Anatomy & Neurobiology 1402 S Grand Blvd Saint Louis MO 63104-1004

YOUNG, PAULA ERNESS, corporate trainer; b. Memphis, Sept. 20, 1957; d. Erneest Leroy and Carrie Louise (Watson) Y. BS, Memphis State U., 1978; MPA, Atlanta U., 1981; EdD in Ednl Adminstrn., U. Cin., 1993. Asst. dir. grants and contracts Nat. Assn. for Equal Opportunity in Higher Edn., Washington, 1981-83, clearinghouse and conf. exhibits mgr., 1981-83; dir rsch. and proposal devel. Clark Coll., Atlanta, 1984-87; asst. v.p. for devel. Johnson C. Smith U., Charlotte, N.C., 1987-88; v.p. instl. advancement Bennett Coll., Greensboro, 1988-90; spl. asst. to dean Coll. Arts and Scis., N.C. Agrl. and Tech. State U., 1990-98; sr. instrl. design specialist Fed. Express Corp., 1998—. Mem. Women of Color Com., 1994; mem. Greensboro Minority/Women Bus. Enterprise Adv. Bd., 1993; mem. Greensboro Human Rels. Commn., 1990; founder African Am. Atelier Art Gallery; vol. Girl Scouts U.S.A., 1985-86; active YWCA, NAACP. Woodrow Wilson fellow, 1981-83, 85-87. Mem. Nat. Assn. Negro Bus. and Profl. Women's Clubs, Nat. Soc. Fund Raising Execs., Toastmasters Internat., Alpha Kappa Alpha. Avocations: ceramic artwork, reading. Address: 7617 Windsong Dr Memphis TN 38125-6513

YOUNG, PHILIP HOWARD, library director; b. Ithaca, N.Y., Oct. 7, 1953; s. Charles Robert and Betty Irene (Osborne) Young; m. Nancy Ann Stutsman, Aug. 18, 1979. BA, U. Va., 1975; PhD, U. Pa., 1980; MLS, Ind. U., 1983. Asst. prof. history Appalachian State U., Boone, NC, 1980-82; reference asst. Lilly Libr. Ind. U., Bloomington, 1982-83; adminstr., info. specialist Ind. Corp. Sci. & Tech., Indpls., 1983-85; dir. Krannert Meml. Libr. U. Indpls., 1985—. Mem.: Archeol. Inst. Am., Am. Libr. Assn., Phi Beta Kappa, Beta Phi Mu, Phi Alpha Theta. Democrat. Home: 4332 Silver Springs Dr Greenwood IN 46142-9623 Office: U Indpls Krannert Meml Libr 1400 E Hanna Ave Indianapolis IN 46227-3630

YOUNG, QUENTIN HAYSE, family counselor; b. Panama City, Fla., Mar. 1, 1944; s. Mayo Beckford Young and Rose Mary Kama; m. Mary C. Grith, June 13, 1964 (div. July 1972); children: Jeff, Samantha; m. Ginger Bialas-Lucas, Aug. 18, 2001. Degree in mech. design, Cen. Design Coll., 1968. Machine operator Plastics Fabrication, Wichita, Kans., 1965-67; metal fabricator Beach Aircraft, 1967-69; with aircraft design dept. Fairchild, San Antonio, 1969-70; mem. bd. design Data Point, 1970-72; officer Ga. Correctional Officer, Alto, 1972-73; dir. rsch. So. Steel, San Antonio, 1973-84; exec. v.p. design ADTEC, 1984-90; sr. design engr. R.R. Brink, Shorewood, Ill., 1990-2000; instr. native Am. Indian studies Coll. of DuPage, Glen Ellyn, 1997—; family counselor Balance Thru the 4 Winds of the Lakota, Winfield, 2000—. Advanced open water instr. Scuba Schs. Internat., 1980—. Patentee lock designs, child restraint. With U.S. Army, 1962-65. Mem. ACA, Monroe Inst. Avocations: rock climbing, scuba diving, art. Home: 0S425 Florida Ln Winfield IL 60190 Office: Balance Thru the 4 Winds of the Lakota PO Box 606 Winfield IL 60190 E-mail: wicasa54@aol.com.

YOUNG, RANDY WILLIAM, lawyer; b. Ft. Wayne, Ind., Oct. 19, 1949; s. Robert Arnold and Genevieve Mary (Obert) Y.; m. Julie Maree Brunson, June 16, 1984; children: Maree Elizabeth, Ann Elaine. BBA, U. Notre Dame, 1972; JD, Ind. U., 1975. Bar: Ind. 1975, U.S. Dist. Ct. (no. dist.) Ind. 1976. Law clk. to judge Ind. Ct. Appeals, Indpls., 1975-76; ptnr. Christoff, Cornelius & Young, Ft. Wayne, 1976-80; sole practice, 1980—. Recipient Silver Beaver award Boy Scouts Am., 1981, dist. award of Merit, 1985, Sagamore of Wabash, Gov. of Ind., 1990. Mem. Allen County Bar Assn. (treas. 1983-85), Allen County Law Library Assn. (treas. 1980-98). Clubs: St. Vincent Men's (Ft. Wayne), Notre Dame of Ft. Wayne (award of the Yr. 1985). Avocations: scouting, skiing, camping, backpacking. Home: 2115 Carroll Rd Fort Wayne IN 46818-8908 Office: 202 W Berry St Ste 710 Fort Wayne IN 46802-2273 E-mail: rwy@svscouts.org.

YOUNG, RAYMOND HENRY, lawyer; b. Boston, Sept. 28, 1927; s. Raymond H. and Clara Elms (Oakman) Y.; m. Louisa Breda, Sept. 1, 1951; children: Christopher, Pamela, Amy. AB, Yale U., 1947, LLB, 1950. Bar: Mass. 1951. Assoc. Warner, Stackpole, Stetson & Bradlee, Boston, 1950-52; pvt. practice, 1952-64; ptnr. Young & Bayle, 1964—. Mem. ABA (past sec. sect. real property, probate and trust law, mem. commn. legal problems of the elderly), Am. Coll. Trust and Estate Counsel (mem. joint editorial bd. for trust and estate acts), Am. Law Inst. (advisor for restatement property 3d donative transfers, cons. restatement trusts 3d), Nat. Commn. on Nat. Probate Ct. Standards, Internat. Acad. Trust and Estate Law (past pres.), Mass. Bar Assn., Boston Bar Assn. (past pres.), Boston Estate Planning Coun. (past pres., Estate Planner of Yr. award 1991), Boston Probate and Estate Planning Forum. Home: 122 Garfield St Watertown MA 02472-4916 Office: Young & Bayle 150 Federal St Boston MA 02110-1713

YOUNG, REBECCA MARY CONRAD, state legislator; b. Clairton, Pa., Feb. 28, 1934; d. Walter Emerson and Harriet Averill (Colcord) Conrad; m. Merwin Crawford Young, Aug. 17, 1957; children: Eve, Louise, Estelle, Emily. BA, U. Mich., 1955; MA in Teaching, Harvard U., 1963; JD, U. Wis., 1983. Bar: Wis. 1983. Commr. State Hwy. Commn., Madison, Wis., 1974-76; dep. sec. Wis. Dept. of Adminstrn., 1976-77; assoc. Wadsack, Julian & Lawton, 1983-84; elected rep. Wis. State Assembly, 1985-99. Translator:

Katanga Secession, 1966. Supr. Dane County Bd., Madison, 1970-74; mem. Madison Sch. Bd., 1979-85. Recipient Wis. NOW Feminist of Yr. award, 1996, Eunice Zoghlin Edgar Lifetime Achievement award ACLU, 1997, Outstanding Legislator award Wis. Counties Assn., 1998, Voice for Choice award Planned Parenthood Wis., 1998, Luan Gilbert award for outstanding activities in domestic violence intervention and prevention Domestic Violence Intervention Svc., 1998. Mem. LWV. Democrat. Avocations: board games, hiking. Home: 639 Crandall St Madison WI 53711-1836 Office: State Legislature-Assembly PO Box 8953 Madison WI 53708-8953

YOUNG, RICHARD ALAN, association executive; b. Oak Park, Ill., Mar. 17, 1935; m. Carol Ann Schellinger, June 28, 1958; children: Steven, Karen, Christopher. BA, U. Iowa, 1958; MS, PhD, Western State U., 2000. Chief engr. Cardox Corp., Chgo., 1958-61; asst. chief engr. Goodman Mfg. Co., 1961-63; plant and environ. engr. Signode Corp., Glenview, Ill., 1963-68; editor Pollution Engring. Tech. Pub. Co., Barrington, 1968-81; exec. dir. Nat. Registry of Environ. Profls., 1988—; pub. Cahners Pub. Co., Des Plaines, Ill., 1990-95. Adj. prof. George Williams Coll.; mcpl. pollution control adviser and enforcement officer for 24 cities and state govts; ofcl rep. and pollution control expert U.S. Govt. at tech. transfer meetings; exec. dir. Internat. Certification Accreditation Bd., 1999—. Editor 26 books on environ. engring.; pollution engring.; series editor, Marcel Dekker Inc., N.Y.C.; contbr. articles to profl. jours.; patentee in field. Recipient Jesse H. Neal certificate for outstanding editorial writing Am. Bus. Press, Inc., 1971, Outstanding Service award Western Soc. Engrs., Charles Ellet award as Most Outstanding Engr. of Yr. 1970; Environ. Quality award EPA, 1976 Mem. Internat. Assn. for Pollution Control (dir.), Am. Soc. Bus. Press Editors (Editl. Excellence award 1980, Design Excellence award 1982), Am. Inst. Plant Engrs. (past nat. chmn. environ. quality), Internat. Congress Environ. Profls. (mng. dir.), Nat. Inst. Hazardous Materials Mgmts. (dir. 1984-88, cert. hazardous materials mgr.).

YOUNG, RICHARD D. state legislator; b. Dec. 2, 1942; m. Elaine Young; 5 children. BA, Vincennes U. Mem. Ind. Senate from 47th dist., 1988—; mem. agr., small bus., edn., fin. and natural resource coms.; minority leader, 1996—. Farmer. Mem. Farm Bur., Crawford County C. of C., Lions.' Democrat. Home: RR 1 Box 106-c Milltown IN 47145-9801 Office: Ind Senate State Capitol 200 W Washington St Indianapolis IN 46204-2728*

YOUNG, RICHARD ROBERT, logistics and transportation educator; b. Passaic, N.J., July 18, 1946; s. William Frederick and Helen Mae (Smith) Y.; m. Mary Frances Braccio, Nov. 27, 1971. BS in Commerce, Rider Coll., 1968; MBA, SUNY, Albany, 1971; postgrad., U. Mass., 1973-77; PhD, Pa. State U., 1993. Admitted to practice FMC. Materials handling engr. Thatcher Glass Mfg. Co., Elmira, N.Y., 1968-69; mgr. customer svc. Cooper Labs., Wayne, N.J., 1971; materials mgr. of contracts Sprague Electric Co., North Adams, Mass., 1971-75, mgr. corp. purchasing, 1975-77; mgr. purchasing adminstrn. Am. Hoechst Corp., Somerville, N.J., 1977-80, mgr. group purchasing, 1980-84; mgr. group distbn. Hoechst Celanese Corp., 1984-89; asst. prof. bus. Pa. State U., University Park, 1989—, dir. logistics exec. program in Singapore, 1996-2000. Bd. dirs. Guildcraft Inc., York, Pa., vice-chmn., 1992-94, chmn., 1995—; mem. adv. com. World Trade Inst., N.Y.C., 1985-98; cons. indsl. and svc. sector clients world-wide 1995—; affiliate rschr. Idaho Inst. Bus. and Environ., 1995-98. Contbr. articles to logistics jours. Bd. dirs. No. Berkshire Child Care Commn., North Adams, Mass., 1972-76; mem. Union Twp. (N.J.) Zoning Bd., 1985-89, vice chmn., 1989; v.p. Union Twp. Rep. Club, 1983-87; alt. mem. Hunterdon County (N.J.) Rep. Com., 1987; ordained Presbyn. elder. Fellow Chartered Inst. Transport (U.K.); mem. Can. Assn. Logistics and Supply Chain Mgmt., Phillipsburg R.R. Historians (co-founder), Acad. Mgmt., Decision Sci. Inst., Nat. Assn. Purchasing Mgmt. (cert.), Am. Soc. Transp. and Logistics (sustaining assoc. examiner 1989-98), Assn. for Psychol. Type, World Futures Soc., Masons, Hamilton Club Lancaster, Delta Sigma Pi. Presbyterian. Avocations: sailing, photography, fgn. travel. Home: 222 Heatherstone Way Lancaster PA 17601-4975 Office: Pa State U 146 Acad Bldg Fogelsville PA 18051 Personal E-mail: rry1@aol.com. Business E-Mail: rry100@psu.edu.

YOUNG, RICHARD WILLIAM, corporate director; b. Ridgewood, N.Y., Oct. 17, 1926; s. Charles Michael and Louise Margaret (Baust) Y.; m. Sheila deLisser, Sept. 11, 1949; children: Christine, Noreen, Brian, Eileen. AB, Dartmouth Coll., 1946, A.M., 1947; PhD, Columbia U., 1950. Sr. rsch. chemist Chemotherapy div. Am. Cyanamid Co., Conn., 1950-56, group leader pesticide chems. Agrl. div., 1956-58, dir. chem. Agrl. div., 1958-60, dir. chem. rsch. cen. rsch. div., 1960-62; asst. dir. rsch. Polaroid Corp., Cambridge, Mass., 1962-69, v.p., 1963-69, sr. v.p. rsch. and devel., 1969-72, sr. v.p., pres. Internat. div., 1972-80, exec. v.p., dir. worldwide mktg., 1980-82; pres. Houghton Mifflin Co., Boston, 1982-85; chmn., CEO Mentor O & O, Inc., Norwell, Mass., 1985-92. Bd. dirs. Bay State Milling Corp., Quincy, Mass., Instron Corp., Canton, Mass., Oceantrawl Inc., Seattle, Mentor Corp., Santa Barbara, Calif. Patentee in field. Chmn. bd. trustees Regis Coll., Weston, Mass.; trustee Mass. Eye and Ear Infirmary, Boston, 1963-90, Trinitas Found., Quincy; mem. corp. Northeastern U., Boston, 1960-92; hon. dir. of sci. Regis Coll., 2002. Mem. Am. Chem. Soc. Home: 4 Scotch Pine Cir Wellesley Hills MA 02481-1222 Office: Trinitas Found 100 Congress St Quincy MA 02169-0906

YOUNG, ROBERT, lawyer; b. Forest Hills, N.Y., Apr. 19, 1945; s. Herbert and Sarah Y.; m. Roslyn Patricia Harlan, July 1, 1972. BA, Duke U., 1966; JD, U. S.C., 1969; LLM in Taxation, NYU, 1974. Bar: S.C. 1969; CPA, S.C. Pvt. practice, Columbia, S.C., 1974-2001; of counsel Turner, Padget, Graham & Laney, P.A., 2001—. Lt. (JAGC) USN, 1969-72. Home: 1312 Greenhill Rd Columbia SC 29206-2810 Office: 1901 Main St Fl 17 Columbia SC 29201-2443 Fax: (803) 799-5837. E-mail: ryl@tpgl.com.

YOUNG, ROBERT A., III, freight systems executive; b. Ft. Smith, Ark., Sept. 23, 1940; s. Robert A. and Vivian (Curtis) Y.; m. Mary Carleton McRae; children: Tracy, Christy, Robert A. IV (dec.), Stephen BA in Econs., Washington and Lee U., 1963. Supr. terminal ops. Ark. Best Freight, Ft. Smith, 1964-65; pres. Data-Tronics Inc, 1965-67; sr. v.p. Nat. Bank of Commerce, Dallas, 1967-70; v.p. fin. Ark. Best Corp., Ft. Smith, 1970-73, exec. v.p., 1973, pres., chief operating officer, 1973-88, chief exec. officer, pres., 1988—; pres. ABF Freight Systems, Inc., 1979-94. Bd. dirs. First Nat. Bank, Ft. Smith. Pres. United Way, Ft. Smith, 1981; chmn. bd. dirs. Sparks Regional Med. Ctr., Ft. Smith, 1995, chair, 1999; bd. dirs. ATA Found., Inc., Ft. Smith Boys Club; chmn. bd. trustees Lyon Coll., Sparks Regional Med. Ctr., Ft. Smith. Recipient Silver Beaver award Boy Scouts Am. Mem. Am. Trucking Assn. (vice chmn.), Phi Delta Theta. Presbyterian. Office: Ark Best Corp PO Box 10048 Fort Smith AR 72917-0048 also: Ark Best Corp 3801 Old Greenwood Rd Fort Smith AR 72903-5937

YOUNG, ROBERT CRABILL, medical researcher, science facility administrator, internist; b. Columbus, Ohio, 1940; MD, Cornell U., 1965. Diplomate Am. Bd. Internal Medicine, subspecialty bds. hematology and med. oncology. Intern N.Y. Hosp., N.Y.C., 1965-66, resident, 1966-67; sr. resident Yale-New Haven Med. Ctr., 1969-70; sr. investigator, attending physician med. br. Nat. Cancer Inst., Bethesda, Md., 1971—, chief med. br., 1974-88; pres. Fox Chase Cancer Ctr., Phila., 1988—. Clin. prof. medicine Georgetown U., from 1974, assoc. prof., 1976-84; clin. prof. medicine George Washington U., 1984—; bd. Sci. Advisors, Nat. Cancer Inst., 1996—; bd. Nat. Cancer Policy, 1997-99; chmn. bd. Nat. Comprehensive Cancer Network. Assoc. editor Jour. Clin. Oncology; chmn. editl. bd. Oncology Times. Sr. surgeon USPHS, 1967-69. Fellow ACP; mem. Am. Soc. Hematology, Am. Assn. Cancer Rsch., Am. Soc. Clin. Oncology (pres. 1990), Am. Cancer Soc. (bd. dir. 1995-99, 1st v.p. 1999-2000, pres. 2002), Internat. Gynecol. Cancer Soc. (pres.-elect 1998, pres. 2000). Office: Fox Chase Cancer Ctr 7701 Burholme Ave Ste 2 Philadelphia PA 19111-2497

YOUNG, ROBERT CRAIG, banker; b. N.Y.C., Mar. 15, 1960; s. Robert J. and Gloria L. (Sandhop) Y.; m. Anke Ott, Dec. 2, 2000. BS cum laude, NYU, 1982, MBA, 1985. Asst. v.p. Chem. Bank, N.Y.C., 1982-86; project mgr. GE Credit Corp., Stamford, Conn., 1986-87; dir. Merrill Lynch & Co., N.Y.C., 1987-94; sr. v.p. Greenwich (Conn.) Capital Markets, Inc., 1994-97; mng. dir. Nomura Securities, N.Y.C., 1997-2001; divsn. dir. Macquarie, 2001—. Home: 98 Revere Rd Manhasset NY 11030-2733 Office: Macquarie 600 5th Ave New York NY 10020 E-mail: reverecap@aol.com.

YOUNG, ROBERT DONALD, physicist, educator; b. Chgo., Apr. 20, 1940; s. Robert Joseph and Nellie Y.; children: Robert Gerald, Jennifer Ann Rolinski; m. BJ Marymont, Feb. 14, 1981; 1 child, Emily Sexton. BS in Physics, Ill. Inst. Tech., 1962; MS in Physics, Purdue U., 1965, PhD in Physics, 1967. Asst. prof. physics Ill. State U., Normal, 1967-73, assoc. prof., 1974-78, prof., 1979-2000, prof. emeritus, 2000—, dir. rsch. Coll. Arts and Scis., 1994-95, assoc. v.p. for rsch., dean grad. studies, 1995-97, chair dept. physics, 1997-2000. Adj. prof. physics U. Ill., Urbana, 1986—. Named Rschr. of Yr., Ill. State U., 1989. Mem. Am. Phys. Soc. Achievements include research on glassy properties of proteins, usage of computer techniques in physics education, individualized modular approach in physics education. Home: 838 N Lone Oak Way Flagstaff AZ 86004-5819

YOUNG, ROBERT EDWARD, computer company executive; b. L.A., Nov. 28, 1943; s. David and Sue Young; m. Lucia Young. Student, E. Los Angeles Coll., 1973, Santa Monica Coll., 1975; BA, UCLA, 1978. Cert. securities analyst N.Y. Inst. Fin., 1972. Computer operator Rocketdyne Corp., Canoga Park, Calif., 1963-65; computer ops. supr. Hughes Aircraft Corp., El Segundo, 1965-67; with investment securities dept. Smith, Tilton & Co., Inc., Santa Ana, 1967-70, Morton Seidel & Co., Inc., L.A., 1970-78; sales mgr. of comml. interior constrn. NICO Constrn. Co., Inc., 1978-80; sales mgr. Strauss Constrn. Co., Inc., 1981-82; v.p., instl. investment officer FCA Asset Mgmt./Am. Savs., Los Angeles, 1982-87; pres., chief exec. officer Avalon Fin. Group, Inc., 1988-90; prin. Robert Young & Co., 1991-2000; pres. youngbob.com, Inc., 2000—. Bd. dirs. RESA Prodns. 1973-80, Edu Care, L.A., 1981-90, ASC Edn. Svcs. Inc., L.A., chmn. fin. com.; mktg. cons. Shehata Enterprises, L.A., 1978-79; sales tng. cons. Versailles Gallery, L.A., Schwartz Constrn., L.A., 1982; cons. PC Etcetera, L.A., 1990-91; guest lectr. Pryor Seminars, 2000—. Photographer: prin. works include Man at Work or Play UN, Geneva, 1976, Cat of Yr. photo, 1977, Photomontage U. So. Calif. Early Childhood Edn. Ctr., 1977; producer weekly pub. affairs prog. for family fin. planning sta. KPOL Radio, 1974, Stocks and Bonds Show KWHY-TV, 1975-78, MacRadio show, Am. Radio Network, 1989, WinRadio Show, 1990, MacWin Radio, 1991-93. Fin. cons. Hofheinz Fund, Houston, 1988. Served with USCGR, 1964-70. Mem. Archtl. Hist. Soc. (life mem. So. Calif. chpt.), Reel Sports Club, Masons, Marine Venice Yacht Club (rear commodore). Avocations: fishing, computers, sailing. Home: 6032 Avenida De Castillo Long Beach CA 90803-2004 Office: YoungBob.Com Inc 8306 Wilshire Blvd Ste 499 Beverly Hills CA 90211-2382

YOUNG, ROBERT LEE, religious studies educator, training services executive, consultant; b. Jefferson, Iowa, Aug. 15, 1922; s. Earl Marion and La Rue Berry Young; m. Inga Møller Smith, Aug. 17, 1963; children: Steven Møller, David Berry, Annalisa, Christopher Robert. BS in Commerce, State U. Iowa, 1947; MA in Econs., Stanford U., 1948, PhD in Edn., 1965. Counselor Stanford (Calif.) Christian Fellowship, 1951—53, Internat. Fellowship Evang. Studies, Buenos Aires, 1954—59, Curitiba, Brazil, 1957—59; prof. Am. U., Beirut, 1965—69; tchr. U. Tehran, Iran; prof. Azusa (Calif.) Pacific U., 1984—; sr. cons. for mulit-cultural tng. Global Exec. Resources, San Francisco, 1998—. Dir., prof. Youth Palace, Tehran, 1968—69; mem. adv. bd. Operation Impact, Azusa, 1997—2002. Author: Student Missions in Mid-East, 1965, God and a Woman of Stanford, 1991, I Will Be With You, 2002. Mem. Incorporation Com., Oakhurst, Calif., 1997—99; tchr. Laubach Literacy Group, 2001; founder Lake Tahoe Internat. Student House Parties, Alianca Biblica do Brasil; sr. pastor 1st Covenant Ch., San Francisco, 1950—52. Lt. j.g. USNR, 1945—46, PTO. Recipient Middle East Rsch. award, Am. U. Beirut, 1966—67; fellow rsch. fellow, U.S. Office Edn., Washington, 1962—63. Mem.: Beta Gamma Sigma. Avocations: hiking, mountain climbing, travel, writing. Home: 39339 Pine Ridge Rd Oakhurst CA 93644 Office: Global Exec Resources PO Box 192941 San Francisco CA 94119-2944

YOUNG, ROGER M. judge; b. Cass City, Mich., Feb. 15, 1960; s. James William and Joyce (Little) Y.; m. Janice Marie Young, Apr. 13, 1984. BS, Bapt. Coll. Charleston, 1980; JD, U. S.C., 1983; LLD (hon.), U. Charleston, 1992; M in Jud. Studies, U. Nev., 2000. Bar: S.C. 1983, U.S. Dist. Ct. S.C. 1984. Pvt. practice, Charleston, S.C., 1983-95; mcpl. judge City of North Charleston, 1988-90, acting city atty., 1995; mem. S.C. Ho. Reps., 1990-94; equity ct. judge Charleston County, SC, 1996—2003; cir. ct. judge Ninth Jud. Cir. of S.C., 2003—. Adj. prof. polit. sci. Charleston S. U., 1986; adj. prof. bus. law So. Wesleyan U., 1996—, U. S.C. Sch. of Law, 2000—. Recipient Order Palmetto Gov. Carroll Campbell, 1994; named Disting. Alumnus of the Yr. Charleston S. U., 1998. Mem. ABA, Am. Judicature Soc., Am. Judges Assn., S.C. Bar Assn. Home: 8121 Greenridge Rd Charleston SC 29406-9769

YOUNG, ROLAND FREDERIC, III, lawyer; b. Norway, Maine, Apr. 8, 1954; s. Roland Frederic Jr. and Marylyn May (Bartlett) Y.; m. Dona Davis Gagliano, Aug. 18, 1979; children: Meghan, Wesley, Taylor. AB, Cornell U., 1976; JD, U. Conn., 1979. Bar: Conn. 1979, U.S. Dist. Ct. Conn., U.S. Tax Ct., U.S. Ct. Appeals (2d cir.). Ptnr. Howard, Kohn, Sprague & FitzGerald, Hartford, Conn., 1984-91, O'Brien, Tanski & Young, Hartford, 1991—. Lectr. Hartford Grad. Ctr., 1991-98. Author (seminar booklet) Confidentiality of Med. Records, 1989, Limiting Damages, 1990; co-author (seminar booklet) Med. Malpractice in Conn., 1992; editor Conn. Risk Mgmt. Assn., 1986-98. Mem. Nat. Assn. Health Attys., Conn. Def. Lawyers Assn., Conn. Hosp. Assn., Hartford County Bar Assn. (medico-legal liaison com.). Avocations: golf. Office: O'Brien Tanski & Young City Place II 16th Fl Hartford CT 06103 E-mail: rf_young@otylaw.com.

YOUNG, RONALD FARIS, commodity trader; b. Schenectady, Dec. 17, 1939; s. James Vernon and Dorothy (Girod) Y.; m. Anne Randolph Kendig, Feb. 23, 1963; children: Margaret Randolph Reynolds, Anne Corbin. BA, U. Va., 1962; MBA, Harvard U., 1966. Grain trader Continental Grain Co., 1966-70; pres. Conti-Commodities, Chgo., 1970; v.p. commodity sales Du-Pont, Glore Forgan, 1971-72; self-employed commodity trader Chgo. Bd. Trade, 1972-78; ind. trader Va. Trading Co., 1978-90, pres., 1978-84, dep. chmn., 1984-89; pres. Randolph Ptnrs., Ltd., 1983-91. Chmn. bd. Chgo. Bd. Trade, 1978, dir., 1975-77, 80 Bd. dirs. Princeton Fund, 1981-82, Lake Forest Hosp., 1981-84, Lake Forest Country Day Sch., 1981-86. Served with USMCR, 1959-65. Mem. Racquet Club (bd. dirs. 1989-97), Onwentsia Club (Lake Forest, Ill., bd. dirs. 1981-90, pres. 1991-93), Everglades Cub (Palm Beach, Fla.), Bath and Tennis Club (Palm Beach). Republican. Episcopalian. Home: 531 N Mayflower Rd Lake Forest IL 60045

YOUNG, RONALD FREDERICK, neurosurgeon; b. Buffalo, Jan. 4, 1939; s. Frederick Earl and Ruth Henrietta (Cowan) Y.; m. Sheila Marie Young, June 23, 1962 (div. 1990); children: Scott Ronald, Anne Louise, Karen Lynn. BA, SUNY, Buffalo, 1961, MD, 1965. Diplomate Am. Bd. Neurol. Surgery. Intern U. Minn Hosp., Mpls., 1965-66; resident in neurosurgery VA Hosp., Longbeach, Calif., 1966-67, SUNY, Syracuse, 1969-73, asst. prof. neurosurgery, 1973-77; assoc. prof. UCLA, 1977-85; prof. neurosurgery U. Calif., Irvine, 1986-93; chief of neurosurgery U. Calif. Med. Ctr., 1986-93; clin. prof. U. Calif., 1993—; dir. N.W. Gamma Knife Ctr. and N.W. Neurosci. Inst. Northwest Hosp., Seattle, 1993—; dir. radiosurgery St. Johns Regional Med. Ctr., Oxnard, Calif., 2000—. Elizabeth Crosby Meml. lectr. U. Mich., Ann Arbor, 1990; med. dir. Am. Gamma Knife Network; med. adv. bd. Trigeminal Neuralgia Assn. Author: Spinal Cord Injury, 1981; contbr. articles to profl. jours. Capt. USAF M.C., 1967-69. Recipient Kongress medal German Neurosurg. Soc., 1982. Fellow ACS; mem. Western Neurosurg. Soc. (v.p. 1990-91, pres. 1993-94), Am. Acad. Pain Medicine (sec. 1991-93), Am. Assn. Neurol. Surg., Congress Neurol. Surgery, Soc. Univ. Neurosurgeons (pres. 1996-97), Santa Fe Neuroscis. Inst. (bd. dirs. 1983—), Am. Acad. Neurosurgery, Soc. Neurol. Surgeons, Internat. Leksell Gamma Knife Soc. (chmn. 1995). Avocations: skiing, tennis, French lessons, horseback riding. Office: Calif Neurosci Inst 1600 N Rose Ave Ste 400 Oxnard CA 93030 E-mail: r.f.young@att.net.

YOUNG, ROY ALTON, university administrator, educator; b. McAlister, N.Mex., Mar. 1, 1921; s. John Arthur and Etta Julia (Sprinkle) Y.; m. Marilyn Ruth Sandman, May 22, 1950; children: Janet Elizabeth, Randall Owen. BS, N.Mex. A&M Coll., 1941; MS, Iowa State U., 1942, PhD, 1948; LLD (hon.), N.Mex. State U., 1978. Tchg. fellow Iowa State U., 1941-42, instr., 1946-47, Indsl. fellow, 1947-48; asst. prof. Oreg. State U., 1948-50, assoc. prof., 1950-53, prof., 1953—, head dept. botany and plant pathology, 1958-66, dean rsch., 1966-70, acting pres., 1969-70, v.p. rsch. and grad. studies, 1970-76, dir. Office for Natural Resources Policy, 1986-90; chancellor U. Nebr., Lincoln, 1976-80; mng. dir., pres. Boyce Thompson Inst. Plant Rsch., Cornell U., Ithaca, N.Y., 1980-86. Mem. Commn. on Undergrad. Edn. in Biol. Scis., 1963-68; mem. Gov.'s Sci. Coun., 1987-90; cons. State Exptl. Stas. divsn. USDA; chmn. subcom. plant pathogens, agriculture bd. NAS-NRC, 1965-68; mem. exec. com. study on problems of pest control, 1972-75; mem. exec. com. Nat. Govs.' Coun. on Sci. and Tech., 1970-74; mem. U.S. com. man and biosphere UNESCO, 1973-82; mem. com. to rev. U.S. component Internat. Biol. Program, NAS, 1974-76; mem. adv. panel on postdoctoral fellowships in environ. sci. Rockefeller Found., 1974-78; bd. dirs. Pacific Power & Light Co., 1974-91, PacifiCorp., 1984-91, Boyce Thompson Inst. for Plant Rsch., 1975-93, Boyce Thompson Southwestern Arboretum, 1981-92, Oreg. Grad. Inst., 1987-94; mem. adv. com. Directorate for Engring. and Applied Sci., NSF, 1977-81; mem. sea grant adv. panel, 1978-80; mem. policy adv. com. Office of Grants, USDA, 1985-86. Trustee Ithaca Coll., 1982-89. Lt. USNR, 1943-46. Recipient Disting. Svc. award Oreg. State U., 1978. Fellow AAAS (exec. com. Pacific div. 1963-67, pres. div. 1971), Am. Phytopathology Soc. (pres. Pacific div. 1957, chmn. spl. com. to develop plans for endowment 1984-86, bd. dirs. 1986-88); mem. Oreg. Acad. Sci., Nat. Assn. State Univs. and Land Grant Colls. (chmn. coun. for rsch. policy and adminstrn. 1970, chmn. standing com. on environment and energy 1974-82, chmn. com. on environment 1984-86), Sigma Xi, Phi Kappa Phi, Phi Sigma, Sigma Alpha Epsilon. Home: 3605 NW Van Buren Ave Corvallis OR 97330-4950

YOUNG, RUSSELL DAWSON, physics consultant; b. Huntington, N.Y., Aug. 17, 1923; s. C. Halsey and Edna (Dawson) Y.; m. Carol Vaughn Jones, Aug. 14, 1954; children: Bessmarie, Gale, Janet, Shari. BS in Physics, Rensselaer Poly. Inst., Troy, N.Y., 1953; PhD in Physics, Pa. State U., 1959. Rsch. assoc. Pa. State U., State College, 1959-61; project leader Nat. Bur. Stds., Gaithersburg, Md., 1961-73, chief optics and micrometrology, 1973-78, chief mech. processing div., 1975-80, ind. sys. div. chief, 1980-81, chief mech. prodn. div., 1980-81; pres. R.D. Young Cons., Pasadena, Md., 1981—. Contbr. articles to profl. jours.; inventor in field of instrumentation. 1st lt. Signal Corps, U.S. Army, 1943-46. Recipient Edward V. Condon award Dept. Commerce, 1974, Silver medal 1979, Gaede-Langmuir award 1994, Presdl. citation 1986, Washington Acad. Scis. award 1988. Fellow Internat. Inst. Prodn. Engring. Rsch., Nat. Inst. Standards and Tech. Avocation: boating. Home: 20 Luana Ct Fort Myers FL 33912-6351 E-mail: cryoung@aol.com.

YOUNG, RUTH BROOKS, retired elementary education educator; b. Balt., Aug. 30, 1933; d. Benjamin Franklin and Ora Estelle Brooks; m. David Donald Young Sr., 1952; children: David Donald Jr. (dec.), Gerard Brooks Sr., Mark Douglas (dec.), Elizabeth Allyson Mack. BS, Coppin State Tchrs. Coll., 1958; MS, Morgan State Coll., 1975. Cert. tchr., Md. Tchr. Balt. City Pub. Schs., 1958-98, supervising tchr., 1968-72, sch. test coord., 1990-96; ret., 1998. Mem. Phi Delta Kappa. Democrat. Lutheran.

YOUNG, SARA ANN, women's health nurse; b. Parkersburg, W.Va., June 5, 1948; d. Jack H. and Jean L. (Ankrom) Y. BSN, W.Va. U., 1970; MS in Nursing, Cath. U. Am., 1977. Cert. bereavement counselor; cert. lactation cons. Staff nurse Camden Clark Meml. Hosp., Parkersburg, 1970-72, head nurse, labor and delivery, 1972-74; staff nurse George Washington U. Med. Ctr., Washington, 1974-78; ob-gyn. clin. nurse specialist Hartford (Conn.) Hosp., 1978—. Clin. assoc. II, U. Conn. Sch. Nursing. Co-recipient Wyeth award, 1989, Profl. award La Leche League of Conn., 2001. Mem. ANA, AWHONN (co-recipient Wyeth Lab. plaque 1989). E-mail: syoungharthos-p.org. Office: Hartford Hosp 80 Seymour St Hartford CT 06102-8000

YOUNG, SARAH MOSKOWITZ, educational and computer consultant, journalist; b. Galveston, Tex., June 10, 1947; d. Irving Leonard and Joyce (Schreiber) Moskowitz; children: Clement Clarke III, Leonard Arthur. B Tech. Edn., postgrad., Nat. U., San Diego, 1984; EdD, Calif. Coast U., San Diego, 1989, postgrad. Adult edn. and community coll. credentials, cert. vision and hearing tech., pers. cons., Calif.; cert. first aid and CPR instr. trainer. Tchr. Vista High Sch., San Diego, 1980-81; project dir. Robert Harrow Co., 1981-82; instr. North County Coll., Eldorado Coll., San Diego County, 1982-84, Bangkok U., Kasesart U., 1985-86; assoc. dean, chmn. dept. edn. Phillips Coll., New Orleans, 1988-89; instr., radio performer Am. Lang. Tng., Jakarta, Indonesia, 1989-90; ednl. cons., journalist various mags. and newspapers, 1980—. Seminar speaker Sci. Rsch. Assocs., 1980; tng. officer Naval Sea Cadets, Monterey, Calif., 1988-89; mem. nat. curriculum com. Am. Assn. Med. Transcriptionists, 1978-88; med. instr. Kelsey-Jenney Coll., San Diego, 1990-91; founder Disabled Individuals Suggesting Computer Solutions. Mem., bd. dirs. Mira Mesa Town Coun., San Diego, 1980-84, sec., 1983-84; bd. dirs. Mira Mesa Community Coun., 1982-84; precinct chmn. San Diego Mayoral Election Com., 1982-84. Scholar Nat. U., 1984. Mem. NAFE, Leadership Edn. Awareness and Devel., San Diego Computer Soc., Mensa (chmn. mayor's adv. com. San Diego 1982-84, career day 1983), San Diego Press Club, Tetra Soc. San Diego (founder), Delta Omicron Epsilon. Avocations: artist, musician, world culturee, languages, animals. Home and Office: 10257 Trails End Cir San Diego CA 92126-3517

YOUNG, SCOTT THOMAS, business management educator; b. Oak Park, Ill., Dec. 28, 1949; s. Thomas Menzies and Grace (Butler) Y.; children: Reginald, Galen; m. Luciana Pagotto. BA, U. Ga., 1974; MBA, Ga. Coll., 1982; PhD, Ga. State U., 1987. Prof. U. Utah, Salt Lake City, 1987—, chmn. mgmt. dept., 1994-97, assoc. dean David Eccles Sch. Bus., 1997-99. Mgmt. cons. to numerous orgns.; lectr., speaker, cons. on ops., quality and project mgmt. Author: Managing Global Operations; contbr. numerous articles to profl. jours. With U.S. Army, 1971-73. Decorated Commendation medal; grantee Nat. Assn. Purchasing Mgmt., 1986. Mem. Decision Sci. Inst., Acad. Mgmt., Prodn. and Ops. Mgmt. Soc. Avocation: marathon running. Office: U Utah David Eccles Sch Bus Salt Lake City UT 84112 E-mail: mgtsty@business.utah.edu.

YOUNG, SEAN (MARY SEAN YOUNG), actress; b. Louisville, Nov. 20, 1959; Appeared in films: Jane Austen in Manhattan, 1980, Stripes, 1981, Blade Runner, 1982, Young Doctors in Love, 1982, Dune, 1984, Baby-Secret of Lost Legend, 1985, Blood and Orchids, 1986, No Way Out, 1987, Wall Street, 1987, The Boost, 1988, Cousins, 1989, Fire Birds, 1990, A Kiss Before Dying, 1991, Once Upon a Crime, 1992, Love Crimes, 1992, Fatal Instinct, 1993, Ace Ventura Pet Detective, 1994, Witness to the Execution, 1994, Even Cowgirls Get the Blues, 1994, Blue Ice, 1994, Dr. Jekyll and Ms. Hyde, 1995, Mirage, 1995, The Proprietor, 1996, Motel Blue, 1997, Exception to the Rule, 1997, The Invader, 1997, Men, 1997, Out of Control, 1998, Special Delivery, 1999. Office: Met Talent Agy 4526 Wilshire Blvd Los Angeles CA 90010-3801

YOUNG, SHARON LAREE, mathematics educator; b. San Bernardino, Calif., Jan. 28, 1945; d. Richard Austin and Freida Belle (Southerland) Uzzel; m. Randall Lee Young, June 19, 1966; children: Gillian, Courtney. BA, U. Redlands, 1966; MA, Denver U., 1976; PhD, U. Colo., 1979. Cert. tchr., Calif. Social worker Los Angeles County, Glendale, Calif., 1966-67; tchr. Spottswood (N.J.) Sch. Dist., 1967-68; tchr., then program specialist North Sacramento Sch. Dist., 1968-74; lectr., tchg. asst. U. Colo., Boulder, 1977-80; author, cons. Addison-Wesley Pub. Co., Menlo Park, Calif., 1980-94; assoc. prof. Seattle Pacific U., 1995-99, 2000—. Vis. asst. prof. W.Va. U., Morgantown, 1981-82; asst. prof. La. State U., Baton Rouge, 1982-86; cons. Ednl. Cons. Assocs, Englewood, Colo., 1976-79, Good Apple, Inc., Carthage, Ill., 1980-83. Author: Harry's Math Books, Set A, 1997, Set B, 1998, Geometry Books, 2001, Addison-Wesley Mathematics; co-author textbooks; contbr. articles to profl. publs. Mem. Nat. Assn. Suprs. Math., Nat. Coun. Tchrs. Math., Assn. Math. Tchr. Educators.

YOUNG, SHIRLEY JEAN, small business owner; b. Galveston, Tex., Mar. 18, 1944; d. Rufus H. and Ena I. (Carter) Y. Diploma in computers, basic programming, Halix Inst., 1988. Histologic technician, med. sec. St. Mary's Hosp., Galveston, 1963-66; clk.-typist Am. Oil Co., Texas City, 1967-68, Am. Nat. Ins. Co., Galveston, 1969-75; med. sec. U. Tex. Med. Br., Galveston, 1975-83; owner WORDS ETC (Software Designer), Galveston, 1983—; cons. Art From The Heart, Livingston, Tex., 1984—. Author: Winning Words, 1987, T-A-C Telephone Area Codes, 1989, STAT-ECG, 1988, Quick-Spread (Mini-Spread Sheet Program), 1990; contbr. articles to bus. publs. Mem. Nat. Fedn.

for Decency, 1984—. Mem. NAFE, Am. Soc. Profl. and Exec. Women, Computer Entrepreneur Assn. Am., Am. Soc. Clin. Pathologists (assoc.), 700 Club, 1000 Club. Baptist. Office: Words Etc 7019 Lasker Dr Apt 1535 Galveston TX 77551-1776

YOUNG, SONIA WINER, public relations director, educator; b. Aug. 20, 1934; d. Meyer D. and Rose (Demby) Winer; m. Melvin A. Young, Feb. 24, 1957; 1 child, Melanie Anne. BA, Sophie Newcomb Coll., 1956; M in Ednl. Psychology, U. Tenn.-Chattanooga, 1966. Cert. speech and hearing specialist Am. Speech and Hearing Assn. Speech therapist Chattanooga-Hamilton County Speech and Hearing Ctr., 1961-66, ednl. psychology, 1966-78; staff psychologist Chattanooga Testing and Counseling Svcs., 1978-80; ins. rep. Mut. Benefit Life Ins. Co., Chattanooga, 1980-84; columnist Chattanooga Times, 1982-84; comty. affairs reporter Sta. WRCB-TV, Chattanooga, 1983-84; pub. rels. and promotions dir. Purple Ladies, Inc., 1984—. Cons. psychology Ga. Dept. Human Resources, also Cheerhaven Sch., Dalton, 1970-78; adj. prof. psychology U. Tenn.-Chattanooga, 1971-80, adj. prof. dept. theatre and speech, 1988—; pres. Speak Out; bd. dirs. M. Young Comm., Vol. Ctr., 1995—, Arthritis Found., 1995-98; spl. projects dir. Chattanooga State Tech. C.C., 1995—; bd. dirs. M. Young Comm.; bd. dirs. Purple Lady, Inc. Author (columnist): (jour.) Lookout Mountain Mirror, Signal Mountain Mirror; contbg. editor: Chattanooga Life and Leisure Mag. Pres. Chattanooga Opera Guild, 1973-74, Chattanooga Opera Assn., 1979-80; bd. dirs., sec. Chattanooga-Hamilton County Bicentennial Libr., 1977-79; pres. Little Theatre of Chattanooga, 1984-90, bd. dirs., 1974—; v.p. Girls Club, Chattanooga, 1979-80; bd. dirs. March of Dimes, 1988, Chattanooga Symphony Guild, Mizpah Congregation, Chattanooga Area Literacy Coun., Chattanooga Cares, 1993—, Tourist Devel. Agy., 1990—; mem. alumni coun. U. Tenn.-Chattanooga; mem. selection com. Leadership Chattanooga, 1984-86; sec. Allied Arts Greater Chattanooga, 1978-80, residential campaign chmn., 1985; bd. dirs. Chattanooga Ctr. for the Dance, Ptnrs. for Acad. Excellence, 1987—, Chattanooga Mental Health Assn., 1988, Chattanooga Symphony Opera Assn., 1999—; chmn. March of Dimes Mother's March, 1988, One of a Kind-the Arts Against AIDS-Chattanooga Cares, 1993, 94; co-chair Am. Heart Assn. Gala, 1994, chmn., 1995; chair Little Theatre Capital Campaign, 1995; chmn. Galactic Gala fundraiser Chattanooga State Coll., 1996, Chattanooga Theatre Ctr. Endowment Campaign, 1998-99, April in Paris fundraiser, Chattanooga St. Coll., 1997, Chattanooga H.S. Ctr. for the Creative Arts fundraising, 1999, chmn. Broadway Lights Broadway Nights, 1999; adv. coun. Hamilton County Magnet Schs., 1999; bd. dirs. Chattanooga Symphony Opera Assn., 1999, 2000, fundraiser Evening in Provence, 2000, 2001, fundraiser Evening in Tuscany, 2001; bd. dirs. Chattanooga Ballet, 2000—, Chattanooga Theatre Ctr., 2002--, AIM Ctr., 2002--, Chattanooga Cares, 2002, Chattanooga Zoo, 2002. Recipient Disting. Citizens award City of Chattanooga, 1975, Steakley award Little Theatre Chattanooga, 1982, Pres. award, 1991, 92, Vol. of Yr., 1995, Woman of Distinction award Am. Lung Assn., 1995, Vol. of Yr. award, 1995, Penney's Golden Rule award Chattanooga Cares, 1994, Vol. of Yr., 1995, Best Actress award Chattanooga Theatre Ctr., 2000. Mem. Phi Beta Kappa (pers. Chattanooga chpt. 1978-79). Jewish. Home: 1025 River Hills Cir Chattanooga TN 37415-5611 Office: U Tenn Theatre & Speech Dept 615 Mccallie Ave Chattanooga TN 37403-2504 E-mail: purplesoni@aol.com.

YOUNG, STEPHEN K. academic administrator; DDS, U. Mo., 1971; MS, U. Mich., 1974. Diplomate Am. Bd. Oral Pathology. Asst. prof., oral and maxillofacial surgery U. Okla., David Ross Boyd prof., adj. prof., pathology, assoc. dean, Coll. Dentistry, dean, Coll. Dentistry, 1999—. Contbr. articles to profl. jours. Chair Nat. Cancer Inst.'s Ad Hoc Cancer Edn. Grant Review Com. Recipient President award, Okla. Dental Assn., 1988. Office: 1001 Stanton L Young Blvd Rm 507 Oklahoma City OK 73190*

YOUNG, STEVEN, former professional football player; b. Salt Lake City, Oct. 11, 1961; JD, Brigham Young, 1993. With L.A. Express, USFL, 1984-85, Tampa Bay Buccaneers, 1985-87; quarterback San Francisco 49ers, 1987—2000; NFL MVP, 1992; NFL Player of the Year, 1994; panelist ESPN Sunday NFL Countdown, 2001—. Founder, manages the Forever Young Found. benefitting Bay Area & Utah youth-oriented charities, 1993-. Davey O'Brien Award, 1983, All-America team quarterback, The Sporting News, 1983; Named NFL's Top-rated quarterback, 1991, named NFL MVP The Sporting News, 1992, NFL All-Pro team quarterback, The Sporting News, 1992, Bay Area Sports Hall of Fame Profl. Athlete of the Year, 1992, Superbowl MVP, 1994. Played in Pro Bowl 1992, 93; highest rated passer NFL, 1991-93. Mailing: Forever Young Foundation PO BOx 527 Park City UT 84060*

YOUNG, SUSAN BABSON, retired library director; b. Boston, June 22, 1939; d. David Leaveau and Katherine Lockhart (Allen) Babson; m. Thomas Herbert Young III, June 17, 1961; children: Thomas Herbert IV, Nathaniel Allen. BA, Vassar Coll., 1961; MLS, SUNY, Albany, 1983. Cert. sch. media specialist, Mass. English and history tchr. St. Anthony's H.S., Long Beach, Calif., 1962-63; asst. dir. Geier Libr. Berkshire Sch., Sheffield, Mass., 1968-72, dir., 1972-95. Contbr. articles to profl. jours. Chair Friends of the Bushnell-Sage Meml. Libr. Capital Fund, Sheffield, Mass., 1995—, trustee, 1994—; mem. Arts Coun., Sheffield, 1983-90, 95-2000; mem. So. Berkshire Regional Sch. Com., 1998—. Mem. Am. Needlepoint Guild (1st pl. Nat. Exhibit award 1980, 85, 2d Internat. Exhibit award 1982), Embroiders Guild Am., Arts Coun., Sheffield, 1983-90, 1995-2000, Sheffield Garden Club (pres. 1996-98), Phi Beta Mu. Republican. Home: 321 Boardman St Sheffield MA 01257-9515 E-mail: syoung@campram.com.

YOUNG, TAYLOR LYNN, special education administrator, consultant; b. Evansville, Ind., Dec. 7, 1952; s. James Taylor and Luvenia (Welborn) Y.; 1 child, Virginia Melin. BS in Edn., Ea. Ill. U., 1975; MS in Edn., Ill. State U., 1980; PhD in Edn., U. Denver, 1988. Tchr. spl. edn. St. Joseph (Ill.)-Ogden High Sch. Dist. 305, 1975-80; dir. Mid-State Spl. Edn. Coop., Hillsboro, Ill., 1980-81; dir. spl. edn. Mountain Bd. Coop. Svcs., Leadville, Colo., 1981-87; sr. cons. on sch. fin., cons. on spl. edn. Colo. Dept. Edn., Denver, 1987-88; prin. Laremont Sch., Spl. Edn. Dist. Lake County, Gurnee, Ill., 1988-89; dir. edn. Colo. Christian Home, Denver, 1989-92; spl. edn. tchr. El Paso County Dist. 11, Colo. Springs, 1992-93, Title 1 literacy supr., 1993—. Cons. Project Choice, Ill. Bd. Edn., Springfield, 1989-90. Mem.: CASE. Republican. Avocations: golf, travel. Home: 4780 Paramount Pl Colorado Springs CO 80918-9030 Office: Schl Dist 11 1115 N El Paso St Colorado Springs CO 80903-2599

YOUNG, TERESA GAIL HILGER, adult education educator; b. Modesto, Calif., Mar. 4, 1948; d. Richard George and Jessie Dennie (Dennis) Long; m. Charles Ray Young, June 22, 1974; 1 child, Gregory Paul. BS in Edn., Abilene (Tex.) Christian U., 1970; MEd in Curriculum, Tarleton State U., Stephenville, Tex., 1976; postgrad., Tex. Tech U., 1990-92. Cert. supr., mid-mgmt., supt., Tex. Tchr. sci. Tex. Youth Coun., Gatesville, 1970-73, Gatesville Ind. Sch. Dist., 1973-81; coord. Edn. and Tng. Ctr., Cen. Tex. Coll., Gatesville, 1983; tchr. Tex. Dept. of Criminal Justice-ID, 1984—. Conf. presenter. Trustee Jonesboro (Tex.) Ind. Sch. Dist., 1988-96. Teacher of the Year for Region II of Tex. Dept. of Criminal Justice, 1997-98. Mem. Am. Fedn. Tchrs., Assn. Tex. Profl. Educators. E-mail: tyoung@htcomp.net.

YOUNG, TERI ANN BUTLER, pharmacist; b. Littlefield, Tex., Aug. 22, 1958; d. Doyle Wayne and Bettie May (Lair) Butler; m. James Oren Young, Aug. 1, 1981; children: Andrew Wayne, Aaron Lee. BS in Pharmacy, Southwestern Okla. State U., 1981. Staff pharmacist St. Mary of Plains Hosp., Lubbock, Tex., 1981-84, West Tex. Hosp., Lubbock, 1984-85, asst. dir. pharmacy, 1985-86; pharmacist cons. for nursing homes Billy D. Davis & Assocs., 1986—; relief pharmacist Prescription Lab., Med. Pharmacy and Foster Infusion Care, 1987-89; staff pharmacist Univ. Med. Ctr., 1990-96, diabetic teaching pharmacist, 1995-99; pharmacist Home Health Preferred Infusion, Lubbock, 1994-98, Covenant Home Infusion, Lubbock, 1999—2000, Covenant Health Care System, Lubbock, 1999—2000, Joe Arrington Cancer Ctr, 2000—. Pharmacist Home Health Preferred Infusion, Lubbock, 1994-98, now Covenant Home Infusion, 1998-2000, Covenent Health Care Sys., Joe Arrington Cancer Ctr. Pharmacy; relief pharmacist West Tex. Hosp., 1986-91, Highland Hosp., 1990-94, Med. Infusion Technology, 1992-94. Mem. Lubbock Area Soc. of Hosp. Pharmacists (sec., treas. 1982-83), Lubbock Area Pharm. Assn., West Tex. Pharm. Assn., Am. Soc. Hosp. Pharmacists, Pilot Internat., Lubbock Genealogical Soc. Lodges: Eastern Star. Republican. Baptist. Avocations: needlework, reading, swimming, aerobics. Home: 7410 Toledo Ave Lubbock TX 79424-2214 Office: Joe Arrington Cancer Ctr Covenant Health Care Sys 4000 24th St Lubbock TX 79410-1130

YOUNG, THOMAS BEETHAM, writer; b. Hartford, Conn., July 16, 1942; s. Earl Raymond and Dorothy (Beetham) Y.; m. Jane Towner, Dec. 2, 1966 (div. Mar. 1975); 1 child, Sarah Alexandra Young West; m. Kathleen Mildred Coyle, May 19, 1979. AB in English, Princeton U., 1964; MFA in Creative Writing, U. Iowa, 1967; PhD in English, Ohio State U., 1973. Instr. of English U. Hawaii, Honolulu, 1967-69; vis. asst. prof. English Mercer U., Macon, Ga., 1973-75; assoc. faculty of writing Pima County C.C., Tucson, 1975-76; asst. prof. English Ctrl. Mich. U., Mt. Pleasant, 1976-79; lectr. of English Ohio State U., Columbus, 1979-82; computer specialist Def. Logistics Agy., 1985-98; freelance fiction writer, 1998—. Contbr. Writers' Workshop, U. Iowa. Author: Binary Alliances, 2000; author over 30 publ. poems, 1973-79. Fundraiser class of '64 Princeton U., Columbus, 1995-98. Old Gold fellow U. Iowa, 1964-65. Mem. Poets & Writers Inc., U. Iowa Alumni Assn. Avocations: spending time with friends and family, meeting people, computer games. Home: 2658 N 4th St Columbus OH 43202-2404 E-mail: tygertom2@cs.com.

YOUNG, THOMAS PAUL, lawyer; b. Jamestown, N.Y., Dec. 11, 1955; s. Burdette R. and Ruth Ann Y.; m. Deborah Ann Schwind, May 23, 1981; 1 child, Amanda Marie. BA, SUNY, Geneseo, 1977; JD, Georgetown U., 1980. Bar: N.Y. 1981, U.S. Dist. Ct. (we. dist.) N.Y. 1981. Assoc. Hodgson, Russ, Andrews, Woods & Goodyear, Buffalo, 1980-81; asst. counsel Gannett Co., Inc., Rochester, N.Y., 1982-84; assoc. Underberg & Kessler, 1984-91, sr. atty., 1991-98; of counsel Harter, Secrest & Emery LLP, 1998-2000; gen. counsel, sec. Xelus, Inc., Fairport, N.Y., 2000—. Mem. Perinton (N.Y.) Rep. Com., 1989—; mem. coun. Bethlehem Luth. Ch., Fairport, N.Y., 1984-90; bd. dirs. Geneseo Found., Inc., 1982—; bd. dirs., sec. Martin Luther Found., Rochester, 1986-89; mem. allocations com. United Way Greater Rochester, 1990-95; mem. zoning bd. appeals, Town of Perinton, N.Y., 1997—. Mem. ABA, N.Y. State Bar Assn. Office: Xelus Inc 290 Woodcliff Dr Fairport NY 14450-4212 E-mail: tom_young@xelus.com.

YOUNG, THOMAS RICHARD, sales management professional; b. Winston-Salem, N.C., May 13, 1959; s. James Lawrence and Jacquolyn (Watts) Y.; m. Susan Elizabeth Woodard Young, June 6, 1999. BBA, N.C. Wesleyan Coll., 1982. Mgmt. trainee Planters Nat. Bank and Trust Co., Rockymount, N.C., 1982-83, br. mgr. Wilmington, 1983-84; sales rep. Dictaphone Corp., Atlanta, 1984-85; account rep. Glasrock Home Healthcare, 1985-86; sr. sales rep. renal divsn. Baxter Healthcare Corp., Birmingham, Ala., 1986-90; dist. mgr. Amgen, Inc., 1990—. Com. mem. Nat. Kidney Found. Polo Benefit, Mobile, Ala., 1988; exec. com. treas. March of Dimes Birth Defects Found., Wilmington, 1984, com. mem. United Way Advanced Gifts div., Rocky Mount, N.C., 1983. Recipient Spl. Merit award Greater Wilmington C. of C., 1984. Mem. Rocky Mount Area C. of C. (life, Pres. award 1983), Amgen Pres.'s Club (pres. 1994, 96-99). Republican. Home and Office: 398 N Lake Rd Birmingham AL 35242-7014 E-mail: tyoung@amgen.com.

YOUNG, THOMAS STEVEN, artist, educator; b. Boston, June 13, 1951; s. Leon and Phyllis (Robins) Young; m. Ann Kerlin Conyngham, Apr. 1, 1982 (div. Oct. 1998); 1 child Sarah Kerlin ; m. Susannah Lee Young, Aug. 5, 2001. BA, Goddard Coll., 1973; MFA, R.I. Sch. Design, 1977. Vis. artist Yale U., New Haven, 1977; tech. asst., instr. R.I. Sch. Design, Providence, 1977-78; prof. art Greenfield (Mass.) Cmty. Coll., 1979—. Vis. artist Tufts U., Medford, Mass., 1989, Marlboro (Vt.) Coll., 1993-99, R.I. Sch. Design, Providence, 1995, Harvard U., Cambridge, Mass., 1995. One-man shows include Williams Coll. Mus. Art, 1990, Fogg Mus. Harvard U., 1990;exhibited in over 70 group shows including Frans Hals Mus., Harlem, Holland, 1988. Exhibition com., bd. mem. Franklin County Arts Coun., Greenfield, Mass., 1988-91, Art Bank, Shelburne Falls, Mass., 1998-99. Fellow, Mass. Coun. for the Arts, Boston, 1981, 1986, artist fellow, Nat. Endowment for the Arts/New Eng. Found. for the Arts, 1995, Mass. Cultural Coun. Artists, 1999. Mem. Soc. Photographic Edn. Democrat. Jewish. Avocation: art. Studio: 42 State St Shelburne Falls MA 01370-1019 Office: Greenfield Community Coll 1 College Dr Greenfield MA 01301-9755 Home: 66 Clesson Brook Rd Charlemont MA 01339 E-mail: youngart@rcn.com.

YOUNG, THOMAS WADE, journalist, pilot; b. Raleigh, N.C., Jan. 16, 1962; s. Bobby Wade and Harriett Thomas (Daniel) Y.; m. Kristen Lucille Gooch, June 7, 1986. BA, U. N.C., 1983, MA, 1987. Part time announcer WCBQ Radio, Oxford, N.C., 1979-83; reporter, news anchor WDNC Radio, Durham, 1984-86; writer, prodr., editor AP, Washington, 1987-98; freelance writer, 1999—; pilot Atlantic Coast Airlines, 2001—. Author of short stories and essays. With Air N.G. Baptist. Home: 1524 Mount Eagle Pl Alexandria VA 22302-2120 Office: AP Broadcast Svcs 1825 K St NW Washington DC 20006-1202

YOUNG, TZAY Y. electrical and computer engineering educator; b. Shanghai, China, Jan. 11, 1933; came to U.S., 1958; s. Chao-Hsiung and Chiu-Ming (Chu) Y.; m. Lily Liu, Dec. 27, 1965; children: Debbie Chia-Pei, Arthur Chia-Kai. BS, Nat. Taiwan U., Taipei, 1955; MS, U. Vt., 1959; DEng, Johns Hopkins U., 1962. Rsch. assoc. Johns Hopkins U., Balt., 1962-63; mem. tech. staff Bell Labs., Murray Hill, N.J., 1963-64; asst. prof. Carnegie-Mellon U., Pitts., 1964-68, assoc. prof., 1968-74; prof. elec. and computer enging. U. Miami, Coral Gables, Fla., 1974—, acting chmn. dept., 1988-91, chmn. dept., 1991-2000. Sr. postdoctoral rsch. assoc. NAS, NASA, Goddard Space Flight Ctr., Md., 1972-73. Author: (with T.W. Calvert) Classification, Estimation and Pattern Recognition, 1974; editor: (with K.S. Fu) Handbook of Pattern Recognition and Image Processing, 1986; editor: Handbook of Pattern Recognition and Image Processing, vol. 2, Computer Vision, 1994; also numerous articles. Rsch. grantee NSF, NASA, FHTIC, also indsl. grants. Fellow IEEE (assoc. editor Trans. Computers 1974-76; editorial bd. Trans. Pattern Analysis and Machine Intelligence 1979-84, adv. bd. 1984-90); mem. Sigma Xi, Eta Kappa Nu, Omicron Delta Kappa. Office: U Miami Dept Elec & Computer Engring Coral Gables FL 33124 E-mail: tyoung@miami.edu.

YOUNG, VERNON LEWIS, lawyer; b. Seaman, Ohio, Oct. 13, 1919; s. Ezra S. and Anna (Bloom) Y.; m. Eileen Humble, Sept. 20, 1941; children: Robert, Loretta, Bettie Jo, Jon W., Denise L. Student, Alfred Holbrook Coll., 1938-39; JD, Ohio No. U., 1942. Bar: Ohio 1942. Employee War Dept., 1942; sole practice West Union, Ohio, 1942-50, 78-81; ptnr. Young & Young, 1959-78, Young & Caldwell, 1978-81, 95—, Young-Caldwell & BUBP, West Union, 1981-95. Spl. counsel Office of Atty. Gen., State of Ohio, West Union, solicitor Cities of Jamestown, Seaman, Winchester, Manchester, Ohio; pros. atty. Adams County, Ohio, 1952-56, acting county judge, 1968-79. Mayor City of Seaman, 1944-46; mem. Adams County Health Bd., West Union, 1968-75; chmn. membership com. Eastern Shore Inst. Lifelong Learning, Fairhope, Ala., 1983-84; mem. Rep. Presdl. Task Force, 1980-94. Mem. Ohio State Bar Assn., Adams County Bar Assn. (former pres.), Masons (32 degree), Lions (pres. 1950-51, dist. gov. 1951-52), Sigma Delta Kappa (chancellor 1940). Avocations: fishing, hunting, gardening. Home: 10 Hickory Dr Seaman OH 45679-9762 Office: 225 N Cross St West Union OH 45693-1266

YOUNG, VICTORIA E. occupational health and pediatrics nurse practitioner, lawyer; b. Concord, Mich., Apr. 20, 1933; d. Arthur Raymond and Edith Louise (Hands) Y. Diploma, Mercy Sch. Nursing, Jackson, Mich., 1954; JD, U. West Los Angeles, Culver City, Calif., 1973; BSN, UCLA, 1960, MPH in Adminstrn., 1966. Bar: Calif., U.S. Dist. Ct., Calif.; RN, Calif.; cert. pub. health nurse, pediatric nurse practitioner. Pub. health nurse L.A. City and Los Angeles County Health Dept.; exec. dir. Santa Monica (Calif.) Vis. Nurse Assn.; sch. nurse practitioner L.A. Unified Schs.; relief nurse L.A. Times. Vol. Moorpark City Hall, Moorpark Sr. Ctr; mem. Disaster Assistance Response Team, Moorpark. Ret. capt. USNR, Desert Storm. Mem. Nat. Assn. Pediatric Nurse Assocs. and Practitioners, Calif. Bar Assn., Fleet Res. Assn., Moorpark Woman's Fortnightly Club (treas. 1998-99). Home: 4359 Brookdale Ln Moorpark CA 93021-2302

YOUNG, VIRGIL MONROE, education educator; b. Santa Rosa, Calif., Sept. 24, 1936; s. Virgil M. and Vesta May (Huyett) Williams; stepson Louis H. Young; m. Katherine Ann Young, Dec. 20, 1964; 1 child, Susan Annette. BS, U. Idaho, 1958, EdD, 1967. Cert. advanced secondary edn. educator, sch. supt., Idaho. Tchr. Moscow (Idaho) Sch. Dist., 1959-63; adminstrv. asst. to supt. Coeur d'Alene (Idaho) Sch. Dist., 1965-67; prof. edn. Boise (Idaho) State U., 1967-96, head dept. edn., 1989-96, prof. emeritus, 1996—. Author: (elem., jr. high textbook) The Story of Idaho, 4 edits.; co-author: The Story of the Idaho Guide and Resource Book, 1993; author: (with others) Year 2000 Grolier Multimedia Encyclopedia, 2000; designer, author ednl. Internet websites, 1999—. Capt. USAR. Mem. N.W. Assn. Tchr. Educators (past pres.), Idaho Assn. Colls. Tchr. Edn. (past pres.), Phi Delta Kappa (past pres.).

YOUNG, WAYNE STEVENS, military officer, human resources administrator; b. Bar Harbor, Maine, Sept. 23, 1950; s. Tracy Hoyt and Frances Evelyn (King) Y.; m. Edith Ann Wurzel, Aug. 27, 1977 (div. 1983); m. Deborah Lynn Iorio, Dec. 27, 1986; children: Samantha, Danielle, Jeffrey. BS, Va. Mil. Inst., 1973; MEd, Fitchburg (Mass.) State Coll., 1979, CAGS, 1981. Exec. officer 187th Med. Co., Lawrence Mass., 1983-86; AMEDD recruiter OTSG, Falls Church, Va., 1986-94; pers. mgr. 2290th USAH, Rockville, Md., 1994-96; dir. RTS-Med., Devens RFTA, Mass., 1996-98; force integrator OCAR, Arlington, Va., 1998-99; dep. ACSOPS NARMC, Washington, 1999—. Editor Key North Ctrl. Alcohol Edn. Newsletter, 1979-80, Caretaker Hosp. Newsltter, 1994-96. Sec. Mass. Alcohol Edn. Coun., Mass., 1979-80; adult leader Boy Scouts Am., Va., 1990-94, Mass., 1997-98, Md., 1998-2000. Col. U.S. Army, 1973-2001. Recipient Army Achievement medal, 1986, Meritorious Svc. medal, 1995, 98, Army Commendation medal, 1987, 96. Mem. Order of Knights Templar, Order of Knights Columbus, St. Andrew's Soc. (pres. 2000-01). Roman Catholic. Avocations: Scottish clan Young regent, genealogy. Home: 101 Foxfield Pass Middletown MD 21769-7846 Fax: (301) 371-0956. E-mail: wsyoung@adelphia.net.

YOUNG, WENDY UNRATH, musician; b. Chgo., July 3, 1965; m. Raymond Michael Young, July 17, 1993. MusB, Roosevelt U., 1987, MusM, 1990. With Triton Coll., River Forest, Ill., 1987-91; assoc. prof. piano Elmhurst (Ill.) Coll., 1991—. Office: Elmhurst Coll Music Dept 190 Prospect Ave Elmhurst IL 60126-3271

YOUNG, WILLIAM BENJAMIN, retired special education educator; b. Wichita, Kans., Jan. 30, 1929; s. Ernest William and Florence Belle (McCann) Y.; m. La Vona P., Feb., 1949 (div. 1973); children: Lynda, David, Timothy; m. Patricia Sue Reber, Aug., 1974. Student, Southwestern Coll., Winfield, Kans., 1947-48; B in Gen. Edn., U. Omaha, 1961; MS in Pers. Counseling, Miami U., Oxford, Ohio, 1965; PhD in Exceptional Edn., Adminstrn. and Counseling, Ohio State U., 1972. Cert. elem. and secondary adminstr., tchr., counselor, psychologist, psychometrist, spl. edn., mental retardation, learning disabled/behavior disordered, emotionally handicapped, Ind.; cert. K-12 guidance counselor and edn. leadership, Fla.; lic sexologist, flight instr.; lic. Coast Guard capt. Enlisted USAF, 1948, commd. 2nd lt., 1955, advanced through grades to capt., 1960, ret., 1966; numerous teaching and counseling positions as civilian, 1966-91; co-owner, instr. Ft. Wayne (Ind.) Ground Schs., 1984-88; marriage and family counselor, pvt. practice, 1966-91; tchr., counselor, behavior specialist Broward County Schs., Ft. Lauderdale, Fla., 1989-99; ret., 1999. Cons., internat. presenter/lectr. learning and behavior problems. Vol. instr. AARP Safe Driving Course; vol. support group leader for dementia caregivers support. Mem. ACA, Coun. for Exceptional Children, Coun. Behavior Disorders, Fla. Counseling Assn., 32 degree Masons. Avocations: travel, golf, swimming. Home and Office: 1101 SW 70th Ter Plantation FL 33317-4135 E-mail: wby130@aol.com.

YOUNG, WILLIAM DAVID, computer scientist; b. Albuquerque, Nov. 22, 1953; s. Youree Harold and Alma Catherine (Callahan) Y. BS in Math. with honors, U. Tex., 1975, BA in Philosophy with high honors, MA in Philosophy, U. Tex., 1976, MA in Computer Sci., 1980, PhD in Computer Sci., 1988; postgrad., U. Notre Dame, 1976-77. Rsch. engring. sci. asst., systems analyst U. Tex., Austin, 1978-87; computing rsch. sci. Computational Logic, Inc., 1987-88, sr. computing rsch. sci., 1988—, also bd. dirs. Part-time instr. Austin C.C., 1978-80, Southwest Tex. State U., San Marcos, 1980-81, 83-86; rsch. sci. Honeywell Secure Computing Tech. Ctr., St. Anthony, Minn., 1984-87; invited lectr., presenter, speaker in field; publ. chair Computer Security Workshop III, 1990, IV, 1991; chmn. panel Symposium Software Analysis, Testing and Verification, 1991, program com., 1991; organizer, chmn. panel computer security founds. Computer Security Workshop II, 1989; bd. dirs. Computational Logic, Inc. Mem. editl. bd. Jour. Computer Security; contbr. articles to profl. jours. papers in field. Mem. IEEE, Assn. Computing Machinery, Abelian Group Investment Club (pres. 1992-96), Phi Beta Kappa, Phi Eta Sigma, Pi Mu Epsilon, Upsilon Pi Epsilon. Office: 7617 Nez Perce Trce Manor TX 78653-9677

YOUNG, WILLIAM EDGAR, religious organization official; b. Whitesburg, Ga., July 28, 1930; s. Edgar Woodfin and Maude Alva (Duke) Y.; m. Mary Todd Watts, Mar. 9, 1963; children: William Jefferson, Todd Woodfin. Student, Warren Wilson Coll., 1951, 54; AB, Mercer U., 1956; MRE, Southwestern Bapt. Theol. Sem., 1958; postgrad., George Peabody Coll. Tchrs., U. Tenn., Nashville, So. Meth. U., U. San Francisco, Lesley Coll. Minister of edn. and music 1st Bapt. Ch., Swainsboro, Ga., 1958-59, Sherman, Tex., 1960-64; tchr. North Cobb H.S., Marietta, Ga., 1959-60; ch. bus. adminstrn. cons., 1964-65; dir. ch. adminstrn. field svcs. Bapt. Sunday Sch. Bd. (Life Way Christian Resources), Nashville, 1965-70, mgr. presch. children's sect. discipleship tng. dept., 1970-92. Childhood edn. and family life cons., 1992—; adj. prof. Sch. Religious Edn., So. Bapt. Theol. Sem., Louisville; adj. prof. childhood edn. Golden Gate Bapt. Theol. Sem., Mill Valley, Calif., 1980, 94, Sch. Ednl. Ministries, Southwestern Bapt. Theol. Sem., Ft. Worth, 1984, 94; guest lectr. creative writing East Tex. State U., Texarkana; adj. prof. New Orleans Bapt. Theol. Sem., 2000. Author: Moses, God's Helper, 1976, Jesus, Lord and Savior, 1984, How to Plan and Conduct a Conference, 1987, Now That I Am a Christian, 1992, Heroes of Missions, 1993; compiler, writer: Developing Your Children's Church Training Program, 1977; contbg. author: The Ministry of Childhood Education, 1985; contbr. chpts. to books; curriculum writer religious publs. Chmn. Dist. II citizens adv. coun. Metro Schs., 1975-76; pres. Stanford PTA, 1974-75, Grassland PTA, 1977-78; lectr. European Bapt. Conv., 1990, 2000; So. Bapt. conv. rep. U.S. Dept. Health and Human Svcs., Nat. Conf. on Child Abuse and Neglect; pres. Franklin High Cmty. Assn.; parent rep. Williamson County curriculum assessment group Mid. Sch. Task Force, 1979; mem. adv. coun. edn. dept. Belmont Coll.; bd. dirs. Tenn. Parents Anonymous. Served with USAF, Korea, 1951-54. Recipient Disting. Svc. award Metro Assn. Religious Edn. Dirs., 1980, Founders award Ga. Ch. Secs. Assn., 1981, Disting. Alumni award S.W. Bapt. Theol. Sem., 1993. Mem. So. Bapt. Religious Edn. Assn. (pres. 1977-78, sec.-treas., bd. dirs. 1984-90, treas., bd. dirs. 1990-95, Disting. Leadership award 1996), Assn. Supervision and Curriculum Devel., Assn. Childhood Edn. Internat. (pub. affairs com., early adolescent com.), Nat. Assn. Edn. of Young Children, So. Assn. for Children Under Six, Am. Soc. Tng. and Devel., Internat. Network Children's Ministry (bd. dirs. 1994—, Excellence in Ministry to Children award 1994, David C. Cook Victor Cory award for Visionary Leadership in Christian Edn. 1997), Nashville Area Assn. for Edn. Young Children (gov. bd. 1999—), Life Way Retirees Fellowship (pres.). Home and Office: 605 Williamsburg Dr Franklin TN 37069-4191

YOUNG, WILLIAM GLOVER, federal judge; b. Huntington, N.Y., Sept. 23, 1940; s. Woodhull Benjamin and Margaret Jean (Wilkes) Y.; m. Beverly June Bigelow, Aug. 5, 1967; children: Mark Edward, Jeffrey Woodhull, Todd Russell. AB, Harvard U., 1962, LLB, 1967; LLD, New Eng. Sch. Law, 2001. Bar: Mass. 1967, U.S. Supreme Ct. 1970. Law clk. to chief justice Supreme Jud. Ct., Mass., 1967-68; spl. asst. atty. gen., 1969-72; chief legal counsel to gov., 1972-74; assoc. firm Bingham, Dana and Gould, Boston, 1968-72, ptnr., 1975-78; assoc. justice Superior Ct., Commonwealth of Mass., Boston, 1978-85; judge U.S. Dist. Ct. Mass., 1985-99, chief judge, 1999—. Mem. budget com., 1987-2001, chmn. economy subcom., 1991-2001; lectr. part time Boston Coll. Law Sch., 1968-90, Boston U. Law Sch., 1979—, Harvard Law Sch., 1979—1990. Served to capt. U.S. Army, 1962-64. Mem. Am. Law Inst., Mass. Bar Assn., Boston Bar Assn., Harvard Alumni (pres. 1976-77) Office: US Courthouse Rm 5710 Boston MA 02210 E-mail: william_young@mad.uscourts.gov., bgbg2y3@earthlink.net.

YOUNG, WILLIAM SHERBAN, investment broker; b. Augusta, Maine, Sept. 19, 1947; m. Jeanne Aschenbrenner, June 20, 1970; 1 child, Stephan Sherban. BA, U. Balt., 1974; MA, Morgan U., 1982. Cert. fin. planner. Account exec. Md. Nat. Bank, Balt., 1974-76; div. mgr. Jefferson-Pilot Co.,

1976-81; ptnr. Stewart-Young & Assocs., 1981-83; dir. equity dept. First Fin. Group, 1983—. Bd. dirs. Balt. Choral Arts, 1990. With U.S. Army, 1965-68. Mem. Inst. Cert. Fin. Planners, Am. Jujitsu Assn., Balt. Coun. on Fgn. Rels. Republican. Avocations: chess, black belt jujitsu. Office: 401 Washington Ave Ste 6 Towson MD 21204-4821 E-mail: wyoung@glic.com.

YOUNG, WILLIAM WEBB, military officer, poet; b. St. Louis, Aug. 4, 1967; s. Raymond Andrew and Betty Rosella (Myers) Young; children: Jamie Elizabeth, Christen Lee, Sara Rayan. Commd. ensign USN, 1987; Gulf War/Cold War vet. Svc. officer Three Rivers Serenity Group, Poplar Bluff, Mo., 1989—2002; dist. 8 spl. needs com. chmn. S.E. Mo. AA, Poplar Bluff, Mo., 2001—. Author numerous poems. Local stream team coord. Mo. Dept. Conservation, Butler County, Mo., 1997—2002, frontiers program leader, 1998—2002; water quality monitoring vol. Mo. Dept. Natural Resources, 1999—2002. Recipient Iliad Lit. award, Internat. Poet of Merit, 1996, Editors Choice award, 1996, Americanism award, Grande Voiture of N.J. Navy, 1990, Loyalty Day award, VFW, 1990, Battle "E" Award Persian Excursion, 1991. Fellow: K.C. (1st degree crusader, Altar Server award 1981); mem.: Internat. Soc. Poets, Disabled Am. Vets. (life Golden Anchor award 1988), Amherst Soc., Gulf of Sidra Yacht Club, Persian Gulf Yacht Club, Am. Legion (honor guard). Roman Catholic. Avocation: art. Home: 201 W Lexington Ave Poplar Bluff MO 63901

YOUNG, YVONNE DELEASE, educator; b. Welch, W.Va., Sept. 19, 1939; d. Albert Neal Sr. and Sylvia Claudine (Brooks) Baker; m. Thomas G. Young, June 9, 1973; 1 child, Tajauna D. Tims. BS in Edn., Wilberforce U., 1964; MEd in Adminstrn., Miami U., Oxford, Ohio, 1977. Tchr. Dayton (Ohio) Pub. Schs., 1964-95; retired, 1995. Coord. Careers in Schs., Dayton. Bd. dirs. Youth Engaged for Success, Dayton, 1973-88; vol tutor Right-to-Read, Dayton, 1970-73; vol. Feeding the Homeless, Dayton; pres. OptiMrs., Dayton, 1974—; nat. pres. Carrousels, Inc., 1999-2001. Jennings scholar U. Dayton, 1974-75. Mem. Carrousel's, Inc. (nat. pres.), Delta Sigma Theta, Phi Delta Kappa, Phi Delta Kappa. Avocations: reading, travel, dancing, crossword puzzles, entertaining family. Home: 4224 Caylor Rd Dayton OH 45418-2406

YOUNGBERG, CHARLOTTE ANNE, education specialist, clergywoman; b. Hampton, Iowa, May 8, 1937; d. Sebo and Marion Bradford (Boutin-Clock) Reysack; m. Paul Gordon Neal, Mar. 29, 1969 (div. Jan. 1984); children: Rachel Elizabeth, Kory Bradford; m. Lyle Edwin Youngberg, June 30, 1990; stepchildren: Lynn Eugene, Lori Ann. BA, U. No. Iowa, 1958; MEd, DePaul U., 1966; postgrad., No. Ill. U.; DD in Christian Counseling, Christian Bible Coll. and Sem., Independence, Mo., 2000. Cert. K-14 tchr. and supr. in guidance, counseling, elem. supervising, K-9 elem. tchr., spl. K-12 learning disabilities. Elem. tchr. Des Moines Ind. Sch. Dist., 1958-59, Glenview (Ill.) Pub. Schs., 1959-61; elem. tchr., psychol. ednl. diagnostician Schaumburg Dist. Schs., Hoffman Estates, Ill., 1961-69; supr. learning disabilities and behavior disorders Springfield (Ill.) Pub. Schs., 1969-73; psycho-ednl. diagnostician Barrington (Ill.) Sch. Dist. 220, 1973-77; ednl. strategist Area Edn. Agy. 7, Cedar Falls, Iowa, 1978-90; tchr. spl. edn., testing evaluator Verona (Mo.) Pub. Schs., 1990—, dir. spl. Edn., 1992-95. Ednl. cons. Spl. Edn. Dist. Lake County, Gurnee, Ill., summer 1968. Mem. Mo. Tchrs. Assn., Phi Delta Kappa. Home: PO Box 147 Verona MO 65769-0147 Office: Verona R7 Sch Dist 101 E Ella St Verona MO 65769-5213

YOUNGBERG, GEORGE ANTHONY, pathology educator; b. Chgo., Mar. 14, 1951; s. Gilbert and Barbara (Hoffmann) Y.; m. Rosemary H. Leu, May 12, 1979. BA, Lake Forest Coll., 1973; MD, Northwestern U., 1977. Asst. prof. East Tenn. State U., Johnson City, 1980-85, assoc. prof., 1985-91, prof., 1991—. Surg. pathologist U. Physicians Practice Group, Johnson City, 1980—, dir. renal biospy svc., 1988—; assoc. chief of staff for rsch. VA Med. Ctr., Johnson City, 1988—. Contbr. articles to profl. jours. Fellow Coll. Am. Pathologists; mem. Am. Acad. Dermatology (affiliate), Renal Pathology Soc., U.S. and Can. Acad. Pathology, Phi Beta Kappa. Office: East Tenn State U Dept Pathology Johnson City TN 37614

YOUNGBLOOD, DEBORAH SUE, lawyer, speech pathology/audiology services professional; b. Fairview, Okla., July 29, 1954; d. G. Dean and Beatrice J. (Hiebert) White. BS with honors, Okla. State U., 1976, MA with honors, 1979; JD cum laude, Boston Coll. Law Sch., 1991; MPH in Health Care Mgmt., Harvard U., 1992. Bar: Colo., N.Mex., U.S. Ct. Appeals (10th cir.). Judicial law clk. Colo. Supreme Ct., 1992-94; assoc. atty. Patton Boggs, L.L.P., Denver, 1994-97, Vaglica & Meinhold, L.L.C., Colorado Springs, 1997-99; pvt. practice atty, speech & lang. pathologist North Conway, NH, 1999—2001; speech-lang. pathologist Sun Valley, Idaho, 2001—; speech-language pathologist, 2001—. Mem. ABA, Colo. Bar Assn., N.Mex. Bar Assn., Minoru Yasui Am. Inns of Ct. (exec. coun. 1995-97), Phi Kappa Phi. Office: 201 Bullion St Hailey ID 83333 E-mail: youngblood@peoplepc.com.

YOUNGBLOOD, ELAINE MICHELE, lawyer; b. Schenectady, N.Y., Jan. 9, 1944; d. Roy W. and Mary Louise (Read) Ortoleva; m. William Gerald Youngblood, Feb. 14, 1970; children: Flagg Khristian, Megan Michele. BA, Wake Forest Coll., 1965; JD, Albany Law Sch., 1969. Bar: Tex. 1970, Tenn. 1978, U.S. Dist. Ct. (no. dist.) Tex. 1971, U.S. Dist. Ct. (so. dist.) Tex. 1972, U.S. Dist. Ct. (mid. dist.) Tenn. 1978, U.S. Dist. Ct. (we. dist.) Tenn. 1998. Assoc. Fanning & Harper, Dallas, 1969-70, Crocker & Murphy, Dallas, 1970-71, McClure & Burch, Houston, 1972-75, Brown, Bradshaw & Plummer, Houston, 1975-76; ptnr. Seligmann & Youngblood, Nashville, 1977-88; pvt. practice, 1988-94; of counsel Ortale, Kelley Herbert & Crawford, 1994—. Contbr. articles to profl. jours. Active Law Day Com. Dallas Bar Assn., 1970—71, Com. for Women in Govt., Dallas, 1969—71; vestry Ch. of Advent, 1991. Fellow: Nashville Bar Found. (fee dispute com. 1990—, vice-chair 1996, bd. dirs. 1996, blvd. bolt com. 1996—97, CLE com. 1996—, L.A.W. 1996—, treas. 1997, publicity, steering com. 1997, chair 1997—); mem.: Nashville Bar Assn., Tenn. Bar Assn., Davidson County Rep. Women's Club, Cable Club Nashville (charter), Phi Beta Phi (AAC 1998—, Christmas Village, bd. sec. 1999—2001, AAU bd., merchant relations 2002, v.p./pres.-elect 2002). Republican. Episcopalian. Address: PO Box 198985 200 Fourth Ave N Fl 3 Noel Pl Nashville TN 37219-8985 E-mail: eyoungblood@ortalekelley.com.

YOUNGDAHL, JAY THOMAS, lawyer; b. St. Louis, May 29, 1952; s. James Edward and Patricia Ruth (Lucy) Y.; m. Mary Ellen Vogler, Dec. 12, 1981; children: Benjamin Douglass, Colleen Alexandra. BS, U. Houston, 1978; JD, U. Tex., 1980. Bar: Ark. 1981, Tex., 1992, D.C. 1993, U.S. Dist. Ct. (ea. and we. dists.) Ark. 1981, U.S. Ct. Appeals (8th, 10th and 11th cirs.) 1981, U.S. Claims Ct. 1992, U.S. Tax Ct. 1981, Tex. 1994. Ptnr. Provost, Umphrey, LLP, Youngdahl, Sadin P.C., Little Rock, 2001—; mng. ptnr. Provost, Umphrey LLP, Youngdahl, Sadin P.C., Friendswood, Tex., 1993—; gen. counsel Vox.com. Adj. instr. Webster Coll., Little Rock, 1983-95; adj. prof. U. Ark., Little Rock Sch. of Law, 1988-90; mem. Ark. Employment Security Div. Adv. Coun., Little Rock, 1980-97, Gov.'s Workers Compensation Study Com., Little Rock, 1985-86. With U.S. Army, 1972-74. Mem. ABA, Ark. Bar Assn. (chmn. labor law sect. 1983-84), ATLA, Ark. Trial Lawyers Assn., AFL-CIO Lawyers Coordinating Com. (adv. bd.), Acad. Rail Labor Attys., Tex. Trial Lawyers Assn., State Bar Tex. (Pro Bono Coll. 1996). Avocations: running, reading, flying, culinary arts. Office: Provost Umphrey LLP Youngdahl Sadin PC 211 E Parkwood Ave Ste 207 Friendswood TX 77546-5155 E-mail: jyoungdahl@provostumphrey.com.

YOUNGDAHL, PAUL FREDERICK, mechanical engineer; b. Brockway, Pa., Oct. 8, 1921; s. Harry Ludwig and Esther Marie (Carlson) Y.; m. Elinor Louise Jensen, Nov. 27, 1943; children: Mark Erik, Marcia Linnea, Melinda Louise. Student Pa. State U., 1938-40; BS in Engring., U. Mich., 1942, MS in Engring., 1949, PhD, 1962. Indsl. and devel. engr. duPont, Bridgeport, Conn., 1942-43, Carneys Point, N.J., 1946-48; dir. research Mech. Handling Systems, Detroit, 1953-62; prof. U. Mich., Ann Arbor, 1962-74; cons. mech. engr., Palo Alto, Calif., 1974—; dir. Liquid Drive Corp., Holly, Mich. Contbr. articles to profl. jours. With USNR, 1943-46. Mem. Mich. Soc. Profl. Engrs., Nat. Soc. Profl. Engrs., ASME, Am. Soc. Engring. Edn., Mich. Assn. Professions, Sigma Xi, Tau Beta Pi, Phi Kappa Phi, Pi Tau Sigma. Methodist. Address: 501 Forest Ave Ph 4 Palo Alto CA 94301-2637

YOUNGE, RICHARD GEORGE, family physician; AB, U. Calif., Santa Cruz, 1973; MD, U. Calif., San Francisco, 1977; MPH, U. Calif., Berkeley, 1977. Diplomate Am. Bd. Family Practice, Am. Bd. Preventive Medicine. Resident in family medicine Montefiore Med. Ctr., Bronx, N.Y., 1977-80; physician USPHS Nat. Health Svc. Corps, N.Y.C., 1980-82; med. dir. Montefiore Family Health Ctr., Bronx, N.Y., 1982-92; prof. family practice SUNY, Bklyn., 1992-96; v.p., chief med. officer Affinity Health Plan, 1996—. Fellow N.Y. Acad. Medicine; mem. APHA, Soc. Tchrs. Family Medicine, Am. Acad. Family Practice. Office: Affinity Health Plan One Fordham Plz Ste E220 Bronx NY 10458

YOUNGER, BETTY NICHOLS, social worker; b. Cleve., 1927; d. Manson E. and Esther L. (McDonald) Nichols; m. Paul A. Younger, 1952 (dec. Mar. 1969); children: Deborah, Rebekah, Sarah, Martha. BA, Otterbein Coll., 1949; MS in Social Adminstrn., Western Res. U., 1951. diplomate Am. Bd. Examiners in Clin. Social Work. Family and youth worker East Harlem Protestant Parish, N.Y.C., 1951-52; home missionary apptd. by Evangelical United Brethren Ch; organizer, parent worker Fidelity Presch., Cleve., 1955, 58-60; community worker YWCA, 1966-67; organizer, dir. Community United Headstart, 1965; social worker Children's Hosp., Columbus, 1968, Mt. Sinai Hosp., Chgo., 1972-73, Billings Hosp. U. Chgo., 1973; supr. Ill. Masonic Med. Ctr., Chgo., 1974-79; counselor Barry County Substance Abuse, Hastings, Mich., 1981-82; organizer, dir. Love, Inc., Barry County, 1983-84; mgr. Cir. Pines Ctr., Delton, 1984-85; therapist Family & Child Svcs., Jackson, 1986, Livonia (Mich.) Counseling Ctr., 1986-89; pvt.psychotherapy practice Livonia, 1988—98. Tchr. Schoolcraft Coll., Livonia, 1987-2001; bus. ptnr. Creating Results, Ann Arbor, Mich., 1990-2000. Mem. ACLU,Sierra Club, Women's Internat. League for Peace and Freedom. Avocations: travel, writing and photography, pottery, piano, gardening.

YOUNGER, DEIRDRE ANN, pharmacist; b. Washington, Oct. 17, 1958; d. Norman Sylvester Jr. and Doris Juanita (Smith) Coram; m. Michael Elmer Younger, May 22, 1982; children: Michael Elmer Jr., Brittney Ann. BS in Pharmacy, Duquesne U., 1981. Registered pharmacist, D.C., Md. Pharmacy assoc. U.S. Pharmacopeial Conv., Inc., Rockville, Md., 1981-82; clin. pharmacist Children's Nat. Med. Ctr., Washington, 1983-84, clin. pharmacist supr., 1984-87, clin. pharmacist team leader, 1987-93; instr. Sch. Pharmacy U. Md., Balt., 1993-2000, clin. asst. prof., 2000—. Adj. asst. prof. Sch. Pharmacy, Howard U., Washington, 1990-93; pharmacy residency preceptor ASHP, Washington, 1984-93; prin. investigator Eutectic Mixture of Local Anesthetics (EMLA) efficacy rsch. Children's Nat. Med. Ctr., 1993; pharmacy coord. Health Ctr. Pharmacy U. Md., College Park, 1993—. Editor: Children's Nat. Med. Ctr. Formulary, 1988-93. Sec. Evans' Ridge Home Owners' Assn., Bowie, Md., 1995-97. Mem.: Am. Coll. Health Assn., Am. Pharm. Assn. Avocations: reading, golf. Office: Health Ctr Pharmacy U Md Rm 1190A Bldg 140 College Park MD 20742-0001 E-mail: younger@health.umd.edu.

YOUNGER, JUDITH TESS, lawyer, educator; b. N.Y.C., Dec. 20, 1933; d. Sidney and Kate (Greenbaum) Weintraub; m. Irving Younger, Jan. 21, 1955; children: Rebecca, Abigail M. BS, Cornell U., 1954; JD, NYU, 1958; LL.D. (hon.), Hofstra U., 1974. Bar: N.Y. 1958, U.S. Supreme Ct 1962, D.C. 1983, Minn. 1985. Law clk. to judge U.S. Dist. Ct., 1958-60; assoc. firm Chadbourne, Parke, Whiteside & Wolff, N.Y.C., 1960-62; mem. firm Younger and Younger, and (successors), 1962-67; adj. asst. prof. N.Y. U. Sch. Law, 1967-69; asst. atty. gen. State of N.Y., 1969-70; assoc. prof. Hofstra U. Sch. Law, 1970-72, prof., assoc. dean, 1972-74; dean, prof. Syracuse Coll. Law, 1974-75; dep. dean, prof. law Cornell Law Sch., 1975-78, prof. law, 1975-85; vis. prof. U. Minn. Law Sch., Mpls., 1984-85, prof., 1985-91, Joseph E. Wargo Anoka County Bar Assn. prof. family law, 1991—. Of counsel Popham, Haik, Schnobrich & Kaufman, Ltd., Mpls., 1989-95; cons. NOW, 1972-74, Suffolk County for Revision of Its Real Property Tax Act, 1972-73; mem. N.Y. Gov.'s Panel To Screen Candidates of Ct. of Claims Judges, 1973-74; mem. Minn. Lawyers' Profl. Responsibility Bd., 1991-93. Contbr. articles to profl. jours. Trustee Cornell U., 1973-78 Mem.: AAUP (v.p. Cornell U. chpt. 1978—79), ABA (council legal edn. 1975—79), Minn. Bar Assn., Assn. of Bar of City of N.Y., Am. Law Inst. (adv. restatement property 1982—84). Home: 3520 W Calhoun Pkwy Minneapolis MN 55416-4657 Office: U Minn Law Sch Minneapolis MN 55455 E-mail: young001@umn.edu.

YOUNG III, HARMON GRIFFITH, music educator; b. Charleston, W.Va., July 29, 1951; s. Harmon Griffith Young II and Phyllis Hall Young. BS, WV Wesleyan Coll., Buckhannon, WV, 1973; MA, W.Va. U., Morgantown, WV, 1974—80; PhD, U. Fla., Gainesville, FL, 1995. Prof. music W.Va. U., Parkersburg, W.Va., 1975—. W.va. pres. Am. Choral Directors Assn., 1993, W.Va., 1993—95; pres. W.Va. Coun. Cultural Coordinators, W.Va., 1995—99; w.va. project dir. and condr. Continental Harmony, W.Va., 1999—2000; chorale condr. W.Va. U., Parkersburg, W.Va., 2002—02, artistic dir. disting. performance series, W.Va., 2002—02. Recipient Academic hon., Omicron Delta Kappa, 1972, Phi Kappa Phi, 1995, Music hon., Pi Kappa Lambda, 1995. Mem.: Internat. Fedn. Choral Music, Soc. Am. Music, Am. Choral Directors Assn. (life). R-Consevative. United Methodist. Achievements include Commissioned and conducted premieres of choral works by seven American composers; Prepared choruses for numerous performances including collaborations with Robert Shaw and Dave Brubeck. Home: 75 Reamer Road Clendenin WV 25045 Office: West Virginia University Parkersburg 300 Campus Drive Parkersburg WV 26104 Office Fax: 304-424-8315. E-mail: hg.young@mail.wvu.edu.

YOUNG-LYON, KAY LYNN, dance educator, small business owner; b. Decatur, Tex., Aug. 7, 1955; d. Cecil V. and Evelyn Jane (Cohron) Y. BS in Dance Edn., U. North Tex., 1977, MS in Dance Edn., 1981. Owner, dir. Kay Lynn's Studio of Dance, Carrollton, Tex., 1977—. Choreographer, dir. in field; mem. Nat. Tap Dance Day com., Artists Helping Artists, 1994—; adv. bd. mem. dance and theatre arts dept. U. North Tex., 1997—. Hostess (cable TV) Kay Lynn's Aerobics, 1985-87, Dallas Dance News, 1989—. Mem. Civic League, Inc., 1997—, sec., 1998-99, asst. fundraising chair, 1999—; mentor Carrollton Farmers Branch; key communicator Carrollton Farmers Br. Ind. Sch. Dist., 1982—; vol. dancer, choreographer and hostess Nat. Svcs. Orgn. of Iwo Jima Battle Survivors, 1993—, C. of C. galas, 1985—. Named one of Outstanding Young Women of Am., 1983; recipient Alumna Honor award U. North Tex. Dance and Theatre Arts Dept., 2000. Mem. AAUW (ednl. v.p. 1983-84, cultural v.p. 1987-88, membership v.p. 1991-93), Dallas Dance Coun. (social v.p. 1988-91, bd. dirs.), Nat. Assn. Dance and Affiliate Artists (sec., treas. 1988-91). Baptist. Avocation: travel. Office: 4339 S Capistrano Dr Dallas TX 75287-4012

YOUNG-MALLIN, JUDITH, writer, archivist; b. Mt. Vernon, N.Y., Aug. 10, 1937; d. Milton and Marion Ethel (Peterfreund) Young; m. Joel Mallin, Aug. 8, 1957 (div. 1985); children: Jennifer Young, Adam Young, Noah Young. Student, Syracuse U., 1955, NYU, 1956, 86, 1956. Researcher Conde-Nast, N.Y.C., 1957-58; lectr. Am. Crafts Mus., 1986; ind. lectr., 1986—. Cons., innovator Surreal Eye Series, N.Y.C., 1986-87; lectr. London-Courtauld Inst. Surrealism in N.Y., 1991, Art Inst. Chgo., 1992, Sch. for Visual Arts, N.Y.C., 1992, Pollock-Krasner Found., 1997, Artists Talk on Art, 1997, Guggenheim Mus., Venice, Italy, 1998; cons. Am. Masters, N.Y.C., 1991; established Young-Mallin Archive; surrealist look new world, 1999-2000. Author: M.F.K. Fisher, Virgil Thomson, 1990, Juliet Man Ray, 1991, Surrealism and Women, Eileen Agar, 1991, View Anth. Index Edn., 1991, Edward James, 1991. Mem. James Beard Soc. (profl. mem.). Avocations: study of creative women and aging, surrealists in N.Y. in 1940s, art and food relationships. Home: 719 Greenwich St New York NY 10014-2586

YOUNGMAN, CHARLES VAN PATTEN, neuroscience educator; b. Williamsport, Pa., June 17, 1936; s. John Crawford and Ruth Allen Y.; m. Lynn Marie Ryan, Mar. 9, 1980; 1 child Ryan. BS in Physiol. Psychology, Tufts U., Medford, MASS, 1954—59; JD, Pa. State U., Carlisle, 1962. Exec. asst. Milton Shapp, Govenor of Pa, Phila., 1964—67; dir. of adult basic edn. Rsch. for Better Schs., 1967—73; criminal def. atty. Youngman and Baker, 1975—89; prof. of psychology Art Inst. of Phila., 1990—. Dir. Adult Literacy Inst., Philadelphia, Pa., 1980—90. Author: (poetry) Microtubules, my ass!, 2002 (1st Prize U. of Ariz. biannual Poetry Slam for Consciousness Studies, 2002). Exec. asst. Milton Shapp Govenor of Pa, Philadelphia, Pa., 1964—67. Mem.: Pen and Pencil Club. D-Liberal. Home: 714 Pemberton St Philadelphia PA 19147 Office: Art Inst Phila 1622 Chestnut St Philadelphia PA Home Fax: 215-928-0608; Office Fax: 215-405-6398. Personal E-mail: greybloon@aol.com.

YOUNGMAN, OWEN RALPH, newspaper executive; b. Chgo., Apr. 24, 1953; s. Ralph Elmer and Charlotte Earldine (Ottoson) Y.; m. Linda Ann Erlandson, Aug. 24, 1975. Sportswriter Ashtabula (Ohio) Star-Beacon, 1969-71; office clk. Chgo. Tribune, 1971-73, transcriber, 1973-75, copy editor, slotman, 1976-79, copy chief, news editor, 1979-83, dep. sports editor, 1984-86, assoc. met. editor, 1986-88, assoc. features editor, 1988-90, dep. fin. editor, 1990-91, assoc. mng. editor, 1991-93, features editor, 1993-95, mng. editor, features, 1995, dir. interactive media, 1996-99, dir. planning and devel., 1999, v.p. devel., 2000—. Bd. dirs. Swedish Covenant Hosp., Legacy.com Mem. Newspaper Assn. Am. New Media Fedn. (bd. dirs.), Am. Soc. Newspaper Editors, Presidents Club of North Park U., Arts Club of Chgo. Avocation: vocal and instrumental music. Home: 40 Kenmore Ave Deerfield IL 60015-4750 Office: Chicago Tribune 435 N Michigan Ave Chicago IL 60611-4066 E-mail: oyoungman@tribune.com.

YOUNGNER, JULIUS STUART, microbiologist, educator; b. N.Y.C., Oct. 24, 1920; m. Tula Liakakis, 1943 (dec. 1963); children— Stuart, Lisa; m. Rina C. Balter, Aug. 3, 1964. BA, NYU, 1939; MS, U. Mich., 1941, ScD, 1944. Diplomate: Am. Acad. Microbiology. Teaching asst. dept. microbiology Sch. Medicine, U. Mich., 1941-43, instr., 1946-47; scientist Nat. Cancer Inst., Bethesda, Md., 1949; asst. prof. Virus Research Lab., U. Pitts., 1949-56, asso. prof. dept. microbiology, Sch. Medicine, 1956-60, prof., 1960—; chmn. dept. microbiology Virus Research Lab., U. Pitts. (Sch. Medicine), 1966-85, chmn. dept. microbiology, biochemistry, and molecular biology, 1985-89, Disting. Svc. prof., 1989—. Vis. prof. dept. microbiology, Faculty Medicine U. Athens, Greece, 1963; F.G. Novy meml. lectr. Sch. Medicine, U. Mich., 1965; nat. lectr. Found. for Microbiology, 1972-73; 6th ann. Lippard meml. lectr. Coll. Physicians and Surgeons, Columbia U., 1980; mem. study sect. virology and rickettsiology USPHS, NIH, 1965-69; mem. bd. sci. councilors Nat. Inst. Allergy and Infectious Diseases, 1970-74, chmn., 1973-74, mem. task force on virology, 1976-77; mem. clin. a fellowship study sect. NIH, 1979-80; mem. adv. group to microbiology program Am. Inst. Biol. Scis., 1970-73; asso. mem. commn. on influenza Armed Forces Epidemiol. Bd., Dept. Def., 1959-69, mem., 1970-73; com. .on biomed. research and research tng. Am. Assn. Med. Colls., 1973-75; cons. to surgeon gen. Dept. Army, 1973-76 Contbr. chpts. to books, articles to sci. jours. Referee Macy faculty scholar award program Josiah Macy, Jr., Found., 1977; mem. study group immunology and infectious diseases Health Research Services Found., 1959-79, chmn., 1978-79; mem. microbiology and virology study group Am. Cancer Soc., 1981-85, chmn., 1985. Served with U.S. Army, 1944-46; with USPHS, 1947-49. E.I. du Pont de Nemours & Co. ednl. aid grantee, 1973 Fellow Hellenic Soc. Microbiology and Hygiene (hon. fgn.); mem. AAAS, AAUP, Am. Soc. Microbiology (chmn. sect. T 1981—, mem. com. med. microbiology and immunology, bd. pub. and sci. affairs 1981-97, chmn. ethical practices com. 1997—), Am. Soc. Virology (pres.-elect 1985-86, pres. 1986-87), Soc. for Gen. Microbiology, Am. Assn. Immunologists, Infectious Diseases Soc. Am., Assn. Med. Microbiology Chmn. (pres.), Am. Acad. Microbiology (bd. govs. 1985-91), Am. Type Culture Collection (trustee 1992-95, vice chmn. 1996—, chmn. bd. sci. dirs. 1995-97), Internat. Soc. Interferon and Cytokine Rsch. (hon.) Office: U Pitts Dept Molecular Genetics & Bi Pittsburgh PA 15261-0001

YOUNGQUIST, WALTER LEWELLYN, consulting geologist; b. Mpls., May 5, 1921; s. Walter Raymond and Selma Regina (Knock) Y.; m. Elizabeth Salome Pearson, Dec. 11, 1943; children: John, Karen, Louise, Robert. BA, Gustavus Adolphus Coll., St. Peter, Minn., 1942; MSc, U. Iowa, 1943, PhD, 1948. Registered profl. geologist, Oreg. Jr. geologist U.S. Geol. Survey, 1943-44; rsch. assoc. U. Iowa, Iowa City, 1945-48; asst. prof. geology U. Idaho, Moscow, 1948-51; sr. geologist Internat. Petroleum Co., Talara, Peru, 1951-54; prof. geology U. Kans., Lawrence, 1954-57, U. Oreg., Eugene, 1957-66; cons. geologist Minerals dept. Exxon Corp., Houston, 1968-73; geothermal cons. Eugene Water & Electric Bd., 1973-92; ind. cons. Eugene, 1992—. Author: Investing in Natural Resources, 1980, Mineral Resources and the Destinies of Nations, 1990, GeoDestinies, 1997; co-author: Ordovician Cephalopod Fauna of Baffin Island, 1954. Ensign, USNR, 1944-45. Recipient Lowden Prize in Geology, U. Iowa, 1943, Journalist award, Am. Assn. Petroleum Geology, 2000. Fellow AAAS, Geol. Soc. Am.; mem. Am. Assn. Petroleum Geologists, Geothermal Resources Coun., N.W. Energy Assn., N.Y. Acad. Scis., Sigma Xi. Lutheran. Avocations: fly-tying, photography, fishing. Office: PO Box 5501 Eugene OR 97405-0501

YOUNGS, DIANE CAMPFIELD, learning disabilities specialist, educator; b. Margaretville, N.Y., Feb. 16, 1954; d. Richard Maxwell and Charlotte June (Rickard) Campfield; m. William H. Youngs, June 30, 1984. BS in Edn., SUNY, Geneseo, 1976, MS in Edn., 1977. Professionally recognized spl. educator. Tchr. educable mentally retarded Tompkins-Seneca-Tioga Bd. Coop. Ednl. Svcs., Ithaca, N.Y., 1978-80; tchr. learning disabled Joint Svcs. for Spl. Edn., Mishawaka, Ind., 1980-97; assoc. faculty Ind. U.-South Bend Grad. Sch. Edn., 1996-98. Vis. lectr. dept. edn. Ind. U., South Bend, 1998-2002, lectr., 2002—; mem. Task Force for Reorgn. Spl. Edn., Mishawaka, 1990-91; coord. Tiny Talkers Summer Speech/Lang. Camp, 1994—. Mem. AAUP, AAUW, Coun. for Exceptional Children, Learning Disabilities Assn., Coun. for Learning Disabilities, Ind. Profs. Reading, Internat. Reading Assn., Nat. Coun. Tchrs. English, Kappa Delta Pi, Psi Iota Xi. Republican.

YOUNGS, JACK MARVIN, cost engineer; b. Bklyn., May 2, 1941; s. Jack William and Virginia May (Clark) Y.; m. Alexandra Marie Robertson, Oct. 31, 1964; 1 child, Christine Marie. B in Engring., CCNY, 1964; MBA, San Diego State U., 1973. Mass properties engr. Gen. Dynamics Corp., San Diego, 1964-68, rsch. engr., 1968-69, sr. rsch. engr., 1969-80, sr. cost devel. engr., 1980-81, cost devel. engring. specialist, 1981-95; prin. estimator Martin Marietta Astronautics, 1994-95; estimating adminstr. Lockheed Martin Astronautics, 1995-96; prin., owner Youngs Group, 1996—. Dist. dir. Scripps Ranch Civic Assn, 1976-79; pres. Scripps Ranch Swim Team, 1980-82, dir., 1986-87; judge Greater San Diego Sci. and Engring. Fair, 1981-98, sweepstakes judge, 1999; mem. Princeton U. Parents Assn. Recipient 5th pl. award World Body Surfing Championships, 1987, 6th pl. award, 1988, 2d pl. award, 1999. Mem. AIAA, N.Y. Acad. Scis., Alumni Assn., CUNY, Bklyn. Tech. H.S. Alumni Assn., Inst. Cost Analysis (cert., charter, treas. Greater San Diego chpt. 1986-90), Soc. Cost Estimating and Analysis (cert. cost estimator/analyst, pres. San Diego chpt. 1990-91), Internat. Soc. Parametric Analysts (bd. dirs. San Diego chpt. 1987-90), Nat. Mgmt. Assn. (space sys. divsn. charter 1985, Award of Honor Convair chpt. 1975), Assn. MBA Execs., San Diego State U. Bus. Alumni Assn. (charter 1986), Convair Alumni Assn., Scripps Ranch Swim and Racquet Club (dir. 1977-80, treas. 1978-79, pres. 1979-80), Beta Gamma Sigma, Chi Epsilon, Sigma Iota Epsilon. Lutheran. Achievements include research in life cycle costing and econ. analysis. Office: 11461 Tribuna Ave San Diego CA 92131-1907 E-mail: youngsgroup@hotmail.com.

YOUNGS, JENNIFER ANN, lawyer; b. Washington, Mar. 4, 1970; d. John Kenneth and Gettine Davis Youngs. BA, U. N.C., 1992, JD, 1996. Law clk. U.S. Bankruptcy Ct. (we. dist.) N.C., Charlotte, 1996-98; assoc. James, McElroy & Diehl, PA, 1998-2001; with McGuireWoods LLP, 2001—. Bd. dirs. Plaza-Midwood Devel., Charlotte, 1998-2000; mem. panel Charlotte Transit com., 1998. Avocations: reading, running, home renovation. Office: McGuireWoods LLP 100 N Tryon St Ste 2900 Charlotte NC 28202-4011 E-mail: jyoungs@mcguirewoods.com.

YOUNGS, ROBERT LELAND, forestry educator; b. Pittsfield, Mass., Feb. 10, 1924; s. Frank Leland and Florence (Wilcox) Y.; m. Esther Louise Stevenson, June 11, 1949; children: Susan, Karen, Steven, Rebecca, Sarah. BS, N.Y. State Coll. Forestry, 1948; MWT, U. Mich., 1950; PhD, Yale U., 1957; D (hon.), U. Nancy I, France, 1998, Moscow Forestry U., 1999. Rschr. USDA Forest Svc., Madison, Wis., 1951-66, assoc. dep. chief Washington, 1966-69, 72-75, dir. So. Sta. New Orleans, 1970-72, dir. forest products lab. Madison, 1975-85; prof. Va. Tech. U., Blacksburg, 1985-95, prof. emeritus, 1995—. Mem. adv. bd. Forest Rsch. Inst. Malaysia, Kuala Lumpur, 1986-90. Author: (with others) Encyclopedia of Wood, 1989, Encyclopedia of Materials, 1993, Forest and Wildlife Sci., 1999; editor Wood & Fiber Sci., 1995-2001. With U.S. Army, 1943-46, ETO. Recipient Presdl. Rank award U.S. Civil Svc., 1984. Fellow Internat. Acad. Wood Sci.; mem. Internat. Union Forest Rsch. Orgns. (hon.), Forest Products Soc., Soc. Wood Sci. and Tech. (pres. 1958-60). Avocations: bicycling, hiking, history, genealogy. Office: Va Tech U Brooks Ctr Blacksburg VA 24061

YOUNGS, ROBERT RIGGS, engineer; b. Riverside, Calif., Aug. 20, 1947; s. James Porter and Gwendolyn Gloria (Miller) Y.; m. Susan Ann Cohen, Feb. 10, 1974; children: Sarah Gwen Cohen Youngs, Noah James Cohen Youngs. BS, Calif. State Poly. Coll., 1967; MS, U. Calif., Berkeley, 1973, PhD, 1982. Staff engr. Pacific Found. Engrs., Bloomington, Calif., 1970-72; staff to project engr. Woodward Clyde Consultants, Oakland, 1974-84; sr. to prin. engr. Geometrix Consultants, 1985—. Contbr. articles to profl. jours. Mem. Am. Soc. Engrs., Seismol. Soc. Am., Earthquake Engring. Rsch. Inst. Avocations: fishing, science fiction. Home: 1147 High Ct Berkeley CA 94708-1624 Office: Geomatrix Consultants 2101 Webster St Fl 12 Oakland CA 94612-3027

YOUNGS, WILLIAM ELLIS, motion picture engineer, projectionist; b. Miami, Fla., Apr. 30, 1916; s. Edward Ray and Maude Myrtle (Burd) Y.; m. Mary Helen Still, Aug. 28, 1948; 1 child, Renee Helen. Student, Nat. Radio Inst., 1952. Film technician Washington Motion Picture Co., 1934-35, U.S. Dept. State, Washington, 1948-53; night service mgr. MGM Film Exchange, 1936-41; mgr., projectionist Calvert Theatre, Prince Frederick, Md., 1941-42; research asst. Exec. Office of the President, Washington, 1942; photo lab technician Office War Info., 1942-43; br. chief, advisor film and equipment USIA, 1953-78; engr., projectionist Motion Picture Assn. Am., 1979-94; photographer, chaplain Vets. Commn., Falls Church, Va., 1997—. Advisor Stephens Coll., Columbia, Mo., 1973-75. Columnist Falls Church (Va.) Sun-Echo, 1953-55. Pres. Greenway Downs Civic Assn., Falls Church, 1953-54; pres. Second (Indian Head) Div. Assn. D.C. br., 1953-57; hon. recruiter USN, 1984; chaplain, photographer Vets. Common, U.S.A., Arlington/Falls Church, Va., 1997—. With U.S. Army, 1943-45, ETO. Fellow Soc. Motion Picture and TV Engrs. (life; nat. membership chmn. 1969, Outstanding Svc. award 1979); mem. Washington Film and Video Coun. (life; pres. 1967-68), Univ. Film and Video Assn., SAR (pres. Fairfax Resolves 1991-92, chaplain emeritus 2002, Va. ofcl. photographer, nat. mem. mag. adv. com. SAR/DAR liaison com. 1990—, historian 1993-94, editor 1994—, Meritorious Svc. medal 1991, Va. medal, 1994, Pres. Gen.'s citation for Disting. Svc. and Silver Good Citizenship medal 1994, Patriot medal 1996), Presbyterian. Avocations: photography, pub. relations, hist. and tech. writing. Home: 1436 Mayflower Dr Mc Lean VA 22101-5614

YOUNGSTEDT, SHAWN DOUGLAS, research scientist; b. Ft. Dix, N.J., Mar. 14, 1964; s. Gene Louis and Eleanor Maxine Youngstedt. BA, U. Tex., 1987; MA, U. Ga., 1991, PhD, 1995. Rsch. assoc. U. Ga., Athens, 1989-94, U. Calif., San Diego, 1994-95, rschr., 1997-99, asst. project scientist, 1999—. Adj. faculty Nat. U., San Diego, 1998—. Mem. editl. bd. Am. Jour. of Medicine and Sports; contbr. articles to profl. jours. Eagle Scout Boy Scouts Am., 1978. Recipient Sleep Rsch. Soc., 1995-97; grantee Sigma Xi, Athens, 1995, NIH, 1999; postdoctoral fellow NIH, San Diego, 1995-97. Mem. Am. Coll. Sports Medicine (New Investigator award 2001), Sleep Rsch. Soc., Soc. Light Treatment and Biol. Rhythms. Democrat. Office: U Calif 9500 Gilman Dr La Jolla CA 92093-5004

YOUNGSTROM, PAUL CLARENCE, anesthesiologist; b. Cedar Rapids, Iowa, Dec. 4, 1950; s. Clarence Swan and Hilda (Konga) Y.; m. Karen Jane Daykin, Aug. 18, 1973; children: Erica, Christiane, Andrew. BA in Econs., Yale U., 1972; MD, McGill U., 1976. Cert. anesthesiology. Intern U. Hosps., Cleve., 1976-77, resident in anesthesiology, 1977-79; staff anesthesiologist Cleve. Clinic, 1993—. Cons. Agy. for Health Care Policy and Rsch., Washington, 1993-94. Author: Operative Obstetrics, Common and Uncommon Obstetric Syndromes and Conditions. Elder St. Peter's Luth. Ch., Shaker Heights, 1994—. Mem. Am. Soc. Anesthesiologists, Am. Soc. for Regional Anesthesia, Internat. Anesthesia Rsch. Soc., Soc. Obstetric Anesthesia and Perinatology. E-mail: paul.youngstrom.es.72@aya.yale.edu.

YOUNGWOOD, ALFRED DONALD, lawyer; b. N.Y.C., Apr. 27, 1938; s. Milton and Lillian (Ginsburg) Y.; m. Judith Goldfarb, June 24, 1963; children: Jonathan David, Stephen Michael. BA magna cum laude, Yale U., 1959; LLB magna cum laude, Harvard U., 1962. Bar: N.Y. 1962, D.C. 1970, U.S. Tax Ct. 1964, U.S. Ct. Appeals (2d cir.) 1969. Law clk. to judge U.S. Dist. Ct. N.Y., 1962-63; assoc. Paul, Weiss, Rifkind, Wharton & Garrison, N.Y.C., 1964-70, ptnr., 1970—, chair, 1999—. Trustee, treas. exec. com. Ctrl. Synagogue, N.Y.C., mem. council on fgn. relations. Fulbright scholar, London, 1963-64. Fellow Am. Coll. Tax Counsel; mem. ABA, N.Y. State Bar Assn. (chmn. tax sect. 1978-79, exec. com. 1971—, ho. of dels. 1979-80), Assn. of Bar of City of N.Y., Coun. on Fgn. Relations. Home: 1125 Park Ave New York NY 10128-1243 Office: Paul Weiss Rifkind Wharton 1285 Avenue Of The Americas New York NY 10019-6064 E-mail: ayoungwood@paulweiss.com.

YOUNG-WRIGHT, LORETTA, school system administrator, social worker; b. Clarks, Sept. 20, 1951; d. James Lee and Elnora Young; m. Lester Wright; 1 child Tyehimba Young. BA, U. Ill., Chgo., 1975, MSW, 1977; EdD, Roosevelt U., 1998. LCSW. Coord. student devel. Chgo. State U., Chgo., 1980—81; lead social worker Chgo. Child Care Soc., 1981—88; coord. LaRabida Children's Hosp., 1988—90; social worker, mgr. Chgo. Pub. Schs., 1990—. Adj. faculty mem. Gov.'s State U., 2000—. Author: Inspiration for Seven Days, My Soul's Connections. Mem. doctoral coms. Roosevelt U., 1999—2001. Recipient cert. of appreciation, Bulls Scholars Steering Com., 2001, Ujima Inc. and Wells Cmty., 2001; scholar, Fulbright Found., 1991. Mem.: ASCD, NASW, Zeta Phi Beta (Pearl award 1995, 1998), Phi Delta Kappa. Avocations: book clubs, writing poetry, travel, aqua aerobics.

YOUNIE, WILLIAM JOHN, special education educator, researcher; b. Boston, July 25, 1932; s. Edward Younie; m. Anne Marie Ring, Sept. 8, 1956; children: Anne Elizabeth, John William. BS in Edn., Boston Tchr.'s Coll., 1953; MEd, Tufts U., 1954; EdD, Columbia U., 1959. Cert. elem. edn., handicapped and learning disabilities tchr., sch. counselor, N.J. Tchr. elem. Delmar (N.Y.) Pub. Schs., 1954-55, Deer Park (N.Y.) Schs., 1955-56; children's libr. Agnes Russel Columbia U., N.Y.C., 1956-57; tchr. Yonkers (N.Y.) Pub. Schs., 1957-59; dir. edn. Southbury (Conn.) Tng. Sch., 1959-63; assoc. prof. Tchr.'s Coll. Columbia U., N.Y.C., 1963-70; dept. chair, prof. William Paterson Coll., Wayne, NJ, 1970—2002, prof. emeritus, 2002—. Cons. Fedn. of the Handicapped, N.Y.C., 1965-70, Abilities Inc., Albertson, N.Y., 1967-70, Elwyn (Pa.) Inst., 1968-84, Vineland (N.J.) Tng. Sch., 1985-89. Author: Introduction to Work Study Programs, 1965, Instructional Approaches to the Slow Learner, 1966, (with others) The World of Rehabilitation, 1970, Basic Speech Improvement, 1975; icon paintings, photograph exhibits at Paramus (N.J.) Cmty. Sch., Paramus Pub. Libr., Art Gallery of Loyola Coll., Md., William Paterson Coll., Wayne, Santa Carving Exhibits, New Milford Pub. Libr. Com. chmn. Boy Scouts Am., Southbury, 1959-63; bd. dirs. State Gov.'s Coun. on Mental Retardation, Trenton, N.J., 1970-71, N.J. Spl. Edn. Instnl. Med. Ctr., Clifton, N.J., 1975-76; mem. adv. bd. Edison State Coll., 1990-96, acad. coun., 1993—. Named Educator of the Yr., Morris chpt. ARC, 1990, N.J. State Assn. for Retarded Citizens, 1990; Fulbright fellow People's Republic of China, 1988. Fellow Am. Assn. on Mental Retardation; mem. Coun. for Exceptional Children (pres. Featherstown chpt. 1978). Avocations: woodworking, painting, photography, model railroads, brewerania collecting. Home: 307 South Dr Paramus NJ 07652-4812 Office: William Paterson University 300 Pompton Rd Wayne NJ 07470-2152

YOUNKER, KATHLEEN TEUBER, pianist, music educator; b. St. Cloud, Minn., Jan. 22, 1947; d. Hans Richard and Philomena (Hortsch) T.; m. Daniel William Younker, July 19, 1968; children: Laura, Jonathan. BA in History and Philosophy, St. Cloud State U., 1968; ARCT in Piano Performance, Royal Conservatory Toronto, Ont., Can., 1983; BA in Music, Bishop's U., Lennoxville, Que., Can., 1984; pvt. piano student, Rose Goldblatt, Montreal, 1985-95; MA in Spl. Studies, St. Cloud State U., 2002. Self-employed piano tchr., Lennoxville, 1978-97, St. Cloud, 1997—; sch. music tchr. Eastern Twps. Regional Sch. Bd., Lennoxville, 1982-86; ch. organist Peace United Ch. of Christ, St. Cloud, 1998-99; accompanist Sauk Rapids (Minn.) Rice HS, 1999—2000. Mem. Music Tchrs. Nat. Assn., Nat. Guild Piano Tchrs., Can. Fedn. Music Tcrs. Assns. (com. mem., ex officio nat. conv. 1997), Minn. Music Tchrs. Assn. (com. mem. state conv. 1999—), Eastern Twps. Music Tchrs. Assn. (pres. 1989-91), Que. Music Tchrs. Assn. (pres. provincial coun. 1993-97). Avocations: home restoration, pets, reading, gardening, cooking, entertaining.

YOUNKIN, RICHARD AMBROSE, state official, air quality specialist; b. Woonsocket, R.I., Nov. 22, 1949; s. Burrows Thomas and Margaret Maude (Seitzer) Y.; m. Robyn Anne Roderigues, July 12, 1986; children: Eden Elizabeth Zhen, April Grace Qi. BA, R.I. Coll., 1977, MA, 1985. Cert. tchr., Mass.; cert. air quality specialist, R.I. Instr. English, C.C. R.I., Lincoln, 1985-92; environ. quality technician R.I. Dept. Environ. Mgmt., Providence, 1993-97, air quality specialist, 1997—. Writer, Earthwatch participant, Chaplain's Asst., Riar Natl. Guard, Tech. Sgt. Author: Checkmate, 1997, Our Good Brother, 1998. Field rschr. on tree populations Jahoda Expn., Zancudo Cocha, Ecuador, 1985, field rsch. on black caiman, Cuyabeno, Ecuador, 1990; tracker black rhinocerous Earthwatch, Sinamatella, Zimbabwe, 1995. Staff sgt. USAFR; mem. R.I. Army N.G., 1991-93, R.I. Air N.G., 1993—. Mem. Brazilian Cultural Ctr., Tang Soo Do Assn. (black belt). Avocations: martial arts, literature, natural science, travel, writing plays. Home: 152 Isabella Ave Providence RI 02908-1208 Office: RI Dept Environ Mgmt Air Resources Dept 235 Promenade St Providence RI 02908-5734 E-mail: ryounkin@dem.state.ri.us.

YOUNKIN, STEVEN G. neuroscientist; b. Camden, N.J., June 9, 1944; s. Stuart G. and Bettibel Wurster Y.; m. Linda H. Younkin, June 14, 1969; children: Sarah, Samuel, Curtis. PhD, U. Pa., 1971, MD, 1972. Resident Case Western Res. U., Cleve., 1982-85. Recipient Zenith award Alzheimer's Disease and Related Disorders Assn., 1991-94, Potamkin prize Am. Acad. of Neurology, 1995. Office: Mayo Clinic 4500 San Pablo Rd Jacksonville FL 32224 E-mail: younkin.steven@mayo.edu.

YOUNOS, TAMIM, academic administrator; b. Kabul, Afghanistan, Nov. 3, 1947; s. M. and Setara Younos; m. Yumiko Ohno Yumiko Ohno; children: Ken, Rona. D of Engring., U. Tokyo, 1976. Interim assoc. dir. Va. Water Resources Rsch. Ctr., Va. Tech., Blacksburg, 2002—. Editor: (book) Advances in Water Monitoring Research, 2002. Mem.: Univs. Coun. on Water Resources (bd. dirs. 1999—). Office: Va Water Resources Rsch Ctr Va Tech 10 Sandy Hall Blacksburg VA 24061-0444

YOUNOSSI, ZOBAIR, health facility administrator, medical educator; b. Afghanistan, Nov. 5, 1959; m. Sanya Younossi; children: Youssef, Issah. BS, George Mason U., 1984; MD, U. Rochester, 1989; MPH, San Diego State U., 1995. Cert. bd. cert. gastroenterology, bd. cert. internal medicine, UNOS qualified trransplant physician. Sr. rschr. Cleve. Clinic Found., 1998; exec. dir. Ctr. for Liver Diseases, Falls Church, Va., 2000—; med. dir. liver transplantation Inova Fairfax Hosp., 2000—. Affiliate prof. biomed. scis. Ctr. for Study of Genomic in Liver Diseases, George Mason U., Fairfax, 2002—. Contbr. book; author: (book) Acute Upper Gastrointestinal Bleeding, 2000, Practical Approach to Hepatitis C; Handbooks in Health, 2002, Alpha-1 Antitrypsin Deficiency. Hepatology: A Practical Approach, 2002. Bd. dirs. Am. Liver Found., Washington, 2001; expert advisor Cleve. Health Mus., 1997; expert hepatologist HCV Coalition's Presentation to the State of Ohio, Columbus, 1999. Named one of Top Drs., Cleve. Mag., 1998. Mem.: Am. Assn. for Study of Liver Diseases (com. mem. 1997), Am. Coll. Gastroenterology (rsch. com. mem. 2001), Alpha Omega Alpha. Office: Ctr for Liver Diseases 3300 Gallows Rd Falls Church VA 22042 Office Fax: 703-698-3481.

YOUNT, GEORGE STUART, paper company executive; b. L.A., Mar. 4, 1949; s. Stanley George and Agnes (Pratt) Y.; m. Geraldine Marie Silvio, July 18, 1970; children: Trisha Marie, Christopher George. Postgrad., Harvard U., 1983-86. Mgmt. trainee Fortifiber Corp., L.A., 1969-71, asst. to v.p. ops., 1971-75, adminstrv. v.p., treas., sec., 1975-85, exec. v.p., sec., CFO, bd. dirs., 1985-90, chmn., CEO, 1991—; pres., dir. Fonzia Corp., 1993—. Bd. dirs. Stanwall Corp., pres., 1989—, Thompson & Co. Ins. Svcs., Pasadena, Calif., 1996—, Parasol Found., 1999—, Tracerton Enterprises, Inc., 2001—; past pres. Hollister Ranch Cattle Coop., Gaviota, Calif., 1986-88; trustee Sierra Nev. Coll., 1999-2002,(vice Chair, 2002). Team leader L.A. United Way, 1981-86; bd. dirs. Big Bros. Greater L.A., 1984-87, L.A. coun. Boy Scouts Am., 1992—; mem. Young Pres. Orgn., 1991, forum moderator, 1993-95, chpt. forum officer, 1997-99; mem. Lake Tahoe Cmty. Trust Bd., 2001—. Mem. Am. Paper Inst. (dir. 1993-95, splty. coaters and extrusion sect. 1990—), Nat. Assn. Corp. Dirs., World Presidents Orgn., Harvard Bus. Club So. Calif., Harvard Owner/Pres. Mgmt. Program Club, Jonathan Club (L.A.), Rotary (bd. dirs. L.A. club 1992-94), Internat. Wine and Food Soc., Chaine des Rotisseurs Food and Wine Soc., Wine and Food Soc., Conferie des Chevaliers du Tastevin Wine and Food Soc. Avocations: scuba diving, electronics, cattle ranching, computers. Office: Fortifiber Corp 1001 Tahoe Blvd Incline Village NV 89451-9309

YOUNT, THOMAS DAVID, writer, columnist; b. Chgo., Jan. 22, 1934; s. Thomas William and Bernice Challe Yount; m. Rebecca Tobin, Oct. 15, 1978; children: Virginia, Lisa, Christina. BA cum laude, Knox Coll., 1956; PhB, St. Paul's Coll., Washington, 1960, MA, 1964; Licentiate in Sacred Theology, Cath. Inst., Paris, 1966; DD, Am. Bibl. Inst., Kansas City, Mo., 1979. Exec. editor West Hartford (Conn.) News, 1966-68; assoc. sec. Amherst (Mass.) Coll., 1970-72; acad. dean Marymount Coll., Arlington, Va., 1972-77; dir. instnl. rels. Assn. Am. Colls., Washington, 1977-79; dir. pub. affairs Atlantic Coun. U.S., 1979-81; exec. v.p. Internat. Pub. Rels., 1981-87; pres. Nat. Press Found., 1987-96; syndicated columnist Scripps Howard, 1996—. Pres. Potomac Assocs., Washington, 1977—; chmn. Coll. Preachers, Washington, 1987-90; mem. exec. com. Nat. Cathedral Found., Washington, 1988-90; vice chmn. Wash. Theol. Consortium, Washington, 2000—. Author: Growing in Faith, 1994 (Book of the Month Club 1994), Breaking Through God's Silence, 1996 (Book of the Month Club Selection 1996), Spiritual Simplicity, 1997 (Book Club Selection 1997), 10 Thoughts To Take into Eternity, 1999 (Book of Month Club 1999), Be Strong and Courageous, 2000 (Quaker Book Club 2000), What Are We to Do?, 2002 (Book Club Selection 2002). Millenium lectr. Chautauqua (N.Y.) Instn., 2000; lectr. Earlham Coll., Richmond, Ind., 2000, Guilford Coll., Greensboro, N.C., 2001. Named one of Outstanding Young Men of Am., 1957; recipient award New Eng. Press Assn., 1968, Thoth award Pub. Rels. Soc. Am., 1982, 84, 86, Lifetime Achievement award Knox Coll., 2002. Mem. Phi Beta Kappa. Office: PO Box 2758 Woodbridge VA 22193 E-mail: dyount@erols.com.

YOUNTS, PATTY LOU, interior design executive, researcher; b. Lexington, N.C., Feb. 20, 1950; d. Wayne Lohr and Rosetta Mae (Myers) Y. BS, U. N.C., Greensboro, 1972; postgrad., Wake Forest U., Winston-Salem, N.C., 1976. Apprentice draftsman and interior designer Paul T. Briggs, AIA, Lexington, 1971, in-house designer, specifer, 1972-74; part-time interior designer Watkins Office Interiors, Winston-Salem, 1972-74; ptnr. IN-Ex Designs, Inc., 1974-75, corp. officer, head, 1975-81, pres., owner, 1981—. Pres. Decorative Panel Koncepts, Inc., 1986—, J.P. Walls, Inc., 1989—, pres., 1990—; bd. dir. Industry Gen. Tire, GF Bus. Systems, Armstrong Industries, Mid-State Tile; guest speaker univs. Adv. bd. Lexington Meml Hosp., 1984— , Western Carolina U., 1983—; mem. N.C. Entrepreneurial Devel. Bd., 1996-99, N.C. Econ. Devel. Bd., 1997-98. Patentee novel wall system, 1990. Recipient N.C. AIA awards for Sch. Planning, 1977, 79; Sperry and Hutchinson scholar, 1968-72, hon. scholar U. N.C., Greensboro, 1971-72. Mem. Inst. Bus. Designers (mem., chmn. various coms., pres. Carolinas chpt. 1977-80, 82-84), Am. Soc. Interior Designers, Color Mktg. Group (chairholder 1985, bd. dirs. 1989-91), Lexington C. of C. (com. chmn. 1980, bd. dirs. 1981-84, 92—, pres. 1990), Rotary. Democrat. Mem. United Ch. of Christ. Avocations: water skiing, golf. Office: Design Cons 302 W Center St Lexington NC 27292-2710 E-mail: pyounts@hotmail.com.

YOUREE, CHERYL ANN, secondary education educator; b. L.A., Oct. 14, 1950; d. James William Catlett and Thelma Dolores (Closs) Courts; m. Thomas Eugene Youree, Jan. 19, 1975 (div. Dec. 1992); children: Anna Louise, Daniel Paul. BA in Drama, Calif. State U., Chico, 1973; MA in Theatre, Tex. A&M, 1990. Secondary tchrs. cert., Tex. Theatre, pub. speaking and English tchr. Bonham (Tex.) H.S., 1985—. Actress (movie) When The Time Comes, 1987; cons. (video) Sam Rayburn, 1995; puppeteer, vocal coach (video) Don't Make That Trash, 1995; dir. (commls.) Fannin County Family Crisis Ctr., 1999. Pres. Fannin County Arts Coun., Bonham, 1983; mem. adv. bd., cmty. svc. chmn. Rotary Club Internat., Bonham, 1991-92, mem., 1991-96; del. to People's Republic of China, People to People Internat., Spokane, Wash., 1993. Mem. Ednl. Theatre Assn., Assn. Tex. Profl. Educators, Tex. Edn. Theatre Assn., Alpha Psi Omega. Avocations: travel, knitting, theatre directing. Office: Bonham HS PO Box 490 Bonham TX 75418-0490 E-mail: c_youree@bhs.bonhamisd.org.

YOURISON, KAROLA MARIA, librarian services professional; b. Berlin, Germany, June 30, 1937; came to U.S., 1962; m. James E. Yourison, Feb. 29, 1992. BA, U. Pitts., 1974, MLS, 1976. Libr. mgr. Siemens Rsch. & Tech. Lab., Princeton, N.J., 1983-85; mgr. libr. svcs. Software Engring. Inst., Carnegie Mellon U., Pitts., 1986—. Mem. IEEE, Spl. Librs. Assn. (chair duplicates exch. com. 1992-94, chair sci.-tech. divsn. 1994-95, past chair sci.-tech. divsn. 1995-96), Assn. Computing Machinery. Office: Software Engring Inst 5000 Forbes Ave Pittsburgh PA 15213-3815 E-mail: kky@sei.cmu.edu.

YOURZAK, ROBERT JOSEPH, management consultant, engineer, educator; b. Mpls., Aug. 27, 1947; s. Ruth Phyllis Sorenson. BCE, U. Minn., 1969; MSCE, U. Wash., 1971, MBA, 1975. Registered profl. engr., Wash., Minn. Surveyor N.C. Hoium & Assocs., Mpls., 1965-68, Lot Surveys Co., Mpls., 1968-69; site layout engr. Sheehy Constrn. Co., St. Paul, 1968; structural engring. aide Dunham Assocs., Mpls., 1969; aircraft and aerospace structural engr., program rep. Boeing Co., Seattle, 1969-75; engr., estimator Howard S. Wright Constrn. Co., 1976-77; dir. project devel. and adminstrn. DeLeuw Cather & Co., 1977-78; sr. mgmt. cons. Alexander Grant & Co., Mpls., 1978-79; mgr. project sys. dept., project mgr. Henningson, Durham & Richardson, 1979-80; dir. project mgmt., regional offices Ellerbe Assocs., Inc., 1980-81; pres. Robert Yourzak & Assocs., Inc., 1982—. Lectr. engring. mgmt. U. Wash., 1977-78; lectr., adj. asst. prof. dept. civil and mineral engring. and mech./indsl. engring. Ctr. for Devel. of Tech. Leadership, Inst. Tech.; mem. strategic mgmt. and orgn. dept., mgmt. scis. dept. Sch. Mgmt., U. Minn., 1979-90, 96—; bd. adv. inst. tech., 1989-93; founding mem., membership com., mem. U. of Minn. com. Minn. High Tech. Coun., 1983-95; instr. principles mgmt. dept. bus. and pub. policy Concordia U., 1997, instr. contsrn. mgmt. Inver Hills C.C., 1998—; adj. instr. ops. mgmt. Hamline U., St. Paul, 2001; spkr. in field. Author: Project Management and Motivating and Managing the Project Team, 1984, (with others) Field Guide to Project Management, 1998. Chmn. regional art group experience Seattle Art Mus., 1975-78; mem. Pacific N.W. Arts Coun., 1977-78, ex-officio adviser Mus. Week, 1976; bd. dirs. Friends of the Rep. Seattle Repertory Theatre, 1973-77; mem. Symphonics Seattle Symphony Orch., 1975-78. Named Outstanding Young Man of Am., U.S. Jaycees, 1978; scholar Boeing Co., 1967-68, Sheehy Constrn. Co., summer 1967. Fellow ASCE (chmn. continuing edn. subcom. Seattle chpt. 1976-79, chmn. program com. 1978, mem. transp. and urban planning tech. group 1978, Edmund Friedman Young Engr. award 1979, chmn. continuing edn. subcom. 1979-80, chmn. energy com. Minn. chpt. 1980-81, bd. dirs. 1981-89, sec. 1981-83, v.p. profl. svcs. 1983-84, v.p. info. svcs. 1984-85, pres. 1986-87, past pres. 1987-89, spkr.), P Project Mgmt. Inst. (cert. project mgmt. prof., spkr., founding pres. 1985, chmn., adv. com. 1987-89, bd. dirs. 1984-86, program com. chmn. and organizing com. mem. Minn. chpt. 1984, spkr., project mgr. internat. mktg. program 1985-86, chmn. internat. mktg. standing com. 1986, long range and strategic planning com. 1988-93, chmn. 1992, v.p. pub. rels. 1987-88, ex-officio dir. 1989, 92, internat. pres. 1990, chmn. bd. 1991, ex-officio chmn. 1992, internat. bd. dirs., chmn. nominating com. 1992, PMI fellow 1995, chmn. exec. dir. selection com. 1996-97, Robert J. Yourzak Scholarship Award established Minn. chpt. 1998—), Inst. Indsl. Engrs. (pres. Twin Cities chpt. 1985-86, chmn. program com. 1983-84, bd. dirs. 1985-88, awards com., chmn. 1984-89, fellow 1999, spkr.); mem. ASTD (So. Minn. chpt.), Am. Cons. Engrs. Coun. (peer reviewer 1986-89), Am. Arbitration Assn. (mem. Mpls. panel of constrn. arbitrators), Minn. Surveyors and Engrs. Soc., Cons. Engrs. Coun. Minn. (chmn. pub. rels. com. 1983-85, vice chmn. 1988, chmn. 1989, program com. chmn. Midwest engrs. conf. and exposition 1985-90, spkr., Honor award 1992), Inst. Mgmt. Cons. (cert. mgmt. cons.), Mpls. Soc. Fine Arts, Internat. Facility Mgmt. Assn., Am. Soc. Engring. Edn., Rainer Club (co-chmn. Oktoberfest), Sierra club, Chowder Soc., Mountaineers, North Star Ski Touring, Chi Epsilon (life). Office: 7320 Gallagher Dr Ste 325 Minneapolis MN 55435-4510

YOUSEF, MONA LEE, psychotherapist; BS in Human Devel. and Family Studies, Cornell U., 1986; MSW, NYU, 1991. Cert. social worker, HIV counselor N.Y.; credentialed alcoholism and substance abuse counselor N.Y., cert. master addictions counselor. Coord. People with AIDS buddy program Home Care Am., N.Y.C., 1987-88; rsch. asst. Gay Men's Health Crisis, 1988; caseworker AIDS assessment program Gouverneur Hosp., 1989; support group facilitator Body Positive, 1989-92; clin. social worker mental health clinic Lower Eastside Svc. Ctr., 1991-93; clin. social worker alcoholism outpatient dept. Project Renewal, Inc., 1993-95; psychotherapist Counseling Ctr., Morris Heights Health Ctr., Bronx, N.Y., 1995-2000. Pvt. practice psychotherapy, N.Y.C., 1993—. Contbg. writer PWA Coalition Newsline. Mem. NASW, Nat. Assn. Alcoholism and Drug Abuse Counselors-Assn. for Addiction Profls., Acad. Cert. Social Workers, Assn. Addiction Profls. of N.Y., Nat. Coun. Sexual Addiction and Compulsivity, N.Y. State Soc. for Clin. Social Work, Stuyvesant H.S. Alumni Assn., Psi Chi (life). Democrat. Avocations: dancing, reading, writing, cooking, fitness. Office: 19 W 34th St Penthouse New York NY 10001

YOUSEFIAN, SHAHRAM, chemist; b. Tehran, Iran, Nov. 4, 1962; came to the U.S., 1978; s. Abbas Yousefian and Batool Yousefian-Khairandish; m. Judy Ileene Harmon, Aug. 11, 1984; children: Laila, Cyrus. BS, Southwest Bapt. U., 1984; PhD, U. Mo., 1990. Cert. Calif. profl. clear single subject tchg. credential Calif. Commn. on Tchr. Credentialing. Rsch. assoc. Washington U., St. Louis, 1991-93, Trinity U., San Antonio, 1994-95; lectr. U. Calif., San Diego, 1995-96; adj. prof. chemistry various instns., 1996—99; instr. chemistry San Diego Unified Sch. Dist., 2000-01, Grossmont Union H.S., 2000—. Mem. Am. Chem. Soc., Gideons Internat., Sigma Xi. E-mail: syousefian@parsmail.com.

YOUSIF, SALAH M. electrical engineer, educator, electrical engineer, consultant; b. Burin, Palestine, Nov. 15, 1938; arrived in U.S., 1965; s. Mohammad Yousif and Aisha Darwish; m. Nancy de Manigold Yousif, Jan. 6, 1938; children: Mariam, Dina, Leila. BSEE, Alexandria (Egypt) U., 1962; MSEE, Middle East Tech. U., Ankara, Turkey, 1964; PhD in Elec. and Electronic Engring., Oreg. State U., 1969. Registered control sys. profl. engr., Calif. Elec. engr. Amman (Jordan) Broadcasting, 1962—63, Kuwait Broadcasting, 1964—65; instr. Mich. State U., East Lansing, 1966—67, Oreg. State U., Corvallis, 1967—69; prof. Calif. State U., Sacramento, 1969—. Cons. in field, Calif., 1969. Contbr. articles to profl. jours. Pres. Palestine Arab Fund, Sacramento, 1982—85; observer mem. Palestine Nat. Coun., 1984—86. Fellow UN fellow, UN RWA, Jordan, 1957—62. Mem.: IEEE (control sys. pres. local chpt. 1966). Moslem. Avocations: swimming, walking, reading. Office: Calif State Univ 6000 J St Sacramento CA 95819

YOUST, DAVID BENNETT, career development educator; b. May 14, 1938; s. Howard Page and Agnes (Bennett) Y.; m. Faye Phillips; children: Stacy Sillen, Shawna Sannier, Liesl Berger, Genny Phillips, Elizabeth Curley. BS, SUNY-Albany, 1959; MS, Syracuse (N.Y.) U., 1961; PhD, Mich. State U., 1969. Cert. career counselor Nat. Bd. Counselor Cert. Tchr. sci. North Syracuse schs., 1959-61; adminstr. student pers. Mich. State U., 1961-63; counselor, prin., program dir. Rochester (N.Y.) schs., 1963-70; sr. rsch. technologist Eastman Kodak Co., Rochester, 1970-72; asst. dean Nat. Tech. Inst. for the Deaf, Rochester Inst. Tech., 1972-74; mem. faculty Empire State Coll., SUNY, Rochester, 1974-78; exec. dir. Career Devel. Coun., Corning, N.Y., 1978-84; mgr. engring. tng. Corning Inc., 1984-90; ptnr. Phillips Tng. Sys., Inc., 1989—. Former adj. faculty Corning C.C., Elmira Coll., C.W. Post Coll.; mediator cmty. dispute resolution; instr. MSF motorcycle safety. Author guide, articles in field; former mem. editl. bd. Career Devel. Quar. Former bd. dirs. 171 Cedar Arts Ctr. Mem. ASTD, ACA, Nat. Career Devel. Assn. (Merit award 1970, 84), Am. Ednl. Rsch. Assn., Assn. Measurement and Evaluation in Guidance. Republican. E-mail: ptsdavid@aol.com.

YOUSUFF, SARAH SAFIA, physician; b. Binghampton, N.Y., Dec. 8, 1960; d. Mohamed and Razia (Sivaramasastry) Y.; m. Donald John Sudy, Aug. 7, 1993. BA in Zoology, U. Tex., Austin, 1982; MD, U. Tex., 1988. Diplomate Am. Bd. Anesthesiology, Am. Bd. Pain Medicine. Fellow in med. mgmt. U. N.C., Chapel Hill, 1992-93; resident in anesthesiology U. Wash., Seattle, 1988-92; staff anesthesiologist Kron Med., Research Triangle Park, N.C., 1992-94; med. dir. dept. anesthesiology Southwest Hosp., Little Rock, 1994-96; pres. Southwest Anesthesia Assocs., 1994-95; ptnr. Pain Cons. Ark., 1995-96; dir. Southwest Pain Mgmt. Clinic, Little Rock, 1995—. Capt. USAR, 1990—. Mem. AMA, Am. Soc. Anesthesiology, Am. Coll. Physician Execs., Ark. Med. Soc., Pulaski County Med. Soc., Internat. Spinal Injection Soc.,

Internat. Assn. for Study of Pain, Am. Acad. of Pain Medicine, Am. Soc. of Regional Anesthesia. Avocations: photography, international travel, computers, international healthcare. Home: 4 Rebel Rd Louisville KY 40206-1411 Office: Southwest Pain Mgmt Clinic 11401 Interstate 30 Little Rock AR 72209-7042

YOUTCHEFF, JOHN SHELDON, physicist; b. Newark, Apr. 16, 1925; s. Slav Joseph and Florence Catherine (Davidson) Y.; m. Elsie Marianne, June 17, 1950; children: Karen Janette, John Sheldon, Mark Allen, Heidi Mary Anne, Lisa Ellen. AB, Columbia U., 1949, BS, 1950; PhD, UCLA, 1953. Registered profl. engr., Calif., D.C. Ops. analyst Gen. Elec. Co., Ithaca, N.Y., 1953-56, cons., engr. missile & space divsn. Phila., 1956-64, mgr. advanced reliability programs, 1964-72; mgr. reliability and maintainability Litton Industries, College Park, Md., 1972-73; program mgr. U.S. Postal Svc. Headquarters, Washington, 1973—. Instr. U. Pa., 1965-66, Villanova U., 1957—. Lt. USAAF, 1943-46; to comdr. USNR, 1946—. Fellow AAAS, Br. Interplanetary Soc., AIAA, Explorers Club; mem. IEEE (sr.), Ops. Rsch. Soc., Rsch. Soc. Am., Am. Math. Soc., Am. Physics Soc., Am. Cehm. Soc., Am. Astron. Soc., Am. Geol. Socl., Nat. Soc. Profl. Engrs., Engring. and Tech. Socs., Coun. Del. Vly. (spkrs. bur.), USCG Aux. (flotilla comdr.), Res. Officers Assn., Am. Legion, Optimists Internat. (pres. Valley Forge chpt. 1970-71). Roman Catholic. Home: 1400 S Joyce St Apt 1406 Arlington VA 22202-1852 Office: L'Enfant Plz Washington DC 20260

YOVANOFF, JAMES, rheumatologist; b. Rochester, N.Y., Sept. 9, 1948; BA, Hobart Coll., 1970; MD, Tufts U., 1974. Diplomate Am. Bd. Internal Medicine/Rheumatology. Intern, resident St. Mary's Med. Ctr., Long Beach, Calif., 1974-77; fellow in rheumatology Walter Reed Army Med. Ctr., 1980-82; chief rheumatology svc. U.S. Army Med. Ctr., Tacoma, 1982-87; pvt. practice rheumatology Glens Falls, N.Y., 1987-2001. Col. U.S. Army, ret. Fellow Am. Coll. Rheumatology; mem. N.Y. State Med. Soc. Office: 52 Park St Glens Falls NY 12801 E-mail: yovanoff@usa.net.

YOVETICH, NANCY ANN, business executive, research scientist; b. Pitts., Oct. 31, 1965; d. George Yovetich and Frances Brant; m. Marty Stanley Kraut, June 11, 1994; children: Hannah Elizabeth Kraut, Nicholas George Kraut. BA, Allegheny Coll., 1987; PhD, U. N.C., 1997. Rsch. assoc. U. Pitts., 1987-88; psychology instr. U. N.C., Chapel Hill, 1989-92; rsch. asst. N.H.-Dartmouth Psychiat. Rsch. Ctr., Lebanon, 1994-95; SAS programmer analyst Rho, Inc., Chapel Hill, 1992-94, 95-97, sr. project mgr., 1997-99, dir. project ops., 1999—. Editor Representative Rsch. in Social Psychology, 1991-92. Recipient Nat. Rsch. Svc. award NIMH, 1993-94, Theodore and Vaida Stanley Rsch. award Theodore and Vaida Stanley Found., 1994-95. Mem. Drug Info. Assn., Phi Beta Kappa. Office: Rho Inc 100 Eastowne Dr Chapel Hill NC 27514-2286 E-mail: nyovetich@rhoworld.com.

YOVICH, DANIEL JOHN, educator; b. Chgo., Mar. 5, 1930; s. Milan D. and Sophie (Dorociak) Y.; m. Anita Barbara Moreland, Feb. 7, 1959; children: Daniel, Amy, David, Julie Ann. Ph.B., DePaul U., 1952; MA, Governors State U., 1975, MS, 1976. Cert. reality therapist, cert. profl. mgr., PMA instr. Formulator Nat. Lead Co., 1950-52, 56-59; researcher Montgomery Ward, Chgo., 1959-62; tech. dir. Riley Bros., Inc., Burlington, Iowa, 1962-66, Mortell Co., Kankakee, Ill., 1966-70; exec. dir. Dan Yovich Assocs., 1970-79; asst. prof. Purdue U., Hammond, Ind., 1979-84, assoc. prof., 1984-90, prof., 1990-2000, prof. emeritus, 2000—. Instr. Army Security Agy. Sch., 1954-56; instr. Napoleon Hill Acad., 1965-66; cons. Learning House, 1964—; instr. Kankakee C. C. Continuing Edn., 1976; assoc. Hill, Zediker & Assocs. Psychologists, Kankakee, 1975-79; mem adv. bd. Nat. Congress of Inventor Orgns., 1984; vis. prof. Grand Valley State U., 2000—, Northwood U., 2001—. Author: Applied Creativity; prdr., moderator: (program) Careers Unlimited, Sta. WCIU-TV, Chgo., 1967; contbr. articles to profl. jours.; patentee game Krypto, coating Sanitane. Mem. community adv. council Governors State U., 1978; mem. Hammond (Ind.) Hist. Soc. Served to 1st lt. AUS, 1952-56. Recipient Outstanding Citizen Award News Pub. Co. Am., 1971, Outstanding Tchr. award Purdue U., 1980, 82, 83, Faculty Service award Nat. U. Continuing Edn. Assn., 1984, Disting. Service award Purdue U.-Calumet Alumni Assn., 1988, Arthur Young award Venture Mag., 1988, Entrepreneurial Edn. award Inc. Mag., 1990, Indiana Spirit of Innovation award, 1996. Mem. World Future Soc., Nat. Mgmt. Assn., Am. Soc. Tng. and Devel., Am. Soc. Profl. Supervision (exec. sec. 1986), Inventors and Entrepreneurs Soc. Am. (founder, exec. dir. 1984), Global Intuition Network, Internat. Creativity Network, Infantry Officer Cand. Sch. Alumni Assn. (life), Napoleon Hill Found., Inst. Reality Therapy, Inst. Contemporary Living, Soc. Am. Inventors (life), Am. Legion, K.C., Vets. of the Battle of the Bulge (historian). Home: 3527 Whispering Brook Dr SE Kentwood MI 49508-3733 E-mail: danyovich@prodigy.net.

YOVITS, MARSHALL CLINTON, computer and information science educator, university dean; b. Bklyn., May 16, 1923; s. Louis Frederick and Rebecca (Gerber) Y.; m. Anita S. Friedman, Aug. 2, 1952; children: Bruce J., Mara F., Steven. BS, Union Coll., Schenectady, 1944, MS, 1948, Yale U., 1949, PhD, 1951. Sr. physicist John Hopkins U., 1951-56; physicist electronics br. Office Naval Rsch., Washington, 1956, head info. systems br., 1956-62; dir. Naval Analysis Group, 1962-66; prof., chmn. dept. computer and info. sci. Ohio State U., 1966-78, prof., 1978-79; prof. computer and info. sci. Sch. of Sci., Ind. U., Purdue U., Indpls., 1980—, dean., 1980-88; prof. emeritus Ind. U., Purdue U., 1993—. Gen. chmn. Computer Sci. conf. NSF, 1973 Editor: (with Scott Cameron) Self-Organizing Systems, Proc. Interdisciplinary Conf., 1960, Large-Capacity Memory Techniques for Computing Systems, 1961 (with George T. Jacobi, Gordon D. Goldstein) Self-Organizing Systems, 1962, (with D.M. Gilford, R.H. Wilcox, E. Staveley, H.D. Lerner) Research Program Effectiveness, 1966, Advances in Computers, Vol. 11, 1971; editor: series Advances in Computers, Vols. 13-40; contbr. rsch. articles to profl. jours. AEC fellow, 1950-51, Indpls. Ctr. Advanced Rsch. fellow, 1988-89; recipient Navy Superior Civilian Service award, 1964; Navy Outstanding Performance award, 1961 Fellow AAAS (chmn. coun. sect. T 1985-88, chmn. 1996-98), IEEE (computer soc. chmn. awards com. 1989, bd. govs. 1988-89, computer pioneer award 1990), Assn. for Computing Machinery (coun., gen. chmn. computer sci. conf. 1982), EDUCOM (nominating com.), Sigma Xi. Home: 9016 Dewberry Ct Indianapolis IN 46260-1527 E-mail: myovits@iupui.edu.

YOZWIAK, BERNARD JAMES, retired mathematics educator and academic administrator; b. Youngstown, Ohio, July 5, 1919; s. Walter J. and Anna (Baluch) Y.; m. Helen A. Mika, Aug. 28, 1943; children— Ruth (Mrs. Charles W. Lewis), John B., Mark S., Bernard P. AB, Marietta Coll., 1940; MS, U. Pitts., 1951, PhD, 1961; LLD, Youngstown State U., 1992. Office clk. Youngstown Sheet & Tube Co., 1940-41, 44-45; instr. math. and sci., prin. Fowler (Ohio) Twp. High Sch., 1941-42, 45-47; prof. math., chmn. math. dept. Youngstown State U., 1947—, dean Coll. Arts and Scis., 1971-92, ret., 1992—. Recipient Watson Distinguished Prof. award, 1961; NSF sci. faculty fellow, 1958-60 Mem. Math. Assn. Am. (chmn. Ohio sect. 1970-71), AAUP, Sigma Xi. Home: 2080 S Schenley Ave Youngstown OH 44511-1271

YRIGOYEN, CHARLES, JR. church denomination executive; b. Phila., Dec. 9, 1937; s. Charles and Erma Mae (Suters) Y.; m. Jeanette Alice Brittingham, Dec. 13, 1958; children: Debra Jean, Charles III. BS in Econs., U. Pa., 1959; BD, Lancaster (Pa.) Theol. Sem., 1962; ThM, Ea. Bapt. Theol. Sem., Phila., 1964; PhD, Temple U., 1973; DD (hon.), Albright Coll., 1987. Ordained to ministry United Meth. Ch., 1960. Pastor various chs. Meth. Ch., Pa., 1958-66, campus min., 1966-68; chaplain, prof. religion Albright Coll., Reading, Pa., 1968-82; gen. sec. Gen. Com. on Archives and History, United Meth. Ch., Madison, N.J., 1982—. Vis. scholar Union Theol. Sem., N.Y.C., 1980, adj. prof., 1982-93, 2000—; adj. prof. ch. history Drew U., Madison, 1982—; adj. prof. Moravian Theol. Sem., Bethlehem, Pa., 1994-02; exec. com. World Meth. Coun., 1986—; bd. dirs. Wesley Works Editl. Project; adj. prof. Luth. Theol. Sem., Phila., 1999. Author: Acts for Our Time, 1987, John Wesley: Holiness of Heart and Life, 1996, Belief Matters: United Methodism's Doctrinal Standards, 2001; editor: Reformed and Catholic, 1978, Catholic and Reformed, 1979, Historical Dictionary of Methodism, 1996, The Global Impact of the Wesleyan Traditions and Their Related Movements, 2002, Meth. History Jour., 1982—. Trustee Ocean City (N.J.) Tabernacle Assn., Epworth (England) Old Rectory, Evangel. Sch. Theology. Masland fellow Union Theol. Sem., 1975, 80. Mem. World Meth. Hist. Soc. (gen. sec. 1987—), Wesley Hist. Soc., Wesleyan Theol. Soc., Am. Soc. Ch. History, Charles Wesley Soc., Oxford Inst. Meth. Theol. Studies, Mercersburg Soc. (bd. dirs.), United Meth. Hist. Soc. Republican. Home: 2 Hemlock Ln Morristown NJ 07960-6774 Office: Gen Com on Archives and History PO Box 127 Madison NJ 07940-0127 E-mail: cyrigoyen@gcah.org.

YSSELDYKE, JAMES EDWARD, psychology educator, dean; b. Grand Rapids, Mich., Jan. 1, 1944; 2 children. Student in psychology, Calvin Coll., 1962-65; BA in Psychology, Biology, Western Mich. U., 1966; MA in Sch. Psychology, U. Ill., 1968, PhD, 1971. Lic. cons. psychologist, Minn. Tchr. spl. edn. Kent County Juvenile Ct. Ctr., Grand Rapids, 1966-67; rsch. asst. U. Ill. Inst. Rsch. on Exceptional Children, 1969-70, tchg. asst. dept. ednl. psychology, 1970; sch. psychology intern Oakland County Schs., Pontiac, Mich., 1970-71; asst. prof. sch. psychology Pa. State U., 1971-75, assoc. prof., 1975, U. Minn., Mpls., 1975-79, prof., 1979-91, dir. Inst. Rsch. on Learning Disabilities, 1977-83, dir. Nat. Sch. Psychology Insvc. Tng. Network, 1977-83, dir. sch. psychology program, 1987-93, dir. Nat. Ctr. on Ednl. Outcomes, 1991-99, assoc. dean for rsch., 2000—. Emma Birkmaier endowed prof. U. Minn., 1998-2000; advisor, cons. and researcher in field. Author: (with J. Salvia) Assessment in Special and Remedial Education, 1985, 8th edit., 2001, (with B. Algozzine and M. Thurlow) Critical Issues in Special and Remedial Education, 1992, 3d edit., 2000, Strategies and Tactics for Effective Instruction, 1997, (with S.L. Christenson) Functional Assessment of Academic Behavior, 1993; editor: Exceptional Children, 1984-90; assoc. editor: The School Psychologist, 1972-75, mem. editorial bd., cons. editor numerous jours.; contbr. chpts. to books and articles to jours. Recipient Disting. Tchg. award U. Minn., 1988, Disting. Alumni award U. Ill. Coll. Edn., 1998; fellow NIMH, 1967-69; grantee in field. Fellow APA (Lightner Witmer award 1973); mem. ASCD, APA, NASP, Am. Ednl. Rsch. Assn., Coun. for Exceptional Children (Rsch. award 1995), Coun. for Ednl. Diagnostic Svcs. Office: Coll of Edn and Human Devel 104 Burton Hall 178 Pillsbury Dr SE Minneapolis MN 55455-0296 E-mail: jim@umn.edu.

YTTREHUS, ROLV BERGER, composer, educator; b. Duluth, Minn., Mar. 12, 1926; s. Chris and Petra (Andal) Y. BA, U. Minn., Duluth, 1950; MusM, U. Mich., 1953; diploma, Acad. Santa Cecilia, Rome, 1962; studies with Nadia Boulanger, Paris, 1954-55; studies with Roger Sessions, Princeton, N.J., 1957-60; studies with, Aaron Copland, Tanglewood, 1958. Instr. music U. Mo., Columbia, 1963-68; asst. prof. Purdue U., West Lafayette, Ind., 1968-69; assoc. prof. U. Wis., Oshkosh, 1969-77; prof. Rutgers U., New Brunswick, N.J., 1977-96; prof. emeritus, 1996—; recorded with Composers Recs., Inc., 1st Edition Records, Centaur Records, MMC Records. Lectr. Internat. Ferienkurse Für Neue Musik, Darmstadt, Germany, 1994. Composer: Music for Winds, Percussion and Viola, 1961, Expressioni Per Orchestra, 1962, Music for Winds, Percussion, Cello and Voices, 1969, Quintet, 1973, Sextet, 1974, Gradus Ad Parnassum, 1979, Sonata for Percussion and Piano, 1983, Explorations for Solo Piano, 1985, Sonata for Cello and Piano, 1988, Raritan Variation (solo piano), 1989, Symphony No. 1, 1998, Espressioni per Orchestra performed by Philharm. Orch., Augsburg, Germany, 1996, Symphony No. 1, 1998 (performed with Warsaw Nat. Philharm. Orch. on Warsaw Autumn Festival 1998), Plectrum Spectrum, 2000; CRI CD 843 the Music of Rolv Yttrehus issued 2000. Served with USN, 1944-46, PTO. Recipient award Minn. Fedn. Music Clubs, 1957, Margaret Lee Crofts award, Tanglewood, Mass., 1958, award N.J. Coun. on Arts, 1989; Fulbright scholar, 1954, scholar Govt. of Italy, 1960-62; fellow Composers Conf., 1971, 72, 75; grantee Nat. Endowment for Arts, 1976. Mem. Internat. Soc. Contemporary Music (bd. dirs. 1979—), Am. Composers Alliance (rec. award 1985), Composers Guild N.J. (pres. 1985-92). Avocation: reading. Home: One Woods Circle East Brunswick NJ 08816 E-mail: yttrehus@rci.rutgers.edu.

YU, AITING TOBEY, engineering executive; b. Chekiang, China, Jan. 6, 1921; came to U.S., 1945, naturalized, 1955; s. H.K. and A. (Chow) Y.; m. Natalie Kwok, Nov. 10, 1951; children: Pamela, Leonard T. BS, Nat. Cen. U., Chungking, China, 1943; SM, MIT, 1946; PhD, Lehigh U., 1949; MBA, Columbia U., 1972. Registered profl. engr., Fla. Asst. prof. engring. NYU, 1949-51; design engr. Hewitt-Robins Inc., 1951-54, chief design engr., 1955-58, engring. mgr., 1958-59, dir. systems engring. N.J., 1967-68, v.p. ops., 1968-71; tech. dir. West S.Am. Overseas Corp., N.Y.C., 1959-67; prin. A.T. Yu Cons. Engrs., 1971-72; co-founder, chmn. Orba Corp., Mountain Lakes, N.J., 1972—, now chmn. emeritus. Contbr. articles to profl. jours; patentee in field. Recipient nat. outstanding engring. achievement awards by ASCE, NSPE, AIME, ASME; inducted into Nat. Mining Hall of Fame, 1998. Mem. NAE, AIME (chmn. minerals processing div., SME pres. 1986), NSPE, Nat. Acad. Engring., Sigma Xi. Home: 36750 Us Highway 19 N Palm Harbor FL 34684-1239 also: 4303A Hana Hwy Haiku HI 96708-5303 Office: Orba Corp 1250 W Sam Houston Pkwy S Houston TX 77042-1916

YU, ANDREW, minister; b. Fu-Yang, Chekian, China, Feb. 28, 1927; came to the U.S., 1972; s. Kung-Chu Yu and Mei-Chen Liu; m. Julie Yu, July 13, 1957; children: Peter, Ruth. BTh, Taiwan Bapt. Theol. Sem., Taipei, 1957; postgrad., Tanghai U., Taichung, Taiwan, 1965; MA in Ministry Studies, Moody Bible Inst., 1991; postgrad., Bibl. Archaeology Soc., 1993, Fuller Theol. Sem., 1996, Fuqua Internat. Sch. Christian Comm., 1998. Cert. pastoral counseling. Jour. clk. Bankers Trust Co., N.Y.C., 1972-80; pastoral coounselor Am. Assn. Christian Counseling, Forest, Va., 1991—; minister Manhattan Chinese Bapt. Ch., N.Y.C., 1980—, sr. pastor, 1986—. Pastorial counselor Am. Assn. Christian Counseling, Forest, Va., 1991—. Author: Rekinling the Fires of Revial, 1993, A Master Piece of Spirituality, 1995; editor Chinese Christian Workers, 1999—. Recipient Lifetime Royal Patronage status Kevin, Prince Regent Princepality of Hutt River Province, Australia, 1994. Mem. Chinese Speaking Writers Abroad, Chinese Writers Assn. N.Y., Poetry Soc. Am. Avocations: reading, writing, music, traveling, collecting. Home: Apt 20E 675 Water St New York NY 10002 Office: Manhattan Chinese Bapt Ch 236 W 72nd St New York NY 10023

YU, ANTHONY C. religion and literature educator; b. Hong Kong, Oct. 6, 1938; came to U.S., 1956, naturalized, 1976; s. P.C. and Norma (Au) Y.; m. Priscilla Tang, Sept. 18, 1963; 1 son, Christopher Dietrich. BA, Houghton Coll., 1960; STB, Fuller Theol. Sem., 1963; PhD, U. Chgo., 1969, DLitt, 1996. Instr. U. Ill., Chgo., 1967-68; asst. prof. U. Chgo., 1968-74, assoc. prof., 1974-78, prof., 1978-88, Carl Darling Buck disting. svc. prof. humanities Div. Sch., Dept. East Asian Langs., Comparative Lit. and East Asian Langs. & Civilizations, English, 1988—. Assoc. vis. prof. Ind. U., Bloomington, 1975; Whitney J. Oates short-term vis. fellow Princeton U., 1986; disting. vis. prof. Faculty of Arts, U. Alta., Can., 1992; mem. joint com. on study Chinese civilization Am. Coun. Learned Socs., 1980-86, bd. dirs., 1986-94; regional chmn. Mellon Fellowship in Humanities, 1982-92; bd. dirs. Ill. Humanities Coun., 1995—; vis. prof. dept. religion Chinese U. Hong Kong, 1997. Asst. editor Jour. Asian Studies, 1975-78; co-editor Jour. Religion, 1980—; author, editor: Parnassus Revisited, 1973; editor, translator: The Journey to the West, 4 vols., 1977-83, Essays on The Journey to the West and Other Studies (in Chinese), 1989; co-editor (with Mary Gerhart) Morphologies of Faith: Essays on Religion and Culture in Honor of Nathan A. Scott, Jr., 1990, Rereading the Stone: Desire and the Making of Fiction in Dream of the Red Chamber, 1997. Recipient Gordon J. Laing prize, 1983; Danforth fellow, 1960-67; Guggenheim fellow, 1976-77; NEH translation grantee, 1977-82; Am. Coun. Learned Socs. sr. fellow, 1986-87; Masterworks Study grant NEH Seminar for Pub. Sch. Tchrs., 1992; elected academician Academia Sinica, 1998; Phi Beta Kappa vis. scholar 2001-02. Fellow Am. Acad. Arts and Scis.; mem. MLA (exec. coun. 1998—2001), Assn. for Asian Studies, Am. Acad. Religion (bd. dirs. 1995-97), Am. Comparative Lit. Assn., Milton Soc. Am., Arts Club. Home: 950 N Clark St Unit G Chicago IL 60610-8702 Office: U Chicago 1025 E 58th St Chicago IL 60637-1509 E-mail: acyu@midway.uchicago.edu.

YU, BIN, statistician, educator; b. Harbin, China, Mar. 18, 1963; arrived in U.S., 1985; d. Dibei Yu, Xiaomin Yu; m. Ke-ning Shen, June 15, 1987; children: Maya Yu Shen, Matthew Yan Shen. BS in Math, Peking U., 1984; MA in Stats., U. Calif. Berkeley, 1987, PhD of Stats., 1990. Asst. prof. U. Wis. Madison, 1990—92; asst. prof., assoc. prof. U. Calif. Berkeley, 1993—2000, prof., 2001—. Postdoctoral fellow MSRI, Berkeley, 1991; vis. asst. prof. Yale U., New Haven, 1993; mem. tech. staff Bell Labs. Lucent, Murray Hill, NJ, 1997—2000. Contbr. Grantee, ARO, 1991, 1994, 1998, NSF, 1994, 1998, 2001. Fellow: IEEE, Inst. Math. Stats.; mem.: Am. Stats. Assn. Achievements include patents for lossless coding and data network tomography. Avocations: reading, walking, swimming, movies. Office: Univ Calif Berkeley 367 Evans Hall #3860 Berkeley CA 94720

YU, CARLOS CHENG, surgeon; b. Zamboanga City, Philippines, Apr. 29, 1940; MD, Far Eastern U., 1966. Diplomate Am. Bd. Surgery. Intern Mt. Sinai Hosp., Milw., 1967-68; resident St. John Hosp., Detroit, 1968-72; pvt. practice New London, Wis. Chmn. dept. surgery New London Family Med. Ctr., 1994—; mem. courtesy staff surgery Appleton Med. Ctr., New London, 1994—, Theda Clark Hosp., Neenah, Wis., 1994—, St. Elizabeth Hosp., Appleton, Wis. Mem. AMA, Am. Soc. Abdominal Surgeons. Office: PO Box 47 1420 Algoma St New London WI 54961-2104

YU, CHACK YUNG, pediatrics educator, molecular biologist; b. Guangdong, People Republic of China, Dec. 24, 1957; s. Hung Ho and Shui-Wo (Kwok) Y.; m. Lai-Chu, Apr. 23, 1987; children: Gayang Heidi, Gakit Richard. BS, Chinese U. Hong Kong, 1981, MPhil, 1983; DPhil, Oxford U., England, 1988. Asst. prof. Ohio State U., Columbus, 1990-96, assoc. prof., 1996—. Contbr. articles to profl. jours. Grantee NIH, Bethesda, Md., 1994—, March of Dimes, 1992-94; postdoctoral fellow Med. Rsch. Coun. Lab. Molecular Biology, Cambridge, England, 1987-90. Mem. AAAS, Am. Assn. Immunologists, Am. Soc. Human Genetics, Am. Soc. Microbiology, Am. Soc. Biochem. & Molecular Biology. Office: Children's Rsch Inst 700 Childrens Dr Columbus OH 43205-2664 E-mail: cyu@chi.osu.edu.

YU, CHARLES X. optical engineer, researcher; b. Shanghai, May 25, 1973; s. Peiwen Jin and Xiaoli Yu. BS, MIT, 1995, MS, 1996, PhD, 2001. Rschr. Hewlett-Packard Labs., Palo Alto, Calif., 1993—94, Tellabs, Hawthorne, NY, 1997, Bell Labs., Holmdel, NJ, 2000—. Contbr. articles to profl. jours. Mem.: IEEE, Optical Soc. Am., Tau Beta Phi, Sigma Xi, Eta Kappa Nu. Home: 805 Knollwood Dr Middletown NJ 07748 Office: Bell Labs Lucent Techs 791 Holmdel-Keyport Rd Holmdel NJ 07733

YU, CHEN, family practice physician; MD, Nat. Chung Cheng Med. Coll., China, 1945; postgrad., Harvard Med. Sch. Diplomate Am. Bd. Family Practice. Intern Chungking (China) Mcpl. Hosp., 1945; resident in gen. surgery Nanking (China) Mcpl. Hosp., 1946; intern Elizabeth (N.J.) Gen. Hosp., 1947; resident in ob.-gyn. Lyingin Hosp., Chgo., pvt. practice family medicine, 1951—. Mem. AMA, R.I. Med. Assn. Address: 18 Blue Ridge Rd Cranston RI 02920-4522

YU, DAVID U.L. physicist, researcher; b. Hong Kong; m. Carolyn Yu; children: Christine, Moutier, Jonathan. BA, Seattle Pacific U., Seattle, WA, 1961; PHD, Wash. U., Seattle, WA, 1964. Tech. services dir. Computer Sciences Corp., Inglewood, Calif., 1972—74; v.p. Basic Tech. Inc., Manhattan Beach, 1975—83; pres. Duly Rsch. Inc., Rancho Palos Verdes, 1983—.

YU, FEI, internist; b. Beijing, China, Mar. 12, 1956; came to U.S., 1990; d. Longshan and Dan (Zheng) Y.; m. Xiangqun Fu, Jan. 7, 1984; 1 child, Danni. MD, Beijing Med. U., 1982; PhD in Med. Sci., Beijing Union Med. Coll., 1989. Diplomate Am. Bd. Internal Medicine. Intern The People's Hosp., Beijing Med. U., 1981-82; resident in internal medicine Jishuitan Hosp., Beijing, 1983-84, Beijing Union Med. Coll. Hosp., 1984-87; clin. fellow hematology dept. internal medicine Beijing Union Med. Coll., Chinese Acad. Med. Scis., 1987-89; rsch. fellow dept. devel. cell biology Sloan-Ketterng Inst. Cancer Rsch., N.Y.C., 1991-93; rsch. fellow dept. internal medicine Columbia U. Coll. Physicians and Surgeons, 1993—95; resident in medicine N.Y. Meth. Hosp. , Bklyn., 1996-99; physician Regal Med. PC, Clifton, N.J., 2000—. Contbr. articles to profl. jours. Mem. AMA, ACP. Avocations: music, swimming, novel reading, travel, stamp collecting. Office: 1114 Clifton Ave Clifton NJ 07013 E-mail: dnffy@aol.com.

YU, FERMIN TONG, retired surgeon; b. Lianga, The Philippines, 1934; came to U.S., 1964; s. Huan Tee and Song (Tong) Y.; m. Carol Ann Swartz, July 15, 1967; children: Christopher, Michael. AA, U. San Carlos, Cebu City, The Philippines, 1954; MD, U. Santo Tomas, Manila, 1962. Diplomate Am. Bd. Surgery, 1970. Intern St. Elizabeth Hosp., Youngstown, Ohio, 1964-65, resident, 1965-69; with St. Joseph Hosp., Warren, ret., 1999. Fellow: ACS.

YU, FU-LI, biochemistry educator, cancer researcher; b. Beijing, May 2, 1934; came to U.S., 1958; s. Ling-Ko and Ying (Chang) Y.; m. Jie Feng, Apr. 20, 1980; children: Jimmy Chan-Ching, Chan-Mei. MS, U. Ala., 1962; PhD, U. Calif., San Francisco, 1965. Asst. prof. biochemistry Jefferson Med. Coll., Phila., 1973-79; asst. prof. biomed. scis. U. Ill. Coll. Medicine, Rockford, 1979-80, assoc. prof., 1980-85, prof., 1985—, head dept., 1988—. Contbr. articles to Proc. NAS, Nature, Jour. Biol. Chemistry, Carcinogenesis. Rsch. grantee NIH, 1974-77, 78-80, 81-90, 95—, Am. Cancer Soc., 1978-81. Mem. Am. Soc. Biochem. and Molecular Biology, Am. Assn. for Cancer Rsch., Am. Chem. Soc. Achievements include discovery of "free" RNA polymerases, Aflatoxin B1 binding to cytosine base in DNA, estrogens as initiators for breast cancer. Office: U Ill Coll Medicine 1601 Parkview Ave Rockford IL 61107-1822

YU, FUSHUN, physiologist, research scientist; b. Changchun, Jilin, People's Republic of China, Sept. 30, 1960; d. Dongxiu and Shunsan (Li) Y.; 1 child, Shi, Andy Piao. MD, Norman Bethune U. Med. Scis., Changchun, 1984, MSc in Med. Biochemistry, 1989; PhD in Cellular and Molecular Muscle Physiology, Karolinska Inst., Stockholm, 1999. Lectr., rsch. assoc. dept. clin. biochemistry Hosp. Dalian Med. U., Liaoning Province, People's Republic of China, 1991-94; lectr. Noll Physiol. Rsch. Ctr. Pa. State U., University Park, 1997-99; post-doctoral rschr. dept. pharmacology Ohio State U., Columbus, 1999-2000; lectr., rsch. scientist Noll Physiol. Rsch. Ctr. Pa. State U., University Park, 2000—. Fellow Karolinska Inst., Stockholm, 1994-97; Doktorand-tjänst scholar Karolinska Inst., 1997-98; recipient Outstanding Young Scientist awards Jilin Biochemistry Soc., People's Republic of China, 1989. Mem. Biophysical Soc., Am. Physiol. Soc., Sigma Xi. Office: Noll Physiol Rsch Ctr Pa State U University Park PA 16802-6900 E-mail: fxy104@psu.edu.

YU, GEORGE TZUCHIAO, political science educator; b. London, May 16, 1931; s. Wangteh and Ying (Ho) Y.; m. Priscilla Chang, Aug. 11, 1957; children: Anthony, Phillip. AB, U. Calif., Berkeley, 1954, MA, 1957, PhD, 1961. Asst. prof. polit. sci. U. N.C., Chapel Hill, 1961-65; assoc. prof. polit. sci. U. Ill., Urbana, 1965-70, prof., 1970—, head dept., 1987-92, dir. Ctr. for East Asian and Pacific Studies, 1992—, dir. grad. studies, 1981-85, chair Asian Am. studies com., 1997—. Vis. sr. lectr. polit. sci. Univ. Coll., Nairobi, 1968. Author: The Chinese Anarchist Movement, 1961, 65, Party Politics in Republican China, 1966, China and Tanzania, 1970, China's African Policy, 1975, Intra-Asian International Relations, 1977, Modern China and Its Revolutionary Process, 1985, American Studies in China, 1993, China in Transition, 1994, Asia's New World Order, 1997, Mongolia and Northeast Asia, 1999. Grantee, Social Sci. Rsch. Coun., 1967—68, 1970—71, NEH, 1978—81, 1984—86, Earhart Found., 1976—77, 1981—83, 1988, Ford Found., 1985—87, 1989, 1992, Freeman Found., 1996, 1997, 1999, 2001. Mem. Assn. Asian Studies. Office: 702 S Wright St Urbana IL 61801-3631 E-mail: g-yu@uiuc.edu.

YU, JEN, medical educator; b. Taipei, Taiwan, Jan. 23, 1943; came to U.S., 1969; s. Chin Chuan and Shiu Lan (Lin) Y.; m. Janet Chen, June 16, 1973; children: Benjamin, Christopher. MD, Nat. Taiwan U., 1968; PhD in Physiology, U. Pa., 1972. Diplomate Am. Bd. Phys. Medicine and Rehab. Intern Phila. Gen. Hosp., 1972-73; resident in phys. medicine and rehab. Hosps. of U. Pa., 1973-75; asst. prof. dept. phys. medicine and rehab. U. Pa. Sch. Medicine, Phila., 1975-76, U. Tex. Health Sci. Ctr., San Antonio, 1976-79, assoc. prof., 1979-81; prof. dept. phys. medicine and rehab. U. Calif. Irvine Coll. Medicine, 1981-82, prof., chmn. dept. phys. medicine and rehab., 1982—. Contbr. articles to profl. jours. Mem. Am. Acad. Phys. Medicine and Rehab., Am. Congress Rehab. Medicine, Assn. Acad. Physiatrists, Am. Assn. Anatomists, Soc. for Neurosci. Office: U Calif Irvine Med Ctr Dept Phys Medicine & Rehab 101 The City Dr Orange CA 92868-3201 E-mail: jyu@uci.edu.

YU, JIRONG, aerospace professional; b. Jiangsu, China, May 4, 1954; came to U.S., 1989; s. Bingchang Yu and Henquan Gong; m. Jianyi Li, Oct. 1, 1981; 1 child, Daijun. BSEE with highest honors, S.E. U., Nanjing, Jiangsu, 1978,

MSEE, 1981; PhDEE, Colo. State U., 1994. Postdoctoral asst. U. Ill., Urbana, 1994, rsch. assoc., 1995; sr. engr. Sci. and Tech. Corp., Hampton, Va., 1996-98; aerospace technologist NASA Langley Rsch. Ctr, 1999—. Presenter progl. confs., 1999-2000. Contbr. articles to sci. jours. Recipient postdoctoral award CEDAR program NSF, 1995. Mem. Soc. Photo-Optical Instrumentation Engrs. (mem. program com. 1st Internat. Aisa-Pacific Symposium 1998), Optical Soc. Am. (Allen prize 1994), Internat. Soc. Optical Engring. Office: NASA Langley Rsch Ctr 5 N Dryden St MS474 Hampton VA 23681-2109 E-mail: jirong.yu@larc.nasa.gov.

YU, JIUN-DER, mechanics researcher; b. Taipei, Taiwan, May 19, 1964; came to U.S., 1990; s. Tzu-I Yu; m. Wei-Li Liu, Jan. 25, 1998. BSE, Nat. Taiwan U., Taipei, 1986; MSE, Nat. Taiwan U., 1990; PhD, Princeton U., 1995. Rsch. assoc. Princeton (N.J.) U., 1995-96; lectr. Nanyang Technol. U., Singapore, 1997-98; sr. mem. tech. staff Epson R & D, Inc., San Jose, Calif., 1998—. Contbr. papers to profl. jours.; patent pending in field. Donator, vol. Gold Sage Temple, San Jose, Calif., 1999. Fu-Chien scholar, 1985, 89; Engring. Sch. Dean's fellow Princeton U., 1990-91, Princeton Honorific fellow, 1995. Mem. IEEE (assoc.), Phi Tau Phi. Office: EPAL 3145 Porter Dr Ste 104 Palo Alto CA 94304-1224 E-mail: yu.jiunder@erd.epson.com.

YU, MAY HUANG, librarian, educator; b. Chengdu, Sichuan, China, June 24; came to the U.S., 1989; s. Dazhou Huang and Jiangzhen Yu; m. Lixin Yu; 1 child, Michael. Student, Beijing U., 1988; LLB, State Normal U. Sichuan, Chengdu, 1982; MLS, SUNY, Albany, 1996. Cert. pub. libr., N.Y. Tchr. Fuxing H.S., Qingcheng, Sichuan, China, 1975-78; asst. prof. State Normal U. Sichuan, Chengdu, 1982-89; libr., instr. Alcorn State U., Lorman, Miss., 1996-97; web developer, metadata libr. Fla. State U., Tallahassee, 1998—2000; libr., instr. Alcorn State (Miss.) U., 2000—, head Instrnl. Media Ctr.; media libr., instr. Alcorn State U., 2000—. Spl. corr. Jour. Ethics, Chengdu, 1985-89; gen. sec. Sichuan State Ethics Assn., Chengdu, 1985-89. Editor: The Dictionary of Ethics, 1987. Named Outstanding Rschr., Assn. Philosophy and Social Scis. Sichuan Province, 1987. Mem. ALA, Internat. Fedn. Libr. Assns. and Instns. Avocations: table tennis, movies, travel. Home: 97 Plantation Dr Vicksburg MS 39183 Office: JD Boyd Libr 1000 ASU Dr Alcorn State MS 39096-7510 Fax: 601-877-3885. E-mail: mhyu.lorman@alcorn.edu.

YU, MEI-YU, medical researcher; b. Chongqing, China, Feb. 21, 1944; d. Wencheng Yu and Xiuying Pan; m. Bo-nan Jiang, Dec. 26, 1968; children: Bo, Hao. MD, Shanghai Med. U., 1968; MA, U. Tex. Austin, 1983, PhD, 1986. Physcian Changha Railway Hosp., Changsha, China, 1969-81; rschr. U. Tex., Austin, 1981-86; post-doctoral fellow U. Mich., Ann Arbor, 1987-89, asst. rsch. scientist, 1990-95, project dir., 1996—. Project dir., Healthy Asian Ams. project, 1996—; adminstr., Internat. Learning program, 1996—. Recipient fellowship, The Population Coun., N.Y., 1983-85, postdoctoral fellowship, NIA, 1987-89. Mem. Nat. Asian Women's Health Orgn's. Nat. Policy Coun., Internat. Coun. Women's Health Issues. Avocations: travel, danicng, music, movies. Office: U Mich Sch Nursing 400 N Ingalls St Ann Arbor MI 48109-0482 Fax: 734-647-9966. E-mail: yujiang@umich.edu.

YU, PETER LEGASPI, rehabilitation physician; b. Jan. 31, 1957; BS, U. Santo Tomas, Manila, 1975, MD, 1979. Diplomate Am. Bd. Ind. Med. Examiners, 1999, U.S. Ednl. Coun. Fgn. Med. Grads., 1980, U.S. Fed. Lic. Examination, 1982, Philippine Med. Bd. Examination, 1980. Intern Vets. Meml. Med. Ctr., Quezon City, The Philippines, 1979-80; resident in gen. surgery St. Clare's Hosp., N.Y.C., 1982-84; resident in phys. medicine U. Ala., Birmingham, 1984—87; pvt. practice, Niles, Mich., 1996—2002, Merrillville, Ind., South Bend, 1988—. Attending physiatrist Meth. Hosp., Gary, Ind., 1989—, Merrillville, 1989—, Porter Meml. Hosp., Ind., 1994—, Meml. Hosp., South Bend, 1988—, Lakeland Med. Ctr., Niles, 1995—, St. Anthony Med. Ctr., Crown Point, Ind., 1992—, St. Mary's Med. Ctr., Hobart, Ind., 1994—, St. Catherines Hosp., East Chicago, Ind., 1994—; rehab. dir. Healthwyn Hosp., South Bend, 1999-2002, Cardinal Nursing and Rehab. Ctr., South Bend, 1999-2001, Silverbrook Manor, Niles, Mich., 1997-2001. Mem. AMA, No. Ind. Rehab. Med. (pres.); Philippine Am. Physiatry Assn., (pres. 1999-2001), Asian Am. Med. Soc. (bd. dirs. 1999-02), Am. Acad. Phys. Medicine and Rehab., Am. Congress Rehab. Medicine, Am. Acad. Electrodiagnostic Medicine, Am. Acad. Exec. Physicians, Ind. Soc. Phys. Medicine and Rehab. Address: 8127 Merrillville Rd Merrillville IN 46410-6158 also: 115 S St Joseph Ave Niles MI 49120-2848

YU, PHILIP S, electrical engineer, researcher; b. Washington D.C., DC, Dec. 10, 1950; s. Kuo-Hwa and Metsung Yu. BSEE, Nat. Taiwan U., 1972; PhD, Stanford U., 1978; MBA, NYU, 1982. Registered Profl. Engr. From rsch. staff to mgr. IBM T.J. Watson Rsch. Ctr., Hawthorne, NY, 1978—96, mgr., 1996—. Editor: IEEE Transactions on Knowledge & Date Engring., 2001—. Fellow: ACM, IEEE. Office: IBM TJ Watson Research Center 19 Skyline Dr Hawthorne NY 10532 Office Fax: 914-784-7455. Business E-Mail: psyu@us.ibm.com.

YU, ROBERT KUAN-JEN, biochemistry educator; b. Chungking, China, Jan. 27, 1938; came to U.S., 1962; m. Helen Chow, July 1, 1972; children: David S., Jennifer S. BS, Tunghai U., Taiwan, 1960; PhD, U. Ill., 1967; Med.ScD. (hon.), Tokyo, 1980; MA (hon.), Yale U., 1985. Rsch. assoc., instr. Albert Einstein Coll. Medicine, Bronx, 1967-72; asst. prof. Yale U., New Haven, 1973-75, assoc. prof., 1975-82, prof., 1983-88; prof. biochemistry, chmn. dept. Med. Coll. Va. Va. Commonwealth U., Richmond, 1988-2000; dir. Inst. Mol. Med. Genetics Med. Coll., Augusta, Ga., 2000—. Mem. study sect. NIH, Washington, 1980-84, 96—; mem. Bd. Lab. Svcs., Va., 1994-98. Editor: Gangioside Structure Function and Biomedical Potential, 1984, New Trends in Ganglioside Research, 1988; contbr. over 500 articles to profl. publs. Josiah Macy scholar, 1979; grantee NIH, 1975—; recipient Va. Outstanding Scientist of Yr. award, 1995, Jacob Javits award NIH, 1984-91, Alexander von Humboldt award, 1990, GRA Eminent scholar, 2000. Mem. AAAS, Am. Soc. Cell Biology, Am. Soc. Neurochemistry (mem. coun. 1983-86, 91-95, pres. 2001—), Internat. Soc. Neurochemistry, Soc. Neurosci., Am. Soc. Biochemistry and Molecular Biology, Am. Chem. Soc., N.Y. Acad. Sci. Home: 821 River Bluff Rd North Augusta SC 29841-6056 Office: IMMAG Med Coll Ga 1120 15th St Augusta GA 30912-0004 E-mail: ryu@mail.mcg.edu.

YU, ROGER HONG, physics educator; b. Shanghai, China, Apr. 19, 1960; came to U.S., 1987; s. Rei Qian and Wei-Zen (Zhang) Y.; m. Ting Shi, Sept. 8, 1990; children: William S., John S. BS, Shanghai U. Sci. & Tech., 1982; MS, U. Mo., 1987; PhD, Mont. State U., 1990. Lectr. physics Shanghai U. Sci., 1982-85; tchg. asst. U. Mo., Kansas City, 1985-86, rsch. asst., 1986-87; tchg. asst. Mont. State U., Bozeman, 1987-88, rsch. asst., 1988-90; prof. physics Ctrl. Wash. U., Ellensburg, 1990—, dist. prof. rsch., chmn. dept. physics, 1997-2000; dean sch. natural scis. St. Edward's U., Austin, Tex., 2000—. Dir. undergrad. rsch. program Ctrl. Wash. U., Ellensburg, 1998—. Contbr. articles to profl. jours.; referee Phys. Rev. B. Mem. Am. Phys. Soc., Acoustic Soc. Am., Coun. Undergrad. Rsch., Associated Western Univs. (rsch. and edn. com.). Office: Sch Natural Scis St Edward's U Austin TX 78704 E-mail: rogery@admin.stedwards.edu.

YU, SHAN, artist; b. Fuzhou, Fujian, China, Oct. 24, 1949; came to the U.S., 1986; s. Yiqiang Chen and Juan Yue Yu; m. Hui Ling Du, Oct. 5, 1980; 1 child, Han. BA, Fujian Art Sch., Fuzhou, 1980; postgrad., Shanghai (China) Theater Acad., 1985-86; MFA, Boston U., 1989. Art tchr. Fujian Art Sch., Fuzhou, 1980-85; chief set designer Visual Design Assn., Cambridge, Mass., 1989-92; sr. set designer V.D.A. Inc., Somerville, 1992-99; pres. Ea. Decor & Art, 1993—. Dir. Watercolor Soc., Fuzhou, 1984-85. One-man show Hong Kong Art Ctr., 1989, The Market Barn Gallery, Falmouth, Mass., 1989, CCI Gallery, Boston, 1993, 98; exhibited in group shows at The East and West Gallery, Chgo., 1990, Creative Arts Workshop Gallery, New Haven, 1992, Hewlett-Packard Co., Andover, Mass., 1994, Kane Gallery, Boston, 1995, Wilson Gallery, Boston, 1997, Am. Watercolor Soc., N.Y.C., 1999; mural artist Children's Mus., Boston, 1995, Mus. Sci., Boston, 1998, 99, 2000, The Children's Mus. at Mus. Ctr., Cin., 1998, Angel Mounds Historic Stie Mus., Evansville, Ind., 2000, Prehistoric Native American mural series Ind. State Mus., Indpls., 2001, three murals Dinosaurs Exhibit Nat. tour, 2002; author: Liaoning Art Press, 1997, Landscape Paintings by Yu Shan, 1997. Fellow Asian Culture Coun., N.Y.C., 1986-89; internat. scholar Boston U., 1989. Mem. Internat. Soc., Nat. Soc. Mural Painters. Avocations: music, drama, film, photography, video. Home: 45 Robinson St Somerville MA 02145 Office: Eastern Decor and Art Ste B 45 Robinson St Somerville MA 02145 E-mail: yushannet1@aol.com.

YU, SHIRLEY SHIU-FANG, economics educator; b. Taoyuan, Republic of China, b. Mar. 21, 1949; came to U.S., 1971, naturalized, 1983; d. Ching-Tseng and Luan (Tseng) Y. BA Nat. Taiwan U., 1971; MS Okla. State U., 1973, PhD 1981. Research analyst Merck Sharp & Dohme, West Point, Pa., 1977-79; asst. prof. Tex. Tech. U., Lubbock, 1981-88, Denison U., 1988—. Contbr. articles to profl. jours. Grantee Pharm. Mfrs. Assn., 1976-77, Pacific Cultural Found., 1987-88. Mem. Am. Econ. Assn., So. Econ. Assn., Omicron Delta Epsilon. Office: Denison U Econs Dept Granville OH 43023

YU, WEI-WEN, retired engineering educator; b. Shandong, China, July 10, 1924; arrived in U.S., 1954; s. Chi-tung and Mong-shih Yu; m. Yueh-hsin Wang, Sept. 6, 1953; children: Julie H.H., Dorothy H.L., Gordon H.I. BS, Nat. Taiwan U., 1950; MS, Okla. State U., 1955; PhD, Cornell U., 1960. Registered profl. engr., Mo. Structural engr. T.H. McKaig & Assocs., Buffalo, 1955—56, 1959—60; rsch. engr. Am. Iron and Steel Inst., N.Y.C., 1960—67; staff engr. TRW Sys., Redondo Beach, Calif., 1967—68; assoc. prof. U. Mo., Rolla, 1968—72, prof., 1972—82, Curator's prof., 1982—92, Curator's prof. emeritus, 1992—. Dir. Ctr. for Cold-Formed Steel Structures, Rolla, 1990—2000; founding dir. Wei-Wen Yu Ctr. for Cold-Formed Steel Structures, Rolla, 2001—; rschr. in field. Author: Cold-Formed Steel Structures, 1973, Cold-Formed Steel Design, 1985, 1991, 2000; guest editor: Spl. Issue on Recent Devels. in Thin-Walled Structures, 1998. Recipient Alumni Merit award, U. Mo. Sch. of Mines and Metallurgy/U. Mo.-Rolla Alumni Assn., 1979, Arch T. Colwell Merit award, Soc. Automotive Engrs., 1988. Fellow: ASCE (Shortridge Hardesty award 2001); mem.: U. Mo.-Rolla Acad. Civil Engrs. (hon.), Chi-Epsilon (chpt. honor). Avocations: reading, gardening. Office: U Mo Rolla Dept Civil Engring Rolla MO 65409

YU, XIAO NAN, dancer; b. Dalian, China; Student, Nat. Ballet Sch., 1995—96. Apprentice Nat. Ballet Can., Toronto, Canada, 1996—2000, first soloist Canada, 2000—. Dancer (ballets) Onegin, Cinderella, Odette/Odile, Swan Lake, Jewels, The Fairy's Kiss, Les Sylphides, Soloist La Bayadère, dancer One Hundred Words for Snow. Office: Walter Carsen Ctr Nat Ballet Canada 470 Queens Quay West Toronto ON Canada M5V 3K4*

YU, YI-YUAN, mechanical engineering educator; b. Tienjin, China, Jan. 29, 1923; came to U.S., 1947, naturalized, 1962; s. Tsi-Chi and Hsiao-Kung (Wang) Y.; m. Eileen Hsiu-Yung Wu, June 14, 1952; children: Yolanda, Lisa. BS, Tienjin U., 1944; MS, Northwestern U., 1950, PhD, 1951. Prof. mech. engring. (Poly Inst. Bklyn.), 1957-66; cons. engr. GE Space Divsn., Valley Forge, Pa., 1966-70; Disting. prof. aero. engring. (Wichita State U.), 1972-75; mgr. components and analysis Rockwell Internat., Rocketdyne, Canoga Park, Calif., 1975-79, exec. engr. Energy Systems, 1979-81; dean engring. N.J. Inst. Tech., Newark, 1981-85, prof. mech. engring., 1981-93, prof. emeritus, 1993—, rsch. prof., 1996-98. Vis. prof. Cambridge U., 1960; advisor Middle East Tech. U., Ankara, Turkey, 1966; lectr. Gen. Electric Co., 1963-73; mem. ad hoc com. on dynamic analysis USN, 1968-69; cons. internat. adv. panel Chinese U. Devel. Project, 1983, David W. Taylor Naval Ship Rsch. and Devel. Ctr., 1987-88; cons. Atty. Gen.'s Office State N.J., 1982-84. Contbr. Handbook of Engineering Mechanics, 1962; author: Vibrations of Elastic Plates, 1997. Guggenheim fellow, 1959-60; Air Force Office Sci. Rsch. grantee, 1956-66; NASA grantee, 1967-69, 74-75 Fellow AIAA (assoc.), ASME (life); mem. Am. Soc. Engring. Edn., Am. Soc. for Composites, Am. Acad. Mechanics (chmn. com. mech. edn. 1993-94), Sigma Xi, Phi Kappa Phi, Pi Tau Sigma, Tau Beta Pi. Presbyterian. Home: 24 Gordon Rd Essex Fells NJ 07021-1604 Office: 24 Gordon Rd Essex Fells NJ 07021-1604 *At the end of each day, let everyone of us ask the question: Have I done the best I can this day to make the world a better place to live for myself and for my fellow human beings? As long as the answer is yes, it does not matter whether one is a teacher, farmer, worker, businessperson or homemaker.*

YU, ZICHENG, paleoclimatologist; b. Changchun, Jilin, China, Nov. 11, 1963; arrived in U.S., 1997; PhD, U. Toronto, Ont., Can., 1997. Instr. Peking U., Beijing, 1988—91; rsch. fellow U. Minn., Mpls., 1997—98, U. Alberta, Alberta, Canada, 1998—2000; rsch. scientist Canadian Forest Svc., Edmonton, Canada, 2000—01; prof. Lehigh U., Bethlehem, 2001—. Contbr. articles to profl. jours. Mem.: Am. Geophysical Union. Office: Lehigh U 31 Williams Dr Bethlehem PA 18015

YU, ZONGCHANG, engineer; b. Wuhe, Anhui, China, Oct. 10, 1961; s. Zuoming Yu and Jianlan Zhang; m. Zhimin Jiang; children: Ryan, James. Bachelor, Hefei (China) Inst. Tech., 1983, Master, 1986; PhD, Harbin Inst. Tech., 1990. Postdoctoral rschr. Beijing U. Aeronautics and Astronautics, 1990-91, assoc. prof., 1991-92; sr. design engr. Microsys. Tech., Kawasaki, Japan, 1992-95, ULVAC Ltd., Chigasaki, Japan, 1995-97; sr. engr. KLA-Tencor Corp., Yokohama, Japan, 1997-2000, San Jose, Calif., 2000—. Assoc. engr. aerospace rsch. Inst. China Aerospace Industry, Beijing, 1986-87. Mem. Internat. Soc. Optical Engring. Avocations: reading, travel. E-mail: zongchang.yu@kla-tencor.com.

YUAN, AIDONG (DAVID YUAN), cell biologist, researcher; b. Zhoukou, Henan, China, Nov. 26, 1963; came to the U.S., 1997; s. Zhenxiang Yuan and Yumei Xiao; m. Susan Shumin Liu, Dec. 29, 1987; children: Helen Lin, Jack Bin. MD, Hunan Med. U., Changsha, China, 1986; PhD, U. Otago, Dunedin, New Zealand, 1997. Physician Xuanwu Hosp., Beijing, 1988-93; rsch. fellow U. Otago, Dunedin, 1993-94; rsch. assoc. U. Nebr., Lincoln, 1997-01; sr. rsch. assoc. and clin. instr. Ctr. for Dementia Rsch. Nathan Kline Inst. NYU Med. Sch., N.Y.C., 2001—. Author: Cardiology Q and A, 1990; contbr. articles to profl. jours. Recipient Math. Competition award Zhoukou City Coun., 1981; rsch. fellow Sandoz Found., Australia, 1992. Mem. Am. Soc. for Cell Biology (Travel award 1996), Physiol. Soc. New Zealand, Dunedin Co. Physiologists, Internat. Dictyostelium Soc. (Travel award 1999), Internat. Soc. for Neurochemistry, Soc. Neuroscience. Avocations: fishing, reading, ping-pong, travel. Office: Ctr Dementia Rsch Nathan Kline Inst NYU Med Sch 140 Old Orangeburg Rd Orangeburg NY 10962 E-mail: dyuan@3721@yahoo.com.

YUAN, CHUN, physicist, educator; b. Beijing, China, Aug. 23, 1957; s. Zhenwu Yuan and Shunying Cheng; m. Tong Zhu, Dec. 17, 1987; children: Eric, Isabelle. BSc, Beijing Normal U., China, 1982; PhD, U. Utah, 1988. Sr. sys. analyst GE Med. Sys., Waukesha, Wis., 1988—91; asst. prof. U. Wash., Seattle, 1991—97, assoc. prof., 1997—2001, prof., 2001—. Adv. bd. Vulnerable Plaque Orgn., Houston, 2001—; vis. prof. The Post Grad. Med. Coll. of People's Liberation Army, Beijing, 2001—. Contbr. articles. Recipient Rsch. Career Develop. award, NIH, 1996—2000, RO1 award, 1998—. Mem.: AAAS, Am. Assn. Physicists in Medicine, Soc. Cardiovasc. Magnetic Resonance (Best Presentation Award 1999), Internat. Soc. Magnetic Resonance in Medicine (student stipend com. 1997—2000). Avocations: skiing, tennis, hiking, bicycling, music. Office: Univ Wash Box 35711 1959 Pacific Ave N Seattle WA 98195 Office Fax: 206-543-3495. Business E-Mail: cyuan@u.washington.edu.

YUAN, JASON XIAO-JIAN, medical researcher, educator; b. Xintian, Hunan, People's Republic of China, May 9, 1963; arrived in U.S., 1988, naturalized, 1998; s. Tian-Lin Yuan and Li-Hua Chen. MD, Suzhou (China) Med. Coll., 1983; PhD in Physiology, Peking Union Med. Coll., Beijing, 1993; postgrad., U. Md., 1993. Intern Suzhou Med. Coll. Hosp., 1982-83; resident Lanzhou (China) Med. Coll. Hosp., 1983-84; mem. sci. cadre Office Sci. and Tech. Gansu Environ. Protection Bur., Lanzhou, 1984; rsch. assoc. dept. environ. medicine Gansu Inst. Environ. Scis., 1984-85; postdoctoral fellow dept. physiology and medicine U. Md. Sch. Medicine, Balt., 1988-93, rsch. asst. prof. dept. physiology, 1993-96, rsch. asst. prof. divsn. pulmonary and critical care med., 1993-96, asst. prof., 1996-98, assoc. prof., 1998-99, U. Calif.-San Diego Sch. Medicine, 1999—. Lectr. in field; ad hoc reviewer grant applications NIH, 1995—, mem. lung biology and pathology study sect. NIH, 2002-; study section mem. Am. Heart Assn., 1995-97, 98—, exec. com. mem., 1999—, editor newsletter, 2001—; ad hoc reviewer rsch. grant applications Wellcome Trust (London), 1995, 98, U.S. Dept. Vets. Affairs, 1995; mem. lung biology and pathology study sect., NHLBI, 2002—.; hon. prof. The Fourth Mil. Med. U., Xian, China, 1999—, China. Acad. of Med. Scis. and Peking Union Med. Coll., 2002—. Author: Olympic Complete Words, 1988; editorial asst. Gansu Assn. Environ. Scis., 1984-85; contbr. articles to profl. jours. Parker B. Francis fellow, 1994-97. Mem. AAAS, Am. Heart Assn. (Md. affiliate rsch. fellow 1990-92, exec. com. 1999—, grantee 1990-92, 93-95, 96-98, Cournand and Comroe Young Investigator award 1995, Best Abstract award 1996, Established Investigator award 1998), Am. Physiol. Soc. (Giles F. Filley Meml. award 1995, Rsch. Career Enhancement award 1995, Lamport award 1998), Am. Thoracic Soc., Biophys. Soc., Chinese Assn. Physiol. Sci. (editl. asst. 1987-88), Soc. Chinese Bioscientists in Am. (Dr. C.W. Dunker award 1993). Home: 3775 Georgia St Apt 301 San Diego CA 92103-7608 Office: U Calif San Diego Med Ctr Divsn Pulmonary CC Medicine 200 W Arbor Dr San Diego CA 92103-1911

YUAN, JEFFREY, bioinformatics scientist; b. N.Y.C., June 14, 1963; s. Shang Wen and Pearl Pei Y.; m. Michele M. Minter, June 15, 1991; children: Brian, Mira. BS, Yale U., 1985; PhD, Rockefeller U., 1991. Biomed. rsch. fellow Princeton (N.J.) U., 1991-97; biotech. cons. Princeton, 1997; bioinformatics rsch. assoc. Merck & Co., Inc., Rahway, N.J., 1997—. Contbr. articles to profl. jours. Office: Merck & Co Inc 126 E Lincoln Ave RY80-A1 Rahway NJ 07065 Fax: 732-594-2929. E-mail: yuanjeff@home.com., jeffrey_yuan@merck.com.

YUAN, JOAN REYNOLDS, community health nurse; b. Providence, Sept. 28, 1952; d. Frank Arthur and Martha (McNiff) Reynolds; m. Albert S. Yuan, May 24, 1974; children: David, Christina, Stephen. BSN, Villanova U., 1974, MSN, 1985. RN, Pa. Dir. edn./quality assessment and improvement Abington Meml. Hosp. Home Care, Willow Grove, Pa., 1984—. Mem. editl. bd. Home Health Digest, 1995-98; contbr. articles to sci. and profl. jours. Mem. ANA, Am. Diabetes Assn. (bd. dirs. S.E. Pa. chpt. 1996-97), Home Healthcare Nurses Assn. (rep. 1997-98), Sigma Theta Tau. Democrat. Roman Catholic. Home: 434 Abington Ave Glenside PA 19038-4812 Office: Abington Meml Hosp Home Care 2510 Maryland Rd Ste 250 Willow Grove PA 19090-1135

YUAN, JUN, computer scientist, educator; b. Nanjing, Jiangsu, China, Nov. 28, 1968; s. Liang Yuan and Xuegin Feng; m. Rui Chen. PhD, Southeast U., Nanjing, Jiangsu, P.R. China, 1995. Asst. prof. Southeast University, Nanjing, China; vis. scholar Hong Kong U. Sci. and Tech., Hong Kong, China, 1996—98; vis. asst. prof. Fla. Internat. U., Miami, 1998—2001; advanced computing technologist The Boeing Company, Seattle, 2001—. Mem.: IEEE Computer Soc. Office: The Boeing Company P.O. Box 3707 MC 7L-70 Seattle WA 98124 Personal E-mail: yuanjun88@yahoo.com.

YUAN, MAY, geographer, educator; b. Chung-Li, Tao-Yuan, Taiwan, Dec. 31, 1964; d. San-Jiun Yuan, Pi-Er Yuan; m. Michael Andrew Magsig; children: Audrey Magsig, Evan Magsig. PhD, SUNY, Buffalo, 1994. Assoc. prof. geography U. Okla., Norman, 1994—.

YUAN, ROBIN TSU-WANG, plastic surgeon; b. Boston, July 2, 1954; s. Robert Hsun-Piao and Grace I. (Chen) Y. AB, Harvard U., 1974, MD, 1978. Diplomate Am. Bd. Plastic Surgery. Resident in gen. surgery UCLA Med. Ctr., 1978-80, Cedars-Sinai Med. Ctr., L.A., 1980-81, 83-84; resident in plastic surgery U. Miami (Fla.)-Jackson Meml. Hosp., 1985-87; pvt. practice L.A., 1987—. Clin. instr. div. plastic surgery UCLA, 1987-98, asst. clin. prof. div. plastic surgery UCLA, 1998—; vice-chief div. plastic surgery Cedars-Sinai Med. Ctr., L.A., 1991—; pres., chief exec. officer, founder Family of Independent Reconstructive Surgery Teams (F.I.R.S.T.), 1990—. Author: Cheer Up...You're Only Half Dead!, Reflections at Mid-Life, 1996; contbr. numerous articles to med. jours. Mem. Am. Soc. Plastic and Reconstructive Surgery, Am. Cleft Palate Assn., Calif. Med. Assn. (del.), L.A. County Med. Assn. (bd. govs. dist. 1), Phi Lambda (co-mgr. 1991—). Avocations: tennis, skiing, golf, creative writing, violin. Office: 150 N Robertson Blvd Ste 315 Beverly Hills CA 90211-2145

YUAN, SHAO WEN, aerospace engineer, educator; b. Shanghai, China, Apr. 16, 1914; came to U.S., 1934, naturalized, 1954; s. Ti An and Chieh-huang (Chien) Y.; m. Hui Chih Hu, Nov. 5, 1950. BS, U. Mich., 1936; ME, Stanford U., 1939; MS, Calif. Inst. Tech., 1937, PhD, 1941. Rsch. engr. Glenn Martin Co., 1942-43; chief of rsch. Helicopter div. McDonnell Aircraft Corp., 1943-45; instr. Washington U., St. Louis, 1944-45; adj. prof. Poly. Inst. Bklyn., 1946-49, assoc. prof., 1949-54, prof., 1954-57; ptnr. von Kármán, Yuan & Arnold Assocs., 1955-63; prof. aerospace engring. U. Tex., 1958-68; prof., chmn. mech. engring. div. George Washington U., 1968-78, chmn. civil, mech. and environ. dept., 1973-78, 80-81, prof. emeritus, 1984; pres. RISE, Inc., 1977-85. Canadair Chair prof. U. Laval, Can., 1957-58; chmn. adv. com. Joint Inst. for Advancement of Flight Sci., 1970-84; hon. prof. Zhejiang U., 1987—; cons. Edo Aircraft Corp., Aerojet Corp., Cornell Aero. Lab., Dept. of Interior, Oak Ridge Nat. Lab., N.Am., Aviation, Inc., Fairchild-Hiller Corp., McDonnell-Douglas Corp., The World Bank; hon. adviser Nat. Center Research of China, Taiwan, 1958-68; chmn., founder 1st U.S.-China Conf. on Energy, Resources, and Environment, 1982; founder Consortium of Univs. for Promoting Grad. Aerospace Studies, 1984; founder Disting. Lecture Series on Founds. of Aerospace Research and Devel., 1986. Author: Foundations of Fluid Mechanics, 1967; Contbr. to: High Speed Aerodynamics and Jet Propulsion series, 1959, Energy, Resources, and Environment: Procs. at 1st U.S.-China Conf., 1982. Founder Yuan Engring. Libr., Zhejiang U., China. Recipient Outstanding Achievements award, Outstanding Contbns. award George Washington U., 1981, Internat. Biog. Ctr. 20th Century Achievement award, Outstanding People of the 20th Century, and the First Five Hundred at the New Millennium, 1998, The One Thousand Great Americans, 2001; named Outstanding Educator of Am., 1970, Outstanding Chinese American, 1983; inducted into Am. Biog. Inst. Hall of Fame, 20th Century Achievement award Five Hundred Leaders of Influence, commemorative medal Man of Yr., 1998. Fellow AAAS, AIAA, Internat. Biog. Assn; mem. ASME (life), Am. Soc. Engring. Edn., Soc. Engring. Sci. (bd. dirs. 1973-78, pres. 1977), Torchbearers Caltech, Founding Grant Soc. of Stanford U. (charter), John Montieth Soc. of U. Mich. (charter), Sigma Xi, Phi Kappa Phi, Phi Tau Phi, Sigma Gamma Tau, Pi Tau Sigma, Tau Beta Pi, Tau Xi Sigma. Achievements include patents in field. Home: 1400 Geary Blvd Apt 1505 San Francisco CA 94109-9309 E-mail: tianyuan@aol.com. *As engineers and scientists, we are concerned with that "something beyond"; consequently, the utmost achievement of an engineer is to create what has never been, for the improvement of quality of life.*

YUAN, SHEN-CHUAN, civil and structural engineer, consultant; b. Hangchow, Chekiang, China, May 10, 1922; came to U.S., 1963; s. Cheng-Ten and Win-Chu (Chou) Y.; m. Hazel Chien, June 11, 1949; children: Alan Y., Brad H., Cary H., Dana I. BS, Nat. Chiao-Tung U., Chungking, China, 1945; MS, U. Colo., 1967. Registered profl. engr., China, Colo., Hawaii, Idaho. Engr. Taiwan Railway Adminstrn., China, 1948-56; chief civil engring. and constrn. Taiwan Fertilizer Plant #6, China, 1956-60; chief soil divsn. Shihmem Devel. Commn., China, 1960-63; project structural engr. Stearns-Roger Engring. Inc., Denver, 1964-85; pres. Y&Y Cons. Engrs., 1986-87; cons. structural engr. Stone & Webster Corp., 1987, 88, 90, 91, 93, 97, 99, ECI, Denver, 1998-2000, Boyle Corp., Denver, 2001—. Contbr. articles to Jour. Irrigation and Drainage. Recipient Dist. Svc. award Rocky Mtn. Chinese Soc. Sci. and Engring., 1991. Fellow ASCE (life). Home: 2766 S Otis St Denver CO 80227-3526

YUAN, XIAO JIE, high technology professional; b. Tianjin, People's Republic of China, Nov. 4, 1957; s. Shu Ji Yuan and Li Xia Guan; m. Fenghong Zhang, July 9, 1988; children: Peijia Yuan. B.Eng., Tianjin U., China, 1982, MSc, 1986; PhD, U. Liverpool, 1995. Engr. Inst. Sensors, Harbin, China, 1982-83; lectr. Tianjin U., China, 1986-91; rsch. assoc. U. Liverpool, 1991-95; sr. engr. Chartered Semiconductor Mfg., Singapore, 1995-96; mem. rsch. staff IMEC, Leuven, Belgium, 1996-2000; sr. engr. Internat. Rectifier, Calif., 2000-2001; staff engr. Xilinx, Inc., 2001—. Contbr. articles to profl. jours. Mem. IEEE. Avocations: music, reading, travelling, sports. Home: 20900 Homestead Road D10 Cupertino CA 95014 Office: Xilinx Inc PO Box 240010 San Jose CA 95154-2410 E-mail: yuanxiaojie@yahoo.com.

YUAN, YUAN, English educator, translator; b. Jinan, Shandong, People's Republic of China, Mar. 2, 1957; s. Yi-ping Yuan and Zheng-yi Cui; m. Ruishan Gao, Mar. 22, 1983; children: Joanna, Erica. BA in Lit., Shandong U., 1981, MA in Lit., 1984; PhD in English, U. Wis., Milw., 1992. Rsch. asst. Inst. Modern Am. Lit., Jinan, Shandong, 1984-85; asst. prof. Calif. State U., San Marcos, 1991-95, assoc. prof., 1995-99, prof., 1999—, dept. chair, 1999-2002.

Referee Assn. Interdisciplinary Studies Arts, 1994—, MELUS, lit., interpreter, theory. Author: The Discourse of Fantasy: Theoretical and Fictional Perspectives, 1994; editor Jour. Fantastic in the Arts, 1996; transl. The Adventures of Augie March, 1992. Fulbright scholar USIA, 1985-90; rsch., scholarship and creativity grantee Calif. State U., 1992-93, 94-95; multicultural studies grantee, Calif. State U. San Marcos, 1992-93, 94-95. Mem. MLA, Internat. Assn. of Univ. Profs. of English, Chinese Assn. (co-founder, bd. dirs. 1993-94), Chinese Cultural Assn. (bd. dirs. 1993-95, sec. 1994-99). Home: 12583 Caminito De La Gallard San Diego CA 92128-2363 Office: Calif State U San Marcos Lit And Writing Studies San Marcos CA 92096-0001 E-mail: yuan@csusm.edu.

YUCELT, UGUR, marketing professional, educator; b. Bursa, Turkey, Dec. 15, 1937; came to the U.S., 1965; s. Nazim and Zisan Yucelt; m. Suna Kuli, Aug. 10, 1967; children: Baris, Onur. Diploma, Istanbul U., 1961; MBA, NYU, 1969; PhD, New Sch. U., N.Y.C., 1980. Instr. Salem (Mass.) State Coll., 1974-78; asst. prof. Norwich U., Northfield, Vt., 1978-82, assoc. prof., 1982-84, Pa. State U.-Harrisburg, Middletown, 1984—. Vis. prof. Oslo Bus. Sch., 1990-91, Mid. East Tech. U., 1992, 96, Al Alhawayn U., Morocco, 1998-99; rsch. assoc. Office Sys. Devel., N.Y.C., 1972-74; book reviewer Macmillan Book Pub., N.Y.C., 1989-90, Prentice-Hall, Inc. Contbr. articles to profl. jours. Lt. Turkish Army, 1962-64. Fellow Advt. Found., 1990, Direct Mktg. Assn., 1989. Mem. Am. Mktg. Assn., Acad. Mktg. Sci., Inst. Mgmt. Scis., Decision Scis., So. Mktg. Assn., Direct Mktg. Assn. Avocations: soccer, swimming, travel, running. Home: 1358 Jill Dr Hummelstown PA 17036-9008 Office: Pa State U Harrisburg Sch Bus Adminstrn Middletown PA 17057

YUDOF, MARK GEORGE, law educator, university president; b. Phila., Oct. 30, 1944; s. Jack and Eleanor (Parris) Y.; m. Judith Lynn Gomel, July 11, 1965; children: Seth Adam, Samara Lisa BA, U. Pa., 1965, LLB, 1968. Bar: Pa. 1970, U.S. Supreme Ct. 1974, U.S. Dist. Ct. (we. dist.) Tex. 1975, U.S. Ct. Appeals (5th cir.) 1976, Tex. 1980. Law clk. to judge U.S. Ct. Appeals (5th cir.), 1968-69; assoc. gen. counsel to ABA study FTC, 1969; rsch. assoc. Harvard Ctr. Law and Edn., 1969-70, sr. staff atty., 1970-71; lectr. Harvard Grad. Sch. Edn., 1970-71; asst. prof. law U. Tex., Austin, 1971-74, prof., 1974—, assoc. dean, 1979-84, James A. Elkins Cent. chmn. in law, 1983-97, dean, 1984-94, exec. v.p., provost, 1994-97, John Jeffers rsch. chair in law, 1991-94; pres. U. Minn., 1997—. Of counsel Pennzoil vs. Texaco, 1987. Author: When Government Speaks, 1983 (Scribes Book award 1983, cert. merit ABA 1983), (with others) Educational Policy and the Law, 1992, (with others) Gender Justice, 1986. Mem. Tex. Gov.'s Task Force on Sch. Fin., 1989-90, Tex. Gov.'s Select Com. on Edn., 1988; bd. dirs. Freedom to Read Found., 1989-91; mem. Austin Cable Commn., 1981-84, chmn., 1982; mem. nat. panel on sch. desegregation rsch. Ford Found., 1977-80; mem. state exec. com. Univ. Interscholastic League, 1983-86; bd. dirs. Jewish Children's Regional Svc., 1980-86; mem. Gov.'s Select Task Force on Pub. Edn., 1995; mem. Telecomms. Infrastructure Fund Bd., State of Tex., 1995-97. Recipient Teaching Excellence award, 1975, Most Meritorious Book award Scribes, 1983, Humanitarian award Austin region NCCJ, 1988, Antidefamation League Jurisprudence award, 1991; hon. fellow Queen Mary and Westfield Coll., U. London. Fellow Tex. Bar Found., Am. Bar Found.; mem. Am. Law Inst., Tex. Bar Assn., Assn. Am. Law Schs. (chmn. law and edn. sect. 1983-84, exec. com. 1988-90), Mpls. Club, Minn. Club, Town & Country Club, Minnikahda Club. Avocation: collecting antique maps. Office: U Minn 202 Morrill Hall 100 Church St SE Minneapolis MN 55455-0110

YUE, AGNES KAU-WAH, otolaryngologist; b. Shanghai, Peoples Republic China, Dec. 1, 1947; came to U.S., 1967; d. Chen Kia and Nee Yuan (Ying0 ; m. Gerald Kumata, Sept. 25, 1982; children: Julie, Allison Benjamin. BA, Wellesley Coll., 1970; MD, Med. Coll. Pa., 1974; postgrad., Yale U., 1974-78. Intern Yale-New Haven Hosp., 1974-75, resident, 1975-78; fellow U. Tex. M.D. Anderson Cancer Ctr., Houston, 1978-79; asst. prof. U. Wash., Seattle, 1979-82; physician Pacific Med. Ctr., 1979-90; pvt. practice, 1991—. Fellow Am. Acad. Otolaryngology; mem. Northwest Acad. Otolaryngology. Avocations: sailing, opera, profl. voice, cooking. Office: 1801 NW Market St Ste 410 Seattle WA 98107-3909

YUE, ALFRED SHUI-CHOH, metallurgical engineer, educator; b. China, Nov. 12, 1920; s. Choy Noon-woo and Sze Man-hun (Tom) Y.; m. Virginia Chin-wen Tang, May 21, 1944; children: Mary, Raymond Yuan, John, Ling Tsao, David, Nancy Chang. BS, Chao-tung U., 1942; MS, Ill. Inst. Tech., 1950; PhD, Purdue U., 1956. Assoc. engr. Taiwan Aluminum Co., 1942-47; instr. Purdue U., 1952-56; research engr. Dow Chem. Co., Midland, Mich., 1956-62; sr. mem. Lockheed, Palo Alto Research Lab., 1962-69; now cons.; prof. engring. and applied sci. U. Calif., Los Angeles, 1969—. Hon. prof. Xian Jiao-tong U., China, 1980; cons. LTV Aerospace Co., Lockheed Missile & Space Co., Atlantic Richfield Co.; Sec.-gen. Chinese Culture Assn. in, U.S.A., 1967, also; bd. dirs. Chinese scholar to U.S.A. Fellow AIAA (assoc.); mem. AAAS, AIME, Am. Soc. Metals, Materials Rsch. Soc., Sigma Xi, Sigma Pi Sigma, Tau Beta Pi, Phi Tau Phi (pres. 1978-82) E-mail: yuealfred@aol.com.

YUE, CHEUNG CHO, physician; b. Kowloon, Hong Kong, Aug. 9, 1951; came to U.S., 1969; s. Siang Hsin Yue and Yung Hwa Chang; m. Janet Ellen Yue, Mar. 17, 1979; children: Andrew, Alexander. AB, Hamilton Coll., 1973; MD with distinction, U. Rochester, 1978. Diplomate Am. Bd. Internal Medicine, Am. Bd. Rheumatology, Am. Bd. Clin. Pathology. Resident in medicine Cleve. Metro. Gen. Hosp., 1978-81, fellow in rheumatology, 1981-83; med. staff fellow Nat. Cancer Inst., Bethesda, Md., 1983-86; physician Metrohealth Med. Ctr., Cleve., 1986—. Avocations: golf, swimming, travel, photography, computing. Office: Metrohealth Med Ctr 2500 Metrohealth Dr Cleveland OH 44109-1900 E-mail: cyue@metrohealth.org.

YUE, HONGYU HENRY, industrial engineer; b. Anyang, Henan, China, June 10, 1970; s. Yongshun Yue and Jiaying Qi; m. Xiang Zhou. B. Eng., Tsinghua University, Beijing, China, 1988—93; M. Eng., Tsinghua U., Beijing, China, 1996; PhD, U. Tex., 2000. Contractor Advanced Micro Devices, Austin, Tex., 1998—2000; engr. tech. staff Tokyo Electron Ltd., 2000—02. Contbr. articles to profl. jours. Achievements include patents in field; patents pending in field. Office: Tokyo Electron 2400 Grove Blvd M/S C-350 Austin TX 78741 Personal E-mail: yue@che.utexas.edu. Business E-Mail: hyue@aus.telusa.com.

YUECHIMING, ROGER YUE YUEN SHING, mathematics educator; b. Mauritius, Feb. 25, 1937; s. James and Marie Yuechiming; m. Renée Bethery, Nov. 9, 1963; children: Françoise, Marianne, Isabelle. BSc with 1st class honours, U. Manchester, Eng., 1964, PhD, 1967. Asst. U. Strasbourg, France, 1967-69; lectr. math. U. Paris VII, 1970—. Participant math. confs. and seminars in numerous countries; referee various math. jours. Contbr. over 80 articles on ring theory to sci. jours. of numerous countries. Mem. French Math. Soc., Am. Math. Soc., London Math. Soc., Belgian Math. Soc., Japan Math. Soc. Achievements include introduction of concept of p-injective modules and the more generalized notion of YJ-injectivity, new approaches in ring and module theory leading to a better understanding of von Neumann regular rings, V-rings, self-injective rings and generalizations. Home: 38 rue du Surmelin 75020 Paris France Office: U Paris VII Unité Mixte de Rsch 9994 CNRS 2 Pl Jussieu 75251 Paris France

YUEH, CHAI-LUN, voice educator, opera singer; b. Beijing, June 28, 1955; came to U.S., 1985; s. Ye Yueh and Zhen-Quan Yu; m. Ai-lan Zhu. Cert. in fine arts, Beijing Western Tchrs. Coll., 1972; MusB, Ctrl. Conservatory Music, Beijing, 1977; artist diploma, U. Hartford, 1987, MusM, 1989. Opera singer, voice tchr. Ctrl. Opera Theatre, Beijing, 1977-84; opera singer, mem. voice faculty Hartt Sch. U. Hartford, Conn., 1988-2001; mem. voice faculty Trinity Coll., Hartford, 1990—, Wesleyan U., Middletown, Conn., 1996—, Ctrl. Conn. State U., New Britain, 1997—; asst. prof. U. Tex., El Paso, 1989-90; chairperson voice dept. Hartford Conservatory. Singer major roles with Conn. Opera, Hartford, 1989-94, Balt. Opera, 1991, Hawaii Opera, Honolulu, 1992, Austin (Tex.) Lyric Opera, 1994. Winner Young Artist Competition, 1985, 1st prize Met. Opera Auditions, 1988. Mem. Nat. Music Honor Soc., Nat. Assn. Tchrs. of Singing. Home: 28 Roma Dr Farmington CT 06032-2157 E-mail: gelargo@aol.com.

YUEN, ANDY TAK SING, electronics executive; b. Wanchai, Hong Kong, Aug. 26, 1952; came to U.S., 1984; s. Yan Chong and Chi Oi (Tse) Y.; m. Kathy Man Kwan Chan, Jan. 29, 1983; children Lambert Hann Shi, Robin Hann Lang. Higher Cert. in Elec. Engring., Hong Kong Poly., 1975; Diploma in Bus. Mgmt., Hong Kong Bapt. Coll., 1976; Diploma in Exec. Devel., Chinese U., Hong Kong, 1981; MBA, Chui Hai Coll., Hong Kong, 1981; PhD in Bus. Mgmt., Calif. Coast U., 1987; diploma in mgmt. High Tech. Cos., Stanford Univ., 1996. Supervising engr. Teledyne Semiconductor Ltd., Kowloon, Hong Kong, 1976-79; ops. mgr. Microsemi (Hong Kong) Ltd., 1979-81, gen. mgr., 1981-84; corp. mgr. Microsemi Corp., Santa Ana, Calif., 1984-89, corp. v.p., 1989—. Corp. dir. Semcon Electronics Pvt. Ltd., Bombay, 1984—. Author (books): Can Quality Circles Bring the Breakthrough to Hong Kong Industrial Management, 1982, Harnessing Japanese Quality Circles in Hong Kong, 1987. Fellow Inst. Sales and Mktg. Mgmt., Brit. Inst. Mgmt., Inst. Elec. and Electronics Inc. Engrs. Office: Microsemi Corp PO Box 26890 Santa Ana CA 92799-6890

YUEN, BENSON BOLDEN, airline management consultant, software executive; b. Hong Kong, Nov. 20, 1960; came to U.S., 1968; s. Eugene Howard and Janet Yuen. BSBA in Fin. summa cum laude, U. Cen. Fla., 1983. Mgr. market planning and automation Fla. Express, Inc., Orlando, 1983-85, dir. pricing, 1986-87; dir. customer svc. Seabrook Mktg., Inc., Houston, 1988-91, v.p. customer svc., 1992-94; v.p. consulting svcs. PROS Strategic Solutions, Inc., 1994-96, sr. v.p. mktg. and consulting svcs., 1996-99; sr. v.p. PROS Revenue Mgmt., Inc., 2000, pres. divsn. travel and transp., 2000—. Cons. airline revenue mgmt., mktg. automation, bus. mgmt., sys. devel. and bus. process engring.; pres. travel and transp. divsn. PROS Revenue Mgmt., Inc., 2000—. Designer (software) Passenger Revenue Forecast and Optimization System, 1989, Group Revenue Optimization and Management System Version 3, 1990-94, Version 4, 1995—, Holiday Mgmt. Module, Network Pricing Analysis Sys., Hub Complex Optimization; contbr. articles to profl. jours. Avocations: travel, music. Office: PROS Revenue Mgmt Inc 3100 Main St Ste 900 Houston TX 77002-9312

YUEN, RICHARD, engineering executive; b. Singapore, Singapore, Oct. 14, 1972; BS in Software Engring. with honors, U. Toronto, 1997; Master of Engring., U. Va., 2001. Tech. specialist Am. Mgmt. Sys. Can., Toronto, Canada, 1997—. Personal E-mail: ryuen@interlog.com.

YUILL, THOMAS MACKAY, academic administrator, microbiology educator; b. Berkeley, Calif., June 14, 1937; s. Joseph Stuart and Louise (Dunlop) Y.; m. Ann Warnes, Aug. 24, 1960; children: Eileen, Gwen. BS, Utah State U., 1959; MS, U. Wis., 1962, PhD, 1964. Lab. officer Walter Reed Army Inst. Rsch., Washington, 1964-66; med. biologist SEATO Med. Rsch. Lab., Bangkok, 1966-68; asst. prof. U. Wis., Madison, 1968-72, assoc. prof., 1972-76, prof., 1976—, dept. chmn., 1979-82, assoc. dean, 1982-93, dir. Gaylord NelsonInst. Environ. Studies, 1993—. Cons. NIH, Bethesda, 1976-86; chmn. Viral Diseases Panel, U.S.-Japan Biomed. Scis. Program, 1979-86, Am. Com. Arbovirology, 1982—; bd. dirs. Cen. Tropical Agrl. Res. Teaching, Turrialba, Costa Rica, 1988-96. Contbr. chpts. to books, articles to profl. jours. Served to capt. U.S. Army, 1964-66. Recipient grants state and fed. govts., 1968—. Mem. Orgn. Tropical Studies (pres. 1979-85), Wildlife Disease Assn. (treas. 19880-85, pres. 1985-87, editl. bd. 1989—), Am. Soc. Tropical Medicine and Hygiene (editl. bd. 1984-96), Nat. Assn. State Univ. Land Grant Colls., EPA Task Force (copchair 1994—), Am. Soc. Virology, Wildlife Soc., Sigma Xi. Avocations: flying, cross-country skiing, music. Office: U Wis Gaylord Nelson Inst Environ Studies 40 Science Hall 550 N Park St Madison WI 53706-1404

YU-LEE, REGINALD TOMAS, consultant executive; b. Dayton, Ohio, May 3, 1964; s. Rudolph Mario and Winifred Earline (Webster) Lee; 1 child, Erin Jeong Mi. B in Engring., U. Dayton, 1987, M in Engring., 1994, PhD in Engring., 1997. Staff engr. Montgomery County, Dayton, 1987; devel. engr. IBM, 1987—91; pres., chief oper. officer Bus. Dynamics & Rsch., 1994—96; from asst. prof. to assoc. prof. Sinclair Coll., 1991—96; sr. cons. Oracle Cons., 1996—97; from mgr. to sr. mgr. Ernst & Young LLP, Cin., 1997—99; dir. strategy Sapient Corp., Atlanta, 1999—2002; pres. The Yu-Lee Co., 2002—. Cons. Sinclair Coll., 1991-94; mentor underpriviledged minority students; cons. Dayton Daily News, 1993-94; guest lectr. Black Leadership Dayton; developer Adopt-a-Class program. Author: (book) Explicit Cost Dynamics: An Alternative to Activity Based Costing, 2001, Essentials of Capacity Management, 2001; contbr. articles to profl. jours. Mem. Parity 2000 Econ. Devel., Dayton, 1995. Mem. Inst. Indsl. Engrs., Soc. Mfg. Engrs., Am. Prodn. and Inventory Control Soc., Omega Psi Phi. Office: The Yu-Lee Company 1266 W Paces Ferry Rd #604 Atlanta GA 30327

YULISH, CHARLES BARRY, public relations executive; b. Cleve., Oct. 14, 1936; s. Isadore and Shirley Yulish; m. Barbara Pearlman, Aug. 22, 1973 (div. 1995); 1 child, Alexi Jules-Nicholas; m. Cynthia Brown Fleek, Oct. 28, 1995. AA in Govt., U. Fla., 1957; BS in Polit. Sci., Kent State U., 1959; MPA, Maxwell Sch., Syracuse U., 1963; postgrad., NYU, 1961-63, New Sch. Social Rsch., 1963-64. Spl. projects officer U.S. AEC, Washington and N.Y.C., 1961-63; pub. affairs mgr. Atomic Indsl. Forum, N.Y.C., 1963-66; pres., chief exec. officer Charles Yulish Assocs. Inc., 1966-83; exec. v.p. Wesley, Brown & Bartle Inc., 1984-87; vice chmn., ptnr. Holt, Ross & Yulish, Edison, N.J., 1988-92; exec. v.p., mng. dir. E. Bruce Harrison Co., Washington, 1993-95; v.p. corp. comm. USEC Inc., Bethesda, Md., 1995—. Writer, dir. (film) Energy: We Have the Choices, 1978 (Golden Eagle award); editor: Hard vs. Soft Energy Paths, 1980; author over 60 articles on classical music. Founder, bd. dirs. Serge Koussevitsky Archives Soc., N.Y.C., 1977; bd. dirs. Imperial Russia Hist. Soc., 1986, U.K. and U.S. Friends of Benjamin Franklin. Maxwell fellow Syracuse U., 1960. Mem. Internat. Assn. Pub. Participation Practitioners, Soc. Profl. Mgmt. Cons. (cert.). Home: 1438 Q St NW Washington DC 20009-3808

YUN, DANIEL DUWHAN, physician, foundation administrator; b. Chinjoo, Korea, Jan. 20, 1933; came to U.S., 1959; naturalized, 1972; s. Kapryong and Woo Im Yun; m. Rebecca Sungja Choi, Apr. 13, 1959; children: Samuel, Lois, Caroline, Judith. BS Coll. Sci. and Engring., Yon-Sei U., 1954, MD, 1958; student, U. Pa., 1963; PhD, Barrington U., 1995. Intern Quincy (Mass.) City Hosp., 1960; resident and fellow Presbyn.-U. Pa. Med. Ctr., Phila., 1961-65; med. dir. Paddon Meml. Hosp., Newfoundland, Labrador, Can., 1965-66; dir. spl. care unit Elkins Park (Pa.) Hosp., 1967-79; founder, pres. Philip Jaisohn Meml. Found., Inc., Elkins Park, Pa., 1975-85, also med. dir., trustee. Clin. prof. medicine U. Xochicalco, 1978; faculty Allegheny U. Health Scis., Phila.; bd. dirs. Elkins Park Hosp. Mem. Bd. Asian Studies Found., U.S. Senatorial Bus. Adv. Bd.; mem. home safety com. Mayor's Commn. on Svcs. to Aging, Phila.; trustee United Way of Southeastern Pa., co-founder Rep. Presdl. Task Force; mem. U.S. Congl. Adv. Bd.; cons. on Korean affairs Phila. City Coun.; hon. mem. adv. coun. Peaceful Unification Policy of Korea; trustee Albright Coll., Reading, Pa., 1997—; chmn. bd. Korean-Am. Christian Broadcasting of Phila.; mem. Phila. Internat. City Coord. Com.; commr. Pa. Human Rels. Commn., 1991—; founder, pres. Korean Heritage Found., 1991—; amb. City of Phila., 1991. Recipient Phila. award Human Rights award, 1981, Disting. Cmty. Svc. award Phila. Dist. Atty., 1981, medal of Merit Presdl. Task Force, 1981, Medal of Nat. Order, Republic of Korea, 1984, Nat. Dong Baek medal Republic of Korea, 1987, award City Coun. Phila., 1987, Gov.'s Pa. Heritage awards, 1990, commendation award Pa. Senate, 1991, award Asian Law Ctr., 1991, Rep. Senatorial Medal of Freedom, 1994; named to Legion of Honor, The Chapel of Four Chaplains; named Amb. City of Phila., 1991. Mem. AMA, Am. Soc. Internal Medicine, Am. Coll. Cardiology, Am. Heart Assn. (mem. coun. on clin. cardiology), Pa. Med. Soc., Phila. County Med. Soc., Royal Soc. Health, Am. Coll. Internat. Physicians, World Med. Assn., Fedn. State Med. Bds., Am. Law Enforcement Officers' Assn., Am. Fedn. Police, Internat. Culture Soc. Korea (hon.), Am. Soc. Contemporary Medicine and Surgery. Home: 3903 Somers Dr Huntingdon Valley PA 19006-1913 Office: 60 Township Line Rd Elkins Park PA 19027-2220

YUN, JAMES KYOON, electrical engineer; b. Andong, South Korea, Oct. 26, 1965; came to U.S., 1973; s. Joh Kyong and Karen Suk (Kim) Y. BSEE, U. Ill., 1987, MSEE, 1989. System engr. GE Co., Syracuse, N.Y., 1989-91, software engr., 1991-93, Martin Marietta Corp., Syracuse, 1993-95; sr. mem. engring. staff Lockheed Martin Corp., Moorestown, N.J., 1995—. Cons. Silver Knight Co., Liverpool, N.Y., 1994—. Inventor seal indicator. Mem. IEEE, Assn. for Computing Machinery, Tau Beta Pi, Eta Kappa Nu.

YUN, LIANG, marine engineer, educator; b. Shanghai, July 15, 1932; s. KunLin and Yun Ya (Sun) Y.; m. Li Hui Qiu, Jan. 1, 1962; children: Gang, Xiao. Grad., Dalian (China) U. Tech., 1953. Asst. prof. Mil. Engring. Acad. China, Harbin, 1953-56, lectr., 1956-66, Harbin Shipbldg. Engring. Inst., 1966-73; dir. air cushion vehicle divsn. Marine Design & Rsch. Inst. China, Shanghai, 1973-85, dep. chief engr., prof., sr. engr., 1980—; tech. dir. China Air Cushion Tech. Corp., 1984-86, Flying Dragon Sci. and Tech. Ltd., Hong Kong, 2000—, Engain Tech Ltd., Hong Kong, 2000—. Prof. Harbin Shipbldg. Engring. U., 1988—, Wu Han (China) Transport Engring. U., 1990—. Author: Theory and Design of Air Cushion Vehicle (in Chinese), 1990, 2000, (in English), 1993, 98. Rcipient 2nd class nat. award nat. Def. Com. China, Beijing, 1980, 2nd class nat. award China State Shipbldg. Corp., Beijing, 1992, 1st class nat. award Kwang-Hua Sci. & Tech. Found., Beijing, 1994. Mem. China Soc. Naval Architects and Marine Engrs. (standing dir. 1993-97, chmn. high performance vehicle subcom. 1984—, vice chmn. ship design com. 1992—). Home: 175 Gao Xiong Rd Apt 501 Shanghai 200011 China Office: Marine Design & Rsch Inst 1688 Xi Zang Nan Rd 200011 Shanghai China E-mail: yunxiao@online.sh.cn., yunxiao@online.sh.cn., yunliang01@att.net.

YUN, MICHELLE WONHE, librarian; b. Seoul, South Korea, July 18, 1936; d. Tchi-Chang and Jinsil Virginia (Sohn) Y.; m. Myungsoo Chun, Aug. 22, 1955 (div. Mar. 1963); m. Yoon-Choo Kim, June 15, 1968 (div. Dec. 1972). Student, Purdue U., 1955-57; BA magna cum laude, U. Pitts., 1974; MLS, Columbia U., 1977. Registered profl. libr., N.Y. English instr. Korean Lang. Sch., N.Y.C., 1978-79; translator, synopsis writer Asian Bilingual Curriculum Devel. Ctr., Seton Hall U., N.J., 1979-82; journalist Korean East Asian Daily News, N.Y.C., 1981-82; translator, lang. officer, analyst U.S. Dept. of Army, 1982-95; ret., 1995. English tchr. Korean Ministry Edn., 1996-98. Vol. Friends of Librs. of Montgomery County, Md., 1995—; mem. Friends of Book Arts Press, Columbia U., 1977—; mem. Montgomery chpt. ARC, 1995. Colby Coll. dean grantee, 1955. Mem. NAFE, Internat. Women's Assn. World Peace, Alumni Assn. U. Pitts., Alumni Assn. Columbia U., Alumni Assn. Kyongki Girls H.S. Avocations: rare books, calligraphy, piano, opera, concerts.

YUN, PETER SUBUENG, economics educator; b. Yong-Wol, Korea, June 7, 1936; s. Sea Young and Soon Oak (Kim) Y.; m. Sandy J. Forsythe, June 21, 1970; children: Amy Rebecca, Peter Jung. B.A., U. Ga., 1966, Ph.D., 1975; M.A., U. Okla., 1968. Asst. prof. econs. Clinch Valley Coll., Wise, Va., 1974-79, assoc. prof., 1979-86, prof., 1986—; chmn. bus. div., 1979-86. Pres., Universal Bus. Services, Wise, 1981-88, East West Quality Assocs., 1991—; dir. Va. Gov.'s Sch for the gifted Clinch Valley Coll., 1987—. Invest-in-America grantee, 1979, 80, NSF grantee, 1991; recipient Outstanding Alumni award Emmanuel Coll., 1984. Mem. Am. Econ. Assn., So. Econ. Assn., Bibl. Archaeology Soc. Home: PO Box 2620 Wise VA 24293-2620 Office: Clinch Valley Coll College Ave Wise VA 24293

YUN, SAMUEL, minister, educator; b. Ulsan, Republic of Korea, June 19, 1958; came to U.S., 1984; s. Eungoh and Chanho (Kim) Y.; m. Kyungim Martha Mah, Jan. 10, 1984; children: Miriam, Joseph, Michelle, John. BTh, Yonsei U., Seoul, Republic of Korea, 1980, MTh, 1984; MA in Religion, U. Dubuque, 1985; ThM, Harvard U., 1987; postgrad., Boston U., 1987-96. Ordained to ministry Korean Presbyn. Ch. in Am., 1987. Preacher Carmel-Peniel Presbyn. Ch., Rewey, Wis., 1984-85; assoc. pastor, dir. edn. Korean Presbyn. Ch. in Boston, Cambridge, Mass., 1985-88; pastor The Peace Ch., Brockton, 1988-90, Korean Presbyn. Garden Ch., Hackensack, N.J., 1990-93, Princeton (N.J.) Korean Presbyn. Ch., 1993—; prof., dean acad. affairs Presbyn. Theol. Sem. in Am., Corona, N.Y., 1986-95. Sec. gen. Coun. Korean Chs. in New Eng., Boston, 1989-90; rec. sec. Coun. Korean Chs. in N.J., 1991-93; adj. prof. New Brunswick Theol. Seminary, 1994—. Author: Living the Word, 1990, Living the Prayer, 1994, Living the Faith, 1997, Footprint and Vision of Korean American Church in U.S.A., Celebrating Centennial Ceremony, 2002; translator The Black Gold and Isram, 1985. Mem. Am. Acad. Religion, Soc. Bibl. Lit. Home: 9 Sayre Dr Princeton NJ 08540-5804 Office: PO Box 7186 Princeton NJ 08543-7186 E-mail: samuelyun@hotmail.com.

YUNE, HEUN YUNG, radiologist, educator; b. Seoul, Korea, Feb. 1, 1929; came to U.S., 1966; s. Sun Wook and Won Eun (Lee) Y.; m. Kay Kim, Apr. 12, 1956; children: Jeanny Kim, Helen Kay, Marc Eany. MD, Severance Med. Coll., Seoul, 1956. Lic. physician, Republic of Korea, Ind.; diplomate Am. Bd. Radiology, Korean Bd. Radiology. Intern Presbyn. Med. Ctr., Chonju, Korea, 1956-57, resident in surgery Korea, 1957-60; resident in radiology Vanderbilt U. Hosp., Nashville, 1960-63, instr. radiology, 1962-64; chief radiology Presbyn. Med. Ctr., Chonju, Korea, 1964-66; from asst. to assoc. prof. radiology Vanderbilt U. Med. Sch., Nashville, 1966-71; prof. radiology Ind. U. Sch. Medicine, Indpls., 1971-91. John A. Campbell prof. radiology, 1991-94, John A. Campbell prof. radiology emeritus, 1994—, dir. residency program, 1985-94, prof. otolaryngology, head and neck surgery, 1992-94, prof. otolaryngology, head and neck surgery emeritus, 1994—. Vis. prof. Yonsei U. Coll. Medicine, Seoul, 1985, Ajou U. Coll. of Medicine, Suwon, 1995-96; active staff Ind. U. Hosps., 1971—, Indpls. VA Hosp., 1971-99, 2000—, Wishard Meml. Hosp., 1971-99, 2000—. Editorial reviewer Am. Jour. Roentgenology, 1975—, Radiology, 1985—, Jour. Vascular and Interventional Radiology, 1989—; contbr. articles to profl. jours. Ordained elder Presbyn. Ch. Capt. Rep. of Korea Army, 1951-55. Decorated Bronze Star, U.S. Army, Wharang medal for meritorious mil. svc., Rep. of Korea Army. Fellow Am. Coll. Radiology; mem Assn. Univ. Radiologists, Radiol. Soc. N.Am., Am. Roentgen Ray Soc., Alpha Omega Alpha, others. Avocations: painting, photography, music appreciation, golf, travel. Home: 2887 Brook Vista Carmel IN 46032-4096 Office: Ind U Med Ctr 500 N University Blvd Indianapolis IN 46202-5149 E-mail: hyyune@pol.net.

YUNG, BABINGTON CHUN-KUEN, radiologist; b. Hong Kong, China, July 30, 1959; s. Kwan Yung and Yip Hin Yeung; m. Donna Yuk-king Mok, June 24, 1984; children: Eva, Helen. MBBS, U. Hong Kong, 1983. Diplomate Am. Bd. Nuclear Medicine, Am. Bd. Radiology. Resident Med. and Health Dept., Hong Kong, 1984-90; clin. and rsch. fellow Johns Hopkins Med. Instns. Johns Hopkins U., Balt., 1990-93; resident, asst. clin. prof. U. South Ala., Mobile, 1993-96; med. and sr. med. officer United Christian Hosp., Hong Kong, 1996-2000; staff radiologist Onslow Meml. Hosp., 2000—02, Quincy Med. Ctr., 2002—. Examiner Hong Kong Coll. Radiologists, 1998; mem. task group on clin. referral guideline on positron emission tomography Hosp. Authority, Hong Kong, 1999. Author: (book) Nuclear Imaging in Drug Discovery, Development and Approval, 1993; contbr. sci. articles to profl. publs. Mem. Soc. Nuclear Medicine, Radiol. Soc. N.Am. Baptist. Avocations: bodybuilding, soccer. Home: Unit 1 10 Bayfield Rd Quincy MA 02171-2060 Office: 317 Western Blvd Jacksonville NC 28546-6338 Fax: 617-376-2030. E-mail: yungbck@earthlink.net.

YUNGINGER, JOHN W. allergist; MD. Exec. sec. Am. Bd. Allergy and Immunology, Phila. Office: Am Bd Allergy and Immunology 510 Walnut St Ste 1701 Philadelphia PA 19106-3601 E-mail: abai@abai.org.

YUNIS, JORGE JOSE, anatomy, pathology, and microbiology educator; b. Sincelejo, Colombia, Oct. 5, 1933; s. José and Victoria (Turbay) Yunis. MD, Complutense U., Madrid, 1956, PhD, 1957; D (hon.), UCLA, 1997. Gen. practice medicine, Barranquilla, Colombia, 1957-59; resident in clin. pathology U. Minn., Mpls., 1959-62, resident in anat. pathology, 1962-64, mem. faculty, 1965-89, prof., 1969-89, dir. grad. studies of lab. medicine, 1969-74, dir. grad. studies of pathology, 1972-74, chmn. human genetics com. for health scis., 1972-77; mem. faculty Hahnemann U., Phila., 1989-92, prof. dept. neoplastic diseases, 1989-92, vice chmn., assoc. dir. Inst. for Cancer and Blood Diseases, 1989-92, dir. Human Genetics and Molecular Biology Div., 1989-92, prof. dept. pathology, 1991-92; prof. depts. anatomy, pathology, microbiology & immunology Thomas Jefferson U. Med. Coll., 1993—; dir. cancer biol., dept. anatomy, pathology, cell biology Thomas Jefferson U. Med. Col., 1993—. Vis. prof. numerous univs. Author: Human Chromosome Method, 1965, 1975, Biochemical Methods in Red Cell Genetics, 1969, Molecular Pathology, 1975; : New Chromosomal Syndromes, 1977, Molecular Structure Human Chromosomes, 1995, Esencia Humana, 1995, Así es la Vida, 1997, The Myth of God, 2002; contbr. more than 250 articles to profl. jours. Named Clin. Prof. of Yr. Harvard Med. Sch., 1987; honored by

Colombian Parliament, Bogota, 1986, 93, Colombian Med. Schs. Assn., 1993. Mem. Leukemia Soc. Am. (trustee 1983-88), Colombian Acad. Medicine. Avocations: poetry, religion, literature, photography. E-mail: jorgeyunis@aol.com.

YURASKO, FRANK NOEL, judge; b. Rahway, N.J., Dec. 22, 1938; s. Frank H. and Estelle (Trudeau) Y.; mm. Mary Byrd, July 23, 1966 (dec. 1991); children: Elizabeth Anne, Suzanne, Frank; m. Rosalee Yurasko, May 1997. BA, Brown U., 1960; cert., London Sch. Econs., 1961; student, Gray's Inn., London, 1960-61; JD, Yale U., 1964. Bar: N.J. 1964, Fla. 1979, U.S. Dist. Ct. N.J. 1965, U.S. Ct. Appeals (3d cir.) 1980, U.S. Supreme Ct. 1969; cert. civil trial atty., N.J. Judge's law clk. N.J. Dept. Judiciary, Trenton, 1964-66; ptnr. Graham, Yurasko, Golden, Lintner & Rothchild, Somerville, N.J., 1966-80; pvt. practice, 1980—. Judge Montgomery Twp. (N.J.) Mcpl. Ct., 1973-84; twp. atty. Hillsborough Twp. (N.J.), 1973—; atty. Green Brook (N.J.) Bd. Adjustment, 1973-2001. Trustee Gill/St. Bernard Sch., Bernardsville, N.J.; mem. alumni bd. trustees Peddie Sch., Hightstown, N.J. Mem. ABA, Am. Jud. Soc., N.J. Bar Assn., Fla. Bar Assn., Somerset County Bar Assn., Mercer County Bar Assn., Assn. Trial Lawyers Am., Trial Attys. N.J., N.J. Fedn. Planning Ofcls., Fed. Bar Assn. Office: PO Box 1041 139 W End Ave Somerville NJ 08876-1809

YURCHAK, KATHERINE SASSO, writer; b. Atlantic Highlands, N.J., June 23, 1921; d. Anthony Sasso and Theresa Sommese; m. Nicholas Yurchak, Feb. 21, 1954; 1 child, John Marshall. BA, Bloomsburg U., 1995. Columnist E. Lycoming Shopper and News, Hughesville, Pa., 1995—; freelance writer monthly periodicals, popular mags. Spkr. in field. Translator (from Italian): Prolific Writings of Giuseppe Petrelli, 1968-1989; contbr. articles to profl. jours. Mem. Soc. Profl. Journalists, Phi Kappa Phi. Avocations: reading, writing, walking.

YURCHENCO, HENRIETTA WEISS, ethnomusicologist, writer; b. New Haven, Mar. 22, 1916; d. Edward and Rebecca (Bernblum) Weiss; m. Basil Yurchenco, June 1936 (div. 1955); 1 child, Peter; m. Irving Levine, 1965 (div. 1979). Student, Yale U., 1935-36; student piano scholarship, Mannes Coll. Music, 1936-38. Radio producer WNYC, WBAI, others, 1939-69; writer, critic, tchr., folk music editor Am. Record Guide and Musical Am., 1959-70. Prof. music Coll. City N.Y., 1962-86, Bklyn. Coll., 1966-69, New Sch. for Social Research, 1961-68; co-dir. project for study of women in music, Grad. Ctr. CUNY. Author: A Fiesta of Folk Songs From Spain and Latin America, 1967, A Mighty Hard Road: A Biography of Woody Guthrie, 1970, !Hablamos! Puerto Ricans Speak, 1971; contbr. articles to profl. jours.; 15 field recs. from Mexico, P.R., John's Island, S.C., Guatemala, Ecuador, Morocco, issued by Libr. Congress, Folkways, Nonesuch, Folkways/Smithsonian, Global Village, Rounder Records; collections in Libr. Congress, Discoteca Hebrew U., Jerusalem, Arais Montana Inst., Madrid, Inst. Nacional Indigenista, Mexico City. Recipient grants-in-aid Am. Philos. Soc., 1954, 56, 57, 65, 67, 89, grants-in-aid CUNY Faculty Research Fund, 1970, 83, 87; NEH grantee, 1984 Mem. Internat. Council Traditional Music (com. on women's studies), Soc. Ethnomusicology, Soc. Asian Music, Sonneck Soc., Internat. Assn. Study of Popular Music, Am. Musicologists Soc. Achievements include research in folk, tribal and popular music for Library of Congress, Mexico, Guatemala, P.R., Spain, Morocco, Balearic Islands, John's Island, S.C., Ireland, 1941-83. Home: 360 W 22d St New York NY 10011-2600 Office: 139th St And Convent Ave New York NY 10031 E-mail: hyurchenco@aol.com.

YURCHUCK, ROGER ALEXANDER, lawyer; b. Amityville, N.Y., June 9, 1938; s. Alexander and Ella Marie (Munley) Y.; m. Sally Ward, Apr. 14, 1961 (div. 1972); children: Scott, Lauren; m. Susan Holland, June 1, 1985. AB cum laude, Northwestern U., 1959; LLB, Harvard U., 1962. Bar: Ohio 1962. Assoc. Vorys, Sater Seymour and Pease, Columbus, Ohio, 1962-68, ptnr., 1969-71, 73—, ptnr. Cin. office, 1984—; v.p., gen. counsel Fed. Home Loan Mortgage Corp., Washington, 1971-73. Vice chmn., bd. dirs. Securities Investors Protection Corp., Washington, 1982-88. Del. Rep. Nat. Conv., 1980, 84. Mem. ABA, Ohio Bar Assn., Phi Beta Kappa. Clubs: Queen City (Cin.). Republican. Episcopalian. Office: Vorys Sater Seymour and Pease 221 E 4th St Ste 2100 Cincinnati OH 45202-5133

YURIST, SVETLAN JOSEPH, mechanical engineer; b. Kharkov, USSR, Nov. 20, 1931; came to U.S., 1979, naturalized, 1985; s. Joseph A. and Rosalia S. (Zoilman) Y.; m. Imma Lea Erlikh, Oct. 11, 1960; 1 child, Eugene. MSME with honors, Poly. Inst. Odessa, USSR, 1954. Engr., designer Welding Equipment Plant, Novaya Utka, USSR, 1954-56; sr. tech. engr. Heavy Duty Automotive Crane Plant, Odessa, USSR, 1956-60, asst. chief metallugist, 1971-78; supr. rsch. lab. Inst. Spl. Methods in Foundry Industry, 1960-66, project engr. sci. rsch., 1966-70; engr. designer Teledyne Cast Product, Pomona, Calif., 1979-81; sr. mech. engr. Walt Elliot Disney Enterprises, Glendale, 1981-83; foundry liaison engr. Pacific Pumps divsn. Dresser Industries, Inc., Huntington Park, 1984-86; casting engr. Superior Industries Internat., Inc., Van Nuys, 1986-89; mech. engr. TAMCO Steel, Ramcho Cucamonga, 1989-96. Contbr. reports, articles to collections All Union Confs. Spl. Methods in Foundry, USSR; USSR patentee permanent mold casting. Recipient award for design of automatic lines for casting electric motor parts USSR Ministry Machine Bldg. and Handtools Mfr., 1966, for equipment for permanent mold casting All Union Exhbn. of Nat. Econ. Achievements, 1966-70. Mem. Am. Foundrymen's Soc. Home: 1718 Downs St Oceanside CA 92054-6191

YURKO, JOSEPH ANDREW, chemical engineer; b. Youngstown, Ohio, Mar. 30, 1955; s. Joseph George and Virginia Mary (Cossentino) Y.; m. Valerie Ann Congdon, Sept. 9, 1992; children: Andrew Dale, Laura Ann. B in BioEngring. Sci., B in Chem. Engring., Cleve. State U., 1981. Lic. profl. engr. Tex. Structural draftsperson HK Ferguson Co., Cleve., 1974-76, architectural draftsperson, 1976-77, process design engr., 1981-84; chem. engr. Chemical Data Systems, Inc., Oxford, Pa., 1984-85; tech. sales engr. Autoclave Data Systems, Inc., Erie, 1985-86; sr. process design engr. Morrison Knudsen Corp., Cleve., 1987—2002, process start up engr., 1988—2002; sr. project engr. Ben Venue Labs., Bedford, 2002—. Cons. EI Dupont de Nemours and Co., Wilmington, Del., 1985-86, Mobil Oil Rsch. Ctr., Princeton, N.J., 1985-86, SmithKline French Labs., Phila., 1985-86, Anheuser-Busch Cos., St. Louis, Dow Corning, Midland Mich., 1996; spkr. in field. Author: (manuals) Aseptic Filtration Tech. Operating Procedure, 1990, Waste Stream Evaporator Tech. Operating Procedure, 1991, Clean-in-Place Process Tech. Operating Procedure, 1992, Viobin Sci. Proten Labs. Pancreatin, Heparin and Blood Processes, 1995; editor: (manual) Natural Water Carbonation Tech. Ops., 1992. Coach track Cath. Youth Orgn. St. Bridgets Cath. Ch., Parma, Ohio, 1977; campaigner Multiple Sclerosis Soc., Cleve., 1978; counselor Soc. Cripplied Children Cuyahoga County, Strongsville, 1979. Mem. Am. Inst. Chem. Engrs. (sec. Cleve. chpt. 1988-89, vice chair Del. Valley chpt. 1986-87), Food Pharm. and Bioengring. Div., Am. Chem. Soc, Cleve. Engring. Soc., Internat. Soc. Pharm. Engring. Republican. Methodist. Achievements include proposed process conversion of carbon dioxide emissions into oxygen and hydroponically grown products for Anheuser-Busch Inc.; ultraviolet photographic study of particle motion in fluid dynamic study of new Autoclave Engrs. microclave reactor with catalyst basket and internals for heterogeneous catalysis, proposition of ceramically encapsulated metallic beads impregnated with catalyst for novel reactor designed to contain catalyst in magnetic zone. Home: 19099 Hunt Rd Strongsville OH 44136-8415 Office: Morrison Knudsen Corp MK Ferguson Plaza 1500 W 3rd St Cleveland OH 44113-1422

YURT, ROGER WILLIAM, surgeon, educator; b. Louisville, June 8, 1945; s. Albert William and Mary Louise (McGrath) Y.; m. Joan A. Terry, Sept. 3, 1971; children: Jennifer, Daniel, Gregory. BS in Biology, Loyola U., New Orleans, 1967; MS, U. Miami, 1972. Diplomate Nat. Bd. Med. Examiners. Intern. Parkland Meml. Hosp.-Southwestern Med. Sch., U. Tex., Dallas, 1972-73, resident, 1973-74; postdoctoral trainee NIH, 1975-77; resident, chief resident N.Y. Hosp.-Cornell Med. Ctr., N.Y.C., 1977-79, acting dir. Burn Ctr., dir. rsch., 1982-83, dir. Trauma Ctr., 1992-99, prof. surgery, 1982-92, 92—, The Johnson & Johnson disting. prof. surgery, 1995—; vice chmn. dept. surgery Cornell U. Med. Coll., 1987—, acting chmn., 1991-93, dir. Burn Ctr., 1995. Acting surgeon-in-chief The N.Y. Hosp., 1991-93; clin. asst. prof. surgery Uniformed Svcs. U. Health Sci., Bethesda, Md., 1980-82; clin. asst. prof. gen. surgery Health Sci. Ctr., U. Tex., San Antonio, 1981-82; chmn. burn com., Regional Emer. Med. Svcs. N.Y., 1982-84, mem. trauma ctr. adv. com., 1984-89, chmn., 1995-98, mem. burn ctr. adv. com., chmn., 1996-2000, mem. sp. ref. ctr. com., chmn., 1996—, N.Y. Bklyn. ACS Com. Trauma, 1994—; dir. Mulhearn Rsch.Lab., N.Y.C., 1982—. Editor: Infections in Surgery, 1981-88; contbr. articles to med. jours. Maj. M.C., U.S. Army, 1979-82. Recipient Irma Hirschl Trust Career Scientist award, 1984-88; grantee United Health Found., 1968-69, NIH, 1984-87; fellow Sch. Medicine, U. Miami, summer, 1969-71, USPHS, 1973-75, postdoctoral fellow medicine Robert B. Brigham Hosp.-Harvard U. Med. Sch., Boston, 1974-77. Mem. Am. Surg. Infection Soc. (charter, chmn. membership com., sec. 1987-90, pres. 1991-92), Assn. Acad. Surgery, Soc. U. Surgeons, Internat. Surg. Soc., Am. Assn. Surgery Trauma, Alpha Omega Alpha, Omicron Delta Kappa. Roman Catholic. Office: NY Hosp Cornell Med Ctr Dir The Burn Ctr 525 E 68th St Rm L-706 New York NY 10021-4885

YURTH, HELENE LOUISE, librarian; b. Cleve., May 21, 1953; d. Joseph Alexander and Helen (Hegedus) Y.; m. William David Birskovich, June 14, 1975. BA in Botany, Kent State U., 1975; MS in Libr. Sci., Clarion U. Pa., 1998. Dir. Bemus Point (N.Y.) Libr., 1988-90, Smith Meml. Libr. at Chautauqua (N.Y.) Instn., 1991—. Avocations: gardening, pets, birds and nature, vegetarianism, reading. Office: Smith Meml Libr 21 Miller Ave Chautauqua NY 14722 Fax: 716-357-3657. E-mail: hyurth@hotmail.com.

YUSHMANOV, VICTOR EVGENIEVICH, biophysicist, researcher; b. Moscow, Oct. 22, 1956; s. Evgeny E.Y. and Anna U. Stepanyants; m. Elena L. Zhukova, July 24, 1987 (div. Feb. 8, 1992); m. Vera Lúcia Lourenço, Nov. 22, 1997; children: Aline, Anna. MS with honors, Moscow Phys.-Tech. Inst., 1979, PhD, 1982; DSc (hon.), Acad. Sci., Moscow, 1992. Rsch. assoc. Inst. Chem. Physics Acad. Sci., 1982-86, sr. scientist, group leader Inst. Chem. Physics, 1986-98. Bd. mem. Inst. Chem. Phys. Acad. Sci., 1986—89; mem., sect. chmn. Coun. Young Scientists, Inst. Chem. Phys. Acad. Sci., 1982—90; reviewer Nat. Inst. Sci. Tech. Info, Moscow, 1983—90; book reviewer MIR Pub., Moscow, 1985—91; guest rschr. U. Parma, Italy, 1994, Nat. Rsch. Coun. , Canada, 1996; vis. prof. U. São Paulo, Brazil, 1992—94, 1995—99, Embrapa Rsch. Ctr., Brazil, 2000; mem. faculty U. Pitts., 2000; mem. edn. bd. Annals of Magnetic Resonance, Rio de Janeiro, 2001—. Contbr. articles to profl. jours.; author chpts. in books. Recipient East Meest West award, European Soc. for Magnetic Resonance in Medicine and Biology, Vienna, 1992, 1993, 1994; grantee, Royal soc. Eng., 1992, Fundação de Amparo a Pesquisa do Estado de São Paulo, 1992, NATO-Italian Consiglio Nazionale delle Ricerche, 1994, Conselho Nacional de Desenvolvimento Cientifico e Tecnológico, Brazil, 1993, 1995, 1996, 1997, 1998. Mem. Internat. Soc. for Magnetic Resonance in Medicine, N.Y. Acad. Sci., Russian Assn. NMR Spectroscopists, Brazilian Assn. Nuclear Magnetic Resonance Users. Avocations: skiing, air pilotage. Office: U Pitts W1309 BSTWR 200 Lothrop St Pittsburgh PA 15213 E-mail: yushmanovve@anes.upmc.edu.

YUSPEH, ALAN RALPH, lawyer, healthcare company executive; b. New Orleans, June 13, 1949; s. Michel and Rose Fay (Rabenovitz) Y.; m. Janet Horn, June 8, 1975. BA, Yale U., 1971; MBA, Harvard U., 1973; JD, Georgetown U., 1978. Bar: D.C. 1978. Mgmt. cons. McKinsey & Co., Washington, 1973-74; adminstrv. asst., legis. asst. Office of U.S. Senator J. Bennett Johnston, 1974-78; atty. Shaw, Pittman, Potts & Trowbridge, 1978-79, Ginsburg, Feldman, Weil and Bress, Washington, 1979-82; gen. counsel Com. on Armed Services-U.S. Senate, 1982-85; ptnr. Preston, Thorgrimson, Ellis & Holman, 1985-88, Miller & Chevalier, Washington, 1988-91, Howrey & Simon, Washington, 1991-97; sr. v.p. ethics, compliance and corp. responsibility HCA, Nashville, 1997—. Coord. Def. Industry Initiative on Bus.., Ethics and Conduct, 1987-97; v.p. Health Care Compliance Assn., 2002; bd. dirs. Health Care Compliance Assn., Ethics Officer Assn. Editor Law and Policy in Internat. Business jour., 1978-79, Nat. Contract Mgmt. Jour., 1988-92; assoc. editor Pub. Contract Law jour., 1987-91. Chmn. bd. of ethics, City of Balt., 1988-96, mem. planning comm. City Balt., 1996-97; mem. bd. Tenn. Repertory Theater, YMCA Mid. Tenn. Camp; mem. bd. Balt. Housing Authority, 1996-97. 1st lt. USAR, 1971-77. Office: HCA One Park Plaza Nashville TN 37203 Address: 3014 Hedriac St #305 Nashville TN 37203 E-mail: alan.yuspeh@hcahealthcare.com.

YUSSOUFF, MOHAMMED, retired physicist, educator; b. Cuttack, India, Aug. 14, 1942; arrived in U.S., 1991; s. Haji and Nurunnisa Fakhruddin; m. Farhana Begum, Apr. 6, 1969; children: Ashraf, Zeenat, Mustafa. MSc, Delhi U., 1963; PhD, Indian Inst. Tech., Kanpur, 1967. Prof. physics Indian Inst. Tech., Kanpur, 1967-90; vis. prof. physics Mich. State U., East Lansing, 1991—; ret., 1999. Guest scientist Ford Rsch., Dearborn, Mich., 1991-97, GM Tech. Ctr., Warren, Mich., 1997-98, Delphi Tech. Ctr., Warren, 1999—; vis. scientist U. Köln, Germany, 1972-74, U. Western Ont., London, Can., 1990-91; Humboldt scientist Atomic Energy Agy, Jülich, Germany, 1979-81; vis. prof. U. Konstanz, Germany, 1986-89; mem. com. physics examination Pub. Svc. Commn., Delhi, India, 1976-86, rsch. grants Univ. Grants Commn., Delhi, 1985-90; dir. Internat. Sch. on Band Structure, Indian Inst. Tech., 1986; creator Slow Pace program for tchg. sci. and engring. to deficient students with poor econ. or sch. backgrounds. Editor: Electronic Band Structure and Its Applications, 1987, The Physics of Materials, 1987. Mem.: Am. Phys. Soc., Internat. Ctr. Theoretical Physics (assoc.). Moslem. Achievements include patents for monitoring the catalytic converters in cars; rsch. in theory of freezing, kinetic model of catalysis, theory of disordered systems, chanelling, clusters, electronic structure, ionic conductors, exhaust gas sensors, superconductors, zeolites, fundamental rate constants of catalytic reactions and foundations of quantum theory. Home: 31011 Grandview St Westland MI 48186-5065 E-mail: yussouf2@hotmail.com.

YUSTER-FREEMAN, LEIGH CAROL, broadcasting executive; b. Trenton, N.J., July 23, 1949; d. Leon Carl and Helen Loretta (Wisniewski) Markiewicz; m. Charles Yuster (div. Apr. 1985); stepchildren: Sarah, Elizabeth, Jared, Alexandra; m. Richard N. Freeman; 1 child, Jessica Lee Freeman. Prof. dancer, 1967-71; editor R.R. Bowker, N.Y.C., 1971-72, from ISBN agy. editl. coord. to dir. prod. devel., 1972-89, dir. product devel., pub. Ulrich's Database, 1989-90, assoc. pub. Bowker Bus. Rsch., A&I Pub. New Providence, N.J., 1990-91, also pub. Ulrich's Database, 1990-91, pub. Broadcasting & Cable Yearbook, 1991-97; mng. dir. Reed Reference Pub., 1992-94, v.p. bibliographies, 1994-96, v.p. directories, 1996; v.p. Database Pub. R.R. Bowker, 1996-99, sr. mng. dir. prodn., 1999-2000; project mgr. workforce devel. NJN Pub. TV, Trenton, NJ, 2000—. Ptnr. Eagle Bakery, Trenton, N.J., 1991-92 Recipient Climate of Excellence award, Cahners Pub. Co., Newton, Mass., 1987, Cert. of Appreciation, Consortium of Univ. Film Ctrs., Kent, Ohio, 1986. Mem. Actors Equity Assn. Jewish. Avocations: gardening, dancing, music, children and children's issues, community services. Home: 19 Theodora Dr Hillsborough NJ 08844-4723 E-mail: lfreeman@njn.org.

YUZEITIS, JAMES RICHARD, information specialist; b. Chgo., Nov. 11, 1942; s. Stanley J. and Amy B. (English) Y.; m. Susan C. London, Oct. 7, 1967; children: Timothy, David, Amy. BA in Econs., Loyola U., Chgo., 1965, MS in Personnel Mgmt., 1968. Personnel adminstr. Chgo. Police Dept., 1965-67; personnel asst. McDonald's Corp., Chgo., 1967-69, ops. trainee Washington, 1969-70, personnel mgr. Detroit, 1970-72, licensing mgr. Columbus, Ohio, 1972-73, internat. personnel cons. Oakbrook, Ill., 1973-80, dir. of human resources, 1980-86, dir. human resources devel., 1986-91; pres. Quality Surveys, Inc., Big Timber, Mont., 1991—. Cons. Ronald McDonald Children's Charities, Chgo., 1986-88. Cons. and vol. Ronald McDonald Houses, Chgo., 1987; vol. Crazy Mont. Mus. Soc., Big Timber, 1991-92; bd. dirs. Pioneer Med. Ctr., Big Timber, 1993—. Recipient medal of Merit Cath. Youth Orgn., Chgo., 1960. Mem. Soc. for Human Resource Mgmt., Human Resource Planning Soc., Indsl. Rels. Rsch. Soc. Avocations: ranch mgmt., fishing, music. Home: PO Box 1244 Big Timber MT 59011-1244 Office: Quality Surveys Inc PO Box 1089 Big Timber MT 59011-1089

YVETTE, JANICE, occupational therapist; b. S.I., N.Y., Oct. 19, 1958; d. James McClain Brown, Jessy Mae (Frances) Brown Walton; m. Michael Murphy, Nov. 23, 1989. BA, Bklyn. Coll.; MA, Coll. of S.I. Home health aide Richmond Home Needs, S.I., 1979—85; personal care aide S.I. Home Health, 1985—2000. Musician Rosewood Club, Cola, SC. Mem.: Rosewood Clubhouse (sec.). Lutheran. Home: 3809 Rosewood Dr Cola SC 29205

Z, CHRIS, internist, medical educator; b. Corning, N.Y., Sept. 10, 1960; s. Chris and Potoula Roulidis; m. Maria Eugenia Hallas, May 24, 1987. BA with distinction, U. Va., 1982, MD, 1986. Diplomate Am. Bd. Internal Medicine. Resident U. Calif., San Francisco, 1988-91; assoc. Yater Med. Group, Washington, 1991-92; asst. clin. prof. Georgetown U., 1993-95; assoc. Duke U. Affiliated Physicians, Durham, N.C., 1995-96; asst. clin. prof. dept. medicine Duke U., 1996-2000, Emory U., Atlanta, 2001—. Gen. Internal Medicine fellow Georgetown U., 1992-93. Fellow ACP; mem. AMA. Avocations: music, piano, flute, bonsai, golf. Office: Emory U 1525 Clifton Rd NE Atlanta GA 30322

ZABEL, CURTIS LEE, artist, rancher; b. Athol, Kans., Feb. 10, 1935; s. Emil Henry and Ruby Jewel Zabel; m. Shirley Marie Zabel, Sept. 16, 1961; chlidren: Kirk Allen, Ty Michael. Grad., Hayden (Colo.) Union H.S., 1953. Mem. trail crew U.S. Forest Svc., Hayden, 1954-57; rancher, 1961—; artist Steamboat Springs, Colo., 1979—. Represented by Hayden-Hays Gallery, Colorado Springs, Knox Gallery, Vail, Colo., Pam Driscoll Gallery, Aspen, Colo., Two Rivers Gallery, Ltd., Steamboat Springs. Bronzes commd. for Meijr Sculpture Garden, 1996, Colo. Farm Bur., 1998, Woodlands, Tex., 2000, Loveland, Colo., 2000; exhibited in group shows at Rocky Mountain Wildlife in Art Exhbn., Littleton, Colo., 1987, Greeley (Colo.) Art Assn. Stampede Art Show, 1987, Eagle Valley Arts Coun. Invitational, Vail, Colo., 1987, C.M. Russell Show, Great Falls, Mont., 1985-87, White Hart Gallery, Steamboat Springs, 1988-89, Cottonwood Prairie Festival, Hastings, Nebr., 1990, Buckaroo Heritage Western Art Round-Up, Winnemucca, Nev., 1991, Rotary Found. Western Heritage Art Fair, Littleton, 1990-91, Eleanor Bliss Ctr. for Arts, Steamboat Springs, 1991, Happy Canyon Western Art Invitational Round-up, Pendleton, Oreg., 1992, Ronald Roebling Soc. of Morton Plant Found., Clearwater, fla., 1993, A.R. Mitchell Mus., Trinidad, Colo., 1994, Zabel/Perry Fine Art Show, Steamboat Springs, 1995, 97-99, Coors Western Art Exhibit & Sale, 1999-, Danada Sculpture Show, Wheaton, Ill., 1995, 96, Benson Park Sculpture Show, 1984—, Colo. Gov.'s Invitational Show, Loveland, 1993-99, numerous others; featured in numerous publs. With U.S. Army, 1958-60. Avocations: horses, farming, hunting, snowmobiling. Home: 39510 RCR 44 Steamboat Springs CO 80487

ZABEL, SHELDON ALTER, lawyer, law educator; b. Omaha, Apr. 25, 1941; s. Louis Julius and Anne (Rothenberg) Z.; m. Roberta Jean Butz, May 10, 1975; children: Andrew Louis, Douglas Patrick, Robert Stewart Warren. AB cum laude, Princeton U., 1963; JD cum laude, Northwestern U., 1966. Bar: Ill. 1966, U.S. Supreme Ct. 1976. Law clk. to presiding justice Ill. Supreme Ct., 1966-67; assoc. Schiff, Hardin & Waite, Chgo., 1967-73, ptnr., 1973—. Instr. environ. law Loyola U., Chgo. Bd. dirs. Chgo. Zool. Soc. Mem. ABA, Chgo. Bar Assn., Chgo. Coun. Lawyers, Order of Coif, Union League Club, Met. Club (Chgo.) Jewish. Avocations: skiing, squash. Office: Schiff Hardin & Waite 7200 Sears Tower 233 S Wacker Dr Ste 7200 Chicago IL 60606-6473 E-mail: szabel@schiffhardin.com.

ZABEL, VIVIAN ELLOUISE, secondary education educator; b. Randolph AFB, Tex., July 28, 1943; d. Raymond Louis and Dolly Veneta (Lyles) Gilbert; m. Robert Lee Zabel, Feb. 18, 1962; children: René Lynne, Robert Lee Jr., Randel Louis, Regina Louise. BA in English and Speech, Panhandle State U., 1977; postgrad., U. Ctrl. Okla., 1987-92. Cert. tchr., Okla. Tchr. English, drama, speech, debate Buffalo (Okla.) H.S., 1977-79; tchr. English, drama, speech Schulter (Okla.) H.S., 1979-80; tchr. English Morris (Okla.) H.S., 1980-81; tchr. speech, drama, debate Okla. Christian Schs., Edmond, 1981-82; tchr. English, drama, debate, speech/debate coach Braman (Okla.) H.S., 1982-83; debate coach Pawhuska (Okla.) H.S., 1983-84; tchr. English, French, drama, speech and debate coach Luther (Okla.) H.S., 1984-95; tchr. debate, forensics, yearbook, newspaper, mag., creative writing, competitive speech Deer Creek H.S., Edmond, Okla., 1995—2001; ret., 2001. Dir. drama Nazarene Youth Impact Team, Collinsville, Okla., 1979-81; tchr. h.s. Sun. sch. class Edmond Ch. of Nazarene, 1991-94; mem. cmty.-sch. rels. com. Luther Pub. Schs., 1991-92, supt.'s adv. com., 1992-94. Editor: Potpourri mag., 1975—77; author (under name Vivian Gilbert Zabel): Reflected Images; author: poetry, short stories, novels. Adult supr. Texas County 4-H, Adams, Okla., 1975-77; double diamond coach NFL; adjudicator and tournament dir. qualifying OSSAA Tournaments. Recipient Disting. Svc. award NFL, 1994, Editor's Choice award for poetry, 1997, 1998, 1999, Tchr. of Excellence, 1996, Outstanding Poet award, 1997, 1998, 1999, 2001. Mem. Nat. Debate Coaches Assn., Nat. Fedn. Interscholastic Speech and Debate Assn., Okla. Speech Theatre Comms. Assn., Okla. Tchrs. English, Internat. Soc. Poets. Republican. Nazarene. Home: 2912 Rankin Ter Edmond OK 73013-5344 E-mail: vzabel@juno.com. *Children are our future, yet we are living in an age of throw-away children. We must find a way to save these children, to give them purpose, training, and love so that they have a promising future, and so will we.*

ZABETAKIS, PAUL MICHAEL, nephrologist, educator; b. Washington, July 30, 1947; s. Michael G. and Rebecca A. (Banakas) Z.; m. Martha Robinson, Oct. 3, 1970; 1 child, Amy Shannon. BA, Washington & Jefferson Coll., 1969; mD, U. Tenn., 1972. Diplomate Am. Bd. Internal Medicine, Am. Bd. Nephrology. Intern in medicine U. Pitts., 1972-73, resident in medicine, 1973-75; fellow in nephrology Yale U., New Haven, 1975-77; asst. chief nephrology-hypertension Lenox Hill Hosp., N.Y.C., 1977-82, assoc. chief nephrology-hypertension, 1978-99, dir. home peritoneal dialysis, 1985-99; asst. prof. clin. medicine N.Y. Med. Coll., Valhalla, N.Y., 1980-88, assoc. prof. clin. medicine, 1988-92; clin. asst. prof. medicine Cornell U., N.Y.C., 1992-93; clin. assoc. prof. medicine NYU, 1993-99; exec. v.p., COO Everest Healthcare Svc., Oak Park, Ill., 1999-2001; CEO Extracorporeal Alliance Fresenius Med. Care, N.Am., 2001—. Mem. editl. bd. Clinical Nephrology, 1979—, Clinical and Experimental Dialysis and Apheresis, 1983-86, Geriatric Nephrology and Urology, 1995—, Advances in Renal Replacement Therapy, 1999—; nephrology cons. Nicholas Inst. Sports Medicine and Athletic Trauma Lenox Hill Hosp., N.Y.C., 1978-99, rsch. physician, 1982-99; mem. hypertension svc. adv. com. ARC, N.Y.C., 1981-99; mem. exec. com. End Stage Renal Disease Network N.Y. Inc., 1986-99, treas., 1992-93, chmn. long-range planning com., 1994; bd. dirs. Physician Hosp. Orgn. Lenox Hill Hosp., chmn. bd. dirs., 1996-99, v.p. med. bd., 1997-99; vice-chmn. quality improvement, med. dir. Everest Healthcare Svcs., Chgo., 1996-99. Contbr. numerous chpts. to books; patentee in field; lectr. in field; contbr. articles to profl. jours. Fellow ACP, Am. Coll. Preventive Medicine, Am. Coll. Sports Medicine; mem. N.Y. County Med. Soc., Med. Soc. of State of N.Y., Am. Heart Assn., Westchester Heart Assn., N.Y. Soc. Nephrology, Am. Soc. Nephrology, Internat. Soc. Nephrology, N.Y. Acad. Scis., N.Y. State Fedn. Profl. Health Educators, Am. Fedn. Clin. Sch., Internat. Soc. Peritoneal Dialysis, Am. Soc. Artificial Internal Organs (program com. 1995-99), Soc. Critical Care Medicine, Am. Coll. Nutrition, Internat. Soc. for Renal Nutrition and Metabolism, Internat. Soc. Geriatric Nephrology and Urology (founding mem., sec-treas. 1994-99). Avocation: sailboat racing. E-mail: paul.zabetakis@fmc-na.com.

ZABETAKIS, THOMAS JOHN, federal agency administrator; b. Balt., Dec. 3, 1955; s. Thomas and Mary Catherine (Potts) Zabetakis; m. Deborah Lynn Wilson, Aug. 12, 1978; children: Jennifer Lynn, Thomas Michael. AA, Anne Arundel CC, Arnold, Md., 1976; BS, U. Balt., 1978, MBA, 1986. Agt. IRS, Balt., 1978-87, mgr., 1987-88; sr. bus. mgr. U.S. Dept. Def., Ft. Meade, 1988—, program mgr., 1998—. Mentor acquisisiotn reform tng. com. U.S. Dept. Def., 1997, mentor bus. mgr. professionalization com., 97, math edn. program, 2000—, subject matter expert, 2001—, bus. mgr. Acquisition Workforce Improvement Act (DAWIA) level 3; level 3 cert. bus. mgr. DAWIA. Nat. tournament dir. PONY, 2001—; Dir. Fast pitch Softball Clinics, Glen Burnie, Md., 1995—; field dir. Pony Softball, Millersville, 1994—, regional field dir., 1999—; v.p. North County Cmty. Girls Softball, 1994—; asst. coach Storm Fast Pitch Softball, Glen Burnie, 1996—99, Angels Fast Pitch Softball, Glen Burnie, 1994—96; v.p. Harundale youth Sports League Travel Softball Teams, Millersville, 1998—; active Balt. and Ohio R.R. Hist. Soc., 1992—; treas. Glen Burnie HS Athletic Boosters, 1997—2000. Mem.: Md. Soc. Accts., Acquisition Mgmt. Assn., Performance Mgmt. Assn. (v.p. publs. 1993—95, v.p. membership 1992—93), Nat. Fast Pitch Coaches Assn., KC (inside guard 1995—96, editor newsletter 1993—99, recorder 1996—99, treas. 1999—, Knight of Month 1994). Avocation: model railroading. Home: 410 Washington Blvd Glen Burnie MD 21061-3882

ZABINSKY, ZELDA BARBARA, operations researcher, industrial engineering educator; b. Tonawanda, N.Y., Oct. 31, 1955; d. Joseph Marvin and Helen Phyllis (Kava) Z.; m. John Clinton Palmer, July 15, 1979; children: Rebecca Ann Zabinsky, Aaron Zeff Palmer. BS, U. Puget Sound, Tacoma,

1977; MS, U. Mich., 1984, PhD, 1985. Tutor math. U. Puget Sound, 1975-77; programmer, analyst Nat. Marine Fisheries, Seattle, 1977, Boeing Computer Svcs., Seattle, 1977-78; sr. systems analyst Vector Rsch. Inc., Ann Arbor, Mich., 1980-84; asst. prof. indsl. engring. U. Wash., Seattle, 1985-93, assoc. prof. indsl. engring., 1993-98, affiliated prof. mech. engring., 1993—, affiliated prof. civil engring., 1996—; prof. indsl. engring., 1998—, affiliated prof. elec. engring., 2000—. Cons. Boeing Corp., Seattle, 1987, Numerical Methods, Inc., Seattle, 1989-90, METRO, Seattle, 1992, Microsoft, Seattle, 1998-99. Contbr. articles to tech. jours. Mem. faculty adv. bd. Women in Engring., U. Wash., 1990—. Recipient E. Goman Math. award, 1977, Rsch. Initiation award NSF, 1992-95; Howarth-Thompson scholar, 1973-77; Benton fellow, 1983-84, Erskine fellow 1998; rsch. grantee NSF, NASA-Langley, FAA, Nat. Forest Svc., NATO, Boeing, 1985—; Excellence in Tchg. award, U. Wash., Seattle, 1999; named Outstanding Professor, 2001. Mem. Ops. Rsch. Soc. Am., Inst. Indsl. Engrs. (sr.), Math. Programming Soc., Mortar Board, Phi Kappa Phi, Alpha Pi Mu. Jewish. Avocations: family activities, camping, skiing, windsurfing. Office: U Wash PO Box 352650 Seattle WA 98195-2650 E-mail: zelda@u.washington.edu.

ZABKA, SVEN PAUL, lawyer; b. Heide, Germany, May 11, 1971; s. Clifton Thomas and Lieselotte A.M. Zabka. BA cum laude with dept. honors in econs., Union Coll., Schenectady, N.Y., 1993; JD, Emory U., 1996. Bar: Ga. 1996, D.C. 1997. Assoc. Smith, Gambrell & Russell, LLP, Atlanta, 1997—. Mem. Emory Law Rev., 1994. Mem. Omicron Delta Epsilon. Avocations: water polo, skiing. Office: Smith Gambrell & Russell 1230 Peachtree St NE Ste 3100 Atlanta GA 30309-3592 E-mail: szabka@sgrlaw.com.

ZABLOCKI, ELAINE, writer; b. Bklyn., June 13, 1942; d. Harry and Anne Finkelstein; m. Benjamin D. Zablocki; 1 child, Abraham M. BA with honors, Swarthmore Coll., 1963. Adminstr. Takilma (Oreg.) Clinic, 1973-80; freelance writer, polit. cons. Oreg., 1981-82; asst. com. adminstr. Oreg. Senate Com. on Human Svcs. and Aging, Salem, 1983; newsletter mgr. New Options, Inc., Washington, 1983-85; writer Craver, Mathews, Smith & Co., Falls Church, Va., 1985-86; freelance writer specializing in healthcare Corona Comms., Arlington, 1986-98, Eugene, Oreg., 1999—. Reporter WebMD, 2000—. Author: Changing Physician Practice Patterns, 1995—; editor Physician Mgr. Newsletter, 1994-95; contbg. editor The Quality Letter for Healthcare Leaders, 1994—; editor Alternative Medicine Business News, 1999; contbr. numerous articles to profl. publs.

ZABOROWSKI, PAUL DAVID, priest; b. Pitts., Dec. 2, 1961; s. Henry Paul and Alice Catherine Zaborowski. BS in Social Work, U. Pitts., 1980; MDiv, Washington Theol. U., 1995. Family counselor Holy Family Inst., Pitts., 1987—89; assoc. pastor Shrine of the Sacred Heart, Washington, 1995—. Chmn. parish social justice com., Washington, 1999—. Mem.: Capuchin Friars. Avocations: painting, crafts, gardening. Home and Office: Shrine of the Sacred Heart Ch 3211 Pine St NW Washington DC 20010

ZABRISKIE, SHERRY LAFOLLETTE, filmmaker, author, actress; b. Madison, Wis., Feb. 22, 1936; d. Philip Fox and Isabel (Bacon) LaFollette; m. George Albert Zabriskie, feb. 10, 1962; children: Oliver LaFollette, Tavia LaFollette. Student, Bennington (Vt.) Coll., 1958, Stella Adler, N.Y.C., 1959, Uta Hagen, 1959. Filmmaker Zabriskie Prodns., N.Y.C., 1962—; profl. chef Sherry's Specialties, Sharon, Conn., 1978—. Actress in Tall Story, Broadway, N.Y.C., 1959, various summer stock, 1953-62, Late Night with Conar O'Brian, N.Y.C., 1998—; Voice of Cheer opposite Alfred Drake as Voice of Gloom in Exxon's Great Energy Answer Hunt, 1975; co-author: (book) Belle Biography of Belle Case LaFollette, 1984, (screenplay) Summerdog, 1977, (cookbooks) Empanadas, 1982, Pancakes, 1983. Justice of the Peace, State of Conn., Salisbury, 1977-82; active fundraising various polit. campaigns. Recipient Golden Eagle award Coun. of Internat. Events, Washington, 1964, Silver Spoon award Woman's Day, 1978; Josephine Bay/Michael Paul Found. grantee, 1988. Mem. Actors Equity, Screen Actors Guild, Am. Fedn. Radio and TV Artists, The Authors Guild. Democrat. Avocations: travel, food, wine, gardening, walking, theater. Home: 14 Schermerhorn St Brooklyn NY 11201-4803 Office: Zabriskie Productions PO Box 21524 Brooklyn NY 11202-1524

ZABSKY, JOHN MITCHELL, engineering executive; b. Joplin, Mo., Apr. 18, 1933; s. Joseph Anthony and Joan (Lucas) Z. AS, Joplin Jr. Coll., 1953; BSME, U. Mo., 1956; MSME, U. Kans., 1965. Profl. engr., Mo. System engr. Bendix KCD, Kansas City, Mo., 1958-62; rsch. engr. Rocketdyne, Neosho, 1962-65, Boeing Co., Huntsville, Ala., 1965-66; prin. rsch. engr., scientist Honeywell Inc., St. Paul, 1966-71; chief engr. Pressure Tank & Pipe Fabrication Co., Nashville, 1971-72, Engring. for Industry, Danville, Va., 1972-73; area mgr. fluid machinery Dresser Adv. Tech. Ctr., Irvine, Calif., 1973-85; v.p. ops. ATI, Laguna Niguel, 1985-93; pres. Cytoprobe, San Diego, 1993-94, v.p. ops., 1994-95. Cons. Oral Care Products, L.A., 1990-92, Kleenair Sys., Inc., Irvine, Calif., 1995—. Patentee in field. Pres. Mpls.-St. Paul Singletons, 1969-72. Mem. AIAA, ASME, Mo. Soc. Profl. Engrs., Soc. Mfg. Engrs. Home: 3640 S Main St Apt C Santa Ana CA 92707-5726 Office: Kleenair Sys Inc 1711 Langley Irvine CA 92614 E-mail: jzabsky@kair.com.

ZACARIAS, FERNANDO R. K. physician; b. Sept. 9, 1944; MD, U. Mexico, Mexico City, 1969; DPH, Harvard U., 1986. Intern St. Francis Gen. Hosp., Pitts.; resident in family medicine U. Miami; resident in internal medicine, infectious diseases Grady Meml. Hosp. Emory U., Atlanta; assoc. researcher Mexican Social Security Inst., 1975-79; prof. cmty. medicine U. Mex., 1978-79; prof. microbiology and parasitology U. Anáhuac, Mexico City, 1976-79; vis. scientist Ctrs. for Disease Control, Atlanta, 1982-84; regional advisor on STD and AIDS Pan Am. Health Orgn., Washington, 1984-89, sr. regional advisor on AIDS/STD, 1989-93, coord. AIDS/STD program, 1993—.

ZACCAGNI, JAMES LOUIS, accountant; b. Springfield, Ill., Oct. 12, 1945; s. Louis Paul and Hazel June (Unland) Z.; m. Jennifer G. Zaccagni, Feb. 25, 1978; children: Zachary, Kirsten, Hayden, Amanda. BSBA, So. Ill. U., 1969. CPA, Ill., Tex. Sr. ptnr. Pehlman & Dold CPA's, Springfield, Ill., 1971-85; pvt. practice San Antonio, 1985-88; sr. tax ptnr. Lowrey, Zaccagni & Crider, 1988—. Treas., v.p. Children's Chorus of San Antonio, 1988—; advisor Women's Aglow fellowship, 1988-92, Full Gospel Bus. Men's fellowship Internat., 1992—, pres. and treas., 1989—; treas. Assn. of Spirit Filled fellowship. Mem. Internat. Assn. of Fin. Planners (officer, bd. dirs. 1991—), Tex. Soc. of CPA's (advanced cert. corp. taxation 1994), AICPA, San Antonio Chpt. of CPA's. Avocations: landscaping, music. Office: Lowrey Zaccagni & Crider 14100 San Pedro Ave Ste 300 San Antonio TX 78232-4362

ZACCARI, STEVEN JOSEPH, secondary school educator; b. Bedford, N.Y., Oct. 28, 1967; s. Angelo Raymond Zaccari and Nora Mary Donnelly. BS in Chemistry, Siena Coll., 1989; MS in Secondary Edn., Coll. St. Rose, 1998. Chemist Adirondack Environ. Svcs., Albany, NY, 1989—98; chemistry tchr. Colonie (N.Y.) H.S., 1998—. Cons. Adirondack Environ., Albany, NY, 1998—. Songwriter: music compact disc The Sound Asylym, 1996. Mem.: NSTA, STANYS. Roman Catholic. Avocations: camping, hiking, writing music, swimming. Home: 403 Shaker Rd Albany NY 12211-1933

ZACCONE, SUZANNE MARIA, sales executive; b. Chgo., Oct. 23, 1957; d. Dominic Robert and Lorretta F. (Urban) Zaccone. Grad. high sch., Downers Grove, Ill. Sales sec. Brookeridge Realty, Downers Grove, 1975-76; sales cons. Kafka Estates Inc., 1975-76; adminstrv. asst. Chem. Dist., Inc., Oak Brook, Ill., 1976-77; sales rep., mgr. Anographics Corp., Burr Ridge, 1977-85; pres., owner Graphic Solutions, Inc., 1985—. Curriculum adv. bd. mem. Sch. Dist. 99, 1997, 1998, 1999, 2000, 2001. Named Supplier of Yr. Through Preferred Supplied, Gen. Binding Corp., 1988—99; recipient Supplier Mem. award, Internat. Bottled Water Assn., 1987—88, Supplier award for excellence U.S., SBA, 1990, Top Performer Supplier award, Cutler Hammer Westinghouse Divsn., 1993, 1994, 1995, 1996, 1997, 1997, 1998, 1999, Blue Chip Enterprise Initiative award, 1994. Mem.: NAFE, World Label Assn. (1st pl. in World Championship 1994, 1995, 1996, 2002), Women in Packaging (exec. bd.), Inst. Packaging Profls., Women Entrepreneurs DuPage County (past pres.), Tag and Label Mfrs. Inst. (chmn. pub. rels. and mktg. com., bd. dirs., pres. 1998-2000) (1st place award in U.S. for Screen Printing 1994, 1995, 1996, 1997, 1999, 2000, 2001, Best Managed Co. award 2001, 2002, 1992, 2001). Avocation: Avocations: reading, sailing, cooking, needlepoint, scuba diving. Office: Graphic Solutions Inc 311 Shore Dr Hinsdale IL 60521-5859

ZACEK, JOSEPH FREDERICK, history educator, international studies consultant, Central and East European culture and affairs specialist; b. Stickney, Ill., Dec. 18, 1930; s. Joseph and Emilie (Dvorak) Z.; m. Judith Ellen Cohen (div. 1975); 1 child, Natalie Ann; m. Jane Perlberg Shapiro; stepchildren: Leslie Helen, Peter Carl. BA summa cum laude, U. Ill., Champaign-Urbana, 1952, MA in History, 1953, PhD in History, 1962; cert., Columbia U. Inst. on East Cen. Europe, 1962. Asst. prof. history Occidental Coll., L.A., 1962-65; asst. prof., dir. Russian & East European Programs UCLA, 1965-68; assoc. prof. SUNY at Albany, 1968-71, dir. Russian & East European Programs, 1968-77, 91-92, prof., 1971—2001, chair dept. history, 1974-77, prof. emeritus, 2001—. Mem. selection com. for East Europe Internat. Rsch. and Exch. Bd., Princeton, N.J., 1978-81; nat. bd. cons. NEH, Washington, 1975—; vis. scholar IREX Comenius U., Bratislava, and Charles U., Prague, Czechoslovakia, 1973, Columbia U., 1977-78, U. Ill, Champaign-Urbana, 1987. Author: Palacky: The Historian as Scholar and Nationalist, 1970; editor, co-author: Frantisek Palacky, 1798-1876: A Centennial Appreciation, 1981, The Enlightenment and the National Revivals in Eastern Europe, 1983, The Intimate Palacky, 1984); also numerous periodical articles and chpts. in multi-authored books. With M.I., U.S. Army, 1954-57. Fgn. Area Tng. fellow Ford Found., Columbia U., 1960-62, Sr. Humanities fellow Rockefeller Found., 1977-78, fellow Russian Rsch. Ctr. Harvard U., 1986-91; rsch. grantee Am. Coun. Learned Soc./Soc. Sci. Rsch. Coun., 1965, Am. Philos. Soc., 1968; recipient Comenius medal Govt. of Czech and Slovak Fed. Republic, 1992, Medal of Comenius Pedagogical Inst. in Prague, 1992, Josef Hlávka medal of Czechoslovak Acad. of Scis. in Prague, 1992; also other grad. and postdoctoral awards and grants. Mem. Am. Hist. Assn., Am. Assn. for Advancement Slavic Studies, Western Slavic Conf., Czechoslovak History Conf., Slovak Studies Assn., Consortium on Revolutionary Europe, Assn. for Study of Ethnicity and Nationalism, Phi Beta Kappa. Avocations: travel, gardening, music. Office: SUNY Dept History Albany NY 12222-0001

ZACH, DEBRA JEAN, social worker; b. Omaha, Apr. 16, 1958; d. Louis Richard and Mary Rose (Roza) Matcha; m. John Paul Zach, Sept. 10, 1988; children: Katie Elizabeth, Abby Morgan. BS, Wayne (Nebr.) State Coll., 1982. Child life assistance Children's Meml. Hosp., Omaha, 1982-84; ind. living advisor League of Human Dignity, Norfolk, 1984-87, Lincoln, 1987-93, tng. cooord., 1993, ind. living svcs. coord. Omaha, 1993-95, dir. Southwest Iowa Ctr. for Ind. Living Council Bluffs, Iowa, 1995—99, Medicaid waiver svcs. dir. Scottsbluff, Nebr., 1999—. Co-chmn. Saunders County Interagy., Wahoo, Nebr., 1987-93, Closing the Gap, Fremont, Nebr., 1987-93, v.p., 1991-93; historian Active Community Team, Wahoo, 1990-93; mem. adv. bd. Kimberly Quality Care Profl., 1993, steering com. Nebr. Parents Ctr., 1993, Lincoln Respite Com., 1993, Coalition for Older Health Promotion, adv. com. NET Captioning, steering com. Project Fremont for Bethpage Group Home, Cass County Agency, Project Help, 1993, Pvt. Indsl. Coun., 1993—, Bd. Strat. Planning Com., 1993—. Mem. DD Coun. 1993-95, MS chpt. Svcs., 1994-95; active Harrison County Preservation Adv., 1995, Pottawattamie County Steering Com., 1995, Human Svcs. Adv. Coun., 1995, IDEAS Project 1995, SILC, 1995, I-Sail, 1995, Interpreter Referral Task Force, 1995. Democrat. Roman Catholic. Avocations: sewing, cross-stitch, bowling, camping, cooking. Home: 2525 Valencia Dr Gering NE 69341-1936

ZACHAI, DOHRN DORIAN, artist; b. Jersey City, Mar. 16, 1932; m. Bill Sax, Aug. 15, 1961 (div. Dec. 1971). Student, Calif. Coll. Arts and Crafts; Assoc. degree, Rochester Inst. Tech., BA, 1960; student, Cooper Union of Sci. and Art. Asst. prof. Boston U. Sch. for Artisrany, Boston, 1976-80, U. Akron, Ohio, 1980-81, U. Oreg., Corvallis, 1975-76; artist in residence Visual Art Ctr. Alaska, Anchorage, 1974-75; condr. numerous workshops, lectr. in field. Represented in collections St. Paul Mus. Art, Am. Craft Mus., N.Y.C., Wustum Mus. Fine Art, Racine, Wis., Milw. Mus. Art; works featured in publs. including The New American Tapestry, The Art Fabric, Objects USA, A Studio of One's Own. Activist for land conservation issues Com. to Save Atsena Otti, Cedar Key, Fla., 1987. NEA grantee, 1976. Avocations: violin, piano, yoga, swimming. Home: PO Box 573 Oxford MD 21654-0573 *From 1960 to 1980 (under the name Dorian Zachai), Dohrn Dorian Zachai created two decades of work using tapestry and woven construction techniques. Fiber and non-traditional weaving materials were used to execute three dimensional, relief, and flat images. Since 1980 (using the name Dohrn Zachai) she has created paintings and drawings. Social awareness/commentary and the man/woman/nature relationship motivate her and are the continuous thread between her Fiber Art and her Fine Art.*

ZACHARIAS, DONALD WAYNE, academic administrator; b. Salem, Ind., Sept. 28, 1935; s. William Otto and Estelle Mae (Newlon) Z.; m. Tommie Kline Dekle, Aug. 16, 1959; children: Alan, Eric, Leslie. BA, Georgetown (Ky.) Coll., 1957, LLD (hon.), 1983; MA, Ind. U., 1959, PhD, 1963. Asst. prof. communication and theatre Ind. U., 1963-69; assoc. prof. U. Tex., Austin, 1969-72, prof., 1972-79, asst. to pres., 1974-77; exec. asst. to chancellor U. Tex. System, 1978-79; pres. Western Ky. U., 1979-85, Miss. State U., Starkville, 1985-97, pres. emeritus, 1998—. Bd. dirs. First Fed. Savs. & Loan Assn., Bowling Green, Ky., Inst. for Tech. Devel., Sanderson Farms, Inc., Miss. Econ. Coun.; dir. John Grisham Libr., Starkville, 1998. Author: In Pursuit of Peace: Speeches of the Sixties, 1970. Bd. dirs. Greenview Hosp.; pres. Southeastern Conf., 1989-91. With U.S. Army, 1959-60. Named Mississippian of Yr. Data Processing Mgmt. Assn.; recipient Teaching award Ind. U. Found., 1963, Cactus Teaching award U. Tex., 1971, Justin Smith Morrill award U.S. Dept. Agriculture, 1992, Disting. Teaching award Honors Program, 2000. Mem. Inst. Tech. Devel. (bd. dirs. 1985-92), Nat. Assn. State Univs. and Land-Grant Colls. (exec. com. 1990-92), Phi Kappa Phi (pres. 1978). Democrat. Episcopalian.

ZACHARIAS, NIKOLAOS MARIOS, obstetrician/gynecologist; b. Athens, Greece; s. Marios Nikolaos and Constantoula Marios Zacharias; m. Ioanna Dimitrios Athanassaki, May 12, 2000. MD, Nat. and Kapodistrian U., Athens, 1995. Gen. practitioner Greek Nat. Health Svc., Vassiliki, Greece, 1996-97; gen. surgery intern Laikon Gen. Hosp., Athens, 1997-98; chief resident in ob-gyn. Baylor U., Houston, 1998—; fellow in maternal-fetal medicine med. br. U. Tex. Med. Br., Galveston, 2002—. Undergraduate Ann. scholar Found. State Scholarships, 1990-94; Papadakis grantee Nat. and Kapodistrian U. Athens, 1990-95, Kontoleon grantee, 1998--. Fellow ACOG; mem. Athens Med. Assn., Gen. Med. Coun., Tex. Med. Assn., Soc. for Maternal-Fetal Medicine. Avocations: swimming, basketball, travel. Home: 6011 Saint Andrews Dr Pasadena TX 77505-4803 Office: U Tex Med Br 3.400 John Sealy Annex Bldg MFM Ste 301 University Blvd Galveston TX 77555 Office Fax: 409-772-5297. E-mail: nmzach@yahoo.com.

ZACHARIAS, THOMAS ELLING, real estate executive; b. Morristown, N.J., Feb. 19, 1954; s. John Elling and Muriel (Eckes) Z.; m. Clelia LeBoutillier, June 22, 1985; children: Clelia Delafield, John Livingston. BArch and Urban Planning, Princeton U., 1976; MBA, Yale U., 1979. Project dir. N.Y. State Urban Devel. Corp., N.Y.C., 1979-81; assoc. Corp. Property Investors, 1981-87, v.p., 1987-98, Corp. Realty Cons., N.Y.C., 1989-98; pres. Brisbane House, Inc., 1994-98; prin. Lend Lease Devel., U.S., N.Y.C., 1998-2000; pres. Lend Lease Manhattan Housing Corp., 1999-2000; sr. v.p. MetroNexus, 2000—02; mng. dir. W.P. Carey & Co. LLC, 2002—. Bd. dirs. Corp. Property Assocs., others. Chmn. Mus. Modern Art Adv. Svc., N.Y.C., 1981-87; mem. steering com. Whitney Mus. Lobby Gallery Assocs., N.Y.C., 1985-92; bd. dirs. Creative Time, N.Y.C., 1982-88, Nat. Acad. Design, 1988-90; bd. overseers Southampton Coll., 1995-96. Fgn. Study grantee McConnel Found., London, 1975. Mem. Nat. Assn. Real Estate Investments Trusts, Internat. Coun. Shopping Ctrs., Urban Land Inst., Meadow Club. Home: 1215 5th Ave New York NY 10029-5209 also: 65 Post Crossing Southampton NY 11968-3446 Office: WP Carey & Co LLC 50 Rockefeller Plz New York NY 10020 E-mail: tzacharias@wpcarey.com.

ZACHARSKI, DENNIS EDWARD, lawyer; b. Detroit, Feb. 25, 1951; s. Edward J. and Margaret R. (Cendrowski) Z.; m. Susan G. Foster, Aug. 8, 1975; children: Jeffrey Alan, Lauren Michelle. BBA, U. Mich., 1973; JD, Mich. State U., 1977. Bar: Mich. 1977, U.S. Dist. Ct. (ea. dist.) Mich. 1977, U.S. Dist. Ct. (we. dist.) Mich. 1982, U.S. Supreme Ct. 1988, U.S. Ct. Appeals (6th cir.) 1990, Ohio, 1993. Atty. Lacey & Jones, Birmingham, Mich., 1977—. Case evaluator Mediation Tribunal Assn., Detroit; arbitrator Am. Arbitration Assn., Southfield, Mich. Mem. Oakland County Bar Assn., Assn. Trial Def. Counsel, Mich. Trial Def. Counsel. Avocations: golf, skiing, soccer, tennis, cycling. Office: Lacey & Jones 600 S Adams Rd Ste 300 Birmingham MI 48009-6827 E-mail: dzacharski@laceyjones.com.

ZACHARY, LOUIS GEORGE, chemical company consultant; b. Aug. 14, 1927; s. George E. and Angelike (Hantsis) Zacharakis; m. Lillie Vletas, Apr. 20, 1955; children: Leslie A., Louis George. Prodn. supr. Dewey & Almy Co., Acton, Mass., 1951-52; salesman chem. divsn. Union Camp Corp., Wayne, N.J., 1952-59, sales mgr. chem. divsn., 1959-62, gen. mgr. chem. ops., 1962-66, gen. mgr. chem. divsn., 1970-78, v.p., 1974-78, Drake Mgmt. Co., N.Y.C., 1966-70; sr. v.p. GAF Corp., 1978-82, mem. office of chmn., 1981-82; cons., 1983-84; chmn., CEO Universal Die Casting, Inc., Saline, Mich., 1984-90; acting pres. chem. divsn. Church & Dwight Inc., 1990-91; v.p. Nat. Exec. Svc. Corp., N.Y.C., 1993-96. Mem. vis. com. chem. engring. dept. Johns Hopkins U., Balt., 1981-83. Co-editor: Tall Oil and Its Uses, 1965. With USN, 1945-46. Mem. Chem. Mfrs. Assn. (dir. 1979-83), Synthetic Organic Chem. Mfrs. Assn., Soc. Chem. Industry, Harvard Club N.J. (exec. com.; trustee 2000—). Home: 227 Oak Ridge Ave Summit NJ 07901-3258

ZACHER, VALERIE IRENE, interior designer; b. Woodland, Calif., Dec. 12, 1942; d. Albert Richard and Laura Ruth (Mast) Z.; m. William Robert Wallace, June 14, 1964 (div. Oct. 1968); 1 child, Jason Zachery Wallace. BA in Polit. Sci., Stanford U., 1964; AS in Interior Design, West Valley Coll., 1982; cert. TESL, U. Calif. Santa Cruz, Santa Clara, 1994. Owner, operator Artefactorage, Fresno, Calif., 1968-77; owner, designer Viz a Viz, Los Gatos, 1978-82; facilities project mgr. Nat. Semiconductor, Santa Clara, 1982-85; project supr. Mervyns, Hayward, 1985-86; interior designer, project mgr. Charles Schwab & Co., San Francisco, 1986-87; small bus. advisor US Peace Corps, Gaborone, Botswana, 1987-89, Swedish Coop. Ctr., Gaborone, 1989-90; English tchr. YCC Am. Club, Yokohama, Japan, 1992-93; interior design cons. Los Gatos, 1993—. Design/facilities cons. Octel Comm. Corp., Milpitas, Calif., 1994-97, Palm, Inc., Santa Clara; interior designer Am. Cancer Soc. Designers Showcase, 1994, 95, 96, San Jose Symphony Designers Showhouse, 1998, 2002. Mem. Internat. Facilities Mgrs. Assn. Avocations: gourmet cooking, gardening, travel. Home and Office: 16721 Madrone Ave Los Gatos CA 95030-4120

ZACHERT, MARTHA JANE, retired librarian; b. York, Pa., Feb. 7, 1920; d. Paul Rodes and Elizabeth Agnes (Lau) Koontz; m. Edward G. Zachert, Aug. 25, 1946; 1 child, Lillian Elizabeth. AB, Lebanon Valley Coll., 1941; MLS, Emory U., 1953; DLS, Columbia U., 1968. Asst. Enoch Pratt Free Library, Balt., 1941-46; head librarian Wood Research Inst., Atlanta, 1947; sch. librarian DeKalb (Ga.) County Schs., 1950-52; head librarian, prof. history of pharmacy So. Coll. Pharmacy, Mercer U., Atlanta, 1952-63; instr. Ga. State Coll., 1962-63, Emory U., summers 1955-59, 1956-57, 59-60; mem. faculty Library Sch., Fla. State U., 1963-78, prof., 1973-78, Coll. Librarianship U. S.C., Columbia, 1973-74, 78-84. Vis. fellow Brit. Library, 1980; cons. So. Regional Med. Library, Emory U., 1976-77, Nat. Library Medicine, 1977, others. Author: Fine Painting in Georgia, 1950s-1960, 1994; assoc. editor Jour. Libr. History, 1966-71, 73-76; mng. editor, 1971-73; cons. editor Jour. Libr. Adminstrn., 1979-86; contbr. numerous articles to profl. jours. Fellow Med. Libr. Assn. (named among 100 Most Notables 1998); mem. ALA, Spl. Librs. Assn. (past pres. Fla. chpt., spl. citation 1977, Hall of Fame 1985), Am. Printing History Assn., Beta Phi Mu (pres. 1974-75). Home and Office: 2018 W Randolph Cir Tallahassee FL 32308-3349

ZACHERT, VIRGINIA, psychologist, educator; b. Jacksonville, Ala., Mar. 1, 1920; d. R.E. and Cora H. (Massee) Z. Student, Norman Jr. Coll., 1937; AB, Ga. State Woman's Coll., 1940; MA, Emory U., 1947; PhD, Purdue U., 1949. Diplomate: Am. Bd. Profl. Psychologists. Statistician Davison-Paxon Co., Atlanta, 1941-44; research psychologist Mil. Contracts, Auburn Research Found., Ala. Poly. Inst.; indsl. and research psychologist Sturm & O'Brien (cons. engrs.), 1958-59; research project dir. Western Design, Biloxi, Miss., 1960-61; self-employed cons. psychologist Norman Park, Ga., 1961-71, Good Hope, 1971-99. Rsch. assoc. med. edn. Med. Coll. Ga., Augusta, 1963-65, assoc. prof., 1965-70, rsch. prof., 1970-84, rsch. prof. emeritus, 1984—, chief learning materials divsn., 1973-84, faculty senate, 1976-84, acad. coun., 1976-82, pres. acad. coun., 1983, sec., 1978; mem. Ga. Bd. Examiners Psychologists, 1974-79, v.p., 1977, pres. 1978; adv. bd. Comdr. Gen. ATC USAF, 1967-70; cons. Ga. Silver Haired Legislature, 1980-86, senator, 1987-93, pres. protem, 1987-88, pres., 1989-93, rep., spkr. protem, 1993-96, spkr., 1997-98, Nat. Silver-Haired Congress rep., 1995—, spkr. 1997-99; govs. appointee White House Conf. on Aging, 1971, 96, Ga. Coun. on Aging, 1988-96; U.S. Senate mem. Fed. Coun. on the Aging, 1990-93; senator appointee White House Conf. on Aging, 1995; Ga. Health Decision's appointee to Ga. Coalition for Health, 1996-98. Author: (with P.L. Wilds) Essentials of Gynecology-Oncology, 1967, Applications of Gynecology-Oncology, 1967. Del. White House Conf. on Aging, 1981, 95. Served as aerologist USN, 1944-46;aviation psychologist USAF, 1949-54. Recipient Jane Kennedy Excellence Aging award, 1999. Fellow AAAS, Am. Psychol. Assn.; mem. AAUP (chpt. pres. 1977-80), Sigma Xi, (chpt. pres. 1980-81) Baptist. Home: 4275 Owens Rd # 403 Evans GA 30809 *It's really quite simple-I find, if I wish to be understood or heard, that simplicity is necessary but not ever easy. Simplicity is basic, essential and always the major factor in my search for truth.*

ZACHMANN, MILO, retired pediatric endocrinologist; b. Basel, Switzerland, June 9, 1936; s. Fritz and Marguerite (Bühler) Z.; m. Charlotte Schreiber, May 19, 1959; children: Claudia, Nicole, Sandra. MD, U. Basel, 1961. Cert. pediatrics, pediatric endocrinology. Asst. pediatric surgery U. Basel, 1962-63; resident Variety Children's Hosp., Miami, Fla., 1963-64; rsch. fellow Jackson Meml. Hosp., 1964-65; sr. lectr. U. Zurich, Switzerland, 1966-78, assoc. prof. dept. pediatrics Switzerland, 1972-78, prof. Switzerland, 1978—. Bd. mem. Ares-Serono Pharm. Co.; hon. cons. U. Warsaw, 1987. Contbr. over 200 articles to profl. jours., chpts. to books. 1st lt. Med. Svc. Swiss Army. Mem. European Soc. Pediatric Endocrinology (sec. gen. 1972-78, Andrea Prader prize 1988), Swiss Pediatric Assn. (sec. gen., Fanconi award 1986), Swiss Endocrine Soc. (coun. mem.), Japanese Soc. Pediatric Endocrinology (hon.). Avocation: flying. Office: U Zurich Dept Pediatrics 75 Steinwiesstrasse 8032 Zurich Switzerland E-mail: zachmann@access.unizh.ch.

ZACHMANN, WILLIAM FRANCIS, computer and communications industry market research company executive; b. Cleve., Oct. 19, 1942; s. Kurt Wilhelm and Jean (O'Konski) Z.; m. Elizabeth Ann Loftus, June 7, 1980. BA, Harvard U., 1966. Programmer, analyst Cambridge (Mass.) Computer Assocs., 1967-69; sys. rsch. officer 1st Nat. Bank, Boston, 1969-74; dir. rsch. Forum Corp., 1974-75; coord. personnel adminstrn. Harvard U., Cambridge, 1976-77; mgr. tech. support CallData Sys., Boston, 1977-79; v.p. tech. assessment Internat. Data Corp., Framingham, 1979-83, v.p. corp. rsch., 1983-87, sr. v.p., 1987-88; pres. Canopus Rsch., Duxbury, Mass., 1988—, v.p. META Group, editor, pub. Canopus report, 1992—, host Canopus rsch. forum, 1992-99; v.p. Meta Group, Stamford, Conn., 2000—02. Mem. Harvard (Boston), Harvard Faculty (Cambridge), Compuserve. Author: Keys to Application Development Productivity, 1981; contbg. editor Computer Industry Report, 1982-88, Communications and Distributed Resources Report, 1983-87, PC World mag., 1987-88; columnist On Communications mag., 1984-86, Software News mag., 1984-86, Computerworld mag., 1986-88, Infoworld mag., 1987-88, Micromarketworld mag., 1985-87, PC Mag., 1988-92, PC Week mag., 1988-92, MacUser mag., 1988-89, Windows World, 1992-95, Ad Week's Marketing Computers, 1993-95, Computing Pro, 1996-99, CIO mag., 1999—; columnist, sr. contbg. editor OS/2 Professional, 1992-94. Mem. City Mgrs. Adv. Com. on Cable TV, Cambridge, 1979-93; mem. Duxbury Econ. Devel. Com., 1992-95; mem. Planning Bd., Duxbury, 1995-2001, vice chmn., 1996-2000. Home: 160 Standish St Duxbury MA 02332-5065 Office: Canopus Rsch Inc PO Box 2805 Duxbury MA 02331-2805 E-mail: wfz@canopusresearch.com.

ZACK, CHRISTINA SALVADORI, social worker; b. Camden, N.J., Sept. 26, 1966; d. Raymond Michael and Claire Irene (Carlson) Salvadori; m. Robert David Zack, July 8, 1989. B in Psychology cum laude, Glassboro (N.J.) State Coll., 1988; MSW, Rutgers U., 1992. Lic. clin. social worker; cert. sch. social worker, bereavement counselor. Counselor Capable Adolescent Mothers Program, Burlington, N.J., 1988-89; outreach worker Crossroads Programs, Inc., 1989-90; clin. social worker Family Svc. of Burlington County, Family Learning Ctr., Mt. Holly, N.J., 1993-94; med. social worker Virtua Meml.

Hosp. Burlington County, 1990-97, coord. child evaluation ctr., 1997-99; sch. social worker Bordentown (N.J.) Regional Sch. Dist., 1999—. Lectr., parenting instr. Virtua Meml. Hosp. Burlington County, Women's Health Network, Mt. Holly, 1995-2000. Vol. domestic violence response team Providence House, Willingboro, N.J., 1994-95; co-chair Healthy Mothers, Healthy Babies of Burlington County, Network on Adolescent Pregnancy, 1993-95; mem. Cmty. Health Assessment Subcom., 1998-2001, sec., 1998, co-chair, 1999; adv. bd. divsn. youth and family svcs. Commn. on Missing and Abused Children, 1998-2001. Mem. NASW, N.J. Edn. Assn., Assn. for Play Therapy E-mail: tina z. Home: 23 Cynwyd Dr Burlington NJ 08016 Office: Bordentown Regional Sch Dist Office of Spl Svcs 50 Dunns Mill Rd Bordentown NJ 08505-4703

ZACK, DANIEL GERARD, library director; b. Waukegan, Ill., Oct. 1, 1943; s. Raymond Gerard and Rosanna Marie (Atkinson) Z.; m. Mary Frances Anthony, Aug. 25, 1966; children: Jennifer Lee, Rebecca Jane. BA in Psychology, Western Ill. U., 1967; MS in Libr. Sci., U. Ill., 1975. Editor IBM Corp., Rochester, Minn., 1968-70, Memorex Corp., Mpls., 1970-74; rsch. assoc. Libr. Rsch. Ctr. U. Ill., Urbana, 1974-75; asst. dir. Portage County Pub. Libr., Stevens Point, Wis., 1976-78; dir. Burlington (Iowa) Pub. Libr., 1978-87, Gail Borden Pub. Libr., Elgin, Ill., 1987—. Trustee Batavia (Ill.) Pub. Libr., 1997—; founder Friends of Ill. Libr., 1990, bd. dirs. 1990-97. Mem. ALA, ACLU, Ill. Libr. Assn. (mgr. pub. libr. forum 1991-92, 2002—, exec. bd. dirs. 1992-95, pub. policy com. 1995-98), Pub. Libr. Assn. (intellectual freedom com. 1993-96), Kiwanis. Office: Gail Borden Pub Libr Dist 200 N Grove Ave Elgin IL 60120-5505

ZACK, GEORGE J. conductor, music director; b. Pine Bluff, Ark., July 8, 1936; s. George Peter and Eugenia (Paschal) Z.; m. Kerry Sheehan, Oct. 4, 1970; children: Katherine Eugenia, Melissa Sheehan. Student, Am. Conservatory Music, Chgo., 1957, 58; MusB cum laude in Music Theory and Composition, Wichita State U., 1958; MusM in Music Theory and Viola, U. Mich., 1960; PhD in Music Theory, Fla. State U., 1972; studies with Dr. Richard Lert, Stella Roberts, Gustav Meier. Instr. music U. Mich., Ann Arbor, 1962-64; assoc. prof. Hiram (Ohio) Coll., 1964-72; music dir. Music Theater Soc., Lexington, Ky., 1972-75, Lexington Philharm., 1972—, Wooster (Ohio) Symphony, 1973-75, Warren (Ohio) Chamber Orch., 1967—. Artist-in-residence Ea. Ky. U., James Madison U.; guest condr. State Orch. Salonika, Greece, 1981, 83-84, 84-85, Louisville Orch., 1978; condr. N.E. Ohio All State Orch., 1969, Men and Boy's Choir Festival, 1975, 76, N.Y. All-State Orch., 1975, Ky. All-State Orch., 1974, 76, South Bend, Inc., Youngstown, Ohio, Albuquerque Chamber Orch., Monterey County Symphony, Calif., Amarillo, Tex., Bridgeport, Conn., Santa Cruz, Calif., Stockton, Calif., Charleston, S.C., Modesto, Calif., Las Vegas, Nev.; guest speaker various civic orgns. Dir. (radio program) George Zack's Enhancement of Music, Sta. WEKU-FM, 1975—; dir., producer (radio program) The Enhancement of Music, Sta. WBKY-FM, 1973-75, (TV program) Form in Music, NBC, 1965; co-host (TV program) Ky. Morning, 1979. Commr. Picnic with The Pops, Lexington, 1982—. Recipient Orpheus award Phi Mu Alpha, 1976, Hellenic award, 1993, Humanitarian award Nat. Conf., 1994, Optimist Cup, 1999; named Gov. Artist of Yr., State of Ky., 1994. Mem. Am. Symphony Orch. League, Condr.'s Guild, Am. Fedn. Musicians (hon. mem. chpt. 554-635 local 118), Cen. Ky. Youth Music Soc. (bd. dirs., condr.), NCCJ (bd. dirs., co-chmn.). Greek Orthodox. Home: 237 Woodspoint Rd Lexington KY 40502-1905 Office: Lexington Philharm Artists Plaza 161 N Mill St Lexington KY 40507-1125*

ZACK, STEVEN JEFFREY, master automotive instructor; b. Middletown, Conn., Oct. 12, 1955; s. Mathias Charles and Sylvia Ann (Berkowitz) Z. AAS, Williamsport Area C.C., 1976. Cert. EPA instr. Automotive technician Bob Sharp Nissan, Danbury, Conn., 1976-79; svc. engr. Ingersoll Rand, Painted Post, N.Y., 1979-85; tech. svc. rep. Chrysler Motor Corp., Metairie, La., 1985-87; automotive instr. Hartford (Conn.) Tech. Inst., 1988-92; master automotive instr. SPX/Automotive Diagnostics, Kalamazoo, 1992-97, SPX/OTC, Owatonna, Minn., 1997—. Tng. cons. Conn. DMV, North Haven, 1994—; with Coun. of Advanced Automotive Trainers, Lisle, Ill., 1995—; master instr. EPA/Coalition Safer Cleaner Vehicles, Albany, N.Y., 1994—. Contbr. articles to trade jours. Mem. Coalition for Safer Cleaner Vehicles. Achievements include designed electric car heat exchanger motor; designed, patent Zack cycle engine; holder 10 copyrights. Avocation: God. Home: 280 East Main St Unit B7 Clinton CT 06413

ZACKEY, CHRISTOPHER ALBERT, mythologist, writer/poet, librarian; b. Brattleboro, Vt., June 12, 1949; s. Albert Walter Jr. and Thelma Eloise Zackey; m. Martha Ann Zackey, Dec. 16, 1973. BA in English, Brandeis U., 1971; MA in English, Ind. U., 1975; MLS, SUNY, Albany, 1987. Cert. libr., N.Y. Libr. tech. asst. Ind. U. Librs., Bloomington, 1974-76; mortgage loan closer and collector U.S. Nat. Bank Oreg., Portland, 1976-80; exam. asst. Nat. Coun. for Interior Design Qualification, N.Y.C., 1982-84; residential mortgage closer Citibank, Troy, N.Y., 1985-86; grad. asst. SUNY, Albany, 1986-87; adult svcs. libr. Jervis Pub. Libr., Rome, 1989—. Author: Chandelier, 1998, The Skylanders, 2002, (chapbooks) An Introduction to the Mythology, 1998, Overworld, 1998, Geodesic Reading, 1999, Pleroma, 2000; author poetry, fiction, creative nonfiction. Mem. Phi Beta Kappa. Democrat. Avocations: reading, writing, listening to music. Home: PO Box 4916 Rome NY 13442-4916 Office: Jervis Pub Libr 613 N Washington St Rome NY 13440-4203

ZACKHEIM, ADRIAN WALTER, editor; b. N.Y.C., Sept. 19, 1951; s. Albert Alex and Mary Elizabeth (Cooper) Z.; m. Sarah Babst Parsons, Sept. 1, 1985; children: Adrian Alex, David Parsons. BA, Grinnell Coll., 1973; MA, U. Toronto, Ont., Can., 1975. Editor St. Martins Press, N.Y.C., 1977-79, Doubleday & Co., Inc., N.Y.C., 1979-84, sr. editor, 1984-85, William Morrow & Co., Inc., N.Y.C., 1986-89, sr. editor, v.p., 1989-90, exec. editor, v.p., 1990-91, editorial dir., v.p., 1991-94; pub. dir., v.p. HarperBus, 1994-97; exec. editor, v.p. Harper Collins, 1994-97, pub. HarperBus., sr. v.p. Harper Collins adult trade, 1997-99; editor-in-chief Harper Info., 1999—2001; pub. Portfolio, Penguin Putnam, Inc., N.Y.C., 2001—. Office: PPI 375 Hudson St New York NY 10014

ZACKHEIM, MARC ALLEN, child psychologist, editor; b. N.Y.C., Oct. 12, 1950; s. Seymour David and Blanche (Kalt) Z.; m. Victoria Fraginals. AA, U. Fla., 1970, BA with high honors, 1972; MS, Fla. State U., 1974, PhD, 1977. Lic. psychologist Fla., Ill., Ind., Ala. Intern Duke U. Med. Ctr., Durham, N.C., 1976; postdoctoral fellow in psychology Fla. State U., 1978; resident in psychology Rush-Presbyn. St. Luke's Med. Ctr., Chgo., 1979; attending child psychologist Assocs. in Adolescent Psychiatry, 1979-85, dir. tng., 1981-85; founder Assocs. in Clin. Psychology and ACP Group Homes, Forest Park, 1985—; v.p. Westlake Hosp., Orlando, Fla., 1985—, Linden Oaks Hosp., Naperville, Ill., 1989—; faculty Auburn (Ala.) U.; attending childpsychologist Riveredge Hosp., Forest Park, Ill., 1979—, Koala Hosp., Plymouth, Ind., 1992—, Lebanon, 1993—. Cons. editor Ednl. and Psychol. Rsch.; contbr. articles to profl. jours., including Readins, A Jour. Am. Orthopsych. Assn. USPHS fellow, 1973-76; apptd. State of Ill. Guardianship and Advocacy Commn. Human Rights Authority, chmn., 1990-94. Fellow Am. Orthopsychiat. Assn.; mem. Am. Psychol. Assn., Ill. Psychol. Assn., Ala. Psychol. Assn., Midwest Psychol. Assn., Fla. Psychol. Assn., S.E. Psychol. Assn. for Psychoanalytic Psychology, Acad. Psychosomatic Medicine. Home: 1801 Shore Acres Dr Lake Bluff IL 60044-1340 Office: Riveredge Hosp 8311 Roosevelt Rd Forest Park IL 60130-2500

ZACUR, HOWARD ARDLEN, reproductive endocrinologist; b. Miami, Fla., July 30, 1947; m. Susan Rawson. AB, Harvard U., 1969; MD, U. Miami, 1973; PhD, Johns Hopkins U., 1979. Diplomate Am. Bd. Reproductive Endocrinology, Am. Bd. Ob-Gyn. Dir. div. reproductive endocrinology Dept. Ob-Gyn. Johns Hopkins U. Sch. Medicine, Balt., 1980—, Theodore and Ingrid Baramki prof., 1980—. Office: Johns Hopkins Hosp Houck 247 601 N Wolfe St Baltimore MD 21287-0004

ZADECK, DONALD JULIAN, oil and gas exploration company executive; b. St. Louis, Sept. 12, 1927; s. Sam Edward and Dorothy (Glatstein) Z.; m. Frances Katzenstein, Nov. 22, 1951; children: Donald J. Jr., Frank Kenneth, Julie. LLB, La. State U., 1950. Pres. Julie Ann Textiles, Shreveport, La., 1970-78, Zadeck Energy Group, Inc., Shreveport, 1978—. Pres. La. State U. Found., Baton Rouge, 1981; mem. La. Bd. Regents, Baton Rouge, 1981-86; chmn. Shreveport Mcpl. Fire and Police Civil Svc. Commn., 1988-98; dir. La. divsn. Am. Heart Assn., 1990, Coun. Alcoholism and Drug Abuse Northwestern La., 1991—; pres. Com. 100, 1980-81; pres. B'nai Zion Congregation, 1970-72; pres. La. State U. Med. Ctr. Shreveport Found., 1998—; chmn. bd. dirs. La. State U. Health Svcs. Found., 1998—. Recipient Mr. Shreveport award, 1981. Mem. Shreveport C. of C. (pres. 1977, Bus. Leader of Yr. 1980), La. Assn. Bus. and Industry (chmn. 1978-79), Shreveport Country Club, Shreveport Club. Republican. Jewish. Avocation: golf. Home: 1 Walton Pl Shreveport LA 71106-1713 Office: Ste 900 401 Edwards St Shreveport LA 71101-5510

ZADOORIAN, MICHAEL CRAIG, writer; b. Detroit, Feb. 26, 1957; s. Norman and Rosemary Zadoorian; m. Rita M. Simmons, Feb. 5, 1983. BA, Wayne State U., 1979, MA, 1995. Copywriter Doner Advt., Southfield, Mich., 1985-89, Campbell-Ewald, Warren, 1991—. Author: (novel) Second Hand, 2000; contbr. short stories to revs. and jours. Recipient Book Sense 76 selection Am. Booksellers Assn., 2000, Discover selection Barnes and Noble, 2000; Loughead-Eldredge scholar Wayne State U., 1991-92. Office: 24700 Northwestern Hwy Southfield MI 48075 E-mail: mzadoori@cecom.com.

ZAEPFEL, GLENN P. psychologist; b. Feb. 15, 1951; s. Walter Henry and Lillian Adair (Kovach) Z.; m. Linda Carrie Grinton, June 1, 1974; children: Peter, Caroline, Christine. BA, U. S.C., 1973; MEd, Ga. State U., 1980, PhD, 1986. Milieu therapist Peachtree-Parkwood Hosp., Atlanta, 1978-80; dir. Roswell St. Counseling Ctr., Marietta, 1980-84; dir. counseling and psychol. svcs. DeKalb Pain Control and Rehab. Ctr., Decatur, 1981-85; pvt. practice Columbia, S.C., 1985—; pres. Columbia Counseling Center, 1985—2001; pres., CEO Barnabas Med.-Behavioral Healthcare, Columbia, 2001—. Founder, program dir. Bapt. Med. Ctr. Pain Mgmt. Program, Columbia, 1985-87; founder, pres. Columbia Counseling Ctr., P.A., 1986—; vis. prof. Reformed Theol. Sem., Orlando. Author: He Wins, She Wins, 1994. Mem. APA, AACD, Christian Assn. for Psychol. Studies, Am. Rehab. Counseling Assn., Am. Bd. Med. Psychotherapists, Sinfonia. Republican. Presbyterian. Avocations: sports, music. Home: 1153 Scotts Hill Rd Chapin SC 29036-8974 also: 601 Polo Rd Columbia SC 29223-2905 also: 122 Powell Dr Lexington SC 29072-9203 Office: # 1301 3790 Fernandina Rd Columbia SC 29210-3864

ZAERA, FRANCISCO, chemistry educator, consultant; b. Caracas, Venezuela, May 11, 1958; s. Francisco and Everys Zaera; m. Encarnacion Montecino. Licenciate, Simon Bolivar U., Caracas, 1975; PhD, U. Calif., Berkeley, 1984. Tchg. asst. Open Univ. divsn. Simon Bolivar U., Caracas, 1975—78, rsch. asst., 1978—79, prof., 1979—80; rsch. asst. U. Calif., Berkeley, 1980—84; asst. chemist Brookhaven Nat. Lab., Upton, NY, 1984—86; prof. chemistry U. Calif., Riverside, Ala., 1986—. Cons. Mex. Inst. Petroleum, Mexico City, 2001—, Venezuelan Inst. Petroleum Tech., Los Teques, Miranda, Venezuela, 1993—98; vis. prof. Venezuelan Inst. Sci. Rsch., Caracas, 1993; Gran Mariscal de Ayacucho vis. prof., 93; presenter in field. Contbr. ; editor: Jour. Molecular Catalysis; assoc. editor: Encyclopedia of Chemical Physics and Physical Chemistry, 1998—2001, guest editor: Jour. Phys. Chemistry, 2001, mem. editl. bd.: Langmuir, 2000. Recipient Innovation Recognition Program award, Union Carbide, 1994, 1995. Fellow: AAAS; mem.: Am. Vacuum Soc., Calif. Catalysis Soc. (pres. 1991—92, sec.-treas. 1990—91), N.Am. Catalysis Soc., Am. Chem. Soc. (treas. colloids divsn. 1997—98, George A. Olah award in hydrocarbon or petroleum chemistry 2001). Office: U Calif Dept Chemistry Riverside CA 92521 Office Fax: 909-787-3962. Business E-Mail: francisco.zaera@ucr.edu.

ZAFERSON, WILLIAM S. philosophy educator, publisher; b. Kalavrita, Greece, Feb. 10, 1925; came to U.S., 1953; s. Steven A. and Katharine (Michael) Z.; m. Toni Adelgunde Humberg, Oct. 15, 1955. BA in Lit. cum laude, U. Athens, Greece, 1952; MA in Classical Langs. and Lit., U. Chgo., 1965; DPhil magna cum laude, U. Athens, 1976; postgrad., Truman Coll., 2000. Asst. prof. U. Upper Iowa, Fayette, 1966-68, Marymount Coll., Salina, Kans., 1968-70; prof. philosophy St. Mary's U., San Antonio, 1970-72. Author: The Meaning of Metempsychosis, 1965, The Universe, Its Elements and Justice, 1974, A Hymn to Health, 1975, The Platonic View of Moral Law and the Influence of the Tragedians on Plato's Thoughts, 1976, The Perfect Family, 1986, The Heraclitean Logos, 1996; author, pub.: The Songs of the Muses for Gods and Men, 1999, (poem and music) Hephaestus, 2000, (poems) Hermes to King Odysseus, 2001, (lyrics and music) Mother Gaea's Reprobation, 2001, (lyrics and music) Pluto and Persephone (A Look into the Elusinian Mysteries), 2002. A. Daniel L. Shorey fellow, U. Chgo., 1955. Mem. AARP, NRTA, AAUP, Am. Philos. Assn. (ctrl. divsn. emeritus), U. Chgo. Alumni Assn., Am. Assn. Learned Socs., Goethe-Institut Chgo., Nat. Assn. Scholars. Avocations: poetry, classical music, opera, hiking, swimming.

ZAFFIRINI, JUDITH, state legislator, small business owner; b. Laredo, Tex., Feb. 13, 1946; d. George and Nieves Pappas; m. Carlos Zaffirini, 1965; 1 child, Carlos Jr. BS, U. Tex., 1967, MA, 1970, PhD, 1978. Committeewoman Tex. State Dem. Exec. Com., 1978-84; mem. Tex. State Senate, 1987—, pres. pro tempore, 1997; owner Zaffirini Comms., Laredo, 1998—. Del. Dem. Nat. Conv., 1980, 84. Recipient Medal of Excellence Nat. League United Latin Am. Citizens, 1987, Jose Maria Morelos y Pavon Medal of Merit for leadership in strengthening U.S.-Mex. rels., 1987; named Woman of Achievement Tex. Press Women, 1980, Gov. of Tex. for a Day, Apr. 19, 1997, Ten Best Legislators Tex. Monthly Mag., 1997, 2001; inductee Nat. Hispanic Hal of Fame, 1987. Democrat. Roman Catholic. Home: PO Box 627 Laredo TX 78042-0627 Office: 1407 Washington St Laredo TX 78040-4411 E-mail: judith.zaffirini@senate.state.tx.us.

ZAFFOS, GERALD, federal agency executive; b. N.Y.C., July 26, 1950; s. Abraham and Lillian (Goldberg) Z.; m. Nydia Picayo, May 10, 1980; children: Aaron Manuel, Gloria Lynn.. BA, CCNY, 1972; MA, Queens Coll., 1976. Clk. typist Presidio of San Francisco, 1975-77, engring. technician, 1977-80; procurement agt. GSA, San Francisco, 1980-83, supervisory procurement agt., 1983-85, chief commodity ops. br., 1985-86, chief procurement br., 1986-88, dep. dir. contracts div., pub. bldgs. svc., 1988-90, dir. contract div. pub. bldgs. svc., 1990-91, spl. asst. office of procurement pub. bldgs. svcs. Washington, 1991-92, dir. procurement policy divsn. pub. bldgs. svc., 1992-95, acquisition exec. pub. bldgs. svc., 1995-97, procurement analyst pub. bldgs. svc., 1997—. Recipient Outstanding Contbns. award Pres.'s Com. for Purchase from Persons Who Are Blind or Severely Disabled, 2001. Mem. ABA, Nat. Contract Mgmt. Assn. Office: GSA 18th And F St NW Washington DC 20405-0001 E-mail: jerry.zaffos@gsa.gov.

ZAFFUTS, GERALD, musician, educator; b. Mt. Pleasant, Pa., May 21, 1953; BA Music Edn., Crane Sch. of Music, Potsdam, NY, 1975; MA Music Performance, U. of No. Colo., Greeley, CO, 1976. Teaching Certificate NY, 1977. Staff musician Starlight Music Theatre, Albany, NY, 1974—98; brass instruments educator Bennington Coll., Bennington, VT, Vt., 1987—94; staff musician Saratoga Performing Arts Ctr., Saratoga Springs, NY, 1974—; dir. Skidmore Jazz Inst., 1987—; dir. of: bands,jazz & music curriculum Averill Pk. H.S., Averill Park, 1992—. Post-session prodr. Dorian Recordings, Troy, NY, 1995—; trombonist New Colombian Brass Band, Danville, Ky., 1995—. Composer: (solo / chamber music) various. Dir. of bands Local VFW, Averill Park, NY, 1992—2002. Recipient Capital Region Outstanding Tchr., BOCES, 1993,1996,2000; grantee Grant for Presenting Maj. Jazz Artists, Nat. Endowment for the Arts, 1999, Grant for Concert Series / Minority Scholarships, NY State Coun. for the Arts, 1996-2002. Mem.: Music Educators' Nat. Conf., Am. Fedn. of Musicians, Internat. Trombone Assn. (life). Achievements include first to founder of Jazz studies at Skidmore College; creator of Jazz Institute at Skidmore College. Avocations: us history, us history. Office: Special Programs / Skidmore College Broadway Saratoga Springs NY 12866

ZAFIRATOS, JAMES A. judge, retired; b. July 17, 1918; s. Anastace and Kalliopi (Georgeopoulos) Z.; m. Anne Sifrer, May 4, 1954; children: James, Carol, Thomas. Assoc., Ctrl. YMCA Coll., Chgo., 1941; LLB, LLM, M Patent Law, John Marshall Sch. Law, Chgo., 1948; postgrad., Reno U., Nev. Bar: Ill. 1948, U.S. Supreme Ct. 1960. Pvt. practice, Chgo., 1948—; asst. corp. coun., 1965—; judge Cir. Ct. Cook County, State Ill., 1965-97; ret., 1997. Cpl. U.S. Army, 1942-45. Decorated Bronze Star, Silver Star; recipient Svc. to Judiciary awards United Am. Congress Am., 1955, United Hellenic Am. Congress, 1957, Svc. and Dedication Hellenic Am. Cmty. award Sparta Soc., 1960. Home: 931 Lathrop Ave River Forest IL 60305-1448

ZAFREN, HERBERT CECIL, librarian, educator; b. Balt., Aug. 25, 1925; s. Morris and Sadie Mildred (Edlavitch) Z.; m. Miriam Koenigsberg, Feb. 11, 1951; children: Ken, Edie. AB, Johns Hopkins U., 1944, postgrad., 1946-49; diploma, Balt. Hebrew Coll., 1944, LittD (hon.), 1969; AM in Libr. Sci, U. Mich., 1950. Jr. instr. Johns Hopkins U., Balt., 1947-49; bibliog. searcher Law Libr. U. Mich., Ann Arbor, 1949-50; libr. Hebrew Union Coll.-Jewish Inst. Religion, Cin., 1950-91, prof. Jewish bibliography, 1968-95, prof. emeritus, 1996—; exec. dir. Am. Jewish Periodical Ctr., 1956-80, co-dir., 1980-96, dir., 1996—; dir. librs. Cin., L.A., N.Y.C., Jerusalem, 1966-94; dir. emeritus librs. Hebrew Union Coll.-Jewish Inst. Religion, Cin., 1994—. Mem. exec. bd. Jewish Book Coun. Am., 1979-96. Editor Studies in Bibliography and Booklore, 1953—2002, Bibliographica Judaica, 1969—; compiler: A Gathering of Broadsides, 1967. With USN, 1944-46. Mem. ALA, Assn. Jewish Librs. (founder, nat. pres. 1965-66), World Coun. on Jewish Archives (v.p. 1977-81), Assn. Jewish Studies, Spl. Librs. Assn. (pres. Cin. chpt. 1953-54), Coun. Archives and Rsch. Librs. in Jewish Studies (pres. 1974-78, 89-91), Am. Hist. Assn., Israel Bibliophiles, World Union Jewish Studies, AAUP (chpt. pres. 1964-68), Grolier Club (N.Y.C.), Phi Beta Kappa, Beta Phi Mu. Office: Hebrew Union Coll- Jewish Inst Religion 3101 Clifton Ave Cincinnati OH 45220-2404

ZAGAR, ROBERT JOHN, psychologist, researcher; b. Great Lakes, Ill., Nov. 26, 1948; s. Anthony John and Helen Gertrude (Kurzynowski) Z.; m. Agata. MS in Psychology, Ill. Inst. Tech., Chgo., 1975; PhD in Psychology, Northwestern U., 1981; MPH in Pub. Health, U. Ill. Med. Ctr., Chgo., 1982; postgrad., DePaul U., 1982-83, Barry U., 1984-85. Clin. psychologist, Ill.; sch. psychologist, Ill. Sch. psychologist Chgo. Pub. Schs., 1991-93; asst. prof. Nat. Louis U., Evanston, Ill., 1991-93; psychologist Juvenile Divsn. Cir. Ct., Chgo., 1985-91; economist Ill. Dept. Labor, 1986-87; pvt. practice Chgo., 1992—. Cons. psychologist But. Disability Determination, Chgo., 1992—, Dept. Children and Family Svcs., 1992—, Jevenile Divsn. Cir. Ct. , 1992—; asst. prof. Ill. Sch. Profl. Psychology, 1989—91; sch. psychologist Aurora Pub. Schs., Ill., 1989—91; asst. prof. Forest Sch. Profl. Psychology, Wheeling, 1988—89; sch. psychology Chgo. Pub. Schs., 1999—2000, Woodstock, 2000—; invited spkr. Nat. Summit Youth Violence, U.S. Dept. Dept. Corrections, others. Contbr. articles to profl. jours. in field of neuropsychol. tests and aggress. Mem. APA, APHA, Am. Psychol. Soc., Fla. Psychol. Assn., Ill. Psychol. Assn., Nat. Assn. Sch. Psychologists. Roman Catholic. Home: 5507 N Winthrop Ave Chicago IL 60640-1412 also: 8642 226th Ave Salem WI 53168-9356 E-mail: drzagar@hotmail.com.

ZAGASKI, CHESTER ANTHONY, JR. author, researcher; b. Manchester, Conn., Mar. 28, 1949; s. Chester Anthony Sr. and Lenora (Zakrzewski) M.; m. Suzanne M. Celata, Apr. 1979 (div. Apr. 1989); children: Jason, Paul, Brian, Matthew. BA, U. S.C., 1971; postgrad., Northeastern U. Sch. Law, Wilbraham, Mass., 1971-72, U. Conn., 1973-75. Career trainee Hartford (Conn.) Ins. Co., 1971; spl. agt. Am. Group, Worcester, Mass., 1973-76; supr. underwriter Interstate Nat./Chgo. Ins., Boston, underwriting mgr. Phila., 1977-79; reins. mgr. N.Am. Reins., 1979-80; asst. v.p. casualty lines Comml. Union Ins. Co., Boston, 1980-82; acct. exec. Frank B. Hall & Co., 1982-84; surplus lines broker Stewart Smith East (USA), 1984-86; sr. underwriting cons. CNA Ins. Co., Quincy, Mass., 1986-89. Former ind. ins. and risk mgmt. cons. to several prominent firms and groups; organizational cons. Omnium Capital, Montreal, 1st Physicians Ins. Co. Vt., 1995, 96; instr., lectr. Inst. Libr. Assn. Boston, Tufts U., 1984-88; former advisor govt. and bus. groups, 1982-90, including New Eng. Coun., Inc., SBA New Eng., Commonwealth of Mass., Dept. Environ. Protection, Joint Ins. Com. of Mass. Legis., U.S. Congl. Subcom., U.S. SEC; lead organizer, cons. A Spl. Purpose Ins. Co., 1983; provider expert testimony before state and fed. legis. coms., among others; workshop and seminar leader; author, rschr. Deer Island Sentinels, 1992, 01. *Chester A. ("Chet") Zagaski Jr., continues his efforts as a free lance author and researcher. Due to the losses and thefts, he closed his selection of collected artifacts and rare coinage of 17th century early Massachusetts Bay. He investigated certain period figures such as secret ancestries of "Chester A. Zagaski," 1620 AD (Warsaw to London to "America"), wife "Alyson Sullivan" 1620 AD (County Cork, Ireland to Leyden, Holland to "America"). They were dispatched along with other settlers and colonizers in 1622-23 AD to Providence as a Crown Colony having special missions. Some of Chester's works in progress are; "Secrets From the Heart Before and Beyond The Legends of the Stones," and "Talking to Stones." "Deer Island Sentinels" is to be completed into three books to be titled upon publication/contract.* Author: Environmental Risk and Insurance, 1992, The Legends of the Lost Treasures, 2001; contbr. articles; involved in prodn. (films) A Civil Action, 1997. Mem. Quincy City Rep. Com., 1989-91; del. State Conv., Boston, 1990; advisor nat. Bush/Quayle Campaigns, 1989, 92; charter mem., sponsor WWII Meml., Washington, 1997. Recipient Citation of Merit Mass. Legis. Spl. Commn. Liability Release Hazardous Materials, 1986. Mem. Harvard Sq. Script Writers, Cape Cod Writers Ctr. Roman Catholic. Achievements include discovery of of Mayflower "coinage" and historical artifacts from that period in a collection of other "proof quality for period" original sets kept for trade and exhibits; Royal Crown artifacts and British East India Tea Co. and Mass. Bay Co. pieces from 1620 with exceptions.

ZAGER, BERNARD SOLOMON, physician, consultant; b. Detroit, Nov. 3, 1926; s. Philip and Lena Zager; m. Denise Acheson, Sept. 11, 1953; children: Robert, Gerald, Martin. BS, Wayne State U., 1947; MD, Northwestern U., 1950. Diplomate Am. Bd. Preventive Medicine and Occpl. Medicine. Intern Detroit Grace Hosp., 1949-50, resident in surgery, 1952-56; chief physician AAD Ford Motor Co., Utica, Mich., 1964-68; med. dir. Nuclear Energy Divsn. GE, San Jose, Calif., 1968-87; occupl. medicine cons. Reno, 1987—. Capt. U.S. Army, 1950-52. Home and Office: 1210 Bridlewood Way Reno NV 89509-7116 E-mail: bernzag@aol.com.

ZAGNOLI, ROLAND CANDIANO, management and marketing consultant, pharmacist; b. Highland Park, Ill., Nov. 6, 1931; s. Valerio Walter and Maria Adalgisa (Solignani) Z.; m. Virginia Louise Rizzo, Oct. 7, 1961; children: Roland Christopher, Lisa Louise, Regina Marie, Laurette Rene, Annia Lynn. BS in Pharmacy, U. Mich., 1955; MBA, Harvard U., 1957; LLB, LaSalle Extension U., 1963. RPh, Fla., Ill., Tenn.; registered consulting pharmacist, Fla. Tech. & adminstrv. rotation trainee Abbott Labs., Inc., North Chgo., 1957-59, corp. product mgr., 1959-63, dir. product mgmt. & new mktg. devel. Ross pediatric div. Columbus, Ohio, 1963-65, dir. product mgmt. internat. div. North Chgo., 1965-67, dir. mktg. & sales diagnostics div. North Chgo. & Los Angeles, 1967-70, dual mgr. Amp-Vial project & mfg. hosp. div. North Chgo. & Rocky Mountain, N.C., 1970-73; pres., gen. mgr. Health Care Industries, Inc., Michigan City, Ind., 1973-76, pres., chmn. bd., CEO, 1976-81; pres., CEO M/PIC Cons., Deltona, Fla., 1982—, Med. Inventors Corp., Orlando, 1988-99. Charter mem. Pharmacy Advancement Com. U. Mich., 1976-91; mem. Cen. Fla. Inventors Coun., Orlando, 1984-89; charter mem., bd. advisors Southtech Growth Fund, Ltd., Orlando, 1988-89; advisor Internat. Med. Techs., Winter Springs, Fla., 1989-92. Inventor Dye Pharm. Chem. (tablets dye-coating stability), 1958; patentee, 1959. Charter mem. Cen. Fla. Coun. High Tech., Orlando, 1984-94; gen. chmn. Notre Dame Parish Festival, Michigan City, 1977-79; pres. Evans Scholars Alumni, 1961-62; mem., cons. Mktg. & Mgmt. Ctrl. Fla. Innovation, Corp. 1995—; fund raiser various orgns. Evans Scholar of Yr. Western Golf Assn., 1954; won 8 golf tournament weekend championships at 7 sites in 4 states; William Douglas McAdams fellow, 1955-57. Mem. Am. Pharm. Assn., Ctrl. Fla. Soc. Hosp. Pharmacists, Fla. Soc. Hosp. Pharmacists, Cen. Fla. Pharmacy Assn. (v.p. 1990-91), Fla. Pharmacy Assn., Assn. Univ. Tech. Mgrs., Walnut Hill County Club (Columbus), Pottawatamie Country Club (Michigan City), Kiwanis, Rotary, Phi Eta Sigma, Rho Chi. Home and Office: 1936 Saxon Blvd Deltona FL 32725-4582 E-mail: megasus@n-jcenter.com.

ZAGOLSKI, FRANCIS, remote sensing expert, executive, researcher; b. Mazingarbe, France, Mar. 9, 1965; s. Casimir and Edwige (Janiak) Z. M in Math. and Physics, U. Lille, France, 1988; DEA degree in space tech., Paul Sabatier U., Toulouse, France, 1990, PhD in Remote Sensing, D in Remote Sensing (hon.), Paul Sabatier U., Toulouse, France, 1994. Rsch. assoc. fellow CESR, Toulouse, 1989-93; rsch. fellow CNES, 1994-96; sr. scientist CARTEL, Sherbrooke, Que., Can., 1996-98; exec. dir. PRIVATEERS (Pvt. Experts in Remote Sensing), St. Maarten, The Netherlands, 1998—; v.p. R&D ParBleu Techs. Inc., Canada, 2001—. Referee, contbr. articles to sci. publs. Cpl. inf.,

French mil., 1988-89. Mem. Planetary Soc. Avocations: travel, sports, music. Home and Office: PRIVATEERS NV 570 Blvd Charest-est #511 Quebec QC Canada G1K 9G3 E-mail: Francis_Zagolski@hotmail.com.

ZAGON, LAURIE, artist, writer; b. N.Y.C., Feb. 4, 1950; d. Jerome and Janet (Rabinowitz) Z.; m. Joseph Sorrentino, Dec. 21, 1991. BFA, Md. Inst. Coll. Art, 1971; MFA, Syracuse U., 1973. Asst. prof. Art CUNY, N.Y.C., 1973-87; color cons. Fieldcrest/Cannon, 1987-88. Spkr. Am. Soc. Interior Designers, Washington, 1993-97—; color, art therapit, Flagstaff, Ariz., 1996, Big Brothers/Big Sisters No. Ariz., 1996. Illustrator (book) It's Never Too Late To Have a Happy Childhood, 1989; one-woman shows include The Nat. Arts Club, N.Y.C., 1989; group exhibits include John Szoke Gallery, N.Y.C., Helio Galleries, N.Y.C., CUNY Abstract Show of Shanghai, China, 1986, L.A. Mcpl. Gallery, 1993, The Brewery Artist Colony, 1996-2000; co-author: Power of Color, 1995. Color/art therapist for AIDS Children, L.A. Children's Hosp., 1994; Martin Luther Hosp., Anaheim, 1990; active painting workshops for the terminally ill, 1995—, City of Hope Nat. Cancer Ctr.; founder, pres. Art and Creativity for Healing, Inc., Laguna Niguel, Calif. Office: 26079 Getty Dr Laguna Niguel CA 92677-1233 Home: 33101 Acapulco Dr Dana Point CA 92629-6003 E-mail: lzagon@aol.com.

ZAGORAC, MICHAEL, communications executive; b. Chgo., Mar. 23, 1941; s. Michael Sr. and Helen Zagorac and Linda Faye, Mar. 7, 1970; children: Christina L., Michael Paul. BS in Pharmacy, Purdue U., 1964; MBA in Mgmt., Am. U., 1973. Lic. pharmacist, Ill., Ind., Fla. Dir. govt. Am. Phamacy Assn., Washington, 1966-68; v.p. Nat. Assn. of Chain Drug Stores, Alexandria, Va., 1968-78, Eckerd Corp., Clearwater, Fla., 1978-94; sr. v.p. Hill & Knowlton, Tampa, 1994—. Dir. Associated Industries Ins. Co., Boca Raton, Fla., 1994—, SMT, Inc., Dunedin, Fla., 1992—; chmn. Fla. Taxwatch, Tallahassee, Fla., 1990-98; chmn. bd. Oasis Inc. Vice-chair Fla. Orch., Tampa, 1994-96, Associated Merchants of Fla., Tampa, 1994—; chmn. Associated Industries of Fla., Tallahassee, 1986-90, Fla. Retail Fedn., Tallahassee, 1984-86; dir. Coun. of Prevention, Tallahassee, 1996—; bd. dirs. Merchants Assn. of Fla. 1st lt. U.S. Army, 1964-66. Recipient Chmns. award for excellence Fla. Retail Fedn., 1997, Outstanding Contbn. Fla. Talkwatch, 1998. Mem. Army-Navy Club, Belleair Country Club, U. Ctr. Club, Govs. Club, Omicron Delta Kappa, Rho Chi. Methodist. Avocations: golfing, skiing, biking, reading. Office: Hill & Knowlton 201 E Kennedy Blvd Ste 1611 Tampa FL 33602-5836 Home: 13300 Indian Rocks Rd Largo FL 33774-2012

ZAGOREN, ALLEN JEFFREY, surgeon; b. Bklyn., May 17, 1947; s. Max and Harriett (Feldman) Z.; m. Gail Marie Sarcinella, Feb. 20, 1977. BA in Biology, Hofstra U., 1969; DO, Phila. Coll. Osteo. Medicine, 1975. Diplomate Am. Bd. Osteo. Surgery, Nat. Bd. Examiners Osteo.-Med. Surgery. Intern Stratford (N.J.) div. John F. Kennedy Meml. Hosp., 1975-76; resident Cherry Hill (N.J.) Med. Ctr., 1976-80; assoc. prof. surgery U. Medicine and Dentistry, Piscataway, N.J., 1980-82; practice osteo. medicine specializing in surgery Des Moines, 1982-2001, Capitol Hill Surgery, 1994-2001; mem. staff Mercy Hosp. Med. Ctr.; practice osteo. medicine specializing in surgery Capitol Hill Surgery; assoc. dean clin. affairs and rsch., prof. surgery/nutrition Western U., Pomona, Calif., 2001—, dean clin. affairs and rsch., 2001—. Chmn. dept. surgery Des Moines Gen. Hosp., 1985-91, Madison County Meml. Hosp., Winterset, Iowa, chmn. surgery dir. Splty. Clinic; clin. prof. surgery and nutrition Des Moines U. Medicine; assoc. prof. pharmacy Drake U.; lectr. in field; sec. Iowa Bd. Med. Examiners, 1997-2001, sec. 1996-98, vice chmn., 1999-2001; program dir. Wound Care Ctr., 1993-2001, dir. med. edn., 1992-2001, dir. postgrad. edn. Des Moines U. Contbr. articles to profl. jours.; creator videotapes (with others). Bd. dirs. Des Moines Gen. Hosp. Found., sec., 1986-95; chmn. bd. dirs. Des Moines Gen. Found., 1991-94; trustee Tiffereth Israel Synagogue, 1992. Grantee SKF Labs., Phila., 1986, Norwich (N.Y.) Eaton Labs., 1986, Ross Labs., 1995-99; recipient J. Swartz award for med. leadership Iowa Osteo. Med. Assn. Found., 1996. Fellow Am. Coll. Osteo. Surgeons (rsch., nutritional support, visual aids coms., chair rsch. com. 1991-92, 1st Prize awards 1982, 83), Am. Coll. Nutrition, Internat. Coll. Surgeons; mem. Am. Osteo. Soc., Am. Soc. Gastrointestinal Endoscopy, Iowa Osteo. Med. Assn. (pres. 1994-95, chmn. constrn. and v.p. bylaws coms. 1992, trustee), Polk County Med. Soc. (treas. 1991-93), Am. Soc. Parenteral and Enteral Nutrition (bd. dirs. 1986, chmn. various coms.), Rhoades Rsch. Found., Iowa and Nebr. Soc. Parenteral and Enteral Nutrition (pres. 1990-92), Iowa Health Leadership Consortium (CEO com., co-chair postgrad. edn. com.), Smithsonian Instn., Airplane Owners and Pilots Assn., Iowa Nebr. Nutrition Soc. (pres. 1990-92). Jewish. Avocations: flying, golf, swimming, skiing, writing. Office: Western U 1300 Des Moines St Des Moines IA 50309 E-mail: drallenz@cs.com.

ZAGOREN, JOY CARROLL, health facility director, researcher; b. N.Y.C., Oct. 31, 1933; d. Murray Morris and Celia (Donner) Rossman; m. Robert H. Zagoren, June 29, 1958 (div. 1988); children: Glenn, Robin; m. Robert Henry Chester, Apr. 1, 1988 (dec. Mar. 1998); children: Peter, Lisabeth, Melinda, Cecily, Kate. BS, NYU, 1957; MS, Adelphi U., 1969; PhD with distinction, NYU, 1981. Sec. sch. faculty Great Neck (N.Y.) Pub. Schs., 1957-71; rsch. scientist Inst. Psychobiol. Studies, Queens Village, N.Y., 1968-71; rsch. assoc. Albert Einstein Coll. Medicine, Bronx, 1971-84; asst. prof. SUNY Sch. Medicine, Stony Brook, 1984-86; dir. Seriatum, N.Y.C., 1991—. Ptnr. Winter Tree Collection; chmn. Esrath Nashim Hosp., 1986—; med. bd. dirs. Sarah Herzog Meml. Hosp. Editor: The Node of Ranvier, 1984; contbr. articles to profl. jours. Chair Peace Corps Svc. Coun., Tri-State, 1965-75; pres. Kidney Found. L.I., N.Y., 1965-77; v.p. United Cmty. Fund L.I., 1970-83; bd. dirs. Jerusalem Mental Health Ctr., N.Y.C., 1986—; med. bd. dirs. Sarah Herzog Meml. Hosp., hon. chair dinner, 1995, chair dinner, 1996, med. chair, 1998, chair membership cocktail party, 2000, chair bd. dirs., 2000—; chmn. mem. N.Y. Acad. Scis., 2000, vice chair Lyceum Club, N.Y. Acad. Scis., 2001. NIH fellow, 1982-84. Svc. awards Kidney Found., Kiwanis, others, 1970-87; named Disting. Alumnus of Yr., Adelphi U., 1986. Mem. AAAS, Nat. Acad. Sci., N.Y. Acad. Sci., Am. Assn. Neuropathology. Democrat. Jewish. Avocations: art, literature, piano, swimming, gardening. Home: 405 E 82nd St New York NY 10028-6038 Office: Seriatum 405 East 82d St New York NY 10028

ZAGORIA, SAM D(AVID), reporter, government official, educator; b. Somerville, N.J., Apr. 9, 1919; s. Nathan and Rebecca (Shapiro) Z.; m. Sylvia Bomse, Dec. 21, 1941; children: Paul, Marjorie Zagoria Isacks, Ronald. BL in Journalism, Rutgers U., 1941. With New Brunswick (N.J.) Daily Home News, 1940-41, N.J. Def. Coun., Trenton, 1941-42; Fed. Office Govt. Reports, Newark, 1942; reporter Washington Post, 1946-55; adminstrv. asst. to Senator Clifford P. Case, Washington, 1955-65; pres. Washington Newspaper Guild, 1953; mem. NLRB, Washington, 1965-69; dir. Labor-Mgmt. Rels. Svc. U.S. Conf. of Mayors, 1970-78; mem. U.S. Consumer Product Safety Commn., 1978-84; ombudsman Washington Post, 1984-86; arbitrator, writer, 1986—2001. Fulbright lectr., Copenhagen, 1987; vis. prof. Fla. Atlantic U., Boca Raton, 1988—91; adj. prof. Wake Forest U., Winston-Salem, NC, 1993—2001. Author: Public Workers, Public Unions, 1972, The Ombudsman: How Good Governments Handle Citizens' Grievances, 1988. Campaign mgr. reelection Senator Case, 1960; campaign mgr. race for gov., former Sec. of Labor James P. Mitchell, 1961. With USAAF, 1942-45. Nieman fellow Harvard, 1954 Mem. Common Cause, Nat. Consumers League, Rutgers U. Alumni Assn. Jewish. Home and Office: 3101 S Ocean Blvd Apt 622 Highland Beach FL 33487-2524 also: 2564 Wynfield Crossing Ln Winston Salem NC 27103-6597 E-mail: SamZagorial@juno.com.

ZAGORIN, JANET SUSAN, legal firm administrator, marketing professional; b. Lakewood, N.J. d. Irving C. and Dorothy (Tarshish) Z. BA, Douglass Coll., 1975; MLS, Rutgers U., 1977. Asst. law libr. N.J. Atty. Gen., Trenton, 1977-78; head of reference sect. Cardozo U. Law Sch., N.Y.C., 1978-79; law and legis. svcs. libr. FTC, Washington, 1979-81; dir. of reference Paul Weiss Rifkind, N.Y.C., 1981-82; libr. dir. Riker Danzig Scherer & Hyland, Morristown, N.J., 1982; libr., profl. devel. dir. Baker & McKenzie, N.Y.C., 1982-96; dir. practice devel. and info. svcs. Stroock & Stroock & Lavan LLP, 1996-98; dir. practice devel. Cadwalader, Wickersham & Taft, 1998-99, Gibson, Dunn & Crutcher, N.Y.C., 1999—2001; dir. mktg. Sidley Austin Brown & Wood, 2001—. Bd. dirs. N.Y. Cares, 1998—. Mem. ABA (vice chmn. standing com. Law Libr. Congress 1995-96, chmn. 1996—, mem. law 2000 steering com. Libr. Congress), Fin. Women's Assn. (mem. bd. dirs. 1993-95, 99—), Bus. Women's Network, Am. Assn. Law Librs. (chair fgn. comparative internat. law com. 1990-91, vice chair pvt. law librs. 1990-91, chair 1991—, chair com. on recruitment 1991), Spl. Librs. Assn., Hadassah. E-mail: jzagorin@sidley.com.

ZAGORIN, PEREZ, historian, educator; b. Chgo., May 29, 1920; s. Solomon Novitz and Mildred (Ginsburg) Z.; m. Honoré Desmond Sharrer, May 29, 1947; 1 son, Adam. AB, U. Chgo., 1941; A.M., Harvard U., 1947, PhD, 1952. Various positions OWI, U.S. Govt., U.P. Syndicate, CIO, 1942-46; instr. Amherst Coll., 1947-49; lectr. Vassar Coll., 1951-53; from asst. prof. to prof. history McGill U., 1955-65; prof. U. Rochester, 1965—, Joseph C. Wilson prof. history, 1982-90, Joseph C. Wilson prof. history emeritus, 1990—, chmn. dept., 1968-69, acting chmn. dept., 1988-89; vis. prof. Johns Hopkins, 1964-65; Amundsen vis. prof. U. Pitts., 1964; William Andrews Clark Meml. Library prof. UCLA, 1975-76. Thompson lectr. history Vassar Coll., 1987. Author: A History of Political Thought in the English Revolution, 1954, 2d edit., 2000, The Court and the Country, 1969, Culture and Politics from Puritanism to the Englightenment, 1980, Rebels and Rulers 1500-1660, 2 vols., 1982, Ways of Lying: Dissimulation, Persecution, and Conformity in Early Modern Europe, 1990, Milton Aristocrat and Rebel: The Poet and His Politics, 1992, Francis Bacon, 1998, The English Revolution: Politics, Events, Ideas, 1998, How the Idea of Religious Toleration Came to the West, 2002; co-editor: Philosophy Science and Religion in England 1640-1700, 1991, Guide to Historical Literature, 1994; contbr. numerous articles in hist. jours.; mem. editl. bd. Jour. of the History of Ideas. Sheldon travel fellow Harvard U., 1949-50, Fulbright fellow 1949-50, faculty rsch. fellow Social Sci. Rsch. Coun., 1958-59, 61-62, sr. rsch. fellow Folger Shakespeare Libr., 1964-65, fellow Inst. Advanced Study, Princeton, N.J., 1972-73, sr. fellow Nat. Humanities Ctr., 1978-79, fellow Ctr. Advanced Study in Behavioral Scis., 1983-84, Guggenheim fellow, 1983-84, Edgar F. Shannon Ctr. for Advanced Studies fellow U. Va., 1994—, Fellow Royal Hist. Soc., Am. Acad. Arts and Scis.; mem. Am. Hist. Assn. (chmn. Gershoy and Schuyler prize com. 1982-84). Home: 2990 Beaumont Farm Rd Charlottesville VA 22901-8717 Office: U Rochester Dept History Rochester NY 14627 E-mail: pz3p@virginia.edu.

ZAGORSKY, CAROL LACCI, information systems project director; b. N.Y.C., Nov. 19, 1942; d. Arthur and Evelyn Marie (Strang) Lacci; m. Eugene Dennis Zagorsky, Jr., May 21, 1983. BBA in Econs., St. John's U., Jamaica, N.Y., 1968. Cert. data processor, quality analyst. Programmer info. systems and services dept. N.Y. Life Ins. Co., N.Y.C., 1967-71, programmer analyst, 1971-74, project leader, 1974-78, project mgr., 1978—, div. head, 1988-89, project dir., 1989—. Conf. spkr. Managing Computer Aided Software Engrng. Implementation; lectr. NYU, Info. Technols. Inst., 1990-92; instr. Am. Mgmt. Assn.-Total Quality Mgmt. for Mgmt. Info. Sys., 1993-94. Trustee Murray Hill Com., N.Y.C., 1977-79, 85-86, v.p. 1979-85. Mem. Women in Data Processing, Quality Mgmt. Assn. N.Y. (pres. 1991—), Nat. Excelerator Users Group (profl. devel. com.), Met. N.Y. Computer Aided Software Engrng. Users Group. Democrat. Episcopalian. Avocations: camping, hiking. Office: NY Life Ins Co 51 Madison Ave New York NY 10010-1603

ZAHARIA, ERIC STAFFORD, health facility administrator; b. Pomona, Calif., Aug. 24, 1948; s. Edgar A. and Dorothy (Stafford) Zaharia; m. Caryle Koentz, Dec. 23, 1967; children: Tye W., Tieg A. BA, Pomona Coll., 1970; MEd, U. Ariz.-Tucson, 1973; PhD, George Peabody Coll., 1978. Mental retardation worker Ariz. Tng. Program, Tucson, 1970-71, unit dir., 1971-73; dir. residential svcs. Willmar State Hosp., (Minn.), 1973-76; rsch. asst. Inst. on Mental Retardation and Intellectual Devel., Nashville, 1976-78; dir. mental retardation program svcs. Dept. Mental Health/Mental Retardation, State of Tenn., 1978-79; dir. Caswell Ctr., Kinston, N.C., 1979-86; program adminstr. Colo. Divsn. of Devel. Disabilities, Denver, 1986-90; dir. Utah divsn. Svcs. for People with Disabilities, Salt Lake City, 1990-95; ind. cons. Park City, Utah, 1995-2000; dir. Ariz. Divsn. Devel. Disabilities, Phoenix, 2000—. Mem. adj. faculty East Carolina U., Greenville, 1979—86; bd. dirs. Neuse Enterprises Inc., Kinston. Chmn. Big Bros./Sisters Kinston Inc., 1980—83; mem. N.C. Coalition for Cmty. Svc., 1982—85. Mem.: Assn. Retarded Citizens, Nat. Assn. Supts., Am. Assn. Mental Retardation, Kinston C. of C. (bd. dirs. 1983—86), Pub. Residential Facilities. Home: 1352 N Hibbert Mesa AZ 85201

ZAHEDI, CAVEH, filmmaker, video artist; b. Washington, Apr. 29, 1960; BA in Philosophy, Yale U., 1981; MFA in Film Prodn., UCLA, 1991. Co-dir.: A Little Stiff; performer: Citizen Ruth, 1996, Treasure Island, 1999, Waking Life, 2001, A Sign From God, 2000; contbr. Named Atlanta Film Festival Best Feature, Image Film and Video Ctr., 1997; recipient Rotterdam Film Festival Critics award, Assn. Dutch Critics, 1994; fellow Guggenheim, 1997, NEA, 1996. Mem.: Film Arts Found.

ZAHL, PAUL FRANCIS MATTHEW, dean; b. N.Y.C., May 24, 1951; m. Mary McLean Cappleman, Dec. 29, 1973; children: John Arthur, David William Franklin, Simeon McLean. Student, U. N.C., 1968-70; AB magna cum laude, Harvard Coll., 1972; MPhil in Theology, U. Nottingham, Eng., 1975; diploma in pastoral studies, St. John's Theol. Coll., Nottingham, 1975; ThD, Eberhard-Karls-Univ., Tübingen, Germany, 1994. Ordained min. Protestant Episcopal Ch., 1976. Deacon in tng. Good Shepherd Episcopal Ch., Silver Spring, Md., 1975-76; curate Grace Ch., N.Y.C., 1976-82; rector St. Mary's Ch., Scarborough, N.Y., 1982-88, St. James' Ch., Charleston, S.C., 1988-92; fellow Episcopal Ch. Found., 1993-95; dean Cathedral Ch. of the Advent, Birmingham, Ala., 1995—. Tchr. Gen. Theol. Sem., N.Y.C., 1979-82, The King's Coll., Briarcliff Manor, N.Y., 1985-88, Coll. Charleston, S.C., 1990-92, U. Tübingen, Germany, 1992-93; vis. scholar Wycliffe Hall, Oxford, Eng., 1994-95. Author: Who Will Deliver Us?, 1983, Die Rechtfertigungslehre Ernst Kasemanns, 1996, Protestant Face of Anglicanism, 1998; co-author: The Collects of Thomas Cranmer, 1999; columnist The Anglican Digest, 1986—; contbr. articles to profl. jours. Mem. Phi Beta Kappa. Office: Cath Church of the Advent 2017 6th Ave N Birmingham AL 35203-2701

ZAHN, ALLAN LEE, emergency physician; b. Wausau, Wis., May 4, 1964; MD, Med. Coll. Wis., 1990. Diplomate Am. Bd. Emergency Medicine. Intern Eastern Va. Grad. Sch., Norfolk, 1990-91, resident, 1991-94; mem. staff Emergency Physicians Tidewater, 1995—. Hosp. appt. Marshal Med. Ctr. N, 1995—. Mem. Am. Coll. Emergency Physicians. Office: Marshal Med Ctr N 8000 Hwy 69 Guntersville AL 35976

ZAHN, CARL FREDERICK, museum publications director, designer, photographer; b. Louisville, Mar. 9, 1928; s. Fred Joseph and Myrtle (Fulks) Z.; m. Betty Jane Woodrow, Nov. 18, 1950 (div. July 1977); children: Lisa, Karen, Richard; m. Felicitas Magdalena Fuhlrott, July 30, 1979 (dec. Mar. 1999). BA, Harvard Coll., 1948. Asst. in conservation Fogg Art Mus., Cambridge, Mass., 1949-50; with art dept. Benton & Bowles Inc., N.Y.C., 1950-51; design asst. Inst. Contemporary Art, Boston, 1951-56; dir. publs. Mus. Fine Arts, 1956—; also dir. exhbns., 1995-96; ret., 1997; co-founder Mus. Pub. Ptnrs., 2000. Exhibitions include: Addison Gallery Am. Art, Andover, Mass., 1959, Am. Inst. Graphic Arts, N.Y.C., 1960—, Rose Art Mus. Brandeis U., Waltham, Mass., 1969; author: Introduction to Hermann Zapf and His Design Philosophy, 1987, Books and Such Designed by Carl Zahn at the Museum of Fine Arts, Boston, 1956-97, 1997; co-author Weston's Westons: Portraits and Nudes, 1989 Mem. Am. Inst. Graphic Arts (v.p. 1971-72), Soc. Printers, Bund Deutscher Buchkünstler, Mink Meadows Golf Club, East Chop Tennis Club (bd. dirs. 1970-72), Longwood Cricket Club. Home: 39 Cedarwood Rd Jamaica Plain MA 02130-3021 also: 1808 Par Pl Sarasota FL 34240-9689 E-mail: czbird@aol.com.

ZAHN, DONALD JACK, lawyer; b. Oct. 24, 1941; s. Jerome and Clara (Zinsher) Z.; m. Laurie R. Hyman, Aug. 19, 1966; children: Lawrence, Melissa. AB, NYU, 1963; LLB, Union U., 1966; LLM in Taxation, NYU, 1967. Bar: N.Y. 1966, U.S. Dist. Ct. (no. dist.) N.Y. 1966, U.S. Tax Ct. 1969, U.S. Ct. Appeals (2d cir. 1970), Tex. 1972, U.S. Ct. Appeals (5th and 11th cirs.). Assoc. Bond, Schoeneck and King, Syracuse, N.Y., 1967-71; ptnr. Haynes and Boone, Dallas, 1971-82, Akin, Gump, Strauss, Hauer & Feld, Dallas, 1982-92; assoc. prof. internat. taxation, fed. income taxation, entities taxation, business associations Tex. Wesleyan Sch. Law, Ft. Worth, 1992-99. Vis. prof. fed. income taxation Baylor U. Sch. Law, 1995, 2000, prof. fed. income taxation and bus. orgns. II; grad. taxation program U. San Diego Sch. Law, 1996—98, fed. income taxation, corp. taxation, current income tax problems, tax ethics; adj. prof. Sch. Law So. Meth U., Dallas, 1972—87, 1990—91. Trustee, sec. mem. exec. and fin. com., nominating com. Greenhill Sch., Addison, Tex., 1980-90; trustee, chmn. budget com., mem. fin. com. Jewish Fedn. Greater Dallas, 1978-89; trustee, chmn. Found. Jewish Fedn., Dallas, 1980-89; trustee, v.p., pres. Dallas chpt. Am. Jewish Com., 1980-92; mem. Tex. World Trade Coun., 1986-87, Dallas Mayor's Internat. Com. Mem. State Bar Tex. (sec. 1982-83, chmn. tax sect. 1984-85, newsletter taxation sect. editor 1980-81), Internat. Bar Assn., Internat. Comte (N.Tex. commn.), Ctr. for Am. and Internat. Law (adv. bd., treas. Internat. and Comparative Law Ctr., lectr. Acad. in Internat. Law), N.Y. State Bar Assn. Address: 11218 Hillcrest Rd Dallas TX 75230-3501 Office Fax: 214-368-5301.

ZAHN, RICHARD WILLIAM, JR. lawyer; b. Richmond, Va., Oct. 1, 1964; s. Richard William and Frances Ellen Z.; m. Kerry Ellen Mahaney, Aug. 7, 1988; children: Ryan William, Allison McKenzie. BA, Washington Lee U., 1986; JD, New Eng. Sch. Law, Boston, 1993. Bar: Va. 1993, U.S. Dist. Ct. (ea. dist.) Va. 1993, U.S. Ct. Appeals (4th cir.) 1994, U.S. Supreme Ct. 2000. Law clk. to Hon. John A. MacKenzie U.S. Dist. Ct., Norfolk, Va., 1993-94; assoc. Taylor & Walker, P.C., 1994—. Bd. dirs., 2d v.p. Big Bros./Big Sisters of South Hampton Roads, Norfolk, 1996—. Mem. Va. Assn. Def. Attys. (bd. dirs. 2000—), Def. Rsch. Inst., Norfolk/Portsmouth Bar Assn. Office: Taylor & Walker PC 555 E Main St Ste 1300 Norfolk VA 23510-2235 E-mail: rzahn@taywal.com.

ZAHND, RICHARD H. professional sports executive, lawyer; b. N.Y.C., July 22, 1946; s. Hugo and Rose (Genovese) Z.; m. Phyllis Beth Workman, Aug. 13, 1978; children: Andrew Richard, Melissa Dawn. AB, NYU, 1968, JD, 1971. Bar: N.Y. 1972. Assoc. Paul, Weiss, Rifkind, Wharton & Garrison, N.Y.C., 1971-74; staff atty. Madison Square Garden Corp., 1974-75; v.p. legal affairs Madison Square Garden Center, Inc., 1975-79; v.p., gen. counsel Madison Square Garden Corp., 1979-86; v.p. N.Y. Knickerbockers Basketball Club, 1979-86, N.Y. Rangers Hockey Club, N.Y.C., 1979-86; ptnr. Morrison & Foerster, 1986-91; exec. v.p., gen. counsel NHL Enterprises, L.P., 1992—. Served to capt. U.S. Army, 1972. John Norton Pomeroy scholar NYU Law Sch., 1969; Mortimer Bishop scholar NYU Law Sch., 1969; Judge Jacob Markowitz scholar NYU Law Sch., 1970; recipient Am. Jurisprudence prize NYU Law Sch., 1969 Episcopalian. Office: NHL Enterprises LP Fl 46 1251 Ave of the Americas New York NY 10020-1104 E-mail: rzahnd@nhl.com.

ZAHNER, ANNE COLETTE, preschool educator; b. Mansfield, Ohio, May 15, 1962; d. Gordon Dean and Mary Anne (Riggle) Z. BS in Journalism, Ohio U., 1984; MS in Teaching, U. Dayton, 1992. Staff writer Huber Heights (Ohio) Courier, 1984-87, editor, 1987; presch. tchr. Cath. Social Svcs., Dayton, Ohio, 1993-97, Butler County Bd. Mental Retardation, Fairfield, 1997—. Reporter Athens Mag., 1983, Athena Yearbook, 1983. Mem. Sigma Delta Chi, Alpha Gamma Delta (house chair 1983-84, corr. sec. 1982-83, newsletter editor 1997). Democrat. Presbyterian. Avocations: travel, photography, exercise. Office: Butler County Bd Mental Retardation Janet Clemmons Ctr 282 N Fair Ave Hamilton OH 45011-4222 Home: 7491 Esther Dr West Chester OH 45069-4140

ZAHNER, DOROTHY SIMKIN, elementary education educator; b. Chengdu, Szechuan, China, May 01; came to U.S. in the 1930s; d. Robert Louis and Margaret Isadore (Timberlake) Simkin; divorced; children: Mary De Avilan, Robert Louis. BA in Sociology, Whittier Coll.; MLS, U. So. Calif., L.A. Cert. tchr. Calif., Ariz. Tchr. L.A. and Pasadena (Calif.) Schs., 1969-93; dir., owner Betty Ingram Sch., North Hollywood, Calif., 1976-79; dir. Foothill Nursery Sch., La Crescenta, 1970s; tchr. L.A. Unified Sch. Dist.; guest tchr. Washington Unified Sch. Dist., Phoenix, 1994-97. Guest tchr. Osborn Sch. Dist., 1998-2000, Madison Sch. Dist., Phoenix, 1999-2001. Author: (poetry) Yucca Poetry Workshop, 1993-94, Treasured Poems of America, 1993, internat. poetry publ., others; poems published in Eng., 1998, 99, 2000, 01. Bd. dirs. Ariz. Tenants Assn., Phoenix, 1994, 95; vol. Am. Friends Svc. Com., Phila., Calif., 1985—, Common Cause, L.A., 1990, Internat. Rescue Com., Dem. Candidates, L.A. and Phoenix. Recipient award for a poem, Ariz. State Poetry Soc., Phoenix, 1995, 2000; honorable mention for poem published Sandcutters, 2000. Mem.: Ariz. State Poetry Soc. (pres. 2002), Alameda Writers Group, Phoenix Poetry Soc. (com. mem., pres. 1998, anthology editl. co. 2001, Poet of Yr. 2000), Phoenix Writers Club (sec. 1998). Avocations: theatre, films, music, swimming, reading.

ZAHNER, MARY ANNE, art educator; b. Dover, Ohio, Mar. 30, 1938; d. Alfred James and Anna Elizabeth (Stewart) Riggle; m. Gordon Dean Zahner, Aug. 27, 1960 (dec. Mar. 1967); 1 child, Anne Colette; m. John Charles Opalek, Aug. 21, 1982. BFA, Ohio U., 1960, MA, 1969; PhD, Ohio State U., 1987. Cert. tchr., Ohio. Instr. art Springfield Twp. Schs., Akron, Ohio, 1960-61, Logan (Ohio) H.S., 1961-62, Dover H.S., 1967-68, chair art dept., 1969-71; teaching asst. Ohio State U., Columbus, 1980-82; from instr. art edn. to asst. prof. U. Dayton, 1971-74, asst. prof., 1974-91, assoc. prof., 1991-2000, prof., 2000—. Faculty rights, governance and svc. com. U. Dayton, 1992-93, arts series com., 1995-98; higher edn. steering com. Ohio Dept. Edn., 1995, adv. com., tchr. preparation programs, 1997; exec. bd. Western Regional Profl. Devel. Ctr., 1996—; reviewer Harcourt, Brace, 1993-98, Prentice Hall Inc., 1996-99. Author: (chpts.) The History of Art Education: Proceedings from the Second Pa. State Conference, 1989, The History of Art Education: Proceedings from the Third Pa. State Conference, 1997; exhibited in group show at Westbeth Gallery, N.Y., 1995. Sec. Kettering (Ohio) Arts Coun., 1990, mem., 1988-93; mem. discretionary support com. Miami Valley Arts Coun., Dayton, 1992; coord. 3d congl. art contest sponsored by Tony P. Hall, Dayton, 1993-95; mem.-at-large edn. com. Culture Works: The Arts and Culture Alliance of the Miami Valley, 1996. Recipient Best of Show award Canton Art Inst., 1969, Inst. Faculty award The Ohio Partnership for the Visual Arts, 1989. Fellow Ohio Art Edn. Assn. (mem. editl. bd. Ohio Art Edn. Jour. 1986—, editor newsletter Artline 1988, workshop coord. 1992, 97, cons. tchr. insvc. for Dayton Pub. Schs. 1995, Outstanding Art Tchr. western dist. 1992, 96); mem. ASCD, Nat. Art Edn. Assn., Assn. Tchr. Educators, Ohio Alliance for Arts Edn., Univ. Coun. for Art Edn., Phi Delta Kappa, Phi Kappa Phi, Delta Kappa Gamma. Democrat. Avocations: music, theater, physical fitness. Office: U Dayton 300 College Park Dayton OH 45469-0001 E-mail: mary.zahner@notes.udayton.edu.

ZAHRADNIK, FREDRIC DOUGLAS, Internet publishing executive; b. Chgo., Sept. 11, 1956; s. Robert Joseph and Grace Eileen (Armstrong) Z.; m. Sally Smith, Oct. 25, 1980; children: Brent Alexander, Alice Janine. BA, Pa. State U., 1980; MBA, DeSales U., Center Valley, Pa., 2002. Assoc. editor Rodale, Inc., Emmaus, Pa., 1982-86, sr. editor, 1987-91; tech. editor Rodale Press, Inc., 1992-94, dir. new media, 1995-96, corp. web site adminstr., 1997, mktg. mgr. online, 1998-99; online dir. men's health brand and men's health on AOL Rodale Inc., 2000—. Invited spkr. Atlanta Super-Show NSGA, 1990, U. Wis., 1995; corr. Outdoor Life Network, 1996; expert, interviewee NBC Olympic Telecast, 1996; corr. bicycling ESPN, 1994; dir. Men's Health co-brand on Am. Online. Author: Cross Country Skiing Guide to Waxing, 1995; editor: Bicycling on America Online, 1994—96; photographs, ; profiled in Circulation Mgmt. mag., 2001; contbr. articles to profl. publs. and newspapers. Soccer coach Lower Macungie Youth Assn., Allentown, 1996—. Named to Min Mag. New Media 50, 2001. Mem. Direct Mktg. Assn., The Assn. for Interactive Media, Internat. Mountain Biking Assn., Trout Unlimited, Hawk Mtn. Sanctuary Assn. Avocations: bicycling, kayaking, fly fishing. Office: Rodale Press Inc 33 E Minor St Emmaus PA 18098-0099

ZAHRLY, JANICE HONEA, management educator; b. Ft. Payne, Ala., Sept. 27, 1943; d. John Wiley and Lillian (McKown) Honea. BA, U. Fla., 1964; MBA, U. Ctrl. Fla., 1980; PhD, U. Fla., 1984. Tchr. Hope Mills (N.C.) H.S., 1964-65, Satellite Beach (Fla.) H.S., 1965-69; realtor-assoc. WD Webb Realty, Melbourne, Fla., 1969-70; realtor Aero Realty, 1970-72, Albert J. Tuttle, Realtor, Melbourne, 1972-74; mktg. mgr. Cypress Woods Devel., Orlando, Fla., 1974-76; regional campaign mgr. Pres. Ford Com., 1976; ednl. researcher Peace Corps, Korea, 1976-78; rsch. analyst, tech. writer Rsch. Sys. Inc., Orlando, 1979-80; rsch. asst., lectr. U. Fla., Gainesville, 1980-84; asst. prof. Wayne State U., Detroit, 1984-89; assoc. prof. Old Dominion U., Norfolk, Va., 1989-94, U. N.D., Grand Forks, 1994—. Mem. Melbourne Bd. Realtors, 1969-76, orientation chair, 1972, pub. rels. chair, 1973, civic affairs chair, 1973, grievance com., 1975; cons. Wayne County Retarded Persons Assn., Detroit, 1985, Gov.'s Conf. on Women Entrepreneurs, Mich., 1986,

Oakland County AAUW Conf. on Women, Mich., 1987, 88, Coll. Bus. and Pub. Adminstrn. Inst. of Mgmt., Old Dominion U., Norfolk, 1990, U.S. Army Corps Engrs., Norfolk, 1990; presenter in field. Contbr. chpts. to books, articles to profl. jours. and procs. Vol. Tidewater AIDS Crisis Task Force, Norfolk, 1990-93, bd. dirs., 1990-92, v.p., 1991, rec. sec., 1992; mem. occupational adv. com. Brevard County Mental Health Ctr., Fla., 1973-74; mem. Brevard County Libr. Bd., 1973-74; bd. dirs. Fla. Dist. 12 Mental Health Bd., 1973-74, sec. 1973-74; bd. dirs. Alachua County Crisis Ctr., Gainesville, 1982-84, chair, 1983-84; vol. Open Door, Detroit, 1986-89; bd. dirs. United Way Grand Forks area, 1996-97; pres. bd. dirs. Cherry Arms Condominium Assn., 1996-97. Recipient Best Paper award Midwest Soc. for Human Resources/Indsl. Rels., 1989, F.W. Lawrence award U. N.D., 1996; rsch. fellow Fed. Mogul Corp., 1987-88; rsch. grantee Wayne State U., 1985-89, Old Dominion U., 1990, U. N.D., 1995, 96, 98. Mem. AAUW (bd. dirs. 1974-75), Acad. Mgmt., Assn. for Rsch. on Nonprofit Orgns./Vols., N.Am. Case Rsch. Assn. (nonprofit track chair 1999-2000, procs. editor 2001), So. Mgmt. Assn., Hampton Rds. Gator Club (co-founder, treas. 1989-91), Alpha Omicron Pi (bd. dirs. alumnae chpt. 1969-73, v.p. 1969-73). Avocations: travel, writing fiction, photography, music. Home: 3424 Cherry St Apt A1 Grand Forks ND 58201-7692

ZAHRT, MERTON STROEBEL, investor; b. Ellington, Wis., May 8, 1910; s. Francis Henry and Anna Barbara (Maves) Z.; m. Genevieve Rosalie Kottler, Aug. 20, 1932 (div. July 1952); children: Barbara Ann, Merton William (dec.), Sally Sue Zahrt-O'Leary; m. Hilda Elizabeth Bouck, Aug. 23, 1952; 1 child, Nancy Joanne Zahrt-Maxwell. MusB, Lawrence U., 1932; MusM, U. Rochester, 1943; EdD, Columbia U., 1950. Prof. music, head dept. Ft. Hays (Kans.) State Coll., 1949-50; assoc. prof. Ithaca (N.Y.) Coll., 1950-52; prof. music Chgo. Mus. Coll., 1952-58, acting chmn. music edn., 1957-58; asst. to dean of students U. Ill., Chgo., 1953-62, asst. dean of men, 1962-65; prof. music edn. U. So. Miss., Hattiesburg, 1965-71, coord. grad. studies in music edn., 1968-71; real estate salesman Hubbard Real Estate, Richmond, Va., 1971-78; profl. investor Zahrt Family Investments, Zahrt Revocable Trust U/A, Dunedin, Fla., 1978-88; trustee, from 1988. Adjudicator sch. music competitions, Ark., Ill., Ind., Kans., Minn., Okla., Wis., 1940-65; conv. chmn. Ill. State Music Tchrs. Assn., Chgo., 1957; ch. choir dir. Coll. Ch., Hampden-Sydney, Va., 1978-79. Contbr. articles to profl. jours. Asst. dir. YMCA Men's Glee Club, Green Bay, Wis., 1935-36; dir. Hays (Kans.) Community Chorus, 1949-50; lay eucharistic min. Ch. Ascension, Clearwater, Fla., 1986-96; music com. mem. Episcopal Ch. of the Ascension, Clearwater, 1988-91. Community music programs grantee U. So. Miss., 1967-68. Mem. Am. Assn. Ret. Persons, State Univs. Annuitants Assn. (Ill.), Lawrence U. Legacy Circle, Guideposts Legacy Circle, The Inst. Econometric Rsch., Phi Gamma Delta, Phi Mu Alpha Sinfonia, Kappa Kappa Psi, Kappa Delta Pi. Republican. Episcopalian. Avocations: travel, golf, music, photography. Home: Palm Harbor, Fla. Died 2001.

ZAHRT, WILLIAM DIETRICH, II, lawyer; b. Dayton, Ohio, July 12, 1944; s. Kenton William and Orpha Catharine (Wagner) Z.; m. Patricia Ann Marek, June 10, 1969; children: Justin William, Alitheia Patricia. BS in Physics, Yale U., 1966, JD, 1969, M of Pub. and Pvt. Mgmt., 1990. Bar: N.Y. 1970, Ohio 1972, Tex. 1982, N.C. 1992, U.S. Ct. Appeals (Fed. cir.) 1977. Assoc. Kenyon & Kenyon, N.Y.C., 1969-71, Biebel, French & Nauman, Dayton, 1971-80; sr. patent atty. Schlumberger Well Svcs., Houston, 1980-82; sole practice Kingwood, Tex., 1982-85, 88-90; patent atty. Shell Oil Co., Houston, 1985-88; sr. patent counsel Raychem Corp., Fuquay-Varina, N.C., 1990-97; asst. gen. counsel Advanced Micro Devices, Sunnyvale, Calif., 1997-2000; assoc. gen. counsel, legal dir. intellectual property Palm, Inc., Santa Clara, 2000—. Mem. ABA, Am. Intellectual Property Law Assn., Tex. Bar Assn., Silicon Valley Intellectual Property Law Assn., Dayton Racquet Club, Masons. Anglican. Home: 629 Villa Centre Way San Jose CA 95128-5138 Office: M/S 9209 5470 Great America Pkwy Santa Clara CA 95054-3644

ZAHS, DAVID KARL, secondary school educator, educational administrator; b. Mt. Clemens, Mich., June 2, 1957; s. William Karl and Shirley Ann Zahs. BEd magna cum laude, U. Toledo, 1982, postgrad. in adminstrn. Student tchr. Waterville Elem. and Monclova Elem. Schs., Ohio, 1982; substitute tchr. Anthony Wayne H.S., Whitehouse, 1982, Bowsher H.S., Toledo, 1982-83; tchr. Toledo Pub. Schs., 1983-88; human svc. program adminstr. vocation, vols. and adult edn. Warrensville (Ohio) Devel. Ctr. MR/DD, 1988-98; substitute tchr., coach girls basketball, boys soccer Garfield Heights (Ohio) H.S., 1989—, head coach, 1989—; boys soccer coach Strongville H.S., 1997; adapted phys. edn. instr. Brunswick (Ohio) City Schs., 1999—; site mgr. HELP Found. Inc., 1999—. Coach soccer and basketball Ctrl. Cath. H.S., Toledo, 1983-88; coach boys' track DeVilbiss H.S., Toledo, 1986-87 (State Champions 1987); coach girl's soccer Brunswick H.S.; referee soccer h.s./USSF Grade 7, 1984-99; instr. Rocket Soccer Camp U. Toledo, 1985-88; asst. Maumee Valley Soccer Sch., 1982-84, head coach girls' team, 1982; dir. Bulldog Basketball Camp, 1992—. Named divsn. 1 Coach of Yr. N.E. Ohio AP, 1997. Mem. AAHPERD, Fellowship of Christian Athletes. Lutheran. Avocations: soccer, distance running. Home: 23215 Chandlers Ln Olmsted Falls OH 44138-3221 Office: Brunswick City Schs 3643 Center Rd Brunswick OH 44212-3619

ZAIDAIN, DAVID ANTHONY, urban planner; b. Dayton, Ohio, Mar. 28, 1974; BS, U. Cin., 1997, M in Cmty. Planning, 1999. Cert. Am. Inst. Cert. Planners. Planner I Warren County Regional Planning Commn., Lebanon, Ohio, 1999—2000; dir. devel. svcs. Anderson Twp., 2000—02; planner Nat. Capital Planning Commn., Washington, 2002—. Mem.: ASPA, Ohio Planning Conf. (treas. Cin. sect. 2001—02), Am. Planning Assn. Avocation: music. Home: 1308 Pennsylvania Ave Washington DC 20003 Office: Nat Capital Planning Commn 401 9th St Ste 500 Washington DC 20576

ZAIDI, EMILY LOUISE, retired elementary school educator; b. Hoquiam, Wash., Apr. 20, 1924; d. Burdick Newton and Emily Caroline (Williams) Johnston; m. M. Baqar Abbas Zaidi, June 12, 1949 (dec. Dec. 1983). BA in Edn. and Social Studies, Ea. Wash. State U., 1948; MEd, U. Wash., 1964, EdD, 1974. Tchr. 4th grade Hoquiam Schs., 1948-49; tchr. grades 5-6 Lake Washington Sch. Dist., Kirkland, Wash., 1949-51; tchr. grades 2-3 Port Angeles (Wash.) Schs., 1951-54; tchr. grade 2 Seattle Schs., 1954-55; tchr., reading specialist Northshore sch. Dist., Bothell, Wash., 1955-69, Sacramento City Schs., 1969-87; ret. Mem. Calif. State Instructional Materials Panel, Sacramento, 1975. Mem. Sacramento Opera Assn., 1986—, Sacramento Ballet Assn., 1987-2000. Fulbright Commn. Exchange Tchr., 1961-62. Mem. Reading Club. Democrat. Avocations: writing, children's literature, reading, travel. Home: 4230 N River Way Sacramento CA 95864-6055

ZAIDI, IQBAL MEHDI, biochemist, scientist; b. Bijnor, India, June 30, 1957; s. Iqbal Haider and Habib (Zehra) Z.; m. Nuzhat Shikoh, Jan. 2, 1993; 1 child, Shan Zehra. BS in Chemistry with honors, Aligarh M. U., 1976, MS in Biochemistry, 1978, PhD in Biochemistry, 1984. Cert. in radiation. Rsch. fellow Indsl. Toxicology Rsch. Ctr., Lucknow, India, 1979-83; rsch. affiliate N.Y. State Health Dept., Albany, 1984-91; scientist Applied Biosystems, Applera Corp., Foster City, Calif., 1991—. Contbr. articles to profl. jours. Mem. AAAS, Am. Chem. Soc. (biochem. tech. div. 1992—), Shia Assn. Bay Area, N.Y. Acad. Scis. Avocations: photography, swimming, travel, natural history. Office: Applied Biosystems 850 Lincoln Centre Dr Foster City CA 94404-1128

ZAIDI, RIAZ HAIDER, aircraft engineer, consultant; b. Baghdad, Iraq, Aug. 25, 1959; s. Syed Ghulam Haider and Ashraf (Razvi) Z.; m. Beenish Zehra, Aug. 17, 2000. AS in Aviation Maintenance Tech., Embry-Riddle Aero. U., Daytona Beach, Fla., 1982, BS in Aero. Studies, 1988, BS in Aircraft Engring., 1990, M in Aero. Sci., 1994; M in Engring. Mgmt., Washington U., St. Louis, Mo., 1998, MS in Tech. and Human Affairs, 1999, postgrad. in engring. and policy, 2000. Lic. FAA Airframe and Powerplant. Engr. T-45 structures McDonnell Douglas Aerospace, St. Louis, 1992-94, sr. engr. T-45 support equipment, 1994-95; sr. engr. F/A-18 mech. sys. Boeing Co., 1995-98, project engr. Phantom Works Joint Strike Fighter program, 1998—2000, project engr./scientist on AH-64D Apache Aircrew Tng. Sys., 2000—. Mem. industry adv. bd. Embry-Riddle Aero. U., 1994—; engring. cons. Britech, St. Louis, 1995-98; bd. dirs. Art2Part Plastics Inc., St. Louis. Vol. Jr. Achievement, St. Louis, 1994—, Embry-Riddle Aero. U. Aces program, 1994—. Achievements include pending patent for heat blanket test panel and test process. Home: 1748 Michaelwood Ct Saint Charles MO 63303-4657 Office: The Boeing Co PO Box 516 Saint Louis MO 63166-0516

ZAIDI, SYED ALI, infectious disease physician; b. Lahore, Pakistan, Jan. 20, 1969; s. Syed Tahir and Shahla Zaidi; m. Sheema Jalil; children: Zoya Syed, Raheen Syed. MD , King Edward Med. Coll., Lahore, 1994. Diplomate Am. Bd. Internal Medicine. Resident in internal medicine U. Pitts. Med. Ctr., McKeesport, Pa., 1997—2000; fellow in infectious diseases/ HIV medicine L.I. Jewish Med. Ctr., New Hyde Park, NY, 2000—. Recipient Physicians Recognition award, AMA, 2000. Mem.: Infectious Diseases Soc. Am. Home: 75-44 263d St 2d Fl Glen Oaks NY 11004 Office: LI Jewish Med Ctr Staff House Rm 226 270-05 76th Ave New Hyde Park NY 11040 Home Fax: 718-470-0637; Office Fax: 718-470-0637. Personal E-mail: szaidi20@hotmail.com. Business E-Mail: szaidi20@hotmail.com.

ZAIKOW, LARRY J. JAMES, painter; b. Red Lake, Ont., Can., Dec. 25, 1951; s. Jim DeMetor and Alice Helen (Dutka) Z. Grad., Red Lake H.S. With Poetry Co., Sacramento, 1987-92. Author: Who's Who in Poetry, 1992. Avocations: writing poetry and songs. Home: 334 Howey St Red Lake ON Canada

ZAIMAN, JOEL HIRSH, rabbi; b. Chgo., Mar. 10, 1938; s. Solomon and Ruth (Levy) Z.; m. Ann Shanok, July 1, 1959; children: Elana Beth, Sarina, Ari Lev. BS, DePaul U., 1957; Master of Hebrew Letters, Jewish Theol. Sem., N.Y.C., 1962. Assoc. rabbi Temple Emanu-El, Providence, 1962-73, sr. rabbi, 1973-80, Chizuk Amuno Congregation, Balt., 1980—. Pres. Balt. Bd. Rabbis, 1985-87; 1st v.p. Synagogue Coun. Am., 1988, pres., 1989-91. Contbr. articles to profl. jours. Chmn. edn. com. Kreiger Schecter Day Sch., Balt., 1983; bd. dirs. Balt. Bd. Jewish Edn., Md. Commn. on Hereditary and Congenital Disorders, Assoc. Jewish Charities and Welfare Fund, Levindale Hebrew Geriat. Ctr. and Hosp., Balt., 1984—, long range planning com.; v.p. Balt. Jewish Coun., 1992-94, pres., 1994-96; chancellors rabbinic cabinet Jewish Theol. Sem.; bd. dirs., patient care adv. com. Sinai Hosp., 1991; bd. dirs., chmn. program com. Inst. Christian and Jewish Studies; adv. coun. Md. Health Care Decisions Act, 1994—. Fellow Pearlstone Inst. Jewish Living (program planning com.); mem. Rabbinical Assembly (exec. council, long range planning com.), United Synagogue Commn. Jewish Edn. (chmn.), Md. Jewish Hist. Soc. (bd. dirs.), Associated Jewish Fedn. Balt. (bd. dirs. 1991—). Home: 1 Talton Ct Baltimore MD 21208-3109 Office: Chizuk Amuno Congregation 8100 Stevenson Rd Baltimore MD 21208-1899 E-mail: jhzaiman@chizukamuno.org.

ZAIMAN, K(OICHI) ROBERT, dentist; b. Cin., Oct. 19, 1944; s. Noboru Gary and Toshiko (Matsuyama) Zaiman; m. Kimberly Ann Sass, Nov. 6, 1976; children: Kara Jean, Matthew Robert. Student, Creighton U., Omaha, 1962-64, DDS, 1968. Asst. prof. Creighton U. Sch. Dentistry, Omaha, 1971-73, assoc. prof., 1973-75; pvt. practice dentistry, 1971—. Dir. Chicano and Native-Am. Free Clinic Creighton U., Omaha, 1970—75. Mem. bd. elders King of Kings Luth. Ch., 1990—95; past v.p., bd. dirs. Japanese-Am. Citizens League, Omaha, 1977—86. Fellow: Acad. Continuing Edn., Acad. Gen. Dentistry (pres. 1976—77, nat. del. 1971—76), Pierre Fauchard Internat. Hon. Acad.; mem.: ADA, Omaha Dental Study Club (pres. 1999—), Nebr. Dental Assn. (del. 1971—94, 1996—), Omaha Dist. Dental Soc. (treas. 1980—85, bd. dirs. 1968, peer rev. 1996—), Delta Sigma Delta (pres. 1973—74). Office: 10841 Q St Ste 109 Omaha NE 68137-3741

ZAISER, KENT AMES, lawyer; b. St. Petersburg, Fla., June 10, 1945; s. Robert Alan and Marion (Brown) Z. AB, Duke U., 1967; postgrad., U. Calif., Berkeley, 1971; JD, U. Fla., 1972. Bar: Fla. 1973, U.S. Dist. Ct. (no. dist.) Fla. 1974, U.S. Supreme Ct. 1978, U.S. Dist. Ct. (so. dist.) Fla. 1980, U.S. Dist. Ct. (mid. dist.) Fla. 1981, U.S. Ct. Appeals (11th cir.) 1981. Rsch. aide Fla. Supreme Ct., Tallahassee, 1973-75, adminstrv. asst. to chief justice, 1975-76; asst. gen. counsel Fla. Dept. Natural Resources, 1976-80; asst. atty. gen. Fla. Dept. Legal Affairs, 1980-85; dep. gen. counsel S.W. Fla. Water Mgmt. Dist., Brooksville, 1985-89, gen. counsel, 1989-92; ptnr. Foley and Lardner, Tallahassee, 1992-93; prin. Kent A. Zaiser, P.A., 1994—. Cons. Fla. State Cts. Adminstr., Tallahassee, 1975; mem. Fla. New Motor Vehicle Arbitration Bd., 1998-99. Contbg. author: Environmental Regulation and Litigation in Florida, 1980-84. Campaign chmn. Vince Fechtel for State Rep. of Fla., Leesburg, 1972. Mem. Tallahassee Bar Assn., Jefferson County Bar Assn., Govs. Club. Democrat. Episcopalian. Home: 3286 Longleaf Rd Tallahassee FL 32310-6406 Office: PO Box 6045 Tallahassee FL 32314-6045

ZAITZEFF, ROGER MICHAEL, lawyer; b. Detroit, June 25, 1940; s. Peter and Mary (Fedchenia) Z.; children: Zachary, Natasha, Zoe, Peter. BA with high honors and high distinction, U. Mich., 1962; MA with distinction, U. Calif., Berkeley, 1963, JD, 1969. Bar: N.Y. 1970, U.S. Dist. Ct. (so. dist.) N.Y. 1975, U.S. Ct. Appeals (2nd cir.) 1975, D.C. 1985. Assoc. Seward & Kissel, N.Y.C., 1969-77, ptnr., 1977-94, Latham & Wakins, N.Y.C., 1994-2000, LeBoeuf Lamb Greene & MacRae, N.Y.C., 2000—02, Swidler Berlin Shereff Friedman, N.Y.C., 2002—. Contbr. articles to profl. jours. Mem. Tribar Opinion Com., 1990-93. Heller grantee U. Mich., 1962; recipient William Jennings Bryan Prize. Mem.: ABA, N.Y. County Lawyers Assn. (spl. com. legal opinions in comml. transactions), N.Y. State Bar Found., Phi Beta Kappa. Office: Swidler Berlin Shereff Friedman 405 Lexington Ave 11th Fl New York NY 10174

ZAJAC, JOHN, semiconductor equipment company executive; b. N.Y.C., July 21, 1946; s. John Andrew and Catherine (Canepa) Z.; m. Vera Barbagallo, Jan. 13, 1973; children: Jennifer, Michelle. AAS, NYU, 1966; BEE, U. Ky., 1968. Project engr. B.C.D. Computing, N.Y.C., 1968-70; v.p. Beacon Systems, Commack, N.Y., 1970-73, E.T. Systems, Santa Clara, Calif., 1973-77; v.p. research and devel. Eaton Corp., Sunnyvale, 1977-81; pres. Semitech/Gen. Signal, Los Gatos, 1981-83; mgr. advanced product div. Tegal/Motorola Inc., Novato, 1983-86; v.p. research and devel. U.S.A. Inc., San Jose, 1986-94; staff scientist Mattson Tech., Fremont, 1994—. Author: The Delicate Balance, 1988, A Thief's Way to Heaven, 1999, Pyramids, Prophecy and 666, 2000; holder of 25 patents in field; guest TV and radio. Office: Mattson Tech 3550 W Warren Ave Fremont CA 94538-6499 E-mail: zajacjohn@aol.com.

ZAJAS, J. JONATHAN R. management consulting company executive, principal; b. Buffalo, Oct. 10, 1954; s. Michael A.A. and Janet J. (Rusch) Z. BA in Humanities, English, Bus. Edn., Canisius Coll. Buffalo, 1975; BS in Liberal Arts, SUNY, Albany, 1977; MA in Humanities, Philosophy, Ethics, Calif. State U., Dominguez Hills, 1976; MBA in Mgmt. and Mktg., U. Tex., Edinburg, 1979; D in Bus. Adminstrn. in Mgmt., Calif. Western U., 1980; MBA in Acctg., Tex. State U., Alpine, 1982; PhD, U. Wyoming, 1985; MA in Profl. Counseling, Liberty U. Va., 1993. Cert. personnel cons., Nat. Assn. Pers. Cons.; cert. profl. supt., prin./supr., Tex.; cert. sch. dist. adminstr., tchr., counselor, N.Y.; accredited prof. in human resources; cert. mediator, arbitrator, Better Bus. Bur.; mem. nat. panel arbitrators Am. Arbitration Assn., cert. fin. svcs. auditor Nat. Assn. Fin. Svc. Auditors, 1998. Tchr. bus., English N.Y. and Tex. Sch. Dists., 1974-80; city adminstr., CFO City of Port Isabel, Tex., 1979-81; asst. prof., MBA dir., chmn. bus. adminstrn. programs Sul Ross State U. Ctr., Alpine and Del Rio, 1981-86; from vis. assoc. to prof. mgmt. Mt. St. Mary Coll., Newburgh, N.Y., 1989-90; pres., dir., sr. cons. The Corp. Mgmt. Group, Del Rio and Nashville, 1984—; sr. prof. bus. adminstrn. U. Mary Hardin Baylor, Belton, Tex., 1992-94; sch. prin., dir. guidance Clymer (N.Y.) Ctr. Sch., 1994-96. Mediator, arbitrator BBB Western N.Y., Jamestown, 1995—; mem. adv. bd. Future Bus. Leaders Am., Clymer, 1994—; sr. mgmt. cons., cons./advisor Border Fed. Credit Union, Del Rio, 1983-85; comml. arbitrator, mem. nat. panel arbitrators Am. Arbitration Assn., N.Y.C., Dallas, 1984-95; Rule 31 mediator Tenn. State Supreme Ct., Alternate Dispute Resolution Commn. Author, editor: Our Moments of Time, 1979 (Excellence in Writing award 1980), A Comparative Analysis of Interpersonal Communication, Leadership and Motivational Styles Among C.E.O.'s, 1981, The Total Career and Life Portfolio: A Guide for Your Success, 1996, The Wee Little Pigs: An Economic Fable, 1997, Jeremy Brown's Wonderful Surprise, 1997, The Pooch that Loves to Mooch, 1997, Creativity and the Art of Problem Solving, 1998, others; co-author: (with O. Church) Applying Telecommunications and Technology from a Global Business Perspective, 1997 (Guest Editor's award 1995); author, editor: The Marketing of Executives & Career Development Success, 1995; spl. editor, Exec. Devel. jours., 1995; contbr. articles to profl. jours. Mem. adv. New Compact for Learning Coun., Clymer Ctrl. Sch. Dist. Wide Com., 1994-96; co-chair, advisor to San Antonio chpt. Cert. Employee Benefits Specialist Bd., 1991; chair, co-chair econ. devel. coun. S.W. Tex. Comm. for Higher Edn., Del Rio, 1987-89; mem. adv. bd., chair fund raising com. Youth For Christ Ministry, Brownsville, Tex., 1978-80; vol. facilitator Am. Summit on Edn. and Cmty. Devel., Rutherford County, Mid. Tenn., 1997-98. Recipient Outstanding Martial Artist of Yr. award U.S. Profl. Martial/Artist Assn., 1975, Outstanding Tchr. of Yr. award U.S. Profl. Martial/Artist Assn., 1976, Master Tchrs. award for Leadership Excellence, Master Tchrs. Coun., 1995, Cert. of Appreciation for Leadership and Svc., Future Bus. Leaders Am., 1995, 96. Mem. Inst. Cert. Profl. Mgrs. (cert. profl. mgr.), Am. Assn. Christian Counselors (charter, profl., assoc.), Nat. Honor Soc., Phi Kappa Phi. Avocations: public speaking, creative writing, hiking, water sports, aerobics. *Have you discovered the joy and the fullness of life? For the essence of life is not found in our mere moments of time, but rather in our timeless moments.*

ZAJICEK, JERONYM, music educator; b. Krasne, Brezno, Czechoslovakia, Nov. 10, 1926; came to U.S., 1952; s. Frantisek Zajicek and Emilie (Lauterkranz) Zajickova. Student, Charles U., Prague, Czechoslovakia, 1946-49; MusB, Roosevelt U., 1957, MusM, 1958; studies with K.B. Jirak, Paul A. Pisk; PhD, Charles U., Prague, 1990. Music program dir. for Czechoslovak sect. Radio Free Europe, Munich, 1950-52; prof. theory and composition Loop Coll., Chgo., 1964-96. Composer numerous works including Clarinet Sonata, 1958, Sinfonietta for Large Orch., 1958, Cello Sonata, 1975; recorded Concertino for Flute and String Orch., 1963, Willie Schwegler Flute and Cologne Radio Orch., String Quartet, 1963, Pater Noster for mixed chorus, 1996, Sonatina for flute, clarinet and bassoon, 1996, Twenty Czech Carols, 2001, Twenty Moravian Carols for four part children chorus, 2002. Oliver Ditson fellow, 1956, 57; 1st prize Internat. Soc. for Contemporary Music (Chgo. chpt. 1964); named hon. citizen Hrochuv Tynec, Czech Republic, 1998. Roman Catholic. Home: 4230 Prescott Ave Lyons IL 60534-1537 Office: Harold Washington Coll 30 E Lake St Chicago IL 60601-2403

ZAJICEK, LYNN ENGELBRECHT, educational administrator; b. Newport News, Va., Mar. 25, 1950; d. Herbert Charles and Lois (Kohler) Engelbrecht; m. Jon M. Zajicek, June 6, 1970; children: Carlye Lynn, Kate Elizabeth. BA, Kearney State Coll., 1971; MEd, U. Nebr., 1973, EdS, 1988. Cert. profl. adminstr./supr., Nebr. Tchr. Lincoln (Nebr.) Pub. Schs., 1971-73; instr. U.S. Army PREP Program, Crailsheim, Germany, 1974-76; subs. tchr. Grand Island (Nebr.) Pub. Schs., 1976-77; mgr., owner rental property Grand Island, 1978—; asst. on survey project U. Nebr., Lincoln, 1987-88; adminstr., edni. diagnostician Nebr. Ctr. for Evaluation of Devel. and Learning, Inc., Grand Island, 1988—. Ctr. dir. Sylvan Learning Ctr., Grand Island; bd. dirs. Reorganized Mark V Mortgage Corp. Bd. dirs. PTA, Grand Island, 1980—, Episc. Ch. Women; supt. Bible Sch. St. Stephen's Ch., Grand Island, 1984-85; mem. Christian edn. com. St. Stephen's, 1985—, subcom. for adult and continuing edn. of strategic planning com. Grand Island Pub. Schs., 1987; coach Odyssey of the Mind Grand Island Pub. Schs., 1986—; active in heart and cancer funds in Grand Island; candidate cmpaign mgr. Rep. Women, 1978; bd. dirs., exec. com. Marque of Nebr., 1989—. Recipient Gen. Arnold scholarship USAF, 1967. Mem. AAUW, Assn. Supervision and Curriculum Devel., Nat. Assn. Secondary Sch. Prins., Nebr. Coun. Sch. Adminstrs., Nebr. Assn. Elem. Sch. Prins., Nebr. Dental Assn. Aux. (numerous offices including pres. 1981-82), Hall County Dental Aux. (sec., treas. 1976—), St. Francis Med. Aux., Nebr. Assn. for Children and Adults with Learning Disabilities, Phi Delta Kappa, Pi Delta Phi, Alpha Mu Gamma, Sigma Tau Delta, Xi Phi. Avocations: reading, jogging, computers. Home: 1618 S Harrison St Grand Island NE 68803-6359 Office: Sylvan Learning Ctr 1508 S Locust St Grand Island NE 68801-8245

ZAJTA, AUREL JOSEPH, software engineer, mathematician; b. Nemesbük, Veszprem, Hungary, Mar. 17, 1926; came to U.S., 1982; s. Joseph and Elisabeth (Daubner) Z.; m. Judith Piroska Répászky, Aug. 15, 1956. MSc in Applied Maths., Eötvös U., Budapest, Hungary, 1960; PhD in Math Analysis, Kossuth U., Debrecen, Hungary, 1964. Prof. math. Kenyatta U., Nairobi, Kenya, 1973-78; prof. applied math. U. Campinas, Sao Paulo, 1978-82; prof. applied math. scis. U. Houston, 1983-85; sr. software engr. Computer Output Printing, Inc., Houston, 1987-91. Vis. prof. math. Lamar U., Beaumont, Tex., 1982-83. Author 2 books; contbr. over 20 articles to profl. jours. Mem. Am. Math. Soc. Achievements include conversion and other utility programs for electronic printing and research in cryptography.

ZAK, BENNIE, pathology educator; b. Detroit, Sept. 29, 1919; s. Morris and Lena (Synder) Z.; m. Doris Kitty Selby; children: Steven Dennis, Deborah Lise Zak Tataranowicz, Marsha Glae. BS, Wayne State U., 1948, PhD, 1952. Jr. assoc. pathology Detroit Receiving Hosp., 1951-59; asst. prof. clin. chemistry in pathology Wayne State U., Detriot, 1957, from asst. prof. to assoc. profl., 1961-63, prof., 1965-91, prof. emeritus, 1991—. Cons. in field. Contbr. articles to profl. jours. Served to 1st lt. USAF, 1941-45. Recipient Faulty Rsch. award Wayne State U., 1973, Disting. Svc. award, 1983; benedetti-Pichlr award Am. Microchem. Soc., 1984. Fellow Nat. Acad. Clin. Biochemists; mem. Am. Chem. Soc., Am. Assn. Clin. Chemistry (Ames award 1974, gen. diagnostics lectr. 1981). Avocation: writing. Office: Wayne State U Sch Medicine 540 E Canfield St Detroit MI 48201-1928

ZAK, JOHN MICHAEL, retired agronomy educator; b. Sunderland, Mass., May 12, 1914; s. John William and Mary (Swaluk) Z.; m. Ruth Symonds, May 5, 1945; children: Karen Elizabeth Zak Benbury, John Merrill, Richard Paul, Rebecca Louise. BS, U. Mass., 1936, MS, 1938. Agronomy U. Mass., Amherst, 1938-84; ret., 1984. Co-founder Mohawk Trout Hatchery, Sunderland. 1960-84. Author pamplets and bulls. in field, including Establishment and Management of Roadside Vegetative Cover in Massachusetts, 1967, Handbooks I and II: A Plant Material's Manual, 1976, Roadside Vegetative Cover for Critical and Eroded Areas, 1976, Massachusetts Roadside Development Researcher, 1977. Grantee Fed. Highway Adminstrn., 1969-80. Mem. Cushman Investment Club (v.p. 1985, pres. 1999), Masons, Sigma Xi, Alpha Tau Gamma. Avocations: beekeeping, fishing, hunting, gardening.

ZAK, PAUL JOSEPH, economist, educator; b. Santa Barbara, Calif., Feb. 9, 1962; s. Donald Edward and Dorothy Dell Zak; m. Lori Darlene Uber; children: Alexandra. Degree summa cum laude, San Diego State U., 1989; PhD, U. of Pa., 1994. Asst. prof. of economics Claremont Grad. U., Claremont, Calif., 1996—2001, assoc. prof. of econ., 2001—. Chmn. econ. dept. Claremont Grad. U., 2001—; rsch. fellow Gruter Inst. for Law and Behavioral Rsch., Portola Valley, Calif., 2000—02; vis. scientist Def. Threat Reduction Agy., Washington, 2001; rsch. fellow divsn. internat. fin. Fed. Res. Bd., Washington. Editor: Monetary Stability and Economic Growth, 2002; author: Currency Crises, Monetary Union, and the Conduct of Monetary Policy: A Debate Among Leading Economists, 1999; contbr. articles to profl. jours. Mem.: Phi Beta Kappa. Office: Claremont Graduate University Department of Economics Claremont CA 91711-6165

ZAK, ROBERT JOSEPH, lawyer; b. Steubenville, Ohio, July 29, 1946; s. Joseph and Pearl (Munyas) Zak; m. Kristy Hubbard Winkler, Sept. 13, 1980; children: Elizabeth Adele, Robert Joseph Jr, Barbara Ann. BS, W.Va. U., 1968, JD, 1975. Bar: WVa 1975, US Dist Ct (so dist) WVa 1975, US Dist Ct (no dist) WVa 1989, US Ct Appeals (4th cir) 1990. Staff atty. Pub. Svc. Commn. of W.Va., Charleston, 1975-76; assoc. Preiser & Wilson L.C., 1976-81, ptnr., 1981-85; sr. ptnr. Zak & Assocs., 1985—. Hearing examiner W.Va. Bd. Regents, Charleston, 1987—90; spl. asst. atty. gen. State of W.Va., Charleston, 1987—90, mem. workers compensation appeals , 1991—97, Charleston, 2001—. With U.S. Army, 1969—71, Vietnam. Fellow: Am Acad Matrimonial Lawyers; mem.: Order Barristers. Republican. Presbyterian. Office: Zak & Assocs 607 Ohio Ave Charleston WV 25302-2228

ZAKANITCH, ROBERT RAHWAY, artist; b. Elizabeth, N.J. s. Andrew and Mary Z. Student, Newark (N.J.) Sch. Fine and Indsl. Art, 1954-57. Vis. artist, lectr. Sch. Art Inst. Chgo., 1976, U. Calif., San Diego, 1974; lectr. numerous univs. One man shows include Henri Gallery, Alexandria, Va., 1965, Reese Palley Gallery, N.Y.C., 1970, 71, Cunningham Ward, N.Y.C., 1973, 74, Holly Solomon Gallery, N.Y.C., 1977, Robert Miller Gallery, N.Y.C., 1978, 79, 81, 84, 85, 88, Galerie Liatowitsch, Basel, Switzerland, 1978, Galerie Rudolf Zwirner, Cologne, Fed. Republic Germany, 1979, Daniel Templon Gallery, N.Y.C., 1980, Bruno Bischofberger Gallery, Zurich, 1980, James Mayor Gallery, London, 1981, Marcus Gallery, 1984, Inst. Contemporary Art, Phila.,

1981, Akira Ikeda Gallery, Nagoya, Japan, 1981, Daniel Templon Gallery, Paris, 1982, 87, 91, McIntosh-Drysdale Gallery, Washington, 1983, Harcus Gallery, Boston, 1984, 87, 89, Delahunty Gallery, Dallas, 1984, Helander/Rubinstein Gallery, Palm Beach, Fla., 1985, 89, Asher Faure Gallery, L.A., 1985, Yares Gallery, Scottsdale, Ariz., 1987, Sidney Janis Gallery, N.Y.C., 1990, Jason McCoy Gallery, N.Y.C., 1994, 1995 (John Simon Guggenheim fellowship grant), Guild Hall, East Hampton, N.Y., 1995, Hirschl & Adler, N.Y.C., 1995, others; group shows include Franklin Gallery, Cornell U., 1978, Va. Mus. Fine Arts, 1979, Palais des Beaux-Arts, Brussels, 1979, Inst. Contemporary Art, U. Pa., 1979, New Mus., N.Y., 1979, Galerie Daniel Templon, Paris, 1980, Nat. Gallery Art, Washington, 1980, Indpls. Mus. Art, 1980, San Francisco Art Inst., 1980, Whitney Mus. Am. Art, N.Y., 1981, Jacksonville Art Mus., 1981, Galeria Civica, Italy, 1982, Mus. Fine Arts, Boston, 1982, Fay Gold Gallery, Atlanta, 1982, High Mus. Art, Atlanta, 1983, Meml. Art Gallery, Rochester, N.Y., 1983, Kuntsmus., Luzern. 1983. Served with U.S. Army, 1958-60. John Simon Guggenheim fellowship grant, 1995. Studio: 119 N 11th St Brooklyn NY 11211-1163

ZAKARAUSKAS, PIERRE, physicist, educator; b. Amos, Que., Can., Dec. 25, 1958; s. Joseph and Réjeanne (Latreille) Z. BSc, U Que., 1980; PhD, U. B.C., Vancouver, 1984. Def. scientist Def. Rsch. Establishment Atlantic, Dartmouth, N.S., 1984-86, Def. Rsch. Establishment Pacific, Victoria, B.C., 1986-95. Rsch. assoc. dept. psychology U. B.C., 1988-93, asst. prof. dept. ophthalmology, 1993—; CTO Wavemakers Inc. Contbr. articles and referee to profl. jours. including Jour. Acoustical Soc. Am., IEEE Transaction on Signal Processing, Neural Network for Ocean Engring., IEEE Proceedings, Hearing Res., Phys. Rev. D. Mem. Acoustical Soc. Am., Can. Acoustical Assn. Achievements include research on ice-cracking noise in Arctic, complexity analysis of nearest-neighbor search, applying neural networks to acoustic localization, computational theories of sound localization, and classification, high-energy particle physics. Home: 655 Moberly Rd Ste 507 Vancouver BC Canada V5Z 2B4 Office: Ste 302 134 Abbott St Vancouver BC Canada V6B 2K4 E-mail: pierre@wavemakers.com.

ZAKHEIM, BARBARA JANE, development professional; b. London, Jan. 31, 1953; d. David Sloma and Sarah Frances (Leifer) Portnoi; m. Dov Solomon Zakheim, Aug. 20, 1972 (div. 1990); children: Keith Samuel, Roger Israel, Scott Elisha; m. Ronald Kleinfeldt, Dec. 13, 1992. BA, Oxford U., Eng., 1974, MA, 1978. Economist Maxima Corp., Silver Spring, Md., 1979, U.S. Dept. Energy, Washington, 1979-80; sr. project analyst Applied Mgmt. Scis., Silver Spring, 1980-83, staff assoc., 1983-85; prin. analyst NUS Corp., Gaithersburg, Md., 1985-87, cons. analyst, 1987-89; pres. Keith R. Scott Assocs., Inc., 1989-96, African Treasures, Inc., 1990-93; dir. policy and econ. studies Sanford Cohen & Assocs., Inc., 1993-96, v.p. info. & comm. svcs. divsn., 1996-2000, COO, 2000—02; dir. devel. Save A Child's Heart Found., U.S., Inc., 2002—. U.S. rep. Coll. Petroleum Studies, Oxford, 1984-93; N.Am. rep. Twirltrade Internat. Ltd., London, 1985—; mem. adv. com. on women in bus. Theodore Roosevelt Nat. Bank, Washington, 1991-92; profl. team mem. Venture Ptnrs. Internat., Inc., N.Y.C., 1990-94. Contbr. articles to profl. jours. Bd. dirs. SE Hebrew Congregation, Silver Spring, 1977-78; sec. Stonington Woods Homeowners' Assn., 1997-98, pres., 1998-99; founder, pres. Greater Washington Jewish Coalition Against Domestic Abuse, 1999—; bd. dirs. Jewish Cmty. Coun. Greater Washington, 2002—. Mem. NAFE, Hadassah, Jewish Women Internat. Republican. Avocations: reading, travel, theater, music, ballroom dancing. Home and Office: 11247 Watermill Ln Silver Spring MD 20902-3439 E-mail: bzakheim@aol.com.

ZAKHEIM, DOV SOLOMON, economist, government official; b. Dec. 18, 1948; s. Zvi Hirsh and Bella (Rabinowitz) Zakheim; m. Barbara Jane Portnoi, Aug. 20, 1972 (div. 1990); children: Keith Samuel, Roger Israel, Scott Elisha; m. Deborah Bing Lowy, May 26, 1991. Student, London Sch. Econs., 1968-69; BA summa cum laude, Columbia U., 1970; DPhil, Oxford U., 1974. Rsch. fellow St. Antony's Coll. Oxford U., 1974; asst. to mng. dir. U.K. br. Internat. Credit Bank Geneva, 1974-75; assoc. analyst Nat. Security and Internat. Affairs Congl. Budget Office, Washington, 1975-78, prin. analyst, 1978-81; spl. asst. to asst. sec. def. (internat. security policy) Dept. Def., 1981-82, spl. asst. to under sec. def., 1982-83, asst. under sec. def. (policy and resources), 1983-85, dep. under sec. def. for planning and resources, 1985-87; exec. v.p. Sys. Planning Corp., Arlington, Va., 1987-90, corp. v.p., 1990-2001; CEO SPC Int Inc, 1998—2001; under-sec. def. (comptr. and CFO) U.S. Govt., 2001—. Consult to secy def and undersecy def, 1987—2000; consult ABC News, 1991; adj prof Nat Def Univ, 1992, Columbia Univ, 1995—96, Yeshiva Univ, 1995—96; adj prof, presidential fellow Trinity Col, Conn., 1998; guest lectr War Coll. Author: (book) Flight of the Lavi; contbr. articles to profl jours. Mem US Comn Preservation Am's Heritage Abroad, 1991—95; mem bd visitors Dept Def Overseas Regulatory Ctrs, 1998; mem Secy Def Task Force Def Reform; mem bd deps Brit Jews, 1971—72; mem Chief Rabbi's Chaplaincy Bd, England, 1971—72; bd dirs Friends of Jewish Chapel, US Naval Acad, 1997—. Fellow, NSF, 1970—73, Kellet, Columbia Col, 1974. Mem.: Royal Inst Int Affairs (UK), Int Inst Strategic Studies, Coun Foreign Relations, United Oxford and Cambridge Univ Club, Columbia Club, Phi Beta Kappa. Home: 817 Lamberton Dr Silver Spring MD 20902-3038 Office: Under Sec of Def (Comptr) 1100 Defense Pentagon Washington DC 20301-1100 E-mail: valentec@osd.pentagon.mil.

ZAKHEIM, NATHAN BARUCIA, conservator; b. Sebastopol, Calif., Dec. 20, 1943; s. Bernard Baruch and Pyllis Wrigtson Zakheim; children: Juliana, Naroitam, Shakuntaia, Kuvaleshaya, Kirtoraja, Dhananjaya, Anangamalini. BA in English, San Francisco State U., 1966; Bhakti Shastri, Iskcon, L.A., 1975. Dir. Nathan Zakheim Assocs., San Francisco, L.A., 1966—; sr. supr. Shaklee, L.A., 1974—80; art dir. Bhaktivedania Book Trust Pub., 1975—80; sales dir. U.S. Sprint, 1988—90. Asst. founder Internat. Soc. for Kristna Consciousness, 1968—86. Recipient Mayoral decree, City of Burbank, Calif., 2001. Fellow: Western States Assn. for Art Conservation, Am. Inst. for Conservation Historic and Artistic Works. Vaishnava. Avocation: theology. Office: Nathan Zakheim Assocs PO Box 11929 Marina Del Rey CA 90295

ZAKI, MAMOON AMIN, political scientist; b. Baghdad, Iraq, Aug. 1, 1939; arrived in U.S., 1965; s. Amin Zaki Ali and Fawziyah Salih; m. Hana Aboud Jayid, Jan. 3, 1980; children: Amin, Jasmine, Miriam. BA, U. Baghdad, 1962; MA, Howard U., 1979; PhD, Calgary (Alta., Can.) U., 1981. Libr., rsch. asst. Libr. Congress, Washington, 1968—75; from asst. to assoc. prof. Le Moyne Queen Coll., Memphis, 1981—; acad. dean U. Ajman, United Arab Emirates, 1996—97. Adj. prof. U. Memphis, 1993—; editl. dir. Jour. Ajman U., Abu Dhabi. Contbr. chpts to books, articles to profl. jours. Recipient Cert. of award, Assn. Advancement in 3d World, 1985, 1990. Fellow: Internat. Assn. Mid. Ea. Studies; mem.: Am. Polit. Sci. Assn. Home: 8365 Sherman Oakes Dr Germantown TN 38139 Office: Le Moyne-Owen Coll 807 Walker Ave Germantown TN 38139 E-mail: mamoon-zaki.lemoyneowen@nile.edu.

ZAKI, MOHAMMED JAVEED, computer scientist, educator; b. Hyderabad, India; s. Mohiuddin and Atiya Zaki. BS, Angelo State U., 1993; MS, U. Rochester, 1995, PhD, 1998. Asst. prof. computer sci. Rensselaer Poly. Inst., Troy, N.Y., 1998—. Editor: Large Scale Parallel Data Mining, 2000. Mem. IEEE, Assn. for Computing Machinery. Avocations: painting, squash. Office: Rensselaer Poly Inst Computer Sci Dept 110 8th St Troy NY 12180 E-mail: zaki@cs.rpi.edu.

ZAKI, WASFY, physician; b. May 19, 1942; MB BCH, Cairo U., 1964. Diplomate Am. Bd. Internal Medicine. Intern in internal medicine Woodhull Med. Ctr., Bklyn., 1989-90, resident in internal medicine, 1990-91, attending physician, 1992—. Fellow ACP; mem. Royal Coll. Physicians (Eng.).

ZAKIAN, MICHAEL, museum director; BA, Columbia U., 1979; MA, Rutgers U., 1984, PhD, 1994. Assoc. curator Palm Springs Desert Mus., 1986—95; dir. Frederick R. Weisman Mus. Art, Malibu, Calif., 1995—. Office: The Frederick R Weisman Art Museum Pepperdine U 24255 Pacific Coast Hwy Malibu CA 90263

ZAKIM, DAVID, biochemist; b. Paterson, N.J., July 10, 1935; s. Sam and Ruth (Sorokin) Zakim; m. Nancy Jane Levine, June 12, 1957 (div. 1976); children: Michael, Eric, Thomas; m. Dagmar Auralia Stanke, July 30, 1978; children: Tamara, Robert. AB in Chemistry, Cornell U., 1956; MD summa cum laude, SUNY, Bklyn., 1961. Diplomate Am Bd Internal Med. Intern N.Y. Hosp., N.Y.C., 1961-62, asst. resident, 1962-63, fellow, 1963-65; asst. prof. to prof. medicine and pharmacology U. Calif., San Francisco, 1968-83; Vincent Astor Disting. prof. medicine Cornell U. Med. Coll., N.Y.C., 1983-2000; prof. biochemistry Cornell U. Grad. Sch. Med. Sci., 1983-2000, prof. emeritus, 2000—; chief scientist, chmn. Zmedix Corp., San Francisco. Contbr. articles to profl jours; editor: (book) Hepatology: A Textbook of Liver Disease, 1982, Hepatology: A Textbook of Liver Disease, 4th ed, 2002, Disorders of Acid Secretion, 1991; ed series: Current Topics in Gastroenterology, 1985; editor: Gastroenterology Med Today, 1992—95. Capt U.S. Army, 1965—68. Named Distinguished Alumnus, SUNY-Brooklyn, 1986. Mem.: Am Soc Biol Chemists, Am Asn Physicians. E-mail: dzakim@pacbell.net., david@zmedix.net.

ZAKIN, JACQUES LOUIS, chemical engineering educator; b. N.Y.C., Jan. 28, 1927; s. Mordecai and Ada Davies (Fishbein) Z.; m. Laura Pienkny, June 11, 1950; children: Richard Joseph, David Fredric, Barbara Ellen, Emily Anne, Susan Beth. BSChemE, Cornell U., 1949; MChemE, Columbia U., 1950; DEng. Sci., NYU, 1959. Chem. engr. Flintkote Research Labs., Whippany, N.J., 1950-51; research technologist, research dept. Socony-Mobil, Bklyn., 1951-53, sr. research technologist, 1953-56, supervising technologist, 1959-62; assoc. prof. chem. engring. U. Mo., Rolla, 1962-65, prof., 1965-77, dir. minority engring. program, 1974-77, dir. women in engring. program, 1975-77; chmn. dept. chem. engring. Ohio State U., Columbus, 1977-94, Helen C. Kurtz prof. chem. engring., 1994-2000, Helen C. Kurtz prof. emeritus, 2000—. Chmn. sci. manpower and resources com. Coun. Chem. Rsch., 1984-86, governing bd., 1986-89; exec. com., 1988-89; adv. bd. State of Ohio Alternative Fuels, 1992-93; vis. prof. Technion, 1968-69, 94-95, Hebrew U., 1987; disting. vis. prof. Mex. Acad. Scis. and Mex.-USA Found. for Scis., 1999. Co-editor: Proc. Turbulence Symposium, 1969, 71, 73, 75, 77, 79, 81, 83; contbr. articles to profl. jours.; patentee in field. Bd. dirs. Rolla Community Concert Assn., 1966-77, 2d v.p., 1975-77; bd. dirs. Ozark Mental Health Assn., 1976-77; trustee Ohio State Hillel Found., 1981-84, treas., 1984-89, pres., 1989-92; trustee Congregation Beth Tikvah, 1983; bd. trustees Columbus Jewish Fedn., 1989-92; co-chmn. Academics and Scientists for Soviet Refuseniks. With USNR, 1945-46. Recipient Outstanding Rsch. award U. Mo., 1970, Josef Hlavka Meml. medal Czechoslovakian Acad. Sci., 1992, Clara M. and Peter L. Scott Faculty award, 1996, Rsch. award Japanese Govt., 2001; named Outstanding Educator of Yr., Ohio Soc. Profl. Engrs., 1994, Tech. Person of Yr., Columbus Tech. Coun., 1987; Am. Chem. Soc. Petroleum Rsch. Fund Internat. fellow, 1968-69, Socony-Mobil Employee Incentive fellow NYU, 1956-59, Sr. Fulbright Rsch. fellow Technion, 1994-95. Fellow Am. Inst. Chem. Engrs.; mem. Am. Chem. Soc., Soc. of Rheology, Am. Soc. Engring. Edn., Sigma Xi, Phi Lambda Upsilon, Phi Eta Sigma, Alpha Chi Sigma, Tau Beta Pi, Phi Kappa Phi. Jewish. Office: Ohio State U 140 W 19th Ave Columbus OH 43210-1110 E-mail: zakin.1@osu.edu.

ZALAQUETT, CARLOS PATRICIO, psychology educator, psychotherapist; b. Valparaiso, Chile; came to U.S., 1987; s. Carlos José Zalaquett and Susana Olivia Montenegro; m. Jenifer Pualuan, July 10, 1982; children: Andrea, Christine. Grad. in Clin. Psychology, P. Cath. U., Santiago, Chile, 1981; MA in Clin. Psychology, Sam Houston State U., 1988; PhD, U. Tex., 1993; hon. diploma, Dept. Edn. Municipal County, Chile, 1998. Lic. clin. psychologist, Chile; cert. neurotherapist, U.S., counselor, Fla. Asst. prof. Cath. U., Santiago, 1981-87, chair clin. psychology, 1985, vice chmn. rsch., 1986-87; counselor Sam Houston State U., Huntsville, Tex., 1993—, asst. dir., 1994—, interim dir., 1999, coord. stress mgmt., 1999—2001. Clin. supr. Sam Houston State U., 1994—; cons. UpBEATT Bilingual Program, Huntsville, 1994—, Nat. Inst. Tng., Santiago, 1996—. Editor: Evaluating Stress, vol. 1, 1987, vol. 2, 1988; author web pages. Founder, 1st pres. Found. for Prevention of Sudden Infant Death Syndrome, Santiago, 1984; counselor The Woodlands (Tex.) Group, 1997-2001; counselor, vol. Cancer Counseling, Houston, 1999. Recipient Best Presentation award Southwestern Comparative Psychology Assn., 1991. Mem. APA, Biofeedback Soc. Tex. (adv. bd. 1999—, Diplomat 1999), Neurotherapy Assn., Chilean Assn. Psychologists (Best Rsch. 1981), Southwestern Psychol. Assn., Chilean Soc. Clin. Psychologists (editor jour. 1981—, Best Contbn. award 1979). Roman Catholic. Avocations: web page creations, painting, writing. E-mail: ccp. Office: U South Fla 4202 E Fowler Ave Edu 162 Tampa FL 33620

ZALAZNICK, SHELDON, editor, journalist; b. Bronx, N.Y., Aug. 6, 1928; s. Samuel and Esther Leah (Schneiderman) Z.; m. Vera Altobelli, Apr. 4, 1953; 1 dau., Andrea. BA, NYU, 1948; MA, Tchrs. Coll. Columbia, 1950. Tchr. English Benjamin Franklin H.S., N.Y.C., 1950-52; assoc. editor Newsweek mag., 1952-56; v.p. Manning Pub. Relations Co., 1956-59; sr. editor Forbes mag., 1959-63, mng. editor, 1976-89; founding editor New York mag. sect. N.Y. Herald Tribune, N.Y.C., 1963-64; Sunday editor N.Y. Herald Tribune, 1964-66; staff writer Gen. Learning Corp., 1966-67; assoc. editor Fortune mag., 1967-69; v.p., editl. dir. New York mag., 1969-76. Home: 458 W 246th St Bronx NY 10471-3330 E-mail: zalaznic@ix.netcom.com.

ZALDASTANI, OTHAR, structural engineer; b. Tbilisi, Republic of Georgia, Aug. 10, 1922; came to U.S., 1946, naturalized, 1956; s. Soliko Nicholas and Mariam Vachnadze (Hirsely) Z.; m. Elizabeth Reily Bailey, June 22, 1963; children: Elizabeth, Anne, Alexander. Diplome d'Ingenieur, Ecole Nat. des Ponts/Chausees, Paris, 1945; Licencie es Scis., Sorbonne, Paris, 1946; MS in Geotech. Engring., Harvard U., 1947, DSc in Aerodynamics, 1950. Registered prof. engr., Mass., R.I. Tenn., Mo., N.H. Mem. faculty Harvard U., Cambridge, Mass., 1947-50; ptnr. Nichols, Norton and Zaldastani, Boston, 1952-63; pres. Nichols, Norton and Zaldastani, Inc., 1976-88, chmn., 1989-97, dir., 1997—, Ga. Coastal Devel. Found. Inc., Boston, 1998—. Gordon McKay vis. lectr. structural mechanics Harvard U., 1961; trustee, 1st v.p. Mass. Constrn. Industry Bd., 1973-76; mem. Mass. Designer Selection Bd., 1976-80. Contbf. author: Advances in Applied Mechanics, vol. 3, 1953; patentee sound-absorbing block, prestressed concrete beam and deck system. Trustee Wheelock Coll., Boston, 1975-81, mem. corp., 1984-93; trustee Boston U. Med. Ctr., 1976—, Brooks Sch., North Andover, Mass., 1986-95. Recipient awards from various ogrns. and agys. including Prestressed Concrete Inst., Cons. Engrs. Coun. New Eng., Am. Inst. Steel Constrn. Fellow ASCE (Ralph W. Horne award), AIAA (assoc.), Am. Concrete Inst.; mem. Georgian Assn. in U.S. (pres. 1958-65, hon. citizen Republic of Georgia 1997), Sigma Xi, Harvard Club, Harvard Faculty Club, Somerset Club (Boston), Country Club (brookline, Mass.), Rolling Rock Club (Ligonier, Pa.). Home: 70 Suffolk Rd Chestnut Hill MA 02467 Office: Zaldastani Assocs Inc 70 Federal St Boston MA 02110-1906 E-mail: otharz@aol.com.

ZALESKE, DAVID JOSEPH, surgeon, scientist, health administrator; b. Feb. 9, 1950; BS, Yale U., 1971; MD, Harvard U., 1975. Diplomate Nat. Bd. Med. Examiners, Am. Bd. Orthop. Surgery. Intern, resident Mass. Gen. Hosp., Boston, 1975-77; orthop. resident Combined Harvard Orthop. Program, 1977-81; chief pediat. orthopedics Mass. Gen. Hosp., 1981—2001; assoc. prof. orthopedics Harvard Med. Sch., 1981—2001; prof. orthopedics George Washington U./Children's Nat. Med. Ctr., Washington, 2001—. Grantee NIH, 1998—. Office: Children's Nat Med Ctr Dept Orthopedics 111 Michigan Ave NW Washington DC 20010-2970

ZALESKI, JAMES VINCENT, electronics executive; b. Kenosha, Wis., Oct. 8, 1943; s. Louis Edward and Lena Louise (Bellotti) Zaleski; m. Beverly Rae Neumann, Nov. 8, 1969. BBA, BSME, U. Wis., 1966, MS, 1967. Project engr. AC Electronics div. GM, Milw., 1968-73; ops. mgr. Applied Computer Sci., Inc., 1970-72; sect. mgr. Delco Electronics div. GM, Santa Barbara, Calif., 1973-84, dept. mgr., 1984-85, chief engr., 1985-87; pres., chief exec. officer Vetronix Corp., 1984—; chief exec. officer Vetronix Japan, Ltd., Kawagoe, Japan, 1990—; pres., chief exec. Vetronix Sales Corp., Santa Barbara, CA, 1997—. Contbr. articles to profl. jours.; patentee in field. Named Entrepreneur of Yr. Greater L.A. Inc. mag., 1995. Mem. Soc. Automotive Engrs., Evans Scholars Assn., Mensa. Avocation: backpacking. Office: Vetronix Corp 2030 Alameda Padre Serra Santa Barbara CA 93103-1716

ZALESKI, JAN FRANCISZEK, biochemist; b. Bytom, Poland, Feb. 3, 1949; came to U.S., 1979; s. Stanislaw and Maria (Fliska) Z.; m. Margaret M. Toczkowska, Dec. 28, 1971; children: Marta, Monika. MS in Biochemistry, U. Warsaw, Poland, 1971, PhD in Biochemistry, 1978. Rsch. assoc., asst. prof., assoc. prof. U. Warsaw Inst. Biochemistry, 1971-82; vis. scientist Roswell Park Meml. Inst., Buffalo, 1979-82; assoc. scientist Okla. Med. Rsch. Found., Oklahoma City, 1982-85; rsch. assoc. U. Pa. Med. Sch., Phila., 1985-88; vis. scientist Great Lakes Lab., Buffalo, 1988; rsch. assoc. prof. Rutgers U. Sch. Pharmacy, New Brunswick, N.J., 1989-97. Cons. J.A. Haley Vets. Hosp., Tampa, 1985, Great Lakes Lab., Buffalo, 1988, Wyeth-Ayerst Rsch., Princeton, 1994. Contbr. articles to profl. jours., chpts. to books. Co-recipient awards Ministry Sci. and Higher Edn., Warsaw, 1978, Polish Acad. Scis., Warsaw, 1979. Mem. AAAS, Internat. Soc. Study of Xenobiotics, Am. Soc. Biochemistry and Molecular Biology. Avocations: antique and modern prints collecting, photography, basketball, gardening. E-mail: jmzaleski@comcast.net.

ZALESKI, JEAN, artist; b. Birkirkara, Malta; d. John M. and Carolina (Micallef) Busuttil; children: Jeffrey, Philip, Susan. Student, Art Students League, N.Y.C., 1955-58, New Sch., 1967-69, Moore Coll. Art, Phila., 1970-71, Parsons Sch. Design, N.Y.C., 1974-75, Pratt Inst., 1976-77. Dir. art Studio 733, Great Neck, N.Y., 1963-67; sr. art instr. Hussian Coll. Art, Phila., 1970-71; dir. Naples (Italy) Art Studio, 1972-74; corp. sec. Women in The Arts, N.Y.C., 1974-75, exec. coord., 1976-78. Adj. lectr. Bklyn. Coll., 1974-75, Hofstra U., 1977-82, Cooper Union, 1986—. One-woman shows include Neikrug Gallery, N.Y.C., 1970, Wallnuts Gallery, Phila., 1971, Il Gabbiano Gallery, Naples, Italy, 1973, Adelphi U., 1975, Women in Arts Gallery, N.Y.C., 1975, Alonzo Gallery, 1979—80, Va. Ctr. for Creative Arts, Sweet Briar, 1981, Hodgell Galleries, Sarasota, Fla., 1982—83, Elaine Starkman Gallery, N.Y.C., 1986, Romano Gallery, Barnegat Light, N.J., 1987—88, Citicorp Ctr., N.Y.C., 1988—89, Z Gallery, 1991, Sweet Briar Coll., 1993, Trinity Coll., Hartford, Conn., 1996, Myungsook Lee Gallery, N.Y.C., 1997—98, Slater Mus., Norwich, Conn., 1999, Westbeth Gallery, N.Y.C., 2000, St. James Cavalier Contemporary Art Ctr., Valletta, Malta, 2002, exhibited in group shows at Art U.S.A., N.Y.C., 1969, Internat. Art Exhbn., Cannes, France, 1969, Frick Mus., Pitts., 1970, Nat. Acad. Design, N.Y.C., 1970—71, Phila. Mus. Art, 1971, Am. Women Artists, Palazzo Vecchio, Florence, Italy, 1972, Internat. Women's Arts Festival, Milan, 1973 (Gold medal), Bklyn. Mus., 1975, Sweet Briar Coll., 1977, CUNY, 1978, Va. Ctr., 1988, Mus. Hudson Highlands, 1982, Pace U. Gallery, N.Y.C., 1982, Bayly Mus., Charlottesville, Va., 1986, Allbright Knox Mus., Buffalo, 1986, E. Starkman Gallery, N.Y.C., 1987, Nabisco, 1989, Queens Coll., N.Y., 1991—92, Mus. City of N.Y., 1993, Nat. Mus. Fine Arts, Malta, 2000, Mediterranean Conf. Ctr., 2001; author: Winged Spirits, 1995; co-author: COW/LINES, 1983; Represented in permanent collections N.Y. Pub. Libr., Met. Mus. Art, Va. Ctr. for Creative Arts, Nat. Mus. Women in Arts, Mus. City of N.Y., Nat. Mus. Malta. Recipient Susan B. Anthony award NOW, 1986; MacDowell fellow, 1971—, Ragdale fellow, 1986—, Va. Ctr. for Creative Arts fellow, 1976—, Tyrone Guthrie Ctr. fellow, 1991; grantee NEA, 1982, Artists Space, 1988; invited to White House by Pres. Carter, 1977. Mem. Artists Equity, Women in the Arts. Democrat. Roman Catholic. Avocations: music, opera, writing. E-mail: valletta@aol.com.

ZALEWSKI, JANUSZ, computer engineer, educator; b. Ciechanow, Poland, Feb. 10, 1949; s. Tadeusz Zalewski, Jadwiga Zalewska; m. Maria M. Zalewska; children: Dominika Zalewska, Dobroslawa Zalewska. PhD, Warsaw (Poland) U. Tech., 1973. Various positions Inst. Nuc. Energy, Warsaw/Swierk, Poland, 1973—89; asst. prof. S.W. Tex. State U., San Marcos, 1989—93; assoc. prof. U. Tex. Permian Basin, Odessa, 1993—94; engr. Lawrence Livermore Nat. Lab., 1994—96; assoc. prof. Embry-Riddle Aeronautical U., Daytona Beach, Fla., 1995—96, U. Ctrl. Fla., Orlando, 1996—. Editor: Advanced Multimicroprocessor Bus Architectures, 1995. Mem.: IEEE Computer Soc., Internat. Fedn. Info. Processing (chmn.working group 5.4 on indsl. software quality 1997—2001), Internat. Fedn. Automatic Control (chmn. tech. com. on safety for computer control sys. 1999—2002). Home: 425 Lagoon Dr Oviedo FL 32765 Office: U Ctrl Fla Computer Engring Orlando FL 32816-2450 Office Fax: 407-823-5835. Business E-Mail: jza@ece.engr.ucf.edu.

ZALEZNAK, BERNARD D. physician; b. Chgo., Nov. 11, 1924; s. Isadore and Fannie (Levine) Z.; m. Eleanor Inkles, Nov. 19, 1949; children: Howard, Robert, Andrew. AB, U. Ill., Urbana, 1945; BS, U. Ill., Chgo., 1945, MD, 1947. Diplomate Am. Bd. Pediatrics. Intern Cumberland Hosp., Bklyn., 1947-48; resident pediatrics Beth-El Hosp., 1948-49; resident infectious diseases Kingston Hosp., 1949-50; chief resident pediatrics N.Y.C. Hosp., 1950-51; dir. pediatrics U.S. Naval Hosp., Portsmouth, N.H., 1952-53; Lt. USNR, 1951-53; pediatrics pvt. practice, Bklyn., 1953-94; pres. med. staff Brookdale Hosp., 1965, 78, 79, attending pediatrics, 1955—. Pres. Bklyn. Pediatric Soc., 1972-73; asst. prof. pediatrics N.Y.U., 1975-80; assoc. prof. pediatrics SUNY, Bklyn., 1980—. Contbr. articles to profl. jours. Lt. USNR, 1944-45, 51-53. Mem. AMA, Am. Acad. Pediatrics, Royal Soc. Health, N.Y. State Med. Soc., Kings County Med. Soc. Avocations: golf, running. Home: 3339 N.W. 53d Cir. Boca Raton FL 33496

ZALEZNIK, ABRAHAM, psychoanalyst, management specialist, educator; b. Phila., Jan. 30, 1924; s. Isadore and Anna (Appelbaum) Z.; m. Elizabeth Ann Aron, June 24, 1945; children: Dori Faith, Ira Harry. AB in econs., Alma Coll., 1945, DLitt (hon.), 1992; MBA, Harvard U., 1947, DCS, 1951; grad., Boston Psychoanalytic Soc. and Inst., 1965; Docteur (honoris causa), U. Montreal, 1999; prof. (honoris causa), Haute Etude Commercial, France, 2001. Research asst. Harvard U. Grad. Sch. Bus. Adminstrn., 1947-48, instr., 1948-51, asst. prof., 1951-56, assoc. prof., 1956-61, prof., 1961—, Cahners-Rabb prof. social psychology of mgmt., 1967-83, Konosuke Matsushita prof. leadership, 1983-90, Konosuke Matsushita prof. leadership emeritus, 1990—; research fellow Boston Psychoanalytic Soc. and Inst., 1965-68, mem. faculty, 1972—; pvt. practice psychoanalysis Boston, 1968—. Cons. to mgmt.; bd. dirs. Timberland Co. Author: Human Dilemmas of Leadership, 1966, (with Manfred F.R. Kets de Vries) Power and the Corporate Mind, 1975, The Managerial Mystique, 1989, An Executive Guide to Motivating People, 1990, Learning Leadership, 1992; contbr. articles to profl. jours. Bd. overseers Beth Israel Hosp., Boston, 1968— . Served with USN, 1942-46. Mem. Boston Psychoanalytic Soc., Am. Psychoanalytic Assn. (cert.), Am. Sociol. Assn., Tavern Club (Boston), Belmont Country Club (Mass.). Home: 170 N Ocean Blvd Palm Beach FL 33480-3946 Office: Harvard University Business School Boston MA 02163 E-mail: azaleznik@hbs.edu.

ZALK, ROBERT H. lawyer; b. Albert Lea, Minn., Dec. 1, 1944; s. Donald B. and Juliette J. (Erickson) Z.; m. Ann Lee Anderson, June 21, 1969; children: Amy, Jenna. BA, Carleton Coll., 1966; JD, U. Minn., 1969. Bar: Minn. 1969, U.S. Dist. Ct. Minn. 1969. Assoc. Popham, Haik, Schnobrich, Kaufman & Doty, Mpls., 1969-72; atty. No. States Power Co., 1972-73, Wright, West & Diessner, Mpls., 1973-84, Fredrikson & Byron P.A., Mpls., 1984-94, Zalk & Assocs., Mpls., 1994-95; ptnr. Zalk & Eayrs, 1995-98, Zalk & Wood, Mpls., 1999, Zalk & Bryant, Mpls., 2000—. Fellow Am. Acad. Matrimonial Lawyers (pres. Minn. chpt. 2000-01), Minn. Bar Assn. (co-chmn. maintenance guideline com. 1991-94), Hennepin County Bar Assn. (co-chmn. family law sect. 1990-91). Office: Zalk & Bryant Sunset Ridge Bus Park 5861 Cedar Lake Rd Minneapolis MN 55416-1481 E-mail: rzalk@zalkbryant.com.

ZALL, PAUL MAXWELL, retired English language educator, consultant; b. Lowell, Mass., Aug. 3, 1922; s. Nathan and Bertha (Rubin) Z.; m. Elisabeth Weisz, June 21, 1948; children: Jonathan, Barnaby, Andrew. BA, Swarthmore Coll., 1948; AM, Harvard U., 1950, PhD, 1951. Teaching fellow Harvard U., 1950-51; instr. Cornell U., 1951-55, U. Oreg., 1955-56; research editor Boeing Co., 1956-57; asst. prof. Calif. State Coll., Los Angeles, 1957-61, asso. prof., 1961-64, prof. English, 1964-86; research scholar, cons. to library docents Huntington Library, San Marino, Calif., 1986-96; acting chmn. dept. Calif. State Coll., 1969-71. Cons. in report writing, proposal preparation and brochures to industry and govt. agys., 1957-99. Author: Elements of Technical Report Writing, 1962, Hundred Merry Tales, 1963, Nest of Ninnies, 1970, Literary Criticism of William Wordsworth, 1966, (with John Durham) Plain Style, 1967, Simple Cobler of Aggawam in America, 1969; (with J.R. Trevor) Proverb to Poem, 1970, Selected Satires of Peter Pindar, 1971, Comical Spirit of Seventy Six, 1976, (with Leonard Franco) Practical Writing, 1978, Ben Franklin Laughing, 1980; (with J.A.L. Lemay) Autobiography of Benjamin Franklin, 1981; Norton Critical Edition of Franklin's Autobiography, 1986, Abe Lincoln Laughing, 1983, 95; (with E. Birdsall) Descriptive Sketches, 1984, Mark Twain Laughing, 1985, Being Here, 1987, George Washington Laughing, 1989, Franklin's Autobiography: Model Life, 1989, Founding Mothers, 1991, Becoming American, 1993, 98, Lincoln's Legacy, 1994, Wit and Wisdom of the Founding Fathers, 1996, Blue and Gray Laughing, 1996, Lincoln on Lincoln, 1999, Dolley Madison, 2001, Franklin on Franklin, 2001,

Jefferson on Jefferson, 2002. Pres. Friends of South Pasadena Library, 1967-70. Served with USAAF, 1942-45, ETO. Am. Philos. Soc. fellow, 1964, 66; John Carter Brown Libr. rsch. grantee, Huntington Libr. rsch. grantee, fellow, 1993. Home: 1911 Leman Ln South Pasadena CA 91030-4628 Office: Huntington Libr San Marino CA 91108 Fax: 626-449-5720.

ZALL, ROBERT ROUBEN, food scientist, educator; b. Lowell, Mass., Dec. 6, 1925; s. Samuel and Sarah (Cohen) Z.; m. Mollie Leah Wiseblood, June 8, 1949; children— Linda Zall Sheffield, Judy Zall Kusek, Jonathan J. BS, U. Mass., 1949, MS, 1950; PhD, Cornell U., 1968. Gen. mgr. Grandview Dairies, Bklyn. and Arkport, N.Y., 1950-66; dairy industry cons. Ithaca, 1966-68; dir. research prodn. Crowley Foods Co., Binghamton, 1968-71; prof. food sci. Cornell U., 1971-92; prof. emeritus, 1992—. Past trustee Milk Industry Pension and Welfare Fund; dairy industry cons., project dir. EPA-Industry demonstration whey processing plant. Author: (with Bela G. Liptak) Environmental Engineers Handbook, 1972; co-contbr. to Food Processing Waste Management, 1979, Food Processing, 15 vols., 1979, Dairy Microbiology, 1981, rev. edit., 1990; contbr. numerous articles to profl. jours., popular mags.; patentee automatic cleaning apparatus, stabilization of milk and improved cheese yield, Rennin-like enzymes from clams, a process for preserving fish and microbial production of acetaldeyde. Served with AUS, 1944-46. Recipient Cert. Appreciation EPA, 1975, 79; Howard B. Marlott award N.Y. State Milk and Food Sanitarians Mem. Internat. Assn. Milk, Food and Environ. Sanitarians, Internat. Dairy Fedn., Inst. Food Technologists, Am. Soc. Agrl. Engrs., Masons, Phi Kappa Phi. Home: 10 Wildflower Dr # A Ithaca NY 14850-6230 Office: Cornell U Dept Food Sci Stocking Hall Ithaca NY 14853-7201 E-mail: rrz1@cornell.edu. *Most people I know, never made a success of themselves by just working forty hours a week. It takes hard work, the love of a good wife, and the willingness to accept challenges.*

ZALLA, LINDA HELEN, artist; b. Detroit, Oct. 29, 1941; d. David and Rose (Schulman) Rubenstein; children: Lisa, Steven. BS in Art, Wayne State U., Detroit, 1963; postgrad., Ctr. for Creative Studies, Detroit, 1963. Cert. tchr. Art tchr. Detroit Schs., 1963-64, Livona (Mich.) Schs., 1964-66, Jewish Cmty. Ctr., West Bloomfield, Mich., 1980-90; art dir. Jewish Assn. Residential Care, 1990—. Spl. advisor bd. trustees Channel 56 Art Auction, Detroit, 1989-90. Featured Cable TV artist Am. Watercolor Linda Zalla, 1986—, Woman on the Move, 1991—; represented in permanent collection City Hall, Livonia, Mich. Bd. mem. sisterhood Congregation Sharrey Zedek, Southfield, Mich., 1965—, head cultural commn., 1984-92 Recipient Woman in Arts award, Wis., 1986, award Mich. Fine Arts Competition, 1989, Jurors award Woman's Caucus Arts, Mich., 1990. Mem. Nat. Mus. Women Artists, Soc. Woman Painters, Bloomfield Art Assn., Soc. Detroit Inst. Arts, Wayne State U. Alumni. Avocations: dancing, music, reading, hiking, theater. Home: 4787 S Chipping Gln Bloomfield Hills MI 48302-2305

ZALLEN, HAROLD, corporate executive, scientist, former university official; b. Boston, Apr. 7, 1926; s. Joseph and Lillian L. (Stahl) Z.; m. Eugenia Malone, Aug. 23, 1959. BS in Pharmacy, Northeastern U., Boston, 1951; EdM in Sci. and Math., Boston U., 1954; MS in Organic Synthetic Medicinal Chemistry, Purdue U., 1959, PhD in Analytical Medicinal Chemistry and Nucleonics, 1960. Registered pharmacist, Mass., Ind. With USAAF, 1943-46, combat flier, sgt. 487th bomb group H, 839th bomb squadron; commd. 1st lt. U.S. Army, 1955, advanced through grades to col.(P), 1986; ret.; mgr. Shoppers World Pharmacy, Inc., Framingham, Mass., 1951-53; asst. prof. phys. sci. Portia Law Sch. Calvin Coolidge Coll., Boston, 1952-54; tchr. physics and chemistry Natick (Mass.) High Sch., 1955-56; asst. prof. microbiology Lowell Gen. Hosp. Sch. Nursing, Mass., 1955-56; grad. instr., asst. radiol. control officer Purdue U., West Lafayette, Ind., 1957-58; assoc. prof. chemistry Coll. Pharmacy Mercer U., Atlanta, 1960-61; assoc. prof. to prof., head dept. radiol. scis., dir. Office Radiol. Safety Auburn U., Ala., 1961-66; specialist phys. sci. rsch. div. higher edn. rsch. Bur. Rsch., U.S. Office Edn., 1966-67, head curriculum higher edn. rsch., 1967; head instructional sci. equipment program, assoc. program dir., then dir. spl. projects program NSF, Washington, 1967-72; asst. dean, dir. rsch. and grad. studies Okla. State U., Stillwater, 1972-73, prof. chemistry, 1972-73, rsch. prof. biochemistry and molecular biology, 1973-75; assoc. v.p. for adminstrn. and fin., CEO Health Scis. Ctr. Campus U. Okla., Oklahoma City and Tulsa, 1973-75, assoc. v.p. for systems planning, procedure devel. and spl. projects, cen. adminstrn. Norman, 1975—; exec. v.p. Acad. World Inc., 1975—; pres., CEO Malone, Zallen & Assocs. div. AcaWorld Corp., Greenville, N.C.; v.p., dir. nuclear divsn. Vachon, Nix & Assocs., Atlanta; pres., CEO Computer Profls. Inc., Computer Distbrs. Corp., Malone Group Internat., Columbus, Ga.; sci. advisor Litton Corp./Army Rsch. Inst., 1991, Omega Tng. Group Inc./GIAT Industries, France, 1992—, Wetzel Internat., Inc., 1994—; chmn. bd. dirs. Cons. Unltd., Columbus, Ga. Asst. dean, dir. rsch. and grad. studies Okla. State U., Stillwater, 1972-73; analytical chemist Communicable Diseases Ctr. USPHS, Atlanta, 1962; spl. lectr. NSF Radiobiology Inst., Tuskegee U., 1963-64, head instrnl. sci. equipment program, assoc. program dir., then dir. spl. projects program, 1967-72; pres. Pres.'s Sci. and Technol. Adv. Commn., Washington; bd. dirs. Internat. Sci. and Engring. Fairs, Sci. Svc., Inc., 1973-85; v.p. Okla. Coll. Osteo. Medicine and Surgery, Tulsa; cons. Okla. State Regents for Higher Edn.; Gov. N.C. primary alt. to So. States Energy Bd., 1984-90, exec. com. bd., 1986; mem. bd. visitors Tex. Christian U., Ft. Worth, 1973-76; cons. in field. Author 4 books in field, 1986-89; editor, pub. Jour. Internat 6800 Computer Ctr.; contbr. articles to profl. jours. Rep. candidate NC Gen. Assembly, 1986. Recipient Mayoralty cert. of merit for outstanding svc. and Key to City, City of New Orleans, 1973, Most Outstanding Alumni award Northeastern U., 1996, Comdg. Gen. award for excellence U.S. Army Inf. Ctr., 1998; GE sci. fellow Union U., Schenectady, NY., 1955, fellow Purdue Rsch. Found., 1958, Elks Cancer Soc., 1959, Am. Cancer Soc., 1960. Mem. Am. Chem. Soc. (bd. dirs., chmn. Auburn sect. 1966), Am. Soc. Engring. Edn. (long range planning com.), Nat. Coun. Univ. Adminstrs., Soc. Rsch. Adminstrs. (pres. So. sect. from 1974, chmn. publs. com.), Health Physics Soc., Greenville (N.C.) Area C. of C. (chmn. rsch.), Columbus Club, Rotary (chmn. bull. com. Auburn 1963, bd. dirs. Auburn 1964, bd. dirs. Stillwater 1972-73, Greenville 1981-86, charter pres. Greenville, N.C. Morning club 1986, Paul Harris fellow), Masons (32 degree), Shriners, Rotary Club of Auburn (chair classification), Sigma Xi, Phi Lambda Upsilon, Rho Chi, Phi Delta Kappa, Delta Sigma Theta, Beta Phi (past nat. sec.). Baptist. Office: Malone Group Internat PO Box 3682 Auburn AL 36831-3682 Fax: 334-887-2085. E-mail: zallen1780@hotmail.com.

ZALLER, ROBERT MICHAEL, history educator; b. N.Y.C., Mar. 19, 1940; s. Abraham Morris and Sylvia (Borenstein) Z.; m. Lili Bita, Jan. 19, 1968; children: Philip (dec.), Kimon. BA, CUNY, 1960; MA, Washington U., 1963, PhD, 1968. Vis. asst. prof. U. Calif., Santa Barbara, 1968-69; asst. prof. to prof. U. Miami, Coral Gables, Fla., 1972-87; prof. history Drexel U., Phila., 1987—. Adv. bd. Yale Ctr. for Parliamentary History, 1983-95, editorial bd. 1997—, Albion Jour., 1992-97. Author: The Parliament of 1621, 1971 (Phi Alpha Theta prize, 1972), Lives of the Poet, 1974, The Cliffs of Solitude, 1983 (Tor House Found. award, 1984), Europe in Transition, 1984; co-author: Civilizations of the World, 1990, 2d edit., 1993, 3d edit., 1997. Mem. steering com. Pennsylvanians United to Abolish the Death Penalty, 2000—. John Simon Guggenheim Found. fellow, 1985-86. Fellow Royal Hist. Soc.; mem. N.Am. Conf. on Brit. Studies, Am. Hist. Assn., Robinson Jeffers Assn. (adv. bd. 1992-95, pres. 1997-2000). Home: 326 Bryn Mawr Ave Bala Cynwyd PA 19004-2822 Office: Drexel University Dept History Philadelphia PA 19104

ZALOZNIK, ARLENE JOYCE, oncologist, retired army officer; b. Pitts., Jan. 30, 1948; d. Ernest and Frances Elizabeth (Augustin) Z. BS, Carlow Coll., 1969; MS, Duquesne U., 1972; MD, Med. Coll. Pa., 1976. Diplomate Am. Bd. Internal Medicine, Am. Bd. Oncology. Commd. U.S. Army, 1976, advanced through grades to col.; intern then resident in internal medicine Madigan Army Med. Ctr., Tacoma, 1976-77; fellow in hematology and oncology Fitzsimons Army Med. Ctr., Aurora, Colo., 1979-81, staff oncology, 1981-82, asst. chief med. oncology, 1982-84, chief hematology and oncology, 1984-86, Brooke Army Med. Ctr., Ft. Sam Houston, Tex., 1986-90; assoc. prof., chief divsn. hematology/oncology divsn. Tex. Tech. U. Health Scis., El Paso, 1997—. Clin. instr. dept. medicine U. Colo. Health Sci. Ctr., 1982-86. Contbr. articles to books and profl. jours. Active profl. edn. com. Aurora-Adams Unit Am. Cancer Soc., 1983-86, pres., 1983-86, active Colo. divsn., 1984-86. Memlow ACP; mem. AMA, Am. Soc. Clin. Oncology. Home: 324 Sharondale Dr El Paso TX 79912-4250 Office: Tex Tech U Health Scis Hematol/Oncol Divsn 4800 Alberta Ave El Paso TX 79905-2709

ZALTA, EDWARD, otorhinolaryngologist, physician; b. Houston, Mar. 2, 1930; s. Nouri Louis and Marie Zahde (Lizmi) Z.; m. Carolyn Mary Gordon, Oct. 8, 1971; 1 child, Ryan David; children by previous marriage: Nouri Allan, Lori Ann, Barry Thomas, Marci Louise. BS, Tulane U., 1952, MD, 1956. Diplomate Am. Bd. Quality Assurance and Utilization Rev. Physicians. Intern Brooke Army Hosp., San Antonio, 1956-57; resident in otolaryngology U.S. Army Hosp., Ft. Campbell, Ky., 1957-60; practice medicine specializing in otolaryngology Glendora, West Covina and San Dimas, Calif., 1960-82. ENT cons. City of Hope Med. Ctr., 1961-76; mem. staff Foothill Presbyn.; past pres. L.A. Found. Cmty. Svc., L.A. Poison Info. Ctr., So. Calif. Physicians Coun., Inc.; founder, chmn. bd. dirs. CAPP CARE, INC.; founder Inter-Hosp. Coun. Continuing Med. Edn.; trustee U.S. Pharmacopeial Conv., Inc.; mem. adv. bd. Global Health Sys., Inc. Author: (with others) Medicine and Your Money; mem. editl. staff Jour. Assn. Managed Healthcare Orgns., Managed Care Interface, Mng. Employee Health Benefits; mem. editl. adv. bd. Inside Medicaid Managed Care, Disease Mgmt. News, Managed Care Outlook; contbr. articles to profl. jours. Pres. bd. govs. Glendora Unified Sch. Dist., 1965-71; mem. Calif. Cancer Adv. Coun., 1967-71, Commn. of Californias, L.A. County Commn. on Economy and Efficiency. Served to capt. M.C. AUS, 1957-60. Recipient Award of Merit Order St. Lazarus, 1981 Mem. AMA, Calif. Med. Assn., Am. Acad. Otolaryngology, Am. Coun. Otolaryngology, Am. Assn. Preferred Provider Orgns. (past pres.), Am. Coll. Med. Quality, L.A. County Med. Assn. (pres. 1980-81), Kappa Nu, Phi Delta Epsilon, Glendora CountryClub, Centurion Club, Sea Bluff Beach and Racquet Club; Center Club (Costa Mesa, Calif.), Pacific Golf Club (San Juan, Capistrano). Republican. Jewish. Home: 3 Morning Dove Laguna Niguel CA 92677-5331 Office: West Tower 4000 Macarthur Blvd Ste 10000 Newport Beach CA 92660-2526

ZALTMAN, MARK ALLEN, federal agency administrator; b. Revere, Mass., Apr. 27, 1948; s. Isadore and Ethel Zaltman; m. Donna Jean Matthews, Jan. 13, 1974; 1 child Rebecca. BA magna cum laude, U. Mass., 1970; MA, Binghamton U., 1974, PhD, 1995. Claims examiner Social Security Adminstrn., Chgo., 1974-90; labor rels. specialist Dept. Housing Urban Devel., 1990-98, Region V human resources coord., 1998—. Tchg. asst. U. Wis., Milw., 1971-72, Binghamton (N.Y.) U., 1972-74; del. Milw. County Labor Coun., 1971-72. Author: Suburban/Rural Conflict in Late 19th Century Chicago, 1998; contbr. articles to profl. jours. Chief steward Am. Fedn. Govt. Employees Local 1395, Chgo., 1974—75, v.p., 1975—79, exec. v.p., 1979—83; mem. adv. bd. fed. sector labor rels. and labor law program Chgo.-Kent Coll. Law, 1998—; bd. dirs. Temple Menorah, Chgo., 2000—. Recipient Achievement award Am. Fedn. Govt. Employees Local 1395, 1976. Mem. Phi Beta Kappa, Phi Eta Sigma. Avocations: reading, traveling.

ZALUTSKY, MORTON HERMAN, lawyer; b. Schenectady, Mar. 8, 1935; s. Albert and Gertrude (Daffner) Z.; m. Audrey Englebardt, June 16, 1957; children: Jane, Diane, Samuel BA, Yale U., 1957; JD, U. Chgo., 1960. Bar: Oreg. 1961. Law clk. to presiding judge Oreg. Supreme Ct., 1960-61; assoc. Hart, Davidson, Veazie & Hanlon, 1961-63, Veatch & Lovett, 1963-64, Morrison, Bailey, Dunn, Cohen & Miller, 1964-69; prin. Morton H. Zalutsky, P.C., 1970-76; ptnr. Dahl, Zalutsky, Nichols & Hinson, 1977-79, Zalutsky & Klarquist, P.C., Portland, Oreg., 1980-85, Zalutsky, Klarquist & Johnson, Inc., Portland, 1985-94; Zalutsky & Klarquist, P.C., 1994—. Instr. Portland State U., 1961-64, Northwestern Sch. of Law, 1969-70; assoc. prof. U. Miami Law Sch.; lectr. Practising Law Inst., 1971—, Oreg. State Bar Continuing Legal Edn. Program, 1970, Am. Law Inst.-ABA Continuing Legal Edn. Program, 1973—, 34th, 37th NYU ann. insts. fed. taxation, So. Fed. Tax Inst., U. Miami Inst. Estate Planning, Southwestern Legal Found., Internat. Foun. Employee Benefit Plans, numerous other profl. orgns.; dir. A-E-F-C Pension Plan, 1994-99, chmn., 1989-99. Author: (with others) The Professional Corporation in Oregon, 1970, 82; contbg. author: The Dentist and the Law, 3d edit.; editor-in-chief (retirement plans) Matthew Bender's Federal Tax Service, 1987-90; contbr. to numerous publs. in field. Mem. vis. com. U. Chgo. Law Sch., 1986-88. Mem. ABA (vice chair profl. svcs. 1987-89, mem. coun. tax sect. 1985-87, spl. coord. 1980-85), Am. Law Inst., Am. Bar Retirement Assn. (trustee, bd. dirs., vice chair 1990-91, chair 1991-92), Am. Coll. Employee Benefits Coun. (charter mem.), Am. Coll. Tax Coun. (charter mem.), Multnomah County Bar Assn., Am. Tax Lawyers (charter mem.), Oreg. Estate Planning Coun. Jewish. Home: 3118 SW Fairmount Blvd Portland OR 97201-1466 Office: 215 SW Washington St Fl 3 Portland OR 97204-2636 E-mail: mort@erisalaw.com.

ZAMAN, MOHAMMAD HAMIDUZ, physician; b. Rangpur, Bangladesh, Dec. 21, 1953; came to U.S., 1981; s. Mohammad Hanif Uddin and Fazila Tun Nesa; m. Rehana Arjumand Zaman, Mar. 26, 1980; children: Tauhid R., Taufiq N. MBBS, Dhaka Med. Coll., 1979; MD, SUNY, Bklyn., 1996. Diplomate in internal medicine and pulmonary and critical care medicine Am. Bd. Internal Medicine. Attending physician, pulmonary and critical care divsn. Bronx Lebanon Hosp., Bronx, N.Y., 1988-90; attending physician, pulmonary divsn. Coney Island Hosp., Bklyn, 1990-93; asst. dir. critical care sect. Brookdale U. Hosp. Ctr., Bklyn., 1993—. Fellow Am. Coll. Chest Physicians; mem. Bangladesh Soc. N.Y. Inc. (pres. 1999-00). Avocation: reading. Home: 64 Central Ave Garden City Park NY 11040 Office: 1 Brookdale Plz Brooklyn NY 11212-3139 also: 137 W 96th St New York NY 10025 E-mail: mzaman1069@aol.com.

ZAMANI, SAEED, gastroenterologist, consultant; b. Isfahan, Iran, June 13, 1958; MD, Shiraz (Iran) U., 1983. Diplomate in internal medicine and gastroenterology Am. Bd. Internal Medicine and Gastroenterology, Iranian Bd. Internal Medicine and Gastroenterology. Sr. advisor Med. Edn., Tehran, 1988-92; asst. prof. medicine Beheshti U., 1990-92; rsch. project scientist U. Calif., San Diego, 1992-94; quality assurance com. U. Pa. Health Sys., Phila., 1995-97; clin. and rsch. fellow Thomas Jefferson U., 1997-2000. Symposium dir. Shiraz U., 1991; consulting gastroenterologist Beheshti U., Tehran, 1990—92. Author: Gastrointestinal Disorders, 1992, Hepatobiliary Disorders, 1992, Pearls of Wisdom in Gastroenterology, 2000, Hepatitis A-G in Common Problems in Gastroenterology, 2001; mem. editl. bd.: The World of Gastroenterology, 1991; contbr. articles to profl. jours. Hon. GI fellow Guy's Hosp., London, 1992. Mem. ACP, AMA, Am. Gastroenterology Assn., Am. Soc. for Gastrointestinal Endoscopy, Am. Coll. Gastroenterology, Am. Soc. Study Liver Disease. Avocations: sports, boating, photography, computer. Office: 20101 Lake Chabot Rd Castro Valley CA 94546 E-mail: szamanimd@aol.com.

ZAMANSKY, JEFFREY IRA, small business owner; b. Chgo., Aug. 16, 1950; s. Abe and Minnette (Levin) Z.; m. Darleen Ellen Chorney, Dec. 26, 1991; 1 child, Jordan. BS, No. Ill. U., 1972; MBA, DePaul U., 1977. Sales Romano Bros. Beverage, Chgo., 1976-80; v.p. mktg., sales Kalkus-Hiro, Inc., Lyons, Ill., 1980-82, Kimball Candy, Chgo., 1982-85; co-owner Silver Coin, Inc., 1985-91, Western Wash, Inc., Chgo., 1985-91, Svc. Coin, Inc., Skokie, Ill., 1996—, A&M Coin Meter, Inc., Skokie, 1993—; pres., owner Alcoin Equipment Co., Wilmette, 1975—. Mem. Am. Mktg. Assn. Avocations: tennis, running, travel, reading.

ZAMBIE, ALLAN JOHN, lawyer; b. Cleve., June 9, 1935; s. Anton J. and Martha (Adamski) Z.; m. Nancy Hall, Sept. 22, 1973. Student, Ohio U., 1953-54; BA, Denison U., 1957; LL.B., Western Res. U. (now Case Western Res. U.), 1960. Bar: Ohio 1960. Assn. firm Hribar and Conway, Euclid, Ohio, 1961-63; staff atty. The Higbee Co., Cleve., 1963-67, asst. sec., 1967-69, sec., 1969-74, v.p.-sec., 1974-88, gen. counsel, 1978-88; v.p., sec., gen. counsel The Lamson & Sessions Co., Cleve., 1989-94; of counsel Conway, Marken, Wyner, Kurant & Kern Co., LPA, 1994-95; v.p.-sec. John P. Murphy Found., 1996-2000, exec. v.p., 2001—. V.p., sec. Kulas Found., 2001. Trustee Cleve. Music Sch. Settlement, pres. bd. trustees, 1980—82, treas., 1996—2001; trustee N.E. Ohio affiliate Am. Heart Assn., 1969—96. Served with U.S. Army, 1960—61. Mem. Ohio Bar Assn., Cleve. Bar Assn., Am. Soc. Corporate Secs. (nat. v.p. 1977—) Home: 2953 Litchfield Rd Cleveland OH 44120-1738 Office: 50 Pub Sq Ste 924 Cleveland OH 44113-2203

ZAMBITO, JOHN R. executive search firm executive; b. Clinton, Iowa, Feb. 17, 1960; s. John R. and Donna (Snell) Z.; m. Jamy S. Nelson, Sept. 14, 1985; children: Molly, Ben, Max. BA in Polit. Sci., Ohio State U., 1985. Salesman Edward Don Co., Columbus, 1985-87, Michaels, Inc., Columbus, 1987-90; acct. exec. MRI (Mgmt. Recruiters, Internat.) of Columbus Downtown, 1990-94, sales mgr., 1994-96, gen. mgr., 1996—. Dir. adv. bd. Mgmt. Recruiters, Inc., Cleve., 1999—. Contbr. articles to mags., newspapers, internet news, radio shows. Fundraiser Upper Arlington (Ohio) Civic Assn., 1997, 99; chief Indian Guides and Princesses YMCA, Upper Arlington, 1996, 97, 99; donor ARC, Upper Arlington, 1985—. Mem. Athletic Club Columbus, Heritage Golf Club, Kiwanis, Rotary, Ohio State U. Alumni Assn., President's Club, Phi Kappa Tau. Avocations: golf, tennis, running, reading, squash. Home: 2705 Abington Rd Upper Arlington OH 43221-3020 Office: MRI 555 S Front St Ste 100 Columbus OH 43215-5668

ZAMBOLDI, RICHARD HENRY, lawyer; b. Kittanning, Pa., Nov. 22, 1941; s. Henry F. and Florence E. (Colligan) Z.; m. Maria Therese Reiser, Aug. 12, 1967; children: Elizabeth M., Richard H. Jr., Margaret B. BBA, St. Bonaventure U., 1963; JD, Villanova U., 1966. Bar: U.S. Dist. Ct. (we. dist.) Pa. 1966, Pa. 1968, U.S. Ct. Appeals (3d cir.) 1970, U.S. Supreme Ct. 1981. Law clk. U.S. Dist. Ct. (we. dist.) Pa., Pitts., 1966-67; atty. Nat. Labor Rels. Bd., 1967-68; assoc. Kanehann & McDonald, Allentown, Pa., 1968-69; ptnr. Elderkin Martin Kelly Messina & Zamboldi, Erie, 1969-90, Knox McLaughlin Gornall & Sennett, Erie, 1990—, pres., 1997—. Author (student articles) Villanova Law Rev., 1964-65, editor, 1965-66. Mem. Pa. Bar Assn., Erie County Bar Assn. Republican. Roman Catholic. Home: 6206 Lake Shore Dr Erie PA 16505-1013 Office: Knox McLaughlin Gornall & Sennett 120 W 10th St Erie PA 16501-1410

ZAMBONE, ALANA MARIA, special education educator, consultant; b. Vineland, N.J., Sept. 17, 1952; d. L. Alan and Joyce (Bernero) Z. AB in Spl. Edn. and Elem. Edn., U. N.C., Chapel Hill, 1974; MS in Human Devel. Liaison, George Peabody Coll. Tchrs., 1978; PhD in Spl. Edn., Vanderbilt U., 1984. Cert. spl. edn., elem. edn., visual impairments, mental retardation, N.C. Tchr., counselor Orange County Assn. for Retarded Citizens, Chapel Hill, N.C., 1973-74; lead tchr. Shelbyville-Bedford (Tenn.) County Adult Svc. Ctr., 1974; program coord. Dickson (Tenn.) County Adult Svcs., 1974-75; dept. head, habilitative svcs. CloverBottom Devel. Ctr., Nashville, 1975-76; exec. dir. Waves, Inc. Adult Svcs., Fairview, 1976-77; from vocat. cons. to liaison, Peabody Tchrs. Coll. Vanderbilt U., 1977-80; chairperson, bd. dirs. Residential Svcs., Inc., Nashville, 1976-80; asst. prof., coord., dept. curriculum N.C. State U., Raleigh, N.C., 1981-84; coord. and asst. prof., div. spl. edn. Minot (N.D.) State U., 1984-86; coord. internat. outreach svcs. Hilton-Perkins Internat. Program Perkins Sch. for the Blind, Watertown, Mass., 1989-94; assoc. prof., dir. Inst. for Visually Impaired Pa. Coll. Optometry, Phila., 1994—. Co-founder, sr. rsch. fellow Walker-Wheelock Inst. for Equity in Edn., sr. project dir. exceptional needs assessment devel. lab. Edn. Devel. Corp., Newton, Mass., 1998—; co-coord. grad. program tchrs. of students with spl. needs, mem. grad. faculty infant toddler program evaluator Danforth cmty. devel. project Wheelock Coll., 1995-98; nat. cons. Am. Found. for the Blind, N.Y.C., 1986-89; adj. asst. prof. div. spl. edn., Columbia U., 1987—; co-dir. model infant/toddler program, sch. medicine, U. N.C., Chapel Hill, 1983-84; project dir., mem. grad. faculty severe and multiple disabilities Simmons Coll., 1990—; bd. dirs. N.D. Coun. for the Arts; adv. bd. Blind Babies Found.; mem. adv. com. Robert E. Miller, Inc., Community Residential Svcs. for Disabled Children; bd. dirs. Specialized Svcs. for Children, Inc.; sch. edn. rep. to fac. N.C. State U., sch. edn. fac. senate, among others. Grantee Busch Found., N.D. Coun. Arts, Nat. Coun. on the Arts, Dean's Grant Program, Burlington/No. Found., Kate B. Reynolds Found., Nat. Rural Spl. Edn. Consortium, U.S. Office Human Devel. Svcs., U.S. Office of Spl. Edn. Mem. Coun. for Exceptional Children (past dir. div. visual handicaps), Assn. for Retarded Citizens, Assn. for Persons with Severe Handicaps, Am. Assn. Mental Deficiency, Am. Assn. for Applied Behavior Analysis, Nat. Assn. for Parents of the Visually Impaired, Internat. Assn. for the Edn. of the Deaf-Blind, Assn. for the Edn. and Rehab. of the Blind and Visually Impaired (pre-sch. div., multihandicaps div., chairperson multiple disabilities div.), Internat. Coun. Educators of Children and Youth Who Are Blinded or Visually Impaired (co-coord. functions curriculum devel. project 1993—). Avocation: scuba diving. Office: Inst for Equity in Schs Affiliate Walker Home & Sch 1968 Central Ave Needham MA 02492-1410 also: Edn Devel Corp 35 Chapel St Newton MA 02458-1010 E-mail: zambone790@earthlink.net.

ZAMBONI, BETH A. statistician, educator; d. Delores J. and William S. Zamboni. BS, U. of Pitts., 1997; MS, Harvard U., 1999. Biostatistician U. of Pitts. Cancer Inst., Pitts., 1997—. Statis. & math. instr. U. Phoenix, Pitts., 2001—. Grantee Tng. grant, NIH, 1997—99, 2001—02. Mem.: Am. Statis. Assn. Personal E-mail: zamboni@upci.pitt.edu.

ZAME, WILLIAM R. mathematician, educator; b. Long Beach, N.Y., Nov. 4, 1945; s. Herbert and Miriam Zame; m. Linda Susan Goettina, Nov. 24, 1997; m. Elaine Bennett, 1989 (dec. 1995). BS, Calif. Inst. Tech., Pasadena, 1965; MS, Tulane U., 1967, PhD, 1970. Instr. Rice U., Houston, 1970—72; asst prof. math. SUNY, Buffalo, 1972—76; assoc. prof. math. Tulane U., New Orleans, 1975—78, SUNY, Buffalo, 1976—81, prof. math., 1981—91; prof. math. and econs. Johns Hopkins U., Balt., 1991—94, UCLA, 1994—. Assoc. editor Jour. Math. Econs., 1988—, Jour. Econ. Theory, 1990—, Econometrica, 1998—; mem. com. on status of women in the econs. profn., 1997—99; co-organizer profl. confs., including Exptl. Econs., Calif. Inst. Tech./UCLA, 1999; vis. prof. Inst. Advanced Study, U. Wash., Inst. Math. and its Applications, Math. Scis. Rsch. Inst., Inst. Mittag-Leffler, U. Copenhagen, Va. Poly. Inst., U. Calif., Berkeley. Contbr. articles to profl. jours., chapters to books. Grantee NSF, 1970—88, 1988—. Fellow: Econometric Soc. (program com. summer mtgs. 1991, 1997, program co-chair summer mtgs. 2002). Office: UCLA Dept Econs 405 Hilgard Ave Los Angeles CA 90095-9000

ZAMECNIK, PAUL CHARLES, oncologist, medical research scientist; b. Cleve., Nov. 22, 1912; married; 3 children. AB, Dartmouth Coll., 1933; MD, Harvard U., 1936; DSc (hon.) , U. Utrecht, 1966, Columbia U., 1971, Harvard U., 1982, Roger Williams Coll., 1983, Dartmouth Coll., 1988, U. Mass., 1994. Resident Huntington Meml. Hosp. Harvard U., Boston, 1936—37; intern U. Hosps., Cleve., 1938—39; Moseley traveling fellow Carlsberg Labs. Harvard U., Copenhagen, 1939—40; Finney-Howell fellow Rockefeller Inst., 1941—42; instr., assoc. prof. medicine Harvard U., 1942—56, Collis P. Huntington prof. oncologic medicine, 1956—79; dir. J.C. Warren Labs., 1956—79; chmn. exec. com. Dept. Medicine Harvard U., 1956—61; emeritus prof. oncological medicine Sch. Medicine, 1979—; prin. sci. Worcester Found. Experimental Biology, 1979—97; physician Mass. Gen. Hosp., 1956—79, hon. physician, 1979—, sr. scientist, 1998—. Vis. fellow dept. chemistry Calif. Tech. U., 1952; vis. Commonwealth scholar in chemistry U. Cambridge, 1962. Recipient Warren Triennial prize, Mass. Gen. Hosp., 1946, 1950, 1999, James Ewing award, 1962, Borden award, 1965, Am. Cancer Soc. Nat. award, 1968, Passano award, 1970, Nat. medal of sci., NSF, 1991, Hudson Hoagland award, 1992, City of Medicine award, Durham, N.C., 1995, Enterprize 2000 award, City of Worcester, Mass., 1996, Lasker Life Sci. award, 1996, Am. Soc. Biochemistry and Molecular Biology-Merck award, 1997. Mem.: NAS, Mass. Med. Soc. (annual lectr. 1998, Ann. Orator award 1998), Nat. Acad. Medicine, Assn. Am. Physicians, Am. Assn. Cancer Rsch. (pres. 1964—65), Am. Soc. Biol. Chemists, Am. Acad. Arts and Scis., Interurban Club. Office: Mass Gen Hosp Charlestown 149 13th St Rm 1494005 Charlestown MA 02129-2020

ZAMFIR, NICOLAE VICTOR, physicist, researcher; b. Brasov, Romania, Mar. 24, 1952; s. Nicolae Zamfir, Livia Zamfir; m. Ecaterina Edita Petre; children: Radu Bogdan, Ioana Livia. Masters Degree, U. Bucharest, Romania, 1976; PhD, Ctrl. Inst. Physics, Bucharest, Romania, 1984. Physicist Inst. Physics and Nuc. Engring., Magurele, Romania, 1978—84, sr. rschr. Bucharest, Romania, 1984—94; physicist Brookhaven Nat. Lab., Upton, NY, 1994—97; sr. rsch. scientist Yale U., New Haven, 1997—. Cons. Clark U., Worcester, Mass., 1992—; mem. adv. com. Internat. Conf. on the Interacting Boson Model, Padova, Italy, 1994, Internat. Conf. on Nuc. Models, Camerino, Italy, 1998; mem. program com. Internat. Symposium on Gamma-ray Spectroscopy, Prague, Czech Republic, 2002—. Contbr. articles to profl. jours.

Recipient Hurmuzescu award in physics, Romanian Acad., 1994. Mem.: Am. Phys. Soc. Office: Yale Univ Physics Dept New Haven CT 06520-8124 Office Fax: 203-432-3522. Business E-Mail: victor.zamfir@yale.edu.

ZAMKA, GEORGE D. astronaut; b. Jersey City, June 29, 1962; s. Conrad and Sofia Zamka; m. Elisa P. Walker; 1 child. BS in Math., U.S. Naval Acad., 1984; MS in Engring. Mgmt., Fla. Inst. Tech., 1997. Commd. 2d lt. USMC, 1984, advanced through grades to lt. col.; with Navy Attack Squadron, Marine All Weather Attacki Squadron, VMA, El Toro, Calif.; squadron weapons and tactics instr.; with Marine All Weather Fighter Attack Squadron VMFA, El Toro; forward air contr. 1st Bn., 5th Marines, Camp Pendleton, Calif.; with 31st Marine Expeditionary Unit, USS Belleau Wood, Western Pacific; test pilot/project officer Naval Strike Aircraft Test Squadron; aircraft maintenance officer VMFA; astronaut NASA, Houston, 1998, with Astronaut Office. Decorated 6 Navy Strike Air medals, Navy Commendation medal with Combat V. Mem.: Soc. Exptl. Test Pilots, Marine Corps Assn., U.S. Naval Acad. Alumni Assn. Achievements include logged over 3,000 flight hours in over 30 different aircraft. Office: Astronaut Office /CB NASA Johnson Space Ctr Houston TX 77058*

ZAMMIT, JOSEPH PAUL, lawyer; b. N.Y.C., May 19, 1948; s. John and Farla (Rudolph) Z.; m. Dorothy Therese O'Neill, June 6, 1970; children: Michael, Paul, Brian. AB, Fordham U., 1968; JD, Harvard U., 1971; LLM, NYU, 1974. Bar: N.Y. 1972, U.S. Dist. Ct. (so. and ea. dists.) N.Y. 1973, U.S. Dist. Ct. (no. dist.) Ala. 1989, U.S. Dist. Ct. (we. dist.) N.Y., 1991, U.S. Ct. Appeals (2d cir.) 1973, U.S. Supreme Ct. 1978, U.S. Dist. Ct. (no. dist.) N.Y. 1983, U.S. Ct. Appeals (11th cir.) 1987, U.S. Ct. Appeals (fed. cir.) 1995. Assoc. Reavis & McGrath, N.Y.C., 1971-74; asst. prof. law St. John's U., Jamaica, N.Y., 1974-76, assoc. prof., 1976-78; assoc. Reavis & McGrath, N.Y.C., 1978-79, ptnr., 1979-88, Fulbright & Jaworski L.L.P. (formerly Fulbright Jaworski & Reavis McGrath), N.Y.C., 1989—. Adj. assoc. prof. St. John's U., Jamaica, 1979-83, adj. prof., 1984—; mem. panel comml. arbitrators tech. panel Am. Arbitration Assn., N.Y.C., 1977—. Bd. editors E-commerce Law and Strategy, 1987—; contbr. articles to profl. jours. Mem. ABA, N.Y. State Bar Assn., Assn. of Bar of City of N.Y. (chmn. com. on computer law 1995-98, chmn. comml. liability subcom. 1981-87, fed. cts. com. 1998-2001), Computer Law Assn., Phi Beta Kappa. Office: Fulbright & Jaworski LLP 666 5th Ave Fl 31 New York NY 10103-0001 E-mail: jzammit@fulbright.com.

ZAMORA-QUEZADA, JORGE C. physician; b. Guadalajara, Jalisco, Mex., Aug. 26, 1956; s. Crescenciano Zamora and Maria de los Angeles Quezada; m. Meisy Silva; children: Tatiana, Alex, Pilar, Victor, Rafael, Lucia, Oscar. MD, U. Guadalajara, Mex., 1980; MPH, Harvard U., 1995. Resident in internal medicine Instituto Nacional de la Nutricion, Mexico City, Salvador Zubiran, Mexico City, Southwestern Med. Sch., Dallas; fellow in rheumatology, immunology Tufts-New Eng. Med. Ctr., 1989; with McAllen Arthritis and Osteoporosis Ctr., Edinburg, Tex. Fellow ACP, Am. Coll. Rheumatology. Office: McAllen Arthritis and Osteoporosis Ctr 2601 Cornerstone Blvd Edinburg TX 78539 E-mail: jczq@aol.com.

ZAMPINO, PHIL, music educator; m. Joanne Muntean. BA Music Ed.?, Armed Forces Sch. of Music, 1965—68. Founder Zampino's Drum Shop, Canton, Ohio. Home: 2415 Bevington St NW Canton OH 44709 Personal E-mail: pazjo@aol.com.

ZANAKIS, STEVE H. management science/information systems educator; b. Athens, Greece, Nov. 16, 1940; came to U.S., 1968; m. Helen Avagianou, 1968; children: Aliki, Christina, Helena. BS in Mech./Elec. Engring., Nat. Tech. U., Athens, 1964; MBA, Pa. State U., 1970, MS in Stats., 1972, PhD in Bus. Adminstrn., 1973. Registered engr., Greece. Indsl. engr. Greek Productivity Ctr., Athens, 1967-68; asst. prof. indsl. engring. and systems analysis W.Va. Coll. Grad. Studies, Charleston, 1972-76, assoc. prof. and dir. indsl. engring. and systems analysis, 1976-80; assoc. prof. mgmt. Coll. of Bus. Adminstrn. Fla. Internat. U., Miami, 1980-82, prof. and founding chmn. dept. decision scis. and info. systems, 1982-86, prof. decision scis. and info. systems., 1986—. Cons. Union Carbide Corp., W.Va. Dept. Hwys., Charleston Area Med. Ctr., Key Pharm. Ryder, U.S. Acad. for Ednl. Devel., City of Miami; instr. exec. mgmt. devel. programs, U.S., Europe, S.Am. Author: Production Operations Management Software for IBM, PC, 1989, Production Planning and Scheduling, 1984, Engineering Economy, 1975, Optimization in Statistics, 1983, Stat-ez: An Easy to Use Statistical Software, 1987, Decision Support System for Conflict Resolution and Strategy Selection, 1991, Decision Support System for Stock Market Trading & Portfolio Management, 1992, Multicriteria Decision Support System for Decontamination Technology Assessment, 1998, Decison Making: Recent Developments and Worldwide Applications, 2000, Medicare Statistical Audit, 2001; guest editor Mgmt. Sci. Jour., 1983, European Jour. Ops. Rsch., 1986, 2002; assoc. editor Decision Scis. Jour., 1990-98; contbr. numerous articles to profl. jours. Recipient Fla. Bd. Regents Teaching award, 1994, Profl. Excellence award, 1997; State of Fla. Hwy. Adminstrn. rsch. grantee, 1984-85, fed. grantee, 1976-77. Mem. Inst. for Ops. Rsch. & Mgmt. Sci., Decision Scis. Inst., Tech. Chamber of Greece. Greek Orthodox. Office: Fla Internat U Dept Decision Scis Info Sys Miami FL 33199-0001 E-mail: zanakis@fiu.edu.

ZANARDELLI, JOHN JOSEPH, healthcare services executive; b. Monongahela, Pa., July 27, 1950; s. John and Linda (Lazzari) Z.; m. Suzanne King, Jan. 29, 1972; children: Brandon John, Stephen William, Robyn Lynn. Student, Davis & Elkins Coll., 1968; AA, C.C. Allegheny Cty, Pitts., 1970; AS in Acctg., C.C. Allegheny Cty., Pitts., 1991; BS in Edn., California State Coll. Pa., 1972; MPH, U. Pitts., 1979, cert. acct., 1994; cert. non-profit mgmt., Harvard U., 1998; cert. gen. mgmt., Carnegie Mellon U., 1999. Rsch. asst. grad. sch. pub. health U. Pitts., 1973-78; adminstrv. resident Ctrl. Med. Ctr. and Hosp., Pitts., 1978-79; vice-chmn., sec., dir. Allegheny Mountain Health Enterprises, Inc., Oil City, Pa., 1985-88; exec. v.p. Oil City Area Health Ctr., Inc., 1979-88; exec. v.p., COO Grane Healthcare, Inc., Pitts., 1988-90; adminstr., COO Southwood Psychiat. Hosp., Inc., 1990-91; exec. dir. Allegheny divsn. Presbyn. Sr.Care, 1991-92; exec. dir., CEO United Meth. Svcs. for Aging, 1993—. Preceptor health adminstrn. program U. Pitts. Grad. Sch. Pub. Health and Bus., 1980—, vis. faculty, 1997—98; adj. asst. prof. health svcs. adminstrn. Grad. Sch. Pub. Health, 1998—2001, adj. assoc. prof. health policy and mgmt. , 2001—; pres. HCCP, Inc., Pitts., 1983—; bd. dirs. Faith-Based Network, Inc., 1998—; co-chair pub. rels. and mktg. com. Davis and Elkins Coll., 2000—; co-chair exec.-in-residence com. U. Pitts. Grad. Sch. Pub. Health, 2001—02, exec. in residence, health adminstrn. program, 2001—; preceptor, Initiative on Social Enterprise, Harvard Bus. Sch., 2001—. Fellow: Am. Coll. Healthcare Execs.; mem.: Delta Omega (Omicron chpt., pres. 2000—01). Home: 2997 Greenwald Rd Bethel Park PA 15102-1615 Office: Asbury Heights 700 Bower Hill Rd Pittsburgh PA 15243-2040 E-mail: johnzan@alumni.pitt.edu, jzanardelli@asburyheights.org.

ZAND, DALE EZRA, business management educator; b. N.Y.C., July 22, 1926; m. Charlotte Edith Rosenfeld, Oct. 16, 1949; children: Fern, Mark, Karen, Jonathan, Matthew. BEE, Cooper Union, 1945; MBA, NYU, 1949, PhD, 1954. Asst. to v.p. Spectator Bags, 1947-49; v.p. Glo-Cold Co., 1949-50; mem. faculty Stern Sch. Bus., NYU, N.Y.C., 1950—, prof. mgmt., 1963—, chmn. dept., 1968—, sr. faculty fellow, 1999—. Cons. to industry, 1951—; bd. dirs. Newfield Exploration Co., Inst. Applied Behavioral Sci. Author: Information, Organization, and Power, 1981, The Leadership Triad, 1997, also articles. Served with USNR, 1945. Ford Found. fellow, 1959-60 Mem. Am. Psychol. Soc., Inst. Mgmt. Sci., Acad. Mgmt., Internat. Assn. Applied Social Scientists. Office: NYU 40 W 4th St # T723 New York NY 10012-0157

ZAND, LLOYD CRAIG, radiologist; b. N.Y.C., May 1, 1942; s. Walter Paul and Estelle Leone Zand; m. Mardan Jeanne Foster, June 9, 1968; children: Jason Matthew, Jory Meagan. AB, U. Ill., 1964; MD, Chgo. Med. Sch., 1968. Intern U. Minn., Mpls., 1968-69; resident in radiology U. Miami, Fla., 1969-70, 72-74, clin. instr., 1973-80; attending radiologist North Shore Med. Ctr., Miami, 1974-97, chmn. dept. radiology, 1989-97, chmn. dept. medicine, 1995-98; pres. Mar-J Enterprises, Inc., 1990—; chmn. Diagnostic Network, Inc., 1993-96. Chmn. Med. Resources Devel. Corp., Miami, 1985—88; mem. adv. bd. 3M Corp., Mpls., 1988—90; bd. dirs. MTR, Inc., Atlanta, Disabled Sports USA. Trustee Zool. Soc. Fla., Miami, 1996—; pres. bd. Cmty. Crusade Against Drugs, 2001—. Lt. comdr. USNR, 1970—72. Mem. AMA, Am. Coll. Radiology, Radiology Soc. of Fla., Soc. Cardiovascular and Interventional Radiology. Avocations: flying, photography. Office: 10501 Snapper Creek Rd Coral Gables FL 33156-3452

ZANDER, ARLEN RAY, physics educator; b. Shiner, Tex., Dec. 12, 1940; s. Elton A. and Lillie G. (Malina) Z.; m. Dorothy Marie Mayer, Feb. 1, 1964; children: Melanie, Aaron, Bryan. BS in Physics, U. Tex., 1964; PhD in Physics, Fla. State U., 1970. Asst. prof. physics East Tex. State U., Commerce, 1970-74, assoc. prof. physics, 1975-79, prof. physics, 1980-89, coord. external grants, 1974-77, asst. dean arts and sci., 1982-86, dean arts and sci., 1986-89; provost, v.p. acad. affairs U. La., Monroe, 1989-2000. Liaison superconducting super collider E. Tex. State U., Commerce, 1987-89; lectr. fgn. countries; commentator weekly radio show Sci. Update, 1981-82. Contbr. articles to profl. jours.; author weekly newspaper column Halley's Comet (Sci. Writing award Coun. for Advancement and Support of Edn. 1986), 1985-86. Campaign chmn. United Way, Commerce, 1988; bd. govs. Monroe Symphony Orch., 1991. Numerous grants various agys.; NATO fellow, 1982. Mem. Am. Assn. Physics Tchrs., West Monroe C. of C. (chmn. 1994), Lions (bd. dirs. internat. youth camp 1983-86), Sigma Xi. Avocations: jogging, reading, racquetball, classical music. Home: 100 Bluff Dr West Monroe LA 71291-9434 Office: U La-Monroe 700 University Ave Monroe LA 71209-9000 E-mail: zander@alpha.ulm.edu.

ZANDER, BENJAMIN, conductor, educator; b. London, Mar. 9, 1939; Diploma, State Conservatory, Cologne, 1960; BA, London Univ., 1964; studied cello with, Gaspar Cassadó. Prof. chamber music, performance and analysis New Eng. Conservatory of Music, Boston, 1967—, condr. Youth Philharm. Orch., 1972—; mus. dir., condr. Boston Philharm. Orch., 1979—; artistic dir. Walnut Hill High Sch. for the Performing Arts. Address: New England Conservatory of Music 290 Huntington Ave Boston MA 02115-5018

ZANDER, DANI S. pathologist, educator; b. Bronx, N.Y., Aug. 1, 1961; d. Ronald Austin and Rona (Pomerantz) Swartz; m. Erik Henry Zander, Mar. 7, 1987. BA, NYU, N.Y.C., 1982; MD, U. Fla., 1986. Diplomate Am. Bd. Pathology, with added qualification in cytopathology. Pathology intern N.Y. Hosp., N.Y.C., 1986-87; resident in pathology U. Fla., Gainesville, 1987-91, asst. prof. pathology, 1991-96, assoc. prof. pathology, 1996—; chief anatomic pathology VA Med. Ctr., 1992—. Contbr. articles to Am. Jour. Clin. Pathology, Cancer, Chest, Am. Jour. Med. Scis., Oral Surgery Oral Medicine Oral Pathology, others. Fellow Coll. Am. Pathologists; mem. AMA, AAAS, U.S. and Can. Acad. Pathology, Pulmonary Pathology Soc., Am. Soc. for Investigative Pathology.

ZANDER, GAILLIENNE GLASHOW, psychologist; b. Bklyn., Apr. 7, 1932; d. Saul and Anna (Karasik) G.; m. A.J. Zander, Aug. 5, 1952; children: Elizabeth L., Caroline M., Catherine A. MusB, U. Wis., 1953, MS, 1970; PhD, Marquette U., 1984. Diplomate Am. Bd. Forensic Examiners, Am. Acad. Pain Mgmt.; cert. Am. Soc. Clin. Hypnosis. Music tchr. Wis. Sch. Systems, 1953-65; psychol. asst. Vernon Psychol. Labs., Chgo., 1965-70; psychologist Milw. Pub. Schs., 1970-92, CESA 19, Kenosha, Wis., 1977-78; pvt. practice psychology Milw., 1980—. Fellow Am. Orthopsychiat. Assn.; mem. APA, Wis. Psychol. Assn. Home: 13750 Carson Ct Brookfield WI 53005-4989 also: A Healing Ctr 20860 Watertown Rd Waukesha WI 53186-1872 E-mail: zanderga@aol.com.

ZANDER, JANET ADELE, psychiatrist; b. Miles City, Mont., Feb. 19, 1950; d. Adelbert William and Valborg Constance (Buckneberg) Z.; m. Mark Richard Ellenberger, Sept. 16, 1979; 1 child, Evan David Zander Ellenberger. BA, St. Olaf Coll., 1972; MD, U. Minn., 1976. Diplomate Am. Bd. Psychiatry and Neurology. Resident in psychiatry U. Minn., Mpls., 1976-79, fellow in psychiatry, 1979-80, asst. prof. psychiatry, 1981—; staff psychiatrist St. Paul (Minn.) Regions Hosp., 1980—, dir. edn. in psychiatry, 1980-94, dir. inpatient psychiatry, 1986—, vice chair Dept. Psychiatry, 1991-96, divsn. head behavioral health, 2002. Bd. dirs. Perry Assurance. Contbr. research articles to sci. jours. Sec. Concentus Musicus Bd. Dirs., St. Paul, 1981-89; mem. property com. St. Clement's Episcopal Ch., St. Paul, 1985. Mem. Am. Psychiat. Assn., Am. Med. Women's Assn., Minn. Psychiat. Soc. (ethics com. 1985-87, women's com. 1985-87, coun. 1994-96), Minn. Med. Assn., Ramsey County Med. Soc. (bd. dirs. 1994-96). Democrat. Avocations: singing, skiing. Home: 230 Crestway Ln West Saint Paul MN 55118-4424 Office: Regions Hosp 640 Jackson St Saint Paul MN 55101-2502 E-mail: janet.a.zander@healthpartners.com.

ZANDER SCHRAGE, MARYANNE ELIZABETH, physician assistant; b. Chgo., May 5, 1944; d. John Charles and Loretta Jane (Rowland) Zander; m. Michael Schrage, Aug. 21, 1965 (dec. Jan. 1991); children: James Michael and Andrew John. AA in Nursing, Prairie State Coll., 1973; BA, Govs. State U., University Park, Ill., 1995; B. in Med. Sci., Midwestern U., Downers Grove, Ill., 1998. RN, Ill.; cert. physician asst. RN, asst. head nurse Little Co. Mary Hosp., Evergreen Park, Ill., 1973-83; RN, ICU-critical care unit staff Osteo. Med. Ctr., Olympia Fields, 1983-96; physician asst., med. staff liaison Rock Creek Ctr. L.P., Lemont, 1998—. Fellow Am. Assn. Physician Assts., Soc. Army Physician Assts., Soc. Emergency Medicine Physician Assts., Ill. Assn. Physician Assts., Am. Assn. Physician Assts. Avocations: sewing, embroidery work, yoga, biking. Office: Rock Creek Ctr LP 40 Timberline Dr Lemont IL 60439

ZANE, ARNIE, performing company executive, choreographer; b. Bronx, N.Y., 1948; Student, SUNY, Binghamton. Co-founder, with Lois Welk Am. Dance Asylum, Binghamton, 1973—82; co-founder, choreographer Bill T. Jones/Arnie Zane Dance Co., N.Y.C., 1982—88. Choreographer (ballets) Blauvelt Mountain, 1980 (co-recipient German Critics award with Bill T. Jones, 1980), How to Walk an Elephant, 1985 (N.Y. Dance and Performance "Bessie" award, 1985). Fellow Creative Artists Public Svc. fellow in Photography, 1973, Creative Artists Public Svc. fellow in Choreography, 1981, in Choreography, N.E.A., 1983, 1984. Died 1988.*

ZANE, N.A. internist; b. 1956; MD, Damascus (Syria) U., 1979. Diplomate Am. Bd. Internal Medicine. House officer in Geriatrics Boston U and Harvard U. Affiliated Hosps., Boston, 1984—86; resident in internal medicine Hahnemann U. Affiliated Program/N.E. Pa., 1986—89; 1sole practitioner internal medicine, Boynton Beach, Fla., 1989—96. Office: PO Box 357541 Gainesville FL 32635-7541

ZANE, PHILLIP CRAIG, lawyer; b. N.Y.C., Sept. 25, 1961; s. Martin I.L. and Rosalind Carol (Siegler) Z.; m. Denise Janine Wydra. BA, Pomona Coll., 1983; postgrad., U. Mich., 1985-88; JD cum laude, NYU, 1991. Bar: Ill. 1991, D.C. 1996, U.S. Dist. Ct. (no. dist.) Ill. 1991, U.S. Ct. Appeals (7th cir.) 1994, U.S. Ct. Appeals (8th cir.) 1993, U.S. Ct. Appeals (9th cir.) 1996, U.S. Fed. Cir. Ct. 1994, U.S. Dist. Ct. D.C. 2000. Assoc. Mayer, Brown & Platt, Chgo., 1991-93; judicial law clerk to Hon. Morris S. Arnold 8th Cir. Ct. Appeals, Little Rock, 1993-94; assoc. Mayer, Brown & Platt, Chgo., 1994-95, Morgan, Lewis & Bockius, Washington, 1996-2000, of counsel, 2000—. Staff editor NYU Rev. of Law and Social Change, 1989-90, critical legal studies editor, 1990-91; editor Sherman Act Almanac, 1998; contbr. articles to profl. jours. Sec. gen. coun. Arthur F. Burns Fellowship program, Inc., 1998—. Fellow Thomas J. Watson Found., 1983-84; fgn. lang. area studies fellow U. Mich., Ann Arbor, 1986, 87-88. Mem. ABA (vice chair Sherman Act sect. one com. 1999-2001), Ill. State Bar Assn. (spl. com. on Law Day in Moscow & Kiev 1992) Democrat. Avocation: legal history. Office: Morgan Lewis & Bockius LLP 1111 Pennsylvania Ave NW Washington DC 20004 E-mail: pzane@morganlewis.com.

ZANE, RAYMOND J. state legislator, lawyer; b. Woodbury, N.J., July 23, 1939; s. Clarence R. and Veronica (Levy) Z.; children: Marybeth, Raymond II, Kenneth. BSBA, St. Joseph's U., 1965; JD, Rutger's U., 1974. Bar: N.J. 1974, N.Y. 1989. Freeholder Gloucester County, Woodbury, N.J., 1971-73; mem. N.J. Senate, Dist. 3, Trenton, 1973—. Mem. N.J. Bar Assn., Gloucester County Bar Assn. Home: 509 Sharp Dr Mickleton NJ 08056-1441 Office: 39 S Broad St Woodbury NJ 08096-7920

ZANE, WILLIAM ANTHONY, chemicals executive; b. Hazleton, Pa., Oct. 15, 1950; s. William Richard and Mary An (Maylath) Z.; m. Jean Marie Holy, Feb 22, 1975; children: William P., Michael J., Andrew A. BSChE, Pa. State U., 1972. Sales rep. Diamond Shamrock Chem. Co., Omaha, Pitts., Dayton, Ohio, 1972-77, mktg. mgr. chlorine Cleve., 1978-80, product mgr. internat., 1981-82, dist. sales mgr., 1982-84, Midwest regional mgr. splty. chem. divsn. Chgo., 1985-87; nat. sales mgr. Cognis Corp. (formerly Henkel Corp.), 1988-89, N.Am. sales mgr. Phila., 1989-94, bus. dir., 1993-94, bus. dir. coating resins and additives, 1994-95, v.p., gen. mgr. plastic and polymer chem. divsn., 1995-98, v.p. coatings and inks divsn. and plastic/polymer divsn., 1998—. Treas. Methacton H.S. Basketball Club, Fairview Village, 1995-96. Mem. Medinah Country Club (non-resident). Republican. Roman Catholic. Avocations: golf, skiing, running, family activities. Home: 3067 Sunny Ayre Dr Lansdale PA 19446-5828 Office: Cognis Corp 300 Brookside Ave Ambler PA 19002-3497 E-mail: waz34869@aol.com., bill.zane@cognis-us.com.

ZANECCHIA, THOMAS EDWARD, financial executive; b. Bklyn., Dec. 29, 1954; s. Armando Luigi and Irma Elda (Martinuzzi) Z.; m. Deborah Sue Newhouse, June 18, 1977; children: Natalie Newhouse, Katie Lynn. BS in Commerce, U. Va., 1976; MBA in Fin., U. Pa., 1981. CPA, Colo. Sr. acct. Coopers & Lybrand, Boston, 1976-79; staff cons. Wharton Applied Rsch. Ctr., Phila., 1979-81; pres., shareholder Asset Mgmt. Group, Denver, 1981-93; founder, pres. Wealth Mgmt. Cons., Inc., 1993—; co-founder, pres. Branzan Investment Advisors, Inc., 2001—. Mem. bd. advisors F&B Mfg., Inc., 1994—; guest lectr. U. Denver, 1996—99; bd. dirs. Am. Materials Corp., 1997—; mem. bd. advisors Denver Family Bus. Forum, 2001—; spkr. nat. seminars Family Firm Inst., Young Pres.' Orgn., other trade assns. Contbr. fin. articles to profl. and fin. publs.; recognized in J.K. Lasser's Estate Planning for Baby Boomers and Retirees. Bd. dirs. Hospice of Metro Denver, 1989-94, bd. advisers, Denver Entrepreneurship Acad., 1992-94; mem. Body of Knowledge com. Family Firm Inst., 1997-98, mem. mentor com., 2001—. Named among Worth Mag.'s Best Fin. Advisors, 1998—2001. Fellow Family Firm Inst.; mem. AICPA, Colo. Soc. CPAs. Avocations: golf, skiing. Home: 4930 S Gaylord St Englewood CO 80110-7129 Office: Wealth Mgmt Cons Inc 475 17th St Ste 570 Denver CO 80202-4015 E-mail: tez1@wealth-manage.com.

ZANES, GEORGE WILLIAM, management, marketing, human resources consultant; b. Laconia, N.H., May 13, 1926; s. Robert Lewis and Mina (Edgerly) z.; m. Anne Schuetz, Dec. 21, 1957 (div. 1970); children: Laura, David, Scott, Hugh; m. Ruth Weissman, June 17, 1970; stepchildren: Glenn, Lee. BS, U. N.H., 1952. Dir. indsl. rels., cons. I.P.C. Inc., Bristol, N.H., 1953-56; dir. spl. projects Am. Rsch. Bur. Inc., Beltsville, Md., 1957-60, Alfred Politz Rsch. Inc., N.Y.C., 1960-62; v.p. Simulmatics Corp., 1962-63; group rsch. mgr. Foote Cone & Belding Inc., 1963-65; v.p. Trendex Inc., 1965-67; pres. Zanes & Assocs. Inc., Ft. Lee, N.J., 1967-80, chmn., chief exec. officer, 1980-88; also bd. dirs., pres. The Mktg. Rsch. Workshop Inc., 1974-88. Cons. Strategic Resource Group Inc., 1988-89; cons., ceo G & R Enterprises, Tallahassee, Fla., Alpharetta, Ga., 1989—, bd. dirs. Ad Net, Inc. Mem. F. Lee Rent Leveling Bd., past pres., Jaycees, Bristol, N.H. With U.S. Army, 1944-47; ETO, capt. USAR, 1947-60. Mem. Am. Mktg. Assn. (v.p. programs Atlanta chpt. 1993-94), Greater North Fulton C. of C., Acacia.

ZANETTI, JOSEPH MAURICE, JR. corporate executive; b. San Francisco, Aug. 3, 1928; s. Joseph Maurice and Lillian Mary (Solari) Z.; m. Marilyn Ruth Parker, Aug. 11, 1956; children: Pamela, Gregory, Geoffrey, Regina. BA, Saint Mary's Coll., 1950; postgrad., U. Calif., Berkeley, 1950-51, 53-55, 56-57; postgrad. in Edn., San Francisco State Coll., 1955-56. Cert. secondary tchr., Calif. Tchr. Piedmont (Calif.) High Sch., 1956-57, Pleasant Hill (Calif.) High Sch., 1957-58; supr. Sandia Labs., Albuquerque, 1958-64; mktg. dir. Ednl. Research Assocs., 1964-66; exec. asst. Sandia Labs., 1966-73; pres. U. of Albuquerque, 1973-75; dir. area devel. Pub. Svc. Co. of N.Mex., 1975-86; pres., chmn. bd. dirs. Rio Grande Trading Co. Inc., 1986-88; pres. Foresight, Inc., 1988-90; v.p. Summa Med. Corp., 1988-91, sr. v.p. Vienna, 1991-92; v.p. Systems Support Agy. Inc., 1992-93; pres. Complexus, Inc., Albuquerque, 1993—. Cons. Pub. Service Co. N.Mex., Albuquerque, 1986-88; ; pres. N.Mex. Internat. Trade and Investment Council Inc., Albuquerque, 1984-89; active Adv. Bd. Coll. and U. Partnership Program, Memphis, 1984-99; sr. v.p. TecMed Inc., 1999—; sr. v.p. Complex Light Valve Corp., 1999—, also bd. dirs. Chmn. adv. bd. N.Mex. Mus. Natural History, Albuquerque, 1985-90; vice chmn., bd. govs. Albuquerque Tech. Vocat. Inst., 1971-77; mem. Bd. Edn., Albquerque Pub. Schs., 1971-77. Capt. USNR, 1948-83. Mem. Res. Officers Assn. (life), Resource Devel. Com., Albuquerque Pub. Schs. (chmn.). Republican. Roman Catholic.

ZANETTI, RICHARD JOSEPH, publisher; b. Weehawken, N.J., Mar. 22, 1939; s. Mario and Lucille (Coco) Z.; m. Norma Diane Nesheim, June 28, 1969; children: Joseph, Michael. BSChemE, Bucknell U., Lewisburg, Pa., 1961, MSChemE, 1964; MBA, Fairfield U., 1998. Technologist Mobil Oil Corp., Bklyn., 1964-66; dept. editor Chem. Week mag., N.Y.C., 1980-84; from assoc. editor to editor-in-chief Chem. Engring. mag., 1984-97, pub., 1997—. Lectr. in field. Producer, dir. documentary film: Standups, 1979. Cons. Manhattan Coll., Riverdale, N.Y., 1989—. 1st lt. U.S. Army, 1964-65. Recipient Hammer award Nat. Performance Rev. Mem. Am. Bus. Press, Tau Beta Pi, Omicron Delta Kappa. Avocations: fiction writing, fishing, stamp collecting. Office: Chemical Week Assoc 110 William St New York NY 10038-3901

ZANFAGNA, PHILIP EDWARD, government executive, urban planner; b. Lawrence, Mass., Dec. 5, 1936; s. Philip Edward and Edna Edith (Hill) Z.; m. Joan Elizabeth Criswell, Sept. 9, 1961; children: Deborah Carol Bass, Gary Philip. BA, Ohio Wesleyan U., 1958; MDiv, Yale U., 1961; JD, George Washington U., 1964. Certified in sr. exec. svcs., acquisition profl. Sr. negotiator USN, Washington, 1964-72; dep. dir. contracts dept. Navy USMC, 1972-80, dir. contracts, 1980-90, asst. chief of staff installations and logistics, 1990—, dep. asst. commandant, 2000. Pres. Lewinsville Inc., McLean, Va., 1980-95. Commr., vice chmn. Fairfax (Va.) County Planning Commn., 1973-77; active Dulles Airport Planning Com., Fairfax, 1975-76, Fairfax Blue Ribbon commn., 1986-87; pres. Dranesville Dist. Coun., McLean, 1982-83; chmn. bd. dirs. McLean Citizens Assn., 1979-81; trustee McLean Found., 1980-86; bd. dirs. McLean Citizen's Assn., 1996—. Recipient Presdl. Rank award for exceptional pub. svc., 1993 98, Disting. Civilian Svc. medal. Mem. Sr. Exec. Assn., Yale U. Alumni Assn., Fed. Exec. Inst. Assn., Nat. Def. U. Alumni Assn., Harvard U. Sch. Govt. Alumni Assn. Presbyterian. Avocations: travel, music, photography, sports, teaching theology. Office: HQMC I & L Dept Code LB 3033 Wilson Blvd # 725 Arlington VA 22201-3843

ZANGRILLI, ALBERT JOSEPH, JR. lawyer; b. Pitts., May 3, 1940; s. Albert Joseph and Regina (DeSimone) Z.; m. M. Ursula McKenzie, Aug. 20, 1977; children: Albert J. III, Mary Catherine, Ursula Therese. AB, U. Notre Dame, 1963; MA, Holy Cross Coll., Washington, 1967; JD, Cornell U., 1972. Bar: Pa. 1972, U.S. Dist. Ct. (we. dist.) Pa. 1972, U.S. Ct. Appeals (3d cir.) 1976, U.S. Supreme Ct. 1988. Ptnr. and co-mng. ptnr. Metz, Cook, Welsh & Zangrilli P.C., Pitts., 1981-92; ptnr. Yukevich, Marchetti, Liekar & Zangrilli, PC, 1992—. Ct. rules com. Allegheny County, Pa., 1974—. Contbr. author: Yearbook of Liturgical Studies, 1964-68. Committeeman Allegheny County Dem. Com., Pitts., 1990—; adv. bd. Notre Dame Club of Pitts., 1990—; mem. Theology Students Com. for Civil Rights, Washington, 1965-66; sec., exec. com. St. Paul Cathedral, 1985-02. Mem. ACBA, St. Thomas More Soc. (pres. 1987-89, gov. 1976—), Pitts. Athletic Assn. (dir. 1989-96), Assn. Mcpl. and Sch. Solicitors (bd. dirs.), Irish Centre of Pitts. (dir. 1992-94). Democrat. Roman Catholic. Office: Yukevich Marchetti Liekar and Zangrilli P C 11 Stanwix St Ste 1024 Pittsburgh PA 15222 E-mail: azangrilli@ymlz.com.

ZANGWILL, SHEILA BETH, nursing administrator; b. Fall River, Mass., Oct. 5, 1951; d. Moses Eli and Harriet Reva Zangwill. Diploma in nursing, Mt. Auburn Hosp., 1972; BS in Psychology and Rehab. Counseling, Emmanuel Coll., 1982. RN Mass., R.I., lic. chem. dependency profl., recognized clin. supr. Clin. dir., nursing supr., rehab. nurse Brighton Clinic/City of Boston Drug Treatment Program, 1975-82; charge nurse McLean Hosp., Belmont, Mass., 1982-90; nurse mgr. St. Luke's Hosp., New Bedford, 1990-91; dir. inpatient and day treatment svcs. Stanley St. Treatment and Resources, Inc., Fall River, 1992-93; nurse mgr. Butler Hosp., Providence, 1994—. Presenter, cons. on substance abuse edn., nutrition, weight control, stress prevention. Author: Home Dialysis Training Manual, 1974, Resource Handbook, 1979; creator board game for substance abuse programs Winning is Just the Beginning, 1986. Recipient Spl. Achievement award VA, 1975, Future Vision CARE award Care New Eng., 1998; (2) Acad. Achievement scholar, 1969.

Democrat. Jewish. Avocations: travel, reading, bicycling, swimming, horseback riding. Home: 124 Joseph Dr Fall River MA 02720-4634 Office: Butler Hosp 345 Blackstone Blvd Providence RI 02906-4829

ZANI, FREDERICK CAESAR, retired corporate consultant; b. Medford, Mass., June 9, 1929; s. John and Catherine (Voluletti) Zani; m. Dorothy Ann Menezes, Feb. 20, 1960; children: Gregory Robert, Elizabeth Ruth. BS, Salem State Coll., 1954; M.Ed., Boston U., 1959, cert. in advanced grad. studies, 1967; PhD (hon.) , World U., 1986. Lic. sch. psychologist. Tchr., 1954—60; tchr. pub. schs. Gloucester, Mass., 1960—65; guidance counselor Attleboro, Mass. public schs., 1965—90; ret. Former owner, exec. dir. Zani Group Internat. Consulting Co., 1990—. Contbr. articles to profl. jours. Recipient Outstanding Svc. award, Bristol County Tchrs. Assn. . Mem.: Ret. State, County and Mcpl. Employees Assn., Boston Children's Hosp. Med. Center Parent Orgn. for Exceptional Children, Attleboro Mental Health Ctr., Mass. Sch. Psychologists Assn., Mass. Ret. Tchrs. Assn., Mass. Tchrs. Assn., Attleboro Tchrs. Assn., Mass. Assn. Children with Learning Disabilities (v.p. Attleboro chpt. 1969—70), Ret. Nat. Educators Assn., Christian Edn. Assn., Internat. Platform Assn. Mem. Assembly Of God. Ch. Home and Office: 115 Holmes Rd North Attleboro MA 02760-4441 E-mail: f.c.zz1@aol.com.

ZANJACOMO, PAULO REGIS, engineering executive; s. Expedicto and Alzira Zanjacomo; m. Hilda Hortensia Valero Tonone, Mar. 27, 1999. BSc in Computer Scis., U. Sao Paulo, 1990, MSc in Applied Math., 1992; PhD in Indsl. Engring., Ga. Inst. Tech., 1998. Asst. prof. U. Sao Paulo, 1992—94; sr. engr. for rsch. and product design Energy Imperium, Atlanta, 1999—99; dir. rsch. and design Altra Energy Technologies, Houston, 1999—2000; chief tech. officer eTiburon Corp., Atlanta, 2000—. Contbr. articles to profl. jours. Mem.: INFORMS.

ZANK, GARY PAUL, phyicist; b. Pietermaritzburg, Natal, South Africa, June 6, 1961; came to U.S., 1989; s. Patrick Petre and Lynnete J. (Nadauld) Z.; m. Lorraine Anne Lipman, Dec. 16, 1983; children: Taryn Caitlin, Janine Nissa. BS, U. Natal, 1982, BS (hon.), 1983, PhD, 1987. Post doctoral physicist Max-Planck Inst. Nuclear Physics, Heidelberg, Germany, 1987-89, Lindau, Germany, 1989, Bartol Rsch. Inst., Newark, 1989-91, asst. prof., 1991-94, assoc. prof., 1994-99, prof., 1999-2001; dir. Inst. Geophysics and Planetary Physics, prof. physics U. Calif., Riverside, 2001—, prof. physics, 2001—. Mem. com. on solar space physics NRC, 2000—. Editor: Particle Acceleration in Cosmic Plasmas, 1992; assoc. editor Jour. Plasma Physics, 1992—; contbr. articles to profl. jours. Recipient Presdl. Young Investigator award NSF, 1993, Zeldovich medal Russian Acad. Sci. and Com. Space Rsch., 1996. Mem. Am. Geophys. Union, Am. Phys. Soc. Office: U Calif Riverside IGPP Riverside CA 92521 E-mail: zank@bartol.ude1.edu.

ZANN, NICHOLAS T. artist; b. N.Y.C., June 7, 1943; s. Ernest Luke and Ellen Rita (Mihalis) Z.; m. Mary Jo Quay, Dec. 27, 1970 (div. 1983). Student, Sch. of Visual Arts, Manhattan, N.Y., 1967-69. Artist covers for Psychology Today; illustrations for Time, Newsweek, N.Y. Times, Esquire, NBC, ABC, CBS, also covers for books, Broadway posters and corp. clients, 1964—; commn. painting An Die Musik, 1995; art work appears in books, mags., TV and advt. campaigns; writer, creator design concepts MAD Mag., Esquire, Scholastic, Grey Advt., others; artist, creator The Answer Deck, 1998; commns. include An Die Musik, 1995; creator (internet comic strip) Spare-Partz, 2000. Recipient Funny Bone award Soc. of Illustrators, 1986. Avocations: rock'n'roll singing, song writing, cooking. Office: 155 W 68th St Apt 1114 New York NY 10023-5817

ZANNA, MARTIN THOMAS, physician; b. Mpls., Apr. 2, 1947; s. Peter J. and Mary L. (Peck) Z. AB, Harvard U., 1969, MPH, 1976; MD, U. Minn., 1973. Diplomate Am. Bd. Preventive Medicine. Resident in pub. health N.J. State Dept. Health, 1974-77, acting dir. chronic disease svcs., 1976-79, dir. chronic disease svcs., 1979-81; med. adminstr. Fla. Dept. Health and Rehab. Svcs., Tallahassee, 1981-82; med. cons. N.J. Medicaid, Trenton, 1982—, chief med. cons., 1990-96; med. cons. N.J. State Dept. Health and Sr. Svcs., 1996—. Mem. Fla. Cancer Coun., 1981-82, Fla. Bd. Med. Examiners, 1982, N.J. Hypertension Study Group, 1977-81; chmn. grad. med. edn. com. N.J. State Dept. Health & Sr. Svcs., 1993—; diabetes adv. coun. exec. com. N.J. Dept. Health, 2001—. Contbr. articles to profl. jours. Participant Fla. Gov.'s Mission to Haiti, 1982; mem. divsn. profl. edn. Am. Cancer Soc., 1976-81. Fellow Am. Coll. Preventive Medicine; mem. APHA, Harvard Club (Boston), Harvard Faculty Club (Cambridge), Harvard Club (Washington). Home: # 11 201 Salem Ct Apt 11 Princeton NJ 08540-7039 Office: NJ State Dept Health & Sr Svcs PO Box 722 Trenton NJ 08625-0722

ZANON, JAMES THOMAS, product designer, private investigator; b. Detroit, May 11, 1947; s. Harold Joseph and Margaret Louise Zanon; m. Suzanne Margaret Poikey, Feb. 11, 1978 (div. Sept. 15, 1994); children: Ricky L., Robert L., Juli A., James H., Thomas C. BA, Ford Motor Coll., Dearborn, MI; police adminstrn., Henry Ford Coll., Dearborn, MI; police acad. (hon.) , Detroit Police Acad., Detroit, MI, 1970. Designer Ford Motor Co., Dearborn, Mich., Am. Motors Corp., Detroit; patrol officer Detroit Police Dept.; contractor Detroit area auto body shops. Sch. bd. Pinellis County Coll. Sch. Bd., St. Petersburg, Fla. Author: (book) America a More Perfect Union. Vice chmn. Mich. Dem. Party, Lansing, Mich., 1980—82. E-5 sgt. U.S. Army, 1966—80, Vietnam. Recipient Citizen Citation For Bravery, Lincoln Pk. Police Dept., 1974. Mem.: Pres. Reagan Presdl. Task Force (advisor), NRA. Conservative-R. Born Again Christian. Avocations: hunting, fishing, camping, boating. Home: PO Box 316 Grosse Ile MI 48138 Personal E-mail: jtzanon@yahoo.com.

ZANONI, MICHAEL R. accountant; b. Laramie, Wyo., Mar. 7, 1969; s. Mickey G. and Barbara J. Zanoni. BS, Pepperdine U., 1991. CPA. Acct. Deloitte & Touche, LLP, Seattle, 1996—. Bd. dirs. Pepperdine U. Alumni Assn. Pacific Northwest, Seattle. Mem. AICPA, Wash. Soc. CPAs. Avocations: cycling, skiing, rowing. Home: 1200 Alki Ave SW # 2 Seattle WA 98116 Office: Deloitte & Touche LLP 700 5th Ave Ste 4500 Seattle WA 98104-5044 E-mail: mzanoni@mail.com.

ZANONI DE LOS SANTOS, JACQUELINE M. artist, curator; b. Zurich, Switzerland, Apr. 11, 1959; BA in Art History, Clark U., 1982; MA in Art History, U. Okla., 1997; postgrad., Trier (Germany) U., U. Florence, Italy. Arts writer The News, Mexico City, 1984-85; visual artist various locations, 1982—; v.p., bd. dirs. Grove St. Art Gallery, Worcester, Mass., 1987-89; artist in residence NEA/Okla. State Artist in Residence Program, 1992-94; grad. tchg. asst. U. Okla., Norman, 1995-96, curatorial intern F.J.J. Mus. Art, 1997; instr., pub. art project coord. Fine Arts Inst., Edmond, Okla., 1992-97; dir. art program St. Mary's Sch., 1995-97; curator The Christian Keesee Collection, Oklahoma City, 1997-2000; ind. curator, 2000—. Pres. bd. dirs. Okla. Visual Artists Coalition, 2001—; adj. prof. art history Oklahoma City U., 2001-2002; vis. curator City Arts Ctr., Oklahoma City, 2001; spkr. Mountain-Plains Mus. Conf., Tulsa, 2001; grant rev. panelist Arts Coun. Okla., 2002. Solo exhbn. at IMARC Gallery, Mexico City, 1987; group exhbns. include IAO Gallery, 1992, numerous others. Active Boy Scouts Am., 1991-97; mentor Will Rogers Elem. Sch., Edmond, 1991-94; Book Fair, PTO Ctrl. Mid. Sch., Edmond, 1997—. N.J. Merit scholar, 1977; Jonas Clark scholar, 1977, 79, 80, 81; Edmond Women's Club scholar, 1995. Mem. Am. Assn. Museums (curators com. 1997—), Okla. Visual Artists Coalition (bd. dirs. 1999—), Nat. Mus. Women in the Arts. Avocations: mountain biking, languages, ypga, travel. Home and Office: 917 Dover Dr Edmond OK 73034-6458 E-mail: jzdls@cox.net.

ZANOT, CRAIG ALLEN, lawyer; b. Wyandotte, Mich., Nov. 15, 1955; s. Thomas and Faye Blanch (Sperry) Z. AB with distinction, U. Mich., 1977; JD cum laude, Ind. U., 1980. Bar: Ind. 1980, Mich. 1981, U.S. Dist. Ct. (so. dist.) Ind. 1980, U.S. Dist. Ct. (no. dist.) Ind. 1981, U.S. Ct. Appeals (6th cir.) 1985, U.S. Dist. Ct. (ea. dist.) Mich. 1987, U.S. Dist. Ct. (we. dist.) Mich. 1990. Law clk. to presiding justice Allen County Superior Ct, Ft. Wayne, 1980-81; ptnr. Davidson, Breen & Doud P.C., Saginaw, Mich., 1981—. Mem. ABA, Mich. Bar Assn., Ind. Bar Assn., Saginaw County Bar Assn. Roman Catholic. Home: 547 S Linwood Beach Rd Linwood MI 48634-9432 Office: Davidson Breen & Doud PC 1121 N Michigan Ave Saginaw MI 48602-4762

ZANOTELLI, WILLIAM DUANE, music educator; b. Trinidad, Colo., May 27, 1950; s. William J. and Valeria M. Zanotelli. MA, Adams State Coll., Alamesa, Colorado, 1973, BA, 1972. Band dir. Trinidad H.S., Trinidad, Colo., 1975—, Trinidad Jr. H.S., Trinidad, 1974—75, Rice Mid. Sch., Trinidad, 1973—74. Band dir. Trinidad Area Cmty. Band, Trinidad, Colo., 2001—02; cmty. jazz band dir. Trinidaires, Trinidad, Colo., 1991—2002. Recipient Excellence in Tchg., Trinidad Hispanic Chamber of Commerce, 2000, Boettcher Found. Winner, Boettcher Found., 1998, Hall of Fame, Colo. Band Masters Assn., 1997. Mem.: Music Educators Nat. Conf., Colo. Bandmasters Assn. (pres. 1973—2002, 1980), Phi Beta Mu, Kappa Chpt. (pres. 1980—2002, 1986). Home: 1120 Western Avenue Trinidad CO 81082-2252

ZANTEK, PAUL F. management scientist, educator; BA, Concordia Coll., 1993; PhD, Purdue U., 1998. Bus. mgr. Tomahawk Scout Reservation, Indianhead Coun., Saint Paul, Minn., 1991—93; asst. prof. of mgmt. sci. and stats. U. of Md., Coll. Pk., Md., 1999—. Cons. Ctr. for Naval Analyses, Alexandria, Va., 2000. Fellow Doctoral Dissertation fellowship, Ctr. for the Mgmt. of Mfg. Enterprises, Purdue U., 1996—97; grantee Rsch. grant, Purdue Rsch. Found., 1996, 1998. Mem.: Inst. for Ops. Rsch. and the Mgmt. Sci., Am. Statis. Assn. Office: University of Maryland Van Munching Hall College Park MD 20742

ZANTOPULOS, WILLIAM THEODORE, sales representative, small business owner; b. Canton, Ohio, Sept. 1, 1962; s. John and Despina Z.; m. Karen Louise Wyler, Sept. 26, 1987; children: William John, Deanna Lee. BSBA, U. Akron, 1986. Mgmt. Rent-A-Ctr., Inc., Newcastle, Pa., 1987-91; mgr. Dollar Tree, Inc., Boardman, Ohio, 1992-94; rt. sales rep. Entenmann's Bakery, Tallmadge, 1994—; owner Computer Experts LLC, Canton, 1999—. Democrat. Avocations: computers, golf, bowling, family. Office: Computer Experts LLC 6704 Orchard Trl NE Canton OH 44721-3803 E-mail: wzantopulos@neo.rr.com.

ZAPAPAS, JAMES RICHARD, pharmaceutical company executive; b. Martinsville, Ind., July 15, 1926; s. James K. and Bertha (Gardner) Z.; m. Patricia A. Ryan, Aug. 30, 1947; children: Marianne Zapapas McGriff, Patricia Zapapas Parry, Gail Zapapas Rodecker, James R., Carol, Julie. BS in Pharmacy, Purdue U., 1947, ScD hon., 1979. Dir. dry products ops. Eli Lilly & Co., Indpls., 1967-70, dir. pers., 1970-73, dir. pers. and pub. rels., 1973-74, v.p. prodn. ops., 1974-75, group v.p., dir., 1976-77, pres. Elizabeth Arden Inc., 1975-76, chmn. bd., 1977-86, ret., 1986. Bd. dirs., group v.p. Eli Lilly & Co., 1976-86. Republican. Roman Catholic. Home: 5025 Plantation Dr Indianapolis IN 46250-1638

ZAPEL, ARTHUR LEWIS, book publishing executive; b. Chgo., 1921; m. Janet Michel (dec.); children: Linda (dec.), Mark, Theodore, Michelle; m. Cynthia Rogers Pisor, 1986; stepchildren: Dawn, Anthony. BA in English, U. Wis., 1946. Writer, prodr. Westinghouse Radio Stas.; film writer Galbreath Studios, Ft. Wayne; creative dir. Kling Studios, Chgo., 1952-54; writer, prodr. TV commls. J. Walter Thompson Advt., 1954-73, v.p. TV and radio prodn., 1954-73; founder, pres. Arthur Meriwether, Inc., 1973-83; pres. Meriwether Pub. Ltd., 1969-90, chmn., 1990-97. Pres. Westcliffe (Colo.) Ctr. for the Arts. Author: Sweet Uncertainty, 2001; illustrator: 'Twas the Night Before, The Jabberwock; created game A Can of Squirms; wrote plays for ednl. use in schs. and chs.; supr. editing and prodn. 2300 plays and musicals, 1970-99; exec. editor 210 books on theater skills for secular and religious use. Founding pres. Art Students League of Colorado Springs, 1992; past pres. Colo. Springs Symphony Coun.; past bd. dirs. Colorado Springs Opera Festival. Recipient numerous awards Freedoms Found., Valley Forge, Art Dirs. Club N.Y., Art Dirs. Chgo., Hollywood Advt., 1960-67, Gold Records Radio Ad Bur., 1959-60, XV Festival Internat. Du Film Publicitaire Venise, 1968, Gold Camera award U.S. Indsl. Film Festival, 1983, Dukane award, 1983, Gold award Houston Internat. Film Festival, 1984, 2d pl. award Best New Fiction, 2002. Office: Meriwether Pub Ltd 885 Elkton Dr Colorado Springs CO 80907-3576 E-mail: merpcds@aol.com., alzart@aol.com.

ZAPF, HERMANN, book and type designer; b. Nuremberg, Germany, Nov. 8, 1918; s. Hermann and Magdalene (Schlamp) Zapf; m. Gudrun von Hesse, Aug. 18, 1951; 1 child Christian Ludwig. Freelance designer, 1938—; type dir. D. Stempel AG, type foundry, Frankfurt, Fed. Republic of Germany, 1947-56; design cons. Mergenthaler Linotype Co., N.Y.C. and Frankfurt, 1957-74; cons. Hallmark Internat., Kansas City, Mo., 1966-73; v.p. Design Processing Internat. Inc., N.Y.C., 1977-86; prof. typographic computer programs Rochester (N.Y.) Inst. Tech., 1977-87; chmn. Zapf, Burns & Co., N.Y.C., 1987-91. Instr. lettering Werkkunstschule, Offenbach, Fed. Republic Germany., 1948-50; prof. graphic design Carnegie Inst. Tech., 1960; instr. typography Technische Hochschule, Darmstadt, Fed. Republic Germany, 1972-81. Author: William Morris, 1948, Pen and Graver, 1952, Manuale Typographicum, 1954, 1968, About Alphabets, 1960, 1970, Typographic Variations, 1964, Orbis Typographicus, 1980, Hora fugit/Carpe diem, 1984, Hermann Zapf and His Design Philosophy, 1987, ABC-XYZapf, 1989, Poetry Through Typography, 1993, August Rosenberger, 1996, (film) The Art of Hermann Zapf, German version Die Welt der Buchstaben von Hermann Zapf, (CD-ROM) The World of Alphabets, 2001; designer types Palatino, Melior, Optima, ITC Zapf Chancery, ITC Zapf Internat., Digiset, Marconi, Digiset Edison, Digiset Aurelia, Pan-Nigerian, URW-Roman and San Serif, Renaissance Roman, Linotype Zapfino. Hon. pres. Edward Johnston Found., Ditchling, Eng.; hon. curator Computer Mus., Boston. Named hon. citizen, State of Tex., 1970, hon. Royal Designer for Industry, London, 1995; recipient Silver medal, Brussels, 1962, 1st prize typography, Biennale Brno, Czechoslovakia, 1966, Gold medal, Type Dirs. Club, N.Y., Frederic W. Goudy award, Inst. Tech. Rochester, 1969, Silver medal, Internat. Book Exhbn., Leipzig, 1971, Gold medal, 1989, Johannes Gutenberg prize, Mainz, Fed. German Republic, 1974, Gold medal, Museo Bodoniano, Parma, Italy, 1975, J.H. Merck award, Darmstadt, 1978, Robert Hunter Middleton award, 1987, Euro Design award, 1994, Wadim Lazursky award, Acad. of Graphic Arts, Moscow, 1996. Mem. Royal Soc. Arts, Am. Math. Soc., Alliance Graphique Internationale, Bund Deutscher Grafik Designer, Internat. Gutenberg Gesellschaft; hon. mem. Type Dirs. Club N.Y.C., Soc. Typographique de France (Paris), Soc. Typographic Arts (Chgo.), Double Crown Club (London), Soc. Scribes and Illuminators (London), Friends of Calligraphy (San Francisco), Soc. Printers (Boston), Soc. Graphic Designers Can., Bund Deutscher Buchkünstler, Grafiska Inst. (Stockholm), Typophiles (N.Y.), Alpha Beta Club (Hong Kong), Soc. of Calligraphy (L.A.), Wynkyn de Worde Soc. (London), Letter Exchange (London), Caxton Club (Chgo.), Monterey Calligrapher's Guild, Washington Calligraphers Guild, Eesti Kalligraafide Koondis (Tallinn, Estonia), Chgo. Calligraphers Guild, Typographers Internat. Assn., Art Dirs. Club Kansas City, Assocs. Stanford U. Librs., Alcuin Soc. (Vancouver), Goudy Internat. Ctr., Brno Biennale Assn., Soc. Scribes N.Y., Dante e.V. (German TEX Group, Heidelberg), Caxton Club (Oregon), Gamma Epsilon Tau.

ZAPFFE, NINA BYROM, retired elementary education educator; b. Independence, Mo., Aug. 17, 1925; d. Richmond Douglas and Nina Belle (Howell) Byrom; m. Robert Glenn Fessler, June 25, 1946 (dec. June 1947); 1 child, Robert Glenn Fessler Zapffe; m. Fred Zapffe, July 1, 1952 (dec. Dec. 1999); children: Paul Douglas, Carl Raymond. BA, So. Meth. U., 1946. Fin. sec. Tyler St. Meth. Ch., Dallas, 1948-49; tchr. Dallas Ind. Sch. Dist., 1949-52, Norman (Okla.) Pub. Schs., 1966-74; cert. chief reader for GED Writing Skills Test Part II GED Testing Svc., Am. Coun. on Edn., Washington, 1990-98. Adv. com. (Acad. Resource Ctr.) Moore-Norman Tech. Ctr., 1988—. Adv. bd. Norman Salvation Army, 1978-90; organizer, historian Norman Salvation Army Womens Aux., 1983-2000; organizer, past pres. Norman Literacy Coun., 1976—; organizing com., past pres. Norman Interfaith Coun., 1974-93; organizing com., past treas. Friends of the Norman Libr., 1979—; mem. McFarlin Meml. United Meth. Ch., historian 2-in-1 Sunday Sch. class, 1990-2002, lay leader, 1980-81. Named Woman of Yr., Norman Bus. and Profl. Women, 1999; named to Literacy Hall of Fame, Pioneer Libr. Sys., Norman, 1995; recipient medal of appreciation, SAR, 2002. Mem. DAR (regent Black Beaver chpt. 1998-2000, state literacy chmn. 2000-02), Nat. Soc. Daus. 1812 (state treas. 1996-2000), Old Regime Study Club (pres. 1998-99), Coterie Club (pres. 1996, 2002), Delta Delta Delta Alumnae. Republican. Avocation: genealogy. Home: 2717 Walnut Rd Norman OK 73072-6940

ZAPHIRIOU, GEORGE ARISTOTLE, lawyer, educator; b. July 10, 1919; came to U.S., 1973, naturalized, 1977; s. Aristotle George and Callie Constantine (Economos) Z.; m. Peaches J. Griffin, June 1, 1973; children: Ari, Marie. JD, U. Athens, 1940; LLM, U. London, 1950. Bar: Supreme Ct. Greece 1946, Eng. 1956, Ill. 1975, Va. 1983. Gen. counsel Counties Ship Mgmt. and R & K Ltd., London, 1951-61; practicing barrister, lectr. City of London Poly., 1961-73; vis. prof. Ill. Inst. Tech.-Chgo. Kent Coll. Law, 1973-76; pvt. practice Northbrook, Ill., 1976-78; prof. law George Mason U. Sch. Law, 1978-94, prof. law emeritus, adj. prof., 1994—. Prof. internat. transactions George Mason U. Internat. Inst., 1992-94; mem. Odin, Feldman & Pittelman P.C., Fairfax, Va., 1994-96; mem. study group on internat. elec. commerce cons. and other pvt. internat. law covs. U.S. Dept. of State. Author: Transfer of Chattels in Private International Law, 1956, U.S. edit., 1981, European Business Law, 1970; co-author: Declining Jurisdiction in Private International Law, 1995; joint editor: Jour. Bus. Law, London, 1962-73; bd. dirs. and bd. editors Am. Jour. Comp. Law of Am. Soc. Comparative Law, 1980-94; contbr. articles to profl. jours. Mem.: ABA (sect. internat. law and practice and dispute resolution), George Mason Am. Inn of Ct. (founder, master, emeritus), Am. Arbitration Assn. (panel comml. arbitrators), Chgo. Bar Assn., Ill. Bar Assn. Home: 400 Green Pasture Dr Rockville MD 20852-4233 Fax: 301-984-1164. E-mail: gzaphiri@gmu.edu.

ZAPINSKI, ROBERT PAUL, lawyer; b. Oak Park, Ill., Oct. 24, 1960; s. Norbert J. and Particia Marie (Celeskey) Z.; m. Susan Marie Sullivan, Aug. 10, 1985; children: Andrew, Kevin, Jennifer, Catherine. BS in Criminal Justice, BS in Psychology, Bradley U., 1982; JD, U. Ill., 1985. Bar: Ill. 1985, U.S. Dist. Ct. (no. dist.) Ill. 1986, U.S. Ct. Appeals (7th cir.) 1987. Law clk. to Hon. Micheal Mihm U.S. Dist. Ct., Peoria, Ill., 1985—87; assoc. Jenner & Block, Chgo., 1984-92, ptnr., 1994—99; corp. counsel Tenneco Automotive Inc., 1999—. Contbg. author: Insurance Coverage, 1996. Soccer coach Westmont Park Dist., Ill., 1994—. Mem. ABA, Ill. State Bar Assn., Chgo. Bar Assn., Order Coif. Roman Catholic. Avocations: camping, whitewater rafting, kayaking, sports, soccer. Home: 336 Blackhawk Dr Westmont IL 60559-1563 Office: Tenneco Automotive Inc 500 N Field Dr Lake Forest IL 60045-2595

ZAPLETAL, JINDRICH, mathematician; b. Tabor, Czech Republic, June 24, 1969; s. Jindrich Zapletal and Milena Zapletalova. PhD, Pa. State U., 1995. Bateman instr. math. Calif. Inst. Tech., Pasadena, 1996—98; John Wesley Young instr. math. Dartmouth Coll., Hanover, NH, 1998—2000; asst. prof. U. Fla., Gainesville, 2000—. Office: U Fla 358 Little Hall Gainesville FL 32611

ZAPOL, WARREN MYRON, anesthesiologist; b. N.Y.C., Mar. 16, 1942; BS, MIT, 1962; MD, U. Rochester, 1966; MA (hon.) , Harvard U., 1990. Cert. in anesthesiology. Intern Harvard Surgical Unit/Boston City Hosp., 1966-67; resident in anesthesiology Mass. Gen. Hosp., Boston, 1970-72, anesthesiologist-in-chief, 1994—; Reginald Jenney prof. anesthesiology Harvard Med. Sch., 1991—. Mem. Am. Heart Assn., Am. Phys. Soc., Am. Thoracic Soc., Am. Soc. Anesthesiologists, Am. Soc. for Artificial Internal Organs, Inst. Medicine. Office: Mass Gen Hosp 55 Fruit St Boston MA 02114*

ZAPP, DAVID EDWIN, infosystems specialist, investment consultant; b. Columbus, Ohio, Dec. 6, 1950; s. Robert Louis and Harriet (Miller) Z.; divorced; 1 child, Heather; m. Grace Lynn Spidell, Apr. 28, 1978. Road freight conductor N&W Ry., Columbus, 1971-77; with Franklin County Welfare, 1977-78; income tax preparer J.E. Wiggins Co., 1978-81; pub. inquiry asst. Ohio Bur. Workers Compensation, 1978-80, auditor, 1980-82, programmer, analyst, 1982-88, infosystems analyst, 1988-94; investment cons. Montano Securities Corp., 1994; ind. registered rep. Quest Capital Strategies, Inc., 1995—; software sys. cons. Optimum Techs., Inc., Worthington, Ohio, 1995—. Council mem. Southside Orgns., Columbus, 1985-86; mem. Gates Street Block Watch, Columbus, 1986. Mem. Nat. Assn. Investors Corp., Am. Assn. Individual Investors, Assn. Sys. Mgrs., Ohio Jaycees (program mgr. 1984-85, #1 individual devel. v.p. 1983-84, dist. dir. 1986—, named Outstanding Dist. Dir. 1986), Southside Columbus Jaycees (mgmt. v.p. 1984-85, pres. 1985-86, senator 1989), Employee Mgmt. Participation (chmn. 1985-86). Avocations: aviation, running, bicycling, personal computers. Home: 299 E Gates St Columbus OH 43206-3627 Office: Quest Capital Strategies Inc PO Box 77680 Columbus OH 43207-7680

ZAPP, JOHN S. retired medical association administrator; Exec. dir. ADA, 1993—2002.*

ZAPPALA, STEPHEN A. state supreme court justice; b. 1932; s. Frank and Josephine Zappala. BA, Duquesne U.; LL.B., Georgetown U., 1958. Bar: Pa. 1958. Solicitor Allegheny County, Pitts., 1974-76; judge Ct. of Common Pleas-Allegheny County, 1980-82; assoc. justice Pa. Supreme Ct., 1982—, judge. Served with U.S. Army. Office: Pa Supreme Ct 2802 Grant Bldg 6 Gateway Ctr Ste 616 Pittsburgh PA 15222*

ZAPPE, JOHN PAUL, city editor, educator, newspaper executive; b. N.Y.C., July 30, 1952; s. John Paul and Carolyn (Pikor) Z.; m. Siobhan Bradshaw, May 30, 1982. JD, Syracuse (N.Y.) U., 1978. Reporter Poughkeepsie Jour., 1973-75, Nev. State Jour., Reno, 1979-80; prin. Am. Media Bold, Oakland, Calif., 1981-83; reporter Press-Telegram, Long Beach, 1983-88, city editor, 1988-97, webmaster PT Connect, 1995-97, mgr. new media, 1997-98; dir. new media Riverside (Calif.) Press-Enterprise, 1998-2000; v.p. new media L.A. Newspaper Group, Woodland Hills, Calif., 2000—. Tchr. Syracuse U., 1976-78, Calif. State U., 1985-87; cons. Am. Media Bold, 1981-83. Chmn. Local 69 Newspaper Guild, Long Beach, 1984-87. Mem. Investigative Editors and Reporters, NAA New Media Fedn. Office: LA Daily News 21221 Oxnard St Los Angeles CA 91367 E-mail: JZappe@LangNews.com.

ZAPPIA, SISTER MARY ROQUETA, retired social services professional, volunteer; b. Clifton, Ariz., Sept. 25, 1915; d. Joseph Rocco and Guilia M. (Casetto) Z. RN, St. Mary's Sch. Nursing, Tucson, 1936; BSNE, San Francisco Coll. for Women, 1946; MSW, Ariz. State U., 1970. RN, Ariz.; joined Sisters of Mercy, Roman Cath. Ch., 1941. Supr. St. Mary's Hosp., San Francisco, 1941-46; social worker St. Mary's Hosp. Clinics, 1941-46; instr. sociology, social problems, supr. St. Joseph's Hosp., Phoenix, 1946-53; supr. St. Joseph's Hosp. Mercy Clinics, 1953-66, med. social worker., 1970-83; social worker, adminstr. St. John's Hosp. Nursing Home, Oxnard, Calif., 1966-68; field instr. social work Ariz. State U., Tempe, 1970—. Cons. Transient Aid Ctr., St. Vincent de Paul, Phoenix, 1983—; mem. Sisters of Mercy, Burlingame, Calif., 1941—. Mem. NASW, St. Vincent de Paul Soc. Democrat. Roman Catholic. Home: 525 W Earll Dr Apt 117 Phoenix AZ 85013-4324 Office: St Vincent de Paul Transien Aid Ctr 420 W Watkins St Phoenix AZ 85003-2830

ZAR, JERROLD H(OWARD), biologist, statistician; b. Chgo., June 28, 1941; s. Max and Sarah (Brody) Z.; m. Carol Bachenheimer, Jan. 15, 1967; children: David Michael, Adam Joseph BS, No. Ill. U., 1962; MS, U. Ill., Urbana, 1964, PhD, 1967. NSF fellow marine sci. Duke U. Marine Lab., Beaufort, N.C., 1965; research assoc. dept. zoology U. Ill., Urbana, 1967-68; asst. prof. dept. biol. scis. No. Ill. U., DeKalb, 1968-71, assoc. prof., 1971-78, prof., 1978—, chmn. dept. biol. scis., 1978-84, vice provost grad. studies and research, dean Grad. Sch., 1984—2002. Vis. scientist Argonne Nat. Lab., 1974; cons. EPA, also other govt. agys. and industries; founder, dir. ENCAP, Inc., 1974-93. Author: Biostatistical Analysis, 1974, 4th edit., 1999. NIH fellow U. Ill. Urbana, 1965-67. Fellow AAAS; mem. Am. Inst. Biol. Scis., Am. Ornithologists Union, Am. Physiol. Soc., Am. Statis. Assn., Biometric Soc., Cooper Ornithol. Soc., Am. Soc. Zoologists, Ecol. Soc. Am., Nat. Assn. Biol. Tchrs., Wilson Ornithol. Soc. Office: No Ill U Dept Biol Scis Dekalb IL 60115 E-mail: jhzar@niu.edu.

ZARAGOZA, LAWRENCE JAY, government manager; b. Santa Maria, Calif., Mar. 4, 1952; s. Julio and Helan Zaragoza; m. Karen Lynn Feldmann, Nov. 9, 1996. BA in Biology, UCLA, 1975; MA, Calif. State U., Long Beach, 1977; D of Environ. Sci. and Engring., UCLA, 1982. Environ. health scientist Office of Air Quality Planning and Standards/EPA, Research Triangle Park, N.C., 1979-86; environ. protection specialist Office of Solid Waster and Emergency Response/EPA, Washington, 1986-89, Office of Emergency and Remedial Response/EPA, Washington, 1989-99, dir. REgions 5/7 Accelerated Response Ctr., 1999—. Co-chair tech. rev. workgroup for lead/EPA, 1997-99. Author articles. Chair archtl. rev. com. Wessynton Homes Assn., Alexandria, Va., 1998-99; v.p. Arlington County Civic Fedn., 1994; chair Air Quality Pub.

Adv. Com., Washington, 1998, 99; pres. Colonial Villages Cmty. Svcs. Assn., Arlington, 1992-95. Recipient Environ. award Arlington County Bd., 1992. Mem. AAAS. Avocations: bicycling, kayak paddling. Office: US EPA 5204 G 1200 Pennsylvania Ave NW Washington DC 20460-0001 Fax: (703) 603-9133. E-mail: Zaragoza.Larry@EPA.Gov.

ZARATE, LENORE BEATRICE, non-profit administrator; b. N.Y.C., Sept. 21, 1937; d. Saul and Ida Sarah (Friedman) Trushin; m. Alvan O'Neil Zarate, Aug. 31, 1958 (div. Aug. 1971); children: Steven A., Jeffrey T., Jason R. BS with distinction, U. Conn., 1958; postgrad., U. Tex., 1965-66; MA, Cen. Mich. U., Mt. Pleasant, 1981. Adminstrv. asst. U. Conn., Storrs, 1959-60; research asst. U. R.I., Kingston, 1960-61, U. Tex., Austin, 1965-66, 66-67, Dept. of Mental Health and Mental Retardation, Austin, 1966; adminstrv. asst. Am. Social Health Assn., Columbus, Ohio, 1971-75, dir. midwest region, 1976-82, dir. no. region, 1982-87, dir. so. region, 1987, dir. United Way activities, 1988-89; exec. dir. Actors' Summer Theatre Co., 1989—. Author curriculum guide VD: Getting the Right Answers, 1976. Steering com. Venereal Disease Action Coalition, Detroit, 1978—; bd. dirs. Columbus VD Hotline, 1976-86. Mem. Am. Pub. Health Assn., Am. Venereal Disease Assn., Nat. Soc. Fund Raising Execs. Democrat. Jewish. Avocations: tennis, bridge, photography. Office: Actors Summer Theatre Co 1000 City Park Ave Columbus OH 43206-2515

ZARBIN, MARCO ATTILIO, ophthalmologist, surgeon, educator; b. Milan, Nov. 20, 1956; came to the U.S., 1958; s. Gino Franco and Adriana Virginia (Corasaniti) Z. BA summa cum laude, Dartmouth Coll., 1978; MD, PhD, Johns Hopkins U., 1984. Diplomate Am. Bd. Ophthalmology. Resident Johns Hopkins Hosp., Balt., 1985-88, fellow vitreoretinal surgery, 1988-89, chief resident opthalmology, 1989, fellow retinal vascular disease, 1990; asst. prof. ophthalmology U. Calif., San Francisco, 1990-93; chair dept. ophthalmology N.J. Med. Sch., Newark, 1994—, prof., 1998—. Mem. sci. adv. bd. Found. Fighting Blindness, Hunt Valley, Md., 1995—. Mem. editl. bd. Investigative Ophthalmology and Visual Sci., Survey of Ophthalmology. Fellow Am. Acad. Ophthalmology (Honor award 1995), Retina Soc. (exec. com. 1998), Macula Soc.; mem. Assn. for Rsch. in Vision and Ophthalmology, Assn. U. Prof. Ophthalmology (bd. dirs. 2000—), Phi Beta Kappa, Alpha Omega Alpha. Avocations: ancient history, opera. Office: NJ Med Sch Dept Ophthalmology 90 Bergen St Newark NJ 07103-2425

ZARCONE, MICHAEL JOSEPH, experimental physicist, consultant; b. Danbury, Conn., Dec. 10, 1950; s. Michael Joseph Zarcone and Mary Elizabeth Belardinelli; children from previous marriage: Cassandra Marie, Sally Marie, Michael Joseph, Christopher Michael. BS in Physics, Fairfield U., 1973; MS in Physics, N.Mex. Inst. Mining and Tech., 1984; PhD in Physics, U. Conn., 1989. Rsch. asst. Radon Lab., Socorro, N.Mex., 1983-84, Vande-Graaff Accelerator Lab., Storrs, Conn., 1985-89; physics instr. Cen. Conn. State U., New Britain, 1989-90; accelerator tech. fellow Brookhaven Nat. Lab., Upton, N.Y., 1990-91, asst. physicist, 1991-93, physics assoc. II, 1993-98, physics assoc. I, 1998—, coord. environ. safety/health, rsch./devel., foil prodn. tng. coord., 1994-99; dir. prodn., cons. Separations divsn. Corning Inc., 1994-99, Whatman Nuclepore, 1999—. Cons. Corning Contbr. articles to profl. jours. including Phys. Rev. A, Nuclear Instruments and Methods in Phys. Rsch., Physics Rev. Letters, Atmospheric Environment, Semiconductor Internat. Mem. Internat. Nuc. Target Devel. Soc., Am. Phys. Soc., Sigma Xi. Avocations: mountain climbing, hiking. Home: 17 Jones St East Setauket NY 11733-2935 Office: Brookhaven Nat Lab Bldg 510A Upton NY 11973

ZARDINI, ELSA MATILDE, botanist, educator; b. La Plata, Buenos Aires, Argentina, June 9, 1949; d. Raul Alberto and Elsa Taccaliti Zardini; m. Alwyn Howard Gentry, Oct. 24, 1984 (dec. Aug. 4, 1993); children: Maria Liana Gentry. MS, Nat. U. La Plata, La Plata, Argentina, 1973; PhD, Nationa U. La Plata, La Plata, Argentina, 1974. Asst. prof. U. Buenos Aires, Buenos Aires, Argentina, 1975—76; prof. U. La Plata, La Plata, Argentina, 1978—84, botany chmn. Argentina, 1982—84; rsch. assoc. Mo. Bot. Garden, St Louis, Mo., 1984—84, asst. curator, 1985—91, assoc. curator, 1991—2002, curator, 2002—. Contbr. articles to profl. jour. Grantee Nat. Geog. Soc. Grantee, Nat. Geog. Soc., 1988-2002. Roman Apostolic Catholic. Achievements include first to created and developed a school of botany in Paraguay. Home: Veteranos Guerra del Chaco 415 Asuncion Paraguay Office: Missouri Botanical Garden PO Box 299 Saint Louis MO 63166 E-mail: elsa.zardini@mobot.org.

ZARE, RICHARD NEIL, chemistry educator; b. Cleve., Nov. 19, 1939; s. Milton and Dorothy (Amdure) Zare; m. Susan Leigh Shively, Apr. 20, 1963; children: Bethany Jean, Bonnie Sue, Rachel Amdur. BA, Harvard, 1961; postgrad., U. Calif., Berkeley, 1961—63; PhD (NSF predoctoral fellow), Harvard, 1964; DS (hon.) , U. Ariz., 1990; DS (hon.) , Northwestern U., 1993; DS (hon.) , ETH, Zürich, 1993, Columbia U., 2000, State U. West Ga., 2001; DP (hon.) , Uppsala (Sweden) U., 2000; PhD U. York (hon.) , 2001. Postdoctoral fellow Harvard, 1964; research assoc. Joint Inst. for Lab. Astrophysics, 1964—65; asst. prof. chemistry MIT, 1965—66; asst. prof. dept. physics and astrophysics U. Colo., 1966—68, assoc. prof. physics and astrophysics, assoc. prof. chemistry, 1968—69; prof. chemistry Columbia, 1969—77, Higgins prof. natural sci., 1975—77; prof. Stanford U., 1977—, Shell Disting. prof. chemistry, 1980—85, Marguerite Blake Wilbur prof. natural sci., 1987—, prof. physics, 1992—. Cons.. Aaeronomy Lab, NOAA, 1966—77; radio standards physics divsn. Nat. Bur. Stds., 1968—77, Lawrence Livermore Lab., U. Calif., 1974—, SRI, Internat., 1974—, Los Alamos Sci. Lab., U. Calif., 1975—; fellow adjoint Joint Inst. Lab. Astrophysics, U. Colo.; sci. adv. com. IBM, 1977—92; chmn. commn. on phys. scis., math. and applications Nat. Rsch. Coun., 1992—95; chmn. bd. dirs. Annual Revs., Inc., 1995—. Contbr. articles to profl. jours.; editor: Chem. Physics Letters, 1982—85. Named Calif. Scientist of Yr., 1997; recipient Fresenius award, Phi Lambda Upsilon, 1974, Michael Polanyi medal, 1979, Nat. Medal Sci., 1983, Spectroscopy Soc. Pitts. award, 1983, Michelson-Morley award, Case Inst. Tech. Case We. Res. U., 1986, ISCO award for significant contbns. to instrumentation for biochem. separations, 1990, Ea. Analytical Symposium award, 1997, Exceptional Sci. Achievement award, NASA, 1997, Space award Aviation Week and Space Tech., 1997, Disting. Svc. award, Nat. Sci. Bd., 1998, Centennial medal, Harvard U., The Welch award, 1999, Faraday medal, Royal Soc. Chemistry, 2001, Bing Fellowship Tchg. award, 1996; fellow Nonresident fellow, Joint Inst. for Lab. Astrophysics, 1970—, Alfred P. Sloan fellow, 1967—69, Christensen fellow, St. Catherine's Coll./Oxford U., 1982, Stanford U., 1984—86. Fellow: AAAS, Inst. of Physics, Royal Soc. Chemistry (hon.), Calif. Acad. Scis. (hon.); mem.: NAS (coun. mem., Chem. Scis. award 1991), Royal Soc. London, Chem. Soc. London, Am. Philos. Soc., Am. Chem. Soc. (Harrison Howe award 1985, Remsen award 1985, Kirkwood award 1986, Willard Gibbs medal 1990, Peter Debye award in phys. chemistry 1991, Linus Pauling medal 1993, The Harvey prize 1993, Dannie-Heineman prize 1993, Analytical Chemistry Divsn. award in chem. instrumentation 1995, Analytical Chemistry award 1998, G.M. Kosalapoff award 1998, E. Bright Wilson award in spectroscopy 1999, Charles Lathrop Parsons award 2001, Madison Marshall award 2001, Nobel Laureate Signature award 2000), Am. Phys. Soc. (Earle K. Plyler prize 1981, Irving Langmuir prize 1985, Arthur L. Scharlow prize in laser sci. 2000), Am. Acad. Arts and Scis., Phi Beta Delta, Phi Beta Kappa. Achievements include research in laser chemistry and chem. physics. Office: Stanford U Dept Chemistry Stanford CA 94305-5080

ZAREM, ABE MORDECAI, management consulting executive; b. Chgo., Mar. 7, 1917; s. I.H. and Lea (Kaufman) Z.; m. Esther Mariam Moskovitz, Oct. 4, 1941; children: Janet Ruth, David Michael, Mark Charles. BS in Elec. Engring, Ill. Inst. Tech., 1939, LL.D. (hon.), 1968; MS in Elec. Engring, Calif. Inst. Tech., 1940, PhD, 1944; LL.D., U. Calif. at Santa Cruz, 1967. Design engr. very high voltage power transmission system Allis Chalmers Rsch. div., 1944; group leader Ultra Micro Time Program Manhattan Dist. Project/CalTech, 1944—45; initiator, group mgr. Microtime & Electro Optical Phys. Rsch., U.S. Naval Test Sta., 1945-48; assoc. dir., mgr. L.A. div. Stanford Rsch. Inst., 1948-56; mem. faculty UCLA, 1956-61; founder, chmn., pres. Electro-Optical Systems, Inc., Pasadena, Calif., 1956-67; v.p. Xerox Corp., L.A., 1963-67, sr. v.p., dir. corp. devel., bd. dirs., 1967-69; mgmt. and engring. cons., 1969-79; founder, chmn. Xerox Devel. Corp., L.A., 1975-80; chmn. strategic bus. planning, techno-econ. and venture capital, pres., owner Abe M. Zarem & Co., 1981—; founder, mng. dir., Frontier Assoc., 1980—. Mem. adv. com. competitive tech. program State of Calif., 1989; mem. Calif. Coun. Sci. and Tech., chmn. advanced sci. & tech. programs com., 1989-97, disting. fellow 1997—; cons., disting. vis. exec. in sci. and tech., sr. advisor on tech. transfer and commercialization and strategic planning studies Jet Propulsion Lab./Calif. Inst. of Tech., 1997—; cons., advisor, chair of sr. adv. bd. UCLA Brain Rsch. Inst., 1997—; mem. adv. bd. dept. urology UCLA, 1994—. Author: Utilization of Solar Energy, 1963. Traffic and parking commr. City of Beverly Hills, 1971-72, planning commr., 1972-73; Bd. dirs. Music Center Opera Assn., Los Angeles, 1968— ; nat. trustee City of Hope; trustee Calif. Inst. Arts, 1973-76. Named Outstanding Young Elec. Engr. in U.S. Eta Kappa Nu, 1948; One of America's Ten Outstanding Young Men U.S. Jr. C. of C., 1950; recipient Albert F. Sperry medal Instrument Soc. Am., 1969 Fellow AIAA, IEEE; sci. mem. (a founder) Solar Energy Soc.; mem. Nat. Acad. Engring. Achievements include inventing World's fastest high-speed camera, automatic oscillograph. Home: 9640 Lomitas Ave Beverly Hills CA 90210-3333 *I have always had a Vision, Mission & Series of Strategic Objectives - The principal one having been instilled by loving parents & family who encouraged me. I was born to identify talent and to challenge it to do more than it would have done if it had not met me. I am mentor and tormentor. I build and stretch people.*

ZAREMBA, LESZEK SATURNIN, mathematics educator; b. Warsaw, Poland, Oct. 16, 1948; s. Jozef and Marianna Zaremba; m. Halina Teresa Galka, Apr. 25, 1981; children: Cezary, Adrian. MSc in Math., Warsaw U., 1972; PhD in Math., Wroclaw (Poland) U., 1978; PhD, Lodz (Poland) U., 1986. Rsch. asst. Polish Acad. Scis., Warsaw, 1972-73; instr. Wroclaw Tech. U., 1973-77; asst. prof. Czestochowa (Poland) Pedag. U., 1977-82; assoc. prof. U. Siedlce, Poland, 1982-86, full prof. math. Poland, 1991-95; exch. prof. Ea. Ill. U., Charleston, 1986-87; assoc. editor Am. Math. Soc., Ann Arbor, Mich., 1987-90; assoc. prof. Meml. U. Newfoundland, St. John's, 1990-91, Polish Acad. Scis., Warsaw, 1996—. Dean faculty of chemistry and math. U. Siedlce, 1993-95; dir. Ctr. for Quantitative Methods in Fin., Polish Open U., Warsaw. Mng. editor ULAM Quar., Breach, N.Y., 1991-98; contbr. articles on math. and fin. to profl. jours. Recipient award of 3rd degree Min. Edn., Warsaw, 1987. Mem. Am. Fin. Assn. Home: Karwinska 9A 02639 Warsaw Poland Office: Polish Acad Scis Newelska 6 01-447 Warsaw Poland also: Polish Open U Domaniewska 37a 02-672 Warsaw Poland Mailing: U Toledo Dept Math 2801 W Bancroft Toledo OH 43606 E-mail: leszek.zaremba@ibspan.waw.pl., lzaremba@kki.net.pl.

ZAREMSKI, MILES JAY, lawyer; b. Chgo., Aug. 16, 1948; s. Samuel and Ann (Levine) Z.; m. Elena Cinthia Resnik, July 19, 1970; children: Jason Lane, Lauren Devra. BS, U. Ill., 1970; JD, Case Western Res. U., 1973. Bar: Ill. 1973, U.S. Dist. Ct. (no. dist.) Ill. 1973, U.S. Ct. Appeals (7th cir.) 1973, U.S. Supreme Ct. 1977, U.S. Ct. Appeals (8th cir.) 1988, U.S. Dist. Ct. Nebr. 1996, U.S. Dist. Ct. (ea. dist.) Tenn. 1997, U.S. Ct. Appeals (6th cir.) 1998, Ind. 2000, Pa. 2000, U.S. Dist. Ct. (no. dist.) Ind. 2001. Spl. asst. state's atty. Lake County, Ill., 1980-82; ptnr. Kamensky & Rubinstein, Lincolnwood, Chgo., 2000—. Arbitrator, mandatory arbitration programs Cook and Lake Counties, Ill., 1990—; asst. prof. med. jurisprudence U. Health Scis./Chgo. Med. Sch., 1991—; adj. faculty U. Chgo. Law Sch., 1999—2001; adj. asst. prof. Case Western Res. Law Sch., 2001—. Editor: Medical and Hospital Negligence, 4 vols., 1988, supplement, 1993, 95-99; contbr. chpts. in books and articles to profl. jours.; author: Reengineering Healthcare Liability Litigation, 1997, supplement, 1999; patentee in field. Oversight com. law sch. Case Western Res. U., Cleve., 1985-99, alumni bd. dirs., 1996-99; mem. exec. com. law sch. ctr for health care Loyola U., Chgo., 1987-89; mem. lakefront commn. City of Highland Park, Ill., 1982-84; bd. dirs., officer Regional Organ Bank Ill., Chgo., 1986-91; bd. dirs. The Lambs, Libertyville, Ill., 1982-84, Jocelyn Ctr. for Mental Health, 1994-96; field play marshall U.S. Olympics Baseball, Atlanta, 1996. Named one of Outstanding Young Men in Am., U.S. Jaycees, 1979. Fellow: Am. Bar Found., Am. Coll. Legal Medicine (assoc. in law 1973—91, chair legal com. 1996—98, chair Amicus com. 1997—2000, editl. bd. Jour. Legal Medicine 1981—, bd. govs., sec. 1999—2000, treas. 2000—01, pres.-elect 2001—02, pres. 2002—); mem.: ABA (various coms. tort and ins. practice sect., vice chmn. 1979—90, chmn. med. and law com. 1984—85, editor-in-chief Forum 1979—81, spl. com. on med. profl. liability 1985, 1991—95, 1998—, chmn. 2000—, editl. bd. Forum on Health Law 1989—91), Ill. Assn. Healthcare Attys., Quality Mgmt. Health Care (editl. bd.), Am. Soc. Writers on Legal Subjects (scribes), Am. Health Law Assn. (vice chair hosp. liability com. 1999—), Am. Soc. Law and Medicine (editor-in-chief 1981—83, bd. editors 1983—86), Lake County Bar Assn., Ill. Bar Assn. (1st and 3d prizes 1978—79). Jewish. Avocations: baseball, soccer, coaching athletic teams. Office: Kamensky & Rubinstein 7250 N Cicero Ave Ste 200 Lincolnwood IL 60712 *"Success is a journey; not a destination." "A man may make many mistakes but he isn't a failure until he starts blaming someone else." John R. Wooden.*

ZARET, BARRY LEWIS, cardiologist, medical educator; b. N.Y.C., Oct. 3, 1940; s. Irving Z. and Beatrice (Fader) Zaret; m. Myrna Zimmerman, June 23, 1963; children: Adam L., Elliot C., Owen M. BS, Queens Coll., 1962; MD, NYU, 1966; MA, Yale U., 1982. Diplomate: Am. Bd. Internal Medicine. Intern Bellevue Hosp., N.Y.C., 1966-67, resident, 1967-79; research fellow John Hopkins U., Balt., 1969-71; asst. prof. medicine Yale U., New Haven, 1973-76, assoc. prof. medicine and diagnostic radiology, 1976, chief sect. cardiology, 1978—, assoc. prof. medicine and diagnostic radiology, 1980-82, prof. medicine and diagnostic radiology, 1982-84, Robert W. Berliner prof. medicine, 1984—, assoc. chair clin. affairs dept. internal medicine, 1994—; mem. staff Yale-New Haven Med. Ctr.; med. dir. Yale-New Haven Med. Hosp. Heart Ctr., 1999—. Mentor cardiovasc. subsplty. bd. Am Bd. Internal Medicine, 2002—. Mem. editorial bd. Am. Jour. Cardiology, 1977—, Jour. Am. Coll. Cardiology, 1986-91, 92-97, Jour. Cardiac Imaging, 1986—, Circulation, 1993; assoc. editor: Yearbook of Nuclear Medicine, 1980-95; editor-in-chief Jour. Nuclear Cardiology, 1993—; contbr. articles to profl. jours. Recipient Casimir Funk award Soc. Mil. Surgeons, 1973; recipient Herrman Blumgart Pioneer award New Eng. chpt. Soc. Nuclear Medicine, 1978, Solomon Berson Alumni Achievement award in clin. sci. NYU Sch. Medicine, 1998. Fellow Am. Coll. Cardiology, Coun. Clin. Cardiology, Am. Heart Assn., Coun. Circulation, Am. Heart Assn., Am. Physiology Soc.; mem. Am. Soc. Clin. Investigation, Am. Fedn. Clin. Rsch., Assn. Am. Physicians, Soc. Nuclear Medicine, Am. Soc. Nuclear Cardiology, Assn. Univ. Cardiologists, Assn. Profs. Cardiology (pres. 1992), Phi Beta Kappa, Alpha Omega Alpha, Interurban Clin. Club. Jewish. Home: 15 Cassway Rd Woodbridge CT 06525-1214 Office: 333 Cedar St # 3fmp New Haven CT 06510-3206 E-mail: barry.zaret@yale.edu.

ZARETTI, JOAN LUCY, music educator; b. Flushing, N.Y., Aug. 18, 1971; d. John Benvenuto and Susan Carol (Tosi) Z. BM, U. Mich., 1993; postgrad., Ind. U., 1996—. Cert. K-12 music tchr. Gen. & vocal music educator Traverse City (Mich.) Area Pub. Schs., 1993-96. Counselor Salvation Army, Canton, Mich., 1989; vol. Shelter Assn., Ann. Arbor, Mich., 1990, Safehouse Shelter for Domestic Violence, Ann Arbor, 1991, Habitat for Humanity, 1990; dir., asst. dir., recreation dir., counselor Interlochen (Mich.) Arts Camp, Interlochen Ctr. Arts, summers 1990-95; choir dir. Ch. of Savior, Livonia, Mich., 1992-93. Mem. Am. Choral Dirs. Assn., Music Educators Nat. Conf., Soc. for Ethnomusicology. Avocations: volleyball, dancing, guitar, reading. Office: Ind U Archives Traditional Music Mornson Hall 117 Bloomington IN 47405-2501

ZARETZKY, JEREMY, computer company executive; s. Joel and Linda Zaretzky. BS in Econs. summa cum laude, Duke U., 1997—2000. Creative svcs. mgr. Duke U. Chronicle, Durham, NC, 1997—2000; founder, pres. MacBrilliance Computer Tng., Boca Raton, Fla., 1996—2000; co-founder, pres. WireSpring Technologies, Inc., 2000—. Dir. WireSpring Technologies, Inc., Boca Raton, 2000. Scholar, JM Rubin Found., 1997. Mem.: Internet-Coast, Phi Beta Kappa. Jewish. Office: WireSpring Technologies Inc 8000 N Federal Hwy Ste 303 Boca Raton FL 33487

ZARICZNYJ, BASILIUS, orthopedic surgeon; b. Ukraine, Aug. 31, 1924; came to U.S., 1951; m. Stefania Pidburny, Aug. 21, 1954; children: Marta, Stephanie Christine, Andrea Maria, Mark B. MD, U. Bonn, Germany, 1951; MD (hon.), Odessa State Med. U., Ukraine, 1996. Diplomate Am. Bd. Orthopedic Surgery. Resident St. Luke's Hosp., Chgo., 1954-56, Univ. Hosps., Oklahoma City, 1955-56; fellow in orthopedics Northwestern U., Chgo., 1957; asst. prof. Sch. Medicine U. Okla., Oklahoma City, 1957-58; orthopedic surgeon Springfield, Ill., 1958—; clin. prof. Sch. Medicine So. Ill. U., 1973-85, acting chmn. divsn. orthopedic surgery, 1972-75, chief sports medicine sect., 1975-82, program chmn. sports injury symposium, 1977-79, 82, 83. Mem. sports medicine com. Ill. State Med. Soc., 1979-80; chmn. dept. orthopedic surgery St. John's and Meml. Hosps., Springfield, 1970-79; program chmn. Med. Congress of World Fedn. of Ukrainian Med. Assn., Dniepropetrovsk, 1994, Odessa, Ukraine, 1996; presenter Am. Acad. Orthopedic Surgeons, Miami, Fla., 1961, N.Y., 1969, San Francisco, 1971, Washington, 1972, Las Vegas, 1973, 77, Anaheim, Calif., 1983, Chgo. Orthopedic Soc., 1967, 76, O'Donoghue Okla. Orthopedic Alumni Assn., Oklahoma City, 1972, 75, 78, Internat. Soc. for Orthopedic Surgery and Traumatology, XII World Congress, Tel Aviv, 1972, Copenhagen, 1975, Kyoto, Japan, 1978, So. Ill U. Sch. Medicine, Springfield, 1977, 79, 80, 82, Ill. State Orthopedic Soc., Chgo., 1978, ACS, Chgo., 1979, Am. Orthopedic Soc. for Sports Medicine, Atlanta, 1980, Big Sky, Mont., 1980, Lake Tahoe, Nev., 1981, Clin. Orthopedic Soc., Chgo., 1987, World Fedn. Ukrainian Med. Assn., Kiev, Ukraine, 1990, U. Lviv, Ukraine, 1990, 11th Congress of Orthopedic Surgeons of Ukraine, Kharkiv, 1991, Congress of World Fedn. of Ukrainian Med. Assn., Kharkiv, 1992, Dnipropetrovsk, 1994, Odessa, 1996, Ukraine, among others. Mem. editl. bd. Jour. Ukranian Med. Assn. N.Am., 1977-95; contbr. articles to profl. jours. and med. textbooks. Fellow Am. Acad. Orthopedic Surgery; mem. AMA, Ill. Orthopedic Soc., Internat. Soc. Orthopedic Surgery and Traumatology, Am. Orthopedic Soc. for Sports Medicine, Internat. Soc. of the Knee, Mid-Am. Orthopedic Assn., Ukrainian Acad. and Profl. Assn. Pres. 1985-89), Sangamon County Med. Soc., Chgo. Orthopedic Soc. Avocations: golfing, walking, chess. Home and Office: 125 Oakmont Dr Springfield IL 62704-3118

ZARIN, JERALD LAWRENCE, pediatrician, physician executive; b. N.Y.C., Feb. 21, 1942; s. Emanuel B. and Esther Zarin; m. Aileen Carole Singer; children: Jason, Randall, Marni. BS, Rensselaer Poly. Inst., 1962; MD, Albert Einstein Coll. Medicine, 1966; MBA, Houston Bapt. U., 1988. Diplomate Am. Bd. Pediatrics, Nat. Bd. Med. Examiners. Intern in pediatrics U. Hosps. Cleve., 1966-67, resident in pediatrics, 1967-69; pvt. practice Houston, 1971-97; pres. Inwood Pediatric Assocs., 1978-96; med. dir. Tex. Children's Health Plan, 1996—. Asst. clin. prof. pediatrics Baylor Coll. Medicine, Houston, 1976—. Maj. USAF, 1969-71. Fellow Am. Acad. Pediatrics; mem. AMA, ACP Execs., Tex. Med. Assn., Tex. Pediatric Soc., Houston Pediatric Soc., Exec. Com. Am. Acad. Pediat. Sec. Adminstrn. Practice Mgmt. Home: 12330 Boheme Dr Houston TX 77024-4902 Office: Tex Childrens Health Plan PO Box 301011 1919 S Braeswood Blvd Houston TX 77230-4412

ZARINS, BERTRAM, orthopaedic surgeon; b. Latvia, June 22, 1942; came to U.S., 1946, naturalized, 1956; s. Richard Arthur and Maria (Rozenbergs) Z. AB in Chemistry, Lafayette Coll., 1963; MD, SUNY, Syracuse, 1967. Diplomate Am. Bd. Orthop. Surgery. Clin. instr. orthop. surgery Harvard Med. Sch., Boston, 1976—, asst. clin. prof., 1982—; orthop. surgeon Mass. Gen. Hosp., 1982-95; assoc. clin. prof. Harvard Med. Sch., 1996—; chief sports medicine svc. Mass. Gen. Hosp., 1982—; team physician Boston Bruins Hockey Team, 1976—. Chmn. edn. com. Sports Medicine Coun., U.S. Olympic Com., 1980-92; team physician New England Patriots football team, 1982— ; head physician USA Olympic teams XIV Winter Olympic Games, Sarajevo, Yugoslavia, 1984. Contbr. articles to profl. jours. Team physician N.E. Revolution profl. soccer team, 1996—. Lt. comdr. M.C., USNR, 1973-75. Fellow ACS, Am. Acad. Orthop. Surgeons (chmn. com. on sports medicine 1993-97), Am. Coll. Sports Medicine; mem. AMA, Internat. Arthroscopy Assn. (bd. dirs. 1991-95), Arthroscopy Assn. N.Am., N.Am. Trauma Assn. (pres. 1977), Internat. Soc. of Arthroscopy, Knee Surgery and Orthopaedic Sports Medicine, Am. Shoulder and Elbow Surgeons, Herodicus Soc., Brookline (Mass.) Country Club, Somerset Club. Office: Mass Gen Hosp Ambulatory Care Ctr Ste 514 Boston MA 02114 E-mail: bzarins@partners.org.

ZARINS, CHRISTOPHER KRISTAPS, surgery educator, vascular surgeon; b. Tukums, Latvia, Dec. 2, 1943; came to U.S., 1946; s. Richard A. and Maria (Rozenbergs) Z.; m. Zinta Zarins, July 8, 1967; children: Daina, Sascha, Karina. BA, Lehigh U., 1964; MD, Johns Hopkins U., 1968. Surgery residency U. Mich., Ann Arbor, 1968-74; asst. prof. surgery U. Chgo., 1976-79, assoc. prof. surgery, 1979-82, prof. surgery, 1983-93, chief of vascular surgery, 1978-93; prof. surgery, chmn. divsn. vascular surgery Stanford (Calif.) U., 1993—, acting chmn. dept. of surgery, 1995-97. Author: Essays In Surgery, 1986, Atlas of Vascular Surgery, 1988; editor Jour. of Surg. Rsch., 1982-95; contbr. articles to profl. jours. Pres. Latvian Med. Found., Boston, 1991. Lt. comdr. USN, 1974-76. Grantee NIH, NSF. Mem. Am. Surg. Soc., Soc. for Clin. Surgery, Soc. for Vascular Surgery (pres. 1998-99), Internat. Soc. for Cardiovascular Surgery, Soc. of Univ. Surgeons, Latvian Nat. Acad. of Scis., Latvian Vascular Surg. Soc. (pres. 1989), Soc. for Vascular Surgery (pres. 1998-99). Avocations: triathlons, skiing. Office: Stanford U Med Ctr Divsn Vascular Surgery 300 Pasteur Dr # H3630 Palo Alto CA 94304-2203

ZARLEY, KARLTA RAE, nurse consultant; b. Des Moines, Apr. 9, 1957; d. Robert Kent and Joyce Eva (Zeman) Z.; m. Keith D. Kastella, 1986; children: Keilor, Kahli. ADN, Rochester Community Coll., 1981; BS, Iowa State U., 1980. RN, Mich., Minn., Iowa. Staff nurse labor and delivery Mary Greeley Med. Ctr., 1981-82; office nurse pvt. neurology and psychology Anchorage, 1982-83; staff nurse postpartum unit, Ambulatory Ob-Gyn. Clinic and antepartum unit U. Hosp., Stony Brook, N.Y., 1983-87; ambulatory ob-gyn. staff nurse Hennepin County Med. Ctr., Mpls., 1988-98; healthcare cons., 1998—. Writer policy and procedures and client edn. materials for high risk OB care, 1988—98; writer, leader health and wellness retreats and workshops, 2001—. Mem.: Healing Touch Internat., Am. Holistic Nurses Assn., Neonatal Nurses (cert. inpatient obstet. 1987—94, cert. high risk obstet. 1993—), Assn. Women's Health, Obstet., Spiritual Dirs. Internat. Office: PO Box 107 Dexter MI 48130 E-mail: kzarley@worldnet.att.net.

ZARNICH, ROBERT E. research scientist; b. Aliquippa, Pa., Apr. 15, 1963; s. Elizabeth Zarnich; m. Elaine B. Burk; children: Hannah, Genevieve. BSEE, Gannon U., 1985; MSEE, George Mason U., 1994, PhD, 2000. Signal processor engr. NAVSEA, PMS412, Std. Signal Processing Office, Arlington , Va., 1985—89; signal processor R&D lead engr. NAVSEA, PMS428, Std. Signal Processing Office, Arlington, 1989—93; common processing and studies project officer PEO(USW) Advanced Sys. and Tech. Office, 1993—96, passive processing project officer Arlington , 1996—2000; undersea warfare chief scientist NAVSEA 93/ASTO, Washington, 2000—. Office: Naval Sea Sys Command SEA93/ASTO-J 614 Sicard St Washington DC 20376-7017

ZARNOWITZ, VICTOR, economist, educator; b. Lancut, Poland, Nov. 3, 1919; came to U.S., 1952, naturalized, 1957; s. Leopold and Bertha (Blumenfeld) Z.; m. Lena Engelman, Jan. 12, 1946; children: Steven L., Arthur H. Student, U. Cracow, Poland, 1937-39; MA in Econs, U. Heidelberg, Germany, 1949, PhD summa cum laude, 1951. Tutor, instr. econs. U. Heidelberg, also Grad. Sch. Bus., Mannheim, Germany, 1949-51; analyst Nat. Bur. Econ. Research, 1952-59, mem. sr. research staff, 1963-78, research assoc., 1979—; lectr., then vis. prof. Columbia, 1956-59; mem. faculty Grad. Sch. Bus., U. Chgo., 1959—, prof. econs. and fin., 1965-90, prof. emeritus, 1990—. Dir. study of bus. cycle indicators, cons. Bur. Econ. Analysis, U.S. Dept. Commerce, 1972-93; rsch. assoc. Ctr. for Internat. Bus. Cycle Rsch., Columbia U., 1979—, co-dir. rsch., 1994-95; dir. rsch. Found. Internat. Bus. and Econ. Rsch., 1995-2000; sr. fellow and econ. counselor The Conf. Bd., 2000—. Author: Unfilled Orders, Price Changes and Business Fluctuations, 1962, An Appraisal of Short Term Economic Forecasts, 1967, The Business Cycle Today, 1972, Orders, Production and Investment, 1973, (with C. Boschan) Cyclical Indicators: An Evaluation and New Leading Indexes, 1975, An Analysis of Forecasts of Aggregate Income, Output, and the Price Level, 1979, Business Cycles and Growth, 1981, (with G.H. Moore) Sequential Signs of Recession and Recovery, 1982, On Functions, Quality, and Timeliness of Economic Information, 1982, The Accuracy of Individual and Group Forecasts from Business Outlook Surveys, 1984, Recent Work on Business Cycles in Historical Perspective, 1985, Rational Expectations and Macroeconomic Forecasts, 1985, (with G.H. Moore) Major Changes in Cyclical Behavior, 1986, (with L.A. Lambros) Consensus and Uncertainty in Economic Prediction; Business Cycles: Theory, History, Indicators and Forecasting, 1992, What is a Business Cycle?, 1992, Has Macro-Forecasting Failed?, 1993, (with Phillip Braun) Twenty Two Years of the NBER- ASA Quarterly Economic Outlook Surveys, 1993, Cyclical Indicators and National Accounts, 1998, (with Alan. L. Montgomery and George Tiao) Forecasting the U.S. Unemployment Rate, 1998, Has the Business Cycle Been Abolished?, 1998, Theory and History Behind Business Cycles: Are the 1990s the Onset of a Golden Age?, 1999, The Old and the New in the U.S. Economic Expansion, 2000; co-author: A More Timely and Useful Index of Leading Indicators, 2001, Time Series Decomposition and Measurement of Business Cycles, Trends and Growth Cycles, 2002; co-author, editor: The Business Cycle Today, 1972; contbr. to books. Fellow Nat. Assn. Bus. Economists, Am. Statis. Assn.; mem. Am. Econ. Assn., Ciret (hon.). Home: 333 E 56th St New York NY 10022

ZARNOWSKI, C(HESTER) FRANK, economics educator; b. York, Pa., Apr. 14, 1943; s. Chester Francis and Getrude (Krout) Z. BS in Econs., Mt. St. Mary's, 1965; MS in Econs., Lehigh U., 1967, ArtsD in Econs., 1978. Prof. econs. Mt. St. Mary's Coll., Emmitsburg, Md., 1967—, dean grad. program bus., 1981-88; prof. econs. The Johns Hopkins U., Balt., 1986; vis. scholar, prof. Dartmouth Coll., 2001—02. Exec. dir. DECA, The Decathlon Assn., Emmitsburg, 1975—; bd. trustees Hagerstown (Md.) Bus. Coll., 1986—; cons. Seoul (Republic of Korea) Olympic Games, NBC, N.Y.C., 1988. Author: The Decathlon, 1989 (ATFS award 1989). Edn. dir. Frederick (Md.) C. of C., 1985-87, Econ. and Community Devel. Com., Frederick, 1984-88; nat. coach The Athletics Congress/USA, Indpls., 1989; pub. address announcer Spl. Olympics Internat., Washington, 1983—, Olympic Games, L.A., 1984. Fellow GE Found., Chgo., 1971, Carnegie Found., Pitts., 1975-77; recipient Gov.'s Citation, Gov. of Md., 1988, 92. Mem. Am. Econs. Assn., Eastern Econ. Assn., Atlantic Econ. Soc. Avocations: Decathlon, running. Home: 58 2nd Ave Emmitsburg MD 21727-9169

ZARNOWSKI, MARJORIE ELIZABETH, music educator; b. Goessel, Kans., Dec. 15, 1925; d. Edward and Elizabeth (Regier) Unruh; m. Clarence Edmund Zarnowski, Sept. 2, 1945; children: Catherine Ann, Joyce Marie, Marian Sue, Roger Edward, Loretta Jane, Susan Paule. BA in Fine Arts, Music Edn., Wichita State U., 1984. Music tchr. self employed, 1964—. Charter mem. Bd. Dirs. Disability Supports of the Great Plains, Inc., McPherson, 1996—. Mem. Harvey County Transition Coun., 1984-92, Kans. State Transition Coun., 1991-95. Mem. MTNA, AARP, Common Cause, Am. Coll. Musicians.

ZARO, BRAD A. research company executive, biologist; b. San Jose, Calif., Dec. 4, 1949; s. Raymond J. and Irene R. Z.; children: Amy C., Kristen E. BA in Zoology, San Jose State U., 1974, MA in Biology, 1981. Chemist, Dept. Drug Metabolism Syntex Rsch., Inc., Palo Alto, Calif., 1976-78, chemist II, Dept. Drug Metabolism, 1978-81, chemist III, Dept. Drug Metabolism, 1981-84, clin. rsch. assoc. I, Inst. of Clin. Medicine, 1984-85, clin. rsch. assoc. II, Inst. of Clin. Medicine, 1985-87, sen. clin. rsch. assoc., Inst. of Clin. Medicine, 1985-87; sen. clin. rsch. assoc. Triton Biosciences, Inc., Alameda, 1988, mgr. clin. trials, 1988; pres., CEO Clinimetrics Rsch. Assoc., Inc., San Jose, 1988—. Contbr. articles to scholarly jours. Mem. AAAS, Am. Coll. Clin. Pharmacology, Am. Soc. Pharmacognosy, Assn. Clin. Rsch. Profls., Drug Info. Assn. Democrat. Roman Catholic. Avocations: scuba diving, skiing, flying airplanes. Office: Clinimetrics Rsch Assocs 5285 Hellyer Ave San Jose CA 95138

ZARR, MELVYN, lawyer, law educator; b. Worcester, Mass., Aug. 29, 1936; m. Gail Sclar, Aug. 29, 1971. AB, Clark U., 1958; LL.B., Harvard U., 1963. Bar: Mass. bar 1964, Maine bar 1973. Staff atty. NAACP Legal Def. & Edn. Fund, Inc., N.Y.C., 1963-69; co-dir. Mass. Law Reform Inst., Boston, 1970-73; prof. law U. Maine, 1973—; U.S. magistrate, Portland, Maine, 1977-82. Mem. Am. Law Inst. Home: 19 Mckinley Rd Falmouth ME 04105-1913 Office: U Maine Sch Law 246 Deering Ave Portland ME 04102-2837 Business E-Mail: mzarr@usm.maine.edu.

ZARRA, ERNEST JOSEPH, III, educator, researcher; b. Montclair, N.J., Dec. 14, 1955; s. Ernest Joseph Jr. and Faith Zarra; m. Susan Sembrat, May 29, 1976; children: Elya Joelle, Jonathan Joseph. BA, Northeastern Bible Coll., 1978; MA, Simon Greenleaf U., 1981; MABS, Grace Grad. Sch., Long Beach, Calif., 1986; MEd, Calif. State U., Bakersfield, 1988; PhD, U. So. Calif., 1999. Cert. tchr., N.J., Calif. Pvt. sch. tchr., 1978-89; pastor Millington Bapt. Ch., Basking Ridge, N.J., 1994-95; tchr., GATE coord. Fruitvale Sch. Dist. Pub. Sch., Bakersfield, Calif., 1989-94, 95-00; tchr. govt. and econs. Centennial H.S., 2000—, girls varsity soccer coach, 2000—. Adj. faculty Calif. State U., Bakersfield, 1998—, Pt. Loma Nazarene U.; lectr. U. Pa., Bakersfield Coll., Fresno Pacific U., U. San Diego, others; presenter in field. Author: It Should Never Happen Here, 1997; contbr. articles to profl. jours. Youth coach Am. Youth Soccer Orgn., Kern County, Calif., 1993—; youth and adults tchr. Laurelglen Bible Ch., Bakersfield, 1984—; presenter to law enforcement officers Kern County Sheriffs Dept., 1988. Named All-Am. Soccer Player Nat. Christian Coll. Athletic Assn., 1978, All-State, All Dist., All Conf.; drafted Dallas Tornado (NASL), 1978. Mem. ASCD, Am. Ednl. Rsch. Assn., Evang. Theol. Soc., Link Inst., Kappa Delta Pi (Character Edn. Partnership). Republican. Mennonite Brethren. Avocations: athletics, writing, travel, ministry, debate. Home: 400 Sinaloa Ave Bakersfield CA 93312-9334

ZARRILLO, MARK JOSEPH, landscape architect, planner; b. Elizabeth, N.J., Nov. 30, 1948; s. Marco Basil and Margaret Rose (Venturo) Z.; m. Cheryl Papio, Nov. 14, 1970; children: Taryn M., Adriana L. BS in Landscape Arch., Rutgers U., 1970; MS in Landscape Arch., Harvard U., 1974. Registered landscape arch., Mass., N.Y., N.J., W.Va., Calif., Maine, Minn., Fla.; cert. planner Am. Inst. Cert. Planners. V.p., dir. landscape arch. and planning The Archs. Collaborative, Inc., Cambridge, Mass., 1973-95; prin. Symmes Maini & McKee Assoc., 1996—. Contbr. articles to profl. jours.; prin. works include Jubail Indsl. City Cmty. Plan, Kingdom of Saudi Arabia, 1977, R4 Permanent Housing, Saudi Arabia, 1979, Kuwait Inst. for Sci. Rsch., 1980, Kulafa Street Streetscape Beautifications, Baghdad, Iraq, 1982, Sharp Electronics, Mawah, N.J., 1984, New Eng. Telephone Hdqrs., Burlington, Vt., 1986, Fla. State Acad. Ctr., Tallahassee, 1990, Regional Postal Sorting Facility, Shrewsbury, Mass., 1991, Internat. Ctr. for Advanced Med. Care, Clydebank, Scotland, 1995, among others. Bd. dirs. Planning Bd., Brookline, Mass., 1995—. Recipient Planning Merit award Boston Soc. Landscape Archs., 1999, Design award Fla. chpt. Am. Soc. Landscape Archs., 1987. Fellow Am. Soc. Landscape Archs., Boston Soc. Landscape Archs.; m. Am. Inst. Cert. Planners, Am. Planning Assn., Brookline Greenspace Alliance, Soc. Coll. Univ. Planners. Avocations: bicycling, golf, baseball, fastpitch softball. Home: 3 Copley St Brookline MA 02446 Office: Symmes Maimi McKee Assocs 1000 Massachusetts Ave Cambridge MA 02138 E-mail: m_zarrillo@smma.com.

ZARRO, JANICE ANNE, lawyer; b. Newark, June 30, 1947; BA, Rutgers U., 1969; JD, IIT-Chgo.-Kent Coll. Law, 1973. Bar: Pa. 1974. Counsel jud. com. U.S. Ho. Reps., Washington, 1973-77; profl. staff mem. counsel labor and human resources com. U.S. Senate, 1977-80; dir. Avon Products, Inc., N.Y.C., 1980-81, Washington, 1982-86, v.p., 1986-90; pres. The Novus Group, Inc., 1990-92; dir. fed. affairs Mallinckrodt Med., 1992—, v.p., 1993-94; v.p. govt. affairs Worldwide Mallinckrodt Inc., 1994-2000. Gen. counsel Nat. Italian-Am. Found., 1989-96, chair bd. trustees, 1996-99; mem. Bus. Govt. Rels. Coun., Washington, 1987—; past chair Women's Fgn. Policy Group. Past chmn. Nat. Capital chpt. Multiple Sclerosis Soc. Recipient Leadership Recognition award Nat. Women's Econ. Alliance, 1984. Mem. ABA, Pa. Bar Assn. E-mail: j6a3n@yahoo.com.

ZARROS, PANAGIOTIS NIKOLAOS, mathematics researcher, financial executive; b. N.Y.C., Feb. 17, 1964; s. Nikolaos Ioannis and Aikaterinh (Photopoulos) Z. B in Elec. Engring., CCNY, 1988, M in Elec. Engring., 1993; PhD in Engring., MPhil, CUNY, 1995. Adj. lectr. CCNY, N.Y.C., 1988-90, Unix sys. adminstr., 1990-94, CS First Boston, N.Y.C., 1994-96; cons. Bond Technologies, 1996-97; parallel batch adminstr. Lehman Bros., 1997—; pres., rschr. P.N. Zarros Rsch., 1995—. Dion fellow Dion Found., N.Y., 1987; grad. fellow B Grad. Ctr. CUNY, N.Y., 1991-94. Mem. IEEE. Achievements include finding of an algorithm which synchronizes parkes arriving from different participants in a multimedia tele-conference without using feedback packets, patent in field. Avocations: athletics, running, philosophical discussions. Office: Lehman Bros 3 Wfc New York NY 10285-0001 Home: Apt 7E 3044 29th St Astoria NY 11102-2526

ZARTMAN, DAVID LESTER, animal sciences educator, researcher; b. Albuquerque, July 6, 1940; s. Lester Grant and Mary Elizabeth (Kitchel) Z.; m. Micheal Aline Plemmons, July 6, 1963; children: Kami Renee, Dalan Lee. BS, N.Mex. State U., 1962; MS, Ohio State U., 1966, PhD, 1968. Cert. dairy cattle specialist, Am. Registry Profl. Animal Scientists. Jr. ptnr. Marlea Guernsey Farm, Albuquerque, 1962-64; grad. rsch. assoc. Ohio State U., Columbus, 1964-68; asst. prof. dairy sci. N.Mex. State U., Las Cruces, 1968-71, assoc. prof., 1971-79, prof., 1979-84, Ohio State U., Columbus, 1984—. Chmn. dept. Ohio State U., Columbus, 1984-99; pres. Mary K. Zartman, Inc., Albuquerque, 1976-84; cons. Bio-Med. Electronics, Inc., San Diego, 1984-89, Zartemp, Inc., Northbrook, Ill., 1990, Recom Applied Solutions, 1993-2000, Am. Registry of Profl. Animal Scientists, 1996—. Contbr. articles to profl. jours.; patentee in field. Recipient State Regional Outstanding Young Farmer award Jaycees, 1963, Disting. Rsch. award N.Mex. State U. Coll. Agr. and Home Econs., 1983, Outstanding Svc. award Ohio Poultry Assn., 1999, Grazier of Yr. award Gt. Lakes Internat. Grazing Conf., 2001; named one of Top 100 Agr. Alumni, N.Mex. State U. Centennial, 1987; spl. postdoctoral fellow NIH, New Zealand, 1973; Fulbright-Hayes lectr., Malaysia, 1976. Fellow AAAS; mem. Am. Dairy Sci. Assn., Am. Soc. Animal Sci., Dairy Shrine Club, Ohio Farm Bur., Sigma Xi, Gamma Sigma Delta, Alpha Gamma Rho (1st Outstanding Alumnus N.Mex. chpt. 1985), Alpha Zeta, Phi Kappa Phi. Home: 7671 Deer Creek Dr Worthington OH 43085-1551 Office: Ohio State U 2027 Coffey Rd Columbus OH 43210-1043 E-mail: zartman.3@osu.edu.

ZARUBA, ALLEN SCOTT HARMON, sculptor, educator; b. Annapolis, Md., Sept. 23, 1952; s. Alvin Bassett and Katherine Audrey (Zaruba) Harmon. A in Fine Art, Long Beach City Coll., Calif., 1974; postgrad., Parsons in Paris, 1986-87; BFA, Otis/Parsons Art Inst., L.A., 1988; MFA, Md. Inst., 1990. Lectr. Towson State U., Md. Tchr. Towson State U., Anne Arundel C.C. Selected exhbns. include: Chesapeake Gallery, Harford C.C., 1996, Sch. 33 Art Ctr., 1996, McDonough Art Ctr., 1996, Rockville Arts Place, 1996, Rosenberg Gallery, Balt., 1996, Art Gallery U. Md., 1997, Montpelier Cultural Arts Ctr., Laurel, Md., 1998, Artscape Ann., 1998, Contemporary Painting, Arona, Italy, 1998, 99, Italy, 2000, Best of Md., Howard County Ctr. for Arts, 1998, Displaced Realities, MAP, Balt., 1999, Eklektikos Gallery, Washington, 1999, Elliott City, Md., 2000, Stone Quarry Sculpture Park, N.Y., 1999, 2000, Grounds for Sculpture, N.J., 2000, Montpelier Invitational, 2000, Martland Inst., 2000, Contemporary Mus., Balt., 2001, Gomez Gallery, 2001, Elizabeth Found., N.Y., 2001, Quiet Waters Park, Annapolis, Md., 2001, Nexus Found., Phila., 2002, Ace Gallery, N.Y., 2002, Korean Embassy, Washington, 2002, numerous others; work collected at Everson Mus., Syracuse, N.Y., Max Landau/Indsl. Plastics, N.Y.C., Air Force Art Collection, Washington, Shanks and Herbert, Alexandria, Va., Exptl. Aircraft Assn. Mus., Oshkosh, Wis., Great Lakes Naval Tng. Facility, Ill., Naval Aviation Mus., Pensacola, Fla., others; author: (books of poetry) Anima, 2000, Aura, 2001. Mem. Internat. Sculpture Ctr. Inst. of Noetic Scis. With USN, 1975-84, Philippines. Recipient awards Md. State Arts Coun., 1992, 97, Vt. Studio Program, 1996, The Pollock-Krasner Fellowship, 1992-93, The Space Program - The Marie Walsh Sharpe Art Found., 1992-93, others; apptd. to The Blue Angels, Navy Flt. Demonstration Squadron, 1980-84; resident Sculpture Space Inc., 1998. Mem. Washington Sculptors Group, Sch. 33 Arts Ctr., Internat. Artists Support Group, Sculptor's Inc., Md. Art Place, Pyramid Atlantic. Liberal. Avocations: poetry, tree peonies, photography, gardening. Home: 5715 Seymour Ave Baltimore MD 21206-3321 Office: Studio 1601 Guilford Ave 5-S Baltimore MD 21202-2877 E-mail: gmaris@mica.edu.

ZARUTSKIE, ANDREW JOHN, town official; b. Newburgh, N.Y., Feb. 16, 1950; s. Steve and Eleanor L. Zarutskie. AA, Orange County C.C., 1969; BA, Am. U., 1971; postgrad., SUNY, New Paltz, 1971-73. Asst. for urban renewal dept. City of Newburgh, N.Y., 1971-72; asst. assessor Town of Newburgh, 1972-73; dist. office asst. U.S. Congressman Benjamin A. Gilman, Newburgh, 1973-77, grants and project coord. Washington, 1977-83, pres. sec., 1983-2001; town clk. Town of Newburgh, 2001—. Contbr. articles to profl. publs. Mem. Orange County Rep. Com., 1971—, exec. com., 1979-83; bd. dirs. Meals on Wheels, Newburgh, 1975-77. Mem. Rep. Comm. Assn., Orange County Hist. Soc., KC, Kiwanis. Roman Catholic. also: PO Box 10185 Newburgh NY 12552

ZARWYN, BERTHOLD, physical scientist; b. Vienna, Austria, Aug. 22, 1921; came to U.S., 1949, naturalized, 1955; s. Joseph and Bronislawa Regina (Unger) Zarwyn. ME, Gliwice, Poland, 1946; ScD, UN Univ., Munich, 1947; PhD, NYU, 1954; ScD in Engring., Columbia U., 1963. Project engr. Curtiss-Wright Corp., Woodridge, N.J., 1951-55; staff scientist AMF Corp., N.Y.C., 1955-57; chief scientist Link Aviation Co., Binghamton, N.Y., 1957-58; head rsch. staff Am. Bosch-Arma Corp., Garden City, 1958-63; corp. cons. Cutler-Hammer Corp., Deer Park, 1963-65; chief engr. Bell Aerosystems Corp., Niagara Falls, 1965-66; sr. cons. Mitre Corp., Bedford, Mass., 1966-68; spl. asst. to commdg. gen., acting chief engr. Hdqs. U.S. Army Materiel Command, Arlington, Va., 1968-71; chief phys. scis. br. U.S. Army Devel. and Readiness Command, Alexandria, 1971-75; phys. scientist U.S. Army Harry Diamond Labs., Washington, 1975-78; chief sys. analysis br. U.S. Army Elec. Rsch. and Devel. Command, Adelphi, Md., 1978-79, chief tech divsn., 1979-81, asst. tech. dir., 1981-85; spl. asst to dep. chief of staff for tech. & program mgmt. U.S. Army Lab. Command, 1985-87; pres. Pan-Tech. Corp., Delray Beach, Fla., 1987—. Adj. faculty, lectr., cons. in field; dir. Film Microelectronics Co. Inc., Burlington, Mass., 1965-67. Mem. editl. bd. Bavarian Soc. Engrs., 1947-49, transl. panel Russian Jour. Applied Math. and Mechanics with Pergamon Inst., 1956-57; inventor nucl. gyroscope, microwave holography, other items. Mem. IEEE, Am. Phys. Soc., N.Y. Acad. Scis., Sigma Xi. Home and Office: Pan-Tech Corp 7589 Mansfield Hollow Rd Delray Beach FL 33446-3314

ZARZOUR, ROBIN ANN, special education educator; b. Parma, Ohio, Apr. 14, 1964; d. Robert Halim and Rosalie Frances (Ezzie) Z. AAS in Early Childhood Edn., Cuyahoga C.C., 1985; BS in Spl. Edn., Cleve. State U., 1990, MA in Early Childhood Spl. Edn., 1993. Early childhood spl. edn. aide Middleburg Spl. Presch., Middleburg Heights, Ohio, 1983-86; counselor Camp Sunshine, Parma, 1986-88; early childhood spl. religious tchr. St. Charles, 1988-89; early childhood spl. edn. tchr. Parma City Sch. System, 1990—. Mem. Cleve. Assn. Mid. Ea. Orgn., 1992—. Recipient Tchr. of Yr. award Cuyahoga Spl. Edn. Svc. Ctr., 1993—. Mem. Coun. for Exception Children, Parma Edn. Assn. (union bldg. rep. 1992—). Democrat. Roman Catholic. Avocations: golf, working out, movies, music.

ZASHIN, ANDREW AARON, lawyer; b. Cleve., Feb. 7, 1968; AB, Brown U., 1990; JD, Case Western Res. U., 1993. Bar: Ohio 1993, Fla. 1994, D.C. 1995; cert. family rels. law specialist. Atty. Zashin & Rich Co., Cleve., 1993—. Notes editor Case Western Res. U. Law Rev. Bd. trustees Congregation Beth Am., 1996—; co-chmn. Israel Bonds, Cleve., 1996-98. Mem.: Cuyahoga County Bar Assn. (treas. family law sect. 2000—01, sec. family law sect. 2001—02), Ohio State Bar Assn. Office: Zashin & Rich Co CPA 55 Public Sq Ste 1490 Cleveland OH 44113-1998

ZASLAVSKY, ROBERT, secondary school educator; b. Phila., Feb. 26, 1942; s. Harry and Sally (Zwick) Z.; div.; 1 child, Cordelia Helena. AB in Philosophy, English Lit., Temple U., 1964; MA in Philosophy, New Sch. Social Rsch., 1969, PhD in Philosophy, 1978; postgrad., Cabrini Coll., 1989-91. Substitute tchr. math. and English Phila. Bd. Edn., 1964; caseworker Phila. Dept. Pub. Assistance, 1964-65, N.Y.C. Dept. Welfare, 1965-68; instr. philosophy Villanova U., 1971-73; instr. philosophy of art Immaculata Coll., 1975; libr. interlibr. loan and reference Bryn Mawr (Pa.) Coll., 1973-86; exec. producer, on-air performer, camera oper. Studio 9 Video Prodns., 1986—; adj. instr. English and religion, student tchr. adviser Cabrini Coll., 1990; instr. lit. Main Line Sch. Night, 1991-95; instr. humanities Akiba Hebrew Acad., Merion Station, Pa., 1990-96; instr. English Marine Mil. Acad., Harlingon, Tex., 1997-99; instr. Latin and English Fort Worth Ind. Sch. Dist., 1999—. Job counselor Kingston (N.Y.) Community Ctr., 1968; presenter seminars; guest lectr. Greek lit. Bryn Mawr Coll., 1976-78, Villanova U., 1978-81; assoc. Greater Phila. Philosophy Consortium, 1983-86; instr. Rittenhouse Acad., 1989, Haverford Twp. Adult Sch., 1989, Valley Forge Mil. Acad., 1989-90; instr. Elderhostel program Cabrini Coll., 1990, 91, Valley Forge Hist. Soc., 1991. Contbr. articles, revs. to lit. publs. Mem. ASCD, MLA, Nat. Coun. Tchrs. English, Core Knowledge Found., Acad. Am. Poets, Am Coun. Tchrs. Fgn. Langs., S.W. Conf. on Lang. Tchg., Tex. Fgn. Lang. Assn., Am. Classical League. Home: 6412 Wildwood Cir S Apt 815 Fort Worth TX 76132-5124 E-mail: RobertZ466@aol.com.

ZASLAVSKY, THOMAS, mathematics educator; b. Bklyn., Jan. 16, 1944; s. Sam and Claudia Z. BS, CCNY, 1965; PhD, MIT, 1974. Staff sci. Arcon Corp., Wakefield, Mass., 1972-73; instr. MIT, Cambridge, 1975-77; asst. prof. Ohio State U., Columbus, 1977-84; visiting researcher U. Evansville (Ind.), 1984-85; assoc. prof. math. SUNY, Binghamton, 1985-88, prof. math., 1988—. Contbr. articles to profl. jours. Office: SUNY Dept Math Scis Binghamton NY 13901

ZASLOWSKY, DAVID PAUL, lawyer; b. N.Y.C., Dec. 30, 1960; s. Daniel N. and Rhoda (Sohn) Z.; m. Lisa Ann Freudenberger, Aug. 26, 1982; children: Amanda Lauren, Michael Joel, Steven Ira. BS in Computer/Info. Sci. summa cum laude, Bklyn. Coll., 1981; JD, Yale U., 1984. Bar: N.Y. 1984, N.J. 1984, U.S. Dist. Ct. (so. and ea. dist.) N.Y. 1985, U.S. Dist. Ct. N.J. 1985, U.S. Cir. Ct. (2d cir.) 1992. Assoc. Baker & McKenzie, N.Y.C., 1984-94, ptnr., 1994—. Author: (with others) Federal Civil Practice, 1989, Transnational Litigation in U.S. Federal Courts, 1991, Litigating International Commercial Disputes, 1996. Mem. ABA (litigation sect.), N.Y. State Bar Assn. (comml. and fed. litigation sect.), Assn. Bar City N.Y. Office: Baker & McKenzie 805 3rd Ave Fl 29 New York NY 10022-7513 E-mail: david.zaslowsky@bakernet.com.

ZATLIN, GABRIEL STANLEY, physician; b. N.Y.C., Dec. 5, 1935; s. Samuel and Bernice (Morgenstern) Z.; m. Linda M. Gertner, Dec. 29, 1959 (div. 1973); children: Jonathan Reid, Andrew Evan; m. Lorna G. Schofield, May 14, 1983; 1 child, Sarah Schofield. BS, U. Miami, Coral Gables, Fla., 1956; MD, Washington U., St. Louis, 1960. Diplomate Am. Bd. Pediatrics, Am. Bd. Family Practice. Intern St. Louis Children's Hosp., 1960-61, resident, 1961-62, Children's Hosp. Med. Ctr., Boston, 1965-66, Downstate Med. Ctr., Bklyn., 1979-81; Epidemiologist Ctrs. for Disease Control, Atlanta, 1962-64; pvt. practice, 1966-73; cons. Pertamina, Jakarta, Indonesia, 1974-76; field dir. African Health Tng. Project, Yaounde, Cameroun, 1976-77; assoc. dir. Brown U. Health Svcs., Providence, 1977-79; asst. prof. Downstate Med. Ctr., Bklyn., 1981-82; assoc. dir. St. Mary Hosp. Family Practice, Hoboken, N.J., 1982-88, dir., 1988-92; clin. assoc. prof. Downstate Med. Ctr., Bklyn., 1992-95, dir. family practice residency program, 1993-95; faculty family practice residency program Beth Israel Hosp., 1997—. Clin. asst. prof. Albert Einstein Sch. Medicine, 1997—. Contbr. articles to profl. jours. With USPHS, 1962-64. Fellow Am. Acad. Pediatrics; mem. Am. Acad. Family Practice, Soc. for Adolescent Medicine. Avocation: gardening. Office: Inst for Urban Family Prac 16 E 16th St New York NY 10003-3105

ZATLIN, PHYLLIS, Spanish language educator, translator; b. Green Bay, Wis., Dec. 31, 1938; d. Frank L. and Ellen Mary (Butler) Z.; m. George Boring Kelly, Aug. 20, 1962; children: William, Lee. BA, Rollins Coll., 1960; postgrad., U. Grenoble, France, 1960-61; MA, U. Fla., 1962, PhD, 1965. Cert. Spanish to English translator Am. Translators Assn. Instr. Rutgers U., New Brunswick, N.J., 1963-66, asst. prof., 1966-71, assoc. prof., 1971-79, assoc. dean, 1974-80, prof. Spanish, 1979—, chair dept. Spanish, grad. dir., 1980-87. Mem. discipline adv. com. Coun. for Internat. Exch. of Scholars, 1990-93; spkr. in field. Co-author: Lengua y Lectura: Un Repaso y Una Continuación, 1970; author: Elena Quiroga, 1977, Víctor Ruiz Iriarte, 1980, Jaime Salom, 1982, Cross Cultural-Approaches to Theatre: The Spanish-French Connection, 1994, The Novels and Plays of Eduardo Manet: An Adventure in Multiculturalism, 2000; editor: (Francisco Ayala) El Rapto, 1971, (Víctor Ruiz Iriarte) El Landó de Seis Caballos, 1979, (Jaime Salom) La Piel del Limón, 1980, (Antonio Gala) Noviembre y un Poco de Yerba. Petra Regalada, 1981, (Francisco Nieva) Combate de Opalos y Tasia. Sombra y Quimera de Larra. La Magosta, 1990, El teatro alternativo español, 2001; co-editor: The Contemporary Spanish Theater. A Collection of Critical Essays, 1988, Homenaje (A Tribute to Martha T. Halsey), 1995; co-editor: Entre Actos: Diálogos sobre teatro español, 1999, Un escenario propio (A Stage of Their Own), 1998; co-guest editor jour. Art Teatral. Cuadernos de Minipiezas Ilustradas, 1996; translator play edits.: (J.L. Alonso de Santos) Going Down to Marrakesh, 1992, Hostages in the Barrio, 1997, (Paloma Pedrero) Parting Gestures (The Color of August, A Night Divided, The Voucher With, Tonight in the Subway, 1999, (Jaime Salom) A Bonfire at Dawn, 1992, (Jean-Paul Daumas) The Elephant Graveyard, 1994, (Eduardo Manet) Lady Strass, 1992, 97, also performances; assoc. editor Estreno, 1992-2001, editor Estreno Plays, 1998—; mem. editl. bd. Western European Stages, Espana Contemporanea, others. State pres. Women's Equity Action League, N.J., 1971-72, nat. bd. dirs., Washington, 1973, 76-77. Fellow Fulbright Found., 1960-61, Woodrow Wilson Found., 1961-62; recipient Profl. award Fgn. Lang. Educators of N.J., 1989. Mem. AAUP (mem. nat. coun. 1987-90), MLA (mem. commn. on status of women 1978-81), Dramatists Guild, Soc. Gen. de Autores y Editores (Profl. award 1997). Democrat. Avocations: biking, jogging, travel. Home: 5 Timber Rd East Brunswick NJ 08816-2941 Office: Rutgers Univ 105 George St New Brunswick NJ 08901-1414 E-mail: pzatlin@spamport.rutgers.edu.

ZATSIORSKY, VLADIMIR MOISEEVICH MICHAILOVICH, biomechanics educator, researcher; b. Leningrad, Russia, Dec. 26, 1932; came to U.S., 1990; s. Moisey T. and Berta L. (Bardenstein) Z.; m. Rita Y. Zatsiorsky, Oct. 27, 1960; children: Betty V. Ulitsky, Michael V. PhD, Lesgaft Inst. Phys. Culture, Leningrad, 1961; DSc, Ctrl. Inst. Phys. Culture, Moscow, 1969; D honoris causa, Acad. Phys. Culture, Wroclaw, Poland, 1999. Asst. prof. Lvov (Ukraine) Inst. Phys. Culture, 1954-57; asst. prof., assoc. prof., prof. Ctrl. Inst. Phys. Culture, Moscow, 1959-90; vis. prof. UCLA, 1990, U. Calgary, Can., 1991; prof. kinesiology Pa. State U., University Park, 1991—. Med. commn. Internat. Olympic Com., 1982—. Author: Science and Practice of Strength Training, 1995, Kinematics of Human Motion, 1998, Kinetics of Human Motion, 2002; editor: Biomechanics in Sport, 2000, Classics in Movement Science, 2001 (all books published in English, Russian, German, Italian, Spanish, Portuguese, Chinese, Japanese, Polish, Romanian, Czech, Serbo-Croatian & Bulgarian). Recipient J. Dyson award Internat. Soc. of Sport Biomechanics, 1992. Fellow: Am. Acad. Kinesiology; mem.: Internat. Soc. Sport Kinetics (hon.). Avocations: reading, music. Office: Pa State U 39 Rec Bldg University Park PA 16802 E-mail: vxz1@psu.edu.

ZATZ, IRVING J. structural engineer; b. May 27, 1953; s. Hyman and Frances Zatz; m. Janet Gwen Share, Aug. 15, 1976; children: Jonathan, Eric. BS, Cornell U., 1975; M in Engring., 1976. Structural engr. Goodkind & O'Dea, Inc., Clifton, N.J., 1976-77, Grumman Aerospace Corp., Bethpage, N.Y., 1977-80; sr. project engr. engring. analysis divsn. Princeton (N.J.) U. Plasma Physics Lab., 1980—. Univ. fellow Cornell U., 1975-76. Contbr. articles to profl. jours. Bd. dirs. Princeton Oaks Homeowners Assn. (v.p. 1992-94, pres. 1994-97); mgr. West Windsor Little League; mem. West Windsor Rd. Design Com., West Windsor Transp. Com. Recipient 1st Pl. award, James F. Lincoln Engring. Design Competition, 1975, Cmty. Svc. award, West Windsor Twp., 1994. Mem. AIAA, ASCE (exec. com. met. sect. 1978-80), Am. Concrete Inst., Tau Beta Pi, Chi Epsilon (chpt. treas. 1974-75, pres. 1975-76). Home: 8 Huntington Dr Princeton Junction NJ 08550-2122 Office: Princeton Plasma Physics Lab PO Box 451 Princeton NJ 08543-0451 E-mail: zatz@pppl.gov.

ZAUDERER, MARK CARL, lawyer; b. Jan. 26, 1946; BA, Union Coll., 1967; JD, NYU, 1971. Bar: N.Y. 1972. Law clk. U.S. Dist. Ct., Newark, 1971-72; ptnr. Solomon, Zauderer, Ellenhorn, Frischer & Sharp, N.Y.C., 1981—. Faculty chmn. Practicing Law Inst. Program., Litigating Comml. Cases up to Trial, N.Y.C. and San Francisco, 1986, faculty mem. Deposition Skills Tng. Program, N.Y., 1986, 88-90; adv. com. on civil practice to Chief Adminstrn. Judge N.Y. State Ctrs., 1992—; trustee bd. advisors Union Coll., 1993—; chief Judge's Task Force on Comml. Cts., 1995—. Author, moderator practising law inst. satellite TV program Deposition Strategy and Tactics, 1989; contbr. articles to profl. jours. Fellow N.Y. Bar Found.; mem. ABA, N.Y. State Bar Assn. (chmn. program strategy and tactics in bus. and comml. litigation N.Y.C., Buffalo and Rochester, N.Y., 1990-91, 94, faculty 1992-94), Assn. of Bar of City of N.Y. (com. state cts. superior jurisdiction 1983-87, profl. discipline com. 1987-88, judiciary com. 1988-91, chmn. com. complex civil litigation, comml. and fed. litigation sect., mem. exec. com. 1991—, chair 1996-97), Fed. Bar Coun. (trustee 1998—). Home: 11 Avon Rd Larchmont NY 10538-1420 Office: 45 Rockefeller Plz New York NY 10111-0100

ZAUNER, CHRISTIAN WALTER, university dean, exercise physiologist, consultant; b. Phila., July 21, 1930; s. Philip Walter and Margaret Helen (Gilmor) Z.; m. Betty Ann Schwenk, Feb. 1, 1957; children: Beth, Ward, Joe. BS, West Chester State, 1956; MS, Syracuse U., 1957; PhD, So. Ill. U., 1963.

Asst. prof. Temple U., Phila., 1963-65; prof. phys. edn. and medicine U. Fla., Gainesville, 1965-84; dir. Sports Medicine Inst., Mt. Sinai Med. Ctr., Miami Beach, Fla., 1984-87; chmn. exercise sci. Oreg. State U., Corvallis, 1987-94; dean health and human performance East Carolina U., Greenville, N.C., 1994-99; retired; data base developer Sports Medicine for Human Kinetics Pubs., 2000—. Cons. in exercise rehab. Hosp. Corp. Am.; cons. in sports medicine State of Kuwait, Arab Gulf; cons. sport sci. curriculum Ministry Edn., Thailand. Contbr. numerous articles to various profl. jours. Served with USN, 1951-54. Grantee U. Fla., 1971, Am. Scandinavian Foun., 1971, Fla. Blue Key, 1978, Nat. Acad. Sci., 1985-86, 88, 90, 94. Fellow: Am. Coll. Sports Medicine; mem.: AAHPERD, Am. Physiol. Soc. Democrat. Roman Catholic. E-mail: czauner@home.com.

ZAVACKY-DEBERTRAND, LYNETTE MICHELE, women's health nurse; b. Wheeling, W.Va., Feb. 2, 1966; d. Sam J. and Linda L. (Cheroka) Z. ADN, Belmont Tech. Coll., 1986; BSN, Ohio U., 1989; MSN, W.Va. U., 1990. RN, Ohio; cert. child birth tchr., inpatient obstetric nurse. Clin. nurse specialist Birthplace Martins Ferry (Ohio), East Ohio Regional Hosp. Part-time clin. instr. W.Va. No. C.C., Wheeling. Home: 67568 Elizabeth St Saint Clairsville OH 43950-9127

ZAVADA, BARBARA JOHANNA, artist; b. Jena, Thueringen, Germany, June 20, 1938; came to U.S., 1953; d. Paul Egon and Johanna Helene (Kuehlich) Weber; m. Gerhard Manfred Grote, Mar. 6, 1971 (div. Jan. 1975); 1 child, Erika Barbara. Cert., Traphagen Sch. Fashions, N.Y.C., 1960; studied with, Karl Bobeck, Berlin, 1962; Assoc., Rochester (N.Y.) Inst. Tech., 1966; postgrad., Art Students League, N.Y.C., 1970. Painter, Europe and U.S.A., 1960—; fashion designer H & U Schmidt, Berlin, 1961-62, Dave Goldberg, N.Y.C., 1967-71; graphic designer Zavada Assocs., Stamford, Conn., 1974-90; now lectr. on abstract expressionism. One-woman shows include Mus. Art Sci. and Industry, 1974, Bruce Mus., 1976, Conn. Women's Bank, Greenwich, 1985, Stamford (Conn.) Landmark Tower Rotunda, 1985, So. Conn. State U., New Haven, 1990, Edge of Cedars Mus., Blanding, Utah, 1996, 1999, We. Colo. Ctr. Arts, 1998, Zavada Fine Art Studio, Gallery Arroyo Seco, N.Mex., 1998—, State of Utah, Iron Mission State Park, 2000—, pmwgallery.com, —, artprice.com, Saint-Romain-au-Mont-d'Or, France. Prodr. Graphics for Scholarship Fund, Greenwich (Conn.) Acad., 1985-90; v.p. Ind. German Lang. Sch., Westport, Conn., 1981-83; search and rescue pilot CAP, Rochester, N.Y., 1964-68, Staten Island, N.Y., 1969-70. Recipient 1st prize N.Y.C. Fashion Competition, 1960, Faber Birren Color award, Stamford, 1981. Mem. Am. Acad. Women Artists, The Art Ctr. at Fuller Lodge, Friends of Contemporary Art, Mus. N.Mex. Found. Avocations: travel, hiking, skiing, gardening. Home: HC 64 Box 3001 Castle Valley UT 84532-9614 also: 24 Meyers Rd Espanola NM 87532-9609 E-mail: zavadabj@yahoo.com.

ZAVADA, MICHAEL STEPHEN, plant science educator; b. Bridgeport, Conn., Aug. 25, 1952; s. Michael Joseph and Helen (Kokoruda) Z.; m. Maria F. Chavez, May 25, 1972 (div. June 1990); children: Yolanda X., M. Rebeca, Sarah M.; m. Jeanne E. Ledford, Aug. 11, 1990. BS in Botany, Ariz. State U., 1974, MS in Palynology, 1976; BA in Russian, PhD in Evol. Botany, U. Conn., 1982. Rsch. assoc. Ind. U., Bloomington, 1982-84, Ohio State U., Columbus, 1984-85; lectr. U. Witwatersrand, Johannesburg, South Africa, 1985-88; asst. prof. U. Southwestern La., Lafayette, 1988-93, assoc. prof., 1993-94; asst. prof. Providence Coll., 1994-96, assoc. prof., 1996-99, chmn. dept. biology, 1996—, prof., 1999—. Contbr. articles to profl. publs. U. Conn. fellow, 1980-82; grantee Fulbright Found., 1976-77, Nat. Geog. Soc., 1986-87, 89. Mem. Am. Assn. Stratigraphic Palynologists, Botanical Soc. Am., Internat. Orgn. Paleobotanists, Orgn. Tropical Studies, Paleontol. Soc. South Africa, South African Soc. Quaternary Rsch., Soc. for Study of Evolution, Sigma Xi, Tri Beta, Alpha Mu Gamma. Avocations: Russian literature, folklore, skiing, basketball, hiking. Office: Providence Coll Providence RI 02908

ZAVALA, ALBERT, research psychologist; b. Chgo., Mar. 10, 1930; s. Edward and Maria Soledad (Herrejon) Z.; div.; children: Camille, Sally, Elena, Jenifer, Alexis. BA, Willamette U., 1959; MA, Mich. State U., 1961; PhD, Kans. State U., 1966. Prof., head life scis. Carlspan, Buffalo, 1967-73; prof. SUNY, 1968-78; exec. dir. Corp. IV, Cheektowaga, N.Y., 1973-77; dir. projects Inpsych, Cupertino, Calif., 1978-80; sr. rsch. psychologist SRI Internat., Menlo Park, 1980-85; sr. staff engr. Lockheed Missiles and Space Co., Sunnyvale, 1985-94; sr. engr. Nova Mgmt. Monterey, 1994-97; bid mgr. Siemens Info. and Network Comm., Inc., Santa Clara, 1997-2000; sr. staff engr. Hernadez Engring., Inc., 2000—. Author: (with J.J. Paley) Personal Appearance Identification, 1972; contbr. numerous articles to profl. jours. Mem. Erie County (N.Y.) Sheriff's Sci. staff, 1972-78. With U.S. Army, 1955-57. Dunlap fellow, 1964, fellow Greater Kans. City Mental Health Found., 1962-63. Mem. APA, Human Factors Soc., Sigma Xi, Psi Chi, Phi Kappa Phi.

ZAVALA, ALBERTO, real estate investment company executive; b. Sept. 29, 1953; Student, U. Tex. Pan Am., Edinburg, 1984-89. Pres., CEO, Alberto Zavala & Assocs., Edinburg, 1980—.

ZAVARZADEH, MAS'UD, sociologist, educator; s. Hossain Zavarzadeh and Koucheck Keyghobadi; m. Teresa L. Ebert, July 23, 1981. PhD, Ind. U., 1973. Prof. Syracuse U., Syracuse, NY, 1979—. Founder The Red Factory, 2000—. Contbr. articles to profl. jours. Fellow Rsch. fellowship, NEH, 1977—78, Nat. Humanities Ctr., 1981—82, Humanities Ctr., U. of California-Davis, 1989—90.

ZAVATSKY, MICHAEL JOSEPH, lawyer; b. Wheeling, W.Va., Dec. 15, 1948; s. Mike and Mary (Mirich) Z.; m. Kathleen Hanson, May 28, 1983; children: David, Emily. BA in Internat. Studies, Ohio State U., 1970; MA in Polit. Sci., U. Hawaii, 1972; JD, U. Cin., 1980. Bar: Ohio 1980, U.S. Dist. Ct. (so. dist.) Ohio 1981, U.S. Ct. Appeals (6th cir.) 1985, U.S. Supreme Ct. 1989. Ptnr. Taft, Stettinius & Hollister, Cin., 1980—. Adj. prof. in trial practice and immigration law U. Cin., 1986— Trustee Internat. Visitors Ctr., Cin., 1984-86; bd. dirs. Cin. Charter Com., 1988-91; bd. dirs., mem. steering com. Leadership Cin., 1994-96. Capt. USAF, 1973-77. William Graham fellow U. Cin., 1979, East West Ctr. fellow U. Hawaii, 1970. Mem ABA, Ohio Bar Assn., Cin. Bar Assn., Am. Immigration Lawyers Assn. (chmn. Ohio chpt. 1987-88, 90-93), Potter Stewart Inn of Ct., Order of Coif. Home: 3820 Eileen Dr Cincinnati OH 45209-2013 Office: 1800 Firstar Tower Cincinnati OH 45202

ZAVATTO, AMY ELIZABETH, freelance/self-employed writer, editor; b. East Rockaway, N.Y., Mar. 20, 1968; d. Michael John and Virginia Louise Zavatto; m. Daniel Calogero Marotta, June 20, 1998. BA in Journalism, NYU, 1992. Copy editor Matthew Bender, N.Y.C., 1990—94; assoc. editor Warren, Gorham, & Lamont, 1994—95; editor The Princeton Rev., 1995—97; acquiring editor Macmillan Pub. (Pearson Edn.), 1997—2000; freelance writer Bklyn., 2000—. Author: The Pocket Idiot's Guide to Family Reunions, 2002; contbr. articles to mags. E-mail: azavatto@earthlink.net.

ZAVON, MITCHELL RALPH, occupational medicine physician; b. N.Y.C., May 9, 1923; s. Irving and Claire (Gutterman) Z.; m. Betty Berthold, June 24, 1976; children by previous marriage: Peter, Dan, Juliet, Barbara. Student, Cornell U., 1940-43, Harvard U., 1943-44; MD, Boston U., 1949; postgrad., Duke U., 1951-52, U. Cin., 1956-58. Diplomate Am. Bd. Med. Examiners, Am. Bd. Prevention Medicine, Am. Bd. Indsl. Hygiene. Intern Wilson Meml. Hosp., Johnson City, N.Y., 1949-50; surgeon USPHS, Washington, 1950-56; from instr. to asst. clin. prof. U. Cin., 1952-74, from asst. prof. to clin. prof. indsl. medicine, 1956-71; asst. health commr. Cin. Health Dept., 1956-74; med. dir. Ethyl Corp., Baton Rouge, 1974-76; dir. health Occidental Chem. Corp., Niagara Falls, N.Y., 1976-86; pres., med. dir. Agatha Corp., Sarasota, Fla., 1968—. Mem., cons., del. Threshold Limits Com., 1962-87; mem., cons. Biol. Indeces Com., 1982-96; pres. Place-to-Be, 1978-83; mem. cons. staff Mt. St. Mary's Hosp., 1980-94; med. dir. Buffalo Union Occupl. Health Ctr., 1996-98. Contbr. articles to profl. jours. Bd. dirs. HART; mem. Cincinnatus Assocs., 1969-77; mem. Niagara County (N.Y.) Bd. Health, 1994-00, pres., 1997. Fellow APHA, Am. Coll. Occupl. and Environ. Medicine, Am. Indsl. Hygiene Assn.; mem. AMA, AAAS, N.Y. State Med. Soc., Niagara County Med. Soc., Am. Conf. Govtl. Indsl. Hygienists. Unitarian Universalist. Home and Office: 4559 Trails Dr Sarasota FL 34232-3450 E-mail: zavonm@cs.com.

ZAVREL, B. JOHN, account executive, museum director; b. Kurim/Gurein, Czechoslovakia, Aug. 2, 1949; came to U.S., 1969; s. Bohuslav and Radoslava (Holubik) Z.; m. Sandra McCracken, May 20, 1972; children: Wesley, Christopher, Thomas. Student, Econ. Sch. Fgn. Trade, Brno/Brünn, 1968; BSBA in Fin., U. Buffalo, 1972; BS in Acctg., Millard Fillmore Coll., 1974; postgrad., U. Buffalo, 1996-97. CPA, N.Y. Dir. Mus. European Art, Clarence, N.Y.; owner B.John Zavrel, PC. Spokesman German-Am. Nat. Congress N.Y.; chmn. Internat. Com. Artists for Ecology (USA); speaker (European Affairs); chmn. Internat. Com. Artists for Ecology (USA); speaker (European Affairs); chmn. Internat. Com. Artists for Ecology (USA); speaker (European Affairs); chmn. Internat. Com. Artists for Ecology (USA); speaker (European Affairs); chmn. Internat. Com. Artists for Ecology (USA); speaker (European Affairs); chmn. Internat. Com. Artists for Ecology (USA); speaker (European Affairs); chmn. Internat. Com. Artists for Ecology (USA); speaker (European Affairs); chmn. Internat. Com. Artists for Ecology (USA); speaker (European Affairs); chmn. Internat. Com. Artists for Ecology (USA); speaker (European Affairs); chmn. Internat. Com. Artists for Ecology (USA); speaker (European Affairs); chmn. Internat. Com. Artists for Ecology (USA); speaker (European Affairs); chmn. Internat. Com. Artists for Ecology (USA); speaker (European Affairs); chmn. Internat. Com. Artists for Ecology (USA); speaker (European Affairs); chmn. Internat. Com. Artists for Ecology (USA); speaker (European Affairs); chmn. Internat. Com. Artists for Ecology (USA); speaker (European Affairs); chmn. Internat. Com. Artists for Ecology (USA); speaker (European Affairs); chmn. Internat. Com. Artists for Ecology (USA); speaker (European Affairs); chmn. Internat. Com. Artists for Ecology (USA); speaker (European Affairs); chmn. Internat. Com. Artists for Ecology (USA); speaker (European Affairs) chair clin. affairs dept. family practice, 1995-97, west regional med. dir. ambulatory care, 1997—. Author: When The Phone Rings My Bed Shakes, 1993. Office: 7300 Dexter Ann Arbor Rd Dexter MI 48130-9512

ZAZULA, BERNARD MEYER, physician administrator; b. Bklyn., July 7, 1941; s. Harry and Clara (Serchuk) Z.; m. Elise Hoch, Aug. 2, 1966; children: Rona, Harold. BA, Yeshiva Coll., 1961; MD, Albert Einstein Coll., 1965; MPH, Columbia U., 1976. Diplomate Nat. Bd. Med. Examiners, Am. Bd. Preventive Medicine; med. lic., N.Y.; cert. in pub. health and gen. preventive medicine. Intern, resident in pediats. Kings County Hosp., Bklyn., 1965-68; sub-dist. med. officer of health Ministry of Health, Jerusalem, 1971-73; dist. health officer N.Y.C. Dept. Health, 1973-74, dir. Bur. for Handicapped Children, 1975-86; med. dir. Medicaid program N.Y.C. Human Resources Adminstrn., 1986—. Cons. staff Flushing (N.Y.) Hosp., 1989-93, hon. staff, 1993—; tchg. staff Wyckoff Heights Hosp., Queens, N.Y., 1993—. Mem., bd. dirs. Queens Valley Homeowners' Civic Assn., Flushing, 1985-91, Young Israel of Kew Gardens Hills, N.Y., 1983-91. Maj. U.S. Army, 1968-70, Vietnam. Fellow N.Y. Acad. Medicine; mem. AMA, APHA, Queens County Med. Soc. (pres. 1995-96, trustee 1996—), Med. Soc. State of N.Y. (chmn. ethics com. 1992—, del. to AMA 2000—), Alumni Assn. Albert Einstein Coll. Medicine (nat. pres. 1991-93). Jewish. Avocations: travel, walking, reading. Home: 14405 70th Rd Flushing NY 11367-1717 Office: Med Assistance Program 330 W 34th St New York NY 10001-2406

ZAZZALI, JAMES R. judge; b. Newark, June 17, 1937; m. Eileen Fitzsimmons; children: Mara, James Jr., Robert, Courtney, Kevin. BA, JD, Georgetown U. Bar: NJ, NY, DC. Law clk. U.S. Dist. Ct. Judge Lawrence A. Whipple, 1964—65; from asst. prosecutor to chief appellate sect. Essex County Prosecutor's Office, 1965—68; ptnr. Zazzali, Fagella, & Nowak, Newark; atty. gen. State of NJ, 1981—82; gen. counsel NJ Sports and Exposition Authority; assoc. justice NJ Supreme Ct., 2000—. Adj. prof. Seton Hall Law Sch., 1984—; commr. NJ State Commn. of Investigation, 1984—94, chmn., 1990—94; vice-chair Disciplinary Rev Bd., 1984—2000. Democrat. Office: NJ Supreme Court Hughes Justice Complex PO BOX 23 Trenton NJ 08625-0023*

ZBAR, LLOYD IRWIN STANLEY, otolaryngologist, educator; b. Jersey City, June 2, 1939; m. Margo Wally, Mar. 25, 1965; children: Ross I.S., Brett I.W. MD, Queen's U., Kingston, Ont., Can., 1964. Cert. in otolaryngology. Intern Beth Israel/Harvard, Boston, 1964; resident in surgery French Hosp., N.Y.C., 1965-66; resident in otolaryngology Bellevue Hosp. Ctr.-NYU, 1966-69, fellow in otolaryngology, 1969-70; chmn. med. edn. com. Mountainside Hosp., Montclair, N.J., 1979-89, dir. otolaryngology, 1990-97, 99—. Sec. med. bd. Mountainside Hosp., Glen Ridge, N.J., 1986-90, clin. assoc. prof. otolaryngology NYU Sch. Medicine. Contbr. rev. to New Eng. Jour. Medicine, 1988. Mem. exec. bd. Boy Scouts of Am., Essex County, N.J., 1984-95; pres. Mountainside Physicians Scholarship Loan Fund, 1972-85. Fellow ACS, Am. Acad. Otolaryngology-Head and Neck Surgery, Royal Soc. Medicine. Office: 200 Highland Ave Glen Ridge NJ 07028-1528 Fax: 973-743-3111. E-mail: lloyd.zbar@verizon.net.

ZBIEGIEN, M. ANDREA, chaplain, religious education educator, consultant, educational administrator; b. Berea, Ohio, May 12, 1944; d. Leopold and Anna Meri (Voskovich) Z. BS in Edn., St. John Coll., 1969; MS in Edn., John Carroll U., 1973; MDiv, Grad. Theol. Union, 1986, D of Ministry, 1988. Tchr. jr. h.s. Diocese of Cleve., 1964-76, instr. dept. religious edn., 1971-82, dir. religious edn., 1976-82; diocesan dir. religious edn. Diocese of Toledo, 1982-87; instr. Dept. Christian Formation Diocese of Savannah, Ga., 1987—2001; dir. religious edn. Diocese of Savannah, 1987—2001; bus. builder/asst. supr. Shaklee Corp., 1978—2001. Substitute tchr., Cleve., also Brunswick, Ga., 1976-2001; cons. Benziger Pub. co., Ohio, 1971-78, Our Sunday Visitor Pubs., 1978-90, Silver Burdett Ginn, St. Augustine Diocese, 1988—; adj. prof. St. John U., Collegeville, Minn., Grad. Theol. Union, San Anselmo, Calif., summers 1978—. Author: RCIA: Parish Team Formation, 1987, Poetic Progress, 2002; producer, author: (videos) RCIA: Parish Team Formation, 1987; contbr. articles to profl. jours. Facilitator Bishop's Task Force Action for a Change, Cleve., 1969-72; adv., facilitator Systematic Techniques of Effective Parenting, 1982—; mem. Bishop's Commn. on Worship, Diocese of Savannah; 1999-2001; vol. Med. Assistance for World's Poor; tour host Ednl. Opportunities. Recipient scholarship KC, Cleve., 1961-69. Mem. AAUW, Nat. Conf. Cathetical Leadership, Nat. Assn. Pastoral Coords. and Dirs., Nat. Cath. Edn. Assn., Sisters for Christian Cmty., Ind. Order Foresters, Shaklee Bus. Builder. Avocations: fiberarts, creative writing, photography, and sketching. Home: 11557 Tyndel Creek LN Jacksonville FL 32223-8706

ZBIKOWSKI, JOHN MICHAEL, education educator; b. Syracuse, N.Y., Aug. 5, 1957; s. John and Anne Zbikowski. AB in English Lit., Syracuse U., 1979, MS in English Edn., 1984; PhD in Curriculum and Instrn., U. Fla., 1991. Tchr. English De La Salle Collegiate H.S., Detroit, 1980-82; rsch. asst. Syracuse U. Reading and Lang. Arts Ctr., 1983-84; tchr. English New Berlin (N.Y.) Cen. Sch., 1984-86; asst. prof. curriculum and instrn. U. Wis., Whitewater, 1989-95, assoc. prof., 1995—. Mem. Internat. Reading Assn., Nat. Coun. Tchrs. English (mem. comm. reading 1994-98), Am. Ednl. Rsch. Assn., Wis. Coun. Tchrs. English (pres. 1999-2000), Wis. State Reading Assn. Home: PO Box 379 Whitewater WI 53190-0379 Office: U Wis 800 W Main St Whitewater WI 53190-1705 E-mail: zbikowsl@mail.uww.edu.

ZDANIS, RICHARD ALBERT, academic administrator; b. Balt., July 15, 1935; s. Albert Francis and Elsie (Kral) Z.; m. Barbara Rosenberger, June 5, 1955; children: Michael Richard, Carole Lynn. BA, Johns Hopkins U., 1957, PhD in Physics, 1960. Rsch. assoc. Princeton (N.J.) U., 1960-61, instr., 1961-62; asst. prof., then assoc. prof. Johns Hopkins U., Balt., 1962-69, prof., 1969-88, assoc. provost, 1975-79, v.p. for adminstrv. svcs., 1977-79, vice provost, 1979-88; provost Case Western Res. U., Cleve., 1988-2000, retired, 2000. Cons. Naval Ordnance Lab., 1967-68, 69-74. Bd. dirs. Great Lakes Mus., 1990—, Cleve. Edn. Found., 1990-96; mem. governing coun. Ohio LINK, 1994-2000; mem. Cleve. Initiative for Edn., 1999—. Mem.: Associated Univs. Inc. (bd. dirs.), Am. Phys. Soc.

ZDEBLICK, MARK JAMES, information technology executive; s. William and Mary Zdeblick; m. Melanie C. Smitt; children: Daniel, Grace. Student, U. Paris, No. III, Versailles, France, 1981—82; B of Fine and Applied Arts, Arch., BSCE, U. Ill., 1982; MS Aeronautics and Astronautics, Stanford U., 1984, PhD, 1988. Founder, dir., chief tech. officer Redwood Microsystems, Menlo Park, Calif., 1989—97; consulting prof. Stanford (Calif.) U., 1997—98; pres. Aspire Tech., Portola Valley, Calif., 1998—2000; chief tech. officer optical switch program K2 Optronics, Inc., Sunnyvale, 2000—01; entrepreneur in residence Spring Ridge Ventures, Atherton, 2001—02; CEO Vivomems, Inc., 2001—02. Contbr. Pres. Ladera Cmty. Assn., 1994—95; judge Santa Cruz County Sci. Fair, 2001, IEEE Sect. 6 for Intel Sci. Fair, 2001; Bd. dirs. Ladera Comty. Assn., 1992—95; bd. dirs. Palo Alto Adult Soccer League, 1990—91. Recipient Commendation for Excellence in Tech. Comms., Laser Focus World, 2001, Trip to Nixon's Inauguration Competition, Park Ridge Newspaper Svc., 1973, Sawyer Cup, Phi Gamma Delta, 1981. Mem.: IEEE, Sensors and Materials Jour. (assoc. editor 1993—2002), Phi Eta Sigma, Tau Beta Pi. Achievements include patents for integrated microminiature electric-to-fluidic valve pressure/flow regulator; method of making an integrated scanning tunneling microscope; microfabricated cantilever stylus with integrated conical tip; microfabricated microscope assembly; integrated variable focal length lens and its application; microfabricated cantilever stylus with integrated pyramidal tip; integrated scanning tunneling microscope; integrated mass storage device. Avocations: soccer, hiking, travel, swimming. Home: 300 La Mesa Dr Menlo Park CA 94028 Office: Vivomems, Inc 3351 El Camino Real Menlo Park CA 94027 Home Fax: 650-854-9198; Office Fax: 650-299-9033. Personal E-mail: mark.zdeblick@stanfordalumni.org. Business E-Mail: mzdeblick@stvc.com.

ZDILLA, ROBYN LYNN, occupational therapist; b. Warren, Ohio, Apr. 15, 1970; d. James Anthony and Suzanne (Lisovich) Z. BS in Occupational Therapy, U. Pitts., 1992; MBA, Waynesburg Coll., 2001. Occupational therapist Allegheny Gen. Hosp., Pitts., 1992-95, Nova Care Inc., Pitts., 1993-95; dir. occupl. therapy Manocare Health Svcs., 1995-99; cluster dir. rehab. HCR Manorcare Health Svcs., various, Pa., 1999—. Participant accreditation for occupl. therapy program as clin. supr. U. Pitts., 1997; item writer Nat. Bd. for Cert. in Occupl. Therapy, 2001—. Mem.: Gold Key Soc. Roman Catholic. Avocations: aerobics. Home: 705 Vermont Ave Pittsburgh PA 15234-1219 Office: HCR Manorcare Health Svcs 1848 Greentree Rd Pittsburgh PA 15220-1851

ZDZINSKI, STEPHEN FRANKLIN, music educator, researcher; b. Buffalo, Sept. 16, 1959; s. Edwin Eugene and Theo Norma Zdzinski. MusB, U. Cin., 1982; M of Music Edn., Ind. U., 1987, PhD, 1993. Pub. sch. music tchr. various sch. dists.; asst. prof. music Wayne State U., Detroit, 1996—99, U. S.C., Columbia, 1999—. Dir. S.C. Music Edn. Rsch. Ctr., Columbia, 2001—; Music Education Representative College Music Society (MidAtlantic Chapter), SC, 2001—02; higher edn. rep. S.C. Visual and Performing Arts Stds. Rev. Bd., Columbia, 2001—; item writer S.C. State Music Assessment, Columbia, 2001—; vis. asst. prof. Ind. U., Bloomington, 1994—96; vis. asst. prof. faculty music U. Toronto, Ont., Canada, 1993—94; vis. lectr. U. Md., College Park, 1992—93. Contbr. articles to profl. jours. Recipient Citation for Outstanding Student Chapter Growth, Music Educators Nat. Conf., 1997—98. Mem.: ASTA with NSOA, MENC SRIGS (Web master 1999—2002), S.C. Music Edn. Assn. (rsch. chair 2001—02, Webmaster 2001—), Soc. for Rsch. in Music Edn., Soc. for Music Tchr. Edn., Soc. for Gen. Music, Internat. Soc. for Music Edn., Coun. for Rsch. in Music Edn., Coll. Music Soc., Assn. for Tech. in Music Instrn., Music Educators Nat. Conf., Mayday Group. United Methodist. Avocations: travel, birdwatching, watercolor painting, tennis. Office: U S C Sch Music Columbia SC 29208 Office Fax: 803-777-6508. Personal E-mail: szdzinski@mozart.sc.edu. Business E-Mail: szdzinski@mozart.sc.edu.

ZEAGER, LLOYD, librarian; b. Elizabethtown, Pa., Sept. 19, 1942; s. Russel S. and Anna Mae (Givens) Z. BA, Goshen Coll., 1976; MS, Drexel U., 1983. Sec., adminstrv. asst. Mennonite Brotherly Aid, Salunga, Pa., 1967-72; asst. libr. Lancaster (Pa.) Mennonite Hist. Soc., 1976-82, libr., 1983—. Author: A York County Givens Family, 1980, Master Alphabetical Compilation of Hymns Appearing in Mennonite Hymn Books, 1980, Mission in the City, 1997. Mem. ALA, Hymn Soc. U.S. and Can. Democrat. Mennonite. Avocations: hymnology, genealogy. Office: Lancaster Mennonite Hist Soc 2215 Millstream Rd Lancaster PA 17602-1429

ZEALEY, SHARON JANINE, lawyer; b. St. Paul, Aug. 30, 1959; d. Marion Edward and Freddie Zealey. BS, Xavier U. of La., 1981; JD, U. Cin., 1984. Bar: Ohio 1984; U.S. Dist. Ct. (so. dist.) Ohio 1985; U.S. Ct. Appeals (6th cir.) 1990; U.S. Supreme Ct. 1990. Law clk. U.S. Atty. for S. Dist. of Ohio, Cin., 1982; trust adminstr. Firstar Bank, 1984-86; atty. UAW Legal Svcs., 1986-88; assoc. Manley, Burke, Lipton & Fischer, 1988-91; mng. atty. and dep. atty. gen. Ohio Atty. Gen. Office, 1991-95; asst. U.S. atty. criminal div. for So. Dist. Ohio U.S. Attys. Office, 1995-97; United States atty. So. Dist. Ohio, 1997—2001; ptnr. Blank Rome Comisky & McCauley, 2001—. Adj. instr. lawU. Cin., 1997—; mem. U.S. Atty. Gen.'s Adv. Com., 1999—2001, chair civil rights subcom., 2001; mem. merit selection com. Sixth Cir. Ct. of Appeals Bankruptcy Ct., 1992—96. Mem. commn. Cin. Cmty. Action Now, 2001—; commr. Tall Stacks Commn., City of Cin., 1990—94, Mayor's Commn. on Children, City of Cin., 1992—94; mem. equal employment adv. rev. panel City of Cin., 1989—91; trustee, bd. visitors U. Cin. Coll. Law, 1992—; trustee Legal Aid Soc. Cin., 1987—92. Named Career Woman of Achievement, Cin. YWCA, 1988; recipient Disting. Alumni award, Friends of Women's Studies, U. Cin., 2001, Theodore M. Berry award for outstanding achievement in politics and in svc. to cmty., Cin. chpt. NACCP, 1998, Nicholas Longworth III Alumni Achievement award for disting. pub. svc., U. Cin. Coll. Law, 1997. Mem. Black Lawyers Assn. of Cin. (pres. 1989-91, round table 1988-), Legal Aid Soc. (sec. 1991-92), ABA, Fed. Bar Assn., Ohio Bar Assn., Nat. Bar Assn. (bd. govs. 1988-1990, Mem. of Yr. region VI 1990), Cin. Bar Assn. (trustee 1989-94), Cin. CAN Commn. Democrat. Episcopalian. Office: 1700 PNC Ctr 201 E 5th St Cincinnati OH 45202 Fax: 513-362-8787. E-mail: zealey@blankRome.com.

ZEARFOSS, HERBERT KEYSER, lawyer; b. Montandon, Pa., Oct. 13, 1929; s. Dean Wilson and Susan Lesher (Keyser) Z.; m. Thelma Mary McCarthy, Dec. 19, 1953 (dec. 1984); children: Timothy McCarthy, Jonathan Andrew, Sarah Creighton; m. Suzanne VanderVeer, Nov. 14, 1992. AB, Bucknell U., 1951; postgrad., Yale U., 1951-53; JD, Am. U., 1958. Bar: Pa. 1959, U.S. Dist. Ct. (mid. dist.) Pa. 1959, U.S. Dist. Ct. (ea. dist.) Pa. 1975, U.S. Supreme Ct. 1975. Ptnr. Fetter & Zearfoss, Lewisburg, Pa., 1959-60; asst. counsel Fidelity Mut. Life Ins. Co., Phila., 1960-67, sr. v.p., gen. counsel, 1978-82; sec., mgr. Ins. Fedn. of Pa. Inc., 1967-68; ptnr. Zearfoss & Campbell, 1968-78; sr. v.p., sec., gen. counsel Provident Indemmity Life Ins. Co. and parent co. Provident Am. Corp., Norristown, Pa., 1982-87; sole practice Radnor, 1987-91; adj. faculty Cabrini Coll., 1988-90; asst. gen. counsel, asst. sec. Teleflex Inc., Limerick, Pa., 1991-2001. Author: The Life Insurance Law of Pennsylvania, 1983; book rev. editor Am. U. Law Rev., 1956-58. Rep. Pa. Gen. Assembly from 167th dist., 1968-78; justice of the Peace, Radnor Twp., Delaware County, Pa., 1966-67; v.p. Valley Forge coun. Boy Scouts Am., 1982-86 (silver beaver award 1989); treas. Netherlands-Am. Amity Trust, Inc., 1981-86. Lt. comdr. USNR, 1954-58. Decorated officer Order of Orange-Nassau (Netherlands), 1992. Mem. ABA, Pa. Bar Assn., Assn. Life Ins. Counsel, Netherlands Soc. Phila. (pres. 1979-83), SAR (pres. Phila. Continental chpt. 1986-87), Colonial Soc. Pa. (gov. 1988-91), Del. Soc. Cin. (pres. 1996-99), Pa. Geneal. Soc. (counsel 1987-91, pres. 1995—), Soc. War 1812 (pres. gen. 1996-99), Mil. Order Loyal Legion U.S. (comdr., Pa. comdr. 1999-2001), Sovereign Mil. Order Temple Jerusalem (grand officer, judge adv.-in-chief 2001—), Priory of Phila. (prior 1994-98), Yale Club of Phila., Phila. Club, Penn Club, Merion Cricket Club, Omicron Delta Kappa, Phi Alpha Delta, Phi Alpha Theta, Tau Kappa Alpha, Pi Sigma Alpha. Republican. Presbyterian. Home: 532 Candace Ln Villanova PA 19085-1702 E-mail: hzearfoss@aol.com.

ZEBERSKY, EDWARD HERBERT, lawyer; b. N.Y.C., May 16, 1966; s. Joseph Zebersky and Patricia (Hirst) Leff. BBA, U. Wis., 1988; JD cum laude, U. Miami, Fla., 1991. Bar: Fla. 1991, U.S. Dist. Ct. (so. dist.) Fla. 1992. Prodn. mgr. Toy Biz Inc., N.Y.C., 1988; assoc. Tripp Scott Conklin & Smith PA, Ft. Lauderdale, 1991-93; dir., mng. ptnr. Zebersky, Zebersky & Guilianti, Plantation, Fla., 1993—; dir. Zebersky & Payne, LLP, Hollywood, 1997, Zebersky, Payne & Kushner, LLP, Hollywood. Cons. Bole Ent Ltd., Oyster Bay, N.Y., 1991-94; staff atty. Broward Lawyers Care, Ft. Lauderdale, 1991—, Fla. Bar Pro Bono Svc., Tallahassee, 1992—, Lawyers for the Arts, Ft. Lauderdale, 1993-94. Deans Honor scholar U. Miami, 1989-9, 90-91. Mem. ATLA, Acad. Fla. Trial Lawyers (chmn. ins. com.), Greater Miami Jewish Fedn., Miami Project Cure Paralysis, Order of Coif. Avocations: mountain climbing, fishing, golf. Office: Zebersky, Payne & Kushner LLP 4000 Hollywood Blvd. Suite 400-N Hollywood FL 33021-6748

ZEBLEY, JOSEPH WILDMAN, III, physician, educator; b. Washington, Aug. 18, 1949; s. Joseph Wildman and Edith Sophie (Schubel) Z.; m. Bernardina Maria Van Eck, Apr. 3, 1971; children: Thomas Edwin, Nicolas Alexander. BA, Johns Hopkins Univ., 1970; MD, Univ. Md., 1976. Residency dept. family medicine Univ. Md., Balt., 1976-79; pvt. practice, 1979-85; medical dir. Towson (Md.) Medical Assocs., 1986-96; physician Greenspring Medical Assocs., Balt., 1997—. Clin. instr. family medicine U. Md., 1979—; cons. UNAFORMEC, Paris, 1991-92, DuPont Pharm., Wilmington, Del., 1994-95; chief divsn. family medicine St. Joseph Hosp., Towson, 1999, clin. dir. Ctr. for Health Enhancement, 1999; mem. spkrs. bur. Lilly Pharm., 2001, GlaxoSmithKline. Contbr. articles to profl. jours. Edn. chmn. Md. Cancer Consortium, Balt., 1992-96; vice spkr. Md. Chirurgical Faculty Md., 1999—. Named Home Care Physician of Yr., Union Meml. Hosp., 1988, Family Physician of Yr., Md. Acad. Family Physicians, 1995, Balt. Best Physician, Balt. mag., 1997, 1999. Fellow: Am. Acad. Family Physicians (del. 1997—); mem.: AMA (del. 2001—02), Balt. City Med. Soc. (pres. 1998), Md. Acad. Family Physicians (past pres.). Lutheran. Avocations: classical music, hiking, camping. Office: Greenspring Med Assocs 2 Hamill Rd Ste 222 Baltimore MD 21210-1815 E-mail: greenspringmedic@earthlink.net.

ZEBROSKI, EDWIN LEOPOLD, risk management consultant; b. Chgo., Apr. 1, 1921; s. Peter Paul and Sophie (Rydz) Z.; m. Gisela Karin Rudolph, Sept. 6, 1969; children: Lars, Zoe, Susan, Peggy. BS, U. Chgo., 1941; PhD, U. Calif., Berkeley, 1947. Registered prof. engr., Calif. Project engr. Gen. Electric Co., Schenectady, N.Y., 1947-53, mgr. devel. engring. San Jose, Calif., 1958-73; mgr. engring. SRI Internat., Menlo Park, 1954-58, dir. systems and materials dept., 1974-79; dir. nuclear safety analysis ctr. EPRI, Palo Alto, 1979-81; v.p. engring. INPO, Atlanta, 1981-83; chief nuclear scientist EPRI, 1983-88; dir. risk mgmt. svcs. APTECH Engring. Svcs., Sunnyvale, Calif., 1988-97; safety and risk mgmt. advisor DOE-Sandia Nat. Lab., 2000—. Vis. prof. Purdue U., West Lafayette, Ind., 1977-78; cons. OTA, Washington, 1980, 82-83, Dept. Energy, Washington, 1985-90, panels Nat. Rsch. Coun., 1990—, Electricite de France, 1986-87, Dept. Interior, Washington, 1987-89, EPRI, Palo Alto, 1988-98, Acad. Sci., USSR, 1987, Karlsruhe Lab., Germany, 1988; mem. commn. engring. edn. NRC, Washington, 1970-73; mem. NAS-NRC Panel on Decision-Making in Govt. Agy., 1997-98; mem. NAS-NRC Panel on High Level Waste R&D, 2001; mem. NAE Panel on Countering Terrorism, 2002--. Contbr. chpts. to books, numerous articles to profl. jours.; patentee in field. Pres. bd. Unitarian Ch., Palo Alto, 1967-68. Recipient Charles A. Coffin award Gen. Electric Co., Schenectady, 1954, Edward Teller award, 2002. Fellow AAAS, Am. Nuclear Soc. (bd. exec. com. 1969-71), Am. Inst. Chemists; mem. NAE (chmn. energy com. 1984-86, chmn. mem. com. 1986-87, policy com. 1995-96), Am. Phys. Soc., Soc. for Risk Analysis. Avocations: safety and risk management, decision analysis, music, writing. Office: ELGIS Consulting 1546 Plateau Ave Los Altos CA 94024-5320 E-mail: edzebroski@worldnet.att.net.

ZECEVIC, ALEKSANDAR I. engineering educator; b. Belgrade, Yugoslavia, Feb. 28, 1961; arrived in U.S., 1988; s. Ilija and Dragoslava Zecevic; m. Jelena Vilotijevic, May 28, 1988; children: Nikola, Stefan. BSEE, U. Belgrade, 1984; MSEE, Santa Clara U., 1990, PhD, 1993. Asst. prof. Santa Clara (Calif.) U., 1994—99, assoc. prof., 1999—. Contbr. articles to profl. jours. Mem.: Alpha Sigma Nu. Home: 3332 Earl Dr Santa Clara CA 95051 Office: Santa Clara U 500 El Camino Real Santa Clara CA 95053

ZECHMAN, DAVID MARK, health system executive, educator; b. Cleve., Jan. 31, 1956; s. Richard Lee Zechman and Marilyn Ann Molter; m. Rhonda Dale Lovett, Aug. 20, 1977; children: Audra, Alyssa. BS, Miami U., Oxford, Ohio, 1977; postgrad. studies in Respiratory Therapy, Northwestern U. Med. Sch., Chgo., 1983; M in Pub. Adminstrn., Cleve. State U., 1989. Biology tchr. and coach St. Bridget Sch. and Holy Name H.S., Cleve., 1982; respiratory therapist St. Luke's Hosp., 1982-83; supr. respiratory therapy Fairview Hosp., 1983-85; supr., clin. instr. respiratory therapy Metrohealth Med. Ctr., 1985-86, staff devel. instr., 1986-87, mgmt. specialist dermatology, renal hemodialysis, 1987-89, acting adminstrv. dir. dept. medicine, 1989, mgr. divsn. cardiology, 1989-91; adminstrv. dir. cardiovascular svcs. St. Vincent Med. Ctr., Toledo, 1991-92; adminstr. Mid-Am. Heart Inst. St. Luke's Hosp., Kansas City, Mo., 1992-97; v.p. cardiovascular svcs. St. Luke's Shawnee Mission Health System, 1997—. Mem. Nat. Fin. Com. United Network for Organ Sharing; faculty presenter Am. Coll. Cardiovascular Adminstrs., Boston, 1991, Anaheim, Calif. 1991, Mpls., Atlanta, 1993; chmn. cardiology adv. com. Novation. H.S. Sunday sch. tchr. 1989-98; bd. dirs. Kansas City chpt. Am. Heart Assn., 1994—; cmty. youth softball coach Blue Valley Recreation, 1994-2000; bd. dirs. Blue Valley Christian Ch., chmn. pastor rels. com., 1995-96; mem. Kansas City Urban League Multicultural Leadership Devel. Inst., 1997, Family Resource Ctr. Bd.; v.p. Jewish Hosp. Healthcare Svcs.; CEO Rudd Heart and Lung Inst. Recipient Disting. Leadership award Nat. Assn. for Cmty. Leadership, 2000; named Bd. Mem. of Yr. Kansas City chpt. Am. Heart Assn., 1998-99. Mem. Am. Coll. Healthcare Execs. (cert. healthcare exec.), Alliance of Cardiovascular Profls. (pres.). Avocations: volleyball, basketball, golf, running. Office: St Luke's Hosp 4401 Wornall Rd Kansas City MO 64111-3220

ZECKHAUSER, RICHARD JAY, economist, educator; b. Phila., Nov. 1, 1940; s. Julius Nathaniel and Estelle (Borgenicht) Z.; m. Nancy Mackell Hoover, Sept. 9, 1967; children: Bryn Gordon, Benjamin Rennell. AB, Harvard U., 1962, PhD, 1969. Jr. fellow Soc. Fellows Harvard U., 1965-68, mem. faculty, 1968—, prof. polit. econ. Kennedy Sch., 1972—, now Frank P. Ramsey prof. polit. economy. Bd. dirs. Comm. Group Ins., Mass.; founder, bd. dirs. Niederhoffer, Cross & Zeckhauser, 1968-84. Co-author: A Primer for Policy Analysis, 1978, Demographic Dimensions of the New Republic, 1981, Joining the Elite: The Early Admissions Game, 2003; editor or co-editor: Benefit-Cost and Policy Analysis, 1974, What Role for Government, 1982, Principals and Agents: The Structure of Business, 1985, Am. Soc. Pub. and Pvt. Responsibilities, 1986; Privatization and State-Owned Enterprise: Lessons from the United Kingdom, Canada and the United States, 1988, Strategy and Choice, 1991, Wise Choices, Games, Decisions, and Negotiations, 1996. contbr. more than 185 articles to profl. jours. and books; rsch. on fin., coll. admissions and healthcare. Bd. dirs. Commonwealth Sch. Fellow Econometric Soc., Assn. for Pub. Policy and Mgmt., Am. Acad. Arts and Scis, Inst. of Medicine/Nat. Acad. Scis. Achievements include winning numerous regional and nat. contract bridge competitions (finalist 1998 world pairs championship). Office: Harvard U John F Kennedy Sch Govt 79 Jfk St Cambridge MA 02138-5801

ZEDROSSER, JOSEPH JOHN, lawyer; b. Milw., Jan. 24, 1938; s. Joseph and Rose (Zollner) Z.; m. Antonina Krass, Sept. 6, 1997. AB, Marquette U., 1959; LLB, Harvard U., 1963. Bar: N.Y. 1964, U.S. Dist. Ct. (so. dist.) N.Y. 1966, U.S. Dist. Ct. (ea. dist.) N.Y. 1971, U.S. Ct. Appeals (2d cir.) 1971, U.S. Ct. Appeals (D.C. Cir.) 1975, U.S. Supreme Ct. 1975. Assoc. William G. Mulligan, N.Y.C., 1964-67, Christy, Bauman, Frey and Christy and successors, N.Y.C., 1967-71; dir. cmty. devel. unit Bedford-Stuyvesant Cmty. Legal Svcs. Corp., 1971-73; assoc. fed. defender svcs. unit Legal Aid Soc., 1973-74; asst. atty. gen. Environ. Protection Bur., N.Y. State Dept. Law, 1974-80; regional counsel EPA, 1980-82; assoc. prof. St. John's U. Sch. Law, 1982-86; ptnr. Rivkin, Radler, Dunne & Bayh, Uniondale, N.Y., 1986-89, Breed, Abbott & Morgan, N.Y.C., 1989-93, Whitman Breed Abbott & Morgan, N.Y.C., 1993-95; v.p. CPR Inst. for Dispute Resolution, 1996; sr. investigative counsel com. on investigations, taxation, and gov. ops. N.Y. State Senate, 1998-99; asst. atty. gen. Environ. Protection Bur. N.Y. State Office Atty. Gen., N.Y.C., 1999—. Lectr., contbr. to course handbooks for courses sponsored by Practicing Law Inst. and other assns. Lt. USNR, 1965-74, USAR, 1963-65. Mem. ABA, Assn. of Bar of City of N.Y., N.Y. State Bar Assn. (mem. Environ. Law Sect. Exec. Com.), Alpha Sigma Nu. Roman Catholic. Home: 45 E End Ave Apt 11F New York NY 10028-7982

ZEE, PHYLLIS C. physician, educator, researcher; b. Hong Kong, June 27, 1954; came to U.S., 1973; d. William and King Di (Wong) Cheung; m. Benjamin Zee; children: David, Caroline, Alex. BA, Mills Coll., 1976; PhD, Chgo. Med. Sch., 1980, MD, 1983. Diplomate Am. Bd. Psychiatry and Neurology, Am. Bd. Med. Examiners, Am. Bd. Sleep Medicine. NIH postdoctoral fellow Northwestern U., Evanston, Ill., 1987-89, asst. prof. neurobiology and neurology Chgo., 1989-95, assoc. prof., 1996—2000, prof., 2001—; dir. Sleep Ctr. Northwestern Meml. Hosp., 1991—. Mem. adv. bd. Enlightened Tech., Md., 1994—; mem. bd. advisors Jour. Biol. Rhythms, 1994—, mem. NIH study sect. Contbr. articles to profl. jours. Fellow Buelher Ctr. on Aging, 1995—, Brookdale Found., 1994; grantee NIH, 1994—. Fellow Am. Sleep Disorders Assn.; mem. Am. Acad. Neurology, Soc. for Neurosci., Soc. Biol. Rhythms, Am. Neur. Assn. Office: Northwestern U 710 N Lake Shore Dr Chicago IL 60611-3006

ZEECK, DAVID, newspaper editor; Exec. editor The News Tribune, Tacoma, 1994—. Office: The News Tribune 1950 South St Tacoma WA 98405 Mailing: PO Box 11000 Tacoma WA 98411 E-mail: david.zeeck@mail.tribnet.com.*

ZEFF, STEPHEN ADDAM, accounting educator; b. Chgo., July 26, 1933; s. Roy David and Hazel (Sex) Zeff. BS, U. Colo., 1955, MS, 1957; MBA, U. Mich., 1960, PhD, 1962; D in Econs. honoris causa, Turku Sch. Econs. and Bus. Adminstrn., Finland, 1990. Instr. U. Colo., 1955-57; teaching fellow, instr. U. Mich., 1958-61; asst. prof. acctg. Tulane U., New Orleans, 1961-63, assoc. prof., 1963-67, prof., 1967-77, W.R. Irby prof., 1977-78; prof. acctg. Rice U., 1978-79, Herbert S. Autrey prof., 1979—. Prof. actg. U. Limburg, The Netherlands, 1992-95; vis. assoc. prof. U. Calif.-Berkeley, 1964-65, U. Chgo., 1966; vis. prof. Instituto Tecnológico y de Estudios Superiores de Monterrey, Mex., 1969, Victoria U., Wellington, New Zealand, 1976, Harvard U., 1977-78, Northwestern U., 1982, 83, U. Tex.-Austin, 1986, Free U. Amsterdam, 1990, 91, U. Nijenrode, 1994-97; spl. lectr., hon. sr. Fulbright scholar Monash U., Australia, 1972. Author: Uses of Accounting for Small Business, 1962, American Accounting Association, Its First 50 Years, 1966,

Forging Accounting Principles in Five Countries: A History and an Analysis of Trends, 1972, Forging Accounting Principles in Australia, 1973, Forging Accounting Principles in New Zealand, 1979, Company Financial Reporting: A Historical and Comparative Study of the Dutch Regulatory Process, 1992, Henry Rand Hatfield: Humanist, Scholar and Accounting Educator, 2000; editor: Business Schools and the Challenge of International Business, 1968, Asset Appreciation, Business Income and Price-Level Accounting: 1918-1935, 1976, The Accounting Postulates and Principles Controversy of the 1960s, 1982, The U.S. Accounting Profession in the 1890s and Early 1900s, 1988; co-editor: Essays in Honor of William A. Paton: Pioneer Accounting Theorist, 1979, Sourcebook on Accounting Principles and Auditing Procedures 1917-1953, 1984, Milestones in the British Accounting Literature, 1996, Accounting Reseach, 1948-58, 1996, Readings and Notes on Financial Accounting, 5th edit., 1997; book rev. editor Acctg. Rev., 1962-66, editor, 1977-82; rev. editor Acctg. Horizons, 1995-97, The Internat. Jour. of Acctg., 1997—; founder, editor Boletín Interamericano de Contabilidad, 1968-71; contbr. articles to profl. jours. Named to Acctg. Hall of Fame, Ohio State U., 2002; recipient Hourglass award, Acad. Acctg. Historians, 1973, 2001. Mem.: AAUP, Fin. Execs. Internat., Inst. Mgmt. Accts., Am. Econ. Assn., European Acctg. Assn. (exec. com. 1981—), Am. Acctg. Assn. (dir. edn. 1969—71, pres. 1985—86, named Outstanding Acctg. Educator 1988, Outstanding Internat. Acctg. Educator 1999), Tex. Soc. CPAs (hon.), Harvard Club. Home: 4545 Acacia St Bellaire TX 77401-3701 Office: Rice University MS 531 PO Box 2932 Houston TX 77252-2932 E-mail: sazeff@rice.edu.

ZEFFIRELLI, LUCIA, dance instructor, music teacher, choreographer, director, dancer, actress; b. Michigan City, Ind., Mar. 18, 1961; d. Vincent J. and Lorraine May (Keen) Strangio; 1 child, Paolo Madden Zeffirelli; m. Scott Grady Madden, Mar. 4, 2000. BA in French and Music, U. Mich., 1984; student, Eastern Mich. U., 1986-87. Piano tchr. self employed, Tucson and Ann Arbor, Mich., 1985-86, 98—; dancer J. Parker Copley Repertory Co., Ann Arbor, 1986-88, Orts Theater of Dance, Tucson, 1994-95, dance instr., 1994—96, Dance Visions Studio, Tucson, 1996—2000, Dance Moves, Tucson, 2000—; founder, artistic dir., choreographer Zeffirelli 8 Dance Co., 1996—. Choreographer/dancer Neptune's Dream, No Exit, 8 of Swords, Night of the Gypsies, Stigmata, A Scream Got Lost, High Priestess, Longing, Sunnyside Up, True Camp, Still Life with Melancholy, Spleen, others. Recipient 1st prize, Concerto Competition, LaPorte (Ind.) Symphony Orch., 1979, Individual Artist grant, Tucson/Pima Arts Coun., 2001. Democrat. Avocations: gardening, laying tile, remodeling, refinishing. Home: 4817 E Eastland St Tucson AZ 85711-4949

ZEGARELLI, EDWARD VICTOR, retired dental educator, researcher; b. Utica, N.Y., Sept. 9, 1912; s. Frank Anthony and Maria Josephine (Ambroselli) Z.; m. Irene Marie Ceconi, June 17, 1939; children: Edward V., David J., Philip E., Peter J. AB, Columbia U., 1934, DDS, 1937, DSc (hon.), 1983; MS, U. Chgo., 1942. Staff Sch. Dental and Oral Surgery, Columbia U., 1937-78, asst. instr., then successively instr., asst. prof., asso. prof., head diagnosis and roentgenology, 1947-58, chmn. com. dental research, 1956-78, Dr. Edwin S. Robinson prof. dentistry, 1958, prof. dentistry, dir. div. stomatology, 1958-78, acting dean, 1973, dean, 1974-78, dean emeritus, 1979—; Edward V. Zegarelli prof. dentistry, 1993—; chmn. sect. hosp. dental services Columbia-Presbyn. Med. Center; dir. and attending dentist dental service Presbyn. Hosp., 1974-79, also mem. exec. com. of med. bd., 1974-76; police surgeon N.Y.C., 1968-89; chmn. exam. com. N.E. Regional Bd. Dental Examiners, 1969-90. Cons. VA, Washington; Weisberger Meml. lectr. Harvard U., 1969, Mershon Meml. lectr., 1970, Ralph L. Spaulding Meml. lectr., 1972; deans com. Montrose VA Hosp.; cons. East Orange, Kingsbridge VA hosps., Westchester Med. Ctr., Valhalla, N.Y., USPHS, Phelps Meml. Hosp., Tarrytown, N.Y., Vassar Bros. Hosp., Poughkeepsie, Bur. Medicine, FDA, Council on Dental Therapeutics; area cons. VA; cons.-lectr. U.S. Naval Dental Sch., Bethesda, Md., 1970-78; pres. N.Y. State Bd. Dental Examiners, 1970-71; chmn. exam. rev. com. N.E. Regional Bd. Dental Examiners, 1969-90; Samuel Charles Miller Meml. lectr., 1976; mem. council deans Am. Assn. Dental Schs., 1973-79; mem. postgrad. edn. com. N.Y.C. Cancer Com.; mem. profl. edn. and grants com. N.Y.C. div. Am. Cancer Soc., 1963-73; chmn. panel on drugs in dentistry NAS, NRC, FDA; mem. N.Y. State Health Research Council, N.Y. Commn. on Health Manpower; chmn. bd. govs. (dental) Gen. Health Ins., N.Y.C. Contbg. author: The Thyroid, Medical Roentgenology, Current Pediatric Therapy, Cancer of Head and Neck; author: (with others) Pharmacotherapeutics of Oral Disease, 1964, Clinical Stomatology, 1966, Diagnosis of Diseases of Mouth and Jaws, 1969, 2d edit., 1978; also articles on mouth, jaw bone disease. Bd. dirs. Hist. Soc. Tarrytowns, 1983, United Way Tarrytowns, 1983, YMCA of Tarrytowns, 1984, Phelps Meml. Hosp. Hospice Agy, 1986. Recipient Austin Sniffen medal 9th Dist. Dental Soc., 1961; Columbia U. Dental Alumni Research award, 1963; Jarvie-Burkhart medal N.Y. Dental Soc., 1970; Samuel J. Miller medal Am. Acad. Oral Medicine, 1976; Henry Spenadel award 1st Dist. Dental Soc., 1979; Man of Yr. award C. of C. Tarrytowns and Irvington, 1983; Man of Achievement award Americans for Italian Migration, 1984; named Disting. Practitioner mem. Nat. Acads. Practice, 1986. Fellow Am. Coll. Dentists (William J. Gies medal 1981), N.Y. Acad. Dentistry, Internat. Coll. Dentists, 9th Dist. Dental Soc.; mem. Am. Acad. Oral Pathology, Am. Assn. for Cancer Edn. (charter), Am. Assn. Dental Examiners (Dentist Citizen of Yr. award 1978), Orgn. Tchrs. Oral Diagnosis, N.Y. Acad. Scis., N.Y. Dental Soc. (chmn. council sci. research 1956-71), Greater N.Y. Acad. Prosthodontics (hon.), Guatemala Dental Soc. (hon.), Am. Dental Assn. (mem. council dental therapeutics 1963-69, vice chmn. 1969), Columbia Dental Alumni Assn., William Jarvie Research Soc., Internat. Assn. Dental Research, AAAS, Nat. Italian-Am. Found., Sigma Xi (chpt. pres. 1974-76), Omicron Kappa Upsilon (sec. treas. Columbia chpt. 1944-57, pres. 1959-60), Sigma Phi Alpha., Knight Malta. Lodges: Rotary (pres. 1985-86) (Tarrytown). Home: 120 Gory Brook Rd Sleepy Hollow NY 10591-1724

ZEGAS, ALAN LEE, lawyer; b. Newark, Oct. 28, 1952; s. Norman and Harriet (Lava) Z.; m. Tina Hannah Burk, Aug. 22, 1976; children: Rachel Sarah, Leah Ariel, Joelle Shira. BS, U. Pa., 1974; MBA, Harvard U., 1978; JD, Rutgers U., 1981. Bar: N.J. 1981, U.S. Dist. Ct. N.J. 1981, N.Y. 1982, U.S. Ct. Appeals (3d cir.) 1982. Law clk. to Hon. H. Lee Sarokin U.S. Dist. Ct. N.J., Newark, 1981-83; assoc. Robinson, Wayne, Levin, Riccio & La Sala, 1983-84; pvt. practice Chatham, N.J., 1984—. Adj. prof. law Rutgers U., Newark, 1983-88; reader N.J. Bd. Bar Examiners, Trenton, 1985; pres. Assn. Criminal Def. Lawyers N.J., 1998-99. Editor-in-chief Rutgers U. Law Rev., 1980-81; editor (pamphlet) Law Tips for the Elderly, 1983. Mem. N.J. Bar Assn. (dist. rep. young lawyers div. 1983-85, vice chmn. 1985-86, trustee 1986-88, chmn. criminal law sect. 1996-97), Essex County Bar Assn. (chmn. lawyers referral service 1986—), Rutgers U. Law Sch. Alumni Assn. (rep. 1983—), U. Pa. Alumni Assn. (sec. 1986-87), Harvard U. Bus. Sch. Alumni Assn., Assn. Criminal Def. Lawyers of N.J. (pres. 1998-99). Home: 476 South St New Providence NJ 07974-2132 Office: 552 Main St Chatham NJ 07928-2120

ZEHEL, WENDELL EVANS, surgeon; b. Brownsville, Pa., Mar. 6, 1934; s. Michael and Emma (Evans) Z.; m. Joan Leasure, Nov. 1, 1958; children: Lori Ann, Wendell Charles. BA, Washington and Jefferson Coll., 1956; MD, U. Pitts., 1960; postgrad. in bioengring., Carnegie-Mellon U., 1968-75. Diplomate Am. Bd. Surgery. Intern Shadyside Hosp., Pitts., 1960-61; resident in surgery U. Pitts., VA Hosp., 1963-66, Wilmington (Del.) Med. Ctr., 1966-68; pvt. practice Pitts., 1968—; surgeon St. Clair Hosp., 1968—. Served with USAF, 1961-63. Fellow ACS; mem. Assn. Advancement of Med. Instrumentation. Home: 553 Harrogate Rd Pittsburgh PA 15241-2028 Office: 110 Fort Couch Rd Ste 3D Pittsburgh PA 15241-1030 Fax: (412) 835-7159.

ZEHLER, LINDA, artist; b. Cambridge, Mass., Nov. 28, 1954; d. Ralph and Ruth Jones; m. Daniel Zehler, Apr. 1, 1978; children: Stephanie, Christina, Kimberly. BS in Radiol. Health Physics, U. Mass., Lowell, 1976; postgrad., U. Hartford, 1989; BFA in Painting with honors, Maine Coll. Art, 1997. Radiation specialist Combustion Engring., Windsor, Conn., 1976-79; pres. Painting by LJZ, Wiscasset, Maine, 1997—, Perry, Ohio, 1997—. Active Maine Art Gallery, Wiscasset, 1995-98; vol. in art classes Perry Middle Sch., 1998-99. One-woman shows include Clapp House-Maine Coll. Art, 1993, 96, Davidson & Daus. Contemporary Art, Portland, Maine, 1996, Elements Gallery, Rockland, Maine, 1998, Ashtabula (Ohio) Art Ctr., 1999; exhibited in group shows Chocolate Ch. Ctr. for the Arts, Bath, 1994-97, Maine Art Gallery, Wiscasset, 1995-98, Maine Coll. Art, Portland, 1996, Danforth Gallery, Portland, 1996, Between the Muse, Rockland, 1997, Maine Coast Artists, Rockport, West Island Gallery, Bath, 1998, others. Active Bath United Meth. Ch., 1989—. Mem. Nat. Mus. Women in the Arts, Cleve. Mus. Art. Avocations: designing houses and landscaping, tennis, swimming, hiking, computers. Home: 3767 Leisurewood Ln Perry OH 44081-9637

ZEHNDER, FREDERICK JOHN, retired automotive executive; b. Detroit, Feb. 11, 1926; s. Frederick Ernest and Katherine Josephine (Raymann) Z.; m. Adele Louise Leslie, May 15, 1970; children: Frederick J. Jr., Leslie, John, Linda. BS, U.S. Merchant Marine Acad., 1947; MBA, U. Mich., 1951. Credit analyst Comerica Bank, Detroit, 1951-53; with Ford Motor Co., 1953—, budget analyst, 1953-64, with sales promotion and tng., 1964-76, used vehicle mgr. truck ops., 1976-80; ops. mgr. Ford Dealer Ops. div. Ford Motor Co., 1980-90, ret., 1990. Served to lt. USNR, 1947-67. Mem. U. Mich. Club, Delta Sigma Pi. Republican. Lutheran. Avocations: boating, photography.

ZEHRING, KAREN, information executive; b. Washington, Dec. 5, 1945; d. Robert William Zehring and Gretchen (Lorenz) Proos; m. George Lang, 1970 (div. 1979); m. Peter Frank Davis (div. 1995); children: Jesse, Antonia; stepsons: Timothy, Nicholas. BA, U. Denver, 1967; postgrad., Yale U., 1967-68. Assoc. pub. mktg. and sales Instl. Investor mag., N.Y.C., 1968-74; co-owner, co-creator Cafe des Artistes Restaurant, 1975-79; owner, pub. The Corp. Fin. Letter, 1976-78; group dir. planning and devel. Bus. Week mag., 1977-78; owner, pub., exec. editor Corp. Fin. Sourcebook The Corp. Fin. Bluebook, 1979-84; chmn., pres., pub., editor-in-chief Corp. Fin. mag., 1986-90; cons. Karen Zehring & Assocs., Castine, Maine, 1990-94; CEO SourceCapital InternetWork, N.Y.C., 1998—2001; mng. ptnr. Creative Devel. Ptnrs., 1995-98, 2001—. Bd. dirs. The Fund for Pub. Advocacy, Inc. Mem.: The Women's Forum. Unitarian Universalist.

ZEHRING, PEGGY JOHNSON, artist; b. Hutchinson, Kans., Jan. 4, 1941; d. Phillip E. and Bernice (Ashley) Johnson; m. R. David Zehring, July 27, 1963; children: Lisa, Geoff. BS, U. Kans., 1963; BA, U. Ill., 1977. Instr. Bellevue (Wash.) C.C., 1979-93, Sch. Visual Concepts, Seattle, 1985-86, Seattle Ctrl. C.C., 1987-97, North Seattle C.C., 1987-97, Coupeville (Wash.) Art Ctr., 1993—. Juror and lectr. Eastside Assn. Fine Art, Mercer Island Visual Arts League, Nat. League Am. Artists & Pen Women; lectr. Women Painters of Washington, Bellevue Art Mus., N.W. Watercolor Soc., Hutchinson Art Assn., Kans. One-woman shows include King County Arts Commn., Seattle, Blake Gallery, Seattle, Bellevue (Wash.) C.C., PACCAR, Bellevue, Pacific N.W. Bell, Seattle, U. Ill., Chgo., Hutchinson Art Assn.; exhibited in group shows at COCA Annual, Seattle, Seattle Art Mus. Sales & Rental Gallery, LewAllen Fine Art, Santa Fe, Bellevue Art Mus., Diablo Valley Coll., Elizabeth Prince Gallery, Prescott, Ariz.; represented in selected collections City of Lynnwood, Wash., Pacific NW Bell, PACCAR, Delitte, Haskins & Sells, Opti-Copy, Kansas City, Harper & Assocs., Bellevue and numerous other pvt. collections; work published in The Artistic Touch I, II and III, The Encyclopedia of Living Artists. Pres. The LaVeta (Colo.) Sch. of Arts. Recipient 1st pl. award Ariz. Internat., Snowgrass Art Inst., Cashmere, Wash., Kans. State Fair, Hutchinson, SPACe, La Veta, Colo., Honorable Mention award W. Wash. State Fair, 2d pl. award Ea. N.Mex. U., Portales, Snowgrass Art Inst., Cashmere, Wash., Merit award Mont. Inst. of the Arts, Butte; named finalist Pierce County Libr. Project, Gig Harbor, Wash., 3rd place Greeley Nat. Juried show. Home: PO Box 967 La Veta CO 81055-0967 E-mail: zehrings@rmi.net.

ZEID, PAULA KLEIN, metals broker; b. Chgo., Oct. 16, 1941; d. Arthur A. and Rosalyn (Davidson) Schwartz; m. Sanford David Klein, Dec. 18, 1960 (div. 1981); children: Gregory Scott, Julie Ann. Student, Mich. State U., 1959-60; BA, Governors State U., 1974, MA, 1975. Mem. editl. staff Okinawa Morning Star, Machinato, 1960-63; exec. dir. Bloom Twp. Com. on Youth, Chicago Heights, Ill., 1975-81; dir. fund devel. and pub. rels. South Chgo. Cmty. Hosp., 1981-84; v.p. South Chgo. Health Care Found., 1982-84; dir. devel. and pub. rels. Chgo. Crime Commn., 1985-88; broker, buyer, trader Universal Scrap Metals, Chgo., 1988—; pres. Klein Trading Co., 1997—; v.p. USM Processing Ltd. Trustee Chgo. Sinai Congregation. Mem. Inst. Scrap Recycling Industries, Indsl. Coun. of N.W. Chgo. Jewish. Home: 1908 N Dayton St Chicago IL 60614-5029 Office: Universal Scrap Metals 2500 W Fulton St Chicago IL 60612-2104 E-mail: pklein@universalscrap.com.

ZEID, PHILIP L. metal recycling executive; b. Chgo., July 27, 1943; s. Samuel P. and Mary S. (Stamler) Z.; m. Donna M. Winston, Dec. 16, 1966 (div. Feb. 1978); 1 child, Jason I.; m. Paula S. Klein, Oct. 13, 1991. BA, Drake U., 1966; postgrad., U. Kans., 1966. Sales mgr. Random House, Inc., Chgo., 1969-74; v.p., dir. mktg. dept. Coronet Films, 1974-82; sr. mgr. MCI Communications, 1982-84; pres. Universal Scrap Metals, Inc., 1984—, also bd. dirs. Pres., bd. dirs. USM Processing Ltd., 1997—. Mem. exec. com. Jewish United Fund. Mem. Assn. Media Producers (statis. com. 1980-82, speakers bur., chmn. trade show com., lobbyist Washington chpt. 1981-82), Sales and Mktg. Execs. Assn., Inst. Scrap Recycling Industries. Avocations: photography, art collecting, skiing, tennis, travel. Home: 1908 N Dayton St Chicago IL 60614-5029 Office: Universal Scrap Metals Inc 2500 W Fulton St Chicago IL 60612-2104

ZEIDENSTEIN, GEORGE, population educator; b. Pitts., July 29, 1929; s. Max and Sophia (Cohen) Z.; m. Sondra F. Auerbach, Jan. 25, 1953; children: Laura, Louis Peter. BA, U. Pitts., 1951; JD cum laude, Harvard U., 1954. Bar: N.Y. 1954. Pvt. practice, N.Y.C., 1954-65; vol. lawyer Lawyers Constl. Def. Com., Holly Springs, Miss., 1964; partner firm Spear and Hill, 1962-65; country dir. Nepal Kathmandu, Peace Corps, 1965-68; regional dir. designate Office E. Asia and Pacific, Washington, 1968; pres. Bklyn. Linear City Devel. Corp., N.Y.C., 1968-69; sr. program officer Asia and Pacific Ford Found., 1969-71, dep. head Asia and Pacific, 1971-72, rep. Bangladesh, 1972-76; pres., trustee Population Council, N.Y.C., 1976-93; disting. fellow Harvard Ctr. Population and Devel. Studies, Cambridge, Mass., 1993—. Chmn. Himalayas coun. Asia Soc., 1970-72; assoc. seminar tradition and change in South and S.E. Asia, Columbia U., 1971-73, assoc. seminar on tech. and pub. issues, 1981-85; coun. Overseas Devel. Coun., 1979-93; chmn. Appraisal Group Global Com. Parliamentarians on Population and Devel., 1985-86; bd. visitors Grad. Sch. Pub. Health, U. Pitts., 1988—; advisor to chair Ind. Commn. on Population and Quality of Life, 1993-95. Vice chmn. bd. trustees, chmn. program com. Save the Children Fedn., 1991-95, Internat. Ctr. Rsch. on Women, 1993—; chmn. Internat. HIV/AIDS Alliance, 1993—; bd. dirs. Earthforce, 1993-95; active Britton Woods Com., 1992—. Decorated knight comdr. Order of Lion (Finland, Senegal). Home: 795 East St N Goshen CT 06756-1130 Office: Harvard Ctr Population Devel Studies 9 Bow St Cambridge MA 02138-5103

ZEIDLER, FRANK P. former association administrator, mayor, arbitrator, mediator, fact-finder; b. Milw., Sept. 20, 1912; s. Michael and Clara (Nitschke) Z.; m. Agnes Reinke; children: Clara, Dorothy, Michael, Anita, Mary, Jeannette. Student, Marquette U., 1930, U. Wis. Extension Div., 1930-70, U. Chgo., 1937; LLD (hon.), U. Wis., 1958, St. Olaf Coll., 1988; LHD (hon.), Carthage Coll., 1983, Mt. Mary Coll., 1993, U. Wis.-Milw., 1990. Dir. Milw. Pub. Schs., 1941-48; mayor City of Milw., 1948-60; dir. Wis. Dept. Resource Devel., 1963-64. Sec. emeritus Pub. Enterprise Com.; mem. U.S. nat. commn. UNESCO, 1953, 56, 59. Author: Shakespeare's plays in modern verse. Pres. Ctrl. North Cmty. Coun.; pres. Greater Milw. UN Assn., pres.; nat. chmn. Socialist Party U.S.A., 1973-83; Socialist Party candidate for Pres. U.S., 1976; convenor Dem. Socialist Conf.; past pres. Luth. Social Action Conf.; bd. dirs. Goethe House, Milw., Milw. Theol. Inst.; mem. exec. coun. Luth. Ch. Am., 1980-82; hon. mem. cabinet Interfaith Conf. Greater Milw.; chmn. Norman Thomas Inst. for Peace and Social Justice. Named One of 10 Outstanding Young Men, Nat. Jr. C. of C., 1949; recipient Eugene V. Debs award, 1977. Mem. Milw. World Federalist Assn. (bd. dirs.), Nat. Model R.R. Assn. (founder). Home: 2921 N 2nd St Milwaukee WI 53212-2411

ZEIDMAN, SETH MICHAEL, neurosurgeon; b. Syracuse, N.Y., Apr. 6, 1962; s. Howard and Sheila Mae Zeidman; m. Eva Karen Pressman; children: Rebecca, Anna, Jessica. Student, Rutgers U., 1980; BS, Duke U., 1984, MD, 1988. Diplomate Am. Bd. Neurol. Surgeons. Chief complex spinal surgery Walter Reed Army Med. Ctr., Washington, 1995—99, U. Rochester (N.Y.) Med. Ctr., 1999—2002; pres. Rochester Brain and Spine Neurosurgery, 2002—. Editor: The Cervical Spine, 3rd edit., 1998, Principles and Practice of Spine Surgery, 2002. Maj. U.S. Army, 1995—99. Office: 400 Red Creek Dr Ste 120 Rochester NY 14623 Office Fax: 585-334-5581. Business E-Mail: seth_zeidman@urmc.rochester.edu.

ZEIEN, ALFRED M. former consumer products company executive; b. N.Y.C., Feb. 25, 1930; s. Alphonse and Betty (Barthelemy) Z.; m. Joyce Valerie Lawrence, Dec. 26, 1952; children: Scott, Grey, Claudia BS, Webb Inst.; MBA postgrad., Harvard U. Group v.p. Gillette Co., Boston, 1973-74; div. gen. mgr. Braun AG, Frankfurt, Federal Republic of Germany, 1974-76; sr. v.p. Gillette Co., Boston, 1978-81, vice chmn., 1981-90, pres., 1990-91, chmn., chief exec. officer, 1991-99; chmn. bd. Braun AG, Frankfurt, Federal Republic of Germany, 1976-78. Bd. dirs. Polaroid Corp., Cambridge, Mass., Raytheon Corp., Lexington, Mass., Mass. Mut. Ins. Co., Springfield, EMC Corp. Trustee Woods Hole Oceanographic Inst. & Marine Biology Lab. Avocations: sailing; tennis.

ZEIGEN, SPENCER STEVEN, architect, consultant; b. Bklyn., Oct. 11, 1924; s. David and Ethel (Katz) Z.; m. Mildred Weinman, Dec. 27, 1952 (dec. Sept. 1992); children: Steven, Scott; m. Lillian Glogau, Oct. 10, 1993; children: Jordan, Laurence, Alexander. BFA suma cum laude, U. Pa., 1952. Registered architect, N.J. Arch. Leo Fischer Arch., South Orange, N.J., 1952-54, Frank Grad Sons Arch., Newark, 1954-64; staff arch. Rutgers State U., New Brunswick, N.J., 1964-74; pvt. practice Highland Park, 1974-78, Jamesburg, 1978-80; arch. Collins, Uhl, Hoisington, Anderson Arch., Princeton, 1978-80; dir. of arch. Brown Hale Arch., Newark, 1980-82, Brown & Mathews, Fords, N.J., 1982-86. Litigation expert witness, 1980—; bd. arch. High Rise Condominiums, Fort Lee, N.J., 1982-89; cons. roofing expert, litigation, expert witness Kipcon, Inc., North Brunswick, N.J., 1980—, bldg. materials analyst, 1988—; instr. arch. Newark Coll. Engring., 1963-69; lectr. Rutgers U., 1961-65. Prin. works include N.J. Divsn. Motor Vehicles Testing Facilities, N.J. Cultural Ctr., Rutgers U. Ednl. Facilities. Bd. dirs. Whittingham Homeowners Assn., Monroe Twp., N.J., 1990-93. Sgt. USAF, 1942-46. Mem. Am. Soc. Arch., Am. Soc. Planners. Democrat. Jewish. Avocations: bridge, tennis, bocci, reading, drawing. Home and Office: 19B Winthrop Rd Monroe Township NJ 08831-2666 Fax: (609) 655-0780. E-mail: lffgz@msn.com.

ZEIGER, DAVID, poet, retired English educator; b. N.Y.C., July 18, 1921; s. Isaac Zeiger and Rose Odessa; m. Lila Anita Leichtling, Nov. 24, 1949; children: Sara, Arnold. BA, Bklyn. Coll., 1943; MA, NYU, 1948. Cert. secondary sch. tchr., N.Y. H.S. sch. tchr. N.Y. pub. schs., 1944-56; English tchr. New Utrecht (N.Y.) H.S., 1944-56; prof. English Fashion Inst. Tech., N.Y., 1956-85; ret., 1985. Vol. instr. English and speech Internat. Ctr., N.Y.C., 1994—. Author: Life On My Breath, 1995. Founder United Coll. Employees, N.Y.C., 1963. Mem. N.Y. State United Tchrs., Poetry Soc. Am. Avocations: dance, chamber music, theater. Home and Office: 9 4th Rd Great Neck NY 11021-1505

ZEIGER, HERBERT EVAN, JR. neurosurgeon; b. Landgale, Ala., Aug. 23, 1949; s. H. Evan Sr. and Imogene (Morris) Z.; m. Margaret Swift Shook, Feb. 25, 1984; children: H. Evan III, Ashley Shook, Douglas Shook. BA, Samford U., 1971; MD, U. Ala., 1974. Diplomate Am. Bd. Neurol. Surgery. Intern Carraway Meth. Med. Ctr., Birmingham, 1975-76; resident Washington U. Med. Sch./ Barnes Hosp., St. Louis, 1976-81; attending neurosurgeon Carraway Meth. Med. Ctr., Birmingham, Ala., 1987—; pres. med. staff, 1992-93, 96, 97; assoc. prof. neurosurgery U. Ala., Brimingham, 1981-87; attending neurosurgeon, chmn. dept. neurosurgery Norwood Clinic, 1987—. Author: Stroke and the Extracranial Vessels, 1983; contbr. articles to profl. jours. Bd. dirs. Ala. Family Alliance, Birmingham, 1989—, Children's Harbor, Birmingham, 1993-96, Salvation Army, Birmingham, 1990—. Fellow U. Western Ont. London, Can., 1981. Fellow Am. Coll. Surgeons; mem. Am. Assn. Neurol. Surgeons, So. Neurosurg. Soc., Neurosurg. Soc. Ala (pres. 1988-90), Birmingham Surg. Soc., Congress Neurol. Surgeons, Jefferson County Med. Soc. (pres. 1997), Rotary (fellow com. 1990). Presbyterian. Avocations: flying, running, family, trout fishing, sailing. Home: 3009 Canterbury Ln Birmingham AL 35223-1241 Office: Norwood Clinic Inc 1528 Carraway Blvd Birmingham AL 35234-1991

ZEIGER, LARRY See KING, LARRY

ZEIGER, LILA L. creative writing educator, poet, fiction writer; b. N.Y.C., Dec. 6, 1927; d. Benjamin Hersh and Sara (Dornbrand) Leichtling; m. David Zeiger, Nov. 24, 1949; children: Sara Ellen, Arnold William. MA in English, Classics, Cornell U., 1949; MLS in Young People's Lit., Pratt Inst., 1957. Tchr. English various N.Y.C. H.S., 1949-56; tchr. libr. N.Y.C. Bd. Edn., 1956-58; tchr. writing Poets in Schs., N.Y.C. and Nassau County, N.Y., 1973-78, 78-84; writing cons., lectr. various orgns., 1984—; creative writing specialist VCC Day Treatment Program, N.Y.C., 1988—. Poet in residence Great Neck Libr., N.Y., 1986-88. Author: The Way to Castle Garden, 1982; contbr. articles to profl. jours. Active Nassau County Office Cultural Devel., 1982—. Fellow MacDowell Colony, 1977, 79, 83; CCLM Fels award Coord. Coun., 1975; grantee N.Y. State CAPS, 1984, Witter Bynner, 1992, others. Jewish. Avocations: gardening, cooking, traveling, Yiddish language. Home: 9 4th Rd Great Neck NY 11021-1505 also: PO Box 4518 Great Neck NY 11023-4518

ZEIGER, MARIA THERESIA, music educator; b. Vienna, Austria, Apr. 28, 1951; came to U.S., 1979; d. Karl Adolf and Maria Theresia Schnuerl; m. William Otis Zeiger, Aug. 28, 1980; children: Chantal, Daniel. BA in English-German Translating, U. Vienna, Austria, 1973; BA in English, German and Secondary Edn., U. Anchorage, 1983, B in Music Edn., 1996. Flight attendant Lufthansa German Airlines, Frankfurt, Germany, 1973-79; tchr. Anchorage (Alaska) Sch. Dist., 1983; pvt. piano tchr. Anchorage, 1983—. V.p. Goldenview PTA, Anchorage, 1997-99. Named Anchorage champion Arctic Bicycle Club, 1988. Mem.: Anchorage Keyboard Tchrs. Assn. (chmn. adjudications 1998—2001, pres. 2001—), Music Tchrs. Nat. Assn. (profl. cert. in piano), Alyeska Masters Ski Club. Roman Catholic. Avocations: bicycling, skiing, hiking, fishing, flying. Home: 941 Maho Cir Anchorage AK 99515-3739

ZEIGER, TIMOTHY DAVID, lawyer; b. Langdale, Ala., June 22, 1953; s. H. Evan and Gene (Morris) Z.; m. Nancy Kay Willis, Aug. 16, 1975; children: David, Matthew, Karolena, Daniel. BA, Samford U., 1975; JD, Baylor U., 1981. Bar: Tex. 1981, U.S. Dist. Ct. (no. dist.) Tex. 1982, U.S. Ct. Appeals (5th cir.) 1983; cert. in civil trial law and civil appellate law Tex. Bd. Legal Specialization. Assoc. Gassaway Gurley Sheets & Michael, Borger, Tex., 1981-84, ptnr., 1985-88, McKinley Dubner Schura & Warner, Dallas, 1988, shareholder, dir., 1989-91, McKinney Hinton Ringer LLP, Dallas, 1991-96, McKinley Ringer Zeiger P.C., Dallas, 1996-99, McKinley & Zeiger LLP, Dallas, 1999—2001. Mem. Nat. Bd. Trial Advocacy (cert. civil trial law). Office: Shackelford Melton & McKuley LLP 10100 N Central Expy Ste 600 Dallas TX 75231-4159

ZEIGLER, ANN DEPENDER, lawyer; b. Spokane, Wash., June 7, 1947; d. F. Norman and Dorothy (Wolter) dePender; m. Paul Stewart Zeigler, June 20, 1970; 1 child, Kate Elizabeth. BA magna cum laude, Ft. Wright Coll. Holy Names, Spokane, 1969; MFA in Creative Writing, U. Mont., 1975; JD, U. Houston, 1984. Bar: Tex. 1984. Course adminstr. legal communications U. Houston, 1982-84; assoc. Dula, Shields & Egbert, 1984-87; ind. project atty., 1987; assoc. Dow, Cogburn & Friedman, 1987-90; assoc. bankruptcy sect./avoidance litigation Hughes, Watters & Askanase, Houston, 1990—. Co-editor: Insurance Guide-Arts Nonprofits, 1993, Basic Issues in Estate Planning-Representing the Artist, 1994, Leading the Arts Nonprofit: Duties of Officers and Directors, 1999; editl. bd. Houston Lawyer, 1999—, guest editor spl. hist. issue 2000, 01; assoc. editor Keeping Up With, 2002-03; contbr. articles to profl. jours. Mem. publs. com., writer Tex. Accts. and Lawyers for Arts, Houston, 1988—; mem. Supreme Ct. of Tex. Unauthorized Practice of Law Com., Houston; vol. Houston Lawyers for Hunger Relief, 1988-90. Mem. ABA, State Bar Tex., Houston Bar Assn. (chair law and the arts com. 1996-97, co-chair ann. fiction contest), Can. Bar Assn., Phi Alpha Delta. Democrat. Home: 4038 Cheena Dr Houston TX 77025-4702 Office: Hughes Watters & Askanase 1415 Louisiana St Fl 37 Houston TX 77002-7360 E-mail: azeigler@hwallp.com.

ZEIGLER, EARLE FREDERICK, physical education-kinesiology educator; b. N.Y.C., Aug. 20, 1919; s. Clarence Mattison and Margery Christina (Beyerkohler) Shinkle; m. Bertha M. Bell, June 25, 1941 (dec. Feb. 1998); children— Donald H., Barbara A; m. Anne K. Rogers, Feb. 27, 1999. AB, Bates Coll., 1940; AM, Yale U., 1944, PhD, 1951; LLD, U. Windsor, 1975; DSc, U. Lethbridge, Alta, Can., 1997. Assoc. phys. dir., aquatic dir. Bridgeport (Conn.) YMCA, 1941-43; instr. German U. Conn., Storrs, 1943-47; coach, instr. phys. edn. Yale U., 1943-49; asst. prof. U. Western Ont. (Can.), London, 1949-50, prof., chmn. dept. phys., health and recreation edn., 1950-56, assoc. prof. Sch. Edn.; supr. phys. edn. and athletics U. Mich., Ann Arbor, 1956-63, chmn. dept. phys. edn. Sch. Edn., 1961-63; prof. dept. phys. edn. for men Coll. Phys. Edn., U. Ill., Urbana, 1963-72, head dept. phys. edn. for men, chmn. grad. dept., 1964-68; prof. dept. phys. and health edn. U. Western Ont., London, 1971-89, prof. emeritus, 1989—, dean faculty phys. edn., 1972-77. Author: A History of Professional Preparation for Physical Education in the United States, 1951, Administration of Physical Education and Athletics, 1959, The Case Method Approach: An Instructional Manual, 1959, Philosophical Foundations for Physical, Health, and Recreation Education, 1964, A Brief Introduction to the Philosophy of Religion, 1965, (with H.J. VanderZwaag) Physical Education: Progressivism or Essentialism, 1968, Problems in the History and Philosophy of Physical Education and Sport, 1968, (with M.L. Howell and M. Trekell) Research in the History and Philosophy of Physical Education and Sport, 1971, Personalizing Physical Education and Sport Philosophy, 1975, Physical Education and Sport Philosophy, 1977, Issues in North American Physical Education and Sport, 1979, Decision-Making in Physical Education and Athletics Administration, 1982, (with G.W. Bowie) Management Competency Development in Sport and Physical Education, 1983, Ethics and Morality in Sport and Physical Education, 1984, (with J. Campbell) Strategic Market Planning: An Aid to the Evaluation of an Athletics/Recreation Program, 1984 , Assessing Sport and Physical Education: Diagnosis and Projection, 1986, (with G. Bowie and R. Paris) Competency Development in Sport and Physical Education Management, 1988, (with A. Mikalachki and G. Leyshon) Change Process in Sport and Physical Education Management, 1988, Introduction to Sport and Physical Education Philosophy, 1989, Sport and Physical Education: Past, Present, Future, 1990, Professional Ethics for Sport Managers, 1992, Critical Thinking for the Professions of Health, Physical Education, Recreation, and Dance, 1994, A Selected, Annotated Bibliography of Completed Research on Management Theory and Practice in Physical Education and Athletics to 1972, 1995, (with G.W. Bowie) Developing Management Competency in Sport and Physical Education, 1995, Who Knows What's Right Anymore?, 2002; author, editor: A History of Sport and Physical Education to 1900, 1973, A History of Physical Education and Sport in the United States and Canada, 1975, (with M.J. Spaeth) Administrative Theory and Practice in Physical Education and Athletics, 1975, History of Physical Education and Sport, 1979, rev. edit., 1988, Physical Education and Sport: An Introduction, 1982, Physical Education and Kinesiology in North America: Professionalism and Scholarly Foundations, 1994; contbr. articles to profl. jours. Recipient Outstanding Tchr. award U. Western Ont., 1987, Disting. Svc. award Internat. Soc. Comparative Phys. Edn. and Sport, 1988; named to Univ. Western Ont.'s Wall of Wrestling Fame, 1991, Univ. Western Ont.'s W Club Hall of Fame, 1995, Univ. Western Ont.'s Swimming Wall of Honor, 2000; named first Human Movement Scis. and Edn. scholar U. Memphis, 1994. Fellow: N.Am. Soc. Health, Phys. Edn., Recreation, Sport and Dance Profls., Am. Acad. Kinesiology and Phys. Edn. (pres. 1981—82); mem.: N.Am. Soc. for Sport Mgmt. (founding mem., hon. past pres. 1986—87), Philosophic Soc. for Study of Sport (pres. 1974—75), Soc. Mcpl. Recreation Dirs. Ont. (Honor award 1956), Ont. Recreation Assn. (v.p., dir. 1955—56), Can. Profl. Schs. Conf. (pres. 1953—55), Internat. Soc. for Comparative Phys. Edn. and Sport (Earle Zeigler award established in his honor), N.Am. Soc. Sport History (life), Nat. Assn. Phys. Edn. in Higher Edn., Am. Philos. Assn., Can. Assn. Health, Phys. Edn. and Recreation (v.p. 1995—96, 1983—85, Honor award 1975, Spl. Presentation citation 1986), Internat. Assn. Profl. Schs. Phys. Edn., Philosophy Edn. Soc., AAHPERD (Alliance scholar 1977—78, Disting. Svc. award 1979, Honor award 1981, Gulick award 1990), Phi Epsilon Kappa (life). Achievements include N.Am. Soc. Sport Mgmt. creating the Annual Earle Zeigler Lecture, 1988. Home: 105 8560 Currie Rd Richmond BC Canada V6Y 1M2 also: PO Box 630 Point Roberts WA 98281-0630 Fax: (604) 270-8414. *Ever since the Platonic tradition split what we once before believed to be a unified organism into mind and body, and then Christianity added a spiritual dimension that shattered a unified concept of the organism even further, purposeful human movement in sport, dance, play, and exercise has been regarded as inferior to so-called intellectual attainments. My life purpose is to work toward redressing that imbalance by promoting a type of education that restores the Greek Classical Ideal.*

ZEIGLER, JOSEPH WILLIAM, surveillance company manager; b. Dayton, July 29, 1948; s. Donald David Zeigler; m. Deborah Marie Whallen, Feb. 2, 1999. Res. peace officer Ohio Law Enforcement, Chillicothe, 1968—2001; owner Joe's Indsl. Counter Surveillance Svcs., 2001—. With U.S. Army, 1967—68, Vietnam. Mem.: VFW (life Cert. Appreciation polit. action com. 2000). Office: Joe's Indsl counter Surveillance Svcs 337 E 7th St Chillicothe OH 45601 Personal E-mail: zeiglerjoseph@hotmail.com. Business E-Mail: zeiglerjoseph@hotmail.com.

ZEIGLER, L(UTHER) HARMON, political science educator; b. Savannah, GA., Mar. 9, 1936; s. Luther H. and Sarah Louise (Betts) Z.; m. Patricia Lynn Duffy, Dec. 20, 1956; children: Michael, Amanda. BA, Emory U., 1957; MA, U. Ill., 1958, PhD, 1960. Asst. prof. Fla. State U., Tallahassee, 1960-61, Emory U., Atlanta, 1961-63, U. Ga., Athens, 1963-64; assoc. prof. U. Oreg., Eugene, 1964-67, prof. dept. polit. sci., 1967-85, chmn., 1982-85; Philip M. Phibbs disting. prof. Am. politics U. Puget Sound, Tacoma, 1985-92. Affiliate prof. U. Wash., 1986-92. Author: The Irony of Democracy, 1970, 10th edit., 1997, 11th edit., 2000, Governing American Schools, 1974, Professionals Versus the Public: Attitudes, Commnication and Response in Local School Districts, 1980, American Politics in the Media Age, 1983, Women, Public Opinion and Politics: The Changing Attitudes of American Women, 1984, Pluralism, Corporatism and Confucianism, 1988, The Political Community, 1990, Political Parties in Industrial Democracies, 1992. Fellow Ford Found., 1969; Guggenheim fellow, 1969-70; Fulbright-Hays grantee W. Germ., 1977; sr. scholar Australia, 1978 Mem. Am. Polit. Sci. Assn. E-mail: harmonzeigler@hotmail.com.

ZEIGLER, ROBERT S. research scientist; b. Bellefonte, Pa., Jan. 3, 1951; s. Martin Luther and Sophia Golden Zeigler; m. Crissan April Spencer; children: Nicholas, Claire, Alison. BSc, U. Ill., 1972; MSc, Oreg. State U., 1978; PhD, Cornell U., 1982. H.s. tchr. Peace Corps, Mokala, 1972—74; maize program adviser, Burundi Internat. Devel. Rsch. Ctr., Ottawa, Canada, 1982—85; rice program leader Internat. Ctr. for Tropical Agr., Cali, Colombia, 1985—91; leader irrigated rice rsch. program Internat. Rice Rsch. Inst., Manila, Philippines, 1991—98; dir. plant Biotech. Ctr., head dept. plant pathology Kans. State U., Manhattan, 1998—. Mem.: AAAS, Sociedad Colombiana Fitopatologia, Am. Phytopathol. Soc. (Ruth Allen award 2001).

ZEILBERGER, DORON, researcher, mathematics educator; b. Haifa, Israel, July 2, 1950; s. Yehuda Heinz and Ruth (Alexander) Z.; m. Jane Deborah LeGrange, June 3, 1979; children: Celia, Tamar, Hadas. BS with first class hons., U. London, 1972; PhD, Weizmann Inst., Rehovot, Israel, 1976. Mem. Inst. for Advanced Study, Princeton, N.J., 1977-78, 93; vis. asst. prof. Ga. Inst. Tech., Atlanta, 1978-79; lectr. U. Ill., Urbana, 1979-80; sr. scientist Weizmann Inst., Rehovot, Israel, 1980-82; lectr. U. Pa., Phila., 1982-83; assoc. prof. Drexel U., 1983-88, prof., 1988-90, Temple U., Phila., 1990-99, Laura H. Carnell prof., 1999-2001; bd. govs. prof. Rutgers U., New Brunswick, N.J., 2001—. Mem. editl. bd. Elec. Jour. of Combinations, others; editor-in-chief Advances in Applied Math.; contbr. numerous articles to profl. jours. Mem. Am. Math. Soc. (Leroy P. Steele Prize 1998), Math. Assn. Am. (Lester R. Ford award 1990). E-mail: zeilberg@math.rutgers.edu.

ZEILE, FRED CARL, oceanographer, meteorologist; b. Phila., Nov. 3, 1950; s. Fred Carl Jr. and Catherine Elizabeth (Wolfrum) Z.; children: Kirche Leigh, Alicia Elizabeth; m. Ingrid Elizabeth Leyrer, Dec. 17, 1988. BS in Oceanography, U.S. Naval Acad., 1973; MS in Meteorology and Oceanography, Naval Postgrad. Sch., 1979; MA in Nat. Security & Strategic Studies, Naval War Coll., 1991. Commd. ensign USN, 1973, advanced through grades to comdr., 1988; meteorologist USS Inchon, Norfolk, Va., 1979-81; oceanography instr. U.S. Naval Acad., Annapolis, Md., 1981-83; commanding officer Oceanographic Unit 4 USNS Chauvenet, Indonesia, 1984-85; dep. asst. chief staff for emerging systems Comdr. Naval Oceanography Command, Stennis Space Center, Miss., 1987-90; commanding officer Naval Oceanography Command Facility, Keflavik, Iceland, 1990-92; tactical oceanography br. head Office of Oceanographer of Navy, Washington, 1992-93; v.p. Anteon Corp., Bay St. Louis, Miss., 1993—. Mem. VWF (life), Am. Meteorol. Soc., Marine Tech. Soc. (chmn. Gulf Coast chpt. 1994), Masons (master Mason), Sigma Xi. Republican. Lutheran. Avocations: fishing, golf. Home: 101 Brushfire Ln Slidell LA 70458-9117 Office: Anteon Corp 294 Thames Ave Bay Saint Louis MS 39520-3730 E-mail: fzeile@anteon.com.

ZEILE, TODD EDWARD, professional baseball player; b. Van Nuys, Calif., Sept. 9, 1965; m. Juliane McNamara. Student, UCLA, 1989. With St. Louis Cardinals, 1995, Chgo. Cubs, 1995, Phila. Phillies, 1995-96, Balt. Orioles, 1996, L.A. Dodgers, 1996, Fla. Marlins, 1996-98; 3rd baseman Tex. Rangers, 1998-99; 1st baseman, infielder New York Mets, 1999—. Holder Nat. League single-season record for fewest putouts by third baseman, 1993, shares Am. League single-game record for most errors by first baseman, 1996; named Midwest League co-Most Valuable Player, 1987. Office: New York Mets 12301 Roosevelt Ave Flushing NY 11368-1699

ZEILER, WILLIAM BARTHOLOMEW, pathologist; b. Pitts., Mar. 21, 1921; s. Edward Peter and Dora Elizabeth (Kern) Z.; m. Geraldine Marie Colby (dec.); children: Anita, Mary, Maura, William, Gerry. BS, U. Pitts., 1942, MD, 1945. Diplomate Am. Bd. Pathology, Am. Bd. Nuclear Medicine. Intern, then resident U. Pitts. Med. Ctr., 1946-51; pathologist Sewickley Valley Hosp., Pitts., 1951-55; dir. pathology various hosps., 1956-84; cons., pathologist Harmarville (Pa.) Rehab. Ctr., 1983—98; assoc. pathologist, dir. lab., pres. Clin. Pathology Facility of Pitts., 1968-91. Emeritus med. dir. Quest Diagnostics, Inc. Contbr. articles to profl. jours. Chmn. bd. Hosp. Utilization Project, 1983-87; chmn. adv. com. Bur. Labs. Health Dept. State of Pa., 1984-90. Served to capt. U.S. Army, 1946-48. Fellow Am. Soc. Clin. Pathologists, Coll. Am. Pathologists (pres. 1987-89, bd. dirs. 1991-99); mem. AMA, Soc. Nuclear Medicine, Pa. Med. Soc., Allegheny County Med. Soc., Am. Pathology Found., World Assn. Socs. of Pathology and Laboratory Medicine (pres. 1997-99), Chartiers County Club. Republican. Avocations: music, piano, photography. Home: 778 Osage Rd Pittsburgh PA 15243-1040 Office: Quest Diagnostics Inc 875 Greentree Rd Pittsburgh PA 15220-3508

ZEILINGER, ELNA RAE, elementary educator, gifted-talented education educator; b. Tempe, Ariz., Mar. 24, 1937; d. Clayborn Eddie and Ruby Elna (Laird) Simpson; m. Philip Thomas Zeilinger, June 13, 1970; children: Shari, Chris. BA in Edn., Ariz. State U., 1958, MA in Edn., 1966, EdS, 1980. Bookkeeper First Nat. Bank of Tempe, 1955-56; with registrar's office Ariz. State U., 1956-58; piano tchr., recreation dir. City of Tempe; tchr. Thew Sch., Tempe, 1958-61; elem. tchr. Mitchell Sch., 1962-74, intern prin., 1976, personnel intern, 1977; specialist gifted edn. Tempe Elem. Schs., 1977-86; elem. tchr. Holdeman Sch., 1986-89; tchr. grades 1-12 and adult reading, lang. arts, English Zeilinger Tutoring Svc., 1991—. Grad. asst. ednl. adminstrn., Iota Workshop coordinator Ariz. State U., 1978; presenter Ariz. Gifted Conf., 1978-81; condr. survey of gifted programs, 1980; reporter public relations Tempe Sch. Dist., 1978-80, Access com. for gifted programs, 1981-83. Author: Leadership Role of the Principal in Gifted Programs: A Handbook, 1980; Classified Personnel Handbook, 1977, also reports, monographs and paintings. Mem. Tempe Hist. Assn., liaison, 1975; mem. Tempe Art League; mem. freedom train com. Ariz. Bicentennial Commn., 1975-76; bd. dirs. Maple Property Owners Assn., 1994—; storyteller Tempe Hist. Mus., 1997-2002; dir. Pageantry-Daughter's of the Nile, 2002. Named Outstanding Leader in Elem. and Secondary Schs., 1976' Ariz. Cattle Growers scholar, 1954-55; Elks scholar, 1954-55; recipient Judges award Tempe Art League, 1970, Best of Show, Scottsdale Art League, 1976. Mem.: Daus. of the Nile (dir. pageantry 2002—). Democrat. Congregationalist.

ZEILTER, WILLIAM M. information technology executive; BS in Math., Gannon U., 1969. Programmer IBM, White Plains, NY, 1969—71, sys. engr. ins. br. office N.Y.C., 1971—80, mgr. sys. engring. NY Securities br. office, 1980—83, regional market support mgr. San Francisco, 1983, several mgmt. positions NY, NC, v.p. mktg. AS/400, 1993—95; v.p. software IBM Asia Pacific, Tokyo, 1995—96; gen. mgr. AS/400 IBM Corp., 1996—97, gen. mgr. server brand mgmt., 1997—98, gen. mgr. worldwide software sales and mktg., 1998—2000, gen. mgr. enterprise servers, 2000, sr. v.p., group. exec. server group, 2000—. Office: IBM 1133 Westchester Ave White Plains NY 10604*

ZEINEDDINE, SAMI K. orthopedist; b. Beirut, May 29, 1974; arrived in U.S., 2000; s. Khalil Abdallah Zeineddine and Mountaha Joseph Amine. BS in Biology, Lebanese U., Beirut, 1994, MD, 1999. Internal medicine doctor Wayne State U., Detroit, 2000; rsch. doctor orthopedics Creighton U., Omaha, 2000—. Author: Renal Angiomyolipoma, 1999; contbr. articles to profl. jours. Mem.: AAAS, AMA, N.Y. Acad. Scis. Achievements include research in testing a new dowel for cervical spine fusion; new procedure (kyphoplacity) for vertebral fracture; testing a new COX2 inhibition drug on ACL reconstruction joints. Avocations: Aikido, swimming, photography, basketball, yoga. Office: Creighton Univ Ste 2300 601 N 30th St Omaha NE 68131

ZEIR, NELL, artist; b. Fairhope, Ala., Jan. 18, 1944; d. James P. Rushing and Minnie Freeman; m. William David Zeir, Nov. 16, 1968; children: John, Jacob. CEO Pioneer Auto Ctr., San Diego, 1984—87. Author: (novel) HaShomer, The Watchmen, 2001 (Nat. Libr. of Poetry:Tranquil Rains of Summer, 1998). Recipient Letters from the Soul Series award, Nat. Libr. of Poetry, 2002. Jewish. Avocation: travel, reading, composing, attending poetry workshops. Personal E-mail: nel.david@mailcity.com.

ZEISEL, GLORIA, real estate company executive; b. Braddock, Pa., June 21, 1920; d. Max and Rachel (Kaufman) Sperling; m. Henry Israel Zeisel, Feb. 1, 1942; children: Cheryl Kramer, Elliot, Howard, Debra Moed. Student, Bklyn. Coll. Pres., founder Adolph Schreiber Sch., Monsey, N.Y., 1954; sec., treas., dir. HiTech Mfg. Co., N.J., 1992—, Real Estate Cos., N.Y., N.J., Fla., 1975—. Founder, life mem. Cmty. Synagogue Monsey, 1954—; founder, bd. trustees Holocaust Ctr., Spring Valley, N.Y., 1988—; bd. govs. Good Samaritan Hosp., Suffern, N.Y., co-chmn. showcase, 1994; vol. United Jewish Appeal. Recipient Outstanding Citizen of Jewish Cmty. Ramapo Town Bd., 1994. Mem. Amit Women Nat. Orgn. (life), Brandies Women Nat. Orgn. (life), Israel Bond Orgn. (bd. dirs., bd. trustees). Home: 18 Hilltop Pl Monsey NY 10952-2808

ZEITELHACK, GLORIA JEANNE, artist; b. San Diego, June 24, 1952; d. Leon Mathew and Claire Irene (Morel) Morissette; m. Don Roger Zeitelhack, Sept. 3, 1977. Student, Nicolet Coll. Artist, Tomahawk, Wis., Alto, N.Mex.; owner Many Moons Jewelry Gallery, Ruidoso. Inventor mother of pearl shell landscapes for jewelery, 1977—. Avocations: art, music, dance. Home and Office: PO Box 419 Alto NM 88312-0419 : Many Moons Jewelry Gallery Time Sq 2501 Sudderth Ruidoso NM 88345

ZEITLAN, MARILYN LABB, lawyer; b. N.Y.C., Sept. 17, 1938; d. Charles and Florence (Geller) Labb; m. Barrett M. Zeitlan, Apr. 14, 1957; children: Adam Scott, Daniel Craig. BA, Queens Coll., 1958, MS, 1970; JD, Hofstra U., 1978. Bar: N.Y. 1979. Tchr. N.Y.C., 1958-61; pvt. practice matrimonial law, Roslyn, N.Y., 1980—. Assoc. editor: Law Rev., Hofstra U., 1977-78; contbr. articles to profl. jours. Commr. East Hills Environ. Commn., 1971-75; co-founder Roslyn Environ. Assn., 1970; v.p. Roslyn LWV, 1974-75. Hofstra Law Sch. fellow, 1976. Mem. Nassau County Bar Assn., N.Y. State Bar Assn., Phi Beta Kappa. Avocation: horseback riding. Office: 1025 Northern Blvd Ste 201 Roslyn NY 11576-1506

ZEITLIN, GERALD MARK, electrical engineer; b. Phila., May 7, 1937; s. David Edward and Charlotte (Freedman) Zeitlin; m. Frances Loretta Scherr, May 17, 1983 (div. 1988); m. Maries-Louise Trabaud, Dec. 13, 1998. BEE, Cornell U., 1960; MSEE, U. Colo., 1969. Electronic engr. Nat. Security Agy., Ft. Meade, Md., 1962-64, Westinghouse Georesearch Lab., Boulder, Colo., 1966-69; owner Sunrise Books, Estes Park, 1969-71; asst. research computer sci. U. Calif., San Francisco, 1972-78, assoc. devel. engr. Berkeley, 1978-82; sr. systems engr. EEG Systems Lab., San Francisco, 1982-86; computer cons., expert systems design Pacific Bell, 1986-87, mgr. microcomputer security San Ramon, 1987-89; dir. Alliance for Innovation tech. devel. ctr., Scottsdale, Ariz., 1990-91; pres. Centauri Secure Computing, 1990; computer security cons. Bedford Cons., San Francisco, 1991; owner, operator Mono Communications, Oakland, 1991—2002, also bd. dirs. Lee Vining and Oakland; ret., 2002. Sr UNIX security analyst Wells Fargo Bank, 1998; sr sys engr Sci Applications Int Corp. Contbr. articles to profl jours. Served to 1st lt., mission transport pilot, comm. officer Civil Air Patrol U.S. Army, 1960—62. Fellow Summer Faculty, NASA-Am Soc Eng Educ, Ames Reasearch Ctr, 1981. Mem.: IEEE. Jewish. Avocation: private airplane pilot. E-mail: gerry@zeitlin.net.

ZEITLIN, HERBERT ZAKARY, retired academic administrator, real estate consultant; b. N.Y.C., Jan. 14, 1919; s. Leonard and Martha Josephine (Soff) Zeitlin; m. Eugenia F. Pawlik, July 3, 1949; children: Mark Clyde, Joyce Therese Zeitlin Harris, Ann Victoria, Clare Katherine. BS, NYU, 1947, MA, 1949; EdD, Stanford U., 1956. Tchr. Mepham High Sch., Bellmore, NY, 1946-47, Nassau County Vocat. Edn. Extension Bd., Mineola; electronics instr., adj. faculty Mephan C.C., 1946-49; tchr., counselor, dir. testing Phoenix Union High Sch. and Coll. Dist., 1949-57; dean eve. coll., prin. high sch. Antelope Valley Union High Sch. and Coll. Dist., Lancaster, Calif., 1957-62; dean instrn. Southwestern Coll., Chula Vista, 1962-64; pres., supt., cons. Triton Coll., River Grove, Ill., 1964—79; dean, pres. West L.A. Coll., 1976-80; pres. Trident Consultants, L.A., mgmt. cons., 1976—; adj. faculty Ariz. State U., Flagstaff, 1953-55, No. Ill. U., DeKalb, 1971-76, U. Calif., Santa Barbara, 1979. Author: (book) Turbulent Birth of Triton College: How a California Dean Overcomes Corruption in the Founding of a Community College in Chicagoland, 2001; editor: in field. Pres. Antelope Valley Breeze & Sage, 1959—60, Bon Vivant Homeowners Assn., 1982—84; mayor Upper Woodland Hills, Calif. With USAAF, 1942—46. Named Adminstr. of the Yr., Triton Coll. Faculty Assn., 1974; recipient Spl. commendation, Chgo. Tribune, Richard Ogilvie, former Gov. Ill., Spl. Achievement award for visionary accomplishment, Ill. Sch. Adminstrs. Assn., 1976. Mem.: Ariz. State Vocat. Assn. (pres. 1952—53), Ariz. Vocat. Guidance Assn. (pres. 1951—52), Maywood Ill. Rotary (pres. 1972—73), Antelope Valley Rotary (pres. 1962). Office: Paramount Properties 21031 Ventura Blvd Woodland Hills CA 91364-1845 Mailing: Trident Cons PO Box 571412 Tarzana CA 91357 Home Fax: 818-884-7854. Personal E-mail: zakywaki@aol.com. *I always felt that being the president of an organization, having held 17 presidencies in my lifetime, was like being the quarterback on the football team. You had a choice of running with the ball and taking some bruises or passing it to someone who should score. I was lucky most of the time in selecting some very fine receivers.*

ZEITLIN, MAURICE, sociology educator, writer; b. Detroit, Feb. 24, 1935; s. Albert J. and Rose (Goldberg) Z.; m. Marilyn Geller, Mar. 1, 1959; children: Michelle, Carla, Erica. BA cum laude, Wayne State U., 1957; MA, U. Calif., Berkeley, 1960, PhD, 1964. Instr. anthropology and sociology Princeton (N.J.) U., 1961-64; rsch. assoc. Ctr. Internat. Studies, 1962-64; asst. prof. sociology U. Wis.-Madison, 1964-67, assoc. prof., 1967-70, prof., 1970-77; dir. Ctr. Social Orgn., 1974-76; prof. sociology UCLA, 1977—; also rsch. assoc. Inst. Inds. Rels. Vis. prof. polit. sci. and sociology Hebrew U., Jerusalem, 1971-72. Author: (with R. Scheer) Cuba: An American Tragedy, 1963, 64, Revolutionary Politics and the Cuban Working Class, 1967, 70, The Civil Wars in Chile, 1984, (with R.E. Ratcliff) Landlords and Capitalists, 1988, The Large Corporation and Contemporary Classes, 1989; (with J. Stepan-Norris) Talking Union, 1996, Left Out: Reds and America's Industrial Unions, 2002; Latin Am. editor Ramparts mag., 1967-73; editor-in-chief: Political Power and Social Theory, 1980-90; mem. editl. adv. bd. The Progressive mag., 1985-96; editor: (with J. Petras) Latin America: Reform or Revolution?, 1968, American Society, Inc., 1970, 1977, Father Camilo Torres: Revolutionary Writings, 1972, Classes, Class Conflict, and the State, 1980, How Mighty a Force?, 1983, Insurgent Workers: The Origins of Industrial Unionism, 1987. Chmn. Madison Citizens for a Vote on Vietnam, 1967-68; chmn. Am. Com. for Chile, 1973-75; mem. exec. bd. U.S. Com. for Justice to Latin Am. Polit. Prisoners, 1977-84; mem. exec. com. Calif. Campaign for Econ. Democracy, 1983-86. Ford Found. fellow, 1965-67, 70-71, Guggenheim fellow, 1981-82; NSF grantee, 1981, 82, 98; recipient Project Censored award Top Censored Story, 1981; named to Ten Best Censored list, 1978; recipient Inaugural Disting. Publ. award in Labor Studies, Soc. for the Study of Social Problems, 1996. Mem. Am. Sociol. Assn. (governing coun. 1977-80, Disting. Contbn. Scholarship award in Pol. Sociology 1992, 96), Internat. Sociol. Assn. (editl. bd. 1977-81). Democrat. Jewish. Office: UCLA Dept Sociology 264 Haines Hall Los Angeles CA 90095-1551 E-mail: zeitlin@soc.ucla.edu. *Personal philosophy: "If I am not for myself who will be? and when I am for myself, what am I?" Hillel, the Elder.*

ZEKMAN, TERRI MARGARET, graphic designer; b. Chgo., Sept. 13, 1950; d. Theodore Nathan and Lois (Bernstein) Z.; m. Alan Daniels, Apr. 12, 1980; children: Jesse Logan, Dakota Caitlin. BFA, Washington U., St. Louis, 1971; postgrad, Art Inst. Chgo., 1974-75. Graphic designer (on retainer) greeting cards and related products Recycled Paper Products Co., Chgo., 1970—, Jillson Roberts, Inc., Calif.; apprenticed graphic designer Helmuth, Obata & Kassabaum, St. Louis, 1970-71; graphic designer Container Corp., Chgo., 1971; graphic designer, art dir., photographer Cuerden Advt. Design, Denver, 1971-74; art dir. D'Arcy, McManus & Masius Advt., Chgo., 1975-76; freelance graphic designer, 1976-77; art dir. Garfield Linn Advt., 1977-78; graphic designer Keiser Design Group, Van Noy & Co., Los Angeles, 1978-79; owner and operator graphic design studio, 1979—. Art and photography tchr. Ctr. for Early Edn., L.A., 1996—, Buckley Sch., Sherman Oaks, 1996—; 3d grade tchr. asst., 1999—. Recipient cert. of merit St. Louis Outdoor Poster Contest, 1970, Denver Art Dirs. Club, 1973

ZELAC, RONALD EDWARD, physicist; b. Chgo., Jan. 22, 1941; BS in Engring. Physics summa cum laude, U. Ill., 1962, MS in Physics, 1964; MS in Environ. Health, U. Mich., 1965; PhD in Environ. Engring., U. Fla., 1970. Diplomate Am. Bd. Health Physics, Am. Bd. Medical Physics. Chief health physicist IIT Rsch. Inst., Chgo., 1965-68; radiation physicist Mercy Medical Ctr., 1967-68; asst., assoc. prof. Temple U., Phila., 1970-92, radiation safety officer, 1970-91; adj. assoc. prof. U. Pa., 1980-86; assoc. vice provost Temple U., 1987-91; sr. physicist and exec. mgr. tech. Landauer Inc., Glenwood, Ill., 1991-97. Adj. prof. Northwestern U., Evanston, Ill., 1991-97, Temple U., 1992—, Purdue U., 1998—; health physicist, tech. asst., sr. asst. to chmn., sr. health physicist, U.S. NRC, Rockville, Md., 1998—; cons. Wyeth-Ayerst Rsch., Radnor, Pa., Princeton, N.J., 1971-94, Presby. U. Pa. Med. Ctr., Phila., 1974-86, Mobile Rsch. Devel. Corp., Paulsboro, Princeton, 1977-95, Rhone-Poulenc Rorer Cen. Rsch., Ft. Washington, Collegeville, Pa., 1986-93, Smith, Kline and French Labs., Phila., 1979-86. Editor: A Guide to Personnel Monitoring, 1993; contbr. articles to profl. jours. Fellow Phi Kappa Phi, 1962-63, U.S. AEC, 1964-65, USPHS, 1968-70. Mem. Health Physics Soc. (com. mem. 1978-79), Campus Safety Assn., Am. Assn. Physicists in Medicine (com. mem. 1995—), Am. Coll. Medical Physics, Sigma Xi (v.p., pres. 1984-88). Home and Office: PO Box 26786 Elkins Park PA 19027-5773 E-mail: rez@nrc.gov.

ZELASKO, NANCY FABER, research scientist educator; b. June 4, 1951; BS, Georgetown U., 1973, MS, 1975, PhD, 1992. Program specialist D.C. Pub. Schs., Washington, 1974-79, project dir., 1979-80; asst. dir. Georgetown U. Bilingual Edn. Ctr., 1980-89; dep. dir. Nat. Assn. Bilingual Edn., 1989-99; sr. rsch. scientist Grad. Sch. Edn. and Human Devel., George Washington U., 1999—; dep. dir. NCBE. Home: 5542 Crossrail Ct Burke VA 22015-1810 E-mail: nzelasko@ncbe.gwu.edu.

ZELBY, LEON WOLF, electrical engineering educator, consulting engineer; b. Sosnowiec, Poland, Mar. 26, 1925; came to U.S., 1946, naturalized, 1951; s. Herszel and Helen (Wajnryb) Zylberberg; m. Rachel Kupfermintz, Dec. 28, 1954; children: Laurie Susan, Andrew Stephen. BSEE, Moore Sch. Elec. Engring., 1956; MS, Calif. Inst. Tech., 1957; PhD, U. Pa., 1961. Registered profl. engr., Pa., Okla. Mem. staff RCA, Hughes R & D Labs., Lincoln Lab., MIT, Sandia Corp., Argonne (Ill.) Nat. Labs., Inst. for Energy Analysis; mem. faculty U. Pa., 1959-67, assoc. prof., 1964-67; assoc. dir. plasma engring. Inst. Direct Energy Conversion, 1962-67; prof. U. Okla., Norman, 1967-95, dir. Sch. Elec. Engring., 1967-71; ret., 1995. Cons. RCA, 1961-67, Moore Sch. Elec. Engring., 1967-68, also pvt. firms. Editor Tech. and Soc. mag., 1990-93; contbr. articles on energy-associated problems and issues to profl. jours. With AUS, 1946-47. Cons. Electrodynamic Corp. fellow Calif. Inst. Tech., 1957,

Mpls.-Honeywell fellow U. Pa., 1957-58, Harrison fellow, 1958. Mem. IEEE, Franklin Inst., Sigma Xi, Tau Beta Pi, Eta Kappa Nu, Pi Mu Epsilon, Sigma Tau, Phi Kappa Phi. Home: 1009 Whispering Pines Dr Norman OK 73072-6912 *To learn as much, and to experience as much as possible, without harm to others; read, study, vary professional and recreational activities within constraints of the system.*

ZELBY, RACHEL, realtor; b. Sosnowiec, Poland, May 6, 1930; came to U.S., 1955; d. Herschel Kupfermintz and Sarah Rosenblatt; m. Leon W. Zelby, Dec. 28, 1954; children: Laurie Susan, Andrew Stephen. Student, U. Pa., 1955, Realtors' Inst., Norman, Okla., 1974; grad., Realtors Inst., Oklahoma City, 1978. Lic. realtor, broker, Okla.; cert. residential specialist, Okla. Realtor, broker, ptnr. Realty World Norman Heritage, 1973-81; realtor, broker Century 21 Parker Real Estate, Norman, 1981—, residential specialist, 1986—. Mem. Jr. Svc. League, Norman, 1980—; charter mem. Assistance League Norman, 1970—; bd. dirs. Juvenile Svcs., Inc., Norman, 1975-76; bd. viss. Coll. Fine Arts U. Okla., 1992—. Mem. Nat. Assn. Realtors, Norman Bd. Realtors, Women's Coun. Realtors (treas. 1985), U. Okla. Women's Assn. (past pres.), Norman C. of C., LWV. Avocations: aerobics, contract bridge, theatre, music, travel. Home: 1009 Whispering Pines Dr Norman OK 73072-6912 Office: Century 21 Parker Real Estate 319 W Main St Norman OK 73069-1312 E-mail: rachelz@telepath.com.

ZELDES, BENJAMIN, optometrist; b. New Britain, Conn., Oct. 23, 1924; m. Edith R. Zeldes. Student, U. Conn., 1945—48; BS, OD, Ill. Coll. Optometry, 1950, postgrad., 1954, Gesell Inst. Child Devel., 1961—62. Pvt. practice, Newington, Conn., 1957—. Optometric cons. Mediplex of Newington and Mediplex of Wethersfield; cons. Hartford (Conn.) Easter Seal Rehab. Ctr., 1970—73, Continuous Progress Ednl. Consultants, 1970—73. Mem. Conn. Comprehensive Health Planning Adv. Coun., 1970—73; mem. adv. bd. Conn. Assn. Children with Perceptual Learning Disabilities, 1966—68; mem. Physicians Task Force on Mental Retardation, 1964—65; chmn. religious sch. com. Temple Sinai, Newington. Fellow: Am. Acad. Optometry; mem.: Nat. Eye Rsch. Found. (fellow internat. orthokeratology sect.), Hartford County Optometric Assn., Conn. Assn. Optometrists (chmn. ins. com. 1959—76, exec. coun. 1970—82, pres. 1976, commn. on personal health svcs., chmn. children's vision), New Eng. Coun. Optometrists (chmn. ins. com. 1965—84, 1986, pres.), Am. Optometric Assn. (ins. com. 1983—84, key person, polit. action com.), Lions (past pres. Newington chpt., chmn. eye rsch.). Home: 107 Lake Shore Blvd Stafford Springs CT 06076 Office: 1268 Main St Newington CT 06111

ZELDES, EDITH R. freelance journalist; b. N.Y.C., Feb. 29, 1928; d. William Shakespeare and Harriet Edith (Pelikan) Herrmann; m. Benjamin Zeldes, July 4, 1948; children: Mildred R. Solomon, Hazel A., Beth E. Margulies, Ross E. BA in Fine Arts, U. Conn., 1948; MEd, Ctrl. Conn. State U., New Britain, 1970. Cert. advanced pilot New Britain Power Squadron chpt. U.S. Power Squadron. Freelance journalist. Writer features for Jour. Inquirer, Middletown Press, Imprint Publs., White Publs. The (New Britain) Herald, The Hartford Courant. Sunday sch. tchr. Temple Sinai, Newington, Conn., Temple B'Nai Israel, New Britain, Conn.; producer, dir., publicist, booking agt., tchr. Newington Children's Theatre; dir., producer, actress, past pres. Theatre Newington On Stage; dir. Tri-Town Players, Vernon, Rockville, Conn.; dir. Aetna Players, Hartford, Conn. Mem. Theatre Newington On Stage (hon. life). Avocations: travel, boating, reading, theater. Home: 107 Lake Shore Blvd Stafford Springs CT 06076-3439 Office: 1268 Main St Newington CT 06111-3038

ZELDES, ILYA M. forensic scientist, lawyer; b. Baku, Azerbaidjan, Mar. 15, 1933; came to U.S., 1976; s. Michael B. and Pauline L. (Ainbinder) Z.; m. Emma S. Kryss, Nov. 5, 1957; 1 child, Irina Zeldes Rieser. JD, U. Azerbaidjan, Baku, 1955; PhD in Forensic Scis., U. Moscow, 1969. Expert-criminalist Med. Examiner's Bur., Baku, 1954-57; rsch. assoc. Criminalistics Lab., Moscow, 1958-62; sr. rsch. assoc. All-Union Sci. Rsch. Inst. Forensic Expertise, 1962-75; chief forensic scientist S.D. Forensic Lab., Pierre, 1977-93. Owner Forensic Scientist's Svcs., Pierre, 1977-93. Author: Physical-Technical Examination, 1968, Complex Examination, 1971, The Problems of Crime, 1981; contbr. numerous articles to profl. publs. in Australia, Austria, Bulgaria, Can., Eng., Germany, Holland, India, Ireland, Israel, Rep. of China, Russia, U.S. and USSR. Mem. Internat. Assn. Identification (rep. S.D. chpt. 1979-93, chmn. forensic lab. analysis subcom. 1991-98, firearm and toolmark identification subcom. 2001—), Am. Soc. Crime Lab. Dirs., Am. Assn. Firearm and Toolmark Examiners (emeritus). Avocation: travel. Home: 5735 Foxlake Dr Apt 1 Fort Myers FL 33917-5661 E-mail: ilyaz@iline.com.

ZELDES, JACOB DEAN, lawyer; b. Galesburg, Ill., Dec. 10, 1929; s. Louis Herman and Sophia Ruth (Koren) Z.; m. Nancy S. Zeldes, Aug. 23, 1953; children: Stephen, Kathryn, Amy. BS, U. Wis., 1951; LLB, Yale U., 1957. Bar: Conn. 1957, U.S. Dist. Ct. Conn. 1958, U.S. Ct. Appeals (2nd cir.) 1959, U.S. Supreme Ct. 1960, U.S. Tax Ct. 1966. Ptnr. Zeldes Needle & Cooper PC, Bridgeport, Conn. Lt. (j.g.) USNR, 1951-53, Korea. Fellow Am. Bar Found., Am. Coll. Trial Lawyers; mem. ABA Assn. Profl. Responsibility Lawyers, Conn. Bar Assn. (lawyer to lawyer dispute resolution com., spl. counsel Conn. Ho. of Reps., select com. to investigate impeachment of probate judge 1985), Conn. Trial Lawyers Assn., Assn. Trial Lawyers of Am., Nat. Assn. Criminal Def. Lawyers, Conn. Criminal Def. Lawyers Assn., Bridgeport Bar Assn. Democrat. Jewish. Avocations: swimming, hiking, travel. Office: Zeldes Needle & Cooper PC 1000 Lafayette Blvd Fl 5 Bridgeport CT 06604-4725 E-mail: jzeldes@znclaw.com.

ZELDIN, MARINA, small business owner; b. Ekaterinburg, Russia, Feb. 12, 1950; arrived in U.S., 1986; d. Vladimir and Sofia Fraden; m. Yuri Zeldin, Oct. 29, 1971; 1 child Eugene. MD magna cum laude, Med. Sch., Ekaterinburg, 1973. Cert. acupuncturist, massage therapist Nat. Bd. Cert. Internist City Hosp., Ekaterinburg, 1973—86; acupuncturist, massage therapist Body Minders, Therapeutic Body Works, New Haven, 1987—92; owner Therma, Wallingford, 1992—. Health cons. Rehab. Ctr., Wallingford, 1992—. Author: Mysterious Nineteenth, 2002. Avocations: travel, writing, reading. Home: 37 Dest Rd Hamden CT 06518

ZELDIN, RICHARD PACKER, publisher; b. Worcester, Mass., Aug. 7, 1918; s. M. and Virginia (Gealt) Z.; m. Virginia Graves, Nov. 25, 1950; children— Elizabeth Ann, Richard Shepherd. BS, West Chester U., Pa., 1942; grad. exec. program bus. adminstrn., Columbia U., 1966. Gen. mgr. profl. and reference book div. McGraw-Hill Book Co., Inc., 1948-68; v.p., publishing dir. Litton Ednl. Pub. Co., Inc., 1968-70; pres. R.R. Bowker Co., 1970-76, Xerox Coll. Pub., Xerox Individualized Pub., 1970-76;; pub. John Wiley & Sons, Inc., 1976-83; v.p. Moseley Assocs. Inc., N.Y.C., 1983—. Sec.-treas. sci., tech. and med. book pubs. group Asso. Am. Pubs., 1966-70; mem. adv. com. comml. publs. AEC, 1966-70 Author: A Tennis Guide to the USA, 1980, Business Forms on File, 1984, Personal Forms on File, 1984 Served to lt. USNR, 1942-46. Recipient Disting. Alumni award West Chester U., 1974. Mem. Info. Industry Assn. (sec. 1973—), IEEE, Am. Soc. Info. Sci., Soc. for Scholarly Pub. Clubs: Dutch Treat (N.Y.C.), Pubs. Lunch (N.Y.C.). Home: 20 Fairfield Dr Eatontown NJ 07724-3114 Office: Moseley Assocs Inc 342 Madison Ave Rm 1414 New York NY 10173-1423

ZELECHIWSKY, BOHDAN JOHN, lawyer; b. Pottsville, Pa., July 6, 1951; s. Bohdan Stephen and Nadia Z.; m. Chrystyna Hawrylak, Sept. 15, 1978 (div. Jan. 1989); children: Sophia, Adrian; m. Anita Louise Walters, Dec. 5, 1993; children: Roman, Zenia. BA, Moravian Coll., 1973; JD, Vt. Law Sch., 1976. Bar: Pa. 1977. Pvt. practice, Bethlehem, Pa., 1978—. Coun. mem. Ukranian Orthodox Ch., N.J., 1993. With USMC, 1971-72. Avocations: skiing, biking. Fax: (610) 866-4626. E-mail: BJZLaw@fast.net.com.

ZELEN, MARVIN, statistics educator; b. N.Y.C., June 21, 1927; m. Thelma Geier, Sept. 10, 1950; children: Deborah, Sandra. BS, CCNY, 1949; MS, U. N.C., 1951; PhD, Am. U., 1957; MA (hon.), Harvard U., 1977. Stat. eng. lab. Nat. Bureau of Standards, 1952-61; assoc. prof. Univ. Md., 1960-61; head, stat. and applied Math. section Nat. Cancer Inst., 1963-66; leading prof. State Univ., Buffalo, N.Y.C., 1967-77; pres. Frontier Sci. and Tech. Rsch. Found., Boston, 1975—; chmn. dept. biostats. Dana Farber Cancer Inst., 1977-98; prof. Harvard U. Sch. Pub. Health, 1977—; chmn. dept. biostat. Harvard U., 1980-90. Vis. prof. Univ. Wis., 1961-63, vis. assoc. prof. Univ. Calif., 1958. Sgt. U.S. Army, 1945-46. Fulbright scholar, 1965-66. Fellow Am. Acad. Arts and Sci., AAAS, Inst. Math. Stats., Am. Statis. Assn.; mem. Internat. Stats. Inst. Home: 230 Eliot St Chestnut Hill MA 02467-1447 Office: Harvard Sch Pub Health 677 Huntington Ave Boston MA 02115-6096

ZELENAK, EDWARD MICHAEL, lawyer, musician; b. Dearborn, Mich., Aug. 28, 1953; s. Edward Patrick and Irene Elaine (Maruska) Z.; m. Angeline Rose Cianfarani, May 24, 1986; children: Amelia Mary Rose and Edward Patrick (twins), Elliott William. BA, Wayne State U., 1975, JD, 1977. Bar: Mich. 1977, U.S. Dist. Ct. (ea. dist.) Mich. 1977, 6th Cir. Ct. of Appeals 1987. Leader Ed Zelenak Orch., Lincoln Park, Mich., 1971—; dir. pub. affairs Sta. WDRQ, Southfield, 1977-83, host talk show, 1978-83; instr. Wayne State Univ., Detroit, 1977-84; pvt. practice, Lincoln Park, 1977—; atty. Cities of Lincoln Park and Southgate (Mich.), 1978—. Hon. consul Slovak Republic, 2001—; corr. RKO Network, 1980-83; host talk show United Cable TV Mich., Woodhaven, 1980—, Sta. WXYT, 1988-94; gen. counsel Pat Paulsen for Pres., 1996; hon. consul Slovakia, 2001. Composer, performer (album) C. B. Polka, 1977. Alt. del. Dem. Nat. Conv., Miami, Fla., 1972, mem. staff Dem. Nat. Conv., N.Y.C., 1976; exec. bd. 16th Dist. Dems., Dearborn, 1975-87; gen. counsel First Cath. Slovak Union U.S. and Can., 1988-99, Pat Paulsen for Pres. Campaign, 1996; spl. counsel City of Ecorse, Mich., 1989—; bd. dirs. People's Cmty. Svcs. of Detroit, 1992-98; dir. Downriver Coun. for the Arts, 1997—; mem. Congress on New Urbanism, Seaside Inst. Recipient Commendation Mich. State Senate, 1982; named One of Five Outstanding Young Michiganders, Mich. Jaycees, 1990. Mem. Am. Fedn. Musicians, State Bar Mich., Wayne State U. Law Sch. Alumni Assn. (dir. 1998—, sec., v.p. 2001), Downriver Bar Assn., Slovak League Am. (nat. dir. 1985—, del. meeting with Vaclav Havel and Alexander Dubcek conf. in Czecho-Slovakia 1990), Wayne State U. Law Alumni Assn. (mem. exec. com., v.p. 2001), Slovak Cath. Sokol Club, Slovak Jednota Club, KC (fin. com. Robert Jones chpt. 1987-96), Kiwanis (pres. local chpt. 1981-82), Rotary Internat. Home: 711 Saint Johns Blvd Lincoln Park MI 48146-4925 Office: 2933 Fort St Lincoln Park MI 48146-2425

ZELENY, ANN DOUGLAS, sculptor; b. Tucson, Dec. 7, 1955; d. Charles Ellingson and Marjorie Ann (Pfeiffer) Zeleny; m. Arthur Jeffrey Munson, Dec. 22, 1974 (div. 1985); 1 child, Frederick Michael Munson Zeleny; m. Carl Douglas Anderson, Nov. 3, 1985; 1 child, Gwyneth Violet Zeleny Anderson. BFA, Va. Commonwealth U., 1977. Songwriter/vocalist Seventh Dawn, Richmond, Washington, 1973-80; archtl. sculptor Monumental Constrn. and Moulding Co., Washington, 1981-86; freelance sculptor, 1986—. Co-creator, set designer, propmaster, puppeteer The Mondo Breakfast Show, Arlington, 1984-86; graphics cons. Gfx, Washington, 1991-95; modelmaker, archtl. ornament cons. (trompe l'oeil murals) Community Bridge, Frederick, Md., 1993-95, (mural) Evang. Luth. Ch., Frederick Md., 2001. Sr. sculptor, sites of installation include: The Nat. Theatre, The Washington Times Bldg., The Hay-Adams Hotel, Phoenix Park Hotel, Phillips Collection Gallery, Casa Casuarina, Miami Beach; songwriter, performer (albums) Sunrise, 1976, Dreams, 1978; creator ceramic or cold cast sculptures including Presence, Purr, Daphne, Leap Dog, Aquarius, and Benevolent Green Man, featured by Design Toscano Galleries; Reflection, Gaia & Green Man Medallion featured by Sacredsource.com, Sylph, Consort, Romeo & Juliet; cameraperson Arlington Weekly News, 1980-85. Vol. graphics The Greens, 1989-92, The Common Market Food Coop., Frederick, Md., 1990-93; vol. set fabrication Beaux Artes Ball, Frederick, 1993; vol. designer, fabricator Delaplaine Visual Arts Ctr., Frederick, Md., 1995. Recipient "Ammy" Craft Award for set design Arlington Community TV, 1985, Ammy for best variety program, 1985, Ammy for humor, 1986. Avocation: metaphysics. Office: PO Box 13 Boonsboro MD 21713-0013 E-mail: zart@erols.com.

ZELENY, MARJORIE PFEIFFER (MRS. CHARLES ELLINGSON ZELENY), psychologist; b. Balt., Mar. 31, 1924; d. Lloyd Armitage and Mable (Willian) Pfeiffer; m. Charles Ellingson Zeleny, Dec. 11, 1950 (dec.); children: Ann Douglas, Charles Timberlake. BA, U. Md., 1947; MS, U. Ill., 1949, postgrad., 1951-54. Vocat. counseling psychologist VA, Balt., 1947-48; asst. U. Ill., Urbana, 1948-50; rsch. assoc. Bur. Rsch., 1952-53; chief psychologist dept. neurology and psychiatry Ohio State U. Coll. Medicine, Columbus, 1950-51; rsch. psychologist, cons. Tucson, Washington, 1954—. Mem. APA, AAAS, DAR, D.C. Psychol. Assn., Southeastern Psychol. Assn., Nat. Soc. Daus. Colonial Wars, Nat. Soc. Daus. Am. Colonists, Nat. Soc. Colonial Dames XVII Century, Nat. Soc. Descendants of Early Quakers, Nat. Soc. Dames of Ct. of Honor, Nat. Soc. U.S. Daus. of 1812, Sons and Daus. Colonial Bench and Bar, Washington Club (Washington), Johns Hopkins Club (Balt.), Mortar Bd., Delta Delta Delta, Sigma Delta Epsilon, Psi Chi, Sigma Tau Epsilon. Roman Catholic. Home: 6825 Wemberly Way Mc Lean VA 22101-1534

ZELEPUKIN, VALERI, hockey player; b. Vosdresensk, Russia, Sept. 17, 1968; married. Hockey player VOSK/USSR, 1984-87, 89-90, CSKA/USSR, 1987-88, SKA/USSR, 1987-88, KHIM/USSR, 1990-91, NJER/NHL, 1991-92, 93-97, 1997-98, EDMO/NHL, 1997-98, RUSS/OLYMP, 1997-98, PHIL/NHL, 1998—, Chgo. Blackhawks, 2000. Recipient ice hockey Silver medal Olympic Games, Nagano, Japan, 1998. Avocation: tennis. Office: Chgo Blackhawks United Ctr 1901 W Madison Chicago IL 60612*

ZELIGER, BERNARD, dean; Provost and dean Touro U. Coll. Osteo. Medicine. Office: 832 Walnut Ave Vallejo CA 94592*

ZELIGS, JOSEPH DANIEL, emergency physician, internist; b. Cin., Apr. 8, 1944; MD, NYU, 1972. Diplomate Am. Bd. Emergency Medicine, Am. Bd. Internal Medicine. Intern U. Utah, Salt Lake City; resident in medicine Walter Reed Army Hosp., Washington; chief emergency med. svc. Walter Reed Army Med. Ctr., 1991—2000, staff emergency medicine physician, 2000—; assoc. prof. medicine Uniform Svcs. U. Health Scis.

ZELIGSON, SHERYL, lawyer; b. Queens, N.Y. BA, Barnard Coll., 1985; JD, Fordham Law Sch., 1988. Bar: N.J. 1988, N.Y. 1989. Assoc. Donovan Leisure Newton & Irvine, N.Y.C., 1989-90, Fulbright & Jaworski LLP, N.Y.C., 1990-92; asst. gen. counsel Hadassah, Women's Zionist Orgn. Am., Inc., 1992—96, gen. counsel, 1996—. Assoc. Kelley Drye & Warren, N.Y.C., 1988-89. Mem.: ABA, NY State Bar Assn., Assn. Bar City of NY (non-profit com. 1999—2002). Office: Hadassah WZOA 50 W 58th St New York NY 10019 E-mail: szeligson@hadassah.org.

ZELIKOW, HOWARD MONROE, management and financial consultant; b. Bklyn., Apr. 17, 1934; s. Herman and Mae (Rebell) Z.; m. Doris Brown, June 10, 1956 (div. Aug. 1987); children: Lori Ann Zelikow Florio, Daniel M.; m. Marcie Peskin Rosenblum, Dec. 12, 1987. BA, Dartmouth Coll., 1955; MBA, Amost Tuck Sch., 1956. Acct. Ernst & Ernst, N.Y.C., 1956-61; controller Kratter Corp., 1961-64; mgr. J.H. Cohn, CPAs, Newark, 1964-65; ptnr. Zelikow & Rebell CPAs, N.Y.C., 1965-70; v.p. Oxbow Constrn. Corp., Port Washington, N.Y., 1970-76; exec. v.p., treas., chief fin. officer Progressive Ins. Cos., Mayfield Village, Ohio, 1976-87; prin. ZKA Assocs., Cleve., 1987-96; ptnr., mng. dir. Kayne Anderson Investment Mgmt., L.A., 1988—. Bd. dirs. FAQ, Inc., Westlake, Calif. Trustee Village of Great Neck Estates, Great Neck, N.Y., 1975-76. Mem. Hillcrest Club, Phi Beta Kappa. Jewish. Home: 10114 Empyrean Way Los Angeles CA 90067-3830 Office: Kayne Anderson Investment Mgmt 1800 Avenue Of The Stars Los Angeles CA 90067-4212

ZELIN, JEROME, retired retail executive; b. Bklyn., Dec. 24, 1930; s. Isidore and Ida (Roffman) Z.; m. Muriel Altsher, Dec. 18, 1955; children— Dorothy, Michael, Steven. BS magna cum laude, N.Y.U., 1952. Acct. Seymour Schwartz CPA, 1954-57; partner firm Schwartz, Zelin & Weiss CPAs, N.Y.C., 1958-61; vice chmn., pres., exec. v.p., treas., financial v.p., dir. Unishops, Inc. (retail co.), Jersey City, 1961-74; exec. v.p. Masters, Inc., Westbury, N.Y., 1974-97; cons. Master's, Inc., 1997-2000; ret. Trustee Temple Sholom of Flatbush. Served with AUS, 1952-54. Mem. N.Y. Soc. CPAs, Am. Inst. CPAs, Beta Gamma Sigma, Tau Alpha Omega. Jewish. Home: 225 Arkansas Dr Brooklyn NY 11234-6901 E-mail: j.zelin1000@aol.com.

ZELINKA, JEFFREY LLOYD, music educator; b. San Diego, June 26, 1960; s. Harry N. and Margo P. Zelinka; m. Gail L. Gandy, Mar. 29, 1998; children: Grant, Collin. MusB, Calif. State U., Northridge, 1983. Music tchr. grades K-12. Musician Air Nat. Guard Band of the S.W., Port Hueneme, Calif., 1989—; music tchr. De Anza Middle Sch., Ventura, 1991—. Condr. De Anza Marching Band, Ventura, 1992—2002. Sgt. U.S. Army, 1984—88. Decorated Army Achievement medal U.S. Army, Army Good Conduct medal, Army Commendation medal. Mem.: So. Calif. Vocal Assn., Music Educators Nat. Conf., So. Calif. Sch. Band and Orch. Assn., Knights of Pythias (prelate 1989—90). Avocation: reading. Office: De Anza Middle Sch 2060 Cameron St Ventura CA 93001 Office Fax: 805-641-5282. Business E-Mail: jzelinka@vtusd.k12.ca.us.

ZELINSKI, JOSEPH JOHN, engineering educator, consultant; b. Glen Lyon, Pa., Dec. 30, 1922; s. John Joseph and Lottie Mary (Oshinski) Z.; m. Mildred G. Sirois, July 22, 1946; children: Douglas John, Peter David. BS, Pa. State U., 1944, PhD, 1950. Grad. fellow Pa. State U., University Park, 1946-50; project supr. applied physics lab. Johns Hopkins U., Silver Spring, Md., 1950-58; staff scientist Space Tech. Labs. (now TRW, Inc.), Redondo Beach, Calif., 1958-60; head chem. tech. div. Ops. Evaluation Group MIT, Cambridge, 1960-62; prin. rsch. scientist Avco Everett (Mass.) Rsch. Lab., 1962-64; prof. mech. engrng. Northeastern U., Boston, 1964-85, prof. emeritus, 1985—; pres. World Edn. Resources, Ltd., Tampa, Fla., 1984—. Cons. Avco Everett Rsch. Lab., 1964-71, Pratt & Whitney Aircraft, East Hartford, Conn., 1966-70, Modern Electric Products and Phys. Scis. Co., Inc., Boston, 1980-82, Morrison, Mahoney and Miller, Boston, 1984; vice-chmn., chmn. exec. com. Univ. Grad. Coun., Northeastern U., Boston, 1980-84, dir. mech. engrng. grad. program, 1982-85; del. 4th World Conf. Continuing Engrng. Edn., Beijing China People to People, Spokane, Wash., 1989. Contbr. articles to profl. jours. Prin. Confraternity Christian Doctrine, Andover, Mass., 1961-64; pres. Andover Edn. Coun., 1962-64; vice chmn. Dem. Town Com., Boxford, Mass., 1980-84. Lt. (j.g.) USNR, 1943-46, PTO. Mem. AAAS, ASME, Am. Chem. Soc., N.Y. Acad. Scis., Combustion Inst. Democrat. Roman Catholic. Achievements include U.S. and foreign patents for coal combustion system for magnetohydrodynamic power generation, for fuel-cooled combustion systems for jet engines flying at high Mach numbers; prediction of optical observables of re-entry vehicles from analysis of decomposition mechanisms of heat-shield materials; invention of high-temperature furnace for production of crystalline graphite; development and verification of a design method for ramjet combustors. Home: Hunters Green 9207 Jubilee Ct Tampa FL 33647-2511

ZELINSKY, DANIEL, mathematics educator; b. Chgo., Nov. 22, 1922; s. Isaac and Ann (Ruttenberg) Z.; m. Zelda Oser, Sept. 23, 1945; children: Mara Sachs, Paul O., David. BS, U. Chgo., 1941, MS, 1943, PhD, 1946. Rsch. mathematician applied math group Columbia U., N.Y.C., 1944-45; instr. U. Chgo., 1943-44, 46-47; Nat. Rsch. Coun. fellow Inst. Advanced Study, Princeton, N.J., 1947-49; from asst. to assoc. prof. dept. math. Northwestern U., Evanston, Ill., 1949-60, prof., 1960-93, prof. emeritus, 1993—, acting chmn. math. dept., 1959-60, chmn., 1975-78. Vis. prof. U. Calif. Berkeley, 1960, Fla. State U., Tallahassee, 1963, Hebrew U., Jerusalem, 1970-71, 85, others; vis. scholar Tata Inst., 1979; mem. various coms. Northwestern U.; lectr. in field. Author: A First Course in Linear Algebra, 1968, rev. edit., 1973; contbr. articles to profl. jours. Fulbright grantee Kyoto U., 1955-56, grantee NSF, 1958-80; Guggenheim fellow Inst. Advanced Study, 1956-57, Indo-Am. fellow, 1978-79. Fellow AAAS (mem. nominating com. sect. A 1977-80, chmn. elect sect. A 1984-85, chmn. 1985-86, retiring chmn. 1986-87), Am. Math. Soc. (mem. coun. 1961-67, editor Transactions of A.M.S. 1961-67, mem. various coms., mem. editorial bd. Notices of A.M.S. 1983-86, chmn. editorial bds. com. 1989, chmn. ad hoc com. 1991-92). Jewish. Home: 613 Hunter Rd Wilmette IL 60091-2213 Office: Northwestern U Dept Math Evanston IL 60208-0001 E-mail: dz@northwestern.edu.

ZELINSKY, PAUL O. illustrator, painter, author; b. Evanston, Ill., Feb. 14, 1953; s. Daniel and Zelda B. (Oser) Z.; m. Deborah M. Hallen, Dec. 31, 1981; children: Anna H., Rachel L. BA summa cum laude, Yale U., 1974; MFA in Painting, Tyler Sch. Art, 1976. Art instr. San Diego State U., 1976; freelance illustrator/author, 1977—. Illustrator: Emily Upham's Revenge, 1978, How I Hunted the Little Fellows, 1979, The History of Helpless Harry, 1980, What Amanda Saw, 1981, Ralph S. Mouse, 1982, The Song in the Walnut Grove, 1982, The Sun's Asleep Behind the Hill, 1982, Zoo Doings, 1983, Hansel and Gretel, 1984, The Story of Mrs. Lovewright and Purrless her Cat, 1985, The Random House Book of Humor for Children, 1988, Strider, 1991, The Enchanted Castle, 1992, Dear Mr. Henshaw, 1993, More Rootabagas, 1993, Swamp Angel, 1994, Five Children and It, 1999, Awful Ogre's Awful Day, 2001; illustrator, adapter: The Maid and the Mouse and the Odd-shaped House, 1981, Rumpelstiltskin 1986, Rapunzel, 1997; illustrator, adapter, designer: The Wheels on the Bus, 1990, Knick-Knack Paddywhack, 2002. Recipient Caldecott Honor for Hansel and Gretel, 1985, Rumpelstiltskin, 1987, Swamp Angel, 1995, Best Illustrated Book N.Y. Times Book Rev., 1981, 85, 94, 2001, Caldecott medal for Rapunzel, 1998. Mem. Graphic Artists Guild, Author's Guild, Soc. Children's Book Writers and Illustrators, Phi Beta Kappa.

ZELIS, ROBERT FELIX, cardiologist, educator; b. Perth Amboy, N.J., Aug. 5, 1939; s. Felix Andrew and Rita Marie (Jurasz) Z.; m. Gail Ann Heelon, Sept. 10, 1960; children: Robert Felix, Kathleen, Karen, David. BS cum laude, U. Mass., 1960; MD with honors, U. Chgo., 1964. Diplomate: Am. Bd. Internal Medicine (cardiovascular disease). Intern, then asst. resident in medicine Beth Israel Hosp., Harvard U. Med. Sch., 1964-66; clin. asso. (lt. comdr. USPHS) cardiology br. Nat. Heart Inst., NIH, Bethesda, Md., 1966-68; mem. faculty U. Calif. Med. Sch., Davis, 1968-74, asst. asso. prof. medicine, 1972-74, chief lab. clin. physiology, 1968-74, asst. chief sect. cardiovascular medicine, 1970-74; prof. medicine and cellular/molecular physiology Milton S. Hershey (Pa.) Med. Center, Pa. State U. Coll. Medicine, 1974—, chief div. cardiology, 1974-84, dir. cardiology research, 1984—. Editor: The Peripheral Circulations, 1975; co-editor: Calcium Blockers, 1982; mem. editorial bd. Annals Internal Medicine, 1976-79, Am. Jour. Physiology, 1976-79, Circulation, 1979-82, Am. Heart Jour., 1980-90, Am. Jour. Cardiology, 1983-86, Jour. Cardiovasc. Pharmacology, 1991—, Jour. Am. Coll. Cardiology, 1994-99; contbr. articles to med. jours. Walter S. Barr fellow, 1960-64; recipient Borden Research award, 1964, Palmer award for Faculty Mentoring Pa. State U., 1997. Fellow A.C.P., Am. Coll. Chest Physicians, Am. Coll. Cardiology (gov. Eastern Pa. 1977-80); mem. Am. Fedn. Clin. Research (pres. 1977-78), Am. Soc. Clin. Investigation (nat. council 1981-85, v.p. 1984-85), Am. Physiol. Soc., Assn. Am. Physicians, Assn. Univ. Cardiologists, Am. Soc. Pharmacology and Exptl. Therapeutics, Am. Heart Assn. (nat. fellow councils circulation, arteriosclerosis, clin. cardiology and epidemiology, v.p. for community programs 1979-81, award of merit 1983 v.p., exec. com. Pa. 1976-79, pres. Pa. affiliate 1979-80, Charles T. Mears Humanitarian award 1984), Western Soc. Clin. Research, Sigma Xi, Alpha Omega Alpha, Phi Eta Sigma. Roman Catholic. Home: 815 Verden Dr Hummelstown PA 17036-9700 Office: MS Hershey Med Ctr Cardiology Divsn HO-47 PO Box 850 Hershey PA 17033-0850

ZELKOWITZ, MARVIN VICTOR, computer science educator; b. Bklyn., Aug. 7, 1945; s. Philip and Tillie Zelkowitz; m. Cindy Sonia Dectrow, May 24, 1970; children: Elena Rochelle, Aaron Daniel. BS in Math., Rensselaer Poly. Inst., 1967; MS in Computer Sci., Cornell U., 1969, PhD in Computer Sci., 1971. Instr. math. Ithaca (N.Y.) Coll., 1970; asst. to assoc. prof. U. Md., College Park, 1971-90, prof., 1990—, assoc. chmn. for edn., 1982-85, acting chmn., 1985, assoc. chmn. for facilities, 1987-88. Systems programmer RCA Computer Systems Divsn., 1969; computer scientist faculty Nat. Inst. Standards and Tech., Gaithersburg, Md., 1976-98; co-dir. Fraunhofer Ctr.-Md., 1997—; cons. various cos.; speaker in field. Series editor: Ablex Software Engineering Series, 1986-97; co-author: Software Specification: Formal Methods, 1994, Programming Languages Design and Implementation, 1996, 4th ed., 2001; editor: Advances in Computers, 1994—; contbr. chpts. to books, articles to profl. jours. Mem. math. adv. com. Howard County, Md., 1992-97. Recipient Software Engrng. Lab. grant NASA/Goddard, 1976—, Cert. Recognition, Nat. Bur. Standards, Gaithersburg, 1981, Cert. Appreciation Navy Next Generation Computing Resources program, Washington, 1993. Fellow Computer Soc. of IEEE (Meritorious Svc. award 1992, 99, cert. of appreciation 1980), Assn. for Computing Machinery (Svc. award 1996, Sigsoft Disting. Svc. award 2000), Nat. Capital Area Skeptics (bd. dirs. 1992—), Tech. Com. on Software Engrng. (chmn. 1981-83), Assn. for Computing Machinery (chmn. spl. interest group on software engrng. 1979-81). Avocations: jogging, model railroading. Office: Univ Md Dept Comput Sci College Park MD 20742-0001 E-mail: mvz@cs.umd.edu.

ZELL, FRAN A. small business owner, writer; b. Cleve., Mar. 1, 1947; BS, Mich. State U., 1968; MA, U. of Ill., 1990. Cert. Tchr. 2002. Feature writer Lansing State Jour., Lansing, Mich., 1968—70, Chgo. Tribune, Chgo., 1970—81; prin., owner, 1981—88; writer Rotary Internat., Evanston, 1988—92; prin., owner Madison, Wis., 1992—. Author: (novels) The Marcy Stories, 2001 (Banta award, 2002), (book) A Multicultural Portrait of The American Revolution, 1996, (plays) Lavender Rose, 2000. Fellow Writing fellowship, Anderson Ctr. for Interdisciplinary Studies, 1999; grantee Writing Residency, Ragdale Found., 1993, 1995, 1997, Travel grant, Wis. Arts Bd., 1998, Barbara Deming Meml. Fund Found., 2000, Writing Residency, Ragdale Found., 2000. Avocation: volunteer work with children.

ZELLER, BEN CRATHERN, actor, writer; b. Manchester, N.H., Dec. 17, 1933; s. William H and Marion Crathern Zeller; m. Evelyn Rita Rios; children: Carl, Janet. Student, U. Alaska, 1956. Homesteader, Chena Ridge, Alaska, 1955—64; forest fire fighter Alaska Forestry Dept., Fairbanks, 1956—58. Guide Arctic Rsch. Lab, Umiat, 1959. (actor, dir., stage designer, art dir.): (plays). Cpl. U.S. Army, 1951—53. Alaskan Independence. Home: PO Box 442 Raton NM 87740 Office: Tinaja Connection Raton NM 87740

ZELLER, CHRISTOPHER LEE, archaeologist; b. Northampton, Pa., Nov. 25, 1956; s. Karl Fredrich and Joan Veron (Hagenbuch) Zeller; m. Christi Joanne Wiggins, Apr. 24, 1982; 1 child Kaeti Grace. BA in Anthropology, Ft. Lewis Coll., 1980. Cert. fireline archaeologist U.S. Forest Svc., 00, dki patroller Nat. Ski Patrol, 82, EMT Colo., 77. Preservation tech., foreman San Juan Stabilization, Mancos, Colo., 1977—81; archaeologist Bur. Land Mgmt., Durango, 1982; stabilization specialist Paul Nickens and Assocs., Montrose, 1983; ind. contractor, stabilization specialist Woods Canyon Archaeol. Cons., Yellow Jacket, 1985—87; ind. contractor, project dir. Four Corners Rsch. Inst., Durango, 1986—87; owner, operator Petro Graphics, 1987—. Ski patroller Durango Mountain Resort, 1974—. Achievements include invention of toboggan platform; conducted over 50 major preservation projects involving over 40 archaeological and historic sites in American Southwest. Avocations: fine art, trout fishing, camping. Office: Petro Graphics Po Box 745 Durango CO 81302

ZELLER, CLAUDE, physicist, researcher; b. Aulnay, Bois, France, Dec. 11, 1940; came to U.S., 1976; m. Elisabeth Kreib, 1962 (div. 1967); 1 child, Frédéric; m. Florence Labour, Oct. 14, 1967; children: Caroline, Elisabeth. PhD, Univ. Nancy, France, 1968. Rsch. physicist Univ. Nancy, France, 1968-76; visiting rsch. faculty Univ. Pa., Phila., 1976-79; sr. physicist Pitney Bowes R&D, Norwalk, Conn., 1979-84, mgr. applied physics, 1984-91; sr. fellow Pitney Bowes, Shelton, 1992—. Adv. bd. CNRS, Paris, 1969-71; sec. scientific bd. Univ. Nancy, 1971-76; cons. Bruker-Spectrospin, Wissembourg, France, 1970-75. Contbr. 78 articles to profl. jours. Recipient sr. fellowship, NATO, 1976. Mem. IEEE, N.Y. Acad. Scis., Am. Phys. Soc., Appalachian Mountain Club, Soc. for Imaging Sci. and Tech., U.S. Jaycees, L'Union Alsacienne (v.p.), Am. Soc. Le Souvenir Français. Roman Catholic. Achievements include pioneer work in electron beam X-Ray microanalysis; early design of soft cast steel electro-magnet yoke for NMR applications; development of advanced materials such as high electrical conductivity intercalated graphite fiber composite materials and very high magnetic permeability amorphous fibers; early investigations of electromagnetic interference with pacemakers; development of digital printing systems for printability and machine readability of information rich, graphically secure, symbologies for postal applications; participant international standard organizations; 9 patents. Home: 97 Fan Hill Rd Monroe CT 06468-1831 Office: Pitney Bowes Inc 35 Waterview Dr Shelton CT 06484-4339 E-mail: czeller@ieee.org.

ZELLER, JOSEPH PAUL, advertising executive; b. Crestline, Ohio, Mar. 19, 1940; s. Paul Edward and Grace Beatrice (Kinstle) Z.; m. Nancy Jane Schmidt, June 17, 1961; children: Laurie, Joe. BA, U. Notre Dame, 1962; MFA, Ohio U., 1963. Mgr.radio/television Drewrys Ltd. USA, Inc., South Bend, Ind., 1963-64; media supr. Tatham-Laird & Kudner, Chgo., 1964-67; v.p. assoc. media dir. J. Walter Thompson Co., 1967-77; v.p. media dir, v.p. Campbell-Mithun, 1977-80; sr. v.p., dir. media, fin., chmn. media coun. D'Arcy Masius Benton & Bowles, 1980-96, sr. v.p., 1996-2000; pres. Fox River Trading Co., East Dundee, Ill., 2000—. Chmn. Z Prop, 1986—; dir. circle Desert Caballeros Mus., 1994-96; founder Native Am. Images web mag., 1999. Pres. Amateur Hockey Assn. Ill., 1985. Mem. Broadcast Pioneers, Chgo. Advt. Club, Moose. Roman Catholic. Avocations: amateur hockey, photography, country music. E-mail: jzeller@prodigy.net., trader@rivertradingpost.com.

ZELLER, MICHAEL EUGENE, lawyer; b. Queens, N.Y., June 19, 1967; s. Hans Ludwig and Geri Ann (Schottenstein) Z. BA, Union Coll., 1989; JD, Temple Law Sch., 1992; LLM magna cum laude, U. Hamburg, Germany, 1994. Bar: N.Y. 1992, U.S. Dist. Ct. (so. and ea. dists.) N.Y. 1995, N.C. 1996. Fgn. intern Bryan Gonzalez Vargas y Gonzalez Baz, Mexico City, 1990; student law clk. Hon. Jane Cutler Greenspan, Phila., 1990-91; fgn. clk. DROSTE, Hamburg, 1991, fgn. assoc., translator, 1992-94; freelance translator Charlotte, N.C., 1995—; mem. Internat. and Corp. Law Group of Moore & Van Allen PLLC, 1995—; owner, restaurateur Salad Garden, LLC. and Salad Garden Café, LLC, 1998—2001; owner Nighttime Entertainment LLC, 1999—2001, BGZ Properties, LLC. Active Charlotte World Affairs Coun., Charlotte Mayor's Internat. Cabinet; bd. dirs. Alemannia Soc., 1996-2000, Young Affiliates of Mint Mus., 1999-2000; bd. dirs., pres. Southgate Commons Homeowners Assn., 1998-2002; vol. atty. Children's Law Ctr. Scholar Fedn. German/Am. Clubs, 1987; named Vol. Lawyer of the Yr. Children's Law Ctr., 1998. Mem. ABA, N.Y. State Bar Assn., N.C. Bar Assn., Mecklenburg County Bar Assn., Gewerblicher Rechtsschutz und Urheberrecht e.V., European Am. Bus. Forum. Avocations: singing, theater, golf, fictional writing. Office: 100 N Tryon St Fl 47 Charlotte NC 28202-4003

ZELLER, MICHAEL EDWARD, physicist, educator; b. San Francisco, Oct. 8, 1939; s. Edward Michael and Marie (Eschen) Z.; m. Linda Marie Smith, June 12, 1960; children: Jeffrey, Daniel. BS, Stanford U., 1961; MS, UCLA, 1964, PhD, 1968. Research assoc. UCLA, 1968-69; instr. physics Yale U., New Haven, 1969-70, asst. prof., 1970-76, assoc. prof., 1976-82, prof., 1982—, chmn., 1989-95, Henry Ford II prof., 1996—. Recipient DeVane medal Phi Beta Kappa, 1980 Fellow Am. Phys. Soc.; mem. N.Y. Acad. Sci., Sigma Xi, Sigma Pi Sigma Democrat. Jewish. Home: 135 Newton Rd Woodbridge CT 06525-1534 Office: Yale U Physics Dept 260 Whitney Ave New Haven CT 06511-8903

ZELLER, MICHAEL JAMES, psychologist, educator; b. Des Moines, Dec. 3, 1939; s. George and Lila (Fitch) Z. BS, Iowa State U., 1962, MS, 1967. Instr. psychology Minn. State U., Mankato, 1967-73, asst. prof., 1974-89; assoc. prof. Minn. State U.-, 1990-2001, prof. emeritus, 2001—. Prof. emeritus Minn. State U.-Mankato, 2001; mem. social sci. edn. coun. Mankato State U., 1976—; ednl. cons. Random House, Scott Foresman, West Pub. Editor: Test Item File to Accompany Introduction to Psychology, 6th edit., 1992; co-author: Test Item File to Accompany Introduction to Psychology, 5th edit., 1989, Test File for Psychology, 3d edit., 1988, Unit Mastery Workbook, 1st edit., 1974, 2d edit., 1976, Test Item File to Accompany Psychology, 1st edit., 1974, 2d edit., 1976, Psychology: A Personal Approach, 1st edit., 1982, 2d edit., 1984; contbr. chpts. to books. With USAR, 1964-70. Mem. APA, Am. Psychol. Soc., Psi Chi (award 1988). Achievements include development and research on educational materials, methods of instruction and career opportunities for psychology majors. Home and Office: PO Box 150 Mc Cormick SC 29835 E-mail: mil9584762@wctel.net.

ZELLER, RONALD JOHN, lawyer; b. Phila., Jan. 28, 1940; m. Lucille Bell; children: John, Kevin, Suzanne. BSBA, LaSalle Coll., 1964; JD, Ohio State U., 1967. Bar: Mich. 1968, Fla. 1971. Ptnr. Patton & Kanner, Miami, Fla., 1973-80, of counsel, 1980-89; pres., chief exec. officer Norwegian Cruise Lines, 1980-86; pres. Twenty First Century Mgmt. Group, Inc., Coconut Grove, Fla., 1986-90, Miami Voice Corp., 1990-92; gen. counsel Splty. Mgmt. Co., Delray Beach, Fla., 1992-93, pres., 1994-96; ptnr. Zeller & Assocs., LLC, Palm Beach, 1996—. Dep. chmn. Cruise Lines Internat. Assoc., N.Y.C., 1981-85, chmn., 1986. Trustee United Way Dade County, 1981-86; pres. Cath. Charities, Archdiocese of Miami 1976-78, Broward County, 1975-76, Excalibur Devel. Ctrs., Inc., 1973-75; mem. citizens bd. U. Miami, 1980-92; mem. exec. bd. New World Sch. Arts, 1986-87; mem. centennial campaign com. Ohio State U. Coll. Law, 1982-92, also mem. nat. coun.; mem. coun. Pres.'s Assocs., LaSalle U., 1982-87; mem. Fla. Postsecondary Edn. Planning Commn., 1986-87; mem. Cmty. Assns. Inst., 1995-2000; chmn. exec. com. Maritime Inst., 1997-99; mem. utility rev. bd. Village of Wellington, 1997-98; mem. gen. counsel Palm Beach Maritime Mus.; mem. Fla. com. Affirm Thy Friendship Campaign, Ohio State U., 1997-2000; mem. cruise line incentive com. Port of Palm Beach, 1997-2000. Mem. ABA (sect. taxation, close corp. com.), Fla. Bar Assn. (lawyers and CPA's com., long range planning com. 2001--), Maritime Law Assn. (proctor in admiralty), Pres.' Club Ohio State U. Office: Zeller & Assocs LLC Esperante Bldg 222 Lakeview Ave Ste 260 West Palm Beach FL 33401 Fax: 561 802-4387. E-mail: zellerlawfirm@juno.com.

ZELLER, THOMAS G. historian; b. 1966; MA, U. Munich, 1995, DPhil, 1999. Vis. asst. prof. Ga. Inst. Tech., Atlanta, 1999—2000, U. Pa., Phila., 2000—01; asst. prof. Oakland U., Rochester, Mich., 2001—. Author: (book) Strasse, Bahn, Panorama, 2002. Mem.: European Soc. Environ. History, Am. Soc. Environ. History, Soc. for History of Tech. (chair Kranzberg com. 2001—02, internat. scholar 1998—99). Office: Oakland U Dept History 378 O'Dowd Hall Rochester MI 48309 E-mail: tzeller@oakland.edu.

ZELLERBACH, WILLIAM JOSEPH, retired paper company executive; b. San Francisco, Sept. 15, 1920; s. Harold Lionel and Doris (Joseph) Z.; m. Margery Haber, Feb. 25, 1946; children: John William, Thomas Harold, Charles Ralph, Nancy. BS, Wharton Sch., U. Pa., 1942; grad., Advanced Mgmt. Program, Harvard U., 1958. With Crown Zellerbach Corp. and subs., 1946-85; officer, dir. Crown Zellerbach Corp., 1960-85. Mem gen. adv. com. fgn. assistance programs AID, 1965-68; pres. Zellerbach Family Fund. Served as lt. USNR, 1942-46. Mem. Nat. Paper trade Assn. (pres. 1970) Clubs: Villa Taverna (San Francisco), Presidio Golf (San Francisco), Pacific Union (San Francisco), Commonwealth (San Francisco); Peninsula Country (San Mateo, Calif.). Office: 120 Montgomery St Ste 2000 San Francisco CA 94104-4323

ZELLERS, ROBERT CHARLES, materials engineer, consultant, speaker; b. Youngstown, Ohio, June 13, 1943; s. Charles Newton and Beatrice Eleanor (Snavely) Z.; m. Patricia Ann Ockerman, Nov. 27, 1965; children: Derek, Shannon, Robyn. BEng in Civil Engring., Youngstown State U., 1967. Registered profl. engr., Pa., Ohio; registered profl. land surveyor, Pa. Materials engr. Standard Slag Co., Youngstown, 1966-72; asst. chief engr. The Duquesne Slag Co., Pitts., 1972-81; exec. sec. Pa. Slag Assn., 1972-81; v.p. engring. Forta Corp., Grove City, 1978-82, exec. v.p., 1983-97; owner, mgr. Zellers Design Group, Mercer, 1982—; owner Zellers Galleries, 1979—; prin. IMTEK, Grove City, Pa., 1988-91; pres. ICEMS, Toledo, 1992-99; v.p. MIZEL, Crowley, Tex., 1994-97; pres. ZELLCO, 1994-97; v.p. mktg. Fibercon Internat. Inc., 1998-99; dir. tech. and engring. Nycon, Inc., Mercer, 1999—2001, v.p. tech. and engring., 2002—. Presenter in field at confs., seminars and profl. orgn. meetings; profl. speaker. Contbr. articles to profl. jours. Dir. Greenville Symphony Orch. Mem. ASCE, ASTM (various coms.), Constrn. Specifications Inst., Internat. Congress Bldg. Ofcls., So. Bldg. Code Congress Internat., Nat. Ready Mixed Concrete Assn., Synthetic Fiber Assn. (co-founder, past pres., v.p.), Transp. Rsch. Bd., Am. Concrete Inst. (various coms.), Lions. Office: Nycon Inc 102 Latonka Dr Mercer PA 16137-9360 E-mail: rzellers@nycon.com.

ZELLNER, ARNOLD, economics and statistics educator; b. Bklyn., Jan. 2, 1927; s. Israel and Doris (Kleiman) Z.; m. Agnes Marie Sumares, June 20, 1953; children— David S., Philip A., Samuel N., Daniel A., Michael A. AB, Harvard, 1949; PhD, U. Calif. at Berkeley, 1957; PhD (hon.), Autonomous U. Madrid, 1986, Tech. U. Lisbon, 1991, U. Kiel, 1998. Asst., then assoc. prof. econs. U. Wash., 1955-60; Fulbright vis. prof. Netherlands Sch. Econs., Rotterdam, 1960-61; assoc. prof., then prof. econs. U. Wis., 1961-66; H.G.B. Alexander disting. service prof. econs. and statistics U. Chgo., 1966-96, prof. emeritus, 1996—; dir. H.G.B. Alexander Rsch. Found., 1973—. Cons. Battelle Meml. Inst., 1964—71; vis. rsch. prof. U. Calif., Berkeley, 1971, Berkeley, 96, adj. prof., 1998—; trustee Nat. Opinion Rsch. Corp., 1973—80; bd. dirs. Nat. Bur. Econ. Rsch., 1980—; seminar leader NSF-NBER Seminar on Bayesian Inference in Econometrics and Stats., 1970—95; vis. prof. Am. U., Cairo, 1997, Hebrew U., 1997, U. Calif., Berkeley, 1997—2002. Co-author: Systems Simulation for Regional Analysis, 1969, Estimating the Parameters of the Markov Probability Model, 1970; author: Bayesian Inference in Econometrics, 1971, Basic Issues in Econometrics, 1984, Bayesian Analysis in Econometrics and Statistics: The Zellner View and Papers, 1997; editor: Economic Statistics and Econometrics, 1968, Seasonal Analysis of Economic Time Series, 1978, Simplicity, Inference and Modelling, 2001; assoc. editor: Econometrica, 1962-68; co-editor: Studies in Bayesian Econometrics and Statistics, 1975, Jour. Econometrics, 1972—, founding editor ASA Jour. Bus. and Econ. Stats., 1983; contbr. articles to profl. jours. Pres. Leonard J. Savage Meml. Trust Fund, Chgo., 1977-2000. Served with AUS, 1951-53. Fellow AAAS, Am. Acad. Arts and Scis., Am. Econ. Assn., Internat. Inst. of Forecasters, Econometric Soc., Am. Statis. Assn. (pres. elect 1990—, pres. 1991—, chmn. bus. and econs. sect. 1980, chmn. Bayesian statis. sci. sect. 1993); mem. Internat. Statis. Inst., Internat. Soc. Bayesian Analysis (co-pres. 1993, pres. 1994-96, Founders award 1998), Soc. Actuaries (trustee, rsch. found., 1994-98). Avocations: golf, tennis, travel, grandchildren. Home: 5628 S Dorchester Ave Chicago IL 60637-1722 Office: U Chgo Grad Sch Bus 1101 E 58th St Chicago IL 60637-1511 E-mail: arnold.zellner@gsb.uchicago.edu.

ZELLNER, KENNETH KERMIT, elementary education educator; b. Allentown, Pa., Sept. 4, 1945; s. Mellis Myron and Thelma Amanda (Bortz) Z.; m. Jean Elizabeth Welsh, June 24, 1978; children: Todd Benjamin, Amanda Elizabeth. BS, Kutztown U., 1967, MEd, 1971. Cert. elementary and secondary edn., environ. edn., supervision elementary edn., Pa. Tchr. Parkland Sch. Dist., Allentown, 1967—, environ. lab. cons., 1980-97. Cooperating tchr. East Stroudsburg (Pa.) U., 1973-97, Lehigh U., Bethlehem, Pa., 1992-94, sci. camp instr. SMART Ctr., 1993-94; faculty mentor Pa. Gov.'s Sch. of Excellence for Teaching Pa. Dept. Edn., Harrisburg, 1992. Contbr. articles to profl. jours. Mem. little Lehigh watershed curriculum task force Wildlands Conservancy, Emmaus, Pa., 1984-97; mem. newspapers in edn. adv. coun. Allentown Morning Call, 1988-89. Recipient Presdl. Award for Excellence in Sci. and Math. Teaching NSF, 1992, Regional Catalyst award for Excellence in Sci. Teaching Chem. Manufacturers Assn., 1994, Nat. Educators award Milken Family Found., 1994, Congrl. Citation for Outstanding Sci. Teaching Pa. Ho. of Reps., 1994. Mem. Pa. Sci. Tchrs. Assn., Nat. Sci. Tchrs. Assn., Coun. for Elem. Sci. Internat., Assn. Presdl. Awardees in Sci. Teaching, Soc. Elem. Presdl. Awardees, Masons (worshipful master 1985). Republican. Lutheran. Avocations: woodworking, antique and classic cars, snow skiing. Home: 9022 Reservoir Rd Germansville PA 18053-2731 Office: Parkland Adminstrn Bldg 1210 Springhouse Rd Allentown PA 18104-2119

ZELLWEGER, RENEE, actress; b. Katy, Tex. BA in English, U. Tex. Actress feature films including Reality Bites, 1994, Love and a .45, 1994, 8 Seconds, 1994, The Low Life, 1995, Empire Records, 1995, The Whole Wide World, 1996, Jerry Maguire, 1996, Texas Chainsaw Massacre: The Next Generation, 1997, Deceiver, 1997, One True Thing, 1998, A Price Above Rubies, 1998, The Bachelor, 1999, Nurse Betty, 2000 (Best Actress in Comedy or Musical Golden Globe award 2000), Me, Myself & Irene, 2000, Bridget Jones's Diary, 2001 (nominee Best Actress SAG award, Broadcast Film Critics Assn. award, Brit. Acad. Award and Acad. award 2001; nominee Best Actress in Comedy or Musical Golden Globe award 2001), White Oleander, 2002, TV including Shake, Rattle and Rock Movie, 1993, Murder in the Heartland mini-series, 1994. Office: Byant Joel CAA 9830 Wilshire Blvd Beverly Hills CA 90212*

ZELMANOWITZ, JULIUS MARTIN, mathematics educator, university administrator; b. N.Y.C., Feb. 20, 1941; s. Morris and Tillie (Holtz) Z.; m. Joan R. Traubel, June 24, 1962; 1 child, Dawn Michèle. AB, Harvard U., 1962; MS, U. Wis., 1963, PhD, 1966. Asst. prof. U. Calif., Santa Barbara, 1966-73, assoc. prof., 1973-77, prof. maths., 1977—, assoc. vice chancellor acad. affairs, 1985-87, assoc. vice chancellor acad. personnel, 1988-98; assoc. prof. Carnegie-Mellon U., Pitts., 1970-71; interim vice provost acad. initiatives U. Calif., 1999-2000, v.p. acad. initiatives, 2000—. Vis. asst. prof. UCLA, 1969-70, vis. assoc. prof. 1973-74; vis. prof. U. Rome, 1977, McGill U., Montreal, Quebec, 1982-83, 87-88, U. Munich, 1983, 88. Contbr. articles to profl. jours. Sr. rsch. grantee Italian Nat. Rsch. Coun., Rome, 1977, Palermo, 1988; named Milw. Prof. of Maths. The Technion, Haifa, Israel, 1979; Fulbright sr. fellow, Munich, 1983. Mem. Am. Math. Soc., Math. Assn. Am. Home: 2040 Franklin St # 1407 San Francisco CA 94109-2982 Office: Off Pres Acad Initiatives 1111 Franklin St Oakland CA 94607-5200 E-mail: julius.zelmanowitz@ucop.edu.

ZELNICK, CARL ROBERT, writer, educator; b. N.Y.C., Aug. 9, 1940; s. David Isadore and Lillian (Ostrow) Z.; m. Pamela Margaret Sharp, Dec. 30, 1967; children: Eva Michal, Dara Yael, Marni Ruth. BS, Cornell U., 1961; LLB, U. Va., 1964. Bar: N.Y. 1965, D.C. 1966. Law assoc. H. Charles Ephraim, Washington, 1966-67; corr./columnist Anchorage Daily News, 1968-76; assoc. editor Environ. Law Reporter, 1971-72; spl. corr. Christian Sci. Monitor, 1973-77; corr./bur. chief Nat. Pub. Radio, Washington, 1972-76; exec. editor Frost/Nixon Interviews, 1976-77; dir. news coverage ABC-TV, 1977-81; dep. bur. chief ABC News, 1981-82, Moscow bur. chief, corr., 1982-84, corr. Israel, 1984-86; ABC News Pentagon corr. Washington, 1986-94; media fellow Hoover Instn., Stanford U., 1998. Mem. Citizens Commn. on Race, 1998—; vis. prof. Boston U., 1998—2000, prof., 2000—, dir. dept. journalism, 2002—. Author: Backfire--A Reporter Looks at Affirmative Action, 1996, Gore--A Political Life, 1999, Winning Florida: How the Bush Team Fought the Battle, 2000; contbr. articles to newspapers and mags. Served with USMC, 1964-65. Recipient Gavel awards Am. Bar Assn., 1969, 74, Du Pont award Columbia U. Sch. Journalism, 1984, Emmy award, 1984, 92; rsch. fellow Hooer Inst., 2001—. Mem. Council on Fgn. Relations, Phi Epsilon Pi, Pi Delta Phi. Jewish. Office: Boston U Coll Comm 640 Commonwealth Ave Boston MA 02215-2422 E-mail: rzelnick@bu.edu.

ZELON, LAURIE DEE, lawyer; b. Durham, N.C., Nov. 15, 1952; d. Irving and Doris Miriam (Baker) Z.; m. David L. George, Dec. 30, 1979; children: Jeremy, Daniel. BA in English with distinction, Cornell U., 1974; JD, Harvard U., 1977. Bar: Calif. 1977, U.S. Ct. Appeals (9th cir.) 1978, U.S. Supreme Ct. 1989. Assoc. Beardsley, Hufstedler & Kemble, L.A., 1977-81, Hufstedler, Miller, Carlson & Beardsley, L.A., 1981-82, ptnr., 1983-88, Hufstedler, Miller, Kaus & Beardsley, L.A., 1988-90, Hufstedler, Kaus & Ettinger, L.A., 1990-91, Morrison & Foerster, L.A., 1991-2000; judge L.A. Superior Ct., 2000—. Contbg. author: West's California Litigation Forms: Civil Procedure Before Trial, 1996; editor-in-chief Harvard Civil Rights and Civil Liberties Law Rev., 1976-77 Bd. dirs. N.Y. Civil Liberties Union, 1973-74. Mem. ABA (chmn. young lawyers divsn. pro bono project 1981-83, delivery and pro bono projects com. 1983-85, subgrant competition-subgrant monitoring project 1985-86, chair standing com. on lawyers pub. svc. responsibility 1987-90, chair law firm pro bono project 1989-91, standing com. legal aid and indigent defendants 1991-97, chmn. 1993-97, mem. ho. dels. 1993—, state del. 1998—, commn. on ethics 2000 1997—), Calif. Bar Assn. (bd. dirs. appellate project 1995-2000, chair commn. on access to justice 1997-99), L.A. County Bar Assn. (trustee 1989-91, v.p. 1992-93, sr. v.p. 1993-94, pres.-elect 1994-95, pres. 1995-96, fed. cts. and practices com. 1984-93, vice chmn. 1987-88, chmn. 1988-89, chmn. judiciary com. 1991-92, chmn. real estate litigation subsect. 1991-92), Women Lawyers Assn. L.A., Calif. Women Lawyers Assn. Democrat. Office: Los Angeles Superior Ct 111 N Hill St Los Angeles CA 90012-3117

ZELONKY, DANIEL, composer; b. Milw., Feb. 10, 1957; s. Barbara J. Zelonky. Student, Foothill Coll., Palo Alto Hills, Clif., 1983—84. Composer: (recs., performances) Wanton Phenomena, 1999 (Yearly Top Ten Wire Mag., 1999). Recipient ASCAP Plus award, ASCAP, 2001. Mem.: Nat. Music Pubs. Assn. Home and Office: 5030 Cleon Ave North Hollywood CA 91601 Personal E-mail: dzelonky@mac.com.

ZELUS, PAUL ROBERT, education researcher; b. Chgo., May 28, 1947; s. Robert J. and Olga C. (Antonacci) Z.; m. Kathryn E. Rehorst, Jan. 15, 1972; children: Jason P., Aaron M. BA, Loyola U., Chgo., 1969, MA, 1972; PhD, Northwestern U., 1975. Asst. prof. sociology SUNY, Geneseo, 1972-79; assoc. prof. sociology Capital U., Columbus, Ohio, 1979-83; asst. prof. sociology Idaho State U., Pocatello, 1983-88, dir. Ctr. for Bus. Rsch., 1988—. Prin. cons. Zelus Assocs., Pocatello, 1995—. Co-author: I Just Went to Work: J.R. Simplot and His Business Career, 1995. Bd. dirs. Greater Pocetello C. of C., 1994-96, Idaho Rural Devel. Coun., Boise, 1995. Fellow Gerontol. Soc. Am.; mem. Rotary Internat. Lutheran. Avocation: genealogy. Office: Ctr for Bus Rsch 1651 Alvin Ricken Dr Pocatello ID 83201-2727

ZEMAN, GREGORY OSWALD, physician; b. Chgo., 1936; MD, Loyola U., 1960. Intern St. Joseph Hosp., Chgo., 1960-61; resident Hines VA Hosp., 1963-65; with MacNeal Hosp., Berwyn, Ill., Hinsdale Hosp., Elmhurst Hosp. Allergy fellow U. Ill. Rsch.-Edn. Hosp., Chgo., 1965-66. Fellow ACP, Am. Acad. Allergy & Immunology, Am. Coll. Allergy & Immunology. Office: 6340 Americana Dr Apt 410 Willowbrook IL 60527-2246

ZEMANIAN, ARMEN HUMPARTSOUM, electrical engineer, mathematician; b. Bridgewater, Mass., Apr. 16, 1925; s. Parsegh and Filor (Paparian) Z.; m. Edna Odell Williamson Zemanian, July 12, 1958; children: Peter, Thomas, Lewis, Susan. BEE, CCNY, 1947; ScD in Engring., NYU, 1953; prof. honoris causa, Dubna (Russia) U., 1996. Registered profl. engr., N.Y. Tutor CCNY, 1947-48; engr. The Maintenance Co., N.Y.C., 1948-52; from asst. to assoc. prof. NYU, 1952-62; prof. SUNY, Stony Brook, 1962-83, leading prof., 1983-98, distinguished prof., 1998—. Author: Distribution Theory and Transform Analysis, 1965, Generalized Integral Transformations, 1968, Realizability Theory for Continuous Linear Systems, 1972, Infinite Electrical Networks, 1991, Transfiniteness for Graphs, Electrical Networks and Random Walks, 1996; Pristine Transfinite Graphs and Permissive Electrical Networks, 2001; co-author: Electronics, 1961; co-founder, editor-in-chief emeritus Circuits, Systems and Signal Processing, 1982—. NSF sr. faculty fellow in sci., 1975-76; recipient Sci. award Armenian Students Assns. Am., 1982; Academician (fgn. mem.) Armenian Acad. Scis., 1990, Academician (fgn. mem.) Armenian Acad. Engrs., 1994. Fellow IEEE, IEEE Circuits and Systems Soc. (Golden Jubilee medal 2000), Am. Math. Soc., Russian Acad. Natural Scis. (fgn. mem.; Kapitsa Gold medal 1996), Sigma Xi, Tau Beta Pi, Eta Kappa Nu. Democrat. Presbyterian. Office: SUNY Electrical Engring Dept Stony Brook NY 11794-0001 E-mail: Zeman@ece.sunysb.edu.

ZEMEL, NORMAN PAUL, orthopedic surgeon; b. Bklyn., Oct. 15, 1939; s. Nathan M. and Mary (Sklarevsky) Z.; m. Mary P. Kane. BSN, Rutgers U., 1961; MD, Thomas Jefferson Med. Sch., 1965. Bd. cert. orthopaedic surgery with added qualification in hand surgery Am. Bd. Orthopaedic Surgery. Orthopaedic surgery resident Northwestern U., Chgo., 1969-73; hand surgery fellow Boyes Hand Fellowship, L.A., 1973-74; hand surgery physician Boyes, Stark, Ashworth, 1974-88, Kerlan-Jobe Orthopaedic Clinic, Inglewood, Calif., 1989—. Clin. assoc. prof. dept. orthopaedics U. So. Calif. Sch. Medicine, L.A., 1977—. Contbr. chpts. to books and articles to profl. jours. Lt. USNR, 1966-68, Vietnam. Mem.: ACS, So. Calif. Soc. Surgery of the Hand (1st v.p.), Calif. Orthopaedic Assn. (sec.-treas. 2000—01, 2nd v.p.), Soc. Internat. Orthopedique et de Traumatologie, We. Orthopaedic Assn. (pres. L.A. chpt. 1993—94), Am. Soc. Surgery of the Hand, Am. Acad. Orthopaedic Surgery (bd. councilors). Avocations: walking, reading, photography. Office: Kerlan Jobe Orthop Clinic 6801 Park Ter Los Angeles CA 90045-1543 E-mail: zemelmd@aol.com.

ZEMM, SANDRA PHYLLIS, lawyer; b. Chgo., Aug. 18, 1947; d. Walter Stanley and Bernice Phyllis (Churas) Z. BS, U. Ill., 1969; JD, Fla. State U., 1974. Bar: Fla. 74, Ill. 75. With fin. dept. Sinclair Oil, Chgo., 1969-70; indsl. rels. advisor Conco Inc., Mendota, Ill., 1970-72; assoc. Seyfarth, Shaw, Fairweather & Geraldson, Chgo., 1975-82, ptnr., 1982—. Mem. Art Inst. Alliance, Chgo., 1993—2002; bd. dirs. Chgo. Residential Inc., 1993—97, pres., 1995—97. Mem. Ill. State Bar Assn., Fla. State Bar Assn., Univ. Club Chgo. (bd. dirs. 1991-94). Office: Seyfarth Shaw 55 E Monroe St Ste 4200 Chicago IL 60603-5863

ZEMOJTEL, ALEXANDER MICHAEL, JR. corporate executive; b. Ware, Mass., Apr. 11, 1952; s. Alexander Michael Sr. and Ruth Helen (Lamay) Z. AA in Biology, Holyoke Community Coll., 1974; AS in Nuclear Medicine, George Washington U., 1984. Nuc. medicine technologist South Shore Hosp., South Weymouth, Mass., 1986-87; supr. nuc. medicine dept. Kent County Meml. Hosp., Warwick, R.I., 1987-89; CFO, ptnr. Apollo Imaging, Inc., Abington, Mass., 1989-91; pres. AMZ Nuc., Providence, 1991-93; supr. nuc. medicine

Wentworth Douglass Hosp., Dover, N.H., 1993—; supr. Hillcrest Bapt. Med. Ctr. Mem. adj. faculty George Washington U., 1984; v.p. St Ze Real Estate, Greenville, R.I., 1986—. Sgt. U.S. Army, 1980—2001, ret. Home and Office: 133 Cieswood Dr Hewitt TX 76643

ZEMPLENYI, TIBOR KAROL, cardiologist, educator; b. Part Lupča, Czechoslovakia, July 16, 1916; came to U.S., 1968, naturalized, 1974; s. David Dezider and Irene (Pollak) Z.; m. Hana Bendová, Aug. 13, 1952; 1 son, Jan. MD, Charles U., Prague, Czechoslovakia, 1946, Docent Habilit., 1966; CSc. (PhD), Czechoslovak Acad. Sci., 1960, DSc., 1964. Clin. asst. with dept medicine Prague Motol Clinic and Charles U., 1946-52; head atherosclerosis rsch. Inst. for Cardiovascular Rsch., Prague, 1952-68; assoc. prof. medicine Charles U., 1966-68, U. So. Calif., L.A., 1969-75, prof., 1975-92, prof. emeritus, 1992—. Attending physician L.A. County- U.So. Calif. Med. Ctr. Author: Enzyme Biochemistry of the Arterial Wall, 1968; editl. bd. Atherosclerosis, 1962-75, Cor et Vasa, 1993—; adv. bd. Advances in Lipid Rsch., 1963-66; contbr. articles to numerous profl. jours. WHO fellow for study in Sweden and Gt. Britain, 1959. Fellow Am. Heart Assn., Am. Coll. Cardiology; mem. Western Soc. for Clin. Rsch., Longevity Assn. (mem. sci. bd.), European Atherosclerosis Group, Italian Soc. for Atherosclerosis (hon.). Office: 3400 Loadstone Dr Sherman Oaks CA 91403-4512

ZEMTSOV, ALEXANDER, dermatology and biochemistry educator, inventor; b. Baku, USSR, Nov. 9, 1959; came to U.S., 1977; s. Ilya and Marya (Dubinsky) Z.; m. Tali Giveon, Oct. 17, 1987; children: Raquel Karen, Gregory Ethan. BA magna cum laude, Temple U., 1981; MSc, U. Pa., 1982; MD with honors, NYU, 1986. Diplomate Am. Bd. Dermatology. Intern, then resident Cleve. Clinic Hosp. Found., 1989-90; assoc. prof. biochemistry and molecular biology Ind. U. Sch. Medicine, Muncie, 1995—. Editor Skin Rsch. and Tech. Jour.; contbr. articles to profl. jours. and books; patentee in field. Recipient Am. Soc. Dermatol. Surgery award, 1989; Cert. Appreciation, Ohio Dermatol. Soc., 1990. Fellow Am. Acad. Dermatology, Am. Contact Dermatitis Soc.; mem. Soc. Magnetic Resonance, Internat. Soc. for Digital Imaging of Skin (pres.), Kiwanis. Jewish. Avocations: stamp collecting, hiking, swimming. Office: University Dermatology Ctr 2525 W University Ave Ste 402 Muncie IN 47303-3409 E-mail: uniderm@aol.com.

ZEN, E-AN, research geologist, educator; b. Peking, China, May 31, 1928; came to U.S., 1946, naturalized, 1963; s. Hung-chun and Heng-chi'h (Chen) Z. AB, Cornell U., 1951; MA, Harvard U., 1952, PhD, 1955. Research fellow Woods Hole Oceanographic Inst., 1955-56, research asso., 1956-58; asst. prof. U. N.C., 1958-59; geologist U.S. Geol. Survey, 1959-80, rsch. geologist, 1981-89. Adj. prof. geology U. Md., 1990—; vis. assoc. prof. Calif. Inst. Tech., 1962; Crosby vis. prof. MIT, 1973; Harry H. Hess sr. vis. fellow Princeton U., 1981; counselor 28th Internat. Geol. Congress. 1986-89. Contbr. articles to profl. jours. Recipient Maj. John Coke medal Geol. Soc. London, 1992, Outstanding Contbn. to Pub. Understanding of Geology award Am. Geol. Inst., 1994, Thomas Jefferson medal Va. Mus. Natural History Found., 1996. Fellow AAAS, Am. Acad. Arts and Scis., Geol. Soc. Am. (councillor 1985-88, v.p. 1991, pres. 1992, Day medal 1986), Mineral. Soc. Am. (coun. 1975-77, pres. 1975-76, Roebling medal 1991); mem. NAS, Geol. Soc. Washington (pres. 1973). Office: U Md Dept Geology College Park MD 20742-0001

ZENDER, JAMES FRANCIS, psychotherapist, researcher, psychoanalyst; b. Upper Sandusky, Ohio, July 3, 1954; s. Joseph Francis and Reva Jean (Barth) Z.; m. Ellen Burns, May 23, 1981 (div. Dec. 1989). Student, Ohio State U., 1972-75, 78-79, 80-81; BA, Antioch Coll., 1977; MA, Antioch U., 1979; PhD, U. Detroit, 1986. Lic. psychologist, Mich.; cert. forensic psychoanalyst, forensic clin. psychologist. Staff psychotherapist Dearborn Heights (Mich.) Human Svcs. Ctr., 1983-84, Cath. Social Svcs., Royal Oak, Mich., 1984-85; staff psychologist Ypsilanti (Mich.) Regional Psychiat. Hosp., 1985-86, Providence Hosp., Southfield, 1986-89; instr. dept. psychiatry Sch. of Medicine Wayne State U., Detroit, 1989—. Pvt. practice, Birmingham, Mich., 1988-92; staff psychologist, dir. clin. psychology tng. Detroit Receiving Hosp./U. Health Ctr., 1989-92; dir. Ctr. for Prevention and Treatment of Psychol. Trauma. Contbr. articles to profl. jours. Mem. AOA, Am. Coll. Forensic Examiners, Internat. Soc. for Traumatic Stress Studies, Nat. Orgn. for Victim Assistance, Mich. Psychol. Assn., Mich. Archaeol. Soc. Avocations: swimming, writing. Office: 67 Cass Ave Ste 406 Mount Clemens MI 48043-2373 Home: 525 Southfield Rd Birmingham MI 48009-1620

ZENDER-BOYKIN, ANGELINA ELIZABETH, social services executive; b. Brighton, Mass., Apr. 19, 1933; d. Sabatino and Giovanina (Beninati) Fantasia; m. Frederick Robert Zender, Dec. 30, 1949 (div. Nov. 1982); children: Richard, Kathryn, James, Nancy, Debra; m. Thomas Julian Boykin, Aug. 25, 1986. AS, U. Wis., Madison, 1973, BS, 1980. Waitress, 1955-66; founder Ricky Zender Meml. Home, Inc., Wausau, Wis., 1973, adminstr., daily living coord., 1973-88, exec. dir., 1988—; mem. Wis. State Service for Oral Exams, 1974-75; bd. dirs. Halfway House Fedn. Wis., 1980-82; mem. task force Wis. Council on Devel. Disabilities, 1987—; mem. adv. com. for long term supports State Dept. Health and Social Svcs., 1991—. Author: (with others) Quality of Life, 1977; mem. rev. com. Guidelines to Community Living Systems for the Developmentally Disabled. Recipient Presdl. citation for community service Apogee, 1975. Mem. Assn. Retarded Citizens (state dir.), Marathon County Assn. Retarded Citizens (treas. 1971, pres. 1973-82), Nat. Assn. Pvt. Residential Facilities for Mentally Retarded (bd. dirs. 1976-85), Nat. Soc. Autistic Children, United Comml. Travelers Aux., United Cerebral Palsy Assn., Wis. Assn. Community Human Services Programs, Am. Assn. Mental Deficiency, Wis. Assn. Residential Facilities (sec. 1982), Nat. Assn. Pvt. Residential Resources (state rep.), Wis. Epilepsy Assn., Wis. Assn. Devel. Disabilities (v.p. 1981), Wausau C. of C. (mem. personnel club, chmn. interclub coordinating council), Assn. for Retarded Citizens (Hall of Honor 1980), Community Living Alliance for Mentally Retarded, Milw. Italian Community Ctr. Clubs: Toastmaster, Toastmistress (pres.). Home: 110 E Moonlite Ave Wausau WI 54401-7731 Office: PO Box PO Box 354 Wausau WI 54402-0354

ZENDLE, HOWARD MARK, software development researcher; b. Binghamton, N.Y., June 8, 1949; s. Abraham and Evelyn (Hershowitz) Z. BA in Physics summa cum laude, SUNY, Binghamton, 1972, MA in Physics, 1976; MSEE, Syracuse U., 1987. With IBM, Owego, NY, 1974—94, staff programmer, 1978-83, mgr. microprocessor application software, 1979-81, mgr. tactical avionics software, 1981-82, adv. programmer, 1983-86, sr. programmer, 1986-94, Loral, Owego, 1994-96, Lockheed Martin, Owego, 1996—. Pres. Fed. Sector div. Mktg. Conf. IBM, 1991. Sec. Men's Club Beth David Synagogue, Binghamton, 1984-85, v.p., 1986-88; bd. dirs. Jewish Cmty. Ctr., Binghamton, 1983-86. Mem. IEEE, Assn. Computing Machinery, Ctrl. Electric Railfan's Assn., Masons, Phi Beta Kappa, Sigma Pi Sigma. Republican. Avocations: railfanning, research into history of industrial development in America. Home: 5 Leigh St Johnson City NY 13790-1608 Office: Lockheed Martin 1801 State Route 17C Owego NY 13827-3998 E-mail: hzendle@stny.rr.com.

ZENEV, IRENE LOUISE, museum curator; b. Albuquerque, Nov. 18, 1948; d. Stanley D. and Louise Marie (Risler) Z.; 1 child, Carson M. Bell. BA, U. N.Mex., 1971. Dir. Umpqua Valley Arts Assn., Roseburg, Oreg., 1978-82; edn. coord. Douglas County Mus., 1985-86, curator history, 1986-98; exhibits curator Benton County Mus., Philomath, Oreg., 1998—; editor Dispatch newsletter Oreg. Mus. Assn., 1995-98. Publs. rschr. Oreg. Mus. Assn., Portland, 1989-92. Reviewer The Roseburg News-Review, 1989-93. Chmn. Douglas County Oreg. Trail Sesquicentennial Celebration Com., 1991-93; mem. Oreg. Coun. for Humanities, 1997-2000, sec. bd., 1998-2000. Mem. Registrar's Com. Western Region (Oreg. state rep. 1995-99), Mus. Assessment Program Peer Reviewer, Am. Assn. Mus., 1997—. E-mail: ilzenev@aol.com.

ZENG, GENGSHENG LAWRENCE, nuclear medicine educator; b. Beijing, Oct. 14, 1960; came to U.S., 1985; s. Yiduo Zeng and Yuqing Lu; m. Ya Li, Aug. 14, 2000; children: Andrew Fang, Kathy Fang, Megan. BS in Applied Math., Xidian U., China, 1982; PhD, U. N.Mex., 1988. Tchr. Xidian U., Xi'An, China, 1982-84; tchg. asst. U. N.Mex., Albuquerque, 1986-88; postdoctoral rschr. U. Utah, Salt Lake City, 1989-91, ltd. term instr., 1992-94, asst. prof., 1994-99, assoc. prof. dept. radiology, 1999—, rsch. assoc. prof. dept. elec. engring., 1999—. Cons. Philips Med. Systems, Cleve., 1999—. Contbr. articles to profl. jours.; patentee in field. Grantee The Whitaker Found., 1991-94; recipient 1st award NIH, 1994-99. Mem. IEEE, IEEE Nuc. Med. and Imaging Scis. Coun., Soc. Nuc. Medicine. Home: 1926 E 3900 S Salt Lake City UT 84124 Office: U Utah MIRL 729 Arapeen Dr Salt Lake City UT 84108-1218 Fax: (801) 585-3592. E-mail: larry@doug.med.utah.edu.

ZENG, HONG, audio system architect, researcher; b. Changchun, Jilin, China, Feb. 20, 1958; arrived in France, 1990; s. Peiwei Zeng and Shige Chen; m. Yuzhi Guo, Jan. 14, 1983 (div. Nov. 2000); 1 child, Yu; m. Jie Li, Aug. 8, 2001. B in Elec. Engring., Changchun Coll. Geology; M in Elec. Engring., U. Pierre & Marie Curie, Paris, 1991, D in Physics, 1996. Asst. engr. Hangzhou (China) Applied Acoustics Rsch. Inst., 1982-85, rsch. engr., dir. magnetic signal processing sect., 1985-90; rsch. engr. French Nat. Sci. Rsch. Ctr., Paris, 1990-95; sys. engr. O1dB Co., Lyon, France, 1995-98; sr. software engr., project team leader ATI Technologies, Inc., Toronto, 1998-2001; audio sys. arch. ViXS Sys. Inc., 2001—. Contbr. articles to profl. jours.; inventor in field. Recipient Sci. and Tech. award China Shipbuilding Industry Corp., Beijing, 1989. Mem. IEEE. Home: 815 Grandview Way Toronto ON Canada M2N 6V5 Office: ViXS Systems Inc 2235 Sheppard Ave E # 1705 Toronto ON Canada M2J 5B5 E-mail: hongzeng@hotmail.com., hzeng@vixs.com.

ZENG, ZHAO-BANG, geneticist, educator; b. Wuhan, China, Dec. 8, 1957; came to the U.S., 1986; s. Guangming and Yulan (Ni) Z.; m. Jia Ma, Sept. 9, 1983; 1 child, Jiemin. BS, Huazhong Agrl. U., 1981; PhD, U. Edinburgh, 1986. Asst. lectr. Huazhong Agrl. U., Wuhan, 1982-83; postdoctoral rsch. assoc. N.C. State U., Raleigh, 1986-90, vis. asst. prof., 1990-91, rsch. asst. prof., 1992-94; rsch. assoc. prof., 1994-99; rsch. prof., 1999—2001; prof., 2001—. Adj. prof. Hunzhong Agrl. U., Wuhan, China, 1995—, Zhejiang U., Hangzhou, 2000—. Assoc. editor Genetics, 1994—, Theoretical Population Biology, 1995-2000; contbr. articles and revs. to profl. jours. Grantee NIH, 1990—, NSF, 1993—, USDA, 1994—. Mem. Am. Soc. Genetics, Soc. for Study Evolution, Biometric Soc., Phi Kappa Phi, Sigma Xi. Avocations: computer games, jogging, classical music, reading. Home: 112 Kirkfield Dr Cary NC 27511-6815 Office: NC State U PO Box 7566 Raleigh NC 27695-7566 E-mail: zeng@stat.ncse.edu.

ZENGER, JOHN HANCOCK, training company executive; b. Salt Lake City, Nov. 13, 1931; s. John H. and L. (Hancock) Z.; m. Dixie Robison, June 1, 1955 (div. 1978); children: Mark R., Robin, Todd R., Blake R., Mitchell R., Drew R.; m. Holly Olsen, June 29, 1979; stepchildren: Roger, Kirk, Lori, Michael. BS, Brigham Young U., 1955; MBA, UCLA, 1957; D in Bus. Adminstrn., U. So. Calif., Los Angeles, 1963. Asst. prof. Grad Sch. Bus. U. So. Calif., L.A., 1966-67; exec. v.p. Blanfield-Smith and Co., Pasadena, Calif., 1965-67; v.p. human resources Syntex Corp., Palo Alto, 1967-77; pres. Zenger-Miller Inc., Cupertino, 1977-92; group v.p. Times Mirror Co., San Jose, 1992-97; vice chmn. Provant, Inc. Chmn. Palo Alto Human Rels. Coun., 1961-66; trustee Utah Valley State Coll.; pres. Midway Boosters, Inc. Ford Found. fellow, 1962-63; recipient Disting. Svc. award Brigham Young U., 1983; named to Human Resources Devel. Hall of Fame, 1994. Mem. Brigham Young U. Alumni Assn. (pres. 1981). Republican. Mem. Lds Ch. Avocation: magic. Home: 275 Luzern Rd Midway UT 84049-1268 E-mail: jack@zenger.net.

ZENILMAN, JONATHAN MARK, medical educator; b. Far Rockaway, N.Y., Apr. 5, 1956; BA, Cornell U., 1977; MD, SUNY, Bklyn., 1981. Diplomate Am. Bd. Internal Medicine, Am. Bd. Infectious Diseases. Intern, resident Kings County Hosp., Bklyn., 1981-84; med. investigator N.Y.C. Med. Examiner, N.Y.C., 1983-85; med. epidemiologist U.S. Ctr. for Disease Control, Atlanta, 1985-89; asst. prof. medicine Johns Hopkins U., Balt., 1989-94, assoc. prof. medicine, 1994—. Infectious diseases fellow Kings County Hosp., 1984-85, Emory U., Atlanta, 1987-88; chief STD control Balt. City Health Dept., 1991-95; cons. WHO, Geneva, 1987, Ctr. for Disease Control, 1989—. Contbr. numerous articles to med. and profl. jours. With USPHS, 1985-89. Recipient Scholar award Am. Found. AIDS Rsch., 1991; grantee NIH. Office: Johns Hopkins U Divsn Infectious Diseases 720 Rutland Ave # 1165 Baltimore MD 21205-2109 E-mail: jzenilma@jhmi.edu.

ZENNER, GRETCHEN HARRIS, finance company executive; b. Buffalo, Jan. 11, 1973; d. Orville Paul and Patricia Louise (Therre) H. BA cum laude, U. Rochester, 1995; MBA, Simon Sch. Bus./U. Rochester, 2001. Asst. to COO Harter, Secrest & Emery, Rochester, N.Y., 1994-97; contract cons. Xerox, 1997; treasury analyst EDS, 1998-99; sr. fin. analyst Harris Corp., 1999—2000, program mgr., 2000—. Cons. Xerox, 1997-99. Soup kitchen vol. Blessed Sacrement Ch., Rochester, 1997—; nursing home vol. Apple Gate Manor, Medina, N.Y., 1996—. Recipient Regents scholarship N.Y. State, 1991, Mildred Burton summer study grant U. Rochester, summer 1992, Alumni scholarship U. Rochester, 1991-95. Mem. Hartford Soc., U. Rochester Career Source (vol.). Episcopalian. Avocations: equestrian events, music, antiques, reading, architecture.

ZENNER, SHELDON TOBY, lawyer; b. Chgo., Jan. 11, 1953; s. Max and Clara (Goldner) Z.; m. Ellen June Morgan, Sept. 2, 1984; children: Elie, Nathaniel. BA, Northwestern U., 1974, JD, 1978. Bar: U.S. Dist. Ct. (no. dist.) Ill. 1978. Assoc. Shadur, Krupp & Miller, Chgo., 1978-80; law clk. to judge U.S. Dist. Ct. (no. dist.) Ill., 1980-81; asst. U.S. atty., dep. chief spl. prosecutions div. No. Dist. of Ill., 1981-89; ptnr. Katten Muchin & Zavis, 1989—. Adj. faculty Medill Sch. Journalism, Northwestern U., 1982-89, Sch. of Law, 1986—; instr. Nat. Inst. Trial Attys., 1989—; mem. practitioners adv. com. U.S. Sentencing Commn.; bd. dirs. Legal Assistance Found. Mem. Phi Beta Kappa. Office: Katten Muchin Zavis Rosenman 525 W Monroe St Ste 1500 Chicago IL 60661-3693

ZENOFF, ELYCE HOPE, legal educator; b. Milw., Feb. 2, 1930; d. Ben and Gertrude (Rothstein) Z.; m. Charles B. Ferster, May 17, 1964; children—William, Andrea, Sam, Warren. B.S., U. Wis., 1951; J.D., Northwestern U., 1954. Bar: Ill. 1954, D.C. 1968, U.S. Supreme Ct. 1961. Research atty. Bar Found. Chgo., 1956-59; atty. AMA, Chgo., 1959-61; counsel U.S. Senate Subcom. on Constl. Rights, Washington, 1961-62; atty. U.S. Commn. on Civil Rights, Washington, 1962-64; faculty George Washington U., Washington, 1964— , prof. law, 1969— . Mem. ABA, D.C. Bar Assn. Democrat. Author: Mental Impairment and Legal Incompetaency, 1968, Readings in Law and Psychiatry, 2d edit., 1975, Sanctions, Sentencing and Corrections, 1982. Contbr. numerous articles to profl. jours. Office: George Washington Law Sch 2000 H St NW Washington DC 20006-4234

ZENTALL, THOMAS R. psychologist, educator; b. Bezier, Herault, France, Sept. 29, 1940; came to the U.S., 1942; s. Robert Sigmund and Elizabeth Aigner Zentall; m. Sydney Snider, Aug. 29, 1965 (div.); m. Melodie Rae, June 4, 1988; children: Gabriel Clay, Shannon Rae. BA, BSEE, Union Coll., 1963; PhD, U. Calif., Berkeley, 1969. Asst. prof. U. Pitts., 1969-75; prof. U. Ky., Lexington, 1975—. Editor: Social Learning, 1988, Animal Cognition, 1993, Stimulus Class Formation, 1996; assoc. editor Psychonomic Bull. and Rev., 1998-2002, Animal Learning & Behavior, 2002-. Fellow APA (exec. com. divsn. 6 1998-2001, exec. com. divsn. 3 1999—), Am. Psychol. Soc., Midwestern Psychol. Assn. (sec.-treas. 1998-2001, pres. 2002—), Psychonomic Soc. (governing bd. 2001--). Office: Dept Psychology Univ Ky Lexington KY 40506-0044 E-mail: zentall@pop.uky.edu.

ZENTHOEFER, SCOTT ALAN, music educator; b. Apr. 28, 1972; s. Steven Alan and Ann Marie Zenthoefer; m. Laura Ann Zima. B of Music Edn., U. Tulsa, 1995, MusM, 1999. Bd. dirs. Tulsa Youth Chorale. Home: 6513 E 90th St Tulsa OK 74133

ZENTMYER, GEORGE AUBREY, plant pathology educator; b. North Platte, Nebr., Aug. 9, 1913; s. George Aubrey and Mary Elizabeth (Strahorn) Z.; m. Dorothy Anne Dudley, May 24, 1941; children: Elizabeth Zentmyer Dossa, Jane Zentmyer Fernald, Susan Dudley. AB, UCLA, 1935; MS, U. Calif., 1936, PhD, 1938. Asst. forest pathologist U.S. Dept. Agr., San Francisco, 1937-40; asst. pathologist Conn. Agrl. Expt. Sta., New Haven, 1940-44; asst. plant pathologist to plant pathologist U. Calif., Riverside, 1944-62, prof. plant pathology, 1962—, prof. emeritus, 1981—, faculty rsch. lectr., 1964, chmn. dept., 1968-73, trustee, 1993-94. Cons. NSF, Trust Ty. of Pacific Islands, 1964, 66, Commonwealth of Australia Forest and Timber Bur., 1968, AID, Ghana and Nigeria, 1969, Govt. South Africa, 1980, Govt. Israel, 1983, Govt. Western Australia, 1983, Ministry Agriculture and U. Cordoba, Spain, 1989, Govt. Costa Rica, 1993; mem. NRC panels, 1968-73. Author: Plant Disease Development and Control, 1968, Recent Advances in Pest Control, 1957, Plant Pathology, An Advanced Treatise, 1977, The Soil-Root Interface, 1979, Phytophthora Cinnamomi and the Diseases it Causes, 1980, Phytophthora: Its Biology, Taxonomy, Ecology and Pathology, 1983, Ecology and Management of Soilborne Plant Pathogens, 1984, Compendium of Tropical Fruit Diseases, 1994; assoc. editor: Ann. Rev. of Phytopathology, 1971—, Jour. Phytopathology, 1951-54, internat. editl. bd. Internat. Jour. Pest Mgmt., 1990—, also jour. articles. Bd. dirs. Riverside YMCA, 1949-58, Friends of Mission Inn, 1981—, pres., 1991-93, Calif. Mus. Photography, 1988—; pres. Town and Gown Orgn., Riverside, 1962; bd. dirs. Riverside Hospice, 1982-85, pres., 1984-85; bd. dirs. Friends U. Calif. Riverside Botanic Garden, 1985-89, 91-95, pres., 1987-89; bd. trustees U. Calif. Riverside Found., 1993-94. Recipient award of honor Calif. Avocado Soc., 1954, spl. award of honor, 1981; recipient Emeritus Faculty award U. Calif., Riverside, 1991, UCLA Alumnus award, 1996; Guggenheim fellow, Australia, 1964-65, NATO sr. sci. fellow, Eng., 1971; NSF rsch. grantee, 1963, 68, 71, 74, 78; Bellagio scholar Rockefeller Found., 1985. Fellow AAAS (pres. Pacific div. 1974-75), Am. Phytopath. Soc. (pres. 1966, pres. Pacific eiv. 1955, found. bd. dirs. 1987—, v.p. 1991—, award of merit Caribbean div. 1972, award of distinction 1983, Lifetime Achievement award Pacific div. 1991), Explorers Club; mem. NAS, Mycol. Soc. Am., Am. Inst. Biol. Scis., Bot. Soc. Am., Internat. Avocado Soc. (hon.), Brit. Mycol. Soc., Australasian Plant Pathology Soc., Philippine Phytopath. Soc., Indian Phytopath. Soc., Assn. Tropical Biology, Internat. Soc. Plant Pathology (councilor 1973-78), Pacific Assn. Tropical Phytopathology, Internat. Avocado Soc. (hon.), Sigma Xi, Gamma Sigma Delta. Home: 5265 Chapala Dr # 212 Riverside CA 92507-5987

ZENTNER, ARNOLD STUART, psychiatrist; b. N.Y.C., Oct. 6, 1925; s. Jay Morris and Lily Zentner; m. Margaret Ann Santomauro, July 3, 1958; children: Lisa, Rena, Gregory, Russell. AB, Columbia Coll., 1945; MD, Columbia Coll. Phys. & Surgs., 1948. Diplomate Am. Bd. Psychiatry and Neurology. Intern Fordham Hosp., Bronx, N.Y., 1948-49; resident and fellow in psychiatry VA Hosp. and Menninger Sch. Psychiatry, Topeka, 1949-52; pvt. practice N.Y.C. and Hartford, Conn., 1953-96; asst. clin. prof. psychiatry NYU, 1962-70, U. Conn., Farmington, 1974-96; chief psychiat. Knickerbocker Hosp. and Morningside Mental Health Clinic, N.Y.C., 1956-70; ret., 1996. Med. expert Social Security Adminstrn., 1994—. Fellow Am. Psychiat. Assn. (life); mem. Conn. Psychiat. Soc. (treas. 1973-74). Avocations: tennis, golf, reading, travel. Home: 9419 Glen Abbey Ln Sarasota FL 34238-5806 E-mail: ASZentner@yahoo.com.

ZENTZ, PATRICK JAMES, artist, rancher; b. Cando, N.D., Jan. 22, 1947; s. Clifford Wayne and Sybil Mae (Dehrer) Z.; m. Susan Grace Hedley, Dec. 7, 1968; children: Keenan, Jesse, Tyson. BA in Biology, Westmont Coll., 1969; MFA in Sculpture, U. Mont., 1974. Juror Nev. State Coun. on the Arts Grants Program, Las Vegas, 1989, Nev. State Coun. on the Arts, Artists Fellowship Program, Reno, 1990, Wash State Commn. on the Arts, Olympia, 1992; artist adv. task force Western States Arts Fedn., Portland, 1991; del. Japan-Am. Grassroots Summit, Tokyo and Kyoto, Japan, 1999; vis. artist program U. Ill., Carbondale, 1994, Oxbow Sch., Napa, Calif., 1999; lectr. in field. Exhibited in group shows Western State Arts Found., Bklyn. Mus., 1986, No. Ariz. U., 1987, Mont. State U., 1987, Washington Project for the Arts, 1987, Curtis Ctr., Phila., 1987, Aspen Art Mus., 1988, Missoula Mus. of the Arts, 1989, Beall Park Art Ctr., Bozeman, Mont., 1989, John Michael Kohler Art Ctr., 1989, Henry Art Gallery, U. Wash., Seattle, 1989, Seattle Art Mus., 1989, The Ctr. on Contemporary Art, Seattle, 1990, Hockaday Ctr. for the Arts, Kalispell, Mont., Contemporary Arts Mus., Houston, 1990, Boulder Art Ctr., 1991, U. Mont., 1992, Beam Art Gallery, U. Nev., 1992, Internat. Sculpture Ctr., Phila., 1992, Cheney Cowles Mus., Spokane, Wash., 1994, San Antonio Mus. of Art, 1994, Rubelle & Norman Schaffer Gallery, Pratt Inst., Bklyn., 1994, Boise Art Mus., 1995, Neuberger Mus. of Art, SUNY, Purchase, 1997, Sheppard Gallery, U. Nev., Reno, 1998, Tarble Art Ctr., Ea. Ill. U., 1998, McAllen (Tex.) Internat. Mus., 1999, Yellowstone Art Mus., Billings, Mont., 1999, Miami U., Oxford, Ohio; represented in permanent collections U. Med. Ctr. U. Wash., Seattle, 1990, Richard Tam Alumni Ctr. U. Nev., Las Vegas, 1991, Snake River Correctional Instn., Ontario, Oreg., 1993, Yellowstone Art Mus., Billings, Mont., 1992, Western State Hosp., Ft. Steilecom, Wash., 1993, Salt Palace, Salt Lake City, 1994, TRI-MET Westside Light Rail Sys., Portland, 1995, Mus. of Fine Art, U. Mont., Missoula, 1997, FDA, College Park, Md., 1999, Edgewood Coll., Madison, Wis., 1999, Miami U., Oxford, Ohio, Reno/Sparks Conv. Ctr., Wash. State U., Spokane, Boise City Arts Commn., Idaho, Weber State U., Ogden, Utah. Grantee Art Matters, Inc., 1988, LEF Found., 1992; fellowship Nat. Endowment for the Arts, 1990.

ZEOBER, LANCE DION, marketing professional; b. Oxnard, Calif., Dec. 10, 1965; m. Celisa Camille Barker; children: Ashely Camille , Alexandria Jewel. BA, Wash. State U., 1989; postgrad., U. Phoenix, 1995. Cert. mktg. exec. 2000. Channel sales dir. Miramar, Seattle, 1992—95; sales dir. Software Labs, Inc., 1995—98; prin. FastMarket Group, Austin, Tex., 2001—. With USAF, 1986—92. Recipient 1st Pl. Advt. Competency, ICDC, 1983, 3rd Pl. Advt. Campaigns, ICDC, 1983. Mem.: Am. Mktg. Assn., Fire and Rescue Explorer Post (Lieutenant 1982—83), DECA, Software Pubs. Assn., Wash. Software & Digital Media Alliance, Austin Software Coun. Office: FastMarket Group 6600 Scrub Oak Ln Austin TX 78759 Business E-Mail: zeober@fast2market.com.

ZEPEDA, GUILLERMO, language educator, speech professional; s. Guillermo Zepeda and Celia Ibarra, Rose Santoyo (Stepmother), Jesus Fierro (Stepfather); m. Rebecca Cecilia Deal. BA, Grand Canyon U., Phoenix, Ariz., 1972; MA in Ch. Music, Southwestern Bapt. Theol. Sem., Ft. Worth, Tex., 1983. Cert. Spanish, ESL, Music Tchr. Ariz., 1995, Humanities, Religion Educator State Bd. Comty. Colls. Ariiz., 1995. Music missionary, Acapulco, Mexico, 1972—74; min. of music Iglesia Bautista Ctrl., Ft. Worth, 1975—81; tchr. citizenship preparation Rosemont Cmty. Sch., 1975—80; tchr. Spanish and English Berlitz Sch. of Languages, Phoenix, 1981—89; tchr. ESL and citzenshp preparation South Mountain Cmty. Coll., 1989—92; tchr. ESL, Spanish and dir. sports info. South Mountain C.C., 1992—. Recipient Human Relation Commn. Award, City of Ft. Worth, 1980, Life Scholarship Honor Soc., San Gabriel H.S., 1962. Mem.: Am. Coun. on the Tchg. of Fgn. Langs. Avocations: guitar, jogging, piano, reading, singing. Office: South Mountain Comty Coll 7050 South 24th St Phoenix AZ 85040 E-mail: guillermo.zepeda@smcmail.maricopa.edu.

ZEPEDA, SUSAN GHOZEIL, foundation administrator; b. N.Y.C., Aug. 8, 1946; d. Harry S. and Anne (Golden) Kantor; m. Isaac Ghozeil, Jan. 29, 1967 (div. Oct. 1979); children: Daniel Jacob, Adam Leo; m. Fernando Zepeda, Jan. 2, 1983 (div. Feb. 1998); children: Paloma Andrea, Sofia Elisa. BA, Brown U., 1967; MA, U. Ariz., 1971, postgrad., 1971-75; PhD, Internat. Coll., 1985. Rsch. assoc. div. bus. and econ. rsch. U. Ariz., Tucson, 1971-73, rsch. assoc. Coll. Medicine, 1975-76; assoc. dir. Pima Alcoholism Consortium, 1976-79, exec. dir., 1979-80; dep. dir. pub. health Orange County Health Care Agy., Santa Ana, Calif., 1980-89, dir. policy, planning, 1989-90; dir. pub. fin. Orange County, 1990-92; dir. San Luis Obispo County Health Agy., 1993-99; exec. dir. The Healthcare Found. for Orange County, Santa Ana, Calif., 1999—. Cons. Tucson Sch. Dist. No. 1, 1973-75, U.S. Dept. Labor, Washington, 1976-79, Indian Health Svc., Rockville, Md., 1984-85; ptnr. Zepeda Assocs., Fullerton, Calif., 1987-93; presenter confs. Mem. Fullerton Planning Commn., 1984-91, chmn., 1990-91; mem. Calif. Task Force on Comparable Worth, 1984-85, Calif. Dist. Appeal Bd. No. 510, L.A., 1986—. Recipient Woman of Achievement award Orange County Bd. Suprs., 1988, Disting. Achievement awards Nat. Assn. Counties, 1985, 86, 87, 89. Mem. APHA, Health Funders Partnership of Orange County (chair 2000-02), County Health Execs. Assn. Calif. (v.p. 1998-99), Nat. Assn. County and City Health Ofcls. (bd. dirs.), Ctrl. Coast Hosp. Coun. (chair 1996), County Alcohol Program Adminstrs. Assn. Calif. (v.p. 1983, pres. 1984-85), So. Calif. Assn. Philanthropy (bd. dirs. 2002-), Rotary Santa Ana (pres. 2001-02). Avocation: fiber arts. Home: 541 Shadow Oaks Irvine CA 92618 Office: The Healthcare Found for Orange County 1450 N Tustin Ave Ste 103 Santa Ana CA 92705-8653 E-mail: szepeda@hfoc.org.

ZEPF, THOMAS HERMAN, physics educator, researcher; b. Cin., Feb. 13, 1935; s. Paul A. and Agnes J. (Schulz) Z. BS summa cum laude, Xavier U., 1957; MS, St. Louis U., 1960, PhD, 1963. Asst. prof. physics Creighton U., Omaha, 1962-67, assoc. prof., 1967-75, prof., 1975—2002, prof. emeritus,

2002—, acting chmn. dept. physics, 1963-66, chmn., 1966-73, 81-93, coord. allied health programs, 1975-76, coord. pre-health scis. advising, 1976-81. Cons. physicist VA Hosp., Omaha, 1966-71; vis. prof. physics St. Louis U., 1973-74; program evaluator Am. Coun. on Edn., 1988—. Contbr. articles and abstracts to Surface Sci., Bull. Am. Phys. Soc., Proceedings Nebr. Acad. Sci., The Physics Tchr. jour., others. Recipient Cert. Recognition award Phi Beta Kappa U. Cin. chpt., 1953, Disting. Faculty Svc. award Creighton U., 1987, Excellence in Teaching award Creighton U., 1997. Mem. AAAS, Am. Phys. Soc., Am. Assn. Physics Tchrs. (pres. Nebr. sect. 1978), Nebr. Acad. Sci. (life, chmn. physics sect. 1985—), Internat. Brotherhood Magicians, Soc. Am. Magicians (pres. assembly #7, 1964-65), KC, Sigma Xi (Achievement award for rsch. St. Louis chpt. 1963, pres. Omaha chpt. 1993-94), Sigma Pi Sigma. Roman Catholic. Office: Creighton U Dept Physics Omaha NE 68178-0001 *The real magic we all have at our disposal - not trickery, not pseudoscience, not spells and incantations - is our ability to comprehend our world, to understand how things behave. Through science we can use that understanding to predict outcomes and exert a measure of control over nature. It's a sacred trust. It makes the scientist a kind of modern day magician.*

ZEPNICK, SEYMOUR, civil engineer, consultant; b. N.Y.C., Mar. 16, 1927; s. Leo and Rose Z.; m. Isabelle Federofsky Zepnick, Dec. 24, 1950; children: Glen Reed, Ira Mark, Eileen Lynda. BSCE, CCNY, 1950. Registered profl. engr., N.Y., N.J., Mass., Conn., W.Va., Del., Calif., Md. Structural engr. Gussow & Skidmore, N.Y.C., 1950-51, H.K. Furgerson, N.Y.C., 1951-53, Vitro Corp., N.Y.C., 1953-55; ptnr. Firm of Dermot Reddy, 1955-88. Ptnr., dir. engring., 1968-74, chief engr., 1967-68, Firm of S. Zepnick; pvt. practice, 1988-96; bd. dirs. Devenco Inc., N.Y.C., 1974-88. Pres. Bnai Brith Colossus Lodge, 1968, 69. Recipient ASCE award, N.Y.C., 1989. Fellow ASCE (chmn. bd. structures 1973, vice chmn. 1972). Home and Office: 6087 Millington Way Delray Beach FL 33484-2487

ZERCHER, D. LOWELL, artist; b. Carlisle, Pa., Dec. 22, 1947; s. Ray Merlin and Ruth Marie (Niesley) Z.; m. Suzanne Jane Bankert, Nov. 11, 1971 (div. Nov. 1975); m. Lucille Anctil, May 26, 1985; 1 child, Tay Anna. BSBA, Elizabethtown (Pa.) Coll., 1971; Assoc. in Fine Woodworking and Furniture Design, Wendell Castle Sch., Scottsville, N.Y., 1986. Indsl. engr. Caterpillar Tractor Co., York, Pa., 1974-75; ptnr. Keystone Constrn. Co., Evergreen, Colo., 1975-80; owner Zercher Constrn. Co., Anchorage, 1980-86; designer/artist D. Lowell Zercher, Waterbury Ctr., Vt., 1986-87, Chugiak, Alaska, 1987—. Exterior sch. clock, courthouse clock, seven interior clocks, ceiling sculpture, 2 mirrors. With U.S. Army, 1971-72. Recipient Best of Show in Woodworking, Anchorage Mus. History and Art, 1990, 2001. Mem. Alaska Creative Woodworkers Assn., (bd. dirs. 1990-92, life), Furniture Soc., N.W. Designer Craftsmen, Collectors of Wood Art. Avocations: photography, hiking, dancing, music. E-mail: zercher@alaska.net.

ZERELLA, JOSEPH T. retired pediatric surgeon; b. Youngstown, Ohio, Mar. 7, 1941; s. Atilio and Ann (Capuzello) Z.; m. Diana Isabelle Talbot, Aug. 5, 1967; children: Ann, Michael, Mark. BS, Northwestern U., 1962, MD, 1966. Diplomate Am. Bd. Surgery, Am. Bd. Pediatric Surgery. Intern Med. Coll. Wis., Milw., 1966-67, resident in surgery, 1967-68, 70-73; tng. fellow in pediatric surgery Children's Hosp. Med. Ctr., Cin., 1973-75; staff pediatric surgeon Phoenix Children's Hosp., 1975—; pvt. practice medicine, specializing in pediatric surgery Phoenix, 1975—. Mem. staff Good Samaritan Hosp., Phoenix, 1975— , sect. chief pediatric surgery, 1979— ; mem. staff St. Joseph's Hosp., Phoenix, 1975— , sect. chief pediatric surgery, 1980—. Contbr. articles to profl. jours. Served as capt. U.S. Army, 1968-70. Served as capt. USAR, 1968—70. Fellow ACS, Am. Acad. Pediatrics, Am. Pediatric Surg. Assn., Pacific Assn. Pediatric Surgeons. Roman Catholic. Office: Saguaro Childrens Surgery Ltd 1301 E Mcdowell Rd Ste 100 Phoenix AZ 85006-2605 Mailing: 8426 N 15th Dr Phoenix AZ 85021

ZERHOUNI, ELIAS ADAM, Federal Agency Administrator, Med educator; b. Algeria, Apr. 12, 1951; s. Mohamed and Yamna (Raahmouni) Z.; m. Nadia Azza, Oct. 25, 1975; children: Djillali, Yasmin, Adam. MD, U. Algiers, 1975. Diplomate Am. Bd. Radiology. Resident in diagnostic radiology Johns Hopkins U., Balt., 1975-79, instr., 1978-79, asst. prof., 1979-81, assoc. prof., 1985-92, prof., 1992—, chmn. dept. radiology, 1995—, exec. vice dean, 1997—; asst. prof. Ea. Va. Med. Sch., 1981-83, assoc. prof., 1983-85; Dir Nat. Inst. of Hlth. Dept HHS, Bethesda, Md., 2002—. Cons. Nat. Cancer Inst., NHLBI, The White House, Washington, 1985-88; centennial lectr. Swedish Royal Acad. Radiology, Stockholm, 1994. Patentee in field. Recipient Lauterbur award for MR Imaging, 1989, 93, Hounsfield award for CT Imaging, 1991. Mem. Am. Heart Assn. (coun. mem.), Radiological Soc. N. Am., Soc. Thoracic Radiology (founding), Soc. Computed Body Tomography, Soc. Magnetic Resonance in Medicine (bd. trustees), Fleischner Soc. Avocations: swimming, windsurfing, music. Office: Dept HHS Nat Inst of Hlth 1 Center Dr MSC 0148 Bldg 1 Bethesda MD 20892-0148*

ZERIN, STEVEN DAVID, lawyer; b. N.Y.C., Oct. 1, 1953; s. Stanley Robert and Cecilie Paula (Goldberg) Z.; children: Alexander James, J. Oliver. BS, Syracuse U., 1974; JD, St. Johns U., 1977. Bar: N.Y. 1978, U.S. Dist. Ct. (so. dist.) N.Y. 1985, U.S. Supreme Ct. 1986. Assoc. Gladstein & Isaac, N.Y.C., 1981-82, Sperry, Weinberg, Wels, Waldman & Rubenstein, N.Y.C., 1982-85; ptnr. Wels & Zerin, 1985—. Trustee, mem. bd. govs. Daytop Village. Mem. ABA (exec. mem. and lectr. family law sect.), N.Y. State Bar Assn. (exec. com. family law sect.), Assn. of Bar of City of N.Y. Democrat. Home: 12 E 88th St New York NY 10128-0535 Office: Wels & Zerin 600 Madison Ave Fl 22 New York NY 10022-1615

ZERINGUE, SANDRA MARIE, school psychologist; b. Lake Charles, La., Apr. 26, 1947; d. Melvin Gordon and Melva Marie (Mayson) Ash; m. Larry Paul Zeringue Sr., Aug. 16, 1968; children: Larry Paul Jr., Marianne Marindia. BS, McNeese State U., 1968; MEd (magna cum laude), Nicholls State U., 1976, MA, 1993. Cert. vocat. evaluation specialist, sch. psychologist; lic. rehab. counselor. Sci. tchr. Calcasieu Parish Sch. Bd., Lake Charles, 1968-70; asst. pers. dir. Lake Charles Meml. Hosp., 1972-73; sci. tchr. Terrebonne Parish Sch. Bd., Houma, La., 1973-76, time-out counselor, 1976-80; mgr. Bayou (La.) Paint Sales, Inc., 1980-82; pvt. practice Houma, 1982-84; vocat. evaluation/specialist Vocat. Svcs. Ctr., Lake Charles, 1984-93, Santa Fe Ind. Sch. Dist., 1994—. Vocat. evaluator ED-U-CARE, Baton Rouge, 1987—, Calcasieu Assn. Retarded Citizens, Lake Charles, 1987-88, Vocat and Rehab. Assocs., Sulphur, La., 1989-90. Ednl. advisor La. Fiscal Reform, Lake Charles, 1988-89; sch. bd. mem. St. Louis High Sch., Lake Charles, 1988-89; pres. St. Louis PTO, Lake Charles, 1988-89. Mem.: Phi Delta Kappa. Republican. Roman Catholic. Avocations: collecting depression glass, reading, collecting antiques. Home: 1702 Orlando St Friendswood TX 77546-6030 Office: Santa Fe Ind Sch Dist PO Box 370 Santa Fe TX 77510

ZERMAN, MELVYN BERNARD, publishing company executive, author; b. N.Y.C., July 10, 1930; s. Abraham and Ida (Belsky) Zirman; m. Miriam Baron, Jan. 2, 1985 (dec.); children: Andrew, Jared, Lenore. BA, U. Mich., 1952; MA, Columbia U., 1953. With Oxford Book Co., N.Y.C., 1953-55; asst. editor Abelard-Schuman, Pubs., 1955-57; office mgr., salesman Harper & Row, 1957-61, sales rep., 1961-69, sales mgr., 1969-79, Random House, Inc., N.Y.C., 1979-83, sales cons., 1983-87; pres., pub. Limelight Edits., 1983—. Mem. exec. com. N.Y.Is Book Country, N.Y.C., 1985—. Author: Call the Final Witness, 1977, Beyond a Reasonable Doubt, 1981 (Freedoms Found. medal 1981), Taking on the Press, 1986. Mem. Phi Beta Kappa. Democrat. Avocations: book collecting, travel. Office: Limelight Edits 118 E 30th St New York NY 10016-7303

ZERNIAL, SUSAN CAROL, educator, consultant, acquisitions editor; b. L.A., July 2, 1948; d. Gus Edward and Gladys Elizabeth (Hale) Z. BA, Calif. State U., Long Beach, 1973; MA, Calif. State U., 1975; EdD, U. San Francisco, 1992. Cert secondary and elementary tchr.; libr. credential. Libr. Clovis (Calif.) Unified Schs., 1975-78; media specialist Anaheim (Calif.) Union High Sch. Dist., 1975; libr. Benicia (Calif.) Unified Sch. Dist., 1978-80; tchr. Atascadero (Calif.) Unified Schs., 1985-93; adj. prof. Edn. Adams State Coll., Alamosa, Colo., 1993—. Sr. acquisitions editor Libs. Unltd./Tchrs. Ideas Press, Englewood, Colo. Recipient Scholarship, Calif. Assn. Sch. Librs., 1974. Mem. ASCD, Am. Rsch. Assn., Phi Delta Kappa. Avocations: camping, hiking, reading, writing.

ZERR, DEAN A. legal assistant; b. Quinter, Kans., Aug. 10, 1947; s. Ludwig and Frances (Selensky) Z. BSN, RN, Ft. Hays State U., 1971, MSN, 1995. RN, Kans.; advanced registered nurse practitioner; cert. nursing adminstr. Staff nurse rehab./pediatrics Hadley Regional Med. Ctr., Hays, Kans., 1971-72, charge nurse surg. floor, 1972-73, head nurse surg. floor, nursing supr., 1976-79; adminstr. Phillips County Health Dept., Phillipsburg, 1974-76, DON Rawlins County Hosp., Atwood, 1979-81; DON Trego County Lempke Meml. Hosp., WaKeeney, 1981-83; staff nurse emergency dept. St. Catherine Hosp., Garden City, 1983-86, charge nurse emergency dept., 1986-87, unit mgr. emergency dept., 1987-91; family nurse practitioner United Meth. Wester Kans. Mex. Am. Mins. Health Clinic, 1991-93; asst. prof. grad. studies program Ft. Hays State U., Hays, Kans., 1993-98; nurse practitioner, clin. dir. Planned Parenthood, 1998-99; legal asst. Ellis County Attys. Office, 1999—. Trustee Kans. Nurses Found. Mem. Emergency Nurses Assn., Kans. State Bd. Nursing (v.p. 1990-91, pres. 1991-93, Kans. del. to Nat. Coun. State Bds. Nursing Ann. Conv. 1990, 92), Kans. State Troopers Assn. (assoc.), Kans. Sheriff's Assn. (hon.), Am. Fedn. Law Enforcement Officers (assoc.), Ft. Hays State U. Alumni Assn. (life), Ft. Hays State U. Nursing Alumni Assn. (founding pres.). Home: 600 Monroe Ellis KS 67637 E-mail: dazerr@ruraltel.net.

ZERUNYAN, FRANK VRAM, lawyer; b. Istanbul, Turkey, Sept. 17, 1959; came to U.S., 1978; s. Jack Hagop and Ayda (Yagupyan) Z.; m. Jody Lynn Forman, May 18, 1986; children: Daniel, Nicole. French Bacalaureat, Coll. Samuel Moorat, Paris, 1978; BA, Calif. State U., Long Beach, 1982; JD, Western State U., Fullerton, Calif., 1985; postgrad., U. Southern Calif., 1988. Bar: Calif. 1989, D.C. 1995, U.S. Dist. Ct. (ctrl. dist.) Calif. 1989, U.S. Dist. Ct. (no. dist.) Calif. 2001, U.S. Ct. Internat. Trade 1994, U. S. Supreme Ct. 2000. V.p. law Internat. Mktg. Alliance, Torrance, Calif., 1985-89; pvt. practice L.A., 1989-92; mng. mem. Yacoubian & Zerunyan, P.C., 1992-95; shareholder Sulmeyer, Kupetz, Baumann & Rothman, 1995—. Instr. law Alex Pilibos Sch., L.A., 1993-99; judge pro tem, L.A. Superior Ct. Editor SKB&R Newsletter, 1995—. Chmn. scholarship com. Orgn. Istanbul Armenians, Van Nuys, Calif., 1992—94; legal counsel and policy adv. com. Armenian Nat. Com. of Am., Armenian Nat. Com. of Am., Washington, 1993—; planning commr., chmn. City of Rolling Hills Estates, 2000—; Bd. dirs. Am. Youth Soccer Orgn., Palos Verdes, Calif., 1995—, referee adminstr., 1995—; bd. dirs., vice-chmn., chmn. Daniel Freeman Hosps. Found., 1998—, chmn., 1998—2002. Mem. ABA, Financial Lawyers Conf. Avocations: golf, soccer. Office: Sulmeyer Kupetz et al 300 S Grand Ave Ste 1400 Los Angeles CA 90071-3124 E-mail: fzerunyan@skbr.com.

ZERVAS, NICHOLAS THEMISTOCLES, neurosurgeon; b. Lynn, Mass., Mar. 9, 1929; s. Themistocles and Demetra P. (Stasinopoulos) Z.; m. Thalia Poleway, Feb. 15, 1959; children: T. Nicholas, Christopher Louis, Rhea. AB, Harvard U., 1950; MD, U. Chgo., 1954. Intern N.Y. Hosp., 1955; resident in neurology Montreal Neurol. Inst., 1956; resident in neurosurgery Mass. Gen. Hosp., Boston, 1958-62; fellow in stereotaxic cerebral surgery U. Paris, 1960-61; asst. attending surgeon, asso. neurosurgery Jefferson Med. Coll., Phila., 1962-67; asso. prof. surgery Harvard U., 1971-77; also chief neurosurg. service Beth Israel Hosp., Boston, 1967-77; prof. surgery Harvard U., 1977-200; also chief neurosurg. service Mass. Gen. Hosp., 1977-2000; Higgins prof. neurosurgery Harvard U., 1986-2000. Contbr. numerous articles to sci. jours. Chmn. Mass. Coun. Arts and Humanities, 1983-91; trustee Boston Symphony Orch., 1990—, vice chmn., 1993—, pres., 1994-2002. Capt. M.C. AUS, 1956-58. Fellow Am. Acad. Arts and Scis.; mem. Am. Acad. Neurol. Surgery (pres. 1990-91), Am. Assn. Neurol. Surgeons, Soc. Neurol. Surgeons, Am. Neurol. Assn., Am. Bd. Neurol. Surgery (chmn. 1990-91), Inst. Medicine Nat. Acad. Scis., Sigma Xi. Home: 100 Canton Ave Milton MA 02186-3507 Office: Mass Gen Hosp Attn Barbara Perrier 32 Fruit St Boston MA 02114-2620

ZERVOUDAKES, ANNETTE DIAN, reinsurance specialist; b. N.Y.C., Sept. 10, 1940; d. Abraham and Margaret (Roth) Dutchen; m. John W. Zervoudakes, June 17, 1966; children: Jason J., Alex R. Student, SUNY, Albany; grad., Career Blazers Inst., 2000. Underwriting asst. Aetna Life and Casualty, Garden City, N.Y., 1962-66; editor Rich Enterprises, Bellmore, 1974-84; sr. reins. specialist William Penn Life, Garden City, 1984-99; hub assoc. Sears Roebuck & Co., Hicksville, NY, Las Vegas, 1999—. Past pres. Mepham and Sawmill PTA Bellmore-Merrick Ctr. H.S. Dist., North Bellmore PTA Coun., Nassau Co. Dist. PTA; past pres., bd. dirs. Bellmore-Merrick Youth Assn.; committeewoman Nassau County Dem. Party; election poll clk., sec. Mid Nassau Dem. Club; polling clk. Clark County Elections, Nev. Recipient Disting. Svc. award, N.Y. State PTA. Mem. W.C. Mepham Alumni Assn. (pres. 1995-99, adv., bd. dirs., Meritorious Svc. award). Democrat. Presbyterian. Avocations: poetry, singing. Office: Sears Roebuck & Co 3450 Maryland Pky Las Vegas NV 89102

ZERZAN, CHARLES JOSEPH, JR. retired gastroenterologist; b. Portland, Oreg., Dec. 1, 1921; s. Charles Joseph and Margaret Cecelia (Mahony) Z.; m. Joan Margaret Kathan, Feb. 7, 1948; children: Charles Joseph, Michael, Kathryn, Paul, Joan, Margaret, Terrance, Phillip, Thomas, Rose, Kevin, Gregory. BA, Wilamette U., 1948; MD, Marquette U., 1951. Diplomate Am. Bd. Internal Medicine. Commd. 2d lt. U.S. Army, 1940, advanced through grades to capt., 1945, ret., 1946, re-enlisted, 1951, advanced through grades to lt. col., M.C., 1965; intern Madigan Gen. Hosp., Ft. Lewis, Wash., 1951-52; resident in internal medicine Letterman Gen. Hosp., San Francisco, 1953-56, Walter Reed Gen. Hosp., San Francisco, 1960-61; chief of medicine Rodriquez Army Hosp., 1957-60, U.S. Army Hosp., Fort Gordon, Calif., 1962-65; chief gastroenterology Fitzsimmons Gen. Hosp., Denver, 1965-66; chief profl. svcs. U.S. Army Hosp., Ft. Carson, Colo., 1967-68; dir. continuing med. edn. U. Oreg., Portland, 1968-73; ptnr. Permanente Clinic, 1973-92, ret., 1992. Assoc. clin. prof. medicine U. Oreg., 1973-97; individual practice medicine, specializing in gastroenterology, Portland, 1968-92; staff Northwest Permanente, P.C., ret., 1992, dir., 1980-83. Decorated Legion of Merit, Army Commendation medal with oak leaf cluster; Meritorious Alumnus award Oreg. Health Scis. U., 1990. Fellow ACP; mem. Am. Gastroenterol. Assn., Oreg. Med. Assn. (del. Clackamas County), Ret. Officers Assn., China-Burma-India Vet. Assn., Burma Star Assn. Republican. Roman Catholic. Home and Office: 6364 SE Mcnary Rd Portland OR 97267-5119

ZESCHUK, GREG, application developer; MD, U. Alta., Can., 1995. Joint CEO BioWare Corp., Edmonton, Canada, 1995—. Software developer (electronic game) Baldur's Gate. Office: BioWare Corp 302 10508 82d Ave Edmonton AB T6E 6H2 Canada*

ZETA-JONES, CATHERINE, actress; b. Swansea, Wales, Sept. 25, 1969; m. Michael Douglas, 2000. Motion picture and T.V. actress. Film appearances include Les 1001 nuits (Italy), 1990, Out of the Blue, 1991, Christopher Columbus: The Discovery, 1992, Splitting Heirs, 1993, Blue Juice, 1995, The Phantom, 1996, The Mask of Zorro, 1998, Entrapment, 1999, The Haunting, 1999, High Fidelity, 2000, Traffic, 2000, America's Sweethearts, 2001, Chicago, 2002 (T.V. films) The Return of the Native, 1994, Catherine the Great, 1995, also mini-series and T.V. guest appearances. Office: c/o ICM 8942 Wilshire Blvd Beverly Hills CA 90211*

ZEUGNER, JOHN FINN, history educator, writer; b. N.Y.C., Oct. 7, 1938; s. Orland Kump and Ethel (Finn) Z.; m. Alice Chatfield Valentine, Sept. 7, 1968; children: Emily Valentine, Maxwell Finn, Laura Ruth. AB, Harvard U., 1959; MA, Fla. State U., 1968, PhD, 1971. Night mgr. Beach Cart, Sarasota, Fla., 1960-67; asst. prof. history Worcester Poly. Inst., Mass., 1971-74, assoc. prof., 1974-82, prof., 1982—; Fulbright lectr. Osaka U., Kobe U., Japan, 1976-78. Vis. prof. Keio U., Tokyo, 1981-83; Bryant Drake guest prof. Kobe Coll., Japan, 1994-95. Contbr. articles, short stores to profl. publs. Served with USCG, 1961-62 Named Paris Fletcher Disting. Prof. Humanities, Worcester Poly. Inst., 1985; grantee NEA, 1970 Mem. Orgn. Am. Historians, Soc. Historians Am. Fgn. Rels., Soc. Historians Tech. Avocations: tennis; chess. Home: 31 William St Worcester MA 01609-2313 Office: Worcester Poly Inst Humanities & Arts Dept Worcester MA 01609

ZEUSCHNER, ERWIN ARNOLD, investment advisory company executive; b. Freiburg, Germany, Nov. 17, 1935; came to U.S., 1936; s. Reinhold Hermann and Helene Barbara (Maas) Z.; m. Christa Elfreide Ellmers, June 20, 1959 (dec. Aug., 1971); children— Peter Erwin, Suzanne Christina, Andrea Ellmers; m. Margaret Anne Finn, Mar. 25, 1972; 1 dau., Elizabeth Nora. BA in Econs., Queens Coll., 1957; MBA in Fin, NYU, 1964. Sr. v.p. Chase Manhattan Bank, N.Y.C., 1970-72; sr. v.p., dir. Chase Investors Mgmt. Corp., 1972-80; sr. v.p. Chase Manhattan Corp., 1970-80; ptnr. David J. Greene & Co. (investment advs.), N.Y.C., 1980—. Trustee Marymount Manhattan Coll., 1997. Served to capt. USAF, 1958-60. Mem. N.Y. Soc. Security Analysts (dir.) Home: 1 Middle Dr Manhasset NY 11030-1414 Office: 599 Lexington Ave New York NY 10022-6030

ZEVIAR-GEESE, GABRIOLE, stock market investor, lawyer; b. L.A., Apr. 10, 1948; d. Harry Lindstedt and Josephine (Conrad) Blom; m. Stephan Otto Geese, Nov. 22, 1992. BA, York U., 1991; JD, Calif. Pacific Sch. Law, 1999. Data base cons., edn. specialist Bull Internat., Toronto, Canada, 1982—91; arbitrator BBB, 1998—2001; pvt. practice Bakersfield, Calif., 2001—. Contbr. articles to profl. jours. Mem.: Consumer Attys. L.A., Kern County Bar Assn., Calif. Bar Assn. Avocations: piano, painting, Tae Kwon Do, Lightarian Reiki master. E-mail: geeselawoffice@aol.com.

ZEVNIK-SAWATZKY, DONNA DEE, litigation coordinator; b. Tulsa, Dec. 15, 1946; d. Robert Joseph Z. and Dorothy Dee (Robertson) Zink; m. Kenneth Sawatzky, May 30, 1965; children: K. Brian, Kaira D. Student, U. Ctrl. Okla., 1977, Okla. State U., 1984. Cert. AIDS educator, State of Okla., 1995-97. Sec. Farmers Ins. Co., Oklahoma City, 1974-80; office mgr. S.A.F.E., Inc., 1980-83; jr. acct. Southeast Exploration Corp., 1983-84; acct. Young Bros., Inc., 1984-88, The Denman Co., Inc., Oklahoma City, 1988-89; litigation coord. ACLU Okla., 1994—; founder, owner Otherwhere Arts, 1999—2001. Bd. dirs. ACLU Okla., 1995—; founder, CEO Otherwhere Arts. Author and illustrator: That Place--Otherwhere, 1994, Something for Otherwhere, 1995; author: At Our House, 1979-83; columnist Putnam City-N.W. News, Warr Acres, Okla., 1979-83; designer stage sets Miss Warr Acres Pageant, 1971-88. Bd. dirs. Miss Warr Acres (Okla.) Pageant, 1984-88, Warr Acres C. of C., 1981-85; treas. ACLU of Okla., 1995—, bd. dirs., 1994—; child welfare advocate Okla. State Dept. Human Svcs., Oklahoma City, 1987-89; coord. AIDS clinic Triangle Assn., Oklahoma City, 1994-97; founder Circle of Friends with Arachnoiditis World Wide Web Chronic Pain Support Group, 1997. Named Honorary Mayor of Warr Acres, 1971, Super Citizen, 1973, Outstanding Vol. Okla. State Dept. Human Svcs., 1988; recipient Svc. award Warr Acres C. of C., 1979, Legis. Commendation State of Okla., 1988, numerous Okla. Newspaper Column of Month awards Okla. Press Assn., Oklahoma City, 1981-82. Mem. NAFE, ACLU (Exec. Dir. Vol. Svc. award 1996), Nat. Notary Assn., Am. Inst. Profl. Bookkeepers, Amnesty Internat., The Interfaith Alliance, Pflag, Human Rights Campaign, Okla. Coalition to Abolish the Death Penalty. Democrat. Methodist. Avocations: painting, writing, photography, family. Office: 3000 Paseo Dr Oklahoma City OK 73103

ZEVOLA, DONNA RUTH, critical care nurse, educator; b. Batavia, N.Y., Dec. 15, 1957; d. Warner E. and Ruth Helen (Forkl) Hopkins; m. James A. Zevola, Sept. 5, 1987. AAS in Nursing, Genesee Community Coll., Batavia, 1978; BSN summa cum laude, Fla. So. Coll., 1983; MSN, U. Fla., 1987. RN N.Y., Fla.; cert. critical care nurse, advanced cardiac life support, clin. nurse specialist, med.-surg. nurse. Staff nurse, med., surg. ICU Fla. Hosp. Med. Ctr., Orlando, 1978-82, staff nurse open heart surgery unit, 1982-86, critical care educator, 1986-87; clin. nurse specialist Westchester Med. Ctr., Valhalla, NY, 1988—. Contbr. articles to profl. jours. Mem. AACN, N.Y. State Nurse's Assn.

ZEVON, SANFORD S. cardiologist, educator; b. Bklyn., Oct. 16, 1932; s. Murray Franklin and Celia (Karlin) Z.; m. Madeline Isaacs, Jan. 17, 1960; children: Paul Rubin, Daniel William, Lawrence Benjamin. BA, U. Ill., 1954; MD, SUNY, Bklyn., 1958. Diplomate Nat. Bd. Med. Examiners, Am. Bd. Internal Medicine; lic. physician N.Y., Calif. Intern Jewish Hsop. Bklyn., 1958-59, resident in internal medicine, 1959-60, Mt. Zion Hosp., San Fracisco, 1960-61, Montefiore Hosp., Bronx, 1961-62, trainee, 1962-67, adj. attending physician, 1967—; asst. clin. prof. medicine Albert Einstein Coll. Medicine, 1981—. Attending physician White Plains (N.Y.) Hosp. Med. Ctr., 1972—, chief divsn. cardiology, 1978-85, chief emeritus, mem. med. bd., 1981-84; cons. in field. Contbr. articles to profl. jours. Trustee Westchester Health Care Found., Inc., 1977-81; physicians chmn. United Way White Plains, 1976-78, bd. dirs., 1978-80; bd. dirs. Main St. Theatre, White Plains, 1980-81. Fellow ACP, Am. Coll. Cardiology, Am. Heart Assn. (coun. clin. cardiology), N.Y. Cardiol. Soc.; mem. N.Y. Med. Soc., Westchester County Med. Soc., Westchester Heart Assn. (med. adv. com. 1977-80). Avocations: skiing, tennis, jogging, golf, computer graphics. Office: 33 Davis Ave White Plains NY 10605-1015

ZEVTCHIN, J. MARK, financial executive, consultant; b. Coatesville, Pa., Oct. 29, 1957; s. Michael Fredrick and Ethel Deloris Zevtchin. BA, Salem (W.Va.) Internat. U., 1980. Pres. Maxwell Industries, Exton, Pa., 1989-90; prin. JMZ Fin. Svcs., Parkersburg, 1984—; contr., adminstrn. mgr. Macke Bldg. Svcs., Bala Cynwyd, 1986; CFO, Brighter Cmty. Inc., York, 1991-92; contr. Pilz Am. Inc., Concordville, 1995-96. Cons. PPL, Allentown, Pa., 1998-2000, JP Morgan Chase, Wilmington, Del., 2000-2001; informal advisor Dept. Def., Washington, 1980—, Dept. Justice, Washington, 1980—, NSC, Washington, 1990—, IRS, Washington, 1995—. Mem. Nature Conservancy, UN Assn., World Affairs Coun. Phila., Internat. Visitors Assn. Avocations: herpetology, ecology, market dynamics, politics, international affairs. Home and Office: 3013 Lincoln Hwy Parkesburg PA 19365 E-mail: jmarkz@ohesco.com.

ZEWAIL, AHMED HASSAN, chemistry and physics educator, editor, consultant; b. Damanhour, Egypt, Feb. 26, 1946; arrived in U.S., 1969, 1982; s. Hassan A. Zewail and Rawhia Dar; m. Dema Zewail; children: Maha, Amani, Nabeel, Hani. BS, Alexandria U., Egypt, 1967, MS, 1969; PhD, U. Pa., 1974; MA (hon.) , Oxford U., 1991; DSc (hon.) , Am. U., Cairo, 1993, Katholieke U., Leuven, Belgium, U. Pa., U. Lausanne, Switzerland, 1997; DU (hon.) , Swinburne U., Australia, 1999; HDA Sc (hon.) , Arab Acad. for Sci. and Tech., Egypt, 1999, Alexandria U., 1999; DSc (hon.) , U. New Brunswick, Canada, 2000; DHC (hon.) , U. Rome, Italy, 2000, U. de Liège, Belgium, 2000. Teaching asst. U. Pa., Phila., 1969—70; IBM fellow U. Calif., Berkeley, 1974—76; asst. prof. chem. physics Calif. Inst. Tech., Pasadena, 1976—78, assoc. prof., 1978—82, prof., 1982—89, Linus Pauling prof. chem. physics, 1990—94, Linus Pauling prof. chemistry and prof. physics, 1995—, dir. NSF Lab. for Molecular Scis., 1996—. Cons. Xerox Corp., Webster, NY, 1977—80, ARCO Solar, Inc., Calif., 1978—81. Editor Laser Chemistry, 1980—85, Jour. Phys. Chemistry, 1985—90, Chem. Physics Letters, 1991—; editor: International Series Monographs on Chemistry, 1992—, Advances in Laser Spectroscopy, 1977—, 1978—, Photochemistry and Photobiology, 1983—, Ultrafast Phenomena , 1990—, 1993—, 1994—, The Chemical Bond: Structure and Dynamics, 1992, Femtochemistry-Ultrafst Dynamics of the Chemical Bond, 1994; contbr. numerous articles to sci. jours., patentee in solar energy field. Recipient Tchr.-Scholar award, Dreyfus Found., 1979—85, Alexander von Humboldt Sr. U.S. Scientist award, 1983, John Simon Guggenheim Meml. Found. award, 1987, King Faisal Internat. prize in sci., 1989, NASA award, 1991, 1st AMM Achievement award, 1991, Nobel Laureate Signature award, 1992, Carl Zeiss award, Cairo U. Medal and Shield of Honor, 1992, U. Qatar medal, 1993, Niles award of honor Bonner Chemiepreis, Germany, 1994, Order of Merit first class, Egypt, 1995, Coll. de France medal Leonardo Da Vinci award of excellence, France, 1995, J.G. Kirwood medal, Yale U., 1996, Beijing U. medal, 1996, Robert A. Welch award in chemistry, 1997, Pitts. Spectroscopy award, 1997, Benjamin Franklin medal, 1999, Paul Karrer Gold medal, Zurich, 1999, Roentgen prize, Germany, 1999, E.O. Lawrence award, U.S. Govt., 1999, Merski award, U. Nebr., 1999, Nobel prize in Chemistry, 1999, Egypt Postage Stamp with portrait issued, 1999, Grand Collar of the Nile, Highest Award, 2000, Order of Zayed, United Arab Emirates, 2000, Ahmed Zewail fellow established, U. Pa., 2000, Order of Cedar, Lebanon, 2000, Order of ISESCO 1st class, Saudi Arabia, 2000, Order of merit, Tunisia, 2000, Insignia Pontifical Acad., Vatican, 2000. Mem.: NAS (Chem. Scis. award 1996), AAAS, Third World Acad. Scis., European Acad. Arts, Scis. and Humanities, Royal Danish Acad. Scis. and Letters, Pontifical Acad. Sci., Am. Phys. Soc. (Herbert P. Broida prize 1995), Am. Philos. Soc., Am. Chem. Soc. (Buck-Whitney medal 1985, Harrison-Howe award 1989, Hoechst prize 1990, Peter Debye award 1997, Linus Pauling medal 1997, 1st E.B. Wilson award 1997, William H. Nichols award 1998, Richard C. Tolman medal 1998), Am.

Acad. Arts and Scis. (Royal Netherlands Acad. Arts and Scis. medal 1993), Sigma Xi (Earle K. Plyler prize 1993, Wolf prize 1993). Office: Calif Inst Tech Divsn Chemistry & Chem Engring Mail Code 127 72 Pasadena CA 91125-0001

ZEX, DAMON, artist; b. Columbus, Ohio, July 11, 1963; s. Arnold Hobart Zaner, Rhoda Lee Zaner. BA, Ohio State U., 1985, MFA, 1991. Sales rep. FAZ Art Products, Columbus, Ohio, 1984—86; dir. gallery Artreach Gallery, 1986—87; designer Contemporary Glass, 1987—88; comml. designer Columbus Arts & Entertainment Mag., 1988—89, Ohio Transmission Corp., Columbus, 1989—91; videographer, tech. dir. Cmty. 21 TV, 1992—2001; co-owner Damon Zex Ltd., 2001—. Expert art witness U.S. Fed. Ct., Columbus, 1999. Actor: Zex TV, 1993—2001 (Comedy award, 1994, Comedy award, 1997, Comedy award, 1998). Avocations: chess, yoga, dancing, astrology, weight training.

ZEXTER, ELEANOR M. secondary education educator; b. Providence, Sept. 7, 1936; d. Morris and Anna Rae (Cantor) Marks; m. D. Ronald Zexter, Dec. 24, 1958; children: Francine Deborah, Judith Blair. BA, Brown U., 1958, MAT, 1962. Cert. tchr. R.I., Calif. Tchr. French and English Hope H.S., Providence, 1959—69, Nathan Bishop Mid. Sch., Providence, 1970—93; tchr. English and social studies Harkham Hillel Hebrew Acad., Beverly Hills, Calif., 1993—99. Mktg. dir. DRZ Sales; grant writer Nathan Bishop Mid. Sch., Providence, 1980-93, choral dir., 1985-93, founder Famous Authors, 1987-93; cons. substance abuse program, Brown U., 1987-93; cons. in field. Vol. tutor Harkham Hillel Hebrew Acad., 1993-99, French club coord., Harkham Hillel Acad., 1993-99. Recipient Citizen Citation for outstanding efforts with Providence children, Mayor, 1990, McClorin award, 1991. Mem. Am. Assn. French Tchrs., Alliance Francaise, R.I. Assn. Foreign Language, Beverly Hills Country Club (tennis team capt.). Avocations: tennis, antique collecting, reading clubs, bridge, travel. Home: 8544 Burton Way Apt 401 Los Angeles CA 90048-3390

ZEYEN, RICHARD JOHN, plant pathology researcher, educator; b. Mankato, Minn., Jan. 17, 1943; s. Clifford John and Eleanor Otilla Zeyen; m. Anita Kozan, June 25, 1967 (div. 1971); m. Carol Breese Van Why, Dec. 10, 1984. Dir. EM facility Minn. Agrl. Exptl. Sta., St. Paul, 1971—2001; asst. prof. plant pathology U. Minn., 1973—75, assoc. prof., 1976—83, prof., 1983—. Cons. Minn. Pollution Control Agy. Contbr. articles to profl. jours. Underwood fellow Agr., Food and Rsch. Coun., U.K., 1993; NATO Scientific Exch. Program fellow, Wales, U.K., 1990-95. Mem. AAAS, Am. Phytopathol. Soc. (chmn. various coms. 1967—), Microscopy Soc. Am., Minn. Microscopy Soc. (past officer, bd. dirs., pres. 1981-82), Minn. State U. Alumni Assn. (bd. dirs. 1974-77), Sigma Xi. Achievements include analytical electron microscopy, X-ray microanalysis applications to biolog. specimens; molecular and biochem. regulation genetically controlled plant disease resistance; cytochemistry diseased plants. Office: U Minn Dept Plant Pathology 495 Borlaug Hall Buford Cir Saint Paul MN 55108 E-mail: richz@umn.edu.

ZGODA, LAWRENCE, artist; b. Chgo., Oct. 27, 1950; s. Alexander John and Augustina Lucille Z. BA, Columbia Coll., 1976. Artist, founder Larry Zgoda Studio, Chgo., 1978—. Creator 11 stained glass works for Our Lady of Angels Chapel, Marian Village, Lockport, Ill., 2000. Recipient Monetary Rsch. award The Graham Found., Chgo., 2000. Avocations: tilemaking, metalsmithing, mosaic, architecture. Office: Larry Zgoda Studio 2117 W Irving Park Rd Chicago IL 60618 E-mail: larryzgoda@studio.com.

ZGUTA, RUSSELL, history educator; b. Ukraine, Oct. 3, 1941; came to U.S., 1949; s. Stephen and Pauline Zguta; m. Nancy Anne Splinter, Aug. 30, 1969; children: Larissa, Gregory, Katherine, Ellen. BA, St. Francis Coll., Pa., 1964; MA, Pa. State U., 1965, PhD, 1967. Asst. prof. history U. Mo., Columbia, 1967-74, assoc. prof., 1974-79, prof., 1979—, chmn. dept. history, 1989-91, chmn. dept. econs., 1991-95. Author: Russian Minstrels, 1978; contbr. articles to profl. jours. Fulbright-Hays fellow, Helsinki, 1969-70, fellow Am. Coun. on Edn., 1986-87; younger humanist grantee NEH, 1974-75, grantee Nat. Libr. Medicine, 1978-79. Mem. Am. Hist. Assn., Am. Assn. for Advancement Slavic Studies, Am. Assn. for History Medicine, Am. Assn. for Ukrainian Studies, Early Slavic Studies Assn., Slavonic and East European Folklore Assn. Avocations: jogging, reading. Home: 500 Thilly Ave Columbia MO 65203-3461 Office: U Mo Dept History Columbia MO 65211-0001 E-mail: zgutar@missouri.edu.

ZHAI, TONGGUANG (TONY ZHAI), educator; b. Hailaer, Nei Mongol, China, Feb. 13, 1962; s. Hongkai Zhai and Guiying Liu; children: Jingxi. PhD, U. Oxford, Eng., 1994. Rsch. assoc. U. Oxford, 1995—2000; asst. prof. U. Ky., Lexington, 2001—. Recipient Buehler Tech. Merit Paper award, Internat. Metallography Soc. and Materials Characterisation, 1994. Mem.: ASM. Office: Univ Ky 177 Anderson Hall Lexington KY 40506 Home Fax: 859-323-1929; Office Fax: 859-323-1929. Personal E-mail: tzhai@engr.uky.edu. Business E-Mail: tzhai@engr.uky.edu.

ZHANG, BI, mechanical engineering educator; b. Yangzhou, China, Sept. 7, 1957; came to U.S., 1990; s. Baoyu and Weizhen Zhang; m. Min Lin, Aug. 23, 1992; children: Deric, Jason. BS, Jiangsu (China) U., 1982; MS, Tokyo Inst. Tech., 1985, PhD, 1988. Rsch. engr. NEC Corp., Tokyo, 1988-89; asst. prof. Shanghai Jiao Tong U., 1989-92; rsch. assoc. Okla. State U., Stillwater, 1990-92; asst. prof. U. Conn., Storrs, 1992-97, program dir. Precision Mfg. Inst., 1992-98, assoc. prof. mech. engring., 1997—. Co-author: Diamond Tool Technology, 1987. Recipient Rsch. Initiation award NSF, 1993. Mem. ASME (Outstanding Reviewer award 1999), Internat. Inst. Prodn. Engring. Rsch. (corr.), Japan Soc. for Precision Engring. Avocations: swimming, tennis. Office: U Conn U-139 191 Auditorium Rd Unit U-139 Storrs Mansfield CT 06269-3139 E-mail: zhang@engr.uconn.edu.

ZHANG, BING, telecommunications industry executive, researcher; b. Wuhe, Anhui, China, May 31, 1965; s. Hegui Zhang, Maoying Zhang; m. Zhanxu Hu; children: Kevin. PhD, Ohio State U., 2001. Policy analyst Ministry Info. Industry China, Beijing, 1991—97. Contbr. articles to profl. jours. Mem.: Internat. Comm. Assn., Internat. Soc. for New Instnl. Econs., Assn. for Pub. Policy Analysis and Mgmt. Home: Apt K 1474 Neil Ave Columbus OH 43201 Office: Ohio State Univ 300 Fisher Hall 2100 Neil Ave Columbus OH 43210 Office Fax: 614-292-7423. Personal E-mail: zhang.214@osu.edu. Business E-Mail: zhang.214@osu.edu.

ZHANG, CHARLES C. financial planner; b. Shanghai; M in Econs. and Finance, Western Mich. U., 1991. ChFC; CFP; CLU; CMFC; CFS. Sr. fin. advisor Am. Express Fin. Advisors, Inc., Kalamazoo, 1991—. Adj. prof. finance Western Mich. U. Mem. Am. Soc. CLU and ChFC, Inst. cert. Fin. Planners, Internat. Assn. Fin. Planning. Office: Am Express Fin Advisors Inc 1302 W Milham Portage MI 49024 E-mail: charles.c.zhang@aexp.com.

ZHANG, CHUNLONG, environmental educator; b. Lanxi, Zhejiang, China, May 4, 1964; s. Yunfeng Pan and Peile Zhang; m. Shuou Zhao; children: Richard; m. Shuou Zhao; children: Richard. PhD, Louisiana State University, Baton Rouge, 1993—97. Assistant professor Hangzhou University, Hangzhou, China, 1986—91, University of Houston-Clear Lake, Houston, 2000—02. Environmental engineering consultant Tyndall Air Force Base, Tyndall, Fl, 1999—99. Author: (original research) Environmental Science and Technology, 2001; : Journal of Hazardous Materials, 2001, Bulletin of Environmental Contamination and Toxicology, 2000; : Journal of Contaminant Hydrology, 1999, Journal of Environmental Science and Health, 1998, Environmental Science and Technology, 1999; : Water Research, 1999; : Journal of Hazardous Materials, 1998; : Journal of Contaminant Hydrology, 1999, (original research) Dissertation, 1997 (Outstanding dissertation in the field of engineering and physical science, 1997), Separation Science and Technology, 1996. Mem.: Society of Environetal Toxicology and Chemistry, American Chemical Society, Association of Environmental Engineering and Science Professors. Office: University Of Houston - Clear Lake 2000 Bay Area Blvd Houston TX 77058 Office Fax: 281-283-3707. Business E-Mail: zhang@cl.uh.edu.

ZHANG, DA-LIN D. meteorologist, educator; b. Yangzhou, Jiangsu, China, Mar. 25, 1952; s. Daoquan D. and Wanzheng W. (Liu) Z.; m. Xiao-Ning X. Zhao, Oct. 18, 1978; children: Jie Jay, Ping Nina. BS in Engring. Mechanics, U. Sci. and Tech. of China, Hefei, 1976; MS in Meteorology, Pa. State U., 1981, PhD in Meteorology, 1985. Rsch. asst. Inst. Atmospheric Physics, Academia Sinica, 1976-80; grad. rsch. asst., rsch. assoc. dept. meteorology Pa. State U., 1980-86; postdoctoral fellow Nat. Ctr. for Atmospheric Rsch., 1986-88; rsch. assoc. dept. physics U. Toronto, Ont., 1988-89; asst. prof. McGill U., Montreal, 1989-94, assoc. prof., 1994-96, U. Md., College Park, 1996-99, prof. meteorology, 1999—. Oversea expert assessor Chinese Acad. Scis., Beijing, 1999—; guest prof. Nanjing U., 1999—; guest sr. scientist Chinese Acad. Meteorol. Scis., 2000—. Assoc. editor Monthly Weather Rev., 1998-2001, Weather and Forecasting, 1992-98; editl. bd. Acta Meteorologica Sinica, 1995—; co-chief editor Advances in Atmospheric Scis., 1999-2002; contbr. numerous articles to profl. jours., chpts. to books. Fellow Royal Meteorol. Soc.; mem. Am. Meteorol. Soc. (Meisinger award 1991). Avocations: ping pont, classical music. Office: Univ of Maryland Dept Meteorology College Park MD 20742 E-mail: dalin@atmos.umd.edu.

ZHANG, DAOWEI, forest economist, researcher, educator; b. Rudian, China, Nov. 6, 1963; s. Qingxiang Zhang; m. Zilun Fan, Sept. 2, 1992; 1 child, Xinrei Zhang. PhD, U. B.C., Vancouver, Can., 1994-99. Asst. prof. forestry Auburn (Ala.) U., 1994-99, assoc. prof. forestry, 1999—. Bd. dirs. Pinchot Inst. Conservation, Washington, 2000—. Recipient award Forestry Ext. Jour. Publ., So. Ext. Forest Resources Specialists, 1997. Mem. Soc. Am. Foresters. Avocation: swimming. Office: Auburn U Sch Forestry&Wildlife Scis Auburn AL 36849 Fax: (334) 844-1084. E-mail: zhangd1@auburn.edu.

ZHANG, DING, management consultant, educator; b. Shanghai, China, Dec. 18, 1958; s. Jinghan Zhang and Peifang Tang; m. Qiong June Dong; children: Alexander, Alena. BS, U. of Sci. and Tech. of China, Hefei, 1981; MS, Tsinghua U., Beijing, 1984; PhD, U. Mass., 1995. Rsch. assoc. U. Mass., Amherst, 1995—96; prof. mgmt. sci. SUNY, Oswego, 1997—. Rsch. fellow Hong Kong Poly. U., 2000—. Author: Projected Dynamical Systems and Variational Inequalities with Applications, 1996; contbr. articles to profl. jours., chapters to books. Mem.: Decision Sci. Inst., Informs. Office: SUNY Oswego Sch Business Oswego NY 13126

ZHANG, GUANG-JIAN, medical researcher, consultant; b. Tianjin, People's Republic of China, Jan. 28, 1955; s. Rui-Zhang Zhang and Xi-Lan Qiao; m. Yan-Li Cao, Dec. 9, 1981; children: Mi. MB, Tianjin Med. Coll., People's Republic of China, 1986, M in Medicine, 1992. Sr. lectr. Tianjin Med. Coll. Inst. Urologic Surgery, Tianjin, China, 1992-95; post-doctoral rsch. fellow and investigator dept. urology U. Iowa, 1995-99; rsch. scientist divsn. urology Med. Coll. Wis., Milw., 1999—. Rsch. asst. Tianjin Med. Coll., 1986-88; lectr. Tianjin Med. Coll. Inst. Urologic Surgery, 1988-92; vis. prof. Second Tchg. Hosp., Tianjian Med. U., 2002; expert reviewer urology, Balt., 2000—; rschr. in field; presenter in field. Contbr. articles including Chinese Jour. Urology, 1994, 96, 98, 2000; cons. Jour. Urology, N.Y., 2000—. Cert. Achievement in sci. and tech. Tianjin Com. Sci. and Tech., 2d class prize Chinese Nat. Sci. and Tech., 2001, 3d class prize Tianjin City Natural Sci., 2001. Mem. Soc. Basic Urologic Rsch. Home: 2312 N 80th St Apt 2 Wauwatosa WI 53213 Office: Med Coll Wis Divsn Urology 9200 W Wisconsin Ave Milwaukee WI 53226 E-mail: gjzhang55@hotmail.com.

ZHANG, G.Z. (GUANGZHI ZHANG), electro-optics engineer; b. Linqu, China, May 23, 1963; came to U.S., 1997; s. Sengjie Zhang and Zhaofend Zeng; m. Hong Gao, May 1, 1989; 1 child, Bohan. BSc, Shandong U., Jinan, China, 1983; MSc, Tsinghua U., Beijing, 1988; PhD in Sci., U. Electro-Comms., Tokyo, 1995. Elec. engr. Ministry Metallogical Industry, Beijing, 1983-91; postdoctoral fellow U. Toronto, Ont., Can., 1995-97; sr. electro-optics engr. New Focus Inc., San Jose, Calif., 1997—. Contbr. articles to profl. jours. Recipient Sci. and Tech. award Ministry of Metallogical Industry, Beijing, 1992, 9. Mem. Optical Soc. Am. Achievements include pioneering a method to produce broad-band frequent tunable single-mode laser with external feedback and mode-hop free orientation; first experimental research on high-conversion efficiency nonlinear optical generations using electromagnetically induced transparency; development and engineering on single-frequency tunable lasers, ultra-low antireflection, optical coating, nonlinear optics, fiber optical components, and optoelectronic instruments for in-situ imaging and metrology. Avocations: sports, fishing, hiking. Office: New Focus Inc Ste 100 5215 Hellyer Ave San Jose CA 95138-1001 E-mail: gzhang@newfocus.com.

ZHANG, HAO, pharmacologist; b. Yu City, China, Oct. 26, 1956; arrived in U.S., 1986; s. Jun-Jie Zhang and Mei-Duan Teng; m. Li Li, Jan. 3, 1986; children: Peter, Mona. MD, Henan Med. Coll., Zhengzhou, China, 1982; M in Med. Sci., Peking Union Med. Coll., Beijing, 1985. Cert. Ednl. Commn. Fgn. Med. Grads. Post doctoral tng. Peking Union Med. Coll., Inst. Antibiotics Chinese Acad. Scis., Beijing, 1982—85, assoc. rschr. Inst. Antibiotics, 1985—86; post doctoral fellow Nat. Cancer Inst., NIH, Bethesda, Md., 1986—89, vis. assoc., scientist, 1989—94; Oak Ridge fellow, staff fellow U.S. FDA, Rockville, 1994—97, reviewing pharmacologist, 1997—. Mem.: Immunotoxicology Com. Achievements include development of palindromic oligonucleotide-directed enzymatic reaction method for measuring deoxyribonucleotide 5'-triphosphates in cells and tissues to improve the evaluation of new antiviral drugs. Avocations: genomic music writing, poetry, swimming, fishing. Home: 14643 Pinto Ln Rockville MD 20850 Office: US FDA 9600 Fishers Ln Rockville MD 20852 Fax: 240-453-0785. E-mail: zhangh@cder.fda.gov.

ZHANG, HARRY, psychologist, human factors engineer, statistician; b. Dongyang, Zhejiang, China, June 15, 1963; came to U.S., 1986; s. Yuchang Zhang and Qine Ni; m. Lucy L. Zhang; 1 child, Joyce. BS, Hangzhou (China) U., 1983; MS, Chinese Acad. Scis., Beijing, 1986; PhD, U. Mich., 1994. Rsch. assoc. U. Mich., Ann Arbor, 1986-94; asst. prof. Ind. U. Kokomo, 1994-2000; statistician Eli Lilly and Co., 2000; human factors engr. Delphi Delco Electronics Sys., Kokomo, Ind., 2000—. Contbr. articles to profl. jours. Summer faculty rsch. fellow Ind. U., 1995, 96. Mem. Am. Psychol. Soc., Psychonomic Soc., Midwestern Psychol. Assn., Ind. Acad. Social Scis. (jr. dir. 2000), Psi Chi. Home: 12514 Spring Violet Pl Carmel IN 46033-9142 Office: Advanced Engring Delphi Delco Electronics Kokomo IN 46904-9003 E-mail: Harry.Zhang@delphiauto.com.

ZHANG, HONG-CHAO, manufacturing engineer, educator; b. Baoding, Hebei, China, Aug. 2, 1953; arrived in U.S., 1989; s. Gefei Xü and Xiaohui Li; m. Hongsi Xie, July 16, 1980; 1 child, Daniel. BSc, Tianjin (China) U. Light Industry, 1976; MSc, U. Aalborg, Denmark, 1986; PhD, Tech. U. Denmark, Lyngby, 1989. Lectr. Tianjin U. Light Industry, 1976-84; rsch. specialist U. Tex., Austin, 1989-90; asst. prof. indsl. engring. Tex. Tech U., Lubbock, 1990-95, assoc. prof., 1995-99, 1999-2000, prof., 2000—. Dir. Ctr. Applied Rsch. in Advanced Mfg. Tex. Tech. U.; presenter in field. Author: Computerized Manufacturing Process Planning Systems, 1993; editor: Advnaced Tolerancing Techniques, 1997, Engring. Design Automation, 1997; author 6 book chpts. and more than 80 articles. Mem. ASME, Soc. Mfg. Engrs., Inst. Indsl. Engrs. (affiliate), Soc. Design Process Sci. (founding.) Avocations: swimming, diving, badminton. Home: 5723 83rd St Lubbock TX 79424-4618 Office: Tex Tech U Dept Indsl Engring Lubbock TX 79409 E-mail: zhang@ttu.edu.

ZHANG, HONGTAO, research scientist; b. Yuzhou, Henan Province, China, Jan. 12, 1966; s. Songpeng Zhang and Zhuanying Liu; m. Huimin Li, Sept. 17, 1966; children: Zhiqi, Jenny, Michael. BS, Zhejiang U., Hangzhou, China, 1988, MS, 1990; PhD, U. Nebr., 2000. Rsch. asst. Zhejiang U., Hangzhou, China, 1988—91; editor China Electric Press, Beijing, 1991—94; vis. rsch. scholar Western Ky. U., Bowling Green, 1994—95; rsch. asst. prof. U. Nebr., Lincoln, 2000—, postdoctoral rsch. assoc., 2000. Editor: A Chinese-English-Russian Dictionary of Fossil-Fired Power Plant Terms, 1994. Recipient Outstanding Scholar award, NASA Nebr. Space Grant Program, 1998—2000, Brooks rsch. fellow, U. Nebr., Lincoln, 2000; fellow Milton E. Mohr rsch. fellow, 1997—99, Martin C. Hemsworth fellow, 1999. Mem.: AIAA, ASME, Combustion Inst. Home Fax: 402-472-1465; Office Fax: 402-472-1465. Business E-Mail: hzhang3@unl.edu.

ZHANG, HUI, research political scientist; b. Tangshan, Hebei, China, Nov. 15, 1962; s. Yuren Zhang and Shuhua Xu; m. Shuqing Bao, Oct. 1, 1987; 1 child, Zhiyi. BS in Physics, Hebei Normal U., Shijiazhuang, China, 1984; MSc, Henan Normal U., Xinxiang, China, 1987; PhD, Inst. Applied Physics and Computational Math., Beijing, 1996. Lectr. Henan Normal U., Xinxiang, China, 1987-93; tchr. physics, rschr. Found. Modern Physics, 1987—93; rsch. assoc. Inst. Applied Physics and Computational Math., 1993-97; postdoctoral rschr. Princeton (N.J.) U., 1997-99; rsch. fellow Kennedy Sch. Govt., Harvard U., Cambridge, Mass., 1999—. Contbr. articles to profl. jours. Social Scis. Rsch. Coun.-MacArthur fellow, 1998. Mem. Arms Control Assn., Inst. Nuclear Materials Mgmt. Office: Harvard U Kennedy Sch Govt 79 JF Kennedy St Cambridge MA 02138 Fax: 617-496-0606. E-mail: hui_zhang@harvard.edu.

ZHANG, JIN, information educator; b. Zheng Zhou, Henan, China, Dec. 3, 1959; came to U.S. 1994; s. Shi Zhang and Lily Yang; m. Yi Hong, Aug. 26, 1987; 1 child, Tian Run. BS, Wuhan (China) U., 1983, MS, 1986; PhD, U. Pitts., 1999. Prof. Wuhan U., 1986-95; asst. prof. U. Wis., Milw., 1999—. Author: Principle of Computerized Information Retrieval System Design, 1994; contbr. articles to profl. jours. Fulbright scholar U.S. Govt., 1994. Mem. Am. Soc. for Info. Sci. (Pratt-Severn Best Student Rsch. Paper award 1994). Avocations: music, reading. Office: U Wis Milw Bolton Hall 532 PO Box 413 Milwaukee WI 53201-0413 Fax: 414-229-4848. E-mail: jzhang@uwm.edu.

ZHANG, JUN, engineering educator, researcher; b. Leshan, Sichuan, China, June 25, 1964; s. Hongji Zhang and Zhilian Ran; m. Yao Han; children: Oliver, Kevin. PhD, George Washington U., 1997. Rsch. scientist Rsch. Computing Ctr., Chengdu, China, 1985—92; rsch. asst. U. Queensland, Brisbane, Australia, 1992—93; dir. Lab. High Performance Sci. Computing and Computer Simulation, Lexington, Ky., 2000—. Tchg. asst. City unviersity of Hong Kong, Hong Kong, 1996—2002, Zhejiang U., Hangzhou, Zhejiang, China, 1995—96, hebei U. of Tech., Tianjin, Tianjin, China, 1992—95. Editor (assoc. editor): (jour.) Korean Jour. Computational and Applied Maths., 2001. Chmn. Chinese Students and Scholars Assn. In HK, Hong Kong, Hong Kong, 1996—. Recipient Faculty Early Career award, NSF, 2001. Mem.: Soc. Indsl. Applied Maths. (2001). Office: U Ky 773 Anderson Hall Lexington KY 40506-0046 Home Fax: 859-323-1971; Office Fax: 859-323-1971. Business E-Mail: jzhang@cs.uky.edu.

ZHANG, JUNSHAN, electrical engineer, educator; b. Xiantao, Hubei, China, Sept. 14, 1972; came to U.S., 1995; s. Yourong and Shui Xiang (Wang) Z.; m. Lingdan Zeng, June 14, 1999. MSc, U. Ga., 1997; PhD, Purdue U., 2000. Tchg. asst. U. Ga., Athens, 1995-96; rsch. asst. Purdue U., West Lafayette, Ind., 1997-2000; asst. prof. Ariz. State U., Tempe, 2000—. Contbr. articles to profl. jours. Mem. IEEE, IEEE Comms. Soc. (chair Phoenix chpt. 2001), IEEE Info. Theory Soc., Internat. Soc. Optical Engring. (tech. com. 2001). Avocations: reading, sports, music. Office: Ariz State U Dept Elec Engring Tempe AZ 85287 E-mail: junshan.zhang@asu.edu.

ZHANG, LI, engineer, researcher; b. Beijing, Nov. 8, 1969; s. Qicheng Zhang and Liuying. MS in Nuclear Engring., MS in Elec. Engring and Computer Sci., MIT, 1996, PhD in Radiol. Scis., 1998. Tchg. asst. MIT, Cambridge, 1993-94, rsch. asst., 1994-98; sys. engr. Robotic Vision Sys., Inc., Hauppauge, N.Y., 1998; tech. mgr. Youngtech Inc., Edison, NJ, 1998—2001; project leader ADP Inc., Parsippany, 2001—. Dir. electronics Beijing Perfect Electronics Engring. Corp., Beijing, 1992-93; project mgr. AT&T, Bedminster, N.J., 1998-99. Mem. AAAS, IEEE, SPIE, Health Physics Soc., Am. Nuclear Soc., N.Y. Acad. Scis., Sigma Xi. Achievements include creation and research for explosive detection and nuclear medicine imaging. Avocations: hiking, computer/internet surfing, travel, movies, Broadway shows. Office: ADP Inc 9 Entin Rd Parsippany NJ 07054 E-mail: lizhang@alum.mid.edu.

ZHANG, MING, policy analyst; b. Jiangsu, China, 1962; arrived in U.S., 1988; m. Jiping Wu, 1993; children: Oak, Sky. BA, Nanjing U., 1983, MA, 1986; cert., Johns Hopkins U.-Nanjing U., 1987; PhD, Purdue U., 1994. Rsch. fellow Nat. Def. U., Washington, 1994—97; rsch. analyst Libr. Congress, 1995—97; dir. rsch. IHS Internat., Arlington, Va., 1998—. Cons. Carnegie Endowment, Washington, 1998—99; non-resident sr. fellow Atlantic Coun. U.S., Washington, 2000—; bd. dirs. Crossroads Initiative LLC, Va.; spkr. in field. Author: Major Powers at a Crossroads, 1995, China's Changing Nuclear Posture, 1999, A Triad of Another Kind, 1999. Grantee Tchg. grant, Rockefeller Bros. Fund, 1991, Travel grant, Am. Polit. Sci. Assn., 1993, Rsch. grant, NDU Found., 1994—97. Mem.: Internat. Studies Assn. Avocations: basketball, travel. Home: 3126 Borge St Oakton VA 22124

ZHANG, MINQUAN, chemistry educator; b. Yixin City, Jiangshu, China, Jan. 29, 1945; s. Peijing Zhang and Fuzheng Cheng; m. Xiaoli Ding, Oct. 25, 1973; children: Yan, Yingna. BS, East China Normal U., Shanghai, 1967, MS, 1981, PhD, 1984; postgrad., So. Ill. U., 1987-90. Cert. tchr., China. Engr. Salt Base Factory, Alta, China, 1968-72; H.S. dir., 1972-76; lectr. Xinjiang Inst. Tech., Urumqi, China, 1976-81, asst. prof., assoc. prof. Urumgi, China, 1981-87, 91-94, prof. China, 1995—; vis. asst. prof. So. Ill. U., Carbondale, 1987-90. Vis. prof. Okla. State U., Stillwater, 1997—. Editor Jour. Xinjiang Inst. Tech., 1994—; contbr. articles to profl. jours.; patentee in field. Scholar China Edn. Com., Beijing, 1987, China Scholarship Coun., Beijing, 1996; recipient Outstanding Profl. award Xinjiang Autonomous Region, Urumgi, China, 1996, New Century Asia 500 award, 2000, New Century Global 500 award, 2001. Mem. AAAS, China Chemistry Soc., N.Y. Acad. Scis., Xinjiang Internat. Assn. for Cooperation of Sci. and Tech., Am. Chem. Soc., Calif. Separation Scis. Soc., Nat. Resources Def. Coun., Planetary Soc. Avocations: table tennis, Chinese chess. Home and Office: Xinjiang Inst Tech 21 N Friendship Rd Urumqi Xinjiang 830008 China Office: Okla State U Food and Atrl Product Rsch & Tech Ctr Stillwater OK 74078-0001 E-mail: mqzhang34@hotmail.com.

ZHANG, NIEN FAN, statistician; b. Shanghai, China, Aug. 25, 1943; came to U.S., 1981; s. Zhong Han Jiang and Ya Li Zhang; m. Di Cheng Sun, July 10, 1970; children: Ning, Jing Yuan. BS, East China Normal U., 1965; MS, Va. Poly. Inst. and State U., 1982, PhD, 1985. Asst. prof. U. Sci. & Tech., Hefei, China, 1978-81; rsch. assoc. So. Meth. U., Dallas, 1985-88; rsch. statistician Shell Oil Co., Houston, 1988-93; supervisory math. statistician Nat. Inst. Stds. and Tech., Geithersburg, Md., 1994—. Contbr. articles to profl. jours. Recipient Silver medal U.S. Dept. Commerce, 1999, award for excellence in tech. transfer Fed. Lab. Consortium, 2000. Office: Nat Inst Stds & Tech Stop 8980 Gaithersburg MD 20899-0001 E-mail: zhang@nist.gov.

ZHANG, QING, mathematics educator; b. Baoding, China, Oct. 20, 1959; s. Fuhua and Yushu Z.; m. Qian Fang, Dec. 23, 1987; children: Sheena, Sean. PhD, Brown U., 1988. Prof. U. Ga., Athens, 1994—. Vis. rsch. prof. U. Toronto, Can., 1993-94. Author: Continuous-time Markov Chains and Applications, 1998, Hierarchical Decision Making in Stochastic Manufacturing Systems, 1994; author more than 150 rsch. papers. Recipient Creative Rsch. medal U. Ga., 2000; rsch. grantee Office Naval Rsch., 1996-98, USAF, 1999-2001. Mem.: IEEE (sr.; TAC assoc. editor 1998—2001), Soc. Indsl. and Applied Math. (assoc. editor SIAM SICON). Home: 130 Buckeye Br Athens GA 30605 Office: U Ga Dept Math Boyd Grad Studies Athens GA 30602 Fax: 706-542-2573. E-mail: qingz@math.uga.edu.

ZHANG, ROBERT, painter; b. Guang Dong, China, Oct. 4, 1941; came to U.S., 1995; s. Xing Heng and Caiying (Peng) Z.; m. Cui Hua Ou, Feb. 17, 1977; 1 child, Yufan. BS, Cen. Acad. Fine Arts, Beijing, 1966. Designer Gina Export Rsch. Inst., Canton, China, 1972-83; freelance artist Robert Fine Arts, N.Y.C., 1985—. Artist Galaxy of Graphics, Ltd., N.Y.C., 1992-97, Posters Internat., Ltd., Toronto, Can., 1996-97. Artist: (oil paintings) Boynton's Gala, 1996, 97, 2001. Avocation: graphic design. Home: 1664 W 6th St Apt 3 Brooklyn NY 11223-1336 Office: Robert Fine Arts 1664 W 6th St # B Brooklyn NY 11223-1336

ZHANG, RUICHONG, civil and mechanical engineer, educator; b. Shanghai, China, Dec. 6, 1962; s. Xianting Zhang and Shoumei Wang; m. Min Zhou, July 1, 1987; children: Vincent, Vivian (Cynthia). BS, Tongji U., 1984, MS, 1987; PhD, Fla. Atlantic U., 1992. Asst. prof. Tongji U., Shanghai, 1987; rsch. asst. U. Colo., Boulder, 1987-88, Fla. Atlantic U., Boca Raton, 1988-92; rsch. assoc. Princeton (N.J.) U., 1992-95; rsch. asst. prof. U. So. Calif., L.A., 1995-97; asst. prof. Colo. Sch. Mines, Golden, 1997-2000, assoc. prof., 2001—. Recipient Jr. Rsch. prize Internat. Assn. Structural Safety Reliability, 1997. Mem. ASME, ASCE, Earthquake Engring. Rsch. Inst., Internat. Assn. Structural Safety Reliability (Jr. Rsch. prize 1997). Home: 16501 W Ellsworth Ave Golden CO 80401-6540 Office: Colo Sch Mines Divsn Engring Golden CO 80401 E-mail: rzhang@mines.edu.

ZHANG, XIAODONG, computer scientist, educator, researcher; b. Beijing, China, July 16, 1958; came to the U.S., 1983; s. Min and Yishan (Jiang) Z.; m. Yan Meng, July 20, 1985; 1 child, Simon. BS, Beijing (China) Poly. U., 1982; MS, U. Colo., 1985, PhD, 1989. Rsch. asst. Beijing (China) Poly. U., 1982-83, Environ. Rsch. Lab., Boulder, Colo., 1983-85, U. Colo., Boulder, 1985-89; tech. staff Toplogix Inc., Denver, 1989; asst. prof. U. Tex., San Antonio, 1989-92, assoc. prof., 1993-97, chair computer sci., 1993, dir. high performance computing and software lab., 1993—; prof. Coll. William and Mary, Williamsburg, Va., 1997—, dir. grad. studies, 1999-2001; prog. dir. NSF, Arlington, Va., 2001—. Vis. scientist Rice U., 1990-91; guest prof. Wuhan U., China, 1995-97; guest rsch. prof. U. Sci. and Tech. of China, 1997—, guest prof. Northwestern Poly. U., China, 1998—; tech. cons. NASA ICASE, 1998—; mem. overseas expert assessor Chinese Acad. Scis., 1999—; adv. panelist NSF, 1995, 96, 97, 99, 2000; program chair 4th Internat. Workshop on Modeling, Analysis and Simulation of Computer and Telecomm. Systems; keynote spkr. 8th Internat. Conf. on Parallel and Distributed Computer Sys., 1996. Co-author: Multiprocessor Performance, 1994; editor Jour. of Parallel Computing, 1994-95; contbr. articles to profl. jours. Recipient Disting. Rsch. Achievement award U. Tex., 1993, Best Paper award 9th Internat. Conf. on Supercomputing, 1995; grantee NSF, 1990—, Southwestern Bell, 1992-97, USAF, 1993-97, AFOSR, 1995—, ONR, 1995-97, Sun Microsystems, 1998. Mem. IEEE (sr., chmn. tech. com. on supercomputing applications, disting. visitor, program coms., program com. 7th Symposium on Parallel and Distributed Processing 1995, 8th Symposium, 1996, 4th Internat. Symposium on High Performance Computer Arch. 1998, Supercomputing '99, others, mem. steering com. Supercomputing '96, '97, 98, 99, High Performance Computing Asia '97, 98, 99, 2000, internat. conf. on parallel processing 2000, editl. bd. Transactions on Parallel and Distributed Sys.), Assn. Computing Machinery (nat. lectr., program coms., program com. 10th Internat. Conf. on Supercomputing), Soc. Indsl. and Applied Math. Office: Coll William and Mary Computer Sci Williamsburg VA 23187

ZHANG, XUEMEI, reliability scientist; b. Qingdao City, Shandong, China, Jan. 16, 1969; parents Fengliang Zhang and Hongzhen Su. M in Mech. and Sys. Engring., Beijing Inst. Tech., 1994; M in Indsl. Engring., Rutgers U., 1997, M in Stats., 1998, PhD in Indsl. Engring., 1999. Rsch. asst. Rutgers U., New Brunswick, N.J., 1996-97, tchg. asst., 1997-98, rsch. asst., 1998-99; reliability scientist Bell Labs., Holmdel, 1999—. Author: (book chpts.) Recent Advances in Reliability and Quality Engineering, 1999, Handbook of Statistics on Reliability, 2000, (modeling and toolkit devel.) Software Reliability Assessment Tools, 1999; contbr. papers to profl. jours. Marion Johnson fellow Rutgers U., 1995-96. Mem. IEEE, Inst. Indsl. Engrs., Inst. Ops. Rsch. and Mgmt. Sci. Office: Bell Labs 101 Crawfords Corner Rd Holmdel NJ 07733-1985 Home: 20 Berkley Ct Morganville NJ 07751-4249 Fax: (732) 949-0019. E-mail: xzhang4@lucent.com.

ZHANG, XUMING, microbiology educator; b. Yueqing, Zhejiang, China, Apr. 7, 1962; came to U.S., 1989; s. Xiaoyin Zhang and Ceir Li; m. Monica Qiaoxia Cai, Oct. 10, 1988; children: Alexander, Jennifer. DVM summa cum laude, Zhejiang Agrl. U., 1982; PhD magna cum laude, Justus-Liebig U., Giessen, Germany, 1988. Lectr. Zhejiang Agrl. U., Hangzhou, 1985-86; rschr. Free U. of Berlin, 1988-89, La. State U., Baton Rouge, 1989-92, U. So. Calif., L.A., 1993-94, asst. prof., 1994-97, U. Ark. for Med. Scis., Little Rock, 1997-2000, assoc. prof., 2001—. Author: Recent Research Developments in Virology, 2001; contbr. articles to profl. jours. Rsch. grantee Am. Cancer Soc., 1998, NIH, 1995, 99, 2000. Mem. AAAS, Am. Soc. for Microbiology, Am. Soc. for Virology. Avocations: reading, classical music, gymnastics, table-tennis. Office: U Ark for Med Scis 4301 W Markham St Little Rock AR 72205 E-mail: zhangxuming@uams.edu.

ZHANG, YANWU, electrical engineer; b. Shaanxi Province, China, June 1969; came to U.S., 1994; s. Hongen and Baochuan Zhang. BSEE, Northwestern Poly. U., 1989, MS in Underwater Acoustics Engring., 1991; postgrad., U. Wash., 1994-95; MSEE and Computer Sci., MIT, 1998; MS in Oceanographic Engring., MIT/Woods Hole Oceanog. Instn., 1998, PhD in Oceanographic Engring., 2000. Rsch. asst. U. Wash., Seattle, 1994-95; rsch. and tchg. asst. MIT, Cambridge, 1995-2000; sys. engr. GE R & D Ctr., Niskayuna, N.Y., 2000; digital signal processing engr. Aware Inc., Bedford, Mass., 2001—. Summer rsch. fellowship Woods Hole Oceanographic Instn., 1997; scholarship 10th Internat. Symposium on Unmanned Untethered Submersible Tech., 1997. Mem. IEEE, Sigma Xi. Achievements include research on the technology of measuring water velocity from an autonomous underwater vehicle (AUV), study of adaptive AUV survey strategy. Avocations: sports, music, sightseeing. Address: c/o Aware Inc 40 Middlesex Turnpike Bedford MA 01730

ZHANG, YIMIN, researcher; b. Shengzhou, China, Dec. 27, 1964; married. PhD, U. Tsukuba, Japan, 1988. Asst. prof. Southeast U., Nanjing, China, 1988-89; sr. mgr. Oriental Sci. Lab., Yokohama, Japan, 1989-95, Comm. Lab., Kawasaki, Japan, 1995-97; rschr. adaptive comm. Rsch. Labs., Kyoto, 1997-98; rsch. assoc. Villanova (Pa.) U., 1998—. Contbr. articles to profl. jours.; patentee in field. Mem. IEEE (sr.). Office: Villanova U Dept Elec & Computer Engr Villanova PA 19085

ZHANG, YING HUA, research scientist; b. Shanghai, Apr. 29, 1936; came to U.S., 1988; d. Han Liang and Xiang E. (Xing) Z.; m. Chu Kun Kuo, Apr. 12, 1960; children: Yale Y. Guo, Jia Guo. BS, East China Inst. Chem. Tech., Shanghai, 1956; PhD, Chinese Acad. Scis., Shanghai, 1978. Assoc. prof. Shanghai Inst. Ceramics Chinese Acad. Scis., 1957-91; sr. scientist, prin. engr., fiber engring. mgr. Polaroid Corp., Boston, 1991-98; sr. staff scientist SDL Inc., San Jose, 1999-2001, JDS Uniphase Corp., San Jose, 2001—. Vis. scientist Rutgers U., Piscataway, N.J., 1989-91. Recipient Nat. Award for Developing Sci. and Tech., China Nat. Com. Sci. and Tech., 1985; named Shanghai Extraordinary Woman Scientist, Shanghai Women's Assn., 1984. Mem. Optic Soc. Am., Photonic Soc. Chinese Am., Polaroid Asia Assn. Achievements include patents and process development for industrial high power fiber lasers and amplifier fibers for telecommunication and speciality optical fibers for fiber optics; research and development of the first optical fiber telecommunication system between local offices in China. Office: JDS Uniphase No 1 Upland Rd Bldg N1 Norwood MA 02062

ZHANG, YINGZE, molecular biologist; b. Chifeng, Mongolia, China, Mar. 15, 1960; d. Kuiwu Zhang and Shuzhin Li; m. Mingui Sun, June 24, 1983; children: Zhipeng Sun, Liann Sun. BS, Liaoning Normal U., DaLian, China, 1982; MS, Duquesne U., 1987, U. Pitts., 1993, PhD, 1997. High sch. tchr. No. 2 High Sch., Chifeng, China, 1982; teaching asst. Duquesne U., Pitts., 1985-87; rsch. specialist U. Pitts., 1987-90, grad. student, researcher, 1990-93, rsch. specialist, 1993-95, lab. mgr., 1995-98, rsch. assoc., 1998-99, asst. prof. rsch., 1999—2002, assoc. prof. rsch., 2002—. Contbr. articles to profl. jours. Mem. AAAS. Home: 3311 Waterford Dr Pittsburgh PA 15238-1151 Office: U Pitts Sch Dental Medicine Pittsburgh PA 15261-0001

ZHANG, YONGXING JOHN, engineering educator; b. Wubu, Shaanxi, China, Oct. 15, 1956; came to U.S., 1984; s. Han-Bin Zhang and Fangzhi Zhao; m. Yen Wang, Feb. 7, 1982; children: Jenniver Jia-Xiao, Jessica Jia-Hui. BS, Shaanxi Inst. Mech. Engring., 1982; MS, Mich. Tech. U., 1986; PhD, Old Dominion U., 1991. Instr., engr. structures and mech. sect. Northwestern Agrl. U., Shaanxi, 1982-84; grad. rsch. asst. Mich. Tech. U., Houghton, 1984-87; grad. rsch. and tchg. asst. Old Dominion U., Norfolk, Va., 1987-91, rsch. assoc. Coll. Engring., 1991-92, adj. rsch. asst. prof. Coll. Health Scis., 1993, rsch. asst. prof. Ctr. for Biotech., 1992—. Presenter in field. Contbr. numerous articles to profl. publs. Rsch. grantee LifeNet Transplant Svcs., 1992, LifeLink Tissue Found., 1992; Collegiate All-Am. Scholar U.S. Achievement Acad., 1990. Mem. ASCE, Chinese Soc. Hydraulic Engrs. Achievements include research in computational structural mechanics, finite element-boundary element methods, large-scale structural dynamics and control, design sensitivity analysis and optimizations, parallel-vector computational methods and algorithms in structural analysis and design, biomechanics and its clinical applications, motion analysis. Office: Old Dominion U Ctr for Biotech Norfolk VA 23529

ZHANG, YOUXUE, geology educator; b. Huarong County, Hunan, China, Sept. 17, 1957; came to U.S., 1983; s. Zaiyi Zhang and Dezhen Wu; m. Zhengjiu Xu; children: Dan, Ray. BS in Geol. Scis., Peking U., Beijing, 1982; MA in Geol. Scis., Columbia U., 1985, MPhil, 1987, PhD in Geol. Scis., 1989. Grad. rsch. asst. Columbia U., N.Y.C., 1983-88; postdoctoral fellow Calif. Inst. Tech., 1988-91; asst. prof. geology U. Mich., Ann Arbor, 1991-97, assoc. prof., 1997—. Contbr. articles to profl. jours. Named Young Investigator, NSF, 1994. Mem. AAAS, Am. Geophys. Union, Geochem. Soc. (F.W. Clarke medal 1993), Mineral. Soc. Am., Sigma Xi. Office: Dept Geol Sci U Mich Ann Arbor MI 48109-1063 E-mail: youxue@umich.edu.

ZHANG, ZHENFANG JOHN, mechanical engineer, educator; b. Lulong, Hebei, China, May 4, 1963; arrived in Can., 1996; s. Mantang Zhang and Guizhen Zhao; m. Hao Zhang, Nov. 12, 1989; children: Yuezhuo, Jeffrey-Tian Liang. BSc in Mech. Engring., Shen Yang Inst. Tech., China, 1983; M in Mech. Engring., Northeastern U., China, 1988; PhD in Materials Engring., U. Sydney, 1996. Mech. engr. Jinshan Machinary Plant, China, 1983-85; lectr. Shen Yang Inst. Tech., China, 1988-91; postdoc. U. Sydney, 1996; mech. engring. educator U. Western Ont., London, Can., 1996-2000; process devel. engr. World Heart Co., Ottawa, Can., 2000—. Equity and Merit scholar Autralian Internat. Devel. Assistance Bur., Sydney, 1991-95. Mem. ASME. Avocation: sports. Office: World Heart Co 1 Laser St Ottawa ON Canada K2E 7V1 E-mail: zhangzf1@yahoo.com.

ZHANG, ZHENGYOU, computer scientist; b. Wenling, China, Apr. 1, 1965; arrived in France, 1986; came to U.S., 1998; s. Qinlan and Xiangfeng (Yang) Z.; m. Ming-Yue Xie, Apr. 22, 1988; children: Shuting Rosaline, Laetitia Xiaoling, Stephanie Xiaoying. BS, U. Zhejiang, 1985; DEA, U. Nancy, 1987; PhD, U. Paris XI, 1990, habilitation, 1994. Asst. rschr. INRIA, Rocquencourt, France, 1987-90, rschr. Sophia-Antipolis, France, 1990-91, sr. rschr. France, 1991-98; rschr. Microsoft Rsch., Redmond, Wash., 1998-99, sr. rschr., 1999—. PhD supr. U. Paris XI, Orsay, 1994-98; program com. mem. Internat. Symposium Young Investigators, Beijing, 1994, IEEE Conf. on Computer Vision and Pattern Recognition, Calif., 1996, IEEE Conf. on Automatic Face and Gesture Recognition, Japan, 1998, IEEE Workshop on Applications of Computer Vision, N.J., 1998, IEEE Conf. on Computer Vision and Pattern Recognition, Colo., 1999, 2000, 2001, Internat. Conf. on Computer Vision, Vancouver, Can., 2001; invited rschr. ATR, Japan, 1996-97; guest rsch. prof. Chinese Acad. Scis.; part-time prof. No. Jiaotong U., Beijing; guest prof., Zhejiang (China) U; adj. assoc. prof. U. So. Calif. Author: 3D Dynamic Scene Analysis: A Stereo Based Approach, 1992, Epipolar Geometry in Stereo, Motion and Object Recognition, 1996, Computer Vision, 1998, (software) Image Matching, 1994; assoc. editor Internat. Jour. Pattern Recognition and Artificial Intelligence, 1997—; action editor Videre: A Jour. Computer vision Rsch., 1998-2000; assoc. editor IEEE Trans. on Pattern Analysis and Machine Intelligence, 2000—; contbr. articles to profl. jours. and chpts. to books. Mem. IEEE (sr.), Chinese Artificial Vision Assn. (founder, chmn. 1993-95), Assn. Computer Machinery. Avocations: sightseeing, walking in nature, table tennis, swimming, tennis. Office: Microsoft Corp One Microsoft Way Redmond WA 98052 E-mail: zhang@microsoft.com.

ZHANG, ZHIWEI, research scientist; b. Wuhan City, China, Oct. 5, 1964; s. Lian Wen and Guang Ming (Tang) Z.; m. Mei X. Zhang, June 18, 1991; children: Jenny, Olivia. BS, Huangzhong U. Sci. and Tech., Wuhan, China, 1985; MS, Va. Commonwealth U., 1994; PhD, Va. Tech., 1999. Sr. rsch. analyst Nat. Opinion Rsch. Ctr., Washington, 1997-98; rsch. scientist Nat. Opinion Rsch. Ctr. U. Chgo., 1999—2000, sr. rsch. scientist Nat. Opinion Rsch. Ctr., 2000—. Author drug use and workplace programs and policies, 1999. Recipient Bur. of Justice Stats. award, 1997; Bur. Labor Stats./Dept. Labor grantee, 1999. Mem. Am. Sociol. Assn. (Clifford C. Clogg award 1996), Am. Stats. Assn. Avocation: tennis. Office: Nat Opinion Rsch Ctr 1350 Connecticut Ave NW Ste 500 Washington DC 20036-1736

ZHANG, ZHONGFEI, computer science educator, researcher, consultant; b. Hangzhou, Zhejiang, China; came to U.S., 1989; s. Yukun Zhang and Ming Song; m. Aiqun Du, Jan. 1, 1997; children: Henry, Andrew. BS cum laude, Zhejiang U., Hangzhou, China, 1984, MS, 1987; PhD, U. Mass., 1996. Mem. rsch. staff Zhejiang U., 1987-89; rsch. asst. U. Mass., Amherst, 1989-95; rsch. scientist SUNY, Buffalo, 1995-99, rsch. asst. prof., 1997-99, asst. prof. computer sci. Binghamton, 1999—. Assoc. editor: Procs. Internat. Conf. on Imaging Sci. Systems and Tech., 1998, Pattern Recognition, 2002—; contbr. articles to sci. jours., including Jour. Robotic Sys., IEEE Transactions on Pattern Analysis and Machine Intelligence, Info. Retrieval, IEEE Multimedia, Library Trends, Pattern Recognition. Achievements include invention of computer based method and apparatus for object recognition. Office: Computer Sci Dept SUNY Binghamton NY 13902 E-mail: zhongfei@cs.binghamton.edu.

ZHANG, ZHONGJIAN, research scientist; b. Zhengzhou, Henan, China, Dec. 14, 1956; s. Weimin Zhang and Guangrong Cui; m. Juan Zhang, Jan. 7, 1986; 1 child, Feipeng. MS, Xian (China) Med. U., 1986; PhD, U. Miami, 1992. Rsch. assoc. U. Miami, 1993-94; intramual rsch. tng. Award fellow NIH, Bethesda, Md., 1994-98, staff rsch. scientist, 1998—. Contbr. articles to profl. jours.

ZHANG, ZHUOMIN, mechanical engineering educator; b. Henan, China, Apr. 14, 1962; came to U.S., 1989, naturalized, 1999; s. Wenbin and Xueqin Zhang; m. Lingyun Wang, Nov. 24, 1988; children: Emmy, Angie, Bryan. BS, U. Sci. Technol. China, Hefei, 1982, MS, 1985; PhD, MIT, 1992. Lectr. U. Sci. Technol. China, Hefei, 1987-89; rsch. assoc. U. Md., College Park, 1992-95; asst. prof. U. Fla., Gainesville, 1995—2000, assoc. prof., 2000—02, Ga. Tech., Atlanta, 2002—. Guest scientist Nat. Inst. Stds. and Tech., Gathersburg, Md., 1992-95. Contbr. articles to profl. jours., chpts. to books. Recipient NSF Career award, 1999, Presdl. Early Career Award for Scientists and Engrs. Mem. ASME, AAAS, AIAA, Am. Phys. Soc., Am. Soc. Engring. Edn., Materials Rsch. Soc., Soc. Photo-Optical Instrumentation Engrs., Sigma Xi. Office: Ga Inst Tech Woodruff Sch Mech Engring 801 Ferst Dr NW Atlanta GA 30332-0405 Fax: 404-894-8496. E-mail: zzhang@sununo.me.gatech.edu.

ZHAO, CONG LONG, physicist; b. Shaanxi, China, Mar. 9, 1944; came to U.S., 1990; m. Diying Yang, Dec. 1971; children: Jean, Ming. BA in Physics, Northwestern U., China, 1970; MS in Atmospheric Physics, Chinese Acad. Scis., 1981, PhD of Atmospheric Physics, 1986. Rsch. asst. Chinese Acad. Scis., Beijing, 1980-82; vis. scientist Wave Propagation Lab. NOAA, Boulder, Colo., 1983-85; rsch. assoc. Chinese Acad. Meteorol. Scis., Beijing, 1986-90; rsch. scientist Climate Monitoring and Diagnostics Lab. U. Colo., Boulder, 1990—. Contbr. articles to profl. jours.; inventor in field. Recipient 1st class nat. award for sci. and tech. Nat. Com. of Sci., Beijing, 1990. Office: NOAA/Climate Monitoring Diagnostics Lab 325 Broadway St Boulder CO 80305-3337 E-mail: czhao@cmdl.noaa.gov.

ZHAO, FANG LI, medical researcher; b. Wugong, Shaan Xi, China, Jan. 3, 1963; s. Huoan Zhao and Yu Ling Zhou; m. Jinzhu Gu, Dec. 19, 1989; children: Guanchao. BA, Shaanxi Teachers U., China, 1984; MA, Xi'an Med. U., China, 1987, PhD, 1997. Asst. rschr. Xi'an Med. U., China, China, 1987—93, China, 1997—98; postdoctoral rschr. Ohio State U., Ohio, 1998—. Contbr. articles to profl. jours. Mem.: Assn. Chemoreception Sci. Avocations: movies, science novels, political news. Office: Oral Biology College of Dentistry 3 at W 12th Avenue Columbus OH 43218-2357

ZHAO, FENG, optical engineer, researcher; b. Yongcheng, Henan, China, Oct. 1, 1961; m. Yun Zhang, May 16, 1988; children: Feng. PhD in Optics, Harbin (China) Inst. Tech., 1991. Assoc. prof. Harbin Inst. Tech., Harbin, 1993—97; vis. prof. Delft (Netherlands) U. of Tech., 1997—98; rsch. fellow U. Tex. , Austin, 1998—. Recipient 2d prize of progress in scis. and tech., Aero-Space and Aviation Ministry of China, 1992. Mem.: AAAS, OSA, IEEE. Office: U Tex at Austin 10100 Burnet Rd #160 Austin TX 78758

ZHAO, GUANG-QUAN, developmental reproductive biologist, researcher; b. Qingdao, Shandong, China, Feb. 21, 1963; came to U.S., 1988; s. Feng-Yue and Xiu-Yun Song Z.; m. Xiaoxia (Sasha) Qi, Dec. 26, 1987; children: Dawn, Erica. MD, Shandong Med. U., 1984; PhD, U. Tex. Grad. Sch. Biomedical Sci., 1993. Clin. resident Shandong Med. Univ., Jinan, China, 1984-88; grad. rsch. asst. Univ. Tex. Anderson Cancer Ctr., Houston, 1988-93; rsch. assoc. Howard Hughes Med. Instit., Nashville, 1993-97; asst. prof. Univ. Mo., Columbia, 1997-2001, Univ. Tex. Southwestern Med. Ctr., Dallas, 2001—. Author numerous jour. articles. Recipient rsch. grant NIH. Mem. Soc. Devel. Biology, Soc. Study Reproduction.

ZHAO, HEQUAN, chemist, researcher; b. Zhengzhou, Henan, China, July 18, 1962; s. Shunzhong and Shuqin (Liang) Z.; m. Guijuan Wang, Aug. 1, 1988; 1 child, Bo. BS, Zhengzhou U. China, 1982, MS, 1988; PhD, Iowa State U., 1997. Asst. prof. Zhengzhou U. China, 1982-88, devel. engr. Catalyst Co., 1988-92; rsch. asst. Ames (Iowa) Lab. of U.S. Dept. Energy, 1992-97; sr. scientist SpectruMedix Co., State College, Pa., 1997—. Contbr. articles to profl. jours. Recipient Sci. Rsch. prize Zhengzhou U. China, 1986, Sci. Rsch. prize Henan Province, China, 1988. Mem. AAAS, Am. Chem. Soc., Phi Kappa Phi (award 1997), Sigma Xi. Achievements include research in Fe-Co spherical catlayst for ammonia synthesis. Office: 2124 Old Gatesburg Rd State College PA 16803-2200 Home: 227 Lexington Dr Phoenixville PA 19460-4222

ZHAO, HONG, chemical engineer, educator; s. Zhao; m. Ying Xu, 1959; children: John, Grant. PhD, Zhejiang U., Hangzhou, China, 1989. From asst. to assoc. prof. Zhejiang U., Hangzhou, China, 1989—91; sr. rschr. Tech. U. of Denmark, Lyngby, Denmark, 1991—94; vis. assoc. prof. U. of Md., College Park, 1994—96; sr. rsch. scientist NeuralWare, Inc., Pitts., 1996—98; sr. technologist Aspen Tech., Inc., Houston, 1998—2002. Author: (Book 2 vols.) Process Control Theory, 1991 (Exemplary Young Tchr. Award, 1991); contbr. articles 15 in peer-reviewed journals. Named Outstanding Prof. and Rschr., US INS, 1996. Mem.: AIChE, IAWQ. Achievements include U.S. patent, 2002. Office: Aspen Technology Inc. 1293 Eldridge Parkway Houston TX 77077 Office Fax: 281-584-4329 281-584-4329.

ZHAO, HONGZHI, research scientist; s. Kechang Zhao and Shuzhenn He; m. Qi Han; children: Yin. Bachelor, Harbin Inst. of Tech., Heilongjiang, China, 1980—84; M in Engring., 1984—87; PhD, Beijing Inst. of Tech., Beijing, China, 1992—95. Lectr. North China Space Inst. of Tech., Langfang, China, 1987—92; rsch. fellow Tsinghua U., Beijing, 1995—97, assoc. prof., 1997—99; rsch. fellow U. of Tex. at San Antonio, San Antonio, 1999—2000, Mass. Gen. Hosp., Boston, 2000—. Contbr. articles to profl. jours. and publs. Mem.: SPIE. Home: 38 Auburndale Ave Newton MA 02465 Office: Mass General Hosp Wellman Lab 55 Fruit St BAR-713 Boston MA 02114 Office Fax: 617-726-4103. Personal E-mail: hongzhi_zhao_utsa@hotmail.com. Business E-Mail: zhaoh@helix.mgh.harvard.edu.

ZHAO, JIAN HUI, electrical and computer engineering educator; b. Nanping, Fujian, China, Aug. 2, 1959; came to U.S., 1983; s. Yumao Zhao and Su Qing Chen; m. Menghan Pan, Apr. 28, 1992. BS in Physics, Amoy U., China, 1982; MS in Physics, U. Toledo, 1985; PhD in E.E., Carnegie Mellon U., 1988. Rsch. asst. Nonlinear Optics Lab. U. Toledo, Ohio, 1983-85; rsch. asst. Solid State Elec. Lab. Carnegie Mellon U., Pitts., 1985-88; asst. prof. electric and computer engring. dept. Rutgers U., New Brunswick, N.J., 1988-93, assoc. prof. electric and computer engring. dept., 1993-99, prof. dept. electric and computer engring., 1999—. Cons. Army Rsch. Lab., Ft. Monmouth, 1991—, Westinghouse, Pitts. Contbr. numerous articles to profl. jours. Henry Rutgers fellow Rutgers U., New Brunswick, N.J., 1989, 90; recipient Initiation award NSF, 1990, Best Teaching Performance award Rutgers Eta Kappa Nu, 1991. Mem. IEEE (sr.), Am. Phys. Soc., Materials Rsch. Soc., N.Y. Acad. Sci. Achievements include patents for InP/InGaAsP optoelectronic high speed thyristor, an AlGaAs/GaAs-based optothyristor for ultra-high power switching, field effect real space transfer transistor, electrical tunable superlattice detector for wavelength division demultiplexing applications. Office: Rutgers Univ Elec & Computer Engring Dept PO Box 909 Piscataway NJ 08855-0909

ZHAO, JIANLIANG LEON, computer scientist, educator, computer scientist, researcher; b. Xinji, Hebei, China, Nov. 24, 1953; married. PhD, Haas Sch. Bus., Berkeley, Calif., 1992. Asst. prof. Coll. William and Mary, Williamsburg, Va., 1992—95; computer scientist Lawrence Berkeley Nat. Lab., Berkeley, 1995—96; asst. prof. Hong Kong U. Sci. and Techn., Hong Kong, China, 1996—99; assoc. prof. U. Ariz., Tucson, 1999—. Mem.: Assn. Info. Sys. Achievements include patents for cool storage supervisory controller.

ZHAO, JINGANG, economist, educator; b. Zhaozai Twp, Yanshi County, Henan Province, China, Nov. 5, 1958; s. ZengGuang Zhao and FengYing Yang; m. Ping Zhang; children: Lisa, Louis. PhD in Econs., Yale U., 1992. Asst. prof. econs. Ohio State U., Columbus, 1992—2000; vis. asst. prof. econs. Iowa State U., Ames, 2000—02; assoc. prof. econs. U. Saskatchewan, Saskatoon, Canada, 2002—. Office: U Saskatchewan 9 Campus Dr Economics Dept Saskatoon SK Canada S7N 5A5 Home Fax: 515-294-0221; Office Fax: 306-966-5232. Personal E-mail: jingang@iastate.edu. Business E-Mail: jingang_zhao@yahoo.com.

ZHAO, JINSONG JASON, engineer, researcher, administrator; b. Beijing, July 14, 1966; came to U.S., 1990; m. Wen Chen. BSME, Tianjin U., 1989; MSME, N.C. A&T State U., 1997. Project mgr. Sinolummus, Inc., 1989-92; sr. mech. engr. Microdyne System, Inc., 1994; mgr. rsch. & engring. IKA Works, Inc., Wilmington, N.C., 1994-98; v.p. CAM Techs., Inc., Schaumberg, Ill., 1998—. Vice-chmn. task com. 3A Sanitary Com., 1997—; bd. dirs. Rotor Stator Mixer Rsch. Adv. Bd. Inventor cleaning in place multistage high shear in-line mixer. Mem. ASME, ISPE, AIChE, NAMF. Office: CAM Techs Inc 1035 Peters Ct Lake Zurich IL 60047-1451 E-mail: jasonzhao@excite.com.

ZHAO, JUN, management educator; b. Chengdu, Sichuan, China, Jan. 10, 1969; came to U.S., 1992; d. Bihui and Zongying (Liao) Z.; m. Hanping Xiao, Aug. 2, 1991; children: Roger Xiao, Andy Xiao. D of Bus. Adminstrn., So. Ill. U., 1998. Asst. prof. mgmt. Western Ill. U., Macomb, 1998-99; prof. mgmt. Govs. State U., University Park, Ill., 1999—. Contbr. articles to profl. jours. Mem. Acad. Mgmt., Strategic Mgmt. Soc. Office: Govs State Univ University Pky University Park IL 60466

ZHAO, JUNSHENG, research scientist, electrical engineer; b. Linqu County, China; s. Liancheng Zhao and Xiuying Sun. BS, Shandong U., Jinan, China, 1985; MS, Second Acad. Min. Astranautics, Beijing, 1988; PhD, Tsinghua U., Beijing, 1995. Engr. Beijing Inst. Radio Measurement, 1988-95; postdoctoral rsch. assoc. U. Ill., Urbana, 1996-99; postdoctoral rsch. fellow Concordia U., Montreal, Que., Canada, 1999; rsch. scientist U. Ill., Urbana, 1999—. Mem. IEEE.

ZHAO, MEISHAN, chemical physics educator, researcher, writer; b. Shanxian, Shandong, People's Republic of China, Nov. 5, 1958; s. Zhong Chen Zhao and Ming Rong Zhang; m. Linlin Cai, Sept. 2, 1983; children: Fang, Yuan, Nan. MS in Physics, U. Minn., 1986, PhD in Chem. Physics, 1989. Lectr. physics S.E. U. China, Nanjing, 1982-84; teaching asst., rsch. asst. U. Minn., Mpls., 1984-89; rschr. James Franck Inst. and dept. chemistry U. Chgo., 1990—, dir. Gen. Chemistry Lab., 1999—. Contbr. articles to profl. jours. Mem. AAAS, Am. Phys. Soc. (internat. editl. bd. Internal. Physics Edn., Chinese ed., 1991-92), N.Y. Acad. Sci. Home: 1443 Keats Ave Naperville IL 60564 Office: Univ Chgo James Franck Inst 5640 S Ellis Ave Chicago IL 60637-1433 E-mail: m-zhao@uchicago.edu.

ZHAO, MINGJUN, physicist, research scientist; b. Shaanxi, China, July 13, 1957; came to U.S., 1994; s. Yong Zhao and Fengying Xue; m. Shihong Chen, July 31, 1984; 1 child, Bowen. BS, Shaanxi Normal U., Xian, 1982; PhD, Xian Inst. Optics/Prec. Mechs., Chinese Acad. Scis., Xian, 1989. Faculty Xian Inst. Petroleum, 1982-86; postdoctoral fellow Xian Inst. Optics & Precision Mechanics Academia Sinica, Xian, 1990-92; Internat. Ctr. for Theoretical Physics fellow Inst. Nat. Optics, Firenze, Italy, 1992-93; rsch. fellow Inst. Phys. and Chem. Rsch., Wako-shi, Japan, 1993-94; rsch. assoc. N.Mex. State U., Las Cruces, 1994-96; rsch. engr. U. Calif., Santa Barbara, 1996; rsch. scientist Phys. Optics Corp., Torrance, Calif., 1996—. Contbr. articles to profl. jours. including Chinese Physics-Letter, Optics Comm., Optics Letter. Recipient 2d pl. natural scis. award Shaanxi Province, 1992, Excellent award Chinese Acad. Scis., 1991, Excellent award of Pres. Scholarship, 1989. Mem. AAAS, Internat. Soc. for Optical Engring., N.Y. Acad. Scis. Achievements include main contribution to nonlinear optics, especially in field of photorefractive multi-wave mixing, phase conjugation, created pertubation approximation theory for analysis of phase distortion in degenerate four-wave mixing, developed photorefractive spatial light modulator base on home-made BSO crystal; realization of self-pumped phase conjugation of diffusely reflected light in a KNSBN crystal, and dynamics pattern formation and storage; demonstrated system which combined ultrasound generation and double phase conjugation for non-destrictive evaluation application, and micro-optical and liquid crystal for 3-D display, optical limiting and optical switching and its applications in communications, and laser plasma diagnostics. Home: Apt 176 39639 Leslie St Fremont CA 94538-2249

ZHAO, QUANSHENG, university administrator, educator; BA, Peking U., 1981; MA, U. Calif., Berkeley, 1982, PhD, 1987. Prof. Fletcher Sch. of Law and Diplomacy, Tufts U., Old Dominion U., Hong Kong U. of Sci. and Tech., Aoyama Gakuin U., Tokyo; assoc.-in rsch. Fairbank Ctr. for East Asian Rsch., Harvard U., 1993—; prof., divsn. dir. Am. U., Washington, 1996—. Chair Asia Coun. Am. U., 2000—, dir. divsn. comparative and regional studies Sch. of Internat. Svcs., 1999—. Author: Interpreting Chinese Foreign Policy, 1996, Japanese Policymaking, 1993 (Outstanding Acad. book Choice), (in Chinese) Understanding Chinese Foreign Policy, 1999; co-editor: Politics of Divided Nations: China, Korea, Germany and Vietnam, 1991; editl. advisor Am. Asian rev., 1992—, Jour. of Strategic Studies, 2000—, Jour. of Contemporary China. Mem. Am. Polit. Sci. Assn. (chair conf. group on China studies 1992—). Avocations: swimming, skiing. Office: CRS/SIS Am U 4400 Massachusetts Ave NW Washington DC 20016

ZHAO, REN WEI, economics educator; b. Jinhua, Zhejiang, China, Mar. 23, 1933; s. Jian guang and Shu jun (Huang) Z.; m. An lin Zhu, Aug. 15, 1965; children: Wen jing, Wen wei. BA in Econs., Beijing (China) U., 1957. Rsch. asst., asst. prof. Inst. Econs., Chinese Acad., Beijing, 1957-79; assoc. prof. Inst. Econs., Chinese Acad. Social Scis., 1979-85, dept. dir., prof., 1985-88, dir., prof., 1988-91, prof. econs., 1991—. Vis. fellow St. Antony's Coll. Oxford (Eng.) U., 1982-83, Columbia U., N.Y.C., 1992-93, Duisburg (Germany) U., 1996, All Souls Coll. Oxford (Eng.) U., 1997. Chief editor Econ. Rsch. Jour., 1989-91; author: Outline of Target Model of China's Economic Reform, 1988; author, editor The Distribution of Income in China, 1993, 99. Recipient Sun Yefang Prizes of Econs. Com. of Sun Yefang Prize, Beijing, 1984, 86, 94; rsch. grantee Ford Found., N.Y.C., 1988, 94, St. Antony's Coll Oxford U., 1983. Mem. Chinese Assn. Hong Kong and Macau Econ. Studies (v.p. 1990-93, hon. cons. 1993—), Chinese Assn. Market Econ. Studies (mem. coun. 1993—), China Devel. Inst. (mem. coun. 1989—), Chinese Assn. Comparative Econ. Studies (v.p. 1986—). Avocations: swimming, gardening. Home: 1 Chang yun gong, Zizhuyan Beijing 100044 China Office: Chinese Acad Social Scis Inst Econs 2 Yuetan Beixiaojie Beijing 100836 China E-mail: rwzhao@public.bta.net.cn.

ZHAO, SEAN ZIXIAN, pharmaceutical company executive; b. Baichen, Jilin, China, Sept. 2, 1955; s. Dejiang and Guiying (Li) Z.; m. Diana S. Zhu, Aug. 14, 1995; children: Amanda S., Oliva S. MD, Beijing Med. U., 1982; MS, U. Hawaii, 1987, PhD, 1992. Sr. rschr. Nova Rsch. Co., Bethesda, Md., 1992—95; assoc. dir. health outcomes G.D. Searle & Co., Skokie, Ill., 1995—98; dir. of epidemiology Pharmacia Corp., Peapack, NJ, 1998—2001, dir. global health outcomes, 2001—. Office: Pharmacia Corp N 100 Rte 206 Peapack NJ 07977 E-mail: sean.z.zhao@pharmacia.com.

ZHAO, WEI, computer science educator, researcher; b. Xian, Shaanxi, China, Sept. 12, 1953; came to U.S., 1982; s. Yousheng Zhao and Zuming Wu; m. Li Chen, Aug. 8, 1980; children: Dacheng, Derek. Diploma, Shaanxi Normal U., 1977; MS, U. Mass., 1983, PhD, 1986. Lectr. Shaanxi Normal U., 1977-82; asst. prof. Amherst (Mass.) Coll., 1986-88; sr. lectr. Adelaide (Australia) U., 1988-90; assoc. prof. dept. computer sci. Tex. A&M U. College Station, 1990-96, prof., 1996—, dept. head, 1997—. Adv. panelist NSF, Washington, 1993—; spkr. in field. Contbr. articles to profl. jours.; editor Jour. Computer Systems and Software, 1992—; patentee in field. Fellow Tex. Engring. Ext. Svc., College Sta. Mem. IEEE (editor IEEE Transactions on Computers 1992-96, Best Paper awards computer soc. 1992, 98). Office: Tex A&M U Dept Computer Sci College Station TX 77843-0001

ZHAO, ZHEN, music educator; b. Tian Jin, China, Aug. 27, 1947; arrived in U.S., 1985; parents Tian Qi Zhao and Pei Ying Gong; m. Yang Zhong Zhang, Apr. 29, 1976; 1 child William Wen Wei Zhang. MusB, U. Tex., 1991, MusM, 1994. Pvt. piano tchr., Austin, Tex., 1995—. Contbr. articles to profl. jours. Mem.: Nat. Guild Piano Tchrs., Music Tchrs. Nat. Assn., Tex. Music Tchrs. Assn., Austin Dist. Music Tchrs. Assn. Avocations: ping pong, tai chi, travel, photography.

ZHARIKOV, ALEXANDER NIKOLAEVICH, trade union federation executive; b. Michailov, Rjazan, Russia, Jan. 2, 1945; s. Nikolaj Philippovich and Claudia Egorovna (Gorodnicheva) Z.; m. Eva Svachova; children: Michail, Anette. Student, Shipbldg. Inst., Leningrad, Russia, 1969. Sec. Student Orgn. Shipbldg. Inst., Leningrad, 1967-70; dir. student dept. Leningrad City Youth Orgn., 1970-71, sec., 1971-74; vice chmn. Com. Youth Orgns. USSR, Moscow, 1974-76; chmn. Student Coun. USSR, 1976-78; v.p. Internat. Union Students, Prague, Czechoslovakia, 1978-84; officer Internat. Dept. Ctrl. Com. CPSU, Moscow, 1984-88; dir. internat. dept All Union Ctrl. Coun. Trade Unions, 1988-90; gen. sec. World Fedn. Trade Unions, Prague, 1990—. Co-author: International Union of Students, 1978. Mem. City Com. Leningrad Youth Orgn., 1970-71, sec., 1971-74; mem. Ctrl. Com. Youth Orgn. USSR, Moscow, 1978-84. Capt. Russian mil., 1962-66. Office: Branická 112 14000 Prague 4 Czech Republic E-mail: wftu@telecom.cz., wftu@login.cz.

ZHDANKIN, VIKTOR VLADIMIROVICH, chemistry educator; b. Sverdlovsk, Russia, June 6, 1956; came to U.S., 1990; s. Vladimir M. and Rimma V. (Lukanina) Z.; m. Olga Y. Geraskina, Sept. 20, 1980; children: Vasili V., Vladimir V. BS, MS, Moscow State U., 1978, PhD, 1981, DSc, 1987. Rsch. fellow Moscow State U., 1982-86; vis. scientist U. Minn., Duluth, 1987-88; rsch. prof. Moscow State U., 1988-89; instr., sr. rsch. assoc. U. Utah, Salt Lake City, 1990-93; asst. prof. U. Minn., Duluth, 1993-96, assoc. prof., 1996-99, prof., 1999—. Panel mem. Internat. Sci. Found., Washington, 1993-95. Contbr. articles to profl. jours.; mem. editl. bd. Russian Jour. Organic Chemistry, 1989-93, Jour. Mendeleev Chem. Soc., 1989-95, Mendeleev Comm., 1998—. Grantee, Rsch. Corp., 1993—96, Petroleum Rsch. Fund/Am. Chem. Soc., 1994—96, NSF, 1995—, Civilian R&D Found., 2000—02, NIH, 2002—. Mem. Am. Chem. Soc., Coun. Undergrad. Rsch., Sigma Xi. Achievements include discovery of new phenomena in physical-organic chemistry; preparation of new iodine reagents; development of organic chemistry of xenon. Avocations: traveling, skiing, reading fiction. Office: U Minn Dept Chemistry 10 University Dr Duluth MN 55812-2403 E-mail: vzhdanki@d.umn.edu.

ZHDANOV, MICHAEL SEMENOVICH, geologist, educator; b. Moscow, Oct. 2, 1946; m. Olga Nikolaevna Zhdanov; children: Elena. MSc in Geophysics, Moscow State Oil and Gas U., 1968; MSc in Math., Moscow State U., 1969, PhD in Physics and Math., 1970, D of Scis., 1978. From asst. to full prof. dept. geophysics Moscow Gubkin State U. of Oil and Gas, 1970—92; head of dept., dep. dir. Inst. Terrestrial Magnetism, Ionosphere and Radio Wave Propagation USSR Acad. Scis., 1978—90; dir. Inst. Geoelectromagnetic Rsch. Russian Acad. Scis., 1991—92; prof. dept. geology and geophysics U. Utah., Salt Lake City, 1993—. Lansdown vis. prof. U. Victoria, B.C., Canada, 1991; Gauss prof. Gettingen Acad. Scis., Gettingen, Germany; vis. prof. Colo. Sch. Mines, Golden. Author: Advanced Theory of Deep Geomagnetic Sounding, 1984, Integral Transforms in Geophysics, 1988, The Geoelectrical Methods in Geophysical Exploration, 1994, Geophysical Inverse Theory and Regularization Problems, 2002; patentee in field. Named Hon. Prof., China Nat. Ctr. of Geol. Exploration Tech., 1997; recipient award for outstanding achievement in the devel. of sci. and tech., Russian Acad. Natural Scis., 2000. Fellow: Acad. Natural Scis. of Russia; mem.: Am. Geophys. Union, Soc. Exploration Geophysics. Office: U Utah 135 S 1460 E Rm 719 Salt Lake City UT 84112

ZHENG, DAWEI, process integration engineer, materials scientist; b. Xianyang, Shanxi, China, Apr. 25, 1970; s. Chengyuan Zheng and Yuying Yang. BS, Fudan U., Shanghai, China, 1990; MS, SUNY, Binghamton, 1995; PhD, UCLA, 1999. Postdoctoral fellow UCLA, 1999-2000; sr. process engr. Intel Corp., Santa Clara, Calif., 2000; prin. engr. Elotechnologies, Inc., Torrance, 2000-2001; sr. process integration engr., materials scientist Lightcross Inc., Pasadena, 2001—. Referee: Applied Physics Letters, Jour. Applied Physics, IEEE Transactions on Components, Packaging and Mfg. Tech.; contbr. more than 30 articles to profl. jours. Recipient Best Paper award Motorola Corp. Mem. IEEE, AAAS, Materials Rsch. Soc. Achievements include patent for resolving stress distribution in patterned thin film for microelectronics applications; residual stress reduction through device processing on thin substrate of membrane properties; sensing and testing chip for monitoring and characterizations of wafer processing; microstress measurement machine; forming an optical mode transformer; method of forming an optical component with reduced stress. Avocations: Kung Fu, karaoke, dance, meditation. Office: Lightcross Inc 2630 Corporate Pl Monterey Park CA 91754 E-mail: dzheng@lightcross.com.

ZHENG, DEYI, epidemiologist; b. Tianjin, China, Jan. 31, 1965; came to U.S., 1991; MB, Shanghai Med. U., 1988; MS, SUNY, 1994; PhD, U. S.C., 1997. Epidemiologist, Dept. Health and Environ. Control, SC, 1996-97; rsch. instr. Med. U. of S.C., 1997—2002, asst. prof., 2002—. Office: 550 Med U SC Coll Medicine 135 Rutledge St 302E Charleston SC 29425-8903

ZHENG, LISA LIQING, computer consultant; b. China; came to U.S., 1990; d. Youzhong Zheng and Siuping Huang. BSEE, Huazhong U. Sci. and Tech., 1988; MSEE, Purdue U., 1992. Asst. engr. Inst. Electronics Chinese Acad. Scis., Beijing, 1988-90; electronics engr., sys. programmer Computer Graphics, Corp., Indpls., 1992-94; programmer Bertelsmann Music Group, Inc., 1994-96; computer cons. SEI Info. Tech., Chgo., 1996—. Avocations: traveling, philately, swimming, bicycling, cooking.

ZHENG, QI-HUANG, chemist, educator; b. Quanzhou, China, Sept. 30, 1964; came to U.S., 1994; s. Yinglin Zheng and Houqing Qiu; m. Yiming Yang, Apr. 2, 1988; 1 child, Xiazhe Zheng. BS, Xiamen (China) U., 1984, MS, 1987; PhD, Zhongshan U., Guangzhou, China, 1990. Asst. prof. Zhongshan U., 1990-92, assoc. prof., 1992-97; rsch. assoc. Ind. U., Indpls., 1997-99, asst. scientist, 1999-2000, asst. prof., 2001—. Vis. scholar U. Chgo., 1994; v.p. Conland Group Co., Zhaoqing, China, 1990-91. Author: Encyclopedia of the Science and Technology Reviews, 1993; contbr. articles to profl. jours. Recipient China Young Chemist prize Chinese Chem. Soc., 1991, Outstanding Tchr. award Guangdong Province, China, 1992, Outstanding Youth award Haizhu Dist., China, 1993; grantee Susan G. Komen Breast Cancer Found., 2000, Nat. Natural Sci. Found. China, 1993. Mem. Am. Chem. Soc. Office: Ind U Dept Radiology 975 W Walnut St Rm 028C Indianapolis IN 46202-5121 E-mail: gzheng@iupui.edu.

ZHENG, ROBERT ZHIWEI, educational technology educator; b. Shanghai, China, May 4, 1958; came to U.S., 1994; s. Zushen Zheng and Yuefeng You; m. Shaowen Hu, May 10, 1992; 1 child, Joanna. BA, Shanghai Tchrs. U., China, 1983; MA, Fudan U., Shanghai, China, 1989; EdD, Baylor U., 1998. Tchr. Shanghai Jian-she H.S., China, 1983—86; lectr. Fudan U., Shanghai, 1989—94; grad. asst. Baylor U., Waco, Tex., 1994—98; instrl. designer Vincennes U., Ind., 1999; asst. prof. edn. in edn1. tech. Marian Coll., Fond du Lac, Wis., 1999—2002; asst. prof. edn. Temple U., Phila., 2002—. Tech. coord. Marian-Chegwin Ptnr. Program, Fond du Lac, 1999-2002. Grantee, U.S. Dept. Edn., 2001—. Mem. Internat. Soc. Tech. Edn., Assn. Ednl. Comm. & Tech., Phi Delta Kappa. Baptist. Avocations: fishing, photography, travelling, reading. Office: Marian Coll 45 S National Ave Fond Du Lac WI 54935 E-mail: rzheng@mariancollege.edu.

ZHENG, SHEN, statistician, consultant; b. Fuzhou, Fujian, China, Nov. 1, 1962; m. Li Li; children: Annie. BS in Math., Xiamen U., Xiamen, Fujian, China, 1983; MS in Math., Xiamen U., Xiamen, Fujian, CHina, 1990; PhD in Stats., U. of Ga., 1996; MS in Computer Sci., So. Poly. State U., 2002. Statis. project mgr. Equifax Decision Solution Dept., Atlanta, 1997—2000, statis. R&D mgr., 2000—. Statis. cons. Statis. Consulting Ctr., Athens, 1994—96. Mem.: Am. Statistician Assn. (Best Student Paper award S.E. Regional Rsch. Conf. 1995). Office: Decision Solution Department Equifax 1525 Windward Concourse Alpharetta GA 30005 Personal E-mail: sz96@yahoo.com.

ZHENG, SHUMING, chemical engineer, educator; b. Nanjing, China; d. Hua-feng Zheng and Wenzhen Jiang; m. Wenjie Zhao, Dec. 11, 1974; 1 child Kevin Zhao. BSChE, Nanjing U. Chem. Tech., 1982; PhD of Chem. Engring., Ill. Inst. Tech., 1989; MPA, Harvard U., 2000. Postdoctoral rsch. assoc. Ill. Inst. Tech., Chgo., 1990—92; vis. prof. U. Ill., 1992—93; prof. Chgo. City Coll., 1994—97, Hampton (Va.) U., 1997—99; prof. engr. Chgo. State U., 2000—. Adj. prof. pharmaceutics U. Ill., Chgo., 1993—97; vis. prof. Med. Sch. Northwestern U., Evanston, Ill., 1995. Author (with R.L. Beissinger, D.T. Wasan, L.R. Sehgal): Emulsions, Foams, and Thin Films, 2000; author: (with R.L. Beissinger, F.J. Martin) Stealth Liposomes, 1995; contbr. Recipient Outstanding Scientist in 20th Century award, 2000. Mem.: Am. Biomed. Engring. Soc., Am. Chem. Soc., Am. Chem. Engring. Inst., Chgo. AIDS Found., Chgo. Harvard Club. Achievements include patents for in field. Home: 5201 W 121st Pl Alsip IL 60803-3172

ZHENG, YUNHAN, research scientist; b. Pujian, Zhoujiang, China, June 19, 1963; s. Keji Zheng and Xianyu Chao; m. Yingxin Liu; children: Chen, Jenny. PhD, U. Wis., Milw., 2000. Sr. rsch. engr. Hohai U., Nanjing, China, 1985—95; vis. scholar Katholieke U. Leuven, Belgium, 1995—96; sr. mech. and thermal engr. 3D Systems, Austin, Tex., 2000—. Mem.: AAAS, ASME (assoc.), Sigma Xi. Home: 8312 Fathom Cir #215 Austin TX 78750 Office: 3D Systems Bldg 2 1611 Headway Cir Austin TX 78754 Home Fax: 512-339-0634; Office Fax: 512-339-0634. Personal E-mail: yunhanz@yahoo.com. Business E-Mail: zhengy@3dsystems.com.

ZHENG, ZHIPING, chemistry educator; b. Jiangle, Fujian, China, July 1, 1967; s. Shuimu Zheng and Zhaodi Yang; m. Lin Deng, Aug. 10, 1990; 1 child, Margaret. BS, Beijing U., 1987, MS, 1990; PhD, UCLA, 1995. Asst. prof. U. Ariz., Tucson, 1997—. Recipient Rsch. Innovation award Rsch. Corp., Tucson, 1998; collaborative rsch./tchg. fellow China Bridge Internat., N.Am., 1999. Office: Dept Chemistry U Ariz 1306 E University Tucson AZ 85721-0001

ZHENG, ZIJIAN, data mining engineer; b. Juye, Shandong, China, May 24, 1964; s. Dahe Zheng and Chunqin Xie; m. Linhui Jia, Mar. 29, 1963; 1 child, Joy Shijie Zheng. B Engring. in Computer Sci./Engring., Beijing U. of Aeronautics and, Astronautics, 1984, M Engring. in Computer Sci., 1987; PhD in Computer Sci., U. Sydney, Australia, 1996. Asst. prof. Beijing U. of Aeronautics/Astronautics, 1987-88, lectr., 1989-91; sr. rsch. fellow Deakin U., Geelong, Victoria, Australia, 1996-99; sr. data mining engr. Blue Martini Software, Inc., San Mateo, Calif., 1999—. Mem. ACM, AAAI, IEEE. Office: Blue Martini Software Inc 2600 Campus Dr San Mateo CA 94403 E-mail: zijian@acm.org.

ZHENG, ZUOXING, food microbiologist; b. Linyi, Shandong, China, Sept. 19, 1965; s. Lianyin and Chongmei (Zhu) Z.; m. Qing Lu, Apr. 28, 1995. BS, Shandong Inst. Light Industry, China, 1985; MS, Tianjin Inst. Light Industry, China, 1988; PhD, U. Mass., 1999. Asst. prof. Tsinghua U., Beijing, 1988-95; rsch. asst. U. Mass., Amherst, 1995-99, tchg. asst., 1997-99; rsch. scientist to Kraft Foods Inc., Glenview, Ill., 1999—. Patentee in field; contbr. articles to profl. jours. Recipient Grad. Rsch. Paper award Inst. Food Technologists, Orlando, Fla., 1997, Atlanta, 1998, Chgo., 1999, fellowship, Chgo., 1998-99, UNESCO, Japan, 1992. Mem. Inst. Food Technologists, Am. Dairy Sci. Assn., Am. Soc. Microbiology, Soc. for Indsl. Microbiology, Phi Kappa Phi, Sigma Xi, Phi Tau Sigma. Office: Kraft Foods Inc R&D 801 Waukegan Rd Glenview IL 60025-4312 E-mail: zzheng@kraft.com.

ZHEUTLIN, DALE, sculptor, educator; b. Newark, July 27, 1948; BFA, R.I. Sch. Design, 1970; MFA, Columbia U., 1972. Group exhbns. include Gallery at Hastings-on-Hudson, N.Y., 1980, Craftsman's Gallery, Scarsdale, N.Y., 1980, 83, Thorpe Intermedia Gallery, Sparkhill, N.Y., 1980, Foundations Gallery, N.Y.C., 1981, Meyer, Breier, Weiss Gallery, San Francisco, 1981, Nat. Arts Club, N.Y.C., 1981, Ten Downtown, N.Y.C., 1981, Hudson River Mus., Yonkers, N.Y., 1981, Holsten Gallery, Palm Beach, Fla., 1982, Robertson Ctr. for Arts and Scis., Binghamton, N.Y., 1982, Cooper/Lynn Gallery, N.Y.C., 1982, Bronx Mus. Arts, N.Y., 1982, Departure Gallery, N.Y.C., 1983, Aldrich Mus., Riegefield, Conn., 1983, Plum Gallery, Kensington, Md., 1984, Newport (R.I.) Art Mus., 1984, Renwick Gallery, Washington, 1984, Ariel Gallery, N.Y.C., 1985, Artquest 1985 L.A., 1985, Greenwich House, N.Y.C., 1985, Henry St. Settlement, N.Y.C., 1986, Hudson River Mus., Yonkers, N.Y., 1986, Palo Alto (Calif.) Cultural Ctr., 1986, Artisan Space, N.Y.C., 1987, Boody Fine Art, St. Louis, 1987, Wita Gardiner Gallery, San Diego, 1987, Joan Robey Gallery, Denver, 1987, Works Gallery, N.Y.C., 1988, Maple Hill Gallery, Portland, Maine, 1988, Castle Mus. Vallauris, France, 1988, Robert Martin Gallery, White Plains, N.Y., 1989, Moviehouse Studio Gallery, Millerton, N.Y., 1989, Katonah (N.Y.) Mus., 1989, Nicolaysen Art Mus., Casper, Wyo., 1989, Tajimi City Spl. Exhbn. Hall, Mino, Japan, 1989, Internat. Ceramics Mus., Faenza, Italy, 1989, San Angelo (Tex.) Mus. Art, 1990, Hudson River Mus., 1991, Wheeler Seidel Gallery, N.Y.C., 1992, Sotheby's, N.Y.C., 1993, Am. Craft Mus., N.Y.C., 1993, Internat. Ceramics Mus., Faenza, Italy, 1995; represented in permanent collections Aetna, Hartford, Conn., Apple Computer, Inc., Norwalk, Conn., Chase Manhattan Bank, N.Y.C., Deloitte and Touche, Wilton, Conn., ITT, Hartford, Peat, Marwick and Main, Indpls., British Airways, IBM, Citibank Tower, others. Recipient Sculpture award Hudson River Mus., Pauline Law prize Nat. Assn. Women Artists.

ZHIGLEVICH, EUGENIA, writer, actress; b. Riga, Latvia, May 7, 1921; naturalized U.S. citizen, 1958; d. Vladimir Zhiglevich and Gertrud (Kupiecki) Melli; m. Boris Filipoff (wid.); children from previous marriages: Anthony Serge Beliajeff, Peter Eugene Sokowski. BA summa cum laude, U. Latvia, 1944. Actress, writer Latvian Drama Ensemble, Riga, 1941-44; actress, reviewer of arts and lit. Radio Riga, 1941-44; actress, translator, writer Voice of Am. (Russian Divsn.), N.Y.C., Washington, 1953-64; co-dir., editor, writer Inter-Lang. Literary Assocs., Washington, 1964-70; regular feature contbr. Russ. émigré weekly "Russkaya Mysl", Paris, 1970-76; freelance writer, 1970—; regular contbr. Russian Lit. Jour. "Poberezhye", Phila., 1992—. Translator/editor Atomic Energy Commn., State Dept., USIA, Washington, 1970-87; translator Russian, English, German and Latvian langs. Editor: Rozanov, Zamyatin, Kandinsky, S. Freud, Zoshchenko, Zabolotsky, Annenkov, Akhmatova, Shkapskaya, Blok, others, 1965-80, F. Stepun's Encounters and Reflections, 1992, others; co-editor: Pasternak, Mandelshtam, Akhmatova, Zamyatin (collective works), Klyuyev, Frank, Tertz, others, 1964-88; graphic artist: (book covers) Rozanov, Zamyatin, Zabolotsky, Filippov, Kandinsky, Freud, Shkapskaya, Blok, 1966-80; translator: T.S. Eliot's Notes Towards the Definition of Culture, 1968 (1st translation into Russian); contbr. articles to profl. jours.; participant drama recitals at Russian Culture Festivals, Riga, varied dramatic arts background in Europe, pre-1950s; regular recitals of Russian prose and poetry to keep Russian culture alive in exile, Washington, 1954—, other major U.S. cities; author: script Journey into the Past-Williamsburg, Va., 1964-65 (Best in Am. Govt. Broadcasting); co-author, producer cassettes on Russian lit. and ideology, 1992; author: Memoirs, 1995, 2d edit., 1997 (Russian Am. prize 2001). Mem. Rep. Senatorial Inner Cir., 1998. Recipient Rep. Senatorial Medal of Freedom, 1999. Mem. Washington Ind. Writers Assn. Avocations: music, film, photography.

ZHITNIK, ALEXEI, professional hockey player; b. Kiev, Russia, Oct. 10, 1972; m. Luda Zhitnik. Defense L.A. Hockey Team, Buffalo Sabres, 1995—. Defense Team russia, World Championships in Austria, 1996, world Cup tournament, 1996, World Championships, Italy, 1993-94; rep. the gold medal Unified Team, 1992 Winter Olympics, Albertville, France. Office: Buffalo Sabres Marine Midland Arena One Seymour H Knox III Plz Buffalo NY 14203*

ZHONG, DALONG, materials scientist, consultant; b. Anren, Hunan, China, Nov. 28, 1970; s. Dashan Zhong; m. Xiaolan Zhang, Nov. 6, 1996. BS in Metallurgy, Ctrl. South U. Tech., Changsha, Hunan, China, 1993, MS in Metallurgy, 1996; PhD in Metallurgy, Colo. Sch. Mines, 2001. Tchg./rsch. asst. Colo. Sch. Mines, Golden, 1997—2001, lab mgr. advanced coatings & surface engring. lab., 1999—, rsch. assoc., 2001—. Pvt. cons. Protonetics Internat. Inc., Golden, COLO., 2001—; referee Thin Solid Films, 2001—, Tribology Internat., 2001—, Jour. Materials Synthesis and Processing, 2001—, Jour. Applied Physics, 2002—, Surface & Coating Tech., 2002—, Acta Materialia, 2002—; presentor at confs. Contbr. articles. Fellow Zhao Tiancong fellow, Ctrl. South U. Tech., 1994, Li Found. fellow, Colo. Sch. Mines, 1997—2000. Mem.: Am. Vacuum Soc., Materials Rsch. Soc., The Minerals, Metals & Materials Soc. Office: Colorado Sch Mines 1500 Illinois St Golden CO 80401 Office Fax: 303-273-3057. Business E-Mail: dazhong@mines.edu.

ZHONG, DAWN HE, chemist; b. Shanghai, China, Aug. 17, 1951; came to the U.S., 1988; d. Qi Wei He and Yu Qin Shi; m. Kai Zhong, Jan. 20, 1987. BS, East China U. Chem. Tech., Shanghai, 1982; MS, Fla. Atlantic U., 1992. Rsch. engr. Shanghai Fiber Reinforced Plastics Rsch. Inst., 1982-88; sr. analytical chemist Motorola, Inc., Boynton Beach, Fla., 1993-2001; sr. engr. Tyco Sensormatic, Boca Raton, 2001—. Contbr. articles to profl. jours. Mem. Am. Chem. Soc., Chinese Assn. Sci., Econs. and Culture South Fla. Achievements include patent in field. Avocations: travel, Chinese cooking, singing, dancing. Office: Sensormatic 6600 Congress Ave Boca Raton FL 33431

ZHONG, MEI, music educator; b. Shanghai, China, Nov. 9, 1954; came to U.S., 1990; d. Xiuming Wang and Huiping Zhong; m. Xiaoge Chu, July 27, 1983; 1 child, Bingbing. BA, Hunan Tchrs. U., China, 1981; Diploma, Shanghai CoOnservatory Music, China, 1986; MFA, UCLA, 1994; DMusical Arts, U. Ill., 1999. Asst. prof. dept. music Hunan Tchrs. U., 1982-97, Jiangshi, dept. music, 1987-90; asst. prof. dept. music Idaho State U., Pocatello, 1998—. Vis. prof. Wuhan (China) Conservatory of Music, 1999—, Hunan Tchrs. U., 1999—, Yueyang Tchrs. U., 1999—. Contbr. articles to ency. and profl. jours. Winner Idaho DIst. Nat. Vocal Competition, Am. Mothers Inc., 1999; Mimi Alpert Feldman scholar, 1993, 94; Atwater Kent scholar, 1993, 94; Phi Bet Kappa scholar, 1993. Mem. Coll. Music Soc., U. Ill. Alumni Assn., Phi Kappa Phi. Office: Idaho State U Dept Music PO Box 8099 Pocatello ID 83209-0001

ZHONG, MIN, chemist; b. Xinfeng, Jiangxi, China, Feb. 28, 1970; s. Chengyao Zhong and Fengju Xiao; m. Liping Guo, Mar. 25, 1997. BS, Sichuan U., Chengdu, China, 1991; MS, East China Normal U., Shanghai, 1994; PhD, Shanghai Inst. Organic Chemistry, Chinese Acad. Scis., 1997. Asst. rsch. prof. Shanghai Inst. Organic Chemistry, Chinese Acad. Scis., 1997-98; postdoctoral fellow Andrew S. Kende group dept. chemistry U. Rochester, N.Y., 1998-99; postdoctoral fellow James P. Collman group dept. chemistry Stanford (Calif.) U., 1999-2001; scientist Sunesis Pharms., Inc., South San Francisco, Calif., 2001—. Presdl. scholar Chinese Acad. Scis., 1997. Mem. AAAS, Am. Chem. Soc. Office: Sunesis Pharms Inc 341 Oyster Point Blvd South San Francisco CA 94080 Fax: (650) 266-3501. E-mail: mzhong@sunesis.com.

ZHONG, YUANZHEN, research chemist; b. Guangzhou, China, May 2, 1947; came to U.S., 1984; s. Yuanfan and Sumei (Zhang) Z.; m. Susan Siying Chen, Nov. 2, 1972; children: Xin, Xun. BS, Jinan U., Guangzhou, China, 1970; MS, Zhongshan U., 1984; PhD, Rutgers U., 1990; MBA, Fairleigh Dickinson U., 2001. Rsch. staff Rsch. Inst., Xin-Yi County, China, 1970-73, 75-78; rsch. asst. Zhongshan U., Guangzhou, 1979-82; rsch. lectr. So. China Normal U., 1982-84; rsch. asst. Rutgers U., New Brunswick, N.J., 1984-90; rsch. chemist Internat. Specialty Products, Wayne, 1990-92, sr. rsch. chemist, 1992-96, rsch. scientist, 1996-2000; sr. chemist L'Oreal USA, Clark, 2001—. Lectr. in field. Contbr. numerous articles to profl. jours.; patentee (8) in field, Mem. Am. Chem. Soc., Soc. Cos. Chem. Avocations: reading, running, collecting stamps. Office: L'Oreal USA 159 Terminal Ave Clark NJ 07066-1386 E-mail: yuanzhen_zhong@yahoo.com.

ZHOU, BING, process scientist; b. Shanghai, China, Dec. 11, 1961; s. Helin and Juxian (Shi) Z.; m. Ruyi Yan; children: Daoshun, Zhou. BSc, Fudan U., China, 1983, MSc, 1988; PhD, Macquarie U., Australia, 1997. Cert. engr. Asst. engr. Shanghai Med. Equipment Factory, China, 1983-85; rschr. Shanghai Inst. Tech. Physics, 1988-92; sr. process scientist Thin Film Device Inc., Anaheim, Calif., 1997-2000; sr. process engr. Internat. Rectifier, El Segundo, 2000—. Co-author: GaN and Related Materials, 1997. Mem. The Internat. Soc. for Optical Engring. Home: 2404 Nutwood Ave Apt H-24 Fullerton CA 92831-3162 Office: Internat Rectifier 233 Kansas St El Segundo CA 90245 E-mail: bingzhou@netzero.net.

ZHOU, BING-NAN, chemist, educator; b. Shanghai, China, Jan. 31, 1934; came to U.S., 1993; m. Xiu-Ying Chen, Feb. 11, 1958; children: Cindy Qin, Hong. BS, Shanghai Med. U., 1954; PhD, Shanghai Inst. Materia Medica, 1962. Vis. scientist Czechoslovak Acad. Scis., Prague, 1962-64; postdoctoral fellow U. Wis., Madison, 1981-83; prof. Shanghai Inst. Materia Medica, 1988—. Reviewer The Sci. Found. for New Drug Rsch. in China, Beijing, 1987-92, NSF of China, Beijing, 1988-94; vis. prof. chemistry U. B.C., Vancouver, Can., 1986, U. Ill., Chgo., 1987-94; dir. dept. phytochemistry Nat. Lab. Drug Rsch., Shanghai, 1989-94; sr. rsch. scientist dept. chemistry Va. Tech., 1994—. Author: Extraction and Separation of Active Compounds from

Chinese Herbs, 2d edit., 1981, Bioactive Natural Products, 1981, The Chemistry of Natural Products, 1993, The Strategies for Development of Natural Organic Chemistry in China, 1995; contbr. over 150 articles to profl. jours. Home: 211 A Landsdowne St Blacksburg VA 24060-5815 Office: Dept Chemistry Va Tech Blacksburg VA 24061-0212 E-mail: bzhou@vt.edu.

ZHOU, HONGHUI, clinical pharmacokineticist; b. Guangzhou, Guangdong, China, Apr. 27, 1967; came to U.S., 1991; s. Rui Li and Liling Zhou; m. Judy Zijie Zhuang, June 11, 1995; children: Rebecca, Emily. BS, China Pharm. U., 1988; PhD, U. Iowa, 1995. Bd. cert. Am. Bd. Clin. Pharmacology. Rsch. pharmacist Guangzhou Inst. Pharm. Rsch., 1988-91; rsch. asst. U. Iowa, Iowa City, 1991-95; postdoctoral fellow Janssen Pharm. and Rsch. Found., Titusville, N.J., 1995-96, scientist, 1996-98; clin. pharmacokineticist Novartis Pharma Co., East Hanover, N.J., 1998-2000; mgr. human pharmacokinetics Janssen Johnson & Johnson, Titusville, 2000—02; assoc. dir. clin. pharmacokinetics Wyeth, Collegeville, Pa., 2002—. Mem. editl. bd. Jour. Clin. Pharmacology. Fellow Am. Coll. Clin. Pharmacology; mem. Am. Assn. Pharm. Scientists, Am. Soc. Clin. Pharmacology and Therapeutics. Avocations: travel, photography, music, tennis, reading. Home: 128 BayHill Dr Blue Bell PA 19422 Office: Wyeth 500 Arcola Rd Collegeville PA 19426 E-mail: zhouhz@wyeth.com.

ZHOU, HUANCHUN, chemist, administrator; b. Shanghai, Oct. 1, 1939; came to U.S., 1985; s. Qingyun and Wanxian (Hu) Z.; m. Qingliang Li, Sept. 5, 1967; 1 child, Fugang. BS equivalent, Fudan U., China, 1962; MS, Shanghai U. Tech., China, 1981; PhD equivalent, U. Fla., 1990. Engr. Wuxi Oil Pump Factory, Jiangsu, China, 1962-67, laborer, analytical technician, 1968-76; faculty Shanghai U. Tech., 1982-84; rschr. dept. chemistry U. Fla., Gainesville, 1985-91; chemist Fla. Dept. Agr., 1991—. Chem. lab. chief Wuxi Oil Pump Factory, 1963-66; chmn. sect. chem. analysis Wuxi Sci-Tech. Assn., 1963-66; lectr. to 201st Am. Chem. Soc. Meeting, 1991. Corr. editor: Jour. Chem. Analysis and Phys. Test, 1964-66; contbr. articles to profl. jours. Co-grantee Office of Naval Rsch., 1991. Achievements include research in determination of phosphorus together with other 6 elements in chrome steel in one solution by using a nonoxidizing acid first in world; searched out of the direct and quantitative relationship between solubility and charges and radii of ions first in world; promotion of simple natural sieve method to prove infinity of prime twins and derivation of simple and most accurate formula in world to estimate number of prime twins; discovery of relationship between phase graphs and differential thermal analysis curves; co-developer chemical polymerization of polyaniline and polypyrrole on Langmuir-Blodgett trough; discovery of method to monitor polymerizations by Langmuir-Blodgett computerized techniques; created a breakthrough software program used to compute the octane number for gasoline using GC data. E-mail: zhouh@doacs.state.fl.us.

ZHOU, JING, finance educator; b. Beijing; m. Xiaohui Li. BS, Peking U., 1987, Master's degree, 1990; PhD U. Ill., 1996. Asst. prof. mgmt. Tex. A&M U., College Station, 1996—2002, assoc. prof. mgmt., 2002—. Mem. editl. bd.: Jour. Mgmt., 2001—; contbr. Fellow Ford Rsch. fellow, Ctr. for Human Resource Mgmt., Tex. A&M U., 2000; scholar Montagne-Ctr. for Tchg. Excellence scholar, Tex. A&M U., 2000. Mem.: APA, Acad. Internat. Bus. (chair microorganl. behavior and human resource mgmt. track 2002), Internat. Assn. Chinese Mgmt. Rsch. (founding mem.), Asia Acad. Mgmt. (founding mem.), Soc. for Indsl. and Orgnl. Psychology, Acad. Mgmt. Avocation: tennis. Office: Tex A&M U Dept Mgmt Lowry Mays Coll and Grad Sch Bus College Station TX 77843-4221 Office Fax: 979-845-9641. E-mail: jing-zhou@tamu.edu.

ZHOU, JINYUAN, physicist, educator; b. Quanzhou, Fujian, China; came to U.S., 1997; s. Gongdang Zhou and Xiao Hong; m. Lihuan Lu, Jan. 5, 1985; children: Tingting, Luwei, Luping. PhD, Wuhan (China) Inst. Physics, 1996; grad., Fujian U., China, 1983. Rschr. Wuhan Inst. Physics, Chinese Acad. Scis., 1985-96; post-doctoral staff Johns Hopkins U. Med. Sch., Balt., 1997-98, faculty, 1999—. Contbr. articles to profl. jours. Outstanding Presdl. scholar Chinese Acad. Scis., 1996. Mem. Internat. Soc. Magnetic Resonance in Medicine, Johns Hopkins Med. and Surg. Assn. E-mail: jzhou@mri.jhu.edu.

ZHOU, JUHUA, molecular biologist; b. Dongyang, Zhejiang, China, Apr. 21, 1963; arrived in U.S., 1994; s. Fude Zhou, Yujuan Shan; m. Yin Zhong; children: Beibei. MS, Zhejiang U., 1988; BS, Zhejiang U., Hangzhou, China, 1983; PhD, U.La., 1999. Assoc. prof. Zhejiang U. (Formerly Hangzhou University), Hangzhou, China, 1988—94; postdoctoral fellow ctr. for cell & gene therapy Baylor Coll. Medicine, Houston, 1999—. Vice dir. divsn. plant physiology Zhejiang U., Hangzhou, Zhejiang, China, 1988—94. Contbr. articles to profl. jours. Grantee, Zhejiang Provincial Natural Sci. Found., 1992, Chinese Natural Sci. Found., 1994. Mem.: AAAS, N.Y. Acad. Sci., Sigma Xi. Home: 5606 Bissonnet Street Apt 114 Houston TX 77081 Office: Baylor College of Medicine One Baylor Plaza N1120 Houston TX 77030 Office Fax: 7137981362. Personal E-mail: juhuaz@hotmail.com. Business E-Mail: jzhou@bcm.tmc.edu.

ZHOU, MIN, sociology educator, researcher; b. Zhongshan, Guangdong, China, July 14, 1956; arrived in U.S., 1984; s. Lei-Ming and Yao-ping (Yao) Z.; m. Sam Nan Guo, Oct. 1, 1982; 1 child, Philip Jia. BA in English, Zhongshan U., China, 1982; MA in Sociology, SUNY, Albany, 1985, PhD in Sociology, 1989. Lectr. Zhongshan U., Guangzhou, 1982-84; asst. prof. La. State U., Baton Rouge, 1990-94; prof. UCLA, 1994—. Spkr., presenter in field; reviewer Am. Jour. Sociology, Ethnic and Racial Studies, Internat. Migration Rev., Social Forces, Social Problems, Social Sci. Quar., Sociol. Quar., Rev. Religious Rsch., Jour. Am. Ethnic History, Sociol. Perspective, Sociol. Forum; cons. youth project Chinatown Hist. Mus., N.Y.C., 1994-95; cons. immigrant family exhibit Bklyn. Hist. Soc., N.Y.C., 1994-96; cultural advisor longitudinal immigration project Grad. Sch. Edn., Harvard U., 1997-99; cons., acad. advisor Sch. Chinese Lang. and Culture, Thousand Oaks, Calif., 1997-2000; expert reviewer Metropolis Expert Comm., Joint Ctr. Excellence for Rsch. on Immigration and Settlement (CERIS), Toronto, Can., 1999. Author: Chinatown: The Socioeconomic Potential of an Urban Enclave, 1992; co-author: Growing Up American: How Vietnamese Children Adapt to Life in the United States, 1998 (Thomas and Znaniecki award 1999, internat. migration sect. Am. Sociol. Assn. award 2000), Straddling Two Social Worlds, 2000; co-editor: Contemporary Asian America: A Multidisciplinary Reader, 2000; contbr. chpts. to books, articles to profl. jours.; cons. editor Am. Jour. Sociology, 2000—; mem. editl. bd. City and Cmty., 2000—. Recipient vis. scholarship Russell Sage Found., 1994-95, Dept. Edn., 2000-01, Nontenured Faculty award Phi Kappa Phi, 1993. Mem. Am. Sociol. Assn., Assn. Asian Am. Studies, So. Sociol. Soc., Population Assn. Am. Avocations: reading, jogging, traveling. Office: UCLA Dept Sociology 265 Haines Hall Box 951551 Los Angeles CA 90095 E-mail: mzhou@soc.ucla.edu.

ZHOU, MING DE, aeronautical scientist, educator; b. Zhejiang, China, June 26, 1937; s. Pin Xiang and Ang Din (Xia) Z.; m. Zhuang Yuhua, Aug. 12, 1936; children: Zhengyu, Yan Zhuang. BS, Beijing U. Aero. and Astron., 1962; MS, Northwestern U. Tech., 1967; PhD, Internat. Edn. Rsch. Found., 1992. Tchr. Harbin (China) U. Tech., 1962-64, 67-73; from lectr. to prof. Nanjing (China) U. Aeronautics and Astronautics, 1973-86, 86—; dean bd. postgrad. studies Nanjing (China) U. Aeros. and Astronautics, 1985-89; nationally qualified PhD advisor China, 1989—; rsch. scientist U. Ariz., Tucson, 1991-93, rsch. prof., 1993—. Vis. scholar Cambridge (Eng.) U., 1980—82; guest scientist Inst. Exptl. Fluid Mechanics, Göttingen, Germany, 1983—84, Göttingen, 1985, Göttingen, 87; sr. vis. scientist Tech. U., Berlin, 1988, Berlin, 90, Berlin, 99; rsch. assoc. U. So. Calif., L.A., 1989—90; adj. prof. Beijing U., 2001—; sr. rsch. scientist State Key Lab. for Studies of Turbulence and Complex Systems, China, 2001—. Author: (with others) Viscous Flows and Their Measurements, 1988, (with others) Introduction to Vorticity and Vortex Dynamics, 1992; mem. editl. com. Chinese Jour. Exptl. Mechanics, 1986-89; contbr. articles to profl. jours. including Jour. Fluid Mechanics, Physics of Fluids, Aero. Jour. U.K., Experiments in Fluids, AIAA Jour., Chinese Jour., Aeronautics. Co-recipient Nat. award Progress in Sci. and Tech. first class, Peoples Republic of China, 1985. Mem. AIAA (sr.), N.Y. Acad. Scis., Am. Phys. Soc., Chinese Soc. Aeronautics, Chinese Soc. Mechanics (mem. acad. group exptl. fluid mechanics 1986-89), Chinese Soc. Aerodynamic Rsch. (acad. group unsteady flow and vortex control 1985-89). Achievements include patent for techniques and device of artificial boundary layer transition. E-mail: zmd@u.arizona.edu.

ZHOU, PING, physical engineer; b. Beijing; came to U.S., 1985; 1 child, Jie Yang. BA, Beijing U. Chem. Tech., 1964; postgrad., U. Sci. & Tech., China, 1978, Beijing U., 1982. Asst. prof. SUNY, Albany, 1985-87; engr. Chinese Acad. Scis., Beijing, 1970-90; rsch. assoc. Stanford (Calif.) U., 1990—. Vis. porf. Stanford U., 1987-88. Mem. Am. Soc. Materials Internat., Materials Rsch. Soc., Am. Vacuum Soc., Am. Phys. Soc. Achievements include development of multilayer Ti-Cu thin films for gravity probe-B gyroscope housings, BSCCO thin films with Tc above 100K; development, manufacturing, and testing of the thin film coatings and the superconducting bearings for the accelerometer for the Satellite Test of Equivalence Principle (STEP) Project. Office: Stanford Univ Hansen Lab Stanford CA 94305 E-mail: ping@relgyro.Stanford.edu.

ZHOU, SOPHIA HUAI, biomedical engineer; b. Huaiyin, Jiangsu, China, Dec. 6, 1953; MS, Dalhousie U., Halifax, Can., 1987, PhD, 1991. Profl. engr., Nova Scotia, Mass. Rsch. assoc. U. Alta., Edmonton, Can., 1991-93, asst. prof. Can., 1993-94, St. Louis U., 1994-95; engring. scientist Hewlett-Packard Co., Andover, Mass., 1995-99, Agilent Techs. Inc., Andover, 1999—2001, Philips Med Sys., 2001—. Contbr. articles to profl. jours. Mem. N.Y. Acad. Sci., Soc. Women Engrs., Internat. Soc. Electrocardiology (Young Investigator's award 1993), Internat. Soc. Computerized Electrocardiology, Am. Heart Assn. Achievements include design and development of automated ECG interpretations. Office: Philips Med Sys 1201 N Rice Ave Oxnard CA 93030 E-mail: sophia.zhou@philips.com.

ZHOU, TAILI, metallurgist; b. Guangzhou, Guangdong, China, Mar. 29, 1937; came to U.S., 1985; s. Bocheng and Huaichen (Xie) Z.; m. Lina Qun Xie, Aug. 28, 1963; children: Enning, Enyu, Enhong. BS in Chemistry, Peking U., Beijing, 1958; PhD in Metallurgy, U. Leeds (Eng.), 1984. Rsch. asst., chemist Guangzhou Rsch. Inst. Chemistry, Chinese Acad. Sci., 1958-62, rsch. metallurg. engr. Changsha Rsch. Inst. Mining and Metallurgy, 1962-79; co-supr. grad. student program Changsha Rsch. Inst. Mining and Metallurgy, 1978-79; project mgr. Guangzhou Rsch. Inst. Non-ferrous Metals, 1980-81; postdoctoral rsch. assoc., rsch. chemist and metallurgist U. Idaho, Moscow, 1985-94, co-prin. investigator, 1990-94; R&D metallurgist The Shepherd Chem. Co., Cin., 1995—. Contbr. numerous articles to profl. jours., chpts. to books. Achievements include development of substituted amide and hydroxamic acid type extractants, and the relevant processes for recovery of rare and scarce metals from numerous soruces; invention substituted pyrazolyl pyridine chelaing extractant, techniques of selective extraction and separtion of cobalt and nickel; development of metal based specialty chemicals. Office: The Shepherd Chem Co 4900 Beech St Cincinnati OH 45212-2398 E-mail: tailizhou@yahoo.com.

ZHOU, WEI, research scientist; b. Qingdao, China, Mar. 12, 1965; BS, Geosci. U. China, Wuhan, 1984; MS, U. Alaska, 1997. Cert. profl. engr. Ministry Elec. Power and Industry China. Asst. engr. Mid-South Design Inst. for Hydroelec. Projects China, Changsha, Hunan, 1984-89, engr., vice head divsn. rock mechs. and found., 1989-94; rsch. asst. U. Alaska, Fairbanks, 1995-96, U. Mo., Rolla, 1997—. Geophys. Inst. travel grantee U. Alaska, 1996. Mem. Am. Geophys. Union, Assn. Engring. Geologists. Achievements include research on high-cut rock slope stability, research on slope stability analysis of creep zone, research on underground excavation monitoring, research on analysis on discontinuous rock. Avocations: cooking, sewing. Home: 243 Nagogami Ter Rolla MO 65401-2173 Office: U Mo Dept Geol Engring 129 McNutt Hl Rolla MO 65409-0001 E-mail: wzhou@umr.edu.

ZHOU, WEIDONG, electrical engineer; b. Jiangsu, China, Feb. 25, 1970; arrived in U.S., 1996; s. Dengguang Zhou and Fengzhu Li; m. Fang Lin, May 28, 1996; 1 child Allen Xu. MS, Tsinghua U., Beijing, 1996; PhD, U. Mich., 2001. Lead engr. Ciena, Lithicum, Md., 2001—. Mem.: IEEE (Grad. Student Fellowship award 2000). Office: Ciena 920 Elkridge Landing Rd Linthicum MD 21090

ZHOU, XIN (JOSEPH ZHOU), pathologist, medical scientist; b. Qingdao, Shandong, China, Sept. 20, 1963; came to U.S., 1988; m. Jian Wang, May 18, 1988; children: Jason K., Jaclyn W. MD, Beijing (China) Med. U., 1986. Diplomate Am. Bd. Pathology. Resident internal medicine China-Japan Friendship Hosp., Beijing, 1986—88; nephrology rsch. fellow U. So. Calif., LA, 1988—90, U. Calif., Irvine, 1990—91, asst. prof., 1991—95, pathology resident and fellow, 1995—98; asst. prof. U. Tex. Southwestern Med. Ctr., Dallas, 1998—2002, assoc. prof., 2002—. Dir. renal rsch. lab. U. Calif., Irvine, Calif., 1990—95; dir. divsn. renal pathology U. Tex. Southwestern Med. Ctr., 1998—. Contbr. chpts. to books and articles to profl. jours. Grantee NIH, 1999—. Mem.: Chinese Am. Soc. Nephrology (pres.-elect 2001—02, pres. 2002—), Internat. Acad. Pathology, Renal Pathology Soc., Coll. of Am. Pathologists (Tng. in Tech. award 1997), Am. Soc. Nephrology, Internat. Soc. Nephrology. Home: 6606 Brentfield Dr Dallas TX 75248-2249 Office: U Tex Southwestern Med Ctr Dept Pathology 5323 Harry Hines Blvd Dallas TX 75390-9073

ZHOU, YAN, chemist; b. Luobei, China, Jan. 23, 1963; came to U.S., 1989; d. Qingshun Zhou and Xi Chen; m. Tao Yuan, Nov. 11, 1987; 1 child, Karen. BS, Heilongjiang U., Harbin, China, 1983; MS, Ji Lin U., Changchun, China, 1986, Auburn U., 1993. Rsch. chemist Harbin Normal Univ., Harbin, China, 1986-89; grad. rsch. asst. Auburn (Ala.) U., 1990-93; prin. rsch. chemist Unilever Rsch. U.S., Edgewater, N.J., 1993—. Contbr. articles to profl. jours., patentee in field. Mem. Am. Chemical Soc. Home: 6 Crest Ter Montville NJ 07045-9608 Office: 45 River Rd Edgewater NJ 07020-1017

ZHOU, YUXIANG, physicist, researcher; b. Jiangsu, China, July 11, 1973; arrived in U.S., 2000; s. Guirong Zhou and Jianzhong Zhang; m. Lingyun Chen, Mar. 1, 1999. BSc in Physics, Nanjing U., 1994; MSc in Physics, S.E. U., China, 1997; PhD in Physics, Hong Kong Bapt. U., 2001. Vis. rsch. scholar Tex. Ctr. for Superconductivity U. Houston, 2000—01, postdoctoral rschr., 2001—. Contbr. articles to profl. jours. Avocations: travel, movies, tennis. Office: U Houston Houston TX 77004-0001

ZHOU, ZHIDE, civil engineer, researcher; b. Beijing, Oct. 20, 1933; s. Ruiting Zhou and Lianyun Wang; m. Wanzhi Feng, Jan. 22, 1963; 1 child, Zhixu. D Engring., Hokkaido U., Sapporo, Japan, 1989. Engr. China Inst. Water Resources and Hydropower Rsch., Beijing, 1958-70, 81-84, Bur. Water Resources, Dingxiang, China, 1971-76, Yellow River Conservancy Commn., Zhengzhou, China, 1977-80; sr. engr. Internat. Rsch. and Tng. Ctr. on Erosion and Sedimentation, Beijing, 1991-94, 95—, dep. sec. gen., 1991-94. Cons. Water and Power Devel. Agy., Lahore, Pakistan, 1991, 95; assoc. project mgr. Regional Tng. Program on Erosion and Sedimentation for Asia, Beijing, 1990-93. Author: Fluvial Processes, 1987 (Best Engring. Book award 1992), Estuarine Processes in China, 1994. Mem. Internat. Assn. Hydraulic Rsch., N.Y. Acad. Scis. Avocations: soccer, music, history, literature. Office: Internat Rsch & Tng Ctr 20 Chegongzhuang Xilu Beijing 100044 China E-mail: itrces@public.bta.net.cn.

ZHU, AI-LAN, opera singer; b. Nanjing, Jiang Su, Peoples Republic of China, Nov. 29, 1956; came to U.S., 1984; d. De-Chang Zhu and Shu-hua Tsao; m. Chai-Lun Yueh, Oct. 30, 1982. MusB, Cen. Conservatory Music, Beijing, 1977; Artist Diploma in Opera, Hartt Sch of Music, U. Hartford, 1986. Appeared in leading opera houses of N.Am.; leading soprano in Tex. Opera Theater, Houston, 1987, 88, Va. Opera Assn., Norfolk, 1987, Met. Opera, 1988, Opera Theater St. Louis, 1989, PepsiCo Summerfare and European tour, N.Y., 1989, Lyric Opera of Boston, 1990, Glyndebourne Opera Festival, 1990, 91, Lyric Opera of Kansas City, 1990, Caramoor Festival, N.Y., 1990, Chautauqua Opera and Orch., 1990, Opera Pacific, L.A., 1991, 92, Dayton, Ohio, 1991, Minn. Opera, 1992, Opera Co. Phila., 1992, Mich. Opera Theater, 1993, Austin Lyric Opera, 1993, 94-99, Scottish Opera, 1994, Conn. Opera, 1995, Atlanta Opera, 1995, Conn. Opera, 1995, 96, 98, Shanghai Symphony, 1996, San Antonio Symphony, 1997, San Diego Opera, 1997, Conn. Opera, 1998, 99, William Hall Master Chorals, L.A., 1998, Opera Caroline, 1999, Opera de Quebec, Chattanooga, 2000, Orlando, Fla., 2000, Opera Regina, Can., 2000, Vancouver Opera, 2000, Opera Toledo, Ohio, 2000, Austin, Tex., 2000, 01, Orlando, Fla., 2001, Conn. Opera, 2001, Vancouver Opera, 2001, Poughkeepsie, NY, 2002, Ariz. Opera, 2002, Montreal (Can.) Opera, 2002; European tour Pellèas et Mèlisande, 1992-93; concert singer Chautauqua (N.Y.) Instn., 1987, Liederkranz Found., N.Y.C., 1989; recital The Theatre Musical de Paris, Chatelet, 1991; concert tour with Sherrill Milnes, Beijing, China, 1993. Finalist Luciano Pavarotti internat. vocal competition, Opera Cos. Phila., 1985; recipient 1st prize Sigma Alpha Iota vocal competition, Chautauqua, N.Y., 1986, 5th prize Liederkranz Found. vocal competition, N.Y.C., 1989. Mem. Am. Guild Mus. Artists. Home: 28 Roma Dr Farmington CT 06032-2157 Office: John J Miller 889 9th Ave Ste 1 New York NY 10019-1781 E-mail: silenzal@aol.com.

ZHU, BO-QING, cardiovascular research specialist; b. Huhan, Hube, China, Feb. 24, 1941; came to U.S., 1986; s. Han-Chang and Zhi-wen (Chen) Z.; m. Jin-Zhen Qiu, Dec. 14, 1967; 1 child, Frank. MD, Shanghai (China) Med. Coll., 1963. Resident Hua Shan Hosp./Shanghai Med. U., 1963-80; attending physician Hua Shan Hosp., Shanghai, 1980-86; vis. prof. U. Calif., San Francisco, 1986-88, asst. rsch. cardiologist, 1988-90, rsch. assoc. specialist, 1990—. Contbr. articles to profl. jours. Fellow Am. Coll. Cardiology. E-mial. Office: U Calif San Francisco 505 Parnassus Ave San Francisco CA 94143-0124 E-mail: zhu@medicine.ucsf.edu.

ZHU, DONGMING, materials scientist; b. Hefei, Anhui, China, Dec. 2, 1962; s. ZhengSe Zhu and Jingjuan Xu; m. Huixiang Deng; children: Shirley. BS, Hefei U. of Tech., China, 1984, MS, 1988; PhD, U. of Minn., 1996. Sec. of rsch. inst. forecast & devel. Hefei U. Tech., Hefei, China, 1988—90, asst. prof., 1988—90; rsch. & tchg. asst. U. Minn., Mpls., 1990—96; sr. materials scientist OAI/NASA Glenn Rsch. Ctr., Cleve., 1996—. Contbr. articles to profl. jours. Bd. dir. Commonwealth Ter. Coop. U. Student Family Housing Sys. U. of Minn., Mpls., 1992—93. Mem.: ASM Internat., Am. Ceramic Soc. (chmn. nominating com. ceramic divsn. 2001, Best Paper award 2002). Home: 1915 Salem Parkway Westlake OH 44145 Office: NASA Glenn Research Center 21000 Brookpark Road Mail Stop 24 1 Cleveland OH 44135 Fax: 216-433-5544. Business E-Mail: Dongming.Zhu@grc.nasa.gov.

ZHU, HUA, biochemist, researcher; b. Xiaogan, Hubei, China, Nov. 5, 1965; came to U.S., 1994; d. Chaoqun Zhu and Yuanying Long; married, May 7, 1997; children: Jessica Xiaoman Yao, Stephanie Xiaoru Yao. BA in Agronomy, Hua Zhong Agrl. U., Wuhan, China, 1985; M in Botany, Northwestern Agrl. U., Yang Ling, China, 1991; PhD in Botany, Chinese Acad. Sci., Beijing, 1994; M in Biochemistry, U. Okla., 1997, PhD in Biochemistry, 2001. Rsch. asst. dept. botany and microbiology U. Okla., Norman, 1994-96, rsch. asst. dept. biochemistry and chemistry, 1996—2001; rsch. scientist Advanced Ctr. for Genome Tech., U. Okla., 2001—02; rsch. assoc. Civil Aerospace Med. Inst., FAA, Oklahoma City, 2002—. V.p. Soc. Chinese Scholar and Students of U. Okla., 1996-97. Mem. AAAS, Am. Chemistry Soc., Microscopy Soc. Am., Botanic Soc. China. Avocations: bedmington, swimming, travel, music, movies. Office: Toxicology Accident Lab CAMI AAM-610 Biochemistry 6500 S MacArthur Blvd Oklahoma City OK 73125 E-mail: zhuhua9863@yahoo.com.

ZHU, JIAN ZHONG, computational engineer; b. Zhengzhou, Henan, China, Oct. 25, 1955; arrived in U.S., 1991; s. Bo Zhu, Jingru Li; m. Song Yu, Aug. 17, 1997; 1 child Jiang Wei. BSc, Harbin Engring. U., China, 1978; MSc, Tianjin U., China, 1982; PhD, U. Coll. Swansea, Eng., 1987. Lectr. Harbin Engring. U., China, 1978—80, Tianjin U., China, 1983; rsch. asst. Univ. Coll. Swansea, 1986—87, sr. rsch. asst., 1987—91; sr. scientist UES-Software, Inc., Annapolis, Md., 1991—. Contbr. articles. Named one of Highly Cited Rschrs., ISI Thomson Scientific, 2000. Mem.: U.S. Assn. for Computational Mechanics, Internat. Assn. for Computational Mechanics, ASME. Mailing: UES-Software Inc 175 Admiral Cochrane Dr #103 Annapolis MD 21401 Home: 6512 Early Lily Row Columbia MD 21044

ZHU, JIANHUA, civil and transporation engineer, researcher; b. NanChang, JiangXi, China, Mar. 15, 1957; s. Yian Zhu and Zhilian Li; m. Xianhua Hou, June 13, 1984; 1 child, Zheng. BS, JiangXi Inst. Tech., Nanchang, 1982; M Engring., Chinese Acad. Sci., Beijing, 1985; MS, U. Hawaii-Manoa, Honolulu, 1995; PhD, U. Okla., 1998. Registered profl. engr., Tex. Rsch. assoc. Inst. Water Resources Rsch., Beijing, 1985-87, engr., 1987-93, sr. engr., 1993-95; rsch. asst. U. Hawaii-Manoa, 1993-95; rsch. engr. U. Okla., Norman, 1995-97; engring. Tex. Dept. of Transp., Bryan, Tex., 1998—. Cons. engr. Bur. Hydropower, Liaoning, China, 1985-89, Bur. Water Resources, Taiyuan, China, 1990-92; supervising engr. Puchen Power Plant, Xian, China, 1991-92; project mgr. Inst. Water Resources Rsch., 1992-93; prin. investigator nat. key rsch. project Min. Water Power, 1993. Author: Theory and Practice in Hydraulic Structure Engineering, 1991 (Kexiejingbu prize 1992); contbr. articles to profl. publs. Recipient Yusiuluwen prize Assn. Hydropower of China, 1991. Avocations: martial arts, cooking, fishing. Office: Tex Dept of Transp 1300 N Texas Ave Bryan TX 77803-2760 E-mail: jzhu@txcyber.com.

ZHU, JIAN-MING, medical physicist, consultant, researcher; b. Hangzhou, Zhejiang, China, Feb. 27, 1963; came to U.S., 1997; s. Jasheng Zhu and Yuzhen Xu; m. Jianya Feng, July 10, 1989; children: Darren, Warren, William. BS, Zhejiang U., Hangzhou, 1983; MS, Chinese Acad. Scis., Shanghai, China, 1986, Saskatchewan U., Saskatoon, Can., 1992; PhD, U. Manitoba, Winnipeg, Can., 1997. Lectr. Zhejiang U., Hangzhou, 1986-89; vis. rschr. Nat. Rsch. Coun. Can., Winnipeg, 1992-97; sr. rsch. specialist U. Ill., Urbana, 1997-98; sr. sys. engr. GE Med. Sys., Waukesha, Wis., 1998—2001; asst. prof. Wake Forest U. Sch. Medicine, Winston-Salem, NC, 2002—. Reviewer Magnetic Resonance Medicine, Phila., 1996-97. Mem. Internat. Soc. Magnetic Resonance Medicine (reviewer 1997-98). Achievements include devel. of clinical MR systems capable of early diagnosis of diseases. Home: 4020 Greenbrier Farm Rd Winston Salem NC 27106 Office: Diagnostic Radiology WFUBMC Medical Ctr Blvd Winston Salem NC 27106 Business E-Mail: jzhu@wfubmc.edu.

ZHU, JIANTING, hydrologist; s. Qiansheng Ying and Meihua Zhu; m. Xuequn Fu, May 17, 1995; children: Daniel, Angela. BS, Zhejiang U., Hangzhou, China, 1978—82; MS, Beijing U., Beijing, China, 1982—85; D of Sci., Beijing University, Beijing, China, 1985—88; PhD, Daltech, Dalhousie University, Halifax, Nova Scotia, Can., 1993—95. Cert. profl. engr., Ontario, Can., 1998. Rsch. engr. Chemistry Inst. Academia Sinica, Beijing, 1988—90; vis. scholar civil engring. dept. Dalhousie U., Halifax, Canada, 1991—93; postdoctoral fellow civil engring. dept. U. of Waterloo, Canada, 1996—98; asst. prof. geol. scis. U. of Saskatchewan, Saskatoon, Canada, 1998—2000; vis. rschr. George Brown Jr. Salinity Lab., Riverside, Calif., 2000—01; asst. rsch. scientist Texas A&M U. Agrl. Engring., College Sta., 2002—. Contbr. articles and scientific papers; reviewer: Water Resources Research, reviewer: Transport in Porous Media, reviewer: The Royal Soc. Proceedings. Recipient Rsch. and Tchg. Assistantship award, Daltech, Dalhousie U., 1993—95, Visiting Scholarship award, 1991—93, Best Thesis award, Zhejiang U., China, 1982; fellow NSERC Postdoctoral fellowship, Natural Sci. and Engring. Rsch. Coun., 1996—98; scholar Bruce and Dorothy Rosetti scholarship, Daltech, Dalhousie U., 1994—95. Mem.: Assn. of Profl. Engineers, Can. Soc. of Civil Engring., Am. Geophysical Union. Avocations: hiking, reading, sports, table tennis. Office: Biol and Agrl Engring Texas A&M University College Station TX 77843-2117 Office Fax: 979-845-3932. Business E-Mail: jzhu@cora.tamu.edu.

ZHU, JIZHONG, engineering educator; b. Sichuan, China, Jan. 17, 1965; married; 1 child. BSEE, Chongqing U., 1985, MSEE, 1987, PhD in Elec. Engring., 1990. Rsch. asst. dept. elec. engring. Chongqing (China) U., 1987-90, lectr., 1990-92, assoc. prof., 1992-96, prof. elec. engring., 1996—. Vis. rsch. fellow Brunel U., U.K., 1995-96; postdoctoral fellow Nat. U. Singapore,1996-97; rsch. fellow Howard U., Washington, 1997—. Contbr. articles to profl. jours., chpts. to books. Recipient Sci. and Tech. Progress prize State Edn. Commn., 1992, 94, Sichuan Province Govt., 1992, 93, 94, Sci. and Tech. New Idea prize Sichuan Province Sci. and tech. Soc., 1992, An Excellent Youth Tchr. prize, Chongqing City Govt., 1992, Nat. Rsch. prize State Edn. Commn. and Huo Yingdong Edn Fund Commn., 1996, others. Mem. IEEE (sr.). Home: 115 150th Ave NE Apt C Bellevue WA 98007-5047 E-mail: zhujz@hotmail.com.

ZHU, JUNYONG, astrophysicist, educator; b. Kunshan, Jiangsu, China, Aug. 25, 1963; arrived in U.S., 1986, naturalized; s. Gui Quan and Meiying Zhu; m. Yana Lu, Aug. 25, 1988; 1 child Jonathan Jiachen. BS, Beijing Inst. Aerospace and Astrophysics, China, 1983; MSc Ariz. State U., 1988; PhD, U.Calif., Irvine, 1991. Scientist Arometrics, Sunnyvale, Calif., 1992—93; asst. prof. Inst. Paper Sci. and Tech., Atlanta, 1993—99, assoc. prof., 1999—. Contbr. articles to profl. jours., chpts. to books. Mem.: Tech. Assn. Pulp and Paper Industry. Achievements include patents for novel flotation drinking tech. Home: 837 Hillwood Dr Marietta GA 30068 Office: Inst Paper Sci & Tech 500 10th St NW Atlanta GA 30318 Office Fax: 509-277-0420. E-mail: junyung.zhu@ipst.edu.

ZHU, KANGMIN, epidemiologist; b. Wuhan, Hubei, China, Nov. 10, 1956; came to U.S., 1988; s. Guangzhong Zhu and Kaiqiong Li; m. Min Dai, Feb. 4, 1985; children: Jingcai, Gene Lee. MD, Tongji Med. U., Wuhan, 1982, MPH, 1985; PhD, U. Wash., 1994. Tchg. asst. Tongji Med. U., 1985-87, lectr., 1987-88; rsch. asst., assoc. U. Wash./Fred Hutchinson Cancer Rsch. Ctr., Seattle, 1988-94; asst. prof. Meharry Med. Coll., Nashville, 1994-98, assoc. prof., 1998-2000, Pa. State Med. Coll., Hershey, 2000—. Rschr. in field. Contbr. articles to profl. jours. Recipient Innovative Devel. and Exploratory award U.S. Dept. Def., 1996, New Investigator award U.S. Dept. Def., 1996, IDEA award U.S. Dept. Def., 1997, Concept award U.S. Dept. Def., 2001. Mem.: Hist. Black Colls. and Univs. (faculty award in cancer rsch. 1998), Am. Assn. Cancer Rsch., Soc. for Epidemiol. Rsch.

ZHU, PETER CHAOQUAN, chemist; b. Jiashan, China, May 8, 1957; came to U.S., 1987; s. Sanguan and Mingbao (Shen) Z.; m. June Zhu, Aug. 7, 1998. BS, Jiangxi Coll. Chinese Medicine, Nanchang, China, 1981, MS, 1987; PhD, Miss. State U., 1993. Instr. Jiangxi Coll Chinese Medicine, Nanchang, China, 1981-85; rsch. scientist 1st Chem. Corp., Mississippi State, Miss., 1990-92; sr. rsch. chemist 3M Health Care, Tustin, Calif., 1994-99, Terumo Med. Corp., Tustin, 1999-2000; prin. scientist ASP, Johnson & Johnson, Irvine, Calif., 2000—. Adj. chemistry prof. Irvine Valley Coll., 1997—; cons. and rschr. in field. Postdoctoral fellow U. Calif., Santa Barbara, 1993-94. Mem. Am. Chem. Soc. (divsn. organic chemistry, divsn. polymer, divsn. medicinal chemistry, divsn. carbohydrate chemistry, divsn. analytical chemistry, divsn. environ. chemistry). Achievements include nanochemistry application, nanobeads chemistry, attachment chemistry, DNA attachment, new chemistry application in molecular biology; development of new chemistry of cyclic ketene acetals, including synthetic procedures and new reactions; invented pure monoacetylation of diols via cyclic ketene acetals; first cationically polymerized cyclic ketene acetals and obtained stable polymers and copolymers; developed new chemistry which led to a chemical oxygen sensor used for open-heart surgery, of new glucose and CO2 chemical sensor for medical use; invented several industrial processes of speciality chemicals; discovered a new silicone reaction; isolated one anti-cancer agent from a plant; development of a new preparative TLC methods, analytical methods of amine in organic and inorganic polymers, a synthetic procedure to introduce PhSe group. Avocations: walking, fishing, piano, pingpong. Office: ASP Biocides Rsch Johnson & Johnson 33 Technology Dr Irvine CA 92618 Fax: 949-450-6850. E-mail: pzhu1@aspus.jnj.com.

ZHU, TULONG, engineer; b. Wujiang, Jiangsu, China, Jan. 27, 1963; s. Xingguan and Xiangbao (Chen) Z.; m. Chaorong Duan, Apr. 30, 1992. BS in Aero. Engring., Northwestern Poly. U., Xi'an, China, 1984, MS in Aero. Engring., 1987; PhD, Ga. Inst. Tech., 1998. From. asst. prof. to lectr. Northwestern Poly. U., Xi'an, 1987-95; rsch. asst. Ga. Inst. Tech., Atlanta, 1995-98; project engr. Aerostructures, Arlington, Va., 1998-99; sr. design analyst Advantek Inter LLC, New Castle, Del., 1999—. Contbr. articles to profl. jours. Dir. composite com. Shaanxi Soc. Aero., Xi'an, 1990-95. Mem. AIAA (sr. mem.), ASME, Gamma Beta Phi. Avocations: sports, music, stamp collecting, photography. Office: Advantek Internat LLC 56 Reads Way New Castle DE 19720-1649 Fax: 302-326-6401. E-mail: tlzhu@yahoo.com.

ZHU, XIANKUI, medical researcher; b. Zhongxiang, Hubei, China, Aug. 29, 1962; s. Mingjing Zhu and Fengying Wu; m. Lin Zhang; children: Julia, Jesse. BS, Hohai U., Nanjing. China, 1984; MS, Hohai U., Nanjing, China, 1987; PhD, Tsinghus U., Beijing, 1995. Rsch. asst. Hohai U., 1984—87; asst. prof. Wuhan U., China, 1987—91; rsch. asst. Tsinghua U., Beijing, 1991—95, postdoctoral rschr., 1995—96; rsch. prof. U. SC, Columbia, 1997—2001. Author: ASTM Special Technical Publications, 1999, 2002. Grantee, NSF, 2001, USAF, 2001, USN, 2001, US Dept. Engring., 2001. Mem.: ASTM, Am. Acad. Mechs. Home: 1035 Comanchee Trail, B-4 West Columbia SC 29169 Office: U SC 300 Main St Columbia SC 29208 Office Fax: 803-777-0106. Personal E-mail: xkuizhu@yahoo.com. Business E-Mail: zhu@engr.sc.edu.

ZHU, XIN LIANG, molecular biologist, researcher; b. Aug. 26, 1930; s. Zhong-Han and Hui-Wen (Wu) Z.; m. Hui Ying Bai; children: Cheng Zhao, Cheng Lang. MD, ZheJiang Med. U., Hang Zhou, 1953; PhD, Shanghai Inst. Cell Biology, 1960. Rsch. instr. Sch. Medicine La. State U., New Orleans, 1991-93; rsch. scientist ARC, Portland, Oreg., 1993-95; rsch. scientist in internal medicine Wash. U., St. Louis, 1995-96; rsch. assoc. in biochemistry Kirksville (Mo.) Coll. Osteo. Medicine, 1996—. Vis. scholar in cell biology Roche Inst. Molecular Biology, Nutley, N.J., 1980-82; vis. scholar in cell genetics Cornell U., N.Y.C., 1982-83; vis. scholar in biochemistry St. Louis U., 1987-91. Mem. editl. bd. Jour. Biochemistry, 1984-87. Mem. Am. Soc. Hematology. Home: 4553 A Gibon Ave Saint Louis MO 63110

ZHU, YONG, research scientist; b. Shanghai, Oct. 30, 1947; s. Shuping Chu and Zhiping Wang; m. Shaokui Wang, Apr. 22, 1977; 1 child, Shenke. B of Engr., East China Inst. Chem. Tech., Shanghai, 1981; postgrad., Tianhin Inst. Textile Engring., 1982; PhD in Organic Chemistry, U. Ill., 1992. Laborer Qingdao (China) Cigarette Manufacture, 1968-72; rsch. asst. Qingdao Inst. Light Industry, 1972-77; asst. prof., head dept. Shandong Inst. Textile Engring., China, 1983-87; vis. scientist U. Ill., Urbana, 1987-88, tchg./rsch. asst., 1988-92, postdoctoral rsch. assoc., 1992-93; scientist Procter and Gamble Far East, Kobe, Japan, 1993-95; sr. staff scientist Procter and Gamble Co., Cin., 1995—. Cons. Qingdao Manufacture of Dyeing Auxiliaries, 1983-87, Jiaonan (China) Manufacture of Fragrances, 1984-87. Patentee in field; contbr. articles to profl. jours. Recipient Edn. scholarship Chinese Edn. Assn., 1987. Mem. Am. Chem. Soc. (vol. in pub. outreach 1991-95), Inter-Am. Photochem. Soc., Chinese Color-Optical Soc., Shandong Textile Engring. Assn. Avocations: sports (volleyball, swimming), music (violin, social dance), travelling.

ZHU, YUDONG, medical imaging researcher; b. Shanghai, China, Feb. 16, 1969; arrived in U.S., 1991; s. Xingzhong Zhu and Wenzhen Yin; m. Yaxing Zhang, Sept. 6, 1994; 1 child Kimberly. Diploma, Shanghai Jiao Tong U., 1991; MSEE, Vanderbilt U., 1993; PhD in Elec. Engring., Stanford U., 1998. Rsch. asst. dept. elec. engring. Vanderbilt U., Nashville, 1992-93; rsch. asst. Lucas MRS Imaging Ctr. Stanford U., Palo Alto, Calif., 1993-98, postdoctoral fellow, 1998; sr. scientist electronic sys. lab. GE Corp. R&D Ctr., Schenectady, N.Y., 1998—. Contbr. . Scholar, Vanderbilt U., 1991. Mem.: IEEE (Trans. Med. Imaging 1996—), Internat. Soc. Magnetic Resonance in Medicine, Sigma Xi. Achievements include three issued patents and 9 pending. Office: GE Corp R&D Ctr Bldg K1 Rm NMR129 Schenectady NY 12309 E-mail: zhu@crd.ge.com.

ZHU, ZHIGANG, computer science educator; b. Zuoquan, Shanxi, China, Oct. 26, 1964; s. Baokui Zhu and Jin Sun; m. Xiaoyan Li, Apr. 8, 1969; 1 child, Marsha. B in Engring., Tsinghua U., Beijing, China, 1988, M in Engring., 1991, PhD, 1997. Aast. prof. Tsinghua U., Beijing, 1991-93, lectr., 1993-96, assoc. prof., 1996—; postdoctoral rschr. U. Mass., Amherst, Mass., 1998—, sr. rsch. fellow, 2001—. Dir. info. processing lab. dept. computer sci. Tsinghua U., 1997-99. Author: Visual Scene Modeling for Robot Navigation, 2001, (with others) Encyclopedia of Computer Science and Technology, 1999; translator: Digital Image Processing, 1998; contbr. articles to profl. jours.; inventor in field. Math. scholarship Tsinghua U., 1997; recipient Sci. and Tech. Achievement award Ministry of Electronics Industry China, 1996. Mem. IEEE, China Image and Graphic Assn. (Best Paper award 1998), Assn. of Computing Machinery. Office: U Mass 140 Governors Dr Amherst MA 01003-4610 E-mail: zhu@cs.umass.edu.

ZHU, ZHIWEI, university educator; b. Shanghai, China, Nov. 23, 1953; arrived in U.S.A., 1982; s. Ji chang Zhu and Shi hua Guo; m. Yiping Xu, Oct. 17, 1982; children: Beth, Kevin. PhD in Industry Mgmt., Clemson U., 1988. Acting dept. head U. La., Lafayette, La., 1989—. Mem. Decision Sci. Inst., Prodn. & Ops. Mgmt. Office: Univ Louisiana Dept Bsat Lafayette LA 70504-0001

ZHUO, MIN, neurobiology educator; b. Xia Pu, People's Republic of China, Nov. 25, 1964; came to U.S., 1988; s. Zi-Jing and Wan-Ru (Huang) Z.; m. Kelly Bin Wei, Apr. 27, 1993; children: Morgan Zhuo, Danielle W. BS, Chinese Inst. Sci. Tech., 1985; MS, Shanghai Inst. Physiology, 1987; PhD, U. Iowa, 1992. Vis. scientist U. Iowa, 1988-89; postdoctoral fellow Columbia U., N.Y.C., 1992-93; rsch. assoc. Howard Hughes Med. Inst. Columbia U., 1993-95, Stanford U., 1995-96; asst. prof. dept. anesthesiology Washington U., St. Louis, 1996-00, assoc. prof. dept. anesthesiology and neurobiology, 2000—. Contbr. articles and abstracts to profl. jours. Recipient first award NIH. Mem. Soc. for Neurosci., Internat. Assn. for Study of Pain (Travel award 1990), Am. Pain Soc. (Travel awards 1990, 91, 92), AAAS. Avocations: painting, fishing, biking, dancing. Office: Washington U Dept Anesthesiology PO Box 8054 Saint Louis MO 63156-8054 E-mail: zhuom@morpheus.wush.edu.

ZHURAVENKO, IGOR N. health services administrator, physician; b. Lvov, Ukraine, Mar. 6, 1959; came to U.S., 1992; s. Naum and Raisa Zhuravenko; m. Svetlana Zhuravenko, Dec. 1, 1990; children: Dimitri, Gary, Richard. MD, Lvov Med. Sch., 1983. Diplomate Am. Bd. Internal Medicine. Physician Gen. Hosp., Rovno, Ukraine, 1984-88, Diagnostic Ctr., Lvov, 1989-92; clin. instr. ultrasound Med. Sch., 1990-92; resident in internal medicine SUNY, Buffalo, 1995-98, clin. asst. instr. medicine, 1995-98. Physician MEDEX, Forest Hills, NY, 1998—99; med. dir. Adult Home Sites/CHS, N.Y.C., 1999—; mem. sci. adv. bd. Nutrition Superstores, Inc., West Palm Beach, Fla., 1999—; pres. Z Best Med. Care, P.C., 1999—; med. dir. Privilege Care a Diagnostic and Treatment Ctr., 1999—2001. Mem. ACP, AMA (Physician's Recognition award 1998). Avocations: chess, reading, computer, internet. E-mail: IZBEST@aol.com.

ZIADEH, FARHAT J. Middle Eastern studies educator; b. Ramallah, Palestine, Apr. 8, 1917; s. Jacob and Nimeh Farah Z.; m. Suad Salem, July 24, 1949; children— Shireen, Susan, Rhonda, Deena, Reema. BA, Am. U., Beirut, 1937; LL.B., U. London, 1940. Bar: Barrister-at-law Lincoln's Inn 1946. Instr. Princeton U., 1943-45, lectr. Oriental studies, 1948-54, asst. prof., 1954-58, asso. prof., 1958-66; magistrate Govt. of Palestine, 1947-48; editor Voice of Am., USIA, 1950-54; prof. U. Wash., Seattle, 1966—, prof., chmn. dept. Near Eastern lang. and lit., 1970-82, dir. Ctr. Arabic Study Abroad, 1983-89. Adj. prof. U. Wash. Law Sch., 1978-87, prof. emeritus, 1987— Author: Reader in Modern Literary Arabic, 1964, Lawyers, The Rule of Law and Liberalism in Modern Egypt, 1968, Property Law in the Arab World, 1979; contbr. articles to profl. jours. Mem. Middle East Studies Assn. (pres. 1979-80), Am. Oriental Soc. (past pres. western br.), Am. Research Center in Egypt (past bd. govs., exec. com.), Am. Assn. Tchrs. Arabic (past pres.) Eastern Orthodox. Office: Univ Wash Mid Eastern Studies Dept Seattle WA 98195-0001

ZIAVRAS, SOTIRIOS GEORGE, computer and electrical engineer, educator; b. Athens, Jan. 2, 1962; came to the U.S., 1984; s. George Spyros and Sofia George Z. Diploma in elec. engring., Nat. Tech. U., Athens, 1984; MS, Ohio U., 1985; DSc, George Washington U., 1990. Rschr. Riso (Denmark) Nat. Lab., 1983; teaching and rsch. asst. Ohio U., Athens, 1984-85; disting. grad. teaching asst. George Washington U., Washington, 1985-89, rsch. asst., 1986; from asst. prof. to assoc. prof. N.J. Inst. Tech., Newark, 1990-2001, prof., 2001—, assoc. chmn. grad. studies, 2001—. Rschr. Walter Reed Army Inst. Rsch., Silver Spring, Md., 1987-88; rsch. asst. U. Md., College Park, 1988-89; vis. prof. George Mason U., Fairfax, Va., 1990; dir. internet engring. program N.J. Inst. Tech., 2000—. Contbr. articles to profl. jours.; assoc. editor; Pattern Recognition Jour., 1994—. Recipient Rsch. Initiation award NSF, 1991, New Millenium Computing Point Design award NSF/DARPA, 1996, 1991, Mem. IEEE (sr.), Assn. for Computing Machinery, N.Y. Acad. Scis. (adv. bd. CIS sect. 1994-97), Eta Kappa Nu. Achievements include development of class of high-performance, low-cost interconnection networks for massively parallel computers called reduced hypercubes; introduction of class of multilevel architectures for high-performance multiresolution image analysis, design of an NSF/Darpa-funded New Millennium Computing Parallel Computer for PetaFLOPS performance by 2007. Office: NJ Inst Tech Elec Computer Engring Dept Newark NJ 07102 E-mail: ziavras@njit.edu.

ZIBART, MICHAEL ALAN, wholesale book company executive; b. Nashville, Mar. 12, 1947; s. Alan Walter and Joy (Hughes) Z.; m. Margaret Anne Boyd, Dec. 27, 1976; children: Emily Joy, Mary Claire. BA, Vanderbilt U., 1969. Mgmt. trainee Zibart Bros. Books, Nashville, 1961-69; property mgr. Pollack Co., 1966-69; buyer Ingram Book Co., 1970-75, mgr. trade dept., 1976, v.p., 1976-85, exec. v.p., 1985-88; founder, pres. ProMotion, Inc., 1988—. Author: Almanac on Bookselling, 3d edit., 1980; pub. (monthly book review) BookPage, 1988—. Office: ProMotion Inc 2143 Belcourt Ave Nashville TN 37212-3503

ZICHEK, MELVIN EDDIE, retired clergyman, educator; b. Lincoln, Nebr., May 5, 1918; s. Eddie and Agnes (Varga) Z.; A.B., Nebr. Central Coll., 1942; M.A., U. Nebr., 1953; D.Litt., McKinley-Roosevelt Ednl. Inst., 1955; m. Dorothy Virginia Patrick, May 28, 1942; 1 dau., Shannon Elaine. Ordained to ministry Christian Ch., 1942; minister Christian chs., Brock, Nebr., 1941, Ulysses, Nebr., 1942-43, Elmwood, Nebr., 1943-47, Central City, Nebr., 1947-83, ret., 1983; rural tchr., Merrick County, Nebr., 1937-40; prin. Alvo (Nebr.) Consol. High Sch., 1943-47; supt. Archer (Nebr.) Pub. Schs., 1948-57; head dept. English and speech Central City (Nebr.) High Sch., 1957-63; supt. Marquette (Nebr.) Consol. Schs., 1963-79. Served as chaplain's asst. AUS, 1942. Mem. Grand Island Ret. Tchrs. Assn. Republican. Home: 2730 N North Rd Grand Island NE 68803-1143

ZICHEK, SHANNON ELAINE, retired secondary school educator; b. Lincoln, Nebr., May 29, 1944; d. Melvin Eddie and Dorothy Virginia (Patrick) Z. AA, York (Nebr.) Coll., 1965; BA, U. Nebr., Kearney, 1968; postgrad., U. Okla., Edmond, 1970, 71, 72, 73, 74, 75, U. Nebr., Kearney, 1980, 81, 82, 89, 92. Tchr. history and English, N.W. H.S., Grand Island, Nebr., 1948-1999, ret., 1999. Republican. Christian. Home: 2730 N North Rd Grand Island NE 68803-1143

ZICHERMAN, DAVID L. lawyer, educator, financial consultant; b. N.Y.C., Oct. 12, 1961; BA in Psychology magna cum laude, W.Va. U., 1984; JD, MPIA, U. Pitts., 1989. Bar: Del. 1990, Pa. 1990, D.C. 1990. Assoc. Richards, Layton & Finger, Wilmington, Del., 1989-92, Klehr Harrison et al, Phila., 1992-94, Kelly Grimes Pietrangelo & Vakil, P.C., Media, Pa., 1994-97. Adj. prof. Widener U. Law Ctr., Wilmington, 1993-95, fin. cons., Merrill Lynch, 1998—. Editor: State Legislation Forum newsletter, 1991-93; editor Delaware County Legal Jour., 1995-97; contbr. chpt. to book, articles to profl. jours. Bd. dirs. Nat. Tay Sachs and Allied Diseases Assn. Delaware Valley, 1998-2001; mem. tech. com. Rose Tree Media Edn. Found., 1998-2000. Avocations: sports, photography, creative writing, travel. Office: Merrill Lynch PO Box 748 Media PA 19063-0748

ZICHICHI, ANTONINO, research and physics educator; b. Trapani, Italy, Oct. 15, 1929; s. Salvatore and Maria (Virgilio) Z.; m. Maria Ludovica Bernardini, Dec. 1958; children; Cosimo, Fabrizio, Lorenzo. D Physics, U. Palermo (Italy), 1953; D Physics (hon.), Beijing U., 1990, Malta U., 1993, U. Buenos Aires, 1994, Bucharest U., 1995, Ariz. U., 1998. Prof. physics U. Bologna (Italy), 1963—; dir. Ettore Majorana Ctr. Scientific Culture, Erice, Italy, 1963—. Pres. Galileo Galilei Found., Rome, 1980—, Internat. Ctr. Sci. Culture World Lab., Geneva, 1986—, Enrico Fermi Ctr. Sci. and Tech., Rome, 2000—; dir. Lepton Assymetry Analyser Project European Orgn. Nuc. Rsch. (CERN), Geneva, 1986—; Italian del. sci. com. NATO, Brussels, 1992—, chmn. panel on disarmament techs., 1993-98. Author: The Infinite, 1988-98, Science and Planetary Emergencies - The Paradox of Modern Era, 1993-97, Subnuclear Physics - The First 50 Years, 1997, Faith and Science, 1999, Creativity and Science, 1999; editor: 38 vols. Subnuclear Physics series, 1963-2000, Academic Press, Editrice Compositori, Plenum, World Scientific; contbr. 500 articles to profl. jours. Pres. Sci. for Peace Internat. Com., pres. European Physical Soc., 1977-79. Named Grand Officer, Order of Merit of Italian Republic, Roma, 1999; recipient Order of Merit, Fed. Republic German, 1993, Poland, 1993, Gold medal, Pres. Rep. Italy, 1981. Mem.: Georgian Acad. Scis. (fgn.), Ukranian Acad. Scis. (fgn.), Pontifical Acad. Scis. Rome, Nat. Inst. Nuc. Physics (pres. 1979—85), World Fedn. Scientists (pres. 1998—). Achievements include idea of the existence of the third lepton; proof that the ultimate brick of matter, the proton, cannot be broken; discovery of the antideuteron, the first example of nuclear antimatter; study of lepton pairs produced in hadronic interaction; invention of new methods for detection of heavy leptons produced in electron positron annihilations; discovery of Universality Features in hadronic interactions; creator Gran Sasso project, the largest underground lab. in the world. Office: CERN 1211 Geneva 23 Switzerland

ZICK, JOHN WALTER, retired accounting company executive; b. Highland Park, Ill., Sept. 21, 1925; s. Walter Ernest and Helen Ann (Wiedenhoeft) Z.; m. Mary Ann Sutter, Dec. 11, 1948; children: Sharon, Catherine, John W. (dec.). BS, Northwestern U., 1948. With Price Waterhouse, Chgo., 1948-73, N.Y.C., 1973-86, partner, 1960-86, partner in charge N.Y.C. office, 1973-76, regional mng. partner, 1976-78, co-chmn., ops., dept. sr. partner, 1978-86. Bd. dirs. Mid-Am. chpt. ARC, 1968-73, Medic Alert Found. U.S., 1994-99; founding mem., elder Winnetka (Ill.) Presbyterian Ch., 1956-67; bd. auditors New Trier Twp., Ill., 1969-73; trustee Carnegie Hall Soc. and Corp., 1980—; mem. corp. Greenwich Hosp. Assn., 1980-89. Served with USN, 1943-46. Mem. AICPA (treas. and dir. 1974-77), Ill. Soc. CPAs (pres. 1971-72) Clubs: Pine Valley Golf; Union League (N.Y.C.); Blind Brook; Burning Tree (Washington).

ZICK, LEONARD OTTO, accountant, manufacturing executive, consultant; b. St. Joseph, Mich., Jan. 16, 1905; s. Otto J. and Hannah (Heyn) Z.; m. Anna Essig, June 27, 1925 (dec. May 1976); children: Rowene Neidow Zick, Arlene (Mrs. Thomas Anton), Constance Mae (Mrs. Hilary Snell), Shirley Ann (Mrs. John Vander Ley) (dec.); m. Genevieve Evans, Nov. 3, 1977 (dec. Nov. 1996); m. Vera H. Helscher, Dec. 6, 1997. Student, Western State U., Kalamazoo, Mich. Sr. ptnr. Zick, Campbell & Rose Accts. (and predecessor firms), South Bend, Ind., 1928-48; sec., treas. C.M. Hall Lamp Co., Detroit, 1948-51, pres., 1951-54; chmn. bd., 1954-56; pres., treas., dir. Allen Electric & Equipment Co. (now Allen Group, Inc.), Kalamazoo, 1957-61; fin. v.p., treas., dir., chmn. bd. Crampton Mfg. Co., 1961-63; mgr. corp. fin. dept. Manley, Bennett, McDonald & Co., Detroit, 1963-68; mgr. Leonard O. Zick & Assocs., Holland, Mich., 1968-88. Contbg. editor: Cost Accountants Hand Book. Former mem. Mich. Rep. Cen. Com.; trustee YMCA Found., Clearwater, Fla., Richard E. Byrd Polar Ctr., Boston; vice chmn. Army-Navy Munitions Bd., 1941-42, asst. to vice chmn. War Prodn. Bd., 1941-43; chmn. Greater Holland United Fund. Mem. Inst. Mgmt. Accts. (past nat. v.p., dir.), Mich. Self Insurers Assn. (past pres.), Fin. Execs. Inst., Stuart Cameron McLeod Soc. (past pres.), Union League (Chgo.), Soc. Automotive Engrs. (chmn. lighting com.), Rotary (Paul Harris fellow), Holland Country Club. Lutheran. Home: 340 W 40th St Holland MI 49423-4600

ZIDE, ARLENE R.K. humanities educator, poet; b. New York City, Ny, Nov. 24, 1940; d. Paul Kirschenbaum and Goldie Schwesky; m. Norman H. Zide, May 18, 1963; children: William Justin, Gregory James. AB, Queens Coll., Flushing, NY, 1957—61; MA, U. Pa, Philadelphia, PA, 1961—63; PhD, U. Chgo., Chicago, IL, 1982. Project asst. Indo-American Munda Languages Project, U. Chgo., India, 1962—63; rsch. asst. Munda Languages Project, U. Chgo., Chicago, Ill., 1965—65, sr. rsch. assoc., 1965—71; vis. prof. Jawaharlal Nehru U., New Delhi, India, 1979—79; rsch. assoc. Munda Languages Project, Dept. South Asian Languages and Civilizations, U. Chgo., Chicago, Ill., 1983—85; assoc. prof. Departments; assoc. prof. fgn. languages and humanities City Colleges Chgo., Chicago, Ill., 1975—. Ctr. coord. NE Wis. Tech. Inst., Fish Creek, Wis., 1974—75; editor Primavera Mag., Chicago, Ill., 1975—81; union rep. Harold Wash. Coll., Chicago, Ill., 1997—, dir. women's studies com., Ill., 1999—. Author: (book) In Their Own Voice: The Penguin Anthology of Contemporary Indian Women Poets; contbr. articles and poetry to profl. jours. and mags. Poetry reader Art Inst. Chgo., Chicago, Ill., 1999, Chgo. Pub. Libr., Chicago, 2000—02. Recipient Sr. Fullbright Rsch. award, Fulbright, 1989-1990, Summer Inst. award, Nat. Inst. Peace, 1997; fellow Fellowship, U. Pa, U. Chgo., Sr. Fellow, Am. Inst. Indian Studies, 1995-1996; grantee Grant to Complete Work on Anthology, AIIS, 1990; scholar Scholarship, U. Pa, U. Chgo. Mem.: CCCHA Host Com. of Harold Wash. Coll., Common Ground Project of Harold Wash. Coll., NCA Com. of Harold Wash. Coll., Rank and Promotion Com. of Harold Wash. Coll., Soglin Scholarship Com. of Harold Wash. Coll., Indian P.E.N., South Asian Lang. Assn., MLA, TESOL, Com. So. Asian Studies, Am. Lit. Translators. Avocations: choral singing, indian cuisine, akido, akido. Home: 1357 E Madison Park Chicago IL 60615 Office: Harold Washington College 30 E Lake Street Chicago IL 60601 Personal E-mail: azide@ccc.edu.

ZIEBARTH, LISA MARIE, medical/surgical nurse; b. Lincoln, Nebr., Dec. 10, 1965; d. Darold E. and Helen Marie Tagge; m. James Ziebarth. BSN, Kearney (Nebr.) State Coll., 1988. RN, Nebr.; cert. med.-surg. nurse. Staff nurse, module leader, dept. supr. med.-surg. and orthopedic units Good Samaritan Hosp., Kearney, 1988—. Mem. ANA, Acad. Med.-Surg. Nurses. Home: RR 1 Box 14 A Wilcox NE 68982-9601

ZIEBARTH, ROBERT CHARLES, management consultant; b. Evanston, Ill., Sept. 12, 1936; s. Charles A. and Marian (Miller) Z.; m. Patience Arnold Kirkpatrick, Aug. 28, 1971; children— Dana Kirkpatrick, Scott Kirkpatrick, Christopher, Nicholas. AB, Princeton, 1958; MBA, Harvard, 1964. With Bell & Howell Co., Chgo., 1964-73, treas., chief fin. officer, 1969-73; mgmt. cons. Ziebarth Co., 1973—. Mem. dirs. adv. bd. Arkwright Boston Ins. Co., devel. com. Nat. Assn. Ind. Schs.; bd. dirs. M.B.A. Resources, Inc., Telemedia, Inc., Corp. Resources, Inc., Nordemann Grimm Inc. Assoc. Community Renewal Soc., Citizens Coun. Gateway House; mem. Ill. Bd. Higher Edn., Ill. Joint Edn. Commn.; trustee Choate Sch.; trustee, pres. Latin Sch.Chgo., Chgo. Maternity Ctr.; bd. dirs. Harvard Bus. Sch. Fund, U.S.O., Inc., Prentice Women's Hosp., Northwestern Meml. Corp., Found. for Reproductive Rsch. and Edn., Endowments Inc., Bond Portfolio Endowments Inc. Served to lt. USNR, 1958-62. Mem. Naval Hist. Found., Art Inst. Chgo., Chgo. Hist. Soc., Mus. Modern Art. Clubs: Mid-Am. (Chgo.), Racquet (Chgo.), Saddle and Cycle (Chgo.), Economic (Chgo.), Executives (Chgo.). Presbyterian. Office: PO Box 4569 Ketchum ID 83340-4569

ZIEGEL, BARI A. marketing professional; b. N.Y.C., Nov. 25, 1959; d. Leonard and Norma (Nemeth) Z.; m. Steven M. Rosman, Sept. 8, 1984; children: Michal Sima Ziegel Rosman, Ilan Chaim Ziegel Rosman. BBA, Hofstra U., 1980. Ops., sales rep. Unitours, Inc., N.Y.C., 1980-82; adminstrv. asst. Bozell and Jacobs Inc., 1982-83, Parfums Stern, Inc., N.Y.C., 1983-85; mgmt. assoc. Citicorp Indsl. Credit, Inc., Harrison, N.Y., 1985-87, mktg. officer Rye, 1987-88; area mgr. Lucent Techs. Product Fin., Plainview, 1988-2000; regional sales dir. Expanets Fin. Svcs., Pt. Washington, 2000—. Mem. NAFE, Women in Equipment Leasing. Jewish. Office: Expanets Fin Svcs 49 Shore Rd Port Washington NY 11050

ZIEGELAAR, BOB W. airport terminal executive; Dir. Bangor (Maine) Internat. Airport, 1991—.

ZIEGELMEIER, PATRICIA KAY, music educator, executive secretary; b. Colby, Kans., July 14, 1944; d. Lon Elmer and Mary Marie (Saddler) Sowers; m. Carl Ernest Ziegelmeier, June 9, 1963; children: Matt, Steve, Lisa, Amy, Lori. BA in Music Edn., U. Wyo., 1967; MS in Ednl. Adminstrn., Ft. Hays State U., 1991. Tchr. music, sub. tchr. Golden Plains Schs., Rexford, Kans., 1969-72; pvt. piano instr. Gem, 1972-87; ch. organist Gem and Colby, 1968—; instr. music Colby C.C., 1988—. Cmty. leader 4-H, Gem, 1980-88, 99—; bd. dirs. Thomas County Ext. Coun., Colby, 1982-86, 94-95. Mem. NEA, Music Tchrs. Nat. Assn., Kans. Music Tchrs. Assn. (bd. dirs. 1981—, exec. sec. 1987—, Outstanding Tchr. award 1994), Western Plains Arts Assn. (exec. dir. 1989—), Northwest Kans. Piano Assn. (clinic chair 1973—). Methodist. Avocations: reading, music listening, playing piano, walking. Office: Kans Music Tchrs Assn 2154 County Road 27 Gem KS 67734-9008 E-mail: patz@colby.ixks.com.

ZIEGENHAGEN, DAVID MACKENZIE, consultant, retired healthcare company executive; b. Mpls., May 25, 1936; s. Elmer Herbert Ziegenhagen and Margaret Ruth (Mackenzie) Kruger; m. Mary Ange Kinsella, Nov. 26, 1966 (div. Dec. 1982); children: Marc, Eric; m. Mary Kinsella, Feb. 7, 2002.

BA, U. Minn., 1962. Assoc. dir. Thailand Peace Corps, Bangkok, 1963-65, Thailand program officer Washington, 1966-67, dir. Western Samoa Apia, 1967-70; exec. dir. Mental Health Assn. Minn., Mpls., 1970-76; co-founder, pres. Current Newspapers, Inc., Burnsville, Minn., 1975-84; sr. program officer The St. Paul Found., 1982-84; pres. DMZ Assocs., Cloverdale, Calif., 1983—; exec. dir. Minn. Bd. Med. Practice, St. Paul, 1985-88; CEO, pres. Stratis Health, Bloomington, Minn., 1988-2000. Field dir. Am. Refugee Com., Bangkok, 1979; dir. Health Edn. Rsch. Found., St. Paul, 1993—99; mem. Citizens League, Mpls., 1975—2000, dir., 1988—95; mem. Adminstrs. in Medicine, Washington, 1985—88; dir. Walk-In Counseling Ctr., Mpls., 1990—99, Ctr. for Clin. Quality Evaluation, Washington, 1990—99. Mem. Cloverdale Planning Commn., 2000—, Sonoma County Civil Grand Jury, 2001—. Mem. Nat. Mental Health Staff Coun. (pres. 1970-76). Avocations: travel, international development, arts.

ZIEGENHORN, ERIC HOWARD, lawyer, legal writer; b. Independence, Mo., Oct. 17, 1957; AB in Econs. with honors, U. Mo., 1979; JD, U. Calif., Berkeley, 1983. Bar: Calif. 1983, Kans. 1986, Mo. 1987. Atty. Law Offices of Richard A. Goodman, Oakland, Calif., 1983-86, Lewis, Rice & Fingersh, Overland Park, Kans., 1986-87; pvt. practice, legal writer Kansas City, Mo., 1987—; sr. staff atty. Midland Loan Svcs., 1991-96. Author: (3-vol. set) Missouri Legal Forms, 1992. Mem. Mo. Bar Assn., Calif. Bar Assn. Office: 104 Vietnam Veterans Memor Dr Kansas City MO 64111-2301

ZIEGLER, ARTHUR P., JR. foundation executive; b. Pitts., June 20, 1937; s. Arthur P. and Vinnie (DeWinter) Z. BA, U. Pitts., 1958, MA, 1959; postgrad., Union Theol. Sem., N.Y.C., 1960, Western Res. U., 1961. Instr. Carnegie Mellon U., Pitts., 1961-64, Pa. State U., Pitts., 1961-63; pres. Cranston Devel. Corp., 1980-87, Pitts. History and Landmarks, 1964—. Trustee emeritus Nat. Trust, Washington; trustee Allegheny Found., Pitts., 1975—, Sarah Scaife Found., 2000—, Walden Trust, 1990—; chmn. Allegheny County Hist. Properties Commn. Author: Historic Preservation of Inner City Areas, 1971, Revolving Funds for Historic Preservation, 1975; co-author: Historic Preservation for Small Towns, 1980, Allegheny, 1975, Landmark Architectur of Allegheny County, 1987; editor: A Critical Edition of Lord of the Flies, 1964. Mem. N.W. regiona and Pitts. adv. coun. Fannie Mae; mem. 10,000 Friends of Pa., Riverlife Task Force, Harbor Gardens; mem. bd. advisors The Waterfront Ctr.; bd. dirs. Preservation Pa. Recipient Crowninshield award Nat. Trust, Nat. Recognition award Ptnrs. for a Livable Cmty., Pvt. Sector award Pres. of the U.S., Man of Yr. in Arts award Pitts. Jaycees, Golden Quill award, Remax Renaissance award. Mem.: HYP Club, City Club. Avocation: gardening. Office: One Station Sq Ste 450 Pittsburgh PA 15219

ZIEGLER, CHARLES EDWARD, political science educator; b. Oct. 17, 1953; BA, Purdue U., 1975; AM, U. Ill., 1977, PhD, 1979. Legis. asst. U.S. Senate, Washington, 1989; exec. dir. Louisville Com. on Fgn. Rels., 1990—; prof., chair dept. polit. sci. U. Louisville, 1998—. Author: Environmental Policy in the USSR, 1987, Foreign Policy and East Asia, 1993, The History of Russia, 1999, The Russian Far East, 2002. Sr. Fulbright scholar Pusan Nat. U., Republic of Korea, 1995, Nat. fellow Hoover Instn., 1985-86, Internat. Affairs fellow Coun. on Fgn. Rels., 1987-88. Office: U Louisville Dept Polit Sci Louisville KY 40292-0001 E-mail: ceziegler@louisville.edu.

ZIEGLER, DANIEL MARTIN, chemistry educator; b. Quinter, Kans., July 6, 1927; s. Anton T. and Clara (Weissbeck) Z.; m. Mary Alice Weir, Aug. 19, 1952; children: Daniel L., Paul W., Mary Claire, James M. BS in Chemistry, St. Benedicts Coll., 1949; PhD in Chemistry, Loyola U., 1955; postdoctoral, U. Wis., 1955-58; DSc (hon.), Benedectine Coll., 2001. Asst. prof. Inst. Enzyme Rsch. U. Wis., Madison, 1958-61; asst. prof. chemistry U. Tex., Austin, 1961-62, assoc. prof. chemistry, 1962-69, prof. chemistry, 1969-97, Roger J. Williams Centennial prof. in biochemistry, 1990-97, prof. emeritus, 1997—. Editor jour. Biol. Chemistry, 1979-83, 85-90, 93-98; mem. editl. bd. Analyt. Biochemistry, 1989-91, Arch. Biochem. Biophys., 1966-71; contbr. articles to profl. jours. Recipient Bernard B. Brodie award Am. Soc. Pharmacol. Exptl. Therapy, 1990, Alexander von Humboldt award, Germany, 1991; estab. investigator Am. Heart Assn., 1960-65. Mem. Internat. Soc. for the Study of Xenobiotics (hon. life). Home: 6704 Shoal Creek Blvd Austin TX 78757-4379 Office: U Tex Dept Chemistry/Biochemistry Austin TX 78712 E-mail: dziegler@mail.utexas.edu.

ZIEGLER, DEWEY KIPER, neurologist, educator; b. Omaha, May 31, 1920; s. Isidor and Pearl (Kiper) Z.; Mar. 30, 1954; children: Amy, Laura, Sara. BA, Harvard U., 1941, MD, 1945. Diplomate Am. Bd. Psychiatry and Neurology (bd. dirs. 1974-83, exec. com. 1978-82). Intern in medicine Boston City Hosp., 1945-46; asst. resident then chief resident in neurology N.Y. Neurol. Inst.-Columbia U. Coll. Physicians and Surgeons, 1948-51; resident in psychiatry Boston Psychopathic Hosp., 1951-53; asst. chief neurol. service Montefiore Hosp., N.Y.C.; and asst. prof. neurology Columbia U., 1953-55; asst. prof. U. Minn., 1955-56; asso. clin. prof. U. Kans. Med. Sch., 1956-64, chief dept. neurology, 1968-85; prof. U. Kans. Med. Center, 1964-89, prof. emeritus, 1989—. Cons. Social Security Adminstrn., 1975— ; mem. com. on certification and co-certification Am. Bd. Med. Specialties, 1979-82 Author: In Divided and Distinguished Worlds, 1942; Contbr. numerous articles to profl. jours. Served to lt., j.g., M.C. USNR, 1946-48. Fellow Am. Acad. Neurology (pres. 1979-81); mem. AMA, Am. Neurol. Assn. (v.p. 1972-73), Am. Headache Assn. Jewish. Home: 8347 Delmar Ln Shawnee Mission KS 66207-1821 Office: Kans U Med Center 3900 Rainbow Blvd Kansas City KS 66103-2918 E-mail: dziegler@kumc.edu.

ZIEGLER, DONALD EMIL, federal judge; b. Pitts., Oct. 1, 1936; s. Emil Nicholas and Elizabeth (Barclay) Z.; m. Claudia J. Chermak, May 1, 1965; 1 son, Scott Emil. BA, Duquesne U., 1958; LL.B., Georgetown U., 1961. Bar: Pa. 1962, U.S. Supreme Ct. 1967. Practice law, Pitts., 1962-74; judge Ct. of Common Pleas of Allegheny County, Pa., 1974-78, U.S. Dist. Ct. (we. dist.) Pa., Pitts., 1978—, chief judge, 1994-2001. Mem. Jud. Conf. U.S., 1997-2000. Treas. Big Bros. of Allegheny County, 1969-74. Mem. ABA, Pa. Bar Assn., Allegheny County Bar Assn., Am. Judicature Soc., St. Thomas More Soc. Clubs: Oakmont Country. Democrat. Roman Catholic. Office: 649 U S Post Office & Courthouse Bldg 7th and Grant St Pittsburgh PA 15219

ZIEGLER, DONALD ROBERT, accountant; b. Lancaster, Pa., Nov. 15, 1932; s. John Jacob and Esther Mae (McKelly) Z.; m. Suzanne Foster; children: D. Rand, Scott F., Kurt J. BS in Econ. Acctg., Franklin and Marshall Coll., 1954. CPA, Pa. Mgr., sr. staff mem. Price Waterhouse, Phila., 1954-67, ptnr., 1967-92, sr. practice ptnr., 1978-92, mng. ptnr. Mid-Atlantic area, 1985-88, vice chmn. S.E. region, 1988-92, mem. policy bd. N.Y.C., 1980-88, mem. mgmt. com., 1986-92. Author: (with others) Managing and Accounting for Inventories, 1980; contbg. author various books in field. Trustee Franklin and Marshall Coll., 1983—, alumni exec. coun., 1979-83, devel. com., exec. com., 1995—, chmn. audit com., 1989—, vice-chmn. bd. trustees, 2002-, Phila. alumni coun.; trustee Pa. Ballet, 1988-92, 94-95, devel. and fin. coms., vice chmn. bd. trustees, 1989-92, chmn. exec. com., 1989-91; bd. dirs. Beebe Med. Ctr., 2000—, Beebe Med. Found., 2001—. With U.S. Army, 1955-57. Recipient Outstanding Soldier award U.S. Army, 1955, Disting. Svc. Alumni medal Franklin and Marshall Coll., 1991. Mem. AICPA (auditing stds. com. 1973-76, chmn. subcom. fraud 1976-80), Pa. Inst. CPAs (Phila. chpt. exec. coun.), Rehoboth Beach Country Club (bd. govs. 2000—), Phila. Aviation Club (bd. govs. and treas. 1969-90), Royal Blackheath Golf Club (U.K.). Home: One West St Dewey Beach DE 19971 Office: PricewaterhouseCoopers LLP Two Commerce Sq 2001 Market St Ste 1700 Philadelphia PA 19103-7042 E-mail: drsfzig@aol.com.

ZIEGLER, EARL KELLER, minister; b. Sheridan, Pa., Mar. 4, 1929; s. Abraham Hoffman and Rhoda Bucher (Keller) Z.; m. Vivian Zug Snyder, Aug. 12, 1951; children: Karen Louise, Randall Earl, Doreen Kay Creighton, Michael Wayne, Konnae Ziegler Berces, Sulien Nicodemus. BA, Elizabethtown (Pa.) Coll., 1951; MDiv, Bethany Theol. Sem., Chgo., 1954; DDiv, Lancaster (Pa.) Theol. Sem., 1982. Ordained to ministry Ch. of the Brethren, 1950. Pastor Woodbury (Pa.) Congregation, Pa., 1954-60, Black Rock Ch. of Brethren, Brodbecks, 1960-70, Mechanic Grove Ch. of Brethren, Quarryville, 1970-83, Atlantic N.E. Dist. Exec., Harrisburg, 1983-89, Lampeter (Pa.) Ch. of the Brethren, 1989-99; moderator Ch. of the Brethren, Elgin, Ill., 1993-94; interim pastor Florin Ch. of the Brethren, Mt. Joy, Pa., 1999—2001. Moderator various dists., Pa., 1959—; mem. Gen. Bd., Ch. of Brethren, 1975-80; chmn. Parish Ministerial Commn., 1979-80; dir. Family Life Inst., 1961, 64, mem. Nat. Korean Cons. Com., 1988-91, Denominational Structure Com., 1990-91, others; adj. prof. ch. history Evang. Sem., Myerstown, Pa., 1988—. Author: Divorce Among the Church of the Brethren Clergy, 1981; contbr. articles to profl. jours. Pres. Manheim Elem. PTA, 1964-65; trustee Elizabethtown Coll., 1965-83; bd. dirs. Cmty. Choir, Lineboro, Md., 1966-70, Solanco Community Men's Chorus, Quarryville, 1976-83, Samaritan Counseling Ctr., Lancaster, Pa., 1992-98, Pa. Coun. Chs., 1983-89, 2000—, Hope Internat. Trustees, 2000—. Recipient Alumni citation, Elizabethtown Coll. Alumni Assn., 1964, award for Outstanding Ch. Planting in Azua Province of Dominican Republic, 1990, Award of Appreciation, Germantown Ch. of Brethren, 1990. Mem. Lampeter Willow St. Ministerium (pres. 1989-91). Republican. *"You shall have what your faith expects," were the words of Jesus to two blind men. These words challenge the potential within each of us, a faith that conquers, a spirit that soars. Between the possible and the impossible is the measure of one's will.*

ZIEGLER, EKHARD ERICH, pediatrics educator; b. Saalfelden, Austria, Apr. 12, 1940; children: Stefan, Gabriele, Lena. MD, U. Innsbruck, Austria, 1964. Diplomate: Am. Bd. Pediatrics. Intern U. Innsbruck, 1966-67, resident in pediatrics, 1967-68 70-71, resident in pharmacology, 1964-66, asst. dept. pediatrics, 1970-73; vis. instr. pediatrics U. Iowa, Iowa City, 1968-70, asst. prof. pediatrics, 1973-76, assoc. prof., 1976-81, prof., 1981—. Mem. nutrition study sect. NIH, 1988-92. Recipient Nutrition award Am. Acad. Pediatrics, 1988. Mem. Am. Soc. Clin. Nutrition, Soc. Pediatric Research, Soc. Exptl. Biology and Medicine, N.Am. Soc. Pediatric Gastroenterology, Midwest Soc. Pediatric Research, Am. Pediatric Soc., The Nutrition Soc., N.Y. Acad. Scis., Am. Acad. Pediatrics., Am. Dietetic Assn. (hon.). Clubs: Univ. Athletic (Iowa City). Office: U Iowa Dept Pediatrics Iowa City IA 52242 E-mail: ekhard-ziegler@uiowa.edu.

ZIEGLER, EVAN FRANK, music educator; b. Hackensack, N.J., Oct. 4, 1970; s. Rudolf and Annette Margaret Ziegler. MusB in Music Edn., U. of Fla., 1994. Cert. Tchr. Fla., 1994. Music specialist Summerfield Elem. Sch., Riverview, Fla., 1994—96; band dir. Progress Village Mid. Sch., Tampa, 1996—98, Rodgers Mid. Sch., Riverview, 1998—. Pvt. music instr., Brandon, Fla., 1999—. Mem.: Fla. Music Educators Assn., Fla. Bandmsters Assn. (honor band chmn. 1998—99), U. of Fla. Alumni Assn., Kappa Kappa Psi (vice president-alpha eta chpt. 1992—93, named Alpha Eta Brother of the Yr. 1993), Phi Mu Alpha (vice president-eta omega chpt. 1991—92). Democrat. Avocations: reading, bicycling, golf, travel, jazz.

ZIEGLER, JACK (JACK DENMORE), cartoonist; b. N.Y.C., July 13, 1942; s. John Denmore and Kathleen Miriam (Clark) Z.; m. Jean Ann Rice, Apr. 20, 1968 (div. 1995); children: Jessica, Benjamin, Maxwell; m. Kelli Joseph, Aug. 1996. BA in Communication Arts, Fordham U., 1964. Free-lance cartoonist, N.Y.C., 1972—; cartoonist The New Yorker, 1974—. Author: Hamburger Madness, 1978, Filthy Little Things, 1981, Marital Blitz, 1987, Celebrity Cartoons of the Rich and Famous, 1987, Worst Case Scenarios, 1990, Mr. Knocky, 1993, The Essential Jack Ziegler, 2000; illustrator: (children's books) Lily of the Forest, 1987, Flying Boy, 1988, Annie's Pet, 1989, Eli and the Dimplemeyers, 1994 (adult books) Waiting Games, 1983, The Joy of Stress, 1984, That's Incurable!, 1984, Modern Superstitions, 1985, The No-Sex Handbook, 1990, There'll Be a Slight Delay, 1991, Byte Me!, 1996. Democrat.

ZIEGLER, JAMES RUSSELL, computer consultant; b. Warren, Pa., Oct. 10, 1922; s. LeRoy Curtis and Daisy (Gesin) Z.; m. Maxine Evelyn Hogue, Feb. 10, 1952 (dec. Nov. 1968); children: Evalinde Aurelia, Charlotte Elaine, Curtis Wayman, Bruce Allan; m. Florence M. Bowler, 1969 (div. 1975); 1 child, Scott. BSEE, Pa. State U., 1943, MA in Math., 1948. UHF wave guide rsch. Norden Corp., N.Y.C., 1943-44; instr. math. Pa. State coll., 1946-48, U. Calif., L.A., 1948-54; rsch. assoc. statistician tchrs. characteristics study Am. Coun. Edn., 1951-54; mgr. programming svcs., electronic computers Nat. Cash Register Co., Hawthorne, Calif., 1954-68; pres. Turn-Key Computer Applications, 1968-75; dir. So. Fed. Savs. & Loan Assn., L.A., 1968-69; adv. dir. Coast Fed. Savs. & Loan Assn., 1969-74; sr. cons. analyst NCR Co., San Diego, 1975-78, San Diego Cash Register Co., 1978-80. Computer cons. Yemen Arab Rep. Nat. Water and Sewerage Authority, 1980-87; tech. cons. Office Naval Rsch. Study; data processing cons. psychol. rsch. projects U. So. Calif., also U. Utah. Author: Time Sharing Data Processing Systems, 1967; contbr. articles to profl. jours. With USMCR, 1944-46; PTO. Mem. Masons, Tau Beta Pi, Sigma Tau, Eta Kappa Nu. Republican. Methodist. Home: 1050 Pinecrest Ave Escondido CA 92025-3853

ZIEGLER, JANET CASSARO, holistic health nurse; b. Bklyn., Oct. 26, 1946; d. Dominic Michael and Rose (Locascio) Cassaro; m. Paul Dennis Ziegler, Nov. 1, 1970; children: Paul Dennis, Daniel Peter, Michael Tyson. BSN, D'Youville Coll., 1968; M in Nursing, U. Pitts., 1975. Instr. Norfolk (Va.) State Coll., 1970-72; pvt. practice in childbirth edn. Va., 1971-72, Pitts., 1972-81; clin. nurse specialist Vis. Nurse Assn. Allegheny County, 1975-83; pvt. practice pvt. practice, 1982—. Educator, cons. Am. Soc. Psychoprophylaxis in Obstetrics, Pitts., 1971-81; practitioner, educator Clin. Hypnosis, Pitts., 1982—, Biofeedback Inst. Am., Wheat Ridge, Colo., 1983—; practitioner, cons., educator Therapeutic Touch, Pitts., 1981—; cons. in field. Lt. USN, 1968-70. Mem.: Inst. Noetic Scis., Aloha Internat., Nurse Healer's Profl. Assocs. Republican. Roman Catholic. Avocations: cooking, boating, reading, dancing. Home: 4566 Dogwood Dr Allison Park PA 15101-1135 Office: 5200 Centre Ave Ste 706 Pittsburgh PA 15232-1311 E-mail: janetziegler@att.net.

ZIEGLER, JOHN ALAN, historian, political scientist, educator; b. Belleville, Ill., Jan. 28, 1933; s. John Wendell and Georgia Elizabeth (Reppel) Z.; m. Carol Ruth Alcorn, June 15, 1963; children: Mimi, Robin. BS, So. Ill. U., 1955, MS, 1956; Rotary Found. fellow, St. Andrews (Scotland) U., 1956-57; PhD, Syracuse U., 1970. Asst. prof. polit. sci. and social sci. Calif. State U., Hayward, 1966-72; lectr. Am. civilization Calif. State Poly. U., Pomona, 1972-74; assoc. prof. polit. sci. Hendrix Coll., Conway, Ark., 1974-84, prof., 1984-91, Harold and Lucy Cabe Disting. prof. history and politics, 1991-98, emeritus prof., 1998—, legendary lectr., 1998. Coord. and founder Hendrix-Oxford program, 1979-98, head social sci. area, 1978-82, chmn. dept. polit. sci. and history, 1974-83; guest lectr. St. Peter's Coll., Oxford U., 1983, 90, 94, Clare Coll., Cambridge U., 1988, 89, Dundee U., 1994; Churchill life fellow Westminster Coll., Fulton, Mo.; participant Wilton Pk. Confs., Wiston House Internat. Conf. Ctr., Sussex, England, 1979—. Author: Experimentalism and Institutional Change, In Search of the Special Relationship with Britain. With AUS, 1957-60. Mem. AAUP, Friends Churchill Meml. (life), Am. Friends Wilton Park, ACLU, Royal Oak Found., Soc. Sussex Downsmen (life), Dundee (Scotland) Curling Club. Mem. United Ch. of Christ. Home: PO Box 1045 Conway AR 72033-1045 Office: Hendrix Coll Conway AR 72032

ZIEGLER, JOHN AUGUSTUS, JR. lawyer; b. Grosse Pointe, Mich., Feb. 9, 1934; s. John Augustus and Monnabell M. Ziegler; m. G. Kay Brubeck; children: John Augustus III, Laura, Lisa, Adeline. AB, U. Mich., JD, 1957. Bar: Mich. 1957. Since practiced in, Detroit; assoc. Dickinson, Wright, McKean & Cudlip, 1957-65, ptnr., 1965-68, Parsons, Tennent, Hammond, Hardig & Ziegelman, 1969-70, Ziegler, Dykhouse & Wise, 1970-77; pres., CEO Nat. Hockey League, 1977-92, chmn. bd. govs., 1976-78; of counsel Dickinson, Wright, PLLC, Bloomfield Hills, 1992—99. Office: 375 Park Ave Ste 2004 New York NY 10152-2099

ZIEGLER, R. W., JR. lawyer, consultant; b. Pitts. children: Caroline, Gretchen, Jeremy, Benjamin, Phoebe, Polly. Student, Carnegie Tech., U. Pitts.; JD, Duquesne U., 1972. Bar: Pa. 1972, Calif. 1981, U.S. Ct. Appeals (3d cir.) 1977, U.S. Dist. Ct. (we. dist.) Pa. 1972, U.S. Supreme Ct. 1977, U.S. Tax Ct. 1978, Calif. 1982, U.S. Dist. Ct. (no. dist.) Calif. 1982, U.S. Ct. Appeals (9th cir.) 1982. Ptnr. Ziegler & Ombres, Pitts., 1973-79; pres. Ziegler Ross Inc., San Francisco, 1979—. Lectr. for Bar Assns. Author: Law Practice Management; editor: Law Office Guide in Computing. Mem. ABA, Am. Mgmt. Assn., Pa. State Bar Assn., Calif. State Bar Assn. Office: 580 Market St Ste 500 San Francisco CA 94104-5413

ZIEGLER, RICK, dean, science educator; Interim dean U. Minn. Sch. Medicine Duluth , 1997—, dean, 1998—. Office: 1035 University Dr Duluth MN 55812*

ZIEGLER, ROBERT F. cardiologist; b. Detroit, Mar. 30, 1916; s. Gustave Adolph and Clara Louise (Niepoth) Z.; m. Grace Charlotte Eberle, Apr. 10, 1951; children: Sally, David, James, Michael. BA, Wayne State U., 1937; MD, U. Mich., 1941. Diplomate Am. Bd. Internal Medicine, Am. Bd. Cardiovascular Disease, Am. Bd. Cardiology, Am. Bd. Pediatric Cardiology. Intern Henry Ford Hosp., Detroit, 1941-42, resident in medicine, 1942-43, resident in cardiovascular disease, 1943-46; resident pediat. cardiology Johns Hopkins Hosp., Balt., 1946-47; adj. prof. biol. sci. Mich. Tech. U., Houghton, 1970-85. Author: EKG Studies in Normal Infants and Chilren, 1951, Cardiac Evaluation in Normal Infants, 1965; contbr. chpts. to books and articles to profl. jours. Pres. Aid Assn. Lutherans, Hancock, 1993-95; bd. dirs. Habitat for Humanity, Hancock, 1996-97, chair ch. rels. com., 1997-2001. Mem. Am. Coll. Cardiology, Am. Coll. Chest Physicians, Am. Heart Assn., Keweenaw Kiwanis.

ZIEGLER, ROBERT OLIVER, retired music and special education educator; b. Cullman, Ala., Sept. 6, 1939; s. Mary Catherine (Taylor) McDonald; adopted Edgar and Kathryn Ziegler; m. Gladys L. Friese, May 3, 1962 (div. Jan. 1970); children: Robert, Edgar, Lesha, Kathy. BS, U. Ala., Tuscaloosa, 1961, MA, 1964, PhD, 1970. Cert. spl. edn. tchr., sch. counselor, music tchr., Ga. Band dir. Phillips Jr. H.S., Mobile, Ala., 1961-62, Wiggins (Colo.) H.S., 1962-63, Eastwood Jr. H.S., Tuscaloosa, 1963-65, McAdory H.S., McCalla, Ala., 1966-70, Calera (Ala.) H.S., 1971-72; prof. music edn. Tift Coll., Forsyth, Ga., 1972-78; jr. H.S. counselor Clayton County Schs., Jonesboro, 1978-80; elem. sch. counselor Rockdale County Schs., Conyers, 1980-82; spl. edn. tchr. Henderson Jr. H.S., Jackson, 1982-87, Clayton County Schs., Jonesboro, 1987-92, gen. music tchr., 1996-99; spl. edn. tchr. City Schs. of Decatur, 1992-96; elem. sch. music tchr. Clayton County Schs., 1996-99. Clarinetist Mobile (Ala.) Symphony Orch., 1961-62; vis. lectr. Stillman Coll., Tuscaloosa, Ala., 1970-71; prof. grad. sch. Mercer U., Macon, 1972-74; vis. lectr. in music Wesleyan Coll., Macon, Ga., 1975-76; acting head music dept. Tift Coll., Forsyth, Ga., 1976-77; curriculum cons. South Metro Psychoedнl. Ctr., Atlanta City Schs., 1989. Contbr. articles to profl. publs. Minister of music, choir dir. United Meth. Ch., 1961-90, lay leader, 1989-94; mem. South Metro Concert Band, Morrow, Ga., 1978—, Tara Wind Band, Jonesboro, Ga., 1987-88. Recipient Cert. of Appreciation United Meth. Ch., 1990, Spl. Mission Recognition award United Meth. Women, 1983; U. Ala. grantee, 1960-61 Mem. Profl. Assn. Ga. Educators (bldg. rep. 1994-96), Soc. for Preservation and Encouragement of Barber Shop Quartet Singing in Am. (founding, co-dir. Fayetteville chpt. 1990, co-founder, 1st dir. So. Crescent Chorus 2001). Avocations: tennis, ragtime piano playing, singing gospel music. Home: 2669 Jodeco Dr Jonesboro GA 30236-5311 E-mail: bobmzieg@aol.com.

ZIEGLER, RONALD LOUIS, former association and government official, writer; b. Covington, Ky., May 12, 1939; s. Louis Daniel and Ruby (Parsons) Z.; m. Nancy Lee Plessinger, July 30, 1960; children: Cynthia Lee Charas, Laurie Michelle Albright. Student, Xavier U., 1957-58; BS, U. So. Calif., 1961; DSc (hon.), Mass. Coll. Pharmacy, 1989, L.I. U., 1993. With Procter & Gamble Distbg. Co., 1961; account rep. J. Walter Thompson Co., 1962-68; press dir. Calif. Rep. Central Com., 1961-62; press aide to Richard Nixon in Calif. gubernatorial campaign, 1962; press aide staff Richard Nixon, 1968-69; press sec. to Pres. Nixon, 1969-74, asst. to, 1973-74; mng. dir., sr. v.p. internat. services Syska and Hennessy, Inc., Washington, 1975-80; pres. Nat. Assn. Truck Stop Operators, Alexandria, Va., 1980-87; pres., CEO, Nat. Assn. Chain Drug Stores, 1987-98; ret., now writer, 1998—. Mem. nat. adv. bd. U. Okla.; adv. coun. Pharm. Found. U. Tex. Writer on current and polit. events. Bd. dirs. Nat. Coun. on Patient Info. and Edn., Nat. Conf. on Pharm. Assns., Richard Nixon Libr. and Birthplace. Mem. Am. Soc. Assn. Execs., Nat. Retail Fedn. (bd. dirs.), Pharmacists Against Drug Abuse, Assn. White House Press Secs., Nat. Orgn. Rare Disorders, Sigma Chi Alumni. E-mail: ronznacds@aol.com.

ZIEGLER, WILLIAM, III, diversified industry executive; b. N.Y.C., June 26, 1928; s. William and Helen (Murphy) Z.; m. Jane Elizabeth Troy, Feb. 22, 1952; children: Melissa Jane, William Troy, Peter Martin, Cynthia Curtis, Helen Matilda, Karl Huttig. BA, Harvard U., 1950; MBA, Columbia U., 1962. Chmn. bd., dir. Swisher Internat. Group, 1966—; pres. Hay Island Holding Corp., Darien, Conn., 1995—. Pres. E. Matilda Ziegler Found. for Blind; v.p. Matilda Ziegler Pub. Co. for Blind; trustee Maritime Aquarium, Norwalk, Conn.; mem. adv. bd. Yale Eye Ctr. Lt. comdr. USNR, 1952-54. Mem. N.Y. Yacht Club, Noroton (Conn.) Yacht Club. Home: 161 Long Neck Point Rd Darien CT 06820-5815 Office: Swisher Internat Group 20 Thorndal Cir Darien CT 06820-5421

ZIEGLER, WILLIAM ALEXANDER, lawyer; b. N.Y.C., July 15, 1924; s. William Alexander and Sally (Cootes) Z.; m. Glenn Crawley, Feb. 10, 1950; children: Richard S., Daryl A. Henning, Susan G. Barrows, W. Thomas. AB, Harvard U., 1944, JD, 1949. Bar: N.Y. 1949, U.S. Tax Ct. 1950, U.S. Dist. Ct. (so. dist.) N.Y. 1949, U.S. Dist. Ct. (ea. dist.) N.Y. 1957, U.S. Dist. Ct. (no. dist.) Ohio 1973, U.S. Dist. Ct. (ea. dist.) Mich. 1983, U.S. Ct. Apppeals (1st cir.) 1963, U.S. Ct. Appeals (2d cir.) 1957, U.S. Ct. Appeals (3d cir.) 1986, U.S. Ct. Appeals (4th cir.) 1979, U.S. Ct. Appeals (5th cir.) 1987, U.S. Ct. Appeals (6th cir.) 1984, U.S. Ct. Appeals (7th cir.) 1992, U.S. Ct. Appeals (8th cir.) 1981, U.S. Ct. Appeals (9th cir.) 1973, U.S. Ct. Appeals (10th and 11th cirs.) 1983, U.S. Ct. Appeals (D.C. cir.) 1972, U.S. Supreme Ct. 1972. Assoc. Sullivan & Cromwell, N.Y.C., 1949-56, ptnr., 1957-89. Bd. dirs. Std. Comml. Corp. Bd. dirs. Wilton (Conn.) Land Conservation Trust. Mem. Assn. Bar City N.Y., Riverside Country Club (Mont.), Harvard Club of N.Y.C., Harvard Club of Fairfield Country (bd. dirs.), Harvard Club Mont.

ZIEHLER, TONY JOSEPH, insurance agent; b. Anderson, Ind., June 20, 1936; s. Joseph Anthony and Julie Ann (Kette) Z.; m. Alice Mae Pattison, Apr. 2, 1956 (div. 1972); children: Susan Z. Brown, Kathryn Z. Dwyer, Jane Z. Bee, Patricia Z. Koty, Michael; m. Barbara Buys Wood, Feb. 28, 1981; stepchildren: David Wayne Wood, Brent Douglas Wood. BSBA, U. Ariz., 1958. CLU. Prin. Ziehler Ins. Group, LLC, Tucson, 1958—. Mem. Fed. Jud. Magistrate Selection Com., 1998—. Employee edn. chmn. So. Ariz. Div. Am. Cancer Soc.; co-chmn. Medic-Alert Found., Pima County, Ariz.; chmn. Tucson Festival Soc.; mem. Salpointe High Sch. Found., others. Recipient William Wisdom award U. Ariz., Tucson, 1958. Mem. Greater Tucson Assn. Life Underwriters (pres. 1963-64, Agt. of Yr. 1975), Ariz. Assn. Life Underwriters (pres. 1970-71, Agt. of Yr. 1980), So. Ariz. CLU Soc. (pres. 1968-69), Salvation Army (pres. adv. bd. 1984-85), Univ. of Ariz. Found. (mem. planned giving com.), Rotary, (com. chmn.), Tucson Conquistadores (pres. 1985-86), Los Charros del Desierto, Golden Key Soc., MIllion Dollar Round Table, Tucson Country Club, others. Republican. Avocations: travel, trail riding, Belgian draft horses, mountain hiking, sports. Home: 8741 E Woodland Rd Tucson AZ 85749-9575 Office: 6992 E Broadway Blvd Tucson AZ 85710-2803

ZIELINSKI, PAUL BERNARD, grant program administrator, civil engineer; b. West Allis, Wis., Sept. 9, 1932; s. Stanley Charles and Lottie Charlotte (Pliszkiewicz) Z.; m. Monica Theresa Beres, July 13, 1957; children: Daniel Paul, Gregory John, Robert Mathias, Sarah Ann. BSCE, Marquette U., 1956; MS, U. Wis., 1961, PhD, 1965. Registered profl. engr., Wis., S.C. Asst. instr. engrng. mechanics Marquette U., Milw., 1956-59, asst. prof., 1964-67; instr. civil engrng. U. Wis., Madison, 1959-64; from asst. prof. to prof. Clemson (S.C.) U., 1967-78, prof. environ. and systems engrng., 1978-82, prof. civil engrng., 1982-90, prof. emeritus, 1991—; dir. S.C. Water Resources Rsch. Inst., Clemson, 1978-90; assoc. dir. associateship grant program Nat. Rsch. Coun., Washington, 1990—. Cons. Am. Pub. Works Assn., Chgo., 1973-76, Nat. Coun. Examiners of Engrng. and Surveying, Clemson, 1973—; cons. swirl devices for storm water separation; com. on exams for profl. engrs. Author numerous publs. on hydraulics and water resources rsch. Chmn. Clemson City Planning Commn., 1971-74; ex-officio mem. S.C. Water Resources Commn., Columbia, 1978-90. Mem. ASCE, Sigma Xi. Roman Catholic. Home: 2111 Wisconsin Ave NW Apt 717 Washington DC 20007-2278 Office: Nat Rsch Coun 2101 Constitution Ave NW Washington DC 20418-0007 E-mail: pzielins@nas.edu.

ZIEMAN, MARK, newspaper editor; VP & editor Kansas City (Mo.) Star, 1997—, mng. editor, 1997—. Office: The Kansas City Star 1729 Grand Blvd Kansas City MO 64108-1458*

ZIEMBA, DAVID LEE, music educator; b. Portsmouth, Va., Oct. 10, 1949; s. Edwin Joseph and Lenita Joyce Ziemba; m. Celtic Renee Skinner, Dec. 17, 2000; children: Rachel, Adam, Jonathan. AA-music, Wingate Coll., Wingate, NC, 1969; BM-music ed., Appalachian State U., Boone, NC, 1972; grad. study, U. of NC, Greensboro, NC, 1973—74, Vandercook Coll. of Music, Philadelphia, PA, 1988—89. Teacher Certification NC. Tchr. Alamance Co. Schools, Mebane, NC, 1972—73, Charlotte-Meck Schools, Charlotte, 1974—78; instr. of music Coll. of the Albermarle, Elisabeth City, 1991—92; tchr. Perquimans Co. Schools, Hertford, 1978—. Mem. Charlotte Symphony Orch., Charlotte, NC, 1974—78, Blues & R&B Group at Beach Resorts, NC, 1992; adjudicator & cons. Sch. Band Field. Performer (cd recording), (book & ed) Arranging Music for the Real World, (cd recording) OBX. Recipient condr. of all-eastern NC Jr. H.S. Band, 1988, guest condr. Walt Disney World Band, 1989, Who's Who Among America's Teachers, 1992, 1994, 1996, 2000. Mem.: NC Band Association-Eastern Dist., NC Music Educators Assn., Music Ed. Nat. Conf. Roman Catholic. Achievements include founding director of bands for the Perquimans Co. Schools-1978; classroom opened 1972, North Carolina School Year on Public Television with Governor Bob Scott; director of Perquimans High School Band at the inauguration of President George Bush, 1989; director of Perquimans High School Band at the inauguration od Governor Jim Hunt, Raleigh, NC, 1981; director of Perquimans High School Band, won National Championship Band at Super Bowl XXV marching band contest, Orlando, FL, 1991; director of Perquimans High School Band, performed in the Boscov Thanksgiving Day Parade, Philadelphia, 1996. Avocations: the arts, the arts, the arts, the arts. Home: 110 Bembury Rd Hertford NC 27944 Office: Perquimans Co Schools PO Box 39 Winfall NC 27985

ZIEMER, JOHN ROBERT, software engineer; b. Berkley, N.J., Jan. 25, 1939; s. John Ziemer Jr. and Doris Catherine (Taylor) Rife; m. Patricia Ann Gable, June 29, 1963 (div. Nov. 1979); children: Brian A., Gary R., Wendy S; m. L. Sue Hayden Boggess, Dec. 29, 1979; 1 child, Marria Lynn Ziemer; stepchildren: Loretta Sue Boggess, Timothy Kent Boggess. Student, Trenton (N.J.) State U., 1964-65, Memphis State U., 1965, U. Mo., 1971, Florissant Valley (Mo.) U., 1973-78. Enlisted USN, 1957, resigned, 1967; simulation engr. Link-Flight Simulation, Binghamton, N.Y., 1967-69, Conductron Electronics, St. Louis, 1969-72; rsch. programmer MacDonnal Douglas Rsch. Lab, 1972-81; software engr. Mastercard Internat., 1981—, sr. software engr., 1998—. Designer antisubmarine warfare tactics trainer, rsch. computer and test facilities. Mem. exec. coun. Boy Scouts Am., St. Louis, 1976-77. Avocations: camping, scuba diving, sailing, flying. Home: 1285 Swallow Ln Florissant MO 63031-3326

ZIEMER, RODGER EDMUND, electrical engineering educator, consultant; b. Sargeant, Minn., Aug. 22, 1937; s. Arnold Edmund and Ruth Ann (Rush) Z.; m. Sandra Lorann Person, June 23, 1960; children: Mark Edmund, Amy Lorann, Norma Jean, Sandra Lynn. BS, U. Minn., 1960, MS, 1962, PhD, 1965. Registered profl. engr., Mo. Research asst. U. Minn., Mpls., 1960-62, research assoc., 1962; prof. elec. engring. U. Mo., Rolla, 1968-83, U. Colo., Colorado Springs, 1984—, chmn. dept. elec. engring., 1984-93; program dir. comms. rsch. NSF, 1998-2001. Cons. Emerson Electric Co., St. Louis, 1972-84, Mid-Am. Regional Coun., Kansas City, Mo., 1974, Motorola, Inc., Scottsdale, Ariz., 1980-84, Martin Marietta, Orlando, 1980-81, TRW, Colorado Springs, summer, 1985, Sperry, Phoenix, 1986, Pericle Communications, summer, 1994, Motorola, Schaumburg, 1995, Scottsdale, 1996, Arlington Heights, 1997. Author: Principles of Communications, 1976, Principles of Communications, 2d edit., 1985, Principles of Communications, 3d edit., 1990, Principles of Communications, 4th edit., 1995, Principles of Communications, 5th edit., 2002, Signals and Systems, 1983, Signals and Systems, 2d edit., 1989, Signals and Systems, 3d edit., 1993, Signals and Systems, 4th edit., 1998, Digital Communications and Spread Spectrum Systems, 1985, Introduction to Digital Communication , 1992, Introduction to Digital Communication, 2d edit., 2001, Introduction to Spread Spectrum Communications, 1995, Elements of Engineering Probability and Statistics, 1997; editor: IEEE Jour. on Selected Areas in Comms., 1989, 1992, 1995, IEEE Comm. Mag., 1991. Served to capt. USAF, 1965-68. Scholar Western Electric, 1957-59; trainee NASA, 1962-65 Fellow IEEE (Third Millenium award 2000); IEEE Disting. Lectr. Program, 2001-; IEEE Fellow Com., 2000-present; mem. Am. Soc. Engring. Edn., Armed Forces Communications and Electronics Assn., Sigma Xi, Tau Beta Pi, Eta Kappa Nu Lutheran. Home: 8315 Pilot Ct Colorado Springs CO 80920-4412 Office: Univ Colo PO Box 7150 Colorado Springs CO 80933-7150 E-mail: ziemer@eas.uccs.edu.

ZIENTARA, JAMES EDWARD, stock brokerage executive; b. Hammond, Ind., Mar. 12, 1943; s. Joseph Edward and Leona Dorothy (Poracky) Z.; m. Frances Elizabeth Gehrke, July 30, 1966; children: Amy Elizabeth, Jeffrey Edward. BS in Math., Purdue U., 1966; MBA in Fin., Ind. U., 1970; cert. investment mgmt. analyst, U. Pa., 1989. Tchr. math. Wilbur Wright Jr. High Sch., Munster, Ind., 1966-68; investment advisor trust dept. Continental Ill. Bank, Chgo., 1970-72; sr. investment officer trust dept. SE Bank Trust, Sarasota, Fla., 1972-75; stock broker Morgan Stanley Dean Witter, Bradenton, 1975—; 1st v.p. investments Dean Witter Reynolds Inc., 1984—, retirement plan coord., 1985—. Grad. asst. Ind. U., Bloomington, 1968. Contbr. Nelson's Guide to Pension Fund Consultants, 1991. Vol. United Way, Bradenton, 1989. Recipient pub. svc. award Am. Radio Relay League, 1965. Mem. Investment Mgmt. Cons. Assn., Bradenton C. of C., Bradenton Country Club, Manatee Personal Computer Users Group (founder), Kiwanis (Kiwanian of Yr. 1999). Republican. Avocations: golf, tennis, personal computers, travel. Home: 416 64th Street Ct NW Bradenton FL 34209-1629 Office: Morgan Stanley Dean Witter 1401 Manatee Ave W Ste 1110 Bradenton FL 34205-6710 E-mail: jimz312@aol.com.

ZIENTARA, SUZANNAH DOCKSTADER, insurance agent; b. Wichita, Kans., Oct. 1, 1945; d. Ralph Walter and Patricia Ann (Harvey) Dockstader; m. Larry Henry Zientara, Oct. 18, 1975; 1 child, Jillian Sue Zientara Cox. Student, U. Kans., 1963-64; BS in Bus. Edn., Ft. Hays State U., 1968; MEd in Secondary Guidance and Counseling, U. Mo., St. Louis, 1973. CLU. Sec. to supt. Wichita Pub. Schs., 1968-69; tchr. bus. edn. Wichita Heights High Sch., 1969-71, Lindbergh High Sch., St. Louis, 1971-72, Holman Jr. High Sch., St. Louis, 1972-75; guidance counselor Pattonville Heights Jr. High Sch., 1975-79; tchr. data processing Lawrence (Kans.) High Sch., 1979-85; ins. agt. State Farm Ins. Cos., Lawrence, 1985-90, agy. mgr. Tulsa, 1990-95, agy. field exec. Topeka, 1995-98, agent, 1999—. Mem. Regional Mgr. Coun., Tulsa, 1992-93; participant Purdue Profl. Mgmt. Inst., West Lafayette, Ind., 1993. Author: Introduction to Data Processing, 1983. Mem. Williams Edn. Fund, U. Kans. Named Outstanding Young Woman of Am., 1974. Mem.: PEO, Soc. Fin. Svc. Profls., U. Kans. Alumni Assn., Mortar Bd., Shawnee Country Club, Pi Omega Pi. Republican. Episcopalian. Avocations: grandchildren, golf, snow skiing, music. Home: 3318 SE 23d Terrace Topeka KS 66605 E-mail: agentz@cox.net.

ZIERDT, ALYSON KATHLEEN, lawyer; b. Milw., Feb. 10, 1947; d. Edward Paul and Alyce Ann (Burt) Dietzmann; m. William Henry Zierdt III, July 12, 1991. Student, St. Norbert Coll., West DePere, Wis., 1964-66; BA, U. Wis., Milw., 1969; JD, Marquette U., 1981. Bar: Wis. 1981, U.S. Dist. Ct. (we. and ea. dist.) Wis. 1981, U.S. Ct. Appeals (7th cir.) 1986. Asst. buyer/sales mgr. Boston Store divsn. Federated Dept. Stores, Milw., 1969-71, buyer, dept. mgr., 1971-78; law clk. Warshafsky, Rotter, Tarnoff, Gesler, Reinhardt & Bloch, S.C., 1979-81, assoc., 1981-86, Mulcahy & Wherry, S.C., Milw., 1986-89, atty./shareholder, 1989-91, Davis & Kuelthau, S.C., Milw., 1991-94, Reff Baivier Bermingham Zierdt & Lim, S.C., Oshkosh, Wis., 1994-2000, Davis & Kuelthau S.C., Oshkosh, 2000—. Mem. dist. III com. Office of Lawyer Regulation, Oshkosh, Fox Valley, 1997—. Co-author: Wisconsin Trial Practice, 1999co-author: The Law of Damages in Wisconsin, 1988, 2d edit. 1994-95, 96. Vol. mediator Winnebago Conflict Resolution Ctr., Oshkosh, 1995—; vols. Irish Fest, Milw., 1990—; bd. dirs., trustee Paine Art Ctr. and Gardens, Oshkosh, 1996—, pres. 2001-02; pres. TEMPO, Milw., 1987-88, bd. dirs. TEMPO Fox Valley, 1995-98, pres. 1995-97; bd. dirs., pres. Women's Fund of Oshkosh Cmty. Found., 1998-2001. Thomas More scholar Marquette U., 1980. Mem. State Bar Wis. (editl. bd. Wis. Lawyer 1988-95, 96-02, bd. dirs. alternative dispute resolution sect., 1996-98), Assn. for Women Lawyers (bd. dirs. 1984-89, pres. 1987-88), Wisc. Assn. Mediators, Wisc. Sch. Attys. Assn., Milw. Bar Assn. (bd. dirs. 1987-88, sec. 1988-91), Oshkosh C. of C. (bd. dirs. 1997—, pres. 1999-2000), Fond du Lac Yacht Club. Office: Davis & Kuelthau PO Box 1278 219 Washington Ave Oshkosh WI 54903-1278 E-mail: ozierate@dkattorneys.com.

ZIERDT, CHARLES HENRY, microbiologist; b. Pitts., Apr. 24, 1922; s. Conrad Henry and Nancy Leora (Harshberger) Z.; m. Margaret May Wise, June 1, 1942 (div. 1962); children: Charles Henry, Jr., Carolyn, Douglas, Richard; m. Willadene Smith, Sept. 30, 1967. BS, Pa. State U., 1943; MS, U. Mich., 1945; Ph.D., George Washington U., 1967. Rsch. assoc. Parke-Davis & Co., Detroit, 1945-48; microbiologist Henry Ford Hosp., Detroit, 1948-53, USPHS, Detroit, 1953-56; rsch. microbiologist NIH, Bethesda, Md., 1956—. Scientist sponsor U. Md., 1975—; instr. Found. Advanced Edn. Scis., Bethesda, 1978—. Author: Glucose Nonfermenting Gram Negative Bacteria in Clinical Microbiology, 1978; Non-fermentative Gram Negative Rods: Laboratory Identification and Clinical Aspects, 1985; McGraw-Hill Yearbook of Science and Technology, 1986; Diagnostic Procedures for Bacterial Infections, 1987; contbr. over 100 articles to profl. jours. Patentee in field. Active PTA. Fellow Am. Acad. Microbiology; mem. Am. Soc. Microbiology (chpt. pres. 1976), U.S. Fedn. Culture Collections (membership chmn. 1985), Avanti Owners Assn. Internat., Mensa, Model A Ford Club of Am. (Fairfax, Va. chpt. pres. 1985), Model T Ford Club Internat., Antique Auto Club Am. (pres. Sugar Loaf Mountain region 1997), Sigma Xi. Republican. Achievements include the classification and pathogenesis of Blastocystis Hominis, an intestinal protozoan parasite of man. Avocations: gardening; antique car restoration, church historian. Home: 4100 Norbeck Rd Rockville MD 20853-1869 Office: NIH Bethesda MD 20816

ZIERING, WILLIAM MARK, lawyer; b. New Britain, Conn., Feb. 4, 1931; s. Jacob Max and Esther (Freedman) Z.; m. Harriet Koskoff, Aug. 20, 1958 (div. Sept. 1993); 1 son, Benjamin. BA, Yale U., 1952; JD, Harvard U., 1955. Bar: Conn. 1955, Calif. 1962. Assoc. Koskoff & McMahon, Plainville, Conn., 1959-60; sr. trial atty. SEC, San Francisco, 1960-65; pvt. practice law, 1965—; ptnr. Bremer & Ziering, 1972-77. Instr. Golden Gate U. Law Sch., San Francisco, 1968-75 Vice pres., bd. dirs. Calif. League Handicapped, 1972— . Served to comdr. USNR, 1955-58. Mem. ABA, Calif. Bar Assn., San Francisco Bar Assn. (past chmn. securities, corps. and banking), Navy League (dir.) Clubs: Commonwealth. Home: 440 Davis Ct Apt 620 San Francisco CA 94111-2418 Office: 440 Davis Ct #620 San Francisco CA 94111

ZIERLER, NEAL, retired mathematician; b. Balt., Sept. 17, 1926; children: Robert Eugene, Joan Mariye, Ann M. AB, Johns Hopkins U., 1945; AM, Harvard U., 1949, PhD, 1959. Mathematician, physicist Ballistic Rsch. Labs., Aberdeen, Md., 1951; mem. tech. staff instrumentation lab. MIT, Cambridge, Mass., 1952-54, mem. tech. staff Lincoln Lab. Lexington, 1954-60; supr. info. processing group of jet propulsion lab. Calif. Inst. Tech., Pasadena, 1960-61; sr. scientist ARCON Corp., Lexington, 1961-62; head sub-dept. process analysis MITRE Corp., Bedford, Mass., 1962-65; tech. staff Ctr. for Comm. Rsch. Inst. Def. Analysis, Princeton, N.J., 1965-96. Patentee error-detecting and -correcting devices; contbr. articles to profl. jours. Lt. USN, 1944-46. Fellow IEEE; mem. Am. Math. Soc., Math. Assn. Am., Am. Physics Soc. Avocations: tennis, skiing, photography. E-mail: nzierler@ieee.org.

ZIESE, DENNIS RUSSELL, protective services official, military officer; b. Bklyn., Jan. 18, 1950; s. Russell Arthur and Joan Elizabeth Ziese; m. Kazuko Katashi, Apr. 23, 1971 (div. June 1985); children: Diane, John, Kathy; m. Linda Nell Pohl, May 18, 1999; children: Eric Pohl, Evan Pohl. AS, Columbia Coll., 1992, BA, 1993; MA, Lincoln U., 1996. Master sgt. USMC, Washington, 1967—89; functional unit mgr. Mo. Dept. Corrections, Jefferson City, 1990—. Recipient Naval Commendation medal, USN, 1971, Conspicuous Svc. medal, State of NY, 1973. Mem.: VFW, USMC League, KC. Republican. Roman Catholic. Avocations: golf, fishing, hunting, reading.

ZIESE, NANCYLEE HANSON, social worker; b. Sioux City, Iowa, July 26, 1938; m. J. A. Ziese; 1 child G. Graham. BA in Sociology, Morningside Coll., 1960; MSW, U. Iowa, 1982, cert. in aging studies, 1986; EFM, U. of the South, 1996. Social worker Florence Crittenton Home, Sioux City, 1960-65, L.A. County, 1965; social worker, supr. Polk County Dept. Social Welfare, Des Moines, 1966-69; social worker, community liaison Tommy Dale Meml., Sioux City, Iowa, 1977-79; dir. internships Briar Cliff Coll., 1981-83; dir. continuing edn. Coe Coll., Cedar Rapids, Iowa, 1983-85; exec. dir. Profl. Women's Network, 1985-87; pvt. practice counselor, consultant, speaker, writer Womanplace Counseling, 1985-87, 99—; adoption coord. Hillcrest Family Svcs., 1987-99. Bd. dirs. Young Parent's Network M.E.L.D., Cedar Rapids, pres., 1994—96; cons. cmty. improvement, recycling; spkr. in field; gov. apptd. mem. Iowa State Citizen Foster Care Review Bd., 2002—. Contbr. articles to newspapers. Mem. steering bd. Iowa Women's Polit. Caucus, 1987—93, pres., 1992—93; dep. gen. conv. ECUSA, 1997, 2000—; past chair Iowa Birth Defects Inst. Adv. Com. Iowa Assn. Adoption Agys.; bd. dirs. Linn County Adolescent Pregnancy Prevention Coalition, treas., 1992—96; steering com. mem. ERA Iowa 1992, 1991—95; gov.'s com. Adoption Reform in Iowa, 1993, 1994; lt. gov.'s com. spl. needs Adoption in Iowa, 1994; bd. dirs., pub. policy chair AAUW, 1995—, pres., 2000—01; co-founder, pres. Iowa Breast Cancer Action, 1998—2000; mem. to chmn. Cedar Rapids Civil Rights Commn., 2000—; cons. med. ethics com. for In-Vitro Fertilization Adoption Program and Adoption Agy. U. Iowa, 1995; mem. gov.'s task force Child Advoccacy Bd., 2002; mem. Cedar Rapids Civil Rights Commn., 2000—, chmn., 2002; bd. dirs. commn. mem. Human Needs, commn. on ministry Episcopal Diocese Iowa, 1996—99, mem. standing com., 2000—; mem., v.p. Sioux City Sch. Bd., 1978—83; bd. dirs., pres. Friends of Iowa Pub. TV, 1978—88; bd. dirs., pres. Family Svc. Boys and Girls Home, Sioux City, 1973—81. Named Woman of Yr., Linn County, Cedar Rapids, 1995; recipient Outstanding Svc. awards, Sioux City C. of C., 1976, Siouxland Arts Coun., 1977. Mem.: Profl. Women's Network Cedar Rapids (bd. mem., Woman of Yr. 1997), NASW, Rotary Internat. Avocation: Avocations: women's movement, human needs advocacy, reading. Home and Office: 1759 Applewood Pl NE Cedar Rapids IA 52402-3321 E-mail: z_nancylee@hotmail.com.

ZIETZ, JOACHIM, economics educator; b. Bergen, Fed. Republic Germany, Oct. 14, 1953; came to U.S., 1978; s. Werner and Gisela (Lehmann) Z.; m. Emily J. Norman, 1996; children: Michael, Olivia. MA, U. Goettingen, Fed. Republic Germany, 1978; PhD, U. Goettingen, 1982. Rsch. asst. Internat. Food Policy Rsch. Inst., Washington, 1979-81; asst. prof. econs. U. Balt., 1981-85; rsch. fellow Kiel Inst. World Econs., Fed. Republic Germany, 1985-87; assoc. prof. U. Detroit, 1987-89; prof. dept. econs. and fin. Mid. Tenn. State U., Murfreesboro, 1989—. Cons. Internat. Food Policy Rsch. Inst., 1981-90, World Food Programme, Rome, 1983-84, World Bank, Washington, 1984, 93, Orgn. for Econ. Coop. and Devel., Paris, 1989. Editor: Jour. Econs. and Fin., 1999—. Mem. Am. Econ. Assn., Royal Econ. Soc., Acad. Econs. and Fin., So. Econ. Assn., Cosmos Club. Office: Mid Tenn State U Dept Econs and Fin PO Box 129 Murfreesboro TN 37132-0129 E-mail: jzietz@mtsu.edu.

ZIETZ, KARYL LYNN KOPELMAN, writer, opera critic, television correspondent, producer, documentary filmmaker; b. N.Y.C., Oct. 11, 1943; d. Bernard and Vera Jean (Wantman) Kopelman; m. Neil J. Stone, Aug. 16, 1970 (div. 1975); m. Joachim Zietz, July 19, 1978 (div. 1994). BA in Chemistry, U. Pa., 1965; MA in Film and Broadcast Journalism, Am. U., 1980; spl. cert., Goettinger U., Germany, 1976. Rschr. Columbia Coll. Physicians and Surgeons, N.Y.C., 1967-70, NIH, Bethesda, Md., 1971-72; producer, writer Am. Chem. Soc., Washington, 1976-78; prodr., rschr. Zweites Deutsches Fernsehen, Mainz, Germany, 1978-89; prodr. ORF-Austrian TV, 1980-84; prodr., reporter European Television Svc., Cologne, Germany, 1985-88; prodr., dir., corr. KOPE Prodns., Washington, 1985—. Lectr. Smithsonian Inst., Arts Club, Chautauqua Instn., 1998, Italian Cultural Soc., 1999, Balt. Opera Guild, 2000, Italian Cultural Inst., Embassy of Italy, 2002; site reporter NEA, 1994-95. Author: Opera! Guide to Western Europe's Great Houses, 1991, Eastern Europe's and USSR's Great Opera Houses, 1992, Opera-Going in South America, 1993, Opera Companies and Houses of the United States: A Comprehensive, Illustrated Reference, 1994, The National Trust Guide to Great Opera Houses in America, 1996, Italian Opera Directory, 1998, Opera Companies and Houses of Western Europe, Canada, Australia, New Zealand: A Comprehensive Illustrated Reference, 1999, Storia dei Teatri d'Opera Italiani, 2001; prodr. (video) An Amish Portrait for USIA; prodr., dir., writer, interviewer documentary films; opera critic, contbr. articles to Opera Now, Orpheus Oper Internat., Toronto Globe and Mail, Opera News, Musica and Arte: Quaderno del Museo Teatrale alla Scala, Opera-Opera. Mem. Music Critics Assn., Coun. Internat. Nontheatrical Events, Internat. Platform Assn., Am. Women in Radio and TV, Author's Guild, Assn. Ind. Video and Filmmakers, Washington Ind. Writers, Contemporary Authors, Cosmos Club. Avocations: sailing, jogging, bicycling, foreign languages. Office: KOPE Prodns Palisades Sta PO Box 40103 Washington DC 20016-0103 E-mail: opera4me123@aol.com.

ZIETZ, STANLEY, mathematics educator; b. N.Y.C., July 23, 1950; m. Elizabeth Zietz; children: Rebekah, Susannah. SB, MIT, 1972; MS, U. Calif., Berkeley, 1974, PhD, 1977; postgrad., Temple U., 1976-79. Asst. prof., then assoc. prof. dept. math. and computer sci. Drexel U., Phila., 1979-99, assoc. dir. biomed. engring., 1986-96; prof., chmn. dept. math., physics and computer sci. U. Scis. in Phila., 1999—. Cons. E.I. Dupont Corp., Wilmington, Del., 1984-86, USN, Warminster, Pa., 1991, San Diego, 1993—. Contbr. over 50 articles to profl. jours. Stanford-NASA faculty fellow, 1992. Mem. Soc. Indsl. and Applied Math., Soc. for Math. Biology, Phi Beta Kappa, Sigma Xi. Avocations: music, photography. Office: U Scis in Phila 600 S 43d St Philadelphia PA 19104 Fax: 215-895-1112. E-mail: s.zietz@usip.edu.

ZIEVE, MICHAEL ERNEST, mathematician; b. Minneapolis, Apr. 15, 1971; s. Franklin Joseph and Sandra Turchick Zieve. AB, Harvard U., 1992; PhD, U. Calif., Berkeley, 1996. Asst. prof. U. of So. Calif., L.A., 1997—99; postdoctoral fellow Math. Sciences Rsch. Inst., Berkeley, 1999; vis. prof. Universiteit Leiden, Leiden, Netherlands, 2000; rsch. staff mem. Ctr. for Comm. Rsch., Princeton, NJ, 2000—. Cons. Ctr. for Comm. Rsch., Princeton, 1992—99. Recipient Postdoctoral Rsch. fellowship, NSF, 1996—99, Math. Scis. Rsch. Inst., 1999. Mem.: Am. Math. Soc. Avocations: tennis, beer, travel. Office: Ctr Comms Rsch 805 Bunn Dr Princeton NJ 08540 E-mail: zieve@idaccr.org.

ZIFCHAK, WILLIAM C. lawyer; b. 1948; BA, Harvard U., 1970; JD, Columbia U., 1973. Bar: N.Y. 1974, U.S. Ct. Appeals (2d cir.) 1975, U.S. Ct. Appeals (3d cir., D.C. cir.) 1983, U.S. Dist. Ct. (so. dist.) N.Y. 1984. Ptnr., co-chair labor and employment law dept. Kaye, Scholer, Fierman, Hays & Handler, N.Y.C. Planning com. NYU Ann. Nat. Conf. Labor, 1991-97. Contbr. articles to profl. jours. Mem. ABA (sect. labor and employment law 1975—, subcom. antitrust, RICO and labor rels. law), Assn. Bar City of N.Y. (sec. com. labor and employment law 1984-87), N.Y. State Bar (comml.-fed. litig. sect. co-chair labor and employment law com. 1995-97). Office: Kaye Scholer LLP 425 Park Ave New York NY 10022-3506

ZIFF, LARZER, English language educator; b. Holyoke, Mass., Oct. 2, 1927; s. Isadore Menden and Sara (Rosenbloom) Z.; m. Ruth Rosalind Geisenberger; children— Joshua, Oliver, Joel, Abigail. Student, Middlebury Coll., 1945-47; MA, U. Chgo., 1951, PhD, 1955; MA (hon.), U. Oxford, Eng., U. Pa. Prof. English U. Calif., Berkeley, 1956-73; univ. lectr. Oxford U., Eng., 1973-78; prof. English U. Pa., 1978-81; Caroline Donovan prof. English Johns Hopkins U., Balt., 1981—, chair dept., 1991-95. Dir. U. Calif. Edn. Abroad Program, U.K., Ireland, 1969-71; cons. and lectr. in field. Author: The Career of John Cotton, 1962; The American 1890's, 1968; Puritanism in America, 1973; Literary Democracy, 1981; Writing in the New Nation, 1991, Return Passages, 2000; also articles, essays in profl. jours.; mem. editorial bds. including ELH, 1981— . Recipient numerous awards for excellence in English including Christian Gauss award, the American 1890's, 1967; Fulbright fellow, 1959-60, fellow Am. Coun. Learned Socs., 1963-64, Newberry Libr., 1964, NEH, 1967-68, Guggenheim fellow, 1977-78, Woodrow Wilson Internat. Ctr. for Scholars, 1986-87; Fulbright Disting. Sr. Lectr., 1993. Fellow Am. Acad. Arts and Scis., Soc. Am. Historians; mem. MLA, Am. Antiquarian Soc. Office: Johns Hopkins U Dept English Baltimore MD 21218 E-mail: lziff@attglobal.net.

ZIFF, MORRIS, internist, rheumatologist, educator; b. N.Y.C., Nov. 19, 1913; s. Benjamin and Ethel (Seldowitz) Z.; m. Jacqueline Mae Miller, Dec. 10, 1978; children: Edward B., David R. BS, NYU, 1934, PhD, 1937, MD, 1948. Intern Bellevue Hosp., N.Y.C., 1948-49, resident in internal medicine, 1949-50, attending physician, 1950-58; asst. prof. medicine NYU, 1954-57, assoc. prof., 1957-58; Ashbel Smith prof. internal medicine U. Tex. Health Sci. Ctr., Dallas, 1958-84, prof. emertus internal medicine, 1984—, Morris Ziff prof. rheumatology, 1982—; dir. Harold C. Simmons Arthritis Rsch. Ctr., 1983-84; attending physician Parkland Meml. Hosp., 1958—. Mem. med. staff Zale-Lipshy Univ. Hosp., Dallas, 1989—; cons. Dallas VA Hosp., Brooke Army Hosp., 1964-75, William Beaumont Army Hosp., 1965-76 Contbr. over 250 articles to sci. jours., chpts. to books. Recipient Heberden medal Heberden Soc. London, 1964, Rsch. Career award USPHS, 1962-84, Marchman award Dallas So. Med. Soc., 1968, Disting. Svc. award Arthritis Found., 1968, Disting. Alumni Sci. award NYU, 1966, Carol Nachman prize in rheumatology, 1974, World Internat. Conf. on Inflammation prize, 1986, Rheuma medal Austrian Soc. Rheumatology, 1996; Morris Disting. Prof. Lectureship award named in his honor, 2000. Fellow ACP; mem. Assn. Am. Physicians, Am. Soc. Clin. Investigation, Am. Assn. Immunologists, Am. Coll. Rheumatology (master, Bunim medal 1982, Gold medal 1988), N.Y. Acad. Medicine (Klemperer medal 1991), Harvey Soc., Phi Beta Kappa, Sigma Xi, Alpha Omega Alpha. Home: 11116 Pinocchio Dr Dallas TX 75229-4031 Office: U Tex Health Sci Ctr Health Sci Ctr 5323 Harry Hines Blvd Dallas TX 75390-9030 Fax: 214-648-9100. E-mail: morris.ziff@utsouthwestern.edu.

ZIFF, PAUL, philosophy educator; b. N.Y.C., Oct. 22, 1920; m. Loredana Vanzetto; 3 children. BFA, Cornell U., 1949, PhD, 1951. Instr. philosophy U. Mich., Ann Arbor, 1952-53; from instr. to asst. prof. Harvard U., Cambridge, Mass., 1953-59; from asst. prof. to assoc. prof. U. Pa., 1959-63; prof. U. Wis., 1964-68, U. Ill., Chgo., 1968-70; Kenan prof. U. N.C., Chapel Hill, 1970-88, prof. emeritus, 1988—; chmn. bd. dirs. Chapel Hill Ctr. Linguistic Rsch. Cons. in field. Contbr. articles to profl. jours. Paul Ziff chair installed in his honor U. N.C., 1994; festschrift Language, Mind and Art pub. in his honor, 1994; grantee Rockefeller Found., spring 1955, Guggenheim Found., Rome, 1962-63. Office: Philosophic Linguistic Rsch 1309 Brigham Rd Chapel Hill NC 27517-3402

ZIGLAR, JAMES W. Federal Agency Administrator, Lawyer; b. Pascagoula, Miss., Dec. 8, 1945; married; 3 children. BA, George Washington U., 1968, JD, 1972. Bar: Va. 1972, D.C. 1973, N.Y. 1975, Ariz. 1977. Staff asst. Senator James Eastland, Washington, 1964-71; spl. asst. Dept. of Justice, 1971-72; law clk. to assoc. justice Harry Blackmun U.S. Supreme Ct., 1972-73; assoc. Mudge, Rose, Guthrie et al, N.Y.C., 1973-77; ptnr. O'Connor, Cavanagh, Anderson et al, Phoenix, 1977-80; sr. v.p. Dillon, Read & Co., N.Y.C., 1980-84; mng. dir. Paine Webber, Inc., Washington, 1984—87, 1990—98; asst. sec. Dept. of Interior, 1987-88; mng. dir. Drexel Burnham Lambert Inc., N.Y.C., 1989-90; sgt. at arms U.S. Senate, Washington, 1998—2001; commr. immigration and naturalization serv. U.S. Dept. Justice, 2001—. Bar: Va. 1972, D.C. 1973, N.Y. 1975, Ariz. 1977. Office: US Dept Justice Immigration and Naturalization Serv 425 Eye St NW Washington DC 20536*

ZIGUN, BENJAMIN JOSHUA, psychiatrist, lawyer; b. Boston, Mar. 3, 1962; s. Charles and Sylvia M. Zigun. BA magna cum laude, Yale U., 1984; MD, U. Conn., 1988, JD with honors, 1997. Diplomate Nat. Bd. MEd. Examiners, Am. Bd. Psychiatry and Neurology; lic. physician, Conn. Bar: Conn. 1997, U.S. Patent and Trademark Office 1998, N.Y. 1999. Intern in internal medicine St. Francis Hosp., Hartford, Conn., 1988-89; resident in psychiatry Yale Sch. Medicine, New Haven, 1989-92, asst. clin. prof. psychiatry, 1993—; attending psychiatrist Elmcrest Psychiat. Inst., Portland, 1992-93, Waterbury (Conn.) Hosp., 1993, Yale Psychiat. Inst./Yale-New Haven Psychiat. Hosp., 1993—; consulting psychiatrist Psychiat. Svcs. Inst., LLC/Psych Svcs., LLC, Hamden, Conn., 1998—. Admitting/attending physician dept. psychiatry Hosp. of St. Raphael, New Haven, 1999—. Contbr. articles to profl. jours. Mem. Am. Radio Relay League, Conn. State Med. Soc., Conn. Bar Assn., Conn. Intellectual Property Law Assn., New Haven County Med. Assn., Phi Delta Phi. Avocation: amateur radio.

ZIKA, BILL, psychologist; b. L.A., Jan. 16, 1946; s. Gilbert Francis Z. and Eleanor (Ames) Abranz; m. Sheryl Corinne Willis, Jan. 6, 1974; children: Kurtis (dec.), Shari, Danielle, Adam. BA, UCLA, 1969; MA, Calif. State U., Northridge, 1974; PhD, Massey U., Palmerston North, New Zealand, 1982. Lic. psychologist, Calif.; registered psychologist, New Zealand. Rehab.

counselor New Horizons SFVAR, Panorama City, Calif., 1973-75; dir. counselling svc. Massey U., Palmerston North, New Zealand, 1975-97; clin., cons. psychologist Bill Zika, Dr. Psychol. Svcs., 1993—97, 1999—; sr. psychologist dept. corrections State of Calif., Soledad, 1997—; sec. med. exec. com. Commn. Bd. Psychology, 2000—01. Cons. psychologist Psychology Clinic Massey U., Palmerston North, New Zealand, 1991-97; provider Accident Comp. Commn., Wellington, New Zealand, 1992-97, Stratos, Ltd., Lower Hutt, New Zealand, 1993-97; clin. supr. Manline Men Against Violence, Palmerston North, 1993-97; clin. advisor Youth Line, Palmerston North, 1995-97; chairperson Marriage Guidance, Palmerston North, 1981. Contbr. articles to profl. jours. Lance cpl. USMC, 1966-67. Mem. New Zealand Coll. Clin. Psychologists. Office: Salinas Valley State Prison Hwy 101 Soledad CA 93960

ZIKAKIS, JOHN P. life scientist, biochemist, nutritionist, educator; b. Piraeus, Greece; came to U.S., 1958; s. Philip J. and Salome J. (Moshou) Z.; m. Kiki K. Matrozos, Aug. 29, 1958; 1 child, Salome J. Assoc. engr., Pythagoras Coll., Piraeus, 1956; BA, U. Del., 1965, MS, 1967, PhD, 1970. Third merchant marine engr. Onassis Shipping Enterprises, Ltd., London, 1956-58; lab. asst. DuPont de Nemours and Co., Newark, 1959-61; rsch. asst. U. Del., 1965-70, asst. prof. animal sci. dept., 1970-75, assoc. prof. animal sci. dept., 1975-81, prof. animal sci. dept., coll. marine studies, 1981-89; acad. indust. cons., 1986—; prof. food sci. U. Del., Newark, 1987-89, prof. emeritus, 1989; v.p. United Chitotechnologies, Inc., 1989-93; chief scientist, marine resource specialist Biopolymer Engring., Inc., St. Paul, 1997—, also bd. dirs. Cons. U. Thessaloniki, Greece, 1972-80; vis. prof. U. Panama, 1984-85, sci. advisor, 1985-89; sci. advisor Govt. of Greece, 1972-74; organizer nat. and internat. sci. confs. and symposia. Author: Chitin, Chitosan and Related Enzymes, 1984, Advances in Chitin and Chitosan, 1992; mem. editorial bd. Jour. Agr. Food Chemistry, 1983-86; contbr. over 125 articles to profl. jours. Patentee in field. Trustee Riverside Hosp., Wilmington, Del., 1977-84; pres. bd. dirs. Maison Grande Condominium Assn., Inc., Miami Beach, Fla., 1990-92; bd. dirs. Holy Trinity Greek Orthodox Ch., Wilmington, 1971-73; pres. bd. govs. Commondore Condominium Assn., Ft. Lauderdale, Fla., 1993-94. 1st lt. Greek Air Force, 1952-56. Sr. Fulbright scholar, U. Panama, 1984-85; recipient Gold medal and cert. U. Patra, 1973, cert. recognition, commendation for excellence in rsch., edn., pub. svc. Pres. of U. Del., 1977. Mem. AAAS, Am. Chem. Soc. (historian div. agrl. and food chemistry 1980-84, chmn. pub. rels. com. 1980-85, chmn. disting. svc. award com. 1987-88, co-founder, editor div. agrl. and food chemistry membership directory 1980-86, chmn. div. agrl. and food chemistry 1986-87, Disting. Svc. award 1991), N.Y. Acad. Scis., Del. Acad. Sci., Inst. Food Technologists, Am. Inst. Biol. Sci., Am. Chitosci. Soc. (co-founder, trustee, pres. 1989—), Am. Dairy Sci. Assn., Sigma Xi. Avocations: tennis, sailing, swimming, gymnastics, travel. Office: 307 SE 14th St Fort Lauderdale FL 33316-1929

ZIKMUND, BARBARA BROWN, minister, church history educator; b. Ann Arbor, Mich., Oct. 16, 1939; d. Henry Daniels and Helen Langworthy Brown; m. Joseph Zikmund II, Aug. 26, 1961; 1 child, Brian Joseph. BA, Beloit Coll., 1961; BDiv, Duke U., 1964, PhD, 1969; D in Div (hon.), Doane Coll., 1984, Chgo. Theol. Sem., 1985, Ursinus Coll., 1989; LHD, U. Hartford, 1998. Ordained to ministry United Ch. of Christ, 1964. Instr. Albright Coll., Reading, Pa., 1966-67, Temple U., Phila., 1967-68, Ursinus Coll., Collegeville, Pa., 1968-69; asst. prof. religious studies Albion Coll., Mich., 1970-75; asst. prof. ch. history, dir. studies Chgo. Theol. Sem., 1975-80; dean and assoc. prof. ch. history Pacific Sch. Religion, Berkeley, Calif., 1981-85, dean and prof. ch. history, 1985-90; pres. Hartford (Conn.) Sem., 1990-2000. Prof. grad. sch. am. studies Doshisha U., Kyoto, Japan, 2000—; chmn. United Ch. of Christ Hist. Coun., 1983-85, mem. coun. for ecumenism, 1983-89; mem. Nat. Coun. Chs. Commn. on Faith and Order, 1979-87, World Coun. of Chs. Programme Theol. Edn., 1984-91, Nat. Coun. Chs. Working Group on Inter-Faith Rels., 1992-96, Nat. Coun. Chs. Commn. on Inter-faith Rels., 1996—, chair Commn. on Inter-faith Rels., 2000—, World Orgn. Confs. Theol. Instns., sec. treas., 1992-96, pres., 1996-2000. Author: Discovering the Church, 1983, Clergy Women: An Uphill Calling, 1998; editor: Hidden Histories in the UCC, 1984, vol. 2, 1987; (with Manschreck) American Religous Experiment, 1976; mem. editl. bd. Jour. Ecumenical Studies, 1987—, Mid-Stream, 1991—; series editor: Living Theological Heritage of the United Church of Christ; contbr. articles to profl. jours. Mem. City Coun., Albion, Mich., 1972-75; elector Wadsworth Atheneum, 1994-2000; corporator St. Francis Hosp., 1994-2000, Hartford Hosp., 1996-2000; pres. Greater Hartford Consortium for Higher Edn., 1994-96. Woodrow Wilson fellow, 1964-66; NEH grantee, 1974-75; vis. scholar Schlesinger Libr. Women's History, Radcliffe Coll., 1988-89, Disting. Alumna, Duke Divinity Sch., 1994; recipient Disting. Svc. Citation Beloit Coll., 1986. Mem. Assn. Theol. Schs. (v.p. 1984-86, pres. 1986-88, issues implementation grantee 1983-84), Am. Soc. Ch. History (council 1983-85, pres. elect 1996-97, pres. 1997-98), Internat. Assn. Women Ministers (v.p. 1977-79), AAUW (v.p. 1973-75), Greater Hartford C. of C. (bd. dirs. 1992-95). Democrat. Office: 5901 Montrose Rd Apt N1109 Rockville MD 20852-4705 E-mail: bbz@hartsem.edu.

ZIL, J. S. psychiatrist, physiologist; b. Chgo. s. Stephen Vincent and Marillyn Charlotte (Jackson) Z.; 1 child, Charlene-Elena. BS magna cum laude, U. Redlands, 1969; MD, U. Calif., San Diego, 1973; MPH, Yale U., 1977; JD with honors, Jefferson Coll., 1985. Med. clk. Clinica de Casa de Todos, Tijuana, Mexico, 1968—70; intern, resient in psychiatry and neurology U. Ariz., 1973-75; fellow in psychiatry, advanced fellow in social, cmty. and forensic psychiatry, Yale cmty. cons. to Conn. State Dept. Corrections Yale U., 1975-77, instr. psychiatry and physiology, 1976-77; instr. physiology U. Mass., 1976-77; unit chief Inpatient and Day Hosp. Conn. Mental Health Ctr. Yale-New Haven Hosp., 1975-76, unit chief, 1976-77; asst. prof. psychiatry U. Calif., San Francisco, 1977-82, assoc. prof. psychiatry and internal medicine, 1982—86, vice-chmn. dept. psychiatry, 1983-86; prof. natural sci. Calif. State U., 1985-87; assoc. prof. bioengring. and internal medicine U. Calif., Berkeley, San Francisco, 1982-92, clin. faculty Davis, 1991-99, legis. liaison Ctrl. Office Berkeley, 1988—. Chief psychiatry and neurology VA Med. Ctr., Calif., 1977—86; prin. investigator Sleep Rsch. & Physiology Lab., 1980—86; chmn. dept. psychiatry and neurology U. Calif., San Francisco; dir. dept. psychiatry and neurology Ctrl. San Joaquin Valley Med. Edn. Program and Affiliated Hosps. and Clinics, 1983—86; chief psychiatrist State Calif. Dept. Corrections, 1986—89, chief forensic psychiatrist, 1986—; chmn. State of Calif. Inter-Agy. Tech. Adv. Com. on Mentally Ill Inmates & Parolees, 1986—92; mem. med. adv. com. Calif. State Pers. Bd., 1986—95; apptd. counciloor Calif. State Mental Health Plan, 1988—93; cons. Nat. Inst. Corrections, 1992—94; invited faculty contbr. and editor Am. Coll. Psychiatrist's Resident in Tng. Exam, 1981—86. Author: The Case of the Sleepwalking Rapist, 1992, Mentally Disordered Criminal Offenders, 5 vols., 1989, 2d edit., 1991, Suicide Prevention Handbook, 1987, 2d edit., 1992, 3d edit., 1996, 4th edit., 1996; contbg. author: The Measurement Mandate: On the Road to Performance Improvement in Health Care, 1993; co-author: Psychiatric Services in Jails and Prisons, 2d edit., 2000; assoc. editor Corrective and Social Psychiatry Jour., 1978-97, referee, 1980—, reviewer, 1981—; contbr. articles in field to profl. jours. Nat. Merit scholar, 1965; recipient Nat. Recognition award Bank of Am., 1965, Julian Lee Roberts award U. Redlands, 1969, Kendall award Internat. Symposium in Biochemistry Rsch., 1970, Campus-Wide Profl. Achievement award U. Redlands, 1994. Fellow Royal Soc. Health, Am. Assn. Social Psychiatry; mem. AAUP, APHA, Am. Psychiat. Assn., Am. Assn. Mental Health Profls. in Corrections (nat. pres. 1978-97), Nat. Coun. on Crime and Delinquency, Calif. Scholarship Fedn. (past pres.), Delta Alpha, Alpha Epsilon Delta. Office: PO Box 160208 Sacramento CA 95816-0208 E-mail: corrmentalhealth@aol.com.

ZILBERT, ALLEN BRUCE, education educator, computer consultant; b. Bronx, N.Y., May 26, 1957; s. Murray and Perla Z.; m. Barbara Dale Palley, July 1, 1984; children: Heather Robynne, Jared Lee. BA in Econ., CUNY, 1978; MBA, St. Johns U., 1980, advanced profl. cert., 1982; MEd in Adminstrv. Computer Systems Edn., Columbia U., 1986, EdD, 1988; post-grad., Kennedy-Western U., 1995—. Instr. bus. computer info. systems & quantitative methods Hofstra U., Hempstead, N.Y., 1981-83; asst. prof. info. systems Pace U. Sch. Computer Sci. and Info. Systems, N.Y.C., 1983-89; dir. ancillary systems Advanced Med. Systems, Rockville Ctr., N.Y., 1989-90; asst. prof. mgmt. Long Island U. Sch. Bus., Coll. Mgmt., Brookville, 1990-94; asst. prof. mgmt. info. sys. Sy Syms Sch. Bus., David Zysman prof. of mgmt. info. sys. Yeshiva U., N.Y.C., 1994-2000; assoc. prof. math./computer sci. Molloy Coll., Rockville Ctr., N.Y., 2000—, dir. computer sci. and computer info. systems programs, 2000—. Mem. curriculum com. Pace U. Sch. Computer Sci. and Info. Sys., 1983-89; chmn. personal computer resources com. Advanced Med. Sys., 1989-90; mem. campuswide computer com. L.I. U., 1991-94, chmn., 1993-94, chmn. scholarship awards com., 1990-91; assembly collegiate schs. bus. curriculum planning com. Coll. Mgmt., 1993-94, chmn. computer needs, usage and stds. com., 1990-93, chmn. mgmt. dept. computer com., chmn. scholar awards com., 1992-93; book and software reviewer. Contbr. articles to profl. jours. Mem. IEEE, Assn. for Computer Tng. and Support, Assn. for Computing Machinery, Assn. of Info. Tech. Profls., Internat. Assn. for Computer Info. Sys., Internat. Assn. Mgmt., Info. Resources Mgmt. Assn. E-mail: azilbert@molloy.edu.

ZILINCIK, JEROME MATTHEW, financial analyst; b. Midland, Mich., Nov. 28, 1968; s. Jerry E. and Sandy J. Z. BSBA, Ctrl. Mich. U., 1990, MBA, 1993. Sr. fin. analyst Johnson Controls, Inc., Plymouth, Mich., 1993—. Mem. Inst. Mgmt. Accts. Home: 22260 Madison Dearborn MI 48124 Office: Johnson Controls Inc 49200 Halyard Dr Plymouth MI 48170 E-mail: jeromez@hotmail.com.

ZILKHA, EZRA KHEDOURI, banker; b. Baghdad, Iraq, July 31, 1925; came to U.S., 1941, naturalized, 1950; s. Khedouri A. and Louise (Bashi) Z.; m. Cecile Iny, Feb. 6, 1950; children: Elias Donald, Donna Zilkha Krisel, Bettina Louise. Grad., Hill Sch., Pottstown, Pa., 1943; AB, Wesleyan U., Middletown, Conn., 1947; LLD (hon.), Wesleyan U., 1987. Dir. Zilkha & Sons, Inc., N.Y.C., NY, 1946—, chmn., pres., 1956—. Dir. Cigna Corp., Phila., 1968—96, INA Life Ins. Co. of N.Y., 1973—87, Heartland Tech., Inc., Chgo., Cambridge Assocs., Boston, 1988—2000, Revlon, Inc., 1981—95, Blyth Eastman Dillon & Co., 1976—79, Chgo. Milw. Corp., 1981—96, Mothercare, Ltd., England, 1970—82; v.chmn. bd. Fortune Bancorp, 1990—94, Handy & Harman, 1969—88; chmn. bd. Fidelity Internat. Bank., 1968—79; chmn. Union Holdings, 1984—90. Chmn. exec. com., former chmn. bd. Internat. Ctr. for Disabled, N.Y.C.; trustee emeritus, former chmn. investment com. Wesleyan U.; hon. chmn., former chmn. investment com. Brookings Inst., Washington; former trustee Spence Sch., N.Y.C., French Inst., N.Y.C., Lycee Francais de N.Y.; trustee Am. Soc. of the French Legion of Honor. Decorated officier Legion d'Honneur, officier Ordre Nat. du Merite (France); recipient Freedom of Human Spirit award Internat. Ctr. for Disabled, 1989, Pilier d'Or award French Inst./Alliance Francaise, 1995. Mem.: Coun. Fgn. Rels., The Brook Club, Polo Club, Travellers Club, Meadow Club, Knickerbocker Club, Racquet & Tennis Club.

ZILKHA, SELIM, energy executive; b. 1927; BA, Williams Coll., 1946. With Zilkha & Sons, 1947—60; founder, chmn., mng. dir. Mothercare, Plc., 1960—82; CEO, dir. Zilkha Energy Co., 1985—98; dir. Sonat Inc., 1998—99, El Paso Corp., 1999—; prin. Zilkha Renewable Energy, Houston. Office: Zilkha Renewable Energy Ste 1740 1001 McKinney Houston TX 77002

ZILLMAN, DONALD NORMAN, law educator, university official; b. Madison, Wis., May 19, 1944; s. Theodore William and Helen Ward Zillman; m. Linda Goforth, June 8, 1968. BS, U. Wis., 1966, JD, 1969; LLM, U. Va., 1973. Staff atty. Defenders, Inc., San Diego, 1970; prof. law Ariz. State U., 1974-79, U. Utah, Salt Lake City, 1979-90; dean, Godfrey prof. law U. Maine Law Sch., Portland, 1991-98, Godfrey prof. law, 1998—; interim provost, acad. v.p. U. Maine, 1999-00. Disting. vis. prof. U.S. Mil. Acad., 1990; interim pres. U. Maine, Ft. Knox, 2001-2002. Co-author: The Military in American Society, 1980, Energy Law, 1983, Constitutional Law for the Citizen-Soldier, 1991, Maine Tort Law, 1993, Energy Law and Policy for the 21st Century, Human Rights in Natural Resources Development, 2002. Special asst. atty. gen. State of Ariz., 1978. Maj. U.S. Army, 1970-74. Mem. Am. Law Inst., Rotary Club. Avocations: athletics, theatre, reading. E-mail: zillman@usm.maine.edu.

ZILLY, THOMAS SAMUEL, federal judge; b. Detroit, Jan. 1, 1935; s. George Samuel and Bernice M. (McWhinney) Z.; divorced; children: John, Peter, Paul, Luke; m. Jane Greller Noland, Oct. 8, 1988; stepchildren: Allison Noland, Jennifer Noland. BA, U. Mich., 1956; LLD, Cornell U., 1962. Bar: Wash. 1962, U.S. Ct. Appeals (9th cir.) 1962, U.S. Supreme Ct. 1976. Ptnr. Lane, Powell, Moss & Miller, Seattle, 1962-88; dist. judge U.S. Dist. Ct. (we. dist.) Wash., 1988—. Judge pro tem Seattle Mcpl. Ct., 1972-80; mem. adv. com. bankruptcy rules U.S. Judicial Conf. Contbr. articles to profl. jours. Mem. Cen. Area Sch. Council, Seattle, 1969-70; scoutmaster Thunderbird Dist. council Boy Scouts Am. Seattle, 1976-84; bd. dirs. East Madison YMCA. Served to lt. (j.g.) USN, 1956-59. Recipient Tuahku Dist. Service to Youth award Boy Scouts Am., 1983. Mem. ABA, Wash. State Bar Assn., Seattle-King County Bar Assn. (treas. 1979-80, trustee 1980-83, sec. 1983-84, 2d v.p. 1984-85, 1st v.p. 1985-86, pres. 1986-87). Office: US Dist Ct 410 US Courthouse 1010 5th Ave Seattle WA 98104-1189

ZILVETI, CARLOS BENJAMIN, preventive medicine physician, pediatrician; b. Sucre, Bolivia, June 14, 1928; came to U.S., 1956; s. Carlos and Marina (De La Reza) Z.; m. Halina J. Daszewski, Sept. 8, 1957 (div. Sept. 1976); 1 child: Carlos Joseph III; m. Vita Palazzolo, Sept. 5, 1987. BS, Sacred Heart Coll., Sucre, Bolivia, 1946; MD, U. San Francisco Xavier, Sucre, Bolivia, 1954; MPH, Yale U., 1966. Physician in rural medicine Bolivian Power Co., La Paz, 1955; intern Hosp. Obrero Victor Paz Estenssoro, 1956; asst. resident in pediats. St. Luke's Hosp., Meml. Cancer Ctr., Woman's Hosp., N.Y.C., 1957-58; resident and chief resident in pediats. Hosp. of St. Raphael, New Haven, 1958-59; pvt. practice New Haven and Branford, 1960-63; dir. maternal-child health New Haven Dept. Health, 1964-74; regional med. officer South and Ctrl. Am. Peace Corps, Bogota, Colombia, 1975-76; regional med. officer, sci. attache in West Africa U.S. Dept. of State, Liberia, Ghana, Togo, Sierra Leone, 1976-79; reserve appt. of maj., advanced to col. USAF, San Antonio, 1979-91, chief environ. medicine Wilford Hall Med. Ctr., 1979-83, cons. preventive and occupl. medicine, 1983-91, cons. aerospace-preventive medicine Wilford Hall Med. Ctr. Lackland AFB, 1984-91, ret. col., 1991. Cons. FDA, HEW, Washington, 1966-75; cons. to Headstart Am. Acad. Pediats., Stanford-Norwalk, Conn., 1968-75; regional med. officer, sci. attache West Africa U.S. Dept. State. Contbr. articles to profl. jours. Chmn. gov.'s task force Conn. State Dept. Health, Hartford, 1969-75. Fellow Am. Acad. Pediats. (emeritus), Am. Coll. Preventive Medicine (emeritus); mem. APHA, AMA, New Eng. Pub. Health Assn., Conn. Acad. Preventive Medicine, Am. Occupl. Med. Assn. Avocations: long distance swimming, tennis, golf, international travel, classical music. Home: 9222 Dover Rdg San Antonio TX 78250-3557

ZIMBARDO, PHILIP GEORGE, psychologist, educator, writer; b. N.Y.C., Mar. 23, 1933; s. George and Margaret (Bisicchia) Z.; m. Christina Maslach, Aug. 10, 1972; children: Zara, Tanya; 1 son by previous marriage, Adam. AB, Bklyn. Coll., 1954; MS, Yale U., 1955, PhD, 1959; D (hon.), U. Peru, 1996; LHD in Clin. Psychology, Pacific Grad. Sch. Psychology, 1996, D (hon.), 1997, Nat. U. of San Martin, 1996, Nat. U. Peru, Thessalonoki, Greece, 1997, Aristotle U., 1998. Asst. prof. psychology Yale U., New Haven, 1959-61, NYU, N.Y.C., 1961-67; vis. assoc. prof. psychology Columbia U., 1967-68; prof. psychology Stanford (Calif.) U., 1968—. Pres. P.G. Zimbardo, Inc., San Francisco; sr. project advisor Exploratorium, 1993; host, writer, gen. acad. advisor PBS-TV series Discovering Psychology, 1987, 2001; cons. NBC. Author: Cognitive Control of Motivation, 1969, Canvassing for Peace, 1970, Psychology and Life, 16th edit., 2000, Shyness, What It Is, What To Do About It, 1977, Influencing Attitudes and Changing Behavior, rev. edit., 1977, The Shyness Workbook, 1979, A Parent's Guide to the Shy Child, 1981, reprinted, 1999, The Psychology of Attitude Change and Social Influence, 1991, Psychology, 3rd edit., 1999. Ctr. for Advanced Study of Behavioral Scis. fellow, 1971; recipient Peace medal Tokyo Police Dept., 1972, City Medal of Honor, Salamanca, Spain, Disting. Tchr. award Am. Psychol. Found., 1975. Fellow APA (pres. 2002—, Presdl. citation Discovery Psychology series 1994, Tchg. award 1999); mem. Am. Psychol. Soc., AAUP, Internat. Congress Psychology, Western Psychol. Assn. (pres. 1985, 2001), Ea. Psychol. Assn., Calif. Psychol. Assn. (Disting. Contbn. to Rsch. award 1978), Soc. for Psychol. Study of Social Issues, Sigma Xi, Phi Beta Kappa, Psi Chi. Roman Catholic. Home: 25 Montclair Ter San Francisco CA 94109-1517 Office: Stanford U Psychology Dept Stanford CA 94305 E-mail: zim@psych.stanford.edu. *One of the few virtues of growing up in a poor urban ghetto is the realization that people are the most important resource we have—to be used wisely, well and as often as possible. The second is the tempering of book learning by street wits. The third is to value a career that allows me to contribute to improving the quality of our lives through research and teaching.*

ZIMBLE, JAMES ALLEN, naval officer, physician; b. Phila., Oct. 12, 1933; s. Nathan Norman and Mary Jay (Klaits) Z.; m. Judith Ann Goldberg, Sept. 17, 1961 (div. Apr. 1970); children: Amy B., Jennifer L.; m. Janet Mary Bailey, June 19, 1970 (dec. Dec. 1994); 1 child, Daniel A.; stepchildren: David T., Jennifer G., Melinda S. Richards; m. Mona C. Melton, Feb. 23, 1996; stepchildren: David P., Findley, Emily E. Zadjura. BS, Franklin and Marshall Coll., 1955; MD, U. Pa., 1959; ScD, SUNY Sch. Medicine, 1990. Diplomate Am. Bd. Ob-Gyn, Nat. Bd. Med. Examiners. Intern U.S. Naval Hosp., St. Albans, N.Y., 1959-60, resident, 1963-66; commd. ensign U.S. Navy, 1956, advanced through grades to vice adm., 1987, med. officer in USS John Marshall, 1961-63; staff U.S. Naval Hosp., Camp Pendleton, Calif., 1966-70, Phila., 1970-72, chief obstetrics and gynecology, dir. clin. services Lemoore, Calif., 1972-76; dir. clin. services Naval Regional Med. Ctr., Long Beach, 1976-78, comdg. officer Orlando, Fla., 1978-81; med. officer Hdqrs. U.S. Marine Corps, Washington, 1981-83; fleet surgeon to comdr. in chief Atlantic Fleet, med. advisor to Supreme Allied Command, Norfolk, Va., 1983-86; dep. asst. sec. of def. for strategic planning and med. program mgmt. Dept. Def., 1986-87; surgeon gen. USN, Washington, 1987-91; chief Bur. Medicine and Surgery, 1987-91; pres. Uniformed Svcs. U. Health Scis., Bethesda, Md., 1991—. Assoc. clin. faculty U. Calif.-Irvine, 1977-78; assoc. prof. dept. mil. medicine Uniformed Svc. U. Health Scis., Bethesda, Md., 1983—. Contbr. articles to profl. jours. Decorated Def. Meritorious Svc. medal (5), Legion of Merit (3), Navy Meritorious Svc. medal, Navy Disting. Svc. medal, Def. Superior Svc. medal; recipient Surgeon Gen.'s medal, Frank Brown Berry prize Fed. Healthcare, 2001. Disting. fellow Am. Coll. Physician Execs.; fellow ACS, Am. Coll. Ob-Gyn, Assn. Mil. Surgeons U.S.; mem. AMA (del.), Uniformed Svcs. U. Health Scis. (bd. regents), Nat. Libr. Medicine (bd. regents), NRA, Interagy, Inst. for Fed. Health Care Execs., U.S. Naval Inst., Rsch. Officers Assn., Naval Hist. Found. (trustee), Armed Forces Radiol. Rsch. Inst. (bd. govs.), Am. Hosp. Assn. (del.). Republican. Jewish. Office: USUHS 4301 Jones Bridge Rd Bethesda MD 20814-4799

ZIMBRAKOS, PAUL WILLIAM, editor; b. Aug. 28, 1935; BA, Roosevelt U., 1956. Reporter, writer, editor City News Bur. Chgo., 1958-99; bur. chief New City News Svc., 1999—. Home: 612 Clinton Pl River Forest IL 60305-1912 E-mail: pzimbrakos@tribune.com.

ZIMBROVSKAYA, NATALIA ARSENJEVNA, physicist, mathematics and physics educator; b. Ekaterinburg, Sverdlovsk, USSR, Sept. 28, 1947; d. Arsenii Nicolaevich Zhukov and Zinaida Alexandrovna Chekalova; m. Grigorii Michailovich Zimobovskii, Feb. 4, 1972; 1 child, Alexander. MA in Physics, Ural's State U., Ekaterinburg, USSR, 1970; PhD in Physics, Inst. Physics of Metals, Ekaterinburg, USSR, 1977; DSc in Physics, U. Nizhni-Novgorod (Russia), 1994. Asst. lectr. Ural's Mining Inst., Ekaterinburg, USSR, 1972-73, asst. prof. Russia, 1986-95; prof. Ural's State Mining and Geol. Acad., 1995-99; rsch. prof. dept. physics City Coll. CUNY, N.Y.C., 1998—2001, prof. dept. physics, 2001—. Author: Local Fermi Surface Geometry and HF Effects in Metals, 1996, English transl., 2001; contbr. numerous articles to profl. jours. Mem. AAAS, Am. Phys. Soc., N.Y. Acad. Scis. Russian Orthodox. Office: City Coll CUNY Convent Ave at 138th St New York NY 10031 E-mail: nzimbov@physlab.sci.ccny.cuny.edu.

ZIMENT, IRWIN, medical educator; b. England, 1936; MB BChir, Cambridge U., 1961. Intern, resident, England, 1961-64, USA, 1964-65; resident Bronx Mcpl. Hosp. Ctr., 1965-66; dir. respiratory therpay Harbor Gen. Hosp., Torrance, Calif., 1968-75; chief medicine Olive View-UCLA Med. Ctr., 1975—2001, med. dir., 1994-97; prof. medicine UCLA Sch. Medicine, 1980—2001, prof. emeritus clin. medicine, 2002—. Contbr. articles to profl. jours. Trustee Chest Found., 2000—. Infectious Disease fellow Wadsworth VA Hosp., L.A., 1966-68. Mem. Am. Thoracic Soc. (clin. problems assembly chmn. 1981-82 , resp. bd. med. advisors 1986-90), Am. Coll. Chest Physicians (mem. editl. bd. 1997-2000), Nat. Assn. Med. Dir. Respiratory Care (founding mem., vice pres. 1978, treas. 1979-81, bd. dirs. 1983-89, 98—), Calif Thoracic Soc. (pres. 1980-81, various coms. 1970-85), L.A. Lung Assn. (various coms. 1969-86). Office: Olive View UCLA Med Ctr Dept Med Rm 2B 182 14445 Olive View Dr Sylmar CA 91342-1437

ZIMET, CARL NORMAN, psychologist, educator; b. Vienna, Austria, June 3, 1925; came to U.S., 1943, naturalized, 1945; s. Leon and Gisela (Kosser) Z.; m. Sara F. Goodman, June 4, 1950; children: Andrew, Gregory. BA, Cornell U., 1949; PhD, Syracuse U., 1953; postdoctoral fellow, Standard U., 1953-55. Diplomate in clin. psychology Am. Bd. Profl. Psychology (trustee 1966-74). Instr., then asst. prof. psychology and psychiatry Yale U., 1955-63; mem. faculty U. Colo. Med. Center, 1963—, prof. clin. psychology, 1965—, head div., 1963—. Mem. Colo. Bd. Psychol. Examiners, 1966-72, Colo. Mental Health Planning Commn., 1964-66; mem. acad. adv. com. John F. Kennedy Child Devel. Center, U. Colo., 1966-68; chmn. Council for Nat. Register of Health Service Providers in Psychology, 1975-85, pres., mem. exec. bd. div. psychotherapy, 1970-89; chair exec. com. Assn. Psychol. Internship Ctrs., 1988-91. Bd. editors: Jour. Clin. Psychology, 1962-91, Jour. Clin. and Cons. Psychology, 1964-73, Psychotherapy, 1967—, Profl. Psychology, 1969-75. With USNR, 1943-46. Recipient Disting. Service award Colo. Psychol. Assn., 1976 Fellow APA (council reps. 1969-72, 73—, bd. dirs. 1985-88, Disting. award for profl. contbn. 1987, div. psychotherapy and div. clin. psychology), Soc. Personality Assessment (pres. 1975-76, bd. dirs., chair gen. psychol. services 1987-97); mem. Am. Acad. Clin. Psychology (pres. 1993—), Denver Psychoanalytic (trustee 1968-71), Med. Sch. Profs. Psychology (pres. 1992-94). Home: 4325 E 6th Ave Denver CO 80220-4939 E-mail: Carl.Zimet@uchsc.edu.

ZIMET, MARC JOSEPH, lawyer; b. N.Y.C., Oct. 3, 1964; s. John Zimet and JoAnn Beth Polakoff. BBA, S.W. Tex. State U., 1987; JD, U. LaVerne Coll., 1996. Law clk. L.A. City Atty.'s Office, 1993-96; atty. Ward, Kroll & Jampol, Beverly Hills, Calif., 1996—. Lectr. L.A. Fair Housing Congress. City coun. mem. San Marcos City Coun. Recipient Am. Jurisprudence award Bancroft-Witney, 1995. Mem. ABA, L.A. County Bar Assn., Calif. State Bar Assn., Phi Kappa Theta (pres. 1985-87). Avocations: skiing, racquetball, boating, cooking. Home: 6209 Pacific Ave Unit 104 Playa Del Rey CA 90293-7551 Office: Jampol & Zimet 815 Moraga Dr Los Angeles CA 90049-1633 E-mail: mjzimet@jzlaw.com.

ZIMET, MATTHEW, graphic arts and science educator; b. Bklyn., Aug. 29, 1947; s. Sidney and Rebecca (Wishnofsky) Z.; m. Yvonne Streisinger, Oct. 16, 1994; children: Timnah, Jacob, Abraham, Nathan. MS, U. Mass., 1976, PhD, 1980. Prof. Vt. Tech. Coll., Randolph, 1984—. Illustrator: Zero, 2000, Black Holes & Timewarps, 1996. Mem. Sigma Xi. Jewish. Avocations: art, canoeing, cross-country skiing. Office: Vt Tech Coll Main St Randolph VT 05061 E-mail: mzimet.fac@vtc.edu.

ZIMIC, STANISLAV, romance language educator; b. Slovenia, Apr. 5, 1930; s. Rafael and Olga Zimic; m. Nereida Samuda Zimic. BA, Univ. Ljubljana, Ljubljana, Slovenia, 1955; MA, Univ. Miami, Coral Gables, FL, 1958; PhD, Duke Univ., Durham, NC, 1964. Instr., spanish Rollins Coll., Winter Park, Fla., 1960—61; instr., spanish/french Wash. and Lee Univ., Lexington, 1961—62; asst. prof. Univ. Tex., Austin, 1962—68, assoc. prof., 1968—77; prof., spanish Univ. Tex., Austin, TX, 1977. Mem.: Academia Norteamericana de la Lengua Espanola. Achievements include author of several books and numerous articles on Spanish Golden Age literature. Home: 4904 Valley Oak Drive Austin TX 78731 Office: Univ Texas Dept of Spanish Austin TX 78712 Personal E-mail: nszim@aol.com.

ZIMM, BRUNO HASBROUCK, physical chemistry educator; b. Woodstock, N.Y., Oct. 31, 1920; s. Bruno L. and Louise S. (Hasbrouck) Z.; m. Georgianna S. Grevatt, June 17, 1944; children: Louis H., Carl B. Grad., Kent (Conn.) Sch., 1938; AB, Columbia U., 1941, MS, 1943, PhD, 1944. Research assoc. Columbia U., 1944; research assoc., instr. Polytech. Inst. Bklyn., 1944-46; instr. chemistry U. Calif. at Berkeley, 1946-47, asst. prof., 1947-50, assoc. prof., 1950-51; vis. lectr. Harvard U., 1950-51; research assoc. research lab. Gen. Electric Co., 1951-60; prof. chemistry U. Calif., San Diego, 1960-91, prof. emeritus, 1991—. Assoc. editor: Jour. Chem. Physics, 1947-49; adv. bd.: Jour. Polymer Sci., 1953-62, Jour. Bio-Rheology, 1962-73, Jour. Biopolymers, 1963—, Jour. Phys. Chemistry, 1963-68, Jour. Biophys. Chemistry, 1973—. Recipient Bingham Medal Soc. Rheology, 1960, High Polymer Physics prize Am. Phys. Soc., 1963; Kirkwood medal Yale U., 1982 Mem. Biophys. Soc., Am. Soc. Biol. Chemists and Molecular Biologists, Am. Chem. Soc. (Baekeland award 1957), Nat. Acad. Scis. (award in Chem. Scis. 1981), Am. Acad. Arts and Scis., Am. Phys. Soc.

ZIMMAN STETSON , NANCY See STUART, NANCY

ZIMMARDI, JAMES ANTHONY, musician, music educator; b. Bklyn., Nov. 3, 1960; s. John Thomas and Sandra Millie (Uria) Z. MusB, New Eng. Conservatory, 1984; cert. McClosky vocal technician, McClosky Inst. Voice. Owner East Coast Music Talent and East Coast Prodns., Watertown, Mass., 1991—, The Healthy Voice, Watertown, 1991—; freelance musician, prodr., tchr. voice. Saxophonist, keyboardist, singer, songwriter. Republican. Roman Catholic. Home and Office: PO Box 317 Newtonville MA 02460-0003 E-mail: jazprod@aol.com.

ZIMMER, DAVID LAWRENCE, retired chemical company executive; b. Buffalo, May 11, 1935; s. James Edward and Helen Rita (Casey) Z.; m. Marilyn Margaret Evans, Apr. 12, 1958; children: Timothy M., Daniel J., Maureen M., Peter D. BS in Chemistry, Canisius Coll., 1956. Process application chemist Allied Chem. Co., Tonawanda, N.Y., 1956-57; tech. rep. BFLO Solvents and Chems. (name now CHEMCENTRAL/Buffalo), 1957-65, sr. tech. rep., 1965-74, sr. customer svc. rep., 1974-83, account mgr., 1983-97, ret., 1997. Cons. Ancient Arts, Inc., Amherst, N.Y., 1974-89. Plant campaign chmn. United Way, Buffalo, 1959-96; pres. St. Vincent de Paul Conf., St. Paul's Roman Cath. Ch., Kenmore, N.Y., 1978-93, treas., 1984—; bd. dirs. Mt. St. Mary Acad., Tonawanda, 1984-93; chmn. bldg. restoration fund St. Paul's Roman Cath. Ch., Kenmore, N.Y., 1986. Capt. USAR, 1956-64. Mem. Am. Numismatic Assn. (life, 25 Yr. award 1988). Avocations: numismatics, philately, gardening, roses, travel.

ZIMMER, DONALD WILLIAM, professional baseball coach, former professional baseball manager; b. Cin., Jan. 17, 1931; s. Harold Lesley and Lorraine Bertha (Ernst) Z.; m. Jean Carol Bauerle, Aug. 16, 1951; children: Thomas Jeffrey, Donna Jean. Student pub. schs., Cin. Baseball player Dodger Farm Clubs, 1949-54, Bklyn. Dodgers, 1954-57, Los Angeles Dodgers, 1958-59, Chgo. Cubs, 1960-61, N.Y. Mets, 1962, Cin. Reds, 1962, Los Angeles Dodgers, 1963, Washington Senators, 1963-65, Toei Flyers, Tokyo, 1966; mgr. Cin. Reds Farm Clubs, Knoxville and Buffalo, 1967, Indpls., 1968, San Diego Padre Farm Clubs, Key West, Fla., 1969, Padre Farm Club, Salt Lake City, 1970; coach Montreal Expos, Que., Can., 1971; mgr. San Diego Padres, 1972-73; coach Boston Red Sox, 1974-76, mgr., 1976-80, Tex. Rangers, 1981-82; coach N.Y. Yankees , 1983, 1986, 1996—2000, N.Y. Yankees, 2001, 2002, Chgo. Cubs, 1984, 85, 86, San Francisco Giants, 1987; mgr. Chgo. Cubs, 1988-91; coach Boston Red Sox, 1992, Colo. Rockies, Denver, 1993-95. Mem. minor league All-Star Teams, Hornell, N.Y., 1950, Elmira, N.Y., 1951, Mobile, Ala., 1952, St. Paul, 1953; player World Series teams 1955, 56, 59; coach World Series teams 1975, 96, 98, 99, 2000, 01. Recipient Bill Stern award NBC, 1949; named St. Paul Rookie of Yr., 1953, All Star Team Player, 1961, All Star Coach, 1978, 81, 90, 97, 99, 2000, 2001, 2002; named Nat. League Mgr. of Yr. 1989. Mem. Profl. Baseball Players Assn. (life), Old Time Ball Players Wis. Office: care NY Yankees Yankees Stadium Bronx NY 10451

ZIMMER, GRETA GAY, secondary school educator, educator; b. Goldthwaite, Tex., Mar. 19, 1941; d. Edwin John and Lillian (Elkins) Drueckhammer; m. Henry Junior Stagemeyer (div.); 1 child, Thomas David Dietrich; m. David LeRoy Zimmer, July 16, 1982. BA, Tex. Luth. U., Seguin, 1963; MS, Kearney (Nebr.) State U., 1969. Tchr. Channing (Tex.) Ind. Sch. Dist., 1963-64, Arapahoe (Nebr.) Ind. Sch. Dist., 1964-65, Loomis (Nebr.) Ind. Sch. Dist., 1965-68, Galena Park Ind. Sch. Dist., Houston, 1969-71, LaPorte (Tex.) Jr. High Sch., 1972-86; tchr. English and German, LaPorte High Sch., 1986-96; ret., 1996. Trainer N.J. Writing Inst. in Tex., LaPorte, 1990-93. Author short stories and poetry. Mem. NEA, Tex. State Tchrs. Assn., LaPorte Edn. Assn. (pres. 1990-91). Lutheran. Home: PO Box 827 La Porte TX 77572-0827

ZIMMER, JANIE LOUISE, mathematics educator, administrator; b. Balt., Sept. 25, 1943; d. Joseph Max and Anna Margaret (Vogtmann) Zimmer; m. Gordon Henry Stills, Jan. 7, 1972 (div. May 1978); 1 child, Sanova Stills; m. William Broaddus Long, Jr., Nov. 17, 1984; children: W. Michael, Calvin, Travon. BA in Math., Trinity Coll., Washington, 1966; MEd, Loyola Coll., Balt., 1973; postgrad., U. Md., 1982—. Tchr. math. Norfolk (Va.) Cath. H.S., 1966-69, Balt. City Pub. Schs., 1969-73, math. specialist, 1980-83; chmn. dept. math. Edmondson H.S., Balt., 1973-80; math. supr. Howard County Pub. Schs., Ellicott City, Md., 1983-91, exec. supr. math., 1991-92, curriculum coord., 1992-2000; math. assoc. Rsch. for Better Schs., Phila., 2000—. Cons. Md. Math. League, 1987-2000; prof. U. Md., Balt. County, 1989-95; clown/mathemagician Md., 1981—. Columnist in math. jour., 1986-98; editor: State Functional Math Guide, 1984; contbr. Mathematical Connections: A Bridge to Algebra and Geometry, 1992. Recipient Outstanding Math. Educator award Md. Coun. Tchrs. of Math., 1991, Outstanding Svc. award Md. Coun. Tchrs. Math., 1985, United Cerebral Palsy, 1974, Citizenship award K.C., 1961, Outstanding Alumna of Yr. award Maryvale Trinity Coll. Prep Sch., 1983. Mem. Md. Assn. Supervision and Curriculum Devel. (bd. mem. 1999-2000), Md. Coun. Tchrs. Math. (rep. 1986-94, pres. 1984-85), Nat. Coun. Tchrs. Math. (regional svcs. com. 1994-97, chair 1997-98, chair regional conf. 1991, bd. dir. 2002—), Nat. Assn. Sci. Tchrs., Pa. Sci. Tchrs. Assn., Nat. Mid. Sch. Assn., Pa. Coun. Tchrs. of Math., Pa. Coun. Suprs. of Math., Nat. Coun. Suprs. of Math., Md. Coun. Suprs. of Math., Clowns of Am. Internat., Freestate Clown Alley, Phi Delta Kappa. Democrat. Roman Catholic. Avocations: clowning, dancing, skiing, reading. Home: 125 N Maple St Woodbury NJ 08096-1838 Office: Rsch for Better Schs 112 N Broad Street Philadelphia PA 19123 E-mail: zimmer@rbs.org.

ZIMMER, JOHN HERMAN, lawyer; b. Sioux Falls, S.D., Dec. 30, 1922; s. John Francis and Veronica (Berke) Z.; student Augustana Coll., Sioux Falls, 1941-42, Mont. State Coll., 1943; LLB, U. S.D., 1948; m. Deanna Langner, 1976; children by previous marriage: Mary Zimmer Quinlin, Robert Joseph, Judith Maureen Zimmer Rose. Bar: S.D. 1948. Pvt. practice, Turner County, S.D., 1948—; of counsel Frieberg, Zimmer, Duncan & Nelson LLP, Parker, S.D., 1992—; states atty. Turner County, 1955-58, 62-64; asst. prof. med. jurisprudence U. S.D.; minority counsel U.S. Senate Armed Services Com. on Strategic and Critical Materials Investigation, 1962-63; chmn. Southeastern Council Govts., 1973-75; mem. U. S.D. Law Sch. adv. council, 1973-74. Chmn. Turner County Rep. Com., 1955-56; mem. S.D. Rep. adv. com., 1959-60; alt. del. Rep. Nat. Conv., 1968; pres. S.D. Easter Seal Soc., 1986-87. With AUS, 1943-46; PTO. Decorated Bronze Star, Philippine Liberation ribbon. Mem. ABA, Fed., S.D. (commr. 1954-57) Bar Assns., Assn. Trial Lawyers Am., S.D. Trial Lawyers Assn. (pres. 1967-68), VFW, Am. Legion, Elks, Shriners, Phi Delta Phi. Home: PO Box 640 Parker SD 57053-0640 Office: Frieberg Zimmer Duncan & Nelson LLPLaw Bldg PO Box 550 Parker SD 57053-0550 E-mail: jhzim@aol.com.

ZIMMER, LARRY WILLIAM, JR. sports announcer; b. New Orleans, Nov. 13, 1935; s. Lawrence W. Sr. and Theodora (Ahrens) Z.; m. Dawn M. Caillouet, June 4, 1955 (div. June 1972); children: Larry III, Tracey; m. Brigitte Bastian, Nov. 17, 1972. Student, La. State U., 1953-55; BJ, U. Mo., 1957. Sports dir. KFRU Radio, Columbia, Mo., 1960-66; asst. mgr. programming WAAM Radio, Ann Arbor, Mich., 1966-71; broadcaster football, basketball, 1966-70; sportscaster, sports dir. KOA Radio, Denver, 1971—; broadcaster Denver Broncos Football, 1971-96; broadcaster football, basketball Colo., 1971—; broadcaster Denver Rockets, 1972-74. Adj. prof. journalism U. Colo., 2001—. Bd. mem. Colo. Ski Mus. and Hall of Fame, Vail, 1981-2000, Opera Colo., Denver, 1985—, Colo. chap. Nat. Football Found; adv. bd. Jefferson Co. Youth Advocacy Ctr. 1st lt. U.S. Army, 1958-60. Named Colo. Sportscaster of the Yr., Nat. Sportscasters and Sportswriters Assn., Salisbury, N.C., 1988, 90, 91, 2001, Broadcaster of the Yr., Colo. Broadcaster's Assn., Denver, 1995; recipient Powerade award for best radio/TV sports story of yr. Nat. Sportscasters and Sportswriters Assn., 2000. Avocations: skiing, jogging, opera. Office: KOA Radio 4695 S Monaco St Denver CO 80237-3403 E-mail: larryzimmer@clearchannel.com.

ZIMMER, LAWRENCE JOSEPH, psychiatrist, internist; b. Port Huron, Mich., Mar. 15, 1946; MD, Wayne State U., 1971; grad., Cin. Psychoanalytic Inst., 2000. Diplomate Am. Bd. Psychiatry, Am. Bd. Internal Medicine and Cardiovascular Disease. Rotating intern U. Cin., 1971-72, resident in internal medicine, 1972-74, 75-76, fellow in cardiology, 1974-75, 76-77, resident in psychiatry, 1986-89; pvt. practice Cin., 1989—2001, Ft. Gratiot, Mich., 2001—. Adj. asst. clin. prof. U. Cin., 1989—2001. Mem.: ACP, Am. Psychoanalytic Assn. Office: 4912 Lakeshore Rd Fort Gratiot MI 48059

ZIMMER, MARKUS BERNHARD, federal court administrator; b. Basel, Switzerland; came to U.S., 1948; s. Max Bernhard and Elisabeth (Sulzmann) Z.; m. Shelley Elaine Melcomian, Jan. 5, 1976; children: Jessica, Christopher. BA in Philosophy, U. Utah, 1971, MA in Philosophy, 1975; MEd, Harvard U., 1977; EdD in Philosophy of Edn., 1980. Teaching fellow U. Utah, Salt Lake City, 1971-72; rsch. asst. Harvard Law Sch., Cambridge, Mass., 1977-78; teaching fellow law and ethics Harvard U., 1977-78; ednl. specialist Divsn. Continuing Edn. and Tng., Fed. Jud. Ctr., Washington, 1978-79, spl. asst. to dir., 1979-82; asst. divsn. dir. Div. Continuing Edn. and Tng., Fed. Jud. Ctr., 1983-84, chief legal svcs. tng. br., 1984-87, chief mgmt. tng. br., 1984-87; adj. assoc. prof. mgmt. U. Md., College Park, 1985-87; clk. of ct., dist. ct. adminstr. U.S. Dist. Ct., Dist. Utah, Salt Lake City, 1987—. Mem. fed. dist. ct. case mgmt. and stats. umbrella group Adminstrv. Office of U.S. Cts. (AOUSC), 1992-98, chair tech. panel on automation, 1999—, dist. ct. efficiencies task force, 1992-93, fed. dist. ct. clks. adv. com. to Adminstrv. Office of U.S. Cts., 1990-96, ct. adminstrn. adv. coun., 1995-96; interagy. adv. group on tng. and devel. Office of Pers. Mgmt., Washington, 1984-87; ABA Ctrl. and East European Law Initiative (ABA-CEELI) ct. adminstrn. cons. Bulgarian Ministry of Justice, Sofia, 1992, USIA, Zagreb, Croatia, 1994; ABA-CEELI adminstrn. cons. Constnl. Ct. Bosnia and Herzegovina, 1995; ABA-CEELI legal specialist, Skopje, Macedonia, 1997; faculty, ABA/CEELI Jud. Tng. Inst., Prague, Czech Republic, 2000; spkr., Workshop on U.S. Jud. Conf., Budapest, Hungary, 1998, jud. reform specialist, Warsaw, Poland, 1998, ct. adminstrn. specialist, Bucharest, Romania, 1999, Bratislava, Slovak Republic, 2000; chair U.S. Dist. Cts. Civil/Criminal User Group, 1995-98; mem. U.S. Cts. ad hoc task force on budget allotment simplification, 1996-98. Contbr. articles to profl. jours. Mem. exec. bd. Utah Combined Fed. Campaign, 1989—, bd. chmn. and statewide campaign dir., 1992. Fulbright fellow, 1972-73; recipient U.S. Cts. Dir.'s award for outstanding leadership, 1994, Roy B. Gibson Freedom of Into. award, Utah chpt. Soc. Profl. Journalists, 2000. Mem. ABA (CEELI ct. adminstrn. working group 1991-94, Russian jury trial working group 1993-94), ASTD (dir. justice sys. trainers 1984-86), Fed. Ct. Clks. Assn. (exec. bd. 1991-92). Office: U S Dist Ct 120 Frank E Moss Courthouse 350 S Main St Ste 150 Salt Lake City UT 84101-2180 E-mail: markus_zimmer@utd.uscourts.gov.

ZIMMER, MICHAEL J. lawyer; married; 3 children. BA in Polit. Sci. cum laude, Providence Coll., 1971; JD cum laude, U. Md., Balt., 1975. Bar: D.C. 1975, Va. 1982. Invited witness various energy and energy tax proposals before congrl. coms., various fed. depts. and agencies, and state commns. and agencies, 1977—; pres., gen. counsel Cogeneration and Independent Power Coalition Am., Inc. (now Electric Power Supply Assn.), 1980-90; mem. Am. Coun. Capital Formation, Am. Cogeneration Assn., Clean Coal Coalition, NAS, Energy Mich., Mid-Atlantic Independent Power Prodrs., Independent Power Prodrs. N.Y., Midwest Gas Assn.; active Am. Gas Assn., 1977-80, staff v.p. govt. rels.; group chair dept. and practice energy and project fin. various nat. law firms; nat. lectr. in field, including Va. Polytechnic Inst., U. Wis., Georgetown U.; invited spkr. N.Y. Soc. Security Analysts. Co-author: Energy Law Transactions, 1990, 2001; contbg. editor Independent Energy mag., 1986—, Electric Light and Power, 1999—; mem. adv. bd. programs McGraw-Hill, Internat. Bus. Forum, Fin. Times. Named Indsl. All-Star, Independent Energy mag., 1993, One of Top Leaders of IPP Industry, Independent Energy mag., 1996. Mem. Fed. Energy Bar Assn. (chmn. cogeneration small power prodn. com. 1986-87). Avocation: youth sports activities. Office: Baker & McKenzie 815 Connecticut Ave NW Washington DC 20006-4078 Fax: 202-452-7074. E-mail: michael.j.zimmer@bakernet.com.

ZIMMER, PAUL GERALD, II, retired community care licensing professional; b. Detroit, Oct. 2, 1946; s. Paul Gerald and Beatrice Mae (Mitchell) Z.; m. Shelly Mardell Hallier, May 23, 1980; children: Paul Gerald III, Carrie Lea. BA in Religion/Social Work, Azusa Pacific U., 1973. Ordained to ministry So. Bapt. Conf., 1985. Vocat. rehab. counselor dept. vocat. rehab. State of Calif., Riverside, 1986-88, intake specialist social svc. cmty. care licensing, 1988-91, licensing program supr. dept. social svc. cmty. care licensing, 1991-2001; ret., 2001. Instr., adv. bd. mem. Riverside County Office Edn.-Family-to-Family, 1993—; mem. Riverside County Dept. Pub. Social Svcs. Child Advocacy Coun., 1994—; co-chair RICKI com. Riverside County Dept. Health-Immunizations, 1996-98; monthly music evangelist L.A. Union Rescue Mission, 1984—; mem. Fontana chpt. Am. Red Cross, 1983-87. Author (booklet) The Age of Becoming, 1977; author (music album) Day-A-Comin', 1989, (lyrics) Flashback Music, 1996. Dist. exec. Boy Scouts Am., Redlands/Victorville, Calif., 1981-83, mem. Order of Arrow, 1963—; mem./instr. Riverside County Office Edn. Child Care Initiative Project for Spanish Speaking Care Providers Indio, 1994—; appointed mem. State of Calif. Equal Employment Opportunity Adv. Com.-Disability Adv. Com., Sacramento, 1999-2000; min. Ch. in the Park, Hemet, Calif., 1996—. With U.S. Army, 1967-68. Recipient Youth Adv. of Yr. award Riverside County Office Edn., 1993. Mem. Inland Empire Parents Anonymous (group facilitator, crisis counselor 1990-93). Avocations: writing/performing Christian music, fitness walking, coin collecting. Home: 1188 Wilson Ave Perris CA 92571-4926

ZIMMER, WILLIE MAE, medical/surgical nurse; b. Knoxville, Tenn., Sept. 18, 1941; d. William Baynoise and Edith Mae (Fain) Bains; div.; children: Sharon Kay Zimmer-Wood, Clifton Leroy Zimmer Jr. Diploma, Knoxville Vocat. Sch., 1977; ASN, Walters State Community Coll., Morristown, Tenn., 1986. Cert. med.-surg. nurse. Supr. Camel Mfg. Co., Knoxville, 1965-77; staff nurse Ft. Sanders Regional Med. Ctr., 1977, charge nurse, 1977—, charge nurse, shift leader med.-surg. respiratory unit, 1991—, physicians asst., office nurse local surgeon, 1990-91, house supr., 1991—. Mem. Beta Sigma Phi. Home: 4717 Maplehill Rd Knoxville TN 37914-2916 E-mail: WillieZimmer@aol.com.

ZIMMERLY, JAMES GREGORY, lawyer, physician; b. Longview, Tex., Mar. 25, 1941; s. George James and Irene Gertrude (Kohler) Z.; m. Nancy Carol Zimmerly, June 11, 1966; children: Mark, Scott, Robin; m. Johanna Bross Huffer, Feb. 14, 1991. BA, Gannon Coll., 1962; MD, U. Md., 1966, JD, 1969; MPH, Johns Hopkins U., 1968; LLD (hon.), Gannon U., 1998. Bar: Md. 1970, D.C. 1972, U.S. Ct. Mil. Appeals 1973, U.S. Supreme Ct. 1973. Ptnr. Acquisto, Asplen & Morstein, Ellicott City, Md., 1970—. Chmn. dept. legal medicine Armed Forces Inst. Pathology, 1971-91; prof. George Washington U., 1972-80; adj. prof. law Georgetown U. Law Ctr., 1972—, Antioch Sch. Law, 1977-80; assoc. prof. U. Md. Sch. Medicine, 1973—; mem. sci. adv. bd. Armed Forces Inst. Path., 1997—; cons. Dept. Def., Dept. Justice, HHS, VA, 1971-91. Editor: Legal Aspects of Medical Practice, 1978-88, Jour. Legal Medicine, 1975-78, Md. Med. Jour., 1977-88, Lawyers' Med. Ency., 1980-90. Chmn. bd. dirs. Balt. Rh Lab., 1984—; med. dir. Monumental Life Ins. Co., 1994—, Aegon Spl. Markets Group, Inc.; chmn. Am. Coll. Legal Med. Found., bd. dirs., 1996—. Fellow Am. Acad. Forensic Scis., Am. Coll. Legal Medicine (pres. 1980-81), Am. Coll. Preventive Medicine; mem. ABA, AMA, Md. Bar Assn., Am. Soc. on Law and Medicine, Am. Coll. Emergency Physicians, Md. Med. Soc. Home: 6300 Old National Pike Bluestone Overlook Boonsboro MD 21713 Office: Monumental Life Ins Co 2 E Chase St Baltimore MD 21202-2559 E-mail: JZimmerly@aegonusa.com.

ZIMMERMAN, AARON MARK, lawyer; b. Syracuse, N.Y., Jan. 28, 1953; s. Julius and Sara (Lavine) Z. B.S., Syracuse U., 1974, J.D., 1976. Bar: N.Y. 1977, Pa. 1977, D.C. 1978, S.C. 1978, Fla. 1978, U.S. Dist. Ct. S.C. 1978, U.S. Dist. Ct. (no. dist.) N.Y. Corp. atty., asst. sec. Daniel Internat. Corp., Greenville, S.C., 1977-79; ptnr. Abend, Driscoll & Zimmerman, 1979-81; Zimmerman Law Office, Syracuse, 1981— . Bd. dirs. Syracuse Friends Ametuer Boxing, 1982-92. Mem. Am. Arbitration Assn. (arbitrator), Workers Compensation Com. N.Y. State Bar (exec. com. 1984—), Workers Compensation Assn. of Cen. N.Y. (charter mem., dir., treas. 1980-95), N.Y. State Bar, S.C. State Bar, D.C. State Bar, Fla. State Bar, ABA. Lodge: Masons. Home: 602 Standish Dr Syracuse NY 13224-2018 Office: 117 S State St Syracuse NY 13202-1103

ZIMMERMAN, AL THOMAS, foundation administrator; b. Portland, Oreg., Oct. 24, 1947; s. Cecil Alva Zimmerman and Edna Loretta (Nelson) Smith; m. Virginia Ann Hawver, July 11, 1969; children: Rebecca, Mark. BA in Christian Edn., Seattle Pacific U., 1969; MDiv, Western Seminary, Portland, 1972; BSBA, Warner Pacific Coll., 1990. Cert. specialist in planned giving, Calif. State U., Long Beach. Minister various chs., Oreg. and Wash., 1972-83; dir. of devel. West Hills Ch. Sch., Portland, 1983-84; sales rep. Magnussen Distbg., 1984-86; dir. ann. giving Warner Pacific Coll., 1986-89; exec. dir. North Lincoln Hosp. Found., Lincoln City, Oreg., 1989-93; dir. planned giving Oreg. Health & Sci. Univ. Found., Portland, 1993—. Pres. Mission Advance N.W. Found., Portland, 1996-98. Author (jour.) Planned Giving Today, 1993. Mem. Nat. Assn. Fundraising Profls. (bd. dirs. 1990-92, 97), Willamette Valley Devel. Officers, N.W. Planned Giving Round Table (v.p. 1987-88, pres. 1988), Kiwanis (v.p. 1992-93). Avocations: photography, backpacking. Office: Oreg Health & Sci Univ Found 1121 SW Salmon St Ste 200 Portland OR 97205-2021 E-mail: zimmeral@ohsu.edu.

ZIMMERMAN, AMY J. producer, director; b. N.Y.C., Nov. 4, 1961; d. Arthur S. and Louise (Weild) Z. BA in Journalism and History, U. So. Calif., 1983. Writer, photographer Thoroughbred of Calif. Mag., Arcadia, 1981-85; prodr. Hammond Prodns., Lexington, Ky., 1985; assoc. prodr. NBC Sports, N.Y.C., 1986—; dir. broadcasting Santa Anita Park, Arcadia, 1986—, acting dir. ops., 1999; prodr., dir. Fox Sports Net, L.A., 1996—; cons. Fox Sports, 1998—. Assoc. prodr. The Breeders' Cup, 1992 (Emmy award Best Live Sports Spl. 1992); exec. prodr. Santa Anita Today, 1996 (Eclipse award honorable mention for local tv), Inside Santa Anita, 1998 (Eclipse award hon. mention for local tv), Santa Anita Tonight: One on One, 1993 (Eclipse award honorable mention for local tv); exec. prodr., dir. Best of Santa Anita, 1999 (Eclipse award for local tv); assoc. prodr., editor: A Cup of Courage, 1988 (Eclipse award honorable mention for local tv). Bd. dirs. U. So. Calif. Panhellenic, 1982-83, Sterling Assn. Aviva Ctr., Hollywood, Calif., 1998—. Recipient Internat. Simulcast award, 2000, 2001, Thoroughbred Racing Assn., 2000—01. Mem. Turf Publicists Assn., Nat. Thoroughbred Racing Assn. (racing and TV task force' Internat. Simulcast award 2000, 01), Alpha Gamma Delta. Office: Santa Anita Park 285 W Huntington Dr Arcadia CA 91007-3439 E-mail: azimmerman@santaanita.com.

ZIMMERMAN, BERNARD, investment banker; b. Bklyn., Dec. 7, 1932; s. Jacob and Pearl (Schechner) Z.; m. Joyce M. Singer, Dec. 24, 1960; children: Wayne Jay, Ellen Holly. BBA, City Coll. N.Y., 1954; MBA, NYU, 1957. CPA, N.Y. Fin. exec. consumer products Spartans Industries, Inc., N.Y.C., 1961-65; sr. v.p. Scheinman, Hochstin, and Trotta, Inc., 1965-72; pres. Bernard Zimmerman and Co., Inc., 1972—. Pres. Beacon Hill Mgmt., Inc., 1994-97; sr. v.p. corp. fin. Gruntal & Co., Inc., 1983-84; pres., chmn. bd., pres. St. Lawrence Seaway Corp., Indpls., 1985-93, fin. cons.; sr. v.p. The Zimmerman Group, Inc., 1991-96; chmn. bd. dirs., pres. Beacon Hill Mutual Fund, Inc., Boston, 1994-97; Liquidating trustee Unity Buying Svc. Co. Liquidating Trust, Hicksville, N.Y.; bd. dirs. Sbarro, Inc., Melville, N.Y.; fin. cons. Beautiful Visions-U.S.A., Ltd., Bethpage, N.Y., Task Mgmt. Co., Ridgefield, Conn., 1998-99. Bd. dirs. Inst. Cancer Rsch. and Molecular Medicine, Temple U., Phila.; trustee Sharro Family Found., Melville, 1993—; mem. Nat. Assn. Corp. Dir. Blue Ribbon Commn. on Corp. Governance-Best Practice Coun., 1997. With AUS, 1955-57. Mem. N.Y. State Soc. CPAs. Home and Office: 18 High Meadow Rd Weston CT 06883-2946

ZIMMERMAN, BERNARD, judge; b. Munich, Fed. Republic Germany, May 31, 1946; came to U.S., 1949; s. Sam and Roza (Spodek) Z.; m. Grace L. Suarez, Oct. 23, 1976; children: Elizabeth, Adam, David, Dara Bylah. AB, U. Rochester, 1967; JD, U. Chgo., 1970. Bar: Calif. 1971, La. 1971, U.S. Supreme Ct. 1975, U.S. Dist. Ct. (no., ea., cen. and so. dists.) Calif., U.S. Dist. Ct. (ea. dist.) La., U.S. Ct. Appeals (9th cir.). Law. clk. chief judge U.S. Dist. Ct. (ea. dist.) La., New Orleans, 1970-71; asst. prof. law La. State U., Baton Rouge, 1971-72; ptnr. Pillsbury, Madison & Sutro, San Francisco, 1972-95; legal cons. 3d Constnl. Conv. Commonwealth of the No. Mariana Islands, Northern Mariana Islands, 1995; U.S. magistrate judge U.S. Dist. Ct. (no. dist.) Calif., 1995—. Dep. pub. defender City of San Francisco, 1975; arbitrator U.S. Dist. Ct., San Francisco, AAA; judge pro tem San Francisco Superior and Mcpl. Cts. Bd. dirs., mem. exec. com. San Francisco Lawyers' Com. on Urban Affairs, 1984-95, treas., 1987; mem. regional bd. Anti-Defamation League, 1989-95. Mem. Phi Beta Kappa. Clubs: Olympic (San Francisco). Democrat. Jewish. Office: 450 Golden Gate Ave San Francisco CA 94102-3661

ZIMMERMAN, BILL, political consultant; b. Chgo., Dec. 26, 1940; s. Sidney W. and Jean Weissman Zimmerman; m. Joan Andersson, Aug. 22, 1974; children: Nico Zimmerman, Emma Andersson. BS, U. Chgo., 1963, PhD, 1967. Asst. prof. Bklyn. Coll., 1967-69; lectr. U. Chgo., 1970-71; exec. dir. Med. Aid for Indochina, Cambridge, Mass., 1971-73; organizing dir. Indochina Peace Campaign, Santa Monica, Calif., 1974-75; pres. Loudspeaker, L.A., 1976-80, Zimmerman, Galaty, Fiman & Dixon, L.A., 1981-90, Zimmerman & Markman, Santa Monica, 1990—. Pres. Frontline Campaigns, Berkeley, Calif., 1990-95; exec. dir. Ams. for Med. Rights, Santa Monica, 1996—, Campaign for New Drug Policies, 1999—. Author: Airlift to Wounded Knee, 1976, Is Marijuana the Right Medicine for You, 1998. Founder, chmn. Med. Aid for El Salvador, L.A., 1981-93. Mem. Am. Assn. Polit. Cons. (Pollie award 1992, 94, 96, 98). Democrat. Avocations: flying, scuba diving. Office: Zimmerman & Markman 1250 6th St Ste 202 Santa Monica CA 90401-1612

ZIMMERMAN, CAROLE LEE, public relations professional; b. Roxboro, N.C., Aug. 28, 1948; d. Ray Richard and Annie Theresa (O'Briant) Z.; m. Richard A. Hoehn, Oct. 26, 1991; 1 child, Kristin Nicole Sizemore. BS in Edn., Fla. State U., 1970; publs. specialist cert., George Washington U., 1980; MA in Pub. Comm., Am. U., 1993. Accredited in pub. rels. Tchr. Gadsden County Pub. Schs., Quincy, Fla., 1971-72, Am. schs., Kaiserslautern and Darmstadt, Germany, 1974-76; editor, writer USLICO Corp., Arlington, Va., 1980-84; dir. communications Bread for the World, Washington, 1984-95; dir. comms. Nat. Coun. for Sci. and Enrivonment, 1995-97; dir. comms. and mktg. Am. Pub. Health Assn., 1997—2002, Am. Pub. Human Svcs. Assn., Washington, 2002—. Bd. dirs. N Street Village, 2000—. Scholar, Pub. Health Leadership Inst., 2001—. Mem.: Washington Met. Soc. for Health Care Mktg. and Pub. Rels., Assn. Women in Comms. (bd. dirs. 1996—98), Pub. Rels. Soc. Am., Am. Soc. Assn. Execs. Democrat. Office: Am Pub Health Assn 800 I St Washington DC 20001-3710

ZIMMERMAN, CONNIE A. human resources specialist; b. Harrisburg, Pa., Nov. 11, 1958; AA, HACC, 1978; BS in Pub. Policy, Pa. State U., 2002. Clk. DER , Harrisburg, Pa., 1988—93, exec. sec., 1993—95, adminstrv. asst., 1995—99; adminstrv. personnel officer PennDOT Bureau of Design, 1999—. Vol. PennDOT Buddy Program, Harrisburg, Pa., 2000—; mem. mktg. com. Ctrl. Pa. Women Execs., 1997—; mem. Women's Legis. Exchange, 2001—. Mem.: Nat. Assn. Women Execs., Am. Soc. Pub. Adminstrn., Mitgleider Deutscher Verein, St. Lawrence Fraternal Union. Roman Catholic. Avocations: golf, dancing, music. Home: 933 Highland St Steelton PA 17113-1537

ZIMMERMAN, DAVID ALAN, cardiologist; b. Akron, Ohio, Sept. 22, 1962; s. Henry Edward and Betty Jane (Young) Z; m. Karlyn Marie Hooton, June 4, 1994. BS summa cum laude, Ohio State U., 1985; MD, Duke U., 1991. Diplomate in internal medicine and cardiovascular disease Am. Bd. Internal Medicine. Intern Ohio State U., Columbus, 1991-92, resident, 1992-94; fellow transplantation cardiology Ochsner Med. Found., New Orleans, 1995-96; fellow in cardiology Tulane U., 1996-2000; cardiologist Kennestone Cardiovasc. Cons., Marietta, Ga., 2000—. Mem. AMA, Internat. Soc. for Heart and Lung Transplantation, Am. Soc. Transplantation, Am. Coll. Cardiology.

ZIMMERMAN, DAVID CARL, controller, corporate financial executive; b. Harrisburg, Pa., July 9, 1957; s. Raymond S. and Alice Hoke Z.; m. Jo Ann G. Zimmerman. BBA, Ga. State U., 1981; MBA, Montclair State U., 2001. Field auditor Grand Union, Atlanta, 1981-89, sr. field auditor Wayne, N.J., 1989-96, acctg. mgr., 1996-99; chief fin. officer, controller Dowel Assocs., Morristown,

NJ, 1999—. Mem. AICPA, N.J. Soc. CPAs, Ga. CPAs, Phi Kappa Phi, Alpha Epsilon Lambda, Beta Gamma Sigma. Methodist. Avocation: golf. Home: 74 Donald Pl Waldwick NJ 07463 Office: Ste 201 25 Lindsley Dr Morristown NJ 07960-4456 E-mail: davidz@dowel.com.

ZIMMERMAN, D(ONALD) PATRICK, lawyer; b. Albany, N.Y., Mar. 20, 1942; s. Bernard M. and Helen M. (Eshelman) Z. BA, Rollins Coll., 1964; JD, Dickinson Sch. Law, 1967. Bar: Pa. 1968, U.S. Supreme Ct. 1971. Atty. Legal Aid, 1968-69; pub. defender Lancaster County, Pa., 1969-72; pvt. practice Lancaster, 1974—. Instr. Ct. Common Pleas for Constables, 1976—; solicitor Lancaster County Dep. Sheriff Assn., 1977—, Lancaster County Constable Assn., 1975—; instr. sheriff's dept. Lancaster County for Dep. Sheriffs, 1978-85; of counsel to Dep. Sheriff Assn. Pa., 1979-81; spl. counsel Pa. State Constables Assn., 1981; chmn. Bd. Arbitrators Lancaster County, 1975-81; spl. counsel Legislative Com. to Constable Assn. Pa., 1982. Author: The Pennsylvania Landlord and Tenant Handbook, 1982, revised edit., 1993; editor (with J. Hatfield and A. Taylor) Pennsylvania Constable Handbook, 1998; contbr. articles to profl. jours. Mem. pastoral coun. St. Anthony's Cath. Ch., 1995-98. Recipient Ofcl. Commendation of Merit, Lancaster County Sheriff's Dept., 1979, Ofcl. Commendation of Merit, F.O.P. State Police Lodge 66, 1985, Disting. Svc. award, 1987. Mem. ABA, ATLA, Pa. Bar Assn., Acad. Family Mediators, Lancaster County Bar Assn., W. Hensel Brown Inn of Ct., Lancaster County Constables Assn. (Outstanding Leadership award 1988, Disting. Svc. award as solicitor 1998, 25 Yrs. Dedicated Svc. award 2000). Office: 214 E King St Lancaster PA 17602-2977

ZIMMERMAN, DORIS LUCILE, chemist; b. L.A., July 30, 1942; d. Walter Merritt and Letta Minnie (Reese) Briggs; m. Christopher Scott Zimmerman, June 5, 1964; children: Susan Christina, David Scott, Brian Allan. BS in Chemistry, Carnegie Mellon U., 1964; MS in Chemistry, Youngstown State U., 1989, MS in Materials Engring., 1992; ABD, Kent (Ohio) State U., 1997. High sch. tchr. Ohio County Schs., Vienna and Campbell, 1983-87; sr. chemist Konwal, Warren, Ohio, 1988-91; limited faculty mem. Kent (Ohio) State U., 1991—; temp. full-time instr. dept. chemistry Edinboro U. Pa., 1995-97, 2000. Substitute tchr. County Schs. of Ohio, Warren, 1972-82; tutor, 1965—; vis. prof. Case Western Res. U., Cleve., 2000-2001; vis. faculty Penn. State, 2001-02; instr. Kent State U., Geauga, 2002-. Instr. water safety ARC, Warren, 1965—; chmn. Trumbull Mobile Meals, Warren, 1977-92, Pink Thumb Garden Club, Warren, 1965—. Recipient Svc. award ARC, 1981, Trumbull Mobile Meals, 1985. Mem. Am. Inst. Chemists, Materials Info. Soc., Soc. for the Advancement Material and Process Engring. (treas. 2002—), Am. Chem. Soc. (sec. 1985-90, chmn. elect 1990, chmn. 1991, alternate councilor 1992—, Commendation award 1990), Carnegie Mellon Alumni Assn. (admissions councilor, Svc. award 1981), Phi Lambda Upsilon, Phi Kappa Phi, Sigma Xi. Republican. Methodist. Avocations: masters' swimming, sailboat racing, tennis, bridge. Home and Office: 1390 Waverly Dr NW Warren OH 44483-1718

ZIMMERMAN, EDWIN MORTON, lawyer; b. N.Y.C., June 11, 1924; s. Benjamin and Tobie (Fuchs) Z.; m. Caroline Abbot, July 3, 1956; children: Sarah Abbot, Lyle Benjamin, Miriam Appleton. AB, Columbia U., 1944, LLB, 1949. Bar: N.Y. 1949, D.C. 1969, U.S. Supreme Ct 1969. With Hoover Commn. Reorgn. Exec. Br., 1948; law clk. to Hon. Stanley F. Reed U.S. Supreme Ct., 1950-51; law clk. to Judge Simon H. Rifkind U.S. Dist. Ct., 1949-50; pvt. practice law N.Y.C., 1951-59; prof. law Stanford U., 1959-69; with Justice Dept., 1965-69, asst. atty. gen. charge antitrust div., 1968-69; mem. Covington & Burling, Washington, 1969-94, sr. counsel, 1994—. Mem. coun. Adminstrv. Conf. U.S., 1975—78; mem. mfg. studies bd. Nat. Acad. Sci., 1983—87; adj. prof. George Washington Sch. Law, 1996—2001. Trustee Textile Mus., 1983—, pres. bd. trustees, 1987-96; mem. Folger Poetry Bd., 1990—; mem. adv. bd. Partisan Rev., 1996—. 1st lt. AUS, 1944-46. Mem. ABA, Assn. of Bar of City of N.Y., Am. Law Inst., Coun. Fgn. Rels., Phi Beta Kappa. Home: 1820 Kalorama Sq NW Washington DC 20008-4022 Office: Covington & Burling PO Box 7566 1201 Pennsylvania Ave NW Washington DC 20004-2401 E-mail: ezimmerman@cov.com.

ZIMMERMAN, EVERETT LEE, English educator, academic administrator; b. Lancaster, Pa., Dec. 9, 1936; s. Amos Wanner and Anna (Sensenig) Z.; m. Muriel Laden, Apr. 28, 1963, children: Andrew, Daniel. BA, Bob Jones U., 1958; MA, Temple U., 1961, PhD, 1966. Lectr. Temple U., Phila., 1961-62; instr. Rutgers U., Camden, N.J., 1962-66, asst. prof., 1966-69, U. Calif., Santa Barbara, 1969-72, assoc. prof., 1972-80, prof. English, 1980—, dean, 1988-89, provost, 1997—2001. Author: Defoe and the Novel, 1975, Swift's Narrative Satires, 1983, The Boundaries of Fiction, 1996; also articles. Dem. committeeman, Phila., 1965-66. Jr. Faculty fellow, 1971, Humanities Inst. fellow, 1975 U. Calif.; NEH grantee, 1986; Guggenheim fellow, 1989-90. Mem. MLA, Am. Soc. 18th Century Studies. Home: 1822 Prospect Ave Santa Barbara CA 93103-1950 Office: U Calif Dept English Office of Provost Santa Barbara CA 93106 E-mail: ezimmer@english.UCSB.edu.

ZIMMERMAN, GAIL MARIE, medical foundation executive; b. Fort Wayne, Ind., June 23, 1945; d. Albert Douglas and Aina Dorothy (Johnson) Z. BA, U. Puget Sound, 1967. Intelligence analyst CIA, Washington, 1970-72; research asst. Arthur Young & Co., Portland, Oreg., 1972-74; emergency med. service planner Marion-Polk-Yamhill Counties, Salem, 1975-76; health cons. Freedman Assocs., Portland, 1976-77; legis. asst. U.S. Senator Bob Packwood, 1977-78; exec. dir. Nat. Psoriasis Found., 1979—. Mem. dermatology panel U.S. Parmacopoeial Conv., 1985-94; lay rep. Nat. Inst. Arthritis, Musculoskeletal and Skin Disease, NIH, 1990-94. Founding bd. dirs. Nat. Abortion Rights Action League, Portland, 1977; pres. bd. dirs. Oreg. Common Cause, Portland, 1977-78 Mem.: Internat. Fedn. Psoriasis Assn. (chair 1995—2001, vice chair 2001—). Avocations: tennis; flute. Office: Nat Psoriasis Found 6600 SW 92nd Ave Ste 300 Portland OR 97223-7195 E-mail: gail@npfupa.org.

ZIMMERMAN, GIDEON K. minister; b. Lehr, N.D., Aug. 18, 1920; m. Eleanor Pekrul; children: Paul, Mark (dec.), Thomas. Diploma, N.Am. Baptist Sem., Rochester, N.Y., 1943; BA, Wesley Coll., U. N.D., 1951; postgrad., Bethany Bibl. Sem., 1958-59, Chgo. Lutheran Sem., 1959-61; BD, N.Am. Bapt. Sem., Sioux Falls, S.D., 1960, DD, 1971. Pastor First Bapt. Ch., Auburn, Mich., 1943-47, Grace Bapt. Ch., Grand Forks, N.D., 1947-51, Temple Bapt. Ch., Milw., 1951-55; gen. sec. dept. Christian edn. N. Am. Bapt. Conf., 1955-68, exec. sec., 1968-79, estate planning counselor, 1979-85. Home: 3721 Bardstown Rd Apt 308 Louisville KY 40218-2261

ZIMMERMAN, GOLDA, lawyer, educator; b. Syracuse, N.Y., Sept. 25, 1949; d. Julius and Sara (Lavine) Z.; m. David C. Kapell, Sept. 18, 1977; children: Jermy S., Bethany R. BS in Edn., Boston U., 1971; MS in Ednl. Adminstrn., U. Kans., 1974; JD, Syracuse U., 1980. Bar: N.Y. 1984, U.S. Dist. Ct. (no. dist.) N.Y. 1984, U.S. Tax Ct. 1984. Elem. tchr. St. John's Sch., Lawrence, Kans., 1971-73; adminstrv. asst. U. Kans., 1973-75; sr. sys. analyst, student data sys. Syracuse U., 1975-77; pvt. practice law Syracuse, 1984—. Adj. prof. adoption law Coll. Law Syracuse U., 1989-99; mem. bd. visitors Syracuse U. Coll. Law, 1988—; spkr. various groups on intercoutry and domestic adoption. Author: (with Sandra Crowther) Five Career Education Module for Pre-Service and In-Service Teachers, 1974, Adoption Law in N.Y., 1997, supplement, 2000; editor-in-chief Adoption Law in New York, 1997. Mem.: Boston U. Alumni Assn., Onondaga County Bar Assn. (bd. dirs. 2002—), N.Y. State Bar Assn. (family law sect.), Women's Bar Assn. State of N.Y. (N.Y. chpt. 1985—87, state dir. 1987—89), Am. Acad. Adoption Attys. Democrat. Office: 711 E Genesee St # 200 Syracuse NY 13210-1540

ZIMMERMAN, HAROLD SAMUEL, retired state legislator, newspaper editor and publisher, state administrator; b. Valley City, N.D., June 1, 1923; s. Samuel Alwin and Lulu (Wylie) Z.; m. Julianne Williams, Sept. 12, 1946; children: Karen, Steven, Judi Jean (dec.). BA, U. Wash., 1947. News editor Sedro-Woolley (Wash.) Courier-Times, 1947-50; editor, pub. Advocate, Castle Rock, Wash., 1950-57; pub. Post-Record, Camas, 1957-80; assoc. pub., columnist, dir. Eagle Publs., 1980-88. Mem. Wash. Ho. of Reps., 1967-80; mem. Wash. Senate, 1981-88, Wash. State Environ. Hearings Bd., Lacey, 1988-93. Mem. Grange, Lions, Kiwanis, Sigma Delta Chi, Sigma Chi. Republican. United Methodist.

ZIMMERMAN, HOWARD ELLIOT, chemist, educator; b. N.Y.C., July 5, 1926; s. Charles and May (Cohen) Zimmerman; m. Jane Kirschenheiter, June 3, 1950 (dec. Jan. 1975); children: Robert, Steven, James; m. Martha L. Bailey Kaufman, Nov. 7, 1975 (div. Oct. 1990); m. Peggy J. Vick, Oct. 1991; stepchildren: Peter Kaufman, Tanya Kaufman. BS, Yale U., 1950, PhD, 1953. NRC fellow Harvard U., 1953-54; faculty Northwestern U., 1954-60, asst. prof., 1955-60; assoc. prof. U. Wis., Madison, 1960-61, prof. chemistry, 1961—, Arthur C. Cope and Hilldale prof. chemistry, 1975—. Chmn. 4th Internat. Union Pure and Applied Chemistry Symposium on Photochemistry, 1972; organizer, chmn. Organic Photochemistry, 1972, Organic Photochemistry Symposium at Pacifichem Honolulu, 1995, Organic Photochemistry Sumposium at Pacifichem, 2000, Honolulu, 00. Author: (book) Quantum Mechanics for Organic Chemists, 1975; mem. editl. bd.: Jour. Organic Chemistry, 1967—71, mem. editl. bd.: Molecular Photochemistry, 1969—75, mem. editl. bd.: Jour. Am. Chem. Soc., 1982—85, mem. editl. bd.: Revs. Reactive Intermediates, 1984—89; contbr. articles to profl. jours. Recipient Halpern award for photochemistry, N.Y. Acad. Scis., 1979, Chem. Pioneer award, Am. Inst. Chemists, 1986, Sr. Alexander vonHumboldt award, 1988, Hilldale award, U. Wis., 1988—89, 1990. Mem.: NAS, Inter-Am. Photochemistry Assn. (co-chmn. orgnic divsn. 1977—79, exec. com. 1979—86), German Chem. Soc., Chem. Soc. London, Am. Chem. Soc. (James Flack Norris award 1976, Arthur C. Cope Scholar award 1991), Phi Beta Kappa, Sigma Xi. Home: 7813 Westchester Dr Middleton WI 53562-3671 Office: U Wis Chemistry Dept 1101 University Ave Madison WI 53706-1322 E-mail: Zimmerman@chem.wisc.edu.

ZIMMERMAN, JAMES M. retail company executive; b. 1944; Chmn. Rich's Dept. Store div. Federated Dept. Stores, 1984-88; pres., COO Federated and Allied Dept. Stores, Cin., 1988-97; chmn., CEO Federated Dept. Stores, 1997—. Office: Federated Department Stores Inc 7 W 7th St Cincinnati OH 45202-2424*

ZIMMERMAN, JAY JAMES, mathematics educator; b. Evanston, Ill., Aug. 10, 1954; s. William Robert and Elsie Lorraine Zimmerman; m. Rebecca Louise Alderson, Dec. 10, 1988. BA, Knox Coll., 1976; MS, U. Ill., 1979, PhD, 1983. Instr. Mich. State Univ., East Lansing, 1983-86; asst. prof. Univ. Ala., Tuscaloosa, 1986-89, Towson (Md.) Univ., 1989—. Contbr. articles to profl. jours. Mem. Am. Math. Soc., Math. Assn. Am. Office: Towson U Math Dept 8000 York Rd Towson MD 21252 E-mail: jzimmerman@towson.edu.

ZIMMERMAN, JEAN, lawyer; b. Berkeley, Calif., Dec. 3, 1947; d. Donald Scheel Zimmerman and Phebe Jean (Reed) Doan; m. Gilson Berryman Gray III, Nov. 25, 1982; children: Charles Donald Buffum and Catherine Elisabeth Phebe (twins); stepchildren: Alison Travis, Laura Rebecca, Gilson Berryman. BSBA, U. Md., 1970; JD, Emory U., 1975. Bar: Ga. 1975, D.C. 1976, N.Y. 1980. Asst. mgr. investments FNMA, Washington, 1970-73; assoc. counsel Fuqua Industries Inc., Atlanta, 1976-79; assoc. Sage Gray Todd & Sims, N.Y.C., 1979-84; from assoc. counsel to sr. v.p., gen. counsel, sec. IBJ Whitehall Bank & Trust Co., 1994-99; sr. v.p., gen. counsel, sec., bd. dirs. IBJ Schroder Bus. Credit Corp., 1996-98, Innovest Capital Mgmt., Inc., N.Y.C., 1997-99; sr. v.p., gen. counsel, sec. Innovest Corp., 1997-99; from gen. counsel, sec. to exec. v.p. ops. and legal ArrowSight, Inc. (formerly Parent-Watch.com), 2001—. From asst. sec. to sr. v.p., gen. counsel, sec., bd. dirs. IBJ Whitehall Bus. Credit Corp., IBJ Whitehall Capital Corp., IBJ Whitehall Securities, Inc., Delphi Asset Mgmt., Inc., Innovest Asset Mgmt., Inc., N.Y.C., 1997-99; from asst. sec. to v.p., gen. counsel, sec. IBJ Schroder Internat. Bank, Miami, Fla., 1989-98; sr. v.p., gen. counsel, sec. Execution Svcs., N.Y.C., 1991-93. Founder, officer ERA Ga., Atlanta, 1977-79; bd. dirs. Ct. Apptd. Spl. Advs., 1988-94. Named one of Outstanding Atlantans, 1978-79; recipient Disting. Alumni award Emory U. Sch. Law, 1999. Mem.: LWV, Am. Soc. Corp. Secs., Inc., Ga. Assn. Women Lawyers (bd. dirs. 1977—79), Assn. of Bar of City of N.Y., ABA, Assn. Emory Alumni (pres. 1999—, bd. govs. 2000—), DAR.

ZIMMERMAN, JO ANN, health services and educational consultant, former lieutenant governor; b. Van Buren County, Iowa, Dec. 24, 1936; d. Russell and Hazel (Ward) McIntosh; m. A. Tom Zimmerman, Aug. 26, 1956; children: Andrew, Lisa, Don and Ron (twins), Beth. Diploma, Broadlawns Sch. of Nursing, Des Moines, 1958; BA with honors, Drake U., 1973; postgrad., Iowa State U., 1973-75. RN, Iowa. Asst. head nurse maternity dept. Broadlawns Med. Ctr., Des Moines, 1958-59, weekend supr. nursing svcs., 1960-61, supr. maternity dept., 1966-68; instr. maternity nursing Broadlawns Sch. Nursing, 1968-71; health planner, community rels. assoc. Iowa Health Systems Agy., Des Moines, 1978-82; mem. Iowa Ho. Reps., 1982-86; lt. gov., pres. of Senate, State of Iowa, 1987-91; cons. health svcs., grant writing and continuing edn. Zimmerman & Assocs., Des Moines, 1991—2000; dir. patient care svcs. Nursing Svcs. Iowa, 1996-98; nurse case mgr. Olsten Health Svcs. (now Gentiva Health Svcs.), 1998—; part-time tour dir. Travel, Inc., 2001—. Ops. dir. Medlink Svcs., Inc., Des Moines, 1992-96. Contbr. articles to profl. jours. Mem. advanced registered nurse practioner task force on cert. nurse mid-wives Iowa Bd. Nursing, 1980-81, Waukee, Polk County, Iowa Health Edn. Coord. Coun., Iowa Women's Polit. Caucus, Dallas County Women's Polit. Caucus; chmn. Des Moines Area Maternity Nursing Conf. Group. 1969-70, task force on sch. health svcs. Iowa Dept. Health, 1982, task force health edn. Iowa Dept. Pub. Instruction, 1979, adv. com. health edn. assessment tool, 1980-81, Nat. Lt. Govs., chair com. on Agrl. and Rural Devel., 1989; Dallas County Dem. Ctrl. Com., 1972-84, 98—; bd. dirs. Waukee Cmty. Sch. Bd., 1976-79, pres. 1978-79; bd. dirs. Iowa PTA, 1979-83, chairperson Health Com., 1980-84; mem. steering com. ERA, Iowa, 1991-92; founder Dem. Activist Women's Network (DAWN), 1992. Mem. ANA, LWV (health chmn. met. Des Moines chpt.), Iowa Nurses Assn., Iowa League for Nursing (bd. dirs. 1979-83), Family Centered Childbirth Edn. Assn. (childbirth instr., advisor), Iowa Cattleman's Assn., Am. Lung Assn. (bd. dirs. Iowa 1988-92), Dem. Activist Women's Network (founder 1992). Mem. Christian Ch. Avocations: gardening, sewing, reading, bridge, breeding British White cattle. Office: Gentiva Health Svcs 3737 Westown Pkwy Ste 2C West Des Moines IA 50266-1028 E-mail: atzzzzz@aol.com.

ZIMMERMAN, JOHN, public relations executive; Dir. pub. and consumer affairs Meijer, Inc., Grand Rapids, Mich., 1994—. Office: Meijer Inc 2929 Walker Ave NW Grand Rapids MI 49544-9428

ZIMMERMAN, JORDAN, marketing professional; Pvt. practice as chmn, CEO, 1984—. Achievements include led Just Say No marketing initiative during the Carter administration which is one of the most recognizable anit-drug campaigns to date. Office: 2200 West Commerical Blvd Fort Lauderdale FL 33309*

ZIMMERMAN, JOSEPH FRANCIS, political scientist, educator; b. Keene, N.H., June 29, 1928; s. John Joseph and May Veronica (Gallagher) Z.; m. Margaret Bernardette Brennan, Aug. 2, 1958; 1 child, Deirdre Ann. BA, U. N.H., 1950; MA, Syracuse U., 1951, PhD, 1954. Instr. govt. Worcester Poly. Inst., 1954-55, asst. prof., 1955-57, assoc. prof., 1957-62, prof., 1962-65; lectr. Clark U., Worcester, Mass., 1957-65; prof. polit. sci. SUNY, Albany, 1965—. Staff dir. N.Y. State Joint Legis. Com. Transp., 1967-68, rsch. dir., 1968-73; rsch. dir. N.Y. State Select Legis. Com. Transp., 1977-82, Legis. Commn. on Critical Transp. Problems, 1982-95. Author: State and Local Government, 1962, The Massachusetts Town Meeting: A Tenacious Institution, 1967, The Federated City: Community Control in Large Cities, 1972, Pragmatic Federalism, The Reassingment of Functional Responsibility, 1976, (with Frank W. Prescott) The Politics of the Veto of Legislation in New York, 1980, The Government and Politics of the Empire State, 1981, Local Discretionary Authority, 1981, (with Deirdre A. Zimmerman) The Politics of Subnational Governance, 1983, State-Local Relations: A Partnership Approach, 1983, 2d edit., 1995 (CHOICE award as outstandin acad. book, 1984), Participatory Democracy: Populism Revived, 1986, Federal Preemption: The Silent Revolution, 1990, Contemporary American Federalism, 1992, (with Wilma Rule) United States Electoral System: Their Impact Upon Women and Minorities, 1992, (with Wilma Rule) Electoral Systems in Comparative Perspective: Their Impact on Women Minorities, 1994, Curbing Unethical Behavior of Government, 1994, Interstate Relations: The Neglected Dimension of Federalism, 1996, The Recall: Tribunal of the People, 1997, The New England Town Meeting: Democracy in Action, 1999; The Initiative: Citizen Law-Making, 1999, (with Wilma Rule) The U.S. House of Representatives: Reform or Rebuild?, 2000, The Referendum: The People Decide Public Policy, 2001; contbr. articles to profl. publs. Pres. Citizens' Plan E Assn., Worcester, 1960-62, Citizens for Neighborhood Improvement Worcester, 1957-59. Served to capt. USAF, 1951-53. Named 1 of 3 Outstanding Young Men Worcester Jr. C. of C., 1959, 61, 1 of 3 Outstanding Young Men Mass, Jr. C. of C., 1961, disting. citizen award Nat. Conf. on Govt., 1986. Mem. Am. Polit. Sci. Assn. (Outstanding Academician sect. intergovtl. adminstrn. 1997), Am. Soc. Pub. Adminstrn. (Outstanding Federalism Academician 1997), Nat. Mcpl. League. Clubs: German-Am. Social. Roman Catholic. Home: 82 Greenock Rd Delmar NY 12054-4414 Office: SUNY Rockefeller College 135 Western Ave Albany NY 12222

ZIMMERMAN, KATHLEEN MARIE, artist; b. Floral Park, N.Y., Apr. 24, 1923; d. Harold G. and Evelyn M. (Andrade) Z.; m. Ralph S. Iwamoto, Nov. 23, 1963. Student, Art Students League, N.Y.C., 1942-44, Nat. Acad. Sch. Fine Arts, 1944-47, 50-54. Tchr. drawing and painting Midtown Sch. Art, N.Y.C., 1947-52 Illustrator (with Ralph S. Iwamoto) Diet for a Small Planet, 1971;one-woman shows include Westbeth Gallery, N.Y.C., 1973—74, St. Mary's Coll., St. Mary's City, Md., 1990, Broome St. Gallery, N.Y.C., 2002, exhibited in group shows at Woodstock Art Gallery, N.Y., 1945, Nat. Arts Club, N.Y.C., 1948—56, 1984, Emily Lowe Award Show, 1951, Contemporary Arts Gallery, N.Y.C., 1952, 1960, Village Art Ctr., 1956—61, Allied Artists Ann., N.Y.C., 1956, 1978, 1980—91, 1993—2002, Studio Gallery, 1957—60, Nat. Assn. Women Artists, N.Y.C., 1957—85, 1987—98, 2000, Art USA, 1958, ACA Gallery, 1958—59, City Ctr. Gallery, 1960, Janet Nessler Gallery, N.Y.C., 1961, Silvermine Guild, Conn., 1962, Pioneer Gallery, Cooperstown, N.Y., 1962—63, Audubon Artists, N.Y.C., 1963—2002, NAD, 1969—2001, Women Artists Award Winners, N.Y.C., 1974, Am. Watercolor Soc., 1975—78, 1980, Cheyenne (Wyo.) Western Galleries, 1975—77, Edward-Dean Mus., Cherry Valley, Calif., 1975—77, Frye Mus., Seattle, 1975—76, 1997, Boise Gallery Art, 1975, Central Wyo. Mus. Art, 1975—76, Willamette U., 1975, Yellowstone Art Ctr., Billings, Mont., 1975, Utah State U., 1975, Applewood Art Gallery, Colo., 1976, Charleston Art Gallery, W.Va., 1976, Kent State U., 1976, Cin. Art Club, 1976, Martello Mus., Key West, Fla., 1976, Buecker Gallery, N.Y.C., 1976, Anchorage Fine Arts Mus., 1976, Davis and Long Gallery, N.Y.C., 1977, Butler Inst. Am. Art, 1978, 2000, Washington Square East Gallery, NYU, 1979, Internat. Festival Women Artists, Copenhagen, 1980, Westbeth Gallery, N.Y.C., 1980, 1983, 1999—2002, City Gallery, 1981, Bergen Cmty. Mus., Paramus, N.J., 1983, Kenkeleba Gallery, N.Y.C., 1985, Adelphi U., Garden City, N.Y., 1987, Lotos Club, N.Y.C., 1987, Temperance Hall Gallery, Bellport, N.Y., 1987, Monmouth Mus., Lincroft, N.J., 1987, Marbella Gallery, N.Y.C., 1989, Knickerbocker Artists, 1990, Brownstone Gallery, N.Y.C., 1993, Viridian Gallery, 1995, Sundance Gallery, Bridgehampton, N.Y., 1996, Mcpl. Art Ctr., Athens, Greece, 1996, ISE Art Found., N.Y.C., 1996, Nat. Soc. Painters in Casein & Acrylic, 1997—2001, Zimmerli Mus., Rutgers U., New Brunswick, N.J., 1998, Gallery OneTwentyEight, N.Y.C., 2001—02, Represented in permanent collections Butler Inst. Am. Art, Youngstown, Ohio, Sheldon Swope Art Gallery, Terre Haute, Ind., Lauren Rogers Mus. Art, Laurel, Miss., U. Wyo. Art Mus., Laramie, U. Miami Lowe Art Mus., Coral Gables, Fla., N.C. Mus. Art, Raleigh, Swarthmore Coll., Pa., Erie Art Ctr., Nat. Acad. Design, N.Y.C., Zimmerli Mus., Rutgers U., New Brunswick, Nat. Mus. Women in the Arts, Washington; bibliography James Mellow, N.Y. Times Art Review, 1973, Hilton Kramer, N.Y. Times Review, 1977, Helen A. Harrison, N.Y. Times Review, 1987, contbr. (bibliography) The Art of Collage, 1978, Mastering Color & Design in Watercolor, 1981; The Collage Handbook, 1985, Painting Without a Brush, 1992, Collage Techniques, 1994. John F. and Anna Lee Stacey scholar, 1954; recipient Nat. Soc. Painters in Casein and Acrylic award 1997, Liquitex Art award, 1999, Winsor & Newton award 2001. Mem.: NAD (Henry Ward Ranger Fund purchase prize 1976, cert. of merit 1980, Henry Ward Ranger Fund purchase prize 1982, L.G. Sawyer prize 1988, Ogden Pleissner Meml. award 1991, William A. Paton prize 1993, 1997, Zellah W. Pike prize 2001), N.Y. Artists Equity Assn. (Dr. Maury Leibovitz award 1985), Allied Artists Am. (Silver medal 1981, Jane Peterson award 1985, Creative Watercolor prize 1989, Silver medal 1991, Creative Watercolor prize 1997, Mary Lou Fitzgerald Meml. award 1998, Gold medal of honor 2001), Nat. Assn. Women Artists (14 prizes 1957—), Am. Watercolor Soc. (Barse Miller Meml. award 1976), Audubon Artists (John Wenger Meml. award 1978, Ralph Fabri medal 1981, J&E Liskin Meml. award 1987, Dick Blick award 1994, Gold medal of honor 2001, Art Students League award 2002). Home: 463 West St Apt 1110A New York NY 10014-2040

ZIMMERMAN, LANCE Y. counselor, musician; b. Reedley, Calif., Sept. 30, 1967; s. G. Wayne and Martha Lee (Yoder) Z.; m. Christina Suzanne Isaac, Nov. 13, '999. BA in Psychology, Bethel Coll., 1989; MEd, Wichita State U., 1997. Lic. profl. counselor Mo. Mental health technician, case mgr. Prairie View, Inc., Newton, Kans., 1992-94; case mgr. specialist cmty. living and support sys. St. Francis Hosp., Wichita, 1994-96; owner, operator Rowan L.L.P. Celtic Music from the Heartland, Lawrence, 1997—; profl. counselor Cath. Charities, St. Joseph, Mo., 2000—01, Samaritan Counseling Ctr., St. Joseph, 2002—. Vol. ch.-based missions to inner city of Toronto, ont., Can. Mennonite. Avocations: weight lifting, hiking, music improvisation, travel. Office: Samaritan Counseling Ctr 207 N 7th St Saint Joseph MO 64501 Fax: 816-232-2607. E-mail: www.cathcahr@ccp.com., lyzimmerman@wildmail.com.

ZIMMERMAN, LARRY JOHN, anthropology educator; b. Anamosa, Iowa, May 24, 1947; s. August Dietrich and Minnie Heiken Zimmerman; m. Karen Louise Pike, July 18, 1970; children: Dietrich, Alice. BA, U. Iowa, 1969, MA, 1976; PhD, U. Kans., Lawrence, 1976. Disting. regents prof. anthropology U. S.D., Vermillion, 1974-96; prof., chair Am. Indian and Native studies U. Iowa, Iowa City, 1998—2001, adj. prof. anthropology, 2001—. Harrington lectr. Coll. Arts and Scis., U. S.D., 1992. Author: (book) Native North America, 2000; editor: (book) Indians and Anthropologists, 1997. Named Tchr. of Yr., U. S.D. Student Assn., 1980, Nat. Lectr., Sigma Xi, 1991-92. Fellow Am. Anthropol. Assn. Avocations: travel, reading. Home: 3916 Freedoms Trail NE Iowa City IA 52240-8175 Office: U Iowa 114 Macbride Hall Iowa City IA 52242-1322 E-mail: larry-zimmerman@uiowa.edu., oneota@earthlink.net.

ZIMMERMAN, LYDIA, retired community health nurse, consultant; b. McMinnville, Oreg., Jan. 12, 1929; d. Frederick H. and Anna Katarina (Beisel) Koch; m. Howard C. Zimmerman, July 14, 1956; children: Sylvia, Angela, Joan, Garth. Diploma in nursing, Emanuel Hosp. Sch. Nursing, Portland, Oreg., 1949; BSN, U. Wash., 1953; cert. sch. nurse practitioner, UCLA, 1977. RN Calif., credentialed sch. nurse. Asst. supr., head nurse surg. Emanuel Hosp., Portland, Oreg., 1949-50; coll. nurse Linfield Coll., McMinnville, 1951-52; public health nurse Lane County Health Dept., Eugene, 1953-57; sch. nurse-counselor Springfield H.S.; staff nurse, asst. supr. maternal-child, mental health Lane County Health Dept., Eugene, Oreg., 1958-63; public health nurse Lucas County Health Dept., Toledo, 1967-69; private nurse Shafter, Calif., 1972-74; sch. nurse Rosedale Sch. Dist., Bakersfield, 1974-76, Beardsley Sch. Dist., Bakersfield, 1974-80, Panama-Buena Vista Union Sch. Dist., Bakersfield, 1974-96; ret., 1996. Lctr. Bakersfield Coll., Calif. State Coll., Bakersfield. Vol. Kern County Collaborative, 1998—2000. Mem.: AAUW, Am. Sch. Health Assn., Learning Disabilities Assn. Am. (pres. Kern County affiliate 1972—74, 1975—78, 1988—94, voting dir. to state bd. dirs. 1993—2000, bd. dirs. Kern County 1993—2002, state nominating chmn. 2000, co-founder, pres. Kern County affiliate 1996—2000), Assn. Children with Learning Disabilities, Calif. Assn. Neurologically Handicapped Children, Ctr. Sci. in Pub. Interest, Nat. Coun. on Family Rels., Sex Info. and Edn. Coun. U.S., Kern County Sch. Nurses Orgn. (pres. 1981—83, 1991—92, co-founder), Calif. Sch. Nurses Orgn., Nat. Assn. Sch. Nurses (Calif. rep. 1986—88), Am. Acad. Nurse Practitioners, Am. Hist. Soc. Germans from Russia, Sigma Theta Tau.

ZIMMERMAN, MARILYN CLAIRE, surgeon; b. San Francisco; m. Robert A. Mickel; children: Samuel, Gabriel. BS, BA, U. Calif. Davis, 1974; MD, UCLA, 1978. MD. Staff physician Olive View-UCLA Med. Ctr., Sylmar, Calif., 1984-95; asst. prof. surgery UCLA Med. Ctr., 1984-95; chief head and neck surgery Olive View-UCLA Med. Ctr., Sylmar, 1989-95; physician pvt. practice San Francisco, 1995—. Contbr. articles to profl. jours. Fellow ACS, Am. Acad. Otolaryngology, Head and Neck Surgery, Am. Soc. for Head and Neck Surgery, Assn. for Rsch. in Otolaryngology, Am. Laryngol., Rhinol. and Otolaryngology Soc. E-mail: zimmickel@earthlink.net.

ZIMMERMAN, MARLIN U., JR. chemical engineer; b. Akron, Ohio, Aug. 2, 1923; s. Marlin Ulrich and Helen (Nelson) Z. BChemE, Johns Hopkins U., 1944; MBA, Harvard U., 1966. Registered profl. engr., Ohio. Jr. engr. Standard Oil Co. (Ohio), Cleve., 1944-46, engr., 1946-48, sr. engr., 1948-49, process engr. Lima (Ohio) refinery, 1949-50, group engr., 1951-55, group supr., 1956-60, supr. process sys. sect., 1961-63, head acrylonitrile task force, 1961, tech. specialist, 1964-66; mgr. long term planning Norton Co., Worcester, Mass., 1966-69; cons. John Van Der Valk & Assocs., N.Y.C., 1970-73; pvt. practice cons. chem. engr. ammonia-urea Hackensack, N.J., 1974—. Head task force to help commercialize Sohio acrylonitrile process. Contbr. articles to profl. jours. Baker scholar, 1966. Mem. AIChE, Johns Hopkins Club, Tudor and Stuart Club, Tau Beta Pi, Omicron Delta Kappa, Beta Theta Pi. Methodist. Achievements include patent for process improvement of Tosco shale process for oil recovery, patent for pig handling for gasoline blender meter testing loop, others. Avocations: travel, photography, reading, investing, computer programming. Home and Office: 229 Union St Hackensack NJ 07601-4225

ZIMMERMAN, MARTIN E. financial executive; b. Chgo., Jan. 28, 1938; s. Joseph and Sylvea Zimmerman; m. Rita Kalifon, June 20, 1961 (div. 1992); children: Jacqueline, Adam. BSEE, MIT, 1955-59; MBA in Fin., Columbia U., 1961. Dir. market research Nuclear-Chgo., Inc. div. G.D. Searle & Co., 1964-67; pres. Telco Mktg. Services, Inc., Chgo., 1967-74; chmn., chief exec. officer Linc Capital, Inc., 1975-2000; chmn. Linc Capital, 1975-2000; chmn., CEO LFC Capital, Inc., 2000—. Contbr. numerous articles on leasing to profl. mags. Bd. overseers Columbia U. Grad. Sch. Bus.; trustee Mus. Contemporary Art, Chgo. Capt. U.S. Army, 1961-63. McKinsey scholar, Kennecott Copper fellow Columbia U., 1959-61. Mem. Equipment Lessors Assn. (bd. dirs.). Clubs: University, Mid-Am. (Chgo.). Avocations: fishing, hunting, skiing, amateur radio. Home: 100 E Bellevue Pl Chicago IL 60611-1157 Office: LFC Capital Inc Ste 207 303 E Wacker Dr Chicago IL 60601-5298

ZIMMERMAN, MARY, performing arts educator; Asst. prof. perforamce studies Northwestern U., Evanston, Ill.; artistic assoc. Goodman and Seattle Repertory Theater; mem. Lookingglass Theater Company, Chicago. Dir.: (plays) The Notebooks of Leonardo da Vinci, The Odyssey, Arabian Nights, Journey to the West, Metamorphoses (Tony award for best director, 2002), Secret in the Wings, Eleven Rooms of Proust, Measure for Measure, Henry VIII, A Midsummer Night's Dream, All's Well That Ends Well. Recipient MacArthur Fellowship, 1998, 10 Joseph Jefferson Awards for best direction. Office: Dept. of Performance Studies Northwestern U 1920 Campus D Evanston IL 60208*

ZIMMERMAN, MELVA JEAN, writer, retired media specialist, educator; b. El Dorado, Ks., Mar. 3, 1941; d. Virgil Leroy Zimmerman and Aldena Berneice Tidball;m. Joe Hudson Yeaman, July 6, 1968 (divorced June 1980). BA, Kansas State U., 1963; MA, U. Colo., 1970, EdS, 1973. Tchr. Jefferson County Schs., Golden, Colo., 1963-71, libr. media splst., 1971-95. Co-chaired 1976 state Conv. Colo. Assn. Sch. Librs., 1976; mem. Colo. Assn. Sch. Librs., 1971-95 (v.p. 1979-80), Jefferson County Ed. Assn. (sec. 1980-82) Lakewood. Colo., 1968-95. Contbr. chpt. to book; columnist Insight, 1983-95. Docent Wichita (Kans.) Art Mus., 1996—; campaign treas. sch. bd. candidate, 1997, Kans. state legis. candidate, 1998, 2000; mem. Sedgwick County Dem. Party. Recipient Lifetime Achievement award, Jefferson County Edn. Assn., Jeffey award for outstanding svc., Statewide Lion award, Colo. Edn. Assn. Mem. AAUW (treas. Wichita chpt. 2000—), Sedgwick County Fedn. Dem. Women's Clubs (sec. 1998-2001, auditor 2001—). Home: 6704 Pepperwood Ct Wichita KS 67226-1609 E-mail: melzimm@southwind.net.

ZIMMERMAN, MICHAEL PHILLIP, management analyst; b. Chehalis, Wash., Dec. 1, 1972; s. Robert Peter and Susan Marie (Sweetingham) Z.; m. Renée Nicole Schelper, Aug. 22, 1995. BA with hons. in Philosophy and Politics, NYU, 1995. Imaging archivist, royalty clk. MPL Comm., Inc., N.Y.C., 1994-96; asst. to exec. dir. Wash. State Bd. Health, Olympia, 1996-99; mgmt. analyst children's svcs. unit Wash. Office Cmty. Devel., 1999—. Mng. editor Coll. Humor Mag., 1992-95. Pres. NYU Parliamentary Debate Soc., N.Y.C., 1994. Mem.: Phi Beta Kappa (Salomonowitz Meml. prize 1995). Avocations: percussion/drums, Asian philosophies, creative/humourous writing, classical music. Office: Wash Office Cmty Devel 906 Columbia St SW Olympia WA 98504-8350 Home: Apt 4B 1157 Mottman Rd SW Tumwater WA 98512-6041 Fax: 360-586-0489. E-mail: LaoTzim@earthlink.net., michaelz@cted.wa.gov.

ZIMMERMAN, NANCY PICCIANO, library science educator; b. Jeannette, Pa., July 29, 1951; d. Daniel Joseph and Helen Elizabeth (Lipinski) Picciano; m. Lee W. Zimmerman, Aug. 10, 1974; children: Matthew, Renée. BA in English, Carlow Coll., Pitts., 1973; MLS in Libr. Sci., U. Pitts., 1974; MS in Computer Edn. and Cognitive Sys., U. North Tex., 1992; PhD in Libr. and Info. Studies, Tex. Woman's U., 1992. Lic. libr. media specialist, K-12, lang. arts/English 7-12. Libr. media specialist Fairfield (Calif.)-Suisun Sch. Dist., 1976-78; reference libr. Pikes Peak Libr. Dist., Colorado Springs, Colo., 1983; libr. media specialist North Pole (Alaska) H.S., 1984-85, Prince William County Schs., Woodbridge, Va., 1985-89; dir. info. retrieval lab. Tex. Woman's U., Denton, 1989-91; adj. prof., rsch. assoc. U. North Tex., 1991-92; from asst. to assoc. prof. Sch. Info. and Libr. Studies SUNY, Buffalo, 1993-99; assoc. prof. Coll. Libr. and Info. Scis. U. S.C., Columbia, 1999—. Nat. stroke and turn ofcl. U.S. Swimming, 1985—. Recipient ALISE rsch. grant award, 1994, SUNY Chancellor's Excellence in Tchg. award, 1998. Mem. ALA (coun. 2000—, chair Libr. Rsch. Round Table 1995-96), Am. Assn. Sch. Librs. (treas. 1996-99, pres. 2002-, exec. bd. 1996-99, 2001-), Internat. Assn. Sch. Librs., N.Y. Libr. Assn. (pres. 1999), Nat. Bd. for Profl. Tchg. Stds. (sch. libr. media com. 1997-2001), Phi Delta Kappa, Beta Phi Mu (nat. exec. coun. 1994-99). Office: U SC Coll Libr and Info Scis 217 Davis Coll Columbia SC 29208-0001

ZIMMERMAN, PAUL ALBERT, retired college president, minister; b. Danville, Ill., June 25, 1918; s. Albert Carl and Hanna Marie (Haffner) Z.; m. Genevieve Emmaline Bahls, June 11, 1944; children— Karmin (Mrs. Raymond Philp), Thomas. Student, Concordia Coll., Ft. Wayne, Ind., 1936-39; BA, Concordia Sem., St. Louis, 1941, M.Div., 1944; MA, U. Ill., 1947, PhD, 1951; D.D., Concordia Sem., Springfield, Ill., 1975; LLD (hon.), Concordia Coll., Ann Arbor, Mich., 1994. Prof. theology and sci. Bethany Coll., Mankato, Minn., 1944-53; prof. Concordia Tchrs. Coll., Seward, Nebr., 1953-54, pres., 1954-61, Concordia Luth. Jr. Coll., Ann Arbor, Mich., 1961-73, Concordia Coll., River Forest, Ill., 1973-83, ret., 1983; pastor St. Luke's Luth. Ch., Harrison, Mich., 1983-88. Author and editor: Darwin, Evolution and Creation, 1959, Rock Strata and the Bible Record, 1971, Creation, Evolution and God's Word, 1972. Chmn. Washtenaw County Red Cross, 1968-70; pres. Ann Arbor Found., 1970-71; mem. Citizens Com. Study Taxation, Ann Arbor, 1972; mem. adv. bd. St. Joseph Mercy Community, 1969-72; chmn. Luth. Ch. Mo. Synod's Bd. for Mission Services, 1982-92, Mission Task Force, 1990-91, adminstrv. asst. pres. Mo. Synod, 1972-73, 93-94, mem. curriculum commn. bd. higher edn., 1963-73, mem. task force constl. revision Mo. Synod, chmn. com. adjudication procedures Mo. Synod, Mo. Synod com. on structure, 1995-98. Fellow Creation Rsch. Assn. Lutheran. Home: 2798 Princeton Dr Traverse City MI 49684-9131

ZIMMERMAN, RICHARD KENT, family physician, preventive medicine specialist; s. Willis and Janys Zimmerman; m. Elizabeth Wellhausen; children: Jonathan, David, Cristy, Hannah. BA in Chemistry, Miami U., Oxford, Ohio, 1982; MD, Ohio State U., 1986; MPH in Epidemiology, U. Minn., 1991. Diplomate Am. Bd. Family Practice, Am. Bd. Preventive Medicine. Intern Grant Med. Ctr., Columbus, Ohio, 1986-87, resident, 1986-89; fellow U. Minn., Mpls., 1989-91; asst. prof. U. Pitts., 1991-98, assoc. prof., 1998—. Author monographs, articles, book chpts. in field. Elder Bellefield Presbyn. Ch., Pitts., 1994-99; bd. dirs. Pitts. Regional Internat. Student Ministry, 1994—, chair, 1995-98. Recipient Spl. Recognition award Assn. Tchrs. Preventive Medicine, 1999. Fellow Am. Acad. Family Physicians (liaison to adv. com. on immunization practices, mem. commn. on clin. policies and rsch. 1996-99), Am. Coll. Preventive Medicine; mem. Soc. Tchrs. of Family Medicine (chmn. group on immunization edn. 1993-98, Best Seminar N.E. region award 1997, Innovation in Family Edn. award 1998). Avocation: jogging. Office: U Pitts 3518 5th Ave Pittsburgh PA 15261-0001

ZIMMERMAN, ROBERT, writer, filmmaker; b. Bklyn., Feb. 5, 1953; s. Milton and Ida Zimmerman. BA, CUNY, 1974; MA, NYU, 1995. Real estate negotiator FAA, Queens, N.Y., 1975-78; freelance movie prodr. and writer, N.Y.C., 1978-97; freelance mag. writer, 1991—. Lectr. NYU, N.Y.C., 1991-96, Stevens Inst. Tech., Hoboken, N.J., 1995-96, New Sch. for Social Rsch., N.Y.C., 1996-97. Author: Genesis, The Story of Apollo 8, The First Manned Flight to Another World, 1998, The Chronological Encylopedia of Discoveries in Space, 2000; contbr. articles to mags., including The Scis., Astronomy, Wall St. Jour., Sky and Telescope, Stardate, Freeman, Invention and Tech., Am. HIstory. Mem. Nat. Speleological Soc. (chmn. Met. Grotto, mem. Balt. Grotto, D.C. Grotto, Bald Eagle Grotto), Potomac Speleological Club, Nat. Assn. Sci. Writers. Avocations: exploration, history, astronomy. E-mail: zimmerman@nasw.org.

ZIMMERMAN, ROGER JOSEPH, fishery biologist; b. Alice, Tex., Dec. 2, 1941; s. Walter George and Laura Virgie (Heine) Z.; m. Domenica Marie DeCaro, Dec. 28, 1976; children: Kathryn, Robert. BS in Biology, Tex. A&I Coll., 1966, MA in Biology and Geology, 1969; PhD in Marine Scis., U.P.R., Mayaguez, 1979. Tchg. asst. biology dept. U. South Fla., Tampa, 1971, rsch. assoc. marine sci. dept. St. Petersburg, 1971-73; rsch. assoc. P.R. Nuclear Ctr. U. P.R., 1974-75, grad. fellow, 1975-78, marine benthic ecologist Ctr. for Energy & Environ. Rsch., 1978-81; fishery ecologist fishery mgmt. divsn. NOAA/NMFS Galveston (Tex.) Lab., 1981-91, divsn. chief fishery ecology divsn., 1991-93, lab. dir., 1993—. Rsch. fellow U.S. Nat. Mus. Natural History, Smithsonian Instn., Washington and Harbor Beach, Fla., summer 1975, 76; vis. instr. marine biology dept. Tex. A&M U., Galveston, summer 1988, 89; vis. instr. biology dept. Corpus Christi (Tex.) State U., 1986; tchg. asst. biology U. South Fla., 1970; lectr.-counselor Tex. A&I U., 1969, lab. coord., tchg. asst., 1968-69; OAS and U.S. AID advisor to Instuto de Pesca de Ecuador, 1985-88; mem. com. coastal ocean estuarine habitat rsch. planning com. NOAA 1987, sci. adv. com., 1989; chair predator-prey com. S.E. Fisheries Sci. Ctr., 1990-91; coord. climate and global change ecol. sys. and dynamics work group NMFS, 1990, spl. asst. to office of sr. scientist, 1990; mem. sci. adv. com. Galveston Bay project Nat. Estuary Program, 1993-96, mgmt. com. Coastal Bend project, 1994-98; bd. dirs. Gulf of Mex. regional marine rsch. program NMFS-SEFSC, 1992-93; rep. programs on coastal fisheries and estuarine ecology SERSC, 1992-95; grad. student advisor, adj. wildlife and fisheries dept. and biology dept. Tex. A&M U., dept. biology Corpus Christi State U., dept. marine scis. La. State U., 1985-89, dept. biology U. Houston, 1983-85; presenter workshops in field. Reviewer for jours. in field, including Fishery Bull., Contbns. to Marine Sci., Marine Ecology Progress Series, Jour. Exptl. Marine Biology and Ecology, Marine Biology, Bull. Marine Sci., Jour. Wetlands Ecology and Mgmt., Estuaries, Coastal and Shelf Sci., also various proposals; editl. reviewer SEFSC Galveston Lab., 1984—; contbr. numerous articles to profl. publs.; author abstracts, revs. in field. Mem. Estuarine Rsch. Fedn., Gulf Estuarine Rsch. Soc., Crustacean Soc., Am. Fisheries Soc., Assn. Marine Labs. of the Caribbean. Office: Nat Marine Fisheries Svc SE Fisheries Sci Ctr 4700 Avenue U Galveston TX 77551-6901

ZIMMERMAN, ROGER MAX, civil engineer; b. Rehoboth, N.Mex., May 15, 1936; s. Ellsworth Willard and Juanita Pauline (Kelley) Z.; m. Mary Elizabeth Nielsen, June 6, 1956; children: Paul Edwin, Michael Lee. BSCE, U. Colo., 1959, MS, 1961, PhD, 1965. Instr. of civil engring. U. Colo., Boulder, 1959-64; from asst. prof. to prof. of civil engring. N.Mex. State U., Las Cruces, 1964-79; vis. scientist Rockwell Internat. Sci. Ctr., Albuquerque, 1979-80; sr. mem. tech. staff Sandia Nat. Labs., 1980-90, dist. mem. tech. staff, 1990—2000; owner Engring. Analyses, LLC, 2000—. Author rsch. papers in field. 1st lt. USAR, 1959-67. Fellow ASCE (state pres. 1974-75); fellow NSPE (chpt. pres. 1991-92, State Engr. of Yr. 1992; nat. dir. 1998-2000; state pres. 1996-97). Achievements include development of new testing method for space shuttle thermal protection tiles; research in rock mass modifications and multiaxial strength of concrete.

ZIMMERMAN, S(AMUEL) MORTON (MORT ZIMMERMAN), engineering executive; b. Paterson, N.J., Mar. 18, 1927; s. Solomon Zimmerman and Miriam (Feder) Glatzer; m. Marion Patricia Boque, Sept. 15, 1951 (dec. 1993); children: Judy, Suzy, Sharon, Dan; m. Rosalie Fitzgerald, June 1, 1998. Student, Ga. Inst. Tech., 1942-44, 46-48, Oglethorpe U., 1948-51; BSEE, Pacific Internat. U., L.A., 1958. Pres. Comml. Electronics Corp., Dallas, 1954-56, Electron Corp. subs. LTV Corp., 1956-65; chmn. bd., pres. Capital Bancshares, Inc., 1965-66; chmn. bd. Capital Nat. Bank Tampa (formerly Springs Nat. Bank), Fla., 1965, Capital Nat. Bank Miami (name now Peoples Downtown Bank), 1966, Merc. Nat. Bank Miami Beach (name now Barnett Bank), 1967, Underwriters Bank & Trust Co. N.Y. (name now Banco Cen.), 1968; chmn. bd., pres. Capital Gen. Corp., 1967, Comml. Tech., Inc., 1977—, Petro Imperial Corp. and subs. DOL Resources and Tech.-Star, Dallas, 1983—; founder, chmn. bd. Atmospheric & Magnetic Tech., Inc., 1997—. Chmn. bd., pres. Tans Exchange Corp., 1965—. Electric & Gas Tech., Inc., 1985—; also chmn. 8 subs. cos.; chmn. bd. Video Sci. Tech., Inc., 1981-92, Interfed. Capital, Inc., 1990—, Dynamic Funding Inc., 2000—, Logic Metals Tech., Inc., 2002—. Patentee: TV camera video amplifier and blanking circuits, electronic thermometer, video x-ray image system and methods, video system and method for presentation and reproduction x-ray film images, electromagnetic radio frequency lighting system, laser display of electronically generated image signal; additional patents pending; U.S. copyrights on electronic atmosphere dew point generator of pure refrigeration drinking water, 2001, hydrogen peroxide electrical power generator, 2001. Petty oficer USN, 1942-45. Recipient Interfaith award City of N.Y. Mem. IEEE, Brookhaven Country Club. Republican. Jewish. Home: 5901 Yardley Ct Dallas TX 75248-2138 Office: Electric & Gas Tech Inc 13636 Neutron Rd Dallas TX 75244-4410 Fax: 972 991-3265.

ZIMMERMAN, SHELDON, foundation administrator, educator; b. Toronto, Ont., Can., Feb. 21, 1942; s. Morris and Helen Z.; m. Judith Elaine Baumgarten, Aug. 9, 1964; children: Brian, Kira, David, Micol. BA, U. Toronto, 1964, MA, 1965; BHL, Hebrew Union Coll., Jewish Inst. Religion, 1969, MAHL, 1970; DDiv, Hebrew Union Coll., 1995. Ordained rabbi, 1970. Asst. rabbi Cen. Synagogue, N.Y.C., 1970-72, sr. rabbi, 1972-85; rabbi Temple Emanu-El, Dallas, 1985-96; pres. Hebrew Union Coll.-Jewish Inst. Religion, N.Y.C., Cin., L.A., 1996-2000, Jerusalem, 2000-01; exec. v.p. birthright israel, Cin. Adj. prof. religious studies So. Meth. U., Dallas, Perkins Sch. Theology; adj. faculty Auburn Theol. Sem.; lectr. liturgy and rabbinics N.Y. Sch. of Hebrew Union Coll.-Jewish Inst. Religion, bd. govs.; lectr. theology Fordham U.; instr. philosophy Hunter Coll. of CUNY; v.p., then pres. Cen. Conf. of Am. Rabbis; bd. trustees Union Am. Hebrew Congregations; mem. Nat. Rabbinic Cabinet of United Jewish Appeal; bd. dirs. World Ctr. for Jewish Unity; bd. govs. Synagogue Coun. Am.; v.p. World Union Progressive Judaism, lectr. in field. Contbr. articles to profl. jours. Bd. dirs. Vis. Nurses Assn. Tex., Children's Med. Found., Jewish Fedn. Dallas, Solomon Schechter Acad. Dallas, S.W. Region of Am. Jewish Congress, Community Outreach Coalition.; adv. bd. CONTACT-Dallas Telephone Counseling Ctr., Downtown Dallas Family Shelter, The AIDS-ARMS Adv. Coun. Dallas, Pastoral Care Adv. Com. of Children's Med. Ctr., Women's Ctr. of Dallas; mem. chaplain's adv. bd. So. Meth. U.; v.p. Jewish Community Rels. Coun. Dallas; bd. govs. ARC, United Way, Cin. Recipient Marshall Hochhauser Meml. Award, Fedn. Jewish Philanthropies, N.Y.C.,Sam Beber Disting. Alumnus award B'nai B'rith Youth Orgn. *We are the sanctifiers-in-process, where we and our lives can make the ultimate difference in the journey to the fulfillment of the promise.*

ZIMMERMAN, SOL SHEA, pediatrician; b. N.Y.C., June 25, 1948; s. Isaac and Estera (Berkowicz) Z.; m. Diana F. Zimmerman, Aug. 8, 1971; children: Jeffrey, Steven, Andrew. AB, Columbia U., 1968; MD, NYU, 1972. Diplomate Am. Bd. Pediats.; pediat. critical care medicine. Intern dept. pediats. NYU-Bellevue Hosp. Ctr., N.Y.C., 1972-73, resident dept. pediats., 1973-75, chief resident dept. pediats., 1977-78, asst. prof. clin. pediats., 1978-83, assoc. prof. clin. pediats., 1983—, dir. pediat. critical care medicine, 1978-98, assoc. dir. dept. pediats., 1985—; assoc. chair dept. pediats. NYU Sch. of Medicine, 1997—. Pres. Pediat. Assocs. N.Y.C., P.C., 1978—; v.p. Univ. Physicians Network, 1996—; chmn. bd. mgrs. Univ. MSO, 1998—. Editor, author: (textbook) Critical Care Pediatrics, 1985. Chmn. com. on heart, health in the young N.Y.C. affiliate Am. Heart Assn., 1987-93. Maj. USAF MC, 1975-77. Fellow Am. Acad. Pediats., Am. Coll. Chest Physicians, Critical Care Medicine; mem. N.Y. Soc. Pediat. Critical Care Medicine (v.p. 1989-91, pres. 1991-93), Alpha Omega Alpha. Office: Pediat Assocs of NYC PC 317 E 34th St New York NY 10016-4974 also: 20 Plaza St E Brooklyn NY 11238-4955

ZIMMERMAN, THOM JAY, ophthalmologist, educator; b. Lincoln, Ill., Oct. 5, 1942; s. Kenneth Earl and Georgia Rosemary (Taylor) Z.; m. Tinker Steiner; 1 child, Jessica. BS in Zoology, U. Ill., 1964; MD, U. Ill., Chgo., 1968; PhD in Pharmacology, U. Fla., 1976. Diplomate Nat. Bd. Med. Examiners, Am. Bd. Ophthalmology. Intern St. Lukes Hosp., Chgo., 1968-69; resident U. Fla. Coll. Medicine, Dept. Ophthalmology, Gainesville, 1971-74, corneal fellow, 1974-75, glaucoma fellow, 1976-77; acting chmn. dept. ophthalmology La. State U., New Orleans, 1977; assoc. prof. ophthalmology and pharmacology Ochsner Clinic, 1977-79; prof. pharmacology and toxicology U. Louisville, 1986-2000, prof., chmn. dept. ophthalmology, 1986-2000; global opthalmic med. dir. global med. affairs Pharmacia & Upjohn, 1999—; emeritus prof. pharmacology and toxicology Univ. Louisville, 2000—. Ophthalmic cons. (glaucoma) USPHS Hosp., New Orleans, 1977-82; cons. Nat. Adv. Eye Council and NEI, 1983; U.S. rep. for exec. com. Pan-Am. Glaucoma Soc., 1983-85; chmn. glaucoma symposium of Nat. Soc. to Prevent Blindness, 1988; guest lectr. numerous profl. socs. and confs. Author 6 books and numerous editorials; contbr. sci. articles to profl. jours.; mem. editorial bd. Jour. Continuing Edn. in Ophthalmology, 1977—, Annals of Ophthalmology, 1978—, Advances in Therapy, 1986—; contbr. book chpts., abstracts. Served with USPHS, 1969-71. Recipient Will F. Lyon award Presbyn.-St. Lukes Hosp., 1969; Robert E. McCormick scholar Research to Prevent Blindness Inc., 1978; grantee Nat. Eye Inst., 1978-84, 85-86; delivered Culler Meml. lecture, Ohio State U., 1986. Fellow Am. Coll. Clin. Pharmacology; mem. AMA (Physician's Recognition award 1971, 73, 75, 77, 79, 81, 83), Assn. for Research in Vision and Ophthalmology, Am. Soc. for Clin. Pharmacology and Therapeutics, Am. Soc. Contemporary Ophthalmology, Internat. Glaucoma Congress, Am. Acad. Ophthalmology, La.-Miss. Ophthalmology Soc., Research to Prevent Blindness Ophthalmologic Assn., So. Med. Assn., Can. Implant Soc., Ky. Med. Assn., Ky. Acad. Eye Physicians and Surgeons, Louisville Acad. Ophthalmology, Jefferson County Med. Soc., Alpha Omega Alpha. Home: 389 Mockingbird Valley Rd Louisville KY 40207-1337 Office: Univ of Louisville Dept Ophthalmology 301 E Muhammad Ali Blvd Louisville KY 40202-1511

ZIMMERMAN, THOMAS FLETCHER, III, medical educator, consultant; b. South Bend, Ind., Feb. 11, 1938; s. Thomas Fletcher and Elizabeth Harriet Z.; m. Marlene Joan Osterman (div. Aug. 1961); children: Thomas Fritzgerald, Jeremy Adam; m. Lynette Marie Ensley, Dec. 17, 1983; 1 child, Ashley Marie. BA, Evangel U., 1959; MS, U. Mo., 1961; PhD, U. Oreg., 1966. Rsch. assoc. Inst. Cmty. Studies, Kansas City, Mo., 1966-68; clin. asst. prof. psychiatry U. Mo. Sch. Medicine, 1966-68; dir. dept. health manpower Am. Med. Assn., Chgo., 1968-71; dean Coll. Assoc. Med. Scis. U. Ill. Med. Ctr., 1972-77, assoc. prof. med. psychology, 1975-80, assoc. vice chancellor, 1977-80; dir. Annenberg Ctr. Eisenhower Med. Ctr., Rancho Mirage, Calif., 1981-90, exec. v.p. edn. and rsch., 1988-91; pres. Interactive Med. Networks, Washington, 1991-95; pres., COO Med. Scholar Digital Networks, Reston, Va., 1996—2001; prof. dept. comparative and internat. studies U. Miami, 1997—. V.p. editl. Physician's Weekly, 2000-2002; contbr. articles to profl. jours., chpt. to book. Mem. higher edn. bd. Gen. Coun. Assemblies of God, Springfield, Mo., 1976-80; bd. dirs. Palm Valley Sch., Palm Springs, Calif., 1989-90, advisor, voluntary health assns., 1981-90. Home: 12523 Summer Pl Oak Hill VA 20171-2474 Office: Telehealth Strategies & Svcs LLC PO Box 12405 Chicago IL 60612

ZIMMERMAN, WILLIAM EDWIN, newspaper editor, publisher, writer; b. Bklyn., Feb. 2, 1941; s. George and Ruth (Edelbaum) Z.; m. Teodorina Bello, Dec. 13, 1969; 1 child, Carlota Pastora. BA, Queens Coll., 1962. Pres. Guarionex Press, Ltd., N.Y.C., 1979—; with Am. Banker, 1962-82, editor, sr. v.p., 1982-89; editor in chief Banking Week, 1986-89; dep. editor Sunday Bus. sect. The N.Y. Times, 1989; spl. projects editor, editor Student Briefing Page Newsday, L.I., N.Y., 1989—. Author: How to Tape Instant Oral Biographies, 1979, A Book of Questions to Keep Thoughts and Feelings, 1984, Make Beliefs, 1987, Life Lines: A Book of Hope, 1990, The Little Book of Joy, 1995, Dogmas: Simple Truths from a Wise Pet, 1995, Make Beliefs for Kids of All Ages, 1996, A Book of Sunshine, 1997, Cat-e-chisms: Feline Answers to Life's Big Questions, 1997, My Life: An Open Book, 2000, Lunch Box Letters, 2000, Idea Catcher for Kids, 2000, Butterfly Wishes. Mem. Am. Oral History Assn., N.Y. Fin. Writers Assn., Am. Soc. Bus. Writers, Overseas Press Club, Deadline Club, Am. Soc. Bus. Press Editors, Dowtown Athletic Club, N.Y. Athletic Club, Sigma Delta Chi. Democrat. Jewish. Office: Newsday Inc 2 Park Ave Rm 601 New York NY 10016-5679

ZIMMERMAN, WILLIAM ROBERT, entrepreneur, engineering based manufacturing company executive; b. Cleve., May 11, 1927; s. Irving and Ella (Berger) Z.; m. Nancy Owen, 1963 (div. 1970); 1 child, Amanda; m. Eileen Samuelson, Nov. 11, 1979. BS, MIT, 1948, MS, 1949. Cons. Kurt Salmon Assocs., Washington, 1949-50, A.T. Kearney and Co., Chgo., 1950-52; mill mgr. Am. Envelope Co., West Carrollton, Ohio, 1952-56; exec. v.p. Avery Internat., Pasadena, Calif., 1956-67; pres. Swedlow, Inc., Garden Grove, 1967-73, Monogram Industries, Inc., Santa Monica, 1973-78. Bd. dirs. Life Script, Orange, Calif., Adept Techs., Los Alamos, OSO Techs., Rancho Cucamonga, Calif., Monitor Products, Inc., Oceanside, Calif., Summa Industries, Fullerton, Calif. Pres. coun. Boy Scouts Am., Painesville, Ohio, 1957-62; exec. com. Jr. Achievement So. Calif., L.A., 1975-77; trustee Los Angeles County Mus. Nat. History, 1987-97, Harvey Mudd Coll., Claremont, Calif., 1983—. Mem.: Calif. (Los Angeles); Valley Hunt, Annendale (Pasadena). Republican. Avocations: tennis, jogging, golf. Office: Zimmerman Holdings Inc PO Box 3570 South Pasadena CA 91031-6570

ZIMMERMAN, ZORA DEVRNJA, English, folklore educator, university dean; b. Marienbad, Czechoslovakia, May 12, 1945; came to U.S., 1951; d. Milutin Devrnja and Dorothea Wohlgemuth; m. Thomas Lee Zimmerman, Sept. 12, 1976; children: Anna, Elizabeth. BA, SUNY, Buffalo, 1967, PhD, 1974. From asst. prof. to assoc. prof. Iowa State U., Ames, 1974-84, prof. English, 1985—, assoc. dean Coll. Liberal Arts and Scis., 1990—. Author: (book) Serbian Folk Poetry: Ancient Legends, Romantic Songs, 1986; editor: (poetry book) Arc from Now, 1978; contbr. articles to profl. jours., chpts. to books. NEH summer fellow Ind. U., 1979. Office: Iowa State U Coll Liberal Arts and Scis 202 Carrie Chapman Catt Hl Ames IA 50011-0001 E-mail: zdzimme@iastate.edu.

ZIMMERMANN, ANN MARIE, lawyer, educator; b. Flint, Mich., July 1, 1963; d. John Fredrick and Maryann Zimmermann; m. David Huerta, Sept. 20, 1998. BA cum laude, U. Mich., 1985; JD, U. San Diego, 1990. Bar: Calif. 1991, U.S. Dist. Ct. (so. dist.) Calif. 1992, U.S. Dist. Ct. (ctrl. dist.) Calif. 1997. Intern Nat. Wildlife Fedn., Washington, 1991-92; atty. L. Brooks Anderholt, El Centro, Calif., 1992—. Tchr. bankruptcy, corps., probate Imperial Valley Coll., El Centro, 1998—; jud. intern 4th Dist. Ct. Appeal, San Diego, 1989. Mem. San Diego Law Rev., 1980-90. Mem. Imperial County Bar Assn. (bd. dirs. 1992-96, pres. 1998), Imperial Valley Breakfast Rotary Club (charter mem.), Order of Barristers. Avocations: scuba diving, skiing, dancing, reading. Home: 740 Drew Rd Calexico CA 92231-9711 Office: Anderholt & Storey 654 Main St El Centro CA 92243

ZIMMERMANN, KARIN E. psychologist; Fellow Am. Coll. Forensic Examiners; mem. APA, Am. Acad. Experts Traumatic Stress. Office: PO Box 84311 Los Angeles CA 90073-0311

ZIMMERMANN, KURT ERIC, music educator, musician; b. Balt., Nov. 16, 1968; s. Delphin and Dianne Zimmermann(Stepmother), Joyce and David Bogert(Stepfather). Bachelor of Music Edn., William Paterson Coll., 1991. Cert. music edn. grades K-12 N.J. Asst. marching band dir. Morris Hills H.S., Rockaway, NJ, 1989—; music educator Copeland Mid. Sch., 1991—; pit orch. dir. spring musical Mountain Lakes H.S., 2000—, Morris Hills H.S., Rockaway, 2000—, Morris Knolls H.S., Denville, 1998. Trumpet player Hanover Wind Symphony, NJ, 92—; musician and staff asst. Hawthorne Caballeros Sr. Drum and Bugle Corps, NJ, 1986—88, NJ, 1991—92, NJ, 1997. Musician (trumpet player) weddings, ch. svcs., cmty. performances; musician: bell choir. Mem.: Music Educators Nat. Conf. Home: 13 Chateau Gardens Rockaway NJ 07866 Office: Copeland Middle School 100 Lake Shore Dr Rockaway NJ 07866 Personal E-mail: z94musik@optonline.net.

ZIMMERMANN, POLLY GERBER, emergency nurse; b. Orrville, Ohio, Apr. 6, 1954; d. Vernon Lee and Paula Mae (Hemple) Gerber; m. Rudolf Zimmermann, May 14, 1988. Diploma in nursing, Aultman Hosp. Sch.

Nursing, Canton, Ohio, 1977; BSN, DePaul U., 1982; MBA, North Park U., 1995, MSN, 1996. RN, Ill.; cert. emergency nurse; cert. ACLS, PALS, ENPC, TNCC, NALS, trauma nurse specialist, instr. ENPC, breath alcohol technician. Staff nurse med.-surg. Columbus Hosp., Chgo., 1977-80, asst. head nurse, 1980-81, staff nurse neonatal ICU, 1981-82, staff nurse emergency dept., 1983-90, clin. nurse dir. emergency dept., 1990-92; staff nurse emergency dept. and occupational health Swedish Covenant Hosp., 1992—2000; assoc. nurse Am. Airlines, 1996—2001; sr. course mgr. Nat. Ctr. for Advanced Med. Edn., Chgo., 1997; assoc. dir. nat. hdqrs. Alzheimer's Assn., 1998; prof. Harry S. Truman Coll., 1998—. Psychiat. nurse Chgo. Lakeshore Hosp., 1983-84; staff triage nurse Michael Reese HMO, 1986-90; presenter in field. Editor: Nursing Management Secrets, 2002; asst. editor, mgr. Manager's Forum; sect. editor, mem. editl. bd. Jour. Emergency Nursing; contbr. chpts. to books, articles to Jour. Emergency Nursing, Nursing, others; mem. editl. bd. Jour. Emergency Nursing. Course co-dir. ARC Ventures, Chgo., 1998; chairperson sci. rev. panel ENA Found. Edn. Exec. Nurse fellow Commonwealth Fund, 1993; named Disting. Writer Sigma Theta Tau, 2000—. Mem.: ANA, Am. Med. Writers Assn., Emergency Nurses Assn. (mem. clin. practice for cert. 1993, CEN test item writer, CEN exam constrn. rev. com., del. and spkr. sci. assembly, CEN test examiner, text item reviewer NCLEX, Gary Sparger Meml. scholar 1994, ENF Leadership Grad. Nursing Edn. scholar 1994), Toastmasters, Delta Epsilon Sigma, Sigma Theta Tau (sec. 1995—96, pres. 1998—2000, past pres. 2001, Grace Peterson scholar 1994). Republican. Home: 4200 N Francisco Ave Chicago IL 60618-2610 E-mail: pzimmermann@ccc.edu.

ZIMMERMANN, ROBERT A. molecular biologist, educator; b. Phila., July 17, 1937; s. William and Margaret (Lukens) Z.; m. Athleen B. Kammerer; 1 child, Hannah Kelly. BA, Amherst Coll., 1959; PhD, MIT, 1964. Rsch. fellow Med. Sch. Harvard U., Boston, 1966-69; rsch. assoc. U. Geneva, 1970-73; assoc. prof. U. Mass., Amherst, 1973-77, prof. dept. biochemistry and molecular biology, 1977—, head dept. biochemistry, 1979-86, dir. program in molecular and cellular biology, 1985-88, dir. NIH chemistry-biology interface tng. program, 1995-2000, adj. prof. dept. chemistry, 2001—. Cons. WHO, Geneva, 1975-78; mem. molecular biology study sect. NIH, Washington, 1978-82; mem. molecular biochemistry panel NSF, Washington, 1994-97. Editor: Ribosomal RNA, 1994; assoc. editor RNA, 1996—; translator, editor: Introduction to Molecular Biology, 1971; contbr. over 90 articles to sci. jours. Participant U.S.-U.S.S.R. Interacad. Exch., 1965-66. Helen Hay Whitney Found. fellow, 1968-71, European Molecular Biology Orgn. sr. fellow, 1971-72; recipient Rsch. Career Devel. award NIH, 1975-80. Mem. AAAS, Am. Chem. Soc., Am. Soc. Biochemistry and Molecular Biology, Am. Soc. Microbiology, Sigma Xi. Office: Univ Mass Dept Biochem and Molec Biol Amherst MA 01003 E-mail: zimmermann@biochem.umass.edu.

ZIMMERMANN, ROBERT LAURENCE, marketing professional; b. Mpls., Jan. 1, 1932; s. Lawrence and Bertha Mabel (Foss) Z. BA, U. Minn., 1954, MA, 1965, PhD, 1970. Asst. prof. psychology U. Winnepeg, Man., Can., 1968-69; research assoc. psychiatry research unit U. Minn., Mpls., 1969-75; sr. scientist biometrics lab. George Washington U., Washington, 1975-76; pvt. cons. research design and data analysis Mpls., 1976-84; sr. research mgr. Maritz Market Rsch., 1984—. Clin. asst. prof. psychiatry dept. U. Minn., Mpls., 1976-90; external rev. officer FDA, Washington, 1974-77. Contbr. numerous articles to profl. jours. Fellow NIMH, 1958, 61, 69-71; merit fellow State of Minn. Mem. AAAS, Com. on Space Rsch., Nat. Space Soc., Nat. Space Found., The Planetary Soc., ACLU, Amnesty Internat., Ctr. Pub. Integrity, Oxfam. Democrat. Avocation: writing. Home: 1920 S 1st St Apt 1104 Minneapolis MN 55454-1048 Office: Maritz Market Rsch Inc 7701 France Ave S Minneapolis MN 55435-5288

ZIMMERMANN, THOMAS CALLANDER PRICE, retired historian, educator; b. Bryn Mawr, Pa., Aug. 22, 1934; s. R.Z. and Susan (Goodman) Z.; m. Margaret Upham Ferris. BA, Williams Coll., 1956, Oxford U., 1958, MA, 1964; AM, Harvard U., 1960, PhD, 1964. Asst. prof. Reed Coll., Portland, Oreg., 1964-67, assoc. prof., 1967-73, prof. history, 1973-77, chmn. dept. history, 1973-75; v.p. acad. affairs Davidson (N.C.) Coll., 1977-86, Charles A. Dana prof. History, 1986-99, Charles A. Dana prof. history emeritus, 1999-2000, ret., 2000. Mem. Oreg. Com. for Humanities NEH, 1971—77; mem. Region 14 selection com. Woodrow Wilson Nat. Fellowship Found., Princeton, NJ, 1967—70. Author: Paolo Giovio: The Historian and the Crisis of Sixteenth-Century Italy, 1995 (Helen and Howard R. Marraro Book prize Am. Hist. Assn. 1996, Presdl. Book award Am. Assn. for Italian Studies 1997); co-editor of collected works of Paolo Giovio, 1985; contbr. articles to profl. jours. Pres. Am. Alpine Club, N.Y.C., 1979-82, bd. dirs., 1975-83; bd. dirs. Charlotte Opera Assn., N.C., 1980-82, N.C. Outward Bound Sch., Morgantown, 1978-81; bd. advisors Lowell Obs., 1988-93; mem. Rome Prize Jury (Post-Classical Humanistic Studies) Am. Acad. in Rome, 1993. Danforth fellow, 1956-62, Fulbright fellow, Italy, 1962-64, Villa "I Tatti" fellow Harvard U. Ctr., 1970-71; Am. Council of Learned Socs. fellow, N.Y.C., 1975-76. Mem. Renaissance Soc. Am., Sixteenth Century Studies Conf., Soc. Italian Hist. Studies, Am. Assn. Italian Studies, Phi Beta Kappa.

ZIMMERS, VIVIAN ELEANOR, development and administrative consultant; b. St. Louis, Oct. 19, 1946; d. John Dominic and Aurea Genevieve (Schottel) Baron; m. John Paul Hargis, Aug. 21, 1964 (div. Mar. 1968); m. Filomeno Mariano Ramos, June 30, 1973 (dec.); children: William S., Kiersten E., Leilani A.; m. Ronald Franklin Zimmers, Sept. 27, 1997. Student, St. Louis U., 1968-69, U. Hawaii, 1986-87; BA in Mgmt., Nat. Louis U., 1991. Co-founder, owner, pres. Batts Ramos and Assocs., Inc., St. Louis, 1991—. Cons. Hawaii Govtl. Affairs Com., Honolulu, 1975-76, Brokers Adv. Com., Honolulu, 1984-85.; govtl. affairs com. St. Louis Assn. Realtors, 1996-97. Mo. Orthopedically Disabled, bd. dirs., 1993—, pres., 1997—; active Assoc. Pres.'s Youth Opportunity Program, St. Louis, 1968; vol. literacy coun., rschr. Vols. in Probation and Parole. Mem. Nat. Assn. Realtors (mem. com. on pub. rels. 1987), St. Louis Real Estate Bd., Mililani Mchts. Assn. (pres. 1985), Rotary Internat. Democrat. Roman Catholic. Home: 70 Willow Dr Eureka MO 63025-2198

ZIMMETT, MARK PAUL, lawyer, educator; b. Waukegan, Ill., July 4, 1950; s. Nelson H. Zimmett and Roslyn (Yastrow) Zimmett Grodzin; m. Joan Robin Urken, June 11, 1972; children: Nora Helene, Lili Eleanor. BA, Johns Hopkins U., 1972; JD, NYU, 1975. Bar: N.Y. 1976, U.S. Dist. Ct. (so. and ea. dists.) N.Y. 1976, U.S. Dist. Ct. (no. dist.) Calif. 1980, U.S. Ct. Appeals (2d cir.) 1980, U.S. Supreme Ct. 1981, U.S. Ct. Appeals (5th cir.) 1986, U.S. Ct. Appeals (9th cir.) 1988. Assoc. Shearman & Sterling, N.Y.C., 1975-83, ptnr., 1984-90; adj. assoc. prof. internat. law NYU, 1986-88; lectr. internat. comml. litig. and arbitration Practicing Law Inst., 2000—02. Author: Letters of Credit, New York Practice Guide Business and Commerical Law, 1990; contbr. articles to profl. jours. Mem. ABA (subcom. on letters of credit, com. on uniform comml. code sect. bus. law), N.Y. State Bar Assn., Assn. of the Bar of the City of N.Y., N.Y. County Lawyers Assn. (com. on bus. bankruptcy law), Citizens Union. Democrat. Jewish. Office: 126 E 56th St New York NY 10022-3613

ZIMMIE, THOMAS FRANK, civil engineer, educator; b. Scranton, Pa., Jan. 24, 1939; s. Thomas and Stella Josephine (Price) Z.; m. Patricia Joyce Kelly, June 8, 1962 (div. 1979); 1 child, David Thomas; m. Judith Anne Braden, July 13, 1989. BSCE, Worcester Poly. Inst., 1960; MSCE, U. Conn., 1962, PhD in Geotech. Engring., 1972. Registered profl. engr., N.Y., Conn. Staff engr. Union Carbide Corp. (Linde div.), Buffalo, 1964-68; profl. engr. Town of Mansfield, Conn., 1968-72; ptnr. Wang and Zimmie Cons., Troy, N.Y., 1973-80; v.p. Arch Engring. Cons., 1984-88; program dir. NSF, Washington, 1988-90; pres., CEO Civrotech Cons. Engrs., Inc., Troy, 1993—; prof. dept. civil engring Rensselaer Poly. Inst., 1973—. Postdoctoral researcher Norwegian Geotech. Inst., Oslo, 1972-73; geotech. engr. N.Y. Dept. Environ. Conservation, Albany, 1983-85; town engr. Town of North Greenbush, N.Y., 1985-88. Editor: Permeability and Groundwater Contamination, 1981. 1st lt. U.S. Army, 1962-64. Fellow Am. Coll. of Forensic Examiner, ASCE (cert., Outstanding Svc. award 1986, 87); mem. ASTM (Spl. Svc. award 1980, Charles Dudley award 1984), Transp. Rsch. Bd., Am. Rd. and Transp. Builders Assn.. Achievements include research in environmental geotechnology. Home: 39 Zelenke Dr Wynantskill NY 12198-8627 Office: Rensselaer Poly Inst Civil Engring Dept Soil Mechanics Lab Troy NY 12180 E-mail: zimmit@rpi.edu.

ZIMMON, DAVID SAMUEL, physician; b. Bklyn., Dec. 2, 1933; s. Louis Harold and Sylvia (Zimmerman) Z.; m. Anita Adelhardt, Sept. 11, 1962; children: Daniel, Rachel, Julian Adam. Student, Emory U., 1951-53; MD, Harvard U., 1958. Diplomate Am. Bd. Internal Medicine and Gastroenterology. Intern Bellevue Hosp. (Cornell II divsn.), N.Y.C., 1958-59; resident Meml. Ctr. for Cancer, 1959-61; fellow gastroenterology Bellevue Hosp., 1961-62; rsch. asst. Royal Free Hosp., London, 1962-63, liver disease rsch. fellow, 1963-64; chief gastroenterology Vets. Hosp., N.Y.C., 1965-84; asst. prof. to prof. clin. medicine NYU Sch. of Medicine, 1965-91; attending physician Bellevue Hosp., 1965-89. Attending physician in medicine, radiology and surgery St. Vincent's Hosp., N.Y.C., 1974-91; vis. prof. Australian Soc. for Gastrointestinal Endoscopy, 1980; pres. N.Y. Soc. for Gastrointestinal Endoscopy, 1976; chmn. Symposium Endoscopic Biliary Surgery, World Congress Gastrointestinal Endoscopy, Stockholm, 1982; chmn. sect. of biliary and pancreatic endoscopy European Soc. for Digestive Endoscopy, Barcelona, Spain, 1984. Editor: Surgical Endoscopy of the Gastrointestinal Tract, 1982; inventor in field; contbr. over 100 articles to profl. jours. Recipient Palmer award William Beaumont Gastrointestinal Soc., 1977. Fellow Am. Coll. Physicians; mem. Internat. Assn. for Study of the Liver, Internat. Biliary Assn., Am. Assn. for the Study of Liver Disease, Am. Gastrointestinal Assn., Am. Soc. for Gastrointestinal Endoscopy. Avocations: tennis, sailing. Office: 38 E 22nd St New York NY 10010-6110

ZIMNY, MAX, labor union administrator, lawyer; b. Bklyn., Mar. 9, 1925; s. Joseph and Rebecca (Nadelman) Z.; m. Bernice Nelson, June 26, 1948; children: Stuart, Andrew. Student, Bklyn. Coll., 1942-47, LLB cum laude, 1950; postgrad., NYU Grad. Sch. Labor Law, 1950-52. Bar: N.Y. 1950, U.S. Dist. Ct. (so. and ea. dists.) N.Y. 1951, U.S. Ct. Appeals (2nd cir.) 1955, U.S. Supreme Ct. 1962, U.S. Ct. Appeals (D.C. cir.) 1968, U.S. Ct. Appeals (4th cir.) 1969, U.S. Ct. Appeals (9th cir.) 1975, U.S. Ct. Appeals (8th cir.) 1980, U.S. Dist. Ct. (no. dist.) N.Y. 1983, U.S. Ct. Appeals (6th cir.) 1987, U.S. Ct. Appeals (7th cir.) 1988, U.S. Ct. Appeals (3rd and 5th cirs.) 1991. Mem. Zimny & Goldberg, N.Y.C., 1950-52; asst. gen. counsel Textiles Workers Union Am., 1952-58, Internat. Ladies' Garment Workers' Union, N.Y.C., 1958-63, assoc. gen. counsel, 1963-72, gen. counsel, 1972-95, Union of Needletrades, Indsl. and Textile Employees, 1995—. Mem. Vladeck, Elias, Vladeck, Zimny and Englehard, N.Y.C., 1976-78; lectr. NYU Sch. Law, Stetson U. Sch. Law, Indsl. Rels. Rsch. Inst., Nat. Acad. Arbitrators. Editor: Labor Arbitrator Development, 1983, Arbitration: A Guide for Advocates, 1990, Arbitration Casebook, 1997. Mediator, fact finder N.Y. Pub. Employment Rels. Bd., 1968—; chmn. Consumer Adv. Coun. City of N.Y.; mem. Levittown (N.Y.) Bd. Edn.; chmn. Profls. for Histadrut, N.Y.C.; arbitrator NYS disciplinary panel; Bd. dirs. Nat. Resources Ctr. for Consumers Legal Svcs., Lawyers Coord. Com. AFL-CIO; bd. dirs. Corsi Labor Mgmt. Inst.; mediator, arbitrator Am. Arbitration Assn.; labor, employment and comml. panels, arbitrator labor and mgmt. panel Fed. Mediation and Concilation Svc.; arbitrator N.Y.C. Office of Collective Bargaining, Electric Boat, Groton, Conn.; mem. nat. adv. coun., chair com. on rules and procedures, chair nat. task force on ADR in employment and due process protocol; mem. steering com. ctr. for Law and Econ. Policy Columbia U. Sch. Law; adv. com. NYU and Fordham Conf. on Labor, 1985—. With U.S. Army, 1943—46. Fellow: Coll. Labor and Employment Lawyers; mem.: ABA (chmn. com. on arbitration 1977—81, coun. labor sect. 1989—, chair labor and employment sect., pub. rels. com.), Commn. Healthcare Dispute Resolution, N.Y. State Bar Assn., Bar Assn. City of N.Y. (labor com.), B'nai B'rith Club (pres. lodge), Order of Coif. E-mail: maxzimny@optonline.net.

ZIMOV, BRUCE STEVEN, software engineer; b. Cin., Oct. 16, 1953; s. Sherman and Sylvia Zimov; m. Cathy Lynn Zimov, July 24, 1999. BS in Physics, U. Cin., 1975, MA in Philosophy, 1979. Physicist Kornylak Corp., Hamilton, Ohio, 1982-83; software engr. Entek Sci. Corp., Cin., 1983-89, project mgr., 1989-95, systems mgr., 1995-2000, AOL tech. mgr., 2000—. Inventor chess variants, table tennis variant. Mem. IEEE, Internat. Neural Network Soc., Tri-State Online Philosophy SIG (founder). Avocations: philosophy, chess, internet, computing, neural networks, economics. E-mail: bzimov@one.net.

ZIMPHER, NANCY LUSK, dean, educator; b. Gallipolis, Ohio, Oct. 29, 1946; d. Aven Denzle and Elsie Gordon (Hammond) L.; 1 child from a previous marriage, William Fletcher Zimpher; m. Kenneth R. Howey, May 8, 1987. BS, Ohio State U., 1968, MA, 1971, PhD, 1976. Cert. K-12 Tchr., Ohio. English tchr. Montgomery County Schs., Md., 1968, Reynoldsburg (Ohio) Schs., 1970; substitute tchr. Rolla (Mo.) City Schs., 1970-71; tchr. Phelps County Schs., Mo., 1971-72; grad. teaching assoc. Coll. Edn. Ohio State U., Columbus, 1972-73; dir. Coll. of Edn. Ohio State U., 1973-74, grad. adminstrn. asst. to dean, 1974-76, dir. field experiences alumni rels., 1976-80, coord. undergraduate programs, 1980-84; asst. prof. Ednl. Policy and Leadership Ohio State U., 1984-86, assoc. prof., 1986-91, full prof., 1991-98, assoc. dean, 1992, dean, 1993, exec. dean, 1994; chancellor, prof. curriculum and instrn. U. Wis., Milw., 1998—. Prin. investigator U.S. Office Edn. Field Devel. Grant, 1981-83, 85-88; co-principal investigator Metro. Life Found. Grant. 1989—, 1992—; cons. The Holmes Group, Lansing, Mich., 1991—. Book rev., editor: Journal of Teacher Education, 1986-89; co-author: Book Profiles of Preservice Teacher Education, 1989, RATE Profiles, 1987-92. Chair Faculty Compensation and Benefits Commn., 1989-90, Fiscal Com., 1991-92, Spousal Equivalency Com., 1990-91, Search Com., v.p. for Fin., 1992, Ohio State U; pres., chair bd. dirs. Holmes Partnership, 1997; chair edn. vision coun. United Way Franklin County, 1997; chair bd. dirs. United Way Franklin County, 1998. Fellow Com. for Instnl. Coop., Acad. Leadership Program. 1989-90; recipient Disting. Rsch. award, Disting. Teacher Educator award Assn. Tchr. Educators, 1990, Adams Professorshi Coll. Edn. Ind. State U., 1990—, Alumni Disting. Teaching award, The Ohio State U., 1992; named YWCA Woman of Achievement, 1997. Mem. AAUP, Am. Edn. Rsch. Assn., Am. Assn. Coll. Teacher Edn. Rsch. Comm., Assn. Tchr. Educators, ASCD, Phi Delta Kappa. Democrat. Episcopalian. Avocations: watercolorist, golf, sewing. Home: 4430 N Lake Dr Milwaukee WI 53211-1775

ZIMRING, FRANKLIN E. law educator, lawyer; b. 1942; BA, Wayne State U., 1963; JD, U. Chgo., 1967. Bar: Calif. 1968. Asst. prof. U. Chgo., 1967-69, assoc. prof., 1969-72, prof., 1972-85; co-dir. Ctr. for Studies in Criminal Justice, 1973-75, dir., 1975-86; prof. law dir. Earl Warren Legal Inst., Univ. Calif., Berkeley, 1985—2002. Author: (with Newton) Firearms and Violence in American Life, 1969; The Changing Legal World of Adolescence, 1982; (with Hawkins): Deterrence, 1973, Capital Punishment and the American Agenda, 1986, The Scale of Imprisonment, 1991, The Search for Rational Drug Control, 1992, Incapacitation: Penal Confinement and the Restraint of Crime, 1995, Crime is Not the Problem, 1997, American Youth Violence, 1998, Punishment and Democracy, 2001. Mem. Am. Acad. Arts and Scis. Office: U Calif Earl Warren Legal Inst Boalt Hall Berkeley CA 94720 E-mail: zimring@law.berkeley.edu.

ZIMRING, STUART DAVID, lawyer; b. L.A., Dec. 12, 1946; s. Martin and Sylvia (Robinson) Z.; m. Eve Axelrad, Aug. 24, 1969 (div. 1981); m. Carol Grenert, May 24, 1981; children: Wendy Lynn Grenert, Joseph Noah, Matthew Kevin Grenert, Dov Shimon. BA in U.S. History, UCLA, 1968, JD, 1971. Bar: Calif. 1972, U.S. Dist. Ct. (cen. dist.) Calif. 1972, U.S. Dist. Ct. (no. dist.) Calif. 1984; U.S. Supreme Ct., 1994; cert. specialist in estate planning, probate and trust law. Assoc. Law Offices Leonard Smith, Beverly Hills, Calif., 1971-73; ptnr. Law Offices Smith & Zimring, 1973-76; assoc. Levin & Ballin, North Hollywood, 1976-77; prin. Levin, Ballin, Plotkin, Zimring & Goffin, A.P.C., 1978-91, Law Offices Stuart D. Zimring, North Hollywood, 1991—. Lectr. Los Angeles Valley Coll., Van Nuys, Calif., 1974-82. Author: Inter Vivos Trust Trustees Operating Manual, 1994, Durable Powers of Attorney for Health Care--A Practical Approach to an Intimate Document, 1995, Reverse Mortgages--An Update, 1996, Cultural and Religious Concerns in Drafting Advance Directives, 1996, Drafting for Multi-Cultural Diversity in Advance Directives, 2000; co-author: California Guide to Tax, Estate and Financial Planning for the Elderly, 2001. Bd. dirs. Bet Tzedek, Jewish Legal Svcs., L.A., 1975-88, chmn. legal svcs. com., 1978-82; bd. dirs. Brandeis-Bardin Inst., Simi Valley, Calif., 1976-80; bd. dirs. Bur. Jewish Edn., L.A., 1973-88, chmn. com. on parent and family edn., 1985-87; trustee Adat Ari El Synagogue, L.A., 1982-2000; bd. dirs. Orgn. for the Needs of the Elderly, 1994, 1st v.p. 1995-97, pres., 1997-2001. Recipient Circle award Juvenile Justice Connection Project, L.A., 1989, Wiley W. Manuel award for pro bono legal svcs., 1994, 95, 96, 97, 98. Fellow: Am. Coll. Trusts and Estates Counsel, Nat. Acad. Elder Law Attys. (pres. So. Calif. chpt. 1997, nat. bd. dirs. 1997—2001, chair nat. tech. com., sec. 2001—); mem.: San Fernando Bar Assn. (trustee 1979—86), State Bar Calif. Democrat. Avocations: music, collecting wine, travel, photography. Office: 12650 Riverside Dr North Hollywood CA 91607-3421 E-mail: zimzim@elderlawca.com.

ZINBERG, DOROTHY SHORE, science policy educator; b. Boston; m. Norman E Zinberg, 1956 (dec.); children: Sarah Zinberg Mandel, Anne. BA, Boston U., 1949, MA, 1958; PhD, Harvard U., 1966. Research chemist Lever Bros., Cambridge, 1950-52; sr. research assoc. Daniel Yankelovich, Inc., N.Y.C., and; Cambridge Center for Research in Behavioral Scis., 1966-68; NSF research sociologist dept. chemistry U. Coll. London, 1968-69; lectr. Harvard U., 1960—. Mem. adv. com. Office Sci. Pers. NRC, Washington, 1971—74, bd. on engring. edn., 1991; spl. adviser Aspen Inst.; cons. MacArthur Found., 1989—93; vis. scholar NAS, China, 1987, Nat. Inst. Sci. and Tech., Tokyo, 1991; vis. lectr. Inst. for Human Scis., Vienna, 1995; mem. adv. bd. Erik Erikson Inst. for Edn. and Rsch., 1996; vis. prof. Imperial Coll., London, 2001—. Columnist: London Times Higher Educ Supplement, 1993—, columnist: NY Times Syndication, 1994—. Mem int sci exchanges NAS, 1994—97, mem comt int relations, 1977—80, mem comt int human resources; chmn adv coun int div NSF, 1978—81; mem coun Int Exchange Scholars, 1978—81; mem comt int exchange engrs NAE, 1987—88; mem adv panel Office Technology Assessment Educ and Employment Scientists and Engrs, 1986—88; trustee Simon's Rock Col, 1971—75; mem panel prioprity area sci and technology policy NATO, 1995—99; bd. dirs. Fine Arts Workshop, Provincetown, Mass., 1970—86, Bill T. Jones Found for Dance Promotion, 1997—99; bd dirs Gen Scanning, Inc, 1998—99; bd dirs eng educ NRC, 1990—95. Fellow: AAAS (mem comt sci freedom and responsibility 1972—74, comt opportunities in sci 1973—76, comt sci, eng, and pub policy 1982—88, comt exchange scientists with Fed Republic Germany 1987—91, 1991); mem.: NAS (mem comt to evaluate Int Sci and Technology Ctr Moscow 1995—97), Int Sci Policy Found (mem adv bd 1988—), Coun Foreign Relations, Fedn Am Scientists (mem coun 1980—85). Home: 3 Acacia St Cambridge MA 02138-4818 Office: Harvard U 79 JF Kennedy St Cambridge MA 02138 E-mail: dorothy_zinberg@harvard.edu.

ZINBERG, STANLEY, physician, educator; b. N.Y.C., Aug. 18, 1934; s. Phillip M. and Etta (Beck) Z.; m. Margaret T. McNally; children: Lloyd M., Randi Ellen, Gregory A. BA, Columbia Coll., 1955; MD, SUNY, 1959; MS, NYU, 1990. Diplomate Am. Bd. Obstetrics and Gynecology. Intern Cornell Med. div. Bellevue Hosp., N.Y.C., 1959-60; resident in ob-gyn. NYU Bellevue Med. Ctr., 1960-64; assoc. prof. ob-gyn. NYU Sch. Medicine, 1966—; chief gynecology Bellevue Hosp., 1975-81; mem. staff NYU Hosp., 1966-93; chief ob-gyn. N.Y. Downtown Hosp., N.Y.C., 1981-93; v.p. practice activities Am. Coll. Obstetricians & Gynecologists, Washington, 1994—. Examiner Am. Bd. Ob-gyn., 1975-98; mem. Residency Rev. Com. for Ob-gyn., 1987-92; chmn. faculty coun. NYU Sch. Medicine, N.Y.C., 1978-79; pres. med. staff N.Y. Downtown Hosp., 1991-92. Contbr. articles to profl. jours. Capt. U.S. Army, 1964-66. Fellow: ACOG (Manhattan sect. chmn. 1979—82), NY Gynecol. Soc., NY Acad. Medicine (chmn. sect. on ob-gyn. 1985—86), NY Obstet. Soc. (pres. 1989—90); mem.: Bellevue Ob-Gyn. Soc. (pres. 1988—92), Am. Coll. Physician Execs. (assoc.), Soc. Alumni Bellevue Hosp., Assn. Profs. of Ob-Gyn. Avocations: painting, photography, tennis. Home: Apt 1416 700 New Hampshire Ave NW Washington DC 20037-2406 Office: Am Coll Ob-Gyn 409 12th St SW Washington DC 20024-2125

ZINDEL, BONNIE, writer; b. N.Y.C., May 3, 1943; d. Jack and Claire (Bromberg) Hildebrand; m. Paul Zindel, Oct. 25, 1973; children: David, Lizabeth. BA in Psychology, Hofstra U., 1964; MS, Columbia U., 1994. Dir. pub. relations The Cleveland Play House, Cleve., 1969-72; producer show Intermission Feature, Boston Symphony, sta. WCLV-FM, Cleve., 1970-72. Author: A Star for the Latecomer, 1980; Hollywood Dream Machine, 1984; playwright I Am A Zoo-Jewish Repetory Theatre-The Troupe Theatre, 1976; Lemons in the Morning, A.M. Back Alley Theatre, 1983, The Latecomer, 1985, Adriana Earthlight-Student Shrink, 1987. Mem. Playwrights Unit-Actors Studio, Women in Film. Office: 200 W 60th St Apt 2E New York NY 10023-8503

ZINDER, NEWTON DONALD, stock market analyst, consultant; b. N.Y.C., Aug. 12, 1927; s. Paul and Jennie (Feld) Z.; m. Clarice Katz, Dec. 26, 1954; children— Marla, Andrea, Pamela. BA, NYU, 1948, MBA, 1957; MA, Columbia U., 1949. Securities analyst Ira Haupt & Co., N.Y.C., 1953-60; securities analyst E.F. Hutton & Co., 1960-63, stock market analyst, 1963-88, Shearson Lehman Bros., N.Y.C., 1988-92; investment cons., 1993—. Served with USN, 1945-46 Mem. Market Technicians Assn. Home: 1734 Roland Ave Wantagh NY 11793-2856

ZINDER, NORTON DAVID, genetics educator, university dean; b. N.Y.C., Nov. 7, 1928; s. Harry Jean and (Gottesman) Z.; m. Marilyn Estreicher, Dec. 24, 1949; children— Stephen, Michael. AB, Columbia U., 1947; MS, U. Wis., 1949, PhD, 1952. Asst. Rockefeller U., N.Y.C., 1952-56, asso., 1956-58, asso. prof. genetics, 1958-64, prof., 1964-99, prof. emeritus, 1999—, John D. Rockefeller Jr. prof., 1977—, dean grad. and postgrad. studies, 1993-95. Cons. genetic-biology NSF, 1962-66, Office Tech. Assessment, Washington, 1979-81, Chas. Pfizer & Co., 1963-67; chmn. ad hoc com. to rev. viral cancer program Nat. Cancer Inst., 1973-74; mem. vis. com. dept. biology Harvard U., 1975-81, sect. virology Yale U., 1975-83, dept. biochemistry Princeton U., 1975-86; mem. sci. adv. bd. Carter-Wallace Inc., 1982-85, Genetic Systems Corp., 1981-86; mem.adv. com. Alliance Internat. Health Care Trust, 1984—; trustee Cold Spring Harbor Lab., 1967-85, sec. to bd., 1980-85; chmn. com. to rev. Army chem. weapons stockpile disposal program, NAS/NRC, 1987-91; chmn. program adv. com. on human genome, NIH, 1988-91, other affiliations; mem. adv. com. Celera Genomics, 1998—. Assoc. editor: Virology; sect. editor Intervirology, 1973-90. Recipient Eli Lilly award in microbiology and immunology, 1962, U.S. Steel Found. award in molecular biology, 1966, medal of excellence Columbia U., 1969, award in sci. freedom & responsibility AAAS, 1982; Am. Cancer Soc. scholar, 1955-58. Fellow Am. Acad. Arts and Scis. (coun. 1984-87); mem. NAS (mem. coun. 1988-91, exec. com. Assembly of Life Scis. 1975-78, bd. army sci. and tech. 1981), Soc. Am. Biol. Chemists, Genetics Soc. Am., Am. Soc. for Microbiology, Council Fgn. Relations, Harvey Soc., Sigma Xi. Achievements include spl. research in microbial genetics. Home: 450 E 63rd St New York NY 10021-7928 Office: Rockefeller U 1230 York Ave New York NY 10021-6399

ZINGALE, ROBERT G. surgeon; b. Bklyn., Feb. 9, 1957; s. Joseph and Theresa Zingale; m. Christine A. Smith, Oct. 4, 1986; children:Jillian, Kara, Alec. BS cum laude, Pace U., 1979; MD, SUNY, Bklyn., 1983. Diplomate Am. Bd. Surgery, Surg. Crit. Care, Nat. Bd. Med. Examiners. Resident Maimonides Med. Ctr., Bklyn., 1983-88; trauma fellow Coney Island Hosp, 1988-89; attending physician, dir. trauma Huntington (N.Y.) Hosp., 1989—; attending physician Nassau County Med. Ctr., East Meadow, N.Y., 1991—; clin. instr. SUNY, Stony Brook, 1991—; assoc. clin. prof. surgery N.Y. Med. Coll./North Shore U. Hosp., Valhalla, 1993—. Dir. surg. svcs. Dolan Health Ctr. Contbr. articles to profl. jours. Fellow ACS, Suffolk Acad. Medicine; mem. AMA, Soc. Laparoendoscopic Surgeons, Am. Soc. Gen. Surgeons, N.Y. Met. Breast Cancer Grop, Med. Soc. N.Y., Suffolk County Med. Soc. Office: 158 E Main St Huntington NY 11743

ZININ, PAVEL V. physicist; b. Moscow, Dec. 20, 1955; s. Valentin F. and Nailya G. (Zinina) Z.; m. Natalia O. Krokhina, Apr. 18, 1987; 1 child, Lisa. BS/MS, Moscow State U., 1973, 80; PhD, Moscow Inst. Physics/Tech., 1987. Rsch. engr. Scientific and Rsch. Inst. for Biol. Testing of Chem., Moscow, 1980-81, rsch. assoc., 1981-83; rsch. scientist N. Semienov Inst. of Chem. Physics/Russian Acad. Scis., 1987-93; Alexander von Humboldt Found. Rsch. fellow Inst. for Material Sci. and Structure Rsch./U. Bremen, 1993-94; rsch. fellow U. oxford, 1995-97; asst. rschr. U. Hawaii, Honolulu, 1998—. Author: (with others) Handbook of the Elastic Properties of Solids, Liquids and Gases, 2000; contbr. chpts. to books and more than 70 articles to profl. jours. Recipient fellowship Alexander von Humboldt, Germany, 1993; grantee NATO, Brussel, 1994-95, Caterpillar Inc., 2000, 01, NSF, 2001. Mem.: Materials Rsch. Soc., Biomech. Soc., Optical Soc. Am. Office: Univ Hawaii 2525 Correa Rd Honolulu HI 96822-2219 E-mail: zinin@soest.hawaii.edu.

ZINK, CHARLES TALBOTT, lawyer; b. Long Beach, Calif., Oct. 27, 1937; s. William Talbott and Nellie Grace (Hoskins) Z.; m. Deborah Sidney Burks, Nov. 26, 1983. AB, Princeton U., 1959; LLB, U. Va., 1965. Bar: Va. 1965, Ga. 1965. Mng. ptnr. Hansell & Post, Atlanta, 1965-89; ptnr. Jones, Day, Reavis & Poque, 1989-93, Long, Aldridge & Norman, Atlanta, 1993—. Lectr. N.W. Ctr. for Profl. Edn., Washington, Atlanta and Tampa, Fla., 1983—; mem. faculty Atlanta Coll. Trial Advocacy, 1985, mem. exec. com., 1984—, pres., 1985, 86. Bd. dirs. Atlanta Humane Soc., 1983—. Lt. (j.g.) USN, 1959-62. Mem. Lawyers Club Atlanta, Atlanta Tax Forum, Capital City Club. Republican. Episcopalian. Office: 1 Peachtree Center Ave NE # 5300 Atlanta GA 30303-3002

ZINK, DAVID DANIEL, retired English educator, writer; b. Kansas City, Mo. s. David Daniel and Virginia (Taylor) Z.; m. Joan Wilson (div. July 13, 1982); children: Laurie Wilson Zink, David Paul Zink; m. Joann Nelson Rocha, Oct. 29, 1982 (filed for dissolution of marriage Dec. 19, 1988); 1 child, Christopher Stewart. BJ, U. Tex., 1952; MA in English, U. Colo., 1957, PhD in Victorian Lit., 1962. Instr./assoc. prof. English USAF Acad., Colo. Springs, Colo., 1957-65; prof. English Lamar U., Beaumont, Tex., 1965-77. Part-time English instr., Pasadena City Coll., Pasadena, Calif., 1984-89; exec. recruiter, L.A., 1980-84. Author: (book) The Ancient Stones Speak: A Photographic and Archaeological Atlas of the Megalithic Sites of the World, 1979, Stones of Atlantis, 1990, on camera cons. Leslie Stephen, 1972; co-author: (with wife Joan) You are the Mystery, 1976; in Bolivia for NBC series In Search of..., 1976, to Cousteau Soc. at Bimini Island for PBS special Calypso's Search for Atlantis, 1976; contbr. to TV specials on Atlantis, 1993-98; co-rschr. Kirlian photography project, 1973. Mem. Internat. Explorers Soc. expdn. to Mosquito Coast, NE Honduras, 1976; led 10 underwater projects (the Poseidia expdns.) to an archaeol. site off Bimini Island, 1974-79. Capt. USAF, 1952-65, comdr. mt. top radio relay detachments, 1953-54, Korea. Explorer of Yr. Internat. Explorers Soc., 1976; appointed dir. of rsch. (hon.) Bahamas Antiquities Inst., Nassau, 1975; Poseidia project listed in Spirit of Enterprise from the Rolex Awards, 1978. Fellow Explorer's Club (N.Y.C.).

ZINK, JOAN WILSON, writer, poet, composer; b. Tulsa, Dec. 17, 1928; d. Paul Almus and Gladys Emily Wilson; m. David Daniel Zink, Feb. 5, 1948; children: Laurie Zink Menard, David Paul; m. Lawrence Eugene Dalen, June 24, 1990. BA, U. Colo., 1958. Contbg. author The Ancient Stone's Speak, 1979, The Stones of Atlantis, 1978; author: (book of poetry) The Road Less Travelled, 1980; co-author (with David Zink): (book) You Are the Mystery, 1976, You Are the Mystery, new edit., 2001; contbr. . Mem.: SPUR. Home: 4011 Saxon Dr New Smyrna Beach FL 32169

ZINK, LEE BERKEY, retired academic administrator, economist, educator; b. Salem, Ind., June 7, 1930; s. Otto C. and Lera (Berkey) Z.; m. Patricia Louise Patton, Aug. 16, 1964; children: Kevin Patrick, Barry Lee. BA in Econs. magna cum laude, Ind. U., 1959; PhD in Econs., Okla. State U., 1967. Field rep. GM Acceptance Corp., Louisville, 1953-54; asst. mgr. Dougherty Motor Sales, Salem, 1954-56; asst. prof. econs. Southeastern State Coll., Durant, Okla., 1964-67, spl. asst. to dir. Tech. Use Studies Ctr., 1964-65, dir., 1965-68, assoc. prof. of Econs., 1967-68; dir., prin. rsch. economist, bur. bus. and econ. rsch. U. N.Mex., Albuquerque, 1968-77; prof. bus. adminstrn. N.Mex. Highlands U., Kirtland, 1974-81; dir. Inst. Applied Rsch. Svcs. U. N.Mex., Albuquerque, 1975-2000, dir. Nat. Energy Info. Ctr. affiliate/U.S. Dept. Energy, 1978-87, assoc. v.p. rsch., bus. and govt. rels., 1988-2000; ret. Mem. Gov.'s adv. com. statis. standards for Okla., 1964-66, sci. and industry Okla., 1965-66, statewide planning com. implemenation of Tech. Svcs. Act, Okla., 1965-66; cons. majority leader U.S. Ho. Reps., 1964-68, So. Okla. Devel. Assn., 1965-68, Gov. Okla., 1965-68, Kiamichi Econ. Devel. Dist., Okla., 1967-68, N.Mex. Corp. Commn., 1969-74, N.Mex. State Planning Office, 1971, Ohio State U. Evaluation Ctr., 1972, others; mem. Gov.'s adv. com. N.Mex. Dept. Devel., 1971; adv. panel spl. tech. assistance program Office Econ. Opportunity, 1972-74; mem. Albuquerque adv. coun. U.S. Small Bus. Adminstrn., 1974-81, chmn. 1977-79; chmn. Gov.'s Coun. Econ. Advisors, 1975-78; sec. econ. devel. Gov.'s Cabinet, 1975-76, policy advisor, 1976-78; econ. devel. task force We. Interstate Commn. Higher Edn., 1979. Mem. edit. review bd. Review of Regional Economics and Business, 1976-85; bd. edit. contbrs. The Albuquerque Tribune, 1979-82; mem. edit. adv. bd. The Southwest Review of Management and Economics, 1981-85; contbr. articles to profl. jours. Organizing pres. Kiamichi Econ. Devel. Dist., Okla., 1966-67; active Monte Vista Christian Ch., 1968—; exec. dir. N.Mex. Coun. Econ. Edn., 1969-75, chmn. operating com., 1976-86; pres. East Holiday Park Neighborhood Assn., 1978-94; adv. coun. city growth and devel. Greater Albuquerque Leadership Devel. Program, 1980-82; adv. bd. U.S. Armed Svcs., 1980-87; adv. bd. econ. devel. City of Albuquerque, 1980-84; community advisor NCAA Vols. for Youth, 1981-85; mem. Bernalillo county Human Svcs. Coalition, 1982-85; apptd. by Gov.-elect Anaya N.Mex. Jobs Task Force, 1982-83; apptd. chmn. by mayor Better Albuquerque Bond Coms., 1983-87, 93-95; trustee U. Albuquerque, 1983-86; bd. dirs. Nat. Tng. Inst. Cmty. Econ. Devel., 1979-82, Inst. Study Cmty. Econ. Devel., 1980-82, Albuquerque Conv. and Vis. Bur., 1984-87, Consumer Credit Counseling Svc. N.Mex., 1985-94, pres. 1989-90, Better Bus. Bur. N.Mex., 1992—; pres. adv. coun. UNICEF, Albuquerque, 1985-95; mem. employment and tng. needs task force City of Albuquerque, 1987-88; evaluation team Congressman Lujan's South Valley task force, 1987; apptd. chmn. by Mayor Saavedra and city coun. pub. forum com. recycling, 1991. 2d lt. U.S. Army, 1951-53, Germany; lt. col. USAR, 1953-71. Fellow Nat. Defense Edn. Act, 1959-62; grantee Nat. Aeronautics and Space Adminstrn., 1964-68, N.Mex. Dept. Devel., 1968-80, HEW, 1968-76, 1971-72, Bank N. Mex., 1969-77, The Albuquerque Model Cities Agy., 1969-70, Four Corners Regional Commn., 1969-80, U.S. Forest Svc., 1974-77, U.S. Dept. Commerce, 1975-79, 1976-2000, N.Mex. Energy Resources Bd., 1976-77, The Navajo Nation, 1976-78, U.S. Army Corps. Engrs., 1976-78, U.S. Dept. Energy, 1978-87. Mem. Am. Assembly Collegiate Schs. Bus. (rsch., statis., publs. com. 1976-77, small bus. adminstrn. liasion com. 1976-78), Am. Soc. Info. Sci. (frontier chpt. exec. com. 1972-73, chmn.-elect 1972, chmn. 1973), Assn. Univ. Bus. and Econ. Rsch. (exec. com. 1971-78, v.p. 1975-76, pres. 1976-77), Mid continent Rsch. and Devel. Coun. (bd. dirs. 1965-69), Fedn. Rocky Mountain States (chmn. bus. rsch. com. 1969-75), Rocky Mountain Coun. Burs. Bus. and Econ. Rsch. (chmn. 1969-77), N.Mex. coun. Econ. Edn. (bd. dirs. 1969-90), Am. Guild Organists (dean Albuquerque chpt. 1996-98), Greater Albuquerque C. of C. (edn. com. 1968-73, bd. dirs. 1970-76, 78-82, chmn. growth com. 1972, v.p. 1973-74, pres. 1981), Phi Kappa Phi, Phi Beta Kappa (alpha chpt. exec. com., sec. 1973-75), Golden Key (hon.). Democrat. Avocation: pipe organs. Home: 3741 Mount Rainier Dr NE Albuquerque NM 87111-4399 E-mail: leezink@unm.edu., drLBZ@aol.com.

ZINK, WALTER EARL, II, lawyer; b. Lincoln, Nebr., Nov. 20, 1947; s. Walter Earl and Marjorie Ellen (Hull) Z.; m. Carol Ann Thomas, June 26, 1971; children: Walter, Robert, Carmela. BA in Edn., Nebr. Wesleyan U., 1970; JD with distinction, Nebr. Coll. Law, 1974. Bar: Nebr. 1974, U.S. Dist. Ct. Nebr. 1974. Ptnr. Baylor, Evnen, Curtiss, Grimit & Witt, Lincoln, 1974—. Adj. prof. law Nebr. Coll. Law, Lincoln, 1978-82; brig. gen., asst. adj. gen. Army, NEARNG. Bd. dirs. Camp Kitaki YMCA, Lincoln, 1980-92. Mem. ABA, Nebr. Bar Assn. (vice chmn. young lawyers 1982-83), Fedn. Inst. Corp. Counsel (workers' compensation chair 1995-97), Assn. Def. Trial Attys., Am. Bd. Trial Advocates, Internat. Assn. Def. Counsel (mem. exec. com., past chair employment law and membership com.), N.G. Assn. U.S., Res. Officers Assn. (v.p. Army 1984-85), Hillcrest Country Club (pres. 1994-96), Blue Key, Kappa Delta Pi. E-mial. Home: 1420 Broadmoore Dr Lincoln NE 68506-1511 Office: Baylor Evnen Curtiss Grimit & Witt 206 S 13th St Ste 1200 Lincoln NE 68508-2077 E-mail: wzink@baylorlaw.com.

ZINKE, MICHAEL DUANE, finance and accountancy manager; b. Mendota, Ill., Oct. 13, 1954; s. Elmer H. and Barbara A. (Williams) Z.; m. Cathy L. Myers, July 22, 1978; children: Duane M., Brian M. AA cum laude, Ill. Valley Community Coll., 1974; BS, No. Ill. U., 1976; MBA, Cen. State U., Edmond, Okla., 1988. Comptr. Office World, Oklahoma City, 1977-79; credit analyst C.I.T. Corp., 1979-80, sr. credit analyst, 1980-81, dist. credit mgr., 1982-84; credit mgr. Macklanburg-Duncan Co., 1984-87, mgr. credit, payroll, accounts payable, gen. acctg., 1987-90; credit mgr. N.Am. Chem. Co., Mission, Kans., 1991-92, N.Am. Salt Co. and N.Am. Chem. Co., Overland Park, 1992—. Chmn. unsecured creditors com. H.E. Leonhardt Lumber, Oklahoma City, 1989-90; mem. unsecured creditors com. O'Hommel Co., Overland Park, Kans., 1991—. Author rsch. papers. Membership drive vol. Oklahoma City C. of C., 1989; rep. Napco Constrn. to Oklahoma City C. of C., 1990-91; dist. sec.-treas. Am. Bus. Clubs, Oklahoma City, 1985-86; bearer of U.S. Olympic Festival Torch, 1989. Mem. Nat. Assn. Credit Mgmt., Nat. Chem. Creditors Assn., Fin. Credit and Internat. Bus. Assn., Internat. Trade Club of Greater Kansas City. Democrat. Lutheran. Avocations: fishing, hunting, reading. Home: 8800 Candlelight Ln Lenexa KS 66215-3432 Office: NAm Salt Co 8300 College Blvd Overland Park KS 66210-1841

ZINKHAM, W. ROBERT, lawyer; b. Balt., May 30, 1955; s. William H. and Claire A. (Rafferty) Z.; m. Theresa McGeehan, July 7, 1985; children: Natalie Anne, Elizabeth Claire. BA, Johns Hopkins U., 1977; JD, U. Md., Balt., 1980. Law clerk to chief judge Md. Ct. Appeals, Balt., 1980-81; assoc. Venable, Baetjer and Howard, 1981-88, ptnr., 1989—. Bd. dirs. Greater Balt. Med. Ctr. Found., 1992—. Editor Md. Law Rev., 1979. Chmn. Johns Hopkins Hosp. Psychiat. Day Hosp., Balt., 1982-92; pres. Mt. Washington Hills Assn., Balt., 1984-87. Mem. ABA, Am. Acad. Hosp. Attys., Nat. Health Lawyers Assn., Md. Bar Assn., Balt. Bar Assn. Republican. Office: Venable Baetjer & Howard 2 Hopkins Plz Ste 2100 Baltimore MD 21201-2982 E-mail: wrzinkham@venable.com.

ZINKHAN, GEORGE MARTIN, III, marketing educator; b. Balt., Feb. 17, 1952; s. George Martin Jr. and Mary Elizabeth (Stoner) Z.; m. Marie Bruce; children: George M. IV, Lydia F., Sam S., M. Elizabeth S., L. James G. BA in English Lit., Swarthmore Coll., 1974; MBA in Ops. Rsch., U. Mich., 1979, PhD in Bus. Adminstrn., 1981. Stats. lab. counselor U. Mich., Ann Arbor, 1978-79, teaching fellow, 1979-81; asst. prof. U. Houston, 1981-86, Conn prof. mktg., 1989-93; Coca-Cola prof. mktg., dept. head U. Ga., Athens, 1994—. Vis. assoc. prof. U. Pitts., 1987-88; mem. exec. com. Faculty Senate, U. Houston, 1991-92; cons. FTC, Washington, 1992-93, San Francisco, 1994-96. Co-author: Electronic Commerce: The Strategic Perspective, 2000, Consumers, 2002; editor: Enhancing Knowledge Developments in Marketing, 1995, Advertising Research: The Internet, Consumer Behavior, and Strategy, 2002; editor Jour. Advt., Richmond, Va., 1991-95, (spl. issue) Jour. Bus. Rsch., 1996, 2d edit. 1999, book rev. editor, mem. rev. bd. Jour. of Mktg., College Station, Tex., 1991—; mem. rev. bd. Jour. Current Issues, 1991—, Jour. Bus. Rsch., 1994—, Jour. MacroMarketing, 1998—. Mem. Am. Mktg. Assn. (track chair 1991-96, v.p. for rsch. 1996-98, pres. advt. spl. interest group 1996—), Am. Acad. Advt. (named one of Top 12 Contbrs. to Advt. 1990, one of Top 10 Contbrs. to Svcs. Advt. 1997, one of top 5 Contbrs. to Advt. Lit., Jour. of Advt., 1998, co-chair Nat. Conf., 2001), Acad. Mktg. Sci. (track chair 1994, track chair electronic commerce 1998), Assn. Consumer Rsch. (session chair 1990, program com. 1996, 2000, Judge Peabody awards 1996—). Democrat. United Ch. of Christ. Avocations: soccer, basketball, swimming, tennis, chess. E-,ail. Home: 372 Chesterfield Rd Bogart GA 30622-1761 Office: Univ Ga Dept Mktg 138 Brooks Hall Athens GA 30602-6258 E-mail: gzinkham@terry.uga.edu.

ZINKIN, LEWIS DAVID, physician; b. N.Y.C., Apr. 28, 1945; s. Solomon B. and Margaret (Tovim) Z.; m. Rochelle Ellen Dershowitz, July 7, 1968; children: Donniel, Ephraim, Gila, Hillel, Adina. BA, Yeshiva U., 1966; MD, N.J. Coll. Med., 1970. Lic. physician, N.J. Surg. intern St. Vincent's Hosp., N.Y.C., 1970-71, gen. surg. resident, 1973-77; colon and rectal surg. fellow Greater Balt. Med. Ctr., 1977-78; attending physician R.W. Johnson U. Hosp., New Brunswick, N.J., 1978—, St. Peters Med. Ctr., New Brunswick, 1978—. Clin. assoc. prof. R.W. Johnson Med. Sch., New Brunswick, 1980-96. Pres. Congl. Ohr Torah, Edison, N.J., 1993-96. Lt. USN, 1971-73. Mem. Am. Cancer Soc. (chmn. N.J.). Jewish. Office: B3 Brier Hill Ct East Brunswick NJ 08816-3330

ZINKLE, STEVEN JOHN, engineer, researcher; b. Prairie du Chien, Wis., Nov. 5, 1958; s. Aloysius Peter and Katherine Edith (Brownlee) Z.; m. Teresa Allen Medford, May 26, 1990; children: Austin Chase, Allen Peter. BS, U. Wis., 1980, PhD, 1985. Rsch. staff Oak Ridge (Tenn.) Nat. Lab., 1985—. Vis. scientist Forschungszentrum Jülich, Germany, 1991-92, Risø Nat. Lab., Roskilde, 1991-92. Recipient Rsch. Publ. award Martin Marietta Energy Systems, Oak Ridge, 1991, David Rose Excellence in Fusion Engrng. award Fusion Power Assocs., Gaithersburg, Md., 1992. Fellow Am. Ceramic Soc. (Nuclear and Environ. Techs. Best Paper award 1994-95); mem. Am. Soc. Metals Internat., Materials Rsch. Soc., Am. Nuclear Soc., Sigma Xi, Phi Kappa Phi. Office: Oak Ridge Nat Lab PO Box 2008 Oak Ridge TN 37831-6138

ZINKON, LANA SUE, occupational health nurse; b. Dover, Ohio, Oct. 19, 1954; d. Jack Eugene and Virginia Louise (Brown) Z.; divorced; children: Amanda Elyse and Emily Suzanne (twins). Diploma, Grant Hosp. Sch. Nursing, Columbus, Ohio, 1976; student, Ashland U., 1991-92. RN, Ohio. Supr. med. Cedar Point Amusement Park, Sandusky, Ohio, 1977-82; shift supr. Nursing Home, Port Clinton, 1978-82; staff nurse Flying Nurses, Calif. La., 1982-83; camp nurse Camp Blue Star, Hendersonville, N.C., summer 1983; staff nurse Med. Pers. Pool, 1983; occupl. health nurse Rockwell Internat., Fletcher, N.C., 1984-88; staff/charge nurse Joel Pomerene Hosp., Millersburg, Ohio, 1988-89, off-shift supr., 1989-93, dir. occupl. health, 1990-94; occupl. health nurse The Timken Co., New Philadelphia, 1989—; dir. on-site svc. for occupl. medcine Ctr. of Tuscarawas County, 1995—. Dir., creator On-the-Job Occupational Program, Joel Pomerene Meml. Hosp., Millersburg, 1990-94. Bd. dirs. John Denver Meml. Peace Cloth, Inc.; active Sugarcreek First United Ch. of Christ. Mem. Am. Assn. Occupational Health Nurses, Ohio Assn. Occupational Health Nurses, Stark Assn. Occupational Health Nurses, Am. Legion Aux. Democrat. Mem. Ch. Christ. Avocation: reading. Office: Occupl Medicine Ctr Tuscarawas Co 306 W High Ave New Philadelphia OH 44663-2134 Fax: 330-339-8858. E-mail: zink73@wilkshire.net.

ZINMAN, DAVID JOEL, conductor; b. N.Y.C., July 9, 1936; s. Samuel and Rachel Ilo (Samuels) Z.; m. Leslie Heyman (dec.); children: Paul Pierre, Rachel Linda; m. Mary Ingham, May 19, 1974; 1 child, Raphael. B.Mus., Oberlin (Ohio) Conservatory, 1958; MA, U. Minn., 1961. Asst. to Pierre Monteux, 1961-64; guest condr. U.S. and Europe; music dir. Netherlands Chamber Orch., 1964-77, Rochester (N.Y.) Philharm. Orch., 1974-85; prin. guest condr. Rotterdam Philharm. Orch., 1977-79, chief condr., 1979-82; prin. guest condr., music dir. designate Balt. Symphony Orch., 1983-85, music dir., 1985—98, Tonhalle Orch., Zurich, Switzerland, 1995; music dir. designate Aspen (Colo.) Music Festival and Sch., 1997; music dir., 1998—; program dir. Am. Acad. Conducting, Aspen, 1998—. Adj. prof. Eastman Sch. Music, Rochester Rec. artist Phillips, Nonesuch, Decca/London, Decca/Argo, Angel/EMI, Telarc, Sony Classical. Recipient Grand Prix du Disque, 1967, 82, Edison award, 1967, 3 Grammy awards, 1990, Grammophone best selling record award, 1993, Grammophone award, 1994, Deutschen Schallplatten prize, George Peabody medal outstanding contbn. music in Am., 1996. Office: 2006 W Peninsula Cir Chandler AZ 85248

ZINN, ALEXANDER NATHAN, retired surgeon; b. Bklyn., July 30, 1927; s. Gerald I. and Lena Y. Zinn; m. Shirley B. Zinn, Dec. 24, 1955 (dec. June 1972); children: Jeffery P., Dale Marie Gaskin; m. Roberta Silver Zinn, Jan. 29, 1989. BA, Hamilton Coll., 1948; MD, Chgo. Med. Sch., 1952. Diplomate Am. Bd. Gen. Surgery. Intern Cook County Hosp., 1952-54; resident in surgery Hines V.A. Hosp., 1954-57; ward surgeon VA Hosp., Saginaw, Mich., 1957-58; pvt. practice Canoga Park, Calif., 1958-93; physician surveyor Joint Commn. on Accreditation Health Care, Oak Brook Terrace, Ill., 1993-2000; surveyor Calif. Med. Assn., Med. Staff Survey Commn., San Francisco, 1972-93; ret., 2000. With USN, 1945-46. Mem. AMA, Calif. Med. Assn. (del. 1990-92), Calif. Med. Assn. (surveyor, med. staff), L.A. County Med. Assn. Avocations: skiing, running. Home: PO Box 3157 Winnetka CA 91396-3157 E-mail: trackdocalex@aol.com.

ZINN, DENNIS BRADLEY, magician, actor, corporate skills trainer; b. Phoenix, Dec. 15, 1957; s. Clarence LaVern and Juanita Alice (Martin) Z.; m. Brenda Ann Puckett, May 25, 1982. Grad. high sch., Phoenix. Actor (movies) Nobody's Fool, To Find My Son, The American Girls, A Fire in the Sky, Assault on Paradise, A Star Is Born; actor (stage) Glendale Little Theatre, Mesa Little Theatre, Scottsdale Little Theatre, Phoenix Little Theatre, Children's Little Theatre, Alhambra High Sch. Drama Dept.; performer numerous comml.s, voice-overs, indsl. films; guest appearances on numerous TV programs; magician appearances at Hollywood Magic Castle and Las Vegas, magician/performer for over 20 talk shows; host, producer The New Variety Arts Show; contbg. author: The Snake Basket; writer Genii mag., Linking Ring mag., ABRA mag., Magician's Weekly. Performer, fundraiser Phoenix Breakfast Civitan Club, 1979-92; mem. Valley Cmty. Access TV, 1990-93; mem. Phoenix and Valley of Sun Visitors and Conv. Bur. Recipient Patrick Henry award for oratory Ariz. Congress for God & Country, 1974, Am. Legion Citizenship award Ariz. Am. Legion, 1975. Mem.: SAG, AFTRA (treas. Ariz. local 1989—90, bd. dir. 1993—95), Magic Castle, Profl. Magicians Assn., Soc. Am. Magicians (v.p. assembly 248 1997—98), Internat. Brotherhood Magicians (pres. local ring 55 1979, ter. rep. 1979—80, Close-Up Magician of Yr. 1976, Internat. Order of Merlin 1997, Ring 55 and Assembly 248 Magician of Yr. 2000). Republican. Avocations: book collecting, golf, travel. Home and Office: Brad Zinn Entertainment Enterprises 4803 W Evans Dr Glendale AZ 85306-4434

ZINN, GROVER ALFONSO, JR. religion educator; b. El Dorado, Ark., June 18, 1937; s. Grover Alfonso and Cora Edith (Saucke) Z.; m. Mary Mel Farris, July 28, 1962; children: Jennifer Anne, Andrew Grover. BA, Rice U., 1959; BD, Duke U., 1962, PhD, 1969; spl. student, U. Glasgow, Scotland, 1962-63. Asst. minister The Barony Ch., Glasgow, 1962-63; instr. in religion Oberlin (Ohio) Coll., 1966-68, asst. prof., 1968-74, assoc. prof., 1974-79, prof., 1979—, Danforth prof. religion, 1986—, chmn. dept. religion, 1980-84, 85-86, 1993-94, 98-00, assoc. dean coll. arts and scis., 2001—. Translator: Richard of St. Victor: The Twelve Patriarchs, The Mystical Ark, and Book Three of the Trinity, 1979; co-editor: Medieval France: An Encyclopedia, 1995; mem. editl. bd. Dictionary of Biblical Interpretation; contbr. articles on medieval Christian mysticism, theology, and iconography. H.H. Powers Travel grantee Oberlin Coll., 1969, 85; Dempster fellow United Meth. Ch., 1965-66, NEH Younger Humanist fellow, 1972-73, Research Status fellow Oberlin Coll., 1972-73, 97-98, Faculty Devel. fellow Oberlin Coll. 1985, Lilly Endowment fellow U. Pa., 1981-82; recipient ACLS Travel award, 1982. Mem. Medieval Acad. Am. (councillor 1983-86), Am. Soc. Ch. History (coun. mem. 1989-92, 95—98, Ecclesiastical History Soc. Democrat. Methodist. Avocations: photography, electronics. Home: 61 Glenhurst Dr Oberlin OH 44074-1423 Office: Oberlin Coll Cox Adminstrn Bldg Oberlin OH 44074 E-mail: grover.zinn@oberlin.edu.

ZINN, KEITH MARSHALL, ophthalmologist, educator; b. Bklyn., Oct. 15, 1940; s. Victor Zinn and Eve (Lane) Z.; m. Elaine H. Kirban, Apr. 8, 1979. Student, NYU, Bronx, 1961; MD, SUNY, Bklyn., 1965. Diplomate Am. Bd. Ophthalmology; lic. physician, N.Y., Calif. Intern St. Lukes Hosp., N.Y.C., 1965-66; research assoc. NIH, Bethesda, Md., 1966-68; post-doctoral fellow Retina Found., Boston, 1968-69; post-doctoral fellow dept. ophthalmology Harvard U. Med. Sch., 1968; asst. resident to chief resident dept. ophthalmology Mount Sinai Hosp., N.Y.C., 1969-71, ednl. fellow dept. ophthalmology, 1971-72; chief clin. fellow retina service Mass. Eye & Ear Infirmary, Harvard U. Med. Sch., Boston, 1972-73, Heed fellow dept. ophthalmology, 1972-73; research assoc. dept. retina research Retina Found., 1972-73; mem. faculty Lancaster Post-Grad. Course in Ophthalmology, Harvard U. Med. Sch., 1970-90; consulting mng. dir. HT Capital Advisors, LLC, 2000—. Guest faculty dept. ophthalmology Harvard U. Med. Sch., Boston, 1969-84; asst. prof. dept. ophthalmology Mt. Sinai Sch. medicine, N.Y.C., assoc. clin. prof., 1976-80, clin. prof., 1980—; attending ophthalmic surgeon N.Y.C., 1980—; attending ophthalmic surgeon Manhattan Eye Ear & Throat Hosp., N.Y.C., 1981—; surgeon cons. Hosp. Joint Diseases, N.Y.C., 1975-83, Patrolmen's Benevolent Assn., N.Y.C., 1977—; lectr. in field. Author: The Pupil, 1972, Ocular Fine Structure for the Clinician, 1973, The Developing Visual System, 1975, The Retinal Pigment Epithelium, 1975; author-editor: The Retinal Epithelium, 1979, Clinical Atlas of Peripheral Retinal Disorders, 1988; numerous audio-visual teaching progs. in ophthalmology; contbg. editor Mt. Sinai Jour. Medicine, 1975—; assoc. mem. editorial bd. Ophthalmic Surgery, 1980-89; mem. faculty editorial bd. Clin. Ophthalmology Update, 1982—; inventor in field. Served to lt. comdr. USPHS, 1966-68. Recipient numerous awards for excellence in medicine, including: Joseph Globus award Mount Sinai Jour. Medicine, 1979, Abraham Kornzweig Teaching award Mount Sinai Sch. Medicine, 1982. Fellow Am. Acad. Ophthalmology, Otolaryngology, ACS, Internat. Coll. Surgeons, Internat. Eye Found., Soc. Eye Surgeons, N.Y. Acad. Medicine, N.Y. Diabetes Assn., N.Y. Heart Assn., N.Y. Soc. Clin. Ophthalmology, Soc. Heed Fellows, Retina Soc., Ophthalmic Soc. U.K., Oxford Ophthal. Congress, Brit. Am. Retinal Group; mem. AMA (Physicians Recognition award 1971, 76, 81, 82, 85), Ophthalmic Laser Surg. Soc. (v.p. 1986-88, pres. 1988-90), Am. Intraocular Lens Implant Soc., N.Y. Acad. Medicine (trustee 1989-90, sec. 1985-86, chmn. ophthalmology sect. 1987-88, David Warfield fellowship com. 1990-92), Am. Bd. Laser Surgery (bd. dirs. 1987—), others. Office: 1044 5th Ave New York NY 10028-0108

ZINN, MICHAEL WALLACE, aerospace engineer; b. Washington, Dec. 30, 1962; s. Wallace Bernard and Frances E. AA, Charles County C.C., La Plata, Md., 1983; BS, Tri-State U., Angola, Ind., 1986. Coop student Naval Ordnance Sta., Indian Head, Md., 1980-86, mine decoy engr., 1986-87, airbreathing propulsion engr., 1987-92; airbreathing propulsion engr. Air/Cruise Missile Br. Naval Surface Warfare Ctr., 1992—. Mem. Joint Army-Navy-NASA-Air Force (JANNAF) airbreathing com., expendable engine subcom., Laurel, Md., 1987—; mem. Internat. Tech. Coop. Program involved in pyrotechnic aging and degradation Key Tech. Area 421, 1994-98. Author several tech. papers for AIAA and JANNAF. Pres. Port Tobacco Players, Inc., La Plata, Md., 1992-93. Mem. AIAA (sr.), Am. Def. Preparedness Assn. (life), Cruise Missile Assn., Internat. Pyrotechnics Soc., Charles County Darts Assn. Achievements include work on aging surveillance programs for expendable gas turbine engines, on aging properties of expendable engines and solid propellant gas generators; assisted in new predictive techniques for ordnance surveillance; assisted in design of mine clearing line charge solid propellant rocket motor. Avocations: volleyball, darts. Home: 4 Somerset St La Plata MD 20646-3923

ZINN, STACIE, writer; b. Phila., July 20, 1965; d. James F. Zinn and Andrea J. Zinn-Carroll. Student, LaSalle U., Phila., 1985; BA in Mass Comm., U. South Fla., 1987. Freelance writer, journalist Zinn Freelance, Inc., Naples, Fla., 1993—. Screenwriter various prodn. cos. Contbr. articles to various publs. Mem.: Naples Press Club (bd. dirs. 1999—2002). Personal E-mail: szinn@comcast.net.

ZINN, WILLIAM, violinist, composer, business executive; b. N.Y.C., Nov. 19, 1924; s. :Philip and Anna (Miller) Z.; m. Sophia Kalish, July 11, 1948; children: Karen Louise Heau, David Benjamin. Student, SUNY, 1952-54. Violinist Balt. Symphony, 1944-45, Indpls. Symphony, 1945-46, Ft. Wayne Philharm., 1946-47, Pitts. Symphony, 1947-49, Mpls. Symphony, 1950-51; concertmaster New Britain (Conn.) Symphony, 1968-90, Queens Symphony, 1969-71, Ridgefield (Conn.) Symphony, 1973-76, Chappaqua (N.Y.) Symphony, 1976, Yonkers Philharm., 1993—. Soloist with orchs. on records, on radio, TV, and in recitals; founder Masterwork Piano Trio, Masterwork Piano Quartet, Classical String Quartet, Zinn's Ragtime String Quartet, Excelsior String Quartet, Queens Festival Orch., Bayside, N.Y., 1965, Assn. Musical William Zinn, Caracas, Venezuela, 1968, Vitametrics of Am., 1976, Internat. Symphony for World Peace, 1978, Big Apple Chamber Pops, 1983, Excelsior Composer's Festival Competition, 1984; tchr. mech. drafting Mondell Inst., 1956; coach ensembles for Chamber Music Assocs., 1973-78; engr. N.Y.C. Bd. Edn., 1951-57, Bodin-Zinn Corp., 1957-58, Chem. Constrn. Corp., 1958-59; pres. Zinn Originals, Inc., 1959-68, Sparx, Inc., Trademark Hall of Fame, Inc., Nice Realty Corp., MFW Restaurant Corp.; co-founder Excelsior Music Pub. Co., Visionary Music Pub. Co., Nat. Music Promotion Agy., Telecomm. Svcs., 1982, Assoc. Sci. Publs., 1985, Barclay House Pubs., 1985, Excelsior Typographers and Engravers Unltd., 1985, Empco Recs. Internat., 1985, Imperial Editions, 1986, Missing Link Publs., 1986, Krazy Klassics Company, 1986, New Age Publs., 1987, Krazy Klassics Komix, 1988, Zinn Pub. Group, 1989, Zinn Comm., 1989, 94, Decca Books, 1993, Arlington House, 1993, Zinn Labs., Inc.; sec. treas Spark Industries, Inc., Music Clearing House, 1989, Innovation Records, 1991, Krazy Klassics Records, 1991, Hanover House, 1991; pres. Zinn Labs., Inc., 1994, Caramoor Press Internat. Corp., 1996, Dunhill Pub. Co., 1996, ZinnPrint Internat., Inc., 1996, Barclay Holdings Group, Inc., 1998; adj. prof. NYU, 1987—; cons. Worldwide Leisure Corp., 1997. Author: (with Edward Gordon) Themography, 1947, (with George S. Grosser) Vitametrics I, The Human Formula for Self-Evaluation, 1976, Vitametrics II, The Human Formula for Self-Improvement, 1978, The Lost

Chord, 1981, To Whom It May Concern, 1995, 1,001 Original Wise Sayings of William Zinn, 1996, 2,600 Wise Sayings, 1997, 3,500 Wise Sayings, 1998, 4,100 Wise Sayings, 1999, 6,000 Wise Sayings, 2000, 6,700 wise sayings, 2001, 10,000 Wise Sayings, 2002; composer (perpetual movement for woodwinds, strings and percussion) Chromatique, 1946, Piccolo Concerto, 1948, Violin Concerto, 1950, String Quartet, 1963, (piano solo) Chopinesque, 1965, (ballet) Night Creatures, 1966, Andante for Strings, 1967, Concerto for Octahorn, 1976, The International Anthem for World Peace, 1977, String Symphony, 1977, Romance for French Horn or Viola and Piano, 1981, Concerto for Violin/Viola/Cello/Double Bass and Orch., 1985, Kol Nidrei Meml. for String Quartet or String Orchestra, 1985, six concert duos for violin and viola, 1988, 15 Leroy Anderson favorites for string quartet or string orch., 1988, also songs including Mia, 1989, Aloha Hawaii, 1989, The Willows, 1990 (winner Hawaiian Nat. Song Contest 1990), Our Song of Love, 1990, Symphony in Ragtime, 1990, In Old Hawaii, 1991, Christmas in Hawaii, 1991, A Tribute to the Masters for String Quartet or String Orchestra (14 original works in the style of Bach, Vivaldi, Mozart, Beethoven, Brahms, Rossini, Chopin, Schubert, J. Strauss, Jr., Tschaikowsky, Dvorak, Debussy, Mendelssohn, Sousa), 1991, A Stroll in a Japansese Garden for Violin, Cello, Harp trio in 24 movements, 1996; arranger numerous operatic arias for string quartet or string orch.; orginator Musiphonics, 1981, 24 Paganini Caprices for String Quartet, 1992, 10 Sousa marches for string quartet, 1992, The Merry Widow Waltz for string quartet or string orch., 1992, Mozart Symphony # 40, 1992; arranger 21 Henry Mancini songs for string quartet/string orch., 1992, 16 Duke Ellington songs for string quartet/string orch., 1993, Gold and Silver Waltz, Skater's Waltz for string quartet and string orch., 8 arias from Porgy & Bess for string quartet/string orch., 1992, A Tribute to Fritz Kreisler for violin and piano, 1994, 16 arrangements of Fritz Kreisler works for string quartet/string orch., 1994, 12 classic Jewish favorites for string quartet/string orch., 1995, 12 Jewish Songs for String Quartet/String Orch., 1995, 6 duets for violin and viola, vol. II, 1996, An elegy for Mother Teresa, 1997, concerto Hebraic for piano ands string orch., Let Freedom Ring, a Tribute to Martin Luther King, Jr., for orchestra, chorus, and narrator; 24 Etudes for solo cello, 1998, Hebraic Lament of Atonement for solo cello and string quartet or string orch., 1999, A Symphonic Portrait of Yonkers, 1999, The Seven Seasons for orchestra: seven symphonic works commemorating the Jewish holidays of Rosh Hashanah, Yom Kippur, Sukkot, Hanukkah, Purim, Passover, Shavuot, 2000, Siegfried Idyll Rhapsody solo violin and orch. (original Wagner orch.), 2001, A Requiem for Jerome G. Sala for soloists, chorus and orch., 2001; 6 Bach cello solo suites converted to duets with original part added, 2002, Dance of the Hours Fantasy for solo violin and orch. or piano, 2002, Meditation for solo violin or flute, harp and string orch., 2002, 28 Betthoven Bagatelles arranged for string quartet or string orch., 2002, Beethoven: Pathetique Sonata, slow movement arranged for string quarter or string orch., 2002; pioneer multi-styles of music for string quartet and string orch.; composer over 500 works; developer numerous products for home, personal, automobile, and novelty use. Chmn., bd. dirs. Let Us Remember to Remember, 1984. Recipient 41st Hawaiian Nat. Song Contest award, 1990, Mayor and City Coun. citations for Yonkers 2000, a Symphonic Portrait. Mem. ASCAP, Internat. Platform Assn., Nat. Coun. Women of U.S., Am. Fedn. Musicians, N.Y. Humanist Assn. Home: 35-19 215th Pl Bayside NY 11361-1725

ZINNEN, ROBERT OLIVER, general management executive; b. Racine, Wis., June 28, 1929; s. Aloys Henry and Mabel Helen (Holy) Z.; m. Darlene Mary Weyers, Aug. 25, 1956; children: Claudia Jane, Robert O. BBA, U. Wis., 1951, JD, 1956. Bar: Wis. 1956, Ill. 1959, Mass. 1982; CPA, Ill. Tax accountant Price Waterhouse, Chgo., 1956-59; mem. firm Tenney & Bentley, 1959-64; assoc. dir. taxes Allstate Cos., Skokie, Ill., 1964-65; v.p. fin. Do-All Co., Des Plaines, 1965-67; dir. taxes Quaker Oats Co., Chgo., 1967-71; internat. atty. Am. Hosp. Supply Corp., 1971-75; fin. cons. Alexander Proudfoot Co., Chgo., 1975-76; v.p. fin. Milton Bradley Co., Springfield, Mass., 1976-82; co-owner, exec. v.p. Roadmaster Corp., Olney, Ill., 1982-88, cons., 1988—. Mem. Housing and Traffic Commns., Highland Park, Ill., 1963-66; chmn. Congl. Action Com., Springfield; bd. dirs. Assoc. Industries, Mass. Served with U.S. Army, 1951-53. Mem. Toy Mfrs. Am. (bd. dirs. 1984-88), Quail Creek Country Club, Longmeadow Country Club. Republican. Roman Catholic. E-mail: cyberzinn@sprintmail.com.

ZINNER, FAITH ORLOFF, social worker, consultant, psychotherapist; b. N.Y.C., Nov. 4, 1932; d. Julius and Cherie (Kotkins) Orloff; m. Elmer Zinner, June 17, 1956; children: Clifford, Tanya, Eric, Renee. BA, U. Pa., 1954; MSW, Bryn Mawr (Pa.) Coll., 1956. Med. social worker Bklyn. VA Hosp., 1956-57; social worker Family & Children's Agy., Springfield, Mass., 1957-59; psychiat. social worker Broome County Mental Health Clinic, Binghamton, N.Y., 1962-80; pvt. practice, 1980—. Supervising social worker alcoholism clinic Broome County, Binghamton, 1963-76; part-time social worker Susquehanna (Pa.) Children's Home, 1966-69, Wyo. Conf. Children's Home, 1970-73; cons. Broome County Nursing Homes, Binghamton, 1975-79; part-time pvt. practice, 1970-80; mem. adj. faculty psychology dept. SUNY, Binghamton, 1981—. Home: 4513 Forest Ln Vestal NY 13850-3804

ZINNER, MICHAEL JEFFREY, surgeon, educator; b. Miami, Fla., Apr. 2, 1945; s. Doran D. and Eve Zinner; m. Rhonda Zinner; children: Darren, Daniel. BEE, Johns Hopkins U., 1967; MD, U. Fla., 1971; postgrad., NIH Found. for Edn. in the Scis., Bethesda, Md., 1973-74. Diplomate Am. Bd. Surgery (bd. dirs. 1988-94). Intern The Johns Hopkins Hosp., Balt., 1971-72, jr. asst. resident in surgery, 1972-73, sr. asst. resident, 1976-79, asst. chief of svc. in surgery, 1979-80; registrar thoracic surgery Frenchay Hosp., Bristol, Eng., 1977; instr. The Johns Hopkins U. Sch. Medicine, Balt., 1978-80; asst. prof. surgery Downstate Med. Ctr., Bklyn., 1980-83, assoc. prof., 1983-85; assoc. dir. surg. residency program, coord. residency program The Johns Hopkins Med. Instns., Balt., 1985-88, assoc. prof., vice chmn. dept. surgery, 1985-88, prof., 1988; prof., chmn. dept. surgery UCLA Sch. Medicine, 1988-94; mem. staff Kings County Hosp., Bklyn., 1980-85, chief gen. surgery and oncology, 1983-85; mem. staff Balt. VA Hosp., 1985-88, Johns Hopkins Hosp., 1985-88, Wadsworth VA Hosp., L.A., 1988-94; chief of surgery UCLA Med. Ctr., 1988-94; surgeon-in-chief Brigham and Womens Hosp., Boston, 1994—; prof. Harvard Med. Sch., 1994—. Contbr. over 150 articles to profl. jours.; lectr. in field. Maj. M.C., U.S. Army, 1973-76. Rsch. grantee NIH, 1982-86, 88—; merit rev. grantee VA, 1988-91; grantee numerous univers., founds., pharm. cos., 1978—. Fellow ACS (com. on rsch. and edn. 1988, adv. com. on gen. surgery 1988); mem. IEEE, NIH (ad hoc, study sect., surgery and biomed. engring. 1986), Am. Fedn. Clin. Rsch., Assn. Acad. Surgery (com. on issues 1980-82, recorder 1982-84, exec. coun. 1982-88, pres. 1985-86), Am. Physiol. Soc., Am. Gastroenterol. Assn., Am. Pancreatic Assn., Soc. Univ. Surgeons (com. on publs. 1984-86, com. on edn., 1986-87, exec. coun. 1986-92, pres. 1987-88), Soc. Critical Care Medicine, Surg. Biology Club, Collegium Internationale Chirugiac Digestival (bd. dirs. 1990-96), Conjoint Coun. Surg. Rsch., Soc. Surgery of Alimentary Tract, Soc. Clin. Surgery, Alpha Omega Alpha. Avocations: fishing, boating. Office: Brigham and Womens Hosp Dept Surgery 75 Francis St Boston MA 02115-6106

ZINNER-KEMP, SUSAN ELIZABETH, medical educator; b. Louisville, July 14, 1961; d. Gilbert and Nancy (Steiner) Zinner; m. Robert Francis Kemp, Aug. 31, 1996. BA, Bellarmine Coll., 1983; MS in Journalism, Northwestern U., 1984; JD, M in Health Adminstrn., Washington U., 1992. Hosp. adminstr. Cook County Hosp., Chgo., 1993-98; asst. prof. Sch. Pub. and Environ. Affairs Ind. U., Gary, 1998—. Adj. prof. Rush U. Coll. Medicine, Chgo., 1995—, U. Ill. Sch. Medicine, Chgo., 1995—, Gov.'s State U., University Park, Ill., 1994—, Nat. Louis U., Chgo., 1996—, U. Chgo., 1999—. Mem. Am. Coll. Healthcare Execs., Am. Soc. Law, Medicine & Ethics, Chgo. Health Execs. Forum, Chgo. Clin. Ethics Forum. E-mail: szinner@iun.edu.

ZINNERMON, SUSAN, writer; b. Coy, Ala., July 29, 1962; d. Gilbert and Ora Dee Zinnermon. Student, Talledega Coll., 1985-87. Substitute chr. Wilcox County, Ala., 1980-87. Contbr. poems to mags. Sunday Sch. tchr. Avocations: writing, reading, sewing, church. Home: Rte 1 Box 132 Coy AL 36435

ZINNES, ALICE FICH, artist, educator; b. Norman, Okla., June 24, 1956; d. Irving I. and Harriet F. (Fich) Z. BA in Art History, Swarthmore Coll., 1977; cert. of merit in painting, N.Y. Studio Sch., N.Y.C., 1977-80; postgrad., Skowhegan (Maine) Sch. Art, 1980; MFA in Painting, Queens Coll., CUNY, 1982. Tchr. Pratt Inst., Bklyn., 1999—. Tchr. N.Y.C. Tech. Coll., CUNY, Bklyn., 1983—88, Bklyn., 1997—, Baruch Coll., CUNY, N.Y.C., 1986, N.Y.C., 1988—97, Coll. S.I., CUNY, 1987—2001, Bklyn. Coll., 1998; guest lectr., vis. critic Millersville (Pa.) U., 1992, 93, 97, Dartmouth Coll., Hanover, NH, 1997; curator Frankel Pariser & Rudder, N.Y.C., 1994—97; vis. critic The N.Y. Studio Sch., N.Y.C., NY, 1997. One-woman shows include The Queens (N.Y.) Coll. Gallery, 1982, Swarthmore (Pa.) Coll., 1987, Frankel Pariser & Rudder, N.Y.C., 1993, Dartmouth Coll., Hanover, 1997, Tribes Gallery, N.Y.C., 1998, 2002, Hopper Horse, Nyack, N.Y., 2002, exhibited in group shows at Millersville U., 1992, Greenwich House, N.Y.C., 1992, Nat. Acad. Design, 1992, 1994, 1996, Tribeca 148 Gallery, 1992, 1996, 2000, N.Y. Studio Sch., N.Y.C., 1993, 1995, 1996, 1997, 1998, 1999, 2000, 2001, The Bowery Gallery, 1993, 1995, Salena Gallery-L.I. U., Bklyn., 1994, 1997, The Art Showcase, The Bond Market, N.Y.C., 1998, Elsa Mott Ives Gallery, 1997, 1999, 2001, Grace Gallery, N.Y.C. Tech. Coll., Bklyn., 1999, Artist Space, N.Y.C., 1999, Simon Gallery, Morristown, N.J., 2000, 55 Mercer Gallery, N.Y.C., 2000, William Paterson U., N.J., 2000, Contemporary Mus. , Balt., 2000, Key Span Corp. Galleries, Bklyn., 2000, Piergo, 2000—, Seton Hall U., Newark, 2000, NYU, 2000, Drawing Ctr. Registry, N.Y.C., 2001—, John Elder Gallery, 2001, Chelsea Pier 60, 2001, Exit Art, 2002. Named Barklie McKee Henry Meml. scholar, Skowhegan Sch. Art, 1980, residency fellow, Va. Ctr. for the Creative Arts, Sweet Briar, Va., 1992, 1997, 1999, 2001, Cummington (Mass.) Cmty. for the Arts, 1993; recipient Julius Hallgarten prize, Nat. Acad. Design, N.Y.C., 1988, 1990. Avocations: swimming, hiking. Home: 457 15th St Apt 5D Brooklyn NY 11215-5734 Office: NYC Tech Coll 300 Jay St Brooklyn NY 11201-1909

ZINNI, HANNAH CASE CASE, foreign language educator; b. Cin., Oct. 10, 1944; d. John Persinger and Althea Kay Case; m. Thomas Arthur Copeland, Aug. 27, 1966 (div. Sept. 1977); m. Chester Samuel Zinni, Sept. 23, 1977; children: Chester, Peter, Meredith. BA, Oberlin Coll., 1966; MA, Northwestern U., Evanston, Ill., 1967, PhD, 1971. Prof. French Slippery Rock (Pa.) U., 1970—. Author: Art and the Artist in the Works of Samuel Beckett, 1975. Coun. mem. Pa. Humanities Coun., Phila., 1996—; founder, pres. French Club New Castle, Pa., 1986—. Recipient Humanities grant Pa. Humanities Coun., 1989, 92, Social Equity grant Commonwealth Pa., 1992. Mem. MLA, Samuel Beckett Found., Am. Assn. Tchrs. French, Pa. Modern Lang., Phi Beta Kappa. Avocations: choral singing, tennis, travel. Office: Slippery Rock U Dept Modern Langs/Cultures Slippery Rock PA 16057 Fax: 724-738-2263. E-mail: hannah.zinni@sru.edu.

ZINS, MARTHA LEE, elementary education educator, media specialist; b. Mankato, Minn., Dec. 14, 1945; d. Hubert Joseph and Rose Marie (Johannes) Z. BS in History, Mankato State U., 1966, BA in English, 1967; MLS, Western Mich. U., 1971; postgrad., U. Minn. Tchr. history Worthington (Minn.) High Sch., 1966-67; sch. media generalist Hopkins (Minn.) West Jr. High Sch., 1967-83, Curren Elem. Sch., Hopkins, 1986—. Mem. Hopkins Dist. Tech. Com., 1986—; co-chair Hopkins Elem. Sci. Com., 1991-94. Contbr. articles to profl. jours.; presenter and speaker at confs. Pres. Saddlewood Patio Homes Assn. Inc., Minnetonka, 1991-95, bd. dirs., 1987-95; mem. various Minn. Gov.'s Task Forces; del. Ngo Forum 95, Beijing; mem. WILPF's Internat. Peace Train (Helsinki to Beijing), 1995; co-chair Minn. Metro WilPF, 1998-99; mem. Metronet Adv. Com., 1994-96. Mem. NEA (bd. dirs. 1976-77, 91-97, Woman Educator of Yr. 1975), ALA, ACLU, Minn. Edn. Assn. (bd. dirs. 1975-86, 91-97, v.p. 1977-83, pres. 1983-86, Human Rels. award 1979), Minn. Civil Liberties Union (bd. dirs. 1982-95), State of Minn. Tchrs. Retirment Assn. (bd. dirs. 1989—), Minn. Ednl. Media Orgn. (co-founder, v.p. 1990), Delta Kappa Gamma (Beta Beta chpt., co-founder, chpt. treas.), Beta Phi Mu, Phi Alpha Theta. Mem. Dem. Farm Labor Party. Roman Catholic. Avocations: travel, reading, photography, volunteer work, environmental/hunger concerns. Home: 17509 Saddlewood Ln Minnetonka MN 55345-2663 Office: Curren Sch Dept Media 1600 Mainstreet Hopkins MN 55343-7409 E-mail: marti_zins@hopkins.k12.mn.us.

ZINTER, STEVEN L. state supreme court justice; m. Sandra Zinter; 2 children. Doctorate, Univ. So. Dakota, 1975, BS, 1972. Judge Supreme Court, 2002—; pvt. practice, 1978—86; practice as asst. atty. gen. State So. Dakota; cir. judge State of So. Dakota, 1987—97; presiding judge Sixth Judicial Cir., 1997—2002. Mem. Harry S. Found.; trustee So. Dakota Retirement Sys.; elect. pres. So. Dakota Corrections Commn. Mem.: Am. Bar Assn. Office: Supreme Court S Dakota State Capital Bldg E Capitol Ave Pierre SD 57501-5070*

ZIOLKOWKSI, RUTH, foundation administrator, postmistress; b. West Hartford, Conn., June 26, 1926; d. Frank Douglas and Lyda Catherine (Miller) Ross; m. Korczak Ziolkowski, Nov. 23, 1950; children: John, Dawn, Adam, Jadwiga, Casimir, Anne, Mark, Joel, Monique, Marinka. Student, Hartford (Conn.) Jr. Coll.; DHL (hon.), S.D. Sch. Mines and Tech., 1991. Vol. asst. to Korczak Ziolkowski on Noah Webster statue, 1941; vol. asst. to Korczak Ziolkowski on Crazy Horse Meml., 1947; pres. Korczak's Heritage, Inc., Crazy Horse, S.D., 1968—; pres., CEO Crazy Horse Meml. Found., 1982—. Owner, asst. dairy farm, lumber mill. V.p. Heritage Village, Crazy Horse, 1996—; postmistress U.S. Post Office, Crazy Horse, 1968—. Recipient Reconciliation award S.D. Native Am. Day, 1990, Disting. Svc. award S.D. Newspaper Assn., 1991, Trailblazer award Old West Trail Found, 1992, Senate Commemoration No. 1 S.D. Legis., 1992, Spirit of Dakota award, 1993, We. Am. award Ctr. We. Studies Augustana Coll., S.D., 1996, Commemoration S.D. Legis., 1997, Free Spirit award Freedom Forum, 1997, Pres.'s award Custer (S.D.) C. of C., 1998, Spl. Achievement award Black Hills Badlands and Lakes Assn., 1998, Doane Robinson award S.D. Hist. Soc., numerous others; co-recipient with family Outstanding Pub. Svc. award S.D. Sch. Mines and Tech., 1998, Commemoration S.D. Legis., 1998, Tom Didier Family Bus. award U. S.D. Sch. Bus., 1998; honoree among 10 South Dakotans The Journal, 1994. Avocations: reading, grandchildren. Home: Ave of the Chiefs Crazy Horse SD 57730-9506 Office: Crazy Horse Meml Found Ave of the Chiefs Crazy Horse SD 57730-9506

ZIOLKOWSKA-BOEHM, ALEKSANDRA, writer; b. Lodz, Poland, Apr. 15, 1949; came to U.S., 1990; d. Henryk and Antonina Zofia (Laskiewicz) Z.; m. C. Norman Boehm Jr., June 8, 1990; 1 child, Thomas J. Tomczyk. M in Lit., U. Lodz, 1973; PhD, U. Warsaw, Poland, 1978. Pvt. asst. Melchior Wankowicz, Warsaw, 1972-74; repertoire rsch. staff Warsaw TV Theater, 1977-81. Author: Blisko Wankowicza, 1975, 1978, 1988, Z Miejsca Na Miejsce, 1983, 1986, 1997, Senator Haidasz, 1983, Dreams and Reality, 1984, Kanada, Kanada, 1986, Diecezja Lodzka I Jej Biskupi, 1987, Moje I Zaslyszane, 1988, Kanadyjski Senator, 1989, Na Tropach Wankowicza, 1989, 1999, Proces M. Wankowicza, 1964, 1990, Nie Tyllko Ameryka, 1992, Korzenie Sa Polskie, 1992, Ulica Zolwiego Strumienia, 1995, Amerykanie Z Wyboru, 1998, The Roots are Polish, 2000, Korespondencja J. Giedroyc-Wankowicz , 2000. Recipient Kontrasty award, 1980, Zloty Leksykon award Ksiaznica Pomorska, 2001; scholar Oxford (Eng.) Lang. Ctr., 1975, Ont. Ministry of Culture, Toronto, 1981-83, Can. Polish Rsch. Inst., Toronto, 1981-83, A. Mickiewicz Found., Toronto, 1981-83, Inst. Internat. Edn., Washington, 1985. Mem. Am. PEN Club, Polish Writers Union, Polish Writers Union Abroad, Polish Inst. Arts and Sci., Zaiks, Kosciuszko Found. (scholar 1990). Avocations: travel, birdwatching, domestic pets. Home: 11 Ridgewood Cir Wilmington DE 19809-2860

ZIOLKOWSKI, JAN MICHAEL, medievalist educator; b. New Haven, Nov. 17, 1956; s. Theodore J. and Yetta (Goldstein) Z.; m. Elizabeth Ann Hillenius; children: Saskia Elizabeth, Ada Margaret, Yetta Joy. AB summa cum laude, Princeton U., 1977; PhD, U. Cambridge, Eng., 1982; MA (hon.), Harvard U., 1987. Asst. prof. Harvard U., Cambridge, Mass., 1981-84, John L. Loeb assoc. prof. of the humanities, 1984-87, prof. medieval Latin and comparative lit., 1987—2002, Arthur Kingsley Porter prof. medieval Latin, 2002—. Editor Comparative Literature Studies. Fellow Guggenheim Found., 1987-88, ACLS, 1986, Rome Prize fellow, Am. Acad. in Rome, 1980-81; Marshall scholar, 1977-80. Mem. Medieval Acad. Am. (councillor 1991-94), Dante Soc. Am., Am. Philol. Assn., Phi Beta Kappa. Home: 930 Centre St Newton MA 02459-1266 Office: Harvard Univ Dept. Medieval Latin/Liter Cambridge MA 02138

ZIOLKOWSKI, THEODORE JOSEPH, comparative literature educator; b. Birmingham, Ala., Sept. 30, 1932; s. Miecislaw and Cecilia (Jankowski) Z.; m. Yetta Bart Goldstein, Mar. 26, 1951; children: Margaret Cecilia, Jan Michael, Eric Josef. AB, Duke U., 1951, AM, 1952; student, U. Innsbruck, Austria, 1952-53; PhD, Yale U., 1957; DrPhil honoris causa (hon.) , U. Greifswald, 2001. Instr., then asst. prof. Yale U., New Haven, 1956-62; assoc. prof. Columbia U., N.Y.C., 1962-64; prof. Germanic langs. and lit. Princeton (N.J.) U., 1964-69, chmn., 1973-79, Class of 1900 prof. modern langs., 1969-2001, prof. comparative lit., 1975-2001, dean Grad. Sch., 1979-92, prof. emeritus, 2001. Vis. prof. Rutgers U., 1966, Yale U., 1967, 75, CUNY, 1971, Bristol U., 1987, U. Munich, 1992; vis. scholar U. Ctr. in Va., 1971, Piedmont U. Ctr., N.C., 1971; Dancy Meml. lectr. U. Montevallo, 1973; Christopher Longest lectr. U. Miss., 1979; Patten Found. lectr. Ind. U., 1980; vis. lectr. Österreichische Akademie der Wissenschaften, 1992; vis. lectr. Korean Ministry of Edn., 1996; chmn. N.Y. State Doctoral Evaluation Program in German, 1975-80; nat. rev. panel for U.S. Nat. Grad. Fellows Program, 1985-87, 91—; chmn. overseers vis. com. on German Harvard U., 1982-88; mem. selection com. for Bennett award, 1988; with German-Am. Acad. Coun., 1993-99; chmn. N.Y. State Humanities Screening Com., 1996; chmn. bd. German-Am. Ctr. for Vis. Scholars, 1997-99; forum assembly spkr. Brigham Young U; mem. evaluation team Rosenzweig Zentrum of Hebrew U., Jerusalem, 1999; mem. search com. for chair in German, Bristol U., 1999; mem. search com. for dean Internat. U. Bremen, 1999-00. Author: Hermann Broch, 1964, The Novels of Hermann Hesse, 1965, Hermann Hesse, 1966, Dimensions of the Modern Novel, 1969, Fictional Transfigurations of Jesus, 1972 (James Russell Lowell prize for criticism), Disenchanted Images, 1977, Der Schriftsteller Hermann Hesse, 1979, The Classical German Elegy, 1980, Varieties of Literary Thematics, 1983, German Romanticism and Its Institutions, 1990, Virgil and the Moderns, 1993, The Mirror of Justice, 1997 (Christian Gauss prize), Das Wunderjahr in Jena, 1998, The View from the Tower, 1998, The Sin of Knowledge, 2000, also articles and revs.; editor: Hermann Hesse, Autobiographical Writing, 1972, Hermann Hesse, Stories of Five Decades, 1972, Hesse: A Collection of Critical Essays, 1972, Hermann Hesse, My Belief: Selected Essays, 1974, Hermann Hesse, Tales of Student Life, 1976, Hermann Hesse, Pictor's Metamorphoses and Other Fantasies, 1982, Hermann Hesse, Soul of the Age: Selected Letters, 1891-1962, 1991; mem. editl. bd. Germanic Rev., 1962-95, Publs. MLA, 1971-75, Arbitrium, 1983—, 17th Century Studies, 1985—, Germanistik, 1987—, Jahrbuch für Internat. Germanistik, 1997—, World Literature Today, 1998—, Etudes Germaniques, 1998—; mem. editl. bd. Princeton U. Press, 1972-75, trustee, 1982-95; translator (with Yetta Ziolkowski): The Poetics of Quotation (Herman Meyer) 1968, Hermann Hesse: A Pictorial Biography, 1975. Decorated comdr.'s cross Order of Merit (Germany), 2000; recipient Howard T. Behrman award for disting. achievement in humanities, 1978, Wilbur Lucius Cross medal Yale U., 1982, Goethe Inst. gold medal, 1987, Henry Allen Moe prize in humanities, 1988, Festschrift Themes and Structures (ed. Alexander Stephan), 1997, Jakob-und-Wilhelm Grimm prize for German Studies, 1998, Humboldt Sr. Rsch. prize, 1998; Fulbright rsch. grantee, 1958-59, grantee Am. Philos. Soc., 1959, NEH grantee, 1978, Guggenheim fellow, 1964-65, Am. Coun. Learned Socs. fellow, 1972, 76; resident fellow Bellagio Study Ctr., 1993. Mem. MLA (exec. coun. 1976-77, pres. 1985), Acad. Lit. Studies, Am. Comparative Lit. Assn., Am. Acad. Arts and Scis., Assn. Lit. Scholars and Critics, Authors Guild, Am. Assn. Tchrs. German (hon. life), Yale Grad. Sch. Assn. (pres. 1974-76), Assn. Grad. Schs. (v.p. 1989-90, pres. 1990-91), Heinrich von Kleist Gesellschaft, Goethe-Gesellschaft, Novalis-Gesellschaft, Internat. Vereinigung für Germanistik (exec. coun. 1985-95, treas. 1990-95), Am. Philos. Soc. (councillor 1991-97), Göttingen Akademie der Wissenschaften, Austrian Akademie der Wissenschaften, Deutsche Akademie für Sprache und Dichtung, Phi Beta Kappa. Home: 36 Bainbridge St Princeton NJ 08540-3902 Office: Princeton U Dept German Princeton NJ 08544-0001 E-mail: tjziol@aol.com.

ZIOMEK, JONATHAN S. journalist, educator; b. Newport News, Va., July 28, 1947; s. Stanley Walter and Joy Carmen (Schmidt) Z.; m. Rosalie Ziomek, Aug. 14, 1977; children: Joseph, Jennifer; 1 stepchild, Daniel. BA in Sociology, U. Ill., 1970, MS in Journalism, 1982. Reporter, labor writer, feature writer, Sun. fin. editor Chgo. Sun-Times, 1970-78; press sec. for U.S. Senate campaign, Chgo., 1979-80; asst. prof. Medill Sch. Journalism, Northwestern U., Evanston, Ill., 1983-88; dir. grad. editl. programs Medill Sch. Journalism/Northwestern U., 1988—, asst. dean, assoc. prof., 1994—. Presenter writing workshops; corp. writing cons. Contbr. articles to various mags.; editor: Chgo. Journalist Newsletter, 1991-93. Participant Internat. Visitors Ctr., Chgo., 1988—; fact-finder USIA, Bulgaria and Yugoslavia, 1990. Mem. Assn. for Edn. in Journalism and Mass Communications, Soc. Profl. Journalists, Nat. Assn. Sci. Writers, Chgo. Headline Club. Home: 2149 Hartrey Ave Evanston IL 60201-2571 Office: Northwestern Univ Medill Sch Journalism Evanston IL 60208-0001

ZIOMEK, STEPHEN PHILLIP, business owner; b. East Chicago, Ind., Nov. 8, 1950; s. John Joseph and Marian Louise Ziomek; m. Jeannine Marie Mayone, Feb. 13, 1993; children: Alexander Stephen, Lucas Andrew. BS, U.S. Coast Guard Acad., 1972; MS, U. So. Calif., 1976. Lic. real estate broker, Ariz.; cert. flight instr., Calif.; RN. Aviation safety officer, rescue pilot U.S. Coast Guard, Chgo. and San Francisco, 1973-82; pres., owner Personal Dynamics, Scottsdale, Ariz., 1982-83; v.p. investments Prudential Securities, Inc., 1983-94; co-founder, chief oper. officer FAS-HOTLINE, Inc., 1989—; chief oper. officer The Ctr. for Mobility Resources, Inc., 1995—, The Homebuyers Fair, Inc., 1996—; crew chief hot air baloon Smang, 1994—. Founder, pres. Scottsdale Bus. Assn., 1986-87; founder, exec. dir. Scottsdale Exec. Alliance, 1987-88; pres. Maricopa Bus. Alliance, Phoenix, 1985-86. Alpine skiing sponsor and fund raiser Ariz. Spl. Olympics Winter Games, Scottsdale, 1992-94; bd. dirs. Scottsdale Boys' and Girls' Club, 1996—. Lt. USCG, 1972-82. Decorated Air medal, USCG commendation medal; recipient numerous awards. Mem. Scottsdale C. of C., Far West Ski Assn. (trustee 1994-95, Man of Yr. 1992-93), Ariz. Ski Coun. (founder, pres. 1991-93), Scottsdale Area Sea and Ski Club (founder, pres. 1986-89), U.S. Coast Guard Acad. Alumni Assn., Desert Coast Guard Assn., Harley Owners Group, Ancient Order of the Pterodactyl. Republican. Roman Catholic. Avocations: skiing, water skiing, scuba diving, hiking and caving, motorcycle touring, flying, hot air ballooning.

ZION, ELLEN C. small business owner; b. Phoenix, Aug. 20, 1975; d. Ruth E. Helein; m. Elizabeth A. Stephens, June 27, 1996. BA in History magna cum laude, U. Mass., 2002. Social worker Alaska Children's Svcs., Anchorage, May Inst., Hadley, Mass., 2000—01; owner No. Lights Cappuccino, 2001—. Mem.: ACLU, Human Rights Campaign. Avocation: fair trade activism. Home: 229 Russell St Hadley MA 01035 Office: No Lights Cappuccino 229 Russell St Hadley MA 01035 Home Fax: 413-586-2587. Personal E-mail: papago@krypto.net.

ZION, ROGER HERSCHEL, consulting firm executive, former congressman; b. Escanba, Mich., Sept. 17, 1921; s. Herschel G. and Helen (Hutchinson) Z.; m. Marjorie Knauss, Feb. 20, 1945; children: Gayle, Scott, Randy. BA, U. Wis., 1943, postgrad., 1944-45. With Mead Johnson & Co., 1946-66, dir. tng. and profl. rels., 1965-66; internat. mktg. mgmt. cons., 1966; mem. 90th-93d congresses from 8th Dist. Ind.; chmn. Rep. Task Force on Energy and Resources; pres. Resources Devel., Inc., Washington, 1975—. Hon. chmn. GoPlus Assn. Author: Keys to Human Relations in Selling, 1963, The Hallowed Howls of Congress, 1994, The Republican Challenge, 1995. V.p. Buffalo Trace council Boy Scouts Am., 1961; Bd. dirs., chmn. Evansville (Ind.) chpt. ARC, 1960-65. Lt. USNR, 1943-46, PTO. Named Toastmaster, Evansville Press Gridiron dinner, 1963; recipient Citizen of Month award New Image Com. of Evansville's Future, 1962 Mem. Nat. Sales and Mktg. Execs. Assn. (pres. Evansville 1962), Wabash Valley Assn., AMVETS (life), Rotary (dir. Evansville club 1964), Evansville Country Club (dir. 1960-65), Alpha Delta Phi (pres. Wis. chpt. 1941-43) Congregationalist. Home: 7938 E Oak St Evansville IN 47715-7214

ZIPAY, JOANNE MARGARET, theatre educator, director, dramaturge; b. Berwyn, Ill., May 1, 1958; d. Michael and Erna (Oldermann) Z.; m. Philip Hernandez, Aug. 18, 1990; 1 child, Mariah Celeste Hernandez. BA in Edn./Theater, SUNY, Oneonta, 1980; MFA in Dramatic Arts, U. San Diego, 1993. Tchg. cert., N.Y. Tchr., dir., adminstr., playwright Children's Arts and Ideas Found., Dallas, 1983-86; tchr., dir., actor, playwright Dallas Theatre Ctr., 1984-87; actor Shakespeare Festival of Dallas, 1988; tchr. youth program Bklyn. Coll., N.Y.C., 1989-90; tchg. artist, adminstr. Theatre for a New Audience, 1989-91, 93-96; actor Old Globe Theatre, San Diego, 1991-93; tchr. Nat. Shakespeare Conservatory, N.Y.C., 1994-98; artistic dir., founder Judith Shakespeare Co., 1995—; tchg. artist Bklyn. Acad. Music, 1997-2000. Guest spkr., tchr., dir. U. San Diego, 1993, SUNY, Oneonta, 1996, 2001, Hofstra U., Hempstead, N.Y., 1997, C.W. Post/L.I. U., Brookville, N.Y., 1999, Mt. Holyoke Coll., 2001, 2002, Collin County C.C., 2001, 2002, Princeton Repertory Shakespeare, 2002; guest spkr. Internat. Dramatology Syposium Mt. Holyoke Coll., 2002. Playwright: (children's play) Tall Texas Tales, 1986; dir., dramaturge, producer, edn. dir. Shakespeare prodns. and new plays (with Judith Shakespeare Co.). Recipient Oobr (off-off-Broadway rev.) award, 1996. Mem. Lincoln Ctr. Dirs.' Lab, Actors' Equity Assn. Avocation: photography. Office: Judith Shakespeare Co PO Box 60 Times Square Sta New York NY 10036 E-mail: judishakes@aol.com.

ZIPES, DOUGLAS PETER, cardiologist, researcher; b. White Plains, N.Y., Feb. 27, 1939; s. Robert Samuel and Josephine Helen (Weber) Z.; m. Marilyn Joan Jacobus, Feb. 18, 1961; children: Debra, Jeffrey, David. BA cum laude, Dartmouth Coll., 1961, B of Med. Sci., 1962; MD cum laude, Harvard Med. Sch., 1964. Diplomate Am. Bd. Internal Medicine, mem. subsplty. bd. cardiovascular disease 1989-99, chmn., 1995-99, chmn. com. cert. in clin. cardiac electrophysiology 1989-96, bd. dirs. 1995—, exec. com. 1999—, chmn. bd. 2002. Intern, resident, fellow in cardiology Duke U. Med. Ctr., Durham, N.C., 1964-68; vis. scientist Masonic Med. Rsch. Lab., Utica, N.Y., 1970-71; asst. prof. medicine Ind. U. Sch. Medicine, Indpls., 1970-73, assoc. prof., 1973-76, prof., 1976-94, prof. pharmacology and toxicology, 1993—, disting. prof. medicine, 1994—; dir. divsn. of cardiology Krannert Inst. Cardiology, Ind. U. Sch. Medicine, 1995—. Bd. dirs. Inst. for Clin. Evaluation; cardiology adv. com NIH, 1991—94; mem. exec. com. on electrophysiology World Heart Fedn. , mem. electrophysiology exec. com.; mem. med. adv. bd. ABCNews.com, 2000—; cons. in field ; mem. dean's coun. Dartmouth Med. Sch. Author: Comprehensive Cardiac Care, 7th edit., 1991; editor: Slow Inward Current, 1980, Cardiac Electrophysiology and Arrhythmias, 1985, Nonpharmacological Therapy of Tachyarrhythmias, 1987, Cardiac Electrophysiology From Cell to Bedside, 1990, 3d edit., 2000; co-editor: Treatment of Heart Diseases, 1992, Ablation of Cardiac Arrhythmias, 1994, 2d edit., 2002, Antiarrhythmic Therapy: A Pathophysiologic Approach, 1994, Heart Disease, A Textbook of Cardiovascular Medicine, 6th edit., 2001; mem. editl. bd. Circulation, 1974-78, 83—, Am. Jour. Cardiology, 1979-82, 88—, Am. Jour. Medicine, 1979-90, Jour. Am. Coll. Cardiology, 1983, 2002-, Am. Heart Jour., 1977-97, PACE, 1977—, Circulation Rsch., 1983-90, Am. Jour. Noninvasive Cardiology, 1985-89, Jour. Electrophysiology, 1987-89, Cardiovascular Drugs and Therapy, 1986-93, Japanese Heart Jour., 1989—, Jour. Cardiovascular Pharmacology and Therapeutics, 1994—, Jour. Cardiovascular Pharmacology, 1995—, Cardiovascular Therapeutics, 1995, Current Clin. Trials, 1995-98, Jour. Interventional Cardiac Electrophysiology, 1996—; editor-in-chief: Progress in Cardiology, 1988-92, Jour. Cardiovascular Electrophysiology, 1990—, Cardiology in Rev., 1992-2002, Contemporary Treatments of Cardiovascular Disease, 1996-98, Am. Coll. Cardiology Extended Learning, 1997—, Ind. Jour. Pacing and Electrophysiology Online, 2001—; contbr. articles to profl. jours.; patentee cardioverter, elec. prevention of arrhythmia, discrimination of atrial fibrillation, fixation of implantable devices, and periocardial delivery of therapeutic and diagnostic agents. Pres., bd. dirs. Indpls. Opera Co., 1983-85; mem. study sect. NIH, Washington, 1977-81; mem. nat. merit rev. bd. VA, 1982-85, Cardiology Adv. Com. NHLBL, 1991-98, chmn. steering com. AVID; chmn. Data and Safety Monitoring Bd. AFFIRM, 1996—; mem. exec. com. on electrophysiology World Health Fedn. Recipient Disting. Achievement award Am. Heart Assn., 1989, Sagamore of the Wabash award, Gov. Ind., 2001. Master Am. Coll. Cardiology (chmn. ACC/AHA subcom. to assess EP studies, chmn. young investigators award com. 1988-94, trustee 1992-97, mem. nominating com. 1993-95, Disting. Scientist award 1996, chmn. devel. com. 1996-2001, sci. sessions program com. 1996-98, v.p. 1999-00, pres.-elect 2000-01, pres. 01-02); fellow ACP, Am. Heart Assn. (exec. com. 1980-88, sci. sessions program 1983-86, chmn. various coms., chmn. 1995, bd. dirs. Internat. Cardiology Found. 1993-98, bd. dirs. 1994-96, chmn. emergency cardiac care com. 1995-96; Herrick award 1997); mem. Am. Soc. Clin. Investigation, Assn. Univ. Cardiologists (v.p. 1994, pres. 1995), Assn. Am. Physicians, Am. Physiol. Soc., Cardiac Electrophysiology Soc. (pres. 1985-86), N.Am. Soc. Pacing and Electrophysiology (pres. 1988-90, trustee 1990—, Disting. Scientist award 1995), InterAm. Soc. Cardiology (1st v.p. 1995-98), Ind. Cardiac Electrophysiology Soc. (founder). Home: 10614 Winterwood Carmel IN 46032-9688 Office: Ind U Sch Medicine 1100 W Michigan St Indianapolis IN 46202-5208 E-mail: dzipes@iupui.edu.

ZIPF, ROBERT EUGENE, JR. legal medicine consultant, pathologist; b. Sept. 18, 1940; s. Robert Eugene and Meriam (Murr) Z.; m. Nancy J. Gaskell, Sept. 11, 1965; children: Karin Lorene, Marjorie Kristine. BA, DePauw U., 1962; MD, Ohio State U., 1966. Diplomate Am. Bd. Pathology. Intern Miami Valley Hosp., Dayton, Ohio, 1966-67; dir. forensic pathology Duke U. Med. Ctr., Durham, N.C., 1967-72; dir. radioisotope pathology Riverside Meth. Hosp., Columbus, 1974-78; dep. coroner, forensic pathologist Franklin County, 1974-78; regional forensic pathologist State of N.C., Rocky Mount, 1978—. Clin. asst. prof. East Caroline U. Med. Sch., Greenville, N.C., 1979—; adj. prof. Atlantic Christian Coll., Wilson, N.C., 1980-89, dir. Sch. Med. Tech., 1983-89; cons. in field. Contbr. articles to profl. jours. Trustee United Fund, 1979-84; mem. Mayor's Com. on Drug and Substance Abuse, 1987—. Maj. USAF, 1972-74. Fellow Am. Soc. Clin. Pathologist, Am. Acad. Forensic Scientists; mem. SMS (clin. adv. bd. 1988-91, lab. advisors bd. 1989-91), Assn. Clin. Scientists, Am. Coll. Nuclear Medicine, N.C. Med. Soc., N.Y. Acad. Scis. (pres. Lab. Users Group 1988-90, 92), Nash County Med. Soc. (pres. 1995). Home: 120 Newby Ct Rocky Mount NC 27804-3322 Office: Nash Gen Hosp Pathology Lab Rocky Mount NC 27804 E-mail: rezpath@email.com.

ZIPKIN, SHELDON LEE, lawyer, educator; b. Washington, June 10, 1951; s. Sol and Selma (Rumerman) Z.; m. Ellen Linda Reitman, July 1, 1973; children: Saul Moshe, Shana Chaya, Joel Mordechai, Abigail Deborah. Student, Hebrew U., Jerusalem, 1970-71; BA, U. Fla., 1973, MA, Cert. in Urban Studies, 1977; JD, Emory U., 1980. Bar: Ga. 1980, Fla. 1980, U.S. Dist. Ct. (so. dist.) Fla. 1983. Assoc. Gladstone Assocs., Miami, Fla., 1973-75; ptnr. Emory Assocs., Atlanta, 1979-80; dep. consumer adv. Metro Dade County, Miami, 1980-81; asst. pub. defender 11th Jud. Cir., 1981-83; ptnr. Roth & Zipkin, 1984-86; pvt. practice, 1986-87, 88-91; chief consumer litigation sect. Fla. Dept. Legal Affairs, Miami and Tallahassee, 1987-88; ptnr. Roth, Zipkin, Cove & Roth, Miami, 1991-95; pvt. practice law, 1995—. Adj. prof. law U. Miami, St. Thomas U., 1998—; pres., chmn. bd. Analytic Prognostication, Inc., Miami, 1988—. Pres., chmn. bd. dirs. Sta. WDNA-FM Pub. Radio, Miami, 1981-82; mem. consumer adv. coun. Fla. Hosp. Cost Containment Bd., Tallahassee, 1988-89. Fellow Soc. for Applied Anthropology; mem. ABA, ATLA, North Dade Bar Assn. (dir. 1997—), Dade County Bar Assn. (dir. 2000), Fla. Bar Assn. (consumer protection com. 1988—), Omicron Delta Kappa. Democrat. Jewish. Avocations: chess, sailing. Office: 2020 NE 163rd St North Miami Beach FL 33162-4927 E-mail: zipkin@aol.com.

ZIPORI-BECKENSTEIN, PNINIT, business administration educator, researcher; b. Tel Aviv, Israel, Oct. 22, 1947; d. Shmaya and Tirza Beckenstein; m. Dov Zipori, June 1, 1971 (div. 1993); children: Sigal, Dan. MSc with honors, Tel Aviv U., 1970; PhD, Weizman Inst. Sci., Rehovot, Israel, 1976; MBA, Bar-Ilan U., Ramat-Gan, Israel, 1985; PhD (hon)., Weizman Inst. Sci., 1977. Researcher Leiden (The Netherlands) U., 1976-78; with software mktg. dept. Med. Corp., Palo Alto, Calif., 1985-87; dir. mktg. Orgenics Ltd., Yavne, Israel, 1987; health editor Globes Econs. Newspaper, Tel Aviv, 1988-90; exec. Med. Mktg., Rehovot, 1988-97; lectr. Sch. Bus. Adminstrn., Israel, 1990-97. Researcher Sheba Med. Ctr., Tel-Hashomer, Israel, 1993-97. Author: Effective Interpersonal Communication, 1996, Effective Coping with Obstacles, 1997; contbr. articles to profl. jours. Mem. municipality edn. com., Rehovot, 1980; mem. leadership com. Meretz Polit. Party, Tel Aviv, 1997; legis. activist for disabled, 1993—. Mem. Biochemistry Soc. Jewish. Avocations: solo travel, swimming, painting. Home: 4 Hagra St 76310 Rehovot Israel Office: Med Mktg Ltd 23A Weizman St 76282 Rehovot Israel

ZIPORYN, TERRA DIANE, writer; b. Chgo., June 1, 1958; d. Marvin Charles and Charlotte Weinberg Z.; m. James Harry Snider, Jun 22, 1986; children: Pallas Amita, Sage Tivona, Solon Abraham. BA summa cum laude, Yale U., 1980; MA, U. Chgo., 1981, PhD, 1985. Assoc. editor Jour. of the Am. Med. Assn., Chgo., 1984-86; freelance writer Severna Park, Md., 1986—; editl. cons./freelance Harvard Med. Sch./Harvard Sch. Pub. Health, Boston, 1986—. Co-author: (books) Alternative Medicine for Dummies, 1998 (AMWA Beth Fonda award for excellence), The Women's Concise Guide to Emotional Well-Being, 1997, The Women's Concise Guide to a Healthier Heart, 1997 (winner Nat. Health Info. award Health Info. Resource Ctr. 1998), The Harvard Guide to Women's Health, 1996 (various awards ALA, others), Future Shop: How New Technologies Will Change the Way We Shop and What We Buy, 1992; author: The Bliss of Solitude, 2002, Time's Fool, 2001, Nameless Diseases, 1992, Disease in the Popular American Press: The Case of Diphtheria, Typhoid Fever, and Syphilis, 1870-1920, 1988; contbr. articles to profl. jours. Recipient numerous awards including Marine Biol. Lab. Sci. Writing fellowship 1997, hon. mention Writer's Digest Mag. Writing Competition, 1996, artist devel. grant Vt. Coun. on the Arts, 1994, scholarship Old Chatham Writer's Conf., N.Y., 1994, writing fellowship Am. Chem. Soc., 1992, AAAS Mass Media Sci. fellowship, numerous others. Mem. Am. Assn. for History of Medicine, Nat. Assn. Sci. Writers, Am. Med. Writers Assn. (Beth Fonda award 1999), Authors Guild of Am., Phi Beta Kappa. Jewish. Avocations: playwriting, creative writing, cello, swimming. E-mail: ziporyn@comcast.net.

ZIPP, JOEL FREDERICK, lawyer; b. Shaker Heights, Ohio, Feb. 12, 1948; s. Jack David and Eleanor Adele Zipp; m. Elizabeth Ann Frieden, Dec. 4, 1976; 1 child Carlyn Leigh. BS, U. Wis., 1970, MS, 1972; JD, Case Western Res. U., 1975. Bar: Ohio 1975, D.C. 1976, U.S. Claims Ct., U.S. Ct. Appeals (D.C. cir.) 1976, U.S. Ct. Appeals (5th cir.) 1979, U.S. Ct. Appeals (11th cir.) 1983, U.S. Supreme Ct. 1983. Trial atty. Fed. Energy Regulation Com., Washington, 1975-79, asst. dir. office of enforcement, 1979; assoc. Morley & Caskin, 1979-80; ptnr. Morley, Caskin & Generelly, 1981-98; mng. ptnr. Cameron McKenna LLP, 1998—; gen. counsel, sec. Portland Natural Gas Transmission Sys., 1993-99. Notes editor: Energy Law Jour., 1990—98; contbr. articles to profl. jours. Bd. dirs. Westmoreland Children's Ctr., Washington, 1987—88, Found. Energy Law Jour., 1999—2001. Fellow Smithsonian, 1969. Mem.: ABA, Energy Bar Assn. (v.p. 1989—99, bd. dirs. 1993—96, past com. chair 1992, 93 ann. meetings, bd. dirs. 2001—02, pres. 2000—01). Jewish. Avocations: skiing, running, bicycling. Home: 9216 Burning Tree Rd Bethesda MD 20817-2251 Office: Cameron McKenna LLP 2175 K St NW Washington DC 20037-1831 E-mail: jzipp@cmcklaw.com.

ZIPP, RONALD DUANE, judge, priest, real estate broker; b. New Braunfels, Tex., Dec. 7, 1946; s. Nolan William and Irene Alyce (Stiba) Z.; children: Robert Andrew, Kristi Nicole; m. Saundra Zipp, Mar. 5, 1989. BBA, Tex. A&M U., 1968; JD, St. Mary U., San Antonio, 1971; MA, Oxford (Eng.) U., 1997. Bar: Tex., U.S. Dist. Ct. (so. dist.) Tex., U.S. Ct. Appeals (5th cir.) 1973, U.S. Supreme Ct. 1974; ordained to ministry Anglican Ch., 1998. Assoc. Kelley, Looney, Alexander & Hiester, Edinburg, Tex., 1971-73; ptnr. Pena, McDonald, Prestia & Zipp, 1973-81; pvt. practice New Braunfels, 1981-82, 89—; real estate broker. Judge Comal County (Tex.) Ct.-at-Law, New Braunfels, 1983—; adj. prof. San Antonio Coll.; real estate broker. Author local newspaper column; contbr. articles to profl. jours. Bd. dirs. New Braunfels Cmty. Svcs., 1992—, prse., 1981-83, 97-98, sec., 1994; bd. dirs. Child Welfare, vice chmn., 1981-82, chmn., 1982-83; dir. Drover-Comal County Fair Assn.; vol. H.O.S.T.S.; vice chmn. Folkfest, 1994, chmn., 1995—; pres. Cmty. Svc. Ctr., 1997; bd. dirs., trustee Sr. Citizens Ctr. and Found.; dir. Comal County Fair Assn.; mentor New Braunfels Ind. Sch. Dist.; clergyman, chancellor Anglican Diocese of S.W. Fellow Coll. of State Bar; mem. ABA, Greater New Braunfels C. of C. (legis. com., resources com., heritage com.), Tex. State Jr. Bar (criminal law com. 1975-76), Tex. Criminal Def. Lawyers' Assn. (bd. dirs. 1976-77, various coms.), Tex. Aggie Bar Assn. (charter), Comal County Bar Assn. (past pres.), Comal County A&M Club (pres., treas.), Hidalgo County Bar Assn. (treas. 1972-75), Opa and Kleine Opa of Wurstfest Assn. (chmn. Folkfest), Hidalgo County A&M Club (pres.), Elks, Kiwanis, Lions (sec. 1996, pres. 1997), Phi Delta Phi. Lutheran/Anglican. Office: 384 Landa St New Braunfels TX 78130-5401 Fax: (830) 629-5754. E-mail: rzipp@nbtx.com.

ZIPPIN, ALLEN GERALD, neurosurgeon; b. Toronto, Ont., Can., Dec. 16, 1937; came to U.S., 1965; s. Sam and Fay (Noble) Z. MD, U. Toronto, 1962. Diplomate Am. Bd. Neurol. Surgery. Intern Mt. Sinai Hosp., Toronto, 1962-63, resident in internal medicine, 1963-64; resident in gen. surgery Jewish Gen. Hosp., Montreal, 1964-65; resident in neurosurgery Albert Einstein Coll. Medicine, Bronx, N.Y., 1965-71; pvt. practice, Smithtown, 1973—. Fellow ACS, Am. Assn. Disability Evaluating Physicians; mem. Am. Assn. Neurol. Surgeons. Jewish. Avocations: tennis, dog shows. Office: Mid Suffolk Neurosurg Assocs 309 E Middle Country Rd Smithtown NY 11787-2829 E-mail: charwin@idt.net.

ZIPPIN, CALVIN, epidemiologist, educator; b. Albany, N.Y., July 17, 1926; s. Samuel and Jennie (Perkel) Z.; m. Patricia Jayne Schubert, Feb. 9, 1964; children: David Benjamin, Jennifer Dorothy. AB magna cum laude, SUNY, Albany, 1947; ScD, Johns Hopkins U., Balt., 1953. Rsch. asst. Sterling-Winthrop Rsch. Inst., Rensselaer, N.Y., 1947-50; instr. biostats. Sch. Pub. Health, U. Calif., Berkeley, 1953-55; asst. to full rsch. biostatistician Sch. Medicine U. Calif., San Francisco, 1955-67, asst. prof. preventive medicine, 1958-60; post doctoral fellow London Sch. Hygiene and Tropical Medicine, 1964-65; prof. epidemiology U. Calif., San Francisco, 1967-91, prof. emeritus, 1991—. Vis. assoc. prof. stats. Stanford U., 1962; adv. WHO, 1969—; vis research worker Middlesex Hosp. Med. Sch., London, 1975; various coms. Am. Cancer Soc. and Nat. Cancer Inst., 1956—; faculty adviser Regional Cancer Centre, Trivandrum, India, 1983—; cons., lectr., vis. prof. in field. Co-author book, book chpts.; author or co-author papers primarily on biometry and epidemiology of cancer; editorial advisor Jour. Stats. in Medicine, Boston, 1981-86. Mem., alt. mem. Dem. Ctrl. Com., Marin County, Calif., 1987-96. Recipient Disting. Alumnus award SUNY, Albany, 1969, also awards, fellowships and grants for work in cancer biometry and epidemiology. Fellow Am. Statis. Assn., Am. Coll. Epidemiology, Royal Statis. Soc. Gt. Britain; mem. Biometric Soc. (mem. internat. coun. 1978-81, pres. Western N.Am. region 1979-80), Calif. Cancer Registrars Assn. (hon.), Internat. Assn. Cancer Registries (hon.), B'nai B'rith (pres. Golden Gate lodge 1970-71, pres. Greater San Francisco Bay area coun. 1974-75), Phi Beta Kappa, Sigma Xi, Delta Omega. Office: Univ Calif Dept Epidemiology Biostats San Francisco CA 94143-0560 E-mail: czippin@itsa.ucsf.edu.

ZIRBES, MARY KENNETH, minister; b. Melrose, Minn., Sept. 4, 1926; d. Joseph Louis and Clara Bernadine (Petermeier) Z. BA in History and Edn., Coll. St. Catherine, 1960; MA in Applied Theology, Sch. Applied Theology, Berkeley, Calif., 1976. Joined Order of St. Francis, Roman Cath. Ch., 1945. Tchr. Pub. Grade Sch., St. Nicholas, Minn., 1947-52; prin. Holy Spirit Grade Sch., St. Cloud, 1953-59, St. Mary's Jr. H.S., Morris, 1960-62; coord. Franciscan Mission Team, Peru, South America, 1962-67, Franciscan Missions, Little Falls, Minn., 1967-70; dir. St. Richard's Social Justice Ministry, Richfield, 1971-80, Parish Community Devel., St. Paul, Mpls., 1980-85; councillor gen. Franciscan Sisters of Little Falls, 1960-62, 67-70; asst. dir. Renew-Archdiocese of St. Paul-Mpls., 1986-89; coord. Parish Social Justice Ministry-Archdiocese of St. Paul-Mpls., 1990-93; minister Franciscan Associates, 1993—; leader of team on evangelical life Franciscan Sisters of Little Falls, 1994-96. Co-developer Assn. of Pastoral Ministers, Mpls., St. Paul, 1979-81, Compañeros/Sister Parishes-Minn. and Nicaragua, 1984-89, Minn. Interfaith Ecology Coalition, 1989-92. Author: Parish Social Ministry, 1985, (manual) Acting for Justice, 1992. Organizer Twin Cities Orgn., Mpls., 1979-80; bd. dirs. Franciscan Sisters Health Care, Inc., Little Falls, 1990-93, Rice-Marion Residents Assn., St. Paul, 1991-92. Named Outstanding chair Assn. Pastoral Ministers, 1981; recipient Five Yrs. of Outstanding Svc. award Companeros, 1989. Mem. Assn. Pastoral Ministers (chair 1979), Amnesty Internat., Voices for Justice-Legis. Lobby, Audubon Soc., Network, Minn. Interfaith Ecology Coalition, Ctrl. Minn. Ecumenical Team on Racism. Avocations: water color painting, birding, golf, reading history and biography. Office: Franciscan Sisters 116 8th Ave SE Little Falls MN 56345-3539 E-mail: mzirbes@fslf.org.

ZIRIN, HAROLD, astronomer, educator; b. Boston, Oct. 7, 1929; s. Jack and Anna Zirin; m. Mary Noble Fleming, Apr. 20, 1957; children: Daniel Meyer, Dana Mary. AB, Harvard U., 1950, AM, 1951, PhD, 1952. Asst. phys. scientist RAND Corp., 1952-53; lectr. Harvard, 1953-55; research staff High Altitude Obs., Boulder, Colo., 1955-64; prof. astrophysics Calif. Inst. Tech., 1964-98, prof. emeritus, 1998—; staff mem. Hale Obs., 1964-80; chief astronomer Big Bear Solar Obs., 1969-80, dir., 1980-97; Disting. Rsch. Prof. N.J. Inst. Tech., 1996—. U.S.- USSR exchange scientist, 1960-61; vis. prof. Coll. de France, 1986, Japan Soc. P. Sci., 1992. Author: The Solar Atmosphere, 1966, Astrophysics of the Sun, 1987; co-translator: Five Billion Vodka Bottles to the Moon, 1991; adv. editor: Soviet Astronomy, 1965-69; editor Magnetic and Velocity Fields of Solar Active Regions. Trustee Polique Canyon Assn., 1977-90. Agassiz fellow, 1951-52; Sloan fellow, 1958-60; Guggenheim fellow, 1960-61 Mem. Am. Astron. Soc., Internat. Astron. Union, AURA (dir. 1977-83) Home: 1178 Sonoma Dr Altadena CA 91001-3150 Office: Calif Inst Tech 264 33 Pasadena CA 91125-0001 E-mail: hz@caltech.edu.

ZIRIN, JAMES DAVID, lawyer; b. N.Y.C., Jan. 10, 1940; s. Morris and Kate (Sapir) Z.; m. Marlene Hess, May 18, 1990. AB with honors, Princeton U., 1961; JD with honors, U. Mich., 1964. Bar: N.Y. 1965, U.S. Supreme Ct. 1978. Asst. U.S. atty. U.S. Dist. Ct. (so. dist.) N.Y., N.Y.C., 1967-70; assoc. Breed, Abbott & Morgan, 1965-67, 70-72, ptnr., 1972-93, Brown & Wood, N.Y.C., 1993-01, Sidley, Austin, Brown & Wood LLP, 2001—. Contbr. articles to London Times, Forbes, Barron's, N.Y., Newsday, N.Y. Law Jour., Washington Times. Bd. dirs. Legal Aid Soc., N.Y.C., 1984-89, exec. com., 1986-89; trustee N.Y. Law Sch., 1996—. Lt. USNR, 1965-70. Fellow Am. Coll. Trial Lawyers; mem. Fed. Bar Coun. (v.p. 1982-84), Assn. of Bar of City of N.Y., Coun. on Fgn. Rels., University Club. E-mail: jzirin@sidley.com.

ZIRIN, RONALD ANDREW, classics educator, psychoanalyst; b. N.Y.C., May 14, 1940; s. Joseph and Sylvia (Srebro) Z.; m. Susan Ona Friedman, Sept. 9, 1962; children; Judith Zirin-Hyman, Joshua, Jeremy. BA, Queens Coll., N.Y.C., 1962; PhD in Psychology, SUNY, Buffalo, 1985; PhD in Linguistics, Princeton U., 1967; diploma, Toronto Inst. Contemporary Psychoanalysis, 1998. Lic. psychology, N.Y. From lectr. to assoc. prof. classics SUNY, Buffalo, 1966-96, prof. emeritus, 1996—; pvt. practice, 1985—. Vis. asst. prof. Ind. U., Bloomington, 1970; jr. fellow Ctr. for Hellenic Studies, Washington, 1973-74. Author: The Phonological Basis of Latin Prosody, 1970. Nat. Def. fellow U.S. Govt., Princeton U., 1962-65, Woodrow Wilson Found. Dissertation fellow Princeton U., 1966-67, NEH fellow U.S. Govt., Washington, 1973-74, Jr. fellow Ctr. for Hellenic Studies, 1973-74. Mem. APA, Psychoanalytis Soc. Upstate N.Y., Assn. Psychoanalytic Self Psychology, Ont. Soc. Contemporary Psychoanalysis. Avocations: wine making, sailing. Home: 275 W 96th St New York NY 10025-6200 E-mail: drdrz@aol.com.

ZIRINSKY, BRUCE R. lawyer; b. N.Y.C., Sept. 6, 1947; BS, Cornell U., 1969; JD, NYU, 1972. Bar: N.Y. 1973, U.S. Dist. Ct. (so. and ea. dists.) N.Y. 1973, U.S. Ct. Appeals (2d cir.) 1974, U.S. Ct. Appeals (1st cir.) 1980, U.S. Ct. Appeals (11th cir.) 1981, U.S. Ct. Appeals (5th cir.) 1986, U.S. Supreme Ct. 1991, U.S. Ct. Appeals (6th cir.), 1995. Mem. Weil, Gotshal & Manges, N.Y.C., 1999; ptnr. Cadwalader, Wickersham & Taft. Mem. ABA (sect. corp., banking and bus. law), N.Y. State Bar Assn. (mem. com. bankruptcy laws banking and bus. law sects. 1979—). Office: Cadwalader Wickersham & Taft 100 Maiden Ln New York NY 10038-4818 E-mail: bruce.zirinsky@cwt.com.

ZIRINSKY, DANIEL, real estate investor, camera collector, photographer; b. Bklyn., Mar. 14, 1927; s. David and Gertrude (Coleman) Z.; m. Ellen Reiss Snyder, Apr. 7, 1957 (div. Aug. 1977); children: Steven George, Mark Allen, Laura Reiss; m. Gilda Schiff, Oct. 12, 1980. BS, Syracuse U., 1949. Pres. Bus. Bldgs. of Am., Inc., Great Neck, N.Y., 1969—; real estate developer and owner/investor, 1950—; photographer, 1950—; pres. Artistry in Photography, Ltd. Judge, lectr. and tchr. photographer; collector and authority of collectable cameras; pictures sold throughout the world. One-man photography shows from 1953-2000 include Great Neck House, Lincoln Savs. Bank, Gould Electronics, Bryant Libr., others; group exhbns. include Great Neck Libr., 1990, 91, 92, 93, 94, 95, 96, 97, 98, 99, 2000, 01, Ind. Art Soc., Long Beach Art League, Chelsea Mansion, others. Treas., founder N. Shore Sci. Mus., Port Washington, N.Y., 1970-78; founder N.Y. Inst. Tech., Old Westbury; v.p., trustee The Advanced Ctr Psychotherapy, 1987—, Advanced Inst. Analytic Psychotherapy, 1987—; mem. Zeiss Hist. Soc., Photographic Hist. Soc. New England, Leica Hist. Soc., Photographic Hist. Soc. N.Y., Nikon Hist. Soc., Photographic Hist. Soc. N.Y. Recipient Photographic Fed. L.I. Color Print of Yr. award, 1st pl. North Shore Univ. Hosp., 1992, 93. Mem. Photog. Soc. Am. (life, 59 medals, 74 hon. mentions in U.S., Eng., Australia, Japan, Can., Mex., France, Yugoslavia, Germany), Photog. Soc. Hong Kong (assoc.), Great Neck Color Camera Club (v.p., Print of Yr. award, Color Print of Yr. award, Color Print of Yr. award 1989-90, 28 awards, 42 hon. mentions), Artists Network Great Neck, Real Estate Bd. N.Y., Sigma Alpha Mu (Eta chpt.). Jewish. Avocations: photography, computer, ham radio, yachting, skiing. Home: 7 Beech Dr Kings Point NY 11024-1230 Office: 60 Cuttermill Rd Great Neck NY 11021-3104 E-mail: camrabug@aol.com.

ZIRKEL, PATRICIA MCCORMICK, retired theology educator, researcher; b. El Paso, Tex., Nov. 2, 1943; d. James Joseph and Lula Marie (Hild) McCormick; m. Gene Zirkel, Apr. 15, 1968; 1 child, George Stephen. BS in Edn., St. Thomas Aquinas Coll., Sparkill, N.Y., 1966; MA in Theology, St. John's U., Jamaica, N.Y., 1978; PhD, Fordham U., 1989. Assoc. prof. theology Coll. of Profl. Studies St. John's U., 1990-2001. Instr. Pastoral Formation Inst., Diocese of Rockville Centre, N.Y., 1991-97. Contbr. articles to profl. jours. Mem. AAUP, Am. Acad. Religion, Coll. Theology Soc. Home: 6 Brancatelli Ct West Islip NY 11795-2502 Office: St John's U 8000 Utopia Pky Jamaica NY 11439-0002

ZIRKIND, RALPH, physicist, educator; b. N.Y.C., Oct. 20, 1918; s. Isaac and Zicel (Lifshitz) Z.; m. Ann Goldman, Nov. 22, 1940; children: Sheila Zirkind Knopf, Elaine Zirkind Gorman, Edward I. BS, CCNY, 1940; MS, Ill. Inst. Tech., 1945; postgrad., George Washington U., 1946-47; PhD, U. Md., 1950; D.Sc., U. R.I., 1968. Physicist Navy Dept., 1945-50, chief physicist, 1951-60; physicist Oak Ridge Nat. Lab., 1950-51, Advanced Research Project Agy., Washington, 1960-63; prof. Poly. Inst. Bklyn., 1963-70, U. R.I., Kingston, 1970-72, adj. prof., 1972—; physicist Advanced Research Projects Agy., Arlington, Va., 1972-74; cons. Advanced Rsch. Projects Agy., 1974—. Lectr. U. Md., 1947-48, 48-50, George Washington U., 1952-53, U. Mich., 1964, 66, Haifa Inst. Tech., 1971; cons. ACDA, Jet Propulsion Lab., Calif. Inst. Tech.; cons. to industry, 1974—. Contbg. author: Jet Propulsion Series, 1952, FAR Infrared Properties of Materials, 1968, NAS Study Biology and Exploration of Mars, 1966; editor: Electromagnetic Sensing of Earth, 1967, Procs. SPIE-Developments in Electronic Imaging Techniques, vol. 32, 1972; mem. editl. bd. Infrared Physics, 1963—; contbr. articles profl. jours. Recipient Meritorious Civilian Svc. award Navy Dept., 1957; Meritorious Civilian Svc. award Dept. Def., 1970; Outstanding Educator of Am. medal, 1972; Maj. Contbn. award BMDO/AIAA, 1994; Spl. Lifetime Achievement Award for Pioneering Work in Sensors, SPIE, 2002. Mem. Am. Phys. Soc., N.Y. Acad. Scis., Sigma Xi, Sigma Pi Sigma (SPIE Aerosense Lifetime Achievement award 2002), Eta Kappa Nu. Home: 820 Hillsboro Dr Silver Spring MD 20902-3202 Office: 4001 Fairfax Dr Ste 700 Arlington VA 22203-1618

ZIRKLE, LEWIS GREER, orthopedist; b. Pittsfield, Mass., July 23, 1940; s. Lewis Greer and Vivian (Shaw) Z.; m. Sara K. Zirkle, Aug. 24, 1963; children: Elizabeth, Molly, Julie. BS, Davidson Coll., 1962; MD, Duke U., 1966. Intern Duke U. Hosp., 1966-67, resident, 1968-73, U.S. Army, Shriner's Hosp., 1967-68; pvt. practice Richland, Wash., 1973—. Chmn. program in Vietnam, Orthopedics Overseas, 1992—; bd. dirs., pres. S.E. Asia helmet program, Surg. Implant Generations Network. Contbr. articles to profl. jours. Maj. U.S. Army, 1968-73. Recipient Kiwanis World Svc. medal, 1997; named Vol. of Yr., Orthopedics Overseas. Presbyterian. Avocations: reading, sports. Home: 2548 Harris Ave Richland WA 99352-1638 Office: NW Orthopedics 875 Swift Blvd Richland WA 99352-3592 E-mail: lgzirkle@sign-post.org.

ZIRKLE, WILLIAM DENMAN, investment company executive; b. Roanoke, Va., Dec. 6, 1938; s. William Isaiah and Dorothy Hutcheson (Smythe) Z.; m. Dagmar Helene Agnes von Maltzahn, Oct. 10, 1970 (dec. Sept. 1987); children: Micaela, Sigrid Anne, Luise Bettina, William Wade. BS, Va. Poly. Inst., 1960; MBA, U. Pa., 1962. Program mgr. IBM Corp., White Plains, N.Y., 1973-76; asst. v.p. Conrail, Phila., 1976-80, asst. treas., 1980-83; mktg. dir. Morgan Stanley Asset Mgmt., N.Y.C., 1983-86; mng. dir. Marinvest, 1986-89; sr. v.p. Lynch & Mayer Inc., 1989-97; exec. v.p. Templeton Worldwide, Ft. Lauderdale, Fla., 1997—. Mem. bus. adv. council Va. Poly. Inst., Blacksburg, 1979-2000, mem. pres.'s adv. coun., 1997-2000. Trustee Randolph-Macon Woman's Coll., 1995-2000; chmn. Prayer Book Soc. Episcopal Ch., 1998-2000. Served to lt. col. U.S. Army, 1960-64, with Res.

1964-86. Mem. Am. Inst. Mktg. and Sales Execs., World Affairs Council Phila., Sons. Confederate Vets., Alpha Kappa Psi, Omicron Delta Kappa. Clubs: Army & Navy (Washington); Merion Cricket (Haverford, Pa.); Phila.; Union (N.Y.). Republican. Anglican. Avocations: tennis, backpacking, fishing. Home: 12097 S Middle Rd Edinburg VA 22824-3847 Office: Templeton Worldwide 500 E Broward Blvd Fort Lauderdale FL 33394-3000 E-mail: wdzirkl@attglobal.net., dzirkle@templeton.com.

ZIRKLE, WILLIAM VERNON, philanthropist; b. Berlin, Germany, Feb. 5, 1959; (parents Am. citizens); s. Michael Neale and Nancy (Behrend) Z. AAS in Electronics, No. Va. C.C., 1980; BA in Humanities, U. Va., 1984. Cert. ETS Praxis series. Cons. designer audio system Uno's Pizzeria, Washington, 1989; cons. crises mgmt. APC, Merrifield, Va., 1993-99; cons. tech. WESCO, Falls Church, 1977—; proprietor Circle Enterprises, Arlington, 1984—, Allco Fin., 1998—; ptnr. Homestead Builders, 2000—. Canvass Children's Defense Fund, Washington, 1991, 92; specializer Md. Sherriff's Youth Ranch, 1991, 92; chair Adult Religious Edn., Falls Church, 1986. Mem. Park Springs Condo Assn. (dir. 1991), Cath. Alumni Club (internat. chair 1990, v.p. 1991, 92), Cath. Young Adults Club (religion com. 1988-89, parliamentarian 1987-88, social justice com. 1992), U. Va. Alumni Club. Independent. Avocations: travel, camping, computers, the arts. Home: PO Box 222051 Chantilly VA 20153-2051

ZIRPS, FOTENA ANATOLIA, psychologist, researcher; b. Pitts., Mar. 27, 1958; d. George T. and Barbara F. (Skinner) Z. BA, U. Akron, 1983, MA, 1987; PhD, Fla. State U., 1990. Sch. psychologist Canton (Ohio) City Schs., 1985-86, Leon County Schs., Tallahassee, 1986-88, program evaluator, 1988-90; cons. Evaluation Systems Design, Inc., 1990-91; pres. Zirps, Vella and Assocs., Inc., 1991—; dir. program evaluation Families First, Atlanta, 1991-94; assoc. prof. Fla. Mental Health Inst. U. South Fla., 1995-97; Fla. mental health coord. Fla. Mental Health Inst.-U. South Fla., 1995-97; coord. spl. studies for children Comprehensive Cmty. Mental Health Program-U. South Fla., 1995-97; pres. Fla. Inst. Quality Improvement, Brandon, 1997-99; dir. standards and evaluation Fla. Dept. Children & Families, Tallahassee, 1999—. Tchr. Fla. State U., Tallahassee, summers 1988-91, grant coord., 1989-90; cons. hild Welfare League Am.; coord. spl. studies Comprehensive Cmty. Mental Health Svcs. Children with Severe Emotional Disturbances; adj. faculty Sch. Social Work, Univ. South Fla. Author: Sun and Moon, 1991, Doing It Right the First Time: A Model Quality Assurance for Human Services Agencies, 1994, rev. edit., 1997, Accountability & Accreditation: A Primer on Outcomes, 1998; (with others) Computer Models of Reading, 1989; author, cartoonist: (slides show/audio tape) Human Rights, 1986; co-inventor: (games) Beauty Pageant, Alien Abduction; editor, co-author: Quality Improvement Program and Program Evaluation in Child Welfare: Managing into the Next Century; panel standards writers Coun. on Accreditation Svcs. for Families and Children, Inc. Chmn. grad. student adv. com. Fla. State, 1986-88. Mem. Am. Psychol. Assn., Am. Evaluation Assn., Am. Ednl. Rsch. Assn. (Disting. Presenter 1991), Nat. Coun. Rsch. in Child Welfare (chair quality improvement subcom.), Fla. Ednl. Rsch. Assn. (Disting. Author 1990). Mem. Soc. Of Friends. Avocations: running, racquetball, tennis, reading. Office: Fla Dept Children & Families 417 Williams St Apt C Tallahassee FL 32303-6381

ZIRPS, GEORGE THOMAS, marine engineer, consultant; b. Nyack, N.Y., Apr. 24, 1932; s. Thomas House and Anna Zirps; m. Barbara Faye Skinner, June 30, 1957; children: Fotena Anatolia, Thomas Christos. B in Marine Engring., Maritime Coll., 1954; A in Computer Engring. Tech., Aiken (S.C.) Tech. Coll., 1999, A in Electronics Engring. Tech., 2000. Registered profl. engr., Pa. Mech. engr. U.S. Naval Shipyard, Bklyn., 1954-55; engring. officer U.S.S. Chambers USN, Newport, R.I., 1955-57; engring. mgr. Westinghouse Plant Apparatus Divsn., Pitts., 1957-69; sr. project engr. Exxon Rsch. and Engring. Co., Florham Park, N.J., 1969-71; program mgr., product devel. mgr., engring. mgr. Babcock & Wilcox Co., Barberton, Ohio, 1971-87; sr. fellow engr., vice chair pressur eqt. protection com. Westinghouse Savannah River Co., Aiken, S.C., 1989-95. Cons. Zirps Consulting, North Canton, Ohio, 1987—. Contbr. articles to profl. jours. including Power, Sci. Am.; inventor vernier throttling/block valves, others. Capt. USNR 1954-84, ret. Mem. ASME (nat. bd. com. for pressure relief devices), Phi Theta Kappa. Democrat. Greek Orthodox. Avocation: computer programming. Home: 4 Inverness St E Aiken SC 29803-5946 E-mail: gtzirps@aol.com.

ZISCHKE, DOUGLAS ARTHUR, foreign service officer; b. Sioux Falls, S.D., May 24, 1929; s. Arthur Gustav and Alice Minetta (Wedeking) Z.; m. Janice Mae Kuehnemann, June 8, 1957; children: Mark Douglas, Deborah Jan, Todd Lincoln. BS in Journalism, U. Wis., 1951, MS cum laude, 1952. Joined U.S. Fgn. Svc., 1957; tech. editor Forest Svc., Madison, 1955-57; asst. info. officer USIS, Montevideo, Uruguay, 1957-58, La Paz, Bolivia, 1958-59; asst. cultural affairs officer, br. pub. affairs officer Mexico, 1960-65; info. specialist Washington, 1965-67; pub. affairs officer Tegucigalpa, Honduras, 1967-69; dep. pub. affairs officer Buenos Aires, Argentina, 1969-71; pub. affairs officer Guatemala, Guatemala, 1971-74; assigned to U.S. Army War Coll., 1974-75; dep. pub. affairs officer Am. embassy Tehran, Iran, 1975-78; cultural coord. USICA, Washington, 1979-80; internat. cons., 1980-86; fgn. affairs advisor State Dept., 1986-98. Author monograph. Bd. dirs. Boy Scouts Am; dir. Lutheran Ch. 1973-74. Served with Signal Corps, AUS, 1953-55. Mem. Diplomatic and Consular Officers Ret.

ZISKIND, ANDREW A. cardiologist, dean; b. Boston, Aug. 31, 1958; s. Alan and Barbara (Schiff) Z.; m. Geraldynn Landry, May 16, 1990; children: Katherine, Rebecca. AB, Bowdoin Coll., 1980; MD, U. Pa., 1984. Diplomate Am. Bd. Cardiology, Am. Bd. Internal Medicine. Intern, resident Mass. Gen. Hosp., Boston, 1984-87, fellow in cardiology, 1987-90; asst. prof. medicine U. Md., Balt., 1990-96, assoc. prof., 1996-99, U. Washington, 1999—, assoc. dean clin. affairs/assoc. v.p. clin specialty program, 1999—. Dir. cardiac catheterization lab. U. Md., 1990-95, dir. cardiac network, 1995-99, v.p. clin. svcs. Univ. Care, 1997-99. Fellow Am. Coll. Cardiology, Am. Coll. Physicians, Soc. Cardiac Angiography & Interventions; mem. Am. Coll. Physicians Execs., Am. Fedn. Clin. Rsch. Avocation: woodworking. Office: Box 356380 C-414 Hlth Sci Seattle WA 98195

ZISKIND, DEBORAH ZISKIND, public relations and legal marketing executive; b. Pitts., Mar. 4, 1961; d. Gerald N. and Norma Jean (Morris) Ziskind. BA in Internat. Rels., Tufts U., 1983. Litigation specialist, sr. case mgr., pub. affairs and client devel. assoc. Weil, Gotshal & Manges, N.Y.C., 1989-94; mgr. mktg. Reed Smith Shaw & McClay, Pitts., Phila., N.Y.C., Washington and Princeton, N.J., 1994-96; pres., CEO, Ziskind Pub. Rels. Assocs., Pitts., 1996—; founder, chmn. The Global Conf. Inst., 1996—. Pub. rels. cons. Pitts. Chamber Music Soc., U. Pitts. dept. music, 1983-85; antitrust case mgr. cons. Dickie, McCamey & Chilcote, 1985-87; exec. May Corp., Pitts., 1987-89. Contbg. columnist The Chronicle, Pitts., 1977—; columnist Resident Publs., N.Y.C., 1991-94, Actor's Resource, N.Y.C., 1992-94; bd. editors Strategies: The Journal of Legal Marketing; mem. Legal Mktg. Assn., 1992—; exec. editor for Yr. 2000, Strategies, The Jour. Legal Mktg. Mem. exec. com. New Leadership bd. Pitts. Symphony Orch., 1994—. MacJannet scholar in internat. law and economics Tufts U. and Ctr. for European Studies, Talloires, France, 1981. Mem. Tufts Media and Comm. Group, Pitts. Filmmakers (bd. dirs. 1996—), Tufts Media and Comms. Group. Avocations: international politics, music, writing, piano performance, legal ethics. Office: 4415 5th Ave Pittsburgh PA 15213-2654

ZISMAN, BARRY STUART, lawyer; b. N.Y.C., Sept. 18, 1937; s. Harry and Florence Rita (Tucker) Z.; m. Maureen Frances Brumond, Dec. 30, 1979; children: Michael Glenn, Marlene Ann. AB, Columbia U., 1958, JD, 1961. Bar: D.C. 1962, N.Y. 1965, Tex. 1986, U.S. Dist. Ct. (ea. and so. dists.) N.Y. 1967, U.S. Ct. Appeals (D.C. cir.) 1967, U.S. Dist. Ct. (no. and so. dists.) Tex. 1986, U.S. Ct. Appeals (5th cir.) 1988, U.S. Supreme Ct. 1967. With U.S. Govt., 1962-66; pvt. practice Syosset, N.Y., 1966-71; sr. counsel CBS Inc., N.Y.C., 1972-75; asst. gen. counsel, asst. sec. M. Lowenstein & Sons, 1975-79; gen. counsel Grumman Allied Indsl. Inc., Bethpage, N.Y., 1979-83; asst. gen. counsel Grumman Corp., 1982-83; sr. atty. FDIC, Dallas, 1984-87; of counsel Arter & Hadden, 1987-88, ptnr., 1988, Winstead, McGuire, Sechrest & Minick, Dallas, 1988-90, Arter & Hadden, Dallas and Washington, 1990-91, Rubinstein & Perry, Dallas, 1991-93, The Zisman Law Firm, P.C., Dallas, 1993—. Advisor in field; vice-chmn. Assn. of Bank and Thrift Receivership Coun. Editor and author: Banks and Thrifts: Government Enforcement and Receivership Law, 1991. With U.S. Army, 1961-62. Home: 905 Murl Dr Irving TX 75062-4441 Office: 1412 Main St Fl 23 Dallas TX 75202 E-mail: zislaw@aol.com.

ZISSER, MARTIN SHEPHERD, fur apparel manufacturer, investor and trader; b. Bklyn., Jan. 30, 1942; s. Irving and Jean (Shepherd) Z. Student, NYU, 1960-63. Wall St. invester and trader. Sec. treas. Fur Dressers Union Local 2A, N.Y.C., 1989-92; v.p. UFCW Local 174, N.Y.C., 1992—. Recipient Ofcl. Brit. Coat of Arms, Queen Elizabeth II. Mem. Internat. Soc. Philosophical Enquiry, Mensa. Republican. Jewish. Avocations: study of history, politics, world current events, economics. Home: 1219 E 80th St Brooklyn NY 11236-4165

ZITO, CHRISTOPHER RICHARD, molecular biologist, biochemist; b. New Haven, Nov. 21, 1975; s. Andrew Richard and Ann (Panico) Zito. BS in Biol. Sci., Albertus Magnus Coll., New Haven, 1997; MS in Cellular and Molecular Biology, U.of New Haven, 1998; postgrad., Wesleyan U., Middletown. Assoc. rsch. scientist Dept. Pharmacology, Yale U., New Haven, 1994—97; ind. rsch. scientist Dept. Ob-Gyn., Yale U., 1997—99; rsch. scientist, tchg. asst. Wesleyan U., Middletown, 1999—. Molecular biology cons. Yale U., New Haven, 1997—, radiation safety lab. cons., 2000—, hazardous waste lab. instr., 2000—. Contbr. Vol. North Haven Rep. Election Com., North Haven, 1994—2000; bd. dirs. St. Tarsius Squire Cir., New Haven, 1994—97, Albertus Magnus Coll. Campus Min., New Haven, 1994—97; counselor K.C., Hamden, 1994—97. Recipient The June Veckerelli Mem.l Award for Academic Excellence in Sci., Albertus Magnus Coll., 1997, Annual Acad. Rsch. Assistantship award, U. of New Haven, 1997—98; fellow Annual Doctoral Acad. Rsch. fellow, Wesleyan U./NIH, 1999—2001. Mem.: K.C. (3rd Degree Member 1994—, Squire Circle Counselor of the Year Award 1996 & 1997). Roman Catholic. Avocations: basketball, classical and contemporary piano, acoustic guitar, computers. Home: 197 Maple Ave North Haven CT 06473-3324 Office: Wesleyan University Lawn Ave Middletown CT 06459 Personal E-mail: crzito@iconn.net. Business E-Mail: czito@wesleyan.edu.

ZITO, GEORGE VINCENT, sociologist, sociology educator; b. N.Y.C., Dec. 5, 1923; s. John Joseph And Margaret (Sapatella) Z.; m. Dorothea Rose Lutz, Apr. 29, 1944; children: Darlene A., George Robinson, Dorothea, Pamela G. BA, Syracuse U., 1970, MA and PhD, 1972. Asst. sr. engr. Bendix Corp., Teterboro, N.J., 1947-69; asst. prof. sociology grad. faculty New Sch. Social Rsch., N.Y.C., 1973-76; assoc. prof. Lemoyne Coll., Syracuse, N.Y., 1976-77, Syracuse U., 1977-94, prof. emeritus, 1994—. Rsch. dir. Law Enforcement Assistance Adminstrn. Victimization, Newark, 1974-75; rsch. assoc. Maxwell Policy Ctr., Syracuse, N.Y., 1977-79; program evaluator history-pub. policy NEH grant U. DC, 1981-83. Author: Methodology and Meanings, 1975, Systems of Discourse, 1984, Sociology of Shakespeare, 1991, The Death of Meaning, 1993, others; contbr. 15 articles to profl. jours. Trustee Northvale (N.J.) Pub. Libr., 1965; advisor Syracuse Taiwan Assn., 1994; mem. Mayor's Neighborhood Com., Syracuse, 1989-94. Invited scholar Taiwan, 1991. Mem. Am. Sociol. Assn., N.Y. State Sociol. Assn. (Leadership scholar 1982, pres. 1980, 92), Ea. Sociol. Assn. (mem. coms. 1975-96), Assn. Sociology of Rels. (chair sessions 1992). Democrat. Mem. Unitarian Ch. Avocations: military miniatures, canoeing, sketching, travel, computers. Home: 822 Lancaster Ave Syracuse NY 13210-2924 Office: Syracuse U Dept Sociology Syracuse NY 13210

ZITRIN, ARTHUR, physician; b. Bklyn., Apr. 10, 1918; s. William and Lillian (Elbaum) Z.; m. Charlotte Marker, Oct. 4, 1942; children— Richard Alan, Elizabeth Ann. BS, City Coll. N.Y., 1938; MS, N.Y. U., 1941, MD, 1945; certificate psychoanalytic medicine, Columbia, 1955. Diplomate: Am. Bd. Psychiatry and Neurology. Research fellow animal behavior Am. Museum Natural History, 1939-42; intern King County Hosp., 1945-46; resident psychiatry Bellevue Hosp., 1948-51; instr. physiology Hunter Coll., N.Y.C., 1948-49; mem. faculty N.Y.U. Sch. Medicine, 1949-97, prof. psychiatry, 1967-97, prof. emeritus, 1997—; mem. staff Bellevue Hosp., N.Y.C., 1951—; dir. psychiatry, 1955-68, N.Y.C. Dept. Hosps., 1962-64; pvt. practice, 1949—; attending psychiatrist Univ. Hosp., N.Y.C. Cons. psychiatrist Manhattan Va Hosp. Author papers in field. Served to capt., M.C. AUS, 1946- 48. Fellow Am. Psychiat. Assn. (life), N.Y. Acad. Medicine; mem. AMA, N.Y. Soc. Clin. Psychiatry (pres. 1966- 67), Am. Psychoanalytic Assn. (life), Sigma Xi, Alpha Omega Alpha. Home: 56 Ruxton Rd Great Neck NY 11023-1529 Office: 550 1st Ave New York NY 10016-6402

ZITSCH, ROBERT PAUL, III, physician, educator; b. Woodbury, N.J., Sept. 28, 1956; s. Robert Paul and Doris Jean (Smith) Z.; m. Mary Gail Hardy, June 11, 1988; children: Whitley Grayson, Georgeanne Emerson, Bradford Paul. BS, U. Ala., Tuscaloosa, 1978; MD, U. Ala., Birmingham, 1982. Diplomate Am. Bd. Otolaryngology. Resident in surgery Carraway Meth. Med. Ctr., Birmingham, 1982-83; resident in otolaryngology U. Ala. Hosp., 1983-87; fellow in head and neck surg. oncology U. Cin. Med. Ctr., 1988-89; assoc. prof. surgery U. Mo. Health Sci. Ctr., Columbia, 1989—. Contbr. chpts. to books and articles to profl. jours. Fellow ACS, Am. Head and Neck Soc.; mem. Soc. U. Otolaryngologists Head Neck Surgeons, Phi Beta Kappa. Republican. Lutheran. Office: U Mo Sch Medicine 1 Hospital Dr Rm MA314 Columbia MO 65201-5276

ZITSMAN, JEFFREY LEONARD, pediatric surgeon; b. Springfield, Ohio, Jan. 17, 1951; s. Bernard Charles and Gloria Rosalie (Levy) Z.; m. Arlene Joy Mellitz, June 24, 1975 (div. Feb. 1987); children: Rachel Hannah, Noah Chaim; m. Elaine Janine Abrams, Oct. 23, 1988; children: Jonah Samuel, Tobias Gabriel. Student, U. Cin., 1968-70; AB in Natural Scis., Johns Hopkins U., 1972; MD, Tufts U., 1976. Diplomate Am. Bd. of Surgery; spl. qualifications in pediatric surgery, surg. critical care. Resident in surgery New Eng. Med. Ctr., Boston, 1976-81; resident in pediatric surgery Babies Hosp., N.Y.C., 1983-85; asst. prof. surgery Robert Wood Johnson Med. Sch., New Brunswick, N.J., 1985-88; asst. clin. prof. surgery Columbia U., N.Y.C., 1988—; asst. prof. surgery N.Y. Med. Coll., Valhalla, N.Y., 1991-97. Contbr. med. articles to profl. jours. and chpt. to book. Mem. ACS, Am. Acad. Pediatrics, Am. Pediatric Surg. Assn. Avocations: running, birding. Phone: (914) 722-6737. Office: Babies Hosp Divsn Pediat Surgery 3959 Broadway New York NY 10032-1590 also: 688 White Plains Rd Scarsdale NY 10583-5059

ZITTO, RICHARD JOSEPH, physics educator; b. Lisbon, Ohio, Sept. 1, 1945; s. Tony Joseph and Olive Lucille (Davison) Z.; m. Pamela Daryl Irons, July 22, 1967; children: Angela Marie, Elena Michelle. BS in Sci. Edn., Ohio State U., 1968, MA in Phys. Sci. Edn., 1978. Tchr. sci. Kenton (Ohio) Jr. H.S., 1968-70; tchr. physics and sci. Kenton Sr. H.S., 1970-76; tchr. physics Boardman H.S., Youngstown, Ohio, 1976-99; physics educator Youngstown State U., 1981—, coord. Physics Olympics, 1994—. Dir. Youngstown Area Physics Alliance, 1987—. Trustee Hardin Meml. Hosp., Kenton, 1971-76; bd. dirs. Blue Cross of Lima, Ohio, 1973-76, Nat. Multiple Sclerosis Soc. N.E. Ohio, 1981-91; trustee Columbiana Pub. Libr., 1990—, pres., 1993-95, 2000—. Recipient Outstanding Young Educator award Kenton Jaycees, 1972, Outstanding Sci. Tchr. Youngstown State U. Sigma Xi, 1980, Career Educator award Ohio State U. Coll. Edn., 1997; A. Jennings scholar Martha Holden Jennings Found. Fellow Ohio Acad. Sci.; mem. ASCD, Am. Assn. Physics Tchrs. (physics teaching resource agt. 1986—, pres. Ohio sect. 1989-90, mem. physics in high schs. com. 1991-94, history and Philosophy com. 1999—), Ont. Assn. Physics Tchrs., Nat. Sci. Tchrs. Assn., N.E. Ohio Edn. Assn. (co-chmn. sci. workshop 1979—), Sci. Edn. Coun. Ohio, United Teaching Profession, Lions, Rotary (sec. 1978-79), Elks. Republican. Presbyterian. Avocations: woodworking, tennis, history of science, collecting antique physics apparatus. Home: 332 W Park Ave Columbiana OH 44408-1242 Office: Physics & Astronomy Dept Youngstown State Univ Youngstown OH 44555-0001 E-mail: rjzitto@cc.ysu.edu.

ZITTRAIN, LESTER EUGENE, lawyer; b. Norfolk, Va., Mar. 27, 1931; s. Leonard and Lee Zittrain; m. Ruth Ann Cohen, Aug. 20, 1957; children: Laura Zittrain Eisenberg, Jeffrey, Jonathan. BA, Washington and Lee U., 1952; JD, U. Va., 1955. Bar: Va. 1955, Pa. 1959, U.S. Supreme Ct. 1970. Ptnr. Zittrain and Zittrain, Pitts., 1959—. Former mem. exec. bd. and trustee Tree of Life Congregation, Pitts. Lt. USN, 1955-58. Fellow: Pa. Bar Found. (life); mem.: ATLA, ABA, Allegheny County Bar Assn. (judiciary com. 1983—86, chmn. 1986, mem. lawyers ins. com. 1984—, bench-bar conf. com. 1986—88, ct. rules com. 1987—, women in law com. 1988—, law libr. com. 1988—, bd. govs. 1988—2001, by-laws com. 1990—, chmn. civil litigation sect. 1986, Amram award 1998), Acad. Trial Lawyers Allegheny County (bd. govs. 1981—85, treas. 1986—88), Pa. Assn. Trial Lawyers, Pa. Bar Assn. (jud. selection reform com., mem. ho. of dels. from Allegheny County). Home: 136 Thornberry Dr Pittsburgh PA 15235-5061 Office: Zittrain & Zittrain 201 Franklin Ctr Profl Bldg 4240 Greensburg Pike Pittsburgh PA 15221-4297 Fax: 412-271-2300. E-mail: razlez@mindspring.com.

ZIVELONGHI, KURT DANIEL, painter, computer graphics artist, designer; b. Barstow, Calif., Oct. 3, 1960; s. Vincent Otto and Beverly Dean (Schwind) Z. Student, Pasadena (Calif.) City Coll., 1984-85, Art Students League, N.Y.C., 1988-89; BFA, Art Ctr. Coll. of Design, 1993. Self employed fine artist, Pomona, Calif., 1990—. Art dir. movies Seagull's Journey, Gizmo LLC, The Innocent Bystander, Mad Dogs Prodns., 1998. One-man show at Coll. of Design Art Ctr., Pasadena, Calif., 1993, two-man show at Flux Gallery, Eagle Rock, Calif., 1993, group show at Art Students League, N.Y.C., 1989, Artexpo, N.Y., 2000, Marbella, Spain, 2000, AR+21, Las Vegas, 2000. Mem. Ctr. for the Study of Popular Culture, Century City, Calif., 1994. Mem. Am. Soc. Portrait Artists. Avocations: piano, weight lifting, theatre, cinema. E-mail: kzivelonghi@earthlink.net.

ZIZI, artist; b. China, 1954; came to U.S., 1985; Grad., Guanzhou Fine Arts Acad., 1979. Chief-in-designer The North Guandong Acad. of Design, China. Hon. curator Borong Mus. Art, China. Exhibited in shows including Fed. Hall Nat. Meml., N.Y.C., 1997, Shogun Chinese Art Mus., China, 1997, Wisser Meml. Libr. N.Y. Inst. of Tech., 1998, Chung Cheng Art Gallery St. John's U., N.Y.C., 1998, others; represented in permanent collections Abney Gallery, N.Y.C., Agroa Gallery, N.Y.C., Kent Gallery, London, Comm. Art Gallery, Phila., Yunbei Fine Arts Mus., China, Xuboreng Fine Arts Mus., China, Ink Painting Mus., Japan, Xin-Shenzhou Gallery, Singapore, Mus. of Arts Collection, Calif., TV Univ., China, Shaogun Tchrs.' Coll., China, Asia Art Sch., London, Guangzhou Fine Arts Acad., China, Modern Art Hall, Paris, Immigrants' Project Theater, Bklyn., Fine Arts Edn. Ctr., N.Y.C., Acad. Oriental Arts, China. Recipient 1st prize in watercolor Queens Artists Alliance's 1st Nat. Exhbn., Award of Excellence Town of Oyster Bay, 2d Pl. Rongwood Manor Arts Assn., Award of Excellence New Age Fine Arts Ctr., Artist Showcase award Manhattan Arts Internat. 5th Ann. Competition, 1st place London Kent Ann. Competition, 1996, Silver medal Chinese Art Exhibition by Comtemporary Famous Artists in China, 1997, Lakeland Bank award Ringwood Manor Arts. Arts's 33rd Annual Exbhn., N.J., 1998, award of excellence Internat. Arts League's 19998 Annual Competition, N.Y., 1998, award for excellence Xin-Shen Zhou Art Inst.'s 5th Internat. Competition, Singapore, 1998. Address: 94-46 85 Rd # 2H Woodhaven NY 11421 Fax: 718-846-6540.

ZIZIC, THOMAS MICHAEL, physician, educator; b. Milw., Dec. 9, 1939; s. Michael Mitchell Zizic and Dorothy (Batas) Ciric; m. Karen Owens, June 15, 1962 (div. Sept. 1967); m. Martha Ann Ardos, Nov. 22, 1967; children: Lara Ann, Kristine Michelle. BS, U. Wis., 1961; MD, Johns Hopkins U., 1965. Intern Johns Hopkins Hosp., Balt., 1965-66, asst. resident, 1966-67, fellow in internal medicine, 1969-71, instr. dept. medicine, 1971-73, asst. prof. medicine, 1971-81, assoc. prof. medicine, 1981—. Pvt. practice, Balt., 1988—; co-dir. Chesapeake Osteoporosis Ctr., Balt., 1988—; dir. med. affairs Murray Electronics, 1993—; v.p. med. quality care Physicians Quality Care, 1995—; pres. U.S. Osteoporosis Network, Inc., 1996—; co-founder, dir. Creative Environ. Solutions, Inc., 1996—; cons. in field. Contbr. numerous articles and abstracts to profl. jours. V.p. Md. chpt. Arthritis Found., Balt., 1976-77; chmn. Md. Commn. on Arthritis and Related Diseases, 1986-90. Fellow Am. Coll. Rheumatology, 1986; Md. Soc. Rheumatic Diseases (pres. 1975-76), D.C. Rheumatism Assn., Balt. City Med. Soc., Johns Hopkins Hosp. Med. Soc., Arthritis Found. (fellow 1971-73, v.p. 1976-77, med. and sci. com. 1977-79, chmn. profl. edn. com. 1977-78, govtl. affairs com. 1979-83), Phi Beta Kappa, Phi Kappa Phi, Phi Eta Sigma. Avocations: skiing, tennis. Office: 5601 Loch Raven Blvd Baltimore MD 21239-2905 *Give 100% today. We have only the present. Plan for the future but don't live in the future. The future never comes. We have only today.*

ZLAKET, THOMAS A. attorney, former state supreme court chief justice; b. May 30, 1941; AB in Polit. Sci., U. Notre Dame, 1962; LLB, U. Ariz., 1965. Bar: Ariz. 1965, U.S. Dist. Ct. Ariz. 1967, U.S. Ct. Appeals (9th cir.) 1969, Calif. 1976. Atty. Lesher Scruggs Rucker Kimble & Lindamood, Tucson, 1965-68, Maud & Zlaket, 1968-70, Estes Browning Maud and Zlaket, 1970-73, Slutes Estes Zlaket Sakrison & Wasley, 1973-82, Zlaket & Zlaket, 1982-92; judge pro tempore Pima County (Ariz.) Superior Ct., 1983—; justice Ariz. Supreme Ct., 1992—2002, vice chief justice, 1996—2002, chief justice, 1997—2002. Fellow Am. Coll. Trial Lawyers, Am. Bar Found., Ariz. Bar Found.; mem. ABA, Pima County Bar Assn., Am. Bd. Trial Advocates, Ariz. Coll. Trial Advocacy, U. Ariz. Law Coll. Assn., Ariz. Law Rev. Assn.*

ZLATKIN, MICHAEL BRIAN, physician; b. Montreal, Que., Can., Mar. 20, 1957; came to U.S., 1986; s. Ralph and Gertrude (Rosen) Z.; m. Paula Roanne Ralph, May 30, 1982 (div. Jan. 1992); children: Nancy, Robert; m. Marilyn Judith Bohan, June 5, 1994; children: Alyssa, Chad. BSc with great distinction, McGill U., Montreal, Can., 1977; MD, Queens U., Kingston, Ont., Can., 1981. Intern Royal Victoria Hosp. McGill U., Montreal, 1981-82, resident diagnostic radiology Jewish Gen. Hosp., 1982-85, chief resident diagnostic radiology Jewish Gen. Hosp., 1985-86; fellow osteoradiology U. Calif., San Diego, 1986-87; asst. prof. radiology Hosp. U. Pa., 1987-89; dir. musculoskeletal imaging Memorial Healthcare System, Fla., 1989-99, Health S. Drs. Hosp., Coral Gables, 1995-97; pres. Specialists in Diagnostic Imaging. PA, Sunrise. Clin. assoc. prof. Sch. Medicine U. Miami, Coral Gables, 1989—. Author: Magnetic Resonance Imaging of the Shoulder, 1991, Clinical Magnetic Resonance Imaging, 2d. edit., 1996. Frances C. C. Lynch scholar Carleton U., 1974-75; Univ. Entrance scholar McGill U., 1975-76, Univ. scholar, 1976-77; named one of Best Drs. in Am., 1998, one of Outstanding Young Men of Am., 1998. Fellow Royal Coll. Physicians (Can.), Am. Bd. Radiology; mem. AMA, Internat. Soc. Magnetic Resonance Imaging Medicine, Internat. Skeletal Soc., Am. Roentgen Ray Soc., Radiologic Soc. N.Am., Am. Coll. Radiologists. Avocations: tennis, swimming, skiing, reading, movies. Address: 2529 Sanctuary Dr Weston FL 33327-1534

ZLATOFF-MIRSKY, EVERETT IGOR, violinist; b. Evanston, Ill., Dec. 29, 1937; s. Alexander Igor and Evelyn Ola (Hill) Z.-M.; m. Janet Dalbey, Jan. 28, 1976; children from previous marriage— Tania, Laura. B.Mus., Chgo. Mus. Coll., Roosevelt U., 1960, M.Mus., 1961. Mem. faculty dept. music Roosevelt U., Chgo., 1961-66. Founding mem., violinist, violist Music of the Baroque, 1971—. Violinist orch. Lyric Opera of Chgo., 1974—; concert master, pers. mgr., 1974—, violinist, violist, Contemporary Chamber Players U. Chog., 1964-82, solo violinist, Bach Soc., 1966-83; violist, violinist, Lexington String Quartet, 1966-81; rec. artist numerous recs., radio-TV and films; solo violinist appearing throughout U.S. Recipient Olive Ditson award Franklin Honor Soc., 1961 Mem. Nat. Acad. Rec. Arts and Scis. Republican. Roman Catholic. Home: 41w743 Hughes Rd Elburn IL 60119-9776 Office: Lyric Opera Chgo 20 N Wacker Dr Chicago IL 60606-2806 E-mail: jdzm@aol.com.

ZLATOS, CHRISTY, librarian; b. Decatur, Ill., June 4, 1956; d. Rudolph and Iva Dene Ebersole Zlatos; m. Michael Boyd Nelson, Dec. 22, 1995. AB, U. Ill., 1978, MSLS, 1979. Reference libr. U. So. Ind., Evansville, 1980-82, Auburn (Ala.) U., 1983-89, Northeastern U., Boston, 1989-91, Wash. State U., Pullman, 1991-92, head edn. libr., 1992-95, head media materials svcs., 1995—. Book rev. editor Jour. Acad. Librarianship, 1995—. Editor: Coming of Age in Reference Services; A Case History of Washington State University Libraries, 1999. Mem. ALA (various coms.). Republican. Episcopalian. Avocation: collecting American pottery. Office: Wash State U Libraries New Library Rm 1 Pullman WA 99164-0001

ZLOCH, WILLIAM J. federal judge; b. 1944; Judge U.S. Dist. Ct. (so. dist.) Fla., Ft. Lauderdale, 1985—. Office: US Dist Ct 299 E Broward Blvd Fort Lauderdale FL 33301-1944

ZLOMEK, ELIZABETH A. customer service/business processes specialist; b. Upstate, N.Y., 1957; d. Frederick and Muriel Zlomek. BA in Polit. Sci., Secondary Edn., SUNY, Cortland, 1980. Legis. asst. U.S. Ho. Reps., Washington, 1979-80; customer svc. mgr. Jordan Kitis Music, College Park, Md., 1980-87; sales mgr. Reines R.V. Ctr., Fairfax, Va., 1987-92; dir. customer svc. Stickley Furniture, Syracuse, N.Y., 1992-2000, sr. bus. analyst, 2000—. Cons. Elanzek Svcs., Silver Spring, Md., 1987-92. Vol. Children's Miracle Network, Syracuse, 1997—, Leukemia Soc. Am.; vol. reader Vols. for Visually Handicapped, Montgomery County, Md., 1979-92. Mem. Jr. League of Syracuse (bd. dirs. 1993-95, fin. chair 1996, treas. 1st Annual Holiday Shoppes Fundraiser), Nat. Assn. of Customer Svc. Mgrs., NAFE, Piano Technicians Guild (assoc.), Pi Sigma Alpha. Avocations: travel, reading, music, computers, needlework. Office: L & JG Stickley Furniture 1 Stickley Dr Manlius NY 13104-2484

ZLOTOLOW-STAMBLER, ERNEST, real estate executive, architectural executive; b. Buenos Aires, Sept. 27, 1943; came to U.S., 1981; m. Laura I. Chotti; children: Dan A., Vanessa E., Paul J. BA, Buenos Aires Nat. Coll., 1960; cert. architecture, U. Buenos Aires, 1968. Lic. architect; registered profl. engr., Argentina. Prof. U. Buenos Aires, 1964-81; mng. ptnr. Zlotolow, Chotti & Assocs., Buenos Aires, 1968-81; pres. Imparsa Corp., 1970-86; mng. ptnr. Archeting Assocs., 1970-81; prof. U. Belgrano, 1976-80; v.p. Playa de la Gruta Corp., Montevideo, Uruguay, 1976-78; project mgr. Kravco Corp., King of Prussia, Pa., 1981-84; chmn. Zlotolow-Evantash-Reider Ltd., Southeastern, 1985—; pres. Meridian Real Corp., Wayne, 1985—, U.S.E.S. Corp., 1989—. Gen. ptnr., One Jenkintown (Pa.) Sta. Assocs., 1984-89. Contbr. articles to profl. publs. Paul Harris fellow, 1987, Guy Gundaker fellow, 1990, Paul Vaughan fellow, 1991. Mem. AIA (assoc.), Urban Land Inst., Nat. Trust Historic Preservation, Pa. Soc. Architects, Sociedad Ctrl. Arquitectos (Argentina), Rotary (pres. 1990-91, chmn. charitable found. 1990-91, chmn. cmty. svc. 1998-), Gundaker Found. (bd. dirs. 1992—, v.p. 1996-97, pres. 1997-98), Green Hills Landowners Assn. (bd. dirs. 1994-97). Avocations: boating, macroeconomics, computer science. Office: Meridian Real Corp PO Box 623 Southeastern PA 19399-0623

ZLOTOWSKI, MARTIN, psychologist; b. Lodz, Poland, Aug. 10, 1934; s. Pawel and Helen Zlotowski; m. Judith Ann Lifschitz, May 17, 1974; children: David, Steven, Laura. BA, NYU, 1955; MA, Mich. State U., 1958, PhD, 1960. Rsch. assoc. Grad. Sch. Pub. Health U. Pitts., 1960-61; rsch. assoc., lectr. Boston U., 1961-62; staff psychologist VA Hosp., Coatesville, Pa., 1962-65, unit chief, 1965-73; clin. dir. St. Mary Providence, 1966-70; assoc. prof. spl. edn. West Chester (Pa.) U., 1973—. Grad. coord., 1987—; dir. Counseling Assocs., Paoli, Pa., 1973-85, exec. dir., 1985—. Pres., bd. trustees Chester County Family Acad., 1999; v.p. Victim Witness Svcs. Chester County, 1976-77. Fellow Phila. Soc. Clin. Psychologists (pres. 1978-79, sec. human svcs. ctr. 1982), Phila. Psychol. Assn., Am. Orthopsychiat. Assn. (life); mem. APA, PFCEC (pres. Pa. divsn. behavior disorders). Democrat. Jewish. Home: 605 Eagle Rd Wayne PA 19087-3437 E-mail: mzlotowski@wcupa.edu.

ZLOWE, FLORENCE MARKOWITZ, artist; b. Allentown, Pa. d. Morris and Anna (Mandel) Markowitz; m. Irwin Zlowe, May 1, 1936. Student, Pa. Mus. Coll. Art, Phila., 1929-33; fine arts courses, NYU, 1950-53. One woman show, Charles Z. Mann Gallery, N.Y.C., 1968, Community Gallery, N.Y.C., 1978; exhibited in group shows, Nat. Acad., Riverside Mus., N.Y., Nat. Arts Club, Pen and Brush Club, Lever House, Jersey City Mus., Norfolk (Va.) Mus., Fort Lauderdale (Fla.) Mus., Joe and Emily Lowe Mus., Fla.; represented in permanent collections, Norfolk Mus., Fort Lauderdale Mus., Joe and Emily Lowe Mus., Wilson Pub. Co., N.Y.C., Phila. Mus. Art, Butler Inst. Am. Art, Minn. Mus. Art, St. Paul, Cooper-Hewitt Mus. Design, Smithsonian Instn., N.Y.C., Tweed Mus., Duluth, Minn., Evansville (Ind.) Mus., Lakeview (Ill.) Center Arts and Scis., Ga. Mus. Art, Athens, Slater Meml. Mus., Norwich, Conn. Mem. Am. Soc. Contemporary Artists (dir., treas.), N.J. Soc. Painters and Sculptors, Nat. Assn. Women Artists (1st prize ann. 1958, 12 additional awards for oils 1958-84), League Present Day Artists, Artists Equity Assn. N.Y. Home: 440 E 57th St New York NY 10022-3045 Studio: 41 Union Sq W New York NY 10003-3208

ZMIJEWSKI, CHESTER MICHAEL, pathology educator; b. Buffalo, June 3, 1932; s. Francis Albert and Sophia Josephine Z.; m. Helen Elizabeth Borkowski, June 2, 1954; children: Michael P., Christopher M., Robert J., David N. BA, U. Buffalo, 1955, MA, 1957, PhD, 1960; MA (hon.), U. Pa., 1978. Instr. bacteriology, immunology U. Buffalo, N.Y., 1961; asst. prof. pathology Med. Coll. Va., Richmond, 1961-63; asst. prof. immunology Duke U., Durham, N.C., 1963-67, assoc. prof. immunology, 1967-70; dir. immunology Ortho Rsch. Found., Raritan, N.J., 1970-73; assoc. prof. pathology U. Pa., Phila., 1975-84, prof. pathology, 1984—97, prof. emeritus pathology, 1997—. Cons. Pa. Jersey Red Cross, Phila., 1978-2002; assoc. dir. William Pepper Labs., Hosp. Univ. Pa., Phila., 1983-1997. Author three text books and numerous book chpts.; contbr. over 100 articles to profl. jours. Mem. Am. Assn. Blood Banks, Am. Assn. Immunologists, Am. Soc. Histocompatibility and Immunogenetics (pres. 1978), Acad. Clin. Lab. Physicians and Scientists, Am. Soc. Transplant Physicians, United Network for Organ Sharing (chmn. histocompatibility com. 1990—). Roman Catholic. Avocation: model railroading.

ZOBEL, HILLER BELLIN, judge; b. N.Y.C., Feb. 23, 1932; s. Hiller and Harriet Selma (Bellin) Z.; m. Deborah Bethell, June 21, 1958; children— John H., David H., Elizabeth T., Sarah B.; m. Rya S. Weickert, Nov. 23, 1973. BA cum laude, Harvard U., 1953, LL.B., 1959; postgrad., Oxford U., 1956. Bar: Mass. 1959, U.S. Ct. Appeals 1960, U.S. Dist. Ct. 1960, U.S. Supreme Ct. 1966. Assoc. firm Bingham, Dana & Gould, Boston, 1959-67; research assoc. Harvard U., 1962-63; assoc. prof. Boston Coll. Law Sch., 1967-69, prof., 1969-79; assoc., counsel firm Hill & Barlow, Boston, 1971-72; partner, counsel firm Brown, Rudnick, Freed & Gesmer, 1972-79; assoc. justice Mass. Superior Ct., 1979—. Reporter Mass. Advisory Com. on Rules of Civil Procedure; spl. asst. atty. gen. Commonwealth of Mass.; spl. counsel Mass. Dept. Pub. Utilities. Author: The Boston Massacre, 1970, reissued, 1996, (with J.W. Smith) Massachusetts Rules Practice, 1974-81, (with S.N. Rous) Doctors and the Law, 1993; editor: (with L.K. Wroth) Legal Papers of John Adams, 1965; contbr. articles to profl. jours., newspapers, mags. Served with U.S. Navy, 1953-55. Recipient Am. Hist. Assn. Littleton-Griswold prize, 1966 Fellow Soc. Am. Historians; mem. Am. Law Inst., Mass. Hist. Soc., Colonial Soc. Mass., Am. Antiquarian Soc., Mass. Bar Assn., Boston Bar Assn., Maritime Law Assn. U.S., Am. Soc. Legal History (v.p. 1970-71), Nat. Conf. State Trial Judges (exec. com. 1990-93). Democrat. Jewish. Office: Superior Ct McCormack Post Office Boston MA 02109 E-mail: honzobe@aol.com.

ZOBEL, JAN A. tax consultant; b. San Francisco, 1947; d. Jerome Fremont and Louise Maxine Zobel. BA, Whittier Coll., 1968; MA, U. Chgo., 1970. Tchr. Chgo. Pub. Schs., 1969-70, San Francisco Pub. Schs., 1971-78; editor, pub. People's Yellow Pages, San Francisco, 1971-81; pvt. practice tax cons. San Francisco, Oakland, 1978—. Tchr. community coll. dist., San Francisco, 1986—; tax lectr. U. Hawaii, 1989—, U. Calif., San Francisco State U., Marin C.C. Author: Minding Her Own Business: The Self-Employed Woman's Guide to Taxes and Recordkeeping, 1997, 3d edit., 2000; editor People's Yellow Pages, 1971-81 (cert. of honor San Francisco Bd. Suprs. 1974), Where the Child Things Are, 1977-80. Named Acct. Adv. of Yr., SBA, 1987; presented Key to City of Buffalo, 1970. Mem. Nat. Assn. Enrolled Agts., Calif. Assn. Enrolled Agts., Nat. Assn. Tax Preparers, Bay Area Career Women. Office: 1197 Valencia St San Francisco CA 94110-3026

ZOBEL, JON D., JR. electrical engineer; b. Colorado Springs, July 7, 1961; s. Jon D. Zobel and Yolanda Jean Billingiere; m. Catherine Anne McKamie, July 21, 1990; 1 child, R.J. BSEE, U. Colo., 1986, MSEE, 1991. Rsch. asst. U. Colo. Control Sys. Lab., 1985—86; rsch. fellow Frank J. Seiler Rsch. Lab., USAF Academy, Colo., 1986; R&D engr. Ford Aerospace Corp., Colorado Springs, 1986—91; sr. elec. engr. TRW Electromagnetic Sys., San Jose, Calif., 1991—. Pubs. chmn. Santa Clara Valley IEEE Electromagnetic Compatibility Soc. EMC '98, Santa Clara, Calif., 1998. Recipient cert. of merit Colo. Engring. Coun., 1986; named Outstanding Young Man of Am., 1987. Mem. IEEE, IEEE Electromagnetic Compatibility Soc., Nat. Assn. Radio and Telecomms. Engrs. (cert. electromagnetic compatibility engr.), Applied Computational Electromagnetics Soc., Eta Kappa Nu (chpt. v.p. 1985-86). Republican. Roman Catholic. Avocations: cycling, golf. Office: TRW Electromagnetic Sys PO Box 530951 6377 San Ignacio Ave San Jose CA 95153-0951 Office Fax: 408-531-2203. E-mail: emc.xprt@ieee.org.

ZOBEL, LOUISE PURWIN, author, educator, lecturer, writing consultant; b. Laredo, Tex., Jan. 10, 1922; d. Leo Max and Ethel Catherine (Levy) Purwin; m. Jerome Fremont Zobel, Nov. 14, 1943; children: Lenore Zobel Harris, Janice A., Robert E., Audrey Zobel Dollinger. BA cum laude, Stanford U., 1943, MA, 1976. Cert. adult edn. and community coll. tchr., Calif. Freelance mag. writer and author, Palo Alto, Calif., 1942—; writer, editor, broadcaster UP Bur., San Francisco, 1943; lectr. on writing, history, travel No. Calif., 1964—; lectr., educator U. Calif. campuses, other colls. and univs., 1969—; writing cons. to pvt. clients, 1969—; editorial asst. Assn. Coll. Unions Internat., Palo Alto, 1972-73; acting asst. prof. journalism San Jose State U., 1976. Keynote speaker, seminar leader, prin. speaker at nat. confs.; cruise/shipboard enrichment lectr. and presenter of travel slide programs; coord. TV shows; TV personality publicity and public rels. campaigns; tchr. corr. classes Writer's Digest Sch.; tchr. online writing classes for Writing-school.com, 1999—. Author: (books) The Travel Writer's Handbook, 1980, (hard cover), 1982, (paperback) 83, 84, 85, rev. edits., 1992, 94, 97, 2002; author, narrator (90 minute cassette) Let's Have Fun in Japan, 1982; contbr. articles to anthologies, nat. mags. and newspapers; writer advertorials. Bd. dirs., publicity chair Friends of Palo Alto Libr., 1985—; officer Santa Clara County Med. Aux., Esther Clark Aux., others; past pres. PTA. Recipient award for excellence in journalism Sigma Delta Chi, 1943, awards Writers Digest, 1967-95, Armed Forces Writers League, 1972, Nat. Writers Club, 1976, All Nippon Airways and Japanese Nat. Tourist Orgn., 1997. Mem. Am. Soc. Journalists and Authors, Travel Journalists Guild, Internat. Food, Wine and Travel Writers Assn., Pacific Asia Travel Assn., Calif. Writers Club (v.p. 1988-89), AAUW (v.p. 1955-57, Nat. writing award 1969), Stanford Alumni Assn., Phi Beta Kappa. Avocations: travel, reading, writing, photography. Home and Office: 23350 Sereno Ct Unit 30 Cupertino CA 95014-6543 E-mail: lzobelwriter@cs.com.

ZOBEL, RYA WEICKERT, federal judge; b. Germany, Dec. 18, 1931; AB, Radcliffe Coll., 1953; LLB, Harvard U., 1956. Bar: Mass. 1956, U.S. Dist. Ct. Mass., 1956, U.S. Ct. Appeals (1st cir.) 1967. Assoc. Hill & Barlow, Boston, 1967-73, Goodwin, Procter & Hoar, Boston, 1973-76, ptnr., 1976-79; judge U.S. Dist. Ct. Mass., 1979—; dir. Fed. Jud. Ctr., Washington, 1995-99. Mem. ABA, Boston Bar Assn., Am. Bar Found., Mass. Bar Assn., Am. Law Inst. Office: US District Ct 1 Courthouse Way Boston MA 02210-3002

ZOBERI, NADIM BIN-ASAD, management consultant, consultant; b. Karachi, Pakistan, July 20, 1951; came to U.S., 1973; s. Asad Ahmad and Nawab Bano Zoberi; m. Samira Khalid, Mar. 24, 1989; 1 child, Noor Jehan. BS in Math., Physics and Chemistry, U. Karachi, 1971; B in Computer Sci., U. Wis., River Falls, 1981, BBA, 1980. Indsl., project engr. ADC Telecommunications, Mpls., 1979-84, supr. prodn. and inventory control, 1984-87; cons. Coopers & Lybrand, 1988-89; dir. mfg. Daig Corp., Minnetonka, Minn., 1989-90; dir. quality internat. op. N.W. Airlines, St. Paul, 1990-92; mgmt. cons. KPMG Peat Marwick, Mpls., 1992-99; prin. IBM Global Svcs., 1999—. Exec. advisor Jr. Achievement, Mpls., 1985-87. Mem. Assn. Mfg. Excellence, Inst. of Indsl. Engrs. Moslem. Avocations: tennis, travel, reading, music, golfing. Home: 1550 Murphy Pkwy Saint Paul MN 55122-1796 Office: IBM Corp 650 3d Ave S Minneapolis MN 55402 E-mail: nzoberi@aol.com.

ZOBL, ELDRED GREGORY, cardiologist; b. Detroit, Sept. 21, 1927; MD, Wayne State U., 1954. Diplomate Am. Bd. Internal Medicine, Am. Bd. Cardiovasc. Medicine. Intern Detroit Gen. Hosp., 1954-55, resident in medicine, 1955-58, fellow in cardiology, 1958-60; clin. assoc. prof. medicine Wayne State U., 1964—; pvt. practice Southfield, Mich., 1968—. Mem. staff Providence Hosp., Southfield. Fellow ACP, Am. Coll. Cardiology, Am. Heart Assn. Office: 22250 Providence Dr Ste 704 Southfield MI 48075-6215

ZOBRIST, BENEDICT KARL, library director, historian; b. Moline, Ill., Aug. 21, 1921; s. Benedict and Lila Agnas (Colson) Z.; m. Donna Mae Anderson, Oct. 23, 1948; children: Benedict Karl II, Markham Lee, Erik Christian. AB, Augustana Coll., Rock Island, Ill., 1946; postgrad., Stanford U., 1946-47; MA, Northwestern U., 1948, PhD, 1953; postgrad., U. Ill., 1961, Tunghai U., Taiwan, 1962, Columbia U., 1962-63, Fed. Exec. Inst., Charlottesville, Va., 1974, Hebrew U., Israel, 1978; LHD, Avila Coll., 1995. Manuscript specialist in recent Am. history Library of Congress, Washington, 1952-53; asst. reference librarian Newberry Library, Chgo., 1953-54; command historian Ordnance Weapons Command, Rock Island Arsenal, 1954-60; prof. history, chmn. dept. Augustana Coll., 1960-69, asst. dean faculty, 1964-69, asso. dean, dir. grad. studies, 1969; asst. dir. Harry S. Truman Libr., Independence, Mo., 1969-71, dir., 1971-94. Exec. sec. Harry S. Truman Libr. Inst., Independence, 1971-94; mem. steering com. Harry S. Truman Statue Com., Independence, 1973-76; dir., regent Harry S. Truman Good Neighbor Award Found., 1974—; mem. Independence Truman Award Commn., 1975-94, Mo. Hist. Records Adv. Bd., 1978—; adj. prof. history U. Mo.-Kansas City, 1975—, Ottawa U., Kansas City, 1977-94, U. Mo. St. Louis, 1987-94; chmn. Independence Commn. Bicentennial of U.S. Constitution, 1987, Uptown Independence, Inc., 1989-94; mem. adv. coun. Truman Little White House State Historic Site, Key West, Fla., 1987-94. Contbr. articles, revs. to profl. jours. Trustee Heritage League of Greater Kansas City, 1981—, Liberty Meml. Assn., Kansas City, Mo., 1990—, Black Archives Mid-Am., Inc., Kansas City, 1992-94; mem. Truman Nat. Centennial Com., 1982-84. Served with AUS, 1942-46. Recipient Outstanding Alumni Achievement award Augustana Coll., 1975, Bronze Good Citizenship medal Kans. SAR, 1986, People's Choice award Independence (Mo.) Neighborhood Councils, 1987, Mid-Am. Regional Council award for contbns. to met. community, 1987, Citizen Achievement award Black Archives of Mid-Am., 1988, Silver Good Citizenship medal Mo. SAR, 1988, Special Recognition award City of Independence, 1988, Outstanding Civic Leader in Independence, 1989, Gold Medal of Honor DAR, 1990, Spl. Commendation award Nat. Park Svc., 1993; named World Citizen of Yr. by Kans. City Mayor's UN Day Com., 1994. Mem. AAUP, Am. Hist. Assn., Jackson County (Mo.) Hist. Soc. (v.p. 1972-82, 93-95), Orgn. Am. Historians, Assn. Asian Studies, Am. Assn. State, Local History, Soc. Am. Archivists, U.S. Power Squadron, Am. Legion, La Societe des 40 Hommes et 8 Chevaux, VFW. Home: 71B T St Lake Lotawana MO 64086-9728

ZOBRIST, GEORGE WINSTON, computer scientist, educator; b. Highland, Ill., Feb. 13, 1934; s. George H. and Lillie C. (Augustin) Z.; m. Freida Groverlyn Rich, Mar. 29, 1955; children: Barbara Jayne, George William, Jean Anne. BS, U. Mo., 1958, PhD, 1965; MS, Wichita State U., 1961. Registered profl. engr., Mo., Fla. Electronic scientist U.S. Naval Ordnance Test Sta., China Lake, Calif., 1958-59; rsch. engr. Boeing Co., Wichita, 1959-60; instr. Wichita State U., 1960-61; assoc. prof. U. Mo., Columbia, 1961-69, U. So. Fla., Tampa, 1969-70; chmn. elec. engring. dept. U. Miami, Coral Gables, Fla., 1970-71; prof. U. South Fla., Tampa, 1971-72, 73-76; prof., chmn. dept. elec. engring. U. Toledo, 1976-79; dir. computer sci. and engring. Samborn, Steketee, Otis, Evans, Inc., Toledo, 1979-82; prof. computer sci. Grad. Engring. Ctr. U. Mo., St. Louis, 1982-85, prof. computer sci. Rolla, 1985-99, chmn. dept., 1994-99, prof. emeritus, 1999—. Rsch. prof. U. Edinburgh, Scotland, 1972-73; lectr. U. Western Cape, South Africa, 1995 summer; cons. Wilcox Electric Co., Bendix Corp., both Kansas City, Mo., 1966-68, ICC, Miami, 1970-71, Def. Comm. Agy., Washington, 1971, 72, U.S. Naval Rsch. Labs., Washington, 1971, Med. Svc. Bur., Miami, 1970-71, NASA, Kennedy Space Ctr., Fla., 1973-76, 88, 89, 93, 94, Prestolite Corp., Toledo, 1977-79, IBM, Lexington, Ky., 1983-86, Wright-Patterson AFB, Ohio, 1986, PAFB, Fla., 1987, McDonnell Douglas, Mo., 1989, Digital Systems Cons., Mo., 1989, Oak Ridge Nat. Labs., 1992. Author: Network Computer Analysis, 1969, Progress in Computer Aided VLSI Design, 1988-90; editor Internat. Jour. Computer Aided VLSI Design, 1989-91, Object Oriented Simulation IEEE Press, 1996, Computer Sci. and Computer Engring. Monograph series, 1989-91, Internat. Jour. Computer Simulation, 1990-96, VLSI Design, 1992—; editor IEEE Potentials Mag., 1996-99; assoc. editor, 1984-96, 99—; contbr. articles to profl. jours. Served with USAF, 1951-55. Named Young Engr. of Yr. ctrl. chpt. Mo. Soc. Profl. Engrs., 1967; NSF summer fellow, 1962, 64; NASA, IBM, DOE, UES/AFOSR, McDonnell Douglas rsch. grantee, 1967-88. Fellow IEEE (life, mem. IEEE Press editl. bd. 1998—); mem. Am. Legion, Rotary, Sigma Xi, Tau Beta Pi, Phi Eta Sigma, Eta Kappa Nu, Pi Mu Epsilon, Upsilon Pi Epsilon. Home: 12030 Country Club Dr Rolla MO 65401-7469 Office: U Mo Rolla Dept Compuer Sci 1870 Miner Cir Rolla MO 65409-0001 E-mail: zobrist@umr.edu.

ZOCCHI, LOUIS JOSEPH, product designer, game company executive; b. Chgo., Feb. 16, 1935; s. Louis Alexander and Martha (Adams) Z.; m. Elissa Lorelei Scott, June 8, 1959 (Sept. 1976); children: David, Suzanne, LaRee, Lisa; m. Sharon Annette Olson, May 25, 1985; 1 child, Heidi Olson. Cert. air traffic controller, 1955, air traffic control instr., 1964. Commd. USAF, 1954, advanced through grades to tech. sgt., air traffic contr. Nebr., 1954, Lincoln AFB, 1955-59, Misawa AFB, Japan, 1959-63, Holloman AFB, N.Mex., 1963-64, air traffic control instr. Keesler AFB, Miss., 1964-70, air traffic contr. Mather AFB, Calif., 1970-71, Kimpo AFB, Korea, 1971-72, George AFB, Calif., 1972-73, Biloxi, Miss., 1973-75, ret., 1975; commd. 1st lt. Miss. State Guard, 1991, advanced through grades to capt., 1993; owner Zocchi Distbrs., Victorville, Calif., 1972—; pres. Gamescience, Inc., Cedarhurst, N.Y., 1974—. Cruise dir. Europa Star cruise ship, 1988; cons. Dupuy Inst., 1995. Designer (games) Battle of Britain, 1968, Star Fleet Battle Manual, 1977 (Gamesday award 1981), Basic and Advanced Fighter Combat, 1980 (H.G. Wells award 1981); inventor Zocchihedron 100 sided dice, 1985. Major Ala. State Guard, 1997—, lt. col., 2000. Recipient Hobbyist award Metro Detroit Gamers, 1979, Spl. Svc. award Strategists Club, 1982, Charles Roberts Adventure Gaming Hall of Fame award, 1987, Gama Honor of Svc. award 1991. Mem. Game Mfrs. Assn. (chmn. membership com. 1978-84, v.p. 1978-84, bd. dirs. 1985), Internat. Brotherhood Magicians (Order of Merlin 2000), Hobby Industry Assn. (pres. gaming div. 1981), Gulf Coast Jazz Soc. (pres.), Soc. Am. Magicians (pres.). Avocations: playing jazz music, ventriloquism, magic. Home and Office: Gamescience Inc 7604 Newton Dr Biloxi MS 39532-2830

ZOCCO, ROSEANNE MARIE, nurse, educator; b. Sioux Falls, S.D., July 15, 1955; d. Rosemarie B. Faini. BS in Nursing, Coll. Mt. St. Joseph on Ohio, Cin., 1977; MSEd, Youngstown State U., 1989. RN, Ohio. Asst. head nurse, then head nurse SICU St. Elizabeth Hosp. Med. Ctr., Youngstown, Ohio; staff devel. coord. Greenville (Pa.) Reg. Hosp., dir. edn. svcs. Mem. ARC, AACN (pres. northeastern Ohio chpt. 1978, 81, sec. 1977), Am. Heart Assn., Am. Soc. Health Edn. and Trainers, Soc. Healthcare Edn. Leaders.

ZODL, JOSEPH ARTHUR, international trade executive, consultant; b. Hackensack, N.J., Aug. 13, 1948; s. Joseph Frank and Edna Josephine (Hokanson) Z. BA in Polit. Sci., Fordham Coll., 1970; MA in Polit. Sci., New Sch. for Social Rsch., N.Y.C., 1991; MBA in Internat. Bus., Wester Internat. U., Phoenix, 1998. Lic. customs broker U.S. Treasury Dept. Export mgr. Savage Universal Corp., Tempe, Ariz., 1984-93; corp. transp. mgr. Nat. Media Corp., Phoenix, 1993—. Adj. instr. internat. bus. Rio Salado C.C., 1989—, Keller Grad. Sch. Bus., 1995—, Scottsdale C.C., 1996—, U. Phoenix, 1999—. Author: Export-Import: Everything You and Your Company Need To Know To Compete in World Markets, 1992, rev., 1995, 4th printing, 1999, rev. 5th printing, 2001; contbr. articles to profl. jours. Vice chmn. Legis. Dist. 20 Dems., 1978-80, chmn., 1980-82; mem. Ariz. State Dem. Com., 1978-89; cand. Ariz. Ho. Reps., 1986. Named Eagle Scout, Boy Scouts Am., 1966. Mem. Am. Polit. Sci. Assn., Ariz. World Trade Ctr., Internat. Transp. Mgmt. Assn. (dir. 1990-91), Phoenix Traffic Club, Phoenix Customs Brokers Assn., Delta Nu Alpha (pres. 1980-81, Ariz. Transp. Man of Yr. 1980), Alpha Phi Omega, Phi Theta Kappa, Delta Mu Delta. Roman Catholic.

ZOELLE, ANDREA MARIE, reference librarian; b. Fond du Lac, Wis., July 21, 1947; d. Edward James and Virginia May (Grabinski) Z. BS in Edn., Marian Coll., 1965-69; MA in Libr. Sci., U. Wis., 1972. Elem. tchr. St. Killian's Grade Sch., Campbellsport, Wis., 1969-70; children's libr. Ela Area Pub. Libr. Dist., Lake Zurich, Ill., 1975-77; mus. libr. Lake County Mus., Wauconda, 1977-78; English conversation tchr. Otsu Catholic Ch., Japan, 1979-81, Echizen English Ctr., Fukui, Japan, 1981-83; reference libr. Desplaines Valley Pub. Libr. Dist., Lockport, Ill., 1986—. Docent Ill. Canal Mus., Lockport, 1987—; vol., resource aide Ill. & Mich. Canal Visitor Ctr., Lockport, 1990—. Mem. Am. Canal Soc., Will County Hist. Soc., Ill. Libr. Assn. E-mail: amzoelle@yahoo.com.

ZOELLER, BETTY ANN, secondary school guidance director; b. Elizabeth, N.J., Aug. 2, 1931; d. Joseph Patrick and Anne Marie (McNamara) Murphy; m. R. Peter Zoeller, Dec. 18, 1971. BA in English, Pace U., 1954; MA in Counseling, Fairfield (Conn.) U., 1966, CAS in Psychol. Examining, 1969. Cert. counselor, N.J. Guidance dir. Preston High Sch., Bronx, N.Y., 1966-68, Lacoudaire Acad., Upper Montclair, N.J., 1969-71, Paul VI Regional High Sch., Clifton, 1971-90; pvt. practice as psychol. examiner Upper Montclair, 1978-79; guidance dir. Paterson (N.J.) Cath. High Sch., 1991—. Mem. Fieldstone Assn., Upper Montclair, 1978—, Zonta Internat., 1983-87; vol. Am. Cancer Soc.; presenter Diocesan Profl. Day, 1991. Mem. AACD, Passaic County Counselors Assn. (exec. bd., program chmn. 1978-84, Recognition award), N.J. Profl. Counselors Assn. Roman Catholic. Avocations: reading, travel, gardening, swimming, golf. Office: Paterson Cath High Sch 764 11th Ave Paterson NJ 07514-1099

ZOELLER, DONALD J. lawyer; b. Queens Village, N.Y., Mar. 18, 1930; s. Henry Adolph and Marion Elizabeth (Brodie) Z.; m. Susan Josephine Campisi, Sept. 3, 1955; children— Paul Joseph, Jean Marie, Diane Marie AB, Fordham Coll., 1951; LL.B., Fordham Sch. Law, N.Y.C., 1958. Bar: N.Y. 1959, D.C. 1967. Law clk. to judge U.S. Dist. Ct. (so. dist.) N.Y., N.Y.C., 1958-59; assoc. Mudge Rose Guthrie Alexander & Ferdon, 1959-68, ptnr., 1968-95, exec. ptnr., 1991-95, chmn. exec. com., 1995; counsel Carter, Ledyard & Milburn, 1995-96, ptnr., 1997-98, of counsel, 1999—. Adj. prof. law Fordham U. Law Sch., 1989—; lectr. in field. Contbr. articles to legal publs. 1st lt. U.S. Army, 1951-53, Korea. Mem. ABA, N.Y. State Bar Assn., Bar Assn. City of N.Y., Nassau County Bar Assn., Inst. Jud. Adminstrn., Am. Judicature Soc., Fed. Bar Coun. Republican. Roman Catholic. Avocations: skiing, swimming, tennis, reading. Office: Carter Ledyard & Milburn 2 Wall St Fl 13 New York NY 10005-2072 Business E-mail: dzoeller@optonline.net. E-mail: zoeller@clm.com. *Notable cases include: Matsushita Electric Indsl. Co. Ltd. et al vs. Zenith Radio Corp. et al, 475 U.S. 574, 89 L. edit. 2d 538, 106, s.ct. 1438.*

ZOELLER, JACK CARL, financial executive; b. Buffalo, Feb. 26, 1949; s. Ronald Carl and Margaret Lillian (Wademan) Z.; m. Kathryn Louise Helmke, Apr. 25, 1981; children: Andrew, Alexander, Charles (dec.). BS, U.S. Mil. Acad., 1970; M of Pub. Policy, Harvard U., 1972; M of Letters, Oxford (Eng.) U., 1974. Program budget officer Army Chief of Staff's Office, Pentagon, Washington, 1978-80; v.p. E.F. Hutton & Co., Inc., N.Y.C., 1982; pres. E.F. Hutton Indemnity Group, 1983-85, Capital Risk Mgmt., Iselin, N.J., 1985-87; exec. v.p., bd. dirs. Comfed Mortgage Co., Lowell, Mass., 1987-88, pres., 1988-91, ComFed Savs. Bank, Lowell, 1990-91; chmn. chief exec. officer ComFed Bancorp., Cambridge, Mass., 1990-95; pres. The Zoeller Group, Washington, 1993-95. Bd. dirs. N.Am. Health Plans, Inc., Amherst, NY, 1995—99; pres. AtlantiCare Risk Mgmt. Corp., 1995—, N.Am. Health & Life Ins., Barbados, 1996—; chmn., CEO AtlantiCare, Inc., 1995—. Mem. exec. com. Lowell Devel. and Fin. Corp., 1989-91, class gift com. U.S. Mil. Acad., 1990-95; youth sports coach, 1990-96; Am. chmn. 750th Ann. Campaign Univ. Coll., Oxford, Eng., 1998-2002; parent group leader Maret Sch., Washington, 1998--. Served to Capt. U.S. Army, 1970-80. Decorated Meritorious Svc. medals; Rhodes scholar Oxford U., 1972. Mem. Self Ins. Inst. Am. (mem. nat. conf. com. 1997-99), DC Captive Ins. Coun., West Point Soc. N.Y. (bd. govs. 1985-87), West Point Soc. D.C., Am. Friends Univ Coll. Oxford, Inc. (v.p. 1999—), Fed. Nat. Mortgage Assn. (N.E. regional adv. bd. 1990-91), New Eng. Hist. Geneal. Soc., Soc. Mayflower Descs. Home: 2810 31st St NW Washington DC 20008-3523 Office: AtlantiCare Inc 1919 Gallows Rd Ste 900 Vienna VA 22182-3964

ZOELLICK, ROBERT BRUCE, federal agency administrator; b. Evergreen Park, Ill., July 25, 1953; s. William T. and Gladys Zoellick; m. Sherry Lynn Ferguson, June 28, 1980. BA with honors, Swarthmore Coll., 1975; M in Pub. Policy, JD magna cum laude, Harvard U., 1981. Bar: D.C. 1981. Spl. asst. to asst. atty. gen. criminal div. U.S. Dept. Justice, Washington, 1978-79; pvt. practice law, 1981-82; law clk. to Judge Patricia M. Wald, U.S. Ct. Appeals for D.C. Cir., Washington, 1982-83; v.p., asst. to chmn. and chief exec. officer of bd. Fannie Mae, 1983-85; from spl. asst. to Dep. Sec., Dep. Asst. Sec. for Fin. Instns. Policy, to counselor to sec. and exec. sec. U.S. Treasury Dept., 1985-88; counselor of Dept. with rank under sec. U.S. Dept. State, 1989-92, under sec. for econ. and agrl. affairs, 1991-92; dep. chief of staff, asst. to Pres. White House, 1992-93; exec. v.p. housing and law Fannie Mae, 1993-97; Olin prof. nat. security U.S. Naval Acad., 1997-98; pres., CEO-designate Ctr.

Strategic & Internat. Studies, Washington, 1998-99; resident fellow German Marshall Fund U.S., 1999—; rsch. scholar Belfer Ctr. Sci. and Internat. Affairs Harvard U.; sr. internat. advisor Goldman Sachs; USTR Off. U.S. Trade Repr. , Wash., 2001—. Bd. dirs. Alliance Capital, Jones Intercable, Said Holdings, Coun. Fgn. Rels., German Marshall Fund U.S., European Inst., Eurasia Found., Nat. Bur. Asian Rsch., Am. Coun. Germany, Am. Inst. Contemporary German Studies, Overseas Devel. Coun. Mem. Trade Deficit Rev. Commn.; dir. strategy group fgn. policy Aspen Inst.; mem. adv. bd. Johns Hopkins Sch. Advanced Internat. Studies, Law & Econs. Ctr. George Mason U.; mem. adv. com. Inst. Internat. Econs. Decorated Knight Comdr.'s Cross (for work on German unification, Germany); recipient Alexander Hamilton award U.S. Treasury Dept., 1988, Disting. Svc. award U.S. State Dept, 1992; fellow Luce Found., Hong Kong, 1980. Mem. D.C. Bar Assn., Phi Beta Kappa.*

ZOELLNER, ROBERT WILLIAM, chemistry educator; b. Marshfield, Wis., May 30, 1956; s. Willard Rudolph and Marie Martha (Prihoda) Z.; m. Barbara Moore, Feb. 5, 1983; children: Joan Moore, Thaddeus Barak. BS, St. Norbert Coll., De Pere, Wis., 1978; PhD, Kans. State U., 1983. Postdoctoral assoc. Cornell U., Ithaca, N.Y., 1983-84; vis. scientist U. Aix-Marseille (France) III, 1984-85; asst. prof. No. Ariz. U., Flagstaff, 1986-92, assoc. prof., 1992-98; sabbatical assoc. Istituto per lo Studio della Stereochimica Consiglio Nazionale delle Ricerche, 1994-95; assoc. prof. Humboldt State U., Arcata, Calif., 1998—2002, prof., 2002—. Mem. AAUP, Soc. for the Advancement of Chicanos and Native Ams. in Sci., Am. Chem. Soc., Internat. Coun. on Main Group Chemistry, Wis. Acad. Sci., Arts and Letters, Sigma Xi, Alpha Chi Sigma, Phi Lambda Upsilon, Delta Epsilon Sigma, Phi Kappa Phi. Office: Humboldt State Univ Dept of Chemistry Arcata CA 95521-8299 E-mail: rwz7001@axe.humboldt.edu.

ZOELLNER, SANDRA ANN, accountant; b. Fond du Lac, Wis., Aug. 25, 1964; d. Daniel Lee and Marguerite Frances (Wildenberg) Z. BS, Okla. State U., 1986. CPA, Tex. Revenue agt. IRS, Dallas, 1987; credit analyst Mercury Marine, 1988-89; asst. controller Leather Ctr., 1989-90; staff acct. TGI Friday's, Addison, 1990-94, Metromedia Restaurant Group, Plano, 1994-98, Pizza Hut, Dallas, 1998—99; acctg. mgr. Time Warner Cable, Flower Mound, 1999—. Distributor Discovery Toys, Dorling Kindersley Family Learning. Mem. NAFE, Dallas Froshinn Women's Orgn. and Damenchor, All Saints Singles Club (v.p.), Alpha Kappa Psi. Republican. Roman Catholic. Avocations: reading, piano, guitar, dancing, teaching religious education. Home: 630 Meadow Crest Dr Highland Village TX 75077 Office: 300 Parker Sq Ste 210 Flower Mound TX 75028

ZOGHBI, HUDA Y. pediatric neurology and genetics educator; b. June 29, 1955; BSc, Am. U. Beirut, 1976; MD, Meharry Med. Coll., 1979. Prof. pediat. neurology and geriatrics Baylor Coll. Medicine, Houston, 1994—; investigator Howard Hughes Med. Inst., 1996—. Elected mem. Inst. of Medicine, 2000. Office: T 807 1 Baylor Plz Houston TX 77030-3411*

ZOGHBY, JAMES FRANCIS, priest; b. Mobile, Ala., June 7, 1945; s. Herbert Michael Zoghby, Sr. and Laurice Haik Zoghby. BA, Notre Dame Sem., New Orleans, 1968, MDiv, 1972. Priest ordained to Roman Cath. ch., 1971. Tchr., priest McGill-Toolen H.S./USA Med. Ctr., Mobile, 1973—77; chaplain Providence Hosp., 1977—81; assoc. pastor St. Mary's Ch., 1981—83, Holy Family Ch., Mobile, 1983—85; pastor Sacred Heart Ch., Grove Hill, Ala., 1985—87, Corpus Christi Ch., Mobile, 1987—. Elected mem. Priests' Pers. Bd., Mobile, 1998—2004, chmn., 1989—95; elected mem. Priests' Coun., Mobile, 1977—2000, rec. sec., 1983—86, corr. sec., 1980—83. Author: (mus., scriptural work) A Proclamation of the Good News, 1983. Mem.: Equestrian Order of Holy Sepulchre of Jerusalem (knight 2001—). Roman Catholic. Home: 6300 McKenna Dr Mobile AL 36608 Office: Corpus Christi Ch 6300 McKenna Dr Mobile AL 36608 Home Fax: 251-342-6313; Office Fax: 251-342-6313. Personal E-mail: CHURCH@CORPUSCHRISTIPARISH.COM. Business E-mail: CHURCH@CORPUSCHRISTIPARISH.COM.

ZOHAR, ZITA, pianist, artistic director, lecturer; b. Bucharest, Romania, May 11, 1949; arrived in Israel, 1962, came to U.S., 1966; d. Marcel and Cecile (Shapira) Finkelstein; m. Adrian Smilovici, Dec. 22, 1972. Diploma, Rubin Acad. Mus., Ramat-Aviv, Israel, 1966; hon. diploma, Chigiana Shc., Siena, Italy, 1970; BS, MS, The Juilliard Sch., 1971. Founder, artistic dir. Festival Chamber Players, L.I., N.Y., 1981—; music dir. Hecksher Series, 1985—; conductor Vanderbilt Orch., 1985-86. Lectr., instr. various schs., 1979—; asst. Dorothy Taubman Sch. at Amherst, 1978-82. Bd. dirs. Musician's Group, Bucharest, Romania, 1961, Music for All, Tel-Aviv, 1968, Festical Chamber Players, N.Y.C., 1985. Recipient First Prize Rep. Commn., 1959, First Prize Bach Competition Israeli Acad., 1965, Silver medal Busoni Competition, 1970. Mem. Chamber Music Am., Juilliard Sch. Alumni Assn., N.Y. Exec. Women. Avocations: jogging, yoga, painting. Home and Office: 205 W 57th St Apt 3db New York NY 10019-2195

ZOHN, MARTIN STEVEN, lawyer; b. Denver, Oct. 22, 1947; s. William and Alice (Lewis) Z.; m. Carol Falender, June 6, 1980; children: David Joseph, Daniel Robert. BA, Ind. U., 1969; JD, Harvard U., 1972. Bar: Calif. 1972, Ind. 1973, U.S. Ct. Claims 1980, U.S. Supreme Ct. 1980, U.S. Ct. Appeals (9th cir.) 1981. Assoc. Cadick, Burns, Duck & Neighbors, Indpls., 1972-77, ptnr., 1977-80. Pacht, Ross, Warne, Bernhard & Sears, Inc., L.A., 1980-86, Shea & Gould, L.A., 1986-89, Proskauer Rose LLP, L.A., 1989—. Pres. Indpls. Settlements, Inc., 1977-79. Bd. dirs. Pub. Counsel, 2001—. Mem. Fin. Lawyers Conf., L.A. County Bar Assn. (exec. com. prejudgment remedies sect. 1985-92), Beverly Hills Bar Assn. (exec. com. bus. law sect. 1985-92), Phi Beta Kappa. E-mail: mzohn@proskauer.com.

ZOIS, CONSTANTINE NICHOLAS ATHANASIOS, meteorology educator; b. Newark, Feb. 21, 1938; s. Athanasios Konstantinos and Asimina (Speros-Blekas) Z.; m. Elyse Stein, Dec. 26, 1971; children: Jennifer, Jonathan. *Great-grandfather Haralambos Zois was a goatherd in Greece. Grandfather A. Blekas went to sea as a cabin boy at age 8. Grandfather Konstantinos Zois was a goatherd in Greece. Blekas eventually came to U.S.A. and worked on the Pennsylvania Railroad. Konstantinos remained in Greece, but his son, Athanasios, came to the U.S.A. in 1918 at age 20. Athanasios met Asimina Blekas at the Washington Florist, where they both worked. They married and had two children, Constantine N.A. Zois and K. Barbara Zois. Constantine N.A. Zois married Elyse Stein in 1971. They had two children, Jennifer and Jonathan.* BA, Rutgers U., 1961; MS, Fla. State U., 1965; PhD, Rutgers U., 1980. Draftsman Babcock and Wilcox Corp., Newark, 1956; designer Foster Wheeler Corp., Carteret, N.J., 1956; instr. Rutgers U., New Brunswick, 1961-62; grad. asst. Fla. State U., Tallahassee, 1962-65; rsch. meteorologist Nat. Weather Svc., Garden City, L.I., N.Y., 1965-67; prof. Kean Coll. N.J., Union, 1967—. Founder meteorology program Kean Coll., N.J.; cons. Connell, Foley and Geiser, Roseland, N.J., 1986-88; chmn. Kean Coll. All-Coll. Promotion com., 1991-93. Author, editor: Papers in Marine Science, 1971; author: Observation of the Newark N.J. Nocturnal Heat Island and Its Consideration in Terms of a Physical Model, 1980, Dynamical and Physical Oceanography, 1988, Atmospheric Dynamics: Exercises and Problems, 1988, Climatology Workbook, 1988, Weather Map Folio, 1989; contbg. author: Outcomes Assessment at Kean College of N.J., 1992, Synoptic Meterology-Exercises and Readings, Vols. 1-3, 1995. Mem. AAAS, Nat. Weather Assn., Am. Meteorol. Soc. (pres. N.J. chpt. 1980-81), N.Y. Acad. Scis. (vice chmn. atmospheric scis. sect. 1986-87, chmn. 1987-88, adv. com. atmospheric sci. sect., 1988—), N.J. Marine Scis. Consortium, Phi Beta Kappa. Republican. Greek Orthodox. Avocations: guitar, banjo, fishing, baseball, snorkeling. Home: 2798 Carol Rd Union NJ 07083-4831 Office: Kean Coll of NJ Dept Meterology Morris Ave Union NJ 07083-7117 *It is water that consecrates the atmosphere as a cathedral of wonderment, as it is water that incarnates the sea as an oasis of life.*

ZOLA, GARY PHILLIP, rabbi, historian, religious educational administrator; b. Chgo., Feb. 17, 1952; m. Stefani Paula Rothberg; children: Amanda Roi, Jorin Benjamin, Jeremy Micah, Samantha Leigh. BA in Am. History with distinction, U. Mich., 1973; MA in Counseling Psychology, Northwestern U., 1976; PhD in Am. Jewish History, Hebrew Union Coll., Cin., 1991. Ordained rabbi, 1982. Dir. informal edn. and youth activities Temple Israel, Mpls., 1973-74; regional youth dir., asst. camp dir. Olin-Sang-Ruby Union Inst., UAHC, Chgo., 1974-77; student pulpit B'nai Israel Congregation, Williamson, W.Va., 1978-79; mem. student pulpit Anshe Sholom Congregation, Olympia Fields, Ill., 1979-80, Columbus Hebrew Congregation, Columbus, Ind., 1981-82; rabbi for high holy days Chgo. Jewish Experience, Chgo., 1982-94; nat. dir. admissions Hebrew Union Coll.-Jewish Inst. Religion, Cin., 1982-89, nat. dean admissions and student affairs, 1989-91, nat. dean admissions, student affairs and alumni rels., 1991-98; exec. dir. Jacob Rader Marcus Ctr. Am. Jewish Archives at Hebrew Union Coll., 1998—; assoc. prof. Am. Jewish Experience Hewbrew Union Coll. Jewish Inst. of Religion. Del. Emerging Leaders Conf., Am. Coun. for Internat. Leadership, 1989, 91; bd. dirs. Am. Jewish Com., Cin., 1982—, mem. exec. com., 1984—; bd. dirs. Hillel U. Cin., 1991-94, Jewish Fedn., Cin., 1993-95; pres. Greater Cin. Bd. Rabbis, 1993-95, Jewish Cmty. Rels. Coun., (bd. dir.,1994—); founding mem. Kehillah of Cin., Jewish Think Tank. Author: Isaac Harby of Charleston, 1994; editor: Hebrew Union College--Jewish Institute of Religion--A Centennial History, 1875-1975, (Michael A. Meyer), 1992, Women Rabbis: Exploration and Celebration, 1996; editor: The American Jewish Archives Jour., 1998—; contbr. numerous scholarly articles to profl. jours.; mem. editl. bd. Reform Judaism. Bd. dirs. ethics com. Jewish Hosp., Cin.; life mem. N.Am. Fedn. Temple Youth; active NCCJ. Mem. Ctrl. Conf. Am. Rabbis, Orgn. Am. Historians, Assn. Jewish Studies, So. Jewish Hist. Soc., Am. Jewish Hist. Soc., N.Am. Fedn. Temple Youth (life). Office: Hebrew Union Coll Jewish Inst Religion 3101 Clifton Ave Cincinnati OH 45220-2404

ZOLA, MICHAEL S. lawyer; b. Madison, Wis., Dec. 15, 1942; s. Emanuel David and Harriet (Sher) Zola; 1 child Emanuel David. BS cum laude, U. Wis., 1964; LLB, Columbia U., 1967. Bar: D.C. 1968, Wis. 1968, U.S. Dist. Ct. (we. dist.) Wis. 1968, Calif. 1969, U.S. Dist. Ct. (no. dist.) Calif. 1969, U. S. Ct. Appeals (9th cir.) 1969, Hawaii 1981, U.S. Dist. Ct. Hawaii 1981. Law clk. to judge U.S. Dist. Ct. (we. dist.) Wis., 1967—68; mng. atty. San Francisco Neighborhood Legal Assistance Found., 1968—70; sole practice Calistoga, 1970—73; directing atty. Mendocino Legal Svcs., Ukiah, 1973—76; state chief of legal svcs. State of Calif., Sacramento, 1976—78, dep. state pub. defender, 1978—79; sole practice Kailua-Kona, Hawaii, 1989—. Mem. adv. bd. Kona Salvation Army, 1993—93; chmn. Mendocino County Dem. Ctrl. Com., Ukiah, 1975—76; pres. Kona Beth Shalom Congregation, 1991—94. Fellow Reginald Heber Smith Poverty Law fellow, 1968—70. Mem.: Legal Aid Soc. Hawaii (bd. dirs. 1985—86), Nat. Assn. Criminal Def. Lawyers, Hawaii Assn. Criminal Def. Lawyers (bd. dirs. 1989—), Rotary Club Kona (pres. 1998—99). Office: 75-5744 Alii Dr Ste 223 Kailua Kona HI 96740-1740 E-mail: zolalaw@aol.com.

ZOLLAR, CAROLYN CATHERINE, lawyer; b. Evanston, Ill., July 5, 1947; d. Maurice Adam and Alice S. (Kelm) Z. BA, Smith Coll., Northampton, Mass., 1969; MA, Columbia U., 1970; JD, Am. U., Washington, 1976. Bar: D.C., Va. Legis. asst. Congressman William Anderson U.S. Ho. of Reps., Washington, 1970-72; planning cons. Nat. Inst. Edn., 1972, legal asst., 1973, asst. for govt. and external rels., 1973-75; assoc. Joe W. Fleming II, P.C., 1975-82; gen. counsel Nat. Assn. Rehab. Facilities, 1982-86, gen. counsel, dir. med. rehab., 1986-94; gen. counsel, v.p. policy Am. Rehab. Assn., 1994-97; v.p. govt. rels. and policy devel. Am Med. Rehab. Providers Assn., 1998—; v.p. Futures Rehab. Mgmt., 1998—. Sec. Am. Rehab. Svcs., Inc., Washington1988, 1988—94; mem. bd. advisors Ind. Living Mag., N.Y.C., 1988—97; mem. Joint Commn. Accreditation Health Care Orgns. Task Force on Rehab. Svcs., 1988; mem. various expert panels on postacute care and rehab. DHHS, 1999—2002. Sec. bd. dirs. Rock Creek Found., Silver Spring, Md., 1983-90; bd. dirs. Affiliated Sante Group, 1993—; chair Nat. Rehab. Caucus, 1991—. Mem. Am. Soc. Assn. Execs., Am. Health Lawyers Assn., Va. Bar Assn., D.C. Bar, Women in Govt. Rels. Episcopalian. Avocations: skiing, golf, singing. Office: Am Med Rehab Providers Assn 1710 W St NW Washington DC 20036-E-mail: czollar@13x.com.

ZOLLER, BETTYE PIERCE, musician, educator, radio and television producer, writer; b. Kansas City, Mo., Jan. 30, 1943; d. Emil J. and Hazel (Cline) Volkart; m. William Raymond Seitz, May 24, 1975; children: Matthew Emil, Jeremy Albert Seitz. MusB, U. Mo., 1964; MusM in Edn., N. Tex. State U., 1986, postgrad., 1986—. Instr. U. Mo., Kansas City, 1964-65; vocalist Les Elgart Band, Lionel Hampton Band, 1966-67; headline performer Cabarets, Supper Clubs, 1968-69; pvt. music tchr., vocal coach, 1972—; creative dir. Ralph Stachon & Assocs., Dallas, 1970-73; writer, producer TV advt. jingles, 1972—; profl. studio singer, announcer, broadcast talent Jingles and Voice-Overs, 1970—; creative dir. Criterion Prodns., 1973-82; recording artist RCA Recording Co. Chet Atkins Prodns., 1977-80; songwriter Screen Gems and EMI, N.Y.C. and London, 1977-80; instr. Dallas County Community Colls., 1980-83; owner Audio-Media Prodns., Dallas, 1987—. Prof. Sch. Adult Continuing Edn. So. Meth. U., 1986—; creative mgr., head writer TM Communications, Inc., Dallas, 1986-90; prof. sch. radio TV U. Tex., Arlington, 1990—; founder ZWL Pub., Inc., 1994. Songwriter published and recorded in Australia, South Africa, England, Can., France; appearances include broadway and roadshow musicals, 1972, 74; Christian Dior show, 1975; headline performer Dallas Symphony, 1988, opening act for Tony Bennett, 1988; featured soloist Dallas Jazz Orch., Fairmont Hotel, Dallas, 1992; author 7 audiobooks including: Speaking Effective English, 1996, Woman Speak, 1997. Commercial Speak, A Guide to Announcing Radio/TV Commercials, 1997. Assoc. Dallas Mus. Art, 1983—; sponsor Dallas Opera, 1985-87; Bronze Bow Stradivarius patron Dallas Symphony, 1987—. Recipient Popular Composer stipend ASCAP, 1978-97, Nat. 1st Pl., Golden Microphone award, 1989, 8 C.L.I.O. awards, 13 A.D.D.Y. awards as writer radio-TV commls. Mem. AFTRA, Am. Bus. Womens' Assn. (Woman of Yr 1997-98), Screen Actors Guild, Nat. Assn. Tchrs. Singing, Symphony Orch. League, Mu Phi Epsilon, Pi Kappa Lambda, Phi Delta Kappa. Avocations: needlepoint, travel.

ZOLLER, JAMES ALEXANDER, educator; b. Nov. 7, 1948; BA, U. N.H., 1971; MA, San Francisco State U., 1973; DA, SUNY, Albany, 1984. Prof. writing and lit. English dept. Houghton (N.Y.) Coll., 1984—. Columnist Wellsville (N.Y.) Daily Reporter, 1997—. Author: Simple Clutter, 1998. E-mail: james.zoller@houghton.edu.

ZOLLER, MICHAEL, otolaryngologist, head and neck surgeon, educator; b. New Orleans, July 21, 1947; s. Harry and Mildred (Daitch) Z.; m. Linda Kramer, Dec. 21, 1974; children: Rebecca, Jonathan. BS, U. New Orleans, 1971; MD, Tulane U., 1972. Resident in gen. surgery Jewish Hosp., St. Louis, Washington U. Sch. Medicine, 1972—74; resident in otolaryngology Mass. Eye and Ear Infirmary, Harvard U. Med. Sch., Boston, 1974—77; pres. Ear, Nose and Throat Assocs., Savannah, Ga., 1977—2002; chmn. Eye, Ear, Nose & Throat Dept. Candler Hosp., 1996—98. Asst. clin. prof. surgery Med. Coll. Ga., Augusta, 1982—96, assoc. clin. prof. surgery, 1996—2002; assoc. prof. surgery Mercer Med. Sch., 2000—02; dir. otology otoneurology dept. St. Joseph's Hosp., Savannah, 1994—2002. Chmn. med. divsn. United Way, Savannah, 1990, chmn. profl. divsn., 1991, 94-2001, vice chmn. campaign, 2002, bd.dirs., 2002, allocation panel, 1997-2002; active Am. Cancer Soc., Savannah, 1993-2000, pres. Chatham County unit, 1996-97, chmn. bd., 1997-98; bd. dirs. Savannah Country Day Sch., 1993-97, chmn. ann. campaign, 1995-96; pres. Savannah Jewish Fedn., 1991-93; active Savannah Jewish Fedn. Endowment Bd., 1995-99; mem. med. adv. bd. South Coll., 1996-2000; mem. parents coun. Washington U., St. Louis, 1997-2001, Tulane U., 2002; bd. dirs. Leadership Savannah, 1996-98. Recipient Young Leadership award Savannah Jewish Fedn., 1985, Boss of Yr. award Savannah Jaycees, 1993, Celebrate Savannah award for outstanding contbns. to Savannah, Ga. Guardian, 1996; Harvard U. Med. Sch. fellow, 1976-77. Fellow: ACS; mem.: AMA, Ga. Soc. Otolaryngology (chmn. bd. trustees 1997—98, editor newsletter 1998—2001), So. Med. Assn., Med. Assn. Ga. (editl. bd. 2001—02, bd. dirs., mem. ho. dels., Ga. Cup award 1993, Ayest-Wyeth Cmty. Svc. award 1996, Cmty. Svc. award 2001), 1st Dist. Med. Assn. (pres. 1987—88), Ga. Med. Soc. (pres. 1992, John B. Rabun Cmty. Svc. award 1995), Am. Neurotology Soc., Am. Soc. Head and Neck Surgery, Am. Acad. Otolaryngology and Head and Neck Surgery (tonsils & adenoids com. 1996—99, sleep disorders com. 1996—2002). Office: Ear Nose and Throat Assocs Savannah 5201 Frederick St Savannah GA 31405-4501 E-mail: MZ47ent@aol.com.

ZOLLINGER, ROBERT MILTON, JR. surgery educator; b. Boston, Feb. 4, 1934; s. Robert Milton and Louise (Kiewitt) Z.; m. Ruth Lois Rice Harold, June 6, 1959; children: Robert W., Raymond H., George R. BA, Harvard U., 1955, MD, 1959. Diplomate Am. Bd. Surgery. Surgery intern, resident, rsch. fellow, chief resident Peter Bent Brigham Hosp., Boston, 1959-67; mem. surgery faculty Harvard Med. Sch., 1968, Case Western Res. U. Sch. Medicine, Cleve., 1969—, now prof. surgery. Co-author: Atlas Surgical Operations, 7th edit., 1993. Bd. dirs. Ctr. for Human Svcs., Cleve., 1983-86, Greater Cleve. Growth Assn., 1981-82, Leadership Cleve., 1984-88, Health Sys. Agy. North Ctrl. Ohio, 1982-91. Fellow: ACS (past pres. Ohio chpt., Disting. Svc. award Ohio chpt. 1998); mem.: Acad. Medicine Cleve. (past pres., Disting. Svc. award 2000), Soc. Internat. Chirurg., Ea. Surg. Soc., Am. Hernia Soc. (bd. dirs. 1999—, pres. 2002—), Soc. Surgery Alimentary Tract, Assn. for Acad. Surgery (Disting. Svc. award 1977), Soc. Univ. Surgeons, Ctrl. Surg. Assn., Am. Surg. Assn. Methodist. Avocations: gardening, electronics, ham radio. Home: 13650 County Line Rd Chagrin Falls OH 44022-4006 Office: Univ Hosp L7 11100 Euclid Ave Cleveland OH 44106-1736 E-mail: rmz3@po.cwru.edu.

ZOLLWEG, WILLIAM GLEN, sociology educator, researcher; b. Detroit, Oct. 2, 1952; s. Albert Walter and Hazel Beatrice Zollweg; m. Barbara Ann Nimmer, June 14, 1990; children: Lillian, Albert. BA, BA, U. No. Colo., Greeley, CO, 1978, MA, 1979; PhD, Western Mich. U., Kalamazoo, MI, 1984. Dir. social rsch. Gove Associates Inc., Kalamazoo, 1979—82; academic staff U. Wis., LA Crosse, Wis., 1982—83, asst. prof., 1983—84, dir. rsch. ctr., 1984—92, assoc. prof., 1990—94, prof., 1994—. Evaluator Drug Ct. Program, LA Crosse, Wis., 2001—, Alternative Justice Programs, Trempealeau County, Wis., 2001—; rsch. cons. CHILEDA Habilitation Inst., La Crosse, Wis., 1995—. Drug ct. staff LA County Drug Ct., La Crosse, Wis., 2001—02. E5 NAVY, 1972—76, Miramar NAS. Achievements include discovery of Findings in the field of autism treatments are noted as seminal for research design. Avocations: dog training (pointers), mule training, bicycle touring. Office: University of Wisconsin 1725 State Street La Crosse WI 54601 E-mail: zollweg.will@uwlax.edu.

ZOLOTOW, CHARLOTTE SHAPIRO, author, editor; b. Norfolk, Va., June 26, 1915; d. Louis J. and Ella F. (Bernstein) Shapiro; m. Maurice Zolotow, Apr. 14, 1938 (div. 1969); children: Stephen, Ellen. Student, U. Wis., 1933-36. Editor children's book dept. Harper & Row, N.Y.C., 1938-44, sr. editor, 1962-70; v.p., assoc. pub. Harper Jr. Books, 1976-81; editorial cons., editorial dir. Charlotte Zolotow Books, 1982-90; pub. emerita, advisor Harper Collins Children's Books, 1991—. Tchr. U. Colo. Writers Conf. on Children's Books, U. Ind. Writers Conf.; also lectr. children's books. Author: The Park Book, 1944, Big Brother, 1960, The Sky Was Blue, 1963, The Magic Words, 1952, Indian Indian, 1952, The Bunny Who Found Easter, 1998, new edit., 1999, In My Garden, 1960, But Not Billy, 1947, 2d edit, 1983, Not a Little Monkey, 1957, 2d edit., 1989, The Man With The Purple Eyes, 1961, Mr. Rabbit and the Lovely Present, 1962, The White Marble, 1963, A Rose, A Bridge and A Wild Black Horse, 1964, 2d edit., 1987, Someday, 1965, When I Have a Little Girl, 1965, If It Weren't for You, 1966, 2d edit., 1987, Big Sister, Little Sister, 1966, All That Sunlight, 1967, When I Have A Son, 1967, My Friend John, 1968, new edit., 1999, Summer Is, 1968, Some Things Go Together, 1969, The Hating Book, 1969, The New Friend, 1969, River Winding, 1970, 79, Lateef and His World, 1970, Yani and His World, 1970, You and Me, 1971, Wake Up and Goodnight, 1971, William's Doll, 1972, Hold My Hand, 1972, 2d edit., 1987, The Beautiful Christmas Tree, 1972, new edit., 1999, Janie, 1973, My Grandson Lew, 1974, The Summer Night, 1974, 3d edit. 1991, The Unfriendly Book, 1975, It's Not Fair, 1976, 2d edit., 1987, Someone New, 1978, Say It, 1980, If You Listen, 1980, 2d edit. 1987, The New Friend, 1981, One Step, Two ..., 1981, The Song, 1982, I Know a Lady, 1984, Timothy Too!, 1986, Everything Glistens, Everything Sings, 1987, I Like to be Little, 1987, The Poodle Who Barked at the Wind, 1987, The Quiet Mother and the Noisy Little Boy, 1988, Something's Going to Happen, 1988, This Quiet Lady, 1992, The Seashore Book, 1992, Snippets, 1992, The Moon was the Best, 1993, Peter and the Pigeons, 1993, The Old Dog, 1995, When the Wind Stops, 1995, Who is Ben, 1997, Wake Up and Goodnight, Some Things Go Together, new edits., 1998, Do You Know What I'll Do?, new edit., 2000, When I Have a Little Girl When I Have a Little Boy, 2000; Overpraised Season, Early Sorrow. Recipient Harper Gold award for editorial excellence, 1974, Kerlan award U. Minn., 1986, Corp. award for children's books Lit. Market Pl., 1990, Silver medallion U. So. Miss., 1990, Tribute for Far Reaching Contbn. to Children's Lit., ALA, 1991, Otter award, 1997; Charlotte Zolotow award for text of disting. picture book U. Wis. named in her honor, 1998. Mem. PEN, Authors League. Home: 29 Elm Pl Hastings On Hudson NY 10706-1703 Office: 10 E 53d St New York NY 10022-5244

ZOMBEK, W. See **LAMANTIA, PAUL**

ZOMBONINI, RON, data processing executive; V.p. rsch. and devel. Cognos Inc., 1989—90, sr. v.p. rsch. and devel., 1990—93, pres., COO, 1993—95, CEO, 1995—. Office: Cognos Inc PO Box 9707 3755 Riverside Dr Ottawa ON Canada K1G 4K9*

ZOMPARELLI, WENDY, newspaper publisher; b. Chgo., 1950; d. Rocco and Eileen Zomparelli; m. André Spies; 1 child, Samuel Z. Spies. BA, Cornell U., 1971. Staff writer Raleigh (N.C.) Times, 1978-80; writer, copy editor Raleigh (N.C.) News and Observer, 1982-84; staff writer Roanoke (Va.) Times, 1984-85, asst. features editor, 1985, features editor, 1985-92, asst. to pres. and pub., 1992-95, editor, 1995-98, v.p., gen. mgr., 1998-2000, pres., pub., 2000—. Mem. Pulitzer Prize journalism awards jury, 1998-99. Mem.: Soc. Profl. Journalists, Am. Soc. Newspaper Editors, Phi Beta Kappa. Office: The Roanoke Times PO Box 2491 201 Campbell Ave SW Roanoke VA 24011-1100 E-mail: wendy.zomparelli@roanoke.com.

ZONA, LOUIS ALBERT, art institute director; s. Patricia Zona; 1 child, Tace. BS in Edn. magna cum laude, Youngstown (Ohio) State U., 1966; MS in Edn., U. Pitts., 1969; DFA, Carnegie Mellon U., 1973. Asst. to dir. The Butler Inst. of Am. Art, Youngstown, 1980-81, exec. dir., 1981—; prof. art history Youngstown State U., 1970—, chmn. art dept., 1978-82. Adj. prof. art and museology Westminster Coll., 1976-80. Contbr. numerous articles to profl. publs. Recipient Gari Melchers medla Artists' Fellowship, N.Y.C., 1996, Gov.'s award for the Arts in Ohio, 1990, Disting. Profl. Svc. award Ohio Steel Valley Art Tchrs. Assn., 1982. Office: Butler Inst Am Art 524 Wick Ave Youngstown OH 44502

ZONGOLOWICZ, HELEN MICHAELINE, education and psychology educator; b. Kenosha, Wis., July 22, 1936; d. Edmund S. and Helen (Ostrowski) Z. EdB, Dominican Coll., 1966; MA, Cardinal Stritch Coll., 1973; EdD, U. No. Colo., 1977. Tchr. elem. schs., Kenosha, 1956-58, Center Line, Mich., 1958-59, Taft, Calif., 1960-61, Lake Wales, Fla., 1962-63, Albuquerque, 1963-65; tchr., asst. prin. St. Mary's Sch., Taft, 1965-69; asst. sch. supt. Diocese of Fresno, Calif., 1969-70; tchr. primary grades Greasewood Boarding Sch., Ganado, Ariz., 1970-72, coord. spl. projects, 1972-75, liaison to parent adv. coun., 1972-75, 1972-75, ltchr. supr., 1972-76; ednl. specialist Ft. Defiance Agy., Navajo Area, Ariz., 1974-75, ednl. diagnostician, 1979-80; asst. prof. Auburn (Ala.) U., 1977-79, U.Mex.-Gallup, 1981-94, prof. edn. and psychology, 1994—, dir. child care ctr., pres. faculty senate, 1995-97; prin. Chuska Sch., 1980-93, chair dept. psychology/edn. CDA dir., 1995-2001, chair behavioral and social scis. dept, 1996—2001, chair psychology/edn. dept., 1995-2001, asst. dean instrn., 2001—. Vis. prof. U. Colo., 1976; mem. N.Mex. State Articulation Task Force, 1994—. Recipient Spl. Achievement award U.S. Dept. Interior, 1971, 73, Points of Light award, 1990, Superior Performance award, 1982, Achievement award Navajo Nation, 1993; named Prin. of Yr. Bur. of Indian Affairs, 1990, Navajo Area Sch. Bd. Assn., 1991. Mem. AAUW, ASCD, NAFE, Nat. Assn. Edn. of Young Children, Nat. Staff Devel. Coun., Am. Assn. Mental Deficiency, Coun. for Exceptional Children, Coun. for Basic Edn., Am. Ednl. Rsch. Assn., Internat. Reading Assn., Assn. for Children with Learning Disabilities, Nat. Coun. Tchrs. of English, Assn. Childhood Edn. Internat., Kappa Delta Pi, Phi Delta Kappa. Address: 604 Mckee Dr Gallup NM 87301-4830 E-mail: drz@gallup.unm.edu.

ZONKA, CONSTANCE ZIPPRODT, public relations executive, marketing professional; b. Evanston, Ill. d. Herbert Edward and Agnes Irene (Turpin) Zipprodt; m. Robert F. Zonka, Aug. 5, 1970; children: Heidi Zapanta, Milo Matthew. BA, U. Fla., 1958; postgrad., U. Chgo., 1960. Account exec. Daniel J. Edelman, Inc., Chgo., 1964-68; pres. Connie Zonka Assocs., 1974-89; dir. coll. rels. Columbia Coll., 1970-89; sr. dir. univ. rels. Roosevelt U., 1990-93; dir. office pub. affairs Gov.'s State U., University Park, 1993—2002. Mem.

NAFE, Pub. Rels. Soc. Am., Publicity Club Chgo., Nat. Assn. Women Bus. Owners, Friends of Downtown, Friends of the Parks. Democrat. Avocations: horseback riding, swimming, theatre, dance, reading. Home: 155 N Harbor Dr Apt 5106 Chicago IL 60601

ZONNEVILLE, ROBERT E. trucking company executive; b. Williamson, N.Y., Jan. 23, 1925; s. Adrian J. and Matie L. Z.; student U. Buffalo, 1949-52; m. Carol A. Alliger, June 7, 1947; children— Bethann, Robin, Kim, David. Dock worker Associated Transport, Buffalo, 1952-53, terminal mgr., 1960-66; terminal mgr. Spector Redball, Cleve., 1966-68, regional mgr., Wis., Minn. and Ill., 1968-71, v.p. central area, Northfield, Ohio, 1971-82; regional mgr., Inway Nationwide, 1982-87, v.p. 1987-89, pres., chief exec. officer, 1989—; v.p. nat. accounts, Landstar, 1995—. Pres. local Presbyn. Ch., Home Owners Assn., Mentor Gardens Home Owners Assn., 1987—; mem. golf com. City of Euclid, Ohio, 1975, com. to elect mayor of Euclid, 1979; sec., bd. dirs. Deercreek Time Share Owners, 1986-87. Served with U.S. Army, 1943-45. Decorated Purple Heart with oak leaf cluster, Bronze Star. Recipient awards for community activities, K.C., 1979. Mem. Western Res. Traffic Club. Clubs: Elks, Masons, Scottish Rite, Shriners. Home: 5803 Mallard Ct Mentor OH 44060-1811 Office: 7350 Palisades Pky Ste 34 Mentor OH 44060-5302

ZONSZEIN, JOEL, endocrinologist; b. Mexico City, Mex., Mar. 15, 1945; came to U.S., 1970; s. Szepsel and Elena (Sheinberg) Z.; m. Anat Arad Zonszein, Aug. 24, 1976; children: Yonatan, Mairav. MD, U. Nacional Autonoma de Mex., 1969. Cert. diabetes educator. Intern Maimonides Med. Ctr., Bklyn., 1970-71, resident, 1971-72, Bronx Mcpl. Hosp., 1972-73; endocrine fellow Northwestern U., Chgo., 1973-74, Georgetown U., Washington, 1974-75; chief endocrinology Bronx (N.Y.) Lebanon Hosp., 1980-93; prof. clin. medicine Albert Einstein Coll. Medicine, Bronx, 1986-2000, dir. Clin. Diabetes Ctr., 1993—, prof. clin. medicine, 2000—. Contbr. articles to profl. jours. Fellow ACP, Am. Coll. Endocrinology; mem. Am. Diabetes Assn. (chmn. Hispanic com. 1987—), Endocrine Soc. Office: 1199 Park Ave Apt 1H New York NY 10128-1713 E-mail: zonszein@aecom.yu.edu.

ZOOGMAN, NICHOLAS JAY, lawyer; b. N.Y.C., Apr. 2, 1947; s. Morris William and Hannah (Stern) Z.; m. Carla Ganz, June 7, 1970; children: Sarah Elizabeth, Peter William. BA, NYU, 1967; MA, Harvard U., 1969, JD, 1973. Bar: N.Y. 1974, U.S. Dist. Ct. (so. and ea. dists.) N.Y. 1974, U.S. Ct. Appeals (2d cir.) 1975, U.S. Supreme Ct. 1979, U.S. Dist. Ct. (ea. dist.) Mich. 1988, U.S. Ct. Appeals (D.C. cir.) 1990, U.S. Ct. Appeals (6th cir.) 1993, U.S. Ct. Appeals (5th cir.) 1997. Assoc. Donovan Leisure Newton & Irvine, N.Y.C., 1973-75; ptnr. Anderson Kill & Olick, 1976-2000; counsel Dickstein Shapiro Morin & Oshinsky, 2000—. Mem. ABA, N.Y. State Bar Assn., Assn. Bar City N.Y., Phi Beta Kappa, Pi Sigma Alpha. Office: Dickstein Shapiro Morin & Oshinsky 1177 Avenue of Americas New York NY 10036-2714 E-mail: zoogmann@dsmo.com.

ZOOK, BERNARD CHARLES, pathology educator, administrator, researcher; b. Beach, N.D., Nov. 1, 1935; s. Frank N. and Elizabeth Ferne (Kramer) Z.; m. Elinore A. Schillo, Oct. 1, 1955; children: Bernita, Melinda, Andrew. BS, Colo. State U., 1962, DVM, 1963; postgrad., Harvard U., 1963-68, Northeastern U., 1966. Diplomate Am. Coll. Vet. Pathologists. From rsch. fellow to asst. in pathology Med. Sch. Harvard U., Boston, 1963-68; from. rsch. fellow to assoc. pathologist Angell Meml. Animal Hosp., 1963-69; asst. prof. George Washington U., Washington, 1969-74, assoc. prof., 1974-83, prof. pathology, 1983—. Cons. comml. orgns. Contbr. articles on heart disease, poisoning, radiation injury, and other med. conditions to profl. jours. Mem. St. John's Choir, 1993—. Rsch. fellow Smithsonian Instn., 1969—; grantee NIH, 1967-68, Murray Corp., 1981-85, Nat. Cancer Inst., 1975-86, Population Coun., 1981-85, Motorola Corp., 1991—. Mem. Am. Coll. Vet. Soc., Soc. Toxicologic Pathologists, Nat. Soc. Med. Rsch. (bd. dirs. 1981-86), Bridge Club, KC, Beta Beta Beta, Phi Zeta. Republican. Roman Catholic. Avocations: music, painting. Office: George Washington U Med Ctr 2300 I St NW Washington DC 20037-2336

ZOOK, ELVIN GLENN, plastic surgeon, educator; b. Huntington County, Ind., Mar. 21, 1937; s. Glenn Hardman and Ruth (Barton) Z.; m. Sharon Kay Neher, Dec. 11, 1960; children— Tara E., Leigh A., Nicole L. BA, Manchester Coll., 1959; MD, Ind. U., 1963. Diplomate Am. Bd. Surgery, Am. Bd. Thoracic Surgery, Am. Bd. Plastic Surgery. Intern Meth. Hosp., Indpls., 1963-64; resident in gen. and thoracic surgery Ind. U. Med. Center, 1964-69; resident in plastic surgery Ind. U. Hosp., 1969-71, asst. prof. plastic surgery, 1971-73; asso. prof. surgery So. Ill. U., Springfield, 1973-75, prof., 1975—, chmn. div. plastic surgery, 1973—. Mem. staff Meml. Med. Center, St. Johns Hosp., Springfield. Contbr. articles to med. jours. Mem. AMA, Assn. Acad. Surgery, Am. Soc. Plastic and Reconstructive Surgery (sec. 1988-91, v.p. 1991-92, pres.-elect 1992-93, pres. 1993-94), Midwestern Soc. Plastic and Reconstructive Surgery (pres. 1986-87), ACS, Sangamon County Med. Soc. (pres. 1987), Am. Cleft Palate Assn., Am. Assn. Plastic Surgery (trustee 1987-90), Plastic Surgery Rsch. Coun. (chmn. 1981), Am. Burn Assn., Ill. Surg. Soc., Am. Soc. Surgery Hand (coun.), Am. Bd. of Plastic Surgery (sec.-treas. 1988-91, chmn. 1991-92), Am. Soc. Aesthetic Plastic Surgery, Am. Soc. Surgery of Trauma, Assn. Acad. Chmn. Plastic Surgery (pes. 1986-87), Am. Surg. Assn., RRC for Plastic Surgery, Sangamo Club, Springfield Med. Club, Island Bay Yacht Club. Clubs: Sangamo, Springfield Med, Island Bay Yacht. Presbyterian. Home: 7235 Mansion Rd Chatham IL 62629-8763 Office: 747 N Rutledge St Springfield IL 62702-6700 E-mail: ezook@siumed.edu. *Do the best possible in all that is possible.*

ZOOK, MARTHA FRANCES HARRIS, retired nursing administrator; b. Topeka, Nov. 15, 1921; d. Dwight Thacher and Helen Muriel (Houston) Harris; m. Paul Warren Zook, July 2, 1948 (dec. 1995); children: Mark Warren (dec.), Mary Elizabeth Zook Hughey. RN, Meriden (Conn.) Hosp./Yale U., 1947; student, U. Kans., 1948-49, Kans. State U., 1960-61, Barton County C.C., 1970-73; BA, Stephens Coll., 1977; postgrad., Ft. Hays State U., 1978-79. Staff nurse Stormont Hosp., Topeka, 1947-48, Watkins Meml. Hosp., Lawrence, Kans., 1948-49; nursing supr. Larned State Hosp., 1949-53, sect. supr., 1956-57, dir. nursing, 1958-61, 83-86; sect. nurse Sedgewick Sect., 1961-76, clin. instr. nursing edn., 1976-77, dir. nursing edn., 1977-83; clinic nurse for podiatrist; sect. supr. Dillon Bldg., Larned, 1957-58; ret., 1986. Mem. DAR, Sacred Heart Altar Soc. Democrat. Roman Catholic. Home: 1109 Johnson Ave Larned KS 67550-2232

ZOOK, MERLIN WAYNE, meteorologist, educator; b. Connellsville, Pa., July 2, 1937; s. Ellrose Durr and Frances Adeline (Loucks) Z.; m. Maxine Beatrice Hartzler, May 1, 1965; children: Kevin Ray, Kathleen Joy. BA, Goshen (Ind.) Coll., 1959; MS, Pa. State U., 1961. Cert. consulting meteorologist. Rsch. assoc. U. Mich., Ann Arbor, 1958; grad. asst. Pa. State U., University Park, 1960-61; audio-visual asst., staff meteorologist Mennonite Cen. Com., Akron, Pa., 1961-63; air quality program specialist Pa. Dept. Environ. Protection, Harrisburg, 1963-2000; ret., 2000. Book reviewer Sci. Edn. Dept. Boston U., 1990-92, Nat. Weather Assn., Temple Hills, Md., 1983-88, book rev. editor, 1988-92; scientist, participant AAAS-Bell Atlantic Found., Washington, 1989-90. Author, contbr.: (chpt.) Behind the Dim Unknown, 1966. Guest lectr. Millersville (Pa.) State U., 1988, 90, Boy Scouts Am., Camp Hill, Pa., 1990, Pa. State U., Middletown, 1990, 91—, Cub Scouts Am., Camp Hill, 1991—. Mem. Am. Meteorol. Soc., Union of Concerned Scientists. Achievements include development of models for the daily prediction of the Air Quality Index of Pa.; collection of cloud type photographs with classifications for study of cloud characteristics/physics; research in mesoscale meteorology and localized forecasting, on the relationship between solar radiation and formation of ozone in urban areas in Pa., research and development of mathematical models for the prediction of ozone episodes in urban areas; on migratory patterns of local birds influenced by meteorological conditions. Home: 105 June Dr Camp Hill PA 17011-5069 E-mail: mwzook@itech.net.

ZOOK, THERESA FUETTERER, gemologist, consultant; b. Barberton, Ohio, Mar. 12, 1919; d. Charles Theodore and Ethel May (Knisely) Fuetterer; m. Donovan Quay Zook, June 21, 1941; children: Theodore Alan, Jacqueline Deborah Zook Cochran. AB, Ohio U., 1941; MA in Pub. Adminstrn., Am. U., 1946. Adminstrv. intern Nat. Inst. Pub. Affairs, Washington, 1941-42; mgmt. intern USDA, 1941-42; adminstrv. analyst Office Emergency Mgmt., 1942-43, Office Price Adminstrn., Washington, 1943-45; founder Zook and Zook Mgmt. Cons., Arlington, Va., 1945-47; tchr. ancient history and U.S. govt. Fairfax County (Va.) Pub. Schs., 1963-64; founder, pres. Associated Gem Cons. Lab., Alexandria, 1974—, Alpha Gate Crafts Ltd., Alexandria, 1977—. Color cons. Internat. Com. on Color in Gems, Bangkok, 1983. Author: Directory of Selected Color Resources Annotated Guide, 1982, Reunion of Descendants of David and Magdalena (Blough) Zook, 1983, Basic Machine Knitting, 1979; contbr. articles to profl. jours. Bd. dirs. Am. Embassy Com. on Edn., Montevideo, Uruguay, 1962; co-founder Workshop of Arts, Santiago, Chile, 1958; mem. Nat. Trust for Hist. Preservation, Nat. Mus. Women in Arts, Nat. Mus. Am. Indian, Am. Horticulture Soc., Textile Mus. Fellow Gemmological Assn. of Gt. Britain (diplomate); mem. AAUW, DAR, Nat. Geneal. Soc., Inter-Soc. Color Coun. (chmn. com. color in gemstones 1982-84, Appreciation cert. 1984), Accredited Gemological Assn. (co-founder, v.p.), Phi Beta Kappa, Tau Kappa Alpha, Kappa Delta Pi. Avocations: garden design, knitting, fabric creation, genealogy, music. Home: PO Box 6310 Alexandria VA 22306-0310

ZOON, KATHRYN CHRISTINE, biochemist; b. Yonkers, N.Y., Nov. 6, 1948; d. August R. and Violet T. (Pollock) Egloff; m. Robert A. Zoon, Aug. 22, 1970; children: Christine K., Jennifer R. BS, Rensselaer Poly. Inst., 1970; PhD, Johns Hopkins U., 1975. Rsch. chemist divsn. biochem. biophys. Bur. Biologics FDA, Bethesda, Md., 1980-84, rsch. chemist divsn. virology, 1984-88, rsch. chemist divsn. cytokine biology Ctr. Biologics, 1988—, divsn. dir., 1989-92; dir. Ctr. Biologics Evaluation and Rsch., 1992—. Lectr. NIH, 1994, Reigelman Lectureship, 1994; chmn. expert com. on biol. standardization WHO, 1997-98, 99, 2000, 01; mem. adv. com. of CMR, 2000-. Contbr. articles to rsch. in biol. chemistry to sci. jours.; sect. editor Jour. Interferon and Cytokine Rsch., 1980—. Bd. dirs., 1st v.p. Found. Advanced Edn. Scis., 1997—; mem. adv. bd. Def. Advance Rsch. Projects Agy., 1998-2000. Recipient Rensselaer Alumni Assn. award, 1997, Person of the Yr. award Biopharm, 1992, Pub. Svc. and Genetic Engring. News award, 1995, Presdl. Meritorious Exec. Rank award, 1994, Grateful Patient award Nat. Assn. Cancer Patients, 1997, Secs. award for disting. svc. Dept. Health and Human Svcs., 2001; N.Y. State Regents fellow, 1970, Interferon rsch. fellow NIH, Bethesda, 1975-77, staff fellow, 1979-80. Mem. Am. Soc. Biochem. and Molecular Biology, Intenat. Soc. Interferon and Cytokine Rsch. (pres. elect 1998-99, pres. 2000-01), Internat. Assn. Biol. Standardization (mem. adv. coun. 2000—). Roman Catholic. Office: CBER 1401 Rockville Pike Rockville MD 20852-1428 Personal E-mail: kzoon@comcast.net. Business E-Mail: zoon@cber.fda.gov.

ZOPF, PAUL EDWARD, JR. sociologist; b. Bridgeport, Conn., July 9, 1931; s. Paul Edward and Hilda Ernestine (Russell) Z.; m. Evelyn Lanoel Montgomery, Aug. 5, 1956; 1 child, Eric Paul. BS, U. Conn., 1953; MS, U. Fla., 1955, PhD, 1966. Asst. prof. sociology Guilford Coll., Greensboro, N.C., 1959-66, assoc. prof., 1966-70, prof., 1970-72, Dana prof. sociology, 1972-93; Dana prof. sociology emeritus, 1993—; chief. coll. marshal, 1997—. Cons. U.S. Dept. Agrl., local govt. agys. Author: North Carolina: A Demographic Profile, 1967, Demography: Principles and Methods, 1970, 76, Principles of Inductive Rural Sociology, 1970, Profile of Women in Greensboro: 1990, 1977, Sociocultural Systems, 1978, Cultural Accumulation in Latin America, 1980, Population: An Introduction to Social Demography, 1984, Income and Poverty Status of Women in Greensboro, 1985, America's Older Population, 1986, American Women in Poverty, 1989, Mortality Patterns and Trends in the United States, 1992; editor Guilford Coll. Self-Study Accreditation Report; contbr. articles to profl. jours. Recipient Teaching Excellence award Guilford Coll., 1978; grantee Kenan Found., 1970-79, Guilford Coll., 1979-93. Mem. Am. Acad. Polit. and Social Sci., Am. Sociol. Assn., Internat. Union Sci. Study Population, So. Sociol. Soc., Rural Sociol. Soc., Population Reference Bur. Mem. Soc. Of Friends. Home: 815 George White Rd Greensboro NC 27410-3317 Office: Guilford Coll Dept Sociology Greensboro NC 27410 *In my role as professor, researcher and author, I have oriented my activities to the service of students, my institution, my professional discipline, and various community agencies. I have found that pursuing various professional processes that I enjoy and can handle adequately, is the real reward. Honors, if they come, are a by-product of that pursuit; they would be elusive and perpetually inadequate if they were the principal reason for my efforts.*

ZORICK, NANCY LEE, artist, actress; b. Chgo., July 24, 1946; d. William Russel and Wilma Beatrice (Fithian) Noble; m. Peter Michael Zorick, Aug. 8, 1980. Student, Art Inst. Chgo., 1965-67, Second City Workshop, Chgo., 1967-68, Am. Acad. Art, 1971. Comml. artist Embosograph Display Co., Chgo., 1964-66, Stevens-Biondi-DiCiccio, Chgo., 1966-68. Illustrator: (book) Making Weight, 1991, (children's book) The Little Acorn, 1996; exhibns. include Fontana (Calif.) Arts Assn., 1988, Riverside County Art Exhibnn., 1990; appeared in plays My Sweet Charlie, Chgo., 1968, Harold, Chgo., 1969, films include Medium Cool, 1968, Jackson County Jail, 1976, Outside Chance, 1978; appeared in commercial Tastee Freeze, 1969. Mem Des Arts, 1981, historian, 1983—85, parliamentarian, 1986—93, 1996—, pres., 1993—95. Named to Taft Alumni Hall of Fame, Chgo., 2000; recipient 1st Place in Fine Arts, Nat. Date Festival, 1983, 2d place, Riverside Nat. Date. Festival, 1993, Riverside Nat. Date Festival, 1996, 2001, Best of Show in Fine Arts, Des-Arts Show, 1988, 1st place, Des Arts, 2000, 2001, Best of Show in Fine Arts, Fontana (Calif.) Arts Assn., 1988. Avocations: teaching Sunday school, ballet and art, volunteering. Home: 51-555 Monroe St #31 Indio CA 92201

ZORIE, STEPHANIE MARIE, lawyer; b. Walla Walla, Wash., Mar. 18, 1951; d. Albert Robert and L. Ruth (Land) Z.; m. Francis Benedict Buda, Apr. 18, 1981 (div. 1985). BA, U. Fla., 1974, JD, 1978. Bar: N.Mex. 1991, Fla. 1978, U.S. Dist. Ct. (so. and mid. dists.) Fla. 1979, U.S. Ct. Appeals (5th cir.) 1979, U.S. Tax Ct. 1980, U.S. Ct. Customs and Patent Appeals 1980, U.S. Customs Ct. 1980, U.S. Ct. Mil. Appeals 1980, U.S. Ct. Claims 1981, U.S. Ct. Internat. Trade 1981, U.S. Ct. Appeals (11th cir.) 1981, U.S. Ct. Appeals (fed. cir.) 1982, U.S. Supreme Ct. 1988; cert. civil ct. mediator Fla. Supreme Ct.; cert. family mediator, N.Mex. Assoc. Richard Hardwich, Coral Gables, Fla., 1978-79, Brown, Terrell & Hogan P.A., Jacksonville, 1979-80, Dorsey, Arnold & Nichols, Jacksonville, 1980-81; sole practice, 1981-84; ptnr. Blakeley & Zorie P.A., Orlando, 1985-86; sole practice, 1986—, Santa Fe. Owner Coyote Cody Co., 1991. Recipient Rep. Claude Pepper award, 1978. Mem. John Marshall Bar Assn., Spanish-Am. Law Students Assn., Phi Alpha Delta (local sec.-treas. 1978-79). Avocations: water sports, needlework, cooking. Office: PO Box 2898 Santa Fe NM 87504-2898 also: PO Box 372118 Melbourne FL 32937-0118

ZORITCH, GEORGE, dance educator, choreographer; b. Moscow, June 6, 1917; came to U.S., 1935; s. Serge and Helen (Grunke) Z. Diploma, Lady Deterding's Russian Sch., Paris, 1933. Mem. Ida Rubinstein Ballet Co., Paris, 1933-34, Pavlova's Co., Eng., W.I., Australia, India, Egypt, 1934-35, Col. W. de Basil's Balle Russe de Monte-Carlo, U.S., Europe, 1935-37; soloist Denham Ballet Russe de Monte-Carlo, U.S., Can., S.Am., Europe, 1938-42; actor, dancer in plays, musicals, concert tours, Broadway and across U.S., S.Am. and Europe, 1943-50; actor 17 movies in Hollywood and Rome; premier danseur noble Grand Ballet de Marquis de Cuevas, Europe, Africa, S.Am., 1951-57, Denham Ballet Russe de Monte Carlo, U.S.A., 1957-62; founder George Zoritch Sch. Classical Ballet, West Hollywood, Calif., 1963-73; prof. fine arts, mem. dance faculty com. fine arts U. Ariz., 1973-87. Freelance engagements, 1973—; symposium panelist New Orleans Internat. Ballet Conf. for A Ballets Russes Celebration, 2000; hon. guest IX Internat. Competition of Ballet Artists, June 2001, courtesy of Bolshoi Theatre, Moscow. Author: (memoir) Ballet Mystique, 2000; editor records: George Zoritch for Classical Ballet, 1962-65. Hon. guest Bolshoi Ballet, Moscow, Russia, 2001. Recipient Key to Jacksonville (Fla.), 1968, Bolshoi Theatre medallion of merit award IV Internat. Ballet Competition, Moscow, 1981, Ariz. Dance Treasures award Ariz. Dance Arts Alliance and Ariz. State U. Dept. Dance, 1992, Merit award Acad. Choreographic Sch. A. Vaganova, 1993, Vaslav Nijinsky medallion of merit award Consulate Gen. of Poland, 1994, Diaghilev House Silver Medallion of Merit award 6th Dance Competition of Paris, 1994, U. Ariz. Spl. Tribute, 2001, Life Time Achievement award Western Mich. U., 2002; named Amb. San Antonio World Hemisphere, 1968. Mem. Ariz. Dance Arts Alliance (hon. life), Phoenix Ballet Gild (hon.), Nat. Soc. Arts and Letters (Medallion of Merit award Valley of Sun chpt. 1990). E-mail: zoritch@dakotacom.net.

ZORKO, MARK A. financial executive; b. Cleve., Mar. 11, 1952; s. Frank A. and Dorothy E. (Bever) Z.; m. Sue A. Langdon, Sept. 6, 1975; children: Jennifer, Andrew. BS in Acctg., Ohio State U., 1976; MBA in Mgmt. Info Systems, U. Minn., 1977. CPA; CPIM. Sr. staff cons. Arthur Andersen & Co., Mpls., 1978-80; fin. mgr. Honeywell, Inc., Mpls. and Brussels, 1980-87; corp. contr. Zenith Data Systems Corp., St. Joseph, Mich., 1987-91; CFO Inverness Castings Group, Inc., Bangor, 1991-93; v.p. fin., sec., CFO Comptronix Corp., Huntsville, Ala., 1993-94; v.p., CFO and chief info. officer Network Svcs. Co., Mt. Prospect, Ill., 1995-99; with Tatum CFO Ptnrs, LLP, Chgo., 2000—. Bd. dirs. Intellimedia Corp. Treas., bd. dirs. United Way, St. Joseph, 1988-93. Sgt. USMC, 1970-73. Mem. AICPA, Fin. Execs. Inst., Nat. Assn. Corp. Treas., Am. Prodn. and Inventory Control Soc., Assn. for Corp. Growth. Methodist. Avocations: sailing, skiing, golf, triathlon. Office: Tatum CFO Partners LLP PMB 3042 125 S Wacker Dr Ste 300 Chicago IL 60606 E-mail: MAZorko@attglobal.net.

ZORN, ELIZABETH C. artist; One-woman shows include Cafe Gallery, Cin., 1994, BASE Art Gallery, Cin., 1996, Enjoy the Arts, Cin., 1998, Suzanna Terrill Gallery, Cin., 1999, Alley Shop, Cin., 1999, Suzanna Terrill Gallery, Cin., 2001; group shows include Cage Gallery, Cin., 1994, 95, Artique Gallery, Middletown, Ohio, 1994, 96, LRC Gallery, Dayton, Ohio, 1995, Phoenix Gallery, Oneonta, N.Y., 1995, Ohio State Fair, Columbus, 1995, Evansville Mus. Art, Ind., 1996, Dairy Barn Cultural Arts Ctr., Athens, Ohio, 1997, Blue Rock Gallery, Cin., 1997, Woman Made Gallery, Chgo., 1997, Fitton Ctr. Arts, Hamilton, Ohio, 1997, Layman's Perspective, Ohio Art League, Columbus, Ohio, 1999, Seeding the Snow, Woman Made Gallery, Chgo., 1999, others; author: It's Happening Again, 1993, (poetry chapbook) The Home Series.; pub., editor Mine's Eye Newsletter. Mem. Nat. Women Writers Guild, Fine Arts Orgn.

ZORN, ROBERT LYNN, education educator; b. Youngstown, Ohio, Mar. 22, 1938; s. Robert S. and Frances L. Zorn; B.S. Ed., Kent State U., 1959; M.Ed., Westminster Coll., 1964; Ph.D., U. Pitts., 1970; m. Joan M. Wilkos, Apr. 26, 1957; children: Deborah Lynn, Patricia Lynn. Tchr., West Branch (Ohio) Schs., 1961-62; elem. prin. Poland (Ohio) Schs., 1962-67, supt. schs., 1976— ; high sch. unit prin. Boardman (Ohio) Schs., 1967-70; dir. adminstrv. services Mahoning County (Ohio) Schs., 1970-73, asst. supt., 1973-76; adj. prof. edn. Westminster Coll., 1985—; chmn. Ohi Adv. Com. to State Dept. Edn.; chmn. McGuffey Hist. Soc. Nat. Educator's Hall of Fame. Chmn. Mahoning County chpt. Am. Cancer Soc.; pres. bd. trustees Poland Methodist Ch.; trustee Mahoning County chpt. Am. Heart Assn. Served to lt. USAF, 1959-61. Mem. Doctoral Assn. Educators (life), Am. Assn. Sch. Adminstrs., Ohio PTA (life; Educator of Yr. 1980-81), Phi Delta Kappa. Republican. Clubs: Fonderlac County, Rotary, Protestant Men's. Author numerous books including Speed Reading, 1989, rev. edit., 1997; contbr. articles to profl. jours. Office: 30 Riverside Dr Youngstown OH 44514-2049

ZORNES, MILFORD, artist; b. Camargo, Okla., Jan. 25, 1908; s. James Francis and Clara Delphine (Lindsay) Z.; m. Gloria Codd, 1935; 1 son, Franz Milford; m. Patricia Mary Palmer, Nov. 8, 1942; 1 dau., Maria Patricia. Student, Otis Art Inst., Los Angeles, 1929, Pomona Coll., 1930-34. Instr. art Pomona Coll., 1946-50; art dir. Vortox and Padua Hills Theatre, Claremont, 1954-66. Exhibited, Calif. Watercolor Soc., Met. Mus., Am. Watercolor Soc., Corcoran Gallery, Bklyn. Mus., Denver Mus., Cleve. Mus., L.A. Mus., Brooks Gallery, London, Bombay Art Assn., Chgo. Art Inst., Butler Mus., Gallery Modern Masters, Washington, Santa Barbara (Calif.) Mus., Cin. Mus., Laguna (Calif.) Art Gallery, Oklahoma City Mus., Springville (Utah) Mus., Claremont (Calif.) Fine Arts, Anderson Art Gallery, Sunset Beach, Calif.; represented in permanent collections at L.A. Mus., White House Collection, Met. Mus., Pentagon Bldg., Butler Mus., UCLA, Nat. Acad., San Diego Mus., L.A. County Fair, Home Savs. and Loan Assn., L.A., Corcoran Gallery, Washington; mem. art com., Nat. Orange Show, San Bernardino, Calif., 1963-65; author: A Journey to Nicaragua, 1977, The California Style: California Watercolor Artists, 1925-1955, 1985; subject of book by Gordon McClelland: Milford Zornes, Hillcrest Press, 1991. Served with U.S. Army, 1943-45, CBI. Recipient Paul Prescott Barrow award Pomona Coll., 1987, David Prescott Burrows award, 1991, A Most Disting. Citizen award So. Utah State Coll., 1988, Am. Artist Achievement award Am. Artist Mag., 1994; named Nat. Academician. Mem. NAD, Am. Watercolor Soc., Southwestern Watercolor Soc., Watercolor West, Nat. Watercolor Soc., Utah Watercolor Soc. Address: 2136 Brescia Ave Claremont CA 91711-1804 *It has been my effort in life to have awareness: not to have all knowledge because no one can encompass all knowledge; not to have only wealth or only success, because there is no dimension of completeness of wealth or success; not to achieve complete goodness, because goodness and right are relative; not to enjoy the epitomy in taste because taste is a gratification of self alone; but rather to seek and achieve understanding of relative values and a concept of the completeness of life. With this as my effort and my inner goal, I find success within the areas of my limited abilities, my meager knowledge, and my frail grasp of the infinite.*

ZORNOW, DAVID M. lawyer; b. N.Y.C., Mar. 31, 1955; s. Jack and Marion (Gilden) Z.; m. Martha Malkin, July 21, 1985; children: Samuel Morris, Hannah Jane, Ethan Lewis. AB summa cum laude, Harvard U., 1976; JD, Yale U., 1980. Bar: N.Y. 1981, U.S. Ct. Appeals (3d cir.) 1982, U.S. Dist. Ct. (so. dist.) N.Y. 1983, U.S. Ct. Appeals (2d cir.) 1984, U.S. Dist. Ct. D.C. 1989, U.S. Ct. Appeals (D.C. cir.) 1989, U.S. Dist. Ct. Ariz. 1990, U.S. Dist. Ct. (ea. dist.) N.Y. 1993. Law clerk to Judge Herbert J. Stern U.S. Dist. Ct. N.J., Newark, 1980-82; assoc. Kramer Levin Kamin Nessen & Frankel, N.Y.C., 1982-83; asst. U.S. atty. so. dist. N.Y. U.S. Atty.'s Office, 1983-87; assoc. counsel Office Ind. Counsel-Iran/Contra Investigation, Washington, 1987-89; ptnr. Skadden Arps Slate Meagher & Flom LLP, N.Y.C., 1989—. Chmn. N.Y.C. Civilian Complaint Rev. Bd., 1994-96; vis. faculty Trial Advocacy Workshop Harvard Law Sch., Cambridge, Mass., 1988. Mem. ABA (com. on white collar crime), Fed. Bar Coun., Assn. of Bar of City of N.Y., N.Y. Coun. Def. Lawyers. Office: Skadden Arps Slate Meagher & Flom LLP 4 Times Sq Fl 33 New York NY 10036-6595 E-mail: dzornow@skadden.com.

ZORNOW, WILLIAM FRANK, historian, educator; b. Cleve., Aug. 13, 1920; s. William Frederick Emil and Viola (Schulz) Z. AB, Western Res. U., 1942, A.M., 1944, PhD, 1952. Vice pres., treas. Glenville Coal & Supply Co., Real Value Coal Corp., Zornow Coal Corp., 1941-45; dep. clk. Probate Ct., Cuyahoga County, Ohio, 1941-43; prodn. planning engr. Hickok Elec. Instrument Co., Cleve., 1943-46; teaching asst. Western Res. U., 1944-47; instr. U. Akron, 1946-47, Case Inst. Tech., 1947-50, Washburn U., 1950-51; lectr. Cleve. Coll., 1948-49; asst. prof. Kans. State U., 1951-58; asst. prof. history Kent (Ohio) State U., 1958-61, asso. prof., 1961-66, prof. history, 1966—. Perpetual hon. fellow Harry S. Truman Libr. Inst., Independence, Mo.; collection corr. Berkshire Loan and Fin. Co., Painesville (Ohio) Security Credit Acceptance Corp., Mentor, Ohio, 1951-60; cons. Karl E. Mundt Library, Dakota State Coll., Madison, S.D.; presenter 1st coll. arts and scis. faculty lecture series Kent State U., 1962. Author: Lincoln and the Party Divided, 1954, rev. edit., 1972, Kansas: A History of the Jayhawk State, 1957, America at Mid-Century, 1959, The Many Faces of Lincoln, 1997; author: (with others) Abraham Lincoln: A New Portrait, 1959, Kansas: The First Century, 1956, The Many Faces of Lincoln, 1997; contbr. articles to encys. and profl. jours.; editor: Shawnee County (Kans.) Hist. Bull, 1950-51; abstractor: America: History and Life: Historical Abstracts, 1964— . Mem. Dir.'s Circle Cleve. Mus. Art, 1989—, Cleve. Clin. Found., 1992—, Soc. Fellows. Faculty rsch. grantee Kans. State U., 1955-57, Kent State U., 1960-64. Mem. AAAS, AAUP, N.Y. Acad. Scis., Soc. Fellow of Cleve. Clinic Found., Am. Acad. Polit. and Social Sci., Am. Assn. State and Local History (award of merit 1958), Am. Hist. Assn., Orgn. Am. historians, Ohio Acad. History (chmn. awards com.), Ohio Hist. Soc. (libr. adv. com. 1969—), Ohio Soc. N.Y., Ctr. Study of Presidency, Acad. Polit. Sci., Lincoln Fellowship of Wis., Sierra Club San Francisco, Delta Tau Delta (4-star coun. 1992—), Pi Gamma Mu, Phi Alpha Theta, Phi Delta Kappa. Home: 7893 Middlesex Rd Mentor OH 44060-7617 Office: Kent State U 305 Bowman Dr Kent OH 44240-4507

ZOROWITZ, RICHARD DAVID, physiatrics educator; b. Teaneck, N.J., Nov. 23, 1958; s. Irving Monroe and Selma Doris Zorowitz; m. Candace Stair, June 25, 1989; children: Samuel, Joel. BS, Northwestern U., 1981; MD, Tulane U., 1985. Diplomate Am. Bd. Phys. Medicine and Rehab. Internal medicine intern L.I. Jewish Med. Ctr., 1986; resident in phys. medicine and rehab. Northwestern U., 1986-89; asst. prof. phys. medicine and rehab. U. Medicine Dentistry N.J.-N.J. Med. Sch., Newark, 1991-95; asst. prof. rehab. medicine U. Pa., Phila., 1995-2001, assoc. prof. rehab. medicine, 2001—; med. dir. Piersol rehab. unit Hosp. U. Pa., 1997—. Dir. stroke svcs. Kessler Inst. for Rehab., East Orange, N.J., 1992-95. Cubmaster pack 36 Cub Scouts Am., Cherry Hill, N.J., 1999. Recipient career achievement award for stroke caregiving Nat. Stroke and Quality of Life Med. Edn. Inst., 1996. Mem. Am. Acad. Phys. Medicine and Rehab., Assn. Acad. Physiatrists, Am. Heart Assn. (fellow stroke coun., Operation Stroke Inst. award S.E. Pa. region 2001, Outstanding Leadership award 2002), Nat. Stroke Assn. (Excellence in Stroke Edn. award 2000), Visionary in Practice Soc., Phi Eta Sigma, Tau Beta Pi. Democrat. Avocations: swimming, music, theatre. Office: U Pa Med Ctr 3400 Spruce St Philadelphia PA 19104-4283

ZORTHIAN, BARRY, communications executive; b. Kutahia, Turkey, Oct. 8, 1920; , naturalized, US, 1930; s. Herbert Peter and Annaly (Markarian) Zorthian; m. Margaret Aylaian, June 6, 1948; children: Gregory Jannig, Stephen Arnak. BA, Yale U., 1941; LLB, N.Y. U., 1953; LLD (hon.), Ind. Inst. Tech., 1970. Bar: NY 1953. Newspaper reporter, 1936-42; newspaper and radio reporter, 1947-48; news and policy editor USIA, 1948-56, program mgr. Voice of Am., 1956-61; dep. pub. affairs. officer USIS, India, 1961-64; min.-counselor for info. Am. Embassy, Vietnam, 1964-68; v.p. Time, Inc., 1969-79, v.p. govt. affairs, 1974-79; pres. Time-Life Broadcast, 1969-73, Washington/Balt. Regional Assn., 1979-81; sr. v.p. Gray and Co., Washington, 1981-84; ptnr. Alcalde & Fay, Arlington, Va., 1984—2001. Bd dirs Am. Univ. Armenia, Armenian Gen Benvolent Union, Internat. Rsch. and Exchs. With USMC, 1942—46, col USMCR, 1946—73. Mem.: Marine Corps Res. Officers Assn., Washington Inst. Fgn. Affairs, Am. Fgn. Svc. Assn., Coun. Fgn. Rels., Congl. Country Club (Washington), Met. Club (Washington), Burning Tree Club (Washington), Century Assn. Club (N.Y.C.). Home: 4201 Cathedral Ave NW Apt 405E Washington DC 20016-4914 Office: Alcalde & Fay 2111 Wilson Blvd Ste 850 Arlington VA 22201-3051 E-mail: barzor2@aol.com.

ZOSIKE, JOANIE FRITZ, theater director, actor; b. Bklyn., July 6, 1949; d. Nathan and Gloria S. (Greenberg) Hieger; m. Godson Zosike. BA in Theatre, NYU, 1980. Actor Living Theatre, N.Y.C., 1990—. Co-dir. DADAnewyork; co-founder Action Racket Theater, N.Y.C.; artist-in-residence Teachers and Writers Collaborative. Author: (stage prodns.) You Told Me That the Carousel Was Crystal, Frames, Inside, 12 Steps to Murder; author: (with Hanon Reznikov) And Then The Heavens Closed; actress (stage prodns.) Chisciotte, Not in My Name, Mysteries and Smaller Pieces, Utopia, Humanity, Body of God, I and I, Midsummer Night's Dream, Mother Courage, Resistance, (solo performances) All Right So I AM the Earth, Harpies Complex, Ereshkigal's Peg, Fritzgabriel Cabaret, Alen Mak Festival (Bulgaria), Festival des Politisches Liedes (Germany), (films) Mass and Masses, Human Flesh; vocalist (radio show) Women on the Edge of Time; contbr. Between Ourselves: Letters Between Mothers and Daughters (edited by Karen Payne), Women in American Theatre (edited by Helen Krich Chinoy and Linda Walsh Jenkins); contbr. poetry and articles to artistic jours. Bd. dirs. N.Y.C. Peoples Life Fund. Mem. War Resisters League, New Yorkers Against the Death Penalty. Office: The Living Theatre 800 West End Ave Ste 5-a New York NY 10025-5467 E-mail: johizo@hotmail.com.

ZOSS, ABRAHAM OSCAR, chemical company executive; b. South Bend, Ind., Feb. 17, 1917; s. Harry and Fannie (Friedman) Z.; m. Betty Jane Hurwich, Dec. 24, 1939; children: Roger, Joel, Hope; m. Magda Szanto, May 26, 1978. BSChemE, U. Notre Dame, 1938, MS, 1939, PhD, 1941. With Gen. Aniline & Film Corp., Easton, Pa., 1941—47, from tech. mgr. to plant mgr. Linden, NJ, 1947—57; from mfr. mfg. adminstrn. to prodn. mgr. chem. divsn. Minn. Mining & Mfg. Co., St. Paul, 1957—60; v.p. Photek, Inc., West Kingston, RI, 1960—62; asst. corp. tech. dir. Celanese Corp., N.Y.C., 1962—65, corp. tech. dir., 1965—66, corp. dir. comml. devel., 1966—69; v.p. corp. devel. Tenneco Chems., Inc., 1969—71, Universal Oil Products Co., Des Plaines, Ill., 1971—72; group v.p. Engelhard Industries divsn. Engelhard Minerals & Chem. Corp., Murray Hill, NJ, 1972—74, v.p. bus. devel., 1974—77; v.p. corp. devel. CPS Chem. Co., Inc., Old Bridge, 1977, dir., v.p., chief adminstrv. officer, 1978—84; pres. Bus. Devel. Internat., N.Y.C., 1984—. Mem. field info. agy. Office Tech. Svc., Commerce Dept., Europe, 1946; tchg. asst. U. Notre Dame, 1939-41. Contbr. articles to profl. jours.; patentee in field. Active Met. Mus. Art., N.Y.C. Recipient Centennial Sci. award U. Notre Dame, 1965, accredited Profl. Chemist, 1980. Fellow AAAS, Am. Inst. Chemists; mem. AIChE, Am. Chem. Soc., N.Y. Acad. Scis., Comml. Devel. Assn., Soc. Chem. Industry, Soc. Plastics Engrs., Soc. Chimie Industrielle (pres. Am. sect.), Chemists Club (N.Y.C.). Home and Office: 333 Elmwood Ave Ste D538 Maplewood NJ 07040-2449 E-mail: aozoss@aol.com.

ZOU, XIAOLEI, meteorologist, educator; b. Jiang Ying, China, May 5, 1960; d. Shixi Zou and Jingan Li; m. Yuanzheng Yao; children: Yimei (Laura) Yao, Yige (Noah) Yao. PhD in Meteorology, Acad. Sinica, Beijing, China, 1988. Fellow U. Ill. Urbana-Champaign, 1989—89, Fla. State U., Tallahassee, 1989—93; scientist Nat. Ctr. Atmospheric Rsch., Boulder, Colo., 1993—97; prof. Fla. State U., Tallahassee, 1997—. Grantee, NOAA, 1997, 2001—, Air Force Office, 1997—99, NSF, 1998—2001, 1999—2002, 2001—, Office of Naval Rsch., 1998—2001, DoD, 1998—2002, NASA, 2000—, 2001—, ONR, 2001—. Mem.: Royal Meteorol. Soc., Am. Geophy. Union, Am. Meteorol. Soc. Office: Fla State Univ 404 Love Bldg Tallahassee FL 32306 Office Fax: 850-644-9642. Business E-Mail: zou@met.fsu.edu.

ZOU, ZHEN, English and Chinese educator, translator and critic, computer technologist; b. Ganzhou, Jiangxi, China, Sept. 12, 1954; came to U.S., 1998; s. Xunqing and Jilie (Li) Z.; m. Ling Wang, Sept. 4, 1982; 1 child, Jia. BA, Jiangxi Normal U., 1982; MA, Peking U., Beijing, 1989, PhD, 1999. Lectr. Jiangxi Normal U., Nanchang, 1982-86; tchg. asst. Peking U., Beijing, China, 1986-89, asst. prof. China, 1989-95, assoc. prof. China, 1997—, dir. grad. English tchg. divsn. China, 1989-91; vis. scholar SUNY, New Paltz, 1991-92; tchg. asst. Purdue U., West Lafayette, Ind., 1995-97, tchr. and rsch. asst., coord., 1998-2000; edn. specialist U. Minn., Mpls., 2000—, lead tchr., 2001—. Chief editor: An English Listening and Speaking Course for Graduate Students, 1996; contbr. articles to profl. jours. Grantee Purdue Rsch. Found., 1999; Winner Translation Contest, English Rev. Mag., 1983; Guanghua award Peking U., 1993-94. Mem. MLA, Chinese Lang. Tchrs. Assn., Peking U. Lit. and Translation Rsch. Soc. (v.p.). Avocations: swimming, skating, table tennis. Office: U Minn Lang Ctr 51 Folwell Hall 9 Pleasant St SE Minneapolis MN 55455 E-mail: zzou6@hotmail.com.

ZOUBAREFF, KATHY OLGA, administrative assistant; b. Hassalt, Belgium; d. Vladimir F. and Kataryna (Sarcov) Z. Grad. in TV acting, J.R. Powers Sch.-Model Agy.; BA in Polit. Sci., Wayne State U.; postgrad., Ann Parsley Sch. Dance, Clinton Twp., Mich., 1990-95, Mary Skiba Sch. Dance, 1995—; A in Gen. Studies, Drama, Macomb Community Coll.; fitness and nutrition cert., Internat. Corr. Schs. Ctr., Scranton, Pa.; voice studies, Ctr. for Creative Studies, Detroit, 1994—; drama studies, Wayne State U., 1994—; broadcasting studies, Macomb C.C., Warren, Mich., 2001. Acct./adminstrv. asst. Univ. Orthopaedic Assocs. Detroit, P.C., 1990-96, office mgr., 1996-98; with The Zoubareff Co., 1998—. Actress, dancer, fashion, TV comml. and photog. model/film screen extra, Hawaiian Tropic Pageants; fragrance model; swimsuit model Ujena; nat. spokesperson Dryell, Physique, Pantene, Oil of O'Lay, Vidal Sassoon, others. Mem. Renaissance Ctr. Fashion Panel, Detroit, 1989-91; rsch. bd. advisors Am. Biog. Inst.; mem. Internat. Biog. Centre Adv. Coun., 1992, St. Clair Shores Players. Avocations: art, drawing, exercising, reading, singing. Home: 38579 Delta Dr Clinton Township MI 48036-1711 Office: Univ Orthopaedics 4707 Saint Antoine St Detroit MI 48201-1427

ZOUFONOUN, AMIR H. electrical engineer; b. Nov. 6, 1959; BSEE, San Jose State U., 1982; MSEE, Santa Clara U., 1986. Devel. engr. Harris Group, 1979-84, engrng. mgr., 1985-89; v.p. engring. Glenayre Western Multiplex, Sunnyvale, Calif., 1989-97, gen. mgr., 1998—.

ZOUHARY, KATHLEEN MAHER, lawyer; b. Greenville, Ohio, June 28, 1951; d. Thomas Richard and Mary (Brown) Maher; m. Jack Zouhary, Oct. 21, 1978; children: Kathleen Marie, Alexis Jacqueline. BA in Polit. Sci. cum laude, Miami U., Oxford, Ohio, 1973; JD cum laude, U. Notre Dame, 1976. Bar: Ohio 1976. Assoc. Fuller & Henry, Toledo, 1976—81, prin., 1981—85; v.p., gen. counsel St. Luke's Hosp., Maumee, 1985—. Bd. dirs. Women Involved in Toledo, 1981—83; trustee Toledo Legal Aid ., 1977—90; bd. trustees Miami U., Oxford, Ohio, 1998—, Toledo Legal Aid Soc., 1977—90; chmn. bd. Notre Dame Acad., 1999—2000; gen. chmn. Tribute to Women and Industry, Toledo, 1984, honoree, 1982. Mem. ABA, Am. Health Lawyers Assn., Ohio Bar Assn., Toledo Bar Assn., Miami Presidents Club, St. Luke's Hosp. Pacesetter Club, Phi Beta Kappa. Office: St Luke's Hosp 5901 Monclova Rd Maumee OH 43537-1899 E-mail: kathleen.zouhary@stlukeshospital.com.

ZOULLAS, DEBORAH DECOTIS, private investor, entrepreneur; b. Salem, Mass., Nov. 13, 1952; d. John and Marie (Mahoney) DeC.; m. Nicholas B. Zoullas, Aug. 15, 1987. BA, Smith Coll., 1974; MBA, Stanford U., 1978. Analyst Morgan Stanley & Co. Inc., N.Y.C., 1974-76, assoc., 1978-81, v.p. London, 1982-84, prin. N.Y.C., 1985-87, mng. dir., 1988-95, adv. dir., 1996—; exec. v.p. Sotheby's Holdings, 1998—2000; dir. Sotheby's Holding Corp., 2000, Armor Holdings Inc., 2002—. Mem. exec. com. spl. projects com. Meml. Sloan Kettering Cancer Ctr. Chair Stanford U. Bus. Sch. Trust; trustee Helena Rubinstein Found. Miller scholar Stanford U., 1978. Home: 160 E 72d St New York NY 10021

ZOUTES, TONYA CASTLEMAN, journalist; b. Flint, Mich., June 15, 1964; d. Thomas Earl and Kay Janis (Corey) Snowball; m. Byron Thomas Castleman, July 29, 1985 (div. 1995); 1 child, Naomi Michelle; m. Edward Peter Zoutes, Oct. 23, 1999. BA in Mass Communications, U. South Fla., 1987. Art specialist U.S. DOD Schs., Fort Davis, Panama, 1986-87; corr. St. Petersburg (Fla.) Times, 1987, copy editor II, 1995-96; tchr. English as a second lang. Colegio Internat., Del Caribe, Panama, 1987-88; sect. editor Fort Campbell (Ky.) Courier, 1989-90; copy editor Ky. New Era, Hopkinsville, 1991-93, Insight Mag., Washington, 1993-94; news editor Washington Times Weekly, 1994-95; info. svcs. tech. writer, documentation splst. Riscorp Ins. Co., Sarasota, 1996-98; freelance journalist Palmetto, Fla., 1996-98; tech. writer Intermedia Comm. Inc., Tampa, 1998—, sr. tech. writer, 1999-2000; owner, founder GeekGirl Jewelry, Palmetto, Fla., 2000—; fashion coord. Weekenders USA, 2000—. Fin. svcs. rep. MetLife Fin. Svcs., Sarasota, 2001. Illustrator: Puzzles for Kids By Kids, 1978; contbr.: Word Puzzles for Kids, 1978, Puzzles for Kids By Kids, 1978. Active dist. communications Cogioba dist. Boy Scouts Am., Clarksville, Tenn., 1990, explorer's leader journalism, 1990. Gov. honors scholar Eckerd Coll., 1981; recipient 1st place award Picnic With the Pops Pennyroyal Arts Coun., 1993; newswriting and editing fellow Poynter Inst. for Media Studies, 1983. Mem. Fla. Craftsmen Guild, Am. Craft Coun., Kappa Delta (parliamentarian Delta Eta chpt. 1985). Republican. Mem. Lds Ch. Avocations: spinning, weaving, embroidery, quilting, gardening. Address: 2625 Terra Ceia Bay Blvd Palmetto FL 34221-5956

ZOWADER, SHERRY LEE, volunteer, artist; b. Washington, Feb. 28, 1946; d. Bertram and Doris (Goldberg) Hersh; m. Donald Alan Zowader, Sept. 7, 1968; 1 child, Seth. AA, N.Y. Phoenix Sch. Design, 1967. Chair N.J. state pub. affairs com., sect. rep. state pub. affairs com., chair Ida Schwartz Meml. Libr., chair Nat. Day Working Parent, nat. bd. dirs. Nat. Coun. Jewish Women; bd. dirs., women's issues dir. Raritan Valley LWV; out door art show coord. Somerset County Art Assn.; bd. dirs., chair Prescriptions for Recovery com. Coun. Human Svcs.; active Women's Agenda N.J., N.J. Commn. Sex Discrimination, Family Planning N.J., Karen Carroll for Congress, Food Bank Ctrl. N.J.; founder N.J. Women & AIDS Network, Homesharing, Choice N.J., N.J. Women's Health Collaborative; vol. art tchr., Oreg., 1981-84. Recipient Hannah G. Solomon Cmty. Svc. award Nat. Coun. Jewish Women, 1994, Somerset County (N.J.) commn. on Women, Woman of Achievement, 1994. Avocation: sculpture.

ZRNIC, DUSAN S. research scientist, educator; b. Belgrade, Serbia, Serbia-Monteneg (Yugoslavia), June 3, 1942; s. Slobodan J. and Vera D. Zrnic. PhD, U. Ill., 1969. Rsch. asst. U. Ill., Urbana, 1965—69; prof. dept. elec. engring. Calif. State U., Northridge, 1969—78. Leader Doppler Radar Project, sr. scientist Nat. Severe Storms Lab., Norman. Author: (R&D, edn.) Doppler Radar and Weather Observations, 1993 (IEEE Harry Diamond award, 1988). Office: NOAA/NSSL 1313 Halley Cr Norman OK 73069

ZRULL, JOEL PETER, psychiatry educator; b. Detroit, Jan. 10, 1932; s. Arthur Benjamin and Mildred (Bazy) Z.; m. Nancy Jane Eichenlaub, June 19, 1954; children: Mark Christian, Lisa Carol. BA with honors, U. Mich., 1953, MD, 1957. Diplomate Am. Bd. Psychiatry, Am. Bd. Child Psychiatry. From instr. to assoc. prof. psychiatry U. Mich. Med. Sch., Ann Arbor, 1962-73; prof., chief child psychiatry Med. Coll. Ohio, Toledo, 1973-75, prof., chmn. dept. psychiatry, 1975-97, prof. emeritus, 1997—. Cons. Monroe (mich.) County Intermediate Sch. Dist., 1961—; pres. Associated Physicians MCO, Inc., Toledo, 1983-84, 87-90; chief of staff Med. Coll. Hosps., Toledo, 1984-86; mem. com. on cert. in child psychiatry Am. Bd. Psychiatry and Neurology, 1986-91, chmn. 1990-91. Editor: Adult Psychiatry: New Directions in Therapy, 1983; contbr. articles to profl. jours. Grantee NIMH, 1974-76, Ohio Dept. Mental Health, 1978-86. Fellow Am. Psychiat. Assn. (life), Am. Acad. Child and Adolescent Psychiatry (chmn. com. tng. 1984-87, chmn. comm. memls. and awards 1992-95), Am. Coll. Psychiatrists, Am. Ortho-Psychiat. Assn.; mem. AMA, Soc. Profs. of Child and Adolescent Psychiatry (sec. treas. 1989-92, pres.-elect 1992-94, pres. 1994-96). Roman Catholic. Avocations: tennis, bridge. Home: 6133 Wyandotte Rd W Maumee OH 43537-1334 Office: Med Coll Ohio Kobacker Ctr 3130 Glendale Ave Toledo OH 43614-5811

ZSCHAU, JULIUS JAMES, lawyer; b. Peoria, Ill., Apr. 1, 1940; s. Raymond Johann Ernst and Rosamond Lillian (Malicoat) Z.; m. Leila Joan Krueger, Aug. 7, 1971; children: Kristen Elisabeth, Kimberly Erna, Kira Jamie, Karla Johanna. BS, U. Ill., Champaign, 1964, JD, 1966; LLM, John Marshall Law Sch., 1978. Bar: Ill. 1966, Fla. 1975. Atty. Ill. Central Gulf R.R. Co., Chgo., 1966-68; assoc. Coin & Sheerin, 1968-70, Snyder, Clarke et al, Waukegan, Ill., 1970-72; counsel Ill. Ctr. Corp., Chgo., 1972-74; v.p., gen. counsel, sec. Am. Agronomics Corp., Tampa, Fla., 1974-76; pres. Sorota & Zschau, Clearwater, 1976-90; shareholder Buynard, Harrell, Ostow & Ulrich PA, 1990-94, Johnson, Blakely, Pope, Bokor, Ruppel and Burns, Clearwater, 1994—. Bd. dirs. Attys. Title Ins. Fund, Inc. (chmn. bd. dirs. 1994-95); chmn. com. on land trusts, sec. exec. com. real property sect., vice chair grievance com., 1985-87, Fla. Bar, chair leadership conf., 1987; chmn. Jud. Nominating Commn. of 6th Jud. Dist., 1991-94. Bd. dirs. Nat. Attys. Title Assurance Fund, Attys. Title Guaranty Fund of Colo., treas.; mem. Pinellas County Exec. Com., Tampa Regional Planning Coun., 1988-92. Served to capt. USNR, 1962-92. Fellow Am. Bar Found. (life); mem. ABA (chmn. land trust com., chmn. standing com. lawyers title guaranty funds 1991-94), Am. Coll. Real Estate Lawyers (chmn. condominium com.), Ill. Bar Assn., Chgo. Bar Assn., Clearwater Bar Assn. (past pres.), Fla. Coun. Bar Assn. (past pres., past chmn. vol. bar liaison com.), Fla. Bar Found. (legal aid to poor com., chmn. judician nominations procedures com. 1992-93), Clearwater C. of C. (bd. govs., exec. com., past pres.). Clubs: Countryside Country (Clearwater, Fla.); Masons, Scottish Rite, Shriners. Republican. Home: 1910 Saddlehill Rd N Dunedin FL 34698-2437 Office: Pennington Moore et al 2701 N Rocky Point Dr Ste 930 Tampa FL 33607 E-mail: jayz@jbpfirm.com.

ZSIGMOND, ELEMER KALMAN, anesthesiologist; b. Budapest, Hungary, May 16, 1930; came to U.S., 1956, naturalized, 1966; s. Elemer Zeykvary and Terez (Kartori) Z.; m. Kathryn Fogarasi, Oct. 19, 1953; 1 son, Zoltan William. MD, U. Budapest, 1955. Diplomate: Am. Bd. Anesthesiology. Intern Med. Clinics, U. Budapest, 1954-55, Allegheny Gen. Hosp., Pitts., 1960-61, resident in anesthesiology, 1961-63, clin. anesthesiologist, dir. anesthesiology research labs., 1966-68; resident in internal medicine Hosp. Sztalinvaros and Cardiac Sanatorium, Balatonfured, Hungary, 1955-56; res. assoc., anesthesia rsch. lab. Mercy Hosp., Pitts., 1957-60; prof. anesthesiology Med. Sch., U. Mich., Ann Arbor, 1968-79, U. Ill. Med. Sch., Chgo., 1979-95, prof. emeritus, 1995—; mem. staff Univ. Hosp., U. Ill. Contbr. over 300 articles on anesthesiology, neuropharmacology, and pulmonary physiology to profl. jours. Fellow Am. Coll. Anesthesiologists, Am. Coll. Clin. Pharmacologists; mem. Am. Soc. Anesthesiologists, Internat. Anesthesia Research Soc., N.Y. Acad. Sci., AAAS, AMA, Ill. Med. Soc., Cook County Med. Soc. Home: 6611 N Longmeadow Ave Chicago IL 60646-3207 Office: U Ill Med Ctr Ste 3214B 1740 W Taylor St Chicago IL 60612-7232 *My father's motto for one of his books has been my principle: "Every man represents as much worth to society as he is willing to give from himself to his fellowman.".*

ZSIGMOND, VILMOS, cinematographer, director; b. Szeged, Hungary, June 16, 1930; came to U.S., 1957, naturalized, 1962; s. Vilmos and Bozena (Illichmann) Z.; children: Julia, Susi. MA, U. Film and Theater Arts, Budapest, Hungary, 1955. Free-lance cinematographer for numerous commls., also ednl., documentary and low-budget feature films, 1965-71; now dir., cinematographer on commls. (winner several nat. and internat. awards); feature films, 1971— ; films include McCabe and Mrs. Miller, 1971; Images, 1972, Deliverance, 1972, The Long Goodbye, 1973, Scarecrow, 1973, Cinderella Liberty, 1973, The Sugarland Express, 1974, Obsession, 1976, Close Encounters of the Third Kind, 1977 (Acad. award 1977), The Last Waltz, 1978, The Rose, 1978, The Deerhunter, 1978 (Acad. award nomination and Brit. Acad. award), Heavens Gate, 1979, The Border, 1980, Blow Out, 1980, Jinxed, 1981, Table for Five, 1982, The River, 1983 (Acad. award nomination), No Small Affair, 1984, Real Genius, 1985, Witches of Eastwick, 1986, Journey to Spirit Island, 1988, Fatman and Little Boy, 1989, Two Jakes, 1989, Bonfire of the Vanities, 1990, Stalin, 1991 (CableAce award, Direction of Photography and/or Lighting Direction in a Dramatic/Theatrical Special/Movie or Miniseries, ASC award, Emmy award), Sliver, 1992; dir. The Long Shadow, 1992, Intersection, 1993, Maverick, 1993, The Crossing Guard, 1994, Assassins, 1995, The Ghost and the Darkness, 1996 (ASC Award nomination), Fantasy for a New Age, 1997, Playing By Heart, 1998, The Body, 1999, The Mists of Avalon, 2000, Life as a House, 2001, (opera film) Bank Ban, 2001. Recipient lifetime achievement award Worldfest, Flagstaff, 1998. Mem. Acad. Motion Picture Arts and Scis., Dirs. Guild, Am. Soc. Cinematographers (lifetime achievement award 1998). Office: Feinstein & Berson 16255 Ventura Blvd Ste 625 Encino CA 91436-2418 E-mail: vzsigmond@adelphia.net.

ZUBER, NORMA KEEN, career counselor, educator; b. Iuka, Miss., Sept. 27, 1934; d. William Harrington and Mary (Hebert) Keen; m. William Frederick Zuber, Sept. 14, 1958; children: William Frederick Jr., Michael, Kimberly, Karen. BS in Nursing, U. Southwestern La., 1956; MS in Counseling, Calif. Luth. U., 1984. Nat. cert. counselor, nat. cert. career counselor; registered profl. career counselor, Calif. Intensive care nurse Ochsner Found. Hosp., New Orleans, 1956-59; career devel. counselor BFC Counseling Ctr., Ventura, Calif., 1984-87; founder, prin., counselor Career & Life Planning-Norma Zuber & Assocs., 1987—. Instr. adult continuing edn. Ventura C.C., 1987—; instr. Calif. State U., Northridge, 1988-89; instr. U. Calif. Santa Barbara, Antioch U.; mem. adv. coun. on tchr. edn. Calif. Luth. U., Thousand Oaks, 1984-87; mem. adv. bd. for development of profl. career counseling cert. program U. Calif., San Diego, 1991—. Co-author: The Nuts and Bolts of Career Counseling: How to Set Up and Succeed in Private Practice, 1992. Chmn. bd. dirs. women's ministries Missionary Ch., Ventura, 1987-90. Recipient profl. contbn. award H.B. McDaniel Found.-Stanford U. Sch. Edn., 1988, Govt. Rels. Com. Cert. of Appreciation, Am. Assn. for Counseling and Devel., Career Devel. Practitioner of the Year award Internat. Career Conf., 1998, Spirit of Networking award Ventura Profl. Women's Network, 2001; featured in Nat. Assn. of Women bus. Owners Bravo award, Ventura, Calif. Mem. NAFE, ACA, Nat. Career Devel. Assn. (western region trustee 1994-97), Calif. Assn. Couseling and Devel. (chmn. legis. task force 1987-89, Jim Saum govt. rels. award 1989), Internat. Platform Assn., Nat. Career Devel. Assn. (western regional trustee 1995-98), Internat. Career Conf. (Career Devel. Practitioner of Yr. 1998), Calif. Career Devel. Assn. (bd. dirs. 1985-98, membership dir. 1991-92, pres. 1992-93, Leadership and Professionaliam award 1988, 89), Calif. Career Conf. (program chair 1993), Ventura County Profl. Women's Network (dir. membership 1990-91, pres. 1998-99), Calif. Registry Profl. Counselors and Paraprofls. (bd. dirs. 1990-94, chair 1995-97), Chi Sigma Iota. Republican. Home: 927 Sentinel Cir Ventura CA 93003-1202 Office: Career and Life Planning Norma Zuber and Assocs 3585 Maple St Ste 237 Ventura CA 93003-9117

ZUBER, RANDOLPH CLARK, urologist; b. Dallas, Apr. 4, 1941; s. Oran H. and Minnie M. (Cuthbertson) Z.; m. Billie Gayle Schumacher, June 20, 1964; children: Randolph Blake, Rustin Kurt. AAPS, Amarillo Jr. Coll., 1961; BA, U. Tex., 1963; MD, U. Tex., Galveston, 1967. Diplomate Am. Bd. Urology. Intern Kans. U. Med. Ctr., 1967-68, resident in urology, 1969-72; practice medicine specializing in urology Kerrville, Tex., 1974—. Bishop Ch. of Christ, 1983-93; mem. urologic cultural exchange to Peoples Republic of China People to People Found., 1987. Founding dir., past pres. Hill County Right to Life; chmn. steering com. Kerr County YMCA, 1990. Served to maj. USAF, 1972-74. Recipient Disting. Leadership award, cert. of excellence Leadership Kerr County, 1989. Fellow ACS; mem. Am. Urol. Assn. (Tex. rep., bd. dirs. south crtl. sect. 1990-96), Tex. Urol. Soc. (pres. 1988-89, bd. dirs. 1996-98), Tex. Med. Assn. Office: 710 Water St Ste 300 Kerrville TX 78028-5338

ZUBKOFF, MICHAEL, medical educator; b. N.Y.C., June 2, 1944; s. Harry and Catherine (O'Brien) Z.; children: Steven, Joel, Lisa; m. Leslee Ann Michaels, 1991. BA, Am. Internat. Coll., 1965, LLD (hon.), 1981; MA, cert. Internat. Fellow program, Columbia U., 1966, PhD, 1968; MA (hon.), Dartmouth Coll., 1980. Research assoc. conservation human resources Columbia U., N.Y.C., 1966-67; assoc. prof. econs. Fisk U., Nashville, 1967-70; assoc. prof. health econs., assoc. chmn. dept. family and community health Meharry Med. Coll., 1967-75; assoc. prof. econs. Vanderbilt U., 1970-75; prof. econs. and mgmt. Amos Tuck Sch. Bus., prof. chmn. dept. cmty. and family medicine Med. Sch. Dartmouth Coll., Hanover, NH, 1975—. Mem. inst. medicine Nat. Acad. Scis., 1982—, mem. assembly engrs. inst. med. com. on tech. and health care, 1977-79, grad. med. ednl. nat. adv. com., 1977-81., com. on grad.-med. edn. programs for mil. services Nat. Acad. Scis., 1980-82., nat. research council commn. on human resources Nat. Acad. Scis., 1980-84, com. on aging soc. Nat. Acad. Scis., 1984-89; corr. com. human rights Nat. Acad. Scis., 1983—, nat. rsch. coun. com. computer tech. and svc. sector productivity Nat. Acad. Scis., 1991-94; instr. econs. Harvard U., Yale U., and Columbia U., 1967-68. Co-author: Urban Health Services: The Case of New York, 1971, Consumer Incentives for Health Care, 1974, Health: A Victim of Cause of Inflation, 1976, Framework for Government Intervention in the Health Sector, 1978, Hospital Cost Containment: Selected Notes for Public Policy, 1980, Problem Based Learning of Social Science & Humanities by Fourth Year Medical Students, 1986, The Medical Outcomes Study: An Application of Methods for Monitoring the Results of Medical Care, 1989, Measuring Functional Status & Well Being: The Medical Outcomes Study Approach, 1992, Health Society & The Physician: Problem Based Learning of Social Sciences & Humanities, 1993; contbr. numerous articles to profl. jours. Del., health spokesman White House Summit on Inflation, 1974. Fellow Woodrow Wilson Found., 1964-66, Fulbright Found., 1967-68, USPHS, 1966-67. Mem. Am. Econ. Assn., Am. Pub. Health Assn. Home: RR 1 Fairlee VT 05045-9801 Office: Dartmouth Med Sch Dept Comty & Family Med HB7250 Hanover NH 03755

ZUBOV, LYNN, special education educator, researcher; b. Bklyn., Dec. 3, 1960; d. David P. Roche III. BS in Spl. Edn., St. John's U., Jamaica, N.Y., 1983; MS in Spl. Edn., St. John's U., 1988, EdS in Supervision and Adminstrn., 1990; PhD in Spl. Edn., Vanderbilt U., Nashville, 1996. Tchr. asst. Little Village Sch., Garden City, N.Y., 1981-82; tchr. of emotionally disturbed J.H.S. 8, Jamaica, 1983-86, Poseidon, Los Angeles, 1986-87; ednl. coord., mainstream coord. P.S. 80, Jamaica, N.Y., 1987-91; rsch. asst. Peabody Coll. Vanderbilt U., Nashville, 1991-95; asst. prof., program dir. Canisius Coll., Buffalo, 1995-99; asst. prof., program coord. Winston-Salem State U., 1999—. Spl. edn. cons. Paul J. Cooper, Bklyn., 1991; mem. project Basics I.H.S. 8, Jamaica, N.Y., 1983-86; sec. Pupil-Pers. Commn., P.S. 80, Jamaica, 1987-91. Cons., instr. How To Use The Apple Computer, How to Make Inclusion Work; co-author: Handbook for the Special Education Paraprofessional, 1990. Mem. CEC, N.Y. State Coun. for Exceptional Children (past pres.). Republican. Roman Catholic. Home: 229 Engleman Ave Burlington NC 27215-4801 Office: Winston-Salem State U 601 Martin Luther King Jr CB 19360 Winston Salem NC 27157 E-mail: zubovle@wssu.edu.

ZUBOV, SERGEI, professional hockey player; b. Moscow, July 22, 1970; Hockey player Rangers, 1992-95, Penguins, 1995-96; defense Dallas Stars, 1996—. Office: Amer. Airlines Center 2500 Victory Lane Dallas TX 75219*

ZUBRIN, JAY ROSS, surgeon; b. Phila., June 11, 1936; BS, Dickinson Coll., 1959; MD, Temple U., 1963. Diplomate Am. Bd. Surgery. Intern San Francisco Gen. Hosp., 1963-64; resident in gen. surgery U. Calif. Med. Ctr., 1964-69; pvt. practice; mem. staff Hoag Meml. Presbyn. Hosp., Newport

Beach, Calif. Mem. ACS, AMA, Calif. Med Assn., Orange County Med. Assn. Office: 351 Hospital Rd Ste 319 Newport Beach CA 92663-3506 E-mail: JZubrin@HoagHospital.org., JZubrin@yahoo.com.

ZUBRITSKY, ALEXANDER NICKOLAEVICH, pathologist; b. Severo-Kurilsk, Sakhalin, Russia, Mar. 14, 1949; s. Nickolay Alexandrovich and Kaleriya Andreevna (Chechulina) Z.; children: Vladimir, Sergey Yashin. MD, Med. Inst., 1974. Hosp. attendant dept. pathology City Hosp. N21, Sverdlovsk, Russia, 1965-67; hosp. attendant Medico-Legal Morgue N1, 1967-68; nurse Sta. of Emergencies Care N1, 1971-72; head pathology dept. Ctrl. Regional Hosp., Neviyansk, Russia, 1975-76; chief pathology dept., head pathologist Sverdlovsk Rd. Hosp., 1976-83; lectr. path. anatomy Med. Sch. Sverdlovsk Rd., 1976-77; chief dept. pathology mcpl. instn. Taldom Ctrl. Regional Hosp., 1983—. Contbr. articles to profl. jours. Recipient award Am. Coll. Chest Physicians, 1990, Pathology Rsch. Pract award , Taldom-Innsbruck, 1993; named Internat. Man of Yr., 1994-95. Mem. European Soc. Pathology, Internat. Union Against Tb and Lung Disease, Internat. Soc. Heart Rsch. (European sect.), Internat. Soc. Diagnostic Quantitative Pathology, N.Y. Acad. Scis. Avocations: music, walking. Home: Prospekt Mira101B/79 129085 Moscow Russia

ZUBRY, BORIS, materials engineer, writer; b. Leningrad, Russia, Apr. 13, 1951; s. Efim Zubry, Adel Zubry. MSME, State U., Leningrad, USSR, 1975. Mgr. Bristol-Myers Squibb, New Brunswick, NJ, 1991—94; dir. Italcom, Bologna, Italy, 1994—99; mgr. West Pharm. Svcs., Lakewood, 1999—2000, GAF Materials Corp., Wayne, 2000—. Author: Chess Master, 2000, Miles of experience, 2002. Member Republican Presidential Task Force, Washington, 1990—2002; Professional Member ASME, New York, NY, 1982—2002, IIOPP, Herndon, VA, 1990—2002. Home: 12 E. Countryside Dr. Princeton NJ 08540 Personal E-mail: boriszubry@home.com.

ZUCARO, ALDO CHARLES, insurance company executive; b. Grenoble, France, Apr. 2, 1939; s. Louis and Lucy Zucaro; m. Gloria J. Ward, Oct. 12, 1963; children: Lucy, Louis, Faye. BS in Acctg, Queens Coll., N.Y.C., 1962. C.P.A., N.Y., Ill. Ptnr. Coopers & Lybrand (and predecessor), Chgo. and N.Y.C., 1962-76; exec. v.p., chief fin. officer Old Republic Internat. Corp., Chgo., 1976-81, pres., 1981—, chief exec. officer, 1990—, also chmn. bd. dirs., 1993—, chmn. of the bd., 1993—. Pres., bd. dirs. Old Republic Life Ins. Co., Old Republic Life of N.Y., Old Republic Ins. Co., Internat. Bus. and Merc. Reassurance Co., Republic Mortgage Ins. Co., Old Republic Nat. Title Ins. Co., Home Owners Life Ins. Co. Editor: Financial Accounting Practices of the Insurance Industry, 1975, 76. Mem. AICPAs. Roman Catholic. Office: Old Republic Internat Corp 307 N Michigan Ave Chicago IL 60601-5311

ZUCCARELLO, MARIO, neurosurgeon, researcher; b. Catania, Italy, Apr. 25, 1952; m. Gabriella Tempesta, May 25, 1985; 1 child, Marco. Undergrad., U. Padova, Italy, 1970-76, MD, 1976. Intern U. Hosp., Padova, Italy, 1976-80, resident in neurosurgery, 1976-80; instr. neurosurgery, 1981-84; rsch. fellow U. Va., Charlottesville, 1984-85; clin. fellow neurosurgery U. Cin., 1985-88, assoc. prof. neurosurgery, 1990-99, prof., 1999—, dir. cerebrovascular surgery; asst. prof. neurosurgery Genova, Italy, 1988-90; chief neurosurgery VAMC, Cin., 1990—. Contbr. articles to profl. jours. Capt. Italian Army, 1981-82. Recipient U. Cin. Rsch. award, 1995; Max Planck scholar, 1977-78, NATO scholar, 1984; VA Merit Rev. grantee Veteran Adminstrn. Med. Ctr., 1991—. Roman Catholic. Avocations: soccer, classical music, skiing, history, geography. Home: 231 Bethesda Ave Cincinnati OH 45229-2827 Office: U Cin 231 Bethesda Ave Cincinnati OH 45229-2827 Fax: 513-558-7702. E-mail: zuccarm@e-mail.uc.edu.

ZUCCHERO, FREDERIC JOSEPH, medical director; b. St. Louis, Dec. 25, 1947; s. Joseph Ernest and Anna Marie (Steinlage) Z.; m. Loretta Christine Hischke, Aug. 11, 1973; children: Theresa Marie, Anthony Joseph. AB in Chemistry, Ripon (Wis.) Coll., 1969; MA in Chemistry, No. Mich. U., 1972; BS in Pharmacy, U. Iowa, 1975. Lic. pharmacist, Iowa, Ill., Mo. Asst. dir. med. affairs Profl. Drug Systems, St. Louis, 1988-89, assoc. dir. med. affairs, 1989-93; med. dir. First DataBank divsn. Hearst Corp., 1993—. Clin. asst. prof. pharmacy St. Louis Coll. Pharmacy, 1990—; assoc. dir. med. affairs U.S.A. divsn. Trimel Corp., St. Louis, 1991-93. Editor: Pocket Guide to Evaluations of Drug Interactions, 1994, Evaluations of Drug Interactions; (newsletter) Medicom Drug Info., 1989-92; contbr. articles to Jour. Emergency Medicine, Jour. Pharmacy Practice. Mem. Am. Coll. Clin. Pharmacy, Am. Soc. Health System Pharmacists (reviewer mid-yr. meeting 1990—, reviewer annual meeting 1990—), others. Home: 1872 Braumton Ct Chesterfield MO 63017-8027 Office: Hearst Corp First DataBank Divsn 530 Maryville Centre Dr Saint Louis MO 63141-5825

ZUCCHI, DONNA MARIE, financial services executive; b. Camden, N.J., May 12, 1953; d. Marion Joseph and Mary (Edgidi) Z.; m. Harold A. Sackeim, Oct. 9, 1977; 1 child, Alexander D. BA, U. Pa., Phila., 1976. Tax cons. Reed Roberts, Inc., Phila., 1976-77; rsch. asst. Tchrs. Ins. and Annuity Assn.-Coll. Ret. Equities Fund, N.Y.C., 1977-80; group ins. analyst TIAA-CREF, 1980-83, adv. officer, 1983-94; dist. mgr. Variable Annuity Life Ins. Co., 1994-98; regional v.p. Am. Internat. Group, Blue Bell, Pa., 1998—. Author: Building Financial Security, 1998. Pres. Lefferts Pl. Block Assn., Clinton Hill, N.Y., 1983; chair Clinton Hill South Hist. Preservation Com., 1984. Fellow Life Office Mgmt. Assn. Avocations: reading, writing, travel, skiing. Office: Am Internat Group/Variable Annuity Life Ins Co Bldg 19 Ste 300 1767 Sentry Pkwy W Blue Bell PA 19422

ZUCCO, RONDA KAY, planning and marketing professional; b. Peoria, Ill., Apr. 3, 1960; d. Richard Leon Zucco. BA, So. Ill. U., 1981. Cert. addictions profl.; cert. relapse prevention specialist. Addictions counselor Parkside at BroMenn, Bloomington, Ill., 1986-89; dir. continuing care/sr. counselor Fla. Hosp. (formerly Parkside), Orlando, Fla., 1989-95; addictions program mgr. Charter Behavioral Health Sys., Kissimmee, 1995-97; coord. outpatient svcs. Heart of Fla. Behavioral Ctr., Lakeland, 1997-99; bus. and industry rep., planning and mktg. dept. Lakeland Regional Med. Ctr., 1999—. Vol. ARC, Carbondale, Ill., 1978—81; crisis hotline vol. Jackson County Cmty. Mental Health Ctr., 1981; mem. AIDS spkrs. bur. BroMenn Healthcare, Bloomington, 1986—89; vol. Alliance for Mentally Ill of Greater Orlando, Fla., 1995—97, Coalition for Homeless, Orlando, 1995—97; mem. exec. bd. Drug Prevention Resource Ctr., Lakeland, Fla., y.p., 1997—; exec. bd. dirs., corr. sec. Imperial Symphony Orch., 2001—. Named Outstanding Profl. of Yr., Fla. Sch. Addiction Studies, 1999; named an Olympic Torchbearer, 2002; recipient State of Ill. scholar, Gen. Assembly, 1977—81, Leadership Lakeland xx award. Mem. Am. Mktg. Assn., Am. Assn. for Counseling and Devel., Am. Mental Health Counselors Assn., Fla. Alcohol and Drug Abuse Assn., Fla. Prevention Assn., Nat. Businesswomen's Leadership Assn., Am. Bus. Women's Assn., Jr. League of Greater Lakeland, C. of C. Greater Lakeland, Fla. Coun. on Crime and Delinquency, Kappa Delta Pi, Chi Sigma Iota. Avocations: reading, running, swimming and diving, travel, the arts. Home: 1100 Oakbridge Pkwy Apt 296 Lakeland FL 33803-5964

ZUCCOTTI, JOHN EUGENE, real estate company executive; b. N.Y.C., June 23, 1937; AB in History, Princeton U., 1959; LLB, Yale U., 1963. Bar: N.Y. 1963, D.C. 1970. Asst. to under sec. and sec. HUD, Washington, 1967-69; sec., counsel Nat. Corp. for Housing Partnerships, 1969-70; spl. counsel to housing subcom. Banking and Currency Com. U.S. Ho. of Reps., 1970-73; ptnr. Tufo, Johnston and Zuccotti, N.Y.C., 1970-72; chmn. N.Y.C. Planning Commn., 1973-75, mem., 1971-73; 1st dep. mayor City of N.Y., 1975-77; sr. ptnr. Tufo, Johnston, Zuccotti and Allegaert, N.Y.C., 1977-86, Brown & Wood, N.Y.C., 1986-89; pres., chief exec. officer Olympia and York Cos. (U.S.A.), 1989—. Impartial arbitrator between MTA/TWU, 1981-90. Office: World Financial Properties Inc 1 Liberty Plz 165 Broadway New York NY 10006-1404

ZUCHMAN, PHILIP ABRIM, artist, educator; b. N.Y.C., Mar. 3, 1942; s. Alexander Asher and Eunice (Slonim) Z.; m. Deborah Gross, Sept. 29, 1974; children: Alexander Eli, William Gross Turner. BA in Philosophy, CUNY, N.Y.C., 1965; MFA, Goddard Coll., Plainfield, Vt., 1973. Prof. Art Inst. Phila., 1984—; painter, printmaker Zuchman Studios, Phila., 1967—; tchr. Brandeis (Calif.) Collegiate Inst., 1997. Artist in residence Brandeis Bardin Inst., Calif., 1997; gallery dir. Art Inst. Phila., 1988-91; mentor Am. Jewish Cultural Project, 1996-97; v.p. Faculty Fedn. Am. Fedn. State, County and Mcpl. Employees, Phila., 1987-92, v.p., 1998—; panelist Phila. Art Alliance, 1989; juror Phila. Celebrates the Arts, 1989, Pa. Coun. on Aging, 1990, Gov.'s Sch. for the Arts, Trenton, N.J., 1993, N.J. State Teen Arts Program, 1993, 94, 96, Rittenhouse Sq. Ann. Outdoor Art Show, 1995; mem. art in embassies program U.S. State Dept., 1983. One-man shows include Ars et Decora Gallery, 1988, English Gallery, Peterborough, N.H., 1991, Brandeis-Bardin Inst., 1997; exhibited in group shows at Goddard Coll., Vt., 1973, Salmagundi Club, N.Y., 1972-75, World Disarmament Conf., Stockholm, 1984, U.S. Embassy, Lagos, Nigeria, 1984, 3d St. Gallery, 1984, U.S. Embassy, Libreville, Gabon, 1984, Washington and Jefferson Coll., 1986, U.S. Embassy, Tegucigalpa, Honduras, 1987, Woodmere Art Mus., 1987, Butler Inst. Am. Art, 1987, Artifacts Gallery, 1987, University City Arts League, 1988, Port of History Mus., 1989, Temple U., 1989, Am. Coll., 1989, U.S. Embassy, Nassau, Bahamas, 1990, Brava Sughera, Italy, 1990, Levy Gallery of Arts, Moore Coll. Art, 1991, Camden County Coll., 1992, Franklin Mint Mus., 1992, U.S. Embassy, Quito, Ecuador, 1992, Goforth Rittenhouse Gallery, 1992, Mill Gallery, 1993, State of Art '93 Nat. Invitational, Boston, 1993, U.S. Embassy, Bangui Ctrl. African Republic, 1995, Berman Mus., Collegeville, Pa., 1995, U.S. Embassy, Addis Ababa, Ethiopia, 1996, Brandeis-Bardin Inst. Gallery, 1997, U.S. Embassy El. Salvador, 2000, Sharjah (United Arab Emirates) Internat. Arts Biennial, 2001, U.S. Embassy, San Salvador, El Salvador, 2001, Snapshot, Mus. of Contemporary Art, Balt., 2001; represented in permanent collections at State Dept. U.S., U.S. Peoples for UN, Fifth Maine Regiment Mus.; also corp. collections. With U.S. Army, 1966-68. Recipient Peter Pauper Press award, 1963, scholarship Salmagundi Club Young Artists, 1971-75, award for oil painting Villanova U., 1983. Mem.: AAUP, Coll. Art Assn. Am., Americans for Arts, Nat. Forum Profl. Artists (pres. 1976—78), Artist Equity (v.p. Phila. chpt. 1988—90), Phila. Water Color Soc. (v.p. 1990—91, 1990—94, exec. bd. 2000—01). Avocations: winemaking, kayaker, travel. Home: 4724 Springfield Ave Philadelphia PA 19143-3515 E-mail: zuchmanstudios@hotmail.com.

ZUCHOWSKI, BEVERLY JEAN, chemistry educator; b. Toledo, Jan. 11, 1950; d. Frank I. and Esther C. (Steinke) Patronik; m. Mark G. Zuchowski, May 21, 1971; children: Caroline H., Mark J., Gregory S., Beverly A. BS in Edn., Bowling Green State U., 1974, MAT in Chemistry, 1989. Cert. tchr. physics, chemistry and math. 7-12, Ohio. Instr. chemistry and physics Eastwood Schs., Luckey, Ohio, 1974-77, Perrysburg (Ohio) Pub. Schs., 1978-88, Owens Tech. Coll., Perrysburg, 1981-88; grad. asst. Bowling Green (Ohio) State U., 1988-89; chemistry instr. Perrysburg Pub. Schs., 1989—. Mem. Ohio Dept. Edn. Sci. Proficiency Content Com., 1995—; tchr. intern Ctr. of Sci. and Industry, Columbus, Ohio, 1987; tchr. chaperone, Young Exptl. Scientist, Columbus, 1988-92, Women in Sci., Bowling Green, 1989-95. Mem. Rossford (Ohio) Bd. Edn., 1988—, v.p., 1991-92, 2000—; mem. Penta County Vocat. Sch. Bd. Edn., 1994-95; leader Girl Scouts U.S., Rossford, 1978-95; precinct worker Wood County Bd. of Elections, 1982-87. Recipient Award of Achievement Ohio Sch. Bd. Assn., 1998, 99, 2000. Mem. NEA, Ohio Edn. Assn., Nat. Sci. Tchrs. Assn., Ohio Coun. Tchrs. Math., Ohio Acad. Sci., Sci. Edn. Coun. Ohio, Perrysburg Edn. Assn. (treas. 1981), Rossford Community Svc. League (sec. 1992), Ohio Womens Caucus, Rossford Lions Club (charter), Toledo Mothers of Twins Club. Democrat. Lutheran. Avocations: camping, gardening, water sports. E-mail: pbhs_st_bz@noeca. Home: 3 Riverside Dr Rossford OH 43460-1130 Office: Perrysburg High Sch 13385 Roachton Rd Perrysburg OH 43551-1363

ZUCK, ALFRED CHRISTIAN, consulting mechanical engineer; b. Ridgefield, N.J., Dec. 16, 1924; s. Frederick William and Margaret Christine (Umland) Z.; m. Vilma Hudson, May 6, 1951; children: Allyson, Jon, Randall. M.E., Poly. Inst. Bklyn., 1960. Registered profl. engr., 21 states including N.Y.; nat. council engrng. examiners; lic. profl. planner, N.J. From designer to sr. v.p. Syska & Hennessy, Inc., N.Y.C., 1946-78; prin. Edwards & Zuck (P.C.), 1978-91, ret., 1991. Mem. nat. panel Am. Arbitration Assn, Nat. Council Engrng. Examiners. Served with AUS, 1943-46; to 1st lt. USAF, 1951-52; to capt. N.J. Air N.G., 1947-56. Decorated Bronze Star (2) Fellow Am. Cons. Engrs. Council (past mem. Nat. Ethical Practices Com.); mem. NSPE, N.Y. State Soc. Profl. Engrs. (past chmn. profl. engrs. in pvt. practice program), Am. Soc. Mil. Engrs., Nat. Council Engrng. Examiners, N.Y. Assn. Cons. Engrs. (past v.p., bd. dirs.), ASHRAE, N.Y. Bldg. Congress. (bd. govs.). Clubs: N.Y. Athletic. Lutheran. Home: 80 N Walnut St Ridgewood NJ 07450-3224 Office: Edwards & Zuck PC 330 W 42nd St Fl 27 New York NY 10036-6949

ZUCK, ALFRED MILLER, public administration educator; b. East Petersburg, Pa., Aug. 27, 1934; s. Walter Newton and Mary (Miller) Z.; m. Geraldine Connelly, July 21, 1957; children: Susan, David. BA, Franklin and Marshall Coll., 1957; MPA, Syracuse U., 1958. Dir. fed. program Presdl. Commn. on Youth Opportunities, Washington, 1967-68; dir evaluation Employment and Tng. Adminstrn., Dept. Labor, 1968-70, dir adminstrn. and mgmt., 1970-75; comptroller U.S. Dept. Labor, 1975-77; exec. dir. Commn. on Exec., Legis. and Jud. Salaries, 1980; asst. sec. Dept. Labor, 1977-83, acting sec., 1981; asst. adminstr. EPA, 1983; exec. dir. Nat. Assn. Schs. of Pub. Affairs and Adminstrn., 1983-97; disting. prof. Am. U., 1996—. Pres. Internat. Inst. Adminstrv. Scis., Brussels, 1989-92, Am. Consortium for Internat. Pub. Adminstrn., Washington, 1984-89; bd. dirs. Pub./Pvt. Venture, Inc., Phila., 1984-90. Recipient Presdl. Disting. Exec. award Pres. of U.S., 1980; Disting. Alumni award Franklin and Marshall Coll., 1980. Fellow Nat. Acad. Pub. Adminstrn. (trustee 1989-95, chmn. bd. trustees 1993-95); mem . Phi Beta Kappa.

ZUCKER, ALEXANDER, physicist, administrator; b. Zagreb, Yugoslavia, Aug. 1, 1924; came to U.S., 1939; s. William and Bertha (Klopfer) Z.; m. Joan-Ellen Jamieson, Nov. 28, 1953; children: Rebecca, Claire, Susannah. BA, U. Vt., Burlington, 1947; MS, Yale U., New Haven, 1948, PhD, 1950. Physicist Oak Ridge Nat. Lab., Tenn., 1950-60, assoc. dir. electro-nuclear div., 1972-75, dir. heavy ion project, 1988, assoc. dir. phys. scis., 1973-88, acting lab. dir., 1988, assoc. dir. for nuclear techs., 1989-93; exec. dir., environ. studies bd. NAS-NAE, Washington, 1970-72; prof. physics U. Tenn., 1996—. Mem. U.S. del. to USSR on Peaceful Uses of Atomic Energy, 1963; Ford prof. physics U. Tenn., Knoxville, 1968-73; U.S. del. to Pugwash Conf., 1971; research coordination council Gas Research Inst., Chgo., 1978-85; com. Army manpower Nat. Research Council, Washington, 1982-83; adv. panel on technologies to reduce U.S. materials import vulnerability Office of Technology Assessment, Washington, 1982-85; council on energy engrng. research Dept. of Energy, Washington, 1983— ; industry, nat. lab. steel initiative White House, Washington, 1984 Editor Internat. Jour. Nuclear Sci. Applications, 1980—; cons. editor Ency. and Yearbook of Sci. and Tech. McGraw-Hill Pub. Co., 1989; mem. editorial bd. Science, 1981-82; contbr. articles to profl. jours. Guggenheim fellow, 1966-67; Fulbright-Hays Research scholar, 1966-67 Fellow Am. Phys. Soc., AAAS, Sigma Xi; mem. ASME, Nat. Acad. Scis. (nuclear physics del. to People's Republic of China 1979), Internat. Union Pure and Applied Physics (mem.-at-large U.S. nat. com. 1976-78) Achievements include research in nuclear physics with heavy ions and protons; accelerators, especially cyclotrons; materials research programs, especially high-temperature materials and surfaces; nuclear power reactors, especially gas-cooled reactors; research reactor with ultra high neutron flux. Office: Oak Ridge Nat Lab PO Box 2008 Oak Ridge TN 37831-2008

ZUCKER, ALFRED JOHN, English language educator, academic administrator; b. Hartford, Sept. 25, 1940; s. Samuel and Rose (Zucker) Z.; m. Sallie Lea Friedheim, Dec. 25, 1966; children: Mary Anne, John James Jr., James Patrick, Patrick Jonathan, Anne-Marie Kathleen, Kathleen Mary. AA, L.A. Valley Coll., 1960; AB in English, UCLA, 1962, AB in Speech, MA in English, 1962, MA in Speech, 1963, PhD, 1966; postgrad., U. So. Calif., Harvard U.; MA in history, 2000. Prof. English and history, chmn. div. humanities L.A. S.W. Coll., 1968-72; prof. English El Camino Coll., 1985—, L.A. Valley Coll., 1989—, chmn. dept. English, honors sponsor, 1997—. Contbr. articles to profl. jours. Mem. L.A. Coll. Dist. Senate, 1969—. Mem. AAUP, L.A. Coll. Tchrs. Assn. (dir.), Calif. Jr. Coll. Assn., Calif. Tchrs. Assn., World Affairs Coun., Calif. Scholarship Fedn., Mensa, KC, Gold Key, Phi Beta Kappa, Phi Delta Kappa (pres. UCLA chpt. 1966-67, v.p. 1967-68), Tau Alpha Epsilon, Phi Theta Kappa, Phi Alpha Theta, Phi Kappa Phi, Phi Delta Gamma. Office: 5800 Fulton Ave Van Nuys CA 91401-4062 E-mail: zuckeraj@iaccd.cc.ca.us.

ZUCKER, ARNOLD HARRIS, psychiatrist; b. Bklyn., July 29, 1930; s. Charles Israel and Bertha (Leff) Z.; m. Marilyn Pistreich, June 10, 1962; children: Harvey, Deborah, Shoshanna, David. BA, Bklyn. Coll., 1950; MD, SUNY, Bklyn., 1954; cert. psychoanalysis, Columbia U. Psychoanalytic Ctr, 1971. Diplomate, Am. Bd. Psychiatry and Neurology. Intern USPHS, Staten Island, N.Y., 1954-55; resident Kings County Hosp., Bklyn., 1955-56, Southwestern Med. Sch., Dallas, 1958-59, Albert Einstein Coll. Medicine, Bronx, N.Y., 1959-60, asst. clin. prof. psychiatry, 1960-72; pvt. practice Mt. Vernon, N.Y., 1960—. Assoc. attending psychiatrist, Mt. Vernon Hosp.; assoc. prof. pastoral counseling, Iona Coll., New Rochelle, N.Y., 1968—. Contbr. articles to profl. jours. Surgeon, USPHS, 1956-58. Fellow Am. Psychiat. Assn. (life), Am. Acad. Psychoanalysis (life); mem. Am. Psychoanalytic Assn., Assn. Psychoanalytic Medicine, AMA, Westchester Psychoanalytic Soc., Phi Beta Kappa. Democrat. Jewish. Avocation: religious studies. Office: 120 E Prospect Ave Mount Vernon NY 10550-2212

ZUCKER, BLANCHE MYRA, civic worker; b. Schenectady, N.Y., July 27, 1925; d. Cassius Alexander and Winifred Estelle (Davis) Millington; m. Nelson Marsh, July 7, 1947 (div. July 1967); children: Kay Patricia, Gary Nelson; m. Reuben Zucker, July 22, 1967 (dec. June 1987); m. Henry Bozarth, Feb. 13, 1994. Grad., Meth. Hosp. Sch. Nursing, Bklyn., 1946; BS in Nursing Edn., Columbia U., 1962; MEd, U. Nev., Las Vegas, 1975. RN, N.Y. Night shift head nurse Meth. Hosp., Bklyn., 1947; floor nurse Carle Meml. Hosp.Clinic, Urbana, Ill., 1947; med. librarian So. Nev. Meml. Hosp (now Univ. Med. Ctr.), Las Vegas, 1963-66; librarian St. Viator Sch., 1968-74. Del. Nev. Gov.'s Conf. on Library and Info. Services, 1978, publicity dir., 1978-79; alt. Nev. del. White House Conf. on Library and Info. Services, 1979. Mem. Univ. Med. Ctr. So. Nev. Aux, 1980—; trustee Univ. Libr. Soc., Las Vegas, 1985—; pres. We Can, 1985—86; mem. Nev. Com. for Protection of Children, 1985—2000, vice chmn., 1987—90, chmn., 1990—95; mem. Citizens Com. Victim Rights, 1986—90. Recipient Svc. award St. Viator Sch., 1975, Adminstrn. for Children, Youth and Families award U.S. Dept. Health and Human Svcs., 1985, Book of Golden Deeds award Las Vegas Exch. Club, 1986, Humanitarian award Las Vegas Women, 1986, Appreciation award We Can, Inc., 1987, Lifetime Achievement in Prevention award/20 Yr. Svc. to Children of Nev., 1994, Blanche Zucker Vol. award, 1990; named Vol. of Yr. Citizens Com. Victim Rights, 1989, Amb. of Courtesy, Las Vegas C. of C. and Las Vegas Conv. and Visitors Authority, 1998. Mem. ALA, Nev. Libr. Assn. (publicity dir. 1979, appreciation award 1979), Friends So. Nev. Librs., Clark County Med. Soc. Aux. (pres. 1971-72), Gen. Fedn. Women's Clubs (chmn. Nev. chpt. child abuse project, 1984-90, mem. Past Pres.'s Club, pres. Mesquite Club 1980-81, 1st place Today's Women -- the Vol. award 1986, mem. Nat. Child Care Action Campaign). Democrat. Avocations: swimming, photography, classical music, opera, creative arts. Home: 2520 Faiss Dr Las Vegas NV 89134-7241

ZUCKER, DAVID I. psychologist; b. N.Y.C., Mar. 26, 1952; s. Jonas J. and Pearl Cele (Kestenbaum) Z.; m. Elizabeth Fay Muler, June 27, 1976; children: Alisha Tamar, Heather Elana. BA, NYU, 1975; MEd, Yeshiva U., 1976; EdD, U. Cin., 1983. Lic. psychologist, Ohio; cert. counselor Nat. Bd. Cert. Counselors. Psychologist Hamilton County Bd. Mental Retardation and Devel. Disability, Cin., 1976—, Behavioral Sci. Ctr., Cin., 1988—; psychologist in pvt. practice, 1988—. Pres. Southeastern Ohio Residences for Persons with Autism, 1994-95; mem. State of Ohio Behavior Mgmt. Rev. Com., 1994-95; mem. behavior support adv. com. Ohio Dept. MR/DD, 2001--. Home: 455 Flemridge Ct Cincinnati OH 45231-4050 Office: Behavioral Sci Ctr 2316 Kemper Ln Cincinnati OH 45206-2611 also: Hamilton Co Bd Mental Retardation 4370 Malsbary Rd Cincinnati OH 45242 E-mail: dzucker@fuse.net.

ZUCKER, HERBERT, retired publishing executive; b. N.Y.C., July 7, 1928; s. Reuben and Bess E. (Kolber) Z.; m. Nancy E. Fine, Nov. 26, 1953 (dec.); children:Bradley Charles, Eileen Sherri(dec.), Amy Diane. BA, NYU, 1950; MS, UCLA, 1953. Regional mgr. TV Guide, Miami, Fla., 1954-61, mgr. nat. merchandising Radnor, Pa., 1961-66, nat. mgr. regional sales, 1966-75, dir. pub. relations, 1975-80, dir. mktg., broadcast and cable, 1980-85, dir. cable mktg., 1985-2000, ret., 2000. Lectr. to trade assns., colls., univs., 1965—. Contbr. articles to TV Guide. Served with U.S. Army, 1951-53. Mem. Advt. Club (v.p. 1957-59). Avocations: tennis, jogging, reading.

ZUCKER, HOWARD, lawyer; b. N.Y.C., June 21, 1952; s. Morris Milton and Sarah Shirley (Spector) Z.; m. Lynn Carol Bierschenk; children: Lauren Heather, Erica Rachael, Monica Juliet. Student, London Sch. Econs., 1973; BS in Econs. summa cum laude, U. Pa., 1973, JD, 1977. Bar: N.Y. 1978. Ptnr. Hawkins, Delafield & Wood, N.Y.C., 1977—. Author: ABCs of Housing Bonds, 5th edit., 1993. Mem. ABA (chmn. pub. fin. com. of state and local govt. law sect. 1996-98), N.Y. State Bar Assn., Nat. Assn. Bond Lawyers (bd. dirs. 1994-2001, pres.-elect 1998-99, pres. 1999-2000), Omicron Delta Epsilon. Office: Hawkins Delafield & Wood 67 Wall St Fl 11 New York NY 10005-3155

ZUCKER, HOWARD ALAN, pediatric cardiologist, intensivist, anesthesiologist; b. N.Y.C., Sept. 6, 1959; s. Saul and Phyllis (Goldblatt) Zucker. BS, McGill U., Montreal, 1979; MD, George Washington U., 1982; JD, Fordham U., 2000; LLM, Columbia U., 2001. Pediatric intern Johns Hopkins Hosp., Balt., 1982-83, pediatric resident, 1983-85; anesthesiology resident Hosp. of U. Pa., Phila., 1985-87; pediatric critical care fellow Children's Hosp. of Phila., 1987-88; asst. prof. anesthesiology and pediatrics Yale U. Sch. Medicine, New Haven, 1988-90; pediatric cardiology fellow Children's Hosp., Harvard Med. Sch., Boston, 1990-92; assoc. prof. clin. pediat. and clin. anesthesiology N.Y. Presbyn. Hosp. and Children's Hosp., N.Y.C., 1992—2001; dir. pediatric transport Columbia Presbyn. Med. Ctr. Babies and Children's Hosp. N.Y., 1992—2001; White House fellow, 2001—01. Adj. assoc. prof. pediat. Cornell U. Weill Coll. Medicine, 2000—01; involved with crew tng. NASA Space Shuttle STS-1 Mission, 1978—80; rsch. affiliate Man-vehicle Lab MIT; White House fellow, 2001—02. Participant med. missions to China Children China Pediat. Found.; chmn. bd. Terre Verte Found., Inc.; bd. dirs. Little Hearts Pediat. Found. Named Person of the Week, ABC World News Tonight, 1993. Fellow: Am. Coll. Critical Care Medicine, Am. Coll. Legal Medicine, Am. Coll. Cardiology, Am. Coll. Chest Physicians, Am. Acad. Pediat.; mem.: AMA, Soc. Critical Care Medicine, Am. Heart Assn., Am. Soc. Anesthesiologists. Jewish. Achievements include research in adaptation to zero gravity, cardiac critical care. Home: 100 Winston Dr Apt 12G Cliffside Park NJ 07010-3240

ZUCKER, JERRY, chemical manufacturing executive; b. Tel-Aviv, Israel, Aug. 24, 1949; s. Leon and Zipora (Shlifkovitz) Z.; m. Anita Goldberg, June 21, 1970; cildren: Jonathan Michael, Andrea Michelle, Jeffrey Mark. BS, U. Fla., 1968, MEE, 1972. Electronics design engr. Vital Industries, Inc., Gainesville, Fla., 1968-71; devel. engrng. group dir. Cons. Engrs., Inc., 1971-73; supr. process engrng. and tech. svcs. Hudson Pulp & Paper Corp. (now Ga. Pacific), Palatka, Fla., 1973-78; dir. mfg. and tech. svcs. Raybestos Manhattan, Inc., North Charleston, S.C., 1978-82; chmn. bd., CEO InterTech Group, Inc.; chmn., CEO Polymer Group, Inc. Bd. dirs. High Tech. Coatings Corp., Advanced Chem. Techs., Inc., Tighitco, Inc., Ecosys, Inc., Polymer Group, Inc., FiberTech Group, Inc., ConX Inc., Tycon Inc., Worthington Products Inc., Aerospace Def. Inc., Technetics Group, Inc., Thantex, Inc., Global Golf, Inc., Fabrene, Inc., Polymer Group, Inc., Daramic, Inc., RemGrit Corp., Polyionix, Inc.; cons. phosphate mining, pulp and paper and sugar industries. Contbr. articles to tech. hours.; patentee in electrochem., mech. and chem. fields. Bd. dirs. Roper Hosp., Trident United Way, Charleston Jewish Fedn.; pres. Hotline Inc., Hebrew Benevolent Soc., Hebrew Orphan Soc., Orgn. Rehab. Tng., S.C. Aquarium; pres. Synagogue Emanuel; trustee S.C. Rsch. Inst., U. S.C., Med. U. S.C. Rsch. Inst. Mem. IEEE, TAPPI (nat. elec. engrng. com. 1977-95), Am. Chem. Soc. Jewish. Home: 16 Buckingham Dr Charleston SC 29407-3455 Office: The InterTech Group Inc PO Box 5205 4838 Jenkins Ave North Charleston SC 29405-4816

ZUCKER, LEONARD CHARLES, trucking executive, rabbi; b. Bronx, N.Y., June 13, 1933; s. Ralph Gilbert and Elsie (Himmelstein) Z.; m. Elaine Trachtman, Dec. 25, 1955 (dec. Aug. 1998); children: Anne, Esther Lynne, Rhea Miriam, Ronald Gary; m. Marilyn Stennstien, Dec. 12, 1999. BA, Yeshiva U., 1951; postgrad., Acad. Advanced Traffic, 1955. Ordained rabbi, 1957. With Charlton Bros. Transp. Co., Inc., Phila., 1953-58; sales mgr.

Phila.-Pits. Carriers, 1958-61; dist. sales rep. Preston Trucking Co., Inc., 1961-65; v.p. Drake Motor Lines Inc., Cherry Hill, N.J., 1965-76; exec. v.p., COO Pinto Trucking Svc., Inc., Phila., 1976-83, pres., 1984-86, L. Zucker Assocs., 1986—. Rabbi Congregation B'nai Tikvah, Turnersville, N.J., 1975-97, Golden Lakes Temple, West Palm Beach, Fla., 1998—; chaplain Fedn. Jewish Agys. of Atlantic County, 1987-93; pres. Tri County Bd. Rabbis, 1995-97; mem. Phila. Bd. Rabbis, Palm Beach County Bd. Rabbis. Author: Why Be a Transportation Specialist, 1971, Safety Guide for the Motor Carrier, 1973. Bd. dirs. Motor Transport Labor Rels., Phila., 1973-76. With U.S. Army, 1953-55. Mem. Assn. ICC Practitioners, Transp. Law Practitioners U.S., Air Cargo Club, Nat. Fedn. Men's Clubs, Fifth Wheel Club, Traffic and Transp. Club, Delta Nu Alpha. Democrat. Jewish. Home: 119 Lake Nancy Dr West Palm Beach FL 33411-9202 Office: PO Box 210064 Royal Palm Beach FL 33421

ZUCKER, LYNNE GOODMAN, sociology educator, consultant; b. Dayton, Ohio, May 10, 1945; d. Robert Alfred and Sieglinde Goodman; m. Joel Steven Zucker, June 5, 1966 (div. Sept. 1991); children: Joshua, Danielle; m. Michael Rucker Darby, Feb. 14, 1992; children: Margaret, David. AB, Wells Coll., 1966; MA, Stanford U., 1969, PhD, 1974. Instr. dept. sociology Stanford U., Palo Alto, Calif., 1972-73; lectr. dept. sociology and urban studies program San Francisco State U., 1974; lectr. dept. sociology UCLA, 1974-75, asst. prof., 1975-81, assoc. prof., 1981-89, prof., 1989—, mem. affiliated faculty Sch. Edn., 1984—, program dir. for orgnl. rsch. Inst. for Social Sci. Rsch., 1986—, prof. policy studies Sch. Pub. Policy and Social Rsch., 1996—, dir. Ctr. for Internat. Sci., Tech. and Cultural Policy, 1996—. Mem. com. on evaluation employment and tng. programs NAS-NRC, 1977-80; mem. vis. faculty dept. sociology U. Chgo., 1982; mem. sociology panel NSF, 1984-87, mem. young presdl. scholar award panel, 1989-91; fellow program on non-profit orgns. Inst. for Social and Policy Studies, Yale U., New Haven, 1986; mem. vis. faculty program in orgnl. behavior Harvard U. Bus. Sch., Boston, 1987; economist stats. of income IRS, U.S. Treasury Dept., Washington, 1989-94; cons. sociologist Am. Inst. Physics, N.Y.C., 1980-95; prin. Dumbarton Group, L.A., 1992—; Hightower lectr. Emory U. Bus. Sch., 1993; rsch. assoc. Nat. Bur. Econ. Rsch., Cambridge, Mass., 1994—. Author: (with Freeman and Jones) Social Problems: A Policy Perspective, 1979, (monograph) The Impact of Proposition 13 on Public Funding and Services for Education and Health in California, 1982, (with Meyer) Permanently Failing Orgniazation, 1989; editor: Institutional Patterns and Organizations: Cultures and Environments, 1988; mem. editl. bd. Am. Jour. Sociology, 1985-87, 95-97, Adminstrv. Sci. Quar., 1982-86, Am. Sociol. Rev., 1980-83, Pacific Sociol. Rev., 1977-83, Symbolic Interaction, 1986-91. Bd. dirs. Opera Assocs., L.A., 1994—. Regents faculty fellow U. Calif., 1976, fellow Calif. Coun. on Sci. and Tech., 2000—. Mem. Macro Orgnl. Behavior Soc., Am. Sociol. Assn. (co-chmn. com. on archives 1994—), Alpha Kappa Delta. Episcopalian. Avocations: art, opera, hiking. Office: UCLA Dept Sociology Box 951441 Los Angeles CA 90095-1551 Fax: 310-454-2748.

ZUCKER, ROBERT A(LPERT), psychologist; b. N.Y.C., Dec. 9, 1935; s. Morris and Sophie (Alpert) Z.; m. Martine Latil; children: Lisa, Alex, Eleanor; m. Kristine Ellen Freeark, Mar. 10, 1979; 1 child, Katherine. B.C.E., CCNY, 1956; postgrad., UCLA, 1956-58; PhD, Harvard U., 1966. Diplomate Am. Bd. Profl. Psychology (clin.); lic. psychologist, Mich. From instr. to asst. prof. psychology Rutgers U., 1963-68; from asst. prof. to assoc. prof. to prof. Mich. State U., 1968-94; prof. psychology in psychiatry and psychology U. Mich., 1994—, dir. Addiction Rsch. Ctr., 1994—, dir. substance abuse divsn. dept. psychiatry, 1994—, rsch. assoc. Inst. for Social Rsch., 1996—. Vis. prof. U. Tex., Austin, 1975; vis. rsch. prof. psychology in psychiatry U. Mich., 1990-91; vis. scholar Nat. Inst. Alcohol Abuse and Alcoholism, 1980; dir. clin. tng. Mich. State U., 1982-94; lectr. Nebr. Symposium on Motivation, 1986; cons. in field. Editor: Further Explorations in Personality, 1981, Personality and the Prediction of Behavior, 1984, The Emergence of Personality, 1987, Studying Persons and Lives, 1990, Personality Structure in the Life Course, 1992, The Development of Alcohol Problems: Exploring the Biopsychosocial Matrix of Risk, 1994, Alcohol Problems Among Adolescents: Current Directions in Prevention Research, 1995, Alcohol Problems and Aging, 1998; contbr. chpts. and articles to profl. publs. Bd. dirs. Nat. Coun. on Alcoholism-Mich., 1978-82; mem. Psychosocial Initial Rev. Group, Nat. Inst. Alcohol Abuse and Alcoholism, 1989-92; mem. HPRB study sect. Ctr. for Sci. Rev., NIH, 1998-2000. Inst. Children Youth & Families fellow Mich. State U., 1993; recipient Blue Cross-Blue Shield Mich. Found. Excellence in Clin. Rsch. award, 1997. Fellow AAAS, APA (pres. addictions divsn. 50 1997-98), APS, Am. Orthopsychiat. Assn.; mem. Midwestern Psychol. Assn., Soc. Personology, Soc. Life History Rsch. in Psychopathology, Rsch. Soc. on Alcoholism (sec. and bd. dirs. 2001—). Office: Univ Mich Addiction Rsch Ctr 400 E Eisenhower Pkwy Ann Arbor MI 48108-3318 E-mail: zuckerra@umich.edu.

ZUCKER, STEFAN, tenor, writer, editor, radio broadcaster; b. N.Y.C. BS, Columbia U., 1967; postgrad., NYU, 1967-72. Freelance tenor concerts and operas in U.S. and Europe, 1965—; tenor RCA Records, N.Y.C., 1972-77; guest singer radio and TV programs U.S. and Europe, 1975—; radio producer, host WKCR-FM, N.Y.C., 1980-94; opera critic N.Y. Tribune, 1983-84; philosophy lectr. Coll. Ins. N.Y.C., 1972; host web radio program Opera Fanatic www.belcantosociety.org, 2002—. Lectr. The Mannes Coll. Music, 2000—. Author: The Origins of Modern Tenor Singing, 1997; appeared in film Opera Fanatic: Stefan and the Divas, 1998; record producer including Rossini's Rivals: Music By Then-Famous, Now-Obscure, Italian Composers, 1984; restorer films of opera singers, 1987—; singer, producer, stage dir., adminstr. various operas, 1967—; editor Opera Fanatic mag., 1986—; commentator and singer (TV series) Bel canto: Tenors of the 78 Era, 1996-97; contbr. articles to Internat. Dictionary of Opera, Opera News, The Opera Quar., Am. Record Guide, Opera Fanatic, Globe & Mail, News World, Professione Musica, others. Pres. Bel Canto Soc., Inc., 1985—. Named Worlds Highest Tenor by Guinness Book of World Records, 1979—; subject of record Stefan Zucker: The World's Highest Tenor, 1981. Mem. NYU Philosophy Assn. (pres. 1969-72, v.p. 1968), Music Critics Assn., Assn. Furtherment Bel Canto (pres. 1967-80). Office: Bel Canto Soc Inc 11 Riverside Dr New York NY 10023-2504

ZUCKER, WILLIAM, retired business educator; b. Bridgeport, Conn., July 21, 1917; s. Meyer and Ida Lena (Elovitz) Z.; m. Kathlyn Saltman, Jan. 16, 1944; children— Peter Bayard, Alison Beth, Jeremy Michael, David Laurence AB, Johns Hopkins U., 1938; AM, Harvard U., 1940, PhD, 1951. Sec. Commerce and Industry Assn. of N.Y., N.Y.C., 1944-59; v.p. Downtown Lower Manhattan Assn., 1959-64; pres. Southeastern Pa. Econ. Devel. Corp., Phila., 1964-73; adj. prof. Wharton Sch. U. Pa., 1972-83, assoc. dir. Entrepreneurial Ctr., Wharton Sch., 1973-83, dir. exec. edn. Wharton Sch., 1977-83, dir. Wharton Real Estate Ctr., 1983-88, Meshulam Riklis prof. creative mgmt. Wharton Sch., 1983-88, prof. emeritus, 1988—; pres. Adviserv Co., Phila., 1993-94. Lectr. CCNY, 1956-58; vis. prof. Columbia U. Grad. Sch. Bus., N.Y.C., 1988-91; adj. prof. Drexel U., PHila., 1997—. Author: Local Development Corporations, 1980, REITS, 1975; editor Real Estate Fin. Jour., 1985-98; contbr. articles to profl. jours. Mem. New Canaan Bd. Edn., Conn., 1961-64, New Canaan Bd. Fin., 1958-61 Democrat. Jewish. Home: Cathedral Village 600 E Cathedral Rd Apt L105 Philadelphia PA 19128-1942 Office: U Pa 2000 Steinberg Dietrich Hal Philadelphia PA 19104

ZUCKER-FRANKLIN, DOROTHEA, physician, educator; b. Berlin, Aug. 9, 1930; came to U.S., 1949; d. Julian J. and Gertrude Zucker; m. Edward C. Franklin (dec.); 1 child, Deborah Julie. BA, CUNY, 1952, PhD in Sci. (hon.), 1996; MD, N.Y. Med. Coll., 1956. Diplomate Am. Bd. Medicine. Intern Phila. Gen. Hosp., 1956-57; resident in internal medicine Montefiore Hosp., N.Y.C., 1957-59, postdoctoral fellow in hematology, 1959-61; postdoctoral fellow in electron microscopy NYU Sch. Medicine, 1961-63, asst. prof. medicine, 1963-67, assoc. prof., 1968-74, prof. medicine, 1974—; assoc. attending physician Bellevue Hosp., 1968-74, attending physician, 1974—. Assoc. attending physician Univ. Hosp., Tisch, 1968-74, attending physician, 1974—; cons. physician Manhattan VA Hosp., 1970—; mem. editl. bd. numerous publs., including Blood, 1963-76, 80-86, Am. Jour. Pathology, 1979—, Ultrastructure Pathology, 1979—, Blood Cells, 1980, Am. Jour. Medicine, 1981-87, Hematology Oncology, 1982—, Jour. AIDS Rsch., 1987—, Hematopathology and Molecular Hematology, 1987—, others; mem. bd. reviewing editors Jour. Lab. and Clin. Medicine, 1990—; mem. hematology panel Health Rsch. Coun. City of N.Y., 1971-74; mem. pathology tng. com. Nat. Inst. Med. Scis., 1971-74; mem. allergy and immunology rsch. com. Nat. Inst. Allergy and Infectious Diseases, 1974-81; mem. U.S.-Israel Binat. Sci. Found., 1980—; mem. ad hoc promotion com. Harvard Med. Sch., 1981, 83; mem. blood products adv. com. FDA, 1981-86; mem. sci. adv. bd. and sci. rev. panel Israel Cancer Rsch. Fund., 1982-90; mem. grant rev. panel VA AIDS Ctr., 1988-89; vis. fellow Assn. Claude Bernard, 1974-75. Co-author: The Physiology and Pathology of Leukocytes, 1962, Amyloidosis, 1986, Atlas of Blood Cells: Function and Pathology, 2 vols., 1981, 3d edit., 2002, Thrombopoiesis and Thrombopoietins: Molecular, Cellular, Preclinical and Clinical Biology, 1996; contbr. over 250 articles to profl. jours. Bd. dirs. Henry M. and Lillian Stratton Found., Inc., 1987-95. Named to Hall of Fame, Hunter Coll., 1977, Internat. Profl. and Bus. Women, 1994. Fellow AAAS, N.Y. Acad. Scis.; mem. Inst. Medicine NAS, Am. Assn. Physicians, Am. Fedn. Clin. Rsch., Am. Soc. Clin. Investigation, Am. Soc. Hematology (program com. 1973, edn. com. 1974-78, chair subcom. on leukocyte physiology 1977, chair subcom. on immunohematology 1984, com. on advanced learning resources 1986—, exec. coun. 1987-91, pres.-elect 1992, pres. 1994-95, chair adv. bd. 1996, com. on govt. affairs, 2001), Federated Socs. Exptl. Biology and Medicine, Am. Soc. Physiology, Am. Acad. Arts & Scis., Am. Assn. Immunologists, Am. Soc. Exptl. Pathology, Am. Soc. Cell Biology (program com. internat. congress 1976), Reticuloendothelial Soc. (program com. 1974-76, nominating com. 1976-78, pres. 1984-85, life mem.), N.Y. Soc. Electron Microscopists (program chair 1984, pres. 1984-85), N.Y. Soc. for Study of Blood (chair program com. 1976-80, pres. 1981-82), Internat. Retrovirology Assn., NTLV and Related Viruses, Phi Beta Kappa, Alpha Omega Alpha. Office: NYU Med Ctr 550 1st Ave New York NY 10016-6402 E-mail: dorothea.zucker-franklin@med.nyu.edu.

ZUCKERMAN, HARRIET, sociologist, educator; b. N.Y.C., July 19, 1937; d. Harry and Anne D. (Wiener) Z; m. Robert K. Merton, 1993. AB, Vassar Coll., 1958; PhD, Columbia U., 1965. Asst. prof. sociology Columbia U., 1965-72, assoc. prof., 1972-78, prof., 1978-92; prof. emerita, 1993—; sr. rsch. scholar, 1993—; chmn. dept. Columbia U., 1978-81; v.p. Andrew W. Mellon Found., 1991-98, sr. v.p., 1998—. Vis. scholar Russell Sage Found., 1971-72, 85-87; mem. adv. bd. Social Sci. Citation Index, Inst. Sci. Information, 1972-98; dir. Annual Revs., Inc., 1974— ; trustee Am. Savs. Bank, 1978-83 Author: Scientific Elite: Nobel Laureates in the United States, 1977, rev. edit., 1996; co-editor: Toward A Metric of Science: The Advent of Science Indictors, 1978, The Outer Circle: Women in the Scientific Community, 1991; mem. editorial bd. Scientometrics, 1977— , Am. Jour. Sociology, 1972-74, 77-79, Am. Sociol. Rev., 1972-74, 87-91, Sci., 1985-86; contbr. articles to profl. jours. Bd. dirs. Social Sci. Rsch. Coun., 1974-76, AAAS, 1980-84, Women's Forum, 1989-91; trustee Ctr. for Advanced Study in Behavioral Scis., 1976-88, 89—; mem. ednl. adv. bd. John Simon Guggenheim Meml. Found., 1986-93, mem. com. on selection, 1989-91. Woodrow Wilson fellow, 1958-59; Center for Advanced Study in Behavioral Scis. fellow, 1973-74; Guggenheim fellow, 1980-81; Phi Beta Kappa vis. scholar, 1982-83; recipient Dean's award for Disting. Achievement Columbia U. Grad. Sch., 1998. Mem. Am. Philos. Soc. (councillor 1997—), Am. Acad. Arts and Scis. (chmn. class III membership com. 1991-94), Soc. Social Studies Sci. (pres. 1989-91), The Century Assn., Coun. on Fgn. Rels.

ZUCKERMAN, HERBERT LAWRENCE, lawyer; b. Newark, June 11, 1928; s. David and Adele Zuckerman; m. Janet Albert, Sept. 10, 1950; children: Julia, Elizabeth, William. BSBA, Lehigh U., 1949; JD, Rutgers U., 1953. Acct. Zuckerman & Black, Newark, 1949-56; pvt. practice law, 1956-71; ptnr. Zuckerman, Aronson & Horn, 1971-81; ptnr., v.p. Sills Cummis, 1981-98, sr.counsel, 1998—. Bd. dirs. Am. Jewish Com., 1990—; vol. The Hospice, Glen Ridge, N.J., 1985—. Fellow Coll. of Tax Counsel; mem. ABA, N.J. Bar Assn., Fed. Bar Assn., Essex County Bar Assn., Mental Health Assn. (bd. dirs. 1997—), Mensa. Avocations: tennis, music, theater, opera, reading. Office: Sills Cummis 1 Riverfront Plz Fl 10 Newark NJ 07102-5401 E-mail: hzuckerman@sillscummis.com.

ZUCKERMAN, JACKIE LYNN, social worker; b. Queens, N.Y., Oct. 11, 1960; d. Alvin and Barbara (Roffis) Lachow; m. Richard K. Zuckerman, Aug. 25, 1984. BA, SUNY, Stony Brook, 1982, MSW, 1984. Cert. social worker, N.Y. Group work supr. Jewish Assn. for Svcs. for Aged, Bklyn.; dir. Multiple Sclerosis Care Ctr., Long Beach (N.Y.) Meml. Hosp. Mem. NASW, Acad. Cert. Social Workers. Home: 3187 Ann St Baldwin NY 11510-4509

ZUCKERMAN, MARC ABRAHAM, accountant, educator; b. N.Y.C., May 30, 1951; s. Henry and Rela (Ast) Z.; m. Sue Carol Kezurer, Dec. 6, 1981; 1 child, Sam David. BA cum laude, CUNY, Bronx, 1973; MA, Columbia U., 1974; MBA, Manhattan Coll., 1984. Cert. mgmt. acct., cash mgr., credit executive. Dir. corp. credit Clinton Swan Clothes, N.Y.C., 1978-80; dir. fin. Lord Jeff, Norwood, N.J., 1980-88; dir. corp. credit Bernard Chaus, Inc., Secaucus, 1988-89; asst. treas. Warnaco, Bridgeport, Conn., 1989; treas. Bernard Chaus, Inc., Secaucus, 1989-95; corp. contr. Precision Custom Coatings, Totowa, N.J., 1996-99; v.p. ops., CFO Triboro Quilt Mfg. Corp., 1999—. Pres. Meadowlands Fin. Group, 1991-95; adj. prof. fin. Contbr. articles to profl. jours. Pack com. mem. Ridgewood Boy Scouts Am., 1997-2000, treas. 1997-2000. Mem. Inst. Mgmt. Accts., Treas. Mgmt. Assn., Treas. Mgmt. Assn. N.J., Nat. Assn. Credit Mgmt., N.J. Corp. Treas. Mgmt. Assn. (treas. 1996—), Nat. Apparel Mfrs. Credit Assn. (bd. dirs. 1993-95), Bergen Rockland Inst. Mgmt. Accts. (bd. dirs. 1996-97). Avocations: jogging, golf. Home: 153 Lincoln Ave Ridgewood NJ 07450-4105 Office: Triboro Quilt Mfg Corp 172 South Broadway White Plains NY 10605

ZUCKERMAN, MARTIN HARVEY, personnel director; b. N.Y.C., Feb. 20, 1942; s. Merwin and Helen (Weinstein) Z.; m. Joyce S. Harris, July 26, 1969; children: Lyle, Evan. BA, NYU, 1963; JD, St. John's U., 1965; LLM, NYU, 1966. Bar: N.Y. 1966. Field atty. Nat. Labor Relations Bd., N.Y.C., 1966-70; sr. atty. Simpson, Thatcher & Bartlett, 1970-80; v.p. compensation and benefits Chemical Banking Corp. (formerly Mfrs. Hanover Trust Co.), 1980-1983, sr. v.p., asst. personnel dir., 1983-85, exec. v.p., personnel dir., 1985-92; exec. v.p., pers. dir. Chem. Banking Corp. (formerly Mfrs. Hanover Trust Co.), 1992-96. Mem. mgmt. com. Chem. Banking Corp., 1994-96; mem. adv. coun. on human resources mgmt. The Conf. Bd., 1992—. Trustee Drs. Hosp., 1984-92, Beth Israel Hosp., 1987-96, Employee Benefit Rsch. Inst., 1989—; treas. Puerto Rican Legal Def. and Edn. Fund, Inc., mem. exec. com., 1985-99, chmn. devel. com., 2000—, mem. fin. com., 1985—. Mem. N.Y. State Bar Assn., N.Y. County Lawyers Assn.

ZUCKERMAN, MARVIN, psychologist; b. Chgo., Mar. 21, 1928; s. Eli and Sophia (Pilder) Z.; children: April B. Zuckerman Schanoes, Steven H. BA, N.Y. U., 1949, PhD, 1954. Research assoc. Inst. Psychiat. Research, Ind. U. Med. Center, 1956-59; asst. prof. psychology Bklyn. Coll., 1959-62; research assoc. Albert Einstein Med. Center, Phila., 1963-69; prof. psychology U. Del., Newark, 1969—. Author: (with C.D. Spielberger) Emotions and Anxiety, 1976, Sensation Seeking: Beyond the Optimal Level of Arousal, 1979, Biological Bases of Sensation Seeking, Impulsivity and Anxiety, 1983, Psychobiology of Personality, 1991, Behavioral Expressions and Biosocial Bases of Sensation Seeking, 1994. Fellow APA, Am. Psychol. Soc.; mem. Eastern Psychol. Assn., Soc. Psychophysiol. Research, Internat. Soc. Study Individual Differences (past pres.). Home: 7 E Rosemont Cir Elkton MD 21921-2067 Office: U Del Dept Psychology Newark DE 19711

ZUCKERMAN, NANCY CAROL, learning disabilities specialist, consultant; b. Jersey City, Aug. 14, 1951; d. Bernard Milton and Shirley (Stepner) Solomon; m. Marshall Howard Zuckerman, Aug. 20, 1978; 1 child, Seth Michael. BA, Rider U., 1973; MEd, William Paterson Coll., 1977. Cert. elem. tchr., spl. edn. and learning disabilities tchr., prin., N.J. Tchr. elem. edn. North Bergen (N.J.) Bd. Edn., 1973-76; tchr. state compensatory edn. Bayonne (N.J.) Bd. Edn., 1977, tchr. cons. learning disabilities, 1977—. Chairperson Child Study Team, Bayonne, 1988—. Mem. adv. bd., sec., asst. pack leader Cub Scouts Pack 35, Bayonne, 1996—; bd. dirs. Temple Beth Am, Bayonne, 1975-79, 97—, edn. chmn., 1975-79. Mem. CEC, Assn. Learning Consultants, Pi Lambda Theta. Jewish. Home: 21 E 35th St Bayonne NJ 07002-3924 Office: Bayonne Bd Edn Bayonne NJ 07002 E-mail: N@LDTC@aol.com.

ZUCKERMAN, RICHARD KARL, lawyer; b. Bay Shore, N.Y., Feb. 23, 1960; s. Jack Irwin and Dorothy Ann (Sugarman) Z.; m. Jackie Lynn Lachow, Aug. 25, 1984. BA summa cum laude, SUNY, Stony Brook, 1981; JD, Columbia U., 1984. Bar: N.Y. 1985, U.S. Dist. Ct. (ea. and so. dists.) N.Y. 1987. Assoc. Rains & Pogrebin, P.C., Mineola, N.Y., 1984-91, ptnr., 1992—. Editor: Discipline and Discharge in Arbitration, 1998, Discipline and Discharge in Arbitration, 1st supplement, 2000, N.Y. State Public Sector Labor and Employment Law, 2d edit., 1st supplement, 2000, 2d supplement, 2002; contbg. author: N.Y. State Public Sector Law and Employment Law, 1998; contbr. articles to profl. newsletters. Chairperson ann. fund. SUNY, Stony Brook, 1986-91, bd. dirs. Alumni Assn., 1990-96. Mem. ABA, N.Y. State Bar Assn. (chair labor and employment law sect. com. on govt. employee rels. law 1998-2002, chair com. on CLE 2002—, chair mcpl. law sect., employment rels. com. 1998—, mem. exec. com. labor and employment law sect, 1998—, mem. exec. com. mcpl. law sect., 2001—). Nassau County Bar Assn., N.Y. State Assn. Sch. Attys. (bd. dirs.). Home: 3187 Ann St Baldwin NY 11510-4509 Office: Rains & Pogrebin PC 210 Old Country Rd Mineola NY 11501-4288

ZUCKERMAN, SIDNEY, retired allergist, immunologist; b. N.Y.C., May 2, 1918; s. Max and Rose (Katz) Z.; m. Irene Elinor Cohen, Oct. 27, 1945; children: Elaine, Laurie, Jed, Amy. BA, Columbia Coll., 1939; MD, N.Y. Med. Coll., 1943. Diplomate Am. Bd. Internal Medicine, Am. Bd. Allergy and Immunology. Chief medicine 172 Sta. Hosp. US Army Med. Corps., Sendai, Japan, 1945-47; med. dir. Ford Instrument Co. divsn. Sperry Corp., N.Y.C., 1947-60; pvt. practice, 1947-91; med. dir. Unysis Corp., Great Neck, NY, 1960-90. Capt. U.S. Army Med. Corps., 1945-47, Japan. Fellow ACP, Am. Coll. Allergy, Asthma and Immunology, Am. Acad. Allergy, Asthma and Immunology, Am. Coll. Occupational and Environ. Medicine, Am. Assn. Cert. Allergists; mem. Masons (jr. warden), Soc. Columbia Grads. Avocations: woodworking, golf. Home: 4140 Bocaire Blvd Boca Raton FL 33487-1148

ZUCKERMAN, STUART, psychiatrist, forensic examiner, educator; b. Syracuse, N.Y., Feb. 18, 1933; s. George and Cassie (Kolsan) Z. Student, U. Kans., 1950-51; BS, U. Ala., 1954; DO, Phila. Coll. Osteo. Medicine, 1958. Diplomate Am. Osteo. Bd. Neurology and Psychiatry, Am. Nat. Bd. Psychiatry, Am. Coll. Forensic Medicine, Bd. Forensic Medicine, Bd. Forensic Examiner; cert. correctional health profl. Rotating intern Hosps. Phila. Coll. Osteo. Medicine, 1958-59; psychiat. fellow, resident Phila. Mental Health Clinic, 1959-62, Psychoanalytic Studies Inst., Phila., 1959-62; chief resident, 1962; chief div. neuropsychiatry Grandview Hosp., Dayton, Ohio, 1962-65; asst. med. dir., chief children's and adolescent's unit N.J. State Hosp., Ancora, 1967-70; chief outpatient dept. Atlantic City, 1970-72; practice specializing in neuropsychiatry Atlantic City, 1965—; founding prof. psychiatry, chmn. dept. Ohio U. Coll. Osteo. Medicine, Athens, 1976-77, clin. prof., 1977—; mem. faculty U. Pa. Sch. Medicine, Phila. Coll. Osteo. Medicine, 1972-76, with Benjamin Franklin scholar spl. studies faculty; lectr. U. Pa., 1977-79; prof. dept. psychiatry, charter faculty Sch. Medicine, Marshall U., 1977-78, clin. prof., 1979-80, N.Y. Coll. Osteo. Medicine, 1979—; chief mental hygiene VA Hosp., Huntington, W.Va., 1978-79; liaison psychiatrist, acting chief VA Med. Center, Perry Point, Md., 1979-80; med. dir. Mental Health Clinic of Ocean County, Toms River, N.J., 1980-85, Ventnor (N.J.) Mental Health Ctr.; chief psychiatrist N.J. Dept. Corrections So. State Correctional Facility, 1985-96. Physician Atlantic City Beach Patrol, 1961-63; attending psychiatrist Atlantic City, Shore Meml., Kessler Meml., Washington Meml., Atlantic County Mental hosps., 1965-76; attending psychiatrist, asst. dir. dept. psychiatry Phila. Gen. Hosp., 1972-76; med. dir. Shawnee Mental Health Center, (Adams, Lawrence, Scioto counties), Portsmouth, Ohio, 1977-78; cons. psychiatrist Athens Mental Health and Mental Retardation Ctr., 1976-77, Scioto Meml., So. Hills, Mercy hosps., Portsmouth, 1977-78, Lansdowne Cmty. Mental Health Center, (Greenup, Carter counties), Ashland, Ky., 1977-78, Atlantic City Med. Ctr., 1984-97, Cmty. Meml. Hosp., Toms River, N.J., 1984-91, So. Ocean County Hosp., Manahawkin, N.J., 1984-91, Paul-Kimball Med Ctr., Lakewood, N.J., 1984-97, Obleness Meml. Hosp., Clin. Services of Athens, Vinton, Hocking Counties, Hudson Health Ctr., Ohio U., 1976-77; cons. Bayside State Prison, Leesburg, N.J., 1989-96, Atlantic County Justice System, Mays Landing, N.J., 1992-93, child study spl. svcs. S. Jersey sch. systems; chmn. profl. adv. com. Atlantic County Mental Health Bd., 1969-71; mem. nominating com. Mental Health Assn., Atlantic County, 1972-75; exam. psychiatrist Jersey Police and Fire depts.; mem. Atlantic County Mental Health Bd.; mem. profl. adv. com. N.J. Dept. Corrections; cons. N.J. Dept. Pub. Advocate; mem. panel med. cons. N.J. State Med. Bd., 1998—. Mem. adv. bd. Osteo. Physician, 1975-98; assoc. editor Bull. Am. Coll. Neuropsychiatrists, 1963-70, Jour. Corr. Health Editl. Bd.; contbr. articles to profl. jours. Bd. dirs. Atlantic County Family Svcs. Assn., 1968-74, Cape May County Drug Abuse Coun., 1973-76, Nat. Comm. Correctional Health Care, 1988-97; mem. Ventnor City Beautification Com., 1996—; sponsor, house physician Friends of the Pops Ocean City (N.J.) Music Pier. Fellow Am. Coll. Forensic Psychiatry, Am. Coll. Neuropsychiatrists (bd. reps.), Am. Acad. Disability Evaluating Physicians (charter), Acad. Psychosomatic Medicine, Acad. Medicine N.J., Coll. Physicians of Phila.; mem. AMA (Physicians Recognition award 1985—), AAUP, Am. Bd. Forensic Examiners (cert. 1994), Am. Coll. Forensic Medicine (bd. cert. 1996), World Psychiat. Assn., Am. Psychiat. Assn., N.J. (confidentiality, pub. psychiatry com., gen. hosp. psychiatry com., law com., mkgt. benefits com.) Psychiat. Assn., Am. Assn. Psychiatrists in Alcohol and Addictions (founder), Am., N.J. pub. health assns., Am. Osteo. Assn. (hosp. inspection team 1971-75, bd. reps.), Am. Assn. CMHC Psychiatrists, Am. Assn. Psychiatrists in Pvt. Practice, Internat. Assn. Med. Specialists, Am. Soc. Law and Medicine, Am. Acad. Clin. Psychiatrists, Corp. Advancement Psychiatry, Am. Med. Writers Assn., Nat. Council Community Mental Health Ctrs., Nat. Alliance Mentally Ill (profl. assoc. mem.), Met. Coll. Mental Health Assn., Am. Soc. Criminology., South Jersey Neuropsychiat. Soc., Psychiat. Outpatients Ctrs. Am., Am. Coll. Legal Medicine, Acad. Psychiatry and Law (pub. info. com., edn. com., internat. affairs com.), Am. Acad. Forensic Scis., Am. Assn. Acad. Psychiatry, Am. Coll. Emergency Physicians (charter mem.), Am. Acad. Psychotherapists, Am. Assn. Mental Deficiency, Am. Assn. Psychiat. Services for Children, N.J. (chmn. com. on confidentiality, liaison com. health human svcs., corrections), Fla. assns. osteo. physicians and surgeons, N.J. Hosp. Assn., Am. Vocat. Assn., Am. Assn. Group Therapy, Am. Soc. Clin. Psychopharmacology, Assn. Mil. Surgeons U.S., Nat. Assn. VA Physicians, Am. Assn. Psychiat. Adminstrs., Am. Assn. Adolescent Psychiatry, World Med. Assn., Am. Assn. Mental Health Adminstrs., Am. Assn. Gen. Hosp. Psychiatrists, Human Factors Soc., Orthopsychiat. Assn., Am. Physicians Fellowship, Assn. for Research Nervous and Mental Diseases, Atlantic County Osteo. Med. Soc. (pres. 1970-72), N.J. Assn. Mil. Surgeons U.S. (v.p.), Am. Assn. Correctional Health Care, Am. Coll. Forensic Psychiatry (diplomate 1984), charter mem. Soc. of Correctional Physicians. N.J. State bd. of Med. Examiners Specialty Adv. Panel, 1998—. Home: 6700 Atlantic Ave Ventnor City NJ 08406-2618

ZUCKMAN, HARVEY LYLE, law educator; b. Mpls., Apr. 14, 1934; s. George and Elizabeth (Polinsky) Z.; m. Charlotte Anne Snyder, Jan. 27, 1962; children: Jill Belinda, Beth Nancy, Michael Scott. AB, U. So. Calif., 1956; LL.B., NYU, 1959. Bar: Calif. 1960, D.C. 1973, U.S. Supreme Ct. 1963. Atty. civil div. appellate sect. U.S. Dept. Justice, Washington, 1963-67; prof. law St. Louis U., 1967-70, Columbus Sch. Law of Cath. U. Am., 1970—; dir. Inst. for Communications Law Studies Columbus Sch. Law, Cath. U. Am., 1981-01; adj. prof. communications Am. U., 1976-81. Cons. Bur. Nat. Affairs., 1974-81 Producer: Am. Law Inst.-ABA Legal Edn. TV series, 1973-74; co-author: Mass Communications Law, 1977, 5th edit., 2000, Modern Communication Law, 3 vols., 1999; editor ABA newsletter Comm. Lawyer, 1981-86. Served with U.S. Army Judge Adv. Gen., 1960-63. Mem. ABA (forum com. on comm. law, co-chmn. nat. celebration of 200th anniversary of 1st amendment 1991), D.C. Bar Assn. (chairperson com. on continuing legal edn. 1975-83), Fed. Comm. Bar Assn., Am. Law Inst. (life), Assn. Am. Law Schs. (sects. family law and mass comm.), Cosmos Club. Democrat. Office: Cath U Am Columbus Sch Law 3600 John Mccormick Rd NE Washington DC 20064-0001 Fax: 202-319-4459. E-mail: zuckman@law.edu.

ZUEGEL, RICHARD A. photographer; b. Oak Park, Ill., Aug. 11, 1935; s. Herbert Henry and Margaret G. Zuegel; m. Barbara B. Zuegel, Sept. 21, 1957; children: Stephen, James, Jonathan. BA, U. Rochester, N.Y., 1957; MBA, Rochester Inst. Tech., 1976. Tech. assoc. Eastman Kodak, Rochester, 1957—89; photographer, owner Photos Unltd., 1989—. Amb. Kodak Co., Rochester, 1993—. Author: Nature Photographer, 1995. Vice chmn. N.Am. Nature Photo Assn. Infinity Found., Denver, 1998-99; v.p. Chautauqua (N.Y.) Ctr. for Art, 2000—. Capt. USAF, 1958-64. Mem. N.Am. Nature Photo Assn.

(founder, bd. dirs. 1993-99, treas. 1998-99, Disting. Svc. award 1999), Photographic Soc. Am., Internat. Assn. Panorama Photos, Kodak Camera Club (fellow, Disting. Svc. award 1983, pres. 1983), Newport Yacht Club (commodore 1980). Home and Office: 35 Minocqua Dr Rochester NY 14617

ZUEHLKE, RICHARD WILLIAM, technical communications consultant, writer; b. Milw., June 17, 1933; s. Harold Babcock and Phoebe Blanche (Frykman) Z.; m. Carol Sue Yates, Dec. 26, 1955; children: Kenneth Richard, William Woodfill, Deanne Elizabeth. BS, Lawrence Coll., 1955; PhD, U. Minn., 1960. Instr. chemistry Lawrence U., 1958-62, asst. prof., 1962-68; Eliphalet Remington prof. chemistry U. Bridgeport, 1968-79, chmn. dept., 1968-73; vis. prof. U. R.I., 1976-77, 79-80, assoc. marine scientist, 1980-85; owner, pres. The Right Connection, Inc., 1983-91; pres. TetraR Cons., Inc., 1985-88. Cons. Kimberly-Clark Corp., 1960-62, United Illuminating Co., 1969-75, Chem. Specialties Corp., 1970-73, Sperry Remington Corp., 1976-79; NSF Sci. Faculty fellow U. Pitts., 1966-67; asst. to dir. Gordon Rsch. Confs., 1990-94; cons., writer in field. Fellow Am. Inst. Chemists; mem. Am. Chem. Soc., AAAS, Rotary, Sigma Xi, Sigma Phi Epsilon. Congregationalist. Home: PO Box 52 Wilmot NH 03287-0052 Office: PO Box 784 New London NH 03257-0784 E-mail: rzuehlke@tds.net.

ZUERLEIN, DAMIAN JOSEPH, priest; b. Norfolk, Neb., May 28, 1955; s. Victor Damian and Elizabeth P. (Wegener) Z. BA, U. St. Thomas, St. Paul, 1977; MDiv, St. Paul Sem., 1981. Ordained priest Roman Cath. Ch., 1981. Tchr. Norfolk Cath. High Sch., 1981-85; asst. pastor Sacred Heart/St. Mary's Parish, Norfolk, 1981-85; assoc. pastor St. Pius X Cath. Ch., Omaha, 1985-88, Mary Our Queen Cath. Ch., Omaha, 1988-90; pastor Our Lady of Guadalupe Parish, 1990—, St. Agnes Parish, Omaha, 1997—2002, St. Francis of Assisi Praish, Omaha, 2002—. Cons. Archdiocesan Vocations Office, Omaha, 1985-95; bd. dirs. Juan Diego Ctr., Omaha, 1990-2000; chmn., co-founder Omaha Together One Cmty., 1991-95; co-founder Weaving, Women's Advocacy Group, Omaha, 1988—. Presenter (video) Loving Your Marriage, 1990, El Matrimonio: Una Jornada Para Todo Una Vida, 1995; co-author: (manual) Hispanic Pastoral Plan, 1991. Bd. dirs. United Cath. Social Svcs., Omaha, 1990-96, Chicano Awareness Ctr., Omaha, 1991-98, Omaha Food Bank, 2000—, Vis. Nurse Assn., 1996-2000, Omaha 100 Inc., 1991-96, chair, 1991-93; advisor Mayor P.J. Morgan, Omaha, 1991-95; mem. Gov. Nelson's Urban Adv. Task Force, 1994; mem. Douglas County Commn. on Domestic Violence (now Domestic Violence Coord. Coun. Gtr. Omaha), 1996—, Nat. Campaign for Human Devel. Adv. Bd., 1997-2000; mem. Nebr. gov.'s task force on immigration, 1999-2000; founder Guadalupe-Ines Mission Sch., 1998-. Mem. Pax Cristi, Amnesty Internat., Fontenelle Forest Assn., Priests for Equality, Greater Omaha Clergy Assn. (pres. 1987-88), South Omaha Neighborhood Assn. (bd. dirs. 1992, pres. 1994—98). Avocations: canoeing the BWCA, skiing, travel, hiking. Home and Office: 2310 O St Omaha NE 68107-2837

ZUERN, ROSEMARY LUCILE, manufacturing executive, treasurer; b. Eureka, Wis., May 28, 1934; d. Kenneth Arthur and Vera Christine (Barnett) George; m. David Lee Zuern, June 30, 1956. Student, U. Wis., 1954-56. With Kimberly-Clark Corp., Neenah, Wis., 1956-78, sales promotion specialist, 1969-71, trade show adminstr., 1971-78; conv. mgr. Smith Bucklin & Assocs., Chgo., 1979-84, account exec., 1984-96; exec. dir. Bakery Equipment Mfrs. Assn., 1984-96, Soc. Gynecologic Oncologists, Chgo., 1984-96; assoc. sec., treas. Internat. Baking Industry Exposition, 1986-98; ret., 1998. Consumer cons. Kimberly-Clark Corp., Neenah, 1969. Mem. World Airlines Hist. Soc., Exptl. Aircraft Assn., Charles A. Lindbergh Collectors Soc. (past pres.). Avocations: philately, philography, music, antiques, historic firehouse restoration. Home and Office: 913 Wylde Oak Dr Oshkosh WI 54904-7633 Fax: 920-231-0396. E-mail: rosyposy@execpc.com.

ZUETEL, KENNETH ROY, JR. lawyer; b. L.A., Apr. 5, 1954; s. Kenneth Roy Sr. and Adelle Francis Z.; m. Cheryl Kay Morse, May 29, 1976; children: Bryan, Jarid, Christopher, Lauren. BA, San Diego State U., 1974; JD, U. San Diego, 1978. Bar: Calif. 1978 U.S. Ct. Appeals (9th cir.) 1979, U.S. Dist. Ct. (ctrl. dist.) Calif. 1979, U.S. Dist. Ct. (so. and no. dists.) Calif. 1980, U.S. Dist. Ct. (ea. dist.) 1981. Clk. to fed. Judge Martin Pence U.S. Dist. Ct. Hawaii, Honolulu, 1978-79; assoc. litigation Buchalter, Nemer, L.A., 1979-83, Thelen, Marrin, L.A., 1983-88; ptnr. Zuetel & Torigian, Pasadena, Calif., 1988—. Superior ct. arbitrator L.A. Superior Ct., 1982-90, superior ct. settlement officer, 1988-93; judge pro tem L.A. Mcpl. Ct., 1983-94, L.A. Superior Ct., 1989-94; guest lectr. Loyola U. Sch. Law, 1986-95; CEB lectr. Author: Civil Procedure Before Trial, 1992; cons. editor: Cal. Civ. Proc., 1992; contbr. articles to profl. jours. Recipient Recognition award L.A. (Calif.) Bd. Suprs., 1988. Mem. State Bar Calif. (mem. adv. com. continuing edn. 1985-88, trial practice subcom. 1985-88, disciplinary examiner 1986), Los Angeles County Bar Assn. (chair trial atty. project 1982-83, mem. L.A. del. conf. of dels. 1986-96, chair L.A. de. conf. of dels. 1995, exec. com. barristers 1984-88, superior ct. com. 1985-88, civil practice com. 1992-94, exec. com. litigation sect. 1989-90), Pasadena Bar Assn., Inns of Ct. (barrister L.A. chpt. 1991-92), Phi Beta Kappa, Phi Kappa Phi, Phi Alpha Theta, Pi Sigma Alpha. Republican. Presbyterian. Office: Zuetel & Torigian 215 N Marengo Ave 3d Fl Pasadena CA 91101 E-mail: krzuetel@ztlaw.net.

ZUG, ELIZABETH E. concert pianist, educator; b. Phila., Oct. 8, 1907; d. Nathan Walter and Amelia Elizabeth (Nelson) Zug. BA in Music, Irving Coll., 1928. Faculty Nat. Guild Piano Tchrs., 1949. Judge Yr. in Music, Nat. Guild Piano Tchrs., 1949. Debut N.Y. Town Hall, 1938; concert pianist, S.Am. tour, 1941. Named Outstanding N.Y. Debut as Pianist, 1938, Judge of the Yr. Nat. Guild Piano Tchrs., 1949. Mem. Music Tchrs. Nat. Assn., Pa. Music Tchrs. Assn. United Ch. Christ. Avocations: writing, designing, landscaping. Office: 12 N 4th St Reading PA 19601-3910

ZUG, ELIZABETH KENDALL, volunteer worker; b. Boston, Oct. 24, 1954; d. Robert Edward Kendall and Diana (Dana) Kendall Fahrney; m. Graham F. Zug, Sept. 8, 1979; children: Keri, Amy, Kelly, Kiersten. BSBA, U. So. Calif., 1976; MBA, U. Pa., 1978, cert. fund raising mgmt., 1997. Fin. analyst FMC Corp., Chgo., 1978-79, sr. fin. analyst, 1979-80, purchasing agt. corp. purchasing, 1980-82; cons. Individual Purchasing Cons., 1984-85; purchasing cons. Beatrice Foods, Chgo., 1984. Mem. long range planning com. bd. trustees Agnes Irwin Sch., Rosemont, Pa., 1994-96, trustee, 1996—; mem. long range planning com. subcom. of vestry Ch. of the Redeemer, Bryn Mawr, Pa., 1995—; adv. com. Bache Lewis Penrose Soc., Children's Hosp. of Phila., 1997—, mem. women's com., 1995—; mem. Gladwyne (Pa.) Libr. League, 1993—, Haverford (Pa.) Civic Assn., 1995—. Wharton scholar, 1976, 77. Mem. Nat. Soc. Fund Raising Execs., Wharton Alumni Club Phila., Alpha Lambda Delta. Avocations: travel, children's health delivery systems, financial investing, swimming, tennis. Home: 127 Rose Ln Haverford PA 19041-1724

ZUGIBE, FREDERICK THOMAS, pathologist; b. Garnerville, N.Y., May 28, 1928; s. Benjamin and Anna (Zarick) Z.; m. Catherine Frances O'Leary, Apr. 7, 1951; children: Frederick T., Thomas P., Cathryn T. Blaber, Theresa A. Mandracchia, Mary E. Raleigh, Matthew M., Kevin J. BS, St. Francis Coll., 1951; MS, U. Chgo., 1954, PhD, 1960; MD, W.Va. U., 1968. Diplomate Am. Bd. Pathology-Anatomic, Am. Bd. Pathology-Forensic, Am. Bd. Family Practice. Rsch. histologist Lederle Labs., Pearl River, N.Y., 1950-52, rsch. chemist, 1953-55; rsch. assoc. ophthalmic rsch. Columbia U., N.Y.C., 1955-56; dir. cardiovascular rsch. U.S. VA, Pitts., 1960—65; chief med. examiner County of Rockland, Pomona, N.Y., 1969—. Adj. assoc. prof. pathology Columbia U., 1972—; bd. dirs. Hudson Techs. Inc., Hillburn, N.Y., Rockland Westchester Found. for Sudden Infant Death, White Plains, N.Y.; med. dir. Rockland County Emergency Med. Svcs. N.Y.S. Dept. Health, Pomona, 1990—; supervising med. officer disaster med. assistance team Nat. Disaster Med. Assistance, Pomona, 1992—. Author: Eat, Drink and Lower Your Cholesterol, 1964, Diagnostic Histochemistry, 1970, The Cross and Shroud: A Medical Inquiry into Crucifixion, 1988, 14 Days to a Healthy Heart, 1986; contbr. numerous articles to profl. jours. and chpts. to books. Named Knight by His Royal Highness Dom Duarte Pio, Duke of Braganca, Head of Royal House Portugal, 2002; named one of 25 people in Rockland County, N.Y. who most influenced this region in the 20th century ; recipient Disting. Citizens award, Assn. Visually Impaired, 1998, Physician Recognition awards, more than 68 law enforcement, govtl. and med. awards, 1971—, numerous others, Presdl. Tribute, 1998, Spl. Congressional Recognition award, 1998. Fellow Coll. Am. Pathologists, Am. Coll. Cardiology, Am. Acad. Forensic Scis., N.Y. Cardiology Soc., Coun. Arteriosclerosis, Am. Heart Assn., Assn. Scientists and Scholars Internat. for the Shroud of Turin (pres., founder), Sigma Xi. Roman Catholic. Achievements include first to describe glycoprotein storage disease (Zugibe-Gilbert Syndrome), the defect in the syndrome of the sea blue histocyte and arthrodentoosteodysplasia. an acroosteolysis syndrome, a mask to eliminate odors of putrefaction, and a demummifaction technique for fingerprinting; invented ac/dc cardiopulmonary resuscitator, many others. Home: 1 Angelus Dr Garnerville NY 10923-2022 Office: Rockland County Health Comp Office Med Examiner Pomona NY 10970 E-mail: fzugibe@msn.com., zugibef@co.rockland.ny.us.

ZUGRAV, MARIA ITTU, research scientist; b. Sibiu, Romania, Apr. 26, 1945; came to U.S., 1988; d. Valeriu and Maria (Badila) Ittu; m. Sylvester Ilie Zugrav, Jan. 22, 1975; children: Dan, Christian. MS in Chemistry, U. Bucharest, 1968; PhD in Chemistry, Poly. Inst., Bucharest, 1982. Rsch. assoc. Inst. Atomic Physics, Bucharest, 1968-72; sr. rsch. scientist Nat. Ctr. Physics, 1972-80, rsch. group leader, 1980-87; rsch. scientist Consortium for Materials Devel. in Space, Huntsville, Ala., 1989-98; rsch. team leader Ctr. for Microgravity and Materials, 1998—. Reviewer manuscripts Jour. Crystal Growth. Contbr. articles to profl. jours.; patentee in field. Recipient Cert. of Appreciation, U. Ala., 1995, 996. Named NASA Female Role Model for Contbns. made to NASA Microgravity Rsch. and Space Product Devel. Programs, 1999. Mem. Am. Assn. Crystal Growth, Internat. Soc. Photo-Optical Instrumentation Engrs. Achievements project scientist for five successful flight missions on board US Space Shuttles on Space Transp. Sys. 40, 57, 59, 69, 77; prin. investigator for numerous NASA contracts; implemented effusive ampoule phys. vapor transport technique for growth of nonlinear optical organic crystals on ground and in space; designed modified hardware manifested to fly on Internat. Space Sta.; discovered novel technique to grow organic thin films on ground, as a result of microgravity rsch.; implemented an innovative measurement sys. of temperature dependence of vapor pressure for thermal stability studies of organic materials; implemented a new solution growth technique with gradual addition of reactant for crystal growth of inorganic materials; designed opto-electronic device using the grown crystals. Avocations: hiking, swimming, reading. Office: Univ of Ala in Huntsville RI D-29 301 Sparkman Dr NW Huntsville AL 35805-1911 E-mail: zugyavm@email.uah.edu.

ZUHDI, NABIL (BILL ZUHDI), lawyer, litigator, consultant, producer; b. N.Y.C., June 8, 1955; s. Nazih and Lamya Zuhdi; child from previous marriage: Noah; m. Darla L. Boyd, May 19, 1984. BS, U. Ctrl. Okla., 1979; JD, U. Okla., 1982. Bar: Okla. 1982, U.S. Dist. Ct. (we. dist.) Okla. 1982, U.S. Ct. Appeals (10th cir.) 1989, U.S. Supreme Ct. 1990, Tex. 1991, U.S. Dist. Ct. (no. dist.) Tex. 1998. Assoc. Linn & Helms, Oklahoma City, 1982-85; ptnr. Zuhdi & Denum, 1985-87; assoc. Law Firm Darrell Keith, Ft. Worth, 1994; pvt. practice Oklahoma City, 1987—. Pres. Zuhdi Entertainment Group, Inc., Okla. City, 1986—, Amerisphere, Inc., Okla. City, 1996—, criminal justice act panel We. Dist. Okla., 1985—, spl. death penalty habeas corpus panel, 1998, criminal justice act voluntary panel No. Dist. Tex., 1998. Producer: (concerts) Frank Sinatra, Julio Igleas. Patron Okla. Heart Ctr., Oklahoma City, 1994—. Mem. ABA, ATLA, State Bar Tex., Oklahoma Bar Assn., Oklahoma County Bar Assn., Phi Alpha Delta, Alpha Chi. Republican. Avocations: boxing, film, prodr. of concerts including Frank Sinatra and others. Office: PO Box 1077 Oklahoma City OK 73101-1077

ZUHDI, NAZIH, former surgeon, administrator; b. Beirut, May 19, 1925; came to U.S., 1950; s. Omar and Lutfiye (Atef) Z.; children by previous marriage: Omar, Nabil; m. Annette McMichael; children: Adam, Leyla, Zachariah BA, Am. U., Beirut, 1946, MD, 1950. Diplomate Am. Bd. Surgery, Am. Bd. Thoracic Surgery. Intern St. Vincent's Hosp., S.I., N.Y., 1950-51, Presbyn.-Columbia Med. Ctr., N.Y.C., 1951-52; resident Kings County SUNY Med. Ctr., 1952-56; fellow SUNY Downstate Med. Ctr., Bklyn., 1953-54; resident Univ. Hosp., Mpls., 1956, Oklahoma City, 1957-58, practice surgery specializing in cardiovascular and thoracic, 1958-87, adminstr., 1985-99, retired, 1999. Founder, dir. Oklahoma Transplantation Inst. (renamed Nazih Zuhdi transplant Inst., Aug., 1999) Bapt. Med. Ctr., 1984-99, chmn. dept. transplantation, 1994-99; transplantation surgeon in chief Bapt. Hosp., Oklahoma City, 1984-99; founder, chmn. Okla. Cardiovascular Inst., Oklahoma City, 1983-84, Okla. Heart Ctr., Oklahoma City, 1984-85 Contbg. author Cardiac Surgery, 1967, 2d edit., 1972; contbr. articles to profl. jours.; developer numerous med. devices, techniques, rsch. and publs. on cardiopulmonary bypass, internal hypothermia, assisted circulation, heart surgery and transplantation of thoracic organs; developer heart-lung machines; designer, use of exptl. plastic bypass hearts; originator use of banked citrated blood for cardiopulmonary bypass for open heart surgery, of clin. non-hemic primes of heart-lung machines producing intentional hemodilution, at present, the universally accepted principle of cardiopulmonary bypass for partial and total body perfusion; researcher in cardiovascular studies. Founder Islamic Ctr., Inc., Oklahoma City. Inducted into Okla. Hall of Fame, 1994. Fellow ACS; mem. AMA, NCCJ (Humanitarian award 1996), Am. Thoracic Soc., Okla. Thoracic Soc., So. Med. Assn., Okla. Med. Assn., Internat. Coll. Angiology, Am. Coll. Chest Physicians, Oklahoma City C. of C., Oklahoma County Med. Soc., Oklahoma City Clin. Soc., Okla. Surg. Assn., Oklahoma City Surg. Soc., Southwestern Surg. Congress, Am. Coll. Cardiology, Am. Soc. Artificial Internal Organs, Soc. Thoracic Surgeons (founding mem.), Am. Assn. for Thoracic Surgery, Internat. Cardiovasc. Soc., Okla. State Heart Assn., Osler Soc., So. Thoracic Surg. Assn., Lillehei Surg. Soc., Internat. Soc. Heart Transplantation, Dwight Harken's Founder's Group Cardiac Surgery, Westaby's Pioneers in Cardiac Surgery, Internat. Soc. Cardiothoracic Surgery (Japan, founding mem.), Am. Soc. Transplant Surgeons, Milestones of Cardiology of Am. Coll. Cardiology, Okla. City Golf and Country Club, Okla. Hall of Fame. Achievements include originating use of banked citrated blood for cardiopulmonary bypass for open heart surgery; invention of clinical non-hemic primes of heart-lung machines producing intentional hemodilution. Home: 7305 Lancet Ct Oklahoma City OK 73120-1430

ZUHDI, OMAR, secondary education educator; b. N.Y.C., Aug. 15, 1951; s. Mohammed Nazih and Lamya (Mujahed) Z.; m. Shelley Howe Rutherford, May 14, 1976; 1 child, Christopher H. BA, Ctrl. State U., 1973; MA, U. Okla., 1975, Johns Hopkins U., 1978. Cert. secondary edn. educator, Okla. Contbg. editor KMT Communications, Fairview, N.C.; tchr. Shawnee (Okla.) Pub. Schs. Author: (novel) Egyptscape, 1982, Chosen of the Sun, 1986; contbr. articles to profl. jours. Mem. Ambucs, Shawnee, 1983-84. Recipient AK Christian fellow U. Okla., 1975, Johns Hopkins U. fellow, 1977-78; named one of Outstanding Young Men in Am., 1978. Republican. Baptist. Avocations: amateur astronomy, sports cars. Home: 2303 Robinwood Pl Shawnee OK 74801-0502 Office: Shawnee H S 1001 N Kennedy St Shawnee OK 74801-4730

ZUICHES, JAMES JOSEPH, academic administrator; b. Eau Claire, Wis., Mar. 24, 1943; s. William Homer and Bronnie Monica (Stich) Z.; m. Carol Ann Kurilo, Aug. 19, 1967; children:; James Daniel, Joseph Kurilo. BA in Philosophy, U. Portland, 1967; MS in Sociology, U. Wis., 1969, PhD in Sociology, 1973. Instr., asst. prof., assoc. prof. sociology Mich. State U., East Lansing, 1971-82, prof., 1982; assoc. program dir. in sociology NSF, Washington, 1979-80, program dir. in sociology, 1980-82; assoc. dir. rsch. Cornell U., Ithaca, N.Y., 1982-86; assoc. dean Coll. Agr. and Home Econs., Wash. State U., Pullman, 1986-94, dir. Agrl. Rsch. Ctr., 1986-94; program dir. food sys. and rural devel. W.K. Kellogg Found., Battle Creek, Mich., 1994-95; dean Coll. Agr. and Home Econs. Wash. State U., Pullman, 1995—. Mem. adv. subcom. NSF, 1977-79; sci. adv. com. USDA Nat. Rsch. Initiative, Washington, 1992-93; com. on future land grant univ. bd. on agr., NRC, Washington, 1994-96; pub. Wash. Land and People Mag., 1987-92. Co-editor: The Demography of Rural Life, 1993; contbr. articles to profl. jours. Pres., bd. dirs. Edgewood Village Children's Ctr., East Lansing, 1978-79. Recipient sustained superior performance award NSF, 1981; rsch. grantee NIMH, 1973, ERDA, 1978. Fellow AAAS; mem. Rural Sociol. Soc. (pres. 1992-93, editor 50th Anniversary Rsch. Series, 5 vols. 1988-93), Am. Sociol. Assn., Population Assn. Am. Roman Catholic. Avocations: skiing, swimming, hiking, reading.

ZUICK, DIANE MARTINA, elementary education educator; b. Gary, Ind., May 19, 1951; d. Arnold and Matilda (Chaimovitz) Herskovic; m. Norman Robert Zuick, Aug. 12, 1973; children: Scott, Amy. BS in Edn., Ind. U., 1972, MS in Edn., 1974. Cert. nat. bd. cert. tchr. early childhood generalist Nat. Bd. for Profl. Tchg. Stds. Tchr. 5th grade George L. Myers Sch., Portage, Ind., 1972-73, tchr. 3d grade, 1973-83, tchr. 1st grade, 1983-90, tchr. 2d grade, 1990—. Mem. prime time com. Portage Twp. Schs., 1991—, mem. reading curriculum com., 1987-88, mem. devel. com., 1987-88, mem. math. curriculum coun., 1999—; mem. adv. K'ton Ton Pre-Sch., Highland, Ind., 1984-86; mem., chairperson adv. group Ind. Profl. Stds. Bd., 1999-2001; mentor candidates Nat. Bd. Cert. for Tchrs., 1999—. Chair sch. bd. Congregation Beth Israel, Hammond, Ind., 1993-95, mem. sch. bd., 1992-95, mem. exec. bd., 1994—; mem. B'nai B'rith, Hammond, 1993—, mem. dist. bd. govs., 1995—. Recipient Ind. Dept. Instrn. Prime Time award, 1988, 89; Portage Twp. Schs. grantee, 1993, 94. Mem. NEA, Ind. State Tchrs. Assn., Portage Assn. Tchrs., Tchrs. Applying Whole Langs., Internat. Reading Assn., Ind. U. Alumni Assn, Delta Kappa Gamma. Avocations: reading, travel, piano, nature, music. Home: 58 Cedar Ln Schererville IN 46375-1107 Office: Portage Twp Schs 6240 Us Highway 6 Portage IN 46368-5057

ZUICK, ERNEST RONALD, JR. career officer, advertising executive; b. San Bernardino, Calif., Nov. 2, 1935; s. Ernest Ronald Sr. and Catherine Louise (Leach) Z.; m. Johnnie Fern Lemons, Aug. 19, 1966. BA, Fresno State U., 1964, MA, 1968; MPA, Auburn U., 1974; postgrad., Air Command and Staff Coll., 1974, Air War Coll., 1982. Cert. tchr., Calif. Joined Calif. Air N.G., 1958, advanced through grades to col., 1984; advt. acct. exec., sports and polit. cartoonist Turlock (Calif.) Jour., 1956-62; advt. acct. exec. Fresno (Calif.) Bee, 1965-76; various assignments Calif. Mil. Dept., Sacramento, 1976-85, dir. legis., 1985-95, spl. projects dir., 1999—2001; dir. Media Svcs., 2001—. Mem. ancillary staff Res. Forces Policy Bd., Office of Sec. of Def., 1982-95. Contbr. articles to profl. jours. Mem. N.G. Assn. Calif. (pres. 1983-84). Avocations: writing, cartooning, video production.

ZUIDEMA, GEORGE DALE, surgeon, educator; b. Holland, Mich., Mar. 8, 1928; s. Jacob and Reka (Dalman) Z.; m. Joan K. Houtman, June 2, 1953; children: Karen Sue, David Jay, Nancy Ruth, Sarah Kay. AB, Hope Coll., 1949, D.Sc. (hon.), 1969; MD, Johns Hopkins U., 1953. Diplomate: Am. Bd. Surgery. Intern Mass. Gen. Hosp., 1953-54, asst. resident surgeon, then chief resident surgeon, 1954, 57, 58, 59; asst. prof. surgery, then assoc. prof. U. Mich. Sch. Medicine, 1960-64; prof. surgery, dir. dept. Johns Hopkins Sch. Medicine; also surgeon in chief Johns Hopkins Hosp., 1964-84; prof. surgery, vice provost med. affairs U. Mich., 1984-94. Cons. Walter Reed Army Med. Center, Sinai Hosp., Balt., Balt. City Hosp., Clin. Center of NIH; chmn. Study on Surg. Services for U.S., 1970-75 Editor: (with O.H. Gauer) Gravitational Stress in Aerospace Medicine, 1961; (with G.L. Nardi) Surgery-A Concise Guide to Clinical Practice, 1961, 4th edit., 1982; (with R.D. Judge and F. Fitzgerald) Physical Diagnosis, 1963, 6th edit., 1997; (with W.F. Ballinger and R.B. Rutherford) Management of Trauma, 1968, 4th edit., 1985; (with L. Schlossberg) Atlas of Human Functional Anatomy, 1977, 4th edit., 1997, Shackelford's Surgery of the Alimentary Tract, 5th edit., 2001; editor Jour. Surg. Rsch., 1966-72, assoc. editor, mem. editl. bd., 1972—; mem. editl. bd. Surgery Ann., 1968-75, Surgery, 1970-97, co-editor in chief, 1975-97. Bd. dirs. Md. divsn. Am. Cancer Soc., 1964-68; trustee William Beaumont Hosp., Royal Oak, Mich., 1984-94, Hope Coll., Holland, Mich, 1987—. Capt. M.C., USAF, 1954-56. John and Mary R. Markle scholar academic medicine, 1961-66; recipient Henry Russell award U. Mich., 1963 Fellow ACS, Royal Coll. Surgeons Ireland (hon.); mem. Assn. Am. Med. Colls., Ctrl. Soc. Clin. Rsch., Soc. Univ. Surgeons, Am. Surg. Assn., So. Surg. Assn., Soc. Clin. Surgery, Soc. Vascular Surgery, Internat. Cardiovascular Surgery, Halsted Soc., Nat. Inst. Medicine, Assn. Acad. Surgeons (pres. 1967-69), Allen O. Whipple Soc., Coun. on Grad. Med. Edn., Phi Beta Kappa, Tri Beta, Alpha Omega Alpha. Home: 983 Willow View Ct Holland MI 49424-6615

ZUIDERVAART, LAMBERT PAUL, philosophy educator; b. Modesto, Calif., Aug. 1, 1950; s. Martin and Tena (Beuving) Z.; m. Joyce Alene Recker, Jan. 8, 1977. BA, Dordt Coll., 1972; MPhil, Inst. Christian Studies, Toronto, Ont., Can., 1975; postgrad., Free U. Berlin, 1977-80; PhD, Free U. Amsterdam, The Netherlands, 1981. Asst. prof. philosophy King's Univ. Coll., Edmonton, Canada, 1981—85; chmn., divsn. humanities, 1982—85; assoc. prof. philosophy Calvin Coll., Grand Rapids, Mich., 1985-89, prof., 1989—2002, chmn. dept., 1991-97, vice chair faculty senate, 1999—2002; prof. philosophy Inst. for Christian Studies, Toronto, 2002—. Dissertation supr. Free U., Amsterdam, 1996-99; vis. prof. Inst. for Christian Studies, Toronto, Ont., Can., 1991, mem. senate, 1993—, chancellor, 1998-2001; treas. bd. dirs. King's Coll. Found., U.S., Grand Rapids, Mich., 1989-95, pres. bd. dirs., 1998-2001 pres., bd. dirs. Urban Inst. for Contemporary Arts, Grand Rapids, 1994-98, chmn. 2.75 Million Dollar Capital Campaign, 1996-99; chmn. organizing com. Art Talks, Toronto, 1996-97; founding secretary-treas., Calvin Coll. Chap., AAUP; pub. lectr. Kendall Coll. Art and Design, 1993, Free U., Berlin, 1994, St. Louis U., 1998, Loft Forum Detroit, 1999, Seattle Pacific U., 2000, Cambridge U., 2001, Edinburgh (Scotland) U., 2001, Kassel U., 2001, Cath. U., Leuven, Belgium, 2001, Wheaton (Ill.) Coll., 2002, King's Univ. Coll., 2002; seminar leader Lang., Truth and Postmodern Culture, Toronto; dir. Civil Soc. rsch. group Calvin Coll., 2001-02. Author: Adorno's Aesthetic Theory, 1991; co-author: Dancing in the Dark, 1991; co-editor: Pledges of Jubilee, 1995, The Semblance of Subjectivity, 1997, The Arts, Community and Cultural Democracy, 2000; contbr. articles to profl. jours. Pres. bd. dirs. Inn Roads Housing Coop., Edmonton, Alta., Can., 1982-85; mem. Politics Meaning Discussion Group, Grand Rapids, 1994-97; mem. Internat. Critical Theory Seminar, 1995—; mem. Coalition to Combat Racism, Grand Rapids, 1997-98; workshop leader Leadership Grand Rapids, Mich., 1993, 94. Grantee STEP Prov. Alberta., Can., 1984, 85, Travel grant Am. Coun. Learned Socs., 1988, Rsch. Visit grant German Acad. Exch. Svc., 1994, 2001; NEH Summer Seminar grantee, 1997; rsch. fellow Calvin Coll., 1990, 93, 94, 96, 98, 99, 2000, McGregor Summer fellow, 1999; NEH fellow, 2002. Mem. Am. Philos. Assn., Am. Soc. Aesthetics, Can. Philos. Assn., Can. Soc. Aesthetics, Internat. Assn. Aesthetics, Soc. Phenomenology and Existential Philosophy. Democrat. Avocations: international travel, music, film, hiking. Office: Inst for Christian Studies 229 College St Toronto ON Canada M5T 1R4 E-mail: zuid@calvin.edu.

ZUIDERVEEN, JEFFREY ALAN, biology educator, toxicology consultant, aquatic toxicologist; b. Kalamazoo, July 17, 1961; s. Larry D. and Alice E. Zuiderveen; m. Kimberly Joy Zuiderveen, Aug. 18, 1984; children: Caleb N., Lydia J., Esther R. BS, Western Mich. U., 1982; PhD, U. Ky., 1994. Analytical chemist Internat. R&D Corp., Mattawan, Mich., 1984-86; tchg. asst., rsch. asst. U. Ky., Lexington, 1986-93, part-time instr., 1993-94; assoc. prof. biology Columbus (Ga.) State U., 1994—. Freshwater mussel cons., 1999—. Head basketball coach Harris County Youth Sports Assn., 2000—; judge Greater Columbus Area Sci. Fair, 1995—; asst. dir. Sci. Olympiad, Columbus, 2000; Awana comdr. Piney Grove Bapt. Ch., Ga., 1998—. Open Competition fellow U. Ky., 1987, 89, Gerontology fellow Ga. Gerontology Consortium, 1998-99. Mem.: AAAS, N.Am. Benthological Soc., Soc. Environ. Toxicology and Chemistry, Am. Chem. Soc. Southern Baptist. Avocations: reading, fishing, tennis, volleyball, treasure hunting. Office: Columbus State U Dept Biology 4225 University Ave Columbus GA 31907-5679 E-mail: jkz@gateway.net.

ZUK, CARMEN VEIGA, psychiatrist; b. Buenos Aires, Argentina, Mar. 5, 1939; came to U.S., 1971; d. Carlos and Carmen Villella Veiga; m. Gerald Harvey, May 7, 1974; children: Cary Elizabeth and Gabrielle Ann (twins). MD, U. Buenos Aires, 1964, cert. psychiatry, 1969. Diplomate Am. Bd. Psychiatry and Neurology. Intern Med. Coll. of Pa., Phila., 1974-75; resident in psychiatry Norristown (Pa.) State Hosp., 1977-79; child psychiatry fellowship Med. Coll. Pa. and Ea. Pa. Psychiat. Inst., Phila., 1979-81; dir. child and adolescent unit Hosp. of Med. Coll. Ga., Augusta, 1981-83; dir. treatment team New Orleans Adolescent Hosp., 1983-85; assoc. Psychiatry Med. Group, Calif., 1985-86; mental health psychiatrist L.A. County Dept. Mental Health San Fernando Mental Health Svcs., 1986-88; psychiatrist-ptnr. So. Calif. Permanente Med. Group, Van Nuys, Calif., 1988-98, ptnr., 1988-98; staff psychiatrist Santa Clarita Child and Family Ctr., 1999—2002. Asst. prof. dept. psychiatry Med. Coll. Ga., 1981-83; clin. asst. prof. dept. psychiatry and neurology Tulane U., 1983-85. Contbr. articles to profl. publs. Mem. AMA, Internat. Soc. for Adolescent Psychiatry. Avocations: reading, cooking, gardening, swimming, music. Home: 7620 Hollister Ave #219 Goleta CA 93117 Office: Santa Clarita Child and Family Ctr 21545 Redview Dr Santa Clarita CA 91350-2617 E-mail: CarmenZuk@msn.com.

ZUK, GERALD HARVEY, psychologist, consultant; b. Chgo., Oct. 25, 1929; s. Albert and Gladys (Gross) Z.; m. Carmen Veiga, May 7, 1974; children: Cary and Gabrielle (twins). BA, L.A. State Coll., 1951; PhD, U. Chgo., 1955. Lic. psychologist, Calif. Asst. rsch. psychologist Inst. Child Welfare/U. Calif., Berkeley, 1955-56; clin. psychologist Pacific State Hosp., Pomona, Calif., 1956-57; chief psychologist St. Christopher's Hosp. for Children, Phila., 1957-61; assoc. dir., dir. tng. program dept. family psychiatry Ea. Pa. Psychiat. Inst., 1961-80; prof. dept. psychiatry, dir. family therapy program Med. Coll. Ga., 1981-83; clin. prof. dept. psychiatry and neurology Tulane U. Sch. Medicine, New Orleans, 1983-85; assoc. and dir. family therapy tng. program Beck Psychiat. Med. Group, Los Angeles County, 1985-86; pvt. practice, 1986—. Cons. and presenter in field. Author: Family Therapy: A Triadic-Based Approach, 1972, 2d edit., 1981, Process and Practice in Family Therapy, 1975, 2d edit., 1986; editor: Family Therapy Approaches for Adolescents, 1985; co-editor: Family Therapy and Disturbed Families, 1967; founding editor Internat. Jour. Family Therapy, 1979-86; mem. editl. bd. Family Process, Psychotherapy: Theory, Rsch. and Practice, Jour. Marriage and Family Counseling, Terapia Familiar; contbr. articles to profl. jours. Fellow APA. Avocation: classical music. Home and Office: Zuk Cons 25316 Pacy St Santa Clarita CA 91321-3343 E-mail: geraldzuk@msn.com.

ZUK, JUDITH, botanic garden administrator; b. Canandaigua, N.Y., Sept. 11, 1951; BA, Rutgers U., 1973; MS, U. Del., 1976. CEO, pres. Bklyn. Botanic Garden, 1990—. Bd. dirs. Botanic Gardens Conservation Internat., Greenwood Cemetery; mem. regional adv. bd. JP Morgan Chase. Mem. Phi Beta Kappa. Office: Bklyn Botanic Garden 1000 Washington Ave Brooklyn NY 11225-1008 E-mail: judithzuk@bbg.org.

ZUKAUKAS, CHARLES LAWRENCE, surgeon; b. Newark, 1921; s. Andrew Joseph and Anna (Naudzeus) Z.; m. Leonora Brust, Aug. 2, 1947; children: Maryanne Tashjian, Andrea Aikins. BA, Rutgers U., 1943; MD, U. Pa., 1946. Diplomate Am. Bd. Surgery. Intern St. Lukes Hosp., N.Y.C., 1946-47; resident in surgery NYU-Bellevue Hosp., 1949-53; ret., 1991; dir. surg. emeritus Monmouth Med. Ctr., Long Branch, N.J., 1992—; prof. surg. emeritus Hahnemann U., 1993—. Cons. in surgery Jersey Shore Med. Ctr., 1970-89, Freehold (N.J.) Med. Ctr., 1977-80. Trustee Monmouth Med. Ctr., 1982-88, YMCA; dir. Long Branch Pub. Health Nursing Assn. Capt. U.S. Army, 1947-49. Named Physician of Yr., Am. Cancer Soc., N.J. divsn., 1977; recipient N.J. C. of C. award. Fellow ACS (pres. N.J. chpt. 1974, gov. at large 1984-87), Acad. Medicine N.J.; mem. AMA, S.E. Surg. Congress, N.J. State Med. Soc. (Golden Merit award), Soc. Surgeons N.J. (pres. 1985-86), Rotary. Roman Catholic. Home: 609 Westwood Ave Long Branch NJ 07740-5008 E-mail: doctorz@home.com.

ZUKERMAN, MICHAEL, lawyer; b. Bklyn., Oct. 3, 1940; s. Charles Morris and Gertrude Ethel Zukerman; m. Claire J. Goldsmith, June 25, 1961 (div. 1986); children: Steven, Amy; m. Elaine DeMasi, Nov. 21, 1986 (div. 1999); children: Jaclyn, Laura; m. Janey Alexander, Feb. 2, 2001. BS, U. Fla., 1961; LLB, St. John's U., 1964; LLM, NYU, 1966. Bar: N.Y. 1965, Pa. 1983, U.S. Tax Ct. 1984. Credit analyst, loan officer Franklin Nat. Bank, 1964-66; assoc. Jaffin, Schneider, Kimmel & Galpeer, N.Y.C., 1966-67; ptnr. Zukerman, Licht & Friedman and predecessors, 1967-79, Baskin & Sears, P.C., N.Y.C., 1979-85, Graubard, Moskowitz, Dannett, Horowitz & Mollen, N.Y.C., 1985-86, Gersten, Savage, Kaplowitz & Zukerman, N.Y.C., 1986-89; of counsel Olsham, Grundman, Frome & Rosenzweig, 1990-95, Graham & James, N.Y.C., 1995-2000, Bryan Cave LLP, 2000—; exec. v.p. Brookhill Group, 1986-89. Pres. First Ptnrs. Credit Corp., N.Y.C., 1988—93; bd. dirs. Interjurist Ltd., Whitestone Realty Capital, Inc., Life Sci. Found. Contbr. articles to profl. jours. Trustee Temple Beth Torah, Melville, N.Y., 1972-80, YMHA Suffolk County, Hauppauge, N.Y., 1980-85; bd. dirs. Dayton Mgmt. Corp., 1974-2001, Suffolk Jewish Cmty. Planning Bd., Hauppauge, 1982-85, Congregation Bnai Elohim, 1994, 2nd v.p., 1995; co-chmn. bus. adv. coun. Town of Greenburgh, 1992. Mem. ABA. E-mail mm. Home: 915 Cherry Ln North Woodmere NY 11581-2722 Office: Bryan Cave LLP 31st Flr 1290 Ave of the Americas New York NY 10104 E-mail: mmzukerman@BryanCave.com.

ZUKERMAN, PINCHAS, concert violinist, violist, conductor; b. Tel Aviv, July 16, 1948; came to U.S., 1962; s. Yehuda and Miriam (Lieberman) Z.; m. Eugenia Rich, May 26, 1968 (div.); children: Natalia, Arianna; m. Tuesday Weld, 1985 (div.). Student, Juilliard Sch. Music, 1965-68; MusD (hon.), Brown U., 1989. Ind. concert violinist, 1968—. With impresario, Sol Hurok, 1967-76; condr., soloist English Chamber Orch., 1974, Mostly Mozart Festival, N.Y.C., 1975; guest condr., soloist Los Angeles Philharm., Boston Symphony, Chgo. Symphony, Pitts. Symphony, Phila. Orch., N.Y. Philharm.; music dir. South Bank Festival, London, 1978-80, St. Paul Chamber Orch., 1980-87, Nat. Arts Ctr. Orch., 1998—; prin. festival condr. Dallas Internat. Summer Music Festival, 1990-94; prin. guest condr. Dallas Symphony, 1993-95; toured with Isaac Stern; mem. trio with Daniel Barenboim and Jacqueline du Pre; (rec. artist) CBS, EMI, Philips Classics labels, RCA Victor Red Seal, BMG Classics. Winner Internat. Levintritt Competition, 1967. Office: care Kirshbaum Demler & Assoc 711 W End Ave Apt 5KN New York NY 10025-6821

ZUKERNICK, HARRY, lawyer; b. N.Y.C., Nov. 25, 1905; s. Jacob and Becky (Meltz) Z.; m. Susan Brower, July 31, 1929; 1 son, Michael. BBA, CCNY, 1926; LLB, Bklyn. Law Sch., 1929. Bar: N.Y. 1930, Fla. 1935, U.S. Ct. Appeals (5th cir.) 1947, U.S. Supreme Ct. 1948. Pvt. practice, N.Y.C., 1930-35, Miami Beach, Fla., 1935—. Chmn. dist. welfare bd. State of Fla. Author chpts. in law books. Mem. pres.'s council Brandeis U.; pres. Miami Beach Lodge, B'nai B'rith; founder Grtr. Miami Jewish Fedn.; trustee Fla. Region Anti-Defamation League. Mem. ABA, Fla. Bar (chmn. real property, probate and trust law sect., bd. govs.), Dade County Bar Assn., Miami Beach Bar Assn. (pres. 1950, merit award 1964), Bklyn. Law Sch. Alumni Assn. (pres. Fla. chpt.), Council Bar Assn. Pres. Fla. (Outstanding Past Local Bar Assn. Pres. award 1981), Miami Beach Civic League (pres. 1940), Anti-Defamation League (nat. vice chmn. deferred gifts com.). Office: 333 W 41st St Ste 506 Miami Beach FL 33140-3608

ZUKOWSKI, BARBARA WANDA, clinical social work psychotherapist; b. Queens, N.Y., Apr. 30, 1957; d. Stanley F. and Domicille K. (Trzebuchowska) Z. BS in Psychology, Bklyn. Coll., 1984; MSW, NYU, 1986; student, Bklyn. Coll. Conservatory Mus., 1982-84; student classical guitar, Am. Inst. Guitar, N.Y.C., 1982-84, 90-97, student Rennaissance, Baroque and classical guitar, 1998—. Cert., registered social worker, N.Y. Clin. social worker on-site program Staten Island (N.Y.) Children's Community Mental Health Soc., 1986-87; clin. social worker Cath. Charities Diocese of Bklyn., 1984-85, 87-89, N.Y.C. Health & Hosps. Corp., Bklyn., 1989-92; child/adolscent therapist Program for Devel. Human Potential Office of Cath. Edn., Diocese of Bklyn., 1992-2000; pvt. practice dream analyst and holistic psychotherapist, 2001—. Part time dream analyst and holistic psychotherapist, Bklyn., 1989—2000; developer children's creative arts therapy groups for social work use Cath. Charities N.Y., 1988—89; therapeutic songwriting for children Program for Devel. Human Potential, Bklyn. Office Cath. Edn., 1996—2000. Singer/songwriter, guitarist, rec. artist, Cosmic Shindig, 1994, Emily, 1996. Music minister Pax Christi Met. N.Y., 1990-94. Mem.: NARAS, NASW. Avocations: singing, songwriting, recording artist, guitarist, study of hagiography. Home and Office: 144 Driggs Ave Apt 3 Brooklyn NY 11222-4202 E-mail: bsjpilgrim@aol.com.

ZUKOWSKY, JOHN ROBERT, curator; b. N.Y.C., Apr. 21, 1948; s. John and Mary (Charchan) Z. BA, Hunter Coll., CUNY, 1971; MA, SUNY, Binghamton, 1974, PhD, 1977. Archtl. archivist Hudson River Mus., Yonkers, N.Y., 1974-76, Art Inst. Chgo., 1978-81, architecture curator, 1981—. Mem. Historic Sites Adv. Council, Springfield, Ill., 1982-83, Landmarks Preservation Council, Chgo., 1982-83; jury mem. Honor awards AIA, Washington, 1987. Co-author: Hudson River Villas, 1985, The Sky's the Limit Chicago Skyscrapers, 1990, Austrian Architecture and Design, 1991; co-author, editor: Mies Reconsidered, 1986, Chicago Architecture: 1872-1922, 1987, Chicago Architecture and Design, 1923-93, 1993, The Many Faces of Modern Architecture, 1994, Karl Friedrich Schinkel, 1781-1841: The Drama of Architecture, 1994, Building for Air Travel: Architecture and Design for Commercial Aviation, 1996, Japan 2000, 1998, Skyscrapers: The New Millennium, 2000, 2001, Building for Space Travel, 2001; editor: A System of Architectural Ornament (Louis H. Sullivan), 1990; author: Space Architecture: The Work by John Frassanito and Associates for NASA, 1999; contbr. articles to profl. jours. Decorated Chevalier des arts and lettres (France), Verdienst/Ehren Kreuz, Austria; recipient Honig award Chgo. chpt. Am. Soc. Appraisers, 1989; postdoctoral rsch. fellow NEH, 1977-78, Rsch. fellow, NEA, 1991. Mem. AIA (hon., Disting. Svc. award Chgo. chpt. 1986), Arts Club Chgo. Office: Art Inst Chgo Dept Architecture 111 S Michigan Ave Chicago IL 60603-6492 E-mail: jzukowsky@artic.edu.

ZULAUF, SANDER WILLIAM, educator, poet; b. Paterson, N.J., Nov. 5, 1946; s. S. William Z. and Marion Ann Zulauf; m. Christianne Beresford, June 15, 1968 (div. 1976); 1 child, Scott; m. Madeline Ruth Slocum, 1979; stepchildren: Michael, Mary Beth. BA, Gettysburg Coll., 1968; MA, Ind. U., 1973. Tchr. Martin Luther King Sch., Paterson, N.J., 1968-69, Hanover Park Regional H.S., East Hanover, 1969-71; prof. County Coll. Morris, Randolph, 1973—. Editor, pub. Ars Poetica, Lake Hopatcong, N.J., 1996-99. Author of poems; editor Jour. N.J. Poets, 1989—. Committeeman County Com., Byram Twp., N.J., 1994—; sec. treas. Forest South Homeowners Assn., Byram Twp., 1989-94; lay eucharistic min. St. Dunstan's Epsicopal Ch., Succasunna, N.J., 1974—. Recipient Allen Ginsberg award Poetry Ctr., Passaic, N.J., 1993, 2001, Excellence in Print award Pub. Radio's Poet and the Poem, 2002; N.J. Arts Coun. grantee, 1992-93; NEH fellow, Princeton, 1987; named 1st Poet Laureate Diocese of Newark, 1999—. Mem. Acad. Am. Poets, Poetry Soc. Am., Poets House, Kenneth Burke Soc., Thoreau Soc., Associated Writing Programs, Skylands Writers & Artists Assn. (sec. treas. 1994-98, v.p. 1999-2000). Democrat. Episcopalian. Avocations: camping, boating, environmental preservation, gardening, travel. Office: County Coll Morris 214 Center Grove Rd Randolph NJ 07869-2007

ZULBERTI, CARLOS ALBERTO, planning executive; b. Bahia Blanca, Argentina, Jan. 22, 1944; s. Carlos and Maria Zulberti; m. Ester Nelida Costanzo, June 13, 1968; children: Florencia and Emiliano (twins). Ingeniero Agronomo, Universidád Catolica, Mar del Plata, 1968; MS, Cornell U., 1971, PhD, 1974. Advisor Internat. Devel. Rsch. Ctr., Bogota, Colombia, 1974-76, Can. Internat. Devel. Agy., Quito, Ecuador, 1976-78; project dir. The SNC Group, San Domingo, Dominican Republic, 1978-81; project assoc. Harvard U., Nairobi, Kenya, 1982-86; cons., advisor Internat. Devel. Rsch. Ctr., 1987-91; dep. chief, tech. cooperation UN Environment Programme, 1992-93; head planning UNEP, 1994-98; cons. Consultative Group on Internat. Agrl. Rsch., 1998—. Cons. Winrock Internat., Nairobi, 1991, FAO, Rome, 1989, UNDP, Nairobi, 1989, World Bank, 1988. Co-author: Living Rural Development, 1978; contbr. articles to profl. jours. George F. Warren grantee, Cornell U., 1971; Ford Found. fellow, N.Y.C., 1968-73. Mem. Internat. Assn. Agrl. Economists, Soc. for Internat. Devel., Internat. Soc. for Ecol. Econs., Am. Agrl. Econs. Assn., Can. Agrl. Econs. and Farm Mgmt. Soc. Address: 2117 L St NW #113 Washington DC 20037-1524

ZULCH, JOAN CAROLYN, retired medical publishing company executive; b. Great Neck, N.Y., Apr. 10, 1931; d. Walter Howard and Edna Ruth (Howard) Z. BS in Biology, Allegheny Coll., 1952; postgrad., Hunter Coll., 1954. Med. sec. E.R. Squibb & Sons, N.Y.C., 1952; with Macmillan Pub. Co., 1952-88, editorial asst. med. dept., 1952-56, asst. editor med. dept., 1956-58, editor med. dept., 1958-61, med. editor coll. and profl. div., 1961-75, sr. editor medicine, coll. and profl. div., 1975-78, exec. editor med. books, profl. books div., 1978-79, editor-in-chief, 1979-80, asst. v.p., editor-in-chief profl. books div., 1980-82, v.p., pub. med., nursing, health sci. dept., 1982-85, v.p., pub. med. books, sci., tech., med. dept., 1985-88. Recipient Best Illustrated Med. Book award Assn. Med. Illustrators, 1977, Outstanding Book in Health Sci. award Assn. Am. Pubs., 1982. Mem. AAAS, AAUW, Post Libr. Assn., L.I.U. (rec. sec. 1990-93, exec. coun. 1990—), Friends of Locust Valley Libr. (pres. 1991-93, 94-96, 98-2000, treas. 1993-94, 96-98, 2000—), Locust Valley C. of C. (bd. dirs. 1997—), Alpha Gamma Delta, Delta Sigma Rho. Republican. Home: 36 Wood Ln Lattingtown PO Box 547 Locust Valley NY 11560-0547

ZULKER, CHARLES BATES, broadcasting company executive; b. Pleasantville, N.J., Dec. 20, 1926; s. William John and Virginia (Carr) Z.; m. Virginia Wright, June 24, 1949; children: Connie Lee, Timothy Scott Charles. Adminstrv. officer Princeton (N.J.) U., 1950-60; asst. mgr. Sta. WPEL, Montrose, Pa., 1960-65; gen. mgr. Sta. WCHR, Trenton, N.J., 1965—. Trustee Princeton Evang. Fellowship, 1973-83; bd. council Word of Life Internat., Schroon Lake, N.Y., 1974-82; mem. exec. bd. Upper Makefield Community Assn., 1972-79; deacon Westerly Rd. Ch., Princeton, 1999—. With U.S. Army, 1945-46. Mem. Wooden Canoe Heritage Assn. of Am., Nat. Religious Broadcasters, Nat. Assn. of Broadcasters, Squam Lakes Assn. (Holderness, N.H.). Office: 1371 Woodside Rd Yardley PA 19067 E-mail: cbzulker@compuserve.com.

ZUMBANO, ANTHONY RALPH, risk, claims management executive; b. Jersey City, May 11, 1947; s. Carl R. and Catherine (Guddemi) Z.; children: Carl Robert, Brian Joseph; m. Kathy E. Kenny, Oct. 7, 1989. BS, St. Peter's Coll., Jersey City, 1969; Dipl. Claims Law, Am. Ednl. Inst., Basking Ridge, N.J., 1973. Supr. Travelers Ins. Co., Morris Plains, N.J., 1969-78; v.p. Marsh & McLennan Inc., N.Y.C., 1978-84; pres., chief exec. officer AMNA Corp., Ft. Lauderdale, Fla., 1984-92; pres., CEO PLCM Group, Inc., 1993-98; pres. Cambridge Profl. Liability Svcs., 1999—. Contbr. articles to profl. jours. Vol. Broward County Spl. Olympics, Ft. Lauderdale, 1991—; bd. pres. Las Olas Villas, Ft. Lauderdale, 1986-88. Mem. Am. Soc. for Healthcare Risk Mgmt., Fla. Med. Malpractice Claims Coun., Tower Club. Republican. Roman Catholic. Avocations: boating, tennis, chess, home restoration. Office: PLCM Group Inc 805 E Broward Blvd Ste 300 Fort Lauderdale FL 33301-2046

ZUMBRUN, ALVIN JOHN THOMAS, law and criminology educator; b. Balt., Aug. 9, 1926; s. Orrell Sylvester Tilton and Mary Kathryn (Sprinkle) Z.; m. Marianne Jane Nolan, Aug. 26, 1950; children: Mary Susan, Alvin J.T. Jr., Steven M., Diane, MaryAnn, Mary Kathleen. BA, U. Md., 1952, MA, 1956; MEd in Spl. Edn., Coppin State U., 1972, MEd in Adminstrn., 1974; JD, U. Balt., 1970. Probation officer Supreme Bench of Balt., 1950-52; budget and program dir. Cmty. Chest, Balt., 1953-55; mng. dir. Criminal Justice Commn., 1956-59; exec. dir., criminologist Md. Crime Investigating Com., 1960-96; dept. chmn., prof. criminal justice Catonsville (Md.) C.C., 1968-94; dept. chmn., dir. grad. program, prof. criminal justice U. Balt., 1974-76. Adj. prof. criminal justice U. Md., Hood Coll., Coppin State U., Md. State Police Acad., Balt. County Police Acad., 1969—; mem. adv. bd. U. Balt. Criminal Justice Program, 1976-94; cons. Am. Edn. Assn., Washington, 1980—; mem. senate Catonsville C.C., 1970-83; mem. Nat. Disaster Med. System, 1993—; mem. acad. stds. senate com. U. Md., College Park, 1997-99. Author: Maryland Crime Report, 5 vols., 1959-94, Directory of Criminal Justice Agencies, 22 vols., 1962-94, Civil Disturbance Riots of 1968, 69, also rsch. in field. Mem. scholarship com. Md. Troopers Assn., Pikesville, 1990-93; mem. adv. bd. articulation com. U. Md., College Park, 1977-94; lay pres., mem. coun. Salem Luth. Ch., Catonsville, 1956-59, 65-68; pres. Maplewoods Home Owners Assn., 1996-97. Lt. (j.g.) USN, 1943-50. Recipient Superior Pub. Svc. award Afro Am. Newspaper, 1962, Excellence in Teaching award Md. State Bd. C.C.s, 1987, Superior Ednl. Svcs. award Balt. County Police Chief, 1994, Gov.'s citation for ednl. achievements Gov. of Md., 1994, Hon. Trooper 25 Yrs. Acad. Teaching Md. State Police, 1995. Mem. VFW (life), Am. Legion (life), Md. Acad. Criminal Justice Profs. (pres. 1971-94), Internat. Soc. Criminology, Nat. Dist. Attys. Assn., Internat. Assn. Chiefs of Police, Maplewoods Homeowners Assn. (pres. 1995-96). Avocations: walking, biking, family activities, world travel. Home: 438 Maple Forest Rd # 9349 Catonsville MD 21228-1783 E-mail: ajtz@juno.com.

ZUMBRUN, KEVIN RONALD, mathematics educator; b. Walnut Creek, Calif., Aug. 11, 1959; s. Ronald Arthur and Ann Hartley Zumbrun. BS in Math., U. Calif., Davis, 1981, MS in Math., 1983; PhD in Math., NYU, 1990. Vis. asst. prof. SUNY, Stony Brook, 1990-92; postdoctoral rschr. Stanford (Calif.) U., 1992; asst. prof. Ind. U., Bloomington, 1992-96, assoc. prof., 1996-99, prof., 1999—. Vis. scholar Mittag-Leffler Inst., Stockholm, 1997, Ecole Normale Superieure, Lyon, France, 1998, 2000, Inst. M. Picare, Rome, 2000; lectr. in field. Editor Ind. Math. Jour.; contbr. articles to profl. jours. Named Navy Young Investigator, Office Naval Rsch., 1994-97; Postdoctoral fellow NSF, 1991-93; grantee NSF, 1994-2000. Mem. Am. Math. Soc., Soc. for Indsl. and Applied Math., Sigma Xi. Office: Dept Math Ind Univ Bloomington IN 47405 E-mail: kzumbrun@indiana.edu.

ZUMBRUNNEN, DAVID ARNOLD, mechanical engineering and materials science educator, consultant; b. Salt Lake City, Sept. 3, 1955; m. Elizabeth Buck. B in Mech. Engring., U. Minn., 1977; MS in Mech. Engring., Purdue U., 1984, PhD in Mech. Engring., 1988. Registered profl. engr., Ind., S.C. Rsch. leader NSF Ctr. for Advanced Engring. Fibers and Films. Lt. USN, 1977-82. Presdl. Faculty fellow The White House/NSF, 1992-97. Mem.: AAAS, AIAA, ASME, SPE, Am. Chem. Soc., AIChemE. Achievements include invention of structured materials formed by chaotic advection. Office: Clemson U Dept Mech Engring Clemson SC 29634-0921 E-mail: zdavid@ces.clemson.edu.

ZUMOFF, BARNETT, endocrinologist, medical researcher; b. Bklyn., June 1, 1926; s. Abraham and Stella (Zumoff) Z.; m. Selma Silver, Nov. 11, 1951; children: Janine, Francine, Linda. AB, Columbia U., 1945; postgrad., Albany Med. Coll., 1945-47; MD, L.I. Coll. Medicine, 1949. Diplomate Am. Bd. Internal Medicine, Am. Bd. Endocrinology and Metabolism. Rotating intern, med. resident Bklyn. Jewish Hosp., 1949-50, 51; straight med. intern Mass. Meml. Hosp., 1950-51; resident pathology Bklyn. VA Hosp., 1954-55; resident medicine univ. svc. Kings County Hosp., 1954-55; spl. fellow medicine, clin. asst. medicine Meml. Ctr., 1955-57; clin. asst. medicine Kings County Hosp., 1957-62; assoc. Sloan-Kettering Inst., 1960-62; asst. medicine James Ewing Hosp., 1959-62, assoc. attending physician div. neoplastic medicine, 1961-63; attending physician dept. oncology, 1963-82; attending physician dept. medicine Montefiore Med. Ctr., 1977-82, 87—, Hosp. for Joint Diseases-Orthopedic Inst., 1981—; attending physician, emeritus chief divsn. endocrinology and metabolism dept. of medicine Beth Israel Med. Ctr., N.Y.C., 2000—; instr. in medicine Cornell U. Med. Coll., 1958-62; attending physician and chief div. endocrinolog and metabolism dept. medicine Beth Israel Med. Ctr., N.Y.C., 1981—2000; asst. prof. Albert Einstein Coll. Medicine, 1965-71, assoc. prof., 1971-78, prof., 1978-82, 94—; vis. prof., 1987-94; prof. Mt. Sinai Sch. Medicine, 1982-94, attending physician, 1982—88, adj. attending physician, 1988—; adj. prof., 1994—. Asst. dir. Clin. Rsch. Ctr., Montefiore Hosp., 1961-76, dir. 1976-81, dir. cancer endocrinology, 1976-84, sr. investigator Inst. Steroid Rsch., 1963-81; vis. physician Rockefeller U. Hosp., 1978-84. Mem. editl. bd. Jour. Clin. Endocrinology and Metabolism, 1971-76, Anticancer Rsch., 1981—, Breast Disease-An Internat. Jour., 1987—; translator Yiddish poetry and prose; contbr. over 250 articles to profl. jours. Pres. Workmen's Cir., 1984-88, 92-96, The Forward Assn., 1991-92, 95—; co-pres. Congress for Jewish Culture, 1989—; active Atran Found., 1987—. With M.C., USAF, 1951-82, brig. gen. Res. ret. Decorated Legion of Merit, Combat Readiness medal, Meritorious Svc. medal, Air Force Commendation medal. Fellow ACP; mem. AMA, AAAS, Am. Heart Assn. (coun. on arteriosclerosis), Am. Soc. Clin. Investigation, Endocrine Soc., Aerospace Med. Assn., Am. Diabetes Assn. (profl. sect.), Am. Fedn. Clin. Rsch., Assn. Mil. Surgeons U.S., Soc. Med. Cons. Armed Forces, Soc. USAF Flight Surgeons, N.Y. Diabetes Assn. Home: 3710 Bedford Ave Brooklyn NY 11229-1704 Office: Beth Israel Med Ctr Div Endocrinolgy Metabolism 1st Ave At 16th St New York NY 10003

ZUMPE, DORIS, ethologist, researcher, educator; b. Berlin, May 18, 1940; came to U.S., 1972; d. Herman Frank and Eva (Wagner) Z. BSc, U. London, 1961, PhD, 1970. Asst. to K.Z. Lorenz, Max-Planck-Inst. für Verhaltensphysiologie, Seewiesen, Fed. Republic Germany, 1961-64; rsch. asst. and assoc., lectr. Inst. Psychiatry, U. London, 1965-72; rsch. assoc. Emory U. Sch. Medicine, Atlanta, 1972-74, asst. prof. psychiatry (ethology), 1974-77, assoc. prof., 1977-87, prof., 1987—. Reviewer NSF, 7 sci. jours. Contbr. over 150 articles to profl. jours. NIMH grantee, 1971-2000. Mem. AAAS, Internat. Soc. Psychoneuroendocrinology, Internat. Primatological Soc., Internat. Soc. for Human Ethology, Soc. Behavioral Neuroendocrinology, Am. Soc. Primatologists, N.Y. Acad. Scis., Earl Music Am., Viola da Gamba Soc. Am. Avocation: music. Office: Emory U Sch Medicine Dept Psychiatry Atlanta GA 30322-0001

ZUMWALT, RICHARD DOWLING, flour mill executive; b. Amarillo, Tex., Dec. 1, 1912; s. Richard Dowling and Cora Bell (Pate) Z.; m. Florine Anita Nelson, Oct. 23, 1938; 1 dau., Alexandra Anita (Mrs. Klaus Schwabe). Student, Met. Bus. Coll., 1930; extension student, Tex. Tech. Coll., 1931, Dallas Coll., 1949. With Pearlstone Mill & Elevator Co., summers 1929/30; With J. C. Crouch Grain Co., 1931-44; with Burrus Mills, Inc., Dallas, 1944-83, exec. v.p., 1956-64, pres., 1964-83; sec.-treas. Zumwalt Inc., 1973—; ret. gen. mgr. Burrus milling dept. Cargill, Inc. Past pres. Bulgur Assos., Washington, Dallas Grain Exchange. Mem. Millers Nat. Fedn., Tex. Mfrs. Assn. (past dir.) Home: 7353 Blairview Dr Dallas TX 75230-5416

ZUMWALT, ROGER CARL, hospital administrator; b. Eugene, Oreg., Oct. 26, 1943; s. Robert Walter and Jean Elaine (Adams) Z.; m. Sharon Marlene Ryan, Aug. 22, 1970; children: Kathryn Nicole Zumwalt Deweber, Timothy Robert. Student, Boise State U., 1963-65; BA, We. Oreg. U., 1969; postgrad., U. Iowa, 1969-71; MA cum laude, Oreg. State U., 1973. Adminstr. Coulee Cmty. Hosp., Grand Coulee, Wash., 1973-75, Eastmoreland Hosp., Portland, Oreg., 1975-81; exec. dir. Cmty. Hosp., Grand Junction, Colo., 1981-97; pres., healthcare cons. accreditation Zumwalt Consulting, Salem, Oreg., 1997—; dir. adminstrv. svcs. divsn. SAIF Corp., 1998—. Chmn., bd. dirs. Alphabet House Pediat. Rehab. and Edn., 1998-2000, Castle Rock Med. Group, Inc., Denver, 1998—; part owner, chmn. bd. dirs. Castle Rock (Colo.) Med. Ctr., 1998--, N.W. Okla. Regional Med. Ctr. Cherokee, 2000; spkr. numerous local and nat. presentations, subjects including healthcare, hosp. mktg./success/costs, 1981-97; CEO Cmty. Med. Plz., 1984-97, Cmty. Health Care Providers Orgn., 1986-97, Cmty. Hosp. Found., 1988-97; guest lectr. Mesa Stae Coll., 1993-98, Colo. Christian Coll., 1996-98. Newspaper columnist, 1973-75; contbr. articles, presentations to profl. publs. Commr. Multnomah County Health Care Commn., Portland, 1978-81; health cons. Grant County Housing Auth., Grand Coulee, 1974-75; mem. pk. bd. City of Tigard, Oreg., 1976-78; caucus rep. Mesa County Rep. Party, Grand Junction, 1988; mem. adv. com., pres.'s office Mesa State Coll., Grand Junction, 1989; bd. dirs. Hospice of Grand Valley, Grand Junction, 1992-97, mem. devel. com., 1993-97, vice chmn. bd. dirs., 1994-97; bd. dirs. Grand Valley Hospice, 1992-96; com. mem. Salem Coalition on Youth Literacy, 2000—. Fellow Coll. Osteo. Healthcare Execs. (bd. dirs. 1985-88, pres. 1987, examiner 1989—, Disting. Svc. award 1989); mem. Am. Osteo. Healthcare Assn. (bd. dirs. 1987-98, treas. 1992-93, 1st v.p. 1994-95, 2d v.p. 1993-94, vice chairperson 1994-95, chmn. 1996-97, chairperson 1997-98, past chmn. 1998), Am. Osteo. Assn. (ex-officio mem. bd. dirs. 1996), Bur. Healthcare Facilities Accreditation (v.p. 1994, advisor 1995-98, accreditation cons. 1995—, accreditation surveyer 1978—, accreditation survey instr. 1994—), Joint Commn. on Am. Healthcare Orgn. (task force on small and rural hosps. 1994-98), Colo. Hosp. Assn. (bd. dirs. 1987-92), Mountain States Vol. Hosp. Assn. (bd. dirs. 1984-98, exec. com. 1991-98, v.p. 1993, vice chmn. bd. dirs. 1992-98), We. Coll. Ind. Practice Assn. (Medicine Mauls Measles com., fin. com. 1991-92), We. Colo. Health Care Alliance (bd. dirs. 1989-94, v.p. 1992, chmn. bd. dirs. 1993, past chmn. bd. dirs. 1994), Mesa County Mental Health Assn. (bd. dirs. 1988-89, 91-92), Grand Junction C. of C. (bd. dirs. 1991-93), Rotary (Grand Coolee Wash. 1973-75, Portland, Oreg. 1975-81, Grand Junction, Colo. 1981-98, Salem, Oreg. 1998—, chair fund raising com. 2000—, bd. dirs. 2001—), Masons, Shriners (pres. Grand Junction club 1989, bd. dirs. El Jebel 1986-90, 1st v.p. Western Colo. club 1989). Republican. Methodist. Avocations: golf, camping, fishing, hunting. Home: 413 NW Heather Ave Sublimity OR 97385-9818 Office: SAIF Corp 440 Church St SE PWB 2 Salem OR 97312-2000 Fax: 503-315-3086. E-mail: Roshzum@cs.com.

ZUMWALT, ROSS EUGENE, forensic pathologist, educator; b. Goodrich, Mich., July 18, 1943; s. Paul Lawrence and Lila Ann (Birky) Z.; m. Theresa Ann Schar, Sept. 12, 1970 (div. Apr. 1988); children: Christopher Todd, Tenley Ann; m. Cheryl Lynn Willman, Sept. 4, 1988; 1 child, David Willman Zumwalt. BA, Wabash Coll., 1967; MD, U. Ill., 1971. Diplomate in anat. and forensic pathology Am. Bd. Pathology. Intern, resident in pathology Mary Bassett Hosp., Cooperstown, N.Y., 1971-73; resident in anat. and forensic pathology Southwestern Med. Sch., Dallas, 1973-76; asst. med. examiner Dallas County, 1974-76; staff pathologist, dir. labs. Naval Regional Med. Ctr., Camp Lejeune, N.C., 1976-78; dep. coroner Cuyahoga County, Cleve., 1978-80, Hamilton County, Cin., 1980-86; assoc. prof. pathology U. Cin. Sch. Medicine, 1980-86; prof. pathology U. N.Mex. Sch. Medicine, Albuquerque, 1987—; chief med. investigator Office of Med. Investigator, 1991—; pres. Am. Bd. of Pathology, Tampa, 2000-. Trustee Am. Bd. Pathology, Tampa, Fla.,

1993—. Lt. comdr. USN, 1976-78. Fellow Am. Acad. Forensic Scis., Coll. Am. Pathologists; mem. AMA, Nat. Assn. Med. Examiners (bd. dirs. 1984-96, pres. 1995-96), Am. Soc. Clin. Pathologists, Am. and Can. Acad. Pathologists. Avocation: golf.

ZUNES, J. STEPHEN, political science educator, speaker, consultant; b. Salisbury, N.C., Nov. 5, 1956; s. John Athas and Helen (Karnes) Z.; m. Nanlouise Wolfe, May 23, 1987; children: Shanti, Kalila, Tobin. BA, Oberlin Coll., 1979; MA, Temple U., 1983, Cornell U., 1987, PhD, 1990. Instr. Temple U., Ambler, Pa., 1981; rsch. asst. Inst. Policy Studies, Washington, 1982-83; asst. prof. Ithaca (N.Y.) Coll., 1987-89, Whitman Coll., Walla Walla, Wash., 1989-91; dir. Inst. for a New Middle East Policy, Seattle, 1991—. Vis. prof. U. Puget Sound, 1993-94; speaker, cons. on U.S. Med. East rels. Contbr. articles to profl. and gen. publs. Rsch. grantee U.S. Inst. of Peace, 1990-91, Inst. for Global Security Studies, 1993—. Mem. Am. Polit. Sci. Assn., Internat. Studies Assn., Caucus for New Polit. Sci., Consortium on Peace Rsch., Edn. and Devel., Middle East Studies Assn. Avocations: folk music, wilderness recreation. Home: 820 Western Dr Santa Cruz CA 95060-6823 Office: Inst Global Security Studies PO Box 10898 Bainbridge Island WA 98110-0898

ZUNG, JONATHAN BRUCE, chemist; b. Suffern, N.Y., Oct. 20, 1964; s. Martin and Ruth Z.; m. Renée L. Sekersky, June 29, 1991; children: Andrew, Ashley. BS, Fla. Inst. Tech., 1986; PhD, Emory U., 1991. Rsch. scientist Pfizer Inc., Groton, Conn., 1991-94, sr. rsch. scientist, 1994-96, project leader, 1996-98, asst. dir., 1998-2000, dir., 2000—01; exec. dir. Bristol Myers Squibb, Princeton, NJ, 2001—. Contbr. chpt. Ency. Analyt. Sci., 1995, numerous manuscripts; patentee in field (2). Mem. Am. Chem. Soc. (intern 1986), Am. Assn. Pharm. Scis. Office: Bristol-Myers Squibb PO Box 4000 Princeton NJ 08543

ZUNG, THOMAS TSE-KWAI, architect; b. Shanghai, China, Feb. 8, 1933; came to the U.S., 1937, naturalized, 1954; 1 child, Thomas Bates. Student, Drew U., 1950-51, Va. Poly. Inst., 1951-53, Columbia U., 1955-57; BArch, U. Mich., 1960; MS in Design Sci., Internat. Coll., 1982. Project arch. Edward Durell Stone, Arch., N.Y.C., 1958, 60-65; arch. Cleve., 1967—. Pres. Buckminster Fuller, Sadao and Zung, Archs., 1979—. Author-editor: Buckminster Fuller, Anthology for the New Millennium; prin. works include City Cleve. Pub. Utilities Bldg., Cleve. State U. Geodesig Elongated Dome, Mayfran, Inc., Sawmill Creek Lodge, U. Akron Guzzetta Hall, Music, Speech and Theater Arts Ctr., Alumni Ctr. Bowling Green State U., U. Akron Master Plan-West, City of East Cleveland, Superior Euclid beautification plan, student recreation ctr. Bowling Green State U., Glenville Pub. Libr., campus bldg. Tex. Wesleyan Coll., recreation, health and phys. edn. bldg. Wittenberg U., Medina Res. Park Office, arena, health, phys. edn. complex U. Akron, Dyke Coll., Lima State Prizon, Cleve. Children's Christian Home, State of Ohio Pre-Release Ctr. Cleve., Lorain-Grafton State Prison, Mayfield H.S., Asian Village Project, Cleve. Metroparks Tropical Rainforest Bldg., Student Union Wittenberg U., YWCA, Salem, Ohio, China Internat. Trade Ctr., People's Rep. China, additions to Cleve. Hopkins Internat. Airport, Ohio State U. Coll. of Dentistry-Postle Hall and Hist. Costume and Textile Mus., Master Plan Schreiner Coll. and Cailloux Student Ctr., Griffin Welcome Ctr., Master Plan Walsh Univ., Walsh Student Union, Columbus, Western Res. Psychiat. Hosp., Ohio, Trumbull State Prison, Ohio Dept. Transp. Prototypical Rest Stop Design; patentee in field. Trustee Pace Assn., 1970-73, Karamu House, 1974-80, Cleve. Inst. Music, 1979-86, Chinese Cultural Assn., 1980-84, Ohio Arts Coun., 1982-84; task force chmn. Greater Cleve. Growth Assn., 1970; mem. Coun. Human Rels., 1972, Leadership Cleve. Class '77; cubmaster local Boy Scouts Am., 1977-79; vestryman St. Christopher-by-River, 1980-83; bd. dirs. Buckminster Fuller Inst., 1983—, Pearl S. Buck Found., 1989-98, cons. arch. hist. house com.; mem. Adv. Coun. Aging, State of Ohio, 1997—. With Signal Corps, U.S. Army, 1953-55. Decorated 4 medals; recipient Pub. Works award State of Ohio, 1971, Design award Korean Inst. Constrn. Tech., 1984, Ohio Valley ABC Design Excellence award Wittenberg U. Student Union, 1989, others. Mem. AIA (dir. Cleve. chpt. 1980, Design award Cleve. chpt. 1972, Design award 1989), Am. Soc. Planning Ofcls., English Speaking Union (trustee 1972-75), Ohio Soc. Archs., Ohio Assn. Minority Archs. and Engrs. (trustee 1982-90), Hermit Club, City Club (dir. 1972-74, v.p. 1974), Rotary. Office: Buckminster Fuller Sadao & Zung 1 Bratenahl Pl Cleveland OH 44108-1181

ZUNICH, JANICE, pediatrician, geneticist, educator, administrator; b. New Kensington, Pa., Sept. 2, 1953; d. Nick and Mary (Zivkovich) Z.; m. Milan Katic, June 20, 1981; children: Nikola Ilija, Milana. BS, Ohio State U., 1974, MD, 1978. Diplomate Am. Bd. Pediat., Nat. Bd. Med. Examiners, Am. Bd. Med. Genetics (clin. genetics, clin. cytogenetics). Lab. technician Cmty. Hosp., Lorain, Ohio, summer 1974, Ohio State U. Hosp., Columbus, 1974-75; intern, then resident in pediat. Columbus Children's Hosp., 1978-81; genetics fellow Luth. Gen. Hosp., Park Ridge, Ill., 1981-83; asst. prof. pediat. W.Va. U. Med. Ctr., Morgantown, 1983-85, assoc. dir. cytogenetics, 1984-85; clin. assoc. prof. med. genetics, dir. Genetics Ctr. N.W. Ctr. Med. Edn., Ind. U. Sch. Medicine, Gary, 1985—. Genetics cons. Cmty. Hosp., Munster, Ind., Porter Meml. Hosp., Valparaiso, Ind., St. Anthony Med. Ctr., Crown Point, Ind., Meth. Hosp., Gary and Merrillville, Ind., St. Margaret Hosp., Hammond, Ind. Contbr. articles to profl. jours. Mem. med. com. Planned Parenthood, N.W.-N.E. Ind., Merrillville, 1987-99; mem. adv. com. N.W. Ind. Sickle Cell Found., Gary, 1987—; mem. med. adv. com. Svcs. for Children with Spl. Health Care Needs, Indpls., 1989-92; mem. adv. bd. Parent Edn. Ctr., Whiting, Ind., 1988-96; chmn. Lake County Task Force on Teen Pregnancy, 1998-2000. Named Person of Yr., Down Syndrome Assn. N.W. Ind., Highland, 1988; Charles F. Whitten fellow Sickle Cell Found. N.W. Ind., 1990. Fellow: AMA, Am. Coll. Med. Genetics (founding fellow), Am. Acad. Pediat.; mem.: Lake County Med. Soc., Ind. State Med. Assn., Am. Soc. Human Genetics, Great Lakes Regional Genetics Group (financing genetics svcs. sub-com. 1988—99), Alpha Epsilon Delta, Phi Beta Kappa. Eastern Orthodox. Avocations: piano, folk dancing, choral singing, travel. Office: NW Ctr for Med Edn 3400 Broadway Gary IN 46408-1101 E-mail: jzunich@iun.edu.

ZUNIGA-GALINDO, WILSON A. mathematician, educator, computer scientist, educator, mathematician, researcher, computer scientist, researcher; b. Bogota , Colombia, Sept. 23, 1964; s. Alvaro Zuniga, Viterba Galindo; m. Maria Elizabeth Carlier; children: Daniela Zuniga-Carlier, Felipe Zuniga-Carlier. BSEE, Francisco Jose de Caldas U., Bogota D.C., Colombia, 1988; BS in Math., Nat. U. Colombia, Bogota D.C., 1988; MSEE, Los Andes U., Bogota D.C., 1991, MS in Math., 1992; PhD, Inst. Pure and Applied Math., Rio de Janeiro, 1996. Rsch. engr. Telecomm. and Electronics Inst., ITEC, Bogota, 1990—91; asst. prof. math. Indsl. U. Santander, Bucaramanga, Colombia, 1996—97; asst. prof. math. and computer sci. Barry U., Miami Shores, Fla., 2001—; dir. sci. computation lab. Autonomous U. Bucaramanga. Vis. prof. Inst. Math. and Computation, Sao Carlos, Sao Paulo, 2000—00. Contbr. articles to profl. jours. Grantee, Colciencias, Colombia, 1998—2000, 2000—02; scholar, Nat. Rsch. Coun. Brazil, CNPq, 1992—96, TELECOM-Colombia, 1989—90. Mem.: Am. Math. Soc. Office: Barry Univ Math and Computer Sci 11300 NE Second Ave Miami Shores FL 33161 Office Fax: 305-899-3610. Business E-Mail: wzuniga@mail.barry.edu.

ZUNZ, OLIVIER JEAN, history educator; b. Paris, July 19, 1946; s. Jean R. and Monique M. (Blin) Z.; m. Christine M. Crommen, July 3, 1970; children: Emmanuel, Sophie. Licence in history and geography, U. Paris X, 1968, M in History, 1969; Doctorat-ès-Lettres, U. Paris I, Panthéon-Sorbonne, 1982. Scientist Ctr. Nat. de la Recherche Scientifique, Paris, 1976-78; asst. prof. dept. history U. Va., Charlottesville, 1978-83, assoc. prof., 1983-88, prof., 1988-99, Commonwealth prof., 1999—. Vis. prof. Ecole des Hautes Etudes en Scis., Sociales, Paris, 1985—, Coll. France, 1997; dir. seminar for Coll. Tchrs. NEH, 1989, 92. Author: The Changing Face of Inequality: Urbanization, Industrial Development, and Immigrants in Detroit, 1880-1920, 1982, Making America Corporate, 1870-1920, 1990, Why the American Century?, 1998; editor, co-author: Reliving the Past: The Worlds of Social History, 1985; co-editor: (with David Ward) The Landscape of Modernity: Essays on New York City, 1900-1940, 1992, (with Leonard Schoppa and Nobuhizo Hiwakari): Social Contracts under Stress: The Middle Classes of America, Europe, and Japan at the Turn of the Century, 2002, (with Alan Sikalan): The Tocqueville Reader: A Life in Letters and Politics, 2002; mem. editorial bd. Revs. in Am. History, 1990-98; contbr. articles, book revs. to profl. jours. Jr. fellow Mich. Soc. Fellows, 1973-76, John Simon Guggenheim Meml. Found. fellow, 1986-87; grantee U. Mich.-Ford Found. Population Devel. Fund, 1974-76, NSF, 1976-78, NEH, 1979-81, 84-87; also recipient numerous rsch. grants. Mem. Am. Hist. Assn., Orgn. Am. Historians, The Tocqueville Soc. (pres. 2001—). Home: 1368 Hilltop Rd Charlottesville VA 22903-1225 Office: U Va Corcoran Dept of History PO Box 400180 Randall Hall Charlottesville VA 22903-4180 Office Fax: 434-924-7891. E-mail: oz@virginia.edu.

ZUO, MINGJIAN, industrial engineering educator; b. Laixi, China, Oct. 16, 1962; s. Wenyuan Zuo and Meiying Zhang; m. Ninghe Hu, Aug. 30, 1987; children: Kevin, Lillian. BSc, Shandong (China) Inst. Tech., 1982; MSc, Iowa State U., 1986, PhD, 1989. Asst. prof. indsl. engring. U. Windsor, Ont., Can., 1989-90; prof. U. Alta., Edmonton, Can., 1990—; assoc. prof. City U. of Hong Kong, China, 1996-98. Guest editor spl. issue Jour. IIE Transactions on Quality and Reliability Engring., 1997; author: Contemporary Engineering Economics: A Canadian Perspective, 1995. Mem. IEEE, Inst. Indsl. Engrs. Avocations: basketball, badminton, travel. Home: 3006-105A St Edmonton AB Canada T6J3A5 Office: U Alberta Dept Mech Engring Edmonton AB Canada T6G2G8

ZUO, YIJUN, statistician, educator; s. Baoyan Zuo and Fadi Zhang; m. Chuanping Yang, Aug. 5, 1993; children: Hanshi, Hanwen. PhD, U. Tex., 1998. Asst. prof. Ariz. State U., Tempe, 1998—2002; assoc. prof. Mich. State U., East Lansing, 2003—. Grantee, NSF, 2000—. Mem.: Am. Statis. Assn.

ZUPERKU, EDWARD JOHN, biomedical engineering educator; b. Chgo., Sept. 14, 1942; s. Edward John Z. and Mary Ann (Sefcik) Driscoll; m. Brenda Marie Seale, May 17, 1975; children: David, Christina, Daniel, James. B of Elec. Engring., Marquette U., 1965, MS in Biomed. Engring., 1967, PhD in Biomed. Engring., 1970. Instr. anesthesiology Med. Coll. Wis., Milw., 1970-74; gen. physical scientist VA Hosp., 1973-76; asst. prof. anesthesiology Med. Coll. Wis., 1974-78; biomed. rsch. engr. VA Hosp., 1976—; assoc. prof. Med. Coll. Wis., 1978-89, rsch. prof. anesthesiology, 1989—. Cons. rsch. & devel. engring. Biochem Internat., Milw., 1976-79, Criticare Systems, Inc., Milw., 1983-88. Contbr. articles to profl. jours. Nat. Merit Rev. grantee VA, 1978—. Mem. Am. Physiological Soc., Soc. Neurosci., Biomed. Engring. Soc. Office: Zablocki VA Med Ctr Rsch Svc 151 Milwaukee WI 53295-0001 E-mail: ezuperku@mcw.edu.

ZUPKO, RAMON, composer, music professor emeritus; b. Pitts., Nov. 14, 1932; s. Michael E. and Frances E. (Bartek) Z.; m. Vonette Sarche, Sept. 14, 1969; 1 child, Mischa. BS in Music, Juilliard, 1956, MS in Music, 1957. Asst. prof. music Chgo. (Ill.) Musical Coll., 1967-71; prof. music Western Mich. Univ., Sch. Music, Kalamazoo, 1971-97. Recipient composition fellowship Guggenheim Found., 1982, Composers awards Am. Acad. and Inst. of Arts and Letters, N.Y., 1982, Disting. Faculty award Mich. Assn. Governing Bds., Lansing, 1984, Composers awards NEA, Washington, 1978-80, 85, Koussevitzky Found. award 1981, Disting. Faculty scholar award Western Mich. U., 1983, Kennedy-Friedheim award, Washington, 1980. Mem. Am. Composers Alliance, Phi Kappa Phi. Avocations: photography, yoga, gardening. Home: 1540 N 2nd St Kalamazoo MI 49009-9375 E-mail: zupko@wmich.edu.

ZURAW, KATHLEEN ANN, special education and physical education educator; b. Bay City, Mich., Sept. 29, 1960; d. John Luke and Clara Josephine (Kilian) Z. AA with high honors, Delta Community Coll., 1980; BS with high honors, Mich. State U., 1984, MA, 1987. Cert. spl. edn., mentally impaired phys. edn. grade K-12, adaptive phys. edn. tchr., Mich. Summer water safety instr. Camp Midicha, Columbia, Mich., 1982, Bay Cliff Health Camp, Big Bay, 1983; summer spl. edn. tchr. Jefferson Orthopedic Sch., Honolulu, 1984, 85, 86, Ingham Intermediate Sch. Dist., Mason, Mich., 1987; spl. edn. tchr. Bay Arenac Intermediate Sch. Dist., Bay City, 1985-87, Berrien County Intermediate Sch. Dist., Berrien Springs, Mich., 1987—. Mem. citizen amb program fitness delegation People's Republic China, 1991. Area 17 coach Mich. Spl. Olympics, Berrien Springs, 1987—; mem. YMCA, St. Joseph, Mich., 1987—, Y-Ptnrs., 1989, Coun. Exceptional Children; participant Citizen Ambassador Delegation to People's Republic of China, 1991. Mem. Am. Alliance Health, Phys. Edn., Recreation and Dance, Phi Theta Kappa, Phi Kappa Phi, Phi Delta Kappa. Roman Catholic. Avocations: sports, crafts. Home: 7306 W S Saginaw Rd Bay City MI 48706

ZURAWSKI, JEANETTE, rehabilitation services professional; b. June 30, 1951; Student, U. Wis., 1969-70, Portland C.C., 1974-78; BS in Chemistry, Portland State U., 1981; MD, Oreg. Health Scis. U., 1985; postgrad. in acupuncture, UCLA, 2000. Diplomate Am. Bd. Phys. Medicine and Rehab. Resident U. Kans. Med. Ctr., Kansas City, 1985-89; med. dir. rehab. svcs. North Miss Med. Ctr., Tupelo, 1989-97; pvt. practice Miss. Past mem. adv. com. Medicare Carrier; presenter in field; bd. dirs. Gilbert's Home Health Care Agy. Past chair pers. com., exec. bd. mem., co-chair fund raising com. Big Brothers/Big Sisters, Lee County, Miss. Mem. AMA, Am. Acad. Phys. Medicine and Rehab. (chairperson edn. com., mem. exec. coun. resident physician sect.), Am. Med. Women's Assn., Am. Bus. Women's Assn. (chair membership com., treas., recipient Woman of the Year), Miss. State Med. Assn., Assn. Acad. Physiatrists, Am. Med. Acupuncture Assn. (bd. eligible), Iota Sigma Pi. Office: 1010 N Eason Blvd Tupelo MS 38804-7532

ZURCHER, VICKIE LEE, geneticist; b. Millersburg, Ohio, Apr. 9, 1956; d. Carl Frederick and Fae Marie (Tressell) Z.; m. David Blaine Joyce, May 29, 1982; children: Katherine Michelle, Michael David. BA in Biology with honors, Coll. of Wooster, 1978; MD, U. Cinn., 1982. Diplomate Am. Bd. Pediatrics, Am. Bd. Med. Genetics. Intern, then resident in pediatrics Children's Meml. Hosp., Chgo., 1982-85, attending physician, 1985-86; mem. staff Children's Meml. Hosp./Prentice Women's Hosp., 1985-86; fellow in clin. genetics U. Hosps. Cleve., 1986-89; instr. in pediatrics Case Western Res. U., Cleve., 1991-95, instr. in genetics, 1992-95. Contbr. articles to profl. jours. Mem. orch. MGP Cmty. Theater, Avon Lake, 1994—; mem. bell choir Avon Lake Presbyn. Ch., 1993—. Fellow Am. Acad. Pediatrics, Am. Coll. Med. Genetics (founding); mem. Am. Soc. Human Genetics, Phi Beta Kappa. Avocations: piano, accordion, clarinet, travel. Address: 31708 Sailors Cv Avon Lake OH 44012-2931 E-mail: DJoycefamily@attbi.com.

ZURHEIDE, CHARLES HENRY, consulting electrical engineer; b. St. Louis, May 9, 1923; s. Charles Henry and Ollie C. (Kirk) Z.; m. Ruth M. Plueck, June 25, 1949; children— Barbara Anne, Pamela S. BS in Elec. Engring, U. Mo., Columbia, 1944. Registered profl. engr., Mo. Distbn. engr. Laclede Power & Light Co., St. Louis, 1944-45; sub-sta. engr., then indsl. engr. Union Electric Co., 1945-51; chief elec. engr. Fruin-Colnon Contracting Co., 1951-54; a founder, treas., v.p. Smith-Zurheide, Inc., 1954-65; pres. Zurheide-Herrmann, Inc., 1965—, chmn. bd., 1988—. Chmn. Elec. Code Rev. Commn., St. Louis, 1965-01, Mo. Bd. Profl. Engrs., 1977-82, St. Louis Indsl. Devel. Commn., 1965-67; mem. adv. panel region 6 GSA, 1977—; plan commn., City of Ferguson, Mo., 1968-73; tech. adv. com. St. Louis C. of C., 1977; mem. Mo. Pub. Svc. Commn. Task Force on Retail Wheeling of Electricity, 1998. Recipient Distinguished Service in Engring. award U. Mo., 1976 Fellow Am. Cons. Engrs. Council; mem. Mo. Soc. Profl. Engrs. (Engr. of Year award 1970), Cons. Engrs. Council Mo., IEEE, Illuminating Engring. Soc., Engrs. Club St. Louis, Tau Alpha Pi. Clubs: Norwood Hills Country, Mo. Athletic. Home: 14336 Spyglass Rdg Chesterfield MO 63017-2140 Office: Zurheide-Herrmann Inc 4333 Clayton Ave Saint Louis MO 63110-1684 E-mail: czurneide@zhideas.com.

ZURICK, JACK, electrical engineer, consultant; b. Bklyn., May 28, 1952; s. Joseph and Edelgard (Wendland) Z.; m. Nenita Cardinal, Apr. 28, 1990. Pre-engring student, Queensborough Community Coll., 1969-71, AAS, 1971-73. Cert. Assoc. Engring. Technician. Elec. designer Ebasco Svcs., Inc., N.Y.C., 1973-76; design engr. Gibbs & Cox, Inc., 1976-78; elec. designer Sci. Design Co., Inc., 1978-85; design engr. Vikonics, Inc., Secaucus, N.J., 1985-87; sr. elec. designer H-R Internat., Inc., Edison, 1988-93; sr. elec. engr. Kleinknecht Elec. Co. of N.J., Maplewood, 1993-94; cons. Rotator Svcs., Inc., East Brunswick, 1994-95; elec. design engr. ICF Kaiser Engrs., Inc., Iselin, 1995-97; sr. elec. engr. Fluor Daniel, Inc., Marlton, 1997, Orbital Engring. Inc., Bensalem, Pa., 1997; design mgr. Automated Control Concepts, Inc., Neptune, N.J., 1998—. Cons. Sherman Svcs., Inc., Somerset, N.J., 1988, Gen. Indsl. Techs., Inc., Valleystream, N.Y., 1987-88, Allied Resources Tech. Cons., Inc., 1997. Mem. Nat. Inst. for Cert. Engring. Technols. (assoc. engring. technician), Tau Alpha Pi (v.p. 1972-73). Avocations: golf, guitar, electronics, scuba diving. Home: 59 Pheasant Run Freehold NJ 07728-7767 Office: Automated Control Concepts 3535 Rte 66 Neptune NJ 07753-2622 E-mail: jzurick@automated-control.com.

ZURICK, JOHN, consultant, former dance company director; MFA in Theatre Arts, Brandeis U. Acting v.p. mktg. InterLearn, Inc.; creator Power of Once; regional mgr./full-time cons. Mills/James Prodns.; co-founder/pres./COO Finis; ptnr. Y&Z Mgmt., Boston; dir. mktg. Cin. Symphony Orch., 1983-88; instr. ESI Internat., Arlington, Va.; founder, past pres. MillennialMinds, Cin.; exec. dir. Cin. Ballet, 1998—2001; consultant Ballet Internationale, Ind., 2001—. Vol. v.p. mktg. Greater Cin. Arts & Edn. Ctr. Office: Ballet Internationale 502 N Capitol Avenue, Suite B Indianapolis IN 46204*

ZURIER, ROBERT BURTON, medical educator, clinical investigator; b. Passaic, N.J., Feb. 19, 1934; s. Milton and Lillian (Matzner) Z.; m. Catherine Elizabeth Miers, June 3, 1962; 1 child, Adam Wheaton. BS, Rutgers U., 1955; MD, U. Tex. Southwestern Med. Sch., Dallas, 1962; MA (hon.), U. Pa., 1981. Intern, then resident in medicine Boston City Hosp., 1962-64; fellow in medicine St. Lukes Hosp., N.Y.C., 1964-66; fellow in rheumatology NYU, 1970-73; pvt. practice internal medicine Holden, Mass., 1967-70; asst. prof. medicine U. Conn., Farmington, 1973-76, assoc. prof., 1976-80; prof., chief. rheumatology U. Pa., Phila., 1980-91; prof. medicine, dir. rheumatology div. U. Mass. Med. Ctr., Worcester, 1991—. Served to capt. USAR, 1956-68. Guggenheim Found. fellow, 1986. Mem. AAAS, Am. Coll. Rheumatology (master), Am. Soc. Clin. Investigation, Interurban Clin. Club (pres. 1989-90). Office: U Mass Med Ctr 55 Lake Ave N Worcester MA 01655-0002 E-mail: robert.zurier@umassmed.edu.

ZURIO, EUGENE JOHN, pharmaceutical executive; b. Plattsburgh, N.Y., June 30, 1937; s. John Theodore and Louise Mary (Di Gioia) Z.; m. Charlotte Rose Ahrens, Aug. 11, 1972; children: Luanne Deirdre, Paul Kurt. BS in Pharmacy, Fordham U., 1958; MBA, L.I. U., 1961. Various positions Baxter Healthcare, Northbrook, Ill.; sr. v.p. Millidore Inc., Bedford, Mass.; COO NYPRO Inc., Clinton, New York Blood Ctr., 1989-94; chmn., founder Alpine Biologics Inc., Orangeburg, N.Y., 1994—. Patentee in field. Chmn. Cath. Radio Assn., Jacksonville, Alliance for Marriage, Washington. Mem. Kiawah Island Club, Heritage Found. Republican. Roman Catholic. Avocations: boating, golfing, travel, history. Home: 4 Nicklaus Ln Kiawah Island SC 29455-5798

ZURKOWSKI, PAUL GEORGE, publisher; b. Milw., Nov. 8, 1932; s. Stanley Frank and Martha (Bednarz) Z.; m. Margaret Ann Becker, July 9, 1960; children: Paul Coleman, Pamela Carol, Patricia Christine, Peggy Catherine, Paula Claire, Peter Christopher. BA, U. Wis., Whitewater, 1954; LLB, U. Wis., Madison, 1957. Bar: Wis. 1957, U.S. Supreme Ct. 1961. Publisher Our Ads (shopping guide), Palmyra, Wis., 1950-55; investigator legal firm Swingen & Stern, Madison, 1955-58; atty. HHFA, Washington, 1958; examiner ICC, 1958-59; congl. legis. asst., 1959-61, 64-69; individual legal practice, also congl. home sec. Madison, 1961; exec. dir. Info. Industry Assn., Washington, 1969, pres., 1972-89. Pub. Holy Redeemer News, 1984-87, Today's Parish, 1987-90, Our Parish Times, 1990—, Family Beach Times, 1995-96, Interparish Community Guide and Business Directory, 1997—. Pres. Parish Cmty. Svcs. Inc., Md., 1991—; founder, lifetime mem. Cath. Bus. Network, 1993, pres., 1993-94, 2000-01, sec., 1994-96, edn. v.p., 1996-97, program v.p. 1997-98, bd. dirs. Prince Georges, 2002, bd. dirs. D.C., 2002--; founder, sec. Holy Land Christian Ecumenical Found., 1999-2000; founder Catholic Bus. Network USA, Nat. Assn. CBNs. Decorated Army Commendation medal; recipient Disting. Alumni Svc. award U. Wis., Whitewater, 1974, Outstanding Svc. award Cath. Bus. Network, 1994; named to Info. Industry Hall of Fame, 1988, Founders award Cath. Bus. Network Montgomery County, 2000. Office: 8027 Ellingson Dr Chevy Chase MD 20815-3029 E-mail: pzurkowski@hotmail.com.

ZURLO, EUGENE JOHN, pharmaceuticals company executive; b. Plattsburgh, N.Y., June 30, 1937; s. John T. and Louise M. (Joy) Z.; m. Charlotte R. Ahrens, Aug. 11, 1962; children: Luanne Deirdre, Paul Kurt. BS in Pharmacy, Fordham U., 1958; MBA, L.I. U., 1960. From entry level to sr. v.p. Hyland Div. Baxter Healthcare, Northbrook, Ill., 1964-75; sr. v.p. Millipore Corp., Bedford, Mass., 1976-82; exec. v.p., COO Nypro, Inc., Clinton, 1982-86, N.Y. Blood Ctr. Inc., N.Y.C., 1987-93; chmn., CEO HemaSure Inc., Marlborough, Mass., 1993-97; founder, chmn. Alpine Biologics Inc., Blauvelt, N.Y., 1993—. Gen. ptnr. Penny Creek Assocs., LLC. Pres. Cath. Radio Assn., Inc. Republican. Roman Catholic. Avocations: travel, sailing, history. Office: Alpine Biologics Inc 33 Kings Hwy Orangeburg NY 10962-1802

ZURLO, JOHN ANTHONY, English educator, writer; b. Takoma Park, Md., Oct. 7, 1941; s. John P. and Marie J. (Gould) Z.; m. Ann Frankland, Nov. 8, 1984; children: Elizabeth Kaitzer, Lynn Wright, Amy Cubbage. BA in History, U. Tex., Arlington, 1963, MA in History, 1976; MA, SUNY, Stony Brook, 1974; PhD in English, E. Tex. State U., 1983. Cert. secondary social studies tchr. N.Y., Tex. Tchr. U.S. Peace Corps, Zaria and Yola, Nigeria, 1965-67, Sayville Pub. Schs., N.Y., 1970-77; asst. instr. E. Tex. State U., Commerce, 1977-80; adj. prof. Lamar U., Beaumont, Tex., 1980-83; instr. Williamsport Area Community Coll., Pa., 1983-84; asst. prof. Lincoln Meml. U., Harrogate, Tenn., 1984-85; asst. dir. Tex. Voices E. Tex. State U., Commerce, 1985-86; asst. prof. Wright State U., Celina, Ohio, 1986—. Contbr. articles, poems and stories to mags. and profl. jours. Advisor student lit. mag. Lincoln Meml. U., 1984-85, Wright State U., 1987—; charter mem. St. Marys Sister City Orgn., 1987; organizer Home Stay for Korei Soc. Koto Band, Wright State U., 1987. With U.S. Army, 1967-70. Recipient Liberal Arts and Scis. Incentive award Lamar U., 1983, Liberal Arts Pubs. award Lamar U., 1982; humanities scholar for book discussion programs Tex. Sesquicentennial 1985, Ohio-Japanese Lit., 1988, NEH Faculty Devel. grantee, 1988-89. Mem. Coll. English Assn., Ohio Coll. English Assn., Conf. on Coll Composition Communication, Nat. Council Returned Peace Corps Vols. Democrat. Avocations: travel, gardening, photography. Office: Wright State U 7600 State Route 703 Celina OH 45822-2952

ZUSCHLAG, NANCY HANSEN, environmental and nature resources educator; b. Montclair, N.J., Dec. 12, 1954; d. Irving Djalmar and Carmen (Del Grippo) Z. BA in Biology cum laude, Coe Coll., 1977; MA in Biology, U. Kans., 1982. Regional conservation educator and coord. Mo. Conservation Dept., Jefferson City, 1982-84; coord. sch. programs Denver Mus. Natural History, 1986-87; program dir. dept. natural resources and environ. edn. Coop. Ext. Colo. State U., 1988-98; dir. ops. and edn. Mad Sci. of Denver, 1998-99; pres. Green Triangle Assocs, Internat., 1997—; instr. and coord. for lower sch. sci. Colo. Acad., 2000—. Instr. environ. educator Mus. Natural History, U. Kans., Lawrence, 1976-82, assoc. pub. edn. dept. , 1986-89; lectr. William Woods Coll., 1982-84; mem. study, rsch. rev. group Canary Islands, 1985; cons. Kongskilde Field Study Edn. Ctr., Soro, Denmark, 1985; bd. dirs. Foothills Nature Ctr., Boulder, Colo., 1987-89; assoc. zool. Denver Mus. Natural History, 1988; cons. and educator Mus. Zool., U. Copenhagen, 1984-85, 95-96; co-dir., sci. coord., instr. Lower Sch. Colo. Acad., 2000—. Author, editor: Back to Ancient Egypt, 1987; (with others) Science - Natur/Teknik, Assessment and Learning Studies and Educational Theory Curriculum, Vol. 22, 1995; editor: (with others) Contributions to Vertebrate Ecology and Systematic; a Tribute to Henry S. Fitch, 1983; contbr. articles to profl. jours. State edn. coord. Colo. Earth Day is Every Day campaign, Boulder, 1990; bd. dirs. Colo. Found. Agr., Denver, 1992-95, mem. edn. bd., 1993; facilitator and presenter UN Program Youth in the Environment, U. Colo., Boulder, 1993; chair environ. and natural resources future's task force com., Colo. State U. Coop. Ext., 1993; mem. nat. natural resources and environ. mgmt. support team coop. states, rsch. ext. edn. sys., USDA, 1993-96; mem. synthesis team and original document writing team, Colo. Environ. Edn. Master Plan, 1994; mem. state steering com. Denver Urban Resources Partnership, 1996—, Denver Youth Naturally Project, 1995. Recipient N.J. award AUW, County Achievement award Nat. Assn. Counties, 1989, Environ. Scholar award USEPA, 1990, region 8 Outstanding Women's Contbns. in Edn. award, 1992, Nat. Environ. Coun. award, 1992, 94, Celebrate Environ. Edn. award, 1992, Environ. Leadership award Colo. State Gov., 1993; scholar Coe Coll., 1973-74; Virginia Harkness-Sawtelle Found. scholar Coe Coll. and U. Kans., 1976-78; Fulbright scholar U. Copenhagen Zool. Mus., 1984-85, Fulbright scholar assoc. Royal Danish Sch. Edn., 1995-96. Mem. Am. Assn. Biol. Scis.,

Nat. Wildlife Fedn. (mem. steering com. Naturlink 1993), North Am. Assn. Environ. Edn., Alliance Environ. Edn., Nat. Assn. Interpreters, Am. Arachnological Assn., Colo. Alliance Environ. Edn. (bd. dirs. 1988-92, pres. 1990-91, adv. bd. 1997), Colo. Assn. Tchrs., Fulbright Alumni Soc., Phi Sigma, Epsilon Sigma Phi (State Early Career Excellence award 1990). Avocations: hiking, writing on Nordic and Celtic myth, nature and culture, jewelry-making, traveling. Office: Green Triangle Assocs Internat PMB 223 4255 S Buckley Rd Aurora CO 80013 E-mail: nhzgreentri@hotmail.com.

ZUSCHLAG, RICHARD EMERY, small business owner; b. Greenville, Pa., Mar. 28, 1948; s. Emery Eugene and Mary Janet (Knapp) Z.; m. Elaine Dupuis; children: Blair, Beth, Blaise. BSEE, Capitol Inst. Tech., 1970. Salesperson Greenville (Pa.) Broadcasting Co., 1968-70; def. training officer Westinghouse Electric Co., Balt. and Lafayette, La., 1970-71; pres. Acadian Ambulance Service, Inc., Lafayette. Bd. dirs. Bank One, Lafayette. Chmn. Lafayette Parish Comm.; bd. dirs. Acadiana Safety Assn., 1978—81; trustee U. La.-Lafayette Found.; chmn. Leadership La.; v.p. Coun. for Better La.; pres., bd. dirs. S.W. La. Edn. and Referral Ctr. Named Businessman of Yr. for State of La. SBA, 1980, Marketer of Yr. Sales and Mktg. Internat. Greater Baton Rouge, 1988; recipient Lafayette Civic Cup award, 1996. Mem. Internat. Elec. Engrs., La. Hosp. Assn. (chmn. ems), La. Press Assn., La. Assn. Broadcasters, Lafayette C. of C. (bd. dirs.), La. Assn. Bus. and Industry. Republican. Roman Catholic. Office: Acadian Ambulance Service Inc 130 E Kaliste Saloom Rd PO Box 98000 Lafayette LA 70509-8000 E-mail: rzuschlag@acadian.com.

ZUSPAN, FREDERICK PAUL, obstetrician, gynecologist, educator; b. Richwood, Ohio, Jan. 20, 1922; s. Irl Goff and Kathryn (Speyer) Z.; m. Mary Jane Cox, Nov. 23, 1943; children: Mark Frederick, Kathryn Jane, Bethany Anne. BA, Ohio State U., 1947, MD, 1951. Intern Univ. Hosps., Columbus, Ohio, 1951-52, resident, 1952-54, Western Res. U., Cleve., 1954-56, Oblebay fellow, 1958-60, asst. prof., 1958-60; chmn. dept. bo-gyn. McDowell (Ky.) Meml. Hosp., 1956-58, chief clin. svcs., 1957-58; prof., chmn. dept. ob-gyn. Med. Coll. Ga., Augusta, 1960-66; Joseph Boliver DeLee prof. ob-gyn., chmn. dept. U. Chgo., 1966-75; obstetrician, gynecologist in chief Chgo. Lying-In Hosp., 1966-75; prof., chmn. dept. ob-gyn. Ohio State U., Columbus, 1975-87, R.L. Meiling prof. ob-gyn. Sch. Medicine, 1984-90, prof. emeritus, 1991—. Founding editor Lying In, Jour. Reproductive Medicine; editor-in-chief Am. Jour. Ob-Gyn. and Ob-Gyn. Reports, (with Lindheimer and Katz) Hypertension in Pregnancy, 1976, Current Developments in Perinatology, 1977, (with Quilligan) Operative Obstetrics, 1981, 89, Manual of Practical Obstetrics, 1981, 90, Clin. and Exptl. Hypertension in Pregnancy, 1979-86, (with Rayburn) Drug Therapy in Ob-Gyn., 1981, 3rd edit., 1992; editor: (with Christian) Controversies in Obstetrics and Gynecology; contbr. articles to med. jours., chpts. to books. Pres. Barren Found., 1974-76. With USNR, 1942-43; 1st lt. USMCR, 1943-45. Decorated DFC, Air medal wth 10 oak leaf clusters. Mem.: Perinatal Rsch. Soc., Soc. Perinatal Obstetrics, Am. Gynecology and Obstetrics Soc. (pres. 1986—87), Internat. Soc. Study of Hypertension in Pregnancy (pres. 1981—83), Soc. Gynecol. Investigation (Pres.'s award 2001), Am. Soc. Clin. Exptl. Hypnosis (exec. sec. 1968, v.p. 1970), Ctrl. Assn. Ob-Gyn. (cert. of merit, rsch. prize 1970), South Atlantic Assn. Ob-Gyn. (Found. prize for rsch. 1962), Assn .Profs. Gynecology and Obstetrics, Am. Coll. Ob-Gyn., Am. Acad. Reproductive Medicine (pres.), Columbus Ob-Gyn. Soc. (pres. 1984—85), Chgo. Gynecol. Soc., Am. Assn. Ob-Gyn., Soc. Gynecol. Investigation, Alpha Omega Alpha, Sigma Xi, Alpha Kappa Kappa. Home: 10520 Button Willow Dr Las Vegas NV 89134-7346 E-mail: FPZUS@aol.com. *The strength of our nation rests in the quality of our offspring. Every fetus has the privilege of being wellborn.*

ZUSSY, NANCY LOUISE, librarian; b. Tampa, Fla., Mar. 4, 1947; d. John David and Patsy Ruth (Stone) Roche; m. R. Mark Allen, Dec. 20, 1986. BA in Edn., U. Fla., 1969; MLS, U. So. Fla., 1977, MS in Pub. Mgmt., 1980. Cert. librarian, Wash. Ednl. evaluator State of Ga., Atlanta, 1969-70; media specialist DeKalb County Schs., Decatur, Ga., 1970-71; researcher Ga. State Libr., Atlanta, 1971; asst. to dir. reference Clearwater (Fla.) Pub. Libr., 1972-78, dir. librs., 1978-81; dep. state libr. Wash. State Libr., Olympia, 1981-86, state libr., 1986—. Chmn. Consortium Automated Librs., Olympia, 1982-97; cons. various pub. librs., Wash. and other U.S. states, Uzbekistan, Russia, 1981—; exec. officer Wash. Libr. Network, 1986-90; v.p. WLN (non-profit orgn.), 1990-93. Contbr. articles to profl. jours. Treas. Thurston-Mason Community Mental Health Bd., Olympia, 1983-85, bd. dirs., 1982-85; mem. race com. Seafair Hydroplane Race, Seattle, 1986—, mem. milk carton derby team, 1994—, announcer, prodr. air show; co-chair Pub. Info. Access Policy Task Force, 1995-96; mem. Gov.'s Work Group on Comml. Access to Govt. Electronic Records, 1996-97; mem. K-20 Telecomms. Oversight and Policy Com., 1996—. Mem. ALA, Assn. Specialized and Coop. Libr. Agys. (legis. com. 1983-86, chmn.. 1985-87, vice chmn. state libr. agys. sect. 1985-86, chmn. 1986-87, chmn. govt. affairs com. Libr. Adminstrn. and Mgmt. Assn., 1986-87), Freedom To Read Found. (bd. dirs. 1987-91), Chief Officers of State Libr. Agys. (bd. dirs.-at-large 1987-90, v.p., pres.-elect 1990-92, pres. 1992-94), Wash. Libr. Assn. (co-founder legis. planning com. 1982—, fed. rels. coord. 1984—), Fla. Libr. Assn. (legis. and planning com. 1978-81), Pacific N.W. Libr. Assn., Rotary (bd. dirs. 1995-96), Phi Kappa Phi, Phi Beta Mu. Avocations: hiking, barbershop chorus/quartet, hydroplane boat racing, cross country skiing. Office: Wash State Libr PO Box 42460 Olympia WA 98504-2460

ZUSY, CATHERINE, curator; b. Washington, May 4, 1958; d. Frederick John and Mary Jane Zusy; m. Samuel Conant Kendall, Sept. 6, 1992. BA, Bucknell U., 1981; MA in History Mus. Studies, SUNY, Oneonta, 1984. Curator of edn. Deland (Fla.) Mus., 1981-82; asst. curator State Capital Pub. Mus., Guthrie, Okla., 1982-83; rsch. asst. dept. Am. decorative arts Mus. Fine Arts, Boston, 1985-87; curator decorative arts The Bennington (Vt.) Mus., 1988-91; chief curator N.H. Hist. Soc., Concord, N.H., 1991-95; exhbn. and interpretation cons., 1996—; project dir., curator Adventures in Light and Color, 2000—. Project dir. for exploratory excavations of the U.S. Pottery Co., Bennington, Vt., 1997, 98; project dir. exhbn. The Bicycle Takes Off, 1998-2000, Faithful Boston, 2000; lectr. L.A. County Mus. Arts, M. H. de Young Mus., San Francisco, Mus. Fine Arts, Boston. Prin. author: Highlights from the Bennington Museum, 1989; author: Norton Stoneware and American Redware: The Bennington Museum Collection, 1992; contbr. author to catalogues; exhbn. Charles Ernick; contbr. articles to profl. jours. Sec. N.H. Visual Arts Coalition, 1992-94; mem. steering com. N.H. Save Outdoor Sculpture, 1992-94; mem. selection com. N.H. % for Art Program, 1994-95; co-organizer Cambridgeport Neighborhood Group. Hist. Deerfield Summer fellow, 1981, Nat. Mus. Act and Norse Found. fellow, 1983-84, Louise du Pont Crowninshield Rsch. fellow Winterthur Mus., 1990; grantee Am. Ceramic Cir., 1993-95, 98; recipient Charles F. Montgomery award Decorative Arts Soc., 1993.

ZUTALI, WUYANBU E. educational assistant, sales executive; b. Canton, Ohio, July 31, 1954; s. Louis and Emma Washington; m. Karen Loutzenheiser Zutali, Dec. 27, 1999; 1 child Nelson. Student, Ctrl. State U., Wilberforce, Ohio, 1974, U. Tex., 1974, U. Akron, 1974. Ednl. asst. Canton City Schs.; journalist, reporter Canton Repository; youth mentor Elsass Teen Ctr., Massillon; factory worker Alpha Security Products, East Canton; sales profl. Best Buy. Mem. music com. Pro Football Hall of Fame, Canton; bd. dirs. Stark County Chess Found. With U.S. Army, 1974—76. Grantee, Stark Cmty. Found., Canton, 1995, Sisters of Charity Found., Canton, 1997, Herbert W. Hoover Found., Canton, 2001. Mem.: Ohio Scholastic Chess Assn. (pres. 2001—), U.S. Chess Fedn. Democrat. Baptist. Achievements include founding of largest scholastic chess program in Ohio. Avocations: chess, music, sports, painting, fine arts. Home: 1215 16th St NW Canton OH 44703 Home Fax: 330-456-2759. E-mail: zutalchess@yahoo.com.

ZVARGULIS, JANIS ELZENS, pediatrician, anesthesiologist; b. Riga, Latvia, 1944; came to U.S., 1951; MD, John sHopkins U., 1969. Intern Childrens Hosp., Pitts., 1969-70, resident, 1970-71, Bronx-Lebanon Hosp., 1973-74, Jefferson U. Hosp., Phila., 1981-83; with Bryn Mawr Hosp., Pa.; asst. clin. prof. Jefferson Med. Coll. Fellow U. of Kans., 1974-75, Children's Hosp., St. Louis, 1975-77. Office: Bryn Mawr Hosp Bryn Mawr PA 19010

ZWAAN, JOHAN THOMAS, ophthalmologist, educator; b. Gorinchem, The Netherlands, Sept. 28, 1934; s. Johan thomas Zwaan and Johanna De Kok; m. Fransje Quakernaat, June 27, 1960 (div. Sept. 1989); m. Karen Beverly Trembowler, Dec. 28, 1989; children: Allegra, Alexander, Andrew. MD, U. Amsterdam, 1960, PhD, 1963. Diplomate Am. Bd. Ophthalmology. Postdoctoral rsch. fellow Johns Hopkins Sch. Medicine, Balt., 1963-64; assoc. prof. anatomy U. Va., Charlottesville, 1964-71; assoc. prof. anatomy and ophthalmology Harvard U. Sch. Medicine, Boston, 1971-89; prof. ophthalmology, cellular biology and pediats. U. Tex. Sch. Medicine, San Antonio, 1989-94, clin. prof. ophthalmology, 1996—; sr. acad. cons. in ophthalmology King Khalid Eye Specialists Hosp., Riyadh, Saudi Arabia, 1994-97. Mem. study sect. NIH, Bethesda, 1973—77; sr. examiner Arab Bd. Ophthalmology, Damascus, Syria, 1996—98; mem. adv. bd. Preventive Blindness Found., San Antonio, 1992—94. Author, editor: book Decision Making in Ophthalmology, 1992, author, editor: book Decision Making in Ophthalmology, 2d edit., 2000, author, editor: book Ophthalmology, Ambulatory Pediatric Care, 1988, author, editor: book Ophthalmology, Ambulatory Pediatric Care, 3d rev. edit., 1999; contbr. chapters to books, articles to profl. jours. Col. USAR, 1982—98. Recipient Rsch. Career Devel. award, NIH, 1972—75; grantee, NSF, Fight for Sight, others. Fellow: Am. Acad. Ophthalmology; mem.: AMA, Tex. Med. Assn., Res. Officers Assn. (life), Assn. Mil. Surgeons (life), Am. Soc. Human Genetics. Avocations: writing, photography, gardening. Home: 9205 Pony Express San Antonio TX 78255 Office: 8038 Wurzbach Rd Ste #520 San Antonio TX 78229 E-mail: johanzwaan@sbcglobal.net.

ZWADIUK, OLEH, radio executive; b. Lviv, Ukraine, Feb. 17, 1934; Grad., Hunter Coll. Sr. corr. Radio Free Europe, Radio Libr., Washington, dep. dir., dir. Washington news bur., 1989—. Office: Radio Free Europe 1201 Connecticut Ave NW Washington DC 20036-2609

ZWAHLEN, FRED CASPER, JR. journalism educator; b. Portland, Oreg., Nov. 11, 1924; s. Fred and Katherine (Meyer) Z.; m. Grace Eleanor DeMoss, June 24, 1959; children: Molly, Skip. BA, Oreg. State U., 1949; MA, Stanford U., 1952. Reporter San Francisco News, 1949-50; acting editor Stanford Alumni Rev., Palo Alto, Calif., 1950; successively instr. journalism, news bur. asst., prof. journalism, chmn. journalism dept. Oreg. State U., Corvallis, 1950-91, prof. emeritus, 1991—. Swiss tour guide, 1991—; corres. Portland Oregonian, 1950-67. Author: (with others) Handbook of Photography, 1984, 5th edit., 2002, Two Centuries of Shadow Catchers, A History of Photography, 1996. Coord. E.E. Wilson Scholarship Fund, 1964-2000; active budget com. Corvallis Sch. Dist., 1979. Recipient Achievement award Sch. Journalism U. Oregon, 1988. Mem. Assn. for Edn. in Journalism and Mass Communications (conv. chmn. 1983, pres.' award 1988), Oreg. Newspaper Pubs. Assn. (hon. life 1998, bd. dirs. 1980-85, student loan fund named in his honor 1988), Soc. Profl. Journalists (nat. svc. citation 1988), Corvallis Country Club, Shriners, Masons, Elks, Moose, Eagles, Delta Tau Delta. Republican. Presbyterian. Avocations: photography, sightseeing, travel. Home: 240 SW 7th St Corvallis OR 97333-4551 E-mail: fredz@peak.org.

ZWAN, BRYAN J. information technology executive; married; 3 children. BS in Physics and Chemistry, U. Houston; PhD in Space Physics, Rice U. Founder Digital Lighthouse, Clearwater, Fla., 1990, arch. flagship product Network Info. Computer, arch. Network Access Agt., chmn. bd., 1990—99, CEO, 1990—98, pres., 1990—96, 1996—98. Office: Digital Lightwave 15550 Lightwave Dr Clearwater FL 33760

ZWASS, VLADIMIR, information systems educator; b. Lvov, USSR, Feb. 3, 1946; came to U.S., 1970, naturalized, 1979; s. Adam and Friderike (Getzler) Z.; m. Alicia Kogut, Apr. 24, 1977; 1 child, Joshua Jonathan MS, Moscow Inst. Energetics, 1969; MPhil, Columbia U., 1974, PhD, 1975. Mem. profl. staff IAEA, Vienna, Austria, 1970; asst. prof. computer sci. Fairleigh Dickinson U., Teaneck, N.J., 1975-79, assoc. prof., 1979-84, prof., 1984—, prof. computer sci. and mgmt. info. sys., 1990—, disting. prof. computer sci. and mgmt. info. sys., 1999—, chmn. com. computer sci., 1976—. Cons. U.S. Govt., Met. Life Ins. Co., Citibank, Diebold Group; seminar assoc. Columbia U., 1986—; speaker nat. and internat. meetings. Author: Introduction to Computer Science, 1981, Programming in Fortran, 1981, Programming in Pascal, 1985, Programming in Basic, 1986, Management Information Systems, 1992, Foundations of Information Systems, 1998; editor-in-chief: Jour. Mgmt. Info. Sys., 1983—, editor-in-chief: Internat. Jour. Electronic Commerce, 1996—, editor-in-chief: monographs Advances in Mgmt. Info. Systems, —; contbr. articles. Columbia U. fellow, 1970-71; Helena Rubinstein Found. scholar, 1971-75; grantee USN, other agys. Mem. IEEE, Assn. Computer Machinery, Assn. for Info. Sys., Sigma Xi, Eta Kappa Nu. Home: 19 Warewoods Rd Saddle River NJ 07458-2712 Office: Sch Computer Sci and Info Sys Fairleigh Dickinson U Teaneck NJ 07666 E-mail: zwass@fdu.edu.

ZWEBEN, STUART HARVEY, information scientist, educator; b. Bronx, N.Y., Apr. 21, 1948; s. Max D. and Ruth (Schwartz) Z.; m. Rochelle T. Small, June 13, 1971; 1 child, Naomi. BS, CUNY, 1968; MS, Purdue U., 1971, PhD, 1974. Systems analyst IBM Corp., Kingston, N.Y., 1969-70; asst. prof. Ohio State U., Columbus, 1974-80, from vice chmn. to acting chmn. computer sci. dept., 1982-84, assoc. prof., 1980-92, prof., 1992—, chmn., 1994—. Pres. Computing Scis. Accreditation Bd., Stamford, Conn., 1989-91, v.p. 1987-89, sec.-treas. 1986-87; sec.-treas. Fedn. on Computing in the U.S., Washington, 1992. Contbr. articles to profl. jours. Rsch. grantee NSF, 1981-83, 88-90, 91-93, 93-97, Army Rsch. Office, 1980-83, Dept. Edn., 1983-85, Applied Info. Tech. Rsch. Ctr., 1990-91, Honda R&D, 1998—; equipment grantee AT&T Bell Labs, 1984, 86-88. Fellow Assn. for Computing Machinery (pres. 1994-96, v.p. 1992-94, coun. mem. 1982-88, chpt. bd. chmn. 1982-85, publications bd. 1988-92, fin. com. 1990-92, nominating com. chmn. 1999-2000, constn. and bylaws chmn. 1988-92, Recognition of Svc. award 1980, 85, 87, 88, Outstanding Contbn. award 1997); mem. AAUP, IEEE Computer Soc. (assoc. editor 1990-98), Computing Rsch. Assn. (bd. dirs. 1997—), Coun. Sci. Soc. Presidents (sec. 1998), Columbus Tech. Coun. (Tech. Person of Yr. award 2000). Avocations: sports, philately. Office: Ohio State U Computer Scis 2015 Neil Ave Columbus OH 43210-1210

ZWECK, RUTH EDNA FEENEY, human services administrator, psychiatric nurse; b. N.Y.C., Apr. 22, 1935; d. Archibald Thomas and Edna Marie (Kaht) Collins; m. Robert M. Zweck; children: Donald C., Diane C., Scott C., Michael C., Thomas C. BSN, Columbia U., 1957; MS in Mental Health Counseling, L.I. Univ., 1984. RN, N.Y., N.J., Nev.; cert. psychiat. and mental health nursing, ANA. Psychiat. nurse St. Dominic's Home, Blauvelt, N.Y., 1975-76; sch. nurse, tchr. Bergen County (N.J.) Sch. Systems, 1974-78; night supr. Rockland Children's Psychiat. Ctr., Orangeburg, N.Y., 1978-79, admission and referral coord., 1979-85; treatment team leader Rockland Psychiat. Ctr., 1985-91, treatment plan coord., 1991-92; clin. nurse coord. partial hospitalization program Montevista Hosp., Las Vegas, 1993-95; nurse clinician Mojave Mental Health Svcs., 1995—. Mem. adv. bd. Dominican Coll. Sch. Nursing, Blauvelt, 1986-92. Mem. Honor Soc. of Nursing (exec. bd. 1987-89), Sigma Theta Tau Internat, dipl. Amer. Brd. Disability Analysts. Avocations: tennis, hiking, sewing, cooking.

ZWEIFEL, DAVID ALAN, newspaper editor; b. Monroe, Wis., May 19, 1940; s. Cloyence John and Uva Lorraine (Skinner) Z.; m. Sandra Louise Holz, Sept. 7, 1968; children: Daniel Mark, Kristin Lynn. BJ, U. Wis., 1962. Reporter The Capital Times, Madison, Wis., 1962-71, city editor, 1971-78, mng. editor, 1978-83, editor, 1983—. Bd. dirs. Swiss Am. Ctr., Friends of Monona Terrace, Capital Times Co., Madison Newspapers Inc., William T. Evjve Charitable Trust. V.p. Alliance for Children and Youth, Madison, 1983—; bd. dirs. United Cerebral Palsy Dane County, Madison, 1984-91. Lt. U.S. Army, 1963-65; col. USNG, ret. Named Investigative Reporter of Yr. Madison Press Club, 1972. Mem.: Soc. Profl. Journalists (Spl. Achievement award 1992, 1996), Wis. Freedom of Info. Coun. (pres. 1986—2000), Wis. AP (pres. 1987—88), Am. Soc. Newspaper Editors (com. freedom of info., Pulitzer Prize juror 2000, 2001), U. Wis. Alumni Assn., Wis. N.G. Assn. (trustee 1975—81), Elks. Avocations: running, bowling, book collecting. Home: 5714 Tecumseh Ave Monona WI 53716-2964 Office: The Capital Times PO Box 8060 Madison WI 53708-8060

ZWEIFEL, DONALD EDWIN, newspaper editor, lobbyist, consultant; b. L.A., Nov. 30, 1940; s. Robert Fredrick and Eugenia Bedford (White) Z.; m. Donna Jean Croslin; 1 son, Phillip Matthew. Student, Orange Coast Coll., 1963-67, 90-92, U. Calif., Irvine, 1968-70, Western State U. Coll. Law, 1973, Irvine U. Coll. Law, 1974-75, Rancho Santiago Jr. Coll., 1988, Chapman U., 1989, 93-97; grad., Aviation Ground Sch., 1990; student, USAF Air U., 1994-95, 2000—. Cert. Student Pilot, 1989, registered lobbyist, Calif. State Legislature. Devel. tech. Hughes Aircraft, Newport Beach, Calif., 1963-64; co-founder Sta. KUCI-FM, Irvine, 1970; owner, mgr. Zweifel Jaguar Car Sales and Svc., Santa Ana, 1975-76; pres. Zweifel & Assocs. Inc., 1977-86, Zweifel South Coast Exotic Cars, Orange, Calif., 1987-96, ret., 1996; assoc. editor Compliance News Pub. Co., Long Beach, 1998—. Co-author: Challenge 2000, Regaining the America's Cup, 1996; editor: (coll. textbook) The Dream Is Alive, Space Flight and Operations In Earth Orbit. Vol. emergency coord. emergency mgmt. div. Orange County Fire Authority, 1985-87, Navy Relief Soc., 1993, 1st lt. CAP Squadron 88 Group VII, 1993-95, sr. programs officer, 1993-94, asst. transp. officer Calif. Wing Hdqrs., 1994-95, Group VII Facilities officer, 1994-95, 2000—, squadron pers. officer, 1993-95, 2000—, Calif. wing rep. to Orange County Vol. Orgns. Active in Disaster, ARC, 1994-95, Calif. wing vol. Office Emergency Svcs., Calif., 1994-96, 2000—, grad. Squadron Leadership Sch., 1993, Wing Supply Officers Sch., 1995, squadron safety officer, pub. affairs officer, asst. aerospace edn. officer, 1998—; program coord. Young Astronaut Coun., 1989-90; cadet CAP, USAF auxiliary, Long Beach, Calif., 1953-59; mem. Orange County Homeless Issues Taskforce, 1994-95, 1997—, Orange County Homeless Svc. Providers for the Reuse of Marine Corps Air Sta., Tustin, Calif., 1994-95; mem. legis. com. Orange County Vets. Adv. Coun., 1998— (Certificate of Commendation 1998) Orange County, Mem. Am Vets post 18, mem. restoration adv. bd., chmn. Tech. Review subcom. Marine Corps Air Sta., El Toro, Calif., 1994—; apptd. to CalEPA DTSC Adv. Group Mil. Base Closure, 1995—, CalEPA Dept. Toxics & Substances Control Adv. Group pro-bono cons., Orange County Citizen's Adv. Commn. and El Toro Local Redevel. Authority, 1996—; vol. mediator Victim-Offender Reconciliation program, 1995-96; restoration adv. bd. MCAS Tustin, 1994—, El Toro, Calif., 2001. With Army N.G. (hon. discharge), 1958-59. Recipient 6 certs. achievement Fed. Emergency Mgmt. Agy., 1989-96, 2 certs. appreciation CAP, 2 certs commendation, 1994, cert. appreciation Southwest Divsn. Naval Facilities Engrng. Commd., 2000, Meritorious Svc. award, Calif. State Assembly Restoration Adv. Bd. Assemblyman John Campbell, 2001. Mem. Air Force Assn. (vice-chmn. civilian recruitment Calif. state membership com. 1988-89, 90-91, v.p. membership, Gen. Doolittle chpt. bd. dirs. 1987-89, 90-92, Exceptional Svc. award Gen. Jimmy Doolittle chpt. 1988, 91, Calif. Meritorious Svc. award 1988, v.p. membership Gen. Curtis E. LeMay Orange County chpt. 2000—), Calif. Assn. for Aerospace Edn. (fellow), Marine Corps Hist. Found. (life), Aerospace Edn. Found. (Gen. Jimmy Doolittle fellow 1988, Gen. Ira Eaker fellow 1989, Pres.'s award 1988), U.S. Naval Inst., AIAA (Cert. of Appreciation 1989, L.A. chpt. hist. com. 1989), Gulf & Vietnam Vets. Strategic Studies Archives (cons., co-founder 1983—, dir.), Marine Corps League (assoc., capt. Heinsey detachment 2000—), U.S. Marine Corps Combat Correspondents Assn. (affiliate), Confederate Air Force (col. 1989, adj. 1st Composite Group detachment 1989), Orange County Peace Officers Assn. (assoc.), Free and Accepted Masons Orange Grove Lodge. Avocations: sailing, bicycle racing, traveling, flying. Home and Office: Apt B 266 Backs Ln Placentia CA 92870-6036 E-mail: zweifel@earthlink.net.

ZWEIFEL, RICHARD GEORGE, curator; b. L.A., Nov. 5, 1926; s. Harold Charles and Kathleen Marguerite (Garland) Z.; m. Frances Ann Wimsatt, July 30, 1956; children: Matthew Karl, Kenneth Paul, Ellen Katrina. BA, UCLA, 1950; PhD, U. Calif. at Berkeley, 1954. Mem. staff Am. Mus. Natural History, N.Y.C., 1954-89, chmn. curator dept. herpetology, 1968-80, curator emeritus, 1989—; sci. attaché Gondwana, 1974-75. Served with AUS, 1945-46. Mem. Soc. Study Amphibious and Reptiles, Am. Soc. Ichthyologists and Herpetologists. Home: PO Box 16354 Portal AZ 85632-1354

ZWEIG, GEORGE, physicist, neurobiologist; b. Moscow, May 20, 1937; came to U.S., 1938; s. Alfred and Rachael (Frölich) Z. BS in Math., U. Mich., 1959; PhD in Physics, Calif. Inst. Tech., 1963. NAS-NRC fellow European Orgn. for Nuclear Rsch., Geneva, 1963-64; asst. prof. physics Calif. Inst. Tech., Pasadena, 1964-66, assoc. prof., 1966-67, prof., 1967-83; staff mem. Los Alamos (N.Mex.) Nat. Lab., 1981-85, fellow, 1985—; founder, pres. Signition, Inc., Los Alamos, 1985—. Vis. prof. physics U. Wis., Madison, 1967-68; mem. Jason div. Inst. for Def. Analysis, Arlington, Va., 1965-72. Recipient MacArthur prize MacArthur Found., 1981, Disting. Alumnus award Calif. Inst. Tech., 1984; Alfred P. Sloan Found. fellow in physics, 1966-74, in neurobiology, 1974-78. Mem. IEEE, AAAS, NAS, Am. Math. Soc., Am. Phys. Soc., Assn. for Rsch. in Otolaryngology. Achievements include discovering quarks, 1963; creating continuous wavelet transform for signal processing, 1975, active model of cochlear mechanics, 1987. Office: LANL MS B276 PO Box 1663 Los Alamos NM 87544-0600

ZWEIG, STEVEN F. statistician; s. Sammuel and Shirley Zweig. BS in Animal Sci., U. of Ga., 1979; MA in Econ., Va. Commonwealth U., 1985; MS in Biostatistics, Med. Coll. of Va., 1993. Retail mgr. Pk. Drug Store, Petersburg, Va., 1980—91; cons. InfoStat Cons., Columbus, 1994—96; statis. Covance, Inc., Princeton, NJ, 1996—2000; sr. statistician Target Rsch. Associates, New Providence, 2000—01; mgr. of biostatistics MDS Pharma Services, King of Prussia, Pa., 2001—. Sec. Columbus Jaycees, Columbus, Ohio, 1994—96. Recipient Dan O'Kane award, Columbus Jaycees, 1996. Mem.: Am. Statis. Assn. Home: 10 Sunflower Lane Trenton NJ 08620 Personal E-mail: stevenfzweig@netscape.net.

ZWEIMAN, BURTON, physician, scientist, educator; b. N.Y.C., June 7, 1931; s. Charles and Gertrude (Levine) Z.; m. Claire Traig, Dec. 30, 1962; children: Amy Beth, Diane Susan. AB, U. Pa., 1952, MD, 1956. Diplomate Am. Bd. Internal Medicine, Am. Bd. Allergy & Immunology. Intern Mt. Sinai Hosp., N.Y.C.; Hosp. U. Pa., Bellevue Hosp. Ctr. Hosp. U. Pa., Bellevue Hosp. Center, 1957-60; fellow NYU Sch. Medicine, 1960-61; mem. faculty dept. medicine U. Pa. Sch. Medicine, Phila., 1963—, prof. medicine, chief allergy and immunology divsn., 1975-98. Cons. U.S. Army, NIH; co-chmn. Am. Bd. Allergy and Immunology, 1979-81 Editor Jour. Allergy Clin. Immunology, 1988-93; contbr. articles to med. jours. Served with M.C., USNR, 1961-63. Allergy Found. Am. fellow, 1959-61 Fellow ACP, Am. Acad. Allergy, Asthma and Immunology (past pres.); mem. Am. Assn. Immunologists, Am. Fedn. Clin. Rsch., Phi Beta Kappa, Alpha Omega Alpha. Office: Hosp U Pa 527 Maloney Bldg 34th & Spruce St Philadelphia PA 19104 E-mail: bzweiman@mail.med.upenn.edu.

ZWEIZIG, DOUGLAS LOUGH, librarian, educator; b. York, Pa., Apr. 3, 1938; s. Charles Russell Zweizig, Grace Lough Zweizig; m. Karen Jane Gielow; children: Walter Clewell. BA, Lafayette Coll., Easton, PA, 1960; MA, Harvard U., 1961; MLS, Rutgers U., 1965; PhD, Syracuse U., 1973. Instr. dept. English U. N.H., Durham, 1961—64; English and speech grad. libr. Ohio tate U. Librs., Columbus, 1965—67; asst. prof. U. Toledo, 1972—75; asst. prof. Sch. Librarianship U. Wash., Seattle, 1975—80; sr. rsch. assoc. King Researcsch., Rockville, Md., 1980—82; prof. emeritus Sch. Libr. and Info. Studies U. Wis., Madison, 1982—. Mem.: ALA (life). Home: 6037 N Finn Rd Evansville WI 53536 Office: Sch Libr and Info Studies 600 N Park St Madison WI 53706 Personal E-mail: dougzweizig@hotmail.com. Business E-Mail: dzweizig@facstaff.wisc.edu.

ZWEMKE, KATHARINE PRISCILLA, dietitian, diabetes educator; b. Rochester, N.Y., Oct. 8, 1948; d. Frederick John Jr. and Priscilla (Pollock) Kolb; m. William J. Zwemke; children: Ingrid Katharine, Donna Marie. BA in Nutrition, Simmons Coll., 1970. Registered dietitian; cert. diabetes educator; notary pub., Mass. Asst. dir. food svc. Franklin Med. Ctr., Greenfield, Mass., 1971-75; prin. dietary/diabetes consulting bus. Ware, 1975—; dietitian, diabetes educator Baystate Nutrition Network, 1995—. Preceptor food svc. certs. U. N.D. Corr. Sch., 1973-83. Pres., treas., sec., mem. Mary Lane Hosp. Aux., Ware, 1974-97. Mem. Am. Dietetic Assn., Am. Assn. Diabetes Educators (sec., newsletter editor Western Mass. chpt. 1983-87), Juvenile Diabetes Assn. Home: 60 Chestnut St Ware MA 01082-1556 Office: Mary Lane Hosp 85 South St Ware MA 01082-1697

ZWERDLING, ALEX, English educator; b. Breslau, Germany, June 21, 1932; came to U.S., 1941, naturalized, 1946; s. Norbert and Fanni (Alt) Z.; m. Florence Goldberg, Mar. 23, 1969; 1 son, Antony Daniel. BA, Cornell U., 1953; postgrad. (Fulbright scholar), U. Munich, Germany, 1953-54; MA, Princeton U., 1956, PhD, 1960. Instr. English Swarthmore Coll., 1957-61;

asst. prof. English U. Calif., Berkeley, 1961-67, asso. prof., 1967-73, prof., 1973-86, prof. English, 1988—, chmn. grad. studies, 1985-86; univ. prof. George Washington U., 1986-88. Vis. prof. Northwestern U., 1977; dir. edn. abroad program U. Calif., London, 1996-98; mem. advanced placement exam. com. Ednl. Testing Svc., 1975-79; mem. fellowship panel Nat. Endowment for Humanities, 1977-82, 84-87, Nat. Humanities Ctr., 1989-90; fellow Ctr. for Advanced Study in Behavioral Scis., 1964-65. Author: Yeats and the Heroic Ideal, 1965, Orwell and the Left, 1974, Virginia Woolf and the Real World, 1986, Improvised Europeans: American Literary Expatriates and the Siege of London, 1998; mem. adv. com. PMLA, 1978-82. Am. Coun. Learned Socs. fellow, 1964-65; NEH fellow, 1973-74; Guggenheim fellow, 1977-78; Woodrow Wilson Ctr. fellow, 1991-92, fellow Nat. Humanities Ctr., 1992-93. Mem. MLA (chmn. 20th Century Brit. lit. div. 1969-70, 85-86) Office: U Calif Dept English Berkeley CA 94720-1030

ZWERDLING, ROBERT G. physician; b. Detroit, Jan. 21, 1942; m. Vicki S. Zwerdling. BA, U. Mich., 1963; MD, Wayne State U., 1967. Intern in pediatrics Bellevue Hosp., NYU, N.Y.C., 1967-69; resident in pediatrics Bronx (N.Y.) Mcpl. Hosp., Albert Einstein Coll. Medicine, 1969-70; resident in pediatric pulmonary disease Children's Hosp., Harvard U., Boston, 1972-74; dir. pediatric pulmonary and cystic fibrosis ctr. U. Mass. Med. Ctr., Worcester, 1981—; prof. pediats. U. Mass. Med. Sch., 1981—. Fellow Am. Acad. Pediatrics, Am. Thoracic Soc.; mem. Nat. Assn. Pediatric Home and Cmty. Care (bd. dirs. 1993—). Office: U Mass Med Ctr Worcester MA 01655

ZWERLING, GARY LESLIE, investment bank executive; b. N.Y.C., Aug. 6, 1949; s. Seymour Joseph and Evelyn Rhoda (Posner) Z.; m. Marierose Miraglia, Aug. 25, 1974; children: Cara Marisa, Craig Harris. BEngring., SUNY, Stony Brook, 1970; MBA, SUNY, Albany, 1972. V.p. Chase Manhattan Bank, N.Y.C., 1972-78; ptnr. Goldman, Sachs & Co., 1978-96; ret., 1996. Mem. bd. overseers Mus. Jewish Heritage-A Living Meml. to the Holocaust; trustee Jewish Fedn. North Jersey; bd. govs. N.Y. chpt. Arthritis Found. Mem. Thoroughbred Owners and Breeders Assn., Nat. Thoroughbred Racing Assn. Jewish. Avocation: skiing. Office: Goldman Sachs & Co 85 Broad St New York NY 10004-2456

ZWERLING, LILLIAN, interior designer; b. N.Y.C., Feb. 24, 1917; d. Morris and Sarah (Dopkin) Schochet; student N.Y. Sch. Interior Design, 1968, Finch Coll., 1970-75, N.Y. U., 1976, also Inst. Fine Arts; m. Robert Zwerling, Oct. 23, 1938; children— Linda Ellen, Diane Judith, Barbara Nan. Asst. estimator J. Kessler Painting Contractor, 1934, Triangle Sheet Metal, Inc., Bklyn., 1935-38; owner, mgr. Lillian Zwerling Interiors, N.Y.C., 1970— ; constructor vacation leisure homes, 1981— .

ZWICK, BARRY STANLEY, newspaper editor, speechwriter; b. Cleve., July 21, 1942; s. Alvin Albert and Selma Davidovna (Makofsky) Z.; m. Roberta Joan Yaffe, Mar. 11, 1972; children: Natasha Yvette, Alexander Anatol. BA in Journalism, Ohio State U., 1963; MS in Journalism, Columbia U., 1965. Copy editor Phila. Inquirer, 1964; night news editor Detroit Free Press, 1965-67; West Coast editor L.A. Times/Washington Post News Svc, 1967-77; makeup editor L.A. Times, 1978—. Adj. prof. U. So. Calif., L.A., 1975-77. Author: Hollywood Tanning Secrets, 1980. NEH profl. journalism fellow Stanford U., 1977-78. Jewish. Avocations: photography, jet skiing, snowmobiling. Office: LA Times Times Mirror Sq Los Angeles CA 90012 E-mail: barryzwick@aol.com.

ZWICK, THOMAS, electrical engineer; b. Ludwigshafen am Rhein, Germany, June 2, 1970; MSEE, U. Karlsruhe, Germany, 1994, PhD in Elec. Engring., 1999. Rsch. asst. Inst. Hoechstfrequenztechnik und Elektronik U. Karlsruhe, 1994—2001; rsch. staff mem. T. J. Watson Rsch. Ctr. IBM, Yorktown Heights, N.Y., 2001—. Contbr. articles to profl. jours. Mem. IEEE. Avocations: playing saxophone, hiking, sports, music. Office: IBM T J Watson Rsch Ctr PO Box 218, Rt 134 Yorktown Heights NY 10598 Fax: 914-945-2141. E-mail: zwick1@us.ibm.com.

ZWICKER, CHARLES, economist, educator, accountant, consultant; b. N.Y.C., Apr. 13, 1912; s. Harry and Sarah Zwicker; m. Mildred Waldman, Oct. 25, 1941; children: Peter, Robert. BS, NYU, 1933, MBA, 1950. CPA, N.Y. Ptnr. Zwicker, Sturmer & Co. CPAs, N.Y.C., 1947-50, Rosenblum, Zwicker & Co., CPAs, N.Y.C., 1950-55, Zwicker & Simon CPAs, Garden City and N.Y.C., 1956-82; prof., prof. emeritus L.I. U., Brookville, 1957-80, dean Sch. Accountancy, 1973-80; dir. First Nat. Bank L.I., Glen Head, NY, 1977—83, Charles Zwicker Tax Inst., Waterbury, Conn., 1980-98; prof. Teikyo Post U., Nat. U., San Diego, 1987-88. Author: (with others) Handbook for Auditors, 1971, Encyclopedia of Accounting Systems, 1976. Mem. nat. adv. bd. Ctr. for Study of Presidency, N.Y.C. and Washington, 1963-99; mem. adv. coun. Coll. of Mgmt., L.I. U., Brookville, 1998—. Recipient Cert. Recognition IRS, 1975-76, Acct. of Yr., Adelphi U., 1974, citations Ctr. Tax Studies, 1968, Teikyo Post U., 1989. Mem. AICPA, N.Y. State Soc. CPA, Sphinx, Quill, Delta Sigma Pi, Kappa Delta Rho. Avocations: golf, reading, travel. Home: 155-B Heritage Village Southbury CT 06488 Office: CW Post/LI U Northern Blvd Greenvale NY 11548

ZWICKLER, ALLEN, investment advisor, educator; b. N.Y.C., Mar. 18, 1958; s. Seymour Zwickler and Sandra Lewin; m. Ellen Karen Pikitch; children: Scott Emlen, Adam, Randi. BS Mgmt., SUNY, Binghamton, 1979; MBA, NYU, 1986. Registered rep. N.Y. Stock Exch., 1979. Rsch. analyst Ladenburg Thalmann, N.Y.C., 1981—89; investment advisor First Manhattan, 1989—. Lectr. NYU Sch. Continuing Edn., N.Y.C., 2000—. Trustee Phil Zwickler Charitable and Meml. Found., N.Y.C., 1992—; bd. dirs. Metro Club Sch. Mgmt. SUNY, Binghamton. Avocations: scuba diving, basketball. Home: 420 E 72 St Apt 12-L New York NY 10021 Office: First Manhattan Co 437 Madison Ave New York NY 10022-7001

ZWICKY, ARNOLD MELCHIOR, JR. linguistics educator; b. Allentown, Pa., Sept. 6, 1940; s. Arnold Melchior and Marcella Ida (Rice) Z.; m. Ann Walcutt Daingerfield, June 16, 1962 (dec. 1985); 1 child, Elizabeth Daingerfield; life ptnr. Jacques H. Transue. AB in Math., Princeton U., 1962; PhD in Linguistics, MIT, 1965. Asst. prof. U. Ill., Urbana, 1965-69; assoc. prof. Ohio State U., Columbus, 1969-71, prof., 1971-89, univ. prof., 1989—, emeritus, 1995—. Vis. prof. Stanford (Calif.) Univ., 1985—, The Linguistic Inst., 1972, 74, 82, 87, 91, 93, 99, Nat. Acad. Scis., Beijing Lang. Inst. China, 1985; trustee Ctr. for Applied Linguistics, Washington, 1979-87. Contbr. articles to profl. jours. Recipient fellowship Guggenheim Found., N.Y.C., 1972-73, Fulbright, Univ. Sussex, Eng., 1977, Ctr. for Advanced Study in the Behavioral Scis., Stanford, 1981-82. Fellow AAAS, Am. Acad. Arts and Scis.; mem. Am. Dialect Soc., Assn. for Computational Linguistics, Linguistic Soc. Am. (exec. com. 1986-88, v.p. 1991, pres. 1992). Home: 722 Ramona St Palo Alto CA 94301-2547 also: 722 Ramona St Palo Alto CA 94301-2547 Office: Ohio State U Linguistics Columbus OH 43210 also: Stanford U Linguistics Palo Alto CA 94305

ZWIEP, DONALD NELSON, mechanical engineering educator, administrator; b. Hull, Iowa, Mar. 18, 1924; s. Daniel and Nellie (De Stigter) Z.; m. Marcia J. Hubers, Sept. 3, 1948; children: Donna J., Mary N., Joan L., Helen D. BSME, Iowa State Coll., 1948, MSME, 1951; DEng (hon.), Worcester Polytech. Inst., 1965. Registered profl. engr., Mass. Design engr. Boeing Airplane Co., 1948-50, sr. tool engr., summer 1953, summer faculty asso., 1955; asst. prof. Colo. State U., 1951-56, assoc. prof., 1956-57; cons. engr. aviation div. Forney Mfg. Co., 1956-57; prof., head dept. mech. engring. Worcester Polytech. Inst., 1957-88, acting head mgmt. engring., 1974-76, chmn. Mfg. Engring. Application Ctr., 1981-88, acting provost, v.p. acad. affairs, 1988-90, prof., dept. head emeritus, 1990—. Constrn. engr. U.S. C.E., summer 1954; cons. engr., acting chief engr. J.J. Malir, Inc., summer 1956 Chmn. bd. trustees James F. Lincoln Arc Welding Found., 1976— . Served as pilot USAAF, World War II, CBI; lt. col. USAFR; cons. and ednl. specialist. Fellow ASME (life, v.p. edn. 1972-74, pres. 1979-80); mem. Am. Soc. Engring. Edn. (life, pres. Colo. State U. chpt. 1954-55, treas. Rocky Mountain sect. 1955, nat. bd. dirs. 1974-75), Am. Assn. Engring. Socs. (chair coun. pre-coll. edn.), Am. Welding Soc., Soc. Mfg. Engrs., Torch Club, Sigma Xi, Omicron Delta Kappa, Tau Beta Pi, Sigma Tau, Pi Tau Sigma. Methodist. Home: 119 2d St SW Orange City IA 51041 Office: Worcester Poly Inst 100 Institute Rd Worcester MA 01609-2247 E-mail: dnzwiep@earthlink.net.

ZWIER, ROBERT, college administrator, political scientist; b. Holland, Mich., June 24, 1950; s. Donald and Ruth L. (Brightrall) Z.; m. Janet Kay Mack, Mar. 25, 1978; children: Michael, Steven. AB, Calvin Coll., 1972; MA, U. Wis., 1973, PhD, 1977. Asst. prof. Emporia (Kans.) State U., 1977-79; from asst. to full prof. Northwestern Coll., Orange City, Iowa, 1979-88, v.p. for acad. affairs, 1988—. Cons., evaluator N. Cen. Assn. Colls. and Schs., Chgo., 1988—. Author: (book) Born-Again Politics, 1982; contbr. articles to profl. jours. Recipient fellowship Ford Found., Madison, Wis., 1973. Mem. Am. Assn. Higher Edn., Am. Polit. Sci. Assn., Assn. for Pub. Justice, Bread for the World. Office: Northwestern Coll 101 7th St SW Orange City IA 51041-1923

ZWIERLEIN, RONALD EDWARD, athletics director; m. Cindy Cromer, Sept. 7, 1968; children: Heidi, Heather, Chad. BS, Bowling Green (Ohio) State U., 1968, MS; PhD in Athletic, Phys. Edn., Recreation, Ohio State U. Head swimming and diving coach Monroe H.S., Rochester, N.Y., Fremont (Ohio) Ross H.S., John Carroll U., University Heights, Ohio, 1975-81, athletic dir., 1977-81; head swimming and diving coach, instr. Bowling Green State U., 1981-1984, assoc. dir. Student Recreation Ctr., 1984--92, dir. recreational sports, 1992-94, dir. intercollegiate athletics, 1994-99, athletic dir., sr. assoc. v.p., 2000—. Mem. Nat. Assn. Collegiate Dirs. Athletics (mem. Mission & Values Com.). Office: Bowling Green State U Perry Stadium Bowling Green OH 43403-0001

ZWIGARD, BRUCE ALBERT, brokerage house executive; b. Newark, Apr. 10, 1948; s. Albert Henry and Doris Emily (Sigmund) Z.; m. Eva Crescencia Lan, June 24, 1973; children: Brian Albert, Bradley William. BA, Rider Coll., 1971; MBA, Fla. Internat. U., 1976. Tchr. physics Wardlaw Sch., Plainfield, N.J., 1971-72, Dade County Schs., Miami, Fla., 1972-77, tchr. gifted, 1977-79; registered rep. Investacorp Inc., Miami Lakes, 1979-80, v.p., 1980-81, pres., chmn. bd. dirs., 1981—; pres. Valor Ins. Agys., 1992—, Investacorp Advisors, Inc., 1997—. Office: Investacorp Inc 15450 New Barn Rd Ste 201 Miami Lakes FL 33014-2199

ZWIKELMAIER, KURT E. pharmaceutical executive; b. Dallas, Dec. 5, 1954; s. Robert and Pearl Zwikelmaier; m. Madeline Axum; children: Virginia, Elise. BS in Chemistry, U. Mo., 1976; MBA, U. New Orleans, 1984. Cert. mgmt. acct. Rsch. chemist Monsanto Co., St. Louis, 1976—79, budget analyst, 1980—81. Cost acct. Monsanto Co., New Orleans, 1981—84, payroll acct., St. Louis, 1985—94, HRIT specialist, 1994—96, mgr. Ctr. for Employee Svcs., 1996—97, HRIT specialist - Europe/Africa, Brussels, 1998—99; sr. mgr. HRIT ops. Pharmacia Corp., St. Louis, 1999—. Sr. warden St. Timothy's Episcopal Ch., St. Louis, 2002. Mem.: Phi Beta Kappa. Episcopalian. Avocations: travel, foreign languages. Home: 11970 Greenwalk Saint Louis MO 63146

ZWILICH, ELLEN TAAFFE, composer; b. Miami, Fla., Apr. 30, 1939; d. Edward Porter and Ruth (Howard) Taaffe; m. Joseph Zwilich, June 22, 1969 (dec. June 1979). MusB, Fla. State U., 1960, MusM, 1962; D Mus. Arts, Juilliard Sch., 1975; studies with Roger Sessions and Elliott Carter; MusD (hon.) , Oberlin Coll., 1987, Converse Coll., 1994; LHD (hon.) , Manhattanville Coll., 1991, Marymount Manhattan Coll., 1994, N.Y. New Sch., Mannes, 1995. Francis Eppes disting. prof. Fla. State U., 1999—. Composer in residence Santa Fe Chamber Music Festival, 1990, Am. Acad. Rome, 1990; first Composer's Chair, Carnegie Hall, 1995-99. Premiere, Symposium for Orch., Pierre Boulez, N.Y.C., 1975, Chamber Symphony and Passages, Boston Musica Viva, Richard Pittman, 1979, 82. Symphony 1, Gunther Schuller, Am. Composers Orch., 1982; violinist Am. Symphony, N.Y.C., 1965-73; composer: Sonata in Three Movements, 1973-74; String Quartet, 1974; Clarino Quartet, 1977; Chamber Symphony, 1979; Passages (for Soprano and Chamber Ensemble), 1981; String Trio, 1982; Symphony 1:3 Movements for Orch., 1982 (Grammy nomination New World Records, 1987); Divertimento, 1983; Einsame Nacht, 1971; Emlekezet, 1978; Im Nebel, 1972; Passages for Soprano and Orch., 1982; Trompeten, 1974; Fantasy for Harpsichord, 1983; Intrada, 1983; Prologue and Variations, 1983; Double Quartet for Strings, Chamber Music Soc. of Lincoln Ctr., 1984; Celebration for Orch., Indpls. Symphony, John Nelson, 1984; Symphony #2 (Cello Symphony) San Francisco Symphony, Edo De Waart, 1985, Symphony #2 Louisville Orch. recording, L.L. Smith (Grammy nomination 1991); Concerto Grosso 1985, Handel Festival Orch., Steven Simon, 1986; Concerto for Piano and Orch., Detroit Symphony, Gunther Herbig, Marc-André Hamelin, 1986; Images for 2 Pianos and Orch., Nat. Symphony Orch., F. Machetti, 1987; Tanzspiel, Peter Martins N.Y.C. Ballet, 1987; Praeludium Boston chpt. AGO, 1987; Trio for piano, violin and cello; Kalichstein, Laredo, Robinson trio, 1987; Symbolon, Zubin Mehta and the N.Y. Philharm., Leningrad and Moscow (USSR), N.Y.C. (Koussevitsky Internat. Rec. award nominee 1990), 1988; concerto for trombone and orch. J. Friedman, Sir Georg Solti, Chgo. Symphony, 1989, concerto for trombone and orch. Christian Lindberg, James De Priest, Malmö Symphony, concerto for flute and orch. D.A. Dwyer, Seija Ozawa, Boston Symphony, 1990, quintet for clarinet and string quartet David Schiffrin, Chamber Music N.W., Lincoln Ctr. Chamber Mus. Soc., 1990; concerto for oboe and orch. John Mack, Christoph von Dohnanyi, Cleve. Orch., 1991; concerto for bass trombone strings, timpani and cymbals Chgo. Symphony Orch. Ch. Vernon, Daniel Barenboim, 1991; concerto for violin, violoncello and orch. Jaime Laredo, Sharon Robinson, Louisville Orch., L. Smith, 1991; the Immigrant Voices Peter Leonard, St. Lukes Orch., N.Y. Internat. Festival ot the Arts Chorus, Ellis Island, 1991, concerto for flute and orch, D.A. Dwyer, J. Sedares, London Symphony Orch., 1992, Symphony # 3 (Grammy nominee 1993), J. Ling, N.Y. Philharmonic, 1993, concerto for bassoon and orch., Nancy Goeres, Lorin Maazel, Pitts. Symphony, 1993, concerto for horn and string Orch., David Jolley, Rochester Philharm., L.L. Smith., 1993, Fantasy for Orch., JoAnn Falletta, Long Beach Symphony Orch., 1994, American Concerto Doc Severinsen, J. Falletta San Diego Symphony, 1994, A Simple Magnificat, 1994, Triple Concerto Kalichstein, Laredo, Robinson Trio Zdenek Macal, Minn. Orch., 1995, for piano and orch., Peanuts Gallery, 1996, violin concerto, Pamela Frank, H. Wolff, 1997; String Quartet # 2, 1998, Emerson Quartet; Upbeat! 1998, Nat. Symphony Orch., conducted by Anthony Aibel, Symphony # 4 (orch., chorus, children's chorus) Mich. State U., L. Gregorian 2000, Lament for solo piano Carnegie Hall, 2000, Millenium Fantasy for Piano & Orch., J. Biegel, J. Cobos-Lopez, Cin. Symphony, 2000, Lament for Cello & Piano, Met. Mus., N.Y.C., 2000, Partita for Violin & String Orch., Carnegie Hall, 2001, Openings for Orch., 2002 JoAnn Falletta Va. Symphony, Clarinet Concerto, D. Shifrin, Chamber Music Soc. of Lincoln Ctr., Buffalo Philharm, 2002; New World Records: Music By Ellen Taaffe Zwilich; N.Y. Philharm. conducted by Zubin Mehta. Bd. dirs. Copland Fund. Named Martha Baird Rockefeller Fund rec. grantee, 1977, 1979, 1982, Guggenheim fellow, 1981; named to, Fla. Artists Hall of Fame, 1994; recipient Elizabeth Sprague Coolidge Chamber Music prize, 1974, Gold medal, G.B. Viotti, Vercelli, Italy, 1975, citation, Ernst von Dohnanyi, 1981, Pulitzer prize, 1983, Composers award, Lancaster Symphony Orch., Arturo Toscanini Music Critics award, 1987, Alfred I. DuPont award, 1991, Performing Arts award, Miami Ctr. Performing Arts, 2000, named, Musical Am. Composer of Yr., 1999. Mem.: AAAL (Acad. award 1984), Guggenheim Found. (bd. dirs.), MacDowell Colony (bd. dirs.), BMI Found., Am. Music Ctr. (bd. dirs., v.p. 1982—84), Am. Fedn. Musicians (hon.; life). Home: 600 W 246th St Bronx NY 10471-3611 Office: care Music Assocs Am 224 King St Englewood NJ 07631-3026

ZWILLING, MARK C. music director; b. Albuquerque, Apr. 5, 1960; s. Daniel Zwilling and June Byles Housiaux. MusB, B in Music Edn., Ea. N.Mex. U., 1982; MusM, DePaul U., 1990. Tchr. Las Lunas (N.Mex.) Schs., 1982—85; music dir. First Presbyn. Ch., Roswell, 1985—87, Trinity-First United Meth. Ch., El Paso, 1987—90, First Presbyn. Ch., Las Vegas, Nev., 1990—99, Cathedral of Hope, Dallas, 1999—2000, St. Andrew United Meth. Ch., Littleton , Colo., 2000—. Music dir. MGM Grand Hotel, Las Vegas, 1994—98; Presbyn. Assn. Musicians exec. nat. bd. mem. Presbyn. Ch. USA, Louisville, 1996—99. Mem.: Music Tchrs., Am. Choral Dirs., Am. Guild Organists. Democrat. Home: 758 Monroe St Denver CO 80206 Office: St Andrew United Meth Ch 6325 S University Blvd Littleton CO 80121

ZWINGE, RANDALL JAMES HAMILTON See RANDI, JAMES

ZWIREN, JANET, holistic professional, educator; b. Orange, N.J., Aug. 3, 1952; d. John Paul and Martha Ann (Gallik) Bachmann; m. Steven Scott Zwiren, Sept. 25, 1971 (div. Feb. 1986); children: Paula Marie, Lisa Michelle. AA in Home Econs., Centenary Coll., Hackettstown, N.J., 1975; BA in Psychology, Coll. St. Elizabeth, Convent Station, N.J., 1987; Reiki master, Unltd. Potential, West Orange. N.J., 1994; grad., Realtors Inst., Edison, N.J., 1994. Cert. residential specialist. Title searcher Chelsea Title, New Brusnwick, N.J., 1972, Stewart Title, Morristown, 1973-75; title searcher, officer Heritage Abstract, 1976-84; mortgage banker Fin. Investement Resources, 1987-88, Greater Metro, Wayne, N.J., 1988; realtor residential sales Weichert Realtors, Succasunna, 1988-91, Re/Max Renown Realty, Randolph, 1991-99; Reiki Master, Shamanic practitioner Universal Life Energy Healing Ctr., Succasunna, 1994—97; dir., Shaman, Reiki master Oasis for the Soul, 1997—. Pvt. cons. Bus. Mktg. and Mgmt., Succasunna, 1995—. Leader Girl Scouts U.S.A., Succasunna, 1993, 1985, 88, Denville, N.J., 1981, 84; town coun. reporter League Women Voters, Randolph, 1975. Mem. Nat. Assn. Realtors, N.J. Assn. Realtors (Million Dollar Club bronze and silver awards 1988-98, Remax Internat. Hall of Fame, 1997), Morris County Bd. Realtors, Residential Spl. Coun., Grad. Realtors Inst., Remax Internat. 100 Club. Democrat. Avocations: sailing, reading, hiking, writing, travel. Home: 16 Meadowview Ave Succasunna NJ 07876-1737 Office: Oasis for the Soul PO Box 85 Succasunna NJ 07876-0085

ZWISLOCKI, JOZEF JOHN, neuroscience educator, researcher; b. Lwow, Poland, Mar. 19, 1922; came to U.S., 1951; s. Tadeusz and Helena (Moscicki) Z.; m. Ruth Gerber, Oct. 29, 1945 (div. May 1954); m. Sylvia Claire Goldman, July 11, 1954 (dec. July 17, 1992); m. Jadwiga M. Morrison, Dec. 2, 1993. Diploma, Fed. Tech. Inst., Zurich, Switzerland, 1944, Sc.D., 1948; D. honoris causa, U. Adam Mickiewicz, Poznán, Poland, 1991. Head electroacoustic lab. dept. otolaryngology U. Basel, Switzerland, 1945-51; research fellow psychoacoustic lab. Harvard U., Cambridge, Mass., 1951-57; dir. Bioacoustic Lab. Syracuse U., N.Y., 1958-63, founder, dir. Lab. of Sensory Communication, 1963-73, founder dir. Inst. for Sensory Research NY, 1973—84, prof. neurosci., 1984—88, disting. prof. neurosci., 1988—92, disting. prof. emeritus, 1992—; prof. communicative disorders dept. spl. edn. Syracuse U. Sch. Edn., 1982—92; research prof. SUNY Health Sci. Ctr. , Syracuse, 1967—. Affiliate prof. bioengring. L.C. Smith Coll. Engring., Syracuse U., 1986-92; Carhart Meml. lectr. Am. Auditory Soc., 1992; mem. exec. coun. Com. Hearing, Bioacoustics and Biomechanics, NRC, Washington, 1965-68, chmn., 1967-68; mem. rev. panel on communicative scis. NIH, Bethesda, Md., 1966-70, chmn., 1969-70; mem. Communicative Disorders Program Project rev. com. NIH, Bethesda, 1971-75; chmn. Bd. Sci. Advs. Ctr. Health Scis., U. Wis., Madison, 1975-78. Inventor acoustic ear simulator, acoustic bridge, several types of ear defenders; contbr. articles to profl. jours. Recipient Faculty Research award Syracuse chpt. Sigma Xi, 1973, Internat. Ctr. Ricerche e Studi Amplifon prize, 1976, Chancellor's citation, Syracuse U., 1980, Javits Neurosci. Investigator award NIH, 1984, Kwiek medal Acoustics Inst., A. Mickiewicz U., Poland, 1991, medal Acoustical Soc. Poland, 1991, Hugh Knowles prize Northwestern U., 1992. Fellow Acoustical Soc. Am. (chmn. tech. com. on psychol. and physiol. acoustics 1962, 63, exec. coun. 1982-85, recipient 1st Bekesy medal 1985, chmn. long-range planning com. 1983-86, nominating com. 1986-87, mem. com. on tutorials 1988-91, com. on meetings 1988-91, chmn. spring meeting, 1989), Am. Speech and Hearing Assn., The Polish Inst. of Arts and Scis. of Am.; mem. NAS, Polish Acad. Scis., Internat. Soc. Audiology (v.p. 1967-72), Internat. Union of Physiol. Scis. (commn. on auditory physiology 1982-89), Internat. Union Pure and Applied Physics (Commn. on Acoustics 1982-89), Collegium Oto Rhino Laryngologicum Amicitiae Sacrum, Assn. for Rsch. in Otolaryngology (award of merit 1988), Hearing Rsch. (editl. bd.). Avocations: skiing, tennis, trout fishing, inventions.

ZWOYER, EUGENE MILTON, retired consulting engineering executive; b. Plainfield, N.J., Sept. 8, 1926; s. Paul Ellsworth and Marie Susan (Britt) Z.; m. Dorothy Lucille Seward, Feb. 23, 1946; children: Gregory, Jeffrey, Douglas. Student, U. Notre Dame, 1944, Mo. Valley Coll., 1944-45; BS, U. N.Mex., 1947; MS, Ill. Inst. Tech., 1949; PhD, U. Ill., 1953. Mem. faculty U. N.Mex., Albuquerque, 1948-71, prof. civil engring., dir. Eric Wang Civil Engring. Rsch. Facility, 1961-70; rsch. assoc. U. Ill., Urbana, 1951-53; owner, cons. engr. Eugene Zwoyer & Assocs., Albuquerque, 1954-72; exec. dir., sec. ASCE, N.Y.C., 1972-82; pres. Am. Assn. Engring. Socs., 1982-84; exec. v.p. T.Y. Lin Internat., San Francisco, 1984-86, pres., 1986-89; owner Eugene Zwoyer Cons. Engr., 1989—2002; COO, treas. Polar Molecular Corp., Saginaw, Mich., 1990, exec. v.p., 1991-92; ret., 2002. Trustee Small Bus. Research Corp., 1976-80; trustee Engring. Info., Inc., 1981-84; internat. trustee People-to-People Internat. 1974-86; v.p. World Fedn. Engring. Orgns., 1982-85. Served to lt. (j.g.) USN, 1944-46. Named Outstanding Engr. of Yr. Albuquerque chpt. N.Mex Soc. Profl. Engrs., 1969, One Who Served the Best Interests of the Constrn. Industry, Engring. News Record, 1980; recipient Disting. Alumnus award the Civil Engring. Alumni Assn. at U. Ill., 1979, Disting. Alumnus award Engring. Coll. Alumni Assn., U. N.Mex., 1982, Can.-Am. Civil Engring. Amity award Am. Soc. Civil Engrs., 1988, Award for Outstanding Profl. Contbns. and Leadership Coll. Engring. U. N.Mex., 1989 Mem. AAAS, ASCE (dist. bd. dirs. 1968-71), NSPE, Am. Soc. Engring. Edn., Am. Concrete Inst., Nat. Acad. Code Adminstrn. (trustee, mem. exec. com. 1973-79), Engrs. Joint Coun. (bd. dirs. 1978-79), Engring. Soc. Commn. on Energy (bd. dirs. 1977-82), Sigma Xi, Sigma Tau, Chi Epsilon. Home and Office: 6363 Christie Ave Apt 1326 Emeryville CA 94608-1940

ZYROFF, ELLEN SLOTOROFF, information scientist, classicist, educator; b. Atlantic City, Aug. 1, 1946; d. Joseph George and Sylvia Beverly (Roth) Slotoroff; m. Jack Zyroff, June 21, 1970; children: Dena Rachel, David Aaron. AB, Barnard Coll., 1968; MA, The Johns Hopkins U., 1969, PhD, 1971; MS, Columbia U., 1973. Instr. The Johns Hopkins U., Balt., 1970-71, Yeshiva U., N.Y.C., 1971-72, Bklyn Coll., 1971-72; libr., instr. U. Calif., 1979, 81, 91, San Diego State U., 1981-85, 94; prof. San Diego Mesa Coll., 1981-95; dir. The Reference Desk Rsch. Svcs., La Jolla, Calif., 1983—; prin. libr. San Diego County Libr., 1985—. V.p. Archaeol. Soc. Am., Balt., 1970-71. Author: The Author's Apostrophe in Epic from Homer Through Lucan, 1971, Cooperative Library Instruction for Maximum Benefit, 1989; contbr. articles to profl. jours. Pres. Women's Am. ORT, San Diego, 1979-81, Zionist Orgn. of Am., San Diego dist., 1997-2000; mem. adv. bd. With Israel Now. Mem.: ALA (chair divsn. and roundtable coms. 1982—), Libr. Congress Cataloging in Publs. Adv. Group, Assn. Jewish Librs., Am. Classical League, Calif. Libr. Assn. (assembly 1993—99, editor Calif. Librs. 1997—99, pres. mgmt. sect. 2000—01), Am. Philol. Assn., Toastmasters, Beta Phi Mu. Office: PO Box 12122 La Jolla CA 92039-2122 E-mail: ezyrofli@sdcl.org.

ZYSKIND, JUDITH WEAVER, molecular biology educator, entrepreneur; b. Cin., July 2, 1939; d. Max Correy Weaver and Mary Catherine Landis; m. George Zyskind, May 2, 1964 (dec. Sept. 13, 1974); children: Aviva, Joy; m. Douglas Wemp Smith, Aug. 16, 1975. BS, U. Dayton, 1961; MS, Iowa State U., 1964, PhD, 1968. Lectr. genetics dept. Iowa State U., Ames, 1970-72, postdoctoral fellow in biochemistry, 1972-74, U. Calif.-San Diego, La Jolla, 1974-77, asst. rsch. biologist, 1977-82; assoc.prof. biology San Diego State U., 1982-86, prof. biology, 1986—; founder, chief sci. officer Elitra Pharms., San Diego, 1997-99, also bd. dirs. Mem. editl. bd. Jour. Molecular Microbiology and Biotech., Norfolk, Eng., 1998—. Contbr. over 60 articles, revs. to profl. publs.; 1 patent in field. Bd. dirs. San Diego State U. Found., 1997—; mem. governing bd. program for edn. and rsch. in biotech. Calif. State U., 1990—. Recipient Women Who Mean Bus. award in biotech. San Diego Bus. Jour., 1997; grantee NIH, NSF, 1983—. Fellow Am. Acad. Microbiology; mem. AAAS, Am. Soc. Biochemistry and Molecular Biology, Am. soc. Microbiology, Assn. for Women in Sci., Sigma Xi. Avocations: backpacking, trekking, photography. Office: San Diego State U Biology Dept 5500 Campanile Dr San Diego CA 92182-4614

ZYSMAN, JOHN ADLER, political scientist, educator; b. Omaha, Mar. 23, 1946; s. Evelyn Zysman; m. Victoria Rehn; children: Lara. PhD of Polit. Sci., MIT, Boston, MA, 1973; BA, Harvard Coll., 1968. Lectr. Dept. Polit. Sci. MIT, Boston, 1973—74; asst. prof. Dept. Polit. Sci. U. Calif.-Berkeley, 1974—82, assoc. prof. Dept. Polit. Sci., 1982—87, prof. Dept. Polit. Sci., 1987—; co-dir. Berkeley Roundtable on Internat. Economy, 1982—. Office: BRIE / Univ. of California 2234 Piedmont Avenue Berkeley CA 94720-2322 Office Fax: (510) 643 6617. Business E-Mail: johnz@socrates.berkeley.edu.

ZYWICKI, CINDY MARY, nurse; b. Chgo., Sept. 22, 1963; d. Robert A. and Barbara J. (Hagerty) Z. BSN and BS in Psychology, Millikin U., 1986. RN Ill.; cert. profl. in utilization Interqual, Inc. Staff nurse, alt. charge nurse Highland

Park (Ill.) Hosp., 1986-95, interim mgr., 1996, utilization rev. outpatient nurse, 1997—, case mgr., 2000. Vol. Fairy Godmother Found. Mem. Bicycle Club Lake County, Single Advantage and Conscious Connections, Alpha Phi Omega, Alpha Tau Delta. Avocations: gymnastics, travel, reading, music, nature. Office: Highland Park Hosp 718 Glenview Ave Highland Park IL 60035-2497 E-mail: CZyW687521@aol.com.

ZYWICKI, ROBERT ALBERT, electrical distribution company executive; b. Chgo., Sept. 23, 1930; s. Martin Albert and Margaret Irene (Mackowski) Z.; m. Barbara Joan Hagerty; children: Robert, Cheryl, Cindy, Carrie. B in Commerce, Northwestern U., 1966. Teller Chgo. Title and Trust Bank, Chgo., 1949-50; painter Getz Molding Co., 1950-51; purchasing agt. Woodworker's Tool Works, 1953-54; serviceman Addressograph Multigraph, 1954-55; mem. Chgo. Fire Dept., 1955-62; v.p. Anixter Bros. Inc., Skokie, Ill., 1955-87; co-owner A-Z Industries, Northbrook, 1987-92, 1992—. Served as cpl. U.S. Army, 1951-53. Mem. Am. Legion (comdr.). Republican. Roman Catholic. Avocations: thoroughbred horse racing, classical music, baseball card collecting, tennis. Home: 1330 Sprucewood Ln Deerfield IL 60015-4771 *Love your family, respect your friends and co-workers, value your customers and suppliers. Always keep each in its proper perspective. Most of all, remember - love, value and respect are all two-way streets.*